FOR USE
IN
LIBRARY
ONLY

D1158265

BENEZIT

DICTIONARY OF ARTISTS

Publisher's guarantee

Whilst a great deal of care has gone into the production of this book, it may contain a printing or manufacturing defect. In the event of such a defect, the book will be exchanged free of charge.

Simply return the book to the place of purchase or write to us at the following address, stating the precise nature of the defect. Your complaint will be dealt with immediately.

Éditions Gründ - 60 Rue Mazarine - 75006 Paris - France

www.grund.fr

ISBN 2 7000 3070 2 (complete set)
ISBN 2 7000 3082 6 (vol. 12)
dépôt légal mars 2006

BENEZIT

DICTIONARY OF ARTISTS

VOLUME 12
ROUCO - SOMMER

GRÜND
2006

NOTES ON THE AUCTION RECORDS SECTION

Never intended to be an exhaustive directory of sales, these listings provide an invaluable record of the movement in prices of an artist's work. Prices are given in the currency of the country of sale (see abbreviations below) as recorded on the date of sale.

The below tables give an indication of the current value of past sales:

- purchasing power of the US Dollar since 1913
- purchasing power of the British Pound since 1901
- purchasing power of the French Franc/Euro since 1901

CURRENCY ABBREVIATIONS (ISO 4217)

ARS	Argentinian Nuevo Peso	**HKD**	Hong Kong Dollar
ATS	Austrian Schilling	**HUF**	Hungarian Forint
AUD	Australian Dollar	**IEP**	Irish Punt
BEF	Belgian Franc	**ILS**	Israeli Shekel
BRL	Brazilian Real	**ITL**	Italian Lira
CAD	Canadian Dollar	**JPY**	Japanese Yen
CHF	Swiss Franc	**MXN**	Mexican New Peso
CZK	Czech Koruna	**NLG**	Dutch Guilder
DEM	German Mark	**NOK**	Norwegian Krone
DKK	Danish Krone	**NZD**	New Zealand Dollar
EGP	Egyptian Pound	**PLN**	Polish New Zloty
ESP	Spanish Peseta	**PTE**	Portuguese Escudo
EUR	Euro	**SEK**	Swedish Krona
FIM	Finnish Markka	**SGD**	Singapore Dollar
FRF	French Franc	**TWD**	Taiwan Dollar
GBP	British Pound	**USD**	United States Dollar
Gns	Guineas	**UYU**	Uruguayan New Peso
GRD	Greek Drachma	**ZAR**	South African Rand

PURCHASING POWER OF THE US DOLLAR SINCE 1913

1 USD in	in USD in 2002
2002	1.000
2001	1.016
2000	1.045
1999	1.079
1998	1.104
1997	1.121
1996	1.147
1995	1.180
1994	1.214
1993	1.245
1992	1.282
1991	1.320
1990	1.378
1989	1.451
1988	1.522
1987	1.583
1986	1.642
1985	1.669
1984	1.728
1983	1.804
1982	1.862
1981	1.975
1980	2.185
1979	2.482

1 USD in	in USD in 2002
1978	2.755
1977	2.966
1976	3.160
1975	3.344
1974	3.649
1973	4.049
1972	4.300
1971	4.435
1970	4.629
1969	4.903
1968	5.167
1967	5.383
1966	5.540
1965	5.694
1964	5.791
1963	5.872
1962	5.942
1961	6.007
1960	6.067
1959	6.164
1958	6.218
1957	6.383
1956	6.615
1955	6.712

1 USD in	in USD in 2002
1954	6.685
1953	6.718
1952	6.772
1951	6.917
1950	7.466
1949	7.541
1948	7.466
1947	8.047
1946	9.200
1945	9.986
1944	10.216
1943	10.394
1942	11.029
1941	12.209
1940	12.817
1939	12.941
1938	12.757
1937	12.520
1936	12.973
1935	13.095
1934	13.424
1933	13.871
1932	13.160
1931	11.804

1 USD in	in USD in 2002
1930	10.766
1929	10.491
1928	10.491
1927	10.351
1926	10.156
1925	10.254
1924	10.513
1923	10.534
1922	10.723
1921	10.045
1920	8.973
1919	10.394
1918	11.933
1917	14.016
1916	16.460
1915	17.703
1914	17.881
1913	18.124

source: US Bureau of Labor Statistics

PURCHASING POWER OF THE BRITISH POUND SINCE 1901

1 GBP in	in GBP in 2003
2003	1.0000
2002	1.0289
2001	1.0461
2000	1.0646
1999	1.0961
1998	1.1130
1997	1.1511
1996	1.1873
1995	1.2159
1994	1.2580
1993	1.2884
1992	1.3089
1991	1.3579
1990	1.4376
1989	1.5736
1988	1.6960
1987	1.7791
1986	1.8533
1985	1.9164
1984	2.0330
1983	2.1343
1982	2.2322
1981	2.4244
1980	2.7122
1979	3.2000
1978	3.6286
1977	3.9297

1 GBP in	in GBP in 2003
1976	4.5525
1975	5.3056
1974	6.5917
1973	7.6492
1972	8.3454
1971	8.9400
1970	9.7839
1969	10.4105
1968	10.9693
1967	11.4799
1966	11.7825
1965	12.2466
1964	12.8172
1963	13.2444
1962	13.4943
1961	14.0787
1960	14.5662
1959	14.7160
1958	14.7769
1957	15.2495
1956	15.7881
1955	16.5940
1954	17.3172
1953	17.6593
1952	18.1985
1951	19.8667
1950	21.6727

1 GBP in	in GBP in 2003
1949	22.3500
1948	22.9968
1947	24.7474
1946	26.4889
1945	27.2977
1944	28.0471
1943	28.8387
1942	29.8000
1941	31.9286
1940	35.4059
1939	41.3410
1938	42.5714
1937	43.0843
1936	44.7000
1935	44.9811
1934	45.2658
1933	45.2658
1932	44.1481
1931	43.0843
1930	41.3410
1929	40.1798
1928	39.7333
1927	39.7333
1926	38.6595
1925	38.4516
1924	38.4516
1923	38.2460

1 GBP in	in GBP in 2003
1922	35.9397
1921	30.9610
1920	28.2688
1919	32.6575
1918	35.9397
1917	43.8773
1916	55.0154
1915	65.0182
1914	72.9796
1913	72.9796
1912	72.2424
1911	74.5000
1910	74.5000
1909	75.2842
1908	76.0851
1907	76.0851
1906	76.9032
1905	76.9032
1904	76.9032
1903	76.9032
1902	77.7391
1901	77.7391

source: British Office for National Statistics

PURCHASING POWER OF THE FRENCH FRANC SINCE 1901 (EURO SINCE 2002)

1 EUR in	in EUR in 2004
2004	1.000
2003	1.021
2002	1.042

1 FRF in	in EUR in 2004
2001	0.16199
2000	0.16468
1999	0.16747
1998	0.16830
1997	0.16947
1996	0.17156
1995	0.17494
1994	0.17796
1993	0.18093
1992	0.18469
1991	0.18907
1990	0.19513
1989	0.20170
1988	0.20899
1987	0.21461
1986	0.22136
1985	0.22724
1984	0.24049
1983	0.25830
1982	0.28315
1981	0.31661
1980	0.35906
1979	0.40772

1 FRF in	in EUR in 2004
1978	0.45158
1977	0.49252
1976	0.53866
1975	0.59046
1974	0.65993
1973	0.75053
1972	0.81968
1971	0.87012
1970	0.91952
1969	0.96747
1968	1.02990
1967	1.07638
1966	1.10572
1965	1.13551
1964	1.16382
1963	1.20384
1962	1.26156
1961	1.32228
1960	1.36597
1959	0.01415
1958	0.01503
1957	0.01729
1956	0.01781
1955	0.01856
1954	0.01874
1953	0.01882
1952	0.01850

1 FRF in	in EUR in 2004
1951	0.02070
1950	0.02406
1949	0.02647
1948	0.02996
1947	0.04755
1946	0.07093
1945	0.10826
1944	0.16078
1943	0.19643
1942	0.24388
1941	0.29331
1940	0.34453
1939	0.40570
1938	0.43410
1937	0.49330
1936	0.62015
1935	0.66785
1934	0.61141
1933	0.58663
1932	0.56377
1931	0.51679
1930	0.49330
1929	0.49897
1928	0.52939
1927	0.52939
1926	0.54950
1925	0.72351

1 FRF in	in EUR in 2004
1924	0.77519
1923	0.88593
1922	0.96468
1921	0.94370
1920	0.81906
1919	1.14238
1918	1.40033
1917	1.80877
1916	2.17052
1915	2.41169
1914	2.89403
1913	2.89403
1912	2.89403
1911	2.89403
1910	3.33926
1909	3.33926
1908	3.33926
1907	3.33926
1906	3.61753
1905	3.33926
1904	3.33926
1903	3.33926
1902	3.33926
1901	3.33926

source: INSEE

GENERAL ABBREVIATIONS

AG Art Gallery
AI Art Institute
AM Art Museum
BNF Bibliothèque nationale de France
CAPC Centre d'Arts Plastiques Contemporains
FAM Fine Art Museum
FMAC Fonds municipal d'Art contemporain
FNAC Fonds national d'Art contemporain
FRAC Fonds régional d'Art contemporain
GA Gallery of Art
Gal. Galerie, Gallery, Galleria, Galeria
GMA Gallery of Modern Art
ICA Institute of Contemporary Art
MA Museum of Art
MAA Museum of Art and Archaeology
MAC Musée d'Art Contemporain, Museo de Arte Contempóraneo, Museu de Arte Contemporânea
MAH Musée d'Art et d'Histoire
MAM Musée d'Art Moderne, Museo de Arte Moderno, Museo d'Arte Moderna
Mamco Musée d'Art moderne et contemporain
MBA Musée des Beaux-Arts, Museo de Bellas Artes, Museo di Belli Arti
MCA Museum of Contemporary Art
MDA Musée des Arts Décoratifs
MFA Museum of Fine Art
MMA Museum of Modern Art
MoCA Museum of Contemporary Art
MoMA Museum of Modern Art
Mus. Musée, Museum, Muséum, Museo, Museu, Museet
Muz. Muzeum, Muzeul, Muzej
NG National Gallery
NGA National Gallery of Art

ROUCO, Martín
Spanish, 17th century.
Active in Tuy during the first half of the 17th century.
Painter.
Martín Rouco was commissioned to paint a statue of *The Virgin* for the collegiate church in Bayonne.

ROUCOLE, Antoine Marie
French, 19th - 20th century.
Born 6 June 1848, in Toulouse; died 22 January 1918.
Painter. History painting, portraits, landscapes.
Antoine Roucole studied at the École des Beaux-Arts in Toulouse and then in Paris under Cabanel from 1871. From 1875 he taught at the École des Beaux-Arts in Toulouse and in 1890 he edited an art methodology handbook entitled *Le Dessin simplifié* (*Drawing Made Simple*). He is remembered for historical paintings such as *Louis XI Receiving the Keys to the City from the Guardians of the Capitol; Procession of the Black Madonna in Faubourg St-Michel; Clémence Isaure and a Troubadour.*
MUSEUMS AND GALLERIES:
TOUL: *Portrait of Nicolas Joly* - TOULOUSE (MBA, Mus. des Augustins): *Chapel of Notre-Dame de Pitié at the Church of the Augustins; Augustinian Chapterhouse* (1894, oil on canvas) - TOULOUSE (Mus. du Vieux Toulouse): *Portrait of Salvayre, Musician.*

ROUCOLLE, André Noël
French, 19th century.
Born 19th century, in Toulouse.
Painter. History painting, portraits.
André Noël Roucolle was a pupil of Cabanel. He first exhibited at the Salon in 1876.
MUSEUMS AND GALLERIES:
TOUL (Mus. municipal): painting.

ROUDE, Matteo. See **RODE**

ROUDENKO-BERTIN, Claire
French, 20th - 21st century.
Born 1958.
Sculptor, video artist. Multimedia.
Claire Roudenko-Bertin lives and works in Lisieux. She is noted for *Anti-Television*, a series permutating sculpture and video which the artist herself describes as 'a controlled skid' involving geographical, linguistic and intellectual elements.

She has exhibited solo on several occasions: in 1990, at the Théâtre de Caen and at the Musée des Beaux-Arts in Le Havre; in 1991, at the Galerie Tugny Lamarre in Paris; and, in 1998, at the Galerie du Dourven in Trédez-Locquémeau.
BIBLIOGRAPHY:
Roudenko-Bertin - Glossaire, exhibition catalogue, Musée des Beaux-Arts André-Malraux, Le Havre, 1990. Giquel, Pierre, "*Claire Roudenko-Bertin*' in *Art Press* n° 151, periodical, Paris, October 1990.

ROUDET, Thérèse
Maiden name: Martel
French, 19th century.
Born 19th century, in St-Malo.
Painter. Landscapes.
Thérèse Roudet was a pupil of Madame Tremisot. She first exhibited at the Salon in 1879, and is best known for landscapes of the area around Rennes and for views of Switzerland.

ROUDNEFF, Georges
French, 20th century.
Born 1933, in Faymoreau (Vendée).
Painter, engraver. Waterscapes, seascapes, landscapes.
Georges Roudneff was awarded the Prix Rencontres in 1973. He is based in Annecy. He featured in the exhibition *De Bonnard à Baselitz - Dix Ans d'enrichissements du cabinet des estampes 1978-1988* (*From Bonnard to Baselitz: A Decade of Acquisitions by the Prints Collection 1978-1988*) at the Bibliothèque Nationale in Paris.
BIBLIOGRAPHY:
Mouizel, Gérard, *Roudneff: bois gravés*, Éd. D'Arnand, Annecy, 1984.
MUSEUMS AND GALLERIES:
PARIS (BNF): *Brighton* (1978, wood in colour).

ROUDNEV, Aleksei
Russian, 20th century.
Born 1914; died 1941.
Painter. Figure compositions, landscapes.
Socialist Realism.
Roudnev studied at the Kharhov art college and became a member of the association of painters of Leningrad (now St Petersburg). He was influenced by the Impressionists. From 1935, his works were exhibited regularly in Moscow and Leningrad.
MUSEUMS AND GALLERIES:
MOSCOW (Ministry of Culture) - MOSCOW (Pushkin MFA) - MOSCOW (State Tretyakov Gal.) - PETROZAVODSK (MFA) - ST PETERSBURG (Gosudarstvennyj Muz. Istorii) - ST PETERSBURG (Gosudarstvennyj Russkij Muz.) - TOMSK (Mus. of Russian Art).
AUCTION RECORDS:
PARIS, 25 March 1991, *Winter at the Dacha* (1940, oil on canvas, 32 x 39 1/4 ins / 81 x 100 cm) FRF 5,500.

ROUDNIEV, Vladimir
Russian, 20th century.
Born 1920, in Moscow.
Painter. Landscapes, portraits.
Roudniev taught at the academy of arts in Moscow. From 1944, he had numerous solo exhibitions, both in the USSR and abroad, including: Lebanon, Czechoslovakia, Germany, Finland and Japan.
MUSEUMS AND GALLERIES:
KRASNODAR - MOSCOW (State Tretyakov Gal.) - ODESSA - RIAZAN - ST PETERSBURG (Gosudarstvennyj Russkij Muz.).
AUCTION RECORDS:
PARIS, 16 June 1991, *Novodievichi Monastery* (oil on canvas, 23 1/2 x 31 1/2 ins / 60 x 80 cm) FRF 4,000.

ROUÈDE, Émile
French, 19th - 20th century.
Born 1850; died 1912.
Painter. Landscapes.
MUSEUMS AND GALLERIES:
AUCH: two Pyrenean landscapes.
AUCTION RECORDS:
RIO DE JANEIRO, 22 March 1982, *Landscape* (oil on canvas, 9 1/2 x 16 1/4 ins / 24 x 41 cm) BRL 750,000.

ROUEL, Alexander. See **ROSWEL**

ROUELLE, Claude de. See **LA RUELLE**

ROUEN, Adolphe Jean Baptiste
French, 19th century.
Born 1814, in Paris.
Sculptor. Genre scenes, animals.
From 1857 to 1877, Adolphe Jean Baptiste Rouen exhibited at the Salon. He mainly painted genre subjects.
MUSEUMS AND GALLERIES:
BAGNOLS-SUR-CÈZE: *Quail Caught in a Trap.*

ROUETTE, Gabriel
French, 18th century.
Painter. Animals.
Rouette was the pupil of Oudry.

Museums and Galleries:
Nantes: *Fox Holding a Rabbit over which a Wild Cat Has Been Fighting.*
Auction records:
Paris, 14 Dec 1979, *Dog in a Kitchen* (1765, oil on canvas, 25½ x 32 ins / 64.5 x 81 cm) FRF 23,000. Paris, 25 Feb 1986, *Dog in a Kitchen* (1765, oil on canvas, 25½ x 32 ins / 64.5 x 81 cm) FRF 35,000. Paris, 23 June 1995, *Water Spaniel Catching a Mallard* (oil on canvas, 23¼ x 36¼ ins / 59 x 92 cm) FRF 20,000.

ROUFF, Daniel Victor
French, 19th century.
Active in Paris.
Painter. Landscapes.
Daniel Victor Rouff exhibited at the Salon from 1844 to 1848. He is particularly noted for his landscapes of Picardy.

ROUFF, Jean
French, 19th century.
Born 19th century, in Lagny-sur-Marne (Seine-et-Marne).
Sculptor.
A pupil of Hubert de Lavigne and of Liénard, Jean Rouff first exhibited at the Salon in 1866. He produced wax reliefs, portraits, medallions, religious subjects etc.

ROUFFET, Jules
French, 19th - 20th century.
Born 18 December 1862, in Paris; died 20 October 1931, in Paris.
Painter. Military subjects.
Jules Rouffet studied under Jean-Paul Laurens. He was party to setting up the Musée de l'Armée (war museum) in Paris.
From 1890 he exhibited at the Salon des Artistes Français, of which he was an associate member, receiving medals in 1890, 1894 and 1900.
Museums and Galleries:
Guéret: *Eagles* - Versailles: *Les Braves Gens (Brave People).*
Auction records:
Paris, 20 Feb 1950, *The Hussar,* FRF 6,000; *Undergrowth* (1903) FRF 650. New York, 24 Feb 1983, *Hussars on Horseback* (1902, oil on canvas, 25½ x 29½ ins / 65 x 75 cm) USD 1,700.

ROUFFET, Marie, or Edmond Marie
French, 20th century.
Painter. Stencil artist, stencil graffiti.
Surface Active.
Marie Rouffet creates paintings and stencils by painting directly onto walls, which serve as his working and exhibition space. His graffiti is not the usual one-dimensional misspelt political invective, but the first in a new genre of stencil art adapted from America and applied to the walls of Paris during a period after 1984.
Auction records:
Paris, 12 Feb 1989, *Whilst Liberating the Horizon* (acrylic/canvas, 51¼ x 37¾ ins / 130 x 96 cm) FRF 4,600. Paris, 10 June 1990, *City Made in Paris* (acrylic/canvas, 51¼ x 63¾ ins / 130 x 162 cm) FRF 7,200. Paris, 28 Oct 1990, *City Monochrome* (acrylic with stencil, 57¾ x 45 ins / 147 x 114 cm) FRF 3,500.

ROUFFIE, Marcelle
French, 20th century.
Born in Clermont-Ferrand.
Painter, sculptor.
Marcell Rouffie has exhibited at the Société Nationale des Beaux-Arts and at the Salon des Tuileries.

ROUFFIO, Paul or Albert Alexandre Paul
French, 19th - 20th century.
Born 1855, in Marseilles; died 15 September 1911, in Viroflay (Yvelines).
Painter, engraver. Religious subjects, nudes, portraits, genre scenes.
Paul Rouffio studied under Alexandre Cabanel and Camille Chazal in Paris. He exhibited at the Salon from 1869, gaining a third class medal in 1879.
He is remembered for *Avarice, Masks* and *Séraphine's Violin.*
Museums and Galleries:
Marseilles: *Samson and Delilah* - Tourcoing.
Auction records:
Paris, 16-17 May 1892, *Trio of Masks,* FRF 320. Paris, 27 Oct 1938, *Folly Unmasked,* FRF 170.

ROUFOSSE, Charles Joseph
French, 19th century.
Born 16 September 1853, in Paris; died 1901, in Paris.
Sculptor.
A member of the Société des Artistes Français, Charles Joseph Roufosse took part in exhibitions, and received an honourable mention in 1884 and 1886 and a third class medal in 1887.
Museums and Galleries:
Paris (Mus. du Petit Palais): *First Thrill* - St-Brieuc: *Lost Illusions.*

ROUGE, Bonabes de (Vicomte)
French, 19th century.
Born 19th century, in Paris.
Sculptor.
Bonabes de Rouge was a pupil of Bonnassieu, and first exhibited at the Salon in 1859. He produced a large number of busts of members of the aristocracy of the Second Empire and of the beginning of the Third Republic.

ROUGE, Fréderic
French, 19th - 20th century.
Born 1867, in L'Aigle (Orne); died 1950, in Ollon.
Painter, illustrator. Landscapes.
Fréderic Rouge studied under Walter von Vigier at the Académie Julian in Paris.
Bibliography:
Fréderic Rouge, peintre 1867-1950, Sion, 1972.
Auction records:
Bern, 28 April 1978, *Items from Heroic Times* (1885, oil on canvas, 41 x 35½ ins / 104 x 90 cm) CHF 4,600. Zurich, 5 June 1996, *The Rhône Valley* (1921, oil on canvas, 32½ x 46 ins / 82.5 x 116 cm) CHF 16,100.

ROUGE, Julie Bonabes de
French, 19th century.
Born in Paris.
Painter. Still-lifes.
Julie Bonabes de Rouge exhibited *Jams* in Angers in 1886.

ROUGE, Regnier La. See **LA ROUGE**

ROUGE, Robert de
French, 19th century.
Born 19th century, in Paris.
Painter. Genre scenes.
Robert de Rouge was a student of Delobbe and he first exhibited at the Salon of 1876.

ROUGEAULT, Jean
French, 16th century.
Active in Bourges in 1508.
Painter.

ROUGELET, Benoît, called Bénédict
French, 19th century.

Born 17 September 1834, in Tournus; died July 1894, in Paris.

Sculptor. Busts, statues, medallions.

A pupil of his father and of Duret, Bénédict Rougelet first exhibited at the Salon in 1876. He received an honourable mention in 1887 and 1889 at the Exposition Universelle and a third class medal in 1892.

Rougelet produced a number of busts, and is noted for *Statue of Greuze* erected in Tournus in 1868 and for stone medallions: *Guerin, Cauchy, La Condamine, Samons, Mlle Mars, Dufresnoy, Lemercier, Quatremere de Quincy, Breton, Lebas,* made for the new Hôtel de Ville in Paris.

Museums and Galleries:

Le Mans: *Cupid* - Tournus: *Greuze; Young Male and Female Fauns; Léon Margue; La promotion de l'aigle.*

Auction records:

Paris, 18 May 1977, *Three Children* (white marble, h. 24 ins / 61 cm) USD 10,350. New York, 1 March 1980, *Echo* (brown-patinated bronze, h. 15 1/2 ins / 39.4 cm) USD 1,000. London, 7 Nov 1985, *Ballerina* (c. 1887, bronze, h. 16 1/4 ins / 41 cm) GBP 950. New York, 19 Jan 1995, *The Dancer* (1887, bronze, h. 16 1/4 ins / 41.3 cm) USD 5,175. Zurich, 2 Dec 1999, *Putti Groups* (marble, h. 28 ins / 72 cm) CHF 70,000. London, 16 April 2002, *Nude Observing Courting Doves* (marble, 30 ins / 75 cm) GBP 19,000. London, 1 Oct 2002, *Standing Cherub Holding a Tambourine* (1880, patinated bronze, h. 24 ins / 60 cm) GBP 2,600. New York, 23 April 2004, *Group of Three Putti* (white marble, h. 27 ins / 68 cm) USD 20,000.

ROUGELET, Émilie Jeanne

French, 19th century.

Born 19th century, in Tournus.

Sculptor.

A pupil of Rougelet her brother, Émilie Jeanne Rougelet first exhibited at the Salon in 1876.

ROUGEMONT, Émilie

Maiden name: Gohin

French, 19th century.

Born 1821, in Paris; died 1859.

Painter. Portraits, genre scenes.

A pupil of Léon Cogniet, from 1848 to 1857 Émilie Rougemont exhibited at the Salon; she received an honourable mention in 1857.

Museums and Galleries:

Strasbourg: two genre paintings.

ROUGEMONT, Guy de

French, 20th century.

Born 1935, in Paris.

Painter, watercolourist, lithographer, sculptor.

Guy de Rougemont studied from 1954 to 1958 under Gromaire at the École des Arts Décoratifs in Paris. He lived in North Africa before staying in Spain on a Casa Velázquez grant, next travelling around the USA before finally settling in Paris.

Abstract and vividly coloured, his acrylic paint treats geometric patterns often inserted within less rigid, gently curved figures reminiscent of clouds. In the 1980s he turned to chalk, pencil and pastel in his series of *Arabic Designs*. In his sculptures, he shaped sensuous volumes before mostly restricting himself to cylinders coloured in sections. He assembled them in ornamental installations such as, in 1977, on a 24-mile (30-kilometre) section of motorway and in 1986 on the forecourt of the Musée d'Orsay. During his solo exhibition at the Musée d'Art Moderne de la Ville de Paris, he translated this principle to the high columns outside the museum which he covered in vinyl of different colours.

He has executed many permanent monumental decorations: at St-Louis hospital in Paris, in a greater Paris Metro Station, on Place Albert-Thomas in Villeurbanne, in 1997 in a 975 feet (300 metre) mural for Nanterre Hospital, at Hakone Open Air Museum in Japan, at the Bonn Hofgarten, in Quito's Parque Metropolitano and in Belfort, Munich, Washington and Los Angeles. Focused on works for the animation of public space, he also produces free-standing pieces where Matisse meets geometry. He has taken part in many collective exhibitions, notably the Biennales in Paris, Venice and Tokyo, the Salon des Réalités Nouvelles in Paris, the Salon de Montrouge and in 1986 *Art construit: Tendances actuelles en France et en Suède* (*Art Construit. Current Trends in France and Sweden*) at the Centre Culturel Suédois in Paris. He has had solo exhibitions in New York, in Paris galleries, including *Rencontre de l'automobile et de la peinture* (*The Motorcar and Painting Meet*) (1967, Musée d'Art Moderne de la Ville de Paris), and in the provinces.

Bibliography:

Bindé, Jérôme, *Rougemont 1962-1982*, Éd. du Regard, Paris, 1984. Gassiot-Talabot, Gérald, *'Odeur du temps'* in *Opus international* n° 132, periodical, Paris, autumn 1993.

Museums and Galleries:

Paris (BNF): *red chalk* (1985, lithograph).

Auction records:

Paris, 19 June 1979, *Composition with Tubes* (acrylic/canvas, 76 3/4 x 51 1/4 ins / 195 x 130 cm) FRF 6,000. Paris, 23 March 1988, *Composition* (gouache/paper, 29 1/2 x 22 ins / 75 x 56 cm) FRF 8,000. Paris, 12 Dec 1999, *Cloud* (steel and aluminium, bench, 28 x 96x28 ins / 70 x 244x70 cm) FRF 21,000. Paris, 24 May 2000, *Untitled* (9 x 12 ins / 23 x 31 cm) FRF 18,000. Paris, 26 March 2003, *Gold* (1967, acrylic on canvas, 59 x 78 ins / 150 x 197 cm) EUR 3,000. Paris, 1 July 2003, *Les couverts d'harlequin* (cutlery in Jagua casket, 118, 13 x 22x13 ins / 33 x 56x34 cm) EUR 2,800. Paris, 15 June 2004, *Cloud* (c. 1970, metal, 18 x 54x43 ins / 45 x 138x110 cm) EUR 37,000. London, 30 June 2004, *Cloud Table* (c. 1969, stainless steel with mirror finish, 15 x 79x35 ins / 39 x 200x90 cm) GBP 12,000.

ROUGEMONT, Jean François

French, 18th century.

Born 1735; died October 1780.

Sculptor.

ROUGEMONT, Philippe de

French, 20th century.

Born 1891; died 1965.

Painter, draughtsman. Figures, nudes.

Auction records:

Göteborg, 7 Nov 1979, *Portrait of Elsa Marianne von Rosen* (oil on canvas, 37 x 22 ins / 94 x 55 cm) SEK 4,000. Göteborg, 18 Oct 1988, *Model* (1943, oil on canvas, 31 1/2 x 28 1/4 ins / 80 x 72 cm) SEK 4,600. Stockholm, 28 Oct 1991, *Nude Model Sitting before a Mirror* (1943, oil on canvas, 30 x 28 3/4 ins / 76 x 73 cm) SEK 7,000. Stockholm, 13 April 1992, *Model - Study for a Nude* (oil on panel, 19 1/4 x 23 1/2 ins / 49 x 60 cm) SEK 4,000; *Nude Girl Reclining on a Sofa* (oil on canvas, 22 x 35 3/4 ins / 56 x 91 cm) SEK 6,500.

ROUGEOT, Charles Antoine

French, 18th century.

Born 1740, in Paris; died 1797, in Tours.

Painter. Landscapes with figures, urban landscapes.

Rougeot painted mainly views of Tours and the surrounding area.

ROUGEOT, Charles Édouard

French, 19th century.

Born 19th century, in Auxonne.

Painter. Landscapes, rustic scenes.

In 1833, 1834 and 1838, Charles Édouard Rougeot exhibited at the Paris Salon. He is known for his scenes around Paris.

ROUGEOT DE BRIEL, Jean
French, 19th century.
Born 19th century, in Allanche (Cantal).
Miniaturist.

Jean Rougeot de Briel was a pupil of Aubrey. He exhibited miniatures at the Salon from 1833 to 1852, mainly copies of famous paintings; he received a third class medal in 1833.

ROUGERON, Christophe
French, 19th century.
Born 19th century, in Recour.
Sculptor.

Christophe Rougeron was a student of Cavelier and Millet. He first exhibited at the Salon of 1874.

ROUGERON, Jules James
French, 19th century.
Born 1841, in Gevray-Chambertin; died 14 July 1880.
Painter, engraver (etching). Figures, genre scenes.

Jules Rougeron was a student of Picot and Cabanel. He exhibited at the Salon from 1869 to 1880. A friend of Henri Regnault, he completed *The Spears*, a work that Regnault left unfinished.

Rougeron worked in Spain and produced a number of sketches in the style of Worms. He also made a contribution to the 'plein-air' (open air) movement of Manet, Renoir and Degas.

MUSEUMS AND GALLERIES:
DIJON: *Bohemian Woman; Taking the Veil* - LANGRES: *Brawl in a Spanish Tavern.*

AUCTION RECORDS:
NEW YORK, 9 April 1929, *Portrait of a Woman*, USD 775. NEW YORK, 25 March 1931, *Wedding in Seville*, USD 1,100. NEW YORK, 14-16 April 1943, *Andalusian Child Awakening*, USD 450. NEW YORK, 16-19 March 1945, *Picnic in Spain*, USD 500. PARIS, 15 Nov 1950, *Spanish Interior* (1876) FRF 45,000. PARIS, 10 Dec 1954, *Wedding in Seville*, FRF 45,000. LONDON, 19 May 1976, *Young Woman at Her Mirror* (oil on canvas, 32 3/4 x 18 1/2 ins / 83 x 47 cm) GBP 650. LONDON, 5 Oct 1979, *Flamenco Dancers* (1871, oil on canvas, 46 x 58 1/4 ins / 117 x 147.9 cm) GBP 1,200. NEW YORK, 1 April 1981, *Young Gypsy Dancer* (1873, oil on canvas, 32 x 23 3/4 ins / 81.3 x 60.3 cm) USD 3,250. PARIS, 30 Nov 1987, *Young Woman with Earrings* (oil on canvas, 21 3/4 x 18 ins / 55.5 x 46 cm) FRF 2,700. AMSTERDAM, 5 June 1990, *Wedding in Seville, Spain* (oil on canvas, 16 1/2 x 27 3/4 ins / 42 x 70.4 cm) NLG 2,070. PARIS, 20 Nov 1991, *Letter* (1877, oil on card/canvas, 17 3/4 x 24 1/4 ins / 45 x 61.5 cm) FRF 28,000. LONDON, 22 May 1992, *Park Bench* (oil on canvas, 13 x 9 1/2 ins / 33 x 24.1 cm) GBP 1,540. NEW YORK, 17 Feb 1993, *Two Young Girls* (oil on canvas, 39 1/4 x 31 1/2 ins / 100 x 80 cm) USD 8,913. NEW YORK, 20 July 1995, *Fashionable Woman with Parasol* (oil on panel, 10 x 6 1/4 ins / 25.4 x 15.9 cm) USD 2,300. LOKEREN, 6 Dec 1997, *Letter* (oil on canvas, 36 1/4 x 29 1/4 ins / 92 x 74 cm) BEF 220,000. LONDON, 26 March 2002, *Mother's Treat* (1877, oil on canvas, 33 x 15 ins / 85 x 37 cm) GBP 14,000.

ROUGERON, Marcel Jules
French, 20th century.
Born 6 October 1875, in Paris.
Active in the USA.
Painter. Landscapes.

Marcel Rougeron is Jules James Rougeron's son. He studied at the Académie Julian, the École des Beaux-Arts, and also under Gérôme and Jehan Georges Vibert. He was a member of the Société des Artistes Français and the Société Royale des Artistes Belges and affiliated to corresponding American organizations. He received an honourable mention in Paris in 1902 and was made an Officier de l'Instruction Publique in 1900.

ROUGET, Alfred
French, 19th century.
Born 19th century, in Magny-St-Médard.
Painter. Landscapes, seascapes.

Alfred Rouget was a student of Bernard and Lequien and he first exhibited at the Salon of 1880.

ROUGET, Claude
French, 16th century.
Active in Paris in 1530.
Medallist.

ROUGET, François
Belgian, 19th century.
Born before 1825, in Nonsons-Thil.
Engraver (wood).

Rouget was the pupil of Andrew. He engraved book illustrations after Raffet and Vernet.

ROUGET, Georges
French, 19th century.
Born 2 May 1784, in Paris; died 9 April 1869, in Paris.
Painter, lithographer. Historical subjects, religious subjects, battles, portraits, genre scenes.

Georges Rouget was a student of David and Garnier and won second prize in the Prix de Rome in 1803. He exhibited at the Salon from 1812 to 1866, winning a second-class medal in 1814, a knighthood in the Légion d'Honneur in 1822 and a first-class medal in 1855.

The titles of Rouget's submissions to the Salon smack a little of sycophancy. Whether his works were produced under the First Empire, the Restoration, Louis-Philippe's reign or the Second Empire, they appear to praise the ruling power of the day. What's more, this obliging quality was rewarded with work. In addition to his works in museums, he produced an *Assumption of the Virgin Mary* at the church of St Germain-l'Auxerrois and *St Louis Pardoning Pierre Duc de Bretagne and Receiving His Homage* at the château of Fontainebleau. Rouget often helped David in his works. For instance, he made a copy of the *Coronation of Napoleon* signed by David and sold as a replica in America.

MUSEUMS AND GALLERIES:
BESANÇON: *General Meunier* - CALAIS: *François I Receives a Delegation from the People of Ghent* - LA ROCHELLE: *François I at La Rochelle* - PARIS (Louvre): *M. de Cailleux, Member of the Institute; Mlles Mollien* - RHEIMS: *Louis XVIII* - ROCHEFORT: *Lolla Montès* - SEMUR-EN-AUXOIS: *Napoleon I* - ST-ÉTIENNE: *Portrait of Mme Rouchon* - ST-OMER: *Portrait of a Man* - VERSAILLES: *Marriage of Napoleon and Marie-Louise at the Louvre; Meeting of Dignitaries in Rouen; Henri IV before Paris; Kellermann; Disembarkation of St Louis in Egypt; Charles III, Known as 'the Simple'; Clovis III; Trivulzio, François l'Hôpital; Pietro Strozzi; De Grouchy; Victor Perrin; Victor Guy Duperré, Sailor in 1792; Bertrand Clausel; Gouvion St-Cyr; La Touche Tréville; François Miranda; Napoleon Presents the King of Rome to the Grand Dignitaries of the Empire; Count Gudin; Marquis d'Armentières; Prince of Hohenlohe-Waldenburg-Bartenstein; St Luc Timoléon d'Espinoy; Schomberg; Dugommier; Gribeauval; Marmont; François Chasseloup-Laubat; Napoleon Receives at St Cloud the Senatus Consulta that Proclaims Him French Emperor; Vicomte de Beauharnais; Gontaut Biron; Death of St Louis; General Houchard; Guébriant; St Louis Receives at Ptolémaïs the Envoys of the Old Man of the Mountain in 1251; St Louis Dispensing Justice under the Oak at Vincennes; St Louis Mediates between the King of England and His Barons.*

AUCTION RECORDS:
PARIS, 24 May 1929, *Louis David, the Painter*, FRF 5,000. PARIS, 8 May 1940, *Portrait of a Man; Portrait of a Woman* (collection) FRF 400. PARIS, 12 March 1941, *Louis XI on His Deathbed* (heightened drawing) FRF 370. PARIS, July 1946, *Portrait of Mme Ravaisson-Mollien*, FRF 20,000. PARIS, 19

May 1950, *Portrait of a Young Woman* (1815) FRF 32,000. PARIS, 21 Nov 1969, *Portrait of Napoleon I, Seated in an Interior*, FRF 7,500. MONACO, 3 Dec 1988, *Bust Portrait of a Gentleman Wearing a Grey Suit* (1817, oil on canvas, 25 1/2 x 21 1/2 ins / 65 x 54.3 cm) FRF 49,540. LONDON, 11 April 1995, *Portrait of Jean-Baptiste Gaspard Roux de Rochelle* (1817, oil on canvas, 23 1/4 x 19 1/4 ins / 59 x 49 cm) GBP 10,350. PARIS, 25 Oct 2001, *Academie d'homme* (oil on canvas, 32 x 26 ins / 81 x 65 cm) FRF 26,000.

ROUGET, Nicolas or Nikolaï
Polish, 19th century.
Born 25 March 1781, in Warsaw; died 24 May 1847, in Warsaw.
Watercolourist, draughtsman, miniaturist, copyist, lithographer, architect. Landscapes.

A student of Kaiser and later of the miniaturist Bechona, Rouget is known for his miniatures, watercolour landscapes, drawings and copies. A particularly notable example is a copy of a landscape by Jacques Ruysddael. He served as an engineer in the army between 1806 and 1835.

ROUGET, Paul
French, 19th century.
Born 1849, in Sens; died 1886, in Mer-sur-Loire.
Landscape artist.

Paul Rouget was a priest.

ROUGEUL, Yves
French, 20th century.
Born 1933, in Varennes-lès-Nevers (Nièvre).
Painter, engraver.

Yves Rougeul took part in 1993 in the exhibition *De Bonnard à Baselitz - Dix Ans d'enrichissements du cabinet des estampes 1978-1988* (*From Bonnard to Baselitz: A Decade of Acquisitions by the Prints Collection 1978-1988*) at the Bibliothèque Nationale in Paris.

MUSEUMS AND GALLERIES:
PARIS (BNF): *Icarus* (1976, etching and aquatint).

ROUGIE, Joël
French, 20th - 21st century.
Born 1957.
Painter. Scenes with figures.

Examples of Joël Rougie's work featured at a group exhibition at the Galerie Hordago in St-Jean-de-Luz in 2003. His composition *Moulin Rouge* comprises three heads of heavily made-up young women set against the cityscape of La Pigalle.

AUCTION RECORDS:
CALAIS, 11 Dec 1994, *Dovecot* (oil on canvas, 28 3/4 x 24 ins / 73 x 61 cm) FRF 7,000. LE TOUQUET, 21 May 1995, *Fashion Parade* (oil on canvas, 28 3/4 x 24 ins / 73 x 61 cm) FRF 6,500.

ROUGIER, Élie François or Jacques.
See **ROGIER**

ROUGIER, Pierre Auguste (Abbé)
French, 19th century.
Born 19th century, in Bellac.
Painter, pastellist.

Pierre Rougier was a student of Paul Delaroche. He exhibited pastels at the Salon in 1843 and 1857.

ROUGIER, Vincent
French, 20th - 21st century.
Born 1948, in Fontenay-sous-Bois.
Painter, engraver. Murals.

Vincent Rougier's work featured in *De Bonnard à Baselitz - Dix Ans d'enrichissements du cabinet des estampes 1978-1988* (*From Bonnard to Baselitz: A Decade of Acquisitions by the Prints Collection 1978-1988*), an exhibition held in 1993 at the Bibliothèque Nationale in Paris.

MUSEUMS AND GALLERIES:
PARIS (BNF): *Secret Valley* (1983, etching and aquatint).

AUCTION RECORDS:
PARIS, 9 April 1989, *Abbadon 1* (oil on canvas, 32 x 25 1/2 ins / 81.5 x 65 cm) FRF 15,000. PARIS, 8 Oct 1989, *Mercury* (mixed media/canvas, 41 1/4 x 28 3/4 ins / 105 x 73 cm) FRF 4,200. PARIS, 26 April 1990, *Crazy Big Fish* (mixed media/canvas, 51 1/4 x 32 ins / 130 x 81 cm) FRF 4,000.

ROUGY, Georges
French, 20th - 21st century.
Born 1947, in Dalat, Vietnam, to French parents.
Painter, engraver.

Georges Rougy lives and works in Brignolles. His work featured in *De Bonnard à Baselitz - Dix Ans d'enrichissements du cabinet des estampes 1978-1988* (*From Bonnard to Baselitz: A Decade of Acquisitions by the Prints Collection 1978-1988*), an exhibition held in 1993 at the Bibliothèque Nationale in Paris.

MUSEUMS AND GALLERIES:
PARIS (BNF): *Portrait of an Engraver in between Two Pages of History* (c. 1980, mezzotint).

ROUHIER, Claude, called Noirot
French, 17th century.
Active in Gray in 1605.
Painter. Armorials.

Claude Rouhier may have been related to the medallist Claude Noirot.

ROUHIER, Louis, or Rouhière
French, 17th century.
Active in Dijon and in Rome c. 1650.
Engraver (burin).

ROUHIER, Pierre
French, 16th century.
Active in Gray in 1559.
Sculptor.

ROUILLARD, Françoise Julie Aldovrandine
Maiden name: Lenoir
French, 19th century.
Born 9 October 1796, in Paris; died 14 July 1833, in Paris.
Miniaturist.

Françoise Rouillard was the student of Jean Sébastien Rouillard, her husband, and Delecluze. She exhibited miniatures at the Salon from 1819 to 1833. She died of cholera.

AUCTION RECORDS:
PARIS, 30 Nov 1 Dec 1923, *Portrait of a Young Woman* (miniature) FRF 1,020.

ROUILLARD, Jean Sébastien or Sébastien
French, 19th century.
Born 1789, in Paris; died 10 October 1852, in Paris.
Painter. History painting, portraits.

Jean Rouillard was the husband of Françoise Rouillard and a student of David. He featured at the Salon from 1817 to 1850, winning a second-class medal in 1822 and a first-class medal in 1827. He was made a Chevalier of the Légion d'Honneur.

He was a portraitist who was very much in fashion under the restoration and during Louis-Philippe's reign.

MUSEUMS AND GALLERIES:
AIX: *Charles X* - AMIENS: *Maréchal de Grouchy* - BLOIS: *General Doguereau* - INNSBRUCK (Tiroler Landesmus. Ferdinandeum): *Dominik Mahlknecht, the Sculptor* - LIMOGES: *Two Portraits of Louis XVIII* - NANCY: *Maréchal Oudinot* - TOURS: *General Donnadieu* - VERSAILLES: *Portrait of Macdonald, Grouchy, Bonaparte as Commander-in-Chief, Dumouriez, Schomberg, Bellefonds, Vandamme, Camille Desmoulins, Marbot.*
AUCTION RECORDS:
PARIS, 27 Nov 1992, *Portrait of General Pauchez's Wife* (1819, oil on canvas, 50 x 37 1/2 ins / 127 x 95 cm) FRF 98,000. PARIS, 2 April 1993, *Portrait of a Young Woman* (1839, oil on canvas, 28 3/4 x 23 1/2 ins / 73 x 60 cm) FRF 7,000. LONDON, 5 April 2001, *Portrait of Mme Auguste Jacobe de Naurois. Portrait of M Auguste Jacobe de Naurois* (1838, oil on canvas, a pair, 46 x 35 ins / 116 x 89 cm) GBP 12,000. PARIS, 2 Dec 2003, *Portrait of Napoleon on the Battlefield* (oil on canvas, 26 x 13 ins / 66 x 34 cm) EUR 4,800.

ROUILLARD, Marie Marcel
French, 19th century.
Born 1860; died 2 June 1881, in Hammam-Mescoutine, Algeria.
Painter, decorative designer.

ROUILLARD, Pierre Louis
French, 19th century.
Born 16 January 1820, in Paris; died 2 June 1881, in Paris.
Sculptor. Animals.
Pierre Rouillard was a student of Cortot. He first exhibited at the Salon of 1837, winning a third-class medal in 1842. He was made a Chevalier of the Légion d'Honneur in 1866.
MUSEUMS AND GALLERIES:
LA ROCHELLE: *Lion Striking down a Boar* (bronze group).

ROUILLER, Albert
Swiss, 20th century.
Born 1938, in Geneva.
Sculptor.
Albert Rouiller studied at the fine arts academy in Geneva and started exhibiting from 1962 (Biel Quadriennale) before going on to show his work at numerous group exhibitions, notably at the Rodin Museum in Paris and in Vienna. Rouiller works with disparate materials, including cast aluminium, polyester and the like. He started out as a non-figurative sculptor; that said, his early work comprises naturally rich plant-like excrescences. His later work, by contrast, sees the development of a personal language based on mechanical elements which he combines, often with considerable humour, to produce ample and at times bizarre forms with a distinctive plasticity.
MUSEUMS AND GALLERIES:
AARAU (Aargauer Kunsthaus): *Relief II* (bronze).

ROUILLERE, Marcel Alexandre
French, 19th - 20th century.
Born 11 October 1868, in Paris.
Sculptor. Busts.
Marcel Rouillere sculpted busts of portraits and architectural ornaments.

ROUILLET, Fériol
French, 19th century.
Born 19th century, in Marcigny.
Painter, draughtsman.
Fériol Rouillet was a student of Allongé and he first exhibited at the Salon of 1872.

ROUILLIER, Paul
French, 20th century.
Born in Paris.
Painter.
Paul Rouillier took part in the Salon d'Automne in Paris.

ROUILLIET, Nicolas Amaranthe
French, 19th century.
Born 2 February 1810, in Varosvre (?); died 1889.
Painter. Portraits, landscapes.
Nicolas Rouilliet was a student at the École des Beaux-Arts in Lyons. He exhibited at the Salon in Paris from 1831.

ROUILLON, Émilie
French, 19th century.
Born 19th century, in Paris.
Painter.
Émilie Rouillon was a student of Couterani and featured at the Salons of 1869 and 1870.

ROUILLON, Moïse
French, 16th century.
Died c. 1601.
Active in Alençon (Orne).
Painter.
Rouillon painted an *Assumption* for the church of Notre-Dame at Alençon.

ROUILLON, Pierre Philibert
French, 19th century.
Born 19th century, in Savigny-le-Temple.
Sculptor.
Pierre Rouillon was a student of Chapu. He exhibited at the Salon from 1865 to 1874, mainly with medallions.

ROUILLY-LE-CHEVALIER, Marie Antoinette
French, 20th century.
Born 1925, in Paris.
Painter, engraver.
Marie-Antoinette Rouilly-le-Chevalier lives and works at La Celle-St-Cloud. She regularly exhibits at the Salon d'Automne in Paris. In 1993, she took part in the exhibition *De Bonnard à Baselitz - Dix Ans d'enrichissements du cabinet des estampes 1978-1988* (*From Bonnard to Baselitz: A Decade of Acquisitions by the Prints Collection 1978-1988*) at the Bibliothèque Nationale in Paris.
MUSEUMS AND GALLERIES:
PARIS (BNF): *Landscape in Reflexion* (1984, etching).

ROUKENS
Dutch, 18th century.
Died before 1750.
Active in Nijmegen.
Draughtsman.
Roukens worked at the Court of the Prince-Elector of the Palatinate, and was also an embosser.

ROUKIN, J. See **ROOUKIN**

ROULAND, Orlando
American, 19th - 20th century.
Born 21 December 1871, in Pleasant Ridge (Illinois); died 1945.
Painter.
Orlando Rouland studied in Germany under Max Thedy and at the Académie Julian in Paris under Jean-Paul Laurens and Benjamin-Constant. He joined the Salmagundi Club in 1901 and was a member of the American Artists Association, Paris and the American Artists Professional League and the American Federation of Arts.
MUSEUMS AND GALLERIES:
MONTCLAIR (New York) - WASHINGTON DC (Smithsonian American AM): *J. J. Shannon, RA* (c. 1910, oil/canvas/fiberboard).

ROULAUD, Claude
French, 20th century.
Born 1945.
Sculptor.
Claude Roulaud works predominantly in copper.

Auction records:
Paris, 30 Jan 1989, *Pelchevant* (welded copper, 55 x 11¾ x 13½ ins / 140 x 30 x 34 cm) FRF 4,000. Neuilly, 3 Feb 1991, *Ventadour* (1990, copper, 61½ x 24½ x 18 ins / 156 x 62 x 46 cm) FRF 7,500. Paris, 3 June 1991, *Vagualam* (1991, welded copper, 45¼ x 17¾ x 15¾ ins / 115 x 45 x 40 cm) FRF 4,700. Paris, 7 Oct 1991, *Urdaxy* (1991, welded and patinated copper, 57¾ x 19¾ x 19 ins / 147 x 50 x 48 cm) FRF 6,000. Paris, 13 May 1996, *Saxilo* (1994, welded and patinated copper, 57¾ x 13¾ x 12½ ins / 147 x 35 x 32 cm) FRF 5,000.

ROULET, Jean
Belgian, 20th century.
Painter (including mixed media). Figures.

Jean Roulet exhibits predominantly in Belgium and, in particular, in Brussels. His extensive travels in Africa, the Middle East and Asia have spawned numerous canvases which capture the features and emotions of varied peoples.

ROULIN, Félix
Belgian, 20th century.
Born 21 August 1931, in Dinant.
Sculptor, painter. Designs for tapestries.
Groupe Axe 59.

Félix Roulin studied at the art school in Maredsous and taught there until 1962, when he moved to Brussels to lecture in metalwork at the La Cambre institute. He was one of the co-founders of the Axe 59 (Axis 59) group. Roulin produced his initial decorative murals during a stay in Rome in 1951. From 1964, he tended to work in co-operation with various architects - notably Jacques Gillet - to produce what he termed 'architectural sculptures'. One notable example of this collaboration with Gillet was the astrophysics centre at Liège University (1965). Roulin worked for many years with molten lead and zinc before turning to the more flexible lost-wax process to turn out pieces in bronze and brass. In addition to his preponderantly abstract architectural sculptures, Roulin also introduced into his work moulded elements in the form of imprints and anatomical references which had the effect of heightening its emotional and symbolic impact. One example of this is where two massive superimposed blocks acquire additional significance by virtue of two hands which seem to reach out from within the sculpture as if to assert their desire for freedom.

Roulin has been the recipient of various awards and distinctions, including runner-up for the Cantü furniture design prize of 1955; the Triennal de la Jeune Sculpture Belge prize and the Rodin Museum Biennale prize (1961); the Berthe-Art sculpture scholarship (1962); the Koopal prize and the runner-up award at the Olivetti sculpture prize (1963); and the critics' prize at the Paris Biennale (1965). His work has featured in group exhibitions, including in 1952 at the exhibition of monumental art held at the Palais des Beaux-Arts in Brussels; in 1955 at the Salon Quadriennal in Mons; in 1958 at the exhibition *Art belge* (*Art in Belgium*), within the framework of the Brussels International Exhibition; in 1959 at the exhibition *European Habitat* in Munich; in 1959 and subsequently at Axe 59 group exhibitions; in 1961 at the Paris Biennale; in 1962 at *Antagonisme de l'objet*, held in the museum of decorative arts in Paris and at the Venice Biennale; in 1963 at *Actualité de la sculpture* (*Sculpture Today*), at the Salon de la Jeune Sculpture held at the Rodin Museum in Paris; in 1964 at an itinerant exhibition of *Artistes primés aux Biennales de Paris* (*Prize-winning Artists of the Paris Biennale*), and in 1964 at *15 Sculptors* in Copenhagen.

Bibliography:
Goyens de Heusch, Serge, *Félix Roulin: métalmythes*, Tandem, 2003 (bilingual French-English edition).

Museums and Galleries:
Brussels (MAM).

Auction records:
Lokeren, 9 Dec 1995, *Composition* (1971, stainless steel and bronze, h. 16½ ins / 42 cm) BEF 55,000. Antwerp, 24 Oct 2000, *Silhouette* (metal, h. 95 ins / 242 cm) BEF 110,000. Lokeren, 15 March 2003, *Composition* (c. 1965, copper and iron, h. 79 ins / 200 cm, w. 21 ins/54 cm) EUR 2,800.

ROULIN, Louis François Marie
French, 19th century.
Painter. History painting, portraits.

Louis Roulin won the second Prix de Rome in 1835. He featured at the Salons of 1838 and 1839.

Museums and Galleries:
Angers: *Tobias Heals His Father*.

Auction records:
New York, 29 Oct 1986, *Portrait of a Man* (1835, pencil, 10 x 7½ ins / 24.5 x 19.2 cm) USD 1,400.

ROULLAND, Jean
French, 20th century.
Born 29 March 1931, in Groix (Nord).
Sculptor, painter, draughtsman, pastellist.

Monster figures dominate Roulland's work. The tormented faces and tortured bodies he brings out of bronze open on a dark world of suffering. He casts the bronze himself using the ancient lost-wax method, which adds to the pathos of his malformed subjects. He exhibited in Roubaix in 1963, then in Lille, Tourcoing and Dunkirk. He showed his work in solo exhibitions in 1966, 1973 and 1975 at the Musée Rodin in Paris and was awarded the Prix Rodin in 1973. In 1969, he exhibited in a number of South American cities.

Roulland

Auction records:
Douai, 13 May 1984, *Head* (bronze, h. 15¼ ins / 39 cm) FRF 10,000. Versailles, 22 April 1990, *Hippocrates* (bronze, h. 9¾ ins / 25 cm) FRF 3,700. Calais, 26 May 1991, *Figure* (pastel and gouache, 42¼ x 28¾ ins / 107 x 73 cm) FRF 3,800. Calais, 13 Dec 1992, *Mask* (gilded bronze, h. 11 ins / 28 cm) FRF 15,000; *Head of a Man* (bronze, h. 22¾ ins / 58 cm) FRF 50,000. Calais, 14 March 1993, *The Cardinal* (1984, pastel, 24¾ x 19 ins / 63 x 48 cm) FRF 4,500. Lille, 16 Dec 2001, *Tribunal of Shadows* (gilt patinated bronze, h. 21 ins / 53 cm) FRF 18,000. Lille, 23 March 2002, *Head of a Shouting Man* (brown-green patinated bronze, 11 x 11x13 ins / 28 x 27x33 cm) EUR 2,900. Calais, 7 July 2002, *Face* (brown-black patinated bronze, h. 17 ins / 42 cm) EUR 4,400. Calais, 14 March 2004, *Head* (patinated bronze, h. 7 ins / 19 cm) EUR 1,600.

ROULLEAU, Jules Pierre or Jean Jules
French, 19th century.
Born 16 October 1855, in Libourne; died 30 March 1895, in Paris.
Sculptor (including bronze). Busts.

Jules Roulleau was a student of Cavelier and Lafon. He first exhibited at the Salon of 1878.

Museums and Galleries:
Amiens: *Leda* - Bucharest (Muz. National de Arta al României): *Léon Gambetta* - Châlons-en-Champagne (Mus. Schiller et Goëthe): *Nicolas Appert* (1892, plaster, bust) - Tours: *Prodigal Son*; *Lazare Carnot*.

Auction records:
Paris, 8 March 1993, *Torrero* (bronze, h. 23½ ins / 60 cm) FRF 6,500.

ROULLEAU, Marcel
French, 20th century.
Sculptor.

Marcel Roulleau featured at the Salon des Artistes Français, being awarded a mention in 1935, a bronze medal in 1936 and a silver medal in 1938.

ROULLEAUX, Thomas
French, 18th century.
Born c. 1688, in Angers; died March 1713, in Angers.
Painter, sculptor.

ROULLET, Auguste
French, 19th century.
Born 19th century, in Angers.
Sculptor.

Auguste Roullet was a student of Barème and Jean Debay. He first exhibited at the Salon of 1866.

ROULLET, Gaston or Marie Anatole Gaston
French, 19th - 20th century.
Born 17 November 1847, in Ars-en-Ré (Charente-Maritime); died 1925, in Paris.
Painter, draughtsman, illustrator. Seascapes, landscapes.

Gaston Roullet studied under Jules Noël. He made his debut at the Salon in 1874. As a correspondant of the *Monde illustré* (*World in Images*), he painted scènes from Africa, Oceania, Indochina and Canada, as well as many sites in Brittany and Normandy. He was the French navy's official painter and was made Chevalier of the Légion d'Honneur in 1895. He featured posthumously in the 2003 collective exhibition *Bretagne, terre des peintres* (*Brittany, Land of Painters*) at the Château de Suscinio and the Musée des Beaux-Arts in Vannes.

BIBLIOGRAPHY:
Delouche, Denise/Le Saux, Marie-Françoise, *Bretagne, terre des peintres*, exhibition catalogue, Musée des Beaux-Arts, Vannes, 2003.

MUSEUMS AND GALLERIES:
GRAY: *View of Nin-Binck* - HENNEBONT (Town Collection): *Vue du port de Hennebont* (*View of the Port of Hennebont*) (oil/panel) - LA ROCHELLE: *Arrival of the Circus (Tonkin, Indochina)*; *Ha Long Bay* - LARMOR-PLAGE (Town Collection): *Le port de Lamor* (*Lamor Harbour*) (1878, oil on canvas) - MONTREAL: *Baie des Morts* - NICE: *Chioggia, the Fish Market* - ROCHEFORT: *Return of the Lifeboat to Le Havre*; *Lagoon at Long-Co* - SAINTES: *On the Red River* - TOULON: *Toulon, View from Six-Fours* - VANNES (collection du conseil général du Morbihan): *St-Cado: Morbihan* (1876, oil on canvas); *Un Clair de lune à Larmor* (*Larmor in Moonlight*) (1878, oil on canvas).

AUCTION RECORDS:
NEW YORK, 8-10 Jan 1909, *In the Venice Arsenale*, USD 165. PARIS, 24 March 1924, *Toulon Harbour*, FRF 155. PARIS, 4 Dec 1926, *Port d'Auray (Brittany)*, FRF 845. PARIS, 15 May 1931, *Giudecca Canal*, FRF 300. PARIS, 20 Feb 1945, *Moonlight Seascape*, FRF 580. PARIS, 7 May 1947, *Étretat*, FRF 1,150. PARIS, 7 Feb 1949, *Tokin Landscape* (watercolour) FRF 550. PARIS, 12 June 1950, *Mediterranean Harbour*, FRF 3,600. PARIS, 6 July 1951, *Treboul (Douarnenez)*, FRF 4,300. VERSAILLES, 1 Feb 1974, *Market Scene Canal S Pietro (Venice)*, FRF 4,500. VERSAILLES, 8 Feb 1976, *Boat in Venice* (oil on canvas, 13 x 18 ins / 33 x 46 cm) FRF 2,000. PARIS, 28 Nov 1977, *Beached Boats* (1898, oil on panel, 6 x 8 1/4 ins / 15.5 x 21 cm) FRF 5,000. ENGHIEN-LES-BAINS, 27 May 1979, *Three-master and Gondola in Venice* (oil on canvas, 28 x 39 1/4 ins / 71 x 100 cm) FRF 14,500. VERSAILLES, 4 Oct 1981, *Venice, Sailing Ships and Gondola before the Doge's Palace* (oil on canvas, 27 1/2 x 41 1/4 ins / 70 x 105 cm) FRF 16,000. PARIS, 6 Nov 1983, *Boats and Gondolas in Venice* (oil on canvas, 17 3/4 x 37 ins / 45 x 94 cm) FRF 22,000. PARIS, 3 Dec 1986, *Seine at Rouen* (1904, oil on canvas, 39 1/4 x 59 ins / 100 x 150 cm) FRF 40,000. VERSAILLES, 20 March 1988, *Ruins of Mohammedia near Tunis* (oil on canvas, 16 1/4 x 25 1/2 ins / 41 x 65 cm) FRF 25,000. PARIS, 8 Nov 1989, *Fort Ste-Marguerite* (oil on canvas, 12 1/4 x 15 3/4 ins / 31 x 40 cm) FRF 15,500. PARIS, 9 March 1990, *Boat at Anchor* (oil on canvas, 11 x 15 ins / 27 x 38 cm) FRF 12,500. PARIS, 11 March 1990, *Venice Canal* (oil on canvas, 14 1/4 x 22 ins / 36 x 56 cm) FRF 24,000. VERSAILLES, 18 March 1990, *Boat at le Tréport* (1876, charcoal and pencil, 27 x 19 3/4 ins / 68.5 x 50 cm) FRF 9,000. PARIS, 16 Nov 1990, *Old Street at Pont de l'Arche* (oil on card, 17 3/4 x 13 3/4 ins / 45 x 35 cm) FRF 4,000. PARIS, 15 Dec 1992, *Venice: Sailing-ships Coming in* (oil on canvas, 30 x 43 3/4 ins / 76 x 111 cm) FRF 20,000. AMSTERDAM, 19 April 1994, *Two-master in Granville Harbour*. PARIS, 13 Oct 1995, *Dordrecht* (oil on canvas, 13 x 18 ins / 33 x 46 cm) FRF 16,000. MONACO, 14-15 Dec 1996, *Belle Poule in Toulon* (1885, oil on canvas, 12 1/4 x 21 1/4 ins / 31 x 54 cm) FRF 8,775.

ROULLET, Jacques Armand
French, 20th century.
Born 17 July 1903, in Sèvres; died 1995.
Painter (gouache), watercolourist, engraver, draughtsman. Landscapes, seascapes.

Jacques Roullet was the official French navy painter Gaston Roullet's grandson. He learnt his art from him. He was also Jules Noël's great-grandson. He studied at the École du Louvre then, on a scholarship, at the École des Beaux-Arts. In 1943, he was appointed chartered conservator of the national museums, then head of the restoration section at Le Louvre. In 1959, he was made a Chevalier of the Légion d'Honneur, becoming an Officier in 1979. He was also a Chevalier des Arts et des Lettres. In 1937, he won a gold medal at the international exhibition of wood engraving.

He also painted, mostly Île-de-Ré landscapes, and specifically Ars-en-Ré, where his family originated.

AUCTION RECORDS:
LA ROCHELLE, 19 July 1989, *Route des Baleines on Ré Island* (1953, oil on canvas, 32 3/4 x 42 1/2 ins / 83 x 108 cm) FRF 17,000; *On the Moor, Ars-en-Ré* (1955, gouache, 9 3/4 x 13 ins / 25 x 33 cm) FRF 3,500.

ROULLET, Jean Louis, or Rollet
French, 17th century.
Born 1645, in Arles; died 15 September 1699, in Paris.
Engraver.

Roullet was the pupil of Jean Lenfant and François de Poilly. He became an associate of the Académie Royale on 28 June 1698. He worked in Italy from 1673 to 1683. On his return to France he settled in Paris, where he produced many portraits. He engraved after Ciro Ferri, Mignard and A. Carracci.

ROULLIER, Alain
French, 20th - 21st century.
Born 18 September 1946, in Nice.
Painter, collage artist, sculptor.
Figuration Libre.

Alain Roullier shows his work at regional group exhibitions, notably in Nice, Marseilles and Arles, and has been awarded a number of regional prizes.

AUCTION RECORDS:
PARIS, 5 June 1992, *Industries* (1991, acrylic/canvas, 38 1/4 x 51 1/4 ins / 97 x 130 cm) FRF 26,000. PARIS, 8 July 1993, *Tribute to James Baldwin* (collage and gouache/card, 25 1/2 x 19 3/4 ins / 65 x 50 cm) FRF 10,000. NEUILLY, 13 Dec 1994, *Justice* (collage/card, 19 3/4 x 23 1/2 ins / 50 x 60 cm) FRF 7,500.

ROULLIER, Christian Henri
French, 19th century.

Born 19th century, in Lyons.
Painter. Portraits, genre scenes.
Christian Roullier was a student of Gérôme. He first exhibited at the Salon of 1878.
AUCTION RECORDS:
TROYES, 24 Jan 1988, *Arab Market Scene* (oil on canvas, 32 1/4 x 39 3/4 ins / 82 x 101 cm) FRF 9,200.

ROULLIER, Jean Chrysostome. See **ROLLIER**

ROULLIERE, A.
French, 17th century.
Active in Paris c. 1650.
Engraver (wood).

ROULLIET, Nicolas Amaranthe.
See **ROUILLIET**

ROUMEGOUS, Auguste François
French, 19th century.
Born 19th century, in Revel.
Painter. Figure compositions, local scenes, landscapes.
Auguste Roumegous was a student of Cabanel and first exhibited at the Salon of 1875.
AUCTION RECORDS:
NEW YORK, 19 July 1990, *Oasis* (oil on canvas, 21 x 31 1/4 ins / 53.3 x 79.4 cm) USD 2,200. NEW YORK, 21 May 1991, *Ladies Playing a Game in the Mosque* (oil on canvas, 28 1/2 x 24 ins / 72.5 x 61 cm) USD 6,600. NEW YORK, 17 Feb 1994, *Perdita (The Winter's Tale, Act IV)* (oil on canvas, 30 x 22 1/4 ins / 76.2 x 56.5 cm) USD 1,840.

ROUMENS, Émile
French, 19th century.
Painter. Portraits, landscapes, still-lifes.
MUSEUMS AND GALLERIES:
CARCASSONNE.
AUCTION RECORDS:
COLOGNE, 23 March 1990, *Mountain Landscape with a Stream* (oil on canvas, 14 1/4 x 21 1/4 ins / 36 x 54 cm) DEM 1,800.

ROUMIER
French, 15th century.
Active in Aix-en-Provence in 1477.
Painter.

ROUMIER, François, or Romié
French, 18th century.
Born in Corbigny (Nièvre); died 27 January 1748, in Paris.
Active in Paris.
Sculptor (wood), engraver (etching/burin).
From 1723 to 1730, Roumier worked in the Dominican church in the St-Germain area of Paris, followed by a lawsuit with the monks over the price of his work. He also produced a series of seven works entitled *Livre de plusieurs coins de Bordures. Inventez et gravez par François Roumier, sculpteur du roi, à Paris chez J. Chereau... 1760.*

ROUMIER, Pierre, or Romié
Italian, 18th century.
Died 1725, in Bergamo.
Active in Carcassonne.
Painter.
This artist painted religious subjects and portraits.

ROUMIEU, Marie Louise
French, 19th century.
Born 19th century, in Douai.
Painter.
Marie Roumieu was a student of Dupuis and exhibited at the Salon from 1881.

ROUPE, Lennart
Swedish, 20th century.
Born 1918.
Painter. Landscapes.
AUCTION RECORDS:
STOCKHOLM, 13 April 1992, *View of Stadsgarden* (1986, oil on canvas, 35 x 35 3/4 ins / 88 x 91 cm) SEK 5,700.

ROUPERT, Louis
French, 17th century.
Born in Metz; died in Paris.
Active during the second half of the 17th century.
Draughtsman, goldsmith. Ornaments.

ROUPI, Jean de. See **JEAN de Cambrai**

ROUQUET, Achille
French, 19th century.
Born 8 January 1851, in Carcassonne.
Engraver (wood), draughtsman, poet.
Aquille Rouquet was the father of Auguste and Jane Rouquet. He engraved magazine illustrations and some landscapes.

ROUQUET, André
French, 20th century.
Painter, watercolourist. Landscapes.
MUSEUMS AND GALLERIES:
NARBONNE (MAH): *The Côte Vermeille*.

ROUQUET, Auguste
French, 20th century.
Born 11 June 1887, in Carcassonne.
Engraver, draughtsman.
Auguste Rouquet was Achille Rouquet's son and assistant.

ROUQUET, Jane
French, 19th - 20th century.
Painter, engraver, draughtsman.
Jane Rouquet worked alongside her father Achille Rouquet. She painted in the pointilliste style after starting as an engraver in the days before the advent of photography, when the demand for prints was great.
AUCTION RECORDS:
PARIS, 24 June 1924, *Landscape* (1906, oil on card, 9 3/4 x 13 ins / 25 x 33 cm) FRF 300.

ROUQUET, Jean André, or André
French, 18th century.
Born 13 April 1701, in Geneva (Switzerland); died 28 December 1759, in Charenton (Seine).
Miniaturist, art writer.
Rouquet went to London, where he worked successfully during the reign of King George II, taking his inspiration from Zincke. He went to Paris and became an associate of the Académie de Peinture on 23 August 1753. He exhibited enamels at the Paris Salon in 1756 and 1757.
MUSEUMS AND GALLERIES:
PARIS (Louvre): *Portrait of the Marquess of Marigny, Commander of the King's Buildings* (enamel).

ROUQUETTE, Antoinette. See **BERTZ Jeanne Françoise Marguerite Esther**

ROURE, Auguste Louis
French, 20th century.
Born 26 April 1878, in Avignon; died 1936.
Painter. Landscapes.
Auguste Roure taught at the École des Beaux-Arts in Avignon. He painted the *garrigue* (Mediterranean brush landscape) in a Fauve style. From 1907, he exhibited at the Salon des Indépendants and the Société Nationale des Beaux-Arts in Marseilles, as well as in Lyons, Geneva, London, New York, Tokyo and Melbourne.
MUSEUMS AND GALLERIES:
AVIGNON (Mus. Calvet) - NÎMES (MBA).

Auction records:
Paris, 4 May 1931, *Rocky Vale*, FRF 60. Avignon, 4 April 1950, *Garrigues*, FRF 6,000.

ROURE, Roland
French, 20th century.
Born 1940, in La Loupe (Eure et Loire).
Sculptor, painter, draughtsman. Marionettes, toys.
Roland Roure has exhibited since 1973, notably at the Brussels Salon d'Art.

His sculptures, of puppets and toys, have a childlike quality. They are assembled out of recycled materials enlivened by touches of colour.

ROURE, Vicente
Spanish, 14th century.
Active in Palma (Majorca) in 1327.
Miniaturist.
Vicente Roure was a priest.

ROURES, Marcos
Spanish, 14th century.
Active in Valencia and Barcelona, in 1331.
Painter.

ROURKE, Nathaniel
Irish, 18th century.
Active in Dublin during the second half of the 18th century.
Portrait artist.
Nathaniel Rourke exhibited in Dublin in 1777.

ROUS, Elizabeth. See **PHILLIPS**

ROUS, John, or Ross
British, 15th century.
Born 1411, in Warwick; died 1491, in Guys Cliff.
Miniaturist, illustrator.
Rous was an academic. He is credited with painting the coat of arms of the counts of Warwick on a parchment preserved in the College of Heralds, together with illustrations for a manuscript now in the British Museum and a *Life of Richard Beauchamp*.

ROUS, Martin
Dutch, 20th century.
Born 1940, in Bandung, Indonesia.
Painter, draughtsman.
Martin Rous studied at the free academy in The Hague and went on to live and work there. Besides abstract painting, he is noted for abstract pen-and-ink studies executed on card. He participated in 1965 at Salon A65 in The Hague, in 1967 in *Contemporary Dutch Art*, an exhibition held within the framework of Expo 67 in Montreal, in 1969 in a travelling exhibition in Britain, in 1973 at the Municipal Van Abbe Museum in Eindhoven and, in 1975, at the Rhineland regional museum in Bonn and in the Paris Biennale. Solo exhibitions by Rous were mounted in 1967 and 1975 in Amsterdam, in 1973 at the municipal museum in The Hague and in 1975 at the Westphalian artists' union in Münster.
Bibliography:
'*Martin Rous*' in *IXe Biennale de Paris*, exhibition catalogue, Idea Books, Musée d'Art moderne de la ville de Paris, Paris, 1975.
Museums and Galleries:
The Hague (Gemeentemus.).

ROUSAUD, Aristide C. L.
French, 19th - 20th century.
Born 7 February 1868, in Rivesaltes (Pyrénées Orientales); died 12 February 1946, in Paris.
Sculptor. Busts, monuments.
Aristide Rousaud studied at the École des Beaux-Arts in Toulouse and then in Paris. He worked for 10 years in Falguière's studio and 12 in Rodin's. He associated with Bourdelle, Despiau and Maillol. He is responsible for busts of Marcel Proust, Victor Hugo, Mahler, Clémenceau and Puvis de Chavannes, among others. After World War I, he worked on war memorials, notably in 1926 a low relief for the war ministry in Paris. In 1927, he sculpted a low relief in Petrarch's honour on the house he lived in at Fontaine-de-Vaucluse. The following year, he produced a bust of Ronsard and contemporary Pleiad poets for the Place Marcelin Berthelot in Paris.

He took part every year as an associate member of the Salon des Artistes Français, Salon des Indépendants and Salon des Tuileries. In 1913 he showed at the Société Nationale des Beaux-Arts, and after his death he featured in exhibitions at the Museum of Modern Art in New York (1963), the Musée d'Art Moderne de la Ville de Paris (1985), the Galeries nationales du Grand Palais (1985-1986, Paris). In 1987, the Musée Rodin in Paris showed nine of his pieces on the occasion of the exhibition *Les Marbres de Rodin* (*Rodin's Marbles*). Received a bronze medal in 1921 and a gold in 1937 for the Exposition Internationale in Paris.

ROUSCHOP, Anny
Dutch, 20th century.
Born 15 September 1929, in Maastricht.
Active in Belgium.
Painter, pastellist, draughtswoman. Figures, portraits, genre scenes, interiors, landscapes, still-lifes, flowers.
Anny Rouschop studied at the Brussels and Etterbeek academies under Albert Philippot and Louis Henno. She was made a Chevalier of the Ordre de la Couronne in 1975. Her work is distinguished by a luminosity reminiscent of the Primitives, the 17th century Dutch Masters, and the Impressionists. She was a regular participant in *Les Arts en Europe* (*Arts in Europe*) exhibitions and exhibited solo from 1962.

ROUSE, Robert William Arthur
British, 19th - 20th century.
Died after 1929.
Painter. Landscapes.
Robert Willliam Arthur Rouse was active from 1882 to c. 1929. He took part in a summer exhibition at the Royal Academy, London, in 1914, with *In the Weald of Kent*.
Bibliography:
'*Royal Academy Exhibitors 1905-1970*' in vol. III, Hilmarton Manor Press, Calne, 1987.
Auction records:
London, 27 June 1978, *Surrey Landscape* (oil on canvas, 39 x 59 ins / 99 x 150 cm) GBP 1,000. London, 18 March 1980, *October* (oil on canvas, 36 x 54 1/4 ins / 91.5 x 138 cm) GBP 1,400. Stockholm, 16 May 1990, *Cattle in a Meadow at the Foot of a Windmill* (oil on panel in grisaille, 18 x 24 ins / 46 x 61 cm) SEK 8,500. New York, 21 May 1991, *Shadow and Sun; Cows in a Meadow by a Stream* (oil on canvas, a pair, 20 x 30 1/4 ins / 50.8 x 76.8 cm) USD 6,050. London, 3 June 1994, *Fish in the Mill Stream* (1888, oil on canvas, 40 x 60 1/4 ins / 101.6 x 153 cm) GBP 4,370. London, 7 June 2001, *Norfolk River Landscape with a Farm and Windmill Beyond* (oil on canvas, 34 x 46 ins / 87 x 116 cm) GBP 1,200. London, 7 Nov 2002, *Cattle Resting in a Meadow. Cattle Watering in a Meadow* (oil on canvas, 18 x 36 ins / 46 x 91 cm) GBP 1,400.

ROUSÉE. See **ROUZÉ**

ROUSIN-FRANÇOIS, Marie
French, 20th century.
Painter. Portraits.
Marie Rousin-François took part in the Salon des Tuileries à Paris.

ROUSOV, Lev
Russian, 20th century.
Born 1926; died 1987.
Painter. Portraits, nudes.

Rousov attended the academy of arts in Leningrad (now St Petersburg), and became a member of the Leningrad association of painters. From 1948, he participated in national and international exhibitions.

Museums and Galleries:
Bratislava (Slovenská Národná Gal.) - Dresden (Gemäldegal.) - Kiev (Chanjenko Mus.) - Moscow (Ministry of Culture) - Moscow (State Tretyakov Gal.) - Osaka (Contemporary Art Center) - Riga (Valsts makslas muzejs/National Art Gallery) - St Petersburg (Academy) - St Petersburg (Gosudarstvennyj Muz. Istorii) - St Petersburg (Gosudarstvennyj Russkij Muz.) - Vologda (MFA).

Auction records:
Paris, 25 March 1991, *Little Girl* (1956, oil on canvas, 15 3/4 x 13 3/4 ins / 40 x 35 cm) FRF 12,500; *In the Café* (1958, oil/hardboard, 47 1/4 x 35 1/2 ins / 120 x 90 cm) FRF 17,000.

ROUSSAUX, Franz, Jakob or Franz Jakob.
See **ROUSSEAU Franz**

ROUSSE, Adolphe Marie Ernest

French, 19th century.
Born 19 September 1844, in La Plaine-sur-Mer; died 1887, in Pornic.
Painter, watercolourist. Seascapes.

Adolphe Rousse was a student of Pradelles. He first exhibited at the Salon of 1879 and appears to have travelled widely. Some of his works portray locations in Brazil, Argentina (La Plata) and Portugal.

Museums and Galleries:
Nantes (MBA): *Entrance to the Port of Pornic, Autumn Evening* (watercolour).

Auction records:
Paris, 15 Feb 1985, *Bay of Montevideo; Yacht in front of Buenos Aires* (1881, watercolour, a pair, 9 1/2 x 17 1/4 ins / 24 x 44 cm and 8 1/4 x 17 ins/21 x 43 cm) FRF 11,500. Monaco, 2 July 1993, *Arrival of a Liner at Rio de Janeiro* (1887, watercolour, 17 1/4 x 24 ins / 44 x 61 cm) FRF 9,990.

ROUSSE, Georges

French, 20th - 21st century.
Born 1947, in Paris.
Painter (including mixed media), draughtsman, watercolourist, environmental artist.

Georges Rousse was awarded a succession of study scholarships - not least among them a Prix de Rome - which enabled him to spend time at the Villa Medici in Rome in 1986-1987 and, in 1988, at the International Center of Photography in New York. He now lives and works in Paris.

He started out as a photographer in a processing laboratory but soon started taking his own photographs. His subject matter was drawn from wastelands, walls weathered by wind and rain and picturesque scenes derived from drawings, sketches and watercolours. Initially, he painted hirsute figures on the walls - in essence, graffiti - but his work became progressively abstract and started to include outsize letters which distorted the overall perspective. He then started to work with optical illusions, where levels and volumes are set off disconcertingly one against the other. Latterly, he has started to produce photographs of these ephemeral views; these are blown up to outsize format and feature subtle plays of light and shadow.

Rousse has participated in numerous group exhibitions: in 1985, at the Siebu Contemporary Art Gallery in Tokyo; in 1985, at the Maison des Arts in Belfort; in 1986, at the Museum of New Mexico; in 1986, at the Guggenheim Museum in New York; in 1986, at the Stedelijk Museum in Amsterdam; in 1986, at the Palazzo Reale in Milan; in 1988, at the Venice Biennale; in 1988, at the Prato Museum of Contemporary Art; in 1988, at the Barbican Art Gallery in London; and, in 1988, at the Kunstmuseum in Lucerne. He has also exhibited solo: in 1982, at the Bibliothèque Nationale in Paris; in 1983, at the CAPC-Musée d'Art Contemporain in Bordeaux; in 1983, 1984 and 1985, at the Galerie Farideh Cadot in Paris; in 1984, at the Musée Municipal in La Roche-sur-Yon; in 1985, at the Musée des Beaux-Arts in Orléans and in San Francisco, Vienna and Montreal; in 1986, 1987 and 1988, at the Farideh Cadot Gallery in New York; in 1987, in London, Bristol and Milan; in 1988, at the French Institute in Innsbruck and at the Caisse Nationale des Monuments Historiques in Paris; in 1993, at the Musée National d'Art Moderne in Paris; in 1994, at the Hôtel Huger in La Flèche (OFAC); in 1998, at the Galerie Durand-Dessert in Paris; and, in 2002, at the Fondation pour l'Art Contemporain C. et J.-M. Salomon at the Château d'Arenthon.

Bibliography:
Georges Rousse, exhibition catalogue, Musée d'Orléans, Orléans, 1985. *Georges Rousse suivi d'un extrait des Chants de Maldoror*, Actes Sud, Arles, May 1986. *Georges Rousse*, exhibition catalogue, Arnolfini, Third Eye Center, Glasgow, 1987. *Georges Rousse - Chemin 1981-1987*, exhibition catalogue, Caisse Nationale des Monuments Historiques et des Sites, Paris Audiovisuel, Paris, 1988. Muntaner, Bernard, '*Une Œuvre de Georges Rousse*' in *coll. Iconoclaste*, Muntaner, Paris, 1993. '*Georges Rousse*' in *coll. Photographes contemporains*, exhibition catalogue, Éd. du Centre Georges-Pompidou, Paris, 1994. *Georges Rousse 1992-1994*, Actes Sud, Arles, Association Information Arts Plastiques en Île-de-France, Centre Photographique d'Île-de-France, Paris, Musées de la Cour d'Or, Metz, 1994. *Georges Rousse 1981-2000*, Bärtschi-Salomon, Paris, 2000.

Museums and Galleries:
Dunkirk (FRAC Nord-Pas de Calais): *Untitled* - Marseilles (Mus. Cantini): *Untitled*.

Auction records:
Paris, 14 Feb 1991, *Brick Wall* (1984, photograph, 43 1/4 x 54 3/4 ins / 110 x 139 cm) FRF 14,500. Paris, 8 Oct 1991, *Untitled* (1984, photo-cibachrome, 48 x 63 ins / 122 x 160 cm) FRF 16,000. Paris, 18 Oct 1992, *Embrasure VIII* (1987, Cibachrome on aluminium, 48 3/4 x 59 ins / 124 x 150 cm) FRF 22,000. Paris, 24 June 1994, *Self-portrait* (1984, Cibachrome) FRF 7,500. Paris, 16 March 1997, *Untitled* (1983, Cibachrome, 57 3/4 x 47 ins / 147 x 118.5 cm) FRF 20,000. Paris, 18 June 1997, *After-Imagery (Remanence) I* (1988, Cibachrome, 61 1/2 x 48 3/4 ins / 156.5 x 124 cm) FRF 21,500. Paris, 20 June 1997, *Biennale Staircase* (1982, Cibachrome, 50 x 61 1/2 ins / 127 x 156 cm) FRF 26,000. Paris, 23 Nov 1997, *Kodachrome* (1962, limited edition of five, 16 1/4 x 19 3/4 ins / 41 x 50 cm) FRF 6,000. Paris, 29 Jan 2001, *Biennale Staircase* (colour cibachrome, 50 x 61 ins / 127 x 156 cm) FRF 20,000. Paris, 23 April 2001, *Embrasure 8, 1987* (cibachrome on aluminium, 49 x 59 ins / 124 x 150 cm) FRF 26,000. Paris, 4 June 2002, *Gallarate V* (1987, cibachrome on aluminium, 49 x 59 ins / 124 x 150 cm) EUR 4,570.

ROUSSE, Robert William Arthur

British, 19th century.
Active in London.
Painter. Portraits, landscapes.

Robert Rousse was a member of the Society of British Artists. He exhibited in London from 1882, notably at the Royal Academy and the Suffolk Street Gallery.

Auction records:
Paris, 27 April 1897, *After a Storm Late in the Day*, FRF 305. London, 13 June 1910, *Heron's Nest* (1889) GBP 11. London, 15 Jan 1974, *Landscape in Surrey*, GBP 500.

ROUSSEAU

French, 17th - 18th century.
Born during the second half of the 17th century, in Paris.
Sculptor.

Rousseau was the father of Franz Rousseau. He settled in Bonn in 1717 and worked in the court of the Prince-Bishop.

ROUSSEAU, Adrien
French, 19th century.
Painter. Landscapes with figures, landscapes.

Adrien Rousseau painted in the forest of Fontainebleau.

MUSEUMS AND GALLERIES:
CARPENTRAS.

AUCTION RECORDS:
PARIS, July 1946, *Landscape*, FRF 5,500. VERSAILLES, 18 March 1990, *Landscapes with Figures* (two oils on panel, 7 x 14 1/4 ins / 17.5 x 36 cm) FRF 6,500. FONTAINEBLEAU, 7 Dec 2003, *Landscape with Tall Trees* (oil on canvas, 21 x 26 ins / 54 x 65 cm) EUR 3,800.

ROUSSEAU, Albert
Canadian, 20th century.
Born 1908; died 1982.
Painter. Figures, nudes, landscapes.

Albert Rousseau was primarily a painter of typical landscapes of Quebec.

A. ROUSSEAU

AUCTION RECORDS:
MONTREAL, 18 Dec 1984, *Village* (oil on canvas, 35 3/4 x 47 1/4 ins / 91 x 120 cm) CAD 3,000. MONTREAL, 17 Oct 1988, *Bernard, Frenchman's Bay* (1960, oil on panel, 30 x 48 ins / 76 x 122 cm) CAD 1,900. MONTREAL, 1 May 1989, *St Simeon* (oil on canvas, 18 x 24 ins / 46 x 61 cm) CAD 1,900. MONTREAL, 30 Oct 1989, *Autumn* (oil on panel, 7 3/4 x 9 3/4 ins / 20 x 25 cm) CAD 990. MONTREAL, 30 April 1990, *Notre Dame Bay* (oil on canvas, 20 x 24 ins / 51 x 61 cm) CAD 1,760. MONTREAL, 5 Nov 1990, *Nude Resting* (oil on canvas, 24 x 35 3/4 ins / 61 x 91 cm) CAD 825. MONTREAL, 4 June 1991, *Houses in the Country* (oil on panel, 15 3/4 x 19 1/2 ins / 40 x 49.5 cm) CAD 1,500; *Notre Dame des Laurentides* (oil on panel, 16 x 20 ins / 40.6 x 50.8 cm) CAD 2,200. MONTREAL, 6 Dec 1994, *Rue St-Gabriel, Quebec* (oil on canvas, 20 x 24 ins / 50.8 x 61 cm) CAD 1,500. MONTREAL, 5 Dec 1995, *Gaspe Peninsula* (1965, oil on canvas, 18 x 24 ins / 45.6 x 61 cm) CAD 1,700. MONTREAL, 26 June 2001, *Fishing Boat* (oil on canvas, 20 x 26 ins / 51 x 66 cm) CAD 2,200. MONTREAL, 30 July 2002, *At the Foot of Cap-Diamant* (oil on canvas, 15 x 30 ins / 38 x 76 cm) CAD 3,000. MONTREAL, 10 Sept 2002, *Montmagny, Qc* (oil on canvas, 20 x 24 ins / 51 x 61 cm) CAD 3,000. MONTREAL, 25 March 2003, *Houses in Winter* (oil on canvas, 16 x 22 ins / 40 x 56 cm) CAD 2,600. MONTREAL, 26 Aug 2003, *Untitled* (oil on canvas, 36 x 48 ins / 91 x 122 cm) CAD 8,100. MONTREAL, 27 Jan 2004, *Baie St Paul* (oil on canvas, 24 x 36 ins / 61 x 91 cm) CAD 3,000. MONTREAL, 27 Jan 2004, *Charlevoix* (oil on canvas, 18 x 24 ins / 46 x 61 cm) CAD 3,000.

ROUSSEAU, Alexandre. See **ROUSSEAU DE CORBEIL**

ROUSSEAU, Alfred Émile. See **ROUSSEAUX**

ROUSSEAU, Alphonse
French, 19th century.
Active in Paris.
Painter. Portraits.

Alphonse Rousseau exhibited portraits, landscapes and still-lifes at the Paris Salon from 1835 to 1849.

ROUSSEAU, André Maurice
French, 20th century.
Born 28 June 1893, in Paris; died November 1980.
Painter. Landscapes, still-lifes, flowers.

André Rousseau was a wrought-iron designer and craftsman and interior decorator. A self-taught painter, he mostly painted flowers. He exhibited at the Salon des Artistes Français, of which he was an associate member. He also showed in other salons, including the Salon des Indépendants.

ROUSSEAU, Antoine
French, 17th century.
Engraver (wood).

Antoine Rousseau sculpted *Christ on the Cross* for the hospital of Meaux, Hôtel-Dieu, in 1643.

ROUSSEAU, Antoine
French, 17th century.
Painter.

Antoine Rousseau was active in Paris and was the ordinary painter in the Court of France, in the service of the widow of Louis XIII. He was the friend of Philippe de Champaigne.

ROUSSEAU, Antoine. See also **ROUSSEAU Jules Antoine**

ROUSSEAU, Charles
French, 18th century.
Born c. 1691; died 10 October 1747, in Paris.
Sculptor.

Charles Rousseau was the son of the sculptor Jacques Rousseau. He was active in Paris and married Magdeleine Mencie on 9 July 1715, in St-Germain-l'Auxerrois. On his marriage he became sculptor to the king, as did his father. In 1706 there was a reference in St-Roch parish register to Jean-Baptiste Roussel, master sculptor, who may have been from the same family.

ROUSSEAU, Charles
Belgian, 19th - 20th century.
Born 1862, in Bruges; died 1916.
Painter. History painting, portraits, genre scenes, landscapes, architectural views.

Charles Rousseau studied at the fine arts academy in Bruges and went on to teach there from 1894.

Ch Rousseau

MUSEUMS AND GALLERIES:
BRUGES: *Samson and Delilah; Patchwork*.

AUCTION RECORDS:
ANTWERP, 10 May 1979, *Sleeping Lacemaker* (1903, oil on canvas, 17 1/4 x 22 ins / 44 x 55 cm) BEF 32,000. NEW YORK, 25 Feb 1988, *In the Studio* (1888, oil on canvas, 27 3/4 x 22 1/4 ins / 70.7 x 56.5 cm) USD 4,400.

ROUSSEAU, Claude
French, 20th century.
Born c. 1880, in the Morvan.
Painter.

A friend of painter Louis Charlot, Claude Rousseau painted in the Realist style.

ROUSSEAU, Clément
French, 19th - 20th century.
Born 2 November 1872, in St-Maurice-la-Fougeureuse.
Sculptor, designer.

Clément Rousseau studied under Léon Morice. Living in Paris, he exhibited at the Salon des Artistes Français from 1921.

AUCTION RECORDS:
PARIS, 6 Feb 1984, *Seller of Second-hand Books* (antique-patinated bronze and ivory, h. 9 ins / 22 cm) FRF 7,000.

ROUSSEAU, Delphine
Maiden name: Guiot
French, 19th century.
Born 19th century, in Paris.
Painter.

Delphine Rousseau's teacher was Desbrosses. In 1865 and 1868, she exhibited still-lifes at the Salon. The museum in Toul owns a work by this artist entitled *Quarter of the Moon*.

ROUSSEAU, Edmé
French, 19th century.
Born 1 June 1815, in Paris; died 15 January or July, 1868, in Paris.
Miniaturist. Portraits.

Edmé Rousseau was a student of Augustin, Picot and Meuret. He exhibited miniatures at the Salon from 1833 to 1857. His output was extensive.

MUSEUMS AND GALLERIES:
COMPIÈGNE (Mus. Antoine Vivenel): *Portrait of the King of Rome* (among eleven miniatures); two self-portraits.

AUCTION RECORDS:
PARIS, 10 June 1938, *Portraits of Young Women* (two canvases) FRF 100. PARIS, 15 Nov 1948, *Woman in Low-Cut Black Dress* (miniature) FRF 1,000. PARIS, 30 Oct 1950, *Portraits of a Man and a Woman* (two miniatures) FRF 4,500. PARIS, 21 Dec 1992, *Young Girl on the Terrace* (1849, oil on canvas, 28 3/4 x 23 1/4 ins / 73 x 59 cm) FRF 13,000. LONDON, 6 Nov 2001, *Theodore Vernes d'Arlande and his Wife Anne* (1853, miniatures, oval, a pair, 4 x ? ins / 11 x ? cm) GBP 3,500.

ROUSSEAU, Émile Alfred. See **ROUSSEAUX**

ROUSSEAU, Émile François
French, 19th - 20th century.
Born 1 November 1853, in Talence near Bordeaux.
Active in Paris.
Engraver (etching).

Émile Rousseau studied under Raphaëlli. He exhibited at the Artistes Français, of which he was an associate member, from 1908, receiving an honourable mention in 1913.

ROUSSEAU, Emmanuel
French, 19th century.
Born 19th century, in Paris.
Painter. Genre scenes.

Emmanuel Rousseau was a student of C. Rousseau and Jules Lefebvre. He featured at the Salon des Artistes Français and received an honourable mention in 1893.

AUCTION RECORDS:
LONDON, 21 March 1984, *Still-life with Musical Instruments* (1888, oil on canvas, 66 1/4 x 83 1/2 ins / 168 x 212 cm) GBP 7,500. ZURICH, 7 June 2000, *Still-life with Onions* (oil on panel, 8 x 15 ins / 21 x 38 cm) CHF 3,000.

ROUSSEAU, Étienne Pierre Théodore. See **ROUSSEAU Théodore**

ROUSSEAU, Fernande
Belgian, 20th century.
Born 19 December 1913, in Biesmes (Namur); died 28 October 1963, in Oburg.
Painter, watercolourist. Portraits, landscapes, still-lifes.

Fernande Rousseau studied under Louis Busseret at the fine arts academy in Mons and under Opsomer and Saverys at the fine arts institute in Antwerp. Her work is rigorously structured and, notably in her later years, attests to a confident treatment of spatial volumes. She was a member of the Artistes Professionels de Belgique, the Artistes de Hainaut and, in Paris, the Union des Femmes Peintres et Sculpteurs. She exhibited in Belgium, France (Paris) and in Moscow.

BIBLIOGRAPHY:
Caso, Paul, *Fernande Rousseau, une double sensibilité*, Fédération du Tourisme et Service des arts plastiques de la province de Hainaut, Mons, 1991.

ROUSSEAU, Franz Jakob. See **ROUSSEAU Jakob**

ROUSSEAU, Franz or Johann Franz, or by error Peter, or Roussaux
German, 18th century.
Born c. 1717, in Bonn (?); died 2 September 1804, in Bonn.
Painter, engraver (etching).

Franz was the father of Jakob Rousseau. He was court painter to the Prince Bishop.

MUSEUMS AND GALLERIES:
COLOGNE (Mus. Rhénan): *Costume Party at the Bonn Court Theatre*.

ROUSSEAU, Gabriel. See **GABRIEL-ROUSSEAU**

ROUSSEAU, Georges, or Geo
French, 20th century.
Born 1901, in Paris.
Painter, draughtsman.

Georges Rousseau took part in the Salon d'Automne in Paris.

ROUSSEAU, Henri
French, 19th century.
Born in Paris.
Painter. Portraits, genre scenes.

Henri Rousseau was the student of Abel de Pujol. He featured at the Salon from 1848.

MUSEUMS AND GALLERIES:
AJACCIO: *Two Rabbits Nibbling Cabbage Leaves*.

AUCTION RECORDS:
PARIS, 10 May 1985, *Old Tomb in Tlemcen* (1887, oil on panel, 17 3/4 x 22 ins / 45 x 55 cm) FRF 70,000.

ROUSSEAU, Henri Émilien
French, 19th - 20th century.
Born 17 December 1875, in Cairo, to French parents; died 28 March 1933, in Aix-en-Provence.
Painter (gouache), watercolourist, draughtsman, illustrator. Local scenes, landscapes.
Orientalism.

Henri Rousseau studied under Gérôme. On a travel grant awarded in 1900, he visited Holland and Belgium and then, a year later, Spain, Tunisia and Algeria. He would return several times to North Africa, working in Morocco from 1920 to 1932. He favoured scenes of nomadic life, horsemen in action, broad landscapes inspired by North Africa or the Camargue. He exhibited at the Salon des Artistes Français and also featured in exhibitions in Belgium, Holland, England, Sweden, Brazil, Argentina and Japan.

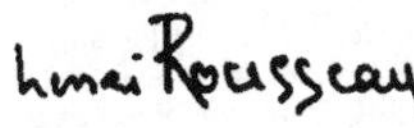

BIBLIOGRAPHY:
Bulletins de l'Association Henri Rousseau, Paris, 1994, 1995.

MUSEUMS AND GALLERIES:
CHAMBÉRY (MBA): *Monastir; The Kasbah* - NANTES: *Low Mass* - PARIS (Louvre).

AUCTION RECORDS:
PARIS, 19 Dec 1932, *Hawking; Word from an Informant* (both) FRF 3,400. PARIS, 22 Jan 1937, *In an Algerian Market*, FRF 4,050. PARIS, 22-23 June 1942, *Fording the River*, FRF 8,700.

PARIS, 19 Feb 1945, *Arab on Horseback in an Oriental Street*, FRF 40,500. PARIS, 16 May 1949, *Arab Encampment*, FRF 24,000. PARIS, 12 March 1951, *Somwhere near Aix* (watercolour) FRF 4,000. PARIS, 16 March 1955, *Arab Hosemen Fording a River*, FRF 56,000. MILAN, 10 Dec 1970, *Gardians* (*Camargue Herdsmen*, ITL 1,000,000. BERN, 6 May 1972, *Harvest Scene*, CHF 3,800. PARIS, 8 Dec 1976, *Arab Horsemen Crossing a Oued* (1928, oil on canvas, 18 x 22 ins / 46 x 55 cm) FRF 10,000. TOURS, 18 April 1977, *Arab Horsemen* (oil on canvas, 15 x 22 ins / 38 x 56 cm) FRF 9,000. PARIS, 16 March 1979, *Arab Horsemen by a Great Wall* (1922, oil on canvas, 23 1/2 x 32 ins / 60 x 81 cm) FRf 11,500. PARIS, 22 Feb 1980, *Fantasia* (gouache, 19 x 24 ins / 48 x 61 cm) FRF 4,200. VERSAILLES, 29 Nov 1981, *Oriental Scene* (1904, oil on wood, 25 1/4 x 22 ins / 64 x 55 cm) FRF 52,000. LONDON, 18 March 1983, *Arabs Back from the Hunt* (oil on canvas, 21 x 17 1/2 ins / 53.2 x 44.4 cm) GBP 7,500. MONTE CARLO, 29 Nov 1986, *La Bocca near Cannes* (watercolour heightened with white, 7 1/4 x 11 ins / 18.5 x 28 cm) FRF 16,000. LONDON, 3 Dec 1986, *Citadel* (c. 1893, oil on card remounted/panel, 18 3/4 x 12 1/2 ins / 47.5 x 32 cm) GBP 32,000. PARIS, 25 June 1987, *Hunting with Dogs* (1924, oil on canvas, 21 1/4 x 28 3/4 ins / 54 x 73 cm) FRF 125,000. LONDON, 24 June 1988, *Hunt in Arabia* (oil on canvas, 17 x 21 3/4 ins / 43 x 55.3 cm) GBP 7,150. AMSTERDAM, 16 Nov 1988, *View from Holland* (1902, oil on canvas) NLG 6,670. PARIS, 17 March 1989, *Horse Traders* (watercolour, 18 3/4 x 25 ins / 47.5 x 63.5 cm) FRF 18,000. LONDON, 7 June 1989, *Street Scene in an Oriental Village* (oil on canvas, 12 1/2 x 9 1/2 ins / 32 x 24 cm) GBP 2,200. LONDON, 4 Oct 1989, *Arab Horsemen in the Desert* (1924, oil on canvas, 23 1/4 x 31 1/2 ins / 59 x 80 cm) GBP 8,800. STOCKHOLM, 15 Nov 1989, *Arab Horses at the Trough* (1915, oil, 38 1/2 x 51 1/4 ins / 98 x 130 cm) SEK 67,000. SCEAUX, 11 March 1990, *Horseman* (oil on panel, 7 x 5 1/2 ins / 18 x 14 cm) FRF 29,000. LONDON, 30 March 1990, *Arab Horseman* (charcoal and watercolour heightened with white, 22 1/4 x 17 1/2 ins / 56.5 x 44.5 cm) GBP 1,760. PARIS, 6 April 1990, *Desert Horsemen* (oil on panel, 18 x 14 3/4 ins / 46 x 37.5 cm) FRF 100,000. PARIS, 27 April 1990, *Arab Nuptials in Tunisia* (1903, oil on canvas, 32 1/2 x 39 1/4 ins / 82.5 x 100 cm) FRF 570,000. NEW YORK, 23 May 1990, *Hawking* (1925, oil on canvas, 19 3/4 x 25 3/4 ins / 50.2 x 65.4 cm) USD 18,700. PARIS, 22 June 1990, *Arab Horsemen and Animals* (1926, watercolour and gouache/bistre-coloured paper, 23 1/2 x 18 1/4 ins / 60 x 46.5 cm) FRF 46,000. PARIS, 8 April 1991, *Horsemen* (1925, oil on canvas, 21 1/4 x 29 ins / 54 x 73.5 cm) FRF 100,000. NEW YORK, 22 May 1991, *Horsemen in the Desert* (1923, oil on canvas, 21 1/2 x 28 1/2 ins / 54.6 x 72.4 cm) USD 18,700. PARIS, 13 April 1992, *Lord Falconer on Horseback* (watercolour and charcoal, 24 x 18 1/2 ins / 61 x 47 cm) FRF 42,000. NEW YORK, 16 July 1992, *Race in the Camargue* (1929, watercolour, gouache and charcoal/paper, 19 x 25 ins / 48.3 x 63.5 cm) USD 1,430. PARIS, 7 Dec 1992, *Arab Encampment* (1922, oil on canvas, 28 3/4 x 39 1/4 ins / 73 x 100 cm) FRF 80,000. PARIS, 5 April 1993, *Horseman* (oil on panel, 6 1/4 x 4 3/4 ins / 16 x 12 cm) FRF 8,000. PARIS, 24 June 1994, *Arab Horsemen* (wax crayon and watercolour, 18 3/4 x 25 ins / 47.5 x 63.5 cm) FRF 9,500. CALAIS, 3 July 1994, *Berber Horseman* (oil on panel, 6 1/4 x 4 3/4 ins / 16 x 12 cm) FRF 12,500. NEW YORK, 20 July 1994, *Horse Market* (gouache, watercolour and charcoal/paper, 19 1/4 x 24 3/4 ins / 48.9 x 62.9 cm) USD 3,450. LONDON, 16 Nov 1994, *Hawking* (oil on canvas, 19 1/4 x 25 1/2 ins / 49 x 65 cm) GBP 26,450. PARIS, 12 Dec 1994, *Ardèche People* (watercolour, 10 x 15 ins / 24.5 x 38 cm) FRF 4,900. NEW YORK, 16 Feb 1995, *Arab Horsemen at the Seaside* (oil on canvas, 21 1/2 x 28 3/4 ins / 54.6 x 73 cm) USD 17,250. PARIS, 13 March 1995, *Horsemen Halt on the High Plain* (oil on panel, 18 x 22 ins / 46 x 55 cm) FRF 52,000. PARIS, 11 Dec 1995, *Flamingo Hunting on Lake Tunis* (1914, oil on canvas, 32 x 46 ins / 81 x 116 cm) FRF 235,000. PARIS, 25 June 1996, *The Pasha and his Standard-bearer* (watercolour and gouache, 24 3/4 x 19 ins / 63 x 48 cm) FRF 45,000. PARIS, 14 Oct 1996, *Horsemen on the Beach* (oil on canvas, 21 1/4 x 28 3/4 ins / 54 x 73 cm) FRF 87,000. PARIS, 8 Dec 1996, *Kaid on Horseback with his Man-servant* (oil on canvas, 25 1/2 x 21 1/4 ins / 65 x 54 cm) FRF 115,000. LONDON, 21 March 1997, *The Fight* (1924, oil on canvas, 21 1/2 x 28 1/2 ins / 54.5 x 72.5 cm) GBP 7,820. PARIS, 10-11 June 1997, *Horsemen on the Banks of Lake Tunis* (oil on canvas, 21 1/2 x 25 1/2 ins / 54.3 x 65 cm) FRF 100,000. PARIS, 17 Nov 1997, *Kaid on Horseback with his Standard-bearer* (oil on panel, 18 x 15 ins / 46 x 38 cm) FRF 95,000. PARIS, 26 March 1998, *Kaid by the Estuary at Rabat* (mixed media, 19 3/4 x 24 1/2 ins / 50 x 62 cm) FRF 90,000. PARIS, 1 April 1998, *Arab Horsemen* (oil on canvas, 18 x 24 ins / 46 x 61 cm) FRF 122,000. STOCKHOLM, 26 May 1999, *Arabian Horsemen in a Desert Landscape* (1904, oil on canvas, 18 x 24 ins / 46 x 61 cm) SEK 56,000. PARIS, 16 Nov 1999, *Arab Shepherds at Dawn* (1907, oil on panel, 18 x 22 ins / 46 x 55 cm) FRF 49,000. PARIS, 3 April 2000, *Falconers on Horseback* (mixed media, 24 x 19 ins / 62 x 48 cm) FRF 110,000. PARIS, 20 Nov 2000, *At the Gate of a Moroccan Town* (1928, oil on canvas, 15 x 22 ins / 38 x 55 cm) FRF 120,000. PARIS, 14 May 2001, *Headscarf Dance* (1922, watercolour and gouache, 18 x 24 ins / 46 x 61 cm) FRF 105,000. PARIS, 23 Nov 2001, *Guardians in Camargue* (1920, oil on canvas, 45 x 76 ins / 114 x 194 cm) FRF 200,000. NEUILLY, 18 June 2002, *Prisoners after the Raid, Morocco* (1923, oil on canvas, 29 x 39 ins / 73 x 100 cm) EUR 30,000. PARIS, 28 Nov 2002, *Chief and Escort* (watercolour and gouache, 24 x 19 ins / 60 x 49 cm) EUR 15,000. PARIS, 19 June 2003, *Fantasy Knight* (oil on canvas, 29 x 24 ins / 73 x 60 cm) EUR 30,000. DEAUVILLE, 13 July 2003, *Horsemen in Camargue* (gouache and watercolour, 16 x 20 ins / 40 x 51 cm) EUR 4,000. PARIS, 7 April 2004, *Chief and Escort* (1924, oil on canvas, 26 x 36 ins / 65 x 92 cm) EUR 51,000. STOCKHOLM, 25 May 2004, *Moroccan Lord* (1925, oil on canvas, 26 x 21 ins / 65 x 54 cm) SEK 140,000.

ROUSSEAU, Henri Julien Félix, called le Douanier
French, 19th - 20th century.
Born 21 May 1844, in Laval (Mayenne); died 2 September 1910, in Paris.
Painter. Figure compositions, scenes with figures, allegorical subjects, figures, portraits, still-lifes, landscapes.

When Henri Rousseau was 19 years old, he joined the French infantry in Angers. His regiment later moved to St-Maur, near Paris. He left the army in 1968 following his father's death (as the main wage-earner of the family he was granted unlimited leave). He did not participate in the Mexican war, as alleged by Guillaume Apollinaire, again for administrative reasons. Instead, he settled in Paris and married Clémence Boitard (who died in 1888) and worked as a bailiff. He was never a douanier (customs officer) but in 1871 got a job collecting customs fees at toll stations (l'Octroi), from the local farmers who brought their merchandise to the Parisian markets.

A self-taught painter, he was encouraged by his neighbour Félix Clément (who had obtained the Prix de Rome), who helped him to obtain a copyist pass to paint in the Louvre and the Luxembourg museums in 1884. He made his debut at the Salon des Indépendants in 1886, introduced by Paul Signac. Camille Pissarro also encouraged him, impressed by his exceptional eye for colours. In 1892, he showed his painting *The War* at the Salon and met the writer Alfred Jarry, also born in Laval, who named him 'Le Douanier' and introduced him to the literary avant-garde. Rousseau accepted an early retirement in 1893 from the Octroi so he could devote himself to art. He married Joséphine Le Tensoret in 1899 (who died in 1903). Unable to sell his paintings, he lived in great poverty and in 1889 wrote a vaudeville, *Une visite à l'Exposition de 1889 et La Vengeance d'une Orpheline Russe* (*A visit to the 1889 Exhibition and the revenge of a Russian orphan*) to try to earn some money - to no avail. In 1902 he decided to give lessons in watercolour, pastels, earthenware and china painting and received his teaching diploma at the Association Philotechnique in 1904. He also gave music and musical notation lessons (he played the violin). He met Guillaume Apollinaire and Robert Delaunay, who defended his work, around 1907. At the end of the same year, he was imprisoned for one month for his naive participation in fraud against the Banque de France. At his trial, one year later, he was given a two-year suspended sentence and lost his teaching job. He then gave lessons in his own home. In 1908, Picasso gave a banquet for Rousseau in his studio, which became known as the *Banquet du Bateau-Lavoir*. Max Weber, a fellow artist and collector of Rousseau's work, who attended the banquet, later organised the first exhibition of Rousseau's works in the USA. Rousseau got a job managing the sales of the *Petit Parisien* (*Little Parisian*) newspaper for a sector of Paris, and this became the main source of his income. This was supplemented by the small amounts he asked from shopkeepers to do their portraits or to teach their children music or elocution. In 1909, Whilelm Uhlde arranged Rousseau's first solo show in a furniture shop in the rue Notre-Dame-des-Champs. In the same year, the dealer Ambroise Vollard bought eleven of his paintings. After that, Rousseau regularly sold his works, but continued to live in poverty.

The greatest and earliest of the so-called modern primitive or naive painters, he was at first much reviled. His early admirers (Signac, Apollinaire, Picasso) were impressed by his guileless yet discriminating eye, which he had acquired through assiduous study of great masters in the Louvre. Le Douanier never doubted his own merits: because his simplicity admitted no understanding of mediocrity; he deemed it natural for an artist to be great. The charge against him was of treating banal themes in an epic style. He rendered nature vividly, in particular in his famous jungle scenes, which he painted from illustrated books and his numerous visits to the Paris zoo and botanical gardens. The trees that abound in many of his outdoor compositions have been associated with diverse sources of inspiration, from Persian and Japanese prints to the paintings of the Barbizon school. The poetry and freshness of his work distinguishes him from other artists. But Rousseau remains an enigma: his legendary naivety was not without guile, and his obsessive determination to improve was hampered by clumsiness. Reportedly uneducated, Rousseau had a sound grounding for a man of his generation and class. He painted with candour and ambition, treating a broad range of subjects and themes, from everyday scenes to vast compositions. Despised by traditionalists, he earned the respect and admiration of the most forward-looking artists, from Brancusi to Tzara. His nature was further obscured by the activities of apologists such as Alfred Jarry, Blaise Cendrars and Guillaume Apollinaire. When Rousseau represented Apollinaire with Marie Laurencin, in *The Muse Inspiring the Poet*, Apollinaire pointedly challenged critics to explain how they had recognised him if, as they claimed, the portrait was such a poor likeness. His masterpieces include: *The Sleeping Gypsy; Liberty Inviting Artists to Take Part in the 22nd Exhibition of the Société des Artistes Indépendants; Tiger Hunt; Old Man Juniet's Cart; Portrait of a Child; The Dream; War; Football Players*.

Henri Rousseau participated in group exhibitions, including: 1886-1910, Salon des Indépendants, Paris; 1906, Salon d'Automne, Paris; 1964, *Le monde des Naïfs*, Musée National d'Art Moderne, Paris.

Solo exhibitions of his work include:1910, Gallery 291, New York; 1911, retrospective, Salon des Indépendants, Paris; 1912, Bernheim-Jeune & Cie, Paris; 1923, 1937, Galerie Paul Rosenberg, Paris; 1933, Kunsthalle, Basel; 1944, *Exposition Commémorative du Centenaire de la Naissance d'Henri Rousseau le Douanier*, Musée National d'Art Moderne, Paris; 1946, *Le Douanier Rousseau*, Museum of Modern Art, New York; 1961, *Henri Rousseau dit 'le Douanier': Exposition de son Cinquantenaire*, Galerie Charpentier, Paris; 1963, Henri Rousseau, Wildenstein Gallery, New York; 1984, Galeries Nationales du Grand Palais, Paris; Museum of Modern Art, New York; 2001, *Henri Rousseau, der Zöllner: Grenzgänger zur Modern*, Kunsthalle, Tübingen; 2005, *Henri Rousseau: Jungles in Paris*, Tate Modern, London.

BIBLIOGRAPHY:

Uhde, Wilhelm, *Henri Rousseau*, E. Figuière, Paris, 1911. Delaunay, Robert, *'Le Douanier Rousseau'* in *L'Amour de l'Art* n° 7, periodical, Paris, 1920. Soupault, Philippe, *Henri Rousseau le Douanier*, Quatre Chemins, Paris, 1927. Apollinaire/Éluard, et al., *Exposition commémorative du centenaire de la naissance d'Henri Rousseau le Douanier*, exhibition catalogue, Musée national d'Art moderne, Paris, 1944. Rich, D. C./Karpel, B., *Le Douanier Rousseau*, Museum of Modern Art, New York, 1946. Rousseau, Henri/Tzara, Tristan (foreword), *Une visite à l'Exposition de 1889 et La Vengeance d'une orpheline russe*, Cailler, Genoa, 1947. Vallier, Dora, *Henri Rousseau*, catalogue raisonné, Flammarion, Paris, 1965 (reprinted coll. Painted œuvre, Flammarion, 1982). Shattuck, Roger, *The Banquet Years: the Origins of the Avant Garde in France, 1885 to World War I: Alfred Jarry, Henri Rousseau, Erik Satie, Guillaume Apollinaire*, Vintage Books, New York, 1968. Vallier, Dora/Arieri, Giovanni, *L'Opera completa di Rousseau il Doganiere*, Rizzoli, Milan, 1969. Keay, Carolyn, *Henri Rousseau: le Douanier*, Academy (ed.), London, 1976. Alley, R., *Portrait of a Primitive: The Art of Henri Rousseau*, Phaidon, Oxford, 1978. Le Pichon, Yann, *The World of Henri Rousseau*, Phaidon, Oxford, 1982 (translation of Le Monde du douanier Rousseau, Laffont, Paris, 1981). Certigny, Henry, *Le Douanier Rousseau en son temps. Biographie et catalogue raisonné*, Bunkazai Kenkyujyo Co., Tokyo, 1984. Shattuck, Roger, et al., *Le Douanier Rousseau*, exhibition catalogue, Gal. nationales du Grand Palais, Réunion des musées nationaux, Paris, 1984. Rubin, William/Hoog, Michel/Béhar, Henri, et al., *Henri Rousseau*, exhibition catalogue, The Museum of Modern Art, New York, 1985. Schmalenbach, Werner, *Henri Rousseau: Dreams of the Jungle*, Prestel Verlag, Munich, New York, 1998 (distributed in the UK by Biblios). Hughes, Robert, *'Henri Rousseau'* in *Nothing If Not Critical: Selected Essays on Art and Artists*, Harvill Press, London, 1999. Adriani, Götz, *Henri Rousseau*, exhibition catalogue, Yale University Press, New Haven and London, 2001.

MUSEUMS AND GALLERIES:

BASEL (Kunsthalle): *The Tropical Forest; The Muse Inspiring the Poet* (*Portrait of Apollinaire and Marie Laurencin*) (1909) - BASEL (Kunstmus.): *Famished Lion; Portrait of Joseph Brummer* (1909) - BUFFALO (Albright-Knox AG): *Bouquet of Flowers with an Ivy Branch* (1909) - CHICAGO (AI): *The Waterfall* (1910) - CLEVELAND (MA): *Jungle* (1909) - DALLAS (MA): *Stroller and Child* (c. 1905-1906, oil on canvas) - LONDON (Courtauld Institute of Art): *Toll gate* (c. 1890, oil on canvas)

- LONDON (NG): *Tiger in a Tropical Storm (Surprised!)* (1891, oil on canvas) - LONDON (Tate Collection): *Bouquet of Flowers* (c. 1909-1910, oil on canvas) - LOS ANGELES (Getty Mus.): *A Centennial of Independence* (1892, oil on canvas) - MERION (Barnes Foundation): *Scout Attacked by a Tiger* (1904, oil on canvas); *Landscape with Tree Trunks* (c. 1887); *Woman Walking in an Exotic Forest* (1905, oil on canvas) - MOSCOW (Pushkin MFA): *Jaguar Attacking a Horse* (1910) - NEW YORK (Metropolitan Mus. of Art): *Spring in the Bièvre Valley* (1908-1910) - NEW YORK (MoMA): *The Sleeping Gypsy* (1897); *The Repast of the Lion* (1904); *Jadwiga's Dream* (1910) - NEW YORK (Solomon R. Guggenheim Mus.): *The Football Players* (1908); *Artillerymen* (c. 1895) - PARIS (Mus. d'Orsay): *Portrait of the Artist's First Wife* (c. 1886-1888); *Portrait of a Woman* (c. 1893-1896); *War, or Discord on Horseback* (1894); *The Representatives of Foreign Powers Coming to Greet the Republic as a Sign of Peace* (1907); *The Snake Charmer* (1907); *Old Man Juniet's Cart* (1908); *Summer, Meadow* - PARIS (Mus. de l'Orangerie): *The Boat in the Storm; The Cliff; The Wedding Party; Anglers* (1909) - PRAGUE (Národní Gal.): *Myself, Portrait-Landscape* (1890) - RICHMOND (Virginia MFA): *Tropical Landscape: An American Indian Struggling with a Gorilla* (1910, oil on canvas) - ST PETERSBURG (Hermitage): *Struggle between Tiger and Bull* (1908, oil on canvas); *The Luxemburg Garden, Monument to Chopin* (1908-1909); *Porte de Vanves, View of the Fortifications* (c. 1909); *Tropical Forest* - TOKYO (MMA): *Liberty Inviting Artists to Take Part in the 22nd Exhibition of the Société des Artistes Indépendants* (1906) - WASHINGTON DC (NGA): *Rendezvous in the Forest* (1889, oil on canvas); *Boy on the Rocks* (1895-1897, oil/linen); *Equatorial Jungle* (1909, oil on canvas); *Tropical Forest for Monkeys* (1910, oil on canvas) - WINTERTHUR: *To Celebrate the Baby* (1903) - ZURICH (Kunsthaus): *Forest Walk* (1886-1890); *Portrait of Pierre Loti* (1910).

AUCTION RECORDS:

PARIS, 30 May 1921, *Portrait of Joseph Brummer,* FRF 11,400; *Child with Cardboard Doll,* FRF 9,000; *Woman in Red in the Forest,* FRF 26,000; *View of Malakoff,* FRF 15,600; *Walk under the Trees,* FRF 17,000. PARIS, 28 Oct 1926, *Sleeping Gypsy,* FRF 520,000. PARIS, 31 March 1927, *The Four Seasons* (four canvases) FRF 132,000. PARIS, 29 April 1927, *Pontoise Landscape,* FRF 27,000; *Boy on the Rocks,* FRF 35,000. PARIS, 16 Dec 1927, *Portrait of Joseph Brummer,* FRF 98,100; *Suburban Landscape,* FRF 39,000. PARIS, 27 April 1929, *Canal,* FRF 28,000. PARIS, 28 Oct 1937, *Garden,* FRF 30,200. PARIS, July 1946, *Small Church,* FRF 150,500. PARIS, 20 June 1947, *Tramp on the Road,* FRF 120,000. GENEVA, 6 May 1950, *Angler,* CHF 3,600. STUTTGART, 10 May 1950, *Lac Daumesnil, Thunderstorm Effect,* DEM 8,000. LONDON, 25 Nov 1959, *Diana's Statue in the Park,* GBP 2,000. NEW YORK, 9 Dec 1959, *View of Saint-Cloud,* USD 25,000. LONDON, 23 Nov 1960, *Football Players,* GBP 37,000. LONDON, 28 June 1961, *Part of the Château de Bellevue,* GBP 8,000. LONDON, 11 April 1962, *View of Fortifications,* GBP 14,000. NEW YORK, 14 Oct 1965, *View of the Fortifications, Boulevard Gouvion St-Cyr,* USD 44,000. LONDON, 30 March 1966, *Landscape with Angler,* GBP 11,000. TOKYO, 27 May 1969, *Parc Montsouris,* GBP 22,192. GENEVA, 12 June 1970, *Ile Saint-Louis, Notre Dame de Paris,* CHF 190,000. NEW YORK, 21 Oct 1971, *Exotic Landscape,* USD 775,000. PARIS, 7 March 1973, *Frumence Biche in Civilian Clothes,* FRF 260,000. NEW YORK, 2 May 1974, *Woman with Sunshade in an Exotic Forest* (1907) USD 325,000. LONDON, 2 July 1974, *Mill* (c. 1896) Gns 28,000. HAMBURG, 4 June 1976, *Portrait of Mr S.* (c. 1898, oil on canvas, 15 3/4 x 12 3/4 ins / 40.1 x 32.5 cm) DEM 96,000. ENGHIEN-LES-BAINS, 2 June 1977, *Flight into Egypt* (c. 1885-1888, oil on canvas, 11 x 13 3/4 ins / 27 x 35 cm) FRF 41,000. NEW YORK, 10 Nov 1978, *War* (1895, black lithograph/red paper, 9 x 12 3/4 ins / 22 x 32.5 cm) USD 2,500. NEW YORK, 16 May 1979, *Portrait of Mr S.* (c. 1898, oil on canvas, 16 1/4 x 13 ins / 41 x 33 cm) USD 40,000. BERN, 22 June 1979, *War* (1894, lithograph/red paper, 9 x 13 ins / 22 x 33 cm) CHF 5,800. TOKYO, 14 Feb 1981, *Portrait of Mrs S.* (c. 1898, oil on canvas, 17 1/4 x 14 ins / 43.5 x 35.5 cm) JPY 9,500,000. NEW YORK, 15 Nov 1983, *View of the Île Saint-Louis from Saint-Nicolas Harbour, Evening* (c. 1888, oil on canvas, 18 x 21 3/4 ins / 46 x 55.2 cm) USD 240,000. LONDON, 15 June 1984, *War* (1894, lithograph/orange paper, 8 1/2 x 12 3/4 ins / 21.4 x 32.3 cm) USD 1,700. LONDON, 26 March 1985, *Stroll at the Buttes-Chaumont* (c. 1908, oil on canvas, 18 x 15 ins / 46 x 38 cm) GBP 170,000. NEW YORK, 20 Nov 1986, *Saint-Cloud Landscape* (1896, oil on canvas remounted on board, 11 3/4 x 9 ins / 29.9 x 22.9 cm) USD 60,000. PARIS, 20 Nov 1987, *Orchard* (after 1886, oil on canvas, 15 x 22 ins / 38 x 56 cm) FRF 2,600,000. PARIS, 15 March 1988, *Dam* (oil on canvas, 14 3/4 x 18 ins / 37.5 x 46 cm) FRF 2,400,000. PARIS, 20 Nov 1988, *Landscape with Castle* (c. 1890-1895, oil on canvas, 13 x 16 1/4 ins / 33 x 41 cm) FRF 3,200,000. PARIS, 1 April 1990, *Flower-Decked Pedestal Table* (oil on canvas, 11 x 7 3/4 ins / 28 x 20 cm) FRF 620,000. LONDON, 3 April 1990, *Vue de la Bièvre à Gentilly* (oil on canvas, 15 x 18 ins / 38 x 46 cm) GBP 880,000. ANGERS, 12 June 1990, *Nymph in an Exotic Forest* (oil on canvas, 20 1/2 x 15 ins / 52 x 38 cm) FRF 3,950,000. LONDON, 5 Oct 1990, *Gathering Cattle* (oil on canvas, 21 1/2 x 27 1/4 ins / 54.6 x 68.9 cm) GBP 3,520. LONDON, 25 June 1991, *View of the Parc de Montsouris* (oil on canvas, 16 x 12 ins / 40.5 x 30.5 cm) GBP 385,000. PARIS, 21 Oct 1993, *Head of a Woman* (oil on canvas, 12 1/2 x 10 1/4 ins / 32 x 26 cm) FRF 300,000. PARIS, 26 Nov 1993, *Still-life with Tropical Fruit* (1908, oil on canvas, 25 1/2 x 32 ins / 65 x 81 cm) FRF 4, 500,000. LONDON, 29 Nov 1993, *Portrait of Joseph Brummer (Portrait-Landscape)* (1909, oil on canvas, 46 x 34 3/4 ins / 116 x 88.5 cm) GBP 2,971,500. PARIS, 14 March 1994, *War* (lithograph/paper, 8 1/4 x 12 1/2 ins / 21 x 31.5 cm) FRF 10,000. NEW YORK, 11 May 1994, *Sketch for the View of the Île Saint-Louis Taken from Quai Henri IV* (oil on paper/canvas, 8 1/2 x 11 ins / 21.9 x 28.2 cm) USD 90,500. PARIS, 13 June 1996, *Landscape and Factory* (c. 1909, oil on canvas, 15 3/4 x 12 1/4 ins / 40 x 31 cm) FRF 400,000. PARIS, 20 June 1996, *View of a Castle* (oil on panel, 14 1/4 x 19 1/4 ins / 36 x 49 cm) FRF 130,000. LONDON, 25 June 1996, *Unemployed Man Playing Music* (c. 1894-1898, oil on canvas, 13 3/4 x 10 3/4 ins / 35 x 27.5 cm) GBP 91,700. PARIS, 19 June 1997, *Arab Horseman Unhorsed by a Tiger* (1903-1904, oil on canvas, 17 x 25 1/2 ins / 43 x 65 cm) FRF 3,050,000. LONDON, 23 June 1997, *Oak-tree Branch* (c. 1907-1908, pen and ink/paper, 6 x 4 ins / 15.5 x 10 cm) GBP 7,820. LONDON, 7 Dec 1999, *Bouquet of Flowers* (1909, oil on canvas, 17 x 14 ins / 44 x 36 cm) GBP 75,000. LONDON, 29 June 2000, *Walkers Approaching a Mountain Chalet* (pencil, crayon and gouache, 14 x 12 ins / 36 x 30 cm) GBP 24,000. PARIS, 14 Dec 2000, *Sailing Boats* (c. 1880, oil on canvas, 39 x 39 ins / 99 x 99 cm) FRF 1,100,000. RENNES, 1 April 2001, *Tiger Cat* (oil on canvas, 13 x 9 ins / 32 x 23 cm) FRF 187,000. LONDON, 26 June 2001, *Tiger Cat* (oil on canvas, 13 x 9 ins / 32 x 23 cm) GBP 60,000. NEW YORK, 8 May 2002, *Landscape with Factory* (c. 1900, oil on canvas, 15 x 18 ins / 38 x 46 cm) USD 320,000. NEW YORK, 9 May 2002, *Ile de la Cite* (c. 1895, oil on canvas, 6 x 9 ins / 15 x 24 cm) USD 70,000. PARIS, 4 April 2003, *Walker in the Countryside with Charcoal Factory* (oil on canvas, 7 x 13 ins / 17 x 33 cm) EUR 45,000. ZURICH, 24 June 2003, *Customs Officer* (oil on panel, 8 x 7 ins / 21 x 19 cm) CHF 38,000. DALLAS, 13 May 2004, *Marine Landscape, the Cliff* (oil on panel) USD 17,000.

ROUSSEAU, J. J., or Rousseaux

Belgian, 19th century.

Active in Namur from 1829 to 1830.

Painter, engraver (burin/etching). History painting.

ROUSSEAU, Jacques

French, 17th century.

Born 1630, in Paris; died 16 December 1693, in London.

Painter, decorative artist, engraver (etching).

Landscapes, architectural views, perspectives.

Jacques Rousseau began his studies in Paris, and then went to Rome. His acquaintance with Herman van Swanevelt and their subsequent friendship had a considerable influence on Rousseau's career. He married Van Swanevelt's sister and rapidly gained a reputation as a skilled painter of landscapes and views. His tastefully executed works were generally decorated with architectural features, and were produced in the style of Nicolas Poussin. On his return to Paris, he was very well received and found work in the royal residences in Marly, St-Germain-en-Laye and Versailles. Although he was a Protestant, he entered the Académie on 2 September 1662, by special permission of the king.

Following the revocation of the Edict of Nantes, he fled to Switzerland. Louis XIV recalled him to France, but he went to Holland and then to England, on the Duke of Montagu's request. He worked on the decoration of Montagu House in London, with Charles de la Fosse and J.B. Monnoyer. He was also employed to paint decorations at Hampton Court Palace, also in London. Even at Mariette's time, there remained almost nothing of his paintings on the exterior walls.

Rousseau's work featured in the 2002 exhibition *Les Mystérieux du XVIIe Siècle. Une Enquête au Cabinet d'Art Graphique* (*Mysteries of the 17th century: An Exploration of the Graphic Art Collection*) at the Musée des Beaux-Arts in Nancy. The exhibition showed works by a group of forgotten artists from the 17th century, whose works are known only from engravings.

Bibliography:

Bouleau, Cécile, '*Jacques Rousseau (1630-1693)*' in *Bulletin de la Société de l'Histoire de l'art français*, Paris, 1994. Paul, Céline/Harent, Sophie, '*Les Mystérieux du XVIIe siècle. Une enquête au cabinet d'art graphique*' in *coll. Lire en filigrane*, Musée des Beaux-Arts, Nancy, 2002.

Museums and Galleries:

Versailles: *Panelling in the Room of Venus*.

Auction records:

London, 15 Dec 1982, *Landscape after Antiquity* (oil on canvas, 38 1/2 x 52 ins / 98 x 132 cm) GBP 4,200. London, 10 July 1992, *Lute Player with an Old Man Holding the Score* (1631, oil on canvas, 48 x 39 3/4 ins / 122 x 101 cm) GBP 52,800. London, 20 April 1994, *Money Changer* (oil on canvas, 28 1/4 x 23 1/2 ins / 72 x 60 cm) GBP 23,000. London, 3 April 1996, *Classical Figures in an Ornamental Park* (oil on canvas, 27 1/2 x 41 3/4 ins / 70 x 106 cm) GBP 2,070.

ROUSSEAU, Jacques

French, 18th century.

Born in Paris; died 12 October 1714, in Angers.

Sculptor.

Jacques Rousseau was the father of Charles Rousseau. He was sculptor to the king, and had lodgings in the Louvre. His wife was from Angers where he married her in 1688 and where he later died during a journey.

ROUSSEAU, Jacques de, or des Rousseaux, or Desrousseaux

Dutch, 17th century.

Born c. 1600, in Tourcoing; died before 5 March 1638, in Leiden.

Painter. Figures, portraits.

Jacques de Rousseau was influenced by Rembrandt.

Museums and Galleries:

Erlangen: *Study of a Head* - Rotterdam (Mus. Boijmans Van Beuningen): *The Father of Rembrandt* - The Hague (Bredius Mus.): *Head of an Apostle*.

Auction records:

Berlin, 4-6 Oct 1937, *Male Bust*, FRF 156,000. London, 14 May 1971, *Portrait of the Father of Rembrandt*, Gns 480. Monte Carlo, 21 June 1986, *St Jerome* (oil on canvas, 28 3/4 x 24 3/4 ins / 73 x 63 cm) FRF 160,000. New York, 30 Jan 1997, *Men and Women Making Music* (1631, oil on canvas, 46 1/2 x 41 ins / 118.1 x 104.1 cm) USD 57,500. London, 25 April 2001, *Old Man Reading a Book* (oil on panel, 17 x 14 ins / 42 x 36 cm) GBP 8,000. Paris, 2 Dec 2003, *Head of an Old Man* (oil on canvas, 26 x 19 ins / 65 x 49 cm) EUR 70,000.

ROUSSEAU, Jakob or Franz Jakob, or Roussaux

German, 18th - 19th century.

Born 1757, in Bonn; died 25 February 1826, in Cleves.

Painter, engraver (etching).

Jakob was the son of Franz Rousseau. He engraved views and portraits.

Museums and Galleries:

Cleves (Provincial Mus.): *Cleves* (four works).

ROUSSEAU, Jean Charles

French, 19th century.

Born 31 December 1813, in Paris.

Sculptor. Mythological figures.

Jean Rousseau featured at the Salon from 1849 to 1874.

Museums and Galleries:

Châlons-en-Champagne: *Ulysses Drawing His Bow*.

ROUSSEAU, Jean François

French, 18th century.

Born c. 1740.

Active in Paris.

Engraver (burin).

Jean François Rousseau engraved portraits and vignettes after Cochin and Gravelot.

ROUSSEAU, Jean Jacques

Swiss, 18th century.

Born 1712, in Geneva; died 1778, in Ermenonville (Oise).

Painter, watercolourist, engraver, draughtsman.

Jean Jacques Rousseau was also a writer and composer, composing *Devin du Village* (*The Village Soothsayer*). However, it is his work as an artist which is of most interest. He invented, without any success, an original notation of music, which he could not have achieved without a knowledge of drawing, a knowledge gained during his apprenticeship to a master engraver in Geneva.

With his great love of nature, Rousseau drew and painted the places he discovered as he collected plants at the country house Les Charmettes and in Montmorency and Ermenonville. He also drew and painted in watercolour some of the plates in his *Dictionnaire de Botanique* (*Dictionary of Botany*), published in 1808. These plates are the work of an artist, in miniature yet with delicate and elegant precision.

ROUSSEAU, Jean Jacques

French, 19th - 20th century.

Born 10 October 1861; died 1911.

Painter, pastellist, engraver. Figures, animals, landscapes.

Jean Jacques Rousseau studied under Desportes, Lehmann, Roll and Ribot, making his debut at the 1878 Salon. He was vice-president the Société Coloniale des Artistes Français and an associate member of the Artistes Français and of the Société Nationale des Beaux-Arts. He was awarded medals in 1889 and 1900, for the Paris Expositions Universelles. He was made a Chevalier of the Légion d'Honneur in 1903.

He helped decorate the former Musée des Colonies in Paris.

Museums and Galleries:

Bern: *Cow in Normandy* - Toulouse: *Before the Storm*.

Auction records:

Paris, 19 May 1919, *Landscape: Road near Vichy*, FRF 65. Paris, 27 Jan 1927, *Cow Taken to Pasture*, FRF 160. Paris, 25

March 1993, *Hong Kong, Night Effect* (1903, oil on canvas, 18 x 24 ins / 46 x 61 cm) FRF 19,500.

ROUSSEAU, Jean Siméon, called Rousseau de la Rottière
French, 18th century.
Born 18 February 1747.
Sculptor.

Jean Siméon Rousseau was the son of Jules Antoine Rousseau. He continued the work of his father.

MUSEUMS AND GALLERIES:
LONDON (Victoria and Albert Mus.): *Boudoir of the Marquis of Sérilly.*

AUCTION RECORDS:
PARIS, 22 Nov 1923, *Imitation of the Antique,* FRF 3,100.

ROUSSEAU, Johann Franz. See **ROUSSEAU Franz**

ROUSSEAU, Joseph
French, 18th century.
Active in Angers at the beginning of the 18th century.
Sculptor.

Joseph Rousseau belonged to the order of Jacobins. He produced several sculptures for the chapel of his monastery.

ROUSSEAU, Jules
French, 19th century.
Active in Paris.
Portrait artist.

Jules Rousseau featured at the Salon from 1836 to 1838.

ROUSSEAU, Jules Antoine
French, 18th century.
Born 7 December 1710, in Versailles; died 30 August 1782, in Lardy (Seine-et-Oise).
Sculptor.

Jules Antoine Rousseau was the son of Alexandre Rousseau, and the father of Jean Siméon and Jules Hugues Rousseau. He worked on the interior decoration of Versailles, Bellevue, St-Cloud, Chambord, Choisy, Compiègne, Fontainebleau, Marly, Meudon and St-Hubert palaces.

AUCTION RECORDS:
LOKEREN, 16 Feb 1980, *Friendship* (bronze, h. 15 ins / 38 cm) BEF 60,000.

ROUSSEAU, Jules Hugues, called Rousseau the Elder
French, 18th - 19th century.
Born 27 February 1743, in Versailles; died 30 April 1806, in Lardy (Seine-et-Oise).
Sculptor.

Jules Hugues Rousseau was the son and assistant of Jules Antoine Rousseau.

ROUSSEAU, Léon
French, 19th century.
Born c. 1825, in Pontoise.
Painter. Portraits, landscapes, still-lifes (flowers/fruit).

Léon Rousseau was a student of Eugène Ciceri and Édouard Pingret. He exhibited at the Paris Salon from 1849 to 1881. He produced a large number of still-lifes that showed an interest in flowers and fruit.

MUSEUMS AND GALLERIES:
ANGERS - BAGNÈRES-DE-BIGORRE - LE PUY-EN-VELAY: *Still-life with Dead Hare* - PONTOISE: *Dead Owl and Dead Magpie* - ROCHEFORT: *Game and Hunting Gear.*

AUCTION RECORDS:
PARIS, 22 Feb 1924, *Hunting Trophy,* FRF 140. PARIS, 30 Dec 1948, *Flowers and Chinese Vase,* FRF 1,500. PARIS, 30 June 1980, *Flowers* (oil on canvas, four companion pieces, 19 3/4 x 55 ins / 50 x 140 cm) FRF 5,200. PARIS, 30 Nov 1981, *Clump of Flowers with Birds* (oil on canvas, 92 1/4 x 59 3/4 ins / 234 x 152 cm) FRF 35,000. NEW YORK, 23 May 1996, *Vase of Flowers* (1853, 45 1/4 x 35 1/2 ins / 115 x 90.2 cm) USD 37,375. PARIS, 24 June 2002, *Garland of Roses* (1855, oil on canvas, 28 x 24 ins / 72 x 60 cm) EUR 6,000. PARIS, 21 May 2003, *Bouquet of Lilacs* (pastel, 39 x 31 ins / 99 x 80 cm) EUR 1,700.

ROUSSEAU, Léon
French, 19th century.
Born in Tours.
Engraver.

Léon Rousseau was the student of John Quartley in Tours and Adolphe F. Pannemaker in Paris. He worked in Paris from 1875 to 1892.

ROUSSEAU, Léonie
French, 19th century.
Born 19th century, in Paris.
Painter. Genre scenes, still-lifes.

Léonie Rousseau was the student of her father Léon Rousseau, the flower painter, and she exhibited at the Paris Salon in 1865, 1868 and 1869.

ROUSSEAU, Lodewyk or Louis
Belgian, 19th century.
Active in Antwerp.
Painter. Genre scenes.

Lodewyk Rousseau was the pupil of Braekeleer in 1839.

ROUSSEAU, Marguerite
Belgian, 20th century.
Born 1888; died 1948.
Painter. Scenes with figures, landscapes, seascapes, still-lifes.

Marguerite Rousseau painted scenes of happy family life in a well-ordered society.

AUCTION RECORDS:
NEW YORK, 23 Feb 1989, *Sea Cliffs at Etretat, Normandy* (1918, oil on panel, 18 1/4 x 25 1/4 ins / 46.3 x 64.2 cm) USD 5,500. NEW YORK, 24 May 1989, *Bathers* (1919, oil on card, 18 x 21 1/4 ins / 45.7 x 54 cm) USD 7,700. NEW YORK, 1 March 1990, *Flower Market* (1920, oil on card, 21 3/4 x 15 ins / 55.3 x 38.1 cm) USD 6,600. VERSAILLES, 22 April 1990, *On the Beach* (1913, oil on canvas, 19 3/4 x 23 1/2 ins / 50 x 60 cm) FRF 23,500. NEW YORK, 21 May 1991, *Pleasures of the Beach* (oil on card, 20 x 25 1/4 ins / 51 x 64 cm) USD 4,620. NEW YORK, 19 Feb 1992, *Regatta* (oil on card, 21 1/4 x 28 1/2 ins / 54 x 72.5 cm) USD 35,200. LONDON, 18 June 1993, *Tennis Match* (oil on card, 15 1/4 x 22 ins / 38.7 x 55 cm) GBP 4,140. BOSTON, 9 March 2001, *Boat Ride* (oil on canvas, 24 x 36 ins / 61 x 91 cm) USD 19,000. BRUSSELS, 6 Dec 2004, *Elegant Ladies on the Balcony. Elegant Ladies at Tennis* (oil on panel, a pair, 21 x 26 ins / 54 x 66 cm) EUR 2,600.

ROUSSEAU, Marina-Maria
Romanian, 20th century.
Born in Russu.
Active in France since 1969.
Painter. Religious subjects.

Rousseau trained at the École du Louvre, and studied traditional Orthodox iconography at the Père Dobrot school in Paris. She has lived and worked in Paris since 1969. She paints icons on wood, borrowing from the naiveté of glass painting. She introduces elements inspired from traditional Romanian popular art.

Rousseau has had shown her work in collective and solo exhibitions in France, Switzerland, Italy, Belgium, Great Britain and the USA.

BIBLIOGRAPHY:
Jianou, Ionel, *Romanian Artists and the West,* American Romanian Academy of Arts and Sciences, Los Angeles, 1986.

ROUSSEAU, Mathurin
French, 17th century.
Active in Angers c. 1602.
Glass painter.

ROUSSEAU, Michel Jean Bernard
French, 20th century.
Born 29 September 1927, in Rheims.
Sculptor, draughtsman, painter. Figures, landscapes. Busts.

Michel Rousseau studied at the École des Beaux-Arts in Rheims and then under Gaumont in Paris until 1947. He also attended the Académie de la Grande Chaumière. He had a studio at La Ruche in Paris as well as one in Catalonia from 1965. He often resided abroad, working in Sweden in 1961, England in 1962, Morocco in 1963, Switzerland in 1964 and in southern France.

He showed at the Salon des Indépendants in Paris in 1948, 1949 and 1950 and in numerous collective exhibitions, notably in 1978 at the Centre National des Arts Plastiques in Paris and in 1985 in the exhibition *Reflets de l'Art en Roussillon* (*Reflections of Art in Roussillon*) in Hanover, Perpignan and Barcelona. He has also shown his works in solo exhibitions in Paris and in the provinces.

Until 1955, he was much in demand for sculptures, low reliefs and busts; in 1954 he turned to painting, working in both disciplines after 1978, showing a predilection for terracotta sculptures. His best known sets of paintings are: *The Loving Ones, The Proud, Sheperdesses, The Messengers, The Virgilian, Deposition, Great Passion.*

BIBLIOGRAPHY:
Elgar, Frank, *'Peintures de Michel Rousseau'* in *Carrefour des Arts*, periodical, Paris, May 1977. Ray, Lionel, *'Michel Rousseau'* in *L'Humanité*, periodical, Paris, May 1977.

MUSEUMS AND GALLERIES:
PARIS (BNF): *Annunciation* (1967, lithograph).

ROUSSEAU, N.
French, 19th century.
Painter. Landscapes.

MUSEUMS AND GALLERIES:
BREST - LOUVIERS (Mus. municipal): *La Varenne St-Maur; La Varenne St-Hilaire at Sunset.*

AUCTION RECORDS:
PARIS, 30 Jan 1929, *Banks of the Marne*, FRF 150. PARIS, 20 Nov 1950, *River*, FRF 8,100. BERN, 12 May 1990, *Forest of Fontainebleau* (oil on canvas, 9 3/4 x 12 1/2 ins / 25 x 32 cm) CHF 4,800. LYONS, 28 March 1999, *Landscape near Gue. Fishermen* (1896, oil on canvas, a pair, 29 x 32 ins / 73 x 82 cm) FRF 16,000. NEW YORK, 30 April 2001, *Washerwomen* (oil on canvas, 29 x 36 ins / 73 x 92 cm) USD 3,500.

ROUSSEAU, Nicolas Louis
French, 19th century.
Active in Paris in 1815.
Engraver (burin).

ROUSSEAU, Odile
French, 20th century.
Born 1939.
Engraver.

Odile Rousseau produces copper engravings, lithographs, woodcuts and engravings on slate. She featured in the exhibition *Gravures contemporaines en relief* (*Contemporary Relief Engravings*) at the Musée du Dessin et de l'Estampe originale in Gravelines in 1987.

ROUSSEAU, P.
French, 19th century.
Painter. Landscapes.

P. Rousseau, who was probably a drawing teacher in Paris, exhibited several *Views of Italy* and some *Studies of Trees* from life at the Salon in 1812, a *Landscape, Site in the Auvergne* in 1831 and a *View from the Coast of Granville* in 1833.

ROUSSEAU, Peter. See **ROUSSEAU Franz**

ROUSSEAU, Philippe
French, 19th century.
Born 22 February 1816, in Paris; died 5 December 1887, in Acquigny.
Painter, watercolourist. Genre scenes, landscapes with figures, animals, farmyard scenes, still-lifes (flowers/fruit).

Philippe Rousseau was the student of Baron Gros and Édouard Bertin. He first exhibited at the Salon of 1834, winning a third-class medal in 1845 and a second-class medal in 1848. He was made a Chevalier of the Légion d'Honneur in 1852 and an officer on 20 June 1870.In the early stages of his career, he painted mainly landscapes, especially in Normandy, where he developed his skills. Following these preliminary exercises, he painted mainly still-lifes of various kinds of game, but he also took inspiration from the animal fables of Florian and La Fontaine in vivaciously drawn sketches with a chiaroscuro, quasi-Caravaggian use of light that is astonishing in the 19th century.

Success came from 1840 onwards. Vaines nicknamed him 'the Raphael of rabbits' in 1847. In his 'Salon' of 1846, Baudelaire had already noticed him: 'I recently saw, at Durand-Ruel's, some ducks by M. Rousseau that were astoundingly beautiful and had all the duck-like mannerisms and gestures'. Subsequently, success and commissions encouraged him to aim higher. His animal still-lifes, which became more ambitious in a pastiche of the 17th century Dutch painters, lost their original purity, which had at first placed him in the intimist tradition of Chardin. These reservations notwithstanding, he remains one of the group of 19th-century 'minor masters' who give a positive redefinition of the term 'simplistic'.In 1993, the Van Gogh museum in Amsterdam showed a collection of his works. In 2002, his work was represented at the exhibition, *'Hommes De Valeur': Henri Fantin-Latour, Odilon Redon En Tijdgenoten* (*'Men of Worth': Henri Fantin-Latour, Odilon Redon and their Contemporaries*) at the Kröller-Müller museum in Otterlo.

Ph. Rousseau

Ph. Rousseau

BIBLIOGRAPHY:
Leeuw, Ronald de, *Philippe Rousseau, 1816-1887*, exhibition catalogue, Van Gogh Museum, Amsterdam, Waanders Uitgevers, Zwolle, 1993.

MUSEUMS AND GALLERIES:
AMIENS: *Still-life* - BAGNÈRES-DE-BIGORRE: *Cornfield* - BORDEAUX: *Turkeys* - CAEN: *Eighteenth-Century Market* - CARCASSONNE: *Two Friends* - CHARTRES: *Farmyard* - DIEPPE: *Plum Preserves* - LA ROCHELLE: *Hunt in the Marsh* - LE MANS: *Still-life* - LILLE: *Kitchen* - LOUVIERS: *Black Hen* - MOSCOW (Rumiantsev Mus.): *Cock and Hen* - NANTES: *Quest for the Absolute* - PARIS (Mus. d'Orsay): *Stork Having a Siesta; Kid-Goat Nibbling Flowers* - ROUEN: *Un canard Chiens; Cheeses* - VALENCIENNES: *Lunch.*

AUCTION RECORDS:
PARIS, 13 March 1877, *Cat Playing with a Mouse*, FRF 3,000. PARIS, 27 June 1900, *Five O'Clock*, FRF 2,100. PARIS, 15 Nov 1906, *After the Hunt*, FRF 860. PARIS, 25-28 March 1912, *Fountain with Doves*, FRF 8,000. PARIS, 4-5 March 1920, *Oysters and Lobster*, FRF 2,500. PARIS, 18 June 1920, *Town Rat and Field Rat*, FRF 10,100. PARIS, 14 Dec 1925, *Farmyard*, FRF 2,500. PARIS, 5 May 1928, *Christ with Roses*, FRF 1,300. PARIS, 22 May 1931, *Yard in the Farm*, FRF 1,150. PARIS, 9 March 1939, *Cat and Her Kittens* (watercolour) FRF 140. PARIS, 23 June 1941, *Hunting Trophy*, FRF 4,100. PARIS, 26 March 1945, *Lemons and Oranges*, FRF 4,800. PARIS, 31 Jan 1949, *Hunting Trophies*, FRF 5,800. PARIS, 10 Feb 1950, *Two*

Hunting Dogs at the Kennels (watercolour) FRF 4,500. PARIS, 8 June 1951, *Dog and Cat*, FRF 5,800. AMSTERDAM, 20 June 1951, *Still-life with Artichokes* (1868) NLG 1,850. LONDON, 27 July 1973, *Still-life*, Gns 450. PARIS, 8 Nov 1974, *Still-life with Hare*, FRF 6,000. LONDON, 9 April 1976, *Wheatsheaves, Flowers and Birds* (oil on panel, 7 1/2 x 11 ins / 19 x 27 cm) GBP 280. AMSTERDAM, 31 Oct 1977, *Still-life with Flowers* (oil on canvas, 29 x 38 3/4 ins / 73.5 x 98.5 cm) NLG 2,000. LONDON, 18 June 1980, *Still-life with Brioche* (oil on panel, 20 3/4 x 25 1/2 ins / 53 x 65 cm) GBP 2,800. STOCKHOLM, 2 Nov 1983, *Still-life with Flowers* (oil on panel, 15 3/4 x 13 1/2 ins / 40 x 34 cm) SEK 19,500. LONDON, 17 June 1986, *Still-life with Flowers* (oil on canvas, 36 1/2 x 48 3/4 ins / 92.5 x 124 cm) GBP 7,500. MONTE CARLO, 6 Dec 1987, *Tribute to Chardin* (oil on canvas, 25 1/4 x 70 1/2 ins / 64 x 179 cm) FRF 110,000. NEW YORK, 9 June 1988, *Group of Pack Dogs near a Wood* (1832, 26 x 38 1/4 ins / 66 x 97.1 cm) USD 8,800. STOCKHOLM, 15 Nov 1988, *Still-life with Game and Hunting Gear* (oil, 39 1/4 x 30 ins / 100 x 76 cm) SEK 35,000. PARIS, 11 Dec 1989, *Still-life with Hare* (canvas, 47 x 33 ins / 118.5 x 84 cm) FRF 83,000. AMSTERDAM, 25 April 1990, *Still-life with a Crow on Some Cheese* (1883, oil on canvas, 28 3/4 x 39 1/4 ins / 73 x 100 cm) NLG 21,850. MONACO, 16 June 1990, *Still-life with Fruit* (oil on canvas, 13 x 18 ins / 33 x 46 cm) FRF 44,400. STOCKHOLM, 29 May 1991, *Still-life with Asters in a Pot* (oil on panel, 19 3/4 x 13 3/4 ins / 50 x 35 cm) SEK 32,000. NEW YORK, 20 Feb 1992, *Post Chaise in a Craggy Landscape* (1841, oil on canvas, 40 1/4 x 47 ins / 102.2 x 119.4 cm) USD 66,000. CALAIS, 5 April 1992, *Still-life with Fish* (oil on canvas, 18 x 24 ins / 46 x 61 cm) FRF 7,000. MONACO, 2 July 1993, *Musical Monkey* (1862, oil on canvas, 22 x 28 1/4 ins / 55 x 72 cm) FRF 72,150. PARIS, 6 Oct 1993, *Still-life with Bouquet of Flowers and Mirror* (1884, oil on canvas, 51 1/4 x 35 ins / 130 x 88 cm) FRF 105,000. AMSTERDAM, 9 Nov 1993, *Still-life with Plate of Sausages* (1873, oil on canvas, 13 1/2 x 20 ins / 34 x 50.5 cm) NLG 12,075. LONDON, 17 June 1994, *Still-life with Roses, Poppies and Other Flowers with a Straw Hat* (oil on canvas, 21 1/4 x 25 1/2 ins / 54 x 64.7 cm) GBP 5,175. LONDON, 21 Nov 1996, *Roses, Peonies and Carnations in Vases* (oil on canvas, 51 x 38 1/2 ins / 129.5 x 97.7 cm) GBP 9,200. NEW YORK, 25 May 1999, *Still-life with Bread and Cheese* (oil on canvas, 11 x 14 ins / 27 x 35 cm) USD 2,700. PARIS, 21 June 1999, *Woman in a Straw Hat* (1847, oil on canvas, 11 x 21 ins / 27 x 54 cm) FRF 28,500. AMSTERDAM, 18 April 2000, *Still-life with Oysters, Lemons and Chrysanthemums in a Vase* (oil on canvas, 39 x 52 ins / 100 x 132 cm) NLG 100,000. BILLINGSHURST, 24 July 2000, *Study of Two Spaniels* (oil on panel, 4 x 4 ins / 10 x 9 cm) GBP 3,200. DOWNINGTON, 23 Feb 2001, *Two Friends, Interior Scene with Cat Sitting on a Chair with a Parakeet* (oil on canvas, 51 x 34 ins / 130 x 86 cm) USD 25,000. LONDON, 30 March 2001, *Peaches in a Wicker Basket on a Marble-topped Commode* (oil on canvas, 29 x 36 ins / 74 x 92 cm) GBP 12,000. PARIS, 25 March 2002, *Still-life with Oranges* (oil on panel, 10 x 13 ins / 26 x 34 cm) EUR 10,000. LONDON, 17 July 2002, *Still-life with Tulips* (oil on canvas, 39 x 52 ins / 98 x 132 cm) GBP 5,800. STOCKHOLM, 4 June 2003, *Heather - Corner of the Studio* (watercolour, 15 x 20 ins / 37 x 51 cm) SEK 29,000. PARIS, 25 June 2003, *Peaches and Robin* (oil on panel, 11 x 14 ins / 28 x 36 cm) EUR 4,500. PARIS, 7 April 2004, *Caged Parrots. Caged Pigeons* (oil on panel, a pair, 13 x 9 ins / 33 x 24 cm) EUR 4,100. NEUILLY, 9 April 2004, *Puppies Feeding* (1864, oil on canvas, 38 x 51 ins / 97 x 130 cm) EUR 11,100.

ROUSSEAU, Pierre

Belgian, 19th century.

Born 1802, in Iseghem; died 1866, in Bruges.

Sculptor (wood), designer of ornamental architectural features.

ROUSSEAU, Robert Louis

French, 20th century.

Painter, draughtsman. Portraits, landscapes.

Robert Rousseau exhibited at the Salon des Artistes Français, winning a silver medal in 1925.

AUCTION RECORDS:

VERSAILLES, 25 Nov 1990, *Screech Owl* (charcoal and yellow chalk, 15 1/4 x 9 ins / 39 x 23 cm) FRF 3,600. PARIS, 22 March 1993, *Valencia* (oil on canvas, 18 x 22 ins / 46 x 55 cm) FRF 4,000.

ROUSSEAU, Théodore Auguste

French, 19th century.

Born c. 1825, in Saumur; died in California.

Painter. Portraits.

Théodore Rousseau was a student of Léon Cogniet. He exhibited at the Paris Salon in 1853.

MUSEUMS AND GALLERIES:

BUCHAREST (Muz. National de Arta al României): *Landscape* - SAUMUR: *Peace Restoring Prosperity* - VERSAILLES: *Portrait of Jean-Baptiste Nompère de Champagne, Duc de Cadore, Minister for Foreign Affairs.*

AUCTION RECORDS:

PARIS, 2 March 1977, *Young Boy Bearing His Sword on His Shoulder* (oil on canvas, 24 3/4 x 20 3/4 ins / 63 x 53 cm) FRF 5,600.

ROUSSEAU, Théodore or Étienne Pierre Théodore

French, 19th century.

Born 15 April 1812, in Paris; died 22 December 1867, in Barbizon.

Painter, draughtsman, engraver (etching). Landscapes. Barbizon School.

Around the age of 14, Théodore Rousseau made a journey to the Jura as assistant to his uncle, the sculptor Lemaire. This first contact with nature made a strong impression on him that endured throughout his life. On his return to Paris, he was unable to resume his studies at college. Another cousin, the landscape artist Pau de St-Martin, accepted Rousseau in his studio. Under his supervision, Rousseau made his first studies, mainly in the Compiègne region, including *View of the Cemetery and the Telegraph Tower on Montmartre*, which Rousseau still held in high regard at the end of his life.

Rousseau was not even 16 when his family decided he should enter the competition for the Prix de Rome. He first went to Rémond's studio to study illustration, later joining Guyon Lethières' studio. This new form of study did not appeal to Rousseau who was attracted to representations of what he saw as the simplicity of nature and not to the classical studies his different masters imposed on him.

After a long period of work in the forest of Compiègne and the Chevreuse valley, Rousseau sought out the forest of Fontainebleau for its romantic views. He began work in the Loing valley and his first subject was that of the *Mill* and the *Footbridge*. This was in 1830, when Rousseau was only just 18.

He spent a summer in the Auvergne and on his return, his works made a powerful impression on Guyon Lethières. In 1832, he tried to reproduce nature in the style of Constable and of Bonington, whose works he admired, and he went to work in Brittany to where these two painters had travelled. He was inspired by the Normandy coast and Brittany, and he especially liked Granville, finding an appeal in the powerful colouring of the cliffs and the violent tonalities of the seaweed at low tide.

Despite his highly individual interpretation of nature, his works convey something of his study of the Dutch masters whom he venerated and sought to imitate as closely as possible. In the Fontainebleau period, the Bellecroix plateau became his favourite place: he would paint there in all weathers. The Louvre owns a small picture from this period; a valuable product of his reflections.

Around 1835 Ary Scheffer invited Rousseau to his studio where he became influenced by the romanticist movement.

Repeated rejections by the official Salon caused a drop in the public's interest in Rousseau's work and he was unable to sell it. He took refuge in the forest of Fontainebleau, where he lived almost all year round, studying nature.

Despite his exile from the Salon, Rousseau had strong supporters among contemporary and successful artists: Diaz, Thoré, Barye and Jules Dupré all appreciated his talent. Around 1842, Rousseau had falled on such hard times that he was working for his inn-keeper when Dupré sent him 500 francs on behalf of Paul Perrier as an advance for one of his canvases.

Dupré had a strong influence on Rousseau at that time and taught him composition. Between 1840 and 1850, the two artists often shared a house. In around 1842, Rousseau made a journey to Berry on Dupré's advice. During these six months of solitude, he produced the bleakest pictures of his entire work such as *Edge of the Wood*. In 1844, another journey to the Landes in the company of Jules Dupré is recalled in his picture *Marsh in the Landes*. In this work, he attains his art of interpreting distances and it is essentially from this point that he interprets light with particular feeling. He brought back from this journey two grisailles, the *Village Oven* and the *Farm in Les Landes*, He painted his *Hoar-Frost Effect* and the *Forest in Winter*.

From around 1848, Rousseau worked to a large extent from previous studies; it was then that he reworked *Farm in the Landes* and the *Village Oven*. It is mainly in his drawings that Rousseau gives free rein to his naturalism. His picture of 1857, *View of the Caves at Apremont*, demonstrates that he does not interpret nature as he feels it but rather with a vision like that of Poussin.

In 1867, the sale of Rousseau's studio brought him a substantial sum and as a result he began acquiring rare proofs by Rembrandt and Japanese prints. He died, a the end of that year, at the height of his success.

Rousseau had obtained the following awards: in 1834, a third-class medal; in 1849, a first-class medal; a knighthood in the Légion d'Honneur on 16 July 1852; a first-class medal in 1855; a medal of honour in 1867; and he was made an officer in the Légion d'Honneur on 7 August 1867.

In 1831, he exhibited for the first time at the Louvre Salon with a *Valley Bordered by the Cantal Mountains*. In 1832, he submitted to the Salon *Coast of Granville*. In spite of his great talent, Rousseau was systematically rejected by the classicists at the Salon. The Salon finally opened its doors to him in 1848 and he was able to show his works to the general public. It was at this moment also that Jeauron procured for him an official commission: *Edge of the Forest of Fontainebleau*, currently at the Louvre, a work which he was paid 4000 francs for. At the Exposition Universelle of 1855, a room was reserved for Rousseau and Decamps' work.

After 1848, Rousseau preferred solitude despite his successes and he moved to Barbizon permanently. Many friends came to visit. Millet, among others, became a close friend.

In the 20th century, he featured in the thematic collective exhibition, *Between Heaven and Earth: Camille Pissarro and the Painters of the Oise Valley* at the Musée Tavet-Delacour, Pontoise, in 2003.

TH.Rousseau

TH. Rousseau THR

Stamps of sale

TH.Rousseau

BIBLIOGRAPHY:

Bouret, Jean, *The Barbizon School and 19th century French Landscape*, London, 1973. Miquel, Pierre, *Le Paysage français au XIXe siècle (1824-1874). L'École de la nature*, periodical, Éd. de la Martinelle, Maurs-la-Jolie, 1975. *The John Tillotson Bequest: paintings and drawings of the Barbizon School*, Fitzwilliam Museum, Cambridge, 1986. *Shadow of the Forest: Prints of the Barbizon School*, British Museum, London, 1993. Adams, Steven, *The Barbizon School and the Origins of Impressionism*, Phaidon Press, London, 1994. Schulman, Michel, *Théodore Rousseau - Catalogue raisonné de l'œuvre graphique*, periodical, Éd. de l'Amateur, Paris, 1996. Schuman, Michel, *Théodore Rousseau, 1812-1867*, group exhibition catalogue, periodical, Paris, 1997. Schulman, Michel, *Théodore Rousseau - Catalogue raisonné de l'œuvre peint*, periodical, Éd. de l'Amateur, Paris, 1999. Thomas, Greg M., *Art and Ecology in 19th century France: the landscapes of Théodore Rousseau*, Princeton University Press, 2000. *Entre ciel et terre, Camille Pissaro et les peintres de la vallée de l'Oise*, group exhibition catalogue, periodical, Musée Tavet-Delacour, Pontoise, Éd. Somogy, Paris, 2003.

MUSEUMS AND GALLERIES:

AMSTERDAM: *Cave with Wolves* - AMSTERDAM (Stedelijk Mus.): *Great Oak*; *Rainbow* - ANN ARBOR (University of Michigan Mus. of Art): 2 drawings - BAYONNE (Mus. Bonnat): *Study of Rocks* - BEAUFORT: *Cottage in Berry* - BESANÇON: *Landscape* - BÉZIERS: *Avenue of Trees* - BOSTON: *Landscape* - BREST (MBA): *Sunset* (attributed) - BRUSSELS: *Paris* - CHANTILLY: *Landscape* - COPENHAGEN (Statens Mus. for Kunst): *Meadow near the Forest*; *Landscape with a Marsh*; *Tree by the Edge of the Water* - DALLAS (MA): *Charcoal-Burners' Cabin* (c. 1850, oil on canvas); *Rock Oaks* (1861, etching) - DETROIT: *Landscape* - DIJON: *Landscape* - GLASGOW: *Heath*; *Forest of Clairbois* - LILLE: *The Seine at Villeneuve-St-Georges* - LONDON (NG): *Sunset in the Auvergne* (1830, oil/wood); others landscapes - LONDON (Wallace Collection): *The Forest at Fountainebleau: Morning* (c. 1850, oil on canvas) - MONTPELLIER: *Pond*; *Edge of the Forest of Clairbois* - MOSCOW (State Tretyakov Gal.): *Barbizon*; *Interior in Forest of Fontainebleau*; *Near a Watering Place* - NANTES: *Meadows and River*; *Cows at the Watering Place* - NEW YORK (Metropolitan Mus. of Art): *River*; *Forest*; *Corner of a Forest*; *Landscape*; *Fontainebleau*; *Trees around a Pond*; *Path through the Rocks* (1861); *Meadow Bordered by Trees* (c. 1845); *Sunset in Winter* - NICE: *Sunset* - PARIS (Louvre): *Sunset at Fontainebleau*; *Le vieux Dormoir au Bas-Bréau*; *Marsh in the Landes*; *River Bank*; *Impression of a Storm*; *Banks of the Loire*; *Ferryman*; *Hillside*; *Landscape*; *Oaks*; *Plain*; *Village under the Trees*; *Spring*; *Fisherboy*; *Pond*; *Landscape with Animals*; *Pond with Oaks*; *Edge of the Forest of Fontainebleau*; *Avenue of Chestnut Trees at the Château in Souliers*; *The Coalmen Hut* (oil on canvas) - PARIS (Louvre, Chauchard Collection): *Avenue, Isle-Adam Forest*; *Pond near the Road*; *Pond at the Foot of the Hillside*; *Footbridge*; *Road in the Forest of Fontainebleau*; *Cart*; *Pond* - RHEIMS (MBA): *Watering Place* (study) - THE HAGUE (Mus. Mesdag): *Descent of the Cattle in the Jura*; *Mountain Landscape*; *Rocky Landscape*; *Small Pond*; *Water-*

course in a Valley in Berry; Old Oak near Fontainebleau; Cut Trees (Fontainebleau); View of a Wood; Landscape with Trees; Great Oaks of Old Bas-Bréau; Road.

AUCTION RECORDS:

PARIS, 1849, *Spring Landscape,* FRF 15,100. PARIS, 1858, *Farm in the Landes,* FRF 4,000. PARIS, 1858, *Group of Oaks in the Forest of Fontainebleau,* FRF 8,200. PARIS, 1868, *Château and Valley of Broglie,* FRF 9,700. PARIS, 1868, *Oaks and Wild Apple Trees at the Shelter in the Caves of Apremont,* FRF 15,000; *Forest in Winter,* FRF 10,000. PARIS, 1868, *Rock Oak,* FRF 18,000. PARIS, 1870, *After the Rain, Berry,* FRF 39,000; *Edge of the Forest at Sunset in Bas-Bréau,* FRF 17,900. PARIS, 1872, *Pond,* FRF 20,000. PARIS, 1872, *Group of Trees near a Watercourse,* FRF 29,200. PARIS, 1873, *Goatherds,* FRF 35,500. PARIS, 1873, *Hoar-Frost,* FRF 60,100; *Women Cutting Wood, Fontainebleau,* FRF 36,000; *Watercourse in Sologne near Romorantin,* FRF 40,000. PARIS, 1878, *Marsh in the Landes,* FRF 38,000; *Charcoal-Burners' Cabin,* FRF 182,500. PARIS, 1881, *Le Vieux Dormoir du Bas-Bréau* FRF 49,000. PARIS, 1881, *Marsh in the Landes,* FRF 129,000; *Farm in the Landes,* FRF 73,000. PARIS, 1883, *Cottage* (drawing heightened with colour) FRF 5,000. NEW YORK, 1885, *Landscape,* FRF 50,000; *Banks of the Oise,* FRF 62,500. PARIS, 1889, *Charcoal-Burners' Cabin,* FRF 75,500. PARIS, 1891, *Pond, View at Fontainebleau,* FRF 82,100. PARIS, 1891, *Pond with Oak,* FRF 90,000; *Footbridge,* FRF 72,000. NEW YORK, 1892, *Forest in Winter at Sunset,* FRF 45,000; *Forest at Compiègne,* FRF 38,500. PARIS, 1893, *Pond at Dagnan on the Bellecroix Plateau,* FRF 40,000. PARIS, 1894, *Under the Wood,* FRF 48,500. PARIS, 1897, *Valley of Tiffauge,* FRF 77, 500. PARIS, 1898, *Fontainebleau Surroundings,* FRF 46,000. PARIS, 1898, *In the Forest* (drawing) FRF 6,000. NEW YORK, 1898, *Marsh in the Landes,* FRF 38,000; *Charcoal-Burners' Cabin,* FRF 182,500. PARIS, 1900, *Village Oven* (watercolour) FRF 6,000. PARIS, 13 March 1902, *Fallow Plain,* FRF 5,300. PARIS, 26-27 May 1902, *Banks of the Oise,* FRF 54,500. PARIS, 26 May 1905, *In the Forest,* FRF 30,000. PARIS, 4-5 Dec 1905, *Pond in the Forest,* FRF 110,000. NEW YORK, 25 Jan 1907, *Impression of Sun,* FRF 108,000; *Landscape in Sologne,* FRF 32,000; *Dusk,* FRF 50,000. NEW YORK, 27 Jan 1907, *Sun Ray,* USD 21,600; *Dusk,* USD 10,000. NEW YORK, 26 Feb 1909, *Farm,* USD 11,700. NEW YORK, 19 March 1909, *Summer Morning in the Oise,* USD 14,500; *Edge of a Wood,* USD 11,000. PARIS, April 1910, *Valley of Tiffauge,* FRF 50,000; *Landscape in Berry,* FRF 130,500. LONDON, 30 June 1910, *Landscape,* GBP 483. PARIS, 8-10 May 1911, *Landscape,* FRF 4,500. PARIS, 5-6 Dec 1911, *Path,* FRF 45,000. PARIS, 2 March 1912, *Landscape, Granville,* FRF 5,300. PARIS, 30 May -1 June 1912, *Avenue of Chestnut-Trees,* FRF 270,000; *Neck of the Sickle,* FRF 67,500. PARIS, 9-11 Dec 1912, *View of the Town of Bressuire,* FRF 5,300; *Landscape,* FRF 20,100. PARIS, 25 Nov 1918, *Bridge at Moret,* FRF 25,000; *Watch-House,* FRF 135,000. PARIS, 26-27 Feb 1919, *Farms in the Trees,* FRF 12,600. PARIS, 16-19 June 1919, *Fontainebleau Surroundings,* FRF 6,700; *Fallow Plain* (watercolour) FRF 8,000; *Cottage in Foliage* (pen and water-colour wash) FRF 2,020. PARIS, 17 Nov 1919, *Greak Oak on the River Bank at Le Fay,* FRF 1,850. PARIS, 26 Nov 1919, *Cottages,* FRF 1,920. PARIS, 6-7 May 1920, *Houses at the Foot of Mont St Michel,* FRF 19,500; *Town of Thiers,* FRF 19,100; *Road,* FRF 9,200. PARIS, 2-4 June 1920, *Barbizon Plain,* FRF 6,500; *Forest* (charcoal) FRF 6,100. PARIS, 30 Nov -2 Dec 1920, *Staircase of the Château de Blois* (watercolour) FRF 3,100. PARIS, 11-12 Feb 1921, *Old Bridge at St-Cloud,* FRF 11,000; *Sea Seen from the Cliffs,* FRF 2,400. PARIS, 4-5 March 1921, *Beeches in the Forest of Fontainebleau* (watercolour) FRF 2,650; *View of the Girard Mountains, Impression of Winter* (pen and wash) FRF 1,050. PARIS, 29 April 1921, *Small Oak Wood* (heightened drawing) FRF 9,400. PARIS, 7 July 1921, *Crossing at the Ford,* FRF 1,300. PARIS, 3-4 Dec 1923, *Landscape* (watercolour) FRF 7,600; *River,* FRF 41,000. LONDON, 15 Feb 1924, *Sunset,* GBP 147. LONDON, 9 May 1924, *Landscape with a Cavalier,* GBP 945. PARIS, 16 June 1925, *Small Wood on the Barbizon Plain* (watercolour) FRF 1,900; *Château de Chenonceaux* (watercolour) FRF 3,220. PARIS, 20 Nov 1925, *Horses at the Stable,* FRF 1,080. PARIS, 22 Jan 1927, *Moonlight at the Clearing, Forest of Fontainebleau,* FRF 4,000. PARIS, 23 May 1927, *Landscape* (lead pencil) FRF 2,700. LONDON, 10 June 1927, *Hunt,* GBP 136. PARIS, 17 June 1927, *Landscape,* FRF 11,200. PARIS, 20 June 1927, *Evening Landscape,* FRF 3,700. LONDON, 8 July 1927, *Crossroads of the White Queen,* GBP 483. LONDON, 22 July 1927, *Forest of Fontainebleau,* GBP 84. LONDON, 30 March 1928, *Rocks,* GBP 105. PARIS, 26 June 1928, *Watercourse Bordered by Trees,* FRF 15,700; *Ruins of a Village in the Auvergne,* FRF 13,000. LONDON, 19 April 1929, *Banks of the Pond* (pastel) GBP 47; *View of Chailly,* GBP 115. PARIS, 6-7 May 1929, *Mont Chauvet, Brûlé Plateau, Forest of Fontainebleau,* FRF 40,000. PARIS, 17 May 1929, *Marsh in Bourgogne,* FRF 23,000. PARIS, 26 June 1929, *Avenue of Chestnut Trees* (drawing) FRF 15,300; *Countryside at Dusk,* FRF 19,100. NEW YORK, 15 Nov 1929, *Storm,* USD 550. NEW YORK, 10 April 1930, *Landscape Study,* USD 600. PARIS, 17 May 1930, *Auvergne Landscape,* FRF 3,500; *Road in the Jura,* FRF 4,500. PARIS, 27 May 1930, *Plain at Chailly,* FRF 64,100. NEW YORK, 12 Nov 1931, *Old Bridge,* USD 1,000; *Sunset after a Rainy Day,* USD 1,900. NEW YORK, 15-16 Jan 1932, *Grazing,* USD 425. PARIS, 4 March 1932, *Corner of a Forest* (lead pencil) FRF 800. PARIS, 9 Dec 1932, *Hilly Landscape* (sepia wash) FRF 1,470. NEW YORK, 7-8 Dec 1933, *Banks of a Lake,* USD 350. PARIS, 8 May 1934, *Study of Trees* (lead pencil heightened with white) FRF 1,250. NEW YORK, 11 May 1934, *Edge of a Wood,* USD 4,200. NEW YORK, 23 Nov 1934, *Copse of Trees,* USD 5,000. PARIS, 7 Dec 1934, *Château de Chambord* (watercolour) FRF 4,500. PARIS, 29 Nov 1935, *Woodcutter,* FRF 23,600. PARIS, 23 June 1936, *Angler,* FRF 28,000. NEW YORK, 3 Dec 1936, *Lake at Dusk,* USD 225. NEW YORK, 3 Feb 1938, *Before the Storm,* USD 370. PARIS, 6 March 1940, *Landscape* (drawing heightened with white) FRF 700. PARIS, 11 July 1941, *Rocks at Fontainebleau,* FRF 30,000. NEW YORK, 17 Jan 1942, *Forest of Compiègne,* USD 3,500. PARIS, 25 March 1942, *Sunset; Landscape at the Riverside* (two sketches) FRF 31,000. PARIS, 23 Dec 1942, *Landscape,* FRF 21,000. NEW YORK, 25 Feb 1943, *Marsh in the Landes,* USD 375. NICE, 25 May 1943, *Mill at Batigny,* FRF 20,500. NEW YORK, 15 Jan 1944, *Road in the Forest,* USD 1,000. NEW YORK, 4 May 1944, *Pond in the Rocks,* USD 725. PARIS, 17 May 1944, *Hay Carts at Sunset,* FRF 39,000; *Pond in the Early Morning,* FRF 150,000. PARIS, 24 Jan 1945, *Road* (pen) FRF 15,000. NEW YORK, 15 March 1945, *Farm,* USD 975; *Barbizon,* USD 500; *Morning,* USD 1,400; *Edge of a Forest,* USD 1,800. PARIS, 22 June 1945, *River* (watercolour) FRF 10,500. NEW YORK, 13 Dec 1945, *Landscape,* USD 425; *Close of Day,* USD 400. NEW YORK, 20-21 Feb 1946, *River Banks,* USD 575. CAIRO, 14-23 March 1947, *Landscape,* EGP 17,100. AMSTERDAM, 15-21 April 1947, *Rock Oak,* NLG 8,200. PARIS, 20 June 1947, *Cows Grazing,* FRF 20,000. PARIS, 24 Dec 1948, *Brulis Wood on the Macherin Plain* (1860, Indian ink and watercolour/panel) FRF 69,000. PARIS, 28 Jan 1949, *Landscape,* FRF 23,000. PARIS, 17 Feb 1949, *Woman Gathering Firewood* (lead pencil) FRF 21,000. PARIS, 23 Nov 1949, *Angler* (lead pencil, light strokes heightened with white) FRF 12,000. PARIS, 1 Feb 1950, *Pavilion by the Waterside* (watercolour) FRF 6,200. PARIS, 20 March 1950, *Landscape* (pen) FRF 37,000. BOBIGNY, 2 April 1950, *Undergrowth,* FRF 13,000. PARIS, 20 Nov 1950, *Evening in the Countryside,* FRF 65,500. PARIS, 27 Nov 1950, *Rocks at Fontainebleau,* FRF 10,000; *Landscape with Pond* (lead pencil) FRF 10,000. PARIS, 11 Dec 1950, *Plain in the Sun* (watercolour) FRF 33,000. PARIS, 5 Feb 1951, *Sunset* (pastel) FRF 24,000. GENEVA, 10 March 1951, *Rocks in the Forest of Fontainebleau,* CHF 750. LONDON, 14 March 1951, *Forest of Fontainebleau,* GBP 200. LONDON, 11 May 1951, *Clearing in the*

Forest of Barbizon, GBP 72. VIENNA, 31 May 1951, *Rocks in the Forest of Barbizon*, ATS 4,500. PARIS, 28 June 1951, *Forest of Fontainebleau* (pen) FRF 15,000. PARIS, 15 June 1954, *Cavalier in a Storm*, FRF 110,000. NEW YORK, 27 March 1956, *Evening*, USD 1,800. PARIS, 3 Dec 1957, *Edge of the Bois de Macherin near the Barbizon Plain* (watercolour) FRF 310,000. LONDON, 9 July 1958, *Marsh in the Landes*, GBP 2,100. LONDON, 25 Nov 1959, *Landscape in the Auvergne*, GBP 600. PARIS, 9 May 1960, *Mountainous Landscape*, FRF 6,100. LONDON, 7 July 1960, *Landscape with Furrowed Fields* (pen and brown ink) GBP 500. PARIS, 23 June 1961, *Auvergne Landscape*, FRF 7,500. LONDON, 28 June 1961, *Valley in the Mountains*, GBP 500. PARIS, 19 June 1963, *Petit Pont (Petit Pont (Small Bridge))* (watercolour) FRF 7,000. NEW YORK, 6 Nov 1963, *Landscape in Berry*, USD 4,750. LONDON, 19 June 1964, *Pond*, Gns 1,800. LONDON, 29 Nov 1967, *Clearing in the Forest*, GBP 3,400. LONDON, 6 Dec 1968, *Village in the Auvergne*, Gns 3,400. LONDON, 3 July 1970, *Landscape*, Gns 1,500. PARIS, 4 Dec 1972, *Clearing*, FRF 135,000. NEW YORK, 2 May 1973, *Landscape with River*, USD 14,000. PARIS, 23 Jan 1974, *Mont Blanc* (watercolour and gouache) FRF 14,000. NEW YORK, 9 Oct 1974, *Troupeau au bord d'un étang* USD 14,000. NEW YORK, 15 Oct 1976, *Forest of Fontainebleau* (oil on panel, 16 x 24 3/4 ins / 40.5 x 63 cm) USD 16,000. MUNICH, 24 May 1977, *Wooded Landscape with Pond* (c. 1845, oil on canvas, 30 x 37 1/2 ins / 76 x 95 cm) DEM 14,500. PARIS, 22 Nov 1977, *Wooded Landscape (Forest of Fontainebleau)* (pen, heightened with watercolour, 4 3/4 x 7 3/4 ins / 12 x 20 cm) FRF 40,000. LONDON, 6 Dec 1977, *Wood at the Edge of an Estuary* (watercolour/black chalk, 8 3/4 x 13 1/4 ins / 22.5 x 33.5 cm) GBP 1,000. NEW YORK, 26 Jan 1979, *Landscape with Cloudy Sky* (oil on panel, 16 3/4 x 20 ins / 42.5 x 51 cm) USD 26,000. PARIS, 16 May 1979, *Sheep Pen near the Road to Chaillly* (Indian ink wash heightened with white, 7 1/4 x 7 ins / 18.5 x 17.5 cm) FRF 16,500. NEW YORK, 11 Feb 1981, *Cows and Sheep in a Landscape* (c. 1855, 16 1/2 x 24 1/2 ins / 42 x 62 cm) USD 26,000. NEW YORK, 27 May 1983, *Path in the Undergrowth* (pen and wash, 7 1/4 x 10 1/2 ins / 18.4 x 26.7 cm) USD 6,000. NEW YORK, 27 Oct 1983, *Wooded Landscape with Pond, Morning* (oil on panel, 11 3/4 x 21 1/4 ins / 29.8 x 54 cm) USD 25,000. NEW YORK, 16 Nov 1983, *Pleasure Boat* (watercolour/pencil outlines, 6 1/4 x 11 ins / 16 x 27.7 cm) USD 10,000. PARIS, 20 Nov 1985, *Landscape* (watercolour, 4 1/4 x 9 1/4 ins / 11 x 23.5 cm) FRF 20,000. NEW YORK, 28 Oct 1986, *Wooded Landscape with Pond* (oil on canvas, 20 x 30 ins / 50.7 x 76.2 cm) USD 19,000. NEW YORK, 3 Feb 1988, *Sunset at Barbizon* (oil on panel, 17 x 25 1/2 ins / 43 x 65 cm) USD 99,000. MONACO, 20 Feb 1988, *Forest of Fontainebleau* (pencil, 5 x 7 3/4 ins / 12.5 x 19.5 cm) FRF 12,765. VERSAILLES, 21 Feb 1988, *Landscape* (pen, 4 3/4 x 6 1/4 ins / 12 x 16 cm) FRF 4,000. PARIS, 11 March 1988, *Pond with Rocks* (oil on panel, 11 1/2 x 17 1/4 ins / 29 x 43.5 cm) FRF 21,000. PARIS, 16 May 1988, *Landscape near Fontainebleau* (watercolour, 5 x 7 ins / 13 x 18 cm) FRF 12,000. COLOGNE, 15 Oct 1988, *Autumn Landscape with Woman Leading Her Cows along the Road* (oil on panel, 8 1/4 x 13 3/4 ins / 21 x 35 cm) DEM 18,000. BERN, 26 Oct 1988, *Mountainous Landscape* (oil on canvas, 17 1/4 x 13 3/4 ins / 44 x 35 cm) CHF 3,200. NEW YORK, 23 Feb 1989, *Women Gathering Firewood in a Wooded Landscape* (oil on panel, 6 x 9 1/4 ins / 15.2 x 23.2 cm) USD 20,900. PARIS, 14 June 1989, *Sunken Lane Leading to a Group of Trees* (oil on paper remounted/canvas) FRF 42,000. LONDON, 20 June 1989, *Figure in a Boat in a Summer Landscape* (oil on canvas, 29 1/4 x 36 1/2 ins / 74 x 93 cm) GBP 93,500. NEW YORK, 25 Oct 1989, *Figure on a Path in a Vast Forest Landscape* (oil on panel, 23 1/2 x 29 ins / 59.7 x 73.7 cm) USD 88,000. NEW YORK, 23 May 1990, *Village of Falgouse in Cantal* (oil on canvas, 11 1/2 x 16 1/2 ins / 28.9 x 41.9 cm) USD 132,000. BARBIZON, 9 June 1990, *Landscape with Pond* (oil and charcoal/paper/canvas, 14 x 20 ins / 35.5 x 50.5 cm) FRF 400,000. PARIS, 22 June 1990, *Avenue of Chestnut Trees* (pen, sepia wash, 7 1/2 x 14 3/4 ins / 18.9 x 37.7 cm) FRF 145,000. NEW YORK, 22 May 1991, *Path in a Clearing on the Heath* (oil on panel, 14 3/4 x 26 1/4 ins / 37.5 x 66.7 cm) USD 55,000. LONDON, 19 June 1991, *Peasant in the Forest of Fontainebleau* (oil on panel, 4 3/4 x 7 1/4 ins / 12 x 18.5 cm) GBP 14,850. MONACO, 6 Dec 1991, *Seine Valley and Paris from the Heights of Meudon* (oil on paper/panel, 8 3/4 x 12 3/4 ins / 22.5 x 32.5 cm) FRF 57,720. PARIS, 3 Feb 1992, *Landscape* (lead pencil and stump, 2 3/4 x 4 3/4 ins / 7.3 x 12 cm) FRF 4,600. NEW YORK, 27 May 1992, *Sunset* (oil on canvas, 10 1/4 x 19 3/4 ins / 26.3 x 50.2 cm) USD 44,000. PARIS, 12 June 1992, *View of a Pond near a Cottage* (pen and wash heightened with watercolour, 5 x 7 1/4 ins / 12.5 x 18.5 cm) FRF 55,000. NEW YORK, 17 Feb 1993, *Sunset in the Landes near Begaar* (oil on canvas, 40 x 34 1/4 ins / 101.6 x 87 cm) USD 123,500. PARIS, 24 Feb 1993, *Site in Berry* (1842, etching) FRF 9,000. PARIS, 2 April 1993, *Shepherdess and Her Flock in the Forest* (1841, oil on panel, 12 1/4 x 16 3/4 ins / 31 x 42.5 cm) FRF 155,000. RIOM, 20 June 1993, *Landscape* (pen, wash, watercolour and gouache, 5 x 7 ins / 13 x 18 cm) FRF 59,500. FONTAINEBLEAU, 28 Nov 1993, *Landscape with Pond, Fontainebleau Area* (oil on panel, 21 x 23 1/2 ins / 53.5 x 60 cm) FRF 300,000. PARIS, 16 Dec 1993, *Woman Gathering Firewood* (lead pencil, 7 x 9 1/4 ins / 18 x 23.5 cm) FRF 100,000. PARIS, 13 June 1994, *Rocks at the Edge of a Forest* (1842, sepia wash heightened with white/paper/canvas, 25 1/4 x 37 ins / 64 x 94 cm) FRF 380,000. LONDON, 15 June 1994, *Road to Paris in the Forest of Fontainebleau* (watercolour and pencil, 5 x 8 1/4 ins / 13 x 21 cm) GBP 17,250. PARIS, 15 Dec 1994, *Undergrowth*. POITIERS, 28 Jan 1995, *Clearing with Figures* (1839, oil on paper/canvas, 12 1/2 x 15 3/4 ins / 32 x 40 cm) FRF 255,000. LONDON, 11 April 1995, *Ploughing in the Arbois Region* (oil on panel, 12 1/2 x 20 1/2 ins / 32 x 52 cm) GBP 45,500. NEW YORK, 2 April 1996, *Farm at Dusk* (oil on panel, 7 x 12 ins / 17.8 x 30.5 cm) USD 26,450. NEW YORK, 22 May 1996, *Mont St Michel* (oil on canvas) USD 59,700. NEW YORK, 23-24 May 1996, *Herdsman near a Pond* (pencil, ink, ink wash and watercolour/paper, 5 x 7 1/4 ins / 13 x 18.1 cm) USD 33,350. PARIS, 20 June 1996, *Study of a Tree* (Indian ink/paper, 5 x 7 ins / 13 x 18 cm) FRF 8,500. LONDON, 21 Nov 1996, *Cottage near Granville, Normandy* (pencil and brown, grey and yellow inks, watercolour, 4 x 13 ins / 10.1 x 32.1 cm) GBP 5,750. PARIS, 26 Nov 1996, *Landscapes* (pen and brown ink, a pair framed together, 4 1/2 x 6 1/4 ins / 11.2 x 15.7 cm; 4 1/4 x 7 1/2 ins/10.7 x 19 cm) FRF 11,000. PARIS, 16 March 1997, *Tall Poplar on the Barbizon Plain, Sunset* (1856-1857, oil on panel, 11 1/2 x 23 1/4 ins / 29 x 59 cm) FRF 30,000. PARIS, 10 June 1997, *View of the Bellecroix Plateau* (1848 or 1849, etching, 7 3/4 x 10 ins / 20 x 25.7 cm) FRF 11,000. LONDON, 11 June 1997, *Woman and Child in a Wooded Landscape* (watercolour heightened with white, 8 1/2 x 13 1/4 ins / 21.5 x 33.5 cm) GBP 16,100. LONDON, 1 Dec 1999, *Bare Trees in an Arid Landscape* (pen and ink wash, 4 x 5 ins / 11 x 13 cm) GBP 8,000. LONDON, 1 Dec 1999, *Landscape with Horse and Cart* (oil on panel, 23 x 28 ins / 59 x 71 cm) GBP 52,000. PARIS, 31 March 2000, *Edge of Bas Breau* (pencil, 19 x 24 ins / 47 x 61 cm) FRF 170,000. NEW YORK, 1 May 2000, *Sunset over the Barbizon Plain* (oil on panel, 16 x 26 ins / 41 x 65 cm) USD 320,000. NEW YORK, 1 May 2001, *Forest at Fontainebleau* (oil on panel, 12 x 15 ins / 30 x 39 cm) USD 50,000. PARIS, 21 Dec 2001, *Pond in the Forest of Fontainebleau* (oil on panel, 13 x 17 ins / 33 x 44 cm) FRF 455,000. NEW YORK, 23 Jan 2002, *Chestnut Avenue* (pencil and ink wash heightened with white, 14 x 7 ins / 36 x 19 cm) USD 14,000. NEW YORK, 24 April 2002, *Pond with Fairies in the Forest of Fontainebleau* (oil on canvas, 23 x 45 ins / 59 x 114 cm) USD 85,000. NEW YORK, 24 April 2003, *Banks of the Oise* (oil on panel, 16 x 25 ins / 41 x 64 cm) USD 85,000. NEW YORK, 28 Oct 2003, *Forest Track* (watercolour and gouache on panel, 11 x 17 ins / 28 x 42 cm) USD 37,500. PARIS, 30 March 2004, *Forest Landscape with Trees and Rocks, Fontainbleau* (pastel and charcoal on panel, 17 x 24 ins / 43 x 62 cm) EUR 12,000. NEW YORK, 23 April 2004, *Sun Setting over the Sands of Jean-de-Paris* (oil on canvas, 35 x 46 ins / 90 x 117 cm) USD 485,000.

ROUSSEAU, Victor

Belgian, 19th - 20th century.

Born 16 December 1865, in Feluy (Ardennes); died 1954, in Brussels.

Sculptor, painter, draughtsman, watercolourist. Figures. Monuments.

Symbolism.

Victor Rousseau studied at the Brussels and St Joost-ten-Node academies before enrolling at the fine arts academy in Brussels, where he studied under Charles van Stappen. He visited France and England and, as a 1894 Prix de Rome laureate, Italy. He went on to teach and subsequently serve as principal of the Brussels academy. In his day, Rousseau was reputed as a sculptor, as exemplified in his *Monument to Belgian Gratitude* in London. His output was considerable, ranging from a *César Franck* monument in Liège to his *Sisters of Illusion*. Rousseau's declared ambition was to translate man's spiritual state into sculpture; that said, his delicate yet sentimental approach was decidedly turn-of-the-century and, as such, his work was largely dismissed by later generations (*Idle Gossip* or *Encounter*, for example). This notwithstanding, he was commissioned to work on numerous public buildings, including the Cinquentenaire monument in Brussels. He took part in exhibitions organised by the Libre Esthétique in Belgium, Art Nouveau in France and the Royal Academy Summer Exhibitions in London (1917 and 1918). His work was also shown at the Exposition Universelle in Paris in 1900. A Rousseau retrospective was organised at the Palais des Beaux-Arts in Brussels in 1933.

MUSEUMS AND GALLERIES:

ANTWERP: *Child* - BERLIN: *Bust of Constantin Meunier* - BRUSSELS: *Demeter; To Life; Memories; Sisters of Illusion; Bust of Constantin Meunier; Awakening; Princess Marie José of Belgium; Marie, Countess of Flanders; Eugène Ysaye, Violinist; Persian Dancer; Secret; Masque of Peace; Summer Figure; Sleeping Child; Woman Kissing Beethoven's Death Mask; Woman Drinking from a Goblet; Young Woman with Flowing Tresses; Delight; Young Woman.*

AUCTION RECORDS:

BRUSSELS, 23 April 1974, *Masked Athlete* (bronze) BEF 44,000. ANTWERP, 19 Oct 1976, *Bust of a Young Woman* (1922, bronze, H.20¾ ins / 53 cm) BEF 30,000. BRUSSELS, 24 Nov 1981, *Bust of a Young Woman* (marble, H.17¼ ins / 44 cm) BEF 46,000. LONDON, 10 Nov 1983, *Fairy Tale* (patinated bronze, h. 26 ins / 66 cm) GBP 1,500. LONDON, 21 March 1985, *Woman with Mandoline* (brown-patinated bronze, h. 30 ins / 76 cm) GBP 1,400. LOKEREN, 19 April 1986, *Dionysos* (1925, green-patinated bronze, h. 30 ins / 76 cm) BEF 300,000. LOKEREN, 28 May 1988, *Young Woman* (1941, terracotta, h. 22 ins / 55 cm) BEF 38,000. LOKEREN, 11 March 1995, *Rapture* (bronze, h. 19¼ ins / 49 cm, w. 16¼ ins/41 cm) BEF 190,000. NEW YORK, 18 March 1998, *Youthfulness* (1906, marble, 24¾ ins / 62.9 cm) USD 9,775. BRUSSELS, 14 June 1999, *Prayer for Peace* (1938, golden patinated bronze, 18 x 25x12 ins / 45 x 63x31 cm) BEF 280,000. BRUSSELS, 14 June 1999, *Rapture* (dark patinated bronze, 20 x 16x9 ins / 52 x 41x22 cm) BEF 290,000. BRUSSELS, 7 Nov 2000, *Standing Teenage Boy* (patinated bronze, h. 11 ins / 28 cm) BEF 210,000. BRUSSELS, 21 Nov 2000, *Nude Seated on a Rock* (brown patinated bronze, h. 10 ins / 25 cm) BEF 210,000. BRUSSELS, 12 Feb 2001, *Innocence* (patinated bronze, h. 15 ins / 39 cm) BEF 350,000. ANTWERP, 11 June 2001, *Woman Laughing* (marble, h. 27 ins / 68 cm, w. 18 ins/45 cm) BEF 760,000. BUENOS AIRES, 3 July 2002, *Instructum laborem* (brown patinated bronze, h. 39 ins / 100 cm) USD 2,850. NEW YORK, 29 Oct 2002, *Man Contemplating a Mask of Beethoven* (brown patinated bronze, h. 16 ins / 41 cm) USD 7,500. BRUSSELS, 9 Sept 2003, *Couple Intertwined on a Cup* (bronze, 12 x 12x8 ins / 30 x 31x21 cm) EUR 8,000. BRUSSELS, 13 Oct 2003, *Draped Male Nude* (black patinated bronze, h. 19 ins / 48 cm) EUR 6,500. PARIS, 1 April 2004, *Intimacy* (patinated bronze, 23 x 16x6 ins / 59 x 40x16 cm) EUR 10,100. BRUSSELS, 12 Oct 2004, *Young Female Nude* (1929, ivory, h. 8 ins / 20 cm) EUR 7,200.

ROUSSEAU, Virginie

Maiden name: Hue de Bréval

French, 19th century.

Active during the first half of the 19th century.

Miniaturist. Portraits.

Virginie Rousseau was a student of Lethiers and Augustin. She exhibited at the Salon from 1810 to 1822.

AUCTION RECORDS:

PARIS, 27-29 May 1929, *Portrait of General de Rougé* (miniature) FRF 1,650; *Portrait of Mlle de Rougé* (miniature) FRF 1,250.

ROUSSEAU DE CORBEIL, Alexandre, called Rousseau

French, 17th century.

Sculptor.

Rousseau de Corbeil was the father of Jules Antoine Rousseau. He was employed to decorate Versailles Palace and Gardens. On the outside of the chapel he sculpted one of the groups of children bearing the attributes of Catholicism, bas-reliefs around the arcade windows. In the gardens, he produced a large Egyptian marble vase, on the chapel side of the northern parterre.

ROUSSEAU-DECELLE, René or René Achille

French, 20th century.

Born 14 June 1881, in La Roche-sur-Yon; died December 1964, in Préfailles (Loire-Atlantique).

Painter. Mythological subjects, portraits, landscapes.

René Rousseau-Decelle studied under Bouguereau, Gabriel Ferrier, Edouard Toudouze and Marcel Baschet. From the teachings of these academic masters he evolved towards more modern forms. A painter of the Parisian smart set, he turned to landscapes when staying in the Vendée. At the end of his life he decorated the Chapel at Préfailles, where he lived. He exhibited at the Salon des Artistes Français, of which he was an associate member from 1903. The Musée Municipal of La Roche-sur-Yon (Vendée) dedicated a retrospective exhibition to him in 1988. He was a Chevalier of the Légion d'Honneur.

MUSEUMS AND GALLERIES:

BEAUFORT-EN-VALLÉE (Mus. Joseph-Denais): *George Sand* - NANTES (MBA): *Silenius in Chains.*

AUCTION RECORDS:

PARIS, 9 Jan 1942, *Shepherds* (two studies) FRF 500. PARIS, 6 Nov 1974, *Palais des Glaces*, FRF 61,000. PARIS, 9 May 1977, *Weighing in at Longchamp* (1910, oil on canvas, 55 x 106¼ ins / 140 x 270 cm) FRF 72,000. PARIS, 1 Dec 1983, *In Parc Monceau* (oil on canvas, 13 x 22 ins / 33 x 55 cm) FRF 16,500. NANTES, 17 June 1992, *Seafront at Biarritz* (oil on panel, 11 x 13¾ ins / 27 x 35 cm) FRF 6,000. AMSTERDAM, 21 April 1993, *Paddling at the Water's Edge* (oil on canvas, diam. 39 ins / 99 cm) NLG 17,250. NEW YORK, 13 Oct 1993, *Swans* (1910, oil on canvas, 18 x 32¼ ins / 46 x 81.9 cm) USD 10,350.

ROUSSEAU-GROLÉE, Nicole
French, 20th century.
Born 1930, in Paris.
Painter.

Nicole Rousseau-Grolée is based in Annecy. In 1993, she featured in the exhibition *De Bonnard à Baselitz - Dix Ans d'enrichissements du cabinet des estampes 1978-1988* (*From Bonnard to Baselitz: A Decade of Acquisitions by the Prints Collection 1978-1988*) at the Bibliothèque Nationale in Paris.

MUSEUMS AND GALLERIES:
PARIS (BNF): *Val-de-Loire* (1984, lithograph).

ROUSSEAUX. See also **ROUSSEAU**

ROUSSEAUX, Émile Alfred, or Rousseau
French, 19th century.
Born 1831, in Abbeville; died 3 December 1874, in Paris.
Draughtsman, engraver (burin).

Émile Rousseaux, who died prematurely, was the son of a cabinetmaker and began his studies at the municipal drawing school in Abbeville. He went to Paris, where he became the student of Henriquel-Dupont and Picot. He first exhibited at the Salon of 1861, with a drawing after Paul Delaroche. His submission to the Salon of 1863, two drawings and an engraving, *Christ* and *St John*, after Ary Scheffer, won him a second-class medal. He continued to exhibit drawings and engravings until his death. He produced three remarkable prints: *Portrait of a Man Attributed to Francia* (Louvre museum), *Christian Martyr*, after Paul Delaroche, and *Marquise de Sévigné* after a pastel by Robert Nanteuil. This last work is possibly the most outstanding.

ROUSSEAUX, Fernand
Belgian, 20th century.
Born 1892, in Chapelle-lez-Herlaimont; died 1971.
Painter, sculptor, engraver. Figures, portraits, interiors, landscapes.

AUCTION RECORDS:
LOKEREN, 12 March 1994, *Birch Trees in the Snow* (oil on panel, 25 1/2 x 32 ins / 65 x 81 cm) BEF 55,000. BRUSSELS, 18 March 2002, *Barges on an Industrial Landscape Background* (oil on canvas, 30 x 35 ins / 76 x 90 cm) EUR 2,000.

ROUSSEAUX, J. J.. See **ROUSSEAU J. J.**

ROUSSEAUX, Jacques des. See **ROUSSEAU Jacques de**

ROUSSEAUX, Jules
French, 17th century.
Active in Angers.
Sculptor.

Jules Rousseaux was sculptor of the king's buildings, in Angers.

ROUSSEAUX VIRLOGEUX, Marcel François
French, 20th century.
Born 6 September 1884, in Decize (Nièvre).
Painter. Murals.

Marcel Rousseau Virlogeux studied under Jean-Paul Laurens and Rochegrosse. He worked in Algeria in the late 1920s. He decorated the council chamber in the town hall at El Biar and exhibited at the Salon des Artistes Français, of which he was an associate member.

ROUSSEEL, Antony or Théodore. See **RUSSEL**

ROUSSEFF, Juliette
Belgian, 20th century.
Born 1913, in Liège.
Painter. Designs for tapestries.

Juliette Rousseff studied at the fine arts academy in Liège and went on to teach tapestry work there. She exhibited on a regular basis in Belgium.

ROUSSEL
French, 18th century.
Active in Paris.
Painter, pastellist.

Roussel was the father of Françoise Roussel. He was a member of the Académie de St-Luc and showed works at the academy's exhibitions in 1752 and 1753. It seems that he painted mainly portraits, particularly in pastels.

AUCTION RECORDS:
PARIS, 7 Nov 1997, *Family Concert* (oil on canvas, 39 1/4 x 52 ins / 100 x 132 cm) FRF 140,000.

ROUSSEL
French, 18th century.
Active in Rheims c. 1760.
Painter.

MUSEUMS AND GALLERIES:
RHEIMS: *Winter, or The Flood* (after the painting by Poussin in the Louvre).

ROUSSEL, Adrien
French, 17th century.
Active during the second half of the 17th century.
Sculptor.

Adrien Roussel worked at Versailles from 1680 to 1686, the former Château Marly from 1688 to 1689, and for the Dôme church at the military hospital, Hôtel des Invalides, in Paris in 1698.

ROUSSEL, Alphonse
French, 19th century.
Born 20 June 1829, in Paris; died 18 September 1868, in Paris.
Painter. History painting, genre scenes.

Alphonse Roussel was a student of Drolling and Picot. He visited Italy and exhibited at the Paris Salon from 1864 to 1869 (in 1869 it was a posthumous exhibition).

ROUSSEL, Amélie
French, 19th century.
Active in Paris.
Painter. Genre scenes, portraits.

Amélie Roussel exhibited at the Paris Salon in 1844 and 1855.

ROUSSEL, André
French, 20th century.
Born 8 June 1888, in Paris; died 3 January 1968.
Painter. Landscapes, architectural views, still-lifes.

Henri Roussel painted landscapes in St-Tropez, Dordrecht and Bruges. He specialized in painting cathedrals. From 1947, he composed still-lifes of silver and glassware on white tablecloths and lace. He exhibited at the Salon de la Société Nationale des Beaux-Arts, of which he became an associate member in 1936, and for whom he judged from 1938. He featured in collective and solo exhibitions in Paris and the provinces as well as Holland and Belgium.

AUCTION RECORDS:
PARIS, 28 April 1980, *St-Tropez Harbour by Night* (oil on canvas, 23 1/2 x 19 3/4 ins / 60 x 50 cm) FRF 4,000.

ROUSSEL, Antony. See **RUSSEL**

ROUSSEL, Armand
French, 20th century.
died during World War I, on the battlefield.
Painter.

Armand Roussel took part in the Salon de la Société Nationale des Beaux-Arts.

ROUSSEL, Charles Emmanuel Joseph
French, 19th - 20th century.
Born 16 February 1861, in Tourcoing; died 1936, in Berck-sur-Mer.
Painter. Seascapes.

Charles Roussel studied under Cabanel, Weerts and Tattegrain at the Académie des Beaux-Arts in Lille. Based in Berck, he worked with Gauguin in Pont-Aven in an Impressionist style. He exhibited at the Salon des Artistes Français, of which he was an associate member from 1887, and at the Salon des Tuileries. He also exhibited in St Petersburg in 1903, at the St Louis World Trade Fair in 1904 and in Buenos Aires in 1909.
MUSEUMS AND GALLERIES:
NICE: *Coastal Barges* - TOURCOING: *Berck-sur-Mer, last preparations before Fishing.*
AUCTION RECORDS:
ENGHIEN-LES-BAINS, 2 June 1977, *Fishermen Hauling an Anchor* (oil on canvas, 206¼ x 14¼ ins / 524 x 36 cm) FRF 3,600. VERSAILLES, 22 June 1983, *The Fishermen's Return* (oil on canvas, 13 x 18 ins / 33 x 46 cm) FRF 13,000. PARIS, 23 June 1988, *Fishermen at Low Tide in Berck* (1902, oil on panel, 9½ x 13½ ins / 24 x 34.5 cm) FRF 26,000. CALAIS, 4 March 1990, *Fishermen Setting off,* FRF 45,000. LE TOUQUET, 11 Nov 1990, *Fishermen Setting off* (oil on canvas, 27½ x 34¼ ins / 70 x 87 cm) FRF 40,000. LE TOUQUET, 19 May 1991, *The Fishermen's Return* (oil on canvas, 13 x 18 ins / 33 x 46 cm) FRF 30,000. CALAIS, 5 April 1992, *Preparation of the Nets* (oil on canvas, 13 x 18 ins / 33 x 46 cm) FRF 34,000. CALAIS, 14 March 1993, *The Fishermen's Return* (oil on canvas, 13 x 18 ins / 33 x 46 cm) FRF 22,000. CALAIS, 3 July 1994, *Fisherman in the Dunes* (oil on canvas, 12½ x 16¼ ins / 32 x 41 cm) FRF 13,500. PARIS, 13 Oct 1995, *Fishermen's Return* (oil on canvas, 13 x 18 ins / 33 x 46 cm) FRF 10,000.

ROUSSEL, Charles Joseph
French, 20th century.
Born 1882, in Meaux; died 1961, in Paris.
Illustrator, draughtsman.

Charles Roussel studied at the École des Beaux-Arts in Paris, working in Gérôme's studio. He travelled in Europe and the USA. He taught art at the École ABC in Paris. He contributed illustrations to *Fantasio* (*Fantasio*), *Le Rire* (*Laugh*), *Le Sourire* (*Smile*) and *Nos Loisirs* (*Leisure*) and illustrated Courteline's *Les Linottes* (*Feather-brains*) and his own *Historique du 13e régiment d'infanterie* (*History of the 13th Infantry Regiment*). He created posters, menus, and covers for music scores and records. He captured stark renderings of the Parisian women he saw as he walked about Montmartre.

ROUSSEL, Félix
French, 20th century.
Painter. Still-lifes.

Félix Roussel lived and worked in Paris. He exhibited at the Salon d'Automne, of which he was an associate member.

ROUSSEL, François
French, 16th century.
Active during the second half of the 16th century.
Sculptor.
Fontainebleau School.

François Roussel was commissioned in 1568 to sculpt a statue entitled *Allegory of Religion,* destined for the château of Fontainebleau.

ROUSSEL, Françoise
French, 18th century.
Active in Paris.
Painter. History painting.

Françoise Roussel was the daughter of the portraitist Roussel. She became a member of the Académie de St-Luc on 4 August 1750, with her painting *Pilgrims of Emmaus.*

ROUSSEL, Fremyre or Frémin
French, 16th century.
Sculptor.
Fontainebleau School.

Fremyre Roussel worked on the château of Fontainebleau.
MUSEUMS AND GALLERIES:
PARIS (Louvre): *Spirit of History* (marble, statue).

ROUSSEL, G.
French, 18th century.
Active c. 1790.
Engraver (etching).

G. Roussel engraved landscapes after St-Quentin and from his own designs.

ROUSSEL, Georges Frederic, called Roussel-Géo
French, 19th - 20th century.
Born 1860, in Beauvais; died 1928, in Paris.
Painter. History painting, genre scenes.

Georges Roussel studied under Cabanel, Maillot and Bouguereau. He took part in the Salon des Artistes Français, of which he was an associate member, and received an honourable mention at the 1889 Paris Exposition Universelle. He was awarded a travel grant in 1892 and medals in 1898 and 1900. He was made a Chevalier of the Légion d'Honneur in October 1908.
MUSEUMS AND GALLERIES:
AMIENS (Mus. de Picardie): *Marceau's Body Handed over to the French Army* - BEAUVAIS: *From a Window* - PARIS (Mus. de l'Armée): *The Emperor.*
AUCTION RECORDS:
MONTE CARLO, 8 Oct 1977, *Thaïs* (c. 1900, white marble and gilded bronze heightened with enamel and turquoise, h. 21¼ ins / 54 cm) FRF 20,000.

ROUSSEL, Henry. See the entry **ROUSSEL Jérome**

ROUSSEL, Jean Baptiste. See the entry **ROUSSEAU Charles**

ROUSSEL, Jean I
French, 17th - 18th century.
Born c. 1643; died 1 December 1723.
Active in Tours.
Sculptor.

Jean Roussel I was the father of Jean Roussel II. He worked for churches in Tours.

ROUSSEL, Jean II
French, 18th century.
Born 24 September 1690; died 26 March 1747.
Active in Tours.
Sculptor.

Jean Roussel II was the son of Jean Roussel I.

ROUSSEL, Jérome
French, 17th - 18th century.
Born 1663; died 22 December 1713, in Paris.
Medallist.

Jérome Roussel has incorrectly been given the forename Henry. He was a medallist at the court of Louis XIV.

ROUSSEL, Ker-Xavier
French, 19th - 20th century.
Born 10 December 1867, in Lorry-les-Metz (Moselle); died 1944, in L'Étang-la-Ville.
Painter, engraver, designer, pastellist. Mythological subjects. Murals.
Symbolism.
Nabis group.

Ker-Xavier Roussel met Édouard Vuillard at the Lycée Condorcet, which they both attended. Together they visited Eugène Ulysse Napoléon Maillard's studio, where Roussel became acquainted with Charles Cottet, going on to study at the Académie Julian under Bouguereau and Jules Lefebvre. There, he became interested in the Synthetism promoted by Sérusier, following Sérusier's heeding of the line Gauguin had adopted in Pont-Aven. He joined the Nabis group. He and his friends form a link between the Impressionists - he knew Cézanne, Degas, Renoir and Monet - and the Fauves and Cubists.

In his earliest paintings, Roussel adopted a dark palette for Realist still-lifes. Later, his work bore the influence of Gauguin, Sérusier, the Nabis and Cézanne, in Intimist scenes painted in flat tints not yet clearly delineated. Their dull, saturated tones are reminiscent of Cézanne. In about 1900 he started painting mythological scenes full of nymphs and fauns and set in his home region of Île-de-France. After a bicycle trip in Provence with Maurice Denis, during which he met Cézanne, he lightened his palette, much taken by the cloudless skies below which he would now set the mythological and idyllic compositions which link him to Poussin and Corot. This wondrous, unreal world found its way into large-scale works, including the stage curtain of the Champs-Élysées theatre in 1913, a large *Pax Nutrix* for the Palais des Nations in Geneva and *Dance* for the Palais de Chaillot in 1937. He is best remembered for: *Silenius' Triumph, Polyphemus, Diana, The Abduction of the Daughters of Leucippus.* The nymphs and fauns of a mythology quite his own appear in clearings and woods from the outskirts of Paris, but the sun they rejoice in is Mediterranean. To capture the vibration of bright colours under a permanent sun, he later turned to pastels. He was more a Symbolist than a Nabi and signed himself *K.-X. Roussel.* He also produced lithographs.

He took part in exhibitions from 1891 with the Groupe des Vingt at le Barc de Bouteville's gallery in Brussels. Then he exhibited in *Les Peintres de la revue blanche* (*Revue Blanche Painters*) in Paris; with the Nabis at Café Volponi in Paris; before World War I with Free Aesthetics in Brussels; from 1901 at the Salon des Indépendants and the Salon d'Automne; in the 1930s in *Les Peintres de la Revue blanche* (*Revue Blanche Painters*) hosted in Paris by designer Bolette Natanson, the daughter of the *Revue Blanche* 's owner. He took part in *Les Maîtres de l'art contemporain* (*The Masters of Contemporary Art*) at the Musée du Petit Palais in Paris, and at the 1938 Venice Biennale and 1939 New York World Fair. He featured posthumously in *Toulouse-Lautrec et les Nabis* (*Toulouse-Lautrec and the Nabis*) at Bern Kunsthalle; *Autour de la revue blanche* (*From the Revue Blanche*) in the Galerie Maeght, Paris, and in Tokyo and Brussels. He had one-man shows in Paris before his death in 1944. Retrospectives were mounted in the 1960s in London and Bremen.

K.X. Roussel.

K.X Roussel

Bibliography:

Couturier, Lucie, *K.- X. Roussel,* Bernheim-Jeune, Paris, 1927. Colombier, Pierre du, *Les Dieux et K.- X. Roussel,* Éd. des Beaux-Arts, Paris, 1942. *K.- X. Roussel,* exhibition catalogue, Gal. Charpentier, Paris, 1947. *K.- X. Roussel,* exhibition catalogue, Wildenstein Gall., London, 1964. *K.- X. Roussel,* exhibition catalogue, Kunsthalle, Bremen, 1965. Salomon, Jacques, *Ker-Xavier Roussel,* La Bibliothèque des Arts, Paris, Lausanne, 1967. Alain, Jacques/Salomon, Antoine, *L'Œuvre gravée de K.- X. Roussel,* Mercure de France, Paris, 1968. Groom, Gloria, et al., *Beyond the Easel. Decorative Painting by Bonnard, Vuillard, Denis and Roussel,* Yale University Press, London, 2001.

Museums and Galleries:

Geneva (Petit Palais): *Haystacks on the Seaside* - Paris (BNF): *Training the Dog; Landscapes* (engraving); *Nymph and Faun* (c. 1895, etching) - Paris (Louvre): *Poject for a Screen* (drawing) - Paris (MNAM-CCI): *The Road* (c. 1905); *The Cyclops* (1908); *Venus and Cupid on the Seafront* (1908); *The Abduction of Leucippus' Daughters* (1911); *Pastorale* (1920); *Diana at Rest* (1923); *Portrait of Vuillard* (1934) - Paris (Mus. d'Orsay): *The Gate* (pastel); *Woman in Profile with Green Hat; In Bed; Félix Valloton; Roussel Reading; The Seasons of Life* - St-Germain-en-Laye (Mus. du Prieuré-Maurice-Denis): *Composition in a Forest* - Toulouse (MBA, Mus. des Augustins): *Our Lady of the Path* - Winterthur: *Autumn* (1916).

Auction records:

Paris, 10 May 1900, *The Lawn,* FRF 160. Paris, 23 Nov 1910, *Secrets,* FRF 960. Paris, 24 Feb 1919, *Euridice with the Snake,* FRF 3,200. Paris, 7 Dec 1923, *Eclogue,* FRF 4,100. Paris, 14 Feb 1927, *Silenius' Travels,* FRF 5,000. Paris, 28 May 1930, *Faun in Ambush,* FRF 20,000. Paris, 28 June 1935, *Acis and Galatea Surprised by Polyphemus,* FRF 1,850. Paris, 15 June 1938, *Spring* (gouache and pastel) FRF 4,800. Paris, 22 Dec 1941, *The Offering* (1921) FRF 28,000. Paris, 26 Feb 1945, *Venus in Cythere* (Dec 1924) FRF 39,100. Paris, 30 May 1949, *Nymph and Satyr* (1919) FRF 46,500. Paris, 11 Dec 1950, *Branch of a Tree in Bloom,* FRF 33,000. Geneva, 10 March 1951, *People and Animals in a Forest* (1915, pastel) CHF 340. Paris, 1 Dec 1959, *Bathers,* FRF 1,900,000. London, 22 March 1961, *The Kiss* (pastel) GBP 230. New York, 24 Nov 1965, *L'Après-midi d'un faune* (*Afternoon of a Faun,* USD 2,750. Versailles, 16 March 1969, *Venus' Repose,* FRF 40,000. Paris, 12 Dec 1973, *Flowers in a Vase* (gouache) FRF 30,000. Versailles, 11 June 1974, *Park in Bloom,* FRF 10,000. Paris, 23 March 1976, *Landscape* (pastel, 9 x 14 1/4 ins / 22 x 36 cm) FRF 1,800. Versailles, 27 June 1976, *Venus' Repose* (oil on canvas, 39 1/4 x 69 3/4 ins / 100 x 177 cm) FRF 17,000. Versailles, 17 March 1977, *Venus Rising from the Water* (oil on canvas, 41 3/4 x 62 3/4 ins / 106 x 159.5 cm) FRF 20,000. Grenoble, 22 May 1978, *Country Lane* (pastel, 17 3/4 x 23 1/2 ins / 45 x 60 cm) FRF 7,800. Enghien-les-Bains, 27 May 1979, *Children in the Meadow* (pastel, 35 x 32 1/4 ins / 88 x 82 cm) FRF 47,000. Enghien-les-Bains, 28 Oct 1979, *Our Lady of the Path* (oil on canvas, 17 3/4 x 12 1/4 ins / 45 x 31 cm) FRF 61,000. Bern, 21 June 1980, *Landscape with House* (1897, coloured lithograph) CHF 2,800. Bern, 25 June 1981, *Training the Dog* (1893, coloured lithograph) CHF 8,800. Versailles, 12 Dec 1981, *Fauns and Satyrs* (oil on panel, 30 3/4 x 41 3/4 ins / 78 x 106 cm) FRF 15,000. New York, 18 March 1982, *Nymphs and Satyrs* (c. 1910, pastel, 13 1/2 x 22 1/4 ins / 34.3 x 56.2 cm) USD 2,800. New York, 19 May 1983, *Faun and Nymphs* (oil on canvas, 41 3/4 x 55 1/2 ins / 106 x 141 cm) USD 14,000. Bern, 23 June 1983, *Training the Dog, or In the Snow* (1893, coloured lithograph) CHF 9,000. London, 26 Oct 1983, *Bathers* (gouache and pastel/charcoal outlines, 30 x 45 ins / 76.2 x 114.3 cm) GBP 2,600. Paris, 15 Dec 1983, *Sleeping Model Seen from Behind* (charcoal and stump heightened with pastels, 8 3/4 x 12 3/4 ins / 22.5 x 32.5 cm) FRF 7,800. London, 13 Feb 1985, *Bather* (pastel, 31 x 43 ins / 78.7 x 109.2 cm) GBP 4,200. Enghien-les-Bains, 13 April 1986, *Our Lady of the Path* (oil on canvas, 21 1/4 x 14 1/2 ins / 54 x 37 cm) FRF 145,000. Paris, 26 June 1986, *Bathers* (pastel, 8 x 14 1/4 ins / 20.5 x 36 cm) FRF 98,000. New York, 18 Feb 1988, *Bathers* (pastel/mounted paper/canvas, 18 x 18 ins / 46 x 44.8 cm) USD 17,600. London, 21 Oct 1988, *Apple Tree* (1924, oil on canvas, 39 1/4 x 25 1/2 ins / 99.7 x 64.8 cm) GBP 7,700. Paris, 22 Nov 1988, *Nudes in a Landscape* (pastel, 9 x 11 3/4 ins / 23 x 30 cm) FRF 19,000. Amsterdam, 10 April 1989, *On the Seaside* (oil on panel, 9 3/4 x 14 1/4 ins / 25 x 36.2 cm) NLG 5,520. New York, 3 May 1989, *Bather* (oil on canvas, 14 1/4 x 19 1/4 ins / 36 x 49 cm) USD 35,520. Paris, 22 Oct 1989, *Young Women in the Undergrowth* (c. 1892, oil on canvas, 10 3/4 x 16 1/4 ins / 27.5 x 41 cm) FRF 131,500. PARIS, 22 Nov 1989, *Diana and Adonis* (pastel/paper, 18 x 26 1/2 ins / 46 x 67.5 cm) FRF 100,000. PARIS, 27 March 1990, *Faun and Nymph* (oil on card, 13 x 28 1/4 ins / 33 x 72 cm) FRF 60,000. PARIS, 30 May 1990, *Sunbathing* (oil on card, 13 x 18 ins / 33 x 46 cm) FRF 80,500. PARIS, 13 June 1990, *Faun in a Landscape* (drawing in wash heightened with gouache, 4 1/2 x 7 3/4 ins / 11.5 x 20 cm) FRF 5,500. PARIS, 2 July 1990, *Landscape with Tree* (pastel, lead pencil and coloured pencil, 16 1/2 x 22 ins / 42 x 55 cm) FRF 9,000. PARIS, 6 Oct 1990, *The Gods' Repose* (pastel, 5 x 7 1/2 ins / 13 x 19 cm) FRF 21,000. CALAIS, 10 March 1991, *Autumn Landscape* (pastel, 16 1/2 x 19 ins / 42 x 48 cm) FRF 18,000. PARIS, 25 Oct 1991, *Fauns and Nymphs* (pastel, 21 x 15 ins / 53.5 x 38 cm) FRF 74,000. NEW YORK, 5 Nov 1991, *Faun with Two Nymphs* (oil on card, 11 x 14 3/4 ins / 27 x 37.5 cm) USD 9,350. ST-ÉTIENNE, 16 Nov 1991, *Women in the Park* (oil on canvas, 14 1/4 x 29 1/2 ins / 36 x 75 cm) FRF 950,000. PARIS, 21 Feb 1992, *Landscape with House* (1897, coloured lithograph, 11 1/2 x 16 1/4 ins / 29 x 41.5 cm) FRF 16,000. PARIS, 3 June 1992, *Bather on the Waterfront* (pastel, 8 1/4 x 13 1/2 ins / 21 x 34.5 cm) FRF 52,000. PARIS, 11 June 1993, *Training the Dog, or In the Snow* (1893, lithograph, 13 x 8 ins / 33 x 20.5 cm) FRF 45,000. LONDON, 13 Oct 1993, *The Runaway* (red chalk, 9 3/4 x 12 1/4 ins / 24.8 x 31.4 cm) GBP 690. PARIS, 25 March 1994, *Village Street* (oil on card, 12 1/4 x 15 1/4 ins / 31 x 39 cm) FRF 20,000. NEW YORK, 9 May 1994, *The Dressmaker* (ink and pencil/paper/paper, 7 1/2 x 4 3/4 ins / 18.8 x 12.1 cm) USD 34,500. PARIS, 21 Sept 1994, *Training the Dog* (1893, coloured lithograph) FRF 31,000. LONDON, 26 Oct 1994, *Landscape* (oil on canvas, 67 1/4 x 29 1/2 ins / 171 x 75 cm) GBP 12,650. PARIS, 24 Nov 1995, *Afternoon of a Faun by Mallarmé* (pastel, 15 3/4 x 24 3/4 ins / 40 x 63 cm) FRF 46,000. PARIS, 21 June 1996, *Fauns* (oil on canvas, 25 1/4 x 18 ins / 64 x 46 cm) FRF 18,000. PARIS, 21 Nov 1996, *Bathers* (1898, lithograph, 10 x 16 3/4 ins / 25.5 x 42.5 cm) FRF 34,000. PARIS, 22 Nov 1996, *Undergrowth* (pastel and gouache/buff-coloured paper, 14 x 21 ins / 35.5 x 53.5 cm) FRF 13,000. LYONS, 2 Dec 1996, *Foxgloves* (pastel, 21 1/2 x 20 1/2 ins / 54.4 x 52.3 cm) FRF 40,000. PARIS, 16 May 1997, *Stable* (pastel/beige paper, 9 1/4 x 11 1/2 ins / 23.5 x 29.5 cm) FRF 47,000. PARIS, 6 June 1997, *Rolling Landscape* (pastel, 12 1/4 x 18 3/4 ins / 31 x 47.5 cm) FRF 16,000. PARIS, 27 Oct 1997, *Bathers* (oil on card, 11 3/4 x 19 ins / 30 x 48 cm) FRF 34,000. PARIS, 16 Dec 1997, *Landscapes* (lithograph, set of six plates, 8 1/2 ins / 21.5 cm-10 x 12 1/2 ins/25.3 x 32 cm-16 1/2 ins/42 cm) FRF 48,000. PARIS, 20 March 1998, *Spring* (pastel, 17 1/4 x 21 1/4 ins / 43.5 x 54 cm) FRF 17,000. PARIS, 6 July 1999, *Prometheus* (oil on canvas, 39 x 41 ins / 100 x 105 cm) FRF 50,000. PARIS, 16 Dec 1999, *In the Snow, or Teaching a Dog* (colour engraving, 13 x 7 ins / 33 x 19 cm) FRF 90,000. PARIS, 9 June 2000, *Fountain at Jovence* (c. 1928, oil on cardboard, 19 x 26 ins / 47 x 67 cm) FRF 95,000. PARIS, 12 July 2000, *Dance: Decoration Project for the Hall of the Palais de Chaillot* (charcoal and pastel, 13 x 13 ins / 33 x 34 cm) FRF 30,000. PARIS, 22 June 2001, *Dance of Bacchus* (oil on panel, 29 x 30 ins / 74 x 77 cm) FRF 500,000. LONDON, 24 Oct 2001, *Forest Interior. Carriage and Tree. Path. Road* (pastel and charcoal on card, four) GBP 5,000. PARIS, 12 July 2002, *Fall of Phaeton* (c. 1910, oil on canvas, 31 x 24 ins / 80 x 60 cm) EUR 19,500. PARIS, 12 Dec 2002, *Landscapes* (lithograph, six, 85 x 126 ins / 215 x 320 cm) EUR 8,500. PARIS, 26 March 2003, *Ancient Scene* (oil on canvas, 26 x 32 ins / 65 x 81 cm) EUR 8,500. LONDON, 22 Oct 2003, *Infant's Bedroom* (pen and ink, 6 x 4 ins / 15 x 11 cm) GBP 9,500. LONDON, 20 Oct 2004, *Faun, Nymph with Yellow Veil and Cupid* (oil on board, 39 x 26 ins / 99 x 66 cm) GBP 11,500.

ROUSSEL, Léon, called Léo
French, 19th - 20th century.
Born 25 November 1868, in Ourches (Meuse).
Sculptor.

Léon Roussel studied under G. J. Thomas and E. Peynot. He sculpted busts, portraits, war memorials and medallions. He exhibited at the Salon des Artistes Français, of which he was an associate member. He received an honourable mention in 1898 and a silver medal in 1931.

MUSEUMS AND GALLERIES:
BAR-LE-DUC - PARIS (Mus. du Petit Palais): *Innocence.*

ROUSSEL, Marius Pascal
French, 19th - 20th century.
Born 7 September 1874, in Sète.
Sculptor.

Marius Roussel studied under Falguière. From 1898 he exhibited at the Salon des Artistes Français. He was an associate member and was declared hors concours. He received a gold medal in 1922 and the Légion d'Honneur in 1935.

ROUSSEL, Modeste
French, 18th century.
Active in Paris in 1752.
Sculptor (ivory).

Modeste Roussel was a member of the Académie de St-Luc.

ROUSSEL, Nicolas
French, 16th - 17th century.
Active in Paris from 1590 to 1624.
Medallist.

ROUSSEL, Paul
French, 17th century.
Active in Paris from 1605 to 1647.
Engraver. Armorials.

Paul Roussel was also a printer and publisher.

ROUSSEL, Paul Marie
French, 19th century.
Born 8 February 1804, in Paris; died 1877.
Painter (including porcelain), glass painter, lithographer.

Paul Marie Roussel was a student of Chenavard. He exhibited at the Salon from 1847 to 1876. He was made a Chevalier of the Légion d'Honneur in 1868. From 1837, he was a stained glass painter at the Sèvres factory but his submissions to the Salon include portraits, subjects from everyday Russian life and Algerian subjects, suggesting that he visited Russia and Algeria.

Paul Marie Roussel produced the stained glass windows at the Louvre after Chenavard, Deveria and Alaux, those in the St Ferdinand chapel after Ingres and those at Dreux and the church of St Louis in Versailles, after Deveria. There is also a lithograph by him - *Russian Peasants before an Icon* - published in *The Artist* in 1836.

AUCTION RECORDS:
PARIS, 1900, *Lawn* (pastel) FRF 100; *Idyll* (pastel) FRF 157.

ROUSSEL, Paul or Hippolyte Paul René, called Paul-Roussel
French, 19th - 20th century.
Born 23 October 1867, in Paris; died 1 January 1928, in Paris.
Sculptor.

Paul Roussel studied under Pierre Jules Cavelier, Louis Ernest Barrias and Jules Félix Coutan. He sculpted war memorials and statues. He judged for the Salon des Artistes Français and the École des Beaux-Arts in Paris. He took the first Grand Prix de Rome in 1895, won a silver medal in 1900, and was declared hors concours the same year. He was an Officier of the Légion d'Honneur.

MUSEUMS AND GALLERIES:
AMSTERDAM: *Little Ones* - LE MANS: *Apollo; Bust of Guynemer; Official Bust for the Republic* - PARIS (Mus. du Petit Palais): *Dancing Nonia* - PARIS (Mus. Galliera): *The Sea.*

ROUSSEL, Pierre
French, 20th century.
Born 4 December 1927, in L'Étang-la-Ville.
Painter, pastellist. Landscapes, seascapes, still-lifes.

Pierre Roussel, a grandson of Ker-Xavier Roussel and great nephew of Vuillard, studied at the École des Arts Décoratifs in Paris in 1945. He published two books of lithographs: one about Japan (1958) and one to celebrate Molière's tricentinary. He took part in exhibitions dedicated to the École de Paris; the Salon des Tuileries; the Menton Biennale; and *Presence of French Figurative Modern Art* in New York in 1969. He showed his works in solo exhibitions in Paris and London from 1953.

MUSEUMS AND GALLERIES:
NEW YORK (MoMA) - PARIS (MAM) - PHILADELPHIA (MA).

AUCTION RECORDS:
PARIS, 22 March 1976, *By the Lakeside* (pastel, 25 1/4 x 18 ins / 64 x 46 cm) FRF 1,600. LONDON, 29 Nov 1976, *Still-life with Fruit* (oil on canvas, 22 x 32 ins / 55 x 81.2 cm) GBP 700. NEW YORK, 8 Aug 1980, *Still-life with Flowers* (oil on canvas, 21 1/4 x 32 ins / 54 x 81.2 cm) USD 1,900. CHICAGO, 11 Sept 1983, *In the Garden* (oil on canvas, 39 x 32 ins / 99 x 81.5 cm) USD 2,200. PARIS, 16 Dec 1987, *Still-life with Pomegranate* (oil on canvas, 11 x 18 ins / 27 x 46 cm) FRF 6,500. PARIS, 12 Oct 1988, *Boats on the Lake in the Bois de Boulogne* (oil on canvas, 22 3/4 x 28 ins / 58 x 71 cm) FRF 12,500. NEW YORK, 9 May 1989, *At the Dressmaker's* (oil on canvas, 25 1/2 x 31 3/4 ins / 64.7 x 80.5 cm) USD 3,960. NEW YORK, 29 Sept 1993, *Still-life with Apples* (oil on canvas, 19 3/4 x 25 1/2 ins / 50.2 x 64.8 cm) USD 1,380. NEW YORK, 7 June 1999, *Summer Landscape* (oil on canvas, 26 x 32 ins / 65 x 81 cm) USD 3,000. NEW YORK, 15 Feb 2000, *Landscape* (oil on board, 18 x 22 ins / 46 x 55 cm) USD 2,800. NEW YORK, 6 Nov 2001, *Oliver and Jacques Working* (oil on panel, 24 x 20 ins / 60 x 51 cm) USD 3,200. NEUILLY, 17 Dec 2001, *Two Children in the Garden* (oil on canvas, 36 x 29 ins / 92 x 73 cm) FRF 12,500. CALAIS, 29 June 2003, *Little Dog* (oil on canvas, 24 x 29 ins / 60 x 73 cm) EUR 1,500. CALAIS, 29 June 2003, *Woman Sewing* (oil on canvas, 39 x 32 ins / 100 x 81 cm) EUR 3,100. NEW YORK, 6 May 2004, *Yvonne in the Theatre Workshop* (gouache, charcoal, pastel and pencil on card, 31 x 21 ins / 79 x 54 cm) USD 2,750. NEW YORK, 29 Sept 2004, *Girl Sitting at a Table* (oil on canvas, 26 x 21 ins / 65 x 54 cm) USD 3,750.

ROUSSEL, Robert
French, 16th century.
Active in Paris from 1541 to 1561.
Glass painter.

Robert Roussel painted stained glass windows for the church of St-Étienne-du-Mont in Paris.

ROUSSEL, Théodore
French, 19th - 20th century.
Born 23 March 1847, in Lorient; died 23 April 1926, in Hastings.
Active in England from 1874.
Painter, engraver. Figures, nudes, scenes with figures, landscapes, seascapes.

Théodore Roussel came to live in England in 1874, settling in Hastings. He worked in Whistler's style. He wrote a study of colours: *L'Analyse chromatique positive* (*Positive Chromatic Analysis*), in which he defines chromatic opposites of each coloured pigment.

MUSEUMS AND GALLERIES:
AMSTERDAM (Stedelijk Mus.) - LONDON (Tate Collection): *The Reading Girl* (1886-1887, oil on canvas).

AUCTION RECORDS:
LONDON, 19 Dec 1946, *Beach Scene in Cannes*, GBP 72. LONDON, 5 March 1980, *A Garden in Fulham* (oil on canvas, 29 1/4 x 24 1/2 ins / 74 x 62 cm) GBP 1,250. LONDON, 23 May 1984, *A Garden in Fulham* (oil on canvas, 30 x 25 ins / 76 x 63.5 cm) GBP 1,700. LONDON, 6 March 1987, *Blue Thames, End of Summer Afternoon, Chelsea* (oil on canvas, 33 x 47 1/4 ins / 84 x 120 cm) GBP 12,000. BERN, 19 June 1987, *Flowers at their Last* (etching, 17 1/2 x 13 3/4 ins / 44.6 x 35 cm) CHF 2,600.

ROUSSEL, Théodore. See also **RUSSEL**

ROUSSEL DE HARMAVILLE
French, 14th century.
Painter.

Roussel de Harmaville was commissioned to paint a retable in the Cathusian monastery of Val-St-Esprit near Gosnay.

ROUSSEL DE PREVILLE, Roger.
See **PRÉVILLE**

ROUSSEL-MASURE
French, 19th - 20th century.
Born 1863, in Paris; died 5 July 1919, in Cagnes-sur-Mer.
Painter. Landscapes with figures, landscapes, waterscapes.

Roussel-Masure studied at the Académie Julian in Paris, alongside Valtat. He enjoyed the friendship of Sisley and Pissarro and the support of Monet and later Renoir. He took to heart the latter's observation: 'To paint well you must paint fast; there is no other way to bring the model to life; don't dwell on details.' Essentially a landscapist, he is remembered for *Éragny, Pontoise Market, The Sea at Bréat, Moret, Antibes, Les Collettes* and *Renoir's House at Cagnes*.

AUCTION RECORDS:
PARIS, 1 May 1889, *La Celle-sous-Moret*, FRF 120. PARIS, 27 Nov 1946, *Château-Gaillard*, FRF 1,500. PARIS, 26 Nov 1948, *The Marne Riverbanks*, FRF 600. PARIS, 20 June 1968, *The Market*, FRF 4,500. VERSAILLES, 4 April 1976, *Village on the Riverbank* (21 1/4 x 28 3/4 ins / 54 x 73 cm) FRF 1,200. VERSAILLES, 4 March 1979, *The Seine at the Vert-Galant* (oil on canvas, 25 1/2 x 21 1/4 ins / 65 x 54 cm) FRF 4,500. STUTTGART, 9 May 1981, *Summer Landscape* (oil on canvas, 11 3/4 x 22 ins / 30 x 55 cm) DEM 3,700.

ROUSSELET, Charles
French, 17th century.
Painter.

Charles Rousselet was the brother of Jean Rousselet.

ROUSSELET, Gilles
French, 17th century.
Born 1610, in Paris; died 15 July 1686, in Paris.
Draughtsman, engraver (burin), print dealer.

Gilles Rousselet was the father of Jean Rousselet. It is not known who was his master, but his style was inspired by that of Bloemaert. It seems that he was highly placed among the engravers and print dealers of his time. His output was considerable, and Le Blanc catalogued 104 works of all genres, after French and Italian masters. He was closely linked to Le Brun, several of whose works he reproduced.

Rousselet became an Academician on 14 April 1663, and exhibited just once, in 1664. He died, blind, at the tapestry factory Les Gobelins on 15 July 1686. His wife, Judith Legout, died several days later and they were buried together in the church of St Hippolyte on 26 July 1686.

BIBLIOGRAPHY:
Lhopiteau, Simon, '*Contrats d'apprentissage de trois graveurs majeurs du XVIIe siècle: Karl Audran, Claude Mellan, Gilles Rousselet (Notes et Documents) par Simon Lhopiteau*' in *Nouvelles de l'Estampe* n° 171, periodical, Bibliothèque nationale de France, Paris, 2000. Meyer, Véronique, *L' Œuvre de Gilles Rousselet graveur parisien du XVII° siècle*, Commission des travaux historiques de la Ville de Paris, 2000.

ROUSSELET, Jean
French, 17th century.

Born 1656, in Paris; died 13 June 1693, in Les Gobelins, Paris.
Sculptor.

Jean Rousselet was the son of the engraver Gilles Rousselet, and the brother of the painter Charles Rousselet. He became an Academician on 28 June 1686.

Museums and Galleries:
Paris (Louvre): *Poetry and Music*.

ROUSSELET, Madeleine Thérèse
French, 18th - 19th century.
Engraver (burin).

Madeleine Rousselet was the sister of Marie-Anne Rousselet.

ROUSSELET, Marie Anne, later Mme Tardieu
French, 18th - 19th century.
Born 6 December 1732, in Paris; died 1826, in Paris.
Engraver (burin).

It is thought that Marie Anne Rousselet belonged to the family of Gilles Rousselet. She was married to Pierre François Tardieu. She engraved several pieces for the works of the French naturalist and writer, Buffon and also produced seascapes after Vernet, Backhuysen, Van Loo and W. van de Velde.

ROUSSELET, Pierre
Flemish School, 18th century.
Active in Liège in 1732.
Illuminator.

ROUSSELIN, Auguste
French, 19th century.
Born 19th century, in Paris.
Painter.

Auguste Rousselin was a student of Gleyre. He first exhibited at the Salon of 1863. He produced portraits and pictures of horses and genre subjects.

Auction records:
Paris, 13 March 1978, *Pau: Horse Market* (1885, oil on canvas, 102 1/4 x 76 3/4 ins / 260 x 195 cm) FRF 7,800.

ROUSSELIN, Joseph Auguste
French, 19th century.
Born c. 1840, in Paris.
Painter. Portraits, genre scenes, landscapes, animals.

Joseph Rousselin was a student of Thomas Couture and Charles Gleyre. He exhibited at the Paris Salon from 1863, as well as at the Salon de la Société des Amis des Arts in Pau. He also posed in 1869 for Manet's famous canvas: *Déjeuner sur l'herbe* (*Picnic on the Lawn*).

Museums and Galleries:
Pau (MBA): *Mule Market* (study).

Auction records:
Paris, 24 Oct 1984, *Mule Market in Pau* (oil on canvas, 101 1/4 x 76 1/2 ins / 257 x 194 cm) FRF 140,000. Paris, 26 Oct 1984, *Mule Market in Pau* (1885, oil on canvas, 101 1/4 x 76 1/4 ins / 257 x 193.5 cm) FRF 140,000. New York, 13 Oct 1993, *St Martin's Fair in Pau* (1885, oil on canvas, 101 x 76 ins / 256.5 x 193 cm) USD 40,250.

ROUSSELIN-CORBEAU DE SAINT-ALBIN, Hortensine Céline
Maiden name: Duhameau
French, 19th century.
Born 1817, in Mayenne; died 1874, in Paris.
Painter. Flowers, fruit.

Hortensine Rousselin-Corbeau de Saint Albin was taught by Jacobber. Under the name of Mme de St-Albin, she featured at the Paris Salon from 1843 to 1874. She often painted on porcelain.

Museums and Galleries:
Alençon: *Flowers and Fruit* - Bagnères: a work.

ROUSSELLE, Hippolyte
French, 19th century.
Born 19th century, in Paris.
Painter, engraver.

Hippolyte Rousselle was a student of Delaunay and of Puvis de Chavannes. He first exhibited at the Salon of 1878. He mainly painted portraits on enamel and earthenware.

ROUSSELOT, Bruno
French, 20th - 21st century.
Born 12 November 1957, in Joinville (Haute-Marne).
Active since 1987 in the USA.
Painter, draughtsman.

Bruno Rousselot has divided his time between New York and Châtillon-sur-Loire since 1987. He is an original exponent of geometrical 'hard-edge' abstraction in the manner of Barnett Newman and Ellsworth Kelly, but he also owes a debt to the Suprematism of Kasimir Malevich. His compositions are a play on diverse forms - rectangles, squares, broken curves, spirals - which are applied by roller and are positioned asymmetrically on the canvas to impart a sense of motion 'which travels nowhere other than towards the painting itself'. Rousselot is noted in particular for several series: *Labyrinths* (1991-1992), *Fragmentations* and *Delta* (both 1993) and *Concorde* (1996).

He has shown examples of his work at various group exhibitions: in 1982, at the Maison des Arts in Créteil; in 1983, at the Musée des Beaux-Arts in Chartres; in 1984, at the Grand Palais in Paris (CNAP); in 1985, at the Kulturhuset in Stockholm; in 1986, 1993 and 1995, at the International Contemporary Arts Fair (FRAC) in Paris; in 1983, at the Paris Salon de Mai; in 1987, at the Salon de Montrouge; in 1991 at Bennington College, Vermont (USA); in 1992 in New York; in 1993, at the Salon Découvertes in Paris; in 1994, at the Musée des Beaux-Arts in Lorient; in 1995, at the Contemporary Art Museum at Tampa University, Florida; and, in 1997, at the 'Le Quartier' Centre d'Art Contemporain in Quimper and at *Abstraction/Abstractions - Géométries Provisoires* (*Abstraction/Abstractions - Provisional Geometry*), held at the Musée d'Art Moderne in St-Étienne. Solo exhibitions by Bruno Rousselot date back to 1981 and include: in 1991, 1993, 1994 and 1996, at the Galerie Zürcher in Paris; in 1992 and 1995, at the Lennon Weinberg Gallery in New York; in 1995, at the École des Beaux-Arts in Valence and at the Centre d'Art Contemporain in Vassivière (Limousin); and, in 1997, at the Atelier Cantoisel in Joigny (Yonne), with Madé.

Bibliography:
Bruno Rousselot - Delta, exhibition catalogue, Gal. Zürcher, Paris, 1994. Piguet, Philippe, "*Bruno Rousselot*' in *Art Press* n° 192, periodical, Paris, June 1994. *Bruno Rousselot*, exhibition leaflet, Centre d'Art Contemporain de Vassivière en Limousin, Beaumont-du-Lac, 1995. Jover, Manuel, "*Bruno Rousselot*' in *Beaux-Arts Magazine* n° 142, periodical, Paris, February 1996. Ceysson, Bernard/Chassey, Éric de/Morineau, Camille, *Abstraction/Abstractions Géométries provisoires*, exhibition catalogue, Musée d'Art Moderne, St-Étienne, 1997.

Museums and Galleries:
Paris (FNAC).

ROUSSELOT, Ernest
French, 19th century.
Born 19th century, in Paris.
Painter. Still-lifes.

Ernest Rousselot exhibited at the Salon in 1869 and 1870.

ROUSSELOT, J. L.
French, 18th century.
Active during the second half of the 18th century.
Sculptor (wood).

J.L. Rousselot sculpted a confessional and stalls in Courtempierre church in 1788.

ROUSSELOT, Lucien
French, 20th century.
Born 21 July 1900, in St-Germain-sous-Doue (Seine-et-Marne); died 4 May 1992, in Fay-les-Etangs (Oise).
Painter. Military subjects.
Lucien Rousselot was an official painter to the French forces.
AUCTION RECORDS:
PARIS, 23 Oct 1992, *Cavalry Batman of 1750* (gouache/card, 25 1/2 x 19 3/4 ins / 65 x 50 cm) FRF 8,000.

ROUSSENCQ, Jean Pierre
French, 18th century.
Died 1756.
Active in Bordeaux.
Potter.
In 1740, Roussencq founded the pottery factory in Marans.
MUSEUMS AND GALLERIES:
PARIS (Mus. National de Céramique Sèvres): several works.

ROUSSET, Françoise
French, 20th - 21st century.
Born 19 April 1952.
Painter. Animals, flowers. Murals.
Françoise Rousset is a painter who also works with children and teaches architecture in St-Étienne. She has painted building-site décors since 1982 and has since received public commissions for schools. She has shown her work in group exhibitions: in 1976, at the Maison de la Culture in St-Étienne; and, in 1989 and 1991 respectively, at *De Georges Matthieu à Charles Belle (From Georges Matthieu to Charles Belle)* and *Sept Artistes d'Aujourd'hui (Seven Contemporary Artists)*, exhibitions held at the R. Mischkind Gallery in Lille. She also exhibited solo in St-Étienne in 1977.

ROUSSET, Helene
German, 19th century.
Born 5 October 1840, in Berlin.
Painter.
Rousset was a pupil of Eschke and Flickel.

ROUSSET, Henri. See **DIDIER DE ROUSSET Henri**

ROUSSET, Jules
French, 19th century.
Born 15 March 1840, in Aillant-sur-Milleron.
Painter. Portraits, waterscapes, landscapes.
Jules Rousset was a student of Léon Cogniet and Isidore Pils at the École des Beaux-Arts in Paris. He exhibited at the Paris Salon from 1867. He painted mainly portraits.
MUSEUMS AND GALLERIES:
AUXERRE: *Banks of the Yonne at Preuilly; Study of a Chimney Sweep* - ORLÉANS: *Head of an Italian Woman* (1873).

ROUSSEV, Svetlin
Bulgarian, 20th century.
Born 14 June 1933, in Pleven.
Painter.
Roussev studied in the studio of Detchko Ouzounovdans at the academy of fine arts in Sofia, where he has taught since 1975 He lives and works in Sofia and is president of the official union of Bulgarian artists. He works in a range of cold blues and purples, often applied in thick blue-green combinations with a knife. He paints obviously anguished figures, which were somewhat out-of-step with the directives of Socialist Realism in the Soviet era.

Roussev has participated in numerous collective exhibitions in Bulgaria, as well as in Budapest, Warsaw, Prague, Berlin, Moscow, Leningrad (now St Petersburg) and Bucharest. He has also shown in Paris at the Salon d'Automne, as well as in Munich, New York, Washington, Tokyo (notably at the Salon Nika Kai). Among the prizes he has received are the gold medal and first prize at the first national exhibition of young artists (1961) and the prize of the first International Biennale of Painting in Sofia (1973).
BIBLIOGRAPHY:
'*Svetlin Roussev*' in *Salon d'Automne*, exhibition catalogue, Paris, 1987.
MUSEUMS AND GALLERIES:
SOFIA (Gradska chudozestvena galerija/Municipal Art Gallery) - SOFIA (Nacionalna chudozestvena galerija/National Gallery of Art).
AUCTION RECORDS:
LONDON, 26 Oct 1989, *In Expectancy* (1988, oil on canvas, 75 1/4 x 72 3/4 ins / 191 x 185 cm) GBP 6,600. LONDON, 18 Oct 1990, *In Expectancy* (1988, oil on canvas, 75 1/4 x 72 3/4 ins / 191 x 185 cm) GBP 14,300.

ROUSSI, Marcel
French, 20th century.
Born 1906; died 1983.
Painter. Landscapes.
Marcel Roussi was a town planner for the city of Paris then for the ministry of public works. He developed urban themes in his art, taking part in the Salon des Indépendants in 1971.
MUSEUMS AND GALLERIES:
NARBONNE (MAH): *Route Nationale 20.*

ROUSSIGNEUX, Charles François
French, 19th century.
Born 4 February 1818, in Paris.
Draughtsman.
Charles Roussigneux exhibited some drawings for the decoration of an edition of the *Gospels* at the Paris Salon in 1868 and 1870.

ROUSSIL, Robert
Canadian, 20th century.
Born 1925, in Montreal.
Active from 1957 in France.
Sculptor. Architectural integration.
Robert Roussil studied at the Montreal School of Fine Art from 1945-1946 and went on to teach there from 1946-1948. He was a member of the Sculptors Association of Quebec.

Early in his career, until around 1954, he primarily sculpted nudes in wood. These often led to accusations of obscenity and caused him a few administrative difficulties. He then moved towards a more symbolic type of expression, though still grounded in the full, supple forms of the human anatomy. He also worked in bronze and concrete. In the works he made shortly before 1970 he introduced a few mobile elements requiring interaction with the spectator. Roussil made sculptures for public places and monumental works, notably for the highway from Ville-Marie to Montreal.

His work was shown in many group exhibitions, including the 1961 Symposium in Yugoslavia, the 1966 Symposium in Quebec, the Symposium in Montreal and *Three Generations of Quebec Art* at the Museum of Contemporary Art, Montreal in 1976. His solo exhibitions included shows in Paris in 1956, Nice in 1961, Montreal in 1962 and 1966 and Cannes in 1968.
MUSEUMS AND GALLERIES:
MONTREAL (MAC): *Flying Bird* (1949) - MONTREAL (Musée des Beaux-Arts): *Family* (1949).

ROUSSILLE, Guy
French, 20th century.
Born 1944, in Castelculier (Lot-et-Garonne).
Painter, engraver, sculptor.
Guy Roussille's work is direct and refreshing, akin to Pop Art and reminiscent of the Ornamentalism of Corneille (Cornelis van Beverloo). He has been involved in various group exhibitions, including the Salon Grands et Jeunes d'Aujourd'hui and the Salon de la Jeune Sculpture. His work featured in *De Bonnard à Baselitz - Dix Ans d'enrichissements*

du cabinet des estampes 1978-1988 (*From Bonnard to Baselitz: A Decade of Acquisitions by the Prints Collection 1978-1988*), an exhibition held in 1993 at the Bibliothèque Nationale in Paris.
MUSEUMS AND GALLERIES:
PARIS (BNF): *Cosmic Meaning* (1979).

ROUSSILLON, Master of the. See **MASTERS**

ROUSSIN
French, 19th century.
Active in Réunion (French Indian Ocean) c. 1860.
Painter, lithographer. Portraits, landscapes.
Roussin illustrated the *Album of La Réunion*.

ROUSSIN, Alfred Victor
French, 19th century.
Born 19th century, in Nantes.
Painter.
Alfred Roussin exhibited at the Paris Salon from 1887.

ROUSSIN, Georges
French, 19th - 20th century.
Born 19 November 1854, in St-Denis (Réunion).
Painter, pastellist. History painting, portraits, genre scenes.
Georges Roussin studied under Cabanel, Jules Lefebvre and Millet. From 1878, he exhibited at the Paris Salon, winning a silver medal in 1920.
MUSEUMS AND GALLERIES:
DIEPPE: *Dieppe Fisherwoman* (pastel) - TOULON: *Laertes and Hamlet Arguing; Portrait of a Lady* (pastel).
AUCTION RECORDS:
LONDON, 25 March 1987, *Florists Watching for Customers* (1891, oil on canvas, 37 1/2 x 50 1/2 ins / 95 x 128 cm) GBP 5,000. PARIS, 30 May 1988, *Portrait of a Woman* (1913, oil on canvas, 41 3/4 x 35 ins / 106 x 89 cm) FRF 4,800.

ROUSSIN, Victor Marie
French, 19th century.
Born 3 March 1812, in Quimper; died c. 1900.
Painter. Genre scenes, landscapes, mountainscapes, waterscapes.
Victor Roussin was a student of François Ricois, Lapito de Simé, Siméon Fort and Évariste Luminais. He settled in Keraval, near Quimper. He featured at the Paris Salon from 1838.

He painted the sites and rugged inhabitants of Armorica. He also produced some views of the Pyrenées.

In 1980, he was represented at the exhibition organised at the Grand Palais by the Musée des Arts et Traditions Populaires.
MUSEUMS AND GALLERIES:
BREST: *Undergrowth; Farm in Penmenez* - LE PUY-EN-VELAY: *Landscape* - NANTES (MBA): *Last Rays* - NICE: *At School; The One Who Hasn't Done Her Homework* - ORLÉANS: *Elderly Woman Unwinding Some Hemp near a Press-House*.
AUCTION RECORDS:
PARIS, 13 Feb 1951, *Exotic Landscape* (1854) FRF 2,800.

ROUSSY, Gilles
French, 20th century.
Sculptor.
Cyber Art.
Gilles Roussy uses computers to create machines which respond to light but also to the human presence. The to-and-froing of the audience triggers off sound and light phenomena.

ROUSSY, Toussaint
French, 19th century.
Born 1847, in Sète.
Painter, draughtsman. Genre scenes, landscapes, waterscapes, still-lifes.
Toussaint Roussy was a student at the École des Beaux-Arts in Paris. He was a curator at the museum in Sète. He exhibited at the Paris Salon from 1877.
MUSEUMS AND GALLERIES:
BÉZIERS: *Cooper's Refreshment Room* - SÈTE: *Fiddler's Lunch; Church Verger; Entrance to the Port of Sète; Time for the Glass of Beer*.

ROUST, Jean Henri
French, 19th century.
Born 1795, in Troyes.
Active in Paris.
Miniaturist.
Jean Roust exhibited pictures of insects at the Salon from 1824 to 1833.

ROUSTAN, Émile
French, 19th - 20th century.
Born in Pnomh Penh, to French parents.
Painter. Landscapes, flowers.
Émile Roustan exhibited at the Salon des Indépendants from 1902.
AUCTION RECORDS:
PARIS, 28 Jan 1943, *The Valley*, FRF 950. PARIS, 16 March 1989, *Still-life of Fruit and Flowers on a Drapery* (1906, oil on canvas, 21 1/4 x 25 1/2 ins / 54 x 65 cm) FRF 4,000.

ROUSTAN, Lucien Paul Marius
French, 20th century.
Born 3 July 1886, in Toulon; died 19 September 1914, in Bar-le-Duc.
Painter.
Lucien Roustan studied under Cormon. He died in action in 1914. He exhibited at the Salon des Artistes Français.

ROUSTAN, Pierre Laurent
French, 20th century.
Born 11 October 1877, in Toulouse.
Sculptor, designer.
Pierre Roustan exhibited at the Salon des Artistes Français, of which he was an associate member from 1917, and Salon de la Société Nationale des Beaux-Arts. He was awarded the Légion d'Honneur in 1926.

ROUSTEAU, Henri (Abbé)
French, 19th century.
Born 28 July 1814, in Bourgneuf-en-Retz; died 10 July 1881, in Nantes.
Draughtsman, sculptor, painter, architect.

ROUTCHINE-VITRY, Sonia
Ukrainian, 20th century.
Born 29 September 1878, in Odessa; died 29 March 1931, in Paris.
Active in France.
Painter. Figures, scenes with figures.
Routchine-Vitry studied with Humbert and Adler. She received a silver medal in 1924 and in 1929. She exhibited *Little Girl in a Red Turban* in London at a summer exhibition of the Royal Academy of Arts in 1914.
BIBLIOGRAPHY:
'*Royal Academy Exhibitors 1905-1970*' in vol. III, Hilmarton Manor Press, Calne, 1987.

ROUTHIER, Maurice
French, 20th century.
Born 4 November 1891, in Rheims; died during World War I, on the battlefield.
Painter.
Maurice Routhier was an architect. He featured at the Salon des Artistes Français and received an honourable mention in 1909.

ROUTIER, Claude
French, 18th century.

Active in Aix-en-Provence in 1729.
Sculptor.

ROUTIER DE LISLE, Jean Henry
French, 18th - 19th century.
Born 21 August 1747, in Paris; died 4 December 1817, in Paris.
Painter. History painting.

Routier de Lisle became a pupil at the school of the Académie Royale, in September 1766, under the patronage of Chardin, and remained there until 1769. He lived at first with his mother, a merchant by the Pont Marie. In 1768 he was the pupil of Monnet and lived in the Rue St-Louis en l'Ile, in the house of Ustache (or, probably, Eustache). He was a history painter and a talented artist whose paintings were very well-regarded; among them was *Jephthah's Sacrifice*. He used colour effectively in rendering the expressions on the faces and the feelings of his figures. He fled Paris in 1793 at the time of the French Revolution as he was sought as a suspect, leaving his fortune, his family papers and his belongings, which were taken or destroyed.

ROUTTIMANN. See **REUTTIMANN**

ROUVE, Jean de
Flemish School, 15th century.
Active in Tournai.
Sculptor.

De Rouve was commissioned in 1475 to sculpt statues of saints for the church of Notre-Dame in Courtrai.

ROUVERET, René
French, 20th century.
Engraver, illustrator. Seascapes.

René Rouveret studied at the École des Beaux-Arts in Nîmes (Gard). He was a sailor before engraving seafaring subjects. He illustrated the *Voyage de Jacques Cartier* (*Jacques Cartier's Voyage*) by E. Peisson, *Le Vieux Port* (*The Old Port*) by Blaise Cendrars.

ROUVEYRE, André
French, 20th century.
Born 29 March 1896, in Paris; died 1962.
Painter, draughtsman, illustrator. Portraits.

André Rouveyre is not easily summed up, having forsaken his pens and pencils in order to write, mostly about other writers such as Remy de Gourmont and Apollinaire. He sustained a voluminous correspondence with Matisse. He furnished satirical papers with brash caricatures, before undertaking his set of *Contemporary Portraits*. In this capacity he proved to be ferociously perceptive. His books treating of women *Le Gynécée* (*The Gynaeceum*) and *Phèdre* (*Phaedra*) show a strange mixture of pity and cruelty.

BIBLIOGRAPHY:
Finsen, Hanne (ed.), *Matisse: correspondance avec André Rouveyre*, Flammarion, Paris, 2001.

AUCTION RECORDS:
PARIS, 27 Nov 1944, *Women at Supper*, FRF 100; *Woman Reclining Seen from Behind* (colouring pencil) FRF 100.

ROUVIER, Noémie, pseudonym: Claude Vignon
Maiden name: Cadiot
French, 19th century.
Born c. 1832; died 10 April 1888, in Nice.
Sculptor, writer.

Noémie Rouvier was a student of Pradier. She executed sculptures at the Louvre, the Tuileries, the St Michel fountain, Montholon square and the church of St Denis-du-St-Sacrement in Paris.

MUSEUMS AND GALLERIES:
CAEN - CHÂTEAU-THIERRY - MARSEILLES - ROMORANTIN.

ROUVIER, Pierre, or Rouvière
French, 18th century.
Born c. 1742, in Aix-en-Provence.
Miniaturist.

Rouvier entered the school of the Académie Royale in January 1770, under the patronage of Dendré-Bardou and recommended by De Marigny. His name is spelt 'Rouvière' on the register of pupils, and 'Rouvier' on the alphabetical list of the same register. He exhibited portraits and genre subjects in miniature at the Salon de la Correspondance in 1779 and 1782. He was probably one and the same as the painter Pierre Rouvier who was in Grenoble around 1774.

AUCTION RECORDS:
PARIS, 28-29 May 1923, *Young Woman Holding a Naked Child in Her Arms* (miniature) FRF 1,905. PARIS, 22 Nov 1926, *Portrait de Jeune Femme Représentée en Source* (miniature) FRF 2,200. PARIS, 13 June 1952, *Portrait of a Young Woman Playing the Guitar*, FRF 113,000. LONDON, 24 May 2000, *Louis Marie Dulieu de Chenevoux in Uniform of Régiment du Roy Infantry* (miniature, h. 2 1/2 ins / 6 cm) GBP 3,000. LONDON, 24 May 2000, *Young Gentleman in Fur-bordered Silk Day Gown* (1780, miniature) GBP 6,000. LONDON, 6 Nov 2001, *Lady in a White Dress with Blue Sash* (1791, miniature) GBP 1,100. LONDON, 22 April 2004, *Lady in a Blue-Grey Dress and Gauze Shawl* (miniature) GBP 2,800.

ROUVIÈRE, Charles Claude Étienne
French, 19th - 20th century.
Born 1866, in Lyons; died December 1924, in Chatou.
Painter. Urban landscapes, landscapes.

Charles Rouvière studied under Pierre Miciol at the École des Beaux-Arts in Lyons. He associated with Garrand, Ravier, Vernay and Terraire. He exhibited at the Salon de la Société Lyonnaise des Beaux-Arts, where he was declared hors concours, having received medals in 1900-1903. He also showed in Buenos Aires in 1909. He has left views of Lyons' historic centre, of its surrounding region, of Savoy and of Corsica. He drew in charcoal on the Front during World War I and decorated cafés and restaurants in Lyons.

MUSEUMS AND GALLERIES:
LYONS (MBA).

ROUVIERE, Daniel
French, 20th century.
Born 6 September 1913, in Paris; died 17 March 1985, in Barbizon.
Painter, engraver, illustrator. Scenes with figures, landscapes, animals.

Daniel Rouviere was trained at the École des Beaux-Arts in Paris and the Académie de la Grande Chaumière. He studied under Maurice Testart, René-Xavier Prinet, Gaston Billoul, Jean de la Hougue and Vaillant. He taught at the École Art et Nature in Barbizon. For 10 years, he worked in the open, closely studying the flora fauna and everyday life of the Barbizon region. They inspired compositions painted on wood panels. His matter-laden, picturesque pieces, often in small formats, add a naive touch to his realistic observations.

From 1933 he exhibited at the Salon de la Société Nationale des Beaux-Arts and in 1938 he was awarded its prize for *The Spanish Revolution*. He also won a prize from the Carnegie Institute in Chicago. He had a one-man exhibition in Paris in 1944.

MUSEUMS AND GALLERIES:
BARBIZON - DAMMARIE-LES-LYS - PARIS (FMAC).

AUCTION RECORDS:
PARIS, 27 June 1990, *Resting* (oil on canvas, 11 x 13 1/2 ins / 27 x 34.5 cm) FRF 8,000.

ROUVIÈRE, Jean Louis Daniel
Swiss, 18th - 19th century.
Born 3 December 1750, in Chêne; died 31 March 1825, in Plainpalais.
Miniaturist.

Rouvière collaborated with F.J. Wolff.

ROUVIÈRE, M.
French (?), 18th century.
Active 1785-1789.
Draughtsman.

ROUVIÈRE, Philibert
French, 19th century.
Born 19 March 1805, in Nîmes; died 19 October 1865, in Paris.
Painter, draughtsman. Allegorical subjects.

Philibert Rouvière studied painting in Baron Gros's studio. A famous comedian of his era, he devoted himself mainly to theatre and, along with Frédérick Lemaire and Bocage, was one of the best interpreters of the dramatists in the Romantic School.

He featured at the Paris Salon from 1831 to 1864. His works include: *Hamlet Forcing His Mother to Contemplate the Portrait of the Late King*, and *The Girondists in Prison*. He fell ill and was financially ruined at the beginning of 1865.

ROUVIÈRE, Pierre. See **ROUVIER**

ROUVILLE DE MEUX, H. J. de
Dutch, 19th - 20th century.
Born 17 November 1863, in Curaçao.
Painter, engraver.

H. J. de Rouville de Meux was a student of Fr. J. Jansen at the academy in The Hague.

ROUVILLOIS, Gwen
French, 20th - 21st century.
Born 1968.
Painter.
Conceptual Art.

Gwen Rouvillois studied from 1988 to 1993 at the École des Beaux-Arts in Paris. She now lives and works in Paris. She was awarded the Gras Savoye Prize in 1994.

Gwen Rouvillois is preoccupied with how painting is currently perceived and conceived. Thus, while producing landscape compositions in a traditional, 'standard' style, she effectively blocks direct access to her work by superimposing extracts from laws and statutory instruments and wrapping the entire work in transparent plastic in order to stress the 'packaged' aspect of art as a neatly-packaged consumer good.

Rouvillois has shown her work at various group exhibitions: in 1993, at the Salon de Montrouge; in 1995, at *Bleu pour les Filles* (*Blue for Girls*), an exhibition at the École des Beaux-Arts in Paris; and, in 1997, at *Philippe Lepeut, Miguel-Angel Molina, Gwen Rouvillois*, held at the Centre d'Art Contemporain in Rueil-Malmaison. She has also exhibited solo, notably in 1996, 1997 and 1998 at the Galerie Zürcher in Paris.

ROUVRE, B. L. M. Philippe de
French, 19th century.
Born 19th century, in Lille.
Sculptor.

B. L. M. Philippe de Rouvre was a student of Bourgeois. He exhibited medallions at the Salon from 1881.

ROUVRE, Yves, pseudonym of Rigolot
French, 20th century.
Born 4 November 1910, in Paris; died July 1996, in Paris.
Painter, watercolourist. Landscapes.

Yves Rouvre was the son of the painter Albert Rigolot. Briefly a student at the École des Arts Décoratifs in Paris, he soon moved on to the free academies. World War II and subsequent stays in Tunisia then Indochina interrupted the association he had initiated with Le Moal, Manessier, Gruber, Tal Coat, Tailleux and Giacometti. He settled in Provence, but worked also in Paris. He did mural decorations in Tunisia. In France, he subjected his art to a radical review in the wake of Tal-Coat's minimalist approach and returned to his studio to paint vibrant, dynamic pieces from watercolours made on site.

He took part in the Salon de Mai and in *L'École de Paris* (*The School of Paris*) at the Galerie Charpentier in 1954. He also showed his works in solo exhibitions in galleries in Paris, particularly with Louise Leiris.

ROUVRE

Rouvre

BIBLIOGRAPHY:
Limbour, Georges (preface), *Yves Rouvre*, exhibition catalogue, Gal. Louise Leiris, Paris, 1961. Joly, Pierre (preface), *Yves Rouvre - Végétation*, exhibition catalogue, Gal. Louise Leiris, Paris, 1975. Harambourg, Lydia, *L'École de Paris 1945-1965 - Dictionnaire des peintres*, Ides et Calendes, Neuchâtel, 1993.

AUCTION RECORDS:
PARIS, 26 May 1989, *Landscape* (1954, oil on canvas, 19 3/4 x 25 1/2 ins / 50 x 65 cm) FRF 6,500.

ROUVROY, Marie von
German, 19th century.
Born 19 July 1826, in Dresden; died 21 July 1893, in Dresden.
Portrait artist.

Von Rouvroy was a pupil of Scholz, Grosse and Böttcher in Dresden.

ROUW, Franz Ludwig. See **RAUFFT**

ROUW, H.
British, 18th - 19th century.
Active in London from 1796 to 1821.
Miniaturist. Portraits, Still-lifes (insects).

H. Rouw exhibited at the Royal Academy on several occasions between 1796 and 1821.

ROUW, Peter I
Flemish School, 18th century.
Died 1807?
Sculptor.

Rouw exhibited wax and marble busts in London from 1787 to 1800. His works are difficult to separate from those of his son Peter Rouw II. He also sculpted tombs.

MUSEUMS AND GALLERIES:
LONDON (Victoria and Albert Mus.): *Portraits of the Family of George III* (attributed).

ROUW, Peter II
British, 18th - 19th century.
Born c. 1771; died 9 December 1852, in Pentonville (London).
Sculptor.

Peter Rouw exhibited wax busts and medallions at the Royal Academy in London from 1795 to 1820. He also sculpted tombs.

MUSEUMS AND GALLERIES:
LONDON (National Portrait Gal.): *James Watt* (1802, wax medallion) - LONDON (Victoria and Albert Mus.): *Matthew Boulton* (medallion).

ROUW, W.
Dutch, 19th - 20th century.
Born 12 May 1874, in Goës.
Painter.

ROUX (maître). See **ROSSO, Il**

ROUX, Alexandre Georges
French, 19th century.

Born in Ganges; died 19th century, in Paris.
Painter. History painting, genre scenes.

Alexandre Roux was a student of Jean Paul Laurens. He exhibited at the Salon from 1880 (Salon of 1882: *Macbeth*) He is comparable with Georges Roux.

MUSEUMS AND GALLERIES:
BÉZIERS: *Macbeth*.

ROUX, Alexandre Théodore
French, 19th - 20th century.
Born 1854, in Paris; died 8 September 1909, in Lisbon.
Painter, designer.

ROUX, André Fernand
French, 20th century.
Born 7 October 1894, in Martinique; died 4 December 1974, in Toulouse.
Painter. Portraits, interiors, landscapes, flowers.

André Roux studied painting in 1912 in Paris at the Académie Julian and at the Grande Chaumière alongside Modigliani. From 1919 to 1964 he lived in Tunisia, where he regularly exhibited. Back in France in 1966, he settled in Toulouse. He exhibited at the Salon des Artistes Français, of which he was an associate member.

ROUX, Anne Marie
French, 20th century.
Born 10 August 1898, in Nevers.
Sculptor, engraver, medallist. Religious subjects.

Anne Marie Roux studied under Victor J. Ségoffin. From 1923 she exhibited at the Salon des Artistes Français and the Salon d'Automne. She also showed at the last Exposition Coloniale in 1931.

ROUX, Antoine
French, 19th century.
Born 19th century, in Combronde.
Painter, watercolourist. Architectural views, landscapes.

Antoine Roux was a student of Devedeux. He exhibited at the Salon from 1863 to 1882. He mainly portrayed sites in the Auvergne. He produced some watercolours.

MUSEUMS AND GALLERIES:
CARCASSONNE: *Courtyard Interior in Davayat*.

ROUX, Antoine or Antoine Mathieu (son)
French, 19th century.
Born 1799, in Marseilles; died 1872, in Marseilles.
Painter, watercolourist. Seascapes.

Antoine Roux was the son of Joseph Ange Antoine Roux.

MUSEUMS AND GALLERIES:
PARIS (Mus. de la Marine).

AUCTION RECORDS:
PARIS, 25 Oct 1933, *Seascapes* (two watercolours) FRF 360. PARIS, 13 Dec 1946, *Yacht at Sea* (watercolour) FRF 20,500. PARIS, 21 May 1951, *Marie-Louise Taking the Pilot to Enter Ruzarchée on 8 April 1864* (1864, watercolour) FRF 11,000. PARIS, 24 Nov 1979, *The Arion, Square Three-Master* (watercolour, 16 1/2 x 22 ins / 42 x 56 cm) FRF 16,000. NICE, 16 Dec 1981, *Portrait of Brig* (1851, watercolour) FRF 13,000. PARIS, 10 July 1983, *Square Three-Master before the Fort of St Jean* (watercolour, 14 1/2 x 20 3/4 ins / 37 x 53 cm) FRF 24,000. PARIS, 19 Oct 1985, *The Brig Aglaea* (watercolour, 17 1/4 x 22 1/2 ins / 44 x 57 cm) FRF 22,000. MONACO, 7 Dec 1990, *The Lucile under Captain Albrand's Command* (1831, lead pencil, brown ink and watercolour, 17 1/4 x 22 1/4 ins / 44 x 56.5 cm) FRF 35,520; *Naval Combat between a Danish Military Brig and Two English Corvettes* (lead pencil, ink and watercolour, 17 1/4 x 23 1/4 ins / 44 x 59 cm) FRF 61,050. LONDON, 20 May 1992, *The Holy Spirit Battling against the Wind* (1817, watercolour and ink, 12 1/2 x 17 ins / 32 x 43 cm) GBP 935. PARIS, 31 Jan 1993, *The Lucile, Journey to Batavia* (1831, watercolour, 17 3/4 x 23 1/4 ins / 45 x 59 cm) FRF 55,000. PARIS, 12 Dec 1997, *Three-Master Boats* (watercolour and gouache, 17 1/2 x 22 1/2 ins / 44.5 x 57 cm) FRF 41,000. PARIS, 30 Jan 2000, *French Threemasters in Sail* (1857, watercolour, 17 x 22 ins / 44 x 57 cm) FRF 38,000. PARIS, 30 Jan 2000, *The Jacques Cartier de St-Malo* (watercolour, 18 x 22 ins / 45 x 57 cm) FRF 70,000. PORTSMOUTH, 18 Aug 2001, *Argus Commanded by C Gilpatrick in a Severe Gale* (1824, watercolour, 7 x 9 ins / 17 x 23 cm) USD 9,000. LONDON, 19 Nov 2003, *The Beatrice of Dundee in Smyrna Bay* (1832, pen, ink and watercolour, 17 x 23 ins / 43 x 58 cm) GBP 1,400.

ROUX, Antoine or Joseph Ange Antoine
French, 18th - 19th century.
Born 1765, in Marseilles; died 1835, in Marseilles.
Painter, watercolourist, draughtsman. Seascapes, landscapes.

Antoine Roux painted mainly seascapes, with a preference for naval battles.

MUSEUMS AND GALLERIES:
DRAGUIGNAN: *Seascapes* - NICE: *Seascapes* - PARIS (Mus. de la Marine): *Seascapes*.

AUCTION RECORDS:
PARIS, 9 Dec 1926, *Fishermen and Boats at a Port Entrance; Boats and Fishermen*, FRF 2,980. PARIS, 30 March 1963, *French Warship at Anchor* (watercolour) FRF 7,100. PARIS, 18 June 1964, *'Achilles', Captain Louis Reynaud; 'Éclair', Schooner of S. M.* (two watercolours) FRF 9,200. PARIS, 6 Dec 1966, *View of the Entrance to the Port of Marseilles from the Embankment of the Square of St-Jean; View of the Entrance to the Port of Marseilles, from the Square of Abbaye St-Victor* (two watercolours) FRF 15,800. PARIS, 15 June 1983, *Battleship 'Hirondelle' Attacking a Spanish Battleship* (1811, watercolour, 17 3/4 x 26 ins / 45 x 66 cm) FRF 58,000. LONDON, 9 July 1985, *Frigate 'Minerva' and Other Ships* (watercolour and pen, 20 1/4 x 33 1/2 ins / 51.7 x 85 cm) GBP 5,500. LONDON, 22 Oct 1986, *'Triton' Arriving in the Port of Marseilles with Prisoners on Board* (1800, watercolour and pen, 14 x 21 ins / 35.5 x 53.5 cm) GBP 2,000. LONDON, 6 May 1987, *Three-master 'Charles' at Sea* (1816, watercolour and pencil heightened with white, 16 x 22 ins / 40.5 x 56 cm) GBP 2,200. LONDON, 17 Nov 1989, *'Bellerophon' Entering Mahon Port* (oil on canvas, 15 x 23 1/4 ins / 37.8 x 59.1 cm) GBP 11,000. MONACO, 7 Dec 1990, *View of the Port of Marseilles and the Harbour* (1831, lead pencil, brown ink and watercolour, 16 3/4 x 22 ins / 42.5 x 55 cm) FRF 83,250; *American Three-master* (1818, lead pencil, ink and watercolour, 16 x 21 ins / 40.5 x 53.3 cm) FRF 53,280; *The Ship 'Zelima' Commanded by Captain Albrand* (1833, lead pencil, brown ink and watercolour, 17 1/4 x 22 1/2 ins / 43.7 x 57.2 cm) FRF 37,740. LONDON, 22 Nov 1991, *Brigantine 'Duc d'Angoulême' off Marseilles* (1818, pencil and watercolour heightened with white, 17 x 23 ins / 43.2 x 58.4 cm) GBP 3,080. PARIS, 10 June 1992, *'Lougre' Rigged as a Schooner and 'Aigle' Seen on the Starboard Side Approaching Marseilles* (1803, pen and watercolour) FRF 75,000. COPENHAGEN, 16 May 1994, *Three-master 'Thetis' off Marseilles* (1807, watercolour, 17 1/4 x 24 1/2 ins / 44 x 62 cm. PARIS, 3 June 1994, *Battle of Navarin* (October 1827, pen and watercolour, 20 1/2 x 28 3/4 ins / 52 x 73 cm) FRF 120,000. LONDON, 30 May 1996, *Frigate 'Révolutionnaire' Sailing* (1820) GBP 3,910. PARIS, 30 Oct 1996, *The Ship 'Éclair'* (1808, pen, black ink and watercolour, 14 1/2 x 22 ins / 37 x 56 cm) FRF 28,500. BOLTON, 28 Feb 1999, *Salange, Capt G Calis, a Brig off Marseilles* (watercolour, 17 x 22 ins / 43 x 56 cm. TROYES, 26 Sept 1999, *The Vittoria d'Algeri* (1795, gouache, 13 x 20 ins / 33 x 51 cm) FRF 28,000. PARIS, 30 Jan 2000, *The Breslaw Capitaine* (1809, watercolour, 19 x 27 ins / 47 x 68 cm) FRF 65,000. BOLTON, 29 Oct 2000, *British Ship Seen Entering the Harbour at Marseilles* (1815, watercolour, 17 x 23 ins / 43 x 58 cm) USD 9,500. PARIS, 4 April 2001, *Battle and Taking of the English Frigate Proserpine* (1817, watercolour, 13 x 20 ins / 34 x 50 cm) FRF 70,000. LONDON, 24 May

2001, *The Delphine, Capt. A. Sene, on her Way to St Thomas* (1820, pencil and watercolour, 17 x 23 ins / 43 x 59 cm) GBP 11,000. Paris, 25 March 2002, *Egide* (1803, watercolour, 17 x 24 ins / 43 x 62 cm) EUR 15,000. Paris, 11 July 2003, *Three-master in Toulon Harbour* (1811, watercolour, 17 x 23 ins / 42 x 58 cm) EUR 8,500. Paris, 3 July 2004, *The Brig St Jean Baptiste Caught in a Gale in the Iles d'Hieres* (1820, watercolour, 17 x 23 ins / 43 x 58 cm) EUR 7,500. Paris, 3 July 2004, *The Armed Brig Amélie, on the Port Tack before the Fort St Jean* (1824, watercolour, 17 x 23 ins / 42 x 58 cm) EUR 8,100.

ROUX, Anton
Austrian, 19th century.
Active in Vienna.
Painter.

ROUX, Auguste
French, 19th century.
Born 19th century, in Combronde.
Painter. Architectural views, landscapes.

Auguste Roux is probably related to Antoine Roux. He was a student of Devedeux and Clermont. He settled in Clermont-Ferrand and featured at the Paris Salon in 1839, 1847 and 1848.

Museums and Galleries:
Clermont-Ferrand: *View of the Royat Valley.*

Auction records:
London, 17 Nov 1993, *Rural Village* (oil on canvas, 26 x 36 1/4 ins / 66 x 92 cm) GBP 4,830.

ROUX, Auguste Jean Simon
French, 19th century.
Painter. Genre scenes, landscapes.

Active in Paris, Auguste Roux exhibited at the Salon in 1846 with *Glazier, Interior at Chatou* and in 1847 with a *View of the Illumination of the City Hall in Paris on 1 May 1847.* He may be the same as the preceding artist.

ROUX, Barthélemy. See **BERMEJO Bartolomé**

ROUX, Charles Louis. See **ROUX Léon Louis Charles**

ROUX, Constant Ambroise
French, 19th - 20th century.
Born 20 April 1865, in Marseilles; died 1929.
Sculptor. Figures. Groups.

Constant Roux studied under Pierre Jules Cavelier and Louis Ernest Barrias. He was made a Chevalier of the Légion d'Honneur in 1923. His style is realistic. He exhibited at the Salon des Artistes Français, of which he was an associate member and where he was declared hors concours. He received an honourable mention in 1892, came first in the Prix de Rome competition in 1894 and was awarded medals in 1898, 1900, 1902, 1911 and 1930 (medal of honour). In 2003, he featured in the thematic collective exhibition *Vénus et Caïn: Figures de la préhistoire 1830-1930* (*Venus and Cain. Prehistoric Figures 1830-1930*) at the Musée d'Aquitaine in Bordeaux. It chartered the rise of prehistory as a scientific discipline and a source of artistic inspiration.

Bibliography:
Lafont-Couturier, Hélène/Dagen, Philippe/Loizeau, Sigolène, *Vénus et Caïn. Figures de la préhistoire 1830-1930*, exhibition catalogue, Musée d'Aquitaine, Bordeaux, 2003.

Museums and Galleries:
Nantes: *General Lamoricière.*

Auction records:
Paris, 16 Nov 1976, *Gladiator* (bronze, h. 23 1/2 ins / 60 cm) FRF 3,100. Lokeren, 9 Oct 1993, *Bust of a Gladiator* (bronze, h. 13 1/4 ins / 33.5 cm, w. 13 ins/33 cm) BEF 180,000. Paris, 18 Feb 2000, *Head of Heracles* (gold patinated bronze and green marble, 18 x 7x19 ins / 45 x 19x48 cm) FRF 18,000. Paris, 23 Nov 2000, *Bust of a Gladiator* (brown patinated bronze, h. 13 ins / 34 cm) FRF 20,000. Paris, 3 June 2002, *Gladiator* (green patinated bronze, h. 33 ins / 84 cm) EUR 6,800. Munich, 20 Sept 2002, *Young Boy* (varnished patinated bronze, h. 18 ins / 46 cm) EUR 2,100. London, 15 Oct 2003, *Achilles Child* (patinated bronze, h. 14 ins / 35 cm) GBP 1,200. New York, 11 Dec 2003, *Gladiator* (bronze, 26 x 16x15 ins / 67 x 41x39 cm) USD 4,000. London, 24 Feb 2004, *Bust of a Phrygian* (bronze, 17 x 15 ins / 44 x 38 cm) GBP 1,900.

ROUX, David Étienne, called Roux-Constantini
Swiss, 18th - 19th century.
Born 20 February 1758, in Geneva; died 10 June 1832.
Miniaturist.

David Étienne was the son and assistant of Jean-Marc Roux.

ROUX, Édouard
French, 18th century.
Active 1723-1748.
Potter.

Édouard Roux worked in Moustiers, Alcora and Lyons.

ROUX, Émile
French, 19th century.
Born c. 1840, in Vannes.
Painter, watercolourist. Landscapes.

Émile Roux featured at the Paris Salon in 1869 and 1870, mainly with watercolours: *Recollections of Journeys.* We think he belonged to the French naval military.

E.ROUX.

Museums and Galleries:
Rochefort: *Landscape* (watercolour).

Auction records:
Bern, 26 Oct 1988, *Quimper* (oil on canvas, 16 1/4 x 11 ins / 41 x 27 cm) CHF 2,000. Neuilly, 23 Feb 1992, *Area around Marseilles* (1889, oil on canvas, 15 1/4 x 23 1/2 ins / 39 x 60 cm) FRF 4,500. Paris, 17 Dec 2001, *Street Scene at Moyen Orient* (oil on canvas, 9 x 7 ins / 24 x 19 cm) FRF 11,000.

ROUX, Fernand
French, 20th century.
Born 3 October 1906, in Toulouse; died 1994.
Painter, watercolourist, draughtsman. Landscapes. Murals, architectural integration.

Fernand Roux fulfilled a number of government commissions, in particular for schools in Orange, Antibes, Dijon, Ars-sur-Moselle and Longwy. He experimented with abstraction as well as producing figurative work. He exhibited at the Salon de l'Art Libre, of which he was an associate member, and in New York, Chicago, Caracas, Bogotá, Havana, Brussels and Madrid.

Museums and Galleries:
Albi - Caracas (MBA) - Havana (Mus. del Tabaco) - Nice (MBA Jules-Chéret) - Pau - Tarbes - Toulouse (MBA, Mus. des Augustins).

ROUX, Francis
French, 20th century.
Born 9 November 1933.
Painter.

Francis Roux took part in numerous collective exhibitions on eroticism. He had solo shows in Paris in 1969 and 1974 and in Brussels in 1971.

ROUX, François Geoffroy
French, 19th century.
Born 21 October 1811, in Marseilles; died 1882.
Painter, watercolourist, draughtsman. Boats.

François Roux was the son of Joseph Ange Antoine Roux. He painted over 60 war vessels.

Auction records:
Marseilles, 30-31 Jan 1947, *The St Jacques* (1841, watercolour) FRF 5,500. Paris, 19 Oct 1985, *Paddle-Steamer Aigle Maritime No. 2 (Sea Eagle 2)* (1842, watercolour, 19 1/4 x 26 3/4 ins / 49 x 68 cm) FRF 36,000. Monte Carlo, 22 Feb 1986, *Boats near the Port; Boats at Sea* (1875, watercolour, a pair, 12 1/2 x 17 ins / 32 x 43 cm) FRF 35,000. Paris, 14 June 1988, *Europa, Captain Cruz* (1857, watercolour, 18 3/4 x 27 1/4 ins / 47.5 x 69 cm) FRF 48,000. Paris, 14 June 1989, *Aimé and Rosette, Captain Pierre Lafon, Coming to Drop Anchor at Île Sacrifice* (1826, watercolour, 17 x 23 ins / 43 x 58.5 cm) FRF 31,000. La Rochelle, 21 July 1990, *The Vessel 'Jacques Langlois de Grand Ville'; the Vessel 'Valeur d'Aubagne'* (1842 and 1860, watercolour, a pair, each 22 3/4 x 30 ins / 58 x 76 cm) FRF 180,000. Paris, 6 Dec 1990, *Eguille and Gates of Étretat, Fishing Boats Returning to Harbour* (1856, watercolour, 7 1/4 x 12 ins / 18.5 x 30.5 cm) FRF 17,500. Monaco, 7 Dec 1990, *The Vessel St Jacques under Captain Durante's Command in 1841* (lead pencil, brown and black ink, wash and watercolour, 17 1/4 x 22 1/4 ins / 44.1 x 56.7 cm) FRF 44,400; *The Vessel Fanny under Captain Albrand's Command* (1836, lead pencil, brown and black ink, wash and watercolour, 17 1/2 x 22 1/4 ins / 44.3 x 56.5 cm) FRF 55,500. Paris, 10 June 1992, *The Alcyon, Transport Brig no. 31, Taking Part in the Morea Expedition* (1830, watercolour and wash, 17 1/4 x 22 1/2 ins / 44 x 57 cm) FRF 80,000. Paris, 22 Nov 1996, *Aigle (Eagle), Paddle-Boat with Sails* (1878, watercolour and gouache, 20 1/2 x 35 1/2 ins / 52 x 90 cm) FRF 58,000. London, 11 Nov 1999, *The French Barque Ganges in Two Positions in the Mediterranean* (1857, pencil, pen, ink and watercolour, 26 x 37 ins / 67 x 93 cm) GBP 20,000. Nice, 14 Nov 2000, *The Threemaster Antilles Leaving Port at Marseilles* (1858, watercolour, 17 x 22 ins / 43 x 57 cm) FRF 65,000. Nice, 14 Nov 2000, *The Threemaster La Valentine* (1850, watercolour, 17 x 22 ins / 43 x 55 cm) FRF 80,000. Paris, 31 May 2002, *Threemaster in Full Sail* (1864, watercolour, a pair, 16 x 21 ins / 40 x 54 cm) EUR 11,800. London, 26 May 2004, *The Francois-Georges Reefed Down in Heavy Seas* (1872, brown ink and watercolour with scratching out, 16 x 23 ins / 41 x 58 cm) GBP 2,700.

ROUX, Frédéric
French, 19th century.
Born 1805, in Marseilles; died 1874, in Le Havre.
Painter, watercolourist, draughtsman. Seascapes.

Frédéric Roux was the second son of Joseph Ange Antoine Roux. He studied in Horace Vernet's studio in Paris. He travelled in Norway and Russia before settling in 1830 in Le Havre, where he opened a hydrographic shop.

Museums and Galleries:
Paris (Mus. de la Marine).

Auction records:
Paris, 29 June 1927, *The Elizabeth Assailed by a Squall* (1837, watercolour) FRF 480. New York, 11 Dec 1970, *The Lawson, Three-Master* (watercolour) USD 2,750. Paris, 30 June 1978, *John Cokerill's Boat* (1838, watercolour) FRF 5,800. La Flèche, 23 March 1980, *The Hamburg* (watercolour, 15 x 22 1/2 ins / 38 x 57 cm) FRF 3,800. Paris, 3 June 1987, *The Schooner Elizabeth Assailed by a Squall* (1837, watercolour, 16 1/2 x 22 1/2 ins / 42 x 57 cm) FRF 35,000. Paris, 15 June 1988, *Paddle Ship on a Calm Sea, Seen from Starboard Bow, Sailing by Steam* (1834, oil on canvas, 11 x 13 3/4 ins / 27 x 35 cm) FRF 30,000. Monaco, 7 Dec 1990, *Military Brig under Repair in the Main Harbour at Marseilles* (1851, lead pencil, pen, ink and watercolour, 15 1/2 x 22 3/4 ins / 39.5 x 58 cm) FRF 24,420; *Two Vessels on a Stormy Sea* (1830, lead pencil, ink, brown wash and watercolour, 12 1/4 x 16 1/4 ins / 31 x 41 cm) FRF 37,740. London, 20 May 1992, *The Theoxena* (1851, watercolour, 16 x 22 ins / 40.5 x 56 cm) GBP 990. Paris, 28 April 1994, *Shore at Edge of the Sea* (1829, oil on canvas, 9 1/2 x 12 3/4 ins / 24.2 x 32.5 cm) FRF 4,200. New York, 9 March 1996, *The Alarm, British Yacht, on the Open Sea* (1867, ink and pencil/card, 11 1/2 x 16 1/4 ins / 29.2 x 41.3 cm) USD 1,035. Paris, 28 Jan 1999, *Schooner Flying American Flag* (1866, 17 x 23 ins / 42 x 58 cm) FRF 18,000. Paris, 24 Sept 2000, *The Port of Toulons and its Masting Machinery* (1832, watercolour, 8 x 11 ins / 21 x 27 cm) FRF 22,000. Nice, 14 Nov 2000, *Ships Sailing at Dawn for Marseilles* (1859, watercolour, 25 x 43 ins / 64 x 109 cm) FRF 95,000. London, 16 Sept 2003, *The British Paddle Steamer St Winifred Cruising off Marseilles* (1824, pen, ink and watercolour heightened with white, 17 x 23 ins / 44 x 58 cm) GBP 2,300. New York, 10 Feb 2004, *Forty-four Gun French Frigate under Reduced Sail in the Mediterranean* (1832, pencil, grey ink and watercolour on board, 23 x 32 ins / 59 x 82 cm) USD 5,000. London, 26 May 2004, *Frigate at Anchor in a Bay Undergoing an Extensive Refit* (1834, pencil, black ink and watercolour, 8 x 13 ins / 20 x 32 cm) GBP 2,500.

ROUX, Gaston Louis, or Le Roux
French, 20th century.
Born 24 February 1904, in Provins (Seine-et-Marne); died 30 March 1988, in Paris.
Painter, engraver, illustrator.

Gaston Roux stood out in his youth for his lively imagination. He studied at the Académie Ranson in Paris under Vuillard, Sérusier and Maurice Denis. In the early 1920s he worked as an assistant decorator with Raoul Dufy. Meeting André Masson in 1924, he developed in his company a light-hearted Surrealism tinged with humorous touches taken from Cubism. He illustrated *Les Exploits d'un jeune Don Juan* (*The Memoirs of a Young Don Juan*) by Apollinaire in 1926, *Les Souvenirs d'égotisme* (*Memoirs of Egotism*) by Stendhal and Mérimée's *Lettres* (*Letters*). His association with the Surrealists lead to the illustration of Robert Ganzo's *Chansons* (*Songs*) in 1942, and Robert Desnos' *État de veille* (*Vigilance*) in 1943.

Drawn to Cubism, he gravitated towards the group Abstraction-Création. In 1932 he took part in the Dakar-Djibouti ethnographic mission with Griaule and Leiris, during which he painted frescoes in the church of Antonios in Ethiopia. He designed the cover of the second issue of the revue *Minotaure* dedicated to the mission, which attracted much interest in French artistic and intellectual circles. His prewar work was highly creative and full of invention. When he resumed work after World War II, he chose interior scenes, landscapes, flowers, trees and gardens. In them, the very occasional figure catches changing light with finesse, but there is none of his early ingenuity.

He took part in *Poetry 32* in Prague alongside Max Ernst, Masson, Miró, Dalí, Tanguy and Sima. He had a number of solo exhibitions in Paris galleries associated with the Surrealists, including Louise Leiris' and Galerie 1900-2000: *Œuvre graphique* (*Graphic Work*). His work was also shown in the Leicester Galleries.

Bibliography:
Phillpotts, B., '*Gaston-Louis Roux (Theo Waddington Gallery, London)*' in *Arts Review* Vol. 33, No. 9, exhibition review, 8 May 1981. Lavell, S., '*Gaston-Louis Roux (Stoppenbach And Delestre, London)*' in *Arts Review* Vol. 34, No. 12, exhibition review, 4 June 1982. *G. L. Roux ou la Force au pouvoir*, exhibition catalogue, Gal. 1900-2000, Paris, 1987 (texts by Gladys C. Fabre and Georges Bataille). Schwartz, Arturo, '*Minotaure: The Pride Of European Culture*' in *Fmr* Vol. 7 No. 31, March-April 1988.

Museums and Galleries:
New York (Mus. of Living Art): painting.

Auction records:
Bern, 22 June 1979, *Still-life* (1931, oil on canvas, 13 x 18 ins / 33 x 46 cm) CHF 1,600. Paris, 23 Nov 1997, *Bust of Diego* (1961, oil/hardboard, 11 x 13 3/4 ins / 27 x 35 cm) FRF 3,800.

LONDON, 3 Dec 1999, *Young Girl with Guitar* (oil on canvas, 14 x 9 ins / 35 x 24 cm) GBP 2,600.

ROUX, Georges, possibly Alexandre Georges Roux
French, 19th - 20th century.
Died 1929.
Painter, draughtsman.

Georges Roux studied under Jean-Paul Laurens. He is noted for his illustrations of Jules Verne's works. He also illustrated Jean Aicard's *Roi de Camargue* (*King of the Camargue*) in 1890 and F. Fabre's *Taillevent* in 1895.
BIBLIOGRAPHY:
Osterwalder, Marcus (ed.), *Dictionnaire des illustrateurs 1800-1914*, Ides et Calendes, Neuchâtel, 1989.
MUSEUMS AND GALLERIES:
BÉZIERS.
AUCTION RECORDS:
PARIS, 1-2 March 1920, *Chatting on the Terrace; In the Cornfield*, FRF 310. PARIS, 26 Dec 1926, *Old Storyteller, Seated*, FRF 450.

ROUX, Guillermo
Argentinian, 20th century.
Born 1929.
Painter, draughtsman, watercolourist. Landscapes.

The Phillips Collection mounted a solo exhibition of the work of Guillermo Roux in Washington in 1988.

Roux's work has a place of its own in Argentinian art.
BIBLIOGRAPHY:
Guillermo Roux, exhibition catalogue, Phillips Collection, Washington DC, 1988.
AUCTION RECORDS:
NEW YORK, 18 May 1988, *The Small Square at Arraial* (1971, watercolour/paper, 21 x 26 ins / 53.3 x 66 cm) USD 2,750.

ROUX, Gustave
Swiss, 19th century.
Born 30 December 1828, in Grandson; died 22 March 1885, in Geneva.
Draughtsman, watercolourist.

Gustave Roux studied in Munich, Geneva and Paris. He worked in Zurich and Geneva.
MUSEUMS AND GALLERIES:
BERN (Kunstmus.): watercolours.

ROUX, Hippolyte
French, 19th century.
Born 16 December 1852, in Ste-Euphémie.
Painter. Landscapes, flowers.

Hippolyte Roux painted many landscapes of the Drôme region.
AUCTION RECORDS:
MUNICH, 30 May 1979, *Cavalier in a Landscape* (oil on panel, 6 3/4 x 14 ins / 17 x 35.5 cm) DEM 1,800.

ROUX, Hubert or Nicolas Hubert
French, 19th century.
Painter.

Hubert Roux worked in Paris from 1831 to 1847. He produced architectural engravings, using chromolithography.

ROUX, Jacques Louis, called Browne
French, 19th century.
Born 16 September 1824, in Bordeaux.
Painter. Portraits, animals.

Jacques Roux was a student of Camille Roqueplan and Belloc. He exhibited at the Paris Salon under the name Browne from 1848 to 1880.
AUCTION RECORDS:
PARIS, 1 July 1949, *General Races* (two watercolours, one dated 1864) FRF 12,000 et 13300.

ROUX, Jakob Wilhelm Christian
German, 19th century.
Born 1775, in Jena; died 1831, in Heidelberg.
Painter, draughtsman, engraver (etching).

Jakob Wilhelm Christian was the father of Karl Roux. He studied in Jena and Dresden. He experimented in painting in wax, obtaining interesting results with this process. An example is his *Head of Venus*, after Titian, which received acclaim. As an engraver, J.W. Roux reproduced picturesque sites with a documentary interest, such as *Tomb of Wieland*, *Goethe's Garden in Weimar* and *Schiller's Garden*. Among his other prints, he is best known for *Students' Revolt in Jena on 17 July 1792*.
MUSEUMS AND GALLERIES:
JENA (Stadtmus.): several works.

ROUX, Jean
French, 18th century.
Active in Nantes c. 1723.
Painter.

ROUX, Jean Marc
Swiss, 18th - 19th century.
Born c. 1735, in Rembert; died 16 March 1812, in Geneva.
Miniaturist.

Jean Marc was the father of David Étienne and Philippe Roux.

ROUX, Johann Friedrich Wilhelm Theodor
German, 19th century.
Born 23 September 1806, in Gotha; died 15 August 1880, in Kassel.
Painter, pastellist, photographer.

Johann Friedrich Wilhelm Theodor Roux mostly worked in pastels.
MUSEUMS AND GALLERIES:
KASSEL (Stadtmus.): several works.

ROUX, Josef Ferdinand
Austrian, 18th - 19th century.
Born 1771; died 30 December 1820, in Vienna.
Engraver (etching).

ROUX, Joseph
French, 19th century.
Born in Gray.
Painter. Genre scenes, portraits.

Joseph Roux was a student of Couture and Léon Cogniet. He settled in his native town. He exhibited at the Paris Salon in 1863, 1864 and 1870.
MUSEUMS AND GALLERIES:
GRAY: *Time for the Breviary; In the High School Grounds.*

ROUX, Joseph Ange Antoine. See **ROUX Antoine**

ROUX, Julien or Julien Toussaint
French, 19th century.
Born 28 July 1836, in St-Michel-Chauveaux; died 1880, in Paris.
Sculptor. Figures.

Julien Roux was a student of Jouffroy. He held a scholarship from his department and first exhibited at the Salon of 1861.
MUSEUMS AND GALLERIES:
ANGERS: *Linnaeus; Jean Louis Charles Daubau; Comedy; Thouvenel.*

ROUX, Karl or Carl
German, 19th century.
Born 14 August 1826, in Heidelberg; died 23 July 1894, in Mannheim.
Painter. Genre scenes, animals, landscapes.

Karl Roux was a pupil of K. Hüber. He worked in Mannheim, Antwerp, Munich, Paris, Düsseldorf and Karlsruhe. He was director of the Mannheim Gallery. He received medals on several occasions in Melbourne.

Museums and Galleries:
Graz: *Scene from the War of 1870* - Hamburg: *Foot Soldiers Resting* - Karlsruhe: *Pillage of a Town; Setting the First Stone of Karlsburg Castle; Herdsman on a High Mountain Pasture* - Mannheim: *Flock in the Mountains*.
Auction records:
London, 6 Dec 1909, *Cattle Grazing*, GBP 6. Lucerne, 23-26 Nov 1962, *Cattle Market in a Meadow*, CHF 7,000. New York, 13 Oct 1978, *Flock beside an Alpine Lake* (oil on canvas, 16 x 31in/40.5 x 79cm) USD 4,250. Munich, 27 Feb 1999, *Two Calves in Bushes* (1870, oil on panel, 20 x 27 ins / 51 x 69 cm) DEM 13,000. Heidelberg, 2 July 1999, *Ferry by Manheim* (oil on canvas, 28 x 54 ins / 71 x 137 cm) DEM 30,000. Zurich, 17 June 2002, *Farmstead with Cows and Herder* (oil on canvas, 16 x 30 ins / 40 x 76 cm) CHF 2,700.

ROUX, Léon Louis Charles

French, 20th century.
Born 15 July 1899, in Nevers.
Painter. Stage costumes and sets.

From 1939 to 1964 Léon Roux designed and produced the models for the sets and costumes for shows, operas and ballets at the Monte Carlo Opera, including *Tosca, Don Giovanni, Cyrano de Bergerac*. He exhibited at the Salon des Indépendants in Paris and also in Rome.

ROUX, Louis François Prosper

French, 19th century.
Born 14 February 1817, in Paris; died 6 April 1903, in Paris.
Painter, watercolourist. Religious subjects, figures, interiors with figures, seascapes, boats.

Louis Roux was a student of Delaroche. He exhibited at the Salon from 1839 to 1877. He won the second Grand Prix de Rome in 1839. He won a third-class medal in 1846 and a second-class medal in 1857 and 1859.

Museums and Galleries:
Avignon: *St Francis of Assisi and the Birds* - Le Puy-en-Velay: *St Thomas Aquinas Reads out the Office of the Holy Sacrament*.
Auction records:
Paris, 1872, *Bernard Palissy Taking a Geology Class*, FRF 5,300. New York, 11 Dec 1970, *The Yacht, Tubal Cain*, USD 2,200. Paris, 19 Oct 1985, *Eighteen-Canon Military Corvette* (watercolour heightened with gouache, 12 3/4 x 18 ins / 32.5 x 46 cm) FRF 16,000. New York, 1 Feb 1986, *The U.S. Harmonia* (oil on canvas, 44 x 70 ins / 111.6 x 177.8 cm) USD 6,250. Paris, 18 June 1986, *Yachts at Sea* (1883, watercolour, 19 3/4 x 29 1/4 ins / 50 x 74 cm) FRF 12,000. Monaco, 20 Feb 1988, *Three-Master* (1864, watercolour, 11 1/2 x 18 ins / 29 x 45.8 cm) FRF 28,860. Paris, 6 Dec 1995, *Languid Woman Dressed in Black, Seated in an Interior* (1854, oil on canvas, 15 3/4 x 12 1/2 ins / 40 x 32 cm) FRF 10,500. Paris, 30 Jan 2000, *Sailing Ships and Boats* (1869, watercolour, 16 x 22 ins / 41 x 57 cm) FRF 45,000. Paris, 30 Jan 2000, *The Steamer Mongibello* (watercolour, 24 x 34 ins / 60 x 86 cm) FRF 50,000. Malmö, 24 Nov 2001, *Ship's Portrait - The Georg Nicolaus Arriving in Marseilles* (1883, watercolour and gouache, 20 x 29 ins / 50 x 73 cm) SEK 44,000. Paris, 21 March 2002, *Portraits* (graphite album, 11 x 13 ins / 27 x 34 cm) EUR 2,200. Hamburg, 7 Dec 2002, *Hamburg Bark - Justine Helene* (1888, watercolour and bodycolour over pen, 20 x 28 ins / 50 x 72 cm) EUR 4,600. London, 12 June 2003, *Spanish Xebec Libertad in the Mediterranean* (1886, pencil, pen, ink and watercolour heightened with bodycolour, 13 x 20 ins / 32 x 50 cm) GBP 2,000. London, 12 June 2003, *The Spanish Trading Schooner Roberto Heading into Marseilles* (pencil, pen, ink and watercolour, 18 x 26 ins / 46 x 65 cm) GBP 2,600. Paris, 24 June 2004, *The Threemaster Svisda Mimubelli* (1877, watercolour, 20 x 28 ins / 50 x 71 cm) EUR 2,500.

ROUX, Marc

French, 18th century.
Active in Aix-en-Provence during the second half of the 18th century.
Sculptor.

Marc Roux produced several sculptures for churches in Toulon.

ROUX, Marcel

French, 20th century.
Born 11 September 1878, in Bessenay (Rhône); died 19 January 1922, in Chartres.
Painter, engraver.

Marcel Roux studied under Paul Borel. He featured in the 1993 exhibition *De Bonnard à Baselitz - Dix Ans d'enrichissements du cabinet des estampes 1978-1988* (*From Bonnard to Baselitz: A Decade of Acquisitions by the Prints Collection 1978-1988*) at the Bibliothèque Nationale in Paris. He did etchings and wood engravings, publishing the print series *Fantasies, Against Alcohol* and *Street Walker*.

Bibliography:
Davenport, Nancy, '*Marcel Roux graveur. L'emprise du péché dans la France fin de siècle*' in *Nouvelles de l'Estampe* n° 164, periodical, Bibliothèque Nationale de France, Paris, 1999.

Museums and Galleries:
Paris (BNF): *Forlorn Worker* (1905, etching from a set); *Danse Macabre*.

ROUX, Marie

French, 19th century.
Born in Paris.
Painter (porcelain), miniaturist. Portraits.

Marie Roux was a student of Lesourd-Beauregard, Barré, Mlle Jacob and Mme de Cool. She exhibited at the Salon from 1868, mainly with portraits on porcelain and miniatures.

ROUX, Michel

French, 20th - 21st century.
Born 1950, in Cotignac (Var).
Draughtsman.

Michel Roux lives and works in Cotignac in the Var region of France. He has been drawing since 1972. He works with Indian ink to produce a plethora of identical signs set into precisely measured squares on equally precisely measured sheets (40 x 50 cm). 'Each sign recurs a specific but undisclosed number of times on each sheet', as one critic (Gilbert Lascault) has since noted.

He has presented examples of his work at various exhibitions since 1976, notably on a regular basis at the Galerie Alphonse Chave in Vence; in 1979, at the Nuremberg Triennial and at the Villa Arson in Nice; in 1980, at the Fréjus Salon; and, in 1981, at the Espace d'Art Contemporain in Lyons and the Centre d'Art Contemporain at the Abbaye de Beaulieu.

Bibliography:
Lascault, Gilbert, *Michel Roux: dessins*, exhibition catalogue, Gal. Alphonse Chave, Vence, 1983. *Écritures dans la peinture*, exhibition catalogue, Villa Arson-Centre National des Arts Plastiques, Nice, April-June 1984.

ROUX, Monique de

French, 20th century.
Active in Spain.
Pastellist, painter (gouache), draughtsman, engraver. Scenes with figures.

Monique de Roux studied under Antonio López García in Madrid's Círculo de Bellas Artes. From 1986 to 1988 she lived in Panama, where she drew figures fixed in their everyday activities and picturesque street scenes imbued with naivety. She exhibited in Belgium in 1992.

ROUX, Nicolas Hubert. See **ROUX Hubert**

ROUX, Oswald
Austrian, 20th century.
Born 31 January 1880, in Vienna.
Painter, engraver. Animals.
Oswald Roux studied at the Akademie der Bildenden Künste in Vienna and was a member of the Viennese Secession. He was an engraver who specialised in etchings of horses.
MUSEUMS AND GALLERIES:
VIENNA (MM): *Injured Horse* - VIENNA (Österreichische Gal. Belvedere): *Cargo of Wood*.

ROUX, Paul Louis Joseph
French, 19th - 20th century.
Born c. 1845, in Paris; died 1918.
Painter, watercolourist, engraver. Landscapes.
Paul Roux studied under Cabanel. He painted scenes in the vicinity of Paris, in the forest of Fontainebleau, and in Brittany and Normandy. Visiting England, he painted the banks of the Thames. He is remembered for *Farm at Fontainebleau-les-Nonnes near Meaux* and *Seine Riverbanks at Tournedas*. He made his debut at the 1870 Salon and continued to show drawings, etchings and oil paintings and watercolours in Paris exhibitions.
AUCTION RECORDS:
PARIS, 27 Nov 1923, *Autumn Landscape* (watercolour) FRF 175. PARIS, 14 March 1925, *Storm on Quiberon*, FRF 110. PARIS, 16 Feb 1931, *Haystacks* (watercolour) FRF 120. PARIS, 22 Nov 1996, *The Forest of Fontainebleau* (oil on canvas, 35 1/2 x 57 3/4 ins / 90 x 147 cm) FRF 10,000.

ROUX, Philippe
Swiss, 18th century.
Born 20 November 1756, in Geneva; died 15 August 1805, in Loex.
Miniaturist.
Philippe was the son and assistant of Jean Marc Roux.

ROUX, Pierre
French, 19th century.
Active in Paris.
Painter, watercolourist. Battles, genre scenes, battles.
Pierre Roux featured at the Salon from 1830 to 1837. He produced mainly seascapes, but also some genre subjects and battles, often in watercolour.
MUSEUMS AND GALLERIES:
VERSAILLES (Mus.): *Battle at Algeciras, 5 July 1801* (two watercolours).
AUCTION RECORDS:
PARIS, 5 Feb 1951, *Brittany Coast* (two watercolours) FRF 4,200.

ROUX, Pierre
French, 20th century.
Born 1932, in Paris.
Painter, sculptor. Scenes with figures, landscapes, urban landscapes, still-lifes, architectural views.
Pierre Roux paints skyscrapers, playing on shapes, lines and reflections, as well as still-lifes and landscapes. He works in great splashes of flat tint, using plain colours, simplifying the shapes. He exhibited at the Salon Comparaisons, Salon d'Automne, Salon des Terres Latines, Salon de la Société Nationale des Beaux-Arts, Salon du Dessin et de la Peinture à l'eau and Salon de Menton. He showed his works in solo exhibitions from 1960, in Paris galleries and in New York.

P-ROUX

MUSEUMS AND GALLERIES:
MINNEAPOLIS.

ROUX, Pol
French, 18th century.
Active in Moustiers in 1727.
Painter (glazed earthenware).

ROUX, Polydore
French, 19th century.
Born 19 July 1792, in Marseilles; died 12 April 1833, in Bombay.
Painter. Seascapes.
AUCTION RECORDS:
MONTE CARLO, 25 June 1984, *Young Painter in a Landscape in Ste-Baume* (1817, oil on canvas, 37 3/4 x 49 1/2 ins / 96 x 126 cm) FRF 160,000.

ROUX, Pompeyo
Spanish, 17th century.
Born to a family originally from France.
Active in Barcelona.
Engraver (burin).

ROUX, Tony Georges
French, 20th century.
Born 3 July 1894, in Fontenay-sous-Bois; died 17 September 1928, in Paris.
Painter, watercolourist. Landscapes.
Tony Roux studied under Flameng and Jean-Paul Laurens.
AUCTION RECORDS:
PARIS, July 1946, *Château of Cabirol* (1916, watercolour) FRF 250. PARIS, 26 Dec 1946, *Pergola on the Mediterranean Coast*, FRF 3,000; *The Cypress*, FRF 3,750. ENGHIEN-LES-BAINS, 25 Oct 1987, *Headless Woman* (charcoal/cream paper, 22 1/4 x 13 1/2 ins / 56.5 x 34.5 cm) FRF 9,000. VERSAILLES, 7 Feb 1988, *Gardens in Bloom near the Palace* (1925, watercolour and gouache, a pair, 29 1/2 x 22 ins / 75 x 56 cm) FRF 3,500. MILAN, 18 March 2003, *Portrait of a Lady with a Stick and a Hat* (oil on canvas, 79 x 61 ins / 200 x 155 cm) EUR 10,000.

ROUX, Vincent
French, 20th century.
Born 1928.
Watercolourist, painter (gouache/mixed media), pastellist. Landscapes, seascapes.
Vincent Roux painted numerous views of Venice.
AUCTION RECORDS:
PARIS, 4 Dec 1987, *The Feluca Hirondelle, Captain H. Bénais in a Northwesterly Gale at Cape de Gruse* (watercolour, 11 x 16 1/2 ins / 27 x 42 cm) FRF 20,000. PARIS, 15 June 1988, *Venice under Snow* (pastel/Cork paper, 11 x 29 1/4 ins / 27 x 74 cm) FRF 26,000. PARIS, 10 Nov 1988, *Venice* (pastel, 11 x 28 3/4 ins / 27 x 73 cm) FRF 20,000. PARIS, 2 July 1990, *Venice* (oil on canvas, 32 x 51 1/4 ins / 81 x 130 cm) FRF 60,000. PARIS, 15 June 1994, *View of Saint Tropez* (pastel and gouache, 28 x 35 1/2 ins / 71 x 90 cm) FRF 7,000. PARIS, 27 Oct 1997, *Venice, Piazza San Marco and Campanile* (oil on canvas, 32 x 51 1/4 ins / 81 x 130 cm) FRF 5,000.

ROUX DE LUC, Félix
French, 19th century.
Born 1820, in Bagnols.
Sculptor. Figures. Busts, statues.
Félix Roux de Luc spent a long period working in Avignon.
MUSEUMS AND GALLERIES:
AVIGNON: *Esprit Raquien* (bust); *Jean Gutenberg* (statue) - BAGNOLS: *Statue of Cassan, the Poet; Medallion Portrait of Léon Alègre, Demosthenes; Bust of M. Léon Alègre*.

ROUX RENARD, Antonin Marius Auguste
French, 19th - 20th century.
Born 16 May 1870, in Orange (Vaucluse).
Painter. Portraits, landscapes.
Antonin Roux Renard studied under E. Delaunay and Gustave Moreau. From 1893, he exhibited at the Salon des Artistes Français, of which he was an associate member. He was awarded the Prix Marie Bashkirtseff in 1898.

Museums and Galleries:
Constantine: *Capture of Constantine* - Paris (former Mus. du Luxembourg): *Villeneuve-lès-Avignon*.

ROUX-CHAMPION, Julien, pseudonym of Julien Hilaire Roux
French, 20th century.
Born 20 May 1920, in Nice.
Painter, watercolourist, draughtsman, illustrator. Landscapes.

Julien Roux-Champion was the son of Victor Roux-Champion and studied under him. A civil servant, his specialist knowledge and his drawings of the region he served are well respected. He exhibited in Langres and Châlons-sur-Marne and was made a Chevalier des Arts et Lettres.

Museums and Galleries:
Champlitte - Digne-les-Bains: a watercolour.

ROUX-CHAMPION, Victor Joseph, pseudonym of Roux Joseph Victor
French, 19th - 20th century.
Born 30 September 1871, in Chaumont; died 7 December 1953, in Vars.
Painter, draughtsman, watercolourist, engraver, potter. Landscapes, flowers, fruit.

Victor Roux-Champion went to Paris to study painting, first at the Académie Colarossi and then under Bouguereau at the Académie Julian until 1892. He studied engraving under Auguste and Eugène Delattre and then spent three years under Gustave Moreau at the École des Beaux-Arts in Paris. He co-founded the society of soft-ground etching engravers. He moved to Champlitte (Haute-Saône) in 1931 and later to Provence.

Besides his activities as engraver and potter, he painted flowers, fruit and numerous landscapes, also working in watercolours. He painted in many regions in France but Paris and his holiday home in Pressigny (Haute-Marne) were his chief inspirations. Associated with the Impressionists and the Nabis, he achieved his most personal expression in the brisk watercolours of his last years.

In Paris, he took part in the Salon d'Automne, Salon des Indépendants and Salon des Arts Décoratifs. In 1897, he had his first solo exhibitions in Paris. He also exhibited in the provinces.

Museums and Galleries:
Alençon (Mus. des Beaux-Arts et de la Dentelle) - Bordeaux (MBA): *Engraved Portrait of A. Marquet* (1928) - Dijon (MBA) - Grenoble (Mus. de Grenoble): *Flowers* (1961) - Narbonne (MAH): *The Painter Laprade in His Studio* (1928); *Self-portrait* (c. 1928) - Paris (MAMVP): *Portrait of an Elderly Woman* (1912) - Paris (Mus. Carnavalet): *View of Champlitte* (engraving) - Paris (Mus. National de Céramique Sèvres): two ceramics - Paris (Mus. Rodin) - Sceaux: two watercolours - Vienna (Albertina Mus.): engravings.

Auction records:
Paris, 20 Nov 1922, *The Pont-Marie* (watercolour) FRF 400. Paris, 26 March 1928, *Pressigny*, FRF 165. Paris, 9 Dec 1931, *Notre Dame, Seen from the Quai de Montebello* (watercolour) FRF 310. London, 28 June 1988, *Figures by a Brook in an Autumn Landscape* (oil on canvas, 18 x 21 3/4 ins / 45.7 x 55.3 cm) GBP 22,000. London, 22 Feb 1989, *Paris, Bridge over the Seine* (oil on canvas/card, 15 x 20 ins / 38.2 x 51 cm) GBP 1,980. Paris, 28 Oct 1990, *Renoir's House at Cagnes* (watercolour and charcoal/bistre-coloured paper, 14 1/4 x 10 1/4 ins / 36 x 26.3 cm) FRF 6,800. Calais, 10 March 1991, *Splash of Flowers in a Landscape* (1897, oil on canvas, 21 1/4 x 25 1/2 ins / 54 x 65 cm) FRF 18,000. New York, 24 Feb 1995, *Notre Dame* (watercolour and charcoal/paper/paper, 9 3/4 x 13 ins / 24.8 x 32.1 cm) USD 1,840. Paris, 13 Oct 1995, *Le Pouldu* (1900, watercolour and pencil, 4 3/4 x 6 ins / 12 x 15.5 cm) FRF 10,000.

ROUX-CONSTANTINI, David Étienne.
See **ROUX David Étienne**

ROUX-COTTAVOZ, Louise
French, 20th century.
Born 30 November 1901, in Grenoble; died 8 January 1977.
Painter, pastellist. Landscapes, flowers.

Louise Roux-Cottavoz studied under André Albertin, Jean Tancrède Bastet and Louise Morel, then at the École des Arts Industriels in Grenoble. In the 1920s, she took part in the Salon de la Société des Amis des Arts in Grenoble, the Salon de la Société Lyonnaise des Beaux-Arts and the Salon des Indépendants in Paris. A retrospective exhibition of her work was mounted in 1980 in Corenc.

Bibliography:
Wantellet, Maurice, *Deux siècles et plus de peinture dauphinoise*, M. Wantellet, Grenoble, 1987.

ROUX-FABRE, Émile
French, 20th century.
Painter.

Émile Roux-Fabre exhibited at the Salon des Tuileries in Paris.

ROUXEL, Louis
French, 19th - 20th century.
Born 5 December 1866, in Paris.
Engraver.

Louis Rouxel exhibited at the Salon des Artistes Français and was declared hors concours. He won a gold medal in 1920.

ROUXEL, Philibert
French, 20th century.
Engraver.

Philibert Rouxel exhibited at the Salon des Artistes Français, sometimes Hors concours. He won a gold medal in 1932.

ROUXELLE, Guy, called Cadet Rousselle
French, 19th century.
Died c. 1820, in Douai.
Silhouettist.

Guy Rouxelle worked in Lille, Cambrai and Douai.

ROUYER, Henry
Swiss, 20th century.
Born 3 March 1928, in Vevey.
Painter, sculptor.

Henry Rouyer's work has featured at various group exhibitions, including the Biennale du Nord in 1959, the Paris Biennale of 1964 and the Salon de la Jeune Sculpture in Paris in 1965. Rouyer has held solo exhibitions in Deauville (1962) and Paris (1962, 1963, 1967, 1969). His work is distinguished by alternating spatial volumes comprised of static and fluid elements.

ROUYER, Louis Victor
French, 19th century.
Active in Paris.
Painter.

Louis Rouyer exhibited landscapes at the Salon from 1842 to 1850.

ROUYR, Jean Antoine
French, 18th century.
Born 1764, in Paris.
Painter, engraver.

Rouyr was the pupil of Lebarbier and Gaucher. He exhibited a drawing, *Portrait of a Young Girl*, at the Salon in 1801.

ROUZAUD, Jean
French, 20th century.
Born 23 November 1923, in Paris.
Painter (mixed media).

Jean Rouzaud studied architecture at the École des Beaux-Arts in Toulouse in 1940 whilst attending Raymond Espinasse's painting classes. In 1943-1944, he worked on theatre and cinema sets. In 1952 he settled in Sète in the south of France. After early figurative works he evolved towards Lyrical Abstraction.

Between informal and action painting, he placed signs on the canvas using a range of materials. He played liquid and compact elements off against each other in rather flat tones. Later he assembled jagged planes in more colourful, more constructed pieces. He has executed mural decorations, low reliefs and murals for public buildings in his region.

He took part in Groupe 57 exhibitions in Béziers and Nîmes, the Festival International d'Art Plastique in Luchon, the Salon d'Automne in Paris and an exhibition at the Maison de la culture in Foix in 1984. Many of his solo exhibitions were in the south of France, in particular in 1987 at the Musée Paul-Valéry in Sète, as well as Paris, Detroit, Barcelona and Frankfurt.

BIBLIOGRAPHY:

Boudaille, Georges, *Rouzaud*, exhibition catalogue, Gal. Massol, Paris, 1969. *Jean Rouzaud peintures*, exhibition catalogue, Musée Paul-Valéry, Sète, 1987.

ROUZE, Ferdinand

French, 19th century.

Born 19th century, in Selles-St-Denis.

Painter. Genre scenes, portraits.

Ferdinand Rouze was a student of Léon Cogniet. He first exhibited at the Salon of 1879 and worked in Paris and in Madrid from 1864 to 1881.

ROUZÉ, Jean, or Rousée

Flemish School, 17th century.

Active in Tournai from 1670 to 1697.

Painter.

Jean Rouzé was the father of Jean Joachim Rouzé.

ROUZÉ, Jean François, or Rousée

Flemish School, 18th century.

Active in Tournai in 1712.

Painter.

ROUZÉ, Jean Joachim, or Rousée

Flemish School, 18th century.

Active in Tournai in 1716.

Painter.

Jean Joachim Rouzé was the son of Jean Rouzé.

ROUZIÈRE DE LA. See **LAROUZIÈRE Antoine de**

ROVALDI STROPPA, Giulia

Italian, 19th - 20th century.

Born in Vercelli; died 19 October 1918, in Verona.

Painter. Flowers.

Rovaldi Stroppa studied under Ferdinando Rossaro and Angelo Dall'Oca Bianca.

ROVEA, Giorgio

Italian, 19th century.

Died before 1892.

Painter. Still-lifes.

Rovea exhibited in Turin from 1843.

MUSEUMS AND GALLERIES:

TURIN (Mus. Civico): *Fruits* (painting, two).

ROVEDATA, Giovanni Battista

Italian, 17th century.

Born in Verona; died after 29 September 1620, in Venice.

Painter.

The son and pupil of Pietro Antonio Rovedata, Giovanni Battista Rovedata worked in Venice and Verona.

MUSEUMS AND GALLERIES:

VERONA (Mus. Civico): *Banquet at the House of Levi; Feast of St Francis [?]*.

ROVEDATA, Pietro Antonio

Italian, 16th century.

Active in Trento (Trentino-Alto Adige) from 1561 to 1570.

Painter.

Pietro Antonio Rovedata was the father of Giovanni Battista Rovedata.

ROVEL, Henri

French, 19th century.

Painter. Figures, landscapes with figures, landscapes, harbour scenes, architectural views. Designs (posters).

In 2002, Henri Rovel's work featured in the collective exhibition *Passing through... the Lorraine Region as Seen by its Painters*, at the Piere-Noël museum in St-Dié-des-Vosges.

MUSEUMS AND GALLERIES:

ÉPINAL: *Evening Harmony* - TOUL: *Pont des Fées near Gérardmer; Woman from the Vosges*.

AUCTION RECORDS:

PARIS, 30 April 1919, *Lights in the Port of Boulogne*, FRF 150. VERSAILLES, 5 March 1989, *Peasant Woman near the Hamlet* (oil on canvas, 8 1/2 x 16 3/4 ins / 21.5 x 42.5 cm) FRF 3,500. PARIS, 23 April 1993, *North African Railway* (oil on canvas, design for a poster, 49 1/4 x 35 1/2 ins / 125 x 90 cm) FRF 19,000. NEW YORK, 22-23 July 1993, *View of Gafsa* (1900, oil on canvas, 31 1/4 x 43 ins / 79.4 x 108.3 cm) USD 3,450. PARIS, 6 April 1994, *Oriental Woman on a Terrace* (1900, oil on canvas, 31 1/2 x 43 1/4 ins / 80 x 110 cm) FRF 23,000.

ROVELA Y BROEANDEL, Hippolito. See **ROVIRA Y BROCANDEL**

ROVELAS, Michel

French, 20th century.

Born 1938, in Capesterre-Bellau (Guadeloupe).

Painter. Scenes with figures.

Nouvelle Figuration.

After a five-year stay in Paris, Michel Rovelas returned to the French West Indies in 1968 and was soon directing the École des Beaux-Arts at the Lamentin in Guadeloupe. He developed a personal style drawing on Nouvelle Figuration, with Expressionist tendencies and signs entirely his own. His painting addresses reality but interferes with standard codes of representation through inversions and shifts. He shows the female body stripped, sacrificed to lust or social pressures. Faces are always spent and indecisive and sometimes gagged.

He took part in the 1976 Cuba Biennale and in *Carifesta* in Barbados and *Peintures du monde noir* (*Paintings from the Black World*) at the Centre Pompidou, Paris in 1985. He has had solo exhibitions in Puerto-Rico, Santo Domingo, Ottawa, Paris, Port of Spain (Trinidad), New York, Seoul, Port-au-Prince (Haiti) (*Manif 95*) and Pointe-à-Pitre (Guadeloupe).

ROVELLI, Antonio

Italian, 17th century.

Sculptor (wood).

Antonio Rovelli sculpted the stalls in the church at Averara.

ROVEN, G.

Painter.

MUSEUMS AND GALLERIES:

GENOA: *Flowers and Fruit*.

ROVERANO, Victor E.

Argentinian, 20th century.

Born 1903, in Buenos Aires.

Painter.

Victor E. Roverano had a very successful solo exhibition in 1923. He travelled in Italy and Spain; exhibited at the 1927

Salon; and received a third national prize from the Buenos Aires City Museum of Fine Art.

His work shows the influence of Édouard Manet.

ROVERE, Gerolamo della

Italian, 16th - 17th century.

Died 1638.

Painter, illuminator. Religious subjects.

Gerolamo della Rovere was the father of Giovanni Battista della Rovere the Younger. He worked for the court of Turin, illuminating heraldic works, and specialised in representations of the Holy Shroud.

ROVERE, Giovanni Battista della, the Elder, called Il Fiammenghino

Italian, 16th - 17th century.

Born c. 1561, in Milan; died after 1627.

Painter, fresco artist, draughtsman. Religious subjects.

Giovanni Battista della Rovere the Elder was the brother of Giovanni Mauro della Rovere, and it is difficult to distinguish between the works of the two brothers. He painted mainly for churches in Milan, for the abbey of Chiaravalle and the church of Sabioncello.

MUSEUMS AND GALLERIES:

CHAMBÉRY (MBA): *Annunciation.*

AUCTION RECORDS:

PARIS, 29 Oct 1980, *People in Debate by a Balustrade* (pen and brown ink wash, heightened with white, 63/4 x 101/4 ins / 17.4 x 26 cm) FRF 15,000. LONDON, 9 Dec 1982, *Martyrdom of a Bishop* (black chalk, pen and wash heightened with white/blue paper) GBP 1,000. LONDON, 2 July 1984, *Lunette Design: Religious Scene* (pen and wash/outline in black chalk, 71/2 x 111/2 ins / 19 x 29.5 cm) GBP 1,150. LONDON, 1 April 1987, *Liberation of St Peter* (black chalk, pen and wash heightened with white, 103/4 x 71/4 ins / 27.2 x 18.5 cm) GBP 1,600. PARIS, 20 Oct 1988, *Ascension of St Albert* (pen and brown wash, 121/2 x 83/4 ins / 31.8 x 22.2 cm) FRF 10,800. TROYES, 19 Nov 1989, *Christ and the Teachers* (1591, pen and brown wash, 91/2 x 7 ins / 24 x 18 cm) FRF 29,000. PARIS, 12 June 1992, *Annunciation* (pen and brown wash, 81/2 x 51/4 ins / 21.5 x 13.5 cm) FRF 3,500. LONDON, 3 July 1995, *Christ in Glory and the Virgin and Two Saints* (ink and wash/chalk, study for a ceiling decoration, 131/2 x 151/4 ins / 34 x 39 cm) GBP 1,150. LONDON, 2 July 1996, *People Arguing by a Balustrade* (black chalk, ink and wash/blue paper, 63/4 x 10 ins / 17.3 x 25.7 cm) GBP 2,990. PARIS, 20 June 1997, *Jesus among the Teachers* (pen and brown ink wash, 103/4 x 9 ins / 27.3 x 22 cm) FRF 24,000. LONDON, 6 July 1999, *Death and Burial of St Dionysus* (chalk/pen/ink wash, 11 x 17 ins / 28 x 43 cm) GBP 2,200. LONDON, 6 July 1999, *Funeral Mass of St Dionysus* (chalk/pen/ink heightened with white, 9 x 13 ins / 24 x 33 cm) GBP 3,200. LONDON, 13 Dec 2001, *Design for a Lunette - The Holy Family Warned by an Angel to Flee* (pen/ink wash heightened with white, 5 x 10 ins / 13 x 26 cm) GBP 1,100. LONDON, 9 July 2002, *Two Angels Appearing to a Priest during Mass* (black chalk ink/heightened with white) GBP 1,700. PARIS, 6 Nov 2003, *Altar* (pen/ink wash, 13 x 9 ins / 34 x 24 cm) EUR 2,700. NEW YORK, 22 Jan 2004, *Marriage of the Virgin* (black chalk/pen/brown ink wash, 10 x 8 ins / 26 x 20 cm) USD 7,000. PARIS, 17 March 2004, *Resurrection of Christ* (pen/brown ink/brown wash heightened with white gouache, 6 x 6 ins / 14 x 15 cm) EUR 1,800.

ROVERE, Giovanni Battista della, the Younger

Italian, 17th century.

Active in Turin.

Painter. Religious subjects, allegorical subjects. Murals.

The son of Gerolamo della Rovere, Giovanni Battista della Rovere was active in Turin, painting the *Allegory of Life* in the church of St Francis of Assisi in Turin.

ROVERE, Giovanni Mauro della

Italian, 16th - 17th century.

Born c. 1575, in Milan; died 1640, in Milan.

Painter, fresco artist, engraver, draughtsman. Religious subjects, allegorical subjects.

Giovanni Mauro della Rovere was the brother of Giovanni Battista della Rovere the Elder, known as Il Fiammenghino. It is difficult to distinguish between the works of the two brothers. He painted for churches in Milan, Como, Brescia, Novara, Padova, Piacenza and Varese, and in the Carthusian monastery in Pavia. He also produced etchings.

MUSEUMS AND GALLERIES:

PARMA (Pinacoteca Giuseppe Stuard): *Baptism of Christ.*

AUCTION RECORDS:

NEW YORK, 16 Jan 1986, *Prophet* (pen and wash/blue-green paper, 81/2 x 103/4 ins / 21.6 x 27.3 cm) USD 3,000. LONDON, 7 July 1987, *Virgin and Child with Cherubs (front), Sketch of a Man in Armour (back)* (black chalk, wash heightened with white/blue paper, 103/4 x 8 ins / 27.6 x 20.6 cm) GBP 5,000. PARIS, 22 Jan 1988, *Death of the Virgin* (pen heightened with white, 141/4 x 93/4 ins / 36 x 24.8 cm) FRF 5,000. NEW YORK, 11 Oct 1990, *Discovery of Moses* (oil on canvas, 361/4 x 33 ins / 92 x 84 cm) USD 19,800. MONACO, 7 Dec 1990, *Baptism of Constantine* (oil on canvas, 211/2 x 281/2 ins / 54.5 x 72.5 cm) FRF 244,200. MILAN, 19 Oct 1993, *St Sebastian Being Cared for by Angels* (oil on panel, 10 x 13 ins / 25.5 x 33 cm) ITL 22,482,000. LONDON, 18 April 1996, *Allegory of Justice in a Pendentive* (ink and wash heightened with white, 9 x 71/4 ins / 23 x 18.7 cm) GBP 747. LONDON, 7 July 1999, *Mary Magdelene Holding Lamp* (pen/ink wash heightened with white, 9 x 6 ins / 24 x 14 cm) GBP 1,300. PARIS, 21 March 2002, *Seated Prophet* (chalk heightened with white, 15 x 10 ins / 37 x 26 cm) EUR 7,500. LONDON, 10 July 2002, *Adoration of the Shepherds* (pen/ink wash heightened with white, 11 x 17 ins / 27 x 42 cm) GBP 8,000. NEW YORK, 21 Jan 2003, *Luxury* (pen/ink wash over chalk heightened with white, 11 x 8 ins / 28 x 20 cm) USD 11,000.

ROVERE, Jan de. See **ROOVERE**

ROVERE, Marco della

Italian, 16th - 17th century.

Active in Milan.

Painter, fresco artist. Religious subjects.

Marco della Rovere was the brother of Giovanni Mauro della Rovere and Giovanni Battista the Elder. He may have worked with Giovanni Mauro della Rovere on frescoes for the church of S Maria della Rosa in Milan.

ROVERIO, Bartolommeo, called Il Genovesino

Italian, 17th century.

Born c. 1577, probably in Genoa.

Active in Milan c. 1620.

Painter.

Bartolommeo Roverio painted several works for the Augustine friars in Milan, in particular a genealogical tree of their order. Oretti refers to a painting by Rovere in the Carthusian monastery of Carignano, signed: *Bartol Roverio D. Genovesino*, dated 1624, and a *Crucifixion* dated 1614. He and the artist Marco Genovesini are believed to have been one and the same person.

ROVEROLLES, Charles de

French, 17th century.

Active in Nantes c. 1655.

Portrait artist.

Roverolles produced a *Portrait of Monsieur de la Pinsonnière, Mayor of Nantes.*

ROVERS, Dio

Dutch, 20th century.

Born 1896.

Painter. Still-lifes.

AUCTION RECORDS:
AMSTERDAM, 18 Feb 1992, *Still-life with Earthenware Jug, Apples in a Bowl and Flowers in a Vase on a Table* (1939, oil on canvas, 38 1/2 x 31 1/2 ins / 98 x 80 cm) NLG 1,955.

ROVESCALLI, Antonio
Italian, 19th - 20th century.
Born 23 December 1864, in Crema.
Painter, watercolourist, draughtsman. Stage sets.
Antonio Rovescalli studied at the Accademia di Belle Arti di Brera in Milan, and produced work for theatres in Milan.
MUSEUMS AND GALLERIES:
MILAN (Mus. Teatrale alla Scala): watercolours; drawings.

ROVETTA, Francesco
Italian, 19th - 20th century.
Born 13 July 1849, in Brescia; died 10 April 1932.
Painter. Genre scenes, landscapes.
Francesco Rovetta studied under M Faustini.
AUCTION RECORDS:
MILAN, 30 Oct 1984, *Landscape with a River* (oil on panel, 8 3/4 x 12 1/2 ins / 22.5 x 32 cm) ITL 1,300,000.

ROVETTA, Ventura
Italian, 18th century.
Born 1687; died 1768.
Active in Brescia.
Sculptor, goldsmith.

ROVETTA, Vincenzo
Italian, 16th century.
Born 1515.
Active in Brescia.
Sculptor, designer of ornamental architectural features.
Vincenzo Rovetta was the pupil of Maffeo Olivieri.

ROVEZZANO, Giovanni di Francesco da. See **CERVELLIERA Giovanni di Francesco del**

ROVIALE. See **RUVIALE**

ROVIGO D'URBINO. See **XANTO AVELLI Francesco**

ROVIOLI, Francesco
Italian, 18th century.
Died 1765.
Active in Ferrara.
Painter.
Rovioli was the pupil of Ercole Graziani.

ROVIRA. See also **RUBIRA**

ROVIRA, José. See **RUBIRA Joseph**

ROVIRA, Nicolás
Spanish, 17th century.
Sculptor.
Nicolás Rovira created the high altar of Tarragona Cathedral in 1682 in collaboration with Fr. Grau.

ROVIRA, Pedro
Spanish, 15th century.
Active in Barcelona from 1427 to 1439.
Painter.

ROVIRA, Pedro Juan
Spanish, 15th century.
Active in Barcelona in 1462.
Painter.

ROVIRA, Riba. See **RIBA-ROVIRA François**

ROVIRA, Toni
Spanish, 20th century.
Painter.
Toni Rovira has exhibited solo in Barcelona (1979), Majorca (1982), Mexico (1985), Gerona (1988) and Tokyo (1989).
BIBLIOGRAPHY:
Catálogo nacional de arte contemporáneo 1990-1991, Ibérico 2Mil, Barcelona, 1990-1991.
MUSEUMS AND GALLERIES:
PORRERES (MAC).

ROVIRA DE CHYPRE, Esteve
Spanish, 14th century.
Active in Cyprus.
Painter.
In 1387, Rovira de Chypre was commissioned to produce a retable behind the high altar of Toledo Cathedral.

ROVIRA SOLER, José
Spanish, 20th century.
Born 1906, in Santiago, Cuba, to Spanish parents.
Painter. Portraits, landscapes, still-lifes, flowers.
Rovira Soler studied at the Escuela de Arte y Oficios in Barcelona before moving to Madrid to study at the Prado Museum. He was awarded a travel scholarship which enabled him to travel not only to France and Italy but also to Cuba and the USA. He took part in various group exhibitions, including the Exposición Nacional de Bellas Artes in Barcelona (1921, 1942, 1944) and the Salón de la Primavera in Madrid (1932, 1933).
BIBLIOGRAPHY:
Arnáiz, José Manuel/López Jiménez, Javier/Merchán Díaz, Manuel (ed.), '*Cien años de pintura en Espana y Portugal (1830-1930)*' in vol. IX, Antiqvaria, Madrid, 1992.

ROVIRA Y BROCANDEL, Hipólito
Spanish, 18th century.
Born 13 August 1693, in Valencia; died 6 November 1765, in Valencia.
Painter, engraver (burin), art restorer (painting). Religious subjects, portraits.
Hipólito Rovira y Brocandel studied in Rome. He was one of the most distinguished exponents of Spanish Baroque painting and worked for the Dominican church in Valencia.

He was chiefly known for his engravings, notably those illustrating Jaime Cervera's sermon *Las Tres Purpuras de Alzira* in 1707. He also engraved the *Allegory of Painting* that Palomino had painted for the frontispiece of the first volume of his *Museo*.
BIBLIOGRAPHY:
Bermudez, C., *Diccionario histórico de los más ilustres profesores de las bellas artes en España*, Madrid, 1800. Kubler G./Soria, M., *Art and Architecture in Spain & Portugal and their American Dominians 1500 to 1800*, Penguin Books, Harmondsworth and Baltimore, 1959. De Orellana, M.A., *Biografía pictórica valentina: o, vida de los pintores, arquitectos, escultores y grabadores valencianos: obra filológica*, Ayuntamiento de Valencia, Valencia, 1967. Gallego, A., *Historia del grabado en España*, Ediciones Cátedra, Madrid, 1979.

ROVIROSA BLANC, Juan
Spanish, 20th century.
Born 1887, in Reus (Catalonia); died 1956.
Painter, watercolourist, draughtsman. Landscapes, mountainscapes, waterscapes, seascapes.
Rovirosa Blanc showed his work in Spain, most notably at an exhibition of regional artists held in Reus in 1981. He painted modest-format landscapes with an extremely low horizon and in a limited range of sober colours. Examples include *Trees, Mountain, Clouds* and *Sea*.
BIBLIOGRAPHY:
Arnáiz, José Manuel/López Jiménez, Javier/Merchán Díaz, Manuel (ed.), '*Cien años de pintura en Espana y Portugal (1830-1930)*' in vol. IX, Antiqvaria, Madrid, 1992.

ROVISI, Leopoldina
Italian, 18th century.

Born 1755, in Moena.
Painter.
Religion provided the inspiration for the paintings of Leopoldina Rovisi, the daughter of Valentino Rovisi.

ROVISI, Valentino
Italian, 18th century.
Born 23 December 1715, in Moena; died 12 March 1783, in Moena.
Painter.
Valentino Rovisi, the father of Leopoldina Rovisi, was a pupil at the Accademia di Belle Arti in Venice and was taught by Tiepolo. He produced numerous religious paintings for churches and individuals in Trentino.

ROVRAIN, Josef. See **ROBRAIN**

ROW, David
American, 20th century.
Painter.
David Row's work belongs to the tradition of American abstract painting, with compositions structured in terms of two-dimensional space and colour, sometimes arranged in several panels. He develops a network of lines governed by an interplay of random symmetries, reminiscent of the sculpture of Brancusi, as in *Endless Column*. His other works include *Who's Afraid of Magenta, Dark Blue and Yellow? Paralaxis* and *Deep Focus*. He held a solo exhibition at the Thaddeus Ropac Gallery, Paris, in 1991.
BIBLIOGRAPHY:
David Row, exhibition catalogue, W. Zimmer Gall., New York, 1987. Ardenne, Paul, *'David Row'* in *Art Press 163*, periodical, Paris, November 1991.
AUCTION RECORDS:
NEW YORK, 19 Nov 1996, *Mars* (1987, oil on canvas, diptych, 32 x 40 ins / 81.2 x 101.6 cm) USD 1,955.

ROWAN, Alexander
British, 19th century.
Active in London.
Painter. History painting.
Alexander Rowan exhibited biblical subjects in London from 1852 to 1859, chiefly at the Royal Academy and the British Institution.

ROWAN, Marian Ellis
Australian, 19th - 20th century.
Born 1848 or 1858, in Melbourne; died 1922.
Painter, watercolourist. Wild flowers, birds, animals, landscapes.
Marian Rowan was largely self-taught. She lived in New Zealand for a while after she married in 1873, and travelled widely, visiting Europe, the USA, India and Papua New Guinea. She endeavoured to find and record every wildflower in Australia.

Ellis Rowan

MUSEUMS AND GALLERIES:
MELBOURNE: watercolours - SYDNEY: watercolours.
AUCTION RECORDS:
LONDON, 1 Dec 1988, *Butterflies* (watercolour and gouache, pair, 12 1/2 x 7 ins / 31.8 x 17.8 cm and 12 1/2 x 7 ins/31.8 x 17.8 cm) GBP 990. SYDNEY, 20 March 1989, *Spring Landscape* (watercolour, 19 1/4 x 11 1/2 ins / 49 x 29 cm) AUD 3,600. MELBOURNE, 29 April 1997, *Still-life with Flowers* (watercolour, 29 1/4 x 21 1/4 ins / 74 x 54 cm) AUD 9,200. MELBOURNE, 27 April 1999, *Kigelia Pinnata, Sausage Tree* (watercolour and gouache, 22 x 15 ins / 57 x 39 cm) AUD 3,500. MELBOURNE, 23 Nov 1999, *Everlasting Daisies* (gouache, 20 x 14 ins / 50 x 36 cm) AUD 3,600. MELBOURNE, 1 May 2000, *Wildflowers* (watercolour and gouache, 15 x 20 ins / 39 x 51 cm) AUD 5,000. MELBOURNE, 29 Nov 2000, *Summer* (watercolour and gouache, 53 x 17 ins / 135 x 43 cm) AUD 5,000. SYDNEY, 28 Aug 2001, *Roses* (watercolour and gouache, 20 x 15 ins / 52 x 37 cm) AUD 3,200. MELBOURNE, 2 May 2002, *Banksias* (gouache, 29 x 21 ins / 73 x 54 cm) AUD 7,000. SYDNEY, 29 Oct 2002, *Floral-leaved Orchid* (gouache, 21 x 14 ins / 53 x 36 cm) AUD 4,000. SYDNEY, 15 April 2003, *Three Flowers* (gouache, 21 x 15 ins / 53 x 38 cm) AUD 4,000. SYDNEY, 15 April 2003, *Red Cedar* (gouache, 21 x 25 ins / 53 x 63 cm) AUD 4,000.

ROWBOTHAM, Charles Edmund, known as Chas
British, 19th - 20th century.
Born 1856, in London; died 1921.
Painter (gouache), watercolourist. Landscapes.
Charles Edmund Rowbotham was the son of Thomas Charles Leeson Rowbotham and, like him, used gouache for many of his landscapes, which were often highly coloured. At the end of his father's career the two often collaborated, with Charles usually painting the figures. He exhibited in London from 1877, at Suffolk Street and at the Royal Institute of Painters in Watercolours.

Chas Rowbotham

MUSEUMS AND GALLERIES:
BOLTON (Mus. and AG): *Messina* (1883) - CARDIFF: *Clifton Bridge* (watercolour).
AUCTION RECORDS:
LONDON, 3 Feb 1976, *Ipswich* (1886, watercolour heightened with white, 5 x 10 1/4 ins / 13 x 26 cm) GBP 280. LONDON, 13 May 1980, *The Chain Pier, Brighton* (1895, heightened with gouache, 8 1/2 x 20 ins / 21.5 x 51 cm) GBP 550. LONDON, 27 April 1982, *Church and Tower of San Giorgio, Lake Como* (1878, watercolour heightened with gouache, 25 x 35 ins / 63.5 x 89 cm) GBP 900. NEW YORK, 29 Feb 1984, *View of Lugano*. LONDON, 14 May 1985, *View of Lausanne* (1884, watercolour and pencil heightened with white, 15 1/2 x 26 ins / 39.5 x 66 cm) GBP 750. LONDON, 22 July 1986, *Bay of Naples* (1895, watercolour heightened with gouache, 25 3/4 x 36 ins / 65.5 x 91.5 cm) GBP 1,600. LONDON, 27 Oct 1987, *Borromean Islands* (1886, watercolour and gouache, 24 1/2 x 35 ins / 62.5 x 88 cm) GBP 2,800. LONDON, 25 Jan 1988, *Dunkeld* (watercolour, 9 x 21 ins / 23 x 53.5 cm) GBP 440. LONDON, 25 Jan 1989, *Shower on the Moorlands* (1859, watercolour and gouache, 9 1/4 x 14 1/4 ins / 23.5 x 36 cm) GBP 550. LONDON, 31 May 1989, *Italian Fishing Boars Moored at a Jetty* (watercolour and gouache, 5 x 7 1/2 ins / 13 x 19 cm) GBP 550. CHESTER, 20 July 1989, *Difficult Sums* (1890, watercolour and gouache, 21 x 15 1/4 ins / 53.5 x 38.5 cm) GBP 3,960. LONDON, 31 Jan 1990, *View on the Rhine* (1887, watercolour heightened with white, 15 3/4 x 25 1/2 ins / 40 x 65 cm) GBP 1,540. LONDON, 14 June 1991, *Lake Garda* (1886, watercolour heightened with gouache, 8 1/2 x 20 ins / 21.3 x 50.5 cm) GBP 2,420. LONDON, 29 Oct 1991, *Figures on the Quay of an Estuary* (pencil and watercolour, 12 3/4 x 17 3/4 ins / 32.4 x 45.2 cm) GBP 660. MONTREAL, 23-24 Nov 1993, *Panoramic View of a Bay with Fishing Boats* (1895, watercolour, 6 x 11 1/2 ins / 15.2 x 29.2 cm) CAD 1,000. LONDON, 30 March 1994, *Bay of Sorrento* (1893, watercolour and gouache, 21 1/4 x 15 ins / 54 x 38 cm) GBP 1,610. LONDON, 10 March 1995, *Italian Landscapes on a Road overlooking a Coastal Town* (pencil and watercolour, 15 x 23 1/2 ins / 38.1 x 60 cm) GBP 2,760. LONDON, 9 May 1996, *Griante, Lake Como* (1893, watercolour heightened with gouache, 12 x 23 1/2 ins / 30.5 x 60 cm) GBP 1,725. LONDON, 17 March 1999, *Bay of Sorrento, Italy* (1890, watercolour and gouache, 12 x 24 ins / 30 x 62 cm) GBP 2,600. HASLEMERE, 1 Sept 1999, *Near Castel a Mare, Bay of Naples. Camero, Maggiore* (watercolour, a pair, 17 x 10 ins / 43 x 25 cm) GBP 3,200. BILLINGSHURST, 24 July 2000, *Chat by the Lakeside* (1894, wa-

tercolour heightened with gouache, a pair, 17 x 13 ins / 43 x 34 cm) GBP 3,000. LONDON, 29 Nov 2000, *Castelmare, Bay of Naples* (1890, watercolour over pencil heightened with white and scratching out, 21 x 40 ins / 54 x 101 cm) GBP 5,200. LEWES, 15 March 2001, *View of Naples from the Hills. Italian Lake Scene* (1881, watercolour, a pair, 10 x 21 ins / 25 x 53 cm) GBP 3,200. LONDON, 28 Nov 2001, *Two Views near Menton* (1882, 1883, watercolour, a pair, 16 x 26 ins / 41 x 66 cm) GBP 3,200. LONDON, 25 June 2002, *Bellagio on Lake Como, Italy* (1883, watercolour and gouache, 13 x 26 ins / 33 x 66 cm) GBP 2,800. LONDON, 17 Oct 2002, *Italian Peasants Resting on a Stone Terrace Path Overlooking a Bay* (1902, pencil and watercolour, 16 x 23 ins / 41 x 59 cm) GBP 2,500. LYMINGTON, 1 Oct 2003, *Italian Lake Scene with Town and Figures. River Scene with Boats* (1886, watercolour heightened with gouache, a pair, 8 x 19 ins / 20 x 49 cm) GBP 2,800. CAMBRIDGE, 22 Oct 2003, *View Across Lake Maggiore, Italy. View by Lake Lugano* (watercolour, a pair, 8 x 19 ins / 20 x 49 cm) GBP 1,800. NEWCASTLE, 23 March 2004, *Figures on a Hillside Overlooking the Bay of Naples* (1894, watercolour, 7 x 19 ins / 19 x 47 cm) GBP 1,500. NEWCASTLE, 23 March 2004, *Figures and Boats on the Shore of an Italian Lake* (watercolour, 7 x 19 ins / 19 x 47 cm) GBP 1,900.

ROWBOTHAM, Thomas Charles Leeson, the Younger

British, 19th century.

Born 21 May 1823, in Dublin; died 30 June 1875, in London.

Watercolourist, painter (gouache), draughtsman. Landscapes.

Thomas Charles Leeson Rowbotham was the son and pupil of Thomas Leeson Scarse Rowbotham the Elder. He began exhibiting in London in 1840 and showed at the Royal Academy, the Suffolk Street Gallery and, above all, the Royal Institute of Painters in Water-Colours until his death in 1875. He was a member of the Royal Institute from 1858. Rowbotham travelled extensively throughout Britain and also spent time in France and in Italy. On the death of his father in 1853, he succeeded him as a teacher of drawing and composition at the Naval Institute in New Cross.

MUSEUMS AND GALLERIES:

BLACKBURN - CARDIFF - LONDON (Victoria and Albert Mus.): six watercolours.

AUCTION RECORDS:

LONDON, 21 Nov 1921, *Island of Ischia from the Bay of Naples* (drawing) GBP 162. LONDON, 9 Dec 1921, *Carnarvon* (drawing) GBP 31. LONDON, 17 March 1922, *Near Sorrento* (drawing) GBP 60. LONDON, 16 June 1922, *Lago di Maggiore* (drawing) GBP 75. LONDON, 16 Feb 1923, *Biebstein on the Moselle River* (drawing) GBP 29. LONDON, 12 March 1928, *Grindelwald* (drawing) GBP 30. LONDON, 30 Oct 1936, *Sorrento, Bay of Naples* (drawing) GBP 89. LONDON, 21 May 1943, *Pallanza* (drawing) GBP 24. LONDON, 17 Sept 1943, *Market Scene, Venice* (drawing) GBP 52. LONDON, 13 June 1978, *Ehrenbreitstein and Coblenz* (1850, watercolour and pencil heightened with white, 9 3/4 x 14 3/4 ins / 25 x 37.5 cm) GBP 600. LONDON, 22 Nov 1979, *Atrani, Gulf of Salerno* (1862, watercolour heightened with white, 28 1/4 x 49 ins / 72 x 124.5 cm) GBP 750. LONDON, 1 April 1980, *Heidelberg Castle and Town View* (1854, oil on canvas, 24 1/2 x 35 1/2 ins / 62 x 90 cm) GBP 1,700. LONDON, 9 Feb 1982, *Edinburgh from Salisbury Crags, Evening* (1848, watercolour and pencil with touches of gouache, 28 x 43 ins / 71.2 x 109.5 cm) GBP 2,600. LONDON, 15 March 1984, *Rouen from St Catherine's Mount* (1849, watercolour heightened with gouache, 27 x 42 ins / 68.5 x 106.5 cm) GBP 4,500. LONDON, 27 Feb 1985, *View of the Como and Lake Como* (1856, watercolour heightened with white, 28 3/4 x 45 ins / 73 x 114 cm) GBP 4,000. LONDON, 16 Oct 1986, *Italian Lake* (1873, watercolour heightened with gouache, 17 x 25 1/2 ins / 43 x 65 cm) GBP 1,300. LONDON, 30 Sept 1987, *Banks of the Rhine* (1860, watercolour and pencil heightened with white, 16 3/4 x 25 ins / 42.5 x 63.8 cm) GBP 2,600. LONDON, 31 Jan 1990, *Fishermen's Huts on the Beach* (1863, watercolour heightened with gouache, 7 1/4 x 22 3/4 ins / 18.5 x 58 cm) GBP 935. LONDON, 25-26 April 1990, *Italian Lake Town* (1873, watercolour and gouache, 16 1/4 x 29 ins / 41.5 x 73.5 cm) GBP 2,200. LONDON, 8 Feb 1991, *Gulf of Calabria* (1871, watercolour heightened with white, 22 x 39 3/4 ins / 55.9 x 101 cm) GBP 4,180. NEW YORK, 15 Oct 1991, *Monastery on a Cliff overlooking the Sea* (1867, watercolour and gouache/card, 9 3/4 x 21 1/2 ins / 25 x 54.5 cm) USD 1,870. PERTH, 31 Aug 1993, *Road in the Highlands; Watercourse in the Highlands* (watercolour heightened with white, each 6 1/4 x 17 3/4 ins / 16 x 45 cm) GBP 1,955. LONDON, 3 Nov 1993, *Bordighera; Bay of Naples* (watercolour and gouache, each 6 1/4 x 11 1/2 ins / 16 x 29.5 cm) GBP 2,530. LONDON, 10 March 1995, *Town in Italy with a Bridge over a River* (1867, pencil, watercolour and gouache, 6 1/4 x 17 3/4 ins / 15.9 x 45.1 cm) GBP 1,035. LONDON, 29 March 1996, *Varenna, Lake Como* (1864, watercolour heightened with white, 10 x 24 1/4 ins / 25.2 x 61.5 cm) GBP 1,725. EDINBURGH, 15 May 1997, *Varenna, Lake Como* (watercolour and gouache heightened with white, 16 x 27 1/2 ins / 40.5 x 70 cm) GBP 3,450. LONDON, 17 March 1999, *Lake Como. Near Sicily* (watercolour and gouache, a pair, 7 x 19 ins / 19 x 47 cm) GBP 1,600. LONDON, 12 July 1999, *Breaking up HMS Imperieuse at Woolwich* (1873, watercolour, 21 x 41 ins / 54 x 103 cm) GBP 2,100. LONDON, 14 June 2000, *Fishermen by Quay* (1865, watercolour, 7 x 18 ins / 17 x 46 cm) GBP 1,400. MANCHESTER, 28 Nov 2000, *View of the Swiss Alps* (1861, watercolour, 10 x 25 ins / 26 x 64 cm) GBP 1,500. BURY ST EDMUNDS, 8 March 2001, *Figures in an Italian Lake Landscape* (1861, watercolour and gouache, 10 x 20 ins / 25 x 51 cm) GBP 2,400. LONDON, 29 Nov 2001, *Mansion in the Highlands* (watercolour over pencil, heightened with gouache, 14 x 20 ins / 35 x 51 cm) GBP 2,600. HASLEMERE, 8 May 2002, *Young Children Fishing, a Punt at the River's Edge and Wooden Bridge* (1873, oil on canvas, 10 x 18 ins / 25 x 46 cm) GBP 1,200. ROME, 26 Nov 2002, *View of Benares* (1872, tempera on card on panel, 30 x 53 ins / 77 x 134 cm) EUR 14,000. LONDON, 9 March 2004, *Rouen from St Catherine's Hill, France* (1849, watercolour, 28 x 43 ins / 70 x 108 cm) GBP 3,000. CHESTER, 17 March 2004, *Eel Bucks on the Thames* (1872, watercolour, 9 x 15 ins / 24 x 37 cm) GBP 1,150.

ROWBOTHAM, Thomas Leeson Scarse, the Elder

British, 19th century.

Born 1783; died 1853.

Painter, watercolourist. Landscapes.

Thomas Leeson Scarse Rowbotham worked in Bath and Bristol and taught drawing and composition at the Royal Naval School in New Cross. He exhibited at the Suffolk Street Gallery in London in 1834.

MUSEUMS AND GALLERIES:

BRISTOL (City Mus. & AG): *The Drawing Room, Leigh Court, Bristol* (c. 1840, oil on canvas) - LONDON (Victoria and Albert Mus.): *Capel Curig, Wales.*

AUCTION RECORDS:

LONDON, 16 July 1987, *Barge on a River at Dusk* (watercolour, 7 1/4 x 9 3/4 ins / 18.5 x 25 cm) GBP 1,000. ST ASAPH, 2 June 1994, *Lake Como* (watercolour, 9 1/2 x 13 3/4 ins / 24 x 35 cm) GBP 2,875. LONDON, 29 Nov 2001, *Frigate in a Stiff Breeze* (watercolour over pencil heightened with gouache and scratching out, 7 x 10 ins / 19 x 26 cm) GBP 1,300.

ROWDEN, Thomas

British, 19th - 20th century.

Born 1842; died 1926.

Painter. Landscapes, animals.

BIBLIOGRAPHY:
Wood, Christopher, *The Dictionary of Victorian Painters*, Antique Collectors' Club, Woodbridge, 1971. Mallalieu, Huon, *The Dictionary of British Watercolour Artists up to 1920*, Antique Collectors' Club, Woodbridge, 1976-1990.
AUCTION RECORDS:
MONTREAL, 1 Dec 1992, *Cattle and Horses Quenching Their Thirst* (watercolour, a pair, each 13 x 12 1/4 ins / 33 x 31 cm) CAD 1,000.

ROWE, Algernon
British, 19th - 20th century.
Painter. Genre scenes.
Algernon Rowe took part in a summer exhibition at the Royal Academy, London, in 1914, with *A Room in Chelsea*.
BIBLIOGRAPHY:
'*Royal Academy Exhibitors 1905-1970*' in vol. III, Hilmarton Manor Press, Calne, 1987.
AUCTION RECORDS:
LONDON, 12 June 1992, *Rehearsal* (oil on canvas, 50 x 30 ins / 127 x 76.2 cm) GBP 2,200.

ROWE, Charles Alfred
American, 20th century.
Born 2 July 1934, in Great Falls (Montana).
Painter.
Charles Alfred Row studied at the University of Montana (1952-1953), the Art Institute of Chicago and the University of Chicago (1957-1960).
His work has been shown in many group exhibitions and also in solo shows, including those in Centerville (Delaware) in 1965, in Philadelphia in 1967, 1968 and 1969, in Washington in 1970 and 1974 and at the Russel Museum, Great Falls, in 1972 and 1973.

ROWE, Clarence Herbert
American, 20th century.
Born 11 May 1878, in Philadelphia; died 17 July 1930, in Cos Cob.
Engraver.
Clarence Herbert Rowe studied under Max Bohm and Bouguereau. He made etchings.

ROWE, Clifford
British, 20th century.
Born 1904, in London; died 1989.
Painter. Scenes with figures.
Artists' International Association.
Clifford Rowe was a communist and in 1930 he spent some time in the Soviet Union. He was one of the founder members of the Artists International Association and took part in demonstrations against fascism.
BIBLIOGRAPHY:
Pagé, Suzanne/Winock, Michel/Michaud, Éric/Vidal, Aline, *Les Années trente en Europe. Le Temps menaçant*, exhibition catalogue, Musée d'Art moderne de la Ville de Paris, Paris musées, Flammarion, Paris, 1997.
MUSEUMS AND GALLERIES:
LEICESTER (New Walk Mus. and AG): *Fried Fish Shop* (1936).

ROWE, Edward
British, 18th century.
Died 2 April 1763.
Stained glass painter.

ROWE, Ernest Arthur
British, 19th - 20th century.
Born c. 1863; died 26 January 1922, in Tunbridge Wells.
Painter. Landscapes.
Ernest Arthur Rowe painted a large number of English gardens, as well as landscapes and views of stately homes. He travelled in Sicily and Capri; his works include a number of Italian landscapes. He participated in the summer exhibitions of the Royal Academy of Arts in 1908, 1910, 1914 and 1917.
BIBLIOGRAPHY:
'*Royal Academy Exhibitors 1905-1970*' in vol. III, Hilmarton Manor Press, Calne, 1987. Hobhouse, Penelope/Wood, Christopher, *Painted Gardens: English Watercolours, 1850-1914*, Atheneum, New York, 1991.
AUCTION RECORDS:
LONDON, 29 Oct 1985, *Garden at Holme Lacy* (1902, watercolour, 19 3/4 x 29 3/4 ins / 50.4 x 75.5 cm) GBP 4,200. LONDON, 16 Dec 1986, *Hampton Court Palace* (watercolour, 12 1/2 x 15 3/4 ins / 32 x 40 cm) GBP 2,400. ORCHARDLEIGH PARK (SOMERSET), 21 Sept 1987, *View of Amalfi* (watercolour, 10 x 14 ins / 25.3 x 35.5 cm) GBP 3,000. LONDON, 1 Nov 1990, *Garden of Mrs Jobob, The Close, Salisbury* (watercolour, 15 3/4 x 22 1/4 ins / 40.1 x 56.5 cm) GBP 3,960. LONDON, 8 Feb 1991, *Garden Path* (watercolour, 7 x 10 ins / 17.8 x 25.4 cm) GBP 1,925. LONDON, 5 June 1991, *Castello from the Hotel Faraglioni, Capri* (1913, watercolour, 11 1/2 x 9 ins / 29 x 23 cm) GBP 1,100. LONDON, 19 Dec 1991, *Below the Terrace at Penshurst* (watercolour, 11 x 15 ins / 28 x 38.4 cm) GBP 1,650. LONDON, 11 June 1993, *Gardens at Chequers Court, Buckinghamshire* (watercolour, 9 3/4 x 14 1/4 ins / 24.8 x 35.9 cm) GBP 2,530. LONDON, 5 Nov 1993, *Rectory at Coddington in Worcestershire* (pencil and watercolour, 9 3/4 x 7 ins / 25 x 17.5 cm) GBP 1,380. LONDON, 21 Jan 1999, *Peacock before Ornamental Archway* (1891, pencil and watercolour, 14 x 10 ins / 35 x 25 cm) GBP 2,000. LONDON, 4 Nov 1999, *Gunn Terrace, Berkeley Castle, Gloucestershire* (pencil and watercolour, 8 x 11 ins / 20 x 28 cm) GBP 1,600. BILLINGSHURST, 1 Feb 2000, *Peacocks in a Terraced Garden. Girl with Peacocks in a Garden* (watercolour, a pair, 7 x 9 ins / 17 x 24 cm) GBP 2,000. BILLINGSHURST, 25 May 2000, *In the Garden. Fountain* (1898, watercolour heightened with gouache, a pair, 9 x 14 ins / 24 x 35 cm) GBP 2,400. LONDON, 21 Nov 2001, *Across the Moat, Hever Castle* (pencil, watercolour and gum arabic, 10 x 14 ins / 25 x 35 cm) GBP 3,800. LONDON, 21 Nov 2001, *Hever Castle from the Rose Garden* (1920, pencil, watercolour and gum arabic, 10 x 14 ins / 25 x 35 cm) GBP 4,000. LONDON, 1 May 2002, *Golders Park, Hampstead* (1919, watercolour, 14 x 9 ins / 35 x 24 cm) GBP 3,000. LONDON, 25 Nov 2004, *Garden at Holme Lacey* (watercolour, 20 x 30 ins / 50 x 75 cm) GBP 23,000.

ROWE, George
British, 19th century.
Born 1797, in Dartmouth; died 1864, in Exeter.
Watercolourist, draughtsman, lithographer. Portraits, landscapes, mountainscapes.
AUCTION RECORDS:
MELBOURNE, 26 July 1987, *The Arapiles* (watercolour/mounted paper, 28 1/2 x 61 1/2 ins / 72.5 x 156 cm) AUD 165,000. MELBOURNE, 27 April 1999, *First Metropolitan Gold Fields Handicap, Ballarat* (1861, watercolour, 9 x 13 ins / 23 x 32 cm) AUD 3,000. MELBOURNE, 16 June 2004, *End of the Rainbow, Golden Square, Bendigo* (watercolour, 12 x 22 ins / 31 x 57 cm) AUD 18,000.

ROWE, George James
British, 19th century.
Died 6 February 1883.
Painter. Genre scenes, landscapes, architectural views.
George Rowe worked in London and exhibited at the Royal Academy between 1830 and 1854.

ROWE, J. Staples
American, 19th century.
Born 1856; died 1 November 1883, in New York.
Portrait artist.

ROWE, Marcos. See **MARCOS ROWE**

ROWE, Michael
British, 20th - 21st century.

Born 1948, in High Wycombe.
Silversmith.

The silversmith Michael Rowe has had a significant impact on the development of 20th and 21st century British applied art. Having trained at High Wycombe College of Art and the Royal College of Art, Rowe went on to set up a London studio in 1972, producing work that frequently moved away from traditional methods of craftsmanship. Drawing inspiration from ancient ceremonial vessels, Rowe's pieces in silver, copper and brass illustrate an innovative approach to concept and form. While the artist's vessels - cups, pomanders, vases and candelabra - are conceived with an explicit function in mind, the abstraction and geometric simplicity of works such as *Conditions for Ornament No. 6* (1988) and *Conical Vessel* (1992) exemplify Rowe's ability to see beyond the decorative aspect that is usually associated with applied arts. Through his writing and research into colouring and patination, many of Rowe's pieces display an acute sensitivity towards both colour and texture. This is indicated in the artist's frequent application of tinning and gold leaf to the surface of his work, a strategy that clearly illustrates Rowe's interest in light and shade.

Rowe became Visiting Lecturer at both Buckinghamshire College of Further Education (1973-1984) and Camberwell College of Art (1976-1982) where he co-researched and published the landmark text, *The Colouring, Bronzing and Patination of Metals* (1982) with Richard Hughes. He became a member of staff at the Royal College of Art in 1984, and was elected a Fellow in 1987. Rowe has shown his work worldwide; notable exhibitions include *Michael Rowe: Objects in Metal* at London's Crafts Council Gallery in 1978 and *Michael Rowe: Retrospective* at the Museem het Princessehof in Leeuwarden, the Netherlands in 1988. He has won numerous awards including Sotheby's Decorative Arts Award in 1993 and the Golden Ring of Honour from the Association of German Goldsmiths (*Die Gesellschaft für Goldschmidekunst*) in 2002.

BIBLIOGRAPHY:

Hughes, Richard/Rowe, Michael, *The Colouring, Bronzing and Patination of Metals*, illustrated book, Crafts Council, London, 1982. Hill, Richard/Margetts, Martina, *Michael Rowe*, exhibition catalogue, Birmingham Museums and Art Gallery in association with Lund Humphries, Birmingham, 2003.

ROWE, Sidney Grant

British, 19th - 20th century.
Born 1861; died 22 July 1928.
Painter, watercolourist. Animals, landscapes.

Sidney Grant Rowe was a member of the Royal Institute of Oil Painters. He took part in the summer exhibitions at the Royal Academy, London in 1912 and 1914. He exhibited in London at the Royal Academy, Suffolk Street and New Water-Colour Society from 1877.

BIBLIOGRAPHY:

'Royal Academy Exhibitors 1905-1970' in vol. III, Hilmarton Manor Press, Calne, 1987.

AUCTION RECORDS:

LONDON, 18 Dec 1909, *Mill on the Moor*, GBP 1. LONDON, 29 July 1988, *Sheep in a Lane* (oil on canvas, 16 3/4 x 22 ins / 42.5 x 55.7 cm) GBP 418. BATH, 2 Dec 2002, *Shepherd, Sheep and a Dog in a Country Lane* (oil on canvas, 24 x 35 ins / 60 x 90 cm) GBP 1,950. BATH, 2 Dec 2002, *Cattle in an Orchard* (oil on canvas, 24 x 35 ins / 60 x 90 cm) GBP 2,300.

ROWE, Thomas Trythall

British, 19th century.
Born 1856.
Painter. Figures, village scenes, landscapes, architectural views, flowers.

Thomas Rowe studied in Paris and went on to exhibit at the Royal Academy in London in 1882, 1885 to 1886, 1888 to 1891, 1893 to 1894 and 1896 to 1899.

ROWE, Thomas William

British, 19th century.
Active in London during the second half of the 19th century.
Sculptor.

Thomas Rowe exhibited at the Royal Academy in London from 1862 to 1878.

ROWELL, John

British, 20th century.
Painter. Landscapes.

John Rowell took part in the summer exhibitions at the Royal Academy, London in 1936 and 1938.

BIBLIOGRAPHY:

'Royal Academy Exhibitors 1905-1970' in vol. III, Hilmarton Manor Press, Calne, 1987. Rowell, Christopher, *'Stained glass by John Rowell and William Price the Younger at the Vyne'* in *The Burlington Magazine*, periodical, London, June 2003.

AUCTION RECORDS:

SYDNEY, 17 April 1988, *Milk Cart* (oil on card, 16 1/4 x 20 ins / 41 x 51 cm) AUD 1,200. SYDNEY, 26 March 1990, *Green Valley and Blue Hills* (oil on card, 18 x 24 ins / 46 x 61 cm) AUD 900. VICTORIA, 12 May 2003, *Holiday Time* (oil on canvas, 9 x 11 ins / 22 x 29 cm) AUD 12,000. VICTORIA, 12 May 2003, *Mornington* (oil on canvas, 9 x 15 ins / 24 x 39 cm) AUD 12,000.

ROWELLE, John

British, 18th century.
Died 2 September 1756, in Reading.
Active in Reading.
Stained glass painter.

John Rowelle painted windows in Hambledon Church.

ROWLAND, William

American, 18th century.
Active in Glasgow during the second half of the 18th century.
Miniaturist.

William Rowland emigrated to America in 1777.

ROWLANDSON, George Derville

British, 19th - 20th century.
Born 1861; died 1928.
Painter. Scenes with figures, sporting subjects, landscapes, animals.

AUCTION RECORDS:

LONDON, 18 March 1980, *A Coach-and-Four Crossing a Bridge* (oil on canvas, 19 1/2 x 29 1/2 ins / 49.5 x 75 cm) GBP 2,200. LONDON, 24 March 1981, *Off to the Derby* (oil on canvas, 28 x 40 ins / 71 x 101.5 cm) GBP 2,000. LONDON, 16 March 1984, *Game of Polo* (1902, oil on canvas, a pair, 20 x 34 ins / 50.8 x 86.3 cm) GBP 10,000. NEW YORK, 6 June 1985, *Hunting Scene* (watercolour/paper, set of 12, 10 1/4 x 14 1/4 ins / 26 x 36 cm) USD 7,250. NEW YORK, 7 June 1985, *Pause for Refreshment Outside the Red Fox Inn* (oil on canvas, 20 x 30 ins / 50.8 x 76.2 cm) USD 4,800. LONDON, 21 March 1990, *Taking a Ditch* (oil on canvas, 20 x 30 ins / 51 x 76 cm) GBP 5,500. NEW YORK, 28 Feb 1991, *Over the Hedge* (oil on canvas, 32 1/4 x 48 1/4 ins / 81.6 x 122.5 cm) USD 20,900. NEW YORK, 7 June 1991, *Over the Fence* (oil on canvas, 24 x 36 ins / 61 x 91.4 cm) USD 6,600. LONDON, 11 Oct 1991, *Over the Ditch; The Kill; Killing* (oil on canvas, a pair, each 24 x 36 ins / 61 x 91.5 cm) GBP 4,400. NEW YORK, 5 June 1992, *Picking up the Scent* (oil on canvas, 20 x 30 1/4 ins / 50.8 x 76.8 cm) USD 6,325. LONDON, 6 June 1996, *Shamrock, a Bay Hunter in Paddock* (1907, oil on canvas, 22 1/2 x 31 ins / 57.2 x 78.7 cm) GBP 920. LONDON, 13 March 1997, *Over the Fence* (1899, oil on canvas, 32 x 48 ins / 81.3 x 122 cm) GBP 13,000. LONDON, 5 Nov 1997,

Jumping a Brook, Leading the Field (oil on canvas, 20 x 30 ins / 51 x 76 cm) GBP 3,220.

ROWLANDSON, Thomas

British, 18th - 19th century.

Born July 1756, in London; died 22 April 1827, in London.

Painter, watercolourist, draughtsman, caricaturist, engraver. History painting, portraits.

Thomas Rowlandson was a tradesman's son who went to live in Paris at the age of sixteen at the invitation of his French aunt by marriage. He had already attended courses at the Royal Academy Schools in London, and his admission to the École de l'Académie Royale in 1772 was supported by Pigalle. He studied there from September 1772 until March 1775. In the course of 1775, he exhibited a *Delilah Visiting Samson in Gaza Prison* at the Royal Academy in London, where he had been re-admitted to complete his studies. During his time spent at school in Paris he acquired a taste for working in a quick and rhythmic style reminiscent of French Rococo.

In 1777, Rowlandson set himself up in a studio in Wardor Street and went on to exhibit portraits at the Royal Academy from 1778 to 1781. A downturn in his father's business caused some financial hardship but his Parisian aunt proved generous to a fault. On her death, he also came into a substantial inheritance. By all accounts, he had acquired a taste for gambling while living in Paris and, for a time at least, he neglected his portraiture in favour of protracted visits to some of London's most notorious gambling dens, where he became known for his self-possession and his stoic acceptance of substantial losses. Once he had gambled away his inheritance, however, he returned to his easel, freely admitting that he had 'played the fool' and now needed to earn some money again. He began to paint caricatures to supplement income from his portrait work and, by 1782, he was effectively no longer a serious artist. However, there was no doubt whatsoever that he was extremely talented and prints of his caricatures were soon very much in demand. He died in 1827 after a protracted illness.

Rowlandson's comic images are on a par with those of William Hogarth in terms of vitality and acute insight into human foibles. His caricatures were typically executed using a reed pen in combination with a delicate colour wash. They were subsequently etched (by Rowlandson) on copper and aquatinted (in most instances by a professional engraver), with the resultant impression then being hand-coloured.

His subject-matter was drawn from familiar social types - old maids, blowsy barmaids, 'Grub Street' hacks, the clergy, street traders, and so on. In most instances he succinctly captures and conveys their essential features, holding their dress sense up to ridicule and mercilessly deflating their pretentious and self-important attitudes and postures. Bosoms and bottoms are generously inflated and facial expressions are as wickedly humorous as they are varied.

His initial series of drawings (*The Schoolmaster's Tour*) was accompanied by verses written by William Combe and published in the *Poetical Magazine* launched by art publisher Rudolph Ackermann. Ackermann was Rowlandson's principal employer and it was Ackermann who published the majority of his caricature series and Combe's verse. Examples of Rowlandson's work include *Museries of Life, Comforts of Bath, Cries of London, The Microcosm of London* (1808), *Tour of Dr. Syntax in Search of the Picturesque* (1812), *The Military Adventures of Johnny Newcome* (1815), *The Great Master or Adventures of Quilli in Hindostan, The English Dance of Death* (1816), *The Dance of Life* (1816-1817), *The Second Tour of Dr. Syntax in Search of Consolation* (1820), *The Third Tour of Dr. Syntax in Search of a Wife* (1821) and *The History of Johnny Quae Genus* (1822). He also illustrated editions of works by Tobias Smollett, Oliver Goldsmith and Laurence Sterne.

Rowlandson 1788

T. Rowlandson

BIBLIOGRAPHY:

Grego, J., *Rowlandson the Caricaturist*, London, 1882. Oppé, Adolf Paul, '*Thomas Rowlandson, his Drawings and Watercolours*' in *Studio*, periodical, London, 1923. Falk, B., *Thomas Rowlandson: His Life and Art*, London, 1949. Hayes, J., *Rowlandson Watercolours and Drawings*, London, 1972. Baskett, J./Snelgrove, D., *The Drawings of Thomas Rowlandson in the Paul Mellon Collection*, London, 1977. Savory, Jerold J., *Thomas Rowlandson's Doctor Syntax Drawings: an Introduction and Guide for Collectors*, Fairleigh Dickinson University Press, Madison (NJ), Cygnus Arts, London, 1997.

MUSEUMS AND GALLERIES:

LONDON (Victoria and Albert Mus.): *The Sacristy of the Parish of Bath* (1784); *Landscape, Cottage and Figures* (1805); *Old Town Hall, Salisbury; Market; Man with a Wooden Leg; York Priory; White Hart Inn, Windsor; The Lawn, Richmond; By the Seaside; Near Helston, Cornwall* (1806); *Picture-Seller; Milk-Seller* (1784); *River Thames near Deptford; Hampton Bridge; Hampton Court Palace; Landscape with Wooden Cart; Portsmouth Harbour* (1794); *Strawberry Hill Castle, Twickenham; Landscape with Figures and Sheep; Knareborough Bridge; St Austell; Kew Palace; Landscape with Riders and Figures; Museum of Ancient Art; Palace Portico; Glastonbury; Illustration for 'The Tour of Dr. Syntax in Search of the Picturesque'; Thames View; Greenwich Fair; Angler; Meir Square, Antwerp; Scene in front of an Inn*; several watercolours, never exhibited - MANCHESTER: *High Life; Roadside Inn; Low Life* - PONTOISE: *Youth and Old Age; Watercolour Caricature*.

AUCTION RECORDS:

PARIS, 1886, *Chevalier d'Eon in a Passage of Arms with Sergeant Liger* (watercolour) FRF 4,000. PARIS, 7 May 1887, *Hunting Accident* (drawing) FRF 470; *Market Scene, London* (drawing) FRF 490. PARIS, 1899, *Visiting Uncle; Visiting Aunt* (two watercolours, pendants) FRF 3,325. PARIS, 1899, *Place de la Victoire* (drawing) FRF 1,450. LONDON, 16 Feb 1922, *Park Gate* (watercolour) GBP 48. LONDON, 24 March 1922, *Market Square, Antwerp* (drawing) GBP 147; *Castle Tavern* (drawing) GBP 99. LONDON, 30 June 1922, *Italian Lake* (drawing) GBP 43. PARIS, 14 and 15 Dec 1922, *Reading the Gazette* (pen and wash) FRF 2,500. LONDON, 16 April 1923, *Party at Boodle's* (drawing) GBP 147; *Bowling Green* (drawing) GBP 48; *The York-Ely Stage* (drawing) GBP 50. LONDON, 12-16 Nov 1923, *Horse Guards' Parade* (watercolour) GBP 140; *Bank Cottery* (watercolour) GBP 79. PARIS, 20 March 1924, *Market Square in a Small Town* (pen and watercolour) FRF 3,300. PARIS, 24 May 1924, *Racing at Newmarket* (watercolour) FRF 1,150. PARIS, 17 Nov 1924, *Bust Portrait (Male)* (pencil) FRF 2,600. LONDON, 22 May 1925, *French Barracks Interior* (drawing) GBP 73; *Drury Lane Theatre* (drawing) GBP 105; *Lady Greeting her Husband* (drawing) GBP 54. LONDON, 7 July 1926, *Coaches at Kew Bridge* (watercolour) GBP 60. LONDON, 18 Feb 1927, *Four Hours in the Country* (drawing) GBP 63; *Dinner*, GBP 78. PARIS, 13 June 1927, *Lauding at Greenwich on Easter Monday* (watercolour and pen) FRF 7,600; *Troop of Strolling Players on the Road* (watercolour and pen) FRF 6,000. LONDON, 16 Dec 1927, *Tavern in Greenwich* (drawing) GBP 99; *Market Square, Brentford* (drawing) GBP 94; *Rag Fair* (drawing) GBP 89. LONDON, 8 Feb 1928, *Oxford Castle* (drawing) GBP 65; *Banbury Fair* (watercolour) GBP 98. London, 10 Feb 1928, *Mr H. Angelo* (drawing) GBP 157; *Market Square, Hertford* (drawing) GBP 157; *Watering-Place* (drawing) GBP 94. London, 23 May 1928, *Windy Day* (drawing) GBP 100. London, 20 Nov 1928, *Large Stairway* (watercolour) GBP 92; *View of the River Camek* (watercolour) GBP 160; *Putney Bridge* (watercolour) GBP 200; *Fox-Hunting* (watercolour) GBP 195. London, 7 Dec 1928, *Market Day, Antwerp* (drawing) GBP 273; *Mail Coach* (drawing) GBP 120; *The Royal Dockyards* (drawing) GBP 141. London, 7 Dec 1928, *Dancers at Covent Garden* (drawing) GBP 183; *Beggars Receiving Alms from Officers* (drawing) GBP 178. London, 13 March 1929, *Thames Barges* (watercolour) GBP 135. Paris, 16 May 1929, *Thatched Cottage by the Water* (watercolour) FRF 3,920. London, 7 June 1929, *Brigadier Hill, Enfield* (drawing) GBP 110. London, 22 Nov 1929, *Market Square, Juliers* (drawing) GBP 147; *Box-Lobby Loungers* (drawing) GBP 199; *Mrs Samuel Howitt* (drawing) GBP 210. New York, 16 April 1930, *Sale of English Beauties to the Indies* (drawing) USD 310; *Spithead* (drawing) USD 375; *Dutch Canal View* (drawing) USD 270. London, 21 July 1931, *Royal Institution Library* (drawing) GBP 135. Paris, 23 Dec 1931, *Card Game* (watercolour) FRF 600. London, 15 Dec 1933, *Market Day, Norwich* (drawing) GBP 79. London, 15 April 1943, *Putney Bridge; Town with Carriages; Figures and Flock; River Scene*. London, 28 April 1944, *Inn Courtyard* (drawing) GBP 99. London, 9 May 1945, *King's Head, Roehampton*, GBP 240; *Harps Farm, Enfield*, GBP 270. New York, 31 May 1945, *Putney Bridge and Church* (watercolour) USD 400; *Amsterdam* (watercolour) USD 470. London, 27 July 1945, *Vauxhall Gardens* (drawing) GBP 2,730. London, 12 Oct 1945, *Eating in the Barn* (drawing) GBP 68. London, 14 Nov 1945, *Stowe Gardens* (drawing) GBP 230; *Four Hours in the Country* (drawing) GBP 120. London, 19 Dec 1945, *Box-Lobby Laughers* (drawing) GBP 480. London, 1 Feb 1946, *Dance at the Pantheon* (drawing) GBP 141. New York, 25-27 April 1946, *Amorous Quaker* (watercolour) USD 225; *Mrs Samuel Howitt* (watercolour) USD 200. London, 24 May 1946, *Thatched Cottage with Figures* (drawing) GBP 73. Paris, July 1946, *Market Square in a Small Town* (watercolour on pen outline) FRF 20,500. London, 31 Jan 1947, *Blackfriars Bridge* (drawing, in collaboration with N. Black) GBP 273. London, 10-12 Feb 1947, *Greenwich* (drawing) GBP 105; *Boats in Estuary* (drawing) GBP 68; *Watercourses, Cornwall* (drawing) GBP 105. London, 6 June 1947, *Pencing Match* (drawing) GBP 52; *Painting Sale at Christie's* (drawing) GBP 157. London, 18 June 1947, *Market Day, Richmond* (drawing) GBP 100; *Thames Scene* (drawing) GBP 150. London, 10 Feb 1950, *Market Square* (drawing) GBP 141. Paris, 5 June 1950, *Cabaret* (pen and wash, attributed) FRF 6,000. London, 16 June 1950, *Old Courtyard, Royal College, Cambridge* (drawing) GBP 105. London, 18 Oct 1950, *Close Game* (drawing) GBP 550. London, 3 Nov 1950, *Horse Market*. London, 24 Jan 1951, *Quarry, Delabole* (drawing) GBP 250; *Cornish Landscape* (drawing) GBP 210. Paris, 24-25 March 1954, *Café* (pen and wash) FRF 180,000. London, 4 Dec 1957, *Old Smithfield Market* (drawing) GBP 900. London, 10 Dec 1958, *Viggen Dam, Amsterdam* (drawing) GBP 420. London, 30 Nov 1960, *Travels in France* (drawing) GBP 900. New York, 21 April 1961, *Filial Affection* (watercolour) USD 1,000. Paris, 13 June 1961, *At the Races* (pen and watercolour) FRF 1,000. Versailles, 25 Nov 1962, *Old Vauxhall Gardens* (watercolour) FRF 11,000. London, 12 Nov 1968, *Peasants Going to Market* (watercolour on pen outline) Gns 1,300. London, 15 June 1971, *Hunting* (watercolour on pen outline) Gns 1,600. London, 20 April 1972, *Wrestlers* (watercolour) GBP 1,000. London, 6 Nov 1973, *The Royal Oak* (watercolour) Gns 5,500. London, 5 March 1974, *Paris Stage* (watercolour and pen) Gns 3,800. London, 18 Nov 1976, *Travellers Arriving in the Market Square* (watercolour, 11 3/4 x 17 3/4 ins / 30 x 45 cm) GBP 1,350. London, 1 March 1977, *The Female Penitentiary* (watercolour and pen, 13 x 10 1/2 ins / 33 x 26.5 cm) GBP 1,400. London, 27 July 1979, *Field Day in Hyde Park* (etching and coloured aquatint, 15 x 21 1/4 ins / 38.3 x 54.2 cm) GBP 520. London, 13 Dec 1979, *St Paul's and Blackfriars from the Thames* (watercolour and pen, 10 3/4 x 16 3/4 ins / 27.3 x 42.5 cm) GBP 7,000. New York, 3 June 1980, *Declaration of Love* (pen, coloured wash and black chalk, 11 1/2 x 9 1/4 ins / 28.9 x 23.5 cm) USD 3,200. London, 19 June 1981, *The Hunt* (etchings and aquatint, 18 1/4 x 23 1/4 ins / 46.6 x 58.8 cm) GBP 4,900. New York, 10 June 1983, *Racing at Epsom* (1823, pencil, pen and watercolour, 11 1/4 x 16 3/4 ins / 28.8 x 42.5 cm) USD 7,000. London, 9 July 1985, *Greenwich at Low Tide* (watercolour and pen, 9 1/4 x 12 ins / 23.8 x 30.6 cm) GBP 7,000. London, 21 Nov 1985, *Thames Barges near Kew Castle* (pen and watercolour/pencil outlines, 11 1/4 x 17 1/4 ins / 28.5 x 44 cm) GBP 2,400. London, 30 June 1986, *Seated Lady* (pen and wash/pencil outlines, 10 1/4 x 7 3/4 ins / 25.9 x 19.6 cm) GBP 3,600. London, 16 July 1987, *George III and Queen Charlotte Passing through Bedford* (watercolour/outlines in pen and ink and pencil, 16 1/2 x 27 1/2 ins / 42 x 70 cm) GBP 75,000. London, 25 Jan 1988, *Venus and Cherub* (ink, 6 1/2 x 8 3/4 ins / 16.5 x 22.5 cm) GBP 2,860; *Prostitutes doing their Housework in a Harbour Setting* (ink, 7 3/4 x 5 ins / 19.5 x 13 cm) GBP 1,045. New York, 25 Feb 1988, *Leda and the Swan* (1797, ink and watercolour, 5 1/4 x 7 1/4 ins / 13.4 x 18.3 cm) USD 1,430. Paris, 18 Nov 1988, *Teacher and Pupil* (1812, pen and watercolour, 11 x 9 ins / 27.8 x 22 cm) FRF 9,500. London, 25 Jan 1989, *Mending the Nets* (ink and watercolour, 6 x 8 1/4 ins / 15 x 21 cm) GBP 825. Paris, 15 March 1989, *Gamblers at a Gaming Table* (pencil, pen, ink, wash and watercolour, 12 3/4 x 17 1/4 ins / 32.5 x 43.5 cm) FRF 140,000. Montreal, 1 May 1989, *Quarrel* (1798, watercolour, 5 x 7 3/4 ins / 13 x 20 cm) CAD 850. London, 25-26 April 1990, *Reapers at Rest* (ink and watercolour, 6 x 9 1/4 ins / 15 x 23.5 cm) GBP 1,760. New York, 24 Oct 1990, *Greenwich Hospital* (1822, watercolour and ink/paper, 12 x 19 ins / 30.5 x 48.5 cm) USD 7,700. New York, 9 Jan 1991, *Fifteen Female Caricatures* (ink and watercolour/paper, 10 x 8 ins / 25.4 x 20.6 cm) USD 3,850. London, 30 Jan 1991, *Dream Merchants* (ink and watercolour, 7 3/4 x 11 ins / 19.5 x 27 cm) GBP 1,320. London, 9 April 1992, *Genius in his Attic* (1805, ink and watercolour, 8 1/2 x 11 1/4 ins / 21.5 x 28.5 cm) GBP 3,300. London, 7 Oct 1992, *At the Races* (ink and watercolour, 5 1/2 x 9 ins / 14 x 23 cm) GBP 1,210. New York, 29 Oct 1992, *Conjugal Love* (watercolour, ink and wash/paper, 7 3/4 x 11 ins / 19.7 x 27 cm) USD 1,760. Paris, 11 Dec 1992, *Fencing Academy, Bond Street* (watercolour and Indian ink, 6 1/4 x 10 ins / 16 x 24.5 cm) FRF 5,300. London, 13 July 1993, *Toll Gate* (ink and watercolour, 5 3/4 x 9 ins / 14.9 x 22.8 cm) GBP 4,600. New York, 11 Jan 1994, *Soldiers Playing Cards* (watercolour, graphite, ink and wash, diam. 12 1/4 ins / 31.2 cm) USD 3,680. New York, 19 Jan 1994, *Officer Strolling in the Garden of a Country Residence in the Company of Two Ladies* (watercolour, ink and pencil/paper, 7 1/2 x 11 ins / 19.1 x 27.9 cm) USD 16,100. London, 9 May 1996, *Nymphs Bathing* (ink and watercolour, 4 1/4 x 6 1/4 ins / 10.5 x 16 cm) GBP 920. Edinburgh, 26 Nov 1997, *Wicked Schoolmarm* (pen and brown ink, watercolour, 5 3/4 x 10 ins / 14.9 x 24.5 cm) GBP 1,380. Paris, 5 Feb 1998, *Distressed Mariners* (pen and wash, 9 x 8 ins / 23 x 20.5 cm) FRF 4,500. London, 15 July 1999, *The City Chop House* (pen, ink and wash over pencil, 11 x 4 ins / 27 x 11 cm) GBP 14,000. London, 9 Nov 1999, *Thomas Stitchwell, Shoemaker from London* (pencil, pen, ink and watercolour, 12 x 19 ins / 31 x 49 cm) GBP 13,000. London, 30 Nov 2000, *King's Buckhounds in Full Cry after a Stag* (pen, ink and watercolour over pencil, 11 x 17 ins / 28 x 42 cm) GBP 7,600. London, 6 Dec 2000, *Caricatures* (etching) GBP 14,000. London, 29 Nov 2001, *Figures Unloading Fishing Boats on the Shore* (pen, ink and watercolour over pencil, 10 x 16 ins / 25 x 41 cm) GBP 6,000. London, 21 March 2002, *Travelling in France* (pen, ink and watercolour over pencil and gouache, 13 x 20 ins / 33 x 52 cm) GBP 18,000. LONDON, 21 Nov 2002, *Happy Family - or the Married Man* (pencil and pen, 10 x 12 ins / 25 x 30 cm) GBP 18,000. LEWES, 29 April 2003, *Dr Syntax at the Auction* (c. 1820, pen, ink and watercolour, 10 x 16 ins / 25 x 41 cm) GBP 9,000. LONDON, 5 June 2003, *Dinner in the Kitchens* (pencil, 11 x 17 ins / 28 x 43 cm) GBP 9,000. LONDON, 1 July 2004, *Furniture Auction* (pen, brown ink and grey wash over pencil, 7 x 10 ins / 19 x 25 cm) GBP 17,000. LONDON, 18 Nov 2004, *The Connoisseurs* (1785, on paper, 13 x 16 ins / 32 x 40 cm) GBP 22,000.

ROWLEY, Frances Richards
Canadian, 19th century.
Active at the end of the 19th century.
Painter. Genre scenes, portraits.
MUSEUMS AND GALLERIES:
MONTREAL: *Parisian Woman.*

ROWNTREE, Kenneth
British, 20th century.
Born 14 March 1915, in Scarborough; died 1997.
Painter, watercolourist, illustrator, designer.
Landscapes, architectural views. Murals.

Kenneth Rowntree studied at Ruskin School, Oxford, under Albert Rutherston from 1930 to 1934, then at the Slade School of Fine Art, London under Schwabe in 1934 and 1935. He was appointed an official war artist. He was a member of the Society of Mural Painters, and taught mural painting at the Royal College of Art (RCA), London from 1948 to 1958. He was also Professor of fine a at Newcastle-upon-Tyne University from 1959 to 1980.

He executed a great many murals, notably for the British pavilion at the Exposition Universelle in 1958. He also illustrated *A Prospect in Wales* (1948).

He held his first exhibition in Leicester in 1946. A retrospective was held at the Hatton Gallery at the University of Newcastle in 2003.

BIBLIOGRAPHY:
Milner, John, *Kenneth Rowntree*, Lund Humphries, 2002.
MUSEUMS AND GALLERIES:
LONDON (Tate Collection): *Guitar Players* (1933).
AUCTION RECORDS:
LONDON, 21 Sept 1989, *Road from Cavendish to Clare* (oil on canvas, 16 x 26 ins / 40.7 x 66.1 cm) GBP 770. LONDON, 20 Sept 1990, *Road from Cavendish to Clare* (oil on canvas, 15 1/4 x 25 1/2 ins / 39 x 65 cm) GBP 792. LONDON, 2 March 1999, *Essex Garden* (oil on board, 17 x 24 ins / 44 x 61 cm) GBP 2,100. LONDON, 14 July 1999, *West Country Landscape* (oil on board, 24 x 30 ins / 61 x 76 cm) GBP 2,400. LONDON, 6 June 2002, *Hereford Cathedral from the Wye* (oil on canvas, 18 x 24 ins / 46 x 61 cm) GBP 3,000. LONDON, 4 July 2002, *Durham* (1963, oil on board, 12 x 16 ins / 31 x 41 cm) GBP 2,000. LONDON, 3 July 2003, *Venice, Evening* (oil on board, 25 x 30 ins / 63 x 76 cm) GBP 1,900. LONDON, 10 Sept 2003, *Designs for the County Guides* (set of eight, 30 x 21 ins / 76 x 53 cm) GBP 2,800. OXFORD, 28 July 2004, *View of a Stately Home* (oil on canvas, 13 x 17 ins / 33 x 43 cm) GBP 1,000. OXFORD, 28 July 2004, *College Barge on the Isis* (oil on canvas, 15 x 19 ins / 38 x 48 cm) GBP 1,800.

ROWSBY. See **RICHARD the Carver II**

ROWSE, Samuel Worcester
American, 19th century.
Born 29 January 1822, in Bath (Maine); died 24 May 1901, in Morristown.
Portrait artist.

Samuel Worcester Rowse moved to Boston in 1852, then settled in New York in 1880.

MUSEUMS AND GALLERIES:
BOSTON: *Mrs Longfellow.*

ROX, Henrik. See **ROHESK Hendrick**

ROX, P.
German, 18th century.
Active at the beginning of the 18th century.
Draughtsman, engraver.
MUSEUMS AND GALLERIES:
BERLIN (Kupferstichkabinet): *Cain Killing Abel.*

ROXAS. See also **ROJAS**

ROXAS Y SARRIO, José de (Count of Casa-Roxas)
Spanish, 19th century.
Active in Alicante during the first half of the 19th century.
Miniaturist.

ROXIN, Antoine Leopold
French, 18th century.
Born c. 1704, in Nancy; died 21 February 1762, in Nancy.
Painter. History painting, portraits, genre scenes.

Roxin was named painter to the City of Nancy in 1758, then painter to the King of Poland.

ROY. See also **LE ROY**

ROY, Abel
French, 20th century.
Painter, watercolourist.

Abel Roy was active in about 1900.

AUCTION RECORDS:
PARIS, 16 Nov 1992, *Falconners* (1900, watercolour, 8 1/4 x 11 1/2 ins / 21 x 29 cm) FRF 4,000.

ROY, Alix
Haitian, 20th century.
Painter. Scenes with figures.

Alix Roy paints picturesque compositions as well as street and market scenes.

AUCTION RECORDS:
NEW YORK, 19 May 1992, *Fruit and Vegetables* (oil/synthetic resin, 23 3/4 x 15 ins / 60.3 x 38 cm) USD 3,960. NEW YORK, 24 Feb 1995, *Market Scene* (oil on canvas, 18 x 23 ins / 45.7 x 58.4 cm) USD 1,265.

ROY, Bartholomäus
German, 17th century.
Active in Danzig in 1612.
Painter.

ROY, Bénigne
French, 17th century.
Active in Dijon in 1675.
Sculptor.

ROY, Dolf van
Dutch, 19th - 20th century.
Born 1858; died 1943.
Painter. Nudes, interiors, landscapes.

MUSEUMS AND GALLERIES:
ANTWERP.
AUCTION RECORDS:
AMSTERDAM, 2 May 1990, *Nude Recling on a Sofa* (oil on panel, 9 x 22 1/4 ins / 23 x 56.5 cm) NLG 6,900. LOKEREN, 9 Oct 1993, *Reclining Nude Smoking a Cigarette* (oil on canvas, 16 1/4 x 27 1/2 ins / 41 x 70 cm) BEF 110,000.

ROY, Donatien
French, 19th - 20th century.
Born 17 April 1854, in Nantes; died 1930, in Nantes.
Painter (gouache), watercolourist. Landscapes, winter landscapes, urban landscapes.

Donatien Roy, the father of Pierre Roy, was a pupil of Joseph René Gouézou.

MUSEUMS AND GALLERIES:
NANTES: *Snow in Nantes; Courtyard in Pornic; Steps, Quai de Turenne, Nantes; St Nazaire.*

ROY, Félix Ernest
French, 19th century.
Born 15 October 1824, in Dijon.
Painter. Genre scenes.

Félix Roy was the student of Drolling. He first exhibited at the Salon of 1865. He produced works with rustic subjects.

ROY, François de. See **DEROY François**

ROY, Françoise
French, 20th - 21st century.
Born 1956.
Painter, engraver.

Françoise Roy lives and works in Paris. She explores the potential of Japanese rice paper, typically by layering it or gluing it to canvas. She uses transparent effects to reveal individual objects - such as pieces in a Go set. Her work has featured in group exhibitions, notably at *En Filigrane - Un Regard sur l'Estampe Contemporaine* (*Beneath the Surface: A Survey of the Contemporary Print*), an exhibition held at the Bibliothèque Nationale in Paris in 1996-1997. She also exhibited at the Biennale de l'Estampe (Prints Biennale) in St-Maur-des-Fossés in 2003.

BIBLIOGRAPHY:
Biennale de l'Estampe de Saint-Maur, exhibition catalogue, Musée de Saint-Maur, St-Maur-des-Fossés, 2003.

ROY, Giovanni
German, 19th - 20th century.
Born 1866, in Heidelberg; died 14 November 1924, in Ferrara, committed suicide.
Active in Italy.
Painter. Portraits.

ROY, Hans, or Le Roi or Le Roy, called Hans von Coblenz
German, 16th - 17th century.
Active in Flanders.
Painter.
Koblenz School.

Roy worked in Koblenz from 1574 to 1603. He is remembered for a panel in the church in Andernach and a triptych in the church at Maria-Laach.

ROY, Hugues
French, 16th century.
Active in Dijon in 1564.
Sculptor.

ROY, Ida de
Belgian, 20th - 21st century.
Born 1946, in Diest.
Potter. Insects, flowers.

Ida de Roy studied at the Provinciaal Hoger Instituut voor Kunstonderwijs in Hasselt and joined the teaching staff. She produces polychrome ceramics of insects and flowers and expressive busts, sometimes laced with vegetation.

ROY, Ignatius J. Van
Flemish School.
Engraver. Religious subjects.

MUSEUMS AND GALLERIES:
AMSTERDAM (Rijksprentenkabinet): *Lamentations of Job.*

ROY, J. Auguste
French, 19th century.
Born 19th century, in Paris.
Portrait artist, engraver (burin).

The student of J. P. Lebas, J. Auguste Roy featured at the Salon of 1800.

ROY, Jacqueline
French, 20th century.
Born 1 November 1898, in Paris.
Painter, sculptor.

Jacqueline Roy, a pupil of Humbert and Suzanne Minier, exhibited in Paris at the Salon des Artistes Français, of which she was a member from 1921 as a painter and from 1926 as a sculptor.

ROY, Jaminy
Indian, 20th century.
Born 1887, in Beliatore (Bangladesh); died 1972, in Calcutta (now Kolkata).
Painter, watercolourist, draughtsman, sculptor.
Religious subjects, mythological subjects, portraits, genre scenes, landscapes.

Roy Jaminy is an extremely famous artist. He studied at the college of art in Calcutta where he received training in Western techniques, and became well known for his academic portraits and his impressionist landscapes in the Western style. In the 1920s his style evolved and he was inspired by folk and village art, particularly Bengali art. As well as works of great purity tending towards abstraction, he produced patterned watercolour landscapes, religious and mythological compositions, and sculptures. He painted subjects of Christian inspiration, in particular the works he sent to the Paris exhibition in 1946: *Christ between the Thieves, The Crucifixion* and *The Virgin and St John*. Roy Jaminy's promoted modern art in India and participated in the international exhibition organized by the United Nations at the Musée d'Art Moderne, Paris, in 1946.

BIBLIOGRAPHY:
Dutta, A. K., *Jamini Roy*, New Delhi, 1973. *Six Indian Painters*, group exhibition catalogue, Tate Galllery, London, 1982. *Jamini Roy: Centenary Exhibition*, exhibition catalogue, National Gallery of Modern Art, New Delhi, 1987. Ströter-Bender, Jotta, *L'Art contemporain dans les pays du Tiers-Monde*, L'Harmattan, Paris, 1995.

ROY, Jas, or Jaes, or Joseph, or Jaspar Coninckx du. See **LE ROY Jas** or **Jaes** or **Joseph**

ROY, Jean
French, 16th century.
Active in Tours in 1566.
Sculptor.

ROY, Jean Baptiste, or de Roy
Flemish School, 19th century.
Born 11 March 1808.
Painter. History painting, portraits, genre scenes.

Jean Baptiste Roy was the pupil of M de Brie. He travelled to Italy, France and England from 1830 to 1838.

ROY, Jean Baptiste de, called de Roy de Bruxelles
Belgian, 18th - 19th century.
Born 29 March 1759, in Brussels; died 7 January 1839.
Painter, engraver (etching). Figures, landscapes with figures, still-lifes, animals.

His father took him to Holland at a very young age, and there trained his talent by the study of the masters of the 17th century, Paul Potter, Cuyp and Berchem, and by working from life. Ommeganck had considerable influence on the style he adopted.

MUSEUMS AND GALLERIES:

GOTHA - LA FÈRE: *Landscape on the Banks of the Meuse* - MAINZ: *Two Paintings of Animals; Landscape with Cattle; Ox in a Meadow* - VIENNA (Albertina Mus.).

AUCTION RECORDS:

PARIS, 1882, *Animals*, FRF 920. PARIS, 27 Nov 1919, *Landscape with Figures and Animals*, FRF 410. PARIS, 22-24 Jan 1923, *Shepherd Guarding His Flock*, FRF 1,610. PARIS, 19 Nov 1928, *The Pasture*, FRF 2,300. PARIS, 20 May 1935, *Flock at Pasture*, FRF 200. LONDON, 18 July 1938, *Peasants*, GBP 7. LONDON, 24 March 1950, *Cows at Pasture* (1792) FRF 5,500. LONDON, 28 Feb 1973, *Pastoral Scene*, GBP 1,400. LONDON, 15 Feb 1980, *Horsemen Halting at the Inn* (oil on canvas, 20 1/2 x 28 ins / 52 x 71.2 cm) GBP 3,800. LONDON, 19 June 1981, *Peasants and Flock in a Landscape* (oil on panel, 20 3/4 x 29 1/4 ins / 52.7 x 74.2 cm) GBP 1,300. LOKEREN, 20 Oct 1984, *Flock near a Cottage* (1811, oil on panel, 32 1/2 x 22 ins / 82.5 x 55 cm) BEF 220,000. AMSTERDAM, 7 May 1992, *Bull and Cows in a Meadow with Peasants Chatting near a Fence and the Château de Laeken in Brussels in the Background* (1794, oil on panel, 31 3/4 x 45 3/4 ins / 80.7 x 116.2 cm) NLG 27,600. LONDON, 6 July 1994, *Landscape with Shepherds and Shepherdesses and Their Animals* (1792, oil on panel, a pair, each 26 1/2 x 21 1/4 ins / 67 x 54 cm) GBP 7,475. AMSTERDAM, 6 May 1996, *Still-life with Flowers in a Vase on an Entablature* (1793, oil on canvas, 21 x 19 ins / 53.5 x 48 cm) NLG 18,880. AMSTERDAM, 9 March 1999, *Cowherd and Cattle near a Waterfall and Peasant Family on a Haycart* (1798, oil on panel, 30 x 43 ins / 76 x 109 cm) NLG 22,000. LONDON, 14 April 1999, *Drover with Cattle on a Track with the Palace of Larckeaw beyond* (1823, oil on panel, 30 x 42 ins / 76 x 106 cm) GBP 7,500. ANTWERP, 21 Feb 2000, *Young Cowherd with Wife and Child* (1825, oil on panel, 15 x 15 ins / 37 x 38 cm) BEF 260,000. LONDON, 19 April 2000, *Cattle and Drovers on a Riverbank. Cattle and Sheep on a Riverbank* (1792, oil on panel, a pair, 15 x 20 ins / 37 x 52 cm) GBP 4,500. LONDON, 26 April 2001, *Pastoral Landscape with Figures and Cattle by a River with Windmill and Drovers beyond* (1791, oil on panel, 19 x 27 ins / 49 x 68 cm) GBP 2,000. LONDON, 26 March 2003, *Dutch Landscape with Drover and Sheep* (1807, oil on panel, 15 x 21 ins / 37 x 54 cm) GBP 3,600. PARIS, 17 Oct 2003, *Cows in Pasture* (1796, oil on canvas, 36 x 52 ins / 91 x 133 cm) EUR 3,000.

ROY, Jeanne Françoise, called Fanny, or König

Swiss, 19th century.

Born 30 April 1837, in Geneva; died 2 March 1899, in Geneva.

Painter. Portraits.

Roy was a pupil of Lugardon and Lamuniere. She settled in Geneva as a portrait painter in oil and on enamel. She also made copies of old masters on enamel, as well as decorative works and fans. She exhibited at various Swiss exhibitions, and at the Salon in Paris in 1845 and 1863.

ROY, José

French, 19th - 20th century.

Active from 1886 to 1905.

Illustrator.

José Roy illustrated many book covers, including Alphonse Daudet's *Lettres de mon moulin* (*Letters from my Windmill*), Méladin's *Corsaires et Flibustiers* (*Pirates and Buccaneers*), and P. Perrault's *Mon Oncle Range-Tout* (*My Uncle Tidy*).

BIBLIOGRAPHY:

Osterwalder, Marcus (ed.), *Dictionnaire des illustrateurs 1800-1914*, Ides et Calendes, Neuchâtel, 1989.

ROY, Jyotirindra

Indian, 20th century.

Born in India.

Painter.

Jyotirindra Roy's painting *The Mother* was shown at the international exhibition organized by the United Nations at the Musée d'Art Moderne, Paris, in 1946.

ROY, Léo van

Belgian, 20th century.

Born 1921.

Active in Brussels.

Painter.

Apport group.

ROY, Louis George Éléanor or Éléonor

French, 19th - 20th century.

Born 22 July 1862, in Poligny; died 1907, in Paris.

Painter (gouache). Scenes with figures, flowers, landscapes.

Louis George Éléanor Roy was a coach at the Lycée Michelet, Vanves, and then at the Lycée Buffon and the Lycée Voltaire, Paris. At the Lycée Michelet he became friendly with Claude Émile Schuffenecker, who invited Roy to take part in the famous exhibition *Groupe impressioniste et synthétiste* (*The Impressionist and Synthetist Group*) that he organised in Paris at the Café Volponi in 1889. Nearly all the exhibitors belonged to the Pont-Aven group centred round Gaugin. The young Nabis were impressed by this 'new style' and its representatives, and the art historian and critic André Mellerio applied the description 'idealist movement in painting' to these artists. Louis Roy exhibited in group and solo shows in Paris, Pont-Aven, Zurich, New York and elsewhere.

MUSEUMS AND GALLERIES:

PARIS (MNAM-CCI).

AUCTION RECORDS:

PARIS, 7 Nov 1977, *Women Gooseherds* (1895, oil on canvas, 15 x 21 3/4 ins / 38 x 55.5 cm) FRF 16,000. BREST, 13 Dec 1981, *Breton Women* (1891, oil on card, 24 x 15 ins / 61 x 38 cm) FRF 86,000. BREST, 12 Dec 1982, *Yellow Field* (gouache, 9 x 11 3/4 ins / 22 x 30 cm) FRF 30,000. ENGHIEN-LES-BAINS, 17 April 1983, *Haymaking* (c. 1895, oil on canvas, 16 1/4 x 11 ins / 41 x 27 cm) FRF 441,500. PARIS, 19 June 1984, *Meal* (1895, gouache, 6 1/2 x 9 ins / 16.5 x 23 cm) FRF 50,000. ENGHIEN-LES-BAINS, 24 March 1985, *Young Women Dressing* (gouache, 5 1/2 x 4 1/2 ins / 14 x 11.5 cm) FRF 25,000. PARIS, 24 June 1988, *Shepherdess or the Saint* (oil on card, 10 x 9 ins / 25.5 x 23 cm) FRF 55,000. PARIS, 2 Nov 1992, *Breton Women by a River* (gouache, 9 x 9 ins / 23 x 23 cm) FRF 70,000. PARIS, 28 Feb 1994, *Landscape* (1895, oil on card, 8 1/4 x 6 3/4 ins / 21 x 17.3 cm) FRF 37,000. PARIS, 20 Nov 1994, *Farm with a Blue Roof* (watercolour, 15 1/4 x 18 3/4 ins / 39 x 47.5 cm) FRF 45,000. PARIS, 30 Oct 1995, *Rose in a Vase* (oil on card, 12 x 9 ins / 30.5 x 22 cm) FRF 20,000. PARIS, 9 Jan 1996, *Small Vase of Flowers (verso), Study of an Interior: The Paraffin Lamp* (1890, oil on canvas, 12 3/4 x 9 3/4 ins / 32.5 x 25 cm) FRF 59,000. NEW YORK, 10 Oct 1996, *Still-life with Flowers* (1890, oil on canvas, 12 3/4 x 9 3/4 ins / 32.7 x 24.8 cm) USD 6,900.

ROY, Lucien

French, 19th century.

Born 4 September 1850, in Nantes.

Watercolourist, architect. Landscapes.

Lucien Roy was the student of Brunet-Debaisne. From 1876 to 1879, he featured at the Salon with watercolours.

ROY, Marie

Maiden name: Jourjon

French, 19th century.
Born 19th century, in Rennes.
Painter.

Marie Roy was the student of her father, the painter Jourjon. She settled in Rennes and produced mainly portraits. She first exhibited at the Paris Salon.

ROY, Marius

French, 19th century.
Born 1833, in Lyons.
Painter. Military subjects, genre scenes.

Marius Roy was the student of Gustave Boulanger and Jules Lefebvre at the École des Beaux-Arts in Paris. He exhibited in Paris from 1880, at the Salon and then at the Salon des Artistes Français.

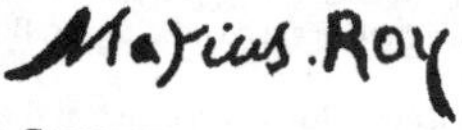

MUSEUMS AND GALLERIES:
LYONS (MBA): *After the Battle of Solferino* - SÈTE: *In the Arms Room, the Night Watch Lesson*; *Recoating*.
AUCTION RECORDS:
PARIS, 25 May 1923, *Piece of Information*, FRF 120; *Recollections*, FRF 230. NEW YORK, 10 Oct 1973, *Soldiers around a Camp Fire*, USD 1,600. NEW YORK, 17 Feb 1993, *Canteen at the Barracks* (oil on panel, 13 x 17 3/4 ins / 33 x 45.1 cm) USD 5,175. LONDON, 15 March 1996, *In Quarters - at Half Past Eight* (1883, oil on canvas, 59 x 78 3/4 ins / 150 x 200 cm) GBP 45,500. ASHVILLE, 22 July 2000, *Soldier in Prone Position Firing Rifle* (oil on canvas, 5 x 9 ins / 13 x 23 cm) USD 1,600. NEW YORK, 29 June 2004, *Mess* (oil on panel, 13 x 18 ins / 33 x 45 cm) USD 5,500.

ROY, Michel

French, 17th century.
Sculptor (wood).

Roy was active in Bourges, in 1647.

ROY, Michel

French, 20th century.
Born 12 July 1938, in Paris.
Sculptor.

Although Michel Roy trained as a wrought-iron worker, as an artist he was self-taught. His abstract works are in iron cut with a blowtorch, which he uses to alter the surface of elements placed at different levels. Some of his large-scale works are part of an exploratory series called *Living Walls*. He showed his work at an exhibition in Cachan.

ROY, Peter van

Flemish School, 17th - 18th century.
Born in Antwerp.
Painter.

Peter van Roy was perhaps the father of Ludwig Roy, a painter in Vienna known only by archive pieces. He worked at the Court of Vienna from 1706 to 1738. He executed portraits and altar paintings in Austrian towns.

ROY, Philéas

French, 19th century.
Born in Loudun (Vienne).
Painter. Landscapes.

Philéas Roy first exhibited at the Paris Salon in 1876. He frequently painted subjects from the area around Paris.
AUCTION RECORDS:
PARIS, 2 Feb 1949, *Landscape*; *Edge of the Canal* (two companion pieces) FRF 1,100. PARIS, 8 March 1950, *Village Road*, FRF 10,200. COMPIÈGNE, 25 Oct 1987, *Mountainous Landscape* (oil on canvas, 25 1/2 x 19 3/4 ins / 65 x 50 cm) FRF 3,600.

ROY, Pierre

French, 19th century.
Born in Troyes; died 1897, in Paris.
Painter.

ROY, Pierre

French, 20th century.
Born 10 August 1880, in Nantes; died 26 September 1950, in Bergamo.
Painter, watercolourist, engraver (wood), illustrator.
Figures, local figures, landscapes with figures, still-lifes, fruit. Stage sets.
Pittura Metafisica (Metaphysical Painting).

Pierre Roy was related to the family of Jules Verne, whose brother read his books to Roy when he was a child. Initially, Roy wanted to be a sailor, but he began work in an architect's studio and there learnt to draw with the precision and meticulousness that was to characterise his later work. He had already received some teaching from his father, Donatien Roy, when he decided to go to Paris. He studied Japanese at the School of Oriental Languages, attended the Académie des Beaux-Arts, and became a pupil of Jean Paul Laurens at the Académie Julian, and then of Eugène Grasset at the École des Arts Décoratifs. At the Académie Julian he was a fellow pupil of Dunoyer de Segonzac and Boussingault. He travelled extensively in England, the Netherlands, Germany and Italy, and died suddenly in Bergamo during an exhibition there of his works.

His early works were influenced by Post-Impressionism, but in about 1910 he made contact with the Fauves and the writers associated with them: André Salmon, Max Jacob and Apollinaire. The collection of coloured woodcuts *Counting Rhymes* that he designed at this time, though not published until 1926, also shows the influence of popular art. It was only after World War I that he radically changed his style and began to paint, with a meticulous and poetic technique, objects not usually juxtaposed. He considered *Adrienne Fishing* of 1919 as the true start of his career. Some consider him an immediate precursor of Surrealist painting. Others think the Surrealism of his unusual juxtapositions to be more a matter of ornamentation. De Chirico's metaphysical period may have had some influence on his development. He was a skilful technician who could render in paint poetical dreams and that spirit of things in which Gerard de Nerval believed. Essentially, he painted everyday objects as faithfully as possible, but created a mysterious and dreamlike effect by bringing them together in a way that raises questions about their real significance. He also painted a few nudes and a series of Hawaiian landscapes that were the result of a strange commission to paint a pineapple for advertising purposes, the client insisting that it be painted on the spot. He illustrated Baudelaire's *Fanfarlo*, J. Supervielle's *Cent Comptines: L'Enfant de la haute mer* (*A Hundred Counting Rhymes: Child of the High Seas*), and many of his paintings were used on covers of the American magazine *Vogue*. He designed the sets for H. Ghéon's *Eau de Vie*, performed at the Vieux-Colombier, Paris, in 1914, and worked with Massine's ballet company, the *Lion in Love* company in London, the Copenhagen opera house, and in the 1945 production of Igor Stravinsky's *Card Game* in Paris.

He first exhibited in Paris at the Société Nationale des Beaux-Arts in 1906, and subsequently at the Salon des Indépendants in 1907-1908. Associated with the Surrealist group, he took part in its first exhibition at the Galerie Pierre, Paris, in 1925, and its exhibition of 1926. He also participated in the Paris Exposition Internationale of 1937 (where he presented six canvases in the exhibition *Maîtres de l'art indépendant* (*Masters of Independent Art*)), in Pittsburgh in 1930, where he was a jury member, in New York in 1932 and 1935, and in San Francisco in 1938. An overall view of his work was presented in Paris in 1934. He was much admired in the USA and frequently visited the country when exhibitions of his painting were being held.

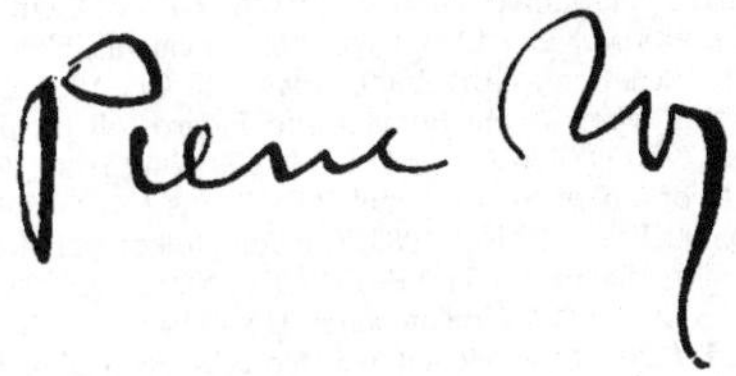

BIBLIOGRAPHY:

Souvenir de Pierre Roy, Musée des Beaux-Arts, Nantes, 1966. Bréhant, Cécile, *Pierre Roy et les marges du surréalisme,* L'Harmattan, Paris, 2001.

MUSEUMS AND GALLERIES:

CASTRES: *Homage to Goya* - HARTFORD (Wadsworth Atheneum): *The Electrification of the Country* (oil on canvas) - LONDON (Courtauld Institute of Art): *Still-life with bottles and Breton bonnets* (c. 1924, oil on canvas) - NANTES (MBA): *Road to the Port* (1943); *Helix and Alley* - NEW YORK (MoMA): *Snakes on the Stairs; Summer Hour; Agricultural Show* - PARIS (MAMVP): *Day in the Country* - PARIS (MNAM-CCI): *Summer in St-Michel* (1932) - PHILADELPHIA (MMA): *The Metric System* (1930) - SAN FRANCISCO (University of California): *The Metric System.*

AUCTION RECORDS:

PARIS, July 1946, *Exotic Fruit,* FRF 10,500. LONDON, 4 Nov 1959, *The Cunard Liner,* GBP 260. PARIS, 27 March 1980, *Barrel Maker* (watercolour, 14 1/2 x 17 3/4 ins / 37 x 45 cm) FRF 4,200. LONDON, 6 Oct 1982, *Still-life with Shellfish* (1928, oil on panel, 15 x 11 3/4 ins / 38.1 x 29.8 cm) GBP 1,800. PARIS, 5 Dec 1983, *Rebuke* (pencil and gouache, 24 x 16 1/4 ins / 61 x 41 cm) FRF 7,000. NEW YORK, 12 Nov 1984, *Homage to Paul Rivet* (oil on canvas, 15 x 24 ins / 38 x 61 cm) USD 13,000. NEW YORK, 11 Nov 1987, *Butterflies* (1932, coloured wax crayons/pencil outlines, 9 1/4 x 7 1/2 ins / 23.7 x 19 cm) USD 3,800. NEW YORK, 18 Feb 1988, *Pink Knot and Shellfish by the Sea; Blue Knot and Ears of Corn near a Château* (oil on canvas, two pendants, each 21 1/4 x 6 1/2 ins / 54 x 16.2 cm) USD 30,800. PARIS, 6 May 1988, *Windmill* (1908, watercolour, 9 x 8 1/4 ins / 22 x 21 cm) FRF 8,000. NEW YORK, 13 Nov 1989, *Amusing Face* (1929, oil on canvas, 36 3/4 x 26 ins / 93.3 x 66 cm) USD 93,500. LONDON, 3 April 1990, *Landscape with Shellfish* (1931, oil on canvas, 9 1/2 x 16 1/4 ins / 24 x 41 cm) GBP 24,200. PARIS, 7 Nov 1990, *Music* (1943, oil on panel, 10 1/2 x 9 1/2 ins / 26.5 x 24 cm) FRF 160,000. NEW YORK, 15 Feb 1991, *Butterflies and Glasses* (oil on canvas, 16 1/2 x 13 ins / 42 x 33 cm) USD 35,750. LONDON, 19 March 1991, *Still-life with Antique Vase* (oil on canvas, 29 x 19 3/4 ins / 73.7 x 50.2 cm) GBP 7,700; *Akaka Waterfall, Hawaii* (oil on canvas, 18 x 12 3/4 ins / 46 x 32.5 cm) GBP 26,400. MONACO, 11 Oct 1991, *Model for the Set of the Ballet 'Game of Cards'* (pencil and gouache, 6 1/4 x 7 3/4 ins / 16 x 20 cm) FRF 24,975. LONDON, 1 July 1992, *Composition with Weights and Measures* (oil on canvas, 36 1/4 x 23 1/2 ins / 92 x 60 cm) GBP 30,800. PARIS, 29 March 1993, *Trompe-l'oeil with Lighthouse* (1930, oil on canvas, 16 1/4 x 12 3/4 ins / 41 x 32.5 cm) FRF 85,000. NEW YORK, 12 May 1994, *Still-life* (oil on canvas, 14 x 10 3/4 ins / 35.6 x 27.3 cm) USD 16,100. LONDON, 28 June 1994, *Still-life by the Sea* (oil on canvas, 9 1/2 x 7 1/2 ins / 24.1 x 19 cm) GBP 6,325. LONDON, 28 June 1995, *Milking* (1923, oil on canvas, 28 3/4 x 19 3/4 ins / 73 x 50 cm) GBP 14,950. LONDON, 25 Oct 1995, *Whale Fishing* (oil on canvas, 16 1/4 x 13 ins / 41 x 33 cm) GBP 13,800. PARIS, 1 April 1996, *Portrait of Madame Draeger* (oil on paper/canvas, study for 'The Belle Marinière', 21 1/2 x 15 ins / 54.8 x 37.8 cm) FRF 25,000. PARIS, 20 June 1996, *Castilian Interior* (pastel/paper, 27 1/4 x 20 3/4 ins / 69 x 53 cm) FRF 7,000. PARIS, 25 May 1997, *Andromeda in Chains, Version III* (c. 1946, oil on canvas, 9 1/2 x 6 1/4 ins / 24 x 16 cm) FRF 20,000.

ROY, Pierre Marcel
French, 19th - 20th century.
Born 1874, in Troyes; died 14 March 1907, in Paris.
Engraver.

Pierre Marcel Roy, a pupil of Gustave Moreau and Henri Lefort, engraved etchings of views of Troyes, Paris, Amsterdam, Antwerp and Bruges.

ROY, Simon
French, 16th century.
Painter.
Fontainebleau School.

Simon Roy was a friend of Clanet, and was working at Fontainebleau in 1548.

ROY, Ulysse. See **ULYSSE-ROY Jean**

ROY DE MAISTRE. See **MAISTRE Leroy Leveson Laurent Joseph de**

ROY DU. See also **DURAY**

ROY-AUDY, Jean-Baptiste
Canadian, 18th - 19th century.
Born c. 1778, in Charlesbourg (Quebec); died c. 1848, in Trois-Rivières (Quebec).
Painter, copyist. Religious subjects, portraits.

Jean-Baptiste Roy-Audy was a pupil of the sculptor François Baillairgé. He trained as a carpenter and cabinet-maker, then started working as a sign painter before moving on to easel paintings. He also made copies of some old religious paintings.

MUSEUMS AND GALLERIES:

MONTREAL - QUEBEC CITY (Mus. du Québec): *Self-portrait.*

ROYAL, Thomas
British, 18th century.
Modeller (wax).

Thomas Royal was active in London in 1770.

ROYANNEZ DE VALCOURT, Adèle (Mme)
19th century.
Painter.

Adèle Royannez de Valcourt exhibited portraits, still-lifes and genre paintings at the Paris Salon in 1814 and 1824.

AUCTION RECORDS:

PARIS, 5 Dec 1979, *The Duchesse de Berry Mourning her Murdered Husband* (1822, oil on canvas, 35 1/2 x 45 3/4 ins / 90 x 116.5 cm) FRF 5,300.

ROYBAERT, Regnier or Reynier, or Royenbart
Flemish School, 17th century.
Sculptor (wood).

Roybaert sculpted the choir screen of the church of Our Lady of Antwerp in the first half of the 17th century.

ROYBET, Ferdinand Victor Léon
French, 19th - 20th century.
Born 12 April 1840, in Uzès; died 10 April 1920, in Paris.
Painter, engraver. Portraits, genre scenes.

Having first learned engraving in Lyons, Ferdinand Roybet came to Paris in 1864 to study under Georges Vibert. He painted a great many figures in period dress. His musketeers, lords, ruffians, women and children in 17th and 18th century costumes attest to a fastidious but undeniably accomplished hand and a genuine flair for colour. In 1871, following visits to Dutch museums, Roybet produced a number of copies from Rembrandt and Franz Hals. He is remembered for his portraits, such as *Madame Gibson* and *Georges de Dramard and Antoine Guillemet,* and some original etchings.

He made his debut in 1865 at the Salon des Champs-Élysées and showed his etchings the same year at the Société des Aquafortistes. His submission to the 1866 Salon, *Fool at*

Henri III's Court, was acquired by Princesse Mathilde. That leading art patron's favour made his name and determined his genre. In 1892 he showed two portraits, one of his pupil *Juana Romani.* He took part in the Salon des Artistes Français, of which he was an associate member and where he was declared hors concours. In 1893 his painting *Sweet Nothings* sold for 100,000 francs and he obtained a medal of honour for *Charles the Bold at Nesles.* He was made a Chevalier of the Légion d'Honneur. He received further medals at the Universal Exhibitions in Antwerp, Berlin and Vienna.

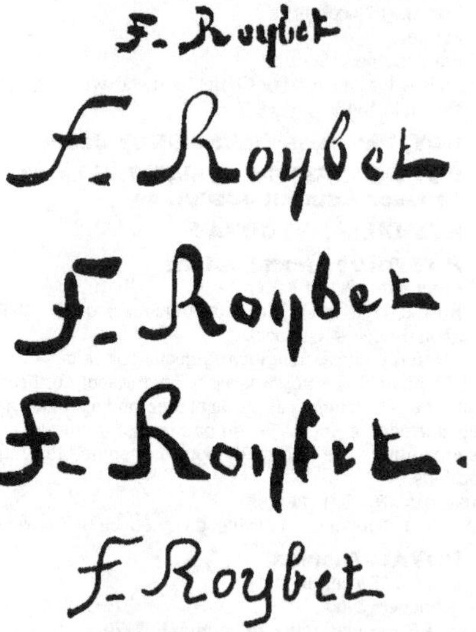

MUSEUMS AND GALLERIES:
AMIENS: *Duke of Urbino* - AVIGNON: *Man with a Glass of Wine* - BAGNOLS: *Study for a Child* - BORDEAUX: *The Geographer* - BUCHAREST (Muz. National de Arta al României): *Portrait of a Man from Senegal* - COLOGNE: *Off to the Hunt* - COURBEVOIE (Mus. Roybet-Fould): several works - DUNKIRK: *Halberdier* - GRENOBLE: *Fool at Henri III's Court* - LYONS: *Arquebusier; Portrait of Hector Brame when Young* - MONTPELLIER: *Flemish Gentleman, 17th Century* - MONTREAL (Learmont Mus.): *Highwayman* - MOSCOW (State Tretyakov Gal.): *Pageboy with Dogs* - MULHOUSE: *The Geographer; The Drinker* - NEW YORK (Metropolitan Mus. of Art): *Game of Cards* - NICE: *Sweet Nothings* - PARIS (former Mus. du Luxembourg): *Girl with Parrot; Little Girl with Doll* - PARIS (Louvre): *The Smoker* - RHEIMS: *Nobleman at Louis XIII's Court in Red Coat* - ROUEN: *Head of Young Man in Henri III Costume.*
AUCTION RECORDS:
PARIS, 12 Feb 1872, *Jester,* FRF 5,710. BRUSSELS, 1878, *Charles I Insulted by Cromwell's Soldiery,* FRF 11,005. PARIS, 1890, *Ensign,* FRF 11,400. PARIS, 9 May 1898, *Model,* FRF 14,000. NEW YORK, 12-14 March 1906, *Philosopher,* USD 2,590. LONDON, 2 April 1910, *Ensign,* GBP 378. PARIS, 4 Dec 1918, *Gentleman,* FRF 6,900. LONDON, 1 June 1923, *Carroussel,* GBP 451. PARIS, 2-3 Dec 1926, *White Lansquenet,* FRF 18,000. PARIS, 26 June 1928, *Gentleman Preparing to Go Out,* FRF 32,500. NEW YORK, 15 Nov 1935, *Horseman in Louis XIII Costume,* USD 550. PARIS, 24 April 1942, *Tableau Vivant,* FRF 26,000. PARIS, 13 June 1947, *The Artist's Studio,* FRF 48,600. PARIS, 17 March 1950, *Musketeer* (1897) FRF 75,000. LONDON, 15 Feb 1961, *Checkmate,* GBP 900. NEW YORK, 24 Nov 1965, *Portrait of a Gentleman,* USD 5,250. LOS ANGELES, 28 Feb 1972, *Portrait of a Gentleman,* USD 4,000. NEW YORK, 12 Jan 1974, *Merrymaking in an Interior,* USD 4,400. NEW YORK, 14 May 1976, *Game of Cards* (oil on panel, 18 x 21 1/2 ins / 46 x 54.5 cm) USD 3,750. GRENOBLE, 9 May 1977, *Tryst* (1885, oil on canvas remounted, 28 3/4 x 36 1/4 ins / 73 x 92 cm) FRF 5,000. LONDON, 3 Oct 1979, *Gypsy* (oil on canvas, 52 x 38 1/2 ins / 132 x 98 cm) GBP 2,600. NÎMES, 15 Oct 1981, *Three Friends, Roybet, Juana Romani and Figaro* (oil on panel, 51 1/4 x 37 3/4 ins / 130 x 96 cm) FRF 75,000. NEW YORK, 26 Oct 1983, *Geographer* (oil on panel, 32 x 21 ins / 81 x 53.4 cm) USD 5,000. PARIS, 28 Nov 1985, *The Song* (oil on panel, 33 1/4 x 39 1/4 ins / 84.5 x 100 cm) FRF 48,000. NEW YORK, 21 May 1986, *Art Lovers* (1883, oil on panel, 31 x 24 1/4 ins / 78.8 x 61.9 cm) USD 8,000. MONTE CARLO, 6 Dec 1987, *Refusal of Taxation* (oil on panel, 77 1/2 x 102 1/4 ins / 197 x 260 cm) FRF 300,000. NEW YORK, 25 Feb 1988, *Man in a Ruff* (oil on panel, 24 x 17 1/2 ins / 61 x 44.4 cm) USD 3,520. VERSAILLES, 15 May 1988, *Book Lovers* (graphite, 7 1/4 x 6 1/4 ins / 18.5 x 16 cm) FRF 1,200. CALAIS, 13 Nov 1988, *Drummer Boy* (oil on panel, 24 x 17 1/4 ins / 61 x 44 cm) FRF 20,000. TORONTO, 30 Nov 1988, *Portrait of Félix Ziem* (oil on canvas, 15 1/4 x 12 1/2 ins / 39 x 32 cm) CAD 2,000. NEW YORK, 23 Feb 1989, *Gentleman, Louis XIII Period* (oil on panel, 32 x 26 1/2 ins / 81.2 x 67.3 cm) USD 5,500. LONDON, 7 June 1989, *Falconers* (oil on canvas, 28 1/4 x 22 1/2 ins / 72 x 57 cm) GBP 1,430. LONDON, 4 Oct 1989, *Gentleman Admiring a Gun* (oil on panel, 32 x 20 3/4 ins / 81 x 53 cm) GBP 3,300. NEW YORK, 28 Feb 1990, *Portrait of Madame Clémenceau in 16th-Century Costume* (oil on panel, 44 x 44 ins / 111.8 x 111.8 cm) USD 7,150. PARIS, 12 June 1990, *Portrait of a Gentleman* (oil on canvas, 38 1/2 x 30 ins / 98 x 76.5 cm) FRF 40,000. NEW YORK, 19 July 1990, *Horseman in a Black Hat* (oil on panel, 32 x 25 ins / 81.4 x 63.5 cm) USD 5,225. PARIS, 6 Dec 1990, *Portrait of a Man in a Red Cape* (oil on canvas) FRF 14,000. AMSTERDAM, 14-15 April 1992, *Portrait of an Officer* (oil on panel, 31 x 24 1/2 ins / 79 x 62.5 cm) NLG 12,075. NEW YORK, 18 Feb 1993, *Young Arab* (oil on panel, 17 x 13 1/2 ins / 43 x 34 cm) USD 9,900. PARIS, 25 June 1993, *Long-haired Woman in Yellow* (oil on panel, 18 1/2 x 14 3/4 ins / 47 x 37.5 cm) FRF 13,000. NEW YORK, 13 Oct 1993, *Standing Musketeer with Harehound* (oil on canvas, 59 x 33 1/2 ins / 149.9 x 85.1 cm) USD 13,800. EDINBURGH, 9 June 1994, *Self-portrait* (oil on panel, 26 1/2 x 22 ins / 67.3 x 55.8 cm) GBP 5,520. PARIS, 2 Dec 1994, *Portrait of a Gentleman with Hound* (oil on panel, 51 x 27 1/4 ins / 129.5 x 69 cm) FRF 45,000. LONDON, 14 June 1995, *Drinking Song* (oil on panel, 35 x 46 1/2 ins / 88 x 118 cm) GBP 13,800. PARIS, 1 Feb 1996, *Page Boys* (oil on panel, 22 x 18 ins / 55 x 45.5 cm) FRF 43,000. NEW YORK, 23-24 May 1996, *Page Boys* (oil on canvas, 22 x 17 3/4 ins / 55.9 x 45.1 cm) USD 25,300. PARIS, 28 June 1996, *Scientists* (1901, oil on panel, 60 1/4 x 38 1/4 ins / 153 x 97 cm) FRF 110,000. NEW YORK, 24 Oct 1996, *Blessing of the French Royal Court* (oil/panel, 35 x 46 ins / 88.6 x 115.9 cm) USD 29,900. LONDON, 22 Nov 1996, *Ensign* (oil on panel, 30 x 20 ins / 76.2 x 50.8 cm) GBP 2,300. LONDON, 21 March 1997, *Odalisque* (oil on canvas, 30 x 68 ins / 76.2 x 173 cm) GBP 28,750. NEW YORK, 23 Oct 1997, *Art Lover in a Studio* (oil on panel, 32 x 25 ins / 81 x 63.5 cm) USD 18,400. NEW YORK, 12 Feb 1998, *Saraband* (1895, oil on canvas, 99 1/4 x 78 3/4 ins / 252.1 x 200 cm) USD 112,500. PARIS, 9 March 1998, *Falconers* (oil on canvas, 18 1/4 x 24 ins / 46.5 x 61 cm) FRF 10,000. LONDON, 17 June 1999, *Odalisque* (oil on panel, 17 x 13 ins / 43 x 33 cm) GBP 28,000. NEW YORK, 29 Nov 1999, *Unexpected Guest* (1878, oil on panel, 31 x 25 ins / 80 x 64 cm) USD 18,000. NEW YORK, 1 May 2000, *Conoisseurs* (1883, oil on panel, 32 x 25 ins / 81 x 64 cm) USD 26,000. NEW YORK, 31 Oct 2000, *Portrait of a Boy in Finery* (oil on canvas, 40 x 29 ins / 101 x 74 cm) USD 11,000. PARIS, 12 June 2001, *Portrait of Carmen de Wendel* (oil on canvas, 50 x 37 ins / 128 x 94 cm) FRF 155,000. PARIS, 7 Dec 2001, *Portrait of Juana Romani* (oil on mahogany panel, 32 x 25 ins / 81 x 64 cm) FRF 63,000. PARIS, 25 March 2002, *Portrait of a Gentleman* (oil on panel, 25 x 32 ins / 64 x 81 cm) EUR 10,000. NEW YORK, 30 Oct 2002, *Recital* (oil on

panel, 19 x 18 ins / 48 x 46 cm) USD 12,000. NEW YORK, 28 Oct 2003, *Troubadours* (1887, oil on panel, 44 x 57 ins / 113 x 146 cm) USD 80,000. LONDON, 3 Dec 2003, *Odalisque* (oil on canvas, 28 x 67 ins / 72 x 170 cm) GBP 16,000. PARIS, 19 March 2004, *Musketeer with White Collar* (oil on panel, 24 x 17 ins / 60 x 44 cm) EUR 9,500. PARIS, 25 May 2004, *Portrait of Juana Romani* (1891, oil on panel, 51 x 27 ins / 130 x 69 cm) EUR 13,000.

ROYE, Barthélemi van
Flemish School, 17th century.
Active in Mechelen during the first half of the 17th century.
Sculptor.

Roye executed works for the church of Our Lady beyond the Dyle at Mechelen.

ROYE, Jozef van de
Belgian, 19th - 20th century.
Born c. 14 March 1861, in Antwerp; died 1941, in Kalmhout.
Painter, designer. Still-lifes, fruit.

Jozef van de Roye studied under L. Schaeffels at the fine arts academy in Antwerp.

MUSEUMS AND GALLERIES:
ANTWERP - MECHELEN - YPRES.

AUCTION RECORDS:
PARIS, 10 March 1955, *Still-life with Melons*, FRF 52,000. ANTWERP, 12 June 2001, *Peonies* (oil on canvas, 31 x 40 ins / 80 x 102 cm) BEF 110,000. LONDON, 28 Nov 2001, *Still-life with Oranges* (oil on panel, 10 x 17 ins / 26 x 43 cm) GBP 2,500.

ROYE, Willem Frederik van. See **ROYEN**

ROYEN. See also **ROOYEN**

ROYEN, A. J. van
Dutch, 19th century.
Active at the beginning of the 19th century.
Painter.

AJ van Royen acquired a certain reputation in her lifetime through her watercolours, which show real quality. On one of them (Gemeentemuseum in The Hague), one can read the signature *Mejonkvr. JA van Royen did this in 1818.*

MUSEUMS AND GALLERIES:
THE HAGUE (Gemeentemus.): *The Buitenhof* (1818, watercolour).

ROYEN, Anna Maria van
Dutch, 19th century.
Born 16 June 1800, in The Hague; died 19 March 1870, in Brussels.
Painter.

Anna Maria van Royen married Corneille Jacques van Assen, a lecturer at the University of Leiden, who died in 1859.

ROYEN, Peter
Dutch, 20th century.
Born 1923, in Amsterdam.
Active in Germany.
Painter (mixed media).
Gruppe 53.

Peter Royen studied at the college of fine arts in Düsseldorf. He lived and worked in Düsseldorf and exhibited both in Germany and abroad, including the *Düsseldorf Artists* exhibition held at the fine arts museum in Ostend in 1962. Royen's work mainly comporises fluid abstract compositions.

AUCTION RECORDS:
LUCERNE, 20 Nov 1993, *Fields* (1977, mixed media in relief/canvas, 16 1/2 x 19 1/4 ins / 42 x 49 cm) CHF 1,650.

ROYEN, Willem Frederik van, or Roye
German, 17th - 18th century.
Born c. 1645 or 1654, in Haarlem (?); died 1723, in Berlin.
Painter, draughtsman. Landscapes, still-lifes, flowers, animals.

Willem Frederik van Royen was a pupil of A. van Ravesteyn in 1661. He was painter to the court of Potsdam in 1689. He then settled in Berlin, where he became director of the Kunstakademie.

MUSEUMS AND GALLERIES:
BERLIN (Imperial Collection): *Bouquet of Flowers; Paintings of Flowers* - BRUNSWICK: *Game* - DARMSTADT: *Poultry and Dove; Poultry and Raptor* - HAMBURG: *Hunter with Dog and Game* - SCHWERIN: *Fruit.*

AUCTION RECORDS:
LONDON, 8 July 1910, *Birds, Parrot and Monkey in a Garden* (signed and dated 1706) GBP 94. NEW YORK, 20 Nov 1931, *Landscape with Birds*, USD 250. PARIS, 8 May 1940, *Flowers and Monkey*, FRF 600. LONDON, 28 Feb 1947, *Flowers in a Sculpted Vase*, GBP 199. PARIS, 7 Dec 1971, *Vase of Flowers*, FRF 11,000. LONDON, 8 Dec 1989, *Large Floral Composition in a Pewter Vase on a Marble Ledge* (1698, oil on canvas, 24 3/4 x 20in/63 x 50.5cm) GBP 60,500. LONDON, 5 July 1991, *Goose with Red Feet Hissilng by a Fountain with Other Geese and Ducks Splashing in the Water* (1701, oil on canvas, 49 x 41in/124.7 x 104cm) GBP 18,700. NEW YORK, 14 Jan 1993, *Floral Composition with Poppies, Tulips, Snowdrops, Roses and Other Flowers in a Sculpted Urn on a Marble Ledge* (oil on canvas, 25 x 20in/63.5 x 50.8cm) USD 66,000. AMSTERDAM, 15 Nov 1995, *Peacock in a Landscape* (ink and wash, 7 3/4 x 6 1/4in/19.5 x 16.4 cm) NLG 3,068. LONDON, 14 April 1999, *Flowers in an Urn on a Ledge* (1700, oil on panel, 9 x 7 ins / 23 x 18 cm) GBP 5,000. SAN FRANCISCO, 15 May 2002, *Cockerels, a Hen and a Crow in a Landscape* (oil on canvas, 41 x 34 ins / 104 x 86 cm) USD 32,500. STOCKHOLM, 29 May 2002, *Still-life with Peaches and Grapes* (oil on copper, 16 x 11 ins / 40 x 28 cm) SEK 135,000. NEW YORK, 23 Jan 2003, *Still-life with Grapes and Peaches on a Marble Ledge* (1714, oil on copper, 16 x 11 ins / 41 x 29 cm) USD 22,000.

ROYEN, Willem van
Dutch, 18th century.
Born 1672; died between 5 August 1738 and le 15 June 1742.
Painter. Animals, still-lifes.

Willem van Royen was active in Amsterdam from 1714. According to Houbraken, he had been the pupil of Melchior Hondecoeter.

AUCTION RECORDS:
NEW YORK, 4 Oct 1996, *A Pheasant, a French Partridge, a Crested Bird and a Dove in Parkland in the Middle of Classical Ruins* (oil on canvas, a fragment, 36 x 28 1/2 ins / 91.5 x 72.4 cm) USD 4,830. AMSTERDAM, 19 May 2004, *Two Silver Pheasants and a Black-crowned Night Heron in a Landscape* (1735, watercolour, gouache and black chalk, 12 x 17 ins / 30 x 44 cm) EUR 8,500.

ROYENBART, Regnier or Reynier.
See **ROYBAERT**

ROYER
French, 19th - 20th century.
Painter.

In his book on naive painting Anatole Jakovsky speaks highly of this painter, about whose life little is known.

BIBLIOGRAPHY:
Jakovsky, Anatole, *Naive painting*, Phaidon, Oxford, 1979.

ROYER, Alain
French, 20th - 21st century.
Born 1947, in Châtillon-sur-Seine.
Draughtsman, engraver.

Alain Royer lives and works in Paris. Examples of his work featured in *De Bonnard à Baselitz - Dix Ans d'enrichissements du cabinet des estampes 1978-1988* (*From Bonnard to Baselitz: A Decade of Acquisitions by the Prints Collection 1978-1988*), an exhibition held in 1993 at the Bibliothèque Nationale in Paris.

MUSEUMS AND GALLERIES:
PARIS (BNF): *False Window* (1984, chisel-point (burin)).

ROYER, Charles
French, 19th century.
Born in Langres.
Painter.

Charles Royer was the student of Dujardin. He settled in his native town and exhibited at the Paris Salon from 1880. He is also reported to have exhibited in Angers in 1886.

MUSEUMS AND GALLERIES:
CHÂLONS-EN-CHAMPAGNE: *Study of a Woman* - LANGRES: *Hare, Still-life; Chrysanthemums* - TOUL: *Early; Triumph of Silenus.*

AUCTION RECORDS:
PARIS, 12 June 1926, *Young Woman Reading,* FRF 300. NICE, 14 Nov 1984, *Fine Supper with the Cardinal* (oil on canvas, 23½ x 35 ins / 60 x 88 cm) FRF 10,800. PARIS, 12 June 2002, *End of a Meal at the Prelates' House* (1903, oil on canvas, 23 x 35 ins / 59 x 89 cm) EUR 3,200.

ROYER, Dieudonné Auguste
French, 19th - 20th century.
Born 31 January 1835, in Troyes; died 22 January 1920, in Troyes.
Painter. Landscapes.

Dieudonné Auguste Royer was a pupil of Dieudonné A. Lancelot. He taught at the École Municipale de Dessin in Troyes, where he was the director. He also taught art at the École Normale des Institutrices. He exhibited at the Paris Salon from 1868 to 1872.

MUSEUMS AND GALLERIES:
TROYES: *The Marsh of Villechétif; Bunch of Chrysanthemums; Avenue du Château des Cours, Saint Julien, near Troyes.*

ROYER, Henri Paul
French, 19th - 20th century.
Born 22 January 1869, in Nancy; died 1938.
Painter, draughtsman, illustrator. Portraits.

Henri Paul Royer was a pupil at the École des Beaux-Arts, Paris, and then attended the classes of Jules Lefebvre, Louis Devilly and François Flemeng at the Académie Julian. He travelled widely in Europe, including Greece and Sicily, and in North and South America. From 1890, he exhibited at the Salon des Artistes Français, of which he was awarded the Hors concours. He won the Prix National in 1898 and a gold medal at the Exposition Universelle of 1900, and was made a Chevalier of the Légion d'Honneur in 1900 and an Officier in 1931.

Henri Royer.

MUSEUMS AND GALLERIES:
BREST: *Young Breton Woman* - LANGRES: *Portrait of M. Jean du Breuil of St-Germain* - NANCY: *Communicants* (1897); *Breton Women Seeing off the Fishing Fleet* - PARIS (former Mus. du Luxembourg): *Saying Grace; Portrait of Léon Bonnat* - QUIMPER: *Ex Voto* - RIO DE JANEIRO: *On the Hill.*

AUCTION RECORDS:
PARIS, 2 June 1943, *View of Monte Carlo* (1890) FRF 1,000. PARIS, 28 May 1945, *Old Man Eating his Soup,* FRF 8,100. PARIS, 22 Dec 1950, *Breton Women,* FRF 14,500. PARIS, 23 June 1954, *Lunch,* FRF 26,000. LONDON, 9 April 1976, *Woman Dressing* (1893, oil on canvas, 16¼ x 12½ ins / 41 x 32 cm) GBP 280. PARIS, 20 April 1979, *Legendary Clearing* (1936, oil on canvas, 18 x 22 ins / 46 x 55 cm) FRF 4,800. LYONS, 18 Dec 1983, *Young Breton Woman* (pastel, 21¼ x 16½ ins / 54 x 42 cm) FRF 8,000. LONDON, 24 June 1987, *Young Model* (oil on panel, 16¼ x 23¼ ins / 41 x 59 cm) GBP 5,800. PARIS, 5 Nov 1991, *Young Woman with Vase* (1897, oil on canvas, 18 x 13 ins / 46 x 33 cm) FRF 30,000. PARIS, 8 March 1993, *The Pardon Festival* (lead pencil, 15¾ x 12¾ ins / 40 x 32.5 cm) FRF 4,100. RENNES, 7 Oct 2003, *Model* (1890, oil on canvas, 32 x 21 ins / 81 x 54 cm) EUR 5,000. PARIS, 26 Jan 2004, *Old Fishermen, Brittany* (oil on canvas, 32 x 26 ins / 81 x 65 cm) EUR 3,000.

ROYER, Jacob S.
American, 20th century.
Born 9 November 1883, in Waynesboro (Pennsylvania).
Painter, engraver.

Jacob S. Royer studied under Robert Olivier and was a member of the American Artists Professional League.

ROYER, Jan
Dutch, 18th century.
Landscape artist.

ROYER, Jean Matthias
German, 18th century.
Born 1755.
Active in Berlin.
Painter, engraver (burin).

Royer studied at the Académie Royale in Paris from 1775 to 1778.

ROYER, Jean-Claude
French, 20th century.
Born 4 November 1923, in Rheims.
Painter.

After taking part in the Salon des Moins de Trente Ans in Paris, Jean-Claude Royer exhibited at the Salon d'Automne and the Salon des Indépendants, of which he was a member.

ROYER, Lionel Noël
French, 19th - 20th century.
Born 25 December 1852, in Château-du-Loir; died 31 June 1926, in Neuilly-sur-Seine.
Painter. Religious subjects, mythological subjects, portraits. Murals.

Lionel Noël Royer was a pupil of Cabanel and Bouguereau. He painted murals for churches, and in Le Mans a *Christ on the Cross* for the cathedral and *Germanicus Paying Last Honours to Varus* for the Town Hall. He exhibited at the Salon of 1874, where he won a second-class medal in 1896, and at the Salon des Artistes Français, of which he was awarded the Hors concours. In 2001, he was represented in the exhibition *Peintres et la Sarthe* (*Painters and the Sarthe Region*), held in Le Mans at the Musée de la Reine Bérangère (19th century) and the Abbaye de l'Épau (20th century).

BIBLIOGRAPHY:
Arpentinier, Jean, *Sarthe, terre d'artistes*, Éd. de la Reinette, Le Mans, 2001.

MUSEUMS AND GALLERIES:
CHARTRES: *Mary Magdalene with the Body of the Dead Christ* - GRAY: *The Hostess's Daughter* - LE MANS: *Portrait of Théodore David; Dian Taken by Surprise; The Choir of Le Mans Cathedral; Daphne Changed into a Laurel Tree; Venus Guarding the Body of Hector; Battle of Auvours, 10 January 1871; Germanicus Discovers the Remains of Varus's Legions* - LE PUY-EN-VELAY: *Vercingetorix Laying his Arms at Caesar's Feet.*
AUCTION RECORDS:
PARIS, 1895, *Death of Manon Lescaut,* FRF 95. NEW YORK, 21-22 Jan 1909, *Arrival at the Élysée Palace,* USD 125. PARIS, 6 March 1950, *Young Girl,* FRF 1,500. PARIS, 27 Dec 1950, *Cliffs,* FRF 1,150. ENGHIEN-LES-BAINS, 25 April 1976, *Judgement of Paris* (oil on canvas, 22 1/2 x 17 ins / 57 x 43 cm) FRF 2,000. PARIS, 10 Feb 1988, *Portrait of Henriette* (oil on panel, 18 x 13 3/4 ins / 46 x 35 cm) FRF 3,200. CALAIS, 14 March 1993, *Woman Selling Flowers in the Place de l'Hôtel de Ville, Paris* (1908, oil on panel, 20 1/2 x 25 1/2 ins / 52 x 65 cm) FRF 28,000. NEW YORK, 15 Oct 1993, *Mandolin Recital* (1901, pastel/paper, 30 1/2 x 28 1/2 ins / 77.5 x 72.4 cm) USD 1,725. NEW YORK, 22 Oct 1997, *Portrait of Robert* (1882, oil on canvas, 51 1/2 x 27 1/2 ins / 130.5 x 69.8 cm) USD 16,100. NEW YORK, 18 March 1998, *Portrait of François Jean-Baptiste Emmanuel Gustave, Count of Adhémar de Gransac* (1890, oil on canvas, 79 x 38 ins / 200.7 x 96.5 cm) USD 9,200.

ROYER, Louis or Lodenvyck
Dutch, 19th century.
Born 19 June 1793, in Mechelen; died 5 July 1868, in Amsterdam.
Sculptor. Mythological subjects, portraits. Statuettes.
Louis Royer was the pupil of Jan Frans van Geel and of Jean Baptiste de Bay in Paris. He stayed for a time in both Paris and Rome. He was appointed Sculptor to the Court at The Hague in 1835, and subsequently Director of the academy in Amsterdam.
MUSEUMS AND GALLERIES:
AMSTERDAM (Mus. Amstelkring): *Bust of Pope Leo XII* - BRUSSELS: *Bust of Philippe van Brèe* - BRUSSELS (Mus. royaux des Beaux-Arts de Belgique): *Flora* (terracotta, statuette) - LONDON (Victoria and Albert Mus.): *Apollo* (1818) - MECHELEN: *Bust of the Prince of Orange; Statue of Mercury with Bacchus as a Child.*

ROYER, Marie François
French, 18th century.
Active during the second half of the 18th century.
Painter.
Marie François Royer was the son of Pierre Alexandre Royer I.

ROYER, Pierre Alexandre I
French, 18th century.
Born c. 1705; died 1787; buried 28 December in Paris.
Painter.
Pierre Alexandre Royer I was the father of Marie François Royer and Pierre Alexandre Royer II. He was painter to the queen.

ROYER, Pierre Alexandre II
French, 18th century.
Active during the second half of the 18th century.
Painter.
Pierre Alexandre Royer II worked in London and Paris, where he exhibited English landscapes and architectural scenes from 1779 to 1796.

ROYER, Pierre I
French, 17th century.
Active in Nantes c. 1635.
Painter, glass painter.

ROYER, Pierre II
French, 18th century.
Born in France.
Active in London and in Paris.
Painter. Landscapes, architectural views.
Little is known about the early career of Pierre Royer II. It seems that he began work in England, and he was established in London from 1774 to 1778. He exhibited landscapes at the Society of Artists and at the Royal Academy. He exhibited views of England at the Salon de la Correspondance in 1779, 1780 and 1786. Although he may not have lived permanently in Paris, he must have visited the city, since Charpentier painted his portrait in 1783. Royer assumed the false title of 'member of the Royal Academy in London'. In 1791 he was settled in Paris, living in the Rue des Quatre-Vents. In the same year he exhibited at the Salon, and subsequently in 1793, 1795 and 1796.

ROYER, Sébastien
French, 17th century.
Active in Nantes 1670-1692.
Painter, glass painter.

ROYER-FORGE, Germaine
French, 20th century.
Born 18 November 1897, in Nancy.
Painter.
Germaine Royer-Forge, a pupil of Henri Royer and Marcel Baschet, exhibited from 1922 in Paris at the Salon des Artistes Français, of which she was a member.

ROYET, H.
French, 19th - 20th century.
Painter. Seascapes, landscapes, interiors.
AUCTION RECORDS:
LA VARENNE-ST-HILAIRE, 23 Oct 1988, *Steamer on the Seine, Paris at Sunset* (oil on canvas, 20 3/4 x 31 1/4 ins / 53 x 79.5 cm) FRF 17,000. LA VARENNE-ST-HILAIRE, 21 May 1989, *Steamer on the Seine* (oil on canvas, 20 3/4 x 31 1/2 ins / 53 x 80 cm) FRF 23,000. LOKEREN, 10 Oct 1992, *Interior* (oil on canvas, 63 3/4 x 45 ins / 162 x 114 cm) BEF 170,000. PARIS, 28 Oct 1996, *Paris Street Scene at Night* (oil on canvas, 14 1/2 x 21 1/4 ins / 37 x 54 cm) FRF 14,500.

ROYLE, Herbert
British, 19th - 20th century.
Died 19 October 1958.
Painter. Landscapes.
School of Liverpool.
Herbert Royle was active from 1892. He belonged to the School of Liverpool and took part in the exhibitions in this city. He participated in the exhibitions at the Royal Scottish Academy from 1900 and at the Royal Academy, London, from 1911.
MUSEUMS AND GALLERIES:
LIVERPOOL: *Harvesting the Hay in the Valley.*
AUCTION RECORDS:
LONDON, 23 April 1974, *Winter Landscape,* GBP 400. LONDON, 19 June 1979, *Landscape at Dusk* (oil on canvas, 24 1/2 x 29 1/2 ins / 62 x 75 cm) GBP 500. LONDON, 24 July 1985, *Hay Cart* (oil on canvas, 20 x 24 ins / 51 x 61 cm) GBP 2,300. PERTH, 27 Aug 1990, *Kyle of Lochalsh* (oil on canvas, 25 1/4 x 30 ins / 64 x 76 cm) GBP 6,600. LONDON, 27 Sept 1991, *Richmond Castle* (oil on canvas, 30 x 40 1/4 ins / 76 x 102 cm) GBP 3,080. LONDON, 3 March 1993, *Haymaking near Ilkley* (oil on canvas, 20 x 24 ins / 51 x 61 cm) GBP 1,725. ST ASAPH, 2 June 1994, *Kyle of Lochalsh* (oil on canvas, 14 1/4 x 18 ins / 36 x 46 cm) GBP 2,070. ILKLEY, 28 April 1999, *Boy Herding Cattle at High Austby Cottage, Ilkley* (oil on canvas, 19 x 23 ins / 48 x 58 cm) GBP 7,000. ILKLEY, 28 April 1999, *Bolton Abbey - Summer's Evening with Figures* (oil on canvas, 24 x 29 ins / 61 x 74 cm) GBP 8,500. AUCKLAND, 19 Sept 2000, *English Country*

Estate and Cattle at a Watering Hole (oil on canvas, a pair, 16 x 24 ins / 40 x 60 cm) NZD 24,000. LEEDS, 14 Nov 2000, *Wharfedale Farmstead* (oil on canvas, 12 x 16 ins / 30 x 40 cm) GBP 6,200. ILKLEY, 15 Aug 2001, *Autumn on the Wharfe, Bolton Abbey* (oil on canvas, 15 x 23 ins / 38 x 58 cm) GBP 9,400. ILKLEY, 5 Dec 2001, *Haytime* (oil on canvas, 19 x 23 ins / 48 x 58 cm) GBP 9,000. ILKLEY, 13 Feb 2002, *Snowscene, Ullswater* (oil on canvas, 35 x 49 ins / 89 x 124 cm) GBP 13,500. LEEDS, 23 July 2002, *Harvest Time* (oil on canvas, 28 x 36 ins / 71 x 91 cm) GBP 15,000. LEEDS, 4 Feb 2003, *Snow Scene Above Nessfield, Ilkley* (oil on canvas, 20 x 24 ins / 51 x 61 cm) GBP 11,200. LEEDS, 18 Nov 2003, *Entrance to Canada Docks* (oil on canvas, 27 x 41 ins / 68 x 103 cm) GBP 24,000. LEEDS, 15 June 2004, *Bluebell Wood, Near Bolton Abbey* (oil on canvas, 23 x 19 ins / 58 x 47 cm) GBP 11,000. ILKLEY, 16 June 2004, *Tree Felling at Denton Hall Woods* (oil on canvas, 27 x 35 ins / 69 x 89 cm) GBP 8,500.

ROYLE, Stanley
British, 20th century.
Born 1888; died 1961.
Painter. Landscapes.

Stanley Royle participated in the exhibitions at the Royal Academy, London from 1913 to 1950, and at the Royal Scottish Academy from 1918 to 1928.

AUCTION RECORDS:
LONDON, 18 Nov 1980, *Bridge Beneath the Ruins* (oil on canvas, 48 x 59 3/4 ins / 122 x 152 cm) GBP 550. LONDON, 25 May 1983, *Lilac Bonnet* (1921, oil on canvas, 28 x 36 ins / 71 x 91.5 cm) GBP 2,600. LONDON, 7 Nov 1985, *Homeward Journey* (1917, watercolour, gouache and pastel, 14 x 21 ins / 35.5 x 53.5 cm) GBP 1,200. LONDON, 12 Nov 1986, *Winter Morning* (1925, oil on canvas, 28 3/4 x 36 1/2 ins / 73 x 93 cm) GBP 7,500. LONDON, 3-4 March 1988, *Young Girl in a Village Street* (1870, oil on canvas, 17 3/4 x 21 ins / 45 x 52.5 cm) GBP 1,870. LONDON, 7 June 1990, *Young Girl Picking Roses* (1910, oil on canvas, 32 x 24 1/2 ins / 81 x 62 cm) GBP 3,300. LONDON, 5 March 1999, *The Mill Barn* (oil on canvas, 25 x 30 ins / 63 x 76 cm) GBP 11,000. PARTRIDGE GREEN, 5 Nov 1999, *Winter Landscape with Shepherd Feeding his Flock* (1926, oil on canvas, 16 x 20 ins / 40 x 50 cm) GBP 4,100. DUBLIN, 6 March 2001, *Driving Home the Sheep* (oil on canvas, 25 x 30 ins / 63 x 76 cm) IEP 7,200. LEWES, 6 Dec 2001, *Farm on the Hill* (oil on board, 11 x 15 ins / 28 x 38 cm) GBP 2,600. LONDON, 14 March 2002, *Fording Along the River* (oil on canvas, 25 x 30 ins / 63 x 76 cm) GBP 9,000. LONDON, 1 May 2002, *Ploughing* (1913, watercolour and gouache, 14 x 20 ins / 36 x 51 cm) GBP 2,900. LEEDS, 25 March 2003, *Feeding the Geese* (oil on canvas, 20 x 24 ins / 51 x 61 cm) GBP 5,000. LONDON, 4 Sept 2003, *Down by the Stream* (1917, oil on canvas, 19 x 24 ins / 48 x 61 cm) GBP 5,600. LEEDS, 16 March 2004, *River Landscape with Buildings in Winter* (1928, oil on board, 11 x 15 ins / 29 x 39 cm) GBP 5,600. LEEDS, 16 March 2004, *Village Scene in the Snow* (1927, oil on board, 11 x 15 ins / 29 x 39 cm) GBP 8,000.

ROYMERSWAELE, Marinus Van.
See **MARINUS VAN ROEJMERSWAELEN**

ROYNARD, Vincent
French, 17th century.
Painter.

Roynard worked for Anne of Austria from 1642 to 1656.

ROYNISHVILI, A.
Russian, 19th century.
Painter.

MUSEUMS AND GALLERIES:
TBILISI (Mus. hist. et ethn.): *Portrait of Sciota Russthalevi.*

ROYON, Louis
Belgian, 20th century.
Born 1 July 1882, in Ostend; died 10 September 1968, in Waulsort.
Painter, draughtsman, illustrator. Seascapes.

Louis Royon embarked on a naval career, starting out as a 15-year-old cabin boy and serving as a lieutenant at 17. He was a self-taught painter who, from an early age, painted ships and seascapes. He also produced poster designs as well as painting naval. His work, which is distinguished by its meticulous attention to detail, was shown at the annual Salon de la Société Belge des Peintres de Mer from its inception in 1934 until 1940.

AUCTION RECORDS:
BRUSSELS, 27 March 1990, *Seascape* (oil on panel, 15 3/4 x 23 1/2 ins / 40 x 60 cm) BEF 65,000.

ROZ, André
French, 20th century.
Born 18 June 1897, in Paris.
Painter. Landscapes.

André Roz, a pupil of J. Adler, J. Bergès and Legrand, exhibited in Paris from 1927 at the Salon des Artistes Français, of which he was awarded the Hors concours, and at the Salon d'Automne, of which he was also a member. He was awarded a silver medal in 1930, a gold in 1932, and the Légion d'Honneur in 1933. A painter from the Franche-Comté, he founded in 1923 the Salon des Annunciades, Pontarlier.

AUCTION RECORDS:
LYONS, 7 Feb 1945, *Landscape,* FRF 16,000. PARIS, 28 Feb 1949, *Skating Rink,* FRF 5,200. BERN, 12 May 1990, *Alpine Lake* (oil on panel, 13 x 18 ins / 33 x 46 cm) CHF 1,400. BESANÇON, 3 June 1990, *The Square in Ornans* (oil on canvas, 23 1/2 x 29 1/4 ins / 60 x 74 cm) FRF 70,000. PARIS, 21 June 1995, *An Open-air Fair in the Jura* (oil on canvas, 15 x 22 ins / 38 x 55 cm) FRF 26,000. PARIS, 3 Dec 1999, *Figure on Mountain Road* (oil on canvas, 20 x 24 ins / 50 x 61 cm) FRF 32,000. SION, 8 June 2001, *Church at Dompierre-les-Tilleuls* (oil on board, 15 x 18 ins / 38 x 45 cm) CHF 3,600. PARIS, 2 March 2003, *Village Festival* (oil on hardboard, 18 x 26 ins / 46 x 65 cm) EUR 5,200.

RÖZ, Stephan. See **REZ**

ROZADILLA, Juan de, or Roçadilla
Spanish, 16th century.
Sculptor.

In 1599, Juan de Rozadilla sculpted capitals for Nuestra Señora de las Angustias in Valladolid.

ROZAIRE, Arthur D.
Canadian, 20th century.
Born 1879, in Montreal; died 26 February 1922, in Los Angeles.
Active in the USA.
Painter. Landscapes.

Arthur D. Rozaire studied under William Brymner and Maurice Galbraith Cullen.

ROZANÈS, Monique
French, 20th century.
Born 9 August 1936, in Bordeaux.
Painter, sculptor.

Monique Rozanès studied at the École Nationale Supérieur des Arts Décoratifs, Paris, in 1955 and then spent a period in the laboratories of the St-Gobain company, where she acquainted herself with synthetic materials. She visited Morocco, Switzerland and the USA. Her sculptures *Stratyls* and *Sphérostratyls* are assemblies of geometrical shapes encased and embedded in opaque, transparent or translucent materials. She has exhibited in France, Spain, Belgium, Italy and the former Yugoslavia. Her many solo shows include: 1959, the Faculty of Letters, Aix-en-Provence; 1972, Museum of Le Mans; 1973, Chartres Museum; 1973, Galerie Liliane François, Paris; 1978, Museum of Chaux-de Fonds; 1987, Galerie Praxis, Buenos Aires; 1989, Galerie Van Eyck, Buenos Aires; 1990, with Torres-Agüero, Centre de l'Art Contemporain, Lycée du Forez, Feurs; and others in Switzerland, Italy and Belgium.

BIBLIOGRAPHY:

Galli, Aldo/orres Agüero, Léopoldo /Sottile, Silvina/Roussel, Dominique, *Monique Rozanès*, Fragments, Paris, 2001.

ROZANOVA, Ol'ga Vladimirovna

Russian, 20th century.

Born 21 June 1886, in Malenki; died 8 November 1918, in Moscow.

Painter, collage artist, draughtswoman, engraver, poet. Futurism, Suprematism.

Groups: Soiuz Molodezhi (Union of Youth), Supremus.

Rozanova studied at the Stroganov school of art and industry in Moscow. She was one of the most active members of the St Petersburg avant-garde. In 1911, she belonged to the Soiuz Molodezhi (Union of Youth) group, and to the Supremus group in 1916. She participated actively in the Revolution in 1917, devoting herself to the artistic life of her lover, the poet and sculptor Aleksei Kuchenykh. She was a poet herself, and also wrote theoretical texts on art. She was influenced by Cubism and by Malevich's Suprematism. She had an individual studio in the Vkhutemas, the higher artistic and technical studios, which replaced the art college in Moscow in 1918.

Early on, Rozanova executed still-lifes and figures in an Expressionist style. From 1912, she illustrated for Futurist reviews, and wrote an article demonstrating the link between Futurist experimentation and the Abstraction of Kandinsky. Collage was a primordial preoccupation in her non-objective experimental works, dating from 1915. The result was a series of woodcuts and collages for the album *Vojna* (*War*). She then drew closer to Suprematism, creating dynamic, original coloured works that were decorative and accentuated flatness. After the Revolution, she created everyday objects.

Rozanova participated in exhibitions of the Soiuz Molodezhi group, in addition to: 1905, Tramway V in Moscow; 1914, International exhibition of free Futurists in Rome; 1915-1916, 0-10 in Moscow; and the exhibitions of the Bubnovy Valet (Jack of Diamonds) group in Moscow. Her work was also included in the following exhibitions: 1977, *Aspects Historiques du Constructivisme et de l'Art Concret* (*Historical Aspects of Constructivism and Concrete Art*), at the Musée d'Art moderne de la Ville de Paris; 2003, exhibition presenting three books created by three Russian artists in the 1910s: *Guerre(s); Natalya Goncharova, Olga Rozanova et Alexsej Kuchenykh: Trois Suites Insignes sur un Thème, 1914-1916* (*War(s); Natalija Gontcharova, Olga Rozanova and Aleksej Kuchenykh: three notable suites on a theme, 1914-1916*), Cabinet des Estampes, Geneva; and 2003, an exhibition around Rozanova's work, associated with that of Aleksei Kuchenykh, entitled *Russie 1913-1922. Un couple dans l'Avant-garde: Ol'ga Rozanova et Aleksej Kruchenykh* (*Russia 1913-1922. A Couple in the Avant-garde: Olga Rozanova and Aleksei Kuchenykh*), at the Cabinet d'Estampes, Geneva.

BIBLIOGRAPHY:

Paris-Moscou, 1900-1930, exhibition catalogue, Éd. du Centre Georges-Pompidou, Paris, 1979. Mason, Rainer Michael, *Guerre (s); Nalalija Gontacharova, Olga Rozanova et Aleksej Kruchenykh: trois suites insignes sur un thème, 1914-1916*, exhibition catalogue, Cabinet des estampes, Genève, Adam Biro, Paris, 2003.

MUSEUMS AND GALLERIES:

GENEVA (Musée d'Art et d'Histoire, Prints Coll.): Rozanova-Kruchenykh donation - SMOLENSK: *Still-life* - ST PETERSBURG (Gosudarstvennyj Russkij Muz.): *Non-Objective Composition (Suprematism)* (c. 1916); *Abstract Composition* (c. 1918, oil on canvas).

AUCTION RECORDS:

MUNICH, 27 Nov 1981, *Composition* (1915, linograph, 14 1/4 x 11 ins / 36 x 27 cm) DEM 3,300. LONDON, 25 June 1985, *Composition with Fish* (1915-1916, collage/paper, 8 1/4 x 11 1/2 ins / 21 x 29.2 cm) GBP 3,000. BERN, 19 June 1987, *He Remembers with Terror* (1916, woodcut, 15 x 10 1/4 ins / 37.2 x 26.2 cm) CHF 3,400. LONDON, 23 May 1990, *Composition* (collage, 17 1/2 x 10 ins / 44.4 x 25.4 cm) GBP 9,900. MADRID, 15 Dec 1999, *Winter Walk* (oil on board, 15 x 20 ins / 37 x 52 cm) ESP 1,750,000. STOCKHOLM, 4 Nov 2003, *Mars' Fight with Scorpion - from The Universal War* (collage on paper, 8 x 12 ins / 21 x 30 cm) SEK 54,000. LONDON, 1 July 2004, *War, Voina* (nine woodcuts, one collage, five pages of text) GBP 30,000.

ROZAS, Alonso de

Spanish, 17th century.

Sculptor.

Alonso de Rozas executed sculptures for the high altar of S Pelayo in Oviedo in 1678.

ROZAS, José de

Spanish, 18th century.

Sculptor.

José de Rozas executed sculptures for the high altar of the church of Jesus of Nazareth in Valladolid in 1702.

ROZAT, Fanny. See **ROZET Fanny**

ROZBICKA-GIZYCKA, Mieczyslawa

Polish, 20th century.

Born 27 November 1891, in Radom; died 4 December 1925, in Warsaw.

Painter.

Rozbicka-Gizycka was a pupil of E. Trojanowski.

ROZDARZS, Fricis

Latvian, 20th century.

Born 8 November 1879, in Riga.

Painter. Genre scenes.

Roždarzs was a painter at the theatre in Riga, and executed paintings for churches in Germany and Lithuania.

MUSEUMS AND GALLERIES:

RIGA (MM) - RIGA (Valsts Makslas Muzejs/National Gallery of Art).

ROZE. See also **LIEMAKERE Nicolaas de**

ROZE, Albert Dominique

French, 19th - 20th century.

Born 4 August 1861, in Amiens.

Sculptor.

Albert Dominique Roze, the son of a mechanical engineer, though of humble origin, came from an old and honourable Amiens family. He was 12 when he entered the École de Dessin, Amiens. After studying sculpture he was awarded a municipal scholarship in 1979 at the age of 18 and went to Paris, where he worked with enthusiasm and success, first in Dumont's studio and then with Bonnassieux. Having failed to win the Prix de Rome, he set off for Rome at his own expense in 1891. He returned from Italy two years later at the age of 32. The mayor of Amiens asked him to become director of the city's École des Beaux-Arts, a post that he filled very actively and with great foresight for 30 years. He was also director of the Picardy Museum for 26 years. During World War II, when he was nearly 80, he defended his city's museum with great spirit. He decided to live in the building night and day and only left the burning town one night in 1940, after sending away in two lorries the masterpieces he had done so much to preserve.

During his long and fruitful career he received many awards: 1891, honourable mention (at the age of 30), 1897, a third-class medal, 1908, a third-class medal, and 1914 a gold medal. He was made a member of the Légion d'Honneur in 1920 and was a member of the Institut de France. His many talented and spiritual works are an adornment of French art; in particular the *Virgin of the Albert Basilica*, which is known throughout the world. This statue was left hanging in space after the building was bombarded at the start of World War I, but Roze subsequently remade it. Also among his works are: *The Holy Women at the Tomb, The Prayer of the Lowly*, the frontage of the Amiens Savings Bank, *The Nest* (1902), *Pietà*, busts of *Franz Liszt* and *Lamarck*, monuments to *Alphonse Figuet, Frédéric Petit, Jules Verne* and *Parmentier*, monuments to the dead of Corvie and Amiens, *The Resistance* (1940-1945), and *The Firstborn*.

ROZE, Janis Stanislavs or Johann Stanislas, or Rosée or Rohsit
Estonian, 19th century.
Born 3 April 1823, in Estonia; died 30 November 1897, in Riga.
Painter. Portraits.

Stanislas Roze studied at the art academy in St Petersburg. He travelled widely throughout Europe, and produced portraits of members of the Russian Imperial family.

MUSEUMS AND GALLERIES:
RIGA (Valsts makslas muz.): *Portrait of Miss Cimze*.

ROZE, Jean
French, 16th century.
Active in Bourges from 1567 to 1585.
Sculptor, architect.

ROZE, Jean Baptiste de
French, 18th century.
Sculptor, painter.

ROZE, Léonard. See **ROSE**

ROZE, Pascal de La. See **LA ROSE**

ROZEK, Celesztin
Hungarian, 19th century.
Born 19 May 1859, in Szólád.
Active in Budapest.
Painter. Figures, landscapes.

ROZEK, Marcin
Polish, 20th century.
Born 8 November 1885, in Kosieczyn, near Zbaszyn.
Sculptor.

Rozek studied in Posen (now Poznan), with P. Gimzicki in Berlin, at the Kunstakademie in Munich and at the Académie des Beaux-Arts in Paris. He sculpted saints and historic statues.

MUSEUMS AND GALLERIES:
KATOWICE: *Madonna with Child* (wood) - POZNAN: *Bust of Kosciuszko* - WARSAW (Muz. Narodowe): *Madonna with Child*.

ROZELIUS, Johan von. See **ROSENHEIM**

ROZEN, Félix, real name: Rosenman
Russian, 20th century.
Born 12 January 1938, in Moscow, to Polish-Jewish parents.
Active since 1966 and naturalised since 1974 in France.
Painter, sculptor, engraver, performance artist. Landscapes.

Rozen first studied electronic engineering and then studied painting and interior architecture from 1959 to 1965, receiving a Master's degree from the academy of fine arts in Warsaw. He visited France regularly, beginning in 1961, and met Zadkine and Chagall. He moved to Montparnasse in Paris in 1966 and lived at the home of Pougny's widow. In 1979-1980, he went to New York. He taught at the school of fine arts in Besançon, the faculty in Vincennes, and the department of fine arts at the Sorbonne.

Rozen began in Warsaw with still-lifes, nudes and landscapes, which he sometimes signed *Rosenman*. Once he had settled in Paris, he collaborated with Xenakis in 1967. He was in charge of exhibitions at the Centre de Royaumont, of architectural projects, and of the Festival de Collias, and executed posters, all the while continuing to paint and sculpt. Though he began with an Expressionist tendency, he turned towards the Informal (in painting more so than in sculpture). He drew his inspiration from the archaic artists up to Giacometti. He has also created performances that are close to Land Art, participated in concerts and musical explorations, and published books and photographic albums. He invented 'pyrocera' engraving, using fire and wax.

Since 1967, Rozen has participated in collective exhibitions in Paris: Salon de la Jeune Sculpture, Salon de Mai, Salon des Grands et Jeunes d'Aujourd'hui since 1976, Salon Comparaisons, Salon des Réalités Nouvelles; as well as: Biennale of graphic art in Brno, 1974, 1976; Musée des Beaux-Arts in Mons, Musée d'Art Contemporain in Dunkirk, Musée des Beaux-Arts in Amiens, 1978; Exhibition of Contemporary Art in Stockholm and International contemporary art fair in Bari, 1981; Municipal library in Genoa and the Biennale of contemporary art in Ibiza, 1982; Kunstmuseum in Silkeborg, 1984, 1989; National museum in Jerusalem and Musée Cantini in Marseilles, 1987; Salon de Montrouge, 1989; and Musée de Boulogne-Billancourt, 1990. He has also had solo exhibitions, including the following: regularly in Paris, notably at the Centre Culturel Suédois in 1981; Auvers-sur-Oise, 1968, 1974; Amsterdam, 1971; Contemporary Art Center, Sorrento, 1977; performance in the snow, Kunstmuseum, Silkeborg, 1980; Maison des Arts et de la Culture, Grenoble, 1981; Living Art Museum, Reykjavik, 1983; and Kunstmuseum, Silkeborg, 1987, 1989.

BIBLIOGRAPHY:
Lévêque, Jean-Jacques, *Rozen*, Pierre-Jean Balbot, Paris, 1975. Lacarrière, Jacques, *Rozen. Œuvres récentes*, exhibition catalogue, Gal. Orsini, Toulouse, 1977. Andersen, Troels, *Rozen Black Tracks*, exhibition catalogue, Kunstmuseum, Silkeborg, 1981 (text in English). Hovdenakk, Per, *Rozen Rosen*, exhibition catalogue, Living Art Museum, Reykjavik, 1983 (text in English and Icelandic). Pleynet, Marcelin/Ragon, Michel, *'L'Art abstrait'* in vol. V, Maeght, Paris, 1989. *Rozen Rosen*, exhibition leaflet, Gal. Artemporel, Montpellier, 1990. Sourd, Gérard, *'Félix Rozen: la mémoire et le signe'* in *Les Nouvelles de l'Estampe*, periodical, Bibliothèque nationale de France, Paris, March 1995.

MUSEUMS AND GALLERIES:
AMSTERDAM (Stedelijk Mus.) - ARLES (Mus. Réattu): *Voyage to Japan* (1975) - BRUSSELS (Bibliothèque royale Albert Ier, Prints Collection) - DUNKIRK (MAC): *Maximal Art* (1977-1978) - GENEVA (MAH) - HØVIKODDEN (Henie Onstad Kunstsenter) - LA JOLLA (MCA of San Diego): *Polypartitas* (1980, lithograph) - LONDON (Tate Collection): *Uncertain Opus* (1981, series of screenprints/paper) - NEW YORK (Brooklyn Mus.) - NEW YORK (Metropolitan Mus. of Art) - NEW YORK (MoMA) - NEW YORK (Solomon R. Guggenheim Mus.) - PARIS (BNF): engravings - PARIS (FNAC): *Mother Spoon* (1971-1976) - PARIS (MNAM-CCI) - PISA (Mus. Nazionale di S Matteo) - SILKEBORG (Kunstmus.): *Closed World* (1978) - TOKYO (MMA) - WASHINGTON DC (NGA): *Three Black Bands (Trois Bandes Noires)* (1979, colour lithograph).

AUCTION RECORDS:
PARIS, 26 March 1995, *'Mysteries' Series* (1993, pigment on embossed paper, 39 1/4 x 39 1/4 ins / 100 x 100 cm) FRF 15,000.

ROZENBURG, C. M. Rutgers von.
See **RUTGERS VON ROZENBURG C. M.**

ROZENDAAL, Nicolas. See **ROSENDAAL**

ROZENSTEIN, Erna
Polish, 20th century.
Born in Lviv.
Painter.
Cracow Group.
Rozenstein was a laureate of the fine arts academies in both Vienna and Cracow. She is one of the promoters of the artistic association of the Cracow group. She participated in the international exhibition of contemporary art in Essen in 1962; the Biennale in São Paulo in 1964; the Exposition Collective d'Art Polonais in Paris in 1960; in the USA in 1962; Belgrade in 1964; Berlin in 1965; and in Cairo and Damascus in 1965. She has had numerous solo exhibitions in Warsaw and Wroclaw.

ROZENTAL, Ira
Latvian, 20th - 21st century.
Born 1959.
Painter.
Ira Rozental attended the academy of fine arts in Moscow. In 1988, she was awarded the gold medal by the Soviet ministry of culture. Her compositions are abstract, gestural.
AUCTION RECORDS:
PARIS, 11 July 1990, *Homage to St Exupéry* (1989, oil on canvas, 38¼ x 30 ins / 97 x 76 cm) FRF 7,800.

ROZENTAL, Roman
Polish, 20th century.
Born 18 October 1897, in Lódz; died 1942, in Treblinka.
Painter.
Rozental studied in Lódz and at the fine arts academies in Vienna and in Paris.
MUSEUMS AND GALLERIES:
LÓDZ (Muz. Historii): *Church in Kazimierz.*

ROZENTALS, Janis, or Rosenthal, Jan
Latvian, 19th - 20th century.
Born 18 March 1866, in Saldus; died 20 December 1916, in Helsinki.
Painter, illustrator.
Rozentals studied in Riga, and at the academy of arts in St Petersburg, where he received teaching from Makovsky. He was the founder of Latvian national painting. He was also an art critic and executed lithographs.
AUCTION RECORDS:
LONDON, 22 March 1984, *Maternity* (charcoal and pencil, 7¼ x 10 ins / 18.5 x 25.5 cm) GBP 720. LONDON, 19 June 1985, *The Artist's Studio* (1895, oil on canvas, 23½ x 16½ ins / 60 x 42 cm) GBP 3,000.

ROZET
French, 18th century.
Born c. 1770.
Active in Marseilles.
Painter. Genre scenes, portraits.
Rozet was painter to the King of Westphalia.
MUSEUMS AND GALLERIES:
MARSEILLES (Mus. Grobet-Labadié): *Old Woman.*

ROZET, Fanny, or Rozat
French, 20th century.
Born 13 June 1881, in Paris.
Sculptor. Figures.
Fanny Rozet, a pupil of Marqueste, exhibited from 1904, mainly at the Salon des Artistes Français, of which she was a member. She was awarded a bronze medal in 1921.
AUCTION RECORDS:
PARIS, 11 March 1988, *Young Dancer* (terracotta, h. 13½ ins / 34 cm) FRF 1,600.

ROZET, René
French, 19th - 20th century.
Born 14 May 1859, in Paris.
Sculptor.
René Rozet, a pupil of Cavelier and Millet, first exhibited at the Salon in 1876. He also exhibited at the Salon des Artistes Français, of which he was awarded the Hors concours, winning a gold medal in 1927. He was awarded the Légion d'Honneur in 1912.
MUSEUMS AND GALLERIES:
LYONS: *Good Evening, Mother.*

ROZET, Roger
French, 20th century.
Born 1912.
Painter, pastellist. Landscapes.
Roger Rozet exhibited in Paris at the Salon des Artistes Français, the Salon of the Société Nationale des Beaux-Arts and the Salon d'Automne. He painted landscapes of Paris, Normandy, Brittany and Ireland. They are characterised by restrained colour and gently evocative drawing.
AUCTION RECORDS:
PARIS, 11 April 1988, *The Tuileries in Snow* (oil on canvas, 19¼ x 28¼ ins / 49 x 72 cm) FRF 2,000.

ROZGONYI, László or Ladislaus
Hungarian, 20th century.
Born 5 March 1894, in Budapest; died 1948, in Budapest.
Painter.

ROZHDESTVENSKY, Vasili Vasilievich, or Roshdestwenski
Russian, 20th century.
Born 1884, in Tula; died 1963, in Moscow.
Painter. Landscapes.
Groups: Bubnovy Valet (Jack of Diamonds), Association of Artists of Revolutionary Russia (AKhRR).
Rozhdestvensky studied from 1900 to 1910 at the Moscow college of painting, sculpture and architecture (MUZhVZ) with Korovin, V. Serov and L. Pasternak. In 1912, he visited Austria and Italy. From 1918 to 1920, he taught at the higher artistic and technical studios (Vkhutemas) in Moscow, and from 1920 to 1922 at the Udomlya school. He painted mostly landscapes of northern Russia and Siberia.

Rozhdestvensky participated in the exhibitions of various groups: Bubnovy Valet (Jack of Diamonds), 1911-1917; Mir Iskusstva (World of Art), 1917-1922; OMKh (Moscow Society of Artists); and AKhRR (Association of Artists of Revolutionary Russia), 1927-1929.
BIBLIOGRAPHY:
Paris-Moscou, 1900-1930, exhibition catalogue, Éd. du Centre Georges-Pompidou, Paris, 1979.
MUSEUMS AND GALLERIES:
MOSCOW (State Tretyakov Gal.): *Still-life with Liquor* (1913).
AUCTION RECORDS:
PARIS, 15 Feb 1982, *Still-life* (1921, oil on canvas, 32 x 25½ ins / 81 x 65 cm) FRF 31,000.

ROZIER, Amédée. See **ROSIER**

ROZIER, Dominique Hubert
French, 19th century.
Born 21 October 1840, in Paris; died 9 November 1901, in Paris.
Painter. Landscapes, interiors with figures, still-lifes (flowers/fruit/game/fish).
Dominique Rozier was the student of Antoine Vollon. He exhibited at the Paris Salon from 1879 and then at the Salon des Artistes Français. He obtained a third-class medal in 1876, a second-class medal in 1880, a bronze medal at the Exposition Universelle of 1889 and another at the Exposition Universelle of 1900.

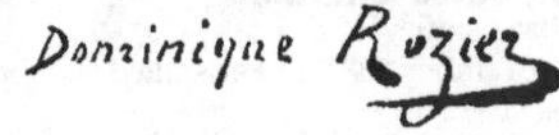

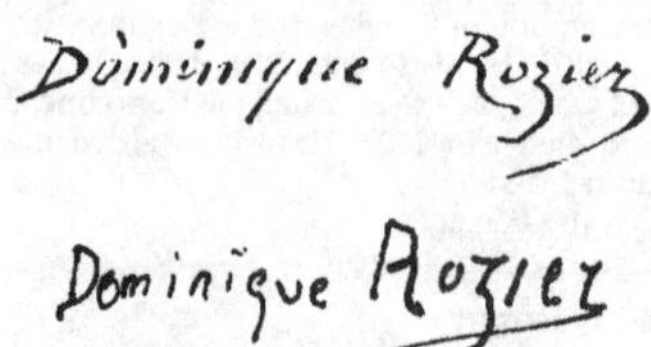

Museums and Galleries:
Bergues: *Grape Harvest* - Bucharest (Muz. National de Arta al României): *Poultry and Hares* - La Roche-sur-Yon: *Fresh Fish at the Central Food Markets* - Lille: *Game* - Lyons: *Haul* - Montpellier: *Sea Fish* - Pontoise: *Still-life and Fruit* - Tourcoing: *At Gargantua's House.*
Auction records:
Paris, 1878, *Still-life,* FRF 240. Paris, 1892, *Seine Valley at Jenfosse,* FRF 400. Paris, 1900, *Fish, Prawns and Mussels,* FRF 145. Paris, 10 Dec 1920, *Auvergne Landscape,* FRF 165. Paris, 18 Dec 1922, *Flowers and Fruit,* FRF 400. Paris, 25 May 1924, *Shellfish and Violets,* FRF 100. Paris, 11 Dec 1926, *Game Birds,* FRF 400. Paris, July 1946, *Still-life with Antique Vase and Fruit,* FRF 450. Paris, 28 Nov 1946, *Flowers* (sold with an unsigned canvas) FRF 1,800; *Flowers* (companion piece of the preceding item) FRF 1,250. Paris, 14 Dec 1949, *Flowers of the Fields,* FRF 6,000. Paris, 15 Dec 1950, *Roses and Goblet,* FRF 5,000. Paris, 11 June 1951, *Kitchen Boy Plucking a Duck,* FRF 10,000; *Flowers in a Pot,* FRF 4,000. Paris, 27 Jan 1977, *Country Bouquet* (oil on canvas, 25 1/2 x 32 ins / 65 x 81 cm) FRF 2,200. Zurich, 16 May 1980, *Bouquet of Flowers* (oil on canvas, 19 x 23 1/4 ins / 48 x 59 cm) CHF 3,500. Vienna, 22 June 1983, *Bouquet of Roses* (oil on canvas, 27 3/4 x 29 ins / 70.5 x 73.5 cm) ATS 50,000. Paris, 5 June 1989, *Roses and Pansies* (oil on canvas, 21 1/4 x 28 3/4 ins / 54 x 73 cm) FRF 14,000. Paris, 5 April 1990, *Still-life with Fruit* (oil on canvas, a pair, each 13 x 16 1/4 ins / 33 x 41 cm) FRF 26,000. Calais, 7 July 1991, *Bowl of Peonies* (oil on canvas, 21 1/4 x 25 1/2 ins / 54 x 65 cm) FRF 26,500. London, 18 March 1994, *Roses in a Vase* (oil on canvas, 22 x 18 1/2 ins / 55 x 47 cm) GBP 4,600. Paris, 16 Dec 1994, *Still-life with Game* (oil on canvas, 55 x 90 1/2 ins / 140 x 230 cm) FRF 37,000. Calais, 23 March 1997, *Still-life with Tureen and Fruit* (oil on canvas, 21 1/4 x 25 1/2 ins / 54 x 65 cm) FRF 15,500. Paris, 5 March 1998, *Still-life with Fruit* (oil on canvas, 21 1/4 x 25 1/2 ins / 54 x 65 cm) FRF 12,500. New York, 13 Sept 2000, *Bowl of Oranges and Violets with a Ewer and a Vase* (print, 22 x 18 ins / 55 x 46 cm) USD 3,200. London, 22 Sept 2000, *Peach and Grapes* (oil on canvas, 18 x 22 ins / 46 x 55 cm) GBP 3,200. Paris, 23 April 2001, *Flask, Oysters and Shrimps. Peaches, Pears and Grapes* (oil on canvas, a pair, 21 x 26 ins / 54 x 65 cm) FRF 20,000. Trieste, 4 Dec 2001, *Large Composition with Flowers* (oil on canvas, 26 x 22 ins / 66 x 56 cm) ITL 9,000,000. Calais, 10 March 2002, *Still-life with Oysters* (oil on canvas, 21 x 26 ins / 54 x 65 cm) EUR 3,200. London, 21 March 2002, *Roses in a Basket with Cherries alongside* (oil on canvas, 26 x 21 ins / 65 x 54 cm) GBP 2,800. Neuilly, 28 March 2003, *Bouquet of Roses* (oil on canvas, 24 x 29 ins / 60 x 73 cm) EUR 3,500. Milwaukee, 26 Jan 2004, *Floral Still-life with Urn, Tazza and String of Pearls* (oil on canvas, 29 x 24 ins / 74 x 61 cm) USD 4,000. Paris, 18 June 2004, *Basket of Roses* (oil on canvas, 24 x 29 ins / 60 x 74 cm) EUR 2,800.

ROZIER, Jean
French, 17th century.
Sculptor.
Rozier sculpted a retable for Caudiès church in 1662.

ROZIER, Jules Charles
French, 19th century.
Born 14 November 1821, in Paris; died October 1882, in Versailles.

Painter, engraver. Genre scenes, landscapes, seascapes. Jules Rozier was the student of Bertin and Delaroche. He exhibited views of the banks of the Seine and Normandy and seascapes in silver-grey tonalities at the Salon from 1839 to 1882.
Museums and Galleries:
Aix: *Bank of the Seine at Vainville* - Clamecy: *View of a Farm* - Dieppe: *Banks of the Seine at Caudebec* - La Rochelle: *Banks of the Seine* - Nantes: *Banks of the Seine at Rolleboise* - Rheims: *Duck Shoot* - Saumur: *Area around Honfleur* - St-Lô: *Cliffs at Villequier; Morning on the Île Chausey.*
Auction records:
Paris, 12-15 May 1902, *Sculpture Studio,* FRF 925. Paris, 8-9 May 1905, *Fisherman,* FRF 380. Paris, 4-5 Dec 1918, *Farms by the Roadside, Impression of Snow,* FRF 230. Paris, 27 May 1920, *Sunset over the River,* FRF 500. Paris, 23-24 Nov 1923, *Road to Le Bout-aux-Pages, Lommoyer,* FRF 950. Paris, 21 Jan 1926, *Plain before the Village,* FRF 245. Paris, 16 Feb 1927, *Towhorse on the Banks of the Seine,* FRF 1,300. Paris, 27 March 1931, *Grazing in Normandy,* FRF 520. Paris, 5 June 1931, *Grazing on the Banks of the Seine,* FRF 200. Paris, 22 Jan 1943, *Washerwomen at the Edge of the River,* FRF 4,000. Paris, 23 June 1943, *Young Angler* (1858) FRF 3,400. Paris, 11 Dec 1944, *Landscape,* FRF 2,000. Paris, July 1946, *Landscape,* FRF 3,800. Paris, 8 Nov 1946, *River Banks,* FRF 5,100. Paris, 17 June 1949, *Troupeau dans les landes* FRF 4,000. Paris, 3 Oct 1949, *Landscape with Pond,* FRF 2,100. Paris, 20 Oct 1949, *Washerwomen* (sold with a canvas by Quinton) FRF 4,100. Paris, 27 Oct 1950, *Farm Scene* (1859) FRF 6,900; *Sheep Grazing* (1860) FRF 6,700. Paris, 4 April 1951, *Seaside Landscape,* FRF 14,000. Paris, 6 July 1951, *Venice at Sunset,* FRF 8,800. Paris, 16 Nov 1953, *Landscape with Washerwoman,* FRF 22,000. Versailles, 16 June 1974, *Washerwoman,* FRF 5,200. London, 29 Sept 1976, *Washerwomen at the Edge of the River* (1862, oil on panel, 11 x 17 3/4 ins / 27 x 45 cm) GBP 850. Paris, 25 Feb 1977, *Farm at the Edge of a Pond* (oil on canvas, 18 x 25 1/2 ins / 46 x 65 cm) FRF 8,400. Paris, 3 March 1978, *Fisherman with Casting Net* (1864, oil on panel, 12 1/4 x 22 1/2 ins / 31 x 57 cm) FRF 10,000. Versailles, 11 June 1978, *Barges* (oil on canvas, 30 x 41 3/4 ins / 76 x 106 cm) FRF 10,000. Paris, 20 May 1980, *Seashore with Figures* (oil on canvas, 39 1/4 x 59 ins / 100 x 150 cm) FRF 21,000. Vienna, 17 March 1981, *Landscape* (oil on canvas, 15 1/4 x 22 ins / 38.5 x 56 cm) ATS 60,000. New York, 25 Oct 1984, *River Landscape with Figures* (1859, oil on panel, 12 1/4 x 22 3/4 ins / 31.4 x 57.8 cm) USD 4,500. Cologne, 20 May 1985, *Wooded Landscape* (oil on canvas, 18 x 15 ins / 46 x 38 cm) DEM 6,000. Paris, 9 Dec 1988, *Landscape with Pasture* (oil on canvas, 10 1/2 x 16 1/4 ins / 26.5 x 41 cm) FRF 4,000. Rheims, 11 June 1989, *Cows Grazing* (oil on canvas, 11 x 16 1/4 ins / 27 x 41 cm) FRF 8,600. Douai, 3 Dec 1989, *Composition* (oil on paper, 14 1/4 x 21 1/4 ins / 36 x 54 cm) FRF 7,800. Paris, 24 May 1991, *Bank of the River* (oil on canvas, 16 x 21 1/4 ins / 40.5 x 54 cm) FRF 21,000. Calais, 7 July 1991, *House by the River Bank* (oil on canvas, 12 1/2 x 18 1/2 ins / 32 x 47 cm) FRF 13,000. Paris, 12 Dec 1991, *Landscape with Pond* (oil on panel, 5 x 9 ins / 13 x 23 cm) FRF 30,000. Paris, 5 Nov 1993, *Le Retour du troupeau; By the River Bank* (oil on panel, a pair, each 9 3/4 x 16 ins / 25 x 40.5 cm) FRF 19,000. Paris, 14 March 1994, *Country Landscape with Shepherd* (oil on panel, 13 1/2 x 22 1/2 ins / 34 x 57 cm) FRF 21,000. Calais, 24 March 1996, *Garden in Bloom* (oil on panel, 14 1/2 x 12 1/4 ins / 37 x 31 cm) FRF 8,000. Paris, 20 Jan 1997, *Low Tide* (1865, oil on panel, 8 1/2 x 15 1/2 ins / 21.5 x 39.5 cm) FRF 11,500. New York, 22 Oct 1997, *Fisherboys* (oil on panel, 14 x 22 1/2 ins / 35.6 x 57.2 cm) USD 9,775. New York, 5 Oct 1999, *Washerwomen by Stream* (oil on panel, 13 x 22 ins / 32 x 57 cm) USD 5,000. Paris, 25 Oct 1999, *Fishing Party* (1858, oil on panel, 11 x 19 ins / 29 x 47 cm) FRF 17,000. Calais, 10 Dec 2000, *Fisherman on the Riverbank* (oil on panel, 12 x 19 ins /

30 x 47 cm) FRF 34,000. MELUN, 10 Dec 2000, *Country Life* (1875, oil on canvas, 24 x 36 ins / 61 x 91 cm) FRF 40,000. COLOGNE, 5 April 2001, *River Landscape in France* (oil on panel, 12 x 22 ins / 31 x 57 cm) DEM 7,000. PONTOISE, 15 Dec 2001, *Snowy Landscape* (oil on canvas, 11 x 16 ins / 27 x 41 cm) FRF 18,000. LONDON, 13 Feb 2002, *Cows in Pasture* (oil on panel, 19 x 29 ins / 47 x 74 cm) GBP 5,500. PORTLAND, 31 July 2002, *Farmhouse* (oil on canvas, 16 x 13 ins / 41 x 32 cm) USD 4,500. HEIDELBERG, 10 May 2003, *Seine Shore with Fishing Boat* (1861, oil on panel, 10 x 16 ins / 26 x 41 cm) EUR 1,600. FONTAINEBLEAU, 11 May 2003, *Shepherd and Sheep on the Riverbank* (1863, oil on panel, 11 x 16 ins / 27 x 41 cm) EUR 2,000. PARIS, 3 June 2004, *Figures on the Riverbank* (oil on panel, 11 x 18 ins / 28 x 46 cm) EUR 3,000. PARIS, 22 June 2004, *Granville, Boat and Fishermen on the Shore* (1878, oil on panel, 8 x 13 ins / 21 x 33 cm) EUR 12,000.

ROZIER, Paule

French, 20th century.
Born 20 December 1910, in Aubusson (Creuse); died 1988.
Painter. Designs for tapestries.

In her home town, Aubusson, Paule Rozier received advice from Martin and Depouthieux, who steered her towards tapestry design. She exhibited at the Salon de l'École Française, the Salon d'Hiver, the Salon de la Marine and the Salon des Artistes Français. Working in Brest, she helped to found the Salon des Artistes Bretons, of which she became vice-president. She created works for the General Hospital and Maritime Prefecture of Brest.

ROZIER, Prosper Roch

French, 19th century.
Born in Dampmart.
Painter. Portraits.

Prosper Rozier was the son of Roch Rozier, the architect, and the student of Glaize. He first exhibited at the Salon in 1877. He produced a large number of portraits.

AUCTION RECORDS:
NEW YORK, 25 May 1983, *Portrait of a Woman in Black* (oil on canvas, 38¾ x 31 ins / 98.4 x 78.7 cm) USD 1,400.

ROZIER, Victor Alexandre

French, 19th century.
Born 19th century, in Paris.
Painter.

Victor Rozier was the student of his father, Jules Rozier. He featured at the Salon in 1864 and 1865.

AUCTION RECORDS:
PARIS, 28 Jan 1924, *Banks of the Seine in Summer*, FRF 280.

ROZMAINSKY, Vladimir

Georgian, 20th century.
Born 12 January 1885, in Tiflis (now Tbilisi); died 16 December 1943, in Paris.
Active in France from 1917.
Painter, draughtsman. Nudes, landscapes, urban landscapes.

Rozmainsky lived in France in 1905. He studied in Nancy, and then at the École des Beaux-Arts in Paris in 1905. He returned to Russia in 1910, but left again upon the outbreak of the Revolution in 1917. He travelled in the Far East before returning to France. He painted nudes, in addition to views of Paris and landscapes.

Rozmainsky participated in the Salon des Artistes Français, Salon des Indépendants, and Salon de la Société Nationale des Beaux-Arts in Paris. He received the first prize for the nude, in 1943, at the Salon de la Société Nationale des Beaux-Arts, and was posthumously attributed the first prize for drawing at the Salon de l'Art Libre in 1956.

ROZMANITH, Antoni Piotr

Polish, 19th century.
Died 1830.
Active in Cracow.
Painter.

Antoni Rozmanith designed and painted architecture.

ROZNIATOVSKA, Antonina

Polish, 19th century.
Born c. 1860, in the Ukraine; died 20 June 1895, in Cracow.
Sculptor.

In 1868, Rozniatovska went to Cracow where she studied with Guyski. Cracow Museum has *Old Lithuanian Priest*, and two busts of women by her.

ROZNIECKI, Eugenjusz.

Polish, 19th century.
Active in Warsaw.
Draughtsman.

The National Museum in Warsaw has some works by this artist.

ROZO, Janik

French, 20th century.
Born 1920, in Belfort.
Painter, draughtsman.

Janik Rozo, who studied at the École des Arts Décoratifs, Paris, lived and worked in Lille from 1972. In 1950 and 1951 he took part in the Salon des Jeunes Peintres, Paris; in 1951 and 1953 the Menton Biennale; in 1956 the Salon de l'Art Sacré, Paris; in 1959 the Paris Biennale; from 1961 to 1967 the Salon Comparaisons, Paris. In 1964 he participated in exhibitions at the museum of Nantes and the Musée des Arts Décoratifs, Paris; in 1970 at the Museum of Modern Art, Legnano, and in 1977 at the Bibliothèque Française, Cracow. He held solo shows in 1956, 1962, 1964, and 1968 at the Galerie La Roué, Paris; in 1961 at the Palais des Beaux-Arts, Brussels; in 1966 at the Cercle des Arts Plastiques, Amiens.

MUSEUMS AND GALLERIES:
AMIENS - NANTES - PARIS (MAMVP).

ROZSA, Imre

Hungarian, 17th century.
Born in Nagyszombat (now Trnava in Slovakia).
Draughtsman.

Bailiff at Garamszebtbenedek, Rozsa illustrated a manuscript in pen drawing listing the duties of the serfs of the place in 1658. It gives among other things pictures of Hungarian serfs and the harvest. He is also known for the cover of a convent rule book and self-portrait coloured in watercolour.

RÓZSAFFY, Dezsö or Desiderius

Hungarian, 20th century.
Born 22 July 1877, in Budapest; died 1937, in Budapest.
Painter. Figures, still-lifes.

Rózsaffy studied with Simon Hollósy in Munich, and with Blanche and Simon in Paris. He wrote about art.

MUSEUMS AND GALLERIES:
BUDAPEST (Magyar Nemzeti Gal.).

ROZSAY, Emil

Slovak, 19th century.
Born 4 March 1839 or 1838, in Kassa (now Košice); died 1891, in Pressburg (now Bratislava).
Painter. Landscapes, animals.

Emil Rozsay was a student of Von Wengheim in Munich.

ROZSNYAY, Kálmán or Koloman

Hungarian, 19th - 20th century.
Born 22 June 1874, in Arad; died 7 November 1948.
Engraver.

ROZTWOROWSKI, Stanislav.
See **ROSTWOROWSKI**

ROZWADOWSKI, Zygmunt
Austrian, 19th - 20th century.
Born 25 January 1870, in Lemberg (now Lviv, Ukraine); died 1950, in Zakopane.
Painter. History painting, military subjects, genre scenes.

Rozwadowski studied in Cracow and Munich, and settled in his home town of Lemberg. He executed mostly genre paintings and battle scenes.

MUSEUMS AND GALLERIES:
LVIV (Picture Gallery).

AUCTION RECORDS:
VIENNA, 13 March 1979, *Light Cart Pulled by Four Horses* (1908, oil on cardboard, 15 1/4 x 19 3/4 ins / 39 x 50 cm) ATS 25,000. BILLINGSHURST, 13 Oct 1999, *Escort* (1904, oil on board, 13 x 16 ins / 32 x 40 cm) GBP 1,200. WARSAW, 5 Oct 2000, *Horse-drawn Carriage* (1904, oil on canvas, 54 x 30 ins / 136 x 76 cm) PLZ 66,000. COLOGNE, 5 April 2001, *Winter Landscape* (1923, oil on board, 13 x 27 ins / 32 x 69 cm) DEM 5,000. WARSAW, 15 June 2003, *Girl Picking Flowers in a Field* (c. 1900, oil on canvas, 18 x 13 ins / 45 x 33 cm) PLZ 8,000.

ROZY, H. L. Bernardus
Flemish School, 19th century.
Active in Ghent c. 1840.
Sculptor.

ROZYNA, Wenzel
Czech, 17th century.
Painter.

Wenzel Rozyna painted the altar picture for Probluz church in 1690.

ROZYNSKI, Kurt von
German, 19th - 20th century.
Born 1 June 1864, in Schippenbeil (now Sepopol, Poland).
Painter.

Kurt von Rozynski studied under Carl Steffek and Emil Neide at the fine arts academy in Königsberg (now Kaliningrad, Russia).

Kurt von Rozynski

AUCTION RECORDS:
COLOGNE, 20 May 1985, *Queen of the Elves* (1901, oil on canvas, 55 x 41 3/4 ins / 140 x 106 cm) DEM 7,000.

ROZZI, Paolo
Italian, 17th century.
Active in Reggio.
Sculptor (ivory).

ROZZOLONE, Pietro, or Ruzzolone or Ruzzulone or Ruzolone or Ruzulone
Italian, 15th - 16th century.
Born in Palermo (Sicily).
Active from 1484 to 1522.
Painter. History painting.

Pietro Rozzolone's works are in Palermo, Chiusi and Alcamo, and he also produced a *Christ on the Cross*, for the church in Termini.

RROTA, Simon
Albanian, 20th century.
Born 23 October 1887, in Shkodër; died 1967 or 27 January 1961, in Shkodër.
Painter. Scenes with figures, genre scenes, landscapes, urban landscapes.

Rrota's painting evokes the everyday experience of cities and the countryside. He approached themes with simplicity: an artisan in his shop, or a family scene.

MUSEUMS AND GALLERIES:
TIRANA (AG): *A Door in Shkoder; At the Village Well.*

RU, Pu. See **PU RU**

RU WENSHU, or Jou Wen-chou or Ju Wen-shu
Chinese, 17th century.
Born in Wuxiang.
Active c. 1600.
Painter.

Ru Wenshu was the grandmother of the painter Mao Xinian. She was known for her landscapes, her flowers and her insects.

RU XIAO-FAN, or Xiao-Fan Ru
Chinese, 20th - 21st century.
Born 1954, in Nanjing.
Active in France.
Draughtsman, painter (wash).

Ru Xiao-Fan obtained his diploma from the higher teacher training college in Nanjing in 1982. In 1983 he followed courses at the École des Beaux-Arts in Paris. He lives and works in Paris. His art is based on a sensitive abstraction in which figures and portraits can be discerned. His compositions have a vertical rhythm and are also an invitation to a world of dream and fantasy.

Ru Xiao-Fan has taken part in collective exhibitions including the Salon des Réalités Nouvelles in Paris in 1985. He exhibits his works in solo exhibitions, including: 1982, Museum of Fine Arts in Nanjing; 1983 and 1984, Arts Promotion in Hong Kong; 1984, Galerie Carrefour de la Chine in Paris; 1986, Espace Vendôme in Paris (with Yan Pei Ming).

RUAIS, Stéphane
French, 20th century.
Born 1945.
Painter. Landscapes.

AUCTION RECORDS:
PARIS, 5 June 1992, *Jardin du Luxembourg* (oil on canvas, 21 1/4 x 25 1/2 ins / 54 x 65 cm) FRF 13,000.

RUANO LLOPIS, Carlo
Spanish, 20th century.
Born 1879, in Orba, near Alicante; died 1950.
Painter, draughtsman. Religious subjects, genre scenes, sporting subjects.

Ruano Llopis studied at the Escuela de Bellas Artes in Valencia. He painted a number of religious subjects but concentrated primarily on bullfighting, collaborating on a number of specialist publications in that field. Examples of his work include *Prophet Isaiah; Prophet Jeremiah; Prophecy of Abraham; Victims of the Fiesta; Brave Bull* and *Skilful work by the Picador*. He showed his work at various exhibitions in Madrid, Valencia and Bilbao (where he was awarded a gold medal in 1909).

BIBLIOGRAPHY:
Arnáiz, José Manuel/López Jiménez, Javier/Merchán Díaz, Manuel (ed.), *'Cien años de pintura en Espana y Portugal (1830-1930)'* in vol. IX, Antiqvaria, Madrid, 1992.

AUCTION RECORDS:
NEW YORK, 22-23 July 1993, *Female Nudes in Matador Postures* (oil on reinforced canvas, four paintings, each 15 x 8 ins / 38.1 x 20.6 cm) USD 6,325. PARIS, 4 Nov 1994, *Two Spanish Women* (oil on canvas, 22 x 27 1/2 ins / 56 x 70 cm) FRF 9,000. MADRID, 10 July 2000, *Bull Performance* (oil on canvas, 40 x 20 ins / 101 x 50 cm) ESP 690,000. MADRID, 20 Nov 2000, *In Lucas' Inn* (oil on canvas, 21 x 24 ins / 54 x 62 cm) ESP 425,000.

RUAO. See first name

RUAZ, Émile Louis de
French, 19th - 20th century.
Born 20 September 1868, in Paris; died 3 December 1931, in Paris.
Painter, engraver.
Émile Louis de Ruaz, a pupil of Blandet, was president of the French society of wood engravers. He exhibited in Paris at the Salon des Artistes Français, of which he was a member, from 1890, and also at the Salon des Indépendants. He was awarded a bronze medal in 1900, and practised both as a painter and a wood engraver.

RUAZ, Georges de
French, 19th - 20th century.
Born 12 May 1871, in Paris.
Engraver.
Georges de Ruaz, a painter and wood engraver, exhibited at the Salon des Artistes Français from 1907.

RUBACH, Wilhelm
German, 19th - 20th century.
Born 1870, in Frankfurt an der Oder; died 23 May 1905.
Painter, engraver. Portraits, landscapes.
Wilhelm Rubach was a student of Max Koner at the fine arts academy in Berlin.

RUBAT DU MÉRAC, Bruno
French, 20th century.
Born 1943, in Marrakech, Morocco.
Sculptor. Figures.
Bruno Rubat du Mérac was an exhibitor in Paris at the Salon des Indépendants of 1987 and the Salon d'Automne of 1988.

RUBATTO. See also **ROBATTO**

RUBATTO, Carlo
Italian, 19th century.
Born 1810, in Genoa; died 1891, in Genoa.
Sculptor.
Rubatto studied under Ignazio Peschiera. He sculpted mostly statues for tombs and busts for cemeteries, churches and public buildings in Genoa.

RUBBENS
Flemish School, 18th century.
Born in Brussels; died 1742, in The Hague.
Sculptor.
Rubbens is probably identical to the sculptor P. Ruebbens.

RUBBENS, Arnold. See **RUBENS Arnold Frans**

RUBBENS, Georgette
Belgian, 20th century.
Painter.
Georgette Rubbens studied at the fine arts academy in Ghent.

RUBBI, John James. See **RUBBY John James**

RUBBIANI, Felice
Italian, 18th century.
Born 30 December 1677, in Modena; died 18 October 1752, in San Pancrazio di Fredo.
Painter. Still-lifes (flowers/fruit), birds.
Rubbiani was the pupil of Domenico Bettini.
AUCTION RECORDS:
NEW YORK, 14 Jan 1993, *Still-life with Parrot Perched on the Edge of a Blue and White Porcelain Bowl Filled with Fruit; Compositions with Flowers and Fruit* (ensemble of four oils on canvas, each 22½ x 38¼in/57.2 x 97.2cm) USD 77,000. ROME, 10 May 1994, *Still-life of a Bowl of Fruit; Still-life of a Vase of Flowers* (oil on canvas, a pair, oval, 45 x 35¾in/114 x 91cm) ITL 64,400,000. MILAN, 15 Oct 1996, *Still-life with Stork and Fruit* (oil on canvas, a pair, each 37¾ x 30in/96 x 76cm) ITL 33,785,000. VIENNA, 7 June 2000, *Still-life with Flowers and Fruit* (oil on canvas, 21 x 17 ins / 54 x 44 cm) ATS 80,000. MILAN, 25 Feb 2004, *Vases with Flowers* (oil on canvas, a pair, 35 x 15 ins / 90 x 39 cm) EUR 35,000.

RUBBILLIARD, Vincenzo, or Rubbligliard
Italian, 18th century.
Died 1778.
Painter.
In 1775, Rubbilliard went to London, where he exhibited in 1776 and 1777.

RUBBIO. See **RUBIO**

RUBBO, A. Dattilio. See **DATILIO Anthony**

RUBBONI, Giovanni. See **RUBONI**

RUBBY, John James, or Rubbi
British, 18th - 19th century.
Born c. 1750, in Plymouth; died 21 August 1812, in Rome.
Portrait artist, draughtsman. Architectural views.
John James Rubby was a pupil of Mengs. He settled in Rome in 1777 and produced sepia drawings of ancient monuments and buildings.
MUSEUMS AND GALLERIES:
COPENHAGEN (Thorvaldsens Mus.): *Golden Age* (in collaboration with F.I. Catel).

RUBCIC, Stanislas
Bosnian, 16th century.
Born in Rubcic, Bosnia.
Illuminator.
Stanislas Rubcic produced heraldic illustrations.

RUBCOV, Aleksandr Aleksandrovich, or Roubtzoff, Alexandre
Russian, 20th century.
Born January 1884, in St Petersburg; died November 1949, in Tunis.
Active in Tunisia from 1914 and naturalised in France from 1924.
Painter, watercolourist, draughtsman. Figure compositions, figures, portraits, urban landscapes. Orientalism.
Rubcov studied at, graduated and received a bursary from the imperial academy of fine arts (later the I.E. Repin institute) in St Petersburg. His aunt, Yekaterina Alexandrovna Wachter, taught him the basics of painting. They travelled together in the Crimea, Poland, Austria, Germany, France, Italy, Estonia and Finland. In 1912, he received the grand prize from the imperial academy of fine arts in St Petersburg, which enabled him to travel and study for four years.

After staying in Spain and France, Rubcov went to Tunis. He was attracted by the quality of light and the picturesque character of the place and its inhabitants. He became interested in Islamic and Bedouin art, and kept a detailed journal of his impressions and reflections between 1915 and 1946. The World War I and the Russian Revolution in 1917 influenced his decision to settle definitively in Tunis. He lived there in the same house up until his death. He learned French, Arabic, Italian and Spanish in order to be able to communicate efficiently during his many travels. He went to Paris annually between 1925 and 1935. He executed monumental paintings, one for the Chambre de Commerce de Tunis, and four for the Résidence Générale de France in Tunisia, now the embassy. The Association Artististique Alexandre Roubtzoff was created in 1980.

Rubcov executed numerous sketches and his work comprises thousands of studies and paintings. Though he also painted many portraits of Europeans living in Tunis, he mostly painted Tunisian architectural scenes and landscapes. He was an attentive observer, sensitive to the warm colours of Tunisian inhabitants, particularly those with elaborate headdresses. The modernisation of Tunis saddened him, which he explained in an article in *Tunisie* in June, 1938. When he was in Paris, he enjoyed synthesising all he saw into his teeming, sometimes humorous compositions: *Paris at Night, The Boulevards, Parisian Cafes, Impressions of Paris*. He remained indifferent to emerging trends, subscribing to the painters of the 19th century from Manet to Puvis de Chavannes, although he was sensitive to Van Dongen. His technique evolved according to the subjects of a perfectionist Academicism and a tempered Post-Impressionism.

Rubcov exhibited in Paris at the Salon d'Automne (1922-1927); Salon de la Société Nationale des Beaux-Arts (1928); Salon des Indépendants (regularly from 1930); Salon de la Société des Peintres Orientalistes; and Salon Artistique de l'Afrique Française. He participated in other collective exhibitions, notably at the Salon Tunisien (Institut de Carthage) annually from 1920, and in diverse group exhibits in numerous provincial cities in France. He also showed some of his paintings in Paris in 1947. After his death, exhibitions dedicated to his work were mounted in 1981 at the Musée Fabre in Montpellier, and in 1984 at the Trianon des Jardins de Bagatelle in Paris.

A. Roubtzoff

BIBLIOGRAPHY:

Sainte-Marie, R. de, *Roubtzoff*, Éd. du Rayonnement, Paris, 1947. Dumas, P., *Roubtzoff, peintre de la lumière*, Privat, Toulouse, 1951. Defianas, L./Boglio, P., *A. Roubtzoff*, exhibition catalogue, Trianon de Bagatelle, Paris, 1984. Hamza, Alya, *Alexandre Roubtzoff*, Alif, Éd. de la Méditerranée, Tunis, 1994. Dubreucq, Patrick, *Les Orientalistes, Alexandre Roubtzoff*, ACR Édition, Courbevoie, 1996.

MUSEUMS AND GALLERIES:

FRONTIGNAN: *Fashion in Juan-les-Pins* (drawing in watercolour) - LUNEL: *Nude Study* - PARIS (Municipal Collection): *View of Paris* (drawing) - PARIS (Mus. Carnavalet): *Old Streets of Paris* (25 works, drawing in watercolour) - PARIS (Mus. du Petit Palais): *Women Weaving a Carpet* (1924) - ST PETERSBURG (Academy): *Grand Duchess Maria Pavlovna* (1911); *Dining Room* (1911) - ST PETERSBURG (Hermitage): *Red Room* (1909); *Yellow Room* (1910); *Interior in Empire Style* (1912) - TUNIS: *Woman with Canoun, Manoubia* (1922); *Rue du Souki Bel-Khir* (1927, drawing with watercolour); *Rue Ghrabel* (1929, drawing with watercolour); *Sidi Bou Said* (1931); *Arabian Girl from Tunis* (1940); *Chadlia, Bedouin Woman* (1948).

AUCTION RECORDS:

PARIS, 18 Feb 1980, *Tunisian Woman* (1917, 31 1/2 x 23 1/2 ins / 80 x 60 cm) FRF 10,500. PARIS, 18 Feb 1980, *Tunisian Woman* (1917, oil on canvas, 31 1/2 x 23 1/2 ins / 80 x 60 cm) FRF 10,500. LONDON, 8 Feb 1984, *Tunisian Woman Preparing a Meal* (1917, oil on canvas, 45 x 62 ins / 114.5 x 157.5 cm) GBP 4,500. LONDON, 8 Feb 1984, *Tunisian Women Preparing a Meal* (1917, oil on canvas, 45 x 62 ins / 114.5 x 157.5 cm) GBP 4,500. PARIS, 27 Feb 1984, *Nightclub in Luchon* (1927, watercolour, 12 1/2 x 19 1/4 ins / 31.5 x 49 cm) FRF 3,500; *Lady in Black* (1936, oil on canvas, 78 3/4 x 54 3/4 ins / 200 x 139 cm) FRF 30,100. MONTPELLIER, 17 Dec 1984, *Fatma with Tatoos* (oil on canvas, 25 1/2 x 19 3/4 ins / 65 x 50 cm) FRF 16,000. PARIS, 27 April 1990, *Katan* (oil on canvas, 57 x 41 1/4 ins / 145 x 105 cm) FRF 65,000. PARIS, 11 Dec 1991, *Reclining Nude* (1923, oil on canvas, 24 1/2 x 54 3/4 ins / 62 x 139 cm) FRF 22,000. PARIS, 16 Nov 1992, *Young Girl with Elegant Pins* (pastel, 28 3/4 x 19 1/4 ins / 73 x 49 cm) FRF 26,000. PARIS, 5 April 1993, *Sidi Bou Said* (1944, oil on cardboard, 14 x 10 ins / 35.5 x 24.5 cm) FRF 15,000. PARIS, 22 April 1994, *Aïda, Bedouin Woman* (oil on canvas, 37 1/2 x 31 1/2 ins / 95 x 80 cm) FRF 110,000; *Teboursouk* (drawing, 12 1/2 x 19 1/4 ins / 32 x 49 cm) FRF 6,500. PARIS, 6 Nov 1995, *Gardens of the Persian Villa in Tunis* (1928, oil on canvas/cardboard, 11 x 14 3/4 ins / 28 x 37.5 cm) FRF 38,000. PARIS, 21 April 1996, *Garden in Flower* (1920, oil on canvas/panel, 6 3/4 x 11 ins / 17.2 x 27 cm) FRF 30,000. PARIS, 5-7 Nov 1996, *View of Sidi Bou Said* (1915, oil on canvas, 22 1/2 x 32 1/4 ins / 57 x 82 cm) FRF 42,000. PARIS, 26 March 1998, *Paris, Boulevard St-Germain* (1928, oil/cardboard, 11 x 15 ins / 28 x 38 cm) FRF -.

RUBCZAK, Jan de, or Rubezak
Polish, 20th century.
Born 18 January 1884, in Stanislawów (now Ivano-Frankivs'k); died 1949 or 27 May 1942.
Painter, engraver. Portraits, landscapes, seascapes, architectural views, flowers.

Rubczak studied at the academy of fine arts in Cracow and at the Académie Colarossi in Paris.

MUSEUMS AND GALLERIES:

CRACOW (Muz. Narodowe): *Luxembourg Palace* - PARIS (Mus. du Petit Palais) - WARSAW (Muz. Narodowe): *Church in Rabka*; *Port in Brittany*.

AUCTION RECORDS:

PARIS, 28 Jan 1943, *Sunken Boats*, FRF 1,000; *Village by the Seaside*, FRF 1,000; *Maritime Pines*, FRF 1,200. PARIS, 20 March 1998, *Boats at Port* (oil on canvas, 23 1/2 x 28 3/4 ins / 60 x 73 cm) FRF 23,500. WARSAW, 7 March 1999, *View of Tarascon* (oil on canvas, 24 x 28 ins / 60 x 70 cm) PLZ 40,000. WARSAW, 14 March 1999, *Noon in French River Landscape* (c. 1920, oil on canvas, 21 x 26 ins / 54 x 65 cm) PLZ 28,000.

RUBCZAK, Jan or Jean
Polish, 19th - 20th century.
Active in France.
Painter, engraver. Landscapes.

Rubczak participated in the open exhibition of Polish artists in 1921 at the Salon de la Société Nationale des Beaux-Arts, where he sent three paintings: *Olive Trees, Road to Collioure*, and *House in Collioure*; and two drawings, *Pont-Neuf* and *Winter*.

RUBCZAK, Marie (Mme)
Polish, 19th - 20th century.
Active in France.
Painter. Figures.

Rubczak sent her *Odalisque* to the open exhibition of Polish artists in 1921 at the Salon de la Société Nationale des Beaux-Arts.

RUBÉ, Auguste Alfred
French, 19th century.
Born 1815, in Paris; died 13 April 1899, in Paris.
Painter, decorative designer. Landscapes. Wall decorations.

Auguste Rubé was a student of Ciceri. He occupied an important position among the set painters of the Second Empire and the beginnings of the third Republic. He carried out some major decorations for the main opera house and for the Opéra Comique. He was made a Chevalier of the Légion d'Honneur in 1869.

RUBECK, Carsten
German, 17th century.
Sculptor (wood).

Carsten Rubeck carved the stalls in the church of St Nicholas in Greifswald from 1625 to 1626.

RUBEI, Emilio
Italian, 19th - 20th century.
Born 11 August 1869, in Aquila.
Portrait artist.

Emilio Rubei worked in Ascoli Piceno from 1902.

RUBEIS. See also **ROSSI** and **ROSSO**

RUBEIS, Giovanni Battista de
Italian, 18th - 19th century.
Born c. 1750, in Udine; died 27 August 1819, in Udine.
Portrait artist, medallist, art writer.
Rubeis studied in Venice and returned to Udine around 1773. He is known for a medal which he made for Countess Virginia Giustinian Tassis.

RUBEL, Georges
French, 20th century.
Born 1945, in Paris.
Painter, engraver, draughtsman.
Georges Rubel lives and works in Paris. His work featured in *De Bonnard à Baselitz - Dix Ans d'enrichissements du cabinet des estampes 1978-1988* (*From Bonnard to Baselitz: A Decade of Acquisitions by the Prints Collection 1978-1988*), an exhibition held in 1993 at the Bibliothèque Nationale in Paris.
MUSEUMS AND GALLERIES:
PARIS (BNF): *Country Scene, Ancient and Modern* (1975-1976, etching, burin, dry-point).

RUBELLA, Robert de
French, 15th - 16th century.
Illuminator.
Rubella worked in Paris and, from 1493 to 1506, in Avignon.

RUBELLES, Albert Auguste
French, 19th century.
Born in Pouzat (Ardèche).
Painter.
Albert Rubelles was a student of Lambinet. He exhibited some landscapes of sites in the department of Eure at the Paris Salon in 1868 and 1870.
AUCTION RECORDS:
PARIS, 5 Nov 1923, *Hunt at the Pond,* FRF 100.

RUBELLI, Ludwig (Baron von Sturmfest)
Austrian, 19th century.
Born c. 1841; died 25 January 1905, in Feldhof, near Graz.
Painter. Seascapes.
AUCTION RECORDS:
LINDAU, 8 Oct 1980, *The Prince of Liechtenstein's Family in a Gondola* (oil on canvas, 27 3/4 x 49 1/4 ins / 70.5 x 125 cm) DEM 6,500. ZURICH, 8 Sept 1999, *Fishermen and Boats in Northern Waters, Mountains Beyond* (1881, oil on card, 14 x 20 ins / 35 x 50 cm) CHF 2,500. VENICE, 7 July 2001, *The Bucintoro at Moonlight* (oil on canvas, 17 x 27 ins / 42 x 69 cm) ITL 11,500,000.

RUBEMPRE, Marie Cozette de
French, 19th century.
Born in Amiens.
Sculptor.
Marie Cozette de Rubempre was a student of Chapu. She first exhibited at the Salon of 1873. She seems to have devoted herself more particularly to ceramics. She is known mainly for some earthenware reproductions of works by Chapu and Prud'hon.

RUBEN, Carl
German, 18th - 19th century.
Born 30 January 1772, in Trier; died 13 February 1843, in Trier.
Painter.
Carl Ruben was the father of Christian Ruben. He is noted for a portrait of *Bishop Karl Mannay of Trier.*

RUBEN, Christian
German, 19th century.
Born 30 November 1805, in Trier; died 8 July 1875, in Inzersdorf, near Vienna.
Active in Munich, Prague and Vienna.
Painter. Genre scenes.
Christian Ruben was a pupil of his father Carl Ruben and also studied under Cornelius at the academy in Düsseldorf. He became director of the academy in Prague in 1848, then of the academy in Vienna in 1852. He executed a series of cartoons produced for the stained glass windows of Regensburg Cathedral (Belvedere Museum in Vienna).
MUSEUMS AND GALLERIES:
MUNICH (Pinakothek): *Cow Girl* - VIENNA: *Battle of Lipany (1434)* - VIENNA (Österreichische Gal. Belvedere): series of cartoons for stained-glass windows.
AUCTION RECORDS:
LONDON, 6 March 1974, *Sirens,* GBP 400.

RUBEN, Dominique. See **RABEN**

RUBEN, Franz Leo
Austrian, 19th - 20th century.
Born 16 August 1842, in Prague; died 18 December 1920, in Munich.
Painter. History painting, genre scenes, landscapes.
Franz Leo Ruben was the son of Christian Ruben. A medal winner in Vienna (1873) and Munich (1883), he painted numerous views of Venice.
MUSEUMS AND GALLERIES:
GRAZ: *Beggar in front of a Church in Venice* - PRAGUE (Národní Gal.): *Idyll* - STUTTGART: *Carnival, Venice* - VIENNA: *Venice Scene*; two watercolours - ZURICH (Kunsthaus): *Venetian Fisherman.*
AUCTION RECORDS:
NEW YORK, 6 April 1960, *Papal Audience,* USD 300. LONDON, 14 April 1967, *Fitting,* Gns 350. LONDON, 16 Oct 1974, *Pigeons on St Mark's Square, Venice,* GBP 1,100. VIENNA, 14 Sept 1976, *Gathering Shellfish in the Venice Lagoon* (1886, oil on panel, 15 1/2 x 23 1/2 ins / 39.5 x 60 cm) ATS 80,000. LONDON, 3 Oct 1979, *Fish Market, Venice* (1880, oil on canvas, 33 3/4 x 56 ins / 86 x 142 cm) GBP 4,200. VIENNA, 14 Sept 1983, *Ducal Palace, Venice* (1884, oil on canvas, 15 x 28 ins / 38 x 71 cm) ATS 160,000. LONDON, 29 Nov 1985, *Fish Market, Venice* (1880, oil on canvas, 34 x 56 ins / 86.4 x 142.3 cm) GBP 6,000. NEW YORK, 25 May 1988, *Fan-seller* (oil on canvas, 34 x 22 1/2 ins / 86.3 x 57.2 cm) USD 8,800. MILAN, 1 June 1988, *Fish-sellers on the Campiello delle Mosche, Venice* (1880, oil on canvas, 35 x 56 1/4 ins / 88 x 143 cm) ITL 22,500,000. NEW YORK, 28 Feb 1990, *Portrait of a Lady in White with a Green Sash* (1885, oil on canvas, 48 x 31 ins / 121.9 x 78.7 cm) USD 25,300.

RUBEN, Ludvig
Swedish, 19th century.
Born 17 February 1818, in Karlskrona; died 31 March 1875, in Stockholm.
Engraver.
Ruben was a pupil of Leo Lehmann in Hamburg. He continued his studies in Paris with Joel Ballin, and in Berlin with E. Mandel.

RUBEN, Mathias
German, 18th century.
Died 11 October 1800, in Trier.
Painter.
MUSEUMS AND GALLERIES:
TRIER (Rheinisches Landesmus.): *Panoramic View of Trier.*

RUBENS, A.
Belgian, 19th century.
Died c. 1824.
Active in Brussels.
Painter.
A Belgian painter of the name of Rubens, probably from the same family, and who claimed to be descended from P.P. Rubens, worked in Paris in the 19th century. He painted portraits, of no artistic value, and copies in the Louvre. He seems to be identical to Jean-Baptiste Rubens.

RUBENS, Albert
Belgian, 20th century.
Born 1944, in Tielt.
Painter, draughtsman.

Albert Rubens studied at Academie St-Lucas in Ghent.

RUBENS, Arnold Frans or Francesco, or Rubbens, known as sometimes Rubens des Batailles
Flemish School, 18th century.
Baptised 22 November 1687 in Antwerp; died 1719; buried 11 June in Antwerp.
Painter. Battles, religious subjects, landscapes.

MUSEUMS AND GALLERIES:
ANTWERP (Carmelite Church): *Crucifix* - ANTWERP (Geelhaud): *Two Battles* - LIÈGE: *Battle under Louis XIV* - ROME (Palazzo Doria Pamphili): *Levantine Seaport; Synagogue of Scala Levantina* - SIBIU: *Two Battles.*

AUCTION RECORDS:
PARIS, 5 May 1949, *Flocks in Landscapes* (two pendants) FRF 11,000. LONDON, 19 March 1982, *Village Scene* (oil on panel, 11 x 13 1/2 ins / 28 x 34.2 cm) GBP 2,800. AMSTERDAM, 11 Nov 1997, *Shepherds Resting near a Classical Tomb in an Italian Coastal Landscape* (oil on panel, 9 1/4 x 11 1/2 ins / 23.3 x 29.4 cm) NLG 11,070. VIENNA, 9 June 1999, *Cavalry Encounter between Imperial and Turkish Troops* (oil on panel, a pair, 6 x 8 ins / 15 x 20 cm) ATS 90,000. PARIS, 3 Dec 2001, *Cavalry Clash* (oil on panel, 11 x 18 ins / 27 x 45 cm) FRF 34,000. MADRID, 17 Dec 2001, *Battle Scene* (oil on canvas, 18 x 23 ins / 45 x 58 cm) ESP 1,200,000.

RUBENS, Bartholomeus, called le Vermeio
Hispano-Flemish School, 15th century.
Born probably in Cordova.
Painter.

Bartholomeus Rubens designed stained glass windows for Barcelona Cathedral in 1494. According to F. de Mély, he was in fact an artist from Ferrara named Bartholomeus Brason. According to Dr Wurzbach, however, it is essential to distinguish between two painters of this name - Bartholomeus Brason I Rubens, known as 'Rosso' (the redhead), who died in 1473 and whose son Dominicus died before 1486, and his grandson Bartholomeus II, who was buried in Ferrara in the church of Our Lady of Life in 1517. There is little to indicate whether or not 'Vermeio of Cordova' was the same artist as one of those two. It should also be noted that the grandfather of Peter Paul Rubens was of Antwerp stock (the legend of his origins in Styria was an 18th century invention) and was also called Bartholomeus. Examples of Bartholomeus Rubens' work include a *Triptych* (in Aqui), a *St Michael* (Musée Calvet in Avignon), a *Pietà* in Barcelona Cathedral, a *St Engracia* (in the Isabella Stewart Museum in Boston), a *St Michael and the Dragon* (in the J. Weenher Collection in London), a *St Catherine* in Pisa's municipal museum, and a *St Veronica* in Ausona Cathedral near Barcelona.

MUSEUMS AND GALLERIES:
AVIGNON (Mus. Calvet): *St Michael* - BOSTON (Isabella Stewart Gardner Mus.): *St Engracia* - LONDON (J. Weenher Collection): *St Michael and the Dragon* - PISA (Mus. Civico): *St Catherine.*

RUBENS, Jean Baptiste or Johannes Baptist
Belgian, 19th century.
Died c. 1824.
Active in Brussels.
Draughtsman, miniaturist.

Jean Baptiste Rubens seems to be confused with A Rubens.

RUBENS, Joes
German, 18th century.
Active in Frankfurt am Main 1727-1742.
Painter.

RUBENS, Josse
Flemish School, 18th century.
Active in Paris in 1786.
Painter. Portraits.

RUBENS, N. N.
Belgian, 18th century.
Active in Brussels.
Sculptor.

NN Rubens was the pupil of Xaverq, and worked in The Hague about 1719.

RUBENS, Peter Paul
Flemish School, 16th - 17th century.
Born 28 June 1577, in Siegen (Westphalia), Germany; died 30 May 1640, in Antwerp.
Painter, engraver (including etching), draughtsman. Historical subjects, figures, nudes, portraits, genre scenes, landscapes. Wall decorations, church decoration, ornaments, designs for tapestries.
Antwerp School.

Peter Pau(we)l Rubens came from a rich bourgeois family from Antwerp. His father Jan Rubens, (b. 13 March 1530, d. 1 March 1587 in Cologne, Germany) was a doctor of civil and canon law, an alderman in Antwerp and a man of considerable culture who had lived in Italy for seven years. On 29 November 1561, he married Marie Pypelynckx (b. 20 March 1538, d. 15 November 1608 in Antwerp) and fathered seven children by her. Although he was born a Roman Catholic, Jan Rubens belonged to the reformed (Calvinist) church. He campaigned against the tyranny of the Duke of Alba and, as a result, was obliged to flee the Low Countries in 1568, seeking refuge in Cologne. Following an affair with his employer's second wife, the Protestant Princess Anna of Saxony, which resulted in a pregnancy, he was banished to Siegen in Westphalia. Rubens was finally allowed to return to Cologne after posting bail to the sum of 6,000 thalers, and on 15 May 1578, he settled his family into a modest house in which he was destined to spend the final nine years of his life - under constant surveillance by the agents of the House of Orange-Nassau. It was during this time that his son, Peter Paul Rubens, commenced his Jesuit education. In the interim, Jan Rubens had had a change of heart and, on his return from imprisonment, abjured Protestantism. On his death in 1587, he was buried at the St Peterskirche in Cologne. His wife Marie left Cologne in March 1589, a virtual pauper as a result of the vindictiveness of the House of Orange-Nassau, and returned to Antwerp with her children.

Peter Paul Rubens entered a Latin school directed by Rombout Verdonck near Antwerp Cathedral. Shortly thereafter, he found a place as a page in the household of a noblewoman named Marguerite de Ligne, widow of the Count de Lalaing, but soon tired of courtly life and left after only a few months in her service. In 1591, he Rubens commenced his artistic studies under a relative on his mother's side, the Mannerist landscape painter Tobias Verhaecht who, although only 29 years old, had already forged himself a considerable reputation. Rubens studied under him for two years, then spent four years in the studio of Adam van Noort. He completed his apprenticeship from 1596 to 1598 under the guidance of Otto van Veen (Otto Vaenius), an Antwerp Romanist who had himself worked in Italy under Zucchero and who was at the time court painter to the Archduke Albert and the Infanta Isabella. In 1598, Peter Paul graduated and was accepted into the Antwerp Guild of St Luke. Following two years of seniority in the Guild, Rubens secured the archduke's permission to visit Italy. He left Antwerp on 8 May 1600, travelling first to Venice, where he met a young gentleman who secured for him the patronage of the reigning duke of Mantua, Vincenzo I Gonzaga, who appointed Rubens painter to the court with a stipend of 400 ducats.

Rubens subsequently accompanied Vincenzo Gonzaga to Florence to attend the wedding of Maria de' Medici to Henri IV, then to Genoa. In July 1601, Rubens left for Rome to paint some copies for his patron Gonzaga. Once there, he worked assiduously, turning out three paintings destined for the altar of St Helena in the church of S Croce di Gerusalemme.

At the time of Rubens' arrival, the art world in Rome was in turmoil, with a bitter dispute raging between the supporters of Caravaggio on the one hand and those of Giuseppe Cesari (the so-called 'Cavalier d'Arpino') and Guido Reni on the other. There appears to have been little doubt in Rubens' mind that the bold approach to art espoused by Caravaggio was preferable to the styles of the others. It is highly doubtful, however, if Rubens and Carvaggio actually met: in the course of 1601, Caravaggio was in Malta and in 1602, Rubens was recalled to Mantua, only to leave again for Spain on 5 March 1603, entrusted with a diplomatic mission on the duke's behalf. 13 March 1603 found Rubens in Valladolid with the Duke of Lerma, whose portrait he painted on several occasions. He was to remain in Spain until November of that year, during which time he painted numerous portraits and historical subjects. He returned to Mantua in 1604, where he started work on three major paintings for the Jesuit church in Mantua: the *Duke of Mantua and his Family Worshipping the Holy Trinity*, the *Baptism of Christ* and the *Transfiguration*.

In 1605-1606, Rubens worked in Genoa, and from 1606 to 1608 he was back in Rome, where he painted an altarpiece for S Maria in Valicella. On 28 October 1608, Rubens wrote to Vincenzo Gonzaga informing him that his mother was seriously ill and that he was leaving immediately for Antwerp. As it turned out, Marie Pypelynckx died on 15 November, which Rubens was to discover on his journey back to Antwerp.

Rubens returned to Antwerp from Italy a comparatively wealthy man. He considered his options and was on the point of returning to Italy when Archduke Albert and the Infanta Isabella persuaded him to remain in Antwerp by appointing him to the post of official painter to the Brussels court. Rubens had another cogent reason for not leaving; Isabella Brandt had caught his fancy, and he married her on 3 (or 13) October 1609, an event he commemorated in his *Portrait of the Artist and his Wife Isabella Brandt*, now in the Alte Pinakothek in Munich. That same year (1609), Rubens joined the Romanist Order of St Peter and St Paul. His first daughter, Clara Serena, was born on 21 March 1611 and, in that year also, he acquired a property in Antwerp which he enlarged and decorated lavishly in the Italian style. This princely mansion would finally be completed in 1618, by which time Rubens is reported to have spent a fortune on its decoration and furnishings. His eldest son, Albert, was born on 5 June 1614 and such was his standing that the Arhduke Albert consented to be the child's godfather. On 28 March 1618 a second son, Nicolas, was born.

As Peter Paul Rubens became established as a major artist, so more commissions came in. In 1612 he painted a *Descent from the Cross*. In 1616 he painted a number of mythological, allegorical and historical subjects, among them a *Rape of the Daughters of Leucippus* (Alte Pinakothek, Munich), a composition whose prancing horses and fleshy nudes presaged much of his later work.

In early 1622, Rubens was called to Paris by Maria de' Medici, the widow of Henri IV, in order to provide decorative compositions for the Palais du Luxembourg. In Paris, Rubens made preparatory sketches for the 21 paintings that comprise the *Destiny of Maria de' Medici*, now in the Louvre. The paintings themselves were produced in his own studio in Antwerp, with some of them being delivered in 1621 and the balance in 1625. Rubens' correspondence alludes to his dissatisfaction with how the incredible amount of work in question was remunerated. Nevertheless, he appeared willing to accept a further commission - to decorate another room in the Palais du Luxembourg with paintings recording the life of Henri IV (a commission Cardinal Richelieu would have preferred to go to the Cavalier of Arpino). In the event, serious delays in the building of the Palais du Luxembourg and the ill-health of the queen mother meant that Rubens failed to progress beyond a few preparatory drawings.

Meanwhile, Rubens' daughter Clara died in 1623 and three years later, on 26 June 1626, his wife Isabella died. In the course of a visit to Paris in 1625, Rubens had met the Duke of Buckingham, whose portrait he promptly painted. One year later, he sold Buckingham - a favourite of Charles I of England - a part of his own collection of paintings, statues and other works of art. It is possible that while Rubens was at work painting Buckingham's portrait a plan was mooted by the former Infanta Isabella, who had governed the Low Countries following the death of Archduke Albert, to send Rubens on a mission to the king of Spain (Philip IV) in a bid to effect a reconciliation between the royal courts of London and Madrid. Rubens was given a warm welcome during this, his first voyage to Madrid in 1628, and he reciprocated by painting numerous compositions, notably a portrait of Philip IV and several copies of works by Titian. He particularly enjoyed the company of Velázquez. Rubens' diplomatic efforts were not in vain and he left Madrid on 28 April 1629 on a mission to England travelling via Brussels and Antwerp to London, reaching the English capital on June 5. There, he was received with all due honours, and his diplomatic skills may have helped to establish a basis for a peace treaty between Spain and England. In acknowledgement of his diplomatic services, Charles I conferred a knighthood on him on 21 February 1630, three days before he left London. Meanwhile, Rubens painted the ceiling of the royal Banqueting House in the Inigo Jones-designed Whitehall Palace on the theme of *Peace and War* (1619-1622). In 1630, Rubens remarried, this time to Helena Fourment, a sister of his late wife's brother-in-law, who was a mere sixteen years old (Rubens was by this time over fifty-three). The second marriage produced five children: Clara Johanna (born on 18 January 1632), Franz (12 July 1633), Isabella Helena (3 March 1635) Petrus Paulus (1 March 1637), and Constantia Albertina (3 February 1641) - the last-named born eight months after her father's death.

In 1633, the Infanta Isabella entrusted him with a further diplomatic mission, this time to the States-General in Holland. Rubens was less happy about this; his health had deteriorated and he was suffering from chronic gout. In 1635, his desire for a less turbulent life prompted him to purchase the château of Steen (Elewijt) between Vilvorde and Mechelen. It was there that he spent his summer months and it was there that he painted his late landscapes, including a *Landscape at Sunset with Wagon* (Boymans-van Beuningen Museum, Rotterdam).

At the end of 1635, Rubens provided decorations for the visit of the new governor of the Low Countries, Archduke Ferdinand. (These were subsequently engraved by Gevaertius in 1642). In 1636, Rubens was appointed painter to the new governor's court. In 1637 he painted a *Helena Fourment with her Two Children* (now in the Louvre) and in the same year, he demonstrated that he had lost none of his technical virtuosity and brio by completing his *Fall of the Titans* (Koninklijke Musea voor Schone Kunsten van België, Brussels) and, just before his death in 1639, he produced his *Three Graces* (Prado, Madrid), a last flourish, as it were, of blond and voluptuous Flemish nudity.

Peter Paul Rubens had no immediate artistic predecessors, and his subsequent influence on painters and painting can only be described as substantial. His roster of pupils, collaborators and imitators included Anthony van Dyck, Justus von Egmard, Theodor van Thulden, Abraham van Diepenbeck, Pieter van Mol, Cornelius Schut, Jan van Hœck, Simon de Vos, Francis Wouters, David Teniers the Elder, David Teniers the Younger, Frans Snyders, Jan Wildens, Lucas van Uden, Josse Momper, Gerard Segers (or Zeghers), Gaspard de Crayer, Jacob Jordaens, Jan Brueghel, Paul de Vos, Jan van den Bergh, Mathys van den Bergh, Gonzales Coques, Job Cossiers, Deodat Delmont, the sculptor Lucas Faydherbe, Lucas Franchois II, Jacob Peter Gonvoi, Samuel Hoffmann, Nicolas van den Horst, Jacob Warmans, Daniel Mytens, Willem Pauweels, Erasmus Quillimus II, the engraver Nicolaes Rickmans, Antoine Sallaert, the painter-engraver Pieter Soutman, Jan Thomas van Yperen, and Victor Walvoet.

Rubens has featured prominently in a large number of major thematic exhibitions, notably those devoted to Flemish Baroque. Examples include: *Rubens and his Age: Treasures from the Hermitage Museum*, which, from 1999 to 2002, travelled between the Palazzo dei Diamanti in Ferrara, the Hermitage in St Petersburg, the Art Gallery of Ontario and the Guggenheim Museum in Bilbao; and *Dans la lumière de Rubens. Peintres baroques des Pays-Bas du Sud* (*In the Light of Rubens. Baroque Painters of the Southern Netherlands*), an exhibition held in 2000 at the Musée des Beaux-Arts in Valenciennes which set out to do justice to minor painters of talent whose work has often been eclipsed by the Grand Masters of Flemish Baroque. Meanwhile, solo Rubens retrospectives have been held on a frequent basis, including *Rubens: Drawing on Italy*, an exhibition mounted in 2002 at the National Gallery of Scotland in Edinburgh.

Peter Paul Rubens died a wealthy man. His eldest son Albert inherited his library (and his his collection of precious stones and medallions) and succeeded to his father's post of Secretary to the Privy Council of the Low Countries. His paintings, on the other hand, were sold off, having been catalogued by Frans Snyders, Jan Wildens and Jacques Moeremans. In addition to a monumental body of paintings and drawings, Rubens also left numerous engravings, studies for jewellery and libraries and tapestry cartoons. The commission in Antwerp entrusted with collating his engravings assembled no fewer than 2,253 items (excluding a further 484 drawings) and it is likely that this figure may grow. In 1968, a new inventory of his work, a *Corpus Rubenianum* was compiled and directed by Ludwig Burchard.

Bearing in mind his diplomatic commitments and the protracted and exhausting missions they entailed, it seems surprising that Rubens found the time to produce such an immense body of work. However, Rubens had assembled in his studio a number of excellent pupils and collaborators who worked from his sketches and designs to prepare paintings to which Rubens himself added the finishing touches. He sold these compositions without dissimulating their provenance, informing his clients that they were priced substantially lower than work executed entirely by his own hand. While this goes some way towards explaining some of the unevenness and inconsistencies in his output, it in no way detracts from the scope and importance of his work in terms of its influence. The particular genius of Rubens may reside in the fact that he worked across the broadest of spectra. His portraits, while subject to the implicit constraints of that genre, exhibit a personal touch that mirrors his perception (and appreciation) of the subject at hand. As well as his large-scale compositions, which are irrefutably masterpieces, he left innumerable mythological works which grace museums and galleries the world over. There are also the preparatory sketches and drawings by his own hand which betray a boldness and freedom of execution that is not found in the more restrained final work. Finally, there are the myriad more discreet and more intimate paintings, sketches and drawings executed by Rubens himself (such as his portrait of Helena Fourment and her children, or his 'private' nudes such as the *The Little Fur (Helena Fourment)* now housed in Vienna).

In sum, Rubens was a master of design and composition. His dazzling technique and his sensuality stamp him as one of the most individualistic artists of the early 17th century.

PPR

PPR 1634 f P P RVBINS.

P P RVBENS F 1613 P.P.RVBENS.F 1614 P.P.R

P.RVBENS.F. 1.6.1.4

PE PA. RVBENS. FE A 1625

BIBLIOGRAPHY:

Held, J.S., *'Thoughts on Rubens' Beginnings'* in *Ringling Mus. A.J. 1983 pp. 14-35.* Piles, Roger de, *La Vie de Rubens*, N. Langlois, Paris, 1681. Burchard, Ludwig, *'Corpus Rubenianum'* in *26 vol.*, Phaidon, London, New York, 1968. Stechow, Wolfgang, *Rubens and the Classical Tradition*, Cambridge (MA), 1968. Martin, J. R., *Rubens: The Antwerp Altarpieces*, London, 1969. Glen, T. L., *Rubens and the Counter-Reformation: Studies in his religious paintings, between 1609 and 1620*, New York, 1977. *The century of Rubens and Rembrandt: seventeenth century Dutch and Flemish drawings from the Pierpoint Morgan Library*, exhibition catalogue, British Museum, London, 1979 (exhibition organised by the British Museum Dept of Prints and Drawings, 27 September 1979 to 13 January 1980). Held, J.S., *The Oil Sketches of P. P. Rubens*, Princeton, 1980 (2 vols). Held, Julius Samuel, *'The Oil Sketches of Peter Paul Rubens: a Critical Catalogue'* in *2 vols*, Princeton University Press, Princeton, 1980. Held, J.S., *Rubens and his Circle*, Princeton, 1982. Vergara, L., *Rubens and the Poetics of Landscape*, New Haven and London, 1982. Alpers, Svetlana, *L'art de dépeindre, la peinture hollandaise au XVII° siècle*, Gallimard, Paris, 1986. Cavalli-Björkman, Görel (ed), *Bacchanals by Titian and Rubens: papers given at a symposium in the Nationalmuseum Stockholm, March 18-19 1987*, Nationalmuseum, Stockholm, 1987. Vlieghe, H., *'Rubens Portraits of Identified Sitters Painted in Antwerp'* in *CRLB, xix/2*, London and New York, 1987. White, C., *Peter Paul Rubens: Man and Artist*, New Haven and London, 1987. Hulst, R.A. d'/Vandenven, M., *'Rubens: The Old Testament'* in *CRLB, ii*, London, 1989. Millen, R.F./Wolf, R.E., *Heroic Deeds and Mystic Figures: A New Reading of Rubens's 'Life of Marie de' Medici*, Princeton, 1989. Goodman, E., *The Garden of Love as 'Conversate à la mode*, Amsterdam, 1992. Sutton, Peter C., *The Age of Rubens*, exhibition catalogue, Ghent, Boston, Museum of Fine Arts, New York, 1993. Van der Meulen, *Rubens: Copies after the Antique*, London, 1994 (3 vols). Alpers, Svetlana, *La Création de Rubens*, Gallimard, Paris, 1997. Oppenheimer, Paul, *Rubens: a portrait: beauty and the angelic*, Duckworth, London, 1999. Vergara, Alexander, *Rubens and his Spanish Patrons*, Cambridge University Press, New York, 1999. Judson, J. Richard, *Rubens: the Passion of Christ*, Harvey Miller, Turnhout, 2000. Limousin, Isabelle/Ramade, Patrick/Cordier, Gaëlle, *Dans la lumière de Rubens: peintres baroques des Pays-Bas du Sud*, exhibition catalogue, Musée des Beaux-Arts, Valenciennes, 2000. Gritsay, Natalia/Babina, Natalia, et al., *Rubens and his Age. Treasures from the Hermitage Museum*, group exhibition catalogue, The Guggenheim Museum Bilbao, Bilbao, 2002.

Museums and Galleries:

Aachen: *Fall of the Damned; Coronation of the Virgin; Portrait of Philip IV of Spain; Lot and his Daughters; Crucifixion* - Aix: *Male Portrait; Female Portrait; Hercules Strangling Antaeus* (sketch, grisaille) - Ajaccio: *Holy Family; Queen Tomyris* - Amsterdam: *Noli Me Tangere; Publicus Cornelius Scipio Africanus; Cimon and Pero (Roman Charity); Helena Fourment; Anne of Austria* (study) - Angers: *Erichthonius as a Child entrusted to the Daughters of Cecrops; Rebecca at the Well; Drunken Silenus* - Angoulême: *Voyage of Maria de' Medici to Ponts-de-Cé* - Antwerp: *Christ between the Two Thieves; Adoration of the Magi; St Theresa Delivering Bernardin de Mendoza from Purgatory; Virgin and Infant Jesus, the Saviour, St John the Apostle and the Virgin* (reverse, grisaille, triptych); *Communion of St Francis; Education of the Virgin; Doubting Thomas; Nicolas Rockox; Coat of Arms of Rockox (verso); Adrienne Rockox née Perez; Coat of Arms of Adrienne Rockox* (triptych); *Virgin with Parakeet; Christ on the Cross; Holy Trinity* (two sketches); *Triumphal Car of Kallo; Christ Lamented by St John and the Saintly Women; Kasper Gavaertuis, Town Secretary of Antwerp; Baptism of Christ; Nobleman; Venus Frigida* - Antwerp (Cathedral of Our Lady): *Descent from the Cross* - Augsburg: *Hunt Scene* - Austin (Jack S. Blanton MA, University of Texas): *Study for the Head of a Youth* (1601-1602) - Avranches: *Beheading of St John the Baptist* - Bayonne (Mus. Bonnat): *Triumph of Venus; Triumphal Entry of Henry IV into Paris* (sketch); *Henri IV at the Battle of Ivry* (sketch); *Salome and Herod; Last Communion for a Dying Warrior* (mythological subject); *Prophet Elijah in the Desert of Horeb receiving Bread and Water from an Angel; Israelites Gathering Manna; Triumph* (sketch); *Bellerophon on Pegasus Piercing the Chimera with his Lance; Raising of the Cross* - Beaufort: *Portrait of the Infanta Claire Isabella Eugenie; Abduction of Hippodamus; Kermesse* - Berlin: *Coronation of the Virgin; Isabella Brandt; Conversion of St Paul; Diana and her Nymphs Surprised by the Fauns; Child Portrait; Penitent Magdalene; Venus and Adonis; Diana Hunting Deer; Neptune and Amphitriton; Bacchanale; Andromeda; Landscape with Tower; Landscape with Shipwrecked Aeneas; Virgin, Infant Jesus and Saints; Raising of Lazarus; Mars, Venus and Eros; Fortuna; Capture of Paris by Henri IV; St Peter; Capture of Tunis by Charles V; St Sebastian; Lamentation of Christ; Virgin and Child Jesus* (sketch) - Berlin (Gemäldegal.): *St Cecilia; Perseus Liberating Andromeda* - Berlin (National Mus.): *Landscape with Man on Gallows; Landscape with Cows and Duck-Hunters; Portraits of Jan van Ghindertalen; Death of Achilles; Three Horsemen* - Besançon: *Two Allegorical Figures; Hercules and the Lion; Nymphs Surprised by a Shepherd* - Bordeaux: *Martyrdom of St George; Martyrdom of St Juste; Bacchus and Ariane; Villagers Dancing in the Country; Christ on the Cross* - Boston: *Thomas Howard, Count Arundel; The Mystic Marriage of St Catherine* - Boston (Isabella Stewart Gardner Mus.): *Portrait of Thomas Howard, Count Arundel* - Brussels: *Road to Calvary; Martyrdom of St Liévin; St Francis Protecting the World; Adoration of the Magi; Assumption; Coronation of the Virgin; Pieta; The Woman Taken in Adultery; Venus in Vulcan's Forge; Posthumous Portrait of Archduke Albert of the Netherlands; Archduchess Isabella of the Netherlands; Archduke Ernest of the Netherlands; Seigneur de Cordes; Jacqueline van Caestre; Theophratus Paracelsus; Four Negro Heads* (studies); *Virgin of the Forget-Me-Nots* (with Brueghel); *Wisdom Triumphing over War and Discord under the Reign of James I of England; Jesus Teaching Nicodemus; Massacre of the Innocents; Landscape with Atalanta Hunting* (sketches); *Martyrdom of St Ursula; Mercury and Argus; Abduction of Hippodaurus by the Centaurs; Fall of the Titans* (1637) - Budapest: *Mucius Scaevola; Holy Family; Meleager and Atalanta; Male Portrait; Study of a Head; Last Judgment* (sketch) - Caen: *Assumption; Portrait of Nicolas Rockox; Portrait of a Man wearing the Order of the Garter* (sketch); *Straw Hat; Melchizedek Offering Abraham Bread and Wine* - Calais: *Judgment of Paris* - Châlons-en-Champagne: *Decapitation of St John the Baptist; Victims of the Plague* (two sketches/wood) - Cologne: *Juno and Argus; Holy Family; St Francis Receiving the Stigmata* - Compiègne (Mus. national du Château): *Diana Returning from the Hunt* - Copenhagen (Statens Mus. for Kunst): *Judgment of Solomon; Matthaeus Yrsselius (1541-1629), Abbot of Sint-Michiel's Abbey in Antwerp; Francis I of Tuscany; Johanna of Austria, wife of Francis I* - Coutances: *Lions and Dogs in Battle* - Darmstadt: *Diana and her Nymphs* - Detroit: *Portrait of the Artist's Brother Philip; Meeting of David and Abigail; St Michael* - Dijon: *Virgin Presenting the Child Jesus to St Francis of Assisi; Entry of Christ into Jerusalem; Jesus Washing the Disciples' Feet; Ganymede Abducted by an Eagle; Isabella Brandt* - Douai: *Grape Harvest* - Dresden: *Hero and Leander; St Jerome; Hero of Virtue Crowned by the Goddess of Victory; Drunken Hercules; Young Girl and Faun; Old Woman at the Fire; Male Portrait; Boar Hunt; Diana Returning from the Hunt; Judgment of Paris; Mercury Surprising Argus; Old Bishop; Blond Woman; Quos Ego; Bathsheba; St Francis di Paola* (sketch) - Dublin: *Vision of St Ignatius* (sketch); *St Francis Receiving the Stigmata; St Dominic; Christ at the House of Martha and Mary* - Dunkirk: *St Francis Kneeling; Marriage of the Virgin; Reconciliation of Jacob and Esau* - Düsseldorf: *Assumption* - Edinburgh (Nat. Gal. of Scotland): *Prudence* (16th century, copy after Raphael retouched by P.P. Rubens) - Florence (NG): *Henri IV at the Battle of Ivry; Triumphal Entry of Henri IV into Paris; Helena Fourment; Isabella Brandt; Bacchante; Two Self-portraits; Hercules between Vice and Virtue; Venus and Adonis; Three Graces, Old Silenus and Fauns* (sketch) - Florence (Palazzo Pitti): *Ulysses on the Island of the Phaeacians; Returning from the Fields; The Artist, the Artist's Brother and the Philosophers Lipsius and Grotius; Consequences of War* (*Aftermath of War*); *St Francis at Prayer; Holy Family* (two); *Nymphs and Fauns; Duke of Buckingham* - Fort Worth (Kimbell AM): *The Martyrdom of St Ursula and the Eleven Thousand Maidens* (c. 1615-1620, oil/panel); *The Duke of Buckingham* (1625, oil/panel, portrait) - Frankfurt am Main: *King David* (two sketches) - Geneva (MAH): *Sleeping Nymphs and Fauns* - Geneva (Mus. Ariana): *Frederick of Nassau on Horseback* - Genoa: *Artist and Wife; Portrait of an Alderman* - Glasgow: *Nature Adorned by the Graces; Boar Hunt; Christ Child and St John* (disputed); *Theseus Battling the Amazons; Portrait of a Lady* (disputed); *Male Portrait* - Grenoble: *St Gregory surrounded by Saints; Head of Old Man; Virgin and Child; Adoration of the Virgin by Angels and Saints* - Hanover: *Nessus the Centaur abducting Dejanira* - Karlsruhe: *Family* - Kassel: *Drunken Hercules with Fauns and Bacchantes; Jupiter and Callisto; Flight into Egypt; Meleager Presenting Atalanta with the Head of the Wild Boar of Calydon; Portrait of a Young Man; Young Girl with Mirror; Allegory: The Victor; Nicolas de Respaigne in Oriental Attire; Diana and her Nymphs Surprised by Fauns; St Francis; Virgin and Sinners; Jupiter and Callisto* - Kassel (Gemäldegal. Alte Meister): *Venus, Eros, Bacchus and Ceres* - La Fère: *Garden of the Muses* - Le Mans: *Male Portrait* - Le Puy-en-Velay: *Adonis Leaving for the Hunt* (landscape by Breugel) - Lille (MBA): *Descent from the Cross; Death of Mary Magdalene; St Francis and the Virgin; St Bonaventure; Ecstasy of St Francis; Abundance;*

Providence (Sketch); *Descent from the Cross* (1616-1617); *Ecstasy of Mary Magdalene* - LONDON: *Daughter of the Artist* (sketch); *Apotheosis of William the Silent; Fall of the Damned; Sorrows of St Paul; Crucifixion; Portrait of a Child; Helena Fourment; Diana and Endymion; Triumph of Silenus; Portrait of a Lady* (four studies) - LONDON (Dulwich Picture Gal.): *Venus mourning Adonis* (before 1614, oil/panel); *Saint Barbara fleeing from her Father* (c. 1620, oil/panel); *Catherine Manners, Duchess of Buckingham (?)* (c. 1625, oil/panel, portrait); *Ceres and Two Nymphs with a Cornucopia* (c. 1625/1628, oil/panel); *Venus, Mars and Cupid* (c. 1630-1635, oil on canvas); *Hagar in the Desert* (after 1630, oil/panel); *The Three Graces* (c. 1636, oil/panel) - LONDON (NG): *The Judgement of Paris* (c. 1600, oil/wood); *St Bavo about to receive the Monastic Habit at Ghent* (before 1612 or 1616-1623, oil/wood, sketch); *A Shepherd with his Flock in a Woody Landscape* (1615-1622?, oil/wood); *The Miraculous Draught of Fishes* (1618-1619, black chalk, pen and oil on paper on canvas); *Portrait of Susanna Lunden (?) ('Le Chapeau de Paille')* (c. 1622-1625, oil/wood); *A Wagon fording a Stream* (c. 1625-1640, black chalk and oil/paper/canvas, unfinished); *Peace and War ('Minerva protects Pax from Mars')* (1629-1630, oil on canvas); *A Roman Triumph* (c. 1630, oil/canvas/panel); *The Birth of Venus* (c. 1632-1633, black chalk and oil/wood, probably a model for a silver basin); *The Judgement of Paris* (1632-1635?, oil/wood); *The Rape of the Sabine Women* (c. 1635-1640, oil/wood); *The Brazen Serpent* (1635-1640?, oil on canvas); *A View of Het Steen in the Early Morning* (1636?, oil/wood); *Sunset Landscape with a Shepherd and his Flock* (c. 1638, oil/wood); *The Horrors of War ('An Allegory showing the Effects of War')* (after 1638, oil/paper/canvas) - LONDON (Wallace Collection): *The Rainbow Landscape* (c. 1636-1637, oil/panel); *Christ's Charge to Peter* (c. 1616, oil/panel); *The Holy Family with Elizabeth and Saint John the Baptist* (c. 1614-1615, oil/panel); *The Union of Henri IV and Marie de Médicis (Henri IV as Prince of Peace)* (c. 1628, oil/panel); *The Birth of Henri IV* (c. 1628, oil/panel); *The Triumph of Henri IV* (c. 1628, oil/panel); *The Defeat and Death of Maxentius* (oil/panel) - LOS ANGELES (Getty Mus.): *Entombment* (c. 1612, oil on canvas) - LYONS: *St Francis, St Dominic and Several Other Saints Protecting the World against the Wrath of Christ; Adoration of the Magi* - MADRID (Prado): *Countess Gavia; Judgment of Solomon; Moses and the Serpent; Adoration of the Three Kings; Holy Family* (three); *Pieta; Resurrected Christ and the Disciples of Ammaus; St George and the Dragon; Relgious Observance of Rudolf of Hapsburg; St Peter the Apostle; St John the Apostle; St James the Elder; St Andrew; St Philip; St Thomas; St Bartholomew; St Matthew; St Mathias; St Simon; St Judas Thaddeus; St Paul; Centaurs and Lapiths; Abduction of Persephone; Terto's Banquet; Achilles Discovered by Ulysses; Atalanta and Meleager; Andromeda and Perseus; Ceres and Pomone; Diana's Nymphs Surprised by Fauns; Nymphs and Fauns near a Brook; Orpheus and Eurydice; Juno Creating the Milky Way; Judgment of Paris; Three Graces* (1639); *Diana and Callisto; Ceres and Pan* (with Snyders); *Mercury and Argus; Fortuna; Flora* (with Brueghel); *Vulcan; Mercury; Saturn Devouring One of his Children; Ganymede Abducted by Jupiter; Heraclitus Weeping; Democritus Laughing; Archimedes Meditating; Archduke Albert in a Brueghelian Landscape; Infanta Isabella in a Brughelian Landscape; Maria de' Medici; Equestrian Portrait of Philip II; Ferdinand of Austria; Thomas More, Chancellor of England; Portrait of a French Princess; Garden of Love; Dance of the Peasants; Adam and Eve; Abduction of Europa* (copy from Titian); *Head of an Old Man; Elders of the Church with St Thomas and St Elisabeth; Tithe; Triumphs of Truth, the Catholic Church, Charity and the Eucharist; Law of Christ Triumphing over Paganism; Four Apostles* (sketches for the decoration of the Torre de la Parada) - MELBOURNE (Nat. Gal. of Victoria): *Descent from the Cross* - MILAN (Pinacoteca di Brera): *Cenacle* - MONTAUBAN: *Thinker* - MONTPELLIER: *Martyrdom of a Saint; Christ on the Cross; Landscape; Episode from a War of Religion; François Franck (Rubens or Van Dyck)* - MOREZ: *St Paul on the Road to Damascus* - MOSCOW (Rumiantsev Mus.): *Mucius Scaevola; Samson Vanquishing the Lion and the Bear; Three Bathers; Resurrection; Abduction; Imaginary Scene* - MUNICH: *Last Judgment; Silvia and Aminta; Hercules and Dejanira; Benediction; St Mary Magdalene; Virgin and Child; St Louis of Gonzaga; Holy Family at the Cradle; Death of Seneca; Triumph of Virtue over Drunkenness and Voluptuousness; Martyrdom of St Lawrence; Crown of Fruits; Crown of Flowers; Sleeping Diana; Diana at Rest after the Hunt; Defeat of Sanherib; Conversion of St Paul; Lion Hunt; Christ in the Clouds with Virgin and Saints; Fall of the Reprobates into Hell; Last Judgment; Woman of the Apocalypse; Nativity; Apostles and the Holy Spirit; Two Fauns; Samson in Prison; Suzannah and the Elders; Christ and the Repentant Sinners; Christ, Peter and John; Christ on the Cross; Holy Trinity; Apostles Peter and Paul; Romans and Sabines Reconciled; War and Peace; Mars (Allegory); Deposition; Shepherd and Young Wife; Herd of Cattle at Pasture; Landscape with Rainbow; St Christopher Carrying the Infant Jesus; St Francis of Paola and Victims of the Plague; Education of Maria de' Medici; Henri IV Accepting the Portrait of Maria de' Medici; Marriage of Maria de' Medici; Entry of the Recently Remarried Queen to the Port of Marseilles; Coronation of Maria de' Medici, 1610; Henri IV Conferring the Regency on his Wife; Adoration of Henri IV; Voyage of Maria de' Medici to Ponts-de-Cé; Reign of Maria de' Medici; Family Alliance between France and Spain; Allegory of the Reign of Maria de' Medici; Coming of Age of Louis XIII; Maria de' Medici Imprisoned in Blois on the Orders of her Son; Maria de' Medici Takes Flight; Peace Accord after the Reconciliation of Louis XIII with his Mother; Louis XIII Meeting his Mother; Funeral Service for Decius Mus; Boar Hunt with Hunters and Dogs; Portrait of the Artist's Brother, the Lawyer Philippe Rubens; Thomas Howard of Arundel and his Wife; Male Portrait; Young Man with a Black Cap; Philippe II; Elisabeth of Bourbon; Equestrian Portrait of Ferdinand of Spain; Infant Don Ferdinand, Cardinal; Franciscan Monk; Old Woman with Black Veil; Young Fair-Haired Girl; Four Portraits of Helena Fourment; Garden Promenade; Jan Brandt, the Artist's Father-in-Law; Doctor Van Thulden; Hippopotamus Hunt* - MUNICH (Alte Pinakothek): *Battle of the Amazon Women; Rape of the Daughters of Leucippus by Castor and Pollux* (1616); *Slaughter of the Children of Bethlehem; Drunken Silenus; Portrait of the Artist and his Spouse Isabella Brandt; Fall of the Rebel Angels* - NANCY: *Transfiguration; Jesus Walking on the Waters; Jonah Thrown into the Sea* - NAPLES: *Portrait presumed to be of Helena Fourment; Triumph of a Warrior (or The Maccabees); Flight into Egypt* (sketch); *Shepherd and Shepherdess* (sketch); *Head of Monk* (sketch) - NARBONNE: *Jesus at the House of Martha and Mary* (with Snyders); *Concluding the Peace* (with Snyders) - NEW YORK (Metropolitan Mus. of Art): *Wolf and Dog Hunt* (c. 1615-21); *Return of the Holy Family from Egypt; Holy Family; Venus and Adonis; Male Portrait* (two); *Portrait of an Old Man; St Teresa of Avila Interceding for Souls in Purgatory* (studio composition) - NEW YORK (Pierpont Morgan Library): *Daniel in the Lions' Den* (drawing) - NICE: *St George and the Dragon; Thetis Accepting the Weapons of Achilles from the hands of Vulcan; Achilles, Victor over Hector* (for a Gobelin tapestry) - OPORTO: *Peasant Man and Woman Going to Market with Fowl and Fruit; Meleager and Atalanta* - PARIS (Louvre): *Lot's Flight; Prophet Elijah in the Wilderness; Adoration of the Magi; Virgin Surrounded by Innocents; Virgin, Infant Jesus and an Angel in a Garland of Flowers; Flight into Egypt; Raising of Lazarus; Christ on the Cross; Triumph of Religion; Tomyris, Queen of Scythia, with the Head of Cyrus; Francesco de'Medici, Grand-Duke of Tuscany and Father of*

Maria de' Medici; Johanna of Austria, Mother of Maria de' Medici; Maria de' Medici as Bellone; Maria de' Medici; Triumph of Truth and the Fates spinning the Destiny of Maria de' Medici; Baron Henri de Vicq, Ambassador of the Netherlands to the Court of France; Elisabeth of France; Helena Fourment and her Children (1637); *Lady of the Boonen Family; Kermesse; Tournament beside a Castle Moat; Three Landscapes; Abraham's Sacrifice; Melchizedek and Abraham; Raising of the Cross; Coronation of the Virgin; Philipoemen Recognised by an Old Woman; Job Tormented by Demons; Peace and War* (study for the ceiling of Whitehall Palace in London); *Head Study for a St John; Portrait Bust of an Old Man; Portrait presumed to be of Suzanna Fourment; Ixion Deceived by Juno; Head Study for St George; Genius Crowning Religion; Raising of the Cross; Landscape with the Ruins on the Palatine Hill in Rome; Portrait of Anne of Austria, Queen of France; Destiny of Maria de' Medici* (compositions painted between 1621 and 1625 for the Medici Gallery in the Palais du Luxembourg); *Birth of Maria de' Medici; Education of Maria de' Medici; Henri IV Receiving the Portrait of Maria de' Medici; Marriage of Maria de' Medici; Maria de' Medici Disembarking in Marseilles; Marriage of Henri IV and Maria de' Medici in Lyons; Birth of Louis XIII; Henri IV Leaves for the German War and Appoints Maria de' Medici as Regent in his Stead; Coronation of Maria de' Medici; Apotheosis of Henri IV; Regency of Maria de' Medici; Governance of Maria de' Medici; Voyage of Maria de' Medici to Ponts-de-Cé; Exchange of Two Princesses on the Hendaye River on 9 November 1615; Blissful Regency of Maria de' Medici; Coming of Age of Louis XIII; Queen Maria Flees to the Chateau of Blois on 21/22 February 1619; Maria de' Medici Reconciled with her Son; Concluding the Peace; Meeting of Maria de' Medici and her Son; Triumph of Truth* - PARIS (Mus. Jacquemart-André): *Hercules Suffocating the Lion of Nemea* - PAU (MBA): *Achilles, Victor Over Hector* (1630) - PHILADELPHIA (MA): *Prometheus Bound* (c. 1611-1612, finished in 1618) - PITTSBURGH (Frick AM): *Charlotte-Marguerite de Montmorency, Princess of Condé* - PRAGUE: *Martyrdom of St Thomas and St Augustine* - RENNES: *Tiger and Lion Hunt* (with Snyders) - RENNES (MBA): *Tiger Hunt* - RICHMOND (Virginia MFA): *Pallas and Arachne* (1636-1637, oil/wood) - ROHRAU (Schlossmus., Graf Harrach'sche Familiensammlung): *Head of a Young Girl; Study for the Head of a Negro* - ROME (Gal. Colonna): *Assumption; Jacob and his Family Take Their Leave of Esau* - ROME (Gal. Nazionale): *St Sebastian* - ROME (Mus. e Gal. Borghese): *Deposition; Visitation of St Elisabeth* - ROME (Palazzo Doria Pamphili): *Franciscan Monk; Portrait of an Old Man* - ROTTERDAM: *All Saints* - ROTTERDAM (Mus. Boijmans Van Beuningen): *Martyrdom of St Lievin; Landscape at Sunset with Wagon* (1630-38); *Story of Achilles; Portrait of a Monk; Three Crosses; Coronation of the Virgin; Minerva and Mars; Diana Bathing* - ROUEN: *Moses Rescued from the Waters of the Nile* - SEATTLE (AM): *Last Supper* (1620-1621, oil on wood) - ST PETERSBURG (Hermitage): *Abraham Sending Hagar Away; Adoration of the Magi; Virgin and Infant Jesus* (two); *Virgin Presenting a Rosary to St Dominic and Other Saints; Jesus at the House of Simon the Pharisee; Descent from the Cross; Coronation of the Virgin; Venus and Adonis; Bacchus; Bacchanale; Perseus and Andromeda; Union of Earth and Water* (with Wildens); *Five Statues of Sovereigns of the House of Hapsburg; King Philip IV of Spain; Elisabeth of France, Queen of Spain; Isabella Brandt; Suzanna Fourment and her Daughter Catherine; Helena Fourment; Old Lady; Cavalier; Portrait of a Lady; Franciscan Monk; Old Man; Warrior; Pastorale; Coachmen; Rainbow; Cimon and Pero (Filial Love); Young Woman; Henri IV, King of France* (two studies) - STOCKHOLM: *Offering to Venus* (freely after a Titian original); *Bacchante in the Open Air; Three Graces; Susanna and the Elders* (sketches) - STRASBOURG: *St Francis; Salvator Mundi* (two sketches); *Female Portrait; Holy Family* - TARBES: *Christ on the Cross; Burgomaster Nicolas Roskow; Last Communion of St Francis of Assisi; Descent from the Cross; Christ on the Cross; Adoration of the Magi; Assumption of the Virgin* (copies) - THE HAGUE: *Helena Fourment; Michel Ophovius; Isabella Brandt; Man's Head* - TOULOUSE: *Christ between the Two Thieves; Queen Tomyris with the Head of Cyrus* - TOURS: *Mars Crowned by Victory; Ex voto* - VADUZ (Fürstliche Sammlungen): *Death of Decius; Triumph in Rome; Assumption; Erechtnius and the Daughter of Cecrops; Two Sons of the Artist; Venus at her Toilette; Ajax and Cassandra* - VALENCIA: *Raising of the Cross* - VALENCIENNES: *Ecstasy of St Francis of Assisi; St Stephen Preaching; Stoning of St Stephen; Burial of St Stephen; Annunciation; Descent from the Cross; Cavalry Charge; Martyrdom of St Stephen* - VERONA (Mus. Civico): *Holy Trinity* - VIENNA: *The Fur Coat (Helena Fourment); Head of Venus (Allegory); Maximilan I; Penitent Magdalene* (votive painting for the Brotherhood of St Ildefonse); *Hero Crowned by Bellone; Five Portraits of Old Men; Lamentation of Christ; Infant Jesus, St John and Two Children; Charles the Bold; Annunciation; Cinion and Iphigenia; Venetian Woman* (after Titian); *Isabella d'Este* (after Titian); *Head of the Medusa* (animal figures by Snyders); *Cardinal St Jerome; Ferdinand, King of Hungary; St Ambrose Refusing Theodosus Entry to the Church; Cardinal Ferdinand as a Child; Man Dressed in Furs; Landscape Study; Male Portrait; Four Corners of the World; Boar Hunt; Atalanta and Meleager; Self-portrait; St Francis-Xavier; Assumption* (two sketches); *St Ignatius Loyola; Dead Saviour; King Ferdinand of Hungary; St Pepin, Duke of Brabant, and his Daughter St Bega; Sleeping Hermit and Angelica; Landscape in Storm and Tempest; Jupiter and Mercury with Philomen and Baucis; Holy Family; Isabella of Spain; Female Portrait; St Andrew* - VIENNA (Akademie der Bildenden Künste): *Bacchanale; Circumcision of Christ; Esther Appearing before Assuerus; Souls in Purgatory; Christ at the Home of Simon the Pharisee; Three Graces; Adoration of the Shepherds; St Jerome; St Cecilia; Ascension; Angels in Adoration of an Image of the Virgin; Annunciation; Apotheosis of Jacob; Head Study of an Old Man; Boreas Abducting Orethia; Christ Carrying the Cross* - VIENNA (Czernin'sche Gemäldegal.): *The Holy Women at Christ's Tomb; Portrait of a Man; Portrait of a Woman* - VIENNA (Kunsthistorisches Mus.): *Ildefonso Altar; The Holy Family under an Apple Tree; The Miracles of St Ignatius* (sketch); *Lamentation of Christ by the Virgin and St John; Feast of Venus; Mary Magdalene and Martha; Archduke Albert; The Castle Garden; Crowning the Heroes of the Victory; Young Girl with a Fan; Charles the Bold* - VIENNA (Schönborn-Buckheim): *Faun carrying a Basket of Fruit* (study of a head) - VIRE: *Samson and the Lion* - YPRES: *Beheading of St John* (two sketches).

AUCTION RECORDS:

AMSTERDAM, 1702, *Cimon and Pero*, FRF 1,150. PARIS, 1742, *St Cecilia*, FRF 10,000. PARIS, 1750, *Atalanta Accepting the Boar's Head from Meleager*, FRF 3,000. PARIS, 1756, *St Cecilia at her Piano*, FRF 20,050; *Landscape with Animals and Human Figures*, FRF 9,905. PARIS, 1770, *One of Ruben's Wives, Seated*, FRF 20,000. PARIS, 1777, *Adoration of the Three Kings*, FRF 10,000; *One of Rubens' Wives*, FRF 18,000. PARIS, 1784, *One of Rubens' Wives with a Child Standing between her Legs*, FRF 20,001. LONDON, 1791, *Nativity*, FRF 11,830. PARIS, 1795, *Christ at the House of Martha and Mary*, FRF 22,005. PARIS, 1800, *Scipio Returning the Betrothed of Allucius*, FRF 21,200; *Queen Tomyris with the Head of Cyrus*, FRF 31,800; *Judgment of Paris*, FRF 53,000. LONDON, 1810, *Pan with Flute (Syrinx)*, FRF 26,250; *Portrait of Rubens Attired as St George, together with Rubens' Two Wives*, FRF 53,800. ANTWERP, 1822, *Portrait known as 'The Straw Hat'*, FRF 71,940. LONDON, 1840, *Judgment of Paris*, FRF 105,000. LONDON, 1846, *Holy Family*, FRF 61,950. LONDON, 1853, *Adoration of the Magi*, FRF 30,000. PARIS, 1856, *Landscape with a Rainbow*, FRF

113,750. LONDON, 1860, *Interior with Portrait of the Balthazar Family*, FRF 187,000. PARIS, 1872, *Apollo and Midas*, FRF 40,000. BRUSSELS, 1873, *Antiope*, FRF 200,000. PARIS, 1881, *Miracles of St Benoit*, FRF 170,000. ANTWERP, 1881, *Venus*, FRF 100,000. LONDON, 1884, *Holy Family with Saints Francis of Assisi, Elisabeth and Joseph*, FRF 131,250; *Conversion of Saul*, FRF 86,625. LONDON, 1886, *Rubens with Wife and Child* (two pendants) FRF 1,375,000; *Venus, Cupid and Adonis*, FRF 189,000. NEW YORK, 17 and 18 March 1909, *Madonna and Child*, USD 1,475. PARIS, April 1909, *Holy Family*, FRF 80,000. LONDON, 19 Feb 1910, *King David and the Elders of Israel Offering a Sacrifice*, GBP 924. LONDON, 8 April 1911, *Maria de' Medici as Bellone* (sketch) GBP 178. LONDON, 25 and 26 May 1911, *Lot and his Family leaving Sodom*, GBP 6,825. LONDON, 4-7 May 1923, *Flight into Egypt*, GBP 2,625; *Death of Hippolytus*, GBP 1,102; *Meeting at Nordlingen between the King of Hungary and the Cardinal-Infanta*, GBP 1,102. LONDON, 6 July 1923, *Count de Werve*, GBP 1,575; *Helena Fourment*, GBP 1,365. PARIS, 2 June 1924, *Triumph of Christ over Sin and Death* (sketch) FRF 220,000; *Ford*, FRF 96,000; *Portrait of the Painter Frans Franken*, FRF 125,000; *Portrait presumed to be of Isabella Brandt*, FRF 275,000. LONDON, 3 Dec 1924, *Old Gentleman*, GBP 1,180. LONDON, 1 May 1925, *Meeting of David and Abigail*, GBP 126. LONDON, 1 May 1925, *Head of an Old Woman*, GBP 2,100. LONDON, 12 June 1925, *Jewish Sacrifice*, GBP 714. PARIS, 27 and 28 May 1926, *Portrait of R.P. Michiel Ophovius*, FRF 75,000; *Abduction of Hippodamia* (sketch) FRF 110,000. LONDON, 29 July 1926, *Female Portrait*, GBP 756. LONDON, 19 Nov 1926, *White Priest*, GBP 420. LONDON, 17 Dec 1926, *Virgin and Child*, GBP 1,732. LONDON, 6 May 1927, *Mars*, GBP 1,995. LONDON, 27 May 1927, *Two Men in Roman Costume*, Gns 500; *Heads of Two Patriarchs*, Gns 270. LONDON, 10 June 1927, *Family Group*, GBP 2,940. LONDON, 8 July 1927, *Lot and his Daughters Leaving Sodom*, GBP 2,205. LONDON, 16 Dec 1927, *Man with Beard*, GBP 325. LONDON, 24 Feb 1928, *Reconciliation between Jacob and Esau*, GBP 1,312. LONDON, 27 April 1928, *Esther before Assuerus*, GBP 840. LONDON, 16 May 1928, *Suzanna Fourment*, GBP 2,650. LONDON, 17 and 18 May 1928, *Helena Fourment* (red chalk) GBP 6,825; *Raising of the Cross*, GBP 5,460; *Martyrdom of St Paul*, GBP 682. LONDON, 8 June 1928, *Anton Triest, Bishop of Ghent*, GBP 9,660. NEW YORK, 10 April 1929, *Head of One of the Three Kings*, USD 4,000. LONDON, 3 May 1929, *Mercury and Argus*, GBP 1,680. BERLIN, 20 Sept 1930, *Shepherd and Shepherdess*, DEM 3,100. NEW YORK, 22 Jan 1931, *St Mark*, USD 1,300; *St Luke*, USD 1,300. NEW YORK, 4 and 5 Feb 1931, *Mystic Marriage of St Catherine*, USD 2,100. NEW YORK, 7 and 8 Dec 1933, *Briseis Returned to Achilles*, USD 2,600. NEW YORK, 18 and 19 April 1934, *Cornelis de Vos and a Sibyl*, USD 1,225; *Victory Crowning a Prince Royal*, USD 1,900; *Village Brawl* (in collaboration with David Teniers) USD 550. LONDON, 1 June 1934, *Reconciliation between Jacon and Esau*, GBP 546. GENEVA, 28 Aug 1934, *Divination of William of Orange*, CHF 3,000. LONDON, 23 Nov 1934, *Heads of Two Peasants*, GBP 1,522. PARIS, 9 June 1936, *Hygieia*, FRF 44,000. LONDON, 10-14 July 1936, *Landscape* (pen and watercolour) GBP 892; *Faun Seated* (black chalk and sepia) GBP 1,102; *Three Studies for a 'Venus'* (pen) GBP 672. LONDON, 18 Dec 1936, *Conversion of Saul*, GBP 115. LONDON, 16 April 1937, *Return to Egypt*, GBP 304; *Princess Brigida Spinola-Doria*, GBP 2,835. LONDON, 28 May 1937, *Adoration of the Magi*, GBP 1,522. MUNICH, 28 Oct 1937, *Isabella Brandt*, DEM 18,000. BRUSSELS, 6 Dec 1937, *Drunken Silenus*, BEF 5,000. PARIS, 12 May 1938, *Prophet Elijah*, FRF 44,000. LONDON, 20 May 1938, *Woman with a Bouquet of Flowers*, GBP 340. LONDON, 31 March 1939, *Battle between Constantine and Maxentius*, GBP 1,575; *Church Interior*, GBP 262. LONDON, 9 June 1939, *Annunciation*, GBP 1,680. LONDON, 18 Dec 1940, *Mythological Scene*, GBP 430. NEW YORK, 17 Oct 1942, *Isabella Brandt*, USD 1,300. LONDON, 11 Dec 1942, *Battle of the Amazon Women*, GBP 1,995. NEW YORK, 5 April 1944, *Eleonora de'Medici*, USD 3,200. LONDON, 9 June 1944, *Pieter Pecquius*, GBP 16,800. NEW YORK, 20 Jan 1945, *Coronation of Roxane*, USD 7,000. NEW YORK, 15 Nov 1945, *Portrait presumed to be of the Artist's Son*, USD 5,800; *David and Goliath*, USD 6,000. NEW YORK, 20 and 21 Feb 1946, *Holy Family*, USD 15,000; *Portrait of a Gentleman*, USD 1,900. LONDON, 17 May 1946, *Holy Family with St Anne*, GBP 2,520. LONDON, 26 June 1946, *Virgin and Child with St Elisabeth and the Child St John*, GBP 1,700. NEW YORK, 24 Oct 1946, *Steer Hunt*, USD 3,800. BRUSSELS, 30 April 1947, *Steen Gardens*, BEF 300,000; *Equestrian Portrait of Philippe II*, BEF 110,000. BRUSSELS, 30 Jan 1950, *Magus of Ethiopia* (study for the painting of the 'Adoration of the Magi' for the church of St John in Malines) BEF 240,000; *Portrait Bust of a Woman*, BEF 50,000. PARIS, 10 Feb 1950, *Adoration of the Shepherds* (pen and wash, school of P. P. R.) FRF 14,000. NEW YORK, 2 March 1950, *Portrait of a Medici Princess* (c. 1604-05, painting) USD 1,200. LONDON, 26 April 1950, *Portrait of a Carmelite*, GBP 4,000. LUCERNE, 17 June 1950, *Boar Hunt* (sketch) CHF 4,500. LONDON, 28 July 1950, *Village Fete*, GBP 800. NICE, 8 Nov 1950, *Holy Family* (school of P. P. R.) FRF 30,000. LONDON, 19 Jan 1951, *Death of Hippolytus*, GBP 682. PARIS, 22 Jan 1951, *Portrait of a Man in Black with a Ruff* (workshop of P. P. R.) FRF 200,000. PARIS, 6 March 1951, *Mythological Scene* (school of P. P. R.) FRF 39,000. PARIS, 9 March 1951, *Young Woman Singing* (school of P. P. R.) FRF 48,000. HAMBURG, 29 March 1951, *Portrait Bust of Madame Goubau* (1614-1615, study for the painting in Tours) DEM 20,500. LONDON, 6 April 1951, *Landscape with Château, Forest, Peasants and Goats*, GBP 1,730. LONDON, 18 April 1951, *Portrait of the Archduke Albert of Austria*, GBP 1,500. PARIS, 20 April 1951, *Presentation (in the Temple)* (workshop of P. P. R.) FRF 29,000. BRUSSELS, 21 May 1951, *Adoration of the Shepherds* (sketch, attributed) BEF 19,000. LONDON, 23 May 1951, *Road to Calvary* (grisaille) GBP 5,000; *Moorish King* (1608-1609, study for an 'Adoration of the Magi' in the Prado) GBP 1,600. PARIS, 30 May 1951, *Frontal Study of a Fair-Haired Man*, FRF 100,000. PARIS, 14 June 1951, *Relaxation in the Country* (school of P. P. R.) FRF 50,000. LONDON, 29 June 1951, *Faun and Family in a Wooded Landscape*, GBP 336; *Death of Abel*, GBP 315. LONDON, 13 July 1951, *Stag Hunt*, GBP 1,995. PARIS, 5 Dec 1951, *Landscape in a Storm*, FRF 6,800,000. PARIS, 7 June 1955, *Roman Charity*, FRF 3,120,000. NEW YORK, 18 April 1956, *St Bartholomew*, USD 3,100. LONDON, 26 June 1957, *Adoration of the Magi*, GBP 14,000. PARIS, 4 June 1958, *Battle between Constantine and Maxentius*, FRF 7,000,000. LONDON, 2 July 1958, *Meeting of Abraham and Melchizedek*, GBP 33,000. LONDON, 24 June 1959, *Adoration of the Magi*, GBP 275,000. LONDON, 25 Nov 1960, *Portrait of Doctor Garnisius*, GBP 11,550. PARIS, 7 March 1961, *Deposition*, FRF 45,000. LONDON, 17 May 1961, *Portrait of an Old Woman*, GBP 2,100. NEW YORK, 24 Oct 1962, *Holy Family*, USD 75,000. LONDON, 2 July 1965, *Portrait presumed to be that of Eléonore de Bourbon, Princesse de Condé*, Gns 29,000. LONDON, 25 Nov 1966, *Judgment of Paris*, Gns 24,000. LONDON, 21 June 1968, *Marriage of Constantine*, Gns 49,000. LONDON, 3 Dec 1969, *Rape of the Sabine Women; Reconciliation between the Romans and the Sabines*, GBP 350,000. LONDON, 8 Dec 1971, *Magnanimity of Scipio Africanus*, GBP 59,000. LONDON, 8 Dec 1972, *Self-portrait*, Gns 130,000. LONDON, 21 March 1973, *Minerva and Hercules Pursuing Mars* (sketch) GBP 50,000. LONDON, 11 Dec 1974, *St Ignatius Loyola*, GBP 140,000. AMSTERDAM, 3 May 1976, *Christ on the Cross* (pen and wash/outline in black chalk heightened with white, 15 1/4 x 8in/38.7 x 20.2cm) NLG 90,000. LONDON, 7 July 1976, *Christ on the Cross* (oil on panel, 41 1/4 x 30in/105 x 76cm) GBP 20,000. AMSTERDAM, 21 March 1977, *Tomyris Presenting the Head of Cyrus* (black and grey ink drawing heightened with white gouache and reddish/black chalk, 15 1/2 x 23 1/2in/39.3 x 59.5cm) NLG 92,000. COLOGNE, 23 Nov 1977, *St Cecilia* (oil on panel, 31 x 22 3/4in/78.5 x 58cm) DEM 300,000. LONDON, 30 March 1979, *Neptune and Amphitriton* (c. 1617, oil on panel, 13 1/2 x 29 1/2in/34.3 x 74.9cm) GBP 38,000. AMSTERDAM, 29 Oct 1979, *Fall of the Damned (Study)* (black and white chalk on grey paper, 12 1/2 x 10 1/4in/32 x 26.3cm) NLG 115,000. BRUSSELS, 28 April 1982, *Portrait of Nicolas Rockox, Burgomaster of Antwerp* (oil on wood, 15 x 11 1/2in/38 x 29cm) BEF 1,000,000. LONDON, 9 Dec 1982, *Nude and Female Heads* (black and red chalk with trace of white chalk on brown/pale grey paper) GBP 100,000. LONDON, 3 July 1984, *Farm Courtyard with Peasant Threshing Wheat near a Cart* (c. 1615-1617, black, red, blue, yellow and pale-green chalk with touches of pen and brown ink on pale-grey paper, 10 x 16 1/4in/25.2 x 41.4cm) GBP 700,000. LONDON, 12 Dec 1984, *Last Supper* (c. 1632, oil on panel, grisaille, 24 1/4 x 19in/61.5 x 48.5cm) GBP 340,000. LONDON, 3 April 1985, *Martyrdom of St Ursula and the Eleven Thousand Maidens* (oil on panel, 25 1/4 x 19 1/2in/64 x 49.5cm) GBP 390,000. LONDON, 2 July 1986, *St Martin Sharing his Cloak* (oil on panel, 14 1/4 x 19in/36 x 48cm) GBP 48,000. LONDON, 6 July 1987, *Left Arm (anatomical study)* (black chalk, pen and brown ink, 10 x 7 1/2in/25.6 x 18.8cm) GBP 40,000. LONDON, 8 July 1988, *Portrait of a Bearded Dignitary Dressed in Black* (oil on panel, 35 3/4 x 29 1/4in/91 x 74.5cm) GBP 68,200; *Bust and Profile of Hercules* (oil on panel, 26 3/4 x 21in/68 x 52.5cm) GBP 506,000. HEIDELBERG, 14 Oct 1988, *St Bernard, supported by Angels, Sees the Apparition of the Mother of God with the Infant Jesus* (black chalk/white finish, 17 1/4 x 12in/44 x 30.5cm) DEM 1,600. NEW YORK, 11 Jan 1989, *Bust Portrait of a Bearded Man* (oil on panel, 27 1/2 x 21in/69.7 x 53.4cm) USD 528,000. NEW YORK, 2 June 1989, *Diana on the Hunt* (oil on panel, 9 1/2 x 21in/24 x 52.5cm) USD 462,000. LONDON, 7 July 1989, *Tears of Clytia* (oil on panel, 5 1/2 x 5 1/4in/14 x 13.3cm) GBP 71,500. LONDON, 8 Dec 1989, *Stag Hunt in a Forest at Daybreak* (oil on panel, 24 1/4 x 35 1/2in/61.8 x 90cm) GBP 3,300,000. LONDON, 14 Dec 1990, *Head and Shoulders of Bearded Man* (oil on panel, 20 x 15 1/4in/51 x 38.5cm) GBP 220,000. LONDON, 24 May 1991, *Fisherman Embracing Peasant Woman* (oil on panel, 31 x 23in/78.5 x 58.4cm) GBP 198,000. NEW YORK, 31 May 1991, *Three-quarters Portrait of a Seated Lady wearing a Gold-Embroidered Back Gown with a Ruff* (oil on canvas, 48 1/2 x 40in/123 x 101.5cm) USD 71,500. LONDON, 5 July 1991, *Portrait Bust of Jan Wildens in a Black Coat with Ruff* (oil on panel, 22 x 19in/56 x 48.3cm) GBP 77,000. AMSTERDAM, 25 Nov 1991, *Dance of Death* (ink and wash heightened with white, album of 44 drawings after Hans Holbein II, 3 1/4 x 4in/8.4 x 10.2 cm and smaller) NLG 713,000. LONDON, 6 July 1992, *Soldiers Demolishing a Bridge* (ink and wash/paper, 15 1/2 x 11 1/4in/39.3 x 28.4cm) GBP 7,480. LONDON, 11 Dec 1992, *Deposition* (oil on canvas, 51 1/2 x 51 1/4in/131 x 130.2cm) GBP 1,045,000. NEW YORK, 19 May 1993, *Head of Bearded Man* (oil on panel, 27 1/2 x 21in/69.7 x 53.4cm) USD 354,000. PARIS, 16 Dec 1993, *Scene from Roman History* (pen and brown ink, 7 3/4 x 11 1/2in/20 x 29.2cm) FRF 520,000. NEW YORK, 13 Jan 1994, *Presentation to the Temple* (oil on panel in grisaille, 24 1/4 x 18 1/2in/61.6 x 46.7cm) USD 1,652,500. MONACO, 20 June 1994, *Parable of the Vintners* (black chalk and ink heightened with white/beige paper, after Andrea del Sarto, 10 1/2 x 14 1/4in/26.5 x 36.5cm) FRF 666,000. AMSTERDAM, 15 Nov 1994, *Back View of Two Figures (study for 'Fall of the Damned')* (black and white chalk on buff-coloured paper, 12 1/2 x 10 1/4in/32 x 26.3cm) NLG 57,500. NEW YORK, 12 Jan 1995, *Portrait of Anthony van Dyck as a Young Man* (oil on panel, 14 1/4 x 10 1/4in/36.2 x 26cm) USD 882,500. LONDON, 6 Dec 1995, *Portrait of Archduke Albert of Austria* (oil on oak panel, 39 3/4 x 29 3/4in/101 x 75.4cm) GBP 111,500. NEW YORK, 30 Jan 1997, *Trophy* (oil on panel, 15 x 11 1/2in/38.1 x 29.2cm) USD 415,000. LONDON, 2 July 1997, *Assumption of the Virgin* (black chalk, pen and brown ink, brown and grey wash heightened with gouache and white and grey oils, black and dark-brown ink with traces of gold on four paper folios, in collaboration with Paulus Pontius, 25 3/4 x 16 3/4in/65.4 x 42.7cm) GBP 441,500. LONDON, 4 July 1997, *Portrait Bust of a Gentleman Dressed in Black* (oil on panel, 23 1/2 x 19 3/4in/59.5 x 50cm) GBP 78,500. AMSTERDAM, 11 Nov 1997, *Castration of Uranus* (pen, brown ink and wax heightened with white and gouache, 10 3/4 x 16 1/4in/27.6 x 41.1cm) NLG 44,840. LONDON, 3-4 Dec 1997, *Head of a Young Warrior* (oil on panel, study, 20 x 16 1/4in/51 x 41.5cm) GBP 265,500; *Male Head* (oil on panel, study, 19 1/4 x 14 1/2in/49.1 x 37cm) GBP 144,500. PARIS, 15 Dec 1997, *Landscape with Allegory of Military Honour and Virtue* (c. 1628?, oil on oak panel, 5 1/2 x 6 3/4in/14 x 17cm) FRF 1,120,000. NEW YORK, Jan 1998, *Salome Presented with the Head of St John the Baptist* (oil on panel, 37 x 40in/94 x 101.8cm) USD 5,502,500. LONDON, 6 July 1999, *Anatomical Studies: Three Nudes* (chalk, pen and ink wash, 11 x 7 ins / 29 x 19 cm) GBP 380,000. LONDON, 9 July 1999, *Bust-length Portrait of Princess Margherita Gonzaga* (oil on canvas, 26 x 20 ins / 65 x 52 cm) GBP 420,000. LONDON, 17 Dec 1999, *Democritus and Heraclitus* (oil on panel, 37 x 49 ins / 95 x 125 cm) GBP 600,000. NEW YORK, 28 Jan 2000, *Portrait of a Man as the God Mars* (oil on panel, 33 x 26 ins / 83 x 66 cm) USD 7,500,000. LONDON, 7 July 2000, *Diana and her Nymphs Hunting a Modello* (oil on panel, 11 x 22 ins / 27 x 57 cm) GBP 2,800,000. NEW YORK, 25 Jan 2001, *Infant Christ and St John the Baptist in an Extensive Landscape* (oil on canvas, 46 x 63 ins / 117 x 161 cm) USD 300,000. LONDON, 11 July 2001, *Last Supper* (pen and brown ink wash heightened with white over black chalk, 12 x 7 ins / 30 x 19 cm) GBP 160,000. LONDON, 12 July 2001, *Pan and Syrinx* (oil on panel, 16 x 24 ins / 40 x 61 cm) GBP 2,000,000. LONDON, 10 July 2002, *Portrait of a Man as the God Mars* (oil on panel, 33 x 26 ins / 83 x 66 cm) GBP 4,000,000. LONDON, 10 July 2002, *Massacre of the Innocents* (oil on panel, 56 x 72 ins / 142 x 182 cm) GBP 45,000,000. LONDON, 8 July 2003, *Young Nude in the Pose of the Spinario* (black and white chalk, 11 x 7 ins / 28 x 19 cm) GBP 150,000. ZURICH, 19 Sept 2003, *Adoration of the Magi* (oil on panel, 19 x 26 ins / 48 x 65 cm) CHF 400,000. ZURICH, 19 Sept 2003, *Adoration of the Magi* (oil on panel, 19 x 26 ins / 48 x 65 cm) CHF 400,000. LONDON, 7 July 2004, *Night Scene with an Old Lady Holding a Basket and Candle* (oil on panel, 31 x 25 ins / 79 x 64 cm) GBP 2,200,000.

RUBENS DES BATAILLES. See **RUBENS Arnold Frans**

RUBENSTEN, or Riebenstein

British, 18th century.

Died c. 1763, in London.

Painter. Portraits, Still-lifes.

Little is known about Rubensten other than that he lived in England for several years and died around 1763 in London. He was a portraitist and still-life painter who appears to have been retained for the main part to paint drapes and soft furnishing in compositions by other better-known artists. He was attached to St Martin's Lane Academy.

RUBERSTEIN, Barnet

American, 20th century.

Painter. Landscapes.

AUCTION RECORDS:

NEW YORK, 21 Feb 1990, *View of 69 Harvey Street, Cambridge (Massachusetts)* (1982, pencil/paper, 22 1/2 x 30 ins / 57.2 x 76.3 cm) USD 2,090.

RUBERT, Joaquin Bernardo

Spanish, 19th century.

Born 1804, in Valencia.

Painter. Flowers.

Joaquin Bernardo Rubert studied at the Valencia academy.

MUSEUMS AND GALLERIES:

VALENCIA: *Flowers*.

RUBERT, Pedro
Spanish, 15th century.
Active from 1402 to 1410.
Painter.
Pedro Rubert produced paintings in the church of S Catalina in Valencia.

RUBERTI, Domenico. See **ROBERTI**

RUBERTI, Giovanni Francesco. See **RUBERTO**

RUBERTO. See also **ROBERTO**

RUBERTO, Giovanni Francesco, or Ruberti, called della Grana
Italian, 15th - 16th century.
Active in Mantua from 1482 to 1526.
Medallist.
Giovanni Francesco Ruberto produced a medal bearing the effigy of Gian Francesco II Gonzaga, dated 1484. He was also a goldsmith.

RUBEUS. See also **ROSSI** and **ROSSO**

RUBEUS, Bartolomeo, or Rosso or Brasone or Braxone
Italian, 16th century.
Died 1517.
Active in Ferrara.
Painter.
Bartolomeo Rubeus was the son of Domenico Rubeus. He worked for Lucrezia Borgia and for Ferrara Cathedral.

RUBEUS, Domenico, or Rosso or Brasoni or Brasone
Italian, 15th century.
Died 1486.
Active in Ferrara.
Painter.
Domenico Rubeus was the pupil of Titolivio da Padova, and the father of the painter Bartolomeo Rubeus. He produced the paintings in the Palazzo Schifanoia, in Ferrara.

RUBEUS, Johann Anton. See **ROSSI Giovanni Antonio de'**

RUBEZAK, Jan de. See **RUBCZAK Jan de**

RUBIALES, Francesco or Pedro de. See **RUVIALE**

RUBIALES, Miguel
Spanish, 17th century.
Born c. 1642, in Madrid; died 1702, in Madrid.
Sculptor.
Miguel Rubiales was a pupil of Alonso de los Ríos. He made a wooden sculpture of the *Descent from the Cross* in the church of Sta Cruz in Madrid.

RUBICANO, Cola or Nicola, or Rabicano or Rapicano or Ribicano
Italian, 15th century.
Born in Amantea (Calabria); died 1488, in Naples.
Illuminator.
Cola Rubicano worked in the court of Naples. Several books illuminated by him are in the Bibliothèque Nationale in Paris and the university library in Valencia. He was the father of Nardo Rubicano.

RUBICANO, Nardo
Italian, 15th century.
Active at the end of the 15th century.
Illuminator.
Nardo Rubicano was the son and pupil of Cola Rubicano. Like his father, he worked in the court of Naples.

RUBIDGE, Joseph William
British, 19th century.
Active in London during the first half of the 19th century.
Miniaturist. Portraits.
Joseph Rubidge was an exhibitor at the Royal Academy in London in 1823 and 1824.

RUBIN, Albert
Bulgarian Jewish, 20th century.
Born 1887, in Sofia; died 1956.
Active in France from 1909.
Painter, pastellist. Figures, portraits, landscapes.
Rubin studied at the school of fine arts in Sofia from 1904 to 1906. He participated in the foundation of the Bezalel school in Jerusalem from 1906 to 1909, under the direction of Professor Schatz. He studied at the École des Beaux-Arts in Paris from 1909 to 1916, and was a pupil in the studio of Fernand Cormon. After World War II, he was a founding member of the Association des Artistes Peintres et Sculpteurs Juifs in France. He executed mostly portraits of well-known figures of his time.

Rubin exhibited at the Salon des Artistes Français, of which he was a member, and received a distinction in 1950. He was a member of several associations.

RUBIN, Auguste, the Younger
French, 19th century.
Born in Grenoble; died 1909, in Paris.
Sculptor.
Auguste Rubin was the student of his brother, Hippolyte Rubin. He first exhibited at the Salon in 1878. He produced some busts.

RUBIN, Francesco
Italian, 18th century.
Active during the second half of the 18th century.
Painter.
Francesco Rubin was a pupil at the academy in Turin and a member of the Accademia di San Luca in Rome in 1797.

RUBIN, Frank
Danish, 20th century.
Born 1918, in Copenhagen.
Painter, engraver.
Frank Rubin participated in *De Bonnard à Baselitz: Dix Ans d'enrichissements du cabinet des estampes 1978-1988* (*From Bonnard to Baselitz: A Decade of Acquisitions by the Prints Collection 1978-1988*), an exhibition held in 1993 at the Bibliothèque Nationale in Paris.
MUSEUMS AND GALLERIES:
PARIS (BNF): *Sunday* (1983, dry-point).
AUCTION RECORDS:
COPENHAGEN, 4 March 1992, *Composition* (1948, oil on canvas, 15 1/4 x 22 ins / 39 x 55 cm) DKK 4,200.

RUBIN, Hippolyte
French, 19th century.
Born 10 May 1830, in Grenoble.
Active in Paris.
Sculptor.
Hippolyte Rubin featured at the Paris Salon from 1857 to 1868. He made a large number of statuettes. His works include the *Bust of Monnier* for the prefecture of l'Isère. He also produced a *Holy Family*, a low relief for the chapel of the Great Charterhouse.

RUBIN, Johann Georg
Austrian, 18th century.
Born 1679; died 1725.
Active in Olmütz (now Olomouc, Czech Republic).
Sculptor.

RUBIN, Reuven

Romanian, 20th century.

Born 13 November 1893, in Galati; died 1974, in Tel Aviv.

Active in Israel from 1912.

Painter (including gouache), watercolourist, engraver (wood), lithographer. Figures, portraits, self-portraits, scenes with figures, landscapes, still-lifes, flowers, animals. Murals, stage costumes and sets, designs for stained glass.

Rubin studied at the Bezalel academy in Jerusalem for a year. Then in 1913-1914, he attended the École des Beaux-Arts and the Académie Colarossi in Paris. Though he went back to Romania for seven years, he resided in New York for several months. He then moved to Tel Aviv definitively in 1922. In 1948, he was named Ambassador of Israel to Romania. He received the Prize of Israel in 1973.

Rubin published an album of wood engravings *The God-Seekers* and an album of lithographs *Faces of Israel*. He directed the production and designed the costumes for Molière's *Le Malade imaginaire* (*The Imaginary Invalid*), H. Berner's *The Deluge*, and R.B. Hoffman's *Jacob's Dream*. He executed a mural painting for the Knesset Building and stained glass windows for the new presidential residence in Jerusalem. During the 1920s, he attracted attention with his pastoral scenes in a Naive style, in which mythological figures from the Old Testament evolve in a timeless Judaea.

Rubin participated in collective exhibitions, including: Tower of David in Jerusalem (1924-1927); Tel Aviv (1926, 1927); Museum of Modern Art, New York (1942); Venice Biennale (1948, 1950, 1952); Institute of Contemporary Art, Boston, Carnegie Institute, Pittsburgh, the Metropolitan Museum of Art, New York, Albright-Knox Art Gallery, Buffalo, Museum of Art, Baltimore, and Los Angeles County Museum of Art (1953); Art Council of Great Britain, London (1958); Musée National d'Art Moderne, Paris (1960); Museum of Israel, Jerusalem (1965, 1972); Museum of Modern Art, Haifa (1965, 1973); and Jewish Museum, New York (1981). He had solo exhibitions of his work, including: New York (1921); Tel Aviv (1923-1924); Tower of David, Jerusalem (1924); Tel Aviv Museum (1933, 1947, 1955); Bezalel Museum, Jerusalem (1938); Los Angeles and San Francisco (1941); New York (1942); Art Center of Oklahoma City (1944); London (1957); Tel Aviv Museum and Museum of Israel in Jerusalem (1966); and Museum of Modern Art, Haifa (1986).

BIBLIOGRAPHY:

Rubin, exhibition catalogue, Muzeon Yisrael, Yerushalayim [Jérusalem], Muzeon Tel Aviv, Tel Aviv, 1966. *Rubin*, exhibition leaflet, Musée d'Art Moderne, Haifa, 1986. Kampf, Avram, *Chagall to Kitaj: Jewish Experience in 20th Century Art*, Barbican Art Gall., London, 1990.

MUSEUMS AND GALLERIES:

TEL AVIV (Rubin Mus.).

AUCTION RECORDS:

NEW YORK, 22 Oct 1976, *Landscape of Israel* (oil on canvas, 26 x 32 ins / 66 x 81 cm) USD 14,000. LONDON, 3 Dec 1976, *Jacob's Dream* (watercolour and pen, 16 1/4 x 11 3/4 ins / 41.5 x 30 cm) GBP 1,000. NEW YORK, 21 Oct 1977, *Orchard Scene* (1958, oil on canvas, 19 3/4 x 25 3/4 ins / 50 x 65.5 cm) USD 13,000. NEW YORK, 18 Oct 1979, *Horses* (mixed media/paper, 26 x 20 ins / 66 x 50.5 cm) USD 4,000. NEW YORK, 8 Nov 1979, *Flute Player* (pen, 12 3/4 x 9 1/2 ins / 32.4 x 24 cm) USD 1,000. NEW YORK, 8 Nov 1979, *Still-life by the Window* (c. 1960, oil on canvas, 36 1/4 x 28 1/2 ins / 92 x 72.5 cm) USD 30,000. LONDON, 1 July 1981, *Three Figures* (1923, oil on canvas, 33 x 27 1/4 ins / 84 x 69.2 cm) GBP 12,000. NEW YORK, 4 Nov 1982, *Landscape of Galilee* (1930, watercolour and gouache) USD 6,000. NEW YORK, 16 Nov 1983, *Olive Harvest* (1967, oil on canvas, 21 1/4 x 28 3/4 ins / 54 x 73.2 cm) USD 36,000. NEW YORK, 15 Dec 1983, *Horses* (Indian ink, 22 1/2 x 31 ins / 57.3 x 79 cm) USD 2,100. NEW YORK, 31 May 1984, *Safed Family* (watercolour/pencil outlines, 20 x 14 3/4 ins / 51 x 37.5 cm) USD 3,700. NEW YORK, 21 Feb 1985, *Rabbi Holding a Torah* (watercolour and Indian ink, 30 x 20 ins / 76.3 x 51.1 cm) USD 3,100. TEL AVIV, 2 June 1986, *Balfour Street, Tel Aviv* (1924, oil on canvas, 23 1/2 x 28 3/4 ins / 60 x 73 cm) USD 47,000. NEW YORK, 18 Feb 1988, *Miracle of the Fishes* (1935, ink/paper, 22 x 15 ins / 56 x 38 cm) USD 2,420. TEL AVIV, 26 May 1988, *Olive Grove* (oil on canvas, 25 1/2 x 32 ins / 65 x 81.5 cm) USD 33,000; *Potato Eaters* (1920, bronze, l. 19 3/4 ins / 50 cm h. 11 1/2 ins/29 cm) USD 6,600. NEW YORK, 6 Oct 1988, *Road to Safed* (oil on canvas, 13 x 16 1/4 ins / 33.2 x 41.4 cm) USD 22,000. LONDON, 19 Oct 1988, *Road to Safed* (oil on canvas, 19 3/4 x 26 ins / 50.2 x 65.2 cm) GBP 14,300. TEL AVIV, 2 Jan 1989, *Masks* (gouache and watercolour, 15 3/4 x 12 1/2 ins / 40 x 31.5 cm) USD 2,200. NEW YORK, 16 Feb 1989, *Road to Safed* (oil on canvas, 21 1/4 x 28 3/4 ins / 54 x 73 cm) USD 44,000. TEL AVIV, 30 May 1989, *Milkman* (1928, oil on canvas, 36 1/4 x 28 3/4 ins / 92 x 73 cm) USD 74,800. LONDON, 28 Nov 1989, *Fisherman* (oil on canvas, 26 x 20 ins / 66 x 51 cm) GBP 33,000. TEL AVIV, 3 Jan 1990, *Gate at Ein Karem* (1929, oil on canvas, 23 3/4 x 29 ins / 60.5 x 73.5 cm) USD 74,800. NEW YORK, 21 Feb 1990, *Florida Landscape* (oil on canvas, 25 1/2 x 33 1/4 ins / 64.8 x 84.2 cm) USD 42,900. TEL AVIV, 31 May 1990, *Spring in Ain Karem* (1956, oil on canvas, 17 3/4 x 32 ins / 45 x 81.5 cm) USD 52,800. PARIS, 21 June 1990, *Landscape* (oil on canvas, 23 1/2 x 29 ins / 60 x 73.5 cm) FRF 220,000. CALAIS, 8 July 1990, *Galilean Fisherman* (watercolour and ink, 25 1/2 x 19 3/4 ins / 65 x 50 cm) FRF 41,000. NEW YORK, 2 Oct 1990, *Arrival in Safed* (oil on canvas, 25 3/4 x 32 ins / 65.4 x 81.3 cm) USD 60,500. TEL AVIV, 1 Jan 1991, *Fisherman* (pastel, 13 x 9 ins / 33 x 23 cm) USD 3,080. NEW YORK, 15 Feb 1991, *Gathering of Olives* (1967, oil on canvas, 25 1/2 x 32 ins / 64.8 x 81.2 cm) USD 35,750. TEL AVIV, 12 June 1991, *Ancient Olive Trees* (oil on canvas, 23 3/4 x 29 ins / 60.5 x 73.5 cm) USD 50,600. CALAIS, 7 July 1991, *Vase of Flowers in Front of the Window* (watercolour, 9 1/2 x 7 1/2 ins / 24 x 19 cm) FRF 28,000. TEL AVIV, 26 Sept 1991, *Maternity* (oil on canvas, 25 1/4 x 29 1/4 ins / 64 x 74 cm) USD 85,800. NEW YORK, 25 Feb 1992, *Self-portrait* (1924, oil on canvas/synthetic resin, 35 3/4 x 25 ins / 90.8 x 63.5 cm) USD 90,200. NEW YORK, 10 Nov 1992, *In the Negev* (1960, coloured ink and wash/paper/cardboard, 31 x 20 1/2 ins / 77.8 x 52 cm) USD 6,600. TEL AVIV, 14 April 1993, *Old Arabian House* (oil on canvas, 20 x 25 3/4 ins / 51 x 65.3 cm) USD 92,700. NEW YORK, 4 Nov 1993, *Purple Lilacs* (1945, oil on canvas, 32 x 26 ins / 81.3 x 66 cm) USD 79,500. TEL AVIV, 4 April 1994, *Vase of Flowers with Hills in the Distance* (oil on canvas, 62 1/2 x 38 1/2 ins / 159 x 97.5 cm) USD 200,500. TEL AVIV, 30 June 1994, *Self-portrait in the Courtyard* (1925, oil on canvas/synthetic resin, 35 1/2 x 24 1/2 ins / 90 x 62.5 cm) USD 177,250. NEW YORK, 10 Nov 1994, *Still-life with Landscape* (oil on canvas, 28 3/4 x 23 1/2 ins / 73 x 59.7 cm) USD 81,700. LONDON, 29 Nov 1994, *Landscape of the Outskirts of Nazareth* (1937, oil on canvas, 25 1/2 x 32 ins / 65 x 81 cm) GBP 34,500. TEL AVIV, 22 April 1995, *Market Scene* (oil on canvas, 25 1/2 x 32 ins / 65 x 81 cm) USD 118,000. TEL AVIV, 11 April 1996, *Storm over the Negev* (oil on canvas, 29 1/2 x 37 1/2 ins / 75 x 95 cm) USD 112,500. NEW YORK, 1 May 1996, *Spring in the Outskirts of Safed* (1966, oil on canvas, 25 1/2 x 36 1/2 ins / 64.8 x 92.7 cm) USD 92,700. TEL AVIV, 30 Sept 1996, *Biblical Apparition* (1968, oil on canvas, 36 1/2 x 28 3/4 ins / 92.5 x 73 cm) USD 68,500. TEL AVIV, 7 Oct 1996, *On the Road to Safed* (watercolour and pencil, 13 1/2 x 11 ins / 34 x 27 cm) USD 14,375; *Jaffa* (c. 1923, oil on canvas, 24 x 18 1/4 ins / 61 x 46.3 cm) USD 67,400. NEW YORK, 14 Nov 1996, *On the Road to Safed* (1965-1966, oil on canvas, 29 x 36 1/4 ins / 73.4 x 92.1 cm) USD

40,250. TEL AVIV, 12 Jan 1997, *Road to Rosh Pinah* (1951, oil on canvas, 23 1/2 x 29 ins / 60 x 73.5 cm) USD 60,650; *Road to Safed* (c. 1955, oil on canvas, 19 3/4 x 27 1/2 ins / 50 x 70 cm) USD 56,250; *Family and Child* (pencil, 9 1/4 x 12 ins / 23.5 x 30.5 cm) USD 4,850. TEL AVIV, 26 April 1997, *Horseman with Bouquet* (1923, oil on canvas, 32 x 26 ins / 81.3 x 66 cm) USD 283,000. NEW YORK, 14 May 1997, *Spring in Galilee* (1965, oil on canvas, 28 1/2 x 36 1/2 ins / 72.7 x 93 cm) USD 48,875. TEL AVIV, 23 Oct 1997, *Scene in the Holy Land* (1923-1924) USD 167,500. TEL AVIV, 25 Oct 1997, *Ruth, the Moabite* (oil on canvas, 18 x 15 ins / 45.9 x 38 cm) USD 28,750.

RUBIN, Yefime or Yefim, or Roubin
Russian, 20th century.
Born 1912 or 1919, in Oriopl.
Painter. Portraits, landscapes, still-lifes.
Socialist Realism.

Rubin studied with Aleksandr Osmerkin at the academy of fine arts in Leningrad (now St Petersburg). He also studied under the direction of Aleksandr Avilov. He was a member of the union of the artists of the USSR.

MUSEUMS AND GALLERIES:
KOSTROMA (Mus. of Russian Art) - MOSCOW (Ministry of Culture) - MOSCOW (State Tretyakov Gal.) - MURMANSK (Mus. of Contemporary Soviet Art) - ROSTOV (MFA) - ST PETERSBURG (Academy) - ST PETERSBURG (Gosudarstvennyj Russkij Muz.).

AUCTION RECORDS:
PARIS, 18 Feb 1991, *I'm Learning to Read* (1948, oil on canvas, 26 1/2 x 32 1/4 ins / 67 x 82 cm) FRF 5,600. PARIS, 6 Dec 1991, *Harvest* (1949, oil on canvas, 29 1/4 x 39 3/4 ins / 74 x 101 cm) FRF 7,000. LONDON, 11 April 1997, *Skiers on the Slopes* (1965, oil on canvas, 38 1/2 x 28 1/2 ins / 97.7 x 72.4 cm) GBP 747.

RUBIN-BEAUFILS, Olga Maria
French, 20th century.
Painter, designer. Designs for tapestries.

RUBINACCI, Pompeo
Argentinian, 20th century.
Born 1893, in Buenos Aires; died 1972, in Geneva.
Painter. Still-lifes.

AUCTION RECORDS:
ROME, 31 May 1990, *Still-life with Books and Trompe-l'Oeil* (oil on canvas, 31 1/2 x 39 1/4 ins / 80 x 100 cm) ITL 3,000,000.

RUBINGHER, Moise
Romanian Jewish, 20th century.
Born 25 April 1911, in Leova.
Active in Germany since 1963.
Painter, draughtsman, illustrator, watercolourist.
Portraits, landscapes. Stage costumes and sets.

Rubingher lived and worked in Düsseldorf. He executed numerous scenic décors, creating sets and costumes for productions ranging from the works of Shakespeare to Tolstoy to Garcia Lorca. As a painter, he depicted mostly portraits and trees. He took part in collective exhibitions in Romania, Germany and Israel. He had solo exhibitions, beginning in 1969, in Düsseldorf and in Israel.

BIBLIOGRAPHY:
Jianou, Ionel, *Romanian Artists and the West*, American Romanian Academy of Arts and Sciences, Los Angeles, 1986.

RUBINI, Agostino
Italian, 16th century.
Died before 25 February 1595.
Active in Vicenza (Veneto).
Sculptor.

Agostino Rubini was the brother of Andrea Rubini and the brother and assistant of Vigilio Rubini. He sculpted the low reliefs, *Virgin* and *Angel of the Annunciation*, on the Rialto Bridge in Venice.

RUBINI, Andrea
Italian, 16th - 17th century.
Active in Vicenza (Veneto).
Painter.

Andrea Rubini was the brother of Agostino and Vigilio Rubini.

RUBINI, Antonio. See **RUBINO**

RUBINI, Giovanni Battista
Italian, 18th century.
Born in Cortemaggiore, near Piacenza; died c. 1752.
Painter.

Giovanni Battista Rubini was a pupil of Santo Prunati. He painted altarpieces for the churches of Castione della Presolana, Piacenza and Verona.

RUBINI, Lorenzo
Italian, 16th century.
Born in Vicenza (Veneto).
Active from 1550 to 1568.
Sculptor.

Lorenzo Rubini was the father of Andrea, Agostino and Vigilio Rubini. He produced sculptures in the Basilica Palladiana, and in the Villa Rotonda in Vicenza.

RUBINI, Pietro
Italian, 18th century.
Born c. 1700; died after 1765.
Painter.

Pietro Rubini worked in Parma and painted altarpieces for churches there.

RUBINI, Vigilio
Italian, 16th - 17th century.
Born in Riva (Trentino-Alto Adige).
Active from 1583 to 1608.
Sculptor.

Vigilio Rubini was the son of Lorenzo Rubini, and the brother of Andrea and Agostino Rubini. He was the pupil of Alessandro Vittoria and was his assistant in Venice. He worked on Vittoria's tomb in the church of S Zaccaria in Venice.

RUBINO
Italian, 17th century.
Active in Piedmont c. 1650.
Painter.

Rubino painted a *Madonna with Saints* for the church of S Vito in Treviso.

RUBINO, Antonio, or Rubini
Italian, 20th century.
Born 15 May 1880, in San Remo; died 1 July 1964
Painter, draughtsman, illustrator. Landscapes.

Antonio Rubino wrote and illustrated a number of fairy stories and tales of imagination as well as providing illustrations for several magazines. He was also a writer.

RUBINO, Edoardo
Italian, 19th - 20th century.
Born 8 December 1871, in Turin; died 1954.
Sculptor.

Edoardo Rubino studied at the academy of fine art in Turin. He carved many statues of eminent people for various Italian towns as well as sculpting tombs and mausoleums.

MUSEUMS AND GALLERIES:
BOLOGNA (Gal.) - FLORENCE (Gal.) - LIMA: *Madonna* - ROME (Gal. Nazionale d'Arte Moderna): *Bust of Signora N. Remmer* - TURIN (Mus. Civico): *Bust of an Inhabitant of the Gressonay Valley*.

AUCTION RECORDS:
ROME, 19 April 1994, *Anna Maria* (gilt bronze, 11 3/4 x 9 3/4 x 4 3/4 ins / 30 x 25 x 12 cm) ITL 1,610,000. MILAN, 5 June 2001, *Face of a Girl* (marble, h. 13 ins / 34 cm) ITL 5,500,000. LON-

DON, 8 July 2003, *Bust of a Woman* (dark brown patinated bronze, h. 16 ins / 40 cm) GBP 8,000. FLORENCE, 9 Dec 2003, *Face of a Woman* (bronze, h. 17 ins / 42 cm) EUR 3,400. SYDNEY, 15 May 2004, *Head of Medusa* (bronze, h. 16 ins / 40 cm, w. 16 ins/40 cm) AUD 14,000.

RUBINO, Giovanni Angelo
Italian, 17th century.
Painter.

Giovanni Angelo Rubino painted altarpieces for churches in Naples in the first half of the 17th century.

RUBINO, Gustavo
Italian, 17th century.
Born in Naples.
Active during the first half of the 17th century.
Landscape artist.

Gustavo Rubino was a pupil of Attilio Simonetti.

RUBINO, Salvatore
Italian, 19th - 20th century.
Born 1847, in Salemi; died 1910?.
Active in Palermo.
Painter, sculptor. Portraits.

Salvatore Rubino studied first at the academy in Palermo thanks to a bursary from the Salemi town council, then with the painter Salvatore La Forte and finally with Morelli in Naples. He specialised in portraits, also painting a number of historical subjects.

RUBINOS, Domingo de
Spanish, 17th century.
Sculptor (wood).

Domingo de Rubinos carved the choir screen in the Franciscan church in Betanzos.

RUBINS, Harry W.
American, 19th - 20th century.
Born 15 November 1865, in Buffalo (New York State); died 1934.
Painter, engraver. Murals.

Harry W. Rubins studied at the Art Institute of Chicago and was a member of the Chicago Society of Etchers. His murals can be seen on many American public monuments.

MUSEUMS AND GALLERIES:
NEW YORK (Public Library).

RUBINS, Nancy
American, 20th - 21st century.
Born 1952, in Naples (Texas).
Draughtswoman, installation artist.

Nancy Rubins obtained her Masters Degree in Fine Arts from the University of California, Davis. She teaches at the University of California, Los Angeles.

Everyday waste items feature in Rubins's work - for example worn out household gadgets, large rubbish containers, concrete blocks, mattresses, pieces of crashed aeroplanes and sometimes dead trees - which explains the monumental scale of her constructions. Rubins works with the balance and dynamic relationship between opposing forces, exploiting points of tension between pieces assembled using the technique of 'tensegrity' developed by the American artist Kenneth Snelson.

Her work has been shown in group exhibitions, including *Helter Skelter* at the Museum of Contemporary Art, Los Angeles in 1992, *Aperto 93* at the Venice Biennale in 1993, *Country-Sculpture* at Le Consortium, Dijon (France) in 1994 and the Whitney Biennial, New York in 1995. Her solo shows include those at the Paul Kasmin Gallery, New York in 1993 and 1997, *Building and Airplane Parts. A Large Growth for San Diego* at the Museum of Contemporary Art, San Diego (California) in 1994 and at the Museum of Contemporary Art, Los Angeles in 2003.

BIBLIOGRAPHY:
Building and Airplane Parts. A Large Growth for San Diego, exhibition catalogue, Museum of Contemporary Art, San Diego (CA), 1994. Volk, Gregory, *'Nancy Rubins'* in *Art News*, periodical, New York, Summer 1995.

MUSEUMS AND GALLERIES:
DIJON (FRAC Bourgogne): *Table and Airplane Parts* (1993).

RUBINSKY, Igor
Russian, 20th century.
Born 1919.
Painter. Portraits, genre scenes.
Socialist Realism.

Rubinsky studied with Sergei Gerasimov at the V.I. Surikov state art institute (MGKhI) in Moscow, and later at the academy of fine arts in Leningrad (now St Petersburg). He was a member of the society of Moscow painters and the union of painters of the USSR.

Rubinsky has painted numerous collective portraits, scenes of World War II, and portraits of Northern Fleet fishermen. His works include: *The Supporters Arrive*, *The War Began*, and *Awarding the Diplomas*. He participated in official exhibitions in the republics and in national exhibitions.

BIBLIOGRAPHY:
Tableaux soviétiques, auction catalogue, Salle Drouot, Paris, 3 October 1990.

AUCTION RECORDS:
PARIS, 23 March 1992, *Basket of Lilacs* (oil on canvas, 23 1/4 x 31 1/2 ins / 59 x 80 cm) FRF 5,200. PARIS, 27 May 1992, *Children in Front of a Dacha* (oil on canvas, 31 1/2 x 48 ins / 80 x 121 cm) FRF 9,500. PARIS, 16 Nov 1992, *Puppy and Children* (oil on canvas, 27 3/4 x 21 3/4 ins / 70.5 x 55.5 cm) FRF 3,800.

RUBINSTEIN, David
Ukrainian, 20th century.
Born 1902, in Odessa.
Painter. Figure compositions, portraits.

Rubinstein studied under T. Dvornikov and I. Mormoné at the school of fine arts in Odessa from 1914 to 1919. He continued in T. Fraerman's studio in at the institute of fine arts in Odessa until 1929. He was a member of the union of painters of the USSR from 1933. He took part in World War II between 1941 and 1945 and settled in Moscow after his military service. His preferred artform was portraiture.

Rubinstein participated in numerous national exhibitions from 1930. Solo exhibitions of his work were presented in 1938, 1954, and 1976.

BIBLIOGRAPHY:
Tableaux soviétiques, auction catalogue, Salle Drouot, Paris, 3 October 1990.

MUSEUMS AND GALLERIES:
MOSCOW (State Tretyakov Gal.) - PERM (MFA) - ST PETERSBURG (Gosudarstvennyj Russkij Muz.) - TASHKENT (Gosudarstvennyj Muzej Iskusstv/National Art Gallery).

AUCTION RECORDS:
PARIS, 3 Oct 1990, *Morning on the Black Sea* (1960, oil on canvas, 23 1/2 x 35 1/2 ins / 60 x 90 cm) FRF 16,000. PARIS, 25 Nov 1991, *Concerto for Violin and Orchestra* (1949, watercolour/paper, 11 3/4 x 16 1/4 ins / 30 x 41 cm) FRF 8,000. PARIS, 20 May 1992, *Woman in Red* (1956, pastel/paper, 20 1/2 x 16 1/4 ins / 52 x 41 cm) FRF 9,500. PARIS, 5 Nov 1992, *Orchestra Conductor* (watercolour/paper, 31 1/2 x 23 1/4 ins / 80 x 59 cm) FRF 7,000.

RUBIO, Antonio
Spanish, 17th century.
Died 2 June 1653, in Toledo.
Painter.

Antonio Rubio was a pupil of Antonio Pizarro. He worked at the chapterhouse in Toledo in 1645.

RUBIO, Joaquín
Spanish, 19th century.
Born 1818, in Algeciras; died 28 December 1866, in Murcia.
Painter.

RUBIO, Luigi or Louis
Italian, 18th - 19th century.
Born at the end of the 18th century, in Rome; died 2 August 1882, in Florence.
Painter. Religious subjects, genre scenes, portraits, figures.

Luigi Rubio began studying in Rome at the Accademia di San Luca, of which he became a member in 1827. He then went to Paris, where he worked with Léon Cogniet, exhibiting paintings, particularly portraits, at the Paris Salon from 1831 to 1867. He lived in Geneva for about 20 years and exhibited there in 1851, 1856, 1859 and 1862. He produced four paintings, including *St Helena, St Stephen* and *Christ and the Virgin*, for the Russian church in Geneva.

Rubio travelled a great deal and while in Constantinople painted the portrait of *Sultan Abdul Medjid Khan*, which was shown at the 1848 Salon. He also visited Russia, where he painted the portrait of the Tsar. In 1870 he was appointed professor at the academy of fine arts in Florence. The famous *Portrait of Frédéric Chopin* in the Alfred Cortot collection is attributed to him.

L Rubio
Genève

MUSEUMS AND GALLERIES:
ANTWERP: *Portrait of the Painter Calame* - FLORENCE (Uffizi): *Self-portrait* - GENEVA: *Orange-picking in Sorrento* - VERSAILLES (Trianon): *The Marriage of Salvator Rosa* - WARSAW (Muz. Narodowe): *Portrait of Leonard Chodzko.*

AUCTION RECORDS:
PARIS, 14 June 1979, *Portrait of Sultan Abdul Medjid Khan* (1847, oil on canvas, 25½ x 22in/65 x 55cm) FRF 6,600. NEW YORK, 19 July 1990, *Odalisque* (oil on canvas, 25¾ x 22in/65.4 x 55.9cm) USD 3,300. PARIS, 24 May 1991, *Woman with Pitcher* (oil on canvas, 28¾ x 36¼in/73 x 92cm) FRF 44,000. PARIS, 13 April 1992, *Portrait of Sultan Abdul Medjid Khan* (1847, oil on canvas, 25½ x 21¼in/65 x 54cm) FRF 68,000.

RUBIO, Ricard
Spanish, 20th century.
Painter (including mixed media). Figures.

Rubio exhibits solo, notably in 1979 at the Galeria d'Art Dau al Set in Barcelona. His figurative compositions and abstract landscapes are inspired by Roman and Byzantine tradition.

RUBIO, Rosa María
Spanish, 20th - 21st century.
Born 1961, in Madrid.
Painter (mixed media). Scenes with figures, landscapes.

Rosa María Rubio was a pupil at the school of fine arts in Madrid. She produces poetic, material compositions using scraping, card collages, paper, plates of wood, cardboard, sand, natural or synthetic pigments, objects and stamps, very much in the tradition of Tápies. Faint drawings and symbols are inscribed on this dense surface, with washed-out shades dominated by white, evoking primitive landscapes, telling 'simple' stories, describing a world close to childhood.

She very frequently exhibits in Madrid, notably in 1986 at the school of fine arts, and has also shown work in Bilbao in 1982; at the municipal museum in Salamanca in 1986; in Valencia in 1988, and in France: Toulouse in 1985 and Paris in 1990. She has received numerous prizes and distinctions in France.

BIBLIOGRAPHY:
Catálogo nacionál de arte contemporaneo 1990-1991, Ibérico 2Mil, Barcelona, 1990-1991.

AUCTION RECORDS:
PARIS, 18 June 1990, *Untitled* (1989, 63¾ x 51¼ ins / 162 x 130 cm) FRF 10,000. PARIS, 9 Dec 1990, *Untitled* (oil and graphite/canvas, 64¼ x 38¼ ins / 163 x 97 cm) FRF 12,000.

RUBIO EL. See **HERRERA**

RUBIO POLO, Enrique
Spanish, 20th - 21st century.
Born 1959, in Valencia.
Painter, sculptor, mixed media.

Enrique Rubio Polo has shown his work in group and solo exhibitions: 1988, fine arts group in Valencia; 1989, Sala Parés in Barcelona; 1990, Granada; and the Salón de la Primavera in Valencia.

RUBIO Y SÁNCHEZ, Adolfo
Spanish, 19th century.
Born March 1841, in Murcia; died 22 January 1867, in Murcia.
Painter. Genre scenes.

Adolfo Rubio y Sánchez was the son and pupil of Joaquin Rubio. There are paintings by him in the Murcia provincial museum.

RUBIO Y SÁNCHEZ, Roberto
Spanish, 19th century.
Born 1845, in Murcia; died 1873, in Havana.
Draughtsman.

Roberto Rubio y Sánchez was the brother of Adolfo Rubio.

RUBIO Y VILLEGAS, José
Spanish, 19th century.
Born in Madrid; died 2 September 1861, in Madrid.
Painter, illustrator.

José Rubio y Villegas was a pupil of J. Aparicio.

MUSEUMS AND GALLERIES:
MADRID (Mus. de Arte Moderno).

RUBIRA, Andrés Nicolas de, or Rovira or Ruvira
Spanish, 18th century.
Born in Escacena del Campo; died 29 February 1760, in Seville.
Painter. Historical subjects, genre scenes, interiors with figures, still-lifes. Church decoration.

Andrés de Rubira studied in Seville under Domingo Martinez and later assisted him in his work. Tradition has it that he designed and drew the sketches for the decoration of the old chapel of Seville Cathedral, the work being completed by Martinez. Rubira went to work in Lisbon and on his return to Seville received some important commissions. These included the chapel of the Holy Sacrament at S Salvador college, a number of paintings at S Alberto college, and various decorations at the convent of the Calced Carmelites. Although considered primarily as a painter of large-scale compositions, Rubira also produced easel paintings, interiors and light-hearted genre pieces.

RUBIRA, Joseph or José de, or Rovira or Ruvira
Spanish, 18th century.
Born 1747, in Seville; died 12 November 1787, in Cádiz.
Painter, sculptor, copyist. History painting.

José de Rubira was the son of Andrés de Rubira. Although only 11 years old when his father died, he is not known to have studied under any other teacher. He is known in particular as an excellent copyist of Murillo.
Museums and Galleries:
Seville (PM): *Holy Family*.

RUBLAGH, Peder, or Rublach or Rüblagh
Swedish, 17th century.
Active at the end of the 17th century.
Painter.
Rublagh's *Portrait of Christian V of Denmark* is in the Nationalmuseum, Stockholm.

RUBLETZKY, Géza
Hungarian, 20th century.
Born 1 July 1881, in Budapest.
Sculptor.
Museums and Galleries:
Budapest (Fövárosi Képtár): *Mother and Child*.

RUBLEV, Andreev or Andreef or Andrei, or Rublef or Rubliov
Russian, 14th - 15th century.
Born during the second half of the 14th century; died between 1427 and 1430, in Moscow.
Icon painter. Frescoes.
Some of Rublev's paintings are in churches in Russia. His work is easily distinguishable from that of earlier icon painters. In the same way that Cimabue, and especially Giotto, released Byzantine painting from its constraining forms and pioneered the use of realistic perspectives, Rublev abandoned the restrictive rules of Eastern illuminators, by the use of more supple draughtsmanship and nuanced colours. The Russians claimed that he painted 'with smoke', and praised his delicate style. His exact date and place of birth is unknown. He was possibly a student of Maxim the Greek, an icon and fresco painter whose known works date between 1370 and 1380. Rublev was a monk at the St Sergei of Radonege convent of the Trinity in Zagorsk. He took part in the decoration of cathedrals, including that of Blagoveschensky, the cathedral of the Annunciation in Moscow in 1405, and the cathedral of the Dormition in Vladimir in 1408. He produced these decorations alongside other artists, including Theophane, the monk Prochor, and Chorny. His principle work was an icon entitled *Trinity*, which was produced for the Zagorsk monastery, and is in the Tretiakov Gallery in Moscow. It is a perfectly balanced and exquisitely delicate work, suffused with harmony, spirituality and lyricism, expressed in an understated graphic style. His works can only be viewed where they currently hang, as they have been judged too fragile to be loaned to exhibitions.
Bibliography:
Hamilton, George Heard, *The Art and Architecture of Russia*, Yale University Press, New Haven, 1983. Talbot Rice, T., *Icons: Art and Devotion*, Bracken Books, London, 1993.
Museums and Galleries:
Moscow (State Tretyakov Gal.): *Trinity* (1411).

RUBLI, Samuel
German, 20th century.
Born 17 July 1883, in Zurich.
Active in Munich.
Painter. Landscapes.

RUBLIOFF, Andréi. See **RUBLEV Andreiev**

RUBNER, Simon
German, 15th century.
Active in Zweibrücken.
Painter.
Simon Rubner painted a picture depicting *The Gifting of the Monastery of Ochsenhausen* in 1481.

RUBO, Frants Alexeevich, or Roubaud, Franz
Ukrainian, 19th - 20th century.
Born 15 June 1856, in Odessa; died 13 March 1928, in Munich.
Painter, watercolourist. Figures, genre scenes, landscapes.
Orientalism.
Rubo worked in Munich and in Tiflis (now Tbilisi, Georgian Republic). He is probably the same artist as the painter cited in the catalogue of the Revoltella museum in Trieste under the name of Francesco Roubaud.

F Roubaud

Museums and Galleries:
Monaco: *Market in the Caucasus* - Munich (Pinakothek): *Wounded; In the Caucasus*.
Auction records:
Paris, 19 April 1950, *Cossack*, FRF 2,000. Paris, 15 May 1950, *Cossack Camp* (1900) FRF 8,800. Cologne, 15 March 1968, *Circassian Horseman*, DEM 5,000. New York, 1 May 1969, *Game of Buzkashi, Samarkand*, USD 3,750. London, 8 Oct 1971, *Cavalry Shock*, Gns 700. Cologne, 15 Nov 1972, *Landscape in the Caucasus*, DEM 17,000. Los Angeles, 28 Nov 1973, *Cossack Crossing a River*, USD 4,250. New York, 14 May 1976, *Workhorses* (oil on canvas, 23 1/2 x 19 1/4 ins / 60 x 49 cm) USD 500. Munich, 26 Nov 1976, *Horseman* (watercolour, 7 x 4 3/4 ins / 18 x 12 cm) DEM 720. New York, 7 Oct 1977, *Standard Bearer* (oil on panel, 13 x 8 1/2 ins / 33 x 21.5 cm) USD 2,100. San Francisco, 4 May 1980, *Troika* (1884, oil on canvas, 25 x 37 ins / 63.5 x 94 cm) USD 9,500. New York, 28 Oct 1981, *North African Bazaar* (1884, oil on canvas, 36 x 22 ins / 91.4 x 56 cm) USD 23,000. New York, 24 May 1984, *Arabs Resting By the Edge of a River* (1885, oil on canvas, 25 x 35 1/2 ins / 63.5 x 90.3 cm) USD 18,000. New York, 15 Feb 1985, *Battle for the Flag* (1892, oil on panel, 15 3/4 x 20 ins / 40 x 50.8 cm) USD 7,500. New York, 22 May 1986, *Arabian Horsemen by the Edge of a Stream* (1885, oil on canvas, 25 x 35 1/2 ins / 63.5 x 90.3 cm) USD 14,000. London, 6 Oct 1988, *Circassians Crossing a River* (oil on canvas, 23 1/4 x 32 3/4 ins / 59 x 83.2 cm) GBP 7,700. New York, 23 Feb 1989, *Cossacks Crossing the Steppes* (oil on panel, 12 1/4 x 20 ins / 31.1 x 50.8 cm) USD 3,850. Calais, 5 July 1992, *Troika* (1885, oil on canvas, 11 1/2 x 15 ins / 29 x 38 cm) FRF 6,500. New York, 30 Oct 1992, *Crossing a Ford* (oil on canvas, 28 x 39 1/2 ins / 70.2 x 100.3 cm) USD 6,600. New York, 17 Feb 1994, *Tunisian Horseman* (oil on panel, 8 1/2 x 4 3/4 ins / 21.6 x 12 cm) USD 1,380. London, 17 March 1995, *Horse Market* (oil on canvas, 30 3/4 x 51 ins / 78.1 x 129.5 cm) GBP 8,280. New York, 23-24 May 1996, *Mongolian Soldier* (oil on canvas, 24 1/2 x 15 1/2 ins / 62.2 x 39.4 cm) USD 6,325. Paris, 25 June 1996, *Circassian Horseman* (watercolour and gouache, 7 3/4 x 5 1/2 ins / 20 x 14 cm) FRF 6,000; *Escaped Stallion* (oil on canvas, 24 1/4 x 15 1/4 ins / 61.5 x 39 cm) DEM 4,800. New York, 22 Oct 1997, *Falconer* (oil on panel, 14 1/4 x 10 1/2 ins / 35.9 x 26.7 cm) USD 9,775.

RUBONE. See **RUBONI**

RUBONI, Giovanni, or Rubboni
Italian, 16th century.
Active in Cremona and in Novellara from 1518 to 1525.
Sculptor.

RUBONI, Giulio I, or Rubone
Italian, 16th century.
Born 1479; died 1539.
Active in Mantua.
Painter.
Giulio Ruboni I painted religious subjects.

RUBONI, Giulio II, or Rubone
Italian, 16th century.
Painter.
Giulio Ruboni II worked in Mantua for the Gonzaga family, from 1555-1587.

RUBOVICS, Márk
Hungarian, 19th - 20th century.
Born 21 November 1867, in Budapest; died 28 October 1947, in Budapest.
Painter. Genre scenes, still-lifes.
Rubovics studied drawing in Vienna and in Paris. He taught at a school of his own creation from 1891.
AUCTION RECORDS:
LONDON, 26 Feb 1988, *Elegant Figure* (oil on canvas, 12 x 8 1/2 ins / 30.5 x 21.5 cm) GBP 880.

RÜBSAM, Josep or Jupp
German, 20th century.
Born 30 May 1896, in Düsseldorf.
Sculptor, engraver. Religious subjects. Funerary monuments, war memorials, religious statuary.

RUBT, Johann
Austrian, 18th century.
Active in Waidhofen.
Sculptor.
In 1713 Johann Rubt sculpted two side altars with figures for the church of Langschlag.

RUBY, René
French, 20th century.
Born 16 November 1908, in St-Jean-de-Moirans (Isère); died 15 October 1983, in Grenoble.
Painter. Portraits, landscapes.
René Ruby, who studied at the Académie Colarossi, Paris, from 1930 to 1934 was a member of the group L'Effort. He painted landscapes, especially of the Isère, and many self-portraits. He exhibited in Paris at the Salon des Indépendants, the Salon d'Automne and the Salon des Tuileries and showed at the Musée Herbert, Paris, and the Château de la Condamine.
BIBLIOGRAPHY:
Wantellet, Maurice, *Deux siècles et plus de peinture dauphinoise*, M. Wantellet, Grenoble, 1987.

RUCABADO GÓMEZ, Leonardo
Spanish, 20th century.
Born 1876, in Castro-Urdiales; died 1918, in Bilbao.
Painter, watercolourist.
Also an architect and author.

RUCH, Christoffer
Danish, 18th century.
Born 1736, in Copenhagen; died 6 December 1804, in Copenhagen.
Miniaturist.
Ruch studied in Copenhagen, Hanover and Berlin. He was a painter at the royal Copenhagen porcelain factory.

RUCH, Jacob or Jakob
Swiss, 19th - 20th century.
Born 12 August 1868, in Glarus.
Painter. Figures, landscapes.
Son of the decorative artist Rudolf Ruch, Jacob Ruch moved to Paris with his family and enrolled at the Académie Julian, where he studied under Bourgeron (1884 to 1885), then at the École des Beaux-Arts, where he studied until 1892 under Gérôme. Ruch visited Switzerland on numerous occasions. He exhibited at the Salon des Artistes Français in Paris, notably showing landscapes with animals.
MUSEUMS AND GALLERIES:
GENEVA (MAH): *Heifer Grazing at Dawn* - GLARIS - LA CHAUX-DE-FONDS - LAUSANNE.

RUCH, Rudolf
Swiss, 19th century.
Born 1839.
Draughtsman, painter.
Rudolf Ruch was the father of Jacob Ruch.

RUCH (VAN RUCH?), T.
Dutch.
Painter.

RUCHENSTEINER, Martin
Swiss, 16th century.
Died before 1556.
Active in Wil (St Gall) from 1534.
Glass painter.

RUCHER
French, 18th century.
Active in Vosnes (near Nuits).
Sculptor.
Rucher sculpted the tomb of Anne Claude de Thiard, marquis of Bissy, in Pierre-en-Bresse church in 1774.

RUCHET, Anna Rosa
Maiden name: Hartmann
Swiss, 19th century.
Born 25 October 1856, in Aarau; died 27 October 1909.
Painter. Animals.
Anna Rosa Ruchet was a pupil of Rud Koller.

RUCHET, Berthe. See the entry **OBRIST Hermann**

RUCHOLLE, Gilles or Egidius, or Russholle
Flemish School, 17th century.
Active in Antwerp from 1645 to 1662.
Engraver.
Gilles Rucholle was probably the son of Peeter Rucholle.

RUCHOLLE, Peeter or Petrus, or Russcholle or Ruscioli
Flemish School, 17th century.
Born 1618, in Antwerp; died 1647, in Antwerp.
Engraver (burin).
Peeter Rucholle was the master of a studio in Antwerp in 1641. He is remembered for: *Annunciation*, after E Quellinus, *Mater Dolorosa*, after Van Dyck, *King Fernand*, *Louis XIV*, after Rigaud, *Melchior Voit*, after M Merian, *Plan of the Battle of Catel* and *Some Horsemen*.

RUCHOMOVSKY, Israel, or Rachoumovski
Russian, 19th - 20th century.
Born 1860, in Mosyr.
Engraver.
Ruchomovsky worked first in Odessa before moving to Paris. He was also a silversmith.

RUCK, Andreas. See **RUEFF**

RUCK, Michael. See **ROEG**

RÜCK, Nicolaus Friedrich
German, 19th century.
Born 1820, in Nuremberg.
Active in Munich.
Painter (porcelain), engraver (etching).
Nicolaus Friedrich Rück was a pupil of Heideloff. He is noted for his views of Nuremberg.

RUCKDESCHEL, Christoph Lorenz
German, 18th century.
Born 1721; died 30 June 1768, in Bayreuth.
Medallist.
Christoph Lorenz Ruckdeschel was medallist to the court of Bayreuth and engraved medals commemorating events at the court.

RUCKDESCHEL, Johann Lorenz
German, 18th century.
Born 1690, in Bayreuth; died 15 April 1742.
Medallist.
Johann Lorenz Ruckdeschel was the father of Christoph Lorenz Ruckdeschel. He engraved a medal bearing the effigy of Margrave Georg Wilhelm of Bayreuth dated 1726.

RÜCKEBUSH, Jean-Marie
French, 20th century.
Born 1916, in La Madeleine (Nord); died 1984, in the Somme.
Painter, watercolourist, draughtsman, decorative designer, architect. Landscapes, seascapes, architectural views, flowers.
Jean-Marie Rückebush studied painting and architecture at the École des Beaux-Arts de Lille, then in that of Paris where he was a pupil of Henri Expert. He settled in Peronne from 1951 where he mainly painted landscapes of Picardy in luminous watercolours, with confident, lively drawings. He was also the principal decorator of the steamboat *Normandy*. After his death, his works appeared in various artists' shows in Picardy, including the Salon des Amis des Arts de la Somme in 1977. Retrospectives of his work have been arranged, for example, in 1988 at the Centre Culturel de la Somme, in Amiens and in 1996 at the Hotel de Ville of Peronne.

RUCKENBAUER, Johann Philipp, or Rhuckerbauer, Ruckerpaur or Rückepaur
Austrian, 17th century.
Born c. 1668.
Painter.
Johann Philipp Ruckenbauer was in Rome from 1698 until 1699, and was active in Sarleinsbach around 1700. He executed frescoes in the abbey of St Florian and altarpieces for several churches in Upper Austria.

RÜCKER, Anton
Austrian, 19th century.
Born 1801; died 19 April 1851, in Vienna.
Sculptor (stone/ivory), lithographer.
Anton Rücker engraved portraits.

RUCKER, Franz
Austrian, 19th century.
Born 1807, in Gnadendorf, near Vienna; died 30 September 1866, in Gnadendorf.
Painter, art restorer. Portraits.
Franz Rucker was a pupil at the academy in Vienna. He concentrated on painting the portraits of prominent personalities of his day.

RÜCKER, Johann Adam
German, 18th century.
Baptised in Mainz 31 August 1752; died 17 September 1776, in Mainz.
Engraver (burin).
Johann Adam Rücker was the son of Wilhelm Christian Rücker. Following his father's death, he continued the almanac of coats of arms started by the former.

RÜCKER, Peter or Johann Peter Andreas
German, 18th century.
Baptised in Mainz 6 April 1757; died after 1807 (?).
Draughtsman, engraver (burin).
Peter Rücker was the son of Wilhelm Christian Rücker. He worked on the almanac of coats of arms started by his father and his brother Johann Adam Rücker, and later concentrated on engraving landscapes.

RÜCKER, Wilhelm Christian, or Rückert
German, 18th century.
Died 1774, in Mainz.
Draughtsman, engraver (burin).
Wilhelm Christian Rücker was the father of Johann Adam and Peter Rücker. He mainly engraved portraits, vignettes, views, and coats of arms.

RUCKERBAUER. See **RUCKENBAUER**

RÜCKERT (Frau). See **GREVE Johanna**

RUCKERT, Fedor Ivanovich, or Feodor
Russian, 19th - 20th century.
Born in Moscow, of German origin.
Active in Moscow.
Jeweller, silversmith, enameller.
Fedor Ruckert is famous as the master jeweller and cloisonné enameller who worked in Moscow from 1898 to 1917 and for Fabergé from 1903. He designed pieces in neo-Russian style.

RÜCKERT, Friedrich
German, 19th century.
Born August 1832, in Hamburg; died November 1893, near Treptow.
Painter. Still-lifes.
Friedrich Rückert studied in Düsseldorf.

RUCKI, Lambert. See **LAMBERT-RUCKI Jean**

RUCKI, Mara
Polish, 20th century.
Born 1888.
Active in France.
Painter.
Rucki was the daughter of the painter Jean Lambert-Rucki.
AUCTION RECORDS:
VERSAILLES, 18 Nov 1990, *Pink Wings* (oil/hardboard, 24 x 19 3/4 ins / 61 x 50 cm) FRF 71,000.

RUCKINSATTEL, Johannes
Austrian, 17th century.
Active in Hermannstadt (now Sibiu, Romania), 1657-1660.
Medallist.

RUCKLE, T. C.
American, 19th century.
Active in Baltimore.
Painter. Genre scenes.
T.C. Ruckle exhibited in London from 1839 to 1840.

RUCKMAN, Johan Gustaf
Swedish, 19th century.
Born 12 December 1780, in Stockholm; died 20 January 1862.
Engraver (burin).
Ruckman engraved portraits and book illustrations.

RÜCKRIEM, Ulrich
German, 20th century.
Born 1938, in Düsseldorf.
Sculptor, draughtsman.
Ulrich Rückriem started out as an apprentice stonemason and was involved in the restoration of Cologne Cathedral. He taught sculpture in Hamburg from 1974. Rückriem worked initially on portrait busts and funerary statuary, but marked his debut as a sculptor with a first geometrical abstract piece entitled *Teilung* (*Division*), produced in 1968. Rückriem was particularly fascinated by the properties of raw materials (wooden beams, sheet metal and, above all, stone - notably dolomite and granite from 1970) and by their structural susceptibility when cut, split or sawn along their inherent force lines. He was also attracted to their formal potential when reduced to blocks, rectangles, squares, triangles and cubes. Over time, he became increasingly preoccupied with the finished surface, which he sometimes left *au naturel* but frequently hammered, polished or worked with a

chisel, making no attempt to camouflage cracks or cuts - the intention being to leave a visible trace of human intervention. Rückriem has produced a number of monumental sculptures which alternate polished and unworked surfaces, among them his 1982 *Heinrich Heine Monument* in Bonn and his 1985 *Bild Stock* at the Centre d'Art Contemporain in Kerguennec.

In 1964, Rückriem participated in an exhibition of 20th century German art in Aachen, then in a 1967 exhibition at the Ostwall Museum in Dortmund. In 1968 and 1990, he took part in exhibitions at the Wilhelm-Lehmbruck Museum in Duisburg; in 1972, 1982, 1987 and 1992 at Documenta in Kassel; in 1974 at the artists' union in Cologne; in 1977 and 1980 at the Westphalian regional museum in Münster, and 1982 and 1985 at the Nationalgalerie in Berlin. He also exhibited abroad, notably in 1971 at the Paris Biennale; in 1973 and 1981 at the Antwerp Biennale; in 1978 at the Venice Biennale; in 1981 at the Musée d'Art Moderne in Paris; in 1982 in *Choix pour aujourd'hui* (*Choices for Today*), at the Musée National d'Art Moderne in Paris; in 1987 at the Castello di Rivoli in Turin; in 1989 at the São Paulo Biennale; in 1993 at FRAC in Amiens; in 1994 at regional fine arts museum in Graz; in 1993 at the Musée du Luxembourg in Paris; in 2003 in *Un tableau dans le décor: Peintures 1970-2000* (*A Painting in the Décor: Paintings 1970-2000*) at the Château des Ducs de Bretagne in Nantes, and also in 2003 at *Esprit des Lieux* (*The Spirit of Places*), an exhibition of contemporary art in contemporary settings, held at the Palais des Papes in Avignon. The latter two exhibitions were held within the framework of the FRAC exhibition *Trésors publics: 20 ans de création dans les Fonds régionaux d'art contemporain (FRAC)* (*Public Treasury, 20 Years of Creation in the Regional Collection of Contemporary Art*).

Rückriem has also had numerous solo exhibitions, beginning in 1964 with the first in a series of regular exhibitions in Cologne (notably in 1987 at the artists' union). He exhibited in 1967 in Antwerp, from 1969 on a regular basis in Düsseldorf (notably at the fine arts gallery in 1987), in 1970 at the Haus Lange Museum in Krefeld, in 1972 and 1979 in New York; in 1973 at the fine arts gallery in Tübingen, in 1973 and 1987 at the municipal museum in Mönchenbgladbach, from 1975 on a regular basis at the Galerie Durant-Dessert in Paris, in 1976 at the Museum of Modern Art in Oxford in 1977 at the Stedelijke Van Abbe Museum in Eindhoven, in 1978 at the Folkwang Museum in Essen, in 1978 at the fine arts museum in Bonn, in 1981 at the Fort Worth Art Museum, in 1983 at the Centre Georges-Pompidou in Paris, in 1985 at the Westphalian regional museum in Münster, in 1985 at the Neue Galerie in Kassel, in 1984 in Tokyo, in 1986 at the Kröller-Müller Museum in Otterlo, in 1987 at the artists' union in Cologne, in 1988 and 1990 in Athens, in 1989 at the Queen Sofia Museum in Madrid, in 1989 at the municipal museum in The Hague, in 1991 at the fine arts museum in Winterthur, in 1991 at the Centre d'Art Contemporaine in Geneva, in 1991 at the Serpentine Gallery in London, in 1993 at the Espai Poblenau Foundation in Essen in 1994 at the museum of Egyptology in Berlin-Charlottenburg and in 2002 at the fine arts museum in Bonn.

BIBLIOGRAPHY:

Ulbricht, G., *Ulrich Rückriem, Skulpturen 1968-1973*, DuMont Schauberg, Cologne, 1973. *Ulrich Rückriem*, exhibition catalogue, Éd. du Centre Georges-Pompidou, Paris, 1983. Soutif, Daniel, '*Ulrich Rückriem*' in *Artstudio* n° 3, periodical, Gal. Templon, Paris, winter 1986-1987. *Ulrich Rückriem*, exhibition catalogue, Donald Young Gall., Chicago, 1987. *Ulrich Rückriem: Skulpturen*, exhibition catalogue, Kunstsammlung Nordrhein-Westfalen, Düsseldorf, 1987. Hohmeyer, Jürgen, *Ulrich Rückriem*, Silke Schreiber, Munich, 1988. Tazzi, Pier Luigi, '*Romancing the Stone*' in *Artforum*, periodical, New York, September, 1990. Batchelor, David, *Ulrich Ruckriem*, exhibition catalogue, Serpentine Gall., London, 1991. Ehrhardt, H., *Ulrich Ruckriem - Arbeiten*, Oktagon, Stuttgart, 1994. Zahm, Olivier (preface), et al., *Trésors publics, 20 ans de création dans les Fonds régionaux d'art contemporain*, Flammarion, Paris, 2003 (text in French and English).

MUSEUMS AND GALLERIES:

AMIENS (FRAC Picardie) - CHÂTEAUGIRON (FRAC Bretagne) - CLONEGAL (Huntington Castle) - DIJON (FRAC Bourgogne): *Untitled* (1978) - DUNKIRK (FRAC Nord-Pas de Calais): *Dolomite* (1977) - KREFELD (Kaiser Wilhelm Mus.) - PARIS (MNAM-CCI): *Dolomite* (1976); *Dolomite* (1982).

AUCTION RECORDS:

NEW YORK, 3 May 1989, *'Pierre Bleue' Stone, Aachen* (1980, granite in two sections, 1 1/2 x 21 3/4 x 43 1/4 ins / 4 x 55.3 x 110 cm) USD 19,800. NEW YORK, 14 Nov 1991, *Untitled* (felt on brown paper with two iron bars, 61 3/4 x 1/2 x 1/2 ins / 157 x 1.5 x 1.5 cm) USD 200. NEW YORK, 19 Nov 1997, *Untitled* (stone, 88 x 33 1/4 x 48 ins / 223.5 x 84.5 x 121.9 cm) USD 14,950. COLOGNE, 12 Nov 1999, *Black-Swedish* (board, 1 x 19x20 ins / 3 x 48x51 cm) DEM 3,600. MUNICH, 2 Dec 2000, *Piece I* (seven granite blocks as one, 39 x 39x12 ins / 100 x 100x30 cm) DEM 38,000. HAMBURG, 14 June 2002, *Iron Ring* (iron, 1 x 5x16 ins / 3 x 12x41 cm) EUR 2,600. COLOGNE, 28 May 2003, *Head* (sandstone, 16 x 12x12 ins / 40 x 30x30 cm) EUR 8,000. COLOGNE, 28 May 2003, *Untitled* (basalt, 26 x 21x16 ins / 67 x 54x40 cm) EUR 10,000.

RUCKSTULL, Frederick Wellington

German, 19th - 20th century.

Born 22 May 1853, in Breitenbach (Lower Rhine); died 1942.

Sculptor. Statues, busts, monuments.

Frederick Wellington Ruckstull went to America when he was very young. He studied at the Académie Julian, Paris, under Boulanger and Lefebvre, and at the Académie Rollins under Mercié. He received many prizes, including an honourable mention at the Paris Salon of 1888.

Ruckstull made statues, busts and monuments in New York and Washington. His works include *John C. Calhoun*, *Uriah M. Rose* and *Wade Hampton*, three marble busts in a naturalist style in the Statuary Hall of the Capitol.

MUSEUMS AND GALLERIES:

NEW YORK (Metropolitan Mus. of Art) - ST LOUIS (AM).

RUCKTÄSCHEL, Emil Richard

German, 19th - 20th century.

Born 11 July 1868, in Dresden.

Painter, etcher.

MUSEUMS AND GALLERIES:

BERLIN (Staatliche Mus.).

RUCKTESCHELL, Eugen von

German, 19th century.

Born 28 November 1850, in Simferopol (Crimea).

Active in Füstenfeldbruck.

Painter.

Eugen von Ruckteschell studied in Munich.

RUCKTESCHELL, Walter von

Russian, 20th century.

Born 12 November 1882, in St Petersburg; died 27 September 1941, in Messina.

Active in Germany.

Sculptor, painter, engraver. Landscapes. Funerary monuments.

Ruckteschell was a pupil of A. Jank. He lived and worked in Dachau. He sculpted monuments commemorating the dead.

MUSEUMS AND GALLERIES:

HAMBURG (Kunsthalle): several paintings.

AUCTION RECORDS:
COPENHAGEN, 12 Nov 1984, *Klosters at Nightfall* (1911, oil on canvas, 32 x 23 1/2 ins / 81 x 60 cm) CHF 6,000.

RUCKTESCHELL-TRUEB, Clara. See **TRUEB Clara**

RUCZ, Lambert. See **RAUTZ**

RUDA, Janós or Johannes
Hungarian, 16th century.
Born in Kassa (now Košice, Slovakia).
Draughtsman.
Janós Ruda drew the town and fortress of Gran (now Esztergom) in 1594.

RUDAKOV, Aleksei Gavrilovich
Russian, 18th century.
Born 1748.
Engraver (burin).

RUDAUX, Edmond Adolphe
French, 19th century.
Born 10 February 1840, in Verdun (Meuse).
Painter, illustrator, engraver (etching). Genre scenes.
Edmond Rudaux was the father of Henri Edmond Budaux. He was the student of Lanielle, Leclaire and Boulanger. He first exhibited at the Salon of 1863.

He mainly produced works with genre subjects. He illustrated various books, such as Loti's *Icelandic Fisherman* and M. Taconet's *Along the Paths*.

AUCTION RECORDS:
PARIS, 1872, *Fishing Trip* (watercolour, fan) FRF 325. PARIS, 10 April 1899, *Spring*, FRF 165. PARIS, 21 Feb 1900, *Fan* (watercolour) FRF 225. PARIS, 30 April 1919, *Shoemaker's Romance*, FRF 135. PARIS, 20 Nov 1989, *Waiting for High Tide* (1882, oil on panel, 9 1/2 x 13 3/4 ins / 24 x 35 cm) FRF 9,500. PARIS, 29 June 2001, *Return from the Hunt* (oil on canvas, 71 x 54 ins / 180 x 137 cm) FRF 36,000.

RUDAUX, Henri Edmond
French, 19th - 20th century.
Born c. 1865, in Paris; died 1925 or 1927, in Paris.
Painter, draughtsman, illustrator. Portraits, genre scenes, seascapes.
Henri Edmond Rudaux was a pupil of his father, Edmond Adolphe Rudaux, and of Benjamin-Constant and Jules Lefebvre. He lived and worked in Paris and exhibited at the Salon des Artistes Français, of which he became a member in 1893. He was awarded an honourable mention in 1897. He was admired at the start of his career for his seascapes, and later for his portrait drawings, which were published mainly in the review *Le Théâtre*.

RUDBECK, Alexander de, or Oscar Thure Gustaf Alexander Fredrik (Baron)
Swedish, 19th century.
Born 21 January 1829, in Stavby; died 24 April 1908, in Stockholm.
Painter, miniaturist. Portraits, genre scenes.
Rudbeck studied at the academies in Düsseldorf and Paris.

MUSEUMS AND GALLERIES:
GÖTEBORG: *Portrait in Miniature of a Young Lady* (paint/ivory).

AUCTION RECORDS:
STOCKHOLM, 16 May 1990, *Barn Interior With Young Girl in Regional Costume Throwing Grain to the Hens* (oil on canvas, 22 3/4 x 17 3/4 ins / 58 x 45 cm) SEK 13,500.

RUDBERG, Gustav
Swedish, 20th century.
Born 1915.
Painter. Landscapes with figures, seascapes, landscapes.
Gustav Rudberg's landscape work is typically Swedish, with its predilection for cloudless clear skies and traces of drifting mist. His discreet colour palette juxtaposes yellow ochres and greens with the gentle blues of the sky.

AUCTION RECORDS:
STOCKHOLM, 14 April 1984, *Summer Day* (oil on canvas, 30 1/4 x 32 1/4 ins / 77 x 82 cm) SEK 25,000. STOCKHOLM, 6 June 1988, *Mountains to the South of Stockholm* (oil, 20 1/2 x 26 3/4 ins / 52 x 68 cm) SEK 18,500. STOCKHOLM, 6 Dec 1989, *Morning Mist at Hven* (1986, oil on canvas, 22 3/4 x 18 1/2 ins / 58 x 47 cm) SEK 28,000. STOCKHOLM, 5-6 Dec 1990, *Green Cliffs at Hven* (oil on canvas, 26 x 32 1/4 ins / 66 x 82 cm) SEK 16,000. STOCKHOLM, 30 May 1991, *Beach and Sea at Hven* (1982, oil on canvas, 30 1/4 x 32 1/4 ins / 77 x 82 cm) SEK 25,000. STOCKHOLM, 28 Oct 1991, *Nämndemansgården, Hven* (oil on canvas, 18 1/2 x 23 1/4 ins / 47 x 59 cm) SEK 8,000. STOCKHOLM, 21 May 1992, *Sea and Seashore* (oil on canvas, 20 1/2 x 33 1/2 ins / 52 x 85 cm) SEK 11,000. STOCKHOLM, 10-12 May 1993, *Seascape, Hven* (oil on canvas, 34 1/4 x 33 3/4 ins / 87 x 86 cm) SEK 41,000. STOCKHOLM, 30 Nov 1993, *May Evening* (oil on canvas, 37 3/4 x 32 3/4 ins / 96 x 83 cm) SEK 47,000. STOCKHOLM, 26 Oct 1999, *Landscape from Hven* (oil on canvas, 35 x 38 ins / 90 x 97 cm) SEK 38,000. STOCKHOLM, 26 Oct 1999, *Heaven and Sea* (oil on panel, 31 x 43 ins / 80 x 110 cm) SEK 47,000. MALMÖ, 8 April 2000, *View across the Harbour, Kyrkbacken, Hven* (oil on canvas, 38 x 38 ins / 97 x 97 cm) SEK 56,000. STOCKHOLM, 7 Nov 2000, *Vessels at Hven* (oil on canvas, 20 x 26 ins / 51 x 65 cm) SEK 64,000. STOCKHOLM, 2 May 2001, *Vessel near Hven* (oil on canvas, 48 x 39 ins / 121 x 98 cm) SEK 260,000. STOCKHOLM, 6 Nov 2001, *Vessel in Hazy Sunshine* (oil on canvas, 34 x 29 ins / 86 x 74 cm) SEK 94,000. STOCKHOLM, 23 April 2002, *Vessel at Anchor in Sundet, Hven* (oil on canvas, 35 x 35 ins / 90 x 90 cm) SEK 47,000. STOCKHOLM, 6 Nov 2002, *Landscape from Hven* (1974, oil on canvas, 38 x 38 ins / 96 x 96 cm) SEK 37,000. STOCKHOLM, 28 April 2003, *Norreborg, Hven* (oil on canvas, 37 x 26 ins / 95 x 65 cm) SEK 58,000. STOCKHOLM, 4 Nov 2003, *Calm Day in Öresund* (oil on canvas, 37 x 31 ins / 95 x 80 cm) SEK 85,000. STOCKHOLM, 2 Nov 2004, *Noreberg's Harbour, Hven* (oil on canvas, 38 x 29 ins / 97 x 74 cm) SEK 100,000. STOCKHOLM, 3 Nov 2004, *Kyrkbacken's Beach and Harbour, Hven* (oil on canvas, 24 x 33 ins / 61 x 83 cm) SEK 43,000.

RUDD, Agnes J.
British, 19th - 20th century.
Painter. Landscapes.
Agnes J. Rudd lived and worked in Bournemouth. She exhibited in London from 1888 to 1926.

RUDD, Charles
British, 19th century.
Painter. Urban landscapes.

MUSEUMS AND GALLERIES:
BIRMINGHAM: *Paradise Street, Birmingham* (c. 1840).

RUDD, Johannes Bruno
Belgian, 19th century.
Born 13 December 1792, in Bruges, of English origin; died 22 February 1870, in Bruges.
Engraver (burin), architect.
Rudd engraved the main monuments of Bruges.

RUDDER, Emile de
Belgian, 19th century.
Born 29 May 1822, in Ghent; died 3 February 1874, in Ghent.
Painter.
Emile de Rudder painted costumes.

RUDDER, Isidore Liévin de
Belgian, 19th - 20th century.
Born 3 February 1855, in Brussels; died 1943.
Sculptor, potter, painter, engraver. Genre scenes.

Isidore Liévin de Rudder studied at the fine arts academy in Brussels and was a Prix de Rome runner-up in 1885.
MUSEUMS AND GALLERIES:
ANTWERP: *Nest.*
AUCTION RECORDS:
LONDON, 21 March 1985, *Bacchante and Four Children* (c. 1870, brown-green patinated bronze, h. 25 1/2 ins / 65 cm) GBP 2,300.

RUDDER, Jan de
Belgian, 19th century.
Active in Paris in 1836.
Painter. Genre scenes.

RUDDER, Louis-Henri de
French, 19th century.
Born 17 October 1807, in Paris; died 11 August 1881, in Paris.
Painter, draughtsman, lithographer. Religious subjects, portraits, genre scenes.

Louis-Henri de Rudder was the student of Baron Gros and Nicolas Charlet at the École des Beaux-Arts in Paris. He exhibited at the Paris Salon from 1835, obtaining a third-class medal in 1840 and a second-class medal in 1848. He was made a Chevalier of the Légion d'Honneur in 1863.
MUSEUMS AND GALLERIES:
AUXERRE: *Portrait of the Prince of Eckmühl* - LA ROCHELLE: *Nicolas Flamel* - ST-ÉTIENNE (Mus. d'Art et d'Industrie): *Ecce Homo [Behold the Man]* - VERSAILLES: *Louis de Lorraine, Cardinal de Guise; Étienne Pasquier.*
AUCTION RECORDS:
PARIS, 9 March 1949, *Portrait of a Woman* (drawing heightened) FRF 600.

RUDE, Anton Christopher, or Ryde
Danish, 18th - 19th century.
Born 1744, in Copenhagen; died 23 April 1815, in Hørsholm.
Painter. Allegorical subjects, battles.

Rüde was a pupil at the Kunstakademi in Copenhagen.
MUSEUMS AND GALLERIES:
HILLERØD (Frederiksborg Slot): *Allegory of the Fight on the Reede.*
AUCTION RECORDS:
STOCKHOLM, 30 Nov 1993, *The Cavalry in Battle* (1794, oil on canvas, 27 1/2 x 40 1/4 ins / 70 x 102 cm) SEK 28,000.

RUDE, François
French, 19th century.
Born 4 January 1784, in Dijon; died 3 November 1855, in Paris.
Sculptor, engraver. Monuments, busts.

François Rude's father owned a business that manufactured stoves, known as 'cheminées à la prussienne' (Prussian-style chimneys), boilers and ironwork, and François became involved with the company from the age of 18. His artistic studies began at 16 under the direction of Devosge, the founder and director of the École des Beaux-Arts in Dijon. Several busts, and in particular one of *Louis-Gabriel Monnier* in 1804, attracted the attention and patronage of M. Frémiet, who had commissioned it from him. From then on, Fremiet regarded Rude with a fatherly affection. When conscription happened in 1805, Frémiet provided the funds for a replacement and Rude was able to go to Paris in 1807 with a recommendation to Denon (this was undoubtedly Vivant Denon), to whom he presented a figure of *Theseus Picking up a Disc.* Denon regarded it as a copy from antiquity and took an interest in Rude, obtaining a place for him in Edme Gaulle's studio, where he may have worked on the low reliefs of the column at Vendôme. Shortly afterwards, Rude left to join Cartellier's studio, later preparing for his entry to the competition for the Prix de Rome. He was accepted as the first in the examination room for the Prix de Rome and he won the second prize. In 1812, Rude was awarded the first Grand Prix de Rome, but did not go to receive it. He left Paris for Brussels, following the Frémiet family who had been forced into exile; he had also fallen in love with Sophie Frémiet. Rude was the uncle and master of Emmanuel Frémiet. He opened a studio in Brussels, where he worked until 1826 and then returned to Paris, where he took part in the exhibitions from 1827. He sent to the Salon: a *Mercury Fastening His Sandal* in 1827 and the *Neapolitan Fisherboy* in 1831. His remarkable talent won him a major medal of honour in 1855 (Exposition Universelle); he was a Chevalier of the Légion d'Honneur from 1833. A museum has been dedicated to him in Dijon, his native town.

He was given many commissions, in particular a *A Virgin Mary* for the church of St Gervais (1827); *Prometheus Bringing the Arts to Life,* low relief at the legislative body; *Gentleness,* a young girl caressing a bird, for Cartellier's tomb in the Père-Lachaise cemetery; *Baptism of Christ,* marble group at the church of Mary Magdalene; *Louis XIII,* silver statue for the Duc de Luynes; *Godefroy Cavaignac* (1847), recumbent statue, bronze, at the Montmartre cemetery; *Gaspard Monge* (1848), bronze statue for the town of Beaune; *Maréchal Bertrand,* bronze statue for the town of Châteauroux; *Maréchal Michel Ney* (1852-1853), bronze statue for the Place de l'Observatoire in Paris, near the site of his execution; *Napoleon Awakening to Immortality* (1847), in Noisot's park at Frisinez-Dijon, Noisot being a former soldier of Napoleon whose worship of the emperor Rude shared; *Poussin* and *Houdon,* stone statues for the Louvre; but Rude's claim to renown among the general public was the way in which he managed to translate French heroism into plastic form in the group *Departure of the Volunteers in 1792* (1835-1836), which adorns the eastern façade of the Arc-de-Triomphe de l'Étoile, a work that has been nicknamed *The Stone Marseillaise.*

Despite an enduringly formal aspect to some of his work that still belongs with classical forms of representation, Rude shocked his contemporaries with his realism, his vitality and sometimes his audacity. His relief on the Arc-de-Triomphe is one of the most convincing testimonies to romanticism in sculpture, through the violence of its expression and the ardour of the impetus that carries along the group of combatants; this is *Departure of the Volunteers in 1792* from the *Song of the Departure* or *The Marseillaise* of the Revolution or of Austerlitz.
BIBLIOGRAPHY:
Fourcaud, Louis de, *Rude sculpteur, ses œuvres et son temps 1784-1855,* Librairie de l'art ancien et moderne, Paris, 1904.
MUSEUMS AND GALLERIES:
BRUSSELS: *Busts of William I of the Netherlands* - CHÂLONS-EN-CHAMPAGNE: *David; Jean-François Galaup de la Pérouse* - DIJON: *Hebe; François Devosge; Young Neapolitan; Mercury; Departure of the Volunteers in 1792; A. M. J. J. Dupin; Love as Conqueror of the World* (two) - PARIS (Louvre): *The Marseillaise; Head of a Young Girl; Young Neapolitan Fisherman; Mercury Fastening His Sandal; Maurice of Saxony; Gaspard Monge; Joan of Arc; Christ on the Cross; Napoleon I; Mme Cabet* - ROUEN: *Death of Cavaignac; Louis David* - SEMUR-EN-AUXOIS: *Hebe* - TOULON: *Young Neapolitan Fisherman; Louis David* - VALENCE: *Young Neapolitan Fisherman* - VERSAILLES: *Marshal of Saxony; L. d'Armagnac, Duc de Nemours; Jean La Pérouse; David.*
AUCTION RECORDS:
PARIS, 4 March 1932, *Allegorical Figure* (pen) FRF 660. PARIS, 12 May 1937, *Moses Brings Forth Water* (pencil heightened with white, drawing of a low relief) FRF 800. PARIS, 25 March 1949, *Study for the Hunt of Meleager* (1856, pen) FRF 8,000. MARSEILLES, 8 April 1949, *Head of an Old Man* (gouache) FRF 20,000. NEW YORK, 1 March 1972, *The Marseillaise*

(bronze) USD 3,600. PARIS, 13 May 1976, *Child with Tortoise* (gilt patinated bronze, h. 12 ins / 30.5 cm, l. 13 1/2 ins/34 cm) FRF 1,500. NEW YORK, 1 March 1980, *Neapolitan Fisherman* (bronze, brown-red patina, h. 13 1/2 ins / 34.3 cm) USD 1,600. PARIS, 20 Nov 1981, *Figure from the Marseillaise* (patinated bronze, h. 14 1/2 ins / 37 cm) FRF 6,100. LONDON, 26 Nov 1986, *Hebe and the Eagle of Jupiter* (c. 1851-1855, patinated brown-red bronze, h. 32 ins / 81 cm) GBP 31,000. NANTES, 17 Dec 1986, *Young Winged Woman Brandishing a Flare* (black patinated bronze, h. 29 1/2 ins / 75 cm) FRF 141,000. PARIS, 24 April 1988, *Neapolitan Fisherman* (patinated bronze medal, l. 14 1/4 ins / 36 cm, h. 12 1/2 ins/31.5 cm) FRF 8,500. NEW YORK, 23 May 1990, *Head of an Old Warrior* (terracotta, h. 23 ins / 58.4 cm) USD 26,400. PARIS, 22 March 1994, *Pietà* (lead pencil, 15 1/4 x 21 1/4 ins / 39 x 54 cm) FRF 8,000. PARIS, 28 June 1996, *Head of a Gaul* (plaster, study, h. 24 3/4 ins / 63 cm) FRF 26,000. PARIS, 13 May 1997, *Head of an Old Warrior* (patinated plaster, h. 24 3/4 ins / 63 cm) FRF 30,000. BRUSSELS, 23 March 1999, *Chagrin. Woman Feeding Birds* (oil on canvas, a pair, 24 x 19 ins / 60 x 48 cm) BEF 140,000. PARIS, 10 Dec 1999, *Bust Representing the Spirit of the Patria* (plaster, h. 19ins / 48cm) FRF 30,000. CALAIS, 28 May 2000, *Neapolitan Fisherman* (brown patinated bronze, 9 x 10 ins / 23 x 26 cm) FRF 23,000. LONDON, 5 July 2000, *Neapolitan Fisherboy* (brown patinated bronze, 13 x 13 ins / 32 x 34 cm) GBP 3,500. LILLE, 17 June 2001, *Fisherboy* (c. 1860, brown patinated bronze, 9 x 10x6 ins / 23 x 26x14 cm) FRF 16,000. BERLIN, 15 June 2002, *Neapolitan Fisherman with Turtle* (brown patinated bronze, 12 x 14x7 ins / 31 x 35x18 cm) EUR 2,200. NEW YORK, 29 Oct 2002, *Head of a Gaul* (black patinated bronze, h. 15ins / 37cm) USD 5,500. LONDON, 9 April 2003, *Neapolitan Fisherboy* (sculpture, 9 x 10 ins / 24 x 25 cm) GBP 2,400. LONDON, 8 July 2003, *Bust of the Old Warrior* (terracotta, h. 24ins / 60cm) GBP 6,000. LONDON, 28 Oct 2003, *Hebe and the Eagle of Jupiter* (patinated bronze, h. 30ins / 77cm) GBP 14,000. LONDON, 9 July 2004, *Head of a Gaul* (patinated bronze, h. 26ins / 55cm) GBP 4,200.

RUDE, Olaf

Danish, 20th century.

Born 26 April 1886, near Rakvere, Estonia; died 1957, in Copenhagen.

Painter. Figures, interiors with figures, landscapes, still-lifes.

School of Bornholm.

Olaf Rude studied at the Kongelige Danske Kunstakademi in Copenhagen and went on to live and work there. He belonged to the Bornholm School, founded in 1911 as the last major artists' colony in Denmark, following those of Skagen and Funen during the latter half of the 19th century. The Bornholm School subscribed to new approaches to painting based on the dictates of form and colour. Rude was a Danish Cubist who devoted his time to painting predominantly landscapes and still-lifes. Peasant and village life were his preferred themes.

Olaf Rude

BIBLIOGRAPHY:

Johansen, Annette, et al., *Danske Kunstnerkolonier: Skagen, Fyn, Bornholm*, group exhibition catalogue, Aarhus Kunstmuseum, Aarhus, 2000.

AUCTION RECORDS:

COPENHAGEN, 6 July 1950, *Man Sitting at a Table*, DKK 2,100. COPENHAGEN, 30 Oct 1950, *Women in a Village Street*, DKK 2,950. COPENHAGEN, 22 May 1951, *Still-life*, DKK 3,000; *Landscape*, DKK 1,800. COPENHAGEN, 5 March 1958, *View from the Artist's Studio*, DKK 8,100. COPENHAGEN, 15 and 16 May 1963, *Fields*, DKK 8,100. COPENHAGEN, 30 June 1965, *Still-life*, DKK 11,000. COPENHAGEN, 13 May 1970, *Woman with an Umbrella*, DKK 15,900. COPENHAGEN, 15 March 1972, *Three Peasant Women*, DKK 21,000. COPENHAGEN, 5 Sept 1973, *September Landscape*, DKK 25,000. COPENHAGEN, 22 May 1974, *Still-life*, DKK 31,000. COPENHAGEN, 25 Nov 1976, *Still-life* (1921, oil on canvas, 17 1/4 x 19 1/4 ins / 44 x 49 cm) DKK 15,000. COPENHAGEN, 8 March 1977, *Landscape* (1923, oil on canvas, 32 x 39 1/4 ins / 81 x 100 cm) DKK 21,000. COPENHAGEN, 11 Oct 1979, *Horsemen* (1918, oil on canvas, 31 1/2 x 39 1/4 ins / 80 x 100 cm) DKK 34,000. COPENHAGEN, 22 Jan 1980, *Still-life* (1940, oil on canvas, 29 1/4 x 39 1/4 ins / 74 x 100 cm) DKK 25,000. COPENHAGEN, 26 Nov 1981, *Studio View, Allinge* (1942, oil on canvas, 39 1/4 x 49 1/4 ins / 100 x 125 cm) DKK 27,000. COPENHAGEN, 11 May 1983, *Harbour Scene* (oil on canvas, 23 1/2 x 36 1/2 ins / 60 x 93 cm) DKK 20,000. COPENHAGEN, 15 Oct 1985, *Still-life with Flowers and Fruit* (oil on canvas, 35 3/4 x 28 3/4 ins / 91 x 73 cm) DKK 78,000. COPENHAGEN, 25 Sept 1986, *Cubist Composition* (1917, oil on canvas, 49 1/4 x 38 1/4 ins / 125 x 97 cm) DKK 250,000. COPENHAGEN, 4 May 1988, *Cubist Composition* (1919, 34 1/4 x 28 ins / 87 x 71 cm) DKK 130,000; *Sea View* (1928, 27 1/2 x 32 ins / 70 x 81 cm) DKK 36,000; *Summer Landscape* (1942, watercolour, 18 x 24 3/4 ins / 46 x 63 cm) DKK 5,000. COPENHAGEN, 10 May 1989, *Summer Landscape with Houses, Bornholm* (1945, oil on canvas, 35 1/2 x 51 1/4 ins / 90 x 130 cm) DKK 28,000. COPENHAGEN, 20 Sept 1989, *House near Østersøn* (oil on canvas, 38 1/4 x 51 1/4 ins / 97 x 130 cm) DKK 30,000. NEW YORK, 21 Feb 1990, *The Artist's Parents* (1934, oil on canvas, 43 1/2 x 47 1/2 ins / 110.5 x 120.7 cm) USD 6,600. COPENHAGEN, 9 May 1990, *Still-life with Ceramic Utensils* (1941, oil on canvas, 32 x 39 1/4 ins / 81 x 100 cm) DKK 60,000. STOCKHOLM, 14 June 1990, *Landscape* (oil on canvas, 25 1/2 x 36 1/2 ins / 65 x 93 cm) SEK 28,000. COPENHAGEN, 31 Oct 1990, *Sea View, Allinge* (oil on canvas, 38 1/4 x 51 1/4 ins / 97 x 130 cm) DKK 44,000. COPENHAGEN, 4 Dec 1991, *Cubist Composition* (1917, oil on canvas, 49 1/4 x 38 1/4 ins / 125 x 97 cm) DKK 250,000. COPENHAGEN, 1 April 1992, *Stormy Weather, Bornholm* (1928, oil on canvas, 39 1/4 x 49 1/2 ins / 100 x 126 cm) DKK 60,000. COPENHAGEN, 20 Oct 1993, *Cubist Composition I* (1918, oil on canvas, 39 1/4 x 49 1/2 ins / 100 x 126 cm) DKK 325,000. COPENHAGEN, 19 Oct 1994, *Interior of the Artist's Studio* (oil on canvas, 35 1/2 x 37 1/2 ins / 90 x 95 cm) DKK 50,000. COPENHAGEN, 17 April 1996, *Still-life* (oil on canvas, 29 1/4 x 35 3/4 ins / 74 x 91 cm) DKK 36,000. COPENHAGEN, 16 April 1997, *View over the Jetty* (1926, oil on canvas, 13 x 16 1/4 ins / 33 x 41 cm) DKK 16,000. COPENHAGEN, 5 Oct 1999, *Still-life with Fruit and Potted Plant* (1945, oil on canvas, 31 x 40 ins / 80 x 101 cm) DKK 60,000. COPENHAGEN, 5 Oct 1999, *Cubist Landscape with Daneborg in the background* (1917, oil on canvas, 31 x 27 ins / 80 x 68 cm) DKK 115,000. COPENHAGEN, 20 June 2000, *Summer Landscape, Bornholm* (1940, oil on canvas, 32 x 46 ins / 82 x 116 cm) DKK 40,000. COPENHAGEN, 3 Oct 2000, *Portrait of a Woman with a Tea Cup* (1917, oil on canvas, 33 x 25 ins / 83 x 64 cm) DKK 120,000. COPENHAGEN, 28 May 2001, *Man Wandering along a Row of Trees, Farm beyond* (1917, oil on canvas, 26 x 32 ins / 67 x 82 cm) DKK 100,000. COPENHAGEN, 2 Oct 2001, *Still-life with Bottle of Wine, Vases and Fruit on a Tablecloth* (oil on canvas, 33 x 36 ins / 83 x 92 cm) DKK 95,000. COPENHAGEN, 10 April 2002, *Still-life with Fruit and Potted Plants* (oil on canvas, 33 x 27 ins / 85 x 69 cm) DKK 50,000. COPENHAGEN, 1 Oct 2002, *Still-life with Jug on a Square Table* (1923, oil on canvas, 41 x 34 ins / 105 x 86 cm) DKK 50,000. COPENHAGEN, 1 April 2003, *Dancer in a Pink Dress on a Green Background* (1917, oil on canvas, 35 x 27 ins / 90 x 69 cm) DKK 180,000. COPENHAGEN, 17 Sept 2003, *Cubist Cow* (c. 1913, oil on canvas, 28 x 34 ins / 72 x 87 cm) DKK 150,000. COPENHAGEN, 29 March 2004, *Lady with Glass: Cubist Figure Composition* (1919, oil on canvas, 34 x 28 ins / 87 x 71 cm) DKK 400,000. STOCKHOLM, 26 April 2004,

Woman with Tea Cup (1917, oil on canvas, 33 x 25 ins / 84 x 63 cm) SEK 165,000.

RUDE, Sophie (Mme)
Maiden name: Frémiet
French, 19th century.
Born 20 June 1797, in Dijon; died 4 December 1867, in Paris.
Also active in Belgium.
Painter, copyist. History painting, religious subjects, mythological subjects, portraits. Murals.

Sophie Rude was the daughter of Emmanuel Frémiet and the wife of François Rude. She was first the student of Anatole Devosge in Dijon, then of Jacques-Louis David in Brussels, where she lived with her family from 1816 to 1827.

She featured at the Salon in Antwerp in 1819 and entered the competition for the main prize at the Salon in Ghent in 1820, winning a medal of honour.

She painted several decorative murals for the castle in Tervuren and the Arenberg residence. Her works, which are slightly theatrical and Davidian in style, include: *Holy Reading* or *Bible Reading; Holy Family; Sleeping Virgin; Beautiful Anthea of Ephesus; Death of Cynos; Charles I's Farewells; Episode from the Fronde*. Her fairly numerous portraits are crisp in construction. She also copied various pictures by David such as *Psyche or the Anger of Achilles*.

Museums and Galleries:
Dijon (MBA): *Rebellion in Bruges in 1436; Holy Family; Meeting of M. le Prince and Mlle de Montpensier in 1652; Mme Rude; Mme Van der Haërt, née Frémiet; Mme Gerbois and Her Daughter; M. Petit; Mme Petit; Mlle Duval; M. Wasset; Mme Wasset; M. Frémiet, the Artist's Father; François Rude, the Artist's Husband; Ariadne Abandoned on the Island of Naxos* (1826) - Paris (Louvre): *Portrait of Bernard Wolf*.

Auction records:
Paris, July 1946, *Venus and Cupid*, FRF 16,500. Brussels, 27 Oct 1976, *Bible Reading* (1819, oil on canvas, 26 3/4 x 33 1/2 ins / 68 x 85 cm) BEF 110,000. New York, 28 Feb 1990, *Death of Cenchirias, Son of Neptune* (oil on canvas, 81 1/4 x 100 1/4 ins / 206.4 x 254.6 cm) USD 137,500. New York, 26 May 1994, *Death of Cenchirias, Son of Neptune* (oil on canvas, 81 1/4 x 100 1/4 ins / 206.4 x 254.6 cm) USD 156,500. New York, 5 April 2001, *Death of Cenchirias, Son of Neptune* (c. 1822, oil on canvas, 81 x 100 ins / 206 x 255 cm) USD 160,000.

RUDEL, Jean Antoine
French, 20th century.
Born 25 October 1917, in Montpellier.
Painter. Nudes, landscapes.
Symbolism.

Jean Antoine Rudel's father was a painter and a teacher at the École des Beaux-Arts in Montpellier. His studies were both artistic and academic. He graduated in history, obtained a doctorate in art history, became a secondary school teacher and then taught at the Sorbonne at a more advanced level than that at which he had studied. As an art historian, he published books on Venice, Italian art, contemporary art, and art techniques. At various times he held posts at the Louvre, with the municipality of St-Germain-en-Laye, UNESCO and the ORTF (the former French broadcasting corporation). Throughout his life his paintings conveyed his feelings about Mediterranean scenery, the sea coasts and marshes of his native region, and of Italy, Greece and Spain, and women bathing on sunny beaches. His reference point is antique sculpture, which combines physical sensuality with harmonious proportions. He had a love of the created world that is expressed in implicitly, sometimes explicitly, religious terms.

He began his artistic career at the Écoles des Beaux-Arts in Marseilles and Paris after World War II and later received advice from Jean Aujame and Roger Chastel. He exhibited in Paris first at the Salon de la Jeune Peinture, and subsequently at the Salon des Indépendants, the Salon of the Société Nationale des Beaux-Arts, the Salon d'Automne, of which he was a member, the Salon Comparaisons, and the Salon du Dessin et de la Peinture à l'Eau, of which he became vice-president. He also took part in group exhibitions in several French towns, in the Biennale Inter-Arts of St-Germain-en Laye, which he founded, and abroad in Tokyo, Rio de Janeiro, and elsewhere. He held solo shows in Paris, Arles and Montpellier. In 1998 the Galerie de l'Ancien Courrier, Montpellier, held an exhibition of the works of Jean Aristide and Jean Antoine Rudel.

Museums and Galleries:
Paris (MAMVP) - St-Germain-en-Laye - Toulon.

RUDEL, Jean Aristide
French, 20th century.
Born 1884, in Montpellier; died 1959, in Montpellier.
Painter, draughtsman. Figure compositions, figures, nudes, portraits, landscapes with figures, seascapes, still-lifes.

Jean Aristide Rudel was a scholar at the École des Beaux-Arts, Montpellier, and from 1917 studied under Jean-Paul Laurens at the École des Beaux-Arts, Paris. He may also have attended the Académie Julian and received advice from Jacques-Émile Blanche. After World War I, in which he was seriously wounded and received the Croix de Guerre, he returned to his art. Although he went to Paris and exhibited there, it was from the countryside of Montpellier that he drew his inspiration, and in Montpellier that he built up a considerable clientele. After 1925, he sold works in the USA, Canada, Australia, Britain and Sweden. In Montpellier and roundabout he took part in a variety of social, charitable and artistic activities, and was involved in museum purchases. Late in life he taught at the École des Beaux-Arts, Montpellier.

Using minimal materials and small formats, he searched ceaselessly for subjects from nature on the beaches and by the ponds of the Montpellier region. He returned with these sketches to work in his studio, but they are perhaps the freest and liveliest of his productions. Initially attracted by Renoir, whose scintillating Impressionism and sensual brushstroke he admired, he came later to value Titian, Delacroix and Courbet. He painted a whole range of subjects - landscapes and seascapes, still-lifes, portraits of people well-known in the region, and even a few commissioned religious pictures. His favourite - for him the quintessence of natural beauty - was the female nude, placed sometimes in groups, sometimes in graceful or relaxed poses, such as bathing or sleeping.

He exhibited in Paris at the Salon des Artistes Français, in Montpellier and in towns of the Mediterranean coast - Perpignan and Nice. In 1986, the Musée Fabre, Montpellier, organised a large retrospective of his work, and in 1998 the Galerie de l'Ancien Courrier, Montpellier, held an exhibition of the paintings of Jean Aristide and Jean Antoine Rudel.

Bibliography:
Rudel, Jean, *J.A. Rudel*, exhibition catalogue, Musée Fabre, Montpellier, 1986.

Museums and Galleries:
Montpellier (Mus. Fabre).

RUDELBACH, C. L.
Austrian, 18th century.
Painter.

C. L. Rudelbach executed a *Portrait of Prince Eugene of Savoy* dated 1718.

RÜDELL, Carl
German, 19th - 20th century.
Born 6 September 1852, in Trier; died 1939, in Berlin.

Watercolourist. Landscapes, urban landscapes.
Carl Rüdell was an architect by profession.

Museums and Galleries:
Cologne (Rheinisches Bildarchiv) - Trier (Rheinisches Landesmus.).
Auction records:
Cologne, 19 Oct 1973, *View of Cologne* (watercolour) DEM 5,500. Cologne, 26 March 1976, *Landscape* (watercolour, 14 1/4 x 9 1/2 ins / 36 x 24 cm) DEM 1,600. Cologne, 19 Oct 1979, *Carnival Scene* (1938, watercolour, 22 x 15 3/4 ins / 56 x 40 cm) DEM 12,000. Cologne, 23 Oct 1981, *Concert in the Park* (watercolour, 9 3/4 x 12 1/4 ins / 25 x 31 cm) DEM 6,000. Cologne, 28 Oct 1983, *Procession in Cologne* (watercolour, 16 1/2 x 11 1/4 ins / 42 x 28.5 cm) DEM 8,000. Cologne, 15 Oct 1988, *Landscape with Windmill* (watercolour, 9 x 14 1/2 ins / 23 x 37 cm) DEM 1,100. Cologne, 20 Oct 1989, *Children's Games in Winter* (watercolour, 8 x 11 1/2 ins / 20.5 x 29 cm) DEM 1,500. Cologne, 23 March 1990, *Summer's Day at the Eigelsteintor* (watercolour, 15 x 11 ins / 38 x 27 cm) DEM 5,500.

RUDELL, Peter Edward
American, 19th century.
Born 1854, in Preston (Ontario); died 20 June 1899.
Active in New York and France.
Painter. Landscapes.
Peter Edward Rudell was a pupil of Alexander Helwig Wyant. He showed work in a number of exhibitions, notably at the following: the Boston Art Club (1881-1883, 1898); the Pennsylvania Academy of the Fine Arts (1881-1882, 1888-1892); the National Academy of Design in New York (1881-1899); the Brooklyn Art Association (1882-1883, 1886, 1891); and the Paris Salon (1885).

RÜDER, Sigismund
German, 16th century.
Active in Burghausen.
Sculptor.
Sigismund Rüder carved mainly tombs and funerary low reliefs.

RÜDER, Wolf. See **RIEDER**

RUDGE, Bradford
British, 19th century.
Painter (gouache), lithographer. Landscapes.
Bradford Rudge exhibited at the Royal Academy in London in 1840 and from 1863-1872.
Auction records:
London, 6 Nov 1995, *Promenade at Ampthill* (1862, gouache, 22 x 16 1/2 ins / 55 x 42 cm) GBP 3,450. London, 29 Nov 2000, *Senate House and St Mary's Church, Cambridge* (watercolour over pencil heightened with gouache, 10 x 16 ins / 25 x 40 cm) GBP 1,800.

RUDGER LUCAS VON OSSEG
Austrian, 13th century.
Illuminator, calligrapher.
A Cistercian monk, he illuminated a missal for the abbess of the convent of Saaz in Moravia.

RUDGERIUS, or Rudgerus
Austrian, 13th century.
Painter.
Rudgerius probably painted some of the frescoes in the west tribune of Gurk Cathedral (Carinthia) in 1218.

RUDGISH, Astrid von
Belgian, 20th century.
Born 1940, in Brussels.
Painter. Portraits, landscapes.
Astrid von Rudgish studied at the higher institute of arts and crafts in Cologne and exhibited in Brussels in 1972 and in Paris in 1973. Her work is essentially linear in structure, with figures and objects more or less geometrically delineated and the canvas built up as a succession of planes which, in some cases, combine to produce a Neo-Cubist effect.

RUDHARDT, Claude Charles
Swiss, 19th century.
Born 27 September 1829, in Geneva; died 22 April 1895, in Paris.
Painter, ceramicist. Figures, landscapes. Decorative schemes.
Claude Charles Rudhardt settled in Paris in 1862.
Auction records:
Paris, 5 April 1993, *Figures by the Pillar of Pompeii; Figures beside an Old Well* (oil on canvas, 20 3/4 x 17 1/4 ins / 53 x 44 cm) FRF 35,000. Paris, 5 April 2001, *Fishing Family on Strike* (oil on canvas, 16 x 35 ins / 40 x 88 cm) FRF 38,000. Paris, 7 Dec 2001, *Neapolitan Country Landscape* (1850, oil on canvas, 11 x 16 ins / 27 x 40 cm) FRF 25,000.

RUDHART, Theresa
Maiden name: Schumm
German, 19th century.
Born 14 August 1804, in Bamberg.
Painter. Portraits, historical subjects.

RUDIEZ, Vicente
Spanish, 18th century.
Died 25 October 1802, in Madrid.
Sculptor.
Vicente Rudiez studied at the Madrid academy and worked as a sculptor for churches in Madrid.

RÜDIGER, Bernhard
Italian, 20th - 21st century.
Born 1964, in Rome.
Active in France.
Installation artist, performance artist, video artist.
Conceptual Art.
Bernhard Rüdiger's art deals with mental concepts and is based on language. He attempts to establish the sense of such ideas as 'beauty', 'truth' and 'looking' by juxtaposing and dispersing objects.

His solo exhibitions include: 1995, at the Galerie Michel Rein, Tours, and the *International Fair of Contemporary Art* in Paris; 1997, at the Espace d'Art Moderne et Contemporain in Toulouse; and 1999 at the Galerie Michel Rein in Tours.
Bibliography:
Rüdiger, Bernhard, *Neuf rêves, un caprice. Écrits sur l'art*, Galerie de Noisy-le-Sec, c. 2001 (published in French and Italian).
Museums and Galleries:
Orléans (FRAC Centre): *Poetry* (1994, plywood, wood glue and bolts).

RÜDIGER, Johann Anton I
German, 18th century.
Active in Halle in the first half of the 18th century.
Painter.
Johann Anton Rüdiger I was the father of Johann Anton Rüdiger II. He painted portraits of professors at the university of Halle and was a painter in the court of Dessau.

RÜDIGER, Johann Anton II
German, 18th century.
Painter.
Johann Anton Rüdiger II was the son of Johann Anton Rüdiger I. He was a painter at the university of Halle around 1750.

RÜDIGER, Johann Friedrich
German, 18th century.
Active in Nuremberg 1710-1720.
Engraver (etching), print publisher. Decorative motifs (chinoiseries).
Johann Friedrich Rüdiger engraved 10 chinoiserie leaves.

RÜDIGER VON DER LAGE, Max von
German, 19th - 20th century.
Born 14 January 1862, in Berlin.
Active in Potsdam.
Painter. Landscapes.

RUDIN, Nelly
Swiss, 20th century.
Born 1928, in Basel.
Painter, sculptor.
Neo-Constructivism.
Concrete Art Group of Zurich.
Nelly Rudin studied at the college of arts and crafts in Basel and started to paint from 1964.
MUSEUMS AND GALLERIES:
GRENOBLE (Mus. de Grenoble).
AUCTION RECORDS:
LUCERNE, 20 May 1995, *Untitled* (oil/two canvases, 8¼ x 16¼ ins / 21 x 41 cm) CHF 900. LUCERNE, 5 June 1999, *Untitled* (1991, oil on canvas, 41 x 47 ins / 104 x 120 cm) CHF 5,000. LUCERNE, 22 Nov 2003, *NO 3809* (1993, acrylic on canvas on board, 31 x 31 ins / 80 x 80 cm) CHF 3,800. ZURICH, 8 June 2004, *Untitled* (oil on canvas, 24 x 24 ins / 60 x 60 cm) CHF 4,200.

RÜDINGER, Albert
Danish, 19th - 20th century.
Born 20 April 1838, in Copenhagen; died 7 April 1925, in Copenhagen.
Painter. Animals, landscapes.
Albert Rüdinger studied under Ole Haslund and Harald Foss. He was also a composer.

RUDINOFF, Willibald Wolf or Morgenstern
Russian, 20th century.
Born 4 August 1866, in Angermünde.
Painter, engraver.
Rudinoff worked in etching. He was active for a certain time in music halls.

RÜDISÜHLI, Eduard
Swiss, 20th century.
Born 26 June 1875, in Basel; died 1938, in Rorschacherberg.
Painter. Landscapes.
Eduard Rüdisühli was a son of Jakob Rüdisühli and a student of his brother Hermann Rüdisühli.
AUCTION RECORDS:
PARIS, 19 Dec 1989, *Island of Death* (oil on panel, 21 x 31½ ins / 52.5 x 80 cm) FRF 50,000. BERN, 12 May 1990, *Autumn* (oil on card, 12¼ x 21½ ins / 31 x 54.5 cm) CHF 1,200. ZURICH, 17-18 June 1996, *Mythological Landscape* (oil on canvas, 52¾ x 77½ ins / 134 x 197 cm) CHF 11,000. BERN, 17 May 1999, *Autumn Landscape* (1915, oil on canvas, 40 x 59 ins / 101 x 151 cm) CHF 3,000. ZURICH, 21 March 2000, *Prosecution of the Penaten* (oil on canvas) CHF 4,400. MUNICH, 4 Dec 2001, *Pirate Island* (oil on canvas, 19 x 41 ins / 48 x 104 cm) DEM 4,000. LINDAU, 8 May 2002, *Memento Mori, Schloss Luxburg* (oil on panel, 20 x 31 ins / 52 x 79 cm) EUR 2,000.

RÜDISÜHLI, Hermann or Traugott Hermann
Swiss, 19th - 20th century.
Born 10 June 1864, in Lenzburg; died 1944.
Painter, sculptor. Landscapes.
Hermann Rüdisühli was the son and student of Jakob Lorenz Rüdisühli. He studied in Basel and Karlsruhe and went on to live and work in Munich. He was influenced by Arnold Böcklin.
MUSEUMS AND GALLERIES:
ELBERFELD (Municipal Mus.) - MAINZ (Landesmus.) - ZURICH (Henneberg Gal.).
AUCTION RECORDS:
VIENNA, 16 Jan 1979, *Autumn Landscape* (oil on panel, 5½ x 11 ins / 14 x 27 cm) ATS 20,000. LOS ANGELES, 16 March 1981, *Landscape with Stormy Sky* (oil on panel, 20 x 27½ ins / 50.5 x 70 cm) USD 1,300. ZOFINGEN, 3 Dec 1999, *Mediterranean Coastal Landscape with Villa* (oil on board, 19 x 28 ins / 49 x 70 cm) CHF 2,800. COPENHAGEN, 29 Feb 2000, *Toteninsel at Night, from the Bay near Perast, Yugoslavia* (oil on canvas, 21 x 27 ins / 54 x 69 cm) DKK 38,000. MUNICH, 27 Sept 2000, *Southern Landscape in Autumn* (1905, oil on board, 22 x 30 ins / 56 x 75 cm) DEM 4,800. MUNICH, 21 March 2001, *Autumnal Meadow Landscape with Cows Grazing* (1906, oil on canvas, 35 x 46 ins / 90 x 118 cm) DEM 6,500. NEW YORK, 30 April 2001, *Enchanted Island* (oil on board, 20 x 27 ins / 52 x 69 cm) USD 5,000. COLOGNE, 17 May 2003, *Late Summer Landscape with Peasants Harvesting Hay* (oil on panel, 26 x 31 ins / 66 x 80 cm) EUR 2,700. MUNICH, 30 June 2004, *Autumn Wood* (1903, oil on board, 20 x 28 ins / 52 x 70 cm) EUR 1,950. WARSAW, 17 Oct 2004, *Sunset Landscape with Two Figures Approaching a House* (oil on canvas, 30 x 48 ins / 75 x 122 cm) PLN 13,000.

RÜDISÜHLI, Jakob Lorenz
Swiss, 19th - 20th century.
Born 13 October 1835, in St Gall; died 25 November 1918, in Basel.
Painter, engraver, lithographer. Landscapes.
Jakob Lorenz Rüdisühli studied lithography in his native St Gall and in Schaffhausen before going on to study engraving in Darmstadt. He made both etchings and engravings, producing a large number of views of Switzerland and the banks of the Rhine. His talent was recognised by Monkaczy, who enabled him to exhibit at the Paris Salon in 1875. Rüdisühli had several children, some of whom went on to become artists in their own right (notably Eduard, Hermann and Louise).
MUSEUMS AND GALLERIES:
BASEL: *Wooded Landscape in the Evening Light; Marshland* - BERN: *Abandoned Castle; Sunset in a Forest Glade* - MAINZ: *Monte Rosa at Sunset.*
AUCTION RECORDS:
BERN, 26 Oct 1985, *Autumn Landscape with a Stormy Sky* (oil on canvas, 15 x 20½ ins / 38 x 52 cm) CHF 4,300.

RÜDISÜHLI, Louise, later Mme Berlinger
Swiss, 19th - 20th century.
Born 1867.
Painter.
Louise Rüdisühli was the daughter and student of Jakob Lorenz Rüdisühli.

RUDL, Siegmund or Zikmund
Austrian, 19th - 20th century.
Born 7 May 1861, in Prague.
Painter. Religious subjects.
Rudl studied under Trenkwald at the academy in Vienna and under Sequens at the academy in Prague. He painted frescoes and altarpieces for churches in Prague, Königsberg (now Kaliningrad, Russia) and Breslau (now Wroclaw, Poland).

RUDLAND, Robert I
British, 17th century.
Stained glass painter.
Robert Rudland I was the father of Robert Rudland II. He produced stained glass windows for Wadham College Chapel, Oxford in the first half of the 17th century.

RUDLAND, Robert II
British, 17th century.
Stained glass painter.
The son of a father by the same name, Robert Rudland II restored stained glass in St Mary's Church, Oxford in the first half of the 17th century.

RUDLOFF, Johann Georg
German, 18th century.
Sculptor.
Johann Georg Rudloff worked on the town hall in Pirna in 1747.

RUDNAY, Gyula or Július
Hungarian, 20th century.
Born 9 January 1878, in Pelsüc; died 4 January 1957, in Budapest.
Painter, engraver. Figures, portraits, landscapes.
Rudnay studied in Munich with Hollósy, in Nagybanya (now Baia Mare), in Rome and in Paris. He engraved in etching. His works are represented in all of the public collections in Hungary.
MUSEUMS AND GALLERIES:
BRUSSELS: *Young Noble Maiden with Riding Master* - GENOA (Modiano Mus.): *Birdsong* - ROME (Gal. Nazionale): *Angelic Greeting* - VENICE (Gal. d'Arte Moderna): *Wedding Procession.*

RUDNEV, Lev
Russian, 20th century.
Born 13 March 1885, in Novgorod; died 19 November 1956, in Moscow.
Sculptor and architect. Monuments.
Rudnev became an architect after studying from 1906 to 1915 under Leonty Benois at the faculty of architecture in the imperial academy of fine arts in St Petersburg. He travelled to Italy, where he was drawn to Neo-Classicism. He worked in the studios of Igor Fomin, who became a strong influence on his work. He taught in the state artistic studios (Vkhutemas) in St Petersburg, and had Viktor Lebedev and Sergei Speransky as pupils.

Rudnev's first project was the Seleznyovka seminary (1912), completed in a style reminiscent of Romanesque architecture. He designed the *Victims of the Revolution* monument (1917-1919) on Marsovo Pole (the Field of Mars) in Leningrad, a spacious construction of large granite blocks. In 1925, he designed the monument to Lenin and the victims of the Revolution in Odessa.
BIBLIOGRAPHY:
Paris-Moscou, 1900-1930, exhibition catalogue, Éd. du Centre Georges-Pompidou, Paris, 1979.

RUDNICKI, Marek
Polish, 20th century.
Born 24 January 1927, in Warsaw.
Painter, draughtsman, illustrator.
Rudnicki studied architecture in Warsaw. He has illustrated the works of Pushkin, Turgenev, Tolstoy, Camus, Maurois, and Gilbert Cesbron. From 1959, he began drawing portraits for a large French daily newspaper. His paintings are in museums in the USA, Canada and Israel. He exhibited in Warsaw and Cracow in 1946 (at the Palace of the Arts), in Amsterdam and Brussels in 1954, in Berlin and in Munich in 1956, in Vienna in 1957, and Paris in 1965 and 1970. He received the special prize in Vienna in 1956 for his portrait of Thomas Mann.
AUCTION RECORDS:
PARIS, 20 March 1988, *Sofer and Scribe* (oil on canvas, 28 3/4 x 23 1/2 ins / 73 x 60 cm) FRF 18,000. PARIS, 8 April 1990, *Shtetl Scene* (watercolour and pen drawing, 20 1/2 x 24 3/4 ins / 52 x 63 cm) FRF 22,000. PARIS, 14 April 1991, *Shtetl* (oil on canvas, 28 3/4 x 23 1/2 ins / 73 x 60 cm) FRF 22,000. PARIS, 17 June 1991, *Shtetl* (oil on panel, 25 1/2 x 21 1/4 ins / 65 x 54 cm) FRF 16,000. PARIS, 4 April 1993, *Shtetl* (pastel ink and watercolour/paper/wood, 22 x 25 1/2 ins / 55 x 65 cm) FRF 14,700.

RUDOLF. See also **RUDOLPH**

RUDOLF, Elsbeth
German, 19th - 20th century.
Born 26 April 1861, in Valk (now Valga, Estonia).
Painter. Portraits.
Elsbeth Rudolf was a student of Azbé. She lived and worked in Dorpat (now Tartu, Estonia).

RUDOLF, Otto Paul
Austrian, 19th - 20th century.
Born 2 July 1867, in Ljubljana.
Painter. Landscapes, portraits.
Otto Paul Rudolf studied in Graz and Munich and went on to live and work in Vienna.

RUDOLF, Robert
Swiss, 20th century.
Born 4 April 1884, in Selzach.
Sculptor. Monuments.
Robert Rudolf was a student of Richard Kissling. He sculpted monuments in Solothurn and Laufen.
MUSEUMS AND GALLERIES:
LE LOCLE (MBA): several works.

RUDOLF, Samuel, or Rudolff or Rudolph
German, 17th - 18th century.
Born 16 April 1639, in Richwiller (Upper Rhine); died 3 April 1713, in Erlangen.
Active in Nuremberg and Erlangen.
Painter. Portraits, landscapes.

RUDOLF I
German, 14th century.
Active in Lüneburg (?).
Sculptor.
Rudolf I sculpted 10 panels depicting *Scenes from the Life of Jesus* for the monastery church of St Michael, Lünenburg.

RUDOLF II
German, 14th - 15th century.
Active in Nuremberg 1392-1400.
Painter.
Rudolf II painted and gilded Schönbrunn Castle in Nuremberg.

RUDOLF VAN ANTWERPEN, or Rudolph, also called Rudolf von Antwerpen
Flemish School, 16th century.
Born 16th century, probably in Antwerp.
Painter. History painting, portraits.
Rudolf van Antwerpen was the same artist as Rudolph Lœsen and in 1553 painted the main altar of the church of St Victorà, Xautlien. The *Portrait of Johan van der Does* in Leiden is also by him.

RUDOLFF, J. Hanns
Austrian, 16th century.
Active in 1588.
Stained glass painter.
MUSEUMS AND GALLERIES:
GRAZ (Landesmus. Joanneum): *Joseph and Potiphar's Wife* (stained-glass window).

RUDOLFI, Pietro
Austrian, 19th century.
Active in Udine at the beginning of the 19th century.
Sculptor.
Pietro Rudolfi sculpted a sarcophagus for the remains of 13 members of the Hapsburg family found in the abbey of St Paul in Carinthia in 1818.

RUDOLPH. See also **RUDOLF**

RUDOLPH, Arthur
German, 20th century.
Born 17 November 1885, in Dresden.
Painter, lithographer.
Arthur Rudolph was a student of Angelo Jank.
MUSEUMS AND GALLERIES:
POZNAN (Muz. Narodowe).

RUDOLPH, Christian Friedrich
German, 18th century.
Born 1692; died 7 February 1754, in Augsburg.
Draughtsman, engraver, goldsmith.

RUDOLPH, Christoph
Austrian, 18th century.
Died before 11 November 1740.
Active in Carinthia.
Sculptor.
Christoph Rudolph sculpted the high altar in the church of the hospital in Klagenfurt.

RUDOLPH, Friedrich Gotthelf Ferdinand
German, 19th century.
Born 16 July 1815, in Meissen (Saxony-Anhalt).
Lithographer.
Friedrich Gotthelf Ferdinand Rudolph was a pupil of Julius Steinmetz.

RUDOLPH, Gotthold
German, 19th century.
Born 1789, in Annaberg.
Painter, lithographer. Portraits, landscapes.

RUDOLPH, J. Philipp
German, 18th century.
Active in the second half of the 18th century.
Painter.
J. Philipp Rudolph painted the *Battle of Lepanto* for the church of Maria Sondheim of Arnstein in 1770.

RUDOLPH, Jakob
German, 20th century.
Born 21 September 1887, in Behlingen.
Sculptor. Monuments.
Jakob Rudolph studied under Balth at the academy in Munich and went on to live and work there. He sculpted war memorials, Calvaries and fountains.

RUDOLPH, Johann Georg. See **RUDOLPHI**

RUDOLPH, Konrad, or Conrado Rodulfo
Austrian, 18th century.
Born 11 December 1732, in Vienna.
Sculptor, architect.
Konrad Rudolph studied in Paris and Rome and spent a long time in Spain. He executed part of the principal door of Valencia Cathedral. He also worked in Barcelona and Vienna.

RUDOLPH, Samuel. See **RUDOLF**

RUDOLPH, Wilhelm
German, 20th century.
Born 22 February 1889.
Painter, engraver. Genre scenes, urban landscapes.
MUSEUMS AND GALLERIES:
CHEMNITZ (MM): *Flight into Egypt* - DRESDEN (Stadtmus.): *Landscape with Local Railway; Tavern Scene around Midnight.*

RUDOLPHI, Johann Georg
German, 17th century.
Born in Brakel; died 30 April 1693, in Brakel.
Painter, draughtsman.
Johann Georg Rudolphi was a painter in the court of Prince Bishop Ferdinand von Furstenberg and mainly executed altar paintings.

RUDOLPHI, Johannes
German, 20th century.
Born 5 October 1877, in Potsdam.
Painter. Portraits, landscapes.
Johannes Rudolphi studied at the fine arts academies of Berlin and Munich. He lived and worked in Berlin.

RÜDORF, Anna Margareta
German, 20th century.
Born 9 March 1879, in Berlin.
Painter. Portraits, landscapes.
Anna Margareta Rüdorf was a student of H. Balechek and Heinrich Knirr. She lived and worked in Jena.

RUDORF, Hermann
German, 19th - 20th century.
Born 27 June 1862, in Wieden (Saxony).
Painter. Landscapes.
Hermann Rudorf studied under Schultz-Naumburg and Gogarten. He lived and worked in Plauen.

RUDOW, Gustav Ludwig or Ludwig
German, 19th century.
Born 29 May 1850, in Merseburg; died 27 July 1907, in Dresden.
Painter.
Gustav Ludwig Rudow was a pupil at the academy in Dresden and a medal-winner there in 1870 and 1873.
MUSEUMS AND GALLERIES:
DRESDEN: *Self-portrait.*

RUDROFF, Alexander
Austrian, 19th century.
Active at the beginning of the 19th century.
Painter.
Alexander Rudroff was a pupil of Johann Martin Schmidt, known as Kremser-Schmidt. In 1807 he executed a painting for the high altar of the church of St Veit an der Gölsen.

RUDROFF, Matyas or Mathias
Hungarian, 18th century.
Born c. 1731; died 25 May 1786, in Ofen (now Buda).
Painter.
Matyas Rudroff painted two altar pictures in 1771 depicting *The Infant Jesus* for St Anne's church in Ofen.

RÜDT, Anton von
German, 20th century.
Born 1883; died 1936, in Munich.
Painter. Landscapes.
AUCTION RECORDS:
COLOGNE, 15 Oct 1988, *Winter Landscape with a Farm in the Snow* (1908, oil on canvas, 39 1/4 x 59 ins / 100 x 150 cm) DEM 7,000.

RUDULPH, Rella
American, 20th century.
Born 1906, in Livingston (Alabama); died 1988.
Active from 1948 in France.
Painter.
Rella Rudulph studied at the Chapelle School of Art in Denver (1928) before studying at the Art Students League of New York in 1933. She travelled to Ecuador, Chile and Mexico before settling in Paris in 1948.

Rudulph's first non-figurative paintings date from 1949. She often painted on aluminium. After her early abstract paintings, in which she was still searching for her own style, she soon developed a very strict geometric abstraction, comparable to that of Soldati or, more particularly, Dewasne.

Her work was shown in group exhibitions, including the Salon des Réalités Nouvelles, Paris, in 1953, 1954 and 1955. Her solo exhibitions include shows in Birmingham (Alabama) in 1940, in New York in 1941, Los Angeles in 1945 and Paris in 1955.

RUDZKI, Aleksander
Polish, 19th century.
Born 1832, in Warsaw; died 6 February 1866, in Warsaw.
Painter. Genre scenes.
Aleksander Rudzki studied in Warsaw; some works by this artist are in the National Museum.

RUDZKI, Jan Wezyk
Polish, 19th century.
Born 11 March 1792, in Witkowice; died 31 January 1874, in Florence.
Sculptor, painter, architect.
Jan Rudzki studied at the Accademia di San Luca in Rome. The National Museum in Warsaw has a bronze medallion depicting *A. Fredro* by this artist.

RUE, Abraham de La. See **LA RUE**

RUE, Aimée-Zoé. See **MIRBEL Lizinka Aimée Zoé de**

RUE, Heinrich
French, 17th century.
Sculptor (ivory).
Rue sculpted the bust of the *Duke of Alba*.

RUE, Jean de
French, 16th century.
Born to a family originally from Picardy.
Sculptor (wood).
In 1540 Jean de Rue carved the stalls of the church of Rue (Somme).

RUE, Louis Félix de La. See **LA RUE**

RUE, Philibert Benoît de La. See **LA RUE**

RUE, Pierre de La. See **LA RUE**

RUEBBENS, P.
Flemish School, 18th century.
Born in Brussels; died 1742, in The Hague.
Sculptor.
P Ruebbens sculpted the tomb of Pompejus de Roovere in the church at Harsinxvelt. He is probably identical to the sculptor Rubbens.

RUEBER, Magnus
German, 17th century.
Born in Amberg; died 1686, in Bamberg.
Painter.
Magnus Rueber was a member of the Franciscan order. He executed altar paintings for the Franciscan churches of Amberg and Bamberg.

RUECKE, Hans
Austrian, 16th - 17th century.
Active in Bohemia.
Medallist.
Hans Ruecke worked in Lünenburg, Bremervörde, Moisburg and Harburg.

RUEDA, Alonso de
Spanish, 16th century.
Active during the second half of the 16th century.
Sculptor.
Alonso de Rueda produced sculptures for Anne of Austria's entry into Madrid, in 1570.

RUEDA, Esteban de
Spanish, 17th century.
Painter.
Esteban de Rueda painted historical subjects in the church of Sta Ana and in the Piedad convent in Granada.

RUEDA, Gabriel de
Spanish, 17th century.
Died 24 December 1640, in Toledo.
Painter.
Gabriel de Rueda worked first in Granada and then at Toledo Cathedral, where he painted the vast fresco of *St Christopher*.

RUEDA, Gerardo
Spanish, 20th century.
Born 1926, in Madrid; died 25 May 1996, in Madrid.
Painter, sculptor, collage artist.
Rueda studied music and taught himself to paint. He lived and worked in Madrid and became a member of the Real Academia de San Fernando in 1995.

He started out as a figurative painter whose collages of the 1940s were influenced by the Cubist aesthetic. Around 1954, his work became more abstract, consisting of solid and more or less geometric forms that were assembled and juxtaposed into balanced and well-ordered compositions painted in thick colour (often applied by palette knife). By 1961 or so, his work had become more spontaneous and fluid; by this time he was painting in freer monochrome blocks. His approach changed again, however, and 1963 saw him working with what were essentially monochrome white low reliefs fashioned from (more often than not, octagonal) blocks of wood of different sizes placed within the frame either parallel to it or on a diagonal. In effect, he was by now working in a manner not unlike a Piet Mondrian - whose influence he acknowledged - or a Ben Nicholson. In Rueda's case, however, the underlying impulse was purely to arrive at abstraction. In other compositions from around this time he experimented with various optical effects already familiar from the work of Victor Vasarely. In 1992 he received a commission to design the two monumental doors to the Spanish Pavilion at the Universal Exhibition in Seville.

He showed at numerous group exhibitions, starting with the Second Hispano-American Biennale in Havana, Caracas and Bogotá in 1953 and going on to include *Recent Spanish Painting* in Fribourg, Basel, Munich and Göteborg in 1959-1960; 1960 Venice Biennale; *Contemporary Spanish Painting* in Tokyo, San Francisco and New York in 1960-1961 and at the Tate Gallery in London in 1962; *Spanish Art Today* held in Bochum and Nuremberg in 1967; the Louisiana Museum in Copenhagen in 1968; and at the Third International Salon of the Galeries Pilotes held at the Cantonal Museum of Lausanne in 1970.

He exhibited solo from 1949 at the Revista del Occidente Gallery in Madrid. This was followed by one-man shows between 1953 and 1995 in major cities throughout Spain and Italy and in Paris and Dublin.

An exhibition of Rueda collages was held in 2001 at the Museo Nacional Centro de Arte Reina Sofia in Madrid, and a retrospective of Rueda's work between 1946 and 1996 was mounted at the Kunsthistorisches Museum in Vienna in 2003.

BIBLIOGRAPHY:
IIIe Salon international des Galeries pilotes, exhibition catalogue, Musée cantonal, Lausanne, 1970. *Rueda*, exhibition catalogue, Gal. Juana Mordo, Madrid, 1971. *Catálogo nacional de arte contemporáneo 1990-1991*, Ibérico 2Mil, Barcelona, 1990-1991. Bonet, Juan Manuel, *Gerardo Rueda*, monograph, Ed. Polígrafa, Madrid, 1993. *Gerardo Rueda: collages 1956-1996*, Ediciones del Umbral, Madrid, 1999. Rose, Barbara (ed.), *Gerardo Rueda, retrospettiva 1946-1996. Pitture e collages*, exhibition catalogue, Palazzo Reale, Naples, 2000 (text in Spanish and English). *Gerardo Rueda. Exposicion retrospectiva, 1941-1996*, exhibition catalogue,

Museo Nacional Centro de Arte Reina Sofía, Madrid, 2001. Guirao Cabrera, José (ed.), *Gerardo Rueda: escultor*, Fundación Eduardo Capa, Alicante, 2002.
MUSEUMS AND GALLERIES:
CAMBRIDGE, MA (Fogg AM, Harvard University) - CUENCA (Mus. De Arte Abstracto Español, Fundación Juan March) - GÖTEBORG (Konstmus.) - LONDON (British Mus.) - MADRID (Mus. Nacional Centro de Arte Reina Sofía) - MANILA (Mus. del Ateneo) - MEXICO CITY (MAC International Rufino Tamayo) - NEW YORK (Brooklyn Mus.) - PARIS (MAM) - PHILIPPINES (National Mus.) - ROCHESTER (Memorial AG, Rochester University) - SEVILLE (Centro Andaluz de Arte Contemporáneo) - VERUCCHIO (Gal. Comunale d'Arte Moderna).

RUEDA, Jeronimo de
Spanish, 17th century.
Active at the beginning of the 17th century.
Painter.
Jeronimo de Rueda painted historical subjects in the church of S Andrés and in the collegiate church in Granada.

RUEDA, Juan de
Spanish, 17th century.
Active in Seville at the beginning of the 17th century.
Painter.
Juan de Rueda carved two altars for Seville Cathedral in 1609.

RUEDA, Nicolas de
Spanish, 18th century.
Sculptor, architect.
Nicolas de Rueda worked for churches in Lorca.

RUEDENAUER, Adolf C.
German, 20th century.
Born 1 September 1896, in Stuttgart.
Painter, engraver, architect.
Ruedenauer studied at the academies in Munich and Berlin.

RUEDORFER, Ildefons
Austrian, 18th century.
Born 3 January 1726, in Kitzbühl; died 16 December 1801, in Rott am Inn.
Painter.
Ildefons Ruedorfer was a member of the Benedictine order.

RUEELE, Jean. See **RUWEEL**

RUEF, Mathias
Austrian, 18th - 19th century.
Born 1745; died 1822.
Active in Volders (Tyrol).
Painter.
Mathias Ruef was a pupil and assistant of M. Knoller in Neresheim and in Volders. He executed frescoes in the churches of Wiesing in 1780 and Kirchbichl in 1784.

RUEFF, Andreas, or Ruck
Austrian, 17th century.
Active in Vienna 1675-1679.
Painter, art critic.
Andreas Rueff worked for Prince Charles Eusebius of Liechtenstein.

RUEFF, Christof
Austrian, 18th century.
Active in Bozen, South Tyrol (now Bolzano, Italy).
Sculptor.
Christof Rueff worked in Eppan in 1757.

RUEFF, Hans Jakob, or Ruoff
German, 17th century.
Died between 1631 and 1650.
Active in Freiberg.
Sculptor.
Hans Jakob Rueff worked in Freiberg Cathedral, Masmunster and Guebwiller.

RÜEGG, Eduard
Swiss, 19th century.
Born 1838, in Wila; died 8 April 1903, in Wengen.
Landscape artist.

RÜEGG, Ernst Georg
Swiss, 20th century.
Born 21 August 1883, in Milan; died 1948, in Männedorf.
Painter, fresco artist, draughtsman, engraver. Genre scenes.
Ernst Georg Rüegg was a student of H. Gattiker and E.A. Stuckelberg. He is noted for frescoes in Schaffhausen town hall.
MUSEUMS AND GALLERIES:
AARAU (Aargauer Kunsthaus): *Little Children's Voices in the Evening* (1919) - GLARIS - OLTEN - WINTERTHUR - ZURICH.
AUCTION RECORDS:
ZURICH, 26 May 1978, *Grape Harvest* (oil on canvas, 56 1/2 x 37 1/2 ins / 143.5 x 95 cm) CHF 3,900. ZURICH, 19 July 1984, *Magician* (1919, oil on canvas, 19 3/4 x 25 1/2 ins / 50 x 65 cm) CHF 4,400. ZURICH, 24 Nov 1993, *Lonely Little Girl* (ink and watercolour/paper, 14 1/2 x 10 3/4 ins / 37 x 27.5 cm) CHF 1,495. ZURICH, 9 June 1999, *Squirrel* (1911, oil on canvas, 15 x 21 ins / 39 x 53 cm) CHF 3,000.

RÜEGG, Jakob or Hans J.
Swiss, 19th century.
Born 26 December 1859, in Dällikon.
Painter, engraver (etching), architect.

RÜEGG, Johann
Swiss, 17th century.
Active in Kempten-Wetzikon 1694-1695.
Engraver (burin).

RUEGGER, Henri
Swiss, 20th century.
Born 8 October 1881, in Geneva.
Landscape artist.
Henri Ruegger taught at the Geneva college of art.

RUEHE, Aegid de. See **RYDE Aegidius de**

RUEL, Gabriel de
Spanish, 17th century.
Died 24 December 1641.
Active in Granada.
Painter. History painting.
Gabriel de Ruel worked at Toledo Cathedral in 1633. Most of his works are in Granada.

RÜEL, Gottfried
German, 17th century.
Glass painter.
Gottfried Rüel settled in Potsdam in 1678.

RUEL, Jean. See **REVEL**

RUEL, Jean-Pierre
French, 20th - 21st century.
Born 1970, in St-Étienne.
Painter.
Jean-Pierre Ruel studied under Velickovic at the École des Beaux-Arts in Paris. He has been involved in various group exhibitions, notably at the Salon de Mai in Paris in 1996 and 1997 and, as a solo artist, at the Galeries Aittouarès in 1998. His work typically features violence as it impacts on everyday life.

RUEL, Johan Baptist de, or Rüll or Rul
Flemish School, 17th century.
Born c. 1634, in Antwerp; died 20 June 1685, in Würzburg.

Painter. History painting, portraits.
Ruel was the pupil of Hohann Thomas van Ypres, called Ipenaer, having started his career as a cantor in Mainz Cathedral. He worked in Heidelberg, Mainz, Würzburg, Augsburg and Vienna, where he executed several altar paintings and portraits.

J.B.R

MUSEUMS AND GALLERIES:
DARMSTADT: *Portrait of Prince Damian Hartard van der Leyen* - GOTHA: *Mary and the Infant Jesus* - HEIDELBERG: *Portrait of Melchior Friedrich von Schönborn and His Wife* - MUNICH (Alte Pinakothek): *Portrait of Bishop Val. Voit von Rieneck* - MUNICH (Bayerisches Nationalmus.): *Madonna and Child* - OBERSCHLEISSHEIM (Neues Schloss Schleissheim, Staatsgal.): *Pierre Philippe de Dernbach* - SPEYER: *Portrait of the Elector Charles Louis.*

RUEL, Pierre Léon Horace
French, 19th century.
Born c. 1845, in Paris.
Painter, watercolourist, draughtsman. Battles, allegorical subjects, figures, portraits, genre scenes, landscapes.
Pierre Ruel was a student of Isidore Pils and Louis Arbant. He exhibited at the Paris Salon, then at the Salon des Artistes Français from 1868 to 1903.
MUSEUMS AND GALLERIES:
ABBEVILLE: *Tribute to Admiral Courbet.*
AUCTION RECORDS:
PARIS, 6 March 1893, *The King is Passing,* FRF 620. PARIS, 17-18 Nov 1943, *Operatic Ballet* (lead pencil, watercolour and gouache) FRF 200. NEW YORK, 29 May 1980, *Pickpocket* (1881, oil on panel, 12 x 9 1/2 ins / 30.5 x 24 cm) USD 2,300. CALAIS, 15 Dec 1996, *Village Festival* (1898, oil on canvas, 29 1/4 x 23 1/4 ins / 74 x 59 cm) FRF 22,000.

RUELA, Juan de. See **LAS ROELAS**

RUELAND. See also **FRUEAUF Rueland**

RUELAND, Theobald
German, 18th century.
Active in the second half of the 18th century.
Draughtsman.
Theobald Rueland was a monk. He drew the church of Sammerei in 1786.

RUELANDT, Christoph
German, 17th century.
Sculptor.
Christoph Ruelandt worked for the Jesuit churches in Munich and Wessobrunn around 1600 as an engraver and stucco artist.

RUELAS, Julio
Mexican, 19th - 20th century.
Born 1870; died 1907.
Painter.
Like other Latin American artists, Julio Ruelas trained in the late 19th century in Europe, in his case in Karlsruhe under the direction of Professor Mayerbeer.

Before going to Europe, he was already collaborating on two avant garde publications, supplying drawings and vignettes to the *Revista Moderna* and to *Los Contemporaneos.*
AUCTION RECORDS:
NEW YORK, 5 April 1978, *La Critica* (etching and dry-point, 9 x 6 1/2 ins / 23 x 16.8 cm; 7 x 5 3/4 ins/17.8 x 14.8 cm) USD 1,600. NEW YORK, 2 May 1990, *Vision of the Conquistadors* (1905, oil on canvas, 35 x 52 ins / 89 x 132 cm) USD 57,750. NEW YORK, 25-26 Nov 1996, *Nude* (c. 1900, gouache/paper, 10 1/4 x 5 1/2 ins / 26 x 14 cm) USD 2,760. MEXICO, 19 Sept 2000, *Implacable* (1901, ink, 5 x 7 ins / 12 x 17 cm) MXP 20,000.

RUELL, Johann Jakob. See **RILL**

RUELLAN, Joseph Alexandre
French, 19th century.
Born 1864, in St-Quay-Portrieux.
Painter. Landscapes.
Joseph Ruellan was a student of Jean Paul Laurens and Benjamin Constant. A member of the Société des Artistes Français from 1901, he featured at this group's Salon, receiving an honourable mention in 1897.
MUSEUMS AND GALLERIES:
ST-BRIEUC.
AUCTION RECORDS:
PARIS, 22 March 1990, *Edge of the Beach* (oil on panel, 9 x 13 ins / 22 x 33 cm) FRF 20,000.

RUELLE, Charles de La. See **LA RUELLE**

RUELLE, Jacques
French, 17th century.
Active in Lyons 1672-1695.
Painter.

RUELLE, Jean, called La Ferté
French, 17th century.
Active in Paris during the second half of the 17th century.
Painter.

RUELLE, Robert
French, 17th century.
Active in Lyons 1631-1649.
Painter.

RUELLES, Jean François de, or Ruwelles
Flemish School, 17th century.
Active in Antwerp during the second half of the 17th century.
Engraver (burin).
Ruelles was the pupil of P. Clouet.

RUELLES, DES. See also **DES RUELLES**

RUEMANN. See **RÜMANN**

RUEP, Johann
Austrian, 18th century.
Died c. 1780, in Bruneck.
Active in Taufers.
Painter.
Johann Ruep painted miniatures on silk canvases in the style of Prunner and Burgmann.

RUEPP
German, 18th century.
Active in Wertingen.
Painter.
Ruepp painted the altarpiece depicting *St Francis of Assisi* in the ancient Capuchin church at Donauwörth.

RUEPP, Jakob
Austrian, 18th century.
Active in Waidhofen an der Thaya in 1721.
Painter.

RUEPP, Richard
Austrian, 20th century.
Born 4 April 1885, in St-Vigil-d'Enneberg.
Active in Vienna.
Sculptor, medallist.
Richard Ruepp studied under H. Fuss in Innsbruck and under Bitterlich in Vienna. He sculpted war memorials, portrait busts and tombs.

RUEPRECHT
Austrian, 16th century.

Active in Klausen (Tyrol) in the first half of the 16th century.
Painter.
Tyrolean School.
Rueprecht worked in the church of Säben in 1516.

RUER, Tommaso, or Ruez or Rerer
Italian, 17th century.
Of German origin.
Sculptor.
Tommaso Ruer worked for several churches in Venice and Brescia.

RUES, Jacob. See **RUSS**

RUES, Lorenz
Austrian, 17th century.
Born c. 1640; died 15 April 1690, in Rome.
Active in Bruneck.
Sculptor.
Lorenz Rues married in Rome. He probably sculpted his aunt's tomb, which is to be found in the church at Bruneck.

RUESCH, Nicolaus or Niklaus, or Rüsch, called Lawelin or Lawlin or Clavin or Clewin
Swiss, 15th century.
Died perhaps between 1453 and 1454, in Basel.
Painter, fresco artist. Religious subjects.
The dates of the birth and death of Nicolaus Ruesch are unknown, but it is known that he worked in Tübingen. In 1405 he was in Basel, where he decorated some cloisters. In 1427 he became a member of the town council and in the same year he painted a fresco of *St Christopher* above the market fountain. In 1429 he painted a *Virgin* for the town hall, in 1438 a *Crucifixion* for the Charterhouse, and in 1441 a *Virgin with the Two St Johns* for the monastery of the Carthusian Fathers. He was probably the master of Konrad Witz. None of his works has survived.

RUESCH, Thaddäus, or Rüesch
Swiss, 18th century.
Active in the second half of the 18th century.
Sculptor.
Thaddäus Ruesch was commissioned to execute sculptures for the altars of St Gall Cathedral in 1772.

RUESCHE
German, 18th century.
Active in Bonn in the second half of the 18th century.
Painter.
Ruesche worked at the castle and town hall in Münster under the guidance of Ferdinand Lipper between 1775 and 1780.

RUESS, or Ruis
Austrian, 17th century.
Active in Vienna.
Painter.
Ruess worked for the prince of Liechtenstein from 1650 to 1652.

RUESS, Jacob. See **RUSS**

RUESSEL, Johann
Austrian, 18th - 19th century.
Born 1746; died 11 February 1810, in Vienna.
Sculptor.

RUEST, Else
German, 20th century.
Born 19 April 1861, in Hanover.
Painter, engraver. Landscapes, flowers.
Else Ruest was a student of V. Roman, Hans Richard Volkmann and Hermann Gattiker.
MUSEUMS AND GALLERIES:
HANOVER: several paintings.

RUESTES, Francesc
Spanish, 20th - 21st century.
Born 1959, in Barcelona.
Painter, draughtsman, mixed media.
Francesc Ruestes underwent classical training in Barcelona's art institutions. His art brings the Surrealist conceptual wave of the 1950s Catalan avant-garde up-to-date. The first exhibition of his work was shown in Barcelona's Alejandro Sales gallery.

RUET, Claude de. See **DERUET**

RUET, Louis
French, 19th - 20th century.
Born 8 March 1861, in Paris.
Engraver.
Louis Ruet, a pupil of Le Rat, was president of the society of French etchers. He won gold medals and awards at salons and exhibited in Paris at the Salon des Artistes Français from 1881. In 2003, his work was represented in the exhibition held at the Musée d'Aquitaine, Bordeaux, *Vénus et Caïn. Figures de la préhistoire 1830-1930* (*Venus and Cain. Prehistoric Figures 1830-1930*), which charted the rise of prehistory as a scientific discipline and a source of artistic inspiration. He engraved etchings.
BIBLIOGRAPHY:
Lafont-Couturier, Hélène/Dagen, Philippe/Loizeau, Sigolène, *Vénus et Caïn. Figures de la préhistoire 1830-1930*, exhibition catalogue, Musée d'Aquitaine, Bordeaux, 2003.

RUETA, José
Spanish, 18th century.
Painter.
José Rueta executed the paintings for the altar of the Virgen de los Dolores in the church of Nuestra Señora in San Sebastián.

RÜETSCHI, Paul
Swiss, 20th century.
Born 23 August 1878, in Suhr, near Aarau.
Painter. Genre scenes.
Paul Rüetschi was a student of Léon Pétua, Karl Raupp and Alexander von Wagner.

RUETTER, W.C. Georg
Dutch, 20th century.
Born 8 March 1875, in Haarlem; died 1966.
Painter, engraver. Portraits, still-lifes, flowers.
W. C. Georg Ruetter was a student of Jan Derek Huibers and August Allebé.
MUSEUMS AND GALLERIES:
ROTTERDAM (Mus. Boijmans Van Beuningen): *Portrait of M.A. Allebé*.
AUCTION RECORDS:
AMSTERDAM, 25 April 1990, *Still-life with Flowers in a Vase* (1958, oil on canvas, 29 x 24 3/4 ins / 73.5 x 63 cm) NLG 18,400. AMSTERDAM, 6 Nov 1990, *Still-life with Flowers* (oil on canvas, 19 3/4 x 24 1/2 ins / 50 x 62 cm) NLG 13,800. AMSTERDAM, 17 Sept 1991, *Still-life with Carnations in a Vase* (1950, oil on canvas, 17 x 18 ins / 43 x 45.5 cm) NLG 3,680. AMSTERDAM, 18 Feb 1992, *Still-life with Roses in a Vase* (1948, oil on panel, 11 3/4 x 10 1/2 ins / 30 x 26.5 cm) NLG 2,300. AMSTERDAM, 28 Oct 1992, *Summer Flowers in a Vase* (1935, oil on canvas, 33 3/4 x 22 1/4 ins / 86 x 56.5 cm) NLG 4,830. AMSTERDAM, 7 Nov 1995, *Still-life with Roses in a Vase* (oil on canvas, 15 3/4 x 13 3/4 ins / 40 x 35 cm) NLG 2,360. AMSTERDAM, 19 Jan 1999, *Carnations in a Glass Vase* (oil on canvas, 18 x 15 ins / 45 x 38 cm) NLG 3,600. AMSTERDAM, 7 June 1999, *Flower Still-life* (oil on canvas, 20 x 20 ins / 50 x 51 cm) NLG 4,400. AMSTERDAM, 4 July 2000, *Summer Flowers in a Faience Vase* (oil on canvas, 12 x 13 ins / 30 x 34 cm) NLG 15,000. AMSTERDAM, 4 July 2000, *Roses in a Blanc de Chine vase* (1957, oil on canvas, 20 x 16 ins / 52 x 41 cm) NLG 18,000. AMSTERDAM, 30 Jan 2001,

White Flowers (oil on canvas, 11 x 13 ins / 29 x 34 cm) NLG 4,800. AMSTERDAM, 30 Jan 2001, *Vase of Roses* (oil on canvas, 21 x 21 ins / 53 x 53 cm) NLG 12,000. AMSTERDAM, 4 March 2002, *Still-life with Flowers, Fruit and Letter* (1950, oil on canvas, 21 x 24 ins / 53 x 61 cm) EUR 1,650. AMSTERDAM, 25 June 2002, *Pink and White Roses in a Glass Vase* (oil on canvas, 20 x 18 ins / 51 x 46 cm) EUR 3,000. AMSTERDAM, 3 Feb 2004, *Pink Carnation in a White Vase* (oil on canvas, 15 x 18 ins / 38 x 46 cm) EUR 2,000. AMSTERDAM, 21 Dec 2004, *Still-life with Magnolia* (1943, oil on canvas, 33 x 28 ins / 85 x 71 cm) EUR 2,800.

RUETZ, Hedwig
Latvian, 20th century.
Born 29 May 1879, in Riga; died 19 November 1966, in Beulwitz.
Active in Germany.
Painter. Portraits, landscapes.

Ruetz was a pupil of R. von Rosen, K. Ritter and H. von Habermann in Karlsruhe and Munich, and studied with Max Liebermann in Berlin. She continued her studies in Paris, before settling in Beulwitz, Saalfeld. She lived and worked in Berlin. Her *Portrait of the President of the Swiss Confederation, M Frey* is preserved in the head office of Communications Téléphoniques in Bern.

RUETZ, Jakob. See **RUEZ**

RUEZ, Arnould de
French, 18th century.
Active in Lille during the first half of the 18th century.
Painter.

Ruez painted two panels, *Scenes from the Life of Jesus*, for the high altar of St-Piat church in Tournai, in 1724.

RUEZ, Jakob, or Ruetz or Rutz
German, 18th century.
Born 30 June 1728, in Wurzach; died 4 November 1782, in Wurzach.
Sculptor, stucco artist.

Jakob Ruez was the son of Johann Ruez. He worked in the church at Hechingen.

RUEZ, Johann
German, 18th century.
Died 1762, in Wurzach.
Active in Strengen am Arlberg.
Sculptor.

Johann Ruez was the father of Jakob Ruez. He executed sculptures in the church of the Holy Cross near Wurzach.

RUEZ, Lambert. See **RAUTZ**

RUEZ, Tommaso. See **RUER**

RUF, Heinrich
German, 19th century.
Born 10 March 1837, in Munich; died 23 January 1883, in Munich, committed suicide.
Active in Basel 1867-1875.
Sculptor.

Heinrich Ruf was a pupil of Widermann and Schwanthaler.

MUSEUMS AND GALLERIES:
BASEL (Bernoullianum): *Bust of Johann Jakob* (marble); *Bust of Daniel Bernoulli* (marble); *Bust of Leonh. Euler* (marble).

RUFANO, Giacomo
Italian, 17th century.
Active in Padua during the second half of the 17th century.
Engraver (burin).

Rufano worked in Trento from 1652 to 1670 and engraved views of this city and the surrounding area.

RUFER, Bendicht, called Hüttenbenz
Swiss, 18th - 19th century.
Born 1756, in Münchenbuchsee; died 14 September 1833, in Münchenbuchsee.
Glass painter, glassmaker.

MUSEUMS AND GALLERIES:
BERN (Stadtbibliothek): four books of sketches for stained-glass windows (1789-1832).

RUFER, Hannes
Swiss, 20th century.
Born 1908.
Painter.

MUSEUMS AND GALLERIES:
AARAU (Aargauer Kunsthaus): *Workers at the Sea* (1954).

RUFER, Jacob. See **RUSS**

RUFF, Andor or András
Hungarian, 20th century.
Born 2 January 1885, in Taksony.
Sculptor.

Ruff studied in Budapest and in Brussels. He lived and worked in Budapest.

AUCTION RECORDS:
NEW YORK, 14 Oct 1993, *Arabian Craftsman Decorating a Jug* (polychrome metal, h. 14 1/2 ins / 37 cm) USD 748. NEW YORK, 17 Jan 1996, *Inkstand with Two Fishermen* (bronze, h. 9 1/2 ins / 24.1 cm, l. 17 3/4 ins/45.1 cm) USD 2,070.

RUFF, Emma
French, 20th century.
Born 12 May 1884, in Paris.
Painter. Portraits, landscapes, still-lifes, flowers.

Emma Ruff, a pupil of F. Lauth, M. Baschet and Henri Royer, exhibited at the Salon des Artistes Français, of which she was a member and where she was awarded a silver medal in 1941.

AUCTION RECORDS:
RHEIMS, 18 June 1995, *Still-life with Apples* (oil on canvas, 28 1/4 x 36 1/4 ins / 72 x 92 cm) FRF 5,500.

RUFF, Johannes
Swiss, 19th century.
Born 1813, in Oberstrass (Zurich); died 21 April 1886, in Weinigen, near Zurich.
Painter, engraver (mezzotint).

Johannes Ruff was a pupil of G. C. Oberkogler.

MUSEUMS AND GALLERIES:
ZURICH (Prints Collection): watercolours; drawings.

RUFF, Thomas
German, 20th - 21st century.
Born 1958, in Zell am Harmersbach.
Active in Düsseldorf.
Photographer. Portraits.

From the 1980s on, Thomas Ruff created several series of portraits that were deliberately deprived of all emotion. He also shot interiors and architecture in the spirit of the architectural photography of the Bauhaus, before producing more politicised work in the 1990s with his series *Nights*, illustrating the Gulf War. He then produced a series entitled *Nudes*, based on pornographic images from the Internet, and continued his experiments with electronic images in his series *Substratum*.

Ruff has taken part in group exhibitions, including: *Moving Pictures*, an exhibition presenting the use of photography, film and video in art since the end of the 1960s, held at the Solomon R. Guggenheim Museum in New York (2002); and *Peter Pan is Back!* at the Galerie Nelson in Paris (2003). His solo exhibitions include *Thomas Ruff: 1979 to the Present* at the Tate Liverpool in 2003.

BIBLIOGRAPHY:
Moving Pictures, exhibition catalogue, Solomon R. Guggenheim Museum, New York, 2002.

MUSEUMS AND GALLERIES:
NEW YORK (Solomon R. Guggenheim Mus.): *Portrait (M. Roser)* (1999, photograph).
AUCTION RECORDS:
LONDON, 23 May 1996, *15h 52m 45°* (1990, colour photograph, 101 1/2 x 74 ins / 258 x 188 cm) GBP 8,625. LONDON, 6 Dec 1996, *16h 30m 55°* (1989, colour photograph, 96 1/2 x 69 3/4 ins / 245 x 177 cm) GBP 5,750; *Untitled* (1987, colour photograph, portrait of Elke Denda, 82 3/4 x 65 1/4 ins / 210 x 165.5 cm) GBP 8,050. NEW YORK, 17 May 2000, *09h 54m/ -25* (1992, colour photo, 102 x 74 ins / 260 x 188 cm) USD 48,000. NEW YORK, 18 May 2000, *O9 H 12 M, 30 degrees* (1991, black and white photo, 99 x 71 ins / 252 x 180 cm) USD 75,000. LONDON, 9 Feb 2001, *Photo 09H 58 Min-40* (1990, photo, Photographs, 79 x 53 ins / 201 x 134 cm) GBP 60,000. LONDON, 23 Oct 2001, *Stars 02h 56m - 65o* (colour photo, 99 x 71 ins / 252 x 180 cm) GBP 70,000. LONDON, 6 Feb 2002, *21h 32m/-60* (1992, colour photo) GBP 50,000. LONDON, 7 Feb 2002, *09H 12M/-30* (1991, colour photo, 79 x 53 ins / 201 x 134 cm) GBP 50,000. LONDON, 22 Oct 2003, *17h 16m/-45* (1990, colour photo, 112 x 73 ins / 285 x 186 cm) GBP 42,000. NEW YORK, 14 Nov 2003, *17H 38M, -30* (photo, 102 x 73 ins / 258 x 185 cm) USD 72,000. NEW YORK, 8 Nov 2004, *Substrat 4III* (photo, three, 73 x 94 ins / 186 x 240 cm) USD 102,000. NEW YORK, 10 Nov 2004, *Substrat 22 III* (2003, photo, 119 x 63 ins / 301 x 160 cm) USD 80,000.

RUFFÉ, Léon Henri
French, 19th - 20th century.
Born 29 April 1864, in Paris.
Engraver, painter.
Léon Henri Ruffé, a pupil of Baude, exhibited in Paris at the Salon des Artistes Français from 1884. He won a gold medal in 1900 and a medal of honour in 1908, and was made an Officier of the Légion d'Honneur in 1927. He was awarded the Hors concours of the Salon des Artistes Français.

RUFFERIUS, Claudius
Swiss, 16th century.
Illuminator.
In 1552 Claudius Rufferius illuminated an antiphonary for Abbot Johann Christoph von Grüth in Muri.

RUFFIER, Noël
French, 19th century.
Born 19th century, in Avignon.
Sculptor.
Noël Ruffier was the student of Guilbert d'Anelle and Dumont. He exhibited at the Salon from 1878 to 1896.
MUSEUMS AND GALLERIES:
AVIGNON (Mus. Calvet): *Bust of Viala; Bust of Bara; Recumbent Woman* (large decorative plaster-cast).
AUCTION RECORDS:
PARIS, 12 March 1984, *Pitcher* (bronze, brown patina, tree-shaped belly, handle decorated with a Bacchic couple, h. 15 1/4 ins / 38.5 cm) FRF 7,500.

RUFFIEUX
Swiss, 17th century.
Active in Fribourg towards the end of the 17th century.
Sculptor.
Ruffieux sculpted chairs and altars in churches in the canton of Fribourg.

RUFFIN, Émile Auguste
French, 19th century.
Born 19th century, in Rouen.
Painter.
Émile Ruffin was a student of Pils and Morin. He first exhibited at the Salon of 1876.

RUFFIN, Johann. See **RUFFINI Joseph**

RUFFIN, Nicolas
French, 16th century.
Active in Toulouse 1557-1566.
Medallist.

RUFFIN, Ritta Pauline
French, 19th century.
Born 19th century, in Cromoisy.
Painter.
Rita Ruffin was a student of Petit and Delacroix. She first exhibited at the Salon of 1877.

RUFFINACO, Jacopo
Italian, 16th century.
Active in Rome.
Sculptor.
Jacopo Ruffinaco sculpted plaster maquettes for Antonio de San Gallo's model of St Peter's Basilica in Rome, in 1546.

RUFFINER, Ruggero, or Ruffino
Swiss, 15th century.
Active in Milan.
Sculptor.
Ruggero Ruffiner carved sculptures for Milan Cathedral.

RUFFINI, Agnese. See **POSTEMPSKA**

RUFFINI, Joseph, or erroneously known as Johann Ruffin
Austrian, 18th century.
Born in Meran (now Merano, Italy); died 7 February 1749, in Augsburg.
Painter.
Joseph Ruffini studied in Munich and decorated the cloisters of the convent in Ottobeuren with 72 paintings. He also worked in the abbey of St Florian (Upper Austria) and the abbey of Lambach.

RUFFINO, Ruggero. See **RUFFINER**

RUFFLE, Teófilo
Spanish, 19th century.
Born 1835, in Paris.
Active in Madrid.
Lithographer.

RUFFO, Marguerite
French, 19th century.
Born 19th century, in Paris.
Painter.
Marguerite Ruffo's teachers were Brandon, Hebert and Barrias. She first exhibited at the Salon in 1877.

RUFFO, Tommaso
Italian, 19th - 20th century.
Born 24 May 1849, in Tropea; died 22 March 1919.
Painter. Genre scenes, flowers.
Tomasso Ruffo was a pupil of Morelli and Mancinelli.

RUFFONI, Giacomo Giuseppe. See **RUPHON Jacopo**

RUFFY, Odette
Swiss, 20th century.
Born 1892, in Bern; died 25 April 1915.
Painter, engraver.
Odette Ruffy was a student of S. Hollosy.

RUFILIONI, Alessandro
Italian, 15th century.
Born c. 1476, in Florence; died c. 1504, in Rome.
Sculptor.

RUFILIONI, Gabriele
Italian, 15th century.
Born c. 1487, in Florence; died c. 1504, in Rome.
Sculptor.

RUFILUS
German, 13th century.
Active c. 1200.
Illuminator.
Rufilus illuminated a legendary with his portrait for the monastery of Weissenau, near Ravensburg.

RUFIN, Maurice, or Ruffin
French, 20th century.
Born 19 January 1880, in Valenciennes; died 4 September 1966, in Valenciennes.
Painter. Religious subjects, portraits, landscapes, still-lifes, flowers.
Maurice Rufin studied initially with Joseph Layraud at the École d'Art, Valenciennes, and then went to the École des Beaux-Arts, Paris. He left after disagreements with his teacher, Léon Bonnat, whom he considered was not open enough to new developments in painting. He also attended the Académie Julian and the classes of Alphonse Chigot and Le Sidaner. Eventually he went back to Valenciennes. He was a friend of the poet Émile Verhaeren. After World War I he drew for *Le Petit Journal* and particularly covered the important treason trials of the period. He was appointed to teach at the École d'Art, Valenciennes, in 1920 and began giving private lessons in 1929. He was made a Chevalier of the Légion d'Honneur. His painting combines colour borrowed from Impressionism and open-air painting with the symbolism of Eugène Carrière. He painted a *Crucifixion* for the church of Notre Dame, Le St-Cordon. He exhibited in Paris at the Salon des Artistes Français from 1920 to 1922, and in 1956 and 1966 the Musée des Beaux-Arts, Valenciennes, organised retrospectives of his work.
MUSEUMS AND GALLERIES:
CAMBRAI - CONDÉ-SUR-L'ESCAUT - HAZEBROUCK - MAUBEUGE - VALENCIENNES (Hôtel de Ville): three still-lifes - VALENCIENNES (MBA): six canvases.

RUFINO D'ALESSANDRIA
Italian, 15th century.
Painter.
Rufino d'Alessandria painted a retable of which the centre panel depicts the *Madonna and Child*, for the church of Marsaglia near Mondovi.

RUFO, Josef or José Martin
Spanish, 18th century.
Born in El Escorial.
Active during the second half of the 18th century.
Painter. History painting, portraits.
Josef Rufo studied at the Real Academia de San Fernando from 1752 to 1763.
MUSEUMS AND GALLERIES:
MADRID (Real Academia de Bellas Artes de San Fernando): *Defence of Morro de la Habana.*

RUFO Y CARILLO, Luis
Spanish, 17th century.
Born 1582, in Cordova; died 18 May 1653, in Cordova.
Painter, poet.
Luis Rufo y Carillo was the son of the poet Juan Rufo. He studied in Rome.

RUFONIO, Giacomo Giuseppe. See **RUPHON**

RUFUS I
1st century.
Active probably at the beginning of the 1st century.
Cameo engraver.
Ancient Roman.
Rufus is known for a cameo showing *Victory Driving Four Horses*, now in the St Petersburg Museum.
MUSEUMS AND GALLERIES:
ST PETERSBURG (Hermitage): *Victory Driving Four Horses* (double layer onyx cameo).

RUFUS II
1st century.
Active during the second half of the 1st century.
Painter.
Ancient Roman.
Rufus is mentioned in an epigram by Lucilius.

RUGA, Alessandro
Italian, 19th century.
Born 1836, in Milan; died 1916
Sculptor.
A pupil of Vela, Alessandro Ruga exhibited in Turin and Milan.
MUSEUMS AND GALLERIES:
BERN (Kunstmus.): *Bust of the Sculptor Vela* - TURIN (Mus. Civico): *Bust of Marchese Roberto d'Azeglio.*

RUGA, Pietro
Italian, 19th century.
Active in Rome.
Engraver. Architectural views.
Pietro Ruga engraved *The Ruins of Pompeii* and *Twenty-five Views of the Gates and Walls of Rome.*

RUGALDIER. See **RUNGALDIER**

RÜGÉ, George. See **RUGUÉ**

RUGEL
German, 18th century.
Active in Waldsee.
Sculptor.
Rugel sculpted a *Christ on the Cross* in the arch of the choir at the chapel of St Nikolaus in Zweifelsberg in 1744.

RUGENDAS, Christian Johann or Johann Christian
German, 18th century.
Born 1708, probably in Augsburg; died 10 July 1781, probably in Augsburg.
Draughtsman, engraver (mezzotint).
Christian Johann Rugendas was a pupil of his father Georg Philipp Rugendas and of J. B. Probst. His engravings were mainly after his father's drawings of battles and other military scenes. His work is quite important and comprises around 100 pieces, 30 or so of which are after his own drawings.

RUGENDAS, Georg Philipp I
German, 17th - 18th century.
Born 27 November 1666, in Augsburg; died 9 March 1742, in Augsburg.
Painter, engraver. Military subjects, battles, genre scenes.
Georg Philipp Rugendas I was a pupil of Isaac Fescher. He quickly earned a reputation working in his master's genre. In 1692 he left for Italy, stopping first in Venice, where he gained valuable advice from Giovanni-Baptista Molinari. He then went to Rome, where he met with great success. He was forced to return to Augsburg in 1695 by the death of his father. The Spanish War of Succession provided him with scenes of carnage from which his talent drew inspiration. He was noted for his composure, particularly during the bombardment and capture of Augsburg by the French and the Bavarians in 1703; he drew several scenes from this, which he later used for a series of etchings. His etched and mezzotint work is significant and comprises military scenes. He was also an editor.

G P Rugendas fec.

Museums and Galleries:
Aachen: *Battle on Horseback* - Avignon: *Battle Scene; After the Battle* - Basel: *Battle between Cavalry Soldiers; After the Battle* - Brest: *A Cavalry Camp under Louis XIV* - Dresden: *Pillaging of Bodies on the Battlefield* - Graz: *Battle between Cavalry Soldiers* - Kaliningrad: *Cavalry Battles* - Mulhouse: *Cavalry Battles* - Nantes: *Taking of a Fortified Town; Battle* - Oslo: *Cavalry Battle* - Périgueux: *Fox Hunt* - Stockholm: *Trotting Horse* (wax sketch) - Stuttgart: *Two Turkish Battles; Battle; Scene in a Camp* - Vienna: *Two Battles* - Vienna (Schönborn-Buckheim): *Cavalry Battle*.
Auction records:
Paris, 1772, *View of a Market in Rome with People and Animals* (pen drawing with Indian ink wash) FRF 72. Paris, 1821, *Cavalry Clash,* FRF 85. Paris, 28 June 1926, *Study Sheet: Women* (Indian ink) FRF 45. Paris, 23 and 24 May 1927, *A Battle* (pen and wash) FRF 1,750; *Cavalry Clash* (brush and wash) FRF 320. Paris, 18 Nov 1935, *Battle Scene,* FRF 205. Paris, 2 Dec 1946, *Wild Boar Hunt; Military Scene* (two pen and wash drawings, one signed 1725) FRF 2,000. London, 28 March 1947, *Two Soldiers,* GBP 63. Paris, 10 June 1949, *Cavalry Clashes* (two watercolours) FRF 6,000. Brussels, 18 Oct 1969, *Battle Scene,* BEF 80,000. Paris, 24 Jan 1980, *Military Staff on Horseback before a Town* (1704, pen and wash/pencil outlines, 6 x 9 3/4 ins / 15.5 x 25 cm) FRF 4,800. Monte Carlo, 25 June 1984, *Romantic Scene in a Riverside Landscape* (oil on canvas, 30 x 23 3/4 ins / 76.5 x 60.5 cm) FRF 23,000. Paris, 26 June 1987, *Battle Scene* (1700, pen and brown wash, 11 1/2 x 24 ins / 29.5 x 61 cm) FRF 12,000. London, 13 May 1988, *Cavalry Preparing for Battle* (oil on canvas, 23 3/4 x 39 1/2 ins / 60.6 x 100.3 cm) GBP 3,080. Milan, 4 April 1989, *Battle between the Christians and the Turks* (oil on canvas, 48 1/2 x 68 1/2 ins / 123 x 174 cm) ITL 21,000,000. London, 2 July 1997, *Cavalry Skirmish* (oil/copper, 8 1/2 x 9 3/4 ins / 21.5 x 24.7 cm) GBP 1,092. Cologne, 15 May 1999, *Before the Battle* (oil on canvas, 23 x 33 ins / 59 x 84 cm) DEM 18,000. Berlin, 26 Nov 1999, *Friedrich Wilhelm I, King of Prussia. Herzog Victor Amadeus II von Savoyen* (ochre, two works, 17 x 14 ins / 43 x 36 cm) DEM 4,200. Munich, 6 Dec 2000, *Cavalry Battle* (oil on canvas, one of a pair, 19 x 27 ins / 48 x 69 cm) DEM 25,000. Paris, 18 Dec 2000, *The Battle of Jean III Sobieski against the Turks in front of Vienna, 1689* (oil on canvas, 37 x 67 ins / 95 x 171 cm) FRF 105,000. Berlin, 18 May 2001, *Muscle Man in Profile* (pen and wash, two works, 11 x 8 ins / 29 x 20 cm) DEM 6,000. Stuttgart, 21 June 2001, *Cavalry Battle Scene* (oil on canvas/panel, 24 x 32 ins / 62 x 82 cm) DEM 14,000. Lucerne, 4 June 2003, *Cavalry Battle* (oil on canvas, 19 x 28 ins / 49 x 71 cm) CHF 3,000. Buenos Aires, 17 July 2003, *Messenger* (oil on canvas/board, 28 x 36 ins / 72 x 92 cm) USD 2,700.

RUGENDAS, Georg Philipp II
German, 18th century.
Born 7 September 1701; died 1774, in Augsburg.
Painter, engraver. Battles, animals.

Georg Philipp Rugendas II was the son of Georg Philipp Rugendas I. He mainly painted animal and battle scenes. He did engravings after his father's paintings. He was also an art editor.
Museums and Galleries:
Augsburg (Maximilianmus.): *Self-portrait.*

RUGENDAS, Jeremias Gottlob
German, 18th century.
Born 1710; died 1772, in Augsburg.
Engraver.

Jeremias Gottlob Rugendas was the son of Georg Philipp Rugendas I. He engraved portraits, religious subjects and views, as well as events that took place during his era.

RUGENDAS, Johann Gottlieb
German, 18th century.
Born c. 1708; died 1736, in Augsburg.
Engraver.

Johann Gottlieb Rugendas engraved a subject commemorating baptism after the drawing by J. H. Hiethe in Weissenburg, Bavaria.

RUGENDAS, Johann Lorenz I
German, 18th century.
Born c. 1730; died 1799, in Augsburg.
Draughtsman, engraver. Historical subjects, portraits, animals.

Johann Lorenz Rugendas I was the son of Georg Philipp Rugendas II. He engraved historical scenes from his era, portraits and animals.
Auction records:
Munich, 29 May 1980, *Frederick the Great at the Parade* (1782, pen drawing heightened with white, 11 1/2 x 17 1/4 ins / 29 x 43.5 cm) DEM 15,000.

RUGENDAS, Johann Lorenz II
German, 19th century.
Born 1775, in Augsburg; died 19 December 1826, in Augsburg.
Painter, draughtsman, engraver. Historical subjects, battles, portraits.

Johann Lorenz Rugendas II was the grandson of Georg Philipp Rugendas II. He was director of the academy in Augsburg. He engraved battles and portraits, and was also an art editor.
Auction records:
Paris, 3 Dec 1985, *Battle of Znaim* (1809, pen and Indian ink wash, 15 x 21 3/4 ins / 38 x 55.5 cm) FRF 28,000. Paris, 20 Dec 1988, *Battle of Eylau, 8 February 1807* (pen and wash, 14 x 20 1/4 ins / 35.7 x 51.5 cm) FRF 34,000.

RUGENDAS, Moritz or Johann Moritz
German, 19th century.
Born 29 March 1802, in Augsburg; died 29 May 1858, in Weilheim.
Painter, watercolourist, draughtsman, lithographer, engraver (etching). History painting, genre scenes, landscapes.

Moritz Rugendas was the son and pupil of Johann Lorenz Rugendas II. He drew landscapes and popular South American designs.

He featured in the exhibition *Expedition Kunst: Die Entdeckung der Natur von C. D. Friedrich bis Humboldt* (*Expedition Art. The Discovery of Nature from C.D. Friedrich to Humboldt*) at the Hamburg Kunsthalle in 2002, an exhibition that demonstrated the links between the natural sciences and the painted landscape.
Bibliography:
Expedition Kunst. Die Entdeckung der Natur von C. D. Friedrich bis Humboldt, exhibition catalogue, Hamburger Kunsthalle, Hamburg, 2002.
Museums and Galleries:
Munich (Pinakothek): *Columbus Claiming America.*
Auction records:
London, 14 Nov 1969, *Scene from Peru,* Gns 400. London, 14 May 1970, *Popular Festivities, Lima,* GBP 1,800. London, 12 Nov 1974, *Gauchos in the Pampa,* GBP 3,500. London, 11 May 1976, *Gauchos Lassoing a Bull* (oil on canvas, 23 x 36 ins / 58.5 x 91.5 cm) GBP 6,500. London, 30 May 1979, *Gauchos Lassoing a Bull* (oil on canvas, 31 1/4 x 39 ins / 79.5 x 99 cm) GBP 13,000. São Paulo, 25 June 1981, *Convoy Travelling to Caete from Diamant (recto); Gathering in Fernambuc (verso)* (pencil, 5 x 7 1/2 ins / 12.7 x 19 cm) BRL 480,000. New York, 29 Nov 1983, *Peasants on Horseback* (c. 1834, oil on canvas, 27 x 36 ins / 68.6 x 91.5 cm) USD 49,000. London, 22 May 1984, *Costumes of Bahia* (1830, sepia wash drawing/pencil outline, 12 1/2 x 10 ins / 32 x 24.5 cm) GBP 3,300. London, 19 Nov 1985, *Mexico City* (oil on canvas, 9 x 14 ins / 22.9 x 35.6 cm)

GBP 7,500. NEW YORK, 20 May 1986, *Mexico: Indian Woman Bathing in a Forest* (1834, oil on canvas, 18¼ x 15 ins / 46.3 x 37.8 cm) USD 11,000. NEW YORK, 21 Nov 1988, *Peruvian Peasant* (1843, oil on canvas, 13½ x 17¾ ins / 34.5 x 45 cm) USD 41,250. NEW YORK, 20 Nov 1989, *Queen of the Fête* (1841, oil on canvas, 20½ x 26½ ins / 52.1 x 67.3 cm) USD 88,000. NEW YORK, 20-21 Nov 1990, *Lake Patzcuaro near Michoacan* (oil on panel, 5¼ x 8¼ ins / 13.6 x 21 cm) USD 22,000. NEW YORK, 19-20 May 1992, *Leaving Church* (oil on canvas, 19½ x 15½ ins / 49.5 x 39.4 cm) USD 57,750. NEW YORK, 23 Nov 1992, *Festival of Archangel St Michael* (watercolour/paper, 7¾ x 11¾ ins / 20 x 30 cm) USD 41,250. NEW YORK, 25 Nov 1992, *Village* (1838, oil on canvas/panel, 9¼ x 12¼ ins / 23.2 x 30.8 cm) USD 28,600. NEW YORK, 18 May 1993, *Last Spanish Warrior* (oil on canvas, 15 x 10¾ ins / 38 x 27.6 cm) USD 20,700. NEW YORK, 1 June 2000, *India Mexicana Banandose en el Rio* (oil on canvas, 18 x 15 ins / 45 x 37 cm) USD 35,000. NEW YORK, 1 June 2000, *Landscape with Wagon* (oil on canvas, 11 x 17 ins / 28 x 43 cm) USD 35,000. LONDON, 21 Sept 2000, *Gentry Visiting an Estate in Brazil* (pencil, pen and ink, 7 x 11 ins / 19 x 27 cm) GBP 4,500. NEW YORK, 19 Nov 2001, *Volcanoes Seen From Puebla* (1831, oil on canvas, 13 x 33 ins / 33 x 85 cm) USD 85,000. MUNICH, 18 April 2002, *Sketch Book of Portraits and Landscapes* (works on paper, also works by other artists) EUR 32,000. LONDON, 15 Nov 2002, *Plaza Mayor, Lima* (oil on canvas, 27 x 36 ins / 68 x 92 cm) GBP 96,000. LONDON, 25 Sept 2003, *Santiago de Chile from the Hill of Santa Lucia, Looking West* (1841, oil on canvas, 23 x 36 ins / 58 x 91 cm) GBP 175,000. NEW YORK, 19 Nov 2003, *Landscapes and Sketches* (1819-1853, graphite, album, 12 x 8 ins / 31 x 21 cm) USD 45,000. COPENHAGEN, 2 March 2004, *Landscape with Oxcart in Valparaiso, Chile* (oil on canvas, 13 x 16 ins / 33 x 41 cm) DKK 200,000. RIO DE JANEIRO, 6 July 2004, *Rancher on Horseback* (watercolour, 10 x 12 ins / 25 x 30 cm) BRL 70,000.

RUGENDAS, Peter
German, 18th century.
Born c. 1734; died c. 1762, in Augsburg.
Engraver (mezzotint).

Peter Rugendas may have been the son of Christian Rugendas.

RUGENDAS, Philipp Sebastian
German, 18th century.
Born 1736; died 1807.
Engraver.

Along with his father Christian Rugendas, Philipp Sebastian Rugendas engraved *The Four Seasons* and *The Four Corners of the Earth*.

RÜGER
German, 16th century.
Died 1519.
Active in Deggendorf.
Painter.

RÜGER
German, 18th - 19th century.
Painter. Landscapes.

Rüger worked for the porcelain factory in Gotha between 1795 and 1803.

RÜGER, Curt
German, 19th - 20th century.
Born 17 March 1867, in Leipzig; died 29 March 1930, in Leipzig.
Painter. Figures, portraits, interiors.

Curt Rüger studied under L. Pohle and J. Scholz. He worked in Munich and in Buch (Lake Ammersee).

RÜGER, Isaac. See **RIGA**

RÜGER, Johannes
German, 19th - 20th century.
Born 1868, in Vienna; died 4 March 1907, in Dresden.
Painter. Figures, portraits.

RUGER, Julius
American, 19th century.
Born c. 1841, in Oldenburg, Germany; died 23 July 1906, in Brooklyn.
Portrait artist.

Julius Ruger emigrated to the USA when he was a young man.

RÜGER, Karl Gottlob
German, 18th century.
Born 1761, in Annaberg; died in Kamsdorf, near Iena.
Painter, engraver (burin), art writer. History painting, landscapes.

Karl Gottlob Rüger worked for the porcelain factories in Gera and Volkstedt.

RUGERI, Girolamo. See **RUGGIERI di Girolamo de Bergamo**

RUGERY, Roger de. See **RUGIERI Rugiero de**

RUGG, Matt
British, 20th century.
Born 8 November 1935, in Bridgwater (Somerset).
Painter. Low reliefs.

Matt Rugg studied at King's College in Newcastle-upon-Tyne under Victor Pasmore, then he was awarded a travelling scholarship. He has been a lecturer in painting at Newcastle-upon-Tyne University since 1962.

He has taken part in group exhibitions, including the Arts Council touring exhibition *Construction: England* 1963. He had his first solo exhibition at the New Art Centre 1963. He was awarded the Royal Academy Prize and Arts Council Award at the *Young Contemporaries* Exhibitions in 1960 and 1961.

MUSEUMS AND GALLERIES:
LONDON (Tate Collection): *Painted Unit Relief* (1963).

RÜGGENBERG, Peter
German, 18th century.
Painter.

Peter Rüggenberg executed an altarpiece depicting the *Farewells of the Princes of the Apostles* dated 1722.

RUGGERI. See also **RUGGIERI**

RUGGERI, Antonio
Italian, 19th century.
Active in Mantua c. 1800.
Painter.

Works by Antonio Ruggeri, a pupil of Giuseppe Bottani, can be found in Mantua in the cathedral and the church of St Leonard.

RUGGERI, Antonio Maria, or Ruggieri
Italian, 18th century.
Active during the first half of the 18th century.
Painter.

Antonio Ruggeri worked for numerous churches in Milan.

RUGGERI, Biagio, or Rugiere
Italian, 18th century.
Died 1721, in Rome.
Active in Rome.
Painter.

Biagio Ruggeri is known for a *Portrait of Pope Innocent XI* painted in 1680.

RUGGERI, Ferdinando, or Ruggieri
Italian, 19th century.
Born September 1831, in Naples.

Painter. History painting, portraits, genre scenes, landscapes.

A pupil of Domenico Caldara, Ferdinando Ruggeri made his debut in 1853. He took part in all the major Italian salons, exhibiting his history paintings. He also painted a number of portraits.

MUSEUMS AND GALLERIES:

NAPLES (Pinacoteca): *V. Alfieri as a Child.*

AUCTION RECORDS:

LONDON, 14 June 1996, *Teasing; Flirtation* (oil on board, a pair, each 16 x 21 ins / 39.7 x 53.3 cm) GBP 8,625.

RUGGERI, Girolamo. See **RUGGIERI di Girolamo de Bergamo**

RUGGERI, Piero

Italian, 20th century.

Born 1930, in Turin.

Painter. Figures.

After studying at Turin academy of fine art, Piero Ruggeri continued to live and work in Turin. From 1955, he painted in an informal expressionist style, somewhat reminiscent of De Kooning in its energy but with a more attractive tonal range.

He took part in many group exhibitions including: 1956 and 1958, Venice Biennale; 1960, Guggenheim Prize, New York; 1961 and 1963, São Paulo Biennale; 1961, Biennale des Jeunes, Paris. He came second in the Morgan's Paint competition in Rimini in 1959, won the Marche Prize in Ancona in 1960 and the second prize awarded by the Republic of San Marino in 1959.

MUSEUMS AND GALLERIES:

BOLOGNA - CASALE MONFERRATO - CESENATICO - FRANCAVILLA AL MARE - LA SPEZIA - ROME - SPOLETO - TURIN.

AUCTION RECORDS:

MILAN, 6 April 1976, *Painting* (1965, oil on canvas, 9 3/4 x 7 3/4 ins / 25 x 20 cm) ITL 150,000. MILAN, 14 Nov 1991, *Composition* (1972, oil on canvas, 31 1/2 x 23 1/2 ins / 80 x 60 cm) ITL 2,000,000. MILAN, 14 April 1992, *Rembrandt's Studio* (1957, oil on canvas, 56 1/4 x 49 1/2 ins / 143 x 126 cm) ITL 18,000,000. MILAN, 6 April 1993, *Window at Dawn* (1970, oil on canvas, 47 1/4 x 39 1/4 ins / 120 x 100 cm) ITL 5,000,000. MILAN, 22 June 1995, *Figure* (oil on canvas, 23 1/2 x 19 3/4 ins / 60 x 50 cm) ITL 2,875,000. MILAN, 26 Oct 1995, *Self-portrait* (1960, oil/plywood, 72 x 28 3/4 ins / 182 x 73 cm) ITL 9,775,000. MILAN, 28 May 1996, *Figure in an Interior* (1964, oil on canvas, 39 1/4 x 31 1/2 ins / 100 x 80 cm) ITL 6,900,000. MILAN, 17 Nov 1999, *Still-life in White* (oil on canvas, 20 x 28 ins / 50 x 70 cm) ITL 4,000,000. MILAN, 16 Dec 1999, *Figure* (oil on canvas, 39 x 33 ins / 100 x 85 cm) ITL 5,000,000. BRUSSELS, 14 Feb 2000, *Musicians* (oil on canvas, 30 x 25 ins / 77 x 63 cm) BEF 300,000. VERCELLI, 16 Dec 2000, *Figures* (oil on masonite, 33 x 30 ins / 85 x 75 cm) ITL 10,000,000. VERCELLI, 17 March 2001, *red chalk* (oil on canvas, 31 x 35 ins / 80 x 90 cm) ITL 10,000,000. MILAN, 5 Dec 2001, *Self-portrait with Dead Ox* (1961, oil on canvas, 79 x 97 ins / 201 x 247 cm) ITL 32,000,000. ROME, 12 Nov 2002, *Paint* (1960, oil on board, 12 x 10 ins / 30 x 25 cm) EUR 2,260. VERCELLI, 23 Nov 2002, *Napoleon* (oil on canvas, 47 x 31 ins / 120 x 80 cm) EUR 2,200. VERCELLI, 1 May 2003, *Figure* (1970-1971, oil on canvas, 35 x 28 ins / 90 x 70 cm) EUR 1,700. TURIN, 17 Nov 2003, *Composition* (1973, oil on canvas, 20 x 16 ins / 50 x 40 cm) EUR 2,000. VERCELLI, 12 June 2004, *Redhead* (1961, oil on canvas, 24 x 20 ins / 60 x 50 cm) EUR 5,200. TURIN, 14 June 2004, *Untitled* (oil on canvas, 24 x 20 ins / 60 x 50 cm) EUR 2,800.

RUGGERI, Quirino

Italian, 20th century.

Born 24 March 1883, in Albacina; died 1955

Sculptor. Portraits. Busts.

Self-taught, Quirino Ruggeri produced mainly portrait busts. He lived and worked in Rome.

MUSEUMS AND GALLERIES:

ROME (former Mussolini Mus.) - ROME (Gal. Nazionale d'Arte Moderna).

RUGGERI DI SAN MARZANO, Pasquale

Italian, 19th - 20th century.

Born 20 December 1851, in San Marzano sul Sarno (Campania); died 11 September 1916, in Naples.

Painter. Genre scenes.

Pasquale Ruggeri di San Marzano exhibited in Naples and Milan.

MUSEUMS AND GALLERIES:

NAPLES (Mus. di Capodimonte).

AUCTION RECORDS:

LONDON, 9 May 1979, *Italian Peasant Couple in an Interior* (oil on canvas, 15 x 19 ins / 38 x 48 cm) GBP 1,200. AMSTERDAM, 16 Nov 1988, *Monk Conversing with Two Women in the Courtyard of a Peasant House in the Summer* (oil on canvas, 25 1/2 x 19 ins / 65 x 48.5 cm) NLG 6,900. NEW YORK, 16 July 1992, *The Letter* (1879, oil on canvas, 18 3/4 x 14 ins / 47.6 x 35.6 cm) USD 7,150.

RUGGERO DI PIETRO. See **RUGGIERO**

RUGGIERI. See also **RUGGERI**

RUGGIERI, Antonio

Italian, 17th century.

Active in Florence.

Painter. History painting, architectural views.

Antonio Ruggieri was the pupil of O. Vannini. He is noted for his *Martyrdom of St Andrew*, which used to hang in the church of SS Michele e Gaetano in Florence.

RUGGIERI, Ercole, called Ercolino del Gessi

Italian, 17th century.

Born c. 1620, in Bologna.

Painter. History painting.

The brother of Giovanni-Battista Ruggieri, Ercole was the pupil of Francesco Gessi, whose style he imitated in such a servile manner that it is difficult to distinguish between his works and those of his master. He is noted for a *Death of St Joseph* in the church of S Cristina di Pietralata and a *Virgin and the Infant Jesus, St Catherine and Various Saints* in the church of the Servite order.

RUGGIERI, Ferdinando, or Ruggeri

Italian, 18th century.

Born c. 1691, in Florence; died 27 June 1741.

Engraver (etching), architect. Architectural views, urban landscapes.

Ferdinando Ruggieri engraved architectural views and views of Florence.

RUGGIERI, Giovanni Battista, called Battistino del Gessi

Italian, 17th century.

Born 1606, in Bologna; died 1640, in Rome.

Painter. History painting.

The brother of Ercole Ruggieri, Giovanni Battista Ruggieri was a pupil of Domenichino and later of Francesco Gessi. He accompanied the latter to Naples and became his collaborator. He visited Rome during the pontificate of Urban VII and was protected by the Marquis Giustiniari. He produced works for the palaces and churches of Naples and Bologna, and is noted in particular for three altarpieces in the church of S Barbaziano in Bologna.

RUGGIERI, Guido, or Ruggeri

Italian, 16th century.

Born in Bologna.

Also active in France.

Painter, engraver, draughtsman.

Fontainebleau School.

Guido Ruggieri was the pupil of Francesco Roibolini for painting, and may have been the pupil of Marcantonio Raimondi for engraving. He went to France with Primaticcio and worked with him on the decoration of Fontainebleau palace.

Ruggieri is known mainly for his engravings, in particular, of several of Primaticcio's drawings. His prints are normally signed with a G and an R, joined by an F, for *fecit*. His style recalls that of Marco da Ravena.

AUCTION RECORDS:
PARIS, 1776, *Figure of a Seated Woman with a Child Nearby* (pen and bistre) FRF 72.

RUGGIERI, Marco. See **ZOPPO**

RUGGIERI, Rugiero de. See **RUGIERI**

RUGGIERI DI GIROLAMO DE BERGAMO, Girolamo or Giovanni, or Rugeri or Ruggeri
Italian, 17th century.
Born 1662, in Vicenza; died 18 December 1707, in Verona.
Active in Verona.
Painter. Battles, landscapes.

Girolamo Ruggieri was the son of the painter Cornelius Dusman of Amsterdam.

MUSEUMS AND GALLERIES:
VERONA (Mus. Civico): *Battle on a Bridge*.

RUGGIERO. See the entry **ROBERTUS**

RUGGIERO, or Roggerius
Italian, 13th century.
Sculptor.

Possibly of Norman origin, Ruggiero is thought to have been working in Benevento (Campania) in 1200. He sculpted three porches of Benevento Cathedral.

RUGGIERO, Pasquale. See **RUGGERI DI SAN MARZANO**

RUGGIERO DA MURO
Italian, 12th century.
Active in the second half of the 12th century.
Sculptor, architect.

RUGGIERO DA TODI, or Ruggero
Italian, 13th century.
Active at the end of the 13th century.
Painter.

He painted a *Madonna with Child* formerly in the abbey church of S Nicola near S Gimignano.

RUGGIERO DA VASTO
Italian, 13th century.
Active at the end of the 13th century.
Sculptor.

Ruggiero da Vasto sculpted the central porch of the church of S Augustino, Vasto.

RUGGIERO DI PIETRO, or Ruggero
Italian, 15th century.
Active during the first half of the 15th century.
Painter.

RUGGIRELLO, Jean-Claude
French, 20th - 21st century.
Born 2 January 1959, in Tunis.
Draughtsman, sculptor.

Jean-Claude Ruggirello lives and works in Marseilles. Jean-Claude Ruggirello's sculpture is intended typically to be hung on walls. It comprises diverse elements - gearwheels, silk screen images, maps, flags and audio tapes - and is presented in a 'neutral' manner, which is to say, without further explanation or background history. The phrase 'My friends' friends are my friends' is inscribed in a large white rectangle which lends its title to one of his pieces from 1989; the whole is interrupted at regular intervals by three vertically-mounted electric switches, the overall impact being to highlight both the validity and the banality of the phrase in question.

He has shown his work at group exhibitions, notably: in 1983, at *L'Après-Midi* (*Afternoon*), hosted by the Fondation Nationale des Art Graphiques (National Foundation for the Visual Arts) in Paris; in 1986, at *Identité Marseille* (*Marseilles Profile*), held at the Vieille Charité in Marseilles; in 1987, at *Affective Machines*, hosted by the Renaissance Society in Chicago; in 1988, at *Les Déchargeurs* (*Unloading*), coordinated by the Regional Fund for Contemporary Architecture (FRAC) in Marseilles; and, in 1988, at the International Pays du Loire Workshops in Fontevrault. Solo exhibitions by Ruggirello include those in 1984, at the Galerie Axe Actuel in Toulouse; in 1985, at the Gallery Circé in Nîmes; in 1987, at the Galerie de Paris; in 1988, at the Galerie Latitude in Nice; in 1989, at the Musée de Poitiers; in 2001, at the Galerie Papillon-Fiat in Paris; and, in 2004, at the 'Creux d'Enfer' Contemporary Arts Centre in Thiers.

BIBLIOGRAPHY:
Bellido, Ramon Tio, "*Principes de physique élémentaire et le Temps élémentaire de l'espace*' in *Identité Marseille*, exhibition catalogue, ARCA Centre d'Art Contemporain, Marseilles, 1986. Ruggirello, J.- C., "*Le Temps de voir*' in *Les Déchargeurs*, Marseilles, 1988. Ollat, Thierry/Valabrèque, Frédéric/Pérenc, Arielle, *In out, J.- C. Ruggirello*, Ateliers d'Artistes-Office de la Culture, Marseilles, 1998.

RUGH, Michael. See **ROEG**

RUGHER, Jan
Dutch, 15th century.
Active in Zwolle during the second half of the 15th century.
Sculptor.

Between 1464 and 1490 Jan Rugher carved decorations for the choir of Utrecht Cathedral.

RUGIA, Francesco
German, 17th century.
Active in the first half of the 17th century.
Painter.

Francesco Rugia worked in Düsseldorf in 1631 and in Cologne in 1635.

RUGIERE, Biagio. See **RUGGERI**

RUGIERI, Rugiero de, or Ruggieri, called Roger de Rogery or Rugery
Italian, 16th century.
Died 1596, in Fontainebleau, France.
Also active in France.
Painter.
First Fontainebleau School.

Rugiero de Rugieri worked first in Bologna and then accompanied Primaticcio to Fontainebleau Palace, where he was superintendent of paintings. His paintings depicting the legend of Hercules were done at Fontainebleau in 1570.

RUGIERO, Kaynoot. See **ROGIER Claes**

RUGUÉ, Georges, or Rügé
French, 17th century.
Active in Jüterbog, Germany.
Painter.

Rugué worked in Bernay from 1628 to 1671, where he produced altarpieces.

RUHALM, Hans
German, 16th century.

Died 14 August 1549, in Forchheim.
Sculptor. Figures.
Hans Ruhalm was a carpenter as well as a sculptor. He carved a self-portrait for the town hall of Forcheim in 1535.

RUHIERRE, Edme Jean
French, 19th century.
Born 29 December 1789, in Paris.
Engraver (burin).
Edme Ruhierre was the student of Boutrois and Malbeste.

RUHIERRE, François Théodore
French, 19th century.
Born 31 October 1808, in Paris; died 29 January 1884, in Paris.
Engraver (burin), painter, medallist.
François Ruhierre was the nephew and student of Edme Jean Ruhierre.
MUSEUMS AND GALLERIES:
MARSEILLES: *Portrait* (four drawings).

RUHIERRE, Marie Marguerite
French, 19th century.
Born 19th century, in Tours.
Painter.
Marie Ruhierre was a student of Mlle Richard.

RUHL, Andreas. See **RIEHL**

RUHL, Johann Andreas. See **RIEHL Jean André**

RUHL, Johann Christian
German, 18th - 19th century.
Born 15 December 1764, in Kassel; died 29 September 1842, in Kassel.
Sculptor, engraver (etching), lithographer.
Johann Christian Ruhl was the father of Julius Eugen and Ludwig Sigismund Ruhl. He worked particularly for the castle of Wilhelmshöhe, near Kassel.

RUHL, Julius Eugen
German, 19th century.
Born 13 October 1796, in Kassel; died 27 November 1871, in Kassel.
Painter, engraver (etching), architect. Landscapes.
Julius Eugen Ruhl was the brother of Ludwig Sigismund Ruhl and the son of Johann Christian Ruhl. He was a pupil of Jussow and worked for the court of Kassel.

RUHL, Leonhard
German, 18th century.
Active in the first half of the 18th century.
Engraver (burin).
Leonhard Ruhl engraved the *Portrait of Lorenz Laelius, Priest of Onolzbach, in 1615*.

RUHL, Ludwig Sigismund or Sigmund Ludwig
German, 19th century.
Born 10 December 1794, in Kassel; died 7 March 1887, in Kassel.
Painter, draughtsman, engraver (etching), writer.
Ludwig Sigismund Ruhl was a pupil of his father Johann Christian Ruhl. He improved his technique in Dresden and Munich and settled in Rome for three years.

The Nazarenes with their Christian inspiration were what could be called 'Italianists', settling in Rome around Overbeck and Cornelius. On the other hand, in the German Romantic movement in painting, a quite separate and at the time far less famous group (which underwent a revival in parallel to the poetic movement of Tieck, Brentano, Arnim and Novalis) was also seeking sources of inspiration in the Middle Ages, but in the German Middle Age. Such was the case with Ludwig Sigismund Ruhl, who practiced the 'troubadour' genre, as reflected in his *Beautiful Melusina at her Toilette* (Mannheim), as well as in a number of his other works. If the inspiration of this group of painters was still attached to the anecdotal and picturesque, it nevertheless seems that it was with them, rather than the Nazarenes, that what was to become German Romantic landscape painting located itself, became defined and developed. Ruhl is also cited to have produced a *Portrait of Schopenhauer*.
BIBLIOGRAPHY:
Brion, Marcel, *La Peinture allemande*, Éd. Pierre Tisné, Paris, 1959.
MUSEUMS AND GALLERIES:
BERLIN (Nationalgal.): *Lost Knight* - KASSEL (Kunsthalle): *Portraits of Two Boys; Mars and Venus* (drawing) - MANNHEIM: *Beautiful Melusina at her Toilette*.
AUCTION RECORDS:
LONDON, 18 Oct 1978, *Girl's First Communion* (1859, oil on canvas, 28 3/4 x 24 ins / 73 x 61 cm) GBP 1,800.

RÜHLE, Clara
German, 20th century.
Born 14 April 1885, in Stuttgart.
Painter, draughtsman.
Clara Rühle was a student of Pötzelberger and Altherr.

RÜHLE, Rütjer
German, 20th century.
Born 1939, in Danzig (now Gdansk, Poland).
Active in Spain and in France.
Painter.
Rütjer Rühle studied between 1963 and 1966 at the fine arts academy in West Berlin. Before settling in Paris in 1970, he spent some years in the Andalucian village of Ugijar, where he still maintains a studio. Andalucia has greatly influenced his choice of materials, and he has largely distanced himself from conventional painting techniques, inasmuch as he more often than not uses his fingers or employs disparate substrates (gates, shutters, pieces of wood and, more recently, sections of tree trunk or slabs of marble). His outsize 'landscapes' are composed from massive layers of rhythmically-applied contrapuntal colour. Rühle has taken part in various group exhibitions, including *Peinture: l'autre nouvelle génération* (*Another New Generation of Painters*) held at the Galeries Nationales du Grand Palais in Paris in 1985, and *Le Style et le Chaos* (*Style and Chaos*), held at the Centre National des Arts Plastiques in the Musée du Luxembourg in Paris that same year. Examples of Rühle's work are on regular display at the Galerie Stadler in Paris.
BIBLIOGRAPHY:
Rütjer Rühle, Gal. Stadler, Paris, 1988.

RÜHLIG
German, 18th century.
Active in Gera c. 1780.
Painter (porcelain).

RUHLMANN, Émile Jacques
French, 19th - 20th century.
Born 26 August 1869, in Paris; died 1933.
Painter, draughtsman, designer. Genre scenes, figures, landscapes. Furniture.
Art Deco.
The many drawings, landscapes, figures and caricatures that Émile Jacques Ruhlmann committed to notebooks are much admired, but his paintings are rarer. He used his talent primarily in the design and making of Art Deco furniture. He exhibited in Paris at the Salon d'Automne, and in Lyons, Strasbourg, Monaco, Ghent and Amsterdam. In 2003, the Galerie Makassar, Paris, held a posthumous exhibition of his work.
BIBLIOGRAPHY:
Camard, Florence, *Émile Jacques Ruhlmann*, Éd. du Regard, Paris, 1983.

Museums and Galleries:
Paris (BNF) - Paris (Mus. des Arts décoratifs): sketchbooks.

RÜHM, F. Oskar Ad
German, 19th - 20th century.
Born 3 March 1854, in Hengelbach, near Paulinzella; died in the summer of 1934, in Hiltpoltstein, near Erlangen.
Sculptor.

This artist studied in Dresden under Schilling and went on to live and work there, producing statues, fountains and portrait busts.

RUHMANN
French, 19th century.
Painter.

Ruhmann featured at the Salon from 1808 to 1812.

RÜHTS. See **RÜTS**

RUHULT
German.
Painter. Genre scenes.

Museums and Galleries:
Orléans: *Justice and Peace Crowned by Genius.*

RÜIJVEN, Pieter Jansz. van, or Reuver
Dutch, 17th - 18th century.
Born 7 March 1651, probably in Delft; died 17 May 1716, probably in Delft.
Painter, engraver.

Rüijven was the presumed pupil of Jac. Jordaens in Antwerp.

P. v. Rüijven. f.

Museums and Galleries:
Amsterdam (Rijksmus.): *Cock and Hens* - Amsterdam (Stedelijk Mus.): *Chimney* - St-Omer: *Apollo and Issa.*

Auction records:
Paris, 5 Dec 1983, *Venus Receiving the Arms of Aeneas from the Hands of Vulcan* (oil on canvas, 59 x 44 ins / 150 x 112 cm) FRF 78,000.

RUILLE, Geoffroy de (Vicomte)
French, 19th - 20th century.
Born 1842; died 1922.
Sculptor. Animals. Statues.

Auction records:
London, 11 May 1977, *Two Officers on Horseback* (bronze, h. 23 1/4 ins / 59 cm) GBP 1,800. Enghien-les-Bains, 10 Oct 1982, *Curvet and Croupade* (brown-patinated bronze, h. 23 1/4 ins / 59 cm) FRF 60,000. London, 8 Nov 1984, *Hurdle Race* (c. 1870, brown-patinated bronze, h. 20 ins / 51 cm) GBP 4,800. London, 5 July 1985, *Two Galloping Horses* (c. 1900, light brown patinated lost-wax bronze, h. 3 1/2 ins / 9 cm) GBP 2,800. Paris, 26 Jan 1991, *Courvet and Croupade* (bronze, h. 22 1/2 ins / 57 cm, l. 22 3/4 ins/58 cm) FRF 140,000; *Master of the Hounds on Horseback* (bronze, h. 22 ins / 56 cm, l. 19 3/4 ins/50 cm) FRF 10,500. Paris, 29 June 1993, *Amazon on Horseback* (bronze, 20 1/2 x 19 3/4 x 6 1/4 ins / 52 x 50 x 16 cm) FRF 66,000. Paris, 29 Nov 1995, *Amazon* (bronze, 19 x 21 1/4 x 4 3/4 ins / 48.5 x 54 x 12 cm) FRF 21,500.

RUIN-TIGERSTEDT, Ingrid
Finnish, 20th century.
Born 15 May 1881, in Pori; died 1956.
Painter. Figures.

Ingrid Ruin-Tigerstedt was a student of Anders Zorn.

Auction records:
Göteborg, 18 May 1989, *'Sagotanten': Figures in a Kitchen* (oil on canvas, 33 1/2 x 28 3/4 ins / 85 x 73 cm) SEK 21,000. Helsinki, 11 Dec 1999, *Doing the Washing* (oil on canvas, 29 x 26 ins / 74 x 65 cm) FIM 17,500. Helsinki, 9 Feb 2003, *Girl on Stones on the Beach* (oil on canvas, 27 x 16 ins / 68 x 41 cm) EUR 1,700. Stockholm, 3 Dec 2003, *Country Girl in the Light of an Open Fire* (1916, oil on canvas, 19 x 15 ins / 47 x 38 cm) SEK 27,000.

RUINA, Gaspare, or Ruini, called Gasparo da Corte
Italian, 16th century.
Engraver (wood), architect.

Gaspare Ruina engraved war subjects and mythological scenes.

RUINART DE BRINANT, Jules
French, 19th century.
Born 1838, in Koblenz; died 26 May 1898, in Rilly-la-Montagne.
Painter. History painting, portraits, genre scenes.

Jules Ruinard de Brinant was the student of Rudolf Jordan at the school of fine arts in Antwerp and of Achenbach in Düsseldorf. He visited Italy, Germany, England, Holland and Belgium. He is generally thought to be French in nationality.

Museums and Galleries:
Rheims: *Study of a Festival; Mme de Rilly; Rock on the Meuse* - Vienna (Czernin'sche Gemäldegal.): *Waiting at the Banks of the Rhine.*

Auction records:
Paris, 1 May 1940, *On the Terrace, in Italy,* FRF 350. Paris, July 1946, *Last Meeting,* FRF 5,300. San Francisco, 8 Nov 1984, *Goose-Keeper* (oil on canvas, 29 1/4 x 23 ins / 74 x 58.5 cm) GBP 2,250. London, 16 June 2004, *Unloading on a French Quay* (1830, oil on panel, 9 x 13 ins / 23 x 34 cm) GBP 1,300.

RUIPÉREZ, Luis
Spanish, 19th century.
Born 1832, in Murcia; died 15 October 1867, in Murcia.
Painter. History painting, portraits, genre scenes.

Luis Ruipérez was a pupil of P. López, C. Lorenzale and E. Meissonier.

Ruiperez

Ruiperez

Auction records:
London, 20 June 1924, *Visit to the Tailor,* GBP 48; *Whist Players,* GBP 73. London, 16 May 1929, *Guardroom,* GBP 54. London, 24 May 1935, *Soldiers Playing Cards,* GBP 56. New York, 18-19 April 1945, *The Rendezvous,* USD 400. London, 11 Oct 1995, *The Guardroom* (1862, oil on panel, 9 1/2 x 13 ins / 24 x 33 cm) GBP 2,875. London, 20 March 2003, *Bookshop* (1861, oil on panel, 13 x 11 ins / 34 x 29 cm) GBP 3,200. Madrid, 14 Sept 2004, *Dutch Interior* (1866, oil on card, 13 x 10 ins / 34 x 26 cm) EUR 2,400.

RUIS. See also **RUIZ** and **RUESS**

RUIS, Hercule
French, 16th century.
Active during the second half of the 16th century.
Glass painter.

In collaboration with Pierre Bacon, Hercule Ruis painted two windows for the church of St Ythier in Sully-sur-Loire.

RUISCH, Rachel. See **RUYSCH**

RUISCHER, Jan, or Ruijscher, Ruyscher, Ruysser, Rousscher, Ruisschairt, Rauscher, called Jorge Herkules
German, 17th century.

Born c. 1625, in Francker; died after 1675, in Germany.
Painter, draughtsman, engraver (etching). Landscapes.
Jan Ruischer was perhaps the son of Johann Rauscher, who was painter to the court of Saxony. A painter called Hans de Ruyster was in the guild in Dordrecht in 1609. Ruischer executed the two engravings *Landscape* and *Landscape with Castle*.

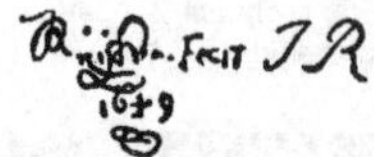

AUCTION RECORDS:
LONDON, 9 May 1929, *Dutch Plain* (drawing) GBP 34. LONDON, 10-14 July 1936, *Landscape* (pen) GBP 126.

RUISDAEL, Isaak, Jakob, Salomon van.
See **RUYSDAEL**

RUITER DE WITT, Maria de
Dutch, 20th - 21st century.
Born 1947, in Breda.
Painter, pastellist.
Maria de Ruiter de Witt was a pupil of Sierk Schroder. On a visit, she met Willem Hofker and was influenced by his work. From 1988, she exhibited in Holland and France, where she won several awards in 1988 and 1989. Her style is in an Impressionist vein.
AUCTION RECORDS:
SINGAPORE, 5 Oct 1996, *Ode to Dancer To Ni Pollok* (1994, pastel/canvas, 32½ x 27¼ ins / 82.5 x 69 cm) SGD 6,900. SINGAPORE, 7 April 2002, *Rebab Player* (oil on canvas, 51 x 47 ins / 130 x 120 cm) SGD 13,000. SINGAPORE, 6 Oct 2002, *Masterclass* (oil on canvas, 67 x 47 ins / 170 x 120 cm) SGD 10,000. SINGAPORE, 18 May 2003, *Two Beautiful Nudes* (oil on canvas, 31 x 39 ins / 80 x 100 cm) SGD 9,600. HONG KONG, 6 July 2003, *Tribute to Ni Pollok* (oil on canvas, 51 x 51 ins / 130 x 130 cm) HKD 75,000. HONG KONG, 25 April 2004, *Girl by the Puri Lukisan* (pastel, 31 x 39 ins / 80 x 100 cm) HKD 38,000.

RUITH, Horace Van
British, 19th - 20th century.
Born 1839; died 1923.
Also active in Italy.
Painter. Figures, portraits, genre scenes, landscapes.
Horace Van Ruith lived and worked in London and Capri. He exhibited regularly at the Royal Academy in London from 1888. He executed a *Portrait of Queen Victoria* after a copy in Windsor Castle.

MUSEUMS AND GALLERIES:
BRISTOL: *Portrait of Queen Victoria* - COLOGNE (Wallraf-Richartz Mus.): *Portrait of a Young Woman*.
AUCTION RECORDS:
LONDON, 22 Nov 1982, *Market in the Street in Bombay* (oil on canvas, 36½ x 67 ins / 93 x 170 cm) GBP 1,300. LE TOUQUET, 8 June 1992, *Beach with Figures* (oil on canvas, 30¼ x 41¾ ins / 77 x 106 cm) FRF 90,000. NEW YORK, 14 Oct 1993, *Arab with a Narguile* (watercolour/paper, 26½ x 20 ins / 67.3 x 50.8 cm) USD 3,450.

RUIZ, Andrés I
Spanish, 16th (?) century.
Illuminator.
Andrés Ruiz I produced the initial letters for a psalter in Seville Cathedral.

RUIZ, Andrés II
Spanish, 16th century.
Active during the second half of the 16th century.
Sculptor, architect.
Andrés Ruiz II designed the high altar of Villacastin church.

RUIZ, Andrés III
Spanish, 17th century.
Active in Seville from 1627 to 1641.
Painter, sculptor (?).
Andrés Ruiz III executed historical paintings and two statues for the Easter monument of Seville Cathedral.

RUIZ, Antonio
Mexican, 20th century.
Born 1897, in Mexico.
Painter.
Antonio Ruiz's father was a doctor and his mother a pianist. He was a significant painter in the first half of the century, but, like Rodríguez Lozano, he was not involved in the great movement of the mural-painters, Rivera, Siqueiros and Orozco, which was so important in bringing Latin American art into the modern world. He was well aware of the social conditions of Mexican people, but did not have the temperament for the violent expression and embattled art so dear to the muralists. His minute and painstaking methods, no doubt the reason for his small output, almost bring him into the naive category of a Douanier Rousseau. He generally painted complex scenes, 'manufactured' landscapes with figures such as the 1938 *Sports Party* and the 1941 *Les Nouveaux Riches*.

RUIZ, Antonio or Anton
Spanish, 16th century.
Painter.
Antonio Ruiz produced a panel for Seville Cathedral, the *Descent of the Holy Spirit*.

RUIZ, Bartolomé
Spanish, 15th century.
Painter.
Bartolomé Ruiz painted an *Entombment*, dated 1450.

RUIZ, Diego
Spanish, 15th century.
Active in Seville.
Sculptor (wood).
Diego Ruiz sculpted the gilded ceiling of the Salón de Embajadores in the Alcazar Palace in Seville, in 1427.

RUIZ, Federico
Spanish, 19th century.
Born 1837, in Madrid; died 4 February 1868, in Madrid.
Painter, illustrator.
Federico Ruiz was a pupil of G. Pérez Villaamil and J. Vallejo.

RUIZ, Francisco
Spanish, 17th century.
Active in Valladolid during the first half of the 17th century.
Sculptor (wood).
Francisco Ruiz collaborated with Marcos Garcia on the altar of the church of S Pedro in Olmos de Esgueva.

RUIZ, Gaspar
Spanish, 16th century.
Active in Seville.
Painter.
Gaspar Ruiz worked on the high altar of Seville Cathedral, in 1574.

RUIZ, Gilberto
Cuban, 20th - 21st century.
Born 1950, in Havana.
Painter.

Gilberto Ruiz studied at the Academia San Alejandro in Havana. In 1980 he left for the USA and now lives in New York. Ruiz is one of the principal members of the 'Mariel Generation' of Cuban artists.

Ruiz has taken part in numerous collective exhibitions in the USA. The Barbara Gillman Gallery held a solo exhibition of his work in Miami in 1993.

AUCTION RECORDS:
NEW YORK, 18 May 1994, *I can swim but I would like to fly* (1986, acrylic/canvas, 60 x 48 ins / 152.4 x 121.9 cm) USD 4,025.

RUIZ, Gregorio
Spanish, 17th century.
Active in Madrid.
Painter.

RUIZ, Jean-Paul
French, 20th - 21st century.
Born 1954, in Poissy.
Sculptor, engraver. Artists' books.

Jean-Paul Ruiz lives and works in Corrèze. He typically uses plastic-coated and painted paper (browns and ochres) as the base material for his compositions. He was a participant at the Uzerche Book Biennale of 1991 and at *l'Art à la Page* (*Art on the Page*), an exhibition mounted in 1992 at Cagnes-sur-Mer. Ruiz has also exhibited solo, notably in 1988 at the Galerie Métamorphose in Paris and, in 1992, at the Hôtel de Région in Aurillac.

RUIZ, Juan I
Spanish, 15th century.
Active in Toledo (Castile-La Mancha) during the first half of the 15th century.
Sculptor.

Juan Ruiz I produced sculptures for the portals and tower of Toledo Cathedral, from 1418-1425. He was identical with the sculptor of the same name, who was in Seville in 1432.

RUIZ, Juan II, or Rois
Spanish, 15th century.
Active at the end of the 15th century.
Painter.

Juan Ruiz II painted an altar for the church of the Preaching Friars in Barcelona, with Nicolas Léonard, from 1496-1497.

RUIZ, Juan III
Spanish, 16th century.
Active in Seville at the beginning of the 16th century.
Painter.

Juan Ruiz III decorated two lecterns for the high altar in Seville Cathedral.

RUIZ, Juan IV
Spanish, 17th century.
Active during the second half of the 17th century.
Sculptor.

Juan Ruiz IV worked on the Puerta Nueva de la Oliva at Seville Cathedral from 1466 to 1469.

RUIZ, Juan Salvador. See **SALVADOR RUIZ**

RUIZ, Koki
Paraguayan, 20th - 21st century.
Born 1957, in San Ignacio, Misiones.
Painter, draughtsman, illustrator. Figures. Murals.

Koki Ruiz entered the faculty of architecture at the Mackensie University, São Paulo, Brazil in 1978 and, in 1979, he worked as an illustrator on the *Diario La Tribuna*, in Asunción. He paints figures (mother and child, madonnas) in warm, contrasting colours on abstract backgrounds. The people are depicted in a very natural and relaxed way. He has made murals for monuments in Paraguay such as the *La Comunión de los Guaranies* (*The Communion of the Guaranis*) San Ignacio, Misiones.

Collective exhibitions include Galería Michele Malingue, Asunción (1985); *II Exposición de Arte Latino americana en Nueva York*, Belenky Gallery, New York (1998); *Présence de la peinture paraguayenne contemporaine* (*The Influence of Contemporary Paraguayan Painting*), Musée École de la Perrine, Laval, France (2000) and with two other Paraguayan artists, Marcelo Medina and Hernán Miranda at the 2002 World Cup in Seoul. Solo exhibitions include the Galería Prepuestas, Asunción (1985); Galería El Viejo Galpón, San Bernadino, Paraguay (1988) and Galería Montalban, Madrid, Spain (1994). He has won many prizes in Paraguay.

RUIZ, Manuel
Spanish, 20th - 21st century.
Born 28 September 1948, in Granada.
Active in Argentina.
Painter.

Manuel Ruiz is an eclectic artist.

MUSEUMS AND GALLERIES:
CARACAS (MAC Sofía Imber) - GUATEMALA CITY (National Mus.) - SALVADOR DA BAHIA (Kennedy MCA).

RUIZ, Martín
Spanish, 15th century.
Active in 1479.
Sculptor.

Martín Ruiz produced sculptures for the Puerta del Perdón in Toledo Cathedral.

RUIZ, Pablo. See **PICASSO**

RUIZ, Valentín
Spanish, 17th century.
Active in 1624.
Glass painter.

Valentín Ruiz executed stained-glass windows for the transept of Burgos Cathedral.

RUIZ AGUA NEVADA, Lope
Spanish, 16th century.
Active during the first half of the 16th century.
Sculptor (wood).

Lope Ruiz Agua Nevada was probably identical with Lope Fernandez Aguanevada. He sculpted a statue of Christ for Seville Cathedral, and an altar for the Franciscan convent in Seville.

RUIZ AGUADO, Francisco
Spanish, 17th century.
Painter.

RUIZ BLASCO, José
Spanish, 19th - 20th century.
Born 1841, in Málaga; died 3 May 1913, in Barcelona.
Painter.

The father of Pablo Picasso (Picasso signed his own early work 'Ruiz'), José Ruiz Blasco's was the son of a leather and glove manufacturer who was supportive of his son's artistic aspirations, as indeed were his two brothers, Pablo - the canon of Málaga Cathedral, and Salvador, a doctor of medicine. As a result, José was free to frequent artistic and political circles in Málaga, where he quickly made a name for himself both for his painting and as a teacher of drawing and composition and curator of the first provincial museum. In 1891, however, financial problems obliged him to leave Málaga. He moved to La Coruña, where he taught at the Instituto da Guarda for four years before leaving for Barcelona to take up a teaching post at the provincial college of fine arts, a position he was to hold until his death in 1913.

Why José Ruiz Blasco stopped painting and reportedly broke his brushes is not known with any certainty; some art historians allege this was because of eye trouble, while others insist he was simply 'making way' for his gifted son Pablo. In his *Picasso: A Portrait and a Memory*, Jaime Sabartès recalls that Picasso once commented that his father 'painted "dining room subjects with partridges and pigeons and rabbits and hares"... His specialities were birds and flowers, above all doves and lilacs. One day, he painted an immense canvas of a dovecote complete with doves sitting on their perch'. One such painting of doves by Ruiz Blasco is now preserved in Málaga Museum. Some other compositions by him are of a religious nature and were commissioned by religious communities.

RUIZ CESAR, Bartolomé
Spanish, 17th century.
Died 1699.
Active in Seville.
Painter.

Bartolomé Ruiz Cesar was at the Seville academy from 1667 to 1672.

RUIZ DE ALMODÓVAR, José
Spanish, 19th century.
Born 5 August 1867, in Granada.
Painter, illustrator. Portraits, landscapes.

José Ruiz de Almodóvar was a pupil of Ferrant.

MUSEUMS AND GALLERIES:
GRANADA (University): portraits.

RUIZ DE AMAYA, Francisco
Spanish, 18th century.
Active in Madrid.
Sculptor.

Francisco Ruiz de Amaya was a member of the Real Academia de San Fernando in 1756.

RUIZ DE ANDENA, Cristóbal, or de Andino
Spanish, 17th century.
Active in Valladolid.
Sculptor.

Cristóbal Ruiz de Andena created the high altar of the church of S Martín in Valladolid. He was a genuine artist yet, like many others, little is known of his life or his work as it has become confused with that of his contemporaries. He was almost certainly a descendant of Pedro Andino.

RUIZ DE CASTANEDA, Juan
Spanish, 17th century.
Active in Toledo at the beginning of the 17th century.
Sculptor.

Juan Ruiz de Castaneda was a pupil of G. Becerra. He worked at Toledo Cathedral and at the church of La Torre de Esteban Hambran.

RUIZ DE EGUINO, Iñaki Moreno
Spanish, 20th century.
Painter.
Neo-Constructivism.

Ruiz de Eguino was awarded the Gran Premio de Pintura Vasca in San Telmo (San Sebastian) in 1974 and first prize and gold medal at the Marseilles Salon d'Automne of 1982. He exhibited solo from 1974, notably in Navarre and Pamplona (1975), Salamanca (1985 and 1987) and at the San Telmo Museum in San Sebastian in 1986.

MUSEUMS AND GALLERIES:
ALICANTE (MAC) - BUDAPEST (Szépmuvészeti Múz.) - GRANADA (MBA) - HUESCA (MCA) - PAMPLONA (Mus. of Navarre) - SAN SEBASTIAN (Mus. Municipal de San Telmo) - TOLEDO (Mus. de Santa Cruz).

RUIZ DE ELVIRA, Cristóbal and Pedro
Spanish, 17th century.
Painters.

Cristóbal and Pedro Ruiz de Elvira were related, possibly brothers. They worked in Daimiel and Manzanares during the first half of the 17th century. In collaboration with Giraldo de Merlo they created the high altar of the church of the Virgen del Prado in Ciudad Real.

RUIZ DE INFANTE, Francisco
Spanish, 20th - 21st century.
Born 1966, in Spain.
Active in France.
Installation artist, video artist.

Francisco Ruiz de Infante won the 9th Ivry Scholarship for Monumental Art in 1994. He held a solo exhibition of his work, *Les Frères de Pinocchio* (*Pinocchio's Brothers*), at the Centre d'Art d'Ivry in 1994, the subject of which was an imaginary dialogue between the worlds of childhood and adulthood.

RUIZ DE LA IGLESIA, Francisco Ignacio
Spanish, 17th century.
Born probably in 1648, in Madrid; died 1704, in Madrid.
Painter, engraver (etching). History painting.

Francisco Ruiz de la Iglesia was a pupil of Francisco Camilo and Juan Carreño de Miranda. In 1689 he was appointed pintor de cámara (court painter) to Charles II of Spain.

BIBLIOGRAPHY:
Bermudez, C., *Diccionario histórico de los más ilustres profesores de las bellas artes en España*, Madrid, 1800. Palomino de Castro y Velasco, A.A., *El museo pictúrico ó escala óptica (1715-23)*, Editorial Poseidon, Buenos Aires, 1944 revised edition. Gallego, A., *Historia del grabado en España*, Ediciones Cátedra, Madrid, 1979. Tomlinson, Janis, *Painting in Spain: El Greco to Goya, 1561-1828*, George Weidenfeld & Nicolson, London, 1997. Brown, J., *Painting in Spain 1500-1700*, Yale University Press, New Haven and London, 1998.

MUSEUMS AND GALLERIES:
BOSTON: *Immaculate Conception* - GUADALAJARA: *St Anthony* - MADRID (Prado): *St John*.

AUCTION RECORDS:
MARSEILLES, 8 April 1949, *Fair near a Fortified Port*, FRF 27,000.

RUIZ DE SARABIA, Andrés. See **SARABIA**

RUIZ DE VALDIVIA, Nicolás
Spanish, 19th century.
Born in Almuñecar; died 21 January 1880, in Madrid.
Painter. Historical subjects, genre scenes.

Nicolás Ruiz de Valdivia was a pupil of C. Ribera and Ch. Gleyre.

MUSEUMS AND GALLERIES:
SARAGOSSA (Ateneo): several works - SARAGOSSA (Diputación Provincial): *Juramento de los defensores de Zaragoza en la plazuela del Carmen* (1866, oil on canvas).

RUIZ DEL ARBOL, Luis
Spanish, 20th century.
Born 1938, in Bilbao.
Painter, sculptor.

Luis Ruiz del Arbol's body of work is very much in line with the Lyrical Abstraction that characterised French painting in the 1960s and is particularly reminiscent of the abstractions of James Guitet. His habit of carving a low relief into the wooden support imbues his paintings with a certain originality.

He participated in group exhibitions from 1964, most notably at *Lines and Figures in Contemporary Spanish Painting* in 1971 in San Juan, Puerto Rico; *Contemporary Spanish Painting* in Havana, Cuba in 1977; at the international Marbella Biennale in 1981-1982 and 1985; and in Madrid in 1987-

1990 (BMW Prize). He also took part in various painting competitions, including those at Mostoles, Alcorcon, the Catalan Circle in Madrid, La Vagueda and at the Madrid Post Office. His solo exhibitions were held in Vina del Mar (Chile) 1964; Bilbao in 1966, and in Madrid (1970, 1971, 1974, 1977 and 1988).

BIBLIOGRAPHY:

Catálogo nacionál de arte contemporaneo 1990-1991, Ibérico 2Mil, Barcelona, 1990-1991.

RUIZ DEL PERAL, Torcuato
Spanish, 18th century.
Born in Granada; died 5 July 1773, in Granada.
Sculptor.

Torcuato Ruiz del Peral worked for churches in Granada and for Cádiz Cathedral.

RUIZ GIJÓN, Bernardo, or Ruiz Gixón
Spanish, 17th - 18th century.
Born c. 1658, in Seville; died c. 1750, in Seville.
Sculptor.

Bernardo Ruiz Gijón studied under his uncle Francisco Antonio Ruiz Gijón. He worked in Seville.

RUIZ GIJÓN, Francisco Antonio, or Ruiz Gixón
Spanish, 17th century.
Born 1653, in Utrera.
Sculptor.

Francisco Ruiz Gijón was a pupil of Andrés Causino, the brother of Juan Antonio and uncle of Bernardo Ruiz Gijón. He was one of the most distinguished sculptors in Seville in the 17th century and carved many statues for churches in the city.

RUIZ GIJÓN, Juan Antonio or Juan Carlos, or Ruiz Gixón
Spanish, 17th century.
Painter.

Juan Antonio Ruiz Gijón was the brother of Francisco Antonio and uncle of Bernardo Ruiz Gijón. He worked in Seville from 1668 to 1672 and is believed to have been a pupil of Herrera the Younger. He certainly took inspiration from Herrera's style, as can be seen in a signed painting of the *Immaculate Conception* which he executed for Seville Cathedral. He is believed to have lived in Andalusia from 1663 to 1677.

RUIZ GIXÓN. See **RUIZ GIJÓN**

RUIZ GONZÁLEZ, Pedro
Spanish, 17th century.
Born 1640, in Araudilla; died 3 May 1706, in Madrid.
Painter.

Pedro Ruiz González was a pupil of Juan Antonio Escalante and Juan Carreño de Miranda. There were three works by him in the church of S Millán which was destroyed by fire in 1720. Ruiz González was also buried there.

BIBLIOGRAPHY:

Palomino de Castro y Velasco, A.A., *El Museo Pictúrico ó Escala Óptica (1715-23)*, Editorial Poseidon, Buenos Aires, 1944 (revised edition). Kubler G./Soria, M., *Art and Architecture in Spain & Portugal and their American Dominians 1500 to 1800*, Penguin Books, Harmondsworth and Baltimore, 1959. Angulo Iniguez, D., *Pintura del Siglo XVII*, Editorial Plus Ultra, Madrid, 1971. Brown, J., *The Golden Age of Painting in Spain*, Yale University Press, New Haven and London, 1991. Brown, J., *Painting in Spain 1500-1700*, Yale University Press, New Haven and London, 1998.

MUSEUMS AND GALLERIES:

FLORENCE (Uffizi): several works - MADRID (Prado): *Christ before Pilate* (1673).

AUCTION RECORDS:

PARIS, 1853, *The Redeemer Tied to a Column*, FRF 275.

RUIZ LUNA, Justo
Spanish, 19th - 20th century.
Born 1865, in Cádiz; died 9 March 1926, in Cádiz.
Painter, watercolourist, pastellist. Historical subjects, battles, figures, portraits, genre scenes, interiors with figures, waterscapes, seascapes.

Ruiz Luna studied at the Escuela de Bellas Artes in Cádiz, then under José Villegas. He spent several periods in Rome, notably in 1882 and 1888.

He painted a wide variety of subjects but was particularly fond of seascapes. Examples of his work include: *Portrait of the Bishop of Cordova; Evening Prayer; Remains of a Shipwreck; Canal in Venice; Christopher Columbus Landing on the Island of Guanahani; Sea Battle off Trafalgar.*

He took part in various group exhibitions from 1884, showing his work at Exposición Nacional de Bellas Artes in Madrid. He went on to exhibit in Madrid (1886, Athenaeum), Munich (1888, 1891), and the Círculo de Bellas Artes in Madrid (1906). He was awarded a medal of honour in 1887, a bronze medal in 1888, a gold in 1890 and a silver in 1891.

BIBLIOGRAPHY:

Perez Mulet, Fernando, *La pintura gaditana (1875-1931)*, Monte de Piedad y Caja de Ahorros de Córdoba y Excmo. Ayuntamiento de Cádiz, Córdoba, 1983. Arnáiz, José Manuel/López Jiménez, Javier/Merchán Díaz, Manuel (ed.), '*Cien años de pintura en Espana y Portugal (1830-1930)*' in vol. IX, Antiqvaria, Madrid, 1992. Ruiz Casas, Carmen, *La Bahía de Cádiz y el pintor Justo Ruiz Luna (1865-1926)*, El Carro del Sol, Barcelona, 1999.

MUSEUMS AND GALLERIES:

CÁDIZ (Mus.) - MADRID (Prado): *Sea Battle off Trafalgar.*

AUCTION RECORDS:

NEW YORK, 11 March 1943, *Interiors with figures*, USD 240. NEW YORK, 26 Feb 1997, *Arab Sentinel* (1881, oil on canvas, 27 x 18 1/4 ins / 68.6 x 46.3 cm) USD 6,325. PARIS, 26 March 1998, *Palace Guard* (oil on canvas, 27 1/4 x 18 1/4 ins / 69 x 46.5 cm) FRF 90,000. MADRID, 26 Oct 1999, *Harem Guard* (oil on canvas, 27 x 18 ins / 69 x 46 cm) ESP 800,000. MADRID, 22 May 2000, *Serenade* (1884, oil on panel, 15 x 15 ins / 39 x 37 cm) ESP 450,000. MADRID, 16 Nov 2000, *Bridge* (oil on canvas, 28 x 17 ins / 70 x 42 cm) ESP 450,000. MADRID, 21 May 2001, *Serrallo Guard* (oil on canvas, 27 x 18 ins / 69 x 46 cm) ESP 950,000. MADRID, 13 Nov 2002, *Coastal Landscape* (oil on canvas, 25 x 31 ins / 64 x 78 cm) EUR 3,000. MADRID, 18 Feb 2003, *Serrallo Guard* (oil on canvas, 27 x 18 ins / 69 x 46 cm) EUR 6,000. MADRID, 24 Feb 2004, *Guard* (oil on canvas, 27 x 18 ins / 69 x 46 cm) EUR 5,000.

RUIZ MELGAREJO, Juan
Spanish, 18th century.
Active in Murcia during the first half of the 18th century.
Painter.

Juan Ruiz Melgarejo executed portraits and frescoes for the church of the Order of St Augustine in Murcia.

AUCTION RECORDS:

LONDON, 11 July 1979, *Views of Naples* (two oils on canvas, 19 1/2 x 54 1/4 ins / 49.5 x 138 cm) GBP 4,500.

RUIZ MOYA, Francisco
Spanish, 18th century.
Sculptor (wood).

Francisco Ruiz Moya was commissioned to carve the stalls in the church of Sta Cruz in Seville. He may be the same as Francisco Moya.

RUIZ PANIAGUA, Francisco
Spanish, 17th century.
Active in Cordova.
Sculptor.

In 1664 Francisco Ruiz Paniagua carved an altar and tabernacle for the church of Canete de las Torres.

RUIZ PULIDO, Cristóbal
Spanish, 20th century.
Born 15 March 1881, in Villacarrillo, near Jaén (Andalusia); died 1962.
Painter. Portraits, landscapes, seascapes.

Ruiz Pulido studied at the college of fine art in Cordova and in Madrid and under Angel Ferrant at the École des Beaux-Arts in Paris. He lived from 1902 to 1914 successively in France, Belgium and the Netherlands.

He was preoccupied with the effects of light and painted in broad swatches of colour with little or no attention to detail. His body of work comprises chiefly landscapes and portraits, among them *Doctor Zavala; My Pupils; Two Little Girls; Jaen Landscape* and *Landscape near Segovia*.

Ruiz Pulido showed his work at various group exhibitions, including Exposición Nacional de Bellas Artes in Madrid in 1910 and 1917; Bilbao (1919, 1920); Madrid (Athenaeum, 1925, Museum of Modern Art, 1925 and Círculo de Bellas Artes, 1930). He was awarded silver medals in 1917 and 1920.

Bibliography:
Arnáiz, José Manuel/López Jiménez, Javier/Merchán Díaz, Manuel (ed.), '*Cien años de pintura en Espana y Portugal (1830-1930)*' in vol. IX, Antiqvaria, Madrid, 1992.

Museums and Galleries:
Madrid (Mus. de Arte Moderno).

Auction records:
Madrid, 11 Nov 1976, *By the Sea* (1954, oil on canvas, 39 1/4 x 49 1/4 ins / 100 x 125 cm) ESP 90,000.

RUIZ REY, José Antonio
Spanish, 18th century.
Born 24 September 1695, in Puente Genil; died 25 October 1767, in Puente Genil.
Painter, sculptor.

José Antonio Ruiz Rey executed frescoes, statues and altars in the churches of Puente Genil.

RUIZ SÁNCHEZ MORALES, Manuel Bernardino
Spanish, 19th - 20th century.
Born 20 March 1857, in Baza, near Granada; died 1922, in Madrid.
Painter, watercolourist, art restorer. History painting, portraits, genre scenes, landscapes.

Ruiz Sánchez Morales studied at the Escuela de Bellas Artes in Granada and received a travel scholarship in 1886 that enabled him to complete his studies in Rome. He settled in Madrid, where he continued to study (under E. Rosales). He is noted for his restoration work of the Goya frescoes in the San Antonio de la Florida monastery. He also painted views of Granada. His technique was characterised by a lightness of touch and a luminosity that reflected the colours of Andalusia. Not least, he painted some portraits and genre compositions, examples of which include *Corpus Christi, Christmas Market; Market in Tangier; Extern Sister Marguerita*.

He showed at various group exhibitions, including the Exposición Nacional de Bellas Artes (1884, 1895, 1897, 1899) and in Granada (1886, 1903) and Madrid (1889).

Bibliography:
Arnáiz, José Manuel/López Jiménez, Javier/Merchán Díaz, Manuel (ed.), '*Cien años de pintura en Espana y Portugal (1830-1930)*' in vol. IX, Antiqvaria, Madrid, 1992.

Museums and Galleries:
Granada (MBA).

RUIZ SORIANO, Juan
Spanish, 18th century.
Born 23 June 1701, in Higuera de Aracena; died 17 August 1763, in Seville.
Painter.

Juan Ruiz Soriano studied under his cousin Midge Tovar. He settled in Seville where he painted historical subjects. He is known for his work on the high altar of Seville Cathedral.

RUIZ Y PICASSO, Pablo. See **PICASSO**

RUIZ-DURAND, Jesús. See **DURAND**

RUIZ-GUERRERO, Manuel
Spanish, 19th - 20th century.
Born 1864, in Granada; died 1917, in Madrid.
Painter, draughtsman. Religious subjects, figures, portraits, genre scenes, landscapes, urban landscapes, still-lifes, flowers.

Ruiz-Guerrero studied at the Escuela de Bellas Artes in Granada and in Madrid and was awarded a study scholarship to Rome in 1881. He went on to teach at the Escuela de Bellas Artes in Málaga and to exhibit his work at the Madrid Exposición Nacional de Bellas Artes of 1884, 1887 and 1892 (silver medal in 1892).

Ruiz-Guerrero's work is a pretext for the study of colour and its application. His technique is generous and characterised by large brushstrokes typically applied with evident vigour (as in *After the Bullfight; Mercenaries; Flowers*). Other examples of his work include *Procession in Granada; The Bull's Last Breath; Customs of Galicia; Gallantry; The Condemned* and *Smoker*.

Bibliography:
Arnáiz, José Manuel/López Jiménez, Javier/Merchán Díaz, Manuel (ed.), '*Cien años de pintura en Espana y Portugal (1830-1930)*' in vol. IX, Antiqvaria, Madrid, 1992.

Auction records:
Paris, 27 April 1988, *Elegant Lady at the Races* (oil on canvas, 33 x 13 1/2 ins / 84 x 34 cm) FRF 80,000. New York, 29 Oct 1992, *Basque Pelota* (oil on canvas, 21 3/4 x 31 1/2 ins / 55.2 x 80 cm) USD 7,150.

RUIZ-PIPO, Manolo
Spanish, 20th century.
Born 1929, in Granada; died 25 September 1998.
From 1954 also active in France.
Painter (including gouache), sculptor (bronze), engraver, illustrator. Figure compositions, figures, portraits, landscapes, still-lifes. Stage sets, puppets.

Ruiz-Pipo studied from 1942 at the Escuela de Arte y Oficios in Barcelona, then in 1944 at the Escuela de Bellas Artes de San Jorge, also in Barcelona; a French Government study scholarship in 1954 enabled him to continue his engraving studies under Goerg at the École des Beaux-Arts in Paris. He met Jaime Sabartès and Pablo Picasso in 1955 and the latter put him in touch with gallery owner Jeanne Castel. Ruiz-Pipo lived mainly in London from 1958 to 1963 where he painted numerous portraits. In 1963 he returned to France, dividing his time between Paris and Bonnaquil in the Lot-et-Garonne. That year, two of his canvases were acquired by the Musée d'Art Moderne de la Ville de Paris. He also lived for a period in Florence in 1968 before moving to Bologna in 1969; thereafter, he divided his time between France and Italy.

In 1964, Ruiz-Pipo produced marionettes for Manuel de Falla's opera *El retablo de Maese Pedro (Master Peter's Puppet Show)*; in 1957 he sculpted a hammered bronze statue, *The Challenge,* for the Théâtre des Nations; and between 1963 and 1965, he illustrated several *Cahiers de la Barbacane*, a series of 'notebooks' containing poems by Jean Cocteau, Jean Follain, André Breton and Jasmin. His work focuses on traditional themes - portraits, landscapes and still lifes - but his treatment of those themes owes something to Cézanne and the post-Cubists and, at times, even to the metaphysical paintings of Giorgio de Chirico.

He participated in group exhibitions, notably at the fine arts Museum in Barcelona (1951-1953); Jeanne Castel Gallery in Paris (1955-1962); 1955 Ibero-American Biennale in Barcelona; Spanish Art Biennale at the Musée Galliéra in Paris in 1968 and at various times in major salons such as the Grands et Jeunes d'Aujourd'hui and the 1985 and 1989 Salons d'Automne in Paris. In 1962, he was selected for the City of Paris Critics' Prize.

He exhibited solo from 1951, when he showed at the Municipiale de Bellas Artes in Barcelona, featuring again there in 1952 and 1953. This was followed by solo exhibitions in Milan (1970); Holland (1971); Sweden (1971); Villeneuve-sur-Lot (retrospective, 1978); Überlingen (1979) and Madrid (1990, 1992). He was awarded the Grand Prix de Peinture at Villeneuve-sur-Lot in 1957 and first prize at the 1990 Salon d'Automne in Paris.

Ruiz Pipó

BIBLIOGRAPHY:

Bailly, Patricia/Buffet-Challié, Laurence, *Ruiz-Pipo*, Charles et André Bailly, Paris, 1992. Harambourg, Lydia, *L'École de Paris 1945-1965. Dictionnaire des peintres*, Ides et Calendes, Paris, 1993.

MUSEUMS AND GALLERIES:

BRIVE-LA-GAILLARDE - PARIS (MAMVP) - VILLENEUVE-SUR-LOT.

AUCTION RECORDS:

PARIS, 27 Nov 1990, *Golden Motherhood* (oil on canvas, 46 x 35 ins / 116 x 89 cm) FRF 125,000. NEW YORK, 12 June 1991, *Child with Cockerel* (1957, oil on canvas, 36 x 28 1/2 ins / 91.4 x 72.4 cm) USD 4,400. CALAIS, 5 April 1992, *Tumblers* (gouache, 22 x 15 ins / 56 x 38 cm) FRF 20,000. PARIS, 26 June 1992, *Peasant Couple* (1959, watercolour and gouache, 19 1/4 x 12 1/4 ins / 49 x 31 cm) FRF 7,300. NEW YORK, 10 May 1993, *Rodrigo with a Chiffon; Rodrigo with Bowls* (oil/synthetic resin, pair, 13 3/4 x 11 ins / 35 x 27 cm) USD 1,840. PARIS, 21 March 1994, *Couple* (1959, gouache, 19 x 12 ins / 48.5 x 30.5 cm) FRF 7,500. LE TOUQUET, 22 May 1994, *Young Dutch Woman Eating Grapes* (oil on canvas, 32 x 25 1/2 ins / 81 x 65 cm) FRF 45,000. PARIS, 28 March 1996, *Figures in the Rain* (oil on canvas, 18 1/4 x 22 ins / 46.5 x 55 cm) FRF 14,000. CALAIS, 7 July 1996, *Conversation at the Fountain* (oil on canvas, 22 x 18 ins / 56 x 46 cm) FRF 12,500. PARIS, 4 Nov 1997, *Children on the Beach, Antibes* (1955, oil on canvas, 18 1/4 x 22 ins / 46.5 x 55 cm) FRF 6,500. PARIS, 4 March 1998, *Village Belfry and Rooftops* (1956, oil on canvas, 22 x 18 ins / 55 x 46 cm) FRF 16,000. PARIS, 15 March 1999, *Two Women at the Fountain* (oil on canvas, 24 x 29 ins / 61 x 73 cm) FRF 36,000. PARIS, 24 June 1999, *Eros Minos* (1979, ink and watercolour, 11 x 15 ins / 28 x 38 cm) FRF 20,000. PARIS, 16 Dec 2000, *Bulls in the Country* (gouache, 21 x 29 ins / 54 x 73 cm) FRF 12,000. PARIS, 24 Feb 2001, *Landscape in La Mancha* (1965, oil on canvas, 28 x 20 ins / 72 x 52 cm) FRF 20,000. PARIS, 21 May 2001, *Portrait of a Lady* (oil on paper on canvas, 19 x 15 ins / 48 x 37 cm) FRF 13,500. AUSTINBURG, 6 Oct 2001, *Head of a Child with Blue Ribbon* (1960, oil on canvas, 21 x 18 ins / 53 x 46 cm) USD 1,500. NORTH BETHESDA, 19 May 2002, *Cows* (oil on canvas, 35 x 57 ins / 89 x 146 cm) USD 1,800. PARIS, 6 Dec 2002, *Children of Paradise* (1956, oil on canvas, 46 x 31 ins / 116 x 80 cm) EUR 2,400. ST-GERMAIN-EN-LAYE, 12 Oct 2003, *Two Bulls in a Field* (gouache and watercolour on paper on canvas, 20 x 26 ins / 50 x 65 cm) EUR 3,700. ST-GERMAIN-EN-LAYE, 12 Oct 2003, *Violaine and Renault Hilleret* (1969, oil on canvas, 51 x 38 ins / 130 x 97 cm) EUR 6,000. ST-GERMAIN-EN-LAYE, 14 March 2004, *Young Girl with Apple* (oil on canvas, 14 x 18 ins / 35 x 46 cm) EUR 3,800. PARIS, 24 June 2004, *Etrangere* (wax crayon, 25 x 19 ins / 63 x 49 cm) EUR 2,200.

RUIZ-SANTILLAN, Luis

Spanish, 20th century.
Born 1903, in Santander.
Painter. Portraits.

Ruiz-Santillan studied at the École des Beaux-Arts in Bordeaux. He was primarily a portrait painter.

RUKENSTAIN, Gregorius

Austrian, 16th century.
Sculptor.

In 1544 Gregorius Rukenstain carved decorative sculptures for the church of St Peter in Dvor, near Ljubljana.

RUKHIN, Evgeny Lvovich or Eugène, or Rouhkine

Russian, 20th century.
Born 1943, in Saratov; died 23 May 1976, in Leningrad (now St Petersburg).
Painter, collage artist. Landscapes, interiors with figures, still-lifes.

Evgeny Rukhin first trained as a geologist, but switched to being a full-time painter in about 1963. He took part in the famous open-air exhibition organised by dissident Modernists in a Moscow suburb that came to be known as the *Bulldozer Exhibition* after the political powers ordered that the show be forcibly broken up with the help of bulldozers. He was linked to the group of artists that also includes Oscar Rubin, Vladimir Nemukhin, Valentina Kropivnitskaya and Lidia Masterkova. He was killed when fire swept through his studio. He was one of the prime movers in the relaunch of modern art in Russia after relations with the West started to thaw. Interested in achieving an understanding of painting in itself, with no ideological or aesthetic references, he steered himself towards an analytical type of Abstraction, closely questioning the texture and the surface of the canvas, in particular, and their relationship with the paint and the paint brush. He neutralised the traditional function of painting through the incorporation of everyday objects or of symbols printed out by means of stencils. In parallel with this, he would paint Russian or Asian landscapes and traditional subjects (villages, bell towers, interiors, still-lifes) in a realist, almost synthetic style, using a generally cool palette. In 1975, he had a solo exhibition of his works in North Carolina at the Art Museum in Raleigh.

BIBLIOGRAPHY:

Eugene Rukhin: A contemporary Russian artist, exhibition catalogue, North Carolina Museum of Art, Raleigh, 1975. *Rukhin*, exhibition catalogue, Gallery 1912, Los Angeles, 1989.

AUCTION RECORDS:

ZURICH, 7 April 1995, *Composition* (1975, collage and oil on canvas, 39 1/4 x 38 1/4 ins / 99.5 x 97 cm) CHF 1,500.

RUL, Andreas. See **RIEHL**

RUL, Andrzej

Polish, 16th century.
Active at the beginning of the 16th century.
Portrait artist.

Andrzej Rul produced a portrait of *King Sigismund August* in 1551.

RUL, Henri or Henry Pieter Edward

Belgian, 19th - 20th century.
Born 2 July 1862, in Antwerp; died 1942, in Viersel.
Painter, engraver. Landscapes.

Henri Rul, one of the co-founders of the Als Ik Kan group, studied in Middelburg under Poulwelsen and in Antwerp under Jospeh van Luppen. He lived and worked in Antwerp and Calmpthout.

MUSEUMS AND GALLERIES:
ANTWERP: *Dunes.*
AUCTION RECORDS:
AMSTERDAM, 14-15 April 1992, *Dune Landscape near Heyst* (oil on canvas, 31 1/2 x 39 1/4 ins / 80 x 100 cm) NLG 4,600. LOKEREN, 4 Dec 1993, *Willow Tree by the Water* (oil on canvas, 15 3/4 x 19 3/4 ins / 40 x 50 cm) BEF 26,000. LOKEREN, 12 March 1994, *Winter Evening* (oil on canvas, 78 3/4 x 39 1/4 ins / 200 x 100 cm) BEF 55,000. BRUSSELS, 17 Jan 2000, *River Scheldt in Holland* (oil on canvas, 40 x 55 ins / 101 x 140 cm) BEF 305,000. BRUSSELS, 9 May 2000, *Landscape at Twilight* (oil on canvas, 31 x 47 ins / 80 x 120 cm) BEF 110,000. LOKEREN, 9 March 2002, *Landscape* (oil on canvas, 39 x 31 ins / 100 x 80 cm) EUR 3,000. ANTWERP, 26 March 2002, *View over a Stream in the Country* (oil on canvas, 0 x 60 ins / 0 x 153 cm) EUR 5,500. ANTWERP, 26 Oct 2004, *Spring* (oil on canvas, 39 x 31 ins / 100 x 80 cm) EUR 1,700.

RULAND, Carl Friedrich
German, 19th century.
Born 1783; died 28 January 1851.
Painter, decorative designer.
Carl Friedrich Ruland was the son of Johannes Ruland

RULAND, Heinrich
German, 19th century.
Born 9 June 1866, in Munich; died 5 April 1900, in Munich.
Painter (including porcelain), lithographer.
Heinrich Ruland was a pupil of Raupp and O. Seitz.
MUSEUMS AND GALLERIES:
BAMBERG (Municipal Mus.): *Portrait of a Municipal Councillor; Scholar; Three Heads* (study).

RULAND, Johann Gerhard
German, 19th century.
Born 13 June 1785; died 27 November 1854.
Painter, engraver (burin), lithographer.
Johann Gerhard Ruland was the son of Johannes Ruland.
MUSEUMS AND GALLERIES:
SPEYER (Historisches Mus. der Pfalz): *View of Speyer; Queen Theresa.*

RULAND, Johannes
German, 18th - 19th century.
Born 2 February 1744, in Speyer; died 20 September 1830, in Speyer.
Painter, draughtsman, engraver (burin/etching).
Landscapes, architectural views.
Johannes Ruland was the father of Carl Friedrich and Johann Gerhard Ruland.
MUSEUMS AND GALLERIES:
SPEYER (Historisches Mus. der Pfalz): *Hares* (painting); *Church of St Bartholomew* (painting); *Order of St John* (painting); *Ruins of Speyer, Frankenthal and Worms* (drawing); *Landscape with Lake Constance* (drawing, two); *View of Schwetzingen Park* (drawing); *Battle of Speyer* (drawing); *General Custine* (drawing); *Erection of the Tree of Liberty* (drawing); *Return of the Hostages* (drawing).

RULAND, Theobald. See **RUELAND**

RULE, Conrad
German, 15th century.
Died after 1478.
Active in Freiberg (Hesse).
Glass painter.
Between 1474 and 1478 Conrad Rule painted windows for the church of Freiberg.

RULE, William Harris
British, 19th century.
Born 15 November 1802, in Penrhyn; died 25 September 1890, in Clyde Road.
Painter. Portraits.
William Harris Rule is best-known as a writer, philologist and, but he started out as a portrait painter. He took several lessons from an itinerant artist and painted portraits in Devonport, Plymouth and Exeter. He appears to have stopped painting after moving to London in 1822.

RULEFINK, Daniel
German, 17th century.
Active in Halle in 1604.
Painter.
Daniel Rulefink painted scenes from the *Passion* on the retable in the church of Löbejün.

RULI, Martín
Spanish, 17th century.
Active in Palma (Majorca).
Painter.
Martín Ruli was in Rome in 1680.

RULL, Antonio
Spanish, 15th century.
Active in Saragossa from 1431 to 1437.
Painter.

RULL, Bernardo
Spanish, 15th century.
Active in Valencia from 1431 to 1436.
Painter.

RÜLL, Johan Baptist de. See **RUEL**

RULL, Juan
Spanish, 15th century.
Active in Valencia from 1408-1436.
Painter.
Valencian School.

RULLENS, Jules
Belgian, 19th - 20th century.
Born 14 May 1850, in Ghent.
Painter. Interiors with figures, flowers, animals.
Jules Rullens studied from 1876 at the fine arts academy in Brussels. He is noted for his paintings of grazing or stabled cattle and horses, together with studio interiors.

RÜLLER, Anton
German, 19th - 20th century.
Born 26 May 1864, in Ascheberg.
Sculptor. Religious subjects. Statues, monuments.
Anton Rüller lived and worked in Münster. He studied under H. Bäumer and went on to sculpt monuments and religious statuary in Münster and Ascheberg.

RULLIER (Mme)
Maiden name: Durand
French, 19th century.
Painter. Portraits.
Mme Rullier exhibited portraits at the Paris Salon from 1812 to 1847.
MUSEUMS AND GALLERIES:
PARIS (Mus. National de Céramique Sèvres): *Portrait of Mme Marie Adélaïde Ducluzeau, the Artist's Sister.*

RULLIER, Jean-Jacques
French, 20th - 21st century.
Born 1962, in Bourg-St-Maurice (Savoy).

Draughtsman, installation artist.
Neo-Conceptual Art.

Jean-Jacques Rullier lives and works in Lyons. Since 1987, his approach has involved arranging and cataloguing various everyday objects and images, such as tools, utensils, posters, glasses, plates and platters. The titles of his compositions, such as *Every Object Beginning with 'C'*, *25 x 4 Businesses*, and *One Hundred Potatoes in One Hundred Plates* reflect his compulsion to document, analyse and interpret his immediate environment and to explore its artistic and poetic values.

He has taken part in various group exhibitions, among them: in 1987, at the Villa Peyzieu in Paris; in 1989, at the Exhibition Centre in Genas; in 1990, at the Bullukian Foundation in Champagne au Mont-d'Or; in 1991, at the Salon Découvertes at the Grand Palais in Paris, representing the Froment Putman Gallery; in 1992, also at Salon Découvertes held at the Grand Palais, this time representing the Jennifer Flay Gallery; in 1992, at *Oh! Cet Echo*, held at the Swiss Cultural Centre in Paris; in 1997, at *Transit - 60 Artistes Nés Après 60 - Œuvres du Fonds National d'Art Contemporain* (*Transit - 60 Artists Born After 60 - Works from the National Collection of Contemporary Art*), a FRAC (Regional Fund for Contemporary Art) exhibition held at the École des Beaux-Arts in Paris; and, in 2000, at *Présumés Innocents: l'Art Contemporain et l'Enfance* (*Presumed Innocent: Contemporary Art and Childhood*), held at the CAPC Musée d'Art Contemporain in Bordeaux.

Solo exhibitions by Rullier include those of 1988, at the Octobre des Arts exhibition in Lyons; 1992, at the Centre d'Arts Plastiques in St-Fons; 1992, at the Robert Walser Museum in Gais, Switzerland; 1993, at *Aide Jean à Trouver le Chemin de sa Maison* (*Help Johnny Find His Way Home*), at the Musée d'Art Moderne de la Ville de Paris; 1993, at the Jennifer Flay Gallery; 1993, at the Bograshov Gallery in Tel Aviv; and, in 1997, at the Centre Pompidou in Paris.

Bibliography:
Huitorel, Jean-Marc, "*Jean-Jacques Rullier. Réinvestir les interstices du monde*' in *Aide Jean à trouver le chemin de sa maison*, exhibition catalogue, ARC Musée d'Art Moderne de la Ville de Paris, Paris, 1993. Bernadac, Marie-Laure/Moisdon-Tremblay, et al., *Présumés innocents: l'art contemporain et l'enfance*, exhibition catalogue, Capc Musée d'Art contemporain, Bordeaux, 2000.

Museums and Galleries:
Carquefou (FRAC Pays de la Loire): *Promenades; Dreams* (1992-1994, numerous coloured drawings) - Marseilles (FRAC Provence-Alpes-Côte d'Azur): *One Hundred and Fifty Cutting Objects* (1989) - Montpellier (FRAC Languedoc-Roussillon): *Air Travel, Walking (Tel Aviv), Walking the Ramparts (Jerusalem), Walking the Frontier, Walking in the Desert* (1993, drawing) - Paris (FNAC): *Bad Dreams* (1993-1994, set of ten Indian ink drawings).

RULLIS, François, or Rulys
French, 16th - 17th century.
Died c. 1643.
Active in Grenoble.
Painter.

RULLMANN, Ludwig
German, 18th - 19th century.
Born 1765, in Bremen; died 1822, in Paris.
Active in Bremen and Paris.
Painter, engraver (etching), lithographer. History painting, portraits.

Ludwig Rullmann studied at the academy in Dresden and was a pupil of David in Paris. He exhibited at the Paris Salon from 1808 to 1822. He was a talented portrait artist.

Museums and Galleries:
Bremen (Kunsthalle): *Resurrection of Christ.*

Auction records:
Paris, 22 March 1991, *Young Man Being Presented to a Young Girl* (watercolour and gouache, 14 1/4 x 17 1/2 ins / 36.5 x 44.5 cm) FRF 8,000. Paris, 22 Nov 2000, *Morning. Afternoon. Evening. Night* (gouache, set of four, 7 x 10 ins / 19 x 25 cm) FRF 17,000. Paris, 8 March 2001, *Abraham, Sara and Hagar* (gouache, 8 x 11 ins / 20 x 28 cm) FRF 13,000.

RULLO
Hungarian, 16th century.
Active in Transylvania in 1548.
Painter.

RULOT, Joseph Louis
Belgian, 19th - 20th century.
Born 29 January 1853, in Liège; died 16 February 1919, in Herstal.
Sculptor, medallist, draughtsman, designer of ornamental architectural features. Religious subjects, historical subjects, allegorical subjects, portraits. Statues, monuments, funerary monuments.

Joseph Louis Rulot studied at the royal academy of fine arts in Liège and subsequently taught there. He authored *Sentiment wallon en sculpture* (*The Walloon Spirit in Sculpture*). Rulot exhibited at the fine arts circle in Liège from 1894 to 1899, showing predominantly statues, portrait busts and decorative works. He also sculpted memorials and funerary monuments.

Museums and Galleries:
Liège (Drawings and Prints Collection) - Liège (Mus. de l'Art wallon) - Paris (Mus. d'Orsay): *Adoration of the Magi.*

RULQUIN, Claude
Flemish School, 17th century.
Born c. 1632; died 12 November 1704.
Active in Liège.
Sculptor.

Rulquin sculpted tombs and religious statues, but no work by this artist has survived.

RULYS, François. See **RULLIS**

RUMANI, Girolamo. See **ROMANINO**

RÜMANN, Wilhelm, or Ruemann
German, 20th century.
Born 30 June 1884, in Schwarzach, near Bregenz.
Painter.

Wilhelm Rümann was the son of Wilhelm von Rümann. He studied under Jean-Paul Laurens in Paris and went on to live and work in Munich.

RÜMANN, Wilhelm von, or Ruemann
German, 19th - 20th century.
Born 11 November 1850, in Hanover; died 6 February 1906, in Ajaccio (Corsica).
Sculptor. Portraits. Monuments, statues, busts.

Wilhelm von Rümann studied at the fine arts academy in Munich and visited England, Italy and France. He went on to teach at the academy in Munich and to sculpt monuments and statues in numerous towns and cities throughout Germany.

Museums and Galleries:
Berlin (Nationalgal.): *Young Woman, Seated* - Hanover (Kestner-Mus.): *Head* (marble) - Hanover (Niedersächsisches Landesmus.): *Rümann Family Tomb* - Munich (Deutsches Mus.): *Stele of Robert Maye, Bust of Bauer.*

RUMBLER, Heinrich or Johann Heinrich
German, 19th century.
Born 28 December 1831, in Frankfurt-Sachsenhausen; died 17 July 1875, in Frankfurt-Sachsenhausen.
Painter, engraver (etching). Genre scenes, landscapes, architectural views.

Heinrich Rumbler was a pupil of Hessemer, Jakob Becker, Steinle and Eissenhardt.

RUMBLER, Paul. See **RUMLER**

RUMBOLD, Karl
Austrian, 19th century.
Active in the first half of the 19th century.
Landscape artist.
Karl Rumbold worked in Klagenfurt in 1827 and in Villach in 1834.

RUMEAU, Jean Claude
French, 18th - 19th century.
Born 18th century, in Paris.
Miniaturist, watercolourist, painter (gouache), painter (porcelain), lithographer. History painting, genre scenes, interiors with figures.
Rumeau was the pupil of David and Isabey. He exhibited at the Paris Salon from 1806 to 1822.
MUSEUMS AND GALLERIES:
MONTPELLIER: *Church Interior.*
AUCTION RECORDS:
MONACO, 20 Feb 1988, *Vert-vert* (1821, watercolour, 4 1/4 x 5 1/2 ins / 11 x 14 cm) FRF 5,550. PARIS, 19 Dec 1994, *Interior of a Cloister: Nuns Going to Night Prayers; Interior of a Charitable Home* (gouache, a pair, each 20 x 23 1/4 ins / 51 x 59 cm) FRF 65,000.

RUMEAU, Jean Maurice
French, 20th century.
Born 1 December 1915, in Pussay.
Painter, sculptor.
Jean Maurice Rumeau was a pupil at the École des Arts Décoratifs, Paris. After exhibiting circus drawings in 1933, he spent two years in Italy, Greece, Egypt and North Africa, getting to know at source the art of the past. He returned to France and pursued his career in the academies of Montparnasse. While abroad he met Marquet, who had a decisive influence on his artistic development. The war and captivity interrupted his work, but he returned again to Paris, where he supported himself by painting commissioned portraits. In 1943 he exhibited in Paris at the Salon des Indépendants, and held several solo shows, including that of 1933 and one of still-lifes and figures in Paris in 1947.

RUMEBERG, Walter Magnus.
See **RUNEBERG**

RUMEL, August I
Austrian, 18th century.
Active in the second half of the 18th century.
Painter. Architectural views.
August Rumel I was an assistant to Maulbertsch in the execution of frescoes in Pápa and Steinamanger.

RUMEL, August II
German, 19th century.
Born 30 November 1805, in Trier.
Active in Vienna.
Painter. History painting.

RUMEL, Johann Paul. See **RUMMEL Paul**

RÜMELIN, Wilhelm, or Nida-Rümelin
German, 20th century.
Born 27 November 1876, in Linz.
Sculptor, painter, architect.
Wilhelm Rümelin studied under Wilhelm von Rümann and worked as an assistant to E. Pleifer. He lived and worked in Nuremberg and supplied decorative paintings and sculpture for several towns in Germany.

RUMELLIN, Louis or Ludwig. See **RIMELLIN**

RUMENT, Jakob. See **ROMENT**

RUMILLY, Victorine Angélique Amélie
French, 19th century.
Born 1789, in Grenoble; died 1849, in Paris.
Painter. History painting, portraits, genre scenes.
Victorine Rumilly was a student of Regnault. She exhibited at the Paris Salon from 1812 to 1839, mainly with portraits.
MUSEUMS AND GALLERIES:
GRENOBLE (Mus. de Grenoble): *Queen Brunnhilde, Fugitive; Historical Scene.*

RUMLER, Jürgen I, or Rundeler
German, 17th century.
Died 1646.
Active in Tönning.
Sculptor (wood).
Jürgen Rumler I was the father of Jürgen Rumler II.

RUMLER, Jürgen II, or Rundeler
German, 17th century.
Active in Tönning.
Sculptor (wood).
Jürgen Rumler II was the son of Jürgen Rumler I. He sculpted a pulpit for the church of Tetenbüll in 1655.

RUMLER, Paul or Poul, Powell, or Romler, Rumbler
Danish, 17th century.
Probably of German origin; died shortly before 25 January 1641, in Copenhagen.
Painter.
Rumler executed mostly decorative paintings and frescoes in the castles of Copenhagen and Frederiksborg.

RUMLER-SIUCHNINSKI, Friedrich
German, 20th century.
Born 15 March 1884, in Pilsen (now Plzen, Czech Republic).
Painter, engraver, designer. Portraits, landscapes.
Friedrich Rumler-Siuchninski studied at the fine arts academy in Paris and under Lovis Corinth at the academy in Berlin. He lived and worked in Berlin.

RUMLEY, Elisabeth (Mrs). See **DAWSON B.**

RUMM, August
German, 20th century.
Born 10 March 1888, in Schwanheim.
Painter, lithographer. Figures, portraits, landscapes.
August Rumm was a student of W. Trübner. He lived and worked in Durlach, painting historical portraits and religious subjects.

RUMMEL, Adolf
German, 19th - 20th century.
Born 15 November 1872, in Hersbruck.
Painter, caricaturist.
Adolf Rummel lived and worked in Munich, where he was an illustrator on the periodical *Jugend* (*Youth*).

RUMMEL, Johann Georg
German, 18th century.
Born 1713, in Au (Bavaria); died 7 September 1796, in Augsburg.
Draughtsman, designer of ornamental architectural features, ironworker.
Johann Georg Rummel drew designs for decorative grilles.

RUMMEL, Paul or Johann Paul
German, 18th - 19th century.
Born 5 June 1774, in Munich; died 28 September 1832, in Munich.
Painter, lithographer. Portraits.
Paul Rummel was a pupil of Bartholomaus Ignaz Weiss.

MUSEUMS AND GALLERIES:
MUNICH (Stadtmus.): *Portrait of Johann Nepomuk Mayrhofer*; three lithographs.

RUMMEL, Peter
German, 19th century.
Born 12 July 1850, in Regensburg.
Sculptor.
Peter Rummel studied at the academy in Munich and was a pupil and assistant of Zumbusch. He settled in Vienna.

RUMMELHOFF, John
American, 20th century.
Born 1942, in Minnesota.
Painter.
John Rummelhoff has been exhibiting since 1964. In the way he enlarges the details of everyday objects and the important role played by reflections and chrome, Rummelhoff's painting is very close to Hyperrealism.
AUCTION RECORDS:
NEW YORK, 13 May 1988, *Evel Knievel* (acrylic/canvas, 60 x 60 ins / 152.5 x 152.5 cm) USD 2,420.

RUMMELSPACHER, Joseph
German, 19th - 20th century.
Born 23 November 1852, in Berlin; died 10 December 1921, in Berlin.
Painter. Landscapes.
Joseph Rummelspacher was a student of Theodore Hagen.
MUSEUMS AND GALLERIES:
BERLIN (Nationalgal.): two watercolours - ROSTOCK (Kunsthalle): *Mountains in Norway*.
AUCTION RECORDS:
LONDON, 19 May 1976, *Landscape with Figures* (1876, oil on canvas, 28 x 42 1/4 ins / 71 x 107 cm) GBP 300. COLOGNE, 23 Oct 1981, *Village View* (oil on canvas, 32 3/4 x 50 1/2 ins / 83 x 128 cm) DEM 5,000. AMSTERDAM, 19 Sept 1989, *Alpine Chalet* (oil on canvas, 26 1/2 x 38 1/2 ins / 67 x 98 cm) NLG 3,220. COLOGNE, 29 June 1990, *Moonlight* (1882, oil on panel, 8 1/2 x 6 1/4 ins / 21.5 x 16 cm) DEM 2,400.

RUMMEN, Jan van, or Ruremonde
Flemish School, 15th century.
Painter.
Jan van Rummen painted a picture and a retable for the church of Leau in 1486.

RUMMLER, Alexander Joseph
American, 19th - 20th century.
Born 25 July 1867, in Dubuque (Iowa); died 1959.
Painter, illustrator.
Alex J. Rummler studied in Paris under Jean-Paul Laurens. He was a member of the Salmagundi Club from 1900 and of the American Federation of Arts.

RUMOHR, Carl Friedrich Ludwig Felix von
German, 19th century.
Born 6 January 1785, in Reinhardsgrimma, near Dresden; died 25 July 1843, in Dresden.
Draughtsman, engraver. Historical subjects, landscapes, animals.
Carl Friedrich Ludwig Felix von Rumohr began his studies in Reinhardsgrimma. In 1804 he visited Rome and Naples. After returning from Italy, he lived successively in Hamburg, Munich and Berlin. In 1827 he became a member of the academy in Berlin.

He mainly drew landscapes, animals and historical scenes and was an art collector.
AUCTION RECORDS:
MUNICH, 28 Nov 1979, *Woodland River Landscape* (1812, pen, 7 3/4 x 10 ins / 20 x 25.5 cm) DEM 7,000. MUNICH, 10 Dec 1992, *Italian Mountain Landscape* (black ink/paper, 10 x 13 3/4 ins / 25.5 x 34.8 cm) DEM 5,650. MUNICH, 22 June 1993, *Mountain Landscape* (ink/paper, 11 x 13 3/4 ins / 27 x 35 cm) DEM 8,050. HAMBURG, 10 June 1999, *Italian Landscape* (1820, pen and brown ink, 9 x 13 ins / 24 x 34 cm) DEM 20,000.

RUMORH, Knut
Norwegian, 20th century.
Born 1916, in Bergen.
Painter, engraver (wood). Designs for tapestries, wall decorations.
Knut Rumorh studied at the Oslo college of design in 1936, and from 1938 to 1941 under Heiberg and Jacobsen at the fine arts academy in Oslo. His woodcut engravings from around 1943 are influenced to some degree by the work of Edvard Munch. It was not until after 1950 that Rumorh started to paint, taking his inspiration initially from Norwegian popular art and literature and developing those themes to the point of abstraction. He is particularly noted for his decorative murals for the Hotel Viking in Oslo. He took part in group exhibitions, notably at the 1962 Venice Biennale.
MUSEUMS AND GALLERIES:
BERGEN - GÖTEBORG - OSLO - STOCKHOLM.

RUMP, Gotfred or Christian Gottfried
Danish, 19th century.
Born 8 December 1816, in Hillerød; died 25 May 1880, in Frederiksborg.
Painter. History painting, portraits, landscapes.
Rump was a pupil of Dund in Copenhagen. He was initially a history painter, executing a *Presentation at the Temple* for the church of Grouholt. From 1846 onwards, he turned to landscapes. In 1855-1856, he travelled in Norway, and he visited Germany and Italy in 1857-1858. In 1866, he became a member of the Kunstakademi, and then a professor in 1874. Rump's paintings can be seen in museums in Aarhus, Apenrade, Kolding, Maribo and Randers.
BIBLIOGRAPHY:
Bramsen, H., *Landskabsmaleriet i Danmark 1750-1850*, Copenhagen, 1935.
MUSEUMS AND GALLERIES:
COPENHAGEN: *Frederiksborg; Early Morning in the Forest; River in the Forest; Swedish Landscape; Part of the Frederiksborg Forest; Spring Landscape; Frozen Stream in a Garden; The Outskirts of Vesterskov; View of Ariccia* - STOCKHOLM (Nationalmus.): *Landscape with Rainbow*.
AUCTION RECORDS:
COPENHAGEN, 18 March 1980, *Swedish Landscape* (1854, oil on canvas, 38 1/4 x 56 3/4 ins / 97 x 144 cm) DKK 10,000. COPENHAGEN, 3-5 Dec 1997, *Winter Day* (oil on canvas, 26 x 20 3/4 ins / 66 x 53 cm) DKK 26,000. COPENHAGEN, 26 May 2000, *Lake Landscape, Skovdammen near Skodsborg* (1876, oil on canvas, 39 x 57 ins / 98 x 144 cm) DKK 26,000. COPENHAGEN, 4 Dec 2000, *The Artist's Three Sisters* (oil on canvas, three) DKK 50,000. COPENHAGEN, 27 Aug 2002, *Farmers by a Marl Pit* (1837, oil on canvas, 25 x 31 ins / 63 x 78 cm) DKK 70,000.

RUMP, Magdalena Sophia
German, 18th century.
Active in the first half of the 18th century.
Painter.
Magdalena Sophia Rump painted a *Crucifixion* and an *Entombment* in the church at Trebbus.

RUMPEL, Karl Ernst Friedrich
German, 19th - 20th century.
Born 21 June 1867, in Potsdam.
Painter, illustrator.
Karl Ernst Friedrich Rumpel studied under Heyser, Max Koch and Max Thedy. He painted frescoes and historically-themed decorations for public buildings in Pomerania.
MUSEUMS AND GALLERIES:
KOLOBRZEG (Municipal Mus.): *Ancient Kitchen*.

RUMPELMAYER, Martin
Austrian, 19th century.
Active in Presburg c. 1800.
Sculptor.
Martin Rumpelmayer sculpted the high altar of the cathedral at Steinamanger and worked for the churches in Pápa and Nagylégh.

RUMPELT, Hedwig
German, 19th - 20th century.
Born 31 May 1861, in Breslau (now Wroclaw, Poland).
Painter. Architectural views, urban landscapes.
Hedwig Rumpelt studied in Munich under Dill, Firle, Marr and Fehr. Her work includes numerous views of old Dresden.
MUSEUMS AND GALLERIES:
DRESDEN (Stadtmus.): *Three Views of Old Dresden.*

RUMPF
German, 19th century.
Active in Berlin in 1834.
Painter. Portraits.

RUMPF, Emil
German, 19th - 20th century.
Born 28 February 1860, in Frankfurt am Main; died 1948, in Kronberg.
Painter, illustrator. Genre scenes.
Emil Rumpf was the son of Philipp Rumpf. He studied at the Düsseldorf and Karlsruhe academies.
MUSEUMS AND GALLERIES:
FRANKFURT AM MAIN (ML): *View of Frankfurt am Main* (c. 1825).
AUCTION RECORDS:
HEIDELBERG, 12 Oct 1991, *Coach Halt* (oil on canvas, 20 1/4 x 31 1/2 ins / 51.5 x 80 cm) DEM 6,500. LONDON, 19 Nov 1993, *Arrival* (oil on canvas, 45 x 70 ins / 114 x 178 cm) GBP 8,970.

RUMPF, Friedrich Carl Georg
German, 20th century.
Born 5 January 1888, in Charlottenburg.
Illustrator, engraver, art writer.
Friedrich Carl Georg Rumpf was the son of Fritz Rumpf. He studied in Berlin and Tokyo (under Igami Bonkotsu) and went on to live and work in Potsdam.

RUMPF, Fritz or Friedrich Heinrich
German, 19th - 20th century.
Born 12 February 1856, in Frankfurt; died 23 July 1927, in Potsdam.
Painter, engraver, writer. Genre scenes, landscapes, architectural views.
Fritz Rumnf was the father of Friedrich Carl Georg Rumpf. An etcher, he studied at the Städel Institute in Frankfurt and the academy in Kassel.
MUSEUMS AND GALLERIES:
FRANKFURT AM MAIN (Historisches Mus.): *Portrait of the Artist's Father.*

RUMPF, Georg Eberhard, or Rumph or Rumphius
German, 17th century.
Born 1627, in Hanau; died 15 June 1702, on Ambon Island.
Draughtsman. Natural history (botanical subjects).
Rumpf was a naturalist, and a long-standing employee of the Dutch Indies Company between 1654 and 1702. He was the celebrated author of *Herbarium Amboinense* (six volumes, 1741-1745, Amsterdam), the first illustrated publication on the botany of the Indonesian islands.

RUMPF, Karl or Anton Karl
German, 19th - 20th century.
Born 24 March 1838, in Frankfurt am Main; died 5 May 1911, in Frankfurt am Main.
Sculptor. Allegorical subjects, figures.
Karl Rumpf was the father of Maria Rumpf. He studied in Frankfurt, Nuremberg and Munich and went on to sculpt statues and allegorical pieces.
MUSEUMS AND GALLERIES:
FRANKFURT AM MAIN (Goethe Mus.): *Goethe as a Young Man; Goethe's Parents; Marianne von Willemer.*

RUMPF, Maria
German, 20th century.
Born 21 January 1884, in Frankfurt am Main; died 10 January 1931, in Frankfurt am Main.
Painter.
Maria Rumpf was the daughter of Karl Rumpf.

RUMPF, Paul August, or Rumphius
German, 17th century.
Active in the second half of the 17th century.
Draughtsman, painter.
Paul August Rumpf is noted for his portrait of his father.
MUSEUMS AND GALLERIES:
FRANKFURT AM MAIN (Historisches Mus.): *Entrance to a Town by a Bridge.*

RUMPF, Philipp or Peter Philipp
German, 19th century.
Born 19 December 1821, in Frankfurt; died 16 January 1896, in Frankfurt.
Painter, engraver (etching). Portraits, genre scenes, landscapes.
Philipp Rumpf was a pupil of Jakob Becker and Dielmann. He travelled through Germany, Italy and France and settled in Frankfurt.
MUSEUMS AND GALLERIES:
FRANKFURT AM MAIN: *Child's Portrait; Nied, close to Rödelheim; Young Girl Reading; Mother and Child* - KALININGRAD: *Lady with Child.*
AUCTION RECORDS:
FRANKFURT AM MAIN, 8 April 1978, *Picnic* (oil on canvas, 7 3/4 x 9 ins / 20 x 23 cm) DEM 7,500. MUNICH, 26 Nov 1981, *Interior Scenes* (watercolour, a pair, 4 1/4 x 3 1/2 ins / 10.5 x 9 cm and 5 x 4 1/2 ins/12.5 x 11.5 cm) DEM 5,200. LONDON, 23 June 1983, *Little Girl Offering Flowers to a Baby* (1862, watercolour and pencil, 5 3/4 x 6 ins / 14.7 x 15.2 cm) GBP 800. BERN, 26 Oct 1988, *Young Woman Preparing to Put her Child to Bed* (1864, oil on card, 9 1/2 x 7 1/2 ins / 24 x 19 cm) CHF 5,500. COLOGNE, 15 May 1999, *Girl Playing with Doll* (oil on canvas, 20 x 16 ins / 50 x 40 cm) DEM 25,000. ZURICH, 7 Dec 1999, *Girl with Handicraft on Steps in Front of House* (watercolour, 22 x 17 ins / 55 x 42 cm) CHF 4,700. MUNICH, 5 July 2000, *Love Letter* (1869, oil on panel, 10 x 7 ins / 25 x 18 cm) DEM 23,000. MUNICH, 5 July 2000, *Young Mother Sewing by Window* (1853, oil on panel, 14 x 12 ins / 35 x 30 cm) DEM 60,000. COLOGNE, 28 June 2001, *Elegant Woman in Park Landscape* (watercolour, 22 x 16 ins / 57 x 41 cm) DEM 6,400. AMSTERDAM, 7 Sept 2004, *Mother Watching Over her Sleeping Child* (1856, oil on copper, 7 x 6 ins / 19 x 15 cm) EUR 3,000. AMSTERDAM, 7 Sept 2004, *Mother and Child* (1856, oil on panel, 9 x 8 ins / 22 x 20 cm) EUR 11,000.

RUMPFER, Jeremias
Austrian, 17th century.
Died in Brixen, South Tyrol (now Bressanone, Italy).
Active 1614-1640.
Painter, gilder. Religious subjects, figures.
Jeremias Rumpfer worked for Brixen Cathedral and other churches in the southern Tyrol.

RUMPHIUS, Paul August. See **RUMPF**

RUMPLER, Franz
Austrian, 19th - 20th century.
Born 4 December 1848, in Tachau; died 7 March 1922, in Klosterneuburg.

Painter. Figures, portraits, genre scenes, landscapes, urban landscapes.
Franz Rumpler studied under Edward von Engerth at the Akademie der Bildenden Künste in Vienna. He then travelled extensively before settling in Vienna.

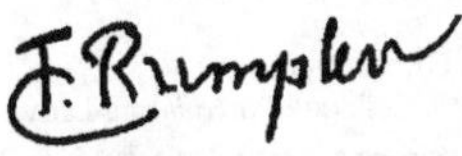

MUSEUMS AND GALLERIES:
VIENNA (MM): *Historical Cortège* (1879) - VIENNA (NM): *Little Patient; Portrait of the Artist's Mother; Sunday at Lundenburg; Drinking Trough*; 14 other paintings.
AUCTION RECORDS:
PARIS, 8-10 Nov 1926, *Young Woman*, FRF 1,250. MUNICH, 11 Dec 1968, *View of Vienna*, DEM 5,200. VIENNA, 19 May 1981, *Young Girl Sitting in a Park* (mixed media, 11 x 10¼ ins / 28 x 26 cm) ATS 25,000. VIENNA, 22 June 1983, *Young Girl (Three-Quarters View)* (oil on panel, 8 x 6¼ ins / 20.5 x 16 cm) ATS 50,000. VIENNA, 12 Sept 1984, *Flowers* (watercolour, 9¼ x 6 ins / 23.5 x 15 cm) ATS 15,000. NEW YORK, 13 Dec 1985, *Young Woman with White Roses* (1879, oil on panel, 20½ x 14½ ins / 52 x 37 cm) USD 3,000.

RUMPLER, Georg
German, 17th century.
Died 27 December 1621.
Active in Forchheim.
Painter.
In 1621 Georg Rumpler painted the ceiling of the church at Leutenbach.

RUMPLER, Johann I
Austrian, 19th century.
Died 1876, in Tachau.
Sculptor (wood).
Johann Rumpler I was the father of Franz Rumpler and Johann Rumpler II. He sculpted a *Christ on the Cross* and a *Calvary* in the chapel at Hohenstein, near Tachau.

RUMPLER, Johann II
Austrian, 19th century.
Born 1846, in Tachau.
Sculptor (wood).
Johann Rumpler II was the son of Johann Rumpler I. He sculpted statues in the churches at Purtschau and Damnau.

RÜMPLER, Wilhelm or Johann Wilhelm
German, 19th century.
Born 26 June 1824, in Frankfurt am Main; died 13 March 1903, in Frankfurt am Main.
Painter.
Wilhelm Rümpler was a pupil of Jakob Becker.
MUSEUMS AND GALLERIES:
FRANKFURT AM MAIN (Städel): *Portrait of the Painter Carl Morgenstern*.

RUMPLER VON LEOWENHALT, Jesaias
German, 17th century.
Active in Strasbourg.
Draughtsman, poet.
Jesaias Rumpler von Leowenhalt did book illustrations.

RUMSEY, Charles Cary
American, 20th century.
Born 1879, in Buffalo (New York State); died 21 September 1922, near Glen Head.
Sculptor.
Charles Cary Rumsey studied at Harvard University and in Paris with Paul Wayland Bartlett.
MUSEUMS AND GALLERIES:
BROOKLYN, NY: *Dying Indian*.
AUCTION RECORDS:
NEW YORK, 29 Sept 1977, *Tigers Walking* (two bronzes, green and brown patina, l. 15 ins / 38.1 cm) USD 850. NEW YORK, 28 Sept 1989, *Miss Eleonora Sears* (bronze equestrian group, h. 20 ins / 50.8 cm) USD 5,280. CLEVELAND, 19 March 2001, *Panther* (bronze, 6 x 15 ins / 15 x 38 cm) USD 2,000.

RUMSTET, Christian. See **ROMSTEDT**

RUMYANTSEVA, Galina
Russian, 20th century.
Born 1927.
Painter. Figures, landscapes with figures, still-lifes.
Rumyantseva studied at the academy of arts in Leningrad (now St Petersburg) and was a pupil of Boris Ioganson at the I.E. Repin institute. She became a member of the association of painters of Leningrad.
AUCTION RECORDS:
PARIS, 15 May 1991, *In the Park* (oil on cardboard, 15¾ x 12½ ins / 40 x 32 cm) FRF 4,800. PARIS, 27 Jan 1992, *Christmas Night* (oil on canvas, 27½ x 35½ ins / 70 x 90 cm) FRF 14,500. PARIS, 3 June 1992, *By the Water's Edge* (oil on canvas, 28½ x 36 ins / 72.5 x 91.5 cm) FRF 4,000. PARIS, 16 Nov 1992, *Nude from the Back* (1958, oil on canvas, 32¼ x 38¼ ins / 82 x 97 cm) FRF 6,100. VIENNA, 16 Nov 1999, *Hour of Leisure* (1973, oil on canvas, 35 x 43 ins / 89 x 109 cm) ATS 45,000.

RUMYANTSEVA, Kapitolina
Russian, 20th century.
Born 1925, in Leningrad (now St Petersburg).
Painter. Scenes with figures, still-lifes.
Rumyantseva studied under the direction of Aleksandr Osmerkin at the I.E. Repin institute in Leningrad (now St Petersburg). She was a member of the Society of Painters of the USSR. She has specialised in the representation of children in flowered gardens, in an Impressionist style. Her works reveal a certain serenity, that of an enclosed world shunning external realities.
MUSEUMS AND GALLERIES:
ST PETERSBURG (Academy) - ST PETERSBURG (Gosudarstvennyj Muz. Istorii) - ST PETERSBURG (Mus. of Performing Arts).
AUCTION RECORDS:
PARIS, 24 Sept 1991, *First Fish* (oil on cardboard, 24 x 32 ins / 61 x 81 cm) FRF 6,000. PARIS, 27 Jan 1992, *Near the House* (oil on canvas, 39¼ x 39¼ ins / 99.5 x 99.7 cm) FRF 10,000. PARIS, 3 June 1992, *Still-life* (oil on canvas, 23¾ x 31½ ins / 60.3 x 80 cm) FRF 4,000. PARIS, 25 Jan 1993, *At the Dacha* (oil on canvas, 26½ x 34½ ins / 67.5 x 87.5 cm) FRF 6,200. PARIS, 13 Dec 1993, *Calendulas* (oil on canvas, 19¾ x 27¼ ins / 50 x 69.5 cm) FRF 4,500. PARIS, 31 Jan 1994, *Summer* (oil on canvas, 31½ x 31¾ ins / 80 x 80.5 cm) FRF 5,000. PARIS, 30 Jan 1995, *Still-life with Watermelon* (oil on canvas, 23½ x 27½ ins / 60 x 70 cm) FRF 4,500.

RUNACHER, Suzanne
French, 20th century.
Born 16 May 1912, in Tientsin, China.
Engraver, painter, draughtswoman.
Suzanne Runacher trained at the École des Beaux-Arts, Paris. In the late 1950s she made a journey round the world and returned with a collection of drawings taken from life. Wishing to engrave them, she made a study of the language of engraving under Friedlander. Her early work was totally figurative, but her engravings became gradually freer, at first combining figurative elements with fleeting abstract visions. Using aquatint, she introduced colour, and then relief by cutting and incising the plates. Eventually, though her work took as its staring point some reality, vision, thought or impression, it became only distantly related to figuration. She exhibited in Paris at the Salon des Artistes Français, where she was awarded a medal in 1938, and she took part

in international biennales and the Paris salons. She also exhibited in Germany and South Africa.

Museums and Galleries:

Berkeley (AM, University of California) - Corvallis, OR, OR (Mus. of Oregon University) - Paris (MNAM-CCI) - Zurich (ETH Graphics Collection).

RUNCIMAN, Alexander

British, 18th century.
Born 15 August 1736, in Edinburgh; died 21 October 1785, in Edinburgh.
Painter, engraver (etching). History painting.

Alexander Runciman is believed to have started out as a coachwork decorator or, possibly, to have been apprenticed to a commercial painter from 1750 to around 1757. He harboured artistic aspirations, however, and eventually went to study in Italy for a five-year period between 1767 and 1771. On his return, he is thought to have stayed for a time in London and perhaps to have been retained by William Hogarth's widow, at whose house he found lodgings. What is certain is that he worked on decorations in Penicuick Castle some time between 1771 and 1772 and was in Edinburgh in 1773. He is also listed as an exhibitor in London from 1772 to 1782, at times at the Royal Academy, at others at the Free Society. Runciman was one of the leading lights at the Academy of Arts. His body of work includes an altarpiece for the Cowgate Episcopal Chapel. His decorations in Penicuick Castle (home of his benefactor James Clark) were inspired by themes from the legendary Gaelic poet Ossian (Oisín) - or Macpherson's version thereof - and it appears that he was among the first in a line of artists who were similarly inspired, including Cotman, Isabey and Ingres.

Runciman's work was overtly classical, but he added a dramatic touch to his canvases by outlining his figures with a dark wash. He was also an etcher, producing several etchings from his own originals.

Museums and Galleries:

Edinburgh (Nat. Gal. of Scotland): *Italian River Landscape with a Hermit* (oil/panel); *Hubert and Arthur* (inspired by Shakespeare's 'King John') - Edinburgh (Scottish National Portrait Gallery): *John Brown and Alexander Runciman reading from Shakespeare's 'Tempest'* (1784, oil on canvas, on loan from the National Museums of Scotland).

Auction records:

London, 10 Dec 1971, *The Poet Ferguson*, Gns 380.

RUNCIMAN, Charles

British, 19th century.
Active in London at the beginning of the 19th century.
Painter. History painting, portraits, genre scenes, architectural views.

Charles Runciman exhibited historical compositions from 1825 to 1867 at the Royal Academy, the British Institution and the Suffolk Street Gallery.

RUNCIMAN, John

British, 18th century.
Born 1744, in Edinburgh; died 1768, in Naples.
Painter, engraver (etching). Religious subjects, portraits.

John Runciman was the younger brother of Alexander Runciman, whom he accompanied to Rome around 1766. He showed early signs of talent but died when barely 24.

Museums and Galleries:

Edinburgh (Nat. Gal. of Scotland): *King Lear in the Storm* (oil on canvas); *Christ with his Disciples on the Road to Emmaus* (oil/copper); *The Flight into Egypt* (oil/panel); *The Temptation of Our Lord* (oil/panel); *Salome Receiving the Head of St John the Baptist* (oil/panel) - Edinburgh (Scottish National Portrait Gallery): *Self-portrait* (1767, oil on canvas, on loan from the National Museums of Scotland).

Auction records:

London, 19 May 1939, *Christ*, GBP 110.

RUNCIMAN, Kate

British, 19th century.
Active at the end of the 19th century.
Miniaturist. Portraits.

Museums and Galleries:

Oxford (Queen's College): *Portrait of a Lady*.

RUNDAL'TSOV, Mikhail Viktorovich, or Rundalizeff

Russian, 19th - 20th century.
Born 1871, in St Petersburg; died 1935.
Active in France from 1922.
Painter, engraver. Portraits, landscapes.

Rundal'tsov was a pupil of Maté and at the art school in Chtiglits.

RUNDELER, Jürgen I or II. See RUMLER

RUNDSTEDT, Eberhard von

German, 19th century.
Born c. 1802; died 22 September 1851, in Schönfeld, near Stendal.
Painter. Genre scenes, portraits, landscapes.

Eberhard von Rundstedt was an officer.

RUNDT, Carl Ludwig

German, 19th century.
Born 1802, in Königsberg (now Kaliningrad, Russia); died 1868, in Wiesbaden.
Active in Rome 1829-1858.
Painter, lithographer. Genre scenes, landscapes, architectural views.

Carl Ludwig Rundt was a pupil at the academy in Berlin.

Museums and Galleries:

Kaliningrad: *Hunter Resting in the Marais Pontins; View of the Church of St Peter and the Castle of the Holy Angel.*

Auction records:

Paris, 27 April 1950, *Terrace in an Italian Palace: The Painting Presented, Rome* (1831) FRF 17,000. London, 17 Feb 1999, *S Maria La Nuova at Naples* (oil on canvas, 25 x 34 ins / 63 x 87 cm) GBP 3,000. Amsterdam, 24 Oct 2000, *The Cloister Garden of Monreale near Palermo* (1864, oil on canvas, 38 x 54 ins / 97 x 136 cm) NLG 6,000. Ahlden, 24 Nov 2000, *Entry of the Lords into St Paul's Cathedral* (1850, oil on canvas, 35 x 28 ins / 90 x 71 cm) DEM 4,000. London, 19 Nov 2002, *Panorama of Rome* (1857, oil on canvas, 11 x 21 ins / 27 x 53 cm) GBP 18,000.

RUNDT, Hans Hinrich

German, 17th - 18th century.
Born c. 1660; died c. 1750, in Hamburg.
Active in Hamburg.
Painter. Religious subjects, portraits.

Hans Hinrich Rundt was a painter and architect. He was registered in 1684 as a pupil of Gérard de Lairesse in Amsterdam, studied in Amsterdam and settled in Hamburg in 1692. He worked for the court of Detmold and painted numerous family portraits of Count Friedrich Adolph and the Detmold family.

Museums and Galleries:

Hamburg (Kunsthalle) - Oldenburg (Landesmus. für Kunst und Kulturgeschichte) - Wolfenbüttel (Herzog August Bibliothek).

Auction records:

New York, 19 March 1981, *Christ in the Garden of Gethsemane* (1729, oil on canvas, 42 1/4 x 52 1/4 ins / 107.5 x 132.5 cm) USD 3,500. New York, 10 Oct 1991, *Christ in the Garden of*

Gethsemane (oil on canvas, 42 1/2 x 53 3/4 ins / 108 x 136.5 cm) USD 7,700.

RUNEBERG, Walter Magnus, or Rumeberg
Finnish, 19th - 20th century.
Born 29 December 1838, in Borga; died 23 December 1920, in Helsinki.
Sculptor.

Walter Magnus Runeberg was the son of the celebrated Finnish poet Johan Ludvig Runeberg. He lived and worked in Paris. One of his portrait busts housed in Stockholm Museum is signed *V.R. bg Paris, jan, 1881*.

MUSEUMS AND GALLERIES:
COPENHAGEN (Statens Mus. for Kunst): *Spirit of the Arts; Aged 16* - HELSINKI: *Achilles and the Centaur Chiron; Finland Defending its Birthright* (sketch); *Silenus and the Cherubs; J. L. Runeberg* (two versions); *R. W. Ekmann, Painter* (medallion); *Werner Hamberg; Apollo and Marsyas; Young Boy Dancing with a Basque Drum; Angel of Peace* (funerary low relief); *Bacchus and Venus; Aged 16; Silenus and the Satyrs; Moon Goblin; Sketch; Miss A. Bredberg; Psyche with Her Lamp; Nils Adolf Erik Nordenskjöld; Spirit of the Arts* - STOCKHOLM: *Anders Fryxell* (two versions); *Nils Adolf Erik Nordenskjöld.*

RUNGALDIER, Anton
Austrian, 19th century.
Born 1814, in Graz.
Watercolourist.

Anton Rungaldier was a pupil at the academy in Vienna.

RUNGALDIER, Ignaz
Austrian, 19th century.
Born 9 July 1799, in Graz; died 20 November 1876, in Graz.
Miniaturist, engraver (burin).

Ignaz Rungaldier began his career as an engraver, firstly as a pupil of Kauperz and later studying at the academy in Vienna from 1816. He reproduced paintings by the German masters in particular. He enjoyed great success as a painter of miniature portraits.

MUSEUMS AND GALLERIES:
GRAZ: *Portrait of Count Johann von Harrach and his Wife.*

RUNGALDIER, Peter
Austrian, 19th century.
Active in St Ulrich (in the Gröden Valley) in the first half of the 19th century.
Sculptor.

Peter Rungaldier sculpted a *Crucifix* at the church of St Ulrich and the altars of the churches of St Kassian and Schenna.

RUNGE, August
German, 19th century.
Active in Berlin in 1832.
Painter. Portraits, genre scenes.

August Runge was a pupil of Carl Kretschmar.

RUNGE, Julius Friedrich Ludwig
German, 19th - 20th century.
Born 28 June 1843, in Röbel; died 14 March 1922, in Lindau-im-Bodensee (Bavaria).
Painter. Seascapes.

Julius Friedrich Ludwig Runge studied at the fine arts academy in Munich and went on to live and work in Munich and Hamburg.

MUSEUMS AND GALLERIES:
ALTENBURG - PRAGUE (Národní Gal.) - ZURICH (Kunsthaus).

AUCTION RECORDS:
LINDAU, 11 May 1977, *Lake Constance* (oil on canvas, 16 3/4 x 27 ins / 42.5 x 68.5 cm) DEM 4,700. LINDAU, 9 May 1979, *Harbour Scene* (oil on canvas, 16 1/2 x 24 ins / 42 x 61 cm) DEM 3,800.

RUNGE, Otto Sigismund
German, 19th century.
Born 30 April 1806, in Hamburg; died 16 March 1839, in St Petersburg.
Sculptor.

Otto Sigismund Runge was the son of Philipp Otto Runge. He was a pupil of J. G. Matthäi in Dresden and of Thorvaldsen in Rome.

MUSEUMS AND GALLERIES:
HAMBURG (Kunsthalle): *A Little Girl Teaching a Small Boy to Fish.*

RUNGE, Philipp Otto or Otto Philipp
German, 19th century.
Born 23 July 1777, in Wolgast; died 2 December 1810, in Hamburg.
Painter, draughtsman, engraver (etching). History painting, portraits, genre scenes, flowers.

Philipp Otto Runge started out as a pupil of Abildgaard at the Kunstakademi in Copenhagen, after which he continued his studies in Dresden. He settled in Hamburg in 1804. There are three reasons why his work is so rare - his early death at the age of 33, his mystical sense of perfection inaccessible to man, which prevented him from completing his projects and, lastly, as with many German Romantics including Blechen, Carus and Friedrich himself, the fire in 1931 that destroyed a large part of the exhibition of Romantic paintings at the Glass Palace in Munich.

Having started out in commerce, Runge was only able to embark upon his artistic career thanks to the devotion of his brother Daniel, who supported him. His main influences were Carstens and Friedrich. His letters to his brother Daniel, as was later the case with Van Gogh's letters, have retained for us the essence of his philosophy of nature and his conception of painting. Like all of the other German Romantics, Runge was completely pantheistic. He was convinced of a deep unity between creatures and the universe. For him, all things in the world were, like man himself, endowed with sensitivity, spirit and soul. Like most of his contemporary artists, sunrises or sunsets or any other magnificent natural spectacle were, for Runge, an expression of God himself, in other words, of the universe as a whole. Everything was an integral part of that overriding notion: 'In the beginning was the word.'

Runge painted flowers with astonishing detail, women with a child-like naivety, and children with adoration. His drawing was precise with pure lines. His sense of composition and his familiarity with the hidden aspect of things, their magic, was something he shared with William Blake. However, these qualities would not perhaps have been sufficient to elevate him to the status of one of the founding fathers of German Romanticism (especially since his works are rare and generally unfinished) if their poetic content had not made a major contribution to the Romantic movement. Like the poet Novalis and the German philosophers from that defining era between the 18th and 19th centuries, Runge believed that everything in the universe was in harmony, and knowledge of this implied succeeding in 'quantifying things'. For his part, Runge applied himself to establishing and illustrating in his work the association between the seasons of the year, the times of the day and night, the seasons of man, the times of his thoughts and heavenly bodies, constellations, flowers, different sorts of shapes and colours. For him, everything gave rise to a symbolic interpretation, everything had to be numbered. Flowers, in particular, seemed to him to be the model of perfection and skill in colour and form.

As a painter, Runge was particularly concerned with this symbolism of colours and his work in this area has remained well-known in Germany: 'Light is the sun, which we cannot look at; but when it sinks towards earth and man, the sky turns red. Blue awakens a certain veneration in us, it is the Father; red is usually the intermediary between heaven and earth. When these two disappear, fire arrives in the night, which is yellow, the comforter that has been sent to us; the moon is also yellow.' As a painter and poet, Runge ascribed great importance to research on colour.

Western Rationalism of the 17th century had shattered the unity of the universe by separating thought from subject. Runge made great endeavours to rediscover this lost unity - the soul of things labelled inert, the materialisation of feelings and thoughts. The small number of portraits that he painted, in particular *We Three* (1805), *The Huelsenbeck Children* (Hamburg, dated 1805-1806), *Portrait of the Artist's Parents* (Hamburg, 1806), *Portrait of the Artist's Wife and Son* (Berlin), *Self-portrait in a Blue Coat* (Hamburg, dated 1805), and *Self-portrait in a Brown Coat* (dated 1810), bore testimony to this state of harmony between man and nature. But it was primarily in his principle work *Times of the Day* that he sought both to provide a complete spectacle, which was a specifically Romantic preoccupation, and to create an illustration of his conviction of the existence of associations between the times of the day, the passage of the seasons and heavenly bodies, the life of man, flowers, plants and colours. This was to be a series of monumental compositions, designed to be placed in a specially constructed building and viewed to the accompaniment of music and poetry. As with many others of his works, this project involving a collection of 'spiritual landscapes' did not progress beyond sketches. These sketches, dating to around 1803, are kept at the Kunsthalle in Hamburg.

Runge's work was shown in 2002 as part of the exhibition *Expedition Kunst. Die Entdeckung der Natur von C.D. Friedrich bis Humboldt* (*Expedition Art. The Discovery of Nature from C.D. Friedrich to Humboldt*) at the Hamburg Kunsthalle, an exhibition that presented links between the natural sciences and the painted landscape. In 2003 his work appeared in the exhibition *The Origins of Abstraction (1800-1914)* at the Musée d'Orsay in Paris. Private and retrospective exhibitions worth mentioning include: Kunsthalle, Hamburg (1960, 1963); with the works of Caspar David Friedrich, Oberes Belvedere, Vienna (1978); *Philipp Otto Runge, Kind und Blume: Zu Zwei Zentralmotiven in seinem Werk* (*Philipp Otto Runge, Child and Flower: Two Leitmotifs in his Work*), Schloss Rantzaubau, Kiel (1980); and *Philipp Otto Runge, Caspar David Friedrich: The Passage of Time*, Van Gogh Museum, Amsterdam (1996).

BIBLIOGRAPHY:

Bisanz, Rudolf M., *German romantisism and Philipp Otto Runge: a study in nineteenth-century art theory and iconography*, 1970. Traeger, Jörg, *Philipp Otto Runge und sein Werk*, monograph, catalogue raisonné, Prestel, Munich, 1975. Langner, Johannes, *Philipp Otto Runge in der Hamburger Kunsthalle*, Amburger Kunsthalle, Hamburg, 1976. Brodersen, Waltraud, *Philipp Otto Runge: historisch-kritische Analysen zu seinem Werk*, Anabas, Giessen, 1978. Hopp, Gisela, *Philipp Otto Runge, Caspar David Friedrich*, exhibition catalogue, Belvedere, Vienna, 1978. Betthausen, Peter, *Philipp Otto Runge*, E.A. Seemann, Leipzig, 1980. Hohl, Hanna, et al., *Philipp Otto Runge, Caspar David Friedrich. the passage of time*, exhibition catalogue, Van Gogh Museum, Amsterdam, 1996. *Philipp Otto Runge: die Zeiten, der Morgen*, exhibition catalogue, Kunsthalle, Hamburg, 1997. *Expedition Kunst. Die Entdeckung der Natur von C.D. Friedrich bis Humboldt*, exhibition catalogue, Hamburger Kunsthalle, Hamburg, 2002. Lemoine, Serge/Rousseau, Pascal, et al., *Aux origines de l'abstraction (1800-1914)*, exhibition catalogue, Musée d'Orsay, Paris, 2003. Littlejohn, Richard/Murray, Chris (ed.), *'Runge, Philipp Otto'* in *Encyclopedia of the Romantic Era, 1760-1850*, Fitzroy Dearborn, New York, 2004.

MUSEUMS AND GALLERIES:

BERLIN (Nationalgal.): *Portrait of the Artist's Wife with Little Boy* (drawing) - HAMBURG (Kunsthalle): *The Nightingale's Singing Lesson; Der Morgen* (*Morning*) (1808); *Children Resting; Child among the Flowers; The Artist and his Family; The Artist's Wife; The Hülsenbeck Children; Portrait of the Artist; Portrait of the Artist's Elder Son; Perth's Pretty Daughter; Portrait of Daniel Runge; The Artist's Parents; Rest during the Flight; Christ on the Sea; Portrait of the Artist's Mother-in-law; Portrait of the Artist's Two Eldest Children; Return of the Sons* (drawing); *Triumph of Love* (drawing); *Scene from the Iliad* (drawing); *Athena with Ulysses and Diomedes* (drawing); *Achilles and Scamander* (drawing); *Joys of Wine* (drawing); *The Four Moments in the Day* (drawing); *Life of Fingal* (drawing); *The Poet and the Source* (drawing); *Moses Laid in the Water* (drawing); *Night* (1807, engraving); *Morning* (1807, engraving) - SZCZECIN: *Portrait of the Artist's Niece; Portrait of M. Mohnike; Sleeping Child* (drawing); *Portrait of the Artist's Brother, Karl Hermann* - VIENNA (Österreichische Gal. Belvedere): *Portrait of the Painter Friedrich August von Klinkowström; Child in the Bloom of Youth.*

AUCTION RECORDS:

HAMBURG, 1 June 1978, *Morning* (1803-1805, engraving/copper) DEM 2,000. MUNICH, 28 Nov 1979, *Lily* (c. 1808-1809, pen and black ink, 11 1/2 x 9 1/4 ins / 29.5 x 23.8 cm) DEM 111,000. MUNICH, 29 Nov 1979, *Morning; Day; Evening; Night* (1803-1806, series of four engravings/copper) DEM 21,000. HEIDELBERG, 3 April 1993, *Child Sleeping in its Cradle* (ink and pencil, 11 x 9 1/4 ins / 27.7 x 23.8 cm) DEM 29,000. MUNICH, 27 June 1995, *Study of a Lily Stem with Details of the Pistil and Stamens* (pencil and black ink/paper, 13 x 10 1/4 ins / 33 x 26 cm) DEM 238,900. HAMBURG, 7 June 2000, *The Day - Noon* (copperplate) DEM 16,000. HAMBURG, 7 June 2001, *Four Seasons* (copperplate, four works, 28 x 19 ins / 71 x 47 cm) DEM 64,000. HAMBURG, 8 May 2002, *Four Seasons* (copperplate, 28 x 19 ins / 71 x 47 cm) EUR 56,000.

RUNGENHAGEN, Friedrich Wilhelm

German, 19th century.
Active in Berlin 1800-1812.
Draughtsman, designer of ornamental architectural features.

RUNGER, Raphaël

Flemish School, 17th century.
Painter.

Runger is remembered for a panel (*Triumph of Apollo*), dated 1687.

RUNGGALDIER. See **RUNGALDIER**

RUNGIUS, Carl

German, 19th - 20th century.
Born 18 August 1869, in Berlin; died 1959.
Active in the USA.
Painter, illustrator. Landscapes, landscapes with figures, animals.

Carl Rungius was a student of Paul Meyerheim in Berlin. He moved to the USA in 1894 and was a member of the Salmagundi Club and the American Arts Federation. He was awarded several prizes and distinctions, among them two Salmagundi Club prizes in 1922 and 1923. Rungius painted landscapes but was first and foremost an animal painter.

AUCTION RECORDS:

NEW YORK, 4 March 1937, *Throwing a Steer*, USD 400. NEW YORK, 24-26 Oct 1946, *Across the Barren Plains*, USD 400. NEW YORK, 11-14 Dec 1946, *Buck*, USD 200. NEW YORK, 14 March 1968, *Landscape with Goats*, USD 3,200. NEW YORK, 19 March 1969, *Horses on a Mountain Path*, USD 5,250. LONDON, 19 Jan 1973, *Landscape with Stag*, Gns 2,200. NEW YORK, 28 Oct 1976, *Sheep* (dark green patinated bronze, h. 16 3/4 ins / 42.5 cm) USD 8,000. NEW YORK, 24 Oct 1979, *Big-*

horn Sheep (1915, brown-patinated bronze, h. 16½ ins / 42.2 cm) USD 9,500. NEW YORK, 17 Oct 1980, *Ibex* (oil on canvas, 24 x 18 ins / 60.9 x 45.7 cm) USD 21,000. PORTLAND, 7 Nov 1981, *Landscape with Moose* (oil on canvas, 30 x 46 ins / 76.2 x 117 cm) USD 37,000. NEW YORK, 21 Oct 1983, *Bighorns in the Field* (pencil sketch, 13½ x 20 ins / 34.3 x 50.8 cm) USD 11,000. NEW YORK, 30 May 1984, *Challenge* (oil on canvas mounted on hardboard, 35¾ x 55½ ins / 90.8 x 141 cm) USD 70,000. NEW YORK, 20 June 1985, *Rocky Mountains Scene* (oil on canvas, 16 x 20 ins / 40.6 x 50.8 cm) USD 13,000. NEW YORK, 29 May 1986, *His Domain* (c. 1916, oil on canvas, 30 x 40 ins / 76.3 x 101.6 cm) USD 26,000. NEW YORK, 28 May 1987, *Mountain Goats* (oil on canvas, 36 x 48 ins / 91.4 x 121.9 cm) USD 35,000. NEW YORK, 23 May 1990, *Large Mouflon* (bronze, h. 16¾ ins / 42.5 cm) USD 60,500. NEW YORK, 24 May 1990, *Ibex in the Mountains* (oil on canvas, 17 x 11 ins / 43.2 x 27.9 cm) USD 20,900. NEW YORK, 30 May 1990, *Three Mouflons in a Mountain Landscape* (oil on canvas, 30 x 40 ins / 76.3 x 101.6 cm) USD 51,700. NEW YORK, 12 April 1991, *Arizona Desert Ram* (1909, oil on canvas, 24 x 18 ins / 61 x 45.7 cm) USD 13,750. NEW YORK, 11 March 1993, *Wyoming: Rocky Mountains Landscape with Green River* (oil on canvas, 30 x 36 ins / 76.4 x 91.5 cm) USD 23,000. NEW YORK, 26 May 1993, *Mountain Ibex at Nigel Pass near the Alberta Border* (1919, oil on canvas, 12¼ x 16 ins / 31 x 40.7 cm) USD 13,800. NEW YORK, 27 May 1993, *Old Man of the Mountains* (oil on canvas, 30 x 45 ins / 76.2 x 114.3 cm) USD 29,900. NEW YORK, 23 Sept 1993, *Last of the Herd* (oil on canvas, 30 x 40 ins / 76.2 x 101.6 cm) USD 34,500. NEW YORK, 1 Dec 1994, *Mountain Landscape* (oil on canvas, 32 x 46 ins / 81.3 x 116.8 cm) USD 71,250. NEW YORK, 14 Sept 1995, *Large Mouflons* (oil on canvas, 30 x 40 ins / 76.2 x 101.6 cm) USD 65,750. NEW YORK, 21 May 1996, *Moose Combat* (pencil/paper, 18 x 24¾ ins / 45.5 x 62.8 cm) USD 3,220. NEW YORK, 3 Dec 1997, *Round-Up Over* (oil on canvas, 52 x 62 ins / 132.1 x 157.5 cm) USD 167,500.

RUNK, Ferdinand
German, 18th - 19th century.
Born 14 October 1764, in Freiburg im Breisgau; died 4 December 1834, in Vienna.
Painter, engraver (etching). Landscapes.

Ferdinand Runk was a pupil at the academy in Vienna. He quickly gained a reputation for his views of the Austrian Tyrol and mountain paintings. Piringer, in particular, engraved several of his works.

MUSEUMS AND GALLERIES:
VIENNA: *View of the Tyrol.*

AUCTION RECORDS:
LONDON, 14 June 1974, *Lake Landscape with Figures*, Gns 1,500.

RUNZE, Wilhelm
German, 20th century.
Born 4 June 1887, in Frankfurt am Main; died 1973.
Painter. Portraits, genre scenes, landscapes.

Wilhelm Runze studied under Wilhelm Amandus Beer and O. Seitz at the Städel Institute in Frankfurt and at the Colarossi academy in Paris.

W Runze.

MUSEUMS AND GALLERIES:
MUNICH (NG): *Gentleman in a Top Hat.*

RUO, Gennaro
Italian, 19th century.
Born 15 March 1852, in Naples; died 15 January 1884.
Miniaturist. Historical subjects, portraits.

MUSEUMS AND GALLERIES:
NAPLES (Mus. di Capodimonte): *Death of Carlo di Durazzo.*

RUOF, Batholomäus
Swiss, 17th century.
Born to a family originally from Valais.
Sculptor (wood).

Batholomäus Ruof collaborated on the stalls of the church of St Valerie in Sion between 1661 and 1664.

RUOFF, Hans Jakob. See **RUEFF**

RUOKOKOSKI, Jalmar or Jalmari, or Ruokokski
Finnish, 20th century.
Born 16 March 1886; died 1936.
Painter. Figures, portraits, landscapes.
November Group.

Ruokokoski studied in Helsinki and in Paris.

MUSEUMS AND GALLERIES:
HELSINKI (Ateneumin Taidemus.): four paintings.

AUCTION RECORDS:
STOCKHOLM, 7 Dec 1987, *Little Girl with Doll* (1911, oil on canvas, 24 x 17¾ ins / 61 x 45 cm) SEK 60,000. LONDON, 24 March 1988, *Portrait of Alma Lömberg* (1913, oil on canvas, 20¾ x 15 ins / 53 x 38 cm) GBP 5,500. HELSINKI, 14 Feb 1999, *Rural Area* (1914, oil on board, 20 x 17 ins / 52 x 43 cm) FIM 20,000. HELSINKI, 21 Oct 1999, *Women on the Beach* (oil on canvas, 13 x 20 ins / 34 x 51 cm) FIM 25,000. HELSINKI, 13 May 2000, *Red Head* (1910, crayon, 11 x 8 ins / 27 x 20 cm) FIM 19,000. HELSINKI, 9 Dec 2000, *View from Hogland* (1926, oil on canvas, 20 x 24 ins / 50 x 61 cm) FIM 20,000. HELSINKI, 11 Feb 2001, *Still-life with Fruit* (1923, oil on canvas, 21 x 26 ins / 53 x 67 cm) FIM 14,000. HELSINKI, 12 May 2001, *Women on the Beach* (1913, oil on canvas, 22 x 19 ins / 56 x 47 cm) FIM 19,000. HELSINKI, 27 April 2002, *Female Nude* (1911, oil on canvas, 30 x 26 ins / 77 x 66 cm) EUR 12,000. HELSINKI, 30 Nov 2002, *Women Bathing* (1917, oil on canvas, 22 x 24 ins / 55 x 60 cm) EUR 2,200. HELSINKI, 3 April 2003, *Sleeping* (oil on canvas, 31 x 18 ins / 78 x 46 cm) EUR 4,800. HELSINKI, 29 Nov 2003, *Chauffeur* (1914, oil on canvas, 26 x 24 ins / 65 x 62 cm) EUR 4,100. HELSINKI, 25 March 2004, *Lady in a Hat* (1935, oil on canvas, 25 x 21 ins / 63 x 53 cm) EUR 1,800. HELSINKI, 25 March 2004, *Girl* (1924, oil on canvas, 22 x 19 ins / 56 x 48 cm) EUR 2,200.

RUOLLZ, Léopold Marie Philippe de (Comte), or Ruolz
French, 19th century.
Born 1805, in Lyons; died in Paris.
Sculptor. Figures. Busts.

Léopold Ruollz featured at the Paris Salon from 1834 to 1838.

MUSEUMS AND GALLERIES:
LYONS: *Bouchet, Surgeon* (bust); *Suchet, Duke D'Albufera* (bust); *J. J. de Boissieu* (bust).

RUOPPOLO, Giovanni Battista, or Ruopolo or Ruoppoli
Italian, 17th century.
Born 1629, in Naples; died 1693, in Naples.
Painter. Still-lifes (flowers/fruit). Murals.
Neapolitan School.

Giovanni Battista Ruoppolo is said to have been the pupil of Paolo Porpora and of Luca Forte, and to have been influenced by Battistello, Ribera and Caravaggio (via Ribera). He was, alongside Giuseppe Recco, the most important still-life painter in the Neapolitan School of the 17th century.

Authoritative studies divide his works into two distinct periods. The first period, from 1650 to 1660, which is naturalistic and restrained, includes the famous still-life in the Ashmolean Museum in Oxford, in which a number of humble objects are placed in clearly defined positions and illuminated by crude, Caravaggesque lighting that cuts sharply through the shadows. In the second period the objects are more select, arranged in abundance so as to cover the entire canvas with flowers, fruit and household utensils. The artist's touch is more alert: forms are revealed by golden light and colours emerge sensuously from the shadows. The influence of Paolo Porpora, Michelangelo Campidoglio and Cerquozzi is particularly evident in the works from this second period.

Ruoppolo featured in a collective exhibition on the theme of still-life in Italy, entitled *Stille Welt. Italienische Stilleben aus drei Jahrhunderten* (*Still World: Three Centuries of Italian Still-life Painting*), held at the Kunsthalle der Hypo-Kulturstiftung in Munich in 2003.

BIBLIOGRAPHY:

La Natura morta italiana, exhibition catalogue, Alfieri & Lacroix, Milan, 1964. Salmi, Mario/Bazin, Germain, *Le Caravage et la Peinture italienne au XVIIe siècle*, exhibition catalogue, Musée du Louvre, Paris, 1965. Gregori, Mina/Prinz, Johann Georg, *Stille Welt. Italienische Stilleben aus drei Jahrhunderten*, exhibition catalogue, Kunsthalle der Hypo-Kulturstiftung, Munich, 2003.

MUSEUMS AND GALLERIES:

HAMBURG (Kunsthalle): *Still-life* - NAPLES (Mus. Nazionale): *Flowers and Fruit* (three items) - NEW YORK (Metropolitan Mus. of Art): *Still-life* - OXFORD (Ashmolean Mus.): *Still-life with Fruit* - ROME (GA Antica di Palazzo Corsini): *Still-life*.

AUCTION RECORDS:

COLOGNE, 11 Nov 1964, *Still-life with Fruit*, DEM 5,000. LONDON, 8 Dec 1965, *Still-life with Fruit* (two pendants) GBP 1,600. ZURICH, 21 Oct 1969, *Still-life with Fruit*, CHF 8,200. MILAN, 1 Dec 1970, *Still-life with Fruit*, ITL 3,500,000. NEW YORK, 19 March 1981, *Still-life with Fruit* (oil/hardboard, 27 1/2 x 37 1/2in/70 x 95.3cm) USD 22,000. LONDON, 12 Dec 1984, *Still-life with Mushrooms and Fruit* (oil on canvas, 38 1/2 x 28in/98 x 71cm) GBP 37,000. NEW YORK, 5 June 1986, *Still-life with Fruit* (oil on canvas, 34 1/4 x 48 3/4in/87 x 124cm) USD 20,000. MILAN, 17 Dec 1987, *Still-life with Fruit* (oil on canvas, 52 1/4 x 79 1/2in/133 x 202cm) ITL 75,000,000. NEW YORK, 14 Jan 1988, *Still-life with Flowers in an Urn Surrounded by Various Fruits in a Landscape* (oil on canvas, 38 1/2 x 46 1/2in/98 x 118cm) USD 27,500. LONDON, 8 July 1988, *Still-life with Cut Pomegranate, Figs and Other Fruit and Various Flowers* (oil on canvas, 18 x 26in/46 x 66cm) GBP 26,400. NEW YORK, 11 Jan 1990, *Still-life with Fruit* (oil, a pair, each 29 1/4 x 39 1/4in/74 x 100cm) USD 297,000. MONACO, 21 June 1991, *Still-life in a Landscape with Oranges, Lemons and a Parrot Perching on a Pot, and Still-life in a Landscape with Bunches of Grapes, Water Melon, Figs and Apples* (oil on canvas, a pair, each 29 1/2 x 40 1/4in/75 x 102cm) FRF 1,554,000. LONDON, 8 July 1992, *Large Still-life of Flowers and Fruit on a Stone Entablature* (oil on canvas, 43 3/4 x 34in/111 x 86.5cm) GBP 41,800. ROME, 14 Nov 1995, *Still-life with Apples, Peaches and Figs; Still-life with Grapes, Quinces and Water Melon* (oil on canvas, a pair, 29 1/2 x 39 3/4in/75 x 101cm) ITL 138,000,000. LONDON, 18 April 1997, *Water Melons, Pomegranates, Lemons, Apples, Pears, Cherries, Figs and Bunches of Grapes* (oil on canvas, 49 1/2 x 69 1/4in/126 x 176.2cm) GBP 155,500. NEW YORK, 24 Jan 2002, *Still-life with Oranges, Lemons and a Parrot in a Landscape* (oil on canvas, 30 x 40 ins / 75 x 102 cm) USD 75,000. LONDON, 11 July 2002, *Still-life of Watermelons, Plums and Other Fruit. Still-life with Figs, Cherries* (oil on canvas, a pair, 23 x 52 ins / 58 x 132 cm) GBP 46,000. AMSTERDAM, 13 May 2003, *Still-life of Fruit in Basket on Stone Ledge* (oil on canvas, 29 x 44 ins / 74 x 111 cm) EUR 90,000. MILAN, 15 Nov 2003, *Still-life with Grapes, Peaches and Apples* (oil on canvas, 24 x 29 ins / 60 x 74 cm) EUR 102,000. MILAN, 25 Feb 2004, *Still-life of Fruit with Grapes, Watermelon and Figs* (oil on canvas, 28 x 41 ins / 71 x 105 cm) EUR 91,000.

RUOPPOLO, Giuseppe, or Ruopolo or Ruoppoli

Italian, 17th - 18th century.

Born c. 1639, in Naples; died 1710, in Naples.

Painter. Still-lifes (flowers/fruit/game/sea shells).

The nephew and pupil of Giovanni Battista Ruoppolo, Giuseppe Ruoppolo was a celebrated flower, fruit and still-life painter. He was represented in the collective exhibition devoted to the subject of still-life in Italy, entitled *Stille Welt. Italienische Stilleben aus drei Jahrhunderten* (*Still World: Three Centuries of Italian Still-life Painting*), held at the Kunsthalle der Hypo-Kulturstiftung in Munich in 2003. His particular forte was the depiction of bunches of grapes.

BIBLIOGRAPHY:

Zimmermann, Katrin, *Die Stilleben von Giuseppe Recco, Giuseppe Ruoppolo und Abraham Brueghel aus der Sammlung D'Avalos*, Berlin Freie Univ., 1998. Gregori, Mina/Prinz, Johann Georg, *Stille Welt. Italienische Stilleben aus drei Jahrhunderten*, exhibition catalogue, Kunsthalle der Hypo-Kulturstiftung, Munich, 2003.

MUSEUMS AND GALLERIES:

STOCKHOLM: *Fish and Oysters*.

AUCTION RECORDS:

MILAN, 12 and 13 March 1963, *Still-lifes* (two pendants) ITL 3,400,000. LONDON, 26 Nov 1971, *Still-life with Flowers and Game*, Gns 3,500. LONDON, 30 Nov 1973, *Fowl and Still-life in a Landscape*, Gns 9,000. RIVAROLO CANAVESE, 14 Nov 1982, *Still-life with Fish* (oil on canvas, 38 1/4 x 49 1/4in/97 x 125cm) ITL 29,000,000. LONDON, 15 April 1983, *Flowers in a Vase on an Entablature* (oil on canvas, 40 x 29 1/2in/101.6 x 75cm) GBP 15,000. ROME, 22 March 1988, *Still-life with Plums, Vegetables, Mushrooms, Vase of Flowers and Copper Pan* (oil on canvas, 21 1/4 x 40 1/2in/54 x 103cm) ITL 70,000,000. COLOGNE, 15 June 1989, *Still-life with Plentiful Arrangement of Fruit* (oil on canvas, 24 x 29 1/4in/61 x 74cm) DEM 6,000. MONACO, 2 July 1993, *Still-life with Fruit, Parrots and Tortoises* (oil on canvas, a pair, each 40 1/2 x 51 1/4in/103 x 130cm) FRF 555,000. NEW YORK, 30 Jan 1997, *Still-life with Grapes, Melons, Pomegranate, Celery, Shellfish and Other Objects* (oil on canvas, 33 x 44 1/4in/84.1 x 112.7cm) USD 51,750. ROME, 24 Oct 2000, *Still-life with Flowers and Strawberries. Still-life with Pears and Cherries* (oil on canvas, a pair, 20 x 25 ins / 50 x 63 cm) ITL 150,000,000. ROME, 24 Oct 2000, *Still-life with Pears and Grapes. Still-life with Peaches and Plums* (oil on canvas, a pair, 20 x 25 ins / 50 x 63 cm) ITL 180,000,000. LONDON, 13 Dec 2001, *Still-life with Fruit and Macaw. Still-life with Fruit and Mushrooms in a Landscape* (oil on canvas, a pair, 41 x 51 ins / 103 x 130 cm) GBP 60,000.

RUOSS, Jacob. See **RUSS**

RUOTTE, Louis Charles (père)

French, 18th century.

Born 1754, in Paris; died c. 1806.

Engraver.

Ruotte engraved religious subjects, genre scenes and portraits. He exhibited at the Salons of 1793, 1795, 1796 and 1804. In 1797 he lived in the Rue St-Lazare, near the Chaussée d'Antin.

RUOTTE, Louis Charles (son)

French, 19th century.

Born c. 1785, in Paris.

Engraver.

Louis Ruotte was the son of Louis Charles Ruotte and probably his student. He also worked at the École des Beaux-Arts, which he entered at the age of 11 on the 13 Brumaire (second month of the French republican calendar) in year V (3rd November, 1796.)

The print entitled *To the Most Beautiful One*, exhibited under the name of Ruotte at the Salon of 1812, must be attributed to him, as his father Ruotte died in around 1806.

RUOZI, Zaverio

Italian, 19th century.

Born 1787, in Reggio Emilia; died 19 February 1870.
Portrait artist, engraver (burin).

RUP, Karl
Austrian, 19th century.
Active in the first half of the 19th century.
Painter.
Karl Rup is noted for an altar painting dated 1820 depicting the *Madonna*, which is to be found in the castle of Gainfarn.

RUPALLEY, Angélique Marie Gabrielle Geneviève, later Mme Le Master
French, 19th century.
Born 1786, in Bayeux; died 26 July 1872, in Le Vernay (Rhône).
Portrait artist.
Angélique Rupalley was the daughter of Gabriel Narcisse Rupalley.
MUSEUMS AND GALLERIES:
BAYEUX: *Portrait of Joachim Rupalley (the Artist's Grandfather); Portrait of the Chevalier du Castel; Portrait of Monseigneur de Rochechouart; Portrait of du Castel, the Canon; Portrait of Monseigneur de Luynes in His Mature Years.*

RUPALLEY, Gabriel Narcisse
French, 18th century.
Born 12 March 1740, in Bayeux; died 17 March 1798, in Bayeux.
Painter.
Gabriel Rupalley was the father of Angélique Marie Gabrielle Rupalley, and the son of Joachim Rupalley. He was a pupil at the École de Peinture in Rouen from 1766 to 1767. His works include a *Portrait of J.-D. de Chelles, Bishop of Bayeux*. In 1780 he became Sovereign Knight Prince of the Rosicrucian Fraternity.

RUPALLEY, Joachim
French, 18th century.
Born 1713, in Bayeux; died 8 October 1780, in Bayeux.
Painter.
Joachim Rupalley was the father of Gabriel Narcisse Rupalley. He was the pupil of J. Restout. Tardieu produced an engraving after Rupalley's 1771 portrait of P.J.C. de Rochechouart, Bishop of Bayeux. Rupalley also painted *Portrait of Marshal de Broglie*.
MUSEUMS AND GALLERIES:
ALENÇON: *St George, Pilgrim Crossing a Landscape* - BAYEUX: *Portraits of the Bishop of Luynes (Two); Portrait of the Bishop of Rochechouart; Portrait of the Canon of Castel; Portrait of the Knight of Castel* - ST-LÔ: *Henri François of Bricqueville; Midday; Midnight; Burgher of Bayeux; Knight of St Louis.*

RUPALLEY, Juliette de
French, 20th century.
Born 24 June 1893.
Painter. Historical portraits.
Juliette de Rupalley became a member of the Salon des Indépendants, Paris, in 1934, and won a silver medal from the city of Paris in 1966. She painted a *Portrait of General De Gaulle*.
MUSEUMS AND GALLERIES:
PARIS (MAMVP).

RUPALLEY, Marcienne de
French, 20th century.
Born 21 April 1928.
Painter.
Marcienne de Ruppalley painted a *Portrait of the Empress of Iran* for which she was awarded a commemorative gold medal by the crown, and a *Portrait of Monseigneur Badré*, Bishop of Bayeux.
MUSEUMS AND GALLERIES:
ST-HIMMER: *Portrait of Pascal.*

RUPERT (Prince), or Ruprecht or Robert, called Prince Rupert of the Rhine
German, 17th century.
Born 27 December 1619, in Prague; died 29 November 1682, in London.
Engraver (mezzotint).
Rupert was the third son of the elector palatine and Princess Elizabeth of England. He was often considered to have invented the engraving process known as 'mezzotint', but in fact he was no more than the propagandist. The discovery was actually made by Ludwig von Siegen, a lieutenant-colonel in the service of the landgrave of Hessen, William IV, who taught the prince the technique during their meeting in Brussels in 1654. Rupert, already adept in etching and burin engraving, was taken with the new method and in 1658, during a visit to Frankfurt for the crowning of Emperor Leopold I, he produced a plate entitled the *Execution of St John the Baptist* after Spagnoletto. In Frankfurt the artist prince met Wallerant Vaillant, the court painter Jan Thomas d'Ypres, and Theodor Caspar von Furstenberg. He taught them the new engraving method and may have received help from them. Having then settled in London, Rupert introduced the English public to his work in 1661 and this communication marked the point of departure for the school of mezzotint engravers, whose works are so avidly sought-after by art-lovers. Rupert's work includes 12 genuine pieces and 6 that are only attributed to him.
MUSEUMS AND GALLERIES:
LONDON (British Mus.): *Mortar on a Boat; Head Study.*
AUCTION RECORDS:
LONDON, 1 Nov 1978, *Standard Bearer* (mezzotint, 11 x 7 1/2 ins / 27.7 x 19 cm) GBP 12,000. LONDON, 17 June 1983, *The Great Executioner* (1658, mezzotint, 14 1/2 x 17 1/2 ins / 36.8 x 44.5 cm) GBP 4,800.

RUPERT, Johann Christian. See **RUPRECHT**

RUPERT, Pedro. See **RUBERT**

RUPERT, Peter
Swiss, 17th century.
Active c. 1617-1636.
Sculptor (wood).
Peter Rupert worked for the new abbey church of Lucerne.

RUPERTI, Madja
Swiss, 20th century.
Born 1903; died 1981.
Painter.
Madja Ruperti lived and worked in Arlesheim. He exhibited at the Salon des Réalités Nouvelles in Paris in 1952 and 1953, showing compositions based on intertwined beams and easel frames or tree trunks and branches.

RUPERTUS
Austrian, 18th century.
Active in 1766.
Sculptor (wood).
Rupertus was a member of the Dominican order. He sculpted the pontifical chair in the church of Podcepitz.

RUPFLIN, Karl
German, 20th century.
Born 1889, in Lindau im Bodensee (Bavaria).
Painter, engraver.
Karl Rupeflin painted frescoes in Lindau, Hildesheim and Augsburg.

RUPHON, Jacopo or Giacomo Giuseppe, or Ruffoni, Ruffone, Rufonio, Rufonus
Italian, 17th century.
Possibly active in Venice during the second half of the 17th century.
Engraver.

RUPIED, Ernestine
French, 19th century.
Active in 1863.
Painter. Flowers.
Ernestine Rupied was the student of Maréchal de Metz.
MUSEUMS AND GALLERIES:
DIEPPE: a pastel.

RUPNIEVSKI, Roman
Polish, 19th century.
Born 1802, in Gnojno; died 1893, in Gnievecin.
Painter. Military subjects.

RUPP
Austrian, 18th century.
Active in Waidhofen an der Thaya in the first half of the 18th century.
Sculptor.
In 1735 Rupp sculpted the statues of *St Roch* and *St Sebastian* for the church of Waidhofen.

RUPP, Henri
French, 19th - 20th century.
Born possibly in 1837; died 18 December 1918, in Paris.
Painter.
Henri Rupp was curator of the Gustave Moreau Museum, Paris.

RUPP, Jakob
German, 16th century.
Active c. 1518.
Engraver (wood).
Jakob Rupp collaborated with Albrecht Dürer on his *Triumph of Emperor Maximilian.*

RUPP, Ladislaus
Austrian, 19th century.
Born 1793, in Vienna; died 7 October 1854, in Vienna.
Draughtsman, engraver (aquatint), mosaicist.
Architectural views.
Ladislaus Rupp was a pupil of Giacomo Raffaelli in Milan, where he spent most of his life.
MUSEUMS AND GALLERIES:
NEW HAVEN (Knights of Columbus Mus.): *Italian Churches* (aquatints, six views).

RUPP, Rudolf
German, 20th century.
Born 18 August 1886, in Frankfurt am Main.
Painter. Portraits, genre scenes, interiors.
Rudolf Rupp studied under Hasselhorst and Anton Burger and at the academy in Karlsruhe.

RÜPPE, C. F. (Mme). See **CHALON Christina**

RÜPPE, Christian Frederik
Dutch, 18th century.
Engraver (etching).
Rüppe was an organist by profession, practising etching as an amateur. The husband of Christina Rüppe, he lived in Leiden in the second half of the 18th century.
MUSEUMS AND GALLERIES:
AMSTERDAM (Rijksprentenkabinet): three prints.

RUPPE, Michael
Austrian, 19th - 20th century.
Born 24 March 1863, in Schäflein, near Nesseltal (Carniole).
Sculptor, painter. Allegorical subjects.
Michael Ruppe was a student of H. Klotz and Adam Hölzel. He lived and worked in Salzburg and is noted for his watercolours of Ljubljana.
MUSEUMS AND GALLERIES:
LJUBLJANA (Narodni Muzej Slovenije): three allegorical statues.

RÜPPEL, Hermann
German, 19th century.
Born 17 November 1845, in Willershausen; died 15 July 1900, in Kassel.
Painter, architect.

RUPPERSBERG, Allen
American, 20th century.
Born 1944, in Cleveland (Ohio).
Installation artist, draughtsman, mixed media.
Conceptual Art.
Allen Ruppersberg lives and works in Los Angeles and New York. As with other conceptual artists, the basis of his work lies in his interest in language and his ability to interpret or dodge reality. He mixes various conceptual media such as posters, books, popular magazines and urban graffiti. Allen Ruppersberg is interested in the duality of fiction and reality and draws the viewer into an endless story. He has written a book on art entitled *23, 24 and 25 pieces*, (2000), published by the Centre National de l'Estampe et de l'Art Imprimé in Chatou. His group exhibitions include: *Nine Young Artists: Theodoron Prize*, Solomon Guggenheim Museum, New York, 1977; *The New Five Foot Shelf*, as part of the show *Play*, at the Musée d'Art Moderne et Contemporain, Geneva, 2001; *L'Altro Mondo*, FRAC Poitou-Charentes, Château d'Orion, Deux-Sèvres, France, 2002; *Une collection de 'chefs-d'œuvre', emprunts, pastiches, copies, citation et interprétations* (*A Collection of 'Masterpieces', Borrowings, Pastiches, Copies, Quotations and Interpretations*), an exhibition dealing with the subject of appropriation in art, mainly from the European standpoint, FRAC Limoges. Solo exhibitions include: Galerie Yvon Lambert, Paris, 1973; *Allen Ruppersberg: The Secret of Life and Death*, Museum of Contemporary Art, Los Angeles, 1985; Galerie Gabrielle Maubrie, Paris, 1991; first retrospective, Le Magasin, Centre d'Art Contemporain de Grenoble, 1997; Kultur-Stiftung des Deutschen Bank Gruppe, Münster, 1997; FRAC (Fonds Régional d'Art Contemporain - Regional Contemporary Art Fund), Poitou-Charentes, Angoulême, 1997; FRAC Limousin, Limoges, 1999.
BIBLIOGRAPHY:
Singerman, Howard/Brown, Julia, *Allen Ruppersberg: The Secret of Life and Death*, exhibition catalogue, Museum of Contemporary Art, Los Angeles, Black Sparrow Press, Santa Barbara (CA), 1985. Brugerolle, Marie de, *Allen Ruppersberg. Where's Al?*, exhibition catalogue, Centre national d'Art contemporain Le Magasin, Grenoble, 1996 (text in French and English). Bussman, Klaus/König, Kasper/Matzner, Florian, *Allen Ruppersberg. Die Best aller möglichen Welten [A Tourguide to the Best of All Possible Works]*, exhibition catalogue, Kultur-Stiftung der Deutschen Bank Gruppe, Münster, 1997 (text in English and German). Ruppersberg, Allen/Paul, Frédéric, *Allen Ruppersberg. Books Inc*, exhibition catalogue, Fonds régional d'Art contemporain du Limousin, Limoges, 1999 (text in French and English, including interview with the artist).
MUSEUMS AND GALLERIES:
LIMOGES (FRAC Limousin): *To Tell the Truth* (1973, photograph) - PARIS (FNAC): *The Long Goodbye* (1990, drawing); *One Way to Write your Novel* (1991, drawing).
AUCTION RECORDS:
NEW YORK, 8 Nov 1993, *Footnote* (1975, colour photograph and pencil/card mounted on card on three panels, in all 50 x 150 ins / 127 x 381 cm) USD 23,000. NEW YORK, 3 May 1994,

Word Game - Collection of Rare Books - Jonathan Swift (1979, wooden case construction with a book, an ink drawing/paper, an index card, satin and Plexiglas, 28 1/2 x 21 3/4 x 27 1/2 ins / 72.1 x 55.4 x 69.8 cm) USD 4,600. NEW YORK, 20 Nov 1996, *Untitled* (1976, pencil/paper, five items, 22 3/4 x 29 ins / 57.8 x 73.7 cm in all) USD 18,400. LOS ANGELES, 30 March 2003, *Searching for passion and sex* (1979, pencil dr. three in one frame, drawings, 3 x 10 ins / 7 x 25 cm) USD 1,900. LOS ANGELES, 30 March 2003, *Searching for Passion and Sex* (1979, pencil, three in one frame, 3 x 10 ins / 7 x 25 cm) USD 1,900. LONDON, 4 Feb 2004, *Art for Mammoth Adventures* (1995, collage on paper, four parts, 80 x 120 ins / 203 x 305 cm) GBP 2,500. LONDON, 4 Feb 2004, *Art for Mammoth Adventures* (1995, collage on paper, four parts, 80 x 120 ins / 203 x 305 cm) GBP 2,500.

RUPPERT. See also **RUPERT, RUPRECHT** and **RUPPRECHT**

RUPPERT, Fritz or Friedrich Karl Leopold

German, 20th century.

Born 15 August 1878, in Karlsruhe.

Painter, watercolourist. Religious subjects, figures, portraits, landscapes.

Ruppert studied under Caspar Ritter in Karlsruhe, under Ferdinand Keller, and in Paris. He painted predominantly religious subjects.

MUSEUMS AND GALLERIES:

GELSENKIRCHEN: a watercolour and ten prints - PFORZHEIM: two landscapes.

RUPPERT, Georg Friedrich

German, 18th century.

Born 17 April 1715, in Wildensorg, near Bamberg; died 13 November 1771, in Bamberg.

Miniaturist.

RUPPERT, Otto von

German, 19th century.

Born 2 August 1841, in Waldshut.

Painter, watercolourist. Landscapes, architectural views, still-lifes.

Otto von Ruppert undertook his preliminary studies in Vienna under August Schäfer and refined his skills in Venice where he lived for several years. After returning to his home country, he made several study trips around Germany and Austria.

MUSEUMS AND GALLERIES:

MUNICH (Municipal Mus.): five watercolours and nine drawings.

AUCTION RECORDS:

COPENHAGEN, 2 Nov 1982, *View of Venice* (1876, oil on canvas, 17 1/4 x 13 3/4 ins / 44 x 35 cm) DKK 14,000. MUNICH, 23 Oct 1985, *Munich Oktoberfest* (1876, watercolour, 11 1/2 x 18 ins / 29.5 x 46 cm) DEM 5,200. NEW YORK, 15 Oct 1993, *Mountain Chalet* (1872, oil on canvas, 16 x 12 1/4 ins / 40.6 x 31.2 cm) USD 805. LONDON, 27 Oct 1993, *Farmyard* (oil on card, 5 x 7 3/4 ins / 13 x 20 cm) GBP 977. BOSTON, 22 Nov 2002, *Tightrope Walker* (oil on panel, 10 x 14 ins / 26 x 35 cm) USD 1,800. MUNICH, 28 March 2003, *Figures by Konigssee* (oil on canvas, 27 x 19 ins / 68 x 47 cm) EUR 2,200. NEW YORK, 30 March 2004, *Nomads Resting by the River with Pyramids beyond* (oil on canvas, 19 x 15 ins / 49 x 39 cm) USD 6,000.

RUPPERT, Sybille

German, 20th century.

Born 1942, in Frankfurt am Main.

Painter, draughtsman, illustrator.

Sybille Ruppert trained at the Werkkunstschule in Offenbach and the Hochschule fur Bildenden Künste in Frankfurt. She has exhibited regularly in Germany and France, notably at the Fantasy Biennale at the Château of Homécourt in 1989. She illustrated the German edition of de Sade's works.

AUCTION RECORDS:

PARIS, 14 Oct 1989, *Bondage* (pencil, 20 x 11 ins / 51 x 27 cm) FRF 9,500.

RUPPRECHT. See also **RUPRECHT, RUPERT** and **RUPPERT**

RUPPRECHT, Adèle. See **RUPRECHT**

RUPPRECHT, Christian I

German, 18th century.

Born in Neuhaldensleben.

Potter.

Between 1737 and 1751 Christian Rupprecht I worked in several earthenware factories, including those at Wrisbergholzen, Fulda, Göppingen and Calw.

RUPPRECHT, Christian II

German, 19th century.

Born 1815, in Memmingen; died 11 February 1900, in Munich.

Painter, engraver (wood).

While in Munich Christian Rupprecht II contributed to the journal *Fliegende Blätter*.

RUPPRECHT, Friederich Carl

German, 19th century.

Born 1779, in Obernzenn; died 25 October 1831, in Bamberg.

Painter, miniaturist, engraver (etching/wood), architect, draughtsman. Portraits, landscapes, architectural views.

Friederich Carl Rupprecht began his education in Nuremberg before going to work in Dresden, where he executed copies after Titian, Claude Lorraine and Paul Potter. He also studied architecture and perspective. In 1802 he travelled in southern Germany where he painted the landscape in a natural style. However, due to the constraints placed on him by war, he was forced to earn a living from portrait painting. His patron was General Drouet, whose effigy he painted and with whom he travelled as an interpreter. He seems to have settled quite early on in Bamberg, where he was employed as an architect on the cathedral restoration. Several of his etchings are dated in this town around 1815 and depict sites to be found there. He also executed minutely detailed watercolours and produced wood engravings and lithographs.

MUSEUMS AND GALLERIES:

BAMBERG (Municipal Mus.): *A Cardinal* (miniature); *Venetian Woman* (miniature, after Titian).

RUPPRECHT, Johann. See **RUPRECHT**

RUPPRECHT, Tini

German, 19th - 20th century.

Born 14 December 1868, in Munich; died 1956.

Painter. Portraits, figures.

Tini Rupprecht was a student of Franz B. Doubek. She is noted for portraits of princesses and society ladies.

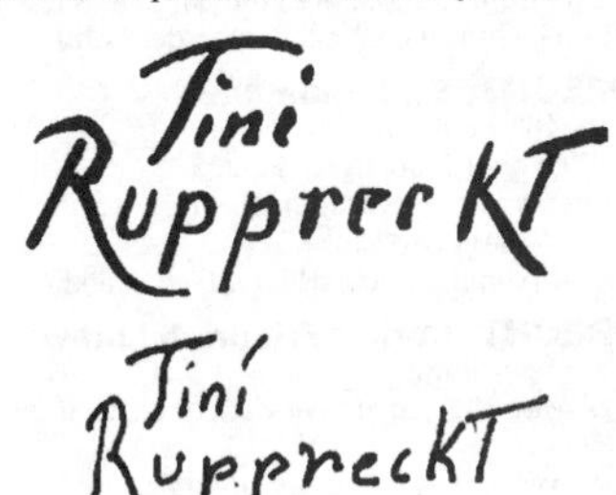

Auction records:
Paris, 15 March 1924, *Woman with a Green Veil* (pastel) FRF 200. Lindau, 5 May 1982, *Mother and Child* (1910, pastel) DEM 3,600. Mexico, 21 June 2000, *Portrait of a Lady in Yellow* (pastel, 35 x 22 ins / 88 x 55 cm) MXP 22,000.

RUPPRECHT, Wilhelm
German, 19th century.
Active in Halberstadt c. 1810.
Painter, lithographer. Architectural views, landscapes.

RUPPRECHT, Wilhelm
German, 19th - 20th century.
Born 15 May 1886, in Stadtprozelten.
Painter, stained glass painter, engraver, designer. Religious subjects.
Self-taught, Wilhelm Rupprecht painted and engraved predominantly religious subjects.
Museums and Galleries:
Detroit: *Genesis and Passion* (stained-glass windows); *Three Kings* (tapestry) - Leipzig (Grassi Mus.): *Trumpeter of Jericho* - Munich (Bayerisches Nationalmus.): *Last Supper*; *Virgin and Angels*; *Christ's Entry into Jerusalem*.

RUPPRECHT, Wilhelm Hugo
German, 20th century.
Born 3 January 1881, in Stuttgart.
Painter, engraver. Portraits, landscapes.
Wilhelm Hugo Rupprecht was a student of Christian Landesberger and Robert Haugs.
Museums and Galleries:
Stuttgart (Gal. der Stadt): *River Landscape*.

RUPRECHT (prince). See **RUPERT**

RUPRECHT
Austrian, 15th century.
Active in Salzburg.
Painter.
Ruprecht painted pictures for the Salzburg church of St Peter between 1457 and 1466. He may have been the same artist who in 1471 started the painting in the town hall of Passau that was finished by Rueland Frühauf.

RUPRECHT. See also **RUPPRECHT, RUPERT** and **RUPPERT**

RUPRECHT, Adèle, or Rupprecht
Austrian, 19th century.
Active 1843-1845.
Painter, illustrator. Portraits, still-lifes.
Adèle Ruprecht was the daughter of Johann Ruprecht.
Auction records:
New York, 19 Oct 1984, *Portrait of the Ruprecht Family* (1839, oil on canvas, 43 1/2 x 31 ins / 110.5 x 78.7 cm) USD 5,750.

RUPRECHT, Anton
German, 18th century.
Active in the first half of the 18th century.
Sculptor (wood).
In 1710 Anton Ruprecht sculpted the pulpit and the grilles of the choir in the church of Weilburg an der Lahn.

RUPRECHT, Bartholomäus
German, 18th century.
Born 1705; died 1756, in Augsburg.
Draughtsman, engraver (burin).
Museums and Galleries:
Augsburg (Maximilianmus.): *Winter* (red chalk).

RUPRECHT, Carl or Friedrich Ludwig Carl
German, 19th century.
Born 22 May 1817, in Halberstadt; died 1 January 1909, in Eisleben.
Painter. Portraits, landscapes, animals.
Carl Ruprecht was a pupil at the academy in Munich. He painted the ceiling of the secondary school in Eisleben.

RUPRECHT, Johann, or Rupprecht
Austrian, 19th century.
Active in Vienna and Budapest 1825-1831.
Portrait artist.
Johann Ruprecht was the father of Adèle Ruprecht.

RUPRECHT, Johann Christian or Christian, or Rupert
German, 17th century.
Born 1600, in Nuremberg; died probably in 1654, in Vienna.
Painter, copyist. Religious subjects.
Johann Christian Ruprecht is mentioned as an excellent copyist of the paintings of Albrecht Dürer and other German old masters. He is also credited with original works, notably a *Raising of Lazarus* in the church of St Sebald in Nuremberg. Emperor Ferdinand III summoned him to Vienna and employed him there.

RUPRECHT, Marx Abraham
German, 18th century.
Born c. 1733; died 1800, in Augsburg.
Engraver (burin), print publisher.
Marx Abraham Ruprecht engraved views of Augsburg, Hanover and Ulm.

RUPRECHT, Otto
German, 19th century.
Born 5 May 1846, in Augsburg; died 7 May 1893, in Munich.
Painter. Genre scenes.
Otto Ruprecht was a pupil of W. von Diez.
Auction records:
Stuttgart, 8 Sept 1979, *Der Batzenbauer* (oil on canvas, 32 x 25 1/2 ins / 81 x 65 cm) DEM 12,000.

RUPRECHT, P.
German, 19th century.
Active in 1823.
Miniaturist.
P. Ruprecht painted portraits of princes and princesses.
Museums and Galleries:
Munich (Stadtmus.): *Portrait of Princess Theresa Charlotte of Saxony Altenberg*.

RURAWSKI, Alfred
Polish, 19th century.
Born 17 October 1841, in Warsaw; died 28 June 1873, in Warsaw.
Painter, watercolourist, engraver (wood). Portraits, landscapes.
Alfred Rurawski studied in Warsaw.
Museums and Galleries:
Warsaw (Muz. Narodowe): *Mountain Dweller* (watercolour).

RURBACH, Wenzel
Austrian, 18th - 19th century.
Born 1745; died 19 October 1827, in Vienna.
Portrait artist.

RUREMONDE, Jan van. See **RUMMEN**

RURIK
French, 20th - 21st century.
Born 1960, in Dieudonné (Oise).
Painter.
'Rurik' is the son of the painter Pierre Dmitrienko. He studied sculpture under César at the École des Beaux-Arts in Paris, and now lives in the French capital.

He has shown examples of his work at group exhibitions, notably in 1981 at the Centre Culturel in Villeparisis. His solo

xhibitions to date have included his first - at the La Cité Gal-
ry in Luxembourg in 1979, and subsequent one-man hows at the International Monetary Fund headquarters in Vashington DC in 1981 and, in 1984, at the Villa Medici in ome.
IUSEUMS AND GALLERIES:
ARIS (FNAC).

RURMOND, Balthasar von, or Rormund or Reumund
German, 16th century.
Active in Cologne 1553-1596.
Sculptor (wood).
Cologne School.

RUSCA, Antonio I
Italian, 17th - 18th century.
Active in Milan.
Painter.
usca painted a *St Maurice* for the church of St Benedict in errara.

RUSCA, Antonio II
Italian, 19th century.
Active in Rancate (Ticino) during the first half of the 19th century.
Sculptor.
he nephew of Grazioso Rusca and pupil of C. Pacetti, Antoio Rusca II worked at Milan Cathedral between 1808 and 821, carving statues of the apostle Simon, eleven saints and our prophets.

RUSCA, Bartolomeo or Bartolomé
Swiss, 18th century.
Born in Rovio, near Lugano; died 1745, in Milan.
Painter.
artolomeo Rusca painted frescoes in the convent of St Aargaret in Lugano. He became painter to the court of Aadrid in 1714.

RUSCA, Carlo Francesco or Francesco Carlo, or Ruschi
Swiss, 18th century.
Born 1696, in Torricella; died 11 May 1769, in Milan.
Painter, draughtsman. History painting, religious subjects, portraits.
Iaving started by studying law, Carlo Francesco Rusca deoted himself to painting and was a pupil of Amiconi in urin. He later went to Venice and travelled in Switzerland nd Germany, with notable stays in Hanover and Berlin, as vell as visiting England. It would appear that he finally setled in Milan.
IUSEUMS AND GALLERIES:
BERLIN (Mus. Hohenzollern): *Frederick II, Heir to the Throne, vith his Three Brothers* - BERN: *Heinrich von Erlach; Mayor saak von Steiger* - BRUNSWICK (Herzog Anton Ulrich-Mus.): *Old Man's Head; Colonel Przovski; Duke Charles I* - ERLACH: *Mayor Jerome von Erlach* - KASSEL: *Monk Reading* - SCHW-ERIN (Staatliches Mus.): *Two Studies of an Old Man's Head* - VENICE: *Jesus and the Woman of Samaria.*
AUCTION RECORDS:
LONDON, 26 Oct 1990, *Portrait of a Gentleman in a Blue Suit and Shirt with White Lace Ruffle and Cuffs* (1735, oil on canvas, 50 1/2 x 38 ins / 128 x 96.5 cm) GBP 4,400. LONDON, 17 Oct 1997, *Portrait of a Turk* (oil on panel, 9 x 6 3/4 ins / 23 x 17 cm) GBP 6,325. PARIS, 25 Oct 2002, *Portrait of an Actor in Don Quixote* (1737, oil on canvas, 19 x 15 ins / 49 x 38 cm) EUR 2,500.

RUSCA, Castello Francesco
Italian, 17th century.
Sculptor.
From 1625 to 1649, Castello Francesco Rusca sculpted 13 busts for the Monastero Maggiore in Milan.

RUSCA, Ernesto
Italian, 19th century.
Born 15 August 1864.
Active in Milan.
Painter, decorative designer, architect.
A pupil of the Accademia di Belle Arti di Brera, Ernesto Rusca studied under C. Boito and L. Cavenaghi. He carved many sculptures for the churches and private and public buildings of Milan and other towns in northern Italy.
MUSEUMS AND GALLERIES:
BERN (Kunstmus.): portraits of famous Swiss artists.

RUSCA, Francesco
Italian, 16th century.
Sculptor.
Francesco Rusca produced some gargoyles on the apse of Como Cathedral, with Bernardo Bianchi.

RUSCA, Francesco. See also **RUSCHI**

RUSCA, Gerolamo
Italian, 19th century.
Active in Milan.
Sculptor.
The son of Grazioso Rusca, Gerolamo Rusca worked at Milan Cathedral between 1823 and 1871.

RUSCA, Giorgio
Italian, 18th century.
Active in Milan towards the end of the 18th century.
Sculptor.
Giorgio Rusca worked at the cathedral in Milan in 1791.

RUSCA, Giovanni Battista
Italian, 18th century.
Born 24 June 1718, in Verona; died 22 October 1808, in Verona.
Portrait artist.
A pupil of Balestra and D. Pecchio, Giovanni Battista Rusca was inspector of fine arts for the city and province of Verona.

RUSCA, Giuseppe
Italian, 18th - 19th century.
Active in Milan from 1789 to 1812.
Sculptor.
Giuseppe Rusca sculpted the low relief adorning the southern pillar of the façade of the cathedral in Milan.

RUSCA, Grazioso
Italian, 18th - 19th century.
Born 1757, in Rancate; died 18 June 1829, in Milan.
Sculptor.
The father of Gerolamo Rusca, uncle of Antonio Rusca and pupil of Stefano Salterio, Grazioso Rusca worked for the cathedral in Milan from 1785 onwards. He also produced sculptures for the cathedral in Cremona and for churches in Piacenza and Altdorf.

RUSCA, Matteo
Italian, 19th century.
Born c. 1809, in Arosio; died 19 January 1886, in Parma.
Stucco artist.
Matteo Rusca executed decorations in stucco in a number of churches in Parma and Piacenza.

RUSCH, Dietrich or Diedrich
German, 19th - 20th century.
Born 29 June 1863, near Hanover.
Painter. Architectural views, landscapes.
Rusch studied in Weimar under Wald. Friedrich and Theodor Hagen.

Museums and Galleries:
Weimar: *Smallholding in the Lower Elbe.*

RUSCH, Heinrich

German, 18th century.
Active in the first half of the 18th (?) century.
Sculptor (wood).

Heinrich Rusch sculpted the pulpit in the church of Villyunen in East Prussia, now Kaliningrad, Russia.

RÜSCH, Jacob. See **RUSS**

RUSCH, Niklaus Lawlin. See **RUESCH**

RUSCHA, Edward Joseph, called Ed

American, 20th century.
Born 16 December 1937, in Omaha (Nebraska).
Painter, engraver, film producer, photographer.
Artists' books.
Conceptual Art.

In 1942 Edward Joseph Ruscha and his family settled in Oklahoma City. Rusha trained as a commercial artist at the Chouinard Art Institute, Los Angeles from 1956. He settled in Los Angeles.

Ruscha started painting in the mid-1950s in a style close to Abstract Expressionism and was later, perhaps wrongly, assimilated into Pop Art, although his early work showed similarities with that of Jasper Johns. In reality Ruscha's work was far more Realist than Pop, depicting neutral images with emotion. He later acknowledged the impact of works by Schwitters and Duchamp. In the early 1960s Ruscha took a long trip to Europe, including two months in Paris. During this time he made small oil paintings on paper representing names (Annie), emblems, signs seen in the street (Métropolitain, Boulangerie) and pictogrammes. From then on his drawings, paintings and engravings fell into two categories: object-images and word-images. Ruscha was seeking neutrality in both these choices of objects (pencils, olives, pills, sachets, golf balls) and also in the style in which he painted them. Ultimately, however, the objects can appear arbitrary, and the same is true of the standardised or vulgarised architecture he painted, including *20th Century Fox, Standard Station* (1966) and *Los Angeles County Museum on Fire* (1965-1968). These are perhaps literally 'commonplaces', whose linguistic counterparts in the form of simple words he set out carefully on coloured grounds, with a great deal of pictorial skill. Apart from the abovementioned *Annie* (1962), these pictures include *Stardust* (1966), *Murder* (1974), *Here* (1983), aphorisms such as *We Humans* (1974) and trompe l'oeil words which look as though they have been written in liquid, including *Adios* (1967) and *Eye* (1969). These 'Wetwords' are remarkable for the contrast between the minute detail of the trompe l'oeil, the striving for transparency, the impression of capillarity and the meaninglessness of the words, some of which return again and again, such as *Spent, Surgical, Hydraulic, Automatic, Adult* and *Sugar*.

Ruscha's works draw strongly on graphics, typography and the aesthetics of the cinema. Many of the commonplaces that he paints are taken from images of the American West and Hollywood.

It was while driving between Oklahoma City and Los Angeles at dusk that he became aware of the extraordinary degree of standardisation of buildings such as petrol stations and restaurants and of the logos to be seen along Route 66. In its carefully studied composition, its standardisation of words and the objectivity of language, Ruscha's work foreshadows conceptual art. From 1969 he began a series of paintings involving a wide range of substances, which he presents and catalogues in the form of simple marks on white paper. In the spirit of a collector he used a variety of organic materials, some edible, such as chocolate, caviar, egg yolk and tea, some inedible. In 1970 he made his first film, *Premium* and, in 1985, created a mural for the Mian Dade Public Library entitled *Words Without Thoughts Neve to Heaven.*

The same impression of neutralised meanings can b found in the books of photographs that Ruscha has mad and published since 1962. The first, *Twenty-Six Gasoline Sta tions*, published in 1962, sets the tone for the rest, all simpl collections of everyday things. With hindsight these works such as *Some Los Angeles Apartments* (1965), *Every Buildin on the Sunset Strip* (1966), *Thirty-Four Parking Lots in Lo Angeles* (1967), *A Few Palm Trees* (1971) and *Hard Ligh* (1978) seem very similar to some approaches of conceptua art, notably that of Huebler. In the spirit also reflected in hi paintings, Ruscha starts by using typographic and cinema ographic codes (framing, credits, subtitles) to combine tex and image in an original way. In 1965 he also worked on th layout of the journal *Art Forum*. He later abandoned text fo images alone, reproducing only things in his books, whic thus become collections of found items. In the English speaking world of art, these books, which are very differen from European books by painters, have now become mode for books by artists.

Ruscha has shown work in group exhibitions, includin *New Painting of Common Objects* at the Pasadena Art Muse um in 1962, *Los Angeles Now* at the Fraser Gallery, Londo in 1966, the 5th Paris Biennale in 1967, the Biennales of Pari and São Paulo and the 5th Kassel Documenta in 1972, *L'Es prit de famille* (*Family Spirit*) at the Villa du Parc, Annemass (France) in 2001, *Les Années 70: l'art en cause* (*The 1970s: A in Question*) at the Cape-Musée d'Art Contemporain, Bor deaux and *Sans commune mesure. Image et texte dans l'ar actuel* (*Without Common Measure: Image and Text in Con temporary Art*) at the Musée d'Art Moderne, Lille Métropole Villeneuve d'Ascq in 2002 and *C'est arrivé demain* (*It Hap pened Tomorrow*) at the Lyons Biennale in 2003. Before 196 most of Ruscha's solo shows were at the Ferus Gallery, Lo Angeles and in San Francisco. He has also had shows i New York, Paris, Munich, London and in 1985 at the Musé St-Pierre, Lyons (France). A travelling exhibition of his wor was launched in 1989 at the contemporary galleries of th Centre Georges-Pompidou, Paris, before going on to th Museum Boymans van Beunigen, Rotterdam, the Fundaci Caixa de Pensions, Barcelona, the Serpentine Gallery, Lon don and the Museum of Contemporary Art, Los Angeles. I 2001 the Museum of Modern Art, Oxford hosted a retro spective of Ruscha's work and there have been many othe exhibitions devoted to him, including *Edward Ruscha. Mad in Los Angeles* at the Museo Nacional Centro de Arte Rein Sofia, Madrid, in 2002 and at the National Gallery of Ar Washington in 2004.

Bibliography:

Ruscha, Edward, *Twenty six gasoline stations*, Cunninghan Press, Alhambra (CA), 1969. Hickey, Dave/Plagens, Peter *The works of Edward Ruscha*, exhibition catalogue, Sa Francisco Museum of Modern Art, San Francisco, 1982. Cu eff, A., *'Edward Ruscha: un monde éloigné'* in *Parkett*, peri odical, Zurich, December 1988. Hulten, Pontus/Cameron Dan/Blistène, Bernard, *'Edward Ruscha'* in *coll. Contempo rains*, exhibition catalogue, Éd. du Centre Georges-Pompid ou, Paris, 1989. Bois, Yve Alain, *Edward Ruscha, romanc with liquids: paintings 1966-1969*, exhibition catalogue, Riz zoli, Gagosian Gall., New York, 1993. Engberg, Siri, *'Edwar Ruscha. Editions, 1959-1999: catalogue raisonné'* in *2 vol.*, ex hibition catalogue, Walker Art Center, Minneapolis, 199 *They called her Styrene*, Phaidon, London Paris, 2000 (collec tion of 600 'words' by the artist). Sprüth, Monika, et al., *E Ruscha: gunpowder and stains*, exhibition catalogue, Monik Sprüth Philomene Magers Galerie, Munich, 2000. Schwartz Alexandra (ed.), *Leave any information at the signal: writings interviews, bits, pages*, MIT Press, Cambridge (MA), 2002.

MUSEUMS AND GALLERIES:
EINDHOVEN (Van Abbe Mus.): *Pure Ecstasy* (1974) - GENEVA (Mamco) - HANOVER (Hood Museum of Art, Darmouth College): *Standard Station Amarillo Texas* (1963) - MARSEILLES (Mus. Cantini): *Here* (1983) - PARIS (MNAM-CCI) - RICHMOND (Virginia MFA): *Noise, Pencil, Broken Pencil* (1963, oil on canvas) - SAN DIEGO (MA): *Eternal Amnesia* (1982, oil on canvas); *End* (1983, oil on canvas); *Please...* (1985, oil on canvas).

AUCTION RECORDS:
LONDON, 1 July 1976, *Flash Fried* (1973, powder/paper, 11 1/2 x 29 1/4 ins / 29 x 74 cm) GBP 480. NEW YORK, 21 Oct 1976, *Keychain Music* (1974, pastel/paper, 23 x 28 ins / 58.5 x 71 cm) USD 1,500. LOS ANGELES, 27 Sept 1977, *Mocha Standard* (1969, brown silk screen print, 19 1/2 x 37 ins / 49.7 x 93.9 cm) USD 800. NEW YORK, 2 Nov 1978, *20th Century Fox with Searchlights* (1962, oil on canvas, 67 x 132 ins / 170 x 335 cm) USD 57,500. NEW YORK, 18 May 1979, *LA* (1971, pastel and powder/paper, 11 1/2 x 29 ins / 29 x 73.5 cm) USD 1,800. NEW YORK, 18 May 1979, *Noise, Pencil, Broken Pencil, Cheap Western* (1966, acrylic/canvas, 71 1/4 x 67 ins / 181 x 170 cm) USD 44,000. LOS ANGELES, 25 Sept 1979, *Cheese Mold Standard with Olive* (1969, silk screen print in colour, 19 3/4 x 37 ins / 50 x 93.8 cm) USD 1,200. NEW YORK, 13 May 1981, *Peeler* (1972, gunpowder/paper, 11 1/2 x 29 ins / 29.3 x 73.7 cm) USD 1,900. LOS ANGELES, 3 Feb 1982, *Hollywood* (1969, grey lithograph, 4 1/4 x 17 ins / 10.5 x 43.2 cm) USD 2,000. NEW YORK, 2 May 1983, *Hollywood with Observatory* (1969, pale blue and black lithograph, 12 1/2 x 29 1/2 ins / 32 x 75 cm) USD 1,400. NEW YORK, 2 Nov 1984, *Chili Draft* (1974, gunpowder/paper, 14 x 22 3/4 ins / 35.7 x 57.6 cm) USD 2,200. NEW YORK, 2 Nov 1984, *Just an Average Guy* (1978, oil on canvas, 22 x 80 ins / 55.8 x 203.2 cm) USD 16,000. NEW YORK, 6 Nov 1985, *Dimple* (1964, tempera and ink/paper, 11 1/2 x 15 ins / 29.3 x 37.2 cm) USD 2,500. NEW YORK, 6 May 1986, *Mint* (1968, acrylic/canvas, 60 x 55 ins / 152.5 x 139.7 cm) USD 29,000. NEW YORK, 6 May 1987, *Protein* (coloured chalks and powder/paper, 23 x 29 ins / 58.4 x 73.7 cm) USD 6,200. NEW YORK, 4 Nov 1987, *Strange Catch for a Freshwater Fish* (1965, oil on canvas, 59 x 55 ins / 149.7 x 139.6 cm) USD 72,500. NEW YORK, 8 Oct 1988, *Went Out for Cigarettes* (1985, varnish and oil on canvas, 64 x 64 ins / 162.5 x 162.5 cm) USD 77,000. NEW YORK, 10 Nov 1988, *Strength* (1983, gunpowder and chalks/paper, 60 x 40 ins / 152.3 x 101.8 cm) USD 33,000. NEW YORK, 2 May 1989, *The Future* (1981, oil on canvas, 22 x 79 3/4 ins / 55 x 202.5 cm) USD 209,000. PARIS, 21 June 1989, *Pressurized Diabolics* (1976, pastel/paper, 22 1/2 x 28 1/4 ins / 57 x 72 cm) FRF 300,000. NEW YORK, 5 Oct 1989, *Jr. 1988* (dry pigment and acrylic/paper, 60 x 40 ins / 152.5 x 101.5 cm) USD 60,500. NEW YORK, 9 Nov 1989, *Honey... I Twist Through More...* (1984, oil on canvas, 72 x 72 ins / 183 x 183 cm) USD 297,000. NEW YORK, 23 Feb 1990, *Flash Fried* (1973, gunpowder/paper, 11 1/2 x 29 ins / 29.2 x 73.7 cm) USD 38,500. NEW YORK, 27 Feb 1990, *You Know the Old Story* (1975, gunpowder and pastel/paper, 13 x 22 3/4 ins / 33 x 57.7 cm) USD 41,250. NEW YORK, 7 May 1990, *Squeezing Dimple* (1964, oil on canvas, 28 x 29 3/4 ins / 71.2 x 75.5 cm) USD 165,000. NEW YORK, 5 Oct 1990, *Halloween 1977* (oil on canvas, 22 x 80 ins / 55.6 x 203.2 cm) USD 165,000. NEW YORK, 1 May 1991, *Artificial Park* (1988, acrylic/canvas, 54 x 120 ins / 137 x 305 cm) USD 187,000. NEW YORK, 12 Nov 1991, *Not a Bad World, Is It?* (1984, oil on canvas, 99 1/4 x 79 3/4 ins / 251.8 x 202.5 cm) USD 132,000. NEW YORK, 5 May 1992, *Days of the Week* (1979, oil on canvas, 22 1/4 x 80 ins / 56.2 x 203.2 cm) USD 77,000. NEW YORK, 18 Nov 1992, *The Study of Friction and Wear on Mating Surfaces* (1983, oil on canvas, 83 3/4 x 124 ins / 213 x 315 cm) USD 71,500. NEW YORK, 23-25 Feb 1993, *Light (Part I)* (acrylic/canvas, 62 x 138 ins / 157.5 x 350.5 cm) USD 112,500. FRANKFURT AM MAIN, 14 June 1994, *Two Glasses* (1993, acrylic/paper, 14 3/4 x 11 1/2 ins / 37.3 x 29 cm) DEM 10,000. NEW YORK, 15 Nov 1995, *City* (1961, oil on paper/card, 8 3/4 x 7 1/4 ins / 22.2 x 18.5 cm) USD 31,050. NEW YORK, 8 May 1996, *Untitled* (1987, acrylic and oil on canvas, 60 x 60 ins / 152.7 x 152.4 cm) USD 51,750. NEW YORK, 9 Nov 1996, *Hollywood* (1968, colour lithograph, 12 1/2 x 40 3/4 ins / 31.8 x 103.7 cm) USD 11,500. NEW YORK, 20 Nov 1996, *The Funneling of You-Know-What* (1985, acrylic and dry pigment/paper, 40 x 60 ins / 101.6 x 152.4 cm) USD 18,400. NEW YORK, 21 Nov 1996, *Dream 1* (1987, acrylic/paper, 17 1/4 x 46 1/4 ins / 43.5 x 117.5 cm) USD 39,100. LONDON, 6 Dec 1996, *PM* (1988, dry pigment and acrylic/paper, 30 x 40 1/4 ins / 76.5 x 102.25 cm) GBP 27,600. NEW YORK, 6 May 1997, *Untitled (Window)* (1984, colour chalks/paper, 23 x 40 1/4 ins / 58.4 x 102.2 cm) USD 6,325. NEW YORK, 8 May 1997, *Little White Girl* (1986, pigment/paper, 58 x 38 ins / 147.3 x 96.5 cm) USD 70,700. LONDON, 27 June 1997, *These are Brave Days* (1989, dry pigment/paper, 40 x 60 ins / 101.5 x 152.5 cm) GBP 13,800. NEW YORK, 19 Nov 1997, *Ripe* (1967, oil on canvas, 59 1/4 x 54 3/4 ins / 150.3 x 139.1 cm) USD 167,500. NEW YORK, 6 and 7 March 1998, *Brews* (1970, colour lithograph, 18 x 26 3/4 ins / 45.7 x 68.2 cm) USD 2,587. NEW YORK, 17 Nov 1999, *Lisp* (1968, oil on canvas, 59 x 55 ins / 150 x 139 cm) USD 420,000. LOS ANGELES, 7 June 2000, *House on 38th St* (1965, oil on canvas, 20 x 22 ins / 51 x 56 cm) USD 130,000. LOS ANGELES, 7 June 2000, *Honk* (1962, oil, black ink and pencil on paper laid on board, 16 x 16 ins / 40 x 41 cm) USD 220,000. NEW YORK, 14 May 2001, *Truth* (1973, oil on canvas, 54 x 60 ins / 136 x 153 cm) USD 240,000. NEW YORK, 14 Nov 2001, *Untitled* (1989, acrylic on canvas, 60 x 112 ins / 152 x 284 cm) USD 620,000. NEW YORK, 13 May 2002, *Untitled* (1963, oil on canvas, 67 x 72 ins / 170 x 183 cm) USD 2,300,000. NEW YORK, 14 May 2002, *Talk About Space* (1963, oil on canvas, 71 x 67 ins / 181 x 170 cm) USD 3,200,000. NEW YORK, 11 Nov 2003, *Mind - Red* (1968, oil on canvas, 60 x 55 ins / 152 x 140 cm) USD 1,400,000. NEW YORK, 12 Nov 2003, *Not Only Securing the Last Letter but Damaging It As Well, Boss* (1964, oil on canvas, 59 x 55 ins / 150 x 140 cm) USD 1,700,000. NEW YORK, 11 May 2004, *News* (1990, acrylic on canvas, 96 x 72 ins / 244 x 183 cm) USD 550,000. NEW YORK, 11 May 2004, *Damage* (1964, oil on canvas, 72 x 67 ins / 183 x 170 cm) USD 3,200,000.

RUSCHE, Richard
German, 19th century.
Born 17 March 1851, in Diesdorf, near Magdeburg.
Painter, draughtsman. Hunting scenes, animals.

Richard Rusche was a pupil of Fritz Schaper. He drew illustrations for hunting books.

RUSCHEL, Hans, or Rischel or Rüschel
German, 17th century.
Born c. 1576; died 27 July 1628, in Breslau (now Wroclaw, Poland).
Painter.

Hans Ruschel was a pupil of Peter Fichtenberger.

RUSCHER, Alois
Austrian, 19th century.
Active in Bizau in the second half of the 19th century.
Sculptor.

In 1870 Alois Ruscher sculpted statues for the churches of Hinterreuthe, Mittelberg and Schnepfau.

RUSCHEWEYH, Ferdinand
German, 19th century.
Born 1785, in Neustrelitz; died 21 December 1846, in Neustrelitz.
Draughtsman, engraver.

Ferdinand Ruscheweyh studied in Berlin under Daniel Berger and in Vienna. He produced engravings after Raphael, Michelangelo and Peter Cornelius.

RUSCHI, Bernardina
Italian, 17th century.
Died 11 September 1649, in Lucca.
Painter.
Bernardina Ruschi was a nun and worked in the convent of St George in Lucca from 1619 onwards.

RUSCHI, Francesco, or Rusca
Italian, 17th century.
Born c. 1600, in Rome; died 1661, in Venice.
Painter, draughtsman, engraver. Mythological subjects, religious subjects.
Francesco Ruschi was active from 1643 to 1656. He was influenced by Pietro da Cortona and for the most part painted religious subjects.
MUSEUMS AND GALLERIES:
TREVISO (Churches) - TREVISO (Mus. Civico L. Bailo): *Banishment of Hagar* - VENICE (Churches) - VICENZA (Churches).
AUCTION RECORDS:
NEW YORK, 17 June 1982, *Hercules and Omphale* (oil on canvas, 41¾ x 49¼in/106 x 125cm) USD 15,000. LONDON, 12 Dec 1990, *Venus Mourning the Death of Adonis* (oil on canvas, 48 x 66¾in/122 x 169.5cm) GBP 27,500. NEW YORK, 31 May 1991, *Crucifixion* (oil on canvas, 60¼ x 40½in/153 x 103cm) USD 18,700. ROME, 9 Dec 1997, *Rebecca and Eleizer* (oil on canvas, 44½ x 63in/113 x 160cm) ITL 23,000,000. NEW YORK, 28 Jan 2000, *Allegory of the Fifth and Sixth Beatitudes, Purity of Heart and Forgiveness* (oil on canvas, 61 x 91 ins / 154 x 232 cm) USD 120,000. MILAN, 12 June 2001, *Moses Saved from the River* (oil on canvas, 46 x 57 ins / 118 x 145 cm) ITL 32,000,000. NEW YORK, 3 Oct 2001, *Hercules and Omphale* (oil on canvas, 38 x 48 ins / 97 x 122 cm) USD 50,000. NEW YORK, 23 Jan 2004, *Venus Mourning the Death of Adonis* (oil on canvas, 58 x 47 ins / 148 x 120 cm) USD 26,000. MILAN, 26 May 2004, *Venus Mourning Adonis* (oil on canvas, 48 x 67 ins / 123 x 170 cm) EUR 46,000.

RUSCHI, Francesco Carlo. See **RUSCA Carlo Francesco**

RUSCHKE, Egmont or Theodor Egmont
German, 19th century.
Born 5 August 1815, in Burg, near Magdeburg.
Lithographer.
Egmont Ruschke was a pupil of L. Veit in Berlin and later of Charles Fuchs in Hamburg.

RUSCHOF, Heinrich
German, 18th century.
Active in Cologne c. 1729.
Glass painter.

RUSCIOLLI. See **RUCHOLLE**

RUSCONE, Giovanni Antonio. See **RUSCONI**

RUSCONI, Albertino and Giacomo. See **RASCONI**

RUSCONI, Benedetto. See **DIANA**

RUSCONI, Camillo
Italian, 17th - 18th century.
Born 14 July 1658, in Milan; died 8 December 1728, in Rome.
Sculptor. Religious subjects. Statues, medallions.
School of Rome.
The pupil of Volpini and Giuseppe Rosnati in Milan, Camillo Rusconi was also influenced by Maratti. He sculpted numerous tombs, statues, medallions and low reliefs in various churches in Rome. He is also said to have been the pupil of Bernini, and evidence that he imitated Bernini's style is apparent in particular in the funeral sculptures of the Paravicini in the church of S Francesco a Ripa in Rome, and also in the high Baroque drama of Rusconi's four *Apostles* among the twelve produced between 1708 and 1718 for the cathedral of S Giovanni in Laterano in Rome. One of his most important works is the *Monument to Pope Gregory XIII*, sculpted entirely in white marble in St Peter's Basilica between 1719 and 1725.

RUSCONI, Franz Karl
Swiss, 18th century.
Born 1693, in Lucerne; died 23 April 1748.
Painter. Coats of arms.
MUSEUMS AND GALLERIES:
LUCERNE (Municipal Mus.): several works.

RUSCONI, Giovanni Antonio, or Ruscone
Italian, 16th century.
Born c. 1520, in Ticino (Switzerland); died 1587, in Venice.
Painter, architect, engineer.
Giovanni Antonio Rusconi was in the service of the city of Venice.

RUSCONI, Giuseppe
Italian, 18th century.
Born 9 November 1687, in Tremona, near Como; died 1737 or 1758, in Rome.
Sculptor.
The pupil and assistant of Camillo Rusconi, Giuseppe Rusconi produced sculptures for St Peter's Basilica and the Basilica of S Giovanni in Laterano in Rome.
MUSEUMS AND GALLERIES:
ROME (Mus. Capitolini, Pinacoteca Capitolina): *Camillo Rusconi* (bust).

RUSCONI, Pietro
Italian, 18th century.
Active in Perugia in 1790.
Stucco artist.

RUSCONI, Pietro Martire
Italian, 18th century.
Born in Sondrio; died 1761, in Milan.
Painter, draughtsman, writer. Landscapes.
Pietro Martire Rusconi was the pupil of P. Ronzoni.

RUSER, Ernst
German, 19th - 20th century.
Born 13 February 1869, in Bleckendorf; died 14 August 1934, in Kohlgrub.
Painter.
Ernst Ruser lived and worked in Erfurt and in Kapellendorf, near Weimar.

RUSERUTI, Filippo. See **RUSUTI**

RUSH, J. A.
British, 20th century.
Painter. Seascapes.
AUCTION RECORDS:
LONDON, 27 Sept 1946, *Ships on a Calm Sea*, GBP 54.

RUSH, Olive
American, 20th century.
Born in Fairmount (Indiana); died 1966.
Painter. Murals.
Olive Rush studied in New York and Paris. She was a member of the New York Watercolorists Club. Her reputation was based largely on her teaching and her encouragement of Indian cultural traditions. She was the first woman to be given a solo exhibition in New Mexico.
BIBLIOGRAPHY:
Cuba, Stanley L., *Olive Rush: A Hoosier Artist in New Mexico*, 1992.

RUSH, William
American, 18th - 19th century.

Born 4 July 1756, in Philadelphia; died 17 January 1833, in Philadelphia.
Sculptor (wood).

William Rush was a pupil of E. Cutbush. He sculpted statues, as well as a fountain and a crucifix, for various churches and public monuments in Philadelphia. Some of the highly original figureheads he produced at the beginning of his career can now be seen in Philadelphia and Annapolis.

MUSEUMS AND GALLERIES:
ANNAPOLIS (Naval Academy Mus.): figureheads - PHILADELPHIA (Independence Hall): figureheads.

AUCTION RECORDS:
NEW YORK, 31 May 1985, *Andrew Jackson* (painted terracotta, h. 20 ins / 50.5 cm) USD 250,000.

RUSHBROKE
British, 18th century.
Draughtsman. Portraits.

MUSEUMS AND GALLERIES:
LONDON (British Mus.): *Portrait of the Actor David Garrick* (two).

RUSHBURY, Henry George (Sir)
British, 20th century.
Born 28 October 1889, in Harborne, near Birmingham; died 1968.
Painter, draughtsman, watercolourist, draughtsman, engraver, illustrator. Urban landscapes, architectural views, designs for stained glass and murals.

The father of the painter Julia Rushbury, Sir Henry Rushbury trained at the Birmingham College of Art (1903 to 1909). He worked as an assistant to Henry Payne and went to live in London in 1912. He travelled to France, Spain and Italy, and later in life settled in Lewes. He was official war artist in both World War I and World War II. He was encouraged by Francis Dodd to take up engraving.

Up to 1920, he etched views and landscapes, then concentrated on buildings, while figures remained rare. He excelled in delineated buildings and the representation of complicated structures, achieving a consistent level of excellence with little development in style. Works include *The Quarry* (1912); *The Harbour, Lowestoft* (1916); *Old Deal* (1920); *Château Gaillard* (1921); *Les Baux, Provence* (1922); *Canale de la Douane, Marseilles* (1930); *Walls of Gerona* (1936).

He exhibited in London at the Royal Academy, the Royal Watercolour Society, the Fine Art Society and the Goupil Gallery.

BIBLIOGRAPHY:
Schwabe, R., '*The Etchings of Henry Rushbury*' in *Print Collectors Quarterly*, no. 10, periodical, 1923 (includes catalogue of works (1912-1923) by H.J.L. Wright). Salaman, M., '*Rushbury*' in *Modern Masters of Etchings* no. 18, periodical, The Studio, London, 1928.

MUSEUMS AND GALLERIES:
LONDON (Courtauld Institute of Art, De Witt Library) - LONDON (Tate Collection): *Forest of Brotonne* (1920, drawing); *Brewery Yard* (1920, drawing); *Palazzo Uguccione, Florence* (1922, drawing); *Ship in Dock* (c. 1925-1926, drawing); *St Paul's* (1930, drawing); *Repairing the Sails* (c. 1923, drawing); *La Rochelle* (c. 1923, drawing).

AUCTION RECORDS:
LONDON, 13 April 1928, *Versailles, the Orangerie* (drawing) GBP 1. LONDON, 17 Dec 1930, *Florence and its Palaces* (drawing) GBP 22. LONDON, 20 March 1936, *Front at Brighton* (pen and coloured chalk) GBP 16. LONDON, 11 Dec 1936, *View of Edinburgh* (drawing) GBP 16. GLASGOW, 7 Feb 1989, *Sanctuary* (watercolour, 7 1/2 x 22 ins / 19 x 55 cm) GBP 1,430. CREWKERNE, 17 Oct 2002, *Godmanchester. The Common, St Ives* (1934, watercolour and pencil, a pair, 18 x 10 ins / 45 x 25 cm) GBP 1,050.

RUSHCHITS, Ferdinand Eduardovich, or Rushits
Russian, 19th - 20th century.
Born 1870; died 1936.
Painter.

Rushchits is the same person as Ferdynand Ruszczyc.

MUSEUMS AND GALLERIES:
MOSCOW (State Tretyakov Gal.): *In Spring; Early Spring.*

RUSHTON, David
British, 20th - 21st century.
Born 1950.
Painter (mixed media), installation artist.
Conceptual Art.
Art & Language group.

RUSHTON, William C.
British, 19th - 20th century.
Born c. 1875; died 1921.
Painter. Landscapes.

MUSEUMS AND GALLERIES:
BRADFORD (Cartwright Hall AG): *In the Crimple Country.*

AUCTION RECORDS:
GLASGOW, 16 April 1996, *Shore at Cramond* (oil on canvas, 12 1/4 x 18 ins / 31 x 46 cm) GBP 747.

RUSIECKI, Boleslav Michal
Polish, 19th - 20th century.
Born 23 November 1824; died 31 January 1913, in Vilno (now Vilnius, Lithuania).
Painter.

Rusiecki was the son of Kanut Rusiecki, and studied with Brüloff and Bruni at the academy of art in St Petersburg. He executed religious paintings for the cathedral in Vilno (now Vilnius) and for churches in Grodno and Trzcianny.

RUSIECKI, Kanuty
Polish, 19th century.
Born 1801, in Lithuania; died 21 August 1860, in Vilna (now Vilnius, Lithuania).
Painter.

Kanuty Rusiecki began his studies in Paris in 1821, under Lethière, and then worked in Rome with Camuccini. He was one of the founders of the modern school of painting in Poland. One of his works, *A Young Italian*, featured in the *Exposition des Artistes Polonais* (*Exhibition of Polish Artists*) held in 1921 at the Salon de la Société Nationale des Beaux-Arts in Paris. The museum in Cracow owns his *Portrait of the Artist's Wife*, the Lubomirski museum in Lviv (Ukraine) owns his *Church of St Anne in Vilnius in Winter*, and the National Museum in Warsaw owns his *Mountain of the Three Crosses near Vilnius*.

RUSIECKI, Ludomir
Polish, 19th century.
Painter.

The National Museum in Warsaw owns a work by Ludomir Rusiecki, *Two Polish Horsemen in 17th-century Dress.*

RUSIÑOL Y PRATS, Santiago
Spanish, 19th - 20th century.
Born 25 February 1861, in Barcelona; died 13 June 1931, in Aranjuez (Castile-La Mancha).
Active in France.
Painter, watercolourist, draughtsman, writer. Portraits, scenes with figures, genre scenes, interiors with figures, landscapes, urban landscapes, gardens.

Santiago Rusiñol studied in Barcelona under Tomás Moragas and spent a long period in Paris, working initially at the Académie Gervex. He settled in Montmartre, where he was closely associated with Miguel Utrillo, Ramón Casas and Zuloaga. His mentors/tutors at the Académie de la Palette included Eugène Carrière and Puvis de Chavannes. He moved in artistic circles and was friendly with Daudet, Toulet, Cumonsky and Erik Satie. He returned to Barcelona in 1894.

Rusiñol must rank among the most important Catalan landscape painters of his day. He was a founder member of Els Quatre Gats, the avant-garde Barcelona group that later attracted Picasso and Nonell. He acquired two paintings by El Greco, one of which - a *Mary Magdalene* - he ceremoniously donated to the Catalan museum in Barcelona. His residence in Sitges (Cau Ferrat) was decorated by him and was a mecca for the avant-garde of the day. It was subsequently converted into a museum dedicated to his work and operated by the Barcelona Museum of Modern Art.

His earliest work was in the realist mode and betrayed the influence of Whistler, Impressionism and Japanese prints. Over time, his painting evolved towards a discreet Symbolism and was subsequently influenced by horticultural aesthetics (notably in his *Deserted Gardens*, published in 1900). The garden theme was a recurrent one and dominates what is widely regarded as his most productive period, when he produced *Path in the Park, Garden in Bloom, Flowering Almond Trees* and *Greenery*, works that were inspired by gardens in Aranjuez, Majorca, Horta (Barcelona) and the Alhambra. He was in the habit of painting at his home in Sitges while surrounded by young and aspiring artists. Together with Ramón Casas, he can be credited with introducing major western European trends into Spanish painting - the English Pre-Raphaelites, the Symbolism of Maeterlinck's *Pelleas*, Expressionist currents from Scandinavia, Whistler's dandyism, 'cosmic' post-Romanticism from Germany and, not least, a sense of sordid realism and moral decline nourished by Forain, Steinlen and Toulouse-Lautrec (in works such as *Café* and *Portrait of Clarasso*). These and other modernist influences would later merge in the work of the architect Antoní Gaudí and have an impact on the work of Picasso and Nonell y Monturiol.

Rusiñol was also a prominent author, playwright, poet and art critic. Examples of his theatrical work include *The Conjurer, The First Card* and *The Feminist*.

He received various awards and distinctions, including a medal of honour in 1904, a gold medal in 1908 and a further gold in 1912. The French government elevated him to the rank of Chevalier of the Légion d'Honneur. He started exhibiting in 1878, in Gerona. His work featured on several occasions at the Parès Salon in Barcelona and he also exhibited in Paris (at the Salon des Artistes Français), Rome, Venice, Buenos Aires and Chicago.

S. Rusiñol

BIBLIOGRAPHY:

Arnáiz, José Manuel/López Jiménez, Javier/Merchán Díaz, Manuel (ed.), *'Cien años de pintura en Espana y Portugal (1830-1930)'* in vol. IX, Antiqvaria, Madrid, 1992.

MUSEUMS AND GALLERIES:

BARCELONA (MAM del Mus. Nacional d'Art de Catalunya): *Utrillo in front of the Moulin de la Galette, Paris* - CASTRES (Mus. Goya): *Orangery* (1904) - MONTPELLIER (Mus. Fabre): *Gardens in Majorca* - NEW YORK (Hispanic Society of America): *Calvary at Sagunto* (1901) - PARIS (Mus. d'Orsay) - SITGES (Mus. Cau Ferrat): *Mystique; Angelus; Nightwatch.*

AUCTION RECORDS:

PARIS, 1 July 1943, *Golden Cypresses*, FRF 11,500; *Soller Valley*, FRF 16,500. PARIS, 4 Dec 1944, *Garden Steps in Barcelona*, FRF 9,200. MADRID, 13 Dec 1973, *Patio with White Columns*, ESP 460,000. BARCELONA, 21 June 1979, *Mountain Landscape* (oil on canvas, 50 x 35¾ ins / 127 x 91 cm) ESP 450,000. BARCELONA, 6 May 1981, *Garden* (oil on canvas, 59 x 47¼ ins / 150 x 120 cm) ESP 700,000. BARCELONA, 19 Dec 1984, *En la fuente* (oil on canvas, 38½ x 61¾ ins / 98 x 157 cm) ESP 2,300,000. MADRID, 19 Dec 1985, *Gardens at Aranjuez* (oil on canvas, 46 x 57¾ ins / 116 x 147 cm) ESP 3,500,000. BARCELONA, 18 Dec 1986, *Garden* (oil on canvas, 40½ x 48½ ins / 103 x 123 cm) ESP 40,000,000. BARCELONA, 17 June 1987, *Garden in Bloom* (oil on canvas, 32¾ x 41 ins / 83 x 104 cm) ESP 7,200,000. NEW YORK, 24 Oct 1989, *Market in Valencia* (oil on canvas, 32 x 39¾ ins / 81 x 101 cm) USD 352,000. MADRID, 22 April 1999, *Evening Waters, Sierra del Montseny* (c. 1928, oil on canvas, 39 x 44 ins / 100 x 112 cm) ESP 13,000,000. MADRID, 25 May 1999, *El cami de ses monjes, Majorca* (oil on canvas, 29 x 39 ins / 74 x 98 cm) ESP 13,000,000. MADRID, 20 March 2000, *Gardens of Spain, Valencia* (oil on canvas, 31 x 39 ins / 80 x 100 cm) ESP 13,000,000. MADRID, 6 Nov 2000, *Landscape in Majorca* (oil on canvas, 37 x 41 ins / 94 x 105 cm) ESP 19,000,000. MADRID, 3 April 2001, *Garden* (oil on canvas, 39 x 27 ins / 99 x 68 cm) ESP 14,500,000. LONDON, 19 Nov 2001, *Jardines of Aranjuez in Autumn* (1919, oil on canvas, 33 x 37 ins / 85 x 95 cm) GBP 70,000. LONDON, 19 Nov 2002, *Fishermen's House, Majorca* (1905, oil on canvas, 35 x 51 ins / 89 x 129 cm) GBP 160,000. MADRID, 21 Jan 2003, *Boat Keeper* (oil on canvas, 32 x 59 ins / 81 x 151 cm) EUR 27,000. LONDON, 18 Nov 2003, *View along the River Jucar, Cuenca* (oil on canvas, 39 x 51 ins / 100 x 130 cm) GBP 120,000. MADRID, 6 Oct 2004, *Dusk in Catalonia* (oil on canvas, 31 x 47 ins / 80 x 120 cm) EUR 70,000.

RUSIOLO, Mercurio

Italian, 16th century.
Born 16th century, in San Ginesio (Marche).
Painter.

Mercurio Rusiolo was the pupil of Domenico Malpiedi.

RUSKIEWICZ, August

Polish, 19th century.
Born 1826, in Warsaw.
Draughtsman. Landscapes.

August Ruskiewicz studied at the school of art in Warsaw. The National Museum in Warsaw owns two of his drawings.

RUSKIEWICZ, Franciszek

Polish, 19th century.
Born 2 April 1819, in Warsaw; died 18 April 1883, in Warsaw.
Painter. Landscapes.

Franciszek was the brother of August Ruskiewicz. The National Museum in Warsaw owns some of his paintings.

RUSKIN, John

British, 19th century.
Born 8 February 1819, in London; died 20 January 1900, in Brantwood.
Painter, watercolourist, draughtsman, art theorist. Architectural views.

John Ruskin was of Scottish stock; his father John James Ruskin was a prosperous wine merchant and his mother a devout evangelical Christian. As a child, Ruskin's health was suspect and he was educated principally at home. He demonstrated a taste for the arts from an early age. He travelled frequently in the company of his parents, visiting most parts of Britain and travelling extensively in Europe (Northern France, Flanders, the Rhineland and Switzerland). He visited Paris in 1825 and started writing poetry and plays the following year, although he only began publishing his verse in 1830. As an artist, he was not, as is sometimes alleged, 'essentially self-taught'. In 1831, he took drawing and composition lessons from Charles Runciman; in 1836, his father arranged for Copley Fielding to tutor him in drawing and composition and introduce him to the art of watercolours; and, in 1841, he received further instruction from John Duffield Harding.

He went up to Christ Church, Oxford in 1836 (and won the 1839 Newgate Poetry Prize). A generous allowance from his father allowed him to live comfortably and, more importantly, to start collecting pictures by J.M.W. Turner and begin his collection of illuminated medieval manuscripts. His studies at Oxford were abruptly interrupted in early 1841 when he suffered a haemorrhage thought to have been brought on by incipient consumption/tuberculosis. He was advised to winter abroad and the family spent time in Italy (Rome, Naples and Venice) and in Switzerland. He was by this time a passionate nature lover; he resolved to commit himself to celebrating the beauties of the natural world in poetry, in painting and in his writings.

He returned to Oxford and graduated in 1842. The family spent that summer in the French Alps (Chamonix-Mont Blanc) and it was there that he began drafting a defence of Turner, whose late style had been scorned by the majority of art critics when he had exhibited that year at the Royal Academy. That defence mutated into the initial volume of *Modern Painters,* a spirited and articulate exposition of 'truth to Nature' in landscape painting. He was only twenty-four years old when the volume was published in 1843.

Two years later, he embarked on a further journey to Italy, this time unaccompanied by his family. The architecture of Northern Italy made a lasting impression on him and the sketches and drawings he made during that visit rank among his best work. He completed the second volume of Modern Painters in April 1846. Two years later, he married Euphemia (Effie) Chalmers Gray; the marriage - which was never consummated - was not a success.

His five volumes of *Modern Painters,* written between 1843 and 1860, elevated art criticism to new heights of excellence. Their impact on English and European art was considerable. Claude Monet would later assert that '90% of the theory of impressionist painting' was to be found in Ruskin's *Elements of Drawing* (1857), and his three-volume *The Stones of Venice* was a masterful account not only of Venice and art but of the city's chequered socio-political history. Like *The Stones of Venice, The Seven Lamps of Architecture,* an incisive analysis of Romanesque and Gothic architecture in Normandy and Northern Italy written in 1849, was splendidly illustrated by Ruskin himself.

He was a public apologist for the Pre-Raphaelites (although he found some of their work immature) and encouraged the likes of Rossetti, Burnes-Jones, Madox Brown and Holman Hunt. Nowhere was he more eloquent and committed, however, than on the social front. His *Four Essays on the First Principles of Political Economy* was a blistering attack on the perceived evils of capitalism and an unequivocal denunciation of the Victorian market economy which he regarded as conducive to a dehumanisation of manufacture and as the root of all evil: bad design, inferior decoration and progressively poor craftsmanship. Ruskin was generous with his time and with his money when it came to addressing social issues. He gave public lectures, notably in Edinburgh in 1853-1854; he taught at the Working Men's College in London (1854-1861); he set up projects designed to promote good workmanship and 'honest toil'; and, while teaching at Oxford as Slade Professor of Art (1869-1979), founded the Ruskin Drawing School. Not least, he was instrumental in the creation of the Oxford Museum and the Museum of St George in Sheffield (known as the Ruskin Gallery from 2001).

It is convenient to assert with the benefit of hindsight that his missionary zeal and utopian visions were as laudable as they were impractical. The scintillating quality of his prose style is also deceptive, concealing as it does views that are at times inconsistent and at other times downright contradictory. But his writings were remarkably popular and did much to disseminate public awareness about art. His influence was not confined to Britain alone, as his honorary membership of the Fine Arts Academies of Venice, Brussels, Florence, Antwerp and America and his election to a wide range of learned societies clearly indicate. He was a frequent visitor to Amiens and wrote at length on the region; his *Amien's Bible* of 1885 was translated into French by Marcel Proust, who was an admirer of Ruskin's prose style.

His art was essentially conceived as a complement to and illustration of his prose. However, examples have recently featured at various thematic group exhibitions, including *Ruskin, Turner and the Pre-Raphaelites,* held at the Tate Gallery in London in 2000; in 2002, at *Expedition Kunst. Die Entdeckung der Natur von C.D. Friedrich bis Humboldt* (*Expedition Art. The Discovery of Nature from C.D. Friedrich to Humboldt*), and exhibition which probed the links between landscape painting and the natural sciences, held at the Fine Arts Gallery in Hamburg; and, in 2003, at *Ruskin-Turner. Dessins et voyages dans la Picardie romantique* (*From Ruskin to Turner: Drawings and Travels in Romantic Picardy*), an exhibition held at the Musée de Picardie in Amiens. There have been few solo exhibitions of his work, but they include: 1954, *John Ruskin: Watercolours and Drawings,* organised in London by the Arts Council of Great Britain; 1983, at the Mappin Art Gallery in Sheffield; 1991, *John Ruskin e le Alpi* (John Ruskin and the Alps), held at the Museo Nazionale della Montagna in Turin; 1996, *Ruskin and the Art of Education,* held at the Ashmolean in Oxford; and 2000, *Remembering John Ruskin,* a presentation at the Grolier Club in New York City.

He published an autobiography, *Praeterita* (1885-1889). By this time, he was in poor health and his eyesight was failing. He died in January 1900 and was buried in Coniston Cemetery in Cumbria. A Ruskin Museum set up in Coniston in 1901 houses an important collection of his writings, paintings, manuscripts and memorabilia.

BIBLIOGRAPHY:

Axon, William E.A., *John Ruskin: a bibliographical biography,* A. Heywood & son, London, 1879. Collingwood, W.G., *The Life and Work of John Ruskin,* Methuen, London, 1893. Abse, Joan, *John Ruskin, the passionate moralist,* Quartet Press, London, 1980. Hilton, Tim, *John Ruskin. the early years, 1819-1859,* Yale University Press, New Haven and London, 1985. Herbert, Robert L. (ed.), *The Art criticism of John Ruskin,* Da Capo, New York, London, 1987 (reprinted, Garden City, New York, 1964). Smith, Lindsay, *Victorian photography, painting and poetry: the enigma of visibility in Ruskin, Morris and the Pre-Raphaelites,* Cambridge University Press, Cambridge, 1995. Hunt, John Dixon, *The Wider Sea,* Phoenix, London, 1998. Hilton, Tim, *John Ruskin: the later years,* Yale University Press, New Haven, 2000. Walton, Paul H., *Master drawings by John Ruskin,* Pilkington, London, 2000. Hewison, Robert, et al., *Ruskin, Turner and the Pre-Raphaelites,* group exhibition catalogue, Tate Gall., London, 2000. Perosa, Sergio, *Ruskin e Venezia,* Olschki, Florence, 2001. *John Ruskin - Werk und Wirkung: internationales Kolloquium,* symposium proceedings, Bibliothek Werner Oechslin, Einsiedeln, 2002. Brix, Michel (ed.), *Proust et Ruskin. De "La Bible d'Amiens" à la "Recherche",* Association Européenne François Mauriac, St-Avold, 2002. *John Ruskin. Werk und Wirking,* symposium proceedings, GTA Verlag, Zurich, 2003 (colloque, Einseideln, August 2000). Gamble, Cynthia/Wildman, Stephen/Pinete, Matthieu, *Ruskin - Turner. Dessins et voyages en Picardie romantique,* group exhibition catalogue, Musée de Picardie, Amiens, 2003. Birch, Dinah (ed.), *John Ruskin: Selected Writings,* Oxford University Press, Oxford and New York, 2004.

Gaskell, Elizabeth, *Lives of Victorian Literary Figures III*, Pickering & Chatto, London, 2005.

MUSEUMS AND GALLERIES:

BIRMINGHAM (Mus. and AG): *Coal Merchant's House in Market Street, Croydon* (c. 1830, drawing); *Lady Glenorchy's Chapel, Edinburgh* (1838, pencil); *Dumbarton* (1838, pencil and watercolour); *View from San Miniato, Florence* (1845, sepia, pencil and wash); *Coast Scene, near Dunbar* (1847, pencil and watercolour); *Cascade de la Folie, Chamonix* (1849, pencil and watercolour); *Folkestone: Hillside and Church as formerly seen from the Pavilion Hotel* (1849, sepia, pencil, ink); *Church Tower, Courmayeur, with the Mont Blanc Range in the Background* (1849, pencil and watercolour); *'Aiguilles' (The Needles), Chamonix* (1849, pencil, watercolour); *Old Houses on the Île de Rhône, Geneva* (c. 1862-1863, watercolour); *Lauffenburg on the Rhine River between Basel and Schaffhausen* (1863, pencil, watercolour); *Alpine Peaks: Jungfrau, Schreckhorn, Eiger and Others* (drawing); *Italian Village* (drawing and watercolour); *Studies of a Primrose* (drawing, study); *Arches and Capitals, Venice* (drawing) - CONISTON (Ruskin Mus.): large collection of works, archives and objects - LANCASTER (Ruskin Library): major collection of graphical works and 150 photographs - LONDON (Victoria and Albert Mus.): *Watercolour* - SHEFFIELD (Ruskin Gal.).

AUCTION RECORDS:

LONDON, 7 July 1922, *Towers of Thun Castle, Switzerland* (drawing) GBP 16; *Ramparts, Lucerne* (drawing) GBP 27; *Alpine Pine Forest* (drawing) GBP 17. LONDON, 20 May 1931, *Grand Canal, Venice* (black chalk) GBP 52; *Lucca Cathedral* (watercolour) GBP 36. LONDON, 20 May 1931, *Venetian Palazzo* (watercolour); *Pass of Killiecrankie* (watercolour, both) GBP 52. LONDON, 21 Nov 1945, *Thatches at Trontbeck* (drawing) GBP 24. LONDON, 10 Jan 1947, *Scenes from the Life of Christ* (drawing) GBP 39. LONDON, 11 July 1972, *Old House, Fribourg* (watercolour) Gns 750. LONDON, 8 June 1976, *Thames seen from Richmond, Winter* (pencil, black ink, watercolour heightened with white/paper, 11 x 14 3/4 ins / 27 x 37.5 cm) GBP 2,800. LONDON, 28 Feb 1979, *Neuchâtel* (pencil and colour wash, 5 x 7 ins / 12.7 x 17.8 cm) GBP 500. LONDON, 18 March 1980, *The Sea at Dusk* (watercolour and pencil heightened with white, 9 1/4 x 12 1/2 ins / 23.8 x 31.5 cm) GBP 4,000. LONDON, 17 Nov 1981, *Schaffhausen* (watercolour and pencil heightened with white, 9 1/4 x 18 1/2 ins / 23.8 x 46.8 cm) GBP 1,500. LONDON, 16 Nov 1982, *View of Rome* (1852 or 1882, pencil and wash, 12 1/4 x 17 3/4 ins / 31 x 45 cm) GBP 4,500. LONDON, 30 March 1983, *Amboise* (1841, watercolour/pencil outlines, 17 1/4 x 11 1/4 ins / 44 x 28.5 cm) GBP 18,000. LONDON, 15 March 1984, *Rocky Bank of a River* (grey wash, pencil and pen heightened with white, 12 3/4 x 18 1/2 ins / 32.5 x 47 cm) GBP 16,000. LONDON, 14 March 1985, *Canal View, Venice* (pencil, 5 1/4 x 8 1/2 ins / 13.5 x 21.5 cm) GBP 1,100. LONDON, 14 March 1985, *River Thames from Richmond Hill* (watercolour/pencil outlines and pen with touches of white/grey paper, 10 1/4 x 14 1/4 ins / 26 x 36.5 cm) GBP 19,000. LONDON, 8 July 1986, *Bridge Studies, Coblenz* (pen, two drawings, one of which is heightened with white, 4 1/4 x 7 ins / 11 x 17.8 cm) GBP 1,100. LONDON, 24 March 1987, *Spanish Steps, Rome* (watercolour and pencil, 8 x 4 3/4 ins / 20.6 x 12.3 cm) GBP 3,000. LONDON, 25 Jan 1989, *Richmond, Yorkshire* (pencil, 7 x 9 1/4 ins / 18 x 23.5 cm) GBP 495. LONDON, 30 Jan 1991, *Königsfeld in the Black Forest, Germany* (pencil, 5 1/4 x 8 1/2 ins / 13.5 x 21.5 cm) GBP 396. LONDON, 9 April 1992, *Val Anzasca, Italy* (ink and watercolour/brown paper, 6 1/4 x 8 3/4 ins / 16 x 22.5 cm) GBP 7,920. NEW YORK, 12 Oct 1993, *View of Neuchâtel, Switzerland* (watercolour and pencil/paper, 5 x 7 ins / 12.7 x 17.5 cm) USD 4,370. LONDON, 8 June 1999, *Lake Lucerne, Switzerland* (pencil, watercolour and scratching out, 11 x 15 ins / 27 x 37 cm) GBP 95,000. LONDON, 12 July 1999, *Head of an Owl* (1871, watercolour over pencil, 9 x 7 ins / 23 x 17 cm) GBP 13,000. LONDON, 30 Nov 2000, *Sandgate Beach* (watercolour heightened with gouache, 5 x 8 ins / 12 x 21 cm) GBP 7,500. LONDON, 30 Nov 2000, *Amboise* (watercolour over pencil heightened with scratching out, 17 x 11 ins / 44 x 28 cm) GBP 30,000. LONDON, 14 June 2001, *Château Colombier, Neuchâtel, Switzerland* (pen and ink over pencil, 5 x 8 ins / 13 x 21 cm) GBP 22,000. LONDON, 29 Nov 2001, *View at Coniston Water* (watercolour over pencil heightened with gouache, 7 x 11 ins / 17 x 27 cm) GBP 24,000. NEW YORK, 25 Jan 2002, *View of a Building and Tower in the Alps* (pen, ink, watercolour and gouache over black chalk, 8 x 7 ins / 21 x 19 cm) USD 25,000. LONDON, 6 June 2002, *Footbridge, Wallington Hall* (pencil and colour wash heightened with white, 8 x 13 ins / 20 x 33 cm) GBP 12,000. LONDON, 20 Nov 2003, *View of Geneva, Switzerland* (1854, pencil, pen, ink and watercolour heightened with white scratching out, 6 x 9 ins / 16 x 23 cm) GBP 13,000. LONDON, 20 Nov 2003, *Bellinzona, Switzerland, Looking North Towards the St Gotthard Pass* (pencil, watercolour and gouache, 20 x 14 ins / 52 x 35 cm) GBP 240,000. LONDON, 3 June 2004, *Oxalis and Heather* (pencil and watercolour heightened with gouache and scratching out, 7 x 11 ins / 18 x 27 cm) GBP 60,000. BANTAM, 14 July 2004, *View of Venice* (watercolour, 5 x 6 ins / 13 x 15 cm) USD 8,750.

RUSLI

Indonesian, 20th century.

Born 1922, in Medan (Sumatra).

Painter. Architectural views, landscapes.

From 1945 to 1949, Rusli was professor at the Taman Siswa Institute. In 1951 he was appointed senior lecturer at the fine arts academy in Yogyakarta, and in 1970 he was elected to the Jakarta Academy. He lives and works in Yogyakarta.

Rusli's work was shown at the 2nd São Paulo Biennale (1953), and he had a solo exhibition at the Palazzo Brancaccio, Rome (1954 to 1956).

AUCTION RECORDS:

SINGAPORE, 5 Oct 1996, *Temple* (1966, oil on canvas, 35 x 45 ins / 89 x 114 cm) SGD 11,500. SINGAPORE, 29 March 1997, *Temple Interior* (1965, oil on canvas, 35 1/2 x 42 1/2 ins / 90 x 108 cm) SGD 25,300. SINGAPORE, 1 April 2001, *House* (1982, oil on canvas, 20 x 24 ins / 51 x 62 cm) SGD 4,500. HONG KONG, 28 April 2002, *Temple Scene* (1964, oil on canvas, 38 x 49 ins / 96 x 124 cm) HKD 60,000. SINGAPORE, 6 Oct 2002, *Temple* (1964, oil on canvas, 39 x 51 ins / 100 x 130 cm) SGD 48,000. SINGAPORE, 18 May 2003, *Boats* (1984, oil on canvas, 20 x 23 ins / 50 x 59 cm) SGD 4,800. HONG KONG, 26 Oct 2003, *Boats by the Beach* (1977, oil on canvas, 24 x 30 ins / 60 x 75 cm) HKD 24,000. SINGAPORE, 3 April 2004, *Odalan* (1969, oil on canvas, 26 x 20 ins / 65 x 50 cm) SGD 7,500. SINGAPORE, 3 April 2004, *Wanita dan Gedang Hijau, Upacara* (1966, oil on canvas, 35 x 46 ins / 90 x 117 cm) SGD 12,000.

RUSNATI, Giuseppe, or Rosnati

Italian, 17th - 18th century.

Died 1713, in Milan.

Sculptor. Religious subjects.

Milanese School.

Giuseppe Rusnati studied in Rome under Antonio Albertino and E. Ferrati. He worked at the cathedral in Milan from 1677 onwards and at the Carthusian monastery in Pavia.

RUSOV, Aleksandr Nikolaevich, or Volkov-Muromzov

Russian, 19th - 20th century.

Born 1844; died 1928.

Painter, watercolourist. Genre scenes, local scenes, landscapes.

Orientalism.

Rusov travelled to Egypt, and moved to Venice. He painted in a deeply personal style. He exhibited in London, notably at the Royal Academy, from 1880.

A. N. Roussoff

MUSEUMS AND GALLERIES:
DERBY: *Oil Merchant in Cairo* - MOSCOW (State Tretyakov Gal.): *Luxor; Street in Cairo; The Nile, After Sunset; Cairo Before the Setting of the Sun; Evening on the Nile; Bought* - SYDNEY: *Funeral of a Child in the Countryside in Chioggia.*
AUCTION RECORDS:
LONDON, 19 May 1922, *Rejected* (drawing) GBP 46. LONDON, 9 July 1949, *Rejected* (drawing) GBP 31. LONDON, 17 Nov 1976, *Cairo Street Scene* (1891, watercolour, 31 3/4 x 19 1/2 ins / 80.7 x 49.6 cm) GBP 400. LONDON, 24 Nov 1983, *Venice Street* (1888, watercolour and pencil, set of five, each 9 3/4 x 4 1/2 ins / 24.8 x 11.5 cm) GBP 1,200. LONDON, 20 June 1985, *Tombs of the Mameluks in Cairo* (1891, watercolour, 10 1/2 x 20 1/2 ins / 26.5 x 52 cm) GBP 850. LONDON, 18 June 1986, *At the Metal Refurbisher's* (1882, oil on canvas, 47 1/2 x 30 ins / 120.5 x 76.5 cm) GBP 10,500. LONDON, 24 June 1988, *Crossing Before the Palazzo Ducale in a Boat* (1887, watercolour, 13 1/2 x 7 ins / 34.3 x 16.9 cm) GBP 275. LONDON, 5 Nov 1993, *Cairo* (1891, pencil and watercolour, 16 x 10 1/4 ins / 40.4 x 26 cm) GBP 1,840.

RUSOVA, Zdenka
Czechoslovak, 20th century.
Born 21 July 1939, in Prague.
Engraver.

Rusova studied from 1958 to 1964 at the school of applied arts in Prague, where she lives and works. She mixes a synthetic simplification of form with the humour of Pop Art. She has participated in group exhibitions, including: *14 Prague Engravers* in Essen at the Folkwang Museum in 1966; and *Young Czech Engravers* in Heidelberg in 1966. She has had solo exhibitions of her work, including in Prague in 1966.

RUSPAGIARI, Alfonso
Italian, 16th century.
Born 1512, in Reggio nell' Emilia; died 1576, in Reggio nell' Emilia.
Modeller (wax), medallist. Portraits.

Alfonso Ruspagiari produced medals depicting famous people of his time, and a self-portrait.

RUSPI, Ercole
Italian, 19th century.
Active in Rome.
Painter.

Ercole Ruspi executed paintings for a number of churches in Rome including 24 medallions with portraits of popes.

RUSPOLI, Francesco
French, 20th - 21st century.
Born 11 December 1958.
Also active in England.
Painter, watercolourist. Portraits, figures, interiors with figures. Stage costumes and sets, frescoes.

Francesco Ruspoli is an economics graduate who has lived and worked in London since 1986. A self-taught artist, his work is strongly influenced by Surrealism. He paints stylised nudes reminiscent of De Chirico's mannequins, typically in contorted and/or intertwined poses against an abstract coloured background. He also designs theatre costumes and stage sets and has adapted several plays.

He has shown examples of his work at various regional venues and has been awarded various medals and distinctions. His group exhibitions include those in Paris - at the 1984 and 1985 Salon des Indépendants, the Salon des Artistes Français of 1985 and the 1986 Salon d'Automne - followed by exhibitions at the Heifer Gallery in London in 1992, 1995, 1996 and 1997. Solo exhibitions by Ruspoli include those of 1985, at the Galerie René Borel in Deauville; 1998, at the Heifer Gallery in London; 1999, at the Galerie La Capitale in Paris; and 2000, at the Sylvia White Gallery in New York.

RUSPOLI, Ilarione
Italian, 16th century.
Active in Florence.
Sculptor.

Ilarione Ruspoli was the pupil of Vincenzo de Rossi. He was in Rome in 1586.

RUSS, Clementine
Austrian, 19th century.
Born c. 1810, in Vienna; died 1850, in Vienna.
Painter.

Clementine Russ was the daughter of Karl Russ. She painted altarpieces for the churches of Atzgersdorf and Zlin, Moravia.

RUSS, Franciscus
Austrian, 18th century.
Born c. 1707, in Lidicz (Bohemia); died 16 May 1749, in Prague.
Painter.

RUSS, Franz I
Austrian, 19th century.
Died after 1888.
Active in Vienna.
Painter.

Franz Russ I was the father of Franz Russ II.

RUSS, Franz II
Austrian, 19th century.
Born 27 March 1844, in Vienna; died 22 November 1906, in Vienna.
Painter, watercolourist. Portraits, genre scenes, architectural views.

Franz Russ II was a pupil at the academy in Vienna and also studied under Christian Ruben. He spent a number of years in Paris and settled in Vienna.
MUSEUMS AND GALLERIES:
LVIV (Lubomirski Mus.): *Portrait of a Lady* - ST GALL: *Unmasked* - VIENNA: *Old Theatre in Vienna* (watercolour).
AUCTION RECORDS:
LUCERNE, 25 Nov 1972, *Young Girl Sitting*, CHF 4,600. VIENNA, 22 May 1973, *Portrait of Empress Elizabeth of Austria*, ATS 55,000. VIENNA, 22 June 1976, *Portrait of an Aristocratic Woman* (1857, oil on canvas, 33 1/2 x 27 1/4 ins / 85 x 69 cm) ATS 45,000. VIENNA, 26 May 1982, *Maternal Joy* (oil on canvas, 31 x 24 3/4 ins / 79 x 63 cm) AST 50,000. VIENNA, 20 March 1985, *Portrait of an Oriental Woman* (1868, oil on canvas, 39 1/4 x 29 1/4 ins / 100 x 74 cm) ATS 90,000. COLOGNE, 20 Oct 1989, *Portrait of Men Seated at a Table* (oil on canvas, 37 x 31 ins / 94 x 79 cm) DEM 2,200. VIENNA, 9 Feb 1999, *Female Nude in Landscape* (oil on canvas, 29 x 39 ins / 73 x 100 cm) ATS 90,000. NEW YORK, 5 May 1999, *The Beauty and the Butterfly* (oil on canvas, 29 x 38 ins / 73 x 97 cm) USD 22,000. VIENNA, 30 Oct 2001, *Madonna with Child* (oil on canvas, 31 x 25 ins / 78 x 63 cm) ATS 40,000. VIENNA, 28 Nov 2002, *Oriental Beauty* (1868, oil on canvas, 39 x 29 ins / 100 x 74 cm) EUR 9,500.

RUSS, Henning. See **REUSS**

RUSS, Ignaz I
Austrian, 18th century.
Active in Trautenau in the second half of the 18th century.
Painter.

Ignaz Russ I was the father of Ignaz Russ II.

RUSS, Ignaz II
Austrian, 18th - 19th century.
Born 1766, in Trautenau; died 23 December 1849, in Trautenau.
Painter.
Ignaz Russ II was the son and pupil of Ignaz Russ I. He painted the altarpiece in the church of Trautenau in 1825.

RUSS, Jacob, or Ruess or Ruoss, or erroneously Rüsch or Rösch or Rufer
Swiss, 15th - 16th century.
Born c. 1455; died c. 1525.
Sculptor.
Lake Constance School.
Jacob Russ worked in Ravensburg, Überlingen and Switzerland.

RUSS, Johan. See **ROST**

RUSS, Karl
Austrian, 19th century.
Born 11 August 1779, in Vienna; died 19 September 1843, in Vienna.
Painter, engraver, lithographer. History painting, mythological subjects, portraits.
Karl Russ was the father of Clementine and Leander Russ. He was a pupil of Kapp, Schmutzer and Maurer. In 1800 he became involved in conservation work on the gallery of the Belvedere in Vienna. It was Adam von Bartsch who initiated him into engraving. He exhibited 37 paintings at the art academy in Vienna in 1822.

He executed a notable series of paintings relating to the Habsburg family. He is still noted for his *Hecuba on the Shore beside the Bodies of her Children* and *Rudolf von Habsburg's Meeting with the Priest.*

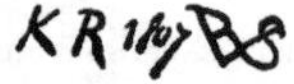

Museums and Galleries:
Vienna (Österreichische Gal. Belvedere): *Self-portrait.*
Auction records:
Vienna, 6 June 1972, *Princely Engagement in Passau,* ATS 40,000. Vienna, 17 March 1981, *Rudolf von Habsburg at the Gates of Vienna* (oil on canvas, 37 1/2 x 49 1/2 ins / 95 x 126 cm) ATS 50,000. Vienna, 29-30 Oct 1996, *Legend of Agnesbründel* (1820, oil on canvas, 20 3/4 x 23 1/2 ins / 53 x 60 cm) ATS 207,000.

RUSS, Leander
Austrian, 19th century.
Born 25 November 1809, in Vienna; died 8 March 1864, in Kaltenleutgeben.
Painter, watercolourist, draughtsman, lithographer. Historical subjects, battles.
Leander Russ was a pupil of his father Karl Russ and studied at the academy in Vienna. He worked in Munich, Italy and Egypt and mainly painted battle subjects in watercolours and Indian ink.
Museums and Galleries:
Vienna: *Attack of the Turks at Lowelbastei*; numerous drawings.

RUSS, Robert
Austrian, 19th - 20th century.
Born 7 March 1847, in Vienna; died 16 March 1922, in Vienna.
Painter, watercolourist. Landscapes with figures, urban landscapes, architectural views.
Robert Russ was the brother of Franz Russ. He studied under Albert August Zimmermann at the academy in Vienna and went on to live and work in Vienna.
Museums and Galleries:
Brno: *Villa Borghese and Gardens, Rome* - Graz: *Forge* - Prague (Národní Gal.): *After the Storm; Mill in South Tyrol* - Stuttgart: *Marketplace, Friesach* - Vienna: *Prison Courtyard at Burgos Castle; Part of Heidelberg Castle;* a watercolour - Vienna (Akademie der Bildenden Künste): *Mals Motif, Tyrol; Eisenherz Motif* - Vienna (Liechtenstein Mus.): *Coast near Gargano; Merano: The Arcades; Klausen on the Brenner Road* - Vienna (Österreichische Gal. Belvedere): *Onset of Spring in Penzing Forest.*
Auction records:
Paris, 14 May 1881, *View of Klaus (Tyrol),* FRF 1,680. Vienna, 17 Nov 1949, *Tyrolean Landscape* (1893) ATS 3,500. Paris, 18 Oct 1950, *Seascape,* FRF 900. Vienna, 17 Sept 1963, *Landscape near Merano,* ATS 90,000. Vienna, 1 and 4 Dec 1964, *Ticino Landscape in the Spring,* ATS 140,000. Vienna, 22 Sept 1970, *Village Street,* ATS 55,000. Vienna, 6 June 1972, *View of Weiszenkirchen* (watercolour) ATS 28,000. Vienna, 4 Dec 1973, *Summer Landscape,* ATS 100,000. Vienna, 12 March 1974, *Church Interior,* ATS 200,000. Vienna, 30 Nov 1976, *Spring* (1918, oil on canvas, 71 1/4 x 54 ins / 181 x 137 cm) ATS 70,000. Vienna, 19 Sept 1978, *Rustic Scene* (1871, oil on canvas, 23 3/4 x 33 ins / 60.5 x 84 cm) ATS 160,000. London, 18 Jan 1980, *Alpine Torrent* (1891, oil on canvas, 69 1/2 x 63 ins / 176.5 x 160 cm) GBP 3,000. Vienna, 17 March 1982, *Hay Wain* (1876, oil on panel, 20 1/2 x 15 1/4 ins / 52 x 39 cm) ATS 220,000. Vienna, 18 May 1983, *Water Mill* (mixed media/paper, 43 1/4 x 55 ins / 110 x 140 cm) ATS 28,000. Vienna, 22 June 1983, *Old Bridge, Tivoli* (oil on canvas, 43 1/2 x 55 1/4 ins / 110.5 x 140.5 cm) ATS 160,000. Cologne, 25 Oct 1985, *Marketplace in Friesach, Karinthia* (1890, oil on canvas, 39 1/4 x 29 1/2 ins / 100 x 75 cm) DEM 50,000. Vienna, 20 March 1986, *Country Road* (watercolour, 11 1/2 x 11 1/2 ins / 29 x 29 cm) ATS 38,000. London, 8 Oct 1986, *Woodland Walk in an Italian Town* (1896, oil on canvas, 52 1/4 x 28 1/2 ins / 133 x 72.5 cm) GBP 26,000. Vienna, 18 March 1987, *Mill by the River* (oil on canvas, 41 1/4 x 53 1/4 ins / 105 x 135 cm) ATS 600,000. Paris, 7 March 1989, *View of Arco Castle near Riga, Lake Garda* (1894, oil on canvas, 66 1/4 x 44 1/2 ins / 168 x 113 cm) FRF 400,000. London, 22 Nov 1989, *Garden* (oil on panel, 6 3/4 x 9 3/4 ins / 17 x 25 cm) GBP 16,500. New York, 28 Feb 1990, *North Italian Landscape* (1894, oil on canvas, 64 1/2 x 43 3/4 ins / 164 x 111 cm) USD 68,750. London, 30 March 1990, *Torrent near a Village* (charcoal and gouache, 11 3/4 x 16 1/2 ins / 29.8 x 42 cm) GBP 2,750. Munich, 22 June 1993, *Gothic Church with Wrought-iron Calvary in Garden* (1870, oil on canvas, 47 x 35 1/2 ins / 119.5 x 90 cm) DEM 63,250. New York, 16 Feb 1994, *View of Capri* (watercolour and gouache/paper, 28 1/2 x 36 ins / 72.4 x 91.4 cm) USD 17,250. Munich, 25 June 1996, *Sunny Path through the Woods* (watercolour/paper/card, 15 1/4 x 11 ins / 39 x 28 cm) DEM 9,000.

RUSSAC-CLAIREFOND, Lucienne
French, 20th century.
Born 13 July 1909, in Fumel.
Painter. Landscapes, urban landscapes. Designs for tapestries.
Lucienne Russac-Clairefond was a pupil of Etcheverry and Michel Paul Dupuy and was married to the painter Jean Clairefond. She abandoned her early style, with its dark and forceful landscapes of Paris, the pigment applied with a knife, to depict landscapes of her native south of France painted with a brush and full of light. In Paris, she was a member of the Salon des Artistes Français and also exhibited at the Salon des Indépendants, the Salon des Paysagistes and the Salon des Femmes Peintres. In 1937, she exhibited tapestry designs at the Paris Exposition Internationale.

RUSSAGNOTI, Carlo Antonio.
See **BUFFAGNOTI**

RUSSANGE, Nicolas I de
French, 15th - 16th century.
Died 1511.
Active in Paris from 1469.
Medallist.

RUSSANGE, Nicolas II de
French, 16th century.
Active in Paris 1545-1561.
Medallist, goldsmith.

RUSSCHOLLE. See **RUCHOLLE**

RUSSE, Paul, or Rosier
Austrian, 18th century.
Active in Vienna in the second half of the 18th century.
Painter.

Between 1750 and 1760 Paul Russe painted five altarpieces for the church of Battelau near Iglau (now Jihlava, Czech Republic).

RUSSEL. See also **RUSSELL**

RUSSEL, Antony, or Rousseel or Roussel
British, 17th - 18th century.
Born c. 1663; died July 1743, in London.
Portrait artist.

Antony Russel was the son of Theodore Russel and (probably) pupil of Riley. J. Smith and Vertue made engravings from Russel originals.

AUCTION RECORDS:
LONDON, 7 July 1967, *Portrait of Charles II*, Gns 750.

RUSSEL, Claudius
Flemish School, 17th century.
Born c. 1606, in Brussels; died 18 August 1629, in Rome.
Painter.

RÜSSEL, Franz
German, 19th century.
Born 10 June 1817, in Mainz; died 15 November 1888, in Mainz.
Draughtsman, lithographer.

Franz Rüssel engraved scenes from the local history of Mainz and vignettes.

RUSSEL, James John
Irish, 18th - 19th century.
Born in Limerick; died October 1827, in Limerick.
Portrait artist.

James Russel exhibited in Dublin from 1804 and in London from 1818-1823.

RUSSEL, Theodore, or Rousseel or Roussel
Flemish School, 17th century.
Born 1614, in London; died 1689.
Painter, copyist. Portraits.

Theodore Russel was the son of Nicolas Roussel and father of Antony Russel. He was the pupil of his uncle Cornelius Jansen, and of Anton van Dyck, whom he accompanied to England. He executed numerous copies of portraits by his famous master and other painters of note. He also painted original works, and had as his protectors Lord Essex and Lord Holland. He is particularly remembered for his portraits, at Woburn Abbey and the Palace of Holyrood respectively, of *Charles II* and *James II*.

MUSEUMS AND GALLERIES:
LONDON (National Portrait Gal.): *James Stuart, 1st Duke of Richmond, and 4th Duke of Lennox* (c. 1640-1649, oil on canvas, attributed).

AUCTION RECORDS:
LONDON, 14 Nov 1979, *Mortimer Menpes, Esquire* (oil on canvas, 48 x 24 1/2 ins / 121 x 62 cm) GBP 10,000. LONDON, 3 Feb 1993, *Portrait of Henry Rich, Count of Holland* (oil on panel, 15 1/2 x 12 1/2 ins / 39.5 x 31.5 cm) GBP 1,840. LONDON, 12 April 1995, *Bust Portrait of a Lady in a Blue Dress* (oil on canvas, 27 3/4 x 22 3/4 ins / 70.5 x 58 cm) GBP 5,290. LONDON, 13 Nov 1996, *Portrait of a Lady* (oil on panel, 15 1/2 x 12 1/2 ins / 39.5 x 31.5 cm) GBP 2,875.

RUSSELL. See also **RUSSEL**

RUSSELL, Ann, later Mrs Jowett
British, 19th century.
Born 1781, in London; died 1851.
Painter, pastellist. Portraits, genre scenes.

Ann Russell was the daughter of John and sister of William Russell. She was influenced by Rosalba Carriera.

AUCTION RECORDS:
LONDON, 25 Jan 1988, *Little Girl holding a Bunch of Grapes* (1811, pastel, 18 x 12 1/2 ins / 46 x 32 cm) GBP 1,045.

RUSSELL, Charles
Irish, 19th - 20th century.
Born 4 February 1852, in Dumbarton; died 12 December 1910, in Blackrock.
Painter. Portraits, genre scenes, landscapes.

Charles Russell worked in Dublin from 1874.

AUCTION RECORDS:
NEW YORK, 16 Oct 1974, *Calling the Horses* (watercolour and gouache) USD 5,000. SLANE CASTLE, 20 Nov 1978, *Repose* (1909, oil on canvas, 35 1/2 x 26 3/4 ins / 90 x 68 cm) GBP 900. NEW YORK, 17 Feb 1994, *A Quiet Spot, Young Woman Seated on Rock Above Pool* (1889, oil on canvas, 30 x 25 ins / 76.2 x 63.5 cm) USD 1,725. NEW YORK, 10 Feb 1998, *Pose in the Garden* (oil on canvas, 18 x 14 ins / 46 x 35.5 cm) USD 3,220.

RUSSELL, Charles Marion
American, 19th - 20th century.
Born 19 March 1864, in St Louis (Missouri); died 24 October 1926, in Great Falls (Indiana).
Painter (including gouache), sculptor, watercolourist, illustrator. Figures, local scenes, equestrian subjects, landscapes with figures, animals. Sculpted groups.

Charles Marion Russell lived in Montana from 1880, initially as a fur trapper and later as a cowboy, although he never missed an opportunity to sketch or to draw as he moved from place to place. He even lived with an Indian tribe for six months. In 1897 he settled in Great Falls. Most of his work focused on the American West of his youth.

Self-taught, Russell was endowed with a sense of composition and an ability to depict backgrounds, landscapes and movement. One of his earliest paintings, *Caught Red Handed* was also his first illustration, published in 1888 in *Harper's Weekly*. He also published in such magazines as *McClures* and *Leslie's*. A penetrating observer of life, Russell also doubled as a talented story-teller, but this was only appreciated after 1905 since before then, and certainly since 1892, he had only worked as a painter. He also illustrated numerous works by other writers, including: *How the Buffalo Lost his Crown* by J.H.Beacom (1898); with Remingington, Wister's *Virginian* (1911); *Indian Why Stories* by Lindermann. He was the author and illustrator of *Studies of Western Life; the Rawhide Rawlins Stories, Back-Trailing on the Old Frontiers, More Rawhides, Trails Plowed Under* and *Good Medicine*.

Russell was also a sculptor and muralist: in 1911 the State of Montana commissioned him to paint a mural for its Chamber of Representatives: *Lewis and Clark Encountering Flathead Indians at Ross Hole*.

His work featured in the exhibition *À la Découverte de l'Ouest Américain* (*Discovering the American West*) held at the Salon d'Automne in Paris in 1987.

CM Russell 1919

BIBLIOGRAPHY:

Keto, Kellie, *Charles M. Russell: The Artist in His Heyday 1903-1926*, University of Washington Press, Seattle, 1995. Taliaferro, John, *Charles M. Russell: Life and Legend of America's Cowboy Artist*, Little Brown, Boston, 1996.

MUSEUMS AND GALLERIES:

FORT WORTH (Amon Carter Mus.): *The Buffalo Hunt No. 39* (*Buffalo Hunt No. 39*) (1919, oil on canvas) - OKLAHOMA CITY (National Cowboy and Western Heritage Mus.): *Redman's Wireless* (*Redman's Wireless*) (1916, oil on canvas).

AUCTION RECORDS:

NEW YORK, 12 Dec 1956, *Pursued Antelope* (watercolour) USD 1,700. NEW YORK, 17 Nov 1966, *Cowboy Threatening a Young Chinese Boy with His Revolver* (patinated bronze) USD 5,000. LONDON, 6 Dec 1967, *Ambush*, GBP 14,400. LONDON, 2 July 1968, *Indians on Horseback Setting Fire to a Mule Train* (watercolour) Gns 11,000. NEW YORK, 19 March 1969, *Indian on Horseback* (bronze) USD 32,000. NEW YORK, 29 Jan 1970, *Cowboy* (chalk) USD 20,000. NEW YORK, 27 Oct 1971, *Death of the Gambler*, USD 100,000. NEW YORK, 19 Oct 1972, *Indians on Horseback* (watercolour and gouache) USD 45,000. LOS ANGELES, 22 May 1973, *Douglas Fairbanks as d'Artagnan* (bronze) USD 3,000. NEW YORK, 4 March 1974, *Will Rogers* (bronze) USD 8,000. NEW YORK, 16 Oct 1974, *The Trail*, USD 60,000. LOS ANGELES, 9 June 1976, *Indian on a White Horse Shooting a Buffalo* (watercolour, 9 1/4 x 14 1/2 ins / 23.5 x 37 cm) USD 22,000; *Where the Best of Riders Quit, Bronze* (brown patina, h. 14 1/4 ins / 36 cm) USD 8,500. NEW YORK, 27 Oct 1977, *Montana Cowboy* (watercolour, 22 x 15 ins / 56 x 38 cm) USD 21,000. LONDON, 27 Sept 1978, *His First Hunt* (watercolour and pencil heightened with gouache, 18 1/4 x 22 1/4 ins / 46.5 x 56.5 cm) GBP 30,000. NEW YORK, 27 Oct 1978, *The Weaver* (brown-patinated bronze, h. 14 1/2 ins / 37 cm) USD 23,000. LOS ANGELES, 18 June 1979, *Smoking to the Spirit of the Buffalo* (1914, bronze, 4 1/2 x 8 1/4 ins / 11.4 x 21 cm) USD 5,000. NEW YORK, 25 Oct 1979, *Crees Coming In to Trade* (1896, watercolour, 19 3/4 x 28 1/4 ins / 50.2 x 71.8 cm) USD 155,000. NEW YORK, 25 Oct 1979, *The Judith Basin Round Up* (1889, oil on canvas, 30 x 48 ins / 76.2 x 122 cm) USD 185,000. NEW YORK, 17 Oct 1980, *Saddling Up* (pen, 6 3/4 x 9 1/2 ins / 17.1 x 24.1 cm) USD 6,500. LOS ANGELES, 9 Feb 1982, *Utica Round Up Camp* (pen and wash, 4 x 7 ins / 10 x 17.5 cm) USD 5,500. NEW YORK, 23 April 1982, *Indian War Party* (1903, watercolour/card, 8 x 20 ins / 20.4 x 50.7 cm) USD 125,000. ZURICH, 13 May 1982, *Sleeping Thunder* (dark-patinated bronze, h. 9 ins / 23 cm) CHF 4,000. NEW YORK, 1 June 1984, *Squaws Moving Camp* (oil on card remounted on board, 12 1/4 x 18 1/2 ins / 30.8 x 47 cm) USD 110,000. NEW YORK, 6 Dec 1984, *Start of the Round Up* (1898, watercolour, 14 1/2 x 20 1/2 ins / 36.8 x 52.1 cm) USD 140,000. NEW YORK, 7 Dec 1984, *The Indians Slid from their Ponies and Commenced Stripping Themselves* (pen, brush, black ink and gouache/paper, 17 x 22 3/4 ins / 43 x 58 cm) USD 30,000. NEW YORK, 5 Dec 1985, *The Buffalo Hunt* (1900, watercolour and gouache/paper, 5 x 6 1/4 ins / 12.7 x 16 cm) USD 35,000. NEW YORK, 4 Dec 1986, *Buffalo Hunter* (ink wash/paper, in grisaille, 4 1/2 x 7 ins / 11.4 x 17.8 cm) USD 20,000. NEW YORK, 28 May 1987, *Belt Knocker* (pencil and wash, 18 1/2 x 23 ins / 47 x 58.4 cm) USD 7,000. NEW YORK, 30 Nov 1989, *At the Head of a Cattle Train* (1905, gouache and watercolour/paper, 13 x 10 3/4 ins / 33 x 27.3 cm) USD 143,000; *Indian Braves Returning from a Skirmish* (1914, oil on canvas, 24 1/4 x 36 1/4 ins / 61.6 x 92.1 cm) USD 1,100,000. NEW YORK, 1 Dec 1989, *Buffalo Hunt* (1897, oil on canvas, 23 3/4 x 35 3/4 ins / 60.3 x 90.8 cm) USD 528,000. NEW YORK, 24 May 1990, *Cowboys Firing Gunshots to Keep the Cattle in a Line* (oil on canvas, 15 1/4 x 21 ins / 38.7 x 53.4 cm) USD 473,000. NEW YORK, 31 May 1990, *Texas Steer* (bronze, h. 4 1/2 ins / 11.7 cm) USD 6,050. NEW YORK, 30 Nov 1990, *Indian Clay Pipe for Invoking the Spirit of the Buffalo* (1914, bronze, 4 1/2 x 8 1/2 ins / 11.2 x 21.6 cm) USD 8,250. NEW YORK, 5 Dec 1991, *Misplaced Confidence* (watercolour grisaille gouache/paper, 12 1/2 x 17 1/2 ins / 31.8 x 44.5 cm) USD 55,000. NEW YORK, 28 May 1992, *Encampment on the Edge of the Lake* (1908, watercolour and gouache/card, 14 x 22 1/4 ins / 35.5 x 56.5 cm) USD 143,000. NEW YORK, 27 May 1993, *The Enemy's Tracks* (bronze, h. 12 ins / 30.5 cm) USD 24,150. NEW YORK, 2 Dec 1993, *Breaking In a Bronco* (1899, watercolour/paper, 14 x 22 ins / 35.6 x 55.9 cm) USD 156,500. LOKEREN, 28 May 1994, *Six Horse Wagon* (bronze, h. 15 3/4 ins / 40 cm, w. 41 1/4 ins/105 cm) BEF 75,000. NEW YORK, 1 Dec 1994, *Cowboys Lassoing a Bull* (1900, watercolour/paper, 20 x 30 ins / 50.8 x 76.2 cm) USD 222,500. NEW YORK, 25 May 1995, *Navajo Indians Capturing Wild Horses* (1919, watercolour and gouache/paper, 13 1/2 x 18 1/2 ins / 34.3 x 47 cm) USD 140,000. NEW YORK, 14 March 1996, *War Cry* (bronze, h. 10 1/4 ins / 26 cm) USD 19,550. NEW YORK, 22 May 1996, *Indians on the Move with Stretchers Made from Branches* (1903, watercolour/card, 7 3/4 x 14 ins / 19.7 x 35.6 cm) USD 101,500. NEW YORK, 3 Dec 1996, *King of the Mountains and King of the Plains* (bronze, a pair, h. 4 3/4 ins / 12 cm) USD 4,830. NEW YORK, 4 Dec 1996, *Weapons of the Weak* (bronze, group, h. 6 ins / 14.3 cm) USD 57,500; *Wet Horses* (watercolour/paper, 14 1/2 x 21 1/2 ins / 36.8 x 54.6 cm) USD 167,500; *When the Redskin Talks of War* (1922, watercolour and gouache/paper, 14 1/2 x 21 1/2 ins / 36.8 x 54.6 cm) USD 442,500. NEW YORK, 26 May 1999, *Price of his Hide* (1915, oil on canvas, 24 x 36 ins / 61 x 91 cm) USD 1,300,000. HAYDEN, 31 July 1999, *Scattering Riders* (1900, watercolour, 21 x 29 ins / 53 x 74 cm) USD 825,000. HAYDEN, 29 July 2000, *Meat for Wild Men* (watercolour, 6 x 9 ins / 15 x 24 cm) USD 1,000,000. NEW YORK, 30 Nov 2000, *Buffalo Hunt* (1899, oil on canvas, 18 x 24 ins / 46 x 62 cm) USD 600,000. HAYDEN, 28 July 2001, *Scouting Party* (oil on canvas, 20 x 14 ins / 51 x 36 cm) USD 850,000. HAYDEN, 28 July 2001, *Disputed Trail* (1898, watercolour, 23 x 18 ins / 58 x 46 cm) USD 2,100,000. NEW YORK, 22 May 2002, *Alert* (1895, oil on board, 24 x 18 ins / 61 x 46 cm) USD 220,000. HAYDEN, 27 July 2002, *Counting Coup* (c. 1920, bronze, h. 11 ins / 28 cm) USD 180,000. HAYDEN, 26 July 2003, *Kindergarten or Storyteller* (oil on board, 10 x 12 ins / 25 x 30 cm) USD 350,000. HAYDEN, 26 July 2003, *Trail of the Iron Horse* (watercolour, 17 x 27 ins / 43 x 69 cm) USD 925,000. HAYDEN, 24 July 2004, *Wild Meat for Wild Men* (1890, oil on canvas, 20 x 36 ins / 51 x 91 cm) USD 370,000. HAYDEN, 24 July 2004, *Navajo Lookout, Surveying the Plains* (watercolour, 15 x 21 ins / 38 x 53 cm) USD 550,000.

RUSSELL, Edwin Wensley

British, 19th century.

Active in London.

Painter. History painting, portraits, genre scenes.

Edwin Russell exhibited in London from 1855 to 1878, notably at the Royal Academy, the British Institution and the Suffolk Street Gallery.

MUSEUMS AND GALLERIES:

BLACKBURN: *Portrait of Miss Nancy Hargreaves*; *Picking Primroses* (watercolour).

RUSSELL, Elisabeth Laura Henrietta, later Mrs Wriothesley

British, 19th century.

Died 5 May 1886.

Engraver (etching).

Elisabeth Russell engraved from originals by Rembrandt and Callot. She was noted for a portrait of *Lord Cosmo Russell*.

RUSSELL, Frances (Lady)
Maiden name: Eva Webster
American, 19th century.
Born 22 September 1856, in Chicago.
Painter. Genre scenes.

Lady Frances Russell was a pupil of John H. Vanderpoel and Martha Baker.

RUSSELL, George Horne
British, 19th - 20th century.
Born 1861, in Banff; died 26 June 1933, in St Stephens.
From 1889 active in Canada.
Painter. Portraits, seascapes.

George Horne Russell trained at the South Kensington Academy in London. He moved to Canada in 1889.

MUSEUMS AND GALLERIES:
OTTAWA (NG. of Canada): several paintings.

AUCTION RECORDS:
TORONTO, 19 Oct 1976, *Fishing Village* (oil on canvas, 17 x 24 ins / 43 x 61 cm) CAD 4,000. TORONTO, 5 Nov 1979, *Gathering Seaweed* (gouache, 12 x 16 3/4 ins / 30.7 x 42.5 cm) CAD 1,700. TORONTO, 26 May 1981, *Mount Pelee, Yellow Head Pass Evening, Mount Pelee*) (oil on canvas, 35 1/2 x 24 1/2 ins / 90 x 62.5 cm) CAD 9,500. PARIS, 7 Nov 1982, *Regattas at St-Tropez* 1910, watercolour, 10 1/4 x 14 1/4 ins / 26 x 36 cm) FRF 22,200. TORONTO, 26 Nov 1984, *Incoming Tide* (oil on canvas remounted on board, 8 1/2 x 10 1/2 ins / 21.3 x 26.9 cm) CAD 2,400. LONDON, 22 Sept 1988, *Yacht out at Sea* (oil on canvas, 14 x 22 1/4 ins / 35.5 x 56.5 cm) GBP 1,045. MONTREAL, 30 Oct 1989, *Morning Mist in St Andrews* (oil on panel, 13 x 18 ins / 33 x 46 cm) CAD 715. MONTREAL, 5 Nov 1990, *Gathering Clams* (oil on panel, 9 x 12 1/4 ins / 23 x 31 cm) CAD 1,925.

RUSSELL, George William
Irish, 19th - 20th century.
Born 10 April 1867, in Lurgan; died 1935.
Painter. Figures, portraits, genre scenes, landscapes.

George Willliam Russell was completely self-taught. He was active in Dublin. He was also a writer.

AUCTION RECORDS:
LONDON, 18 Nov 1977, *Bathing Off the Rocks* (oil on canvas, 21 x 32 ins / 53.5 x 81.5 cm) GBP 900. LONDON, 9 June 1988, *Fairies of the Peat Bog* (oil on canvas, 15 3/4 x 19 3/4 ins / 40 x 50 cm) GBP 1,650. BELFAST, 28 Oct 1988, *Apple Pickers* (oil on board, 18 1/2 x 24 1/4 ins / 47 x 61.5 cm) GBP 3,850; *Sea Nymphs* (oil on canvas, 15 x 21 ins / 38.2 x 53.4 cm) GBP 1,650. DUBLIN, 12 Dec 1990, *The Big Oak of Raheen in the County of Galway* (oil on canvas, 29 x 40 1/2 ins / 73.6 x 102.9 cm) IEP 9,200. DUBLIN, 26 May 1993, *Self-portrait* (oil on canvas, 18 x 15 ins / 45.7 x 38.1 cm) IEP 1,760. LONDON, 2 June 1995, *The Sultry Children of the Air* (oil on canvas, 16 1/4 x 21 ins / 41 x 53.5 cm) GBP 5,520. LONDON, 9 May 1996, *Swing* (oil on canvas, 21 x 32 ins / 53.3 x 81.5 cm) GBP 16,100. LONDON, 21 May 1997, *Lordly Ones Appearing to a Turf Cutter* (oil on canvas, 21 x 32 ins / 53.3 x 81.3 cm) GBP 10,350.

RUSSELL, Gyrth
Canadian, 20th century.
Born 13 April 1892, in Dartmouth, Nova Scotia; died 8 December 1970, in Penarth, Wales.
Active in Canada to c. 1918, in England and Wales after c. 1918.
Painter, watercolourist, etcher, engraver (aquatint, dry point). Military subjects, marine scenes, landscapes, railways.
Langham Sketching Club.

Gyrth Russell studied at the Victoria School of Art and Design in Halifax, Nova Scotia, and also in Paris at the Académie Julian and Atelier Colarossi (1912-1914) and in Boston. He was keenly interested in printmaking from the beginning, and displayed a strong technical talent for this work. During World War I he was appointed an official war artist to the Canadian War Memorial Fund for the Canadian government, being assigned the rank of Lieutenant. He completed a set of drypoint etchings of action at the front for the Fund, which also employed the artists A.Y. Jackson, Cyril Barraud and James Kerr Lawson. After the war Russell settled in Britain, living in Topsham in Devon and later at Penarth in Wales. His coloured aquatints show a stylistic relationship to the Impressionists. He also wrote books on art technique and illustrated the book *Unknown Devon*.

Russell's war etchings were shown at the Canadian War Memorials Exhibition at Burlington House in London in 1919, touring to New York, Montreal and the Canadian National Exhibition Fine Art Gallery in Toronto. He also exhibited at the Howard Roberts Gallery in Cardiff (1956), at Penarth in Glamorgan, at the Royal Institute of Oil Painters and at the Royal Glasgow Institute of Fine Arts. In 1999 his work was included in *From the Collections*, Art Gallery of St Francis Xavier University, Antigonish.

BIBLIOGRAPHY:
Du Garde Peach, L., *Unknown Devon*, illustrated book, John Lane, London, 1927 (illustrated by Gyrth Russell). Russell, Gyrth, *An Introduction to Oil Painting*, Winsor & Newton, London, 1959. Russell, Gyrth, *See and Paint, A Guide to Picture Construction*, illustrated book, Winsor & Newton, London, 1959.

MUSEUMS AND GALLERIES:
ANTIGONISH, NOVA SCOTIA (Art Gallery of St Francis Xavier University) - HALIFAX (Dalhousie Art Gallery): *Fishing Village with Stone Houses* (oil); *Mansands, South Devon* (c. 1920, oil) - OTTAWA (Canadian War Mus.): *Crest of Vimy Ridge* (1918) - OTTAWA (NG): *The Aerodrome* (1918, dry-point); *Mine Crater, Vimy Ridge* (1918, dry-point); *Estaminet at Cambligneul* (1918, dry-point); *Hôtel de Ville, Arras* (c. 1918-1919, etching); *Le Grand Place, Arras* (1918, dry-point); *Le Havre, Globe Trotters* (1916, ink); *Napoo Corner* (1917-1918, dry-point); *Lane in Spring* (oil); *The Rother at Rye* (1915, etching); *The White Barn, Montarlot* (1916, aquatint).

AUCTION RECORDS:
LONDON, 12 May 1989, *Houses at Mevagissey Harbour* (oil on canvas, 25 1/2 x 29 1/2 ins / 65 x 75 cm) GBP 1,100. LONDON, 5 Oct 1989, *Newlyn Harbour* (oil on canvas, 21 1/4 x 28 ins / 53.9 x 70.2 cm) GBP 5,500. NEW YORK, 21 May 1991, *Exe Valley at Exminster* (oil on canvas, 16 1/4 x 21 1/4 ins / 41.3 x 53.9 cm) USD 1,540. LONDON, 5 March 1999, *Polperro, Cornwall* (oil on board, 15 x 17 ins / 39 x 43 cm) GBP 3,500. LONDON, 30 Sept 1999, *Summer's Morning, Moored Boats* (oil on board, 15 x 21 ins / 38 x 53 cm) GBP 5,500. LONDON, 13 July 2000, *Busy Harbour* (oil on canvas laid on board, 15 x 20 ins / 39 x 51 cm) GBP 2,500. EASTBOURNE, 22 Nov 2000, *Quayside Scene with Moored Boats* (oil on canvas, 19 x 29 ins / 48 x 74 cm) GBP 1,150. LONDON, 21 Nov 2001, *St Ives, Unloading the Catch* (oil on canvas, 21 x 30 ins / 53 x 76 cm) GBP 5,000. NEW YORK, 5 Dec 2001, *Boats at Mevagissey Harbour, Cornwall* (oil on canvas, 23 x 29 ins / 58 x 74 cm) USD 4,250. DUBLIN, 8 May 2002, *Ballinaboy* (oil on canvas, 13 x 30 ins / 33 x 76 cm) EUR 1,600. LONDON, 17 May 2002, *Carraroe, Connemara* (oil on canvas, 15 x 20 ins / 38 x 51 cm) GBP 1,200. LONDON, 26 Feb 2003, *French Harbour* (oil on canvas, 13 x 18 ins / 34 x 45 cm) GBP 3,200. LONDON, 6 June 2003, *Polperro* (oil on board, 26 x 39 ins / 67 x 100 cm) GBP 4,800. LONDON, 15 Sept 2004, *Harbour* (oil on canvas, 15 x 21 ins / 38 x 53 cm) GBP 1,600. LONDON, 15 Sept 2004, *Mannin Bay, Connemara* (oil on canvasboard, 6 x 15 ins / 16 x 38 cm) GBP 1,800.

RUSSELL, John
British, 18th - 19th century.
Born 29 March 1745; died 20 April 1806, in Hull.

Active in Guildford (Surrey).

Painter, pastellist, engraver (burin), writer. Portraits.

John Russell, father of Anne and William Russell, came from a Yorkshire family. His father and grandfather were booksellers and print dealers in Hull. His family background and his youthful talent pointed him in the direction of an artistic career. He was a pupil of the academic painter Francis Cotes.

Russell began exhibiting in 1760, at the Society of Artists. By 1767, he was working independently, although he remained in frequent contact with his mentor, Cotes. In 1770, he married the daughter of a map and prints dealer, Miss Hanna Foden - a beautiful young woman whose portrait he subsequently painted in pastel. Although his skill was widely recognised - not least at the level of the Royal Academy, where he had been an exhibitor since the foundation of that institution in 1768 - his life was not without its disappointments and frustrations. Much of this can be ascribed to his intransigent religious convictions, an aspect of his character that would cause a rupture in his relationship with Cotes.

He was admitted to associate membership of the Royal Academy in 1772 but did not become a full member until 1778. He travelled extensively in England, spending time in Cambridge and Brighton in 1772, in Kidderminster and Shrewsbury in 1777, in Worcester in 1780 and in Wales in 1781. Some of his best (and rare) landscapes date from after 1781.

He came into a substantial inheritance in 1768 and was by that time earning a considerable amount from his portrait work. On the other hand, he had seven children to feed and clothe. In 1790, however, he was retained as a painter to George III, a position which afforded him access to leading figures in English society. He painted numerous portraits of the English royal family.

Towards the end of his career, he retired to the provinces, most notably to the Yorkshire town of Leeds. A bout of cholera in 1803 left him deaf. Then, in April 1806, he contracted typhoid fever, and died several days later.

Russell was a remarkable portraitist, whose draughtsmanship and colour sense were widely agreed in his day to rival those of Sir Joshua Reynolds. Excellent as his oils may be, it is for his pastel work that he will be best remembered. He was a hard worker who encouraged his pupils to 'learn all there is to learn about the human anatomy - and then forget it'. His main strength lay in his child portraits, but his delicate rendering of flowers and fabrics also deserves particular mention. He wrote several technical treatises on painting and toiled for over two decades using a telescope and engraving tools to produce a lunar map.

JR

Museums and Galleries:

BATH (Holburne Mus. of Art): *Love Songs and Matches* (oil on canvas) - BRIGHTON (Mus. & AG): *Portrait of John Godbold* (1794, pastel); *Portrait of Robert Darling Wills* (1789, pastel) - LEEDS (City AG): *Portrait of William Wilberforce* (oil on canvas); *Portrait of Alexander Turner* (oil on canvas); *Portrait of Anthony Knowles* (oil on canvas) - LONDON (British Mus.): *Portrait of Emperor Leopold I* - LONDON (Dulwich Picture Gal.): *Samuel Moody* (pastel/paper) - LONDON (Tate Collection): *The Fortune-Teller* (exhibited in 1790, pastel/paper) - LONDON (Victoria and Albert Mus.): nine pastels - PARIS (Louvre): *Child with Cherries* (pastel).

Auction records:

LONDON, 1896, *Anne Bonar*, FRF 2,700; *Mr Bonar's Two Children*, FRF 3,000. PARIS, 1 Feb 1896, *Portrait of Sir George Beaumont*, FRF 2,375. LONDON, 1899, *Portraits of Madame Earle* (pastel) FRF 8,125. LONDON, 1899, *Pig in a Poke* (pastel) FRF 19,675; *Incredulity* (pastel) FRF 78,750. LONDON, 1899, *Portrait of the Misses Earle in White* (pastel) FRF 19,625. LONDON, 1 July 1899, *Persian Sibyl*, FRF 30,175. PARIS, 16-18 May 1907, *Portrait of Miss Colighby*, FRF 5,000; *Portrait of Lady Boyd*, FRF 6,900. NEW YORK, 12 March 1908, *Out of the Garden*, USD 460. LONDON, 24 Feb 1910, *Portrait of Colonel Schipley* (1771) GBP 21. PARIS, 15 Feb 1911, *Portrait of a Great Lady*, FRF 4,100. LONDON, 28 April 1922, *Portrait of the Misses May*, GBP 945; *Mr May*, GBP 168. LONDON, 26 May 1922, *Lady Hill* (pastel) GBP 44. LONDON, 22 June 1922, *Gentleman in Blue* (drawing) GBP 50. LONDON, 23 March 1923, *Mrs Austin* (drawing) GBP 141. LONDON, 11 May 1923, *Lady Arabella Montagu* (pastel) GBP 147. LONDON, 18 July 1924, *Mrs Rawlins* (pastel) GBP 33. LONDON, 18 July 1924, *Match-Seller*, GBP 462. LONDON, 26 June 1925, *Sir James Duff*, GBP 136. LONDON, 18 Dec 1925, *Mrs Grant and Daughter* (pastel) GBP 210. LONDON, 28 July 1926, *Mrs Vyner* (pastel) GBP 199; *Miss Laura Glover*, GBP 199. LONDON, 15 June 1928, *Little Match-Seller*, GBP 504. LONDON, 13 July 1928, *Dr R. Darling Willis* (pastel) GBP 147; *Admiral Richard Willis* (pastel) GBP 199. PARIS, 10 and 11 Dec 1928, *Portrait of General Sir William Pawcett* (pastel) FRF 26,100. LONDON, 14 Dec 1928, *Miss Darby with a Little Girl* (pastel) GBP 756; *Miss Sarah White as Hebe* (pastel) GBP 294; *John Bonar's Two Children* (pastel) GBP 210; *Little Lace-Makers* (pastel) GBP 262; *Love Songs and Matches* (pastel) GBP 651; *Persian Sybil* (pastel) GBP 819. PARIS, 19 Dec 1928, *Little Girl with a Lamb*, FRF 6,150. LONDON, 24 May 1929, *Portrait of a Gentleman* (pastel) GBP 304; *Age of Innocence*; *Cake in Danger* (two pastels) GBP 1,102. LONDON, 21 June 1929, *Sophia Margaret Penn* (pastel) GBP 173. LONDON, 9 May 1930, *Sir John Frederick* (pastel); *Lady Frederick* (pastel) GBP 199. LONDON, 11 July 1930, *Colonel Eidington* (pastel) GBP 210. LONDON, 20 March 1931, *Mrs Adams* (pastel) GBP 126. NEW YORK, 2 April 1931, *Two Sisters*, USD 275. LONDON, 4 and 5 Feb 1932, *Earl of Harrington as a Child*, GBP 475. LONDON, 29 April 1932, *Female Portrait* (pastel) GBP 250. NEW YORK, 14 Nov 1934, *Mathew Smith*, USD 330. PARIS, 15 March 1935, *Child with Soap Bubble* (pastel) FRF 32,000. LONDON, 29 March 1935, *Mrs Higginson and Son* (pastel) GBP 126. LONDON, 31 May 1935, *Child Portrait of Philip Stanhope, Earl of Chesterfield*, GBP 131. PARIS, 5 March 1936, *Portrait presumed to be of one of the Sibley-Braithwaite Children* (pastel) FRF 2,000. NEW YORK, 21 Oct 1937, *Portrait of a Gentleman*, USD 370. LONDON, 18 July 1941, *Portrait of a Gentleman*, GBP 94. PARIS, 30 March 1942, *Female Portrait* (1787) FRF 32,500. NEW YORK, 14-16 Jan 1943, *Portrait of a Gentleman*, USD 450. NEW YORK, 17 Feb 1944, *Susan Warren* (pastel) USD 900. LONDON, 31 March 1944, *Dr Thomson's Children*, GBP 273. NEW YORK, 24 May 1944, *Female Portrait* (pastel) USD 225. PARIS, 9 June 1944, *Child with Bonnet* (pastel) FRF 35,000. LONDON, 31 Jan 1945, *George IV as Prince Regent* (red and black chalk) GBP 96. LONDON, 14 Dec 1945, *Miss Reid* (drawing) GBP 78. NEW YORK, 25-27 April 1946, *Portrait of a Lady*, USD 200. LONDON, 3 May 1946, *Young Girl with Dog* (pastel) GBP 31. PARIS, 4 June 1947, *Portrait of Madame Morgan and her Daughter* (light watercolour wash) FRF 6,400. PARIS, 11 March 1949, *Young Girl Sitting under a Tree* (attributed) FRF 9,500. PARIS, 8 July 1949, *Portrait presumed to be that of Sir William Garrow* (attributed) FRF 65,000. PARIS, 21 March 1952, *Portrait of a Gentleman* (pastel) FRF 300,000. LONDON, 24 June 1960, *Portrait of Lieutenant-General Sir James Duff*, GBP 504. NEW YORK, 7 April 1961, *The Wormald Children, York*, USD 11,000. PARIS, 14 March 1964, *Child Portrait of Lady Georgina Cavendish* (pastel) FRF 11,000 LONDON, 13 March 1970, *Match-Seller*, Gns 420. VERSAILLES, 13 May 1973, *Portrait of a Lady of Quality* (pastel) FRF 6,000. VERSAILLES, 2 Dec 1973, *Cliffs at Belle-Ile*, FRF 7,500. LONDON, 18 July 1974, *Portrait of Emily de Visme* (pastel) GBP 500. LONDON, 18 Nov 1976, *Child Portrait of Henrietta Rice* (pastel, 22 1/2 x 17 1/4 ins / 57 x 44 cm) GBP 1,900. LONDON, 30 Nov 1978, *Portrait of a Young Girl* (1788, pastel, oval, 23 x 17 1/4 ins / 58.5 x 43.5 cm) GBP 900. NEW YORK, 30 May 1979, *Mountain Land-*

scape with Dead Game (oil on canvas, 41 1/2 x 66 ins / 105.5 x 167.5 cm) USD 2,000. LONDON, 19 June 1979, *Thomas Pitt's Two Sons* (1804, pastel, 29 1/2 x 24 1/2 ins / 75 x 62.5 cm) GBP 12,000. PARIS, 30 March 1981, *Little Boy and Dog* (1792, oil on canvas, 51 1/4 x 35 1/2 ins / 130 x 90 cm) FRF 270,000. LONDON, 16 March 1982, *Fortune-Teller* (1795, pastel, 31 1/4 x 27 1/4 ins / 79.5 x 69.5 cm) GBP 2,600. LONDON, 8 June 1983, *Still Life* (oil on canvas, 27 x 47 1/4 ins / 68.5 x 120 cm) GBP 2,000. LONDON, 20 March 1984, *Young Woman with a Silver Chalice* (pastel/mounted paper/canvas, 24 x 18 ins / 61 x 45.7 cm) GBP 7,000. LONDON, 14 March 1985, *Thomas Pitt and his son William* (1799, pastel, 30 x 25 ins / 76 x 63.5 cm) GBP 7,500. TROYES, 16 Oct 1988, *Portrait of a Young Girl* (pastel, 24 1/2 x 19 1/4 ins / 62 x 49 cm) FRF 15,000. NEW YORK, 21 Oct 1988, *Portrait of the Artist's Daughter* (1778, pastel/paper/canvas, 24 x 20 1/4 ins / 61 x 51.5 cm) USD 10,450; *Portrait of a Little Girl with a Basket of Flowers* (pastel, 23 1/4 x 18 1/2 ins / 59 x 47 cm) GBP 660. PERTH, 28 Aug 1989, *Sea Lions and a Sea Trout* (oil on canvas, 36 x 40 1/4 ins / 91.5 x 102.5 cm) GBP 2,750. NEW YORK, 13 Oct 1989, *Male Portrait* (1767, oil on canvas, 29 1/4 x 24 1/2 ins / 74 x 62 cm) USD 7,150. LONDON, 17 Nov 1989, *Young Peasant Woman holding a Duck* (oil on canvas, 23 3/4 x 18 ins / 60.3 x 45.6 cm) GBP 7,700. PARIS, 15 Dec 1989, *Profile Portrait of a Lady* (pastel, 24 x 18 ins / 61 x 46 cm) FRF 40,000. LONDON, 14 Feb 1990, *Waiting for the Mistress to Return* (oil on canvas, 20 x 29 ins / 50.8 x 73.6 cm) GBP 8,250. PARIS, 10 April 1990, *Portrait of a Woman wearing a Lace Bonnet* (1789, pastel, 23 1/2 x 17 1/4 ins / 60 x 44 cm) FRF 24,000. NEW YORK, 19 July 1990, *Portrait of a Lady* (pastel/paper/canvas, 35 1/2 x 27 ins / 90.3 x 68.6 cm) USD 2,090. LONDON, 14 Nov 1990, *Portrait of a Lady and Child at the Harpsichord* (1798, oil on canvas, 39 x 30 ins / 99 x 76 cm) GBP 4,950. MONACO, 21 June 1991, *Portrait of Mr Lee* (1795, pastel, 23 1/2 x 17 1/4 ins / 60 x 44 cm) FRF 28,860. PERTH, 26 Aug 1991, *Trout* (oil on panel, 10 1/4 x 18 ins / 26 x 46 cm) GBP 1,320. GLASGOW, 4 Dec 1991, *Two Salmon* (oil on canvas, 14 1/2 x 29 1/2 ins / 37 x 75 cm) GBP 2,860. EDINBURGH, 28 April 1992, *Salmon* (oil on canvas, 17 3/4 x 35 1/2 ins / 45 x 90 cm) GBP 2,310. NEW YORK, 21 May 1992, *Portray of a Young Nobleman presumed to be Robert Grosvenor, Viscount Belgrave and Marquis of Westminster* (1788, oil on canvas, 12 x 10 ins / 30.5 x 25.4 cm) USD 8,250. NEW YORK, 5 June 1992, *The Day's Catch* (1871, oil on canvas, 31 3/4 x 47 1/2 ins / 80.6 x 120.7 cm) USD 11,550. PERTH, 31 Aug 1993, *Sea Trout* (oil on canvas, 14 3/4 x 29 3/4 ins / 37.5 x 75.5 cm) GBP 2,185. LONDON, 10 March 1995, *Trout on a Rocky River Bank* (1871, oil on canvas, 16 x 22 ins / 40.6 x 55.8 cm) GBP 7,475. LONDON, 3 April 1996, *Portrait of Caroline Sackville in a White Gown with a Blue Belt* (oil on canvas, 29 1/4 x 24 1/2 ins / 74 x 62 cm) GBP 2,185. LONDON, 6 June 1996, *Netting Salmon* (oil on canvas, 17 1/2 x 36 ins / 44.5 x 91.5 cm) GBP 1,725. LONDON, 17 Oct 1996, *The Day's Takings* (oil on canvas, 21 x 40 1/2 ins / 53.4 x 103 cm) GBP 2,990. LONDON, 15 April 1997, *Banks of the River* (oil on canvas, 35 3/4 x 28 ins / 91 x 71 cm) GBP 5,290. LONDON, 12 Nov 1997, *Portrait of Micoc and his son Tootac, New World Eskimoes brought to England by Commodore Palliser* (oil on canvas, 29 3/4 x 24 ins / 75.5 x 61 cm) GBP 33,350. LONDON, 12 July 1999, *Portrait of Young Boy. Portrait of Young Girl* (oil on canvas, oval, a pair, 15 x 13 ins / 39 x 33 cm) GBP 12,000. LONDON, 9 Nov 1999, *Boy Blowing Bubbles Identified as the Artist's Son William* (pastel, 24 x 17 ins / 60 x 44 cm) GBP 3,800. LONDON, 8 June 2000, *Portrait of Lady in a White Dress with Blue Ribbons* (pastel, 23 x 17 ins / 59 x 44 cm) GBP 7,000. LONDON, 15 June 2000, *Portrait of Mr Wilson Wearing Blue Coat and White Cravat* (pastel, 24 x 18 ins / 61 x 46 cm) GBP 3,800. LONDON, 21 Nov 2001, *Portrait of Girl, Half-length in White Dress and White Fichu* (1784, pastel, 24 x 18 ins / 60 x 45 cm) GBP 19,000. LONDON, 29 Nov 2001, *Portrait of Anne and Maria Russell* (pastel, 40 x 30 ins / 101 x 76 cm) GBP 28,000. LONDON, 21 March 2002, *Portrait of Dr Francis Willis* (pastel, 23 x 17 ins / 59 x 44 cm) GBP 7,200. LONDON, 28 Nov 2002, *Portrait of Miss E. and Miss L. Earle with a Lamb* (pastel, 29 x 24 ins / 74 x 62 cm) GBP 10,800. LONDON, 22 May 2003, *Lady Wearing White Dress with Cream Waistband* (miniature) GBP 6,500. NEW YORK, 30 May 2003, *Portrait of a Gentleman, Half-length, in a Blue Coat* (pastel on paper on board, 30 x 22 ins / 75 x 57 cm) USD 8,000. CHICHESTER, 27 April 2004, *Portraits of Miss Paterson and Mr Hardcastle* (1785, pastel, oval, a pair, 24 x 18 ins / 60 x 45 cm) GBP 3,400. LONDON, 14 July 2004, *Portrait of a Young Lady with a Bonnet* (1801, pastel, 24 x 18 ins / 61 x 45 cm) GBP 6,500.

RUSSELL, John Peter

Australian, 19th - 20th century.

Born 16 June 1858, in Sydney; died 1930 or 1931, in Sydney.

From 1882 to 1921 active in France.

Painter. Portraits, landscapes with figures, landscapes.

John Peter Russell left Australia for England in 1881. He studied at the Slade School of Fine Art, London, then he went to France in 1882 where he worked in the studio of Fernand Cormon in Paris. He made the acquaintance of Carrière and Toulouse-Lautrec. He lived in France for 40 years: in Picardy, Paris, the Paris region and finally in Belle-Île from 1886, where he built a house. He knew Monet in Belle-Île in 1886, and also encountered Sisley and Rodin who sculpted a bust of his wife. But he was particularly friendly with Van Gogh and painted a portrait of him. He also knew the young Matisse and gave him painting lessons. He returned to Australia in 1921. He was a wealthy man and sold very few works during his lifetime. In 1997, the Jacobin Museum in Morlaix dedicated an exhibition to him.

He painted a great variety of subjects in an Impressionist style, but very freely and instinctively.

MUSEUMS AND GALLERIES:

AMSTERDAM (Rijksmus.): *Portrait of Van Gogh* - MORLAIX (Mus. des Jacobins): on loan from the Louvre (Orsay collection) - PARIS (Mus. d'Orsay) - PARIS (Mus. Rodin) - SYDNEY.

AUCTION RECORDS:

LONDON, 17 March 1976, *Mountainous Winter Landscape* (watercolour and pencil, 6 3/4 x 9 1/2 ins / 17 x 24 cm) GBP 340. LONDON, 16 Nov 1977, *Spire, Winter Sun* (1903, oil on canvas, 25 x 25 ins / 63.5 x 63.5 cm) GBP 6,900. LONDON, 2 Nov 1979, *Trafalgar Square* (1914, watercolour and gouache, 17 1/2 x 22 1/2 ins / 44.4 x 57.2 cm) GBP 800. LONDON, 25 June 1980, *Belle-Ile* (1905, oil on canvas, 26 x 32 ins / 66 x 81 cm) GBP 11,500. LONDON, 19 May 1982, *Rocks in Belle-Ile* (oil on panel, 9 1/4 x 13 ins / 23.5 x 33 cm) GBP 2,800. LONDON, 4 Nov 1987, *Belle-Île, Brittany* (oil on canvas, 15 1/4 x 18 ins / 38.5 x 46 cm) GBP 13,500. LONDON, 1 Dec 1988, *Landscape* (1912, pencil and watercolour, 7 x 9 3/4 ins / 18 x 25 cm) GBP 3,850; *Idyll* (oil on canvas, 22 1/2 x 28 1/2 ins / 57.2 x 72.4 cm) GBP 60,500. LONDON, 30 Nov 1989, *Portrait of a Man* (pencil, 11 1/4 x 5 1/2 ins / 28.3 x 14 cm) GBP 1,540. CHALON-SUR-SAÔNE, 21 April 1991, *Dunes at Belle-Île* (charcoal and pastel, 7 x 9 3/4 ins / 17.5 x 25 cm) FRF 15,000. LONDON, 28 Nov 1991, *Misty Evening in Belle-Île* (1910, watercolour, 9 3/4 x 13 3/4 ins / 25 x 35 cm) GBP 3,300. ANGERS, 12 Dec 1995, *Goulphar Point in Belle-Île* (1901, painting/canvas, 21 1/4 x 25 1/2 ins / 54 x 65 cm) FRF 310,000. MELBOURNE, 20-21 Aug 1996, *The Needle, Winter Sun, Belle-Île* (1903, canvas, 24 3/4 x 24 3/4 ins / 63 x 63 cm) AUD 266,500. PARIS, 31 March 1998, *Belle-Île on Sea* (oil on canvas, 18 x 22 ins / 46 x 55 cm) FRF 315,000.

RUSSELL, John Wentworth

Canadian, 20th century.

Born 28 August 1879, in Binbrook, near Hamilton (Ontario); died 1959.

Painter. Figures, portraits, urban landscapes.

John Wentworth Russell studied at the Hamilton Art School before continuing his studies in New York and Paris.

MUSEUMS AND GALLERIES:

OTTAWA (Nat. Gal. of Canada): *Mother and Son*.

AUCTION RECORDS:
TORONTO, 12 June 1989, *Honfleur Harbour in France* (oil on card, 12 1/2 x 15 1/2 ins / 31.8 x 39.4 cm) CAD 3,600. TORONTO, 25 Feb 2002, *Girl in a Hammock* (oil on panel, 13 x 19 ins / 32 x 49 cm) CAD 3,000. TORONTO, 3 June 2002, *Fruit and Glass* (1908, oil on canvas, 26 x 32 ins / 65 x 81 cm) CAD 6,800.

RUSSELL, Morgan

American, 20th century.
Born 25 January 1886, in New York; died 1953, in Broomall (Pennsylvania).
Active between 1909 and 1946 in France.
Painter.
Symbolism, Synchromism.

Morgan Russell lived in Paris in 1906 and was drawn to the work of the Impressionists. On his return to America he enrolled at the Art Students League of New York and was the pupil of Robert Henri, a Realist painter who in 1908 exhibited with the American Ashcan Painters. He returned regularly to Paris and went to live there in 1909, working with Matisse on a number of sculptures. Through his connections with Leo and Gertrude Stein he met a large number of innovative artists of the time. In 1911-1912 he met Macdonald Wright, with whom he set up a movement they named Synchromism. Until 1946 Russell lived in Aigremont, a quiet village in Burgundy.

Macdonald Wright and Russell were close to Kupka, Picabia and in particular Delaunay, painters whom Apollinaire called 'Orphists'. The relationship between Russell's early Synchromist paintings and Picabia's *Procession to Seville* of 1912 and his *Udnies* series of 1913 cannot be denied. In the preface to the catalogue for the exhibition they jointly held at Bernheims in 1913, which marked the official arrival of Synchromism, they tried to dissociate themselves from the Orphists, also prominent in 1913 following the appearance of Apollinaire's *Cubist Painters*. While Russell's work features a crowding together of Cubist-type shapes - with echoes both of Picabia and Delaunay's contrasting polychromy - as a Synchromist he aimed to exploit the synthesis between form and colour: 'We dream of a more noble role for colour. This is the same quality of form that we attempted to express and reveal, and for the first time here, colour appears in this role. It is the painter's duty to deepen the mysterious relationships between colour and form, between colours and the nature of the form.' Russell himself offers a more subtle explanation: 'In *Synchromy in Dark Blue*, I have worked solely on the colour, its rhythms, its contrasts and certain directions motivated by masses of colour. There is no subject to be found here in the ordinary sense of the word: its subject is the dark blue... This is a range of colours balancing around a generator colour that must shoot out from the form.' The preoccupation with a synaesthesia of colours, particularly when combined with spatial planes and three-dimensional forms, was common to the majority of painters of the time, particularly Delaunay, Kandinsky, Jawlensky and Léger. Russell, however, achieved a certain purity in his concept of Abstraction: 'It is intentional that there is no subject (image), in order to exalt other regions of the spirit', a remark that set him on the same level as Mondrian, Kandinsky, Delaunay, Kupka and Malevich. From 1916 he all but renounced Abstraction altogether, painting mainly scenes from the Bible in the Symbolist style as seen in works by Maurice Denis, moving on to fairly conventional crucifixions. Even the late-flowering of the movement, which Russell observed almost as a stranger, did not encourage him to return to his former style (unlike Macdonald Wright). He preferred instead the sincerity of painting religious compositions. Yet Russell's influence and that of the Synchromist Movement was nonetheless very real, as the works of Thomas Benton, Marsden Hartley and Patrick Henry attest.

His work featured at the 1910 Salon d'Automne in Paris and then at the Salon des Tuileries. Russell and Macdonald Wright exhibited several Synchromist works in 1913 at the Neue Kunstsalon in Munich, at the Galerie Bernheim-Jeune in Paris, and at the Salon des Indépendants. Russell's work was included in the historic *Armory Show* of 1913, along with that of Patrick Henry Bruce and Macdonald Wright. He and Macdonald Wright held a Synchromist exhibition in New York in 1916, and Russell featured in the *Abstract Painting and Sculpture in America* exhibition held at the Museum of Modern Art in New York in 1951. In 2003 he was posthumously represented at the collective exhibition *Aux origines de l'abstraction (1800-1914)* (*The Origins of Abstraction, 1800-1914*) at the Musée d'Orsay, Paris. After a solo exhibition in 1950 in the USA, he had his first retrospective in 1953 at the Rose Fried Gallery in New York.

BIBLIOGRAPHY:
Wright, Willard Huntington, *Modern Painting, its Tendency and Meaning*, John Lane, New York, 1915. *Three American Pionneers: Russell, Mac Donald-Wright, Bruce*, exhibition catalogue, Rose Fried Gall., New York, 1950. Ritchie, Andrew Carnduff, *Abstract Painting and Sculpture in America*, Museum of Modern Art, New York, 1951. *Morgan Russell: in Memoriam*, exhibition catalogue, Rose Fried Gall., New York, 1953. Kushner, Marilyn S., *Morgan-Russell*, Hudson Hills Press, New York, 1990. Lemoine, Serge/Rousseau, Pascal, et al., *Aux origines de l'abstraction (1800-1914)*, exhibition catalogue, Musée d'Orsay, Paris, 2003.

MUSEUMS AND GALLERIES:
BUFFALO (Albright-Knox AG): *Synchromy to Form: Orange* (1914) - NEW YORK (MoMA).

AUCTION RECORDS:
PARIS, 14 May 1925, *Paris, L'Arc de Triomphe and La Place de l'Étoile*, FRF 105. PARIS, 2 March 1934, *Torso of a Young Boy*, FRF 50. PARIS, July 1946, *La Place de l'Étoile*, FRF 1,700; *Le pont Alexandre* (*Alexandre Bridge*, FRF 1,400. NEW YORK, 9 Dec 1959, *Still-life with Apples*, USD 1,600. LOS ANGELES, 6 Nov 1978, *Seated Nude* (oil on canvas, 36 x 28 1/2 ins / 91.4 x 72.4 cm) USD 2,600. LOS ANGELES, 23 June 1981, *Two Nudes* (oil on canvas, each 20 x 20 ins / 51 x 51 cm) USD 3,000. NEW YORK, 22 June 1984, *Seated Nude* (oil on canvas, 21 x 25 3/4 ins / 53.3 x 65.4 cm) USD 1,300. NEW YORK, 28 May 1987, *Abstraction* (1914, oil on canvas, 12 1/2 x 9 1/2 ins / 31.8 x 24.1 cm) USD 29,000. PARIS, 27 Oct 1988, *Adam and Eve* (1927, two oils on canvas, 13 3/4 x 9 1/2 ins / 35 x 24 cm) FRF 10,500. PARIS, 26 April 1990, *Adam and Eve* (two oils on canvas, 13 3/4 x 9 1/2 ins / 35 x 24 cm) FRF 8,500. NEW YORK, 16 May 1990, *Synchromy No. 2 Towards the Light* (1912, oil on canvas, 13 x 9 1/2 ins / 33 x 24.2 cm) USD 176,000. NEW YORK, 17 Dec 1990, *Family* (oil on canvas, 53 x 36 ins / 134.6 x 91.6 cm) USD 4,950. NEW YORK, 31 March 1993, *Untitled* (oil on canvas, 16 1/2 x 13 1/4 ins / 41.6 x 33.7 cm) USD 1,265. NEW YORK, 15 Nov 1993, *Landscape* (oil on canvas, 23 x 29 ins / 58.3 x 73.6 cm) USD 2,990. NEW YORK, 3 Dec 1993, *Synchromy* (oil on canvas, 32 x 10 ins / 81.3 x 25.4 cm) USD 31,050. PARIS, 20 Dec 1995, *Self-portrait* (oil on canvas, 32 1/4 x 25 1/2 ins / 82 x 65 cm) FRF 8,000. PARIS, 24 Nov 1996, *Self-portrait with Palette* (oil on canvas, 28 3/4 x 21 1/4 ins / 73 x 54 cm) FRF 5,500. PARIS, 20 March 1998, *Still-life with Cup* (oil on canvas, 23 1/2 x 28 3/4 ins / 60 x 73 cm) FRF 2,900. NEW YORK, 5 May 1999, *Synchromy* (oil on canvas, 16 x 13 ins / 41 x 33 cm) USD 8,500. NEW YORK, 26 May 1999, *Synchromy in Blue-violet* (1912, oil on canvas laid on board, 13 x 9 ins / 33 x 24 cm) USD 270,000. SAN FRANCISCO, 24 Oct 2000, *Still-life with Blue Jug* (oil on canvasboard, 24 x 21 ins / 61 x 54 cm) USD 10,000. NEW YORK, 29 Nov 2000, *Synchromist Still-life* (oil on canvas, 17 x 13 ins / 42 x 33 cm) USD 80,000. PARIS, 6 April 2001, *Synchromy* (c. 1912, oil on canvas on card, 13 x 9 ins / 32 x 24 cm) FRF 310,000. NEW YORK, 29 Nov 2001, *Synchromist Nude* (1913, oil on canvas, 24 x 20 ins / 60 x 50 cm) USD 180,000.

RUSSELL, Moses
American, 19th century.
Active in 1832.
Miniaturist.

RUSSELL, Walter
American, 20th century.
Born 19 May 1871, in Boston (Massachusetts); died 1963.
Painter, sculptor, illustrator. Portraits.

Walter Russell was the pupil of Albert Munsell and Ernest Major in Boston, of Howard Pyle in Wilmington and Jean-Paul Laurens in Paris. He was a member of the Spanish academy of arts and letters and of the Royal Academy, of which he was an associate since 1920. He lived and worked in New York and Washington. In 1900 he was given a special mention at the Turin exhibition in Italy. He painted many portraits of children and illustrated many children's books.

MUSEUMS AND GALLERIES:
LONDON (Tate Collection): several works.

AUCTION RECORDS:
NEW YORK, 17 Dec 1990, *Roman Villa* (1906, oil on canvas, 25 x 30 ins / 63.5 x 76.3 cm) USD 1,650. NEW YORK, 4 Dec 1992, *At the Beach* (1898, oil on canvas, 28½ x 36¼ ins / 72.5 x 91.8 cm) USD 77,000. BOSTON, 12 Nov 1999, *Ipswich Willows, Autumnal Landscape* (oil on canvas, 25 x 30 ins / 63 x 76 cm) USD 4,750.

RUSSELL, Walter Westley (Sir)
British, 19th - 20th century.
Born 31 May 1867; died 16 April 1949.
Painter, engraver (etching), illustrator. Figures, portraits, interiors, landscapes, architectural views.

Walter Westley Russell trained at Westminster School of Art. He taught at Slade School of Fine Art, London from 1895 to 1927, He was elected a Royal Academician in 1935, and was knighted in the same year.

He was notably appreciated as a portraitist, and also made etchings. He contributed to the following publications: *Illustrated London News, Daily Chronicle, The Graphic* and *Pall Mall Magazine*.

He exhibited in London from 1891. He appeared at the exhibitions at the Royal Academy, London, the Royal Hibernian Academy and the New English Art Club, and in Liverpool in 1909.

MUSEUMS AND GALLERIES:
DUBLIN (GMA) - LIVERPOOL (Walker AG) - LONDON (Grosvenor Gallery) - LONDON (Tate Collection) - PIETERMARITZBURG.

AUCTION RECORDS:
LONDON, 18 Feb 1911, *In the Orchard,* GBP 1; *Lady with a Muff,* GBP 21. LONDON, 8 and 9 April 1943, *Bathing Tents* GBP 39. LONDON, 19 Oct 1945, *Hampstead Heath* GBP 94. LONDON, 25 June 1980, *Poole Harbour* (oil on canvas, 23½ x 35½ ins / 60 x 90 cm) GBP 900. LONDON, 12 March 1982, *Coutances Landscape* (oil on canvas, 28½ x 36 ins / 72.5 x 91.5 cm) GBP 1,000. LONDON, 14 Nov 1984, *Firelight* (oil on canvas, 30 x 40 ins / 76 x 101.5 cm) GBP 4,500. NEW YORK, 24 May 1995, *Beach Cabins* (oil on canvas, 28 x 36 ins / 71.1 x 91.4 cm) USD 34,500. LONDON, 4 June 1999, *The Square at Etaples* (oil on canvas, 28 x 36 ins / 71 x 91 cm) GBP 2,400. LONDON, 4 June 1999, *The Grand Canal, Evening* (oil on canvas, 24 x 36 ins / 61 x 91 cm) GBP 7,200. LONDON, 28 June 2001, *Children at Croquet* (oil on canvas, 28 x 36 ins / 71 x 91 cm) GBP 2,800. LONDON, 28 June 2001, *Fishing Boats in a Sunlit Harbour* (oil on canvas, 28 x 36 ins / 71 x 91 cm) GBP 3,900. LONDON, 3 July 2002, *Under the Apple Trees* (oil on canvas, 23 x 30 ins / 58 x 76 cm) GBP 20,000. LONDON, 26 Nov 2002, *Firelight* (oil on canvas, 30 x 40 ins / 76 x 102 cm) GBP 7,500.

RUSSELL, William
British, 19th century.
Born 1780, in London; died 14 September 1870.
Painter, pastellist. Portraits, genre scenes.

William Russell was the son and pupil of John Russell. He worked in London and exhibited at the Royal Academy and at the British Institution in 1805 and 1809.

MUSEUMS AND GALLERIES:
LONDON (National Portrait Gal.): *Sir John Bayley, 1st Bt* (c. 1808, oil on canvas).

AUCTION RECORDS:
LONDON, 11 July 1930, *Mrs. Grave and Saint Agnes* (pastel) GBP 22. LONDON, 27 April 1951, *Portrait of a Young Woman,* FRF 450,000.

RUSSELL, William George
American, 19th - 20th century.
Born 6 February 1860, in Chatam.
Painter, watercolourist. Landscapes, seascapes.

William George Russell settled in Atlantic City.

RUSSENBERGER, Jacob.
See **RAUSSENBERGER**

RUSSI. See also **RUSSO**

RUSSI, Francesco di Giovanni de, or Rossi, called Franco Ferrarese
Italian, 15th century.
Active in Mantua.
Illuminator.

Francesco di Giovanni de Russi was the pupil of Guglielmo Giraldi, and was influenced by C. Tura. He also worked in Urbino and Venice. His illuminations are in the British Museum, London and in the Vatican Library, Rome.

AUCTION RECORDS:
PARIS, 28 and 29 June 1926, *Annunciation* (pen and bistre) FRF 1,400. LONDON, 15 July 1927, *Woman Wearing a White Dress,* GBP 210. GENOA, 27 Oct 1934, *Portrait of a Man,* ITL 4,100.

RUSSI, Gennaro
Italian, 18th - 19th century.
Born 20 September 1770, in Castelli; died 23 December 1850.
Potter.

RUSSI, Mattia
Italian, 18th century.
Born 1717, in Castelli; died 1790.
Potter.

RUSSO, Alfred
Austrian, 19th - 20th century.
Born 22 September 1868, in Vienna.
Active in Germany.
Painter. Portraits, genre scenes.

Alfred Russo studied in Leipzig, Berlin, Munich and Paris (under Bouguereau). He lived and worked in Berlin, notably as a restorer.

RUSSO, Cristoforo
Italian, 18th century.
Active in Naples during the first half of the 18th century.
Painter. Landscapes. Wall decorations.

Cristoforo Russo collaborated with F. Malerba on the ceiling of the great hall of the Girolamini library in Naples.

RUSSO, Domenico
Italian, 19th century.
Born 2 July 1832, in Nicotera; died 13 January 1907, in Nicotera.
Painter.
Domenico Russo studied with Auria, Mancinelli, Guerra and Domenico Morelli, producing works in a retro-Romantic style.
MUSEUMS AND GALLERIES:
NAPLES (Mus. di San Martino): *Garibaldi outside Rome.*

RUSSO, Francesco Maria
Italian, 18th century.
Painter.
Francesco Maria Russo was active in Naples. In 1749, he produced the paintings representing the *Glory of the Holy Spirit* in the dome of the old Sansevero chapel of S Maria di Pietà dei Sangro, as well as the Rococo trompe l'œil decoration with grey-green cameo medallions depicting the six saints honoured by the family. The restrained palette, the greys and ochres, and the use of marble in the same limited spectrum mark out this church (originally built as a private chapel at the end of the 16th century and then converted into a church in the 17th and 18th centuries) as one of the most successful of the numerous 18th-century churches in Naples, most of which fail to observe the same degree of discipline. The church is also famous for the quality of its sculptures, by Giuseppe Sammartino, Antonio Corradini, Francesco Queirolo and Francesco Celebrano.

RUSSO, Gaetano
Italian, 19th century.
Born 19th century, in Messina.
Active in Rome.
Sculptor.
From 1880, Gaetano Russo exhibited works in Rome, Turin and Venice.

RUSSO, Giacomo
Italian, 16th century.
Born to a family originally from Messina, Sicily.
Illuminator. Maps.
Between 1521 and 1528, Giacomo Russo produced two painted maps, now in the Biblioteca Estense in Modena, and a decorated topographical map of the Mediterranean, now in Birmingham Museum.
MUSEUMS AND GALLERIES:
BIRMINGHAM: map of the Mediterranean - MODENA (Biblioteca Estense): two maps.

RUSSO, Giovanni Pietro
Italian, 17th century.
Born c. 1600, in Capua; died 1667.
Painter.
Having studied in Rome, Bologna and Florence, Giovanni Pietro Russo produced paintings in several churches in Capua.

RUSSO, Jacopo
Italian, 17th century.
Active in Naples during the first half of the 17th century.
Painter. Still-lifes.

RUSSO, Lorenzo
Italian, 17th - 18th century.
Died 1718.
Active in Naples.
Painter. Still-lifes.
Lorenzo Russo was a member of the guild in 1694.

RUSSO, Michelangelo
Italian, 19th century.
Born October 1817, in Polistena.
Sculptor.

RUSSO, Muzio. See **ROSSI**

RUSSO, Nicolo or Nicola Maria, or Rosso or (erroneously) Rossi
Italian, 17th century.
Born c. 1647, in Naples; died 15 July 1702.
Painter, draughtsman. Historical subjects, religious subjects, genre scenes, interiors with figures, animals. Church decoration, murals.
The pupil and imitator of Luca Giordano, Nicolo Russo painted decorative works from his master's drawings in the royal chapel in Naples. He also worked in Vienna.
MUSEUMS AND GALLERIES:
CAEN: *Animals; Interior of a Stable* - NAPLES: *Ascension of a Blessed Woman.*
AUCTION RECORDS:
PARIS, 7 March 1986, *Devotion of St Philip (Neri)* (pen and wash/outlines in black chalk, study for a ceiling) FRF 16,000. NEW YORK, 27 Jan 1999, *Triumph of Amphitrite* (oil on canvas, 30 x 40 ins / 75 x 101 cm) USD 15,000. VIENNA, 30 March 2000, *Apollo and the Four Seasons, Preparation Painting for Ceiling* (oil on canvas, 18 x 22 ins / 46 x 57 cm) ATS 120,000. NEW YORK, 29 May 2001, *Pagan Offering with an Angel Hovering with a Cross* (chalk, pen and ink wash, 12 x 9 ins / 31 x 22 cm) USD 2,000.

RUSSO, Raül
Argentinian, 20th century.
Born 1912, in Buenos Aires; died 5 December 1984, in Paris.
Painter.
Raül Russo visited Europe in 1959. He taught at the National School of Fine Art in Buenos Aires.

His work featured in collective exhibitions, including some put on by the new school of Argentinian painting such as the 1960 *International Exhibition of Modern Art* in Buenos Aires and the 1961 *150 Years of Argentinian Painting.*

He had a number of solo exhibitions, including: at the Society of the Friends of Art in Buenos Aires (1942); in Preuser (1946); in Witcom (1952); and several others in Buenos Aires.

He was awarded the Palanza Prize by the National Academy of Fine Art.

RUSSOFF, Alexander. See **RUSOV Aleksandr Nikolaevich**

RUSSOLO, Luigi or Guido
Italian, 20th century.
Born 30 April 1885, in Portogruaro (Veneto); died 1947, in Cerro di Laveno (Lake Maggiore), in 1941 according to some sources.
Active in France.
Painter, watercolourist, collage artist, engraver (etching/aquatint), musician. Figures, portraits, self-portraits, landscapes, still-lifes. Stage sets.
Futurism.
Luigi Russolo studied music but became a self-taught painter. He frequented avant-garde literary circles and was a contributor to the review *Poesia.* After meeting Boccioni and Carra in 1909 he joined the Futurist movement, signing the Futurist Manifesto of 1910. After 1913, he abandoned painting almost entirely in order to devote himself to musical research. He volunteered to fight in World War I. Wounded in the head in 1917, he underwent trepanation and it is believed that he never really recovered from this procedure. After the war, in 1927, he settled in Paris.

His early works continued to be influenced by Art Nouveau and Symbolism and centred around images of women, despite the strongly virile emphasis of Marinetti's Futurist theories that was to lead the movement to collude with the

Fascist regime. Examples are his *Perfume* of 1909-1910 or *Tina's Hair* of 1911. Nevertheless, he wholeheartedly embraced the Futurists' ideas on movement, noise and simultaneity and he painted an important series of canvases devoted to central themes of the movement with titles such as *Revolt* (1911), *Dynamism of a Car* (1911), *Memories of a Night* (1911), where his Futurism is enriched by a dreamlike quality, *Plastic Synthesis of the Movements of a Female Figure* (1912), *Energy Lines of Lightning* (1912), *Solidity of Mist* (1912) and *Compenetration of Houses + Light + Sky* (1913). This last-named work is notable for the strictly Futurist formulation of its title. Alongside these Futurist abstract paintings, his musical studies led him to turn away from subjects inspired by reality towards visual compositions directly derived from music in which interpenetrating planes and the superimposition of volumes in space recall the arrangement of musical elements in the dimension of time. An example is his painting *Music*, but it is also apparent in some of the previously mentioned works such as *Energy Lines of Lightning*. This frequent use of music as a basis for his paintings allowed him to detach himself from reality to a greater extent than many of his contemporaries, making him one of the very first precursors of truly abstract art. He was responsible for the development of Futurism into the realm of sound, publishing a *Manifesto for the Art of Noise*, which he called *Bruitisme* (Noise-Sound) and which was to anticipate future developments in *musique concrète*, the only representative of which at that time being the almost unknown Edgard Varèse. He also invented a new musical instrument, the *Intonarumori* ('Noise Intoner or Noise Tuner') which he made in collaboration with Ugo Piatti. It was capable of producing and modulating new sounds and was demonstrated a number of times from 1914.

In June 1922, when Tzara, Eluard, Péret and other members of the Dadaist movement were organising the 'Dada Salon', the Futurists put on a *Soirée Bruitiste* at the Théâtre des Champs-Élysées. During the evening, Marinetti and Russolo attempted to present their *bruitiste* works in the face of violent opposition from a deputation of Dadists (possibly because of the political orientation of the Futurists). It is perhaps to be regretted that the evening was disrupted because this was one of the very first presentations of phonetic poetry and *musique concrète*. In 1927, Russolo collaborated with Prampolini on the production of a Futurist pantomime at the Théâtre de la Madeleine in Paris. He also invented another musical instrument, the *Rumorharmonium* (Noise Harmonium).

In 1930, he was a member of the Cercle et Carré group of abstract artists founded by Michel Seuphor. Attracted to occultism, in 1938 Russolo published a work entitled *Beyond Matter*. In 1941, he began to paint again, but this time in a figurative style, as if his Futurist past had never happened, yet this was the man who had worked tirelessly for Futurists productions, writing parts for *Grande Ville* (Big Town) and *Eating on the Kursaal Terrace*, conducting orchestras, inventing and building musical instruments and painting stage sets.

Bibliography:

Seuphor, Michel, *Le Style et le Cri*, Éd. du Seuil, Paris, 1965.

Museums and Galleries:

Basel (Kunstmus.): *Compenetration of Houses + Light + Sky* (1913) - Grenoble (Mus. de Grenoble): *Plastic Synthesis of the Movements of a Female Figure* (1912) - Paris (MNAM-CCI): *Dynamism of a Car* (1912-1913) - The Hague (Gemeentemus.): *Revolt* (1911).

Auction records:

Milan, 21 and 23 Nov 1962, *Self-portrait*, ITL 2,200,000. Rome, 16 Dec 1976, *Portrait of Gino Severini* (1912, watercolour, pastel and collage, 11 1/4 x 7 3/4 ins / 28.5 x 20 cm) ITL 1,700,000. Milan, 14 June 1983, *Chestnut Tree* (oil on panel, 15 x 11 3/4 ins / 38 x 30 cm) ITL 2,200,000. Rome, 3 Dec 1985, *Futurist Figure* (1927, tempera collage on board, 7 3/4 x 11 ins / 20 x 28 cm) ITL 4,400,000. Milan, 9 April 1987, *Still-life with Bottle of Wine and Bunch of Grapes* (1929, oil on canvas, 24 x 19 3/4 ins / 61 x 50 cm) ITL 15,000,000. Milan, 14 Dec 1988, *Still-life with Flask of Wine and Bunch of Grapes* (1929, oil on canvas, 24 x 19 3/4 ins / 61 x 50 cm) ITL 13,000,000. Paris, 18 June 1989, *Still-life with Flask and Bunch of Grapes* (1929, oil on canvas, 24 x 19 3/4 ins / 61 x 50 cm) FRF 90,000. New York, 16 May 1990, *Perfume* (oil on canvas, 26 1/4 x 25 1/4 ins / 66.4 x 64 cm) USD 462,000. Rome, 13 May 1991, *Flood* (tempera/paper, 9 3/4 x 13 3/4 ins / 25 x 35 cm) ITL 15,525,000. Milan, 21 May 1992, *Morning* (aquatint etching, 8 x 10 ins / 20.5 x 25.3 cm) ITL 1,400,000. Milan, 23 June 1992, *Poplar Tree in Moonlight* (1945, oil on panel, 15 3/4 x 11 ins / 40 x 28 cm) ITL 5,500,000. Rome, 13 June 1995, *Study for 'Revolt'* (1911, red and blue pencil/yellow paper, 9 3/4 x 12 3/4 ins / 24.6 x 32.5 cm) ITL 7,935,000. London, 28 June 1999, *Untitled* (1912, colour crayon, 7 x 20 ins / 19 x 52 cm) GBP 75,000. Exeter, 1 July 2003, *Nocturnal Landscape* (oil on board, 9 x 11 ins / 23 x 29 cm) GBP 3,900. Milan, 24 May 2004, *Woman, Tree and Cloud* (1944, oil on board, 25 x 33 ins / 64 x 84 cm) EUR 5,500. Berlin, 19 June 2004, *Composition in Blue* (oil on canvas/board, 26 x 32 ins / 66 x 81 cm) EUR 2,000.

RUSSOM, R.

Draughtsman.

In 1898 the Art Society of New South Wales bought a sketch by Russom (now in the Museum of Sydney).

Museums and Galleries:

Sydney: a sketch.

RUSSUTI, Filippo. See **RUSUTI**

RUST, Franz

Italian, 18th century.

Born 20 October 1720, in Rome; died after 1807.

Engraver (burin), architect.

Franz Rust, the father of Giovanni Rust, engraved a picture of the procession in Rome on the occasion of the feast of Corpus Christi.

RUST, Giovanni

Italian, 19th century.

Active in Rome from 1830 to 1855.

Miniaturist.

The son of Franz Rust, Giovanni Rust was keeper at the Musei Capitolini in Rome.

RUST, Johan Adolph

Dutch, 19th - 20th century.

Born 13 April 1828, in Amsterdam; died 28 July 1915, in Amsterdam.

Painter. Landscapes, seascapes, boats, harbour scenes.

Johan Adolph Rust was a student of Cornelis Springer. He lived and worked in Amsterdam.

J.A. Rust

Museums and Galleries:

Amsterdam: *View from the Hooge Sluis Bridge, Amsterdam* - Courtrai: *Admiral Ruyter's Vessel moored in the Texel Estuary* - Montreal: *Naval Arsenal in Veere Harbour*.

Auction records:

New York, 11 May 1972, *Boats at Anchor*, Gns 4,800. Amsterdam, 22 Oct 1974, *Fishing Boats in Open Sea* (watercolour) NLG 2,600. Paris, 13 Dec 1976, *Yachts at the Quayside* (oil on canvas, 15 1/4 x 22 3/4 ins / 39 x 58 cm) FRF 23,000. London, 30 Nov 1977, *Boats in Open Sea off the Coast* (oil on canvas, 19 1/2 x 31 ins / 49.5 x 79 cm) GBP 1,600. Enghien-les-Bains, 27 May 1979, *Three-Master in a Dutch Harbour* (oil on canvas, 15 1/2 x 22 3/4 ins / 39.5 x 58 cm) FRF 46,000. New York, 27 May 1982, *View of a Dutch Port* (1867, oil on canvas,

25 x 39 ins / 63.5 x 99 cm) USD 6,500. LONDON, 16 March 1983, *Yachts in Open Sea off the Coast* (oil on canvas, 18 x 24 ins / 45.7 x 61 cm) GBP 3,000. LONDON, 10 Oct 1986, *Yachts in an Estuary* (1865, oil on panel, 15 3/4 x 22 1/2 ins / 40 x 57 cm) GBP 6,500. AMSTERDAM, 16 Nov 1988, *Coastal Landscape with Figures on a Transporter Bridge with a Three-Master in the Background* (oil on canvas, 20 x 32 ins / 51 x 81.5 cm) NLG 8,625. AMSTERDAM, 23 April 1991, *Figures among the Dunes* (oil on canvas, 9 1/2 x 12 3/4 ins / 24 x 32.5 cm) NLG 2,875. NEW YORK, 29 Oct 1992, *Sailing the Estuary* (oil on canvas, 12 x 16 3/4 ins / 30.5 x 42.5 cm) USD 3,080. LONDON, 18 Nov 1994, *Dutch Vessels Anchored in an Estuary* (oil on canvas, 17 1/4 x 23 1/2 ins / 43.7 x 60 cm) GBP 13,800. LONDON, 17 March 1995, *Steamer and Sailing Ships on a Calm Sea* (oil on panel, 12 x 16 ins / 30.5 x 40.5 cm) GBP 10,580. AMSTERDAM, 5 Nov 1996, *Vessel Coming Alongside, with Figures on the Quay* (oil on panel, 12 1/2 x 18 ins / 32 x 46 cm) NLG 35,400. LONDON, 21 Nov 1997, *Repairing the Nets* (oil on canvas, 24 3/4 x 38 1/2 ins / 62.9 x 98.1 cm) GBP 7,130.

RUST, Karolina
German, 19th century.
Born 11 October 1850, in Bodenmais.
Sculptor.
Karolina Rust was a pupil of Rudolf Maison.

RUST, Richard
German, 20th century.
Born 7 December 1878, in Brunswick.
Painter, designer. Portraits, landscapes.

RUST, Rudolf
Swiss, 19th century.
Born 12 April 1848, in Solothurn; died 6 March 1892, in Solothurn.
Portrait artist.

RUSTAN, E. Layne
American, 20th century.
Painter. Landscapes.
E. Layne Rustan painted mostly seascapes using a generously applied paste-like paint in glaucous shades.

RUSTE, Charles, or Rustre
French, 18th century.
Active in Paris during the first half of the 18th century.
Sculptor.
Ruste worked in Russia from 1717 to 1722, and decorated the castle in Stockholm in 1732.

RUSTEM, Jan
Polish, 18th - 19th century.
Born 1762, in Costantinople; died 21 June 1835, in Vilna (now Vilnius, Lithuania).
Painter. Portraits, genre scenes.
Jan Rustem began studying in Warsaw, in Norblin's workshop, and later in Bacciarelli's workshop. In 1798 he became a teacher of painting at the University of Vilna. The two sepia paintings entitled *Old Polish Men* and *Reading* that he showed at the *Exposition des Artistes Polonais* (*Exhibition of Polish Artists*), held at the Salon de la Société Nationale des Beaux-Arts in Paris in 1921, are typical examples of his style.
MUSEUMS AND GALLERIES:
CRACOW (Muz. Narodowe): *Portrait of T. Kosciuszko* - DRESDEN (Prints Collection): *Self-portrait* - LVIV (Lubomirski Mus.): *The Poet J. Slowacki Dressed as Love* - LVIV (Municipal Mus.): *Portrait of a Woman* - POZNAN (Mielzynski Mus.): *Self-portrait; Turkish Horseman* - VILNIUS (Municipal Mus.): *J. Shiadecki; P. Slawinski* - WARSAW (Muz. Narodowe): *Diana Resting; Self-portrait; J. Glowacki.*

RUSTEN, Maurice van der.
See **VANDERRUSTEN Maurice**

RUSTI, Olav, or Rusten
Norwegian, 19th - 20th century.
Born 29 March 1850, in Søndmøre; died 1920, in Bergen.
Painter, draughtsman.
Olav Rusti studied under Eckersberg and at the fine arts academies of Copenhagen and Munich. He worked for 11 years at Maulbronn monastery.
MUSEUMS AND GALLERIES:
HELSINKI (Ateneumin Taidemus.) - OSLO (Nasjonalgal.): *Portrait of Fredrikke Gram.*

RUSTI-HOECK, Frieda
Maiden name: Hoeck
German, 19th - 20th century.
Born 1861, in Karlsruhe.
Painter. Portraits, genre scenes.
The wife of Olav Rusti, Frieda Rusti-Hoeck studied under Paul Borgmann in Karlsruhe, under Gussow in Berlin, and under Merson in Paris. She exhibited in Berlin from 1885.
MUSEUMS AND GALLERIES:
BERGEN (Kunstmus., Billedgal.): *Self-portrait.*

RUSTICELLI, Tommaso
Italian, 17th - 18th century.
Active in San Giovanni in Persiceto, from 1690 to 1720.
Painter.
The pupil of Giovanni Viani, Tommaso Rusticelli worked in Bologna.

RUSTICHINO, Il. See **RUSTICI Francesco**

RUSTICI, Cristoforo or Cristofano, called Il Rusticone
Italian, 17th century.
Born 1650, in Siena; died 1690.
Painter, fresco artist, illuminator. Decorative motifs (grotesques).
The son and pupil of Il Rustico, whose style he imitated, this artist produced paintings in several churches in Siena.

RUSTICI, Francesco, called Il Rustichino or Rusticino
Italian, 17th century.
Born c. 1592, in Siena; died 16 April 1626.
Painter. Religious subjects, allegorical subjects.
Francesco Rustici, the son of Vicenzo Rustici, appeared full of promise. He was first inspired by Michelangelo da Caravaggio and by Gérard Honthorst. He also studied the works of Annibale Carracci and Guido Reni in Rome, but died before he was able to make his mark. Some of his biographers give the date of his death, probably erroneously, as 1652.
BIBLIOGRAPHY:
Auffret-Duriez, Isabelle, '*Saint Sébastien soigné par Irène et sa servante par Francesco Rustici au musée de Picardie à Amiens*' in *Revue du Louvre* n° 4 p. 55, periodical, Paris, October 2001.
MUSEUMS AND GALLERIES:
AMIENS (Mus. de Picardie): *St Sebastian Tended by Irene and Her Servant Woman* - CHAMBÉRY: *St Margaret of Cortona* - FLORENCE (Palazzo Pitti): *Death of Mary Magdalene* - GRAZ: *Painting; Sculpture* - ROME (Mus. e Gal. Borghese): *St Irene Removing the Arrows from the Body of St Sebastian; Entombment.*
AUCTION RECORDS:
ROME, 12 Nov 1986, *St Peter and the Angel* (oil on canvas, 48 3/4 x 67 3/4in/124 x 172cm) ITL 10,000,000. PARIS, 31 March 1993, *Christ and God the Father Surrounded by Angels* (pen and brown wash, 12 1/2 x 10 1/2in/31.5 x 26.5cm) FRF 9,000. ROME, 9 Dec 1997, *Olindo and Sophronia* (oil on canvas, 77 1/2 x 64 1/4in/197 x 163.4cm) ITL 283,800,000.

RUSTICI, Gabriello di Girolamo
Italian, 16th century.
Died 7 December 1562.
Active in Florence.
Painter.
Gabriello di Girolamo Rustici was a pupil of Fra Bartolomeo.

RUSTICI, Giovanni Francesco
Italian, 15th - 16th century.
Born 13 November 1474, in Florence; died 1554, in Tours, France.
Sculptor, painter.
Giovanni Francesco Rustici was influenced by Verrocchio and Leonardo da Vinci. He was called to the court of François I at Fontainebleau in 1528.

Rustici's works include the bronze statues, *Preaching of St John the Baptist* (1506-1511), above the north door of the Baptistery in Florence, and terracotta battle scenes often attributed to Da Vinci.

MUSEUMS AND GALLERIES:
FLORENCE (Mus. Nazionale del Bargello): *Virgin* - PARIS (Louvre): *Battle Scenes* (terracotta, often attributed to Da Vinci).

RUSTICI, Lorenzo, called Il Rustico
Italian, 16th century.
Born 1521, in Siena; died 10 June 1572.
Painter, stucco artist. Decorative motifs (grotesques).
Lorenzo Rustici was the father of Vicenzo Rustici and is thought to have been the pupil of Sodoma. He painted exclusively decorative subjects.

RUSTICI, Vicenzo
Italian, 16th - 17th century.
Born 1556, in Siena; died 1632.
Painter.
Vicenzo Rustici was the son of Lorenzo Rustici, and the pupil of Casolano. He was commissioned to produce an altarpiece in 1594 and armorial bearings in 1613.

RUSTICO
Italian, 11th century.
Active in Florence in 1066.
Painter.
Florentine School.

RUSTICO, Il. See **RUSTICI Lorenzo**

RUSTICONE, Il. See **RUSTICI Cristoforo**

RUSTICUS. See **BAUER Marius Alexander Jacques**

RUSTIGASSI, Bartolomeo
Italian, 14th century.
Born in Piacenza; died 1384, in Piacenza.
Painter.
Bartolomeo Rustigassi painted a fresco in S Giovanni monastery, in Piacenza.

RUSTIGE, Heinrich Franz Gaudenz von
German, 19th century.
Born 11 April 1810, in Werl (Westphalia); died 15 January 1900, in Stuttgart.
Painter, engraver (etching). History painting, portraits, genre scenes.
Heinrich Franz Gaudenz von Rustige was a pupil of Schadow at the academy in Düsseldorf. He taught at the Städelsches Kunstinstitut in Frankfurt and at the school of fine arts in Stuttgart. After a spell in Paris, he accepted the post of curator at the museum in Stuttgart. He was also a writer.

MUSEUMS AND GALLERIES:
BERLIN (Nationalgal.): *Prayer during the Storm; Flood* - DÜSSELDORF (Kunstmus.): *Alfred Rethel and his Fellow Students in Düsseldorf* - KARLSRUHE: *Interrupted Meal; Children Feeding the Chickens* - STUTTGART: *Bohemian Prophecy; Duke of Alba at the Castle of Rudolstadt; Emperor Othon, Conqueror of the Danes; Little Villagers on the Way to School.*

AUCTION RECORDS:
COLOGNE, 3 March 1967, *The Arndst Family,* DEM 6,000. BERN, 6 May 1972, *Scene in a Tavern,* CHF 5,000. LOS ANGELES, 27 May 1974, *Circus Folk,* USD 2,600. COLOGNE, 25 Nov 1976, *The Cavalier and the Cook* (1861, oil on canvas, 24 3/4 x 22 ins / 63 x 56 cm) DEM 9,000. COLOGNE, 17 March 1978, *At the Village Magistrate's* (1859, oil on panel, 11 x 13 3/4 ins / 27 x 35 cm) DEM 4,400. COLOGNE, 30 March 1984, *Interior of an Inn* (1887, oil on canvas, 19 1/4 x 25 1/2 ins / 49 x 65 cm) DEM 13,000. LONDON, 17 Nov 1993, *Skaters* (1857, oil on canvas, 23 1/2 x 30 3/4 ins / 60 x 78 cm) GBP 3,450. CONNECTICUT, 15 Nov 1999, *Proud Hunter* (oil on canvas, 24 x 36 ins / 61 x 91 cm) USD 9,250. STUTTGART, 2 Dec 1999, *Clouds Gathering over Alpine Lake* (1836, oil on canvas, 18 x 22 ins / 45 x 55 cm) DEM 8,500. MUNICH, 21 March 2001, *Farmstead by Mountain Lake* (1836, oil on canvas, 18 x 22 ins / 46 x 56 cm) DEM 14,000. MUNICH, 7 Nov 2001, *Battle in Village, Soldiers Tending Wounded Man* (1851, oil on canvas, 12 x 16 ins / 30 x 40 cm) DEM 6,500. STUTTGART, 18 Sept 2003, *Drinker* (oil on canvas, 17 x 22 ins / 43 x 55 cm) EUR 3,000.

RUSTIN, Jean
French, 20th century.
Born 3 March 1928, in Montigny-les-Metz.
Painter. Figures, nudes.
Jean Rustin was a pupil at the École des Beaux-Arts, Paris, from 1947 to 1953. In 2002, the Rustin Foundation opened in Berchem, Belgium. Rustin's early work is in the style of International Lyrical Abstraction, but later his forms take on semiological meanings and in about 1966-1967 they begin to depict in lively organisation and colour a real world inspired largely by Pop Art in the manner of Allan Davie and the Frenchman Daniel Humair. Drawing and the humorous or incisive line play an important role in his language and explain his frequent use of rapidly drawn watercolour. From 1971, painted figures and faces appear more frequently, gradually appearing in a context emptied of any decorative element. It was a break with the earlier work that Rustin commented on a few years later: 'I painted a lot of abstracts, played with paint, then one day I refused to play any longer with prettiness; I wanted to express something more precise, deeper, and I did so by using bodies.' However, it was only in the mid-1970s that the real theme emerged: the naked body, male and female, placed in enclosed interiors, faces full of horror, though the features are sometimes scarcely outlined, and with broken flesh that seems to carry the heavy burden of their entrails. It is an unreal and unhealthy world, an existential chaos, the only result of which seems to be a miserable exhibition of bodies to the gaze of others.

He participated in salons from 1956, including from 1957 the Salon Comparaisons, Paris; from 1960 to 1976 the Salon des Réalités Nouvelles, Paris; from 1963 the Salon de Bagnolet; in 1965 and 1966 the Salon Schèmes, Paris; from 1970 the Salon de Mai, Paris; in 1971 the Biennale at Villeneuve-sur-Lot; from 1974 the Salon de la Jeune Peinture, Paris. In 1980, he participated in *Figure de l'enfermement* (*Metaphor of Confinement*) in Lyons; in 1982 in *Hommage à Bataille* (*Homage to Battle*); in 1983 in *Le Corps* (*The Body*) at the Musée des Beaux-Arts, Nancy. His solo shows have included: 1959, 1961, 1962 (watercolours), 1964, 1965, 1968, Galerie La Roue, Paris; 1962, Auvernier-Neuchâtel; 1971, ARC, Musée d'Art Moderne, Paris; 1972, Maison de la Culture, St-Étienne; 1976, Galerie L'Œil de Bœuf, Paris; 1981,1984, 1985, Galerie Isy Brachot, Paris; 1994, Museum of Modern Art, São Paulo; 1997, Museo de Arte Contemporaneo, University of Chile, Santiago; 2000, Vlanis Frissiris Museum, Athens; 2001, *Pein-*

tures 1971-2001 (*Paintings 1971-2001*), Halle St-Pierre, Paris; 2004, Galerie Dominique Polad-Hardouin, Paris.

Rustin

BIBLIOGRAPHY:

Troche, Michel/Noël, Bernard/Le Bot, Marc, *Jean Rustin*, Équinoxe, Paris, 1984. Smith, Edward Lucie, *Rustin*, Heneage, London, 1991. Meray, Agnès, *Regard sur l'œuvre de Jean Rustin*, dissertation, Université de Paris I Panthéon-Sorbonne, Paris, 1992. Mandagot, Daniel, *La Quête de la figuration. Entretien avec Daniel Mandagot*, À la Croisée, Bernin, 1999.

MUSEUMS AND GALLERIES:

ALGIERS (Mus. National des Beaux-Arts) - AMSTERDAM (Stedelijk Mus.) - BARCELONA (Mus. Nacional d'Art de Catalunya) - BIRMINGHAM (Mus. and AG) - CAMBRIDGE (Fitzwilliam Mus.): *Portrait of a Young Man* (1991, oil on canvas) - CHRISTCHURCH (AG Te Puna o Waiwhetu) - CRÉTEIL (FDAC Val-de-Marne) - DÔLE (MBA) - GRENOBLE (Mus. de Grenoble) - HAMBURG (Kunsthalle) - LONDON (British Mus.) - NANTES (MBA) - NEW ORLÉANS (AM) - OBERHAUSEN (Ludwig Gal.) - PARIS (CNAC) - PARIS (MAMVP) - PRINCETON (AM, Princeton University) - SANTIAGO (Mus. de la Solidaridad Salvador Allende) - SÃO PAULO (MAC, Universidade) - VILLEURBANNE (FRAC Rhône-Alpes) - WASHINGTON DC (Hirshhorn Mus. and Sculpture Garden): *Pres De La Porte Ouverte (Near The Open Door)* (1993, acrylic/canvas).

AUCTION RECORDS:

PARIS, 27 Jan 1992, *Reclining Nude* (1971, oil on canvas, 15 x 18 ins / 38 x 46 cm) FRF 42,000. PARIS, 12 Feb 1992, *Nude* (1971, oil on canvas, 16¼ x 13 ins / 41 x 33 cm) FRF 29,000. VERSAILLES, 28 Feb 1993, *In the Kitchen* (1955, oil on canvas, 15¾ x 15¾ ins / 40 x 40 cm) FRF 53,000. PARIS, 6 Dec 1993, *Portrait of a Man* (1985, oil on canvas, 16¼ x 11 ins / 41 x 27 cm) FRF 22,000; *Portrait of a Woman* (1985, oil on canvas, 28¾ x 23½ ins / 73 x 59.5 cm) FRF 40,000. PARIS, 6 Feb 1994, *Apparition* (1971, acrylic/paper/canvas, 28¾ x 39¼ ins / 73 x 100 cm) FRF 56,000. LOKEREN, 8 Oct 1994, *Portrait* (1989, acrylic/canvas, 13¾ x 11 ins / 35 x 27 cm) BEF 220,000. LOKEREN, 10 Dec 1994, *Naked Man* (1993, oil on canvas, 16¼ x 11 ins / 41 x 27 cm) BEF 210,000. PARIS, 7 Dec 1995, *Composition with Figures* (oil on canvas, 25½ x 32 ins / 65 x 81 cm) FRF 12,800. VERSAILLES, 21 Nov 1999, *In the little Room* (1987, oil on canvas, 39 x 32 ins / 100 x 81 cm) FRF 20,000. AMSTERDAM, 29 Nov 1999, *Portrait of Old Couple* (oil on canvas, 45 x 35 ins / 115 x 88 cm) NLG 36,000. CALAIS, 5 Nov 2000, *The Green Room* (oil on canvas, 22 x 18 ins / 55 x 46 cm) FRF 51,000. LYONS, 4 March 2001, *The Green Room* (oil on canvas) FRF 20,000. VERSAILLES, 28 April 2002, *Untitled* (1989, oil on canvas, 14 x 11 ins / 35 x 27 cm) EUR 4,600. AMSTERDAM, 3 June 2003, *Portrait of a Man* (1990, oil on canvas, 25 x 21 ins / 64 x 54 cm) EUR 7,500. PARIS, 28 June 2004, *Friends* (1973, oil on canvas, 64 x 51 ins / 162 x 130 cm) EUR 16,500. PARIS, 17 Oct 2004, *Portrait* (1994, oil on canvas, 14 x 11 ins / 35 x 27 cm) EUR 3,900.

RUSTING, Johannes
Dutch, 17th century.
Painter.

Rusting painted the portrait of *Johannes Pistorius* in the Lutheran church at Woerden.

RUSTRE, Charles. See **RUSTE**

RUSU, Alla
Moldavian, 20th - 21st century.
Born 12 December 1965.
Active in France from 1994.
Painter. Figures, figure compositions, still-lifes.

Alla Rusu's canvases are loaded with thick materials and saturated with clashing colours. In her more mature works, the style appears to be slightly less distant from that Expressionism, and contains reminiscence of Léger and Picasso. Rusu first studied at the academy of fine arts in Tallinn, Estonia, then later at its counterpart in Bucharest, Romania, from which she graduated in 1993. She has exhibited in both countries. In 1994 she went to Paris and took a studio at the Cité Internationale des Arts. That same year she submitted works to the Salon Grands et Jeunes d'Aujourd'hui. In 1996, the Galerie Élysée-Miromesnil held a solo exhibition of her work.

RUSUTI, Filippo, or Rusiti or Rizuti or Rossuti or Russuti or Ruzuti or Ruseruti
Italian, 14th century.
Active in Rome c. 1300.
Painter, mosaicist.

Filippo Rusuti produced mosaics depicting *Christ Blessing* and *Legend of the Foundation of S Maria Maggiore Church* in S Maria Maggiore, around 1308, and effigies of saints. The frescoes in the vault of the upper church of S Francesco in Assisi are attributed to him. Although he went to France after 1308, he contributed to the release of the Byzantine hold on Italian painting at the beginning of the 14th century.

RUSZ, Károly or Karl
Hungarian, 19th century.
Active in Budapest during the second half of the 19th century.
Engraver (wood).

Károly Rusz studied under J. Mihalovics, and worked for periodicals.

RUSZCZYC, Ferdynand, or Rushchits, Ferdinand
Polish, 20th century.
Born 27 November 1870, in Bohdanów, near Vilnius; died 3 October 1936, in Vilnius.
Painter, engraver, illustrator, scenographer.
Landscapes, urban landscapes.

Ruszczyc studied at the academy of fine arts in St Petersburg from 1890. He was professor at the academy of fine arts in Warsaw from 1904 to 1907, and at that in Cracow from 1907 to 1908. He travelled in the Crimea, the Baltic, and to Berlin, Cologne, Paris, Ostend, Brussels, Milan, Venice and Vienna. He worked as an illustrator on the review *Chimera*, and was a member of the artists' association, the Sztuka. He participated in the creation of the faculty of fine arts at Vilnius University, of which he was the Dean, beginning in 1919. He lived and worked in Vilnius.

Ruszczyc painted mostly Polish landscapes and views of Vilnius. He structured his compositions with low or aerial points of view, in such a way that the earth seemed at odds with the menacing sky, as in *Earth*, 1898.

Ruszczc exhibited his works in Moscow, St Petersburg, Warsaw, Cracow and Vilnius. In 1921, he presented *Earth; Mill in Winter; Vision of Winter; Spring Breeze* at the open exhibition of Polish artists at the Salon de la Société Nationale des Beaux-Arts in Paris. A retrospective paying homage to his work was presented in 1937-1938 in Cracow, Torun, Warsaw and Vilnius. It showed famous paintings that had disappeared during World War II. An enormous exhibition of his work took place in Warsaw in 1964. In 2001, he was included in the exhibition *L'Avant-printemps. Pologne 1880-1920* (*Early Spring. Poland 1880-1920*) at the Palais des Beaux-Arts in Brussels. In 2002, a second retrospective of his work entitled *Ferdynand Ruszczyc 1870-1936: Zycie i Dzielo* (*Ferdynand Ruszczyc 1860-1936: Life and Works*) was organised by the Muzeum Narodwe in Cracow, and then travelled to the Muzeum Okregowe in Torun, the Muzeum Norodwe in Warsaw, and to the Lietuvos Daïles Muziejus in Vilnius.

Bibliography:
Wystawa posmiertna prac malarskich i rysunkowych Ferdynand da Ruszczyca, exhibition catalogue, Vilnius, Warsaw, Cracow, Torun, 1937-1938. Bulhak, Jan (ed.), *Ferdynand Ruszczyc: zycie i dielo, ksiega zbiorowa*, Sklad glówny w ksiegarni psw Wojciecha, Vilnius, 1939 (with an essay in French by Marjan Morelowski). *Ferdynand Ruszczyc, 1870-1936: katalog*, Muzeum Narodowe, Warsaw, 1964. Ruszczycowna, J., *Ferdynand Ruszczyc 1870-1836: Pamietnik wystawy*, essay, Warsaw, 1966. Ruszczyc, E., *Ferdynand Ruszczyc: Dziennik*, Warsaw, 1994. Morawinska, Agnieszka/Clegg, Elisabeth/Poprzecka, Maria/Crugten, Alain van, *L'Avant-printemps. Pologne 1880-1920*, exhibition catalogue, Palais des Beaux-Arts, Tempera, Brussels, 2001. *Ferdynand Ruszczyc 1870-1936: Zycie i Dzielo*, exhibition catalogue, Muzeum Narodowe w Krakowie, Cracow, 2002.
Museums and Galleries:
Paris (former Mus. du Jeu de Paume) - Poznan (Muz. Narodowe): *Storm Cloud* (1902, oil on canvas) - Torun (Muzeum Okregowe/Regional Museum): *Banks of the Wilejka* (1900, oil on canvas) - Vilnius (Lietuvos Daïles Muziejus): *Nec Mergitur* (1904-1905, oil on canvas) - Warsaw (Muz. Literatury im. Adama Mickiewicza): *Evening on the Wilejka* (c. 1900, oil on canvas) - Warsaw (Muz. Narodowe): *Earth* (1898, oil on canvas).

RUSZELAK, Josef
Czechoslovak, 20th century.
Born 1938.
Painter, pastellist, engraver, illustrator, designer. Stage sets.
Josef Ruszelak first attended the school of art in Zlín in southern Moravia, then trained at the higher college of decorative arts in Uherské Hradište where he was taught by Vladimir Hroch, Jan Blazek and Karel Hofman.
Josef Ruszelak was mainly carried a graphic artist producing decorative work and illustrations. He was inspired by nature, particularly by the effects of light; his work has an ethereal atmosphere with light and fluffy shades.

RUSZKOWSKI, Zyslav or Zdzislaw
Polish, 20th century.
Born 1907; died 1990.
Active in England.
Painter. Nudes, landscapes, still-lifes.
Zyslav Ruszkowski studied in Cracow and Warsaw then settled in Paris in 1934. During World War II he was in England where he joined the allied forces and eventually settled.
A figurative artist, he took shortcuts, extending shapes as far as he could, playing on contrasts. He was endowed with a deep, dramatic sense which he applied through shapes, colours and light to everyday scenes. His works include still-lifes, nudes and landscapes of Cornwall. Zyslav Ruszkowski exhibited in London.
Auction records:
London, 14 May 1992, *View From the Boatyard* (oil on canvas, 41 3/4 x 29 3/4 ins / 106 x 75.5 cm) GBP 1,980. London, 23 Oct 1996, *Landscape* (1944, oil on canvas, 16 x 24 ins / 40.5 x 61 cm) GBP 2,070. London, 14 July 1999, *Lyme Regis Beach* (oil on canvas, 30 x 20 ins / 76 x 51 cm) GBP 1,200. London, 3 Nov 1999, *Still-life with Fruit* (oil on canvas, 20 x 24 ins / 51 x 61 cm) GBP 1,000. London, 28 April 2000, *Nude Standing in Interior* (oil on canvas, 50 x 33 ins / 127 x 84 cm) GBP 1,000. London, 2 Nov 2000, *In Front of the Grocer's Shop* (1946, oil on board, 16 x 19 ins / 40 x 49 cm) GBP 1,100. London, 13 June 2001, *Seaside Cafe* (oil on canvas, 30 x 55 ins / 76 x 140 cm) GBP 1,500. London, 13 June 2001, *Lola Leaning on a Table* (oil on canvas, 24 x 30 ins / 61 x 76 cm) GBP 1,700. London, 4 Dec 2002, *Still-life* (oil on canvas, 21 x 26 ins / 53 x 67 cm) GBP 2,800. London, 4 Dec 2002, *Irish Coast, Stradbally, County Waterford* (oil on canvas, 23 x 34 ins / 59 x 86 cm) GBP 4,200. London, 3 July 2003, *Surreal Landscape* (oil on canvas, 22 x 32 ins / 55 x 81 cm) GBP 5,800. London, 3 Dec 2003, *Portrait of Doris Pamela Hodin* (oil on canvas, 24 x 20 ins / 61 x 51 cm) GBP 1,600. London, 11 March 2004, *Landscape from Iceland* (oil on canvas, 30 x 20 ins / 76 x 51 cm) GBP 6,500.

RUSZNAK, Nandor or Ferdinand
Hungarian, 20th century.
Born 8 July 1880, in Lucenec.
Painter. Figures, landscapes.
Nandor Rusznak studied in Munich and Paris.

RUSZTI, Gyula or Julius
Hungarian, 20th century.
Born 8 October 1885, in Lucenec; died November 1918.
Painter. Figures.
Gyula Ruszti studied in Budapest and Munich.

RUTA, Clementi or Clemente, or Rutta
Italian, 18th century.
Born 9 May 1685, in Parma; died 11 November 1767.
Painter. Religious subjects.
Clementi Ruta studied under Spolverini and Carlo Cignani in Bologna and accompanied Charles of Bourbon to Naples. He worked for churches in Piacenza and Parma and for the cathedral in Mantua. By the time of his death, he had gone blind.
Museums and Galleries:
Parma (GA): *St Vincent Ferrer*.
Auction records:
Rome, 28 May 1985, *Infanta Maria Isabella of Bourbon* (oil on canvas, 24 1/2 x 30in/62 x 76cm) ITL 9,000,000. Rome, 8 March 1990, *Holy Family* (canvas/panel, oval, 8 3/4 x 7 1/2in/22.5 x 19cm) ITL 3,400,000. Monaco, 19 June 1994, *Religious Scene* (oil on canvas, 18 x 13 1/2in/46 x 34cm) FRF 19,980.

RUTAERT, Daniel I
Flemish School, 15th century.
Died shortly before 7 February 1486.
Active in Ghent.
Sculptor.
Daniel Rutaert I was the father of Daniel Rutaert II.

RUTAERT, Daniel II, or Ruutaert or Ruuthaert, called Van Lovendeghem
Flemish School, 16th century.
Died before 17 March 1540.
Active in Ghent.
Sculptor.
Daniel Rutaert II was the son of Daniel Rutaert I. In 1511 he carved a rood screen for the Carmelite church of Ghent. He also worked for other churches in the city and for the church of Auweghem.

RUTAI, or Ju-t'ai or Jou-t'ai
Chinese, 14th - 15th - 16th century.
Born in Huating (Jiangsu, China).
Active during the Ming dynasty (1368-1644).
Painter.
Rutai was a monk painter and a well-known figure in Shanghai. A river landscape in blue and green is extant.

RUTATI, Pier Maria
Italian, 17th century.
Active in Pistoia, Italy.
Sculptor (wood).
Pier Maria Rutati sculpted a *Christ on the Cross* in the church of the Madonna dell'Umiltà in Pistoia.

RUTAULT, Claude
French, 20th century.
Born 25 October 1941, in Trois-Moutiers (Vienne).
Painter.
Conceptual Art.

Claude Rutault studied politics and law before going on to work as a painter. He started out as an abstract painter, producing composition in bands of colour which frequently employed a Y-configuration. His work quickly assumed strong political overtones, however, notably with panels such as his *France Indicted* and *Vietnam*, and his participation in the *Aspects of Racism* exhibition of 1970. His political commitment is also exemplified in compositions such as his *Le Monde* series of 1972, where he juxtaposes clippings from the French daily newspaper (*Le Monde* and drawings representing the daily, the notion being to point up the 'progressive disappearance of external meaning (i.e. information) and the paper's descent into 'scribbles' (drawings) which create a mere illusion of the newspaper itself'. In the interests of maintaining a figurative component in his work, Rutault then embarked on an extended series entitled *Marelle* (*Hopscotch*); this series served a dual purpose, enabling him not only to reflect on social, religious and art-related issues but also to indulge in an analysis of painting per se in terms of perspective and the interplay between text and image, photograph and drawing. His preoccupation with the redefinition of painting subsequently led him to abandon a figurative approach entirely and begin producing canvases stretched over frames painted in colours matching the wall on which they are hung, stressing that 'a canvas of the same colour as the wall is not a monochrome'. In other words, his intention was to redefine painting by reducing it to a set of basic objective criteria.

In essence, Claude Rutault's subsequent work - although not strictly speaking 'conceptual', as canvas, frame and painting remain - applies variations to the basic principle set out in his *Définitions/Méthodes* (*Definition and Method*), where he describes painting that is 'irrespective of the physical presence of the artist'. That said, the participation of the viewer (or, for that matter, of institutions) emerges as a constituent of the work itself: his first article of faith in *Définition/Méthode* (*Definition and Method*) is entitled *Toiles à l'Unité* (*The Canvas as a Unit*), where he remarks that 'a canvas stretched over a frame painted in the same colour as the wall to which it is attached admits all standard formats currently available, be they rectangular, square, round or oval'. A further example of Rutault's work is his *Suicidal Painting*, the surface of which reduces almost imperceptibly year by year. Meanwhile, Rutault's exhibits at *Transit* at the Centre de Création Contemporaine in Tours comprised a pile of canvases and frames, a sort of 'warehouse' for future installations.

Rutault's obsession with the independence and specificity of a composition in terms of where and how it is exhibited and with the analysis of form and function ultimately leads him to question the validity of the composition itself and of art in general. Rutault's originality arguably lies in his awareness of the limits to art and artistic intention. As he notes in his *Définitions/Méthodes* (*Definition and Method*), the artist's intention may often be frustrated by external circumstances beyond his control. This point is of particular relevance to exhibition organisers or, indeed, to private collectors, whose 'positioning' of a particular work may in effect call into question its intrinsic nature and identity.

He exhibited at major thematic group exhibitions such as *Présumés innocents: l'art contemporain et l'enfance* (*Presumed Innocent: Contemporary Art and Childhood*), held at the CAPC Musée d'Art Contemporain in Bordeaux in 2000 or, in 2003, at *Un tableau dans le décor. Peintures 1970-2000* (*A Painting in the Décor: Paintings 1970-2000*), an exhibition held at the Château des Ducs de Bretagne in Nantes to celebrate two decades of funding by the FRAC (Regional Fund for Contemporary Art).

Rutault has also exhibited solo, notably in 1983, at the Musée d'Art Moderne de la Ville de Paris; in 1989, at the Galeries Contemporaines in the Centre Pompidou in Paris; in 1990 at the Musée Ste-Croix in Poitiers; in 1992, at Grenoble Museum; in 1992, at the Musée National d'Art Moderne in Paris; in 1992, at the Consortium in Dijon; in 1993 and 1997, at the Centre de Création Contemporaine in Tours; in 1994, at the Musée des Beaux-Arts in Nantes; in 1997, at the Galerie Martine et Thibault de la Châtre in Paris; in 2001, at *176, International d/m*, held at the Museum of Modern and Contemporary Art in Geneva; and, in 2002, at *Claude Rutault: les Saisons* (*Claude Rutault: Seasons*), an exhibition held at the Centre d'Art Contemporain et Parc de Sculptures in Vassivière, where Rutault painted the Art Centre walls in a different colour chosen by a different person to represent each season (covering in the process the existing facsimiles of *Seasons* engraved by Nicolas Poussin).

BIBLIOGRAPHY:

Gauthier, Michel, *Mutations, sur neuf aspects du travail de Claude Rutault*, Musée Sainte-Croix, Poitiers, 1990. Gauthier, Michel, *Claude Rutault 'à titre d'exemple'*, exhibition catalogue, Musée des Beaux-Arts, Nantes, 1994. Gauthier, Michel, ''*L'Isochrome à l'icône (sur une 'légende' de Claude Rutault)*' in *Art Présence*, periodical, Éd. Alpa, Pléneuf-Val-André, January 1997. Mollet-Viéville, Ghislain, ''*Claude Rutault. La peinture définie avec méthode*' in *Art Press* n° 226, periodical, Paris, July-August 1997. Rutault, Claude, *Définitions-méthodes. Le livre, 1973-2000*, catalogue raisonné, Centre de Création Contemporaine, Tours, 2000. Bernadac, Marie-Laure/Moisdon-Tremblay, et al., *Présumés innocents: l'art contemporain et l'enfance*, exhibition catalogue, Capc Musée d'Art Contemporain, Bordeaux, 2000.

MUSEUMS AND GALLERIES:

AMIENS (FRAC Picardie): *AMZ* (1987) - DUNKIRK (FRAC Nord-Pas de Calais): *Van Meegeren's Dream* - GENEVA (Mamco): two Definition and Method articles on permanent display; *Untitled* (Tee-shirt) - METZ (FRAC Lorraine): *Floor/Wall/Ceiling/Wall: Definition and Method No. 103* (1979) - PARIS (MAMVP).

RUTCHIEL, Henri Joseph. See **RUXTHIEL**

RUTELLI, Mario

Italian, 19th - 20th century.

Born 4 April 1859, in Palermo, Sicily; died 1941 or 1943.

Sculptor. Busts.

Mario Rutelli first worked in Palermo, then went to Rome to continue his studies. He took part in the Italian salons from 1875 and exhibited work at the Exposition Universelle in Paris in 1878.

MUSEUMS AND GALLERIES:

ROME (Gal. Nazionale d'Arte Moderna): *Bust of Domenico Morelli*.

AUCTION RECORDS:

ROME, 1 June 1983, *Naiad* (bronze, a pair, h. 15 1/4 ins / 39 cm and 17 1/4 ins/44 cm) ITL 6,500,000. MILAN, 6 June 1991, *Bust of Domenico Morelli* (1893, bronze, h. 26 3/4 ins / 68 cm) ITL 5,000,000. ROME, 12 Dec 2001, *Sicilian Woman* (patinated bronze, h. 12 ins / 31 cm) ITL 4,000,000. ROME, 5 June 2002, *Family of Cats* (1883, white marble, 11 x 26x16 ins / 28 x 66x40 cm) EUR 1,600.

RUTENZWIG, Bartholomäus

Swiss, 15th century.

Active in Basel during the second half of the 15th century.

Painter, glassmaker.

Bartholomäus Rutenzwig was the son of Hans Rutenzwig. He was a member of the guild in 1474.

RUTENZWIG, Hans

Swiss, 15th century.

Active in Basel.

Painter, goldsmith (?).

Hans Rutenzwig was the father of Bartholomaüs Rutenzwig.

RUTENZWIG, Peter
Swiss, 16th century.
Active in Bern in 1508.
Painter.

RÜTER, Hans Jakob, or Rütter or Reutter
Swiss, 17th century.
Active in Zurich 1610-1613.
Glass painter.
Hans Jakob Rüter was in Nuremberg in 1605.

RÜTER, Hans Peter, or Rütter
Swiss, 16th - 17th century.
Born c. 1550; died 1610.
Active in Zurich.
Glass painter.

RÜTER, Heinrich
German, 20th century.
Born 22 April 1877, in Bergedorf.
Painter.
Heinrich Rüter was a student of P. Janssen and E. von Gebhard. He lived and worked in Düsseldorf and painted frescoes for churches in Bochum, Bielfeld, Anholt, Dortmund-Hörde and Hamm.

RÜTGER, Christian
German, 19th century.
Born 12 January 1821, in Cologne; died 8 October 1846, in Bensberg, near Cologne.
Sculptor.
Christian Rütger was a pupil of L. von Schwanthaler.

RUTGERS, Abraham, called the Elder, or de Oude
Dutch, 17th century.
Born 1632, in Amsterdam; died 1699.
Draughtsman, watercolourist. Landscapes, landscapes with figures.
Abraham Rutgers was the pupil of L. Bakjuysen, and worked from 1660 to 1690.

His watercolours and pen-and-ink drawings are well composed and vigorously executed.

MUSEUMS AND GALLERIES:
AMSTERDAM - BERLIN - LONDON - ROTTERDAM - VIENNA.

AUCTION RECORDS:
PARIS, 8 Dec 1938, *The Hunter* (pen and bistre wash) FRF 1,320. AMSTERDAM, 6 Nov 1978, *Skaters at Dusk* (pen and wash, 3 x 7 1/4 ins / 7.9 x 18.2 cm) NLG 7,800. AMSTERDAM, 16 Nov 1981, *View of Gouda* (pen and wash, 7 3/4 x 12 1/2 ins / 19.5 x 31.8 cm) NLG 7,800. NEW YORK, 16 Jan 1985, *Village beside a Frozen Canal, with Figures* (pen and wash heightened with white, 7 3/4 x 12 ins / 19.5 x 30.6 cm) USD 6,750. PARIS, 4 March 1988, *Track Lined with Trees near a Pond with a House* (brush and brown wash, 3 1/2 x 5 3/4 ins / 9.2 x 14.5 cm) FRF 10,000. AMSTERDAM, 10 May 1994, *View of Gouda* (ink and wash, 7 1/2 x 12 1/2 ins / 19.3 x 31.6 cm) NLG 4,600. PARIS, 28 Oct 1994, *Fisherman beside the Vecht* (pen and brown wash, 4 1/4 x 7 3/4 ins / 11 x 20 cm) FRF 90,000. AMSTERDAM, 12 Nov 1996, *River with a Figure Looking over the Parapet, with Houses and Windmills in the Background* (pen, brown ink and wash/black chalk, 4 1/2 x 8 1/4 ins / 11.4 x 21 cm) NLG 8,496. NEW YORK, 22 Jan 2004, *View of Gouda from the South East* (black chalk, brown ink and colour wash, 7 x 13 ins / 19 x 32 cm) USD 42,000.

RUTGERS VON ROZENBURG, C. M.
Dutch, 19th century.
Active in Amsterdam.
Miniaturist.
C.M. Rutgers Von Rozenburg was a lady artist who exhibited in Amsterdam from 1828 to 1830.

RUTHART, Karl Andreas or Carl Borromäus Andreas
German, 17th century.
Born in Danzig (now Gdansk, Poland) (?); died after 1703, in L'Aquila.
Painter, engraver (etching). History painting, hunting scenes, animals.
Karl Andreas Ruthart became a master of the guild of Antwerp in 1636. He worked in Regensburg in 1664, then probably in Graz and Styria. After 1672 he went to Italy and joined holy orders as a Celestine monk at the monastery of St Eusebius in Rome. Certain biographers distinguished between a Karl Andreas and an Andreas, although they would appear to be one and the same artist. Although a monk, he still painted profane subjects such as hunting scenes and animal fights. It was only later on in life, when he had retired to the monastery of the Abruzzi, that he devoted himself to depicting hermits and other saintly personages at prayer.

C: RVTHART 1663

CRH

CRH

MUSEUMS AND GALLERIES:
BUDAPEST: *Wolf and Wild Boar Fighting; Stag Hunt* - DRESDEN: *Odysseus and Circe; Stag and Heron; Stag Hunt; Bear and Dog Fight* - FLORENCE (Palazzo Pitti): *Wild Beasts; Stag Overwhelmed by Savage Beasts* - GRAZ: *Stag Hunt* (two); *Lions and Tigers Fighting over a Dead Stag* - INNSBRUCK: *Stag Hunt; Leopard Ravine* - OBERSCHLEISSHEIM (Neues Schloss Schleissheim, Staatsgal.): *Bear Hunt; Stag Attacked by Dogs* - OLDENBURG: *David Called before the Prophet Samuel* - PARIS (Louvre): *Bear Hunt* - POZNAN (Muz. Mielzynskich): *Stags and Elks* - PRAGUE: *Lion and Tiger* - ROHRAU (Schlossmus., Graf Harrach'sche Familiensammlung): *Rocky Shore with Deer, Stag and Hare* - STOCKHOLM: *Savage Beasts in a Crevice; Stag Hunt; Three Stags Resting in a Rocky Place* - VIENNA: *Stag Hunt; Donkey Drivers* - VIENNA (Czernin'sche Gemäldegal.): *Darius in a Landscape; Stags in a Mountainous Region; Bears Chased by Dogs; Stag Hunt* - VIENNA (Liechtenstein Mus.): six works - VIENNA (Schönborn-Buckheim): *Bear Hunt*.

AUCTION RECORDS:
PARIS, 1897, *Lion Hunt; Tiger Hunt* (two pendants) FRF 105. PARIS, 29 Oct 1948, *Lions and Tigers Fighting* (two pendants) FRF 22,000. VIENNA, 17 March 1970, *Bear Attacked by Dogs*, ATS 32,000. VIENNA, 16 March 1971, *Tiger Devouring a Hind*, ATS 28,000. LONDON, 21 March 1973, *Leopards Attacking a Stag; Wolves Attacking a Wild Boar* (two pendants) GBP 1,800. LONDON, 21 May 1976, *Boar Hunt* (oil on canvas, 26 1/2 x 33 1/2 ins / 67.5 x 85 cm) GBP 2,200. COPENHAGEN, 2 Nov 1978, *Hunting Scene* (oil on canvas, 31 1/2 x 40 1/2 ins / 80 x 103 cm) DKK 19,000. LONDON, 19 April 1985, *Tigers Attacking a Stag in a Steep Landscape* (oil on canvas, 37 1/2 x 45 ins / 95.2 x 114.3 cm) GBP 16,000. LUCERNE, 11 Nov 1987, *Wildcats Fighting Over Prey* (oil on canvas, 26 3/4 x 22 3/4 ins / 68 x 58 cm) CHF 43,000. LONDON, 20 May 1993, *Studies of Woodland Animals and Wild Birds* (oil on canvas, 19 1/4 x 30 1/4 ins / 48.7 x 76.6 cm) GBP 56,300. PARIS, 7 March 1994, *Bear Hunt* (oil on canvas, 24 3/4 x 34 1/4 ins / 63 x 87 cm) FRF 25,000. LONDON, 9 Dec 1994, *Dogs Attacking a Young Stag in a Mountainous Landscape* (oil on canvas, 43 x 60 1/4 ins / 109.5 x 153 cm) GBP 9,200. LONDON, 8 Dec 1995, *Studies of Two Hunting Dogs, an Ibis, Three Bats and Two Swallows* (oil on canvas, 6 3/4 x 17 1/2 ins / 17.2 x 44.5 cm) GBP 17,250. LONDON, 13 Dec 1996, *Stags*

Resting in a Clearing with Ducks, a Rabbit and a Beaver near a Waterfall; Leopards Attacking a Stag and an Elk in a Clearing with Rocks, a Lion, Vultures and a Fox (oil on canvas, a pair, each 38 x 52¼ ins / 96.5 x 132.7 cm) GBP 84,000. VIENNA, 6 Oct 1999, *Fight between Leopard and Zebra in Wooded Landscape* (oil on canvas, 20 x 26 ins / 52 x 66 cm) ATS 160,000. COLOGNE, 29 June 2000, *Hunting Scene* (oil on canvas, 26 x 33 ins / 66 x 85 cm) DEM 7,000. LONDON, 7 July 2000, *Lion and Tiger Fighting over a Fallen Stag before Sarcophagus in a Cave* (oil on canvas, 38 x 45 ins / 97 x 114 cm) GBP 50,000. LONDON, 12 Dec 2001, *Bears and Hounds Fighting in a Landscape* (oil on canvas, 28 x 35 ins / 71 x 88 cm) GBP 28,000. MUNICH, 20 March 2002, *Hunting Dog with Dead Rabbit* (oil on canvas, 17 x 13 ins / 42 x 32 cm) EUR 2,000. ANTWERP, 27 May 2002, *Deers Playing* (oil on panel, 19 x 25 ins / 49 x 64 cm) EUR 3,200.

RUTHENBECK, Reiner
German, 20th century.
Born 30 June 1937, in Velbert (Rhineland).
Sculptor, painter. Multimedia.
Antiform.

Reiner Ruthenbeck studied under Joseph Beuys in Düsseldorf in 1962. His work carries the clear imprint of Beuys in that it points up the link between art and attitude, and between execution and creative intention. His quasi-religious approach presents a direct challenge to conventional attitudes to art, but is actually less revolutionary than it might appear at first sight. His first 'transformations' of 1966-1967 have a workmanlike quality about them and are strongly reminiscent of the Poor Art movement spearheaded by Beuys in Germany. In practice, his exhibits include piles of sand or shreds of paper. The initial impact is perhaps intended to surprise and shock but, on closer examination, his work betrays an attempt to comment on man's links with his immediate environment and his distant past. His work is essentially 'elemental' and it is in this spirit that one must approach his cruciform 'floating canvases' replete with symbolism. From 1979, Ruthenbeck started to produce works with an inherent chromatic duality to which certain elemental values may be assigned - hot versus cold, active versus passive, and so on. He also integrates video and film components into his work.

Ruthenbeck's resolutely avant-garde output has featured at events and exhibitions designed to explore the limits of artistic creativity. Typical events have included those at the fine arts museum in Bern in 1969 (*When Attitudes Become Form*); a 'happening' at the museum in Lucerne alongside Beuys, Palermo and Polke; Documenta V in Kassel in 1972; and the Concrete Art Show at Mouans-Sartoux in 1996. Ruthenbeck has also exhibited more recently at *Les Années 70: l'art en cause* (*The 1970s: Art in Question*), held at the Capc Musée d'Art Contemporain in 2002 and at *Esprit des Lieux* (*The Spirit of Places*), an exhibition held at the Palais des Papes in Avignon in 2003 within the framework of *Trésors publics, 20 ans de création dans les Fonds régionaux d'art contemporain (FRAC)* (*Public Treasury, 20 Years of Creation in the Regional Collection of Contemporary Art*) an exhibition designed to explore contemporary art in contemporary contexts and settings. Ruthenbeck's work has also been the subject of solo exhibitions in Düsseldorf, Antwerp, Berlin, Munich and Copenhagen.

BIBLIOGRAPHY:

Liesbrock, Heinz, *Reiner Ruthenbeck, Fotografie 1956-1976*, Cantz, Stuttgart, 1991. Bee, Andreas, *Reiner Ruthenbeck*, Museum für Moderne Kunst, Frankfurt am Main, 1996. *Reiner Ruthenbeck: Zeichnungen*, exhibition catalogue, Hamburger Kunsthalle, Hamburg, 2000. Fréruchet, Maurice, et al., *Les Années soixante-dix: l'art en cause*, exhibition catalogue, Capc musée d'Art contemporain, Bordeaux, 2002. Zahm, Olivier (preface), et al., *Trésors publics, 20 ans de création dans les Fonds régionaux d'art contemporain*, Flammarion, Paris, 2003 (text in French and English).

MUSEUMS AND GALLERIES:

DIJON (FRAC Bourgogne): *Tuch mit Spannrahmen* (*Cloth with Tension Frame*) (1976) - DUNKIRK (FRAC Nord-Pas de Calais): *Floor Frame* (1971).

AUCTION RECORDS:

NEW YORK, 14 Nov 1991, *Untitled* (felt pen and graphite/four sheets of paper, in all 16¼ x 23½ ins / 41.3 x 59.5 cm) USD 1,100. LONDON, 29 June 1999, *Board with White Corners* (1988, painted aluminium panel, 79 x 39 ins / 200 x 100 cm) GBP 6,500. LONDON, 29 June 1999, *Board with White Edges* (1988, painted aluminium panel, 79 x 39 ins / 200 x 100 cm) GBP 6,500.

RÜTHER, Hermann
German, 20th century.
Born 20 February 1885, in Münster.
Painter. Architectural views.

Hermann Rüther was a student of Soetebier.

MUSEUMS AND GALLERIES:

MÜNSTER: *Lugger Old Gate; Münster seen from the Southeast* (1810).

RÜTHER, Hubert Josef Anton
German, 20th century.
Born 11 April 1886; died 16 September 1945.
Painter. Religious subjects.

Hubert Josef Anton Rüther studied decorative painting in Dresden before enrolling at the Dresden arts and crafts college and then, from 1919, at the fine arts academy, where he studied under R. Müller, O. Zwintscher, G. Kuchl and O. Gussman. In 1934, the Nazi regime prohibited him from exhibiting on account of the fact that he was married to a Jew. He was sent to a labour camp in 1944. Examples of Rüther's work featured at a major exhibition in 2001 at the cultural and historical museum of Osnabrück. That exhibition, *Verfemt, Vergessen, Wiederentdeckt: Schicksale expressiver Bildkunst im 20. Jahrhundert* (*Condemned. Forgotten. Rediscovered. The Fate of Expressive Art in the 20th Century*)) was expressly designed to highlight the work of German and Austrian-born artists of the 1920s and 1930s whose work was banned by the Nazis and largely ignored after the war. He is also noted for compositions painted for the cemetery chapel in Dresden-Friedrichstadt.

BIBLIOGRAPHY:

Hubert Rüther, exhibition catalogue, Haus der Heimat Freital, 1987. *Verfemt. Vergessen. Wiederentdeckt. Schicksale expressiver Bildkunst im 20. Jahrhundert. Sammlung Gerhard Schneider*, exhibition catalogue, Kulturgeschichtiches Museum, Osnabrück, Osnabrück, 2001.

RÜTHER, Irene
Maiden name: Rabinowicz
German, 20th century.
Born 22 September 1900, in Cologne.
Painter.

The wife of Hubert Rüther, Irene Rüther lived and worked in Dresden and was a student of O. Gussmann.

RUTHER, Salomon, or Rütter or Ritter or Reuter
German, 17th century.
Born c. 1645; died 1691.
Active in Danzig.
Painter.

RÜTHER-RABINOWICZ, Irena
German, 20th century.
Born 22 September 1900, in Cologne.
Painter. Portraits.

Irena Rüther-Rabinowicz was the wife of Hubert Rüther. She moved to Dresden in 1916 and enrolled at the fine arts academy three years later - their first female student. Both rena and her husband were proscribed by the Nazi authorities in 1934 and she was subsequently sent to a labour camp.

RUTHERFORD, A.
British, 18th - 19th century.
Engraver (etching).
A. Rutherford was an engraver of views and portraits.

RUTHERFORD, Violet Mary.
See **CHARLESWORTH Violet Mary**

RUTHERSTON, Albert Daniel, or Rothenstein
British, 20th century.
Born 5 December 1881, in Bradford (Yorkshire); died 14 July 1953, in Ouchy (Lausanne), Switzerland.
Painter, draughtsman, poster artist, illustrator, writer. Figures, landscapes.
Albert Daniel Rutherston was the brother of William Rothenstein. He was a pupil of Fred Brown. Although his landscapes are traditional in style, he developed a personal style in his design work. He staged plays by Shakespeare and Bernard Shaw, and illustrated volumes of Shakespeare and Maeterlinck.
MUSEUMS AND GALLERIES:
BRADFORD (Cartwright Hall AG): title of a poem by Thomas Hood*The Song of the Shirt* (1902, oil on canvas) - LONDON (National Portrait Gal.): *Spencer Frederick Gore* (1902, oil on canvas); *James Dickson Innes* (1908, pencil) - LONDON (Tate Collection): *Laundry Girls* (1906, oil on canvas); *The Pump, Nash End* (1931, oil on canvas).
AUCTION RECORDS:
LONDON, 25 June 1980, *Nude in a Landscape* (watercolour/silk, 23 x 14 ins / 57.5 x 35.5 cm) GBP 420. LONDON, 29 July 1988, *Extensive Hilly Landscape* (1910, watercolour and gouache, 9 3/4 x 13 3/4 ins / 25 x 35 cm) GBP 748.

RUTHIEL, Henri Joseph. See **RUXTHIEL**

RUTHS, Amélie
German, 20th century.
Born 28 April 1871, in Hamburg.
Painter, engraver. Architectural views, interiors, still-lifes.
Amélie Ruths was a niece and student of Johann Valentin Georg Ruths.

RUTHS, Johann Valentin Georg
German, 19th century.
Born 6 March 1825, in Hamburg; died 17 January 1905, in Hamburg.
Painter, lithographer. Seascapes, landscapes.
Johann Valentin Georg Ruths started his studies in Düsseldorf and Karlsruhe. He spent some time in Italy and returned to Germany in 1857, at which time he settled in Hamburg. In 1869 he became a member of the academies of Vienna and Berlin. He was a gold medal winner in Berlin in 1872.
MUSEUMS AND GALLERIES:
BERLIN: *Twilight* - BREMEN: *Walking in the Outskirts of a Small Town* - DRESDEN: *Autumn Morning in Southern Switzerland* - HAMBURG: three works - KALININGRAD: *Forest Spring* - WROCLAW: *Holstein Landscape*.
AUCTION RECORDS:
COLOGNE, 29 March 1974, *Alpine Landscape,* DEM 7,000. HAMBURG, 1 June 1978, *Traveller in a Landscape* (oil on panel, 13 x 20 1/2 ins / 33 x 52 cm) DEM 3,800. HAMBURG, 7 June 1979, *Mountain Landscape* (oil on mounted card/panel, 13 x 20 ins / 33.3 x 50.6 cm) DEM 2,400. HAMBURG, 11 June 1981, *Mountain Landscape at Twilight* (1870, oil on panel) DEM 4,000. HAMBURG, 4 Dec 1987, *Woodland Landscape, Oldenburg* (1878, oil on canvas, 39 1/4 x 66 1/4 ins / 100 x 168 cm) DEM 19,000. LONDON, 15 Feb 1991, *Flüela Pass* (oil on panel, 14 x 20 1/2 ins / 35.6 x 52.1 cm) GBP 1,980. DÜSSELDORF, 31 Jan 2000, *Riders by Lake in Roman Countryside* (1869, oil on canvas, 23 x 39 ins / 58 x 100 cm) DEM 30,000. DÜSSELDORF, 31 Jan 2000, *Landscape in Thuringen* (1868, oil on canvas, 39 x 62 ins / 99 x 158 cm) DEM 45,000. HAMBURG, 15 June 2002, *Friedrichsruh with Angler by Steam and Farmer in the Distance* (1885, oil on panel, 13 x 19 ins / 34 x 47 cm) EUR 2,500. HAMBURG, 7 Dec 2002, *Spring* (chalk heightened with white, 33 x 24 ins / 84 x 61 cm) EUR 3,800.

RUTHVEN, Mary (Lady)
Maiden name: Hamilton Campbell
British, 19th century.
Painter. Architectural views.
MUSEUMS AND GALLERIES:
EDINBURGH (Nat. Gal. of Scotland, Print Room): *Temple of Theseus* (watercolour); *Temple of Jupiter at Olympus* (watercolour).

RUTHXIEL, Henri Joseph. See **RUXTHIEL**

RUTILENSI, Piero
Italian, 17th century.
Active in Florence during the first half of the 17th century.
Sculptor.
Piero Rutilensi is known for a depiction of St Matthew painted around 1620.

RÜTIMAN, Emil
Swiss, 20th century.
Born 9 August 1878, in Zurich.
Painter, architect.

RÜTIMANN, Christoph
Swiss, 20th - 21st century.
Born 1955.
Installation artist, performance artist. Multimedia. Conceptual Art.
Christoph Rütimann lives and works in Lucerne. In the field of multimedia installation, his work is unclassifiable. The artist appropriates certain scientific phenomena to link, disentangle and measure the relationships between things and show them off in their visual, audio and psychological dimensions. He exhibited from 1981 in Germany, Italy, Holland and Sweden, and represented Switzerland at the Venice Biennale. He had solo shows at the Galerie Mai 36, Lucerne, La Criée Centre d'Art Contemporain, Rennes (1993), the Galerie Philippe Rizo, Paris (1995), and the Galerie Mai 36, Zurich (2001).

RÜTIMEYER, Friedrich or Nikolaus Friedrich
Swiss, 19th century.
Born 7 May 1797, in Schwarzenegg (Bern); died 8 February 1847, in Mett.
Active in Bern.
Medallist.

RUTKOWSKI, Helene
German, 20th century.
Born 24 January 1862, in Stettin (now Szczecin, Poland).
Painter. Portraits, landscapes.
Helene Rutkowski was a student of Gussow, Gustaf Graef and Herterich.
MUSEUMS AND GALLERIES:
WARSAW (Muz. Narodowe): *Landscape during a Storm*.

RUTKOWSKY, Szczesny
Polish, 20th century.
Born 15 August 1887, in Szptal Górny, near Wloclawek.
Painter, art writer.
Szczesny Rutkowsky studied in Rome and Paris and was influenced by Henri Rousseau. The Muzeum Narodowe in Warsaw has his *Landscape in a Storm*.

RUTLAND, Violet of (Duchess). See **GRANBY**

RUTLEDGE, William
British, 19th century.
Painter. Portraits, landscapes.
William Rutledge worked in Sunderland and exhibited in London from 1881 to 1892, notably at the Suffolk Street Gallery.
MUSEUMS AND GALLERIES:
SUNDERLAND: *Portrait of the American Poet Walt Whitman*.
AUCTION RECORDS:
MONTREAL, 1 May 1989, *London Bridge* (oil on canvas, 32 x 41 ins / 81 x 104 cm) CAD 850.

RUTLINGER, Johannes
British, 16th century.
Probably of German origin.
Engraver (burin), medallist.
Johannes Rutlinger engraved maps and the *Portrait of Queen Elizabeth* that is in the British Museum, London.

RÜTLINGER, Kaspar, or Reutlinger
Swiss, 16th - 17th century.
Born 1562, in Zurich; died 8 November 1610, in Zurich.
Painter, calligrapher.
Zurich School.
Kaspar Rütlinger was a master in 1583.

RUTS. See also **RUTZ**

RUTS, Adriaen
Dutch, 17th century.
Died 1619, in Leeuwarden.
Active in Bremen.
Painter.
Adriaen Ruts worked in Amsterdam from 1593, and set up in Leeuwarden in 1597. He was probably the father of Cornelis Ariensz. Ruts.

RUTS, Cornelis
Flemish School, 16th century.
Active in Antwerp.
Painter.
Cornelis Ruts was made a burgher of Amsterdam in 1586. According to Dr Wurzbach, he may have been the same artist as Cornelis Rutz, called Baerts.

RUTS, Cornelis Ariensz.
Dutch, 17th century.
Born 1594, in Leeuwarden.
Painter.
Cornelis Ariensz. Ruts was probably the son of Adriaen Ruts. He worked in Leeuwarden in 1621.

RÜTS, Helene von
German, 20th century.
Born 11 August 1868, in Naumburg; died 1 November 1933, in Leipzig.
Painter. Portraits.
Helene von Rüts studied under Georg Ludwig Meyn in Berlin, in Paris and in Leipzig under H. Soltmann.
MUSEUMS AND GALLERIES:
LEIPZIG: *Marguerite*; *Portrait of the Artist's Mother*; drawing.

RÜTS, Karl Rudolf von
German, 19th century.
Born 31 May 1790; died 9 August 1875, in Rüdersdorf, near Berlin.
Painter. Portraits.
Karl Rudolf von Rüts painted actors in costumes from the time of Wallenstein.

RUTSCH, Alexander
Austrian, 20th century.
Born 1916, in Vienna; died 1997.
Active in the USA.
Painter, sculptor.
Alexandre Rusch cannot be assigned to any particular school or movement. His body of work ranges from outright realism to total abstraction. He does not limit himself to painting or sculpture, and is also involved in music and cinema. Typically, Rutsch welds hallucinatory human and animal figures, but he has explored a wide variety of other techniques.

RUTSCHELL, Henri Joseph. See **RUXTHIEL**

RUTTA, Clementi. See **RUTA**

RUTTE, E. A.
German, 19th century.
Active in Berlin in 1826.
Painter. Flowers.
E. A. Rutte was a pupil of K. Rötigs.

RUTTEN, Anne
Belgian, 20th century.
Born 1898, in Lanaken; died 1981, in Waterschei.
Painter. Figures, genre scenes, still-lifes.
Anne Rutten was a student of J. Damien.
AUCTION RECORDS:
LOKEREN, 10 Oct 1992, *Still-life* (oil on canvas, 33¾ x 27½ ins / 86 x 70 cm) BEF 55,000.

RUTTEN, Jan or Johannes
Dutch, 19th century.
Born 31 July 1809, in Dordrecht; died 10 October 1884, in Dordrecht.
Painter, draughtsman. Landscapes, urban landscapes.
Jan Rutten was the pupil of A van Stry, whose granddaughter he married, and of GA Schmidt.
MUSEUMS AND GALLERIES:
DORDRECHT: *Views of Old Dordrecht* (more than 700 drawings).
AUCTION RECORDS:
LONDON, 21 Oct 1970, *Street Scene*, GBP 2,700. LONDON, 26 March 1982, *The Bourse, Copenhagen* (oil on canvas, 25 x 33 ins / 63.5 x 84 cm) GBP 8,000. LONDON, 22 June 1984, *View of a Town in Holland* (oil on panel, 16½ x 21½ ins / 42 x 54.5 cm) GBP 6,500. AMSTERDAM, 10 Feb 1988, *A Village Fantasy with a Pleasure Boat Approaching, near Fishing Boats* (oil on canvas, 25½ x 19½ ins / 65 x 49.5 cm) NLG 3 680. AMSTERDAM, 30 Oct 1996, *View of Dordrecht with the Grote Kerk in the Distance* (oil on panel, 23 x 32¼ ins / 57.5 x 81.8 cm) NLG 36,902.

RUTTENZWIG. See **RUTENZWIG**

RÜTTER, Hans Jakob and Hans Peter. See **RÜTER**

RÜTTER, Salomon. See **RUTHER**

RÜTTGERS. See **RÜTGERS**

RÜTTIMANN, A.
Swiss, 18th - 19th century.
Painter.
A. Rüttimann painted a *St Eloise* and a *St Francis Xavier* in the chapel of Ried in Lachen.

RUTTKAY, György
Hungarian, 20th century.
Born 1898; died 1974.
Painter, watercolourist.
György Ruttkay trained in Košice. He made friends with Kassak, to whom he sent his first drawings and watercolours during World War I; these were later exhibited on several occasions at the MA group exhibitions and in the accompanying magazine. After the war, he continued studying at the academy of fine art in Bucharest. In 1922-23, Ruttkay went on a study trip to Germany. He featured in *L'art en Hongrie - 1905-1930 - art et révolution* (*Art in Hungary 1905-*

1930. Art and Revolution), Musée d'Art et d'Industrie in St-Étienne (1980).
MUSEUMS AND GALLERIES:
BUDAPEST (Magyar Nemzeti Gal.): *Composition with Owl* (1923, watercolour); *Sleep* (watercolour, 1923) - PÉCS (Janus Pannonius Mus.): *Composition* (1910, watercolour); *Self-portrait* (1923).

RUTXHIEL, Henri Joseph. See **RUXTHIEL**

RUTY, P. M.
French, 19th - 20th century.
Born 1868, in Paris.
Painter, draughtsman, illustrator. Figures, genre scenes, architectural views.
P. M. Ruty, a pupil of Lechevellier-Chevignard and the architect Rocque, illustrated, among other books, G. Frenay's *Mon Chevalier* (published 1896), Hugo's *Eviradnus*, 1900, and, with Mucha, J. Gautier's *Mémoires d'un éléphant blanc* (*Memoirs of a White Elephant*) (published 1924). He was a contributor to the *Petit Français Illustré*
BIBLIOGRAPHY:
Osterwalder, Marcus (ed.), *Dictionnaire des illustrateurs 1800-1914*, Ides et Calendes, Neuchâtel, 1989.
MUSEUMS AND GALLERIES:
LIMOGES: *Château de Blois* (drawing); *Town Entrance, Breton Scene* (drawing).

RUTZ, Caspar
Flemish School, 16th century.
Active during the second half of the 16th century.
Painter.
Caspar Rutz fled Mechelen in 1567 and settled in Cologne, where he engraved a *Last Supper* after Cornelius Cort. He also published engravings.

RUTZ, Cornelis, called Baerts
German, 16th century.
Active during the second half of the 16th century.
Painter.
Cornelis Rutz was possibly the son of Caspar Rutz. He may have been the same person as Cornelis Ruts.

RUTZ, Gustav
German, 19th - 20th century.
Born 14 December 1857, in Cologne.
Sculptor.
Gustav Rutz studied under Julius Geertz in Düsseldorf and under A. Hess in Munich. He went on to sculpt statuary and fountains for several towns in Germany.

RUTZ, Jakob. See **RUEZ**

RUTZ, Jean
French, 16th century.
Died at the end of 1606, in Laon, or at the beginning of 1607 according to some sources.
Active in Laon.
Painter.
Jean Rutz was possibly of German origin and the first master of Antoine and Louis Lenain. He worked for Laon Cathedral.

RUTZ, Maximilian
German, 18th century.
Active in Cologne in the second half of the 18th century.
Painter.

RUTZ, P.
German, 17th century.
Active in Cologne in 1650.
Engraver (burin).

RUUTAERT, Daniel. See **RUTAERT**

RUVIALE, Francesco, called Il Polidorino, known mistakenly as Pedro de Rubiales
Spanish, 16th century.
Born in Extremadura.
Active in Naples from 1527 to 1560.
Painter. History painting, religious subjects.
Neapolitan School.
Francesco Ruviale grew up in Naples, where he saw works by Polidoro da Caravaggio (when the latter was in refuge in the city following the sack of Rome by the Imperial Army), and became the pupil of this famous disciple of Raphael. He imitated his master so successfully that he was given the nickname Polidorino. He also worked with Varsori.
Ruviale's works include *Dead Christ*, in the chapel of the Tribunal in Naples, and *Deposition*, in the chapel of the Vicaria Criminale.

RUVIRA. See **RUBIRA**

RUVOLO, Felix
American, 20th century.
Born 1912, in New York; died 1992.
Painter. Wall decorations.
Felix Ruvolo spent his childhood in Sicily, but lived in Chicago from 1926-1948, studying at the Art Institute. He lived and worked in Walnut Creek (California). He was commissioned to paint several murals in Chicago.
He held his first solo exhibition in 1947, and in the same year exhibited at the Carnegie Foundation in Pittsburgh a work entitled *Duel of the Entomologist*, which was midway between Abstract and Surrealist in inspiration. His work subsequently featured in many private and public exhibitions in the USA.

RUWEEL, Jean, or Rueele
Flemish School, 15th century.
Sculptor (wood).
In 1411 and 1412 Jean Ruweel carved a retable for Courtrai Cathedral, and between 1413 and 1415 executed another for the church of St Martin in the same city.

RUWEL, Alexander
Flemish School, 17th century.
Active in Bruges from 1675 to 1684.
Painter.

RUWEL, Alexander. See also **ROSWEL**

RUWELLES, Jean François de. See **RUELLES**

RUWERSMA, Wessel Pieters
Dutch, 18th - 19th century.
Born 1750, in Korlum (Friesland); died 1827, in Buitenpost.
Painter. Portraits, landscapes.
Ruwersma was the master of W-H van der Kool and A-G Zuvart.

RUWOLDT, Hans Martin
German, 20th century.
Born 15 February 1891, in Hamburg; died 16 October 1969, in Hamburg.
Sculptor (stone/bronze), draughtsman, watercolourist, lithographer. Animals, figures, landscapes.
Jugendstil.
Hans Martin Ruwoldt studied initially at the College of Sculpture in Rostock, where he was instructed in the craft of modelling and casting. He completed his studies under Richard Luksch at the hamburg arts and crafts college from 1911 to 1914. He was taken prisoner in France during World War I. After the war, he embarked on a series of study visits, notably to France (1930), Italy (1932, in the company of Wilhelm Grimm and Karl Kluth) and Denmark (1934). Like many artists of his generation, he became a member of the free fine arts academy in Hamburg at the beginning of the 1950s. He taught sculpture at the fine arts academy in Hamburg from 1955 to 1959. He was awarded the City of Hamburg Ed-

win-Scharff Prize in 1956 and the Joost van den Vondel Prize in 1967. Examples of his work were exhibited from 1921 within the framework of the Hamburg Secession, a group he formally joined in 1928.

Ruwoldt is thought of primarily as an animal sculptor. Several of his works are on show in public places in Hamburg: *Polar Bear* and *Panther* are in Hamburg's Stadtpark (municipal gardens) and the city boasts a number of other sculptures by him, including *Cheetah* and a *Figure of a Walking Woman*. Ruwoldt is generally considered to be an Expressionist (not least, perhaps, because of his preference for exotic animals not native to Western Europe), but his numerous drawings attest to the fact that he was also fascinated by the human body and its different poses. He was also a successful painter of watercolour landscapes.

His first solo exhibition was held in Berlin in 1926. Since his death in 1969, other exhibitions have been dedicated to his work, most recently in 2003 at the Haspa (Hamburger Sparkasse) Gallery in Hamburg.

BIBLIOGRAPHY:

Clausen-Gaedke, Renate, *Der Bildhauer Hans Martin Ruwoldt (1891-1969). Werkmonographie und œuvre der Plastik*, thesis, Kunsthistorisches Institut der Universität Kiel, 1991.
Bruhns, Maike, *Hans Martin Ruwoldt (1891-1969). Plastik, Zeichnungen, Graphik*, exhibition catalogue, Hamburger Sparkasse, Galerie in der Zentrale, Hamburg, 2003.

MUSEUMS AND GALLERIES:

HAMBURG (Mus. für Kunst und Gewerbe): several works - SALZBURG (Rupertinum).

RUXTHIEL, Henri Joseph, or Rutchiel or Rutxhiel or Ruthiel or Ruthxiel or Rutschell
Belgian, 19th century.
Born 4 July (or June) 1775, in Lierneux, near Liège; died 15 September 1837, in Paris.
Sculptor.

Ruxthiel started his career as a shepherd, but moved to Paris, where he was the pupil of Devandre, Houdon and David. He was second in the prize called the Grand Prix de Rome in 1804, and won first prize in 1808. He exhibited at the Salon from 1814 to 1827.

Stamps of sale

MUSEUMS AND GALLERIES:

BOURGES: *Pandora* - DIJON: *Charles Antoine d'Angoulême* - LIÈGE: *Grètry* - NANTES (MBA, Clarke-de-Feltre Collection): *Elfride Clarke de Feltre* - PARIS (Louvre): *Zephyr and Psyche* - VERSAILLES: *Duke of Berry; Suffren; Napoleon I.*

RUY, Alphonse or Joseph Alphonse
French, 19th century.
Born 5 July 1853, in Paris.
Watercolourist, architect. Landscapes.

Alphonse Ruy was the student of Vaudremer, L. J. André and Brunet-Debaines.

RUYCK, Roger de
Belgian, 20th century.
Born 1918, in Merelbeke.
Draughtsman, illustrator, watercolourist.

Roger de Ruyck studied at the academy of St Luke and the college of arts in Ghent.

RUYER, Jean
French, 20th century.
Born in Rouen.
Painter.

Jean Ruyer exhibited at the Salon d'Automne, Paris.

RUYL, L. F. G. van der
Flemish School, 18th century.
Active in 1789.
Painter. Portraits.

MUSEUMS AND GALLERIES:

DUNKIRK: *Portrait of the Artist; Portrait of J. Emmery, Mayor of Dunkirk.*

RUYS, Simon or Symen, or Ruysch
Dutch, 17th century.
Active during the second half of the 17th century.
Painter, draughtsman. Portraits.

Ruys was possibly the pupil of W Vaillant, a member of the guild at The Hague in 1679, 1685 and 1688. He is remembered for: *Johannes Camprich van Cronefeldt* (in Amsterdam).

RUYSCH, Aletta Jacoba Joséphine, later Thol-Ruysch
Dutch, 19th - 20th century.
Born 6 August 1860, in the Netherlands; died 1931.
Painter. Still-lifes.

Aletta Jacoba Joséphine Ruysch studied initially in Holland before visiting England in 1879 and France in 1880. She also studied in Antwerp under Eugène Joors. She married Henrick Otto Thol. She exhibited in The Hague in 1890.

MUSEUMS AND GALLERIES:

THE HAGUE (Gemeentemus.): *Still-life* (signed: Aletta Ruysch) - VERVIERS (Mus. communal des Beaux-Arts et de la Céramique): *Benedicite* (oil on canvas).

RUYSCH, Anne or Anna Elisabeth
Dutch, 18th century.
Died after 1741.
Painter. Still-lifes (flowers/fruit), animals.

Anne Ruysch, who was the sister of Rachel Ruysch, is said to have been active from 1680 to 1741. Dr von Wurtzbach mentions a painting by her as having appeared in the Brand von Cabour sale which took place at Breukalen in 1849.

MUSEUMS AND GALLERIES:

KARLSRUHE: *Reptiles and Flowers.*

AUCTION RECORDS:

LONDON, 24 Nov 1971, *Still-life with Fruit*, GBP 1,850. NEW YORK, 15 Jan 1993, *Still-life with Two Peaches and Bunches of Grapes on a Red Cloth* (1685, oil on canvas, 13 1/2 x 12 ins / 34.3 x 30.5 cm) USD 28,750.

RUYSCH, Fredericus or Frederich
Dutch, 17th - 18th century.
Born 23 March 1638, in The Hague; died 12 or 22 February 1731, in Amsterdam.
Painter. Flowers.

Fredericus Ruysch was the father of Anne and Rachel Ruysch. He was a lecturer in anatomy and botany in Amsterdam.

RUYSCH, J.
Dutch, 17th century.
Active in The Hague at the end of the 17th century.
Landscape artist.

J. Ruysch is mentioned in 1699, as a member of the Guild of St Luke.

RUYSCH, Johann
German, 16th century.
Born in Utrecht; died 1533, in Cologne.
Painter. Religious subjects.

Johann Ruysch was both an astrologer and a painter. A Benedictine, he collaborated from 1508 with Sodoma on the *stanze* of the Vatican in Rome.

RUYSCH, Rachel, or Ruisch
Mme Juriaen Pool
Dutch, 17th - 18th century.

Born 1664 or 1665, in Amsterdam; died 12 August 1750, in Amsterdam.

Painter. Still-lifes (flowers/fruit), insects.

Rachel Ruysch was the daughter of the lecturer in anatomy Fredericus Ruysch, and the pupil of Willem van Alst. She was so enthusiastic about her work that for a long time she refused to marry despite being rich and beautiful, to avoid the worries of running a household. However, in 1695 she decided to marry the painter Juriaen Pool, two years her junior, whom she outlived. Moreover Pool, enthralled by the talent of his wife who had just entered the academy at The Hague, in 1701, soon stopped all artistic activity and devoted himself to the lace trade. Ruysch, on the other hand, never stopped painting, and was showered with honours and presents. One of her ten children was held at the font in Düsseldorf by the Elector Palatine, to whose service she had been attached since 1708. He made her a present of a gold medal, in addition giving her 'a silver dressing-table set, of 28 pieces, to which he added six candlesticks of the same metal'. On the death of the prince in 1716, she returned to Amsterdam.

Rachel Ruysch always signed her works in her maiden name. She painted almost exclusively still-lifes, copying the objects in front of her down to the tiniest detail. In the 17th century she had a considerable reputation as a painter of flowers, which she depicted in bouquets placed in niches or on a table, together with butterflies or insects. Ruysch spent her whole life copying flowers and birds in minute detail, casting aside, it would seem out of scruple, any originality, and the extreme care she took with each work explains their rarity in spite of such a long career.

Museums and Galleries:

Aachen: *Bouquet* - Aix: *Still-life* - Amsterdam: *Bouquet; Three Flower Paintings* - Bonn: *Flowers* - Brunswick: *Flowers and Fruit* - Brussels: *Flowers and Fruit* - Budapest: *Flowers* - Cheltenham (AG and Mus.): *Flowers in a glass vase* (c. 1700, oil on canvas) - Cherbourg: *Bouquet of Flowers* - Cologne: *Flowers* - Darmstadt: *Flowers* - Dresden: *Fruit and Kite; Flowers; Flowers in front of a Rock* - Florence (Palazzo Pitti): *Fruit, Flowers and Insects; Flowers and Fruit* - Florence (Uffizi): *Flowers and Fruit; Flowers in a Basket* - Frankfurt am Main: *Bouquet of Flowers* - Geneva (Mus. Ariana): *Bouquet of Various Flowers* - Glasgow: *Flowers; Vase of Flowers* - Karlsruhe: *Bouquet; Fruit* - Kassel: *Flowers* - La Fère: *Painting Reminding of the Inevitability of Death* - London (NG): *Flowers in a Vase* (1690, oil on canvas) - Munich: *Flowers on a Marble Table; Melon, Grapes, Peaches at the Foot of a Tree; Flowers on a Marble Table, Butterflies and Caterpillars* - New York (Metropolitan Mus. of Art): *Flowers and Butterflies* - Nice: *Monkeys Plundering a Dessert; Crayfish and Grape* - Rotterdam: *Flowers* - The Hague: *Flowers; Bouquet* - Vienna: *Large Bouquet* - Vienna (Czernin'sche Gemäldegal.): *Flowers on a Stone Table; Fruit, Melons, etc. on a Table* - Vienna (Liechtenstein Mus.): *Flowers and Fruit* - Wiesbaden: *Vase with Flowers* - Wroclaw: *Flowers.*

Auction records:

Amsterdam, 22 April 1709, *Vase of Flowers,* FRF 580. Paris, 1777, *Flowers and Pomergranates; Grapes, Peaches, Plums and Other Fruit* (collection) FRF 3,000. London, 1840, *Peaches, Grapes and Other Fruit,* FRF 7,185; *Bouquet of Flowers,* FRF 5,250. Paris, 1865, *Vase of Flowers,* FRF 1,500; *Fruit,* FRF 1,200. Paris, 1867, *Bouquet of Flowers,* FRF 4,450. London, 1876, *Vase of Flowers,* FRF 10,500. Brussels, 1882, *Flowers,* FRF 3,200. Paris, 1897, *Garland of Flowers,* FRF 800. Paris, 1898, *Flowers,* FRF 2,300. London, 22 July 1910, *Flowers in a Vase,* GBP 43. London, 25 and 26 May 1911, *Melon, Pears and Other Fruit* (1707) GBP 262. London, 16 June 1911, *Fruit, Bird's Nest and Insects,* GBP 89. Paris, 12-15 Jan 1921, *Still-life,* FRF 4,600. London, 23 June 1922, *Vase of Flowers, Glass of Wine and Peeled Orange,* GBP 136. London, 23 March 1923, *Fruit and Bird's Nest,* GBP 136. London, 29 Jan 1926, *Flowers in a Vase,* GBP 96. London, 11 June 1926, *Flowers in a Vase on a Marble Table,* GBP 194. London, 20 May 1927, *Flowers in a Glass Vase,* GBP 210. New York, 1 May 1930, *Vase of Flowers,* USD 900. Paris, 18 June 1932, *Fruit at the Base of a Stone Vase,* FRF 2,400. London, 12 July 1935, *Vase of Flowers and Insects,* GBP 94. London, 2 July 1937, *Flowers in a Cup,* GBP 693. Paris, 30 June and 1 July 1941, *Vase of Flowers with Butterflies and Insects* (attributed) FRF 4,600. Paris, 10 Feb 1943, *Vase of Carnations; Vase of Flowers* (two panels, attributed) FRF 9,200. London, 4 March 1943, *Flowers, Lizard and Butterflies,* GBP 92. Paris, 12 March 1943, *Vase of Flowers* (attributed) FRF 6,800. Paris, 17 March 1943, *Fruit, Flowers and Macaw* (school of Rachel Ruysch) FRF 22,000. London, 7 May 1943, *Flowers in a Vase,* GBP 105. London, 14 Dec 1945, *Flowers and Fruit; Bird and Reptile,* GBP 241. New York, 20 and 21 Feb 1946, *Flowers,* USD 275. Utrecht, 8-11 Oct 1946, *Flowers,* NLG 2,100. London, 11 Oct 1946, *Flowers in a Vase,* GBP 997. London, 5 Feb 1947, *Roses, Tulips and Poppies,* GBP 520. Paris, 19 June 1947, *Flowers and Butterflies,* FRF 92,500. Paris, 12 May 1950, *Bouquet of Flowers* (attributed) FRF 55,000. London, 23 June 1950, *Vase of Flowers* (1716) GBP 441. Lucerne, Nov 1950, *Vase of Flowers,* CHF 1,500. Amsterdam, 13 March 1951, *Still-life with Flowers,* NLG 1,800. London, 11 May 1951, *Flowers and Fruit* (two pendants) GBP 198. Paris, 12 Dec 1953, *Flowers and Insects,* FRF 200,000. London, 25 Feb 1959, *Still-life,* GBP 880. London, 1 April 1960, *Floral Composition,* GBP 3,780. Paris, 24 April 1961, *Vase of Roses,* FRF 15,200. London, 30 June 1961, *Poppies, Thistles and Columbine,* GBP 1,995. London, 27 June 1962, *Still-life with Fruit; Still-life with Flowers* (painting/metal) GBP 2,800. London, 4 Dec 1964, *Still-life with Flowers,* Gns 3,800. London, 29 March 1968, *Still-life with Flowers,* Gns 4,000. London, 27 June 1969, *Still-lifes with Flowers and Fruit* (two canvases) Gns 5,600. London, 26 Nov 1971, *Still-life with Flowers,* Gns 8,000. London, 23 March 1973, *Flowers on an Entablature,* Gns 30,000. London, 28 June 1974, *Still-life with Flowers,* Gns 3,800. Paris, 22 Oct 1976, *Still-life with Fruit and Insects* (oil on canvas, 35 1/2 x 30 ins / 90 x 76 cm) FRF 45,000. London, 1 Dec 1978, *Flowers, Snakes and Insects beside a Pond* (1686, oil on canvas, 44 1/2 x 33 3/4 ins / 113 x 85.7 cm) GBP 30,000. London, 29 June 1979, *Still-life with Flowers* (1682, oil on canvas, 20 x 15 ins / 51 x 38 cm) GBP 24,000. London, 9 Dec 1981, *Still-life with Flowers* (oil on canvas, 22 3/4 x 20 ins / 58 x 51 cm) GBP 19,000. Paris, 29 April 1982, *Vase of Flowers and Fruit on an Entablature* (oil on canvas, 32 1/4 x 27 1/2 ins / 82 x 70 cm) FRF 68,000. New York, 9 June 1983, *Vase of Flowers* (oil on canvas, 24 1/2 x 19 3/4 ins / 62 x 50 cm) USD 70,000. London, 3 April 1985, *Still-life with Flowers* (1695, oil on canvas, 12 1/4 x 9 1/2 ins / 31 x 24 cm) GBP 74,000. London, 12 Dec 1986, *Still-life with Flowers on an Entablature* (oil on canvas, 30 x 25 1/4 ins / 76.2 x 64.1 cm) GBP 48,000. Paris, 14 April 1988, *Flowers Scattered on an Entablature* (oil on panel, 6 1/2 x 6 3/4 ins / 16.5 x 17 cm) FRF 45,000. New York, 11 Jan 1989, *Still-life of Fruit with a Bird and Its Nest, a Lizard and Insects* (oil on canvas, 24 3/4 x 21 1/4 ins / 63 x 54 cm) USD 165,000. London, 6 July 1990, *Branch of a Plum Tree, Daffodil and Other Spring Flowers with Insects on a Marble Entablature* (oil on canvas, 10 1/4 x 8 1/4 ins / 26 x 21 cm) GBP 68,200. Amsterdam, 13 Nov 1990, *Important Floral Composition with Tulips, Roses, Honeysuckle, Peonies and Other Flowers in a Vase near a Nest on an Entablature* (1739, oil on canvas, 20½ x 16½ ins / 52 x 42 cm) NLG 943,000. MONACO, 7 Dec 1990, *Bouquet of Flowers on an Entablature* (oil on canvas, 22 x 17¾ ins / 56 x 45 cm) FRF 832,500. AMSTERDAM, 14 Nov 1991, *Still-life with Poppy, Carnations, Cornflower, Mushrooms and Insects on a Mossy Forest Floor* (1683, oil on canvas, 25¼ x 20¼ ins / 64 x 51.6 cm) NLG 172,500. BOLOGNA, 8-9 June 1992, *Floral Composition in a Vase on a Stone Entablature* (oil on canvas, 30¾ x 24¾ ins / 78 x 63 cm) ITL 63,250,000. LONDON, 11 Dec 1992, *Carnation, Convolvulus and Hibiscus with a Butterfly on an Entablature* (oil on panel, 13½ x 10¾ ins / 34.4 x 27.2 cm) GBP 154,000. NEW YORK, 12 Jan 1994, *Bunch of Grapes with Hollyhocks, Iris, African Marigolds, Clematis, a Chestnut and Mulberries Hanging in a Niche* (1681, oil on canvas, 25¾ x 20 ins / 65.5 x 50.8 cm) USD 96,000. LONDON, 8 Dec 1995, *Tulips, Roses, Peonies, Honeysuckle and Other Flowers on a Marble Entablature with Butterflies and Insects* (oil on canvas, 24½ x 21 ins / 62.3 x 53.2 cm) GBP 342,500. LONDON, 5 July 1996, *Large Still-life of Fruit with a Bird's Nest, a Lizard and Insects* (1710, oil on canvas, 34¼ x 27¼ ins / 87 x 69.5 cm) GBP 210,500. LONDON, 18 April 1997, *Honeysuckle, Sweet Peas, Lilies, Peonies, Hyacinths, Passion Flowers and Other Flowers, a Pineapple and a Cactus in a Boettger Stone Urn with a Pale Yellow Butterfly on a Marble Entablature* (oil on canvas, 35¼ x 27¾ ins / 89.5 x 70.5 cm) GBP 40,000. LONDON, 3 Dec 1997, *Bouquet of Roses, Marigolds and a Larkspur with a Red-Admiral on a Marble Entablature* (1686, oil on canvas, 13½ x 11½ ins / 34 x 29 cm) GBP 199,500. VIENNA, 24 March 1999, *Still-life with Tulip, White Rose and Carnation in a Glass Vase* (1716, oil on canvas, 22 x 21 ins / 57 x 54 cm) ATS 280,000. LONDON, 8 July 1999, *Still-life with Summer Flowers Including Roses, Marigolds and Antirrhinums* (oil on canvas/panel, 22 x 17 ins / 56 x 43 cm) GBP 210,000. MUNICH, 21 June 2002, *Still-life with Fruit and Stone Vase* (oil on canvas, 36 x 27 ins / 91 x 69 cm) EUR 440,000. LONDON, 12 Dec 2002, *Still-life with Roses, Poppies and Other Flowers in a Glass Vase* (1716, oil on canvas, 19 x 15 ins / 48 x 39 cm) GBP 600,000.

RUYSCH, Simon. See **RUYS**

RUYSCHER, Jan. See **RUISCHER**

RUYSDAEL, Isaac or Isaack van, or Ruisdael
Dutch, 17th century.
Born 1599, in Naarden; died 1677; buried 4 October in Haarlem.
Painter. Landscapes with figures, landscapes.

Isaac Ruysdael was the brother of Salomon and father of Jakob Ruysdael. He was not only a painter, but also a dealer in paintings and a frame-maker. In 1642 he married in Haarlem, where he had settled.

He specialised in painting landscapes in a style similar to his brother's, but foreshadowing his son's. His canvases are executed with precision and in a small range of colours.

MUSEUMS AND GALLERIES:

BERLIN: *Landscape with Peasants* - MUNICH: *Sandy Slope* - VIENNA (Akademie der Bildenden Künste): *Landscape with Fencing.*

AUCTION RECORDS:

PARIS, 14 June 1891, *Landscape,* FRF 3,600. AMSTERDAM, 14 Nov 1990, *Figures on Tracks in the Country with a Farm in the Background* (1638, oil on panel, 20¾ x 42 ins / 53 x 106.5 cm) NLG 26,450. NEW YORK, 11 Jan 1995, *Wooded Landscape with Travellers near a Cottage and a Mill in the Background* (oil on panel, 19¼ x 26 ins / 49.2 x 66 cm) USD 63,000. LONDON, 11 July 2001, *Dune Landscape with Figures by a Farm and Church Spires in the Distance* (1638, oil on panel, 22 x 42 ins / 56 x 106 cm) GBP 26,000.

RUYSDAEL, Jakob Isaakszoon van or Jacob, or Ruisdael
Dutch, 17th century.
Born 1628 or 1629, in Haarlem; died 1682, in Amsterdam, buried 14 March in Haarlem.
Painter, draughtsman, engraver (etching). Landscapes, winter landscapes, seascapes.

Jakob Ruysdael's master is not known: it has been said to be his uncle Salomon van Ruysdael, or Allardt van Everdingen, or Wynans, or Jan Cornelisz. Vroom. It has also been said that his father, a frame dealer, was a painter, and taught his son. However it seems probable that Ruysdael taught himself by studying nature and his immediate surroundings, which would explain a sometimes naive and experimental approach. He entered the Haarlem Guild in 1648 and went to Amsterdam in 1657, obtaining citizenship in 1659, but his work met with little success. During his time there he may have met Rembrandt. He visited Westphalia, Guelder and Hanover in 1650, but it seems that he never went to Norway even though he painted Scandinavian landscapes, probably after those of Allart van Everdingen who had been there. He was fascinated by the austere and tormented wilderness and perpetually dark vegetation.

Ruysdeal's will indicates that he must have suffered from 'chronic melancholy' from which he may have wanted to cure himself; this is sometimes perceived as the reason why he took up medicine and was received as a doctor at the University of Caen in 1676. It seems that he returned to Haarlem in poverty in 1681 and died there in hospital.

He was represented at the exhibition *Twee gouden eeuwen: schilderkunst uit Nederland en Denemarken* (*Two Golden Ages: Masterpieces of Dutch and Danish Painting*) at the Rijksmuseum, Amsterdam, in 2001. The Kunsthalle in Hamburg staged an exhibition in 2002 on the theme *Jacob van Ruisdael Oder die Revolution der Landschaft* (*Jacob van Ruisdael or The Revolution in Landscape Painting*).

Ruysdael's first works were etchings such as *Landscape with Trees,* 1646. In 1647 he painted *Sandy Track* in quite a thick medium, which he made more fluid from 1650. From 1657, and this change may be attributed to the possible influence of Rembrandt in Amsterdam, Ruysdael subjects his landscapes to a meticulously detailed, carefully planned composition. He is above all restrained in the means he employs; his use of colour avoids anything eye-catching or bright, and red, amongst other colours, is banished. Only occasionally do figures - added at the request of purchasers and often painted by other artists - break the perfect unity of the work. Hobbema may have been one of his pupils at the end of his career. His paintings were also embellished with figures by van Ostade, V. Berchem, Philippe Wouverman, Br. D'Helst, J. Vecton, and J. Vonck.

Deeply attached to his native country, Ruysdael did not paint landscapes in the Italian style like those of Jean Both and others; the light effects which often appear in his paintings are characteristic of the Zuider Zee. He also painted a large number of dramatic seascapes: the Louvre has one in which the colour of the water turns yellow with the approach of a storm, depicting apprehension at the prospect of the storm rather than the storm itself. At a time when so many painters emphasised the picturesque aspect of the countryside, Ruysdael was pursuing the elusive spirit of nature itself. Each element of the landscape was included more for its symbolic value than for its actual appearance. A constant reminder of the inevitability of death is also present in his Vanitas still-lifes as the changing appearances of things in light and darkness. In the years 1660-1670, Ruysdael painted two versions of the *Jewish Cemetery.* In these works he created a realistic vision of the ruined tombs in the Jewish cemetery in Amsterdam dominated by imaginary ruins. In one of the works a storm is looming; in the other, a rainbow reconciles earth and sky.

Ruysdael's work imposes an entirely subjective point of view, and he is often perceived as the inventor of picturesque landscape, in contrast to the Classical style of Poussin and Claude Lorraine. His body of work is considerable and includes the famous *Mill at Wijk, near Duurstede* which even at its most peaceful is subject to an underlying anxiety. A pantheist, Ruysdael fuses the actual reality of the landscape with the divine essence of things. Johann Wolfgang Goethe saw in him a painter of 'visionary landscapes'. For Ruysdael landscape painting is a reflection of a state of mind.

BIBLIOGRAPHY:

Bartsch, Adam von, *'Ruysdaël'* in *Le Peintre graveur 21 vol.*, J. V. Degen, Vienna, 1801-1821 (J. A. Barth, Leipzig, 1854-1876, G. Olms, Hildesheim, 1970). Dutuit, Eugène, *'Manuel de l'amateur d'estampes. Écoles flamandes et hollandaises'* in *3 vol.*, A. Lévy, Paris, Dulau, London, 1881-1885 (G. W. Hissink, Amsterdam, 1970-1972). Cundall, Frank, *The Landscape and Pastoral Painters of Holland: Riusdael, Hobbema, Cuijp, Potter*, London, 1891. Wurzbach, Alfred von, *'Niederländisches Künstler-Lexikon'* in *3 vol.*, Halm und Goldmann, Leipzig, Vienna, 1906-1911. Hofstede de Groot, Cornelis, *Verzeichnis der Werke. Holländische Maler'* in *10 vol.*, P. Neff, Esslingen, 1907-1928. Rosenberg, Jakob, *Jacob Van Ruisdaël*, Bruno Cassirer, Berlin, 1928. Simon, K.E., *Ruisdaël*, Berlin, 1930. Riat, G., *Ruysdaël*, Laurens, Paris, 1935. Hollstein, Friedrich Wilhelm Heinrich, *'Ruysdaël'* in *Dutch and Flemish Etchings, Engravings and Woodcuts, ca. 1400-1700* vol. II-XVI, Menno Hertzberger, Amsterdam, 1949-1974. Levey, Michael, *Jacob van Ruisdael and Other Painters of His Family*, National Gallery, London, 1977. Walford, John E., *Jacob van Ruisdael and the Perception of Landscape*, Yale University Press, 1991. Gibson, Walter S., *Pleasant places: The Rustic Landscape from Bruegel to Ruisdael*, University of California Press, 2000. Slive, Seymour, *Jacob van Ruisdael: A Complete Catalogue of His Paintings, Drawings, and Etchings*, Yale University Press, 2001.

MUSEUMS AND GALLERIES:

AACHEN: *Landscape in the Dutch Plain; Landscape with Field of Corn* - AIX-EN-PROVENCE: *Landscape* - AMSTERDAM (Rijksmus.): *View of Haarlem; Corner of a Wood; Sandy Track* (1647); *Mill at Wijk, near Duurstede* (c. 1670, two landscapes); *Waterfall; Rocky Site; Winter Landscape; The Castle at Bentheim; View of an 'Overboom'; Track in the Wood; Ford* - ANGERS: *Landscape* - ANTWERP: *Landscape; Waterfall in Norway; Storm at Sea* - AVIGNON: *Undulating Landscape* - BEAUFORT: *Landscape* - BERGAMO (Accademia Carrara): *Landscape* - BERLIN: *Rough Sea; Ruins of a Convent; Landscape; Forest; Hills; Haarlem Seen from the Dunes near Overveen; The Damplatz in Amsterdam; Extended View of the Dunes near Overveen; Village on the Side of a Hill; Oak Forest; Wooded Banks of a River; Landscape with Farm* - BESANÇON: *Seascape; Pond under a Cloudy Sky* - BONN (Rheinisches Landesmus.): *Thick Forest; Farms on a Mountain Slope* - BOURG: *Forest Bisected by a River Where Cattle Have Just Drunk* - BREMEN: *View of a Castle* (uncertain attribution) - BRUNSWICK: *Waterfall with a Castle* - BRUSSELS: two landscapes; *Flock Beside the Forest; Haarlem Lake; Clearing* - BUDAPEST: *Pond near a Forest; Landscape with Brook; Waterfall* (uncertain) - CARCASSONNE: *Landscape* - CHANTILLY: *Beach and Dunes at Scheveningen* - COLOGNE: *Landscape* - COPENHAGEN (Statens Mus. for Kunst): *Stream; Waterfall; Track through the Thicket; Oaks beside the Pond* - DARMSTADT: *Landscape in the Forest* - DETROIT (IA): *Jewish Cemetery* (1660-1670) - DIJON: *Forest Track; Landscape* - DRESDEN (Gemäldegal.): *Hunt, Landscape; Ford; Monastery; Waterfall in front of a Castle; Waterfall and Wooded Hillside* (two works); *Oaks on a Hill; Track in the Forest; Waterfall and Pines; Jewish Cemetery* (1660-1670); *Village in Woodland behind the Dunes; Canal* - DRESDEN (Gemäldegal. Alte Meister): *Jewish Cemetery; Castle at Bentheim; Waterfall in front of a Wooded Hill* - DUBLIN: *Forest Landscape; Forest Scene near The Hague* (figures and animals by Th. de Kayser) - EDINBURGH: *Riverbanks; Forest Scene* - ÉPINAL: *Forest Interior with Footbridge* - FLORENCE (NG): *Landscape after Rain* - FLORENCE (Palazzo Pitti): *Landscape* - FORT WORTH (Kimbell AM): *Rough Sea at a Jetty* (c. 1650, oil on canvas) - FRANKFURT AM MAIN: *Wooded Landscape; Wooded Hills* (two winter landscapes); *Waterfall; Dunes; Seaside* - GENEVA (Mus. Ariana): *Winter Landscape, Desolate Country Ravaged after a War; Rough Sea; Landscape with Figures* - GENOA: *Landscape* - GLASGOW: *View of the Town of Kativyk; Landscape with Figures; Castle at Brederode; Wooded Landscape; Landscape, River, Sheep and Figures* - HAARLEM: *Dutch Dunes; Landscape* - HAMBURG: *Forest Pond; Mountain Chapel; Track near a Lake in a Forest; Wooded Higher Slopes; Winter Landscape; Peasant House; Group of Trees on a Higher Slope; Landscape; Hut; Sunny Landscape; Castle on the Higher Slope* - HANOVER: two landscapes; *Dunes and Seaside; Oak Forest; Beech Forest* - HELSINKI: *Sunlit Hill, Ford; Huts in the Dunes; Wood Hill with Church Tower; Forest Interior, Fishermen and Shepherds* - KARLSRUHE: *Watercourse in the Forest* - KASSEL: *Wooded Landscape; Waterfall; Beach and Dunes* - LA FÈRE: seven landscapes - LE MANS: *Landscape* - LEIPZIG: *Landscape with Wood* - LILLE: two landscapes - LONDON (Dulwich Picture Gal.): *A Waterfall* (late 1660s, oil on canvas) - LONDON (NG): *A Bleaching Ground in a Hollow by a Cottage* (1645-1650, oil/wood); *A Cottage and a Hayrick by a River* (1646-1650, oil/wood); *Two Watermills and an Open Sluice at Singraven* (1650-1652, oil on canvas); *A Ruined Castle Gateway* (1650-1655, oil/wood); *A Rocky Hill with Three Cottages, a Stream at its Foot* (1650-1660, oil on canvas); *A Landscape with a Ruined Building at the Foot of a Hill by a River* (c. 1655, oil/wood); *Vessels in a Fresh Breeze* (1660-1665, oil on canvas); *A Landscape with a Waterfall and a Castle on a Hill* (1660-1670, oil on canvas); *A Waterfall in a Rocky Landscape* (1660-1670, oil on canvas); *A Waterfall at the Foot of a Hill, near a Village* (1665-1670, oil on canvas); *A Torrent in a Mountainous Landscape* (1665-1670, oil on canvas); *A Road leading into a Wood* (1655-1660, oil on canvas); *A Landscape with a Ruined Castle and a Church* (1665-1670, oil on canvas); *The Shore at Egmond-aan-Zee* (c. 1675, oil on canvas); other paintings - LONDON (Wallace Collection): *Rocky Landscape* (c. 1650s, oil on canvas); *Landscape with Waterfall* (c. 1660s, oil on canvas); *Landscape with a Village* (c. 1650-1655, oil on canvas); *Sunrise in a Wood* (c. 1670s, oil on canvas) - LOS ANGELES (Getty Mus.): *Two Watermills and an Open Sluice* (1653, oil on canvas) - LUGANO (Thyssen-Bornemisza Collection): *Seascape* - LYONS: *Brook; Norwegian Site; Sun Effect after the Storm* - MADRID: *Hunting; Wood with Lake and Boats* - MAINZ: *Forest* - MONTAUBAN: *Landscape* - MONTPELLIER: *Waterfall; Storm; Landscape* - MONTREAL (Learmont): *Waterfall* - MOSCOW (Rumiantsev Mus.): *Fallen Trees in the Forest* - MULHOUSE: *Forest Entrance* - MUNICH: *Sandy Hill, Trees, Path; Forest Landscape at the Approach of the Storm; Marshy Landscape; Mountain Landscape with Triple Waterfall; Forest with Oaks and Beeches, Pond with Duck and Water Lilies; Village during the Thaw; Oak Tree, Beech Trees, Stream; Landscape with Waterfall* - NANCY: *Two Oaks; Hut* - NEW YORK (Metropolitan Mus. of Art): *Track through the Corn Fields* - ORLÉANS: *Landscapes* - PARIS (Louvre): *Forest; Country Road; Storm by the Dutch Dykes; Landscape called The Bush* (1647); *Landscape called Sunlight; Landscape; Entrance to a Wood* - PARIS (Mus. Jacquemart-André): *Ruin of a Castle in a Plain* - POITIERS: *Landscape* - ROTTERDAM: *Cornfield; Sandy Track; View of the Dam, Taken from the Damrak* - ROUEN: *Stream; Landscape with Figures* - ST PETERSBURG (Hermitage): *Country Road at the Edge of a Wood; River in a Wood* (four landscapes); *Small Houses in a Wood; Farm; Landscape in Norway; Near Groningue; Marsh* - STOCKHOLM: *Road through a Clump of Trees; Small Dutch Town on the Dunes* - STRASBOURG: *Mills; Rough Sea* - THE HAGUE: *Waterfall; Haarlem Seen from the Dunes at Overveen; Beach; The Nigverberg at The Hague* - VIENNA: *Waterfall; Wooded Landscape* - VIENNA (Akademie der Bildenden Künste): *Pond in the Forest; Landscape* - VIENNA (Czernin'sche Gemäldegal.): *Storm at Sea* (two landscapes with waterfalls) - VIENNA (Kunsthistorisches Mus.): *Great Forest* - VIENNA (Schönborn-Buckheim): *Landscape, Pasture and Cows; Bentheim Castle* - WARRINGTON: *Landscape with Waterfall* - WEIMAR: *Summer Landscape; Watermill* - WORCESTER, MA (AM): *View of the IJ on a Stormy Day* (c. 1660, oil on canvas) - WROCLAW: *Forest Clearing* - ZURICH (Kunsthaus): *Panoramic View of Haarlem*.

AUCTION RECORDS:

Dunes, FRF 37,000; *Pond*, FRF 25,500. PARIS, 1772, *View of Scheveningen; Seashore Bordered by Dunes* (collection) FRF 1,701. PARIS, 1777, *Landscape*, FRF 1,200. PARIS, 1786, *Ruins in a Flat Landscape*, FRF 2,300. PARIS, 1795, *Bridge*, FRF 4,331. LONDON, 1802, *Landscape: View of the Castle at Bentheim*, FRF 7,870. PARIS, 1816, *Wood Crossed by a Lake* (figures by van den Velde) FRF 10,000; *Landscape*, FRF 5,000. PARIS, 1826, *Landscape, Evening Effect*, FRF 8,700. PARIS, 1828, *Peasants and a Flock*, FRF 10,335. PARIS, 1841, *Waterfall*, FRF 16,000. PARIS, 1843, *Waterfall: Storm Effect*, FRF 25,000. LONDON, 1852, *View of a Forest*, FRF 18,370. BRUSSELS, 1861, *Stream*, FRF 38,000; *View of Holland* (figures by Adrien van den Velde) FRF 19,000. PARIS, 1865, *Stream*, FRF 12,500; *Landscape*, FRF 30,100. PARIS, 1868, *Dunes at Scheveningen*, FRF 60,000. AMSTERDAM, 1872, *Norwegian Landscape*, FRF 53,550. PARIS, 1873, *Norwegian Chapel*, FRF 37,100. LONDON, 1876, *Mill*, FRF 46,000; *Woodland Scene with River*, FRF 30,450. PARIS, 1888, *Waterfall*, FRF 30,000. PARIS, 1890, *Lock*, FRF 37,000. PARIS, 1893, *Mills in Ruins*, FRF 44,620; *Landscape: Old Cottage under a Clump of Trees*, FRF 31,500. LONDON, 1893, *View of the Town of Mayden*, FRF 44,620; *View of Scheveningen*, FRF 76,080. PARIS, 1896, *Ruins*, FRF 26,100. LONDON, 1899, *Area around Haarlem*, FRF 22,100. PARIS, 26-29 April 1904, *Old Oak*, FRF 8,500. PARIS, 16 May 1904, *Stream*, FRF 9,500. BRUSSELS, 12 and 13 July 1905, *Wooded Bank of a Watercourse*, FRF 12,000. NEW YORK, 22 and 23 Feb 1907, *Waterfall*, USD 3,300. PARIS, 28 May 1907, *Track Coming Down from the Hill*, FRF 33,000; *Footbridge over the River*, FRF 18,000. NEW YORK, 9 and 10 April 1908, *Mountain in Norway*, USD 4,300. LONDON, 18 Feb 1910, *Rocky River Bank*, GBP 1,260. NEW YORK, April 1910, *Landscape*, FRF 10,500. PARIS, 21 April 1910, *Stream in Norway*, FRF 9,600. PARIS, 17 June 1910, *Stream*, FRF 15,800. LONDON, 22 July 1910, *River with Waterfall*, GBP 267. LONDON, 10 Dec 1910, *River Bank, Peasants, Sheep and Goats*, GBP 2,370. LONDON, 11 Feb 1911, *Seascape*, GBP 357. LONDON, 3 April 1911, *Wooded Road near a River*, GBP 168. LONDON, 19 May 1911, *Wooded Landscape with Figures*, GBP 220. PARIS, 9 June 1911, *Valley*, FRF 41,000; *Stream*, FRF 34,000; *Flood*, FRF 60,000; *River in the Forest*, FRF 42,000; *Hillock*, FRF 40,500. PARIS, 2-4 May 1912, *Stream*, FRF 8,500. PARIS, 16-19 June 1919, *River*, FRF 117,100. PARIS, 8-10 June 1920, *Dutch Landscape* (pen) FRF 15,400. LONDON, 31 March 1922, *Edge of a Wood*, GBP 210. LONDON, 31 March 1922, *Watermill*, GBP 2,625. LONDON, 26 May 1922, *Landscape with Stream*, GBP 304. LONDON, 14 June 1922, *Dutch Landscape*, GBP 200. LONDON, 13 April 1923, *Landscape with Castle and Waterfall*, GBP 525; *Landscape with Watermill*, GBP 2,415. LONDON, 4-7 May 1923, *Landscape with Houses*, GBP 1,890; *Harvest Landscape*, GBP 1,102; *Rough Sea*, GBP 892. PARIS, 11 May 1923, *Pond Fishing*, FRF 42,000. LONDON, 6 July 1923, *Forest Landscape*, GBP 945; *Waterfall*, GBP 714. PARIS, 22 May 1924, *Watermills*, FRF 59,500. PARIS, 2 June 1924, *Laundries at Brederode*, FRF 51,000; *Track to the Village*, FRF 130,000. LONDON, 20 June 1924, *Forest Scene*, GBP 472. LONDON, 1 May 1925, *Town on a Frozen River*, GBP 315. LONDON, 22 May 1925, *Waterfall*, GBP 1,417. LONDON, 12 June 1925, *Forest Landscape*, GBP 787. PARIS, 27 and 28 May 1926, *Hillock*, FRF 145,000; *Little House on a Hill*, FRF 27,000. PARIS, 12 June 1926, *Pond*, FRF 20,000. LONDON, 8 July 1927, *Rough Sea*, GBP 1,050. LONDON, 17 and 18 May 1928, *Sunlight*, GBP 6,300. LONDON, 7 June 1928, *View of the Dunes at Overveen*, GBP 1,520. LONDON, 15 June 1928, *River Scene and Waterfall*, GBP 1,155; *Waterfall*, GBP 1,417; *Seascape*, GBP 189. LONDON, 2 Aug 1928, *Fishing Boats on the Estuary of a River*, GBP 183. LONDON, 13 March 1929, *Landscape with Washerwomen*, GBP 880. PARIS, 13 and 15 May 1929, *Old Castle* (drawing) FRF 21,000. NEW YORK, 25 March 1931, *Cottages*, USD 925. NEW YORK, 20 Nov 1931, *Romantic Landscape*, USD 7,000. PARIS, 14 Dec 1933, *Sunny Meadow*, FRF 180,000. LONDON, 23 March 1934, *River Lined with Houses, a Church and Trees*, GBP 1,050. BERLIN, 29 and 30 May 1934, *Ruin in a Forest*, DEM 7,800. GENEVA, 9 June 1934, *Landscape*, CHF 4,100. GENEVA, 28 Aug 1934, *Landscape with Waterfall*, CHF 2,500. STOCKHOLM, 7 and 9 Nov 1934, *Landscape*, DKK 1,460. LONDON, 21 Nov 1934, *Winter Landscape*, GBP 500. STOCKHOLM, 11 and 12 April 1935, *Wooded Landscape*, DKK 1,700. GENEVA, 25 May 1935, *Landscape*, CHF 3,550. LUCERNE, 2-7 Sept 1935, *Winter Landscape*, CHF 8,500. LONDON, 5 March 1937, *River Scene*, GBP 756. LONDON, 30 April 1937, *Wooded Landscape near Muiderberg*, GBP 5,460. LONDON, 28 May 1937, *Landscape at Harvest Time*, GBP 1,050; *Storm on the Dutch Coast*, GBP 892. LONDON, 18 June 1937, *Winding Stream*, GBP 1,522. LONDON, 2 July 1937, *Wooded Landscape*, GBP 1,102; *Norwegian Landscape*, GBP 735. LONDON, 22 July 1937, *Entrance to the Old Meuse*, GBP 780. MUNICH, 28 Oct 1937, *Large Landscape*, DEM 18,000. LONDON, 27 May 1938, *Quiet Stream*, GBP 399. AMSTERDAM, 15 Nov 1938, *Amsterdam*, NLG 12,200. LONDON, 18 Nov 1938, *Garden of a House in the Country*, GBP 1,680. NEW YORK, 20 Jan 1945, *Three Old Oaks*, USD 5,000. LONDON, 12 July 1946, *Watermill*, GBP 2,730. LONDON, 11 Oct 1946, *Wooded Landscape*, GBP

,470. AMSTERDAM, 21-28 Jan 1947, *Landscape,* NLG 12,000. STOCKHOLM, 31 Jan 1947, *Landscape,* DKK 14,000. BRUSSELS, 0 April 1947, *Uprooted Tree,* BEF 26,000. PARIS, 25 May 949, *Winter Landscape,* FRF 3,200,000. LONDON, 21 Oct 949, *River Scene,* GBP 2,100. NEW YORK, Jan 1950, *Landscape with Waterfall,* USD 2,400. LONDON, 17 Feb 1950, *Seaide near Scheveningen,* GBP 6,195; *River Passing under Trees,* GBP 3,360. AMSTERDAM, 11 July 1950, *Lock,* NLG ,200. LONDON, 19 July 1950, *Wooded Landscape Crossed by Stream,* GBP 650. LUCERNE, Nov 1950, *Flock at Pasture* 1657) CHF 1,250. COLOGNE, 3 Nov 1950, *Stream,* DEM 9,000. AMSTERDAM, 21 Nov 1950, *Flock at the Edge of a Forest,* NLG ,100. PARIS, 7 Dec 1950, *Panoramic Landscape* (attributed) FRF 160,000. LONDON, 19 Jan 1951, *Bridge,* GBP 2,635. PARIS, 3 Feb 1951, *Landscape* (school of J. I. R.) FRF 47,000. AMSTERDAM, 13 March 1951, *Path under Trees with Figures,* NLG 1,150. PARIS, 25 April 1951, *Waterfall,* FRF 750,000; *Stream,* FRF 690,000. LONDON, 4 May 1951, *Flock in a Landscape with Waterfall, Dusk,* GBP 630. PARIS, 5 Dec 1951, *Marsh,* FRF 2,000,000. NEW YORK, 18 April 1956, *Landscape with Waterfall,* USD 2,600. COPENHAGEN, 11 Feb 1957, *Wooded Landscape,* DKK 23,500. LONDON, 24 Oct 1958, *River Landscape Lined with Trees,* GBP 2,730. LONDON, 8 July 959, *Wooded Landscape,* GBP 1,100. PARIS, 3 Dec 1959, *Landscape with Waterfall,* FRF 1,600,000. LONDON, 1 April 960, *Castle at Kostverloren, near Amsterdam,* GBP 8,400. LONDON, 21 June 1961, *Wooded Landscape,* GBP 5,300. LONDON, 23 Nov 1962, *Landscape with Numerous Figures,* Gns ,000. LONDON, 27 March 1963, *Town in Winter,* GBP 8,500. LONDON, 30 Nov 1966, *Landscape with Birch,* GBP 9,500. LONDON, 10 July 1968, *Landscape with Field of Corn,* GBP 3,000. LONDON, 3 Dec 1969, *Wooded Landscape with an Estuary,* GBP 20,500. LONDON, 30 June 1971, *Landscape with Castle and Waterfall,* GBP 23,000. LONDON, 6 Dec 1972, *Landscape with River,* GBP 64,000. LONDON, 29 June 1973, *Landscape with Fields of Corn,* Gns 110,000. LONDON, 29 March 974, *River Landscape with Waterfall and Old Mill,* Gns 5,000. AMSTERDAM, 26 April 1976, *Wooded Landscape* (oil on canvas, 20 1/4 x 23 ins / 51.2 x 58.4 cm) NLG 310,000. AMSTERDAM, 9 June 1977, *Boats in a Heavy Sea* (oil on canvas, 18 x 25 1/4 ins / 46 x 64 cm) NLG 200,000. LONDON, 1 Nov 1978, *Cornfield* (etching, 4 x 6 ins / 10.4 x 15.2 cm) GBP 9,000. NEW YORK, 11 Jan 1979, *Norwegian Landscape with Waterfall* (oil on canvas, 25 1/2 x 21 ins / 65 x 53.5 cm) USD 90,000. LONDON, July 1980, *Track beside a Marsh* (etching, 7 1/4 x 10 1/4 ins / 8.4 x 26.1 cm) GBP 4,200. NEW YORK, 9 Jan 1981, *Wooded Landscape with Flock beside a Road* (oil on canvas, 15 x 20 ins / 38 x 51 cm) USD 22,000. NEW YORK, 7 June 1984, *Steep Wooded Landscape* (c. 1650, oil on canvas, 38 3/4 x 49 1/2 ins / 8.5 x 125.5 cm) USD 470,000. NEW YORK, 9 May 1985, *Wooded Landscape with Waterfall* (oil on canvas, 20 3/4 x 3 1/2 ins / 52.6 x 59.6 cm) USD 280,000. LONDON, 11 April 986, *Wooded Landscape with Cottage and Peasants beside a Stream* (oil on canvas, 24 3/4 x 31 ins / 63 x 78.5 cm) GBP 0,000. NEW YORK, 3 June 1988, *Landscape with a Stream* (oil on canvas, 26 1/4 x 21 ins / 66.5 x 52.5 cm) USD 77,000. HEIDELBERG, 14 Oct 1988, *Cottage on a Hill* (etching, 7 1/2 x 11 ins / 19.3 x 27.7 cm) DEM 2,400. NEW YORK, 11 Jan 1989, *River Landscape with a Rider on a Track and Haarlem in the Background* (oil on panel, 20 1/2 x 26 3/4 ins / 52 x 67.8 cm) USD 440,000. NEW YORK, 2 June 1989, *Wooded Mountain Landscape* (oil on canvas, 38 3/4 x 49 1/2 ins / 98.5 x 125.5 cm) USD 297,000. PARIS, 27 June 1989, *Three Fishermen in a River Landscape* (canvas, 33 1/4 x 38 1/2 ins / 84.5 x 98 cm) FRF ,000,000. LONDON, 8 Dec 1989, *Peasant, His Son and a Dog Moving Towards a Wooden Bridge under a Large Oak, under a Dark Sky* (oil on panel, 21 x 26 1/2 ins / 52.5 x 67.5 cm) GBP 1,500. MONACO, 15 June 1990, *Wooded Landscape with a Traveller Seated beside a Track* (1647, oil on panel, 12 1/4 x 5 3/4 ins / 31 x 40 cm) FRF 466,200. LONDON, 13 Dec 1991, *Wooded Landscape with a Peasant on the Track across the Dunes* (oil on panel, 18 3/4 x 25 ins / 47.6 x 63.7 cm) GBP 20,900. LONDON, 15 April 1992, *Wooded Landscape with a Couple of Herdsmen Chatting near a River* (oil on canvas, 20 1/4 x 24 ins / 51.5 x 61.2 cm) GBP 180,000. LONDON, 8 July 1992, *Wooded Landscape with Figures near a Stream* (oil on canvas, 25 1/4 x 32 ins / 64.2 x 81.2 cm) GBP 44,000. LONDON, 8 Dec 1993, *Figures on a Vast Beach with Dunes and a Tower in the Background* (oil on canvas/panel, 21 1/2 x 27 ins / 54.7 x 68.5 cm) GBP 45,500. NEW YORK, 19 May 1994, *Wooded Landscape with a Large Oak and Two Fallen Birch Trees* (oil on canvas, 26 3/4 x 30 1/4 ins / 67.9 x 76.8 cm) USD 68,500. LONDON, 6 July 1994, *Wooded Landscape with Figures Resting beside a Track* (1647, oil on panel, 25 1/2 x 24 ins / 65 x 61 cm) GBP 102,700. NEW YORK, 11 Jan 1995, *Wooded Mountain Landscape with Cottages beside a Stream and a Dead Tree in the Foreground* (1653, oil on canvas, 26 1/2 x 32 1/2 ins / 67.3 x 82.6 cm) USD 552,500. LONDON, 6 Dec 1995, *Dunescape with a Peasant and His Dog on a Path Leading to a Village* (1647, oil on wood panel, 27 1/4 x 35 3/4 ins / 69.3 x 91 cm) GBP 419,500. NEW YORK, 11 Jan 1996, *River Landscape with a Waterfall* (oil on canvas, 27 x 21 ins / 68.6 x 53.3 cm) USD 772,500. AMSTERDAM, 7 May 1996, *Stream at the Foot of the Castle at Bentheim, with Travellers on a Footbridge* (oil on canvas, 26 1/2 x 20 ins / 67.3 x 50.8 cm) NLG 460,000. PARIS, 28 June 1996, *View of Hooge Lock from the River Amstel* (lead pencil and grey wash, 5 3/4 x 8 1/4 ins / 14.5 x 21 cm) FRF 1,000,000. LONDON, 3 July 1996, *Landscape with a Stream at the Edge of a Wood and Travellers on a Road* (oil on canvas, 22 x 24 1/2 ins / 55.6 x 62.3 cm) GBP 73,000. LONDON, 3 July 1997, *Wooded Landscape with Cattle Crossing a Stream in the Background* (c. 1655, oil on canvas, 41 x 51 1/2 ins / 103.2 x 130.5 cm) GBP 89,500. LONDON, 3 Dec 1997, *Scandinavian Landscape with a Mill* (oil on canvas, 40 1/4 x 34 1/2 ins / 102.2 x 87.6 cm) GBP 47,700. LONDON, 3-4 Dec 1997, *Wooded Mountain Landscape with Figures on a Track near a Watercourse* (oil on canvas, 42 1/4 x 50 1/2 ins / 107 x 128.5 cm) GBP 95,000. NEW YORK, Jan 1998, *Winter Landscape with a Frozen Canal, Farms and Windmills Behind* (oil on canvas, 15 1/2 x 17 1/4 ins / 39.4 x 43.8 cm) USD 1,322,500. NEW YORK, 29 Jan 1999, *River Landscape with Waterfall, Rustic Cottage beyond* (oil on canvas, 21 x 24 ins / 53 x 60 cm) USD 1,000,000. AMSTERDAM, 9 Nov 1999, *Man Leading Two Dogs outside a Cottage* (black chalk, grey wash, pen and black ink, 6 x 8 ins / 15 x 20 cm) NLG 90,000. NEW YORK, 27 Jan 2000, *Wooded Landscape with Traveller Resting on a Path* (oil on panel, 16 x 21 ins / 40 x 53 cm) USD 480,000. LONDON, 6 July 2000, *Wooded Landscape with Shepherd and Shepherdess Resting with Their Flock by a River* (oil on canvas, 20 x 24 ins / 51 x 61 cm) GBP 350,000. NEW YORK, 24 Jan 2001, *Two Oak Trees in an Extensive Landscape with Deer Leaping beyond* (black pencil, black chalk, brush, grey ink and grey wash with framing lines, 8 x 13 ins / 20 x 32 cm) USD 42,000. LONDON, 12 July 2001, *Dune Landscape with Two Figures by a Fence* (1647, oil on panel, 13 x 17 ins / 32 x 44 cm) GBP 290,000. LONDON, 10 July 2002, *Landscape with Torrent at the Margins of a Wood and Figures on a Road* (oil on canvas, 22 x 24 ins / 56 x 62 cm) GBP 75,000. LUCERNE, 20 Nov 2002, *Farmstead in a Winter Landscape under a Cloudy Sky* (oil on canvas, 11 x 13 ins / 28 x 33 cm) CHF 155,000. ZURICH, 19 Sept 2003, *Extensive Landscape with Figures* (oil on canvas, 19 x 23 ins / 48 x 58 cm) CHF 38,000. BERLIN, 27 Nov 2003, *Hillside Huts* (etching, 7 x 11 ins / 19 x 28 cm) EUR 8,000. LONDON, 6 July 2004, *Landscape with Farmhouse by a River* (black chalk, brush and ink wash, 4 x 6 ins / 9 x 14 cm) GBP 10,000. ZURICH, 22 Sept 2004, *View of the Castle at Bentheim* (oil on canvas, 14 x 17 ins / 35 x 42 cm) CHF 58,000.

RUYSDAEL, Jakob Salomonsz. van, or Ruisdael
Dutch, 17th century.
Born c. 1630, in Haarlem; died 1681; buried 13 November in Haarlem.
Painter. Landscapes with figures, landscapes.

Jakob Salomonsz. van Ruysdael was the pupil of his father Salomon Ruysdael, and cousin of Jakob. He entered the guild at Haarlem in 1664, and the same year married Geertruyt Pieters, of Alkmaar. In 1665, his former servant Sara Harmons accused him of having seduced her and made her pregnant. In 1666 he left for Amsterdam, and in 1673 was married for the second time, to Annetje Jans Colgns. His monogram is often confused with the monogram of Jan van Kessel III and also of his illustrious cousin.

MUSEUMS AND GALLERIES:
AMSTERDAM: *Area around Haarlem* - BESANÇON: *Pond* - BRUSSELS: *Inn* - BUDAPEST: *Landscape with Cows* - COPENHAGEN: *Spyck Manor* - KASSEL: *Flock at the Entrance to the Forest* - LONDON (NG): *A Waterfall by a Cottage in a Hilly Landscape* (1650-1681, oil on canvas) - ROTTERDAM: *Landscape* - STRASBOURG: *Rough Sea* - TOURS: *Mountain Landscape with Waterfall.*

AUCTION RECORDS:
PARIS, 21 Nov 1918, *Pond,* FRF 7,600; *Dutch Landscape,* FRF 3,400. PARIS, 22 May 1919, *Stream,* FRF 15,300; *Huts near a Wood* (drawing in Indian ink wash) FRF 1,000. PARIS, 8-10 June 1920, *Dutch Landscape* (pen drawing) FRF 15,400; *Landscape Broken up by Canals* (pencil drawing) FRF 1,650. PARIS, 21 Nov 1922, *Return of the Flock* (watercolour) FRF 1,150. PARIS, 17 and 18 March 1927, *Road at the Edge of a Wood* (black chalk and Indian ink wash) FRF 2,310. PARIS, 18 June 1930, *Halt near a River,* FRF 20,000. PARIS, 16 Oct 1946, *Landscape with Figures* (attributed) FRF 37,500. NEW YORK, 26 and 27 Feb 1947, *Landscape with Figures and Flock,* USD 400. LONDON, 9 July 1947, *Forest Stream,* GBP 95. COLOGNE, 27 Nov 1969, *Landscape,* DEM 28,000. LUCERNE, 28 Nov 1970, *Wooded Landscape,* CHF 20,000. LONDON, 19 July 1974, *Wooded Landscape with Figures,* Gns 3,800. COLOGNE, 14 June 1976, *Shepherd and Flock in a Wooded River Landscape* (oil on panel, 33 1/2 x 39 1/4 ins / 85 x 100 cm) DEM 60,000. LONDON, 6 April 1977, *Flock in a Wooded Landscape* (oil on panel, 14 1/2 x 20 ins / 37 x 50.5 cm) GBP 2,500. LONDON, 29 June 1979, *The Beach at Egmond-aan-Zee with Figures* (1652, oil on panel, 20 1/4 x 32 ins / 51.4 x 81.3 cm) GBP 60,000. LONDON, 6 July 1984, *River Landscape with Fishermen in Their Boats* (1641, oil on panel, 15 1/4 x 21 1/2 ins / 39 x 54.6 cm) GBP 42,000. NEW YORK, 5 June 1985, *Travellers and Flock in a Wooded Landscape* (1665, oil on panel, 32 x 44 1/2 ins / 81.2 x 113 cm) USD 25,000. NEW YORK, 15 Jan 1986, *Flock at a Drinking Trough in a Wooded Landscape* (1649, oil on panel, 16 1/2 x 26 ins / 42 x 66 cm) USD 24,000. NEW YORK, 13 Oct 1989, *Landscape with Cattle in a Clearing near a Track* (oil on panel, 20 x 26 3/4 ins / 51 x 68 cm) USD 16,500. NEW YORK, 10 Jan 1990, *Cattle near a Stream and Herdsmen Seated under a Tree near a Village* (oil on canvas, 19 3/4 x 25 1/4 ins / 50.2 x 64.2 cm) USD 66,000. LONDON, 12 Dec 1990, *Wooded Landscape with Cattle Drinking in a River* (oil on canvas, 60 3/4 x 43 ins / 154.5 x 109 cm) GBP 20,900. NEW YORK, 10 Jan 1991, *Landscape with Travellers Crossing a Ford* (oil on canvas, 42 3/4 x 53 1/2 ins / 108.5 x 136 cm) USD 330,000. NEW YORK, 20 May 1993, *Landscape with Cattle in a Clearing near a Track* (oil on panel, 20 x 26 3/4 ins / 50.8 x 67.9 cm) USD 18,400. PARIS, 28 Oct 1994, *Tree beside a Track* (grey wash and lead pencil, 8 1/4 x 7 1/2 ins / 21 x 19 cm) FRF 820,000. AMSTERDAM, 6 May 1996, *Wooded River Landscape* (oil on panel, 22 x 33 ins / 56 x 84 cm) NLG 18,880. NEW YORK, 15 May 1996, *Wooded Landscape with a Shepherd Watching His Flock* (oil on panel, 21 3/4 x 32 1/4 ins / 55.3 x 81.8 cm) USD 17,250. NEW YORK, 28 May 1999, *Landscape with Cattle Resting in a Clearing* (oil on panel, 20 x 27 ins / 51 x 68 cm) USD 23,000. MUNICH, 1 Dec 1999, *River Landscape with Peasant Couple and Sheep Crossing a Bridge* (oil on canvas, 22 x 30 ins / 56 x 76 cm) DEM 15,000. NEW YORK, 25 May 2000, *Wooded River Landscape with Shepherd* (oil on canvas, 19 x 25 ins / 47 x 63 cm) USD 20,000. LONDON, 12 Dec 2000, *Wooded River Landscape with Cowherd and Livestock Resting by a Path and Waterfall beyond* (1647, oil on panel, 32 x 46 ins / 81 x 116 cm) GBP 25,000. LONDON, 25 April 2001, *Wooded Landscape with Herders Resting and Cattle and Sheep Grazing* (1655, oil on panel, 20 x 27 ins / 52 x 69 cm) GBP 7,500. LONDON, 10 July 2001, *Wooded Landscape with Cattle Grazing on a Path* (oil on panel, 13 x 17 ins / 33 x 43 cm) GBP 9,000. LONDON, 17 April 2002, *Shepherd and Dog Resting in a Wooded Landscape* (oil on panel, 26 x 36 ins / 67 x 92 cm) GBP 8,000. AMSTERDAM, 18 May 2004, *Wooded Landscape with Shepherd Watering His Flock in a Wallow* (1656, oil on panel, 33 x 45 ins / 84 x 115 cm) EUR 80,000. VIENNA, 29 Sep 2004, *Summer Day in a Wooded River Landscape* (oil on panel, 30 x 42 ins / 76 x 107 cm) EUR 45,000.

RUYSDAEL, Salomon van, or Ruisdael
Dutch, 17th century.
Born c. 1600 or 1601, in Naarden; died 1670; buried 1 November in Haarlem.
Painter. Genre scenes, village scenes, landscapes, landscapes with figures, winter landscapes, seascapes.

Salomon van Ruysdael was the uncle and perhaps master of Jakob Ruysdael. He may have been the pupil of Van Schoeff and Jan van Goyen, or, according to some writers, of Esaias van de Velde. In 1623 he entered the guild at Haarlem, where he lived. He had H. Psz. de Hont as a pupil in 1637.

Houbraken relates that Salomon Ruysdael discovered a method of producing marble of every colour, and working it into vases and objects of all sorts. In particular, he was the friendly rival of Van Goyen, thanks to a skilful technique and his ability to react to the fashion of the moment. Although he adopted several genres, he is especially known for his views of the rivers in Haarlem and the surrounding area, mingling realism and fantasy. In fact, his views are hardly identifiable, being more the evocation of a place or a point in time. Several of his paintings were adorned with figures by Esaias van de Velde.

BIBLIOGRAPHY:
Stechow, Wolfgang, *Salomon Van Ruysdaël, eine Einführung in seine Kunst,* 1938 (published in Belgium). Stechow, Wolfgang, *Salomon van Ruysdael: Dutch Landscape Painting of the Seventeenth Century,* London, 1966. Stechow, Wolfgang, *Salomon van Ruysdael,* catalogue raisonné, Berlin, 1975. Brown, C. (ed.), *Dutch Landscape, the Early Years: Haarlem and Amsterdam, 1590-1650,* exhibition catalogue, National Gallery, London, 1986. Sutton, P. C. (ed.), *Masters of Seventeenth-century Dutch Landscape Painting,* exhibition catalogue, Museum of Fine Art, Boston, 1987 (pp. 466-475).

MUSEUMS AND GALLERIES:
AACHEN: *Sailing Boats; Scheveningen Beach* - AMIENS: *Setting Sun; Cows by a River; View of the Meuse; River in Holland; Small Landscape with River; Village beside Water* (two works); *Small Seascape; Landscape with Animals; Mill* - AMSTERDAM: *Coaching Inn; Village Inn; View of a River; Village Panorama* - ANTWERP: *Calm Water; Landscape with River* - BASEL: *Landscape with Flock and Figures* - BERLIN: *Landscape with River; Dutch Plain; Dutch Landscape; Landscape with Sailing Boats* - BONN (Rheinisches Landesmus.): *Halt at the Inn* - BORDEAUX: *Landscape* - BRUSSELS: two landscapes; *Ferry* - BUDAPEST: *Inn at Haarlem; Halt at the Inn; Landscape after Rain; The White Swan Inn* - CAEN: *Maritime Landscape* - COLOGNE: *Inn on the Shore* - COPENHAGEN: *Beside the River; Landscape* - DARMSTADT: *Forest Landscape with Carriage and Travellers* - DETROIT (IA): *Seascape* - DIJON: *Dutch Landscape* - DRESDEN: *Village under the Trees; Trees by a River; Banks of a River* - DUBLIN: *View of Alkmaar, Skaters; Halt* - FRANKFURT AM MAIN: *Ferry; Fresh Breeze* - GENEVA (Mus. Ariana): *Fisherman beside a Watercourse* - GLASGOW: *Landscape* - GRENOBLE: *Seascape* - HAMBURG: *Mouth of a River; Grey Day* - KASSEL: *Wide Mouth of a River and Boats* - LA FÈRE: *Skaters* (three seascapes); *Landscape* - LEIDEN: *Skating; Cavalry Skirmish* - LEIPZIG: *Canal; Wooded Landscape; Dutch Landscape* - LILLE: two landscapes - LONDON (NG): *River Scene* (1632, oil/wood); *A River with Fishermen drawing a Net* (1630-1635, oil/wood); other landscapes - MAINZ: *Spring; Shore; River; Beach near Scheveningen* - MUNICH: *Canal; Mouth of a River; Dutch Landscape with River; Landscape with Watchtower on a Road* - NEW YORK (Metropolitan Mus. of Art): *Marine* (1650); *Fishermen; Country Road* (1648); *View of Haarlem* - PARIS (Louvre): *Ferry; Large Tower; River Bank* - ROTTERDAM: *The Meuse above Dordrecht* - ROUEN: *Landscape* - ST PETERSBURG (Hermitage): *River* - STOCKHOLM: *Dutch River Landscape with Boats; Plain, Shepherd and Shepherdess near a River* - STRASBOURG: *River Landscape* - THE HAGUE: *Dutch Landscape; View of a River* - VIENNA (Czernin'sche Gemäldegal.): two seascapes with boats - VIENNA (Kunsthistorisches Mus.): *Festival under a May Tree; Winter Landscape; Landscape beside a Canal* - WEIMAR: *Summer Landscape, Flock by the Brook* - WROCLAW: *Landscape, River.*

AUCTION RECORDS:
PARIS, 1831, *Landscape,* FRF 1,160. PARIS, 1840, *View of a Canal in Holland,* FRF 1,050. PARIS, 1846, *Maritime Landscape,* FRF 1,170. PARIS, 1868, *Seascape,* FRF 1,100. PARIS, 1870, *Landscape with Figures,* FRF 8,000; *An Arm of the Meuse,* FRF 3,050. PARIS, 1873, *Dutch Canal,* FRF 6,300. PARIS, 1880, *Beside the Meuse,* FRF 25,100; *The Halt,* FRF 15,000; *The Stream,* FRF 13,000. PARIS, 1881, *The Ferry,* FRF 32,000. PARIS, 1884, *The Town Road,* FRF 6,800. PARIS, 1886, *The Watering Place, Landscape with Figures and Animals,* FRF 9,250. LONDON, 1893, *View of a River,* FRF 22,830. LONDON, 1899, *Scheveningen,* FRF 22,880. PARIS, 9-11 April 1902, *View of a Dutch River,* FRF 5,000. PARIS, 25-28 May 1907, *Banks of a River in Holland,* FRF 11,000. NEW YORK, 9 and 10 April 1908, *River and Waterfall,* USD 600. LONDON, 8 July 1910, *River Bank,* GBP 346. PARIS, 9 June 1911, *The Prisoners,* FRF 33,000; *The Ferry,* FRF 26,500; *The Beach at Scheveningen,* FRF 11,500; *The Watering Place,* FRF 51,200; *The Mill,* FRF 18,300; *The Banks of the River,* FRF 22,100. PARIS, 30 May and 1 June 1912, *The Quay beside a Canal,* FRF 25,100. PARIS, 17-19 Nov 1919, *Shepherd Taking His Flock to the Watering Place,* FRF 7,100. LONDON, 3 Feb 1922, *Fishing Scene on a River,* GBP 94. LONDON, 8 and 9 March 1922, *River Scene,* GBP 290. LONDON, 10 May 1922, *An Estuary with Boats,* GBP 145. LONDON, 23 June 1922, *Horse Fair,* GBP 525. LONDON, 19 July 1922, *Dutch Landscape,* GBP 165. LONDON, 28 July 1922, *Market Day in the Village,* GBP 504; *River Scene,* GBP 483. LONDON, 2 March 1923, *Village Scene,* GBP 1,680. PARIS, 11 May 1923, *The Ship Repair Yard,* FRF 41,000. LONDON, 13 July 1923, *Ferry Boat,* GBP 892. PARIS, 30 April 1924, *Watercourse Criss-crossed by Small Boats,* FRF 8,500. LONDON, 9 May 1924, *River Scene,* GBP 787. PARIS, 2 June 1924, *The Watering Place,* FRF 53,000; *View of a Town,* FRF 130,000. PARIS, 5 June 1924, *The Keep,* FRF 37,750. LONDON, 21 July 1924, *River Scene,* GBP 1,732. PARIS, 12 Dec 1925, *Stag Hunting,* FRF 38,500. LONDON, 21 April 1926, *Dutch River,* GBP 420. LONDON, 20 May 1927, *The Ferry Boat,* GBP 2,940. LONDON, 22 Dec 1927, *The Ferry Boat,* GBP 2,205. LONDON, 16 May 1928, *River with Vessels,* GBP 3,000. LONDON, 14 Dec 1928, *Landscape with Farm,* GBP 126. LONDON, 1 Feb 1929, *The Ferry,* GBP 3,150. LONDON, 15 March 1929, *Winter in Dordrecht,* GBP 3,465. LONDON, 18 July 1930, *River Scene,* GBP 3,360. LONDON, 12 Dec 1930, *The Ferry,* GBP 241. NEW YORK, 22 Jan 1931, *The Poachers,* USD 1,400. PARIS, 23 March 1931, *The Plain,* FRF 39,000. GENEVA, 9 June 1934, *Landscape,* CHF 3,600. LONDON, 5 July 1934, *River Scene,* GBP 460. GENEVA, 28 Aug 1934, *Landscape,* CHF 4,500. LONDON, 22 Feb 1935, *River Scene with Ferry,* GBP 199. LONDON, 22 Feb 1935, *The Ferry,* GBP 504. GENEVA, 25 May 1935, *The River and the Old Tower,* CHF 5,875. LONDON, 13 Dec 1935, *Ferry Boat,* GBP 1,365. LONDON, 15 May 1936, *Village on the Dutch Coast,* GBP 199. NEW YORK, 15 Jan 1937, *Landscape with Flock,* USD 400. LONDON, 9 April 1937, *River Scene in Holland,* GBP 1,050. LONDON, 12 April 1937, *Fort near a River* (drawing) GBP 462. PARIS, 26 May 1937, *Fishermen's Hamlet,* FRF 24000. LONDON, 18 March 1938, *River Scene,* GBP 472. PARIS, 31 March 1938, *River Estuary,* FRF 100,000. LONDON, 8 April 1938, *River Scene with Ferry,* GBP 819. LONDON, 18 Nov 1938, *River Scene with Ferry,* GBP 4,200. LONDON, 25 Nov 1938, *River Scene,* GBP 2,520. LONDON, 19 May 1939, *Landscape, near Haarlem,* GBP 609; *Valley Scene,* GBP 131. LONDON, 3 July 1940, *River Scene in Holland,* GBP 500. NEW YORK, 5 Feb 1942, *Landscape,* USD 500. NICE, 21-22 and 23 Dec 1942, *Landscape near Haarlem* (1667) FRF 200,000; *Landscape with Figures* (1643) FRF 266,000. NEW YORK, 26 May 1943, *River Scene,* USD 650. LONDON, 28 Jan 1944, *River Scene,* GBP 3,465. LONDON, 18 Feb 1944, *Village Inn,* GBP 840. LONDON, 14 April 1944, *River Scene,* GBP 1,575. PARIS, 4 Dec 1944, *Landscape* (bistre wash) FRF 12,000. LONDON, 26 Oct 1945, *River Scene with Ferry,* GBP 1,195. LONDON, 12 Dec 1945, *Wooded Landscape with River and Fishermen,* GBP 400. NEW YORK, 20 and 21 Feb 1946, *River Scene with the Town of Haarlem in the Middle Distance,* USD 1,900. LONDON, 25 Oct 1946, *River Scene,* GBP 525. PARIS, 18 Dec 1946, *The Ferryman* (school of Salomon van Ruysdael) FRF 550,000. AMSTERDAM, 21-28 Jan 1947, *Banks of a River,* NLG 4,000; *Boats on the Sea,* NLG 6,500. BRUSSELS, 30 April 1947, *River Bank,* BEF 110,000. LONDON, 30 May 1947, *Wooded Road,* GBP 315. PARIS, 2 Dec 1948, *Town on the Estuary of a River* (pen and wash) FRF 12,000. PARIS, 8 Dec 1948, *The Halt in front of the Inn* (1644) FRF 1,600,000. PARIS, 22 Dec 1948, *River Bank* (school of Salomon van Ruysdael) FRF 35,000. PARIS, 25 May 1949, *View of Weesp* (1650) FRF 2,100,000. LONDON, 28 Oct 1949, *River Scene,* GBP 1,470. LUCERNE, 17 June 1950, *River Scene,* CHF 3,100. LONDON, 23 June 1950, *River Estuary,* GBP 336. PARIS, 23 June 1950, *River near a*

Watercourse (attributed) FRF 490,000. AMSTERDAM, 11 July 1950, *Winter Pleasures near a Church,* NLG 8,600. COLOGNE, 3 Nov 1950, *The Ferry,* DEM 5,200. PARIS, 3 Nov 1950, *Hunters in a Large Landscape* (attributed) FRF 48,000. PARIS, 20 Nov 1950, *Hunter in a Wooded Landscape* (attributed) FRF 290,000. PARIS, 7 Dec 1950, *The Landing Stage* (1635) FRF 3,000,000. PARIS, 20 Dec 1950, *Figure and Flock in the Countryside* (1633, attributed) FRF 320,000. AMSTERDAM, 13 March 1951, *View of Beverwyk: Two Carts on a Country Road,* NLG 15,000; *Banks of a River and Fishermen,* NLG 11,000. LONDON, 20 April 1951, *Figure and Horsemen in a Wooded Landscape with a Castle and a Watercourse,* GBP 945. PARIS, 25 April 1951, *Skating Scene within Sight of Arnhem* (1652) FRF 2,500,000. PARIS, 4 May 1951, *Village Scene beside a Canal* (black chalk, bistre wash and Indian ink wash) FRF 132,000. PARIS, 30 May 1951, *The Hamlet beside the Water* (attributed) FRF 220,000. PARIS, 1 June 1951, *A Tower beside a River* (1665) FRF 900,000. PARIS, 6 June 1951, *The Ferry* (1648) FRF 950,000. LONDON, 29 June 1951, *River Scene,* GBP 525; *Wooded Landscape* (1658) GBP 441. PARIS, 5 Dec 1951, *The Ferry,* FRF 2,300,000. PARIS, 28 March 1955, *Winter Landscape,* FRF 1,851,000. PARIS, 29 Jan 1957, *River Bank,* FRF 2,000,000. LONDON, 27 Nov 1957, *Landscape,* GBP 1,100. PARIS, 21 March 1958, *The Basket of Birds,* FRF 700,000. LONDON, 28 Nov 1958, *Wooded River Scene,* GBP 7,350. LONDON, 24 June 1959, *View of Ysel,* GBP 10,500. PARIS, 3 Dec 1959, *River Landscape,* FRF 2,900,000. PARIS, 31 March 1960, *Sailing Boars on a River,* FRF 82,000. LONDON, 1 April 1960, *The Ferry,* GBP 15,750. AMSTERDAM, 6 June 1961, *River Landscape,* NLG 13,000. LONDON, 4 April 1962, *An Estuary with Sailing Boats,* GBP 7,200. LONDON, 27 March 1963, *River Scene,* GBP 10,800. LONDON, 25 Nov 1966, *River Landscape with Ferry,* Gns 6,000. LONDON, 19 April 1967, *Landscape with a View of The Hague in the Background,* GBP 8,500. LONDON, 10 July 1968, *Wooded Landscape with a Church,* GBP 16,000. LONDON, 5 Dec 1969, *River Landscape,* Gns 50,000. LONDON, 26 June 1970, *River Landscape,* Gns 16,000. LONDON, 8 Dec 1971, *The Coast at Egmond-aan-Zee,* GBP 30,000. LONDON, 6 Dec 1972, *River Landscape,* GBP 89,000. LONDON, 29 June 1973, *Landscape with River and Figures,* Gns 35,000. LONDON, 27 March 1974, *River Landscape with a Castle,* GBP 35,000. AMSTERDAM, 26 April 1976, *Winter Landscape with Skaters* (1661, oil on panel, 20 x 26 3/4 ins / 51 x 68 cm) NLG 480,000. LONDON, 14 Dec 1977, *View of an Estuary* (oil on panel, 8 x 12 1/2 ins / 20.5 x 32 cm) GBP 38,000. AMSTERDAM, 7 Nov 1978, *River Landscape with Boats and Figures* (oil on panel, 16 1/4 x 14 1/2 ins / 41.5 x 37 cm) NLG 740,000. COLOGNE, 11 June 1979, *Hunters in a Boat* (oil on panel, 21 1/4 x 30 1/4 ins / 54 x 77 cm) DEM 145,000. NEW YORK, 8 Jan 1981, *Alkmaar Seen from the Banks of the River* (1657, oil on panel, 21 1/4 x 33 1/2 ins / 54 x 85 cm) USD 240,000. LONDON, 6 July 1983, *Winter Landscape with Figures on the Outskirts of a Town* (1653, oil on panel, 22 x 31 1/2 ins / 56 x 80 cm) GBP 220,000. LONDON, 3 July 1985, *River Landscape with Boats and a Castle* (1645, oil on panel, 24 3/4 x 36 1/4 ins / 63 x 92 cm) GBP 330,000. NEW YORK, 14 Jan 1988, *Nijmegen with the Castle of Valkhof and the Ferry Boat Crossing the Waal* (1652, oil on panel, 27 1/4 x 36 1/4 ins / 69.5 x 92 cm) USD 907,500. NEW YORK, 7 April 1988, *Fishing Boats Pulled up on the Shore and Fishermen Unloading Their Catch* (1636, oil on canvas, 29 x 39 1/4 ins / 73.5 x 100 cm) USD 33,000. LONDON, 22 April 1988, *Troop of Cavalry Repelling Infantry at the Bridge* (1653, oil on panel, 16 x 20 1/2 ins / 40.5 x 52 cm) GBP 46,200. AMSTERDAM, 18 May 1988, *Fishermen Hauling in a Net Behind A Sailing Boat, on the River Meuse* (1643, 19 3/4 x 27 ins / 50.4 x 68.8 cm) NLG 207,000. NEW YORK, 3 June 1988, *Horseman in the Dunes and Figures among the Rocks* (1628, oil on panel, 10 1/4 x 16 1/4 ins / 26 x 41 cm) USD 88,000. LONDON, 8 July 1988, *Peasants and Cattle on the Ferry Boat, Alkmaar in the Background* (1657, oil on panel, 21 1/4 x 33 1/2 ins / 54 x 85 cm) GBP 121,000. NEW YORK, 11 Jan 1989, *Wooded River Landscape with Travellers on the Track* (oil on panel, 14 1/2 x 25 3/4 ins / 36.8 x 65.5 cm) USD 49,500. NEW YORK, 12 Jan 1989, *Sailing Boats in a Calm Sea* (oil on panel, diam. 12 1/2 ins / 31.5 cm) USD 407,000. PARIS, 27 June 1989, *River Landscape in Holland with the Arrival of a Ferry in front of an Abbey* (canvas, 20 1/2 x 28 1/4 ins / 52 x 72 cm) FRF 980,000. LONDON, 8 Dec 1989, *River Landscape with Hunters in a Boat and Fishermen Tending Their Nets and the Church of Nordosten in the Background* (1641, oil on panel, 21 1/2 x 30 1/4 ins / 54.3 x 76.8 cm) GBP 165,000. PARIS, 12 Dec 1989, *Horsemen on a Bridge* (canvas, 23 1/2 x 32 1/4 ins / 60 x 82 cm) FRF 1,750,000. AMSTERDAM, 22 May 1990, *River Landscape with Fishermen in the Foreground and the Ferryman in the Background Awaited by an Ox-cart on the Bank* (oil on panel, 11 x 16 1/2 ins / 27 x 42 cm) NLG 40,250. NEW YORK, 1 June 1990, *The Ferryman at the Entrance to a Village* (1646, oil on canvas, 19 3/4 x 18 1/2 ins / 50 x 47 cm) USD 104,500. LONDON, 6 July 1990, *Wooded Landscape with Peasants and Cattle in a Ferry and Fishermen in a Boat and a Sailing Boat in the Background* (1644, oil on canvas, 39 3/4 x 49 1/4 ins / 101 x 125 cm) GBP 93,500. LONDON, 11 Dec 1991, *View of the Rhine Towards Arnhem with Sailing Boats and Cattle Drinking* (1652, oil on panel, 24 1/2 x 37 ins / 62 x 94 cm) GBP 63,800. AMSTERDAM, 6 May 1993, *Peasants and Cattle in a Ferry Approaching the Bank Where Travellers and a Cart are Waiting under Trees* (1637, oil on canvas, 39 3/4 x 55 1/4 ins / 101 x 140.5 cm) NLG 218,500. LONDON, 9 July 1993, *Winter Landscape with Skaters and a Horse-drawn Sleigh near Fishermen's Houses with a Town in the Background* (oil on panel, 20 x 26 3/4 ins / 51 x 68 cm) USD 705,500. NEW YORK, 14 Jan 1994, *Skaters on a Canal Near Plomptoren in Utrecht* (oil on panel, 15 1/2 x 23 1/4 ins / 39.4 x 59.1 cm) USD 277,500. AMSTERDAM, 10 May 1994, *Peasants and Shepherds near a Ferry* (1637, oil on panel, 29 1/4 x 43 ins / 74.5 x 109 cm) NLG 414,000. NEW YORK, 11 Jan 1995, *River Landscape with Cows Drinking, Fishermen in a Boat near a Windmill and a Church in the Distance* (oil on panel, 13 x 12 1/4 ins / 33 x 31 cm) USD 134,500. LONDON, 5 July 1995, *Fishing Boat and Other Small Dutch Craft on the River Waal with the Town of Gorinchem to the Right* (1659, oil on panel, 16 1/2 x 14 3/4 ins / 42 x 37.3 cm) GBP 1,541,500. AMSTERDAM, 7 May 1996, *Fishermen in a Boat and Ferryman Disembarking His Passengers on a Cloudy Summer's Day* (1641, oil on panel, 24 1/2 x 35 ins / 62 x 89 cm) NLG 207,000. NEW YORK, 15 May 1996, *River Landscape with a Barn in Trees, a Ferryman Transporting Passengers and Cattle, Fishermen, Sailing Boats and a Village in the Distance* (oil on canvas, 26 x 33 ins / 66.3 x 84.1 cm) USD 244,500. LONDON, 13 Dec 1996, *Small Boat in an Estuary, Two Fishermen in a Boat in the Foreground, a Church in the Background* (oil on panel, 16 1/4 x 14 ins / 41 x 35.5 cm) GBP 183,000. LONDON, 3 July 1997, *Winter Landscape with Skaters and Sledges on a Frozen Lake in front of a Town* (oil on panel, 16 1/4 x 25 1/2 ins / 41.5 x 64.9 cm) GBP 441,500. LONDON, 4 July 1997, *River Landscape with Fishermen Hauling in Their Nets* (oil on panel, oval, 9 1/4 x 20 ins / 23.5 x 49.9 cm) GBP 36,700. AMSTERDAM, 10 Nov 1997, *Dead Songbirds, a Dead Pheasant, a Duck, a Pigeon and Other Game on a Stone Table, the Barrel of a Gun Placed on the Table at the Back* (oil on panel, 13 3/4 x 12 ins / 35.2 x 30.5 cm) NLG 109,554. LONDON, 3-4 Dec 1997, *Extensive River Landscape* (1644, oil on panel, 24 1/2 x 35 3/4 ins / 62 x 91 cm) GBP 2,311,500; *Arnhem Seen from the South-West with the Main Church and St Walburgskerk, a Broad Beamed Boat and Other Small Dutch Craft on the Rhine* (oil on panel, 15 x 21 1/4 ins / 38.2 x 54 cm) GBP 254,500. NEW YORK, 30 Jan 1998, *River Landscape with Two Sailing Boats and Other Dutch Craft in an Estuary* (oil on panel, 12 3/4 x 17 1/4 ins / 32.7 x 43.8 cm) USD 772,500. PARIS, 31 March 1998, *Pastoral Landscape near a Dutch Town* (oil on oak panel, 10 3/4 x 16 1/4 ins / 27.5 x 41.5 cm) FRF 750,000.

LONDON, 9 July 1999, *River Landscape with Fishermen in Rowing Boats and Peasants on the Shore* (1644, oil on panel, 20 x 33 ins / 52 x 84 cm) GBP 460,000. LONDON, 17 Dec 1999, *Beach at Egmond-aan-Zee with Figures and Boats on the Shore* (1662, oil on panel, 14 x 22 ins / 35 x 56 cm) GBP 340,000. NEW YORK, 25 Jan 2001, *Estuary with a Wijdschip and Other Smallcraft* (oil on panel, 15 x 13 ins / 37 x 32 cm) USD 1,000,000. LONDON, 11 July 2001, *River Landscape with Figures on a Wooded Bank* (1651, oil on panel, 20 x 33 ins / 52 x 84 cm) GBP 720,000. LONDON, 11 April 2002, *River Landscape with Fishermen Laying Out Nets and Pots* (1641, oil on panel, 15 x 21 ins / 39 x 54 cm) GBP 120,000. LONDON, 12 Dec 2002, *River Landscape with Cattle Ferry* (1656, oil on panel, 22 x 32 ins / 57 x 81 cm) GBP 260,000. LONDON, 9 April 2003, *Philip and the Eunuch* (1630, oil on canvas, 30 x 38 ins / 77 x 97 cm) GBP 13,000. LONDON, 9 July 2003, *River Landscape with the Pellecussenpoort neat Utrecht and Five Cattle Wading in the Foreground* (1663, oil on panel, 29 x 24 ins / 74 x 60 cm) GBP 300,000. LONDON, 7 July 2004, *Wooded River Landscape with Figures on a Bank Awaiting the Ferry* (1651, oil on panel, 20 x 33 ins / 52 x 83 cm) GBP 680,000. LONDON, 8 July 2004, *Sandy Landscape with Travellers* (1642, oil on panel, 24 x 33 ins / 61 x 85 cm) GBP 55,000.

RUYSSEN, Nicolas Joseph

French, 18th - 19th century.

Born 17 March 1757, in Hazebrouck; died 18 May 1826.

Painter. History painting.

Ruyssen was the drawing master to the royal princesses of England, under King George III.

RUYSSEVELT, Jozef van

Belgian, 20th century.

Born 1941; died 20 March 1985.

Painter, engraver.

Jozef van Ruyssevelt trained at the Hoger Instituut voor Schone Kunsten in Antwerp, where he was the pupil of René de Coninck and Jos Hendrickx. He subsequently joined the teaching staff at the Koninklijke Academie voor Schone Kunsten in Antwerp. He won several prizes and awards, including the Oscar Nottebohm Prize in 1959. His painting is in a Post-Impressionist vein.

RUYSTER, Hans. See **RAUSCHER Johann**

RUYT, Jacobus de

Dutch, 18th - 19th century.

Born 1771, in Amsterdam; died 27 September 1848, in Alkmaar.

Painter, draughtsman. Landscapes, architectural views, flowers.

Ruyt was the pupil of CV Glashorst. He sketched *Views of Alkmaar*.

RUYTAERTS, Daniel. See **RUTAERT**

RUYTEN, Jean or Jan Michael, or Ruyters

Belgian, 19th century.

Born 9 April 1813, in Antwerp; died 12 November 1881, in Antwerp.

Painter, engraver. Historical subjects, scenes with figures, genre scenes, interiors with figures, landscapes with figures, winter landscapes, urban landscapes, waterscapes, seascapes, architectural views.

Ruyten was the pupil of Wynand Jan Joseph Nuyen and Petrus van Regemorter. He set up in the town of his birth.

Ruyten painted numerous works: market scenes, streets and squares with figures, and the canals of Antwerp, in which he often seeks to depict the effects of light.

Jm Ruyten

J. Ruyten

MUSEUMS AND GALLERIES:

ANTWERP (Koninklijk Mus. voor Schone Kunsten): *Main Square in Antwerp in 1875; Canal des Brasseurs in Antwerp in 1875; Canal aux Charbons in Antwerp in 1875* - BRUGES (Stedelijke Mus.) - COURTRAI: *Former Fish Market in Antwerp; Occupation of Bersken-Guelder by the Troops of Martin Schenck* - KALININGRAD: *Borgenhout Gate in Antwerp; Market Scene* - STUTTGART: *Travellers outside an Inn* - TOULOUSE: *Street Corner in Flanders* - TRIESTE: *Seascape.*

AUCTION RECORDS:

BRUSSELS, 21 May 1951, *Lovers' Meeting* (1851) BEF 15,000. VIENNA, 17 March 1970, *Winter Landscape*, ATS 25,000. LONDON, 28 July 1972, *Winter Landscape with Skaters*, BEF 180,000. ANTWERP, 7 May 1974, *Dock in Antwerp*, BEF 280,000. LONDON, 22 July 1977, *Procession in Antwerp* (1848, oil on canvas, 15 x 19 3/4 ins / 38 x 50 cm) GBP 5,000. NEW YORK, 26 Jan 1979, *Antwerp Market* (1865, oil on canvas, 31 1/2 x 39 ins / 80 x 99 cm) USD 25,000. AMSTERDAM, 17 Nov 1981, *Market Scene, Antwerp* (1865, oil on canvas, 30 1/2 x 38 1/4 ins / 77.5 x 97 cm) NLG 26,000. NEW YORK, 29 June 1983, *View of Antwerp* (oil on panel, 15 x 11 ins / 38 x 28 cm) USD 6,500. LOKEREN, 25 Feb 1984, *Binnerhaven* (1837, watercolour, 9 x 11 ins / 22 x 28 cm) BEF 60,000. LONDON, 27 Nov 1985, *The Itinerant Doctor* (1843, oil on panel, 26 1/2 x 34 1/4 ins / 67 x 87 cm) GBP 7,000. AMSTERDAM, 28 May 1986, *Distress* (1857, oil on panel, 31 x 23 3/4 ins / 78.5 x 60.5 cm) NLG 35,000. CALAIS, 8 Nov 1987, *Village Festival* (oil on panel, 23 1/4 x 19 1/4 ins / 59 x 49 cm) FRF 58,500. AMSTERDAM, 3 May 1988, *River with Barges, the Ferryman and Washerwomen* (oil on panel, 16 1/4 x 11 3/4 ins / 41 x 30 cm) NLG 23,000. LONDON, 28 March 1990, *Sale of Game near a Port* (1847, oil on panel, 17 3/4 x 20 1/2 ins / 45 x 52 cm) GBP 8,800. AMSTERDAM, 20 April 1993, *Small Craft in the Port of Antwerp* (1869, oil on canvas, 10 1/2 x 13 1/2 ins / 26.5 x 34 cm) NLG 16,100. NEW YORK, 22-23 July 1993, *Village Family Celebrating* (oil on panel, 23 1/2 x 20 ins / 59.7 x 50.8 cm) USD 5,750. NEW YORK, 17 Feb 1994, *Elegant Figures in a Garden* (oil on canvas, 15 1/4 x 15 1/2 ins / 38.7 x 39.4 cm) USD 4,025. AMSTERDAM, 19 April 1994, *Citizens on the Bank of a River near Antwerp* (1843, oil on panel, 26 1/2 x 22 ins / 67.5 x 55 cm) NLG 24,150. LOKEREN, 7 Dec 1996, *The Farrier* (1844, oil on panel, 26 1/2 x 34 ins / 67 x 86.5 cm) BEF 850,000. GRAVENHAGE, 28 April 1999, *Pleasures of the Ice* (1856, oil on canvas, 13 x 19 ins / 34 x 49 cm) NLG 6,000. GRAVENHAGE, 28 April 1999, *Winter Landscape with Figures on the Ice* (1852, oil on canvas, 19 x 26 ins / 47 x 65 cm) NLG 54,000. COLOGNE, 4 Dec 1999, *River Landscape* (1839, oil on canvas, 16 x 24 ins / 40 x 60 cm) DEM 16,000. LOKEREN, 7 Oct 2000, *Arrival of Willem of Orange in Antwerp* (1855, oil on canvas, 20 x 24 ins / 51 x 62 cm) BEF 650,000. BRUSSELS, 20 March 2001, *Skaters on a Frozen Canal* (1867, oil on canvas, 14 x 20 ins / 36 x 52 cm) BEF 140,000. MONTREAL, 12 Dec 2001, *Busy Street in Antwerp* (1866, oil on canvas, 19 x 24 ins / 47 x 60 cm) CAD 21,500. AMSTERDAM, 22 Oct 2002, *Figures on the Ice near a Dutch Town* (1857, watercolour, 11 x 15 ins / 27 x 38 cm) EUR 3,500. BRUSSELS, 19 Nov 2002, *Busy Market in the Main Square in Antwerp* (1877, oil on panel, 17 x 21 ins / 44 x 54 cm) EUR 20,000. LYONS, 9 Feb 2003, *Busy Poultry Market* (1874, oil on canvas, 19 x 24 ins / 49 x 60 cm) EUR 15,500. AMSTERDAM, 28 Oct 2003, *Bustling City Life around the Vleeeshal in Antwerp* (1870, oil on canvas, 39 x 31 ins / 100 x 80 cm) EUR 19,000. STAUFEN, 25 March 2004, *Fishing Boats and Busy Harbour Town* (oil on canvas, 28 x 39 ins / 71 x 98 cm) EUR 9,500.

RUYTENBACH, E.

Dutch, 17th century.

Active during the second half of the 17th century.
Painter. Landscapes.

AUCTION RECORDS:
PARIS, 10 May 1982, *Village Scenes* (oil on panel, in pairs, 23 1/4 x 32 3/4 ins / 59 x 83 cm) FRF 60,000. NURNBERG, 23 Nov 2000, *People and Horses before an Inn* (oil on panel, 7 x 10 ins / 18 x 25 cm) DEM 6,000.

RUYTENBACH, J.
Dutch, 17th century.
Active during the second half of the 17th century.
Landscape artist.

RUYTENBURG, A. Van
Dutch.
Painter.
A painting by van Ruytenburg, *Diana and Callisto*, was included in the Jan de Vries sale in Amsterdam, in 1738.

RUYTENSCHILD, Leendert
Dutch, 18th century.
Active in Amsterdam in 1723.
Painter.

RUYTENSCHILDT, Abraham Jan or Johannes
Dutch, 19th century.
Born 22 April 1778, in Amsterdam; died 13 May 1841, in Amsterdam.
Painter. Genre scenes, landscapes with figures, landscapes.
Ruytenschildt was the pupil of Jandriessen and P Barbiers. He was an art teacher.

AUCTION RECORDS:
AMSTERDAM, 7 Nov 1995, *Cows Drinking in a Landscape* (oil on panel, 12 1/4 x 16 1/4 ins / 31 x 41 cm) NLG 1,298.

RUYTER, Jan
Dutch, 18th century.
Active from 1733 to 1741.
Engraver.
Jan Ruyter engraved *Views of Nijmegen* and book illustrations.

RUYTER, Jan de
Dutch, 19th century.
Active in Amsterdam in the first part of the 19th century.
Painter. Portraits, genre scenes.

MUSEUMS AND GALLERIES:
AMSTERDAM (Rijksmus.): *Woman Preparing Fish.*

AUCTION RECORDS:
AMSTERDAM, 2 Sept 1997, *An Old Woman Selling Game to a Young Woman in a Stone Niche* (oil on canvas, 15 1/4 x 12 ins / 38.6 x 30.7 cm) NLG 3,228.

RUYTER, Lisa
American, 20th - 21st century.
Born 24 June 1968, in Washington DC.
Painter. Figures, landscapes, cityscapes.
Lisa Ruyter studied at the MCPS Art Center in Maryland (1982-1986) before continuing her studies with a BFA at the School of Visual Arts in New York, completed in 1990. From 1991 to 1992 she completed the graduate fine arts programme at Hunter College.

Ruyter works with bright acrylic paints, strong yellows, blues, greens, reds and pinks, but has also experimented with pastel shades. She paints the outlines of figures and landscapes and applies the colours flatly to the canvas, creating a two-dimensional feel. Her work has a strong decorative quality.

She has been part of several group shows and solo exhibitions, including shows at the following: Ace Gallery in Los Angeles (1999); the Dorothee DePauw Gallery in Brussels (1999); the Pierre Huber Gallery in Geneva (2000); the Georg Kargl Gallery in Vienna (2001, 2003); the Leo Koening Inc. in New York (2002); the MoMA in New York (2002); and the Galerie Thaddaeus Ropac in Paris (2004).

BIBLIOGRAPHY:
Dailey, Meghan, '*Jeff Elrod/Lisa Ruyter*' in *Artforum*, Summer 1999. Ise, Claudine, '*Lisa Ruyter at Ace*' in *The Los Angeles Times*, 5 March 1999. Nickas, Bob, '*Interview*' in *Index*, November-December 1999. Hunt, David, '*Lisa Ruyter, Leo Koenig Inc.*' in *Flash Art*, no. 220, p 103, Milan, 2001.

RUYTER, Nicaise de
Dutch, 17th century.
Born 1646 (?).
Engraver.
Nicaise de Ruyter is remembered for his *Diana and Callisto*, of 1688, and *Children Dancing*.

RUYTER, Salomon. See **RUTHER**

RUYTER, Viktor de
German, 20th century.
Born 2 September 1870, in Kerkberg.
Painter. Seascapes, landscapes, interiors.
Viktor de Ruyter was a student of Frank Spenlove-Spenlove. He was active in Berlin and Hamburg.

RUYTER, Willem. See **REUTER**

RUYTERS, Jean or Jan Michael. See **RUYTEN**

RUYTINX, Alfred
Belgian, 20th century.
Born 18 April 1871, in Schaerbeek (Brussels).
Painter. Landscapes, still-lifes, flowers.
Alfred Ruytinx was a nephew and student of the painter Privat Livemont. He started exhibiting in 1896 and went on to exhibit in Brussels and Antwerp.

AUCTION RECORDS:
LONDON, 19 March 1986, *Woman Plucking a Cockerel* (1903, oil on canvas, 68 1/2 x 78 1/4 ins / 174 x 198.5 cm) GBP 7,000. PARIS, 29 June 1988, *Vase of Flowers* (oil on canvas, 35 x 24 1/2 ins / 89 x 62 cm) FRF 13,000. NEW YORK, 25 Oct 1989, *Vase of Chrysanthemums* (oil on canvas, 48 3/4 x 32 1/4 ins / 123.8 x 82 cm) USD 8,800. NEW YORK, 24 Oct 1990, *Vase of Chrystanthemums* (oil on canvas, 48 3/4 x 32 1/4 ins / 123.8 x 82 cm) USD 4,400. PARIS, 15 Dec 1994, *Farm Interior* (oil on canvas, 74 3/4 x 92 1/4 ins / 190 x 234 cm) FRF 38,000. NEW YORK, 18 March 1998, *Geese* (oil on canvas, 59 x 98 1/2 ins / 149.9 x 250.2 cm) USD 19,550. MADRID, 20 Dec 1999, *Harbour* (oil on canvas, 16 x 20 ins / 40 x 50 cm) ESP 550,000. ANTWERP, 4 April 2000, *Still-life* (oil on canvas, 20 x 28 ins / 50 x 70 cm) BEF 150,000. BRUSSELS, 9 May 2000, *Kitchen Scene with Game, Fruit and Vegetables* (oil on canvas, 58 x 86 ins / 147 x 218 cm) BEF 340,000. LONDON, 20 March 2003, *Mixed Summer Flowers in a Blue Vase on a Table* (oil on canvas, 37 x 45 ins / 95 x 115 cm) GBP 3,000.

RUYZ. See **RUIZ**

RUZAN, Élie
French, 19th century.
Born in Labeaudière; died 4 November 1861, in Labeaudière.
Draughtsman, lithographer. Portraits, landscapes.
Élie Ruzan was the student of Pico, Pils and Hippolyte Flandrin.

RUZHEINIKOV, Piotr
Russian, 20th century.
Born 1916, in Krasnodar.
Painter. Scenes with figures, flowers.

Ruzheinikov completed his studies at the Krasnodar polytechnic institute in 1937.

AUCTION RECORDS:

PARIS, 3 June 1992, *Peonies and Jasmine* (oil on canvas, 32 x 30 ins / 81 x 76 cm) FRF 4,800. PARIS, 23 Nov 1992, *Hunters in Winter* (oil on canvas, 26 1/2 x 39 1/4 ins / 67.3 x 100 cm) FRF 3,500.

RUZIC, Branko

Croat, 20th century.
Born c. 1920.
Sculptor.

After an initial period when he was still associated with tradition, the threefold influence of Yugoslav medieval art, Henry Moore's sculpture and Picasso's work led Branko Ruzic to rethink both materials and processes of creation. Ever since his *First Trilogy* (1959), he made just one figure out of three, giving the impression of a crowd swarming. Later he subjected the human figure to ever more pronounced synthetic distortions, the logical development of which can be observed particularly in the series of creations from 1960 which he devoted to an often symbolic representation of Cézanne. He worked first with bronze, then cement, as in *Cathedral* (1960), copper plate, as in a number of versions of *Cézanne*, and with other unconventional materials, before discovering wood. Apart from works inspired by human figures, Branko Ruzic was inspired from 1963 onwards by objects characteristic of daily life in his native country, particularly the white gates in the fields of Slovenia, as in *White Trinity* (1964), the characteristic layout of the geometrical furrows of a field of maize, as in *Reunion* (1964). In later years Branko Ruzic dealt with other themes including stumps associated with seasonal floods, strongholds and ships.

RUZICKA, Antonin Josef

American, 20th century.
Born 1891, in Racine (Wisconsin); died 18 October 1918, in France.
Painter, illustrator.

Antonin Josef Ruzicka studied at the Chicago Art Institute.

RUZICKA, Othmar

Austrian, 20th century.
Born 7 November 1877, in Vienna; died 1962.
Painter. Portraits, genre scenes, landscapes with figures.

Othmar Ruzicka studied at the Akademie der Bildenden Künste in Vienna and painted scenes of everyday life in Moravia.

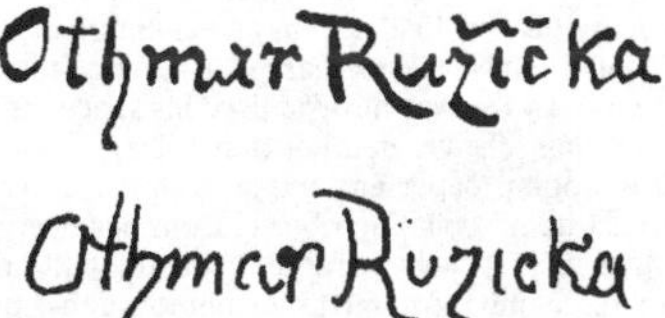

AUCTION RECORDS:

VIENNA, 17 March 1976, *Larder* (oil on canvas, 29 1/2 x 24 3/4 ins / 75 x 63 cm) ATS 20,000. BERN, 6 May 1977, *Café-Concert* (oil on canvas, 23 1/2 x 31 1/2 ins / 60 x 80 cm) CHF 2,700. LONDON, 7 June 1989, *Young Peasant Woman with Sunflowers in a Garden* (1912, oil on panel, 32 1/4 x 27 1/4 ins / 82 x 69 cm) GBP 2,200. SALZBURG, 27 March 2002, *Goose Maid* (oil on board, 12 x 14 ins / 30 x 35 cm) EUR 4,500. VIENNA, 12 Oct 2004, *Girl with Goose* (oil on plywood, 17 x 13 ins / 43 x 34 cm) EUR 3,200.

RUZICKA, Rudolf

German, 20th century.
Born 26 June 1883, in Bohemia; died 1978.
Active in the USA.
Engraver, illustrator.

Rudolf Ruzicka studied in Chicago and New York and eventually settled in Dobbs Ferry. He illustrated numerous publications with woodcuts and etchings and also produced an ex libris design for art collector Philip Hofer based on a drawing of Tantalus by Holbein the Younger.

RUZISKAY, György or Georg

Hungarian, 20th century.
Born 16 August 1896, in Szarvas.
Painter, collage artist, draughtsman.
Symbolism.

György Ruziskay trained between 1922 and 1924 at the academy of fine art in Munich under L. Herterich, Gröber and Dörner, then in Rome (1925) and Paris (from 1927).

György Ruziskay was known in Hungary in the 1930s for his paintings in an Expressionist style he had discovered during his time in Germany. His main theme was the world of hard labour, of humanity enslaved to the machine. He evolved from an obvious ideological Naturalism to a Symbolism with romantic overtones and also executed large-scale figure compositions. From 1965 onwards, he produced paintings and collages under the term 'Biopainting' a reflection of nature's inner workings and published a manifesto on this occasion. He produced several albums of drawings including: *Looking for Love* (1935); *Towards the Light* (1936) and *The Life of Samuel Tessedik* (1938).

György Ruziskay took part in collective exhibitions including: National Exhibitions, Budapest (regularly from 1947); Salon d'Automne, Paris (1957); Salon Grands et Jeunes d'Aujourd'hui, Paris (1958); New York; Glasgow; Moscow; Vallauris;: International Illustration Competition, Edinburgh (1959); Grand Prix International de Peinture, Deauville (1961).

Solo exhibitions include: Oradea (1924, 1927); as part of the National Exhibition, Budapest (1927); Ernst Museum, Budapest (1932, 1966); Arad (1934); Bucharest (1935); Cluj (1936); Utrecht (1939); Musée de Toulon (1961); Poitiers (1965); Galerie Saxe, Paris (1967); Hungarian National Gallery; Paris (1976). He was awarded a number of distinctions including the Gold Medal for Work, Budapest (1971). A member of the Federation of Hungarian Artists, in 1976 György Ruziskay became 'Artist Emeritus' of the Republic of Hungary.

BIBLIOGRAPHY:

Gal-Gyorgy, Sandor, *Gyorgy Ruzicskay*, Éd. Népszava, 1948.

MUSEUMS AND GALLERIES:

BÉKÉSCSABA (Munkácsy Mihály Múz.) - BUDAPEST (Kiscelli Múz.) - BUDAPEST (Magyar Nemzeti Gal.) - BUDAPEST (Munkasmozgalmi Mus.) - HERZLIA (MA) - ORADEA (Koros Videke Mus.) - ORADEA (Muzeul Tarii Crisurilor) - TOULON (MA) - UTRECHT (Centraal Mus.).

RUZO, Victor, real name: Victor Rutz

Swiss, 20th century.
Born 22 December 1913, in Straubenzell (St Gall).
Painter, draughtsman, illustrator. Portraits.
Symbolism.

Victor Ruzo started out as a poster artist and went on to paint portraits, landscapes and still-lifes. His personal universe is a product of symbolic Surrealism in a Salvador Dali vein, with interspersed religious and metaphysical allusions. In 1947, he painted a series of portraits and other works on the theme of concentration camps. In 1952, he produced a *Revolving Painting* and, in 1964, he authored a decorative fresco for the Swiss Pavilion at the New York International Exhibition. From 1968, he worked in emulsion paint on aluminium in order to generate disturbing and hyper-realist images. He exhibited solo in the USA and also on a regular basis at the Galerie du Vieux Pressoir in Onnens.

BIBLIOGRAPHY:

Ruzo, L. P. Kuperman, New York, 1956. *Ruzo*, monograph, F. Depret, Paris, 1962. Neuburg, Hans/Wirz, Adolf, *Ruzo: von der realistischen zur spirituellen Malerei*, ABC Verlag, Zurich, 1982.

RUZOLONE, Pietro. See **ROZZOLONE**

RUZUTI, Filippo. See **RUSUTI**

RUZZOLONE, Pietro. See **ROZZOLONE**

RY. See also for second names **starting with the letters RIJ**

RY, Danckerts de. See **DANCKERTS de Ry Peter**

RYABUSHINSKY, Nikolai Pavlovich

Russian, 20th century.

Born 1876; died 1951.

Painter. Landscapes with figures, still-lifes, flowers. Symbolism.

Nikolai Pavlovich Ryabushinsky was the son of the wealthy industrialist Pavel Ryabushinsky and an important patron of the arts during Russia's Silver Age. In 1906 he founded the magazine *Zolotoe runo* (*Golden Fleece*), which promoted painters of all styles, and organised exhibitions in Moscow of French and Russian Symbolists.

A talented painter himself, he exhibited with K. Granov in 1933.

AUCTION RECORDS:

PARIS, 28 March 1949, *Still-life* (1924) FRF 200; *Garden*, FRF 300. PARIS, 13 Oct 1949, *Vase of Flowers*, FRF 1,100.

RYABUSHKIN, Andrei Petrovich, or Rjabuschkin or Rabuchkine

Russian, 19th century.

Born 17 October 1861; died 27 April 1904.

Painter (gouache), illustrator. History painting, religious subjects, genre scenes. Murals.

Peredvizhniki (Wanderers) group.

Andrei Petrovich Ryabushkin studied at the school of painting, sculpture and architecture in Moscow under Vasili Perov, E. Sorokin and Ilarion Pryanishnikov from 1875 to 1882. He later attended lessons at the academy of fine arts from 1882 to 1890. He showed his work in exhibitions organised by the Association of Travelling Exhibitions, and by the World of Arts society, as well as at exhibitions in Paris. He was awarded a commendation at the 1900 Paris Exposition Universelle.

He visited many historical towns in Russia, where he painted many mural compositions in churches. His works often looked back at Russia's history in his painting of historical scenes, but more often in genre scenes. He showed a delicate touch in his painting of female silhouettes. He was among the artists chosen to produce paintings to mark the coronation of Tsar Nicholas II, and his work featured in the official coronation album.

BIBLIOGRAPHY:

L'Art russe des Scythes à nos jours, exhibition catalogue, Gal nationales du Grand Palais, Paris, 1967.

MUSEUMS AND GALLERIES:

MOSCOW (State Tretyakov Gal.): *A Muscovite Woman and Young Girls at Church; Peasant Wedding; Peter the Great's Soldiers at an Inn; Crucifixion* - ST PETERSBURG (Gosudarstvennyj Russkij Muz.): *Arrival; Young Muscovite Girl in the 17th Century*.

AUCTION RECORDS:

AMSTERDAM, 9 Nov 1994, *Hare in the Snow* (1935, oil on canvas, 10 x 13 1/4 ins / 25.5 x 33.5 cm) NLG 1,380. LONDON, 15 June 1995, *Sketch of a Scene from the Coronation in 1896* (gouache/pencil, 12 1/2 x 17 3/4 ins / 31.5 x 45 cm) GBP 3,910.

RYALL, Henry Thomas

British, 19th century.

Born August 1811, in Frome; died 14 September 1867, in Cookham.

Painter, engraver. Figures, genre scenes.

Henry Ryall was a pupil of S. Reynolds. He engraved prints, including *Conservative Statesmen* and *Stages of Feminine Beauty*.

RYAN, Adrian

British, 20th century.

Born 3 October 1920, in London.

Painter. Portraits, landscapes, still-lifes.

Adrian Ryan is the son of the painter Vivian D. Ryan. He trained at the Architectural Association from 1938 to 1939, and at the Slade School of Fine Art, London from 1939 to 1940. He went to paint in Cornwall from 1943 to 1948, to France from 1948 to 1950, and painted in Suffolk from 1951 to 1957. He taught at Goldsmiths College from 1950.

He exhibited with the London Group in 1942 and 1943, and at the Royal Academy from 1949. He showed his works in solo exhibitions, the first one was held in 1951.

MUSEUMS AND GALLERIES:

LONDON (Tate Collection): *Flowers on a Chair* (1958).

RYAN, Anne

American, 20th century.

Born 1889, in Hoboken (New Jersey); died 1954, in Morristown (New Jersey).

Painter, collage artist, engraver, watercolourist. Portraits, genre scenes, still-lifes.

Anne Ryan was a self-taught artist who was also a poet, writer and sculptor. Between 1930 and 1933 she lived in Majorca, then in Paris. On her return to New York she opened a restaurant, The Hearthstone, in the artists' quarter (Greenwich Village) where she encountered Jackson Pollock, Barnett Newman, Tony Smith and Hans Hofmann. From 1937, while continuing to write poems and novels, she began experimenting with different techniques and researching into form and pictorial material.

Having enrolled in Stanley William Hayter's Studio 17 in the early 1940s, she experimented with watercolours and in particular with wood engravings, producing several Cubist compositions, portraits, still-lifes, religious, street and circus scenes. Developing her sensitive response to the texture of paper, colours, surfaces and finishes, she gradually abandoned Figuration for Abstraction. Her discovery of the art of Kurt Schwitters in 1948 during an exhibition at the Pinacotheca Gallery in New York marked a turning point for Ryan. Influenced by the way he organised his spaces and by his use of materials, she created her first collage using several types of wrapping paper and the ends of waxed canvases. She then set about collating objects from her everyday life (public transport tickets, wrapping paper, cuttings from newspapers, stamps, fragments of photographs, pieces of leather, fabrics) in order to create compositions marked by their dominant geometry in the form of sets of shapes, materials and tangles. Her early collages still made use of symbols, with pieces of typed text and fragmented words that served as decorative items. Little by little she opted for a more supple style, bringing form and movement together and incorporating biomorphic forms, as in her *College Number 376*.

From the 1950s she changed direction again with a series of ovals, squares and rectangles. Her pictorial language took on a more rigorous formalism, the various elements being laid out according to a rigid, rhythmic composition with several juxtapositions of planes (*Number 453* of around 1952).

Anne Ryan exhibited for the first time in 1941, at the Pinacotheca Gallery, and her engravings featured at the Marquie Gallery in New York. She was later to take part in many collective and solo exhibitions in the USA, Mexico and Paris, inclding: 1948, Galerie Denise Severin; 1949, Petit Palais (at the time of the Exposition Internationale de la Gravure Contemporaine). Her work featured in several posthumous retrospectives, including: 1979, *Anne Ryan, Collages 1948-1954*, André Emmerich Gallery, New York; 1980, *Anne Ryan: Collages and Prints*, Museum of Fine Arts, Houston; 2001 retrospective of her collages at the Musée d'Art Américain in Giverny.

BIBLIOGRAPHY:

Gibson, Éric, *Anne Ryan, collages 1948-1954*, exhibition catalogue, André Emmerich Gall., New York, 1979. McCandless Rooney, Judith, *Anne Ryan: Collages and Prints*, exhibition catalogue, Museum of Fine Arts, Houston, 1980. Armand, Claudine, *Anne Ryan: Collages*, exhibition catalogue, Musée d'Art américain, Giverny, Terra Foundation for the Arts, Evanston (IL), 2001 (text in French and English).

MUSEUMS AND GALLERIES:

NEW HAVEN (AG, Yale University): *Number 97* (c. 1950, collage); *Number 524* (1951, collage); *Number 421* (1952, collage); *Number 426* (c. 1952, collage) - NEW YORK (Metropolitan Mus. of Art): *Number 6: 'Rumpelmayer'* (c. 1948, collage); *Number 319* (1949, collage); *Number 57* (c. 1950, collage); *Number 587* (1952, collage); *Number 30* (1953, collage); *Number 547* (1954, collage) - NEW YORK (MoMA): *Number 353* (1949, collage); *Number 156* (1950, collage); *Collage 141* (1951); *Number 413* (1951, collage); *Number 495* (1951, collage); *Collage 283* (1952); *Number 518* (1953, collage); *Number 706: Red Collage III* (1954, collage).

AUCTION RECORDS:

NEW YORK, 17 May 1979, *Untitled* (collage, 12 x 9 1/2 ins / 30.5 x 24 cm) USD 2,000. NEW YORK, 13 May 1981, *Untitled* (c. 1950, paper, fabric and string, collage, 7 3/4 x 6 3/4 ins / 20 x 17 cm) USD 4,000. NEW YORK, 9 Nov 1983, *Collage* (1953, paper, fabric and silver/card, collage, 16 x 12 3/4 ins / 40.5 x 32.5 cm) USD 5,500. NEW YORK, 4 Nov 1987, *Untitled* (tempera and collage/hardboard, 6 3/4 x 5 ins / 17 x 12.8 cm) USD 3,200. NEW YORK, 11 March 1993, *Untitled Collage* (collage of paper, 7 x 5 1/4 ins / 17.5 x 13.3 cm) USD 3,450. NEW YORK, 4 May 1993, *Grey and White Collage* (1953, sacking, paper, silver sheet/synthetic resin, 16 3/4 x 13 3/4 ins / 42.5 x 34.9 cm) USD 7,475. NEW YORK, 23 Feb 1994, *Collage No. 552 (Majorca)* (collage of different sorts of paper/card, 18 3/4 x 23 3/4 ins / 47.6 x 60.3 cm) USD 8,050. NEW YORK, 15 Nov 1995, *Untitled No. 115* (paper and sacking/paper, 8 1/2 x 7 1/4 ins / 21.6 x 18.4 cm) USD 5,750. NEW YORK, 22 Feb 1996, *Untitled* (paper/paper, collage, 6 3/4 x 5 1/4 ins / 17.1 x 13.3 cm) USD 6,325. BOSTON, 12 March 1999, *Composition* (collage on paper, 6 x 6 ins / 16 x 15 cm) USD 3,750. DETROIT, 15 Dec 2000, *Untitled - Abstract* (collage on paper, 21 x 15 ins / 53 x 38 cm) USD 2,500. NEW YORK, 13 May 2004, *Untitled No 236* (c. 1950, paper, thread, silver foil and fabric collage on paper, 8 x 6 ins / 20 x 16 cm) USD 7,500. NEW YORK, 13 May 2004, *Untitled No 10* (printed paper, sand, paper and fabric collage on Howell paper, 7 x 5 ins / 18 x 13 cm) USD 11,000.

RYAN, Arlette (Mme)

Maiden name: Warrain
French, 20th century.
Born 9 April 1892, in Paris.
Painter, pastellist. Figures, portraits.

Arlette Ryan, who studied with Marcel Baschet and at the Académie Julian, Paris, exhibited from 1938 at the Salon des Artistes Français, where she was awarded an honourable mention in 1939 and a silver medal in 1941. Among her works are portraits of *Francis Warrain, René Baschet, The Count of Anadia, Princess Andrée Aga Khan and Her Son Prince Sadri, Mme Y. L. C. Fabre*, and *Mme Paul Cocteau*.

RYAN, Charles J.

British, 19th century.
Active in Ventnor.
Painter, watercolourist. Landscapes, flowers.

Charles Ryan exhibited in London from 1885 to 1892, notably at the Royal Academy. He served for a time as principal of Leeds Art College.

MUSEUMS AND GALLERIES:

LONDON (Victoria and Albert Mus.): *Hawthorn Bush* (watercolour).

RYAN, David

Irish, 20th - 21st century.
Born 1960, in Cork.
Active in Nantes.
Painter.

David Ryan studied at the École des Beaux-Arts in Bordeaux. He usually paints figures, making careful use of iconographic elements. His work is somewhat in the tradition of Giorgione, Watteau and Tiepolo in its openness to meaning or image being transformed by the 'invisible alchemy' of colour.

Ryan has taken part in group exhibitions, including at the following: the Galerie Pier Peyverges in Bordeaux (1982); the Salon de Montrouge in Paris (1983); *Ateliers 84* (*Studios 84*) at the ARC Musée d'Art Moderne de la Ville de Paris (1984); *Quatre Français en Amérique* (*Four Frenchmen in America*) at the American Center in Paris (1985); the Ateliers Internationaux de l'Abbaye Royale de Fontevraud at the Fonds Régional d'Art Contemporain (FRAC) in the Pays de la Loire (1987); and the Collection du Fonds National d'Art Contemporain at the Fondation Nationale des Arts Graphiques et Plastiques in Paris (1989).

Ryan has also shown his work in solo exhibitions, including at the following: the Contre Exposition in Bordeaux (1983); the Galerie Gillespie Laage Salomon in Paris (1983); the CAPC Musée d'Art Contemporain in Bordeaux (1984); the PS1 Institute of Art in New York (1984, 1987); the Abbaye de la Sauve Majeur at the Fonds Régional d'Art Contemporain in Aquitaine (1985); the Galerie des Beaux-Arts in Nantes (1987); *L'Inversion du Temps* (*Inversion of Time*) at the Galerie de l'Ancien Collège in Châtellerault (1991); *Entre Charybde et Skylla* (*Between Charybdis and Scylla*) at the Salon d'Angle in Nantes (1991-1992); the Galerie Gilles Peyroulet in Paris (1993); and *David Ryan: Pilot* at the Centre d'Art Passerelle in Brest (2003).

RYAN, Francis

Irish, 18th century.
Active in Dublin from 1756 to 1788.
Painter. Portraits.

RYAN, Gregory

American, 20th - 21st century.
Born 1967, in Philadelphia.
Painter (mixed media).

Gregory Ryan studied at the Parsons School of Design and then at the École Nationale des Beaux-Arts in Paris. He exhibited at the Galerie Kunst Akademie in Munich in 1988 and at the Hôpital Éphémère in Paris in 1991.

AUCTION RECORDS:

PARIS, 14 April 1991, *Self-portrait* (1989, rolled sheet metal and painted card, 22 x 28 3/4 ins / 56 x 73 cm) FRF 4,000.

RYAN, I.

Irish, 18th century.
Active at the end of the 18th century.
Painter.

RYAN, Thomas
British, 20th century.
Born 1929.
Painter. Landscapes.

AUCTION RECORDS:
DUBLIN, 24 Oct 1988, *Surrounding Area of Ashbourne* (oil on card, 24 x 20 ins / 61 x 50.8 cm) IEP 1,430.

RYAN, Tom
American, 20th century.
Born 1922, in Illinois.
Painter.

Tom Ryan's work featured in the exhibition *À la Découverte de l'Ouest Américain* (*Discovering the American West*) held at the Salon d'Automne in Paris in 1987. He painted compositions depicting the lives of cowboys on the American prairies. His work was traditional in both style and technique.

AUCTION RECORDS:
NEW YORK, 18 Sept 1980, *The Cocked Gun* (oil on canvas, 22 1/4 x 17 ins / 56.5 x 43.1 cm) USD 2,100. SANTA FE, 19 May 2001, *Trouble at the Creek* (oil on board, 20 x 30 ins / 51 x 76 cm) USD 35,000. HAYDEN, 28 July 2001, *Cowgirls Around the Campfire* (pastel, 11 x 22 ins / 29 x 55 cm) USD 22,500. SANTA FE, 18 May 2002, *Big Enough* (oil on canvas, 24 x 36 ins / 61 x 91 cm) USD 60,000. SANTA FE, 18 May 2002, *Ghost Town* (oil on canvas, 24 x 30 ins / 61 x 76 cm) USD 74,000. SANTA FE, 23 May 2003, *Torn Chaps* (pencil, 16 x 10 ins / 41 x 25 cm) USD 9,500. SANTA FE, 1 Nov 2003, *Texas Dust* (oil on board, 22 x 15 ins / 56 x 38 cm) USD 35,000. SANTA FE, 15 May 2004, *Two Horses* (pastel, 8 x 12 ins / 20 x 30 cm) USD 2,400. HAYDEN, 24 July 2004, *Sundown Farm* (oil on canvasboard, 12 x 16 ins / 30 x 41 cm) USD 2,000.

RYAZHSKY, Georgi Georgeevich, or Riajski, Riajsky, Rjasky
Russian, 20th century.
Born 1895, in Ignatievo, near Moscow; died 1952, in Moscow.
Painter.
Association of Artists of Revolutionary Russia (AKhRR).

Georgi Ryazhsky studied under M. Leblanc, R. Baklanov, M. Severov, A. Golubkina and K. Malevich. He was a member of the New Society of Painters (NOZh) who joined the Association of Artists of Revolutionary Russia (AkhRR) in 1923. He was an active member of MOSSKh in 1932 and later the USSR academy of arts. His painting *Woman in Charge* won the Grand Prize at the International Exhibition *Art and Technology in the Modern World* in Paris, 1937.

Several of his works were included in the exhibition *Paris-Moscou*, held in the Centre Georges-Pompidou, Paris in 1979.

BIBLIOGRAPHY:
Shchekov, N., *G. Ryazhski*, Leningrad, 1935. Yuravlev, V., *G.G. Ryazhski*, Moscow, 1952. Yuravlev, V., *G.G. Ryazhski, Album*, Moscow, 1958. Halturin, Aleksandr/Hulten, Pontus/Gunar, Karl (ed.), *Paris-Moscou*, group exhibition catalogue, Éd. du Centre Georges-Pompidou, Paris, 1979.

MUSEUMS AND GALLERIES:
MOSCOW (State Tretyakov Gal.): *Chairwoman* (1928, oil on canvas); *A Delegate* (1927).

RYBACK, Issachar Ber
Ukrainian, 20th century.
Born 1897, in Elisavetgrad (now Kirovhrad); died 1935, in Paris.
Also active in France.
Painter (including gouache), watercolourist, sculptor (including bronze), engraver, lithographer, ceramicist.
Figure compositions, figures, portraits, scenes with figures, rustic scenes, flowers. Figurines, stage sets.

Issachar Ber Ryback trained at the academy of fine art in Kiev. He taught drawing after the Revolution in 1917 and worked for the studio of Jewish theatre in Kiev and the Yiddish theatre in Moscow as well as in the Jewish agricultural communities of the Ukraine; he joined the November Group in 1921. Ryback settled in Paris in 1926 and exhibited at the Salon des Tuileries; he was well regarded and on the way to success. Georges Wildenstein a famous dealer, prepared a retrospective of his work, but Ryback died suddenly on the eve of the opening.

During the time he was teaching in the Ukraine, Ryback compiled a book of drawings entitled *In the Jewish Fields of the Ukraine*, painting the rebirth of Jews liberated from the ghettoes. The subject of the death of his father, murdered by the Cossacks, obsessed him for a long time. He created ceramic figurines of characters typical of Jewish life. The themes of his series of engravings were almost always associated with the history of the Jewish people: *Pogrom, Little Town, Jews of the Ukraine*. Ryback was perhaps influenced by the Expressionists, but the strongest influence on him, particularly in his Parisian period, was the influence of Chagall's tempered, dream-like Cubism, although his own work was dark and tragic.

J Ryback

BIBLIOGRAPHY:
Schiratzki, Berit, *'Målaren Issachar Ryback'* in *Judisk tidskrift*, 1932-1935. *Mané-Katz. Issachar Ryback*, Haifa, 1993 (text in Hebrew). Nieszawer, Nadine/Boyé, Marie/Lanzmann, Claude (preface), *Peintres juifs de l'école de Paris 1905-1939*, Denoël, Paris, 2001.

MUSEUMS AND GALLERIES:
BAT YAM (Ryback Mus.) - HAIFA (University, Reuben and Edith Hecht Mus.) - TEL AVIV (MA): *The Old Synagogue* (1917).

AUCTION RECORDS:
PARIS, 4 June 1943, *Village Market*, FRF 1,000. PARIS, 28 Nov 1971, *Donkey Cart*, FRF 8,000. PARIS, 8 Nov 1976, *On the Banks of the Seine* (oil on canvas, 19 3/4 x 25 1/2 ins / 50 x 65 cm) FRF 6,800. LONDON, 9 Dec 1977, *Peasant Farmer Gathering His Ducks* (oil on canvas, 15 x 22 ins / 38 x 55 cm) GBP 750. BOURG-EN-BRESSE, 25 Nov 1979, *Village Wedding in the Ukraine* (oil on card, 14 1/2 x 17 3/4 ins / 37 x 45 cm) FRF 23,000. LONDON, 20 Feb 1985, *Blind Jewish Violinist* (watercolour and gouache, 13 1/2 x 10 ins / 34.5 x 25.5 cm) GBP 1,100. GENEVA, 24 Nov 1987, *Portrait of Raya Garbusoya* (1931, oil on canvas, 47 1/4 x 39 1/4 ins / 120 x 100 cm) CHF 36,000. PARIS, 20 March 1988, *Icecream Seller* (oil on canvas, 25 1/2 x 19 3/4 ins / 65 x 50 cm) FRF 55,000. TEL AVIV, 26 May 1988, *Jewish Theatre* (gouache and watercolour, 14 1/4 x 19 1/2 ins / 36.5 x 49.5 cm) USD 3,850. TEL AVIV, 2 Jan 1989, *Portrait of a Jew* (watercolour, 17 1/4 x 10 1/2 ins / 43.5 x 26.5 cm) USD 3,960. PARIS, 16 April 1989, *Church* (oil on canvas, 25 1/2 x 21 1/4 ins / 65 x 54 cm) FRF 22,000. TEL AVIV, 30 May 1989, *Sleigh in the Snow in Russia* (oil on canvas, 25 1/2 x 36 1/4 ins / 65 x 92 cm) USD 24,200. LONDON, 5 Oct 1989, *Abstract Composition: Head* (red chalk/paper, 17 3/4 x 13 ins / 45 x 33 cm) GBP 6,600. TEL AVIV, 3 Jan 1990, *Well in the Steppes* (oil on card, 20 x 25 3/4 ins / 50.5 x 65.5 cm) USD 14,300. TEL AVIV, 19 June 1990, *Jewish Figures* (sepia, 16 x 10 1/4 ins / 40.5 x 26 cm) USD 660. TEL AVIV, 20 June 1990, *Chicken Seller* (bronze, h. 10 3/4 ins / 27.5 cm) USD 2,310. LONDON, 10 Oct 1990, *Felix, the Happy Wanderer* (watercolour heightened with white/paper, 17 1/2 x 11 ins / 44.5 x 28 cm) GBP 3,080. ST-DIÉ, 18 Nov 1990, *Chokhet, the Poultry Seller* (bronze, h. 11 ins / 28 cm) FRF 22,000. TEL AVIV, 1 Jan 1991, *Young Woman with White Scarf* (oil on canvas, 18 x 15 ins / 46 x 38 cm) USD 8,800. TEL AVIV, 26 Sept 1991, *Portrait of Raya Garbusoya* (oil on canvas, 39 1/4 x 31 3/4 ins / 100 x 80.5 cm) USD 13,200. AM-

STERDAM, 11 Dec 1991, *Grape-picker* (1920, oil on canvas, 39 1/4 x 32 ins / 100 x 81 cm) NLG 10,350. TEL AVIV, 6 Jan 1992, *Chicken Seller* (bronze, h. 10 3/4 ins / 27.5 cm) USD 1,650. NEW YORK, 9 May 1992, *Young Boy with Yeshiva* (watercolour/paper, 12 3/4 x 9 3/4 ins / 32.4 x 24.8 cm) USD 2,860. TEL AVIV, 20 Oct 1992, *Matchmaker* (oil on canvas, 13 x 9 1/2 ins / 33 x 24 cm) USD 9,900. PARIS, 16 Nov 1992, *Vase of Flowers* (watercolour, 17 1/4 x 12 1/2 ins / 44 x 32 cm) FRF 10,500. PARIS, 4 April 1993, *Villagers' Dance* (bronze, h. 13 3/4 ins / 35 cm) FRF 13,000. TEL AVIV, 25 Sept 1994, *Two Musicians* (oil on canvas, 22 x 15 ins / 55 x 38 cm) USD 12,650. TEL AVIV, 27 Sept 1994, *Harvest* (sepia chalk/buff-coloured paper, 26 3/4 x 21 1/2 ins / 68 x 54.5 cm) USD 2,875. NEW YORK, 24 Feb 1995, *Chicken Seller* (bronze, h. 10 3/4 ins / 27.6 cm) USD 1,725. PARIS, 24 March 1996, *Rest* (oil on canvas, 25 1/2 x 18 ins / 65 x 46 cm) FRF 28,000. TEL AVIV, 11 April 1996, *Cubist Composition* (gouache, 27 1/2 x 19 1/4 ins / 70 x 49 cm) USD 70,700. NEW YORK, 10 Oct 1996, *The Bride* (oil on canvas, 13 x 9 1/2 ins / 33 x 24.1 cm) USD 4,600. TEL AVIV, 26 April 1997, *Jewish Musicians* (oil on panel, 12 1/2 x 17 1/4 ins / 32 x 44 cm) USD 50,600. TEL AVIV, 8 April 1999, *Hariette Louise* (c. 1928-30, oil on canvas, 36 x 25 ins / 92 x 64 cm) USD 25,000. AMSTERDAM, 1 Dec 1999, *Young Peasant Girl* (oil on canvas, 11 x 9 ins / 27 x 22 cm) NLG 5,000. TEL AVIV, 16 Jan 2000, *Musicians* (oil on canvas, 18 x 15 ins / 46 x 38 cm) USD 6,000. PARIS, 15 March 2000, *Vase of Flowers* (gouache and watercolour, 19 x 13 ins / 47 x 32 cm) FRF 14,000. COLOGNE, 4 Dec 2001, *Cubist Composition* (Indian ink, watercolour over pencil, 12 x 9 ins / 30 x 22 cm) DEM 14,000. LONDON, 20 March 2003, *Flowers of the Field* (oil on canvas, 36 x 25 ins / 92 x 63 cm) GBP 7,000. CINCINNATI, 7 March 2004, *Peasants with Goat* (1918, oil on paper, 11 x 15 ins / 28 x 38 cm) USD 18,000. NEW YORK, 5 May 2004, *Cubist Composition* (1918, gouache, watercolour, 13 x 9 ins / 32 x 24 cm) USD 32,000.

RYBAK, Jaromir
Czech, 20th century.
Sculptor.
Jaromir Rybak makes glass sculptures. He has exhibited at the Galerie Clara Scremini, in Paris, and in 1991 at the Galerie Transparence, Brussels.

RYBAKOV, Gavriil Fedorovich
Russian, 19th - 20th century.
Born 1859.
Painter. Genre scenes.
MUSEUMS AND GALLERIES:
MOSCOW (State Tretyakov Gal.): *Blind Man's Buff* (1884); *Home From School* (1885).

RYBICKA, Jósef
Bohemian School, 19th century.
Born 9 February 1817, in Prague; died 1872, in Prague.
Engraver (burin).
Jósef was the son of Karl Rybicka, and studied at the art academy in Prague under Hellich, Führich and Klandler.

RYBICKA, Karl or Karel
Bohemian School, 19th century.
Born 27 December 1783, in Lysá; died 27 December 1853, in Prague.
Engraver (burin).
Karl Rybicka was the father of Jósef Rybicka, and studied under J. Balzer.

RYBIN, Sven
20th century.
Painter.
Sven Rybin lives and works in Antibes. He exhibited at the 1990 Salon d'Automne in Paris.

Rybin's work is abstract and influenced by Rayonism. He draws inspiration from the modern world and technological progress.

RYBINSKI, Feliks
Polish, 19th century.
Active in Warsaw.
Lithographer.
The National Museum in Warsaw owns a work by Feliks Rybinski entitled *Turk with a Horse*.

RYBKIEWICZ, Jósef
Polish, 19th century.
Died 27 August 1831.
Active in Cracow.
Painter.
Jósef Rybkiewicz painted portraits and was made a master painter on 13 March, 1793.

RYBKOVSKI, Jan
Polish, 19th century.
Born 1812, in Wólka Tarlowska; died 1852, in Warsaw.
Portrait artist.
Jan Rybkovski was the father of Tadeusz Rybkovski. He studied in Cracow, and worked in Kielce and, from 1850, in Warsaw. His works include a *Self-portrait*, and a portrait of the musician *Antoni Mecinski*.

RYBKOVSKY, Thadeusz
Polish, 19th - 20th century.
Born 30 March 1848, in Kielce; died 16 September 1926, in Lemberg (now Lviv, Ukraine).
Painter, designer, illustrator. Genre scenes.
Thadeusz Rybkovsky trained at the school of fine art in Cracow, then worked in Vienna with Loffler and Macort. He was appointed a teacher of decorative art in 1893 at the higher commercial college in Lemberg.
MUSEUMS AND GALLERIES:
CRACOW: *Am Hof Square in Vienna*.

RYBON, François. See **RIBON**

RYCERSKI, Aleksander
Polish, 19th century.
Born 15 November 1825, in Speranda, near Sandomierz; died 30 November 1866, in Paris.
Painter.
Aleksander Rycerski studied at the art academy in Warsaw, and was forced to leave Poland for political reasons in 1863. He was influenced by Delaroche. The Mielzynski museum in Poznan owns one of his works, entitled *Old Woman with a Book*, and the National Museum in Warsaw owns his *Portrait of an Old Woman*.

RYCHALS, François. See **RYCKKALS**

RYCHE, Paul, or Riche
British, 18th century.
Active in 1740.
Portrait artist.
MUSEUMS AND GALLERIES:
LONDON (British Mus.): *Portrait of Mr Deisel*; *Portrait of J. Faber*; *Portrait of an Unknown*.

RYCHTARSKY, Adam
Polish, 20th century.
Born 17 December 1885, in Olchowa.
Painter.
Adam Rychtarsky trained at the academy of fine art in Warsaw and Munich with Hollósy.
MUSEUMS AND GALLERIES:
WARSAW: two landscapes.

RYCHTER, Tadeusz
Polish, 20th century.
Painter, draughtsman.
The husband of Bronislava Rychter-Janovska, Tadeusz Rychter worked from 1900 to 1906 and produced many drawings for ex-libris.

RYCHTER-JANOVSKA, Bronislava
Maiden name: Janovska
Polish, 19th - 20th century.
Born 13 July 1868, in Cracow.
Painter. Figures.
Bronislava Janovska trained with her brother, Stanislas Janovsky, in Cracow, with Azbé and Hollósy in Munich and at the Florence academy.
MUSEUMS AND GALLERIES:
CRACOW (Muz. Narodowe): *Portrait of the Artist J. Wegrzyn* - LÓDZ (Muzeum Historii): *Interior; Italian Landscape* - LVIV (Picture Gallery): *Interior; Mill; Polish Nobleman's Castle* - PRAGUE: *St John* - VATICAN (Mus. Vaticani): *Home From Church* - WARSAW (Muz. Narodowe): *Portrait of W. Rozycky von Rosenwerth.*
AUCTION RECORDS:
AMSTERDAM, 9 Nov 1994, *Woman in an Interior* (oil on card, 12 1/2 x 18 1/4 ins / 32 x 46.5 cm) NLG 1,725. WARSAW, 22 Oct 2000, *Manor House in Garden* (oil on board, 14 x 19 ins / 35 x 49 cm) PLZ 9,000.

RYCK. See also **RYCKX**

RYCK, Aertszoon. See **AERTSZ. Lambert Ryck**

RYCK, Cornelia de, or Rijck
Dutch, 17th century.
Born 1656, in Delft.
Painter. Animals, birds, farmyard scenes.
Cornelia de Ryck married the painter Van Goor in Amsterdam, then the painter Simon Schynvoet. She had Gerard Rademaker as her pupil. She painted numerous farmyard birds, and she is particularly remembered for her *Farmyard* (Budapest).

RYCK, Guilliam de. See **DERYKE William or Willem**

RYCK, J. van, or Rijck
Dutch, 17th century.
Painter. Genre scenes.
J van Ryck painted a work, *Musical Gathering,* which was sold in Cologne in 1894 with the Clavé Boubaven Collection.
AUCTION RECORDS:
GLASGOW, 25 Aug 1997, *Peasants Chatting near a Cottage with a Donkey, Cows, Goats and Sheep* (oil on canvas, 19 3/4 x 23 ins / 50.2 x 58.5 cm) GBP 1,610.

RYCK, Johann von
German, 18th century.
Active at the beginning of the 18th century.
Sculptor.
Johann von Ryck worked with his master J.F. van Helmont on sculptures for a chapel in the church of St Mary in Cologne. He also sculpted a *St Bruno* in the council chapel in Cologne.

RYCK, Katharina
Flemish School, 17th - 18th century.
Painter.
Katharina Ryck was the daughter of Willem Ryck.

RYCK, Lambert. See **RYCKX Lambrecht**

RYCK, Nicolaes van, or Rijck
Dutch, 17th century.
Died 1666.
Painter. Hunting scenes, fruit.
Nicolaes van Ryck was a member of the guild at Delft in 1652. He was Burgomaster of Waelivyck.

RYCK, Paul de
Belgian, 20th - 21st century.
Born 1953, in Aalst.
Painter, engraver, draughtsman.
Paul de Ryck studied at the academies of fine arts in Aalst and Ghent. The dramatic, mysterious world he conjures up shows him more as a painter of chiaroscuro effects than as a colourist.

RYCK, Pieter Cornelisz. van, or Rijck
Dutch, 16th - 17th century.
Born 1568, in Delft; died probably 1628; after 1635 according to some sources.
Painter.
Pieter Cornelisz. van Ryck was a pupil of Jacob Willemsz. Delff in Delft and of H. Jaz Grimani, with whom he went to Italy. He was in Haarlem in 1604. Among his works are *Kitchen* (attributed) in Amsterdam, *Large Kitchen* in Brunswick, *Kitchen* in Haarlem, and *Adoration of the Shepherds* in Münster.

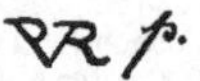

AUCTION RECORDS:
PARIS, 4 Dec 1963, *Preparations for the Feast,* FRF 14,000.

RYCK, William or Willem de. See **DERYKE**

RYCKAERT, Aertszoon. See **AERTSZ. Richard**

RYCKAERT, David I, or Rijckaert or Rickaert
Flemish School, 16th century.
Born 1560, in Antwerp; died c. 1607, in Antwerp.
Painter, art dealer.
Antwerp School.
In 1585 David Ryckaert I appears on the guild list as a paint mixer and canvas stretcher, so he must have worked for other painters. He married Catharina Rem in 1585 and his three sons, David, Martin and Paul, were also his pupils. It is thought that he was especially employed in painting figures into the paintings of his colleagues. Among his works is *Three Smokers Sitting on a Barrel* (Lerins Collection, Antwerp).

AUCTION RECORDS:
LONDON, 26 June 1959, *Pickpockets,* GBP 682.

RYCKAERT, David II
Flemish School, 17th century.
Born 1586, in Antwerp; died 1642; buried 3 October in Antwerp.
Painter. Genre scenes, interiors, landscapes, still-lifes.
David Ryckaert II was the pupil of his father David Ryckaert I. He was the master of a studio in Antwerp, and married Catharina de Meere in 1608. His elder daughter married Gonzales Coques.

Although David II seems, like his father, to have painted figures and interiors, he is mentioned especially as a painter of mountains, and he is remembered in particular for his *Rag Merchant* (Lerins Collection, in Antwerp) and *Man Laughing* (Court of the Béguines). He was also an art dealer.

Auction records:
Paris, 28 Feb 1945, *Village Interior* (school of David Ryckaert) FRF 9,000. Paris, 20 April 1945, *Hunter Resting,* FRF 2,800. London, 5 April 1946, *Hunter's Return,* GBP 252. Brussels, 27 Jan 1947, *Kitchen Interior,* BEF 14,000. Stockholm, 15 Nov 1989, *Interiors with Figures Seated near a Table* (oil, 9¾ x 13 ins / 25 x 33 cm) SEK 12,000. Amsterdam, 6 May 1993, *Elderly Bearded Lute Player Seated in front of a Table* (1642, oil on panel/panel, 13¾ x 11¼ ins / 35.2 x 28.7 cm) NLG 43,700. London, 8 Dec 1995, *Gold Objets d'art, Nautilus, Pieces of Porcelain with Shellfish, Coral and Jewels on a Table Covered with a Cloth* (1616, oil on canvas, 40¾ x 53½ ins / 103.5 x 136 cm) GBP 139,000. Ahlden, 28 Sept 2001, *Satyr and Peasants* (oil on canvas, 44 x 60 ins / 111 x 153 cm) DEM 38,000. New York, 25 Jan 2002, *Jupiter and Mercury in the House of Philemon and Baucis* (1639, oil on canvas, 31 x 53 ins / 79 x 134 cm) USD 16,000.

RYCKAERT, David III, the Younger

Flemish School, 17th century.
Born 1612, baptised 2 December in Antwerp; died 11 November 1661, in Antwerp.
Painter. Genre scenes, interiors with figures, landscapes.
Antwerp School.

David Ryckaert III, the Younger, was the third son and pupil of David Ryckaert II. He was a master in the Antwerp Guild in 1636 and its Dean in 1652. He married Jacoba Pallemaus in 1647.

He started as a landscape painter, but the prevailing fashion for the works of Brouwer and Teniers seems to have led him to treat the familiar subjects dear to these two great artists. He was no less successful, being able to blend soft and dazzling colours. He also painted tavern scenes, painters' studios and subjects from fantasy. He was protected by Archduke Leopold William and had so many commissions that he had difficulty keeping up. He had as a pupil his brother-in-law Gonzales Coques.

Museums and Galleries:
Aachen: *Workshop of a Shoemaker* - Aix-en-Provence: *Guard* - Amiens: *Singer* - Amsterdam: *Shoemaker's Workshop* - Antwerp: *Peasants' Meal; War Scene* - Arras: *Tavern Interior* - Berlin: *The Village Idiot* - Besançon: *Still-life* (attributed) - Bonn: *In the Inn* - Bourg: *Tobacconist's* - Brussels: *Chemist in His Laboratory; Children's Party; Old Man near the Hearth* - Budapest: *Inn Interior; Adoration of the Shepherds; Alchemist; Old Man Singing* - Chalon-sur-Saône: *Scientist Studying* - Cologne: *Shoemaker and His Wife* - Copenhagen (Statens Mus. for Kunst): *Inn Parlour with Guests; Rural Banquet; Concert* - Dijon: *Painter in His Studio* - Dresden: *Peasant Bedroom* (two genre subjects); *Still-life and Cat; Still-life with a Child and Its Top* - Dunkirk: *Woman Spinning* - Florence: *Temptation of St Antony* (two works) - Frankfurt am Main: *Butcher* - Geneva (MAH): *Flemish Inn* - Graz: *Scene from Everyday Life* - Hanover: *Jolly Company* - Leipzig: *Alchemist and His Wife; Shoemaker and His Assistant at Work* - Lille: *Mussel Seller* - Lyons: *Avarice* - Madrid: *Alchemist* - Mainz: *Inn Scene* - Montpellier: *Tooth-puller* - Munich: *Twelfth Night* - New York (Metropolitan Mus. of Art): *Farm* - Nice: *Dressing the Wound* - Oberschleissheim (Neues Schloss Schleissheim, Staatsgal.): *Peasants Drinking* - Paris (Louvre): *Studio Interior* - Rohrau (Schlossmus., Graf Harrach'sche Familiensammlung): *Pillage of a House* - Rome (Palazzo Doria Pamphili): *Old Lute Player* - Schwerin: *Peasant Interior; Family Concert* - St Petersburg (Hermitage): *Old Woman with Cat; Peasant with Dog* - Stockholm: *Cottage Interior with Rustics Smoking and Drinking* - Valenciennes: *Surgeon* - Vienna: *Parish Patronal Festival; Witch; Kitchen; Scientist at His Work Table; Pillage of a Village* - Vienna (Czernin'sche Gemäldegal.): *Peasants in an Inn; Musical Conversation - Two Works* - Vienna (Liechtenstein Mus.): *Adoration of the Shepherds; Musical Entertainment* - Wroclaw: *Evening Meal in the Village* - Ypres: *Knife-grinder; Rustic Interior; Kitchen Interior; Farm Interior.*

Auction records:
Paris, 19 Oct 1772, *Kitchen Utensils and Vegetables,* FRF 805. Paris, 1831, *The Painter in His Studio,* FRF 3,102. Paris, 1859, *Jolly Company,* FRF 1,105. Paris, 1870, *Inn Interior,* FRF 1,650. Paris, 20 May 1873, *Lunch,* FRF 2,010. Paris, 1890, *Kitchen Interior,* FRF 1,900. Amsterdam, 1892, *The Shoemaker,* NLG 1,375. Paris, 1899, *Kitchen Interior,* FRF 1,900. Paris, 7 Feb 1907, *Kitchen Interior,* FRF 705. London, 6 May 1910, *Inn Interior,* GBP 199. Paris, 26-28 June 1919, *The Alchemist's Laboratory,* FRF 2,700. Paris, 7 July 1926, *Studio Interior,* FRF 1,850. Paris, 17 June 1927, *Old Woman Holding a Jug and a Glass,* FRF 2,700. New York, 4 and 5 Feb 1931, *The Inn,* USD 275. Paris, 23 May 1932, *Interior of a Bar,* FRF 2,000. Paris, 16 June 1932, *The Musicians,* FRF 280. Paris, 14 Dec 1933, *The Picture Gallery,* FRF 6,000. London, 12 March 1937, *Interior with Peasants Smoking* (drawing) GBP 39. Brussels, 28 and 29 March 1938, *The Meal,* BEF 4,200. Paris, 4 Dec 1941, *Scene at a Tobacconist's* (attributed) FRF 3,600. Paris, 8 July 1942, *Inn Interior: The Dice Players* (attributed) FRF 3,200. Paris, 15 June 1949, *Couple in a Tavern* (attributed) FRF 8,000. Paris, 28 Oct 1949, *Rustic Interior* (school of Ryckaert) FRF 10,100. Paris, 2 June 1950, *Figures in a Rustic Interior* (attributed) FRF 10,500. Paris, 8 Nov 1950, *Peasant Holding a Jug* (attributed) FRF 11,000. Paris, 22 Dec 1950, *The Lute Player* (attributed) FRF 9,000. Paris, 14 Feb 1951, *Drinkers at the Tavern* (attributed) FRF 16,000. Paris, 9 March 1951, *Peasant Interior,* FRF 24,000. Brussels, 5-6-7 May 1965, *Interior with Happy Family Group.* London, 10 April 1970, *Scene Featuring Elegant Lovers in an Idealised Rural Setting,* Gns 1,300. Rome, 11 June 1973, *Peasant Smoking,* ITL 3,500,000. Brussels, 27 Oct 1976, *Tavern Scene* (oil on wood, 22 x 29¼ ins / 56 x 74 cm) BEF 525,000. Amsterdam, 22 Nov 1977, *Peasants Drinking and Singing* (oil on panel, 14¼ x 18 ins / 36 x 46 cm) NLG 21,000. Lucerne, 30 May 1979, *Interior* (1642, oil on panel, 19¾ x 27¼ ins / 50 x 69 cm) CHF 24,000. Paris, 18 March 1981, *Family Reading a Letter* (oil on canvas, 23 x 37½ ins / 58.5 x 95 cm) FRF 65,000. New York, 9 June 1983, *Tavern Scene* (1637, oil on canvas, 25 x 31¼ ins / 63.5 x 79.5 cm) USD 7,500. London, 13 Feb 1985, *The Shoemaker's Shop* (oil on panel, 21 x 28¾ ins / 53.5 x 73 cm) GBP 5,000. London, 9 April 1986, *Witch Chasing Devils* (oil on panel, 18 x 23½ ins / 45.5 x 60 cm) GBP 5,000. Paris, 14 April 1988, *Cellar Interior* (oil on canvas, 33 x 45 ins / 84 x 114 cm) FRF 150,000. Amsterdam, 18 May 1988, *Bootmaker at Work in a Barn, a Woman Carrying a Jug and Peasants near a Fire in the Background* (oil on panel, 22¾ x 32½ ins / 58 x 82.5 cm) NLG 23,000. Amsterdam, 18 May 1988, *Bootmaker at Work in a Barn, a Woman Carrying a Jug and Peasants near a Fire in the Background* (oil on panel, 22¾ x 32½ ins / 58 x 82.5 cm) NLG 23,000. Milan, 4 April 1989, *Card Players* (oil on panel, 21 x 25¼ ins / 53.5 x 64 cm) ITL 19,000,000. Paris, 12 April 1989, *Children Playing at Being Married: The May Queen* (oil on panel, 15¼ x 16¼ ins / 38.5 x 41.5 cm) FRF 300,000. London, 20 July 1990, *A Shoemaker* (oil on panel, 25½ x 33½ ins / 64.7 x 85 cm) GBP

11,000. NEW YORK, 22 May 1992, *Game of Cards in an Interior* (oil on panel, 23 1/2 x 31 1/2 ins / 59.7 x 80 cm) USD 7,150. PARIS, 30 March 1998, *The First Pipe* (oak panel, 19 3/4 x 25 3/4 ins / 50 x 65.5 cm) FRF 140,000. LONDON, 16 April 1999, *Gentleman Drinking in an Inn* (1649, oil on canvas, 23 x 30 ins / 59 x 77 cm) GBP 21,000. LONDON, 9 July 1999, *Peasants Smoking and Drinking in an Inn* (oil on panel, 19 x 25 ins / 48 x 64 cm) GBP 12,000. VIENNA, 30 March 2000, *Drinking in a Tavern* (oil on panel, 19 x 15 ins / 48 x 39 cm) ATS 400,000. LONDON, 5 July 2000, *Peasants Playing Cards in a Tavern* (oil on canvas, 18 x 24 ins / 46 x 61 cm) GBP 13,000. LONDON, 25 April 2001, *Alchemist in His Study at Night* (oil on panel, 24 x 30 ins / 61 x 77 cm) GBP 19,000. LONDON, 14 Dec 2001, *Peasant Smoking in a Tavern* (oil on panel, 22 x 31 ins / 56 x 79 cm) GBP 19,500. MADRID, 21 Jan 2003, *Inn Interiors with figures and Still-life* (oil on board, 16 x 20 ins / 41 x 52 cm) EUR 9,000. ZURICH, 8 Dec 2003, *Inn with Drinking and Smoking Peasants* (1638, oil on panel, 16 x 22 ins / 40 x 57 cm) CHF 21,500. PARIS, 26 March 2004, *Drinkers in a Tavern* (oil on panel, 23 x 32 ins / 59 x 81 cm) EUR 7,000. ZURICH, 22 Sept 2004, *Picture Collector* (oil on panel, 15 x 11 ins / 37 x 28 cm) CHF 12,000.

RYCKAERT, David IV

Flemish School, 17th century.
Born 1649, in Antwerp.
Painter (?).

David Ryckaert IV was the son of David Ryckaert III.

RYCKAERT, Friedrik

Flemish School, 16th century.
Painter.
Antwerp School.

Friedrik Ryckaert was a member of the guild of St Luke in Antwerp in 1550, and painted a large altarpiece for the church of St James in 1570.

RYCKAERT, Martin, Marten or Maerten

Flemish School, 17th century.
Baptised 8 December 1587 in Antwerp; died 1631; buried 11 October in Antwerp.
Painter. Landscapes, landscapes with figures, mountainscapes, waterscapes.
Antwerp School.

Martin or Marten Ryckaert was the pupil of his father David Ryckaert I, and Tobais Verhaecht. He had only one arm. He went to Italy, where he spent several years, returning to Antwerp in 1611. He entered the guild in Antwerp, and was a close friend of Anton van Dyck.

Ryckaert's landscapes, with figures often painted by Jan Brueghel, were very much appreciated in his time.

MUSEUMS AND GALLERIES:

CHAMBÉRY (MBA): *Landscape* - FLORENCE: *Waterfalls at Tivoli* - HANOVER: *Italian Landscape* - LONDON (NG): *Landscape with Satyrs* (c. 1626, oil/wood) - MADRID: *Landscape* - ST PETERSBURG: *Landscape*.

AUCTION RECORDS:

BRUSSELS, 27 Jan 1947, *Landscape with Watercourse*, BEF 15,000; *St John on Patmos*, BEF 16,000; *Sower of Cornweeds*, BEF 33,000. LONDON, 3 July 1963, *Mountain Landscape*, GBP 750. LONDON, 17 Nov 1965, *Rest on the Flight into Egypt; Village Scene*, GBP 1,600. VIENNA, 1 Dec 1970, *River Landscape*, ATS 60,000. LONDON, 29 March 1974, *Steep Landscape with Waterfall*, Gns 7,000. LONDON, 7 July 1976, *Artist Sketching in a Landscape* (oil on panel, 36 1/4 x 49 1/2 ins / 92 x 125.5 cm) GBP 10,000. LONDON, 8 July 1977, *Winter Landscape with Skaters* (oil on panel, round, diam. 6 1/4 ins / 15.9 cm) GBP 12,000. LONDON, 30 Nov 1979, *Travellers in a Wooded Landscape* (oil on panel, 9 3/4 x 13 1/2 ins / 24.7 x 34.3 cm) GBP 5,500. BRUSSELS, 28 Oct 1981, *Sower of Corn-weeds* (1616, oil/copper, 9 x 11 3/4 ins / 23 x 30 cm) BEF 1,100,000. AMSTERDAM, 14 Nov 1983, *Banks of the Rhine with Figures Repairing a Boat* (gouache/parchment, 5 1/2 x 8 ins / 14.1 x 20.6 cm) NLG 5,200. LONDON, 12 Dec 1984, *River Landscape with Figures* (oil on panel, 21 1/2 x 29 1/2 ins / 54.5 x 75 cm) GBP 36,000. LONDON, 19 April 1985, *Peasants and Travellers in a Wooded Landscape* (oil on panel, 11 1/2 x 17 1/4 ins / 29.2 x 43.9 cm) GBP 20,000. LONDON, 23 May 1986, *Steep Landscape with Figures* (oil/copper, 7 3/4 x 11 ins / 19.7 x 28 cm) GBP 21,000. LONDON, 8 July 1988, *Tinkers on a Track beside a Dammed River with Mills, and a Town in the Distance* (oil on panel, 3 1/4 x 7 ins / 8.5 x 17.5 cm) GBP 13,200. PARIS, 12 April 1989, *Monks Clearing the Hill* (oil on panel, 8 3/4 x 10 1/2 ins / 22.5 x 26.5 cm) FRF 90,000. LONDON, 21 April 1989, *Extensive Wooded Landscape with Figures, a River and a Bridge in the Foreground and a Village and Castle in the Distance* (oil on panel, 17 1/4 x 23 1/4 ins / 43.7 x 59 cm) GBP 55,000. PARIS, 30 June 1989, *Walkers in a Wooded Avenue* (copper, 7 3/4 x 11 ins / 19.5 x 27 cm) FRF 26,000. LONDON, 7 July 1989, *Foundry on a River in the Alps* (oil/copper, 12 1/2 x 16 1/4 ins / 31.5 x 41.5 cm) GBP 49,500. PARIS, 11 Dec 1989, *Fall of Icarus* (copper, a pair, each 2 3/4 x 7 1/2 ins / 7 x 19 cm) FRF 100,000. PARIS, 22 Dec 1989, *Walkers in an Avenue* (oil on card, 7 3/4 x 11 ins / 19.5 x 27 cm) FRF 95,000. LONDON, 9 April 1990, *River Valley with a Swineherd Seated under a Tree and a Hamlet in the Distance* (oil on panel, 23 x 15 1/4 ins / 58.5 x 39 cm) GBP 137,500. LONDON, 14 Dec 1990, *Wooded River Landscape with a Peasant Woman Cooking for Soldiers on a Camp Fire* (oil on panel, 14 1/2 x 19 3/4 ins / 36.7 x 50 cm) GBP 29,700. LONDON, 11 Dec 1991, *Figures on the Banks of a River* (oil on panel, 11 x 13 1/2 ins / 27 x 34.4 cm) GBP 33,000. PARIS, 15 Dec 1992, *Landscape with Shepherd* (oil on panel, 15 1/4 x 8 3/4 ins / 38.5 x 22.5 cm) FRF 12,000. NEW YORK, 20 May 1993, *Landscape with Hunters near a Brook* (1622, oil/copper, 8 x 11 ins / 20.3 x 27.9 cm) USD 79,500. LONDON, 10 Dec 1993, *Rocky River Valley with Goatherds and Their Goats near a Waterfall* (1628, oil on panel, 19 x 28 ins / 48 x 71.4 cm) GBP 16,100. PARIS, 27 May 1994, *River Landscape* (oil/copper, 17 1/4 x 22 1/4 ins / 44 x 56.5 cm) FRF 600,000. MONACO, 19 June 1994, *Landscape* (oil/copper, 6 1/2 x 8 3/4 ins / 16.5 x 22.5 cm) FRF 88,800. NEW YORK, 12 Jan 1996, *River Landscape in the Mountains with Woodmen in the Foreground* (3 1/2 x 7 1/4 ins / 9 x 18.2 cm) USD 12,650. LONDON, 30 Oct 1996, *Travellers in an Extensive Mountain Landscape* (oil on canvas, 35 x 51 1/4 ins / 89 x 130 cm) GBP 20,700. LONDON, 13 Dec 1996, *Italian Landscape with Shepherds and Goatherds Leading Their Flocks, and the Evening Meal at Emmaus in the Distance* (oil on panel, 20 1/2 x 31 ins / 51.8 x 78.8 cm) GBP 36,700. LONDON, 3 Dec 1997, *Extensive River Landscape with the Flight into Egypt and Fishermen on a Bridge, and a Town in the Distance; Extensive River Landscape with Travellers Resting beside a Cross by the Roadside, and Stag-hunting in the Distance* (oil/copper, a pair, 5 x 6 1/2 ins / 13 x 16.5 cm) GBP 24,150. LONDON, 8 July 1999, *Panoramic Campagnan Landscape with Herders and Goats* (1625, oil on canvas, 39 x 55 ins / 98 x 139 cm) GBP 55,000. LONDON, 16 Dec 1999, *Rocky Wooded Landscape with Coastal Town* (oil on panel, 10 x 17 ins / 25 x 44 cm) GBP 62,000. LONDON, 6 July 2000, *Wooded Landscape with Travellers Resting beside a Pool* (oil on panel, 6 x 10 ins / 16 x 25 cm) GBP 13,500. LONDON, 14 Dec 2000, *Mountain Landscape with Shepherds Piping and Tending Their Goats* (oil on panel, 20 x 26 ins / 50 x 66 cm) GBP 55,000. MADRID, 14 Nov 2001, *Flight into Egypt* (oil on canvas, 29 x 35 ins / 74 x 89 cm) ESP 4,600,000. BRUSSELS, 20 Nov 2001, *Figures on the Edge of a Forest. Figures on a Riverbank* (oil on copper, a pair, 7 x 9 ins / 17 x 22 cm) BEF 700,000. NEW YORK, 24 Jan 2002, *Pastoral Landscape with Swineherd Resting under a Tree* (oil on panel, 15 x 24 ins / 39 x 60 cm) USD 140,000. LONDON, 12 Dec 2002, *Classical Landscape with Satyr's Family* (oil on panel, 22 x 35 ins / 56 x 88 cm) GBP 52,000. LONDON, 9 April 2003, *Wooded Landscape with Travellers and Cart* (oil on panel, 13 x 18 ins / 32 x 46 cm) GBP 18,000. LONDON, 9 July 2003, *Extensive Italianate Landscape with Goatherds, Shep-*

herd and Their Flocks (1625, oil on canvas, 39 x 55 ins / 98 x 139 cm) GBP 50,000. LONDON, 21 April 2004, *Wooded River Landscape with Goatherds Resting with Their Goats and Dogs by a Waterfall* (1626, oil on panel, octagonal, 9 x 11 ins / 23 x 28 cm) GBP 15,000.

RYCKAERT, Paul or Pauwel
Flemish School, 17th century.
Born 1592, in Antwerp; died 1649 or 1650.
Painter.

Paul Ryckaert was the son and pupil of David Ryckaert I.

RYCKE. See also **RYCKERE**

RYCKE, Daniel de, or Ryckere
Flemish School, 16th - 17th century.
Born 22 April 1568, in Antwerp; died before 1614.
Painter.

Daniel de Rycke was the son and pupil of Bernaert de Ryckere.

RYCKE, Daniel de. See also **RYKE**

RYCKE, Jacques Zachée de
Flemish School, 18th century.
Born 23 August 1723, in Bruges; died 30 November 1792, in Bruges.
Painter. History painting, portraits.

Rycke was the pupil of M de Visels and J Gaeremyn.
MUSEUMS AND GALLERIES:
BRUGES (Academy): *St Luke Surrounded by Angels.*

RYCKE, William or Willem de. See **DERYKE**

RYCKEBUSCH, or Ryckebus
French, 19th century.
Active in Paris 1850-1872.
Illustrator, engraver (wood).

RYCKEMANS, Nicolaes. See **RYCKMAN**

RYCKEN, Henrik
Dutch, 16th century.
Active in Haarlem, and in Amsterdam in 1585.
Engraver. Maps.

RYCKENHOVEN, Jasper van, called Jasper Jaspers
Dutch, 17th century.
Active in Leiden in 1628.
Painter.

RYCKENROYEN, Jan van. See **REKENROY Jean van**

RYCKERE, Abraham de, or Rycker or Rycke
Flemish School, 16th century.
Baptised 5 July 1566 in Antwerp; died before 19 August 1599.
Painter.

Abraham de Ryckere was the son of Bernard de Ryckere. In 1591 he painted a triptych depicting *Christ on the Cross between the Two Thieves* for the church of St James in Antwerp. The central panel was destroyed in 1807, but the two side panels show that he was a painter of some skill.
MUSEUMS AND GALLERIES:
AIX: *Marie Le Batteur* - ANTWERP: *Lodewijk Clarys* (wings from a triptych); *Virgin and Jesus* (reverse grisaille); *Marie Le Batteur; St Louis the King* (reverse grisaille).

RYCKERE, Bernard or Bernaert de, or Rycke or Rycker, called B. van Rues
Flemish School, 16th century.
Born c. 1535; died 1 January 1590, in Antwerp.
Active in Courtrai.
Painter.
Antwerp School.

In 1561 Bernard de Ryckere was a member of the guild of Antwerp. He married Maria Boots in 1563 and in 1589 was one of the experts appointed to examine the *Last Judgement* by Raphael van Coxie in Ghent. He founded a shop for the copying of old master paintings, and was assisted in this by his sons and pupils Abraham and Daniel, the latter of whom was born in 1568 and died in 1614. Among his works are the following: *Beheading of St Matthew* (church of Notre Dame, Antwerp); *Diana and Actaeon* (Budapest); *Pentecost, Creation of Adam* and *Baptism of Christ* (triptych); and *Carrying of the Cross, with St Agnes* (church of St Martin, Courtrai).

RYCKERE, Daniel de. See **RYCKE** and **RYKE**

RYCKERS
Dutch, 18th century.
Active at the beginning of the 18th century.
Painter. Landscapes.

RYCKEVORSEL, Jacobus Josephus van (Baron)
Dutch, 16th century.
Born 7 February 1485, in 's Hertogenbosch.
Glass painter, draughtsman.

Jacobus Josephus van Ryckevorsel was the father of Joannes Ryckevorsel.

RYCKEVORSEL, Joannes
Dutch, 19th century.
Glass painter.

Joannes Ryckevorsel was the son of Jacobus Ryckevorsel, and was a priest.

RYCKKALS, Francoys or Frans or François, or Rijckhals
Dutch, 17th century.
Born c. 1600, in Middelburg; died 1647, in Middelburg.
Painter. Genre scenes, interiors, landscapes, still-lifes.
Middelburg School.

Ryckkals was, like his grandfather, a member of the guild at Middelburg, the town where he studied. After a brief period in Rotterdam at the start of the 1630s he became a member of the guild at Dordrecht in 1633, then returned to the town of his birth in 1642.

The style of Ryckkals reveals contact with the Saftleven Group. L.J. Bol suggests that he was a pupil of Adriaen van de Venne. He played an important part in establishing rustic still-life in Holland, characterised by a pile of household utensils and vegetables in carefully arranged disorder.

BIBLIOGRAPHY:
Bol, Laurens Johannes, *"Goede onbekenden": hedendaagse herkenning en waardering van verscholen, voorbijgezien en onderschat talent*, Tableau, Utrecht, 1982.
MUSEUMS AND GALLERIES:
BERLIN (Bodemus.): *Crockery on a Table* - BRUSSELS: *Barn* - BUDAPEST (Szépmuvészeti Múz.): *Still-life in front of the Cowshed* (1641) - HAARLEM: *Interior* - IXELLES: *Fish on the Beach* - KALININGRAD: *Interior of a Barn* - KARLSRUHE: *Two Barn Interiors* - ST PETERSBURG: *Farm.*
AUCTION RECORDS:
BRUSSELS, 6 Dec 1937, *Landscape*, BEF 1,700. BRUSSELS, 27 Jan 1947, *Kitchen Interior*, BEF 11,000. PARIS, 7 Dec 1954, *At-*

tic, FRF 170,000. COLOGNE, 14 June 1976, *Kitchen Interior* (oil on panel, 10 1/4 x 12 1/2 ins / 26 x 31.5 cm) DEM 6,500. PARIS, 26 Feb 1979, *Barn Interior* (oil on wood, 15 x 19 1/2 ins / 38 x 49.5 cm) FRF 24,300. COLOGNE, 20 March 1981, *Rustic Interior* (oil on wood, 14 1/4 x 18 3/4 ins / 36 x 47.5 cm) DEM 11,000. AMSTERDAM, 25 April 1983, *Wooded Landscape* (black chalk, 7 3/4 x 11 3/4 ins / 19.8 x 29.7 cm) NLG 5,200. LONDON, 30 Nov 1983, *Jacob with the Flock of Laban* (oil on canvas, 49 1/4 x 83 ins / 125 x 211 cm) GBP 10,000. PARIS, 14 Dec 1987, *Kitchen Still-life* (watercolour and pencil, 10 x 13 1/2 ins / 25.2 x 34.2 cm) FRF 8,000. AMSTERDAM, 29 Nov 1988, *Pile of Pots, Pans and Vegetables in a Barn with a Couple of Peasants in the Background* (1631, oil on panel, 12 1/2 x 20 ins / 32 x 51 cm) NLG 14,950. PARIS, 6 April 1990, *Still-life of Provisions in a Farm Interior* (oil on panel, 15 x 21 1/4 ins / 38 x 54 cm) FRF 59,000. PARIS, 9 April 1991, *Still-life in a Cowshed* (oil on panel, 15 1/4 x 21 1/4 ins / 38.5 x 54 cm) FRF 60,000. LONDON, 11 Dec 1992, *Still-life with a Herring, Oysters, Mussels, a Lobster and a Crab with Silver Objets d'art on an Entablature Covered with a Cloth* (oil on canvas, 21 1/2 x 25 ins / 54.6 x 63.5 cm) GBP 8,250. AMSTERDAM, 17 Nov 1993, *Still-life with a Crayfish, a Crab and Cheese near a Jug and Gold Objets d'art on an Entablature* (1644, oil on panel, 30 3/4 x 41 ins / 78 x 104 cm) NLG 178,250. LONDON, 5 April 1995, *Barn Interior with Peasants Seated* (oil on panel, 15 x 16 1/2 ins / 38.2 x 42 cm) GBP 7,475. LONDON, 31 Oct 1997, *Fish and Seafood on an Entablature* (1641, oil on panel, 23 x 32 3/4 ins / 58.4 x 83.2 cm) GBP 4,600. PARIS, 25 June 1999, *Dutch Farmer in a Scullery* (oil on panel, 13 x 11 ins / 34 x 28 cm) FRF 30,000. NEW YORK, 23 Jan 2001, *Landscape with Cattle and Two Figures* (black chalk, 3 x 8 ins / 8 x 20 cm) USD 4,000. VIENNA, 3 Oct 2001, *Woman Washing Dishes in a Barn* (1638, oil on panel, 23 x 32 ins / 59 x 81 cm) ATS 110,000. AMSTERDAM, 5 Nov 2002, *Barn Interior with Kitchen Still-life, Goat and Sheep* (oil on panel, 13 x 15 ins / 32 x 38 cm) EUR 2,500. AMSTERDAM, 4 Nov 2003, *Study of Trees* (black chalk, 7 x 6 ins / 18 x 15 cm) EUR 6,500. PARIS, 24 June 2004, *Stable Interior* (oil on panel, 4 x 6 ins / 11 x 15 cm) EUR 8,000.

RYCKMAN, Nicolas or Claes, or Ryckmans or Ryckemans
Dutch, 17th century.
Born c. 1595, in Edam.
Engraver.

Ryckman was the pupil of P Rubens. He reproduced, using a burin and with considerable talent, several important paintings by Rubens, and is considered to be one of the good interpreters of the famous master.

RYCKX, Jan I, or Rycx
Flemish School, 17th century.
Born 1585, in Bruges; died 19 September 1643.
Painter.

Jan Ryckx is mentioned only as the father of the painters Jan II, Karl, Paul I, Mathias and Nicolas Rycx or Ryckx, but otherwise nothing is known about either his life or his works.

RYCKX, Jan II
Flemish School, 17th century.
Died 6 December 1646, in Delft.
Painter.

Jan Ryckx II was the son of Jan Ryckx I.

RYCKX, Karl
Flemish School, 17th century.
Born c. 1650.
Active in Bruges.
Glass painter.

Karl Ryckx was the son of Jan Ryckx I.

RYCKX, Lambrecht, called Robbesant
Flemish School, 16th century.
Active in Antwerp.
Painter.

Lambrecht Ryckx was the son of Aertsz. Lambert Ryck. He worked in Sweden from 1557 to 1572.

RYCKX, Matthias
Flemish School, 17th century.
Died 1649.
Active in Bruges.
Painter.

Matthias Ryckx was the son of Jan Ryckx I.

RYCKX, Nicolaes, or Rycx
Flemish School, 17th century.
Born 1637, in Bruges; died after 1672, in Bruges.
Painter. Landscapes.

Nicolaes Ryckx was the pupil of Van der Kabel. He returned home in 1664, after a period in Palestine, and was a member of the guild at Bruges in 1667. During his journey to the East, he executed numerous studies and rough drawings of Jerusalem and its surrounding area, as well as Oriental subjects and costumes. This material was used by him, on his return to Holland, in the execution of paintings which were very sought after.

AUCTION RECORDS:
PARIS, 25 June 1996, *Procession of Turks* (oil on canvas, 28 1/4 x 39 1/4 ins / 72 x 100 cm) FRF 310,000.

RYCKX, Paul, the Elder, or Ricx
Flemish School, 17th century.
Born 1612, in Bruges; died 5 March 1668.
Painter. History painting.

Paul Ryckx the Elder was the father of Paul Ryckx the Younger, and the son of Jan Ryckx, as well as probably being his pupil. He was admitted to the guild in Bruges in 1635. In the church of St Saviour in Bruges can be seen his *St Jerome*, signed *P Rycx did this in 1644*.

RYCKX, Paul, the Younger
Flemish School, 17th century.
Born 1649, in Bruges; died 27 March 1690, in Bruges.
Painter.

Paul Ryckx the Younger was the son of Paul Ryckx the Elder, and a member of the guild of painters in the town of his birth. His name is mentioned between 1672 and 1677.

RYCKX, Pieter. See **RYCX**

RYCX, Jan, Lambrecht, Nicolaes and Paul. See **RYCKX**

RYCX, Pieter, or Ryckx or Rijck or Ricx
Dutch, 17th century.
Died in Amsterdam.
Active in Bruges and in Rotterdam from 1658 to 1672.
Sculptor.

Pieter Rycx was very probably related to Jan Rycx. He was in the guild at Delft in 1658, returned to Rotterdam in 1666 and executed there in 1669 the mausoleum of the widow of Cornelis de Witte in the church of St Lawrence. He is remembered for: *St Jerome in the Desert* (Bruges Cathedral) and *Admiral Cornelis de Witte* (Rotterdam).

RYD, Carl Magnus
Swedish, 20th century.
Born 13 August 1883, in Lekaryd; died 1958.
Active in Paris 1909-1911.
Painter. Landscapes.
Unga Group.

AUCTION RECORDS:
GÖTEBORG, 29 March 1973, *Wooded Landscape*, SEK 5,600. GÖTEBORG, 7 Nov 1984, *View of Hamburg* (1918, oil on canvas, 37 1/2 x 43 1/4 ins / 95 x 110 cm) SEK 15,100. STOCKHOLM, 5-6 Dec 1990, *Landscape with Trees and Rocks* (1919, oil on canvas, 31 1/2 x 39 1/4 ins / 80 x 100 cm) SEK 9,500. STOCK-

HOLM, 28 Oct 1991, *After the Storm* (1948, oil on canvas, 14 1/2 x 17 3/4 ins / 37 x 45 cm) SEK 7,000. STOCKHOLM, 13 April 1992, *Snow-Covered Firs* (1925, oil on canvas, 21 1/4 x 17 3/4 ins / 54 x 45 cm) SEK 7,000. STOCKHOLM, 27 Nov 2000, *Landscape with Buildings, Cagnes* (1921, oil on canvas, 26 x 30 ins / 67 x 76 cm) SEK 17,000.

RYDBERG, Gustaf
Swedish, 19th - 20th century.
Born 13 September 1835, in Malmö; died 11 October 1933, in Malmö.
Painter. Landscapes.

Gustaf Rydberg studied at the fine arts academies in Copenhagen and Stockholm. His work was influenced by Corot and by the Impressionists. He is noted particularly for his landscapes of the Skåne region in Sweden.

MUSEUMS AND GALLERIES:
GÖTEBORG - KRISTIANSTAD - LINKÖPING - MALMÖ - NORRKÖPING - STOCKHOLM: *Spring Landscape in Skåne; Tithed Cottage, Skåne; Swedish Landscape.*

AUCTION RECORDS:
STOCKHOLM, 30 Oct 1946, *Mountain Landscape,* DKK 6,200. STOCKHOLM, 31 Jan 1947, *Landscape,* DKK 16,400. STOCKHOLM, 16 Nov 1949, *Farmyard at Dusk,* DKK 2,715. STOCKHOLM, 11 Oct 1950, *Snow-covered Cart* (1874) DKK 3,475. STOCKHOLM, 8 Nov 1972, *River Landscape,* SEK 10,700. GÖTEBORG, 9 Nov 1977, *Railway Station* (1905, oil on canvas, 11 3/4 x 18 ins / 30 x 46 cm) SEK 22,000. GÖTEBORG, 7 Nov 1979, *River Landscape* (1879, oil on canvas, 22 1/2 x 35 ins / 57 x 89 cm) SEK 43,500. STOCKHOLM, 27 Oct 1981, *Landscape with Farm* (1892, oil on canvas, 17 x 24 ins / 43 x 61 cm) SEK 28,000. STOCKHOLM, 30 Oct 1984, *Winter Landscape with Mill* (1873, oil on canvas, 31 1/2 x 44 ins / 80 x 112 cm) SEK 150,000. STOCKHOLM, 17 April 1985, *Village Street with Mill* (1903, oil on canvas, 18 1/2 x 29 1/4 ins / 47 x 74 cm) SEK 76,000. STOCKHOLM, 22 April 1986, *Summer Landscape* (1905, oil on canvas, 20 1/2 x 33 1/2 ins / 52 x 85 cm) SEK 180,000. STOCKHOLM, 13 Nov 1987, *Winter Landscape with Mill* (oil on panel, 9 3/4 x 13 3/4 ins / 25 x 35 cm) SEK 77,000. STOCKHOLM, 15 Nov 1988, *Seaside and Fishermen* (oil, 9 3/4 x 11 ins / 25 x 28 cm) SEK 8,000. LONDON, 16 March 1989, *Coastal Landscape* (1900, oil on canvas, 14 1/4 x 22 ins / 36.1 x 55.8 cm) GBP 6,050. STOCKHOLM, 16 May 1990, *Cattle Slaking Their Thirst at a Tree-lined Stream* (oil on canvas, 14 1/2 x 20 1/2 ins / 37 x 52 cm) SEK 55,000. STOCKHOLM, 14 Nov 1990, *Summer Landscape in Sweden with a Small House Surrounded by Trees* (oil on canvas, 15 3/4 x 24 1/2 ins / 40 x 62 cm) SEK 33,000. STOCKHOLM, 29 May 1991, *Summer Landscape with a Thatched Cottage amongst Trees* (oil on canvas, 15 3/4 x 24 1/2 ins / 40 x 62 cm) SEK 35,000. STOCKHOLM, 19 May 1992, *Young Girl with a Sled on a Snow-covered Path* (oil on panel, 14 1/4 x 17 3/4 ins / 36 x 45 cm) SEK 22,000.

RYDE, Aegidius de, or Rye or Ruehe
Flemish School, 16th century.
Born in the Netherlands; died 30 November 1605.
Painter, fresco artist. Religious subjects.

Aegidius de Ryde painted frescoes in the chapel of Duke Charles I's castle in Graz.

Ey. de Ryd 1597

MUSEUMS AND GALLERIES:
VIENNA (Kunsthistorisches Mus.): *Entombment of St Catherine* (1597).

RYDEN, Henning
Swedish, 19th - 20th century.
Born 21 January 1869, in Sweden.
Active in the USA.
Painter, medallist. Portraits, landscapes.

Henning Ryden studied at the Art Institute of Chicago and also in Berlin and London. He was a member of the Salmagundi Club (1908) and the American Arts Federation. Examples of his work featured at the American Society of Numismatology.

RYDER, Albert Pinkham
American, 19th - 20th century.
Born 19 March 1847, in New Bedford (Massachusetts); died 28 March 1917, in Elmhurst (New York).
Painter, writer. Figures, landscapes, seascapes. Symbolism.

Albert Pinkham Ryder was born and brought up in the whaling port made famous by Herman Melville, but came with his family to New York in 1867. He received advice from the engraver William E. Marshall, who had studied in Paris. In 1972 he enrolled at the National Academy in New York. In 1877 he was one of the founders of the Society of American Artists; in 1902 became an associate member of the National Academy and a full member in 1906. He was awarded a silver medal in Buffalo in 1901. He travelled to Europe on several occasions but gradually abandoned painting.

A contemporary of Van Gogh and of Gauguin, Ryder did not belong to any movement, although he was closest to the syntheticism of the Nabis and Symbolists. His trips to Europe do not appear to have opened his eyes in any significant way to the pictorial movements of the age. He remained obdurately independent, refusing to ask for advice, inventing adventurous techniques - even painting directly on to panels torn from his bed when he had no canvases left. Always unhappy with his results, he refused to sell his paintings and would rework them again and again, so that of the 150 or so of his works that remain, none has survived intact. These include dream scenes, tumultuous seas, patches of mysterious undergrowth - as in *Forest of Arden, Siegfried and the Rhine Maidens* - often inspired by the literary works of Chaucer, Edgar Allen Poe and Shakespeare. His subject-matter functions purely as a symbol for his own feelings, in the same way that his use of colour and the play between shades of different intensities acts as a synaesthetic expression of his emotions. Totally indifferent to the way colours can imitate reality, Ryder expressed himself instead through tragic landscapes, transmuting the profundity of nature and dramatic scenes, as in his portrayal of the suicide of a friend. Reality is made to conform to the simple lines of his essential rhythms, which come close to Abstraction. Significantly, Jackson Pollock acknowledged Ryder as the sole American painter in whose work he was interested. Typical works include Death on a *Pale Horse and Moonlight Over the Sea.*

BIBLIOGRAPHY:
Price, Frederic Newlin, *Ryder, 1847-1917: a study in appreciation*, W.E. Rudge, New York, 1932. Goodrich, Lloyd, *'Albert P. Ryder'* in *coll. The Great American artists series*, G. Braziller, New York, 1959. Broun, Elizabeth/Jones, Eleanor L., *Albert Pinkham Ryder*, exhibition catalogue, National Museum of American Art, Smithsonian Institution Press, Washington DC, 1989. Homer, William Innes, *Albert Pinkham Ryder: Painter of Dreams*, Abrams, New York, 1989. Zalesh, Saul, *'Ryder among the writers: friendship and patronage in the New York art world'* in *2 vol.*, dissertation, University of Delaware, 1992. Johnson, Diane Chalmers, *American Symbolist Art. Nineteenth-Century Poets in Paint: Washington Allston, John La Farge, William Rimmer, George Inness and Albert Pinkham Ryder*, Edwin Mellen Press, Lewiston (NY), 2004.

MUSEUMS AND GALLERIES:
BOSTON (MFA): *Constance* - BUFFALO (Albright-Knox AG): *Temple of the Spirit* (1885) - CLEVELAND (MA): *Racecourse or Death on a Pale Horse* (1895-1910) - DETROIT (IA): *Storm* - NEW YORK (Metropolitan Mus. of Art): *Curfew; Toilers of the Sea; Moonlight Over the Sea* (1870-1890); *Forest of Arden* - WASHINGTON DC (NGA): *Mending the Harness* (1875-1879, oil on canvas); *Siegfried and the Rhine Maidens* (1888-1891,

oil on canvas) - WASHINGTON DC (Phillips Collection): *Dead Bird* - WASHINGTON DC (Smithsonian American AM): *Panel for a Screen: Woman with a Deer* (c. 1876, oil/gilded leather); *Moonlight* (1887, oil on mahogany, cradled); *Pastoral Study* (1897, oil/canvas/fiberboard) - WORCESTER (AM): *The Wood Road* (*The Wood Road*) (oil on canvas); *Joan of Arc* (*Joan of Arc*) (oil on canvas); *Pegasus* (*Pegasus*) (oil on canvas).

AUCTION RECORDS:

NEW YORK, 10 and 11 April 1907, *Dancing Dryads,* USD 350; *In the Stable,* USD 325; *Pegasus,* USD 1,225. NEW YORK, 11 and 12 March 1909, *Curfew Time,* USD 560; *Rising Moon,* USD 1,000. NEW YORK, 27 and 28 March 1930, *Sailboats in the Moonlight,* USD 1,600. NEW YORK, 7 Nov 1935, *Autumn Idyll,* USD 1,100. NEW YORK, 14 Jan 1938, *Stone House in Autumn,* USD 650. NEW YORK, 18-20 Nov 1943, *Sea by Moonlight,* USD 1,800. NEW YORK, 4 May 1945, *Landscape,* USD 300; *Homecoming,* USD 1,650. NEW YORK, 24 Jan 1946, *Moonlight Over the Sea,* USD 6,200; *Siegfried and the Rhine Maidens,* USD 23,500. NEW YORK, 20 and 21 Feb 1946, *Storm,* USD 7,000. NEW YORK, 26 and 27 Feb 1947, *Spirit of Autumn,* USD 850. NEW YORK, 9 and 10 April 1947, *Hay Meadow,* USD 1,150. LONDON, 22 April 1959, *Merlin and Vivien,* USD 200. LONDON, 26 July 1961, *Merlin and Vivien,* USD 850. NEW YORK, 15 Nov 1967, *Landscape,* USD 13,500. LONDON, 24 Oct 1968, *Farmer in His Field,* USD 15,000. LONDON, 27 June 1972, *Seascape,* Gns 16,000. NEW YORK, 11 April 1973, *Plodding Homeward,* USD 14,500. MUNICH, 24 May 1976, *Farmyard* (watercolour, 6 3/4 x 9 1/4 ins / 17.2 x 23.3 cm) DEM 4,300.

RYDER, Chauncey Foster

American, 19th - 20th century.

Born 29 February 1868, in Danbury (Connecticut); died 1949.

Painter, engraver. Landscapes.

Chauncey Foster Ryder studied at the Chicago Art Institute and at the Académie Julian in Paris, and was also the pupil of Collin and Jean-Paul Laurens. He was a member of the Salmagundi Club and of the American Arts Federation. He lived and worked in New York. He specialised in painting winter landscapes. He also produced etchings.

He won several prizes, including an honourable mention at the Salon de Paris in 1907, and a silver medal at the San Francisco Exhibition in 1915.

MUSEUMS AND GALLERIES:

NEW YORK (Metropolitan Mus. of Art): *Mount Mansfield, Vermont* - WASHINGTON DC (NGA): *French Hill* (1942, drypoint).

AUCTION RECORDS:

NEW YORK, 21 Nov 1945, *Path in the Middle of the Fields,* USD 650. NEW YORK, 26 and 27 Feb 1947, *A Valley,* USD 400. LOS ANGELES, 5 March 1974, *Sailboats in Harbour,* USD 650. NEW YORK, 30 Jan 1976, *House in a Clearing* (oil on canvas, 32 x 40 ins / 81.5 x 101.5 cm) USD 1,900. NEW YORK, 18 Nov 1977, *Seaside* (oil on canvas, 25 x 30 ins / 63.5 x 76.2 cm) USD 1,800. LOS ANGELES, 17 March 1980, *Glade* (oil on canvas, 40 x 32 ins / 101.5 x 81 cm) USD 5,000. NEW YORK, 24 April 1981, *Black Mountain* (oil on canvas, 28 1/4 x 36 ins / 71.7 x 91.7 cm) USD 7,000. NEW YORK, 3 June 1983, *Road to Raymond* (oil on canvas/panel, 28 1/4 x 36 1/4 ins / 71.5 x 92.1 cm) USD 32,000. NEW YORK, 6 Dec 1985, *Tyringham Valley* (oil on canvas, 24 3/4 x 29 3/4 ins / 62.7 x 75.7 cm) USD 15,000. NEW YORK, 14 March 1986, *The Sand Hill* (oil on canvas, 32 x 44 ins / 81.4 x 112 cm) USD 8,000. NEW YORK, 20 March 1987, *Unaka Forest, Tennessee* (oil on canvas, 28 x 36 ins / 71.4 x 91.7 cm) USD 9,000. NEW YORK, 24 June 1988, *Cabin at Bear Creek* (oil on canvas, 24 1/2 x 29 1/2 ins / 62.5 x 75 cm) USD 12,100. NEW YORK, 24 Jan 1989, *Moonlight* (oil on canvas, 15 3/4 x 19 3/4 ins / 40 x 50 cm) USD 7,700. NEW YORK, 25 May 1989, *Squaw Mountain* (oil on canvas, 32 x 40 ins / 81.5 x 101.6 cm) USD 13,200. NEW YORK, 16 March 1990, *On the Edge of the Wood* (oil on canvas, 32 x 39 1/2 ins / 81.3 x 100.3 cm) USD 23,100. NEW YORK, 27 Sept 1990, *Onset of Winter* (oil on canvas, 28 x 36 1/4 ins / 71 x 91.8 cm) USD 7,480. NEW YORK, 14 March 1991, *Waterville Farm* (oil on canvas, 22 1/4 x 28 1/4 ins / 56.5 x 72 cm) USD 5,500. NEW YORK, 26 Sept 1991, *Deep Valley* (oil on canvas/panel, 25 x 30 ins / 63.5 x 76.5 cm) USD 9,900. NEW YORK, 18 Dec 1991, *Path Leading to the Hay Field* (oil on canvas, 12 x 16 ins / 30.5 x 40.6 cm) USD 2,310. NEW YORK, 12 March 1992, *Hills in Autumn* (oil on canvas/synthetic resin/panel, 21 x 30 ins / 53.6 x 76.2 cm) USD 6,600. NEW YORK, 28 May 1992, *The Old Road* (oil on canvas/synthetic resin, 25 x 30 ins / 63.7 x 76.5 cm) USD 8,800. NEW YORK, 3 Dec 1993, *Spring Landscape, Old Lyme, Connecticut* (oil on canvas, 25 x 30 ins / 63.5 x 76 cm) USD 19,550. NEW YORK, 14 March 1996, *Hoosatonic Mountain* (oil on canvas, 32 x 44 ins / 81.3 x 111.8 cm) USD 9,775. NEW YORK, 3 Dec 1996, *Landscape* (oil/Masonite, 12 x 16 ins / 30.5 x 40.5 cm) USD 3,450; *On the Beach* (oil on panel, 9 3/4 x 13 ins / 24.8 x 33 cm) USD 8,625. NEW YORK, 30 Sept 1997, *In April* (oil on canvas, 20 x 24 ins / 50.8 x 61 cm) USD 9,200. NEW YORK, 26 May 1999, *U Road Pastures, 1927* (oil on canvas, 25 x 30 ins / 64 x 76 cm) USD 6,750. NEW YORK, 29 Sept 1999, *Mount Lovewell* (oil on canvas, 44 x 56 ins / 112 x 143 cm) USD 9,500. MILFORD, 11 May 2000, *Early Fall* (oil on canvas, 24 x 20 ins / 61 x 51 cm) USD 7,500. NEW YORK, 15 June 2000, *Low Tide at Cape Porpoise* (oil on canvas, 25 x 30 ins / 63 x 76 cm) USD 7,500. LOS ANGELES, 2 May 2001, *Hilltops* (oil on canvas, 25 x 30 ins / 63 x 76 cm) USD 8,000. NEW YORK, 13 June 2001, *Brick House, Mount Vernon, New Hampshire* (oil on canvas over panel, 10 x 28 ins / 26 x 71 cm) USD 6,500. PHILADELPHIA, 23 June 2002, *Mountain Range with Trees in the Foreground* (oil on canvasboard, 12 x 16 ins / 30 x 41 cm) USD 3,750. DETROIT, 18 Oct 2002, *Landscape* (oil on canvas, 12 x 16 ins / 30 x 41 cm) USD 4,000. SAN FRANCISCO, 11 June 2003, *Amherst Road* (oil on canvas, 12 x 16 ins / 30 x 41 cm) USD 10,000. NEW YORK, 9 Oct 2003, *Village in the Valley* (oil on canvas over panel, 25 x 30 ins / 63 x 76 cm) USD 8,500. NEW YORK, 11 March 2004, *Sand Hill* (oil on canvas, 32 x 44 ins / 82 x 112 cm) USD 15,000. BOSTON, 10 Sept 2004, *Pastures of Egremont* (oil on canvas, 28 x 36 ins / 71 x 91 cm) USD 9,000.

RYDER, Platt Powell

American, 19th century.

Born 11 June 1821, in Brooklyn; died 1896, in New York.

Painter. Portraits, genre scenes.

Plath Powell Ryder studied under Léon Bonnat in Paris, and became an associate of the National Academy of Design in New York in 1868.

MUSEUMS AND GALLERIES:

NEW YORK (Metropolitan Mus. of Art): *Portrait of George P. Putnam.*

AUCTION RECORDS:

NEW YORK, 8 Feb 1907, *Giving Instructions,* USD 30. NEW YORK, 21 Oct 1982, *Portrait of a Black Nanny* (1887, oil on board, 12 1/4 x 9 1/4 ins / 31.1 x 23.2 cm) USD 2,800. SAN FRANCISCO, 21 June 1984, *In the Corner of the Fire* (1881, oil on canvas, 12 x 14 ins / 30.5 x 35.5 cm) USD 4,750. NEW YORK, 17 March 1988, *Woman Knitting by a Window* (watercolour and gouache, 7 1/2 x 11 1/4 ins / 19.3 x 28.7 cm) USD 2,530. NEW YORK, 14 Sept 1995, *Mamma Lecturing her Son* (1868, oil on canvas, 17 x 14 ins / 43.2 x 35.6 cm) USD 7,475. PARIS, 19 Feb 1996, *Woman in a Chair Reading* (oil on canvas, 26 x 19 1/4 ins / 66 x 49 cm) FRF 22,000.

RYDER, Thomas I

British, 18th - 19th century.

Born 1746, in London; died 1810.
Engraver (burin).
Thomas Ryder was the father of Thomas Ryder and pupil of James Basire. He was an exhibitor at the Free Society in London in 1766 and 1767, and was noted for a portrait of *Queen Charlotta Sophia*.

RYDER, Thomas II
British, 18th - 19th century.
Engraver (burin).
Thomas Ryder II was the son of Thomas Ryder.

RYDGE, Richard
British, 16th century.
Active in London c. 1535.
Engraver (wood).
Richard Rydge worked at the court of the King Henry VIII of England.

RYDING, Caroline Mathilde
Danish, 19th century.
Born 1780, in Copenhagen.
Painter. Flowers.
Caroline Ryding worked in Christianfeld in Slesvig.

RYDINGSVÄRD, Johan Henrik
Swedish, 19th century.
Born 27 September 1796, in Färgelanda; died 8 January 1839.
Painter.
Records show that in 1831, Rydingsvärd was a member of the Kungliga Akademi för de Fria Konsterna in Stockholm.

RYE, Aegid de. See **RYDE Aegidius de**

RYE, Andres Pedersen
Norwegian, 19th century.
Sculptor (wood).
Pedersen sculpted decorative figures in wood for the church in Valdres, in 1850.

RYE, Margriete van. See **RIE Marguerite van**

RYE, William Brenchley
British, 19th century.
Born 26 January 1818, in Rochester; died 21 December 1901, in West Norwood.
Engraver (etching).
The British Museum houses three volumes of illustrations by Rye, produced in part to accompany his own writings.
MUSEUMS AND GALLERIES:
LONDON (British Mus.).

RYERSON, Margery Austen
American, 20th century.
Born 15 September 1886, in Morristown; died 1989, in Rye Brook (New York).
Painter, engraver.
Margery Austen Ryerson was the pupil of Robert and Charles W. Hawthorne. She was a member of the Washington Watercolorists Club.
MUSEUMS AND GALLERIES:
FLORENCE (Uffizi) - PARIS (BNF).

RYFF, Andreas
Swiss, 16th century.
Active in Basel at the end of the 16th century.
Miniaturist.
Andreas Ryff decorated a Swiss chronicle (dated 1597) with miniatures and coats of arms.

RYFFEL, Martin
Swiss, 19th century.
Born c. 1795, in Stäfa; died 1839, in Trieste (?).
Miniaturist. Portraits.

RYGIER, Maria
French, 20th century.
Painter (gouache), engraver, sculptor. Landscapes. Murals.
Maria Rygier was a pupil of Georges d'Espagnat, Ducos de la Haille, Charles Despiau, Bertrand, Cami, Jaudon, and of the École des Beaux-Arts, Paris, and the Académie de la Grande Chaumière. During World War II she worked on subjects related to the Resistance, Paris under the occupation and the liberation. She carried out many public commissions, including mural decoration and mosaics for nursery schools. She exhibited in Paris from 1939 at the Salon des Indépendants, from 1953 at the Salon d'Automne, in 1975 at the Salon des Femmes Peintres and in 1978 at the Salon des Artistes Français. In 1980, she exhibited at the Office Culturel in Brie. She exhibited solo from 1942 in Paris, mainly at the Galerie Marcel Bernheim, in 1968 at the Centre Municipal in Argenteuil, in 1965 and 1968 in Banyuls-sur-Mer, in 1971 in Bonn and in 1972 in London.
MUSEUMS AND GALLERIES:
PARIS (Mus. Carnavalet) - PARIS (Mus. National du Sport) - WARSAW (Muz. Narodowe): *Lavandou Landscape*.

RYGIER, Theodor or Teodor
Polish, 19th - 20th century.
Born 9 November 1841, in Warsaw; died 18 December 1913, in Rome.
Sculptor. Monuments.
The Mickiewicz monument in Cracow is by Theodor Rygier.
MUSEUMS AND GALLERIES:
CRACOW: *Queen of Heaven*; *Bacchante*; *Bust of Meleiko* (marble); *Bust of Krasrevski* (bronze); *Bust of Copernicus* (bronze); *Bust of a Woman* - LVIV (Gallery of Paintings): *Modesty*; *Lute Player* - POZNAN (Muz. Mielzynskich): *Busts of J. Kossak and T. Lenartowicz* - WARSAW (Muz. Narodowe): *Busts of Copernicus and King Stanislas Augustus*; *The Architect A. Corazzi*.

RYK. See **RYCK**

RYKAERT, David I. See **RYCKAERT**

RYKE, Catharina de. See the entry **DERYKE William** or **Willem**

RYKE, Daniel de, or Rycke or Ricke or Rike or Ryckere or Ricken
Flemish School, 15th century.
Born in Ghent.
Active 1440-1482.
Painter.
Daniel de Ryke was a member of the guild in 1440 and was made a juror in 1455. He worked for the marriage celebrations of Charles the Rash in 1468 and for his visit to Ghent in 1469. According to Michiels, the Munich *Annunciation* usually attributed to Hugo van der Goes is in fact by Daniel de Ryke.

RYKE, William or Willem de. See **DERYKE**

RYKENROYEN, Jean van. See **REKENROY**

RYKENS, Pieter
Dutch, 17th century.
Active in Dordrecht in 1682.
Painter.

RYKR, Zdenek
Czech, 20th century.
Born 20 October 1900, in Chotebor; died 1940.
Painter. Stage costumes and sets.
Zdenek Rykr studied philosophy and archaeology and travelled widely in Europe. His pictorial compositions were often inspired by stage sets and costumes, placing poorly defined figures in situations inspired by Surrealism. Zdenek Rykr exhibited on several occasions, particularly in Prague,

including an important exhibition in 1937; he featured in exhibitions abroad notable at the Exposition Internationale, Paris (1937).

BIBLIOGRAPHY:

Fifty years of Czechoslovak Painting from the Collections of the Galleries, 1918-1958, exhibition catalogue, Slovenska Narodna Gal., Bratislava, 1968 (in commemoration of the 50th anniversary of the Republic of Czechoslovakia).

RYLAND, Adolfine

British, 20th century.
Born 14 March 1903, in Windsor.
Sculptor.

Adolfine Ryland trained at Heatherley's School of Art from 1920 to 1925. She exhibited at the Women's International Art Club from 1927, and became a member in 1936.

MUSEUMS AND GALLERIES:

LONDON (Tate Collection): *Isaac Wounds Jacob* (1933).

RYLAND, Edward

British, 18th century.
Born in Wales; died 26 July 1771, in London.
Engraver, printer.

Edward Ryland was the father of William Wynne Ryland.

RYLAND, Henry

British, 19th - 20th century.
Born 1856, in Biggleswade; died 23 November 1924, in London.
Painter, draughtsman, watercolourist. Figures, genre scenes.

Henry Ryland studied in Paris under Benjamin-Constant, Boulanger, Lefebvre and Ferdinand Cormon. He was influenced by Rossetti and the Pre-Raphelites. He contributed to the *English Illustrated Magazine.*

HENRY RYLAND

AUCTION RECORDS:

LONDON, 25 June 1926, *Gathering Oranges* (drawing) GBP 14. NEW YORK, 28 April 1977, *The Dreamer* (1901, oil on canvas, 56 x 22 ins / 142 x 56 cm) USD 2,250. NEW YORK, 23 Jan 1980, *Beatrice* (1907, watercolour/plaster background, panel, 26 x 17 1/2 ins / 66 x 44.5 cm) USD 7,000. LONDON, 15 June 1982, *Dorothea and the Roses* (oil on panel, 20 x 14 1/2 ins / 51 x 37 cm) GBP 5,000. ENGHIEN-LES-BAINS, 24 March 1984, *Woman at the Fountain* (watercolour and gouache, 30 x 14 ins / 76 x 35.5 cm) FRF 65,000. LONDON, 30 May 1985, *Woman and Child Making Laurel Wreaths* (watercolour heightened with white/mounted paper/card, 30 x 19 ins / 76 x 48 cm) GBP 2,200. LONDON, 16 Dec 1986, *Oceanid* (1899, watercolour and pencil heightened with white, 28 3/4 x 21 ins / 73 x 53.5 cm) GBP 2,000. LONDON, 21 June 1989, *Dante's Vision* (gouache, 7 x 10 ins / 18 x 25.5 cm) GBP 2,200. LONDON, 1 Dec 1989, *St Cecilia* (ceramic on terracotta, 10 3/4 x 7 1/2 ins / 27.5 x 19 cm) GBP 2,420. LONDON, 8 Feb 1991, *The Little Goatherd* (watercolour/card, 17 x 8 1/4 ins / 43.3 x 21.2 cm) GBP 1,540. LONDON, 29 Oct 1991, *Surprised* (pencil and watercolour, 14 1/2 x 20 3/4 ins / 36.9 x 52.7 cm) GBP 1,320. LONDON, 3 June 1992, *Greeting* (watercolour, 14 1/2 x 20 3/4 ins / 37 x 53 cm) GBP 4,400. NEW YORK, 29 Oct 1992, *Archangel* (1887, oil on panel, 19 1/2 x 9 1/4 ins / 49.5 x 23.5 cm) USD 7,150. LONDON, 8-9 June 1993, *Compliment* (watercolour, 14 1/2 x 20 3/4 ins / 37 x 53 cm) GBP 5,290. NEW YORK, 15 Oct 1993, *Dancing to Song* (watercolour and pencil/paper, 15 1/4 x 21 1/2 ins / 38.5 x 54.3 cm) USD 2,530. LONDON, 2 Nov 1994, *Dreamer* (1901, oil on canvas, 57 x 22 ins / 145 x 56 cm) GBP 20,700. LONDON, 4 Nov 1994, *Iris (Irises, Portrait of a Young Woman)* (pencil and watercolour, 14 1/2 x 8 1/4 ins / 36.9 x 21.2 cm) GBP 3,220. LONDON, 14 March 1997, *Idle Moments* (pencil and watercolour heightened with white, 14 1/2 x 30 3/4 ins / 37 x 78.2 cm) GBP 17,250. LONDON, 6 June 1997, *Reflections* (pencil and watercolour, 20 1/4 x 14 3/4 ins / 51.5 x 37.5 cm) GBP 6,325. NEW YORK, 22 Oct 1997, *Summer Afternoon* (watercolour/paper, 15 x 21 1/4 ins / 38.1 x 54 cm) USD 14,375. LONDON, 5 Nov 1997, *Torn Robe* (watercolour, 22 x 15 ins / 56 x 38 cm) GBP 6,900.

RYLAND, Joseph

British, 18th century.
Active in London in 1775.
Miniaturist. Portraits.

Joseph Ryland is in all likelihood identical with the wax sculptor, cold-chisel engraver and portraitist J. Ryland who is on record as having been active in London between 1757 and 1790.

RYLAND, Robert Knight

American, 20th century.
Born 10 February 1873, in Grenada (Mississippi); died 1951, in Washington DC.
Painter, fresco artist, illustrator.

Robert Ryland studied at the Bethel College in Kentucky, the Art Students League, the National Academy of Design in New York and the American academy in Rome. His reputation was enhanced as a result of his contribution to New York World's Fair in 1939-1940. He was a member of the Salmagundi Club.

MUSEUMS AND GALLERIES:

NEWARK.

AUCTION RECORDS:

NEW YORK, 13 June 1980, *Female Bather* (1922, oil on canvas, 36 1/4 x 25 ins / 92.1 x 63.5 cm) USD 4,000. NEW YORK, 30 Sept 1988, *Striped Dress* (1940, oil on card, 25 x 20 ins / 63.5 x 51 cm) USD 2,090. NEW YORK, 12 March 1992, *No Room in Manhattan* (oil on card, 16 x 13 ins / 40.7 x 33 cm) USD 2,200.

RYLAND, William Wynne

British, 18th century.
Born 1732, in London; died 29 August 1783, in London, sentenced to death.
Engraver, illustrator.

William Wynne Ryland was a most accomplished artist. Initially a pupil of François Ravenet, who had settled in London at the time, Ryland subsequently went to Paris and worked with Roubillac and J.P. Lebas. He lived in Paris for five years before returning to London, where he enjoyed virtually overnight success and was retained as an engraver to the court.

He employed etching, cold-chisel, pencil-point and pointillist techniques to engrave from originals by the likes of Angelica Kauffmann and Cipriani. He contributed no fewer than 57 engravings to the splendid *Collection of Prints in Imitation of Drawings,* a two-volume work published by Charles Rogers.

Ryland appeared to have no financial worries, bearing in mind his generous retainer from the crown and a considerable income from the sale of his etchings. He spent an exorbitant amount of money on a young lady, however, and was foolish enough to forge banknotes. He was arrested and convicted of what was at the time a capital offence. Despite the intercession of his friends, he was hanged on August 29, 1783 in London.

MUSEUMS AND GALLERIES:

LONDON (British Mus.): illustrations in Indian ink for Fielding's 'Tom Jones'.

AUCTION RECORDS:

LONDON, 13 Nov 1997, *Britannia dedicating Painting, Sculpture and Architecture to the Munificence of the Crown* (drypoint engraving, mezzotint, fifteen items) GBP 3,680.

RYLANDER, Carl Isak
Swedish, 19th century.
Born 1779; died 1810, in Göteborg.
Miniaturist.
Rylander is known to have been a pupil at the Kungliga Akademi för de Fria Konsterna in Stockholm.
MUSEUMS AND GALLERIES:
GÖTEBORG: *Portraits of the Consul Wendler and His Wife* - STOCKHOLM: *Portrait of General H. Morner Aged 57; Portrait of an Unknown Lady*.

RYLANDER, Hans Christian
Danish, 20th century.
Born 1939, in Copenhagen.
Painter. Figures.
Hans Christian Rylander studied between 1965 and 1968 under Egill Jacobsen at the Kongelige Danske Kunstakademi in Copenhagen. He became a member of the Colorists group in 1968 and of the Decembrists group from 1969. His paintings are disturbing and even morbid - disjointed and superficially coarse compositions where perspectives are dislocated and faces and figures depersonalised. Rylander's work has featured at group exhibitions, starting with the Copenhagen Autumn Salon of 1963 and followed by appearances at *Danish Art*, held at the Haus am Lützowplatz in West Berlin in 1967, *Contemporary Art* at the Athenaeum in Helsinki in 1968, the 1969 Youth Biennale (where he was an award winner), and *Art Danois* (*Danish Art*), held in 1973 at the Galeries Nationales du Grand Palais in Paris.
BIBLIOGRAPHY:
Galy-Carles, Henry, *Art danois, 1945-1973*, exhibition catalogue, Gal. nationales du Grand Palais, Paris, 1973.
MUSEUMS AND GALLERIES:
COPENHAGEN (Statens Mus. for Kunst): *Shrew Store* (1968-1969) - RANDERS (Kunstmus.): *Theatrical Pose in a Landscape Setting* (1967).

RYLE, Arthur Johnston
British, 19th - 20th century.
Born 10 September 1857; died 25 March 1915, in Dornoch.
Painter, watercolourist. Landscapes, portraits.
The son of the Bishop of Liverpool, John Charles Ryle, himself a portrait painter, Arthur Johnston Ryle was educated at Eton and for a short time at New College, Oxford. He lived in London and in Dornoch.
Ryle showed *Torish, Helmsdale* in 1891 and *Harbour and Hillside* in 1903 at the Royal Academy, London. He also featured in exhibitions of the Society of British Artists and of the New Gallery in London.

RYLEY. See also **RILEY**

RYLEY, Charles Reuben, or Riley
British, 18th century.
Born c. 1752, in London; died 1 October 1798, in London.
Painter, illustrator, engraver (burin). History painting.
Charles Ryley started out as a moderately successful engraver before going on to study painting under Mortimer. He exhibited at the Royal Academy from 1780. He taught drawing and composition and illustrated several works. He is noted above all for his decorations at the Earl of Richmond's residence, Goodwood House.
MUSEUMS AND GALLERIES:
LONDON (British Mus.): five drawings.
AUCTION RECORDS:
NEW YORK, 15 Feb 1973, *Battle Scene (Bender)*, USD 2,500.

RYLEY, Edward
British, 19th century.
Active in London from 1833 to 1837.
Sculptor. Figures. Busts.
MUSEUMS AND GALLERIES:
LIVERPOOL: *Bust of the Reverend James Martineau*.

RYLEY, John. See **RILEY**

RYLEY, Thomas
British, 18th century.
Active from 1744 to 1755.
Engraver (mezzotint).

RYLL, Andreas. See **RIEHL**

RYLOV, Arkadi Aleksandrovich, or Ryloff
Russian, 20th century.
Born 1870, in Istobenskoe; died 1939, in Leningrad (now St Petersburg).
Painter. Figure compositions, landscapes.
Socialist Realism.
Association of Artists of Revolutionary Russia (AKhRR).
Arkadi Aleksandrovich Rylov trained first at the Stieglitz School 1888, at the Society for the Encouragement of the Arts in St Petersburg from 1888 to 1891, then with Arkhip Kuindzhi at the art academy in St Petersburg from 1894 to 1897. He was a member of the Mir Iskusstva (World of Art) and of the Association of Artists of Revolutionary Russia (AKHRR) and travelled to Germany, France and England in 1898. He painted landscapes as well as scenes from the Revolutionary period and from life in a Socialist society.
Rylov took part in collective exhibitions with a number of groups including: 36 Artists (1901-1902); Mir Izkousstva Mir Izkousstva (World of Art) (1901 to 1911); New Association of Russian Artists (1905 to 1909); Community of Artists (1908); Sixteen (1922 to 1927); Association of Artists of Revolutionary Russia (1926); A. Kuindzhi Society (1919-1920). He featured in: *Paris-Moscow*, Centre Georges-Pompidou, Paris (1979); *Les Années trente en Europe. Le temps menaçant* (*Europe in the 1930s: The Gathering Storm*), Musée d'Art moderne de la Ville de Paris (1997). He occasionally signed his work *Rylof*.
BIBLIOGRAPHY:
Paris-Moscou, 1900-1930, exhibition catalogue, Éd. du Centre Georges-Pompidou, Paris, 1979. Pagé, Suzanne/Winock, Michel/Michaud, Éric/Vidal, Aline, *Les Années trente en Europe. Le Temps menaçant*, exhibition catalogue, Musée d'Art moderne de la Ville de Paris, Paris musées, Flammarion, Paris, 1997.
MUSEUMS AND GALLERIES:
MOSCOW (State Tretyakov Gal.) - ST PETERSBURG (Gosudarstvennyj Russkij Muz.): *Lenin at Sunset in 1917* (1934); *Islet* (1922); *Mouth of the River Orlinka* (1928).
AUCTION RECORDS:
LONDON, 15 June 1995, *Seaside* (gouache and pencil, 10 x 13 1/4 ins / 25.5 x 33.5 cm) GBP 1,610. LONDON, 7 July 2000, *Wooded Landscape with River* (oil on canvas on board, 12 x 16 ins / 30 x 40 cm) GBP 2,200. PARIS, 9 June 2004, *Country Landscape* (1925, oil on cardboard, 13 x 19 ins / 33 x 47 cm) EUR 4,100.

RYLSKI
Polish, 18th century.
Active c. 1769.
Painter. Religious subjects.
The church in Sieciechóv owns one of his works, *Ten Thousand Martyrs*, signed *Pinxit Rylski An. 1769*.

RYLSKY, François
French, 20th century.
Born 1901, in Paris.
Painter.
François Rylsky exhibited at the Salon d'Automne and the Salon des Indépendants, Paris.

RYM, Jacques I
Flemish School, 15th - 16th century.
Active in Ghent.
Sculptor.
Jacques Rym I was the father of Jacques Rym II.

RYM, Jacques II, or Remey or Remyn
Flemish School, 16th century.
Active in Ghent during the first half of the 16th century.
Sculptor.
Jacques Rym II was the son of Jacques Rym I. He carved the stalls in the church of Axel in 1519.

RYMAN, Robert
American, 20th century.
Born 1930, in Nashville (Tennessee).
Painter, engraver.
Minimal Art.
Robert Ryman arrived in New York in the 1950s after completing his military service, hoping to follow a career as a jazz musician. Self-taught, his initiation into contemporary art was due primarily to his job as a museum guard at the prestigious Museum of Modern Art in New York. There he met Dan Flavin and Sol Le Witt and struck up a friendship with them both. He also enrolled in the Black Mountain College. In about 1955 he decided to become a professional painter.

Since his early years as a painter, Ryman chose to pursue Abstract art. In his first paintings, small format works on canvas or paper, he superimposed colour upon colour. The style of his works was gestural, punctuated with brushstrokes or regular lines, the paint thick or scumbled. This sort of experimentation helped him to establish his direction: he insisted that 'The question is never one of knowing what to paint but only how to paint. The how of painting has always been the image.' Some people deduce from this that Ryman therefore reduced his art to a process - the square as a measure of the format and often shape, the colour white used exclusively to work the surfaces, rapidly determining the broad orientations of his art. He sometimes exploited the constituent elements of the picture, such as his signature and the year of execution, which are made bigger, centered or inserted along the sides. He also concerns himself with the borders of the image, incorporating the edges of the picture into the canvas itself (1958) or folding the traditionally fixed edges of the canvas over and behind the frame (1962).

Meanwhile, he frequently changed the medium of his surfaces: from 1976 Ryman perfected a visible hanging system, a series of small metallic rods by which he could play with the relationships within the picture itself or between the picture and the wall. Some of these supports even transformed his works into three-dimensional objects. From 1965 his painting evolved in a more systematic fashion. Between 1967 and 1975, perhaps under the influence of Minimal Art, Ryman executed several series of paintings on metal or using white paint on wooden panels. Also at this time he began to give titles to his works, using names unrelated to their subject-matter, such as *Essex*, 1968; *Criterion*, 1976; *Archive*, 1980; *Dial*, 1980.

With Ryman, the colour white in itself has no value, or rather it exists in an infinite variety of different shades depending on the different textures, the way in which it is applied and the medium on to which it is applied. This colour also reacts with subtle variations and in close relationship with the environment in which his paintings are hung. The combinations are constantly renewed. Ryman likes to vary the media he uses - fabric, linen, cotton, paper, wood, metal, Plexiglas or glass fibre - which in turn influence the texture of the pigment (oil, gouache, casein, enamel).

Ryman began painting at the height of the Abstract Expressionist period, the so-called post-pictorial era in the USA, at a time when Minimal Art was already making an appearance. His primarily concern was with Minimalism, even though he never proclaimed any related theories; in fact, some point to an absence of ideology in Ryman. In fact, all Ryman's artistic output points a conscientious analysis of the pictorial elements. Ryman himself affirms that 'The poetry of painting is from the domain of emotion. It must be a sort of revelation, a venerable experience even.'

Since 1964 Ryman has taken part in numerous collective exhibitions, including: 1965, American Abstract Artists Association, Riverside Museum, New York; 1966, *Systemic Painting*, Solomon R. Guggenheim Museum, New York; 1967, *A Romantic Minimalism*, Institute of Contemporary Art, University of Pennsylvania, Philadelphia; 1968, *The Square in Painting*, travelling exhibition in the USA; 1969, *When Attitudes Become Form: Works-Concepts-Process-Situations-Information*, Kunsthalle, Bern; 1975, *Critiques-Théorie-Art* (*Critiques-Théorie-Art*), Galerie Rencontres, Paris; 1978, Venice biennale; 1989, *Geometric Abstraction and Minimalism in America*, Solomon R. Guggenheim Museum, New York; 2002, *Painting on the Move*, showcasing a century of contemporary painting simultaneously at the Kunstmuseum, the Kunsthalle, and the Museum für Gegenwartskunst, Basel.

He has also shown his works in solo exhibitions, including: 1967, Paul Bianchini Gallery, New York; 1968, 1969, 1971, 1972, Heiner Friedrich gallery, Munich; 1969, Galerie Yvon Lambert, Paris; 1970, 1971, 1972, Solomon R. Guggenheim Museum; 1974, Stedelijk Museum, Amsterdam; 1974, Palais des Beaux-Arts, Brussels; 1977, Whitechapel Art Gallery, London; 1981, Musée National d'Art Moderne, Paris; 1986, Leo Castelli Gallery, New York; 1990, 1993, The Pace Gallery, New York; travelling retrospective, 1993-1994, seen at the Tate Gallery, London, Museum of Modern Art, San Francisco, Museo Reina Sofia, Madrid, Museum of Modern Art, New York, Walker Art Center, Minneapolis. From 1983 the Hallen für Neue Kunst in Schaffhouse, Switzerland, have hosted a permanent exhibition of his work..

BIBLIOGRAPHY:
Rose, Barbara, '*ABC Art*' in *Art in America*, periodical, New York, October-November, 1965. Ryman, Robert, *Robert Ryman*, exhibition catalogue, Whitechapel Art Gallery, London, 1977. Ryman, Robert, *Robert Ryman*, Dia Art Foundation, New York, 1988. Sauer, Christel, '*Robert Ryman, peintre*' in *Robert Ryman*, exhibition catalogue, Espace d'Art contemporain Renn Productions, Paris, 1991 (text in French, English and German). Bois, Yve-Alain, '*Robert Ryman. Surprise et sérénité*' in *Galeries Magazine 49*, periodical, Paris, June-July 1992. Serota, Nicholas/Storr, Robert, *Robert Ryman*, travelling exhibition catalogue, Tate Gall., London, Museum of Modern Art, Harry N. Abrams, New York, 1993. Bürgi, Bernhard Mendes, et al., *Painting on the Move*, exhibition catalogue, Kunstmuseum, Kunsthalle, Museum für Gegenwartskunst, Basel, 2002. Ryman, Robert, *Robert Ryman*, Pace Wildenstein, New York, 2004.

MUSEUMS AND GALLERIES:
AMSTERDAM (Stedelijk Mus.) - HARTFORD (Wadsworth Atheneum): *Winsor* (1966) - NEW YORK (Guggenheim Mus.): *Classico IV* (1968, acrylic on handmade Classico paper, mounted on foamcore); *Surface Veil I* (1970, oil and blue chalk on linen); *Surface Veil II* (1971, oil and blue chalk on linen); *Surface Veil III* (1971, oil and blue chalk on canvas) - PARIS (MNAM-CCI): *Untitled* (1974); *Chapter* (1981) - SAN FRANCISCO (MoMA): *Unitled (A)* (1991, aquatint); *A Painting of Twelve Strokes, Measuring 11 1/4" x 11 1/4"* (signed at the bottom 1961, oil and gesso on canvas); *Untitled (E)* (1965, white enamel on linen canvas); *Archive* (1979, oil on steel); *Untitled* (1958, oil on canvas); *An All White Painting, Measuring 9 1/2" x 10" and signed on the left side with white umber* (1961, oil on linen canvas); *Surface Veil* (1970-1971, oil on fibreglass).

UCTION RECORDS:

ONDON, 3 April 1974, *Composition* (1961) GBP 8,750. LON-ON, 7 Dec 1977, *Untitled* (1961, oil on canvas, 74 3/4 x 74 3/4 ns / 190 x 190 cm) GBP 26,000. LONDON, 5 Dec 1979, *Untitled* 1965, acrylic/canvas, 10 1/4 x 10 1/4 ins / 26 x 26 cm) GBP ,300. NEW YORK, 9 May 1984, *26 Square* (1963, oil plaster nd pencil/canvas, 26 x 26 ins / 65.8 x 65.8 cm) USD 35,000. IEW YORK, 6 Nov 1985, *Untitled* (1965, oil on canvas, 10 1/4 x 0 1/4 ins / 26.2 x 26.2 cm) USD 30,000. NEW YORK, 5 May 986, *Channel* (1982, enamel lacquer/fabric, 35 x 35 ins / 88.8 . 88.8 cm) USD 33,000. NEW YORK, 5 May 1987, *Untitled* 1973, five panels of enamelled copper, 9 1/2 x 10 1/2 ins / 24.2 26.7 cm each) USD 75,000. NEW YORK, 8 Oct 1988, *Untitled* 1965, oil on canvas, 11 1/4 x 11 1/4 ins / 28.3 x 28.3 cm) USD 48,500. NEW YORK, 3 May 1989, *Untitled* (1969, oil/synthetic esin, 18 x 18 ins / 45.7 x 45.7 cm) USD 121,000. NEW YORK, 5)ct 1989, *Untitled* (1969, oil/fibreglass, 19 3/4 x 20 ins / 50 x 0.5 cm) USD 143,000. NEW YORK, 9 Nov 1989, *Untitled* (1969, il/fibreglass, 18 1/2 x 18 1/2 ins / 47 x 47 cm) USD 154,000. IEW YORK, 7 May 1990, *Signet 20* (1966, oil on canvas, 62 x 62 ıs / 157.5 x 157.5 cm) USD 1,760,000. NEW YORK, 3 Oct 1991, *Jntitled* (1961, oil/fabric, 13 x 13 ins / 33 x 33 cm) USD 88,000. IEW YORK, 13 Nov 1991, *Director* (1983, oil/fibreglass and luminium, 94 x 84 ins / 238.5 x 213.5 cm) USD 330,000. NEW 'ORK, 3 May 1993, *Empty Surface* (oil/fibreglass, 19 1/4 x 19 1/4 ıs / 48.9 x 48.9 cm) USD 40,250. NEW YORK, 4 May 1993, *Un-tled* (1965, oil/fabric, 10 1/4 x 10 1/4 ins / 26 x 26 cm) USD 2,700. NEW YORK, 9 Nov 1993, *Marker* (oil/fabric/fibreglass, 2 x 42 ins / 106.7 x 106.7 cm) USD 134,500. NEW YORK, 2 Nov 994, *Media* (1981, oil/aluminium, 59 3/4 x 59 3/4 ins / 151.8 x 51.8 cm) USD 288,500. NEW YORK, 8 May 1996, *Report* 1983, oil and lacquer/fibreglass with a montage on alumin-ım legs, 79 3/4 x 72 ins / 202.6 x 182.9 cm) USD 387,500. NEW 'ORK, 20 Nov 1996, *Untitled* (1974, polymer/vinyl/fibreglass, ollection of ten panels, each 21 x 21 ins / 53.6 x 53.6 cm) USD 34,500. LONDON, 6 Dec 1996, *Untitled* (1969, oil/fibreglass, 8 1/2 x 18 1/2 ins / 47 x 47 cm) GBP 36,700. NEW YORK, 7 May 997, *Untitled* (1960, oil on canvas, 59 1/4 x 59 1/4 ins / 150.5 x 50.5 cm) USD 464,500. NEW YORK, 19 Nov 1997, *Capital* 1977, vinyl/canvas/wooden panel, 72 x 72 ins / 182.9 x 182.9 m) USD 343,500. NEW YORK, 16 Nov 1999, *Manual* (1993, oil, namelac on Lumasite, 48 x 48 ins / 122 x 122 cm) USD 70,000. NEW YORK, 17 Nov 1999, *Van Dyke 9H No 1* (1996, raphite on paper) USD 22,000. NEW YORK, 17 May 2000, *Vhitney Revision Painting I* (1969, Enamelac on corrugated ard, 120 x 120 ins / 305 x 305 cm) USD 270,000. NEW YORK, 7 May 2000, *Manager* (1980, rust preventative on canvas, 32 30 ins / 82 x 76 cm) USD 350,000. NEW YORK, 15 May 2001, *1essenger* (Lascaux and acrylic on fibreglass panel, 34 x 34 ıs / 86 x 87 cm) USD 300,000. NEW YORK, 17 May 2001, *Ad-ance* (1976, oil and Elvacite on canvas, 35 x 34 ins / 90 x 86 m) USD 130,000. NEW YORK, 15 May 2002, *Uncle Up* (1963, il and gesso on linen, 74 x 74 ins / 189 x 189 cm) USD ,800,000. NEW YORK, 13 Nov 2002, *Untitled* (1965, oil on can-as, 10 x 10 ins / 26 x 26 cm) USD 340,000. NEW YORK, 15 May 003, *Instructor* (1985, oil and enamel on fibreboard with luminum brackets, 52 x 48 ins / 131 x 121 cm) USD 230,000. EW YORK, 12 Nov 2003, *Region I* (1978, oil and elvacite on ıen on canvas with four fasteners bolts, 32 x 30 ins / 81 x 76 m) USD 450,000. NEW YORK, 12 May 2004, *Part 9* (1993, oil n card with screws and tape, 15 x 15 ins / 38 x 38 cm) USD 0,000. NEW YORK, 13 May 2004, *Eagle Turquoise 6H 2* (1966, encil on Chemex coffee filter paper, 12 x 12 ins / 31 x 31 cm) SD 20,000.

RYMER, James
British, 18th century.
Active in Edinburgh from 1773 to 1791.
Engraver (burin).

RYMSDYCK, Andreas van
Dutch, 18th century.
Died 1786, in Bath.
Painter, engraver.

Andreas van Rymsdyck set up in London about 1767, exhibiting portraits, still-lifes and scenes from Shakespeare in 1769, 1775 and 1776.

RYMSDYCK, Jan van, or Remsdyke
Dutch, 18th century.
Painter, engraver, draughtsman. Anatomical subjects, portraits.

Jan van Rymsdyck was the father of Andreas Rymsdyck. He lived in Bristol, England, from 1760 to 1770, and worked on the anatomical drawings of Dr W Hunter. He is remembered for his: *Frederick Henry of Orange* and *Emile van Solms*, after Jordaens, sheets for *The Gravid Uterus* by Hunter, and sheets for *The British Museum* (engraved with his son Andreas).

RYN, Jan van, or Rijn or Reyn
Flemish School, 17th century.
Born 1610, in Dunkirk; died 20 May 1678, in Dunkirk.
Portrait artist.

Jan van Ryn was the pupil of Van Dyck, whom he accompanied to London, returning to Dunkirk after his death. Summoned to Paris by Marshal de Grammont, he did not find the protection there that he had hoped for, so he returned to set up definitively in Dunkirk.

J ENYAN Ryn.

J·ENYAN Ryn·.
J de Reyn.

MUSEUMS AND GALLERIES:

BAMBERG: *Portrait of a Woman* - BERGUES: *Ecstasy of St Casimir* - BROOKLYN, NY: *Portrait of a Lady* - BRUSSELS: *Portrait of a Young Lady* - CAMBRIDGE (Fitzwilliam Mus.): *Shop of a Game Dealer* - DUNKIRK: *Portrait of a Nobleman in a Spanish Costume; Portrait of a Nobleman in a Ruff; Admiral Mathieu Rombout; St Alexander Liberated by the Angels* (triptych); *Christ on the Cross; Portrait of Admiral Colaert and his Wife, Jeanne Pierens; Louis XIII; Head of a Young Man; Head of a Woman with a Wig; Count of Estrade; Portraits of Jean Leys and His Wife* - HANOVER (Haussmann): *Patrician* - LILLE: *Madonna with Donor* - MADRID: *Wedding of Tethys and Peleus* - ROME (GA Antica di Palazzo Corsini): *Resurrection of Christ* - ROME (Gal. Nazionale d'Arte Antica di Palazzo Barberini): *Henrietta of France, Wife of Charles I of England.*

RYN, Titus Rembrandtsz. van, or Rhyn or Rijn
Dutch, 17th century.
Born 1641; died 4 September 1668.
Painter.

Titus Rembrandtsz. van Ryn was the only son of Rembrandt and Saskia van Uylenburgh. He was the pupil of his father, and married Magdalena van Loo in 1668. Some paintings by him are mentioned in the inventory of works by Rembrandt of 1656.

RYNBOUT, Joannes or Jan, or Rijnboutt
Dutch, 19th century.
Born 29 January 1839, in Utrecht; died 9 December 1868, in Utrecht.
Sculptor.

Joannes Rynbout is remembered for his statues in the church at Harmelen and in the Palace of Justice in Utrecht.

RYNBOUT, Johannes Jacobus, or Rijnbout
Dutch, 19th century.
Born 16 June 1798, in Utrecht; died 12 August 1849, in Utrecht.
Modeller, sculptor.
Johannes Jacobus Rynbout was the brother of Johannes Rynbout.

RYNBOUT, Johannes or Joannes Everardus, or Rijnbout
Dutch, 19th century.
Born 12 July 1839, in Utrecht.
Painter.
MUSEUMS AND GALLERIES:
UTRECHT (Centraal Mus.): *Beside the Lake.*

RYNE, Johannes or Jan van
Dutch, 18th century.
Born c. 1712, in the Netherlands; died c. 1760.
Draughtsman, engraver (burin).
Ryne worked in London about 1754. He is remembered for his: *View of Batavia; Fort St Georges on the Coast of Coromandel; Fort William in Bengal; Bombay from the Malabar Coast; Island of St Helena; Cape of Good Hope.*

RYNEMAN, Pieter
Dutch, 18th century.
Active in Leiden in 1723.
Painter.
Pieter Ryneman was the master of Matthias van der Eyck.

RYNEN, Thierry van
Flemish School, 17th century.
Active in 1613.
Glass painter.
Rynen executed some stained glass windows in the north transept of the church of St Saviour in Bruges.

RYNENBURG, Nicolaes, or Rijnenbourg or Reinenbourg or Reynenbourg
Dutch, 18th century.
Born c. 1713, in Leiden.
Painter. Portraits, genre scenes.
Rynenburg studied in Leiden, and then worked in Amsterdam and Delft. He is particularly remembered for his *Anatomy Lesson*, mentioned by C Tosmert.
AUCTION RECORDS:
LONDON, 13 May 1988, *Woman Filling a Basket with Herrings. Woman at Table with a Glass of Beer* (oil on canvas, a pair, 8¾ x 7 ins / 22.2 x 17.8 cm) GBP 4,950. AMSTERDAM, 9 May 2000, *Man Cleaning Fish by a Table in an Interior. Woman Seated by a Table Counting Money* (1761, oil on panel, a pair, 10 x 8 ins / 25 x 21 cm) NLG 15,000.

RYNEVELT
Dutch, 17th century.
Painter.
Rynevelt is remembered for his *Isaac and Rebecca.*

RYNG, Pieter de. See **RING**

RYNGHEL, Jan de
Flemish School, 15th century.
Active in Bruges in 1410.
Glass painter.

RYNGHELE, Antonis, or Ringhel
Flemish School, 15th century.
Glass painter.
Bruges School.
In 1463 Antonis Rynghele was a senior member of the guild of Bruges, a city where he had been working since 1441.

RYNJUM, Hjarand Asmundson
Norwegian, 18th - 19th century.
Born 1738; died 1822.
Active in Seljord.
Sculptor (wood), architect.

RYNSBURCH, Cornelis van
Flemish School, 17th century.
Active in Middelburg from 1642 to 1647.
Painter.

RYNSOEVER, Gerrit, or Rynsouwer
Dutch, 17th century.
Born c. 1639.
Active in Rotterdam and Delftshaven.
Painter. History painting.

RYNT, J. J.
Austrian, 17th century.
Active in Prague in 1675.
Painter. History painting.

RYNTJES, E. H.
Dutch, 19th century.
Active c. 1870.
Painter. History painting.
Ryntjes executed some works mentioned in Leiden.

RYNVISCH, Evert, or Rijnvisch
Flemish School, 17th century.
Active in Kampen from 1617 to 1653.
Painter. Winter landscapes, landscapes.
Rynvisch painted in the style of Velvet Brueghel. The Boymans Museum in Rotterdam has his *Winter Landscape.*

Ew R.

RYOEN, real name: Hoin Ryoen Sasakino
Japanese, 12th century.
Sculptor.
Ryoen was a *Dai busshi* (master sculptor). He followed the tradition of Jocho (died in 1057) and left several known works: the Buddha Amida (Sanskrit Amitabha) in the Daisen-ji Temple in Tottori, completed in 1131; ten statues of each of the following divinities: Aizen Myoo (Sanskrit Raga), Fudo Myoo (Sanskrit Acala) and Sonsho O, executed for the emperor and completed in 1147; and an Amida dated 1171.
BIBLIOGRAPHY:
Kuno, Takeshi, *A Guide to Japanese Sculpture*, Mayuyama, Tokyo, 1963.

RYOIN. See **UMPO**

RYON, Bernard
French, 20th century.
Born 22 February 1937, in Châlons.
Painter. Landscapes.
Bernard Ryon, who studied at the École des Beaux-Arts, Toulouse, lives and works in Toulouse. He tought in secondary schools there and at the École des Beaux-Arts. He exhibits in regional group exhibitions such as the Société des Artistes Méridionaux, of which he became president in 1992, and in the many solo shows he has held in the Toulouse area and the south-west of France.
BIBLIOGRAPHY:
Cent-vingt ans de gravure toulousaine, exhibition catalogue, École des beaux-arts de Toulouse, Toulouse, 1986.

RYOSEN I
Japanese, 14th century.
Painter. Religious subjects.
Ryosen I painted scenes from Buddhism.

RYOSEN II, real name: Ryosen Kojima, pseudonym: Ekkei, Hakushi
Japanese, 16th century.
Born in Echizen, now Fukui Prefecture.

Active during the first half of the 16th century.
Painter.
Ryosen II was a painter of the ink painting school (*suiboku*) in the Muromachi period.

RYOTAI, real name: Ryosoku Tatbe, original name: Kitamura, nickname: Kingo, pseudonyms: Ryotai, Kan Yosai, Ayatari, Kyuroan, Ayata
Japanese, 18th century.
Born 1719, in Mutsu, now Iwate Prefecture; died 1774.
Painter.
Ryotai was a painter of the Nanga school (literati painting). He settled in Kyoto in his youth and became a monk in the Tofuku-ji Temple.

RYOZEN. See **RYOSEN**

RYP, Abraham de
Dutch, 17th century.
Born c. 1644.
Active until 1705.
Painter. Portraits, landscapes.
Ryp married Isabella Jonderville in 1674.

RYPINSKI, Karol
Polish, 19th century.
Born 1808; died 29 August 1892, in Vilna (now Vilnius, Lithuania).
Miniaturist, watercolourist, draughtsman. Portraits.
Karol Rypinski studied at the art academy in Warsaw under Rustem.
MUSEUMS AND GALLERIES:
WARSAW (Muz. Narodowe): *Portrait of a Lady*.

RYS, Bernard
Flemish School, 18th century.
Born 1690, in Tournai; died 26 January 1769, in Tournai.
Sculptor, decorative designer.
Rys was the son of Jean Rys. He executed some decorations in the Municipal Archives of Tournai.

RYS, Jean
Flemish School, 17th - 18th century.
Active in Tournai.
Sculptor.

RYSBRACK, Gerard or Geerard, or Rysbraeck
Flemish School, 17th - 18th century.
Born 1696, baptised 19 December in Antwerp; died 25 May 1773, in Antwerp.
Painter. Hunting scenes, landscapes, still-lifes, animals.
Gerard Rysbrack was the son of Pieter Rysbrach. He was master of a studio in Antwerp in 1726, but died blind and in poverty.
MUSEUMS AND GALLERIES:
COMPIÈGNE: *Stag-hunting* - GRENOBLE: *Diana and Nymphs*.
AUCTION RECORDS:
PARIS, 2 April 1941, *Duck, Basket of Peaches, Asparagus and Pomegranates on a Landscape Background*, FRF 4,000. PARIS, 17 and 18 Dec 1942, *Flowers, Fruit and Game* (1757) FRF 100,000. PARIS, 31 March 1995, *Pointer in front of a Hare* (oil on canvas, 35 x 49 3/4 ins / 88 x 126.5 cm) FRF 72,000.

RYSBRACK, Jacques or Jacob Cornill, or Rysbraeck
Flemish School, 18th century.
Born 1685; died 22 February 1765, in Paris.
Painter.
Jacques Rysbrack may be the son of Pieter Rysbrack. He went to Paris about 1729.
AUCTION RECORDS:
VERSAILLES, 9 Dec 1973, *Large Ferry at the Mouth of a River*, FRF 13,000.

RYSBRACK, Jean Michel or John Michael
Flemish School, 18th century.
Born 24 June 1693, in Antwerp; died 8 January 1770, in Antwerp.
Sculptor. Busts, statues, monuments.
Jean Michel Rysbrack was the son of Peter Rysbrack, and studied sculpture under the direction of Michel van der Voort. None of his works executed in Flanders has survived. He enjoyed success from his arrival in England in 1720, and remained one of the masters of the golden age of English sculpture until his retirement in 1764.

Jean Michel Rysbrack sculpted numerous busts, statues and tombs in several towns and cities in England, one of his major pieces being a marble *Hercules*.

M.R

Stamp of sale

MUSEUMS AND GALLERIES:
BRUSSELS: *Bust of Lady Jemima Dutton; John Howard* - LONDON (British Mus.): *Bust of Sir Robert Walpole; Sunna* (c. 1728-1730); *Thuner; Daniel Finch, 2nd Earl of Nottingham* (1723).
AUCTION RECORDS:
CHARLBURY, 22 May 1967, *Bust of Cromwell* (bronze) Gns 1,200. LONDON, 28 Nov 1968, *Allegory of Victory* (model in terracotta) GBP 3,400. LONDON, 14 June 1983, *Proposal for a Monument for a Military Hero* (pencil, pen and wash heightened with white, 14 1/2 x 11 ins / 37 x 27 cm) GBP 2,200. LONDON, 22 April 1986, *Bust of Daniel Finch, Earl of Winchelsea and Nottingham* (c. 1744, white marble, h. 23 1/4 ins / 59 cm) GBP 48,000. NEW YORK, 13 Jan 1993, *Group of Women Carrying a Basket and an Urn on Their Heads* (chalk, ink and wash, 7 1/2 x 5 ins / 19.1 x 12.6 cm) USD 1,210. NEW YORK, 12 Jan 1995, *Saul and the Witch of Endor* (black and red chalk, ink and wash/brown paper, 13 1/2 x 10 1/4 ins / 34.5 x 26.1 cm) USD 4,830. LONDON, 8 June 1999, *Joseph's Brothers Show His Bloodied Coat to Their Father* (colour ink and colour wash heightened with white, 11 x 16 ins / 28 x 40 cm) GBP 1,700. LONDON, 27 Nov 2003, *Designs for the Monument to Earl Stanhope in Westminster Abbey* (pen and ink heightened with white and bodycolour, a pair, 15 x 10 ins / 38 x 26 cm) GBP 8,200.

RYSBRACK, Ludovicus, or Rysbraeck
Flemish School, 18th century.
Painter. Mythological subjects, allegorical subjects, landscapes with figures.
Ludovicus Rysbrack was probably the nephew of Michael Rysbrack, and possibly the son of Pieter. The Liechtenstein Gallery in Vienna has two landscapes with mythological figures by him.
AUCTION RECORDS:
PARIS, 22 May 1974, *Allegory of the Arts*, FRF 21,000.

RYSBRACK, Peter or Pieter, or Rysbraeck
Flemish School, 17th - 18th century.
Baptised 25 April 1655 in Antwerp; died 1729, in Brussels.
Painter, engraver (etching). Mythological subjects, landscapes with figures, landscapes, animals.
Peter Rysbrack was the pupil of Philips Augustyn Immenraet in 1672, and the master of a studio in 1673. He went to London in 1675, then to Paris with Francisque Millet, whom certain biographers give as his master. There he married Geneviève Compagnon, widow of the sculptor P. Buysters. He returned to Antwerp in 1692, and went to Brussels on the death of his wife in 1719. He had as pupils his sons, and Karel and Frans Breydel.

Peter Rysbrack's style is inspired by the styles of Francisque Millet and Gaspard Dughet. He engraved interesting etchings.

MUSEUMS AND GALLERIES:

ANTWERP - ASCHAFFENBURG - BAMBERG - BERLIN - COPENHAGEN - DARMSTADT - DESSAU - DRESDEN: *Mountain Landscape with Castle* - HAMBURG: *Southern Landscape in a Storm* - INNSBRUCK - LA FÈRE: *Landscape and Animals; Landscape* - POZNAN - TOULOUSE.

AUCTION RECORDS:

PARIS, 1852, *Landscape with Flocks*, FRF 200. PARIS, 1890, *Landscape*, FRF 720. PARIS, 24 May 1944, *Herdsmen and Animals in a Landscape* (attributed) FRF 2,000. BRUSSELS, 27 Oct 1976, *River Landscape with Figures* (oil on canvas, 22¾ x 33 ins / 58 x 84 cm) BEF 195,000. LONDON, 10 May 1983, *Gardens of Chiswick House* (oil on canvas, a pair, 24 x 42¼ ins / 61 x 107 cm) GBP 28,000. BERN, 30 April 1988, *Pastoral Scene Beside a Lake in a Mountainous Landscape* (oil on canvas, 17 x 20¾ ins / 43 x 53 cm) CHF 7,500. LONDON, 23 March 1990, *Bacchanalia in an Extensive Wooded Landscape* (oil on canvas, 40¼ x 51¼ ins / 102.5 x 130 cm) GBP 20,900. LONDON, 18 May 1990, *Girls Guarding Goats in a Classical Landscape with a Palace Beside a Lake in the Background* (1691, oil on canvas, 25½ x 32 ins / 64.5 x 81.2 cm) GBP 8,800. MONACO, 7 Dec 1990, *Offering to Diana* (oil on canvas, 62¼ x 91¼ ins / 158 x 232 cm) FRF 188,700. AMSTERDAM, 17 Nov 1994, *Peasants Selling Vegetables near Classical Ruins with a Man Pushing a Wheelbarrow* (oil on canvas, 25½ x 35 ins / 64.5 x 88 cm) NLG 9,775. LONDON, 27 Oct 1999, *Maidens Dancing by a Sarcophagus. Making Music by a Sarcophagus* (oil on canvas, a pair, 24 x 29 ins / 60 x 73 cm) GBP 23,000. MILAN, 24 Nov 1999, *Landscape with Animals* (oil on canvas, 39 x 49 ins / 99 x 125 cm) ITL 17,000,000. STOCKHOLM, 29 May 2000, *Hunting Still-life in a Landscape* (oil on canvas, 33 x 44 ins / 83 x 113 cm) SEK 210,000. LONDON, 4 July 2000, *Elegant Hunting Party beside a Statue of Diana* (oil on canvas, 30 x 27 ins / 77 x 68 cm) GBP 2,900. LONDON, 24 April 2001, *Italianate Landscape with Peasant Family Resting by a Fountain* (oil on canvas, 32 x 48 ins / 82 x 122 cm) GBP 4,000. CORK, 28 June 2002, *Still-life with Fish and Crustaceans* (oil on canvas, 24 x 43 ins / 61 x 109 cm) EUR 5,750. PARIS, 25 June 2003, *View of a Fortress by a River* (oil on canvas, 17 x 22 ins / 42 x 55 cm) EUR 11,000. STOCKHOLM, 2 Dec 2003, *Landscape with Hunting Still-life* (oil on canvas, 33 x 44 ins / 83 x 113 cm) SEK 250,000.

RYSBRACK, Peter or Pieter Andreas, the Younger, or Rysbraeck

Flemish School, 18th century.

Born 1690, in Paris; died 1748, in London.

Painter. Genre scenes, landscapes, still-lifes, animals.

Peter Rysbrack the Younger was the son and pupil of Peter Rysbrack. He was master of a studio in Antwerp in 1709.

MUSEUMS AND GALLERIES:

SIBIU: two works - VIENNA (Liechtenstein Mus.): *Cave with a Lioness.*

AUCTION RECORDS:

LONDON, 19 Feb 1910, *Landscape* (in collaboration with Begyn) GBP 9. LONDON, 27 Feb 1963, *Birds in a Park*, GBP 570. NEW YORK, 30 May 1979, *Richmond Ferry at Kew Gardens* (oil on canvas, 35 x 46 ins / 89 x 117 cm) USD 12,500. NEW YORK, 18 June 1982, *The Thames at Deptford* (oil on canvas, 10¼ x 15½ ins / 26 x 39.5 cm) USD 4,000. ZURICH, 3 June 1983, *Still-life with Fruit* (1745, oil on canvas, 26 x 40¼ ins / 66 x 102 cm) CHF 12,000. MONACO, 19 June 1988, *Exotic Birds in a Tropical Landscape* (oil on canvas, 36½ x 56¾ ins / 93 x 144 cm) FRF 333,000. LONDON, 8 Dec 1989, *Vegetable Stall near a Fountain Topped with a Sculpture in an Italian Landscape; Artist and His Pupil Sketching an Outdoor Entertainment in a Park* (oil on canvas, a pair, 27½ x 35 ins / 70 x 88 cm) GBP 13,200. PARIS, 6 Nov 1991, *Drawing Lesson; Market Scene* (oil on canvas, a pair, 27½ x 35 ins / 70 x 88 cm) FRF 125,000. LONDON, 15 April 1999, *Still-life with Swan, Duck, Partridge, Snipe and Pheasant* (oil on canvas, 46 x 57 ins / 117 x 145 cm) GBP 7,000. NEW YORK, 25 May 1999, *Fruit, Dead Songbirds and Kestrel on a Forest Floor with River beyond* (oil on panel, 19 x 22 ins / 49 x 55 cm) USD 8,000. LONDON, 18 April 2000, *Still-life with Birds and Powder Case in a Wooded Landscape* (oil on canvas, 30 x 29 ins / 76 x 74 cm) GBP 11,000. LONDON, 19 April 2000, *Pheasant, Pigeon, Owl, Basket with a Partridge, Duck, Lapwing and Woodcock* (oil on canvas, 30 x 38 ins / 76 x 96 cm) GBP 14,000.

RYSBROECK, Jacob van. See **REESBROECK**

RYSCAK, L. or P.

Flemish School, 19th century.

Active during the first half of the 19th century.

Portrait artist.

RYSEN, Warnard or Werner or Wernerus van, or Ryssen or Ryzen

Dutch, 17th century.

Born c. 1625, in Zaltbommel; died after 1665, in Spain.

Painter. Religious subjects, landscapes with figures.

Rysen was the pupil of Cornelius Poelenburg. He visited Italy, and on returning to Holland, painted landscapes with historical personages, in the style of his master. In 1664, he had Gerard Hoet as his pupil in Zaltbommel. About 1665 he gave up painting for dealing in diamonds, and went to Spain.

MUSEUMS AND GALLERIES:

KASSEL: *Penitent Magdalene.*

AUCTION RECORDS:

VIENNA, 17 March 1981, *Rest during the Flight into Egypt* (oil/copper, 8½ x 10¼ ins / 21.5 x 26 cm) ATS 110,000. PARIS, 16 Dec 1992, *Cavernous Landscape in the Countryside around Rome* (oil on canvas) FRF 12,000. AMSTERDAM, 5 Nov 2002, *Nymphs Bathing and Washerwoman near Ruins in a Southern Landscape* (oil on panel, 8 x 11 ins / 21 x 29 cm) EUR 8,000.

RYSER, Peter

Swiss, 20th century.

Born 1939, in Eriswil.

Painter, watercolourist, draughtsman.

Peter Ryser studied at the college of arts and crafts in Lucerne and made extended visits to Paris and Munich, ultimately settling in Munich. Ryser's work comprises drawings heightened with acrylics, watercolours and wax pastels. His technique is at times meticulously detailed and hyper-realist, at times fragmentary and cursory. In essence, his work is concerned less with the image *per se* than with the emotion it seeks to convey. In 1972, Ryser's work featured at *Kunst: 28 Schweizer* (*28 Swiss Artists*), an exhibition held at the Raeber Gallery in Lucerne. He had already exhibited solo at the same gallery in 1970.

BIBLIOGRAPHY:

Kneubühler, Theo, *Kunst: 28 Schweizer*, exhibition catalogue, Gal. Raeber, Lucerne, 1972.

MUSEUMS AND GALLERIES:

AARAU (Aargauer Kunsthaus): *Rainbow Settling into a Curve* (1971).

RYSERMANN, Peter

German, 15th - 16th century.

Active in Kalkar from 1498 to 1500.

Sculptor.

Peter Rysermann collaborated with Loedevich de Kalkar on the central low relief of the high altar of the church of St Nicholas in Kalkar.

RYSSE, Ulrich, or Risse or Rissi
Swiss, 17th century.
Active in Wil.
Painter.

Ulrich Rysse may have been the son or grandson of Ulrich Rissi.

MUSEUMS AND GALLERIES:
ZURICH (Schweizerisches Landesmus.): *Madonna.*

RYSSEL, Paul Van (Dr). See **GACHET Paul**

RYSSELBERGHE, Théodore van, called Théo
Belgian, 19th - 20th century.
Born 23 or 28 November 1862, in Ghent; died 13 December 1926, in St-Clair (Var).
Painter, watercolourist, designer, draughtsman, engraver, illustrator, lithographer. Figures, landscapes, urban landscapes, seascapes, flowers. Murals.
Groups: Les XX, Libre Esthétique.

Théodore van Rysselberghe was born into a family whose members included several architects. He studied under Canneel at the academy in Ghent, and then under Portaels in Brussels. Van Rysselbeghe was extremely well-off and could afford to travel extensively, painting and exhibiting as he went. He lived for several years in Paris, spending his summers by the Channel, in accordance with the Impressionist and Neo-Impressionist custom. He participated in the establishment of the Franco-Belgian artistic exchange group The 20 (Les XX) and in its various exhibitions. He was also a founder member of the Libre Esthétique movement. He exhibited at the Salon des Indépendants in Paris on several occasions. At that juncture, his painting was on the conventional side, fleshy and sombre, betraying some orientalist elements inherited perhaps from Portaels.

Van Rysselberghe visited Spain and Morocco on several occasions from 1884, painting his *Arab Storyteller* and *Fantasia*. His colours gradually lightened and he began to emerge as a portrait artist. He was on intimate terms with Émile Verhaeren, and it was the latter who invited him to Paris, where van Rysselberghe was greatly impressed by Seurat's *La Grande Jatte*. He was not entirely convinced, however, by the scientific approach the Divisionists derived from the theory of colour expounded by Chevreul and espoused to a greater or lesser degree by Signac, Cross and Pissarro.

From 1887, van Rysselberghe began painting in the Neo-Impressionist manner, becoming virtually the only artist to apply this approach to portraiture. Paintings such as *Madame Oc. Ghysbrechts*, *Octave Maus* (1885) and *Madame Maus* (1890) date from around this time. Van Rysselberghe also painted a number of landscapes, among them *Promenade* and *Tartan Vessels at Sète*. Around 1895, he joined Henry van de Velde in a bid to resuscitate the decorative arts. He designed posters, furniture, typographical elements and jewellery in the 'new style' and painted a large number of decorative panels specifically commissioned by architects.

In 1898, he left Brussels and settled in Paris, where he moved in Symbolist literary circles. His wife - 'Madame Théo' or 'The Little Lady' - played an important role in the life of André Gide. In 1903, van Rysselberghe painted his celebrated *Reading*, where a large number of writers are depicted in a group surrounding Verhaeren, including Gide, Maeterlinck and Fénéon. He continued to paint essentially in the Neo-Impressionist manner, using visual effects achieved by juxtaposed patches of colour, with a predominance of violets, mauves and blues. While residing at St-Clair in Provence, however, he felt a need for a greater repertoire in terms of technique and colour. He duly abandoned the strict tenets of Neo-Impressionism and began painting in the Fauvist manner, using more intense colours in his seascapes and bathing scenes, where the female bathers' bodies are fleshed out by the strong colours of sea and sun.

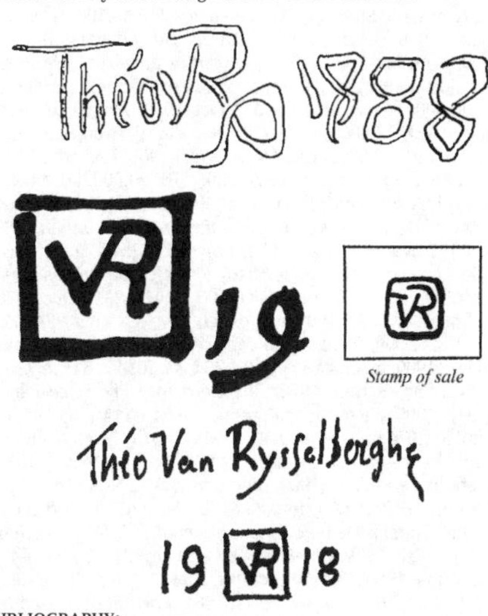

Stamp of sale

BIBLIOGRAPHY:
Chabot, *Van Rysselberghe*, exhibition catalogue, Museum voor Schone Kunsten, Ghent, 1962 (in commemoration of his centenary). Hoozee, Robert/Lauwaert, Helke, *Théo van Rysselberghe*, Pandora, Brussels, 1993. Palmer, Michel, *D'Ensor à Magritte - Art belge de 1880 à 1940*, Éd. Racine, Brussels, 1994. Feltkamp, Ronald, *Théo van Rysselberghe: monographie et catalogue raisonné*, Racine, Paris, 2003.

MUSEUMS AND GALLERIES:
AMSTERDAM (Rijksmus.): *Aquarium with Fish and Crayfish* - BRUSSELS (MBA): *Woman Reading and a Young Girl*; *Mademoiselle Z.*; *Promenade*; *Émile Verhaeren, Poet*; *Mandolinist*; *Octave Maus* (1885); *Madame Maus* (1890); *Fantasia* (before 1884) - ESSEN (Folkwang Mus.): *Moonlight in Boulogne* - GHENT (Mus. voor Schone Kunsten): *Reading*; *Dario de Regoyos, Spanish Painter* - HELSINKI (Ateneumin Taidemus.): *Midi Landscape* - HYÈRES: *Portrait of Madame Deman* - LEIPZIG: *Venetian Woman* - OSTEND (Mus. voor Schone Kunsten) - OTTERLO (Kröller-Müller Mus.): *Per-Kinder Point* (1889); *Pines at Cavalière* (1904) - PARIS (Mus. d'Orsay): *Estuary with Sailing Vessels* (1892-1893); *Portrait of Émile Verhaeren, Poet* (1915, oil on canvas) - ROTTERDAM (Mus. Boijmans Van Beuningen): *Mirror* - WEIMAR: *Fiery Sky.*

AUCTION RECORDS:
PARIS, 29 Oct 1926, *Morning Sun*, FRF 2,400. PARIS, 3 Dec 1928, *Young Woman Seated in an Armchair*, FRF 1,300. PARIS, 6 May 1932, *Woman Brushing Her Hair* (red chalk) FRF 300. PARIS, 31 Jan 1938, *Vase of Flowers*, FRF 1,000. PARIS, 5-6 and 7 Nov 1941, *Handful of Flowers*, FRF 7,500; *Fountain*, FRF 4,100. PARIS, 15 April 1944, *Nude Seen from Rear* (red chalk) FRF 400. PARIS, 29 June 1945, *Arno River, Florence*, FRF 10,100. PARIS, 18 Dec 1946, *Bathers*, FRF 28,000. PARIS, 26 March 1947, *Entrance to Boulogne Harbour* (1900, watercolour) FRF 2,200. PARIS, 30 May 1947, *Rowboats, Honfleur* (watercolour) FRF 7,500. PARIS, 3 May 1949, *Landscape* (1891) FRF 18,500. PARIS, 10 June 1949, *Pines by the Sea* (1916) FRF 10,500. PARIS, 30 June 1950, *Dancer* (1909, wash) FRF 6,000. PARIS, 7 Feb 1951, *Carriage on the Boulevard*, FRF

8,500. PARIS, 30 April 1951, *Yacht on the River* (1892) FRF 20,000. PARIS, 10 June 1955, *Arno River, Florence,* FRF 350,000. PARIS, 25 Feb 1957, *Landscape at Le Pouldu,* FRF 270,000. PARIS, 7 June 1961, *Peach Trees in Blossom,* FRF 7,000. LONDON, 5 July 1961, *Young Women in a Park,* GBP 900. NEW YORK, 16 May 1962, *Back Yard,* USD 3,000. GENEVA, 2 Nov 1963, *Sunset at Ambleteuse,* CHF 64,500. GENEVA, 26 Nov 1966, *Young Female Nude, Seated* (pastel) CHF 10,000. LONDON, 2 Dec 1966, *Portrait of the Artist's Mother,* Gns 2,800. VERSAILLES, 7 June 1967, *Portrait of Alice Sethe,* FRF 90,000. ANTWERP, 1 and 2 Oct 1968, *Landscape with Houses,* BEF 820,000. PARIS, 9 Dec 1968, *Portrait of Jeanne Pissarro,* FRF 17,000. LONDON, 30 April 1969, *Portrait of Madame Paul Dubois (née Alice Sethe),* GBP 20,000. LONDON, 9 July 1971, *Nude with Mirror* (pastel) Gns 2,800. VERSAILLES, 31 May 1972, *Young Women Bathing in the Fountain,* FRF 130,000. LONDON, 3 April 1974, *Portrait of Irma Sèthe,* GBP 18,500. LONDON, 1 Dec 1976, *Shady Pines* (oil on canvas, 33 3/4 x 43 1/4 ins / 86 x 110 cm) GBP 8,500. COLOGNE, 3 Dec 1976, *Pine Forest* (watercolour and pencil, 9 1/2 x 13 ins / 24 x 33 cm) DEM 4,300. ZURICH, 20 May 1977, *Fields of Summer Flowers* (1900, oil on canvas, 40 x 20 ins / 101.5 x 51 cm) CHF 18,000. BERN, 8 June 1978, *Shepherd in a Provence Landscape* (c. 1890, pastel/pencil outline, 16 3/4 x 11 3/4 ins / 42.4 x 30 cm) CHF 4,000. ANTWERP, 8 May 1979, *Model* (pastel, 37 1/2 x 13 ins / 95 x 33 cm) BEF 37,000. LONDON, 4 July 1979, *Bathers at Cap Bénat* (1909, oil on canvas, 28 x 45 ins / 71 x 114.5 cm) GBP 11,000. BRUSSELS, 22 Nov 1979, *Portrait of Madame Eugène Demolder, Daughter of Félicien Rops* (colouring pencil, 26 3/4 x 32 3/4 ins / 68 x 83 cm) BEF 65,000. MUNICH, 3 June 1980, *Dancer* (etching, 10 x 11 3/4 ins / 25.3 x 30.1 cm) DEM 6,500. PARIS, 18 March 1981, *Portrait of Alexandre Charpentier* (charcoal, 37 x 27 1/2 ins / 94 x 70 cm) FRF 9,600. ANTWERP, 29 April 1981, *Daydream* (1901, pastel, 36 1/4 x 30 ins / 92 x 76 cm) BEF 140,000. LONDON, 2 Dec 1981, *Café-Concert* (1896, etching, 10 x 11 3/4 ins / 25.1 x 30 cm) GBP 1,150. LONDON, 1 July 1982, *Bathers* (1911, oil on canvas, 82 3/4 x 98 1/2 ins / 210 x 250 cm) GBP 15,000. LONDON, 22 March 1983, *Seated Bather* (pastel, 24 3/4 x 19 3/4 ins / 63 x 50 cm) GBP 5,500. NEW YORK, 19 May 1983, *Evening with the Three Sèthe Sisters by Lamplight* (1889, pencil with touches of gouache/Ingres paper remounted on board, 19 3/4 x 26 ins / 50.2 x 66 cm) USD 19,000. NEW YORK, 19 May 1983, *Regatta* (1892, oil on canvas, 25 1/4 x 33 ins / 64.2 x 83.7 cm) USD 180,000. BERN, 23 June 1983, *Fishing Fleet* (1894, etching, 9 x 11 ins / 22.6 x 28 cm) CHF 1,900. LONDON, 26 June 1985, *Female Portrait* (1898, pastel, colouring pencil and graphite, 21 1/4 x 26 3/4 ins / 54 x 68 cm) GBP 3,600. LOKEREN, 19 April 1986, *Anthemis* (1910, oil on canvas, 28 3/4 x 39 1/4 ins / 73.3 x 100 cm) BEF 5,600,000. NEW YORK, 10 Nov 1987, *Regatta* (1892, oil on canvas, painted wooden frame, 25 1/2 x 33 ins / 64.5 x 83.8 cm) USD 400,000. FONTAINEBLEAU, 21 Feb 1988, *Poster for the 4th Salon of the Libre Esthétique* (coloured lithograph, 37 x 29 1/4 ins / 94 x 74 cm) FRF 28,000. VERSAILLES, 20 March 1988, *Nude* (oil on canvas remounted on board, 10 1/2 x 13 3/4 ins / 26.5 x 35 cm) FRF 24,000. PARIS, 22 April 1988, *Reclining Nude* (pastel, 15 x 19 1/4 ins / 38 x 49 cm) FRF 6,500. LOKEREN, 28 May 1988, *White Roses* (oil on canvas, diam. 26 1/2 ins / 67 cm) BEF 750,000. PARIS, 24 June 1988, *Riders on the Beach at Morgat* (1904, oil on card, 15 x 22 ins / 38 x 55 cm) FRF 90,000. LONDON, 28 June 1988, *Bather* (oil on canvas, 50 x 37 ins / 127 x 94 cm) GBP 22,000; *Houseboats on the Escaut* (1892, oil on canvas, 22 x 25 1/2 ins / 55 x 65 cm) GBP 418,000. LONDON, 19 Oct 1988, *Female Head* (1901, pastel, 16 1/2 x 13 3/4 ins / 42 x 35 cm) GBP 8,250. LONDON, 29 Nov 1988, *Fishing Boats Setting Out to Sea* (1887, oil on canvas, 22 x 26 1/2 ins / 56 x 67 cm) GBP 176,000. PARIS, 14 Dec 1988, *Reclining Nude* (charcoal drawing heightened with white chalk, 13 1/2 x 23 1/2 ins / 34 x 60 cm) FRF 11,500. PARIS, 12 Feb 1989, *Nude on a Beach* (oil on canvas, 24 x 19 3/4 ins / 61 x 50 cm) FRF 145,000. LONDON, 27 June 1989, *Seated Nude* (1908, oil on canvas, 39 1/4 x 25 1/2 ins / 100 x 65 cm) GBP 28,600. NEW YORK, 18 Oct 1989, *Canal, Flanders* (1894, oil on canvas, 23 1/2 x 31 1/2 ins / 60 x 80 cm) USD 770,000. LE TOUQUET, 12 Nov 1989, *Young Woman in a Green Dress* (oil on panel, 9 x 16 1/4 ins / 23 x 41 cm) FRF 32,000. LONDON, 28 Nov 1989, *Near the Rocks at Per-Kindec* (oil on canvas, 12 1/2 x 15 3/4 ins / 32 x 40 cm) GBP 220,000. NEW YORK, 26 Feb 1990, *Female Portrait* (1911, oil on panel, 45 1/4 x 30 1/4 ins / 115 x 77 cm) USD 85,250. LONDON, 2 April 1990, *Mill at Kalf* (1894, oil on canvas, 31 1/2 x 27 ins / 80 x 68.5 cm) GBP 275,000. AMSTERDAM, 10 April 1990, *Anemones* (oil on canvas, 18 x 15 ins / 46 x 38 cm) NLG 69,000. BRUSSELS, 9 Oct 1990, *Woman in Blue* (oil on panel, 17 3/4 x 13 ins / 45 x 33 cm) BEF 160,000. NEW YORK, 14 Nov 1990, *Isle of Levant Seen from Cap Bénat* (oil on canvas, 17 3/4 x 25 1/2 ins / 45.1 x 65 cm) USD 550,000. PARIS, 7 Dec 1990, *Elisabeth Sleeping* (pastel, 14 1/2 x 12 1/4 ins / 37 x 31 cm) FRF 15,000. AMSTERDAM, 13 Dec 1990, *Straits of Messina Seen from Taormina* (oil on card, 13 1/2 x 16 1/4 ins / 34.5 x 41.5 cm) NLG 71,300. NEW YORK, 9 May 1991, *Woman with Mirror* (1907, oil on canvas, 31 x 35 1/2 ins / 78.7 x 90.2 cm) USD 99,000. AMSTERDAM, 22 May 1991, *Female Nude before a Mirror* (1906, red chalk heightened with white/brown paper, 43 1/2 x 34 1/2 ins / 110.5 x 87.5 cm) NLG 34,500. AMSTERDAM, 23 May 1991, *Rossignol Point* (1912, oil on canvas, 18 x 22 ins / 46 x 55 cm) NLG 59,800. LONDON, 25 June 1991, *Bathers by the Seaside* (oil on canvas, 66 1/4 x 107 3/4 ins / 168 x 274 cm) GBP 68,200. LOKEREN, 23 May 1992, *Elisabeth Sleeping, Aged Four* (pastel/card, 14 3/4 x 12 1/2 ins / 37.5 x 31.5 cm) BEF 150,000. PARIS, 22 June 1992, *Portrait of Émile Verhaeren* (graphite, 9 x 7 3/4 ins / 23 x 19.5 cm) FRF 4,800. LONDON, 1 July 1992, *Female Nude before a Mirror* (1905, pastel/buff-coloured paper/canvas, 23 x 28 ins / 58.5 x 71.2 cm) GBP 16,500. PARIS, 8 April 1993, *Floral Composition* (oil on panel, two sides, 16 x 13 ins / 40.5 x 33 cm) FRF 8,500. PARIS, 2 June 1993, *Émile Verhaeren Reading* (watercolour and graphite, 12 1/2 x 10 ins / 32 x 25.5 cm) FRF 21,000. LOKEREN, 9 Oct 1993, *Young Moroccan Woman* (1880, oil on panel, 18 x 15 ins / 46 x 38 cm) BEF 330,000. NEW YORK, 3 Nov 1993, *Model's Siesta* (1920, oil on canvas, 26 x 29 1/2 ins / 66.3 x 75.2 cm) USD 90,500. LONDON, 30 Nov 1993, *Mansour El Hay Portal, Meknès (Morocco)* (1887, oil on canvas, 16 x 24 ins / 40.6 x 61 cm) GBP 34,500. LOKEREN, 8 Oct 1994, *Woman with Bowl* (1908, oil on canvas, 58 1/4 x 45 1/4 ins / 148 x 115 cm) BEF 5,700,000. NEW YORK, 8 Nov 1994, *Race Track at Boulogne-sur-Mer* (1900, oil on canvas, 30 x 34 1/2 ins / 75.9 x 87.9 cm) USD 189,500. AMSTERDAM, 8 Dec 1994, *Red-haired Woman* (1911, oil on canvas, 21 3/4 x 18 1/4 ins / 55.5 x 46.5 cm) NLG 14,950. PARIS, 16 Dec 1994, *Female Portrait* (1907, oil on canvas, 19 1/4 x 16 1/2 ins / 49 x 42 cm) FRF 34,000. PARIS, 3 April 1995, *Nude (Posterior View)* (1916, oil on canvas) FRF 149,000. LONDON, 28 June 1995, *River Arno, Florence* (1909, oil on canvas, 28 3/4 x 23 1/2 ins / 73 x 60 cm) GBP 80,700. LOKEREN, 7 Oct 1995, *Pink Necklace* (1907, oil on canvas). AMSTERDAM, 6 Dec 1995, *Beach at Morgat, Brittany* (1904, oil on canvas, 18 x 22 ins / 46 x 55 cm) NLG 43,700. PARIS, 1 April 1996, *Young Woman in an Oak Wood (Daughter of Jean Schlumberger and Suzanne Weiler)* (oil on canvas, 18 x 15 ins / 46 x 38 cm) FRF 66,000. NEW YORK, 1 May 1996, *Female Nude, Seated* (1908, oil on canvas, 39 1/4 x 25 1/2 ins / 100 x 65 cm) USD 25,300. NEW YORK, 12 Nov 1996, *Female Nude, Arms Raised* (1911, oil on canvas, 21 3/4 x 18 ins / 55.4 x 45.8 cm) USD 9,200. NEW YORK, 14 Nov 1996, *Young Woman with Vases of Flowers* (oil on canvas, 39 x 30 1/4 ins / 99 x 76.9 cm) USD 57,500. PARIS, 21 Nov 1996, *Café-concert* (1896, etching, 10 x 11 3/4 ins / 25.2 x 29.9 cm) FRF 20,000. AMSTERDAM, 10 Dec 1996, *Nude* (1890, oil on card, study, 14 1/2 x 17 3/4 ins / 37 x 45 cm) NLG 21,910. PARIS, 12 Dec 1996, *Beach at Ambleteuse* (1900, oil on canvas, 21 1/4 x 25 1/2 ins / 54 x 65 cm) FRF 320,000. NEW YORK, 19 Feb 1997, *Cherries* (watercolour and pencil/paper/card, 9½ x 13 ins / 24.1 x 33 cm) USD 12,650. CALAIS, 23 March 1997, *Mediterranean Littoral* (watercolour, 5½ x 9 ins / 14 x 23 cm) FRF 9,000. AMSTERDAM, 4 June 1997, *Woman before the Mirror* (1905, oil on canvas, 28¾ x 23½ ins / 73 x 60 cm) NLG 149,916. PARIS, 19 Oct 1997, *Portrait of Émile Verhaeren, Poet* (pencil/paper, 9½ x 12¼ ins / 24 x 31 cm) FRF 19,000. LONDON, 22 Oct 1997, *Window* (oil on canvas, 28¾ x 23½ ins / 73 x 60 cm) GBP 21,850. NEW YORK, 13 Nov 1997, *Evening at Low Tide on Ambleteuse Beach* (1900, oil on canvas, 21½ x 25¾ ins / 54.6 x 65.4 cm) USD 85,000. PARIS, 24 March 1998, *Young Women* (1902, red chalk, study for 'Reading in the Garden', 33½ x 22 ins / 85 x 56 cm) FRF 90,000. LONDON, 28 June 1999, *Little Denise* (1889, oil on canvas, 40 x 24 ins / 102 x 60 cm) GBP 420,000. LONDON, 30 June 1999, *Bathers under the Pines by the Sea* (1926, oil on canvas, 46 x 35 ins / 116 x 90 cm) GBP 45,000. LONDON, 7 Dec 1999, *Coastal Scene* (oil on canvas, 20 x 24 ins / 51 x 61 cm) GBP 300,000. BRUSSELS, 16 May 2000, *Study of Bathers* (gouache on cardboard, 20 x 26 ins / 51 x 65 cm) BEF 1,400,000. LONDON, 28 June 2000, *Pines and Eucalyptus at Cavaliere* (1905, oil on canvas, 26 x 32 ins / 65 x 81 cm) GBP 100,000. LONDON, 5 Feb 2001, *Rocks at Antheor* (1906, oil on canvas, 18 x 22 ins / 46 x 56 cm) GBP 95,000. LONDON, 7 Feb 2001, *Summer Landscape* (oil on canvas, 20 x 30 ins / 51 x 77 cm) GBP 120,000. NEW YORK, 5 Nov 2002, *Sailing Boats on the Scheldt* (1892, oil on canvas on painted liner, 27 x 35 ins / 68 x 90 cm) USD 2,400,000. LONDON, 22 Oct 2003, *Two Bathers under the Pines by the Sea* (1925, oil on canvas, 46 x 35 ins / 116 x 89 cm) GBP 36,000. LONDON, 22 Oct 2003, *Bay at St Clair* (1923, oil on canvas, 29 x 36 ins / 73 x 91 cm) GBP 36,000. NEW YORK, 4 Nov 2004, *Vallee de la Sambre* (1890, oil on canvas, 21 x 26 ins / 54 x 67 cm) USD 650,000. NEW YORK, 5 Nov 2004, *Pointe du Rossignol, Cap Layet* (1905, oil on canvas, 29 x 33 ins / 73 x 85 cm) USD 410,000.

RYSSEN, Warnard or Werner or Wernerus van. See **RYSEN**

RYSSENS DE LAUW, Joseph Martin
Belgian, 19th century.
Born 30 September 1830, in Antwerp; died 2 April 1889, in Antwerp.
Painter, architect. Flowers.

RYSSER, Mathes. See **REISER**

RYSSUKHIN, Yuri, or Rissukhin
Kazakhstanian, 20th - 21st century.
Born 1947, in Uiuk (Djambul, Kazakhstan).
Painter. Figure compositions, figures, portraits, landscapes with figures.

Yuri Ryssukhin studied at the school of art in Krasnodar, graduating in 1971. He became a member of the union of Soviet artists in 1975. He lives and works in Orenburg. His painting falls somewhere between stylised decorative and naive, but is not without Symbolist influences. He depicts lively scenes of everyday life. He has been exhibiting since 1974. In 1980, he won a first prize from the union of Soviet artists.

MUSEUMS AND GALLERIES:
KAZAN (AM) - KOURGAN - MAGNITOGORSK - MOSCOW (State Tretyakov Gal.) - ORENBURG (Mus. Iso) - PERM (PG).

AUCTION RECORDS:
PARIS, 25 Nov 1991, *Carnival in Orenburg* (1990, oil on panel, 46½ x 64¼ ins / 118 x 163 cm) FRF 10,000. PARIS, 16 Feb 1992, *Painter in January* (oil on panel, 46½ x 64¼ ins / 118 x 163 cm) FRF 18,000.

RYSWYCK, Dirk van
Dutch, 17th century.
Born 1596; died 1679.
Active in Amsterdam.
Medallist, goldsmith. Military subjects, figures. Medals.

D. V. R.

MUSEUMS AND GALLERIES:
AMSTERDAM (Rijksmus.): *Siege of Amsterdam in 1650* (medal); *Admiral Martin Tromp* (medal).

RYSWYCK, Edward van
Belgian, 20th century.
Born 1871.
Active in Antwerp.
Painter. Still-lifes (flowers/fruit).

Ryswyck lived and worked in Antwerp. He was a painter of the Belgian school, often executing still lifes of both fruits and flowers. He was known to have exhibited at the Walker Art Gallery in Liverpool in 1908.

AUCTION RECORDS:
NEW YORK, 29 Oct 1992, *Still-life with Melon* (oil on canvas, 47¼ x 63¼ ins / 120 x 160.7 cm) USD 8,800. LOKEREN, 18 May 1996, *Peonies* (oil on canvas, 27½ x 39¾ ins / 70 x 101 cm) BEF 52,000. LONDON, 21 Nov 1996, *Bouquet of Peonies* (oil on canvas, 27¾ x 40 ins / 70.3 x 101.4 cm) GBP 5,175. AMSTERDAM, 1 Sept 1999, *Still-life with Peaches, Melons and Grapes* (oil on canvas, 35 x 45 ins / 90 x 115 cm) NLG 10,000. AMSTERDAM, 1 Sept 1999, *Autumn Still-life with Grapes and Bindweed* (oil on canvas, 28 x 39 ins / 70 x 100 cm) NLG 19,000. LOKEREN, 13 May 2000, *Still-life with Fruit and Shell* (oil on canvas, 28 x 40 ins / 70 x 101 cm) BEF 220,000. STOCKHOLM, 29 May 2000, *Still-life with Poppies and Japanese Doll* (oil on canvas, 28 x 39 ins / 70 x 100 cm) SEK 40,000. BRUSSELS, 16 Jan 2001, *Roses on a Table* (oil on canvas, a pair, 8 x 20 ins / 20 x 50 cm) BEF 120,000. ANTWERP, 22 April 2002, *Still-life with Chestnuts and Oak Leaves* (oil on canvas, 26 x 39 ins / 66 x 98 cm) EUR 3,000. ANTWERP, 21 Oct 2002, *Still-life with Tulips and Peonies* (oil on canvas, 28 x 39 ins / 70 x 100 cm) EUR 3,600. NEW YORK, 23 April 2003, *Pink Rose and Irises on a Stone Ledge* (oil on canvas, 36 x 28 ins / 91 x 71 cm) USD 13,000. ANTWERP, 26 April 2004, *Still-life with Flowers, Lobster and Samovar* (oil on canvas, 50 x 37 ins / 128 x 93 cm) EUR 1,800. BRUSSELS, 11 May 2004, *Still-life with Mandarins and Tambourine* (oil on canvas, 24 x 31 ins / 61 x 80 cm) EUR 1,700.

RYSWYCK, Theodor van
Belgian, 19th century.
Born 8 July 1811, in Antwerp; died 7 May 1849, in Antwerp.
Engraver (etching), draughtsman, poet.

RYSZKIEWICZ, Jozef
Polish, 19th - 20th century.
Born 19 November 1856, in Warsaw; died 19 May 1925, in Warsaw.
Painter.

Jozef Ryszkiewicz trained at the academies in Warsaw, St Petersburg and Munich.

He favoured battle scenes and horses and executed genre paintings as well. He was influenced by French Impressionism from 1890.

RYTHER, Augustine
British, 16th century.
Born in Leeds.
Active 1579-1592.
Engraver (burin), print publisher.

Augustine Ryther engraved maps and historical scenes.

RYTSERE, Willem de or Le, or Ritsere, called Willem van Lombeke
Flemish School, 14th - 15th century.
Died before 26 May 1447.
Active in Ghent from 1395.
Painter. Figures.

Willem de Rytsere painted decorative works for palaces and churches in Ghent. He also painted coats of arms.

RYTZ-FUETER (Mme). See **FUETER Charlotte**

RYUEI, real name: Morimitsu Momoda, nickname: Buzaemon, pseudonyms: Ryuei and Yukosai
Japanese, 17th century.
Born 1647; died 1698.
Active in Edo (now Tokyo).
Painter.

Ryuei was a pupil of Tan'yu (1602-1674). He belonged to the Kano School in Kyoto. The National Museum of Kyoto has in its collection one of his portraits of Tan'yu, a hanging scroll in ink and light colours on paper, which is on the register of Important Cultural Possessions.

MUSEUMS AND GALLERIES:
KYOTO (National Mus.): *Portrait of Tan'yu*.

RYUHO I, real name: Chikashige Hinaya, original name: Nonoguchi, nicknames: Shoemon Beniya, Ichibei, Jirozaemon, Sozaeman, pseudonyms: Ryuho, Shoo
Japanese, 17th century.
Born 1599, in Kyoto; died 1669.
Painter, poet.

After studying haiku composition with Teitoku, Ryuho I became known first and foremost as a poet, and painted only as a pastime.

RYUHO II, real name: Nei Fkushima, nickname: Shichoku, nickname: Shigejiro, pseudonyms: Ryuho, Mokudo, Mokushin, Sodo
Japanese, 19th century.
Born 1820; died 1889.
Active in Tokyo.
Painter.

Ryuho II was a painter of landscapes, flowers and birds. He began his career as a pupil of Zeshin and subsequently turned to literati art.

RYUKO, real name: Takatsune Takahisa, original name: Hata, nickname: Jutsuji, nickname: Onoshiro, pseudonyms: Ryuko, Baiju, Baisai, Ekiu, Kiryu, Mudo Dosha, Udo
Japanese, 19th century.
Born 1801, in Shimotsuke, now Tochigi Prefecture; died 1859.
Painter.

Ryuko painted historical subjects. He was the adopted son of Aigai. At a mature age he settled in Kyoto where he studied painting in the *yamato* (Japanese painting) style with Kiyoshi and Ikkei.

RYUKOSAI, real name: Jokei Taga, nickname: Jihei
Japanese, 18th - 19th century.
Born 1772; died 1816.
Print artist.

Ryukosai was active in the region of Osaka between 1770 and 1809.

AUCTION RECORDS:
NEW YORK, 21 March 1989, *Potrait of the Actor Ichikawa Danzo in Costume and Mask* (Hosoban print, 12 1/2 x 6 ins / 31.9 x 14.3 cm) USD 77,000.

RYUSAI. See **HIROSHIGE I**

RYUSHI, Kawabata. See **KAWABATA Ryushi**

RYX. See **RYCKX**

RYZEN, Warnard or Werner or Wernerus van. See **RYSEN**

RZAKULEV, Alikper
Russian, 20th century.
Born 1903, in Baku.
Engraver, illustrator.

Alikper Rzakulev illustrated picturesque scenes of the life of Russian peasants in a traditional style. He apparently avoided subjects too edifying or moralistic.

BIBLIOGRAPHY:
L'Art russe des Scythes à nos jours, exhibition catalogue, Gal. nationales du Grand Palais, Paris, 1967.

MUSEUMS AND GALLERIES:
MOSCOW (Mus. of Eastern Art): *Shoeing Bullocks* (linocut).

RZEBETZ, Hieronymus
Austrian, 18th century.
Active in Kukuksbad (Bohemia) c. 1744.
Engraver (burin).

Hieronymus Rzebetz was a pupil of M. Rentz.

RZECKI, Stanislav
Polish, 20th century.
Born 19 October 1888, in Warsaw.
Painter, engraver, sculptor.

Stanislav Rzecki trained at the academies in Cracow and Paris; he shared the Pre-Raphaelites' taste for Gothic art and the early Renaissance.

MUSEUMS AND GALLERIES:
WARSAW (Muz. Narodowe): *Woman's Head* (bronze); two oil paintings; etchings.

RZEPINSKY, Czeslaw
Polish, 20th century.
Born 8 February 1905, in Strusov.
Painter. Landscapes, still-lifes. Murals.

Czeslaw Rzepinsky trained at the academy in Cracow from 1924 to 1934 with W. Weiss and Felician Kowarski, and with Jozef Pankiewicz in Paris. One of the founders of the School of Fine Arts in Katowice in 1937, he taught at the academy of fine art in Cracow from 1945. Influenced by French Post-Impressionism and one of the representatives of the colourist and outdoor movement in Polish painting, Rzepinsky painted landscapes and still-lifes in particular. He also executed murals, notably at Wawel Castle, Cracow (1933) and in Katowice (1938).

Czeslaw Rzepinsky exhibited in Paris in 1932. He held five solo exhibitions between 1938 and 1961, including: Cracow; Warsaw; London (1960); and Vienna (1961). He was awarded the City of Cracow Art Prize in 1958 and was selected for the S. Guggenheim award in New York in 1960.

MUSEUMS AND GALLERIES:
WARSAW (Muz. Narodowe): *Still-life*.

AUCTION RECORDS:
PARIS, 20 Nov 1994, *Composition in Pink* (oil on canvas, 32 x 25 1/2 ins / 81 x 65 cm) FRF 4,000. WARSAW, 19 Nov 2000, *Still-life with Fruit* (oil on canvas, 33 x 39 ins / 85 x 100 cm) PLZ 14,000. WARSAW, 22 Feb 2001, *Woman Playing Lute* (1954, oil on canvas, 36 x 25 ins / 91 x 64 cm) PLZ 10,000. WARSAW, 29 March 2001, *Portrait Study* (oil on canvas, 20 x 24 ins / 50 x 61 cm) PLZ 12,500. WARSAW, 21 April 2002, *Still-life with Fruit on Dish* (oil on canvas, 21 x 26 ins / 54 x 65 cm) PLZ 12,000.

RZEWUSKI, Vincenty
Polish, 19th century.
Born 1803; died 1866.
Active in Warsaw.
Miniaturist.

Vincenty Rzewuski studied under Marszalkiewicz. The National Museum in Warsaw owns one of his works, *Portrait of Aniela Radziminska*, dated 1842.

RZHESHEVSKAYA, A. Z.
Russian, 19th - 20th century.
Born 1861.
Painter. Genre scenes, figures.
MUSEUMS AND GALLERIES:
MOSCOW (Rumiantsev Mus.): *Orphans*; *Gay Minute*.

RZHEVSKAYA, Antonina Leonardovna
Russian, 19th - 20th century.
Born 1861; died 1934.
Painter.
MUSEUMS AND GALLERIES:
MOSCOW (State Tretyakov Gal.).

RZYSZCZEWSKI, Aleksander
Polish, 19th century.
Born 6 December 1823, in Krzemieniec (now Kremenets, Ukraine); died May 1891, in Stary Oleksiniec.
Miniaturist.
Aleksander Rzszczewski was the son of Gabriel Rzyszczewski. He studied at the University of Warsaw. His works include *Portrait of the Artist's Mother, née Princess Czatoryska*.

RZYSZCZEWSKI, Gabriel
Polish, 19th century.
Born 1780, in Zukowice; died 1857, in Zukowice.
Painter.
Gabriel Rzyszczewski was a general and the father of Aleksander Rzyszczewski. He studied under D. Saint in Paris. He painted a *Transfiguration* for the church of Dederkaly in Volynia.

S.
Initial of an engraver.
The initial 'S.' is listed in Ris-Paquot.

S.
German.
Initial of an engraver.
This 'S', which is listed in Ris-Paquot, is to be found on a number of prints: *Adam and Eve, The Soldiers Offering Jesus Wine to Drink Before Crucifying Him, Jesus on the Cross, The Beheading of St John the Baptist, Temptation of St Anthony, St George, Standing Saint, Man and Woman Walking Together, Fencer, Sheath.*

S

S., MASTER WITH THE INITIALS.
See **MASTER S.**

S. A. D.
Flemish School, 15th - 16th century.
Active at the end of the 15th or the beginning of the 16th century.
Monogram of a painter.
S. A. D. is referred to by Ris-Paquot.

MUSEUMS AND GALLERIES:
ANTWERP.

S. A. V. H.
German.
Initials of an engraver.
The initials S.A.V.H. are listed in Ris-Paquot. They are to be found on prints of the *Crucifixion* and *Virgin with Monkey* (after Dürer).

SAVH

S. B.
16th century.
Initials of an engraver.
S.B. is known for *View of Buildings*.

SB

S. C.
German.
Initials of an engraver.
The initials S.C. are listed in Ris-Paquot. They are to be found on a print of *Adam and Eve*.

S. C.
German, 16th century.
Monogram of an engraver.
S.C. is referred to by Ris-Paquot. The monogram appears on *Peasants at Market* (1584), a copy of a print by Hans-Sebald Beham.

S. C., MASTER OF THE INITIALS
German, 16th century.
Active in Augsburg during the first half of the 16th century.
Engraver.
S.C. was a talented artist. Among his engravings are *St John at Patmos* (1517), *Wild Pair* and *Standard Bearer.*

S. E. V.
Flemish School, 16th century.
Monogram of an engraver.
S. E. V. is mentioned by Ris-Paquot. This monogram is found on aquatints after Birck van Staren dated 1540 and 1543.

S. F.
German.
Monogram of an engraver (wood).

S.F. is mentioned by Ris-Paquot; he worked in the style of Virgile Solès, Tobie Stimmer, Josse Amman and others.

S. F.
German, 16th century.
Monogram of a draughtsman.
S.F. is referred to by Ris-Paquot and was active about 1580. Two biblical subjects by him, engraved by an unknown artist, were included in Martin Luther's German Bible, which was printed in Frankfurt in 1565.

S. G.
Italian.
Monogram of an engraver.
S.G. is mentioned in Ris-Paquot.

S. H. G.
German.
Monogram of an engraver.
S.H.G. is mentioned in Ris-Paquot. This monogram was discovered on an ornamental panel depicting the grotesque.

S. I.
German.
Monogram of an engraver.
S.I. is mentioned in Ris-Paquot. These initials were discovered on a wooden engraving depicting a group of three oriental figures, one of which is making a sign to an apostle on a boat preaching to peasants on the seashore.

S. K.
Monogram of a sculptor (ivory).
S.K. is mentioned in Ris-Paquot.

S. P. M.
Monogram.
The initials S.P.M., discovered on certain engravings, stand for Sanctus Petrus, martyr: they were found on engravings by, or are imitations of, Marc Antoine, as mentioned in Ris-Paquot.

S. R.
16th century.
Monogram of a sculptor (ivory).
These initials, mentioned in Ris-Pacquot, were found on a diptych.

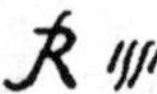

S. W.
German.
Monogram of an engraver.
The initials S.W. have been found on several pieces of artwork, including one of *The Passion of Christ*, a sequel of 12 prints copied from the works of Schongauer. The artist is mentioned in Ris-Paquot.

SA, Aernance de
Portuguese, 19th century.
Born in Avintes.
Sculptor.
Aernance de Sa was a pupil of Puech and Falguière. He settled in Paris where he exhibited his work and was awarded a bronze medal at the Exposition Universelle of 1900.

SA, Fernandes de. See **FERNANDES de SA Antonio**

SA DULA, or Sa Tou-la or Sa Tu-la, nickname: Tianxi, pseudonym: Zhizhai
Chinese, 14th century.
Born in Yenmen (Shanxi).
Active c. 1315-1340.
Painter.
Sa Dula was born into a Mongol family during the Yuan dynasty. He was also known as a calligrapher and a poet. He held the rank of *jinshi* (presented scholar) and held the position of provincial judge.
MUSEUMS AND GALLERIES:
TAIPEI (National Palace Mus.): *Two Birds on a Plum Tree* (1315, with a poem by the painter); *The Yen Guang Cliff Overhanging the River* (1339).

SA TOU-LA. See **SA DULA**

SA-NOGUEIRA, Rolando
Portuguese, 20th century.
Born 1921, in Lisbon.
Painter. Urban landscapes.
Rolando Sa-Nogueira spent much of the 1960s in London and was influenced by contemporary English painting; on his return to Portugal, he was also inspired by contemporary American trends.

SAA, Antonio
Spanish, 18th century.
Died 1790, in Seville.
Medallist, engraver. Coins.
Antonio Saa was chief engraver at the Seville mint.

SAABYE, August Vilhelm
Danish, 19th - 20th century.
Born 7 July 1825, in Skivholme (Aarhus); died 12 November 1916, in Copenhagen.
Sculptor. Mythological subjects, figures. Busts.
August Vilhelm Saabye exhibited in Paris and won a gold medal at the Expositions Universelles of 1889 and 1900.
MUSEUMS AND GALLERIES:
COPENHAGEN (Statens Mus. for Kunst): *Dancing Satyr, Faun and Little Bacchus* (1859); *Susanna before the Consul; Lady Macbeth* (1891); *Little Fisherman* (1856) - HILLERØD (Frederiksborg Slot): nine busts and a low relief.

SAABYE, Carl Anton
Danish, 19th century.
Born 26 August 1807, in Copenhagen; died 25 April 1878, in Copenhagen.
Painter. Landscapes.
Saabye studied in Copenhagen with Christian August Lorentzen and Christopher Wilhelm Eckersberg. He went on to study in Düsseldorf, Dresden and Munich.

SAAGMOLEN, Martinus, or Saeghmeulen, Zaagmolen, Zaegmolen, Zogmoolen
Flemish School, 17th century.
Born c. 1620, in Oldenburg; died 1669; buried 1 November in Amsterdam.
Painter, engraver. Religious subjects.

Saagmolen was a painter in Leiden in 1640, where he was one of the founders of the guild in 1648. He went to Amsterdam in 1654, and obtained the right of citizenship in that city in 1664. He had as his pupils N Piemont, J van Luyken and M van Musscher. Houbraken mentions his *The Last Judgment*, and he also realised etchings.

SAAL, or Sall
Hungarian, 18th century.
Born 8 July 1714, in Buda.
Sculptor.

Saal carried out restoration work at the church of St Anne in Budapest in 1746.

SAAL, Georg Eduard Otto
German, 19th century.
Born 11 March 1818, in Koblenz (Rhineland-Palatinate); died 3 October 1870, in Baden-Baden (Baden-Württemberg).
Painter. Genre scenes, landscapes, mountainscapes, waterscapes.
Barbizon School.

In 1842 Georg Eduard Otto Saal was a pupil of Johann Wilhelm Schirmer in Düsseldorf. In 1848 he went to Heidelberg, then to Baden-Baden, where he was appointed court painter. He regularly stayed in the Barbizon region of France. In 1870 he went to Paris but did not stay there long on account of the Franco-German war.

He painted mountain scenes, fjords and views of the forest at Fontainebleau. He is noted for his *Morning Landscape* and *Evening Landscape*.

He featured in the Exposition Universelle in Paris in 1867.

Museums and Galleries:
Amsterdam: *Moonlight* - Bremen: *Midnight Sun over the Northern Cape* - Frankfurt am Main: *Mountain View on the Hardang Fjord* - Karlsruhe (Staatliche Kunsthalle): *Avenue near Fontainebleau; Path near Fontainebleau* - Leipzig: *Midnight Sun in Norway; A Fjord in the Midnight Sun; Sea of Ice* - Mulhouse: *Moonlight Study* - Munich: *Moonlit Landscape in Norway*.

Auction records:
Paris, 17 Feb 1902, *The Crow and the Fox*, FRF 125. Paris, 30 April 1926, *River by Moonlight*, FRF 1,210. Neuilly-sur-Seine, 13 May 1950, *Mountain View*, FRF 2,700. Cologne, 17 March 1978, *Norwegian Landscape* (1863, oil on canvas, 15 1/4 x 21 1/4 ins / 39 x 54 cm) DEM 3,500. Munich, 29 May 1980, *Woodland Landscape with Lake* (1864, oil on canvas, 14 1/4 x 19 ins / 36.5 x 48 cm) DEM 2,600. New York, 28 May 1981, *Young Peasant Couple by Moonlight* (1864, oil on canvas, 29 1/2 x 40 3/4 ins / 75 x 103.5 cm) USD 3,500. Copenhagen, 8 Nov 1983, *Hinds in a Wooded Landscape* (oil on canvas, 29 1/2 x 37 ins / 75 x 94 cm) DKK 26,000. London, 26 Nov 1986, *Centenary Anniversary* (1865, oil on canvas, 32 3/4 x 49 1/4 ins / 83.5 x 125 cm) GBP 9,000. Rome, 25 May 1988, *Funeral on a Lake in the Alps* (oil on canvas, 39 x 51 1/2 ins / 99 x 131 cm) ITL 10,000,000. Cologne, 23 March 1990, *Garmish in the Tyrol* (1867, oil on canvas, 19 x 24 3/4 ins / 48 x 63 cm) DEM 2,200. New York, 24 Oct 1990, *Approach of the Storm* (1846, oil on canvas/card, 37 x 50 1/4 ins / 94 x 127.7 cm) USD 9,350. Amsterdam, 24 April 1991, *River Landscape with a Sailing Boat in the Moonlight* (1865, oil on canvas, 20 x 31 1/2 ins / 50.5 x 80 cm) NLG 5,520. London, 18 Jan 2000, *Shepherds Coming Home* (1868, oil on canvas, 40 x 60 ins / 102 x 152 cm) GBP 7,500. Oslo, 22 May 2001, *Norwegian Landscape with Two Farmers* (1855, oil on canvas, 35 x 55 ins / 90 x 139 cm) NOK 100,000. Oslo, 22 March 2004, *Landscape from Finnmark* (1852, oil on canvas, 24 x 39 ins / 60 x 98 cm) NOK 45,000. Cologne, 22 May 2004, *Norwegian Fjord* (1853, oil on canvas, 15 x 21 ins / 38 x 54 cm) EUR 2,500.

SAAL, Isaak
German, 17th century.
Active in Danzig (now Gdansk, Poland).
Engraver (burin).

Isaak Saal engraved the portraits of the scholars and pastors of Danzig between 1673 and 1678.

SAALBORN, Louis, called Loe
Dutch, 20th century.
Born 1890 or 1891, in Rotterdam; died 1957.
Painter. Portraits, landscapes, architectural views.

Louis Saalborn studied under K. van Leeuwen. He was a friend and erstwhile pupil of Piet Mondrian, whom he worked alongside in 1914-1915. His subsequent work clearly displays Mondrian's influence.

Bibliography:
Louis Saalborn, exhibition catalogue, Stedelijk Museum, Amsterdam, 1919.

Auction records:
Amsterdam, 29 Oct 1980, *View of a Church* (1916, oil on card, 27 1/2 x 19 1/2 ins / 70 x 49.5 cm) NLG 4,400. Saumur, 16 Nov 1986, *Satie's Saraband* (1917, oil on canvas, 32 x 42 1/2 ins / 81 x 108 cm) FRF 112,500. Paris, 9 April 1989, *Satie's Saraband* (1917, oil on canvas, 31 1/2 x 42 1/2 ins / 80 x 108 cm) FRF 450,000. Amsterdam, 24 May 1989, *Portrait Bust of a Woman in front of a Bay Window* (1915, black chalk and ink, 27 1/2 x 20 1/2 ins / 70 x 52 cm) NLG 4,140. Amsterdam, 22 May 1990, *Church of Cunera* (oil on canvas, 27 1/2 x 20 ins / 70 x 51 cm) NLG 18,400. Amsterdam, 22 May 1991, *Shells on a Beach* (oil on card, 24 3/4 x 29 1/4 ins / 63 x 74.5 cm) NLG 2,760. Amsterdam, 23 May 1991, *Farms near Heerden* (1949, oil on card, 19 3/4 x 23 1/2 ins / 50 x 60 cm) NLG 3,450. Amsterdam, 11 Dec 1991, *Farmyard* (1949, oil on canvas, 25 1/4 x 30 ins / 64 x 76 cm) NLG 4,025. Amsterdam, 18 Feb 1992, *Self-portrait* (1941, oil on canvas, 29 1/2 x 35 1/2 ins / 75 x 90 cm) NLG 1,092. Amsterdam, 21 May 1992, *Bergen Church and Lake* (1950, oil on canvas, 28 3/4 x 36 1/4 ins / 73 x 92 cm) NLG 4,370. Amsterdam, 9 Dec 1992, *View of a Town* (1922, oil on canvas, 23 3/4 x 23 3/4 ins / 60.5 x 60.5 cm) NLG 13,800. Lokeren, 4 Dec 1993, *Young Woman* (black chalk and wash, 27 1/2 x 20 1/2 ins / 70 x 52 cm) BEF 38,000. Amsterdam, 8 Dec 1994, *Portrait of a Lady* (1915, oil on canvas, 32 1/4 x 25 1/2 ins / 82 x 65 cm) NLG 17,250. Amsterdam, 4-5 June 1996, *Chrysanthemums* (1916, pencil, ink and watercolour/paper, 22 1/2 x 16 1/2 ins / 57 x 42 cm) NLG 1,035; *House with Pond* (oil on canvas, 19 1/4 x 25 1/2 ins / 49 x 65 cm) NLG 1,416. Amsterdam, 7 June 1999, *Still-life with Flowers* (oil on canvas, 41 x 35 ins / 105 x 90 cm) NLG 7,500. Amsterdam, 1 Dec 1999, *Mountain Landscape in Spring* (oil on canvas on board, 23 x 29 ins / 59 x 74 cm) NLG 7,500. Amsterdam, 7 June 2000, *Sailing Boat at Sea* (oil on canvas, 20 x 28 ins / 50 x 70 cm) NLG 4,000. Amsterdam, 4 Dec 2001, *Elegant Lady in the City at Night* (oil on panel, 8 x 11 ins / 20 x 27 cm) EUR 2,800. Amsterdam, 1 Sept 2004, *Seated Woman* (oil on board, double-sided, 32 x 24 ins / 82 x 60 cm) EUR 1,700.

SAALHAUSEN, Antonius von.
See **SALHAUSEN**

SAAN, P. de
British, 19th century.
Painter. Genre scenes.

Museums and Galleries:
Nottingham (Castle Mus. & AG): *Figures at Table, Singing*.

SAANE, Pieter. See **SANE**

SAAR, Alison

American, 20th - 21st century.

Born 1956, in Los Angeles.

Draughtswoman, installation artist, sculptor, engraver (including wood). Figures, animals.

Alison Saar studied at Scripps College, Claremont (California), and at the Otis Art Institute, Los Angeles. She is Betye Saar's daughter. She dwells on themes of the African diaspora in installations and sculptures where her figures can assume the dimension of fetishes. She brings together found objects, string, dust, all sorts of materials which, within her constructions or assemblages, take on ritualistic connotations. Her work also reflects ironically the role of women in a patriarchal society. She has produced monumental pieces in response to official commissions, notably for the subway station on 125th Street in New York. She has taken part in the Whitney Biennial, and *Making the Body in Contemporary Sculpture*, Allen Memorial Art Museum, Oberlin (Ohio). She has shown her works in solo exhibitions in museums and galleries in New York and Los Angeles.

BIBLIOGRAPHY:

Dallow, Jessica K., *Family Legacies/race, gender and inheritance in the art of Betye and Alison Saar*, dissertation (University of North Carolina, Chapel Hill (USA,NC), 2000). Lewis, Samella, *African American Art and Artists*, University of California Press, Berkeley, 1990. Adams, B., '*Alison Saar*' in *Art In America* vol. 80 n° 12, periodical, New York, December 1992. *Alison Saar, Fertile Ground*, exhibition catalogue, High Museum of Art, Atlanta, 1993. Brooks, R., '*Alison Saar*' in *ArtForum* vol. 37, n° 7, periodical, New York, March 1999.

MUSEUMS AND GALLERIES:

ATLANTA (High Mus. of Art) - BALTIMORE (MA) - HONOLULU (Contemporary Mus.) - KANSAS CITY (Nelson-Atkins MA): *Subway Preacher* (1984, installation) - LOS ANGELES (Getty Mus.): *Afro-Deity* (2000, installation) - NEW ORLÉANS (MA): *Travelin' Light* (1999, sculpture) - NEW YORK (Metropolitan Mus. of Art) - NEW YORK (Whitney Mus. of American Art) - NEWARK (Mus.) - OBERLIN (Allen Memorial AM): *Lave Tête* (2001, mixed media) - PROVIDENCE (Rhode Island School of Design): *Ulysses* (1994, engraving) - RICHMOND (Virginia MFA) - SANTA BARBARA (MA) - WASHINGTON DC (Hirshhorn Mus. and Sculpture Garden): *Snake Charmer* (1985).

SAAR, Alois von

Austrian, 19th century.

Born 1779, in Traiskirchen; died after 1840.

Painter (?), watercolourist, lithographer. Landscapes, architectural views.

Alois von Saar was a cousin of Karl von Saar. He was a pupil at the academy in Vienna. He is noted for his *View of Moldau Bridge in Prague* (Vienna Museum).

SAAR, Betye

American, 20th century.

Born 30 July 1926, in Los Angeles.

Painter, sculptor, assemblage artist, installation artist, illustrator.

Identity Art.

Betye Saar is the mother of Alison Saar. She studied at the University of California and the University of Southern California in Los Angeles, California University in Long Beach and Northridge, as well as at the American Film Institute in Los Angeles. She taught at the Otis Art Institute of the Parson School of Design in Los Angeles from 1976. She was awarded honorary doctorates from the California College of Arts and Crafts in Oakland in 1991; the Otis Art Institute of the Parson School of Design in Los Angeles; the San Francisco Art Institute in San Francisco, and from the Massachusetts College of Art in Boston in 1992; and from the California Art Institute in Los Angeles in 1995. She lives and works in southern California.

Saar assembles *objets trouvés* for her constructions, which evoke both the boxes created by Joseph Cornell and the ritual coffins used in the Afro-Cuban cults of La Santeria. She has been influenced by Simon Rodia, the creator of a monumental sculpture put together from *objets trouvés* entitled *Watts Tower* (1921-1954) which stands in the Black quarter of Los Angeles. She oscillates between being a militant artist, denouncing the condition of American Blacks oppressed as a consequence of slavery and pursuing a spiritual quest to pursue anything that makes up the collective Afro-American memory. She thus attempts to give positive depictions of racial stereotypes or popular symbols such as the American flag. In her famous assemblage *The Liberation of Aunt Jemima* (1972) she transformed the stereotype of the fat Black nanny into a woman armed with a rifle in one hand and a bayonet and a grenade in the other. Aunt Jemima is also clenching a raised fist in the style of the Black Panthers. She illustrated *A Secretary to the Spirits* (Ishmael Reed, NOK Publishers, New York, 1978).

She has participated in many collective exhibitions, including: 1977, *Painting and Sculpture in California: The Modern Era*, National Art Gallery, Smithsonian Institute, Washington DC; 1999, *The American Century: Art and Culture 1900-2000*, Whitney Museum of American Art, New York; 2000, *Strength and Diversity: A Celebration of African American Artists*, Carpenter Center, Harvard University, Cambridge (Massachusetts). Solo exhibitions have included: 1977, San Francisco Museum of Modern Art, San Francisco; 1980, Studio Museum in Harlem, New York; 1984, 1990, Museum of Contemporary Art, Los Angeles; 2000, 2002, Michael Rosenfeld Gallery, New York.

BIBLIOGRAPHY:

Clothier, Peter, *Betye Saar*, exhibition catalogue, Museum of Contemporary Art, Los Angeles, 1984. Shepherd, Elizabeth (dir.)/Lippard, Lucy, et al., *The Art of Betye and Alison Saar: Secrets, Dialogues, Revelations*, Wight Art Gallery, University of California, Los Angeles, 1990. *The Art of Betye Saar and John Otterbridge*, exhibition catalogue, Biennial of São Paulo, São Paulo, 1994. Patton, Sharon F., *African-American Art*, Oxford University Press, Oxford, 1998. Carpenter, Jane H., *Betye Saar*, Pomegranate, San Francisco, 2003.

MUSEUMS AND GALLERIES:

BERKELEY (AM): *The Liberation of Aunt Jemima* (1972, mixed media) - LOS ANGELES (California African American Museum) - NEW YORK (Metropolitan Mus. of Art) - NEW YORK (Studio Mus. in Harlem) - NEW YORK (Whitney Mus. of American Art) - OAKLAND (Mus. of California) - SAN FRANCISCO (FAM) - SAN FRANCISCO (MoMA): *The Time In Between* (1974, wooden box containing photographs, magazine illustration, paint and envelope) - ST LOUIS (AM) - TRENTON (New Jersey State Mus.) - WASHINGTON DC (Corcoran Gal. of Art).

SAAR, Karl von

Austrian, 19th century.

Born 22 August 1797, in Vienna; died 23 March 1853, in Vienna.

Painter, watercolourist. Portraits.

Karl von Saar was a cousin of Alois von Saar. He was a pupil at the academy in Vienna. He mainly painted miniatures.

MUSEUMS AND GALLERIES:

VIENNA: a portrait.

AUCTION RECORDS:

PARIS, 26 Jan 1949, *Portrait of a Young Woman in a White Dress Wearing a Large Hat* (1823, miniature) FRF 7,000. PARIS, 3 March 1950, *Young Woman in a White Dress* (1825, miniature) FRF 15,000; *Young Girl with Curly Hair* (1838, miniature) FRF 5,900. VIENNA, 23 Feb 1989, *Portrait of a Lady* (1833, watercolour/ivory, 4 1/4 x 3 1/4 ins / 10.5 x 8.3 cm) ATS

66,000. LONDON, 22 Nov 1999, *Countess Kinsky in White Dress with Gauze Veil* (miniature, 3 x 2 ins / 7 x 6 cm) GBP 1,100. VIENNA, 2 Oct 2001, *Portrait of Girl with Roses in Hair* (watercolour on ivory, miniature, 5 x 4 ins / 12 x 9 cm) ATS 55,000. LONDON, 6 Nov 2001, *Young Boy in a Brown Coat and Spotted Blue Tie* (miniature, oval, h. 4 ins / 9 cm) GBP 6,500. LONDON, 24 July 2002, *Young Lady in a Low Cut Dress* (1840, miniature, h. 3 ins / 8 cm) GBP 2,300.

SAARBURCK, Bartholomäus.
See **SARBURGH**

SAARBURG, Ludwig
German, 19th century.
Born 18 August 1778, in Trier.
Portrait artist, draughtsman.

Ludwig Saarburg was a pupil of Peter Schmid. He settled in Hamburg in 1809.

SAARI, Peter
American, 20th - 21st century.
Born 1951, in New York.
Sculptor (mixed media).

Peter Saari graduated from the Yale University School of Art in 1976. He also studied at the School of Visual Arts in New York and at the Tyler School of Art in Rome.

AUCTION RECORDS:
NEW YORK, 6 Nov 1985, *Untitled* (1983, casein, plaster and canvas mounted/panel, 29 x 45 ins / 73.8 x 114.3 cm) USD 2,750. NEW YORK, 7 Nov 1985, *Untitled* (1975, plaster and tempera/shaped canvas, 57 x 120 x 2 1/4 ins / 144.7 x 305 x 5.5 cm) USD 4,200. NEW YORK, 10 Oct 1990, *Untitled* (1986, wall relief, casein, gesso and plaster/canvas and card, 78 1/2 x 41 1/2 ins / 199.6 x 105.4 cm) USD 5,225. NEW YORK, 30 June 1993, *Untitled Mural Relief* (1986, casein, gesso and plaster/canvas and card, 78 1/2 x 41 1/2 ins / 199.4 x 105.4 cm) USD 6,325.

SAAS, Joseph
German, 19th century.
Active in the first half of the 19th century.
Sculptor.

Joseph Saas was the son of Michael Saas. He sculpted pulpits in Neudorf and Philippsburg and altars in Oberhausen, near Bruchsal.

SAAS, Michael
German, 18th century.
Died 1789.
Active in Bruchsal.
Sculptor, designer of ornamental architectural features.

Michael Saas was the father of Joseph Saas.

SAAS, Peter Anton
German, 19th century.
Active in Rastatt in the first half of the 19th century.
Sculptor. Religious furnishings.

Peter Anton Saas was the son or brother of Joseph Saas.

SAATHAAS, Laurenz
Swiss, 18th century.
Born 29 March 1721.
Active in Schaffhausen.
Modeller (wax), goldsmith.

Laurenz Saathaas produced wax sculptures.

SAAVEDRA, Alejandro
Spanish, 17th century.
Sculptor (wood).

Alejandro Saavedra carved the high altar of the old cathedral of Cádiz in 1650.

SAAVEDRA, Francisco de
Spanish, 16th century.
Sculptor (wood).

Francisco de Saavedra sculpted the tabernacle for the altar of the Virgin in S Pedro in Seville, with Pedro de Heredia, in 1541.

SAAVEDRA Y RAMIREZ DE BAQUEDANO, Ángel (Duke of Rivas)
Spanish, 19th century.
Born 10 May 1793, in Cordova; died 22 June 1865, in Madrid.
Painter. History painting, portraits, still-lifes.

Ángel Saavedra y Ramirez de Baquedano was a Spanish general who took refuge in Orléans during the Restoration and gave painting lessons in the town. He later became president of the parliament and duke of Rivas.

MUSEUMS AND GALLERIES:
ORLÉANS: *Bread, Radishes, Bottle and Coffeepot* (signed in Arabic).

SABADINI. See **SABATINI** and **SABBATINI**

SABADINI, Giovanni Battista. See **SABATINI**

SABAN, Ody or Odet
Turkish, 20th - 21st century.
Born 1953, in Istanbul.
Active in France.
Painter, watercolourist, draughtswoman, sculptor, mixed media, performance artist.
Art Brut.
Art-Cloche Group.

Saban studied restoration in Istanbul, sculpture in Tel Aviv and painting in Haifa, and from 1977 to 1980 at the École des Beaux-Arts in Paris. She was a member of the Art-Cloche group, which was established in 1981 and occupied a squat in the Rue Arcueil in Paris; this informal group claimed Dada and Fluxus as its sources of inspiration. She spent time in New York in 1980, and lives and works in Paris.

In her meticulous coloured paintings and Indian ink drawings heightened with watercolour, Saban creates surrealist compositions in which figures and writing enter into a game of decorative arabesques, influenced by miniatures and Turkish calligraphy. She portrays an organic, teeming universe in which order and disorder combine.

Saban has taken part in collective exhibitions in Tel-Aviv (1977); regularly in Paris, especially at the Salon de la Jeune Peinture and the Salon d'Automne (from 1978), the Salon des Indépendants (1980) and the Musée des Arts Décoratifs (1982); in Art-Cloche events in Paris, Venice and Bologna (regularly from 1980); in Istanbul (1986, 1987); at the Bibliothèque Municipale, Amiens (1987); at the national museum of painting and sculpture, Ankara (1990); and in *Noir sur Blanc. Mondes Intérieurs* (*Black on White: Inner Worlds*), Halle St-Pierre, Paris (2001). She has shown her works in solo exhibitions in Paris (regularly since 1977), in Istanbul (1986) and in Ankara (1987).

BIBLIOGRAPHY:
Chevrefils Desbiolles, Annie, '*Odet Saban, les chiffres*' in *Fonds National d'Art Contemporain*, catalogue, Centre national des Arts plastiques, Paris, 1989. *Art cloche. Élément pour une rétrospective. Squatt artistique*, auction catalogue, Maître Pierre Cornette de Saint-Cyr, Paris, 30 January 1989. *Ody Saban*, exhibition catalogue, Gal. Procréart, Paris, 1990. Monnin, Françoise, '*Ody Saban, racines iconoclastes et fleurs de lune*' in *Artension* n° 16, periodical, Rouen, July-August 1990. Gallien, Antoine/Lusardy, Martine/Pons, Louis, *Noir sur Blanc. Mondes intérieurs*, exhibition catalogue, La Halle Saint-Pierre, Paris, Travioles, Paris, 2001 (text in French and English).

MUSEUMS AND GALLERIES:
ANKARA (National Library) - AUVERS-SUR-OISE (Mus. Daubigny) - PARIS (BNF) - PARIS (FNAC): *Numerals* (1979).

Auction records:
Paris, 10 June 1990, *Icon of the Bride's Trousseau* (watercolour and Indian ink/paper, 30 1/4 x 22 1/2 ins / 77 x 57 cm) FRF 3,700.

SABARTÈS, Jaime

Spanish, 20th century.
Born 1880, in Barcelona; died c. 1970, in Barcelona.
Active in France.
Painter, sculptor.

Jaime Sabartès met Pablo Picasso in Barcelona in 1889 and decided to devote himself to the master, acting as his secretary/factotum and chronicling major events in the artist's life. Picasso painted several portraits of Sabartès, who lived and worked in Paris except for time spent in the USA during World War II.

SABAS, Christian

French, 20th - 21st century.
Born 21 January 1953, in Pointe-à-Pitre, Guadeloupe.
Painter. Figures.
Groupe Art-cloche.

Christian Sabas is a self-taught painter and ex-psychiatric nurse who moved to Paris in 1973 and began painting a decade later. He was a member of the Art-Cloche Group of artists founded in 1981, an informal grouping of Dada and Fluxus-inspired artists who 'squatted' in a building in the Rue de l'Arcueil in Paris.

Christian Sabas paints lone or group figures which populate an indeterminate universe conjured up from untreated canvas and scraps of paper covered with a network of lines and tracings and punctured by nails.

Sabas took part in Art-Cloche group exhibitions in Berlin and Paris (1989), Hamburg (1990), at Salons in Vitry and Bagneux, and at the Salon de Montrouge (1991). He exhibited solo in 1992 at the Galerie Mostini Bastille in Paris.

Bibliography:
Art cloche. Élément pour une rétrospective. Squatt artistique, auction catalogue, Maître Pierre Cornette de Saint-Cyr, Paris, 30 January 1989. Monnin, Françoise, *Sabas*, Gal. Mostini Bastille, Paris, 1992.

Auction records:
Paris, 4 April 1993, *Untitled* (mixed media/canvas, 46 1/2 x 51 1/4 ins / 118 x 130 cm) FRF 3,500. Paris, 21 Nov 1993, *Untitled* (mixed media/canvas, 46 1/2 x 51 1/4 ins / 118 x 130 cm) FRF 4,800. Paris, 4 Oct 1994, *Composition* (1990, oil on canvas, 57 x 45 ins / 145 x 114 cm) FRF 7,800.

SABATÉ JAUMA, Pablo

Spanish, 20th century.
Born 1872, in Reus (Catalonia); died 1957.
Painter, watercolourist, engraver, draughtsman.
Landscapes.

Sabaté Jauma moved to Barcelona, where he initially studied architecture before entering the Escuela de Bellas Artes. He served as president of the Agrupació d'Aquarellistes de Catalunya (The Association of Catalan Watercolorists) from 1927 to 1936. His own watercolours comprise mainly Barcelona street scenes, together with designs for costumes. He also worked as a book illustrator.

Bibliography:
Arnáiz, José Manuel/López Jiménez, Javier/Merchán Díaz, Manuel (ed.), *'Cien años de pintura en Espana y Portugal (1830-1930)'* in vol. IX, Antiqvaria, Madrid, 1992.

SABATELLI, Francesco

Italian, 19th century.
Born 22 February 1803, in Florence; died 1829, in Milan.
Painter, fresco artist, engraver (etching). Historical and mythological subjects.

Francesco Sabatelli was the son and pupil of Luigi Sabatelli. He continued his studies in Rome and Venice. He was summoned to Florence by Grand Duke Leopold II in 1823 and was appointed professor at the academy there. He produced a number of etchings.

Museums and Galleries:
Prato (Mus. Civico): *Ajax, Son of Oïleus, Scrambling Ashore, Sees the Sinking of his Fleet* (painting); *Hector Preparing for Battle* (fresco).

Auction records:
Milan, 21 April 1986, *Mythical Subjects* (pen, nine drawings on a page from a sketchbook, 13 1/4 x 18 ins / 33.7 x 46 cm) ITL 1,500,000. Milan, 12 June 1989, *Scene from a Classical Tragedy* (oil on canvas, 18 1/4 x 31 ins / 46.5 x 79 cm) ITL 4,500,000.

SABATELLI, Gaetano

Italian, 19th century.
Painter. History painting.

The son of Luigi Sabatelli I, Gaetano Sabatelli was active in Milan until 1893.

Museums and Galleries:
Prato (Mus. Civico): *Cimabue, Dismounting from his Horse, Sees the Child Giotto Drawing a Goat on a Stone.*

Auction records:
Rome, 4 Dec 1990, *Double Portrait* (1880, oil on canvas, 11 1/2 x 10 ins / 29 x 24.5 cm) ITL 3,500,000.

SABATELLI, Giovanni

Italian, 15th century.
Sculptor.
Sienese School.

Giovanni Sabatelli worked on the tomb of the bishop Carlo Bartoli in Siena Cathedral, in 1444.

SABATELLI, Giuseppe

Italian, 19th century.
Born 24 June 1813, in Milan; died 27 February 1843, in Florence.
Painter. History painting, portraits.

The son and pupil of Luigi Sabatelli, Giuseppe Sabatelli was appointed professor at the Accademia di Belle Arti in Florence in 1834.

Museums and Galleries:
Florence (Uffizi): *Self-portrait* - Milan (Gal. d'Arte Moderna): *Othello and Desdemona* - Prato (Mus. Civico): *Farinata degli Uberti at the Battle of the Serchio River.*

SABATELLI, Luigi I

Italian, 18th - 19th century.
Born 19 or 21 February 1772, in Florence; died 29 January 1850, in Milan.
Painter, engraver (etching). History painting.

Luigi Sabatelli was the pupil of Pietro Pedroni at the academy in Florence, and worked in Rome and Venice between 1788 and 1797. In 1808 Eugène de Beauharnais made him a teacher at the academy in Milan. He produced paintings for many public monuments. His works include *Abigail before David*, in the chapel of the Virgin in Arezzo; *Christ Blessing the Children*, in the Palazzo Paroni in Genoa; *The Four Great Prophets*, in S Gaudenzio church in Novara; *Olympic Games*, in the Pitti Palace in Florence; *Marriage of Cupid and Psyche*, in Busca Serbelloni Palace in Milan; *Adoration of God by the Prophets and Patriarchs*, in Valmadrera church in Lucca; and *Coronation of the Virgin*, in S Firenze church in Florence.

His son Luigi Sabatelli the Younger often assisted him in his work. He produced many fresco paintings, and engraved genre scenes and mythological subjects.

Museums and Galleries:
Florence: drawings - Florence (Uffizi): *Self-portrait* - Lille: drawings - Milan: drawings - Rome: drawings.

AUCTION RECORDS:
MILAN, 25 May 1978, *Battle Scene* (oil on card, 23 1/2 x 35 1/4 ins / 60 x 89.5 cm) ITL 1,000,000. MILAN, 4 Nov 1986, *Il Carroccio della Battaglia di Montaperti* (pen and black ink, 4 1/2 x 19 1/4 ins / 11.2 x 49 cm) ITL 2,600,000. LONDON, 7 July 1987, *Death of Brutus and Aruns* (1832, black chalk, pen and brown ink, 12 3/4 x 16 1/2 ins / 32.2 x 42.1 cm) GBP 2,600. MILAN, 14 Nov 1990, *Christ and the Tribute Money* (oil on canvas, 42 3/4 x 48 1/2 ins / 108.5 x 123 cm) ITL 28,500,000. ROME, 11 Dec 1990, *Woman with a Book* (1848, pencil, 9 1/2 x 7 ins / 24.2 x 17.5 cm) ITL 1,265,000. LONDON, 2 July 1996, *Crucifixion* (black chalk, ink and wash heightened with white/brown treated paper, 20 3/4 x 14 1/4 ins / 52.9 x 36.4 cm) GBP 3,220. LONDON, 21 Nov 1996, *Charon Ferrying Souls* (pen and brown ink, 17 1/2 x 24 1/4 ins / 44.2 x 61.8 cm) GBP 4,600.

SABATELLI, Luigi II
Italian, 19th century.
Born 12 February 1818, in Milan; died 5 May 1899, in Milan.
Painter, fresco artist. Religious subjects.

The son and assistant of Luigi Sabatelli I, he specialised in fresco painting. His work can be found in many churches in Milan and other northern Italian cities.

SABATER SALABERT, Daniel
Spanish, 20th century.
Born 13 December 1888, in Valencia; died 27 December 1951, in Barcelona.
Painter, miniaturist, pastellist. Scenes with figures, religious, allegorical, and military subjects, nudes, portraits. Fans.

Sabater Salabert began working in a fan designer's studio before travelling to Madrid, where he was exposed to the work of Spanish masters such as Velázquez, Goya and Ribera. Early in his career he painted militiary themes but when he moved to Paris in 1912, where he remained about a year, he was commissioned to paint religious compositions for the convent church of St Vincent-de-Paul, which he executed in luminous colours. On his return to Spain his canvases featured macabre scenes peopled by witches and monsters and his colour palette darkened and took on a sickly blue-green tinge. He spent morning after morning in various mortuaries in Madrid, taking corpses as his models. His output earned him the nickname 'witches' painter'. He was beset by family problems and affairs of the heart to the point where his painting became increasingly morbid in outlook. His work was received with increasing disfavour in his native Spain and he removed to the Americas, where he travelled extensively in both the north and south, returning to Spain only in 1923.

Sabater exhibited his work at the Sociedad Nacional de Bellas Artes in Madrid in 1910 and also exhibited in Uruguay and Brazil.

BIBLIOGRAPHY:
Daireaux, Max, *Daniel Sabater, Peintre des sorcières*, Per Orbem, Paris, no date (1930?). Arnáiz, José Manuel/López Jiménez, Javier/Merchán Díaz, Manuel (ed.), '*Cien años de pintura en Espana y Portugal (1830-1930)*' in vol. IX, Antiqvaria, Madrid, 1992.

MUSEUMS AND GALLERIES:
HAVANA (Mus. Nacional, Palacio de Bellas Artes) - PARIS (MNAM-CCI).

AUCTION RECORDS:
PARIS, 1 Feb 1943, *Allegory of Luxury*, FRF 6,300. PARIS, 29 Jan 1945, *Nudes* (two oils on canvas) FRF 4,800. PARIS, July 1946, *Nude (Isn't Life Wonderful?)*, FRF 7,000. PARIS, 8 Nov 1946, *Nude and Monsters*, FRF 4,200. MADRID, 20 Dec 1976, *Good and Evil* (1934, oil on panel, 18 1/2 x 15 ins / 47 x 38 cm) ESP 105,000. PARIS, 6 May 1981, *Spanish Woman on the Planet Mars* (1931, oil on card, 26 3/4 x 32 1/4 ins / 68 x 82 cm) FRF 8,000. PARIS, 1 July 1988, *Tender Hearts, Eastern Quack Doctors* (oil/hardboard, 16 x 13 ins / 40.5 x 33 cm) FRF 6,800. VERSAILLES, 25 March 1990, *Earth Mother* (oil on canvas, 25 1/2 x 39 1/4 ins / 65 x 100 cm) FRF 34,000. PARIS, 4 March 1992, *Heatwave* (oil on canvas, 25 1/2 x 32 ins / 65 x 81 cm) FRF 7,500. PARIS, 19 Nov 1993, *Bath* (oil on canvas, 39 1/4 x 32 ins / 100 x 81 cm) FRF 9,000. PARIS, 24 March 1995, *Civilising Influence, Paris* (oil on canvas, 18 x 22 ins / 46 x 55 cm) FRF 7,000. PARIS, 1 April 1998, *Land of Good Intentions* (oil on canvas, 25 1/2 x 36 1/4 ins / 65 x 92 cm) FRF 13,500. MADRID, 23 March 1999, *Figures with Guitar* (1929, oil on canvas, 26 x 21 ins / 65 x 54 cm) ESP 575,000. CALAIS, 7 Nov 1999, *Still-life with Fruit and Vegetables* (oil on canvas, 20 x 26 ins / 50 x 65 cm) FRF 14,000. COPENHAGEN, 6 Sept 2000, *Sunbathing from a Boat* (oil on canvas, 22 x 30 ins / 56 x 75 cm) DKK 14,000. MADRID, 6 Nov 2000, *And Now They Will Not Find the Dove. The Devil's Tickles* (oil on board, a pair, 16 x 13 ins / 40 x 33 cm) ESP 550,000. PARIS, 6 April 2001, *Spanish Woman in the Lost Country* (1934, oil on panel, 24 x 31 ins / 60 x 80 cm) FRF 18,500. STOCKHOLM, 2 May 2001, *Fantastic Landscape with Figures* (1931, oil on canvas, 29 x 35 ins / 73 x 90 cm) SEK 30,000. MADRID, 12 March 2002, *Phydias and His Models* (1940, oil on canvas, 32 x 39 ins / 81 x 100 cm) EUR 3,500. LONDON, 19 Nov 2002, *Pretty Spanish Woman* (oil on canvas, 26 x 363 ins / 65 x 921 cm) GBP 3,000. PARIS, 26 June 2003, *Boat* (oil on canvas, 24 x 30 ins / 60 x 75 cm) EUR 1,900. MADRID, 23 Sept 2003, *Love of St Teresa of Avila* (oil on canvas, 39 x 32 ins / 100 x 81 cm) EUR 4,000. MADRID, 26 Jan 2004, *A Little Kiss and Nothing Else* (1935, oil on canvas, 39 x 31 ins / 98 x 78 cm) EUR 4,000. MADRID, 21 Sept 2004, *Spring* (1939, oil on canvas, 32 x 26 ins / 82 x 65 cm) EUR 7,000.

SABATER Y MUR, José
Spanish, 20th century.
Born 9 May 1875, in Barcelona.
Painter. Landscapes, waterscapes.

Sabater y Mur was a pupil of José Cusachs. Examples of his work include *Railway Platform; Garden; Springtime; Lake.* He exhibited at the Parès Salon in Barcelona and at the 1924 Madrid Salón de Otoño.

BIBLIOGRAPHY:
Arnáiz, José Manuel/López Jiménez, Javier/Merchán Díaz, Manuel (ed.), '*Cien años de pintura en Espana y Portugal (1830-1930)*' in vol. IX, Antiqvaria, Madrid, 1992.

SABATER Y PUCHADES, Vicente
Spanish, 19th century.
Born c. 1835, in Valencia.
Painter. Figures.

Vicente Sabater y Puchades was a pupil of F. Aznar.

SABATERII, Laurent
French, 14th century.
Glass painter.

Laurent Sabaterii was the son of Pierre Sabaterii and a very talented artist. He assisted his father and succeeded him.

SABATERII, Pierre
French, 13th century.
Active in Montpellier c. 1298.
Glass painter.

Sabaterii's stained glass windows for Montpellier Cathedral are renowned.

SABATIER, Aglaé Appoline (Mme)
French, 19th century.
Born in Mézières (Ardennes).
Painter, miniaturist.

Aglaé Sabatier was a student of Meissonier. She exhibited miniatures at the Paris Salon in 1861 and 1864.

SABATIER, Anne-Marie
French, 20th - 21st century.
Born 1947, in Paris.

Painter, illustrator. Landscapes, urban landscapes, landscapes with figures.

Anne-Marie Sabatier is a self-taught painter who started out as a street artist in Paris and St-Tropez. She produces illustrations for newspapers and women's magazines, together with posters and postcards. She was involved in two collaborative art naive compilations: *Paris et les Naïfs* (*Paris and the Naïfs*) of 1982 and *Chats Naïfs* (*Naïf Cats*) of 1984. Her work exhibits features common to most successful naive artists - a discerning eye, an ability to accumulate and faithfully capture detail, and a strong narrative sense. Anne-Marie Sabatier appears particularly at ease in the city, and she is adept at painting bustling canals and harbours and Parisian street scenes, including sweeping panoramas of the busy squares and shopping streets of the French capital painted from a vantage point high up on the rooftops.

She has shown examples of her work at group exhibitions: in 1985 and 1986, at the Salon International d'Art Naïf in Paris, in Honfleur, New York and New Jersey; and, on a regular basis, at the Salon Femmes Peintres et Sculpteurs, the Salon d'Automne and the Salon de la Marine in Paris. She has also exhibited solo, notably in specialist Parisian galleries such as Galerie Antoinette, Galerie Naïfs et Primitifs, and the Galerie Naïfs du Monde.

SABATIER, Étienne

French, 19th century.

Born c. 1810, in Montpellier.

Painter, draughtsman. Genre scenes, landscapes, landscapes with figures.

Étienne Sabatier was a student of Baron Gros and Alexandre Decamps. He exhibited regularly at the Paris Salon from 1831 to 1861.

MUSEUMS AND GALLERIES:

VILLENEUVE-SUR-LOT (Mus. Rapin): *Farmyard.*

AUCTION RECORDS:

PARIS, 20-22 May 1920, *Cavaliers in a Rocky Landscape,* FRF 1,000.

SABATIER, François Victor

French, 19th century.

Born 1823, in Agen.

Painter, watercolourist, draughtsman. Architectural views.

François Sabatier was the student of Hippolyte Le Bas and Decamps. He began as an architect. He exhibited at the Paris Salon from 1853 to 1881.

He produced a large number of drawings and watercolours, mostly representing views and churches in Paris and Nice.

AUCTION RECORDS:

PARIS, 24 Jan 1945, *Old Bridge of St Michel,* FRF 11,800. PARIS, July 1946, *New Louvre in 1858* (sepia wash/pen outlines) FRF 3,000. PARIS, 18 Oct 1946, *Pont Royal and Pavillon de Flore* (1855, pen and sepia wash) FRF 4,900. MONACO, 21 June 1991, *View of the Conciergerie Prison in Paris* (1856, brown ink wash, 13 3/4 x 22 ins / 35 x 55 cm) FRF 6,105.

SABATIER, Jean Baptiste

French, 19th century.

Painter. Portraits.

Jean Baptiste Sabatier featured at the Salon from 1831 to 1841. He was principally a miniaturist.

AUCTION RECORDS:

PARIS, 14 Feb 1951, *Young Woman in Green* (1831, miniature) FRF 6,200.

SABATIER, Josefa

Maiden name: Loubeur

Spanish, 19th century.

Active in Madrid in 1804.

Painter, miniaturist. Portraits.

SABATIER, Léo

French, 19th century.

Born 1826, in La Réole.

Draughtsman.

Léo Sabatier was a drawing teacher in Vire.

MUSEUMS AND GALLERIES:

VIRE.

SABATIER, Léon

French, 20th century.

Born 23 April 1891, in Toulon; died 2 October 1965, in Tourettes-sur-Loup.

Painter, fresco artist. Portraits, landscapes, seascapes.

Léon Sabatier, initially a building decorator, was a pupil at the École des Beaux-Arts, Toulon, when Bonny was the director. In 1911, he obtained a scholarship that enabled him to enter the École des Beaux-Arts in Paris, under Raphaël Colin, and the École des Arts Décoratifs, where he was awarded the Minister's prize. He served in the army in Avignon, and after the World War I he returned to Paris. He spent some time in Toulon in 1930 and finally settled there. He learnt the art of fresco painting with De Signori and Morreira and decorated the chapel of St-André (Nièvre) and the church of Toulon. He exhibited in Paris at the Salon des Independents and the Salon d'Automne, of which he was a member, and in 2003 was represented in the exhibition *José Mange,* held at the Musée d'Art, Toulon. In 1966, the same museum organised a retrospective of his works.

BIBLIOGRAPHY:

José Mange, exhibition catalogue, Musée d'Art, Toulon, 2003.

SABATIER, Léon Jean Baptiste

French, 19th century.

Born in Paris; died July 1887, in Paris.

Painter, engraver, draughtsman. Landscapes, architectural views.

He was a student of the Baron Taylor and Bertin. He exhibited at the Salon from 1827 to 1870, obtaining a third-class medal in 1839.

He produced a large number of illustrations: *Picturesque Views; Travels in Ancient France; Travels in Scandinavia;* by P. Gaymard; *Asia Minor; Constantinople; The Seine; European Sea Port; Paris in its Glory; Paris and its Ruins* (1872); *Paris through the Ages.* He also produced lithographs.

AUCTION RECORDS:

PARIS, 27 March 1950, *The Louvre* (1858, sepia) FRF 1,000. PARIS, 8 April 1991, *Market in Timgad* (drawing in watercolour, 12 1/2 x 20 1/2 ins / 32 x 52 cm) FRF 25,000. NEW YORK, 25-26 Nov 1996, *View of the Bay at Rio de Janeiro* (1850, oil on canvas, 32 x 44 1/2 ins / 81.3 x 113 cm) USD 59,700.

SABATIER, Louis Anet

French, 19th century.

Born in Gannat.

Painter.

Louis Sabatier exhibited landscapes at the Paris Salon from 1880. He was a member of the Société des Artistes Français from 1898.

AUCTION RECORDS:

PARIS, 18 March 1904, *On the Way,* FRF 150. PARIS, 21 Dec 1994, *The Fashionable Women Leaving* (pen with Indian ink and watercolour, 14 x 11 ins / 35.5 x 28 cm) FRF 6,500. BRUSSELS, 10 Dec 2001, *China Town* (oil on canvas, 35 x 26 ins / 90 x 66 cm) BEF 90,000.

SABATIER, Roland

French, 20th century.

Born 1942, in Toulouse.

Painter, engraver.

Lettrism.

Roland Sabatier lives and works in Paris. He has authored several books and novels and has worked alongside Alain Satié. When Sabatier initially joined the Lettrist group in 1963, his compositions featured exclusively Latin calligraphy. He quickly adapted, however, incorporating into his *Hypergraphics* characters taken from various alphabets which completely covered the surface of his canvases. As of 1969, he introduced foreign elements into his compositions in the form of specific 'constraints' - bandages, folds, tears, erasures, even partial destruction. By the 1980s, he had become preoccupied with Taoism (the *Talismans* series) and was producing 'diagrammatic' compositions akin to ideograms.

Sabatier has shown examples of his work at various Lettrist group exhibitions in Paris, exhibiting on a regular basis at the Galerie Michel Broomhead (1986, 1989), the Galerie Rambert (1987, 1988), the Galerie 1900-2000 (1988), and the International Contemporary Arts Fair (1988, 1989). He has also shown abroad, notably in Chicago and Florence in 1989 and at the Modern Art Gallery in Bologna in 1990.

BIBLIOGRAPHY:

Lettrisme: les débuts, 1944-1966. Isidore Isou, Gabriel Pomerand, Maurice Lemaître, Roland Sabatier, Alain Satié, Gal. Rambert, Paris, 1987.

MUSEUMS AND GALLERIES:

PARIS (BNF): *Italian Suite.*

AUCTION RECORDS:

PARIS, 4 June 1989, *Lettrist Composition* (1987, oil and gouache/paper, 31 1/2 x 37 ins / 80 x 94 cm) FRF 26,000. DOUAI, 2 July 1989, *History of Architecture: Circus No. 4* (1987, oil on canvas, 22 x 18 ins / 55 x 46 cm) FRF 8,000. PARIS, 18 Feb 1990, *Lettrist Composition* (1987, gouache, 31 1/2 x 37 1/2 ins / 80 x 95 cm) FRF 25,000. PARIS, 14 June 1990, *Hypergraphy with Allusions* (1989, acrylic/canvas, 23 1/2 x 28 3/4 ins / 60 x 73 cm) FRF 28,000. DOUAI, 1 July 1990, *Composition* (mixed media/paper, 21 x 19 3/4 ins / 53.5 x 50 cm) FRF 15,000. PARIS, 23 Oct 1990, *Solence, Error No. 5* (1963, oil on panel, 22 x 28 1/4 ins / 56 x 72 cm) FRF 41,000. PARIS, 17 March 1994, *Hypergraphy with Silent Gestures* (1964, black ink wash/paper, 25 1/2 x 19 3/4 ins / 65 x 50 cm) FRF 6,000. PARIS, 23 March 1998, *Lettrist Composition* (1964, gouache/paper, 28 x 20 3/4 ins / 71 x 53 cm) FRF 3,800. PARIS, 27 Nov 2002, *Multiplication Hyperthestine* (1966, acrylic, ink and oil, 53 x 43 ins / 134 x 109 cm) EUR 4,000.

SABATINI. See also **SABBATINI**

SABATINI, Giovanni Battista, or Sabadini
Italian, 18th century.
Active in Pavia.
Painter.

At one time, Giovanni Sabatini worked in the Jesuit church in Nevers. He also produced several paintings for churches in Pavia.

SABATINI, Luigi
Italian, 19th century.
Born 1840
1895
Painter. Religious subjects, genre scenes.

Sabatini was a pupil of Silvio Valeri in Perugia. He executed five paintings of saints for the high altar in the church of S Fortunato in Todi during the second half of the 19th century.

AUCTION RECORDS:

NEW YORK, 16 Feb 1995, *The Book of Poetry* (oil on canvas, 26 x 16 3/4 ins / 66 x 42.5 cm) USD 8,050. LONDON, 21 Nov 1997, *Afternoon Concert* (oil on canvas, 27 1/2 x 19 3/4 ins / 70 x 50 cm) GBP 12,650. ROME, 21 Nov 2000, *Miracle* (oil on canvas, 30 x 39 ins / 75 x 100 cm) ITL 6,000,000.

SABATINI, Marina
Spanish, 18th century.
Active in Madrid during the second half of the 18th century.
Pastellist.

Marina Sabatini was a member of the Real Academia de San Fernando in 1790.

SABATO, Gabriele de, or Sabbato
Italian, 18th century.
Active during the first half of the 18th century.
Painter.

In 1720, Gabriele Sabato painted ten pictures representing the *Life of St Bernard Tolomeo* in the church of S Maria di Monteoliveto in Naples.

SABATOWICZ, Jan
Polish, 17th century.
Active during the first half of the 17th century.
Painter, engraver. Portraits.

SABATTE, Fernand
French, 19th - 20th century.
Born 14 May 1874, in Aiguillon; died 1940.
Painter, sculptor. Portraits, landscapes, architectural views, church interiors, architectural interiors.

Fernand Sabatte, a pupil of Gustave Moreau, taught at the École des Beaux-Arts, Paris. He exhibited in Paris at the Salon des Artistes Français, of which he was a member and where he was awarded an honourable mention in 1896, a third-class medal in 1897, a second-class in 1898, and a silver during the Paris Exposition Universelle of 1900. He won the Prix de Rome in 1900, and became a Chevalier of the Légion d'Honneur in 1912 and an Officier in 1920. He received the Medal of Honour in 1926 and was appointed to the Institut de France in 1935.

MUSEUMS AND GALLERIES:

BORDEAUX: *Church Interior; My Grandmother* - BUCHAREST (Muz. National de Arta al României): *St-Germain-l'Auxerrois* - PARIS (former Mus. du Luxembourg): *Portrait of the Artist's Grandmother; Interior of the Church of St-Germain-des-Prés* - PARIS (MAM): *Interior of the Manor House of Champigny* - PARIS (Mus. du Petit Palais): *Old Tombs.*

AUCTION RECORDS:

PARIS, 31 Oct 1941, *Self-portrait,* FRF 4,200. PARIS, 27 April 1945, *Reclining Nude,* FRF 10,000. PARIS, 17 Nov 1948, *Under a Church Porch* (1899) FRF 2,000. PARIS, 19 March 1951, *Nude on a Divan,* FRF 3,200. PARIS, 18 Nov 1973, *Coming Out of the Cathedral* (36 1/2 x 43 1/4 ins / 93 x 110 cm) FRF 3,900.

SABATTIER, Louis Rémy
French, 19th - 20th century.
Born in Annonay.
Painter, illustrator. Portraits.

Louis Rémy Sabattier, a pupil of Gérôme and Boulanger, exhibited in Paris at the Salon des Artistes Français, of which he was a member from 1890 and where he was awarded an honourable mention in 1894. Among his works were posters advertising toothpaste.

AUCTION RECORDS:

PARIS, 3 April 1950, *German Guns on the Place de la Concorde in 1918,* FRF 4,000.

SABBADINI, Giuseppe, or Sabbatini
Italian, 18th century.
Sculptor (wood).

Giuseppe Sabbadini stayed for a time in Venice and was active in Padua around 1793. He produced a sculpture of *St Jerome Kissing the Cross* for the tabernacle of the church of S Giustina in Rovigo.

SABBAGH, Georges Hanna
Egyptian, 20th century.
Born 10 August 1887, in Alexandria; died 9 December 1951, in Paris.

Active in France and naturalised from 1930.
Painter, pastellist, watercolourist, engraver, decorative artist. Nudes, portraits, landscapes, still-lifes.
Orientalism.

Georges Hanna Sabbagh left Egypt in 1906 for Paris, where he was the student of Maurice Denis, Paul Sérusier and Félix Valloton. He became a professor at the Académie Ranson in Paris and at the school of fine arts in Cairo from 1926. He associated with the artists of Montparnasse, including Modigliani. In spite of extended periods in Egypt, his career progressed mainly in France.

Sabbagh was both an elegant and a robust painter of portraits, figures, nudes, landscapes in Brittany and Cairo, and still-lifes. Influenced by the Nabis, Cézanne and Cubism, he forged an individual style in intimate canvases that were structured through geometrisation of the volumes. Working with a thick paste, he simplified the planes, adopting a restrained palette with few contrasts (ochre and earth tones) and conferring a monumental quality on his works. In the 1930s, he maintained a simplicity of composition but his works became more Expressionist through a greater spontaneity and his palette was enriched with a wider variety of colours.

Sabbagh exhibited in Paris at the Salon d'Automne, of which he was a member, the Salon des Indépendants and the Salon des Tuileries. He took part in exhibitions in Amsterdam, Brussels, Ghent, Geneva, Lausanne, London and Stockholm. The Salon d'Automne in Paris devoted a major retrospective exhibition to his work in 1952 and in 1987, and his work has also been exhibited in Cairo and Alexandria (1953); at the Centre Culturel Égyptien in Paris (1982); at the Salon des Indépendants in Paris (1984); at the town hall in Perros-Guirec (1988); at the Musée de Boulogne-Billancourt (1990); and in Toulon (1991). He was made a Chevalier of the Légion d'Honneur in 1928.

BIBLIOGRAPHY:

Sabbagh, Jean/Sabbagh, Pierre, *Georges Sabbagh*, Beauchesne Éd., Paris, 1981. *Georges Sabbagh 1887-1951*, exhibition catalogue, Musée municipal, Boulogne-Billancourt, 1990. Sabbagh, Pierre/Sabbagh, Jean, et al., *G. H. Sabbagh. Tout l'œuvre peint*, AFOSA, Paris, 1995.

MUSEUMS AND GALLERIES:

AUTUN (Musée des Ursulines) - BEAUVAIS (Mus. départemental de l'Oise): *Synthesis of Ploumanac'h* (1920); *Landscape in Brittany* - BEIRUT (Sursock Mus.): *Nude Lying on the Beach* (1924) - BOULOGNE-BILLANCOURT (Mus. des Années 1930): *Human Life* (1919); *Venus Anadyomene* (1922) - CAIRO (Egyptian MMA): *Village beside the Nile* (1928); *Storm on the Brittany Coast* (1933); *Coptic Convent in Maadi, near Cairo* (1936) - GENEVA (Petit Palais): *Tree* (1949) - GRENOBLE (Mus. de Grenoble): *The Sabbaghs in Paris* - LE HAVRE: *Seascape* (1931) - PARIS (MAMVP): *Sailing Boats at Aswan* (1930) - PARIS (MNAM-CCI): *Family: The Sabbaghs in La Clarté* (1920); *Monte Forno at Majola* (1929) - ST-GERMAIN-EN-LAYE (Mus. du Prieuré-Maurice-Denis): *Portrait* - VERDUN (Musée de la Princerie): *Allegory of Peace*.

AUCTION RECORDS:

PARIS, 21 Jan 1924, *Still-life: Marigolds and Books*, FRF 400. PARIS, 26 April 1928, *Banks of the Nile*, FRF 720. PARIS, 14 June 1934, *Naked Woman with a Shawl*, FRF 1,050. PARIS, 9 July 1942, *Port of Ploumanac'h*, FRF 900. PARIS, 12 Dec 1946, *Nude*, FRF 3,800. PARIS, 18 Nov 1949, *Landscape*, FRF 24,000. PARIS, 2 April 1952, *Landscape in Savoie* (oil on canvas) FRF 40,000. PARIS, 20 Nov 1953, *Village in Provence* (oil on canvas) FRF 40,000. PARIS, 28 Nov 1955, *Sunset at Ploumanac'h* (1920, watercolour) FRF 25,000. PARIS, 14 Feb 1966, *House in the Country* (oil on canvas) FRF 200. PARIS, 14 Oct 1974, *Impression of Snow* (oil on canvas) FRF 400. PARIS, 20 Feb 1975, *Stacks of Gorse in Brittany* (1921, oil on canvas) FRF 420. PARIS, 30 June 1975, *Quai des Bergues in Geneva* (1949, oil on canvas) FRF 600. PARIS, 28 Feb 1976, *Le Buffet* (1918, oil on canvas) FRF 900. PARIS, 17 March 1978, *Landscape in Brittany* (oil on canvas) FRF 950. PARIS, 29 May 1979, *Old Sycamore at Rod el Farag (Cairo)* (1920, oil on canvas) FRF 550. PARIS, 7 May 1980, *Sunset on the Sound* (1920, oil on canvas) FRF 1,700. PARIS, 19 June 1982, *Nude in an Interior* (oil on canvas) FRF 2,100. PARIS, 26 Oct 1983, *Impression of Fog at Champgattin (Crozant)* (1925, oil on canvas) FRF 5,000. PARIS, 6 April 1987, *Mill by the Sea at Ploumanac'h* (1928, oil on canvas) FRF 35,000. PARIS, 4 Dec 1987, *Nude with Pink Slipper* (c. 1924, oil on canvas) FRF 13,000. PARIS, 24 Jan 1990, *Staircase at Brélévenez in Lannion* (1918, oil on canvas) FRF 15,000. PARIS, 7 Feb 1990, *Recumbent Nude* (oil on canvas) FRF 8,000. PARIS, 8 April 1990, *Maritime Pines at La Clarté (Perros-Guirec)* (1918, oil on canvas) FRF 36,500. PARIS, 7 June 1991, *Feluccas at the Port of Old Cairo* (1921, oil on canvas) FRF 70,000; *Nude with Red Sheet* (1923, pastel) FRF 5,000. PARIS, 3 Feb 1992, *Model Resting* (1923, pastel, 18 x 24 1/4 ins / 46 x 61.5 cm) FRF 5,000. CALAIS, 5 April 1992, *Recumbent Nude* (1923, pastel, 18 x 24 ins / 46 x 61 cm) FRF 13,000. PARIS, 8 April 1993, *Seated Nude* (oil on canvas, 18 x 15 ins / 46 x 38 cm) FRF 6,500. PARIS, 6 Oct 1993, *Still-life* (1920, watercolour and charcoal, 17 1/2 x 13 1/2 ins / 44.5 x 34 cm) FRF 4,200; *Arabian Village near Palm Trees* (1920, oil on card, 12 1/2 x 16 ins / 32 x 40.5 cm) FRF 4,200; *Seated Nude with Fur* (1921, oil on canvas, 24 x 19 3/4 ins / 61 x 50 cm) FRF 11,500. PARIS, 25 Feb 1996, *Peasant Woman of Cairo* (1928, oil on canvas, 29 x 21 1/4 ins / 73.5 x 54 cm) FRF 18,000. PARIS, 23 June 1997, *Landscape at Ploumanac'h (Côtes-d'Armor)* (1927, oil on canvas, 13 x 22 ins / 33 x 55 cm) FRF 5,000; *Seascape (St-Guénolé)* (1928, oil on canvas/card, 11 x 16 ins / 27 x 40.8 cm) FRF 4,500. PARIS, 7 Dec 1997, *Village in the Desert* (1939, oil on canvas, 8 1/4 x 12 1/2 ins / 21 x 31.5 cm) FRF 2,300.

SABBATINI, Andrea, or Sabatini, called Andrea da Salerno or Sabbatini da Salerno
Italian, 16th century.
Born c. 1487, in Salerno (Campania); died 1530, in Gaeta (Latina).
Painter (gouache), draughtsman. Religious subjects.

Andrea Sabbatini followed his father, a rich merchant, to Naples, and was brought up in the city by Raimo Epifanio. He was traditionally thought to have gone to Rome and to have been the pupil of, and subsequently worked with, Raphael. In this capacity he would have worked on frescoes in the Vatican and in S Maria della Pace. However, modern biographers claim that he never left Naples.

It seems clear that Sabbatini held some influential position. He produced an important decoration, now destroyed, in S Maria delle Grazie, Salerno; paintings in the vestibule and interior courtyard of S Gennaro dei Poveri, Naples; *Assumption of the Virgin* in Naples Cathedral; *Adoration of the Magi* in S Spirito di Palazzo, Naples; *Virgin and Infant Jesus* in S Dominico Maggiore, Naples, and *Mei Pietà* in Salerno Cathedral.

MUSEUMS AND GALLERIES:

BUDAPEST: *Death of the Virgin* - METZ: *Virgin, Infant Jesus and St John the Baptist* - NAPLES: *Miracle of St Francis by the City Walls of Gubbio*; *Miracle of St Nicolas*; *St Benedict* (two paintings); *Martyr*; *John the Baptist*; *St Benedict Welcoming Novices*; *Holy Carthusian Monk*; *The Magi*; *St Benedict Giving Holy Orders to Novices*; *St Paul* - ROHRAU (Schlossmuseum, Graf Harrach'sche Familiensammlung): *Virgin and Infant Jesus* - SALERNO: polyptych with four panels.

AUCTION RECORDS:

PARIS, 1855, *Holy Family*, FRF 1,150. PARIS, 1863, *Virgin and Infant Jesus*, FRF 600. PARIS, 19 April 1865, *Untitled* (pen and bistre) FRF 10. PARIS, 1895, *Christ among the Apostles*, FRF 45. NEW YORK, 12-14 April 1909, *Virgin on Throne*, USD 475. LONDON, 29 Feb 1910, *Coronation of the Virgin*, GBP 3. PARIS,

10 Feb 1950, *Figures of Apostles or Popes* (pen and wash, heightened with gouache, six drawings in the same frame) FRF 2,000. LONDON, 10 April 1981, *Virgin and Child with Sts Giovanni Guadalberto, Bernardo degli Uberti and Don Biagio Milanesi* (1522, oil on panel, 142 1/4 ins / 361 cm) GBP 22,000. NEW YORK, 17 June 1982, *Virgin and Child with St John the Child* (tempera/panel, gilt ground, 21 1/2 x 17 1/2 ins / 54.5 x 44.5 cm) USD 32,000. NEW YORK, 11 Jan 1990, *Virgin with Child and St John the Baptist* (tempera/panel with gilt ground, 21 1/2 x 17 1/2 ins / 54.5 x 44.5 cm) USD 52,250. NEW YORK, 16 May 1996, *Virgin with Child Surrounded by a Garland of Angels Appearing to St Sebastian and St Roch* (tempera/panel/canvas, 70 x 47 1/2 ins / 177.8 x 120.7 cm) USD 68,500. LONDON, 3 Nov 2000, *St Anthony Abbot* (oil on panel, 56 x 21 ins / 143 x 54 cm) GBP 3,000.

SABBATINI, Angelo
Italian, 16th - 17th century.
Active in Orvieto from 1590 to 1650.
Mosaicist.

Angelo Sabbatini assisted Provenzale in the production of mosaics for the cupola of St Peter's Basilica, Rome.

SABBATINI, Francesco
Italian, 17th century.
Active in Orvieto in 1632.
Painter.

Francesco Sabbatini copied the frescoes of B. Gozzoli in the church of S Rosa in Viterbo.

SABBATINI, Gaetano, or Sabadini, called Il Mutolo
Italian, 18th century.
Born 1703, in Bologna; died 1732, in Bologna.
Painter.

Gaetano Sabbatini, who was deaf and dumb, was also the pupil of Francesco Monti, D.M. Viani and C.A. Rambaldi. He painted a *St Benedict with St Scholastica* in the church of St John the Baptist of the Celestines in Bologna.

SABBATINI, Giuseppe. See **SABBADINI**

SABBATINI, Lorenzo, or Sabatini, Sabadini, Sabattini, called Lorenzino da Bologna
Italian, 16th century.
Born c. 1530, in Bologna; died 2 August 1576, in Rome.
Painter, draughtsman. History painting, religious subjects, portraits.
Bolognese School.

Lorenzo Sabbatini studied in Bologna with Tibaldi. Having produced many works in Bologna, he visited Rome under the pontificate of Pope Gregory XIII. He painted several scenes from the *Life of St Paul* in the Pauline chapel (Capilla Paulina) in the Vatican, with Federico Zuccaro, and *Triumph of Faith* in the royal hall (Sala Regia) in the Vatican. These works won him the position of superintendent of decoration in the Vatican.

Sabbatini also produced *Virgin and Saints* in S Pietro e S Paulo; *Crucifixion* in S Maria delle Grazie; *St Joachim* and *St Anne* in S Martino Maggiore and *St Michael Striking the Devil*, *The Four Evangelists* and *The Four Fathers of the Church* in S Giacomo, all in Bologna.

It appears that Sabbatini's studies of Raphael's work influenced his own style greatly, as he often took inspiration from the master. His work is also reminiscent of that of Parmigianino.

MUSEUMS AND GALLERIES:
BORDEAUX: *Holy Family* - BUDRIO: *Madonna with Child; St Catherine; St Lucy* (fragments of frescoes) - CHAMBÉRY (MBA): *Mystical Marriage of St Catherine* - DRESDEN: *Betrothal of St Catherine* - LA FÈRE: *Rest of the Virgin* - MILAN (Pinacoteca di Brera): *Virgin, Jesus and Saints* - PARIS (Louvre): *Holy Family* - PARMA (Pinacoteca Giuseppe Stuard): *Portrait of a Man; Portrait of a Woman* - ROME (Mus. e Gal. Borghese): *Portrait of a Woman* - ST PETERSBURG (Hermitage): *Mystical Marriage of St Catherine; Madonna and Child.*

AUCTION RECORDS:
PARIS, 1858, *Crossing the Red Sea* (pen with indigo wash heightened with white) FRF 20. PARIS, 4 Feb 1924, *Holy Family and an Angel,* FRF 4,100. LONDON, 13 July 1945, *Presentation to the Temple,* GBP 94. MONTE CARLO, 26 Nov 1979, *Virgin and Child* (pen, wash and touches of red, 13 x 9 1/4 ins / 32.8 x 23.2 cm) FRF 6,000. NEW YORK, 30 April 1982, *Angel* (pen and wash heightened with white/blue paper) USD 4,000. NEW YORK, 6 June 1984, *Adoration of the Shepherds* (oil on canvas, 10 1/4 x 44 1/2 ins / 25.8 x 113 cm) USD 4,000. MILAN, 6 June 1985, *Virgin with Patrons of the City of Bologna Surrounded by Angels* (oil on canvas, 46 x 32 3/4 ins / 116 x 83 cm) ITL 10,500,000. LONDON, 26 June 1985, *Christ Dead Carried by Two Angels* (etching, 10 1/2 x 8 1/2 ins / 26.7 x 21.4 cm) GBP 4,000. MILAN, 12 Dec 1988, *Circumcision* (oil on canvas, 67 x 96 1/2 ins / 170 x 245 cm) ITL 8,500,000. LONDON, 5 July 1989, *Virgin and Child Holding Fruit* (oil on canvas, 48 x 38 ins / 121 x 96.5 cm) GBP 48,400. NEW YORK, 10 Oct 1991, *Annunciation* (oil on canvas, 41 1/4 x 33 1/4 ins / 105 x 84.5 cm) USD 16,500. LONDON, 22 April 1994, *Holy Family with St Anne and the Infant St John the Baptist* (oil on panel, 38 1/2 x 29 3/4 ins / 97.9 x 75.6 cm) GBP 45,500. ROME, 23 May 1996, *Holy Family and St John* (oil on panel, 39 1/4 x 28 ins / 100 x 71 cm) ITL 57,500,000. LONDON, 17 Dec 1999, *Holy Family with SS Anne and Infant John Baptist* (oil on panel, 39 x 30 ins / 98 x 76 cm) GBP 22,000. NEW YORK, 23 May 2001, *St Jerome in the Wilderness* (oil on copper, 10 x 6 ins / 25 x 16 cm) USD 36,000. NEW YORK, 25 Jan 2002, *Madonna and Child with St Petronius* (black chalk, 15 x 10 ins / 38 x 25 cm) USD 6,500. MILAN, 14 May 2003, *Study of Angel* (pen/ink/watercolour, 12 x 7 ins / 30 x 19 cm) EUR 2,000.

SABBATINI, Niccolo
Italian, 16th - 17th century.
Born c. 1574, in Pesaro (Marche); died 25 December 1634, in Pesaro.
Painter, architect. Stage sets.

Niccolo Sabbatini worked in Urbino, in the service of the duke Francesco Maria II, for many years.

BIBLIOGRAPHY:
Hewitt, Bernard (ed.), *The Renaissance Stage: Documents of Serlio, Sabbatini and Furttenbach*, University of Miami Press, Coral Gables (FL), 1958.

SABBATO, Gabriele de. See **SABATO**

SABBIDES, Symeon
Greek, 19th - 20th century.
Born 1859, in Tokaj, Hungary; died 1927.
Active in Germany.
Painter. Genre scenes, landscapes.

Symeon Sabbides trained at the academy in Munich under Alexander Straethuber, Gyuia Benczur, Nicolas Gysis, Ludwig von Loefftz and Wilhelm von Diez. He worked in Munich.

MUSEUMS AND GALLERIES:
ATHENS (Gal.).

AUCTION RECORDS:
LONDON, 6 Oct 1989, *Landscape with Palm Trees* (oil on canvas, 13 x 9 3/4 ins / 33 x 25 cm) GBP 1,650.

SABBIONETA. See **PISENTI**

SABEL, Mans
Danish, 17th century.
Active in Alsen towards the end of the 17th century.
Painter.

SABEL, Petter
Danish, 17th century.
Active in Alsen in 1694.
Painter.

Sabel painted versions of *The Last Supper*, using portraits of contemporary people.

SABELIS, Huilbert
Dutch, 20th century.
Born 28 February 1942, in Wageningen.
Active in Canada from 1963.
Painter. Figures, scenes with figures, still-lifes.

Of Dutch-Indonesian origin, Huilbert Sabelis lived in Medan (Indonesia) from 1948 to 1952. From 1968, he lived in Canada, where he married a Filipina, and then he lived in Los Angeles from 1976 to 1977. He works in acrylics, lithography and silkscreens. Blending American, Indonesian and Philippine cultures, he paints flat, sketchy figures, stylised moving silhouettes and symbolic biomorphous forms on an often monochrome background. He sometimes envelopes his subjects with bundles of lines, using a supple linearity that is dominated by a play of curves. Examples include *Discussion, Young Lovers, The Lesson.*

He exhibited in Canada, the USA and Tokyo regularly from 1967, and was also represented in the exhibition *De Bonnard à Baselitz: Dix ans d'enrichissements du cabinet des estampes 1978-1988* (*From Bonnard to Baselitz: A Decade of Acquisitions by the Prints Collection 1978-1988*) at the Bibliothèque Nationale in Paris in 1992.

BIBLIOGRAPHY:
Grubisic, Vinko, *Sabelis*, exhibition catalogue, Keen Gall., New York, 1979.

MUSEUMS AND GALLERIES:
LOS ANGELES (City Mus.) - PARIS (BNF): *Geese* (1977) - TORONTO (Royal Ontario Mus.).

SABELLA, Giuseppe
Italian, 19th century.
Born 1779, in Sciacca; died 1845, in Sciacca.
Painter.

Giuseppe Sabella executed paintings for the churches and palazzi of Sciacca.

SABIELLO, Parmen Petrovich, or Zabello
Russian, 19th century.
Born 1830, in Monastyrchino.
Sculptor.

Sabiello studied at the art academy in St Petersburg. He sculpted statues and bust portraits.

SABIN, Joseph F.
French, 19th century.
Born 1846.
Engraver (etching), illustrator.

Joseph Sabin spent a long period in New York.

SABIN, Philippe
French, 20th - 21st century.
Born 1954, in Lille.
Sculptor.

Philippe Sabin was an exhibitor at the Paris Salon d'Automne of 1988. He works in polyester resins to produce 'primitive forms'.

SABINESE, Il. See **GENNAROLI Andrea**

SABIRZYANOV, Farkhat
Russian, 20th century.
Born 30 May 1933.
Painter (gouache). Portraits, still-lifes, flowers, landscapes.
Socialist Realism.

Farkhat Sabirzyanov trained at the Surikov Institute Moscow. He was influenced by Cézanne. His *On the Volga, Self-portrait in Autumn, Woman with Agave* can be quoted along with portraits of Lenin. He featured in exhibitions in Perm, Moscow, Leningrad (now St Petersburg) and Lviv.

AUCTION RECORDS:
PARIS, 25 Nov 1991, *Lenin at the Kremlin* (oil) FRF 14,000; *Dacha* (1987, oil on canvas, 32 1/4 x 23 1/2 ins / 82 x 60 cm) FRF 5,200. PARIS, 11 Dec 1991, *October 17 in St Petersburg* (oil on canvas, 39 1/4 x 35 1/2 ins / 100 x 90 cm) FRF 9,000; *Lenin at the Kremlin* (oil on canvas, 35 1/2 x 32 3/4 ins / 90 x 83 cm) FRF 14,000. PARIS, 16 Feb 1992, *Singer* (1962, oil on canvas, 42 1/2 x 46 ins / 108 x 117 cm) FRF 6,000. PARIS, 16 Nov 1992, *Still-life with Impatiens* (1959, oil on canvas, 35 x 39 3/4 ins / 89 x 101 cm) FRF 8,000.

SABIS, Juan
Spanish, 17th century.
Active in Granada.
Painter.

Juan Sabis painted landscapes for the archbishop's palace in Granada in 1636.

SABLÉ, André
French, 20th century.
Born 13 December 1921, in St-Thomas-de-Courceriers.
Painter, pastellist, draughtsman, sculptor.
Groupe Réalité Seconde.

In Paris, André Sablé studied painting with Aujame and sculpture with Rivière. He went on to live and work in Paris as a member of the Réalité Seconde group. His paintings are full of movement created by spontaneous gestures and squirts of paint. Greys, reds and oranges leap from the dark to reveal turmoil, the primal chaos. He has also carried out monumental works, including mosaics for school complexes in Laval and Sens, sculptures, rest areas and lighted walls. He exhibited in Paris at the Salon Comparaisons, of which he became a committee member, the Salon de la Jeune Peinture, the Salon d'Automne, the Salon des Indépendants, the Salon de Mai, the Salon du Dessin et de la Peinture à l'Eau, and the Salon d'Art Sacré, as well as in London, Brussels, Tokyo, Bangkok, Vienna, and Rio de Janeiro. He held solo shows regularly in Paris from 1957, and in 1957 at the Alliance Française, Montevideo, in 1987 in Le Mans, Lourdes and Chamalières, and in 1993 in Laval.

BIBLIOGRAPHY:
Réalité Seconde, group exhibition catalogue, Gal. d'Art contemporain, Chamalières, 1986. *André Sablé*, exhibition catalogue, Gal. Méduane, Laval, 1993.

MUSEUMS AND GALLERIES:
CHAMALIÈRES (MAC) - PARIS (MAMVP) - PARIS (MNAM-CCI).

SABLERY, Véronique
French, 20th century.
Draughtswoman, engraver, sculptor, installation artist.

Véronique Sablery lives and works in Caen. She creates works on the subjects of Mary Magdalene, weight, and gravitation using black and white photographs of clouds fixed between two plates of glass, suspended by cord or attached to metal structures, and from drawings, engravings and sculptures. In 1992, she was represented in the exhibition *De Bonnard à Baselitz - Dix Ans d'enrichissements du cabinet des estampes 1978-1988* (*From Bonnard to Baselitz: A Decade of Acquisitions by the Prints Collection 1978-1988*), held at the Bibliothèque Nationale, Paris. In 1995, she held a solo show of her works at the Artothèque, Caen, and the École des Beaux-Arts, Cherbourg.

BIBLIOGRAPHY:
Chalumeau, Jean-Luc, '*Véronique Sablery*' in *Opus international*, n° 134, periodical, Paris, autumn 1994.

MUSEUMS AND GALLERIES:
PARIS (BNF): *Blue Resonance* (1988).

SABLET, François Jean or Jean François, called The Roman
Swiss, 18th - 19th century.

Born 23 November 1745, in Morges; died 24 February 1819, in Nantes, France.

Painter, watercolourist, engraver, draughtsman.

History painting, portraits, genre scenes, landscapes, still-lifes.

François Jean Sablet was the son of the painter and art dealer Jacob Sablet, known as Jacques. He demonstrated remarkable talent from an early age. In 1767 he went to Paris and became a pupil of Vien. He later went to Rome and worked there successfully, acquiring the nickname 'The Roman', which stayed with him all his life. In 1777 he returned to Paris and obtained a grant from the town of Bern to continue his studies. On 20 November of the same year he married Madeleine Borel. The first events of the Revolution led him to return to Switzerland, but he stayed there only a short time before returning to Paris in August 1793. He exhibited two landscapes, two interiors and two portraits at the Salon in 1798, 1804, 1817 and 1819 (in a posthumous exhibition). In 1805 Sablet, a naturalised Frenchman, settled in Nantes and gained a good position there. He executed six large grisaille paintings for the city recalling the passage of Napoleon I to Nantes in 1809. These paintings, which were completed in 1812 and removed from the great hall of the stock exchange during the Restoration, were sold to America. A number of his works can be found in private collections in the Nantes region.

He was regarded as an excellent portraitist and collaborated with Madame Vigée Lebrun. He executed the figures and she painted the clothes.

Museums and Galleries:

Nantes (MBA): *Tivoli and the Roman Countryside Seen from the Appian Way; Gateway to Savoy; View of Italy; Vue de la Cale de la Machine près des Salorges à Nantes; Man in Nankeen Breeches in a Landscape; Madame Peccot; Mathurin Michel Peccot; François Peccot; Antoine Peccot; The Architect J. B. Ceineray; The Painter Pierre René Cacault; Female Portrait; The Artist* - Nantes (Mus. Dobrée): *Portrait of Th. Dobrée; Madame Dobrée.*

Auction records:

Paris, 1861, *View of a Grotto and an Ancient Temple near Rome* (drawing) FRF 42. Paris, 1897, *An Old Woman* (drawing) FRF 25. Paris, 18-20 March 1920, *Portrait of a Young Man,* FRF 200. Paris, 13 Nov 1924, *Hunter* (wash heightened with watercolour) FRF 320. Paris, 25 and 26 June 1926, *Female Portrait,* FRF 750. Paris, 23 Nov 1927, *Nymphs and Satyrs* (pen and wash) FRF 260. Paris, 12 Feb 1941, *Child's Swing* (1781) FRF 59,000. London, 21 June 1968, *Thomas Hope Playing Cricket,* Gns 9,500. Lucerne, 17 June 1977, *Landscape with Waterfall* (oil on canvas, 40 1/4 x 54 3/4 ins / 102 x 139 cm) CHF 12,500. Zurich, 12 Nov 1982, *Child's Swing* (1784, oil on canvas, 28 3/4 x 26 ins / 73 x 66 cm) CHF 50,000. Lille, 20 May 1984, *Cavalier and his Horse* (oil on canvas, 25 1/2 x 32 ins / 65 x 81 cm) FRF 38,000. Monte Carlo, 22 June 1985, *Portrait of a Man in front of a Castle* (1813, oil on canvas, 23 1/2 x 19 1/4 ins / 60 x 49 cm) FRF 140,000. Paris, 2 Oct 1985, *Gate of Vevaix in Switzerland* (grey wash, 12 1/2 x 10 1/4 ins / 32 x 26 cm) FRF 8,500. Monaco, 17 June 1989, *Male Portrait* (oil on canvas, 8 3/4 x 7 1/2 ins / 22.5 x 19 cm) FRF 19,980. Paris, 18 April 1991, *Portrait of a Child Wearing Earrings* (oil on canvas, 9 1/2 x 8 ins / 24 x 20.5 cm) FRF 28,000. New York, 12 Jan 1995, *Portrait of Charles Gruy Holding a Hoop next to his Dog, his Parents in the Background* (1796, oil on panel, 10 x 7 ins / 24.5 x 18 cm) USD 12,650. Paris, 24 Nov 1995, *View of the Gardens of the Villa Borghese in Florence* (watercolour, 17 x 24 3/4 ins / 43 x 63 cm) FRF 6,200. Zurich, 4 June 1997, *Still-life with Game and a Vulture* (oil on canvas, 21 1/2 x 26 ins / 54.5 x 66 cm) CHF 20,700.

SABLET, Jacob, called Jacques (père)

Swiss, 18th century.

Born 4 April 1720, in Morges; died 29 April 1798, in Lausanne.

Painter, art dealer.

Jacob Sablet père started out as a house painter. He was the father of François and Jacques Henri Sablet who were children of an earlier marriage. He married his third wife, the painter Lizette Maselier, and devoted himself to art, gaining some success. He became established as an art dealer in Lausanne.

SABLET, Jacques or Jacob or Jacques Henri (fils), or Jacques Sablet the Younger, called 'The Painter of the Sun'

Swiss, 18th century.

Born 28 January 1749, in Morges; died 4 April 1803, in Paris.

Painter, engraver, draughtsman. History painting, portraits, genre scenes, landscapes.

Jacques Sablet fils was the son of Jacob Sablet père and the younger brother of François Sablet. He worked with his father to begin with, but was then placed with the decorators Lyonnais and Cochet. He later rejoined his elder brother in Vien's studio. In 1775 Sablet left for Italy in the company of his master, who had been appointed master of the academy in Rome. He stayed there until 1794, having earned a distinguished position among the painters there. In 1781 he executed a painting of note entitled *City of Bern Represented by a Woman Giving her Hand to Minerva and Protecting Painting and Sculpture.* This work earned Sablet a bonus of 100 crowns. In 1791 he competed for the Rome Prize by submitting a painting on the subject *Venus Preventing Aeneas from Killing Helen;* he won second prize. Sablet never neglected his native country and he is believed to have spent time there on one or more occasions. From 1791 he exhibited at the Paris Salon. He was awarded a prize of 4000 francs following the 1795 Salon. On returning to Paris in 1794 he got married. However, it was an unhappy union that broke up 11 months later. He obtained a government pension and accommodation in the Louvre. He seems to have had close links to the Bonaparte family. Cardinal Fesch was a great admirer of Sablet's works and acquired a significant number of them for his renowned collection. In a sketch kept at the museum in Nantes, *Interior of the Hall of the Five Hundred at St-Cloud on the Evening of the 18th Brumaire,* Sablet is shown offering his arm to Pauline Bonaparte, then married to General Leclerc. He also painted her portrait as Princess Borghese and accompanied Lucien Bonaparte to Spain as ambassador.

Sablet possessed remarkable qualities as a draughtsman and colourist. His paintings, like some of those of Prud'hon, have unfortunately suffered from craquelure due to the underlying bitumen. The marquis of Granges de Surgère mentions this in his handbook *The Sablets.* Sablet also produced some interesting etchings.

In 2001 Sablet was represented at the exhibition *Un Paese Incantato: Italia Dipinta da Thomas Jones a Corot* (*An Enchanted Country. Italy Depicted by Artists from Thomas Jones to Corot*) at the Centro Internazionale d'Arte e di Cultura di Palazzo Te in Mantua.

Bibliography:

Van de Sandt, Anne, *Les frères Sablet (1775-1815): peintures, dessins, gravures,* exhibition catalogue, Musées départementaux de Loire-Atlantique, Nantes, Centre culturel français, Éd. Carte Segrete, Rome, 1985. Ottani Cavina, Anna (ed.), *Un Paese incantato. Italia dipinta da Thomas Jones a Corot,* exhibition catalogue, Electa, Milan, 2001.

Museums and Galleries:

Bern (Library): *City of Bern Represented by a Woman Giving her Hand to Minerva and Protecting Painting and Sculpture* - Lausanne (Cantonal MFA) - Morges (Salle de la Municipalité): *Justice* - NANTES: *Portrait of the Artist; Old Man Sitting Reading; Italian Washerwomen; Grape Harvests in Italy; Interior of the Hall of the Five Hundred at St-Cloud on the Evening of the 18th Brumaire, Year VIII* (sketch); *François Cacault Walking in his Garden* - SEMUR-EN-AUXOIS: *Woman Sitting in a Kitchen* - ZURICH (Kunsthaus): *Conrad Gessner in a Landscape* (oil on canvas).

AUCTION RECORDS:

PARIS, 21 Feb 1919, *Stage Coach* (Indian ink) FRF 60. VIENNA, 22 Sept 1970, *The Sablet Brothers Meeting at the Grave of a Friend*, ATS 55,000. LOS ANGELES, 28 Feb 1972, *Lovers*, USD 2,000. LONDON, 10 July 1979, *At the Antiquary* (1788, pen and gouache, 12 x 16 ins / 30.2 x 39.7 cm) GBP 3,300. MONTE CARLO, 22 Feb 1986, *Couple Drawing in the Countryside* (oil on canvas, 26 x 20 1/4 ins / 66 x 51.5 cm) FRF 350,000. NEW YORK, 28 Jan 1999, *Alban Peasants in Park near Rome* (1793, oil on canvas, 24 x 29 ins / 62 x 73 cm) USD 340,000. PARIS, 27 June 2002, *Portrait of Madame Danloux when Pregnant* (oil on canvas, 17 x 14 ins / 42 x 35 cm) EUR 27,000.

SABLIN, Nikolai Yakovlevich, or Ssablin
Russian, 18th century.
Born 1730; died 11 July 1808, in St Petersburg.
Engraver (burin).

Sablin studied under Ivan Sololov, G.F. Schmidt and A. Radigues. He engraved portraits, views, contemporary events, almanacs and book illustrations.

SABLJAK, Peter, or Srecko
Serb, 20th century.
Born 19 November 1892, in Zemun.
Painter, sculptor, engraver (wood).

Peter Sabljak trained in Zagreb, Budapest and Paris and practised wood engraving.

SABLON, Pierre
French, 17th century.
Born 1584, in Chartres.
Draughtsman, engraver.

Four prints by Sablon are worthy of attention: a copy of the engraving *Lamech and Cain* by Lucas de Leyde, which he produced at the age of 18 in 1602; *Portrait at 23 Years of Age*, produced in 1607; *Portrait of Rabelais*; and *Good Samaritan*. He may have died young.

SABLUKOV, Ivan Semenovich, or Sablukov or Ssablukov
Russian, 18th century.
Born c. 1735; died 17 December 1777, in Kharkov.
Portrait artist.

Sablukov studied under I. Argunov in St Petersburg.

MUSEUMS AND GALLERIES:

MOSCOW (State Tretyakov Gal.): *Portrait of M. Juryev.*

SABOGAL, José
Peruvian, 20th century.
Born 1888, in Cajabamba; died 1956, in Lima.
Painter. Scenes with figures, landscapes.

José Sabogal visited Europe and North Africa, then studied at the art school in Buenos Aires. While in Mexico he met Orozco and Rivera, whose influence he felt. He taught at the Lima art school.

He was an expressionist painter who wanted to increase awareness and appreciation of Amerindian traditions using simple compositions and vivid colours. His works include: *Amerindian Women of Quechua, Panorama: High Sierra* and landscapes.

AUCTION RECORDS:

NEW YORK, 7 May 1980, *Arab Horse no. 9* (1950, oil on canvas, 26 x 30 ins / 65.8 x 75.36 cm) USD 1,300. NEW YORK, 30 Nov 1983, *Indio* (1925, oil on canvas remounted on board, 26 3/4 x 24 3/4 ins / 68 x 63 cm) USD 1,800. NEW YORK, 23 Nov 1999, *Indian 'Chanca'* (1936, burlap, 29 x 24 ins / 74 x 60 cm) USD 2,000.

SABOIA, José
Brazilian, 20th - 21st century.
Born 1949, in Almadina.
Painter. Scenes with figures.

José Saboia took part in the Salão Nacional de Artes Plásticas in Ceara in 1969 and 1971. He received prizes for his work at the April Salon in Fortaleza in 1970. He exhibits regularly in Rio de Janeiro; much of his work is based on popular Brazilian themes.

AUCTION RECORDS:

NEW YORK, 18-19 May 1993, *Group of Musicians* (oil on canvas, 13 3/4 x 11 ins / 34.9 x 27 cm) USD 3,105.

SABOLOTSKY, Piotr Efimovich, or Zabolotski
Russian, 19th century.
Born 1804; died 28 February 1866.
Painter. Portraits, genre scenes.

Piotr Efimovich Sabolotsky was the father of Piotr Petrovich Sabolotsky. He studied at the art academy in St Petersburg.

MUSEUMS AND GALLERIES:

MOSCOW (State Tretyakov Gal.): *Portrait of Lermontov in Hussar Uniform.*

SABOLOTSKY, Piotr Petrovitch, or Zabolotski
Russian, 19th century.
Born 1842.
Portrait artist.

Piotr Petrovitch Sabolotsky was the son of Piotr Efimovich.

SABON, Laurent
French, 19th century.
Born 1852, in Nîmes.
Painter, watercolourist, decorative designer.
Landscapes. Stage sets.

Laurent Sabon's parents were from Geneva but he settled early in Paris, where he became the student of Lavastre, whom he later helped to paint sets for the Opera. In 1876, he was summoned to Geneva to paint the sets for the town theatre.

Sabon exhibited watercolours and views of Switzerland at the Paris Salon, winning a third-class medal in 1893. He also took part in the Geneva exhibitions. He produced many oil paintings and watercolours of the Geneva area.

The catalogue for the Salon of 1880 mentions a watercolourist by the name of Clément Sabon, born in Nîmes and a student of Cheret and Lavastre, who exhibited watercolours of the Geneva area. It seems likely that this is the same artist as Laurent.

MUSEUMS AND GALLERIES:

GENEVA (MAH): *Banks of the River Aire.*

SABORIT Y AROZA, Enrique
Spanish, 19th century.
Painter. Genre scenes.

MUSEUMS AND GALLERIES:

MADRID (Gal. of Modern Painters): *In Peril.*

SABOURAUD, Émile
French, 20th century.
Born 17 November 1900, in Paris; died 1996.
Painter. Figures, landscapes, still-lifes. Murals.
Poetic Reality.
School of Algiers.

Just after World War I, Émile Sabouraud became one of the first pupils of Othon Friesz at the Académie Moderne. He was a scholar at the Villa-El-Tif in Algeria, where he won the prize in 1935. He then visited Spain, the Canaries, Italy and the USA. He taught at the Académie Julian from 1946, and from 1954 at the École des Arts Décoratifs. He made very individual use of the sensuous brushstroke and acid, Fauviste colour of his teacher, Othon Friesz. He painted murals for the national open-air school at Salon-de-Provence in 1952, and for the Lycée Claude Bernard, Enghien. He exhibited regularly at Salon d'Automne and the Salon des Tuileries, of which he was a committee member, the Salon des Indépendants, the Salon Comparaisons, and the Salon des Peintres de Leur Temps. In 2003, he was represented in the exhibition *L'École d'Alger* (*The School of Algiers*), held at the Musée des Beaux-Arts, Bordeaux. After his first private exhibition at Zborowski's in 1928, he held solo shows in most of the Parisian galleries, including: until 1967, the Galerie Bernier, then the Galerie Ambroise, from 1973 the Galerie Articurial. Abroad, he exhibited solo in Algiers from 1935 to 1936 and at the Carnegie Foundation and in New York in 1951. He was the winner of the first Menton Biennale in 1951, of the Sestri Levante Biennale in 1952, and he was awarded the Wildenstein prize in 1970. He was made a Chevalier of the Légion d'Honneur.

BIBLIOGRAPHY:
Salmon, André (preface), *Sabouraud*, exhibition catalogue, Gal. Zborowski, Paris, 1928. *Sabouraud raconte Sabouraud*, Mame, Tours, 1988. Harambourg, Lydia, *L'École de Paris. Dictionnaire des peintres*, Ides et Calendes, Neuchâtel, 1993. Cazenave, Elisabeth/Dalia, Mahammed-Orfali/Vidal-Bué, Marion, *L'École d'Alger*, exhibition catalogue, Musée des Beaux-Arts, Bordeaux, 2003.

MUSEUMS AND GALLERIES:
ALGIERS (Mus. National des Beaux-Arts): *The Admiralty, Algiers* - NARBONNE (MAH): *Water Taxis* - PARIS (MAMVP) - PARIS (MNAM-CCI).

AUCTION RECORDS:
PARIS, 30 May 1945, *Still-life with Violin*, FRF 1,050. PARIS, 19 Feb 1954, *Bois de Boulogne*, FRF 38,000. PARIS, 27 March 1974, *Young Girls in a Garden*, FRF 5,500. NEW YORK, 25 Sept 1980, *River Landscape with Figures* (oil on canvas, 21 1/4 x 32 ins / 54 x 81 cm) USD 900. PARIS, 16 Dec 1987, *The Yellow Paper* (oil on canvas, 32 x 23 1/2 ins / 81 x 60 cm) FRF 9,500. PARIS, 22 April 1988, *Landscape* (oil on canvas, 19 3/4 x 26 ins / 50 x 66 cm) FRF 4,500. PARIS, 16 Oct 1988, *Still-life* (oil on canvas, 25 1/2 x 32 ins / 65 x 81 cm) FRF 11,000. CALAIS, 13 Nov 1988, *The Belfry, Calais* (oil on canvas, 32 x 25 1/2 ins / 81 x 65 cm) FRF 13,500. PARIS, 12 Feb 1989, *Mediterranean Landscape* (oil on canvas, 21 1/4 x 32 ins / 54 x 81 cm) FRF 17,500. PARIS, 7 April 1989, *Woman Seated in a Pink Armchair* (oil on canvas, 27 1/2 x 27 1/2 ins / 70 x 70 cm) FRF 15,000. PARIS, 18 June 1989, *Vase of Flowers* (oil on canvas, 17 x 13 ins / 43 x 33 cm) FRF 8,000. NEUILLY, 5 Dec 1989, *Rue St-Pierre, Milly* (oil on canvas, 19 3/4 x 24 ins / 50 x 61 cm) FRF 16,000. PARIS, 19 June 1990, *Landscape* (oil on canvas, 21 1/4 x 28 3/4 ins / 54 x 73 cm) FRF 13,000. PARIS, 2 July 1990, *Reclining Nude* (oil on canvas, 24 3/4 x 36 1/2 ins / 63 x 93 cm) FRF 34,500. PARIS, 10 Dec 1990, *The River Marne at Nogent-l'Artaud* (oil on canvas, 23 1/2 x 28 3/4 ins / 60 x 73 cm) FRF 9,500. PARIS, 6 Dec 1991, *Light-boat in Dunkirk* (oil on canvas, 23 1/2 x 36 1/4 ins / 60 x 92 cm) FRF 14,000. LE TOUQUET, 8 June 1992, *Portrait of Woman in a Red Hat* (oil on canvas, 32 x 23 1/2 ins / 81 x 60 cm) FRF 15,000. PARIS, 16 Oct 1992, *Still-life* (oil on canvas, 21 1/4 x 25 1/2 ins / 54 x 65 cm) FRF 14,500. PARIS, 26 Oct 1994, *Still-life* 1941, oil on canvas, 25 1/2 x 29 1/4 ins / 65 x 74.5 cm) FRF 3,500. NEUILLY, 9 May 1996, *Steamer Moored at a Quay* (oil on canvas, 23 1/2 x 29 1/4 ins / 60 x 74 cm) FRF 9,000. NEUILLY, 27 Nov 1997, *Table with Fruit* (1944, oil on canvas, 26 3/4 x 28 ins / 68 x 71 cm) FRF 19,000. ENGHIEN, 14 March 1999, *Still-life with Fruit and Book* (oil on canvas) FRF 14,000. ENGHIEN, 14 March 1999, *Trawlers at Dieppe* (1961, oil on canvas, 32 x 39 ins / 81 x 100 cm) FRF 14,000. OAK PARK, 2 Dec 2001, *Boats at the Dock* (oil on canvas, 27 x 32 ins / 69 x 81 cm) USD 1,600. PARIS, 17 Feb 2002, *Corner of the Studio* (1929, oil on canvas, 21 x 32 ins / 54 x 81 cm) EUR 2,800. PARIS, 10 April 2002, *Dam at Chezy-sur-Marne* (oil on canvas, 21 x 29 ins / 54 x 73 cm) EUR 3,300. ST-GERMAIN-EN-LAYE, 23 March 2003, *Still-life with Yellow Coffee Pot* (oil on canvas, 32 x 21 ins / 81 x 54 cm) EUR 2,800. PARIS, 16 June 2003, *Man Leaning* (oil on canvas, 26 x 19 ins / 66 x 47 cm) EUR 2,000.

SABOURAUD, Raymond Jacques
French, 19th - 20th century.
Sculptor.

Raymond Jacques Sabouraud was a doctor of medicine and an art lover whose collection was justly well-known. He exhibited in Paris at the Salon d'Automne and was a Commandeur of the Légion d'Honneur.

SABOURDY, Cécile
French, 20th century.
Born 6 March 1893, in Janailhac (Haute-Vienne); died 27 April 1970, in St-Priest-Ligoure.
Painter. Scenes with figures, landscapes.

Cécile Saboundy depicted the landscapes and villages of the Limousin simply and naturally. She exhibited at the Exposition des Artistes Limousin and at the Salon des Arts, Sciences et Lettres, Limoges, and in 1937 in the Limousin-Marche-Quercy-Périgord pavilion of the Exposition Internationale des Arts et Techniques, Paris. A posthumous retrospective of her work was held in Limoges in 1981. She was awarded the bronze medal of the Société Lorraine des Beaux-Arts in 1934 and 1935 in St-Dié and Strasbourg.

MUSEUMS AND GALLERIES:
WARSAW (French Institute): *Fenaison in the Limousin*.

SABOUREUX D'ARCHEVILLE
French, 18th century.
Portrait artist.

MUSEUMS AND GALLERIES:
DIJON: *Portrait of Bernard de La Monnaye* (1721) - RHEIMS: *Portrait of the Abbot Lebrun*.

SABOURIN, Denise
French, 20th century.
Painter.

Denise Sabourin, a pupil of the École des Beaux-Arts, Bordeaux, and that of Paris, lives and works in Poitiers, where she founded the Artothèque. She creates gestural paintings consisting of graphic signs similar to those of Far Eastern calligraphy. In 1989, she took part in an exhibition organised by the Galerie des Beaux-Arts, Bordeaux. Solo shows have included: 1983,1986, 1987 Poitiers; 1985 Perpignan; 1987 Bordeaux and Osaka; 1988, Toulouse and Montreal. She was awarded the Prize for Young Artists at the Biennale des Arts, Niort.

BIBLIOGRAPHY:
Cinq Artistes en 1989, exhibition catalogue, Gal. des Beaux-Arts, Bordeaux, 1989.

SABRAN-PONTEVÉS, Edmond Marie Zozine
French, 19th century.
Born in Marseilles.
Painter. Landscapes.

Edmond Sabran-Pontevés was the student of P. Colin. He first exhibited at the Salon of 1869.

SABRAN-PONTEVÈS, Éléazar Charles Antoine de (Duc)
French, 19th century.
Born 19 April 1840, in Marseilles; died 6 April 1894.
Painter, watercolourist. Landscapes.

As an amateur, Éléazar Sabran-Pontevès followed the courses of P. Martin and E. Soulet. He first exhibited at the Salon of 1880.

MUSEUMS AND GALLERIES:
BÉZIERS: *View of the Pond at Bages* - NARBONNE: *View of the Pond at Bages*.

SABRI BERKEL. See **BERKEL Sabri**

SABRIER, Jean
French, 20th - 21st century.
Born 1951, in Cestas (Gironde).
Painter, sculptor, installation artist.

Jean Sabrier lives and works in Bordeaux. He juxtaposes art and science (mathematics and information technology), setting side by side work by Renaissance painters and research by Marcel Duchamp in his installations. He is particularly fascinated by the interaction between the act of observing and the object observed. This is exemplified in his image of the mazzocchio (an article of Florentine headwear) which he identifies in the paintings of Paolo Uccello, Piero della Francesca and Leonardo da Vinci, rediscovers subsequently in Duchamp's *Chocolate Bean Grinder*, and then uses himself in his *Anamorphic Lamp* of 1989. Sabatier also produces books accompanied by objects and films.

He has been involved in various group exhibitions: in 1983, at the Musée Municipal in La Roche-sur-Yon; in 1993, at *Haptisch, une érotique du regard* (*Haptisch: An Erotic Exchange of Glances*), at the Musée de l'Abbaye Ste-Croix in Les Sables d'Olonne; and, in 2003, at *Une Collection de 'Chefs-d'œuvre', Emprunts, Pastiches, Copies, Citations et Interprétrations* (*A Collection of 'Masterpieces', Borrowings, Pastiches, Copies, Quotations and Interpretations*), an exhibition focusing on appropriation in (predominantly European) art, coordinated in Limoges by the Regional Fund for Contemporary Art (FRAC). Sabrier has also exhibited solo, notably in 1982, at the Galerie Janus in Bordeaux; in 1991, at *Faire Voir* (*Making Visible*), an exhibition held at Angoulême Museum; in 1992, at the French Institute in Athens; in 1993, in Bordeaux; and, in 1995, at the Musée du Périgord in Périgueux.

BIBLIOGRAPHY:
Jean Sabrier, exhibition catalogue, Gal. Janus, Bordeaux, 1982. Arnaudet, Didier, "*Jean Sabrier, le système du regard*" in *Art Press* n° 182, periodical, Paris, July-August 1993. Vanel, Hervé, "*Jean Sabrier prend du champ*" in *Beaux-Arts Magazine* n° 130, periodical, Paris, January 1995.

MUSEUMS AND GALLERIES:
PARIS (FNAC): *Constellation* (1990, installation).

SABUGO
Spanish, 16th century.
Active in Burgos (Castilla y León).
Sculptor (wood).

Sabugo worked on the stalls of Burgos Cathedral, from 1550-1557.

SABY, Bernard
French, 20th century.
Born 1925, in Pommard; died 4 July 1975, in Paris.
Painter (including gouache), pastellist.

After studying science and musical composition, Bernard Saby devoted himself from 1947 to the painting that, in fact, he had been practising since childhood. He always painted little and slowly, and for several years he gave up painting to study Chinese and Far Eastern philosophy. He came back to art only in 1974. Passionate about the natural sciences and obsessed with the study of lichens, for a long time he painted, almost as a miniaturist, transparent landscapes in small format. Later, his style broadened and became more complex. His works, often structurally indecipherable, evoked a world of dreams and infinite reflections. His deeply personal art was fully contemporary and earned him the respect and friendship of the poet Henri Michaux, the painter Zao-Wou-Ki, the musician Pierre Boulez and the writer Michel Fardoulis Lagrange. He was remembered by his friends as a person who was as enigmatic and reserved as his paintings. He exhibited at the Salon de Mai in 1953 and his first solo show was held in 1955 at the Galerie du Dragon, Paris, where he exhibited again in 1956 and 1974. In 1974, he presented his last exhibition of paintings, pastels and gouaches a few months before his premature death.

BIBLIOGRAPHY:
Jouffroy, Alain, *Saby ou le Labyrinthe*, Gal. du Dragon, Paris, 1955. Solier, René de, *Saby*, Gal. du Dragon, Paris, 1956. *Saby - Peintures, pastels, dessins*, exhibition catalogue, Gal. du Dragon, Paris, 1974. *Saby*, exhibition catalogue, Musée d'Art moderne de la ville de Paris, Paris, 1986. Harambourg, Lydia, *L'École de Paris. Dictionnaire des peintres*, Ides et Calendes, Neuchâtel, 1993. *Conversation de Bernard Saby avec Michel Butor*, Gal. de l'Œil, Paris, 1996.

AUCTION RECORDS:
PARIS, 20 March 1988, *Untitled* (1958, oil on canvas, 46 x 35 ins / 116 x 89 cm) FRF 20,000. PARIS, 20 Nov 1988, *Untitled* (1957-1958, tempera and wax/paper/canvas, 36 1/4 x 28 3/4 ins / 92 x 73 cm) FRF 37,000. PARIS, 18 Feb 1990, *Abstraction* (1964, oil on canvas, 18 x 22 ins / 46 x 55 cm) FRF 28,000. PARIS, 8 April 1990, *Small Flower in Magnosc* (oil on panel, 21 1/4 x 25 1/4 ins / 54 x 64 cm) FRF 45,000. PARIS, 8 Oct 1991, *Untitled* (oil on canvas, 28 3/4 x 39 1/4 ins / 73 x 100 cm) FRF 25,000. PARIS, 10 April 1992, *Untitled* (1964, gouache/paper/canvas, 32 x 39 ins / 81 x 99 cm) FRF 4,800. PARIS, 12 Dec 1992, *Untitled, VI-64* (1964, pastel/card/canvas, 37 3/4 x 51 1/4 ins / 96 x 130 cm) FRF 25,000. PARIS, 19 March 1993, *Composition* (1957-1962, oil on canvas, 51 1/4 x 63 3/4 ins / 130 x 162 cm) FRF 36,000. PARIS, 29 March 1995, *Untitled* (oil on canvas, 36 1/4 x 28 1/2 ins / 92 x 72.5 cm) FRF 12,000. PARIS, 24 March 1996, *Untitled* (1955, oil on canvas, 28 3/4 x 23 1/2 ins / 73 x 60 cm) FRF 11,000. PARIS, 19 Oct 1997, *Painting* (1960, oil on paper remounted/panel, 39 1/4 x 31 1/2 ins / 99.7 x 80.3 cm) FRF 6,000. PARIS, 3 March 1999, *Untitled* (oil on canvas, 18 x 22 ins / 46 x 55 cm) FRF 10,000. PARIS, 15 March 2000, *Composition* (oil on canvas, 52 x 39 ins / 132 x 98 cm) FRF 13,000. PARIS, 15 March 2000, *Composition* (1961, oil on canvas, 57 x 45 ins / 146 x 114 cm) FRF 19,000. PARIS, 4 June 2002, *Composition* (1963, pastel on paper on canvas, 37 x 50 ins / 95 x 128 cm) EUR 2,300. PARIS, 3 July 2002, *Composition* (1961, acrylic on canvas, 46 x 35 ins / 116 x 89 cm) EUR 3,300. PARIS, 29 April 2003, *Untitled* (1961, oil on canvas, 58 x 45 ins / 147 x 114 cm) EUR 3,800.

SABY-VIRICEL, Philippe. See **ARTIAS**

SACAILLAN, Edoyard or Edward
Greek, 20th century.
Active in France from 1985.
Painter. Interiors.

Edoyard Sacaillan trained at the school of fine art in Athens and with Cremonini in Paris. He practised figurative painting full of biographical elements and references, accumulating details and matterist effects. Edoyard Sacaillan exhibited in Paris.

BIBLIOGRAPHY:
Sacaillan, exhibition catalogue, Gal. Eonnet-Dupuy, Paris, 1990-1991. Perrot, Raymond, *'Edouard Sacaillan'* in *Artension*, Rouen, November 1990.

SACCA, Filippo, or Sache or Sacchi or de Sacchis, called dal Sacco
Italian, 15th century.
Active in Cremona in 1488.
Sculptor (wood), marquetry worker.

Filippo Sacca may have been identical with Filippo Morari. He probably sculpted the central portal of S Maria delle Grazie church in Brescia.

SACCA, Giacomo
Italian, 15th century.
Active in Cremona in 1498.
Sculptor (wood).

Giacomo Sacca sculpted the door and the window frames of the chapel of the choir in S Domenico basilica in Cremona.

SACCA, Giovanni Antonio
Italian, 16th century.
Born c. 1497.
Active in Cremona.
Sculptor (wood).
Giovanni Sacca was the son of Imero Sacca. He worked with his uncle, Paolo Sacca.

SACCA, Giuseppe
Italian, 16th century.
Active in Cremona from 1520 to 1554.
Sculptor (wood).
Giuseppe Sacca was the son of Paolo Sacca. He worked for the cathedral and various churches in Cremona.

SACCA, Imero
Italian, 16th century.
Died before 1519.
Active in Cremona.
Sculptor (wood).
Imero Sacca was the son of Tommaso Sacca, with whom he worked in 1496 on the stalls of the Carthusian monastery in Asti. He was the father of Giovanni Antonio Sacca.

SACCA, Paolo
Italian, 16th century.
Born in Piadena; died 31 May 1537, in Cremona.
Sculptor (wood), architect.
Paolo Sacca was the father of Giuseppe Sacca and the brother of Imero Sacca. He sculpted stalls and doors for churches in Cremona, Bologna and Vercelli.

SACCA, Tommaso, or Sacha, Sacchi or de Sacchis
Italian, 16th century.
Born in Cremona; died before 1517.
Sculptor (wood).
Tommaso Sacca was the father of Imero and Paolo Sacca. He worked in Parma from 1465. He sculpted lecterns for the cathedral and S Lorenzo church in Cremona and, with Imero, produced stalls in the Carthusian monastery in Asti.

SACCACCINO
Italian, 16th century.
Active in Carpi from 1503 to 1531.
Painter.
Saccaccino worked with Ugo da Carpi.

SACCADELLI, Francesco
Italian, 17th - 18th century.
Born c. 1670, in Casalmaggiore; died c. 1736.
Landscapist.

SACCAGGI, Cesare
Italian, 19th - 20th century.
Born 1868, in Tortona (Piedmont); died 1934.
Active in France.
Painter, watercolourist, pastellist. Portraits, genre scenes.
After studying at the Accademia Albertina di Belle Arti in Turin, Cesare Saccaggi moved to Paris where he exhibited works at the Salon des Artistes Français. He was awarded a bronze medal at the Exposition Universelle of 1900 and a third-class medal in 1903. He exhibited from 1895 to 1927.
MUSEUMS AND GALLERIES:
TURIN (Mus. Civico).
AUCTION RECORDS:
PARIS, 4 Feb 1925, *Baptism of St John the Baptist*, FRF 2,005. NEW YORK, 14 May 1976, *Bouquet of Mimosa* (oil on canvas, 23 1/2 x 15 3/4 ins / 60 x 40 cm) USD 1,800. PARIS, 4 April 1979, *Soul Nature Bird* (pastel/mounted paper, 31 1/2 x 51 1/4 ins / 80 x 130 cm) FRF 45,000. MILAN, 17 June 1981, *Samson as Prisoner of the Philistines* (oil on canvas, 36 1/4 x 46 1/2 ins / 92 x 118 cm) ITL 9,500,000. NEW YORK, 19 May 1987, *Procession* (oil on canvas, 12 1/2 x 18 ins / 31.5 x 46 cm) USD 12,000. LONDON, 24 June 1988, *Best Friends* (1928, oil on canvas, 58 1/4 x 38 ins / 148 x 96.5 cm) GBP 3,520. MILAN, 14 March 1989, *Travelling Players* (oil on panel, 11 3/4 x 9 3/4 ins / 30 x 25 cm) ITL 6,000,000. MILAN, 5 Dec 1990, *Flirtation* (watercolour/paper, 26 x 17 1/2 ins / 66 x 44.5 cm) ITL 5,700,000. LONDON, 19 June 1991, *Crowd Mocking a Prisoner* (oil on canvas, 37 x 50 1/2 ins / 94 x 128 cm) GBP 7,700. ROME, 9 June 1992, *Waterfall in the Susa Valley* (oil on panel, 11 x 15 3/4 ins / 27 x 40 cm) ITL 3,800,000. MILAN, 17 Dec 1992, *Portrait of a Woman* (oil on panel, 32 1/2 x 25 ins / 82.5 x 63.5 cm) ITL 1,800,000. MILAN, 29 March 1999, *At Prayer* (oil on canvas, 57 x 73 ins / 146 x 186 cm) ITL 82,000,000. VENICE, 16 Dec 2001, *Seascape* (1931, oil on board, 8 x 11 ins / 20 x 29 cm) ITL 5,500,000. PARIS, 24 May 2002, *Alma natura ave* (pastel, 32 x 52 ins / 81 x 131 cm) EUR 21,000. ROME, 27 May 2002, *Chioggia, Madonna delle Grazie* (oil on panel, 12 x 15 ins / 31 x 38 cm) EUR 2,800. ROME, 21 May 2003, *Portrait of a Young Woman* (oil on board, 26 x 21 ins / 65 x 54 cm) EUR 3,495.

SACCARDO
Italian, 19th - 20th century.
Born 16 February 1858, in Vicenza; died 7 May 1919, in Ceriano Laghetto.
Painter. Landscapes.
Saccardo was also an architect and engineer.

SACCARO, John
American, 20th century.
Born 1913, in San Francisco; died 1981, in San Francisco.
Painter, watercolourist.
School of San Francisco.
John Saccaro enrolled in the easel painters and murals sections of the government-sponsored PWAP (Public works of Art Project) in the 1930s, and in World War II he served in the French Army. From 1951-1955 he studied at the California School of Fine Arts in San Francisco, and from 1963-1964 taught at UCLA. He has held many solo exhibitions at the San Francisco Museum of Art, De Young Museum and the Oakland Art Museum. He was a major figure in the movement towards Abstract Expressionism in San Francisco.
MUSEUMS AND GALLERIES:
SAN FRANCISCO (FAM): *Ballet Chinoise* (oil on canvas); *Pleiades Suite, No. 1* (1954, oil on canvas).
AUCTION RECORDS:
LOS ANGELES-SAN FRANCISCO, 12 July 1990, *Rainy Landscape with Horses Under the Downpour* (1979, watercolour/paper, 17 1/2 x 23 1/2 ins / 44.5 x 60 cm) USD 1,045. SAN FRANCISCO, 26 Oct 1999, *Untitled, from the Dreams and Lies Series* (1955, on paper, 37 x 32 ins / 95 x 81 cm) USD 2,250. CINCINNATI, 23 May 2004, *Untitled* (1956, oil on canvas, 49 x 39 ins / 124 x 99 cm) USD 8,000.

SACCATORE, Giovan Domenico, or Saccataro
Italian, 16th - 17th century.
Active in Naples from 1596 to 1613.
Sculptor (wood).
Saccatore sculpted panels and organ cases for churches in Naples.

SACCELLA
Italian, 17th century.
Active in Lovere in 1657.
Sculptor (wood).
Saccella sculpted carved stalls in the church of S Maria in Valvendra.

SACCHETTI, Alessandro
Italian, 15th - 16th century.
Born 1474, in Brescia.
Painter.

SACCHETTI, Antonio
Italian, 19th century.

Born 8 January 1790, in Venice; died 15 April 1870, in Warsaw.
Painter, lithographer, decorative designer. Urban views. Stage sets.
The son and pupil of Lorenzo Sacchetti, Antonio Sacchetti painted stage sets for theatres in Brno, Prague, Dresden, Berlin and Warsaw.
MUSEUMS AND GALLERIES:
CRACOW (Muz. Narodowe): model of theatre set - WARSAW (Muz. Narodowe): *View of Warsaw*.

SACCHETTI, Enrico
Italian, 19th - 20th century.
Born 28 February 1874 or 1877, in Rome.
Painter, illustrator. Portraits.
MUSEUMS AND GALLERIES:
FLORENCE (Palazzo Pitti): *Portrait of a Woman* - FLORENCE (Uffizi) - TRIESTE (Civico Mus. Revoltella).

SACCHETTI, Francesco
Italian, 15th century.
Active c. 1465.
Painter.
Francesco Sacchetti was the brother of Giacomo Sacchetti.

SACCHETTI, Giacinta
Italian, 18th century.
Painter.
In 1734, Giacinta Sacchetti painted several pictures for the church of S Maria a Cellaro in Naples. She was a nun.

SACCHETTI, Giacomo
Italian, 15th century.
Born c. 1444.
Active in Verona from 1473 to 1492.
Painter.
Giacomo Sacchetti was the brother of Francesco Sacchetti. He drew geographical maps and reliefs.

SACCHETTI, Giovanni Battista, or Saqueti or Zacchetti
Italian, 18th century.
Born in Turin; died 3 December 1764, in Madrid.
Painter, architect, goldsmith.
A pupil of F. Juvara, Giovanni Battista Sacchetti went to Spain in 1736 and became a professor at the San Fernando academy in Madrid.

SACCHETTI, Giovanni Francesco, or Zacchetti
Italian, 17th century.
Active in Turin during the second half of the 17th century.
Painter.
Giovanni Francesco Sacchetti painted altarpieces for churches in Turin, Chieri, Lanzo and Chambéry.
MUSEUMS AND GALLERIES:
VIENNA (Albertina Mus.): *Denarius* (drawing).

SACCHETTI, Lorenzo
Italian, 18th century.
Born 22 June 1759, in Padua.
Painter, lithographer, fresco artist, engraver. Stage sets.
The brother of Vincenzio and father of Antonio Sacchetti, Lorenzo was the pupil of Domenico Cerato and Domenico Fossati in Venice. He produced frescoes in palaces in Padua and engraved sets for the opera *Coriolanus* at the opera house in Vienna.
AUCTION RECORDS:
LONDON, 11 Dec 1985, *Stage Set: Adonis with Hunting Party* (black chalk, pen and wash, 8 3/4 x 13in/22.4 x 33cm) GBP 700.

SACCHETTI, Vincenzio
Italian, 18th - 19th century.
Born in Padua; died possibly in Naples.
Painter, decorative designer. Stage sets.
With his brother Lorenzo, Vincenzio Sacchetti made stage sets for the opera house in Vienna.

SACCHETTINI, Simone
Italian, 17th century.
Active in Florence during the first half of the 17th century.
Painter.
In 1613, Simone Sacchettini painted the Holy Rosary altarpiece for the church of St Agatha in Mugello.

SACCHETTO, Attilio
German, 20th century.
Born 18 May 1876, in Munich.
Draughtsman. Portraits, landscapes, architectural views, interiors.

SACCHETTO, Bartolameo
Italian, 15th century.
Active in Trento (Trentino-Alto Adige) in the second half of the 15th century.
Painter.
Bartolameo Saccheto produced paintings for the episcopal palace in Trento, in 1477.

SACCHETTO, Cristoforo
Italian, 15th century.
Active in Trento (Trentino-Alto Adige) in the second half of the 15th century.
Painter.

SACCHETTO, Giacomo
Italian, 15th century.
Active in Trento (Trentino-Alto Adige) in 1478.
Painter.
Giacomo Sacchetto may have been the son of Lorenzo Sacchetto.

SACCHETTO, Lorenzo
Italian, 15th century.
Active in Verona in 1490.
Painter.
Lorenzo Sacchetto may have been the father of Giacomo Sacchetto.

SACCHI. See also **SACCA** or **SACCO**

SACCHI, Andrea, called Ouche
Italian, 17th century.
Born shortly before 30 November 1599, in Nettuno, near Rome; died 21 June 1661, in Rome.
Painter. History painting, religious subjects, allegorical subjects, mythological subjects, portraits.
Andrea Sacchi was the son and pupil of Benedetto Sacchi. He then worked with Francesco Albano and studied Raphael, Polidoro da Caravaggio and the artists of antiquity. He later trained numerous pupils, most notably Lauri, Gazzi and Carlo Maratti.

Sacchi was the protégé of Cardinal Barberini, who employed him to work in his palace and procured for him major public works commissions in Rome. Between 1629 and 1633, Andrea Sacchi produced for his patron the *Triumph of Divine Wisdom*, inspired by Raphael's *Parnassus*. Other notable works include *S Romuald and His Monks*, a work long considered one of the most remarkable paintings in Rome, the *Death of St Anne* at the church of S Carlo in Cativari, the *Mass of St Gregory and Clement VIII* in the Vatican, the *Angel Appearing to St Joseph* at S Giuseppe and *St Andrew* at the Quirinale.

Collective thematic exhibitions in which Sacchi's work has been featured include the 2002 exhibition *Cieux en gloire* (*Celestial Glories*) held at the Fesch museum in Ajaccio, which evoked the great decorative commissions of the Roman Baroque through sketches and models. A solo exhibition was mounted in 1999 in Forte Sangallo.

BIBLIOGRAPHY:

Sutherland Harris, Ann, *Die Handzeichnungen von Andrea Sacchi und Carlo Maratta*, catalogue raisonné, Kunstmuseum Düsseldorf, Düsseldorf, 1967. Harris, A. Sutherland, *Andrea Sacchi*, Oxford, 1977. *Andrea Sacchi, 1599-1661*, exhibition catalogue, De Luca Editore, Rome, 1999. Olivesi, Jean-Marc (ed.), *Cieux en gloire*, exhibition catalogue, Musée Fesch, Ajaccio, 2002.

MUSEUMS AND GALLERIES:

AMIENS: *Saint* - ANGERS: *Self-portrait* - ÁSCOLI PICENO (Pinacoteca Civica): *Holy Family* - BAGNÈRES-DE-BIGORRE: *St Romuald and his Companions* - BERLIN (National Mus.): *Drunkenness of Noah; Presumed Portrait of Alessandro del Borro; Allegory* - CAMBRAI: *Crucifixion* - DRESDEN: *Rest during the Flight into Egypt* - FORLÌ (Pinacoteca Civica Melozzo degli Ambrogi): *St Peter* - GENOA: *Daedalus and Icarus* - MADRID: *Francesco Albani; Self-portrait; St Paul the Hermit and St Anthony the Abbot; Feast of Lupercalia; Birth of St John the Baptist* - NANCY: *Pope Alexander VII Borne Aloft at the Procession of Corpus Domini; Trinity* - NANTES: *Funeral Procession of a Bishop; St Romuald and His Disciples* - ORLÉANS: *Raising of Lazarus* - OTTAWA (NG. of Canada): *Portrait of Cardinal Angelo Giori* - PERUGIA (Gal. Nazionale dell'Umbria): *Presentation* - PRATO: *Mary Magdalene* - RENNES: *The Muse Euterpe* - ROME (Church of S Giuseppe): *Angel Appearing to St Joseph* - ROME (Gal. Nazionale d'Arte Antica di Palazzo Barberini): *Cain and Abel; Divine Wisdom* - ROME (Mus. e Gal. Borghese): *Don Horace Giustiniani* - ROME (Palazzo del Quirinale): *St Andrew* - ROME (Palazzo Doria Pamphili): *Daedalus and Icarus* - ST PETERSBURG (Hermitage): *Hagar in the Desert; Triumph of Wisdom; Venus Resting* - STRASBOURG: *Portrait of a General* - VATICAN (Mus. Vaticani): *Mass of St Gregory and Clement VIII; St Gregory the Great; St Romuald* - VERSAILLES: *St Bernard, Abbot of Clairvaux* - VIENNA (Schönborn-Buckheim): *Cyclops.*

AUCTION RECORDS:

PARIS, 1772, *Dead Christ in the Arms of Mary Magdalene* (pen and bistre drawing) FRF 128; *Penitent Saint* (drawing in red chalk) FRF 71. PARIS, 1781, *Adoration of the Shepherds*, FRF 400. PARIS, 1785, *Bearing of the Cross* (pen and bistre drawing) FRF 119. PARIS, 1793, *Bearing of the Cross*, FRF 3,750; *Adam Mourning the Death of Abel*, FRF 500. PARIS, 1859, *Ascension of the Virgin*, FRF 5,200. PARIS, 1862, *Virgin and Child*, FRF 1,480. PARIS, 1899, *Portrait of a Prelate*, FRF 480. LONDON, 19 Feb 1910, *Ascension of the Virgin*, GBP 33. LONDON, 4 July 1924, *Holy Family and St John*, GBP 105. PARIS, 28 Oct 1927, *St Francis and St Bonaventura as Children* (pen) FRF 100. PARIS, 10 Oct 1941, *Portrait of a Man* (attributed) FRF 8,500. LONDON, 12 April 1983, *Studies of a Young Man (possibly Maffeo Barberini), of a Black Man, Hands and Arms (recto)* (red and white chalk); *Monk Standing (verso)* (black and white chalk, 10 x 13 1/4in/25.2 x 33.4cm) GBP 4,500. ROME, 27 May 1986, *Study of Two Men's Heads* (oil on canvas, 19 3/4 x 26 1/2in/50 x 67cm) ITL 7,000,000. LONDON, 6 July 1992, *Virgin and Child with St Jerome* (red chalk, 5 1/2 x 6 1/2in/14.2 x 16.7cm) GBP 3,960. LONDON, 18 April 1994, *Christ Crowned with Thorns* (red chalk and wash, 5 1/4 x 6 1/2in/13.3 x 16.3cm) GBP 4,600. LONDON, 8 July 1994, *Half-length Portrait of Francesco Albani in a Brown Suit* (oil on paper/canvas, 19 x 14 1/2in/48 x 37cm) GBP 11,500. LONDON, 2 July 1996, *Young Gentleman Holding a Plumed Hat, and Young Black Page Leaning over a Parapet, and Studies of Jesuits at Prayer (verso); Priest Kneeling (recto)* (red chalk and black or white chalk, 10 x 13 1/4in/25.2 x 33.4cm) GBP 10,925. LONDON, 10 July 2002, *Studies for a Figure of Apollo. Figure and Drapery Studies* (red chalk heightened with white, double-sided, 11 x 16 ins / 28 x 40 cm) GBP 14,000. LONDON, 7 July 2004, *Daedalus and Icarus* (oil on canvas, 54 x 39 ins / 136 x 98 cm) GBP 150,000.

SACCHI, Andrea, or Sacco
Italian, 17th century.
Sculptor.

Andrea Sacchi collaborated with his brother and with Carlo Sacchi in Pavia at the end of the 17th century. He was also a mosaicist.

SACCHI, Antonio
Italian, 17th century.
Born c. 1650, in Como; died 1694, in Como.
Fresco artist.

Antonio Sacchi studied in Rome and died in 1694, reputedly of a broken heart, having painted a cupola in Como with the wrong proportions.

SACCHI, Bartolomeo or Zohan Bartolomeo di, called Domenedio
Italian, 15th - 16th century.
Born 1456; died 1 July 1542.
Active in Mantua.
Painter.

Bartolomeo di Sacchi was the father of Roberto di Sacchi. He was the pupil of Mantegna and the assistant of Giulio Romano.

SACCHI, Battista
Italian, 16th century.
Died 1528.
Active in Genoa.
Painter.

Battista Sacchi was the younger brother, pupil and assistant of Pier Francesco Sacchi.

SACCHI, Benedetto
Italian, 16th - 17th century.
Active in Nettuno near Rome.
Painter.

Benedetto Sacchi was the father and first master of Andrea Sacchi. No works by him survive.

SACCHI, Bernardino, or Sacco
Italian, 17th century.
Active in Pavia at the end of the 17th century.
Sculptor.

In collaboration with Giovanni Battista Sacchi, Bernardino Sacchi painted an altarpiece in the chapel of St John the Baptist at the Carthusian monastery in Pavia.

SACCHI, Biagio
Italian, 19th century.
Born in Busseto; died 1878.
Engraver (burin).

Biagio Sacchi was a pupil and assistant of P. Toschi.

SACCHI, Carlo
Italian, 17th century.
Born 1616 or 1617, in Pavia; died 1706 or 1709, in Pavia.
Painter, engraver (etching). Religious subjects.

Having first studied as the pupil of Rossi in Milan, Carlo Sacchi worked in Rome and finally settled in Venice, where his style seems to have been formed as a result of imitating Paolo Caliari. He is noted in particular for a painting in the Osservanza in Pavia of *St James Reviving a Dead Man*, the style of which is reminiscent of Veronese.

AUCTION RECORDS:

LONDON, 5 Dec 1985, *Adoration of the Shepherds* (etching, 20 1/2 x 15 1/4in/51.8 x 38.7cm) GBP 3,500.

SACCHI, Carlo Battista
Italian, 17th century.

Active in Pavia at the end of the 17th century.
Sculptor, mosaicist.

Carlo Battista Sacchi was the brother of Andrea Sacchi. He worked in the Carthusian monastery at Pavia, where he produced altarpieces and choir screens.

SACCHI, Filippo or Pietro, called lo Spagnuolo
Italian, 18th century.
Died c. 1750; young.
Active in Cremona.
Painter.

Filippo Sacchi studied in Bologna and painted a picture in Cremona of *San Egidio, San Omobono and San Liberio*. His legacy also includes a *Glory of the Virgin*.

SACCHI, Gaspare, called Gaspare da Imola
Italian, 16th century.
Active in Imola (Emilia-Romagna) during the first part of the 16th century.
Painter.

Gaspare Sacchi was the pupil of Francia. He produced many paintings in Ravenna and in the former province of Romagna. In particular, he painted an altarpiece signed and dated 1517 in the sacristy of Castel S Pietro, in Imola, and a work dated 1521 in S Francesco-in-Tavala, in Bologna.

MUSEUMS AND GALLERIES:
BOLOGNA (Pinacoteca Nazionale): *Marriage of the Virgin* - IMOLA (Municipal Mus.): *Virgin with Four Saints* - MILAN (Pinacoteca di Brera): *Adoration of the Magi and Shepherds with the Portrait of J. B. Botrigari on the Right* (1521).

SACCHI, Giovanni Angelo
Italian, 16th century.
Born c. 1476.
Painter.

Giovanni Angelo Sacchi was the brother of Pier Francesco Sacchi.

SACCHI, Giovanni Antonio.
See **PORDENONE**

SACCHI, Giovanni Battista, or Sacco
Italian, 17th century.
Active in Pavia at the end of the 17th century.
Sculptor.

Giovanni Battista Sacchi collaborated with Bernardino Sacchi on an altarpiece in the chapel of St John the Baptist in the Carthusian monastery at Pavia.

SACCHI, Giulio
Italian, 18th century.
Active in Casalmaggiore during the first half of the 18th century.
Sculptor (wood).

Giulio Sacchi was the pupil of Bertesi. He was active in Cremona and also worked for a time in Spain.

SACCHI, Giuseppe
Italian, 17th century.
Active in Rome.
Painter. History painting, portraits.

Giuseppe Sacchi was the son and pupil of Andrea Sacchi. He may have painted the *Sibyl* in Warsaw attributed to Giuseppe Sacconi. He became a monk in the Franciscan order and painted *The Holy Apostles* in the sacristy of his monastery in a manner reminiscent of his father's style.

SACCHI, Giuseppe
Italian, 18th century.
Sculptor (wood).

Giuseppe Sacchi worked for the Badia Fiorentini, a Benedictine church in Florence, in 1780.

SACCHI, Luigi
Italian, 19th century.
Born in Milan.
Painter. Portraits, genre scenes.

Luigi Sacchi exhibited works in Rome and Milan. His paintings include a *Portrait of King Umberto I*.

SACCHI, M., called Il Sacchi
Italian, 17th century.
Born in Casale.
Painter. History painting, genre scenes.

He is noted for a curious painting in the church of S Francesco in Casale of *The Lottery of Marriage*, and for a *Virgin and Saints* in the church of S Agostino containing numerous portraits of members of the Gonzaga family.

SACCHI, Pier Francesco, or Sacchio or Sacchius or Sacco or Saccus, called Il Pavese or Pietro or Pier Francesco di Pavia
Italian, 16th century.
Born 1485, in Pavia; died July (?) 1528, in Genoa.
Painter.
Pavia School.

Very little is known about Pier Francesco Sacchi, and critics are not in agreement. According to Lamasso he was one of the painters flourishing in Milan during the reign of Francesco Sforza. He has been identified with the Master of Maretto because of similarities in style and the polished detail of their works. His first known work, *St John the Baptist Leaving His Parents*, in S Maria oratory in Genoa, is dated 1512.

In 1514, Sacchi painted the *Crucifixion*, now in the museum in Berlin, and *The Four Fathers of the Church*, now in the Louvre. In July 1520 he was on the council of the Corporation of Painters in Genoa. In 1526 he completed a *Glory of the Virgin* in S Maria church in Castello.

Sacchi's masterpieces were a *Deposition*, in S Nazzaro e S Celso in Multedo near Pegli, and the remarkable *St George Striking the Dragon*, in the Chiesa dei Frati Minori in Levanto, near Spezia. He also produced decorative frescoes *The Fathers of the Church* and *Prophets* in S Michele in Pavia.

MUSEUMS AND GALLERIES:
BERLIN: *Christ on the Cross and Saints* (1514); *St Martin, St Jerome and St Benedict* (attributed) - BORDEAUX: *Adam and Eve* - PARIS (Louvre): *The Four Fathers of the Church* (1514) - ROME (GA Antica di Palazzo Corsini): *Apotheosis of St Bernard of Siena*.

AUCTION RECORDS:
PARIS, 20 Dec 1962, *Holy Family*, FRF 9,000. PARIS, 15 Dec 1980, *Entering the Tomb* (oil on wood, 78¾ x 62¼ ins / 200 x 158 cm) FRF 45,000.

SACCHI, Roberto di
Italian, 16th century.
Born c. 1489; died 4 December 1569.
Active in Mantua.
Painter.

Roberto di Sacchi was the son of Bartolomeo di Sacchi, and the assistant of Giulio Romano.

SACCHI, Valerio, or Sacco
Italian, 17th - 18th century.
Active in Pavia.
Sculptor.

Valerio Sacchi sculpted altars in the Carthusian monastery at Pavia.

SACCHIENSE-CORTICELLI, Giovanni Antonio (chevalier). See **PORDENONE**

SACCHIO, Pier Francesco. See **SACCHI**

SACCHIS, Filippo de. See **SACCA**

SACCHIS, Giovanni Antonio de. See **PORDENONE**

SACCHIS, Tommaso de. See **SACCA**

SACCO. See also **SACCA** and **SACCHI**

SACCO, Carlo Orazio
Italian, 16th - 17th century.
Painter, draughtsman. Religious subjects.

Carlo Sacco was the assistant of Guglielmo Caccia, in Moncalvo.

AUCTION RECORDS:
PARIS, 16 March 1994, *St John the Baptist in the Desert* (brown ink and wash, 7 1/4 x 9 1/2 ins / 18.6 x 24.2 cm) FRF 9,200.

SACCO, G.
French, 19th century.
Painter, miniaturist. Portraits.

G. Sacco exhibited at the Paris Salon in 1833 and 1848 and in London from 1852 to 1854, and again in 1857 and 1865.

SACCO, Gaetano
Italian, 17th - 18th century.
Active from 1691 to 1712.
Sculptor.

Gaetano Sacco produced works for churches in Naples, Aversa, Cava dei Tirreni and Salerno.

SACCO, Luca
Italian, 19th - 20th century.
Born 22 January 1858, in San Remo; died 18 July 1912, in Brooklyn (New York).
Active in the USA.
Painter. History painting, portraits.

SACCO, Scipione, or Sacchi
Italian, 16th century.
Born 1494 (?), in Cesena (Emilia-Romagna); died 1557.
Painter. History painting.

It is believed that Scipione Sacco was the pupil of Raphael Sanzio, whose style he imitated. His painting *St Gregory*, dated 1545, is in Cesena, and *Death of St Peter of Verona* is in S Domenico, Cesena.

SACCO OYTANA, Alessandro Gustavo
Italian, 19th - 20th century.
Born 5 November 1862, in Montferrato (Piedmont); died 3 January 1932, in Turin.
Painter. Figures, portraits, landscapes.

Sacco Oytana studied at the Turin academy of art under Giacomo Grosso and also at the academies in Milan and Rome.

SACCOCCIA, Cola
Italian, 15th century.
Active in Rome, from 1464 to 1494.
Painter.
School of Rome.

Saccoccia painted banners for the coronations of Popes Paul II and Sixtus IV.

SACCOMANNO, Santo
Italian, 19th - 20th century.
Born 1833, in Genoa; died 1914.
Sculptor, medallist. Figures. Statues.

Santo Saccomanno studied at the academy in Genoa under Varni and then worked as an assistant to Giuseppe Gaggini. He carved statues of *Giuseppe Mazzini* and his followers and also produced medals and tombs, the majority of which are in Vienna.

SACCONI, Carlo
Italian, 17th - 18th century.
Active in Florence.
Painter.

The son of Francesco Sacconi and brother of Marco, Carlo Sacconi produced paintings for the church in Pescia and for churches in Florence.

SACCONI, Francesco
Italian, 17th century.
Florentine, active towards the end of the 17th century.
Painter.

The father of Carlo and Marco Sacconi, Francesco produced paintings in the Palazzo Riccardi in Florence.

SACCONI, Giuseppe
Italian, 18th century.
Active in Florence during the second half of the 18th century.
Painter.

The son of Marco Sacconi, Giuseppe worked for the Carthusian monastery of Calci, near Pisa.

SACCONI, Marco
Italian, 18th century.
Born c. 1690, in Florence; died 1762, in Florence.
Painter. Landscapes, architectural views.

Marco Sacconi was the son of Francesco and the father of Giuseppe Sacconi. He worked mainly in the palaces of Genoa.

SACCOROTTI, Oscar
Italian, 20th century.
Born 1898, in Rome; died 1989
Painter.

Oscar Saccorotti studied at the Accademia Ligustica in Genoa, where he lived and worked.

SACEDA, Pedro
Spanish, 16th century.
Active during the second half of the 16th century.
Sculptor (wood).

Pedro Saceda worked on the stalls in Cuenca Cathedral, in 1578.

SACEDO, Juan Bautista
Spanish, 16th century.
Active during the second half of the 16th century.
Glass painter.

Juan Bautista Sacedo worked for Utiel church in 1569, with Miguel Toran.

SACERDOTE, Anselmo
Italian, 20th century.
Died 1926, in Turin.
Painter. Landscapes.

AUCTION RECORDS:
ROME, 14 Dec 1988, *Forest Path* (1913, oil on panel, 17 1/2 x 14 ins / 44.5 x 35.5 cm) ITL 900,000.

SACERDOTE, Rosy
Italian, 19th - 20th century.
Born 7 November 1872, in Turin.
Painter, decorative designer. Landscapes, flowers.

Rosy Sacerdote was a pupil of C. Pollonera.

SACERER, Michael or J. M. F.. See **SACKERER**

SACHA, Tommaso. See **SACCA**

SACHA GUITRY. See **GUITRY Sacha**

SACHAROFF, Olga Nicolaevna.
See **SACHAROV**

SACHAROV, Konstantin
Russian, 20th century.
Born 1920.
Painter (including mixed media).

AUCTION RECORDS:
ZURICH, 22 June 1990, *Kolkhoz Market* (mixed media/wood, 22¼ x 31 ins / 56.5 x 78.5 cm) CHF 1,100.

SACHAROV, Olga Nicolaevna, or Sacharova, Zakharova
Georgian, 20th century.
Born 29 May 1889, in Tiflis (now Tbilisi); died 1967 or 1969, in Barcelona, Spain.
Active in France, then Spain.
Painter (gouache), watercolourist, engraver. Figures, portraits, genre scenes, landscapes, still-lifes, flowers, animals.

Olga Sacharov trained at the school of fine art in Tiflis. She worked in France from 1910 to 1916 then travelled to Munich, Florence and Rome before finally settling in Barcelona. She was married to the painter Otto Lloyd.

Olga Sacharov was influenced in Paris by Rousseau, from whom she learned a certain naivety; she portrayed the countryside and its inhabitants with an anecdotal style and also produced portraits. She featured in collective exhibitions including: Paris (Salon d'Automne, Salon des Tuileries and Salon des Indépendants); Barcelona (receiving a gold medal in 1964); Madrid; London; Munich; Florence; Rome; Buenos Aires; and New York.

BIBLIOGRAPHY:
Arnáiz, José Manuel/López Jiménez, Javier/Merchán Díaz, Manuel (ed.), '*Cien años de pintura en Espana y Portugal (1830-1930)*' in vol. IX, Antiqvaria, Madrid, 1992.

MUSEUMS AND GALLERIES:
BARCELONA (MAM del Mus. Nacional d'Art de Catalunya).

AUCTION RECORDS:
PARIS, 18 Nov 1925, *Maid's Room*, FRF 300. PARIS, 29 Oct 1926, *Amazon*, FRF 1,100. PARIS, 24 March 1930, *Family Portrait*, FRF 170. PARIS, 31 May 1972, *Family Picnic*, FRF 8,000. MADRID, 1 April 1976, *River Landscape* (oil on canvas, 28¾ x 36¼ ins / 73 x 92 cm) ESP 250,000. MADRID, 22 May 1978, *Little Girl with Flowers* (oil on canvas, 26 x 21¼ ins / 66 x 54 cm) ESP 360,000. BARCELONA, 21 June 1979, *Landscape* (oil on panel, 13 x 15½ ins / 33 x 39.5 cm) ESP 290,000. BARCELONA, 29 Jan 1981, *Florero* (oil on panel, 36 x 27½ ins / 91.5 x 70 cm) ESP 360,000. BARCELONA, 26 May 1983, *Waterfall* (oil on canvas, 56¾ x 44½ ins / 144 x 113 cm) ESP 320,000. BARCELONA, 18 Dec 1985, *Loggia* (oil on canvas, 28¾ x 36¼ ins / 73 x 92 cm) ESP 775,000. MADRID, 18 Dec 1986, *Alameda* (oil on panel, 22¾ x 32¼ ins / 58 x 82 cm) ESP 900,000. MADRID, 12 Jan 1999, *Vase of Flowers against Landscape* (oil on canvas, 26 x 21 ins / 65 x 54 cm) ESP 2,900,000. MADRID, 9 Feb 1999, *Vase of Flowers, Landscape Beyond* (oil on canvas, 26 x 21 ins / 65 x 54 cm) ESP 2,500,000. MADRID, 5 June 2000, *Vase of Flowers* (oil on canvas, 29 x 24 ins / 73 x 60 cm) ESP 1,800,000. LYONS, 8 Oct 2000, *Family Meal* (c. 1910, oil on canvas, 39 x 31 ins / 98 x 79 cm) FRF 192,000. MADRID, 3 April 2001, *Portrait of Woman with Vase of Flowers* (oil on canvas, 31 x 24 ins / 78 x 62 cm) ESP 3,700,000. LYONS, 15 May 2001, *Vase of Flowers on Entablature* (c. 1925, oil on canvas, 26 x 21 ins / 66 x 54 cm) FRF 135,000. AMSTERDAM, 3 Dec 2002, *Danspartij - Dancing* (oil on canvas, 26 x 32 ins / 65 x 81 cm) EUR 75,000. PARIS, 17 Dec 2002, *Lovers* (oil on canvas, 29 x 36 ins / 73 x 92 cm) EUR 45,000. LYONS, 15 June 2003, *Vase of Flowers* (oil on cardboard, 16 x 13 ins / 41 x 33 cm) EUR 17,000. MADRID, 27 April 2004, *Women with Spanish Shawls* (watercolour, 13 x 17 ins / 33 x 43 cm) EUR 6,500. PARIS, 17 May 2004, *Bouquet* (oil on panel, 9 x 7 ins / 22 x 18 cm) EUR 1,900.

SACHAROV-ROSS, Igor
Russian, 20th century.
Born in Khabarovsk.
Active in Germany from 1978.
Sculptor, painter. Multimedia.

Igor Sacharov-Ross had very ambitious intentions, aiming, at providing no less than a symbolic, complete view of the world and of man's place in it. He used resources liberally as well as modern technology to produce complex, monumental installations. The Musée des Beaux-Arts in Tourcoing and the Goethe Institut in Lille organised a presentation of his work (1997).

SACHAULT, Étienne
French, 17th century.
Died before 1634.
Active in Dôle.
Painter, gilder.

Sachault produced paintings for Mont-Roland church in Dôle.

SACHE, Filippo. See **SACCA**

SACHERI, Giuseppe
Italian, 19th - 20th century.
Born 8 December 1863, in Genoa; died 1950, in Pianfei.
Painter. Seascapes.

Giuseppe Sacheri studied in Ravenna with Moradei and at the Accademia Albertina di Belle Arti in Turin.

MUSEUMS AND GALLERIES:
GENOA (Gal. d'Arte Moderna) - MILAN (Gal. d'Arte Moderna) - ROME (Gal. Nazionale d'Arte Moderna).

AUCTION RECORDS:
MILAN, 15 March 1977, *Full Moon* (1900, oil on canvas, 39¾ x 55 ins / 101 x 140 cm) ITL 950,000. ROME, 11 Dec 1990, *Peasants in a Landscape* (oil on board, 9 x 12¼ ins / 22 x 31 cm) ITL 4,600,000. MILAN, 12 March 1991, *The Sea at Pieve Ligure* (oil on board, 15¼ x 18 ins / 39 x 46 cm) ITL 6,500,000. MILAN, 6 June 1991, *Seascape* (oil on board, 12 x 15¾ ins / 30.5 x 40 cm) ITL 2,800,000. MILAN, 7 Nov 1991, *Seascape near Nervi* (1930, oil on panel, 9¼ x 13 ins / 23.5 x 33 cm) ITL 2,700,000. ROME, 14 Nov 1991, *Gust of Wind on the Sea* (oil on board, 15¼ x 17¼ ins / 39 x 44 cm) ITL 5,750,000. MILAN, 3 Dec 1992, *Seascape* (oil on board, 11¾ x 9 ins / 30 x 22 cm) ITL 2,260,000. ROME, 27 April 1993, *Gust of Wind on the Sea* (oil on board, 15¼ x 17¼ ins / 39 x 44 cm) ITL 5,630,200. ROME, 2 June 1994, *Sea in Winter* (oil on canvas, 27½ x 43¾ ins / 70 x 111 cm) ITL 16,675,000. ZURICH, 22 March 1999, *Coastal Landscape with Stormy Sea* (mixed media, 16 x 18 ins / 41 x 45 cm) CHF 2,700. VENICE, 14 April 2000, *Porto Corsini* (oil on canvas, 11 x 17 ins / 29 x 44 cm) ITL 7,500,000. ROME, 23 May 2000, *Ligurian Countryside* (oil on canvas, 38 x 47 ins / 96 x 120 cm) ITL 24,000,000. ZURICH, 16 Sept 2002, *Coastal Landscape with Pines* (oil on paper, 18 x 22 ins / 46 x 57 cm) CHF 3,600. TURIN, 20 Oct 2003, *White Mill* (oil on card, 12 x 15 ins / 31 x 39 cm) EUR 1,900. TURIN, 22 March 2004, *Harbour* (1896, oil on canvas, 9 x 14 ins / 22 x 35 cm) EUR 4,000. VERCELLI, 1 May 2004, *White Mill* (oil on cardboard, 12 x 15 ins / 31 x 39 cm) EUR 2,300.

SACHETTI. See **SACCHETTI**

SACHIENSE. See **PORDENONE**

SACHIS, Giovanni Antonio de.
See **PORDENONE**

SACHOT, Octave
French, 19th century.
Born in Montigny-Lencoup.
Sculptor, medallist.

Octave Sacho was a student of Petit. He exhibited at the Salon from 1861 to 1878. He was a Chevalier of the Légion d'Honneur.
MUSEUMS AND GALLERIES:
SENS: *M. Fillemin; Mme de la E.; Mme X; M. Petitgand; M. Henri Mamet; Mételin's Greek Wife; The Artist; Georges Sachot; M. Charles Carré; Mme X.*

SACHOWICZ, Grzegorz
Polish, 19th century.
Active in Warsaw in the middle of the 19th century.
Miniaturist, photographer.
The National Museum in Warsaw owns a miniature by Grzegorz Sachowicz, *Portrait of a Lady*.

SACHOWICZ, Jacek or Jecenty
Polish, 19th century.
Born 1813, in Ilza; died 14 February 1875, in Warsaw.
Painter.
Jacek Sachowicz studied at the art academy in Warsaw under A. Blank and A. Brodowski and at the art academy in Dresden. He worked in Kielce and Warsaw.

SACHS (Mrs). See **HOLLAND Ada R., Miss**

SACHS, Adolf
Austrian, 19th century.
Active c. 1840.
Painter. Portraits, costume studies.
Adolf Sachs painted regional costumes.

SACHS, Antoinette
French, 20th century.
Born 1904, in Paris.
Painter, draughtsman. Figures, landscapes, still-lifes.
Antoinette Sachs exhibited regularly in Paris at the Salon des Indépendants, the Salon d'Automne, and the Salon des Tuileries. Her robust and uncompromising art was strongly influenced by Soutine, and she received advice from Othon Friesz. Nevertheless, she escaped from these influences and developed her own language for conveying her lucid vision of landscapes, still-lifes and, above all, the figures at which she excelled.

SACHS, Balthasar
German, 19th century.
Active in Sulzthal at the beginning of the 19th century.
Sculptor (wood), cabinet maker.
Balthasar Sachs sculpted the pulpit, confessional and side altars in the church of Brebersdorf.

SACHS, Clara
German, 19th - 20th century.
Born 6 February 1862; died 1 January 1921.
Painter. Landscapes, still-lifes, flowers.
Clara Sachs studied under Herbert Bayer, Carl Schirm, Julius Jacob and Carl von Marr. She worked also as a lithographer.
MUSEUMS AND GALLERIES:
WROCLAW.

SACHS, Gottfried
German, 18th century.
Active in Wittenberg during the second half of the 18th century.
Painter (porcelain).
Gottfried Sachs worked at the porcelain factory in Meissen in 1772.

SACHS, Gottfried
German, 18th century.
Active in Siegmundsburg during the second half of the 18th century.
Painter.
Gottfried Sachs worked in Limbach in 1781.

SACHS, Hans
Austrian, 14th century.
Active in Vienna in 1386.
Painter.
Hans Sachs was court painter to Duke Albert III of Austria.

SACHS, Heinrich
Swiss, 16th century.
Active in Basel in 1521.
Glass painter.

SACHS, Heinrich
German, 19th century.
Born 18 April 1831, in Berlin; died 10 October 1901, in Königsberg (now Kaliningrad, Russia).
Engraver (burin/etching).
Heinrich Sachs was a pupil of L. Buchhorn and E. Mandel and taught at the academy in Königsberg.

SACHS, I. Liborius
German, 18th century.
Active in 1760.
Painter.
I. Liborius Sachs executed frescoes and altarpieces in several Bavarian churches.

SACHS, Johanna
German, 19th century.
Active in Berlin in 1828.
Painter.

SACHS, Konrad
German, 15th century.
Active in Nuremberg 1418-1448.
Painter.

SACHS, L.
German, 19th century.
Active in Mannheim in 1847.
Portrait artist.
L. Sachs was a pupil of Götzenberger and J. Weber.

SACHS, Michael Emil
German, 19th century.
Born 1836, in Hadamar; died 9 July 1893, in Partenkirchen.
Active in Wiesbaden 1860-1865.
Sculptor (wood). Landscapes.
Michael Emil Sachs was a pupil of J.W. Schirmer in Karlsruhe and of O. Achenbach in Düsseldorf. He founded the school of wood sculpture in Partenkirchen.

SACHS, Richard
German, 19th - 20th century.
Born 9 January 1875, in Plauen.
Painter. Genre scenes, landscapes.
AUCTION RECORDS:
NEW YORK, 29 Oct 1992, *Mandolin Serenade* (oil on panel, 10 1/4 x 8 ins / 26 x 20.3 cm) USD 1,540.

SACHS, Tom
American, 20th - 21st century.
Born 1966, in New York.
Active in New York.
Sculptor (mixed media), installation artist.
Tom Sachs grew up in Westport in Connecticut and was encouraged by his mother, who later became his business manager, to take an interest in crafts. He trained at Bennington College in Vermont and at the Architectural Association in London in 1987.

Sachs plays with the notions of seriality, commercialism and trendiness pervading our popular culture and plays with the idea of consumerism through a combination of extraordinary logic and aggressive wit in his work. He has taken on design teams, public relations departments and creative think-tanks of the 'high fashion' industry, offering an alternative 'low fashion' model using hot glue guns, foamcore and materials from DIY stores. His breakthrough came in 1994 with the provocative *Hello Kitty Nativity Scene* designed for Barney's department store in New York. It included three Bart Simpsons as the Wise Men and the singer Madonna as the Virgin. It created a scandal but drew the critics' attention to Allied Cultural Prosthetics, his workshop in Lower Manhattan, where he had been producing his sculptures since the early 1990s.

Works include: *Prada Toilet* (1997); *Chanel Chainsaw* and a fully functioning *Chanel Guillotine* (1998); *Super Dynamite Soul* (1998); and *Chanel Value Meal* (1999). The elements of *Hello Kitty and Miffy*, a project with the Art of the Century Gallery in New York, were conceived in foamcore and glue, then cast in bronze and painted to mimic the original foamcore model. The contradiction between art and reality stands at the heart of Sachs's approach.

From single objects Sachs moved on to installations. His *Nutsy's*, shown at the Bohen Foundation in New York (2002-2003) and at the Deutsche Guggenheim in Berlin (2003), is a 15,000 square foot (1,400 sq metre) 1:25 representation of a world complete with a model of Le Corbusier residential complex, MacDonalds restaurant, ghetto, sculpture park and so on. Modernism and bricolage act as a kind of foil for each other in *Nutsy's*, with the resourcefulness of bricolage standing in contrast to the grandiosity of scheme.

Group exhibitions in which he participated from 1994 include *Materials, Metaphors, Narratives: Work by Six Contemporary Artists* at the Albright-Knox Art Gallery in Buffalo in New York (2003) and *Sculptural Sphere* at the Sammlung Goetz in Munich (2004). Solo exhibitions from 1995 include *American Bricolage* at the Sperone Westwater Gallery in New York (2000) and one at the Galleria Cardi & Co in Milan (2001).

Bibliography:

Sachs, Tom, *Sony Outsider*, Santa Fe, 1999. Sheets, Hilarie M., '*Chic to Cheeks*' in *Artnews*, journal article, summer 2000. Hanhardt, John G., *Tom Sachs: Nutsy' s*, exhibition catalogue, Guggenheim Museum, New York, 2003. Sachs, Tom/Hanhardt, John G./Villaseñor, Maria-Christina, *Tom Sachs: Nutsy's*, Solomon R. Guggenheim Foundation, 2003. Vincent, Steven, '*Tom Sachs*' in *Art+Auction*, journal article, summer 2003. MacDonough, Tom, '*A Day at the Races*' in *Art in America*, journal article, July 2003.

Auction records:

New York, 17 Nov 1999, *Bulletproof Diaper* (Yellow Pages, nylon straps, hanger, tape and sheet metal, 22 x 20x14 ins / 56 x 51x36 cm) USD 3,500. New York, 18 May 2000, *Key Kabinet Kontrol* (keys, plastic tag, battery powered clock and Plexiglas, 23 x 18x7 ins / 58 x 45x17 cm) USD 13,000. New York, 15 May 2001, *Uncle Tom's Kitchen* (commercially produced cardboard and thermal adhesive, three parts, 25 x 25x3 ins / 63 x 63x8 cm) USD 8,000. New York, 15 May 2001, *Chanel Happy Meal* (1999, Chanel shopping bag, glue and tissue paper, 4 x 14x10 ins / 11 x 36x26 cm) USD 18,000. New York, 14 May 2002, *Hermes Hand Grenade* (1995, tissue paper and glue, 5 x 3x3 ins / 13 x 7x7 cm) USD 5,800. New York, 15 May 2002, *357 Magnum* (1997, oil, cloth, tape, wood and metal hardware, 7 x 11x3 ins / 18 x 27x7 cm) USD 9,500. New York, 16 May 2003, *Falling* (1996, duct tape on plywood, 36 x 36 ins / 91 x 91 cm) USD 14,000. Paris, 3 July 2003, *Clock* (1998, painted wood, metal and Coca-Cola bottles, 19 x 20x6 ins / 48 x 50x15 cm) EUR 8,000. New York, 14 May 2004, *Miffy* (2002, acrylic and cast bronze, 9 x 4x4 ins / 24 x 11x11 cm) USD 18,000. New York, 10 June 2004, *Untitled: Come Out with Your Hands Up You French Fuck* (1997, pen, ink and felt tipped pen, 11 x 9 ins / 28 x 22 cm) USD 2,500.

SACHS-PAVARD, Lucienne

French, 20th century.
Born in Jargeau (Loiret).
Painter. Landscapes.

Lucienne Sachs-Pavard was first a pupil at the École des Arts Décoratifs, Paris, then at the École des Beaux-Arts. She went with her husband to live in Morocco. She took part in group exhibitions, including, in 1984, that of the Société Nationale de l'Armée, where she was a guest of honour.

SACHSE, Emil Eugen, or Sachsse

German, 19th century.
Born 23 January 1828, in Dresden; died 27 November 1887, in Plauen, near Dresden.
Painter, draughtsman. History painting.

Emil Eugen Sachse was a pupil at the academy in Dresden. He painted religious subjects and drew illustrations for historical works.

SACHSE-SCHUBERT, Marta

German, 20th century.
Born 26 July 1890, in Siebenbrunnen, near Markneukirchen.
Painter. Figures.

Marta Sachse-Schubert was the granddaughter of the sculptor Hermann Schubert. She produced silhouettes.

SACHSENHEIM, Klara. See **SOTERIUS von Sachsenheim**

SACHSSE, Emil Eugen. See **SACHSE**

SACHSSE, Walter Max

German, 19th - 20th century.
Born 24 December 1870, in Bautzen.
Sculptor, medallist. Monuments.

Walter Max Sachsse studied in Dresden under Friedrich Offerman and August Hudler. He sculpted a war memorial in Dresden.

Museums and Galleries:

Dresden: *Portrait of E. von Schuchs* (medallion).

SACHTLEVEN. See **SAFTLEVEN**

SACHY, Henri Émile de

French, 19th century.
Born in Paris.
Landscape artist.

Henri Sachy was a student of Colin, Cabanel, Dubufe and Mazerolle. He first exhibited at the Salon of 1869 with *Area around Fécamp at Low Tide*.

Museums and Galleries:

Digne-les-Bains: *Sunset in the Forest of Fontainebleau*.

SACILOTTO, Luis

Brazilian, 20th century.
Born 1924.
Painter.

Luis Sacilotto belonged to the Ruptura group, which produced a manifesto and had an exhibition in the Museum of Modern Art in São Paulo in 1952. In the 1960s he joined the Association of New Movements which promoted optical art and kinetic art and had its first exhibition in São Paulo in 1963.

Through his work on movement his style developed from strictly geometric concrete art forms towards kineticism.

SACIO, F. E.

Italian, 19th century.
Active during the first half of the 19th century.
Miniaturist.

Sacio painted a portrait miniature of *Ferdinand II, King of the Two Sicilies* in 1836.

SACK, Alexander

Austrian, 19th century.
Born 1807, in Vienna; died 13 December 1885, in Vienna.
Painter, engraver (etching). Landscapes.

lexander Sack was the son of Franz Sack and a pupil of ;sellhofer and Wegmayr.

UCTION RECORDS:

IONACO, 14-15 Dec 1996, *Interior View* (1843, watercolour, 2 x 10¼ ins / 30.7 x 26 cm) FRF 84,240.

SACK, Eduard

German, 19th - 20th century.
Born 6 March 1857, in Boppard; died 25 February 1913, in Hamburg.
Painter, designer. Genre scenes, landscapes.

:duard Sack studied under Kaspar Kögler and Ferdinand :eller and at the fine arts academy in Berlin. He was also an istorian and a caricaturist.

SACK, Franz

Austrian, 18th - 19th century.
Born 1765, in Troppau (now Opava, Czech Republic); died 9 June 1825, in Vienna.
Draughtsman, engraver (etching). Landscapes.

'ranz Sack was the father of Alexander Sack and a pupil of . Mössmer. He engraved around 77 plates copied from na- ire or after Ruisdael, Brand, Molitor and Waterloo.

SACK, Gottlieb

Austrian, 19th century.
Born 1791, in Vienna.
Sculptor, lithographer.

;ottlieb Sack was a pupil at the academy in Vienna from 808 to 1817. He engraved illustrations for La Fontaine's *Fa- les.*

SACK, Ludwig August

German, 18th century.
Born 25 October 1759, in Görlitz; died c. 1797, in St Petersburg.
Painter. History painting, portraits.

udwig August Sack studied under Schenau in Dresden.

SACK, Wolfgang

Austrian, 18th - 19th century.
Born 1748, in Vienna; died 22 August 1815, in Vienna.
Sculptor.

Volfgang Sack was sculptor to the Viennese court.

SACK, Wolfgang

Austrian, 19th century.
Active in Vienna c. 1838.
Painter.

SACKER, Amy M.

American, 20th century.
Born 17 July 1876, in Boston; died 1965, in Boston.
Painter, illustrator, engraver.

my M. Sacker was the pupil of Joseph Rodefer de Camp nd Joseph Lindon Smith. She also studied in Rome. She /as a member of the American Arts Federation. She found- d her own school in 1901, later called the Sacker School of esign and Interior Decoration.

SACKERER, Michael or J. M. F., or Sacerer

German, 17th century.
Active in 1614.
Engraver (burin).

Iichael Sackerer engraved the *Death of Abel* and *Christ and ie Woman Taken in Adultery* after J.M. Kager.

SACKH, A.

Hungarian, 17th century.
Active in Kremnitz (now Kremnica, Slovakia) at the beginning of the 17th century.
Medallist.

. Sackh made a medal to commemorate the election of Iathias II, dated 1617.

SACKH, Franciscus

Austrian, 17th century.
Active in the first half of the 17th century.
Sculptor.

Franciscus Sackh sculpted two windows at the abbey of Klosterneuburg near Vienna.

SACKH, Michael

Hungarian, 17th century.
Active in Kremnitz (now Kremnica, Slovakia) from 1601 to 1615.
Medallist.

He engraved medals commemorating the reign of Mathias II.

SACKLARIAN, Stephen

American, 20th century.
Born 1899, in Varna, Bulgaria, to American parents; died 1983.
Painter, sculptor.

Stephen Sacklarian was born in Bulgaria but emigrated to the USA at the age of 10. He worked as a professional boxer, an electrician and graduated in finance from the University of Pennsylvania while at the same time studying at Philadelphia College of Art, at the Academy of Fine Arts in Pennsylvania and working as a painter with Paul Manship and as a sculptor with Francis Speight, Daniel Garber and Franklin Watkins.

He exhibited in the USA, notably at the Moravian College of Bethlehem (Pennsylvania), Country Museum of Art, Greenville, the Everson Museum of Art in Syracuse, New York State. From 1940-1950 he painted in a realist style, then from 1950-1960 began to produce expressive sculptures made from wood. In 1968 his style changed again as he began to work in acrylics. At the end of his life one can discern several paintings relating to his origins, expressing the hopes and the heartbreak of his people.

MUSEUMS AND GALLERIES:

BOSTON (Institute of Contemporary Art) - COLUMBIA (Musuem of Art) - DENVER (AM) - GREENVILLE (County Museum of Art) - JACKSON (Museum of Art) - LONG BEACH (Museum of Art) - MEXICO CITY (Museum of Modern Art) - MINNEAPOLIS (IA): *Genesis No.2* (1969, oil on canvas) - NORFOLK (Chrysler MA) - PASADENA (Norton Simon Mus.) - PHILADELPHIA (MA) - RICHMOND (Virginia MFA): *Genesis* (*Genesis*) (oil on canvas) - SALT LAKE CITY (Utah MFA) - SOFIA (Nacionalna chudozestvena galerija/National Gallery of Art) - ST PAUL (Minnesota Museum of American Art) - SYRACUSE (NEW YORK CITY) (Everson Museum of Art): *Untitled* (1970, gouache); *Reality of Unreality, No. XXXVII* (*Reality of Unreality, No. XXXVII*) (1976, acrylic) - WASHINGTON DC (Smithsonian American AM): *Light Green* (c. 1957-1967, acrylic/canvas).

AUCTION RECORDS:

NEW YORK, 18 Dec 1985, *Nocturnal Gray* (oil on canvas, 73 x 53½ ins / 185.5 x 136 cm) USD 20,000. NEW YORK, 13 Nov 1986, *Untitled* (oil on canvas, 30¾ x 24¾ ins / 78.1 x 62.9 cm) USD 16,000. NEW YORK, 6 May 1987, *Reality of Unreality-Genesis* (acrylic/canvas, 74 x 53 ins / 188 x 134.6 cm) USD 48,000. NEW YORK, 7 May 1991, *Reality of Unreality XVI* (1975, acrylic/canvas, 40 x 51 ins / 101.6 x 129.4 cm) USD 605.

SACKSICK, Gilles

French, 20th century.
Born 1942, in Paris.
Painter, engraver.

Gilles Sacksick's work featured in *De Bonnard à Baselitz - Dix Ans d'enrichissements du cabinet des estampes 1978-1988* (*From Bonnard to Baselitz: A Decade of Acquisitions by the Prints Collection 1978-1988*), an exhibition held in 1993 at the Bibliothèque Nationale in Paris.

Museums and Galleries:
Paris (BNF): *Apples and Cleaver* (1979, etching).

SACO, Amalia
Spanish, 19th century.
Active from 1820 to 1838.
Miniaturist.

SACONHAC, Auguste de
French, 19th century.
Born 1844; died 28 December 1907, in Labordes, near Toulouse.
Painter.

SACONIDES
6th century BC.
Active in the middle of the 6th century BC.
Vase painter.
Ancient Greek.
Saconides decorated vases with female heads and mythological subjects.
Museums and Galleries:
Berlin: vase signed by Saconides - Cambridge: vase signed by Saconides - Munich: vase signed by Saconides - Taranto: Vase signed by Saconides.

SACQUESPER, Adrien
French, 17th century.
Born 17 July 1629, in Caudebec-en-Caux (Seine-Maritime); died after 1688.
Painter, poet. History painting.
Sacquesper was the pupil of François Garnier in Paris. He was influenced by Lesueur and Poussin.
Museums and Galleries:
Rouen: *Martyrdom of St Adrian; St Bruno at Prayer; Monks at Mont St-Bernard; Deposition.*

SACRÉ, Émile
Belgian, 19th century.
Born 1 January 1844, in St-Gilles-les-Bruxelles; died 22 or 23 November 1882, in Ixelles (Brussels).
Painter. Portraits, genre scenes.
Émile Sacré was the pupil of Alfred Cluysenaar in Brussels.

Emile Sacré

Museums and Galleries:
Brussels (MBA): *The Woman with the Fan; Portrait of the Artist; The Father of the Artist; The Mother of the Artist* - Liège: *The Milliner.*
Auction records:
Paris, 26 March 1904, *The Woman with the Fan,* FRF 360. Amsterdam, 14-15 April 1992, *The Woman with the Fan* (oil on panel, 21 3/4 x 14 3/4 ins / 55.5 x 37.5 cm) NLG 4,830. Lokeren, 11 Dec 1999, *Young Woman with a Fan* (oil on panel, 19 x 22 ins / 48 x 55 cm) BEF 90,000. Antwerp, 26 May 2003, *Woman with Dog* (oil on panel, 18 x 13 ins / 45 x 34 cm) EUR 2,600.

SACRE, Jacques
Belgian, 19th - 20th century.
Born 1870, in Liège; died 1941.
Painter. Figures, portraits.
Jacques Sacre taught at the fine arts academy in Liège and exhibited at the Cercle des Beaux-Arts of Liège from 1894 to 1920.
Museums and Galleries:
Liège (Mus. de l'Art wallon): *Old Man.*

SACRE, Joseph
Belgian, 19th century.
Born in Ghent.
Painter. Genre scenes, interiors.
Joseph Sacre began to show his works in public from 1829. He came to Paris in 1837.
Museums and Galleries:
Douai: *Return from the Market.*
Auction records:
London, 20 June 1984, *Kitchen Interior* (1844, oil on canvas, 21 x 25 ins / 53.5 x 63.5 cm) GBP 3,500. Brussels, 10 Dec 2001, *Itinerant Merchant in a Snowy Landscape* (1887, oil on canvas, 20 x 24 ins / 50 x 60 cm) BEF 145,000.

SACRE, Marie Clara (Mme)
French, 19th century.
Born in Paris.
Painter. Portraits.
Marie Sacre first exhibited at the Salon of 1875.

SACRE, Marie José
Belgian, 20th - 21st century.
Born 1948, in Battice.
Painter (gouache), pastellist, draughtsman, illustrator, sculptor. Scenes with figures, landscapes.
Marie José Sacre has painted landscapes of the Ardennes.

SACX, Thomas, or Schackt
Dutch, 17th century.
Born in The Hague.
Sculptor.
Sacx was the pupil of Rombout Verhulst, and a member of the guild at The Hague in 1668.

SADA, Angelo
Italian, 20th century.
Painter. Landscapes, seascapes.
A self-taught artist, Angelo Sada began to paint in 1958. Beginning with landscapes and seascapes, he then began to produce his characteristic *Flowerbeds.* While out playing golf one day, he was inspired to try to recreate the grass of the golf course, drawing sections of it and adding flowers. Although in no way scientifically accurate, these works seek to convey the poetry of nature.

SADAFUSA, nicknames: Osawa and Utagawa, pseudonyms: Gokitei, Gofutei, Gohyotei, Tochoro and Shinsai
Japanese, 19th century.
Active c. 1830-1840.
Print artist.
Sadafusa was originally from Edo (now Tokyo), and subsequently settled in Osaka, specialising in prints on the world of the theatre. According to a print dated 1830 he was the pupil of Shigeharu.

SADAHARU, nickname: Hasegawa, pseudonyms: Goryutei and Goshotei
Japanese, 19th century.
Active at the end of the 1830s in Osaka.
Print artist.

SADAHIRO I, real name: Sadahiro Utagawa, original name: Nanakawa, pseudonyms: Ukiyo, Gochotei, Gorakutei, Gosotei, Gokitei, Kogado
Japanese, 19th century.
Print artist.
It is possible that Sadahiro I may be one and the same artist as Hirosada. According to the records, his seals carry the various names Tamikuni (1830), Hiro (1834), and Sada (1836). He was active in the Osaka region around 1830-1851.

SADAHIRO II, real name: Matasaburo, first name: Hirokane, nickname: Mitani, pseudonym: Shokotei
Japanese, 19th - 20th century.
Born 1840, in Osaka; died 1910.
Active from 1864 to 1876.
Print artist.

After studying the pictorial style of the Maruyama School, Sadahiro II took this name following the death of his master Hiromasa.

SADAKAGE, real name: Sadakage Utagawa, original name: Kojima, nickname: Shogoro, pseudonym: Gokotei
Japanese, 19th century.
Painter, draughtsman. Portraits, genre scenes.

Sadakage came from Edo (now Tokyo) but he worked in Osaka around 1820-1830, where he was known for his portraits of actors and his 'surimono' (limited edition prints used as greeting or cards announcing events such as births, marriages and deaths).

AUCTION RECORDS:
LONDON, 9 Nov 1988, *Large Plan of a Woman's Face Disguised as Daruma with a Red Scarf on her head* (print, 7 3/4 x 7 ins / 19.7 x 17.5 cm) GBP 1,870. NEW YORK, 15 June 1990, *Two Courtesans Reading with Another Smoking a Pipe* (print ona tate-e, triptych, 14 1/2 x 10 ins / 37 x 25.5 cm) USD 4,950. NEW YORK, 27 March 1991, *The Actor Danjuro VII in the Role of Matsunaga Daizen and Sagawa Kikunojo in the Role of Yukihime* (Kakubuan print surimono, diptych, 8 1/4 x 7 1/4 ins / 20.9 x 18.1 cm) USD 2,200.

SADAKATSU
Japanese, 19th century.
Active in the Osaka region in 1834, more likely in 1852.
Print artist.

The few examples of prints by Sadakatsu may possibly be the works of other artists.

SADAKAZU, pseudonyms: Kudarado, Isshinsai and Shinsai
Japanese, 19th century.
Active in the Osaka region in 1826.
Print artist.

SADAMARO. See **SADAMARU**

SADAMARU, first name: Sadamaro, nickname: Utagawa
Japanese, 19th century.
Active in the Osaka region in 1833.
Print artist.

SADAMASA, real name: Hasegawa
Japanese, 19th century.
Active in the Osaka region c. 1834-1840.
Print artist.

According to a print dated March 1834 Sadamasa was the pupil of Toto Kunisada, whilst according to another undated work, he was the pupil of Hasegawa (Sadanobu).

SADAMASU, real name: Sadamasu Utagawa, pseudonym: Gohotei
Japanese, 19th century.
Active in the Osaka region in 1849.
Print artist.

Sadamasu was the pupil of Kunimasu.

BIBLIOGRAPHY:
Guth, Christine, *Japanese Art of the Edo Period*, Calmann & King, 1996.

SADANOBU, real name: Sadanobu Kano, nicknames: Sakon, Sakon Shoran, Shirojiro, Toshinobu, Ukyonosuke
Japanese, 17th century.
Born 1597; died 1623.
Painter.
Kano School.

Sadanobu was the son of Mitsunobu (1565-1608) and succeeded him as director of the Kano School.

SADANOBU I, real name: Bunkichi Hasagawa, original name: Tokubei, pseudonyms: Nanso, Nansoro, Sekkaen, Shin'o, Shinten'o, Yuen Ryokuitsusai, Kinkado (1843) and Ranko (as a singer of joruri), seals: Fujinomiya and Shinten'o
Japanese, 19th century.
Born 1809; died 1879.
Active from 1834 to 1879.
Print artist.

SADANOBU II, real name: Tokutaro, first name: Konobu I, nickname: Hasagawa
Japanese, 19th century.
Born 1848; died 1886.
Active from 1867 to 1880.
Print artist.

Sadanobu II was the son of Sadanobu I, and the second of five generations of artists of the Hasegawa family who have continued to work right up to the present day.

SADATAKA
Japanese, 19th century.
Born in Edo, now Tokyo.
Print artist.

Sadataka worked in Osaka in the 1830s.

SADATSUGU, pseudonym: Gochotei
Japanese, 19th century.
Active in the Osaka region c. 1835-1839.
Print artist.

Sadatsugu was a pupil of Kunisada.

SADAYOSHI, real name: Sadayoshi Yoshikawa
Japanese, 18th century.
Active in the Osaka region c. 1760.
Print artist.

SADAYOSHI, real name: Sadeyoshi Utagawa, nickname: Higoya Sadashichiro, pseudonyms: Baisoen, Gofutei, Gohyotei, Kaishuntei, Kokuhyotei and Baisoen Kinkin
Japanese, 19th century.
Active in the Osaka region from 837 to 1853.
Print artist.

SADAYOSHI, nickname: Utagawa
Japanese, 19th century.
Active in the Osaka region c. 1850.
Print artist.

SADAYUKI
Japanese, 19th century.
Active in the Osaka region c. 1839-1840.
Print artist.

Sadayuki was the pupil of Sadamasu.

SADD, Henry S.
American, 19th century.
Born at the beginning of the 19th century, in England.
Engraver.

Henry S. Sadd moved to New York in 1840, and also spent time in Australia. He chiefly engraved portraits.

SADDLER, John
British, 19th century.
Born 1813; died 29 March 1892, in Wokingham.
Engraver (burin).

John Saddler studied under George Cooke and went on to make a name for himself as an engraver of originals by Turner, Landseer, Rosa Bonheur, Millais, Gustave Doré and H. Dawson. He was also a prolific illustrator. He exhibited his work from 1862. He committed suicide in 1892 after a fit of depression.

SADEE, E.
French, 19th century.
Painter. Genre scenes.

MUSEUMS AND GALLERIES:
SYDNEY: *Moments of Anxiety* (watercolour).

SADEE, Philippe Lodowyck Jacob Frederik

Dutch, 19th century.

Born 7 February 1837, in The Hague; died 14 December 1904.

Painter. Genre scenes, landscapes.

Sadee was the pupil of J.E.J. van den Berg, and also studied at the academy in The Hague. He travelled to France and Italy.

MUSEUMS AND GALLERIES:
AMSTERDAM: *Women Gleaning Potatoes* - AMSTERDAM (Stedelijk Mus.): *On the Beach; On the Dunes; Return from Selling Fish* - BAUTZEN: *On Scheveningen Beach* - BREMEN: *War Scene in Holland* - DORDRECHT: *After the Departure of the Fishing Boats* - LEEUWARDEN: *Sale of Fish* - SHEFFIELD: *The End of the Day* (two paintings) - THE HAGUE (Gemeentemus.): *The Poor Man's Lot; Station of the Dutch Company at The Hague* - THE HAGUE (Mus. Mesdag): *Interior.*

AUCTION RECORDS:
LONDON, 1871, *Leaving Church,* FRF 8,840. LONDON, 1884, *Poor Man's Lot* (drawing) FRF 1,942. LONDON, 1899, *Waiting for the Fishing Boats,* FRF 2,750. LONDON, 13 June 1910, *Fishwives Chatting,* GBP 105. LONDON, 17 March 1922, *Fishermen in the Dunes,* GBP 63. LONDON, 12 May 1922, *Sale of Fish,* GBP 39. LONDON, 27 April 1923, *Fishermen in the Pas-de-Calais,* GBP 105. LONDON, 2 May 1924, *Waiting for Father,* GBP 157. LONDON, 14 Nov 1924, *Fishermen Returning Home,* GBP 173. LONDON, 4 March 1932, *Waiting for Fishing Boats,* GBP 86. LONDON, 2 Feb 1945, *Fishermen on the Beach,* GBP 183; *Bereaved,* GBP 131. LONDON, 22 April 1966, *Fishermen on the Beach,* Gns 450. AMSTERDAM, 24 April 1968, *Return of the Fishermen,* NLG 8,900. LONDON, 14 June 1974, *Breton Fishermen on the Beach,* Gns 550. LONDON, 24 Nov 1976, *Women Gathering Wrack* (oil on panel, 9 1/4 x 7 1/4 ins / 23.5 x 18.5 cm) GBP 1,900. NEW YORK, 28 April 1977, *Gallant Conversation* (1867, oil on canvas, 24 3/4 x 20 3/4 ins / 63 x 53 cm) USD 3,750. AMSTERDAM, 24 April 1979, *Fish Market* (1890, oil on canvas, 31 x 50 3/4 ins / 79 x 129 cm) NLG 37,000. NEW YORK, 28 May 1981, *Fishermen's Families Returning* (1881, oil on canvas, 34 1/2 x 51 1/2 ins / 87.5 x 131 cm) USD 21,000. LONDON, 16 March 1983, *Fisherman's Return* (oil on canvas, 27 x 38 3/4 ins / 68.5 x 98.5 cm) GBP 5,800. AMSTERDAM, 3 May 1988, *Fishwives Bringing Back the Baskets of Fish* (oil on canvas, 28 3/4 x 38 1/4 ins / 73 x 97 cm) NLG 27,600. STOCKHOLM, 15 Nov 1989, *Fisherman's Family Working on the Shore* (oil, 6 1/4 x 11 ins / 16 x 27 cm) SEK 41,000. NEW YORK, 1 March 1990, *Fisherman's Farewell* (oil on canvas, 22 x 27 1/2 ins / 55.8 x 69.8 cm) USD 26,400. LONDON, 28 Nov 1990, *Waiting for the Fishermen to Return* (oil on canvas, 20 3/4 x 29 1/2 ins / 53 x 75 cm) GBP 12,100. AMSTERDAM, 24 April 1991, *Farewell to Father* (1889, oil on canvas, 27 1/2 x 23 3/4 ins / 70 x 60.5 cm) NLG 28,750. LONDON, 18 June 1993, *Waiting for the Boats* (1881, oil on canvas, 27 3/4 x 22 ins / 70.5 x 55 cm) GBP 10,580. NEW YORK, 13 Oct 1993, *After the Boats Have Departed* (1881, oil on canvas, 31 1/2 x 51 ins / 80 x 129.5 cm) USD 19,550. AMSTERDAM, 21 April 1994, *Harvest* (1877, oil on panel, 8 1/2 x 12 1/2 ins / 21.5 x 32 cm) NLG 12,650. LONDON, 15 June 1994, *Watching Fishermen in the Distance* (1875, oil on canvas, 26 1/2 x 48 ins / 67 x 121 cm) GBP 43,300. AMSTERDAM, 8 Nov 1994, *Fishermen's Families on the Shore* (oil on canvas, 8 1/4 x 12 1/4 ins / 21 x 31 cm) NLG 40,250. LONDON, 17 March 1995, *On the Beach* (oil on canvas, 22 x 27 3/4 ins / 56 x 70.4 cm) GBP 13,800. AMSTERDAM, 5 Nov 1996, *Mother and Child Waiting for the Fishing Boat to Return* (watercolour, 13 1/2 x 19 ins / 34 x 48 cm) NLG 14,160. LONDON, 21 March 1997, *Mending the Nets* (oil on canvas, 21 1/2 x 32 ins / 54.6 x 81 cm) GBP 26,450. LONDON, 13 June 1997, *Fisherman's Family Returns* (oil on canvas, 27 1/2 x 40 ins / 70 x 101.5 cm) GBP 28,750. LONDON, 17 Feb 1999, *Beach Scene* (watercolour, 11 x 20 ins / 29 x 51 cm) GBP 1,500. AMSTERDAM, 27 April 1999, *Lighting the Stove: Kitchen Interior* (1884, oil on paper/panel, 14 x 20 ins / 35 x 50 cm) NLG 12,000. LONDON, 7 April 2000, *Fisherfolk* (oil on canvas, 22 x 28 ins / 56 x 70 cm) GBP 80,500. AMSTERDAM, 18 April 2000, *Motherly Love* (oil on canvas, 2[illegible] x 28 ins / 57 x 70 cm) NLG 110,000. AMSTERDAM, 24 April 2001, *Arrival of the Fleet* (1903, oil on canvas, 29 x 44 ins / 7[illegible] x 112 cm) NLG 48,000. NEW YORK, 28 June 2001, *Waiting for His Return* (oil on canvas, 28 x 22 ins / 70 x 55 cm) USD 26,000. AMSTERDAM, 23 April 2002, *View of the Central Station, Amsterdam* (oil on panel, 14 x 20 ins / 35 x 51 cm) EUR 25,000. AMSTERDAM, 24 April 2002, *Strandjutters* (oil on canvas, 22 x 28 ins / 55 x 70 cm) EUR 20,000. AMSTERDAM, 2[illegible] April 2003, *Anticipating the Return* (oil on canvas, 28 x 22 ins / 71 x 57 cm) EUR 26,000. BETHESDA, 13 Dec 2003, *Welcoming the Boats* (1896, oil on canvas, 29 x 39 ins / 74 x 99 cm) USD 46,000. AMSTERDAM, 20 April 2004, *Return of the Fishing Fleet at Katwijk* (1896, oil on canvas, 29 x 40 ins / 74 x 10[illegible] cm) EUR 95,000. LONDON, 16 June 2004, *Looking out to Se[a]* (1886, oil on canvas, 22 x 27 ins / 55 x 68 cm) GBP 8,500.

SADELEER, Jacques de

Belgian, 20th century.

Born 1920, in Haaltert.

Painter, draughtsman, watercolourist, pastellist. Genre scenes, landscapes.

Jacques de Sadeleer studied at the St Luke Institute in Schaerbeek and went on to paint landscapes of Provence, Andalusia and the Belgian plains.

SADELER, A.

German, 18th century.

Painter.

A. Sadeler painted a *St Sebastian* in 1738 for the church of Lindenfels.

SADELER, Aegidius or Egidius I

Flemish School, 16th - 17th century.

Engraver.

Antwerp School.

Aegidius Sadeler I was the father of Aegidius Sadeler II and the brother of Jean I and Raphaël I. He became a master of the guild of Antwerp in 1580. He was also a seller of prints.

BIBLIOGRAPHY:
Limouze, Dorothy A., *The Sadelers: Engravers from the Golden Age of Antwerp and Prague,* exhibition catalogue, Philadelphia Museum of Art, Philadelphia, 1989. Ramaix, Isabelle de, *Les Sadeler,* exhibition catalogue, Bibliothèque royale de Belgique, Brussels, 1992.

SADELER, Aegidius or Egidius or Gillis II

Flemish School, 16th - 17th century.

Born 1570, in Antwerp; died 1629, in Prague.

Active also in Italy and Germany.

Painter, engraver. Religious subjects, mythological subjects, allegorical subjects, portraits, interiors with figures.

Antwerp School, Prague School.

Aegidius Sadeler II was the son of Aegidius Sadeler I. He was the nephew of Jean and Raphaël Sadeler and a pupil of theirs in 1585, when he entered the guild of Antwerp as an engraver. He went to Germany, then in 1593 to Rome and in 1595 to Munich, where he met Joris Hoefnagel. Some writers say that he went to Munich in 1590 and then moved on to Venice, Florence, Bologna and Rome. Summoned to the Prague court, he worked for Emperor Rodolphus II, Emperor Mathias and Ferdinand II. He was a friend of B. Sprange[r] and was dubbed the 'Phoenix of Engravers'. His output was large and very varied in the technical means used. He often engraved from his own drawings and his treatment of portraits was usually interesting. His engraving is notable for the clearness of the cutting and the chiaroscuro achieved by hatching.

Sadeler's work has been extensively represented in thematic exhibitions, including some devoted to the work of the Sadeler family: *The Sadelers: Engravers from the Golden Age of Antwerp and Prague* at the Philadelphia Museum of Art (1989); *Les Sadeler* (*The Sadelers*) at the Royal Library of Belgium (1992); and *Praga Magica. L'Art à Prague au Temps de Rodolphe II* (*Praga Magica. Art in Prague under Rudolph II*) at the Musée Magnin in Dijon (2002).

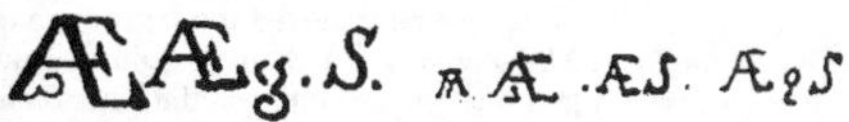

Bibliography:

Hollstein, Friedrich Wilhelm Heinrich, *Dutch and Flemish Etchings, Engravings and Woodcuts ca. 1450-1700*, Menno Hertzberger, Amsterdam, 1949-1974. DaCosta Kaufmann, Thomas, *L'École de Prague*, Flammarion, Paris, 1985. Limouze, Dorothy A., *The Sadelers: Engravers from the Golden Age of Antwerp and Prague*, exhibition catalogue, Philadelphia Museum of Art, Philadelphia, 1989. Limouze, Dorothy A., *Aegidius Sadeler. Drawings, prints and art theory*, dissertation, UMI Research Press, Ann Arbor, 1990 (Princeton University). Ramaix, Isabelle de, *Les Sadeler*, exhibition catalogue, Bibliothèque royale de Belgique, Brussels, 1992. Ramaix, Isabelle de, *Aegidius Sadeler II*, Abaris Books, New York, 1997.

Museums and Galleries:

Cologne (Roland Palace): *Christ and the Pilgrims of Emmaus*
Vienna (NM): *St Sebastian and Parnassus.*

Auction records:

Paris, 15 March 1983, *View of the Great Hall of Hradchyn Palace, Prague* (oil on wood, 25 3/4 x 25 3/4 ins / 65.5 x 65.5 cm) FRF 39,000. Berlin, 26 Nov 1999, *Portrait of Emperor Matthias of Austria* (copper engraving, 26 x 16 ins / 66 x 41 cm) DEM 14,000. Berlin, 26 Nov 1999, *King Ferdinand II on Horseback* (copper engraving, two, 35 x 24 ins / 88 x 62 cm) DEM 14,000. Berlin, 26 May 2000, *Kaiser Rudolph on Horseback* (copperplate, 20 x 15 ins / 50 x 38 cm) DEM 12,000. Berlin, 26 May 2000, *Bartholomaus Spranger and his Wife Christian Muller* (copperplate, 11 x 16 ins / 29 x 41 cm) DEM 78,000. Berlin, 18 May 2001, *Synal Chaen, Persian Ambassador at Prague Court* (copperplate, 9 x 6 ins / 23 x 15 cm) DEM 3,500. London, 3 Dec 2001, *Emperor Mathias* (engraving, 27 x 19 ins / 68 x 47 cm) GBP 7,200. New York, 6 May 2004, *Bartholomacus Spranger and his Wife Christina Muller* (engraving, 12 x 17 ins / 30 x 43 cm) USD 3,800.

SADELER, Franz

German, 17th century.
Born 1629, in Munich.
Engraver.

Franz Sadeler was the son of Philipp Sadeler.

Bibliography:

Ramaix, Isabelle de, *Les Sadeler*, exhibition catalogue, Bibliothèque royale de Belgique, Brussels, 1992.

SADELER, Gillis. See SADELER Aegidius II

SADELER, Jean or Johann or Hans II, the Younger

Flemish School, 17th century.
Died 1665, in Munich.
Engraver.

Jean Sadeler the Younger was the son of Raphaël Sadeler. He worked in Vienna, and in 1652 in Munich.

Bibliography:

Ramaix, Isabelle de, *Les Sadeler*, exhibition catalogue, Bibliothèque royale de Belgique, Brussels, 1992.

SADELER, Jean or Johann or Jan or Hans I, the Elder

Flemish School, 16th century.
Born 1550, in Brussels; died August 1600, in Venice.
Active also in Germany and England.
Draughtsman, engraver (burin), print dealer.

Jean Sadeler I's father was an inlaid metal worker and Jean was trained for this profession. However, he devoted himself at an early age to the study of the human figure. When he was about 20 he began to engrave on copper and in 1572 he was admitted as a master to the guild of St Luke. It has been said that he travelled in Germany and worked in Cologne from 1580 to 1587. The facts, or at least the dates, may not be correct, because according the guild archives, Gillis Sadeler was a pupil of his in 1585. In 1587 he is referred to in Frankfurt, and in 1589 in Munich, where Duke William II of Bavaria granted him a pension of 200 gold florins. He went to Rome in 1593 or 1595, and finally to Venice. During these travels he engraved a large number of plates and his overall output was considerable.

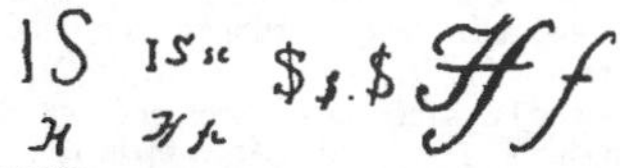

Bibliography:

Ramaix, Isabelle de, *Les Sadeler*, exhibition catalogue, Bibliothèque royale de Belgique, Brussels, 1992.

SADELER, Justus or Josse

Flemish School, 17th century.
Born 1583, in Antwerp; died 1620, in Venice, after 1620 in Leiden according to some sources.
Engraver, art dealer.

Justus Sadeler was the son of Jan Sadeler the Elder. He went with his father to Italy, and was in Venice is 1596, where he died in 1620. According to Gaudellini, he married in 1620 and died in Amsterdam in 1629, but according to others, he returned to Holland in 1620 with a Dutch ambassador, and fell ill in Leiden, where he died.

Bibliography:

Limouze, Dorothy A., *The Sadelers: Engravers from the Golden Age of Antwerp and Prague*, exhibition catalogue, Philadelphia Museum of Art, Philadelphia, 1989. Ramaix, Isabelle de, *Les Sadeler*, exhibition catalogue, Bibliothèque royale de Belgique, Brussels, 1992.

SADELER, Marcus Christoph

Flemish School, 17th century.
Born 1614, in Munich.
Engraver, publisher.

Marcus Christoph Sadler was the son of Jan Sadeler the Elder. He was active in Prague and Venice, where the Sadeler family was apparently firmly established. Marcus published a number of prints by Jan Raphael and Gillis Sadeler, from plates which he seems to have inherited, since his name appears on the second impressions only. He seems to have been active mainly as a dealer. A series of 16 counter-proofs after Dürer's *Passion* is attributed to him, thought to have been published between 1606 and 1613; the name Marcus appears on the second impression only.

Bibliography:

Limouze, Dorothy A., *The Sadelers: Engravers from de Golden Age of Antwerp and Prague*, exhibition catalogue, Philadelphia Museum of Art, Philadelphia, 1989. Ramaix, Isabelle de, *Les Sadeler*, exhibition catalogue, Bibliothèque royale de Belgique, Brussels, 1992.

SADELER, Philipp
Flemish School, 17th century.
Active in Munich.
Engraver.

Philipp Sadeler was the son of Raphaël Sadeler. In 1624, in Munich, he married Regina, the daughter of the painter P. Candid. He was an engraver of religious subjects, portraits and landscapes.

BIBLIOGRAPHY:
Ramaix, Isabelle de, *Les Sadeler*, exhibition catalogue, Bibliothèque royale de Belgique, Brussels, 1992.

SADELER, Raphaël I, the Elder
Flemish School, 16th - 17th century.
Born 1560 or 1561, in Antwerp; died 1628 or 1632, in Munich.
Active also in Italy and Germany.
Painter, engraver. Religious subjects, portraits.
Antwerp School.

Raphaël Sadeler I was the younger brother of Jean Sadeler I. He was a member of the guild of Antwerp in 1582. He went with his father Jan to Germany and Italy, and in 1604 he was summoned by Prince Maximilian to leave Venice and go to Munich, where he was granted a pension of 105 florins.

Sadeler produced a considerable body of work. Le Blanc catalogued 126 engravings, some of which, especially the portraits, are remarkable in execution.

BIBLIOGRAPHY:
Limouze, Dorothy A., *The Sadelers: Engravers from the Golden Age of Antwerp and Prague*, exhibition catalogue, Philadelphia Museum of Art, Philadelphia, 1989. Ramaix, Isabelle de, *Les Sadeler*, exhibition catalogue, Bibliothèque royale de Belgique, Brussels, 1992.

MUSEUMS AND GALLERIES:
WROCLAW: *Visitation*.

SADELER, Raphaël II, the Younger
Flemish School, 17th century.
Born 20 December 1584, in Antwerp; died 1632, in Munich.
Painter, engraver. Religious subjects.

Raphaël Sadeler the Younger was the son of Raphaël Sadeler. He joined the Antwerp guild in 1610. *Bryan's Dictonary* records him as active in Venice in 1596, but this is clearly due to a confusion of his works with those of Raphaël Sadeler the Elder. Given the documented dates available, it seems much more likely that he moved from Antwerp to Munich, where he collaborated with his father on engravings of Rader's *Bavaria Sancta et Pia*. He is best known for a *Holy Family*, dated 1613.

BIBLIOGRAPHY:
Limouze, Dorothy A., *The Sadelers: Engravers from de Golden Age of Antwerp and Prague*, exhibition catalogue, Philadelphia Museum of Art, Philadelphia, 1989. Ramaix, Isabelle de, *Les Sadeler*, exhibition catalogue, Bibliothèque royale de Belgique, Brussels, 1992.

SADELER, Tobias
17th century.
Engraver.

Tobias Sadeler was the son of Egidius Sadeler II. He worke in Vienna (1670-1675) and Prague.

BIBLIOGRAPHY:
Limouze, Dorothy A., *The Sadelers: Engravers from th Golden Age of Antwerp and Prague*, exhibition catalogue Philadelphia Museum of Art, Philadelphia, 1989. Ramaix, Isabelle de, *Les Sadeler*, exhibition catalogue, Bibliothèqu royale de Belgique, Brussels, 1992.

SADELER, Valérius de. See **SAEDELER**

SADEQUAIN
Pakistani, 20th century.
Born in Amroha; died 10 February 1987, in Karachi.
Painter, calligrapher. Murals.

Sadequain spent his early years in Delhi before settling i Pakistan in the 1950s, where he received the patronage o the Pakistani Prime Minister Hussain Shaheed Suhrawardy He travelled widely in the 1960s, exhibiting at the Paris Bien nale in 1961. In Pakistan he became well-known as a mural ist, painting many murals on public buildings in Karachi. H also made his name as a calligrapher, turning his attentio to this art in the 1970s. His work attracted controversy an led to protests and even violence in reaction to the nudit and political elements of his art.

His painting depicts cubist-like figures, seascapes and land scapes, covering moral and political issues, often satirically One of his best-known works is the mural representing *Th Dignity of Labour* on the Mangla Dam near Islamabad. He i also noted for his series of paintings featuring cacti which h produced during a period of recuperation by the sea in Gad dani.

Sadequain was awarded fisrt prize at the Pakistan Nation al Exhibition in 1960. In 2002 a retrospective exhibition wa held at the Mohatta Palace in Karachi called *The Holy Sinne Sadequain 1954-1987*. Much of his work is held in privat collections.

BIBLIOGRAPHY:
Hashimi, S./Haroon, H., *The Holy Sinner*, exhibition cata logue, 1987.

MUSEUMS AND GALLERIES:
LAHORE (Central Museum) - NEW YORK (Metropolitan Mus of Art): Calligraphic Panel (1980, paint on wood).

SADKOWSKY, Alexander, or Alex
Swiss, 20th century.
Born 1934.
Painter, draughtsman, sculptor.

Alexander Sadkowsky lived and worked in Zurich in 195 and 1957 as a pupil of W. Jonas and C. Kissling before goin on to study at the Real Academia de Bellas Artes de San Car los in Valencia in Spain. His work borders on fantasy and a compendium of aesthetic and metaphysical invention. H exhibited in Zurich (1957, 1959, 1961, 1968), in Stuttga (1967, 1969), and in Berlin, London and Amsterdam (1970).

BIBLIOGRAPHY:
Lutz, Hans-Rudolf/Billeter, Fritz, *Werkkatalog Alex Sadkowsk Graphik 1954-1967*, Hans-Rudolf Lutz, Zurich, 1968. Lutz Hans-Rudolf, *Werkkatalog Alex Sadkowsky Malerei*, Hans Rudolf Lutz, Zurich, 1974.

MUSEUMS AND GALLERIES:
AARAU (Aargauer Kunsthaus): *Emancipation II* (1972, oil o canvas).

AUCTION RECORDS:
ZURICH, 23 Nov 1977, *Man Lying Awake* (1964, oil on canvas 32 x 45 1/4 ins / 81 x 115 cm) CHF 9,500. ZURICH, 3 Nov 197 *Swiss Man* (1968, acrylic/paper, 19 3/4 x 27 1/2 ins / 50 x 70 cm CHF 1,700. ZURICH, 9 Nov 1983, *Titine* (1973-1975, acryl ic/canvas, 70 3/4 x 47 1/4 ins / 180 x 120 cm) CHF 8,000. ZUR ICH, 18 Oct 1990, *Lovers* (oil and distemper/Bristol boar 19 1/2 x 27 1/4 ins / 49.5 x 69.5 cm) CHF 3,000. ZURICH, 21 Jun 1991, *Spanish Tales* (1963, oil on canvas, 36 1/4 x 23 1/2 ins / 9

60 cm) CHF 1,200. ZURICH, 13 Oct 1993, *Young Woman* ıcrylic/canvas, 25 1/2 x 21 1/4 ins / 65 x 54 cm) CHF 6,000. ZU-ICH, 13 Oct 1994, *Bouquet of Flowers* (1962, oil on canvas, 5 1/2 x 21 1/4 ins / 65 x 54 cm) CHF 2,400. ZURICH, 17-18 June 996, *Child Dancer* (acrylic and oil on paper, 39 1/4 x 27 1/4 ins 100 x 69 cm) CHF 2,800. LUCERNE, 27 Nov 1999, *Alex the Pi-nist* (oil on paper, 39 x 28 ins / 100 x 70 cm) CHF 3,000. ZU-ICH, 15 May 2001, *Woman Kissing* (1982, oil on canvas, 29 x 1 ins / 73 x 54 cm) CHF 4,400. ERLENBACH, 31 March 2004, *'oetess* (1984, acrylic on pavatex, 19 x 17 ins / 48 x 44 cm) :HF 3,500. ZURICH, 8 June 2004, *Woman with Scar* (1973, oil n canvas, 50 x 34 ins / 128 x 87 cm) CHF 4,200.

SADLER, Dendy. See **SADLER Walter Dendy**

SADLER, Fernande
French, 19th - 20th century.
Born 7 July 1869, in Toul.
Painter, engraver.
'ernande Sadler exhibited in Paris at the Salon des Artistes 'rançais from 1894.

SADLER, Jakob or Johann Jakob.
See **SATTLER**

SADLER, John
British, 18th century.
Born c. 1720, in Melling; died 10 December 1789, in Liverpool.
Engraver (burin), potter.
ohn Sadler is on record as having been active in Liverpool rom 1748.
IUSEUMS AND GALLERIES:
ONDON (British Mus.) - LONDON (Victoria and Albert Mus.).

SADLER, Joseph. See **SATTLER Josef Ignaz**

SADLER, Karóly or Karl
Hungarian, 19th century.
Active in Budapest during the first half of the 19th century.
Engraver (burin).
:aróly Sadler exhibited in Vienna from 1838 to 1840, and in ·udapest in 1844.

SADLER, Philipp. See **SATTLER**

SADLER, Rupert
Irish, 19th century.
Born 1810; died 5 September 1892, in Dublin.
Painter. Genre scenes.
Rupert Sadler was the son of William Sadler II.

SADLER, Thomas
British, 17th century.
Born c. 1647; died c. 1685.
Miniaturist. Portraits.
homas Sadler made a name for himself in London during ıe reigns of Charles II and James II.
IUSEUMS AND GALLERIES:
ONDON (National Portrait Gal.): *John Bunyan* (1684, oil on anvas).

SADLER, Walter Dendy
British, 19th - 20th century.
Born 12 May 1854, in Dorking; died 13 November 1923, near St Ives.
Painter. Genre scenes.
Valter Dendy Sadler was the son of a lawyer. He studied in ondon and Düsseldorf.

He exhibited in London from 1872 at the Royal Academy nd Suffolk Street. He was a member of the Royal Society of ·ritish Artists and Royal Institute of Oil Painters.

He frequently handled 18th-century subjects, and intro-uced furniture and accessories into his paintings which were painted with the exactitude of a connoisseur. His works have been frequently copied.

WDS

MUSEUMS AND GALLERIES:
BRADFORD (Cartwright Hall AG): *A Prisoner of the State* (1885, oil on canvas) - LIVERPOOL (Walker AG): *Friday* (1882); copy*Darby and Joan* - LONDON (Tate Collection): *Thursday*; *Good Story*.

AUCTION RECORDS:
LONDON, 22 April 1911, *Autumn Scene* (1889) GBP 304. NEW YORK, 17 Jan 1914, *Genre Subject*, USD 750. LONDON, 9 Dec 1921, *Popular Candidate*, GBP 357. LONDON, 22 June 1923, *Called to Account* GBP 115. LONDON, 18 June 1926, *His Favourite Box*, GBP 141. LONDON, 26 July 1929, *The Queen, God Bless Her*, GBP 241. LONDON, 2 Dec 1938, *Marriage by Proxy*, GBP 94. LONDON, 5 Dec 1941, *Tea and Scandal*, GBP 220. LONDON, 14 April 1944, *Autocrat in front of His Lunch*, GBP 199. LONDON, 7 Feb 1947, *Marriage by Proxy*, GBP 409. LONDON, 26 April 1968, *Bagman's Toast to Sweethearts and Wives*, Gns 420. LONDON, 28 Nov 1972, *Dummy Whist with Figures*, GBP 1,350. LONDON, 27 July 1973, *Figures in an Interior*, Gns 1,600. LONDON, 26 April 1974, *Old Crusted*, Gns 1,600. LONDON, 25 Oct 1977, *Chance Companions* (oil on canvas, 37 1/4 x 49 1/2 ins / 94.5 x 126 cm) GBP 2,600. LONDON, 16 Jan 1979, *Oh, For a Bite* (1886, oil on canvas, 25 1/2 x 20 ins / 65 x 51 cm) GBP 650. NEW YORK, 28 Oct 1981, *Old Friends* (oil on canvas, 33 1/2 x 47 1/2 ins / 85.1 x 120.6 cm) USD 8,000. NEW YORK, 26 Oct 1983, *Home Sweet Home* (oil on canvas, 52 x 68 ins / 132 x 172.5 cm) USD 14,500. NEW YORK, 24 May 1985, *For He's a Jolly Good Fellow and So Say All of Us* (oil on canvas, 38 1/4 x 50 ins / 97.1 x 127 cm) USD 17,000. NEW YORK, 27 Feb 1986, *The Cellar's Best* (oil on canvas, 34 x 48 ins / 86.3 x 122 cm) USD 14,500. NEW YORK, 28 Feb 1990, *Widow in Her Garden* (oil on canvas, 26 1/4 x 34 ins / 66.6 x 86.4 cm) USD 11,000. LONDON, 13 Feb 1991, *Squire's Song* (oil on canvas, 39 x 50 ins / 99 x 127 cm) GBP 19,800. LONDON, 14 June 1991, *Expert* (oil on canvas, 16 x 20 ins / 40.8 x 51 cm) GBP 1,980. LONDON, 3 Feb 1993, *By the River* (1883, oil on canvas, 20 x 30 ins / 51 x 76 cm) GBP 3,220. NEW YORK, 27 May 1993, *Chorus Gentlemen* (oil on canvas, 38 x 50 ins / 96.5 x 127 cm) USD 25,300. LUDLOW, 29 Sept 1994, *Nearly Done* (oil on canvas, 37 1/2 x 49 1/2 ins / 95 x 125.5 cm) GBP 24,150. LONDON, 29 March 1996, *After Dinner, Rest Awhile* (oil on canvas, 34 x 48 ins / 86.3 x 122 cm) GBP 31,050. LONDON, 5 June 1996, *Temptation* (oil on canvas, 24 1/2 x 32 ins / 62.5 x 81 cm) GBP 4,140. NEW YORK, 26 Feb 1997, *Nightcap* (oil on canvas, 22 x 16 ins / 55.8 x 40.6 cm) USD 2,530. LONDON, 6 June 1997, *Meeting of Creditors* (oil on canvas, 38 1/2 x 50 1/2 ins / 98 x 128 cm) GBP 27,600.

SADLER, William I
Irish, 18th century.
Born in England; died c. 1788.
Painter, engraver, draughtsman. History painting, portraits, landscapes.
William Sadler studied in Dublin.
MUSEUMS AND GALLERIES:
DUBLIN: *Portrait of the Actor John Kemble* (chalk drawing).
AUCTION RECORDS:
LONDON, 15 July 1988, *Landscape with Anglers near a Waterfall* (oil on panel, 8 3/4 x 13 ins / 22.3 x 33 cm) GBP 1,980. LONDON, 16 May 1990, *View of Dublin with the Wellington Memorial, St Patrick's Cathedral and the Royal Kilmainham Hospital* (oil on canvas, 11 x 16 1/2 ins / 28 x 42 cm) GBP 3,520. BELFAST, 30 May 1990, *Battle of the Boyle, with Stackallan House in the Distance* (oil on panel, 22 1/2 x 34 1/2 ins / 57.1 x 87.9 cm) GBP 7,700. LONDON, 31 Oct 1990, *Fishing in the Dar-*

gle River, Co. Wicklow (oil on panel, 8¼ x 13¼ ins / 21 x 33.5 cm) GBP 990. LONDON, 3 Feb 1993, *View of Dublin from Phoenix Park, with the Xallington Memorial* (oil on canvas, 22 x 33½ ins / 56 x 85 cm) GBP 747. LONDON, 11 Oct 1995, *View of the Killarney Hills* (oil on panel, 10¾ x 17 ins / 27.5 x 43 cm) GBP 690. LONDON, 16 May 1996, *River Landscape with Horsemen and a View of Clonleigh Church at Lifford, Co. Donegal* (oil on panel, 17 x 24 ins / 43 x 61 cm) GBP 1,495. DUBLIN, 11 Oct 1999, *Seven Churches, Glendalough* (oil on panel, 19 x 29 ins / 48 x 74 cm) IEP 3,700. DUBLIN, 8 Dec 1999, *Meeting of the Waters* (oil on panel, 8 x 12 ins / 20 x 30 cm) IEP 4,600. VENICE, 13 May 2000, *Vesuvius Erupting* (oil on panel, 22 x 32 ins / 55 x 81 cm) ITL 9,000,000. DUBLIN, 1 May 2001, *Near Dunmore East, Co. Waterford* (oil on panel, 5 x 10 ins / 13 x 25 cm) IEP 2,000. DUBLIN, 5 Dec 2001, *St Patrick's Cathedral, Dublin* (oil on panel, 10 x 11 ins / 26 x 28 cm) IEP 5,500. LONDON, 16 May 2002, *Harbour Scene* (oil on panel, 10 x 15 ins / 25 x 37 cm) GBP 1,400. CASTLECOMER, 4 March 2003, *Seven Churches, Glendalough* (oil on panel, 19 x 28 ins / 49 x 72 cm) EUR 18,000.

SADLER, William II
Irish, 18th - 19th century.
Born c. 1782; died 19 December 1839, in Ranelagh.
Painter. History painting, genre scenes, landscapes.
William Sadler worked in Dublin.

AUCTION RECORDS:
LONDON, 26 March 1976, *The Eagle's Nest, Killarney* (oil on panel, 16 x 21½ ins / 40.5 x 54.5 cm) GBP 550. LONDON, 17 March 1978, *View of Dun Laoghaire, Dublin* (oil on panel, 22½ x 35 ins / 57 x 89 cm) GBP 3,000. LONDON, 23 Nov 1979, *Dublin Bay* (oil on panel, 14¼ x 22¼ ins / 36.2 x 56.4 cm) GBP 4,200. LONDON, 26 June 1981, *Canoeing at the Mouth of the Liffey, Dublin* (oil on panel, 16½ x 23½ ins / 42 x 59.7 cm) GBP 4,800. LONDON, 15 July 1983, *The Powerscourt Waterfall; Shipping at the Pigeon House; The Two Sugar Loaves and a Thatched Cottage; Salmon Leap at Leixdip; Ruined Church with the Sugar Loaf; Wooded River Landscape near Dublin* (oil on panel, series of six, 8¼ x 13 ins / 21 x 33 cm) GBP 6,500. LONDON, 13 March 1985, *View of Dublin Park from Magazine For Hill* (oil on canvas, 17½ x 23 ins / 44.5 x 58.5 cm) GBP 4,800. DUBLIN, 24 Oct 1988, *Donnybrook Fair* (oil on panel, 21½ x 35¾ ins / 54.7 x 90.8 cm) IEP 27,500. BELFAST, 28 Oct 1988, *Soldiers Amusing Themselves in a Clearing* (oil on panel, 8¼ x 12¼ ins / 21.2 x 31.2 cm) GBP 418. DUBLIN, 12 Dec 1990, *View near Bray on the River Dargle with the Sugarloaf beyond* (oil on panel, 14½ x 19¾ ins / 36.8 x 50.2 cm) IEP 4,200. LONDON, 8 April 1992, *Duke of Wellington at the Battle of Waterloo* (oil on panel, 13 x 22½ ins / 33 x 57 cm) GBP 2,640. DUBLIN, 26 May 1993, *Sackville Street from Carlisle Bridge* (1813, oil on canvas, 24¾ x 30½ ins / 62.8 x 77.5 cm) IEP 11,550. LONDON, 2 June 1995, *River Landscape with Anglers* (oil on panel, 9¼ x 13½ ins / 23.5 x 34.5 cm) GBP 4,025. LONDON, 20 May 1999, *Lower Lake Killarney with Eagle's Nest* (oil on panel, 11 x 16 ins / 29 x 41 cm) GBP 2,700. LONDON, 20 May 1999, *View of Dublin Bay* (oil on panel, 22 x 15 ins / 57 x 37 cm) GBP 13,000. LONDON, 19 May 2000, *View of Deputy Master's House at Royal Hospital* (oil on panel, 15 x 24 ins / 37 x 61 cm) GBP 24,000. DUBLIN, 31 May 2000, *Dublin Harbour* (oil on panel, 8 x 12 ins / 20 x 30 cm) IEP 4,800. DUBLIN, 28 March 2001, *Seven Churches, Glendalough* (oil on board, 19 x 28 ins / 49 x 72 cm) IEP 11,000. LONDON, 17 May 2001, *View of Dublin Bay with Kingstown Harbour. View in Co. Wicklow with Elegant Figures* (oil on panel, a pair, 9 x 13 ins / 22 x 34 cm) GBP 10,500. DUBLIN, 25 Sept 2002, *Salmon Leap* (oil on board, 8 x 12 ins / 21 x 31 cm) EUR 2,300. DUBLIN, 3 Dec 2002, *House of Lords, Portico of Parliment House from Collage Street, Dublin* (oil on board, 8 x 13 ins / 21 x 32 cm) EUR 16,000. DUBLIN, 28 May 2003, *Street Scene, Possibly Blarney, Co. Cork* (oil on panel, 13 x 20 ins / 32 x 50 cm) EUR 8,000. LONDON, 29 Oct 2003, *Capriccio River Landscape with a Classical Town in the Distance at Sunset* (oil on panel, 24 x 36 ins / 60 x 92 cm) GBP 5,200. DUBLIN, 31 March 2004, *Entrance to Dublin Port with Shipping* (oil on panel, 8 x 10 ins / 21 x 26 cm) EUR 5,600. DUBLIN, 27 April 2004, *Distant View of Powerscourt Waterfall, C. Wicklow, with Horseman* (c. 1830, oil on panel, 11 x 17 ins / 28 x 43 cm) EUR 4,200.

SADLER, William III
Irish, 19th century.
Born 1808.
Painter. Landscapes.
William Sadler III was the son of William Sadler II.

SADLEY, Wojciech
Polish, 20th century.
Born 3 April 1932, in Lublin.
Painter. Designs for tapestries.
Wojciech Sadley produced tapestries, outside the traditional context of this technique. His works evoke soft sculptures, spreading over the ground according to the laws of gravity and chance. Executed with great freedom of composition, these tapestries make references to humanity with their evocative titles: *Man, Suzy, He-on.*

Wojciech Sadley featured in collective exhibitions including: International Contemporary Textile Art Fair, Musée de Lausanne (1962, 1965, 1967, 1969, 1971 and 1973); Mannheim museum (1964); São Paulo Biennale (1965); Konsthalle, Lund (1967); Museum of Modern Art, New York (1968); Museo de Arte Moderno, Mexico City, Stedelijk Museum, Amsterdam and the Royal Academy of Arts, London (1969); Maison de la Culture, Grenoble, and the National Museum, Stockholm (1970). Solo exhibitions include: Lausanne (1963); Warsaw (1967); Torun (1968); Cracow (1969); Zurich and Ulm (1973), New York and Oklahoma City (1974); Hartford and Gallery of Contemporary Art, Bialystck (1975).

MUSEUMS AND GALLERIES:
ŁÓDZ (Centralne Muzeum Wlokiennictwa) - MEXICO CITY (MMA) - OSAKA (National MA) - PRAGUE (Národní Muz.) - WARSAW (Muz. Narodowe) - ZURICH (Mus. Bellerive).

SADOCHI, Giorgio de', also known as Aleotti, called da Modena
Italian, 15th - 16th century.
Painter.
Giorgio de' Sadochi was the brother of Maurello de' Sadochi. He was a painter at the court of Ferrara from 1490.

SADOCHI, Maurello de', also known as Aleotti, called da Modena
Italian, 15th - 16th century.
Active in Modena.
Painter.
Maurello de' Sadochi was the brother of Giorgio de' Sadochi. He was a painter at the court of Ferrara from 1490. The two brothers may have been connected with Antonio Aleotti.

SADOLETO, Lodovico, or Sadoletti
Italian, 16th century.
Died 20 March 1533.
Active in Modena.
Painter. Architectural views.

SADOLIN, Anne-Suzette
Danish, 20th century.
Born 1943.
Painter. Figures.
Anne-Suzette Sadolin trained at the Kongelige Danske Kunstakademi in Copenhagen (1979-1986). One of her starting points is the observation: 'Where in history have woman painters exhibited nude paintings and sketches of their own husbands or lovers?' She painted a series of large format

featuring male nudes in various poses. Using an Expressionist touch and rapid line, she shapes silhouettes on her grounds, which she hastily paints in colour or leaves unpainted to show the texture of the canvas. She has taken part in many collective exhibitions in Denmark (Aalborg, Odense, Aarhus and elsewhere). She has had regular solo shows at Galerie C in Aarhus and exhibited at the Galerie Birthe Laursen in Paris (1998, 2001).

Bibliography:

Anne-Suzette Sadolin, exhibition catalogue, Gal. Birthe Laursen, Paris, 2001.

SADOLIN, Ebbe Benedikt

Danish, 20th century.
Born 19 February 1900, in Copenhagen.
Painter, designer.

Ebbe Benedikt Sadolin was a pupil of P. Rostrup Boyesen. He married the painter Mana Sadolin.

Museums and Galleries:

Chemnitz - Copenhagen - Leipzig - New York (Brooklyn) - Stuttgart.

SADOLIN, Gunnar Asgeir

Danish, 19th - 20th century.
Born 5 February 1874, in Valloby.
Active in Dragør, near Copenhagen.
Painter.

Gunnar Asgeir Sadolin studied under P.H. Kristian Zahrtmann.

SADOLIN, Mana

Maiden name: Van Hausen
Danish, 20th century.
Born 27 January 1898, in Christiania (now Oslo).
Painter.

Mana Sadolin was the wife of the painter Ebbe Sadolin.

SADOT

French, 18th century.
Active in Paris during the second half of the 18th century.
Sculptor (wood).

In 1777, Sadot sculpted the organ case of the church of St-Sulpice in Paris, with Duvet.

SADOUK, Abdallah

Moroccan, 20th - 21st century.
Born 1950, in Casablanca.
Active in France.
Painter, engraver.

Abdallah Sadouk studied decoration in the sculpture department at the École des Arts Décoratifs in Paris and drawing at the École des Beaux-Arts. He has taken part in collective exhibitions at the École des Beaux-Arts and Institut de France, Paris (1974); the Galeries Nationales du Grand Palais, Paris (1982); and at the Foire Internationale, Rennes (1985). He has shown his works in solo exhibitions in Paris.

SADOUX, Eugène

French, 19th century.
Born 1841, in Angoulême; died November 1906, in Tunis.
Painter, lithographer, engraver (etching).

Eugène Sadoux was a student of E. May. He produced a substantial number of plates of picturesque architecture, such as the *City Hall in Paris* (1884), *Château de Chantilly* (1887), *Carp Pool at Fontainebleau* and others. His contribution to the plates for Palustre's *Renaissance in France*, in three volumes (1879 to 1885), is also worth mentioning.

SADOVNIKOV, Konstantin Fedor Petrovitch, or Saadovnikov, Ssadovnikov

Russian, 19th century.
Born 25 December 1824; died 1875.
Painter. History painting, portraits.

Konstantin Fedor Sadovnikov studied at the academy of fine arts in St Petersburg.

SADOVNIKOV, Vasili Semenovich

Russian, 19th century.
Born 1800; died 1879.
Painter (gouache), watercolourist. Landscapes with figures, waterscapes, urban landscapes, architectural views.

Auction records:

London, 6 Oct 1988, *View of the St Nicholas Bridge over the Neva in St Petersburg* (1852, watercolour and ink/paper, 9 3/4 x 14 1/2 ins / 25 x 37 cm) GBP 2,200. New York, 12 Jan 1994, *The House of Pavlino with Boating on the River in the Foreground* (watercolour/black chalk, 10 1/4 x 15 1/4 ins / 26.2 x 39 cm) USD 2,990. London, 14 Dec 1995, *View of the Winter Palace in St Petersburg* (gouache and pencil, 6 x 8 3/4 ins / 15 x 22.5 cm) GBP 3,220.

SADR, Behdjate

Iranian, 20th century.
Born 1924, in Tehran.
Painter, collage artist.

Behdjate Sadr studied at the faculty of fine arts in Tehran, then at the Accademia di Belle Arti in Rome (1956) and in Naples (1957). She then studied methods of teaching painting from 1967 to 1968 with Singier at the École des Beaux-Arts in Paris, before becoming a teacher at the university of art in Tehran.

Influenced by Soulages, Sadr is a representative of Informal painting, executing large lyrical and calligraphic compositions that are made up of contractions and bursts of colour. Since 1980, she has produced collages based on colour photographs of landscapes or details of landscapes, which she 'frames' with painting, for example with thick black parallel strokes.

Sadr has taken part in collective exhibitions, including the Venice Biennale (1956, 1962); in New Delhi (1961); at the School of Art in Minneapolis (1962); at the São Paulo Biennale and Salon Comparaisons in Paris (1963); at the Palais des Beaux-Arts in Brussels and Salon d'Automne in Paris (1973); at the museum of modern art and the Iranian-American cultural centre in Tehran (1977); at the Salon de Montrouge (1986); and at the UNESCO exhibition in Paris (1989). She has shown her works in solo exhibitions in Rome (1957, 1958); Tehran (1967, 1991); at the Cité Internationale des Arts in Paris (1975); and in Paris (1984, 1986, 1990). She won the prize for painting at the biennial in Tehran in 1962.

Bibliography:

Ragon, Michel, '*L'Art abstrait*' in vol. IV, Maeght, Paris, 1974.
Tapié, Michel, *Behdjate Sadr*, exhibition catalogue, Gal. Cyrus, Paris, 1975.

Museums and Galleries:

Paris (FNAC) - Tehran (Honarhaye Moaser).

SADUN, Piero

Italian, 20th century.
Born 1919, in Siena; died 1974, in Rome.
Painter.

Piero Sadun was originally of student of classics but went on to painting. From 1957, he taught at the Istituto d'Arte in Rome, where he lived and worked.

Originally expressionist in style, his work evolved into neo-Cubism and, after 1955, a kind of Intimism which, in his rendering of planes in space, derives from aspects of Mondrian's Neo-Plasticism and is combined with the colour values of Morandi.

After his first exhibition in 1945, he took part in many collective events including the Rome Quadriennale of 1948 and the Venice Biennale in 1950 and 1960. In 1959, he won the AGIP Prize at the Marche awards in Ancona. In 1954,he was appointed to the chair of graphic arts at the art college of Urbino.

MUSEUMS AND GALLERIES:
LONDON - ROME.

AUCTION RECORDS:
ROME, 18 May 1976, *Composition* (1957, oil on canvas, 31 1/2 x 23 1/2 ins / 80 x 60 cm) ITL 360,000. ROME, 24 May 1979, *Untitled* (1958, oil on canvas, 38 1/2 x 77 1/2 ins / 98 x 197 cm) ITL 800,000. ROME, 11 June 1981, *Cat. IV, no. 14* (1972, oil on canvas, 45 1/4 x 41 1/4 ins / 115 x 105 cm) ITL 5,000,000. ROME, 22 May 1984, *Untitled* (1963, oil on canvas, 29 1/4 x 36 1/4 ins / 74 x 92 cm) ITL 3,000,000. MILAN, 20 March 1989, *Untitled* (1973, oil on canvas, 41 1/4 x 37 1/2 ins / 105 x 95 cm) ITL 2,800,000. ROME, 28 Nov 1989, *Hypothesis No. 7* (1961, oil on canvas, 35 x 31 1/2 ins / 88 x 80 cm) ITL 6,500,000. BRUSSELS, 13 Dec 1990, *Composition* (1959, oil on canvas, 27 1/2 x 24 1/4 ins / 70 x 61.5 cm) BEF 43,320. ROME, 3 Dec 1991, *Untitled* (1972, oil on canvas, 47 1/4 x 43 1/4 ins / 120 x 110 cm) ITL 10,000,000. ROME, 12 May 1992, *Plastic Space* (1959, oil on canvas, 46 x 40 ins / 117 x 101.5 cm) ITL 4,800,000. ROME, 14 Dec 1992, *Composition* (1959, oil on canvas, 27 1/2 x 24 1/2 ins / 70 x 62 cm) ITL 1,840,000. ROME, 30 Nov 1993, *Still-life* (1956, oil on canvas, 19 3/4 x 23 1/2 ins / 50 x 60 cm) ITL 1,725,000. ROME, 14 Nov 1995, *Untitled* (1969, oil on canvas, 31 1/2 x 29 3/4 ins / 80 x 75.5 cm) ITL 8,625,000. MILAN, 28 May 1996, *Untitled* (collage and oil on canvas, 57 x 65 ins / 145 x 165 cm) ITL 5,175,000. ROME, 12 April 2001, *Dialogue Number 4* (oil on canvas, 45 x 41 ins / 115 x 105 cm) ITL 5,000,000. MILAN, 24 Nov 2003, *Composition in Grey* (oil on canvas, 31 x 39 ins / 80 x 100 cm) EUR 2,600. NEW YORK, 25 Feb 2004, *Identity* (1957, oil on canvas, 38 x 45 ins / 96 x 114 cm) USD 3,000. MILAN, 8 June 2004, *Transparency 2* (oil on canvas, 45 x 41 ins / 115 x 105 cm) EUR 2,000.

SADURNY Y DEOP, Celestino

Spanish, 19th century.
Born 1830, in Ripoll (Catalonia); died 20 October 1896, in Barcelona.
Engraver.

Celestino Sadurny y Deop studied at the fine arts academy in Barcelona. In 1881 he exhibited at the exhibition of the national fine arts society of Madrid with his engraving *Uno de Tantos* (*One of Many*), a frontispiece for Cervantes's *Don Quixote*. He worked as a line engraver and is known for his piece entitled *¿Qué Ha Sucedido?* (*What's Happened?*).

BIBLIOGRAPHY:
Arnáiz, José Manuel/López Jiménez, Javier/Merchán Díaz, Manuel (ed.), '*Cien años de pintura en Espana y Portugal (1830-1930)*' in vol. IX, Antiqvaria, Madrid, 1992.

SAEBYE, Poul

Danish, 20th century.
Born 19 September 1889, in Copenhagen.
Painter, engraver. Murals.

Poul Saebye was a pupil of Joachim Skoogaard. He painted decorative compositions in Copenhagen.

SAEDELEER, Elisabeth de

Belgian, 20th century.
Born 1902; died 1972.
Painter. Scenes with figures, landscapes.

AUCTION RECORDS:
BREDA, 26 April 1977, *Spring* (oil on canvas, 33 1/2 x 37 1/2 ins / 85 x 95 cm) NLG 6,200. BRUSSELS, 13 June 1979, *Winter Landscape* (oil on canvas, 33 x 37 1/2 ins / 84 x 95 cm) BEF 90,000. LOKEREN, 23 May 1992, *Landscape with Farm* (oil on canvas, 15 3/4 x 19 3/4 ins / 40 x 50 cm) BEF 80,000. LOKEREN, 11 March 1995, *Procession* (1930, oil on canvas, 33 1/2 x 37 1/2 ins / 85 x 95 cm) BEF 120,000. PARIS, 17 Dec 2001, *Couple* (1927, oil on canvas, 15 x 18 ins / 39 x 46 cm) FRF 26,000.

SAEDELER, Valerius de, or Saedeleer

Belgian, 19th - 20th century.
Born 10 August 1867, in Aalst; died 1941 or 1942, in Leupegem.
Painter, draughtsman. Landscapes. Designs for tapestries.
Symbolism.
Laethem-St-Martin Group (First School).

Valerius de Saedeler studied at the fine arts academies of Aalst and Ghent, then under Frans Courtens in Brussels. He lived from 1895 to 1898 in Lissewege but settled in Laethem in 1908. He spent the years of World War I in London, but returned to Belgium after the war and set up a tapestry studio and workshop in Etikhove. He was a member of the royal academy of Belgium.

De Saedeler was initially influenced by Gustave Courbet. He belonged to the Laethem School, so called after a village near Ghent where a number of artists had elected to live and work; among them were the sculptor Georges Minne and the painters Constant Permecke and Albin van den Abeele (who was actually born there). The emergence of the Laethem School at the beginning of the 20th century effectively closed the chapter on Belgian Impressionism (which had not, in any event, been particularly influential) and marked a transition to a type of painting that was more 'spiritual' in terms of content and more structured in terms of form, very much in the tradition of the Flemish Primitives.

As a landscape painter, De Staedeler started exhibiting in 1878, showing canvases inspired by the meticulously observed and structured Flemish Masters. To a degree, his landscape work is reminiscent of that of Bruegel.

MUSEUMS AND GALLERIES:
GHENT (Mus. voor Schone Kunsten): *An Overcast Day Draw[s] to a Close* (1907).

AUCTION RECORDS:
BRUSSELS, 12 Nov 1937, *Mill at Tieghem*, BEF 3,600. BRUS[SELS], 25 Jan 1947, *Landscape*, BEF 28,000. BRUSSELS, 2[...] March 1950, *Orchard under Snow*, BEF 28,000. ANTWERP[,] 30-31 March 1965, *Winter*, BEF 270,000. ANTWERP, 14 Oc[t] 1969, *Winter Landscape*, BEF 360,000. BRUSSELS, 25 Oc[t] 1972, *Flemish Landscape*, BEF 200,000. ANTWERP, 22 Oc[t] 1974, *Etikhove in Spring*, BEF 300,000. ANTWERP, 6 Apr[il] 1976, *Winter Landscape* (watercolour, 13 3/4 x 37 3/4 ins / 35 [x] 96 cm) BEF 440,000. BRUSSELS, 27 Oct 1976, *Winter Landscape near Etikhove* (oil on canvas, 11 3/4 x 13 3/4 ins / 30 x 3[...] cm) BEF 340,000. BREDA, 26 April 1977, *Landscape with Mi[...]* (oil on canvas, 19 3/4 x 15 3/4 ins / 50 x 40 cm) NLG 30,000. LOKEREN, 31 March 1979, *Landscape* (drawing, 27 1/4 x 37 ins / 6[...] x 94 cm) BEF 40,000. BRUSSELS, 28 Oct 1981, *Landscape under Snow* (oil on canvas, 22 3/4 x 26 3/4 ins / 58 x 68 cm) BEF 900,000. BRUSSELS, 24 Oct 1984, *Winter Landscape* (oil on canvas, 34 x 37 3/4 ins / 86.5 x 96 cm) BEF 1,800,000. LOKEREN[,] 20 April 1985, *Landscape near Etikhove* (c. 1935, oil on canvas, 15 3/4 x 19 3/4 ins / 40 x 50 cm) BEF 260,000. ANTWERP, 2[...] April 1986, *Weaver's Cottage* (oil on canvas, 22 3/4 x 27 1/4 ins / 58 x 69 cm) BEF 2,200,000. LOKEREN, 8 Oct 1988, *Café Inte[...]*

ior with Peasants (oil on canvas, 16 x 21 3/4 ins / 40.5 x 55.5 m) BEF 450,000. LONDON, 19 Oct 1989, *Winter Landscape* oil on canvas, 16 x 20 ins / 40.5 x 50.5 cm) GBP 26,400. AMTERDAM, 13 Dec 1990, *Winter Landscape* (oil on canvas, 34 x 7 1/2 ins / 85.5 x 95 cm) NLG 195,500. LOKEREN, 23 May 1992, *ummer Light at Leupegem* (oil on canvas, 16 x 20 ins / 40.5 51 cm) BEF 850,000. LOKEREN, 10 Oct 1992, *View of the Ieule at Lissewege* (oil on canvas, 17 3/4 x 11 1/4 ins / 45 x 28.7 m) BEF 90,000. LOKEREN, 5 Dec 1992, *Winter in Flanders* (oil n canvas, 30 3/4 x 31 1/2 ins / 78 x 80 cm) BEF 2,250,000. AMTERDAM, 27-28 May 1993, *Enclosure behind a Church* (oil on anvas, 14 x 16 1/4 ins / 35.5 x 41 cm) NLG 43,700. LOKEREN, 4 Dec 1993, *Landscape with Farm* (oil on canvas, 11 3/4 x 25 1/2 ns / 30 x 65 cm) BEF 1,300,000. LOKEREN, 12 March 1994, *andscape and Farm in the Snow* (1941, oil on canvas, 23 1/2 x 7 1/2 ins / 60 x 70 cm) BEF 1,850,000. LOKEREN, 11 March 995, *Church of Laethem* (1893, oil on canvas, 39 1/4 x 30 1/4 ns / 100 x 77 cm) BEF 650,000. LOKEREN, 18 May 1996, *Sumner Landscape* (1892, oil on canvas, 16 1/4 x 20 1/2 ins / 41 x 52 m) BEF 185,000. LOKEREN, 6 Dec 1997, *Summer Landscape vith Impending Storm* (c. 1912, oil on canvas, 29 3/4 x 35 1/2 ns / 75.5 x 90 cm) BEF 1,700,000. AMSTERDAM, 12 Oct 1999, *Road on the Plain in Winter* (1931, oil on canvas, 67 x 74 ins / 70 x 188 cm) NLG 240,000. PARIS, 13 Dec 1999, *Flemish Countryside* (oil on canvas, 16 x 19 ins / 40 x 49 cm) FRF 10,000. BRUSSELS, 9 May 2000, *Landscape in the Flemish Ardennes* (drawing, 23 x 27 ins / 58 x 69 cm) BEF 80,000. LOKEREN, 13 May 2000, *Summer Landscape* (oil on canvas, 12 14 ins / 30 x 36 cm) BEF 1,650,000. LOKEREN, 6 Oct 2001, *arge Hilly Landscape* (oil on canvas, 33 x 38 ins / 85 x 96 cm) BEF 3,300,000. BRUSSELS, 18 Dec 2001, *Village in the Snow* pencil and watercolour, 7 x 12 ins / 19 x 31 cm) BEF 280,000. ANTWERP, 22 Oct 2002, *Walloon Landscape* (oil on canvas, 9 24 ins / 24 x 61 cm) EUR 12,000. LOKEREN, 15 March 2003, *Summer Landscape with Mill* (oil on canvas, 11 x 14 ins / 27 x 6 cm) EUR 7,000. BRUSSELS, 1 Dec 2003, *Mills at Sunrise* (oil on canvas, 19 x 31 ins / 49 x 78 cm) EUR 8,000. LOKEREN, 9 Oct 2004, *Landscape with Two Mills* (oil on canvas, 26 x 37 ns / 65 x 95 cm) EUR 9,000. BRUSSELS, 6 Dec 2004, *Walloon Landscape at Etikhove* (watercolour and crayon on paper laid down, 12 x 14 ins / 30 x 35 cm) EUR 9,000.

SAEFVENBOM, Johan. See **SEVENBOM**

SAEGER, François de. See **SAGGERE**

SAEGHER, Rodolphe de

Belgian, 19th - 20th century.

Born 1871, in Gavere; died 1941, in Ghent.

Painter, pastellist. Landscapes.

Rodolphe de Saegher studied at the fine arts academy in Ghent.

MUSEUMS AND GALLERIES:

GHENT.

AUCTION RECORDS:

LOKEREN, 21 March 1992, *Summer* (pastel, 9 3/4 x 13 3/4 ins / 25 35 cm) BEF 44,000. LOKEREN, 8 March 1997, *Evening* (pastel, 10 1/2 x 13 1/4 ins / 26.5 x 33.5 cm) BEF 14,000. BRUSSELS, 2 Feb 1999, *Lys* (pastel, 25 x 27 ins / 63 x 69 cm) BEF 190,000. LOKEREN, 8 Dec 2001, *Snow* (1927, pastel, 28 x 39 ins / 70 x 98 m) BEF 130,000. CANNES, 30 Dec 2001, *Gardens near a Village* (oil on canvas, 20 x 29 ins / 52 x 73 cm) FRF 19,000. BRUSSELS, 13 May 2002, *Fjord in Norway* (pastel, 24 x 16 ins / 60 x 0 cm) EUR 6,600. BRUSSELS, 11 Nov 2002, *Fjord in Norway* 1897, oil on canvas, 14 x 10 ins / 35 x 25 cm) EUR 2,000.

SAEGHER, Romain de

Belgian, 20th century.

Born 1907, in St-Amand-sur-Escaut; died 1986.

Painter (including gouache), watercolourist, pastellist. Religious subjects, interiors, landscapes.

Romain de Saegher was self-taught. He painted *Stations of the Cross* for churches in Brugge and St-Amand.

MUSEUMS AND GALLERIES:

OSTEND (Mus. of Religious Art).

AUCTION RECORDS:

LOKEREN, 19 Oct 1985, *Pietà* (1966, gouache, 14 1/4 x 16 1/4 ins / 36 x 41 cm) BEF 55,000. LOKEREN, 22 Feb 1986, *Pietà* (1972, gouache, 44 x 32 1/4 ins / 112 x 82 cm) BEF 90,000. LOKEREN, 28 May 1988, *Pietà* (1966, gouache, 11 1/2 x 16 1/2 ins / 29.5 x 42 cm) BEF 30,000. LOKEREN, 21 March 1992, *Christ Walking on Water* (1982, gouache, 19 1/2 x 27 1/2 ins / 49.5 x 70 cm) BEF 48,000. LOKEREN, 23 May 1992, *Bridge over a River* (1976, watercolour, 19 1/4 x 20 ins / 49 x 51 cm) BEF 33,000. LOKEREN, 15 May 1993, *River Scheldt near St-Amand* (1972, gouache, 17 x 24 ins / 43 x 61 cm) BEF 30,000. LOKEREN, 4 Dec 1993, *Calvary* (1967, watercolour, 19 3/4 x 22 ins / 50 x 55 cm) BEF 28,000. LOKEREN, 10 Dec 1994, *Christ and the Fishermen* (1982, gouache, 19 3/4 x 27 1/2 ins / 50 x 70 cm) BEF 33,000.

SAEGHMEULEN, Martinus. See **SAAGMOLEN**

SAEGMOLEN, Martinus. See **SAAGMOLEN**

SAEIJS, Jakob Ferdinand. See **SAEY**

SAEKI, Masaaki. See **GANKU**

SAEKI, Yuzo

Japanese, 20th century.

Born 1898, in Osaka; died 1928.

Painter. Landscapes.

In 1923 Yuzo Saeki obtained a diploma from the department of western painting from the University of Fine Arts in Tokyo. He left for France where he worked for some time with Vlaminck. He executed many views of Paris and landscapes.

He exhibited at the Salon d'Automne in Paris in 1925 and also several times at the Nikka kai Salon in Japan.

SAEMANN, Johann Christian

German, 18th century.

Born 1753, in Königsberg (now Kaliningrad, Russia); died 1799.

Painter, draughtsman. Urban landscapes.

Johann Christian Saemann was the brother of Johann Gottlieb Saemann. He drew and painted views of Königsberg.

SAEMANN, Johann Gottlieb

German, 18th century.

Born 1761, in Königsberg (now Kaliningrad, Russia); died 1807.

Draughtsman.

Johann Gottlieb Saemann was the brother of Johann Christian Saemann. He taught drawing in Königsberg.

SAEMISCH, Andreas

German, 19th century.

Born 16 October 1849, in Karith, near Magdeburg.

Active in Ratibor (now Racibórz, Poland).

Painter. History painting, portraits.

Andreas Saemisch was a pupil at the academies of Berlin and Düsseldorf and studied under Biermann and Gussow.

MUSEUMS AND GALLERIES:

SCHWERIN (Staatliches Mus.): *Portrait of the Landscape Artist T. Martens.*

SAEN, Egidius or Gillis van or de

Dutch, 17th century.

Active c. 1600.

Painter. History painting, landscapes.

SAENE, Jan M. J. van

Belgian, 20th - 21st century.

Born 23 September 1947, in Ninove.

Painter, pastellist, draughtsman.

Jan van Saene studied psychology and political and social science, then went on to the state school of sculpture in Anderlecht. He developed a style of painting with signs, using an abstract calligraphy. He has taken part in many collective exhibitions and has regularly had solo shows in Belgium from 1971.

SAENE, Maurice van, or Mauritz
Belgian, 20th century.
Born 1919, in Ninove.
Painter.

Maurice van Saene studied initially at St Luke's Academy in Brussels before enrolling at the École des Beaux-Arts in Paris. He worked at the Belgian Academy in Rome in 1947. He is noted for having painted the large fresco for the Holy See Pavilion at the 1958 Exposition Universelle in Brussels. His first solo exhibition was held in Ninove in 1943 and was followed by numerous others both in Belgium and abroad.

AUCTION RECORDS:
ANTWERP, 19 Oct 1976, *Mountains in Spain* (oil on canvas, $31\frac{1}{2}$ x $39\frac{1}{4}$ ins / 80 x 100 cm) BEF 55,000. LOKEREN, 14 May 1977, *Seascape* (oil on canvas, $31\frac{1}{2}$ x $39\frac{1}{4}$ ins / 80 x 100 cm) BEF 50,000. LOKEREN, 17 Oct 1981, *Landscape* (oil on canvas, $39\frac{1}{4}$ x $47\frac{1}{4}$ ins / 100 x 120 cm) BEF 65,000. LOKEREN, 18 Oct 1986, *Reclining Nude* (charcoal, $27\frac{1}{4}$ x 39 ins / 69 x 99 cm) BEF 50,000. LOKEREN, 12 March 1994, *Seated Nude* (tempera/paper, 37 x $24\frac{3}{4}$ ins / 94 x 63 cm) BEF 40,000. LOKEREN, 15 May 1999, *Reclining Nude* (gouache, 16 x 25 ins / 40 x 64 cm) BEF 80,000. LOKEREN, 9 March 2002, *After the Bath* (oil on canvas, 22 x 15 ins / 57 x 39 cm) EUR 2,600. LOKEREN, 13 Dec 2003, *Seascape* (oil on canvas, 31 x 39 ins / 80 x 100 cm) EUR 5,000. LOKEREN, 9 Oct 2004, *Seascape* (oil on canvas, 24 x 28 ins / 60 x 70 cm) EUR 1,900. ANTWERP, 25 Oct 2004, *Seacape* (mixed media, 28 x 39 ins / 70 x 100 cm) EUR 2,000.

SAENGER, Lucy von, married name Miram
Latvian, 20th century.
Born 1 December 1902, near Riga.
Painter. Portraits, still-lifes.

Lucy von Saenger studied in Riga, and in Munich with Lossow.

SAENREDAM, Jan Pietersz., or Sanredam or Zaenredam
Dutch, 16th - 17th century.
Born 1565, in Zaandam; died 6 April 1607, in Assendelft.
Painter, engraver, draughtsman.

Jan Pietersz. Saenredam was the father of Pieter Jansz. Saenredam and was initially a basket-maker. He was a pupil of J. de Gheyn and Hendrick Goltzius. He produced a large number of engravings after his own drawings, those of his masters, and the works of Dutch painters of the period.

In 2002 works by Saenredam were included in the exhibition *Masken der Schönheit: Hendrick Goltzius und das Kunstideal um 1600* (*Masks of Beauty: Hendrick Goltzius and the Artistic Ideal around 1600*) at the Kunsthalle in Hamburg.

BIBLIOGRAPHY:
Masken der Schönheit. Hendrick Goltzius und das kunstideal um 1600, exhibition catalogue, Hamburger Kunsthalle, Hamburg, 2002.

AUCTION RECORDS:
LONDON, 16 May 1980, *Stranded Whale* (1602, engraving/copper, 16 x $23\frac{1}{2}$ ins / 40.9 x 59.5 cm) GBP 800.

SAENREDAM, Pieter Jansz. or Janszoon
Dutch, 17th century.
Born 9 June 1597, in Assendelft; died 16 August 1665, in Haarlem.
Painter, engraver, draughtsman. Architectural views, church interiors.
Assendeflt School.

Pieter Jansz. Saenredam was the son of the engraver Jan Pietersz. Saenredam. He was born with restricted growth and curvature of the spine. He studied art with his father and, following the latter's death, entered the Haarlem studio of the engraver Frans Pieter de Grebbern, where he worked alongside the young Jacob van Campen, the painter and architect of Amsterdam's town hall. Van Campen's friendship was a source of encouragement and moral support for Saenredam throughout his life.

Saenredam's paintings are both a product of their age and country, and yet strikingly original, particularly in view of the broad range of influences to which Dutch artists were exposed in the 17th century, thanks to widely published translations and engravings of the work of mathematicians, architects and painters alike - especially collections of engravings after works by masters of the Antwerp School. Saenredam's first church interior was painted at the age of 31, in 1628; in this, he seems to have been influenced by Van Campen's architectural training and knowledge of Italian perspective (the latter had returned from a six-year sojourn in Italy in 1624). Saenredam joined the Assendelft guild in 1623 and was appointed secretary in 1635. From 1628 to 1663 he painted the interiors of churches in Utrecht (hence his nickname, the 'painter of Utrecht'), Assendelft, Haarlem, Rhenen, 's Hertogenbosch and Alkmaar. These constitute the bulk of his work, although he also painted occasional outdoor scenes, including a series of four Roman views after drawings by Marten van Heemskerck, around 1632, and a view of Van Campen's Amsterdam Town Hall. In 1638 he married Aefjen Gerrits. He travelled little, and for short periods only, but spent six months in Utrecht where he painted the majority of the city's Romanesque and Gothic churches.

Fifty-five paintings by him survive, together with some 140 drawings, providing a valuable insight into his methods and technique. The drawings include a number of plant studies and city views (a popular genre at the time); all witness his extraordinarily meticulous approach. Drawings made *in situ* were transposed and modified in the studio according to careful calculations of proportion and perspective, often incorporating additional sight-lines. Characteristically, this subtle reworking is not immediately apparent: the paintings seem at first glance to be straightforward, faithful reproductions of natural perspective. In fact, he exaggerates the height of the structures depicted, emphasising their soaring columns and vertiginous vaults. At the same time, he diminishes the relative size of the few human figures haunting these vast, impersonal spaces. Perhaps inevitably, given his own physical characteristics, Saenredam's perspective reconstructs the churches' interior volumes around a low horizon and vanishing point, augmenting their monumentality and creating a stereoscopic effect in his treatment of objects and figures in the foreground.

Saenredam excels in conveying the tactile values of powdery, chalk-white stone tinted gold or silver by the changing rays of the sun, or the soft, diffuse light filling the spaces between the columns, with subtle notes of ivory-yellow, yellow-green or dawn pink, darkening to brown in the shadows. His light is the light of Vermeer - the Vermeer of the 'little patch of yellow wall' in the 1658 *View of Delft*. He shares Vermeer's vision, and his fate: too often celebrated simply for the precision and optical accuracy of his paintings, their essential discourse on the nature of interiority and illusion is frequently undervalued. Saenredam's precision and detail are functionally important, but of no intrinsic significance: they serve to cloak his distorted proportions with a semblance of reality, just as his palpable, disingenuously natualistic light serves to counter the viewer's dizzying, implicit ealisation of the scale of human insignificance.

Saenredam usually painted his own figures, albeit few and xaggeratedly diminished in relation to their surroundings; n accordance with contemporary practice, however, some vere occasionally painted by Adrien van Ostade or Jan oth. We may be surprised by the presence in church of donestic animals, promenaders, dice players or a mother servng food and drink to a group of children who have evidently een playing; in fact, Holland's former Catholic churches ad been taken over by the Calvinists, cleared of their decoations and white-washed. Some painted decoration was alowed, and the buildings were furnished with simple benches, a ectern for the choir-master and - most importantly - a pulpit or the preacher. On weekdays, the benches were moved side to provide a space for strolling and conversation,parcularly welcome in view of the Dutch climate. In this sense, aenredam's views provide an accurate record of daily life n the churches of his time.

His work featured in the exhibition *Twee gouden eeuwen: childerkunst uit Nederland en Denemarken* (*Two Golden Ages: Masterpieces of Dutch and Danish Painting*), at the ijksmuseum in Amsterdam in 2001. A retrospective of his vork, organised by the Utrecht Centraal Museum, was held t the J. Paul Getty Museum in 2002.

IBLIOGRAPHY:
willens, P.T.A., *Pieter Janszoon Saenredam, schilder van Iaarlem, 1597-1665*, De Spieghel, Amsterdam, 1935. Bremner, Henricus Petrus, *P. J. Saenredam: achttien lichtdrukken*, i.J. Nieuwenhuizen Segaar, The Hague, 1938. Hollstein, riedrich Wilhelm Heinrich, *Dutch and Flemish Etchings, ngravings and Woodcuts ca. 1450-1700*, Menno Hertzbergr, Amsterdam, 1949-1974. Leymarie, Jean, *La Peinture hollndaise*, Skira, Paris, Geneva, 1956. Swillens, P.T.A., *Pieter anszoon Saenredam*, exhibition catalogue, catalogue raionné, Centraal Museum, Utrecht, 1961. *Saenredam*, exhibion catalogue, Institut néerlandais, Paris, 1970. Helmus, iesbeth M./ Groot, Arie de, *Pieter Saenredam, The Utrecht Vork*, exhibition catalogue, J. Paul Getty Museum, Los Angeles, 002.

IUSEUMS AND GALLERIES:
LKMAAR (Stedelijk Mus.) - AMSTERDAM (Rijksmus.): *Interior f the Church of St Bavo, Haarlem* (1626); *Interior of the Church of St Bavo, Haarlem; Interior of the Church of St Iary, Utrecht* (1637 and 1641, two paintings); *Interior of St)dolphus' Church, Assendelft* (1649); *Amsterdam Town Hall* 1657) - BANBURY (Upton House, Nat. Trust) - BERLIN (Bodeius.): *Church Interior* - BOSTON (MFA) - BRUNSWICK (Herzog nton Ulrich-Mus.) - BUDAPEST (Szépmuvészeti Múz.): *Interior of the Nieuwerkerk, Haarlem* - FORT WORTH (Kimbell M): *Interior of the Buurkerk, Utrecht* (1645, oil/panel) - LASGOW (AG and Mus.): *Church Interior* - HAARLEM (Frans Ialsmus.): *Interior of the New Church of St Anne, Haarlem* 1652) - HAMBURG (Kunsthalle) - KASSEL (Staatliche Kunstammlungen): *Interior of the Church of St Mary, Utrecht* - ONDON (NG): *The Interior of the Grote Kerk at Haarlem* 1636-1637, oil/wood); *The Interior of the Buurkerk at Utrecht* 1644, oil/wood) - LOS ANGELES (Getty Mus.): *The Interior of t Bavo, Haarlem* (1628, oil/panel) - MUNICH (Alte Pinaothek): *Interior of the Church of St James, Utrecht* (1636) - PHILADELPHIA (MA) - ROTTERDAM (Mus. Boijmans van Beuningen): *Interior of the Church of St Peter, Utrecht* (1644); *Interior of the Church of St Lawrence, Alkmaar* (1661); *Sankt Marien, Utrecht* (1663); *Interior of St Janskerk, Utrecht* - THE HAGUE (Mauritshuis) - TURIN (Gal. Sabauda) - UTRECHT (Centraal Mus.) - WARSAW (Muz. Narodowe) - WASHINGTON DC (NGA): *Church of Santa Maria della Febbre, Rome* (1629, oil/panel); *Cathedral of Saint John at 's-Hertogenbosch* (1646, oil/panel) - WORCESTER, MA (AM): *Interior of the Choir of St Bavo's Church at Haarlem* (1660, oil/panel).

AUCTION RECORDS:
PARIS, 1804, *The Entry of Prince Maurits into the City of Haarlem*, FRF 1,210. AMSTERDAM, 1872, *Church of St Mary*, FRF 2,205. PARIS, 26 and 27 March 1924, *Church Interiors* (two drawings) FRF 620. LONDON, 4 Feb 1927, *Scene in Front of a Church; Church Interior* (pair) GBP 546. PARIS, 28 Nov 1934, *Church Interiors* (pen and watercolour, two drawings. PARIS, 23 April 1937, *Church Interior* (pen and wash) FRF 2,010. PARIS, 5 Dec 1951, *Interior of the Church of St Bavo*, FRF 4,200,000. LONDON, 27 March 1963, *Interior of the Church of St Bavo, Haarlem*, GBP 36,000. AMSTERDAM, 15 Nov 1976, *Church Interior, Utrecht* (1651, oil on panel, 19 x 14 1/4 ins / 48 x 36 cm) NLG 230,000. LONDON, 16 April 1980, *Interior of the Cunerakerk, Rhenen* (oil on panel, 19 3/4 x 27 1/4 ins / 50 x 69 cm) GBP 52,000. LONDON, 18 June 1982, *The Parable of the Wise and Foolish Virgins* (series of five copperplate engravings, 10 1/2 x 14 1/2 ins / 26.6 x 36.7 cm) GBP 1,000. LONDON, 12 Dec 1984, *Haarlem Town Hall* (oil on panel, 15 1/2 x 19 1/2 ins / 39.5 x 49.5 cm) GBP 140,000. LONDON, 26 June 1985, *Sine Cerere et Libero Friget Venus* (engraving/copper, 10 1/2 x 8 ins / 26.8 x 20.1 cm) GBP 3,200. AMSTERDAM, 14 Nov 1988, *Interior of the Church of St Bavo, Haarlem* (1635, ink and watercolour, 14 3/4 x 15 1/2 ins / 37.5 x 39.1 cm) NLG 2,127,500. BERLIN, 18 May 2001, *Annunciation to the Shepherds* (copperplate, after Abraham Bloemaert, 22 x 16 ins / 56 x 40 cm) DEM 17,000. NEW YORK, 5 Nov 2001, *Christ at the Feast of Simon* (c. 1600, engraving on three joined sheets, after Veronese, 17 x 35 ins / 43 x 89 cm) USD 3,200. NEW YORK, 22 Jan 2004, *Haarlem, Interior of the Nieuwe Kerk* (1658, oil on panel, 12 x 12 ins / 30 x 31 cm) USD 1,650,000.

SAENS, Jan or Hans. See **SOENS**

SAENS, Juan

Mexican, 18th century.
Active in Mexico during the second half of the 18th century.
Painter. Church decoration.

Juan Saens was a pupil of José de Aguirre y Acuna and of R. Ximono. He was one of the most important painters of the Mexican School; works of his are in Mexico City Cathedral.

SAENZ, María

Ecuadorean, 20th century.
Painter.

María Saenz sent *Procession*, a nationalist work distinguished at the exhibition opened in Paris in 1946, to the Museum of Modern Art by way of the United Nations.

SAENZ DE TEJADA Y LEZAMA, Carlos

Spanish, 20th century.
Born 22 June 1897, in Tangiers; died 24 February 1958.
Painter, draughtsman, illustrator. Murals.

Carlos Saenz grew up in Oran, where his father was Spanish Consul, and studied painting first under Daniel Cortès, then under Sorolla, López Mezquita and Álvarez de Sotomayor at the Escuela de Bellas Artes in Madrid, before completing his studies in Paris. During the Spanish Civil War, he was in charge of artistic propaganda for the Nationalist side. He went on to teach from 1948 at the Escuela de Bellas Artes in Madrid.

He worked as an illustrator for various periodicals, including *La Libertad (Liberty), La Ilustractión (Illustration), Blanco y Negro (White and Black)* and *ABC*, and produced illustrations for literary and academic works, among them a *Historia de la Cruzada Española (History of the Spanish Crusades)* by Joaquin Arraras, Larreta's *Zogoili*, and *(Por Dios, por la Patria y el Rey (For God, King and Country)* by José María Pemán. Saenz produced a number of energetic schemata celebrating Spanish history and also painted a number of decorative murals.

Carlos Saenz featured at a number of group exhibitions, including the Exposición de Artistas Ibericos of 1927 and the 1947 exhibition of decorative arts in Madrid (where he was awarded a gold medal).

BIBLIOGRAPHY:

Arnáiz, José Manuel/López Jiménez, Javier/Merchán Díaz, Manuel (ed.), '*Cien años de pintura en Espana y Portugal (1830-1930)*' in vol. X, Antiqvaria, Madrid, 1993.

SAENZ HERMUA, Eduardo, called Mecachis

Spanish, 19th century.

Born 1859, in Madrid; died 1898, in Madrid.

Illustrator.

Eduardo Saenz Hermua produced illustrations for magazines such as *Madrid Cómico* and *La Caricatura.*

SAENZ Y SAENZ, Pedro

Spanish, 19th - 20th century.

Born 1867, in Málaga; died 1927.

Painter. Religious subjects, allegorical subjects, figures, nudes, portraits, genre scenes.

Saenz y Saenz studied under Bernardo Ferrandiz and at the Escuela de Bellas Artes in Madrid, completing his studies in Rome and Paris. His body of work focuses on women and aspects of womanhood. In the main, he painted nudes which exhibit a subtle eroticism: *Through the Window; Gypsy Woman; Poet's Tomb; Temptation of St Anthony; Portrait of the Artist's Son; Butterfly.*

Pedro Saenz showed his work at the Exposición Nacional de Bellas Artes in Madrid, receiving a bronze medal in 1887, a silver in 1897 and a gold in 1901.

BIBLIOGRAPHY:

Arnáiz, José Manuel/López Jiménez, Javier/Merchán Díaz, Manuel (ed.), '*Cien años de pintura en Espana y Portugal (1830-1930)*' in vol. IX, Antiqvaria, Madrid, 1992.

MUSEUMS AND GALLERIES:

MADRID (Prado): *Chrysalid; Innocence.*

AUCTION RECORDS:

NEW YORK, 28 May 1982, *At the Opera* (oil on canvas, 40¾ x 25¼ ins / 103.5 x 64.2 cm) USD 2,000. LONDON, 8 Feb 1984, *At the Opera* (oil on canvas, 40½ x 25 ins / 103 x 63.5 cm) GBP 1,000. MADRID, 22 Oct 1985, *Dream* (oil on canvas, 23½ x 41¼ ins / 60 x 105 cm) ESP 300,000. MADRID, 23 March 1999, *Woman* (oil on canvas, 28 x 22 ins / 70 x 55 cm) ESP 350,000. MUNICH, 5 Nov 2003, *Vestalin* (oil on canvas, 51 x 31 ins / 129 x 80 cm) EUR 2,800.

SAËS, Jakob Ferdinand. See **SAEY**

SÆTHER, Anders Olsen

Norwegian, 18th century.

Sculptor (wood).

From 1780 until 1790, Saether sculpted altarpieces with figures, and a *Last Judgement* for the churches of Brottum and Veldre.

SÆTTERDALEN, Jakob

Norwegian, 18th - 19th century.

Born c. 1740; died c. 1820.

Sculptor (wood).

Saetterdalen sculpted both the chair and choir vault for a church in Lom.

SAETTI, Bruno

Italian, 20th century.

Born 21 February 1902, in Bologna; died 1984.

Painter, watercolourist, pastellist, fresco artist.

Bruno Saetti studied at the academy of art in Bologna. He held the chair of painting at the academy of fine art in Venice, where he lived and worked.

His style is figurative but not naturalistic, based on a post-Cézannian sense of construction with references to the stylisation of Byzantine and Roman art. This can be seen particularly in the large frescoes he painted in Padua University.

He began to exhibit work in 1925 and took part in many important exhibitions: the Venice Biennale from 1928-1956 and then in 1962; the Rome Quadriennale from 1931-1959, the São Paulo Biennale in 1953 and 1957; the Carnegie Prize exhibition at the Pittsburgh International Exhibition in 1955. He won the Quadriennale Prize in Rome in 1939, the prize awarded by the Venice council at the 26th Venice Biennale in 1952, the Micchetti Prize at Francavilla al Mare in 1956 and the Fiorino Prize in Florence in 1959.

AUCTION RECORDS:

MILAN, 10 Dec 1970, *Still-life* (gouache and watercolour) ITL 900,000. MILAN, 2 Dec 1971, *Sun* (tempera) ITL 1,000,000. MILAN, 29 Oct 1974, *Painted Wall,* ITL 3,200,000. MILAN, 16 March 1976, *Landscape* (1956, gouache, 9¼ x 13½ ins / 23.5 x 34.5 cm) ITL 200,000. ROME, 18 May 1976, *Landscape with Sun* (1955, mixed media/canvas, 22 x 27½ ins / 55 x 70 cm) ITL 2,000,000. MILAN, 18 Dec 1979, *Still-life* (1961, fresco/canvas, 25½ x 30 ins / 65 x 76 cm) ITL 4,800,000. MILAN, 25 Nov 1980, *Sun* (mixed media/mounted on board, 13¾ x 19 ins / 35 x 48 cm) ITL 1,200,000. MILAN, 16 June 1981, *Still-life* (1944, oil on canvas, 13 x 16¼ ins / 33 x 41 cm) ITL 4,500,000. VENICE, 28 Oct 1983, *Sun* (1981, mixed media/canvas remounted/panel, 40½ x 30 ins / 103 x 76 cm) ITL 6,000,000. MILAN, 18 Dec 1984, *Maternity* (pen on artboard remounted on canvas, 19¾ x 13¾ ins / 50 x 35 cm) ITL 1,200,000. MILAN, 11 June 1985, *The Piano* (pen, 12¾ x 17 ins / 32.5 x 43 cm) ITL 1,100,000. MILAN, 16 Oct 1986, *Still-life with Fish* (1955, frescoes/canvas, 30¼ x 22 ins / 77 x 56 cm) ITL 13,000,000. MILAN, 8 June 1988, *Landscape with Sun* (1978, mixed media, 19¾ x 27½ ins / 50 x 70 cm) ITL 4,500,000. MILAN, 20 March 1989, *Circus* (1931, oil on board, 15½ x 11¾ ins / 39.5 x 30 cm) ITL 15,500,000. ROME, 8 June 1989, *Venice* (water paints/canvas, 19¾ x 15¾ ins / 50 x 40 cm) ITL 15,000,000. LONDON, 20 Oct 1989, *Virgin and Child with a Dove* (1951, gouache/paper/canvas, 47¼ x 29½ ins / 120 x 75 cm) GBP 7,700. ROME, 28 Nov 1989, *Basket of Fruit* (1938, fresco, 13¾ x 18 ins / 35 x 45.5 cm) ITL 19,500,000. MILAN, 1[illegible] June 1990, *Flowers* (oil on panel, 19¾ x 17¾ ins / 50 x 45 cm) ITL 10,500,000. MILAN, 14 Nov 1991, *Masks* (1934, oil on panel, 17½ x 25½ ins / 44.5 x 64.5 cm) ITL 11,000,000. MILAN, 19 Dec 1991, *Sun* (1968, fresco/canvas, 9½ x 12¼ ins / 24 x 31 cm) ITL 5,000,000. ROME, 25 March 1993, *Maternity* (oil on canvas/panel, 34½ x 27½ ins / 87.5 x 70 cm) ITL 11,500,000. MILAN, 16 Nov 1993, *Watermelon* (1944, oil on canvas, 13 x 16 ins / 33 x 40.5 cm) ITL 8,050,000. ROME, 1[illegible] April 1994, *Maternity*. MILAN, 22 June 1995, *Landscape* (1968, tempera/paper, 12½ x 19 ins / 32 x 48.5 cm) ITL 1,380,000. MILAN, 27 May 1996, *White Fruit Bowl* (1971, sand and oil on canvas, 20 x 22 ins / 51 x 55 cm) ITL 16,100,000. MILAN, 2[illegible] Nov 1996, *Untitled* (1980, fresco/canvas, 17¾ x 22 ins / 45 x 56 cm) ITL 8,050,000. VENICE, 13 Nov 1999, *Landscape with Sun* (1980, mixed media on paper/canvas, 28 x 39 ins / 70 x 100 cm) ITL 12,600,000. VENICE, 13 Nov 1999, *Athletes* (oil on canvas, 24 x 20 ins / 60 x 50 cm) ITL 18,500,000. VENICE, 1[illegible] April 2000, *Landscape with Sun* (oil on board, 8 x 13 ins / 20 x 32 cm) ITL 15,500,000. PRATO, 10 Nov 2000, *Musical Instruments* (tempera on paper/canvas, 20 x 15 ins / 50 x 38 cm) ITL 5,000,000. PRATO, 1 Dec 2001, *Tired Player* (1933, oil on canvas, 30 x 45 ins / 76 x 114 cm) ITL 44,000,000. VENICE, 16 De

2001, *Red Sun* (1975, fresco, 19 x 23 ins / 47 x 59 cm) ITL 17,500,000. FLORENCE, 16 May 2002, *Still-life with Bottle* (oil on canvas, 22 x 22 ins / 55 x 57 cm) EUR 13,500. MILAN, 21 May 2002, *Still-life* (fresco on canvas, 27 x 33 ins / 68 x 85 cm) EUR 14,000. MILAN, 26 May 2003, *Composition of Fruit and Trumpet* (1980, fresco on canvas, 24 x 24 ins / 60 x 60 cm) EUR 10,000. PRATO, 14 Nov 2003, *Sunny Landscape* (mixed media on paper/canvas, 18 x 22 ins / 45 x 55 cm) EUR 2,200. MILAN, 16 March 2004, *Still-life with White Bottle* (1944, oil on canvas, 16 x 24 ins / 41 x 60 cm) EUR 12,500. PRATO, 29 May 2004, *Ants' Ferry* (1975, fresco on canvas, 37 x 51 ins / 95 x 130 cm) EUR 21,000.

SAEVENBOM, Johan. See **SEVENBOM**

SAEY, Jacobus or Jacques or Jakob Ferdinandus, or Saeys, Saeijs, Saës or Saiss

Flemish School, 17th - 18th century.

Born 1658, in Antwerp (?); died 1725, in Vienna.

Painter. Genre scenes, architectural views.

Jacobus Saey was a pupil of W. van Ehrenberg in 1672, in Antwerp, where he became a guild master in 1680. He was active in Mechelen in 1684. In 1694, he married Maria van Risman, in Vienna. Some authors identify two painters with the name Saey, citing documents recording the activity of a painter of this name (first name unknown), as early as 1660 - possibly a relative of Jacobus.

MUSEUMS AND GALLERIES:

ANTWERP: *Church of the Jesuits, Antwerp* (painted in collaboration with Janssens) - SIBIU: *Hall with Columns; Fountain with a Pyramid.*

AUCTION RECORDS:

BRUSSELS, 18 Dec 1938, *The Messenger's Return*, BEF 2,200. COLOGNE, 14 June 1976, *Architecture* (1719, oil on canvas, 27 x 33½ ins / 68.5 x 85 cm) DEM 2,200. VERSAILLES, 23 May 1978, *Figures on the Terrace of a Palace* (oil on canvas, 30¼ x 36½ ins / 77 x 93 cm) FRF 16,000. LONDON, 16 April 1980, *Palace Interior* (1719, oil on canvas, 26¼ ins / 66.5 cm33 ins/84 cm) GBP 4,400. PARIS, 10 March 1981, *Peristyle of a Palace, with Figures in Oriental Costume* (oil on canvas, 48 x 56¾ ins / 122 x 144 cm) FRF 39,500. STOCKHOLM, 10-12 May 1993, *Palace Courtyard with a Troupe of Musicians* (oil on canvas, 32¾ x 47¼ ins / 83 x 120 cm) SEK 37,000. NEW YORK, 18 May 1994, *Colonnade with an Elegant Couple Conversing Beside a Fountain* (1719, oil on canvas, 27 x 23 ins / 68.3 x 58.2 cm) USD 16,100. PARIS, 20 Dec 1994, *Architectural Fantasy with Turkish Figures* (oil on canvas, 59¾ x 65¾ ins / 152 x 167 cm) FRF 140,000. NEW YORK, 12 Jan 1995, *Promenaders in Front of a Double Portico with Fountains* (oil on canvas, 47 x 67¼ ins / 119.4 x 170.8 cm) USD 57,500. LONDON, 18 April 1997, *Classical Palace in a Park, with Elegant Figures* (oil on canvas, 32¾ x 46¼ ins / 83.2 x 117.5 cm) GBP 32,200. LONDON, 3 Dec 1997, *Courtyard of a Baroque Palace, with an Oriental Queen and Other Figures* (oil on canvas, 41¼ x 58 ins / 104.9 x 147.3 cm) GBP 19,550. NEW YORK, 29 Jan 1998, *Loggia of a Mansion Surrounded by a Moat, with Elegant Figures Beside a Flotilla of Gondolas* (oil on canvas, 25 x 37 ins / 63.2 x 94 cm) USD 23,000. NEW YORK, 28 Jan 1999, *Elegant Figures Strolling in Palace Garden* (1719, oil on canvas, 31 x 51 ins / 80 x 129 cm) USD 20,000. NEW YORK, 14 Oct 1999, *Imaginary Loggias* (oil on canvas, a pair, 23 x 31 ins / 58 x 79 cm) USD 30,000. VIENNA, 30 March 2000, *Renaissance Palace in Southern Port with Boats and Figures* (oil on canvas, 28 x 37 ins / 71 x 94 cm) ATS 160,000. MADRID, 8 May 2000, *Architectural Capriccio with Lazarus* (oil on canvas, 42 x 39 ins / 106 x 99 cm) ESP 3,500,000. LONDON, 12 July 2001, *Architectural Capriccio with Elegant Figures Promenading* (oil on canvas, 36 x 49 ins / 92 x 125 cm) GBP 9,500. PARIS, 18 March 2002, *Moses Saved from the Waters Before a Renaissance Palace* (oil on canvas, 33 x 44 ins / 84 x 113 cm) EUR 55,000. NEW YORK, 7 June 2002, *Classical Portico with an Elegant Company Gathered by a Fountain* (1694, oil on canvas, 37 x 29 ins / 93 x 73 cm) USD 10,000. PARIS, 25 June 2003, *Festival Before the Façade of a Renaissance Palace* (1683, oil on canvas, 22 x 33 ins / 56 x 83 cm) EUR 8,000.

SAEY, René

Belgian, 20th century.

Born 1913, in St-Joris-ten-Distel.

Painter, watercolourist, pastellist, draughtsman.

René Saey studied at the fine arts college in Buenos Aires.

SAEYS, Jacob Ferdinand. See **SAEY**

SAEZ DIEZ, Luis

Spanish, 20th century.

Born 1925, in Burgos.

Painter.

Saez Diez studied at the Escuela de Bellas Artes in Madrid and travelled extensively in France and Switzerland. After a figurative period which lasted until 1957 or so, he developed an abstract lyrical style based on intersecting geometric elements.

SAEZ GARCÍA, Ángel

Spanish, 19th century.

Born March 1811, in Pradillo de Cameros.

Painter.

Ángel Saez García was a pupil of J. Galvez.

SAEZ GARCÍA, Benito

Spanish, 19th century.

Born 21 March 1808, in Pradillo de Cameros; died 27 June 1847, in Madrid.

Painter. Figures.

Benito Saez García was the brother of Ángel and Pedro Saez. He studied under J. Galvez before going to Rome to continue his studies. Working with Galvez he executed frescoes in the Escorial and the palace of El Pardo near Madrid.

SAEZ GARCIA, Pedro

Spanish, 19th century.

Born 29 April 1805, in Pradillo de Cameros.

Painter, art restorer.

Pedro Saez Garcia was a pupil of J. A. Ribera.

SAFF, Vojtech Edward, or Schaff

Czech, 19th - 20th century.

Born 17 June 1865, in Policka; died 26 December 1923, in Prague.

Sculptor.

Vojtech Saff trained at the academy of fine art with Kundmann. He sculpted monuments and produced low reliefs, the subjects of which were borrowed from Bohemian legend.

MUSEUMS AND GALLERIES:

PLZEN: two low reliefs - PRAGUE: *Air; Earth.*

SAFFARD

French, 17th century.

Active in Orbec in 1664.

Sculptor (wood).

SAFFARO, Lucio

Italian, 20th century.

Born 1929, in Trieste.

Painter.

AUCTION RECORDS:

MILAN, 27 Sept 1990, *The Hypothesis of Micenus* (1969, acrylic/canvas, 51¼ x 43¼ ins / 130 x 110 cm) ITL 2,000,000.

SAFFER, E. F.

German, 18th century.

Active in Leipzig at the beginning of the 18th century.

Portrait artist.

Museums and Galleries:
Leipzig (Stadtbibliothek): *Portrait of Councillor Gottfried Christian Goetze* (1709).

SAFFER, Hans Konrad
German, 19th - 20th century.
Born 16 October 1860, in Bamberg.
Painter.

Hans Konrad Saffer was the brother of the painter Heinrich Saffer. He studied in Munich under Alexander von Liezen-Mayer, Wilhelm Durr the Younger and Martin Feuerstein.

Museums and Galleries:
Bamberg (Municipal Gal.): *Head of an Apostle; Portrait of Konrad Funk.*

SAFFER, Heinrich
German, 19th century.
Born 8 October 1856, in Bamberg.
Active in Cuxhaven.
Painter.

Heinrich Saffer was the brother of Hans Konrad Saffer. He painted altarpieces and decorations.

SAFFREY, Henri Alexandre
French, 19th century.
Born in Montvilliers.
Painter, engraver (etching). Landscapes.

Henri Saffrey was a student at the municipal school in Le Havre. He exhibited at the Salon from 1870 to 1881. He mainly produced etchings of views of Paris and the surrounding area.

Museums and Galleries:
London (Victoria and Albert Mus.): prints.

Auction records:
Paris, 18 Nov 1946, *Panorama of Paris* (watercolour) FRF 3,000; *Sketchbook; Boat* (pen drawing) FRF 160.

SAFFREY, Lydie Marie
French, 19th century.
Born in Cherbourg.
Painter. Portraits.

Lydie Saffrey was a student of Mme Allier de Clairières de Seinemont and Mlle Kron-Méni. She first exhibited at the Salon of 1880.

SAFFT, Jan Karel Willem
Dutch, 19th century.
Born 4 October 1778, in Amsterdam; died 1849 or 1850, in Amsterdam.
Painter, draughtsman. Religious subjects, genre scenes, landscapes.

Jan Karel Safft was a pupil of Pieters Barbiers; he was also an art dealer. In 1822, he was appointed to a professorship at the Amsterdam academy of fine art.

Museums and Galleries:
Brussels (MBA): *Virgin and Child* - Warsaw: *St Philip Baptising the Faithful.*

SAFIR, Raya
French, 20th century.
Born 1912.
Painter (gouache). Scenes with figures, interiors with figures.

Raya Sabir's colours are soft to the point of paleness, and she chooses to depict peaceful family scenes: *Young Woman Seated in a Garden, Conversation in an Interior* and *Breakfast.* In 1996, the Galerie dans la Cour, Paris, exhibited a collection of her gouaches.

SAFOKHIN, Anatoli, or Saphokine
Russian, 20th century.
Born 1928, in Simonovo.
Painter, illustrator, draughtsman. Portraits, genre scenes, landscapes, still-lifes.
Socialist Realism.

Anatoli Safokhin trained at the Surikov Institute in Moscow and became a member of the Association of Painters of the USSR. He belonged to the pictorial tradition of the Bubnovy Valet (Jack of Diamonds) group and was interested in the painting of Cézanne, Matisse and Derain. He often painted landscapes outdoor. Safokhin took part in regional, national and international exhibitions in France, Sweden and Finland. He held solo exhibitions in Moscow.

A.CAФ.64

Bibliography:
Tableaux soviétiques, auction catalogue, Salle Drouot, Paris, 3 October 1990.

Auction records:
Paris, 6 Feb 1993, *Evening in Pereslavl* (oil on canvas, 29 1/2 x 41 ins / 75 x 104 cm) FRF 3,000. Paris, 29 Nov 1993, *Fishing Boats* (1961, oil on canvas, 39 1/4 x 35 1/2 ins / 100 x 90 cm) FRF 10,200. Paris, 1 June 1994, *Portrait of a Woman* (1962, oil on canvas, 43 1/4 x 29 1/2 ins / 110 x 75 cm) FRF 12,500.

SAFONT, Lorenzo
Spanish, 16th century.
Painter.

Lorenzo Safont worked in Palma de Majorca Cathedral, in 1328.

SAFT, J. C. W.. See **SAFFT**

SAFTLEVEN, Abraham, or Sachtleven or Zachtleven
Dutch, 17th century.
Born 1612 or 1613, in Rotterdam.
Painter.

Abraham Saftleven was the son of Herman Saftleven I and brother of Cornelis and Herman Saftleven II. He was a pupil of Abraham van der Linden.

SAFTLEVEN, Cornelis, or Sachtleven or Zachtleven
Dutch, 17th century.
Born 1607, in Gorkum; died 1681; buried on 4 June in Rotterdam.
Painter, watercolourist, engraver (etching), draughtsman (including ink). Religious subjects, figures, genre scenes, interiors with figures, rustic scenes, landscapes with figures, landscapes, ruins, animals.

Cornelis Saftleven was the brother and pupil of Herman Saftleven II. He married Catharina Dirksz. van der Heyde in 1649, and lived in Rotterdam from 1648 to 1674. He married his second wife, Elisabeth van der Avondt, in 1655, and was appointed director of the Rotterdam guild in 1667. His pupils included Ludolf de Jonge. Although not the equal of his brother, Cornelis's work is highly interesting: his genre paintings recall those of Teniers and Brouwer, and he produced a remarkable body of etchings.

.C.S

C Saftleven

Museums and Galleries:
Amsterdam: *Group of Villagers; Landscape with Cattle; Annunciation to the Shepherds; Trucidata Innocentia; Johan van Oldenbarneveld and his Judges* - Brunswick: *The Flight into Egypt* - Budapest: *Stable* - Dresden: *Scene in a Stable; Peasant Musicians; Feeding Chickens in a Peasant Cabin; Still-life*

in a Peasant Cabin - DUBLIN: *Interiors with figures* - HAARLEM: *Oldenbarneveld and his Judges as Animals* - HAMBURG: *Rhine Landscape* - HANOVER: *Interior of a Peasant House* - KARLSRUHE: *Surgical Operation; Job and his Comforters* - OBERSCHLEISSHEIM (Neues Schloss Schleissheim, Staatsgal.): *Annunication to the Shepherds; Adoration of the Shepherds; The Angel Taking Leave of Tobias's Family* - PARIS (Louvre): *Portrait of a Painter* - ROTTERDAM: *Peasant Looking over a Hedge at a Recumbent Ram and a Standing Goat* - ST PETERSBURG (Hermitage): *Livestock Market; Farm Animals, Resting* - STOCKHOLM: *Bamboccio in Front of a Country Tavern; Landscape with Animals and Figures* - VALENCIENNES: *Livestock Market* - VIENNA: *Peasants' Bedchamber* (figures by Teniers the Younger) - VIENNA (Liechtenstein Mus.): *Livestock Market.*

AUCTION RECORDS:

PARIS, 1842, *Interior with Numerous Household Utensils,* FRF 70. PARIS, 1853, *Rustic Interior with a Group of Three Figures,* FRF 415. PARIS, 1865, *Seated Woman; A Dog at her Side* (watercolour) FRF 61. PARIS, 1891, *Animals,* FRF 430. PARIS, 31 March 1900, *Temptation of St Anthony,* FRF 200. PARIS, 19 June 1925, *Wounded Fawn* (pen and watercolour wash) FRF 310. PARIS, 10-11 May 1926, *Ruins of a Castle Above a River with Craft* (black chalk and bistre) FRF 1,050. PARIS, 17 and 18 March 1927, *Study of a Young Boy Asleep on a Bank* (black chalk with highlights) FRF 220. PARIS, 8 Dec 1938, *Animals at Pasture* (black chalk and wash) FRF 550. PARIS, 20 June 1939, *Seated Peasant Woman* (black chalk) FRF 1,030. LONDON, 4 June 1943, *Interior of a Barn,* GBP 136. PARIS, 25 April 1951, *Wooden Bridge,* FRF 175,000. LONDON, 27 March 1968, *Kitchen Scene,* GBP 500. NEW YORK, 15 March 1974, *Adoration of the Shepherds,* USD 12,500. AMSTERDAM, 18 April 1977, *Seated Young Man, Seen From the Back* (1643, black chalk and grey wash, 11 1/2 x 8 ins / 29.5 x 20.2 cm) NLG 18,000. LONDON, 28 Oct 1977, *Parade of Monsters* (1627, oil on panel, 18 1/2 x 24 1/4 ins / 47 x 61.5 cm) GBP 4,800. COLOGNE, 11 June 1979, *Farmyard* (oil on panel, 29 1/4 x 42 ins / 74 x 106.5 cm) DEM 17,000. AMSTERDAM, 16 Nov 1981, *Camel* (black and white chalk, 7 1/2 x 9 1/2 ins / 19 x 24 cm) NLG 15,000. LONDON, 17 Dec 1982, *Interior of a Stable* (oil on panel, 18 x 26 1/4 ins / 45.6 x 66.7 cm) GBP 3,800. AMSTERDAM, 26 Nov 1984, *Roaring Lion* (black chalk and rouge and watercolour, 15 1/2 x 12 3/4 ins / 39.2 x 32.4 cm) NLG 55,000. LONDON, 3 July 1985, *Livestock Market Near a Church* (c. 1660, oil on panel, 20 3/4 x 26 3/4 ins / 53 x 68 cm) GBP 23,000. LONDON, 8 April 1986, *Standing Figure of a Man* (1666, black chalk, 11 1/4 x 6 1/2 ins / 28.8 x 16.4 cm) GBP 1,300. LONDON, 10 April 1987, *Tavern Scene* (1635, oil on panel, 19 1/4 x 28 1/2 ins / 49 x 72.5 cm) GBP 20,000. AMSTERDAM, 30 Nov 1987, *Boy Walking With Arms Outstretched* (1641, black chalk and grey wash, 8 1/4 x 6 ins / 21.1 x 15.5 cm) NLG 12,000. AMSTERDAM, 14 Nov 1988, *Riverscape with Ruined Castle* (wash and chalk, 5 3/4 x 8 ins / 14.9 x 20.2 cm) NLG 6,440. MONACO, 17 June 1989, *Kitchen Scene, With a Cat* (oil on panel, 6 3/4 x 9 ins / 17 x 22 cm) FRF 77,700. AMSTERDAM, 20 June 1989, *Juno Commanding Argus to Watch over Io* (oil on panel, 17 x 22 1/2 ins / 43.4 x 57 cm) NLG 9,775. LONDON, 12 Dec 1990, *Livestock Market on the Banks of a Canal on the Edge of a Dutch Village* (oil on panel, 23 1/4 x 32 1/4 ins / 59 x 82 cm) GBP 52,800. NEW YORK, 8 Jan 1991, *Seated Young Man Playing the Trombone* (1637, black chalk, 9 3/4 x 7 1/2 ins / 25 x 19.1 cm) USD 35,200. AMSTERDAM, 25 Nov 1991, *The Ruins of Huis te Spangen at Overschie, Near Rotterdam* (1649, black chalk and wash, 7 3/4 x 12 1/4 ins / 20 x 31.1 cm) NLG 9,775. AMSTERDAM, 12 May 1992, *Shepherd and Shepherdesses with their Flock in Front of a Barn* (oil on panel, 29 1/4 x 40 1/2 ins / 74 x 103 cm) NLG 18,400. NEW YORK, 20 May 1993, *Card-players in a Tavern* (oil on panel, 14 1/2 x 22 1/2 ins / 36.8 x 57.2 cm) USD 13,800. AMSTERDAM, 16 Nov 1993, *Peasants and their Children in a Kitchen* (oil on panel, 10 x 13 1/2 ins / 24.5 x 34.5 cm) NLG 44,850. NEW YORK, 11 Jan 1994, *Adolescent Standing in a Doorway* (1662, black chalk, 11 1/2 x 7 ins / 29 x 18 cm) USD 6,900. NEW YORK, 12 Jan 1994, *Livestock Market on the Banks of a Canal on the Outskirts of a Town* (oil on panel, 23 x 32 1/4 ins / 58.3 x 82.2 cm) USD 134,500. NEW YORK, 12 Jan 1995, *Swineherd on the Banks of a River with a Cow and a Foal, a Farm and Ruins in the Distance* (oil on panel, 22 x 35 ins / 55.9 x 88.9 cm) USD 51,750. LONDON, 3 April 1995, *Study of a Gentleman with a Hat, His Right Arm Extended* (white and black chalk with touches of red/buff-coloured paper, 11 1/2 x 6 1/2 ins / 28.9 x 16.5 cm) GBP 3,680. AMSTERDAM, 14 Nov 1995, *Cat Keeping Watch Over a Fence* (oil on panel, 4 1/4 x 5 1/4 ins / 11 x 13.5 cm) NLG 413,000. NEW YORK, 2 April 1996, *Figures on a Riverbank, With a Hill-top Village in the Background* (oil on panel, 23 1/2 x 33 ins / 59.4 x 83.8 cm) USD 6,325. AMSTERDAM, 11 Nov 1997, *Cat* (black chalk, pen and brown ink, study, 3 3/4 x 5 ins / 9.7 x 12.8 cm) NLG 51,920. AMSTERDAM, 8 Nov 1999, *Couple Embracing by Farmhouse, the Prodigal Son among Swine Beyond* (1656, oil on panel, 19 x 26 ins / 47 x 65 cm) NLG 38,000. AMSTERDAM, 10 Nov 1999, *Country Market with Dovecote* (1676, chalk and watercolour, 8 x 13 ins / 20 x 32 cm) NLG 30,000. NEW YORK, 28 Jan 2000, *Standing Peasant Holding a Hat and Stick* (black chalk and grey wash, 11 x 7 ins / 27 x 17 cm) USD 9,000. LONDON, 4 July 2000, *Seated Man Playing a Sackbut* (1637, black chalk, 10 x 7 ins / 25 x 19 cm) GBP 10,000. LONDON, 2 Nov 2001, *Barn Interior with Cattle, Pigeons and a Dog Barking at a Peasant* (oil on panel, 18 x 27 ins / 46 x 68 cm) GBP 8,000. LONDON, 13 Dec 2001, *Summer Landscape with Harvesters Resting* (1644, oil on panel, 19 x 25 ins / 49 x 63 cm) GBP 7,500. STOCKHOLM, 28 May 2002, *From an Outhouse with Well, Figures and Still-life of Vegetables and Kitchen Utensils* (oil on panel, 23 x 26 ins / 59 x 65 cm) SEK 105,000. AMSTERDAM, 5 Nov 2002, *Farmstead near a Stream, with a Horse, Sheep and Goat* (oil on panel, 29 x 41 ins / 73 x 105 cm) EUR 30,000. COLOGNE, 20 Nov 2003, *Fairytale Interior* (oil on canvas, 33 x 42 ins / 85 x 106 cm) EUR 40,000. STOCKHOLM, 3 Dec 2003, *Interior Scene with Figures* (1637, oil on panel, 20 x 30 ins / 50 x 75 cm) SEK 170,000. MUNICH, 25 June 2004, *Outdoor Musicians with Dancer and Dancing Dog* (oil on panel, 17 x 15 ins / 42 x 38 cm) EUR 7,900. LONDON, 8 July 2004, *Huntsman Feeding Dogs under Porch* (oil on panel, 15 x 22 ins / 39 x 56 cm) GBP 22,000.

SAFTLEVEN, Herman I

Dutch, 17th century.

Died March 1627, in Rotterdam.

Painter.

Herman Saftleven I was a painter and art dealer, the son of an artist of the same name. His first wife, Lyntje Cornelis, bore him three sons, all painters: Cornelis (born in 1608), Herman II (1609) and Abraham (1613). He married his second wife, Lucretia de Beauvais, in 1626.

SAFTLEVEN, Herman II or III, or Zachtleven or Sachtleven or Saftleben

Dutch, 17th century.

Born c. 1609, in Rotterdam; died 5 January 1685, in Utrecht.

Painter, engraver (etching). Landscapes.

This artist was the son of Herman Saftleven I and a pupil of Jan van Goyen. He married Anna van Vliedt in 1633 and lived in Utrecht from 1632, serving as director of the city's guild from 1655 to 1667. In 1635 he worked with his brother Cornelis at the castle of Houselaersdyk. His pupils included W. van Bemmel, J. Vorsterman and J. van Bunnik. Some catalogues mention a Herman Saftleven III, who can in fact be identified as Herman II.

His work falls into three broad periods: the first combines the monochrome style of Jan van Goyen with the dramatic light of Hercules Seghers; the second features Romantic ruins and nostalgic views along the Rhine and the Mosel; the third is characterised by small, meticulously painted landscapes in brilliant colours, in the Italianising tradition of the Utrecht School.

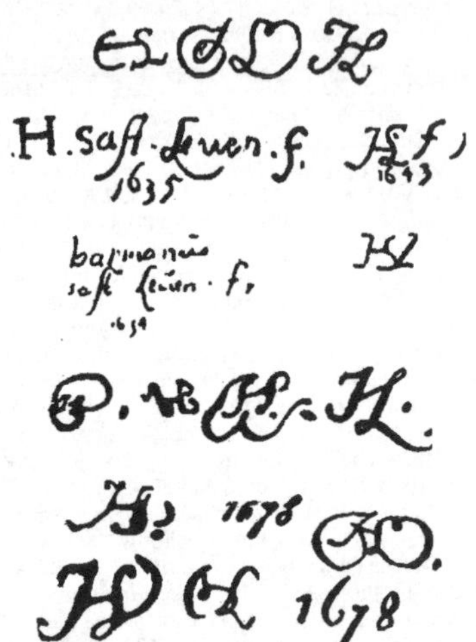

BIBLIOGRAPHY:

Heirich Hollstein, Friedrich Wilhelm, *Dutch and Flemish Etchings, Engravings and Woodcuts ca. 1450-1700*, Menno Hertzberger, Amsterdam, 1949-1974.

MUSEUMS AND GALLERIES:

AIX: *Interior of a Thatched Cottage* - AMIENS: *Banks of the Rhine* - AMSTERDAM: *Village on the Banks of a River; View of a River; Ferry on a Broad Stretch of Water; View Painted near Boppard; Mountainous Landscape; Banks of the Rhine; View of a River in a Mountainous Setting* - AUGSBURG: *Landscape with a Mountain Stream* - BERLIN: *Silvio Presenting the Arrow to the Wounded Dorinda* - BRUNSWICK: *Riverscape; Landscape* - BRUSSELS: *Barn* - BUDAPEST: *Landscape on the Banks of the Rhine* - COPENHAGEN: *Grape Harvest on the Banks of the Rhine; Rocky Countryside; Ruin on a Rocky Outcrop; View of Utrecht; Autumn in the Rhineland* - DOUAI: *Landscape; Farmyard* - DRESDEN: *Grape Harvest in a Mountain Setting; Festive Scene in a Valley; Castle Overlooking a River Valley; Festive Scene on the Rhine* (two paintings); *Mountain Landscape with a Small Chapel; Village Church in a Rocky Valley; Valley; Rhineland Landscape with High Mountains; Mountainous Countryside; Rhineland Landscape; Landscape; View of Utrecht; Countryside around Briey; Lighthouse; Riverscape; Riverscape with Waterfall* - DUBLIN: watercolour - EDINBURGH (Nat. Gal. of Scotland): *Christ Preaching from a Boat* (oil/panel) - FRANKFURT AM MAIN: *Valley* (two paintings); *Rhineland Landscape* - GLASGOW: *Riverscape* - GOTHA: *Mountainous Landscape* - HANOVER: *Two Riverscapes; Scene in the Rhineland; Interior of a Peasant Dwelling* - KARLSRUHE: *Mountain Landscape* - KASSEL: *Skaters Before the Ramparts of Utrecht; Banks of the Mosel; Eslach, on the Rhine* - LEIPZIG: *Dutch Landscape with River; Landscape* - LONDON (NG): *Christ teaching from St Peter's Boat* (1667, oil/wood) - MAINZ: *Riverscape* - MUNICH: *Rhineland Landscape; Hembach: A Boat on the Rhine* - NANCY: *Swineherds* - NIORT: *Skaters* - PARIS (Louvre): *View of the Banks of the Rhine* - ROTTERDAM: *Landscape in Southern Holland; Mountain Landscape with Figures; Banks of the Rhine; In the Dunes* - SCHWERIN: five views of the Rhine - ST PETERSBURG (Hermitage): *View of the Rhine; Landscape; The Mäuseturm near Bingen*; two views of the banks of the Rhine; *Interior of a Peasant Cabin* - STOCKHOLM: *Site in the Rhineland, with a Market Square* - STRASBOURG: *Rhineland Landscape* - THE HAGUE: *Landscape with Animals* - UTRECHT: *Landscape* - VIENNA: *Landscape with a View of the Rhine Valley* (three paintings); *Autumn Landscape; Sunset; Cows* - VIENNA (Czernin'sche Gemäldegal.): *Landscape with Trees; Landscape on the Edge of a Forest* - VIENNA (Liechtenstein Mus.): *Landscape with Mountain Stream* - VIENNA (Schönborn-Buckheim): *Landscape; Temptation of St Anthony* - YPRES: *Virgin, Child and St Katherine.*

AUCTION RECORDS:

PARIS, 13 May 1705, *Summer Landscape*, FRF 460. AMSTERDAM, 12 Sept 1708, *View of the Rhine*, FRF 360. PARIS, 1773, *Ruin Above the City of Utrecht* (chiaroscuro drawing) FRF 150; *View of the Rhine* (drawing) FRF 118. PARIS, 1846, *Farm Interior*, FRF 402. ANTWERP, 1853, *Landscape with Animals*, FRF 820. COLOGNE, 1862, *Hunter Shooting Duck in the Marshes*, FRF 619. PARIS, 1875, *Landscape with a Large Tree* (lead pencil and bistre wash) FRF 215; *Rocky Outcrop Forming an Archway Opening Onto a Landscape with Boules Players in the Foreground; Entrance to a Village* (lead pencil and bistre wash, collection) FRF 100. PARIS, 1881, *Barn*, FRF 4,050. PARIS, 1899, *Rustic Interior*, FRF 8,100. LONDON, 27 Nov 1909, *Landscape*, GBP 4. PARIS, 8-10 June 1920, *Landscape with Thatched Cottages* (pen) FRF 4,700. PARIS, 17 and 18 June 1924, *Harvest*, FRF 2,900. PARIS, 30 March 1925, *Landscape with Figures* (black chalk and wash) FRF 480. BERLIN, 20 Sept 1930, *Still-life*, DEM 850. PARIS, 10 June 1932, *Christ on the Sea of Galilee*, FRF 1,000. LONDON, 28 May 1937, *Landscape on the Rhine*, GBP 84. PARIS, 8 Dec 1938, *View of Utrecht and the Church of St Mary* (black chalk and bistre wash) FRF 900. PARIS, 13 Feb 1939, *Bridge over a Canal* (black chalk and bistre wash) FRF 900. PARIS, 1 July 1942, *Christ Giving Succour to the Blind* (no forename given, attributed) FRF 3,600. PARIS, 12 April 1943, *Flirtatious Old Man* (follower of Herman Saftleven) FRF 10,500. PARIS, 2 Dec 1946, *Dogs* (two drawings in black chalk heightened with white, attributed) FRF 750. PARIS, 24 Dec 1948, *Tower on the Banks of a River* (attributed) FRF 3,500. PARIS, 19 June 1950, *View of a River in a Mountain Setting*, FRF 40,000. PARIS, 14 Feb 1951, *Riders Hunting in a Mountainous Landscape Traversed by a Stream*, FRF 40,000. PARIS, 25 April 1951, *River* (1652) FRF 160,000. PARIS, 27 June 1951, *Landscape on the Banks of the Rhine*, FRF 33,000; *Bridge over a River* (attributed) FRF 6,500. AMSTERDAM, 3 July 1951, *Mountainous Landscape*, NLG 1,350. LONDON, 26 June 1964, *Rhine Landscape with Numerous Figures*, Gns 1,700. LONDON, 1 July 1966, *Banks of the Mosel*, Gns 1,200. LONDON, 19 April 1967, *Riverscapes* (two pendants) GBP 1,700. LONDON, 5 Dec 1969, *Landscape with a Castle*, Gns 2,800. PARIS, 2 June 1971, *View, thought to be of Linz*, FRF 30,000. LONDON, 23 March 1972, *Flower* (watercolour) GBP 850. LONDON, 21 March 1973, *Flower Studies* (watercolour) GBP 1,400. LONDON, 27 March 1974, *Riverscape*, GBP 7,000. ZURICH, 28 May 1976, *Landscape with Figures* (1667, oil/copper, 6 x 9 1/4 ins / 15 x 23.8 cm) CHF 92,000. LONDON, 8 Dec 1976, *Fishing Boat Returning to Port* (watercolour and black chalk, 6 1/2 x 9 1/4 ins / 16.6 x 23.5 cm) GBP 900. AMSTERDAM, 26 April 1977, *Mountain Landscape* (1650, oil on canvas, 26 3/4 x 37 1/2 ins / 68 x 95.5 cm) NLG 52,000. PARIS, 13 June 1978, *Steep Track* (oil on panel, 10 3/4 x 17 1/4 ins / 27.5 x 43.5 cm) FRF 40,000. LONDON, 4 May 1979, *Hunters in a Mountain Landscape with a Castle* (oil on canvas, 16 1/2 x 23 1/2 ins / 42 x 59.6 cm) GBP 8,500. AMSTERDAM, 29 Oct 1979, *Landscape with the Ruined Castle at Montfoort* (black chalk and wash, 14 1/4 x 11 1/2 ins / 36.5 x 29.4 cm) NLG 5,300. LONDON, 9 April 1981, *Woman on a Drawbridge* (black chalk, watercolour and white gouache, 11 3/4 x 17 1/2 ins / 30 x 44.3 cm) GBP 5,000. AMSTERDAM, 25 April 1983, *Boules Players at the Entrance to a Cave* (1648, black chalk and wash, 8 1/2 x 11 ins / 21.5 x 27.8 cm) NLG 7,400. LONDON, 2 Dec 1983, *Landscape with Figures* (oil/copper, 6 x 8 1/2 ins / 15.2 x 21.5 cm) GBP 29,000. COLOGNE, 23 May 1985, *Landscape with Figures and Boats* (1674, oil on wood, 10 x 12 ins / 24.5 x 30.5 cm) DEM 110,000. AMSTERDAM, 18 Nov 1985, *Travellers in a Wood* (1647, black and brown wash heightened with white, 11 ins / 28 cm, 2 x 9 1/4 ins/5 x 23.4 cm) NLG 23,000. NORFOLK (ENGLAND), 22 Oct 1986, *Imaginary Landscape on the Banks of the Rhine, with Figures* (1667, oil on panel, 11 x 13 3/4 ins / 27 x 35 cm) GBP 22,000. NEW YORK, 14 Jan 1988, *Vast Imaginary Landscape with a Clifftop Village Overlooking the Rhine* (1650, oil on canvas, 20 3/4 x 28 ins / 53 x 71 cm) USD 121,000. AMSTERDAM, 14 Nov 1988, *Wooded Landscape with Figures in a Clearing* (1630, ink and white chalk, 8 1/4 x 10 1/2 ins / 21 x 26.5 cm) NLG 13,800. NEW YORK, 11 Jan 1989, *The De Bok Tower and the West Postern Gate at Weert, near Weertpoort, in the Region of Utrecht* (1650, chalk and wash, 18 1/4 x 12 1/4 ins / 46.6 x 31.3 cm) USD 39,600. LONDON, 7 July 1989, *Rhine Landscape with Grape-pickers and Pilgrims, a Cross and a Fortified Town in the Background* (1678, oil on panel, 11 x 15 ins / 28 x 37.8 cm) GBP 33,000. AMSTERDAM, 28 Nov 1989, *Shepherd Asleep Amidst Herd of Goats* (oil on panel, 12 1/2 x 15 3/4 ins / 31.5 x 40 cm) NLG 27,600. NEW YORK, 10 Jan 1990, *Wooded Riverscape with Figures in a Clearing and a Sailing-boat at Anchor* (oil on panel, 10 1/4 x 8 1/4 ins / 26 x 21 cm) USD 15,400. LONDON, 6 July 1990, *Boat-building Site on an Estuary* (1682, oil on canvas, h/p 8 x 11 ins / 20.4 x 28 cm) GBP 126,500. AMSTERDAM, 14 Nov 1990, *Rhineland Landscapes* (1677, oil on panel, a pair, each 8 1/2 x 11 ins / 21.5 x 28 cm) NLG 201,250. NEW YORK, 11 April 1991, *Rocky Valley with Figures on a Track* (oil on panel, 14 1/2 x 18 3/4 ins / 37 x 47.5 cm) USD 9,900. AMSTERDAM, 2 May 1991, *Peasants Merry-making outside an Inn, in an Extensive Mountain Landscape in the Siebengebirge* (1663, oil/copper, 11 x 14 3/4 ins / 28.2 x 37.6 cm) NLG 178,250. MONACO, 21 June 1991, *View of the Rhine* (1669, oil/copper, 6 x 6 3/4 ins / 14.3 x 17.4 cm) FRF 299,700. LONDON, 2 July 1991, *Peasant Carrying a Rod, Seen From the Rear* (black chalk, brown wash, 12 1/4 x 8 ins / 31 x 20.3 cm) GBP 11,000. LONDON, 13 Sept 1991, *Riverscape with Figures, Overlooked by a Farm* (1671, oil on panel, 8 3/4 x 10 1/4 ins / 22.2 x 26 cm) GBP 12,650. AMSTERDAM, 14 Nov 1991, *Extensive Rhineland Landscape with River Rraffic and a Village on the Opposite Bank* (1655, oil on panel, 7 x 9 1/4 ins / 18 x 23.2 cm) NLG 74,750. NEW YORK, 15 Jan 1992, *Peasant Walking wth a Rucksack on his Back* (black chalk and wash, 11 3/4 x 7 1/4 ins / 29.8 x 18.4 cm) USD 10,450. LONDON, 6 July 1992, *Rhine Landscape with Boats at Anchor and Figures in the Foreground* (black chalk and brown wash, 6 1/2 x 10 ins / 16.8 x 25.3 cm) GBP 4,950. AMSTERDAM, 10 Nov 1992, *Christ Preaching on the Shore of the Sea of Galilee* (1648, oil on panel, 28 1/2 x 40 1/4 ins / 72.4 x 102.2 cm) NLG 25,300; *Rhine Landscape with Peasants at Work Near a Farm, at Twilight* (1675, oil on panel, 8 1/4 x 11 ins / 21 x 27.8 cm) NLG 43,700. NEW YORK, 13 Jan 1993, *Rolling Landscape with Travellers* (black chalk and wash, 7 3/4 x 11 ins / 19.9 x 27.8 cm) USD 5,175. LONDON, 21 April 1993, *Rhine Landscape* (oil on panel, 14 1/2 x 18 3/4 ins / 37 x 47.5 cm) GBP 13,800. PARIS, 28 June 1993, *Landscape in the Rhine Valley with a Ferry About to Leave* (1665, oil on canvas, 6 x 9 1/2 ins / 15.2 x 24 cm) FRF 280,000. MONACO, 2 July 1993, *View of the Rhine* (1674, oil on panel, 18 x 25 ins / 46 x 63.5 cm) FRF 377,400. PARIS, 5 March 1994, *Riverbank Scene with Figures* (oil on panel, 8 1/4 x 11 ins / 21 x 28 cm) FRF 90,000. AMSTERDAM, 15 Nov 1994, *Ruins with Figures near Gildbrug, Utrecht* (1674, black chalk and wash, 7 3/4 x 5 3/4 ins / 19.8 x 14.9 cm) NLG 5,980. LONDON, 7 Dec 1994, *Capriccio of Extensive Rhine Landscape* (1673, oil/copper, 14 x 18 1/2 ins / 35.6 x 47.3 cm) GBP 91,700. NEW YORK, 12 Jan 1995, *Travellers on the Banks of a River Overlooked by Ruins, Extensive Landscape beyond* (1634, oil on panel, 13 1/4 x 18 1/4 ins / 33.7 x 46.4 cm) USD 32,200. PARIS, 12 June 1995, *Landscape in the Rhine Valley* (oil on panel, 8 1/2 x 10 3/4 ins / 21.5 x 27.5 cm) FRF 50,000. AMSTERDAM, 13 Nov 1995, *Rhine Landscape with Boats at Anchor, Merchants and Sailors in the Foreground* (1666, oil on panel, 12 3/4 x 16 ins / 32.2 x 40.6 cm) NLG 80,500. AMSTERDAM, 7 May 1997, *Rhine Landscape with Merchants and Traders; Rhine Landscape with a Barge Loaded with Hay* (1665, oil on panel, a pair, each 6 x 9 1/2 ins / 15 x 24 cm) NLG 276,768. LONDON, 31 Oct 1997, *River Landscape with Mountains at Sunset, Fishermen Pulling in Nets, Barge and Peasants on the Bank* (1684, oil on panel, 8 1/4 x 11 ins / 21.2 x 27.9 cm) GBP 10,350. AMSTERDAM, 11 Nov 1997, *Mountain Landscape With a River and Town* (black chalk and wax, 7 x 7 1/4 ins / 17.5 x 18.5 cm) NLG 6,490. PARIS, 12 Dec 1997, *Landscape on the Banks of the Rhine* (copper, 10 1/4 x 13 1/2 ins / 26 x 34.5 cm) FRF 180,000. NEW YORK, 29 Jan 1998, *Rhine Landscape With Traders Unloading Merchandise at the River's Edge* (1651, oil on canvas, 29 x 35 1/4 ins / 73.7 x 89.5 cm) USD 32,200. LONDON, 15 April 1999, *Extensive Rhenish River Landscape with Fishermen* (1652, oil on panel, 13 x 18 ins / 34 x 45 cm) GBP 18,000. NEW YORK, 28 May 1999, *Rhenish River Landscapes* (1664, oil on panel, a pair, 6 x 9 ins / 16 x 24 cm) USD 120,000. LONDON, 7 July 2000, *Rhenish Landscape with Fishermen and Peasants on a Quayside, Town Beyond* (oil on panel, 11 x 15 ins / 28 x 37 cm) GBP 50,000. LONDON, 14 Dec 2000, *Wooded Landscape with Figures Picnicking, Others Harvesting Beyond* (1655, oil on panel, 11 x 16 ins / 29 x 40 cm) GBP 28,000. NEW YORK, 23 Jan 2001, *Young Herdsman Leaning on his Houlette* (black chalk and brown wash, 11 x 7 ins / 27 x 18 cm) USD 48,000. NEW YORK, 5 Oct 2001, *Landscape with Travellers* (1633, oil on canvas, 11 x 15 ins / 27 x 37 cm) USD 42,500. LONDON, 11 July 2002, *Rhenish River - Landscape Capriccio* (1681, oil on panel, 16 x 20 ins / 40 x 51 cm) GBP 28,000. AMSTERDAM, 6 Nov 2002, *Rhenish Landscape with Peasants Dancing Around a Maypole* (1682, oil on canvas, 15 x 18 ins / 38 x 46 cm) EUR 44,000. UPPSALA, 25 May 2003, *Rhine Landscape with Boats and Figures* (1670, oil on panel, 11 x 15 ins / 29 x 38 cm) SEK 270,000. LONDON, 11 Dec 2003, *Rhenish River Landscape with Figures Unloading Barges and Sailboats* (1664, oil on oak panel, 9 x 13 ins / 23 x 32 cm) GBP 33,000. NEW YORK, 21 Jan 2004, *Sheet of Studies of Peasants, Riders and Wagons* (black chalk and brown wash, 11 x 8 ins / 29 x 20 cm) USD 10,000. LONDON, 21 April 2004, *Extensive River Landscape with a Monastery on a Cliff* (1672, oil on panel, 17 x 23 ins / 43 x 58 cm) GBP 9,000.

SAFTLEVEN, Sara
Dutch, 17th century.
Born after 1633, in Utrecht.
Painter.

Sara Saftleven was the daughter of Herman Saftleven II. She painted watercolours of flowers.

SAFVENBOM, Johan. See **SEVENBOM**

SAGAU Y DALMAU, Félix
Spanish, 19th century.
Born 1786, in Barcelona.
Active in Madrid.
Medallist.

SAGAUD
French, 18th century.
Painter. Portraits, genre scenes.

Sagaud exhibited at the Salon in 1793.

SAGAZAN, Olivier de
French, 20th - 21st century.
Born 1959, in Brazzaville, Congo.
Sculptor, painter, draughtsman, performance artist.
Figures.

After studying biology and philosophy, Olivier de Sagazan turned to the visual arts and began exploring different techniques. He now lives and works in St-Nazaire. His sculptures might best be described as figures in search of an identity. They comprise disparate mineral (clay, laterite, slate and kaolin) and organic (cinders, hemp, bone gelatine) elements. His figures are single nudes or nude pairs of different heights and girths, typically caught in poses connoting expectation, prostration or shock and amazement, their wrinkled, parched earth-like features a sign of the passage of time. Like his sculpture, his paintings typically show nude couples rendered against an empty monochrome background, their form and colour dictated by the primordial slime from which they emerge. De Sagazan's performance video *Face to Flesh* (2001) is a further example of this use of mud and slime to achieve heightened dramatic impact.

He is a regular participant in group exhibitions: in 1994, at the Centre Culturel Scène Nationale in St-Nazaire; in 1997, at the Galerie du Rayon Vert in Nantes; in 1998, at the Chapelle St Anne in La Baule and the town hall in Nevers; in 1999 and 2000, at the Salon Linéart in Ghent (as part of the Galerie Pierre Marie Vitoux exhibit); and, in 1999, at the Salon Grands et Jeunes d'Aujourd'hui in Paris.

He has also exhibited solo with compositions and 'performances': in 1996, at *Avec et sur Bernard Noël* (*With and on Bernard Noël*), performed at the Galerie du Rayon Vert, Nantes; in 1997, at *Aqua ça sert* (*What's the point?*) (a pun on 'A quoi ça sert?'), a performance held at the Panonica in Nantes; in 1998, at *L'Innommable* (*Unnameable*) and, in 1999, at *Hommes de Boue* (*Mud Men*), both at the Galerie Pierre Marie Vitoux in Paris; and, in 2001, at *Êtres Chairs* (*People Dear to my Heart*) (a pun on 'Êtres Chers'), held at the Atelier d'Estienne in the Espace d'Art Contemporain in Pont-Scorff (Morbihan).

BIBLIOGRAPHY:

'Olivier de Sagazan' in *Les Cahiers du Rayon Vert* n° 3, periodical, Gal. du Rayon Vert, Nantes, June 1997. *Corps - Textes*, exhibition catalogue, Gal. des Franciscains, St-Nazaire, 2000. Sagazan, Olivier de, *Êtres chairs*, exhibition catalogue, Gal. Pierre Marie Vitoux, Paris, 2001.

SAGE, Auguste Jules

French, 19th century.
Born 16 March 1829, in Paris; died 1908.
Painter. History painting, portraits.

Auguste Sage was a student of Picot at the École des Beaux-Arts. He first exhibited at the Salon in 1870.

SAGE, Cornelia Bentley, Mrs Quinton W. W.

American, 20th century.
Born 3 October 1876, in Buffalo; died 1936, in Santa Barbara (California).
Painter.

Cornelia Bentley Sage studied at the Art Students League of New York under John Henry Twachtman, Carroll Beckwith, Irving Ramsey Wiles and Robert Reid. She was decorated with the Legion of Honour in 1921, appointed leader of the Groupe des Peintres et Sculpteurs Américains in Paris, and was the recipient of many other honorary titles in the USA.

SAGE, Kay, Mme Tanguy Yves

American, 20th century.
Born 25 June 1898, in Albany (New York State); died 7 January 1963, in Woodbury (Connecticut).
Active in France.
Painter.

Kay Sage spent her childhood in Europe. She studied at the Corcoran Art School in Washington, then at the British Academy in Rome in 1920. She lived in Italy from 1900-1914, returning there from 1919-1937, and to Paris from 1937-1939. During this period the work she had submitted to the Salon des Surindépendants was spotted by André Breton and Yves Tanguy, and she soon became attached to the Surrealist group. In 1939 she married Yves Tanguy, and together they left France for Connecticut. She committed suicide a few years after her husband's death.

Before discovering Surrealism in Paris in 1937 Sage produced geometric abstract paintings. Subsequently, her paintings became populated with mannequins, shadows, familiar yet unidentifiable shapes, biomorphic figures, set in a pallid light in the midst of geometric compositions and architectural antiquities. By the 1950s her canvases began to look deserted, with depictions of urban places populated with ghostly scaffolding, flags, sky-scrapers, sets of lines and planes, the effects of perspective.

She took part in several collective exhibitions: 1938 Salon des Surindépendants, Paris; 1942 Council of French Relief Societies, New York; 1954 Wadsworth Atheneum, Hartford, Connecticut; 1955 Whitney Museum, New York; 1958 Contemporary Art Museum, Houston and Foire Artistique Mondiale in Brussels; 1961 Museum of Modern Art, New York. Her work was also shown on many occasions at the Carnegie Foundation in Pittsburgh. En 1962, she exhibited one of her works at the Salon des Réalités Nouvelles in Paris. She had her first solo exhibition in Milan in 1936 at the Galeria del Milione, then regularly in New York: 1940 Pierre Matisse Gallery; 1944 and 1947 Julian Levy Gallery; 1950, 1952, 1956, 1958, 1960, 1961 Catherine Viviano Gallery. Also: 1941 Museum of Art, San Francisco, 1953 Rome and Paris, 1965 Mattatuck Historical Society Museum, Waterbury.

BIBLIOGRAPHY:

Sage, Kay, *Kay Sage: Retrospective*, exhibition catalogue, Catherine Viviano Gallery, New York, 1960. Miller, Stephen R., *'The Surrealist Imagery of Kay Sage'* in *Art International 3*, periodical, Lugano, October, 1983. Vieuille, Chantal, *Kay Sage ou le surréalisme américain, biographie 1898-1963*, Complicités, 1995. Suther, Judith D., *Kay Sage, a house of her own, solitary surrealist*, University of Nebraska Press, Lincoln (NE), 1997.

MUSEUMS AND GALLERIES:

CHICAGO (AI) - MINNEAPOLIS (Walker Art Center) - NEW HAVEN (AG, Yale University): *Danger, Construction Ahead* (1940) - NEW YORK (Metropolitan Mus. of Art): *Tomorrow Never Comes* (1955) - NEW YORK (MoMA): *Union Treaty* (1954) - NEW YORK (Whitney Mus. of American Art): *No Overtaking* (1954) - NEWARK: *At the Appointed Hour* (1942) - SAN FRANCISCO (California Palace of the Legion of Honor): *Untitled* (c. 1947, lithograph/smooth, woven paper) - SAN FRANCISCO (De Young Mus.): *The Hidden Letter* (1943, oil on canvas) - WATERBURY (Mattatuck Museum): *Vorticist* (c. 1935); *My Room with Two Doors* (1939).

AUCTION RECORDS:

NEW YORK, 1 Nov 1978, *Point of Intersection* (1951/52, oil on canvas, 38 3/4 x 32 ins / 98.7 x 81.5 cm) USD 19,000. NEW YORK, 6 Dec 1985, *Count the Stars* (1939, oil on canvas, 12 3/4 x 16 ins / 32.3 x 40.5 cm) USD 3,000. NEW YORK, 30 May 1986, *Other Answers* (1945, oil on canvas, 16 1/4 x 13 ins / 41.2 x 33.2 cm) USD 6,000. NEW YORK, 28 May 1987, *The Upper Side of the Sky* (1944, oil on canvas, 23 x 28 ins / 58.5 x 71.2 cm) USD 11,000. NEW YORK, 20 Feb 2001, *This Morning* (1939, oil on canvas, 11 x 14 ins / 27 x 35 cm) USD 16,000. NEW YORK, 20 Feb 2001, *Apostrophe* (1951, oil on canvas, 16 x 13 ins / 41 x 33 cm) USD 18,000. PARIS, 14 April 2003, *Untitled* (1941, oil on canvas, 30 x 40 ins / 76 x 102 cm) EUR 38,000. NEW YORK, 18 May 2004, *Les Rouleax* (1937, oil on canvas, 26 x 20 ins / 65 x 50 cm) USD 14,000.

SAGE, P. Le. See **LE SAGE**

SAGER, Ernst

German, 19th century.
Active 1810-1838.
Painter. Genre scenes, landscapes, still-lifes.

Ernst Sager was a pupil of O. Völcker at the academy in Berlin where he was a frequent exhibitor. He often painted on porcelain.

SAGER, Hans
Norwegian, 18th century.
Active in Bergen in the first half of the 18th century.
Painter. Religious subjects, portraits. Decorative schemes.

SAGER, Jakob
German, 18th century.
Active in Landshut at the beginning of the 18th century.
Sculptor (wood).
Along with three other artists, Jakob Sager sculpted the stalls in the church of St Martin in Landshut.

SAGER, Otto
German, 19th - 20th century.
Born 19 September 1870, in Stettin (now Szczecin, Poland).
Active in Berlin.
Painter, engraver (etching).

SAGER, Xavier
French, 20th century.
Painter, draughtsman, illustrator. Landscapes.
Xavier Sager is best known for his postcards.

SAGER-NELSON, Olof or Johan Olof Gudmund
Swedish, 19th century.
Born 13 September 1868, in By; died 11 April 1896 or 1898, in Biskra.
Painter. Portraits, landscapes.
Sager-Nelson was a pupil of Bruno Liljefors, Johann Ericson and Anna Gardell-Ericson. Above all a portrait artist, he was influenced by Gauguin and van Gogh. His works are imbued with mysticism and the figures are evoked primarily through their outline, in the manner of fresco painting. He wanted to strip figures of their humanity, in order to attain a quality of unrealness. His art was that of a visionary, though somewhat morbid, mind.
BIBLIOGRAPHY:
Kent, N., *The Triumph of Light and Nature: Nordic Art, 1740-1940*, monograph, Thames and Hudson, London, 1987.
AUCTION RECORDS:
STOCKHOLM, 31 Jan 1947, *Coastal Scene*, DKK 1,650. STOCKHOLM, 24 April 1984, *Seashore* (oil on panel, 16 1/4 x 9 3/4 ins / 41 x 25 cm) SEK 42,000. STOCKHOLM, 28 Oct 1985, *Interior with Three Figures* (1894, oil on canvas, 22 x 18 ins / 55 x 46 cm) SEK 350,000. STOCKHOLM, 19 Oct 1987, *The Village Street* (1893, oil on canvas, 24 x 19 3/4 ins / 61 x 50 cm) SEK 820,000. STOCKHOLM, 5-6 Dec 1990, *Portrait of Esther Wallerstedt* (oil on canvas, 18 x 12 1/2 ins / 46 x 32 cm) SEK 15,500. STOCKHOLM, 16 May 2000, *The Lesson* (oil on canvas, 18 x 22 ins / 46 x 55 cm) SEK 280,000. STOCKHOLM, 28 May 2002, *Mother Nursing Baby* (oil on canvas, 18 x 14 ins / 45 x 35 cm) SEK 60,000. STOCKHOLM, 26 May 2003, *Small Girl in the Green Grass* (oil on canvas, 13 x 16 ins / 33 x 40 cm) SEK 68,000. STOCKHOLM, 4 June 2003, *Bleke Avenue, Gaarda* (oil on canvas, 10 x 10 ins / 25 x 25 cm) SEK 250,000. STOCKHOLM, 26 May 2004, *Summer Landscape with Girl* (oil on canvas, 13 x 16 ins / 33 x 40 cm) SEK 150,000.

SAGERT, Hermann or Carl Hermann
German, 19th century.
Born 1 January 1822, in Berlin; died 20 April 1889, in Friedenau, near Berlin.
Engraver. Portraits, genre scenes.
Hermann Sagert was a pupil of Hans Fincke. He engraved illustrations for Goethe's *Iphigenia in Tauris*.

SAGET
French, 19th century.
Sculptor. Busts.
Saget exhibited at the Salon in 1834 and 1837.
MUSEUMS AND GALLERIES:
TOULOUSE: *Bust of General Darmagnac.*

SAGET, Guillaume
French, 19th - 20th century.
Born 17 September 1873, in La Réole.
Sculptor.
Guillaume Saget, a pupil of Barrias, exhibited in Paris from 1904 at the Salon des Artistes Français, of which he was a member and where he was awarded an honourable mention in 1908.

SAGETTE, Louis
French, 18th century.
Active in Avallon in 1732.
Sculptor (wood).

SAGGERE, François de, or Saeger or Ager or Saghere
Flemish School, 17th century.
Active in Antwerp.
Sculptor.
François de Saggere was assistant to his brother-in-law, Artus Quellinus the Elder. He carved a portrait bust and decorative sculpture for the cathedral at Schleswig.

SAGIO, Lucano, or Zagio, called Lucano da Imola
Italian, 16th century.
Active in Imola (Emilia-Romagna).
Painter.
Lucana Sagio may have been the pupil of Lorenzo Lotto. He worked in Bergamo from 1519-1548, and was still alive in 1568.

SAGLIANO, Francesco
Italian, 19th century.
Born 17 November 1826, in Capua; died 26 January 1890, in Naples.
Painter. Religious subjects, genre scenes.
A pupil of N. Palizzi, G. Bonoli and A. Vertunni, Francesco Sagliano exhibited paintings in Parma, Milan and Turin. He painted works for several churches in Naples.
MUSEUMS AND GALLERIES:
NAPLES (Mus. Civico): *Burial of Conradin in the Church of the Carmine in Naples* - NAPLES (Mus. di Capodimonte): *Children* - NAPLES (Provincial Mus.): *Flower Festival; Sarno Boatman.*
AUCTION RECORDS:
ROME, 16 April 1991, *Farmyard Scenes with Figures* (oil on panel, a pair, 11 3/4 x 6 3/4 ins / 30 x 17 cm) ITL 6,900,000. LONDON, 16 June 1993, *Pleasures of Pompeii* (1880, oil on canvas, 32 1/4 x 53 1/4 ins / 82 x 135 cm) GBP 6,900.

SAGLIO, Camille
French, 19th century.
Born 1804, in Paris or in Strasbourg; died October 1889, in Paris.
Landscape artist, illustrator.
Camille Saglio was a student of Holivard and Roqueplan. He exhibited at the Salon from 1839 to 1875, obtaining a second-class medal in 1846. He produced a large number of works depicting the banks of the Rhine and the Rhône. He illustrated Adolphe Badin's book *Caves and Caverns* (Éditions Hachette, Paris, 1876).
MUSEUMS AND GALLERIES:
AUTUN: *View from the Area around Cività Castellana.*

SAGLIO, Edward or Édouard
French, 19th - 20th century.
Born 1867, in Versailles.
Painter. Nudes, portraits, genre scenes.
Edward Saglio, a pupil of Jean-Paul Laurens, was awarded an honourable mention at the Paris Exposition Universelle of 1900. He exhibited at the Salon of the Société Nationale des Beaux-Arts, of which he was an associate member.

Museums and Galleries:
Munich (Pinakothek): *Tea Party.*
Auction records:
Paris, 11 Dec 1935, *Béatrix,* FRF 20. Paris, 5 Feb 1943, *Wooden Horses,* FRF 200. Paris, 1 June 1945, *Bust of a Female Nude,* FRF 420.

SAGLOVA, Zorka
Romanian, 20th century.
Born 1942, in Humpolec.
Active in Czechoslovakia from 1961.
Painter, performance artist.

Zorka Saglova studied at the school of applied arts in Prague, where he settled in 1961. In his early years, his style was close to Constructivist Abstraction, but he moved on to portraying momentous events which he set down in photographs and film, particularly: *Homage to Gustav Oberman* and *Hanging the Sheets* in 1970, *550th Anniversary of the Battle of the Hussites with the Armies of the Counter-Reformation: Homage to Fafejta* in 1972. He took part in collective exhibitions in Czechoslovakia and was invited to the Paris Biennale in 1973. He had his first solo exhibition in 1969 in Prague.

SAGMÜLLER, Berhard
Austrian, 18th century.
Active during the first half of the 18th century.
Sculptor (wood).

Berhard Sagmüller was a member of the Cistercian order. He worked in the monastery of Heiligenkreuz near Vienna, where he sculpted a pulpit and several altars.

SAGNE, August Eugen
German, 19th century.
Born 29 October 1815, in Munich; died 12 November 1842, in Munich.
Painter. Genre scenes.

SAGNOWSKI, Karol Rafal
Polish, 19th century.
Born 1836, in Cracow; died 17 March 1879, in Lemberg (now Lviv, Ukraine).
Painter.

Karol Sagnowski studied at the art academies in Cracow and Vienna. The National Gallery in Cracow owns his *St Sebastian,* and the National Gallery in Lviv owns his *Self-portrait.*

SAGODY VON NEMESSAGOD, József
Hungarian, 19th century.
Born 1810; died after 1895, in Pressburg (now Bratislava).
Painter, architect.

SAGORSKA. See **ZAGORSKA**

SAGORSKY, Nikolai Petrovich, or Zagorskii
Russian, 19th century.
Born 20 November 1849; died 30 December 1893.
Painter. Genre scenes, portraits.

Museums and Galleries:
St Petersburg (Gosudarstvennyj Russkij Muz.): *Ravaged Courtyard.*

SAGOT, Émile
French, 19th century.
Born 1805, in Dijon; died c. 1875.
Painter, draughtsman, illustrator, lithographer.
Landscapes, architectural views.

Émile Sagot was a major architect. He illustrated Baron Taylor's *Picturesque Journeys.* He also drew some views and churches in Normandy, Brittany and Bourgogne.

SAGRAMORO, Jacopo, real name: Jacopo da Soncino or Soncini, called Sagramoro
Italian, 15th century.
Died 1456 or 1457, in Ferrara.
Painter.

Jacopo Sagramoro worked in the court of Ferrara, and also painted religious subjects.

SAGRERA, Francisco
Spanish, 15th century.
Active in Palma (Majorca).
Sculptor, architect.

Francisco Sagrera was the son and assistant of Guillen Sagrera. He sculpted the *Tomb of Raimundo Lulio* in S Francisco church in Palma de Majorca, in 1487.

SAGRERA, Guillen or Guillermo
Spanish, 15th century.
Born in Inca (Majorca); died 19 August 1456, in Naples.
Sculptor, architect.
Majorca School.

Guillen Sagrera was the father of Francisco Sagrera. He worked in Palma de Majorca Cathedral from 1420-1447.

SAGRESTANI, Giovanni Camillo
Italian, 17th - 18th century.
Born 1660, in Florence; died 1730 or 1731, in Florence.
Painter, fresco artist. Religious subjects, allegorical subjects, portraits, local scenes.
Florentine School.

During his frequent travels in Italy, Giovanni Camillo Sagrestani worked with a number of painters who influenced him, notably Antonio Giusti and Romolo Panfi in Florence and Cignani and Crespi in Bologna. However he felt more of an affinity with the painting of his friend Sebastiano Ricci. He created a series of sketches of the *Four Sections of the Earth* for the Grand Duke's tapestry manufactory, where he was employed between 1704 and 1730. He wrote an account of the *Lives* of contemporary artists, and was also a poet. His work is soft and hazy, illuminated by a delicate light.

Bibliography:
Arrigucci, G., '*G. C. Sagrestani*' in *Commentari,* periodical, Florence, 1954. *La Peinture italienne au XVIIIe siècle,* exhibition catalogue, Association française d'action artistique, musée du Petit Palais, Paris, 1960-1961.

Museums and Galleries:
Florence (Church) - Florence (Uffizi): *Self-portrait; Rest during the Flight into Egypt.*

Auction records:
Milan, 29 Oct 1964, *Oriental Scene,* ITL 650,000. London, 30 March 1979, *Last Judgement* (oil on canvas, oval, 29 1/4 x 24in/74.2 x 61cm) GBP 3,800. Rome, 28 April 1981, *Rest during the Flight into Egypt* (oil on canvas, 37 1/2 x 55in/95 x 139.5cm) ITL 5,500,000. London, 20 Nov 1984, *San Luigi dei Francesi* (oil on canvas, 61 3/4 x 48 1/2in/157 x 123cm) ITL 11,000,000. New York, 3 June 1988, *Woman Sleeping with Her Servant beside Her* (oil on canvas, 20 1/4 x 28 3/4in/51.5 x 73cm) USD 4,400. London, 31 Oct 1990, *Diana Bathing* (oil on canvas, 33 3/4 x 41 3/4in/86 x 106cm) GBP 9,020. Rome, 8 April 1991, *Allegorical Scene with a Blind Man Discovering a Statue by Touch* (oil on canvas, 34 x 46in/86.5 x 116cm) ITL 57,500,000. New York, 9 Oct 1991, *Triumph of Galatea* (oil on canvas, 45 1/2 x 34 1/2in/115.6 x 87.6cm) USD 12,100. New York, 20 May 1993, *Interior with Two Turks Playing Draughts* (oil on canvas, 17 1/4 x 11 3/4in/43.8 x 29.8cm) USD 4,600. Milan, 21 Oct 1999, *Dido Abandoned* (oil on glass, 12 x 9 ins / 30 x 24 cm) ITL 5,500,000. London, 18 April 2000, *Bacchanalian Scene with Figures Dancing in a Wooded Landscape* (oil on canvas, 45 x 64 ins / 115 x 163 cm) GBP 15,000. London, 2 Nov 2000, *Madonna and Child Adored by the Kneeling Saints* (oil on canvas, 16 x 14 ins / 41 x 35 cm) GBP 4,600. Vienna, 24 March 2004, *Finding of Moses* (oil on canvas, 36 x 30 ins / 91 x 75 cm) EUR 14,000. London, 29 Oct 2004, *Crucifixion* (oil on canvas, 24 x 13 ins / 61 x 33 cm) GBP 4,800.

SAGSTÄTTER, Hermann or Gottfried Hermann
German, 19th century.
Born 1811, in Munich; died 25 December 1883, in Munich.
Painter. History painting, genre scenes, figures.
Hermann Sagstätter was a pupil of P. Cornelius at the academy in Munich.

After initially painting historical subjects, he devoted himself to representing scenes from rustic life in Bavaria and gained numerous successes.

AUCTION RECORDS:
NEW YORK, 16 Feb 1993, *Profile of an Elegant Young Woman* (oil on panel, 13 x 9 1/2 ins / 33 x 24.1 cm) USD 3,520.

SAHAGUN, Alfonso Fernandez de. See **FERNÁNDEZ de SAHAGUN**

SAHAGUN, Matias de
Spanish, 18th century.
Active during the first half of the 18th century.
Painter.
Matias de Sahagun painted a *Virgin* for the chapel of the Virgen del Santuario at Toledo Cathedral in 1714.

SAHDEV, Inderjeet
Indian, 20th century.
Born 1938, in Sialkot.
Active in France.
Sculptor.
Sahdev studied painting and sculpture at the college of arts and crafts in New Delhi. Together with other artists, notably Rajendra Dhawan, he was a founder member of the Unknown group. In 1963, he was awarded a French government grant and studied at the École des Beaux-Arts in Paris, in Collamarini's studio. He subsequently taught sculpture at the college of art in New Delhi. He lives and works in Paris.

His work has been shown at collective exhibitions including: Montreal Sculpture Symposium (1967); 1st Biennale of Artists from Quebec, Montreal (1977); and Musée National des Monuments Français, Paris. Sadhev has held regular solo exhibitions including: Lalit Kala Academy, New Delhi (1962); the USA; Canada (1966 to 1981). He was awarded the national sculpture prize in 1962.

BIBLIOGRAPHY:
Artistes indiens en France, exhibition catalogue, Centre national des Arts plastiques, Paris, 1985.

SAHIB, pseudonym of Lesage, Louis Ernest, also known as Ned
French, 19th - 20th century.
Born 1847, in Paris; died 1919, in Paris.
Painter, draughtsman, illustrator, caricaturist. Genre scenes.
Sahib, who first exhibited at the Salon of 1872, drew illustrations, especially caricatures. He worked as an illustrator for *La Vie parisienne* (*Paris Life*) and the *Journal de la presse*, and wrote and illustrated *La Frégate, l'Incomprise* (*The Frigate 'Impenetrable'*) (1882).

BIBLIOGRAPHY:
Osterwalder, Marcus (ed.), *Dictionnaire des illustrateurs 1800-1914*, Ides et Calendes, Neuchâtel, 1989.

SAHIFA BANU
Hindu School, 17th century.
Active between 1605 and 1627.
Painter.

MUSEUMS AND GALLERIES:
LONDON (Victoria and Albert Mus.): *King Shah Tamasp* (miniature).

SAHLBERG, Joh. Fr.
Swedish, 18th century.
Active in Stockholm, during the second half of the 18th century.
Sculptor (wood).
Sahlberg worked in the Frederik-Adolf church in Stockholm.

SAHLEN, Artur Oliver Julianus
Swedish, 20th century.
Born 16 February 1882, in Säm.
Engraver, painter.
Artur Oliver Julianus Sahlen studied at the Académie Colarossi in Paris and went on to produce several series of woodcut engravings.

SAHLER, Helen
American, 20th century.
Born 1877, in Carmel (New York); died 1950.
Sculptor.
Helen Sahler studied at the Art Students League of New York with Enid Yandell and H.A. MacNeil. She was a member of the American Arts Federation.

SAHLER, Otto Christian. See **SALER**

SAHLI, Abderrazak
Tunisian, 20th century.
Born 31 December 1941, in Hammamet.
Also active in France since 1970.
Painter (mixed media).
Abderrazak Sahli was a student at the school of fine arts in Tunis, then attended the Cité Internationale des Arts in Paris in 1970 and 1980. He has lived and worked in Paris since 1970. In his early work, he was concerned with exploring colour, which he wanted to be sparse and violent. He then became increasingly interested in the material, and constructed his pictures by making the pictorial processes spill over the frame of the canvas. His painting is difficult to define: with a luxuriant matterist construction and cursory brush-strokes, his works seem intended to hint at realities without identifying them. Through its deliberate appearance of poor execution, it resembles the 'Bad Painting' of the 1980s.

Sahli has taken part in collective exhibitions devoted to contemporary Tunisian Arabic painting, including the Paris Biennale (1971, 1980); the Salon de Mai and the Salon de la Jeune Peinture (1976-1977); and the Arab Biennial in Rabat and UNESCO in Paris (1980). He has shown his works in solo exhibitions in Tunis (1970, 1975, 1977); Paris, Nantes and Hammamet (1980); and the Centre Culturel in Fontenay-aux-Roses (1984).

SAHLSTROM, Anna
Swedish, 19th - 20th century.
Born 7 January 1876, in Fryksände.
Engraver, painter.
Anna Sahlstrom was a member of the Originalträsnitt Engravers' Association.

SAHLWEINER, Andreas, or Sahlwein
German, 18th century.
Painter. Religious subjects.
Andreas Sahlweiner was a pupil of J. E. Holzer in Augsburg, where he settled. He also worked in Weissenhorn and painted altarpieces.

SAHM, Hermann
German, 19th - 20th century.
Born 19 January 1867, in Königsberg (now Kaliningrad, Russia).
Painter. Portraits, genre scenes.
Hermann Sahm was a pupil of Heydeck and Steffeck. He is noted for an Indian ink drawing depicting a *Chamber in Königsberg Castle*.

SAHOL, Claude, or Saholle
French, 17th - 18th century.
Born at the end of the 17th century, in Nancy.
Sculptor.

SAHRAOUI, Schems-Eddine, pseudonym of Schems
Tunisian, 20th - 21st century.
Born 13 June 1948, in Tunis.
Active especially in France since 1969.
Painter, watercolourist, pastellist, engraver. Local scenes, landscapes with figures, urban landscapes. Orientalism.

Schems was the student of Ridha Bettaïeb in Tunis; he then worked in public studios in Paris, including at the Académie de la Grande Chaumière. He depicts typical places using a traditional technique, though in certain scenes with figures, his stroke becomes freer, more incisive and luxuriant, leading to a certain Expressionist tendency.

Schems has taken part in collective exhibitions, including *La Peinture Arabe Hier et Aujourd'hui* (*Arabic Painting Then and Now*) (1995) in Paris, where he was the representative of Tunisia; and *Tunisian Painting in France* in Carthage (1996). He mainly presents his works in solo exhibitions, such as at the Ligue Arabe in Paris (1995), and in cultural centres on the suburbs.

SAHUT, Francine
French, 20th century.
Born 1919, in Marly-lez-Valenciennes.
Painter.

Francine Sahut studied in Valenciennes and then in Paris with Jean Souverbie.

She exhibited in Paris at the Salon of the Société Nationale des Beaux-Arts, the Salon des Artistes Français, of which she was a member, the Salon des Indépendants, the Salon d'Automne, and the Salon des Femmes Peintres, as well as outside France. A figurative painter, she created powerful works using a range of warm colours.

MUSEUMS AND GALLERIES:
ST-DENIS DE LA REUNION.

SAHUT, Marcel
French, 20th century.
Born 1906 or 24 July 1901, in Grenoble; died 12 April 1990, in Milles (Bouche-du-Rhône).
Painter, watercolourist, draughtsman, lithographer. Portraits, landscapes, seascapes, still-lifes, flowers. L'Effort group.

The son of a stonecutter and sculptor, Marcel Sahut first studied with the painters Édouard d'Apvril and Fournier-Gabriel and then went to the École des Arts Industriels, Grenoble. He married Louise Morel in 1920 and towards the end of his life settled in Aix-en-Provence. He was a founder and president of the group L'Effort. He was a lithographer as well as a painter of Norwegian and Spanish landscapes characterised by large, open spaces and contrasts between the black of the soil and the trees and the white of the snow. His style is abstract in its use of forms, materials and light. He exhibited at the salon of L'Effort in Grenoble and at the Salon des Tuileries, Paris. His solo shows included: 1959, the museum of Toulon and then Grenoble; 1967, Centre Français, Wedding, Berlin; 1981, the Château de la Condamine, Corenc, and the Orangerie of the Jardins du Luxembourg; 1976, a retrospective at the Musée Granet, Aix-en-Provence, where he held another exhibition in 1982.

BIBLIOGRAPHY:
Sahut, exhibition leaflet, Orangerie du Luxembourg, Paris, Musée Granet, Aix-en-Provence, 1981-1982. Wantellet, Maurice, *Deux siècles et plus de peinture dauphinoise*, M. Wantellet, Grenoble, 1987.

MUSEUMS AND GALLERIES:
AIX-EN-PROVENCE (Mus. Granet) - GRENOBLE (Mus. de Grenoble) - TOULON: *Still-life* - VOLVIC (Mus. Marcel Sahut): several works.

AUCTION RECORDS:
PARIS, 10 March 1949, *African Landscape*, FRF 2,500.

SAIA, Pietro
Italian, 19th century.
Born 1779, in Sessano; died July 1833, in Naples.
Painter.

Pietro Saia studied at the Accademia di Belle Arti in Naples and with Tischbein.

MUSEUMS AND GALLERIES:
NAPLES (Mus. di Capodimonte): *Death of Hector*; *Cassandra*; *Vestal Virgin Buried Alive*; *Tancredi and Clorinda*.

SAIAN
Japanese, 16th century.
Monk, painter.

Saian practised ink painting (*suiboku*) during the Muromachi period. He lived in the Shokoku Temple in Kyoto.

SAÏD. See **LÉVY Alphonse Jacques**

SAÏD, Anne
British, 20th century.
Born 19 August 1914, in Hook (Hampshire); died 1995.
Painter, draughtsman.

Anne Saïd studied at Queen's College, London, from 1925 to 1930. She trained occasionally under Ozenfant in Paris from 1938 to 1939, and designed fabrics in order to pay for her art studies. She worked in Egypt from 1941 to 1955, and taught in the company of her husband, Hamed Saïd, forming a group of students there, whose work was exhibited in Cairo in 1948 and 1955. She had her first solo exhibition in 1957.

MUSEUMS AND GALLERIES:
LONDON (Tate Collection): *Wild Wood of Jo* (1961).

SAIDI, Aboul Ghasem
Iranian, 20th century.
Born 1925, in Arak.
Painter.

Aboul Ghasem Saidi came from a family of carpet-makers, and thus knew traditional decorative techniques from an early age. He went to Paris in 1950, and studied for four years at the École des Beaux-Arts in the studio of Eugène Narbonne. He then travelled in Italy and in Iran.

After his early work, which was characterised by his admiration for the Impressionists, Saidi developed in the direction of intimism in the style of Bonnard. He subsequently moved towards a vibrantly coloured decorative art, in a style inspired by Gustav Klimt. He decorated the buildings for the Iranian television service.

Saidi exhibited in Paris at the Salon de la Jeune Peinture, the Salon d'Automne, the Salon des Peintres Témoins de Leur Temps and the Salon de l'École de Paris in 1961. He took part in many group exhibitions, in particular at the Tehran and São Paulo Biennials, and in Belgium, Spain and Switzerland. He won the Prix de la Jeune Peinture in Paris in 1959, and prizes in 1960 and 1966 at the Tehran Biennial.

BIBLIOGRAPHY:
Six peintres contemporains iraniens, exhibition catalogue, Gal. Guiot, Paris, 1973.

SAIER, Joseph
German, 19th century.
Active in Rottweil during the first half of the 19th century.
Painter.

Joseph Saier is noted for his *Dying Capuchin* dated 1834.

SAIETZ, Gunnar
Danish, 20th century.

Born 1936.
Painter. Landscapes.

Saietz

AUCTION RECORDS:
COPENHAGEN, 7 April 1976, *Surrealist Landscape* (1972, oil on canvas, 33¾ x 54¾ ins / 86 x 139 cm) DKK 3,000. COPENHAGEN, 30 May 1990, *Nights* (1964, oil on canvas, 28¾ x 36¼ ins / 73 x 92 cm) DKK 4,000.

SAIGET, Gillet
French, 14th - 15th century.
Active 1395-1405.
Sculptor, goldsmith.

SAIGNES, Jean Jacques
French, 20th century.
Born 1932, in Paris.
Painter, watercolourist. Tapestries, murals.

Jean Jacques Saignes is both a painter and a writer. He has worked with Jacques Lagrange, mainly on tapestries and murals, and has restored buildings with Fernando Lerin. From the early 1960s, he worked mainly in white, endlessly nuanced, full of internal movement, with framed shapes appearing and disappearing in relation to changes of light. His paintings are sometimes diptyches or triptychs, and he also makes charcoal drawings and *Boxes*, the insides of which he paints. He has exhibited in group exhibitions held at the abbey of Beaulieu-en-Rouergue, Ginals: 1973, *L'Espace lyrique* (*Lyrical Space*), 1980, *Autour d'une collection* (*From a Collection*), 1984, retrospective, 1990, *Collection de Beaulieu* (*The Beaulieu Collection*). In 1974, 1976, 1986 and 1989, he exhibited at the Salon des Réalités Nouvelles, Paris; in 1976 and 1981 at the Galerie Regards, Paris; in 1981 in the exhibition *Le Clair et l'obscur* (*Light and Shade*) at the museum of Évreux, then Perpignan, Clamency and Bourges; in 1982 in Caylus; in 1990 at the Ingres Museum, Montauban, and the museum of Pau. Solo shows have included: 1974, Galerie Regards, Paris; 1974, Galerie Le Scribe, Montauban; 1984, the abbey of Beaulieu-en-Rouergue, Ginals; 1994, Temple-de-Caussade; 1996, Galerie Larock-Granoff, Paris.

BIBLIOGRAPHY:
White, Kenneth/Baxter, Alice/Bonnefoi, Geneviève/Olgiati, Gaspard, *Blancs-seings pour Jean Jacques Saignes*, Babel Éd., Mazamet, 1980. *Saignes*, exhibition catalogue, Abbaye de Beaulieu-en-Rouergue, Ginals, 1984.

MUSEUMS AND GALLERIES:
PARIS (FNAC).

SAIKALI, Nadia, or or Saikaly
Lebanese, 20th century.
Born 1936, in Beirut.
Painter, watercolourist, mixed media, sculptor.

Nadia Saikali trained at the Lebanese Academy of Fine Arts, where she taught during the 1960s, and at the École des Beaux-Arts, in Paris, where she studied engraving under Henri Goetz at the Académie de la Grande-Chaumière. She also taught at the Fine Arts Institute of Beirut University. In 1962, she visited Iran and in 1974 was awarded a Lebanese government scholarship, which she used to study mural tapestry at the École des Arts Décoratifs, Paris.

She was one of the first Arab artists to make kinetic sculptures, using her knowledge of physics and drawing on the help of specialist technicians. She also made a number of very lyrical pieces in ink or watercolour on Japan paper, playing on graduations of colour and 'craquelé' effects, creating a geometrical structure out of floating horizontal rectangles reminiscent of Rothko. Noteworthy among her works are: *Sanctuary of Silence* and *The Enigma of Time*.

She has exhibited in group and solo exhibitions since 1956. Her group shows include: 1961, 1963 Paris Biennale; 1962 Alexandria Biennale; 1965 São Paulo Biennale; 1961, 1965, 1968, 1974, 1988 Sursock Museum Salon, Beirut; 1970 *Seven Lebanese Painters*, Smithsonian Institute, Washington; 1972, 1973, 1974 Salon des Réalités Nouvelles, Paris; 1972, 1974 Salon Comparaisons, Paris. Her solo exhibitions include Beirut, 1956 UNESCO Centre, 1959 French Cultural Centre, 1962, 1963 Juliana Larsson Gallery; Frankfurt, 1964; Paris: 1964 Galerie Marcel Bernheim, 1978 Centre Georges Pompidou; Lausanne, 1985; Athens: 1987. Among her prizes were the Carreras First Prize for Painting in London (1967) and honourable mentions at the Sursock Museum Salon, Beirut (1965 and 1968).

BIBLIOGRAPHY:
Liban - Le Regard des peintres, exhibition catalogue, Institut du Monde Arabe, Paris, 1989.

MUSEUMS AND GALLERIES:
BEIRUT (Sursock Mus.) - PARIS (FRAC Île-de-France).

SAIKINA, Aleksandra
Russian, 20th century.
Born 1925.
Painter. Landscapes, still-lifes, flowers.

Aleksandra Saikina trained at the school of fine art in Kharkov where she was taught by Aleksandr Besedin.

AUCTION RECORDS:
PARIS, 12 Dec 1992, *Delphiniums* (oil on canvas, 31½ x 27¼ ins / 80 x 69 cm) FRF 15,000. PARIS, 20 March 1993, *Still-life With Samovar* (1965, oil on canvas, 33¾ x 31½ ins / 86 x 80 cm) FRF 3,800. PARIS, 4 May 1994, *Composition with Window* (1965, oil on canvas, 37½ x 27½ ins / 95 x 70 cm) FRF 6,200.

SAIKO, real name: Tahoko Ema, nickname: Ryokugyoku, pseudonyms: Saiko, Kizan, Shomu
Japanese, 19th century.
Born 1787, in Mino, now Gifu; died 1861.
Painter.
Nanga School.

Saiko specialised in flowers. He lived in Kyoto.

SAILA, Pauta
Canadian, 20th century.
Born 2 May 1916, near Cape Dorset (Baffin Island).
Sculptor (stone); engraver. Animals, figures.

Pauta Saila, usually known simply as Pauta, lived most of his life as a semi-nomadic hunter. He is married to the graphic artist Pitaloosie Saila, and lives in Cape Dorset on Baffin Island. He began sculpting in the 1950s, and made his first print in 1962 at the Cape Dorset art co-operative where James Houston initiated the Inuit print-making movement.

Pauta is primarily a sculptor, working in the local steatite or soapstone. He was one of the first Inuit sculptors to gain widespread recognition in Canada and internationally, and his dancing bears, powerful-looking animals balanced on one foot, are particularly well known. He has also done drawings for stonecut and stencil prints, or has incised copper plates for engravings, producing more than forty prints. His approach to drawing and printmaking reflects his view as a sculptor, as his graphics tend to be strong massive images, such as the stonecut *Eskimo Girl Juggling* (1967).

In 1967, Pauta was invited to create a large sculpture (now in the McMichael Collection at Kleinburg) for the sculptural festival sponsored by the City of Toronto for Canada's Centennial year. His work has been shown in many exhibitions such as the *Sculpture/Inuit* touring exhibition (1971-1973); *The Inuit Print*, National Museum of Man, Ottawa (1977, touring); many exhibitions at the Winnipeg Art Gallery; and shows at Feheley Fine Art, Toronto, including *Old Friends: Graphics from the Klamer Family Collection of Inuit Art* (1997), *The Ryan Collection* (1998), *Cross Currents: Cape Dorset in the 1960s* (2001), *The Discreet Collector* (2002), and *The Inuit Icon* (2003).

BIBLIOGRAPHY:
Swinton, George, *Sculpture of the Eskimo*, McClelland and Stewart, Toronto, 1972. *The Inuit Print*, exhibition catalogue, National Museum of Man, Ottawa, 1977. *Zazelenchuk Collection of Eskimo Art*, exhibition catalogue, Winnipeg Art Gallery, Winnipeg, 1978.

MUSEUMS AND GALLERIES:
KLEINBURG (Art Gallery of Ontario): *Polar Bear* (1967, stone sculpture) - OTTAWA (Nat. Gal. of Canada): *Bear* (1963, engraving); *Bird* (c. 1966, stone sculpture); *Composition* (1967, stonecut print); *Dancing Bear* (1968, stone sculpture); *Hunters and Large Animals* (1980, stonecut print); *Owl* (c. 1966, stone sculpture); *Owl on Cairn* (1967, stonecut print); *Standing Bear* (1962, stone sculpture); *Startled Owl* (1966, stonecut print); *Untitled* (1962, copper engraving) - REGINA (MacKenzie AG): *Bear and Seal* (c. 1960, stone sculpture) - TORONTO (AG of Ontario): *Dancing Bear* (stone sculpture).

AUCTION RECORDS:
TORONTO, 3 Nov 2003, *Polar Bear Standing with Head Raised* (mottled green soapstone, h. 19 ins / 48 cm) CAD 12,000. TORONTO, 3 Nov 2003, *Dancing Polar Bear with Its Mouth Open* (marbled green soapstone, h. 17 ins / 43 cm) CAD 15,000. TORONTO, 26 April 2004, *Bird* (marbled green soapstone, h. 13 ins / 33 cm) CAD 2,800.

SAILER, Daniel
German, 16th - 17th century.
Born c. 1571; died 1645.
Active in Augsburg.
Medallist, goldsmith.

SAILER, Johann Georg. See **SEILLER**

SAILER, Martin. See **SAILLER Johann Martin**

SAILER, Peter
Austrian, 19th century.
Born 1778, in Vienna; died 18 June 1845, in Vienna.
Painter. History painting.

SAILER, R.
German, 18th century.
Active in Dettingen in 1766.
Painter.

R. Sailer painted the *Virgin with St Leonard and St Joseph* for the chapel of St Leonard in Dettingen.

SAILLANT, Giovanni (Fra), or de Saillans or Saliano
French, 17th century.
Died towards the middle of the 17th century, in Avignon.
Painter, draughtsman.

Saillant was an Augustinian monk. He visited Rome and Florence and worked in Avignon from 1620 to 1635. He produced mainly miniatures.

SAILLAR, Louis or Lewis, or Sahler or Sailliar
French, 18th century.
Born 1748, in Paris; died c. 1795, in London.
Engraver.

Saillar went to live in London and worked on Boydell's Shakespeare Gallery. He produced plates after Van Dyck, Reynolds and Gerrit Dou, among others.

SAILLARD, Robert
French, 20th century.
Painter, lithographer. Architectural views.

In 1992, Robert Saillard was represented in the exhibition *De Bonnard à Baselitz - Dix Ans d'enrichissements du cabinet des estampes 1978-1988* (*From Bonnard to Baselitz: A Decade of Acquisitions by the Prints Collection 1978-1988*), held at the Bibliothèque Nationale, Paris.

MUSEUMS AND GALLERIES:
PARIS (BNF): *Notre Dame, La Roche Bercaille* (1978, lithograph).

SAILLART, Jehan
French, 15th century.
Active in 1452.
Cameo engraver.

SAILLAUX, Jean
French, 17th century.
Active in Angers c. 1671.
Glass painter.

SAILLER, Johann Martin
German, 18th century.
Born c. 1694, in Oberammergau; died 23 October 1774, in Freising.
Active in Freising.
Sculptor, stucco artist.

Johann Martin Sailler executed sculptures for several churches in Bavaria, notably the one in Freising.

SAILLOUR, Michel
French, 20th century.
Born 20 April 1931, in Cravigny near Évreux.
Painter, engraver, potter, sculptor, watercolourist.

Michel Saillour attended free courses at the École Nationale des Beaux-Arts, Paris, in about 1950. In 1952, he met Vlaminck painting in the open-air in the Eure valley, in 1961 Jacques Villon, and in 1981 André Masson. He was the founder of the Société des Peintres Indépendants de l'Eure. He was awarded the Charles Pacquement prize at the Musée Nationale d'Art Moderne, Paris.

He took part regularly from 1953 in the Salon des Andelys; in 1959 and 1962 in the Salon de la Jeune Peinture, Paris; in 1963 in the exhibition *La Jeune école de Paris* (*The Young School of Paris*) at the Musée d'Art Moderne, Paris, which then travelled to the USA; in 1971 in the Salon de Rouen; in 1976 in the exhibition *Hommage à Odilon Redon* (*Homage to Odilon Redon*) at the Grand Palais, Paris. Solo exhibitions have included: 1961, Galerie Étienne Pépin, Paris; 1962, Galerie du Fleuve, Bordeaux; 1966, Maison de la Culture, Le Havre; 1967, Galerie Simonde Badinier, Paris.

SAILLY, Laure Louise Jehanne
French, 19th - 20th century.
Born 22 December 1871, in Beauvais.
Miniaturist, engraver.

Laure Louise Jehanne Sailly, a pupil of Robert-Fleury, Jules Lefebvre and Humbert, exhibited in Paris from 1897 at the Salon des Artistes Français, of which she was a member, and of which she was later awarded the Hors concours. She was awarded an honourable mention at the Paris Exposition Universelle of 1900, another in 1907 for lithography, a silver medal in 1924, and a gold in 1926 for engraving. She received the Légion d'Honneur in 1937.

SAILMAKER, Isaac, or Sailmacker
British, 17th - 18th century.
Born c. 1633, in England (?); died 28 June 1721.
Painter. Landscapes, seascapes.

Isaac Sailmaker was a pupil of George Geldrop. He was noted for a *Fleet off Mardyke in 1657* (commissioned by Oliver Cromwell) and a *Fleet under Admiral Sir George Rooke's Command, 1714*.

AUCTION RECORDS:
LONDON, 17 Nov 1967, *View of Greenwich*, Gns 2,800. LONDON, 17 July 1974, *Vessels off the Dover Coast*, GBP 750. NEW YORK, 2 Dec 1976, *View of Greenwich* (oil on canvas, 19½ x 29½ ins / 49.5 x 75 cm) USD 3,800. LONDON, 6 June 1984, *Vessels off Portsmouth* (oil on canvas, 34 x 30½ ins / 85.5 x 77.5 cm) GBP 3,500. LONDON, 20 April 1990, *The 98-Canon, Full-Rigged 'Britannia' and other Warships* (1683, oil on can-

vas, 30 x 46 3/4 ins / 76.2 x 118.7 cm) GBP 41,800. NEW YORK, 11 April 1991, *Greenwich seen from the Thames with the Royal Observatory in the Distance* (oil on canvas, 19 3/4 x 29 1/2 ins / 50 x 75 cm) USD 22,000. PARIS, 13 Dec 1996, *Seascape: Off Dover* (oil on canvas, 23 1/2 x 35 3/4 ins / 60 x 91 cm) FRF 42,000. LONDON, 11 Nov 1999, *Squadron of the Red in Coastal Waters Possibly off Tangiers* (oil on canvas, 11 x 14 ins / 29 x 35 cm) GBP 2,400. LONDON, 11 May 2000, *HMS Gloucester Aground on Sandbank, off Great Yarmouth with Other Ship* (oil on canvas, 35 x 41 ins / 89 x 105 cm) GBP 4,500.

SAILO, Albinus, or Alpo, Léopold
Finnish, 19th - 20th century.
Born 17 November 1877, in Tavastehus (now Hämeenlinna).
Sculptor.

Albinus Sailo studied in Helsinki, Florence and Budapest.

MUSEUMS AND GALLERIES:
HELSINKI (Ateneumin Taidemus.): three busts.

SAIN, Edouard Alexandre de
French, 19th century.
Born 13 May 1830, in Cluny; died 27 June 1910, in Paris.
Painter. History painting, portraits, scenes with figures, genre scenes.

Edouard Sain was a student of Picot at the Académie des Beaux-Arts in Paris and at the academy in Valenciennes. He lived and worked in Écouen, making regular trips to Brittany, the Basque country and Italy.

He exhibited at the Paris Salon from 1853 to 1910 and at the Salon des Artistes Français; he was a member of this society from 1883. From 1890 to 1910, he exhibited at the Salon de la Société Nationale des Beaux-Arts, of which he was also a member, as well as in Toulouse, Périgueux, Lyons, Amsterdam, Antwerp, London, Vienna, Chicago and Melbourne. He received a medal in 1886, a third-class medal in 1875 and, at the Exposition Universelle in Paris, a silver medal in 1889 and a bronze medal in 1900. He was made a Chevalier of the Légion d'Honneur in 1877.

He began with history paintings, then produced a large number of compositions inspired by Rome and Naples.

E. Sain
E. Sain
Edouard Sain

MUSEUMS AND GALLERIES:
AUTUN: *Payment, Recollection of the Piazza Montanara in Rome* - DIEPPE: *Félia Litvinne at the Opera* - LONDON, CANADA: *Young Girl from the Island of Capri* - PARIS (former Mus. du Luxembourg): *Excavations at Pompeii* - PÉRIGUEUX: *Jeannette* - RHEIMS: *Napoleon III* - VALENCIENNES: *Wedding Feast in Capri; Portraits of Lambrecht, Delsart and Constant Moyaux* - VAUCOULEURS: *Family.*

AUCTION RECORDS:
PARIS, 23 Dec 1918, *Portrait of a Man in Costume of Henri IV,* FRF 45. PARIS, 20 April 1928, *Model,* FRF 205. PARIS, 28 Dec 1942, *Mussels Merchant,* FRF 3,800. PARIS, 14 March 1945, *Portrait of a Woman,* FRF 2,600. PARIS, 18 Oct 1946, *Landscape,* FRF 1,800. PARIS, 11 April 1949, *Woman Raking,* FRF 3,000. BERN, 3 May 1979, *Reverie* (1883, oil on canvas, 19 3/4 x 15 1/2 ins / 50 x 39.5 cm) CHF 2,100. NEW YORK, 28 Oct 1981, *Wedding* (1871, oil on canvas, 37 3/4 x 58 ins / 96 x 147.5 cm) USD 9,500. L'ISLE-ADAM, 20 Feb 1983, *Portrait of a Young Woman* (oil on canvas, 21 1/4 x 18 ins / 54 x 46 cm) FRF 12,000. LONDON, 7 Feb 1986, *Portrait of a Fashionable Woman* (oil on canvas, 77 x 51 1/4 ins / 195.7 x 130 cm) GBP 4,500. NEW YORK, 29 Oct 1987, *Fashionable Woman with Red Parasol* (oil on canvas, 77 1/4 x 51 1/2 ins / 196 x 131 cm) USD 21,000. PARIS, 7-12 Dec 1988, *Cliffs at Étretat; Sunken Lane in Normandy* (black chalk and chalk/blue paper, 9 x 14 1/4 ins / 23 x 36 cm) FRF 15,000. COPENHAGEN, 25 Oct 1989, *Hunting Scene with Four Dogs at the Foot of a Tree on which a Groom's Outfit and a Hunting Horn are Hanging* (1885, oil on canvas, 22 3/4 x 17 ins / 58 x 43 cm) DKK 32,000. PARIS, 12 June 1990, *Road Scene* (oil on panel, 18 x 14 1/4 ins / 46 x 36 cm) FRF 18,000. NEW YORK, 22 May 1991, *Excavations at Pompeii* (1866, oil on canvas, 42 1/2 x 33 1/2 ins / 108 x 85.1 cm) USD 27,500. NEW YORK, 17 Oct 1991, *Rosina* (oil on canvas, 41 1/2 x 25 ins / 105.1 x 63.5 cm) USD 9,900. NEW YORK, 22 Oct 1997, *Neapolitan Peasants Taking a Break* (1898, oil on canvas, 53 3/4 x 35 ins / 136.5 x 88.9 cm) USD 16,100. PARIS, 19 Nov 1999, *Virgin* (oil on canvas, 16 x 11 ins / 41 x 27 cm) FRF 38,000. ZURICH, 20 June 2000, *Coastal Landscape with Seated Girl* (1883, oil on canvas, 15 x 20 ins / 39 x 50 cm) CHF 2,700. LONDON, 5 April 2001, *Neapolitan Girl Carrying Fruit and Wine* (oil on canvas, 16 x 11 ins / 41 x 27 cm) GBP 2,000. PARIS, 28 June 2002, *The Digs at Pompei* (cardboard, 8 x 13 ins / 20 x 32 cm) EUR 2,800. LILLE, 20 Oct 2002, *Mussel Fishermen at Bourg d'Ault, Somme* (oil on canvas, 58 x 44 ins / 147 x 112 cm) EUR 12,500. VIENNA, 10 April 2003, *Head of a Girl* (oil on canvas, 13 x 10 ins / 33 x 25 cm) EUR 1,500. MUNICH, 17 March 2004, *Maid Looking at her Reflection in Shop Window* (1858, oil on panel, 13 x 11 ins / 32 x 27 cm) EUR 3,500. PARIS, 24 June 2004, *View of Capri. View of Pompei* (oil on canvas/cardboard, 8 x 13 ins / 21 x 32 cm) EUR 6,000.

SAÏN, Marius Joseph
French, 20th century.
Born 18 October 1877, in Avignon.
Sculptor.

Marius Joseph Saïn, a pupil of Thomas, Félix Charpentier, Injalbert and Allouart, exhibited in Paris at the Salon des Artistes Français, of which he was a member from 1903. He was awarded an honourable mention in 1903, a third-class medal in 1906 and a second-class in 1910. He was made a Chevalier of the Légion d'Honneur in 1926. He sculpted many monuments to the dead.

MUSEUMS AND GALLERIES:
AVIGNON: *Harmony; Drinking Song; The Flagellation* - PARIS (Mus. du Petit Palais): *Young Arab Shepherd.*

AUCTION RECORDS:
PARIS, 13 June 1980, *Greek Water-carrier* (1912, gilded patinated bronze, h. 17 1/4 ins / 44 cm) FRF 3,800. ENGHIEN-LES-BAINS, 16 Oct 1983, *Two Young Berbers* (gilded patinated bronze with brown tones, a pair, h. 14 1/4 ins / 36 cm) FRF 80,000. ORLÉANS, 17 Oct 1985, *Venus Anadyomene* (white marble, h. 103 1/2 ins / 263 cm) FRF 145,000.

SAÏN, Paul Étienne
French, 20th century.
Born 27 October 1904, in Paris.
Sculptor, designer.

Paul Étienne Saïn, a pupil of Jules Félix Coutan, Paul Maximilien Landowski, Carli and his father Marius Saïn, exhibited from 1923, mainly at the Salon des Artistes Français, of which he was a member and where he was awarded a bronze medal in 1924.

AUCTION RECORDS:
PARIS, 11 April 1988, *Vase and Flower* (lacquered panel, 55 1/2 x 47 1/4 ins / 141 x 120 cm) FRF 18,500. LONDON, 13 March 1996, *Figure on a Road into a Village* (oil on canvas, 15 1/4 x 21 3/4 ins / 38.5 x 55.5 cm) GBP 1,035.

SAÏN, Paul Jean Marie
French, 19th century.
Born 5 December 1853, in Avignon; died 6 March 1908, in Avignon.
Painter. Landscapes, seascapes.

Paul Saïn was the student of Guilbert, Anelle and Gérôme. He lived in Saint Cicéry in Orne, then in Southern France. He first exhibited at the Salon of 1879, receiving an honourable mention in 1883 and a third-class medal in 1886. He received a bronze medal at the Exposition Universelle in Paris in 1889, a second-class medal at the Salon in 1893 and a bronze medal at the Exposition Universelle in Paris in 1900. He was made a Chevalier of the Légion d'Honneur in 1895.

MUSEUMS AND GALLERIES:
ALENÇON: *The Sarthe and St-Cénery* - AVIGNON: *Morning on the Banks of the Rhône; Dusk in November, Île de la Barthelasse* - CARPENTRAS: *View of Avignon from Barthelasse; View of Avignon from the Road to Villeneuve; Tower of Philippe Le Bel; Road with the Green Oak; Ste-Garde, near St-Didier* - DOUAI: *Study of a Head* - MONTPELLIER: *Banks of the Sarthe at St Céneris* - PARIS (former Mus. du Luxembourg): *The Bridge at Avignon* - PARIS (Louvre): *Dusk in Normandy* - SÈTE: *Dusk at the Bridge in Avignon.*

AUCTION RECORDS:
PARIS, 6 Dec 1916, *Villeneuve-les-Avignon,* FRF 180. PARIS, 11 Feb 1919, *Toga, in the Bastia Area,* FRF 300. PARIS, 20 Nov 1925, *Corsican Landscape,* FRF 650. PARIS, 22 March 1933, *Landscape with Tree,* FRF 42. PARIS, 13 Nov 1942, *Working-Class Scene,* FRF 3,000. PARIS, 26 April 1944, *Reading by the Roadside,* FRF 2,000. PARIS, 2 Nov 1948, *Edge of the Lake,* FRF 1,500. PARIS, 18 Dec 1950, *Landscape in Southern France,* FRF 1,200. PARIS, 9 Feb 1955, *In the Countryside,* FRF 8,100. PARIS, 16 March 1972, *Boat* (16 1/2 x 20 1/2 ins / 42 x 52 cm) FRF 550. BERN, 25 Oct 1979, *Autumn Landscape* (1884, oil on canvas, 24 x 18 ins / 61 x 46 cm) CHF 2,200. LYONS, 4 Dec 1985, *Les Béni-ramesses près de Constantine* (oil on canvas, 28 3/4 x 39 1/4 ins / 73 x 100 cm) FRF 19,500. PARIS, 29 June 1988, *On the Road to Draveil* (oil on canvas, 16 1/4 x 22 ins / 41 x 55 cm) FRF 10,000. LYONS, 21 March 1990, *Mediterranean Landscape* (oil on canvas, 18 x 24 ins / 46 x 61 cm) FRF 17,500. LONDON, 11 May 1990, *June Morning on the Banks of the Sarthe in the Alençon Area* (oil on canvas, 34 3/4 x 52 ins / 88.5 x 132 cm) GBP 7,150. PARIS, 16 Nov 1990, *Country Lane* (oil on canvas, 13 x 19 ins / 33 x 48 cm) FRF 6,800. PARIS, 26 June 1992, *Young Woman at the Edge of the River* (oil on canvas, 18 x 23 1/2 ins / 46 x 60 cm) FRF 7,900. PARIS, 6 Oct 1995, *Young Woman Reading* (oil on canvas, 14 1/4 x 21 ins / 36.5 x 53.5 cm) FRF 12,000. PARIS, 19 April 1996, *Area around the River* (oil on canvas, 11 x 16 ins / 27 x 40.5 cm) FRF 6,000. NEW YORK, 9 Feb 1999, *Stream Through Undergrowth* (oil on canvas, 29 x 46 ins / 73 x 116 cm) USD 10,000. LYONS, 17 Oct 1999, *Evening on the Banks of the Sarthe* (oil on canvas, 35 x 52 ins / 90 x 131 cm) FRF 75,000. ZURICH, 14 March 2000, *Southern Landscape with Houses and Farmers* (oil on canvas, 15 x 22 ins / 38 x 55 cm) CHF 3,000. NEW ORLEANS, 29 July 2000, *Peasant Family Picking Fruit* (oil on canvas, 15 x 22 ins / 38 x 56 cm) USD 5,250. PONTOISE, 16 Dec 2000, *Farm Scene in the Afternoon* (oil on canvas, 15 x 22 ins / 38 x 55 cm) FRF 16,500. PARIS, 6 April 2001, *Seashore in the South of France* (oil on canvas, 13 x 18 ins / 33 x 46 cm) FRF 13,500. LUCERNE, 15 May 2002, *Part of L'Orne near Alencon* (oil on canvas, 35 x 52 ins / 88 x 131 cm) CHF 36,000. NEW ORLEANS, 17 May 2003, *Le Havre seen from the Top of La Heve* (oil on canvas, 15 x 21 ins / 38 x 53 cm) USD 2,200. NEUILLY, 27 June 2003, *Seashore at Houlgate* (oil on panel, 9 x 13 ins / 22 x 33 cm) EUR 11,000.

SAIN, Petrus Sinan
Bosnian, 20th century.
Born 1885, in Mostar.
Painter.

Petrus Sain trained in Vienna, Munich, Berlin and Paris and settled in Sarajevo.

SAINCTIER, Lidoire
French, 16th century.
Active in Tours 1581-1584.
Sculptor, architect. Coats of arms.

SAINCTON. See **SAINTON**

SAINSBURY, Everton
British, 19th century.
Born 1849; died October 1885.
Active in Clapham.
Painter. Genre scenes.

SAINSOT, Louise Victoire
Maiden name: Charpentier
French.
Born in St-Prest; died in St-Prest.
Painter. Landscapes.

MUSEUMS AND GALLERIES:
CHARTRES: *Landscape: Effect of Snow.*

SAINT, Daniel
French, 19th century.
Born 12 January 1778, in St-Lô; died 23 May 1847, in St-Lô.
Painter, watercolourist, miniaturist. Portraits, genre scenes.

Daniel Saint was a student of Jean-Baptiste Regnault, Jean-Baptiste Augustin and Aubry. He exhibited at the Salon from 1804 to 1839, obtaining a second-class medal in 1806 and a first-class medal in 1808; he was made a Chevalier of the Légion d'Honneur in 1839. He produced a large number of miniatures, mainly portraits of women.

MUSEUMS AND GALLERIES:
LONDON (Wallace Collection): *Empress Josephine* (miniature); *Napoleon I* (miniature); *Portrait of a Woman* (miniature); *Louis-Napoleon, King of Holland* (miniature) - NARBONNE: *Beautiful Greek Woman* (miniature) - PARIS (Louvre): *Mme E. Jullien, née Beauvalet* (miniature); *Young Lady in Black* (miniature) - ST-LÔ: *Two Portraits of Women and a Portrait of a Man* (ivory, miniatures); a watercolour - VIRE: *Hoop Factory in La Mauffe* (miniature).

AUCTION RECORDS:
PARIS, 1862, *Young Girl in a Park* (miniature) FRF 955; *Young Woman Seated near a Window to the Countryside* (miniature) FRF 1,970. PARIS, 1872, *Half-length View of a Young Woman* (miniature) FRF 2,400. PARIS, 1886, *Portrait of the Empress Josephine* (miniature) FRF 2,500. PARIS, 1898, *Portrait of the Empress Josephine* (miniature) FRF 4,700. PARIS, 18-22 April 1910, *Portrait of a Woman; Portrait of a Young Boy* (two miniatures decorating the top and inside of a lid on an ancient gold-carved musical box) FRF 2,550. PARIS, 8 April 1919, *Portrait of a Woman* (miniature) FRF 2,300. PARIS, 6 July 1920, *Half-length Portrait of a Young Woman* (miniature) FRF 1,150. PARIS, 26 April 1923, *Portrait of a Queen* (miniature) FRF 5,000. PARIS, 2 Dec 1925, *Portrait of Charles X* (miniature) FRF 2,800. PARIS, 27 June 1935, *Young Woman* (miniature) FRF 2,000. PARIS, 5 March 1937, *Young Woman in White Dress and Blue Belt* (miniature) FRF 900; *Portrait of King Charles X* (large miniature) FRF 7,000. PARIS, July 1946, *Portrait of a Woman* (miniature) FRF 36,000; *Portrait of a Man* (miniature) FRF 11,500. PARIS, 17 May 1950, *Portrait of the Comte d'Artois* (1824, miniature) FRF 60,000; *Portrait of an Officer* (miniature) FRF 17,000. PARIS, 13 June 1952, *Portrait of a Young Woman in a White Dress,* FRF 102,000. PARIS, 8 Nov 1996, *Marcelle Clary, Countess Tascher de la Pagerie* (watercolour and gouache, 2 3/4 x 2 1/4 ins / 7 x 5.5 cm) FRF 30,000. LONDON, 21 June 1999, *Emperor Napoleon I in National Guard Uniform and Orders* (1813, miniature, oval, h. 2ins / 5cm) GBP 1,300. LONDON, 22 May 2001, *Young Lady in*

a White Dress with a Coral and Gold Tiara in her Hair (miniature, h. 2ins / 6cm) GBP 3,500. PARIS, 20 June 2001, *Portrait, thought to be Charlotte Bonaparte* (miniatures, 2 x 2 ins / 6 x 4 cm) FRF 130,000. LONDON, 28 May 2002, *Young Lady in a White Dress* (miniature, h. 2ins / 6cm) GBP 2,200. LONDON, 25 June 2002, *Lady with Lace-trimmed Bonnet* (miniature, oval, h. 3ins / 7cm) GBP 2,300. PARIS, 21 May 2003, *Empress Josephine* (miniature, 2 x 1 ins / 5 x 3 cm) EUR 7,800. PARIS, 26 Nov 2003, *Portrait of Napoleon Bonaparte* (miniature, oval, 5 x 4 ins / 12 x 9 cm) EUR 2,600. LONDON, 22 April 2004, *Colette de Reiset, Baroness de Beurnonville* (miniature, oval, h. 3ins / 8cm) GBP 3,400.

SAINT, J. D.
French, 18th century.
Draughtsman, designer of ornamental architectural features.

SAINT, Jean Pierre
French, 20th century.
Born 1938, in Lisieux.
Draughtsman, pastellist.

Jean Pierre Saint regularly exhibited in Paris at the Salon d'Automne during the 1980s and 1990s, as well as at the Salon de Montrouge, the Salon Grands et Jeunes d'Aujourd'hui, Paris, and the MAC Salon of 2000. Among his works is *Monkey and Ball: Various reactions of a Monkey*

SAINT, Lawrence
American, 20th century.
Born 29 January 1885, in Sharpsburg (Pennsylvania); died 1961.
Painter, draughtsman, engraver, illustrator. Designs for stained glass.

Lawrence Saint was the pupil of William Merritt Chase, Cecilia Beaux, Henry Rankin Poore and William Sergeant Kendall and also studied in Europe.

He specialised in the decoration of stained-glass windows and illustrated a number of books.

MUSEUMS AND GALLERIES:
LONDON (Victoria and Albert Mus.) - PITTSBURGH (Carnegie MA): numerous watercolours.

SAINT, Louise Anne (Mlle)
French, 19th - 20th century.
Born 14 April 1865, in Évreux.
Painter. Genre scenes.

Anne Louise Saint, a pupil of Jouffroy, exhibited in Paris at the Salon des Artistes Français, Paris, of which she was a member. She was awarded an honourable mention in 1904 and a third-class medal in 1910.

MUSEUMS AND GALLERIES:
PARIS (Mus. du Petit Palais).

SAINT, Willem
Dutch, 18th century.
Draughtsman, engraver (burin).

Willem Saint was active in Amsterdam.

MUSEUMS AND GALLERIES:
AMSTERDAM (Rijksprentenkabinet): one drawing.

SAINT..., Master of. See **MASTERS**

SAINT AGRICOL
French, 5th century.
Born at the beginning of the 5th century 5th century.
Painter. Religious subjects.

Saint Agricol was bishop of Chalon-sur-Saône. He is said to have built the cathedral and to have embellished it with paintings and mosaics.

SAINT ANDRÉ, Simon Bernard de (Sieur de), or erroneously known as Simon Renard
French, 17th century.
Born 1613 or 1614, in Paris; died 13 September 1677, in Paris.
Painter, engraver. Allegorical subjects, portraits, still-lifes, vanitas.

Simon de Saint André was the pupil of Louis Beaubrun, and worked in Rome. He became painter to the king in 1646, and Academician on 28 May 1663. At first, he produced portraits of the royal family, then went on to depict his figures in allegorical forms. He also produced still-lifes and vanitas still-lifes inspired by the Dutch painters Jacques de Claeuw and Jan Vermeulen.

The similarity between the names suggest a relationship between this artist and the engraver Bernard de St-André who worked in Paris around 1695.

StA.

MUSEUMS AND GALLERIES:
PONTOISE: *Still-life* - VERSAILLES: *Portrait of the Queen Mother, Anne of Austria; Portrait of the Reigning Queen; Marriage of Louis XIV and Marie-Thérèse; Meeting of Louis XIV and Philip IV; Louis XIV Visiting the Gobelins Factory.*

AUCTION RECORDS:
VERSAILLES, 19 July 1981, *Vanitas* (oil on canvas, 28 x 23 3/4 ins / 71 x 60.5 cm) FRF 13,800. PARIS, 31 Oct 1984, *Vanitas* (oil on canvas, 22 3/4 x 18 1/2 ins / 58 x 47 cm) FRF 40,000. MONTE CARLO, 29 Nov 1986, *Allegory of Charles I of England and Henrietta of France in a Vanitas* (oil on canvas, 57 1/2 x 47 1/4 ins / 146 x 120 cm) FRF 58,000. MONTE CARLO, 6 Dec 1987, *Vanities of the World* (oil on canvas, 45 1/4 x 66 1/4 ins / 115 x 168 cm) FRF 290,000. NEW YORK, 14 Jan 1988, *Allegory of Charles of England and Henrietta of France in a Vanitas* (oil on canvas, 57 1/2 x 47 1/4 ins / 146 x 120 cm) USD 55,000. NEW YORK, 12 Jan 1989, *Allegory of the History of the Gauls* (oil on canvas, 35 1/4 x 28 1/2 ins / 89.5 x 72.5 cm) USD 187,000. PARIS, 12 June 1995, *Vanitas* (oil on canvas, 14 1/2 x 18 1/4 ins / 37 x 46.5 cm) FRF 130,000. LONDON, 6 Dec 1995, *Vanitas with a Palette and Paintbrushes, Sculptures, a Coral Branch, an Open Book and Other Objects* (oil on canvas, 21 x 24 1/4 ins / 53.2 x 61.4 cm) GBP 20,700. NEW YORK, 29 Jan 1999, *Vanitas: Skull, Violin, Music Score, Pipe, Hourglass* (oil on canvas, 26 x 21 ins / 65 x 54 cm) USD 50,000. MUNICH, 19 Sept 2003, *Vanitas Still-life* (oil on canvas, 10 x 8 ins / 25 x 21 cm) EUR 5,800. ROME, 17 May 2004, *Vanitas* (oil on canvas, 10 x 8 ins / 25 x 21 cm) EUR 5,700.

SAINT ÉTIENNE (Mme)
French, 19th century.
Painter. Interiors, flowers.

Mme Saint Étienne exhibited at the Paris Salon in 1835 and 1836.

SAINT LUC. See **SANTO LUCA**

SAINT MARC. See **MONNAUD Émile**

SAINT MARY MAGDALENE, Master of. See **MASTER OF MARY MAGDALENE**

SAINT PAULL
Australian, 20th century.
Active in France.
Painter. Figures.

AUCTION RECORDS:
PARIS, 10 Nov 1987, *Portrait of a Woman with a Hat* (oil on canvas, 36 1/4 x 28 3/4 ins / 92 x 73 cm) FRF 2,500.

SAINT VIL, Murat
Haitian, 20th - 21st century.
Born 1955.
Painter. Landscapes.

AUCTION RECORDS:
PARIS, 13 June 1994, *Imaginary Garden* (oil on canvas, 23 1/4 x 35 ins / 59 x 89 cm) FRF 8,000; *Landscape with Tree* (oil on

canvas, 16 1/4 x 20 ins / 41 x 51 cm) FRF 6,000. PARIS, 12 June 1995, *Landscape with Flowers* (oil on canvas, 20 x 24 ins / 51 x 61 cm) FRF 7,200. PARIS, 25 May 1997, *Waterfall* (acrylic/panel, 8 1/4 x 10 1/4 ins / 21 x 26 cm) FRF 3,500.

SAINT-ACHER, F.
17th century.
Painter. Genre scenes, still-lifes.
Saint-Acher is known for *Partridge* (in Berlin) and *Fruit and Silverware* (in The Hague).

SAINT-ALBAN, Michel de
French, 20th century.
Born 1921 or 1923.
Painter, sculptor. Landscapes, waterscapes.
Pre-Impressionist in style and still suggestive of Corot, Michel de Saint-Alban's paintings heighten the pale colours of river scenes. He also painted landscapes of Sologne and a series devoted to Venice. He exhibited at the Salon d'Art Libre from 1955, the Salon des Artistes Français from 1970, the Salon des Indépendants from 1972, and the Salon d'Automne from 1970 to 1984. He held solo exhibitions at: 1947, 1949, the Galerie de France, Paris; 1951, 1952, the Galerie Riquelme, Biarritz; 1984, the Château-Musée, Blois; 1986, 1987, the Galerie Vendôme, Paris.

SAINT ALBAN

AUCTION RECORDS:
NEUILLY, 3 Feb 1991, *Stillness* (1989, bronze, 11 3/4 x 7 ins / 30 x 18 cm) FRF 12,000. ST-JEAN-CAP-FERRAT, 16 March 1993, *Storm on a Lake* (1966, oil on canvas, 39 1/4 x 57 3/4 ins / 100 x 147 cm) FRF 18,000.

SAINT-ALBIN, Hortensine de.
See **ROUSSELIN-CORBEAU DE SAINT-ALBIN**

SAINT-AMAND, Robert de
French, 19th century.
Born in Chartres.
Painter. History painting.
Robert de Saint-Amand was a student of Paul. Delaroche. He first exhibited at the Salon of 1869.
AUCTION RECORDS:
PARIS, 13-14 Dec 1897, *Lolotte's Foreboding*, FRF 65.

SAINT-AMOUR, de
French, 18th century.
Painter.
De Saint-Amour worked in 1753. He painted *Virgin and St Anne* in the church of St Germain in Sully-sur-Loire.

SAINT-AMOUR, Jean de
French, 18th century.
Active c. 1711.
Draughtsman. Equestrian portraits.
MUSEUMS AND GALLERIES:
LONDON (British Mus.): *Riders* (four drawings).

SAINT-AMOUR, Pierre Louis Jules de
French, 19th century.
Born 5 June 1800, in Zutkerque; died 11 December 1861, in St-Omer.
Painter. Urban landscapes.
MUSEUMS AND GALLERIES:
ST-OMER: *Place de Béthune*.

SAINT-ANDRÉ, Ambroise de Lignereux
French, 19th - 20th century.
Born 6 July 1861, in Paris.
Sculptor.
Ambroise de Lignereux Saint-André, a pupil of Barrias, exhibited from 1909 at the Salon des Artistes Français, of which he was awarded the Hors concours. He was awarded medals and made a Chevalier of the Légion d'Honneur.

SAINT-ANDRÉ, Bernard de
French, 17th century.
Painter, engraver. Religious subjects, genre scenes.
Bernard de Saint-André produced engravings of 46 sculptures, dating from 1695, after Le Brun's *Apollo Gallery*.

SAINT-ANGE, Pierre. See **POTERLET**

SAINT-ANGE CHASSELAT, Henri Jean.
See **CHASSELAT Henri Jean Saint-Ange**

SAINT-ANGE-DESMAISONS, Louis or Ange Henri Louis
French, 19th century.
Born 30 April 1780, in Paris; died after 1831.
Draughtsman, engraver (burin).
Louis Saint-Ange-Desmaisons was a student of David, Percier, Brongniart and Vaudoyer. He was a draughtsman at the Sèvres factory. He engraved after Giraudet and also produced some book illustrations. He may be the same as the Desmaisons to whom the following plates are attributed: *Harcourt's Tomb* and five plates for the *Picturesque Journey in Constantinople*, after Melling, as well as many lithograph portraits.
AUCTION RECORDS:
LONDON, 25 June 1981, *Composition for the Canons of the Cathedral of St-Denis* (1827, gouache/parchment, sketch, 19 3/4 x 26 ins / 50 x 66 cm) GBP 900.

SAINT-ANGEL, Pierre Charles Gabriel de
French, 19th century.
Born in Montbreton.
Sculptor.
Pierre Saint-Angel was a student of Dumont, Bonnasieux and Maggesi. He first exhibited at the Salon in 1868.

SAINT-ARMAND, the Elder
French, 18th century.
Born 1723.
Painter (porcelain). Landscapes, birds.
Saint-Armand the Elder worked at the porcelain factory in Sèvres from 1745 to 1755.

SAINT-ARMAND, the Younger
French, 18th century.
Born 1725.
Painter (porcelain). Flowers.
Saint-Armand the Younger worked in the porcelain factory in Sèvres from 1745 to 1755.

SAINT-AUBERT, Antoine François
French, 18th century.
Born 9 April 1715, in Cambrai; died 11 April 1788, in Cambrai.
Painter.
Antoine Saint-Aubert was the son of a gardener. He was sent to Paris by the Archbishop of Saint-Aubin, in order to complete the study of art which he had begun under the local painter and engraver Antoine Taisne. He returned to his home town, where he married in 1741. After a successful career, he proposed the creation of an art school to the Estates General of the Cambrésis region. He became the school's first teacher.

Saint-Aubert appears to have been influenced mainly by Gillot and his school, painting comic and devilish scenes. His colours were somewhat pale, but his design was witty and very pleasing.

St Aubert 1765

Museums and Galleries:
Arras: *Interior of a Tavern; Interior Scene* (two paintings) - Avesnes-lès-Aubert (Church): *Baptism of Clovis* - Cambrai: *View of Cambrai Main Square, during Mardi Gras; Fantasy Scene; Zémire et Azor; Diabolical Scene; Witch's Lair; Self-portrait* - Lille: *Departure for the Hunt; Inside the Village* (two drawings in red chalk).

SAINT-AUBERT, Antoine Louis

French, 19th century.
Born 1 September 1794, in Cambrai; died 16 September or November 1854, in Cambrai.
Painter. Seascapes.

Antoine Saint-Aubert was the student of his father, Louis-Joseph Saint-Aubert.

Museums and Galleries:
Cambrai: *Normandy Coast; Impression of Snow.*

Auction records:
Paris, 7 Dec 1927, *Yacht before the Castle at Dover* (pen and wash) FRF 230.

SAINT-AUBERT, Louis Joseph Nicolas

French, 18th - 19th century.
Born 13 May 1755, in Cambrai; died 12 November 1810, in Cambrai.
Painter. History painting.

Louis Saint-Aubert was the pupil of his father, Antoine Saint-Aubert, and succeeded him at the École de Dessin (school of drawing).

Museums and Galleries:
Cambrai: *Self-portrait; Christ in the Tomb.*

SAINT-AUBIN, Augustin de

French, 18th - 19th century.
Born 3 June 1736, in Paris; died 9 November 1807, in Paris.
Painter (gouache), watercolourist, pastellist, engraver, draughtsman, illustrator.

Augustin de Saint-Aubin was the brother of Charles Germain and Gabriel de Saint-Aubin. The latter taught him before he became the pupil of Fernand and Laurent Cars.

His first exhibited work was an etching, *Indiscretion Avenged*, in 1752. He became acquainted with Gravelot, and engraved the fleurons in the *Decameron*. In 1764 he married Louise Nicolle Gondeau, who may have been his model for *Reciprocal Homage* and *At Least Be Discreet*. He had already become famous for his works *Games of Little Rascals in Paris* and *Fashionable Dress*. Courtois engraved after his drawings *Walk along the Ramparts* and *Fashionable Portraits*.

Saint-Aubin became an associate of the Académie Royale in 1771, and in the same year he exhibited four portraits, drawn from nature, and 18 portraits engraved after Cochin. He never finished his reception pieces, *J.-B. Le Moyne*, after Tocqué, and *Silvestre*, after Greuze. In 1773 he exhibited further portraits and the drawings *Concert* and *Decorated Ball*. In 1776 he was made engraver to the King's library. The following year he sent red chalk and wash drawings to the Salon, after engraved stones from the study of the Duke of Orléans. From that point, he produced drawn or engraved portraits almost without interruption. In 1793 he exhibited *Jupiter and Leda*, after Veronese, and *Venus Anadyomene*, after Titian.

Of the many portraits engraved by Saint-Aubin, those produced after Cochin deserve a special mention, including *Madame de Pompadour, Moreau the Younger, Fombert, Cars* and *Mariette*. He engraved his own works, the most famous of which are *At Least Be Discreet* and *Count on My Word*. Duclos engraved *Concert* and *Decorated Ball* after Saint-Aubin.

Saint-Aubin's considerable output comprised more than 1,300 works which have been catalogued by E. Bocher.

Bibliography:
Viatte, Françoise, '*Le Livre des Saint-Aubin au département des Arts graphiques*' in *Revue du Louvre* n° 3 p. 19, periodical, Paris, June 2001.

Museums and Galleries:
Paris (Louvre): drawings from 'Livre des St-Aubin'.

Auction records:
Paris, 1880, *Young Prince Driving a Plough* (pen and Indian ink) FRF 780. Paris, 1883, *Walk on the Paris Ramparts* (pen drawing with bistre wash, heightened with white) FRF 12,200. Paris, 1894, *Walk on the Ramparts* (sepia) FRF 14,500. Paris, 1896, *St-Cloud Ball at Griel's; Fireworks at Griel's* (two pen and sepia drawings heightened with white) FRF 11,100. Paris, 15-17 Feb 1897, *Portrait of Augustin de St-Aubin* (bistre/outlines in pen and ink) FRF 15,100; *At Least Be Discreet* (lead pencil drawing; body lightly coloured in watercolour) FRF 18,500. Paris, 1898, *Portrait of the Princess of Lamballe* (stump drawing coloured with carmine) FRF 8,100. Paris, 1899, *Woman in a Muff* (drawing) FRF 10,100; *Portrait of Mlle de Fursy* (drawing) FRF 6,400. Paris, 16-19 June 1919, *Portrait of a Young Woman* (black chalk) FRF 4,000. Paris, 8 March 1920, *Portrait of a Woman* (pencil) FRF 2,000. Paris, 18 June 1920, *Portrait of the Artist's Wife* (lead pencil) FRF 5,000. Paris, 29-30 Nov 1920, *Full-length Portrait of a Young Woman, Wearing Court Dress; Queen's Gown, Lady's Hat* (two drawings) FRF 25,000. Paris, 15 April 1921, *Portrait of Mme de St-Aubin* (lead pencil heightened with watercolour) FRF 20,300. Paris, 12 March 1926, *Portrait of Mme Salmon* (lead pencil) FRF 530. London, 6 May 1926, *Le Duo* (gouache) GBP 250. Paris, 1 June 1928, *Reciprocal Homage* (pencil heightened) FRF 40,000; *Portrait of a Lady* (lead pencil) FRF 8,000. London, 24 April 1929, *Madame de Genlis* (black chalk attributed) GBP 32. Paris, 13-15 May 1929, *Portrait of the Artist; Portrait of the Artist's Wife* (two drawings) FRF 12,000; *Portrait of the Artist's Wife* (drawing) FRF 90,000; *Walkers in the Gardens of the Colisée, Paris* (drawing) FRF 76,000; *Portrait of Charles de St-Aubin* (drawing) FRF 11,500. Paris, 1-2 Dec 1932, *Walkers in the Gardens of the Colisée in Paris* (pencil and wash lightly watercoloured) FRF 46,000. Paris, 14 Dec 1935, *Portrait of a Young Woman* (lead pencil) FRF 5,200. Paris, 14 May 1936, *Portrait of Corinville the Elder, of the Théâtre Patriotique* (black chalk) FRF 1,000. Paris, 14 Dec 1936, *Painter in Love* (red chalk) FRF 1,020. Paris, 22 Feb 1937, *Portrait of Gluck* (pencil) FRF 9,500. London, 24 June 1938, *Portrait of the Artist* (drawing) GBP 35. Paris, 13 Feb 1939, *Solemn Procession at Versailles for the Opening of the Estates General* (pen and Indian ink wash) FRF 2,000. Paris, 30 June-1 July 1941, *Embroidery Seller* (pen and wash) FRF 22,100. Paris, 3 July 1941, *Walk on the Ramparts in Paris* (1760, lead pencil and black chalk) FRF 70,000. Paris, 20 Nov 1941, *Bust of a Young Woman* (black chalk and stump, lightly heightened with sanguine) FRF 2,600. Paris, 28 Nov 1941, *Smallholding* (pen and ink wash) FRF 6,600. Paris, 31 March 1943, *Louis XVI Ploughing* (chalk and sepia wash) FRF 5,600. Paris, 4 Dec 1944, *Young Woman in Profile* (black chalk heightened with vermilion) FRF 4,000. Paris, 8 Feb 1945, *Walk on the Ramparts of Paris* (1760, lead pencil and black chalk) FRF 230,000; *Embroidery Seller* (pen and wash) FRF 100,000. Paris, 8 July 1949, *Sleeping Woman* (lead pencil, attributed) FRF 5,200. Paris, 23 June 1950, *Venus and Cupid* (lead pencil, heightened with pastel, watercolour and wash) FRF 380,000. Paris, 15 Jan 1951, *People at the Entrance to a Cave* (bistre wash and Indian ink, attributed) FRF 190,000. Paris, 21 March 1952, *Portrait Presumed to be of Madame Helman*, FRF 380,000. Paris, 4 June 1958, *Self-portrait of Augustin de St-Aubin* (pen, wash) FRF 650,000. Paris, 28 March 1963, *Maternal Tenderness; Maternal Concern* (two watercolours) FRF 15,500. London, 13 Dec 1984, *Portrait of the Artist's Wife* (pencil and touches of red chalk and watercolour,

7 3/4 x 5 1/2 ins / 19.9 x 13.8 cm) GBP 5,000. PARIS, 29 Nov 1985, *Portrait of a Woman* (1776, lead pencil and outlines in red chalk, oval, 5 x 4 1/4 ins / 12.5 x 11 cm) FRF 5,100. PARIS, 12 Dec 1988, *Portrait of the Baroness of... (Louise-Émilie)* (black chalk and watercolour, 6 1/4 x 5 1/4 ins / 15.6 x 13.2 cm) FRF 55,000. NEW YORK, 15 Jan 1992, *Portrait Presumed To Be of the Artist's Wife; Self-portrait* (1767, lead pencil heightened with white, each 3 1/4 x 2 1/4 ins / 8.3 x 5.8 cm) USD 5,500. LONDON, 6 July 1992, *Portrait of a Man in Profile* (black chalk, diam. 5 ins / 12.7 cm) GBP 2,420. PARIS, 9 Dec 1992, *Queen's Gown and Lady's Hat; Court Gown Adorned with Interlaced Gauze* (lead pencil and watercolour, a pair, 9 3/4 x 7 1/4 ins / 25 x 18.5 cm) FRF 30,000. NEW YORK, 11 Jan 1994, *Portrait of a Young Woman Wearing a White Bonnet, Left Profile* (black chalk and ink, 6 1/4 x 4 3/4 ins / 15.9 x 12.2 cm) USD 4,600. LONDON, 4 July 1994, *Design for a Medal Celebrating the Birth of the Dauphin* (ink and white chalk, 7 x 7 ins / 18 x 17.5 cm) GBP 4,830. PARIS, 22 March 1995, *Bust of a Young Woman* (lead pencil, diam. 2 1/2 ins / 6.5 cm) FRF 10,000. PARIS, 25 Nov 1997, *Portrait of a Young Woman in Profile* (black chalk, diam. 2 1/4 ins / 6 cm) FRF 3,000. NEW YORK, 23 Jan 2001, *Portraits of the Artist and his Wife in Clandestine Communication* (black chalk, watercolour and colour wash, two, 8 x 6 ins / 20 x 15 cm) USD 10,000. PARIS, 14 Dec 2001, *Commissionnaire* (black chalk, 7 x 5 ins / 19 x 13 cm) FRF 70,000. PARIS, 6 Feb 2002, *Portrait of Gluck* (crayon, miniature) EUR 1,900. LONDON, 11 April 2002, *Studies of Young Women Undressing, Nude, Eating at their Toilet* (black lead, 8 x 7 ins / 21 x 17 cm) GBP 2,800. PARIS, 24 March 2003, *Embroidery Seller* (pen and ink wash, 5 x 3 ins / 12 x 7 cm) EUR 4,500. NEW YORK, 22 Jan 2004, *Bare-breasted Woman Leaning over a Pedestal, a Woman in the Background* (black chalk and graphite, 7 x 5 ins / 18 x 13 cm) USD 3,200. PARIS, 23 June 2004, *Portrait Presumed to be of the Engraver Nicolas Cochin* (1769, graphite) EUR 3,500.

SAINT-AUBIN, Catherine Louise

French, 18th century.

Born 5 April 1727; died 8 January 1805.

Engraver, draughtswoman.

Catherine Saint-Aubin engraved in particular views of Mont Saint-Michel.

SAINT-AUBIN, Charles Germain de

French, 18th century.

Born 17 January 1721, in Paris; died 6 March 1786, in Paris.

Painter, watercolourist, draughtsman, engraver (etching), decorative designer. Genre scenes, interiors with figures, flowers. Designs (embroidery).

Charles de Saint-Aubin was firstly the pupil of his father, the embroiderer Gabriel-Germain de Saint-Aubin. He then worked in Dutro's studio, where he studied ornamental decoration. He worked with his father until 1745, when he left the family home and moved to the Rue de la Vellerie. In 1751 he married Françoise Trouvé, and became costume designer to the king; in 1759 he lost his wife. He went to Flanders in 1770 and visited art collections, and in the following year he went to Lyons and Provence.

Saint-Aubin had the patronage of Madame de Pompadour, who ordered a box of Chinese colours for him. When he was not producing decorative works, he studied flowers. He spent 40 years producing 250 watercolour studies, brought together in *Livre de Fleurs* (*Book of Flowers*), depicting imaginary flowers beside many pages painted from nature.

Like his brothers Gabriel and Augustin, Charles de Saint-Aubin was an engraver. He signed two series of plates entitled *Mes Petits Bouquets* (*My Small Bouquets*) and *Les Fleurettes* (*Little Flowers*). He also produced two series of etchings, *Essais de Papillonneries Humaines*, in which the bizarre mingles with the graceful. His portrait by a girl from the Saint-Aubin family was engraved by J. de Goncourt.

He produced one of the most famous collections of the 18th century, known as *Livre des Saint-Aubin* (*Book of the Saint-Aubin Family*), which brought together the work of three generations of artists, 180 drawings from the studios of his six brothers and sisters, as well as those of his daughters.

BIBLIOGRAPHY:

Viatte, Françoise, '*Le Livre des Saint-Aubin au département des Arts graphiques*' in *Revue du Louvre* n° 3 p. 19, periodical, Paris, June 2001.

MUSEUMS AND GALLERIES:

PARIS (Bibliothèque Mazarine): about 100 sketches - PARIS (Louvre): drawings from 'Livre des St-Aubin'.

AUCTION RECORDS:

PARIS, 1883, *Inside the Artist's Studio* (pen, bistre wash and Indian ink, heightened with white) FRF 292. PARIS, 1896, *Panels with Trophies* (lead pencil heightened with white, two drawings) FRF 185. PARIS, 19 March 1924, *Embroidery Pattern* (watercolour) FRF 130. LONDON, 27 Feb 1925, *Presentation*, GBP 157. MONTE CARLO, 11 Feb 1979, *Butterfly Musician* (pen and brown ink and grey wash, 8 1/4 x 6 3/4 ins / 21 x 17 cm) FRF 11,000. PARIS, 26 March 1996, *My Little Bouquets* (etching, dedicated to the Duchess of Chevreuse) FRF 35,000.

SAINT-AUBIN, de

French, 19th century.

Painter. Landscapes with figures, landscapes.

De Saint-Aubin exhibited a *View of the Main Road to Melun in the Forest of Fontainebleau* at the Salon in 1808 and a *Forest Interior* in 1833.

It is believed that this artist, who lived on the Rue des Moulins and whose first name is not recorded, is also Jacques Louis de Saint-Aubin.

Jacques Louis de Saint-Aubin was born in Paris in 1779 and entered the École des Beaux-Arts on the 19 Germinal (seventh month in the French Republican calendar) in year III (April 1795), as a student of Saint-Martin, a landscape painter who lived on the Rue de la Lune. There is another Saint Aubin, called Jean Denis. He was born in Paris in 1786 and entered the École des Beaux-Arts on 20 Fructidor (12th month in the French Republican calendar) in year IX (September 1801); he was a former student of Defresne's free school accepted by Houdon. However, this would make the artist very young to have been accepted by the Salon seven years later in 1808, at the age of 22. Also, he does not appear to have been a student of Saint-Martin.

MUSEUMS AND GALLERIES:

ST-OMER: *Landscape with Figures* (given by the artist in 1833).

SAINT-AUBIN, Françoise de

Maiden name: Trouvé

French, 18th century.

Born to a family originally from Lorraine; died 1759, in Paris.

Draughtswoman.

Françoise Trouvé became Françoise de Saint-Aubin when she married Charles Germain de Saint-Aubin in 1751.

AUCTION RECORDS:

PARIS, 13-15 May 1929, *Portrait of Charles de St-Aubin* (drawing) FRF 5,200.

SAINT-AUBIN, Gabriel Jacques de

French, 18th century.

Born 14 April 1724, in Paris; died 14 February 1780, in Paris.

Painter (gouache), watercolourist, engraver, draughtsman, illustrator. History painting, portraits, genre scenes, landscapes.

Gabriel de Saint-Aubin drew firstly at Sarrasin's studio and then at the Académie Royale under Jeaurat, Colin de Vermont and Boucher. In 1750 he won second prize in the Prix de Rome competition. In 1752 he was not placed, and the competition was won by Fragonard, ahead of Monnet. Monnet won the following year and Saint-Aubin was again placed only second. In 1754 he failed again and did not try again, devoting himself in future to drawing.

From 1750 he produced etchings of *Two Lovers, Market of Fat Oxen, Fair at Bezons* and *Merope*. His *Allegory on the Marriages Made by the City of Paris* was produced in 1751, and in 1752 he engraved his competition piece *Reconciliation of Absalom and David, Allegory on the Birth of the Dauphin* and *Nouvellistes*. In 1753 he reproduced his *Laban* on copper, and signed what was arguably the most charming original French etching of the 18th century, *View of the Louvre Salon*.

From that point, Saint-Aubin devoted himself to works of fantasy and his love of contemporary life.

Above all, he drew, covering the margins of sales catalogues and the margins or flyleaves of Piganiol de la Force's eight-volume *Description de Paris* (*Description of Paris*) with sketches. He also engraved *Four Vases, Charlatan, Petite Poste, Tuileries Show*, and *Street Show* in 1760. In 1761 he exhibited his gouache painting *Open-air Café*. His work *Ball at Auteuil* is dated 1761, the ten etchings of *Fire at the Foire Saint-Germain* are dated 1762, *View of the Salon* is dated 1765, *Arrest* is dated 1770, *Festival at the Colisée*, in gouache, is dated 1772, and *Fire at the Hôtel-Dieu*, in gouache, is dated 1774. At around the same time, he painted *Académie Particulière*, in oil, a small graceful masterpiece, after which he produced an excellent etching. In 1778 he painted another important work, *Naumachia in Monceau Park*.

Saint-Aubin was one of the greatest French masters of draughtsmanship and engraving. His best works link fantasy with a confident style, and both his etchings and his drawings for his own amusement reveal his knowledge of chiaroscuro and his ability to use strong and light touches of his pencil.

BIBLIOGRAPHY:

Dacier, Émile, *Catalogue de ventes et livrets de salons illustrés par Gabriel de Saint-Aubin*, Société de reproduction de dessins de maîtres, Paris, 1909-1921. Dacier, Émile, *L'Œuvre gravé de Gabriel de Saint-Aubin*, Société pour l'Étude de la gravure française, Paris, 1914. Dacier, Émile, *'Gabriel de Saint Aubin, peintre, dessinateur et graveur. Catalogue raisonné'* in *2 vol.*, G. Van Oest, Brussels and Paris, 1929-1931. Dacier, Émile, *Le Carnet de dessins de Gabriel de Saint-Aubin conservé à la Bibliothèque Royale de Stockholm*, F. de Nobele, Paris, 1955. Viatte, Françoise, *'Le Livre des Saint-Aubin au département des Arts graphiques'* in *Revue du Louvre* n° 3 p. 19, periodical, Paris, June 2001.

MUSEUMS AND GALLERIES:

LONDON (Wallace Collection): *A Fête at the Colisée* (1772, ink, water and bodycolour/paper) - PARIS (Collection Destailleur) - PARIS (Collection J. Doucet) - PARIS (Louvre): *View of the 1779 Salon* - PARIS (Mus. Carnavalet).

AUCTION RECORDS:

Jupiter and Leda; Jupiter and Io (black chalk, red chalk and wash, four designs for supra portas) FRF 22,800; *Nymph by Houdon* (pencil) FRF 14,600; *Portrait of a Woman* (pastel) FRF 3,400. PARIS, 1855, *Portrait of Mlle Bordier, from the Nicolet Theatre* (drawing in black pencil heightened with pastels) FRF 5,000. PARIS, 20 May 1873, *Romantic Conversation* (watercolour) FRF 900. PARIS, Feb 1877, *Salon of 1787* (watercolour) FRF 915. PARIS, 1883, *Flower Market* (red chalk heightened with white) FRF 2,500. PARIS, 1896, *Portrait of a Young Woman* (drawing in coloured chalks and pastel) FRF 3,000; *L'Académie Particulière* (lead pencil heightened with watercolour) FRF 4,000. PARIS, 15-17 Feb 1897, *Sundays at St-Cloud* (1792, drawing) FRF 2,100; *Construction of Shops on the Arches of the Pont-Neuf* (1775, red chalk and black chalk, with pen) FRF 7,100. PARIS, 28-29 March 1898, *Seizure by the Bailiff* (drawing heightened with colour) FRF 6,200; *Romantic Conversation* (watercolour) FRF 1,700. PARIS, 17 May 1898, *Allegory of Marriage* (pen drawing with lead pencil, gouache and pastel) FRF 3,305. PARIS, 1899, *Auction Room*, FRF 6,550; *Crowning of Voltaire* (drawing) FRF 5,100; *Staircase* (drawing) FRF 9,000; *Adresse de Périer* (drawing) FRF 6,000. PARIS, 8 May 1919, *Scene from the Opera 'Pyramus and Thisbe'* (pencil heightened with Indian ink and sepia) FRF 1,400; *Allegory on the Erection of the Statue of Louis XV* (lead pencil with touches of wash over tracing of etching) FRF 11,500; *Young Woman Standing on the Seat of a Coach*, FRF 2,000. PARIS, 26-27 May 1919, *View of the Dôme from Panthémont Abbey Built to the Designs of N. Coutant* (1779, pen and watercolour wash) FRF 2,500; *Portrait of the Artist* (black chalk, with scumble and wash) FRF 5,950. PARIS, 19 Dec 1919, *Staircase* (wash) FRF 5,100. PARIS, 6-8 Dec 1920, *Fire at Loges Festival* (drawing) FRF 3,500; *Minuet* (red chalk) FRF 6,700. PARIS, 7-8 May 1923, *Portrait of the Painter Pierre Antoine de Machy* (black chalk and pastel) FRF 8,200; *Jupiter and Antiope; Jupiter and Danae*. LONDON, 28 May 1924, *Allegory of the Birth of the Duke of Berri* (pen and wash) GBP 390. PARIS, 17-18 June 1925, *Sheet from an Album* (pencil, red, pen, wash and watercolour) FRF 7,700; *Dream, Voltaire Writing 'The Maid of Orleans'* (painting/engraving remounted) FRF 76,000. PARIS, 12 March 1926, *Study for the Apotheosis of Romulus* (black chalk and wash) FRF 5,500. LONDON, 6 May 1926, *Troop Inspection* (black chalk, pen and watercolour) GBP 370. PARIS, 21 March 1927, *Meeting at the Tuileries* (drawing) FRF 13,100; *Calumny* (pen and wash) FRF 10,200; *Parisian Sketches* (pencil heightened) FRF 14,000. PARIS, 13 May 1927, *Gathering in the Hall of a Palace*, FRF 40,250. PARIS, 28 March 1928, *Mademoiselle Duthé at the Champs-Élysées* (drawing) FRF 13,100. PARIS, 23 May 1928, *Design for a Bowl* (black chalk) FRF 4,800. PARIS, 10 and 11 Dec 1928, *Fire at the Hôtel-Dieu* (drawing) FRF 75,000. LONDON, 9 May 1929, *Design for a Watch* (pen and wash) GBP 165. PARIS, 13-15 May 1929, *Portrait of Augustin de St-Aubin as a Child* (drawing) FRF 20,000; *Gardener and His Master* (drawing) FRF 19,000. NEW YORK, 11 Dec 1930, *Harp Concert*, USD 1,400. PARIS, 25 June 1931, *Two Heads of Women; Street with a Person* (pen and wash, album page) FRF 3,600. LONDON, 31 May 1932, *Three Studies of Women Getting Dressed* (black chalk) GBP 42. PARIS, 1 and 2 Dec 1932, *Interior of a Show Hall* (pen and bistre wash) FRF 35,000. PARIS, 1 Dec 1933, *Allegory* (drawing with bistre wash heightened with watercolour and gouache) FRF 3,000. PARIS, 7 Dec 1934, *Concert Hall* (drawing in black pencil) FRF 6,100. LONDON, 4 Dec 1935, *Two Women in an Interior* (black chalk) GBP 385; *Romantic Gardener* (black chalk) GBP 78; *Scene at the Tuileries* (black chalk) GBP 110. PARIS, 14 May 1936, *Young Mother* (pen and watercolour) FRF 5,300; *Sacrifice of Iphigenia* (black chalk, pen and wash) FRF 3,000. PARIS, 12 June 1936, *Family Scene* (black chalk) FRF 5,000. PARIS, 30 Nov-1 Dec 1936, *Sage the Chemist's Classes at the Paris Mint* (1779, black chalk with Indian ink) FRF 73,000; *Visit of Christian VII, King of Denmark, to the school of the Académie Royale de peinture et de sculpture* (pen, pencil, Indian ink wash heightened with gouache) FRF 31,000. PARIS, 22 Feb 1937, *Harp Lesson* (pen and sepia wash/lead pencil) FRF 6,000. PARIS, 26 May 1937, *Portrait of a Man* (watercolour) FRF 2,450. PARIS, 15 June 1938, *Open-air Café on the Outskirts of Paris* (pen and bistre wash) FRF 57,000; *Gardener and His Master*, FRF 8,200. LONDON, 24 June 1938, *G. and*

Rose de St-Aubin (drawing) GBP 173; *L'académie Particulière*, GBP 399. PARIS, 9 March 1939, *Andromeda at the Rock; Roger and Angelica; Young Woman at the Spring; Bust of a Young Woman with Inclined Head; Statue* (black chalk, sheet of sketches) FRF 1,300. PARIS, 3 July 1941, *Allegory* (1772, pen and Indian ink) FRF 34,000. PARIS, 20 Nov 1941, *Book of Sketches by Gabriel de St-Aubin* (drawing, collection comprising 108 pages) FRF 860,000; *Catalogue of Paintings and Sculptures by Le Quesnoy and Other Masters* (dated 1774, drawings or sketches in black chalk, 58 illustrated pages containing around 180 works) FRF 115,000. PARIS, 6 July 1942, *Catalogue of Works, Prints etc. from the Office of the President of Lyert, Lord of Andilly and Other Places* (black chalk, illustrated with around 40 sketches in the margins) FRF 24,500. PARIS, 5 March 1943, *Sultanas in a Palace* (Indian ink) FRF 8,000; *Catalogue of Works, Prints, etc. from the Office of the President of Lyert*, FRF 40,000. PARIS, 7 Jan 1947, *View of Paris with Figures* (drawing, attributed) FRF 20,000. PARIS, 8 July 1949, *Portrait Presumed to Be of the Countess of Choiseul, Wearing Hunting Clothes* (black chalk) FRF 42,000. PARIS, 1 March 1950, *France Nourishing the Geniuses of the Arts* (1760, pen and wash) FRF 70,000. PARIS, 9 March 1951, *Salon at the Louvre* (pen, watercolour wash heightened with white) FRF 800,000. PARIS, 3 Dec 1957, *Meeting at the Tuileries near the Statue of Antinous* (lead pencil and pen) FRF 1,250,000. PARIS, 21 March 1958, *The Académie d'architecture Entering the Louvre* (pencil, Indian ink and touches of watercolour) FRF 2,050,000. LONDON, 10 June 1959, *Seated Woman Reading* (pencil, black chalk, pen and brown ink) GBP 1,100. LONDON, 10 May 1961, *Ceremony in Notre-Dame in Paris* (wash, pen and ink/charcoal) GBP 300. LONDON, 26 June 1963, *L'Académie Particulière*, GBP 5,000. VERSAILLES, 23 June 1968, *Bridal Procession*, FRF 41,000. LONDON, 7 June 1974, *Self-portrait*, Gns 950. MONTE CARLO, 11 Feb 1979, *Salon of 1757 at the Louvre* (watercolour and gouache, 5 1/2 x 6 1/2 ins / 14 x 16.2 cm) FRF 85,000. MONTE CARLO, 26 Nov 1979, *La Régence Coffee House in 1771* (pen and wash heightened with black chalk, 7 1/2 x 6 ins / 19.1 x 15.3 cm) FRF 60,000. BERN, 20 June 1980, *View of the Fair at Bezons near Paris* (1750, etching) CHF 5,200. PARIS, 9 Dec 1981, *Draughtsmen* (1780, black chalk and stump, 6 3/4 x 9 ins / 17 x 23 cm) FRF 43,000. LONDON, 27 June 1984, *Market of Fattened Oxen* (etching and dry-point, 5 1/2 x 6 3/4 ins / 13.9 x 17.1 cm) GBP 10,000. MONTE CARLO, 8 Dec 1984, *Nude: Studio of a Draughtsman* (oil on canvas, 22 3/4 x 18 ins / 58 x 46 cm) FRF 80,000. LONDON, 13 Dec 1984, *'Le retour desiré...'* (black chalk, blue, pink and yellow pastel/blue paper, 9 x 11 ins / 22 x 28.2 cm) GBP 8,000. PARIS, 23 Oct 1985, *Draughtsman* (black chalk and coloured pencil, 6 x 4 1/4 ins / 15 x 11 cm) FRF 110,000. PARIS, 4 Dec 1986, *Poet's Reward* (oil on canvas, 37 3/4 x 51 1/4 ins / 96 x 130 cm) FRF 3,100,000. PARIS, 4 Dec 1986, *Poet's Reward* (1759, oil on canvas, 37 3/4 x 51 1/4 ins / 96 x 130 cm) FRF 3,100,000. LONDON, 4 Dec 1987, *Roman Procession* (etching, 9 x 15 3/4 ins / 22.8 x 40.2 cm) USD 4,500. PARIS, 19 Feb 1988, *Allegory on the Marriage of the Count of Provence* (1771, etching) FRF 57,000. LONDON, 2 July 1990, *Gardener and His Master from Sedaine* (ink and wash/black chalk, frontispiece, sketch, 5 x 3 ins / 12.5 x 7.9 cm) GBP 24,200. NEW YORK, 9 Jan 1991, *Young Lord Lying, His Hands and a Flower* (black and white chalk, red chalk and ink, study, 5 x 7 3/4 ins / 13 x 20 cm) USD 154,000. NEW YORK, 22-23 March 1991, *Portrait of the Count of Artois Carrying the Duke of Angoulême as a Baby* (1776, black chalk and ink, 6 1/4 x 4 ins / 16.1 x 10.4 cm) USD 26,400. NEW YORK, 14 Jan 1992, *Apollo and Mars Arguing over a Game of Chess Surrounded by Jupiter, Juno and Other Gods Brandishing Chess Pieces With Time on the Left* (1775, ink and wash, 5 x 6 3/4 ins / 12.5 x 17.4 cm) USD 46,200. PARIS, 19 Nov 1992, *Scene from Ancient History* (brown ink and grey wash, 9 1/2 x 7 ins / 24 x 18 cm) FRF 13,000. PARIS, 3 Feb 1993, *Damian the Villain* (etching, 5 3/4 x 5 ins / 14.7 x 12.8 cm) FRF 8,000. NEW YORK, 10 Jan 1996, *La Régence Café in 1771, with J.J. Rousseau Reading in the Foreground* (ink and wash, 7 1/2 x 6 ins / 19.1 x 15 cm, 1 1/4 ins/3 cm) USD 20,700. PARIS, 22 March 1996, *Nude Man Seated* (lead pencil, six studies, 9 x 12 3/4 ins / 22 x 32.2 cm) FRF 19,000. PARIS, 27 Nov 1997, *View of the Louvre Salon in 1753* (etching, first proof of four, 5 1/4 x 6 3/4 ins / 13.6 x 17.3 cm) FRF 155,000. NEW YORK, 28 Jan 1999, *Interior Scene, Woman and Two Children Received by Gentlemen* (oil on canvas, 41 x 37 ins / 105 x 94 cm) USD 25,000. PARIS, 26 Nov 1999, *Scene of Ancient Sacrifice* (1769, black chalk, stump and grey wash, 8 x 7 ins / 21 x 18 cm) FRF 40,000. PARIS, 31 March 2000, *The Little Milliner, with Repeat of the Head* (crayons squared with red chalk, 7 x 5 ins / 19 x 13 cm) FRF 290,000. PARIS, 6 Dec 2000, *Three Girls Drawing* (black chalk and brown ink) FRF 170,000. PARIS, 23 March 2001, *Paris Welcoming King Christian VII of Denmark* (1768, black crayon, 4 x 7 ins / 10 x 17 cm) FRF 190,000. PARIS, 23 March 2001, *Pfaff's 'Birth of Venus', Sculptural Sketch, Seated Woman, Young Man* (black crayon, colour ink, gouache, watercolour and red chalk, 9 x 6 ins / 22 x 15 cm) FRF 820,000. PARIS, 21 March 2002, *Design for a Vignette* (1767, chalk, pen and ink wash, 5 x 7 ins / 12 x 18 cm) EUR 110,000. PARIS, 21 March 2002, *Regattas* (chalk, pen, ink wash, 9 x 7 ins / 22 x 17 cm) EUR 150,000. PARIS, 27 March 2003, *Officer on the Stairs* (chalk and wash, 7 x 5 ins / 17 x 13 cm) EUR 5,000. PARIS, 31 March 2003, *Warm Hand* (pen and ink wash, 4 x 6 ins / 10 x 16 cm) EUR 5,200. PARIS, 19 March 2004, *Battle of Ecnomus Won at Sea by the Romans* (watercolour, gouache, pen, colour ink, black pencil, 8 x 16 ins / 21 x 40 cm) EUR 155,000. PARIS, 19 March 2004, *Triumph of Pompey in Rome* (watercolour, gouache, pen, black ink, pencil, 8 x 15 ins / 21 x 39 cm) EUR 265,000.

SAINT-AUBIN, J.
British, 18th - 19th century.
Painter. Portraits.

J. Saint-Aubin exhibited in London from 1795 to 1802, showing predominantly miniatures.

SAINT-AUBIN, Jacques Louis de. See the entry **SAINT-AUBIN de**

SAINT-AUBIN, Jeanne de. See **PEYRE Jeanne**

SAINT-AUBIN, Louis
French, 19th century.
Draughtsman.

Louis St Aubin was the nephew of Augustin Saint-Aubin. He settled in Russia. The library of the Winter palace in St Petersburg owns 34 drawings by him.

SAINT-AUBIN, Louis Michel de
French, 18th century.
Born 20 March 1731, in Paris; died 24 December 1779, in Paris.
Painter.

In 1764 Louis de Saint-Aubin worked at the porcelain factory in Sèvres as a porcelain painter.

SAINT-AUBIN, Pougin de. See **POUGIN DE SAINT AUBIN**

SAINT-AUBIN Y BONNEFON, Alejandro
Spanish, 19th - 20th century.
Born 20 January 1857, in Madrid; died 24 May 1916, in Madrid.
Painter. Genre scenes, figures.

Pupil of Lizcano; also worked as an art critic.

MUSEUMS AND GALLERIES:
MADRID (Prado): *Deceived and Defeated*.

SAINT-AUBYN, Catherine
British, 18th - 19th century.

Born 6 September 1760, in London; died 21 October 1836, in Truro.
Engraver (etching).
Catherine Saint-Aubyn engraved landscapes and portraits.

SAINT-AULAIRE, Félix Achille
French, 19th century.
Born 1801, in Vercelli.
Painter, lithographer. Seascapes.
Felix St-Aulaire was a student of Garnerey and his son. He exhibited at the Salon in 1827 and 1838. He mainly produced seascape lithographs.

SAINT-BEAUSSANT, Alphonse de
French, 19th century.
Born 1842.
Pastellist.
Alphonse de Saint-Beaussant was a student of Maréchal.
MUSEUMS AND GALLERIES:
NANCY (MBA): *Pines* (Italian landscape).

SAINT-BOMRET, Gabrielle de, or Bonnais
French, 19th century.
Born in Paris.
Painter. Landscapes.
Gabrielle Saint-Bomfret was a student of Cassagne, Mme Laston, Lalaisse and Prosper Guerrin. She first exhibited at the Salon in 1865.

SAINT-BRICE, Robert
Haitian, 20th century.
Born 1898; died 1973.
Painter. Figures, portraits, scenes with figures.
Robert Saint-Brice showed work in the collective exhibitions of Haitian art *Haitian Art in the Angela Gross Collection* at the Woodmere Art Museum in Philadelphia (1984-1985) and in *Masters of Haitian Painting in the Siri von Reis Collection* in the Los Angeles Museum of Afro-American Art (1984-1986).

He was a Voodoo painter, using flour and coffee dregs to sketch the scenes inducing a trance state, before turning to painting.
AUCTION RECORDS:
PARIS, 29 June 1976, *Face* (oil on canvas, 30 x 24 ins / 76 x 61 cm) FRF 3,100. NEW YORK, 30 May 1984, *Untitled* (1954, oil on card, 27 1/4 x 21 1/4 ins / 69.4 x 53.8 cm) USD 1,600. NEW YORK, 15 May 1991, *Woman* (oil on canvas/card, 60 x 32 ins / 152.5 x 81.5 cm) USD 8,800. NEW YORK, 19-20 May 1992, *The Loas Twins* (1955, oil on canvas, 68 x 35 ins / 172.7 x 88.9 cm) USD 9,350. PARIS, 17 May 1993, *Loa* (1971, oil, 24 x 20 ins / 61 x 50.5 cm) FRF 57,000. NEW YORK, 15 Nov 1994, *Adam and Eve* (1959, oil/synthetic resin, 30 3/4 x 26 1/2 ins / 78.3 x 67 cm) USD 3,450. NEW YORK, 24 Feb 1995, *Witchdoctor* (1955, oil/synthetic resin, 24 x 20 ins / 61 x 50.8 cm) USD 2,990.

SAINT-CLAIR, Jean Nicolas
French.
Born in Arras.
Painter.
MUSEUMS AND GALLERIES:
CHERBOURG: *Vows of Love by the Fountain* (oil on canvas).

SAINT-COLUMKILLE. See **COLUMBA**

SAINT-CRICQ, Robert
French, 20th century.
Born 21 December 1924, in Paris.
Painter, assemblage artist.
Robert Saint-Cricq studied at the École des Beaux-Arts in Paris, where he lives and works. He first exhibited in 1950. His output falls into two categories: paintings and 'boxes' that are assemblages of the most varied materials. In both, but most evidently in the paintings, Saint-Cricq seems concerned to depict the human silhouette. In a new version of the Platonic cave image, Saint-Criqc presents allusions, indefinite and hiding shadows that inhabit a space that is also hypothetical. These ghosts and ectoplasmic figures are very characteristic of his paintings. His *Boxes* are suggestive of ex-votos and sometimes recall landscapes, especially in the *Bathing Huts* series.

SAINT-CYR, Yvonne de
French, 20th century.
Born in Paris.
Painter. Local scenes, scenes with figures.
Yvonne de Saint-Cyr travelled extensively, specialising in Tahitian scenes. She exhibited in Paris in the Colonial Section from 1930, at the Salon des Artistes Français, the Salon d'Automne, the Salon des Indépendants from 1931, and in Noumea, Sydney, Tahiti and, at the Colonial Exhibition of 1931, in New York.
MUSEUMS AND GALLERIES:
PARIS (former Mus. des Colonies).

SAINT-DALMAS, F. Emeric de
British, 19th century.
Active in Guernsey.
Draughtsman, engraver (etching).
Emeric de Saint-Damlas exhibited in London from 1872 to 1880, notably at the Royal Academy and the Suffolk Street Gallery, and published a number of etchings in *The Etcher* and *English Etching*.
MUSEUMS AND GALLERIES:
LONDON (Victoria and Albert Mus.): nine etchings.

SAINT-DÉLIS, Henri Liénard de
French, 20th century.
Born 4 April 1878, in Marconne; died 15 November 1949, in Honfleur.
Painter, watercolourist. Landscapes with figures, landscapes, seascapes.
Henri Liénard de Saint-Délis was the son of a Dragoons officer who died young. The family went to live in Le Havre in 1885. At his lycée, Henri Saint-Délis was in the same class as Othon Friesz and they became life-long friends. Both Friesz and he studied at the École des Beaux-Arts, Le Havre, where they were pupils of Charles Lullier, a former pupil of Ingres, and it was there they met Jongkind. He also met Dufy, Braque, Lecourt and Copieux. When Dufy left for Paris, Henri de Saint-Délis followed him, but he stayed there only a year, attending Jean Paul Laurens's studio in 1900, visiting the museums and discovering the Impressionists. He returned to Le Havre and lived a cheerful life with his companions until, in 1905, he contracted tuberculosis and had to spend 12 years in a Swiss sanatorium. His brother René used to visit him and bring back his paintings of the mountains to show to his old studio colleagues. Most of his Swiss output was destroyed during a bombardment of Le Havre in 1944. When he returned to Normandy in about 1920 he moved from Le Havre to Honfleur. It is a pity his Swiss paintings were almost entirely destroyed; from what remains, it seems this period was influenced by Fauvism, maybe as a result of his friendship with Friesz. The colour is lively and the composition organised in broad arabesques. He painted the main body of his work in Honfleur - a few portraits and still-lifes, but above all landscapes depicting the coast, the countryside and the port. He also produced a watercolour every day. His Honfleur paintings are alert and fresh, their drawing deliberately sketchy. We could say that Saint-Délis was to Honfleur what Mathieu Verdilhan was to the coast of Marseilles.

He seems to have exhibited regularly at the Salon des Indépendants, Paris, from 1905. Two solo shows of his work were held during his lifetime - in Paris in 1945, and in Rouen in 1948. Retrospectives were held in 1950 at the École des Beaux-Arts, Le Havre, in 1953 at the Hôtel de Ville, Honfleur, in 1954 in Paris, in 1955 in London, in 1961 in Paris, in 1963 in Paris, Honfleur and Le Havre and in 1965 and 1971 in Honfleur.

H. de St Delis

BIBLIOGRAPHY:
Fischer, Jean, *Henri de Saint-Délis*, exhibition catalogue, Grenier à Sel, Honfleur, 1965.
MUSEUMS AND GALLERIES:
ROUEN: *Port of Honfleur.*
AUCTION RECORDS:
PARIS, 3 April 1925, *View of Honfleur*, FRF 65. PARIS, 13 July 1942, *Three-masters in Port*, FRF 800. PARIS, 20 Dec 1948, *Toys*, FRF 1,200. PARIS, 10 Nov 1954, *Fishing Port at Low Tide* (watercolour) FRF 24,000. LE HAVRE, 30 April 1966, *'The Normandie' Leaving, the Blue Ribbon*, FRF 9,000. VERSAILLES, 6 Dec 1970, *Coastal View of Honfleur*, FRF 8,200. HONFLEUR, 25 Feb 1973, *Public Garden in Honfleur*, FRF 15,500. VERSAILLES, 19 May 1976, *The 14th of July* (watercolour and gouache, 13 1/4 x 18 3/4 ins / 33.5 x 47.5 cm) FRF 4,150. LE HAVRE, 25 June 1976, *Swiss Landscape* (oil on canvas, 21 1/4 x 25 1/2 ins / 54 x 65 cm) FRF 16,000. HONFLEUR, 17 July 1977, *Former Wooden Jetty of Honfleur* (oil on canvas, 15 x 22 ins / 38 x 55 cm) FRF 12,000. ROUEN, 18 March 1979, *Church of Leysin in Snow* (watercolour, 12 1/2 x 19 3/4 ins / 32 x 50 cm) FRF 5,500. HONFLEUR, 15 July 1979, *Port of Fécamp* (oil on canvas, 23 1/2 x 28 1/4 ins / 60 x 72 cm) FRF 30,000. HONFLEUR, 19 April 1981, *Exit from the Port of Honfleur* (oil on panel, 9 x 13 1/2 ins / 23 x 34 cm) FRF 11,500. PARIS, 15 Dec 1982, *Boats in Honfleur* (oil on panel, 11 1/2 x 28 1/4 ins / 29.5 x 72 cm) FRF 25,000. HONFLEUR, 3 April 1983, *Capital in the Old Square of Honfleur* (watercolour, 18 1/2 x 24 ins / 47 x 61 cm) FRF 19,000. VERSAILLES, 11 Dec 1983, *Honfleur, Boats in the Port* (oil on canvas, 15 x 18 ins / 38 x 46 cm) FRF 18,000. HONFLEUR, 7 April 1985, *Swiss Landscape in Snow* (1912, watercolour, 9 x 11 1/2 ins / 22 x 29 cm) FRF 11,000. PARIS, 10 Dec 1986, *Fishing Port* (oil on canvas, 18 x 22 ins / 46 x 55 cm) FRF 60,000. HONFLEUR, 12 July 1987, *House and Garden of the Painter Gernez* (oil on canvas, 20 x 26 ins / 51 x 66 cm) FRF 70,000. PARIS, 7 Dec 1987, *Honfleur, Boats Moored in front of the White Horse* (watercolour, 12 x 17 1/4 ins / 30.5 x 44 cm) FRF 9,000. CALAIS, 4 March 1990, *Three-masters in Port* (watercolour, 17 3/4 x 24 ins / 45 x 61 cm) FRF 23,000. PARIS, 11 March 1990, *Fishing Boats in the Port of Honfleur* (watercolour, 12 1/4 x 19 1/4 ins / 31 x 49 cm) FRF 31,000. SCEAUX, 10 June 1990, *Entrance to the Port of Honfleur* (oil on canvas, 11 x 13 1/2 ins / 28 x 34 cm) FRF 51,000. PARIS, 29 May 1991, *Boats at the Quay, Honfleur* (watercolour, 18 1/2 x 24 1/2 ins / 47 x 62 cm) FRF 18,000. PARIS, 26 Oct 1992, *'The Normandie' Leaving Le Havre* (woodcut, 12 1/4 x 16 1/2 ins / 31 x 42 cm) FRF 5,500. PARIS, 23 June 1993, *Honfleur, St Catherine's Market Square* (watercolour, 11 3/4 x 17 1/4 ins / 30 x 44 cm) FRF 11,000. LE TOUQUET, 22 May 1994, *Village Square* (watercolour, 9 1/2 x 12 1/4 ins / 24 x 31 cm) FRF 7,500. PARIS, 15 June 1994, *Interior of a Haberdasher's Shop* (oil on canvas, 19 3/4 x 28 3/4 ins / 50 x 73 cm) FRF 9,200. DEAUVILLE, 19 Aug 1994, *Place Ste-Catherine, Honfleur* (watercolour and ink, 7 1/2 x 5 1/2 ins / 19 x 14 cm) FRF 4,800. PARIS, 15 Nov 1994, *Fishing Boat* (oil on canvas, 19 x 25 1/4 ins / 48 x 64 cm) FRF 42,000. PARIS, 14 June 1996, *Honfleur, View of the Port* (watercolour, 9 1/2 x 12 ins / 24 x 30.5 cm) FRF 8,800. PARIS, 21 March 1997, *In the Port of Honfleur* (watercolour, 11 1/2 x 18 ins / 29 x 46 cm) FRF 21,000. PARIS, 6 June 1997, *Honfleur, the Port* (watercolour, 11 3/4 x 17 ins / 30 x 43 cm) FRF 11,500. DEAUVILLE, 4 April 1999, *Honfleur, Boats at the Quai* (watercolour, 13 x 20 ins / 34 x 50 cm) FRF 25,000. CALAIS, 12 Dec 1999, *Fishing Boats* (oil on panel, 13 x 13 ins / 34 x 34 cm) FRF 25,000. DEAUVILLE, 23 April 2000, *Honfleur, entrance of the Port* (watercolour, 9 x 12 ins / 24 x 31 cm) FRF 27,500. DEAUVILLE, 23 April 2000, *Honfleur, Sailing Boats at the Quai* (watercolour, 13 x 18 ins / 32 x 45 cm) FRF 29,000. DEAUVILLE, 17 Aug 2001, *Honfleur, Entrance of the Port* (watercolour, 11 x 15 ins / 28 x 37 cm) FRF 35,000. PARIS, 9 Dec 2001, *Boats with Flags for 14 July* (watercolour, 18 x 23 ins / 46 x 59 cm) FRF 57,000. LE HAVRE, 21 April 2002, *Havre Port, Boats at the Quai* (oil on panel, 10 x 12 ins / 25 x 31 cm) EUR 10,000. PARIS, 5 June 2002, *Lake at Honfleur* (oil on canvas, 26 x 31 ins / 65 x 80 cm) EUR 14,800. PARIS, 30 June 2003, *Beach* (oil on canvas, 29 x 36 ins / 73 x 92 cm) EUR 42,000. LE HAVRE, 21 July 2003, *Le Vevey, Switzerland, Landscape with Figures* (oil on canvas, 29 x 37 ins / 73 x 93 cm) EUR 51,400. LE HAVRE, 7 March 2004, *Le Havre, Approach to the Port* (oil on canvas, 29 x 36 ins / 73 x 92 cm) EUR 8,000. DEAUVILLE, 17 July 2004, *Sailing Boats at the Quai, Honfleur* (watercolour, 12 x 10 ins / 30 x 25 cm) EUR 5,000.

SAINT-DÉLIS, René LIÉNARD de
French, 20th century.
Born 1873, in St-Omer; died 1958, in Étretat.
Painter, watercolourist, draughtsman. Landscapes, seascapes, still-lifes.

René Liénard de Saint-Délis, the brother of Henri de Saint-Délis, was a pupil of Othon Friesz and exhibited at the Salon des Indépendants from 1905. He belonged to the Le Havre School and was initially influenced by Boudin and the Impressionists, but later painted in a more realist style. He depicted seascapes, landscapes and still-lifes, but his treatment was somewhat coarse.
MUSEUMS AND GALLERIES:
FÉCAMP (Mus. des Terre-Neuvas et de la Pêche): *Caique Returning to Port* (ink on paper); *Caique Being Launched* (oil/card); *Repairing Nets near Upturned Boats Made into Shoreside Shanties* (charcoal and watercolour on paper); *Last Capstan of Antifer* (charcoal/paper).
AUCTION RECORDS:
PARIS, 31 March 1976, *Estuary of the Seine from the Côte de Grace* (22 x 18 ins / 55 x 46 cm) FRF 6,100. PARIS, 3 March 1989, *Normandy Landscape* (1910, oil on card, 11 x 13 1/2 ins / 28 x 34.5 cm) FRF 4,500. PARIS, 16 Nov 1990, *Normandy Coast* (oil on canvas) FRF 32,000. PARIS, 27 Nov 1992, *Seascape with Beached Boats* (watercolour, 12 1/4 x 19 1/2 ins / 31 x 49.5 cm) FRF 24,000. CALAIS, 15 Dec 1996, *Still-life with Jugs and a Cup* (oil on panel, 12 1/4 x 15 3/4 ins / 31 x 40 cm) FRF 5,100. CALAIS, 30 Sept 2001, *Fishermen* (oil on panel, 14 x 19 ins / 35 x 48 cm) FRF 15,500. PARIS, 5 Dec 2001, *Honfleur, Returning Boats* (watercolour, 9 x 12 ins / 24 x 31 cm) FRF 12,000.

SAINT-DIDIER, Hubert de Balthazar.
See **HUBERT DE SAINT-DIDIER**

SAINT-EDME, Clémentine.
See **TROUILLEBERT**

SAINT-EDME, Louise (Mme). See **FAUQUET Louise**

SAINT-EDME, Ludovic Alfred de
French, 19th century.
Born 30 September 1820, in Paris.
Painter, draughtsman. Figures, portraits, landscapes.

Ludovic Saint-Edme was the student of Darondeau and Duran-Brager. He first exhibited at the Salon in 1848.
AUCTION RECORDS:
PARIS, 30 April 1919, *Beach at Yport*, FRF 46. PARIS, 10 Dec 1926, *Grisettes* (lead pencil, two drawings) FRF 720. BERN, 26 Oct 1988, *Summer Cornfield* (1875, oil on canvas, 13 1/4 x 21 1/4 ins / 33.5 x 54 cm) CHF 2,400. AMSTERDAM, 2 May 1990, *Park at Vittel* (1876, oil on canvas, 15 3/4 x 23 1/2 ins / 40 x 60 cm) NLG 2,530.

SAINT-ELOY, Jehan de
French, 14th century.
Painter.

In 1377 Jehan de Saint-Eloy worked with Perin de Dijon in the library of the duke of Orléans.

SAINT-ÉTIENNE, Francisque de, or Francisc, or Louis Francisc Hippolyte Bessodes de Roquefeuille

French, 19th century.

Born 1824, in Montpellier; died 20 April 1885, in Montpellier.

Painter, engraver (etching). Landscapes.

Francisque de Saint Étienne was a student of Jules Laurens. He exhibited at the Salon from 1857 to 1863. He also participated in the international exhibition in London in 1862, showing four landscape etchings. After his return to Montpellier in 1863, he no longer exhibited in Paris but only at the regional exhibitions of the artists' society in Hérault. His style was strongly influenced by J. P. Laurens. He was principally an etcher.

MUSEUMS AND GALLERIES:

CARPENTRAS: *Old Castle of Granada* - MONTPELLIER: a painting.

SAINT-ÈVE, Jean-Marie

French, 19th century.

Born 9 June 1810, in Lyons; died 4 September 1856, in Paris.

Engraver.

Jean-Marie Saint-Ève was the student of V. Vibert and Richomme. He exhibited at the Salon from 1847 to 1855, and won the first Grand Prix de Rome in 1840. He engraved portraits and religious subjects. He died just as he was beginning to reap the benefits of his extensive studies.

SAINT-ÈVRE, Gillot

French, 19th century.

Born 1791, in Bault-sur-Suippe; died 1858, in Paris.

Painter, engraver. History painting, portraits, genre scenes.

Gillot Saint-Èvre was an artillery officer at first; he then abandoned his military career to devote himself to art. He exhibited at the Paris Salon between 1822 and 1844, obtaining a second-class medal in 1824 and a first-class medal in 1827. He was made a Chevalier of the Légion d'Honneur in 1833.

His works include: *Don Quixote*. He also produced some lithographs on genre subjects.

He was ranked among the Romantics but this artistic notion did not suit his temperament particularly well.

MUSEUMS AND GALLERIES:

ANGERS: *Sleeping Cavalier* - COMPIÈGNE: *Joan of Arc before Charles VII* - GUÉRET: *Coronation of Baudouin, Count of Flanders, as Emperor of Constantinople in 1204* (1839) - SOISSONS: *Job and His Friends* - VERSAILLES: *Anne of Brittany; Philippe de Villiers of l'Isle-Adam* (two works); *Montrevel; Philippe III le Hardi (the Bold); Philippe I; Charles VI; Charles VIII; César Choiseul; Marriage of Charles VIII and Anne of Brittany; Signing of the Treaty of Vervins, 1598; Foundation of the King's Library in Paris in 1379; Charles V; Meeting of Philip Augustus and Henri II at Gisors, 1188; Andrew of Hungary Joins the Order of St John of Jerusalem; Crossing the Bosphorus; Alexis Comnène Receives Peter the Hermit at Constantinople, 1096* - VERSAILLES (Trianon): *Charlemagne Establishing Alcuin at the Louvre; Mary Stuart at the Louvre.*

AUCTION RECORDS:

PARIS, 22 May 1897, *Historical Subject,* FRF 30. PARIS, 24 Nov 1922, *Isabella of Bavaria,* FRF 190. MARSEILLES, 18 Feb 1950, *Joan of Arc and Charles VII,* FRF 19,750. LOS ANGELES, 12 March 1979, *Joan of Arc before Charles VII* (1850, oil on canvas, 29 1/4 x 36 3/4 ins / 74 x 93.4 cm) USD 5,000. SAN FRANCISCO, 14 May 2003, *Joan of Arc before Charles VII* (1860, oil on canvas, 29 x 37 ins / 74 x 93 cm) USD 2,750. PARIS, 1 Dec 2003, *Don Quixote at the Inn* (1823, oil on canvas, 20 x 24 ins / 50 x 61 cm) EUR 2,800.

SAINT-EXUPÉRY, Antoine de

French, 20th century.

Born 29 June 1900, in Lyons; died 31 July 1944, near Marseilles.

Draughtsman.

The novelist and aviator, Antoine de Saint-Exupéry, author of *Courrier sud* (*Southern Mail*) and *Vol de Nuit* (*Night Flight*) and the essays *Terre des Hommes* (*Wind, Sand and Stars*) and *Citadelle* (*Citadel*), liked to heighten his manuscripts with watercolours and decorate his letters with drawings. He illustrated his *Petit Prince* (*The Little Prince*) with fresh and poetic watercolours. Some youthful letters with coloured drawings to his friend Renée Sanssine were published in 1953 under the title *Lettres à une amie inventée* (*Letters to an Imagined Friend*). He was declared missing after a flight in World War II. The Bibliothèque Nationale, Paris, exhibited several of his watercolours and drawings at an exhibition organised in 1954.

BIBLIOGRAPHY:

Saint-Exupéry, Antoine de, *A sense of life,* Funk & Wagnalls, New York, 1965 (translated from Un sens de la vie). Curtis, Cate, *Antoine de Saint Exupéry,* Putnam, New York, 1970. Schiff, Stacy, *Saint Exupéry: A biography,* A. A. Knopf, New York, 1994.

AUCTION RECORDS:

PARIS, 20 May 1976, *Illustration for 'The Little Prince'* (11 pen drawings with captions, 8 1/4 x 11 ins / 21 x 27 cm) FRF 40,000. PARIS, 6 July 1984, *The Little Prince Seated on his Planet* (pencil/one quarto page) FRF 18,200. LONDON, 10 Dec 1985, *The Little Prince* (watercolour and pen, 10 x 8 ins / 25.2 x 19.4 cm) GBP 7,000. PARIS, 2 July 2002, *Figure from a Fantasy* (pen, wash, 11 x 8 ins / 28 x 21 cm) EUR 2,200. PARIS, 9 June 2004, *Seated Woman* (crayon, 11 x 6 ins / 27 x 15 cm) EUR 2,000.

SAINT-FAR, J. L. Eustache, or Saint-Phar

French, 18th - 19th century.

Born 1746 or 1747, in Paris; died 1822, in Mantes (Yvelines).

Painter, watercolourist, engraver. Portraits, landscapes.

Saint-Far was the pupil and assistant of J.R. Perronet. He produced burin engravings of views and landscapes. He was also an architect and engineer.

AUCTION RECORDS:

PARIS, 18 Dec 1940, *Portrait of a Man* (1772, watercolour) FRF 3,100.

SAINT-FLEUR, Michel

Haitian, 20th century.

Painter. Flowers.

AUCTION RECORDS:

PARIS, 12 June 1995, *Bowl of Flowers* (oil on canvas, 20 x 30 ins / 51 x 76 cm) FRF 3,800.

SAINT-FLEURANT, Louisianne

Haitian, 20th century.

Born 1924, in Petit-Trou de Nippes.

Painter.

Louisianne Saint-Fleurant inspired the Saint-Soleil New School of Painters, created under the direction of Tiga, Garoute, and Maude Robbart, promoters of this movement in Soisson-la-Montagne.

AUCTION RECORDS:

PARIS, 17 May 1993, *Children of the Peristyle* (1972, oil, 24 x 24 ins / 61 x 61 cm) FRF 39,000. PARIS, 1 April 1996, *Embryonic Woman* (oil on canvas, 24 x 24 ins / 61 x 61 cm) FRF 4,500.

SAINT-FRANÇOIS, Léon Joly de

French, 19th century.

Born c. 1822, in Clermont (Oise); died 21 August 1886, in Paris.

Painter. Genre scenes, landscapes.
He made his debut at the Salon in 1848.

Museums and Galleries:

Bernay: *The Signal* - Béziers: *Mount Atlas.*

Auction records:

Paris, 1899, *The Return* (charcoal drawing heightened with white) FRF 20.

SAINT-GAUDENS, Augustus

American, 19th century.

Born 1 March 1848, in Dublin, Ireland; died 3 August 1907, in Cornish.

Sculptor.

Symbolism.

Augustus Saint-Gaudens' father was from Gascony (southwest France) and his mother was Irish. His family emigrated to the USA before he was a year old. He studied at the National Academy of Design in New York, then went to Paris from 1867 to 1870, where he was a pupil of Jouffroy at the École des Beaux-Arts. Saint-Gaudens moved to Italy during the Franco-Prussian war of 1870, and was initiated into the Neo-Classical style that dominated Europe at the time, notably by Canova and Thorvaldsen. As soon as he returned to the USA he was enormously successful. He went back to France in 1880, and again in 1897, to serve on the international jury at the Exposition Universelle in Paris. He was also a correspondent member of the Académie des Beaux-Arts in Paris. Saint-Gaudens was involved in founding the liberalist Society of American Artists, and exhibited there, as well as at the Paris Salon. In Paris he was awarded an honourable mention in 1880, and the Grand Prix in 1900 at the Exposition Universelle.

Saint-Gaudens started out engraving cameos. He was an associate of the architects Stanford White and Charles F. MacKin, so received numerous commissions through them. He also sculpted a large number of monuments, notably the following: *President Lincoln* in New York; *Admiral Farragut*, a statue of the admiral standing on the bridge of his ship, erected in Madison Square in New York in 1881; a monument in memory of *General Sherman* in Central Park in New York; a monument to *Robert Shaw* on Beacon Street in Boston; and *The Adams Memorial* at Rock Creek Cemetery in Washington DC. Among the numerous low reliefs he produced, the best known are those of *Mary Schuyler van Rensselaer, Robert Louis Stevenson* and *Samuel Gray Ward.* His works bear the influence of 19th-century French sculpture and the Italian Renaissance.

In 2003 the North Carolina Museum of Art presented a retrospective of Saint-Gaudens' works entitled *Augustus Saint-Gaudens: American Sculptor of the Gilded Age.*

Bibliography:

Dryfhout, John H., *The Work of Augustus Saint-Gaudens,* University Press of New England, Hanover (NH), 1982. Greenthal, Kathryn, *Augustus Saint-Gaudens,* Metropolitan Museum of Art, New York, 1985. Rodriguez Roque, Oswaldo (introduction), *Arts des États-Unis,* Gründ, Paris, 1989 (by the curators of the Metropolitan Museum of Art). Dryfhout, John H./Duffy, Henry, *Augustus Saint-Gaudens: American Sculptor of the Gilded Age,* exhibition catalogue, North Carolina Museum of Art, 2003.

Museums and Galleries:

Buffalo: eight caryatids - Chicago (AI): *Angel* - New York (Metropolitan Mus. of Art): *Children of Jacob H. Schiff; Bronze Head; Victory* - Northampton, MA (MA, Smith College) - Paris (Mus. d'Orsay): *Amor Caritas* (bronze high relief) - Philadelphia (MA): *Diana* - Pittsburgh (Carnegie MA): *Victory* (1892-1903, gilded bronze, probably cast after 1912) - Washington DC: *Bust of D. J. Hill* - Washington DC (NGA): *Charles Stewart Butler and Lawrence Smith Butler* (1880-1881, plaster); *Diana of the Tower* (1892-1893 (conception)).

Auction records:

New York, 5 March 1970, *Puritan,* USD 2,200. New York, 5 March 1970, *Puritan,* USD 2,200. New York, 29 April 1976, *Robert Louis Stevenson* (brown-patinated bronze, medallion, diam. 17 3/4 ins / 45 cm) USD 5,000. New York, 29 Sept 1977, *Puritan* (1899, bronze, h. 31 ins / 78.8 cm) USD 13,000. New York, 25 Oct 1979, *Puritan* (1890, brown-patinated bronze, h. 30 1/2 ins / 77.5 cm) USD 10,000. New York, 3 June 1982, *Psyche of Capua* (c. 1874, marble, h. 34 1/4 ins / 87 cm) USD 5,000. New York, 1 June 1984, *Diana of the Tower* (bronze, h. 39 ins / 98.2 cm) USD 120,000. New York, 31 May 1985, *Diana of the Tower* (1899, brown-patinated bronze, h. 29 3/4 ins / 75.5 cm) USD 50,000. New York, 5 Dec 1986, *Amor Caritas* (1898, green-patinated bronze, h. 40 ins / 101.3 cm) USD 160,000. New York, 26 May 1988, *Diana of the Tower* (1984, bronze, h. 28 3/4 ins / 73 cm) USD 187,000. New York, 24 May 1989, *Relief Portrait of Robert Louis Stevenson* (1887, bronze, diam. 12 ins / 30.5 cm) USD 6,600. New York, 1 Dec 1989, *Allegory of Victory* (gilt bronze, h. 42 1/4 ins / 107.5 cm) USD 242,000. New York, 23 May 1990, *Diana of the Tower* (1899, bronze, h. 22 ins / 55 cm) USD 242,000. New York, 27 Sept 1990, *Diana of the Tower* (bronze bust, h. 8 ins / 19.4 cm) USD 7,700. New York, 30 Nov 1990, *Amor Caritas* (1899, gilt bronze relief, h. 40 ins / 101.3 cm) USD 165,000. New York, 6 Dec 1991, *Diana of the Tower* (bronze with red-brown patina, total h. 37 ins / 93.7 cm, h. of the figure 22 ins/55 cm) USD 242,000. New York, 28 May 1992, *Portrait of Robert Louis Stevenson* (bronze tondo, diam. 17 3/4 ins / 45.1 cm) USD 17,600. New York, 4 Dec 1992, *Amor Caritas* (bronze relief, h. 40 ins / 101.6 cm) USD 99,000. New York, 27 May 1993, *Portrait of Robert Louis Stevenson* (bronze relief, diam. 17 1/2 ins / 44.5 cm) USD 11,500. Paris, 8 Dec 1993, *Bust of a Woman* (marble, h. 19 3/4 ins / 50 cm) FRF 46, 000. New York, 25 May 1994, *Puritan* (bronze, h. 31 ins / 78.7 cm) USD 57,500. New York, 4 Dec 1996, *Diana of the Tower* (bronze, h. 39 1/4 ins / 99.7 cm) USD 145,000. New York, 27 May 1999, *Diana of the Tower* (brown patinated bronze, h. 30 ins / 75 cm) USD 110,000. New York, 7 Dec 1999, *Portrait of Robert Louis Stevenson* (1887, bronze, h. 12 ins / 30 cm) USD 7,750. New York, 10 Oct 2001, *Bust of Davida Johnson Clark* (plaster, h. 11 ins / 27 cm) USD 37,500. Milford, 25 Oct 2001, *Robert Louis Stevenson* (bronze, h. 17 ins / 43 cm) USD 8,500. New York, 13 Feb 2002, *Samuel Johnson* (1874, plaster, h. 29 ins / 74 cm) USD 13,000. New York, 22 May 2002, *Diana of the Towers* (gilded bronze, h. 80 ins / 203 cm) USD 150,000. New York, 21 May 2003, *Puritan: Deacon Samuel Chapin* (weathered green patinated bronze, h. 30 ins / 77 cm) USD 115,000. New York, 4 Dec 2003, *Amor Caritas* (1890, patinated bronze, h. 40 ins / 102 cm) USD 130,000. New York, 27 Sept 2004, *Homer St-Gaudens* (bronze plaque, 20 x 10 ins / 50 x 25 cm) USD 65,000.

SAINT-GENYS, Marie Camille Arthur de

(Marquis)

French, 19th century.

Born in Angers; died 1887.

Painter. Genre scenes, landscapes.

He was a pupil of Aligny, Biennoury and Pignerolles. He first exhibited at the Salon in 1857.

Museums and Galleries:

Angers: *Solitude: Memory of Forez.*

Auction records:

Paris, 1872, *A Path in Spa Park,* FRF 100.

SAINT-GEORGE, Charles

French, 20th century.

Born 22 February 1907, in Paris.

Painter, draughtsman, illustrator. Urban landscapes.

A self-taught painter, Charles Saint-George studied architecture at the École des Beaux-Arts, Paris, and was also a pupil of the poster artist Paul Colin. He was a figurative artist attracted especially by urban landscapes, especially the Paris suburbs, for which he invented a unique mother-of-pearl effect that expresses the essential poetry of his painting. He exhibited in Paris at the Salon des Indépendants and the Salon des Artistes Français (a member and committee member of both), the Salon of the Société Nationale des Beaux-Arts, the Salon d'Hiver, the Salon d'Automne, the Salon de l'École Française, and outside Paris at the salons of Versailles, Fontainebleau, Nevers and Asnières, where he was awarded the Grand Prize for painting in 1870). He won a silver medal at the Salon des Artistes Français and the Taylor prize.

MUSEUMS AND GALLERIES:

PARIS (MAMVP).

SAINT-GERMAIN, Gault de (Mme). See the entry **RAJECKA Anna**

SAINT-GERMAIN, Jean Baptiste Prosper

French, 19th century.

Painter, watercolourist, draughtsman. Genre scenes.

His master was Alexander Colin. He debuted at the Salon in 1863.

MUSEUMS AND GALLERIES:

BREST (MBA): *Return of the Pardon.*

AUCTION RECORDS:

PARIS, 1897, *Village Fair* (watercolour/pen outline) FRF 340.

SAINT-GERMAIN, Prosper

French, 19th century.

Born in Brest.

Painter, engraver. Genre scenes.

This artist was a pupil of Leloir, and was primarily a lithographer. He exhibited at the Salon in 1841 and 1850.

SAINT-GERMIER, Joseph

French, 19th - 20th century.

Born 19 January 1860, in Toulouse; died 5 June 1925.

Painter. Religious subjects, nudes, scenes with figures, genre scenes, interiors with figures, landscapes, urban landscapes, architectural views, church interiors.

Joseph Saint-Germier, a pupil of Cabanel and Bonnat, painted many pictures of Venice. He exhibited in Paris at the Salon des Artistes Français, of which he was a member from 1888. He was awarded an honourable mention in 1888, a travel scholarship in 1889, a bronze medal at the Paris Exposition Universelle of 1889, a second-class medal in 1894, and a gold medal at the Paris Exposition Universelle of 1900. He was made a chevalier of the Légion d'Honneur in 1896.

J. Saint-Germier.

MUSEUMS AND GALLERIES:

BAYONNE: *The Navaja* - MONTPELLIER: *A Guild Meeting in the Baptistery of St Mark's, Venice; The Keeper of the Seals, Venice* - PARIS (former Mus. du Luxembourg): *Burial in Venice; Secret Relationship* - PAU.

AUCTION RECORDS:

PARIS, 14-15 May 1902, *Study*, FRF 220. PARIS, 3 Feb 1919, *Adriatic Festival in Venice*, FRF 160. PARIS, 28 June 1923, *Meeting of the Council of 10, Venice*, FRF 260. PARIS, 12 June 1926, *Interior of a Venetian Church*, FRF 300. PARIS, 9 March 1939, *Gondolas in Venice*, FRF 190. PARIS, 8 March 1943, *Spanish Workshop*, FRF 300. PARIS, 26 Feb 1947, *Arab Woman*, FRF 2,000. PARIS, 28 Feb 1951, *Venice*, FRF 3,100. PARIS, 20 March 1970, *Venice* (28 3/4 x 38 1/4 ins / 73 x 97 cm) FRF 100. TOULOUSE, 1 Dec 1975, *Lunch in the Open Air* (20 3/4 x 31 ins / 53 x 79 cm) FRF 2,300. PARIS, 12 Oct 1983, *Venice, Leaving for the Ball* (oil on panel, 25 1/2 x 32 1/4 ins / 64.5 x 81.8 cm) FRF 11,000. PARIS, 13 March 1989, *Corrida in Seville* (oil on panel, 11 x 13 3/4 ins / 27 x 35 cm) FRF 8,000. STOCKHOLM, 15 Nov 1989, *Canal, Venice* (1887, oil, 10 1/4 x 13 1/2 ins / 26 x 34 cm) SEK 10,500. PARIS, 13 Dec 1989, *The Banderillo* (oil on paper, 16 1/4 x 12 3/4 ins / 41 x 32.5 cm) FRF 7,000; *Arena, Seville* (oil on paper, 11 x 13 3/4 ins / 27 x 35 cm) FRF 12,000. PARIS, 3 July 1991, *Statue of Colleoni, Venice* (oil on panel, 36 1/4 x 29 1/4 ins / 92 x 74.5 cm) FRF 20,000. NEUILLY, 19 March 1994, *Meditation* (oil on canvas, 19 1/4 x 23 1/4 ins / 49 x 59 cm) FRF 4,800. PARIS, 22 March 1995, *Young Mother and Child in a Drawing Room* (1899, oil on canvas, 33 1/2 x 43 1/4 ins / 85 x 110 cm) FRF 37,000. PARIS, 16 March 1996, *Reclining Nude* (1887, oil on canvas, 15 x 23 1/2 ins / 38 x 60 cm) FRF 13,000. PARIS, 12 Dec 1997, *In the Studio* (1886, oil on panel, 13 3/4 x 11 ins / 35 x 27 cm) FRF 11,000. NEW YORK, 18 March 1998, *Masked Ball* (oil on canvas, 36 x 46 ins / 91.4 x 116.8 cm) USD 18,400.

SAINT-GERVAIS, Charlotte de

Maiden name: Comtesse de La Salle

French, 19th - 20th century.

Born April 1860, in Nantes.

Sculptor.

Charlotte de Saint-Gervais, a pupil of Hélène Berteaux, first exhibited at the Salon in 1876.

SAINT-HILAIRE, de

French, 18th century.

Probably active in Frankfurt am Main in 1759.

Engraver (burin).

SAINT-HILAIRE, Julien B. L.

French, 20th century.

Painter.

Julien B.L. Saint-Hilaire was awarded an honourable mention at the Salon des Artistes Français in 1935.

SAINT-HILL, Antoine

French, 18th century.

Born 1731, in Paris.

Engraver (burin/etching).

Saint-Hill engraved after Berchem and Joseph Vernet.

SAINT-HILL, Loudon. See **SAINTHILL**

SAINT-HILLIER, Renée

French, 20th century.

Born in Lyons.

Painter, draughtswoman, sculptor, illustrator.

Renée Saint-Hillier studied in Paris at the Académie Frochat in the studio of René Audebès and P. Metzinger. She exhibited her work in Paris from 1966 and also in Japan. She explored Romanesque art, Cubism and Far Eastern art, combining these sources of inspiration in a somewhat naive style. She illustrated Martin Grey's *Les Pensées de notre vie* (*Our Life Thoughts*).

SAINT-IGNY, Jean de, or Saint-Ygny

French, 17th century.

Born c. 1600, in Rouen; died between 9 November and 10 December 1647.

Painter, sculptor, engraver. History painting, figures, portraits.

There is evidence that in 1614 Jean de Saint-Igny had a painting apprenticeship in Rouen and there exists a legal document that refers to 'the honourable master painter and sculptor Jean de Saint-Isigny, living in Paris, parish of St-Sulpice, Faubourg and rue St-Germain, at the house showing the sign of the Great Turk'. In 1631 he returned to Rouen and was one of the co-signatories to a request made in the church of St-Herbland for the incorporation of a guild of St-Luc. He also left a treatise on portrait painting.

According to Philippe de Chennevières, De Saint-Igny must have been a pupil of Daniel Rabel in Paris. However, between 1610 and 1630 the most fashionable workshop in Paris was Lallemand's, and we might equally suppose that it was there that De Saint-Igny, like Claude Vignon, acquired the stylistic elegance that suggests a meeting of the influence of the Second Fontainebleau School with the almost strange Mannerism of the Lorraine engravers, especially Jacques

Bellange, and with the Baroque graces of Georges Lallemand. In this aspect, some of the paintings of De Saint-Igny and Claude Vignon presage the minor masters of the 18th century such as De Troy, Van Loo and the Coypels. It has been possible to study the stylistic similarities between De Saint-Igny, Claude Vignon and Lallemand because of the large number of De Saint-Igny's drawings that have survived.

BIBLIOGRAPHY:

Hedou, J., *Jean de Saint-Igny, peintre, sculpteur et graveur rouennais*, E. Augé, Rouen, 1887. Beaurepaire, Ch. de, *Notes sur le peintre Saint-Igny*, Cagniard, Rouen, 1905. Sterling, Charles/Jamot, Paul, *Les Peintres de la réalité en France au XVIIe siècle*, exhibition catalogue, Musée de l'Orangerie, Paris, 1934.

MUSEUMS AND GALLERIES:

PARIS (Mus. National du Moyen Age): *Scenes of Roman Antiquity* (seven panels) - ROUEN: *Adoration of the Shepherds; Adoration of the Magi; Allegories* (two panels in grisaille).

AUCTION RECORDS:

PARIS, 28 Nov 1928, *Footman Wearing a Cloak* (drawing) FRF 1,550. LONDON, 2 July 1991, *Three-quarter Head of a Woman Seen from Behind* (red chalk, 6 1/2 x 5 1/2 ins / 16.6 x 14.2 cm) GBP 1,650. MONACO, 5-6 Dec 1991, *Studies of Heads* (red chalk, a pair, 9 x 6 3/4 ins / 23 x 17 cm) FRF 55,500. PARIS, 21 Nov 2001, *Bust of Young Man* (red chalk, 7 x 5 ins / 17 x 13 cm) FRF 35,000. NEW YORK, 21 Jan 2003, *Head of Bearded Saint Looking Down* (chalk, 7 x 5 ins / 18 x 13 cm) USD 2,500. PARIS, 27 March 2003, *Two Elegant Couples with Pages in a Landscape* (chalk, 7 x 13 ins / 18 x 32 cm) EUR 11,000.

SAINT-JACQUES, Camille

French, 20th - 21st century.
Born 1956, in Bièvres (Aisne).
Painter, pastellist, sculptor, mixed media, installation artist, screen printer.

Camille Saint-Jacques was a pupil of Marc Devade and subsequently wrote a thesis on the latter's life and work.

Camille Saint-Jacques initially worked in inks to produce geometrical abstractions which espoused the somewhat Expressionist style of the Support/Surfaces Group. He went on to work in pastels, producing predominantly black compositions and, in the process, distancing himself progressively from the influence of Devade. He then started painting in oils and producing lithographs drawn on various substrates, including rubber. He also produced paintings on wooden panels featuring tiny drops of colour. Saint-Jacques' subject matter, like his techniques, appears to have come in distinct phases, starting with his early abstracts and progressing towards resolutely figurative work which contains overtones of Courbet, Hogarth and his contemporary, David Hockney.

Saint-Jacques has been a participant in various group exhibitions over the years: in 1985, at the FIAC (Foire Internationale d'Art Contemporain) in Paris; in 1987, at the Festival International de Dessin at the Grand Palais in Paris; in 1988, at the Ziem Museum in Martigues, the Centre Culturel in Boulogne Billancourt, and the Centre d'Art in Saint-Priest; in 1992, at *Singularités* (*Peculiarities*), an exhibition at the Galerie Marwan Hoss in Paris; and, in 1995, with François and Fabrice Hybert, at the Galerie François Mitaine in Paris. He has also exhibited solo on a number of occasions: in 1985, 1988 and 1992 in Paris; in 1988, in Lyons; in 1992, in Brussels; in 1994, at the Chailloux Maison d'Art Contemporain in Fresnes and at the Hôtel de Ville in Paris; and so on. In 1991, Saint-Jacques was awarded the Gras-Savoye Prize and his painting was put on exhibition at the École des Beaux-Arts in Paris.

BIBLIOGRAPHY:

Suchère, Éric, "*Camille Saint-Jacques*' in *Beaux-Arts Magazine* n° 128, periodical, Paris, November 1994.

MUSEUMS AND GALLERIES:

PARIS (FNAC): *Story of Judas XXXI 220* (1988).

SAINT-JEAN. See **DIEU Jean de**

SAINT-JEAN

French, 18th century.
Painter. Murals.

Saint-Jean was commissioned to produce three panels above the doors to the mint, Hôtel de la Monnaie, in Paris in 1741.

SAINT-JEAN

18th century.
Miniaturist, painter (gouache), watercolourist, draughtsman. Genre scenes.

Saint-Jean was a member of the Académie de Saint-Luc and exhibited at the Academy's Salon from 1770 to 1777.

AUCTION RECORDS:

PARIS, 20 Nov 1925, *Drinker* (watercolour) FRF 660. PARIS, 22 March 1991, *Return of the Warrior* (watercolour and gouache, 14 1/4 x 17 1/2 ins / 36.5 x 44.5 cm) FRF 9,000. MONACO, 22 June 1991, *Departure of the Young Soldier* (black chalk, ink and watercolour, 11 1/2 x 14 1/4 ins / 29 x 36.5 cm) FRF 7,700.

SAINT-JEAN, Gérard de. See **GÉRARD de Saint-Jean**

SAINT-JEAN, Gustave or Jean Gustave Pierre

French, 19th century.
Born 1844, in Muret (Haute-Garonne); died 22 April 1888, in Paris.
Sculptor.

His masters were Guillaume, Decret and Cavelier. He made his Salon debut in 1869, and won a second-class medal in 1873.

MUSEUMS AND GALLERIES:

LA ROCHELLE: *Cupid and Psyche.*

SAINT-JEAN, Henry de

French, 20th century.
Painter.

Henry de Saint-Jean exhibited in the various annual Paris salons.

SAINT-JEAN, Louis Honoré

French, 19th century.
Born 1793, in Dunkirk.
Painter. Genre scenes, portraits.

This artist was a pupil of Senave.

SAINT-JEAN, Paul

French, 19th century.
Born 1842, in Lyons; died October 1875, in Paris.
Painter. Figures, portraits, genre scenes, flowers.

He was taught to paint by his father, Simon Saint-Jean. He began exhibiting at the Paris Salon in 1866.

MUSEUMS AND GALLERIES:

GRAY: *Young Girl in a White Bonnet* - ROUEN (MBA): *Reading* - UTRECHT: *Flowers.*

AUCTION RECORDS:

PARIS, 12 May 1923, *Young Woman,* FRF 180. LONDON, 15 March 1996, *Spanish Beauty* (oil on canvas, 39 1/4 x 32 ins / 100 x 81 cm) GBP 17,825. NEW YORK, 23 April 2003, *Girl Dreaming* (oil on canvas, 47 x 37 ins / 120 x 93 cm) USD 18,000. LYONS, 28 March 2004, *Pretty Andalusian Girl* (oil on canvas, 39 x 31 ins / 99 x 80 cm) EUR 23,000.

SAINT-JEAN, Simon

French, 19th century.
Born 14 October 1808, in Lyons; died 3 July 1860, in Ecully near Lyons.
Painter. Still-lifes (flowers/fruit).

Simon Saint-Jean was a pupil of François Lepage and Augustin Thierriat at the École des Beaux-Arts in Lyons. He exhibited at the Salon between 1834 and 1859, winning a third-class medal in 1834, and second-class medals in 1841 and 1855.

Simon Saint-Jean enjoyed deserved success as a painter of flowers and fruit during his lifetime, but his works are now no longer particularly sought after.

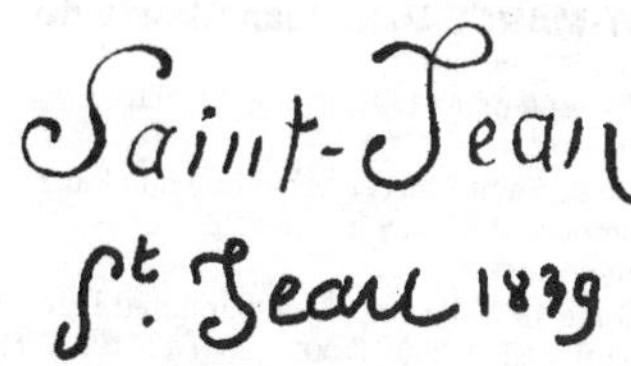

MUSEUMS AND GALLERIES:

AMSTERDAM (Stedelijk Mus.): *Flowers* - LONDON (Wallace Collection): *Flowers and Fruit* (1848 and 1853, oil on canvas, two versions); *Flowers and Grapes* (1844 and 1846, oil on canvas, two versions) - LYONS: *Flowers and Fruit; Young Girl Carrying Flowers; Various Flowers; Eucharistic Emblems; Offering to the Virgin Mary; Vase of Flowers and Fruit* - PARIS (Louvre): *Flowers among the Ruins; Harvest: Grapes, Peaches, Plums and Melons; Flowers and Fruit; Madonna of the Roses* - ROUEN: *Flowers in a Hat.*

AUCTION RECORDS:

PARIS, 1858, *Oranges and Grapes,* FRF 2,180. PARIS, 1863, *Flowers and Fruit,* FRF 4,500. PARIS, 1869, *Fruit and Flowers,* FRF 16,500. PARIS, 6-9 March 1872, *Flowers on the Ground,* FRF 17,900; *Flowers and Fruit,* FRF 9,700. PARIS, 1873, *Plums,* FRF 4,100. PARIS, 1876, *White Roses,* FRF 20,100; *Bouquet of Flowers in a Vase,* FRF 25,100. PARIS, 15 March 1877, *Fruit and Game,* FRF 10,200. LONDON, 1880, *Still-life,* FRF 18,375. PARIS, 1880, *Flowers and Fruit,* FRF 15,000. PARIS, 1889, *Flowers and Fruit,* FRF 12,850. PARIS, 27 Feb 1892, *Bouquet of Flowers on the Ground,* FRF 6,050. PARIS, 1896, *Roses,* FRF 1,300. PARIS, 30 May 1912, *Flowers and Fruit,* FRF 3,700. PARIS, 20-22 May 1920, *Flowers and Fruit,* FRF 1,000. PARIS, 30 May 1924, *Oranges, Pomegranates and Grapes,* FRF 300. PARIS, 3 March 1926, *Roses, Pansies and Forget-me-nots* (watercolour) FRF 1,500. PARIS, 2 and 3 Dec 1926, *Flowers,* FRF 7,200. PARIS, 11 May 1931, *Various Roses and Flowers,* FRF 1,700. PARIS, 4 June 1941, *Overturned Basket of Fruit at the Base of a Stone Pillar* (1850) FRF 780. PARIS, 13 March 1942, *Still-life with Peaches,* FRF 1,000. PARIS, 31 May 1943, *Vase of Flowers,* FRF 2,350. PARIS, 10 May 1950, *Still-life with Game and Fruit,* FRF 900. PARIS, 9 March 1951, *Apples on an Earthenware Dish* (1856) FRF 6,500. PARIS, 7 June 1968, *Bouquet,* FRF 6,500. NEW YORK, 28 April 1977, *Still-life with Fruit* (oil on canvas, 60 x 46 1/2 ins / 152.5 x 118 cm) USD 1,200. LYONS, 8 June 1982, *Bouquet of Peonies, Mimosas and Anenomes* (1843, oil on panel, 18 x 15 ins / 46 x 38 cm) FRF 14,000. PARIS, 15 June 1983, *Still-life with Fruit* (1855, oil on canvas, 18 x 21 1/4 ins / 46 x 54 cm) FRF 30,000. MONTE CARLO, 8 Dec 1984, *Flowers* (1839, watercolour, 19 x 13 3/4 ins / 48 x 35 cm) FRF 6,000. MONTE CARLO, 20 June 1987, *Bouquet of Flowers* (oil on canvas, 28 1/2 x 23 ins / 72.5 x 58.5 cm) FRF 200,000. ST-DIÉ, 7 May 1988, *Basket of Fruit and Flowers* (1850, oil on canvas, 36 1/4 x 28 1/4 ins / 92 x 72 cm) FRF 20,000. ST-DIÉ, 7 May 1988, *Basket of Fruit and Flowers* (1850, oil on canvas, 36 1/4 x 28 1/4 ins / 92 x 72 cm) FRF 20,000. CALAIS, 10 Dec 1989, *Bouquet of Flowers* (oil on panel, 21 1/4 x 16 1/2 ins / 54 x 42 cm) FRF 190,000. LONDON, 28 March 1990, *Still-life with Flowers and Fruit* (oil on canvas, 20 1/2 x 17 1/4 ins / 52 x 44 cm) GBP 6,050. PARIS, 7 Oct 1991, *Still-life* (1857, oil on card, 7 3/4 x 11 3/4 ins / 19.5 x 30 cm) FRF 75,000. NEW YORK, 17 Oct 1991, *Still-life with Roses, Carnations, Grapes and Peaches on a Forest Floor* (1853, oil on canvas, 18 x 24 ins / 45.7 x 61 cm) USD 20,900. PARIS, 29 Nov 1991, *Still-life* (oil on canvas, 17 1/2 x 21 ins / 44.5 x 53.5 cm) FRF 25,000. MONACO, 18-19 June 1992, *Group of Partridges* (1839, oil on canvas, 28 3/4 x 37 1/2 ins / 73 x 95.5 cm) FRF 105,450. LONDON, 17 Nov 1993, *Major Floral Composition with Wild Raspberries on a Table* (1845, oil on canvas, 48 x 36 1/2 ins / 122 x 93 cm) USD 96,100. LONDON, 11 June 1997, *Wild Roses* (1846, watercolour/pencil outlines/paper, study, 21 1/4 x 16 ins / 54 x 40.5 cm) GBP 13,225. PARIS, 3 April 1998, *Bouquet of Flowers Arranged on a Pedestal Table* (1851, lead pencil/beige paper, 9 x 6 1/2 ins / 22 x 16.5 cm) FRF 2,500. BRUSSELS, 23 March 1999, *Still-life with Game, Flowers and Fruit* (1853, oil on canvas, 51 x 39 ins / 130 x 100 cm) BEF 420,000. PARIS, 7 April 2000, *Fruit, Vine Branches, Vase of Flowers, Hare and Pheasant* (1853, oil on canvas, 51 x 39 ins / 130 x 100 cm) FRF 140,000. LYONS, 4 March 2001, *Offering to the Virgin* (oil on canvas) FRF 13,000. PARIS, 16 Dec 2001, *Roses in a Nest* (1850, oil on canvas, 18 x 15 ins / 46 x 38 cm) FRF 40,000. NEW YORK, 29 Oct 2002, *Still-life with Roses* (1858, oil on canvas, 30 x 24 ins / 76 x 60 cm) USD 22,000. NEW YORK, 30 Oct 2002, *Bouquet of Roses, Daisies and Violets with a Butterfly on a Mossy Bank* (1850, oil on canvas, 19 x 24 ins / 49 x 62 cm) USD 24,000. NICE, 8 April 2003, *Bouquet of Flowers* (oil on canvas, 37 x 29 ins / 93 x 73 cm) EUR 2,400. PARIS, 2 Dec 2003, *Fruit on a Terrace with a Low Relief Showing Silenus* (1843, oil on canvas, 33 x 46 ins / 83 x 117 cm) EUR 18,000.

SAINT-JEAN-GIRARD. See **GIRARD de Saint-Jean**

SAINT-JOIRE, Jehan de. See **JEAN de Saint-Yore**

SAINT-JOLY, Jean

French, 19th century.

Born in Toulouse; died towards the end of 1904.

Sculptor.

This sculptor was a pupil of Toussaint. He first exhibited at the Salon in 1863, and received an honourable mention in 1885 for a group entitled *The Archery Lesson.* His *Town of Marseilles* can be seen on the façade of the Hôtel de Ville in Paris. He showed his work for the last time in 1887.

SAINT-LANNE, Georges

French, 19th century.

Born in Bordeaux.

Painter. Genre scenes.

He was a pupil of Delacroix, and made his Salon debut in 1878.

SAINT-LANNE, Louis

French, 19th century.

Born in St-Sever.

Sculptor.

His work appeared at the Salon of the Société des Artistes Français; he received an honourable mention in 1893.

SAINT-LAURENT, Jean de

French, 18th century.

Sculptor.

Jean de Saint-Laurent worked on the decoration of the chapel in Versailles, in 1708. He settled in Russia in 1717.

SAINT-LAURENT, Paul de

French, 18th century.

Sculptor, designer of ornamental architectural features.

Paul de Saint-Laurent was a member of the Académie Saint-Luc in Paris in 1740. In 1764 he worked in the castle in Stockholm.

SAINT-LEGER, Léon Geille de. See **GEILLE DE SAINT-LÉGER**

SAINT-LÉGER-ÉBERLÉ, Abastenia.
See **ÉBERLÉ SAINT LÉGER**

SAINT-LIGIÉ, de
French, 18th century.
Miniaturist.

Saint-Ligié was active during the second half of the 18th century. He worked in The Hague in 1783.

MUSEUMS AND GALLERIES:
AMSTERDAM (Mus.): *Portrait of a Young Woman.*

SAINT-LOU, Maurice
French, 20th century.
Born 24 October 1897, in Paris.
Also active in the USA.
Painter. Portraits, landscapes, still-lifes.

Maurice Saint-Lou exhibited in many exhibitions in both France and the USA. Among his numerous distinctions, he was a Commander of Nichan-Iftikar and was awarded an Arts, Science and Literature gold medal. He adhered to the French form of Expressionism.

SAINT-LOUIS, Blaise
Haitian, 20th century.
Painter. Figures, scenes with figures.

AUCTION RECORDS:
NEW YORK, 9 July 1981, *Meeting between Toussaint Louverture and Henri Christophe* (1979, oil/hardboard, 24 x 30 ins / 61 x 76 cm) USD 2,400. PARIS, 12 June 1995, *Woman with Crossed Hands* (oil on canvas, 7¾ x 11¾ ins / 20 x 30 cm) FRF 18,000. PARIS, 1 April 1996, *The Three Graces* (oil on canvas, 29¾ x 22 ins / 75.5 x 55 cm) FRF 70,000.

SAINT-MARCEAUX, Charles René de, or René
French, 19th - 20th century.
Born 23 September 1845, in Rheims; died 23 April 1915, in Paris.
Sculptor (terracotta). Genre scenes. Busts, monuments.

Charles René de Saint-Marceaux, a pupil of Jouffroy, was influenced by the Italian Renaissance and distanced himself from the academicism of the period in order to work more boldly. Among his principal monuments in Paris are *Alexandre Dumas the Younger* in the cemetery of Montmartre, *Alphonse Daudet* in the Champs-Élysées, *Berthelot* at the Collège de France; in Bern *Creation of the Postal Union*. He also made masks that are suggestive of Symbolism. He first exhibited at the Salon of 1868, and later at the Salon des Artistes Français, of which he was a member from 1885. He was awarded a second-class medal in 1872, a first-class in 1879, and a gold at the Paris Exposition Universelle of 1889. He was made a Chevalier of the Légion d'Honneur in 1880, an Officier in 1889, a member of the Paris Institut in 1905, and an Hors-concours jury member at the London World Exhibition of 1908.

MUSEUMS AND GALLERIES:
BUCHAREST (Muz. National de Arta al României): *Harlequin* - LYONS: *Communicant* - PARIS (Mus. d'Orsay): *Bust of Dagnan Bouveret; The Youth of Dante; Spirit Guarding the Secret of the Tomb* (1879); *Mask of a Young Man; Head of a Man; Mask of a Young Girl; Mask of a Young Woman; Portrait of a Stallholder* - RHEIMS (MBA): *Harlequin*; collection of items.

AUCTION RECORDS:
PARIS, 15 May 1931, *Spirit Leaning on an Urn,* FRF 420. PARIS, 23 Nov 1936, *Gabriel d'Annunzio* (bronze) FRF 1,020. PARIS, 22 Feb 1937, *Harlequin* (wax) FRF 820. PARIS, 28 Feb 1977, *Harlequin* (1879, patinated bronze, h. 35½ ins / 90 cm) FRF 4,700. ANGERS, 25 June 1980, *Harlequin* (1879, silvered bronze, h. 27¼ ins / 69 cm) FRF 3,800. PARIS, 3 Dec 1985, *Harlequin Wearing a Horned Headdress, his arms folded* (1879, plaster original, h. 67 ins / 170 cm) FRF 250,000. PARIS, 27 June 1986, *Harlequin* (1879, bronze) FRF 7,100. PARIS, 23 June 1988, *Harlequin with a Sword* (patinated bronze, h. 34 ins / 85.5 cm) FRF 18,000. PARIS, 16 Oct 1988, *Leda and the Swan* (brown-patinated lost-wax bronze, h. 7 ins / 18 cm without plinth) FRF 4,000. PARIS, 1 Dec 1992, *Portrait of Jean de St-Marceaux* (1880, terracotta, h. 8 ins / 20.5 cm) FRF 12,000. PARIS, 24 March 1995, *Bather* (lost-wax bronze, h. 5½ ins / 14 cm) FRF 4,000. NEW YORK, 23 May 1996, *Harlequin* (1879, plaster, h. 100 ins / 254 cm) USD 68,500.

SAINT-MARCEAUX, Jean Claude de
French, 20th century.
Born 15 September 1902, in Cuy-St-Fiacre.
Sculptor.

Jean Claude de Saint-Marceaux exhibited in Paris at the Salon d'Automne and the Groupe de XII.

AUCTION RECORDS:
PARIS, 16 June 1982, *Parrot* (black-patinated bronze, h. 7¾ ins / 20 cm) FRF 8,200. DIJON, 23 Oct 1983, *Harlequin* (bronze) FRF 9,900.

SAINT-MARCEL, Émile Normand
French, 19th century.
Born 11 July 1840, in Paris.
Painter, draughtsman. Genre scenes, landscapes, landscapes with figures, animals.

He studied under Decamp, Pils, and his father, Charles Edme Saint-Marcel. He began exhibiting at the Salon in 1864.

AUCTION RECORDS:
PARIS, 22 April 1898, *Women* (red chalk) FRF 103. PARIS, 27 Jan 1923, *Snow Effect,* FRF 150. PARIS, 18 June 1926, *Winter Landscape: The Hunter,* FRF 400. PARIS, July 1946, *Towhorses* (1875, two canvases) FRF 9,600; *The Wheat Cart,* FRF 3,000. PARIS, 30 Jan 1947, *Workhorses,* FRF 2,800. VIENNA, 16 March 1971, *Harvest in Normandy,* ATS 25,000. PARIS, 17 Nov 1992, *Horse Market* (oil on canvas, 23¼ x 55 ins / 59 x 140 cm) FRF 5,600. FONTAINEBLEAU, 5 Dec 1999, *Harvest* (1903, oil on canvas) FRF 12,000.

SAINT-MARCEL-CABIN, Charles Edme or Edme
French, 19th century.
Born 20 September 1819, in Paris; died 15 February 1890, in Fontainebleau.
Painter, engraver (etching). Landscapes, animals.

Charles Edme Saint-Marcel-Cabin's masters were Eugène Delacroix and Aligny. He made his Salon debut in 1848. He worked with Delacroix and also assisted him in his decorative works. However, Saint-Marcel's own output is extremely interesting in itself. Behind his landscapes and animals there is evidence of a man with an intense personal vision and a remarkable power of expression. His lions have a majestic yet simple character, which places him on a level with Barye. Although for many years his works were scorned by art lovers, today they are highly sought after.

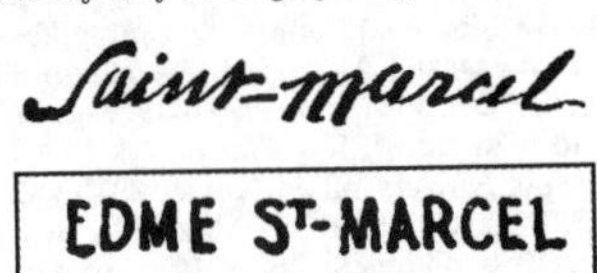

Stamp of sale

EDME S^T-MARCEL

MUSEUMS AND GALLERIES:
BAYONNE (Mus. Bonnat): *Recumbent Lion* (drawing); *Tiger Stretched out on the Ground* (drawing); *Recumbent Tiger* (drawing); *Two Wolves* (drawing) - CHÂLONS-EN-CHAMPAGNE: *View of the Gorge aux Loups (Fontainebleau)* - PONTOISE: 7 drawings of animals and landscapes.

AUCTION RECORDS:
PARIS, 1872, *Recumbent Lion* (watercolour) FRF 120. PARIS, 1899, *Recumbent Lion* (pencil, heightened with pastels) FRF 30. PARIS, 20-22 May 1920, *Doe Lying on Her Side* (pencil) FRF 100. PARIS, 2-4 June 1920, *Recumbent Tiger* (watercolour) FRF 460. PARIS, 31 May 1928, *Woman Reading; Study of Hands* (two drawings) FRF 250. PARIS, 26 June 1929, *Lioness Ready to Pounce* (drawing) FRF 250; *Lioness Walking* (drawing) FRF 450. PARIS, 28 June 1935, *Panther on the Look-out* (drawing in black pencil) FRF 45. PARIS, 14 Dec 1936, *Lion Crouching* (pen and Indian ink wash) FRF 120. PARIS, 4 Nov 1937, *Tiger with a Frog* (black chalk, heightened with watercolour) FRF 105. PARIS, 12 March 1941, *Lion and Lionesses* (pen drawing) FRF 450. PARIS, 24 Feb 1943, *Two Tigers* (watercolour) FRF 5,000. PARIS, July 1946, *Family of Lions* (pen drawing) FRF 1,050. PARIS, 30 March 1949, *Faun Seated; Nudes* (two watercolour) FRF 400. PARIS, 9 June 1949, *Flock Crossing a River in a Mountainous Landscape* (pastel) FRF 300. NEW YORK, 24 May 1985, *Recumbent Male Nude* (red and black chalk, 10 x 17 ins / 25.7 x 43.2 cm) USD 600. LONDON, 11 July 2001, *Portrait of Eugene Delacroix* (pen/brown ink, 8 x 5 ins / 20 x 13 cm) GBP 1,900. NEW YORK, 25 Jan 2002, *In the Forest* (graphite, colour pencil and gouache, 11 x 16 ins / 27 x 40 cm) USD 2,000.

SAINT-MARD, Yvan
Belgian, 20th century.
Born 1939.
Painter. Figures.

Yvan Saint-Mard studied at the fine arts academies of Brussels and Watermael-Boisfort.

SAINT-MARTIN
French, 17th - 18th century.
Active in Caen.
Painter.

Saint-Martin may have been one and the same as Jean Chemelat. His works include *Portrait of William the Conqueror*, a copy of a portrait dated 1522, produced when William's tomb was opened in 1708.

SAINT-MARTIN, Alexandre and Pierre Alexandre. See **PAU de Saint-Martin**

SAINT-MARTIN, de (Mlle)
French, 18th century.
Died c. 1761.
Painter. Portraits, genre scenes.

Mlle de Saint-Martin was a member of the Académie de Saint-Luc. She exhibited at the academy's Salon from 1751 to 1756.

SAINT-MARTIN, Henry
French, 20th century.
Born 13 June 1907, in Paris.
Painter. Nudes, landscapes.

Henry Saint-Martin, a pupil of Louise Hervieu, exhibited in Paris at the Salon des Artistes Français, the Salon des Indépendants and the Salon d'Automne.

SAINT-MARTIN, Marie Hélène
Maiden name: Domain
French, 20th century.
Born 3 February 1881, in Royan; died 5 July 1935, in Pavillon-sous-Bois.
Painter. Portraits, seascapes.

Marie Hélène Saint-Martin, a pupil of Jean-Baptiste Olive, exhibited from 1921 mainly in Paris at the Salon des Artistes Français, of which she was a member and where she was awarded a silver medal in 1924.

SAINT-MARTIN, Paul de
French, 19th century.
Born 24 September 1817, in Bolbec (Seine-Maritime).
Painter (?), lithographer. Landscapes, waterscapes, winter landscapes.

His master was Paul Delaroche. He showed his work at the Salon from 1846 to 1870.

MUSEUMS AND GALLERIES:
CAMBRAI: *View from the Environs of Meaux* - DIEPPE: *Ford* - LOUVIERS: *Canal at Fontaine-les-Nonnes; Snow Effect.*

AUCTION RECORDS:
PARIS, 22 March 1943, *Landscape*, FRF 400.

SAINT-MAUR
French, 20th century.
Born 9 December 1906, in Bordeaux; died December 1979.
Painter, sculptor.

In 1939 Saint-Maur went to the East Indies and Southeast Asia. Because of the war he was not able to return to France until 1947. Having made a reputation as a painter, he learnt the technique of oriental lacquer-work. He then gave up painting completely in order to concentrate on sculpture. He was the first to experiment with layered and heat-metalled polyester, creating forms of Brancusian restraint, transparent or opaque, matt or shining, the surfaces of which coloured the light before reflecting it. He was a master of the materials he sculpted into abstract, self-enclosed forms, portraits, windows, baptisteries, fountains. Later, he explored the use of polyurethane foam, which was more flexible and lent itself to the construction of baroque, but practicable, objects. He exhibited in Paris at the Salon d'Art Mural, which he founded in 1935, the Salon de la Jeune Peinture and the Salon des Réalités Nouvelles from 1954 as well as group exhibitions in Cannes and at the University of Caracas. He held solo shows in 1947, 1951 and 1961 in Paris and in 1956 in Brussels. In 1947, he showed his lacquered panels at the Musée Curnushi in Paris.

BIBLIOGRAPHY:
Saint-Maur, exhibition catalogue, Gal. Roux-Hentschel, Paris, 1947. *Saint-Maur*, exhibition catalogue, Gal. Raymond Creuze, Paris, 1951.

SAINT-MAURICE, P. de
French, 18th century.
Active in Paris 1720-1732.
Engraver (etching).

Saint-Maurice engraved after S. Bourdon and L. Le Nain.

SAINT-MEMIN, Charles Balthazar Julien Févret de
French, 18th - 19th century.
Born 12 March 1770, in Dijon; died 23 June 1852, in Dijon.
Painter, draughtsman, engraver (burin).

Saint-Memin emigrated at the time of the French Revolution. He stayed in Switzerland and Germany and then lived in America from 1793 to 1814, when he returned to France. There are around 200 of his drawings in existence, mostly in American museums. He was curator of Dijon Museum.

MUSEUMS AND GALLERIES:
WASHINGTON DC (NGA): drawings and prints - WORCESTER, MA (AM): *Thomas Jefferson* (1804, charcoal and chalk/paper, portrait in profile).

AUCTION RECORDS:
NEW YORK, 26-29 April 1944, *Pierre Michael Grain* (pastel) USD 350. NEW YORK, 4 Feb 1978, *Portraits of Henry Foxhall and His Wife* (around 1805, two pencil drawings, 21 1/2 x 15 1/2 ins / 54.5 x 39.5 cm) USD 14,500. NEW YORK, 13 Oct 1983, *Portrait of Barclay Haskins* (1803, pastel, 21 1/4 x 16 1/2 ins / 54 x 42 cm) USD 5,800. NEW YORK, 16 Jan 1998, *Portraits: a Man and a Woman (and Two Other Couples)* (1795, paper cut out and pasted on white paper, 2 1/2 x 2 1/4 ins / 6.37 x 5.59 cm) USD 1,955.

SAINT-MICHEL, Joseph de (Comte), or San Michel, Giuseppe
French, 18th century.
Painter, pastellist.

Saint-Michel was active from 1756 to 1778. He was painter in the court of the King of Sardinia.

MUSEUMS AND GALLERIES:
RHEIMS: *Portrait of Louis Desjardins de Courcelles, Captain of the Arquebusiers.*

AUCTION RECORDS:
PARIS, 8 April 1924, *Portraits of Men* (two pastels) FRF 400. PARIS, 27 March 1942, *Portraits of a Woman Wearing a Turban* (1775, pastel) FRF 350. PARIS, 9 Dec 1991, *Young Officer Wearing a Red Coat with a Blue Lining* (1777, pastel, 19 1/2 x 16 ins / 49.5 x 40.5 cm) FRF 5,500.

SAINT-MORIEN, de
French, 19th century.
Active in Paris during the second half of the 19th century.
Engraver (burin).

He made engravings of furniture and architectural views, which are dated 1788 and 1789.

SAINT-MORIN, de
French, 17th century.
Active in Paris in 1624.
Painter.

SAINT-MORYS, Charles Paul Jean-Baptiste Bourgevin de Vialart de (Comte)
French, 18th century.
Died 1795.
Draughtsman, engraver (etching).

SAINT-NON, Richard de, or Jean Claude Richard (Abbé)
French, 18th century.
Born 1727, in Paris; died 25 November 1791, in Paris.
Draughtsman, engraver (etching/aquatint).

Richard de Saint-Non was born in Paris in 1727. His family wanted him to enter the church and made him become a subdeacon. However, he doubted his vocation and obtained the office of clerical adviser to the Parliament in Paris in 1747 and tried, ineffectively, to discharge his duties. He was interested only in art and artists. He was exiled to Poitiers with some members of Parliament, following the troubles caused by the Papal bull *Unigenitus*.

Saint-Non lived in Poitiers from 1752 to 1757, dedicating himself to learning engraving - in particular, to applying the procedures recently invented by Prince Rupert, which led to the creation of mezzotint. With Parliament no longer in exile, he returned to Paris in 1759 to hand in his resignation to the chancellor and sell his office. Soon afterwards, he went to England and then to Italy. In Rome he met Fragonard and Hubert Robert, and travelled throughout the country with them. He had now found his calling. He was the master of the engraving process which he applied to Fragonard and Robert's interpretations of Italian nature, ruins and art, and became a close friend of these two great artists. In aquatint, he fixed their numerous charming drawings, transforming their scribbles into clear pictures.

He may have been unaware of the value of these mezzotints for, on his return to Paris, he wanted to try something different. With the help of an important group of painters, architects and engravers, Saint-Non undertook the publication of *Voyage Pittoresque de Naples et de Sicile* (*Picturesque Voyage to Naples and Sicily*), which appeared in five folio volumes from 1781 to 1786. It was a luminously illustrated work, containing 542 etched plates, and an impressive example of the typographic art. Saint-Non's aquatints are worthy of attention, more delicate and refined than some of Fragonard's drawings reproduced in *Voyage* by burin etching by Macret, Carl Gutenberg, Henriquez and Lemire.

Saint-Non gave to etching a smoothness, a felicitous imprecision and an enticing softness which had been lacking. He was the poet of mezzotint. There was a short mention of him by the abbot Brizard, in 1792. However, Louis Guimbaud has since published a more complete biography. Saint-Non's scribblings appear to have been published under the title *Selected Fragments from the Most Interesting Paintings and Works in the Palaces and Churches in Italy*. Series One and Two are entitled *Rome*, Series Three *Bologna*, Series Four *Naples*, Series Five *Venice*. The work was then completed with *Selection of Parts of Antique Paintings from Herculaneum, from Portici Museum* and published in Paris in quarto, undated.

AUCTION RECORDS:
PARIS, 26 Feb 1900, *Bacchanalian Dance* (drawing) FRF 141. PARIS, 7 and 8 May 1923, *Park in Italy* (red chalk) FRF 1,100; *Convent in Italy* (red chalk) FRF 330. PARIS, 30 April 1924, *Fountain, Vases and Balustrade, in the Gardens of an Italian Villa* (red chalk) FRF 1,305. PARIS, 26 Oct 1925, *Monastery in Italy* (red chalk) FRF 220. PARIS, 29 Jan 1927, *Fauns and Bacchante* (pencil) FRF 700. PARIS, 21 May 1928, *Fountains at the Villa Pamphili* (pencil) FRF 360. PARIS, 7 and 8 June 1928, *Dance of the Bacchantes; Women Holding a Cupid* (two drawings) FRF 2,000. PARIS, 25 June 1931, *Nero's Aqueduct at Tivoli Subiaco* (red chalk) FRF 950. PARIS, 10 June 1949, *Palace and Park in Italy* (drawing) FRF 2,000. PARIS, 4 and 5 Feb 1954, *Pastoral Scene by a Mill* (red chalk) FRF 5,000.

SAINT-OGAN, Alain
French, 20th century.
Draughtsman. Comic strips.

Alain Saint-Ogan exhibited in Paris at the Salon des Humoristes. He was the creator of *Zig, Flea* and *Alfred the Penguin*.

SAINT-OMAERS, Jan van. See **JEAN DE SAINT-OMER**

SAINT-OMER, Guillaume or Willemot
French, 14th century.
Active at the beginning of the 14th century.
Sculptor.

Guillaume Saint-Omer worked in 1304 at the Château d'Hesdin.

SAINT-OMER, Jacques
French, 14th century.
Died c. 1350.
Active in Tournai.
Sculptor (wood), architect.

Jacques Saint-Omer worked for the churches of Tournai and was one of the best wood sculptors of his time.

SAINT-OMER, Jean
French, 13th - 14th century.
Active in St-Omer 1299-1323.
Sculptor.

Jean Saint-Omer carved sculptures and decorations in the Château de Mahaut d'Artois.

SAINT-OMER, Martin
French, 14th century.
Active at the end of the 14th century.
Sculptor.

Martin Saint-Omer worked in Tournai Cathedral and, in 1391, on the belfry of Douai.

SAINT-OMER, Simon
French, 14th century.
Sculptor.

Simon Saint-Omer carried out restoration work in the abbey church of Saint-Jean in Valenciennes.

SAINT-OMER, Simon
French, 16th century.
Active in Beauvais in 1507.
Sculptor, architect.

Simon Saint-Omer worked with Martin Chambiges in Troyes Cathedral.

SAINT-OURS, Jacques
Swiss, 18th century.
Born 22 November 1708, in Geneva; died 1773, in Geneva.
Enameller, engraver, carver.

Jacques Saint-Ours was the father of Jean Pierre Saint-Ours.

SAINT-OURS, Jean Pierre
Swiss, 18th - 19th century.
Born 4 April 1752, in Geneva; died 6 April 1809, in Geneva.
Painter. History painting, portraits, genre scenes.

The father of Jean Pierre Saint-Ours, Jacques Saint-Ours, sent him to Paris at the age of 16, where he entered the school of the Académie Royale and Vien's studio. He was awarded several prizes in 1772 and 1774, carrying off second place in the Grand Prix of 1778 and first place in 1780. Saint-Ours, a foreigner and Protestant, was not entitled to a Rome allowance. He went to the city at his own expense, but still enjoyed the teaching and privileges usually granted. Saint-Ours produced serious studies, painting historical compositions that earned him the patronage of the cardinal of Bernis and the marquis of Créqui, but the climate in Rome profoundly affected his health. He returned to Geneva in 1792 and settled there for good. The Revolution dealt a serious blow to history painters. Saint-Ours felt the impact of this and was forced to devote himself almost exclusively to portrait painting. In 1803 he took part in the competition set up by the French government to celebrate the Concordat. Saint-Ours gained a certificate of merit from this and was appointed a member of the Institut de France. Most of his paintings were collected by Genevese art-lovers.

BIBLIOGRAPHY:
Ruoss, Mylène, *Zur Genfer Historienmalerei von Jean-Pierre Saint-Ours 1752-1809*, P. Lang, Bern, Berlin, 1995.

MUSEUMS AND GALLERIES:
BURGHAUSEN: *Samnite Fiancée* - GENEVA (MAH): *Olympic Games; Earthquake*; study; *Madame Lissignol, at the time Mademoiselle Simard; Abraham Lissignol; Pan-Sarasin; Four Subjects from The Levite of Ephraim* (sketch); *Tronchin of Les Délices; Fable Reading* - GENEVA (Mus. Ariana): *Battle between the Romans and the Barbarians; Portraits of Councillor de La Rive Billiet, Jean Revilliod and Jean Louis Revilliod* - MULHOUSE: *Male Study* - MUNICH (Alte Pinakothek): *Court of the New-borns in Sparta* - NEUCHÂTEL: *Madame St-Ours with a Child; The Concordat Allegory* - VERSAILLES (Trianon): *David Learning of the Death of Saul.*

AUCTION RECORDS:
PARIS, 1814, *Phryne Found Innocent by her Judges* (pen drawing with bistre wash) FRF 22. PARIS, 10 Feb 1899, *Psyche and Zephire*, FRF 102. PARIS, 21 Feb 1919, *Blind Boy* (red chalk) FRF 35. ZURICH, 20 May 1977, *Portrait of Princess Portia* (1803, oil on canvas, 46 x 38 1/4 ins / 116 x 97 cm) CHF 18,500. ZURICH, 12 Nov 1982, *Triumph of Beauty* (oil on canvas, 42 1/2 x 74 1/2 ins / 108 x 189 cm) CHF 12,000. PARIS, 21 Nov 1984, *Family of Darius Begging Alexander for Clemency* (1780, pen and brown wash heightened with white/pencil outlines, 14 x 28 1/4 ins / 35.5 x 71.5 cm) FRF 33,000. BERN, 26 Oct 1985, *Orpheus* (oil on panel, 19 x 15 ins / 48.5 x 38 cm) CHF 4,300. ZURICH, 8 Dec 1994, *Homer Singing the Odyssey at the Entrance to a Village in Greece* (oil on canvas, 16 1/4 x 12 ins / 41 x 30.5 cm) CHF 14,950. ZURICH, 10 Dec 1996, *St-Laurent-hors-les-murs; Ancient Roman Monuments* (pen/paper, a pair, 12 1/4 x 18 ins / 31 x 45.5 cm) CHF 2,990. ZURICH, 8 Dec 1999, *Fight between Horatio and the Curiacs* (oil on panel, 11 x 16 ins / 28 x 40 cm) CHF 22,000. PARIS, 1 Dec 2000, *Study of a Man with Drapery* (charcoal, colour wash heightened with white, 13 x 9 ins / 34 x 24 cm) FRF 50,000. GENEVA, 18 Nov 2001, *Untitled* (drawings, 13 in one frame) CHF 3,200. PARIS, 13 Dec 2002, *Inhabitants of Alba Longa* (pen and ink wash heightened with gouache, 22 x 37 ins / 56 x 93 cm) EUR 13,000. SWITZERLAND, 13 June 2003, *Portrait of a Young Woman* (1806, oil on canvas, 24 x 19 ins / 60 x 49 cm) CHF 4,500.

SAINT-PAUL, Claude
French, 17th century.
Born 3 January 1614, in Nancy.
Painter. History painting.

Claude Saint-Paul was the son of Jean Saint-Paul, and worked for the Duke of Lorraine.

SAINT-PAUL, Claude, or Saint-Pol or Simpol
French, 17th - 18th century.
Born c. 1666, in Clamecy (Nièvre); died 31 October 1716, in Paris.
Painter, draughtsman. Religious subjects.

Claude Saint-Paul was the pupil of Louis de Boullogne. He worked as a draughtsman for burin engravings.

MUSEUMS AND GALLERIES:
PARIS (Louvre): *Christ at the House of Martha and Mary.*

SAINT-PAUL, Édouard
French, 20th century.
Sculptor.

Édouard Saint-Paul exhibited at the Salon d'Automne, of which he was a member, and the Salon des Tuileries.

SAINT-PAUL, Hermance
French, 19th century.
Born in Paris.
Painter. Portraits.

She was a pupil of Chaplain, and made her Salon debut in 1868.

SAINT-PAUL, Jean
French, 17th century.
Painter. Portraits, genre scenes.

Jean Saint-Paul was the father of Claude Saint-Paul. He worked for the city of Nancy and for the Duke of Lorraine between 1614 and 1623. He produced several portraits, and also painted coats of arms.

SAINT-PAUL, Jean
French, 20th century.
Born 4 September 1897, in Paris.
Painter, illustrator. Designs for tapestries.

Jean Saint-Paul exhibited in Paris at the Salon d'Automne, the Salon des Indépendants and the Salon des Tuileries. He was best known for his illustration of the works of Pierre Loüys.

SAINT-PAULET, Pierre de (Marquis).
See **GAUTERI**

SAINT-PÈRE, Claude
French, 18th century.
Active in Dijon c. 1736.
Sculptor, designer of ornamental architectural features.

SAINT-PHALLE, Niki de, pseudonym of Fal de Saint Phalle, Catherine Marie-Agnès
French, 20th century.
Born 29 October 1930, in Neuilly-sur-Seine; died 22 May 2002, in San Diego (California), USA.
Sculptor, painter (including gouache), watercolourist, collage artist, engraver, draughtswoman, performance artist. Figures. Stage sets, artists' books, designs (jewels/objets d'art).

Nouvelle Figuration.
Nouveaux Réalistes group.
Niki de Saint-Phalle was educated at the Sacred Heart Convent in New York, where she lived from 1933 to 1951. In 1952 she went to live in Paris with her husband, Harry Matthews, and travelled in Europe. She was a self-taught painter who painted her first canvases in 1953 and then turned to sculpture. In 1960 she met Jean Tinguely, whose companion she became. In the same year Pierre Restany founded the Nouveaux Réalistes group and Niki de Saint-Phalle joined it in 1961.

She began to paint as a therapy after treatment in a psychiatric hospital, and initially she used collage techniques, with simultaneous references to Surrealism, Abstract Expressionism and Art Brut. From 1956 the collage technique led her to include objects and plaster additions in her paintings, which were baroque and fanciful in character. In 1960, using the symbolic and parodic theme of the *Martyrdom of St Sebastian*, she included cork targets in these assemblages and the viewers were provided with small arrows so they could participate in a work in progress. This led to other gestures aimed at leaving a mark on what she conceived to be an unfinished work. In 1961 she incorporated in her *Tableaux-surprises* (*Surprise Paintings*) containers of paint intended to be burst by the viewers, so that the colours flowed over the surface of the pictures and modified both their appearance and formal structure. She saw the spontaneous, violent and aggressive action as a way of demythologising art. At the same time, it would seem to have been a satirical comment on the excesses of American Tachism, which had by then become a sort of international academicism. In 1961 Pierre Restany organised a demonstration of this activity under the title *Feu à volonté* (*Free Shoot*), the assemblages to be shot at by the viewers being wisely set up in an armoured shooting-gallery. It drew huge crowds and Niki de Saint-Phalle's name was soon known nationally and internationally.

Once these semi-scandalous events had drawn attention to her, she almost completely abandoned the shooting procedure, with its arbitrary colour and spectator involvement, and her next period was devoted to exorcising a variety of personal and collective obsessions. As Pierre Restany so neatly says, 'midway between Louise Nevelson and Robert Rauschenberg', Niki de Saint-Phalle assembled strange altarpieces, almost blasphemous, piling up crucifixes, statues of the Sacred Heart, toy pistols, monstrous animals, celluloid dolls, covering them with a shell of silver paint, as in *Blasphemous Episodes*, and avoiding both the totemism of Louise Nevelson and the aestheticism of Rauschenberg. In the *Everyday Mythologies* of 1964 she exhibited a triptych devoted to *The Bride*, a subject she had already used, and which gives point to her earlier works; doubtless the ridiculous marriage ceremony seemed to her especially characteristic of the everyday mythologies that Gassiot-Talabot had suggested should be targets. In 1965 she began to create *Nanas*, gigantic and farcical female statues, related both to the age-old *Lespugna Venus* and the *Bal des Quat-z'arts*, black and wearing either, in the earliest examples, multi-coloured garments made from rags, or, later, bright polyester fabric. With reference to the *Nanas*, Pierre Restany has spoken of 'Dubuffet reviewed and corrected by Appel' and 'Art Brut and the CoBrA style'. Niki de Saint-Phalle was aiming to make her buxom and cheerful *Nanas* a symbol of the mother-goddess of our time.

In 1966, in collaboration with Tinguely, she built a reclining *Nana* thirty-five metres long in the Moderna Museet, Stockholm. The entrance was a door between the thighs of *Cathedral Nana* and inside there was a bar, an exhibition room and a restaurant. In 1967, at the Montreal Exposition Universelle, she organised on the roof of the French Pavilion a war-like confrontation between her *Nanas* and Tinguely's infernal machines. In the 1980s the *Skinnys* were a counterpoint to the *Nanas*; small lights were attached to these hollow, spindly silhouettes. While still sticking to her favourite subjects - woman, motherhood, love, dreaming - she then moved to the monsters of the *Paintings Burst Open* of 1990. Moving images are superimposed on a brightly coloured background, the levels interpenetrating to tell a story. 'I like the idea of the form bursting and coming back to its first form after passing through abstraction. For that I wanted movement, but no visible mechanical system.' For these works she worked with computer experts to develop a system for animating the canvas.

She made many open-air sculptures: 1966, *Hon* with Tinguely and Ultvedt (now destroyed) and *The Fantastic Paradise* for the Moderna Museet, Stockholm; 1967, *Nana Dream House* at the Stedelijk Museum, Amsterdam and at the Fondation Maeght in Saint-Paul-de-Vence; from 1970 to 1993, *The Cyclops*, with Tinguely in Milly-la-Forêt; 1972, *Golem* in Jerusalem; 1973, *The Dragon* in Knokke-Het-Zoute; 1973-1974, *Swimming Pool Nana* in St Tropez; 1974, *Caroline, Charlotte, Sophie*, three giant Nanas in Hanover, *the Poet and his Muse* in the University of Ulm; since 1979 (unfinished in 1996) *The Tarot Garden*, inspired by the cards of the tarot pack, in Garavicchio (Southern Tuscany); 1983, *The Stravinsky Fountain* with Tingueley in Paris, *Sun God* in the University of Southern California, San Diego; 1988, *Château-Chinon Fountain* with Tinguely at the town hall of Château-Chinon; 1988-1989, *Serpents' Heads Fountain* at the Long Island Medical Center, (New York); 1990, funerary monument for the Tinguely tombe in the Montparnasse cemetery, Paris, and *The Ideal Temple* for an ecumenical church in Nîmes; 1991, installation of a Niki Art Museum in Nasu (Tochigi prefecture); 2001, inauguration in Jerusalem of the *Noah's Ark*, a park of sculptures in the shape of animals. She has also been involved with performances, designed stage sets (1966, *Éloge de la folie* (*In Praise of Folly*), a ballet by Raymond Petit), artists' books and many decorative objects (jewellery, perfume bottles).

Beyond their monstrousness, their ogress-like voracity, and their many psychoanalytical meanings, Niki de Saint-Phalle's creatures are figures in a carnival, jokers full of vitality and a poetic *joie de vivre*. 'I have no ideas about works of art. I didn't go to art school. For me sculpture is not culture, but a way of living. My artistic education came from cathedrals, Facteur Cheval [a postman who, over 25 years of delivering letters, constructed a 'palace' from stones he picked up] and the architect Gaudí.'

She exhibited in group exhibitions, including regularly in Paris: 1961, 1962 at Salon Comparaisons, 1963 Biennale; 1964, *Mythologies Quotidiens* (*Everyday Mythologies*) and 1965, *Narrative Figuration*, organised by Gassiot-Talabot at the Musée d'Art Moderne; 1965, Salon de Mai; 1968, *Expansions-Environnement* at the Musée Galliera, organised by P. Restany; 1977, Musée National d'Art Moderne; and 1961, 1962, 1981, Stedelijk Museum, Amsterdam; 1961, 1968, Museum of Modern Art, New York; 1963, 1966, 1972, Museum of Fine Arts, Houston; 1966, Moderna Museet, Stockholm and the Kunsthalle, Bern; 1966, 1985, Art Institute, Chicago; 1967, Exposition Universelle, Montreal, and the Carnegie Institute, Pittsburgh; 1968, ICA (Institute of Contemporary Art), London; 1968, 1969, 1985, Museum of Contemporary Art, Chicago; 1969, 1973, Kunstverein, Hannover; 1980, Whitney Museum of American Art, New York; 1988, the Venice Biennale; 1989, the Musée Cantonal des Beaux-Arts, Lausanne; 1990, the Russian Museum, St Petersburg and the Museum of Modern Art, Rijeka; 1991, Royal Academy of Arts, London; 2001, exhibition on the unreal, the transreal and the reconstruction of reality, *Hypermental*, Kunsthalle, Hamburg.

Her solo shows include: 1956, Saint-Gall; 1962, Galerie Rive Droite, Paris; from 1965, regularly at the Galerie Alexander Iolas, Paris, New York, Geneva, Milan; 1967, Stedelijk Museum, Amsterdam; 1969, Kunstverein, Hanover, Kunstmuseum, Lucerne; 1975, Palais des Beaux-Arts, Brussels; 1976, Museum Boymans Van Beuningen, Rotterdam, Nordjyllands Kunstmuseum, Aalborg; 1979, travelling exhibition in the USA; 1980, Musée National d'Art Moderne, Paris, Wilhelm Lehmbruck Museum des Stadt, Duisbourg, Kunsthalle, Nuremberg; 1980-1981, 1982-1983, 1986, Space Niky, Tokyo; 1987, Kunsthalle von Hypo-Kultursiftung, Munich; 1987-1988, Nassau County Museum of Fine Art, New York; 1988, Dominican Monastery, Canterbury; 1990-1991, Musée des Arts Décoratifs, Paris; 1992, Kunst und Ausstellungshalle, Bonn; 1993, Musée d'Art Moderne de la Ville de Paris, Musée d'Art et d'Histoire, Fribourg; 1996, Galerie Vidal-Saint Phalle, Paris, prints; 2001, *La Vie Joyeuse des Objets (The Joyful Life of Objects)*, the artist's gift of a collection of twenty pieces, Musée des Arts Décoratifs, Paris; 2002, retrospective, Musée d'Art Moderne et d'Art Contemporain, Nice; 2002, *From Niki Mathews to Niki de Saint Phalle*, Sprengel Museum, Hanover; 2003, The Birth of the Nanas: Niki de Saint Phalle's Works from the 1960s, Sprengel Museum, Hanover.

BIBLIOGRAPHY:

Restany, Pierre (preface), *Art moral, art sacré*, exhibition catalogue, Gal. Rive droite, Paris, 1962. Descargues, Pierre, *Les Nanas*, exhibition catalogue, Gal. Alexandre Iolas, Paris, 1965. Restany, Pierre, *Les Nouveaux Réalistes*, Éd. Planète, Paris, 1968. *Niki de Saint-Phalle*, exhibition catalogue, Gal. Alexandre Iolas, Paris, 1970. Hahn, Otto, "*Les Nanas aux Halles*' in *L'Express*, periodical, Paris, 23 March 1970. *Niki de Saint-Phalle*, exhibition catalogue, Éd. du Centre Georges-Pompidou, Paris, 1980. *Niki de Saint-Phalle*, exhibition catalogue, Wilhelm-Lehmbruck-Museum, Duisburg, 1980. Ponsio, Giuseppe, *Tarot Cards in Sculpture by Niki de Saint-Phalle*, Gimpel Fils, London, Milan, 1985. Eubel, Paul, ed, *Pictures for the Sky: Art Kites*, Prestel, Munich, 1992. *Niki de Saint-Phalle*, exhibition catalogue, Musée d'Art moderne de la Ville de Paris, Paris, 1993. Thomas, Mona, "*Niki de Saint-Phalle - L'Invitation au musée*' in *Art Press* n° 183, periodical, Paris, September 1993. Saint-Phalle, Niki de, *Mon secret*, La Différence, Paris, 1994. Grosenik, Uta/Hulten, Pontus, *Niki de Saint-Phalle*, Stuttgart: Gerd Hatje, 1995 (also in English). Remer, Abby, *Pioneering Spirits: the Lives and Times of Remarkable Women Artists in Western History*, Davis Publications, Worcester (MA), 1997 (last two chapters). Saint-Phalle, Niki de, *Traces. Remembering (1930-1949)*, Acatos, Lausanne, 1999. *Niki de Saint-Phalle. Peintures, tirs, assemblages, reliefs, 1949-2000*, Acatos, Lausanne, 2001. *Niki de Saint-Phalle: la Donation au Musée d'Art contemporain et d'Art moderne de Nice*, G. Naef, Geneva, 2002. Carrick, Jill, '*Phallic Victories? Niki de Saint-Phallle's 'Tirs'* in *Art History UK*, vol 26, no. 5, Nov 2003.

MUSEUMS AND GALLERIES:

AMSTERDAM (Stedelijk Mus.) - HANOVER (Sprengel Mus.): 400 works - HOUSTON (MFA): *Gorgo in New York* - MARSEILLES (Mus. Cantini): *Seated Nana, Negress* (1971) - NEW YORK (Whitney Mus. of American Art): *Black Venus* (1967) - NICE (Mus. d'Art Moderne et d'Art Contemporain): 63 paintings and sculptures, 112 works on paper (donated by the artist in 2001) - PARIS (BNF): *Last Night I Had a Dream* - PARIS (MNAM-CCI): *Crucifixion; The Bride, Eva Maria* (1963); *The Waldaff* (1965) - PARIS (Mus. des Arts décoratifs): rug*Nana* (sisal); *Nana and Man* (sisal, rug); *Charly* (1981, painted polyester, chair); *Oval Table* (1990, mosaic of glass and mirror on wood); *Thread of the Discourse* (1980, painted polyester, iron base, electrical parts, lamp); *Death Mask* (1997, polyester, mosaic of mirrors on wood, iron, lamp); *Frog with Helmet* (1988, painted polyester, vase); *Angel* (1993, painted polyester and iron, vase) - STOCKHOLM (Moderna Mus.).

AUCTION RECORDS:

PARIS, 4 Nov 1971, *Nana* (Polyester) FRF 8,000. PARIS, 18 March 1972, *Napoleon, you've got a spider on the ceiling* (mask) FRF 30,000. LOS ANGELES, 22 Jan 1973, *Nana*, USD 3,750. NEW YORK, 6 June 1974, *Nana* (plaster) USD 3,000. NEW YORK, 28 May 1976, *Nana* (1976, mixed media/cut paper, 20 x 22 ins / 51 x 56 cm) USD 550. PARIS, 22 March 1977, *Snake* (Polyester, 67 x 32¾ x 4 ins / 170 x 83 x 10 cm) FRF 4,000. LONDON, 5 April 1979, *Nana* (c. 1967, painted polyester, h. 30¾ ins / 78 cm) GBP 1,400. LONDON, 3 July 1980, *Woman in a Multi-Coloured Interior* (oil on canvas, 28¾ x 36 ins / 73 x 91.5 cm) GBP 700. NEW YORK, 1 Nov 1984, *snake* (plaster with acrylic paint, 19¾ x 24½ ins / 50 x 62 cm) USD 9,500. LONDON, 13 Feb 1985, *Here's to you, Pablo* (felt pen, 21½ x 29½ ins / 54.8 x 74.8 cm) GBP 1,600. NEW YORK, 3 May 1985, *Jane* (1965, fabric and coloured string/papier mâché, 42¼ x 30¾ x 26¼ ins / 107 x 78 x 66.5 cm) USD 9,000. LONDON, 26 June 1986, *Nana* (painted fibreglass, 111 x 67 x 39¼ ins / 282 x 170 x 100 cm) GBP 22,000. NEW YORK, 4 Nov 1987, *Untitled* (c. 1978, acrylic and gold paint/plaster, h. 90 ins / 228.7 cm) USD 60,000. PARIS, 4 Dec 1987, *Blind Man in a Field* (1978-1979, painted plaster) FRF 60,000. NEW YORK, 20 Feb 1988, *Man reading the Newspaper, Seated on a Snake* (1980, painted ceramic, 6 x 9½ ins / 15 x 24 cm) USD 2,200. LONDON, 25 Feb 1988, *Double Creature* (painted polyester, 5½ x 9½ x 7¾ ins / 14 x 24 x 20 cm) GBP 4,620. LOKEREN, 8 Oct 1988, *Elephant* (painted polyester, h. 11¾ ins / 30 cm) BEF 190,000. NEW YORK, 8 Oct 1988, *Lady and the Dragon* (painted polyester, 5¼ x 9 x 10 ins / 13.6 x 22.8 x 25.3 cm) USD 13,750. PARIS, 21 Nov 1988, *Study for a Large Tapestry* (c. 1970, acrylic/mounted paper, 85 x 120 ins / 215 x 305 cm) FRF 130,000. LONDON, 6 April 1989, *Snake* (painted polyester, h. 65¼ ins / 165.5 cm) GBP 22,000. NEW YORK, 3 May 1989, *Sun Goddess with Nana* (1980, moulded and painted Polyester, feathers and electric lightbulbs, 66¼ x 35 x 13½ ins / 168 x 89 x 34 cm) USD 82,500. PARIS, 24 May 1989, *Frog* (polychrome in Polyester, sculpture) FRF 21,000. PARIS, 12 June 1989, *Nana* (painted resin, sculpture, h. 24¾ ins / 63 cm) FRF 380,000. PARIS, 13 Oct 1989, *Pink Heart* (1964, mixed media, 25½ x 31½ ins / 65 x 80 cm) FRF 300,000. NEW YORK, 9 Nov 1989, *Camel* (painted polyester, 62 x 66 ins / 157.5 x 167.5 cm) USD 104,500. PARIS, 13 Dec 1989, *Nana* (sculpture in painted plaster, h. 7½ ins / 19 cm) FRF 65,000. PARIS, 8 April 1990, *Nana* (pencil, felt and collage/card, 18 x 12¼ ins / 46 x 31 cm) FRF 52,000. NEW YORK, 8 May 1990, *Palais de Justice* (1979, acrylic and pencil/Polyester, h. 31½ ins / 80 cm) USD 66,000. COPENHAGEN, 30 May 1990, *Painted Road* (1960, diam. 6¼ ins / 16 cm) DKK 22,000. LONDON, 28 June 1990, *Seated Nana* (1968, hand-painted polyester, 28¾ x 32 x 30½ ins / 73 x 81.2 x 77.5 cm) GBP 99,000. COPENHAGEN, 14-15 Nov 1990, *Object* (1961, painted frying pan, diam. 12¼ ins / 31 cm) DKK 25,000. PARIS, 16 Dec 1990, *Armchair with Snakes* (stratified Polyester and coloured polyurethane varnish, h. 40½ ins / 103 cm, l. 32 ins/81 cm, w. 28¼ ins/72 cm) FRF 315,000. COPENHAGEN, 30 May 1991, *Nana* (painted polyester, h. 9¾ ins / 25 cm) DKK 46,000. LONDON, 17 Oct 1991, *Table* (acrylic/fibreglass, h. 28¾ ins / 73 cm) GBP 13,200. PARIS, 2 Dec 1991, *Large Armchair with Snake* (painted polyester, h. 40½ ins / 103 cm, w. 32¼ ins/82 cm, prof. 28 ins/71 cm) FRF 125,000. PARIS, 4 Dec 1991, *Dancer* (1966, plaster original, h. 25¼ ins / 64 cm) FRF 175,000. LOKEREN, 21 March 1992, *Nana* (painted polyester) BEF 950,000. PARIS, 1 Oct 1992, *Cathedral* (1961, rifle shooting on an assemblage of objects, skulls, ornamental figures and toys, 28 x 24¼ ins / 71 x 61.5 cm) FRF 80,000. LONDON, 15 Oct 1992, *Tree of Life* (1991, painted aluminium, Polyester and iron, 27½ x 14½ x 11¾ ins / 70 x 37 x 30 cm) GBP 5,500. PARIS, 26 Nov 1992, *Snake Armchair* (1982, polychrome polyester, 40½ x 32¼ x

23½ ins / 103 x 82 x 60 cm) FRF 120,000. LONDON, 3 Dec 1992, *Nana with Dog* (1987, painted polyester, h. 15¾ ins / 40 cm) GBP 10,450; *Nana* (painted polyester, wall relief, 56 x 50½ x 3¾ ins / 142.4 x 128 x 9.5 cm) GBP 39,600. AMSTERDAM, 9 Dec 1992, *Untitled* (1968, painted plaster, h. 6 ins / 15.5 cm) NLG 21, 850. NEW YORK, 4 May 1993, *Table and Footstool* (table: 28½ x 32 x 24 ins / 72.4 x 81.3 x 61 cm; tabouret: 15 x 15 x 12½ ins/38.1 x 38.1 x 31.8 cm) USD 25,300. STOCKHOLM, 10-12 May 1993, *Bull* (varnished plaster, h. 15¾ ins / 40 cm, l. 24½ ins/62 cm) SEK 55,000. COPENHAGEN, 3 June 1993, *Bull* (painted polyester, h. 15¾ ins / 40 cm, l. 23½ ins/60 cm) DKK 65,000. PARIS, 18 June 1993, *Cow and Man Reading a Newspaper* (1974, synthetic resin and vinyl gouache, collection of two sculptures, man 9 x 7½ x 5 ins / 22 x 19 x 13 cm; cow 24¾ x 17¾ x 6 ins/63 x 45 x 15 cm) FRF 150,000. LONDON, 24 June 1993, *Shooting Gallery* (assemblage of plaster, metal and wood/panel with gold spray paint, 31½ x 27 x 5 ins / 80 x 68.5 x 12.7 cm) GBP 31,050. ZURICH, 24 June 1993, *Dear Daniel Claude* (1975, mixed media, collage, watercolour and pencil, 8¼ x 10¾ ins / 21.2 x 27.5 cm) CHF 9,000. LOKEREN, 9 Oct 1993, *Cow* (painted polyester, h. 21½ ins / 54.5 cm, w. 25½ ins/64.5 cm) BEF 230,000. STOCKHOLM, 30 Nov 1993, *Female figure* (1968, polychrome painted clay, h. 8 ins / 20.5 cm) SEK 67,000. NEW YORK, 25-26 Feb 1994, *Untitled* (painted polyester, cow 26 x 16 x 18 ins / 66 x 40.6 x 45.7 cm; man 8½ x 5¼ x 7 ins/21.6 x 13.3 x 17.8 cm) USD 18,400. PARIS, 24 June 1994, *Little Heart* (1967, collage and mixed media/canvas, 24½ x 20¾ ins / 62 x 53 cm) FRF 180,000. AMSTERDAM, 31 May 1995, *Fish* (glazed terracotta/iron base, l. 32 ins / 81 cm) NLG 12,980. LOKEREN, 7 Oct 1995, *Snake-Vase* (bronze, h. 20¾ ins / 53 cm, w. 10¾ ins/27.5 cm) BEF 200,000. LONDON, 26 Oct 1995, *Clarice Chair Woman* (painted polyester, 46¾ x 45 x 33 ins / 119 x 114 x 84 cm) GBP 27,600. NEW YORK, 16 Nov 1995, *Sphynx* (painted polyester, 11½ x 16½ x 11 ins / 29.2 x 41.9 x 27.9 cm) USD 17,250. PARIS, 13 Dec 1995, *Shooting Range with Aircraft* (1961, assemblage of objects/panel with drips of paint, 51¼ x 76¾ ins / 130 x 195 cm) FRF 135,000. COPENHAGEN, 12 March 1996, *Composition* (1968, watercolour, gouache and soft chalks, 25½ x 18½ ins / 65 x 47 cm) DKK 29,000. PARIS, 10 June 1996, *Model for a Swimming Poll Nana* (pencil, 15¾ x 11½ ins / 40 x 29 cm) FRF 13,600. LONDON, 26 June 1996, *The Poet and his Muse* (1973, painted polyester, 94½ x 56 x 22½ ins / 240 x 142 x 57 cm) GBP 166,500. PARIS, 29 Nov 1996, *Footballers* (1993, resin and stratified Polyester, 13¾ x 23 x 16¼ ins / 35 x 58.5 x 41 cm) FRF 130,000. AMSTERDAM, 10 Dec 1996, *Nana* (c. 1967, painted plaster, sculpture, h. 8 ins / 20.5 cm) NLG 20,757. LONDON, 29 May 1997, *Clarice Chair Woman*; *Clarice Chair Man* (1981-1982, painted polyester, a pair, 47½ x 45 x 33 ins / 120.7 x 114.3 x 83.8 cm and 52½ x 47 x 33 ins/133.4 x 119.4 x 83.8 cm) GBP 36,700. LONDON, 25 June 1997, *The Bride* (1963, assemblage, 72 x 70 x 39¼ ins / 182 x 178 x 100 cm) GBP 128,000. LONDON, 23 Oct 1997, *Garden of Goddesses* (1988, ceramic, glass and mosaic, 23 x 72¼ ins / 58.5 x 183.5 cm) GBP 19,550. ZURICH, 18 Nov 1997, *Wandering Knight* (1962, assemblage, 24½ x 19¼ ins / 62 x 49 cm) CHF 50,000. PARIS, 18 Sept 1999, *The Prophet* (1990, polyester, golden leaves, 106 x 28x28 ins / 270 x 70x70 cm) FRF 450,000. LONDON, 8 Dec 1999, *Nana* (papier mache, wool, string, resin, oil, collage on wood, 41 x 35x19 ins / 104 x 88x47 cm) GBP 60,000. PARIS, 27 Oct 2000, *Gwendoline* (coloured paster, 15 x 10x7 ins / 37 x 25x19 cm) FRF 310,000. PARIS, 27 Oct 2000, *Nana, Bathroom* (coloured polyester, 102 x 79x79 ins / 260 x 200x200 cm) FRF 1,100,000. NEW YORK, 15 May 2001, *White and Black Altar* (1962, oil, plaster, elements, metal wire, taxidermied owl, 98 x 79x14 ins / 250 x 200x35 cm) USD 65,000. LONDON, 28 June 2001, *Monkey and Child* (1998, painted polyester, 45 x 35 ins / 114 x 88 cm) GBP 30,000. LONDON, 27 June 2002, *Lou Lou and Mimi* (1965, fabric, paper, string, collage, fiberglass, wood, h. 82 ins / 208 cm) GBP 85,000. NEW YORK, 12 Nov 2002, *Bathers* (1984, polychromed polyester, fiberglass, 108 x 112x120 ins / 274 x 284x304 cm) USD 175,000. AMSTERDAM, 28 May 2003, *Little Horse* (1963, plastic toys, fabric, cotton thread, h. 13 ins / 32 cm) USD 95,000. NEW YORK, 12 Nov 2003, *Moon* (1987, glass tile, mirror tile, painted polyester, 118 x 48x41 ins / 300 x 121x103 cm) USD 320,000. LONDON, 24 June 2004, *Large Chair with Snake - Table, Stool and Urn* (painted polyester) GBP 50,000. PARIS, 18 July 2004, *Vie en rose* (1968, painted polyester, 107 x 91x25 ins / 272 x 230x64 cm) EUR 360,000.

SAINT-PHAR, J. L. Eustache. See **SAINT-FAR**

SAINT-PIERRE, Gaston Casimir

French, 19th - 20th century.

Born 12 May 1833, in Nîmes; died 18 December 1916, in Paris.

Painter, pastellist. Portraits, genre scenes.

Gaston Casimir Saint-Pierre, a pupil of Léon Cogniet and Charles François Jalabert, is best known for his large decorative panels. During his lifetime the state bought from him several paintings that can now be seen in public collections. Casimir first exhibited at the Salon de Paris in 1861. He then exhibited at the Salon des Artistes Français, of which he was a member from 1883 and became an out-of-competition member and a member of the committee and jury. He was awarded a second-class medal in 1881 and was made a Chevalier of the Légion d'Honneur in 1881 and an Officier in 1903.

MUSEUMS AND GALLERIES:

AMIENS: *Woman Thinking* - BAYONNE: *Bacchante* - BORDEAUX (MBA): *Daphne* - CHÂTEAUROUX: *Venus Making Fun of Love* - LIMOGES: *Tenderness and Indifference* - LYONS: *Saadia* - PARIS (Mus. d'Orsay): *Mme Claude Vignon* - TARBES: *Portrait of Madame X* - TOURCOING: *Arab Woman*.

AUCTION RECORDS:

PARIS, 1890, *Head of a Woman* (North African costume) FRF 300. PARIS, 1898, *Oriental Woman*, FRF 300. PARIS, 5 Dec 1936, *Glass of Absinthe* (pastel) FRF 290. PARIS, 17 April 1950, *Bust of a Brunette*, FRF 2,700. VIENNA, 12 March 1974, *Oriental Dancer*, ATS 15,000. NEW YORK, 3 May 1979, *Odalisque* (oil on canvas, 43 x 61 ins / 109 x 154 cm) USD 16,500. ENGHIEN-LES-BAINS, 22 Nov 1981, *Young Oriental Girl with a Crutch* (oil on canvas, 55½ x 35¾ ins / 141 x 91 cm) FRF 22,000. BARBIZON, 24 July 1983, *Young Oriental Girls* (oil on canvas, 21¼ x 25½ ins / 54 x 65 cm) FRF 11,500. NEW YORK, 24 May 1985, *Street Musicians* (oil on canvas, 40 x 29¼ ins / 101.6 x 74.5 cm) USD 5,000. LONDON, 28 Nov 1986, *Diana the Huntress* (oil on canvas, 77¼ x 51 ins / 196 x 129.5 cm) GBP 31,000. PARIS, 28 May 1991, *Song of the Oleander* (oil on canvas, 33½ x 20¾ ins / 85 x 53 cm) FRF 230,000. PARIS, 7 Dec 1992, *Halima* (oil on canvas, 22 x 18 ins / 56 x 46 cm) FRF 40,000. LONDON, 17 March 1993, *Flora and Zephyr* (oil on canvas, 29¼ x 37 ins / 74 x 94 cm) GBP 12,075.

SAINT-PIERRE, Germain de. See **GERMAIN DE SAINT-PIERRE**

SAINT-PIERRE DE MONTZAIGLE, Edgard de. See **MONTZAIGLE DE SAINT-PIERRE**

SAINT-PLANCARD, Émélie Albertine

French, 19th century.

Born in Paris.

Painter.

Her teachers were Madame Caille and Madame Tremblaye. Her first Salon exhibition was in 1879.

SAINT-POL, Claude. See **SAINT-PAUL Claude**

SAINT-PRIEST, Charles
French, 19th century.
Painter.
He exhibited his work at the Salon between 1846 and 1848.

SAINT-PRIEST, Jehan de
French, 15th - 16th century.
Active in Lyons.
Sculptor, medallist.
Jehan de Saint-Priest was the father of Laurent de Saint-Priest. He worked for the city of Lyons. Among his works is a medal depicting *Louis XII and Anne of Brittany*.

SAINT-PRIEST, Laurent de I
French, 16th century.
Active in Lyons 1515-1548.
Sculptor.
Laurent de Saint-Priest I was the son of Jehan de Saint-Priest and the brother of Nicolas Saint-Priest.

SAINT-PRIEST, Laurent de II
French, 16th century.
Active in Lyons 1518-1530.
Sculptor.

SAINT-PRIEST, Marguerite Cerval de
(Vicomtesse, Comtesse de Lavergne)
French, 19th century.
Born 1844, in Sarlat (Dordogne); died 1883, in Paris.
Sculptor.
A pupil of Robinet and Harel, she made her Salon debut in 1875.
MUSEUMS AND GALLERIES:
PÉRIGUEUX: *Primavera*.

SAINT-PRIEST, Nicolas
French, 16th century.
Active in Lyons in 1523.
Sculptor.
Nicolas Saint-Priest was the son of Jehan de Saint-Priest and the brother of Laurent de Saint-Priest I.

SAINT-QUENTIN, Désiré de
French, 19th century.
Born in Valenciennes.
Painter.
He was a pupil of Abel de Pujol, and for a time was director of the Écoles Académiques in Tourcoing, north-east France. He exhibited at the Salons of 1847 and 1848.
MUSEUMS AND GALLERIES:
TOURCOING: *Still-life with Vases and Fruit* (pastel).

SAINT-QUENTIN, Jacques Philippe Joseph de
French, 18th century.
Born 1738, in Paris.
Painter, draughtsman, engraver (etching). Genre scenes, landscapes.
Little is known about Saint-Quentin. He was the pupil of François Boucher, and was a very promising student at the École de l'Académie. In 1757 he won a second-class medal, in 1760 a first-class medal and in 1762 the first prize for painting, which normally gave the winner the right to study at the academy in Rome for three years. It is not known whether he took up his prize. It appears that Saint-Quentin remained Boucher's assistant at his studio. Following the death of his master, he must have set up on his own, since he exhibited decorative paintings and coloured pencil drawings at the Colisée in 1776. Some biographers say he was active until 1780.

AUCTION RECORDS:
PARIS, 20 March 1890, *Young Girl Asleep* (drawing in coloured pencils) FRF 410. PARIS, 1897, *Allegory of the Accession of Louis XVI and Marie-Antoinette* (drawing in Indian ink wash and lead pencil) FRF 205. PARIS, 15-17 Feb 1897, *Wash House* (drawing) FRF 700. PARIS, 8-10 June 1920, *Head of a Young Woman* (pencil) FRF 1,300. PARIS, 7 and 8 May 1923, *Little Gardeners* (black chalk heightened) FRF 4,020. PARIS, 12 June 1929, *Two Cupids on Clouds* (drawing) FRF 3,200; *Young Farmer's Wife*; *Young Girl Setting a Trap* (two drawings) FRF 15,500. PARIS, 17 Dec 1935, *La Petite Fermière*; *Little Bird Catcher* (lead pencil, heightened with white, two drawings) FRF 4,100. PARIS, 28 Nov 1941, *La Petite Fermière*; *Cat's Rest* (red chalk, matching pair) FRF 2,900. PARIS, 8 July 1949, *Wagon in Mud* (pen, wash heightened with gouache, attributed) FRF 1,000. VERSAILLES, 16 May 1971, *Reclining Bacchante* (pastel) FRF 5,000. VERSAILLES, 19 Dec 1982, *La Petite Fermière*; *Little Bird Catcher* (black chalk, heightened with white, two drawings forming a pair, 12 3/4 x 9 3/4 ins / 32.5 x 25 cm) FRF 24,100.

SAINT-QUENTIN, Pierre de. See **BERTON Pierre**

SAINT-RÉMY, Victor
French, 19th century.
Painter.
He exhibited at the Salon between 1836 and 1838.

SAINT-ROMAIN, Jean de. See **JEAN de Saint-Romain**

SAINT-SAËNS, Camille
French, 19th - 20th century.
Born 1835, in Paris; died 1921.
Painter. Landscapes.
Camille Saint-Saëns, the famous composer, pianist and organist, was also an amateur painter.
AUCTION RECORDS:
NEUILLY, 11 June 1991, *The Seine in Paris* (oil on canvas, 15 x 18 ins / 38 x 46 cm) FRF 4,100.

SAINT-SAËNS, Marc
French, 20th century.
Born 1 May 1903, in Toulouse; died 20 December 1973, in Toulouse.
Painter, fresco artist, designer. Mythological subjects. Murals, designs for tapestries.
Marc Saint-Saëns was a pupil at the École des Beaux-Arts, Toulouse, and then at that in Paris. From 1947 to 1973 he was a professor at the École des Arts Décoratifs, Paris, and with Lurçat and Jean Picart Le Doux he founded the association of tapestry painters and designers.

He was deeply interested in the problems posed by decorating walls, and he painted a number of frescoes, the most important of which are to be found in Toulouse in the municipal library and the Théâtre du Capitole, and in Nîmes in the Palais du Travail. It was his meeting with Lurçat in 1934 that drew him to tapestry. He designed large tapestries that were published by Denise Majorel's association of painters and designers, of which he was vice-president. Among his most important designs are *Theseus and the Minotaur* (1943), *Diana*, *Foolish virgins* and *The Commedia dell'Arte*.

Marc Saint-Saëns exhibited regularly in Paris at the Salon des Indépendants and the Salon d'Automne.

MARC-SAINT-SAENS

MUSEUMS AND GALLERIES:
ALBI - CARCASSONNE - GENEVA - OSLO - PARIS (MAMVP): *Theseus and the Minotaur* (1943) - PARIS (MNAM-CCI) - ST-DENIS - TOULOUSE.

AUCTION RECORDS:
LONDON, 22 Oct 1997, *The Alarm Clock* (wool tapestry, 74 3/4 x 76 3/4 ins / 190 x 195 cm) GBP 2,875.

SAINT-SAËNS, Mme
French, 19th century.
Died c. 1890, in Paris.
Watercolourist. Birds, flowers, fruit.

This artist was the mother of the composer Camille Saint-Saëns.

MUSEUMS AND GALLERIES:
DIEPPE: watercolours of flowers, birds and fruit.

SAINT-SIGNY, pseudonym of Gallet, Nelly
French, 20th century.
Born 12 March 1883, in Paris.
Painter, miniaturist. Portraits. Designs for tapestries.

Saint-Signy, a pupil at the Rome school of fine art and of F. M. Roganeau, exhibited in Paris at the Salon des Artistes Français from 1912, in many French provincial towns and in Rome.

She painted *Aubusson* tapestry designs, the technique characterised by a large stitch and low warp.

SAINT-SILVESTRE, Antonio
Portuguese, 20th - 21st century.
Born 1946, in Nampula, Mozambique.
Active in Paris since 1971.
Sculptor. Figures, animals.

Antonio Saint-Silvestre is a self-taught artist whose artistic career began when he arrived in Paris in 1971. His sculptures made from reinforced papier mâché take us through a visionary universe that owes a lot to his native Africa: dragons, lizards, dragonflies, grasshoppers, made more comical than alarming by their coloured, decorative aspect. He produces 'insect jewellery' in the same spirit, including brooches and necklaces in the shape of fantastic animals.

At his first solo exhibition in 1988, he presented paintings on kromekote folded into an accordion. He also participates in numerous group exhibitions in Parisian galleries (Lefor Openo gallery, Treger gallery) and in the salons (Salon d'Automne in 1997).

SAINT-SIMON, Christophe, called Simon
French, 18th century.
Born 30 January 1679, in Angers.
Sculptor, architect.

Christophe Saint-Simon was the brother of Jacques Saint-Simon. They worked together on the church in La Meignanne, in which they produced statues which are still in existence. They also worked for the Ursuline convent in Angers and for Villemaisant and Chantocé churches. Christophe was still living in 1747, when he worked in the church of St Pierre in Saumur.

SAINT-SIMON, Jacques
French, 18th century.
Born c. 1684, in Angers.
Sculptor.

Jacques Saint-Simon was the brother of Christophe Saint-Simon, and he worked with his brother until 1723. After that date, there are no records of him. On his own, he produced sculptures in Andigné church, and in the church of St Maurille in Ponts-de-Cé.

SAINT-SIMON, Lucretia de
German, 17th century.
Active in Oldenburg.
Painter.

Lucretia de Saint-Simon executed three religious paintings for the church of Rastede near Oldenburg in 1636.

SAINT-SIMON, Peter de
German, 17th century.
Painter.

Peter de Saint-Simon painted nine portraits of *Count Anton Günther of Oldenburg*, as well as horses.

SAINT-SIMON, Wilhelm de
German, 17th century.
Painter.

Wilhelm de Saint-Simon was in the service of the counts of Oldenburg and painted history scenes and portraits.

SAINT-SORNY, Pierre
Belgian, 20th century.
Born 1914, in Brussels.
Painter.

Pierre Saint-Sorny studied at the academies of Ixelles, Mons (Bergen) and Brussels.

SAINT-SURIN, Adrien
Haitian, 20th - 21st century.
Born 1961.
Painter. Local scenes.

AUCTION RECORDS:
PARIS, 14 Dec 1992, *Hat Seller* (1991, oil on canvas, 24 x 36 ins / 61 x 91.5 cm) FRF 3,500.

SAINT-URBAIN, Claude
French, 17th century.
Born 1628, in Nancy; died 6 October 1698.
Medallist.

SAINT-URBAIN, Claude Augustin
French, 18th century.
Born 19 February 1703, in Rome; died 1761.
Engraver.

Claude Augustin Saint-Urbain was the son and pupil of Ferdinand Saint-Urbain. He engraved medals of *François III of Lorraine* and *Philip V of Spain*.

SAINT-URBAIN, Élisabeth Dominique
Maiden name: Mantenais
French, 18th century.
Born in Rome; died 10 January 1738, in Nancy.
Painter. Landscapes, flowers, fruit.

Élisabeth Saint-Urbain was the wife of Ferdinand Saint-Urbain.

SAINT-URBAIN, Ferdinand
French, 17th - 18th century.
Born 30 June 1658, in Nancy; died 10 January 1738, in Nancy.
Medallist.

Ferdinand Saint-Urbain was the father of Claude Augustin Saint-Urbain. He was a medallist for the Holy See in Rome, and from 1703 was an engraver of medals and coins in Nancy. He produced over 100 medals and coins.

SAINT-URBAIN, Marie Anne, later Mme Vaultoin
French, 18th century.
Born 3 January 1711, in Nancy; died after 1789.
Sculptor, engraver.

Marie Saint-Urbain was the daughter and pupil of Ferdinand Saint-Urbain. She engraved in Nancy and Vienne and also produced wax sculptures.

SAINT-VIDAL, Francis de
French, 19th century.
Born 16 January 1840, in Milan, Italy, to French parents; died 18 August 1900, in Paris.
Sculptor. Statues.

This artist was a pupil of Carpeaux. He debuted at the Salon in 1875 and became a life member of the Société des Artistes Français. He was also a medallic artist.
MUSEUMS AND GALLERIES:
BORDEAUX: *Bust of Beethoven* - VERSAILLES: *Carpeaux* (statue).
AUCTION RECORDS:
NEW YORK, 12 Oct 1994, *Night* (1884, marble, h. 49 ins / 124.5 cm) USD 74,000.

SAINT-YGNY, Jean de. See **SAINT-IGNY**

SAINT-YON, Ernestine Hardy de
French, 19th century.
Portrait painter.
She exhibited her work at the Salons of 1839 and 1841.

SAINT-YVES, Pierre de
French, 17th - 18th century.
Born 1666, in Rocroi (Ardennes); died 20 March 1716, in Paris.
Painter. History painting.
Saint-Yves became an Academician on 28 January 1708.
MUSEUMS AND GALLERIES:
TOURS: *Jephthah's Sacrifice*.

SAINTAIN. See **SAINTIN**

SAINTAIRE, Hippolyte
French, 19th century.
Born in Pouancé.
Painter. Portraits.
Hippolyte Saintaire was the student of Pils and Léon Cogniet. He first exhibited at the Salon of 1878.

SAINTARD, Marguerite
French, 20th century.
Born in Harcourt.
Miniaturist.
Marguerite Saintard exhibited in Paris at the Salon des Artistes Français from 1900.

SAINTE-AGATHE, Jean Madeleine de
French, 18th - 19th century.
Born 11 January 1761, in Besançon; died 1 March 1837, in Besançon.
Engraver (burin), printer.

SAINTE-ANNE, Victor de
French, 17th century.
Active in Niort during the second half of the 17th century.
Sculptor (wood).
Ste-Anne was a monk in La Flocellière monastery, and sculpted doors and the pulpit in the monastery church.

SAINTE-CATHERINE, Jehan de
French, 14th century.
Active in Lille 1337-1343.
Sculptor, painter.
Jehan de Ste-Catherine was the father of Pierre Ste-Catherine. He carved sculptures for the churches of Lille and painted banners.

SAINTE-CATHERINE, Marie de, called La Poindresse
French, 14th century.
Active in Lille in 1347.
Painter.
Marie de Ste-Catherine did paintings for the bell tower of the church of St-Étienne in Lille.

SAINTE-CATHERINE, Pierre, Peter or Pieter de
French, 14th century.
Died c. 1387.
Active in Lille 1351-1363.
Painter. History painting.
Pierre de Ste-Catherine was the son of Jehan de Ste-Catherine. He painted an altarpiece for the high altar of the church of St-Maurice. His wife was also a painter.

SAINTE-CHAPELLE, Laurence de
French, 19th century.
Landscape artist.
Laurence Ste-Chapelle exhibited at the Salon in 1839 and 1840.

SAINTE-FOY, Hervé de
French, 20th - 21st century.
Born 26 June 1948, in Baden-Baden, Germany.
Painter. Landscapes, seascapes, architectural views, architectural interiors. Murals, decorative panels.
Hervé de Sainte-Foy studied at the Académie Charpentier in 1967 and 1968 before enrolling at the École des Beaux-Arts. He has taught visual arts from 1973 and was appointed an official painter to the French army in 1982.

Sainte-Foy painted a fresco for the hall of the French General Staff headquarters in Berlin in 1973 and a decorative mural for the École Militaire (Military College) in Paris in 1974. He has also produced various decorative panels for a number of military installations. In addition to these formal commissions, Hervé de Sainte-Foy paints on his own account, typically producing seascapes, architectural themes and interiors rendered in an essentially Realist style and with a pronounced affection for light effects and overall 'atmosphere'.

SAINTE-MARIE, Alfred
French, 19th century.
Born in Paris.
Painter. Genre scenes, landscapes.
He was a pupil of Louis Roux. He exhibited at the Paris Salon between 1853 and 1870.
AUCTION RECORDS:
ST-DIÉ, 14 Feb 1988, *The Pack* (oil on canvas, 15 1/4 x 20 3/4 ins / 39 x 53 cm) FRF 8,000.

SAINTE-MARIE, Élisabeth Hélène
Maiden name: de Nielle
French, 19th century.
Landscape painter.
She exhibited at the Salon between 1846 and 1849.

SAINTE-MARIE DE QUILLEBOEUF. See **QUILLEBOEUF**

SAINTHILL, Loudon or Louden, or Saint Hill
Australian, 20th century.
Born 1919; died 1969.
Painter (mixed media), watercolourist. Local figures, genre scenes.
Loudon Sainthill gave an example of his style by sending *Pierrette's Costume* to the exhibition organised by the United Nations at the Musée d'Art Moderne in Paris in 1946.
AUCTION RECORDS:
MELBOURNE, 11-12 March 1971, *Clown* (gouache) AUD 800. SYDNEY, 10 March 1980, *Yuri Larjorsky in Petrushka* (mixed media, 23 1/4 x 19 1/4 ins / 59 x 49 cm) AUD 1,100. MELBOURNE, 26 July 1987, *Portrait of Yua Lazousky in Petrushka* (1939, mixed media, 23 1/4 x 19 1/4 ins / 59 x 49 cm) AUD 5,000. LONDON, 8 Sept 1988, *Winter: Head in Profile* (watercolour chalk and ink/card, diam. 19 3/4 ins / 50.2 cm) GBP 1,430. SYDNEY, 3 July 1989, *Theatrical Allegory* (oil on card, diam. 22 ins / 56 cm) AUD 1,000. LONDON, 28 Nov 1991, *Figure with a Guitar* (1950, ink, watercolour, black chalk and gouache, 30 x 22 1/4 ins / 76 x 56.5 cm) GBP 1,980. PADDINGTON, 16 Aug 1999, *The Juggler* (oil on cardboard, 19 x 15 ins / 49 x 39 cm) AUD 10,500. MELBOURNE, 22 Nov 1999, *Esplanade* (watercolour and gouache, 10 x 14 ins / 25 x 36 cm) AUD 20,000. MELBOURNE, 3 May 2000, *The Musicians* (gouache, pen and ink,

15 x 11 ins / 39 x 28 cm) AUD 14,000. MELBOURNE, 22 Aug 2000, *Tamara Toumanova* (1940, watercolour and gouache, 28 x 20 ins / 70 x 50 cm) AUD 3,000. MELBOURNE, 26 Nov 2001, *Sisters* (1949, pencil, 24 x 19 ins / 60 x 48 cm) AUD 3,000. MELBOURNE, 16 June 2004, *Strange Creatures of Shemakhan, Bridal Procession, Act III* (watercolour and gouache, 18 x 28 ins / 45 x 71 cm) AUD 4,000.

SAINTILAN, Marie Françoise

French, 20th century.

Born 9 July 1912, in St-Brieuc.

Painter. Portraits, landscapes.

Marie Françoise Saintilan exhibited portraits, mother-and-child paintings and landscapes at the Salon des Tuileries in 1938, and thereafter at the Salon des Indépendants. In 1940, she took part in an exhibition of French art in Tokyo.

MUSEUMS AND GALLERIES:

TOKYO.

SAINTIN, Henri or Louis Henri

French, 19th century.

Born 13 October 1845, in Paris; died July 1899.

Painter. Genre scenes, landscapes.

This artist was taught by Pils, Segé, Cointepoin and St-Marcel. He made his Salon debut in 1867, and won a third-class medal in 1882.

Henri Saintin.

BIBLIOGRAPHY:

Delouche, Denise/Michaud, Jean-Marc, et al., *Bretagne, terre des peintres*, exhibition catalogue, Musée des Beaux-Arts, Vannes, 2003.

MUSEUMS AND GALLERIES:

AUXERRE: *Evening at Cernay Pond* - BAYONNE (Mus. Bonnat): *Torrent, Hills and Mountains* - BESANÇON: *Sluice Gate* - CHAMBÉRY: *The Gardener's Wife* - MONTPELLIER: *Path through the Forest* - MORLAIX (Mus. des Jacobins): *Snow in November* (1884, oil on canvas) - RENNES: *Erquy Cove* - TARBES: *Rochegouets Valley* - TOUL: *Interior of a Garden; Landscape* - TOURCOING: *Autumn Evening.*

AUCTION RECORDS:

PARIS, 11 July 1896, *Rochegouets Valley*, FRF 200. PARIS, 19 Dec 1899, *The Road to the Farm: Evening*, FRF 200; *Tinker*, FRF 900; *Rochegouets Valley: Morning*, FRF 1,100; *The Big Wheel at Arcueil*, FRF 7,000; *Cernay Pond: Morning*, FRF 465; *Woman in a Hammock* (Salon of 1893) FRF 1,100. PARIS, 17-21 May 1904, *Head of a Young Girl*, FRF 105. PARIS, 28 Nov 1919, *Rouen Quays*, FRF 215. PARIS, 14 and 15 Dec 1925, *Duck Pond*, FRF 360. PARIS, 19-21 April 1926, *The Château de Ponchartrain*, FRF 220. PARIS, 14 June 1944, *White Frost near Gréhérel*, FRF 750. PARIS, 21 Feb 1945, *Landscape*, FRF 2,500. PARIS, 19 March 1945, *The Grand Canal in Venice*, FRF 2,800. PARIS, 18 Nov 1946, *The Avenue*, FRF 1,000. PARIS, 18 Dec 1946, *Snowy Landscape*, FRF 3,000. PARIS, 28 Jan 1949, *Landscape*, FRF 2,600; *The Val André*, FRF 1,100. PARIS, 4 April 1949, *Military Camps* (two pendants) FRF 5,200. PARIS, 4 July 1949, *Manoeuvres in the Countryside* (two pendants) FRF 2,800. PARIS, 10 Feb 1950, *Marsh Fishing* (1874, two pendants) FRF 5,000. PARIS, 6 Oct 1950, *Farm Courtyard in the Rain at Pont-Réau* (1880) FRF 6,300. PARIS, 25 June 1951, *Riverbank: St-Germain Valley*, FRF 4,900; *Woman Suckling a Child in a Boat*, FRF 4,000. PARIS, 11 July 1951, *Military Manoeuvres* (two pendants) FRF 6,000. DÜSSELDORF, 13 Nov 1973, *St-Geramin-l'Axis*, DEM 3,000. PARIS, 16 March 1976, *The Eiffel Tower at the Exposition Universelle of 1889* (oil on panel, 11 x 13 3/4 ins / 27 x 35 cm) FRF 4,100. PARIS, 26 April 1978, *Floods* (oil on canvas) FRF 5,500. PARIS, 4 Nov 1980, *Farmyard in Pleheren* (oil on canvas, 21 1/2 x 28 3/4 ins / 54.5 x 73 cm) FRF 14,500. BARBIZON, 1 Nov 1981, *Stream beneath the Willows* (oil on canvas, 18 x 13 ins / 46 x 33 cm) FRF 16,100. BARBIZON, 27 Feb 1983, *Cottages near the Cove on the River* (1887, oil on canvas, 25 3/4 x 39 1/4 ins / 65.5 x 100 cm) FRF 15,000. VERSAILLES, 25 Nov 1990, *Windmills of Dordrecht on the Meuse* (oil on canvas, 25 1/2 x 39 3/4 ins / 65 x 101 cm) FRF 18,000. NEW YORK, 21 May 1991, *Still-life with Pitcher, Flowers and Japanese Fan* (oil on canvas, 20 1/2 x 16 ins / 52 x 40.8 cm) USD 4,180. LONDON, 4 Oct 1991, *By the Watermill in Springtime* (1888, oil on canvas, 71 1/4 x 52 ins / 181 x 132 cm) GBP 1,980. NEW YORK, 17 Feb 1994, *Windmill near a Stone Bridge* (oil on canvas, 12 3/4 x 18 ins / 32.5 x 46 cm) USD 1,150. PARIS, 23 June 1995, *Walking in Rennes* (1881, oil on canvas, 18 1/2 x 28 3/4 ins / 47 x 73 cm) FRF 15,000. PARIS, 5 March 1998, *Sailing Ship at the Landing Stage* (1869, oil on panel, 11 1/2 x 19 1/4 ins / 29.5 x 49 cm) FRF 10,200. STOCKHOLM, 24 Nov 1999, *French Shore Landscape* (1875, oil on canvas, 36 x 19 ins / 91 x 48 cm) SEK 57,000. NEW YORK, 15 Dec 2000, *Mending the Nets* (1875, oil on canvas, 35 x 59 ins / 90 x 151 cm) USD 8,000. PARIS, 21 June 2001, *Reverie* (oil on canvas, 15 x 24 ins / 38 x 61 cm) FRF 29,000. AHLDEN, 28 Sept 2001, *Female Angler on Lily Pond* (1889, oil on canvas, 22 x 29 ins / 55 x 74 cm) DEM 22,500. PARIS, 13 Dec 2002, *Encampment* (oil on canvas, 15 x 22 ins / 38 x 56 cm) EUR 2,000. PARIS, 22 June 2004, *Stalk. Heron. Crane. Flamingo* (1883, oil on canvas, 50 x 19 ins / 128 x 49 cm) EUR 6,200.

SAINTIN, Jules Émile

French, 19th century.

Born 14 August 1829, in Lemée (Aisne); died 14 July 1894, in Paris.

Also active in the USA.

Painter, pastellist, draughtsman. History painting, portraits, genre scenes.

Jules Émile Saintin entered the École des Beaux-Arts in Paris in 1845, and was taught in the studios of Michel Drolling and François Édouard Picot. He exhibited first at the Paris Salon (from 1848), then at the Salon of the Société des Artistes Français. He won medals in 1866, 1870 and 1886. He was also decorated with the title of Chevalier of the Légion d'Honneur.

He spent almost ten years in America, painting the Native Americans, their dress and way of life.

MUSEUMS AND GALLERIES:

NICE: *Study of a Head* - ST-BRIEUC: *After the Storm at Portrieux.*

AUCTION RECORDS:

PARIS, 1872, *Rag Pickers: the Chiffonniers of New York*, FRF 2,700. PAR IS, 1878, *Young Woman Picking a Rose*, FRF 1,220. PARIS, 1883, *Leda* (drawing) FRF 300. PARIS, 7 Dec 1918, *The Model*, FRF 200. PARIS, 21 Oct 1936, *Memories*, FRF 520. PARIS, 15 Dec 1950, *Young Woman with an Umbrella* (1872) FRF 9,100. LONDON, 2 Nov 1973, *Young Woman at a Window*, Gns 1,400. BRUSSELS, 19 Jan 1974, *A Visit to the Glover*, BEF 310,000. LONDON, 6 May 1977, *A Visit to the Glover* (1872, oil on canvas, 36 1/4 x 25 1/2 ins / 92 x 65 cm) GBP 3,800. LONDON, 26 Nov 1980, *Young Elegant Woman Seated in an Interior* (1872, oil on canvas, 28 1/4 x 21 ins / 72 x 52.5 cm) GBP 6,800. LONDON, 20 March 1981, *A Visit to the Glover* (1872, oil on canvas, 36 1/4 x 25 3/4 ins / 92 x 65.5 cm) GBP 3,200. FONTAINEBLEAU, 17 June 1984, *Young Fisherwoman* (oil on canvas, 26 x 17 ins / 66 x 43 cm) FRF 31,000. NEW YORK, 19 July 1990, *Head of a Young Chinese Man* (1860, oil on canvas, 9 x 6 1/2 ins / 22.9 x 16.5 cm) USD 4,950. NEW YORK, 27 May 1993, *A Visit to the Glover* (1872, oil on canvas, 36 1/4 x 25 1/2 ins / 92.1 x 64.8 cm) USD 29,900. PARIS, 28 June 1993, *Young Woman Sewing* (1826, oil on canvas, 18 x 14 ins / 46 x 35.5 cm) FRF 24,000. PARIS, 6 July 1993, *Portrait of a Woman in Russian Dress* (1851, wash, 10 1/2 x 8 ins / 26.5 x 20.5 cm) FRF 3,500. NEW YORK, 13 Oct 1993, *Housewife* (1886, oil on canvas, 18 x 14 ins / 45.7 x 35.6 cm) USD 32,200. NEW YORK, 20 July 1995, *The Balcony* (oil on panel, a pair, 6 1/2 x 4 1/4 ins / 16.8 x 10.5 cm) USD 8,050. HELSINKI, 25 April 1999, *Woman in Interior* (1871, oil on canvas, 30 x 22 ins / 75 x 55 cm) FIM 61,000. AMSTERDAM, 24 Oct 2000, *Fair Glance* (1877, oil on canvas, 32 x 23 ins / 81 x 59 cm) NLG 70,000. PARIS, 30 March 2001, *Young Woman* (1890, oil on canvas, 22 x 13 ins / 56 x 34 cm) FRF 40,000. NEW YORK, 5 March 2003, *Thoughtful Young Woman on a Balcony* (1880, oil on canvas, 24 x 17 ins / 62 x 43 cm) USD 6,500. LONDON, 18 June 2003, *Elegant Lady with Book of Japanese Prints* (1879, oil on canvas, 24 x 17 ins / 62 x 44 cm) GBP 7,500. PARIS, 1 April 2004, *Italian Woman* (oil on canvas, 21 x 19 ins / 54 x 49 cm) EUR 2,200. PARIS, 24 June 2004, *Italian Woman* (oil on canvas, 21 x 19 ins / 54 x 49 cm) EUR 2,200.

SAINTON, Charles P.
British, 19th - 20th century.
Born 28 June 1861, in London; died 3 December 1914, in New York.
Painter. Portraits.

SAINTON, Étienne, or Saincton
French, 17th century.
Died 22 March 1629.
Active in Fontainebleau.
Painter.

Étienne Sainton was active from 1613 to 1621.

SAINTON, Gabriel Henry
French, 19th century.
Born 31 January 1854, in Nieul-sur-Mer (Charente).
Painter. Seascapes.

He first exhibited at the Salon of the Société des Artistes Français in 1922. He was made an Officer of the Légion d'Honneur.

SAINTON, Jean I, or Saincton
French, 17th century.
Active in Fontainebleau 1645-1648.
Painter.

SAINTON, Jean II, or Saincton
French, 17th century.
Painter.

Jean Sainton II was a pupil at the academy of Paris and Académie de France in Rome in 1696.

SAINTON, Nicolas, or Saincton
French, 17th century.
Painter.

Nicolas Sainton produced paintings on the rood screen of the Grande Chapelle in Fontainbleau Palace in 1640 and 1641. He was also a gilder.

SAINTURIER, Louis
French, 19th - 20th century.
Born in Le Teil (Ardèche).
Painter. History painting, religious subjects, mythological subjects.

As a very young man Louis Sainturier went to Alès to study drawing, and when he was fourteen he entered the École des Beaux-Arts, Nîmes, where he was successively offered a municipal and a state scholarship. These enabled him to go to Paris, where he became a pupil at the École des Beaux-Arts. He was enthusiastic about antique art, which he studied conscientiously, and which gave him later the conviction needed for a painter treating heroic subjects. He travelled extensively in Europe, Algeria and Egypt, and became acquainted with the Italian, Flemish and Dutch schools. He returned to Nîmes as a professor at the École des Beaux-Arts, a post he resigned to take part in World War I. After demobilisation he lived in Dijon for a while, but finally settled in Paris. It was in the special, post-war artistic atmosphere of the city that he did his main work. From his earlier training he retained a taste for biblical scenes and historical and mythological subjects, which he treated in a spirit quite detached from current trends. His was a very independent artistic personality.

AUCTION RECORDS:
PARIS, 30 May 1945, *Flowers*, FRF 500.

SAINXON, Jean. See **POUZAY Jean de**

SAINZ, Casimirio. See **SAINZ Y SAINZ**

SAINZ, Francisco
Spanish, 19th century.
Born in Lanestosa; died 12 June 1853, in Madrid.
Painter, illustrator. Portraits, genre scenes.

Francisco Sainz was a pupil of J. Madrazo and also studied in Rome.

SAINZ, María del Carmen
Spanish, 19th century.
Active in Madrid during the first half of the 19th century.
Engraver (burin).

In 1816 María del Carmen Sainz engraved a series of 12 heads after Raphael.

SAINZ DE LA MAZA RUIZ, Francisco
Spanish, 20th century.
Born 1900 or 1901, in Burgos; died 1984.
Painter, draughtsman. Portraits, genre scenes, landscapes, seascapes.

Sainz de la Maza Ruiz studied in San Sebastián and in Madrid, spending a year in Barcelona (1917) before settling in Madrid. He was awarded a travel scholarship at the Exposición Nacional de Bellas Artes of 1926.

Examples of his work include a *Portrait of King Alfonso XIII; Corpus Christi Procession*.

His paintings featured at numerous group exhibitions, including the 1918 Salón de la Primavera in Madrid, in Barcelona, and at the Círculo de Bellas Artes in Madrid in 1923, and at the International Exhibition in Barcelona in 1929.

BIBLIOGRAPHY:
Arnáiz, José Manuel/López Jiménez, Javier/Merchán Díaz, Manuel (ed.), *'Cien años de pintura en Espana y Portugal (1830-1930)'* in vol. X, Antiqvaria, Madrid, 1993.

MUSEUMS AND GALLERIES:
BARCELONA (MAM del Mus. Nacional d'Art de Catalunya): *Violinist* - MADRID (Prado).

SAINZ DE MORALES, Gumersindo
Spanish, 20th century.
Born 1900, in Madrid; died 1976, in Barcelona.
Painter, watercolourist, draughtsman, illustrator. Urban landscapes.

Sainz de Morales studied at the Escuela de Bellas Artes de San Fernando in Madrid and showed his work at various group exhibitions in the Spanish capital, elsewhere in Spain and abroad.

He worked as an illustrator on a number of periodicals, including *Imatges (Images)*. Examples of his work include *Street Market; Farmyard*, sketch-like compositions executed in pallid ochres, beiges and greys which record typical street scenes. His watercolours are signed *Gumsay*.

BIBLIOGRAPHY:
Arnáiz, José Manuel/López Jiménez, Javier/Merchán Díaz, Manuel (ed.), '*Cien años de pintura en Espana y Portugal (1830-1930)*' in vol. X, Antiqvaria, Madrid, 1993.

SAINZ Y GIL, Gil, or Saiz y Gil
Spanish, 20th century.
Born 1 October 1876, in Colmenar de Oja (Andalusia).
Painter. Portraits, scenes with figures, genre scenes, landscapes.

Sainz y Gil studied under Joaquin Sorolla at the school of painting in Madrid and participated in the Exposición Nacional de Bellas Artes 1895-1910. He painted numerous decorative compositions for public buildings, including *El Sermon del Abuelo (The Grandfather's Sermon); Una Desgracia en la Cantera (An Accident in the Quarry).*

BIBLIOGRAPHY:
Arnáiz, José Manuel/López Jiménez, Javier/Merchán Díaz, Manuel (ed.), '*Cien años de pintura en Espana y Portugal (1830-1930)*' in vol. X, Antiqvaria, Madrid, 1993.

SAINZ Y OCEJO, Luis
Spanish, 19th - 20th century.
Born in Madrid; died 1920, in Madrid.
Painter, watercolourist, illustrator, decorative designer. Portraits, landscapes.

Sainz y Ocejo was a pupil of José Cala y Moya. He showed his worked at the Madrid Círculo de Bellas Artes exhibitions.

SAINZ Y SAINZ, Casimiro
Spanish, 19th century.
Born 4 March 1853, in Matamorosa; died 19 August 1898, in Madrid.
Painter. Genre scenes, landscapes.

Casimiro Sainz y Sainz was a pupil of V. Palmaroli y Gonzalez but mainly studied under the Belgian Carlos de Haes, who became a naturalised Spaniard and succeeded Ferrant as professor of landscape painting at the Madrid academy.

MUSEUMS AND GALLERIES:
MADRID (Prado): *Model Resting; By a Convent; Tavern Interior.*

AUCTION RECORDS:
MADRID, 13 Dec 1973, *The Egyptian Fountain in the Retiro Park in Madrid,* ESP 70,000. MADRID, 17 May 1974, *View of the Retiro Park in Madrid,* ESP 110,000. PARIS, 21 May 1999, *Orchard* (1879, oil on canvas, 15 x 24 ins / 38 x 60 cm) FRF 44,500. MADRID, 24 Jan 2000, *River Landscape* (oil on canvas, 19 x 11 ins / 47 x 28 cm) ESP 650,000. MADRID, 18 Dec 2000, *Rural Landscape* (1875-1880, oil on canvas, 21 x 34 ins / 53 x 86 cm) ESP 8,500,000. MADRID, 27 May 2003, *Chulas Santanderinas* (*Pretty Girls in Santander*) (1877, oil on panel, a pair, 14 x 10 ins / 36 x 25 cm) EUR 25,000. MADRID, 16 Dec 2003, *Landscape* (oil on board, 6 x 9 ins / 14 x 23 cm) EUR 4,200.

SAIR VASFI
Turkish, 15th century.
Miniaturist.

Sair Vasfi was a noted representative of the Brousse School. He lived during the reign of Sultan Murad III.

SAIRBOT, or Sarbot
French, 17th century.
Born 1624.
Engraver (etching).

SAITER, Abraham. See **SEUTTER**

SAITER, Daniel. See **SEITER**

SAITER, Geoffroy. See **SEUTER**

SAITER, Johann Gottfried. See **SEUTTER**

SAITO, Eiichi
Japanese, 20th century.
Born 1920.
Active from 1936 in France.
Painter, watercolourist, draughtsman. Seascapes, landscapes.

In 1936 Eiichi Saito moved to Alsace to study chemistry. His encounter with the painter René Kuder was significant for his own painting, which he pursued at the same time as scientific research. In 1975 he studied ink painting technique under the guidance of the calligrapher Ung No Lee. From 1983 he devoted himself entirely to painting. He exhibited in Alsace, notably in 1985 in the Municipal Library of Strasbourg and in Paris. He specialised in the landscapes of Alsace, Brittany, Venice, the Alps and Provence.

SAITO, Juichi
Japanese, 20th century.
Born 1931, in Kanagawa Prefecture.
Engraver.

In 1958 Juichi Saito went to France for a year and worked in S.W. Hayter's Studio 17. His works on copper were presented at the Biennale des Jeunes Artistes de Paris and in exhibitions of the Shunyo-kai. In 1960 he won a prize at the Shell exhibition. He was represented at the Tokyo International Print Biennale in 1960, 1962 and 1964 as well as at the International Engraving Biennale in Ljubljana in 1963 and 1965. He frequently held personal exhibitions in Tokyo.

SAITO, Kiyoshi
Japanese, 20th century.
Born 1907, in Sakamoto (Fukushima); died 1997.
Painter, engraver.
First Thursday Society.

Kiyoshi Saito studied western painting at the Hongo Institute of Painting. After exhibiting paintings at the Kokuga-Kai and Nika-Kai Salons he gradually turned towards wood engraving. In 1943 he met the engraver Onchi Koshiro and became part of his group, the First Thursday Society, as well as the Japanese Engraving Association (*Nihon Hanga Kyokai*). He was a member of the Kokuga-Kai (the national painting academy). He spent some time in the USA in 1956. He received several awards in international group exhibitions, notably the São Paulo Biennale in 1951 and in Yugoslavia. He was made citizen of honour in the town of Yanaizu, where a museum is dedicated to him.

Mingling western and traditional styles, Saito painted in oils and in ink (*suiboku ga*), and produced wood engravings and collagraphs. He experimented with the textures of papers or different woods, influenced by the *susaku hanga* movement. He is famous for his stylised landscapes (notably the series on the town of Aizu) in which he experiments with geometric patterns and contrasting colours while conserving a gentle effect in the movement of the contours.

Saito exhibited with Unichi Hiratsuka and Hide Kawanishe in Tokyo at the end of World War II, then in 1948 at the Spring Salon in Tokyo. From 1951 he held a solo exhibition every year in his own country and overseas. In 2002 his work was included in the exhibition *Japanese Prints Under the Allied Occupation 1945-1952* at the British Museum in London.

BIBLIOGRAPHY:
Statler, Oliver, *Modern Japanese Prints: An Art Reborn*, Charles E. Tuttle Co., Rutland (VT), 1956. Petit, G./Arboleda, A., *Evolving Techniques in Japanese Woodblock Prints*, Kodansha International, Tokyo, 1977. Harada, Minoru, *The Life and Works of Kiyoshi Saito*, Abe Shuppan, Tokyo, 1990. Merrit, Helen/Yamada, Nanako, *Guide to Modern Japanese Woodblock Prints: 1900-1975*, University of Hawaï Press, Honolulu, 1992. Smith, Lawrence, *Modern Japanese Prints, 1912-1989*, The British Museum Press, London, 1994. Smith, Lawrence, *Japanese Prints during the Allied Occupation, 1945-1952: Onchi Kôshirô, Ernst Hacker and the First Thurs-*

day Society, exhibition catalogue, The British Museum Press, London, 2002.

Museums and Galleries:

Chicago (AI) - Cincinnati (AM) - Fukushima (Prefectural Mus. of Art) - Kamakura (MMA) - New York (Public Library) - Philadelphia (MA) - San Francisco (Achenbach Foundation for Graphic Arts) - Yanaizu (Saito Kiyoshi Mun. Mus.): important collection of works.

Auction records:

New York, 29 March 1990, *Cat* (print, 30 x 17 ins / 76.5 x 43.2 cm) USD 5,500. Paris, 16 June 1993, *Biyakuje-ji Temple Nara* (1970, wood in colour, 14 3/4 x 21 ins / 37.5 x 52.5 cm) FRF 5,200. New York, 5 May 1999, *Profile of Woman with Camellias* (c. 1960, colour woodcut, 23 x 17 ins / 59 x 44 cm) USD 9,000. Shaker Heights, 11 Dec 1999, *Pansy* (1964, colour woodblock, 21 x 15 ins / 53 x 38 cm) USD 3,000. San Francisco, 25 Oct 2000, *New Mexico* (1965, colour woodcut, 21 x 27 ins / 54 x 69 cm) USD 5,000. San Francisco, 25 Oct 2000, *Shop Girl, Cardin, Paris* (1960, colour woodcut, 24 x 18 ins / 60 x 45 cm) USD 5,500. Cleveland, 23 April 2001, *Cat* (colour woodcut, 29 x 16 ins / 74 x 41 cm) USD 4,600. San Francisco, 14 Oct 2002, *Cats* (colour woodcut, 22 x 26 ins / 55 x 66 cm) USD 3,500. San Francisco, 22 April 2003, *Red Flower* (1952, colour woodcut, 21 x 16 ins / 53 x 41 cm) USD 3,500. San Francisco, 10 May 2004, *Autumn* (print, 33 x 21 ins / 84 x 54 cm) USD 3,750. San Francisco, 10 May 2004, *Steady Gaze* (1957, print, 33 x 22 ins / 84 x 55 cm) USD 4,000.

SAITO, Shin'ichi

Japanese, 20th century.
Born 6 July 1922, in Kurashiki.
Painter.

Shin'ichi Saito studied at the school of Fine Arts in Tokyo. His studies were interrupted by World War II when he was drafted into the navy. At the end of the war he took up his studies again until 1948, then taught design while continuing to paint. He displayed his works in a solo exhibition for the first time in 1970, then again in 1972 and 1974.

In 1959, during a trip to Europe, he discovered gypsies, and on his return to Japan saw in the Goze itinerant folk singers a Japanese equivalent of the gypsy phenomenon. He set off to follow them and capture their way of life in painting.

Auction records:

Paris, 24 Nov 1996, *The Woman* (c. 1956, oil on canvas, 36 1/4 x 25 1/2 ins / 92 x 65 cm) FRF 12,300.

SAITO, Takako

Japanese, 20th century.
Born 1929, in Sabae-Shi.
Draughtswoman, collage artist, photomontage artist, performance artist. Artists' books.
Fluxus.

After studying in Japan, Takako Saito went to the USA in 1963 where she made the acquaintance of George Maciunas and completed her education at the Brooklyn Museum Art School. In 1968 she went to France and made contact with George Brecht and Robert Filliou. She spent time in England and then in Italy. From 1979 she lived and worked near Düsseldorf in Germany.

She has taken part in collective or thematic exhibitions, including: 1992, *De Bonnard à Baselitz - Dix ans d'enrichissements du cabinet des estampes 1978-1988* (*From Bonnard to Baselitz: A Decade of Acquisitions by the Prints Collection 1978-1988*), Bibliothèque Nationale, Paris; 2002, *Eine lange Geschichte mit vielen Knoten. Fluxus in Deutschland 1962-1994* (*A Long Story with Many Threads. Fluxus in Germany 1962-1994*), Kunsthalle Fridericianum, Kassel; 2003, Galerie Lara Vincy, Paris.

Bibliography:

Fluxus in Deutschland 1962-1994, exhibition catalogue, Kunsthalle Fridericianum, Kassel, 2002.

SAITO, Teruaki

Japanese, 20th century.
Born 1942, in Soma, Fukushima Ken.
Active since 1970 in France.
Painter, engraver.

Teruaki Saito lives and works in Bagneux. In 1992 he took part in the exhibition *De Bonnard à Baselitz - Dix ans d'enrichissements du cabinet des estampes 1978-1988* (*From Bonnard to Baselitz: A Decade of Acquisitions by the Prints Collection 1978-1988*) at the Bibliothèque Nationale in Paris.

Museums and Galleries:

Paris (BNF, Prints Collection): *Composition 1* (aquatint).

SAITO, Toyo

Japanese, 20th century.
Active in France.
Painter.

The works of Toyo Saito were shown in Paris at the Salon des Tuileries in 1930.

SAITO, Yoshishige

Japanese, 20th century.
Born 4 May 1904, in Tokyo; died June 2001.
Painter, installation artist.

While still very young, Saito Yoshishige met the artist Nakashino Toshio at school and began to paint in oil; he then saw an exhibition of Italian futurist painting which confirmed him in his vocation. Until the age of 30 he hardly practised painting at all, as he found himself more attracted to international literature. The American Occupation, with its attendant Americanisation of Japanese culture, caused him to despair of ever having a way of life that was specifically Japanese. After trying to express his bitterness through his paintings, he stopped painting for five years, withdrawing from the Bijutsu Bunka Kyokai group (a committed movement which claimed to be partly influenced by surrealism) of which he had been one of the founders, after attempting to convince its members to dissolve it completely. In 1954 he settled in the fishing village of Urayasu near Tokyo. At first he continued not to paint, observing the men, the sea and shores uncovered by the tide as it went out. He worked on three novels which remain incomplete. He taught at the Tama College of Art in Tokyo from 1964 to 1973 and then travelled to Europe, trying to restore those of his works from the end of the 1930s which had been destroyed during the war. He also joined the Surugadai avant-garde centre for Western painting, where he worked with Koga Harue and Togo Seiji.

Saito began painting in a neo-cubo-futurist tradition, in opposition to the trend towards surrealism. In 1930 he began to use various materials that were to become the key element of his painting throughout his career. He created reliefs by mixing pigments and applying this paste directly onto wood, concentrating on constructivist principles. In the immediate post-war years, while still poor and unknown, he painted in a style which tended towards surrealism combined with pre-abstraction. From 1954 to 1957 he stopped painting and later began again in Urayasu. The inhabitants of this village had a reputation for organising boisterous festivities and Saito regarded their drollness as a manifestation of the ancestral spirit. Initially he produced legible evocations whose titles clearly indicate their source, such as *Fishing Village, Fisherman*. Also from this period is *Oni* (*Demon*). In his later, still figurative works the elements taken from reality or from legend are often inscribed in an elliptical manner, appropriately reminding us that the ideogrammatic characters of Chinese script were, to begin with, also taken schematically from the representation which they depicted.

From this period Saito attained the height of his creative powers, and his painting represented from then on a great unity of style. The last traces of figuration which still remained in his formal vocabulary were rejected, and thereafter he based his whole language on the inexhaustible reserve of expression of Oriental calligraphy, in the perfection of its gesture and not in its signification. He also drew on the most traditional source materials of Japanese civilisation - clay and rustic enamels, 'chawans' (bowls for the tea ceremony), seals, and so on - anticipating the direction which would soon after be taken by his compatriot and contemporary Kei Sato. In the 1980s he executed installations which highlighted contrasting geometric forms in lacquered wood as well as the balance and precision of the composition.

Saito Yoshishige is one of the few Japanese artists to have been drawn quite early on to contemporary plastic expression and to have practised abstraction relatively early. In these respects he played an important role in the artistic evolution of Japan, which at that time was on the one hand preoccupied with maintaining traditional calligraphic and painting techniques and, on the other, aping mediocre Western landscape art. As a consequence, his painting and sculpture were not immediately accepted by the public.

Saito held his first exhibition in 1936 at the Nika Kai Salon in Tokyo. He took part in collective exhibitions from 1939 to 1953 with the cultural group Bijutsu Bunka Kyokai. He subsequently exhibited at the following: 1957, *New Artists of Today* in Japan, with *Work No. 2*; 1958 and 1982, Carnegie International exhibition at the Carnegie Institute in Pittsburgh; 1959, 1961 and 1985, at the São Paulo Biennale; 1960, at the Venice Biennale and the Guggenheim International Exhibition at the Guggenheim Museum in New York; 1963, First International Salon of Pilot Galleries of the World in Lausanne; 1965, Zurich Kunsthaus; 1966 and 1973, Museum of Modern Art in New York; 1968 and 1973, National Museum of Modern Art in Tokyo; 1970, Museum of Fine Arts in Osaka; 1974, Düsseldorf Kunsthalle; 1975, Louisiana Museum of Modern Art in Denmark; 1976, 1981 and 1984, Metropolitan Art Museum in Tokyo; 1983, the Musée Rath and the Musée d'Art et d'Histoire in Geneva; 1985, Oxford Gallery of Modern Art; 1986, *Japon des Avant-Gardes 1910-1970* at the George Pompidou Centre in Paris; 1989, *Europalia 89* at the Brussels Museum of Modern Art with Yamaguchi Takeo.

He displayed his works in many personal exhibitions: regularly from 1958 in Tokyo; 1965, Kunstverein in Freiburg; 1978, National Museum of Modern Art in Tokyo; from 1986 at Annely Juda Fine Art in London; 1984, a touring exhibition in Japan; 1989, Moderne Kunst in Basel; 1993, at two retrospectives entitled *Yoshishige Saito - Time, Space, Wood* at the Yokohama Art Museum and the Tokushima Museum of Modern Art. He won many awards, including: 1957, the prize of the Fourth International Exhibition of the 'Mainichi' with *Oni* (*Demon*); 1958-1959, the AICA prize in Paris with *Painting E*; 1960, first prize at the Exhibition of Contemporary Japanese Artists and the Guggenheim Prize in New York; in 1959 a painting prize and in 1961 the international painting prize at the São Paulo Biennale with *Work No. 10*; 1963, the main prize at the Tokyo Biennale; from 1965 to 1967, the prize at the exhibition *New Painting and Sculpture in Japan* in the USA; and in 1984, the Asahi prize.

BIBLIOGRAPHY:

Saito, exhibition catalogue, Annely Juda Fine Art, London, 1992.

MUSEUMS AND GALLERIES:

FUKUOKA (AM) - GIFU (MFA) - HOUSTON (MFA) - KAMAKURA (MMA) - KURASHIKI (Ohara MA): *Work 13* (1961) - KYOTO (National Mus. of Modern Art) - NAGAOKA (Niigata MMA) - OSAKA (National MA) - OTTERLO (Kröller-Müller Mus.) - TOKYO (Metropolitan Art Mus.) - TOKYO (National MMA): *Asymmetry, Square Nos. 1 and 2* - TOYAMA (MMA).

AUCTION RECORDS:

NEW YORK, 27 April 1994, *Untitled (Red)* (1962, oil on wood, 71 3/4 x 47 3/4 ins / 182.2 x 121.3 cm) USD 376,500. NEW YORK, 31 Oct 1995, *Work* (1964, oil on wood panel, 54 1/4 x 48 ins / 137.7 x 121 cm) USD 101,500. LONDON, 24 June 1999, *Composition in Blue* (1961, chalk on panel, 71 x 48 ins / 181 x 121 cm) GBP 92,000. NEW YORK, 23 March 2004, *Untitled* (1965, oil on wood, 12 x 10 ins / 31 x 25 cm) USD 10,000.

SAIVE, Franz de, or Savius or La Saive, called Franciscus de Namur
Flemish School, 16th - 17th century.
Painter. History painting.
Antwerp School.

Franz de Saive was a master in the guild of Antwerp in 1599 and possibly the brother of Jean Baptiste de Saive. The art gallery of Schleissheim has a *Lamentations of Christ* by him.

SAIVE, Jean Baptiste de, or Sayve or Le Save, called Jean de Namur the Elder
Flemish School, 16th - 17th century.
Born c. 1540, in Namur; died 6 April 1624, in Mechelen.
Painter. History painting.
Mechelen School.

Jean Baptiste de Saive was perhaps a pupil of Lambert Lombard. He worked in Namur until after 1578, and in 1590 he was court painter to the prince of Parma in Brussels and keeper of the vineyards to the court. He soon returned to Namur and married the daughter of the painter Bouverie, working in 1594 for Archduke Ernest and in 1597 for the town hall of Namur. In 1603 he went to Mechelen, entered the guild and worked for the cathedral of St-Rombaut and the church of Notre-Dame au-delà de la Dyle. Among his works are *Martyrdom of St Catherine* (in Notre-Dame au-delà de la Dyle, Mechelen), *Triumph of David, Judith and Holofernes, Sacrifice of Abraham, Baptism of Christ* (in the church of St-Rombaut), and *Portrait* (E. Neeffs Collection). There are other works by him in the churches of Tamise, Elewyt and Bouheyden.

AUCTION RECORDS:

LONDON, 3 July 1997, *January; February* (1591, oil on canvas, two works, 86 1/2 x 42 3/4 ins / 219.5 x 108.5 cm) GBP 89,500. NEW YORK, 28 Jan 2000, *Fruit and Vegetable Seller's Stall* (oil on canvas, 62 x 89 ins / 157 x 227 cm) USD 80,000. ANTWERP, 2 Dec 2002, *Kitchen Scene before a Palace Banquet in Renaissance Interior* (oil on canvas, 61 x 94 ins / 154 x 240 cm) EUR 18,000. MADRID, 4 Nov 2003, *Market Scene* (oil on canvas, 56 x 87 ins / 141 x 222 cm) EUR 200,000. LONDON, 21 April 2004, *Annunciation* (oil on panel, 33 x 22 ins / 85 x 55 cm) GBP 3,500.

SAIVE, Jean de, known as Jean de Namur the Younger
Flemish School, 17th century.
Born 1597, in Mechelen.
Painter. History painting, landscapes.

Jean de Saive was the son of Jean Baptise Saive. He is recorded as a guild master in 1621. He is best known for a *Beheading of St Barbara* in the church of St Barbara, in Mechelen.

MUSEUMS AND GALLERIES:

RHEIMS: *Market scene*.

SAIVE, Marianne
Belgian, 20th century.
Born 1941, in Hornu.
Sculptor, potter. Figures, animals.

SAJEVIC, Johann
Slovene, 20th century.
Born 21 October 1891, in Stara vas Postumia.

Sculptor, painter.
Johann Sajevic trained in Vienna with Müllner.

SAJNU
Guler School, 19th century.
Active at the beginning of the 19th century.
Painter.
Sajnu painted 21 illustrations for the *Hamir Hath.*
BIBLIOGRAPHY:
Khandavala, K. Pahari, *Miniature Painting*, Bombay, 1958. Archer, W.G., *Indian Paintings from the Punjab Hills*, London, 1973. Khandavala, K. Pahari, *Miniature Paintings in the N.C. Mehta Collection*, Ahmadabad, 1983.
MUSEUMS AND GALLERIES:
BANARAS (Hindu University).

SAJO, Ferenc
Hungarian, 20th century.
Born 1936, in Miskolc.
Active in France from 1975.
Painter, engraver.
Ferenc Sajo featured in *De Bonnard à Baselitz - Dix ans d'enrichissements du cabinet des estampes 1978-1988* (*From Bonnard to Baselitz: A Decade of Acquisitions by the Prints Collection 1978-1988*), Bibliothèque Nationale de France, Paris (1992).
MUSEUMS AND GALLERIES:
PARIS (BNF, Prints Collection): *Macabre Dance* (1985, line-engraving).

SAJOSY, Lajos or Alois
Hungarian, 19th century.
Born 11 September 1836, in Gyöngyös; died 24 May 1901, in Eger.
Painter. History painting, genre scenes.
Lajos Sajosy studied in Budapest, Vienna, Brussels and Venice. The art gallery in Eger owns some of his paintings.

SAJOUS, Louis
French, 19th century.
Born in Toulouse.
Sculptor.
He exhibited at the Salon of the Société des Artistes Français, receiving an honourable mention in 1906.

SAJZEV, Ivan Kondrateevich
Russian, 19th century.
Born 1805; died 1887.
Painter, watercolourist. Portraits.
Sajzev studied under Stupin.
MUSEUMS AND GALLERIES:
ST PETERSBURG (Gosudarstvennyj Russkij Muz.): three watercolours.

SAKAI, Kasuya or Kazuya
Argentinian, 20th century.
Born 1927, in Buenos Aires.
Painter, illustrator.
Born to Japanese parents, Kasuya Sakai studied in Japan and then returned to Argentina in 1951. He lives and works in Buenos Aires. He has won a number of prizes, including a first prize from the Pipino and Márquez Foundation in Córdoba in 1960 and in 1962 he received a grant to go to Paris.

His work has featured in several collective exhibitions: 1959, *South American Art Today* in Dallas; 1960, *Five Argentinian Painters* in the National Museum of Buenos Aires; 1960, the São Paulo Biennale; 1961, the Venice Biennale 2000, *Octavio Paz Illustré par les Peintres* (*Octavio Paz Illustrated by Painters*) in the Maison de l'Amérique Latine in Paris. He has put on solo exhibitions in Buenos Aires since 1962.
MUSEUMS AND GALLERIES:
PARIS (BNF): *Chromatology II.*
AUCTION RECORDS:
NEW YORK, 17 May 1989, *The Little Theatre* (1964, acrylic and mixed media/canvas, 50 x 50 ins / 127 x 127 cm) USD 3,300. NEW YORK, 18-19 May 1992, *From the Series Black and White* (1958, oil on canvas, 43 1/4 x 39 1/4 ins / 109.8 x 100 cm) USD 5,500. MEXICO, 10 Aug 2000, *Sidewinder* (acrylic, 43 x 51 ins / 110 x 130 cm) MXP 22,000. BUENOS AIRES, 17 July 2003, *Yin* (1961, oil on canvas, 45 x 57 ins / 114 x 146 cm) USD 5,830. NEW YORK, 3 Dec 2003, *Painting no.53* (1960, oil and acrylic, 59 x 45 ins / 149 x 114 cm) USD 4,000. BUENOS AIRES, 29 June 2004, *Untitled* (1960, ink, 21 x 15 ins / 53 x 39 cm) USD 25,000. BUENOS AIRES, 5 Oct 2004, *Painting* (1958, oil on canvas, 24 x 31 ins / 60 x 80 cm) USD 9,700.

SAKAI, Tadamoto. See **HOITSU**

SAKAKI, Shinen. See **HYAKUSEN**

SAKESLAN, Jean
Painter. Portraits.
MUSEUMS AND GALLERIES:
ARRAS: *Portrait of the Metropolitan of Tiflis (Tbilisi).*

SAKHANOV, Aleksandr or Alexander
Russian, 20th century.
Born 1914; died 1989.
Painter. Landscapes.
Aleksandr Sakhanov trained at the Surikov in Moscow. He was a member of the Association of Artists of the U.S.S.R. and Artist Emeritus of the U.S.S.R.
AUCTION RECORDS:
PARIS, 6 Feb 1993, *Frosty Hills* (1966, oil on canvas, 37 1/2 x 26 1/2 ins / 95 x 67 cm) FRF 5,000.

SAKHAROV, Aleksandr Grigorievich, or Zakharov
Russian, 18th century.
Born 1754; died after 1800.
Miniaturist.
Aleksandr Grigorievich Sakharov studied at the academy of fine arts in St Petersburg and, in Paris, he studied under P.A. Machy.

SAKHAROV, Aleksandr I., or Zakharov
Russian, 18th century.
Died 1738.
Painter. History painting, portraits.
Aleksandr Sakharov was sent on educational visits to Holland and Italy by Tsar Peter the Great. He could also have been known as Mikhail Sakharov.

SAKHAROV, Aleksandr II, or Zakharov
Russian, 18th century.
Painter. Historical subjects. Murals.
Aleksandr Sakharov was active in the first half of the 18th century. He worked at palaces in and around St Petersburg from 1720 to 1742.

SAKHAROV, Mikhail, or Zakharov
Russian, 18th century.
Painter. Figures. Murals.
Mikhail Sakharov was active in the first half of the 18th century. He was sent to Florence to learn painting by Tsar Peter the Great, and worked for the Russian Court from 1724 to 1732. He could also have been known as Aleksandr I Sakharov.

SAKHAROV, Piotr Sakharovich or Zakharovich, or Sakarov-Chetchenets
Russian, 19th century.
Born 1816; died 1852.
Painter. Portraits, group portraits.
MUSEUMS AND GALLERIES:
MOSCOW (State Tretyakov Gal.): *Portrait of the Doctor F.I. Inozemtsev; Portrait of Ermolov's Children; Portrait (Identity*

Unknown); Portrait of the Historian J.N. Granovsky; Portrait of N.A. Postnikov; The Postnikov Family, the Teacher I.P. Matiochenkov, the Doctor S.A. Smirnov, the Painter P.Z. Zakharov and the Composer P.P. Bulakhov (drawing, group portrait) - ST PETERSBURG (Gosudarstvennyj Russkij Muz.): *Portrait of the General Ermolov.*

AUCTION RECORDS:
LONDON, 14 May 1980, *Portrait of an Officer* (1842, oil on card) GBP 440.

SAKHAROV, Semen Loginovich, or Zakharov
Russian, 19th century.
Born 1821, in Kholm; died 22 August 1847, in St Petersburg.
Engraver.

Semen Loginovich Sakharov studied under Pavel P. Utkin at the academy of fine arts in St Petersburg.

SAKHINI, Nicos
Greek, 20th century.
Born 1920, in Thessalonica.
Painter.

Nicos Sakhini was a self-taught painter. For a time he followed Informal and Expressionist Abstraction then went back in the 1960s to introducing object as a point of reference point in the pictorial fabric.

He featured in collective exhibitions including: Greece; Paris; the USA; and Germany. He held solo exhibitions in Greece (1954, 1958, 1959 and 1963).

SAKIC, Aleksandar
Serb, 20th century.
Born 28 May 1920, in Vinkovci.
Sculptor, draughtsman. Figures. Monuments.

Aleksandar Sakic trained at the school of fine art in Belgrade; he lived and worked in Niš from 1950. He executed monuments commemorating the battle to liberate the former Yugoslavia. His stone sculptures of fighters, rabbis, wives and satyrs with emaciated faces and prominent noses, evoke an ancestral world, an epic saga. He also executed drawings in ballpoint pen representing hieratic, sculptural figures, a grotesque view of an insolent crowd inspired by traditional tales.

Aleksandar Sakic took part regularly in collective exhibitions. He held a number of solo exhibitions including: Niš (regularly from 1954); Belgrade (1980); Yugoslav community centre gallery, Paris (1982).

MUSEUMS AND GALLERIES:
BELGRADE (Mus.) - NOVI SAD (Mus.) - ZAGREB (Mus.).

SAKIER, George
American, 20th century.
Born 1900, in New York.
Active in France.
Painter.

George Sakier began painting at a very young age in New York, but lived in Paris from 1925-1930. Returning to the USA, he busied himself as a designer and was one of the first artists to use industrial shapes. From 1950 Sakier concentrated on painting, adopting a traditional international abstract style, his works made up of large geometric shapes in dull shades, occasionally reminiscent of Piaubert.

He took part in many group exhibitions in New York (Metropolitan Museum, Museum of Modern Art, Brooklyn Museum) and the Brooklyn Museum in Philadelphia. In 1963 he also took part in the first Salon des Galeries Pilotes at the regional museum in Lausanne. He had a number of solo exhibition, notably in Paris in 1963.

SAKO, Yuzuru
Japanese, 20th century.
Born 1930, in Kagoshima.
Painter.

Sako Yuzuru obtained a diploma from the National Conservatory of Music and Art in Tokyo in 1953 and taught in Tokyo from 1966. He mounted his first personal exhibition in Tokyo in 1962 and 1966. He paints in a very free figurative style.

SAKON, real name: Hasegawa Sakon
Japanese, 17th century.
Active during the first half of the 17th century.
Painter.

Sakon was the son of Tohaku (1539-1610).

SAKURAI, Makoto
Japanese, 20th century.
Born 1943.
Painter, engraver.

Sakurai Makoto has taken part in the activities of the Japanese Engraving Association since 1969 and became a member in 1974. In 1970 his work was represented at the Colour Engraving Triennial in Grenchen, Switzerland, and in 1974 at the *Japanese Art Today* exhibition at the Museum of Contemporary Art in Montreal.

SAKURAI, Takami
Japanese, 20th century.
Born 1928, in Fukuoka.
Painter.

Sakurai Takami works in large format, adopting a primitive style in colourful compositions. He took part in collective exhibitions from 1955, at the Museum of Modern Art in San Francisco, the Municipal Museum in Tokyo, and the Cagnes International Festival. He has presented his works in personal exhibitions in 1959 and from 1974 annually in Tokyo, 1966 in San Francisco, 1977, 1981, 1982 and 1986 in Paris.

SAL, Antonio Luigi del
Italian, 20th century.
Born 1928, in Venice.
Painter. Nudes.

AUCTION RECORDS:
ROME, 10 April 1990, *Pink Nude* (1973, oil on canvas, 31 1/2 x 31 1/2 ins / 80 x 80 cm) ITL 3,600,000.

SALA, Alessandro
Italian, 18th - 19th century.
Born 10 September 1771, in Brescia; died 18 June 1841, in Brescia.
Painter, engraver (burin).

Alessandro Sala's notable works include his illustrations for books on art treasures and public monuments in Brescia.

SALA, Annamaria and Marzio
Italian, 20th century.
Mario born in 1930 in Merano, Annamaria born in 1928 in Turin.
Active in Germany.
Sculptors.

After studying cybernetics and music, Annamaria and Marzio Sala have worked together since 1963 in Hödingen. They have participated in many collective exhibitions and also held solo exhibitions in Turin, Venice and Milan in 1966, Kreuzlingen in 1968, Cologne in 1970 and at the Musée d'Art Moderne in Villeneuve-d'Ascq in 1986.

They work with materials such as aluminium, polyester and coloured Plexiglas, creating spatial animations that are both austere and stimulating.

BIBLIOGRAPHY:
Ier Salon international des Galeries Pilotes, exhibition catalogue, Musée cantonal, Lausanne, 1970. *Sala*, exhibition catalogue, Musée d'Art moderne, Villeneuve d'Ascq, 1986.

SALA, Antonio
Spanish, 15th century.
Glass painter.

Antonio Sala produced stained glass windows for Palma de Majorca Cathedral, in 1441.

SALA, Carlos. See **SALAS**

SALA, Elia
Italian, 19th - 20th century.
Born April 1864, in Milan; died 10 January 1920, in Gorla-Precotto.
Sculptor, painter.

Elia Sala was also an architect. He worked mainly in Russia.

SALA, Eliseo
Italian, 19th century.
Born 2 January 1813, in Milan; died 24 June 1879, in Truggio.
Painter, sculptor. History painting, portraits.

A pupil of Luigi Sabatelli, Elisio Sala continued his studies in Venice and Rome.

MUSEUMS AND GALLERIES:

BRESCIA (Pinacoteca Tosio-Martinengo): *Portrait of Manzoni* - MILAN (Gal. d'Arte Moderna): *Portrait of Giuseppe Corridoni Guenzati; Portrait of Mauro Conconi; Portrait of Vittoria Cima della Scala.*

AUCTION RECORDS:

MILAN, 16 March 1971, *Portrait of a Woman*, ITL 1,900,000. MILAN, 16 June 1980, *Portrait of a Woman* (oil on canvas, 23 1/4 x 19 3/4 ins / 59 x 50 cm) ITL 1,800,000. ANGERS, 8 Dec 1984, *Levee* (1846, oil on canvas, 65 x 49 1/4 ins / 165 x 125 cm) FRF 38,000. MILAN, 21 April 1986, *Portrait of the Artist's Family with a View of Lake Como in the Background* (oil on canvas, 74 3/4 x 82 3/4 ins / 190 x 210 cm) ITL 20,000,000. MILAN, 8 June 1993, *Group of Three Children* (bronze, h. 11 3/4 ins / 30 cm) ITL 1,400,000. MILAN, 29 Oct 2003, *Portrait of Man with Cigar* (oil on canvas, oval, 39 x 32 ins / 98 x 81 cm) EUR 5,600. MILAN, 29 Oct 2003, *Portrait of Lady with Fan* (1835, oil on canvas, oval, 39 x 32 ins / 98 x 81 cm) EUR 8,800.

SALA, Eugène de, pseudonym of Salomonsen Oswald Lykkeberg
Danish, 20th century.
Born 29 August 1899, in Randers.
Active in Copenhagen.
Painter (mixed media), lithographer. Still-lifes.

AUCTION RECORDS:

COPENHAGEN, 25 Sept 1985, *Still-life* (1927, oil on canvas, 48 x 35 3/4 ins / 122 x 91 cm) DKK 28,000. COPENHAGEN, 4 May 1988, *Composition* (1927, wood, h. 29 1/4 ins / 74 cm) DKK 28,000. COPENHAGEN, 30 May 1990, *Still-life* (paint/wood, 27 1/2 x 30 ins / 70 x 76 cm) DKK 5,800. COPENHAGEN, 2-3 Dec 1992, *Bantam Cock* (oil on panel, 23 1/2 x 11 1/2 ins / 60 x 29 cm) DKK 8,500. COPENHAGEN, 10 March 1993, *Still-life* (1928, paint and chalks, 15 1/4 x 15 1/4 ins / 39 x 39 cm) DKK 8,000. COPENHAGEN, 6 Dec 1994, *Face* (oil on canvas, 33 1/2 x 27 1/2 ins / 85 x 70 cm) DKK 4,500. COPENHAGEN, 12 March 1996, *Still-life with Fruit* (oil on canvas, 25 1/4 x 32 ins / 64 x 81 cm) DKK 4,000.

SALA, Eugenio
Italian, 19th - 20th century.
Born 1866, in Milan; died 8 October 1908, in Desenzano.
Painter. Landscapes.

Eugenio Sala was the brother of the painter Paolo Sala.

SALA, Francesco
Italian, 18th century.
Active in Como.
Sculptor.

Sculptures by Francesco Sala can be found in the churches of the Madonna del Sasso near Locarno and the Madonna dei Miracoli in Saronno.

SALA, Georges Augustin or George Augustius
British, 19th century.
Born 24 November 1828, in London; died 8 December 1895, in London.
Painter, draughtsman, engraver.

George(s) Sala studied as a fourteen year-old under the miniaturist painter Carl Schiller. The following year, he was earning a living painting stage sets for the Princess Theatre and the Lyceum Theatre in London. His reputation built gradually following his illustrations for Alfred Bunn's *Word uit Peusch* (1847) and *The Man in the Moon* (1848). He went on to produce four large lithographed panoramas of the 1852 Exhibition. He also worked alongside Henry Alken on a panoramic view of the funeral of the Duke of Wellington. He devoted his later years to journalism and art criticism.

SALA, Gerard
Spanish, 20th century.
Born March 1942, in Tona (Catalonia).
Painter, draughtsman, engraver, potter. Murals.

Gerard Sala was a pupil at the Massana school in 1957. In 1961 he won the first national design prize in Madrid. He joined the school of mural painting at the national institute of Sant Cugat del Vallès. He has been awarded various prizes: 1963, first prize for painting in Alicante; 1964, first prize for drawing from the board of fine arts; 1965, first prize for design at the autumn Salon in Palma, Majorca; 1967, first prize for painting at the Ciudad de Hospitalet. In 1962 he started producing ceramic murals and in 1966 he completed a mural in Vic. He practises an Expressionist figuration strongly influenced by Pop Art.

He has taken part in group exhibitions since 1961, notably at the young artists' Salon in Barcelona in 1962, as well as in numerous cities in Spain. He has shown his work in solo exhibitions, notably for the first time in 1972 in Barcelona.

BIBLIOGRAPHY:

Gérard Sala, exhibition catalogue, Gal. Adria, Barcelona, 1972.

SALA, Giosuè
Italian, 18th century.
Active in Milan at the end of the 18th century.
Painter.

Two altarpieces by Giosuè Sala can be seen in the church in Brignano Gera d'Adda.

SALA, Giovanni Angelo, called Petritto
Italian, 17th century.
Active in Lugano, Switzerland.
Sculptor, stucco artist.

Giovanni Angelo Sala worked in Bergamo from 1653 to 1676.

SALA, Giuseppe
Italian, 17th - 18th century.
Active in Pavia.
Sculptor.

SALA, Grau. See **GRAU SALA**

SALA, Ignacio Gil
Spanish, 20th century.
Born 1912.
Painter. Genre scenes, landscapes, urban landscapes, architectural views.

AUCTION RECORDS:

BARCELONA, 17 March 1981, *Roman Temple, Djemila* (oil on canvas, 32 x 39 1/4 ins / 81 x 100 cm) ESP 105,000. LONDON, 29 Nov 1982, *The Reading Lesson; The Writing Lesson* (two oils on canvas, 12 1/4 x 10 ins / 31 x 25.5 cm) GBP 1,300. BARCELONA, 28 Nov 1985, *Plaza de la Garduna, Barcelona* (oil on canvas, 43 x 35 ins / 109 x 89 cm) ESP 340,000. NEW YORK, 16 Feb

1994, *Sunny Day* (oil on canvas, 28 3/4 x 36 1/4 ins / 73 x 92.1 cm) USD 5,520.

SALA, Juan or Jean

Spanish, 19th - 20th century.

Born 1867, in Barcelona; died 6 June 1918, in Paris.

Painter. Genre scenes, landscapes.

Juan Sala exhibited in Paris, where he was awarded a bronze medal at the 1900 Exposition Universelle.

Jean. SALA

Jean SALA

AUCTION RECORDS:

PARIS, 16-17 May 1892, *Surprise*, FRF 320. NEW YORK, 8-10 Jan 1909, *Sunbeam and Light Breeze*, USD 145. PARIS, 22 March 1970, *Flower-Seller on the Pont-Neuf*, FRF 6,300. LONDON, 23 April 1971, *Flower-Seller on the Pont-Neuf*, Gns 650. PARIS, 4 May 1990, *Sunday in the Country* (1893, oil on canvas, 32 x 39 1/4 ins / 81 x 100 cm) FRF 330,000. NEW YORK, 19 Feb 1992, *Afternoon Tea by the River* (oil on canvas, 19 3/4 x 24 1/4 ins / 50.2 x 61.6 cm) USD 11,000. PARIS, 22 May 1992, *Elegant Lady in a Blue Hat* (pastel, oval, 51 1/4 x 35 ins / 130 x 88 cm) FRF 13,500. NEW YORK, 16 Feb 1995, *Provocation* (1912, oil on canvas, 51 1/4 x 71 1/4 ins / 130.2 x 181 cm) USD 34,500. PARIS, 12 Dec 1997, *Profile of Seated Acrobat* (oil on canvas, 39 1/4 x 28 ins / 100 x 71 cm) FRF 20,000.

SALA, Juan or Jean

Spanish, 20th century.

Born 7 January 1895, in Barcelona.

Active in France.

Painter, pastellist. Figures, portraits, landscapes.

Designs for stained glass.

Juan Sala lived and worked in Paris. He exhibited at the Salon des Indépendants, the Salon des Tuileries and the Salon des Décorateurs.

AUCTION RECORDS:

PARIS, 29 Oct 1918, *Carmen*, FRF 285; *Frisson*, FRF 580; *Bridge and Church of St James, Dieppe* (each) FRF 125; *Green Shawl* (pastel) FRF 300. LONDON, 17 Jan 2002, *Salome* (oil on canvas, 39 x 28 ins / 99 x 71 cm) GBP 5,500. LONDON, 23 Sept 2004, *Coquette* (oil on panel, 23 x 17 ins / 59 x 42 cm) GBP 2,000.

SALA, Louis

French, 20th century.

Painter.

Louis Sala exhibited in Paris at the Salon des Indépendants.

SALA, Mario

Italian, 19th - 20th century.

Born 1874, in Milan; died 24 April 1920, in Milan

Stage sets.

Mario Sala worked at the opera house of La Scala from 1898.

SALA, Marzio. See **SALA Annamaria** and **Marzio**

SALA, Miguel

Spanish, 17th century.

Born 1627, in Cardona; died 1704, in Barcelona.

Sculptor.

Miguel Sala was a pupil of Francisco de Santa Cruz. He executed paintings for churches in Barcelona and Cardona. There is a statue by him of *St Cajetan* in the provincial museum in Barcelona.

SALA, Paolo

Italian, 19th - 20th century.

Born 14 January 1859, in Milan; died 20 December 1929 or 1924, in Milan.

Painter, watercolourist. Portraits, genre scenes, landscapes, seascapes, still-lifes.

Paolo Sala was the brother of the painter Eugenio Sala. He exhibited works in Naples, Rome, Venice and Milan.

PSala

Paolo Sala

AUCTION RECORDS:

PARIS, 19-21 March 1928, *Venetian Canal* (watercolour) FRF 600. MILAN, Feb 1950, *Landscape*, ITL 120,000. MILAN, 4 June 1970, *Shepherd* (watercolour) ITL 650,000. MILAN, 16 March 1972, *Figures by a Lake* (two panels) ITL 1,600,000. BUENOS AIRES, 14-15 Nov 1973, *View of London*, ARS 40,000. MILAN, 20 Nov 1973, *London Street* (watercolour) ITL 1,350,000. MILAN, 28 Oct 1976, *Mountainous Landscape* (oil on canvas, 26 1/2 x 41 1/4 ins / 67 x 105 cm) ITL 950,000. LONDON, 20 April 1979, *View of the Thames* (oil on panel, 7 3/4 x 11 3/4 ins / 20 x 30 cm) GBP 3,200. MILAN, 17 June 1981, *Lucia* (oil on panel, 13 3/4 x 9 3/4 ins / 35 x 24.7 cm) ITL 4,200,000. MILAN, 22 April 1982, *Piazza della Scala; Via Manzetti* (two watercolours, 7 x 10 ins / 17.5 x 24.5 cm) ITL 11,500,000. MILAN, 21 April 1983, *Figures in a Park* (watercolour, 14 1/4 x 20 1/2 ins / 36 x 52 cm) ITL 2,000,000. MILAN, 29 May 1984, *Piazza San Marco in Venice* (oil on canvas, 29 1/4 x 42 1/4 ins / 74 x 107 cm) ITL 16,000,000. LONDON, 28 Nov 1985, *Dogs around a Fireplace* (1895, watercolour, 19 1/4 x 25 1/2 ins / 49 x 65 cm) GBP 2,600. MILAN, 28 Oct 1986, *Tottenham Street, London* (oil on panel, 9 x 5 1/2 ins / 22 x 14 cm) ITL 8,500,000. MILAN, 9 June 1987, *Lake Mergozzo* (oil on canvas, 39 1/4 x 26 ins / 100 x 66 cm) ITL 23,000,000. LONDON, 25 March 1988, *The Strand, London* (oil on panel, 8 x 12 ins / 20.3 x 30.5 cm) GBP 10,450. MILAN, 14 March 1989, *Bridge over the Cannaregio Canal, Venice* (oil on panel, 22 3/4 x 13 1/2 ins / 58 x 34 cm) ITL 12,500,000. MILAN, 14 June 1989, *Gardens on Lake Maggiore* (oil on canvas, 8 1/2 x 11 3/4 ins / 21.5 x 30 cm) ITL 3,300,000. MILAN, 19 Oct 1989, *Church of St Mary on The Strand, London* (watercolour on artboard, 19 3/4 x 27 1/4 ins / 50 x 69 cm) ITL 10,500,000. LONDON, 28 March 1990, *Oxford Street, London* (watercolour, 14 1/4 x 11 ins / 36.5 x 27 cm) GBP 3,740. MONACO, 21 April 1990, *View of St Paul's Cathedral from Ludgate Street, London* (watercolour, 22 x 15 1/2 ins / 55 x 39.5 cm) FRF 38,850; *In the Park* (oil on canvas/panel, 21 1/2 x 14 1/4 ins / 54.5 x 36 cm) FRF 66,600. NEW YORK, 23 Oct 1990, *Still-life with Flowers and Murano Glassware*. ROME, 11 Dec 1990, *London* (watercolour and tempera, 18 1/4 x 11 3/4 ins / 46.5 x 30 cm) ITL 5,750,000. MILAN, 12 March 1991, *The River Lambro* (1927, watercolour/card, 27 1/4 x 38 1/2 ins / 69 x 98 cm) ITL 8,000,000. MILAN, 6 June 1991, *Nievsky Prospect, St Petersburg* (1895, watercolour on paper mounted to board, 19 3/4 x 13 ins / 50 x 33 cm) ITL 6,500,000. NEW YORK, 15 Oct 1991, *St Paul's Cathedral, London* (watercolour/paper, 9 x 13 ins / 22.9 x 33 cm) USD 1,980. MILAN, 7 Nov 1991, *Landscape with Lake* (oil on canvas, 38 1/2 x 58 1/4 ins / 98 x 148 cm) ITL 28,000,000. LONDON, 29 Nov 1991, *Thames Embankment with Cleopatra's Needle and Waterloo Bridge* (oil on panel, 7 3/4 x 12 ins / 19.5 x 30.5 cm) GBP 9,350. MILAN, 19 March 1992, *Morning in Venice* (oil on canvas, 10 x 15 3/4 ins / 25.5 x 40 cm) ITL 10,000,000. NEW YORK, 27 May 1992, *Spring Dance* (watercolour on paper mounted to board, 38 1/2 x 26 1/2 ins / 97.7 x 67.3 cm) USD 5,500. LONDON, 17 June 1992, *Parliament*

Square, London (watercolour, 13 3/4 x 20 1/4 ins / 35 x 51.5 cm) GBP 4,180. NEW YORK, 29 Oct 1992, *The Grand Canal with Palazzo Pisani, Venice* (watercolour/paper, 14 x 20 3/4 ins / 35.3 x 52.7 cm) USD 5,280. MILAN, 29 Oct 1992, *Departure of the Stagecoach* (watercolour/paper, 27 1/4 x 40 1/4 ins / 69 x 102 cm) ITL 11,500,000. LONDON, 25 Nov 1992, *Path on a Hillside with Figures* (oil on panel, 8 1/4 x 14 1/2 ins / 21 x 37 cm) GBP 1,650. LONDON, 27 Nov 1992, *The Strand, London* (1888, oil on panel, 8 x 12 ins / 20.3 x 30.5 cm) GBP 12,100. NEW YORK, 17 Feb 1993, *Pretty Servant Girl* (oil on canvas, 39 1/2 x 49 1/2 ins / 100.3 x 125.7 cm) USD 34,500. MILAN, 16 March 1993, *Cossack Camp* (1909, oil on canvas, 46 x 76 ins / 117 x 193 cm) ITL 40,000,000. ROME, 27 April 1993, *London Street* (watercolour on artboard, 26 x 38 1/2 ins / 66 x 98 cm) ITL 9,000,000. NEW YORK, 27 May 1993, *Horse Riders in a Park* (watercolour on paper mounted to board, 10 3/4 x 18 ins / 27.3 x 45.7 cm) USD 4,830. MILAN, 9 Nov 1993, *The Artist's Family in the Garden of the Villa at Mergozzo* (watercolour on paper mounted to board, 26 1/2 x 38 3/4 ins / 67.5 x 98.5 cm) ITL 13,225,000. LONDON, 16 Nov 1994, *Broad Sanctuary and Westminster, London* (oil on panel, 11 x 7 3/4 ins / 27 x 20 cm) GBP 20,700. ROME, 5 Dec 1995, *Cart in the Countryside* (watercolour, 42 1/4 x 29 1/4 ins / 107 x 74 cm) ITL 8,250,000. LONDON, 12 June 1996, *View of the Church of S Maria della Salute, Venice* (watercolour, 9 3/4 x 14 1/4 ins / 25 x 36 cm) GBP 3,220. MILAN, 18 Dec 1996, *London Street in the Rain* (1919, watercolour/paper, 26 1/2 x 38 1/4 ins / 67 x 97 cm) ITL 22,135,000. LONDON, 13 June 1997, *Strand, London* (1885, oil on panel, 8 1/2 x 5 1/4 ins / 21.6 x 13.3 cm) GBP 8,625. LONDON, 29 April 1999, *Twilight* (oil on canvas, 48 x 68 ins / 123 x 173 cm) GBP 20,000. BUENOS AIRES, 24 Nov 1999, *View of London with Big Ben and Westminster* (1919, oil on canvas, 30 x 46 ins / 76 x 118 cm) USD 48,000. PARIS, 30 Jan 2000, *View of Venise* (watercolour, 14 x 9 ins / 35 x 24 cm) FRF 19,500. MILAN, 31 Oct 2000, *Mountainous Landscape* (oil on canvas, 47 x 67 ins / 119 x 169 cm) ITL 25,000,000. MELBOURNE, 8 May 2001, *Beach Scene* (oil on board, 27 x 39 ins / 68 x 98 cm) AUD 18,000. LONDON, 19 June 2001, *Boating on Lago Maggiore, Isola Bella beyond* (watercolour, 14 x 21 ins / 35 x 53 cm) GBP 5,500. MILAN, 22 May 2002, *Grand Canal, Venice* (1900, oil on canvas, 11 x 18 ins / 27 x 46 cm) EUR 8,500. MILAN, 22 May 2002, *Crevasse* (watercolour, 53 x 30 ins / 135 x 76 cm) EUR 18,500. BRISTOL, 22 July 2003, *Broad Sanctuary, London* (watercolour, 20 x 8 ins / 52 x 21 cm) GBP 3,800. LONDON, 1 Oct 2003, *Piazza San Marco, Venice* (watercolour, 19 x 13 ins / 49 x 32 cm) GBP 2,000. MILAN, 24 March 2004, *Lake Landscape* (oil on board, 5 x 9 ins / 12 x 24 cm) EUR 10,500. LONDON, 6 July 2004, *Grand Canal with S Maria della Salute, Venice. Doge's Palace and the Molo* (pencil and watercolour heightened with white, a pair, 14 x 21 ins / 36 x 53 cm) GBP 5,500.

SALA, Vitale

Italian, 19th century.

Born 18 April 1803, in Cernusco, near Brienz; died 22 July 1835, in Milan.

Painter. History painting.

Vitale Sala was a student at the Accademia di Belle Arti di Brera in Milan. Examples of his work can be found in a number of churches in Milan, Vigevano, Novara, Bosisio and Desio.

MUSEUMS AND GALLERIES:

MILAN (Gal. d'Arte Moderna): *Portrait* - MILAN (Pinacoteca di Brera): *Paolo and Francesca; Funeral of Patrocles.*

AUCTION RECORDS:

MILAN, 5 April 1979, *Departure of Atilius Regulus for Carthage* (oil on canvas, 64 1/4 x 89 3/4 ins / 163 x 228 cm) ITL 1,700,000.

SALA Y FRANCÉS, Emilio

Spanish, 19th - 20th century.

Born 20 January 1850, in Alcoy, near Alicante; died 14 April 1910, in Madrid.

Also active in France.

Painter, watercolourist, engraver, draughtsman, illustrator, poster artist. History painting, religious and mythological subjects, portraits, genre scenes, still-lifes, landscapes. Murals.

Sala y Francés studied under his cousin Placido Francés and under Salustiano Asenjo at the Escuela de Bellas Artes in Valencia before settling in Madrid, where he initially complemented his studies by copying works by Goya and Velázquez. He went on to teach at the school of painting in Madrid from 1907.

His output was nothing short of immense. He worked across many genres, although he favoured portraits and historical subjects (typically featuring episodes drawn from the history of Valencia). Examples include: *Afternoon Tea, Reading Lesson, Gathering Flowers, María Guerrero as a Little Girl, Young Fisherman, Portrait of Don Carlos Fornos* and *Portrait of Ana Colin de Perinat.* Emilio Sala painted decorative murals for the Madrid Casino and for the palacio of the Infanta Isabella. He also produced posters for national festivals and illustrations for the periodical *Blanco y Negro (White and Black).* His written work includes a *Grammar of Colour* and various articles contributed to the periodical *Spanish and American Illustration.*

Sala showed his work at the Exposición Nacional de Bellas Artes in Madrid; 1889 Exposition Universelle in Paris; Berlin Universal Exhibition of 1892 and at the museum of fine arts in Barcelona in 1906. He was awarded a bronze medal in Valencia in 1867 and gold medals in 1978, 1881 and 1892.

BIBLIOGRAPHY:

Espi Valdes, Adrian, *Pintor Emilio Sala y su obra*, Servicio de estudios artísticos, Institución Alfonso el Magnanimo, Caja de ahorros y Monte de piedad de Valancia, Valencia, 1975. Arnáiz, José Manuel/López Jiménez, Javier/Merchán Díaz, Manuel (ed.), *'Cien años de pintura en Espana y Portugal (1830-1930)'* in vol. X, Antiqvaria, Madrid, 1993.

MUSEUMS AND GALLERIES:

BARCELONA (Mus. Nacional d'Art de Catalunya) - BUENOS AIRES (National Mus.) - GRANADA (MBA) - MADRID (Prado): *Expulsion of the Jews from Spain in 1492* - NEW YORK (Hispanic Society of America): portrait*Ramón María de las Mercedes de Campoamor y Campoosorio* (1883-1885) - VALENCIA (MBA San Pío V).

AUCTION RECORDS:

PARIS, 1892, *Surprise*, FRF 320. PARIS, 27 Nov 1899, *Grand Canal, Venice* (two pendants) FRF 610. PARIS, 14 Dec 1925, *Male Portrait in Louis XIII Costume*, FRF 400. MADRID, 13 Dec 1973, *Swing*, ESP 120,000. NEW YORK, 24 May 1985, *Gathering Flowers* (1888, oil on canvas, 25 x 20 ins / 63.3 x 51 cm) USD 9,000. LONDON, 22 June 1988, *Among the Roses* (oil on canvas, 7 1/4 x 10 3/4 ins / 18.5 x 27.5 cm) GBP 1,870. LONDON, 17 Feb 1989, *Young Girl with Bunch of Flowers* (1906, oil on canvas, 10 3/4 x 13 1/2 ins / 27.5 x 34 cm) GBP 7,700. LONDON, 21 June 1989, *Pretty Dressmaker* (oil on canvas, 30 1/4 x 22 ins / 77 x 55 cm) GBP 11,000. NEW YORK, 17 Jan 1990, *Judgement of Solomon* (oil on canvas, 17 1/2 x 22 ins / 44.6 x 55.9 cm) USD 2,310. LONDON, 15 Feb 1990, *Killing Time* (oil on canvas, 18 x 31 ins / 45.8 x 78.7 cm) GBP 11,000. NEW YORK, 28 Feb 1991, *Portrait of Suzanne Caillet* (1897, oil on canvas, 28 1/2 x 18 3/4 ins / 72.4 x 47.7 cm) USD 14,300. LONDON, 18 June 1993, *In the Meadow* (oil on canvas, 20 1/2 x 13 3/4 ins / 52 x 35 cm) GBP 8,050.

SALA-JULIEN, Manuel

Spanish, 19th century.

Born september 1833, in Cádiz.

Painter, lithographer. Portraits, genre scenes.

SALABERT, Firmin
French, 19th century.
Born 1811, in Gaillac (Tarn).
Painter, draughtsman. Figures, portraits, landscapes.
Firmin Salabert was a pupil of Ingres. He made several trips to London, where his actor brother lived, and he also visited Italy. He exhibited at the Paris Salon from 1833 to 1880, and at the Royal Academy in London from 1836 to 1845.

He painted portraits of various actors, dancers and singers in London. He also painted views of the Savoy and Dauphiné regions of France.

MUSEUMS AND GALLERIES:
GAILLAC.

SALADIN, Alphonse
French, 20th century.
Born 6 February 1879, in Épinal; died 1956.
Sculptor (bronze/plaster). Figures. Busts, statuettes, monuments.
Alphonse Saladin, a pupil of Mengué, exhibited in Paris at the Salon des Artistes Français, of which he was a member. He was awarded an honourable mention in 1909, a third-class medal in 1910, a silver in 1920, and the Légion d'Honneur in 1932.

MUSEUMS AND GALLERIES:
FÉCAMP (Musées): *Dr Dufour* (plaster, bust); *Monument to Dr Dufour* (stone, bronze, positioned in the museum's public grounds); *Monument to the Soldiers of Fécamp* (model); *André-Paul Leroux* (bronze, bust) - TROYES: *Bust of the Poet Albert Méral; Bust of Houdain; Bust of Thenissen; Bust of Rodin.*

SALADINI, Achille
French, 19th century.
Born in Lyons; died 1895.
Painter. Landscapes.
A pupil of Kellerhoven, he debuted at the Salon of 1879. He exhibited his work in Paris, at the Salon of the Société des Artistes Français, and was a life member of this group.

Saladini

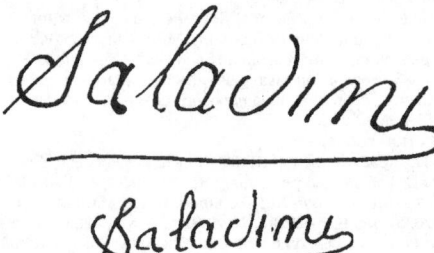

Saladini

AUCTION RECORDS:
MILAN, 21 Dec 1993, *Peasant Family around a Table* (oil on panel, 11 1/2 x 8 1/4 ins / 29 x 21 cm) ITL 8,625,000.

SALADINO, Vincenzo
Italian, 16th century.
Active during the second half of the 16th century.
Miniaturist, illuminator.

MUSEUMS AND GALLERIES:
PALERMO (Biblioteca Centrale della Regione Sicilia): psalter decorated with initials.

SALADO, Pedro
Spanish, 17th century.
Died 27 October 1700, in Saragossa.
Active in Saragossa.
Sculptor. Religious furnishings.
Pedro Salado was the father-in-law of the sculptor Antonio Mesa.

SALAERT, Anthoine
Flemish School, 15th - 16th century.
Active in Ghent 1484-1530.
Sculptor.

SALAERT, Jean
Flemish School, 16th century.
Died 1532.
Active in Ghent.
Sculptor.
Jean Salaert worked on the ceiling of the Great Council Room of Ghent town hall and sculpted a retable for the church of Haeltert near Alost.

SALAI, Andrea, or Salaino or Sallai or Salario, called Gian Giacomo de' Caprotti
Italian, 16th century.
Born c. 1480; died before 10 March 1540, in Milan.
Active in Milan.
Painter. History painting.
Andrea Salai was one of Leonardo da Vinci's most distinguished pupils, mentioned from 1495 onwards. In 1503 he was referred to in Da Vinci's accounts, and Da Vinci later provided a dowry for Salai's sister. When Da Vinci went to Rome in 1514, Salai followed him but, according to some sources, he refused to follow the master to France. Other sources say that he accompanied Da Vinci to Cloux, in Val de Loire, with Melzi and Battista de Vallanis.

Salai lived in Milan and nothing is known about the end of his life. It is believed that Da Vinci finished several of Salai's works and that he even allowed Salai to use his drawings. It seems that Salai prepared replicas or produced copies in his master's studio. According to some critics, the *Virgin and St Anne*, in the Louvre, is one such work.

MUSEUMS AND GALLERIES:
DIJON: *Virgin and Child* - MILAN (Ambrosiana): *St John in the Desert* - MILAN (Pinacoteca di Brera): *Madonna, Jesus and St John; Madonna, Jesus, St Peter and St Paul.*

AUCTION RECORDS:
PARIS, 1756, *Bust of a Sorowful Virgin*, FRF 401. PARIS, 1843, *Virgin and Child*, FRF 1,900; *Herodias*, FRF 780. PARIS, 3 April 1868, *Virgin and Infant Jesus*, FRF 9,600. PARIS, 1881, *Diana*, FRF 4,100. LONDON, 1886, *Beauty, Portrait of a Lady*, FRF 4,200. LONDON, 21 Feb 1910, *Virgin*, GBP 56. LONDON, 8 April 1938, *Virgin and Child*, GBP 102. LONDON, 26 June 1964, *Salvator Mundi*, Gns 450.

SALAIE, Jean Lambert. See **SALÉE**

SALAINO, Andrea. See **SALAI**

SALAKHOV, Tair
Russian, 20th century.
Born 1928, in Baku; died after 1960.
Painter.
An uncritical follower of the retrograde doctrine of Socialist Realism, mixing Populism and popular education, Tair Salakhov depicted the inhabitants of Azerbaijan and oil-well workers of the Caspian Sea; he also painted portraits in a more personal style. He was one of the official artists recognised by the Soviet government and represented Russian art at the Venice Biennale (1962).

SALAKHOVA, Aidan
Russian, 20th - 21st century.
Born 1964, in Moscow.
Painter.
In 1987, Aidan Salakhova graduated from the Surikov art institute. In 1989-1992, she became the joint owner of the First Gallery in Moscow, and in 1992 she founded the Aidan Gallery. In 1987, she took part in the national exhibition of

young artists, Moscow; in 1987-1988 in the *War and Peace* international exhibition in Moscow and Hamburg; in 1988 in *Avant-garde Painters*, in Moscow, in *Labyrinthe* at the young peoples' palace in Moscow and in *New Art Forms* in New York; in 1989 in *Up to 33* at the young peoples' palace in Moscow and in *Rauschenberg to Us, Us to Rauschenberg* at Gallery One in Moscow. In 1999, she took part in *Mata Hari* and *Cult of Culture and Communication* (curator G. Nickich) at the Moscow International Forum for Art Initiatives, in *Suspense* at the Museum of 20th-Century Art, Kemerovo, Siberia, in *After the Wall* at the Moderna Mnseet, Stockholm, in *Inspiration of Lightness* at the Moscow Center for Art, and in *Memories, Mistakes of Memory* at the Exhibition Hall of Russian State Hemane University in Moscow; in 2000 in Klava's *Lovers* and *Art Moscow 2000* at the artists' house, Moscow, and at Zverev's centre for contemporary art, Moscow. In 1997 she exhibited solo in *Antonymous* at the New Academy in St Petersburg; in 1998 in *Diva* at the XL Gallery, Photobiennale-98 at the Central Exhibition Hall, Moscow, and in *Suspense* at the XL Gallery; in 2000 in *Tea in the Desert* at Invogue in Moscow, in *The Sleeping Beaty* at the XL Gallery (supported by European Galleries Projektgesellschaft mbH) and at the Kunstlerhaus Bethanie; and in 2001 in *Alive Paintings* at Gallery D137 in St Petersburg and in *Habibi* at Gallery D137.

Museums and Galleries:
Moscow (State Tretyakov Gal.) - New York (Berman-E. N. Gallery) - New York (Faridek Cadot Gal.) - St Petersburg (Gosudarstvennyj Russkij Muz.) - Tsereteli (Museum of Modern Art).

Auction records:
Paris, 1 March 1993, *15 December 1987* (1987, oil on canvas, diptych, each section 67 x 47¼ ins / 170 x 120 cm) FRF 30,000.

SALAMAN, Julia (Mrs). See **GOODMAN Julia**

SALAMAN VON DANZIG
German, 18th century.
Painter.

Museums and Galleries:
Budapest (Mus.): *Self-portrait.*

SALAMANCA, A.
Spanish, 20th century.
Born 1926, in Valencia.
Active from 1946 in France.
Painter. Portraits. Murals.

Salamanca moved to France in 1946 and settled in the southwest. Examples of his work include a *Portrait of Arthur Rubinstein* and a number of frescoes at the Château Segalas-Rabat in Sauternes. He exhibited in group exhibitions from 1949, notably at the Salon des Terres Latines in Paris, starting in 1959 and solo in Bordeaux and Paris in 1964 and 1966.

SALAMANCA, Alonso de. See **ALONSO DE SALAMANCA**

SALAMANCA, Antonio
Italian, 16th century.
Born c. 1500, in Milan; died 1562, in Rome.
Engraver, print publisher.

Antonio Salamanca produced a *Pietà* after Michelangelo, a portrait after Bandinelli, and *The Creation of Animals*, after Raphael. These works are dated from 1545 to 1548.

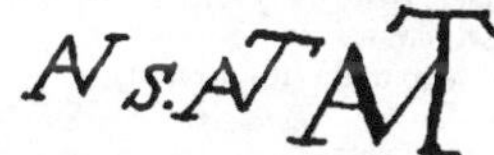

SALAMANCA, Bartolome de.
See **BARTOLOMÉ de Salamanca**

SALAMANCA, Cristobal de. See **CRISTOBAL de Salamanca**

SALAMANCA, Jeronimo da. See **JERONIMO da Salamanca**

SALAMANCA, Pedro de. See **PEDRO de Salamanca**

SALAMBIER, Henri. See **SALLEMBIER**

SALAMON
French, 19th century.
Active in Toulouse.
Sculptor.

Museums and Galleries:
Toulouse: *Gérard, Roger and Odon de Pins; Count Raymond V of Toulouse; Bernard d'Armagnac.*

SALAMON, Iosif
Romanian, 20th century.
Born 5 April 1932, in Cluj.
Active in Denmark from 1959.
Sculptor, engraver. Architectural integration.

Iosif Salamon trained with Risa Propst-Kraid in Romania, with Marcel Ianco in Israel, with Marino Marini and Giacomo Manzú at the Accademia di Belle Arti di Brera, Milan, then worked for a short time at the Accademia di Belle Arti in Rome. In 1957 he received a grant from the Italian government. Salamon executed many outdoor sculptures including: *Relief in Copper*, Regencentralen, Copenhagen (1964); bronze group, museum park, Siegen (1971); stone sculpture, Cologne university (1975); *Family*, Jerusalem (1982); fountain, town hall, Halmstad (1982). He worked with marble or granite as well as with bronze or copper and gave his abstract works evocative titles reminiscent of nature and life: *Tree of Life, Wind Rose, Sunrise*. He had a great concern for harmony and preferred simplified and balanced shapes. He was awarded many prizes including the Assens Art Prize in Denmark (1992) and engraving prize in Seul (1984).

Iosif Salamon held solo exhibitions including: Galleria Nazionale d'Arte Moderna, Rome (1961); Kunsternes Kunsthandel, Copenhagen (1962); New Art Gallery, Odensee (1964); Municipal Gallery, Halmstad (1969, 1971, 1975, 1983); Kunstmuseum, Siegen (1970); Paris (1973); Stockholm (1975); and Berlin (1983).

Bibliography:
Jianou, Ionel, *Romanian Artists and the West*, American Romanian Academy of Arts and Sciences, Los Angeles, 1986.

SALAMON, Petrus
Italian, 17th century.
Active in Venice at the beginning of the 17th century.
Sculptor (wood).

Petrus Salamon worked in Dalmatia and produced an altarpiece in the Dominican church in Zara (now Zadar, Croatia) in 1609.

SALAMON VON ALAP, Gza
Hungarian, 19th century.
Born 9 April 1842, in Alap; died 2 June 1870, in St Andraspuszta.
Painter.

Gza Salamon von Alap studied in Budapest and Munich. His works include altarpieces, paintings of animals, and portraits.

SALAMONE, Giacomo Domenico
Italian, 16th century.
Active in Naples from 1542 to 1549.
Painter.

Giacomo Domenico Salamone produced triptychs for churches in Naples.

SALANDRI, Liborio
Italian, 19th century.

Active in Venice from 1830 to 1850.
Mosaicist.
Liborio Salandri worked as a mosaicist at St Mark's Basilica in Venice.

SALANDRI, Vincenzo
Italian, 19th century.
Born 9 February 1838, in Rome.
Engraver (burin).
Vincenzo Salandri worked in collaboration with L. Fabri.

SALANSON, Eugénie Marie
French, 19th century.
Born in Albert (Somme).
Painter. Portraits, genre scenes.
Her masters were Crocher, Léon Cogniet and Bouguereau. She made her Salon debut in 1864 and exhibited at the Royal Academy in London in 1892.

E SALANSON

MUSEUMS AND GALLERIES:
CHÂTEAUROUX: *Portrait of a Young Girl* - MONTREAL: *Woman Fishing.*
AUCTION RECORDS:
PARIS, 27 Nov 1899, *Woman Fishing,* FRF 250. PARIS, 3-4 May 1923, *Young Woman Fishing,* FRF 80. PARIS, 25 March 1927, *Woman Fishing,* FRF 260. PARIS, 30 Jan 1950, *Fishermen Waiting,* FRF 4,800. ROUBAIX, 4 March 1979, *The Beach at Dieppe* (oil on canvas, 29 1/2 x 41 1/4 ins / 75 x 105 cm) FRF 26,000. LONDON, 26 Nov 1981, *Young Peasant Woman* (1887, oil on canvas, 34 1/2 x 23 1/4 ins / 87.5 x 59 cm) GBP 1,200. NEW YORK, 27 Feb 1986, *Reverie* (1887, oil on canvas, 35 x 23 3/4 ins / 89 x 60.4 cm) USD 8,250. NEW YORK, 28 May 1992, *Lobster in the Creel* (1884, oil on canvas, 53 x 34 ins / 134.6 x 86.4 cm) USD 11,550. LONDON, 16 June 1993, *Fisherman's Daughter* (1891, oil on canvas, 43 x 27 1/4 ins / 109 x 69 cm) GBP 6,325. PARIS, 5 Nov 1993, *Fisherman's Young Daughter* (1886, oil on canvas, 24 3/4 x 15 3/4 ins / 63 x 40 cm) FRF 12,500. DETROIT, 16 Nov 2001, *French Girl with Fishing Basket* (oil on canvas, 27 x 16 ins / 69 x 41 cm) USD 9,000. PARIS, 10 Dec 2002, *Italian Girl by a Fountain* (oil on canvas, 24 x 17 ins / 60 x 44 cm) EUR 4,000.

SALANSON, G.
French, 19th century.
Painter. Genre scenes.
AUCTION RECORDS:
PARIS, 29 May 1897, *The Little Chestnut Seller,* FRF 90. NEW YORK, 25 Feb 1988, *Stopping to Buy Flowers* (oil on panel, 17 3/4 x 21 1/2 ins / 45 x 54.5 cm) USD 3,850.

SALARIER, Jean. See **CÉLARIER Jean**

SALARIO, Andrea. See **SALAI**

SALARIO DA MONCALVO
Italian, 18th century.
Active during the second half of the 18th century.
Sculptor.
Salario da Moncalvo carved the stalls in the cathedral in Asti in 1768.

SALAS
Spanish, 16th century.
Sculptor.
Salas worked on the tabernacle of the high altar of Toledo Cathedral, in 1503.

SALAS, Alonso de
Spanish, 16th century.
Active from 1542 to 1553.
Painter.
Alonso de Salas was commissioned to produce paintings for the house of Melchor Cornieles in Seville, in 1553.

SALAS, Antonio
Ecuadorean, 19th century.
Born 1795, in Quito; died 1860.
Painter. Religious subjects, portraits.
Antonio Salas was a colonial artist,and is best known for his religious paintings such as *St Peter's Denial* in Quito Cathedral and scenes from the Life of the Virgin painted for the Augustinian Order. He also painted portraits of heroes of the struggle for independence like Simon Bolivar.
AUCTION RECORDS:
NEW YORK, 18-19 May 1993, *Indigenous Indio Yumbo* (oil on canvas, 16 x 14 ins / 39.7 x 35.6 cm) USD 5,175.

SALAS, Carlos
Spanish, 18th century.
Born 1728, in Barcelona; died 30 March 1780, in Saragossa.
Sculptor.
Carlos Salas studied in Madrid under F. de Castro and G. D. Olivieri, and also in Rome. He worked for churches in Las Fuentes, Madrid, Saragossa, Tarragona and Tudela.

SALAS, Esteban de
Spanish, 16th century.
Active in Valladolid (Castilla y León).
Sculptor.
Esteban de Salas was an artist of merit, who worked especially under the orders of Pedro Gonzalez de León. Salas was a witness for the latter in a lawsuit between Berruguete and Gonzalez de León.

SALAS, Juan de
Spanish, 16th century.
Sculptor.
Juan de Salas worked in the cathedrals of Jaca and Palma de Majorca.

SALAS, Juan de
Spanish, 16th century.
Active from 1527 to 1549.
Sculptor.
Juan de Salas was the assistant and successor of Diego de Siloe in works for Sta Maria del Campo, in Burgos.

SALAS, Tito
Venezuelan, 20th century.
Born 1887, in Caracas.
Active in France.
Painter. Landscapes.
Tito Salas studied at the Caracas art school and with Raphael Collin, Jean Paul Laurens and Simon in Paris, where he settled. He showed his work at the Salon des Artistes Français, winning a third-class medal in 1907.

SALAS-PÉREZ, Rafael
Ecuadorean, 19th century.
Born in Quito.
Painter.
Rafael Salas-Pérez showed work in exhibitions in Paris and received an honourable mention in the 1900 Exposition Universelle.

SALASSA, Simone
Italian, 19th - 20th century.
Born 12 March 1863, in Montanaro Canavese; died 16 October 1930, in Ivrea (Piedmont).
Painter. Genre scenes, landscapes.

SALASZAR, Basilio de, or Salazar
Spanish, 16th century.
Active at the end of the 16th century.
Miniaturist.
MUSEUMS AND GALLERIES:
LEIDEN (Stedelijk Mus. De Lakenhal): *Portrait of General Francisco de Valdez.*

SALATA, Achille
Italian, 19th century.
Born in Milan.
Sculptor.
Achille Salata is known for a number of bronze statuettes of genre subjects. The faces of his figures are highly expressive. He exhibited works in Milan, Turin and Livorno.

SALATHÉ, Frédéric or Friedrich
Swiss, 19th century.
Born 11 January 1793, in Binningen, near Basel; died 12 May 1860, in Paris.
Painter, watercolourist, engraver, draughtsman.
Landscapes, architectural views.
Frédéric Salathé was a pupil of Peter and Samuel Birmann in Basel. He went to Rome in 1815 in the company of Samuel Birmann and remained in Italy until 1820, when he returned to Basel. He went to Paris and earned a name for himself as a wash engraver. Washington Irving speaks of Salathé in his *Tales of a Traveller*.

Salathé painted numerous watercolour views of Switzerland, like those he had produced of Italy during his travels, gaining inspiration from the style of Alexandre Calame. He collaborated on *Excursion along the Coasts and through the Ports of Normandy*, 40 colour views after Luttringausen, Bonington, Noël, Grenier and Regnier. He also produced wash engravings and etchings of views and panoramas after his own drawings, including: *Battle of Navarino; Trip through the Chamonix Valley* (40 pieces); *Views of Bordeaux, Marseilles, Toulon and Cherbourg; Panorama, Taken from the Cupola of the Palais de l'Industrie* (two leaves, c. 1835); *Views of Venice, Turin, Baden and Leipzig; Castle and Museum of Berlin; Rio de Janeiro*; as well as *Lyons* after Brascassat (two pieces); and *Niagara Falls* after Seleron (two large pieces).

AUCTION RECORDS:
PARIS, 30 June 1943, watercolour and wash, 30 drawings) FRF 3,200.

SALATI, Bernardo (Don), called de Bentivegnis
Italian, 15th - 16th century.
Active in Parma.
Calligrapher, miniaturist, painter.
Bernardo Salati worked for Delfino della Pergola, bishop of Parma.

SALAÜN, Théophile
French, 19th - 20th century.
Born 21 August 1857, in Louannec; died 1 July 1909, in Guingamp.
Painter, draughtsman. Portraits, landscapes.
Théophile Salaün, a pupil of Gérome, taught drawing at the Collège Notre-Dame, Guingamp. He worked in Meissonier's studio and with Carrier, where he was responsible for the illustration of the newspaper *Le Pèlerin*.

He exhibited in 1877 at the Salon de Paris; in 1887 in the exhibition of the École des Beaux-Arts, Rennes, where he was awarded an honourable mention; and in 1896 at the Salon des Artistes Français, Paris, where he won a prize.

Among his works are *Daytime Beggars; Oranges; Portrait of Mme Harscouet; Marquis de Trogoff.* He painted many Breton landscapes.

BIBLIOGRAPHY:
Le Trocquer, Louis, ''*Théophile Salaün*' in *Celta* no. IV, periodical, Centre d'études littéraires touristiques et artistiques de Bretagne, January 1947.

SALAVERRIA ICHAUDAURRIETA, Elias
Spanish, 20th century.
Born 17 April 1883, in Lezo, near Guipúzcoa (Basque Country); died 16 July 1952, in Madrid.
Painter. Religious subjects, portraits, genre and rustic scenes, interiors.
Salaverria studied at the Escuela de Arte y Oficios in San Sebastián and then at the Escuela de Bellas Artes in Madrid, where he worked under the direction of Alejandro Ferrant and Menéndez Pidal. He also spent time in Paris in 1909. He was subsequently appointed to a teaching post at the Madrid school of painting (1934) and, after a sabbatical spent travelling, resumed teaching from 1944 at the Academia de Bellas Artes de San Fernando in Madrid. Salaverria was also appointed to a teaching post at the Escuela de Bellas Artes in Madrid.

His body of work comprises principally genre compositions, typically religious feast days with crowd scenes. Examples of his work include *Corpus Christi Procession in Lezo; St Ignatius de Loyola; Brother Garate and María Joaquina.*

Salaverria's work featured at various group exhibitions, including the Exposición Nacional de Bellas Artes in Madrid (from 1904); 1910 Universal Exhibition in Buenos Aires; Munich (1913) and in Panama (1916). He was the recipient of various awards and distinctions, including an honourable mention in 1904, bronze medals in 1906 and 1908, a gold medal at the Exposición Nacional de Bellas Artes in Madrid in 1912, and a further gold in 1913.

BIBLIOGRAPHY:
Arnáiz, José Manuel/López Jiménez, Javier/Merchán Díaz, Manuel (ed.), '*Cien años de pintura en Espana y Portugal (1830-1930)*' in vol. X, Antiqvaria, Madrid, 1993.

AUCTION RECORDS:
MADRID, 30 Oct 1979, *Back from the Fields* (1907, oil on canvas, 82 x 115 ins / 208 x 292 cm) ESP 400,000. MADRID, 26 Oct 1999, *Great Captain* (oil on canvas, 52 x 49 ins / 133 x 125 cm) ESP 300,000. MADRID, 29 Feb 2000, *Oxherd* (1927, oil on board, 9 x 7 ins / 24 x 19 cm) ESP 500,000. MADRID, 17 July 2000, *Still-life* (oil on canvas, 19 x 13 ins / 49 x 34 cm) ESP 400,000.

SALAZAR, Abel
Portuguese, 20th century.
Born 1889; died 1946.
Painter, watercolourist, engraver, draughtsman.
Portraits, genre scenes.
Abel Salazar was a professor in the medical faculty of the University of Oporto and a well-known author, art critic and painter. He painted voluminous caryatid-like women, typically carrying large burdens or portrayed at their labours. His compositions are to a degree unstructured but are full of detail. Examples include: *Women of Oporto; Women Carrying a Burden on their Backs*. He also produced numerous etchings.

BIBLIOGRAPHY:
Arnáiz, José Manuel/López Jiménez, Javier/Merchán Díaz, Manuel (ed.), '*Cien años de pintura en Espana y Portugal (1830-1930)*' in vol. X, Antiqvaria, Madrid, 1993.

SALAZAR, Ambrosio de
Spanish, 16th century.
Died 1604.
Illuminator.
Ambrosio de Salazar worked on the decoration of choir books for S Lorenzo and was then commissioned to continue work on two missals, begun by Juan Martinez de los Corrales, for Toledo Cathedral. His work is remarkable for ingenious arrangement of the decorations, confident lines and beautiful colouring. He may have been identical with Juan Salazar.

SALAZAR, Basilio de. See **SALASZAR**

SALAZAR, Carlos
Colombian, 20th - 21st century.

Born 1957.
Painter.

AUCTION RECORDS:
NEW YORK, 17 May 1989, *Tantric Tanagra* (1988, oil on canvas, 67 x 59 ins / 170 x 150 cm) USD 4,675. NEW YORK, 1 May 1990, *Tarot Cards* (1989, oil on canvas, 69 x 59 ins / 175 x 150 cm) USD 4,400. NEW YORK, 20-21 Nov 1990, *Niki in a Kimono* (1988, oil on canvas, 38 1/4 x 33 ins / 97 x 84 cm) USD 3,300. NEW YORK, 15 May 1991, *Cupid and Pysche* (1990, oil on canvas, 70 x 66 1/2 ins / 178 x 169 cm) USD 3,520.

SALAZAR, Cristóbal de
Spanish, 17th century.
Active in Murcia from 1635 to 1640.
Sculptor.
Cristóbal de Salazar carved the wooden statues in the church of Alcantarilla.

SALAZAR, Enrique de
Spanish, 19th - 20th century.
Born 23 February 1861, in Bilbao; died 22 March 1922.
Painter. Figures, scenes with figures, genre scenes, landscapes.
Enrique de Salazar studied under Antonio Lecuonan and Casto Plasencia. He exhibited at National Fine Arts Exhibitions and was awarded a medal at the Biscay Provincial Exhibition of 1882. Towards the end of his life, Salazar painted in an Expressionist vein, producing mainly compositions featuring bullfighting, fires and local landscapes.

BIBLIOGRAPHY:
Arnáiz, José Manuel/López Jiménez, Javier/Merchán Díaz, Manuel (ed.), *'Cien años de pintura en Espana y Portugal (1830-1930)'* in vol. X, Antiqvaria, Madrid, 1993.

SALAZAR, Esteban de
Spanish, 16th century.
Active c. 1585.
Illuminator.
Esteban de Salazar was employed by Philip II to produce choir books for S Lorenzo, and worked at the Escorial Palace.

SALAZAR, Francisco
Venezuelan, 20th century.
Born 1937, in Quiriquire.
Active since 1967 in France.
Painter.
Francisco Salazar studied at the School of Fine Arts in Caracas. From 1960 to 1964 he taught in the faculty of architecture in Caracas, and from 1964 to 1967 he was head of the art school in Maracyaragua. Since 1967 he has lived and worked in Paris.

He has held frequent exhibitions of his work: in Caracas regularly since 1957, especially at the Fine Arts Museum in 1967, and at the Museum of Contemporary Art in 1980, 1981 and 1989; and similarly in Paris. His prizes and distinctions include: 1967, first prize at the Biennale des Jeunes in Paris; 1968, first prize at the Latin-American Biennale in Buenos Aires; 1969, second prize at the Latin-American Biennale in Madellin.

Since 1960 he has been engaged in research into optical art. His white-on-white linear reliefs produce a reaction from the retina, although his effects are so delicate that he remains just outside the boundaries of optical art, which is often so much more strident. The slight touches which affect these reliefs, erasures or minimal changes across the whole surface, reveal the path of a line which does not exist. They are not unlike Fontana's crevices.

SALAZAR, Francisco de
Spanish, 17th century.
Active at the beginning of the 17th century.
Sculptor.
Francisco de Salazar created bronze statues for the Escorial palace near Madrid.

SALAZAR, Ignacio
Mexican, 20th - 21st century.
Born 1947, in Mexico City.
Painter. Historical figures.
Ignacio Salazar has shown his work in solo exhibitions in Mexico City: in 1981 at the museum of modern art and in 1987 at the Galeria de Arte Mexicano.

AUCTION RECORDS:
NEW YORK, 21 Nov 1988, *Dauphin II* (1987, acrylic/canvas, screen made of four painted panels, 94 1/2 x 94 1/2 ins / 240 x 240 cm) USD 5,500.

SALAZAR, Joseph D.
American, 18th century.
Active in New Orleans c. 1792.
Portrait artist.

SALAZAR, Juan
Spanish, 16th century.
Active at the beginning of the 16th century.
Sculptor (wood).
Juan Salazar worked on the high altar of Sta Maria Magdalena in Saragossa, from 1506-1514.

SALAZAR, Juan
Spanish, 16th century.
Died 1604, in Toledo (Castile-La Mancha).
Illuminator.
The Salazars were a 16th-century family of artists, including painters, sculptors and, especially, illuminators. The illuminators worked mainly on choir books for the Escorial Palace and on mass books for Toledo Cathedral. According to some authors, both Juan and Ambrosio died in 1604. The similarity in their work, skill and date of death suggest they may have been one and the same artist.

SALAZAR, Juan de
Spanish, 16th century.
Active in Valladolid (Castilla y León).
Painter.
Juan de Salazar painted the retable of the high altar of the church of La Calzada, in Valladolid, with Francisco de Labaino, in 1519.

SALAZAR, Juan José
Spanish, 18th century.
Died 1790, in Granada.
Active in Granada.
Sculptor.
Juan José Salazar carved statues for churches in Granada and for Malaga Cathedral.

SALAZAR, Luis
Spanish, 20th century.
Born in the Basque Country.
Active in Belgium.
Collage artist.
Luis Salazar held solo exhibitions on several occasions in Belgium, mainly with abstract compositions juxtaposing zones of white and black and scraps of bright coloured paper.

SALAZAR, Miguel
Spanish, 16th century.
Active in Santo Domino de la Calzada.
Painter.
Miguel Salazar painted and gilded the high altar of S Asensio de Logroño.

SALAZAR, Pedro de
Spanish, 16th century.
Painter.

Pedro de Salazar produced paintings for the Hospital de los Reyes Católicos in Santiago de Compostela.

SALAZAR, Pedro de
Spanish, 17th century.
Painter.
Pedro de Salazar executed paintings for the high altar of the church of S Miguel in Valladolid.

SALAZAR, Solange
Venezuelan, 20th century.
Born in Caracas.
Painter, engraver. Landscapes.
Work by Solange Salazar was included in the exhibition *De Bonnard à Baselitz - Dix Ans d'enrichissements du cabinet des estampes 1978-1988* (*From Bonnard to Baselitz: A Decade of Acquisitions by the Prints Collection 1978-1988*) at the Bibliothèque Nationale in Paris.
MUSEUMS AND GALLERIES:
PARIS (BNF, Prints Collection): *Landscape* (1981).

SALAZARO, Demetrio
Italian, 19th century.
Born 18 October 1822, in Reggio di Calabria; died 18 May 1882, in Pozzuoli.
Painter, art critic.

SALB, Baptista
Austrian, 16th century.
Active in Vienna.
Painter.
In 1569, in collaboration with Domenico de Pozzo, Baptista Salb painted pictures in the Imperial Palace of Vienna.

SALB, Jakob
German, 16th century.
Active 1561-1578.
Painter.

SALBERG, Frederik
German, 19th - 20th century.
Born 6 January 1876, in Düsseldorf; died 16 May 1909, in Voorburg.
Painter. Portraits, architectural views, flowers.
Frederik Salberg was a pupil of Willem Joannes Schütz, Henry Muhrmann and Marinus van der Maarel.

SALBETH, Mariette, or Gassel
Belgian, 20th century.
Born 5 July 1929, in Anderlecht.
Draughtswoman, engraver, watercolourist, painter (gouache/mixed media). Figures, portraits, landscapes, seascapes.
Mariette Salbeth studied at the Académie Royale des Beaux-Arts in Brussels, then at the Brussels college of architecture and decorative arts and the art college of Anderlecht. She worked in gouache, watercolours and Indian ink and painted predominantly portraits and trees. She also produced stained glass designs and albums of engravings, and painted murals for a day-care centre for autistic children. She exhibited at the fine arts museum in Ixelles and the town hall in Brussels. Her first solo exhibition was held in Brussels in 1965, followed by many others, including in Knokke-le-Zoute in 1968.
MUSEUMS AND GALLERIES:
BRUSSELS (Bibliothèque royale Albert Ier).

SALCEDO, Bernardo
Colombian, 20th century.
Born 12 August 1941, in Bogotá.
Painter, assemblage artist.
Bernardo Salcedo studied architecture at the national university of Colombia in Bogotá, where he later taught. He travelled regularly in Italy and Spain from 1970, in France in 1974 and in Great Britain in 1974-1975. Salcedo creates objects that reflect a black, surrealist humour for example boxes filled with pieces of dolls and then painted entirely in white, to suggest a sterile universe. He also produces assemblages based on photographs.

Bernardo Salcedo has taken part in exhibitions, including: Museo de Arte Moderno, Bogotá (1965, 1974 and 1975); Musée Rodin, Paris and Museo de Arte Moderno, Cali (1966); institute of contemporary art, Lima (1967); Museu de Arte Moderna, Buenos Aires (1968 and 1971); Musée d'Art Moderne, Paris (1969); Museo Nacional de Artes Visuales, Montevideo, São Paulo Biennale and Museo de Arte Moderno, Santiago (1971); FIAC (Foire Internationale d'Art Contemporain), Paris, presented by the El Museo gallery, Bogotá (1995). He has also shown his work in solo exhibitions: Museo de Arte Moderno, Bogotá (1966, 1967 and 1969); centre for art and communication, Buenos Aires (1971); International Cultureel Centrum, Antwerp, Palais des Beaux-Arts, Brussels and Institute of Contemporary Art, London (1974); Louisiana Museum, Humlebaek (1976). Awards received include the first prize for painting, international Dante competition (1965); prize and commendation, Salon of the Americas, Cali (1969); second prize at the American art Biennale, Medellín (1970); first prize, national fine arts Salon, Bogotá (1972).
MUSEUMS AND GALLERIES:
BOGOTÁ (MAC) - BOGOTÁ (MAM) - BUENOS AIRES (MAM) - CALI (MAM La Tertulia) - CARACAS (MBA) - HAVANA (MMA) - NEW YORK (MoMA).

SALCEDO, Diego de
Spanish, 16th century.
Active in Burgos (Castilla y León) in 1542.
Painter.

SALCEDO, Diego de, or Salzedo or Saucedo or Sauzedo
Spanish, 17th century.
Born in Seville; died between 1614 and 1622, in Seville.
Painter, gilder.
Diego de Salcedo was the son of Juan de Salcedo. He produced a number of altars in churches in Seville and the surrounding area.

SALCEDO, Doris
Colombian, 20th century.
Installation artist.
Doris Salcedo had a first solo exhibition in New York in 1994. Especially notable is the series *Casa Viuda* in which she displays the history of her country and the destruction of families by means of fragments of old worn-out furniture.
BIBLIOGRAPHY:
Harris, Susan, '*Doris Salcedo*' in *Art Press* n° 193, periodical, Paris, July-August 1994. Cameron, Dan/Merewether, Charles, *Doris Salcedo*, exhibition catalogue, New Museum of Contemporary Art, New York, 1998.

SALCEDO, Ignacio de Léon. See **LEÓN Y SALGEDO**

SALCEDO, Juan de, or Salzedo or Saucedo
Spanish, 17th century.
Died before 1626, in Seville.
Active in Granada (?).
Painter, gilder.
Juan de Salcedo was the father of Diego de Salcedo. He executed many paintings, decorations and gilded work for churches in Seville and the surrounding area. He may be the same as Juan de Sancedo.

SALCEDO, Martin de
Spanish, 16th century.
Active during the second half of the 16th century.
Sculptor.

Martin de Salcedo worked for Toledo Cathedral, from 1583-1586.

SALCES GUTIÉRREZ, Manuel
Spanish, 19th - 20th century.
Born 24 April 1861, in Suano (Cantabria); died 1 December 1932, in Madrid.
Painter. Landscapes, waterscapes.
Manuel Gutiérrez started studying drawing and composition at the age of thirty or so. He settled in Madrid from 1912 and exhibited on a regular basis at National Fine Arts Exhibitions and at the 1914 Iturrioz Salon of 1914. His body of work comprises primarily views of Madrid and the surrounding countryside. Examples of his work include *Torrent, Monastery, Pines, My Village* and *Downpour.*
BIBLIOGRAPHY:
Arnáiz, José Manuel/López Jiménez, Javier/Merchán Díaz, Manuel (ed.), *'Cien años de pintura en Espana y Portugal (1830-1930)'* in vol. X, Antiqvaria, Madrid, 1993.
MUSEUMS AND GALLERIES:
MADRID (Mus. de Arte Moderno): *Downpour.*

SALCHETTI, Francesco
Italian, 19th century.
Born 1811, in Zara (now Zadar, Croatia).
Painter.
Francesco Salchetti painted works for the churches of S Maria and S Francesco in Zara.
MUSEUMS AND GALLERIES:
FLORENCE (Uffizi): *Self-portrait.*

SALCI, Gabriele or Gabriello
Italian, 18th century.
Active in Rome during the first half of the 18th century.
Painter. Still-lifes (including flowers/fruit).
Gabriele Salci was influenced by the Dutch painters.
MUSEUMS AND GALLERIES:
SIBIU (Muz. National Brukenthal): *Still-life with Pitcher; Still-life with Vase.*
AUCTION RECORDS:
ROME, 3 April 1984, *Still-life with Fruit and Flowers* (oil on canvas, a pair, 24 1/2 x 28 1/4in/62 x 72cm) ITL 47,000,000. MILAN, 21 April 1986, *Still-life with Fruit and Flowers* (oil on canvas, 25 1/2 x 17in/65 x 43cm) ITL 11,500,000. BOLOGNA, 8-9 June 1992, *Still-life of a Basket of Vegetables with Two Cabbages, a Basket of Fruit and Dead Birds* (oil on canvas, 37 3/4 x 52 1/4in/96 x 132.5cm) ITL 27,600,000. ROME, 22 May 2001, *Deer and Dead Game* (oil on canvas, 37 x 53 ins / 95 x 135 cm) ITL 18,000,000. ROME, 4 Dec 2001, *Still-life with Dead Game in Landscape* (oil on canvas, 38 x 52 ins / 97 x 132 cm) ITL 15,000,000. MILAN, 4 June 2003, *Still-life with Musical Instruments, Flowers, Fruit and Vegetables* (oil on canvas, 52 x 39 ins / 131 x 100 cm) EUR 28,000.

SALCILLO. See **ZARCILLO Y ALCARAZ**

SALCMAN, Martin
Czech, 20th century.
Born 7 May 1896, in Druzdova.
Painter.
Martin Salcman trained at the academy of fine art in Prague from 1914 to 1920 then with Loukoty from 1922 to 1924. He continued his training in Paris from 1926 to 1928 and from 1945 taught in Prague where he frequently exhibited from 1936.

His landscapes evade too narrow a representation in favour of poetic expression, coming close to the virtually Abstract Synthetism of Josef Sima.
BIBLIOGRAPHY:
Fifty years of Czechoslovak Painting from the Collections of the Galleries, 1918-1958, exhibition catalogue, Slovenska Narodna Gal., Bratislava, 1968 (commemorating the 50th anniversary of the Republic of Czechoslovakia).
MUSEUMS AND GALLERIES:
PRAGUE (Národní Gal.).

SALCOVSKY, Ana
Uruguayan, 20th - 21st century.
Born 1947.
Collage artist.
Ana Salcovsky uses collage and a bright palette. She bo rows her technique from advertising, producing works th are figurative, dynamic and expressionist.

SALDANHA, Ione
Brazilian, 20th century.
Born 1921.
Painter.
Neo-Constructivism.
Ione Saldanha's main theme is the horizontal band on ba boos and wooden slats.

SALDIVIA, Martín, or Caldiuia
Spanish, 16th century.
Active during the first half of the 16th century.
Sculptor.
Martín Saldivia worked on the town hall in Seville fr 1527-1534.

SALDO, Robert
French, 20th century.
Born 4 January 1877, in Menton.
Painter, engraver.
Robert Saldo exhibited in Paris at the Salon des Artis Français and the Salon des Indépendants.

SALDOERFFER, Conrad
German, 16th century.
Active in Nuremberg 1563-1583.
Painter, engraver (etching/burin).
Conrad Saldoerffer engraved religious subjects and illust tions for travel books.

SALÉ, François
French, 17th century.
Painter. Religious subjects.
François Salé was active in Mans (Sarthe) in the first half the century. Among his known works are several pictures the church of Cérans-Foulletourte such as a *Baptism Christ* (1634) and a *Virgin of the Rosary* (1644) kept in t church of Saint-Rémy at Marolles-les-Braults.

SALE, Giuseppe del. See **SOLE Giovanni Giuseppe dal**

SALE, Mathieu
French, 16th century.
Active in St-Quentin in 1589.
Medallist.

SALE, Niccolo, or Salé
Italian, 17th century.
Of French origin.
Sculptor.
Niccolo Sale worked in Rome from 1635 to 1650, where assisted Bernini in producing the *Fontana dei Quattro Fiu* in the Piazza Navona and in decorating the pillars in St P ter's Basilica.

SALE, Pietro
Italian, 16th century.
Active in Naples during the second half of the 16th century.
Sculptor.

Pietro Sale sculpted statues and a fountain in Vico Equense park, near Naples, in 1570.

SALEE, Jean Lambert or Johannes Lambertus
Belgian, 19th century.
Born 21 March 1788, in Ans, near Liège; died 24 October 1833, in Liège.
Sculptor. Busts.

Jean Lambert Salee was a pupil of Franck and Lemot, in Paris. He produced mainly portrait busts.

SALEEBY, Khalil, or Saliby
Lebanese, 19th - 20th century.
Born 12 March 1870, in B'Tallun, Mount Lebanon; died 7 July 1928, in Suq al Gharb.
Painter. Figures, nudes, portraits, landscapes. Orientalism.

Khalil Saleeby studied at what would later be the American University of Beirut, returning to teach there in 1900. He then went to Edinburgh to complete his training, encountering John Singer Sargent, who advised him to go to the USA. After following Sargent's advice, Saleeby went on to England and France, where he studied under Puvis de Chavannes and discovered Renoir. In 1900 he returned to Lebanon for good, teaching students in his studio. He travelled frequently to Paris, London, New York and Chicago.

Saleeby specialised in portraits, principally of his wife Carrie. He also painted clients and friends. Among his more famous works are his portraits of *Najib Jumblatt* and *The Archbishop Gerassimos Messarra.*

He exhibited at the Edinburgh Salon, winning a medal in 1889, and at the Salon des Indépendants in Paris and at Durant-Ruel.

BIBLIOGRAPHY:
Liban - Le Regard des peintres, exhibition catalogue, Institut du Monde Arabe, Paris, 1989.

SALEH, Radeaa Bastaman, or Raden (Sarief)
Javanese School, 19th century.
Born 1807 or 1814, in Samarang (Java), Indonesia; died 22 April 1880, in Buitenzorg (Java), Indonesia.
Painter. Hunting scenes, animals.

Saleh was a descendant of a noble family of the ruling class. The title 'Sarief' indicates that he was of Arab origin. He was a pupil of A.A.J. Payneu in Batavia (now Jakarta), and of A. Schelfhout and C. Kruseman in The Hague.

MUSEUMS AND GALLERIES:
AMSTERDAM: *Fight to the Death* - THE HAGUE (Gemeentemus.): *The Guardhouse in the Woods at The Hague.*

AUCTION RECORDS:
PARIS, 1865, *Stag Hunt*, FRF 36; *Shipwreck*, FRF 140. AMSTERDAM, 6 Nov 1990, *St Jerome in a Lanscape* (1838, oil on panel, 5 3/4 x 4 1/2 ins / 14.5 x 11.5 cm) NLG 7,130. AMSTERDAM, 30 Oct 1991, *Three-masted Ship in Trouble* (1869, oil on canvas, 30 3/4 x 48 ins / 78 x 122 cm) NLG 39,100. NEW YORK, 29 Oct 1992, *Figures in an Exotic Landscape* (1867, oil on canvas, 48 x 64 1/2 ins / 121.7 x 163.8 cm) USD 55,000. AMSTERDAM, 23 April 1996, *Portrait of a Small Girl with her Dog* (1856, oil on canvas, 31 x 26 1/2 ins / 78.5 x 67.5 cm) NLG 106,200. SINGAPORE, 29 March 1997, *Animals Fighting* (c. 1850, oil on canvas/panel, 27 1/4 x 39 ins / 69 x 99 cm) SGD 773,750. SINGAPORE, 27 Sept 1997, *Portrait of Matthijs Eliza Verstege* (1834, oil on canvas, 39 1/4 x 31 1/2 ins / 100 x 80 cm) SGD 17,825. PARIS, 30 April 1999, *Buffalo Fighting a Tiger* (1847, oil on canvas, 12 x 17 ins / 31 x 43 cm) FRF 660,000. SINGAPORE, 2 April 2000, *Seascape with Ship* (1842, oil on canvas/board, 15 x 18 ins / 39 x 45 cm) SGD 55,000. COPENHAGEN, 6 Sept 2000, *Desert Landscape with Bedouin and Horse* (1843, oil on canvas) DKK 165,000. SINGAPORE, 30 Sept 2001, *Combat between Buffalo and Tiger* (1847, oil on canvas, 13 x 17 ins / 32 x 44 cm) SGD 80,000. HONG KONG, 28 April 2002, *Lion Hunt* (1840, oil on canvas, 33 x 55 ins / 85 x 140 cm) HKD 3,900,000. HONG KONG, 27 Oct 2002, *Last Embrace of Foes: Bedouin Horseman Attacked by a Lion* (1844, oil on canvas, 13 x 20 ins / 33 x 51 cm) HKD 380,000.

SALELLES, Francisco
Spanish, 14th century.
Active in Barcelona in 1336.
Painter.

SALEMANN, Georg, or Saleman
Danish, 17th - 18th century.
Born c. 1670, in Tallinn; died 1729, in Copenhagen.
Miniaturist.

Salemann worked for the court in Copenhagen. Self-portraits by this artist are extant, as are portraits of a lady from the Reventlow family in the Frederiksborgmuseet.

SALEMANN, Hugo Romanovich or Robertovich, or Zaleman
Russian, 19th century.
Born 7 June 1859.
Sculptor.

Hugo Salemann studied at the art academy in St Petersburg.

MUSEUMS AND GALLERIES:
ST PETERSBURG (Gosudarstvennyj Russkij Muz.): *Les Cimbres.*

SALEMANN, Robert Karlovich, or Zaleman
Estonian, 19th century.
Born 16 June 1813, in Reval (now Tallinn); died 12 September 1874, in St Petersburg.
Sculptor.

Robert Salemann studied under Rietschel in Dresden and Schwanthaler in Munich.

MUSEUMS AND GALLERIES:
HELSINKI: *Bust of Nicolas I* (hammered zinc); *Bust of the Count A. Armfelt* - ST PETERSBURG (Gosudarstvennyj Russkij Muz.): *Nicolas I of Russia* (statue).

SALEMBIER, Henri. See **SALLEMBIER**

SALEMBIER, Marèze
French, 20th century.
Born 1936, in Bruay-sur-Escaut (Nord).
Painter, pastellist, draughtsman, sculptor, medallist, potter. Nudes, portraits, landscapes, animals.

Marèze Salembier spent her youth in Fribourg, Switzerland, and then went to Paris, where she studied in the Sculpture Department of the École des Beaux-Arts.

She exhibited at group exhibitions in Paris: 1960, 1973, 1975, Salon de la Société Nationale des Beaux-Arts; 1968, 1971, 1974, 1976, Salon d'Automne; Salon des Indépendants; 1968 to 1975, Salon Terres Latines; 1977 to 1980, Salon des Artistes Français; and also in the provinces and Brussels: 1979, Salon International des Femmes Peintres. She held solo shows regularly in Paris from 1960, and in Copenhagen, Venice and Strasbourg.

She designed medals for the Paris Mint.

MUSEUMS AND GALLERIES:
PARIS (BNF): *By a Pond* (1980).

SALEMI, Perrino
Italian, 16th century.
Active in Ferrara during the first half of the 16th century.
Painter.

Perrino Salemi worked in Trento from 1513-1535.

SALEMME, Antonio
American, 20th century.
Born 1892, in Gaeta, Italy; died 1995, in Easton (Pennsylvania).
Sculptor.

Antonio Salemme moved with his family to Newton, Massachusetts, in 1904. At the age of 13 he began his studies at the Eric Pape Art School and later continued at the Boston Museum of Fine Arts School, under George L. Noyes. While in Boston he began to study sculpture, and in 1910 furthered his studies in Spain and France. He then studied in Rome in 1912 as a protégé of Angelo Zanelli.

AUCTION RECORDS:

NEW YORK, 29 Sept 1977, *Adam and Eve* (1923, grey and green patinated bronze, h. 17 1/4 ins / 43.8 cm) USD 700. NEW YORK, 27 Sept 1990, *Lucifer, Male Nude* (bronze, h. 21 1/4 ins / 53.7 cm) USD 4,620. NEW YORK, 14 June 1995, *Ginger* (1932, bronze on a marble base, h. 35 1/4 ins / 89.5 cm) USD 2,300.

SALEMME, Attilio

American, 20th century.

Born 11 October 1911, in Chestnut Hills (Massachusetts); died 24 January 1955, in New York.

Painter.

Attilio Salemme is best known for the Surrealist canvases he produced after 1950. His rectangular figures, reminiscent of Wilfredo Lam's triangular figures, hark back to totems or funerary statues. Another influence, that of Klee before 1920, is evident in Salemme's use of line. Using acidic colours built up against brighter backgrounds, there is nonetheless something tragic about these works and occasionally a somewhat warped humour. Salemme took part in several collective exhibitions in the USA and in Italy, notably the Venice biennale. He also showed his works in many solo exhibitions in the USA.

AUCTION RECORDS:

NEW YORK, 11 Nov 1959, *Joys of the Architect*, USD 650. NEW YORK, 16 Feb 1961, *Lovers*, USD 700. NEW YORK, 28 May 1976, *Abstraction* (1946, oil on canvas, 22 x 34 ins / 56 x 86.5 cm) USD 5,000. NEW YORK, 24 March 1977, *Daughters of the Sun* (1944, oil on canvas, 20 x 30 ins / 51 x 76.2 cm) USD 3,000. NEW YORK, 22 March 1979, *Lovers* (1951, oil on canvas, 30 x 23 ins / 76 x 58.5 cm) USD 5,000. NEW YORK, 16 Oct 1981, *Formal Expectancy* (1948, oil on canvas, 40 1/4 x 61 ins / 102.3 x 155 cm) USD 5,000. NEW YORK, 7 Nov 1985, *Red Wall* (1947, watercolour and pen, 6 1/2 x 10 ins / 16.3 x 25.3 cm) USD 1,000. NEW YORK, 7 May 1990, *Happy Times* (1954, oil on canvas, 22 x 34 ins / 55.9 x 86.4 cm) USD 6,050. NEW YORK, 12 June 1991, *Untitled* (1947, oil on canvas, 18 x 36 1/4 ins / 45.7 x 92.1 cm) USD 11,550. NEW YORK, 12 June 1992, *Assignation* (1952, oil on canvas, 47 x 59 ins / 119.4 x 149.9 cm) USD 17,600. NEW YORK, 8 Nov 1993, *Echo of a Dream* (1945, oil on canvas, 22 x 40 ins / 56 x 101.6 cm) USD 3,450. NEW YORK, 24 Feb 1995, *Happy Occasion; Saintly Beings* (1950, watercolour/paper, a pair, each 8 1/2 x 11 ins / 21.6 x 27.9 cm) USD 4,025.

SALEMON, Michelet. See **SAUMON**

SALENDRE, Georges and not Maurice

French, 20th century.

Born 1 March 1890, in Lyons; died 30 March 1985, in Lyons.

Sculptor. Figures.

Georges Salendre studied at the École des Beaux-Arts, Lyons, where he was awarded the first prize for sculpture and a gold medal. He gained his reputation mainly in the Lyons area.

He exhibited with Lhote and Gromaire in a group exhibition held in 1937 at the Musée des Beaux-Arts, Lyons. He also showed his works between 1925 and 1935 at the Galerie Georges Petit, Paris, the Galerie Moos, Geneva, and in 1965 at the Musée d'Art Moderne, Paris. He won the Grand Prix for sculpture in 1937.

He worked in stone and bronze. M. Mermillon praised the natural soundness of his rustic creations and his deliberate simplification of forms. Raymond Cogniat also refers to him. He admired the works of Maillol and worked in the same spirit, celebrating the female body. He sculpted the stone *Watchman* that stands in the Place Bellecour, Lyons.

MUSEUMS AND GALLERIES:

AVIGNON - BASEL - BOLLÈNE - LYONS - PARIS (MNAM-CCI): *Bust of Maurice Utrillo; Young Girl with a Bird.*

AUCTION RECORDS:

LYONS, 25 Oct 1972, *Nude* (patinated bronze) FRF 4,500. PARIS, 22 May 1989, *Female Torso* (granite, h. 55 ins / 140 cm) FRF 19,000. LYONS, 29 Nov 1999, *Bather* (brown-patinated bronze, h. 40 ins / 101 cm) FRF 32,000. PARIS, 31 March 2000, *Naked Woman Kneeling, Veiling her Face* (green-patinated bronze, 39 x 16 ins / 100 x 40 cm) FRF 39,000.

SALENIER. See **SALINIER**

SALENTIJN, Kees

Dutch, 20th - 21st century.

Born 1947, in Amsterdam.

Painter.

Kees Salentijn studied at the Gerrit Rietveldt Academie and the academy of fine arts in Amsterdam. He lives and works in Venlo. His works have featured in exhibitions in Holland, Germany, Belgium, Switzerland and the USA. His painting style is abstract and gestural.

MUSEUMS AND GALLERIES:

BERLIN (Nationalgal.) - HUMLEBÆK (Louisiana Mus. for Moderne Kunst).

AUCTION RECORDS:

AMSTERDAM, 10 Dec 1992, *Composition* (1988, oil on canvas, 47 1/4 x 39 1/4 ins / 120 x 100 cm) NLG 1,725.

SALENTIN, Hans

German, 20th century.

Born 1925, in Düren.

Active in Cologne.

Sculptor, collage artist, draughtsman.

Hans Salentin studied at the fine arts academy in Düsseldorf from 1950 to 1954. His work evokes the technology age in sculptures and designs which feature objects 'borrowed' from hi-tech sectors such as aerospace, the automotive industry and optics.

He began showing work in group exhibitions in 1957, notably at the following: the International Art Biennale in San Marino (1963); the Institute of Contemporary Art in Philadelphia (1964); the Gallery of Modern Art in Washington DC (1965); the Museum am Ostwall in Dortmund and the Goethe Institute in Brussels, Paris and Lille (1967); the Lehmbruck Museum in Duisburg (1968); the Kunstverein (Artists' Union) in Heidelberg (1969); the Kunstverein in Frankfurt am Main (1974); Documenta in Kassel (1977); the Deutsches Museum in Munich (1979); and *Zero aus Deutschland: 1957-1966. Und Heute* (*Zero out of Germany: 1957-1966. And Today*) at the municipal gallery in Esslingen (2000).

Salentin also exhibited solo on a number of occasions, notably in Düsseldorf (1962, 1976), Cologne (1967, 1969, 1974, 1975, 1979), Nuremberg (Fine Arts Gallery, 1972), Brussels (1973) and Witten (Märkisches Museum, 1978).

BIBLIOGRAPHY:

Hans Salentin Technoide Fiktionen, exhibition catalogue, Kunsthalle, Nürnberg, 1972. Winkler, Gerd, *Denkmale für die Zukunft - Hans Salentin und die Aluminiumzeit*, Belser Verlag, Stuttgart, 1973. Wiehager, Renate, *Zero aus Deutschland: 1957-1966. Und heute*, group exhibition catalogue, Gal. der Stadt, Esslingen, 2000.

SALENTIN, Hubert

German, 19th - 20th century.

Born 15 January 1822, in Zulpich; died 7 July 1910, in Düsseldorf.

Painter. Genre scenes.

Hubert Salentin studied in Düsseldorf under Schadow, Carl Sohn and Tidemand and then settled in Düsseldorf. He won a medal in Vienna in 1873.

H. Salentin

Museums and Galleries:
Besançon: *Blind Child* - Bremen: *Children and Shepherds; Forest Path* - Cologne: *Pilgrims; Foundling* - Düsseldorf: *Village Church; Espied; Head Study* - Hamburg: *On the Way to Church* - Montreal: *Artist; Grandmother's Pancakes* - Münster: *Evening Prayers*.
Auction records:
Paris, 21 Oct 1936, *Bridal Procession with Children Playing,* FRF 1,950. New York, 24 May 1944, *Reception for a Young Prince,* USD 1,350. New York, 18 Oct 1944, *On the Way to Mass,* USD 400. London, 25-26 Feb 1946, *Cathedral Interior,* GBP 177. London, 9 Dec 1959, *View of Dresden,* GBP 2,000. Cologne, 7 June 1972, *Two Young Girls Looking at a Portrait,* DEM 3,400. Düsseldorf, 13 Nov 1973, *May Queen,* DEM 32,000. New York, 14 May 1976, *Forbidden Fruit* (oil on canvas, 36 x 30 ins / 91.5 x 76 cm) USD 6,500. Cologne, 16 June 1977, *Grandmother Reading* (1869, oil on canvas, 32 x 26 1/2 ins / 81 x 67.5 cm) DEM 20,000. New York, 26 Jan 1979, *Church Entrance* (1875, oil on canvas, 35 x 50 1/2 ins / 88 x 128 cm) USD 21,000. New York, 29 May 1981, *Little Girls Listening to an Old Man Reading Out Loud* (1870, oil on canvas, 30 3/4 x 41 ins / 78.1 x 104.1 cm) USD 28,000. New York, 19 Oct 1984, *Foundling* (oil on canvas, 34 x 41 ins / 86.4 x 104.2 cm) USD 18,000. New York, 13 Feb 1985, *Village Smithy* (1860, oil on canvas, 27 x 22 ins / 68.5 x 55.8 cm) USD 5,000. New York, 26 Feb 1986, *Waiting for a Ferry* (1871, oil on canvas, 32 x 25 1/2 ins / 81 x 64.8 cm) USD 17,000. London, 28 March 1990, *Two Children in the Woods* (1901, oil on canvas, 25 1/2 x 19 1/4 ins / 64.5 x 49 cm) GBP 9,900. New York, 24 May 1995, *Classroom* (1870, oil on canvas, 31 x 39 1/4 ins / 78.7 x 99.7 cm) USD 23,000. London, 11 June 1997, *Foundling* (oil on canvas, 33 3/4 x 41 ins / 86 x 104 cm) GBP 25,300.

SALENTINY, Jeanne
German, 20th century.
Born 1924, in Julich.
Active in Belgium.
Painter. Figures, portraits, landscapes.
Jeanne Salentiny married the painter Luc Perot. She studied at the fine arts academy in Namur in Belgium.

SALER, J.
German, 18th century.
Draughtsman.
J. Saler illustrated the 1790 *Almanac* for Ebner in Augsburg.

SALER, Otto Christian, or Sahler
German, 18th - 19th century.
Born c. 1723, in Augsburg; died 7 July 1810, in Berlin (?).
Engraver (burin), modeller (wax). Portraits.
Otto Christian Saler produced wax sculptures of members of the Prussian royal family and the Russian imperial family.

SALERNITANO, Francesco
Italian, 17th century.
Active in Naples during the second half of the 17th century.
Painter.
Works by Francesco Salernitano, who was the pupil of Domenico Gargiulo, can be found in several churches in the province of Naples.

SALERNITANO, Michele
Italian, 16th century.
Active at the end of the 16th century.
Sculptor (wood).
Michele Salernitano sculpted 20 statues for S Croce di Palazzo church in Naples, in 1594.

SALERNO, da. See first name

SALERNO, Giuseppe. See **ZOPPO di Gangi**

SALERNO, Nicola Maria
Italian, 18th century.
Active in Naples c. 1740.
Painter, poet.
Nicola Maria Salerno was the pupil of F. Solimena.

SALERNO DI COPPO DI MARCOVALDO.
See the entry **COPPO di Marcovaldo**

SALES, André Pierre, or Sallès
French, 19th - 20th century.
Born 14 January 1860, in Perpignan.
Sculptor, medallist, painter.
Orientalism.
With the aid of a scholarship, André Pierre Sales studied in Paris under Augustin Dumont and Paul Dubois. He exhibited in Paris at the Salon des Artistes Français from 1876.
Museums and Galleries:
Perpignan: *Woman Bathing* (1881).
Auction records:
Sceaux, 11 March 1990, *Algerian Woman* (1897, oil on canvas, 15 1/4 x 9 3/4 ins / 39 x 25 cm) FRF 19,000. Paris, 26 March 1998, *Young Oriental Woman with a Pink Scarf* (oil on panel, 7 1/2 x 5 ins / 19 x 13 cm) FRF 5,500.

SALES, Carl von
Austrian, 19th century.
Born 5 November 1791, in Koblenz; died 4 November 1870, in Fürstenfeld.
Active in Vienna.
Painter. Portraits.
Carl von Sales executed *Portraits of Emperor Francis I and his Family* which can be found in the castle at Laxenburg, and a *Portrait of the Duke of Reichstadt,* exhibited in his bedroom at the castle of Schönbrunn.
Museums and Galleries:
Munich (Pinakothek): *Portrait of Charlotte Caroline Augusta, Empress of Austria* - Stuttgart (Staatsgal.): *Portrait of King William I of Württemberg.*
Auction records:
Monte Carlo, 14 Feb 1983, *Portrait of Emperor Franz I* (1818, oil on canvas, 26 1/2 x 19 3/4 ins / 67.5 x 50 cm) FRF 20,000. Boston, 12 Sept 2003, *Portraits* (1817, oil on canvas, a pair, 28 x 22 ins / 70 x 56 cm) USD 2,700. Toronto, 14 June 2004, *Portrait of a Lady in Empire-period Dress* (1814, oil on canvas, 26 x 21 ins / 66 x 53 cm) CAD 2,800.

SALES, José Vicente. See **SALLES**

SALES, Juan de. See **JUAN de Sales**

SALES, Jules Gabriel
French, 19th century.
Born in Paris.
Painter.
A pupil of Vineaux and Flameng, this artist debuted at the Salon in 1876.
Auction records:
Paris, 22 May 1897, *Young Girl Sleeping,* FRF 85.

SALES, Pierre
French, 15th century.
Active in 1473.
Sculptor (wood).
Pierre Sales carved the door of the main porch of the church of Notre-Dame des Tables in Montpellier.

SALES BELLMONT, Bartolomé
Spanish, 18th century.

Active in Valencia during the first half of the 18th century.
Sculptor.

Bartolomé Sales Bellmont assisted his teacher Konrad Rudolph in the execution of the statue of the Virgin in the chapel of Nuestro Señor de los Desamparados.

SALES ROVIRALTA, Francesco, or Francesc, Francisco
Spanish, 20th century.
Born 1904, in Barcelona; died 1977.
Active in France from 1939.
Painter, draughtsman, illustrator. Portraits, landscapes, urban landscapes, still-lifes.

Francesco Sales Roviralta originally planned to serve in the merchant navy but enrolled instead at the Fine Arts Circle in Barcelona and set his sights upon becoming a painter. He studied first at the college of arts and crafts in Barcelona, then at the college of fine arts. He started exhibiting as of 1930. In 1939 he moved to France, settling in Paris in 1944.

He showed his works at major Parisian Salons; his first solo exhibition was held in Madrid in 1934, following which he exhibited solo in Madrid, Paris and Perpignan. He painted very much in the style of the day, but his work is nonetheless straightforward and attractively sincere. He was best known for his landscapes of Madrid. His work is not revolutionary in any sense of the term, but it is solid and effective.

BIBLIOGRAPHY:
Arnáiz, José Manuel/López Jiménez, Javier/Merchán Díaz, Manuel (ed.), *'Cien años de pintura en Espana y Portugal (1830-1930)'* in vol. X, Antiqvaria, Madrid, 1993.

AUCTION RECORDS:
PARIS, 10 April 1989, *Still-life* (oil on canvas, 18 x 22 ins / 46 x 55 cm) FRF 7,800. PARIS, 29 Nov 1989, *Still-life with Watermelon and Black Pitcher* (1959, oil on canvas, 9 x 11 ins / 22 x 27 cm) FRF 6,000. NEW YORK, 26 Feb 1993, *Portrait of a Matador* (1952, oil on canvas, 24 x 18 ins / 61 x 45.7 cm) USD 1,610. PARIS, 10 April 1996, *Young Herdsman* (oil on canvas, 28¾ x 23½ ins / 73 x 60 cm) FRF 5,000. MADRID, 9 March 1999, *Still-life* (oil on canvas, 20 x 25 ins / 50 x 64 cm) ESP 250,000. MADRID, 22 Nov 1999, *Cardboard Horse* (1962, oil on canvas, 35 x 45 ins / 89 x 115 cm) ESP 530,000. MADRID, 21 Feb 2000, *Blue Mountains* (1962, oil on canvas, 25 x 31 ins / 63 x 79 cm) ESP 275,000. PARIS, 25 April 2003, *Doves* (1968, oil on canvas, 16 x 31 ins / 40 x 80 cm) EUR 1,600.

SALESA, Buenaventura
Spanish, 18th - 19th century.
Born 1756, in Borja; died 21 October 1819, in Saragossa.
Painter, engraver (burin). Portraits, genre scenes.

Buenaventura Salesa studied in Madrid and Rome.

SALESA, Cristóbal
Spanish, 18th century.
Born c. 1750, in Borja.
Sculptor. Low reliefs.

Cristóbal Salesa was a pupil of J. de Mena.

MUSEUMS AND GALLERIES:
MADRID (Real Academia de Bellas Artes de San Fernando): one low relief.

SALESSES, J. B.
French, 19th century.
Born 2 November 1817, in Toulouse; died 20 March 1873, in Orléans.
Sculptor, painter, draughtsman, musician. Religious subjects, portraits. Busts, statuettes.

MUSEUMS AND GALLERIES:
ORLÉANS: *Portrait of Meyerbeer* (plaster bust); *Christ* (plaster statuette).

SALFI, Enrico
Italian, 19th - 20th century.
Born 27 November 1858, in Cosenza (Calabria); died 14 January 1935.
Painter. Genre scenes.

Enrico Salfi was a student of the Istituto di Belle Arti in Naples. He exhibited in Turin, Naples and Rome.

MUSEUMS AND GALLERIES:
NAPLES (Mus. di Capodimonte): *The Marriage of Pompeii* - NAPLES (Mus. Provinciale): *Licet?*.

SALGADO, José Mario VELOSO. See **VELOSO SALGADO**

SALGADO, Roque
Spanish.
Sculptor. Religious subjects.

Roque Salgado carved a number of wooden sculptures for church altars in Galicia, notably in Orense.

SALGE, Martinien Gustave
French, 20th century.
Born 29 July 1878, in Marseilles; died 1946, in Jouques.
Painter, watercolourist, engraver, designer, illustrator. Interiors with figures, landscapes. Panoramas.

Martinien Gustave Salge started work with an engraver in Marseilles, received advice from the illustrator Paul Maurou, and attended the École des Beaux-Arts. He received a scholarship that enabled him to study under Gérome and Gabriel at the École des Beaux-Arts, Paris, and another to promote French art in the colonies. He founded the first school of painting in Hanoi. He took part in World War I as a conscript and in 1922 was put in charge of the Indo-Chinese section of the Marseilles Exposition.

He exhibited in Paris at the Salon des Artistes Français, of which he was a member, and at the colonial exhibition of 1931, where he showed a diorama 56 metres long. He was awarded an honourable mention in 1908 and a third-class medal in 1911, also exhibited in Grenoble and New York, and was made a Chevalier of the Légion d'Honneur in 1932.

He depicted with accuracy the light and atmosphere of South-East Asia and Provence.

SALGE, Michel
French, 20th century.
Born 1 March 1932, in Oubone, Thailand.
Painter. Scenes with figures.

Michel Salge was initially an accountant. He first exhibited in Laos and subsequently at various group exhibitions in France (Nice, Marseilles, the Salon International d'Art Naïf, Paris) and in Milan and New York.

AUCTION RECORDS:
PARIS, 28 June 1976, *First Meditation* (1974, oil on canvas, 15 x 18 ins / 38 x 46 cm) FRF 2,600.

SALGEDO, Ignacio de Léon. See **LEÓN Y SALGEDO Ignacio de**

SALGEN, Andres, or Sallge or Salligen or Solliger
German, 17th century.
Died at the beginning of 1612, in Slesvig (now Schleswig).
Sculptor (wood).

Andres Salgen worked for the duchess of Slesvig in the castle of Gottorp.

SALGHETTI-DRIOLI, Angelica
Maiden name: Isola
Italian, 19th century.

Born 30 October 1817; died 20 September 1853, in Zara (now Zadar, Croatia).
Painter.
Angelica Salghetti-Drioli was the wife of Francesco Salghetti-Drioli.

SALGHETTI-DRIOLI, Francesco
Italian, 19th century.
Born 19 March 1811, in Zara (now Zadar, Croatia); died 15 July 1877, in Zara.
Painter.
Francesco Salghetti-Drioli studied with Solferino in Trieste and at the Accademia di Belle Arti in Venice.
MUSEUMS AND GALLERIES:
ZAGREB (Strossmayerova Galerija Starih Majstora Hrvatske Akademija Znanosti i Umjetnosti): *Christopher Columbus in Chains; Pharaoh's Dream; King Dusan and Vila.*

SALGUES, Pierre de. See **SARGUES**

SALHAUSEN, Antonius von, or Saalhausen
Austrian, 17th century.
Born 17 February 1588, in Bensen, Bohemia; died c. 1625.
Sculptor.
Antonius von Salhausen was a pupil of Mich. Schwenke. He executed sculptures for the church of Pirna.

SALHOFER, Wolf
German, 17th century.
Active in Würzburg c. 1600.
Sculptor.
Wolf Salhofer executed sculptures for doors and pediments for the Ehehalten house in Würzburg.

SALIANO, Giovanni (fra). See **SAILLANT**

SALIBA, da. See first name

SALIBY, Khalil. See **SALEEBY Khalil**

SALICATH, Oernulf
Norwegian, 20th century.
Active c. 1937.
Painter.

SALICE, P.
German, 18th century.
Active in Hirschberg (now Jelena Góra, Poland) 1750-1770.
Painter. Portraits.
MUSEUMS AND GALLERIES:
JELENIA GÓRA: portraits of town tradesmen and their wives.

SALICE, Pietro Giacomo
Italian, 17th century.
Active in Milan during the second half of the 17th century.
Painter. Religious subjects, flowers.
Pietro Giacomo Salice was in Rome in 1678.

SALICETI, Jeane
French, 19th - 20th century.
Born 1873, in Tarbes (Hautes-Pyrenées); died 1950, in Tarbes (Hautes-Pyrenées).
Painter. Landscapes, still-lifes, flowers.
Jeane Saliceti must have studied at the École des Beaux-Arts, Paris, about 1900, and she probably visited the Louvre. She returned to Tarbes, where she settled permanently. Two exhibitions of her work were organised in Paris after her death. A modest private income enabled her to devote her life to painting baskets of fruit, vases of flowers, and tranquil landscapes - though never mountains.
AUCTION RECORDS:
VERSAILLES, 19 Oct 1975, *Painting,* FRF 2,000. VERSAILLES, 21 Dec 1975, *Vase of Flowers,* FRF 1,800.

SALICETTI. See **SALIETTI**

SALIÈRES, Paul Narcisse
French, 19th century.
Born in Carcassonne.
Painter, engraver. Genre scenes.
Paul Salières' master was Paul Delaroche. He exhibited at the Salon between 1848 and 1870. In 1853 he sent a dissertation to the Société d'Encouragement pour l'Industrie Nationale (society for the encouragement of national industry), entitled: *Diaphanous Engraving: A New Procedure Relevant to All Painters and Draughtsmen.*
BIBLIOGRAPHY:
Salières, Paul-Narcisse, *Gravure diaphane, nouveau procédé à la portée de tous les peintres et de tous les dessinateurs,* Imprimerie de Bochin, Montpellier, 1853.
MUSEUMS AND GALLERIES:
MONTPELLIER: *Man Selling Laments.*
AUCTION RECORDS:
PARIS, 9 April 1986, *The Earthenware Restorer* (oil on canvas, 24 x 25 ins / 61 x 63.5 cm) FRF 60,000. NEW YORK, 17 Oct 1991, *Twins* (oil on canvas, 63 1/2 x 44 1/4 ins / 161 x 112.1 cm) USD 22,000. PARIS, 6 June 2002, *Portrait of a Child* (oil on canvas, 57 x 39 ins / 145 x 100 cm) EUR 7,500.

SALIÈRES, Sylvain
French, 19th - 20th century.
Born 1865, in Escorneboeuf (Gers).
Sculptor, medallist.
Sylvain Salières, a pupil of Falquière and Marqueste, exhibited at the Salon des Artistes Français, where he was awarded a third-class medal in 1896, a bronze at the Exposition Universelle of 1900, and a second-class in 1901.
MUSEUMS AND GALLERIES:
PARIS (MBA): *April Romance.*

SALIETTI, Alberto
Italian, 20th century.
Born 15 March 1892, in Ravenna; died 1961, in Chiavari.
Painter, draughtsman, watercolourist, engraver, lithographer. Figures, nudes, portraits, scenes with figures, interiors with figures, landscapes, urban landscapes, seascapes, animals, still-lifes, flowers.
Alberto Salietti was born into a family of decorative artists and was a pupil of Cesare Tallone and of Giuseppe Mentessi at the Accademia di Belle Arti di Brera, Milan from 1908 to 1914. He was one of the founders of the group Novecento in which he was the secretary. He was part of the board of directors of the Fascist Syndicate of the Fine Arts of Milan from 1925 to 1932, and in this position he organised the first exhibition of Novecento in Milan in 1926. In 1928 he founded the group Sette pittori moderni (Seven Modern Painters) in Milan, with Bernasconi, Carrà, Funi, Marrusig, Sirroni and Tosi. He settled finally in Chiavari, near Genoa, in 1941. He won first prize for painting at the Venice Biennale in 1936 and received many honours and titles, including the French Légion d'Honneur and the Order of the Vasa of Sweden. He was also a member of the Cherubini National Academy of Florence.

From 1917 he made several landscapes of the Ligurian coast, during frequent summer holidays at Chiavari where he settled in 1941. He also tried divisionism at that time, but abandoned it in the 1920s in favour of antique figure painting, then changed to a magic realism that he adapted to many influences. He remained nevertheless a naturalist, faithful to Post-Impressionist precepts, creating peaceful atmospheres in sensuous textures, using a sharp and bold brushstroke in his method of building up coloured skies, and also quotations from Matisse. Among his animated pictures, there is *Young Girl at the Window; Spring Morning in Liguria; La Pavoncelle.* He offered mural decorations for the Palais de Congrès where the Universal Exhibition of Rome would take place in 1942. He illustrated several works, such as the collection of Diego Valeri, *Poesie Piccole* (*Little Poems*) (Insegna del Pesce d'Oro, Milan, 1969).

Salietti's group exhibitions included in 1916, *Espozizione d'arte degli alleati* (*Exhibition of the Art of the Allies*), Milan; 1917, *Esposizione nazionale di Belle Arti* (*National Exhibition of the Fine Arts*), Accademia di Belle Arti di Brera, Milan; from 1917 annually, Palazzo della Permanente et Famiglia Artistica, Milan; 1920-1952 (except 1938), Venice Biennale; 1922, Bottega di Poesia, Milan; 1927, International Exhibition of the New Century Group, Paris; 1927, *Sette pittori moderni* (*Seven Modern Painters*), Milano Gallery, Milan; 1931, Pesaro Gallery, Milan; 1936, Milan Triennale; 1939, Rome Quadriennale.

His posthumous group exhibitions included: 1999, *Scoperta del Mare. Pittori Lombardi in Liguria tra '800 e '900* (*Discovering the Sea: Lombard Painters in Liguria between 1800 and 1900*), Ducal Palace, Genoa; 2002, *Under Mussolini. Decorative and Propaganda Arts of the Twenties and Thirties*, Estorick Collection, London; 2002, *Semeghini e gli amici di Bagutta* (*Semeghini and the Friends of Bagutta*), Ponte Rosso Gallery, Milan; 2003 *I Novecento italiano*, Spazio Oberdan, Milan. His solo exhibitions included, 1923, Ca'Pesaro, Venice; 1933, Vitelli Gallery, Genoa; 1942, Milan. Among posthumous retrospectives were 1964, Palazzo della Permanente, Milan; 1967, 1969, Gian Ferrari Gallery, Milan; 1971, Cortina Gallery, Milan; 1972, Palazzo Torriglia, Chiavari; 1992, 1997, Museo di Villa Croce, Genoa.

Bibliography:

Nebbia, Ugo, *Alberto Salietti*, Hoepli, Milan, 1925. De Grada, Raffaele/Borghese, Leonardo, *Mostra commemorativa di Alberto Salietti*, exhibition catalogue, Palazzo della Permanente, Commune di Milano, Milan, 1964. Cicogna, Linko (ed.)/Valsecchi, Marco (introduction), *Alberto Salietti 1892-1961: catalogo delle opere grafiche*, catalogue, G. Sansoni, Milan, 1971. Mastrolonardo, Enotrio, *Alberto Salietti: i diari pittorici*, catalogue, Società economica di Chiavari, Chiavari, 1985. Giubbini, Guido, *ALberto Salietti*, exhibition catalogue, Museo di Villa Croce, Genoa, 1992. Ragazzi, Franco/Gian Ferrari, C./Giubbini, Guido, *Alberto Salietti. Un artista di Novecento*, exhibition catalogue, Museo di Villa Croce, Skira, Genoa, 1997. Ginex, Giovanna/Rebora, Sergio, *Scoperta del Mare. Pittori lombardi in Liguria tra '800 e '900*, group exhibition catalogue, Palazzo Ducale, Genova, Mazzetta, Milan, 1999. Barisione, Silvia, et al., *Under Mussolini. Decorative and Propaganda Arts of the Twenties and Thirties*, group exhibition catalogue, Estorick Collection, London, Gabrielle Mazzotta, Milan, 2002.

Museums and Galleries:

Cleveland (MA): *The Country Woman* (1925) - Florence (Gal. d'Arte Moderna) - Milan (Gal. d'Arte Moderna) - Paris (former Mus. du Jeu de Paume) - Rome (Gal. Nazionale d'Arte Moderna): *Pomeriggio domenicale* (*Sunday Afternoon*) (1937, oil on canvas) - Vatican (Mus. Vaticani): *Le amiche* (*Girl Friends*) (1931).

Auction records:

Paris, 30 March 1949, *Bunch of Flowers*, FRF 4,000. Milan, 4 Dec 1969, *Still-life*, ITL 700,000. Milan, 12 Dec 1974, *Young Woman Reading*, ITL 1,300,000. Milan, 7 June 1977, *Landscape, Valdarno* (1937, oil on panel, 29 1/2 x 35 1/2 ins / 75 x 90 cm) ITL 1,100,000. Milan, 18 April 1978, *Landscape* (1927, tempera/canvas, 30 x 35 1/2 ins / 76 x 90 cm) ITL 1,600,000. Milan, 6 April 1982, *View of Lavagna* (tempera/panel, 19 3/4 x 23 1/2 ins / 50 x 60 cm) ITL 1,700,000. Milan, 24 March 1988, *Houses and Kitchen Gardens* (oil on canvas, 20 x 24 ins / 51 x 61 cm) ITL 4,000,000. Milan, 26 March 1991, *The Pink Dress* (1955, oil and tempera/mounted paper, 39 x 28 1/4 ins / 99 x 72 cm) ITL 13,500,000. Milan, 23 June 1992, *Andorra Landscape* (1927, oil on canvas, 47 1/4 x 31 1/2 ins / 120 x 80 cm) ITL 12,500,000; *Carnival in Venice* (oil/synthetic resin, 52 x 50 ins / 132 x 127 cm) ITL 17,000,000. Milan, 15 Dec 1992, *Still-life with Fungi* (1931, oil on panel, 19 1/4 x 23 1/2 ins / 49 x 60 cm) ITL 12,000,000. Milan, 16 Nov 1993, *Two Sisters* (1922, oil on canvas, 36 1/2 x 43 1/4 ins / 93 x 110 cm) ITL 26,450,000. Milan, 12 Dec 1995, *Harlequin and a Ballerina* (termpera/plywood, 57 3/4 x 55 ins / 147 x 140 cm) ITL 13,800,000. Milan, 23 Oct 1996, *Home from Fishing* (1914, oil on panel, 11 3/4 x 15 3/4 ins / 30 x 40 cm) ITL 12,815,000. Milan, 11 April 2000, *Wild Mushrooms* (oil on board, 24 x 29 ins / 60 x 74 cm) ITL 14,500,000. Bern, 10 May 2000, *Woman from Ciociaria* (1926, oil on board, 35 x 30 ins / 90 x 75 cm) CHF 17,000. Vercelli, 21 April 2001, *Spring in Chiavari, Italy* (oil on canvas, 28 x 35 ins / 70 x 90 cm) ITL 15,000,000. Milan, 21 June 2001, *Portrait of a Girl* (wax crayon, 16 x 13 ins / 41 x 32 cm) ITL 4,800,000. Vercelli, 2 March 2002, *Spring in Chiavari* (oil on canvas, 28 x 35 ins / 70 x 90 cm) EUR 8,500. Milan, 21 May 2002, *Portrait of a Young Woman* (1948, oil on board, 35 x 30 ins / 90 x 75 cm) EUR 7,500. Milan, 26 March 2003, *Interior with Girl and Vase of Flowers* (1921, oil on cardboard, 31 x 24 ins / 79 x 60 cm) EUR 22,000. Milan, 20 Nov 2003, *Roman Peasant Woman* (oil on board, 26 x 20 ins / 66 x 50 cm) EUR 4,400. Milan, 15 Sept 2004, *Landscape in Liguria* (oil on canvas, 24 x 20 ins / 60 x 50 cm) EUR 7,000.

SALIGER, Ivo, pseudonym of Ovid Scralgi

Austrian, 20th century.

Born 21 October 1894, in Königsberg (now Kaliningrad, Russia); died in Vienna.

Painter, draughtsman. Figure compositions.

National Socialist Art.

Ivo Saliger studied in Vienna under Ludwig Michalek, Rudolf Jettmar and Ferdinand Schmutzer. His training was strictly along academic lines in terms of drawing, composition and use of colour and must have been a delight to dogmatic academicians such as Max Nordau (who cited Jean-Martin Charcot's research into visual impairment among the hysterical and the degenerate when 'evaluating' the Impressionists) or Professor Adolf Ziegler who, in 1920, dismissed the Dadaists as 'swine'. In short, Saliger had an artistic arsenal at his disposal that was ideally suited to his adoptive masters, the Nazi regime. Predictably, Saliger was in the vanguard of those painters who declared their fervent opposition to anything that smacked of Cubism, Fauvism, Expressionism, Dadaism or Abstract art. As such, he was a darling of the Nazi regime and a shining example of what passed for 'art' as opposed to the 'Degenerate Art' (Entartete Kunst) personally repudiated by the Führer at the eponymous - and now notorious - Munich exhibition of 1937.

His sculptor counterpart Arno Breker celebrated antiquity, whereas Saliger opted for the bucolic; Breker put virility on a pedestal, whereas Saliger celebrated female beauty (often with a subtext hinting at 'the warrior's reward'). One of Saliger's most popular paintings, his *Judgement of Paris*, shows three well-endowed and immaculately complexioned blonde nudes in the process of offering their buxom and unequivocally Aryan bodies to a Paris who is appropriately attired for the occasion in a brown shirt and Tyrolean *Lederhöschen*.

Bibliography:

Hahn, Otto, *'Vive l'art dégénéré'* in *L'Express*, periodical, Paris, 14 April 1989.

Auction records:

Vienna, 10 April 1984, *Youth 32* (1932, oil on canvas, 55 1/2 x 51 1/4 ins / 141 x 130 cm) ATS 28,000. Ahlden, 23 April 1999, *Contemplation by the Sea at Evening* (1941, oil on board, 48 x 44 ins / 121 x 111 cm) DEM 7,200. Vienna, 6 March 2001, *Sleeping Nude* (oil on panel, 26 x 37 ins / 67 x 94 cm) ATS 22,000. Munich, 25 June 2004, *Three Female Nudes* (oil on canvas, 55 x 55 ins / 139 x 139 cm) EUR 4,800.

SALIGO, Charles Louis
Belgian, 19th century.
Born 1804, in Geraardsbergen, Flanders.
Painter. Figures, portraits, interiors.

Charles Louis Saligo was a pupil of Van Huffel and A.J. Gros. He was active in Paris, and exhibited at the Salon from 1827 to 1842.

MUSEUMS AND GALLERIES:
AMSTERDAM: *Self-portrait.*

AUCTION RECORDS:
GHENT, 1856, *Night Scene: A Chemist Working in his Laboratory*, FRF 31. ANTWERP, 13 Dec 1999, *Holly Lady* (1856, oil on canvas, 32 x 25 ins / 82 x 64 cm) BEF 150,000. ANTWERP, 18 Nov 2002, *Portrait of a Lady* (1859, oil on canvas, 71 x 44 ins / 180 x 111 cm) EUR 20,000.

SALIM, Jawad
Iraqi, 20th century.
Born 1920, in Ankara; died 22 January 1961, in Baghdad.
Painter.

Jawad Salim came from a family of painters. He was awarded government scholarships which enabled him to stay in Paris and Rome from 1938 to 1940, and he then worked at the archaeological museum in Baghdad during World War II. He studied at the Slade School of Fine Art in London from 1946 to 1949; on his return to Iraq, he taught at the sculpture department at the institute of fine arts in Baghdad. In 1951, he was one of the founders of the group Modern Art in Baghdad, along with Mohamed Ghani and Hassan Shakir. He was commissioned to produce the *Monument of Liberty* in Baghdad.

BIBLIOGRAPHY:
Jabra, J.I., *Jawaad Saliim wa nasab al-hurriyya (Jawad Salim and the Monument of Liberty)*, Baghdad, 1973 ((Arabic text)). Ali, W., *Contemporary Art from the Islamic World*, London, 1989. Al-Khalil, S., *The Monument: Art, Vulgarity and Responsibility in Iraq*, London, 1991.

SALIM, Saraochim
Indonesian, 20th century.
Born 1908, in Medan (Sumatra).
Active in France, Switzerland and the Netherlands.
Painter.

Saraochim Salim was adopted by a Dutch family, who brought him to Europe. He studied in France, spending two years in Fernand Léger's studio and coming into contact with Western artists of all trends, including Cubism. He assimilated their techniques, but developed his own personal style. He also worked in Switzerland and in the Netherlands, where he became a member of the 'De Onafhankelijken' art society. Although he lived like an European, he remained emotionally attached to his native country. In 1951, the first exhibition of the paintings he had produced in France took place, in Jakarta and subsequently travelled to Bandung and Yogyakarta.

BIBLIOGRAPHY:
Holt, Claire, *Art in Indonesia. Continuities and change*, Cornell University, Ithaca (NY), 1981.

AUCTION RECORDS:
AMSTERDAM, 30 May 1995, *Landscape* (1949, oil on canvas, 19 3/4 x 24 ins / 50 x 61 cm) NLG 4,000.

SALIM QULI
Hindu School, 17th century.
Active at the beginning of the 17th century.
Painter.

Salim Quli painted two miniatures in the *Anvari i Suhaili* (*Lights of Canopus*) manuscript, now in the British Museum, London.

SALIMBENE, Gennaruccio
Italian, 15th century.
Active in San Severino (Marche) at the beginning of the 15th century.
Painter.

Gennaruccio Salimbene painted a *Saviour with Two Apostles* in S Maria della Misericordia church in San Severino, in 1404.

SALIMBENI, Arcangelo di Leonardo
Italian, 16th century.
Born probably in Siena; died after 1580, probably in Siena.
Painter. History painting, religious subjects.
Sienese School.

Arcangelo di Leonardo Salimbeni was a representative of the Siena School. He is known mainly for his friendship with Federigo Zuccaro, whose style he copied. On 20 April 1567 he married Battista Morelli, widow of Eugenio Vanni and daughter of the art lover and goldsmith, Giulian Morelli, who was the friend of Vasari and Beccafumi. This marriage must have lent Salimbeni an unusual importance. He trained two artists who became rightly famous, his son Ventura and his stepson Francesco Vanni.

Salimbeni's most important works include a *Nativity*, begun by Bartolomeo Neroni, which he completed in the Carmelite church in Siena; paintings for the St Bernard congregation in S Lucia and S Catarina in Fontebranda, *Death of St Peter Martyr* in S Domenico church and a *Crucifixion with Mary Magdalene, St Roch and St Francis*, which he painted in 1579 in the parish church of Luseignano in Siena. His paintings are also in SS Giovanni e Geraro in Siena.

AUCTION RECORDS:
NEW YORK, 31 Jan 1997, *Virgin and Infant Jesus with St John the Baptist and St Catherine of Siena* (oil on panel, tondo, diam. 26 ins / 66 cm) USD 90,500.

SALIMBENI, Luigi, or Salimen, Salimei
Italian, 16th century.
Sculptor.

Luigi Salimbeni worked in the Villa Borghese in Rome.

SALIMBENI, Simondio di Ventura, called Bevilacqua
Italian, 17th century.
Born 1597, in Siena; died 11 September 1643.
Painter. History painting.
Sienese School.

The son of Ventura Salimbeni, and his pupil until Ventura's death in 1613, Simondio Salimbeni subsequently worked with Rutilo Manetti, whose style he initially adopted. He was ranked among the best painters of the Sienese School in that era, and was frequently employed to decorate churches in Siena. In 1619, he married Teodora Vettori, who brought him a generous dowry. One of their two daughters had a similarly generous dowry on her marriage to Giovanni Maria Sarta on 14 June 1646, three years after the sudden death of her father, from which we may conclude that Simondio Salimbeni left a considerable fortune. The Salimbeni dynasty came to an end when Simondio died.

Salimbeni is documented as having painted a *Death of St Joseph* in the church of S Pietro Ovile, which apparently survives in the sacristy there, as well as five frescoes in the church of S Rouo in Siena, one of which he signed: *Bevillacqua*. He lost a court case in 1642 concerning paintings he produced for the chapel of Santa Catarina in Fontebranda, and the pictures had to be removed.

SALIMBENI, Ventura di Arcangelo, called Bevilacqua
Italian, 16th - 17th century.

Born January or February 1568, in Siena; died 1613, in Siena.
Painter, engraver (etching). History painting, religious subjects.
Sienese School.

Ventura di Arcangelo Salimbeni was the son of Arcangelo Salimbeni and Battista Morelli. With his half-brother Francesco Vanni, he learnt his style from his father. After his father's death in 1580 he travelled in Lombardy and studied the works of Correggio. In 1585 he painted a figure representing St George on the façade of S Giorgio church, after a drawing by his half-brother. The painting is now in the church sacristy. That year he went to Rome and found work there. In 1591, he married Antonia Focari, in Rome, and they had seven children, the eldest of whom was Simondio.

In 1592, Salimbeni produced several paintings in S Maria della Pace, and *Life of the Virgin* in S Maria Maggiore. He returned to his home town in 1595 and worked in S Pietro church, in Montaleino, in 1599. Cardinal Bevilacqua, papal legate in Perugia, called him there to decorate the Cassinese church, San Pietro. Bevilacqua was so impressed by his work that he made him Knight of the Order of the Golden Spur, and authorised him to take the name Bevilacqua.

At around the same time Salimbeni produced paintings for S Maria degli Angeli church, near Assisi. In 1602 he was back in Siena, completing the ceiling of S Trinita chapel. From 1602 to 1603 he was in Pisa, where he worked on the ceiling of the great hall of S Stefano dei Cavalieri church, and painted a figure personifying the city of Pisa in the Palazzo Communale. After a stay in Rome, during which he worked on Gesù church, he returned to Siena, where several similar works awaited him. In 1605 he worked on frescoes to decorate the cloister of Annunziata church in Florence, with Bernardino Poccetti, which he completed in 1608.

Salimbeni returned to Siena in 1606, to paint the *Crucifixion* in the Colombini chapel in S Domenico. He also completed a *Nativity*, begun by Alessandro Casolani, in Refugio church, where he painted several other works with Francesco Vanni. He worked in Pisa, in the churches of S Cecilia, S Frediano and S Francisco in 1607, and, after a stay in Florence, painted an altarpiece for Pisa Cathedral, in 1608.

In October 1608 he returned to Siena to paint four frescoes in the cathedral. On account of his work in Rome, particularly the *Circumcision* in S Simeone Lancellati church, he was made Knight of the Order of Christ by Pope Paul VIII. He also went to Genoa to decorate several churches and the palace, Casa Adorno, but, dissatisfied with the reception he received, he returned to Siena to complete his work at the cathedral. He also produced the design of a monument commemorating the rectors of S Maria della Scala hospital, which was executed by the sculptor Ascanio di Cortona.

Salimbeni was a skilled draughtsman and his works are very personal. He engraved with spirit, religious subjects only.

VSS

Museums and Galleries:

Budapest: *Annunciation* - Florence (Palazzo Pitti): *Holy Family* - Florence (Uffizi): *Apparition of St Michael to St Galgano the Hermit*; *Self-portrait* - Montpellier: *Virgin's Head* - Pisa: *Allegory of the City of Pisa*.

Auction records:

Paris, 1756, *St Cecilia Lying in a Tomb* (drawing in red chalk) FRF 64. Paris, 1776, *St Cecilia Receiving the Martyr's Crown* (pen drawing with bistre wash) FRF 272. Paris, 1881, *St Cecilia Receiving the Martyr's Crown* (pen drawing with bistre wash) FRF 272. Paris, 23 May 1928, *Marriage of the Virgin* (drawing) FRF 850. Paris, 31 March 1943, *Family of the Virgin* (pen and wash, heightened with gouache) FRF 400. Paris, 5 May 1949, *Study for a Fresco* (pen and wash, heightened) FRF 2,000. London, 24 March 1965, *Calvary*, GBP 500. London, 3 July 1980, *Adoration of the Magi* (black chalk, $7\frac{1}{2}$ x $9\frac{1}{2}$ ins / 19.1 x 24.4 cm) GBP 800. Paris, 21 Oct 1983, *Birth of the Virgin* (pen and red chalk wash heightened with white, $13\frac{1}{4}$ x 9 ins / 33.5 x 23 cm) FRF 151,000. London, 26 June 1985, *Baptism of Christ* (etching, 23 x 17 ins / 57.5 x 43.4 cm) GBP 900. Milan, 4 Dec 1986, *Study for a Portrait of a Woman* (red chalk, 7 x $4\frac{1}{2}$ ins / 17.5 x 11.5 cm) ITL 2,400,000. London, 25 Oct 1988, *Dispute of St Catherine of Alexandria with the Philosophers* (oil on panel, $25\frac{1}{2}$ x $25\frac{1}{4}$ ins / 65 x 64 cm) ITL 20,000,000. Rome, 27 Nov 1989, *Venus and Cupid* (oil on canvas, $51\frac{1}{4}$ x 46 ins / 130 x 116 cm) ITL 11,500,000. Monaco, 2 Dec 1989, *Jesus Delighting the Heart of St Theresa* (oil on canvas, $49\frac{1}{4}$ x $32\frac{1}{4}$ ins / 125 x 82 cm) FRF 222,000. London, 2 July 1991, *Pope Innocent IV Blessing St Clare on Her Deathbed* (black chalk, brown ink and wash heightened with white, $10\frac{1}{4}$ x $9\frac{3}{4}$ ins / 25.8 x 24.8 cm) GBP 35,200. Paris, 15 May 1993, *Annunciation* (1594, etching in the form of a lunette in the upper part, $11\frac{1}{2}$ x $6\frac{1}{2}$ ins / 28.9 x 16.5 cm) FRF 3,200. London, 5 July 1993, *Study of Two Seated People in Profile* (black chalk/paper, $7\frac{3}{4}$ x $7\frac{1}{4}$ ins / 19.9 x 18.7 cm) GBP 1,035. New York, 7 Oct 1993, *Virgin with Child with St Catherine of Siena* (oil on panel, $24\frac{3}{4}$ x 20 ins / 62.9 x 50.8 cm) USD 9,200. Paris, 21 Feb 1996, *Stoning of St Stephen* (ink, $8\frac{3}{4}$ x $5\frac{1}{2}$ ins / 22.5 x 14 cm) FRF 45,000. London, 18 April 1996, *Four Saints before a Holy Image* (ink and wash/black chalk, $12\frac{1}{2}$ x $8\frac{3}{4}$ ins / 31.7 x 22.4 cm) GBP 2,070. Paris, 18 Dec 1996, *Holy Family and St Catherine of Siena* (oil on canvas, $31\frac{1}{2}$ x $23\frac{3}{4}$ ins / 80 x 60.5 cm) FRF 30,000. New York, 27 Jan 1999, *Study of Young Man Holding Stick in Each Hand* (9 x 6 ins / 23 x 14 cm) USD 6,000. London, 28 Oct 1999, *Tiburtine Sibyl and the Emperor Augustus* (oil on canvas, 46 x 32 ins / 118 x 82 cm) GBP 13,000. Paris, 20 Nov 2000, *Lunette with Two Saints in Adoration* (pen/brown ink wash, 6 x 13 ins / 16 x 32 cm) FRF 95,000. London, 26 April 2001, *Holy Family with the Infant St John the Baptist* (oil on panel, 25 x 19 ins / 64 x 49 cm) GBP 30,000. New York, 23 May 2001, *Holy Family with St Jerome* (oil on copper, 15 x 11 ins / 39 x 29 cm) USD 57,500. London, 9 July 2002, *Madonna and Child* (oil on canvas, 30 x 24 ins / 77 x 61 cm) GBP 8,500. Rome, 4 Dec 2002, *Annunciation* (pencil/ink/watercolour, 9 x 7 ins / 23 x 19 cm) EUR 6,000. Milan, 4 June 2003, *St Catherine of Siena and Mary Magdalene* (oil on canvas, 17 x 12 ins / 44 x 30 cm) EUR 3,200. London, 9 July 2003, *Madonna and Child* (oil on canvas, 30 x 24 ins / 75 x 61 cm) GBP 13,000.

SALIMBENI DI SALIMBENE, Jacopo, called da San Severino
Italian, 15th century.
Born in San Severino (Marche); died after 1427.
Painter.
Umbrian School.

Jacopo Salimbeni di Salimbene was the brother and collaborator of Lorenzo Salimbeni di Salimbene.

SALIMBENI DI SALIMBENE, Lorenzo, called da San Severino
Italian, 14th - 15th century.
Born c. 1374, in San Severino (Marche); died before 1420.
Painter, fresco artist. Religious subjects.
Umbrian School.

Lorenzo Salimbeni di Salimbene was the brother of Jacopo Salimbeni di Salimbene. He may have been the pupil of Zanino di Pietro. His *Mystical Marriage of St Catherine*, a triptych dated 1400, reveals his knowledge of Lombardy art and Scandinavian influences. His frescoes, *Virgin and Child, Martyrdom of St Stephen and St Ginesius, Scenes from the Life of St Blaise*, in the crypt of S Ginesio collegiate church, date from 1406.

Salimbeni di Salimbene used refined colours in his narrative art, which bordered on the miniature, as in *Virgin and St Anne*, in the Vatican. He also collaborated on many works with his brother and it can be difficult to distinguish their respective contributions. This is particularly the case in the frescoes; *Scenes from the Life of St John the Evangelist* in a chapel at the Duomo Vecchio, San Severino; *Calvary, Madonna of Paradise, Madonna with St John the Baptist and St Sebastian* and 12 scenes from the *Life of St John the Baptist*, dated 1416, in S Giovanni oratory in Urbino. These frescoes are signed *M.C.C.C.C.X.V.I. die XVII Julii. Laurentius, de Santo-Severino. et Jacobus, frater, ejus, hoc. opus. fecerunt.* They are painted with a picturesque liveliness, great detail in the clothing, vegetation and architecture, an elegance of line and a richness of colour which define the artists as representatives of the International Gothic style, in the same manner as Gentile da Fabriano.

Museums and Galleries:
San Severino: *Betrothal of the Virgin with Saints* (triptych); *Mystical Marriage of St Catherine; Head of Madonna; Head of the Infant Jesus; Four Fragments of a Crucifixion* - Urbino (Gal. Nazionale Delle Marche): *St Clare* - Vatican (Pinacoteca Vaticana): *Virgin and St Anne*.

Auction records:
London, 27 April 1927, *Agony in the Garden* (watercolour, attributed) GBP 235. New York, 10 Jan 1990, *Virgin with Child* (oil on canvas, 17 3/4 x 12 1/2 ins / 45 x 31.8 cm) USD 9,350.

SALIMEI, Luigi. See **SALIMBENI**

SALIMI, Homayon

Iranian, 20th - 21st century.
Born 1948, in Tehran.
Active in France since 1973.
Painter.

Homayon Salimi has lived and worked in Paris since 1973. He paints Abstract compositions, deploying motifs from traditional Persian earthenware, weaving and architecture. In 1992, he took part in the exhibition *De Bonnard à Baselitz: Dix Ans d'Enrichissements du Cabinet des Estampes 1978-1988* (*From Bonnard to Baselitz: A Decade of Acquisitions by the Prints Collection 1978-1988*) at the Bibliothèque Nationale in Paris, and in 1988 showed his works at the Cité Internationale des Arts in Paris.

Museums and Galleries:
Paris (BNF, Prints Collection): *Brick* (1982).

SALINAS, Marcel Charles Laurent

Egyptian, 20th century.
Born 9 April 1913, in Alexandria.
Active in France.
Painter. Seascapes.

Marcel Charles Laurent Salinas settled in Paris, where he studied under André Lhote. He featured regularly in the Salon des Surindépendants in Paris, which meant that he was prevented by regulations from exhibiting in other salons. He also exhibited a collection of his works in a Parisian gallery in 1950.

Museums and Galleries:
Paris (BNF): *Pleasure Boats* (c. 1979).

SALINAS, Tommaso. See **SALINI**

SALINAS Y TERUEL, Agustín, or Augustín

Spanish, 19th - 20th century.
Born 1861 or 1862; died 1923.
Painter. Religious subjects, portraits, genre scenes, landscapes, landscapes with figures, seascapes.

The brother of Juan Pablo Salinas, Agustín Salinas studied first in Madrid and then, from 1883, in Rome. He took part on a regular basis in national fine arts exhibitions in Madrid from 1881 and also exhibited at the 1892 International Fine Arts Exhibition in Munich.

He painted mainly biblical themes and landscapes with figures, using small touches of paint in the Impressionist manner. Examples of his work include: *Beach at Terracina, Ravine of Death, Reapers, Elijah in the Wilderness Consoled by an Angel* and *Cain's Remorse*.

Bibliography:
Garcia Guatas, M., *'La Diputación de Zaragoza y la creacion del pensionado de Pintura en el Extranjero'* in *Seminario de Arte Aragonés XXXIII*. Arnáiz, José Manuel/López Jiménez, Javier/Merchán Díaz, Manuel (ed.), *'Cien años de pintura en Espana y Portugal (1830-1930)'* in vol. X, Antiqvaria, Madrid, 1993.

Museums and Galleries:
Bautzen (Stadtmus.): *Festival in Granada* - Wroclaw (Muz. Narodowe): *Boudoir*.

Auction records:
London, 26 July 1961, *Celebration*, GBP 560. London, 1 March 1972, *Roman Song*, GBP 350. London, 13 June 1973, *Roman Song*, GBP 400. New York, 14 May 1976, *Spanish Dancer* (oil on panel, 9 1/2 x 15 3/4 ins / 24 x 40 cm) USD 8,750. London, 23 Feb 1977, *Dancer with Castanets* (oil on panel, 9 1/2 x 15 3/4 ins / 24 x 40 cm) GBP 2,600. London, 5 July 1978, *Fiesta in Seville* (oil on canvas, 9 1/4 x 15 3/4 ins / 23.5 x 40 cm) GBP 3,400. London, 20 June 1979, *Marriage Proposal* (1888, oil on panel, 7 1/4 x 12 1/2 ins / 18.5 x 32 cm) GBP 480. London, 18 Jan 1980, *Gypsy Dancers* (oil on panel, 9 x 15 3/4 ins / 22.8 x 40 cm) GBP 1,200. New York, 27 Oct 1982, *The Gift* (1883, oil on canvas, 15 3/4 x 9 1/2 ins / 40 x 24.2 cm) USD 2,400. Milan, 23 March 1983, *Drying the Nets* (oil on panel, 5 1/4 x 9 1/4 ins / 13.5 x 23.5 cm) ITL 7,700,000. London, 27 Nov 1985, *Grape Harvest* (oil on panel, 9 1/4 x 15 3/4 ins / 23.5 x 40 cm) GBP 6,000. London, 17 Feb 1989, *Classical Beauty* (oil on panel, 13 1/2 x 7 1/4 ins / 34.3 x 18.3 cm) GBP 3,850. New York, 24 Oct 1990, *Venice Lido in August* (1895, oil on panel, 6 3/4 x 10 1/2 ins / 17.1 x 26.7 cm) USD 7,150. London, 19 June 1991, *Spanish Festival on a Terrace* (oil on panel, 9 1/2 x 15 3/4 ins / 24 x 40 cm) GBP 7,700. Rome, 24 March 1992, *Portrait ofa Young Woman with a Hat* (1885, oil on canvas, 39 1/4 x 23 1/2 ins / 100 x 60 cm) ITL 4,370,000. Rome, 9 June 1992, *Bay of Anzio* (oil on canvas, 9 3/4 x 19 3/4 ins / 25 x 50 cm) ITL 3,500,000. London, 27 Oct 1993, *Regatta off Anzio, Italy* (1913, oil on canvas, 9 3/4 x 19 3/4 ins / 25 x 50 cm) GBP 1,840. Rome, 6 Dec 1994, *Portrait of a Little Rascal* (oil on canvas, 22 x 15 ins / 55 x 38 cm) ITL 3,300,000. Rome, 23 May 1996, *Roman Landscape* (oil on canvas, 9 3/4 x 13 ins / 25 x 33 cm) ITL 1,495,000.

SALINAS Y TERUEL, Juan Pablo, or Pablo

Spanish, 20th century.
Born 1871, in Madrid; died 1946, in Rome.
Painter. Religious subjects, allegorical subjects, figures, nudes, portraits, scenes with figures, genre scenes, interiors with figures.

The brother of Agustín Salinas y Teruel, Juan Pablo Salinas studied at the Escuela Especial de Pintura, Escultura y Grabado in Madrid and, subsequently, at the Accademia Chigi in Rome. He was in Rome in 1886 (his brother had been living there since 1883) before moving to Paris. He was awarded a bronze medal in 1885.

He painted a number of orientalist compositions. He appears to have been fascinated by court scenes and produced genre compositions featuring luxurious Spanish and Italian interiors. His meticulous technique offers a fascinating contemporary record of dress and furnishings of the age, including details of lacework and of women's complexions. Examples of his work include: *Cleopatra and Mark Anthony, Who Are You?, Returning from the Grape Harvest, Cardinal's Supper, Wedding in Aragon* and *Visit to the Cardinal*.

Bibliography:
Arnáiz, José Manuel/López Jiménez, Javier/Merchán Díaz, Manuel (ed.), '*Cien años de pintura en Espana y Portugal (1830-1930)*' in vol. X, Antiqvaria, Madrid, 1993.
Museums and Galleries:
Madrid (Prado): *View of the Roman Campagna.*
Auction records:
London, 16 Feb 1923, *Cardinal,* GBP 50. Lucerne, 17 June 1950, *Marriage Contract,* CHF 7,000. Munich, 24-25-26 June 1964, *Spanish Wedding,* DEM 14,500. London, 10 June 1966, *At the Hairdresser,* Gns 750. Milan, 4 June 1968, *Wedding Feast,* ITL 2,400,000. London, 1 March 1972, *Arrival of the Duke,* GBP 1,900. Vienna, 22 May 1973, *Market Scene, Venice,* ATS 140,000. Milan, 12 Dec 1974, *Brindisi,* ITL 4,000,000. London, 24 Nov 1976, *Recital* (oil on canvas, 10 x 15 1/2 ins / 24.5 x 39.5 cm) GBP 3,400. New York, 7 Oct 1977, *Audience with His Eminence* (oil on canvas, 19 1/4 x 28 ins / 49 x 71 cm) USD 26,000. Zurich, 25 May 1979, *Market Scene, Venice* (oil on panel, 15 3/4 x 9 1/4 ins / 40 x 23.5 cm) CHF 21,000. Milan, 6 Nov 1980, *Visit to the Cardinal* (oil on panel, 13 3/4 x 9 3/4 ins / 35 x 25 cm) ITL 6,500,000. Milan, 16 Dec 1982, *Card Game* (oil on panel, 11 3/4 x 15 1/2 ins / 30 x 39.5 cm) ITL 11,000,000. New York, 27 Oct 1983, *Courtly Discourse* (oil on canvas, 11 1/2 x 11 3/4 ins / 29.4 x 30 cm) USD 15,000. New York, 31 Oct 1985, *Wedding Reception* (oil on canvas, 24 x 32 ins / 61 x 81.5 cm) USD 35,000. Montevideo, 14 Aug 1986, *Flamenco Dancer* (oil on canvas, 15 1/4 x 21 1/4 ins / 39 x 54 cm) UYU 5,008,500. Montevideo, 2 Dec 1987, *Flamenco Dancer* (oil on canvas, 15 3/4 x 22 ins / 40 x 55 cm) UYU 8,457,000. London, 22 June 1988, *Recital* (oil on canvas, 15 1/2 x 26 1/4 ins / 39.5 x 66.5 cm) GBP 36,300. London, 23 Nov 1988, *Portrait of a Cardinal* (oil on panel, 9 1/2 x 7 ins / 24 x 18 cm) GBP 2,090. London, 23 Nov 1988, *Suzanna* (oil on panel, 9 1/2 x 13 ins / 24 x 33 cm) GBP 14,300. London, 17 Feb 1989, *Portrait of the Daughter of the Artist Pippi* (oil on canvas, 18 1/4 x 17 ins / 46.3 x 43.2 cm) GBP 3,300. New York, 23 Feb 1989, *The Letter* (oil on canvas, 10 x 9 ins / 24.5 x 22 cm) USD 11,000. Milan, 14 March 1989, *Cardinal* (oil on panel, 7 1/2 x 6 1/2 ins / 19 x 16.5 cm) ITL 10,000,000. London, 22 Nov 1989, *Standing Nude* (oil on panel, 15 3/4 x 9 ins / 40 x 23 cm) GBP 6,600. Rome, 14 Dec 1989, *Card Game* (oil on panel, 9 3/4 x 14 1/2 ins / 25 x 37 cm) ITL 40,250,000. London, 14 Feb 1990, *Audience with the Cardinal* (oil on canvas, 17 1/2 x 23 1/4 ins / 44.5 x 59 cm) GBP 2,860. New York, 23 May 1990, *Taking Tea with the Cardinal* (oil on canvas/panel, 15 1/2 x 26 ins / 39.3 x 66 cm) USD 44,000. Rome, 16 April 1991, *Toast to the Cardinal* (oil on panel, 13 3/4 x 20 ins / 35 x 51 cm) ITL 34,500,000. New York, 22 May 1991, *Visit to the Cardinal* (oil on panel, 20 x 31 1/2 ins / 50.8 x 80 cm) USD 63,800. Milan, 12 Dec 1991, *Card Game* (oil on panel, 9 x 15 ins / 23 x 38 cm) ITL 31,000,000. London, 29 May 1992, *Piece of Advice* (oil on panel, 5 1/2 x 9 1/2 ins / 14 x 24 cm) GBP 18,700. Rome, 9 June 1992, *Gypsies* (oil on canvas, 15 3/4 x 26 ins / 40 x 66 cm) ITL 5,000,000. Paris, 22 June 1992, *At the Cardinal's* (oil on canvas, 11 1/2 x 18 ins / 29 x 46 cm) FRF 86,000. New York, 27 May 1993, *Private Viewing* (oil on canvas, 28 1/4 x 50 1/2 ins / 71.7 x 128.3 cm) USD 79,500. New York, 12 Oct 1994, *Audience with the Cardinal* (oil on panel, 12 1/2 x 8 ins / 31.8 x 20.3 cm) USD 18,400. London, 20 Nov 1996, *Flirt* (oil on panel, 13 1/2 x 18 ins / 34.5 x 46 cm) GBP 18,400. New York, 26 Feb 1997, *Toast* (oil on panel, 9 1/4 x 15 3/4 ins / 23.8 x 40 cm) USD 18,400. New York, 23 Oct 1997, *Wedding Night* (oil on canvas, 29 x 50 3/4 ins / 73.7 x 128.9 cm) USD 134,500. London, 25 March 1999, *After the Christening* (oil on canvas, 16 x 27 ins / 41 x 68 cm) GBP 58,000. New York, 1 Nov 1999, *Wedding Party* (oil on canvas, 15 x 26 ins / 39 x 67 cm) USD 100,000. London, 22 June 2000, *The Duke's Arrival* (oil on canvas, 16 x 26 ins / 40 x 66 cm) GBP 50,000. London, 27 Oct 2000, *Matador's Triumph* (oil on canvas, 29 x 51 ins / 73 x 129 cm) GBP 80,000. New York, 1 May 2001, *Fiesta Time* (oil on canvas, 18 x 30 ins / 46 x 76 cm) USD 110,000. Milan, 22 May 2001, *Marriage Agreement* (oil on canvas, 35 x 53 ins / 90 x 135 cm) ITL 230,000,000. Madrid, 12 March 2002, *Merrymaking* (oil on canvas, 15 x 26 ins / 39 x 67 cm) EUR 55,000. London, 13 June 2002, *Conversation* (oil on panel, 18 x 13 ins / 45 x 34 cm) GBP 24,000. Madrid, 27 May 2003, *Jolgorio* (oil on canvas, 15 x 26 ins / 39 x 67 cm) EUR 55,000. Madrid, 23 Sept 2003, *Bacia de Oro, Spain* (oil on canvas, 15 x 26 ins / 39 x 66 cm) EUR 90,000. New York, 23 April 2004, *Valuation of Jewels* (oil on canvas, 15 x 26 ins / 39 x 66 cm) USD 70,000. New York, 27 Oct 2004, *The Christening* (oil on canvas, 36 x 44 ins / 92 x 113 cm) USD 95,000.

SALINCORNO, pseudonym of Mirabello di Antonio Cavalori, also called da Salincorno
Italian, 16th century.
Born 1535, in Florence; died 27 August 1572, in Florence.
Active c. 1565-1572.
Painter, draughtsman. Religious subjects, figures.

According to Bottari and Lanzi, Salincorno was in his youth the pupil of Ridolfo Ghirlandaio. He was one of the artists employed to produce paintings for the funeral of Michelangelo.
Bibliography:
Feinberg, L., *The Works of Mirabello Cavalori,* dissertation, Harvard University, Cambridge MA, 1986.
Museums and Galleries:
Florence (Palazzo Pitti): *Head of St John Carried to Herod's Feast.*
Auction records:
Paris, 1859, *St Joseph* (drawing) FRF 14. Monte Carlo, 20 June 1987, *Study of a Young Man Carrying a Stick* (red chalk, 7 1/4 x 3 3/4 ins / 18.5 x 9.7 cm) FRF 130,000. London, 8 July 1994, *Isaac Blessing Jacob* (oil on panel, 22 3/4 x 17 1/4 ins / 58 x 43.5 cm) GBP 397,500.

SALING, Paul E.
German, 19th - 20th century.
Born 19 July 1876.
Active in the USA.
Painter.

Paul E. Saling studied in Germany and went on to become a member of the Salmagundi Club and the American Arts Federation.

SALINGRE, Eugène Édouard
French, 19th century.
Born 19 November 1829, in Soissons (Aisne); died 27 September 1892, in Soissons (Aisne).
Painter. Landscapes, still-lifes, architectural views.

He began exhibiting at the Salon in 1859. He painted still-lifes (birds and game), views of the monuments in Soissons (Picardy) and views of the landscape around Soissons.
Museums and Galleries:
Soissons: several works.

SALINI, Alessandro
Italian, 18th century.
Born 30 June 1675, in Sulmona; died 1764.
Painter. History painting.

Several works by Alessandro Salini can be found in churches in Sulmona.

SALINI, Tommaso, called Mao, or Salinas, Solini
Italian, 17th century.
Born c. 1575, in Rome; died 13 September 1625, in Rome.
Painter. Religious subjects, mythological subjects, landscapes with figures, still-lifes (flowers/fruit).

The son of a Florentine sculptor, Tommaso Salini was the pupil of Baccio Pintelli and was influenced by Caravaggio. His work featured in a collective exhibition on the theme of

Italian still-life, entitled *Stille Welt. Italienische Stilleben aus drei Jahrhunderten* (*Still World: Three Centuries of Italian Still-life Painting*), held in 2003 at the Kunsthalle der Hypo-Kulturstiftung in Munich. He also painted altarpieces.

Bibliography:

Koster Dance, Suzanne, *Tommaso Salini: a window into early seicento painting*, dissertation, University of London, Courtauld Institute of Art, 1999. Gregori, Mina/Prinz, Johann Georg, *Stille Welt. Italienische Stilleben aus drei Jahrhunderten*, exhibition catalogue, Kunsthalle der Hypo-Kulturstiftung, Munich, 2003.

Museums and Galleries:

Rome (Church of S Agostino): altar painting - Rome (Church of S Lorenzo in Lucina): altar painting.

Auction records:

Milan, 15 May 1962, *Still-life*, ITL 1,900,000. Milan, 6 April 1965, *Still-life with Fruit; Still-life with Flowers* (two pendants) ITL 6,000,000. New York, 7 June 1978, *Still-life with Flowers and Fruit* (oil on canvas, 28 x 51 1/2in/71 x 131cm) USD 36,000. Milan, 24 Nov 1983, *Still-life* (oil on canvas, 17 1/4 x 31in/44 x 79cm) ITL 36,000,000. London, 31 Oct 1990, *Still-life with Fruit, Vegetables and Game* (oil on canvas, oval, 30 x 27 1/4in/76 x 69cm) GBP 10,450. London, 24 May 1991, *Young Boy astride a Ram with His Dog Running alongside Him in a Wooded Landscape* (oil on canvas, 67 1/4 x 48 1/2in/171 x 123cm) GBP 35,200. New York, 10 Oct 1991, *Education of Jupiter* (oil on canvas, 63 1/4 x 44in/160.7 x 111.8cm) USD 55,000. Paris, 15 Oct 1991, *Young Woman Tying up a Goat* (oil on canvas, 65 x 45 1/4in/165 x 115cm) FRF 360,000. Paris, 15 Oct 1991, *Young Woman Tying Up a Goat* (oil on canvas, 65 x 45 1/4in/165 x 115cm) FRF 360,000. Paris, 20 Dec 1994, *Still-life with Basket of Apples and Pears, Celery and Grapes* (oil on canvas, 19 x 26 1/2in/48 x 67.5cm) FRF 650,000. London, 9 July 1999, *Girl Feeding Cockerels with Cat on Basket, Goose, Duck and Other Birds* (oil on canvas, 48 x 67 ins / 122 x 171 cm) GBP 48,000. Paris, 22 Nov 1999, *Still-life with Asparagus and Cabbages* (oil on canvas, 26 x 38 ins / 67 x 97 cm) FRF 900,000. Venice, 18 Oct 2000, *Still-life with Fruit and Vegetables* (oil on canvas, 37 x 51 ins / 95 x 129 cm) ITL 195,000,000. London, 14 Dec 2000, *Still-life of Fruit in a Straw Basket, with Asparagus, Cardoons and Duck* (oil on canvas, 28 x 38 ins / 71 x 96 cm) GBP 28,000. Milan, 24 March 2001, *Kitchen Interior with Woman Plucking a Cock and Scolding a Young Boy Holding a Kitten* (oil on canvas, 55 x 76 ins / 139 x 194 cm) ITL 105,000,000. Paris, 13 June 2001, *Young Man Preparing Dish of Fruit* (oil on canvas, 45 x 56 ins / 115 x 142 cm) FRF 270,000. Vienna, 2 Oct 2002, *St Roch* (oil on canvas, 43 x 57 ins / 110 x 146 cm) EUR 30,000. Rome, 17 Dec 2003, *Bacchus* (oil on canvas, 39 x 29 ins / 100 x 74 cm) EUR 37,000.

SALINIER, or Salenier

French, 18th century.

Active in Rodez during the second half of the 18th century.

Painter.

Salinier painted 26 portraits of saints in the Franciscan church in Rodez.

SALIOLA, Antonio

Italian, 20th century.

Born 1939, in Bologna.

Painter. Interiors, landscapes.

A self-taught painter, Antonio Saliola also studied law. His works show verdant gardens and the vibrations of light, painted with small and dense touches (*Six O'Clock: Evening Walk in the Kitchen Garden* 1982, *Afternoon Tea* 1991) or childlike visions (*Masters of the Night* 1991). The viewer is drawn into his minutely detailed compositions and their silent, richly harmonious poetic world, where humans are absent but leave behind them traces of their presence in a half-eaten fruit, a bench or a table.

Solo exhibitions of his work have been held in Turin 1970, 1972, 1975, 1976, 1982; Florence 1972, 1978; Padua 1972, 1976; Verona 1972, 1976; Bologna 1973, 1977; Milan 1974, 1980, 1982; Rome 1976; Paris 1978, 1980, 1982; Amsterdam 1978, and in Frankfurt and Hamburg 1981.

Bibliography:

Chalumeau, Jean-Luc (preface), *Antonio Saliola*, exhibition catalogue, Gal. Liliane François, Paris, 1982-1983. *Antonio Saliola*, exhibition catalogue, Gal. Liliane François, Paris, 1991.

Auction records:

Milan, 5 May 1994, *Gates of Paradise* (1989, oil on canvas, 59 x 47 1/4 ins / 150 x 120 cm) ITL 5,175,000. Milan, 21 June 1994, *Love Lesson Among the Roses* (oil on canvas, 59 x 78 3/4 ins / 150 x 200 cm) ITL 9,775,000. Milan, 9 Nov 1999, *Signor Pilot Cycling* (1970, oil on canvas, 39 x 39 ins / 100 x 100 cm) ITL 7,500,000. Florence, 26 Nov 2003, *Park Tales* (1986, oil on canvas, 28 x 24 ins / 70 x 60 cm) EUR 2,000.

SALIS, Carl von. See **SALES**

SALIS, Carlo

Italian, 18th century.

Born 1680, in Verona; died 1763, in Verona.

Painter. History painting.

The pupil of Antonio Balestra and later of Giovanni dal Sole, whose style he adopted, Carlo Salis is noted for an altarpiece in Bergamo depicting *St Vincent Healing a Sick Man*.

SALIS, David

Panamanian, 20th - 21st century.

Born 1953, in Panama.

Also active in France from 1975.

Painter. Landscapes with figures, still-lifes.

David Salis studied at the faculty of architecture and then at the school of visual arts in Panama. He paints in oils but with the fluidity of watercolour. Since 1992 he has taken part in the Panama Painting Biennale and shows regularly at the Berthet-Aittouares gallery. In 1977 he took part in the Salon des Grands et Jeunes d'Aujourd'hui.

SALIS, Pierre de

Swiss, 19th century.

Painter. Landscapes with figures, landscapes.

Museums and Galleries:

Neuchâtel: *End of Winter; End of Autumn*.

Auction records:

Paris, 25 March 1983, *Mountain Path in Winter* (1878, oil on canvas, 32 3/4 x 26 1/2 ins / 83 x 67 cm) FRF 11,000. London, 22 Feb 1995, *Wood Gatherer with his Dog in a Snow-covered Forest* (1878, oil on canvas, 27 1/2 x 23 1/2 ins / 70 x 60 cm) GBP 2,300.

SALIS, Rodolphe

French, 19th century.

Born 1852; died 1897.

Draughtsman, caricaturist.

Rodolphe Salis founded the famous 'Chat Noir' cabaret club in Montmartre, Paris. The self-styled 'gentleman innkeeper' seems to have been a profiteering cafe owner who exploited the talents of his residents, although he did not treat them harshly. However, without his help, quite a few of them would probably never have come to prominence. The club was home to many famous painters and draughtsmen, including Caran d'Ache, Willette, Steinlen, and many others.

SALIS Y CAMINO, José

Spanish, 19th - 20th century.

Born 1 December 1863, in Santoña (Cantabria); died 30 December 1926, in Irún (Basque Country).

Painter. Genre scenes, landscapes, landscapes with figures, seascapes.

José Salis studied in Madrid, then under Van Ammée in Brussels and, from 1886 to 1888, at the Académie Julian in Paris; he settled in the Basque region in or around 1895.

He took part in various collective exhibitions including: National Fine Arts Exhibition in Madrid (1884 to 1926), Saragossa (1885), San Sebastián (1886), Circolo delle Belle Arti, Rome (1887), Brussels (1897), Salon des Artistes Français in Paris on several occasions and especially in 1900 for the Exposition Universelle, Bilbao (1901) and Toulouse (1913). He received a bronze medal in 1885 and honourable mentions in 1895 and 1900. Examples of his work include: *Lolita Reading, Snow in the Garden of Beraun, High Seas, Forest in Winter, Late Spring* and *English Channel*.

BIBLIOGRAPHY:

Arnáiz, José Manuel/López Jiménez, Javier/Merchán Díaz, Manuel (ed.), '*Cien años de pintura en Espana y Portugal (1830-1930)*' in vol. X, Antiqvaria, Madrid, 1993.

SALIS-SOGLIO, Albert

Italian, 20th century.
Born 6 December 1886, in Turin; died 1941
Painter.

Albert Salis-Soglio studied at the academies of Karlsruhe and Munich under Angelo Janck.

SALIS-SOGLIO, Pierre de (Count)

Swiss, 19th century.
Born 22 November 1827, in Neuchâtel; died 1919, in Neuchâtel.
Painter, engraver (etching). Landscapes with figures.

Pierre de Salis-Soglio grew up in England. He studied at the academy in Düsseldorf in 1852 and 1853 under the guidance of the animal painter Friedrich Happel. He was curator of the museum of fine arts in Neuchâtel from 1885.

He painted pictures depicting children, often accompanied by animals. Despite the evident 50 year divergence in their dates of birth, he may have been the same person as Pietro von Salis-Soglio.

MUSEUMS AND GALLERIES:

COIRE: several works - NEUCHÂTEL: several works.

SALIS-SOGLIO, Pietro von

Swiss, 19th - 20th century.
Born 1877, in Coire.
Sculptor, engraver.

SALISBURY, Alda West

American, 20th century.
Born 1879; died 1933.
Painter. Landscapes.

The New Rochelle Art Association was founded in 1912 when a number of artists living in the city met informally in the studio of Alda West Salisbury.

AUCTION RECORDS:

LOS ANGELES-SAN FRANCISCO, 12 July 1990, *Landscape with Eucalyptus Trees* (oil on canvas, 30 x 25 ins / 76 x 63.5 cm) USD 1,430.

SALISBURY, Frank Owen

British, 19th - 20th century.
Born 1874; died 1962.
Painter.

Frank Owen Salisbury was a pupil at the Royal Academy Schools in London.

AUCTION RECORDS:

LONDON, 17 April 1959, *Portrait of Sir Winston Churchill*, GBP 157. LONDON, 1 April 1980, *Eternal Victory* (1915-1917, oil on canvas, 29 1/4 x 24 1/2 ins / 74.5 x 62 cm) GBP 400. LONDON, 11 March 1981, *By the Pond* (1914, oil on canvas, 63 1/2 x 48 1/2 ins / 161 x 123 cm) GBP 1,750. LONDON, 25 Sept 1985, *Benediction at the Coronation of His Majesty King George VI and Her Majesty Queen Elizabeth* (watercolour, charcoal and coloured chalk, 22 1/2 x 42 1/2 ins / 57.1 x 107.9 cm) GBP 1,500. LONDON, 13 Nov 1986, *Portrait of a Mother and Her Daughter* (oil on canvas, round, diam. 47 1/4 ins / 120 cm) GBP 3,800. LONDON, 5 March 1987, *The Field Mice Nutbrown Maidens, the Twins* (1910, oil on canvas, 64 x 49 1/4 ins / 162.5 x 125 cm) GBP 5,500. LONDON, 29 July 1988, *Monsall Dale in Derbyshire* (1933, oil on card, 14 3/4 x 19 3/4 ins / 37.5 x 50 cm) GBP 352. LONDON, 21 Sept 1989, *Iris* (1942, oil on canvas, 35 x 27 ins / 89 x 68.6 cm) GBP 770. LONDON, 30 March 1994, *Field Mouse* (1909, oil on canvas, 63 3/4 x 48 3/4 ins / 162 x 124 cm) GBP 13,800.

SALISBURY, J.

British, 18th century.
Active from 1783 to 1784.
Painter. Portraits.

J. Salisbury exhibited at the Royal Academy in London in 1784.

SALIZE, Karl

Austrian, 19th century.
Born c. 1785; died 24 November 1856, in Vienna.
Portrait artist.

SALKELD, Cecil French

Irish, 20th century.
Born 1908; died 1968.
Painter. Landscapes.

Cecil Salkeld studied art in Germany during the 1920s and 1930s, where was influenced by the work of Otto Dix and the New Objectivity Movement. When he returned to Dublin, he became one of the leading figures in avant-guard Irish art. He exhibited with the Waddington Galleries in 1945.

AUCTION RECORDS:

DUBLIN, 24 Oct 1988, *House near a Lake in a Wood* (oil on card, 16 x 20 ins / 40.7 x 50.7 cm) IEP 880. DUBLIN, 12 Dec 1990, *Old Man Walking along a Road* (1935, oil on canvas, 24 x 18 ins / 61 x 45.7 cm) IEP 380. CASTLECOMER, 9 March 1999, *Glencree, Figures on Road* (oil on canvas on board, 13 x 9 ins / 33 x 24 cm) IEP 1,300. DUBLIN, 31 March 1999, *Music by Moonlight* (oil on canvas, 23 x 18 ins / 58 x 46 cm) IEP 1,600. DUBLIN, 8 May 2002, *Figures in Moonlight* (oil on canvas, 24 x 19 ins / 61 x 47 cm) EUR 3,000. DUBLIN, 19 Nov 2002, *Figure Composition - An Allegory of Temptation* (1923, watercolour, gouache and gold ink, 12 x 9 ins / 30 x 23 cm) EUR 3,600. DUBLIN, 26 March 2003, *Connemara* (oil on board, 15 x 20 ins / 39 x 50 cm) EUR 4,000. DUBLIN, 28 May 2003, *Portrait of a Medical Gentleman* (oil on canvas, 36 x 28 ins / 91 x 71 cm) EUR 3,800.

SALKIN, Emile

Belgian, 20th century.
Born 1900, in St-Gilles (Brussels); died 1977, in Cotignac (Var).
Painter, engraver.

Emile Salkin studied in Paris and went on to teach at and ultimately become principal of the fine arts academy of Anderlecht and the La Cambre college of architecture and the decorative arts in Brussels.

He was an etcher and a dry-point and burin engraver whose painted work progressed from Fauvism to something close to Abstraction. His work betrays an excellent sense of humour, not least with regard to the theme of the automobile which he perceived as a growing menace to city life. He also produced a series of canvases dedicated to the tango entitled *Antigenesis Tango*.

A Salkin retrospective was held in 2002 at the Museum of Modern Art in Ostend.

BIBLIOGRAPHY:

Van den Bussche, W./Nyssen, Hubert, et. al, *Emile Salkin*, exhibition catalogue, PMMK Museum voor Moderne Kunst, Ostend, 2002 (text in Dutch and French).

SALKIN, Fernand or Ferdinand
French, 19th - 20th century.
Born 27 June 1862, in Montélimar; died 1914.
Painter. Landscapes, waterscapes, seascapes.

Fernand Salkin was appointed an official painter to the French navy. He exhibited in Paris at the Salon des Artistes Français, in Aix-en-Provence, Lyons and Brussels. In 1911-1912 a retrospective of his work, entitled *Au pays de Mistral (In the Country of Mistral)*, was held at the Galerie Georges Petit, Paris. He was made an Officier of the Légion d'Honneur. He painted views of French North Africa, but specialised mainly in Provencal landscapes.

AUCTION RECORDS:
PARIS, 23 Dec 1949, *Calvary*, FRF 150. PARIS, 2 July 1951, *Cypress Farm in Sanary*, FRF 1,400. PARIS, 21 Nov 1995, *Sanary* (1901, oil on canvas, 18 x 24 ins / 46 x 61 cm) FRF 4,000.

SALL. See **SAAL**

SALLAERT, Antoine or Anthonis
Flemish School, 17th century.
Born between 1580 and 1585, in Brussels; died 1650.
Painter, engraver. Religious subjects, portraits.

Antoine Sallaert was a pupil of Michel de Bordeaux and, possibly, Rubens. He joined the Brussels guild in 1606, becoming a master in 1613, and Dean from 1633 to 1648. He executed numerous drawings for woodcuts and etchings (these relatively lucrative activities constitute the bulk of his work) and a far smaller number of paintings - regrettably so, since he was by far the most entertaining and instructive painter of daily life in Flanders, especially Brussels, in the early 17th century.

His pictures generally feature a multitude of figures, depicted with great accuracy and humour. His paintings of religious fraternities, such as the *Processions of Notre-Dame des Sablons*, are exemplary in their genre, and quite unlike the drab counterparts of his contemporaries. His good-hearted, cheerful work is too often misinterpreted as a precursor of later Naïve painting; he was, in fact, an artist of considerable sophistication. His lively paintings were executed in response to specific but unsolicited commissions: indeed, Sallaert seems to have eschewed the protectorship of a regular patron.

ANT SALLAERT. A S.AS

MUSEUMS AND GALLERIES:
ANTWERP: *The French Fury* - BRUSSELS: *The Infanta Isabella attending the Grand Sermon in 1615; Procession of the Virgins of the Sablons; Allegory*; a study in pierre d'Italie (black chalk), attributed, preparatory sketch for a figure in the Procession of clergy and religious fraternities - MADRID: *Judgement of Paris* - MADRID (Prado): *Procession of Clergy and Religious Fraternities* - TURIN: *Procession of the Virgins of the Sablons.*

AUCTION RECORDS:
BRUSSELS, 1865, *Portrait of a Young Woman in Black*, FRF 210. PARIS, 1884, *Feast of Our Lord*, FRF 400. LONDON, 1898, *Festive Scene in Tervueren Park, Brussels*, FRF 3,525. MONACO, 2 Dec 1989, *Christ in Glory with Four Saints* (oil on paper/panel, 11½ x 8 ins / 29.5 x 20.5 cm) FRF 21,090. NEW YORK, 23 Jan 2001, *Standing Man Holding a Plumed Hat and Staff* (black chalk, 7 x 4 ins / 19 x 10 cm) USD 1,700. MILAN, 27 March 2002, *Crucifixion* (oil on copper, 11 x 17 ins / 29 x 44 cm) EUR 10,500. NEW YORK, 30 May 2003, *Glorification of the Name of Jesus* (oil on panel, 14 x 10 ins / 36 x 25 cm) USD 14,000.

SALLAERT, Jean Baptiste
Flemish School, 17th century.
Born 1612, in Brussels.
Painter.

Jean-Baptiste Sallaert was the son and, probably, the pupil of Antoine Sallaert. Little is known of his work. He painted a *Beheading of St John the Baptist* for the altar of the parish church at Releghem in 1633.

SALLAH, Alphonse
Togolese, 20th - 21st century.
Born 10 December 1972, in Afagnan.
Painter.

Alphonse Sallah trained with Sallah Mawuto. He paints abstracts, mixing coloured, black, white or green geometric shapes and small scriptural signs. He has taken part in numerous group exhibitions, including 1992, Palais des Congrès, Lomé; 1994, 1996, 2000, International contemporary art encounters, Ewolé, French Cultural Centre, centre Artistik, Lomé; 1999, Salon Grands et Jeunes d'Aujourd'hui, Paris; 2001, *Artistes Togolais d'aujourd'hui. L'École de Lomé (Togolese Artists Today: the Lomé School)*, Espace St-Jean, Melun. He has also had a number of solo exhibitions, such as 1994, Goethe Institut, Lomé; 1998, French Cultural Centre, Lomé, Coco-cocktail, Cotonou (Benin).

BIBLIOGRAPHY:
Persin, Patrick-Gilles, *L'École de Lomé. Artistes togolais d'aujourd'hui*, exhibition catalogue, Association Grands et Jeunes d'Aujourd'hui, Paris, 2001.

SALLAÏ, Andrea. See **SALAI**

SALLAN, Serge
French, 20th - 21st century.
Born 1951.
Sculptor (mainly marble).

Serge Sallan sculpts predominantly in marble. He produced a monumental work for the town of Théoule-sur-Mer in 1988, and another for the Bouches-du-Rhône Regional Council in 1990. Sallan has taken part in a number of group exhibitions, among them the exhibition held in 1982-1983 at the Centre National d'Art Contemporain in Paris. He exhibits solo on a regular basis in Toulouse.

AUCTION RECORDS:
PARIS, 28 Oct 1990, *Bird* (sculpture in Hérault marble, h. 9 ins / 23 cm, l. 22½ ins/57 cm, w. 9 ins/23 cm) FRF 9,000. PARIS, 17 Dec 1990, *Sandstorm* (1987, carved directly in pink marble, h. 25½ ins / 65 cm) FRF 8,000. PARIS, 4 Feb 1991, *Apostacy* (marble, 35¾ x 13 x 11 ins / 91 x 33 x 27 cm) FRF 8,000. PARIS, 3 June 1991, *Profile* (pink marble, 22 x 12½ x 11 ins / 55 x 32 x 28 cm) FRF 9,500. PARIS, 18 May 1992, *Sensation* (1992, Arguenos marble, 14½ x 9¾ x 9½ ins / 37 x 25 x 24 cm) FRF 6,000. PARIS, 5 Oct 1992, *Ino* (Pyrenean marble, 22 x 9 x 8¼ ins / 56 x 22 x 21 cm) FRF 8,500.

SALLANDRA
Italian, 18th century.
Active in Castelli.
Painter (majolica).

SALLANTIN, Marie
French, 20th - 21st century.
Born 1946, in Paris.
Painter.

Marie Sallantin studied under Jean Bertholle at the École des Beaux-Arts in Paris. In 1984, she was awarded a FIACRE scholarship. She started out as an abstract painter but figures started to appear in her work from the late 1990s, together with masks, individual words, and allusions to Matisse, Picasso and Gauguin. Sallantin works under a number of self-imposed constraints, using a finite number of 'acceptable' colours. She is noted for her *Metamorphoses* series, which features compositions painted predominantly in black, white and ochre.

She has shown examples of her work at various group exhibitions: in 1979, at the Maison des Beaux-Arts in Paris; in

1984 and 1986, at the Salon de Montrouge; in 1984, at the International Festival in Cagnes-sur-Mer; and, in 1987, at the Salon de la Jeune Peinture and the Salon des Réalités Nouvelles in Paris. She has exhibited solo on a number of occasions, including in 1981 in Rheims and, as of 1983, on a regular basis in Paris, notably at the Galerie Nicole Ferry (since 1988).

BIBLIOGRAPHY:
Marie Sallantin, exhibition catalogue, Gal. Nicole Ferry, Paris, 1988. Chalumeau, Jean-Luc, ''*Marie Sallantin, les métamorphoses*' in *Opus international* n° 106, periodical, Paris, January-February 1988. Debecque-Michel, Laurence, ''*Marie Sallantin - Des masques pour démasquer la forme*' in *Opus international* n° 118, periodical, Paris, March-April 1990.

MUSEUMS AND GALLERIES:
PARIS (FNAC).

SALLARD, Annie

French, 20th century.
Born 23 April 1935, in Paris.
Painter, draughtsman. Figures, nudes, interiors with figures, still-lifes.

Annie Sallard, who lives and works in Paris, has exhibited at the Salon de la Société Nationale des Beaux-Arts, the Salon d'Automne, and the Salon des Independents. She has held solo shows in Paris since 1953, including 1968, the Galerie St-Placide; 1977, Le Carré d'Art; 1979, La Touriale; 1985, the Galerie Jean André, and, 1988, the Galerie Étienne de Causans.

She draws and paints a silent world (an urban landscape, a nude in an interior, glasses on a table (catching the permanence of situations with restraint, but acuteness.

SALLBERG, Harald

Swedish, 20th century.
Born 1895; died 1963.
Painter. Landscapes.

AUCTION RECORDS:
STOCKHOLM, 6 June 1988, *View of Stockholm and the Riddarholm Church* (1935, oil, 14 1/2 x 17 3/4 ins / 37 x 45 cm) SEK 4,700. STOCKHOLM, 3 Dec 2002, *View towards Kungsholmen from Langholmen* (1907, oil on canvas, 19 x 24 ins / 49 x 62 cm) SEK 14,500.

SALLE, Abraham

French, 17th century.
Active during the first half of the 17th century.
Sculptor.

Abraham Salle sculpted the statues of *Henry IV* and *Marie de' Medici* for the chapel of the Hôpital St-Louis in Paris.

SALLE, Adelin

Belgian, 20th century.
Born 21 April 1884, in Liège.
Sculptor. Statues.

Adelin Salle sculpted pieces for churches and public buildings in his native Liège.

MUSEUMS AND GALLERIES:
LIÈGE.

SALLE, Anatole

French, 19th century.
Painter. Genre scenes.

He was a pupil of Manet. His most famous work, *Father Jean*, was shown at the Salon of 1886.

SALLÉ, André Augustin

French, 20th century.
Born 9 September 1891, in Longueau (Somme).
Sculptor.

André Augustin Sallé, a pupil of Jules F. Coutan and Auguste H. Carli, exhibited from 1923 at the Salon des Artistes Français, of which he was a member. He was awarded a bronze medal in 1923, the Prix de Rome in 1924, and a silver medal in 1931.

SALLE, David

American, 20th - 21st century.
Born 28 September 1952, in Norman (Oklahoma).
Painter (including mixed media), watercolourist, collage artist, draughtsman. Figures, nudes. Stage sets.
Bad Painting, Neo-Conceptual Art, Appropriation Art.

David Salle studied at the California Institute of the Arts in Valencia, California, where he was taught by John Baldessari. He worked on the American magazine *Stag*. He appeared on the New York scene in the1980s, with what was, considering the forms of expression of the time, a traditional approach in his paintings on canvas, borrowing iconography from a variety of periods from Flemish painting to Abstraction. He was easily identifiable from his divided-up composition, avoiding perspective, which quickly brought him success. The predominantly dark shades, with artificial colours, are reminiscent of photography, a medium which inspired him in the early days of his career and which he also practices. Works mainly playing with the effects of superimposition and transparency. In his large-format works, usually diptychs and triptychs, he alternates figurative and geometric or gestural abstract areas, and monochrome and polychrome fields. Images of different scales are placed side-by-side or juxtaposed one within another. Each image is 'contained' within the classic frame of the painting - a square, rectangular or oval format, with a generally neutral background. It then becomes one of the components of a strict abstract structure, combining abstract forms, and resembles the work of someone like Hans Hoffman. This composition also bestows a very strong autonomy on each 'component' while revealing the ambiguity of the images brought in contact with each other.

In Salle's works two distinct types of iconographic references continually confront each other: firstly art itself and secondly the media society symbolised by stereotypical images taken from magazines, film, comic strips or advertising. Artistic references include reproductions of pictures figurative compositions such as still-lifes and landscapes o abstract paintings, by Hobbema, Watteau, Géricault, Manet, Picabia, Picasso, de Kooning, Rauschenberg, Rosenquist (as in the 1993 series *Pre-Fab*), Johns, Polke, Warho (with *Ghost Paintings*, 1992) or of sculptures, primitiv works or artists like Giacometti. Borrowings from the media, especially the erotic press, include the recurrent imag of the stylised woman, particularly her legs and breasts, a an object of desire 'ready to be consumed' which he interprets personally alongside references to everyday life, suc as furniture (a chair) (*Marking through Weber*, 1987) an decoration (vases), pets (a dog), food (bread in *Yellow Brea* 1987), fish or vignettes of comic strips. Salle freely associate images and sometimes incorporates words and fragmen of texts or mixes styles. He also uses a reduced palette, ofte predominately ochre and grey, but few pure colours, preferring the black and white photography technique of matching tones, sepia and grey. He photographs bodies, usin models, like Karol Armitage, whom he shows in often ve unnatural poses - far from conventional pornography. H continues these clichés in painting and grisalle, emphasisin brush strokes and thus showing his distance from Hyperr alism, and the exact vision of reality with which he operate Sexual violence emanates from his female nudes who powerful contours are counterbalanced by the predom nantly faded greyish tint that lends a certain 'neutrality' the whole work.

In a baroque vein Salle 'composes' with the technique o musician and plays with the effects of rhythm, alternati the steady state and movement, the calmness off a still-l and the violence of a naked body. He plays with eclecticis and invites the eye to wander over the huge canvas and breach the frontiers of this carefully cloistered world, where each component retains its identity. The work cannot be understood as a whole, and created as it is from free association, it appears elusive with no possible links.

Collective exhibitions include the Nouvelle Biennale de Paris, 1985. Solo exhibitions include: Fondation de Corps de Garde, Groningen, Netherlands, 1976-1980; De Apple Foundation, Amsterdam, 1977 and 1980; Mary Boone Gallery, New York, regularly from 1981; Museum Boymans Van Beuningen, Rotterdam, 1983; Galerie Michael Werner, Cologne, regularly from 1985; Galerie Daniel Templon, Paris, 1985 to 1993; Museum of Contemporary Art, Chicago, 1985; Museum am Ostwall, Dortmund, Institute of Contemporary Art, University of Pennsylvania, Philadelphia, 1986; Caja de Pensiones, Madrid, 1988; Galerie Thaddeus Ropac, Paris, 1996; and a retrospective at the Stedelijk Museum, Amsterdam, 1997.

D.S. 87

Bibliography:

David Salle, Works on Paper, exhibition catalogue, Museum am Ostwall, Dortmund, Institute of Contemporary Art, Boston, 1986. Kardon, J./Phillips, L., *David Salle*, exhibition catalogue, Institute of Contemporary Art, University of PA, Philadelphia; Whitney Gallery, New York; Museum of Contemporary Art, Los Angeles; and elsewhere, 1986-1988. *David Salle*, Vintage Books, New York, 1987 (illustrated book). Vaudey, Marc, *'De l'ironie, d'une rhétorique neutre, inquiétante et familière: David Salle'* in *Artstudio* n° 11, periodical, Gal. Templon, Paris, winter 1988. *David Salle*, exhibition catalogue, Fund. Caja Pensiones, Madrid, 1988 (essays by K. Power and C. Schulz-Hoffmann). Millet, Catherine, *'Interview: David Salle entre composition et désignation'* in *Art Press* n° 129, periodical, Paris, October 1988. Jouannais, Jean-Yves, *'David Salle'* in *Art Press* n° 171, periodical, Paris, July-August 1992. Liebmann, Lisa, *David Salle*, Rizzoli, New York, 1994. Cortez, David, *David Salle: Early Product Paintings*, exhibition catalogue, Gagosian Gallery, New York, 1994. *David Salle: Pastoral*, exhibition catalogue, Gagosian Gallery, New York, 2001.

Museums and Galleries:

Los Angeles (MCA): *Brother Animal* (1983) - Paris (MNAM-CCI): *Blue Paper* (1986) - Richmond (Virginia MFA): *Good Bye D* (1982, acrylic/canvas).

Auction records:

New York, 12 Nov 1982, *Untitled* (1981, acrylic/paper, 60 x 42 ins / 152.5 x 106.5 cm) USD 4,000. New York, 9 May 1984, *The Name Painting* (1982, acrylic and oil on canvas, 98 x 196 ins / 249 x 497.8 cm) USD 22,000. New York, 1 Nov 1984, *Untitled* (1983, watercolour, 18 x 24 ins / 46 x 61 cm) USD 6,000. New York, 2 Nov 1984, *Untitled (airplane and nude)* (1978, coloured chalk and graphite, 22 x 30 ins / 56 x 76 cm) USD 4,200. New York, 2 May 1985, *Untitled* (1978, coloured chalk and graphite, 29 1/2 x 41 1/2 ins / 75 x 105.5 cm) USD 2,200. New York, 22 Feb 1986, *Untitled* (1978, pastel/paper, 29 1/2 x 41 1/4 ins / 74.9 x 104.8 cm) USD 4,000. New York, 5 Nov 1987, *How Close the Ass of a Horse Was to Actual Glue and Dog Food* (1980, acrylic and pencil/canvas, 72 1/4 x 48 ins / 183.2 x 121.9 cm) USD 57,000. New York, 8 Oct 1988, *Ordinary Sentences* (1982, oil on canvas, 96 x 56 ins / 243.8 x 142.3 cm) USD 66,000. New York, 3 May 1989, *Shirts* (1984, collage of material and oil on canvas, 52 x 72 ins / 132 x 183 cm) USD 66,000. New York, 5 Oct 1989, *In the Documentary Style* (1981, acrylic collage and charcoal /canvas, 86 x 100 1/2 ins / 218.5 x 255 cm) USD 77,000. New York, 7 Nov 1989, *Tennyson* (1983, oil, acrylic and wood, 78 x 117 1/4 x 5 1/2 ins / 198 x 298 x 14 cm) USD 550,000. New York, 5 Oct 1990, *Never the Instruments of Love* (1979, acrylic/canvas, 42 x 58 ins / 106.7 x 147.3 cm) USD 33,000. New York, 1 May 1991, *In the Bar* (1989, acrylic and oil on canvas, 100 x 130 ins / 254 x 330.2 cm) USD 8,525. Paris, 15 Dec 1991, *Untitled* (1987, watercolour/paper, 23 1/4 x 30 1/4 ins / 59 x 77 cm) FRF 55,000. New York, 7 May 1992, *Embarrassing Page* (1984, acrylic, sacking and oil on canvas with wooden objects, 84 1/4 x 100 1/4 ins / 214 x 254.6 cm) USD 143,000. New York, 17 Nov 1992, *Poverty Is No Disgrace* (acrylic, chair and oil on canvas, in three panels, 98 x 205 ins / 248.9 x 520.7 cm) USD 104,500. New York, 3 May 1993, *By Chance I Missed my Cousin Jasper* (1980, acrylic/canvas, two panels, 48 x 72 ins / 121.9 x 182.9 cm) USD 107,000. New York, 16 Nov 1995, *Untitled* (1989, acrylic and oil on canvas, 78 x 48 ins / 198.1 x 121.9 cm) USD 34,500. London, 30 Nov 1995, *False Queen* (1992, felt hat, acrylic and oil on canvas, 96 x 72 ins / 244 x 183 cm) GBP 51,000. New York, 9 May 1996, *An Illustrator was There* (acrylic/canvas, 84 x 60 ins / 213.4 x 152.4 cm) USD 68,500. New York, 19 Nov 1996, *Untitled* (1978, graphite and oil on canvas, 34 x 50 ins / 86.3 x 127 cm) USD 9,200. New York, 20 Nov 1996, *Acrobat* (1988, acrylic/canvas, 78 x 192 ins / 198.2 x 487.6 cm) USD 189,500. New York, 6 May 1997, *Untitled* (1982, brush and black ink/paper, 27 1/2 x 39 1/4 ins / 70 x 100 cm) USD 6,325. New York, 8 May 1997, *Entertainers* (1986, two acrylic and oil on canvas, 60 x 100 ins / 152.3 x 254 cm) USD 57,500. London, 23 Oct 1997, *Don't Go Home* (1988, oil and acrylic/canvas, 41 3/4 x 61 ins / 106 x 155 cm) GBP 19,550. New York, 19 May 1999, *Couple of Centuries* (1982, oil and acrylic on canvas, diptych, 110 x 160 ins / 279 x 407 cm) USD 70,000. New York, 19 May 1999, *Lola Remake* (1993, oil and acrylic on canvas, 102 x 122 ins / 260 x 311 cm) USD 80,000. New York, 17 May 2000, *Skintight Worldwide* (1983, oil and acrylic on canvas, 88 x 113 ins / 224 x 288 cm) USD 210,000. New York, 18 May 2000, *Maid of Germany* (acrylic on fabric canvas on wood, diptych, 108 x 148 ins / 274 x 376 cm) USD 130,000. New York, 17 May 2001, *An Agreement* (acrylic, oil and graphite on canvas with candle wax, 66 x 90 ins / 168 x 229 cm) USD 150,000. New York, 15 Nov 2001, *Young Krainer* (1989, oil and acrylic on canvas with three inserts, 84 x 85 ins / 213 x 216 cm) USD 80,000. New York, 16 May 2002, *Untitled* (1981, acrylic on canvas, two parts, 70 x 127 ins / 178 x 323 cm) USD 50,000. New York, 16 May 2002, *Lazy Outer Rings* (1984, oil and acrylic fabric on canvas, 52 x 75 ins / 132 x 190 cm) USD 80,000. New York, 15 May 2003, *Making the Bed* (oil, acrylic and wood on canvas, diptych, 120 x 94 ins / 305 x 239 cm) USD 80,000. New York, 13 Nov 2003, *Smells Burns is Vacant* (oil and acrylic on canvas, 66 x 92 ins / 168 x 234 cm) USD 42,500. New York, 13 May 2004, *We Back Them Up* (1979, acrylic and charcoal on canvas, 40 x 58 ins / 102 x 147 cm) USD 60,000. Paris, 18 July 2004, *Flagrant Eyeball* (1987, acrylic, charcoal and oil on canvas, 52 x 106 ins / 132 x 268 cm) EUR 65,000.

SALLE, François

French, 17th - 18th century.

Active in Le Mans.

Sculptor.

François Salle sculpted statues for Mareschė, Assé and Lude churches, from 1696 to 1725.

SALLÉ, François, for François Antoine, or

Sallé de Chou

French, 19th century.

Born 27 May 1859, in Bourges; died March 1929, in Lyons.

Painter. Figure compositions, landscapes.

François Sallé had an honorific title as a baron of the Empire but rarely used the part of his name 'de Chou'. He was a pupil of Luminair and lived and worked mainly in Bourges but also in Paris where he owned an apartment. He went to Algeria in 1895. He was a society member of the Salon des Artistes Françaises, in Paris, in the last fifteen years of the

19th century. His *Anatomy Lesson at l'École des Beaux-Arts de Paris* won him a third class medal. Among his other works exhibited at the Salon were *Plain-Chant; Le Pressoir* (*Wine Press*); *Arius at the Council of Nicea; 'Alerte'* (*'Warning'*); *Entry to the Arab Cemetery; Pines; Pigeons; Pond of Saint-Bonnet-le-Desert*

Museums and Galleries:
Bourges: *Pond of Saint-Bonnet-le-Desert; Forest of Troncais, Allier* - Sydney: *Anatomy Lesson at the École des Beaux-Arts de Paris.*

SALLÉ, Henri
French, 17th century.
Active in Amiens during the first half of the 17th century.
Sculptor (wood).

Sallé sculpted a rood screen for Corbie abbey and St-Michel altar in Amiens Cathedral.

SALLE, Jacques
French, 17th century.
Active in Paris at the beginning of the 17th century.
Sculptor.

Jacques Salle worked at the Louvre in Paris, in 1604.

SALLE, Modeste Joseph de
Dutch, 19th century.
Born 7 September 1826, in The Hague; died 17 February 1877, in 's Hertogenbosch.
Painter. Portraits, still-lifes.

Modest de Salle was a pupil of Van den Berg at the academy of The Hague, and also studied under Schmidt, in Delft, in 1845. He was active in Rotterdam in 1850, where he pursued an unsuccessful career as a portrait-painter. He eventually settled in Amsterdam, as a hotelier.

Auction records:
Amsterdam, 16 March 1976, *Still-life with Fruit* (oil on canvas, 41¼ x 32¾ ins / 104.5 x 83 cm) NLG 4,400.

SALLE, Pierre
French, 17th century.
Sculptor. Religious subjects.

Pierre Salle sculpted *Transfiguration* in wood, around 1600, for St-Étienne chapel in Amiens Cathedral.

SALLÉ, Pierre
French, 19th century.
Born 10 May 1835, in Bordeaux; died 1899, in Lyons.
Painter. Portraits, genre scenes, landscapes.

Pierre Sallé was a pupil of Claude Bonnefond at the École des Beaux-Arts in Lyons, then of Hippolyte Flandrin at the École des Beaux-Arts in Paris. He exhibited at the Lyons Salon from 1861 to 1899, at the Paris Salon from 1864 onward, then finally at the Salon of the Société des Artistes Français, where he was made a life member.

Museums and Galleries:
Lyons (MBA): *Portrait of a Woman.*

SALLÉ, Sébastien Eugène
French, 19th century.
Born 29 February 1812, in Metz.
Active in Paris.
Engraver (burin).

SALLÉ DE CHOU, François
French, 19th century.
Painter. Landscapes.

This artist appears to have been a relative of François Sallé, or they may even have been one and the same person.

Museums and Galleries:
Bourges: *Pond at St-Bonnet Le Désert; Forest of Tronçais, Allier.*

SALLEMBIER, Henri, or Salembier or Sallambier
French, 18th - 19th century.
Born c. 1753, in Paris; died 1 October 1820, in Paris.
Draughtsman (including red chalk), watercolourist, engraver. Architectural views. Ornaments, decorative panels.

Sallembier's drawings and ornaments exerted a considerable influence over the style of the period of Louis XVI.

Museums and Galleries:
Amsterdam: *Two Façades of a Princely Palace.*

Auction records:
Paris, 1888, *Arabesques with Figures of Women and Cupids* (pen, Indian ink wash and watercolour) FRF 206. Paris, 1896, *Large Vase* (pen and watercolour) FRF 200; *Ceiling Design* (pen and sepia) FRF 160. Paris, 21-22 Feb 1919, *Stairway in the Ruins; Small Monument* (two drawings in red chalk) FRF 250. Paris, 31 May 1920, *Chalice Design* (pen) FRF 85. Paris, 22 March 1928, *River Bank with an Old Willow Tree* (black chalk heightened) FRF 600. Paris, 10-11 April 1929, *Window* (pen) FRF 1,550. Paris, 30 June and 1 July 1941, *Tight-rope Walker* (decorative panel, attributed) FRF 210. Paris, 21-22 Feb 1945, *Paris and Helen* (Series of three decorative compositions) FRF 40,000; *Cupid and Psyche,* FRF 42,000; *Cupid Crowning Psyche,* FRF 30,000. Paris, 12 May 1950, *Meeting; Crowning; Kiss* (series of three compositions, attributed) FRF 56,000. Paris, 14 June 1950, *Décoration à Personnages, Volatiles et Rinceaux* (*Decoration with People, Winged Creatures and Foliage*) (series of ten panels from the end of the 18th century, after Henri Sallembier) FRF 75,000. Paris, 11 April 1951, *Sketches of Decorations with Garlands of Flowers* (matching pair, attributed) FRF 30,000. Monte Carlo, 26 Nov 1979, *Grand Trophée de Vases* (*Large Trophy of Vases*) (pen and wash/three sheets, 21 x 43 ins / 52.5 x 109 cm) FRF 45,000.

SALLÈS, André Pierre. See **SALES**

SALLES, Francis
French, 20th century.
Born 12 August 1926, in St-Maur-des-Fossés.
Painter. Figures, still-lifes.

Francis Salles began to study at the École du Louvre in 1945, but in 1947 he became an actor and worked in films and on the stage. It was not until 1953 that he finally decided to become a painter. In 1956 the critic Michel Tapié included him in the group of painters he supported. He lived and worked in the USA during 1962.

From 1953 to 1957 he painted abstracts based on the clash of pure colour. Without any transition period, he decided to abandon his success in this style and turned to the figurative painting that had already been heralded by the CoBrA painters and was soon to be confirmed by Nouvelles Figurations. He painted only a few works each year and returned to the same figures again and again: speechless puppets, pitiful clowns, their faces streaked with dirty black and pallid white like circus clowns, their highly-coloured costumes crying out in contrast with their smeared features: *Fantasy Figure, Agamemnon, Clytemnestra, The Fly, The Widow.* Salles belongs to the school of the absurd and anguish, and says that not only are his figures mad, but that he himself is.

His exaggerated distortions, the faces eaten away, the manipulated paint, and the cruel clash of impossible colours place Francis Salles (with Goya and Soutine) among the Expressionists - as, indeed, he admits.

Group exhibitions in which Salles participated include: 1956 Paris, *À propos Hultberg, Moreni, Salles* (*Hultberg, Moreni, Salles*), Galerie Rive Droite; 1957 New York, *Incantations,* Kootz Gallery; 1959 Vienna, *Junge Maler der Gegenwart* (*Young Painters of Today*); 1960 Paris, *Antagonismes* (*Antagonisms*), Musée des Arts Décoratifs, and Washington, *New Trends in French Painting by Julien Alvard,* Franz Bader Gallery; 1961 Basel, *The Dotremont Collection,* Kunsthalle; 1962 Paris, *Une nouvelle figuration* (*New Figuration*), Galerie

Mathias Fels, among others. He held solo shows in: 1965 Paris, Galerie Europe; 1976 Paris, Galerie Ariel; 1989 Paris, Galerie J. Barbier, C. Beltz.

F. Salles

BIBLIOGRAPHY:
Alvard, Julien/Ashbery, John, *Francis Salles*, exhibition catalogue, Gal. Europe, Paris, 1965. Boudaille, Georges, *Francis Salles: un cri silencieux*, exhibition catalogue, Gal. Ariel, Paris, 1976. Beltz, Caroline, "*Francis Salles*' in *Cimaise* no. 198, periodical, Paris, January-February 1989.

AUCTION RECORDS:
PARIS, 10 April 1992, *Composition* (1952, oil on canvas, 51 1/4 x 35 ins / 130 x 89 cm) FRF 8,000. PARIS, 28 June 1994, *Mask* (1984, oil on canvas, 39 1/4 x 32 ins / 100 x 81 cm) FRF 6,000. PARIS, 17 May 1995, *Woman Wearing a Pink Hat* (oil on canvas, 51 1/4 x 38 1/4 ins / 130 x 97 cm) FRF 4,200. PARIS, 19 Nov 1995, *Still-life* (1961, oil on canvas, 39 1/4 x 32 ins / 100 x 81 cm) FRF 4,000. PARIS, 20 March 1998, *Sketch for the Destruction of Sodom* (1957, oil on canvas, 39 1/4 x 31 1/2 ins / 100 x 80 cm) FRF 3,200.

SALLES, José Vicente
Portuguese, 19th century.
Active in Lisbon.
Engraver (burin).

José Vicente Salles was a pupil of G.F. de Queiroz and continued his studies in Paris.

SALLES, Jules, or Salles-Wagner
French, 19th century.
Born 14 June 1814, in Nîmes; died 1898 or 1900, in Nîmes.
Painter. History painting, genre scenes, figures, portraits.

After embarking upon a commercial career in the silk industry, Jules Salle-Wagner entered the École des Beaux-Arts in Nîmes, where he became a pupil of Numa Boucoiran. He then went to Paris and studied under Paul Delaroche. He visited the museums of Venice, Rome and Naples, and returned there many times. He was widowed in 1859, then married the painter Adélaïde Wagner in around 1865. It is worth noting that he added his wife's patronymic name to his own. His wife was a more established artist than he, and he admired her talent - something that spurred him on in his own work. The couple were heavily involved in the Paris art scene, and for a time lived in the apartment-cum-studio previously occupied by Édouard Detaille. In 1890 Salles was widowed again, left Paris and returned to Nîmes. He bequeathed around a hundred of his wife's paintings and watercolours to the Musée de Nîmes, along with about twenty of his own. He had always played an active part in the cultural life of the town and in 1894 opened an art gallery there, which he named after himself. The gallery has since become an extremely popular cultural attraction.

His first exhibition was in Nîmes, in 1841. He debuted at the Paris Salon in 1859. In 1983 the Musée de Nîmes organised a comprehensive retrospective exhibition of his work.

Although he painted very few landscapes, he would regularly sketch those that caught his eye during his travels around Italy, in pencil or charcoal, with precision and sensitivity. Since Paul Delaroche was his teacher, his work is characterised by the influence of Ingres, and by references to Raphael - particularly his genre scenes, which were popular during this period. They offer a form of idealised realism underpinned by a moral, as can be seen in *Perrette and the Milk Pail* and *Lyther with his Family*. He was particularly fond of painting young Italian peasant women, and women either engaged in their daily activities, or simply daydreaming.

MUSEUMS AND GALLERIES:
BAGNOLS: *A Guide to Eaux-Bonnes* - CARPENTRAS: *Young Girl with Fruit* - LA ROCHELLE: *Waiting* - NÎMES: *The Signal: Young Girl from Capri* (c. 1885); *Self-portrait; Meeting between Jean Cavalier and Marshal de Villard*; other works - SÈTE: *Coming out of Church*.

AUCTION RECORDS:
PARIS, 14 Feb 1949, *The Young Romantic* (1856) FRF 1,500. VIENNA, 19 Sept 1972, *Portrait of a Young Woman*, ATS 25,000. PARIS, 28 June 1991, *Young Girl at the Spinning Wheel* (oil on canvas, 29 1/4 x 21 1/4 ins / 74 x 54 cm) FRF 8,500. PARIS, 27 Nov 1991, *Woman Bathing in a Park* (1851, oil on card, 12 3/4 x 9 1/2 ins / 32.5 x 24 cm) FRF 3,900. NEW YORK, 23 Oct 1997, *Young Mother* (oil on canvas, 45 x 36 ins / 114.6 x 91.4 cm) USD 20,700.

SALLES, Léon Auguste
French, 19th - 20th century.
Born 31 December 1868, in Paris.
Painter, engraver.

Léon Auguste Salles, a pupil of Auguste Boulard, exhibited in Paris at the Salon des Artistes Français, of which he was a member from 1893 and where he was awarded an honourable mention in 1894, a third-class medal in 1896, a bronze medal at the Exposition Universelle of 1900, and a second class medal in 1902. He was out-of-competition and a member of the engraving jury, and was made a Chevalier of the Légion d'Honneur. He engraved etchings.

SALLES, Manuel Germano
Portuguese, 19th - 20th century.
Born in Lisbon.
Sculptor.

Manuel Germano Salles received an honourable mention at the 1908 Salon des Artistes Français in Paris.

SALLÈS, Pierre-Alexandre
French, 19th - 20th century.
Born 1867, in St-Denis-du-Sig (Algeria); died 1915, in Algiers.
Painter.
School of Algiers.

Pierre-Alexandre Sallès featured in *L'École d'Alger* (*The School of Algiers*), Musée des Beaux-Arts, Bordeaux (2003).

BIBLIOGRAPHY:
Cazenave, Elisabeth/Dalia, Mahammed-Orfali/Vidal-Bué, Marion, *L'École d'Alger*, exhibition catalogue, Musée des Beaux-Arts, Bordeaux, 2003.

MUSEUMS AND GALLERIES:
ALGIERS (Mus. National des Beaux-Arts).

SALLES, Robert
French, 19th - 20th century.
Born 17 May 1871, in Lisieux; died 21 November 1929.
Painter. Historical subjects, figures, portraits, scenes with figures, genre scenes, urban landscapes.

Robert Salles, a pupil of Alexandre Cabanel at the École des Beaux-Arts, exhibited in Paris at the Salon des Artistes Français from 1907, where in that year he was awarded a third-class medal and the Maguelone Lefebvre-Glaize prize, and in 1921 an out-of-competition medal.

MUSEUMS AND GALLERIES:
LISIEUX: *Lisieux during the Plague of 1630; Portrait of the First Principal of the Lisieux College*.

AUCTION RECORDS:
SEMUR-EN-AUXOIS, 29 Jan 1984, *Woman Wearing Breton Head-dress* (oil on canvas, 25 1/2 x 21 1/4 ins / 65 x 54 cm) FRF 13,000. PARIS, 8 April 1993, *Portrait of a Seated Man* (1893, oil on canvas/panel, 18 x 14 3/4 ins / 46 x 37.5 cm) FRF 4,800.

SALLES-WAGNER, Adelaïde
Maiden name: Wagner
German, 19th century.

Born 1825, in Dresden; died 2 July 1890, in Paris.
Active in France.
Painter. History painting, religious subjects, mythological subjects, allegorical subjects, portraits, genre scenes.

Adelaïde Salles-Wagner was the sister of the painter Puyroche-Wagner. She was a pupil of Claude Jacquand in Lyons and of Joseph Bernhardt either during her stay in Paris or at his school in Munich. She went to work in Paris and married Jules Salles, dividing her life between Nîmes and Paris. From 1866 she exhibited at the Paris Salon, in 1873 in Vienna, and in 1879 in Munich.

She painted the subjects of her compositions with an assured, unequivocal touch, against backgrounds that offered a discrete setting.

Museums and Galleries:
Brest: *Truth Inveigled by Falsehood* - Castres: *The Fates* - Lyons (MBA): *Elijah in the Desert* - Narbonne: *Addio Teresa* - Rheims: *Reading Lesson* - Sète: *Pifferaro* - Toulon: *St Magdalene Cradled by Angels*.

Auction records:
Brussels, 24 March 1976, *Two Destitute Girls* (oil on canvas, 53¾ x 37½ ins / 134 x 95 cm) BEF 40,000.

SALLET, Jacques
French, 20th century.
Born 23 April 1938, in Neuilly-sur-Seine.
Painter. Landscapes, still-lifes, flowers.

From 1960 to 1966 Jacques Sallet was a pupil of Raymond Legueult and Jean Aujame at the École des Beaux-Arts, Paris, where he was an entrant for the Prix de Rome in 1964 and graduated in 1966. He constructs his landscapes and still-lifes in receding planes of wide, flat, delicate and transparent colour. He has spent several periods in the USA, and took part in a number of group exhibitions, including 1965 the Salon d'Automne, Paris, 1967 the Salon d'Avignon, and various exhibitions in the provinces and New York. He has held solo shows, mainly in alternative venues such as banks and hotels, and in New York in 1972 and 1977.

SALLGE, Andres. See **SALGEN**

SALLHER, Franz
Austrian, 18th century.
Active in Schlierbach c. 1750.
Sculptor (wood).

Franz Sallher was a member of the Cistercian order. He sculpted stalls and cupboards in the church of Schlierbach.

SALLI, Gabriele. See **SALCI**

SALLIETH, Mathias de
Austrian, 18th century.
Born 1749, in Prague; died 1791, in Rotterdam.
Engraver (burin). Landscapes with figures, naval battles.

Mathias de Sallieth was a pupil of J. E. Mansfeld in Vienna and of J. P. Le Bas in Paris. He lived in Rotterdam from 1778. He worked most notably on the *Picturesque Tour of Greece* by Choiseul-Gouffier, the *Picturesque Tour of France* and the *Lebrun Gallery*. He engraved numerous subjects of naval battles.

SALLIG, Andres. See **SALGEN**

SALLINEN, Tyko Konstantin
Finnish, 19th - 20th century.
Born 14 March 1879, in Nurmes; died 18 September 1955.
Painter. Local figures, nudes, portraits, scenes with figures, landscapes.
November Group.

Tyko Konstantin Sallinen was educated in Helsinki and Paris. He came to recognition prior to 1918 with a composition entitled *Little Country Tailor*, and followed this in 1918 with painting destined for the Hihulite religious sect. Salliner art is populist and violent, with a pronounced social conte

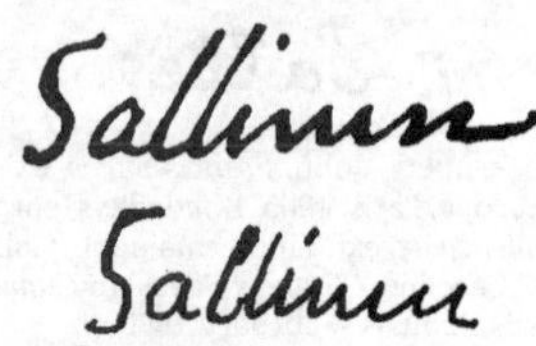

Museums and Galleries:
Copenhagen - Göteborg - Hamburg - Helsinki: *Nude*; *Po trait of the Artist*; several landscapes - Stockholm.

Auction records:
Stockholm, 14 Nov 1990, *Landscape with Small Village or Hillside* (oil on canvas, 18 x 23¼ ins / 46 x 59 cm) SEK 35,00 Stockholm, 10-12 May 1993, *Environs of Cagnes* (1920, on canvas, 22 x 18 ins / 56 x 46 cm) SEK 72,000. Helsinki, April 1999, *From Terhila* (1925, oil on canvas, 20 x 24 ins / x 61 cm) FIM 21,000. Stockholm, 26 May 1999, *Old Cagn* (1920, oil on canvas, 22 x 18 ins / 56 x 46 cm) SEK 128,00 Helsinki, 6 May 2000, *Landscape from Valamo* (1924, oil canvas, 22 x 18 ins / 57 x 46 cm) FIM 48,000. Helsinki, 3 D 2000, *Landscape* (1919, oil on canvas, 18 x 20 ins / 45 x 50 c FIM 25,000. Helsinki, 10 May 2001, *Summerhouse* (oil canvas, 20 x 24 ins / 50 x 61 cm) FIM 16,000. Helsinki, 10 M 2001, *Landscape* (oil on board, 20 x 17 ins / 51 x 43 cm) FI 22,000. Helsinki, 27 April 2002, *Landscape* (oil on board, x 17 ins / 51 x 43 cm) EUR 6,200. Helsinki, 28 April 200 *Winter Landscape* (1914, oil on board, 14 x 10 ins / 36 x cm) EUR 8,200. Helsinki, 29 Nov 2003, *Summer's Day in t Country* (1939, oil on canvas, 13 x 18 ins / 33 x 46 cm) EU 3,400. Helsinki, 29 Nov 2003, *Two Girls in the Sauna* (194 oil on canvas, 39 x 32 ins / 100 x 81 cm) EUR 4,000. Helsin 13 Dec 2003, *View from Berghall, Helsinki* (1917, oil on ca vas, 18 x 20 ins / 46 x 51 cm) EUR 6,400. Helsinki, 8 M 2004, *Evacuees* (1940, oil on canvas, 39 x 32 ins / 100 x 81 c EUR 5,000.

SALLING, Andreas
Danish, 17th century.
Active during the second half of the 17th century.
Sculptor.

Salling executed sculptures for the church of St Peter Copenhagen from 1681 until 1683.

SALLING, Henning
Danish, 17th century.
Active during the second half of the 17th century.
Sculptor.

Salling worked in Copenhagen from 1634 until 1639.

SALLIOR, Marie Augustin
French, 19th century.
Born 6 April 1788, in Paris.
Painter. Portraits.

He was a pupil of Regnault, and entered the École d Beaux-Arts in Paris on 3 September 1813. He exhibited the Salon between 1810 and 1812.

SALLOS
French, 18th century.
Active in Paris during the first half of the 18th century
Sculptor.

Sallos was a pupil at the Académie Royale in Paris. He w first prize in 1738.

SALLOS, Emmanuel
French, 18th - 19th century.
Painter.

Emmanuel Sallos studied at the academy in Paris from 1775 to 1781. He worked in Rome from 1787 to 1810.

SALLOUM, Jayce
Canadian, 20th century.
Active in the USA.
Installation artist. Multimedia.

Jayce Salloum came from Lebanese stock. He lived and worked in New York.

In 1996 he produced the installation *Kan ya ma Kan* (There Was, There Isn't Any More) which occupies an entire room in an exhibition dedicated to the Lebanon and is composed of a range of objects, such as images, photographs and typed documents. He showed his works in several solo exhibitions, including 1996, Montreal.

BIBLIOGRAPHY:

Couëlle, Jennifer, *'Jayce Salloum - Karilee Fuglem - Karin Trenkel'* in *Art Press 222*, periodical, Paris, March 1997.

SALLWIRK, Leonhard
German, 15th century.
Active in Günzburg during the second half of the 15th century.
Miniaturist.

Leonhard Sallwirk also worked in Augsburg and illuminated bibles.

SALLWÜRK, Ernst Sigmund von
German, 19th - 20th century.
Born 12 April 1874, in Baden-Baden.
Active in Halle.
Painter, engraver.

Ernst Sigmund von Sallwürk studied in Munich under Karl de Kalckreuth and in Mannheim under Julius Fehr.

SALLY. See **SALY**

SALM, Abraham, Adam, Adriaen van, or van der
Dutch, 17th - 18th century.
Born c. 1660; died 1720.
Painter, draughtsman. Seascapes, boats, naval battles, landscapes with figures.

The name Abraham van Salm apparently refers to several members of the same family who produced work of similar style and quality. Reynier van Salm can be positively identified as active at the end of the 17th century, while Abraham, Adam and Adriaen van Salm (or Van der Salm) may refer to one or several artists, since their documented dates and subject-matter are closely similar, if not identical. Auction records tend to use the name Adriaen. He was active in Delftshaven from 1706 to 1719. *Bryan's Dictionary* gives an earlier date, towards the middle of the 17th century.

The Van Salms (including Reynier) specialised in grisaille paintings of marines and naval battles; their much rarer landscapes depict typically Dutch rural scenes, featuring windmills and skaters on canals. Their seascapes frequently feature ships in difficulty on stormy seas.

MUSEUMS AND GALLERIES:

LONDON (British Mus.): *Ships* (four pen drawings).

AUCTION RECORDS:

PARIS, 9 May 1949, *Seascape* (grisaille) FRF 63,000. AMSTERDAM, 13 March 1951, *Naval Combat in 1705*, NLG 2,600; *Naval Combat in the Mediterranean*, NLG 2,500. LONDON, 1 May 1963, *Whaling Ship* (grisaille/panel) GBP 380. LONDON, 10 July 1968, *Naval Battle* (grisaille) GBP 1,900. LONDON, 3 Dec 1969, *Sailing-ships in the Arctic*, GBP 8,000. LONDON, 8 Dec 1971, *The 'Province of Gelderland' and other Ships on the High Sea*, GBP 5,500. AMSTERDAM, 16 Nov 1981, *Ships in High Seas* (pen and wash, 6 1/2 x 9 1/2 ins / 16.4 x 24.3 cm) NLG 4,000. LONDON, 19 Dec 1985, *Arctic Expedition* (oil on panel, in grisaille, 30 1/4 x 55 1/2 ins / 77 x 141 cm) GBP 18,000. AMSTERDAM, 28 Nov 1989, *Winter Landscape With a Couple in a Horse-drawn Sleigh and Numerous Skaters on a Frozen Canal Near a Village* (oil on panel in grisaille, 17 3/4 x 24 1/4 ins / 45.2 x 61.3 cm) NLG 184,000. LONDON, 11 April 1990, *Navigation in High Seas* (oil on panel in grisaille, 27 1/2 x 35 1/4 ins / 70 x 89.5 cm) GBP 6,600. AMSTERDAM, 10 Nov 1992, *The 'Vrijheyt', a Dutch Frigate at Anchor Near a Frost-bound Coast, With Whalers at Their Work* (oil on panel, 24 1/4 x 30 1/2 ins / 61.8 x 77.4 cm) NLG 48,300. AMSTERDAM, 25 Nov 1992, *A Yacht and Other Ships in a Strong Wind on the High Sea; Fishing Boats Near a Jetty* (ink and wash, a pair, 6 1/4 x 9 ins / 16 x 22 cm) NLG 7,475. AMSTERDAM, 18 Nov 1993, *Dutch Whalers in the Arctic* (oil on panel, 21 1/4 x 29 ins / 54 x 72.8 cm) NLG 218,500. LONDON, 3 July 1997, *Ships on a Choppy Sea* (oil on panel, 7 x 9 3/4 ins / 18 x 25 cm) GBP 25,300. NEW YORK, Jan 1998, *Dutch Whalers in the Arctic* (ink/panel, 21 1/4 x 31 1/2 ins / 54 x 80 cm) USD 112,500. NEW YORK, 26 May 2000, *Naval Engagement between English and Dutch Men-of-war* (pen, ink and oil on panel, 14 x 19 ins / 36 x 49 cm) USD 100,000. NEW YORK, 26 May 2000, *Dutch Galley Frigates and Other Shipping in Choppy Seas* (pen, ink and oil on panel, 14 x 19 ins / 36 x 49 cm) USD 100,000. NEW YORK, 26 Jan 2001, *Dutch Men-o-war and Frigates with a Galley and Rowing Boats off a Coastline - Penschilderji* (ink on panel, 23 x 33 ins / 58 x 83 cm) USD 50,000.

SALM, B. Nicolas
German, 19th century.
Born 1810, in Cologne; died 1883, in Aachen.
Painter, draughtsman. Portraits, genre scenes.

B. Nicolas Salm studied in Cologne. In 1835 he decorated the Gürzenich with carnival scenes. He was highly regarded as a portrait painter and drawing teacher. He settled in Aachen.

SALM, Isaac
Dutch, 19th century.
Born 14 August 1812, in Amsterdam.
Painter (?), collector. Landscapes.

Isaac Salm was a pupil of Verschuur. His works are to be found in Haarlem.

SALM, Jenny. See **SALM-REIFFERSCHEIDT Johanna**

SALM, Leopold
Hungarian, 18th century.
Sculptor.

Leopold Salm was active in the second half of the 18th century. He settled in Pest in 1791, and produced sculptures for the church of St Christina in Buda.

SALM, Lorens
Danish, 17th century.
Engraver of reproductions.

Salm was active from 1676 until 1681. He engraved in burin, in the style of Abraham Wuchters and Joh. Husman.

SALM, Reynier van
Dutch, 17th century.
Painter. Seascapes.

Reynier van Salm was active in Amsterdam in 1688.

MUSEUMS AND GALLERIES:

MEININGEN - ROTTERDAM (Historisch Mus. Rotterdam).

AUCTION RECORDS:

LONDON, 24 March 1971, *A Whale Hunt* (grisaille) GBP 1,700. LONDON, 9 Dec 1994, *Frigate, Warships and Fishing Boats in a Light Sea Breeze* (oil on panel, 14 x 24 ins / 35.5 x 61 cm) GBP 3,450. NEW YORK, 26 Jan 2001, *Dutch Whalers Groenlandia and Duroux Leonora with Other Shipping in Arctic Waters* (ink on panel, 24 x 30 ins / 61 x 77 cm) USD 42,000.

SALM-REIFFERSCHEIDT, Johanna or Jenny
Maiden name: Countess Pachta-Rayhofen
Austrian, 19th century.

Born 18 March 1780, in Prague; died 13 September 1857, in Prague.
Painter.

MUSEUMS AND GALLERIES:
PRAGUE (Národní Gal.): *Landscape.*

SALMASIO, Chiara, Enea and Francesco. See **TALPINO**

SALMENBACH, Georg
German, 16th century.
Active in Saalfeld in 1509.
Painter.

SALMERON, Cristóbal and Francisco. See **GARCÍA Y SALMERON**

SALMERON, J. Sánchez
Mexican, 17th century.
Active c. 1670.
Painter.

SALMERÓN, José
Spanish, 18th century.
Active during the second half of the 18th century.
Sculptor (wood).
José Salmerón executed sculptures in the church of Sta Ana in Granada in 1785.

SALMERÓN, Juan
Spanish, 18th - 19th century.
Sculptor.
Juan Salmerón carved the tabernacle on the high altar of the church of S Nicolas in Granada. He worked in the city from 1797 to 1802.

SALMERON, Melchior de
Spanish, 16th century.
Active in Toledo (Castile-La Mancha) from 1531 to 1540.
Sculptor.
Melchior de Salmeron produced sculptures in the transept, the King's Chapel and on the façade of Toledo Cathedral.

SALMERON Y GARCIA, Exoristo, pseudonym Tito
Spanish, 20th century.
Born 1877, in Paris; died June 1925, in Madrid.
Painter, humorist artist.

SALMEZZA, Chiara, Enea and Francesco. See **TALPINO**

SALMIER, Josse. See the entry **HERREGOUTS David**

SALMINCIO, Andrea
Italian, 17th century.
Born in Bologna.
Engraver.
The pupil of G.L. Valesio, Andrea Salmincio engraved on copper and on wood. The monogram he used is similar to that of A. Sallaert. He was also a bookseller.

SALMON
British, 18th century.
Active from 1700 to 1715.
Modeller (wax).

SALMON. See also **SALMSON**

SALMON, A.
French, 20th century.
Painter. Landscapes with figures, seascapes.

AUCTION RECORDS:
PARIS, 5 May 1944, *Returning from Fishing,* FRF 1,600. PARIS, 23 Feb 1945, *Landscape with Pond and Washerwoman,* FRF 1,650.

SALMON, Adrien Alphonse
French, 19th century.
Born 6 March 1802, in Paris.
Painter, art restorer. Portraits, genre scenes, landscapes.
He was taught by his father and also by Lecourt. He entered the École des Beaux-Arts on 10 September 1819, and exhibited at the Salon from 1824 to 1848. He was best known for restoring paintings.

SALMON, André Joseph
French, 18th century.
Active in Paris in 1776.
Painter. Mythological subjects, nudes, portraits.

SALMON, Charles
French, 19th century.
Born in Cepoy (Loiret).
Painter. Flowers.
He exhibited at the Salon between 1842 and 1852.

SALMON, Émile Frédéric
French, 19th - 20th century.
Born 15 June 1840, in Paris; died 12 June 1913, in Forges-les-Eaux (Seine-Maritime).
Sculptor, watercolourist, engraver, reproductions engraver. Animals.
Émile Frédéric Salmon was the son of the painter Théodore Frédéric Salmon and the father of the poet and art critic André Salmon. He was a pupil of Barye, Edmond Hédouin and Léon Gaucherel. He gave up sculpture for etching. He first exhibited at the Salon de Paris in 1859, and when living in St Petersburg in 1898 showed a collection of his engravings, watercolours and drawings.

As a sculptor he created small bronzes, often of animals, and he engraved many plates for the state and the Municipality of Paris. At the Hermitage Museum, St Petersburg, he engraved *Abraham's Sacrifice* after Rembrandt.

SALMON, Françoise
French, 20th century.
Born c. 1920, in Paris.
Sculptor, draughtsman. Figures, nudes. Busts, monuments.
From 1939 to 1940 Françoise Salmon was a pupil at the École des Beaux-Arts, Paris. There are written documents that imply she was deported to concentration camps in Germany.

Her work ranges widely and includes sensuous nudes, popular and humorous figurines, and portraits such as the expressive busts of the poets *Paul Éluard* and *Eugène Guillevic* and the critics *Paul Besson* and *René Barotte*. As a monumental sculptor she created a large piece for a nursery in La Courneuve, works for various school complexes, the *Memorial of Neuengamme*, and the *Auschwitz Monument* in the Père Lachaise Cemetery, Paris. These tragic and realistic memorials express the weight of her personal experience.

She exhibited in Paris at the Salon d'Automne, of which she was a member, the Salon de la Jeune Sculpture, regularly at the Salon Comparaisons, the Salon de la Société Nationale des Beaux-Arts, and regularly at the Salon des Peintres Témoins de Leur Temps; 1959 at the first Biennale *Formes humaines* (*Human Forms*) at the Musée Rodin; 1964 with the *Groupe des neufs*, Galerie Vendôme; 1965, exhibition of her sculpture for the *International Memorial of Neuengamme* at the Musée National d'Art Moderne, Paris, and the Kunsthalle, Hamburg; 1966 at the exhibition *Vingt-deux sculpteurs témoignent de l'homme* (*Testimony of Twenty-Two Sculptors* to *Mankind*) at the Museum of St-Denis, and in *Dessins de sculpteurs de Rodin à nos jours* (*Drawings by Sculptors from Rodin to the Present Day*) at the Musée des Beaux-Arts, Strasbourg; 1967 at the first festival of contemporary sculpture at the château of St-Ouen; 1970 in *René Iché et grands sculpteurs contemporains* (*René Iché and Great Contemporary Sculptors*) at the museum of Narbonne; also, *Sculpture dans un parc* (*Sculpture in a Park*) in St-Ouen; *Octobre à Villepreux* (*October in Villepreux*) at the Floralies, Orléans and *Vingt sculpteurs* (*Twenty Sculptors*) at the Centre d'Études Nucléaires, Saclay. In 1957 she was awarded the Prix Fénéon, and she also won prizes from the Municipalities of Montreuil and Taverny.

Bibliography:

Dessins de sculpteurs de Rodin à nos jours, exhibition catalogue, Musée des Beaux-Arts, Strasbourg, 1966. *René Iché et grands sculpteurs contemporains*, exhibition catalogue, Musée de Narbonne, Narbonne, 1970.

SALMON, Gabriel

French, 16th century.

Born in Lunéville.

Active in Nancy 1522-1542.

Painter, engraver. Religious subjects. Wall decorations.

Gabriel Salmon was herald at arms to Duke Antoine and decorated the Franciscan chapel and the chapel of the Château de Gondreville.

SALMON, Jacques Pierre François

French, 19th century.

Born 16 August 1781, in Orléans; died 10 March 1855, in Orléans.

Painter, lithographer. Historical subjects, landscapes with figures, landscapes, urban landscapes, architectural views.

Jacques Salmon was taught by Bardin and Regnault, and became a teacher at the École Centrale in Loiret, central France; he then taught drawing at the Collège d'Orléans. He painted a great many views of Orléans and the surrounding area, several of which were engraved or lithographed.

Museums and Galleries:

Orléans: *View of the Motte House on the Banks of the Loiret*.

Auction records:

Paris, 8 Dec 1996, *Ox in a Meadow* (1845, oil on panel, 7 x 9½ ins / 17.5 x 24 cm) FRF 15,000.

SALMON, John Cuthbert

British, 19th - 20th century.

Born 28 February 1844, in Colchester; died 2 November 1917, in London.

Painter (gouache), watercolourist. Figures, landscapes.

Auction records:

London, 7 Sept 1976, *Waterfall* (1872, oil on canvas, 13½ x 11½ ins / 34 x 29 cm) GBP 120. London, 25 Jan 1989, *Lynton in Devon* (1870, watercolour and gouache, 20¼ x 30¾ ins / 51.5 x 78 cm) GBP 2,310. Paris, 8 Nov 1989, *Eccentric Knight* (1885, watercolour, 22½ x 16¼ ins / 57 x 41 cm) FRF 5,000.

SALMON, John Francis

British, 19th - 20th century.

Born c. 1808; died 1886.

Painter, watercolourist. Landscapes.

John Francis Salmon lived in Gravesend. A number of his works including *London, the Upper Pool* (1838) showing the port of London and St Paul's, and *Quadrant, Regent Street, London* (c. 1838), a view of the Piccadilly Circus end of Regent's Street, were engraved by John Wood and published in his *History of London illustrated by Views in London and Westminster*.

Salmon exhibited at the Royal Academy in 1849 and 1853 and at the Royal British Institution and the Society of Painters in Watercolours in the period between 1838 and 1873.

Auction records:

London, 16 Jan 2002, *Small Boats Running with the Swell Below the Old Tynemouth Lighthouse* (1850, watercolour over pencil heightened with gouache, scratching out, 20 x 30 ins / 52 x 75 cm) GBP 1,000.

SALMON, Louis Adolphe. See **SALMSON**

SALMON, Michèle

French, 20th - 21st century.

Born 21 September 1946.

Painter. Figures.

Michèle Salmon was born in Lorraine and was a pupil of Jacques Despierre and Georges Rohner at the l'École des Arts Décoratifs in Paris.

Michèle Salmon is a painter of sensations and atmosphere. Her acute imagination aligns her with the Surrealists. Her hairless and expressionless figures appear against a background interplay of light and shade and, as a result, are imbued with a mysterious quality.

She has exhibited in Paris, notably at the Salon d'Automne of 1969 and the 1970 Salon des Artistes Français. She held her first solo exhibition in 1972.

M Salmon

Auction records:

Versailles, 25 Sept 1988, *Three Pears* (oil on canvas, 21¼ x 25½ ins / 54 x 65 cm) FRF 5,000; *Little Fair-Haired Girl in a Red Chair* (oil on canvas, 22 x 18 ins / 55 x 46 cm) FRF 4,000. Versailles, 10 Dec 1989, *Two Women* (oil on canvas, 21¼ x 32 ins / 54 x 81 cm) FRF 8,000.

SALMON, Michelet. See **SAUMON**

SALMON, Pierre

French, 14th century.

Miniaturist, illuminator. Historical subjects.

Pierre Salmon was one of the regular illuminators employed by Charles VI at the end of the 14th century.

Museums and Galleries:

Paris (BNF): *The Demands of King Charles VI* (manuscript decorated with miniatures).

SALMON, Robert

American, 18th - 19th century.

Born c. 1775; died c. 1844 or 1845.

Painter. Landscapes, seascapes.

Robert Salmon worked as a painter in England and Scotland before moving to Boston in 1828, where he acquired a reputation as a painter of seascapes, boats and landscapes. He painted a panoramic view of Boston, and the curtain of the city theatre. A large number of his canvases can be seen in the museums of Boston. He renders sky, earth and sea in a free and luminous manner, while his representations of ships are always executed with precise detail, something that is greatly appreciated by specialist collectors and seafarers alike.

Museums and Galleries:

Annapolis (Naval Academy Mus.): *Port of Boston from Constitution Quay*.

Auction records:

New York, 19 March 1969, *Port of Boston*, USD 62,500. London, 10 Dec 1971, *Seascape*, Gns 9,500. London, 13 Dec 1972, *English Corvette*, GBP 9,000. New York, 11 April 1973, *Three-master off the Coast*, USD 20,000. London, 22 March 1974, *Naval Battle*, Gns 6,000. London, 26 March 1976, *Boats off Liverpool* (oil on canvas, 26½ x 42½ ins / 67.3 x 108 cm) GBP 7,000. New York, 21 April 1977, *View of Greenock* (1816, oil on canvas, 26¼ x 44¼ ins / 66.5 x 112.5 cm) USD 7,500. New York, 25 April 1980, *Frigate from the Baltic Fleet off the Coast of Greenock* (1818, oil on canvas, 23¼ x 37¼ ins / 59 x 94.6 cm) USD 27,000. NEW YORK, 22 Oct 1981, *Boats off the Coast of Liverpool* (1809, oil on canvas, 26½ x 42½ ins / 67.3 x 108 cm) USD 77,500. NEW YORK, 24 Oct 1984, *Schooner with View of Boston* (1832, oil on board, 16½ x 24 ins / 42 x 61 cm) USD 92,500. LONDON, 19 July 1985, *Merchantman of the Jardine Matheson Line, and Other Shipping off Liverpool* (oil on canvas, 33¼ x 51 ins / 84.5 x 129.5 cm) GBP 55,000. LONDON, 19 Nov 1986, *Custom House, Greenock, on the River Clyde, with Shipping by the Quay* (1820, oil on canvas, 23 x 37 ins / 58.5 x 94 cm) GBP 43,000. NEW YORK, 25 May 1989, *Stormy Scene* (1839, oil on panel, 16½ x 24 ins / 41.9 x 60.9 cm) USD 115,500. LONDON, 14 March 1990, *Capel Curig, Looking towards Mount Snowdon; Environs of Castle Dolbadarn with Llyn Padarn and Llyn Peris* (1822, oil on canvas, each 17½ x 23½ ins / 44.5 x 60 cm) GBP 5,280. NEW YORK, 30 Nov 1990, *Port of Liverpool* (oil on panel, 8 x 10 ins / 20.3 x 25.4 cm) USD 19,800. NEW YORK, 12 March 1992, *Sailing off the Coast of Greenock* (1826, oil on panel, 20 x 30 ins / 50.6 x 76.2 cm) USD 28,600. NEW YORK, 3 Dec 1992, *Two Vessels off the Coast of Greenock* (1820, oil on panel, 19½ x 31 ins / 49.5 x 78.7 cm) USD 27,500. LONDON, 20 Jan 1993, *Launch of a Ship from the Yards of Greenock, Scotland, in 1822* (oil on canvas, 16¾ x 25½ ins / 42.5 x 65 cm) GBP 16,100. NEW YORK, 4 June 1993, *Raging Sea* (1802, oil on canvas, 18 x 24 ins / 45.7 x 61 cm) USD 34,500. NEW YORK, 17 March 1994, *Boston Lighthouse* (oil on canvas, 15 x 18¼ ins / 38.1 x 46.4 cm) USD 26,450. EDINBURGH, 9 June 1994, *Lifeboats in a Storm Drawing alongside a Frigate Washed up on the Shore* (1814, oil on panel, 8 x 10 ins / 20.3 x 25.3 cm) USD 5,175. LONDON, 12 April 1995, *Naval Battle off the Coast of Dunkirk on 7 July 1800* (1800, oil on canvas, 18 x 28 ins / 46 x 71 cm) GBP 8,050. LONDON, 3 May 1995, *18-cannon Warship Arriving in a Port on the Clyde on the Bank Opposite the Rosneath Peninsula* (1815, oil on canvas, 23 x 36¼ ins / 58.5 x 92 cm) GBP 38,900. NEW YORK, 14 March 1996, *Great Orme Headland near Liverpool* (1836, oil on canvas, 51 x 78 ins / 129.5 x 198.1 cm) USD 48,875. PARIS, 13 Dec 1996, *Coastal Landscape with Boat Run Aground* (1836, oil on panel, 7¾ x 10½ ins / 20 x 26.5 cm) FRF 60,000. NEW YORK, 16 Jan 1998, *Boat Heading into Port* (oil on panel, 16½ x 24¼ ins / 41.9 x 61.6 cm) USD 74,000. NEW YORK, 26 May 1999, *English Cutter and Lugger off North Shields* (1840, oil on panel, 17 x 24 ins / 42 x 61 cm) USD 60,000. NEW YORK, 30 Nov 1999, *View of Greenock Scotland and the Bay of St Lawrence* (oil on canvas, 16 x 23 ins / 40 x 59 cm) USD 26,000. ZURICH, 22 Sept 2000, *English Sailing Boat* (1798, oil on canvas, 27 x 41 ins / 68 x 103 cm) CHF 48,000. LOS ANGELES, 13 Dec 2000, *Port of Liverpool* (oil on canvas, 30 x 43 ins / 77 x 108 cm) USD 35,000. PORTSMOUTH, 18 Aug 2001, *Along the Shore* (1825, oil on canvas, 6 x 9 ins / 16 x 24 cm) USD 48,000. BOSTON, 16 Nov 2001, *Vessels in a Harbour, probably Royal Naval Fort at Milford Haven* (1839, oil on panel, 9 x 12 ins / 24 x 31 cm) USD 46,000. NEW YORK, 21 May 2002, *Schooner with a View of Boston* (oil on panel, 16 x 24 ins / 41 x 61 cm) USD 460,000. NEW YORK, 21 May 2002, *View of Boston Harbour* (oil on panel, 9 x 11 ins / 24 x 29 cm) USD 500,000. NEW YORK, 21 Jan 2003, *Fifth Rate Ship of the Line on the River Mersey* (1808, oil on canvas, 27 x 43 ins / 68 x 110 cm) USD 110,000. PORTLAND, 8 Aug 2003, *Harbour, Liverpool* (oil on panel, 12 x 16 ins / 31 x 41 cm) USD 90,000. NEW YORK, 18 May 2004, *English Cutter* (1832, oil on panel, 17 x 24 ins / 42 x 62 cm) USD 65,000. PORTLAND, 6 Aug 2004, *Departing Brig off Maryport Harbour, Cumbria* (oil on canvas, 31 x 45 ins / 79 x 114 cm) USD 120,000.

SALMON, Théodore Frédéric

French, 19th century.
Born 14 April 1811, in Paris; died 5 August 1876, in Herblay.
Painter. Figures, genre scenes, animals.

This artist was the father of Émile Frédéric Salmon. In 1837 he travelled round France and Italy, visiting Bologna, Florence, Rome, Milan, Venice, Cremona and Sardinia, and returned to Paris via Valais (southern Switzerland). Besides his figure paintings, he also signed a number of small canvases with farm animals as the subject.

Although he is not well known, he was undoubtedly a talented painter. He produced some moving paintings of mothers with their children in rustic settings. Stylistically, his works contain elements of both classical art and Realism, so in this respect he was not unlike the painters of the Barbizon School.

MUSEUMS AND GALLERIES:

ARRAS: *Pastureland in Brittany* - AVIGNON: *Returning from the Fields* - CHARTRES: *The Gleaners* - RHEIMS: *Convent Staircase*.

AUCTION RECORDS:

PARIS, 16-17 May 1892, *The Turkey Keeper*, FRF 340. PARIS, 1899, *The Housewife*, FRF 150. PARIS, 2 May 1900, *Return of the Flock*, FRF 150. PARIS, 30 Nov 1923, *Shepherdess Carrying a Lamb*, FRF 550. PARIS, 6 Feb 1929, *Chickens near a Fountain*, FRF 1,300. PARIS, 10 Oct 1949, *Bust of a Young Farmer's Wife*, FRF 7,000. PARIS, 22 June 1950, *Cows in Pasture*, FRF 4,800. PARIS, 26 June 1950, *The Mender*, FRF 2,800. PARIS, 6 July 1951, *Rest*, FRF 1,500. PARIS, 30 March 1955, *The Shepherdess*, FRF 15,000. AMSTERDAM, 14 Sept 1993, *The Turkey Keeper* (oil on panel, 16¼ x 12½ ins / 41 x 32 cm) NLG 1,840. PARIS, 14 April 2000, *Girl Putting on her Stockings* (oil on panel, 13 x 10 ins / 34 x 26 cm) FRF 16,000. FONTAINEBLEAU, 11 May 2003, *Feeding the Animals* (1854, oil on panel) EUR 3,700.

SALMSON. See also **SALMON**

SALMSON, Abraham

Swedish, 19th century.
Born 1806; died 1857, in Paris.
Medallist.

Abraham Salmson was the son of Sem Salmson.

SALMSON, Anton

Swedish, 19th century.
Born 1831.
Sculptor, medallist.

Anton Salmson was the son of Abraham Salmson.

SALMSON, Axel Jakob or Sem Jakob

Swedish, 19th century.
Born 1807; died 1876.
Engraver, draughtsman.

Salmson studied at the Kungliga Akademi för de Fria Konsterna in Stockholm. He engraved a series of lithographs with figures of the Thirty Years War, in addition to portraying the kings of Sweden.

SALMSON, Hugo Frederik

Swedish, 19th century.
Born 7 July 1844, in Stockholm; died 1 August 1894, in Lund.
Painter. Figures, portraits, genre scenes, landscapes.

Salmson was a pupil of Ch. Cointe. He settled in Paris and first exhibited at the Salon of 1870. He received a third class medal in 1879, and was made a Chevalier of the Légion d'Honneur that same year. He was made an Officer in 1889. He is known for *Odalisque*, 1872; *Memory of Picardy* for the Exposition of 1878; and *In the Fields*, 1879.

Salmson was particularly interested in portraying rustic life in Picardy and in Sweden. He had the ability to translate rustic charm with great acuity of vision. He was one of the most notable painters of the Swedish school at the end of the 19th century.

HUGO SALMSON

HUGOSALMSON

Museums and Galleries:
Amiens: *An Arrest in Picardy; The Little Swedish Girl* - Nantes: *The Little Gleaner* - Paris (former Mus. du Luxembourg): *At the Wall of Dalby, Sweden* - Sète: *In the Vegetable Garden* - Stockholm: *The Little Gleaner.*

Auction records:
New York, 1895, *The Battle,* FRF 2,450. New York, 4 Jan 1935, *In the Fields,* USD 400. London, 31 July 1935, *The Little Swedish Girl,* GBP 66. Pontoise, 2 Oct 1948, *Little Peasant Girl With Bouquet,* FRF 5,600. Stockholm, 11 Oct 1950, *The Young Card Players,* DKK 12,200. London, 22 Jan 1960, *Swedish Peasant Children Playing by a Gate,* GBP 294. Copenhagen, 9 Sept 1966, *The Fish Net,* DKK 6,700. London, 9 May 1979, *Country Works* (oil on panel, 26 1/4 x 36 ins / 66.5 x 91.5 cm) GBP 5,000. London, 20 March 1981, *Children in a Field* (oil on canvas, 35 1/2 x 45 1/2 ins / 90.2 x 115.5 cm) GBP 5,500. Stockholm, 1 Nov 1983, *Interior* (oil on canvas, 18 1/2 x 26 ins / 47 x 66 cm) SEK 86,000. Stockholm, 14 Nov 1984, *Portrait of the Blixen-Finecke Sisters* (pastel, 62 1/2 x 58 1/4 ins / 159 x 148 cm) SEK 146,000. Stockholm, 22 April 1986, *Young Woman and Little Girl in a Garden* (oil on panel, 19 x 24 1/2 ins / 48 x 62 cm) SEK 220,000. London, 25 March 1987, *Children By a Wall* (pen, 10 x 9 ins / 24.5 x 22 cm) GBP 2,500. London, 25 Nov 1987, *A Little Bouquet of Flowers in the Fields* (oil on canvas, 30 x 24 ins / 76 x 61 cm) GBP 16,000. Paris, 29 Nov 1989, *The Ball Game* (oil on canvas, 29 1/4 x 39 1/4 ins / 74 x 100 cm) FRF 140,000. London, 4 Oct 1991, *On the Road to the House* (oil on panel, 26 1/2 x 37 ins / 67.3 x 94 cm) GBP 2,090. London, 16 June 1993, *Portrait of a Little Girl in a Hat* (oil on canvas, 23 1/4 x 17 3/4 ins / 59 x 45 cm) GBP 3,105. Stockholm, 30 Nov 1993, *Two Children Gathering Flowers in a Field* (oil on canvas, 18 x 13 3/4 ins / 46 x 35 cm) SEK 29,000. London, 12 May 1999, *Oriental Nude* (oil on canvas, 95 x 54 ins / 242 x 137 cm) GBP 7,200. Stockholm, 25 Nov 1999, *Cottage Interiors with figures and Fortune-teller* (oil on canvas, 18 x 26 ins / 46 x 66 cm) SEK 61,000. Stockholm, 5 Dec 2000, *In the Garden* (oil on canvas, 13 x 17 ins / 33 x 42 cm) SEK 80,000. Uppsala, 10 Dec 2000, *Young Woman in Deep Thought* (oil on panel, 13 x 9 ins / 33 x 24 cm) SEK 66,000. Stockholm, 29 May 2001, *Girl in Flower Meadow* (oil on panel, 9 x 14 ins / 23 x 35 cm) SEK 20,000. Stockholm, 18 June 2001, *Girl Combing her Hair - Mythological Allegory* (oil on canvas, 43 x 29 ins / 110 x 73 cm) SEK 25,000. Stockholm, 28 May 2002, *Small Girl Picking Flowers* (oil on canvas, 31 x 25 ins / 78 x 63 cm) SEK 130,000. Stockholm, 3 Dec 2002, *The Small Hill - Young Girl Seated Holding Flowers* (oil on canvas, 46 x 31 ins / 118 x 80 cm) SEK 80,000. Stockholm, 4 June 2003, *Young Mother Holding Small Child in Russian Interior* (oil on canvas, 39 x 24 ins / 100 x 60 cm) SEK 90,000. Stockholm, 3 Dec 2003, *Boy Playing Flute for Girls in Summer Meadow* (oil on canvas, 19 x 14 ins / 47 x 36 cm) SEK 22,000.

SALMSON, Jean Baptiste

French, 19th century.
Born 1807, in Stockholm, Sweden; died 1866, in Paris.
Medallist, cameo engraver.

He was a pupil of Bosio, and the father of Jean Jules Salmson.

SALMSON, Jean Jules

French, 19th century.
Born 18 July 1823, in Paris; died 7 May 1902, in Coupvray (Seine-et-Marne).
Sculptor, medallist, illustrator. Statues.

Jean Joules Salmson's teachers were Dumont, Ramey and Toussaint. He made his Salon debut in 1859, and won second-class medals in 1863 and 1867; he was also made a Chevalier of the Légion d'Honneur in 1867. In 1876 the government of Geneva appointed him director of the École des Arts Industriels (School of Industrial Arts). In this capacity he proved himself to be both talented and committed, artistically and administratively, and his contribution was key to the success of the institution. In 1891 he was appointed correspondent of the Institut de France. In 1892 he published an illustrated book entitled *Between Two Strokes of the Chisel: Memoirs of a Sculptor.* He also sculpted the fireplace in the foyer of the Geneva theatre.

Museums and Galleries:
Chamonix: *Monument to H. B. de Saussure and Balmat* (1887) - Geneva (MAH): *Model for a Statue of J-J Rousseau* - La Rochelle (Hôtel de Ville): *Henri IV* (1876, bust) - Paris (Bibliothèque-Mus. de l'Opéra): *Handel* (statue) - Paris (Théâtre du Vaudeville): *Caryatids: Folly, Comedy, Satire, Music* - Paris (Tribunal de Commerce): *Prudence* (1865, statue).

Auction records:
Enghien-les-Bains, 26 June 1983, *Arab Warrior* (varied brown patinated bronze, h. 23 1/4 ins / 59 cm) FRF 76,000. London, 21 March 1985, *Arab Standing; Arab Woman Standing* (brown-patinated bronze, a pair, h. 22 ins / 56 cm and 20 3/4 ins/53 cm) GBP 2,100. London, 20 March 1986, *Young Man with a Bow and His Lady* (c. 1880, light-brown patinated bronze, h. 32 ins / 81 cm) GBP 2,400. Paris, 8 Dec 1989, *Water Carrier* (patinated bronze medal, h. 22 ins / 55 cm) FRF 18,000. New York, 14 Oct 1993, *Arab Warrior* (bronze, h. 22 ins / 56 cm) USD 2,530. New York, 20 July 1994, *Pandora* (bronze, h. 21 1/2 ins / 54.6 cm) USD 1,840. New York, 5 May 1999, *Arab Warrior and Woman* (brown patinated bronze, 22 ins / 56 cm) USD 9,500. New Orleans, 4 Dec 1999, *Horsemen* (bronze, a pair, h. 22 ins / 56 cm) USD 3,400. Detroit, 11 Feb 2000, *Two Female Figures* (gold patinated bronze, h. 9 ins / 22 cm) USD 3,250. Mexico, 21 June 2000, *Painter and Writer* (bronze, 24 ins / 61 cm) MXP 85,000. Amsterdam, 16 May 2001, *Statuettes of Van Dyck and Rubens* (brown patinated bronze, a pair, h. 23 ins / 59 cm) NLG 8,000. Paris, 3 Dec 2001, *Arab Warrior* (brown patinated bronze, h. 22 ins / 57 cm) FRF 37,000. London, 13 March 2002, *North African Warrior and a Woman Carrying Water* (dark brown patinated bronze, a pair, 22 ins / 55 cm) GBP 4,800. London, 28 Oct 2002, *Arab Figures* (painted bronze, a pair, 16 ins / 41 cm) GBP 3,500.

SALMSON, Johan or Isak

Swedish, 19th century.
Born 1799, in Stockholm; died 1859, in Paris.
Sculptor, medallist.

Salmson was a son of Sem Salmson. He sculpted low reliefs and medals for the Swedish royal family.

SALMSON, Louis Adolphe, or Salmon

French, 19th century.
Born 1806, in Paris; died September 1895, in Paris.
Painter, engraver, watercolourist. History painting, portraits.

A pupil of Ingres and Henriquel-Dupont, Louis Adolphe Salmson came second in the Prix de Rome in 1830, and won the first prize for engraving in 1834. He first exhibited at the Salon in 1852, and won second-class medals in 1853 and 1886. He was made a Chevalier of the Légion d'Honneur in 1867. He went to Italy and made many watercolour copies of the classical old masters. He also painted portraits, which were extremely popular with Roman high society. However, he is chiefly remembered as an engraver.

SALMSON, Sem
Swedish, 18th - 19th century.
Born 1767, in Prague; died 1822, in Stockholm.
Engraver.

SALMSON, Sem. See also **SALMSON Axel Jakob**

SALMSON, Semmy
Swedish, 19th century.
Born 1812; died 1860.
Engraver.
Salmson was a son of Sem Salmson, and was an engraver at the Swedish court.

SALMSON, Théodore Frédéric. See **SALMON**

SALMUSMÜLLER. See **SALOMUSMÜLLER**

SALO, Domenico da. See **GRAZIOLI da Salò Domenico di Pietro**

SALO, Pietro da. See **GRAZIOLI da Salo Pietro di Lorenzo**

SALÓ Y JUNQUET, José
Spanish, 19th century.
Born 24 November 1810, in Mataró; died 3 September 1877, in Cordova.
Painter, sculptor, art restorer. Religious subjects.
José Saló y Junquet was a pupil of Fr. Lopez, D. Campeny and S. Mayol. He produced paintings for Cordova Cathedral and the church of Adamuz.

SALÓ Y PRIETO, Nicolás
Spanish, 19th century.
Born 30 May 1834, in Cordova; died 22 May 1854, in Madrid.
Painter.
Nicolás Saló y Prieto studied under his father José Saló and under Federico de Madrazo.

SALODINI, Francesco Carlo
Italian, 20th century.
Born in Brescia.
Painter.
In 1948, Francesco Salodini was the first artist to receive the newly created Prix Montparnasse awarded under the auspices of the city of Paris to an Italian artist resident in Italy and consisting of a bursary to travel in France. This prize was set up to match the Italian Villa d'Este Prize.

SALOGNE (Mlle)
French.
Painter. Historical portraits.
MUSEUMS AND GALLERIES:
VERSAILLES (Mus.): *Portrait of Charles V of Lorraine.*

SALOMAN, Geskel, or Salomon
Swedish, 19th century.
Born 1 April 1821, in Tondern; died 5 July 1902, in Båstad.
Painter, engraver. Historical subjects, figures, portraits, genre scenes, interiors with figures.
Saloman was a pupil of Eckersberg and Lund at the Kunstakademi in Copenhagen. He then went to Paris and worked with Couture. In 1860 and 1861, he travelled to Algeria. He is known to have exhibited at the Salon de Paris, and received honourable mentions for the work he showed there in 1861 and 1863. He settled in Sweden, becoming a member of the Kungliga Akademi för de Fria Konsterna, in Stockholm, in 1871. He became painter to the Swedish court in 1876, and was decorated with the Order of Gustav Vasa in 1869.
MUSEUMS AND GALLERIES:
COPENHAGEN: *The Daughters of Marsk Stig* - GÖTEBORG: *News From the Crimea* - STOCKHOLM: *Interior With Weavers in Bohuslän; Young Girl Reading a Letter.*
AUCTION RECORDS:
GÖTEBORG, 7 Nov 1979, *The Bouquet* (1900, oil on canvas, 18 x 14 1/2 ins / 46 x 37 cm) SEK 9,600. STOCKHOLM, 15 Nov 1989, *Man By the Shore of a Lake Watching Over a Cauldron* (1896, oil on canvas, 14 1/2 x 12 1/4 ins / 37 x 31 cm) SEK 5,500. LONDON, 17 Oct 1997, *Rest on the Seashore* (oil on canvas, 30 3/4 x 46 ins / 78 x 117 cm) GBP 18,400. LONDON, 18 March 1999, *Moving Melody* (oil on canvas, 28 x 25 ins / 72 x 63 cm) GBP 1,000. STOCKHOLM, 18 May 1999, *Women in Coastal Landscape* (1892, oil on canvas, 20 x 29 ins / 50 x 73 cm) SEK 17,000.

SALOMÉ, real name: Wolfgang Cilarz
German, 20th - 21st century.
Born 1954.
Painter.
New Fauves.
In 1977, Salomé, Fetting, Middendorf, B. Zimmer and Castelli set up the Galerie am Moritzplatz in Berlin, where they exhibited their own works. Salomé also took part in other collective exhibitions, including at CAPC Musée d'Art Contemporain in Bordeaux, along with Castelli, Fetting and Luciano.
BIBLIOGRAPHY:
Salomé by Salomé, Cantz Verlag, Stuttgart, 1992.
AUCTION RECORDS:
NEW YORK, 3 May 1985, *Swimmers* (1982, gouache, 38 x 73 3/4 ins / 96.5 x 187.4 cm) USD 9,000. LONDON, 26 June 1986, *Naked Green* (1981, powder paint/canvas, 94 1/2 x 78 3/4 ins / 240 x 200 cm) GBP 11,000. PARIS, 16 Oct 1988, *Sumo Wrestler: Red Circle* (1982, mixed media/canvas, 78 3/4 x 94 1/2 ins / 200 x 240 cm) FRF 130,000. NEW YORK, 8 Nov 1989, *Nina 15* (1980, acrylic/canvas, 78 3/4 x 94 3/4 ins / 200 x 240.5 cm) USD 15,400. NEW YORK, 7 May 1990, *The Big Shower* (1988, acrylic/canvas, 84 x 60 ins / 213.3 x 152.6 cm) USD 12,650. PARIS, 20 Nov 1991, *Romantic Scene* (1983, acrylic/canvas, 72 x 108 3/4 ins / 183 x 276.5 cm) FRF 35,000. NEW YORK, 24 Feb 1993, *Boys in Jeans II* (1987, acrylic/canvas, 77 x 52 1/2 ins / 195.6 x 133.3 cm) USD 5,500. NEW YORK, 3 May 1994, *Swimmers* (1983, tempera/canvas, 63 x 101 1/4 ins / 160 x 257.2 cm) USD 9,775. LONDON, 30 Nov 1995, *Black Swimmers* (1990, synthetic resin/canvas, 31 1/2 x 39 1/4 ins / 80 x 100 cm) GBP 4,370. LONDON, 6 Dec 1996, *The Naked Way of Life* (1981, acrylic/canvas, 94 1/2 x 78 3/4 ins / 240 x 200 cm) GBP 6,325. ZURICH, 18 Nov 1997, *Melancholy* (1980) CHF 9,500. BERLIN, 5 June 1999, *Water* (1988, acrylic on canvas, 56 x 79 ins / 141 x 200 cm) DEM 33,000. BERLIN, 27 Nov 1999, *Lily Pond* (1985, acrylic on canvas, 87 x 180 ins / 220 x 456 cm) DEM 57,000. BERLIN, 27 May 2000, *Heightened Ascension* (1981, acrylic on calico, 94 x 79 ins / 240 x 200 cm) DEM 24,000. BERLIN, 27 May 2000, *Moonlit Swimmers* (1989, acrylic on canvas, 59 x 83 ins / 150 x 210 cm) DEM 30,000. AMSTERDAM, 12 June 2001, *Waterlilies* (1988, oil on canvas, 48 x 60 ins / 122 x 152 cm) NLG 14,000. MUNICH, 15 Nov 2001, *Lily Pond* (1987, mixed media on board, 39 x 25 ins / 98 x 64 cm) DEM 4,000. BERLIN, 8 June 2002, *Pond with Lilies* (1994, acrylic on canvas, 63 x 79 ins / 160 x 200 cm) EUR 10,000. BERLIN, 30 Nov 2002, *Spring. Summer. Autumn. Winter* (1997, oil on canvas, four, 39 x 39 ins / 100 x 100 cm) EUR 10,000. BERLIN, 29 Nov 2003, *Waterlilies* (1994, acrylic on canvas, 63 x 79 ins / 160 x 200 cm) EUR 9,000. COLOGNE, 13 Dec 2003, *Ultramarine* (1989, acrylic on canvas, 39 x 40 ins / 100 x 101 cm) EUR 40,000. COLOGNE, 4 June 2004, *Autumn Swimmers* (1988, acrylic on canvas, 55 x 63 ins / 140 x 160 cm) EUR 6,500. NEW YORK, 29 Sept 2004, *Overpowered Black Attack* (mixed media, 72 x 72 ins / 183 x 183 cm) USD 6,000.

SALOMÉ, Émile
French, 19th century.
Born 13 December 1833, in Lille; died 25 August 1881, in Lille.
Painter. Genre scenes, landscapes.

This artist was the son of Louis Salome. He studied with Souchon and Colas at the Écoles Académiques in Lille, northeast France. In 1862 he was the Wicar resident in Rome. He exhibited at the Paris Salon from 1861 to 1881.

E. Salomé

MUSEUMS AND GALLERIES:
LILLE: *The Mont-Noir Broom-maker*; *The Mont-Noir Broom-maker* (sketch); *La Dascuccia*; *The House of Thérèse* - NEUCHÂTEL: *Head of a Lacemaker from the Nord Département*.
AUCTION RECORDS:
PARIS, 1889, *Solitude*, FRF 300. NEW YORK, 28 Oct 1982, *Young Girl with a Tambourine* (1864, oil on canvas, 31 1/2 x 23 3/4 ins / 80 x 60.5 cm) USD 2,500.

SALOMÉ, Louis
French, 19th century.
Born 6 April 1812, in Bailleul; died 10 October 1863, in Lille.
Engraver (burin).

He was the father of Émile Salome.

SALOMON
Polish, 17th century.
Painter. Portraits.

In 1695, Salomon settled in Italy. His paintings tend to be humorous.
MUSEUMS AND GALLERIES:
FLORENCE: *Portrait*.

SALOMON
German, 18th century.
Active in Königsberg (now Kaliningrad, Russia) towards the end of the 18th century.
Painter. Landscapes.

SALOMON, A., called Le Tropézien
French, 20th century.
Painter. Landscapes, seascapes.
AUCTION RECORDS:
NEUILLY, 20 Oct 1991, *Tartane in St Tropez* (oil on canvas, 21 1/4 x 25 1/2 ins / 54 x 65 cm) FRF 7,000. NEUILLY, 12 Dec 1993, *St Tropez* (1926, oil on canvas, 19 3/4 x 24 ins / 50 x 61 cm) FRF 4,500.

SALOMON, Adam. See **ADAM-SALOMON Antony Samuel**

SALOMON, Anne Élodie
French, 19th century.
Born in Marseilles.
Painter. Still-lifes.

Her teachers were Seleron, Léon Cogniet and Troyon. She exhibited at the Salons of 1859 and 1861.
MUSEUMS AND GALLERIES:
PROVINS: *The Bittern*.

SALOMON, Benedikt
Russian, 19th century.
Died 1810.
Active in Polotsk (Belarus).
Engraver. Portraits.

SALOMON, Bernard, called Le Petit Bernard, Bernardus Gallus and Bernardo Gallo
French, 16th century.
Born between 1506 and 1510, in Lyons; died c. 1561, in Lyons.
Painter, illustrator, engraver.

There is some dispute about Bernard Salomon's place of birth, but it is certain that he lived in Lyons towards the middle of the 16th century. It is claimed that he was a pupil of Jean Cousin, which would establish that he worked in Paris at one time. He illustrated several very attractive volumes printed in Lyons and Paris towards the end of the 16th century, including: *Illustrated Bible*; *Ovid's Metamorphoses, Illustrated*, a work published in Lyons in 1557-1558; and *The Book of Hymns of These Times*, printed in Lyons around 1560. He also engraved a series of 19 plates that make up a *Book of Terms* (1572), and the decorations for a book that is in the possession of the Bibliothèque Nationale in Paris.

Salomon and his followers had a considerable influence on the development of book illustration. Paul Jamot noted that Velázquez took the general compositional arrangement of *Lances* from one of Salomon's engravings for Canon Claude Paradin's *Stories from the Bible in Verse*, published in Lyons in 1560. This engraving depicts the meeting of Abraham and Melchizedek and the similarities with the work by Velázquez are undeniable. Tradition has it that Salomon had a son, Jean Bernard, who like him was an engraver and who was known as Giovanni Gallus or Johanus Gallus.

BB

BIBLIOGRAPHY:
Rosen, Jean (ed.), *Majoliques européennes: reflets de l'estampe lyonnaise XVIe-XVIIe siècles*, Faton, 2003 (symposium proceedings). Sharratt, Peter, *Bernard Salomon, illustrateur lyonnais*, Droz, Geneva, 2005.

SALOMON, Charlotte
German, 20th century.
Born 1917, in Berlin; died 1943, in Auschwitz, during deportation.
Painter (gouache), draughtswoman.

Examples of Charlotte Salomon's work featured in *Inside the Visible*, an exhibition devoted to female creative artists held at the Whitechapel Art Gallery in London in 1996. Earlier, in 1992, the graphic arts section of the Centre Beaubourg in Paris exhibited 170 gouaches selected from her highly original *Life? Or Theatre?*, a suite of nearly 1000 gouache drawings in the form of an illustrated autobiography distinguished by its bold permutation of incisive text and striking image, charting a life lived in the shadow of anti-Semitic repression.

SALOMON, Geskel. See **SALOMAN**

SALOMON, Jean
French, 16th century.
Active in Lyons 1548-1559.
Painter, engraver.

Jean Salomon was the son of Bernard Salomon.

SALOMON, Jean-Claude
French, 20th century.
Born 4 December 1928, in Paris.
Painter, watercolourist, pastellist, draughtsman. Nudes, still-lifes, flowers.

Jean-Claude Salomon, a pupil of Jean Souverbie at the École des Beaux-Arts, Paris, created an allusive pictorial style in which, both in his nudes and his still-lifes, light is the true subject of his painting. Valérie Salomon writes of him: 'Objects as such are no longer important; they are only a pretext for the real subject of the painting, which is the expression of the feeling that objects arouse in us'.

He exhibited in Paris at the Salon des Surindépendants, the Salon des Indépendants, the Salon d'Automne, the Salon Comparaisons, and the Salon de Mantes-la-Jolie; also in group exhibitions in 1972, in Rohan (Cher), 1986 in Grenoble, 1987 in Romans (Isère), and in galleries in Paris, Mulhouse, St-Marcellin, Strasbourg, Miami and Papeete. His solo shows have included: 1959, 1967 Galerie Vidal, Paris; 1971 Galerie des Capucines, Paris; 1980 Galerie Armine, Paris; 1982, 1983, 1986, 1987 Fresneaux-Montchevreuil (Oise); 1983, Beauvais Theatre; Galerie Aktuarius, Strasbourg; 1985 Galerie de Sèvres, Paris; La Rochelle, Galerie Lhote; 1987 Château de Gisors; and 1989 Galerie Sculptures, Paris. In 1971 he was short-listed for the Prix de la Critique.

BIBLIOGRAPHY:

Xuriguera, Gérard, *Le Dessin, le pastel, l'aquarelle dans l'art contemporain*, Éd. Mayer, Paris, 1987.

MUSEUMS AND GALLERIES:

BEAUVAIS (Mus. départemental de l'Oise) - GENEVA (Petit Palais).

SALOMON, Joseph
Austrian, 19th century.
Active in Vienna 1822-1844.
Painter. Mythological subjects.

AUCTION RECORDS:

LONDON, 8 Dec 1995, *Choice of Hercules* (oil on canvas, 28 3/4 x 22 1/2 ins / 73 x 57.2 cm) GBP 5,750.

SALOMON, Louis
French, 19th century.
Born 1815; died 1903, in Bordeaux.
Active in Bordeaux.
Painter.

His masters were Dauzat, Brascassat and Delaroche.

SALOMON, Master of. See **MASTER OF THE KINGS' HEADS**

SALOMON, Robert
British, 19th century.
Active in Liverpool c. 1824.
Painter.

MUSEUMS AND GALLERIES:

LIVERPOOL: two paintings.

SALOMON, Simeon. See **SOLOMON**

SALOMON DE DANTZIG. See **SALOMONE DI DANZICA**

SALOMON DE MORBEYQUE
French.
Probably born in Morbecque, France.
Sculptor. Statues.

Salomon de Morbeyque worked on the statues in the Great Hall of the Château de Germolles in Châlon.

SALOMON LAUGIER. See **LAUGIER Marius François**

SALOMON LE TROPEZIEN, pseudonym of André Salomon
French, 19th - 20th century.
Painter. Seascapes, landscapes with figures.

MUSEUMS AND GALLERIES:

ST-TROPEZ (Mus. de l'Annonciade): *Fréjus Cloister* (1938).

SALOMONE, Gaetano
Italian, 18th century.
Active in Naples during the second half of the 18th century.
Sculptor.

Gaetano Salomone worked for the church of the Annunciation in Naples and for the palace and park at Caserta.

SALOMONE, Giovanni
Italian, 19th century.
Born 28 November 1806, in Naples; died 15 February 1877.
Painter.

Giovanni Salomone painted altarpieces for a number of churches in Naples.

SALOMONE, Yvan
French, 20th - 21st century.
Born 1957, in St-Malo.
Painter, watercolourist, draughtsman. Urban landscapes.
Neo-Conceptual Art.

Yvan Salomone lives and works in St-Malo. He worked initially as a conceptual artist in the mould of Edward Hopper. He paints extremely dense watercolours with little or no transparent effects. His dominant themes are dockyards and harbour installations which he photographs prior to painting.

He has participated in a number of group exhibitions: in 1987 and 1988, at the Salon de Montrouge; in 1988, at *Made in France*, an exhibition held at the Galerie A. Candau in Paris; in 1990, at *Intérieur-Extérieur* (*Interior-Exterior*), held at the Galerie Froment-Putman in Paris; in 2000, at *La Mer pour Sujet* (*The Sea as Subject 2*), hosted by TNB-FRAC Bretagne in Rennes; and, in 2002, at *Maquis*, held at Le Plateau in Paris. His solo exhibitions have included those in 1992 at the La Criée Gallery in Rennes; in 1993, at *Witte de With*, held at the Centre for Contemporary Art in Rotterdam; in 1994, at the FIAC (Foire Internationale d'Art Contemporain) in Paris (as part of the Galerie Praz-Delavallade exhibit); in 1994, at *Rennes 120*, held at the Galerie J. Dutertre in Rennes; in 1995, under the auspices of the egional Collection of Contemporary Art (FRAC) at the Château-Musée in Dieppe; in 1995, at the Musée de Rochechouart in Paris; in 1996, at *Copie* (*Copy*), held at the Espace Croisé in Lille together with Gilles Mahé; in 1996, at the Albert Baronian Gallery in Brussels; in 1997, at *Toulouse 227*, at the Galerie Sollertis in Toulouse; in 1997, at the Le Spot Gallery in Le Havre; and, in 2002 (together with Jim Isermann) and 2003 (solo) at the Galerie Praz-Delavallade in Paris.

BIBLIOGRAPHY:

Lamarche-Vadel, Bernard/Miloux, Yannic, *Yvan Salomone*, Éd. Praz-Delavallade, Paris, 1992. Jover, Manuel, ''*Yvon Salomone*' in *Beaux-Arts Magazine*, periodical, Paris, March-April 1993. Sterckx, Pierre, ''*Yvan Salomone. Les Enjeux de l'eau*' in *Art Press* n° 228, periodical, Paris, October 1997.

MUSEUMS AND GALLERIES:

AMIENS (FRAC Picardie): *Untitled* (1993, two drawings); *Untitled* (1994, six watercolours) - CHÂTEAUGIRON (FRAC Bretagne): watercolours - SOTTEVILLE-LÈS-ROUEN (FRAC Haute-Normandie): *Untitled* (1995, eight watercolours).

SALOMONE DE GRASSI. See **GRASSI Salomone de'**

SALOMONE DI DANZICA
17th century.
Born possibly in Danzig (now Gdansk, Poland); died in Milan.
Painter.

Salomone di Danzica moved to Italy in about 1695. His work, generally of comic subjects, is remarkable for its precision and finish. His portrait, by Gregori, is in the Museo Fiorentino.

SALOMONS, Edward
British, 19th - 20th century.
Died 1906.
Painter, watercolourist, architect. Urban landscapes.

Edward Salomons was a member of the Society of British Architects. He exhibited a *View of Venice* at the Grosvenor Gallery in 1880.

MUSEUMS AND GALLERIES:
MANCHESTER: *Verona* (watercolour).

SALOMONSEN, Oswald Lykkeberg. See **SALA Eugène de**

SALOMUSMÜLLER, Ernst Gottfried, or Salmusmüller
German, 18th century.
Born 1700, in Augsburg; died 1771, in Augsburg.
Medallist, engraver.

SALOMUSMÜLLER, Georg Wilhelm
German, 18th century.
Born c. 1689; died 1722, in Augsburg.
Engraver (burin).

SALOMUSMÜLLER, Matthäus Sigmund, or Salmusmüller
German, 18th century.
Born c. 1696; died 1731, in Augsburg.
Draughtsman, engraver (burin).

Matthäus Sigmund Salomusmüller engraved portraits and views of Augsburg.

SALONI, Agostino
Italian, 17th century.
Active in Brescia in 1699.
Painter.

SALONIER, Carl
Belgian, 18th century.
Active in Liège at the end of the 18th century.
Painter.

Carl Salonier was the brother of Franz Salonier. He exhibited four miniatures and a self-portrait in Dresden, from 1797 to 1799.

SALONIER, Franz
Flemish School, 18th - 19th century.
Painter, engraver (etching). Genre scenes, landscapes.

Franz Salonier was the brother of Carl Salonier. He was active in Liège from 1790 to 1810, and lived for a long period in Dresden.

SALOUN, Ladislav or Ladislaus
Czech, 19th - 20th century.
Born 1 August 1870, in Prague.
Sculptor. Statues, monuments.

A pupil of Bohuslav Schnirch and Thomas Seidan in Prague, Ladislav Saloun sculpted statues for public buildings in Prague and the *Monument to Jan Huss*, which stands alone in the main square in Prague.

SALPION
1st century BC.
Active in Athens during the 1st century BC.
Sculptor.
Ancient Greek.

Salpion is represented by a marble krater decorated with low reliefs, now in the Naples Museum.

SALPIUS, Ulrich von
German, 19th century.
Active in the second half of the 19th century.
Sculptor.

Ulrich von Salpius was an officer.

SALSET, Bartolomé
Spanish, 15th century.
Died 13 March 1418, in Valencia.
Painter.

SALSTERNO. See **SOLSERNUS**

SALT, Henry
British, 19th century.
Born 30 October 1780, in Lichfield; died 30 August 1827, in Dessuke, near Alexandria.
Draughtsman.

Henry Salt studied in Lichfield. He accompanied Lord Valentia on his voyage to India and Sri Lanka, as well as areas that are now in Ethiopia and Eritrea. In 1802, assuming responsibility for the illustrations included in the latter's account of his travels published in 1809. Salt was subsequently commissioned by the English Crown to bear gifts to the Emperor of Abyssinia in order to cement an alliance between the two countries. In the course of his explorations, he was able to assemble the elements needed to publish *Twenty-four views in St Helena, the Cape, India, Ceylon, the Red Sea, Abyssinia and Egypt* in 1809. He was appointed English Consul general to Egypt and made full use of every opportunity to produce some interesting studies of Egyptian antiquity.

SALT, John
British, 20th century.
Born 1937, in Birmingham.
Active since 1967 in the USA.
Painter (mixed media), lithographer.

John Salt initially studied at Birmingham College of Art, then at the Slade School of Fine Art in London. He taught at various different English colleges from 1960 to 1967, and then, having settled in the USA, at the Maryland Institute of Art in 1967 and 1968.

Salt's style of painting in his very early work was strictly abstract, although he often used machines as subject-matter. Once he arrived in the USA, he joined the Hyperrealist movement. Its original objective was principally the disillusioned observation of American civilisation. He began by discovering the possibilities offered by photographs, which he used as the starting point for his paintings. First of all, he used 'artistic' photographs, then, soon judging them to be artificial, he began to simply copy photographs. As for the majority of Hyper Realists, his photographs were copied as faithfully as possible. The objective was perhaps not so much about giving the illusion of reality itself but rather to paint an image, which had already had media coverage of this reality. Symbolic of civilisation, the car dominated Salt's paintings. He chose the car because it was a neutral subject. 'The car [is] so obvious, ugly, invasive and unnecessary.' In order to paint cars without romanticising the style, he used a spray painting method, along the lines of the actual technique used for painting cars. He preferred old and abandoned cars with battered seats and broken window, ready for the scrapyard. He framed the view of the whole car, but could only paint details of it. He often painted the interiors, conjuring up the filth and deterioration, or keeping traces of an accident. His participation in Documenta V determined his international fame. John Salt's paintings were shown in exhibitions dedicated to the Hyperrealist movement of the time, and benefited from the craze that they then triggered.

Salt began exhibiting in Birmingham in 1965 and 1967. Once he was in New York, he participated in group exhibitions which established Hyperrealism: 1971, *Radical Realism*, Museum of Contemporary Art, Chicago, and the Paris Biennale; 1972, *Sharp Focus Realism* in New York, and Documenta V in Kassel; 2003, *Hyperréalismes USA 1965-75*, Musée d'Art Moderne et Contemporain, Strasbourg. He had his first solo exhibition in 1969 in New York, then in Detroit in 1970; in Hamburg in 1972 and again in New York in 1973.

BIBLIOGRAPHY:
Lebensztejn, Jean-Claude, et al., *Hyperréalismes USA 1965-75*, group exhibition catalogue, Musée d'Art moderne et contemporain, Strasbourg, Hazan, Paris, 2003.

AUCTION RECORDS:
LONDON, 3 Dec 1974, *Montego* (1969) Gns 6,000. NEW YORK, 4 May 1982, *Green Chevy in Green Fields* (1973, oil on canvas, 49 1/4 x 72 ins / 125 x 183 cm) USD 17,000. NEW YORK, 2 May 1985, *Demolished Vehicle (S.T.O. with Trash)* (1971, oil on canvas, 51 x 73 ins / 129.5 x 185.5 cm) USD 7,500. NEW YORK, 9 May 1990, *School Bus and Red Delivery Truck* (1973, oil on canvas, 49 x 72 ins / 124.5 x 182.8 cm) USD 46,750. NEW YORK, 3 Oct 1991, *Suburban Pastoral* (1972, oil on canvas, 46 x 57 3/4 ins / 116 x 147 cm) USD 19,800. NEW YORK, 6 May 1992, *Abandoned Vehicle with Torn Seats* (1970, oil on canvas, 51 3/4 x 76 1/2 ins / 131.7 x 194.3 cm) USD 11,000. ZURICH, 21 April 1993, *Car* (1969, mixed media and collage/paper, 23 3/4 x 33 3/4 ins / 60.5 x 86 cm) CHF 1,500. LUCERNE, 20 Nov 1993, *Elektra* (1969, oil on canvas, 53 1/4 x 69 ins / 135 x 175 cm) CHF 16,000. AMSTERDAM, 30 May 1995, *Wreck in the Desert* (coloured lithograph, 22 x 32 ins / 55 x 81 cm) NLG 1,063. NEW YORK, 13 Nov 2002, *Albuquerque Wreck Yard - Sandia Auto Electric* (oil on canvas, 48 x 72 ins / 122 x 183 cm) USD 25,000. PARIS, 27 May 2004, *Untitled* (watercolour, 11 x 17 ins / 29 x 43 cm) EUR 4,200. NEW YORK, 29 June 2004, *Arresting Vehicle with Decomposing Seats* (1972, oil on canvas, 53 x 79 ins / 134 x 200 cm) USD 6,000.

SALTAMACCHIA, Placido
Italian, 16th - 17th century.
Active in Messina, Sicily, from 1595 to 1616.
Painter. Religious subjects, portraits.
Messina School.
Placido Saltamacchia was the pupil of D. Guinaccia and G.S. Comandé, and an imitator of Alonso Rodriguez.

SALTANOV, Bogdan or Ivan, or Saltanov
Armenian, 17th century.
Born in Armenia, of Persian origin.
Active in Moscow from 1667 to 1702.
Painter.
Bogdan Saltanov worked for the court and churches in Moscow.

SALTARELLO, Damaso, or Saltarelli
Italian, 17th century.
Active in Florence from 1600 to 1625.
Painter.
Damaso Saltarello was a monk of the Cistercian order.

SALTARELLO, Luca, or Sartarelli or Saltaregli or Saltarelli
Italian, 17th century.
Born c. 1610, in Genoa; died probably c. 1655, in Rome, young.
Painter. History painting.
Luca Saltarello was the pupil of Domenico Fiasella. He showed great promise, and is noted for his painting in the church of S Stefano in Genoa of the *Miracle of St Benedict*, as well as the *Martyrdom of St Andrew* in the church of S Andrea. In 1655, he went to Rome, where he is said to have died shortly afterwards from overwork.

SALTER, John William
British, 19th century.
Born 1825, in North Tawton; died 1891, in Torquay.
Watercolourist. Landscapes, coastal scenes.
John Salter lived in Torquay in Devon. His works show that he visited Portsmouth, the Isle of Wight, Brighton, Hastings, London, Yarmouth, Yorkshire, Northumberland, Ireland, Wales and Italy. He exhibited between 1848 and 1875. He may be identified with John William Salter, fellow of the Royal Geographical Society, who worked on the geological surveys of the UK and of Canada from the 1840s to 1860s.
AUCTION RECORDS:
EXETER, 2 July 2002, *Dittisham* (1875, watercolour, 14 x 21 ins / 36 x 53 cm) GBP 2,000.

SALTER, William
British, 19th century.
Born 26 December 1804, in Honiton (Devon); died 22 December 1875, in London.
Painter. History painting, religious subjects, portraits.
William Salter moved to London in 1822 and studied under Northcote before travelling to Italy and spending time in Florence, Rome and Parma. He returned to England in 1833. He exhibited in London from 1822 to 1875, notably at the British Institution and the Suffolk Street Gallery. He was a member of the British Society of Artists and served as its vice-president. He was also a member of the Accademia di Belle Arti of Florence. He painted themes drawn from Shakespeare and from the lives of the Stuarts. He is possibly the same artist as William Salter Herrick.
AUCTION RECORDS:
STOCKHOLM, 19 May 1992, *Virgin and Child with Saints Jerome and Mary Magdalene* (oil on canvas, 76 3/4 x 57 ins / 195 x 145 cm) SEK 20,000. LONDON, 15 Dec 1993, *Portrait of an Italian Officer wearing the Cross of St Maurice and St Lazarus and the Order of St Gregory and Francis I of Sicily* (1837, oil on canvas, 44 1/4 x 33 3/4 ins / 112.1 x 85.7 cm) GBP 3,450. LONDON, 6 Sept 2001, *Portrait of Eleanor and Mary Ann Rickards with Flowers in a Basket, in a Landscape* (oil on canvas, 44 x 34 ins / 112 x 86 cm) GBP 2,200. LONDON, 5 Sept 2002, *Portrait of General Sir Arthur Clifton* (oil on canvas, 94 x 58 ins / 240 x 148 cm) GBP 4,000. DETROIT, 13 Dec 2002, *Reclining Female and 2 Bacchantes* (oil on canvas, 18 x 21 ins / 46 x 53 cm) USD 1,750.

SALTERIO, Stefano, or Saltieri
Italian, 18th century.
Sculptor. Religious subjects.
Stefano Salterio worked in Laglio. He produced stucco ornaments and statues for churches in Mantua and the church in Schwyz, Switzerland.

SALTES, Giorgio
Italian, 17th century.
Active in Genoa in 1621.
Painter.

SALTFLEET, F.. See the entry **SALTFLEET J.**

SALTFLEET, J.
British, 19th century.
Painter, watercolourist. Landscapes, seascapes.
J. Saltfleet is possibly the artist identified as 'F. Saltfleet' in the 1892 catalogue of the Royal Institute of Painters in Water-Colours and recorded as having exhibited a landscape.
MUSEUMS AND GALLERIES:
BRISTOL: *Rising Tide* (watercolour); *London Bridge at Sunset* (watercolour).

SALTI, Giulio
Italian, 20th century.
Born 21 July 1899, in Barberino di Mugello; died 1984
Painter. Portraits, genre scenes, landscapes, still-lifes.
Giulio Salti was a self-taught painter.
AUCTION RECORDS:
LOS ANGELES, 10 June 1976, *Young Woman by the Sea* (oil on board, 19 x 12 1/2 ins / 48.2 x 32 cm) USD 500. PRATO, 2 March 2003, *Herring* (oil on board, 16 x 20 ins / 40 x 50 cm) EUR 2,000. PRATO, 2 April 2004, *Still-life with Roses and Violin* (oil on board, 17 x 24 ins / 44 x 60 cm) EUR 1,600.

SALTIERI, Stefano. See **SALTERIO**

SALTINI, Pietro
Italian, 19th - 20th century.
Born 21 February 1839, in Florence; died October 1908, in Florence.
Painter. Genre scenes.

Pietro Saltini was a pupil of Tito (?) Lessi and then of Enrico Pollastrini at the Accademia di Belle Arti in Florence. He became a corresponding professor of the academy.

Museums and Galleries:

Liège: *Old Cobbler with his Cat* - Trieste (Civico Mus. Revoltella): *Between Friends; Grandmother's Story.*

Auction records:

New York, 25 Nov 1908, *Card Game*, USD 320; *The Favourite Cat*, USD 80. London, 30 Nov 1984, *At the Cobbler's* (oil on canvas, 33 x 27 ins / 83.8 x 68.5 cm) GBP 8,500. New York, 13 Feb 1985, *Puppets* (oil on canvas, 24 x 40 ins / 61 x 101.5 cm) USD 19,000. London, 16 March 1994, *Humorous Magazine* (oil on canvas, 33 x 27 1/2 ins / 84 x 70 cm) GBP 13,800. London, 16 Nov 1994, *Playing with Baby* (oil on canvas, 21 1/4 x 18 1/2 ins / 54 x 47 cm) GBP 17,825. New York, 2 May 2000, *Oriental* (oil on canvas, 25 x 20 ins / 63 x 50 cm) USD 5,000.

SALTO, Axel Johann

Danish, 20th century.

Born 17 November 1889, in Copenhagen.

Painter, sculptor, potter, lithographer, illustrator.

History painting, landscapes with figures.

Axel Johann Salto was the husband of Kamma Salto and a pupil of Holger Grönvold, P. Rostrup Boyesen and Julius Paulsen. He worked chiefly as a sculptor/ceramist, producing stone vases and glazed pottery.

Auction records:

Copenhagen, 9 May 1990, *Large Glazed Stone Vase* (h. 15 1/4 ins / 39 cm) DKK 13,000. Copenhagen, 31 Oct 1990, *Glazed Stone Vase with an Ox-blood Coating* (1957, h. 7 ins / 18 cm) DKK 4,300. Copenhagen, 21 April 1993, *Christian IV at the Battle of Barenberg in 1626* (1918, oil on canvas, 74 1/2 x 99 1/4 ins / 189 x 252 cm) DKK 19,000. Copenhagen, 20 Oct 1993, *Large Glazed Stone Vase* (h. 15 1/4 ins / 39 cm) DKK 9,500. Copenhagen, 13 April 1994, *Landscape with Fallow Deer and a Volcano* (painting/synthetic resin, 61 x 98 ins / 155 x 248 cm) DKK 13,000. Copenhagen, 19 Oct 1994, *Pottery Vase with a Glazed Floral Motif* (h. 20 3/4 ins / 53 cm) DKK 18,000. Copenhagen, 19 June 2001, *Eroctic Composition with Figures and Animals in a Landscape* (oil on canvas, 65 x 94 ins / 165 x 240 cm) DKK 22,000. Copenhagen, 10 Oct 2001, *Christian IV in the Battle of Lutter by Barenberg 1626* (1918, oil on canvas, 74 x 99 ins / 189 x 252 cm) DKK 180,000. Havnen, 30 Nov 2002, *Landscape with Vulcano and Antelopes* (oil on panel, 61 x 97 ins / 154 x 247 cm) DKK 18,000. Copenhagen, 29 March 2004, *Crazy Turk* (c. 1938, oil on canvas, 27 x 41 ins / 69 x 105 cm) DKK 52,000.

SALTO, Diego del

Spanish, 16th century.

Born in Seville.

Painter. Religious subjects.

Diego del Salto was an Augustinian monk. He painted a *Deposition*.

SALTO, Kamma, short for Anna Camilla

Maiden name: Thorn

Danish, 20th century.

Born 13 July 1890, in Hammersholm.

Painter.

Kamma Salto was the wife of Axel Johann Salto.

SALTO, Naja

Danish, 20th century.

Born c. 1945.

Painter, designer, designer, scenographer. Murals, designs for tapestries, designs for mosaics, designs for stained glass, stage costumes and sets, painted glass.

Born to an artist family, Naja Salto started out as a stage designer in Danish theatres. These beginnings accustomed her to large formats. Using various techniques - oil on canvas, tapestry, mosaic, stained glass, painted glass - she has displayed a fertile talent as a decorative artist in a range of styles, though floral and marine ornamental motifs are recurrent.

From 1968, she took part in numerous collective exhibitions in Denmark, Sweden and Norway. In 1982, she took part in exhibitions in New York and Los Angeles, in 1983 in Tilburg, Holland, and in Hanover. In 1984, she took part in *Design in Denmark* at the Château in Biron (Dordogne) and in an exhibition at the Musée des Beaux-Arts Nancy. In 1988, she tok part in exhibitions at the Musée des Arts Décoratifs in Lyons, at the Musée des Beaux-Arts in Caen and at the 6th International Triennale in Lódz. She took part in an exhibition at the Nordjyllands Kunstmuseum, Aalborg in 1989, and at Charlottenborg, Copenhagen in 1992.

Solo shows have included Copenhagen (1967), Galerie Linart, Amsterdam (1980, 1984), Copenhagen (1983), Kunstindustrimuseet, Copenhagen (1987), Herning Museum (1988), *Axis Mundi*, Skissernas Museum, Lund (1990), Aarhus (1994), *Naja Salto: Copenhague-Aubusson aller-retour* (*Return Ticket: Copenhagen-Aubusson*), Maison du Danemark, Paris (1994).

Bibliography:

Naja Salto - Copenhague-Aubusson aller-retour, exhibition catalogue, Maison du Danemark, Paris, 1994.

SALTOFT, Edvard Anders Christian

Danish, 20th century.

Born 3 September 1883, in Copenhagen.

Painter, pastellist, lithographer. Figures, portraits, still-lifes, flowers.

Edvard Anders Christian Saltoft studied under Holger Grönvold, Peter Severin Kröyer and Laurits Regner Tuxen.

Auction records:

New York, 28 Oct 1988, *Still-life with Flowers* (pastel/card, 38 3/4 x 31 ins / 98.4 x 78.7 cm) USD 1,320. Copenhagen, 28 March 2000, *Still-life with Flowers in a Vase on a Tray* (oil on canvas, 32 x 25 ins / 82 x 63 cm) DKK 15,000.

SALTORELLI, Luca. See **SALTARELLO**

SALTZA, Carl Fredrik de (Baron)

Swedish, 19th - 20th century.

Born 29 October 1858, in Ortomta; died 10 December 1905, in New York.

Painter. Portraits, genre scenes.

Carl Fredrik de Saltza studied at the fine arts academy in Stockholm and completed his studies in Brussels and Paris.

SALTZER. See **SALZER**

SALTZMANN, Anna

French, 19th century.

Born in Colmar (Upper Rhine).

Painter. History painting.

Her brother was Auguste Saltzmann.

Museums and Galleries:

Colmar: *Resurrection; Crucifixion; Bacchanals.*

SALTZMANN, Auguste

French, 19th century.

Born 15 April 1824, in Ribeauvillé (Haut-Rhin).

Painter, archaeologist. Landscapes.

He was taught by his brother, Henri Gustave Saltzmann. He exhibited at the Salon between 1847 and 1850.

Museums and Galleries:

Colmar: views of Corsica, Paestum and the Gulf of Naples.

SALTZMANN, Carl

German, 19th - 20th century.

Born 23 September 1847, in Berlin; died 14 January 1923, in Berlin.

Painter (gouache). Seascapes.

Carl Saltzmann studied at the fine arts academy in Berlin and subsequently under Hermann Heschke. In 1878 he accompanied Prince Heinrich of Prussia on a world tour and in 1888 he travelled to Russia in the company of Kaiser Wilhelm II. He took part in group exhibitions and was a medal winner in Berlin (1887), Chicago (1893) and Paris at the Exposition Universelle of 1900.

Museums and Galleries:

Berlin: *The Frigate 'Leipzig' off Saint Helena; Naval Manoeuvres* - Wroclaw: *Borja Bai, Tierra del Fuego.*

Auction records:

New York, 29 May 1984, *View of Acapulco* (1879, oil on canvas, 21 x 16 1/2 ins / 53.5 x 42 cm) USD 6,000. Heidelberg, 14 Oct 1988, *View of the Island of Heligoland on a Stormy Day* (1902, gouache, 15 x 22 3/4 ins / 38 x 58 cm) DEM 1,750.

SALTZMANN, Henri Gustave, or Salzmann

French, 19th century.

Born 31 August 1811, in Colmar (Upper Rhine); died 28 November 1872, in Nyon.

Active in Switzerland.

Painter. Landscapes.

Henri Gustave Saltzmann was a pupil of Charles Caïus Renoux and Alexandre Calame. He was married in Geneva in 1856, and set up his studio in nearby Lancy. He exhibited at the Paris Salon from 1846 to 1865; his work was also shown in Geneva during the same period.

He was particularly attracted to landscapes with strong light and stark contrasts: for example the Savoy region, the Roman countryside, Provence and Corsica.

Museums and Galleries:

Colmar: *View from Savoy; Memory of Corsica; The Aqueducts of the Roman Countryside* - Geneva (MAH): *Environs of Rome.*

Auction records:

Paris, 21 Feb 1975, *Italian Countryside: Fountain* (oil on canvas, 14 1/4 x 26 ins / 36 x 66 cm) FRF 2,100.

SALUCCI, Alexandro (Cavaliere), or Saluzzi

Italian, 17th century.

Born 1590, in Florence; died after 1657, in Rome.

Painter, watercolourist. Mythological subjects, urban landscapes, ruins.

Salucci was a member of the Accademia di San Luca in Rome in 1648.

Museums and Galleries:

Basel: *Heliodorus Ransacking the Temple; Lake at Bethesda.*

Auction records:

Paris, 31 March - 1 April 1924, *View of Monuments* (watercolour) FRF 150. Milan, 12-13 March 1963, *View of Constantine's Triumphal Arch; View of an Imaginary Castle*, ITL 4,000,000. Rome, 1 June 1982, *Architectural View with Figures* (oil on canvas, 70 1/2 x 104in/179 x 264cm) ITL 16,000,000. Rome, 28 April 1992, *Architectural Capriccio of the Galleries of a Palace* (oil on canvas, 29 1/4 x 39 1/4in/74 x 100cm) ITL 40,000,000. Lugano, 1 Dec 1992, *Landscape with Roman Ruins* (oil on canvas, 27 x 20 1/2in/68.5 x 52cm) CHF 2,800. Paris, 26 April 1993, *Mediterranean Port with Figures* (oil on canvas, 33 1/2 x 47in/85 x 119.5cm) FRF 170,000. New York, 12 Jan 1995, *Capriccio of a Mediterranean Port with Figures on the Steps of a Classical Building (Possibly Ulyssess Bidding Goodbye to Penelope)* (oil on canvas, 36 3/4 x 49 1/2in/93.3 x 125.7cm) USD 51,750. Rome, 21 Nov 1995, *Abduction of Helen* (oil on canvas, 38 1/4 x 53 1/4in/97 x 135cm) ITL 51,854,000. Lyons, 8 March 1998, *Ruins with Numerous Figures by the Riverside* (oil on canvas, 48 3/4 x 59 1/2in/124 x 151cm) FRF 150,000. Rome, 5 Oct 1999, *Architectural Capriccio of Harbour with Figures* (oil on canvas, figures painted by Jan Miel, 25 x 38 ins / 63 x 96 cm) ITL 31,399,000. New York, 26 Jan 2001, *Elegant Figures in Architectural Landscapes* (oil on canvas, a pair, 29 x 39 ins / 74 x 99 cm) USD 26,000.

SALUZZO, Cesare da. See **CESARE di Piemonte**

SALVA, Guillermo

Spanish.

Active in Majorca.

Sculptor.

Guillermo Salva carved the marble pedestal of the Choir Screen in the Basilica El Pilar, Zaragoza.

SALVA SIMBOR, Gonzalo

Spanish, 19th - 20th century.

Born 1845, in Paris; died 14 January 1923, in Valencia.

Painter. Portraits, landscapes.

Gonzalo Salva Simbor was a pupil of Rafael Montesinos.

Museums and Galleries:

Valencia.

Auction records:

London, 30 May 1984, *Courtyard with Figures* (1870, oil on panel, 11 x 17 3/4 ins / 27 x 45 cm) GBP 1,500.

SALVADO, Jacinto

Spanish, 20th century.

Born 17 October 1892, in Montroig (Tarragona); died 27 August 1983, in Montroig.

Active in France from 1918.

Painter (including gouache), watercolourist, ceramicist. Designs for stained glass.

Jacinto Salvado studied painting at the colleges of fine arts in Barcelona, Marseilles and Paris (where he lived in the 1920s). In 1924, his work was singled out by the art critic Waldemar George and, by 1927, Wilhelm Uhde and Georges Charensol were also singing his praises. While in Paris, Salvado made friends with Picasso, Gargallo, Julio González, Juan Gris and Georges Braque. In the 1930s, Salvado settled in Le Castellet, north of Toulon. Around 1935, his friendship with Jean (Hans) Arp was perhaps the single greatest influence on Salvado's work. In 1939, Salvado moved to Zurich where he met and exhibited alongside Max Bill. He settled in Paris after the war.

Having started out as a figurative painter, he was introduced by André Derain to Fauvism and to Cézanne, whose *Bathers* encouraged him to adopt the form/colour permutations of El Greco. By 1924, Waldemar George had pronounced Salvado one of the finest painters of his generation, and Wilhelm Uhde and Georges Charenton were unstinting in their praise for his work when it was exhibited at the Galerie Bing. Waldemar George may have been instrumental in nudging Salvado towards Expressionism, but Cubism was soon to prove the decisive influence on his work. By 1936, he was painting abstracts influenced by the constructivist geometry of Wassily Kandinsky; he sustained this approach over the long term, producing compositions not unlike those of Auguste Herbin. In 1961, he contributed ceramics and stained glass for architect Maurice Novarina's church at La Forclaz. In the final years of a long and productive life, he continued to be a well-liked and well-respected artist in and around the St-Paul district where he lived, but the art world at large showed a diminishing interest in him and his work.

Over the years, Salvado's work featured at a large number of collective exhibitions: Salon des Tuileries, Paris (1924-1927); Salon d' Autumne, Paris (1925-1957); Salon des Indépendants, Paris (1926-1960); Salon des Artistes Espagnols, Musée du Jeu de Paume, Paris (1936); Salon des Réalités Nouvelles, Paris (1948-1956 and 1982); 1957 Menton Biennale; Salon Comparaisons, Paris (1959, 1960); *Trends in Contemporary Abstract Painting*, Centre Culturel de la Villedieu, St-Quentin-en-Yvelines. Posthumous collective exhibitions include: *Art Construit*, Espace Belleville, Paris (1986) and *José Mange*, Musée d'Art de Toulon (2003).

He also exhibited solo on a regular basis: Dalmau Gallery, Barcelona (1921); Galerie Bing, Paris (1927-1929); Galerie Worms-Billiet, Paris (in the 1930s); in Paris, Madrid, Alicante and Barcelona (1956, 1960, 1961, 1971 and 1974); Châteauvallon near Toulon (1968); Simone Heller Gallery, Paris (1971); *Salvado - Drawings and Reliefs*, Galerie Carmen Martinez, Paris (1978); Galerie Ralph, Paris (1978 and 1979); Goya Gallery, Saragossa (1982); S Francisco Gallery, Lisbon (1983). A Salvado retrospective was held in 2002 at the Museo Nacional Centro de Arte Reina Sofia in Madrid.

BIBLIOGRAPHY:

Salvado, exhibition catalogue, Gal. Simone Heller, Paris, 1971. in *Le Courant d'art*, n° 1, periodical, Carmen Martinez, Paris, February-March 1978. Gómez-Ferrer, Guillermo (ed.), *Jacinto Salvadó*, exhibition catalogue, Museo Nacional Centro de Arte Reina Sofía, Madrid, 2002.

MUSEUMS AND GALLERIES:

MEXICO CITY (Mus. Cuauthemoc) - PARIS (MAMVP) - VILLAFAMÉS (Mus. Popular de Arte Contemporáneo).

AUCTION RECORDS:

PARIS, 26 April 1926, *Carnival* (watercolour) FRF 260. PARIS, 3 May 1930, *Composition* (gouache) FRF 150. VERSAILLES, 2 May 1976, *Clown* (oil on canvas, 28 3/4 x 23 1/2 ins / 73 x 60 cm) FRF 2,500. PARIS, 29 Jan 1988, *Light Transmission* (1970, oil on panel, 28 3/4 x 23 1/2 ins / 73 x 60 cm) FRF 5,000. PARIS, 29 June 1990, *Cubist Portrait* (oil on canvas, 32 x 21 1/4 ins / 81.5 x 54 cm) FRF 11,000. PARIS, 2 July 2002, *Composition* (1975, oil on canvas, 39 x 20 ins / 100 x 50 cm) EUR 5,200. MADRID, 22 June 2004, *Composition* (1959, oil on canvas, 51 x 35 ins / 130 x 89 cm) EUR 3,000. MADRID, 22 June 2004, *Abstract* (1958, oil on canvas, 35 x 52 ins / 89 x 131 cm) EUR 3,250.

SALVADOR
Spanish, 15th century.
Painter.

Salvador painted the panels on the high altar of Plasencia Cathedral, in 1424.

SALVADOR, pseudonym of Palet Salvador Carlos
Spanish, 20th century.
Born 14 February 1912, in Barcelona.
Active in France from 1917.
Painter, poster artist, caricaturist. Figures, landscapes. Stage sets.

Salvador moved to Marseilles in 1917 and attended secondary school and the college of fine arts. Around 1930 he settled in Paris and contributed caricatures to various periodicals. He spent time with Jean Cocteau and his circle of friends and worked as a poster artist, decorator and theatre-set designer. He returned to Spain and was sent on military service to Tunisia, after which he returned to Paris and started working again as a set designer in Paris and on the Côte d'Azur. During World War II, Salvador found refuge at Ste-Segolène in the Upper Loire region. After the war, he embarked on a chequered career, travelling extensively in Australia, New Guinea and New Caledonia and working among other things as a crocodile hunter, a farmer and a ship's captain. All the while, however, he continued to paint, exhibiting with undoubted success in Australia. He spent some fifteen years on the move before returning to France to settle at St-Cyr-sur-Mer in the Var.

Salvador's career as a painter did not get off the ground until the outbreak of World War II, when he sought refuge in a small village and started to paint what he saw around him - farms, peasants and aspects of rural life. Using a pseudonym, he started producing so-called naive paintings. He then embarked on a series of trompe l'œil canvases which brought him to the attention of the public.

SALVADOR, Antonio
Spanish, 17th century.
Died 1 September 1644, in Valladolid.
Sculptor.

SALVADOR, Antonio, called El Romano de Valencia
Spanish, 18th century.
Born 20 February 1685, in Onteniente; died 22 July 1716, in Valencia.
Sculptor.

Antonio Salvador was a pupil of L. Capuz and C. Rusconi. He carved a statue of *Christ* for the church of La Misericordia in Valencia and various *Pietàs* for churches in Valencia and the surrounding area.

SALVADOR, Pedro
Spanish, 17th century.
Active in Valencia.
Painter.

Pedro Salvador painted a number of works for the church of Bocairente in 1645.

SALVADOR, Ruiz Juan. See **SALVADOR RUIZ Juan**

SALVADOR CARMONA, Anna Maria. See **MENGS**

SALVADOR CARMONA, José
Spanish, 18th century.
Born in Nava del Rey; died before 1800, in Ontova.
Sculptor (wood).

José Salvador Carmona studied under his uncle Luis Salvador and was the brother of Manuel Carmona. He painted an *Immaculate Conception* for the church of S Luis in Madrid and a *St Francis Xavier* for the church of S Sebastián, also in Madrid.

SALVADOR CARMONA, Juan Antonio
Spanish, 18th century.
Died 20 January 1805, in Madrid.
Engraver (burin).

Juan Salvador Carmona studied under his brother Manuel and was a member of the Real Academia de San Fernando in 1770.

SALVADOR CARMONA, Luis
Spanish, 18th century.
Born 1709, in Nava del Rey; died 3 January 1767, in Madrid.
Sculptor (stone/wood).

Luis Salvador Carmona studied under Juan Alonso Villa Brille y Ron. There are wooden sculptures by him in churches in Azpilcueta, Cuenca, León, Madrid, Nava del Rey, Oviedo, El Paular, Priego de Cuenca, Segura de Guipúzcoa, Salamanca, Valverde and Vergara.

BIBLIOGRAPHY:

Bermudez, C., *Diccionario histórico de los más ilustres profesores de las bellas artes en España*, Madrid, 1800. Martin González, J.J., *Escultura Barroca en España 1600-1770*, Cátedra, Madrid, 1983. Martin González, J.J., *Luis Salvador Carmona escultor y académico*, Alpuerto, Madrid, 1990.

SALVADOR CARMONA, Manuel
Spanish, 18th - 19th century.
Born 20 May 1734, in Nava del Rey; died 15 October 1820, in Madrid.
Engraver (burin), draughtsman.

According to some sources, Manuel Salvador Carmona lived from 1707 to 1774. He studied under his uncle Luis Salvador and under Nicolas Gabriel Dupuis in Paris. He engraved portraits and mythological and religious subjects and was married to Anna Maria, the daughter of Anton Raphael Mengs.

BIBLIOGRAPHY:
Gayguer, L., *Retratos de los españoles ilustres con un epítome de sus vidas*, En la Imprenta Real de Madrid, Madrid, 1791. Carderera y Solano, V., *Manuel Salvador Carmona*, Editorial Castalia, Valencia, 1950.
AUCTION RECORDS:
LONDON, 1853, *The Foolish Virgins*, FRF 750; *The Wise Virgins*, FRF 900.

SALVADOR DE VALENCIA

Spanish, 15th century.
Active c. 1450.
Painter.

Salvador de Valencia worked with Benozzo Gozzoli in Rome. His patron was Pope Calixtus III.

SALVADOR GÓMEZ, Luciano

Spanish, 17th century.
Active in Valencia c. 1662.
Painter. History painting.

Luciano Salvador Gómez was a pupil of Jacinto de Espinosa and may have been the brother of Vicente Salvador y Gómez.

SALVADOR RUIZ, Juan

Spanish, 17th century.
Died after 1704.
Painter. Landscapes.

Juan Salvador Ruiz studied at the Seville academy and worked in the city for the churches of Espera and Lora del Río. He also worked in Naples and was a gilder as well as a painter.
AUCTION RECORDS:
LONDON, 24 May 1991, *View of Messina* (oil/silvered copper, 8 1/4 x 16 1/2 ins / 21 x 41.7 cm) GBP 24,200. ROME, 31 May 1994, *Caprice of a Night Festival in Naples near Castel Nuovo with Fireworks* (oil/silvered copper, 7 x 15 ins / 17.7 x 38 cm) ITL 42,426,000. LONDON, 5 July 1995, *Panoramic View of Naples from the Bay with the Molo in the Centre; Panoramic View of Naples from Mergellina with Castel dell'Ovo on the Right and Vesuvius in the Background* (oil on canvas, a pair, each 13 3/4 x 41 ins / 35 x 104 cm) GBP 69,700.

SALVADOR Y GÓMEZ, Vicente

Spanish, 17th century.
Born 1637 or 1645, in Valencia; died 1680 or 1698.
Painter, draughtsman. Religious subjects, animals, architectural views.

Vicente Salvador y Gómez studied under Jacinto de Espinosa. He began to paint at the age of 14 and produced a series of scenes from the life of St Ignatius Loyola which established his reputation and won him many commissions from churches and monasteries in Valencia and the surrounding area. In 1670 he was made director of the academy that met in the monastery of Sto Domingo. In 1675 he is known to have produced a series of ten scenes from the life of S Juan de Mala and St Felix de Valois for the choir of the church of El Remedio.

He was a prolific artist producing skilful paintings of birds, animals and architectural views in addition to his history compositions.
BIBLIOGRAPHY:
Kubler G./Soria, M., *Art and Architecture in Spain & Portugal and their American Dominians 1500 to 1800*, Penguin Books, Harmondsworth and Baltimore, 1959. Perez Sánchez, A.E., '*Vincente Salvador Gómez: a propósito de una obra adquirida para el Prado*' in *Boletín del Museo del Prado*, vol 2, 1980.
MUSEUMS AND GALLERIES:
MADRID (Prado): *Christ Driving the Money Lenders from the Temple*.
AUCTION RECORDS:
PARIS, 6 June 1978, *Christ Driving the Merchants from the Temple* (oil on canvas, 52 3/4 x 39 1/4 ins / 134 x 100 cm) FRF 40,000. NEW YORK, 10 Jan 1995, *Madonna of the Rosary* (ink, 12 3/4 x 9 1/2 ins / 32.3 x 24 cm) USD 4,025. PARIS, 27 Nov 2002, *Infant Jesus Appearing to St Anthony of Padua* (pen and brown ink, 7 x 5 ins / 18 x 13 cm) EUR 7,500.

SALVADORE D'ANTONIO, or Salvatore

Italian, 15th century.
Active in Messina at the end of the 15th century.
Painter.

Salvadore d'Antonio painted a panel depicting *St Francis Receiving the Stigmata*, in S Niccolo in Messina. According to some authors, he was the father of Antonello da Messina, but it seems likely that he was just his pupil.

SALVADORI, Aldo

Italian, 20th century.
Born 1905, in Milan; died 2002
Painter. Portraits.

Aldo Salvadori was a pupil at the Accademia di Belle Arti in Florence.
AUCTION RECORDS:
MILAN, 24 June 1980, *Portrait of a Woman* (oil on canvas, 11 3/4 x 15 1/4 ins / 30 x 39 cm) ITL 2,400,000. MILAN, 19 Nov 2002, *Woman* (1975, oil on canvas, 20 x 24 ins / 50 x 60 cm) EUR 7,000. MILAN, 26 March 2003, *Seated Nude* (1970, oil on canvas, 39 x 28 ins / 100 x 70 cm) EUR 5,200. MILAN, 11 June 2003, *Young Woman* (1970, oil on canvas, 39 x 25 ins / 99 x 64 cm) EUR 10,000.

SALVADORI, Andrea

Italian, 17th century.
Active in Florence in 1625.
Draughtsman, engraver(?). Ornaments.

SALVADORI, Giacomo

Italian, 19th - 20th century.
Born 1858, in Trento.
Painter, sculptor, architect.

Giacomo Salvadori worked chiefly as an architect.

SALVADORI, Marcello

Italian (?), 20th century.
Sculptor, environmental artist.
Lumino-Kinetic Art.

Marcello Salvadori set up the Centre for Advanced Study of Science in Art in London. This was a group of technically well-equipped laboratories available for use by artists wishing to carry out special projects. In 1967, he designed a lumino-kinetic building made of stainless steel in the shape of an asymmetric dodecahedron covered with plastic panels. Some of these were intended to reproduce the colours of the prism, varying in intensity according to the time of day, while others, of photometric glass, would grow darker as the daylight increased in intensity. Polaroid glass was also to be used for montages of real movements (it being the characteristic of Polaroid glass to produce all the colours of the spectrum and select them according to its position in relation to light rays). It is not known whether this project was ever realised.
BIBLIOGRAPHY:
Popper, Frank, *L'Art cinétique*, Gauthier-Villars, Paris, 1970

SALVADORI, Remo

Italian, 20th - 21st century.
Born 1947, in Cerreto Guidi (Florence).
Sculptor (mixed media).

Remo Salvadori used a wide variety of objects and methods - sheets of lead cut out and carefully folded, the foot of a camera stand cast in bronze, painted cups and so forth - with the apparent intention of making observers consider the symbolic purpose of the works he set before them.

His work was shown at the 1973 Paris Biennale; at Documenta 7 in Kassel in 1982; and at the 1986 Venice Biennale. He also had solo exhibitions, including: 1971 and 1973, Turin and 1991 at the Magasin in Paris.

SALVADORI, Riccardo
Italian, 19th - 20th century.
Born 24 February 1866, in Piacenza; died 25 November 1927, in Milan.
Painter, watercolourist, illustrator. Genre scenes, landscapes.

Riccardo Salvadori was a pupil at the academy in Lucca and at the Istituto di Belle Arti in Naples. He worked for many years for the periodical *L'Illustrazione Italiana*.

SALVAIRE, Édouard Jules Victor
French, 19th century.
Born 5 December 1831, in Algiers; died 19 October 1889, in Le Mans.
Painter. Landscapes.

He studied under E Guilbert, Charles Valette, Appian and Allonge. He made his Salon debut in 1876. He was a life member of the Société des Artistes Français, and a Chevalier of the Légion d'Honneur.

MUSEUMS AND GALLERIES:
CASTRES: paysages.

SALVAN, Paul Louis
French, 20th century.
Born 10 May 1877, in Paris; died 28 October 1962, in Sanary-sur-Mer (Var).
Painter. Landscapes, seascapes.

Paul Louis Salvan, a pupil of the disabled painter François de Montholon and Louis Henri Foreau, exhibited in Paris at the Salon des Artistes Français, of which he was a member from 1926, the Salon des Indépendants, the Salon d'Automne, the Salon d'Hiver, and in private galleries. He also exhibited in many provincial towns, including Lorient, Nantes, Quimperlé, Dax, Bayonne, Cannes, and, from 1956 to 1962, Sanary-sur-Mer. He received a number of awards and was an official painter to the French navy.

MUSEUMS AND GALLERIES:
DAX - LORIENT - RENNES.

SALVANA, John
Australian, 19th - 20th century.
Painter, draughtsman. Landscapes with figures, landscapes.

John Salvana was active in Sydney, and was a member of the Royal Art Society of New South Wales.

MUSEUMS AND GALLERIES:
SYDNEY: *Trees in the Forest* (drawing).

AUCTION RECORDS:
ROSEBERY, 29 June 1976, *Flock Grazing* (1947, oil on card, 10¼ x 11½ ins / 26 x 29.5 cm) AUD 280. SYDNEY, 10 Sept 1979, *With Necks to the Yoke Bent Low* (oil on canvas, 38¼ x 48 ins / 97 x 122 cm) AUD 1,900. SYDNEY, 29 June 1981, *Mountain Road, Burragorang* (1935, oil on canvas, 30¼ x 40¼ ins / 77 x 102 cm) AUD 3,400. SYDNEY, 4 June 1984, *By the River* (oil on card, 11¾ x 17 ins / 30 x 43 cm) AUD 2,200. SYDNEY, 3 July 1989, *Morning in Yarramalong* (oil on card, 12¼ x 11¾ ins / 31 x 30 cm) AUD 700; *Summer Mist* (oil on card, 9 x 13½ ins / 23 x 34 cm) AUD 850.

SALVANELLO
Italian, 13th century.
Active in Siena in 1274.
Painter.

SALVANH, Antoine, or Salvahn or Salvainh or Salvant or Salvart
French, 15th - 16th century.
Born c. 1478, in Vabrette; died 1552.
Sculptor.

Antoine Salvanh worked in Rodez Cathedral and carved the portals of the churches of St John the Baptist and St Cosmas in Espalion.

SALVANH, Jean, or Salvahn or Salvainh or Salvant or Salvart
French, 16th century.
Active 1561-1580.
Sculptor.

Jean Salvanh sculpted the portal of the church of St Martial in Rodez, and worked in other churches of the city and region.

SALVART, Jean
French, 15th century.
Died 21 September 1447.
Sculptor.

Jean Salvart worked in Rouen Cathedral and the church of St-Jean in Rouen.

SALVAT, François Martin
French, 20th century.
Born 12 July 1892, in Amélie-les-Bains (Pyrénées-Orientales); died 1974.
Painter, engraver, illustrator. Landscapes, urban landscapes, landscapes with figures. Stage sets.

François Martin Salvat studied in Paris with Fernand Cormon. He was an advertising artist and became a director of the publishing house Éditions Grasset. He exhibited in Paris at the Salon d'Automne and the Salon de la Société des Peintres-Graveurs, and was a member and committee member of both. In 1935 he was awarded a diploma at the international exhibition of engraving on wood held in Warsaw. In 1949 he exhibited at the Exposition Internationale de la Gravure held at the Petit Palais, Paris. He also exhibited his paintings in solo shows at Paris galleries.

He is best known as an illustrator of Madame de la Fayette's *La Princesse de Clèves*, Victor Hugo's *Notre-Dame de Paris*, the Abbé Prévost's *Manon Lescaut*, Balzac's *Le Père Goriot*, and Henri de Monterlant's *Les Célibataires* (*The Bachelors*).

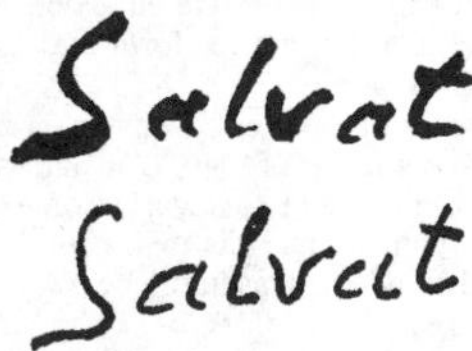

MUSEUMS AND GALLERIES:
NARBONNE (MAH): *The Terrace of Eleusis* - PARIS (MAMVP).

AUCTION RECORDS:
PARIS, 31 Jan 1944, *Landscape in the South of France*, FRF 5,400. PARIS, 7 Dec 1987, *Landscape and Labourer* (oil on canvas, 15 x 21½ ins / 38 x 54.5 cm) FRF 1,800. PARIS, 18 May 1989, *Avenue de Saxe, Paris, seen from the Place de Breteuil* (oil on card, 13 x 16¼ ins / 33 x 41 cm) FRF 3,800.

SALVATELLI, Paulus. See **PAOLO ROMANO**

SALVATERRA, Giovanni Pietro
Italian, 18th century.
Born c. 1687, in Verona; died 2 May 1743, in Verona.
Painter.

The pupil of G. Bellotti, Giovanni Salvaterra painted altarpieces for several churches in Verona.

SALVATIERRA Y BARRIALES, Valeriano
Spanish, 19th century.
Born c. 1790, in Toledo; died 24 May 1836, in Madrid.
Sculptor.

Valeriano Salvatierra y Barriales was the son of Mariano and father of Ramón Salvatierra. He studied under Canova and Thorvaldsen in Rome and became curator of the Prado museum in Madrid. He carved statues for churches and public buildings in Madrid.

SALVATIERRA Y MOLERO, Ramón
Spanish, 19th century.
Born 19 February 1829, in Madrid.
Painter.

Ramón Salvatierra y Molero was a pupil of Vincente Lopez and Juan Battista Ribera and the son of Valeriano. He painted religious subjects for churches in Madrid as well as seascapes.

MUSEUMS AND GALLERIES:
MADRID (Mus. Naval): portraits.

SALVATIERRA Y SERRANO, Mariano de
Spanish, 18th - 19th century.
Born 1752, in Toledo; died 1814, in Toledo.
Sculptor.

Mariano de Salvatierra y Serrano was the father of Valeriano. He worked mainly for Toledo Cathedral and the university of Toledo.

SALVATOR ROSA. See **ROSA Salvator**

SALVATORE, pseudonym of Messina Salvatore
Italian, 20th century.
Born 1916, in Palermo; died 1982
Sculptor.

The son of a sculptor, Salvatore learned the art of carving marble when very young. He studied at the Palermo academy of fine art and then spent periods in Trieste and Milan. In the early part of his career, his work was figurative and much influenced by the work of Arturo Martini. His low relief of *The Family*, which he exhibited at the 1940 Venice Biennale, dates from this period. After 1945, his work offered a freer interpretation of reality, as in *Torso* of 1945. After 1948, influenced by Brancusi and Arp and then by his visit to the USA in 1952-1953, he turned to abstraction, producing his 'exploded' pieces, where he attempted to reveal the occupation of space by the concrete envelope of a sculpture that 'explodes' out of its interior form and can be viewed from many different angles.

His work appeared in many collective exhibitions both in Italy - the Venice Biennales of 1940, 1956 and especially 1964 when a room was devoted to his work; Rome Quadriennale of 1960 where again he had his own room - and abroad, most importantly while he was in the USA.

AUCTION RECORDS:
COLOGNE, 21 May 1976, *Nike* (green-patinated bronze, h. 16 ins / 40.5 cm) DEM 1,900.

SALVATORE, Anna
Italian, 20th century.
Born 1923, in Rome; died 1978.
Painter. Local figures, portraits.

A pupil of Ottone Rosai at the academy of fine art in Florence, Anna Salvatore followed and emphasised the Realism of her teacher, allying herself with the Realist movement and choosing subjects from the world of the common people.

She took part in a number of collective exhibitions: Venice Biennale in 1948, 1950, 1952, 1954, 1956; Rome Quadriennale from 1948. In 1953, she won the Cesenatico Prize and, at the 28th Venice Biennale in 1956, the Drawing Prize awarded by the Venice city council.

MUSEUMS AND GALLERIES:
RICHMOND - ROME - VENICE.

AUCTION RECORDS:
MILAN, 19 Dec 1991, *Young People in the Countryside* (oil on canvas, 61 1/2 x 102 1/4 ins / 156 x 260 cm) ITL 10,000,000. ROME, 30 Nov 1993, *Dreaming Beauty* (mixed media/panel, 63 3/4 x 31 3/4 ins / 162 x 80.5 cm) ITL 2,300,000.

SALVATORE, Nino di
Italian, 20th century.
Born 1924, in Verbania Pallanza.
Painter, sculptor.

Nino di Salvatore's work, both in painting and sculpture, is abstract and geometric in style. Curves are cut through by straight lines that define planes of colour or sections of space. He was appointed director of the school of fine art in Domodossola in 1949.

He participated in several group exhibitions both in Italy and also in France, including the Salon des Réalités Nouvelles in Paris, 1951-1955. He held solo exhibitions in Italy from 1944.

AUCTION RECORDS:
MILAN, 21 June 1994, *Composition* (1952, oil on canvas, 27 1/2 x 35 ins / 70 x 89 cm) ITL 8,625,000.

SALVATORE D'ANTONIO. See **SALVADORE D'ANTONIO**

SALVATORE DA FIESOLE. See **FERRUCCI Salvestro di Michelangelo**

SALVATORE DA VERONA
Italian, 17th century.
Active in Reggio Emilia from 1642 to 1654.
Sculptor.

SALVATORE DI GIOVANNI SALVATORE
Italian, 15th century.
Born in Valencia.
Painter.

Salvatore di Giovanni Salvatore worked in Rome from 1451 to 1458, and painted coats of arms.

SALVATORI, Carlo
Italian, 19th century.
Born c. 1811, in Senigallia; died 6 November 1883, in Rome.
Sculptor.

He was the pupil and son-in-law of L. Bienaimé.

SALVATORI, Enrico
Italian, 19th - 20th century.
Born 1852, in Naples.
Sculptor.

Enrico Salvatori studied under Stanislao Lista at the Istituto di Belle Arti in Naples. He participated in the Italian Salons and also exhibited in London and Paris, including the Salon des Artistes Français of 1885.

SALVATORI, Salvator
Italian, 16th century.
Born in Florence.
Active in Lyons, France, from 1533 to 1536.
Sculptor, painter, architect.

SALVATORI D'AQUILA, or Aquilano
Italian, 15th century.
Sculptor.

Salvatori d'Aquila was the pupil of Nicola Ariscola. He worked on the *Deposition of St Bernard of Siena* with his master in L'Aquila.

SALVATORIELLO, Il. See **OLIVIERI Salvatore**

SALVENDY, Frieda
Austrian, 20th century.
Born 4 January 1887, in Vienna.
Painter, watercolourist, engraver. Urban landscapes, landscapes.

Frieda Salvendy studied in Vienna under Albin Egger-Lienz and Felix Albrecht. She was a member of the Hagenbund group of painters.
MUSEUMS AND GALLERIES:
BELGRADE: *Monte Rosso* - BRATISLAVA: watercolours - CLEVELAND: watercolours - KOŠICE: watercolours - PRAGUE (Národní Gal.): *Village Street in Hrusov* - VIENNA (Albertina Mus.): watercolours.

SALVER, Johann I
German, 17th - 18th century.
Born c. 1670, in Forchheim; died 1738, in Forchheim.
Engraver.
Johann Salver I produced a series of burin engravings depicting the *Bishops of Bamberg* and the *Grand Masters of the Teutonic Order.*

SALVER, Johann II
German, 18th century.
Active 1729-1740.
Painter, engraver. Portraits.
Johann Salver II was the son of Johann Salver I. He mainly engraved portraits of princes and German nobility.

SALVER, Johann Octavian
German, 18th century.
Born 19 May 1732; died 23 April 1788.
Engraver.
Johann Octavian Salver engraved portraits of the nobility of the German empire.

SALVESTRINI, Bartolommeo
Italian, 17th century.
Born in Florence; died 1630; of plague.
Painter. Religious subjects.
Florentine School.
The pupil of Matteo Rosselli and imitator of Biliverti, Bartolommeo Salvestrini is known for a number of paintings in churches in Florence, notably the *Martyrdom of St Ursula* in the church of S Orsola. He died young.
AUCTION RECORDS:
LONDON, 1 July 1986, *Apotheosis of St Ursula* (black chalk, pen and wash, 18 1/4 x 14 1/2in/46.4 x 36.6cm) GBP 1,100.

SALVESTRINI, Cosmo or Cosimo, or Silvestrini
Italian, 17th century.
Florentine, active c. 1650.
Sculptor.
Cosmo Salvestrini, the pupil of R. Curradi, produced works for the Boboli gardens in Florence and sculpted a bust of *Andrea del Sarto.*

SALVESTRO DI MICHELANGELO.
See **FERRUCCI Salvestro di Michelangelo**

SALVESTRONI
Italian, 16th century.
Active in Venice (?) at the end of the 16th century.
Painter.
Salvestroni painted *Triumphant Church* in the sacristy of the Franciscan church in Zara (now Zadar, Croatia).

SALVETTI, Antonio
Italian, 19th - 20th century.
Born 25 September 1854, in Colle di Val d'Elsa; died 30 October 1931, in Colle di Val d'Elsa.
Painter, pastellist. Portraits, landscapes.
A student at the Istituto di Belle Arti in Florence, Antonio Salvetti worked for some time in Paris before returning to settle in Italy. He produced a large number of portraits.

AUCTION RECORDS:
MILAN, 5 April 1979, *Harvest Scene* (1909, pastel, 35 x 54 3/4 ins / 88 x 139 cm) ITL 800,000. MILAN, 6 Dec 1989, *San Gimignano near Siena* (1925, oil on card, 14 1/4 x 7 ins / 36.5 x 18 cm) ITL 1,000,000. FLORENCE, 4 Oct 1999, *Canal at Viareggio* (1890, oil on panel, 19 x 31 ins / 49 x 79 cm) ITL 5,800,000. MILAN, 24 March 2004, *Fisherman* (1888, oil on board, 18 x 11 ins / 45 x 29 cm) EUR 3,600.

SALVETTI, Francesco Maria
Italian, 18th century.
Born 1691; died 1758.
Painter, engraver (etching).
Francesco Salvetti was the pupil and friend of Antonio Domenico Gabbiani.
AUCTION RECORDS:
PARIS, 26 June 1950, *Resurrection of Christ* (wash, heightened with white (attributed)) FRF 1,000.

SALVETTI, Giuseppe
Italian, 18th century.
Born 30 August 1730, in Verona; died 14 May 1796, in Verona.
Painter.
Giuseppe Salvetti was the pupil and friend of Felice Cignaroli.

SALVETTI, Giuseppe Maria
Italian, 18th century.
Florentine, active from 1706 to 1739.
Sculptor.
Giuseppe Salvetti was a monk.

SALVETTI, Lodovico
Italian, 17th century.
Florentine, active c. 1630.
Sculptor.
The pupil of P. Tacca, Lodovico Salvetti sculpted the statues of *St Mark* and *St Matthew* for the church of S Marco in Florence.

SALVI, Bernardino de'. See **DE'SALVI**

SALVI, Domenico
Italian, 17th century.
Active in Pisa c. 1650.
Painter. Religious subjects.
Pisan School.
Domenico Salvi is said to have been the pupil of Guido Reni. He produced paintings for the churches of S Lorenzo, S Maria del Pontenovo and S Sisto in Pisa.

SALVI, Emilio
Italian, 19th century.
Active during the first half of the 19th century.
Engraver (burin).
He was a pupil of A. Perfetti.

SALVI, Filippi de'. See **DE'SALVI**

SALVI, Giovanni Battista, called Il Sassoferrato
Italian, 17th century.
Born 29 August 1609, in Sassoferrato (Marche); died 8 August 1685, in Rome.
Painter. Religious subjects.
School of Rome.
The son and pupil of Torquinio Salvi, Giovanni Battista Salvi, known as Sassoferrato, is generally regarded as a member of the school founded by the Carracci brothers. He spent most of his life in Rome. An altarpiece entitled *Madonna of the Rosary with St Catherine and St Dominic* is considered one of his best works, and he is also noted for free copies of works by Raphael, Titian and Perugino in which his virtuosity is evident.

In evaluating Sassoferrato's work, it is perhaps important to dispense with the deference normally accorded to historical painters and to realise that he concentrated essentially on commissions of private devotional paintings, especially Madonnas. His technique, which could be considered to lack originality, derives from the eclecticism of the Carracci brothers. He also seems to have been greatly influenced by the works of Domenico Zampieri.

Museums and Galleries:

Aix: *Virgin and the Infant Jesus; Virgin at Prayer* - Avignon: *Virgin Holding the Sleeping Infant Jesus on Her Knees* - Bergamo (Accademia Carrara): *Virgin* (two) - Berlin: *Christ Mourned; Holy Family* - Bordeaux: *Virgin* - Budapest: *Virgin and the Infant Jesus* - Chambéry: *Virgin and the Infant Jesus* - Chantilly: *Holy Family* - Darmstadt: *Christ Mourned* - Douai: *Virgin and the Infant Jesus* - Dresden: *Virgin and the Infant Jesus with Heads of Angels* (twice); *Bust of the Virgin at Prayer* - Dublin: *Virgin and the Infant Jesus in the Clouds; Head of the Virgin* - Florence: *Suffering of the Virgin; The Artist* - Frankfurt am Main: *Madonna; Virgin Adoring the Infant Jesus* - Genoa: *Madonna; Virgin with the Sleeping Infant Jesus* - Glasgow: *Holy Family* - Haarlem: *Madonna* - Karlsruhe: *Virgin at Prayer* - Kassel: *Virgin and the Infant Jesus* - Le Havre: *Madonna* - Leipzig: *Virgin and the Infant Jesus* - London (NG): *The Virgin in Prayer* (1640-1650, oil on canvas); *The Virgin and Child Embracing* (after 1660, oil on canvas) - London (Wallace Collection): *The Virgin and Child* (oil on canvas, two versions); *The Mystic Marriage of St Catherine* (c. 1650's, oil on canvas) - Lyons: *Jesus' Slumber; Jesus Asleep in His Mother's Arms* - Madrid (Prado): *Virgin in Contemplation; Virgin and the Sleeping Infant Jesus* - Mannheim: *Holy Family* - Milan (Pinacoteca di Brera): *Immaculate Virgin and the Infant Jesus* (twice) - Montpellier: *Virgin at Prayer; Young Martyr* - Moscow (Rumiantsev Mus.): *Virgin Adoring the Infant Jesus; Virgin Praying* - Munich: *Virgin Praying* - Nancy: *Virgin and the Infant Jesus; Virgin with Cloak* - Nantes: *Head of the Virgin in Adoration; Old Woman Saying Her Rosary* - Naples: *Madonna and Jesus; St Joseph* - Narbonne: *Virgin with Clasped Hands* - New York (Metropolitan Mus. of Art): *Madonna* - Niort: *Virgin of the Passion* - Paris (Louvre): *Virgin and Child; Slumber of the Infant Jesus; Assumption; Holy Family, after Raphael; Annunciation, after Barocchi* - Perugia (Gal. Nazionale dell'Umbria): *Madonna* - Pesaro: *Madonna* - Pommersfelden: *Madonna* - Rohrau (Schlossmus., Graf Harrach'sche Familiensammlung): *Virgin at Prayer* - Rome (Dominican Chapel of S Sabina): *Madonna of the Rosary with St Catherine and St Dominic* - Rome (Gal. Colonna): *Virgin* - Rome (Gal. Nazionale): *Portrait of Ottaviano Proti; Madonna with Child* - Rome (Mus. e Gal. Borghese): *Virgin with Her Son* - Rome (Palazzo Doria Pamphili): *Virgin at Prayer; Virgin, Jesus and St Joseph* - St Petersburg (Hermitage): *Virgin with Bird; Holy Family; Madonna; Virgin and Infant Jesus* - Stuttgart: *Mater Dolorosa* - Tarbes: *St Margaret* - The Hague: *Virgin at Prayer* - Turin (Pinacoteca): *Madonna with Child; Madonna della Rosa* - Vatican (Mus. Vaticani): *Virgin and the Infant Jesus* - Venice: *A Saint* - Vienna (Czernin'sche Gemäldegal.): *Holy Family* - Vienna (Kunsthistorisches Mus.): *Madonna with Sleeping Child* - Vienna (Liechtenstein Mus.): *Virgin.*

Auction records:

Paris, 1767, *Architectural View with View of the Sea,* FRF 1,000. Paris, 1772, *Embarkation of Helen,* FRF 1,420. London, 1801, *Virgin and Child with Cherubim,* FRF 19,685. Paris, 1834, *Virgin in Meditative Pose,* FRF 2,500. Paris, 1841, *Virgin and the Infant Jesus,* FRF 3,400. London, 1844, *Virgin and Child,* FRF 5,385. Paris, 1850, *Virgin and Child,* FRF 6,240. London, 1856, *Marriage of St Catherine,* FRF 26,900. Paris, 1861, *Virgin and Child,* FRF 5,800. Paris, 1869, *Virgin at Prayer,* FRF 2,000. London, 1874, *Madonna,* FRF 10,500. Paris, 1882, *Madonna at Prayer,* FRF 9,600. London, 1892, *Virgin and Child,* FRF 6,240. Paris, 3-5 June 1907, *St Antony of Padua and the Infant Jesus,* FRF 1,150. New York, 1-3 April 1909, *Virgin and Child,* USD 975. London, 8 July 1910, *Madonna,* GBP 21. London, 14 July 1911, *Crucifixion,* GBP 52. Paris, 27 Nov 1919, *Virgin and Sleeping Child* (attributed) FRF 280. London, 4-7 May 1923, *Portrait of the Virgin,* GBP 56. London, 4 July 1924, *Virgin and Child and the Infant St John,* GBP 67. London, 28-29 July 1926, *Portrait of a Cardinal,* GBP 89. London, 15 July 1927, *Virgin and Child Surrounded by Saints,* GBP 462. New York, 5 May 1932, *Virgin and Child,* USD 275. New York, 13 July 1945, *Virgin and Child,* USD 147. Paris, 19 Dec 1949, *Virgin at Prayer,* FRF 135,000. London, 17 May 1961, *Madonna and Child,* GBP 420. London, 4 Dec 1964, *Virgin and Child,* Gns 450. London, 26 Nov 1965, *Virgin and Child,* Gns 1,600. London, 29 Nov 1968, *Virgin and Child,* Gns 1,800. London, 8 Dec 1971, *Virgin and Child* (after Guido Reni) GBP 3,200. London, 25 March 1977, *Virgin and Child* (oil on canvas, 28¼ x 22in/72 x 56cm) GBP 8,500. London, 28 March 1979, *Virgin and Child* (oil on canvas, 52¾ x 37in/134 x 94cm) GBP 7,500. London, 10 Dec 1982, *Virgin and Child* (oil on canvas, 18½ x 14¾in/47 x 37.5cm) GBP 5,500. New York, 18 Jan 1984, *St Barbara* (oil on panel, octagonal, 11 x 7¼in/28 x 18.3cm) USD 26,000. London, 13 Dec 1985, *Virgin and Child* (oil on canvas, 29¾ x 39¾in/75.5 x 101cm) GBP 5,500. London, 1 July 1986, *St Joseph Standing, Leaning against a Table* (black and white chalk/grey paper, 10¼ x 7¼in/26 x 18.3cm) GBP 13,000. New York, 14 Jan 1988, *Mother of God* (oil on canvas, 18 x 14in/46 x 35.5cm) USD 24,200. London, 20 April 1988, *Virgin at Prayer* (oil on canvas, 28¼ x 22½in/72 x 57cm) GBP 11,550. London, 8 July 1988, *Virgin Bidding St John the Baptist to Be Silent and Not Wake the Infant Jesus* (oil on canvas, 24 x 39¼in/61 x 99.5cm) GBP 41,800. Paris, 7-12 Dec 1988, *Virgin at Prayer* (oil on canvas, 26½ x 22in/67 x 56cm) FRF 130,000. New York, 11 Jan 1989, *Madonna and the Infant Christ Holding a Goldfinch* (oil on canvas, 39 x 31½in/99 x 80cm) USD 24,200. New York, 1 June 1989, *Virgin and Child* (oil on canvas, 22¾ x 28in/57.7 x 71.1cm) USD 37,400. Milan, 12 June 1989, *Virgin at Prayer* (oil on canvas, 19¾ x 16¼in/50 x 41cm) ITL 15,000,000. Stockholm, 16 May 1990, *Saint* (oil on canvas, 25¼ x 19in/64 x 48cm) SEK 9,200. London, 12 Dec 1990, *Virgin Praying* (oil on canvas, 19¼ x 15¼in/49 x 38.5cm) GBP 22,000. New York, 10 Jan 1991, *St Barbara* (oil on panel, octagonal, 11 x 7in/28 x 18cm) USD 40,700. London, 5 July 1991, *Virgin and Child* (oil on canvas, 26¼ x 19¾in/66.5 x 50cm) GBP 28,600. Monaco, 5-6 Dec 1991, *Virgin* (oil on canvas, 16½ x 13¾in/42 x 35cm) FRF 27,750. Paris, 11 Dec 1991, *Virgin with Clasped Hands (also called the 'Virgin at Prayer')* (oil on canvas, 29¼ x 23¼in/74 x 59cm) FRF 410,000. Paris, 10 Feb 1992, *Virgin with Child* (oil on canvas, 25½ x 19in/64.5 x 48.5cm) FRF 160,000. Rome, 28 April 1992, *Madonna* (oil on canvas, 19¼ x 15in/49 x 38cm) ITL 19,500,000. New York, 13 Jan 1993, *Hands Clasped in Prayer* (black and white chalk/blue paper, 5¼ x 8in/13.5 x 19.4cm) USD 3,520. London, 9 July 1993, *Virgin with Child Surrounded by Cherubs* (oil on oval canvas, 29¼ x 38½in/74 x 97.8cm) GBP 29,900. Poitiers, 17 Oct 1993, *Virgin with Child* (oil on canvas, 19 x 14¾in/48.5 x 37.5cm) FRF 81,000. Milan, 2 Dec 1993, *Virgin* (oil on canvas, 19 x 14½in/48 x 37cm) ITL 17,250,000. London, 19 April 1996, *St Barbara* (oil on canvas, 26¼ x 20in/66.7 x 50.8cm) GBP 41,100. New York, 16 May 1996, *Virgin and Child with Angels* (oil on canvas, 29½ x 23¾in/74.9 x 60.3cm) USD 101,500. New York, 3 Oct 1996, *Mary Magdalene* (oil on canvas, oval, 17¼ x 13in/43.8 x 33cm) USD 6,900. London, 11 Dec 1996, *Madonna* (oil on canvas, 20¼ x 15¼in/51.5 x 38.5cm) GBP 11,500. New York, 30 Jan 1997, *St Barbara* (oil on panel, octagonal, 11 x 7in/27.9 x 17.8cm) USD 31,625. New York, 31 Jan 1997, *Madonna at Prayer before a Land-*

scape (oil on canvas, 25¾ x 18¾in/65.4 x 47.6cm) USD 118,000. NEW YORK, 22 May 1997, *Holy Family* (oil on panel, 23¼ x 30¾in/59.1 x 78.1cm) USD 29,900.

SALVI, Niccolo
Italian, 18th century.
Born 6 August 1697, in Rome; died 8 February 1751, in Rome.
Sculptor, architect.

Niccolo Salvi studied painting and architecture under Antonio Canevari in Rome, and took charge of the latter's studio in 1727. He competed for both of the major architectural commissions organised in 1732 by Pope Clement XII, and although his plans for the façade of S Giovanni in Laterano were rejected, his designs for the Trevi Fountain were chosen over a significant number of rival projects. Salvi worked on the fountain, eventually completed by Giuseppe Pannini in 1762, for the remainder of his life, involving himself with every aspect of the work. This focus led him to decline numerous other commissions, although he was responsible for the remodelling of the interior of S Maria dei Gradi in Viterbo and also for the expansion of Bernini's Palazzo Odescalchi in Rome, and contributed to his poor health following 1744. The standard of his work was recognised in his election to the Accademia di S Luca in 1733 and the Congregazione dei Virtuosi in 1745, and the Trevi Fountain, with its elaborate combinations of both Baroque and Rococo elements, remains one of the most recognisable landmarks in Rome.

BIBLIOGRAPHY:

Cooke, L.H., *The Documents Relating to the Fountain of Trevi*, A. Bull, 1956. Pinto, J., *he Trevi Fountain*, Yale University Press, New Haven, 1986. Kieven, E., '*Rome in 1732: Alessandro Galilei, Nicola Salvi, Ferdinando Fuga*' in *Papers in Art History from the Pennsylvania State University II*, Pennsylvania State University, University Park (PA), 1987.

SALVI, Tarquinio
Italian, 16th century.
Born in Sassoferrato (Marche).
Painter.

Tarquinio Salvi was the father and first master of G.B. Salvi. He painted the *Rosary*, dated 1553, in Eremitani church in Rome.

SALVI BARILI. See **BARILI Salvi d'Andrea di Domenico**

SALVIANER, Matthias
Austrian, 17th century.
Active in 1680.
Sculptor (wood).

Matthias Salvianer sculpted the organ case in the church of Strasswalchen.

SALVIATI, Antonio
Italian, 19th century.
Born 1816, in Vicenza; died 25 January 1890, in Venice.
Mosaicist.

Antonio Salviati restored the mosaics at St Mark's Basilica in Venice. He also worked in London and Aachen.

SALVIATI, Francesco. See **ROSSI Francesco Salviati del**

SALVIATI, Giuseppe. See **PORTA Giuseppe della** or **Joseph**

SALVIATI, Giuseppe de
Italian, 18th century.
Born possibly in 1751.
Active in Germany.
Sculptor (ivory), cameo engraver.

Giuseppe de Salviati was active in Berlin in the second half of the 18th century and is probably the same person as Karl Benjamin Salviati.

SALVIATI, Karl Benjamin
Probably Italian, 18th century.
Born 1751.
Active in Germany.
Sculptor (ivory), cameo engraver.

Karl Benjamin Salviati was active in Berlin and is probably one and the same as Giuseppe de Salviati, who is said to have adopted Germanic forenames while working in Germany.

SALVIGNOL, Alfred Jules
French, 19th - 20th century.
Born in Pertuis (Vaucluse).
Sculptor.

Alfred Jules Salvignol exhibited in Paris at the Salon des Artistes Français, where he was awarded a third-class medal in 1903.

SALVIN, Anthony
British, 19th century.
Born 1799; died 17 December 1881, in Hallemere.
Painter, draughtsman. Architectural views.

Anthony Salvin was a distinguished architect and a remarkable draughtsman. He produced a large number of drawings of English ruins accompanied by meticulously detailed views of their reconstruction. His daughter was a landscape painter who exhibited at the Royal Academy in 1869.

SALVINI, Francesco
Italian, 18th century.
Active in Milan during the first half of the 18th century.
Sculptor.

Francesco Salvini sculpted the statue of *St Bartholomew* in the church in Sciedi in 1729.

SALVINI, Mario
Italian, 19th - 20th century.
Born in Reggio Emilia.
Sculptor.

He exhibited work in Venice, Florence and Bologna.

SALVINI, Prospero
Italian, 17th century.
Active in Parma in 1653.
Painter.

Prospero Salvini painted religious subjects.

SALVINI, Salvi
Italian, 17th century.
Active at the end of the 17th century.
Painter.

Salvi Salvini painted an altarpiece for the church of the Madonna of the Olive Trees in 1695.

SALVINI, Salvino
Italian, 19th century.
Born 26 May 1824, in Livorno; died 4 June 1899, in Arezzo.
Sculptor.

A student at the academy in Florence and in Rome, Salvino Salvini carved the statue of *Nicola Pisano* in Pisa, the equestrian statue of *Vittorio Emanuele II* in Florence and the statue of *Cardinal Valeriani* on the façade of the Duomo in Florence.

He exhibited in Florence, Naples, Bologna, Rome and Turin and also in Paris. He was awarded a silver medal at the Exposition Universelle in 1889.

MUSEUMS AND GALLERIES:

FLORENCE (Gal. d'Arte Moderna): *Bust of G. Rossini*.

SALVIONI, Angelo
Italian, 18th century.

Active in Ancona, Italy.
Painter.
Angelo Salvioni was the pupil of Ferdinando Galli Bibiena.

SALVIONI, Giuseppe
Italian, 19th - 20th century.
Born 1822, in Lugano, Switzerland; died 21 March 1907, in Turin.
Engraver (wood).
He studied in Paris, Geneva and Turin.

SALVIONI, Rosalba Maria
Italian, 18th century.
Born in Rome.
Active from 1716 to 1736.
Painter. History painting.
The pupil of S. Conca, Rosalba Salvioni became an honorary member of the Clementi academy in Bologna in 1730. She is known for a *St Catherine* in the Minorite church in Frascati.

SALVIONI, Saverio
Italian, 18th - 19th century.
Born 15 September 1755, in Massa; died 6 May 1833, in Massa.
Painter, engraver (etching).
Saverio Salvioni was taught by Tempesti in Pisa and by Maron and Corvi in Rome.

SALVITTI, Nicola
Italian, 14th century.
Active in Sulmona (Abruzzi) towards the end of the 14th century.
Sculptor.
Nicola Salvitti sculpted the pediment of the church of St Pamphilus, in Sulmona.

SALVO, or Gian Salvo di Antonio, called Salvo da Messina
Italian, 15th - 16th century.
Active in Messina, Sicily, from 1493 to 1525.
Painter.
Salvo was the nephew of Antonello da Messina. He became well known by taking inspiration from Raphael. His works include *Death of the Virgin*, in Messina Cathedral.

SALVO, pseudonym of Mangione, Salvator
Italian, 20th - 21st century.
Born 1947, in Leonforte (Sicily).
Painter, collage artist. Figures, portraits, architectural views, still-lifes.
Conceptual Art, Body Art.
Salvator Mangione, known as Salvo, settled in Turin. In 1969 in his *12 Self-portraits* he added pieces cut from photographs to his own painted portrait so that he appeared as an American soldier in Vietnam, a German SS officer or a Cuban guerrilla. During this period, working in a conceptual mode, he engraved his name or statements about his name on precious metals. After 1973, working as a follower of Citazionismo, he painted new versions of famous pictures, mainly figures and landscapes with ruins, from the history of art.

His solo exhibitions include, in 1982, *Salvo, Paintings 1973-1982* at the Kunstmuseum in Lucerne and the Nouveau Musée in Villeurbanne (Lyons), and in 1988, *Salvo, Paintings 1975-1987* at the Museum Boymans-Van Beuningen, Rotterdam.

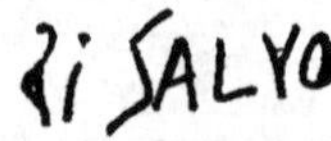

BIBLIOGRAPHY:
Kunz, M./Maubant, J.L., *Salvo, peintures 1973-1982*, exhibition catalogue, Kunstmuseum, Lucerne, Le Nouveau Musée, Villeurbanne, 1982. *Salvo, Paintings 1975-1987*, exhibition catalogue, Museum Boymans Van Beuningen, Rotterdam, 1988.

AUCTION RECORDS:
MILAN, 10 March 1986, *Landscape* (1985, oil on canvas, 31 1/2 x 27 1/2 ins / 80 x 70 cm) ITL 11,500,000. LONDON, 25 Feb 1988, *Untitled* (oil on canvas, 31 1/2 x 39 1/4 ins / 80 x 100 cm) GBP 5,500. MILAN, 24 March 1988, *Nocturne* (1977, oil on paper/canvas, 15 3/4 x 11 ins / 40 x 28 cm) ITL 4,000,000; *Mountainous Landscape* (1986, oil on panel, 13 3/4 x 11 3/4 ins / 35 x 30 cm) ITL 3,000,000. ROME, 7 April 1988, *Still-life with Cup and Cafetière* (oil on canvas, 9 3/4 x 11 3/4 ins / 25 x 30 cm) ITL 2,600,000; *Town* (1983, oil on card, 9 3/4 x 7 3/4 ins / 25 x 20 cm) ITL 3,000,000. MILAN, 8 June 1988, *Vase of Flowers* (1988, oil on canvas, 11 3/4 x 8 ins / 30 x 20.5 cm) ITL 2,600,000. MILAN, 14 Dec 1988, *Moonlight* (1988, oil on canvas, 19 3/4 x 13 3/4 ins / 50 x 35 cm) ITL 7,500,000. NEW YORK, 3 May 1989, *Untitled* (1985, oil on card, 13 3/4 x 9 3/4 ins / 35 x 24.8 cm) USD 3,575. NEW YORK, 9 May 1989, *Untitled* (1984, oil on canvas, 23 1/2 x 12 ins / 60 x 30.2 cm) USD 4,620. MILAN, 6 June 1989, *Still-life* (1980, 35 1/2 x 47 1/4 ins / 90 x 120 cm) ITL 13,000,000. MILAN, 8 Nov 1989, *Sicilians* (1976, oil on panel, 37 1/2 x 41 ins / 95.5 x 104 cm) ITL 40,000,000. MILAN, 27 March 1990, *Nocturne* (1989, oil on canvas, 39 1/4 x 31 1/2 ins / 100 x 80 cm) ITL 18,500,000. AMSTERDAM, 12 Dec 1990, *Tropical Forest* (black chalk/paper, 13 x 9 ins / 32.8 x 22 cm) NLG 1,725. MILAN, 13 Dec 1990, *St George and the Dragon* (oil on canvas, 102 1/4 x 83 1/4 ins / 260 x 211.5 cm) ITL 51,000,000. MILAN, 14 Nov 1991, *Landscape* (1985, oil on card, oval, 9 1/2 x 7 ins / 24 x 18 cm) ITL 3,200,000. ROME, 9 Dec 1991, *Untitled* (1990, oil on card, 20 1/4 x 14 1/4 ins / 51.5 x 36 cm) ITL 4,830,000. MILAN, 14 April 1992, *Landscape* (1991, oil on canvas, 31 1/2 x 39 1/4 ins / 80 x 100 cm) ITL 14,000,000. MILAN, 23 June 1992, *Town* (oil on canvas, 39 1/4 x 31 1/2 ins / 100 x 80 cm) ITL 7,000,000. NEW YORK, 17 Nov 1992, *Untitled* (1985, oil on panel, 24 1/4 x 12 1/4 ins / 61.9 x 31.4 cm) USD 3,520. MILAN, 6 April 1993, *Minaret and Street Lamp* (1990, oil on canvas, 23 1/2 x 27 1/2 ins / 60 x 70 cm) ITL 6,500,000. LONDON, 3 Dec 1993, *Interior, Exceptional Fusion* (1980, oil on canvas, 23 1/4 x 17 1/4 ins / 59 x 44 cm) GBP 5,175. ROME, 19 April 1994, *Workshop* (1987, oil on canvas, 15 3/4 x 11 3/4 ins / 40 x 30 cm) ITL 5,750,000. LONDON, 1 Dec 1994, *Interior, Exceptional Fusion* (1990, oil on canvas, 31 x 27 1/4 ins / 79 x 69.5 cm) GBP 9,200. MILAN, 9 March 1995, *Still-life* (1980, oil on canvas, 19 3/4 x 27 1/2 ins / 50 x 70 cm) ITL 11,500,000. MILAN, 28 May 1996, *Untitled* (oil on canvas, 19 3/4 x 23 1/2 ins / 50 x 60 cm) ITL 7,475,000. NEW YORK, 19 Nov 1996, *Untitled* (1984, oil on canvas, 32 1/2 x 24 1/2 ins / 82.5 x 62.2 cm) USD 4,025. LONDON, 21 Oct 1999, *Sunset* (1984, oil on panel, 51 x 37 ins / 130 x 93 cm) GBP 18,000. LONDON, 25 Oct 2000, *Ruins* (1978, oil on canvas, 20 x 13 ins / 50 x 34 cm) GBP 15,000. PRATO, 24 Nov 2000, *Disco* (1988, oil on canvas, 129 x 81 ins / 328 x 205 cm) ITL 70,000,000. VERCELLI, 21 April 2001, *Landscape* (1987, oil on canvas, 31 x 24 ins / 80 x 60 cm) ITL 20,000,000. VERCELLI, 15 Dec 2001, *Lunigiana, Italy* (1993, oil on canvas, 31 x 39 ins / 80 x 100 cm) ITL 24,000,000. FLORENCE, 16 May 2002, *Night Scene with Trees and Lampost* (oil on canvas, 76 x 43 ins / 192 x 110 cm) EUR 20,000. LONDON, 21 Oct 2002, *Interno con funzioni straordinarie* (1990, oil on canvas, 59 x 39 ins / 150 x 100 cm) GBP 15,000. MILAN, 27 May 2003, *Night, Street, Lamp-post* (1981, oil on canvas, 76 x 43 ins / 192 x 110 cm) EUR 25,000. VERCELLI, 6 Sept 2003, *Winter* (oil on canvas, 35 x 28 ins / 90 x 70 cm) EUR 14,000. MILAN, 16 March 2004, *Church in the Woods* (1979, oil on canvas, 39 x 47 ins / 100 x 120 cm) EUR 30,000. LONDON, 19 Oct 2004, *Fifty-seven Italian Painters* (1975, oil/pencil on panel, 37 x 31 ins / 95 x 79 cm) GBP 40,000.

SALVO, G. B. de
Italian, 20th century.
Born 1903, in Savona.
Painter.

SALVODI, Jérôme, called Girolamo Bresciano
Italian, 16th century.
Born in Brescia.
Active at the beginning of the 16th century.
Painter.
Jérôme Salvodi may have been identical with either Giovanni Girolamo Savoldo, known as Girolamo da Brescia, or Girolamo or Jérome da Brescia.

SALVOLINI, Alessandro
Italian, 18th century.
Active in Bologna in 1768.
Sculptor, designer of ornamental architectural features.

SALVOLINI DE'. See **EPISCOPIO Giustino**

SALVOTTI-FRATNIK, Anna de, or de'
Italian, 19th century.
Born in Gorizia; died after 1834, in Trento.
Painter. History painting.
She studied in Venice and Rome and exhibited work in Vienna in 1834.

SALVUCCI, Matteo
Italian, 17th century.
Born 1576, in Perugia; died 24 December 1627, in Perugia.
Painter.
MUSEUMS AND GALLERIES:
PERUGIA (Gal. Nazionale dell'Umbria): *Christ in Glory with St Benedict and St Scholastica*.

SALVUCCI, Valerio
Italian, 17th century.
Active in Perugia.
Painter.
Valerio Salvucci painted a *Visitation* and a *Coronation of the Virgin* for the church of St Crispin in Perugia.

SALWAY, N.
British, 18th century.
Active c. 1760.
Engraver. Portraits.

SALWIRK, Franz Josef, or Sallwürk
Italian, 18th - 19th century.
Born 3 February 1762, in Mollenberg; died 11 December 1820, in Milan.
Medallist, engraver. Coins.
Salwirk worked at the Milan mint from 1779 to 1819.

SALY, Jacques François Joseph, or Sally
French, 18th century.
Born 20 June 1717, in Valenciennes; died 4 May 1776, in Paris.
Sculptor, engraver (etching).
Saly was the pupil of Pater, and of Gilis in Valenciennes and Coustou the Younger in Paris. He won the Prix de Rome in 1738, and stayed in Italy from 1740 to 1748. He became a member of the Académie de Peinture et Sculpture in Paris in 1751, with *Fawn Holding a Goat*, now in the Cognacq-Jay museum. He produced the statue of *Louis XV* for the town of Valenciennes in 1752, but the statue was destroyed during the French Revolution. He was then called by the King of Denmark to produce an equestrian statue of the king in Copenhagen, on which he worked from 1753 to 1768. He was director of the Royal Danish academy of art, then returned to Paris in 1774. He also produced ornamental engravings.
MUSEUMS AND GALLERIES:
AMSTERDAM: *Bust of Alexandrine d'Etiolles, Daughter of Madame de Pompadour* - BERLIN: *Bust of Alexandrine d'Etiolles, Daughter of Madame de Pompadour* - COPENHAGEN (Statens Mus. for Kunst): *Bust of Frederick V; Diogenes* - PARIS (Louvre): *Allegory of Sorrow* - PARIS (Mus. Cognacq-Jay): *Fawn Holding a Goat* - PARIS (Mus. Jacquemart-André): *Frederick V of Denmark* - VALENCIENNES: *Bust of the Sculptor Antoine Pater; Diogenes.*
AUCTION RECORDS:
PARIS, 1776, *Two Drawings* (after a statue of Frederick V) FRF 72. PARIS, 1776, *Draped Women* (two drawings in red chalk) FRF 75. PARIS, 22 March 1928, *Three Vases* (three drawings in one frame) FRF 460. NEW YORK, 17 Jan 1964, *Venus and Cupid* (marble) USD 1,000.

SALZANO, Tommaso
Italian, 17th century.
Active in Naples from 1684 to 1690.
Sculptor.

SALZANO, Tommaso
Italian, 18th century.
Died April 1723.
Active in Naples.
Painter.
Tommaso Salzano was a member of the confraternity of painters in Naples in 1697.

SALZARD, Pierre Louis Renaud
French, 19th century.
Born in La Fère (Aisne).
Painter.
His masters were Hestent and Paul Delaroche. He exhibited at the Salons of 1831 and 1855.

SALZEDO
Portuguese, 16th century.
Active in Belem.
Painter.
Several paintings in Los Jerónimos monastery in Belem are attributed to Salzedo.

SALZEDO. See also **SALCEDO**

SALZEDO, Diego de and Juan de.
See **SALCEDO** and **SANZEDO**

SALZEDO, Michel
20th century.
Painter.
Michel Salzedo was the half-brother of Roland Barthes.

SALZEDO, Paul Élie
French, 19th - 20th century.
Born in Bordeaux; died January 1910, in Castelmoron-on-Lot (Lot).
Painter. Genre scenes.
Paul Élie Salzedo, a pupil of Léon Bonnat, first exhibited in Paris at the Salon of 1873, which became the Salon des Artistes Français in 1881, and where he was awarded an honourable mention in 1883 and bronze medals during the Expositions Universelles of 1889 and 1900.
MUSEUMS AND GALLERIES:
BORDEAUX: *Case before an Appeal Court.*

SALZER, Friedrich
German, 19th century.
Born 1 June 1827, in Heilbronn (Baden-Württemberg); died 14 May 1876, in Heilbronn.
Painter. Landscapes.
Friedrich Salzer was a pupil of Baumain. He went to work in Munich. In 1863 he abandoned painting in favour of his father's business.
MUSEUMS AND GALLERIES:
STUTTGART: *Winter Landscape.*

SALZER, Ignaz, or Saltzer
Austrian, 18th century.
Active in Prague.
Engraver (burin).
Ignaz Salzer was the brother of Johann Nepomuk and Karl Salzer.

SALZER, Johann Nepomuk, or Saltzer
Austrian, 18th century.
Active in Prague.
Engraver (burin).
Johann Nepomuk Salzer was the brother of Ignaz and Karl Salzer.

SALZER, Karl, or Saltzer
Austrian, 18th century.
Born 1740, in Prague.
Engraver (burin).
Karl Salzer was the brother of Ignaz and Johann Nepomuk Salzer.

SALZES, P. de. See **FURNIUS Pieter Jalhea**

SALZILLO. See **ZARCILLO Y ALCARAZ**

SÄLZLIN, Johann. See **STÖLZLIN Johann**

SALZMANN. See also **SALTZMANN**

SALZMANN, Alexander Gustav von
Georgian, 19th - 20th century.
Born 1870, in Tiflis (now Tbilisi); died 3 March 1933, in Paris.
Active in Germany.
Painter, watercolourist. Genre scenes, landscapes.
Designs (furniture/fabrics).
Alexander Gustav von Salzmann was a pupil of the academy of fine arts in Moscow and of the Akademie der Bildenden Künste in Munich, a city where he settled. He contributed to the review *Die Jugend* and associated with artists of Der Blaue Reiter (the Blue Rider). He joined with the painters Adelbert Niemayer and Carl Strathmann. Towards 1910 he worked for the Dresdener Werkstätten für Handwerkskunst (Dresden Studios) and designed furniture. He specialised in lighting systems; the best known included the Dalcroze Institute at Hellerau, and that of the Dresden-Hellerau theatre in 1913, then after the war, the theatre of the Champs-Elysées in Paris. He and his wife became, towards the end of their lives, disciples of the mystic, Gurdjieff.

BIBLIOGRAPHY:
Kern, Andrea, et al., *Jugendstil in Dresden, Aufbruch in die Moderne*, exhibition catalogue, Staatliche Kunstsammlungen, Dresden, 1999.

MUSEUMS AND GALLERIES:
BREMEN: *Sad Time*; *Huntress* - DRESDEN (Kunstgewerbemus.): *Cushion*; *Several Pieces of Furniture* (1912).

SALZMANN, Gottfried
Austrian, 20th century.
Born 1943.
Also active in France.
Painter, watercolourist. Landscapes, urban landscapes.
Initially, Gottfried Salzmann was primarily a watercolourist, exploiting the fluid character of the technique to produce very evanescent landscapes. Subsequently, though still in the medium of watercolour, he used a photographic support, or sometimes worked on canvas using acrylics that were no doubt very diluted, succeeding in reconciling the most transparent and fluid media with the opaque rigidity of urban architecture treated geometrically. He thus became essentially a painter of urban views, in which he displays remarkable skill. In his compositions, he deploys the mise-en-abyme beloved of critics and teachers very adeptly - the phenomenon of reflections on reflections that echo and repeat the image to infinity. His deconstruction of urban sites and multiple facets is reminiscent of the Cubist prismatic kaleidoscope, buffing up against the frontiers of Abstraction.

He had solo shows at the Galerie Étienne de Causans, Paris (watercolours and charcoal drawings, 1988), Galerie Flak, Paris (1995, 1999), Galerie La Tour des Cardinaux, L'Isle-sur-la-Sorgue (2000). *Gottfried Salzmann: Regards sur 30 ans de création* (*Gottfried Salzmann: Looking Back on 30 Years of Creativity*), a retrospective, was held at the Musée de St-Maur (Villa Médicis), La Varenne-St-Hilaire in 2001. He exhibited solo at the Museum Carolino Augusteum, Salzburg, in 2003.

BIBLIOGRAPHY:
Gottfried Salzmann. Aquarelle und Zeichungen, exhibition catalogue, Graphische Sammlung Albertina, Vienna, 1982.
Heller, Erich R., *Gottfried Salzmann. Stadtlandschaft, Naturlandschaft*, exhibition catalogue, Oberösterreischisches Landesmuseum, Linz, 1991.

SALZMANN, Louis Henri
Swiss, 20th century.
Born 11 December 1887, in Vallorbe; died 19 May 1955, in Geneva.
Painter. Portraits, urban landscapes, landscapes.
Louis Henri Salzmann studied at the fine arts school in Geneva from 1904 to 1908 and then settled in Geneva. He became gravely ill and was hospitalised, continuing to paint from his room in the Geneva Cantonal Hospital until his death in 1955.

Salzmann worked in wrought iron and furnished pieces for the Palais des Nations in Geneva. As a painter, he favoured landscapes and portraits and painted in a style reminiscent of the mature works of André Derain. He left numerous paintings of the Geneva Cantonal Hospital. He was also responsible for the design of postage stamps dating from between 1920 and 1930.

He showed his work at the Federal Fine Arts Exhibition of 1919 and at the National Exhibition of 1931, and a posthumous exhibition of his work was held at the Musée Rath in Geneva in 1955.

SALZMANN, M.
Austrian, 18th century.
Active probably at the beginning of the 18th century.
Painter.

SALZMANN, Michel
French, 20th - 21st century.
Born 1948.
Painter (including mixed media). Figures.

AUCTION RECORDS:
PARIS, 29 Sept 1989, *Bonhomme* (1989, mixed media/paper, 25 1/2 x 19 3/4 ins / 65 x 50 cm) FRF 5,500. PARIS, 26 Oct 1990, *Untitled* (oil on card, 49 1/4 x 57 ins / 125 x 145 cm) FRF 18,000.

SALZMANN, Wilhelm
German, 18th century.
Active at the end of the 18th century.
Painter. Natural history (animals).
Wilhelm Salzmann painted illustrations for natural history works.

SAM, Christiana Maria. See **ELLIGER**

SAM, Engel or Angelo
Dutch, 18th century.
Born 15 June 1699, in Rotterdam; died 4 March 1769, in Amsterdam.
Painter. Genre scenes, portraits.
Engel Sam replicated Van der Werff's style and technique with such exactitude that he succeeded in fooling the experts on more than one occasion. He also made perfect copies after Metsu.

SAMACHINI, Orazio, or Sammachini or Somacchini
Italian, 16th century.
Born 20 December 1532, in Bologna; died 12 June 1577, in Bologna.
Painter, fresco artist, engraver, draughtsman. Religious subjects.
Bolognese School.

Orazio Samachini was the pupil of Pellegrino Tibaldi and studied the works of Correggio. He was commissioned to paint the frescoes in the large chapel by the cupola decorated by Allegri. He went to Rome and was employed by Pope Pius IV to decorate the Sala Regia in the Vatican, with Mario da Siena. He also worked in Bologna and Cremona.

Horatio / 1572.

MUSEUMS AND GALLERIES:

BOLOGNA (Church of S Giacomo Maggiore): *Purification of the Virgin* - BOLOGNA (Church of SS Narborre e Felice): *Coronation of the Virgin* - BOLOGNA (Mus. della Certosa): *Last Supper* - BOLOGNA (Palazzo Lambertini): *Fall of Icarus* - BOLOGNA (Pinacoteca Nazionale): *Annunciation; Adoration of the Kings* - CREMONA (S Abbandio): frescoes on vault - DRESDEN: *Holy Family* - MODENA (Gal. Estense): *Madonna with Child* - PARIS (Louvre): *Diligence Warding off Enmity and Capturing Hatred* (drawing) - PARMA (Pinacoteca Giuseppe Stuard): *Sacra Conversazione* - TURIN (Pinacoteca): *Perseus Delivering Andromeda* - VATICAN (Mus. Vaticani): *Liutprand Confirming the Donation of Aribert.*

AUCTION RECORDS:

PARIS, 1767, *St John the Evangelist, Several Saints* (pen drawing with ink wash) FRF 34. PARIS, 1776, *Soldiers Fleeing from Justice* (pen and bistre) FRF 72. NEW YORK, 22 Jan 1931, *Holy Family Surrounded by Saints,* USD 800. MILAN, 10 May 1967, *Virgin and Child with St Catherine and St Jerome,* ITL 1,500,000. LONDON, 30 Oct 1980, *Noah and the Ark* (pen and wash heightened with white/outline in black chalk/blue paper, 9 x 4 ins / 22.9 x 10.2 cm) GBP 540. LONDON, 18 Nov 1982, *Study of Christ* (black chalk, 14 1/2 x 10 ins / 37 x 25.4 cm) GBP 1,000. LONDON, 5 July 1985, *Philosopher between Virtue and Vice* (oil on canvas, 59 x 41 1/4 ins / 149 x 105 cm) GBP 15,000. NEW YORK, 16 Jan 1986, *Angels Trying to Save St Catherine* (pen and wash/ black chalk outline, 11 1/4 x 7 1/4 ins / 28.3 x 18.2 cm) USD 3,100. LONDON, 8 July 1988, *Holy Family with St Francis, St Margaret and St Catherine* (oil on panel, 40 1/4 x 34 ins / 102 x 86.5 cm) GBP 99,000. NEW YORK, 11 Jan 1990, *Putto Holding the Papal Keys* (ink/black chalk, 10 1/2 x 7 3/4 ins / 26.4 x 19.5 cm) USD 17,600. PARIS, 25 June 1990, *Virgin and Infant Jesus, St Elizabeth, St John the Baptist and the Four Evangelists* (pen, brown ink, brown wash heightened with white gouache, 13 3/4 x 11 ins / 35 x 27 cm) FRF 30,000. PARIS, 15 Dec 1991, *Virgin and Child Crowning St Cecilia between St Jerome and St Francis* (oil on canvas, 56 3/4 x 46 ins / 144 x 116 cm) FRF 90,000. MILAN, 3 Dec 1992, *Mystical Marriage of St Catherine* (oil on canvas, 36 1/2 x 32 ins / 93 x 81 cm) ITL 56,500,000. NEW YORK, 12 Jan 1994, *Prometheus* (black chalk, 14 1/2 x 8 ins / 36.9 x 19.4 cm) USD 13,800. LONDON, 2 July 1996, *Putto Standing Holding the Papal Keys, Study for a Lunette* (black chalk, ink and wash, 10 1/4 x 7 1/2 ins / 26.2 x 19.3 cm) GBP 6,900. LONDON, 5 July 2000, *Madonna and Child with St Bartholomew, St Cecillia and St John the Baptist* (pen/pencil/ink wash, 8 x 7 ins / 21 x 18 cm) GBP 8,000. NEW YORK, 25 Jan 2001, *Holy Trinity* (pen/ink/wash, 15 x 11 ins / 39 x 27 cm) USD 1,500. NEW YORK, 25 Jan 2002, *King David* (pen/brown ink wash over black chalk heightened with white, 10 x 4 ins / 25 x 10 cm) USD 40,000. PARIS, 21 March 2002, *Introduction at the Temple* (pen/ink wash, 9 x 5 ins / 22 x 13 cm) EUR 22,000. MILAN, 15 Nov 2003, *Holy Family* (oil on board, 26 x 23 ins / 67 x 58 cm) EUR 74,000.

SAMAIN, Eugène
Belgian, 20th century.
Born 1935, in Quevaucamps.
Painter, draughtsman, illustrator, graphic artist, designer. Scenes with figures. Designs for stained glass.

Eugène Samain studied at the St Luke Academy and the fine arts academy in Mons. His compositions are full of fantasy, with landscapes and nude figures (typically female) combining to produce a sense of esoteric disquiet.

SAMAIN, Louis
Belgian, 19th century.
Born 4 July 1834, in Nivelles; died 24 October 1901, in Ixelles.
Sculptor. Statues, busts, monuments.

Louis Samain was a pupil at the Brussels academy of fine art; he exhibited with the Société des Artistes Français in Paris in 1895 (highly commended). He was awarded a gold medal at the Paris Exposition Universelle of 1889, and became a Chevalier de l'Ordre de Léopold II. He executed a number of monuments and decorative works in Brussels, notably the façade of the City Hall.

MUSEUMS AND GALLERIES:

ANTWERP: *Gun carriage* - BRUSSELS: *Bust of the Architect J. van Ruysbroeck.*

SAMAKH, Erik
French, 20th - 21st century.
Born 1959, in St-Georges de Didonne (Charente-Maritime).
Installation artist. Multimedia.

In 1993 Erik Samakh spent a year as a scholar at the Villa Medici, Rome. He lives and works in the Hautes-Alpes.

Although Samakh's installations, from the point of view of location, could be considered sculpture, his real purpose is quite different: what he provides is to be heard, not seen. The sound of water, bird-song, the croaking of frogs that he has recorded or produced himself, these are the work itself. However, the sounds, songs and cries intensify the spirit of the place, which is the visual element that he takes over and integrates to his creation. He calls the objects that he places in a natural setting 'autonomous acoustic modules', and their autonomy comes from solar panels that enable them to work independently.

He has taken part in group exhibitions that include: 1989, the Barcelona Biennale; the *Africus* Biennale, Johannesburg; 2002, *La Voie abstraite* (*The Abstract Way*), Fondation d'Art Contemporain Daniel et Florence Guerlain, Les Menuls (Yvelines). He normally creates installations in spaces that are made available to him: 1989, *L'île aux oiseaux* (*Bird Island*), Niort; 1990, *Grenouilles électronique* (*Electronic Frogs*) in the Parc de la Villette, Paris; 1994, *Fontaines solaires* (*Solar Fountains*) in the gardens of the Villa Medici, Rome; 1994, Gétigné-Clisson, *Fontaines solaires*, Villa Lemot, Rome; 1995, Centre d'Art, Le Crestet; 2003, *Erikh Samakh: les rèves de Tijuca (après l'orage ou lumières à planter)* Centre National d'Art et du Paysage, Vassivière-en-Limousin.

BIBLIOGRAPHY:

Le Mouëllic, Maria, ''*Érik Samakh: écoutez voir...*' in *Beaux-Arts Magazine* no. 127, periodical, Paris, October 1994.

SAMARAN, U. M.
French, 19th - 20th century.
Born in Montevideo (Uruguay), to French parents.
Painter. Figures, genre scenes, interiors.

U. M. Samaran was probably a pupil of Nicolas Gysis at the school of fine arts, Athens, and of Franz von Lenbach in Munich; certainly of Raphaël Collin in Paris. He settled in Paris and exhibited at the Salon des Artistes Français, of which he was a member from 1888 and where he was awarded a bronze medal during the Exposition Universelle of 1889. He mainly painted female figures depicted indoors and going about their daily occupations.

AUCTION RECORDS:

PARIS, 21 April 1947, *Women Sitting on a Verandah,* FRF 13,100; *Woman Seated with an Old Man in a Drawing Room,* FRF 8,000; *Woman Painter in her Studio with a Customer,* FRF 13,000. PARIS, 2 Dec 1949, *Woman with Roses on a Plate and a Greyhound,* FRF 2,200. NEW YORK, 28 May 1981, *Young Woman Reading to her Daughter* (oil on canvas, 35 x 39 1/4 ins / 88 x 100 cm) USD 6,500.

SAMARAS, Lucas

Greek, 20th century.
Born 14 September 1936, in Kastoria.
Active in the USA from 1948.
Painter, watercolourist, pastellist, happenings artist, sculptor of assemblages, photographer, mixed media.
Neo-Dadaism.

In 1948 at the age of 12, Samaras arrived in the USA with his family. He became acquainted with Allan Kaprow and George Segal, a major factor in his development, at Rutgers University between 1955 and 1959.

In his early years, Samaras had painted in oils, watercolours and pastels. He abandoned oils and watercolours, in 1959 after meeting Allan Kaprow and George Segal. He took part in 1960 in many happenings with Claes Oldenburg, Jim Dine, Allan Krapow and Red Groom, using his own body, the forerunner of Body Art. Then he began to produce his first plaster-covered objects, reconstituting slices of cake, hot dogs and other typically American foods. He was obviously very close to the Pop Art emerging at the time, though his objects lack the clear evidence of the objects of Pop Art. This 'otherness' was reinforced particularly in the many interpretations of *Dinner,* assemblages in the form of meals, of diverse, often threatening objects and in *Paper Bag,* which consisted of paper bags containing a number objects, both unusual and yet 'impoverished', banal. The first *Boxes,* saturated with plaster, also confirmed this distance with the Pop Art style. Samaras introduced a major theme of his work in about 1960 with these boxes, a theme he reworked in the most unexpected ways. The boxes have a secret, sacred aspect. Formally, this was a profusion of the most diverse materials and colour; he added fabrics, pieces of plastic and feathers to the plaster of his early years. In 1962 the box took on hostile appearances, bristled with needles, nails, knives, scalpels and razor blades, evoking some sadistic practice.

Later, as Samaras often played the attraction/repulsion ambiguity, he included the most diverse elements in the boxes (mirror fragments, pearls, furs, sequins, cotton wool, hair, paste, strands of wool worked in the style of Mexican crafts, costume jewellery and stuffed birds). The box wears make-up, dresses up, arrays itself. Having become a pagan icon of a narcissistic cult, the box seems to contain secret caches, sometimes beginning to look like a labyrinth, sometimes unfolding and opening out like an accordion or is modified by totally extravagant aspects.

In view of the polymorphous handling of the same theme, it is tempting to consider the three rooms *Room I, Room II, Room III,* one in Los Angeles (1964), one for the exhibition in Buffalo (1966) and the third for Documenta IV (1968), equivalent to gigantic boxes. These rooms, the last two of which were totally covered in mirrors, an element that Samaras had often used, have sometimes been seen as the pursuit of Optical Art because they produce 'in-depth' reflections, but appear much more as yet another narcissistic tribute to reflection.

Samaras started on the long series *Transformation* in about 1965. In it he elaborated on the same theme as for *Boxes,* disguising the object, distorting it, but also revealing it under totally unusual, strange and bewitching exteriors. *Chair* and its numerous variations, are the main example. Built on perspective planes, completely unbalanced, covered with materials as diverse as mirrors (again), pins, wools, artificial flowers, they are like thousand of slightly mad extrapolations of the same concept. In the same frame of mind Samaras also produced transformations in *Spectacles, Place Settings, Knives, Scissors.* Never able to resist the most spectacular decorative effects, Samaras seemed to cultivate the multiple manifestations of his fantasies as though for pleasure. Seldom has work appeared so totally introverted. *Autopolaroids,* a series he undertook in 1970 consisting of photographic self-portraits that he had tampered with, deleting superimposing and enriching with illuminations, merely confirm this reading. Striking often acrobatic poses, bending his body to the pursuit of his own expressiveness, Samaras returned to the practices of Body Art, but he favoured the charms of a voluptuously decadent aestheticism instead of the hard facts of physical tolerance. In a further u-turn in around 1977, he produced a number of Abstract pictures contained in the series *Reconstruction,* in contrast to the 1965 series *Transformation,* made up of strips of multicoloured fabrics, like patchwork and undoubtedly also referring to this typically American product, machine sewn and rather aesthetically treated. In 1981, he went back to using pastel for copulation scenes. In 1986, the *Wire Hanger Chair* series took up the theme of the chair again, covering it in a proliferation of objects of all kinds and artificial flowers. While he had been tempted at this point to establish a chronology of themes in his work, it had only been for the sake of convenience, some of the media of his inexhaustible inventions reappeared at any moment (the box, chair and self-portrait).

Greek by birth, Samaras wrote of this heritage in his autobiography: 'Greece is my prehistory, my *pre-literate* past, my unconscious, my fantasy. America is my history, my reality, my adult life' This baroque fantasy, which he regarded as Greek, was symptomatic of his unconscious and only America was able to allow him to externalise it so freely in his works. Samaras' work, varied and apparently inexhaustible, arouses fascination and repulsion. Questioning the obsessions of the time, he seemed to be involved in all those artistic pursuits centred on transformations (Pop Art, Art Brut, Art Povera, Psychedelic Art, Body Art). Elusive, defying classification and better than many other artists who based themselves on the same source, Samaras, with his more fruitful and virtually unpredictable inventiveness, is undoubtedly an authentic restorer of Dada.

He featured in many collective exhibitions including: Documenta IV and V, Kassel (1968 and 1972); Venice Biennale (1970). Solo exhibitions include: Albright Knox Art Gallery, Buffalo (1966); Museum of Modern Art, New York (1969); Museum of Contemporary Art, Chicago (1971); retrospective, Whitney Museum for American Art, New York (1972); Galerie Renos Xippas, Paris (regularly from 1991).

BIBLIOGRAPHY:

Levin, Kim, *Lucas Samaras,* Abrams, New York, 1975. Bataillon, Françoise, *'Lucas Samaras menaçant'* in *Beaux-Arts Magazine,* periodical, Paris, October 1991.

MUSEUMS AND GALLERIES:

ATLANTA (High Mus. of Art): *Photo Transformation, November 12* (1973, polaroid) - BUFFALO (Albright-Knox AG) - NEW YORK (MoMA) - NEW YORK (Whitney Mus. of American Art).

AUCTION RECORDS:

NEW YORK, 2 Dec 1970, *Great Plate* (1961) USD 850. NEW YORK, 17 Nov 1971, *Nail Box* (bronze nails) USD 3,100. NEW YORK, 26 Oct 1972, *Transformation: Flowers,* USD 6,000. NEW YORK, 18 Oct 1973, *Box I,* USD 20,000. NEW YORK, 27-28 May 1976, *Transformation: Scissors* (1986, mixed media,

51 1/2 x 36 1/2 x 36 1/2 ins / 131 x 92.5 x 92.5 cm) USD 13,000; *Untitled* (c. 1960, pastel, 9 x 12 1/4 ins / 23 x 31 cm) USD 1,350. NEW YORK, 18 May 1978, *Chicken Wire Box* (1972, iron wire basket with plaster and acrylic, 12 x 9 x 10 ins / 30.5 x 23 x 25.5 cm) USD 4,000. NEW YORK, 19 Oct 1979, *Untitled* (1958, pastel, 11 3/4 x 8 1/2 ins / 29.8 x 21.6 cm) USD 1,500. NEW YORK, 12 Nov 1980, *Wool Box No. 20* (1964, wood, wool, acrylic and plastic with steel wire, 12 x 26 x 16 ins / 30.5 x 66 x 40.5 cm) USD 11,000. NEW YORK, 27 Feb 1981, *Untitled* (1965, mixed media and a wooden box, construction, 19 x 10 3/4 x 27 1/2 ins / 48.3 x 27.4 x 69.8 cm) USD 4,500. NEW YORK, 11 May 1983, *Untitled* (1962, coloured chalks/black paper, 12 x 9 ins / 30.5 x 23 cm) USD 5,000. NEW YORK, 8 May 1984, *Box No. 4* (1963, construction, 18 1/4 x 24 1/2x11 3/4in/46.5x62.5x29.7cm) USD 58,000. NEW YORK, 6 Nov 1985, *Box No. 55* (1966, wooden box with coloured spiral steel wire, a birds head, bits of glass and oil, 12 1/4 x 16 x 12 ins / 31 x 40.5 x 30.5 cm) USD 50,000. NEW YORK, 7 Nov 1985, *Head No. 178* (1981, coloured chalks, 17 1/2 x 11 1/2 ins / 44.5 x 29.2 cm) USD 8,000. NEW YORK, 11 Nov 1986, *Box No. 25* (1964, mixed media/felt in a box covered with artificial hair, 12 1/2 x 13 x 13 3/4 ins / 31.8 x 33 x 35 cm closed and 12 x 31 x 13 3/4 ins/30.5 x 78.8 x 35 cm open) USD 23,000. NEW YORK, 13 Nov 1986, *Reconstruction No. 86* (sewed fabric, 72 x 81 ins / 183 x 205.8 cm) USD 21,000. NEW YORK, 5 Nov 1987, *Pin Drawing* (1966, pin holes and X-rays/panel, 29 x 25 ins / 73.7 x 63.5 cm) USD 12,000. NEW YORK, 8 Oct 1988, *Untitled No. 2* (1961, pastel/paper, 12 x 9 ins / 30.5 x 22 cm, 3 1/2 ins/9 cm) USD 4,400. NEW YORK, 10 Nov 1988, *Jewellery Box* (mixed media, 4 1/4 x 6 1/4 x 6 1/4 ins / 10.8 x 15.9 x 15.9 cm) USD 26,400. NEW YORK, 2 May 1989, *Transformation - Binoculars* (1966, mixed media in two sheets of transparent acrylic, base de 58 1/2 x 12 x 15 ins / 148.5 x 30.5 x 38.2 cm each) USD 132,000. NEW YORK, 21 Feb 1990, *I Like Cutting* (1968, cut paper and pencil mounted between two sheets of Plexiglas, h. 25 ins / 63.5 cm) USD 3,080. NEW YORK, 27 Feb 1990, *Transformation, Chairs 9* (acrylic/wood, 40 x 25 x 25 ins / 101.5 x 63.5 x 63.5 cm) USD 79,750. NEW YORK, 6 Nov 1990, *Untitled* (1958, oil on reinforced canvas, 24 x 18 ins / 61 x 45.8 cm) USD 3,850. NEW YORK, 15 Feb 1991, *Transformation* (plates, assemblage of polyester resin, 17 1/2 x 17 1/2x4in/44x44x10cm) USD 28,600. NEW YORK, 1 May 1991, *Presentation Box 35* (wood, naturalised bird, pins, thread, bronze, glass egg, 15 1/2 x 14x18in/49.4x35.5x48.2cm) USD 88,000. NEW YORK, 6 May 1992, *Presentation Box No. 94* (1976, wood construction, wool, steel pins, acrylic and nine knives, 13 x 13 x 26 ins / 33 x 33 x 66 cm) USD 46,750. NEW YORK, 8 Oct 1992, *Untitled* (1974, coloured chalk/paper, 13 x 10 ins / 33 x 25.4 cm) USD 11,000. NEW YORK, 4 May 1993, *Untitled* (14 août 1961, pastel/paper, 12 x 9 ins / 30.5 x 22.9 cm) USD 16,100. NEW YORK, 11 Nov 1993, *Shoe Box* (1965, wooden construction, yarns of wool, a shoe and steel spikes, 10 1/2 x 15 1/2 x 11 ins / 26.7 x 39.4 x 27 cm) USD 46,000. LONDON, 26 Oct 1995, *Untitled* (1962, pastel/paper, 11 3/4 x 8 3/4 ins / 30 x 22.2 cm) GBP 4,255. NEW YORK, 7 May 1996, *July 8* (1962, coloured chalk/paper, 12 x 9 ins / 30.5 x 22.8 cm) USD 4,830. NEW YORK, 19 Nov 1996, *Head 6* (1981, coloured chalks/paper, 17 1/2 x 11 1/2 ins / 44.4 x 29.2 cm) USD 9,775. NEW YORK, 21 Nov 1996, *Art Critic* (1985, acrylic/canvas, five paintings, 36 x 120 ins / 91.4 x 305 cm) USD 11,500.

SAMARAYEV, Gavril Tikhonovich, or Samaraiev, Zamaraev
Russian, 18th - 19th century.
Born 1758; died 1823.
Sculptor.

Gavril Tikhonovich Samarayev studied at the art academy in St Petersburg, and under L.P. Mouchy in Paris.

SAMARDZISKI, Ljupco
Yugoslav, 20th century.
Painter.
Figuration Libre.

Ljupco Samardziski explored the possibilities of art history through the juxtaposition of numberless accounts. Colour is to him an outpouring, the canvas multi faceted and references inexhaustible. He showed his work in solo exhibitions including at the Galerie Nicole Ferry, Paris (1990).

SAMARINA, Ekaterina
Maiden name: Rachmanova
Russian, 19th - 20th century.
Born 15 January 1854, in Moscow.
Painter.

Ekaterina Samarina trained under Gabriel Ferrier and William Bouguereau at the Académie Julian in Paris.

SAMARITAN (GOOD), Master of the.
See **MASTER OF VALENCIENNES**

SAMARTINO, Edoardo
Italian, 20th century.
Born 16 October 1901, in Perosa Canavese (Turin).
Painter. Figures, scenes with figures, still-lifes.

Edoardo Samartino went to Paris in 1924 where he worked in the free academies in Montparnasse, particularly that of La Grande Chaumière. He copied the works of Rembrandt and Manet in the Louvre but his chief interest was in the Italian Primitives. In his work he sought to reconcile a sense of formal grandeur with the art of Africa. Possibly in imitation of Leonardo da Vinci, he often used accidental or deliberate blotches to inspire his imaginative compositions.

He rarely took part in the traditional annual salons in Paris but held two solo exhibitions there in 1950 and 1952.

AUCTION RECORDS:
ZURICH, 29 Oct 1983, *Still-life* (c. 1972, oil on canvas, 32 x 39 1/4 ins / 81 x 100 cm) CHF 5,500.

SAMBA, Chéri, pseudonym of Samba Wa Mbimba
Congolese, 20th - 21st century.
Born 30 December 1956, in Madimba, Belgian Congo (now Kinto M'vuila, Democratic Republic of Congo).
Painter. Scenes with figures.

Chéri Samba's father was a smith. After leaving school, Samba went to Kinshasa in 1972, making a living producing shop signs. In 1975, he set up under his own name. Self-taught as a painter, he lives and works in Kinshasa in a rudimentary studio, working practically in public in front of the local population and hanging his latest works outside. Very well known in Kinshasa from 1975, he was overwhelmed with commissions for ceremonial occasions - marriages and the like - and employed workmen assistants. He has travelled widely, in Central Africa (1976-1977, 1978, 1980, 1984-1985 and 1986). He also visited Belgium (1988) and Germany (1989-1990). He became known outside his homeland in 1982, after the French magazine *Actuel* invited him to Paris for the first time. He returned to France in 1982-1983, again in 1986 for the Avignon Festival, for the exhibition *Les Magiciens de la Terre* (*Magicians of the Earth*) (1988-1989) and at the invitation of the Fondation Cartier (1990).

After shop signs, he specialised in the reproduction of photographic portraits. He also did comic strips for *Bilenge-Info*, which he co-ordinated from 1984 to 1988. Subsequently, he painted narrative compositions in the style of advertising comic strips, with texts carefully written in block letters clarifying and commenting on the images. To get the message aross, the figures are shown in a highly didactic style. The three principles underlying his notion of painting are to improve work, display humour and tell the truth, which for him means painting as accurately as possible, exaggerating the characters and delivering a message. This message is often a criticism accompanied by a moral, either of a political nature (for example, African leaders are accused of as much corruption as the colonial powers), or a social nature (for example, criticising the hypocrisy of local customs, such as regarding it as unseemly to show a naked woman or a couple kissing). To get his message across, he explains it in a text in French and Lingala.

He has taken part in collective exhibitions, initially in Congolese cultural centres, then in *Art in Zaire*, Stockholm (1984), at the Avignon Festival (1986), in the exhibition *Les Magiciens de la Terre* (*Magicians of the Earth*), Centre Beaubourg, Paris (1989), an exhibition of seven Zairean artists at the Palais des Beaux-Arts, Charleroi (1996), and others. He has had solo shows outside Zaire at the Galerie J.M. Patras, Paris (1990) PMMK- Provinciaal Museum voor Moderne Kunst, in Ostend and at the Chicago Museum of Contemporary Art (1990-1991), at the Fundació Miró, Barcelona, at Portikus, Frankfurt, at the Musée National des Arts d'Afrique et d'Océanie, Paris (1997), at Le Parvis Centre for contemporary art, at Ibos near Pau (2001), at the Royal Museum of Central Africa, Tervuren (2003), and at the Fondation Cartier, Paris (2004).

BIBLIOGRAPHY:

Marcadé, Bernard, *'Entretien avec Chéri Samba'* in *Galeries Magazine*, periodical, Paris, February-March 1991. Marcadé, Bernard, *Chéri Samba*, La Différence, Paris, 1992 (?). Martin, Jean-Hubert/Jewsiewicki, Bogumil/Lavigne, Emma/Garcia de la Rosa, Philippe, *Chéri Samba*, Hazan, Paris, 1997. Boubès, Carol, *'Chéri Samba'* in *Art Press* n° 227, periodical, Paris, September 1997.

AUCTION RECORDS:

LOKEREN, 21 March 1992, *Papiwata* (1978, oil on canvas, 17 3/4 x 25 1/2 ins / 45 x 65 cm) BEF 33,000. PARIS, 23 March 1992, *Love Transferred* (1981, oil on canvas, 37 x 35 ins / 94 x 88 cm) FRF 16,000. FRANKFURT AM MAIN, 14 June 1994, *Portikus* (1994, acrylic/canvas) DEM 10,000. NEW YORK, 24 June 1998, *Tax* (1992, acrylic, 48 x 73 ins / 123 x 185 cm) USD 4,000. PARIS, 10 Oct 1998, *Bindo Promotion* (1991, acrylic, 27 x 34 ins / 68 x 87 cm) FRF 23,000. LONDON, 24 June 1999, *A Successful Life* (1995, acrylic, 51 x 77 ins / 130 x 195 cm) GBP 8,000. ANTWERP, 4 April 2000, *The Hour of Democracy in Africa* (1990, oil on canvas, 59 x 79 ins / 150 x 200 cm) BEF 270,000. PARIS, 26 Nov 2000, *Kinchasa After the Speech on 24 April 1990* (acrylic, 35 x 47 ins / 90 x 120 cm) FRF 27,000. PARIS, 26 May 2004, *Transferred Love* (1981, oil on canvas, 37 x 35 ins / 94 x 88 cm) EUR 2,500. BRUSSELS, 7 June 2004, *Struggle Against the Mosquitos* (oil on canvas, 35 x 43 ins / 90 x 109 cm) EUR 2,200.

SAMBACH, Christian or Johann Christian

Austrian, 18th century.
Born 1761, in Vienna; died 27 March 1797, in Vienna.
Painter, sculptor, illustrator.

Christian Sambach was the son and pupil of Franz Gaspard Sambach.

MUSEUMS AND GALLERIES:

POZNAN (Muz. Mielzynskich): *Portrait of Philippo Buonarotti* (miniature) - VIENNA (Albertina Mus.): *Crucifixion* (drawing).

AUCTION RECORDS:

PARIS, 24 June 1929, *Two Children's Heads* (drawing) FRF 20.

SAMBACH, Franz Gaspard or Caspar

German, 18th century.
Born 6 January 1715, in Breslau (now Wroclaw, Poland); died 27 February 1795, in Vienna.
Painter. History painting.

Franz Gaspard Sambach started out as a pupil of Reinert and L'Epée before going to work in Vienna with Donner. In 1762 he became a teacher of architecture at the academy in Vienna and in 1772 director of painting at the same academy. He frequently painted mock low reliefs in the style of Geeraerts and J. de Wit. He executed frescoes in the Jesuit church of Stuhlweissenburg and an altarpiece in the church of the Franciscans in Comischa.

C Sambach. 1778.

MUSEUMS AND GALLERIES:

GRAZ: *Virgin and Shepherds Adoring the Child Jesus* - LÜBECK: *Presentation at the Temple* - SIBIU: *Descent from the Cross* - VIENNA (Kunsthistorisches Mus.): *Children's Bacchanalia* - VIENNA (Österreichische Gal. Belvedere, Barockmuseum): *Death of St Francis Xavier*.

AUCTION RECORDS:

VIENNA, 4 Dec 1962, *St Stephen at Prayer before the Virgin*, ATS 38,000.

SAMBARBIERO, Pietro

Italian, 17th century.
Active in Naples during the second half of the 17th century.
Sculptor.

A pupil of Cosimo Fanzago, Pietro Sambarbiero worked in the church of the Carthusian monastery of St Martin and in the churches of Gesù Nuovo and S Lorenzo Maggiore in Naples.

SAMBAT, Jean Baptiste

French, 18th - 19th century.
Born c. 1760, in Lyons; died 29 February 1827, in Paris.
Miniaturist.

Sambat exhibited at the Salon in 1793.

MUSEUMS AND GALLERIES:

BORDEAUX: *Portrait of a Man*.

SAMBEECK, Augustyn van

Dutch, 16th - 17th century.
Active in Utrecht c. 1600.
Painter.

Augustyn van Sambeeck was a pupil of Albrecht Blœmaert before 1590.

SAMBERGER, Leo

German, 19th - 20th century.
Born 14 August 1861, in Ingolstadt; died 1949.
Painter. Portraits.

Leo Samberger studied at the fine arts academy in Munich. He went on to exhibit in that city from 1886 to 1897, securing a medal in 1891. He also exhibited in Paris, where he won a silver medal at the Exposition Universelle of 1900.

MUSEUMS AND GALLERIES:

BREMEN (Kunsthalle): *The Prophet Jeremiah* - LEIPZIG: *Portrait of Lenbach as an Old Man* - MUNICH (Bayerisches Nationalmus.): *Self-portrait; Portrait of the Artist's Father; The Sculptor Josef Flossmann; Councillor von Reber; The Sculptor Balthazar Schmitt* - MUNICH (Municipal Mus.): *The Musician Bennat* - OBERSCHLEISSHEIM (Neues Schloss Schleissheim, Staatsgal.): *Hubert von Heyden; Professor Bruno Becker* - STUTTGART: *Self-portrait* - WUPPERTAL: *Head Study*.

AUCTION RECORDS:

MUNICH, 20 Oct 1983, *Christ and the Crown of Thorns* (oil on canvas, 25 1/2 x 33 ins / 65 x 84 cm) DEM 5,000. MUNICH, 24 Nov 1999, *Portrait of Genevras von Eichtal* (1904, oil on canvas, 41 x 33 ins / 105 x 84 cm) DEM 3,500. MUNICH, 1 Dec 1999, *Portrait of a Woman in Black* (oil on canvas, 39 x 33 ins / 99 x 83 cm) DEM 4,000. MUNICH, 5 Nov 2003, *Portrait of Graf Arcos* (oil on canvas, 41 x 28 ins / 104 x 72 cm) EUR 1,500.

SAMBFLIID, Antonius. See **SANDFELDT**

SAMBIEX, Félix van. See **SAMBISE**

SAMBIN, Bénigne
French, 16th century.
Active in Salins 1584-1594.
Painter.
Bénigne Sambin was the son of Hugues Sambin. He painted an *Adoration of the Shepherds* in the church of Coulans.

SAMBIN, Hugues
French, 16th century.
Born between 1515 and 1520, in Gray; died 1601, in Dijon.
Sculptor (wood), draughtsman, engraver, architect.
Architectural views.
The exhibition *Hugues Sambin: Un Artiste de la Renaissance Française* (*Hugues Sambin: An Artist of the French Renaissance*), held in the National Museum of the Renaissance in Écouen in 2001, stimulated a new interest in Hugues Sambin, of whose life little is known, but whose influence was considerable in the Burgundy region. He was interested in the art of his time and went to Fontainebleau, where he met the greatest artists of the period. He engraved a magnificent series of plates relating to the art of sculpture which were published in 1572 and dedicated to Eleonor Chabot, the governor of Burgundy. Sambin made his reputation directing his father-in-law's joinery shop throughout his life.

There are also references to a Hugues Sambin who was born in Vienne and died in Dijon at the end of the 16th century, who was a pupil and friend of Michelangelo. He may have been related to Sambin, or the two may even have been the same artist given two different places of birth. Whatever the case, it would seem that there must have been some connection between them.

BIBLIOGRAPHY:
Erlande-Brandenburg, Alain/Bruno, Francois/Aubert, Gerard, *Hughes Sambin. Un créateur au XVIe siècle*, exhibition catalogue, Musée national de la Renaissance, Écouen, 2001.
MUSEUMS AND GALLERIES:
ÉCOUEN (Mus. national de la Renaissance): item of furniture.
AUCTION RECORDS:
PARIS, 1896, *Cartouche* (pen drawing with blue wash) FRF 60. PARIS, 2 March 1929, *Apollo and Mercury; Cherub's Head and Amorous Games* (two drawings) FRF 300.

SAMBISE, Félix van, or Sambix or Sambiex
Flemish School, 16th - 17th century.
Born 1553, in Antwerp.
Active in Rotterdam in 1590, and in Delft 1600-1602.
Engraver (burin), calligrapher.
Félix van Sambise was called the 'Maître de la Plume Couronnée'.

SAMBLA, Anechino
Italian, 15th century.
Active in Saluzzo (Piemonte) at the end of the 15th century.
Sculptor.
Anechino Sambla sculpted a baptistery for Pinerolo Cathedral, and worked in S Giovanni church in Saluzzo.

SAMBO, Eduardo
Italian, 20th century.
Born 12 December 1884, in Trieste; died 1966
Painter. Figures, portraits.
After first studying in Venice, Eduardo Sambo became a pupil of Carl von Marr at the Munich academy of fine art. He was the director of the Museo Revoltella in Trieste.

SAMBORSKI, Stefan, pseudonym of Nacht, Arthur or Stefan
Polish, 20th century.
Born 1898, in Cracow.
Active in France from 1924 to 1939.
Painter.
Kapists group.
Stefan Samborski studied at the academy of fine art in Cracow from 1918 to 1921. He spent some time in Paris from 1924 to 1939 when he also took trips to Spain. Samborski's painting is reminiscent of that toned down Post-Cubism characteristic of a large part of the Paris School of the interwar period. He was perhaps significant more for his teaching that for his own work. He taught at the higher school of plastic art in Sopot in 1946 and later at the academy of fine art in Warsaw. A member of the Paris Committee, or Kapists group, with whom he exhibited in Paris, Geneva and also in Poland, he also featured in the Venice Biennale in 1958. Solo exhibitions include: Paris (1930) and Argentina (1960).

SAMBOURNE, Edward Linley
British, 19th - 20th century.
Born 4 January 1845, in London; died 3 August 1910, in London.
Painter, engraver, humorist artist, illustrator.
Edward Linley Sambourne was initially apprenticed to a manufacturer of nautical instruments. From 1875 he exhibited humorous subjects at the Royal Academy and the Fine Art Society in London. He also participated in the Salon des Artistes Français in Paris. He was awarded a bronze medal for the Exposition Universelle in 1889, and was a member of the jury for engraving for the Exposition Universelle in 1900. He contributed to *Punch*, sending in caricatures inspired by John Tenniel, and then became the latter's successor. Books he illustrated include: *New History of Sandford and Merton* by Burnand in 1872; *Royal Umbrella* by Harcourt in 1880; *The Water Babies* by Kingsley in 1885; *Friends and Foes from Fairyland* by Brabourne in 1886; *The Real Robinson Crusoe* by Burnand in 1893; and *Three Tales* by Hans Christian Andersen in 1910.

SAMBUCETO, Gerolamo
Italian, 16th century.
Active in Genoa during the second half of the 16th century.
Sculptor (wood).
Gerolamo Sambuceto was the father of Leonardo and Maria Sambuceto.

SAMBUCETO, Leonardo
Italian, 16th century.
Active in Genoa during the second half of the 16th century.
Sculptor (wood).
Leonardo Sambuceto was the son of Gerolamo Sambuceto.

SAMBUCETO, Maria
Italian, 16th century.
Active in Genoa during the second half of the 16th century.
Sculptor.
Maria Sambuceto was the daughter of Gerolamo Sambuceto.

SAMBUGNAK, Sándor or Alexander
Hungarian, 20th century.
Born 22 April 1888, in Zemun.
Painter, sculptor.
Sándor Sambugnak trained in Budapest, Munich and Paris.

SAMELING, Benjamin. See **SAMMELING**

SAMENE, Abraham
Swiss, 18th century.
Born 19 March 1723, in Geneva; died 16 April 1755, in Geneva.
Enameller.

SAMENGO, Ambrogio
Italian, 17th century.
Born in Sestri Levante (Liguria); died before 1672.

Painter. Figures, landscapes, flowers, fruit.
Ambrogio Samengo was the pupil of G.A. Ferrari. He died at an early age, and very few of his works are still in existence.

SAMER, Johann
Austrian, 17th century.
Active in Znaim (now Znojmo, Czech Republic) during the second half of the 17th century.
Painter.
Johann Samer sculpted altars in the church of St Nicholas at Fuglau (Lower Austria) in 1680.

SAMFLEET, Antonius. See **SANDFELDT**

SAMFLEET, Cornelius
Danish, 16th century.
Active in 1574.
Painter. Portraits.
Cornelius Samfleet painted a series of portraits of Danish kings.

SAMHAMMER, Johann Jakob
German, 18th century.
Born 1728; died 1787.
Painter.
Johann Jakob Samhammer was a pupil of J. C. Fielder in Darmstadt and painter to the court of Saarbrücken.

SAMICO, Gilvan
Brazilian, 20th century.
Born 1928.
Engraver, illustrator.
Gilvan Samico was one of those who re-engaged with figurative work as a means of action in social conflict, after Joao Goulart seized power in Brazil in 1961 and left-wing parties called for a militant Socialism. Samico's wood engravings and book illustrations are inspired by popular regional tales; they mix rusticity with the fantastic in order to evoke the problems that people face in daily life.

SAMIN, Louis. See **SAMAIN**

SAMINIATI, Benedetto
Italian, 16th century.
Active in Lucca at the end of the 16th century.
Architectural draughtsman, architect. Perspectives.
Benedetto Saminiati designed architectural and decorative schemes.

SAMITA
Dutch, 20th century.
Born 1905, in Weert.
Painter. Scenes with figures, nudes, landscapes, seascapes, flowers, fruit.
Samita did not make his mark until after World War II. The superabundant detail in his vividly coloured paintings is such that he seems intent on re-creating the Garden of Eden, peopling it with happy nude innocents wandering amidst a plethora of flowers and exotic fruits.

SAMIVEL, pseudonym of Gayet-Tancrède, Paul
French, 20th century.
Born 11 July 1907, in Paris; died 18 February 1992, in Grenoble.
Painter, draughtsman, watercolourist, illustrator. Mountainscapes, sporting subjects. Humorous cartoons.
Samivel took as a pseudonym the nick-name of a character in a novel by Charles Dickens (Samuel Weller in *The Pickwick Papers*). He was also a film maker and a writer. He made mountaineering films and was a member of the first French expedition to Greenland. He lived in Provence (in St-Paul from 1930 to 1946, in Vence from 1946 to 1992). In 1933 he created an association called 'The Friends of Samivel'.

He was best known for his largely humorous drawings and illustrations of mountains and mountain sports, such as *L'Amateur d'abîmes* (*Lover of Abysses*) (Éditions Hōebeke, Paris, 1974) and *Les Albums de Samivel* (*The Samivel Albums*) (Éditions Delagrave, Paris, 1994). He wrote and illustrated modern fables such as *La Dame du puits* (*The Lady of the Wells*) (Éditions de l'Age d'Homme, Lausanne, 1991) and children's books: *Bon voyage, Monsieur Dumolet* (Éditions Delagrave, Paris, 1978) and *Goupil* (*Fox*) (Éditions de l'École des Loisirs, Paris, 1981.

Samivel exhibited in Paris at the Salon des Peintres de Montagne and his solo and retrospective shows included: 1937, Galerie Drouant, Paris; 1981, Musée Savoisien, Chambéry; 1987, *Samivel: Poet und Humorist der Berge* (*Samivel: Mountain Poet and Humorist*), Schweizerisches Alpines Museum, Bern.

BIBLIOGRAPHY:
Samivel (preface), *Art et montagne: les maîtres savoyards et valdôtains*, exhibition catalogue, Ville de Sallanches et l'Administration valdôtaine, Sallanches, 1978. Barréa, Monique, *Samivel*, exhibition catalogue, Musée Savoisien, Chambéry, 1981. Samivel, *Il y aura de l'eau pour les cygnes*, Albin Michel, Paris, 1983 (roman).

SAMLICKI, Martin Franciszek or Marcin
Polish, 20th century.
Born 23 October 1878, in Bochnia.
Painter. Portraits, landscapes.
Martin Franciszek Samlicki trained under Jozef Unierzyski and Jan Stanislavski at the school of fine art in Cracow. He worked in France and featured in the Exhibition of Polish Artists at the Salon de la Société Nationale des Beaux-Arts, Paris (1921) with *A Painter; View of Sèvres; View of Martigues*.

MUSEUMS AND GALLERIES:
CRACOW - KATOWICE - PRAGUE - TARNÓW - WARSAW.

SAMM, pseudonym of Mandelbaum, Sam
Polish, 20th century.
Born 26 October 1924, in Gryhow.
Active from 1932 in France.
Painter, draughtsman. Scenes with figures.
Samm was the son of a Russian father and a Spanish mother. He settled in Paris during World War II and was deported to the Nazi camps, where his father and mother and other members of his family disappeared. He lived a Bohemian life in post-war Montparnasse painting, or more often drawing, small formats at random, probably through lack of materials. He led a restless existence and eventually ended in a monastery and apparently stopped painting.

Graphic techniques suited Samm better than the purely pictorial disciplines for expressing the spiritual echoes of his inspiration. His intent was to convey visually the essence of the great passion of modern humanity and the sufferings of the Jewish people in an Expressionist style. A universal optimism tends to sublimate his message of fear into a message of hope.

SAMMACCHINI, Orazio. See **SAMACHINI**

SAMMARTINO, Gennaro. See **SANMARTINO**

SAMMARTINO, Giuseppe. See **SANMARTINO**

SAMMARTINO, Marco. See **SAN MARTINO**

SAMMELING, Benjamin, or Sammelins, Sameling
Flemish School, 16th century.
Born 1520, in Ghent; died after 1604.
Painter.
Ghent School.
Benjamin Sammeling was the son of Jan Sammeling and a pupil of Frans Floris. He was a senior member of the guild in

Ghent in 1598. Attributed to him are an allegory on the birth of Charles V (in the library in Ghent) and paintings after drawings by Lucas de Heere (in the Jansenist church of Ghent).

SAMMELING, Jan, or Sammelins
Flemish School, 16th century.
Died before 21 June 1558.
Active in Ghent.
Painter.

Jan Sammeling was the son of Josse Sammeling. In 1541 he painted an altarpiece for the church of Laarne and another for the church of Kapryke.

SAMMELING, Josse, or Sammelins
Flemish School, 16th century.
Died between 3 February 1543 and 9 January 1544.
Active in Ghent.
Painter, art dealer.

Josse Sammeling was the father of Jan Sammeling. There were two Ghent painters of this name, one a master in 1476, the other in 1481. There was also a painter called Jean Sammeling in Ghent in 1550.

SAMMINUZI, Marino di Antonio, or Samminucci
Italian, 16th century.
Died after 10 February 1575, probably in Perugia.
Active mainly in Perugia, also in San Severino (Marche), from 1502.
Painter.

Marino di Antonio Samminuzi was the pupil of Bernardino di Mariotto della Stagno, and the father of Tiburtino Samminuzi.

SAMMINUZI, Tiburtino
Italian, 16th century.
Active in Perugia from 1563 to 1586.
Painter.

Tiburtino Samminuzi was the son of Marino Samminuzi.

SAMMYAKUIN. See **NOBUTADA Konoe**

SAMOGGIA, Gaetano
Italian, 19th - 20th century.
Born 23 April 1859, in Bologna.
Painter, decorative designer.

SAMOGGIA, Luigi
Italian, 19th century.
Born 1 November 1818, in Bologna; died 18 February 1904, in Bologna.
Painter, decorative designer.

SAMOGIT, Adam
Lithuanian, 20th century.
Born 1936, in Vilimiske.
Active in France.
Sculptor.

Adam Samogit trained at the academy of fine art in Vilnius in 1955. He went on study trips between 1956 and 1968, then attended the academy in Cracow in about 1968. He was a student of Jack Lipchitz from 1968 to 1973, working with Carrara marble and bronze in Pietra Santa in 1970. Samogit's inspiration came from an internalised knowledge of the anatomy. His sculptures are not the pursuit of pure abstraction and always show the anthropomorphic theme. He expressed the fullness of human forms, their tension, with a vigour and sensuality not dissimilar to Hindu art and was also apparently heavily influenced by archaic art. One can see the evocation of a female body in the interplay of full and empty spaces, in his tight, polished forms

Samogit featured in collective exhibitions from the age of 21 when he showed in Moscow and Leningrad (now St Petersburg). These include: Salon de la Jeune Sculpture, Paris (from 1969); Paris Biennale (1969); Modern Art Fair, Basel (1971); *Fantastica*, Basel (1972); Salon de Mai, Paris (from 1973); Salon des Réalités Nouvelles, Paris (from 1974). Solo exhibitions include: in Vilnius (1956) and Basel (1972).

Museums and Galleries:
Le Havre - Paris (CNAC) - Paris (MAMVP).

Auction records:
Paris, 22 Dec 1989, *Woman Orchestra* (1971, bronze, 20 1/4 x 18 1/4 x 5 ins / 51.5 x 46.5 x 13 cm) FRF 7,500. Lucerne, 21 Nov 1992, *Surrealist Woman* (bronze, h. 10 1/2 ins / 26.5 cm) CHF 1,000.

SAMOKHVALOV, Aleksandr Nikolaevich, or Samakhvalov
Russian, 20th century.
Born 1894, in Bejetsk (Kalinin); died 1971, in Leningrad (now St Petersburg).
Painter (gouache). Scenes with figures, figures, nudes.
Socialist Realism.

Aleksandr Nikolaevich Samokhvalov trained at the academy of fine art in St Petersburg from 1914 to 1918, working under Kuzma Petrov-Vodkin and also attended the Higher Institute of Art and Technology in Moscow from 1920 to 1923. He lived in Leningrad (now St Petersburg) and belonged to the : Mir Izkousstva (October Group). He exhibited with various groups including: World of Art (1917); Circle of Artists (1926 to 1929); and October Group 1930. He was a member of the Association of Artists of the U.S.S.R. and People's Artist.

Bibliography:
Strougatski, Nota Zalarovitch, *AlekSan dr Samokhvalov*, Ogiz Izogiz, Moscow, 1933. Samokhvalov, A., *Ma voie créatrice*, Leningrad, 1977. Pagé, Suzanne/Winock, Michel/Michaud, Éric/Vidal, Aline, *Les Années trente en Europe. Le Temps menaçant*, exhibition catalogue, Musée d'Art moderne de la Ville de Paris, Paris musées, Flammarion, Paris, 1997.

Museums and Galleries:
Moscow (Pushkin MFA) - Moscow (State Tretyakov Gal.) - Novokouznsk (Museum of Soviet Art) - St Petersburg (Gosudarstvennyj Russkij Muz.): *Komsomol Shooting Practice* (1932); *Metro Driver with Pneumatic Hammer* (1933) - Volgorod (MFA).

Auction records:
Paris, 25 Nov 1991, *Girl in Straw Hat* (1963, oil on canvas, 53 1/2 x 44 1/2 ins / 136 x 113 cm) FRF 34,000; *Parisian Woman* (1963, oil on canvas, 57 3/4 x 35 ins / 147 x 88 cm) FRF 28,000. Paris, 20 May 1992, *Model* (1965, oil on canvas, 54 3/4 x 23 1/4 ins / 139 x 59 cm) FRF 10,000. Paris, 5 Nov 1992, *Oksana* (1970, oil on canvas, 19 1/4 x 13 3/4 ins / 49 x 35 cm) FRF 28,000. Milan, 10 Nov 1992, *For a Manifesto* (tempera/paper, four projets, 4 1/2 x 3 1/4 ins / 11.3 x 8.1 cm and 4 1/2 x 3 1/4 ins/11.2 x 8 cm and 4 1/2 x 3 1/4 ins/11.6 x 8.5 cm and 4 1/2 x 3 1/4 ins/11.3 x 8 cm) ITL 1,500,000.

SAMOKISH, Nikolai Semenovich, or Samokich N. Semionovitch
Russian, 19th - 20th century.
Born 13 September 1860, in Neshin; died 1944.
Painter, watercolourist, engraver, illustrator. Battles, scenes with figures, genre scenes, landscapes.

Nikolai Samokish trained at the academy of fine art in St Petersburg. He was the official painter at the Russian-Japanese war in 1904-1905, and later explored themes linked to the Red Army as a military painter. He took part in the Salon des Artistes Français in Paris, obtaining a silver medal at the 1889 Exposition Universelle.

Museums and Galleries:
Moscow (State Tretyakov Gal.): study; *Walk*.

Auction records:
New York, 27 Feb 1982, *Officer Attacking Three Revolutionaries* (watercolour, pencil and pen, 19 x 33 1/2 ins / 48 x 85.1 cm) USD 1,500. New York, 21 Jan 1983, *Float at the Corona-*

tion of Tsar Nicholas II (watercolour, pen and pencil, 15 x 20½ ins / 38.4 x 51.8 cm) USD 1,300. PARIS, 28 Feb 1984, *Troika* (oil on canvas, 27¼ x 52 ins / 69 x 132 cm) FRF 11,200. LONDON, 6 Oct 1988, *Under the Silver Birches* (1884, oil on canvas, 9¼ x 15½ ins / 23.5 x 39.5 cm) GBP 8,800. NEW YORK, 16 July 1992, *Cart Passing at High Speed in a Village Market* (watercolour and Indian ink/card, 11½ x 8¾ ins / 28.9 x 22.2 cm) USD 1,100. LONDON, 17 July 1996, *Military Camp in the Caucasus* (1888, oil on canvas, 15¾ x 27¼ ins / 40 x 69 cm) GBP 5,175. LONDON, 17 Dec 1999, *Ox-cart in a Farmyard* (oil on canvas, 52 x 82 ins / 131 x 208 cm) GBP 4,200. LONDON, 20 Nov 2001, *Trotting Buggy* (oil on canvas, 32 x 42 ins / 81 x 106 cm) GBP 8,000. LONDON, 20 Nov 2001, *Grey* (oil on canvas, 35 x 49 ins / 88 x 125 cm) GBP 10,500. LONDON, 22 May 2002, *To Victory!* (oil on canvas, 31 x 43 ins / 78 x 108 cm) GBP 28,000. LANDSKRONA, 15 Dec 2002, *Military Force* (oil on canvas) SEK 60,000.

SAMOKISH-SUDKOVSKAYA, Elena
Russian, 19th - 20th century.
Born 1860; died 1924.
Painter, illustrator, poster artist, draughtswoman.

Elena Samokish trained under of Vasili Petrovich Vereshchagin at the school of art in Helsinki. She travelled to Paris and then settled in St Petersburg. She produced drawings for magazines, including *Niva* as well as post cards and posters. Elena Samokish featured in collective and solo exhibitions from 1889.

BIBLIOGRAPHY:
Paris-Moscou, 1900-1930, exhibition catalogue, Éd. du Centre Georges-Pompidou, Paris, 1979.

MUSEUMS AND GALLERIES:
GORKI (AM) - KIROV (Regional Mus. of Art) - KURSK (PG).

SAMOLOV, Vasily Vasilevich, or Samoïlov
Russian, 19th century.
Died 1886.
Painter, draughtsman.

MUSEUMS AND GALLERIES:
ST PETERSBURG (Gosudarstvennyj Russkij Muz.): drawing.

SAMOSTRZELNIK, Stanislas
Polish, 16th century.
Born c. 1485, in Cracow; died 1541, in Mogila.
Illuminator, painter, fresco artist.

Stanislas Samostrzelnik was a monk in the Cistercian abbey in Mogila. He was a well-known illuminator of manuscripts, and worked for the court. He executed frescoes at the abbey and also produced paintings, such as the portrait of *Piotr Tomicki* around 1530. He may be the same artist as Stanislaw of Cracow, who worked as an illuminator at the beginning of the 16th century.

SAMPAIO, Fausto
Portuguese, 20th century.
Born 1893, in Anadia near Coimbra; died 1956.
Painter. Landscapes.

Deaf from birth, Fausto Sampaio was sent to a special school before being granted a scholarship which enabled him to study at the Julian, Renard and Grand-Chaumière Academies in Paris. From 1934 onwards, he visited Santo Tomé, Macao, Timor, Singapore, Hong Kong, Indochina, the Philippines and, in 1974, Africa, notably Mozambique.

Sampaio painted numerous views of rural Portugal and the country's far-flung colonies. His work is characterised by a remarkable sensitivity to his natural surroundings and by his rendering of subtle variations of light. He exhibited at the Salon des Artistes Français in Paris.

BIBLIOGRAPHY:
Arnáiz, José Manuel/López Jiménez, Javier/Merchán Díaz, Manuel (ed.), *'Cien años de pintura en Espana y Portugal (1830-1930)'* in vol. X, Antiqvaria, Madrid, 1993.

MUSEUMS AND GALLERIES:
AVEIRO - CALDAS DA RAINHA - FERNANDO DE CASTRO - FIGUEIRA DA FOZ - LISBON (Mus. do Chiado) - OPORTO.

SAMPAIO, Marcio
Brazilian, 20th century.
Born 1941.
Painter, draughtsman.
Conceptual Art.

Marcio Sampaio also works as an art critic.

In his early career Marcio Sampaio used the speed offered by drawing to produce conceptual pieces. Later, notably with the *Anthropophagic Gallery* series, inspired by the work of Oswald de Andrade, he returned to painting.

SAMPAOLO, Ettore
Italian, 19th - 20th century.
Born 1 September 1852, in Città di Castello; died 1910, in Florence.
Painter.

SAMPIETRA, Francisco, or Sampietro
Italian, 19th century.
Born 2 June 1815, in Garlasco; died 1 August 1892, in Turin.
Painter. History painting.

A pupil of Giovita Garavaglia, Francisco Sampietra made his debut in 1839 in Milan before going to work in Rome and Venice. In 1860, he was appointed professor at the Accademia Albertina. He showed work at all the major Italian salons.

SAMPIETRI, Luigi
Italian, 19th century.
Born 1802, in Pontevico; died 1853, in Brescia.
Painter.

He was a pupil of F. Hayez.

MUSEUMS AND GALLERIES:
BRESCIA (Pinacoteca Tosio-Martinengo): *Self-portrait.*

SAMPIETRO, Stefano
Italian, 18th century.
Born 23 December 1715, in Milan.
Sculptor.

Stefano Sampietro worked in the cathedral in Milan.

SAMPLE, Paul Starett
American, 20th century.
Born 1896, in Louisville (Kentucky); died 1974, in Hanover (New Hampshire).
Painter (gouache), watercolourist, draughtsman. Still-lifes, landscapes, landscapes with figures.

Paul Sample was the pupil of Jonas Lie. He is best known for his landscapes with their delicate snow effects. In 1930 he won first prize from the Los Angeles Museum; in 1931, second Hallgarten prize from the National Design Academy. His work featured in several exhibitions at the Carnegie Foundation in Pittsburgh.

AUCTION RECORDS:
NEW YORK, 13 Dec 1972, *Good Farming - Good Living*, USD 2,100. LOS ANGELES, 5 March 1974, *Mountainous Landscape*, USD 1,000. LOS ANGELES, 3 May 1982, *Fishing Boats* (oil on canvas, 16 x 20 ins / 40.5 x 51 cm) USD 2,200. NEW YORK, 26 June 1985, *Vue of a Harbour* (oil on canvas, 36 x 40 ins / 91.5 x 101.7 cm) USD 8,000. NEW YORK, 14 March 1986, *Cafe Scene, Paris* (oil on canvas, 43 x 63 ins / 109 x 160 cm) USD 7,000. NEW YORK, 20 March 1987, *Manhattan Island* (oil on canvas, 24 x 48 ins / 61 x 121.9 cm) USD 15,000. NEW YORK, 17 March 1988, *Still-life with Poppies* (oil on canvas, 15¾ x 19¾ ins / 40 x 50 cm) USD 3,575. NEW YORK, 1 Dec 1989, *Snow on New England* (oil on canvas, 30 x 36 ins / 76.2 x 91.4 cm) USD 19,800. NEW YORK, 24 Jan 1990, *Saw Mill* (watercolour and pencil/paper, 14¾ x 20 ins / 37.4 x 50.8 cm) USD 2,640. NEW YORK, 16 March 1990, *Remembrance Rock* (tem-

pera/card, 16 1/2 x 24 ins / 41.9 x 60.9 cm) USD 17,600. Los Angeles-San Francisco, 12 July 1990, *Landscape* (oil on card, 16 1/4 x 20 ins / 41 x 51 cm) USD 1,100; *Beach Huts and Palm Trees* (watercolour/paper, 10 x 14 1/2 ins / 25.5 x 37 cm) USD 2,090. New York, 18 Dec 1991, *Hay Harvest* (oil on canvas, 16 x 20 ins / 40.6 x 50.8 cm) USD 3,300. New York, 10 June 1992, *Fox Approaching a Stream in a Snowy Landscape* (oil on canvas, 20 1/4 x 26 1/4 ins / 51.4 x 66.6 cm) USD 5,720. New York, 10 March 1993, *Newark Village, Vermont* (acrylic/canvas, 20 x 31 ins / 50.8 x 78.7 cm) USD 4,600. Downington, 19 June 1999, *Rural New England Landscape* (1939, watercolour, 11 x 15 ins / 28 x 38 cm) USD 2,600. New York, 1 Dec 1999, *Good Farming-Good Living in New Hampshire* (oil on canvas, 34 x 36 ins / 86 x 91 cm) USD 70,000. San Francisco, 14 June 2000, *Vermont Landscape near Brownington* (acrylic on canvas, 12 x 20 ins / 30 x 51 cm) USD 8,000. Washington, 16 Sept 2000, *Before the Squall, Caribbean* (watercolour, 9 x 12 ins / 23 x 30 cm) USD 1,700. New York, 22 May 2001, *Hillside Houses* (oil on canvas) USD 13,000. Byfield, 11 Aug 2001, *New England Scene* (watercolour, 10 x 14 ins / 25 x 36 cm) USD 6,750. Boston, 22 March 2002, *Two White Horses at Brownington* (oil on canvas, ? x ? ins /? x ? cm) USD 42,500. New York, 17 July 2002, *Silent Country No. 2, The River* (oil on canvas, 34 x 50 ins / 86 x 127 cm) USD 18,000. Boston, 16 May 2003, *Field* (watercolour, 13 x 20 ins / 32 x 50 cm) USD 9,000. Plainfield, 1 Sept 2003, *Winter Landscape* (watercolour, 12 x 23 ins / 30 x 58 cm) USD 17,600. New York, 31 March 2004, *October Meadows* (oil on canvas, 26 x 38 ins / 66 x 96 cm) USD 19,000. San Francisco, 8 June 2004, *Town near Hills* (oil on board, 12 x 17 ins / 30 x 43 cm) USD 11,000.

SAMPOLI, Aurelio
Italian, 16th century.
Born 1548.
Active in Brescia.
Painter.
Aurelio Sampoli painted *St Dominic Burning Heretical Books* for the refectory of S Domenico monastery in Brescia.

SAMPOLO, Nicola, or Sanpolo
Italian, 16th - 17th century.
Active in Reggio nell'Emilia from 1571 to 1625.
Sculptor, marquetry worker.
Nicola Sampolo was the pupil of Prospero Spani. He worked for the cathedral and churches of Reggio nell'Emilia.

SAMPSON. See **STRONG Sampson**

SAMPSON, Thomas
British, 19th century.
Painter, miniaturist. Portraits.
Thomas Sampson exhibited in London from 1838 to 1853.
Auction records:
London, 20 Nov 1986, *Portrait of Members of the Horsley Family of Derby* (1845, watercolour/pencil outlines heightened with gouache, 39 x 54 1/4 ins / 99 x 138 cm) GBP 5,800.

SAMPSOY
French, 18th century.
Active 1755-1763.
Miniaturist.
Sampsoy was a painter in the court of St Petersburg.

SAMSO, Juan
Spanish, 19th - 20th century.
Born 1834, in Gracia; died 1908, in Madrid.
Sculptor. Religious subjects. Statues.
Juan Samso sculpted pieces for churches in Madrid, Barcelona and Covadonga (Asturias).

SAMSON. See also **SANSON**

SAMSON, Arnoulet
French, 16th century.
Sculptor (wood).
Arnoulet Samson carved the rood screen of the church of Creil.

SAMSON, Gustave
French, 19th - 20th century.
Born in Granville; died 1929, in Granville.
Painter. Portraits, genre scenes, interiors, landscapes.
Gustave Samson, a pupil of Léon Bonnat, exhibited in Paris from 1902 at the Salon des Artistes Français, from 1903 at the Salon des Indépendants, and also in Fontainebleau, Marseilles and Menton.

SAMSON, Jacques, or Sanson
French, 17th century.
Active during the second half of the 17th century.
Sculptor.
Samson produced decorative sculptures for Clagny, Fontainebleau and Versailles palaces, as well as for the Palais Royal in Paris.

SAMSON, Jean
French, 16th century.
Active in Fontainebleau.
Painter. History painting.
Jean Samson worked in 1533 at the Château de Fontainebleau. Bryan's Dictionary says 'at the Château de Versailles', but Versailles did not exist at this time. He may have been the same artist as Jehan Samson.

SAMSON, Jeanne, later Mme Fichel Benjamin Eugène
French, 19th century.
Born in Lyons.
Painter. Genre scenes.
She was the pupil, and subsequently the wife, of Benjamin Eugène Fichel. She made her debut at the Paris Salon in 1869.

SAMSON, Johann Ulrich
Swiss, 18th century.
Born 13 October 1729, in Basel; died 25 March 1806, in Basel.
Medallist, cameo engraver.
Johann Ulrich Samson was influenced by J.K. Hedlinger.

SAMSON OF LAACH, Master of the.
See **MASTERS**

SAMSONOV, Evgeny
Russian, 20th century.
Born 1926, in Irkutsk.
Painter. History painting.
Evgeny Samsonov studied at the Surikov Institute Moscow graduating in 1948. He became People's Artist Emeritus in Russia.
Museums and Galleries:
Moscow (State Tretyakov Gal.) - St Petersburg (Gosudarstvennyj Russkij Muz.).
Auction records:
London, 2 May 1996, *Birth of a Revolution* (oil on canvas, 27 1/2 x 23 1/2 ins / 70 x 60 cm) GBP 1,150.

SAMSONOV, Igor
Russian, 20th - 21st century.
Born 1963, in Voronezh.
Painter. Genre scenes, landscapes.
Igor Samsonov studied at the Repin Institute in St Petersburg from 1989. He graduated in 1996. He works in various genres and has painted a series of nudes in elegant hats, in the form of allegorical compositions. Warm colouring and virtuoso brushwork mark his style.
Auction records:
Paris, 27 March 1994, *Young Girl with Fan* (oil on canvas, 19 1/4 x 21 1/2 ins / 49 x 54.5 cm) FRF 6,500. Paris, 3 Oct 1994,

Morning (oil on canvas, 25 1/2 x 21 3/4 ins / 65 x 55.5 cm) FRF 4,500. TEL AVIV, 1 Sept 2004, *Still-life with Grapes* (2001, oil on canvas, 28 x 36 ins / 72 x 91 cm) USD 2,350. TEL AVIV, 1 Sept 2004, *Still-life with Landscape through the Window* (2002, oil on canvas, 30 x 36 ins / 77 x 92 cm) USD 2,900.

SAMSONOV, Marat
Russian, 20th century.
Born 1925.
Painter.

Marat Samsonov trained at the school of fine art in Moscow and became an Artist of the People.

AUCTION RECORDS:
PARIS, 5 Nov 1992, *Young Painter* (1949, oil on canvas, 17 3/4 x 14 1/2 ins / 45 x 37 cm) FRF 9,000.

SAMSTAG, Gordon
American, 20th century.
Born 1906, in New York; died 1990.
Painter.

Gordon Samstag studied at the National Academy of Design and the Art Students League of New York with Charles Hawthorne. During the 1930s he participated in the government-sponsored PWAP project. He was director of the American Art School in New York City from 1951-1961 and of the South Australian School of Art from 1961-1971. His work featured in exhibitions held by the Carnegie Foundation in Pittsburgh.

SAMTA
Algerian, 20th - 21st century.
Born c. 1950, in Constantine, now Qacentina.
Also active in France.
Painter, engraver.

Samta was a student at the École des Beaux-Arts in Algeria, possibly in Constantine (modern Qacentina), from 1970 to 1973, and then at the École des Arts Décoratifs in Paris from 1974 to 1979. In 1988-1989, he took a postgraduate diploma in fine arts at the University of Paris VIII. From 1983 to 1988, he was professor of engraving at the school of fine arts in Algiers.

Since 1983, Samta has taken part in collective exhibitions, including *Jeunes Créateurs de la Méditerranée* (*Young Artists of the Mediterranean*) (1985), Musée de la Vieille Charité, Marseilles; *Contemporary Algerian Painting* (1986), national museum of fine arts, Algiers; Biennale of Contemporary Art, Havana; *Peinture Contemporaine Algérienne* (*Contemporary Algerian Painting*) (1987), Centre National des Arts Plastiques, Paris; *Tribute to Picasso*, national museum of fine arts, Algiers; and *Hommage à Picasso* (*Tribute to Picasso*) (1988), Antibes. He has shown collections of his works in solo exhibitions, at the Goethe Institute, Berlin (1986); the Goethe Institute, Algiers; and the Centre Culturel Algérien, Paris (1991).

SAMUDIO, Antonio
Colombian, 20th century.
Born in Bogotá.
Painter, engraver.

Antonio Samudio studied at the art college in Bogotá. His work has been shown in collective exhibitions in Colombia since 1961.

SAMUEL
Romanian, 17th century.
Sculptor (wood).

Samuel worked for the church in Curtea de Arges.

SAMUEL
Polish, 17th century.
Active in 1696.
Painter.

Samuel painted a *Portrait of Maria Casimira d'Arquien, the Queen of Poland*.

SAMUEL, Charles
Belgian, 19th - 20th century.
Born 29 December 1862, in Brussels; died 1939, in Brussels.
Sculptor, medallist. Figures, historical figures. Busts, monuments.

Charles Samuel studied under Louis Eugène Simonis, Jean Joseph Jaquet and Charles van der Stappen at the fine arts academy in Brussels and also served an apprenticeship as a goldsmith. He worked in bronze, stone, marble, ivory and wood. In 1894 he sculpted the *Monument to Charles de Coster* for the Ixelles Ponds in Brussels. He is also responsible for the *Brabançonne* monument in Brussels which celebrates the Brabant figure immortalised in Belgium's national anthem.

He exhibited his work at the Salon des Artistes Français in Paris, securing a silver medal at the Exposition Universelle of 1889 and a gold at that of 1900.

MUSEUMS AND GALLERIES:
BRUSSELS: *Bust of Queen Elisabeth of Belgium* - PARIS (Mus. d'Orsay): *Bust of Charles Hayem* (bronze).

SAMUEL, Gabriel
French, 18th century.
Born 10 May 1689, in Huelle; died 21 November 1758, in Le Puy (Puy-en-Velay), Haute-Loire.
Sculptor.

Samuel was the pupil of Bonfils.

SAMUEL, George
British, 18th - 19th century.
Died 1823; as the result of an accident.
Painter, watercolourist, draughtsman. Landscapes.

George Samuel was an exhibitor at the Royal Academy and the British Institution from 1785 to 1823. He was killed when a wall collapsed on him.

MUSEUMS AND GALLERIES:
LONDON (Victoria and Albert Mus.): a watercolour - NOTTINGHAM (Castle Mus. & AG): *Haz Castle* (1793).

AUCTION RECORDS:
LONDON, 8 July 1929, *Thames Frozen Over in the Great Frost* (drawing) GBP 18. NEW YORK, 7 Oct 1977, *Hampstead Heath* (1820, oil on canvas, 30 1/4 x 25 ins / 77 x 63.5 cm) USD 10,000. LONDON, 18 June 1980, *Hunting Scene* (1794, watercolour, 17 1/2 x 24 1/2 ins / 44.5 x 62.5 cm) GBP 550. LONDON, 14 July 1983, *Porlock Bay from above Bessington, Somerset* (1818; *A View on the Barle, Somerset* (1822, oil on canvas, pair, 36 x 48 ins / 91.5 x 122 cm) GBP 8,800. LONDON, 12 March 1986, *Picnic by the Tamar Estuary* (oil on canvas, 21 x 30 ins / 53.5 x 76.5 cm) GBP 5,600. LONDON, 14 Nov 1990, *View of the River Barle near Dulverton, Somerset* (1822, oil on canvas, 35 x 47 1/4 ins / 89 x 120 cm) GBP 6,050.

SAMUEL, Juliette. See **BLUM-SAMUEL**

SAMUEL, Kornel
Hungarian, 20th century.
Born 10 April 1883, in Szilagykovesd; died 2 October 1914, at Uzhok pass, on the front.
Sculptor.

Kornel Samuel trained in Budapest and Munich.

MUSEUMS AND GALLERIES:
BUDAPEST (Municipal Mus.): *Fortune* - BUDAPEST (Szépmuvészeti Múz.): *Eve*; *Love*; *Little Boy Naked*.

SAMUEL, Richard
British, 18th century.
Painter, engraver. History painting, portraits.

Richard Samuel exhibited at the Society of Artists and at the Royal Academy in London from 1768 to 1785. He is also noted for an engraving from one of his originals, *The Nine Living Muses*, a compendium work that includes portraits of Mrs Sheridan, Mrs Montagu, Angelica Kauffmann and oth-

ers. In 1773, Samuel was awarded a Society of Arts prize for developing a new drilling approach to mezzotint engraving.
Museums and Galleries:
London (National Portrait Gal.): *The Nine Living Muses of Great Britain: portraits in the characters of the Muses in the Temple of Apollo* (1778, oil on canvas); *Robert Pollard* (1784, oil on canvas).

SAMUELS, Daniel
British, 20th century.
Born 1917, in London.
Painter, illustrator, designer. Genre scenes. Stage sets.
Daniel Samuels had his first solo exhibition in London in 1970 followed by others in Washington, New Orleans and Dayton. He was initially a designer of stage sets. From 1935 classical antiquity influenced his life and work. He worked as an illustrator until 1969 and then devoted himself to painting.

SAMUELSON, Mauritz, for Carl Gustav Mauritz
Swedish, 19th century.
Born 22 December 1806, in Stockholm; died 12 March 1872, in Stockholm.
Painter. History painting, portraits.
Samuelson studied at the Kungliga Akademi för de Fria Konsterna in Stockholm and with Gustaf Erik Hasselgreen. He was influenced by Johan Gustaf Sandberg.

SAMULOVICH, Sacharija
Russian, 18th century.
Active in Kiev.
Engraver (burin).

SAMWELL, Mrs. See **COLE Augusta**

SAMWELSON, Ulrik
Swedish, 20th century.
Born 1935, in Norrköping.
Painter. Scenes with figures, urban landscapes.
Ulrik Samwelson was one of the participants in *Eight Swedish Artists*, an exhibition which brought together eight of Sweden's young avant-garde. His work is Neo-Surrealist and clearly influenced by Pop Art. His 'urban environments' emphasise the impact of advertising on today's consumer-driven societies.

SAMWORTH, Joanna
British, 19th century.
Born in Hastings.
Painter, draughtsman.
Joanna Samworth studied in France under Ary Scheffer's brother Henry and under Rosa Bonheur and John Skinner Prout. She exhibited her work from 1867 to 1874.

SAMYON, family of artists
French, 16th century.
Active in Beauvais.
Sculptors (wood).

SAN, Gerard de, or Gerhardus Xaverius
Flemish School, 18th - 19th century.
Born 31 May 1754, in Bruges; died 9 February 1830, in Groningen.
Painter. History painting, portraits.
Gerard de San was a pupil of Légillon; he travelled from France to Rome in 1781, and remained in the city until 1785. In 1790, he was director of the drawing academy in Bruges. He moved to Groningen in 1795.

SAN, Karel de. See **DESAN Karel** or **Charles**

SAN, Master of. See **MASTERS**

SAN ALBERTO, María de. See **SOBRINO María**

SAN ANTONIO, Bartolomé de (Fray), real name: Rodríguez
Spanish, 18th century.
Born 24 August 1708, in Ciempozuelos; died 8 February 1782, in Madrid.
Painter. History painting.
At the age of 15 Bartolomé de San Antonio entered the discalced Trinitarian order and, after studying theology and philosophy, went to Rome in 1734 to study painting. He spent six years in Italy before returning to his monastery in Madrid where he contributed to the decoration. When the Real Academia de San Fernando was founded, San Antonio painted an allegory showing Ferdinand VI and the Catholic religion and this work gained him membership of the new academy. There are a number of his works in the church of the Trinitarian monastery.

SAN BIAGIO, Fedele da
Italian, 18th century.
Active in Sicily.
Painter, writer. Self-portraits.
A Capuchin friar, Fedele da San Biagio was taught by Olivio Sozzi in Palermo and later in Rome by Conca, whose style he imitated.
Museums and Galleries:
Palermo: *Self-portrait.*

SAN CLERICO
Italian, 19th century.
Painter, decorative designer.
San Clerico worked in Milan around 1823 where he painted the ceiling of the Casino degli Negozianti.

SAN DANIELE, Pellegrino da. See **MARTINO DI BATTISTA**

SAN FELICE, Ferdinando, or Sanfelice
Italian, 18th century.
Born 18 February 1675, in Naples; died 2 April 1748, in Naples.
Painter, architect. History painting, genre scenes, landscapes, urban landscapes, still-lifes.
Ferdinando San Felice, the pupil of Solimena, occupies an honourable place among Neapolitan painters, and was particularly successful at painting landscapes and perspectival views. With the help of his master, he also produced some good altarpieces. He was a rich man, and Solimena decorated a gallery in his house, which was later to become an academy for young painters.

SAN GIL, Francisco de
Spanish, 16th century.
Sculptor.
Francisco de San Gil was active in Valladolid and Burgos. He worked on the sculpture of wood panelling on the choir of Sto Domingo de la Calzada church, from 1521 to 1523.

SAN GIORGIO, Eusebio da. See **EUSEBIO DI JACOPO DA SAN GIORGIO**

SAN GIOVANNI, A.
18th century.
Active in Naples in the early 18th century.
Painter. Still-lifes.
A. San Giovanni is known only as a signature on a pair of canvases, one of which is dated 1716. Luigi Salerno now considers him to have belonged to the Tuscan school, revising his earlier view that San Giovanni was Neapolitan.
Bibliography:
Salerno, Luigi, *Natura morta italiana: tre secoli di natura morta italiana, la raccolta Silvano Lodi*, group exhibition catalogue, Bayerische Staatsgemäldesammlungen Alte Pinakothek, München, Centro Di, Florence, 1984. Salerno,

Luigi, *Nuovi studi su la natura morta italiana*, Ugo Bozzi Editore, Rome, 1989.
AUCTION RECORDS:
MONACO, 7 Dec 1990, *Bouquet of Flowers* (oil on canvas, 16 x 13 1/2 ins / 40.5 x 34 cm) FRF 66,600. NEW YORK, 10 Oct 1991, *Still-life with Flowers in an Urn, with fruit and a bird in a landscape* (oil on canvas, 19 1/4 x 24 1/4 ins / 48.9 x 61.6 cm) USD 15,400.

SAN GIOVANNI, Bernardino, or Sangiovanni
Italian, 17th century.
Painter. Religious subjects.
Bernardino San Giovanni was taught by Pietro Faccini. Around 1610, he was painting religious subjects for churches in Bologna.

SAN GIOVANNI, Ercole. See **MARIA Ercole di**

SAN GIOVANNI, Giovanni da.
See **MANNOZZI Giovanni**

SAN GIOVANNI, DA. See first name

SAN GREGORIO, Giancarlo
Italian, 20th century.
Born 1925, in Milan.
Sculptor.
A student at the Accademia di Belle Arti di Brera in Milan, Giancarlo San Gregorio lived and worked in Milan.

His sculptures consist of an assemblage of more or less geometric elements, made of contrasting textures, often wood and stone or marble.
MUSEUMS AND GALLERIES:
OSTEND (Mus. voor Schone Kunsten): *Sculpture* (1981, wood and marble).

SAN IGNACIO PARAMO, María de
Spanish, 17th century.
Born 2 February 1592, in Madrid; died 17 October 1660, in Madrid.
Draughtswoman.
María de San Ignacio Paramo was a nun of the Order of St Augustine.

SAN JOSE, Simon de, also known as Saint Joseph
Portuguese, 16th century.
Illuminator, copyist.
Simon de San Jose was commissioned by Don Luis de Sanzo, archbishop of Lisbon, to produce some of the illuminations of the Registry of Armorial Bearings, in the royal archives, Torre do Tombo.

SAN JUAN, the Younger
Spanish, 16th century.
Sculptor.
San Juan the Younger worked in the town hall in Seville, in 1534.

SAN JUAN, Antonio
Spanish, 17th century.
Active in Entrambasaguas at the end of the 17th century.
Painter.
Antonio San Juan went to Rome in 1680.

SAN LEOCADIO, Pablo de. See **AREGIO**

SAN MARTI, Baltasar
Spanish, 16th century.
Active in 1507.
Painter.
Baltasar San Marti was the son of Martin de San Marti.

SAN MARTI, Gaspar, or Sant Marti
Spanish, 16th - 17th century.
Born c. 1574, in Lucena (Cordova); died 8 April 1644, in Valencia.
Sculptor, architect.
Gaspar San Marti was a Carmelite monk, and worked in the Carmelite church in Valencia.

SAN MARTI, Martin de
Spanish, 15th century.
Active during the second half of the 15th century.
Painter.
Martin de San Marti was the father of Baltasar San Marti. He produced paintings for the high altar of Valencia Cathedral.

SAN MARTIN, Diego de
Spanish, 16th century.
Active in Saragossa.
Painter.
Diego de San Martin sculpted altars for the church of St Anthony in Saragossa and for Tardienta and Tauste churches.

SAN MARTIN, José
Spanish, 19th century.
Active in the first half of the 19th century.
Painter.
José San Martin executed paintings for the high altar of the church of S Ginés in Madrid.

SAN MARTIN, José
Spanish, 20th - 21st century.
Born 1951, in Villagarcia de Arousa.
Active then naturalised in France.
Collage artist, pastellist, engraver, illustrator, draughtsman.
José San Martín spent his childhood in Spain before his family moved to France. Having gained a degree in architecture he later devoted himself to painting, engraving and typography.

A painter and engraver, he has produced and edited several limited edition books in collaboration with the poet Ramón Safon: *Le Sillage du nu* (*The Track of the Nude*), 1976; *Scènes et Lieux* (*Symbols and Places*), 1980; *L'Œil glacé de la planète* (*The Planet's Frozen Eye*), 1982; *Kir Ker Gal*, 1985, a book printed by the Guy Levis Mano association; *Chapiteau d'enfance*, 1988; *Scénario d'une absence* (*Scenario of Absence*), 1991, with Michel Méresse; *Ainsi que Voyelles* (*As well as Vowels*), 1981, on the poem of Arthur Rimbaud and *Mandragora*, 1984, a poem by Orlando Jimeno-Grendi; *L'Île de Giulia* (*The Island of Giulia*), 1994, poems by Pierre-Marc Levergeois and engravings by Léon Diaz-Ronoa. He also illustrated issue three of the journal *Hélice* (*Helix*) (Annecy, 1994) and issues three and ten of *L'Art du Bref* (*The Art of the Brief*) (Paris, 1995, 1996). Since 1993 he and various poets and modellers have undertaken a collection of 'written books', including: *Coeur Coquillier* (*Heart of Shell*), 1994, a poem by Robert Marteau; *Le Dernier* (*The Last*), 1994, a poem by Emmanuel Pernoud, painting by Miguel Buceta; *Extrait du Règlement* (*Extract from the Rules*), 1996, a text by Yannick Haenel (bound by Antonio Pérez-Noriega).

San Martín is especially known for his work as an engraver, in which he has varied his technique since the 1970s, changing from embossing in white in 1978 to colour engraving on Gerflex and wood, then on to the exclusive use of wood. He also paints, draws and works in pastels. His work is characterised firstly by its qualities of composition, which were doubled in the 1990s by research into the effects of material. The surface is close to the pattern. Broken up into planes but without any depth, mostly closed, it is structured by black rings or tracings and a contrasting use of colour, especially ochre, red and blue.

He has participated in group exhibitions including: the Salon Le Trait, Paris, regularly since 1979; *Xylon-Pluriel*, wood engravings, Corbeil-Essonnes in 1982; *Xylon-France*, wood engravings, Oxford in 1984; Premio de Grabadeo Máximo

Ramos, El Ferrol in 1985, 1986, 1987 and 1995; Salon de Mai, Paris in 1986-1987; Jeune Gravure Contemporaine, Paris in 1987; *Le Bois gravé en Chine et en Occident* (*Wood Engraving in China and the West*), Boulogne-Billancourt in 1987; *Xylon France and Quebec*, Michèle Broutta gallery, Paris in 1987; regularly at the Salon des Arts Graphiques Actuels (SAGA) from 1987 until 1993; at *Xylography aujourd'hui* (*Xylography Today*), Élancourt in 1988; at *Ten Young French Engravers*, stamp museum, Mexico in 1989; *Artists' Books*, IFAL gallery, Mexico in 1991; *10 ans d'enrichissement du cabinet des estampes* (*10 Years of Enrichment of the Print Room*), Paris in 1992; Biblioteca Nacional, Madrid in 1993; Brita Printz gallery, Madrid in and *Artists' Books*, Estampa, Madrid in 1994; *Wood Engraving*, Anne Robin gallery, Paris in 1995.

He has shown his work in solo exhibitions including: 1977, Édourd Manet, Gennevilliers; 1978, Hôtel Plamon gallery, Sarlat; 1980, Jules Sandeau gallery, Aubusson; 1982, rotunda of the city theatre, Rennes; 1982, Claude Hemery gallery, Paris; 1983, 1984 and 1986, James Mayor gallery, Paris; 1988, Anne Blanc gallery, Paris; 1989, Museum und Werkstätten, Schwetzingen; 1989, Vermeer gallery, Nantes; 1991, travelling exhibition organised by the centre for contemporary engraving in La Coruña; 1990, 1993 and 1995 (painting), Médiart gallery, Paris; 1991 and 1995, Art + Vision gallery, Bern; 1992, Artothèque, Compiègne; 1992, Torculo gallery, Madrid; 1994, Hof Ten Doeyer gallery, Ghent; 1994, Du Verneur gallery, Pont-Aven; 1996, Lettres et Images gallery, Paris.

BIBLIOGRAPHY:

Leroy-Crèvecœur, Marie, *Graveurs contemporains*, Fondation du Crédit Lyonnais, Paris. Méresse, Michel, "*La Patience créatrice de José San Martin*' in *Poésimage* n° 7, periodical, 1984. Safon, Ramon (preface), *Jose San Martin*, exhibition catalogue, Museum und Werkstätten, Schwetzingen, 1989. Méresse, Michel, *Jose San Martin - Xilografías*, catalogue, Centre de gravure contemporaine, La Coruña, 1990 (engravings). Sousa, Jorge de, *L'Estampe de la gravure à l'impression*, Fleurus, Paris, 1991. "*Jose San Martin*' in *Le Bois Gravé* n° 17, periodical, Paris, February 1991 (special edition).

MUSEUMS AND GALLERIES:

GRAVELINES (Mus. du Dessin et de l'Estampe originale) - MADRID (Biblioteca Nacional) - MEXICO CITY (Mus. Nacional de la Estampa) - PARIS (BNF).

SAN MARTIN, Julián

Spanish, 18th century.

Born 1762, in Valdelacuesta; died 29 November 1801, in Madrid.

Sculptor.

Although Julián San Martin belonged to the decadent period, he was a highly talented artist. He is known for his statue of *St Dominic* installed in the cathedral in 1789.

SAN MARTIN DE LA SERNA, Juan

Spanish, 19th - 20th century.

Born 21 April 1830, in Santiago de Compostela; died 11 November 1918.

Sculptor.

Juan San Martin de la Serna was a pupil of José Piquer y Duart; he sculpted public monuments in Madrid.

SAN MARTINO, Marco, or Sammartino, Sanmarchi

Italian, 17th century.

Born in Venice or in Naples.

Active in Rimini c. 1680.

Painter, engraver (etching). History painting, landscapes.

There is disagreement among the sources as to whether Marco San Martino was born in Venice or Naples. He is definitely known to have lived in Rimini, where the vast majority of his works are to be found. He specialised in painting landscapes peopled with perfectly drawn figures. He also executed paintings for churches, in particular a *Baptism of Constantine* in the cathedral in Rimini and a *Saint Preaching in the Wilderness* in the college of S Vincenzio in Venice. He engraved religious subjects, genre scenes and mythological subjects.

SAN MICHELE, Matteo, or Sanmichele

Italian, 16th century.

Born c. 1480, in Porlezza; died after 31 October 1528.

Sculptor, architect. Funerary monuments.

Matteo San Michele worked mainly in Casale Monferrato (Piedmont), where he sculpted many tombs.

MUSEUMS AND GALLERIES:

SALUZZO (Mus. Civico Casa Cavassa): *Sarcophagus of Galeazzo Cavazza*.

SAN MIGUEL, Pedro de

Spanish, 16th century.

Active at the beginning of the 16th century.

Sculptor.

Pedro de San Miguel worked on the tabernacle of the high altar of Toledo Cathedral from 1503 to 1504.

SAN MIGUEL, Raul

Cuban, 20th century.

Born 25 November 1932, in Havana.

Painter.

Raul San Miguel studied architecture at Havana University, then did scenographic work and also painted. From 1957 onwards he concentrated on painting. His work is abstract and springs from the abstract Tachiste movement (part of the Art Informel movement).

SAN OR SANTA, Master of. See **MASTERS**

SAN PEDRO, Rodrigo de

Spanish, 15th century.

Active during the second half of the 15th century.

Painter.

Rodrigo de San Pedro worked at Aranjuez for Isabella of Castile, in 1489.

SAN PERPETUA, Valentino di. See **VALENTINO DI SAN PERPETUA**

SAN PIETRO, Cagnaccio di. See **CAGNACCIO DI SAN PIETRO**

SAN PIETRO, Stefano. See **SAMPIETRO**

SAN ROMAN Y CODINA, Diego de

Spanish, 18th century.

Active in Seville from 1751 to 1785.

Engraver (burin).

SAN SEVERINO, Jacopo di. See **SALIMBENI DI SALIMBENE**

SAN SEVERINO, Lorenzo di, the Elder. See **SALIMBENI DI SALIMBENE**

SAN SEVERINO, Lorenzo di, the Younger

Italian, 15th century.

Painter. History painting.

Lorenzo di San Severino the Younger is thought to have been the son of Lorenzo di San Severino the Elder. Three works are attributed to him dating from 1481 to 1483: one in the sacristy of a church at Pausola near Macerata; a fresco in the collegiate church of Sarnano and a painting in the National Gallery in London.

MUSEUMS AND GALLERIES:

LONDON (NG): *The Marriage of St Catherine of Siena* (1481-1500, tempera and oil/wood).

AUCTION RECORDS:
LONDON, 3 Dec 1969, *St George and the Dragon*, GBP 4,800.
LONDON, 26 June 1970, *St Augustine*, Gns 1,100.

SAN VICENTE, Vicente de. See **SANT Vicente de**

SAN'YO, real name: Rai Jo, nickname: Shisei, nickname: Kyutaro, pseudonyms: San yo and Sanjuroppo gaishi
Japanese, 19th century.
Born 1780, in Aki (Hiroshima); died 1832.
Painter.
Nanga School.

San'yo was the son of Rai Shunsui, the famous Confucianist of Hiroshima. San'yo himself began as a poet and calligrapher in Hiroshima. He soon left his position as a Confucian official and settled in Kyoto, where his career as a literati painter unfolded from then on. He opened a school there and although a minor landscape painter, at the beginning of the 19th century he found himself at the head of the Nanga School in Kyoto and at the centre of a circle of artists who became first-rate such as Shunkin, son of Gyokudo, and especially Aoki Mokubei (1767-1833) and Tanomura Chikuden (1777-1835).

SANAVIO, Antonio
Italian, 19th century.
Active in Padua.
Sculptor.

The brother of Natale Sanavio.

SANAVIO, Natale
Italian, 19th century.
Born 9 September 1827, in Padua; died 28 December 1905, in Padua.
Sculptor (stone/wood).

The brother of Antonio Sanavio and pupil of Luigi Ferrari, Natale Sanavio carved several statues for the town of Padua.

MUSEUMS AND GALLERIES:
PADUA (Musei Civici): *B. Belzoni* (statue).

AUCTION RECORDS:
LONDON, 20 March 1984, *Busts of a Male and a Female Moor* (coloured basalt marbles, a pair, h. 33 3/4 ins / 86 cm) GBP 23,000.

SANCASCIANI. See **GHERARDI Filippo**

SANCHA, José
Spanish, 20th century.
Painter. Urban landscapes.

José Sancha painted views of Montmartre, the Latin Quarter, the London suburbs and landscapes in Mexico.

SANCHA Y LENGO, Francisco
Spanish, 20th century.
Born 16 August 1874, in Málaga; died October 1936, in Oviedo.
Active in England from 1901 to 1922.
Painter, draughtsman, illustrator, caricaturist. Figures, portraits, genre scenes, landscapes.

Francisco Sancha y Lengo studied under Joaquin Martínez de la Vega (probably in his native Málaga) then under Moreno Carbonero at the college of fine arts in Madrid and lived for a time in Paris, then in London (1901-1902).

He painted some portraits but is remembered primarily as a caricaturist working on Spanish and French periodicals such as *La Vie Littéraire, Comic Madrid,*

ABC, Blanc et Noir, Le Rire, Le cri and *L'assiette au beurre*. Examples of his work include: *Church of St Sebastian, His Eminence Out Walking, Tavern, Old Cobbler* and *Stroking the Dogs*. He showed his work at the national fine arts exhibition in Madrid, securing an honourable mention in 1897. In 1924, he exhibited more than a hundred works at a gallery in Madrid.

BIBLIOGRAPHY:
Arnáiz, José Manuel/López Jiménez, Javier/Merchán Díaz, Manuel (ed.), *'Cien años de pintura en Espana y Portugal (1830-1930)'* in vol. X, Antiqvaria, Madrid, 1993.

SANCHES, José Diaz
Portuguese, 20th century.
Born 4 June 1902, in the Algarve.
Watercolourist.

José Diaz Sanches was active in Lisbon.

SANCHES, Rui
Portuguese, 20th - 21st century.
Born 1954, in Lisbon.
Sculptor of assemblages, installation artist.

Rui Sanches was a pupil at Goldsmith's College of Art in London and at Yale University in the USA. He lives and works in Lisbon. His works gather together and juxtapose geometric elements attributed to the composition of classical paintings or to the exhibition site, and fragmentary, organic elements such as parts of the human body, heads, trunks and animal paws.

He has participated in group exhibitions, including: 1986, *The 20th Century in Portugal* in Brussels; 1987, *Portuguese Contemporary Art*, museum of contemporary art in Madrid; 19th São Paulo Biennale; 1988, *Lisbonne aujourd'hui* (*Lisbon Today*) at Toulon museum; 1990, *Final Frontier*, Centro de Arte Santa Mónica in Barcelona; 1992, *Portuguese Contemporary Art in the ILAD Collection*, Gulbenkian foundation in Lisbon; and elsewhere. He has shown collections of his work in solo exhibitions including in Lisbon in 1984, 1986, 1987 and 1989; in Oporto in 1990; in Lisbon at the centre of modern art, Gulbenkian foundation in 1991; in Rome; and in Paris, Chapelle de la Salpétrière in 1993.

SANCHEZ, Albert Ernest
French, 20th century.
Born 24 April 1878, in Paris.
Sculptor. Animals.

Albert Ernest Sanchez, a pupil of Falguière, Antonin Mercié and Georges Gardet, exhibited in Paris at the Salon des Artistes Français, where he was awarded an honourable mention in 1904 and a medal in 1912.

AUCTION RECORDS:
PARIS, 15 April 1988, *The Three Mice* (brown-patinated bronze, h. 2 1/4 ins / 5.5 cm base 5 1/2 x 2 3/4 ins/14 x 7 cm) FRF 3,000.

SÁNCHEZ, Alfon
Spanish, 15th - 16th century.
Painter, engraver.

Alfon Sánchez worked at the Casa de la Moneda (mint), in Seville. He gave his daughter a dowry by a deed dated 10 August 1500.

SANCHEZ, Alonso. See **SÁNCHEZ LEONARDO Alonso**

SÁNCHEZ, Alonso
Spanish, 15th century.
Active in Seville at the beginning of the 15th century.
Painter.

Alonso Sánchez painted coats of arms for the castles of Encinasola and Utrera, in 1406.

SÁNCHEZ, Alonso
Spanish, 15th century.
Sculptor.

Alonso Sánchez worked on the Puerta de los Leones of Toledo Cathedral, from 1459 to 1469.

SÁNCHEZ, Alonso
Spanish, 15th century.

Active in Arganda near Madrid.
Sculptor.
Alonso Sánchez worked on the high altar of Toledo Cathedral, in 1499.

SÁNCHEZ, Alonso
Spanish, 15th - 16th century.
Active from 1498 to 1533.
Painter. Frescoes, church decoration.
Alonso Sánchez painted frescoes in the university of Alcalá de Henares, on the order of Cardinal Cisneros. In 1498 he received payment for decorative work on the cloister of Toledo Cathedral. In 1508 he worked on the cathedral again, with Diego Lopez.

SÁNCHEZ, Alonso
Spanish, 16th century.
Active in Toledo in 1526.
Sculptor.
Alonso Sánchez sculpted medallions for Toledo Cathedral.

SÁNCHEZ, Alonso
Spanish, 16th century.
Active in Seville during the second half of the 16th century.
Painter.
Alonso Sánchez took part in the decoration of floats for the Corpus Christi celebrations on 15 June 1583.

SÁNCHEZ, Alonso
Spanish, 17th century.
Active during the first half of the 17th century.
Sculptor, writer, architect.
Alonso Sánchez carved many altars for churches in Seville. On 14 December 1622 he was commissioned by the parish church of S Miguel in Seville to carve a candlestick for the Tenebrae services of Holy Week.

SÁNCHEZ, Alvar
Spanish, 15th century.
Active in Seville during the first half of the 15th century.
Painter.
Alvar Sánchez produced paintings on the ceiling and doors of the former town hall of Seville, in 1440.

SÁNCHEZ, Alvar
Spanish, 15th century.
Active in Seville from 1480 to 1494.
Painter.

SÁNCHEZ, Alvar
Spanish, 16th century.
Active in Seville.
Painter.
Alvar Sánchez was referred to in 1540.

SÁNCHEZ, Andrés
Spanish, 15th century.
Active at the end of the 15th century.
Painter.
Andrés Sánchez worked on the Puerta de las Ollas of Toledo Cathedral, in 1496.

SÁNCHEZ, Andrés
Spanish, 16th - 17th century.
Born in Portilla.
Painter. History painting.
Andrés Sánchez was a pupil of El Greco. In 1600 Franciscan missionaries commissioned him to decorate churches they had built in the Spanish colonies.

SÁNCHEZ, Anton
Spanish, 15th - 16th century.
Died before 31 May 1509.
Painter.
Anton Sánchez worked in Seville from 1496. He may have been related to Anton and Juan Sánchez de Castro.

SÁNCHEZ, Antonio Bernardino
Spanish, 19th century.
Born 20 May 1814, in Peñaranda de Bracamonte.
Active in Ávila.
Painter.

SÁNCHEZ, Bartolomé
Spanish, 15th century.
Active during the first half of the 15th century.
Sculptor.
Bartolomé Sánchez worked on the tower of Toledo Cathedral, in 1425.

SÁNCHEZ, Bartolomé
Spanish, 15th century.
Active in Seville in the middle of the 15th century.
Sculptor (wood).
Bartolomé Sánchez was the father of Nufro Sánchez.

SÁNCHEZ, Bartolomé
Spanish, 16th century.
Active in Valladolid (Castilla y León).
Painter.
Bartolomé Sánchez was commissioned to assess important frescoes and to organise their restoration in 1555, under the orders of Berruguete, in the church of Concepción monastery in Valladolid.

SÁNCHEZ, Clemente
Spanish, 17th century.
Active in Valladolid in 1620.
Painter.
Clemente Sánchez worked for the Dominicans in Aranda de Duero.

SÁNCHEZ, Cristóbal
Spanish, 16th century.
Active during the second half of the 16th century.
Sculptor.
Cristóbal Sánchez sculpted a *Crucifixion* for Santo Domingo church in Granada, in 1580.

SÁNCHEZ, Diego
Spanish, 15th century.
Active in Seville in 1467.
Illuminator.
Diego Sánchez may have been identical with the painter of *View of Malaga*.

SÁNCHEZ, Diego
Spanish, 15th century.
Active in Seville during the second half of the 15th century.
Painter.
Diego Sánchez painted *View of Malaga* with Anton Sánchez de Guadalupe I, in 1487.

SÁNCHEZ, Edgar
Venezuelan, 20th century.
Born 1940.
Painter. Figure compositions, figures.
The painting of Edgar Sánchez derives from the incisive technique and exalted atmosphere of the early style of his elder and compatriot Hector Poleo. At first he painted young people in ordinary contemporary situations. In his second period he painted areas of human skin on which nothing could be seen but a mouth twisted in grief, the rest of the face disappearing, barely roughed out against the background. Eventually, while keeping his trademark of expanses of skin, he reverted to painting almost complete figures. These were set in heavy, mysterious compositions, their faces closed and enigmatic and partly concealed by folds of fabric. His 'pictorial design' is soft and fuzzy and yet powerful at

the same time. Following on from the great Hector Poleo, the personality of Edgar Sánchez long dominated the Venezuelan art world.

AUCTION RECORDS:

NEW YORK, 17 May 1988, *Changes in Skin Colour* (acrylic/canvas, 45 x 57 1/2 ins / 114 x 146 cm) USD 6,050. NEW YORK, 1 May 1990, *Skin Gestations* (1986-1989, acrylic/canvas, 67 x 78 1/2 ins / 170.1 x 199.5 cm) USD 7,700. NEW YORK, 15-16 May 1991, *Imaginations-Vision 10013* (1989, acrylic/canvas, 45 x 57 1/2 ins / 114 x 146 cm) USD 8,250. NEW YORK, 20 Nov 1991, *Image, Vision B2000* (acrylic/canvas, 55 x 67 ins / 140 x 170 cm) USD 9,900. NEW YORK, 18-19 May 1992, *Face and Skin 202* (1989, acrylic/canvas, 59 x 59 > ins / 150 x 150 cm) USD 9,350. NEW YORK, 25 Nov 1992, *Face, Image 3003* (1989, acrylic/canvas, 47 1/4 x 47 1/4 > ins / 120 x 120 cm) USD 10,450. NEW YORK, 18 May 1994, *Face, Image 30028* (1993, acrylic/canvas, 47 1/4 x 47 1/4 ins / 120 x 120 cm) USD 6,900. NEW YORK, 1 June 2000, *Personnage of Venice* (acrylic, 47 x 47 ins / 120 x 120 cm) USD 11,000.

SÁNCHEZ, Emilio

Cuban, 20th century.
Born 1921 or 1928.
Painter. Urban landscapes, interiors.

Emilio Sánchez was born in Cuba. He moved to New York in 1952.

His work features in a number of collective exhibitions both in the USA and in Latin America; venues include the Metropolitan Museum and the Museum of Modern Art in New York, the Boston Museum of Fine Art and Philadelphia Museum.

AUCTION RECORDS:

NEW YORK, 17 Oct 1979, *The Entrance* (pen, 35 1/2 x 41 3/4 ins / 90.1 x 106 cm) USD 1,600. NEW YORK, 17 Oct 1979, *The Red Door* (1979, acrylic/canvas, 71 1/2 x 48 1/4 ins / 181.5 x 122.8 cm) USD 3,000. NEW YORK, 7 May 1981, *A White House* (oil on canvas, 23 3/4 x 24 > ins / 60.3 x 60.7 cm) USD 2,100. NEW YORK, 12 May 1983, *Street Scene* (1982, watercolour, 25 x 39 1/2 ins / 63.5 x 100.4 cm) USD 2,100. NEW YORK, 29 May 1984, *Varadero's Cabin* (oil on canvas, 72 x 72 ins / 183 x 183 cm) USD 7,500. NEW YORK, 29 May 1985, *Montego Bay, Jamaica* (1951, watercolour, 22 x 29 1/2 ins / 55.6 x 75 cm) USD 1,800. NEW YORK, 22 May 1986, *House with a Green Door* (oil on canvas, 48 x 72 ins / 122 x 183 cm) GBP 5,000. NEW YORK, 17 May 1988, *Untitled* (oil on canvas, 48 x 48 > ins / 122 x 122 cm) USD > 6,600. NEW YORK, 21 Nov 1988, *House* (oil on canvas, 79 x 79 ins / 200.5 x 200.5 cm) USD 6,600. NEW YORK, 20 Nov 1991, *Green Bungalow* (1979, acrylic/canvas, 54 x 38 ins / 137 x 96.5 cm) USD 6,600. NEW YORK, 18-19 May 1992, *Untitled* (oil on canvas, 48 x 48 ins / 122 x 122 cm) USD 4,400. NEW YORK, 18-19 May 1993, *Large French Window* (1971, oil on canvas, 70 x 49 3/4 ins / 177.8 x 126.4 cm) USD 11,500. NEW YORK, 18 May 1994, *The Big House* (1971, oil on canvas, 72 x 72 ins / 182.9 x 182.9 cm) USD 12,650. PARIS, 7 July 2004, *Window* (1973, oil on canvas, 72 x 36 ins / 184 x 92 cm) EUR 2,000.

SÁNCHEZ, Enrique

Colombian, 20th century.
Born 1938 or 1940, in Bogotá.
Painter, engraver. Figures, landscapes.

Work by Enrique Sánchez has featured in various international collective exhibitions, including: 1961, the São Paulo Biennale; the Biennale of Young Artists in Paris; the Latin-American Biennale of Drawing and Engraving in Buenos Aires; 1962, the Worldwide Biennale in Tokyo; 1966, the 15th National Painting Exhibition in Brooklyn; 1966, 1967, 1968 the American Arts Federation, and others.

He painted landscapes and events of Latin America. His wood engravings were inspired by work of the greatest artists of all time: Cimabue, Leonardo, Titian, Rembrandt, Velázquez, Goya, Manet and Picasso.

AUCTION RECORDS:

NEW YORK, 17 May 1989, *In Mexico Valley* (1986, acrylic/canvas, 17 3/4 x 33 1/2 ins / 45 x 85 cm) USD 4,400. NEW YORK, 21 Nov 1989, *Mexico Valley* (1986, acrylic/canvas, 25 1/2 x 49 1/4 ins / 65 x 125 cm) USD 8,800. NEW YORK, 1 May 1990, *Landscape* (1979, acrylic/canvas, 39 1/4 x 50 3/4 ins / 100 x 129 cm) USD 7,150. LOKEREN, 10 Dec 1994, *Picking Oranges* (oil on canvas, 39 3/4 x 30 ins / 101 x 76 cm) BEF 130,000. MEXICO, 25 April 2002, *Landscape in Mexico* (1985, oil on canvas, 28 x 51 ins / 70 x 130 cm) MXP 68,000. MEXICO, 24 July 2002, *Evening over the Valley of Mexico* (oil on canvas, 16 x 26 ins / 40 x 65 cm) MXP 20,000.

SÁNCHEZ, Esteban

Spanish, 16th century.
Active in Granada.
Sculptor.

Esteban Sánchez worked with Pedro Machuca. He sculpted tabernacles, altars and ceilings for several churches in Granada.

SÁNCHEZ, Esteban

Spanish, 16th century.
Active c. 1581.
Sculptor (wood).

Esteban Sánchez sculpted an altar in Sta Maria la Blanca church, in Seville.

SANCHEZ, Fabian

Swiss, 20th century.
Sculptor of assemblages.
Kinetic Art.

Fabian Sanchez was an exponent of the Kinetic Art fad that proved so popular in the 1970s. His light-hearted approach was to take everyday items and apply them to situations and uses other than those for which they were originally intended.

MUSEUMS AND GALLERIES:

LAUSANNE (Cantonal MFA): *Made in England (The Singer Manufacturing Company)* (1973, sculpture); *Pfaff* (1974, sculpture).

SÁNCHEZ, Felipe

Spanish, 16th century.
Active during the first half of the 16th century.
Painter.

Felipe Sánchez worked on the Hospital de los Reyes Católicos in Santiago de Compostela between 1524 and 1525.

SÁNCHEZ, Ferran

Spanish, 15th century.
Sculptor.

Ferran Sánchez produced sculptures for the Puerta del Perdón and the chapel of St Peter in Toledo Cathedral.

SÁNCHEZ, Francisco

Spanish, 15th century.
Active during the first half of the 15th century.
Painter.

Francisco Sánchez worked with Diego Fernandez on the Easter chandelier in Seville Cathedral, in 1434.

SÁNCHEZ, Francisco

Spanish, 15th century.
Active in Baeza (Andalusia) in 1482.
Painter.

SÁNCHEZ, Francisco

Spanish, 15th - 16th century.
Active in Seville, from 1479 to 1506.
Painter.

SÁNCHEZ, Francisco

Spanish, 16th century.

Active in Seville from 1552 to 1560.
Sculptor (wood).
Francisco Sánchez was the assistant of P. de Becerril.

SÁNCHEZ, Francisco
Spanish, 16th century.
Active in Granada.
Sculptor.
Francisco Sánchez assisted Esteban Sánchez in the execution of the ceiling and the sacristy doors of the church of St Scholastica, in Granada.

SÁNCHEZ, Francisco
Spanish, 17th century.
Sculptor.
Francisco Sánchez created a ceremonial table for Toledo Cathedral in 1644.

SÁNCHEZ, Gaiamo
Spanish, 15th century.
Active in Seville during the first half of the 15th century.
Painter.
Gaiamo Sánchez worked in Palermo from 1422 to 1425.

SÁNCHEZ, Hernando or Hernan
Spanish, 16th century.
Active in Seville from 1547 to 1559.
Painter, gilder.
Hernando Sánchez painted the sides of the principal retable in Seville Cathedral, in 1559.

SÁNCHEZ, Jeronimo
Spanish, 16th century.
Painter. Religious subjects.
Jeronimo Sánchez produced two paintings, *St Francis* and *St Dominic*, for the portal of the Treasury of San Marco in Venice, in 1578. He was also a mosaicist.

SÁNCHEZ, Jesualda. See **SANCHIS**

SÁNCHEZ, José
Spanish, 17th century.
Sculptor.
Between 1635 and 1637 José Sánchez executed several statues and coats of arms for the screen of the Puerta del Perdón in Toledo Cathedral.

SÁNCHEZ, José
Spanish, 19th century.
Born in Cordova.
Active in Cordova from 1804 to 1827.
Engraver (burin).

SÁNCHEZ, Juan
Spanish, 15th century.
Active in Seville.
Painter.
Juan Sánchez painted a *Crucifixion* panel in Seville Cathedral.

SÁNCHEZ, Juan
Spanish, 15th century.
Painter.
Juan Sánchez painted an *Annunciation* in the Patio de los Muertos, in the church of Santiponce.

SÁNCHEZ, Juan
Spanish, 15th century.
Active in Seville from 1413 to 1431.
Painter.
Juan Sánchez may have been identical with Juan Hispalense, and father of Juan de Sánchez de Castro.

SÁNCHEZ, Juan
Spanish, 15th century.
Active in Valencia during the first half of the 15th century.
Illuminator.
Juan Sánchez worked on the Book of Privileges in Valencia, in 1414.

SÁNCHEZ, Juan
Spanish, 15th century.
Sculptor.
Juan Sánchez worked with other artists, including Martin Sánchez, on the Puerta del Perdón in Toledo Cathedral in 1418.

SÁNCHEZ, Juan
Spanish, 15th century.
Active in Fromista (Castilla y León) during the first half of the 15th century.
Painter, sculptor.
Juan Sánchez worked on Burgos Cathedral, from 1427.

SÁNCHEZ, Juan
Spanish, 15th century.
Active in Seville in 1435.
Painter.
Juan Sánchez may have been identical with Juan Sánchez de Castro, or Juan Sánchez de Santroman.

SÁNCHEZ, Juan
Spanish, 16th century.
Active in Seville.
Painter.
In 1513, Juan Sánchez received payment for his paintings for the high altar, in 1519 he painted four shields of royal coats of arms for the bed of the king, Don Fernando, and in 1543 he gilded the wooden crown sculpted by Gomez de Horozco, above the crucifix in S Pablo chapel, in Seville.

SÁNCHEZ, Juan
Spanish, 16th century.
Active in Seville during the first half of the 16th century.
Sculptor.
Juan Sánchez sculpted altars for churches in Seville, El Coronil and Villaverde del Rio, from 1527 to 1539.

SÁNCHEZ, Juan
Spanish, 16th century.
Born c. 1529, in Segovia (Castilla y León).
Active in Avila (Castilla y León) during the second half of the 16th century.
Sculptor.
Juan Sánchez was highly regarded by the great masters of his time. He was a witness for Pedro Gonzalez de León on 11 March 1553 in a disagreement between him and Berruguete.

SÁNCHEZ, Juan
Spanish, 16th century.
Glass painter.
Juan Sánchez produced the stained glass lattice windows of Cordova Cathedral, in 1598.

SÁNCHEZ, Justo
Spanish, 16th century.
Active in Toledo (Castile-La Mancha) in 1575.
Painter.
Justo Sánchez painted frescoes in Santiago del Arrabal church, in Toledo.

SÁNCHEZ, Lorenzo, called Lorencio Florentin
Spanish, 16th century.
Miniaturist.
Lorenzo Sánchez was the son of the sculptor Francisco Florentin. He worked in Granada from 1521, and illuminated four psalters in the Capilla Real.

SÁNCHEZ, Lorenzo
Spanish, 17th century.
Painter.

In 1643 Lorenzo Sánchez was commissioned to execute paintings and gilding work for the St Agnes altar in the church of the discalced Trinitarians in Madrid.

SÁNCHEZ, Luis
Spanish, 16th century.
Active during the first half of the 16th century.
Illuminator.

In 1516, Luis Sánchez worked on the choir books of Seville Cathedral, which were even more beautiful than the books at the Escorial.

SÁNCHEZ, Luis
Spanish, 17th century.
Active in Madrid in 1611.
Draughtsman.

SÁNCHEZ, Luis, or Sánchez Martínez
Spanish, 20th century.
Born 2 April 1913, in Bilbao.
Painter. Nudes, portraits, landscapes, still-lifes.

Luis Sánchez lived and worked in Bilbao, where he was one of the founders of the Nueva Bohemia (New Bohemia) association. He showed work in collective exhibitions in Madrid and was the recipient of several awards and distinctions. He exhibited solo for the first time in Bilbao in 1955 and also in Valencia, Pamplona, Madrid and Valladolid. His work comprises principally landscapes, with a particular fondness for meticulously detailed panoramic views.

BIBLIOGRAPHY:
Luis Sánchez, Gran Enciclopedia Vasca, Bilbao, 1973. *Luis Sánchez*, exhibition catalogue, Galeria Caledonia, Bilbao, 1975.

SÁNCHEZ, Manuel
Spanish, 16th century.
Active during the second half of the 16th century.
Sculptor (wood).

Manuel Sánchez worked on sculptures on the organ case in Seville Cathedral, in 1571.

SÁNCHEZ, Manuel
Spanish, 17th century.
Active in Toledo at the beginning of the 17th century.
Sculptor.

Manuel Sánchez carved the altar plinth in the church of the monastery of Nuestra Señora de Guadalupe.

SÁNCHEZ, Manuel
Spanish, 18th century.
Active in Murcia during the first half of the 18th century.
Painter.

Francisco Zarcillo studied under Manuel Sánchez, who was a priest and painted portraits and religious subjects for churches in Murcia and the surrounding area.

SÁNCHEZ, Marcelo
Spanish, 16th century.
Active at the end of the 16th century.
Sculptor.

Marcelo Sánchez sculpted the pulpit handrail in Plasencia Cathedral, in 1594.

SÁNCHEZ, Mariano Ramón
Spanish, 18th - 19th century.
Born 1740, in Valencia; died 8 March 1822, in Madrid.
Painter. Landscapes.

Mariano Ramón Sánchez studied at the Real Academia de San Fernando and was appointed painter to King Charles IV.

SÁNCHEZ, Martín
Spanish, 15th century.
Active in 1418.
Sculptor.

Martín Sánchez worked with Juan Sánchez on the Puerta del Perdón at Toledo Cathedral.

SÁNCHEZ, Martín
Spanish, 15th century.
Active during the second half of the 15th century.
Sculptor (wood).

Martín Sánchez sculpted the stalls of Miraflores Carthusian monastery, near Burgos, from 1486 to 1489.

SÁNCHEZ, Miguel
Spanish, 15th century.
Sculptor.

Miguel Sánchez worked on the Puerta del Perdón and Puerta de los Leones at Toledo Cathedral, from 1463 to 1493.

SÁNCHEZ, Miguel
Spanish, 16th century.
Active in 1562.
Illuminator.

Miguel Sánchez produced miniatures in the psalters at Seville Cathedral.

SÁNCHEZ, Miguel
Spanish, 17th century.
Sculptor.

Miguel Sánchez executed sculptures in the great chapel and the presbytery of the abbey church of Guadalajara.

SÁNCHEZ, Nufro or Nufrio
Spanish, 15th century.
Active during the second half of the 15th century.
Sculptor (wood).

Nufro Sánchez was the son of the wood sculptor Bartolomé Sánchez. He was in service to the city of Seville, and worked on stalls in the cathedral from 1475.

SANCHEZ, Pauline Stella. See **STELLA SANCHEZ Pauline**

SÁNCHEZ, Pedro
Spanish, 15th century.
Active in Toledo (Castile-La Mancha) during the first half of the 15th century.
Illuminator, calligrapher.

Pedro Sánchez produced psalters for Toledo Cathedral, from 1418 to 1432.

SÁNCHEZ, Pedro
Spanish, 15th century.
Active in Toledo (Castile-La Mancha).
Painter.

Pedro Sánchez worked in Toledo Cathedral in 1462.

SÁNCHEZ, Pedro
Spanish, 15th century.
Painter. Religious subjects.
Andalusian School (Seville).

Pedro Sánchez worked in Seville, during the second half of the 15th century. It is difficult to tell whether works were by the painter from Seville or the painter from Toledo. It is possible that the two painters were one artist who worked in both towns.

MUSEUMS AND GALLERIES:
BUDAPEST: *Entering the Tomb* (attributed) - SEVILLE: *God the Father Causing Lightning to Strike* (attributed).

SÁNCHEZ, Pedro
Spanish, 16th century.
Born in Villalon (Andalusia).
Active during the first half of the 16th century.
Sculptor.
Pedro Sánchez was a Cistercian monk. He sculpted altars for Sahagun and Sandoval churches.

SÁNCHEZ, Pedro
Spanish, 17th century.
Active in Santiago de Compostela.
Painter. Figures.
Pedro Sánchez was commissioned to provide the paintings for the altar of Sta Maria in the church of Sta Maria de Reza.

SÁNCHEZ, Pedro
Spanish, 17th century.
Active c. 1612.
Painter.
Pedro Sánchez was commissioned to provide the paintings that decorate the altar in the church of Arevalo.

SÁNCHEZ, Pedro
Spanish, 17th century.
Active in Seville during the second half of the 17th century.
Painter.
Pedro Sánchez was a member of the Seville academy in 1669.

SÁNCHEZ, Pero
Spanish, 15th century.
Painter. Religious subjects.
Pero Sánchez was probably identical with Pedro Sánchez from Seville. A canvas from the end of the 15th century in the Museo Arqueologico, in Seville, of a strange composition, is signed *Pedro Sánchez*.

SÁNCHEZ, Rui
Spanish, 15th century.
Sculptor.
Rui Sánchez worked on several portals of Toledo Cathedral, from 1459 to 1479.

SANCHEZ, Salvador. See **BARBUDO MORALES Salvador Sánchez**

SÁNCHEZ, Tomás
Spanish, 16th century.
Active in Seville from 1525 to 1536.
Painter.

SÁNCHEZ, Tomás
Spanish, 18th century.
Active in 1714.
Engraver (burin).

SANCHEZ, Tomas
Cuban, 20th - 21st century.
Born 1948.
Painter. Landscapes.
Tomas Sanchez studied at the Academia Nacional de Bellas Artes San Alejandro and the national school of arts in Havana. During the 1960s he was associated with the Neo-Figurative movement. He spends much of his time in the south of Florida.

In his work, Sanchez' idyllic landscapes are contrasted with critical descriptions of environmental pollution. He is known for his meticulous approach to detail of tropical landscapes, which are nevertheless unusual for their Surrealism and the use of geometric forms and angles. Sanchez was awarded the Joan Miró prize.

AUCTION RECORDS:
NEW YORK, 17 May 1988, *Lagoon and the Sea* (1988, oil on canvas, 43 1/2 x 59 1/4 ins / 110.5 x 150.5 cm) USD 7,150. NEW YORK, 20 Nov 1991, *Cloud and its Shadow* (1988, oil on canvas, 43 x 59 ins / 109.3 x 149.7 cm) USD 33,000. NEW YORK, 18-19 May 1992, *Meditation* (1987, acrylic/canvas, 42 1/2 x 59 ins / 108 x 149 cm) USD 66,000. NEW YORK, 24 Nov 1992, *Ojo de las Aguas* (*The Eye of Las Aguas*) (1987, acrylic/canvas, 43 1/2 x 59 1/2 ins / 110.5 x 151.2 cm) USD 66,000. NEW YORK, 18 May 1993, *Landscape with Low Cloud* (1987, acrylic/canvas, 43 1/4 x 59 ins / 110 x 150 cm) USD 79,500. NEW YORK, 23-24 Nov 1993, *Orilla* (*Shore*) (1988, acrylic/canvas, 43 1/2 x 59 ins / 110.2 x 150 cm) USD 74,000. NEW YORK, 18 May 1994, *Cloud and its Shadow* (1989, acrylic/canvas, 58 3/4 x 42 3/4 ins / 149.5 x 108.9 cm) USD 68,500. NEW YORK, 16 Nov 1994, *Looking for a Place in the Moonlight* (1990, acrylic/canvas, 35 1/2 x 48 ins / 90.2 x 122 cm) USD 79,500. NEW YORK, 20 Nov 1995, *Agaucero a La Orilla* (*Downpour at La Orilla*) (1989, acrylic/canvas, 52 x 62 ins / 132 x 157.2 cm) USD 74,000. NEW YORK, 15 May 1996, *Diptych of Day and Night* (1989, acrylic/canvas, 31 1/2 x 23 1/2 ins / 80 x 60 cm) USD 51,750. NEW YORK, 25-26 Nov 1996, *Worship at the Waterfall* (1991, acrylic/canvas, 42 1/4 x 58 ins / 107 x 147.6 cm) USD 101,500. NEW YORK, 26-27 Nov 1996, *Shore* (1989, acrylic/canvas, 78 3/4 x 98 1/2 ins / 200 x 250.2 cm) USD 178,500. NEW YORK, 28 May 1997, *Aerial Landscape* (1989, acrylic/canvas, 59 x 39 1/4 ins / 150 x 100 cm) USD 57,500. NEW YORK, 29-30 May 1997, *In Praise of Moonlight* (1991, acrylic/canvas, 30 x 40 ins / 76.2 x 101.3 cm) USD 68,500. NEW YORK, 24-25 Nov 1997, *Beach and Storm* (1988, acrylic/canvas, 43 x 57 1/4 ins / 109 x 145.5 cm) USD 68,500. MIAMI, 10 Jan 1999, *Clear Night* (1990, oil on canvas, 31 x 39 ins / 79 x 98 cm) USD 60,000. NEW YORK, 2 June 1999, *Nightfall over the Cliff* (1996, tempera on paper, 23 x 30 ins / 58 x 77 cm) USD 35,000. NEW YORK, 1 June 2000, *Nubes sobre laguna* (*Clouds over Lagoon*) (1996, oil on canvas, 77 x 95 ins / 196 x 242 cm) USD 280,000. NEW YORK, 20 Nov 2000, *Night Reflections* (1998, acrylic on canvas, 48 x 60 ins / 121 x 152 cm) USD 140,000. NEW YORK, 19 Nov 2001, *Contemplador de la cascada* (*Waterfall Admirer*) (1996, acrylic on canvas, 24 x 30 ins / 61 x 76 cm) USD 140,000. NEW YORK, 20 Nov 2001, *Autorretrato en la orilla* (*Self-portrait on the River Bank*) (1993, acrylic on canvas, 48 x 48 ins / 122 x 122 cm) USD 200,000. NEW YORK, 29 May 2002, *Llegar al mar* (*Getting to the Sea*) (2001, acrylic on canvas, 22 x 28 ins / 57 x 71 cm) USD 60,000. NEW YORK, 29 May 2002, *Forest* (1987, acrylic on canvas, 32 x 39 ins / 81 x 99 cm) USD 80,000. NEW YORK, 28 May 2003, *Contemplando al contemplador* (*Contemplating the Contemplator*) (2001, acrylic on canvas, 24 x 20 ins / 60 x 50 cm) USD 60,000. NEW YORK, 18 Nov 2003, *Oidor de aguas* (*Listening to the Water*) (1996, acrylic on canvas, 30 x 40 ins / 76 x 101 cm) USD 110,000. NEW YORK, 26 May 2004, *Worshipping a Tree* (2003, acrylic on canvas, 20 x 24 ins / 51 x 61 cm) USD 80,000. PARIS, 10 June 2004, *Meditating by Canal* (1995, acrylic on canvas, 30 x 40 ins / 76 x 101 cm) EUR 90,000.

SÁNCHEZ ALEMAN, Juan
Spanish, 15th century.
Of German origin.
Active in Toledo.
Sculptor.
Juan Sánchez Aleman sculpted the statues for the Puerta de los Leones and Puerta del Perdón of Toledo Cathedral from 1462 to 1466.

SÁNCHEZ ARACIEL, Manuel
Spanish, 19th - 20th century.
Born 21 October 1851, in Murcia; died 24 May 1918.
Sculptor. Busts, low reliefs.
Manuel Sánchez was the son and pupil of Francisco Sánchez Tapia; he sculpted busts and a *Way of the Cross series* for the Madrid church of St Cajetan.

SÁNCHEZ ARTIGUES, Tomás
Spanish, 17th century.
Died at the end of the 17th century, in Madrid.
Sculptor.

Tomás Sánchez Artigues executed sculptures for Valencia Cathedral and for churches in the city. He was probably related to Tomás Artigues.

SÁNCHEZ BARBA, Juan
Spanish, 17th century.
Born c. 1615, to a family originally from the mountains near Burgos (Castile-Leon); died 1670, in Madrid.
Sculptor.

Juan Sánchez Barba carved a *Crucifix* on a scale larger than life in the Caballero del Garcia oratory in Madrid.

SÁNCHEZ BARBUDO MORALES, Salvador.
See **BARBUDO MORALES Salvador Sánchez**

SÁNCHEZ BLANCO, Pedro
Spanish, 19th century.
Born 21 January 1833, in Madrid; died 1902, in Madrid.
Painter, engraver.

Pedro Sánchez Blanco was a pupil of C. L. Ribera. He painted altarpieces for churches in Madrid and San Ginés and also a portrait of *N. M. Rivero* for the Athenaeum in Madrid.

SÁNCHEZ CID, Agustín
Spanish, 20th century.
Born 25 April 1886, in Seville.
Sculptor. Monuments.

Agustín Sánchez studied in Seville under José García y Ramos; he lived and worked in Seville, where he sculpted monuments to *J. Martínez Montanés*.

SÁNCHEZ COELLO, Alonso
Spanish, 16th century.
Born c. 1531-1532, in La Alqueria Blanca, Benifayo (Valencia); died between 1588 and 1590, in Madrid.
Painter. Portraits.

Alonso Sánchez Coello was born in Spain and lived in Portugal from the age of ten. He was educated in Portugal and Flanders. During his travels he met the Flemish painter Anton van Mor, who became his master and patron. He returned to Portugal in 1552, and entered the service of the royal family in Lisbon. In 1555 he moved to Valladolid in Spain, where he was employed by the Infanta Juana, and after 1559 he was attached to the court of Philip II at Madrid.

In 1557 Sánchez Coello returned to Valladolid. He went into service to the king when Antonio Moro fell out of favour, and was the perfect courtier, sharing the private lives of princes and patronised by the king who, in his correspondence, referred to him as 'his very dear son'.

Sánchez Coello was mediocre as a painter of religious compositions but a good and perceptive portrait painter. He did not follow the classical rules governing Spanish painting during the time of Philip II as he had a liking for an Italian style midway between Romanism and Mannerism, so his portraits are endowed with subtle life. He painted the king, princes and royal children, but also deformed people and dwarves, producing portraits as strange as that of the attractive *Princess Eboli*, in which the princess wears a eye patch.

BIBLIOGRAPHY:

Roman, F. de, *Alonso Sánchez Coello*, Lisbon, 1938. Hinkhouse, Forest M., *Vida y obra de Alonso Sánchez Coello*, dissertation, Facultad de Filosofia y Letras, Madrid, 1952. Cueco Mascarós, Rosa, *Alonso Sánchez Coello: lugar de su nacimiento, su vida y su obra*, dissertation, Universidad Literaria de Valencia, Valencia, 1955. Doménech, Fernando Benito, *La pintura religiosa en Alonso Sánchez Coello*, Museo del Prado, Madrid, 1990. *Alonso Sánchez Coello y el retrato en la corte de Felipe II*, Museo del Prado, Madrid, 1990. Mulcahy, Rosemarie, '*Alonso Sánchez Coello and Cardinal Alessandro Farnese*' in *Burlington Magazine, 84*, 1992. Mulcahy, Rosemarie, *Philip II of Spain, Patron of the Arts*, Four Courts Press, Dublin, 2003.

MUSEUMS AND GALLERIES:

BERLIN: *Portrait of Philip II* - BILBAO (MBA): *Joanna of Austria* - DUBLIN: *Portrait of a Young Man, Probably a Spanish Prince* - ÉPINAL: *Portrait of a Child* - MADRID: *Portrait of the Infanta Isabella Clara; Portrait of Philip II; Portrait of the Infanta Catherine Micaela; Portrait of Prince Don Carlos; Mystical Marriage of St Catherine* (1578); *St Sebastian between St Bernard and St Francis* (1582); *Portrait of a Spanish Noblewoman Holding a Chinese Fan* (c. 1550-1565, executed in his studio) - WROCLAW: *Portrait of Don Juan*.

AUCTION RECORDS:

PARIS, 1852, *St Paul and St Anthony, First Hermits in the Desert*, FRF 300. LONDON, 1853, *Joanna of Austria*, FRF 2,750; *Marie of Austria*, FRF 2,625; *Margaret of Austria*, FRF 2,250; *Nine Paintings* (subjects not given) FRF 9,450. LONDON, 1855, *Anne Marie of Austria, Queen of Spain*, FRF 5,390. PARIS, 1867, *Portrait of Hernán Cortés*, FRF 8,700; *Portrait of a Young Gentleman*, FRF 4,600. LONDON, 1882, *Portrait of the Duke of Alba*, FRF 10,500. PARIS, 1890, *Portrait Thought to Be of Dona Juana, Sister of Philip II*, FRF 7,000. LONDON, 1892, *Dona Maria, Infanta*, FRF 14,300. PARIS, 1899, *Solitude*, FRF 7,100; *Don Fernand of Austria*, FRF 8,750; *Patrician Lady*, FRF 9,000. NEW YORK, 1900, *Portrait of the Wife of Admiral de L'Ordes*, FRF 7,750. PARIS, 30 April 1900, *Portrait of Elizabeth of France, Queen of Spain*, FRF 5,800. PARIS, 12 April 1901, *Portrait Thought to Be of Cosimo de Medici*, FRF 460. PARIS, 11 and 12 April 1904, *Portrait of Elizabeth of Bohemia*, FRF 210. PARIS, 17-21 May 1904, *Portrait of a Spanish Royal Child*, FRF 430; *Portrait of Philip IV*, FRF 1,840. PARIS, 8-16 June 1904, *Portrait of a Woman*, FRF 400. NEW YORK, 1905, *Portrait of Isabella Clara*, USD 7,500. PARIS, 8 May 1906, *Portrait of Dona Juana, Infanta*, FRF 700. NEW YORK, 1909, *Duchess Margaret of Parma*, USD 775. PARIS, 27 and 28 Feb 1919, *Portraits of a Woman* (two oils on canvas, school of Alonso Sánchez Coello) FRF 235. PARIS, 10 April 1919, *Portrait Thought to Be of Archduke Albert, Governor of the Netherlands* (attributed) FRF 520; *Portrait Thought to Be of Archduchess Isabella, Daughter of Philip II* (attributed) FRF 980. PARIS, 21 Nov 1919, *Portrait of a Princess* (attributed) FRF 1,000. PARIS, 19 Dec 1919, *Portrait of a Royal Child* (attributed) FRF 1,610. PARIS, 14 Feb 1920, *Portraits of Spanish Princes* (attributed) FRF 900. PARIS, 20 Oct 1920, *Portrait of a Woman* (attributed) FRF 455. PARIS, 14 Dec 1921, *Portrait of a Queen* (school of Alonso Sánchez Coello) FRF 425. PARIS, 4 Feb 1922, *Bust of a Princess Wearing a Ruff* (school of Alonso Sánchez Coello and after him) FRF 135. PARIS, 9 March 1922, *Portrait of a Prince* (attributed to the school of Alonso Sánchez Coello) FRF 280. PARIS, 15 May 1922, *Portrait Thought to be of Infanta Joanna of Austria* (school of Alonso Sánchez Coello) FRF 4,000. LONDON, 19 June 1922, *Ferdinand II de Medici*, GBP 10. LONDON, 19 Jan 1923, *Lady in an Embroidered Dress*, GBP 31. PARIS, 21 Dec 1923, *Portrait of Duke Alessandro Farnese*, FRF 400. PARIS, 30 March 1925, *Young Girl with a Toy* (attributed) FRF 1,230. PARIS, 26 Jan 1927, *Portrait of a Princess* (attributed) FRF 6,500. LONDON, 20 May 1927, *Charles V of Spain; Queen Isabella, His Wife* (two panels) GBP 1,575. PARIS, 25 Nov 1927, *Portrait Thought to Be of Philip II, King of Spain* (school of Alonso Sánchez Coello) FRF 520; *Portrait of a Princess* (school of Alonso Sánchez Coello) FRF 600. PARIS, 20 Jan 1928, *Portrait of a Young Princess* (attributed) FRF 290. PARIS, 2 March 1928, *Portrait of a Lady of Quality* (school of Alonso Sánchez Coello) FRF 500. PARIS, 19 Dec 1928, *Portrait of a Woman Holding a Handkerchief* (school of Alonso Sánchez Coello) FRF 6,000. PARIS, 24 April 1929, *Portrait of a Gentleman Wearing a Ruff* (attributed) FRF 1,150. PARIS, 10 Feb 1933, *Portrait Thought to Be of Marie de Medici* (school of Alonso Sánchez Coello) FRF 1,250; *Portrait of a Royal Princess* (school of Alonso Sánchez Coello) FRF 1,250. PARIS, 26 Feb 1934, *Young Woman Wearing a Lace Ruff* (school of Alonso Sánchez Coello) FRF 300. NEW YORK, 18 and 19 April 1934, *Philip II of Spain*, USD 750. LONDON, 5 April 1935, *Anne Marie of Austria, Wife of Philip II of Spain* (1575) GBP 110. LONDON, 22 Dec 1937, *Anne of Austria*, GBP 58. PARIS, 4 Dec 1941, *Portrait of a Woman* (attributed) FRF 1,800. PARIS, 20 March 1942, *Portrait of a Princess*, FRF 9,100. NEW YORK, 27-29 Oct 1943, *Portrait of a Woman*, USD 775; *Daughter of Philip II of Spain*, USD 680. LONDON, 8 March 1944, *Gentleman*, GBP 34. PARIS, 11 April 1962, *Portrait Thought to Be of Dona Juana, Sister of Philip II*, FRF 24,000. LONDON, 3 July 1963, *Dona Juana, Sister of Philip II of Spain*, GBP 1,600. LONDON, 29 May 1992, *Portrait of Hernan Cortés Wearing Black and with a Sword and a Dagger by His Side, Holding a Glove* (oil on canvas, 48¼ x 41 ins / 122.7 x 104 cm) GBP 264,000. NEW YORK, 20 May 1993, *Portrait of a Child, Catherine, Aged One, in Her Wheeled Chair* (oil on canvas, 40 x 30½ ins / 101.6 x 77.5 cm) USD 40,250. NEW YORK, Jan 1998, *Portrait of Elizabeth of Valois* (oil on panel, 18½ x 16 ins / 47 x 40.6 cm) USD 85,000.

SÁNCHEZ COELLO, Isabel or Isabella Herrera
Spanish, 16th - 17th century.
Born 1564, in Madrid; died 6 February 1612, in Madrid.
Painter. Portraits.

Isabel Sánchez Coello was the daughter and pupil of Alonso Sánchez Coello. She was a distinguished portrait painter and was equally skilled in poetry and music. She married Francisco de Herrera y Saavedra.

SÁNCHEZ COELLO, Jeronimo
Spanish, 16th century.
Active at the end of the 16th century.
Painter.

In 1591, Jeronimo Sánchez Coello was commissioned to produce the high altar of Trinidad abbey in Seville.

SÁNCHEZ CORDOBÉS, Juan
Spanish, 17th century.
Active in Cordova.
Sculptor.

Juan Sánchez Cordobés was a pupil of P. de Mena. He carved a statue of the city's patron saint for the church of Sta Maria Madalena in Granada.

SÁNCHEZ COTÁN, Alonso
Spanish, 17th century.
Born in Alcázar de San Juan.
Sculptor.

In 1612 Alonso Sánchez Cotán worked with his brother Damián in Toledo.

SÁNCHEZ COTÁN, Damián
Spanish, 17th century.
Active during the first half of the 17th century.
Painter.

Damián Sánchez Cotán worked in Toledo with his brother Alonso Sánchez Cotán.

SÁNCHEZ D'AVILA, Andrés
Spanish, 18th century.
Born 1701, in Toledo; died 1762, in Vienna.
Painter. Portraits.

As a young man Andrés Sánchez d'Avila worked in Paris, but he later settled in Vienna.

SÁNCHEZ DE BONIFACIO, Martín, or Bonifacio
Spanish, 15th century.
Active in Toledo (Castile-La Mancha) from 1479 to 1484.
Sculptor, architect.

Martín Sánchez de Bonifacio worked on the Puerta del Perdón of Toledo Cathedral, in 1479.

SÁNCHEZ DE CALIZ, Juan
Spanish, 16th century.
Active in Seville from 1532 to 1599.
Sculptor, architect.

Sánchez de Caliz produced sculptures for the town hall in Seville.

SÁNCHEZ DE CASTRO, Anton
Spanish, 15th century.
Died 1509.
Painter.

Anton Sánchez de Castro was the brother of Juan Sánchez de Castro from Seville. He was in Seville from 1478.

SÁNCHEZ DE CASTRO, Anton
Spanish, 16th century.
Active in 1518.
Painter.

Anton Sánchez de Castro produced paintings for the Alcazar Palace in Seville.

SÁNCHEZ DE CASTRO, Juan
Spanish, 15th century.
Painter.
Andalusian School (Seville).

Juan Sánchez de Castro founded the Andalusian School and was head of the School of Seville. He must have been born during the first half of the 15th century. Little is known of his many works.

Céan Bermendez referred to a Gothic retable painted by Sánchez de Castro in 1445, damaged and almost destroyed by very poor repair work, in S José chapel in Seville Cathedral, two frescoes of St Christopher in S Julian parish church, a fresco of St Ildefonsus, still visible but badly damaged, and the painting *Annunciation*, in existence during Pacheco's time, in S Isidro de Campo monastery.

The remarkable panel discovered behind an altar in S Julian church in 1878, and now in Seville Cathedral, as well as another panel in the Santuario de la Virgen del Águila, in Alcalá de Guadaira, depicting the *Birth of Christ* give an indication of the quality of Sánchez de Castro's work.

MUSEUMS AND GALLERIES:
ALCALÁ DE GUADAÍRA (Santuario de la Virgen del Águila): *Birth of Christ* - SEVILLE (Cathedral).

SÁNCHEZ DE CASTRO, Juan
Spanish, 16th century.
Painter.

Juan Sánchez de Castro worked in the Augustinian monastery in Casbas de Huesca, in 1514.

SÁNCHEZ DE CASTRO, Pedro
Spanish, 15th century.
Active in Seville in 1480.
Painter.

Pedro Sánchez de Castro may have been the brother of Juan Sánchez de Castro.

SÁNCHEZ DE GRELA, Antonio
Spanish, 17th century.
Sculptor.

In 1656 Antonio Sánchez de Grela was commissioned to create an altar for the church of S Salvador in Villar de Sarrià.

SÁNCHEZ DE GUADALUPE, Anton I
Spanish, 15th century.

Born in Santa Maria de Guadalupe (Cáceres); died 1506, in Seville.
Painter. Landscapes.
Anton Sánchez de Guadalupe I was the father of Anton Sánchez de Guadalupe II. He painted *View of Malaga* with Diego Sánchez, in 1487.

SÁNCHEZ DE GUADALUPE, Anton II
Spanish, 16th century.
Active in Seville from 1510 to 1561.
Painter. Religious subjects.
Anton Sánchez de Guadalupe II was the son of Anton Sánchez de Guadalupe I. He produced many altarpieces and painted statues for churches in Seville and other cities in Spain.
AUCTION RECORDS:
NEW YORK, 19 May 1994, *Crucifixion; St Jerome on the Left; Holy Monk with a Prisoner on the Right* (oil on panel, triptych, centre, 31 1/2 x 22 ins / 80 x 55.9 cm each side, 31 1/2 x 9 1/2 ins/80 x 24.1 cm) USD 57,500.

SÁNCHEZ DE GUADALUPE, Miguel
Spanish, 16th century.
Active in Seville from 1505 to 1530.
Painter.
Miguel Sánchez de Guadalupe worked for the Hospital de San Sebastian, in Seville.

SÁNCHEZ DE LA BARBA, Juan
Spanish, 17th - 18th century.
Sculptor, architect.
Juan Sánchez de la Barba was probably related to the sculptor Juan Sánchez Barba.

SÁNCHEZ DE LA PEÑA, Luis
Spanish, 19th - 20th century.
Born probably, in Granada.
Painter. History painting, figures, portraits, landscapes.
Luis Sánchez de la Peña was a pupil of Manuel Dominguez y Sánchez at the Escuela Especial de Pintura, Escultura y Grabado in Madrid, gaining honourable mentions in 1895 and 1904. He was awarded a silver medal at the Exposition Universelle in Brussels. Luis Sánchez de la Peña painted historical subjects (*Return of the Queen's Vessel*); landscapes (*Landscapes and Plantations of Pardo*); figures (*Head of a Cheeky Woman*); and portraits (*Portrait of the Corpse of Don Mariano Fernández; Portrait of the Corpse of Don Antonio Pérez Rubio*).
BIBLIOGRAPHY:
Arnáiz, José Manuel/López Jiménez, Javier/Merchán Díaz, Manuel (ed.), '*Cien años de pintura en Espana y Portugal (1830-1930)*' in vol. X, Antiqvaria, Madrid, 1993.
AUCTION RECORDS:
PARIS, 22 Feb 1936, *Bust of a Young Girl*, FRF 50. PARIS, 31 March 1947, *Portrait of a Woman with Bare Shoulders*, FRF 400.

SÁNCHEZ DE MONTALVA, Juan
Spanish, 16th century.
Active at the beginning of the 16th century.
Illuminator, calligrapher.
Juan Sánchez de Montalva produced psalters for Valencia Cathedral, from 1502 to 1510.

SÁNCHEZ DE MORA, Mateo
Spanish, 17th century.
Active in Seville.
Sculptor (wood), cabinet maker.
In 1671 Mateo Sánchez de Mora was commissioned to create the St Anne altar in the church of Aracena.

SÁNCHEZ DE PALENCIA, Francisco
Spanish, 17th century.
Active in Lugo (Galicia).
Sculptor (wood).
In 1619 Francisco Sánchez de Palencia was commissioned to make an altar with tabernacle for the church of Sta Maria de Dodro.

SÁNCHEZ DE PARIAS, Diego
Spanish, 15th century.
Died before 28 February 1502.
Active in Seville.
Painter.
There were at least three painters called Diego Sánchez active in Seville during the 15th century, and it is easy to confuse them. Diego Sánchez de Parias was the son of the famous Juan Sánchez de Castro, considered the patriarch of the Seville School. He married Ana de Montoja on 9 October 1472.

SÁNCHEZ DE SANTROMAN, Juan
Spanish, 15th century.
Active in Seville.
Painter. Religious subjects.
Juan Sánchez de Santroman mainly painted retables.

SÁNCHEZ DE SEGOVIA, Antón
Spanish, 13th century.
Active in the second half of the 13th century.
Painter.
Sanchez de Segovia painted decorative murals in the old cathedral of Salamanca in 1262.

SÁNCHEZ DE SEGURA, Diego
Spanish, 17th century.
Active in Murcia.
Sculptor (wood), architect.
Diego Sánchez de Segura carved the wooden ceiling of the ceremonial hall of the Trinitarian monastery in Murcia. Part of this work is now kept in the Murcia museum.

SÁNCHEZ DE TOLEDO, Francisco
Spanish, 15th century.
Active in Segovia (Castilla y León).
Sculptor.
Francisco Sánchez de Toledo was commissioned to produce seven low reliefs depicting armorial bearings, in Sta Maria del Parral church.

SÁNCHEZ DÍAZ, Leopoldo
Spanish, 19th century.
Born 1830, in Villafranca del Bierzo.
Active in Madrid.
Painter.
Leopoldo Sánchez Díaz executed allegorical paintings for the cemetery of S Nicolás in Madrid.

SÁNCHEZ FERNÁNDEZ, Juan Miguel
Spanish, 20th century.
Born 18 August 1899, in Puerta di Santa Maria near Cádiz.
Painter, poster artist. Portraits, landscapes. Murals.
Juan Sánchez was a pupil of the painter Gustavo Bacarisas; he exhibited at various collective exhibitions including: Seville (from 1922), Madrid (from 1926), San Sebastián (1939) and Barcelona (1942). In 1925, he won first prize in a nationwide poster design competition; he also won a bronze medal in 1926, a silver in 1945 and a gold in 1948. Examples of his work include *Golden Trees* and *Blue-Eyed Gypsy*.
BIBLIOGRAPHY:
Arnáiz, José Manuel/López Jiménez, Javier/Merchán Díaz, Manuel (ed.), '*Cien años de pintura en Espana y Portugal (1830-1930)*' in vol. X, Antiqvaria, Madrid, 1993.

SÁNCHEZ GONZÁLEZ, Antonio
Spanish, 19th century.
Died 1825, in Madrid.
Active in the Canary Islands.
Painter.

Antonio Sánchez Gonzalez founded a school of painting in Santa Cruz de Tenerife.

SÁNCHEZ IZQUIERDO, Juan
Spanish, 15th century.
Active in Granada and in Seville during the second half of the 15th century.
Painter.

Juan Sánchez Izquierdo worked in Seville from 1496 to 1497, and in Granada in 1499.

SÁNCHEZ LEONARDO, Alonso
Spanish, 16th century.
Active in Seville from 1578 to 1596.
Painter.

Alonso Sánchez Leonardo produced paintings for the town hall in Seville.

SÁNCHEZ MARTÍNEZ, Francisco
Spanish, 18th century.
Active during the first half of the 18th century.
Glass painter.

Francisco Sánchez Martínez worked for Toledo Cathedral from 1713 to 1721.

SÁNCHEZ MARTINEZ, Luis. See **SÁNCHEZ Luis**

SÁNCHEZ NARVÁEZ, Antonio
Spanish, 19th - 20th century.
Born 1850, in Madrid.
Painter.

Antonio Sánchez Narváez was a pupil of Victor Manzano y Mejorada.

SÁNCHEZ PÉREZ, Alberto
Spanish, 20th century.
Born 8 April 1895, in Toledo; died 12 October 1962, in Moscow.
Active in Russia from the beginning of 1938.
Painter, sculptor, engraver, draughtsman, poster artist.
Portraits, figures, genre scenes, landscapes, still-lifes.
Busts, figurines, low reliefs, stage sets.

Alberto Sánchez Pérez served his apprenticeship as a shoemaker but went to work for a stonemason-sculptor in his native Toledo. In 1922, he made friends with the Uruguayan painter Rafael Barradas and, with the latter's help, secured a scholarship from the Toledo municipal council that enabled him to work as a full-time artist. He went on to teach at the institute of public works in Valencia. He was in Moscow in 1938, where he taught drawing and composition to the children of Spanish parents working there.

He started out sculpting busts and figures, including works commissioned to decorate a square in Madrid. His geometric sculptures have a structural flexibility and subtlety complemented by low reliefs of sets of symbols (parallel lines, circles, crosses and points) inscribed on them. He also produced etchings, posters and theatre stage sets, notably for the Moscow productions of *La Zapatera Prodigiosa* and *Bodas de sangre* by Lorca (Theatre Romen), *Carolina* by Carlo Goldoni and *La Gitanilla* by Cervantes in César Arconadas' dramatisation.

Sánchez Pérez took part in various collective exhibitions, including the National Exhibition of Iberian Artists, Madrid (1925), Madrid Athenaeum Exhibition (1930), a Constructivist group exhibition organised by the Uruguayan Torres García, Palacio del Retiro in Madrid (1931) and the Union of Painters, Sculptors and Set Designers exhibition, Moscow (1959). In 2002, the Museu Nacional d'Art de Catalunya mounted a Sánchez Pérez retrospective in Barcelona; it featured in excess of one hundred sculptures, paintings, drawings and set designs.

BIBLIOGRAPHY:
Bozal, Valeriano, *El Realismo plástico en España de 1900 a 1936*, Ed Península, Madrid, 1967. Chávarri, Raúl, *Mito y realidad de la Escuela de Vallecas*, Ibérico Europea de Ediciones, Madrid, 1975. Arnáiz, José Manuel/López Jiménez, Javier/Merchán Díaz, Manuel (ed.), *'Cien años de pintura en Espana y Portugal (1830-1930)'* in vol. X, Antiqvaria, Madrid, 1993.

SÁNCHEZ PERRIER, Emilio
Spanish, 19th century.
Born 15 October 1855, in Seville; died 13 September 1907, in Alhama de Granada.
Painter, watercolourist. Local scenes, landscapes, landscapes with figures, urban landscapes, waterscapes.

Emilio Sánchez Perrier studied at the school of fine arts in Seville and later at the school of fine arts in Madrid. In 1871 he lived in Granada with Martin Rico, where he became friends with Mariano Fortuny. In 1879 he lived in Paris and studied at the studios of Auguste Bolard, Léon Gérome and Félix Ziem.

He exhibited at various group exhibitions: In 1878 at the exhibition of the national fine arts society of Madrid; in 1879 at the Cádiz regional exhibition, where he was awarded a gold medal; and from 1880 at the Salon des Artistes Français, receiving a commendation in 1886 and a silver medal at the Exposition Universelle of 1889. He was made a member of the Seville fine arts academy.

Sánchez Perrier painted views of Paris and verdant landscapes, mainly of river views populated with small figures. He is known for his *Lake with Boats*, *Alcazar Kitchen Garden*; *Winter*; and *Andalusia*. He also produced Orientalist paintings that reveal the influence of Fortuny. His watercolours achieved rapid popularity in England.

E Sanchez Perrier

BIBLIOGRAPHY:
Arnáiz, José Manuel/López Jiménez, Javier/Merchán Díaz, Manuel (ed.), *'Cien años de pintura en Espana y Portugal (1830-1930)'* in vol. X, Antiqvaria, Madrid, 1993.

MUSEUMS AND GALLERIES:
PONTOISE: *Banks of the River Oise* (1896).

AUCTION RECORDS:
NEW YORK, 21-22 Jan 1909, *The Zoco Grande in Tangier*, USD 200. NEW YORK, 30-31 Oct 1929, *Lake Landscape*, USD 425. PARIS, 16-17 May 1945, *By the River*, FRF 10,400. NEW YORK, 23 Feb 1968, *Market Place in Tangier*, USD 1,600. LONDON, 2 Nov 1973, *River Landscape*, Gns 2,200. NEW YORK, 15 Oct 1976, *Washerwomen, Gisors* (oil on panel, 13 x 18 ins / 33 x 46 cm) USD 6,000. NEW YORK, 31 Oct 1980, *River Landscape with Oarsman* (oil on panel, 13 3/4 x 10 1/2 ins / 35 x 26.7 cm) USD 9,000. NEW YORK, 28 May 1981, *River Bank, Osny* (oil on panel, 10 1/4 x 13 1/4 ins / 26 x 33.5 cm) USD 16,000. NEW YORK, 26 Oct 1983, *River Landscape* (oil on canvas, 23 x 34 1/4 ins / 58.5 x 87 cm) USD 18,000. NEW YORK, 30 Oct 1985, *S Juan Mill in Alcalá* (1884, oil on panel, 18 1/4 x 11 ins / 46.3 x 27 cm) USD 25,000. NEW YORK, 22 May 1986, *Fishermen in a Boat by a River* (oil on panel, 10 1/2 x 13 3/4 ins / 26.6 x 35 cm) USD 12,000. NEW YORK, 24 May 1988, *Young Boy in Undergrowth* (1888, oil on panel, 18 x 10 ins / 45.7 x 25.4 cm) USD 20,900. LONDON, 22 June 1988, *Figures by a River* (oil on panel, 13 3/4 x 11 ins / 35 x 27 cm) GBP 5,500. NEW YORK, 23 May 1989, *River Bank in Seville* (oil on panel, 14 3/4 x 18 1/4 ins / 37.5 x 46.2 cm) USD 26,400. LONDON, 21 June 1989, *Harvesters outside a Village* (1876, oil on canvas, 12 1/2 x 20 3/4 ins / 32 x 53 cm) GBP 9,350. NEW YORK, 25 Oct 1989, *River Oise in Auvers* (oil on panel, 16 1/2 x 13 ins / 41.9 x 33 cm) USD

35,200. LONDON, 14 Feb 1990, *River Landscape with Figures* (1884, oil on panel, 8 3/4 x 14 ins / 22.5 x 35.5 cm) GBP 12,100. NEW YORK, 28 Feb 1990, *Campfire by a River* (oil on panel, 12 x 22 ins / 30.5 x 55.9 cm) USD 28,600. NEW YORK, 23 May 1990, *On the Riverbank in Summer* (oil on canvas, 16 x 22 ins / 40.6 x 55.9 cm) USD 33,000. NEW YORK, 17 Oct 1991, *River Alcalá* (oil on panel, 14 x 21 3/4 ins / 35.6 x 55.2 cm) USD 29,700. NEW YORK, 20 Feb 1992, *On the River Huelva near Seville* (oil on panel, 8 3/4 x 16 ins / 22.2 x 40.6 cm) USD 25,300. LONDON, 29 May 1992, *Figures in a Wooded River Landscape* (oil on panel, 14 1/2 x 9 1/2 ins / 36.8 x 24.2 cm) GBP 7,700. NEW YORK, 14 Oct 1993, *Landscape outside Tangier* (1887, oil on panel, 13 3/4 x 10 1/2 ins / 34.9 x 26.4 cm) USD 27,600. NEW YORK, 1 Nov 1995, *Boats on a Stream* (oil on panel, 10 x 20 ins / 25.7 x 50.5 cm) USD 19,550. LONDON, 15 March 1996, *Vigo, Spain* (1879, oil on panel, 8 x 13 1/4 ins / 20.5 x 33.6 cm) GBP 17,250. NEW YORK, 23-24 May 1996, *The Orange Harvest* (1880, oil on panel, 9 3/4 x 16 ins / 24.8 x 40.6 cm) USD 26,450. NEW YORK, 23 Oct 1997, *Boat Excursion* (oil on panel, 10 1/2 x 13 1/2 ins / 26.7 x 34.3 cm) USD 26,450. LONDON, 22 June 1999, *In the Orange Grove* (1881, oil on panel, 10 x 10 ins / 25 x 26 cm) GBP 30,000. NEW YORK, 2 Nov 1999, *Stream and Meadows* (oil on canvas, 20 x 36 ins / 52 x 91 cm) USD 42,500. NEW YORK, 2 May 2000, *The Guadalquivir in Seville* (oil on canvas, 13 x 22 ins / 33 x 55 cm) USD 12,000. NEW YORK, 31 Oct 2000, *Calm Waters at Chaponval* (oil on panel, 9 x 16 ins / 24 x 41 cm) USD 22,000. NEW YORK, 30 April 2001, *On the Pond* (oil on panel, 13 x 16 ins / 32 x 41 cm) USD 15,000. LONDON, 9 Nov 2001, *Orchard* (1880, oil on panel, 15 x 11 ins / 37 x 27 cm) GBP 13,000. NEW YORK, 23 April 2002, *Figures in a Boat in a River Landscape with a Village Beyond* (oil on panel, 10 x 20 ins / 25 x 50 cm) USD 30,000. BUENOS AIRES, 3 July 2002, *October in Andalusia* (oil on board, 13 x 17 ins / 32 x 43 cm) USD 14,250. MADRID, 27 May 2003, *Outskirts of Venice* (1885, oil on canvas, 14 x 21 ins / 35 x 54 cm) EUR 27,500. NEW YORK, 29 Oct 2003, *River Landscape in Pontoise* (oil on panel, 11 x 14 ins / 27 x 35 cm) USD 32,000. SEVILLE, 19 May 2004, *View from the Alhambra in Granada* (1881, oil on board, 9 x 6 ins / 24 x 16 cm) EUR 9,000. SEVILLE, 19 May 2004, *Stream in Guillena* (oil on board, 7 x 14 ins / 19 x 35 cm) EUR 27,500.

SÁNCHEZ PESCADOR, José

Spanish, 19th century.
Born 30 January 1839, in Madrid.
Painter.

José Sánchez Pescador was a pupil of Federico de Madrazo.

MUSEUMS AND GALLERIES:
MADRID (Artillery Mus.): paintings.

SÁNCHEZ PICAZO, Pedro

Spanish, 19th - 20th century.
Born 6 August 1863, in Balsapintada, near Murcia; died 12 January 1952.
Painter. Religious subjects, still-lifes, flowers.

Pedro Sánchez studied under Alejandro Seiquer at the college of fine arts in Madrid. He showed examples of his work at national fine arts exhibitions in Madrid from 1899 and at the International Exhibition in Murcia in 1900. He was awarded a gold medal in 1900 and received an honourable mention in 1904. He was appointed curator of the fine arts museum in Murcia in 1922. His output comprises principally still-lifes of flowers.

BIBLIOGRAPHY:
Arnáiz, José Manuel/López Jiménez, Javier/Merchán Díaz, Manuel (ed.), '*Cien años de pintura en Espana y Portugal (1830-1930)*' in vol X, Antiqvaria, Madrid, 1993.

SÁNCHEZ SANTAREN, Luciano

Spanish, 19th - 20th century.
Born 9 January 1864, in Mucientes near Valladolid; died 1945, in Valladolid.
Painter. History painting, religious subjects, portraits, genre scenes.

Luciano Sánchez Santaren studied painting in Lugo (Galicia) under Leopoldo Villaamil before enrolling at the Escuela Especial de Pintura, Escultura y Grabado in Madrid. He settled in Valladolid, where he taught at the college of fine arts from 1893 before going on to serve as principal of the college of arts and crafts from 1931.

Examples of his work include a *Baptism of Christ* for the Valladolid church of St Michael and various religious compositions for the transept of St Mary's Convent. He produced work across the full spectrum of genres, however, and mention should be made of his *Conquered and Captured, Nero Contemplating the Dead Body of Agrippina, Cervantes by the Bay of Algiers, Head Study, On My Patio* and *Two Brothers*. He exhibited in Valladolid in 1890.

BIBLIOGRAPHY:
Arnáiz, José Manuel/López Jiménez, Javier/Merchán Díaz, Manuel (ed.), '*Cien años de pintura en Espana y Portugal (1830-1930)*' in vol. X, Antiqvaria, Madrid, 1993.

SÁNCHEZ SARABIA, Diego

Spanish, 18th century.
Died 1779, in Madrid.
Painter, sculptor, draughtsman. Genre scenes, architectural views.

Diego Sánchez Sarabia was a member of the Real Academia de San Fernando in 1762. At the academy's request he executed various drawings of the Alhambra and the palace of Charles V in Granada. The drawings are still kept by the academy.

SÁNCHEZ SOLA, Eduardo

Spanish, 19th - 20th century.
Born 25 June 1869, in Madrid; died 1949, in Granada.
Painter, watercolourist, draughtsman, illustrator.
Portraits, genre scenes, animals.

Eduardo Sánchez Sola studied under Alejandro Ferrant and Luis Taberner at the college of fine arts in Madrid and went on to teach at the college of arts and crafts in Granada. He contributed to the periodical *La Ilustración Española y Americana* (*Spain and America Illustrated*). His painting comprises mainly genre compositions painted from nature, including *Young Choristers, Patio in Andalucia, Woman with Rose, Sad News, Requited Husband, Village Mayor, Pearl Necklace, Cats, Weaning* and *Nest*.

He showed his work at various national exhibitions, securing an honourable mention in 1895, a bronze medal in 1897 and a further honourable mention in 1904.

BIBLIOGRAPHY:
Arnáiz, José Manuel/López Jiménez, Javier/Merchán Díaz, Manuel (ed.), '*Cien años de pintura en Espana y Portugal (1830-1930)*' in vol. X, Antiqvaria, Madrid, 1993.

SÁNCHEZ TAPIA, Francisco

Spanish, 19th century.
Born in Murcia; died 1 January 1902, in Murcia.
Sculptor.

Francisco Sánchez Tapia was a pupil of S. Baglietto. He executed sculptures for churches in Murcia, Aljucer, Jamilla and Novelda.

SÁNCHEZ VARONA, Conrado

Spanish, 20th century.
Born 14 February 1876, in Malpartide de Plasencia, near Cáceres.
Painter. Religious subjects, portraits.

Conrado Sánchez Varona studied at the college of fine arts in Madrid, then at the college of arts and crafts in Cáceres. He was primarily a portrait painter (*Alfonso XII* and *Portrait of the Artist's Mother*), but he also painted a *St Joseph* and a *St Francis Xavier* for the Jesuit College of Villanueva de los

Barros. He exhibited on a regular basis at the national fine arts exhibition in Madrid, where he secured honourable mentions in 1897 and 1904.

Bibliography:

Arnáiz, José Manuel/López Jiménez, Javier/Merchán Díaz, Manuel (ed.), '*Cien años de pintura en Espana y Portugal (1830-1930)*' in vol. X, Antiqvaria, Madrid, 1993.

SÁNCHEZ Y COTÁN, Juan (Fray), or Sánchez Cotán
Spanish, 16th - 17th century.
Born 1560 or 1561, in Orgaz (Castile-La Mancha); died 8 September 1627, in Granada.
Painter. Religious subjects, still-lifes.

Juan Sánchez y Cotán was apprenticed to a modest painter, Blas del Prado, in Toledo, then the centre of Spanish artistic life. Although he mainly painted *bodegones* (still-lifes), the authority of his style and his mastery of tenebrism are evident from his earliest works. His *Still-life with Cardoon*, is famous for having been much copied.

Sánchez y Cotán became a Carthusian monk relatively late in life, in 1604, and was first sent to the Carthusian monastery of El Paular, near Segovia. While there he painted several versions of *The Passion* and *Madonna Crowned with Flowers*, which confirmed his reputation. It seems that he continued to paint still-lifes, which had a distinctive style and which were in demand throughout Europe.

From 1612 Sánchez y Cotán was in Granada, where he produced a group of paintings illustrating the life of St Bruno and other saints of his Order for the walls of the cloister of his new monastery, from 1615 to 1617. He also worked for Seville, and in his later years was in contact with painters from Seville, in particular Roelas, whose influence may be discerned in the *Vision of St Francis*, which Sánchez y Cotán painted in 1620 for Seville Cathedral. In 1623 he painted the *Virgin of Good Fortune* for the former monastery of St Augustine in Seville.

At the turn of the 16th century his contemporaries El Greco and Ribalta took prominence over Sánchez Cotán. Art histories nearly always refer to his *Still-life with Cabbage* which, while beautiful and enigmatic, is not representative. His still-lifes put him in the same category as a lesser Flemish master of the 17th century, but he was also a painter of important religious compositions. He proved himself able to produce the chiaroscuro light effects which characterised much European painting from the beginning of the century. Perhaps his greatest achievement was to herald the spirit of Zurbaran's art. In his great composition *English Carthusian Monks before their Judges*, the architectural landscape which reveals a raised curtain in the background, soberly but resolutely lit, heralds the calm, white architectural backgrounds which were to provide the psychological finishing touch to Zubaran's great religious compositions.

In all his works, but especially in his still-lifes, Sánchez Cotán began to define some of the characteristics which were soon to mark European painting. For example, he gave prominence to every figure or object by setting them apart and arranging them rhythmically between areas of shade, in contrast to seeking rich effects by cumulative arrangement, before painters such as Zurbaran, the Le Nain brothers and Chardin. He ennobled the most humble objects in the spirit of the Caravaggesque movement. Thus he may be credited with the creation of tragic naturalism in Spanish painting, heralding not only Zubaran, but also Velázquez and Murillo.

Museums and Galleries:
Granada: *Still-life with Cardoon* (c. 1603, several other works) - San Diego (MA): *Quince, Cabbage, Melon and Cucumber* (c. 1602, oil on canvas); *St Sebastian* (oil/copper).

Auction records:
London, 6 July 1966, *Still-lifes* (matching pair) GBP 3,200. New York, 9 June 1983, *Still-life with Melon, Peach and Fig* (oil on canvas, 20 1/2 x 25 3/4 ins / 52 x 65.5 cm) USD 20,000. Madrid, 19 May 1992, *Holy Family with St John* (oil on canvas, 67 x 51 1/2 ins / 170 x 131 cm) ESP 5,000,000. Madrid, 25 Feb 1993, *Holy Family with St John* (oil on canvas, 67 x 51 1/2 ins / 170 x 131 cm) ESP 4,830,000. Madrid, 30 July 2001, *Virgin* (oil on canvas, 57 x 41 ins / 145 x 103 cm) ESP 3,500,000. Barcelona, 21 May 2002, *Immaculate Conception* (oil on canvas, 57 x 41 ins / 145 x 104 cm) EUR 6,000.

SANCHIS. See also **SÁNCHEZ**

SANCHIS, Francisco
Spanish, 18th century.
Died 8 September 1791, in Valencia.
Sculptor. Religious subjects.

Francisco Sanchis worked for Valencia Cathedral in 1777.

Museums and Galleries:
Madrid (Real Academia de Bellas Artes de San Fernando): *Transfiguration of Christ; Allegory of Sculpture.*

SANCHIS, Jesualda, or Sánchez
Spanish, 17th century.
Active in Valencia from 1650 to 1660.
Painter.

SANCHIS, Salvador
Spanish, 20th century.
Painter. Figures, nudes.

Salvador Sanchis painted mainly female figures and nudes.

SANCHIS HERRAEZ, Salvador
Spanish, 19th century.
Born 1844, in Chiva.
Active in Valencia.
Painter.

SANCHIZ, Juan
Spanish, 16th century.
Active in Valencia in 1513.
Illuminator.

SANCHO
Spanish, 10th century.
Active in the second half of the 10th century.
Illuminator, priest.

Sancho was a priest. In collaboration with Florencio, he illuminated a Bible belonging to the Collegiate Church of S Isidoro, León.

SANCHO
Spanish, 16th century.
Active in Valladolid (Castilla y León).
Sculptor (wood).

Sancho worked on the sculpture of the famous wood panelling of the choir of Sto Domingo de la Calzada church in Valladolid, in 1523.

SANCHO, Antonio
Spanish, 15th century.
Active during the second half of the 15th century.
Sculptor.

Antonio Sancho produced stucco reliefs for the choir of Sta Maria la Mayor church, in Morella.

SANCHO, Antonio
Spanish, 17th century.
Active in Palma (Majorca), at the end of the 17th century.
Sculptor.

Antonio Sancho carved processional statues in 1699.

SANCHO, Dionisio
Spanish, 18th - 19th century.
Born 1762, in Ciempozuelos; died 7 May 1829, in Mexico.

Sculptor (ivory), medallist. Low reliefs.
Dionisio Sancho settled in Mexico in 1810. The Prado Museum in Madrid has some ivory low reliefs carved by him.
MUSEUMS AND GALLERIES:
MADRID (Prado).

SANCHO, Estéban, called Maneta
Spanish, 18th century.
Born in Majorca; died 30 October 1784, in Majorca.
Painter.
Estéban Sancho was the father of Salvador Sancho and a pupil of P. J. Ferrer. He worked for churches in Majorca. He was known as Maneta because he had lost his right hand.

SANCHO, Jeronimo
Spanish, 16th century.
Active in Lérida.
Sculptor (wood).
Jeronimo Sancho sculpted the organ case in Tarragona Cathedral, with Parris Austriarch, from 1562 to 1564.

SANCHO, Julian
Spanish, 15th century.
Active in Valencia during the first half of the 15th century.
Sculptor (wood).
Julian Sancho worked on the ceiling of the gilded hall in Valencia town hall, in 1428.

SANCHO, Pedro
Spanish, 15th century.
Active at the end of the 15th century.
Painter.
Pedro Sancho painted an altar for Carpesa church, in 1490.

SANCHO, Salvador
Spanish, 19th century.
Died 11 March 1814, in Palma (Majorca), Balearics.
Painter.
Salvador Sancho studied under his father Estéban. He painted religious subjects for churches in Palma de Mallorca, Soller and Andraix.

SANCHO CANARDO
Spanish, 15th century.
Active in Jaca (Aragon).
Sculptor (wood).
In 1457, Sancho Canardo was commissioned to produce stalls in Jaca Cathedral.

SANCHO DE ZAMORA
Spanish, 15th century.
Sculptor.
Sancho de Zamora produced sculptures for the altar of St James in Toledo Cathedral, in 1488 or 1498.

SANCHO GALEGO, Jorge
Portuguese, 20th - 21st century.
Born 31 July 1961, in São Bras de Alportel.
Active in France.
Painter (mixed media), engraver, draughtsman, sculptor. Figures, still-lifes, seascapes.
Jorge Sancho Galego's family settled in France in 1966. Essentially self-taught, he nevertheless took a number of courses in design and painting in Paris between 1982 and 1984. He lives and works in Paris. Preoccupied with ecology, he paints 'marine compositions' that tend towards abstraction, inspired by the knots and markings in wood, but especially, since 1992, by tree leaves. He works on the idea of the weeping of leaves threatened by pollution, which he represents by allowing the paint to run. He then tackles a more joyful image with leaves in the form of a painted heart on Altuglas: this transparent synthetic material permits new artistic solutions, notably front and back views. He also creates dream compositions from stains, metal run-out and pulverised materials (*The Clairvoyant with Silver Balls...*; *The Man with Original Ideas*). For sculptures representing figures of musicians, he uses different recycled materials, such as cut, painted aluminium and corrugated cardboard. He himself defines his style as 'free, poetic figuration'.

He has participated in group exhibitions in Paris, notably: 1985-88, Salon des Indépendants; 1987-89, Salon de la Figuration Critique; 1998, Salon des Artistes Naturalistes. He has also shown his work in solo exhibitions: since 1996, permanent exhibition at the Espaço de Arte Contemporânea in São Bras de Alportel; 1997-98, *Les Pluies acides ou Les Feuilles qui pleurent* (*Acid Rain or Crying Leaves*), Unesco building and Buci gallery, Paris; since 2000, permanent exhibition at the Un Poisson dans l'Arbre gallery in Annemasse. He also shows some of his works on the internet.

SANCHO GONTIER, or Sancius Gonterii
French, 15th century.
Active in Avignon c. 1400.
Illuminator.
Sancho Gontier was a monk. He illuminated for Pope Benedict XIII a pontifical now in the Bibliothèque Nationale in Paris.

SANCHO PIQUÉ, José
Spanish, 19th - 20th century.
Born 1872, in Tarragona.
Painter.
José Sancho was a pupil of Antonio (?) Graner.

SANÇON, Mahiet
French, 14th century.
Active in 1384.
Sculptor (ivory).

SANCTIS. See also **SANTI** or **SANTIS**

SANCTIS, Erminia de
Italian, 19th - 20th century.
Born 1840, in Rome.
Painter. Flowers.
She was the sister of Guglielmo de Sanctis.

SANCTIS, Fabio de
Italian, 20th century.
Born 1931, in Rome.
Sculptor. Furniture.
Phases group.
Fabio de Sanctis studied architecture in Rome, qualifying in 1956. In 1963, together with Ugo Sterpini, he founded the Ufficina Undici (Office Eleven), a studio/workshop. In 1964, he met André Breton and the Surrealist group.

At the Ufficina Undici, he designed and made his 'irrational furniture', pieces that, while still respecting their utilitarian function as shelving, a bar or a desk, took on fantastic anthropomorphic, metamorphic or metaphorical forms. Since 1971, he had been producing 'furniture-luggage'. These composite pieces are exquisitely made from luxury materials and look back to the age of François-Xavier Lalanne, evoking movement, travel, memories, nostalgia and dreams through the suggestion of suitcases, racing cars and ships. But instead of being reassuring, the appearance of these objects is at best confusing and generally deeply disturbing.

He took part in collective exhibitions including: *L'Écart Absolu*, an international exhibition of Surrealist art, Galerie L'Oeil, Paris, 1965; *The Object Transformed*, MoMA, New York, 1966; *The Surrealist Vision*, Baukunst Gallery, Cologne, 1971; 38th Venice Biennale, 1976; *L'Unité Composée*, Galerie du Dragon, Paris, 1984; 18th Sculpture Biennale, Middelheim Museum, Antwerp, 1985; *André Breton et la Révolution Surréaliste du Regard*, Cahors Museum, 1986; *Die Surrealisten*, Schirm Kunsthalle, Frankfurt, 1990; *André Breton - La beauté convulsive* (*André Breton: Convulsive Beau-*

ty), Pompidou Centre, Paris, 1991; *Le Mouvement Phases de 1952 à l'horizon 2001* (*The Phases Movement from 1952 to the New Millennium*), Kiosque Centre Culturel, Mayenne, and the Centre Noroit, Arras, 2000.

Fabio de Sanctis has also exhibited his creations in solo exhibitions: in Naples, Venice and Rome, 1946; Milan, 1969; Ferrara, 1972; Amsterdam, 1973, 1977; Paris, 1979 and again, at the Galerie du Dragon, 1982; in Brussels, 1984; Geneva in the gallery at the town hall, 1987, 1988; Paris, at the Galerie du Dragon, 1991; Paris, at the Galerie J.C. Riedel, 1993.

BIBLIOGRAPHY:

Fabio de Sanctis, exhibition catalogue, Gal. du Dragon, Paris, 1991 (documentation).

SANCTIS, Filippo de

Italian, 19th century.
Born 1843, in Rome.
Painter, engraver.

SANCTIS, Francesco de

Italian, 16th century.
Active during the first half of the 16th century.
Painter.

Francesco de Sanctis painted *St Mark* and *St Bartholomew* in Servi di Maria oratory in Sorrento, in 1612.

SANCTIS, Giuseppe de

Italian, 19th - 20th century.
Born 21 June 1858, in Naples; died 1924, in Naples.
Painter, mixed media, pastellist, draughtsman. Genre scenes, figures, portraits, landscapes, still-lifes.

A pupil of Domenico Morelli at the Istituto di Belle Arti in Naples, Giuseppe de Sanctis was awarded a first prize in 1880. He stayed in Paris for a number of years, settling in Naples on his return to Italy.

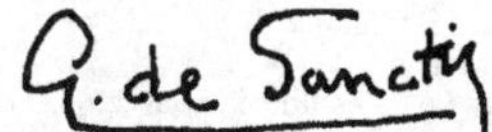

MUSEUMS AND GALLERIES:

MELBOURNE: *Jubilee of Queen Victoria* - NAPLES (Gal. Provinciale): *Fatima* - ROME (Gal. Nazionale d'Arte Moderna): *The Marne*.

AUCTION RECORDS:

ROME, 14 Dec 1988, *Villa in the Trees* (mixed media/paper, 13 1/2 x 18 1/2 ins / 34.5 x 47 cm) ITL 700,000. ROME, 11 Dec 1990, *The 'Parisienne'* (pastel, 18 x 11 1/2 ins / 46 x 29 cm) ITL 2,990,000. ROME, 19 Nov 1992, *Scugnizzo* (1880, charcoal heightened with white, 16 1/4 x 9 1/4 ins / 41.5 x 23.5 cm) ITL 1,150,000. LUGANO, 8 May 1993, *Path to the Villa Communale in Naples in the Snow* (1893, oil on panel, 7 3/4 x 12 ins / 20 x 30.5 cm) CHF 20,000. ROME, 11 Dec 2003, *Red Hat* (oil on canvas, 24 x 18 ins / 60 x 45 cm) EUR 4,200.

SANCTIS, Guglielmo de

Italian, 19th - 20th century.
Born 8 March 1829, in Rome; died 1911 or 1924, in Rome.
Painter. Historical subjects, religious subjects, portraits. Frescoes, church decoration.

A pupil of Tommaso Minardi at the Accademia di San Luca in Rome, Guglielmo de Sanctis went on to enjoy a successful and distinguished career and took part in many exhibitions.

His first works were of religious subjects and included two frescoes in the basilica of San Paolo fuori le Mura; an oil painting of *St Vincent of Paul* for the Mission church; altarpieces for the Ospedale di S Spirito and the Fatebenefratelli Hospital (also known as the Hospital of S Giovanni di Dio); a large painting of *Francesco Saverio Preaching* for the cathedral of Porto Maurizio. His history paintings include *Michelangelo and Ferruccio, Galileo Demonstrating his Telescope* and *Emmanuel Philibert Exhibiting his Infant Son in the Hall of his Castle at Rivoli*. He also painted portraits, including those of *King Umberto* and *Queen Margherita* to hang in the Italian Senate.

MUSEUMS AND GALLERIES:

FLORENCE (Palazzo Pitti): *Self-portrait* - PRATO (Mus. Civico): *Portrait of Marco Tabarrini* - ROME (Gal. Nazionale d'Arte Moderna): *Olimpia Pamphily Doria* - ROME (Palazzo del Quirinale): *Emmanuel Philibert Exhibiting his Infant Son in the Hall of the Rivoli Palace* - TURIN: *Michelangelo and Ferruccio* - VENICE (Gal. Giovanelli): *Galileo Demonstrating his Telescope*.

AUCTION RECORDS:

MILAN, 1 Dec 1970, *Place Blanche, Paris*, ITL 800,000. MILAN, 5 April 1979, *Portrait of a Woman* (1892, oil on panel, 16 1/4 x 11 3/4 ins / 41 x 30 cm) ITL 1,100,000.

SANCTIS AQUILANUS, Horace de

Italian, 16th century.
Active c. 1573.
Engraver.

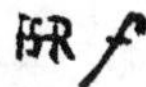

SANCY, Ernest de

French, 19th - 20th century.
Born in Argentan (Orne).
Painter.

Ernest de Sancy first exhibited at the Salon de Paris in 1861.

SAND, Aurore, pseudonym of Dudevant, Aurore; also known as Padilla, Claudio

French, 19th - 20th century.
Born 1866, in Nohant (Indre); died September 1961.
Painter, watercolourist. Local scenes, landscapes.

Aurore Sand, a granddaughter of the French novelist George Sand, married the painter Frédéric Lauth. She exhibited in Paris at the Salon des Orientalistes and the Salon des Indépendants, and mainly painted Spanish subjects.

AUCTION RECORDS:

PARIS, 29 May 1979, *Château of the Seven Daggers, Auvergne* (watercolour, 6 x 7 1/2 ins / 15.5 x 19 cm) FRF 5,400.

SAND, Georg Balthasar von

German, 18th century.
Born 22 June 1718, in Coburg.
Painter.

Georg Balthasar von Sand was painter to the court of the duke of Saxe-Coburg. He painted history subjects and portraits.

SAND, George, pseudonym of Aurore Amantine Lucile Dupin, later Baronne Dudevant

French, 19th century.
Born 1 July 1804, in Paris; died 8 June 1876, in Nohant (Indre).
Painter (gouache), watercolourist, draughtswoman, writer. Portraits, landscapes.

Though best known as a writer, George Sand was also an accomplished artist. Her grandfather, Dupin de Francueil, drew fairly well; as did her father, Maurice Dupin, and her mother, whose maiden name was Sophie Victoire Delaborde. When she left her convent, the Filles Anglaises, in 1831, George Sand went to live in Paris where she began earning her living by decorating boxes and cases made of what was called 'Spa wood'. Collective exhibitions of her paintings and drawings have been held in 1977, at the Bibliothèque Nationale, and in 1992, at a gallery in Paris.

She mostly drew portraits of her friends, and painted watercolours of the landscapes she encountered: particularly on her travels through Italy, in 1833-1834 with the writer Alfred de Musset, and in 1855 with her son Maurice. She would draw caricatures of her travel companions - who included Musset and Stendhal - and of herself. In later years, she and her son Maurice helped to decorate the theatre and puppet theatre in Nohant. It was during her time in Nohant, and also when she was convalescing in Savoy in 1861, that she made what she called her 'dendrites'. This was a term borrowed from the language of crystallography, which she used to describe the abstract imaginary landscapes, the visions of 'empty space', that she would make with splodges of gouache, pressed with a small cylindrical object onto a piece of paper, or between two sheets of paper, which are comparable to some of the visionary wash drawings made by Victor Hugo.

Bibliography:

Lubin, Georges, *Album Sand*, Gallimard, 1973. Bernadac, Christian, *George Sand. Dessins et Peintures*, Belfond, Paris, 1992.

Museums and Galleries:

Nohant-Vic (Maison de George Sand).

Auction records:

Paris, 28 March 1955, *Torrent* (watercolour) FRF 17,000. Monaco, 19 June 1994, *Landscape with Lake* (charcoal and watercolour, 4 1/2 x 6 ins / 11.7 x 15 cm) FRF 4,995. Paris, 12 Dec 1997, *Gabrielle, Aurore Sand and Fadet the Dog in a Landscape* (1876, dentrite, watercolour, gouache, 4 1/4 x 6 ins / 11 x 15 cm) FRF 8,000. Paris, 9 March 1999, *Landscape* (1873, 6 x 9 ins / 16 x 24 cm) FRF 12,500. Calais, 14 March 1999, *Balearic Island Landscape* (watercolour and gouache, 6 x 9 ins / 15 x 23 cm) FRF 21,000. Paris, 23 May 2000, *Self-caricature with Delacroix* (black ink, 6 x 4 ins / 15 x 10 cm) FRF 24,000. Paris, 2 July 2002, *Soft Sandstone Ridge* (3 x 4 ins / 8 x 11 cm) EUR 6,000. Paris, 28 Nov 2002, *Two Children in a Landscape* (watercolour heightened with gouache, 4 x 6 ins / 11 x 15 cm) EUR 2,300. Paris, 19 Dec 2003, *Several Views of the Berry* (watercolour, album of ten) EUR 21,000. Paris, 9 June 2004, *Big Sea Cliff* (watercolour, 3 x 4 ins / 8 x 11 cm) EUR 2,600. Paris, 9 June 2004, *Dead Tree by a Pond* (watercolour, 4 x 5 ins / 9 x 13 cm) EUR 3,300.

SAND, Karl Ludwig

German, 19th - 20th century.
Born 10 May 1859, in Munich.
Sculptor. Portraits. Statues.

Karl Ludwig Sand studied under Joseph Eberle. He sculpted predominantly statues of famous people.

SAND, Maurice, pseudonym of Jean François Maurice Dudevant, (Baron)

French, 19th century.
Born 30 June 1823, in Paris; died 1889, in Nohant (Indre).
Painter, watercolourist, engraver, sculptor, draughtsman, illustrator, decorative designer. Marionettes.

Maurice Sand was the son of George Sand and the father of Aurore Lauth-Sand. He received artistic guidance from Eugène Delacroix because of his family connections. Some of his paintings were exhibited at the Paris Salon. The following are mentioned in the records: in 1857, *Leander and Isabelle* and *The Werewolf*; in 1859, a drawing entitled *The Wolf Driver*; and in 1861, *Mule-drivers* and a watercolour entitled *Market in Pompeii*.

He had novels and short stories published in the *Revue des Deux Mondes*, and by other publishers. These include: *Six Thousand Leagues Full Steam Ahead* in 1862; *Callirhoe* in 1863; *Raoul de la Chastre* in 1865; *The Don Juans of the Village* in 1866 (co-written with his mother); *The Cock with Golden Hair* in 1867; *Miss Mary* in 1868; *Mademoiselle Azote* in 1870; *Mademoiselle de Cérignan* in 1874; *The Monkey's Daughter* in 1886; *The Puppet Theatre* in 1890; and *Augusta*, illustrated by Rochegrosse, in 1900. He also wrote an essay on the characters of the Commedia dell'arte, and provided illustrations for the Magasin Pittoresque. He illustrated several of his mother's novels: the *Story of the Real Gribouille*, *The Miller of Angibault* and *Cora*, all in 1851. He also contributed illustrations to a book of *Popular Songs of the French Provinces*. He illustrated some of his own works too, including, in 1859: *Masks and Clowns*; *The World of Butterflies*; and *The Life of Bees*. He was passionate about theatre, and in the Château de Nohant he built and decorated a proper theatre, where visiting friends would dress up and perform. Then, in 1858, he built a puppet theatre. He designed and sculpted the wooden marionettes (the 'pupazzi') himself, giving them faces typical of the local peasants of the Berry region, and wrote plays in verse for them to perform.

His paintings and illustrations show Maurice Sand to be a consistently faithful observer of nature, sometimes demonstrating a sharp sense of humour, and at other times a romantic sensibility.

M. SAND

Bibliography:

Osterwalder, Marcus (ed.), *Dictionnaire des illustrateurs 1800-1914*, Ides et Calendes, Neuchâtel, 1989.

Museums and Galleries:

Nohant-Vic (Maison de George Sand): *Legends of Berry* (set of charcoal drawings) - Paris (BNF): watercolours - Paris (Mus. Carnavalet): *Landscape in Crozant* (drawing).

Auction records:

Paris, 16 Nov 1981, *Portrait of Mademoiselle Rachel* (1853, charcoal, 6 x 6 ins / 15.5 x 15 cm) FRF 4,200.

SANDALINAS FORNAS, Juan

Spanish, 20th century.
Born 1903, in Barcelona.
Painter. Portraits.

Juan Sandalinas Fornas studied in Barcelona and featured at various collective exhibitions, among them the 1923 Spring Salon and the 1948 and 1949 Autumn Salons in Barcelona; also exhibited at Granollers Museum. He is noted for his Surrealism-inspired *Landlocked Sailor*.

Bibliography:

Arnáiz, José Manuel/López Jiménez, Javier/Merchán Díaz, Manuel (ed.), '*Cien años de pintura en Espana y Portugal (1830-1930)*' in vol. X, Antiqvaria, Madrid, 1993.

SANDARS, Thomas, or Sanders

British, 18th century.
Born in Rotterdam.
Engraver.

Thomas Sandars was the son of a Rotterdam painter. He left for London at an early age and enrolled at the St Martin's Lane Academy. He went on to exhibit at the Royal Academy in 1775. He engraved from originals by Vernet and also produced 15 views of town markets in Worcestershire.

SANDBACK, Fred

American, 20th century.
Born 1943, in Bronxville (New York); died 23 June 2003.
Sculptor of assemblages, installation artist.
Conceptual Art, Land Art, Minimal Art.

Fred Sandback studied at the Yale School of Art and Architecture in New York. He took his own life in 2003. In 1967, he was creating sculptures, from steel wire and elastic bands. From 1973, he restricted himself to acrylic wool yarn of many colours, stretching his threads across the walls and floors of the venues in which he exhibited. He took part in collective exhibitions, especially those dedicated to Conceptual Art, such as *Prospect 68* in Düsseldorf, also in Bern, Berlin, at the Museum of Modern Art in New York, as well as in

Detroit and at the Sydney Biennial. In 2002, he took part in *Les Années 70: l'art en cause* (*The 1970s: Art in Question*), CAPC-Musée d'Art Contemporain, Bordeaux. He showed his works in solo exhibitions from 1968 in Düsseldorf, Paris, New York, Munich, and at Kettle's Yard, Cambridge, England, in 2005.

BIBLIOGRAPHY:

IIIe Salon international des Galeries Pilotes, exhibition catalogue, Musée cantonal, Lausanne, 1970. *Fred Sandback: Werkverzeichnis der Druckgrafik*, catalogue raisonné, Gal. Fred Jahn, Munich, 1987. *Fred Sandback: sculpture*, exhibition catalogue, Yale University Art Gall., New Haven, 1991. *Fred Sandback, sculpture*, Dia Center for the Arts, New York, 1996. Fréruchet, Maurice, et al., *Les Années soixante-dix: l'art en cause*, exhibition catalogue, Capc musée d'Art contemporain, Bordeaux, 2002.

MUSEUMS AND GALLERIES:

CHÂTEAUGIRON (FRAC Bretagne): *Untitled* (1969) - GRENOBLE (Mus. de Grenoble) - KREFELD (Kaiser Wilhelm Mus.) - NEW YORK (MoMA) - NEW YORK (Whitney Mus. of American Art).

AUCTION RECORDS:

NEW YORK, 5 Nov 1985, *Untitled* (1968, stainless steel, four items, 36 x 180 x 36 ins / 91.5 x 457.5 x 91.5 cm) USD 6,250. NEW YORK, 8 May 1990, *Untitled* (1968, steel wire and fluorescent blue elastic, 90 x 30 ins / 228.6 x 76.2 cm) USD 38,500. NEW YORK, 17 Nov 1992, *Untitled* (1990, acrylic/weave, 20 1/4 x 16 x 7 1/2 ins / 51.5 x 40.6 x 19 cm) USD 1,650. NEW YORK, 22 Feb 1996, *Untitled* (1990, graphite and acrylic/paper, 36 1/4 x 48 1/4 ins / 92.1 x 122.5 cm) USD 1,150. ZURICH, 19 June 2001, *Untitled - Vertical Corner Piece* (mixed media, 112 x ?x? ins / 284 x ?x? cm) CHF 17,000. LONDON, 26 June 2002, *Untitled* (1989, watercolour, 29 x 21 ins / 74 x 54 cm) GBP 1,800. VIENNA, 20 May 2003, *Untitled* (1992, pencil, 11 x 15 ins / 28 x 38 cm) EUR 3,000. VIENNA, 26 Nov 2003, *Drawing* (1967, pencil, 8 x 11 ins / 20 x 28 cm) EUR 3,400. NEW YORK, 15 Sept 2004, *Il Terzo del Quattro Olltremare Diagonali* (1974, pastel and pencil, 11 x 15 ins / 29 x 39 cm) USD 4,500. NEW YORK, 15 Sept 2004, *Il quarto del quattro oltremare diagonali* (1974, pastel and pencil, 11 x 15 ins / 29 x 39 cm) USD 6,000.

SANDBERG, Aron Simon

Swedish, 19th - 20th century.

Born 5 January 1873, in Gränna.

Sculptor. Figures, decorative motifs. Busts.

Aron Simon Sandberg was the brother of Gustaf Emil Sandberg.

SANDBERG, Einar

Norwegian, 19th - 20th century.

Born 17 October 1876, in Fredrikstad.

Painter.

Einar Sandberg studied under Erik T. Werenskjold, Johan Nordhagen and P. H. Kristian Zahrtmann and, for a time, under Henri Matisse in Paris.

MUSEUMS AND GALLERIES:

GÖTEBORG - OSLO.

SANDBERG, Gustav Emil

Swedish, 19th - 20th century.

Born 12 January 1876, in Gränna.

Sculptor. Monuments.

Gustav Emil Sandberg was the brother of Aron Simon Sandberg. He is noted for numerous public monuments in Stockholm and other Swedish towns and cities.

SANDBERG, Hialmar or Bror Erick Hialmar

Swedish, 19th century.

Born 5 September 1847, in Stockholm; died 12 April 1888, in Stockholm.

Painter. Genre scenes, landscapes with figures, landscapes.

Sandberg studied in Stockholm and in Paris.

MUSEUMS AND GALLERIES:

BERGEN - STOCKHOLM (Nationalmus.).

AUCTION RECORDS:

LONDON, 21 March 1980, *A Street in Vichy* (oil on panel, 14 1/2 x 22 ins / 37 x 55 cm) GBP 750. STOCKHOLM, 15 Nov 1988, *Small House in an Orchard With a Little Girl at the Entry, Summer* (oil on canvas, 14 1/2 x 17 3/4 ins / 37 x 45 cm) SEK 19,000.

SANDBERG, Johan Gustaf

Swedish, 19th century.

Born 13 May 1782, in Stockholm; died 26 June 1854, in Stockholm.

Painter. History painting, genre scenes.

Sandberg was a pupil at the Kungliga Akademi för de Fria Konsterna in Stockholm. He painted frescoes and scenes of popular Swedish life.

MUSEUMS AND GALLERIES:

DRESDEN (Prints Collection): *Portrait of the Artist* - STOCKHOLM: *Gustav-Adolf at the Battle of Stuhm; Young Vingaker Peasant; Young Peasant Woman of the Same Place in Party Dress; The Landscapist Fahlerantz Aged 54; The Artist* - WARSAW (Muz. Narodowe): *Portrait of Prince Poniatovski; The Arrest of Johan III of Sweden and of Catherine on the Order of Erik XIV.*

AUCTION RECORDS:

STOCKHOLM, 28 Oct 1980, *Portrait of King Karl XIV Johan* (1821, oil on canvas, 33 3/4 x 29 1/2 ins / 86 x 75 cm) SEK 18,000. STOCKHOLM, 23 Nov 1999, *Portrait of Gustav Vasa* (1826, oil on canvas, 15 x 12 ins / 38 x 30 cm) SEK 14,000. STOCKHOLM, 16 May 2000, *Five Artists - Poussin, Raphael, Rubens, Dürer and Rembrandt* (1828, oil on canvas, 19 x 24 ins / 48 x 60 cm) SEK 34,000. STOCKHOLM, 29 May 2000, *Portrait of Crownprince Oscar* (1830, oil on canvas, 28 x 23 ins / 71 x 59 cm) SEK 20,000. STOCKHOLM, 4 Dec 2001, *Portrait of the Sculptor Berngt Erland Fogelberg* (oil on canvas, 11 x 8 ins / 27 x 21 cm) SEK 17,000. VENICE, 7 March 2003, *Christ in the Olive Grove* (1842, oil on canvas, 18 x 28 ins / 46 x 72 cm) EUR 2,700.

SANDBERG, Ragnar

Swedish, 20th century.

Born 1902, in Sanne (Bohuslän); died 1972.

Painter. Figure compositions, scenes with figures, landscapes, landscapes with figures, still-lifes.

Ragnar Sandberg studied under Tor Bjurström at the fine arts college in Valand. He travelled to France and spent time there in 1926 and 1936. He was appointed to a senior teaching post at the fine arts academy in Stockholm in 1947.

In the 1930s his work was influenced by the intimiste Post-Impressionism typified by Pierre Bonnard. Sandberg's technique was fluent although his draughtsmanship was (albeit intentionally) on the casual side. Over time, however, he came to adopt a more structured approach to his favourite themes: bathers, street scenes, football matches and the like. That said, he also painted still-lifes in a manner reminiscent of Poussin, Cézanne and Jacques Villon.

He took part in various group exhibitions, including in London in 1945, having already exhibited solo there in 1939.

R. S.
Sandberg

MUSEUMS AND GALLERIES:

GÖTEBORG - STOCKHOLM.

Auction records:
Stockholm, 31 Jan 1947, *Landscape,* SEK 2,100. Stockholm, 6 April 1951, *Landscape* (1944) SEK 3,000. Göteborg, 22 Nov 1973, *Landscape,* SEK 11,000. Göteborg, 26 March 1974, *Bathers,* SEK 5,600. Stockholm, 23 April 1980, *Chaise Longue* (oil on canvas, 24 3/4 x 28 1/4 ins / 63 x 72 cm) SEK 34,000. Stockholm, 22 April 1981, *Summer Morning* (oil on canvas, 26 3/4 x 32 ins / 68 x 81 cm) SEK 44,000. Stockholm, 26 April 1983, *Returning from Market* (oil on canvas, 28 x 36 1/2 ins / 71 x 93 cm) SEK 70,000. Stockholm, 20 April 1985, *View of Paris* (1931, watercolour, 12 1/2 x 12 1/4 ins / 32 x 31 cm) SEK 10,200. Stockholm, 9 Dec 1986, *Gathering Potatoes* (1951, oil on canvas, 11 3/4 x 22 ins / 30 x 55 cm) SEK 134,000. Stockholm, 7 Dec 1987, *Bathers III* (oil on canvas, 19 x 24 1/2 ins / 48 x 62 cm) SEK 255,000. Stockholm, 6 June 1988, *Road to Perstorp in Summer* (1944, oil, 11 3/4 x 15 ins / 30 x 38 cm) SEK 40,000. Stockholm, 6 Dec 1989, *Lighthouse at Kyrkesund* (mixed media/panel, 11 x 15 ins / 27 x 38 cm) SEK 27,000. Stockholm, 14 June 1990, *Bryggan* (oil on panel, 11 x 13 1/2 ins / 27 x 34 cm) SEK 36,000. Stockholm, 5-6 Dec 1990, *Umbrellas* (oil on canvas, 16 1/4 x 25 1/2 ins / 41 x 65 cm) SEK 200,000. Stockholm, 30 May 1991, *Football Pitch* (oil on canvas, 33 1/2 x 40 1/2 ins / 85 x 103 cm) SEK 145,000. Stockholm, 30 Nov 1993, *Embarkation* (1934, oil on canvas, 19 3/4 x 25 1/2 ins / 50 x 65 cm) SEK 200,000. Stockholm, 17 May 1999, *Bathers* (1933, oil on canvas, 25 x 31 ins / 64 x 80 cm) SEK 380,000. Stockholm, 26 Oct 1999, *Figures in a Rowing Boat* (1935, oil on canvas, 15 x 19 ins / 38 x 48 cm) SEK 325,000. Stockholm, 2 May 2000, *Bathers* (1937, oil on canvas, 25 x 33 ins / 63 x 85 cm) SEK 160,000. Stockholm, 15 May 2000, *On the Balcony* (oil on canvas, 20 x 24 ins / 50 x 61 cm) SEK 370,000. Stockholm, 2 May 2001, *Horse-swing in Jardin du Luxemburg* (1937, oil on canvas, 16 x 28 ins / 41 x 70 cm) SEK 550,000. Stockholm, 21 May 2001, *Gate* (oil on canvas, 14 x 20 ins / 36 x 50 cm) SEK 485,000. Stockholm, 23 April 2002, *Blue Roller Blind: Interior with Female Nude* (oil on canvas, 28 x 35 ins / 71 x 88 cm) SEK 250,000. Stockholm, 6 Nov 2002, *Thawing: Street Scene from Drottningtorvet in Göteborg* (1939, oil on canvas, 20 x 30 ins / 52 x 75 cm) SEK 280,000. Stockholm, 28 April 2003, *American Launch* (oil on canvas, 17 x 39 ins / 43 x 98 cm) SEK 350,000. Stockholm, 4 Nov 2003, *Football Players* (1937, oil on canvas, 16 x 24 ins / 41 x 60 cm) SEK 255,000. Stockholm, 2 Nov 2004, *Cyclists* (1930s, oil on canvas, 17 x 25 ins / 42 x 64 cm) SEK 670,000. Stockholm, 2 Nov 2004, *Girl in the Pear Tree* (1942, oil on canvas, 41 x 41 ins / 104 x 104 cm) SEK 1,300,000.

SANDBICHLER, Mathäus

Austrian, 19th - 20th century.
Born 1877, in Imst.
Sculptor. Monuments.

Mathäus Sandbichler sculpted funerary statuary and war memorials.

SANDBICHLER, Peter

Austrian, 20th - 21st century.
Born 1964, in Kufstein (Tyrol).
Painter (mixed media).

Peter Sandbichler uses materials borrowed from daily life or manufactured, making them unrecognisable and turning them into receptive surfaces for light. He has participated in collective exhibitions of recent Austrian painting - for example, *Young Painters' Works,* Akademie der Bildenden Künste, Vienna (1988), *60 Tage* (*60 Days*), Museum der XX. Jh., Vienna (1989). He took part in an exhibition at the Salon Découvertes, Paris in 1992. He had solo shows at the Galerie Krinzinger, Innsbruck (1988), and the Galerie Grita Insam, Vienna (1990).

Museums and Galleries:
Vienna (Mus. Moderner Kunst Stiftung Ludwig).

SANDBY, Paul

British, 18th - 19th century.
Born 1725, in Nottingham; died 1809, in London.
Painter (including gouache), watercolourist, engraver, draughtsman. Genre scenes, landscapes, landscapes with figures.

Paul Sandby moved to London at the age of 16 and worked initially as an apprentice decorator at the court. The Duke of Cumberland then retained him to accompany engineer David Watson on a topographic survey mission to Scotland. In his free time, he sketched a considerable number of well-known sights, from which he subsequently produced etchings that were later published by Ryland and Bryce. Shortly after his return to London, he and his brother went to Windsor, where he drew views of the royal residence and its surroundings near Eton. These drawings and watercolours were immediately acquired by Sir Joseph Banks, and Sandby was invited to accompany the latter on a visit to Wales. He was also retained by Sir Walkin William Wynne to draw some of the more notable sites in Wales. The results exceeded Wynne's wildest expectations and Snadby's reputation was firmly established.

In 1768, Sandby and his brother Thomas were founder members of the Royal Academy. He had already exhibited in London from 1760, notably at the Society of Artists and at the Free Society. In 1768, he was appointed to a teaching post at the Military College in Woolwich and he worked there until his retirement in 1799.

Sandby is widely regarded as the pioneer of topographical watercolours painted directly from nature and, as such, is the precursor of the many watercolourists of subsequent generations. Charles Grevelle passed on the secrets of aquatint engraving he had acquired from J.B. Leprince and Sandby used this process to reproduce his landscapes. His prints were avidly collected. No fewer than 125 of his compositions were exhibited at the Royal Academy between its foundation in 1768 and the artist's death in 1809.

Bibliography:
Sandby, Paul, *The Virtuosi's Museum, Containing Select Views, in England, Scotland and Ireland, Drawn by P. Sandby, Esq. R.A.*, London, 1778, 1781. Sandby, William, *'Thomas and Paul Sandby: Royal Academicians,* Seeley, London, 1892. Oppé, Adolf Paul, *The Drawings of Paul and Thomas Sandby in the Collection of His Majesty the King at Windsor Castle,* Phaidon, London, 1947. Herrman, Luke, *Paul and Thomas Sandby,* Victoria and Albert Museum, London, 1986.

Museums and Galleries:
Birmingham: *Forest View, Warwick Castle* (two views); *Lutow Castle; Beddley, Worcestershire; Landscape* - Birmingham (Mus. and AG): several watercolours - Cape Town: two landscapes - Cardiff: two Italian landscapes; *Pembroke Castle; West Gate, Cardiff; Church in Cambridge; Coity Castle; L. Lamphey's Manor House* - Dublin: two views of Hyde Park, London; *Eltham Palace; Windsor Castle* - Edinburgh (Nat. Gal. of Scotland, Print Room): *Bothwell Castle, Lanakshire, from the South* (gouache); *Bothwell Castle, South View* (pencil and wash) - Glasgow: two views of Windsor Castle; *Episode from Allan Ramsay's 'Gentle Shepherd'* (painting) - Leeds (City AG): drawings and watercolours - Leicester: *Elizabeth Gate, Windsor; Landscape* - Liverpool: *Carnarvon Castle; View of the River Dee; Old Windsor seen from the South; Woolwich; Landscape* - Liverpool (Walker AG): *Conway Castle* (1776) - London (Victoria and Albert Mus.): *Conway Castle; View from the Terrace* (painting); *L. Landoff's 'Cathedral'; Temple* (1788); *Chystow Castle; Warwick Castle; Village Street; Windsor Forest; Old Tead Garden, Bayswater; Old Bridge, Shrewsbury; Meddleton; Easton Park; Hubertson Priory; Road through Windsor Forest; Huddesdon; Rochester; Old Swan Inn, Bayswater; Windsor Castle* (1800); *Eton College; Corregcennin Castle; The Three Daughters of the*

Earl of Waldegrave - MANCHESTER: six landscapes; *River Thames with a View of St Paul's Cathedral* - NORWICH (Castle Mus. and AG): *View of Ipswich* (watercolour); *Garlinge near Margate* (watercolour) - NOTTINGHAM (Castle Mus. & AG): *View of Bengow* (1776); *View of Richmond Castle* (1763); *View of Windsor* (1760) - VICTORIA: four landscapes.

AUCTION RECORDS:

PARIS, 20 March 1901, *Windsor Castle, View from the Terrace*, FRF 630. LONDON, 16 Feb 1922, *Windsor Castle* (gouache) GBP 37; *Bayswater Turnpike* (gouache) GBP 39; *Panormic View of Windsor Castle* (watercolour) GBP 29. LONDON, 16 March 1923, *Warwick Castle* (two gouaches) GBP 31. LONDON, 14 May 1923, *Welsh Bridge* (gouache) GBP 25. LONDON, 30 Nov 1923, *Going to Market* (gouache) GBP 14. LONDON, 7 Dec 1925, *Escarpments* (drawing) GBP 50. LONDON, 12 March 1926, *Landscape with Cricketers* (drawing) GBP 115. LONDON, 9 July 1926, *Hyde Park* (drawing) GBP 189. PARIS, 18 Nov 1926, *Windermere Water* (pen with blue and mauve wash) FRF 490. LONDON, 4 Feb 1927, *Bow Church* (drawing) GBP 31. LONDON, 16 March 1928, *Chippenham; Salt Hill* (two drawings) GBP 46. LONDON, 24 May 1929, *Italian Coastal Town* (gouache) GBP 71. LONDON, 7 June 1929, *St Paul's, Covent Garden* (drawing) GBP 57. LONDON, 31 July 1929, *River Thames at Chelsea* (drawing) GBP 71. LONDON, 9 Dec 1929, *Entrance to Bayswater Turnpike* (gouache) GBP 67. LONDON, 10 Nov 1933, *Newark* (gouache) GBP 47. LONDON, 4 April 1935, *Nuneham* (watercolour) GBP 34. LONDON, 5 April 1935, *Seven Sisters*, GBP 126. LONDON, 16 April 1937, *Old Harbour, Staines* (drawing) GBP 69. LONDON, 25 April 1940, *Spread Eagle Inn* (drawing) GBP 304. LONDON, 5 June 1942, *Eagle Tower and Carnarvon Castle* (drawing) GBP 136. LONDON, 7 Aug 1942, *Morning; Afternoon; Evening; Night* (four gouaches) GBP 241. LONDON, 18 Sept 1942, *Cricket Match* (gouache) GBP 63. LONDON, 12 Jan 1945, *Windsor* (gouache) GBP 66. LONDON, 26 July 1946, *Rocks Overlooking a River* (drawing) GBP 50. LONDON, 1 Nov 1946, *Wooded Landscape* (gouache) GBP 78; *Melrose Abbey; River Scene* (two gouaches) GBP 131. LONDON, 12 March 1947, *Tunbridge* (drawing) GBP 64. LONDON, 9 July 1947, *Rochester* (drawing) GBP 250. LONDON, 9 Dec 1949, *View of Eton College from the South Bank* (gouache) GBP 766. LONDON, 2 March 1951, *View of Chepstow Castle* (drawing) GBP 100. LONDON, 26 May 1959, *Full-length Portrait of Lady Maynard, Knitting* (pencil and red pencil) GBP 609. LONDON, 18 Nov 1960, *Extended River Scene with Ladies and Gentlemen Out Walking*, GBP 2,100. LONDON, 19 April 1961, *St Augustine Abbey and Canterbury Cathedral* (drawing) GBP 600. LONDON, 14 March 1962, *Eton College* (gouache) GBP 2,800. LONDON, 28 June 1963, *View of Warwick Castle* (watercolour) Gns 1,600. LONDON, 13 July 1965, *Windsor Castle: North Terrace* (gouache) Gns 8,400. LONDON, 29 April 1971, *Road to Tonbridge* (watercolour) GBP 1,700. LONDON, 20 July 1972, *St George's Gate, Canterbury*, GBP 5,400. LONDON, 6 Nov 1973, *Dartmouth Castle* (gouache) Gns 5,500. LONDON, 16 June 1974, *Welsh Bridge, Shrewsbury* (gouache) GBP 3,000. LONDON, 9 Nov 1976, *Miltary Encampment, Hyde Park* (1780, watercolour and pen, 8 x 12 ins / 20.5 x 30.5 cm) GBP 4,000. LONDON, 24 Nov 1977, *Mountain Loch, Scotland* (1801, watercolour, 25 1/4 x 35 3/4 ins / 64 x 91 cm) GBP 5,200. LONDON, 13 Dec 1979, *Two Women with Parasols* (pencil and wash, 4 3/4 x 3 1/4 ins / 12.2 x 8 cm) GBP 500. LONDON, 10 July 1980, *Windsor Castle: North Terrace* (gouache/mounted paper/card, 18 1/2 x 24 1/2 ins / 47 x 62 cm) GBP 5,200. LONDON, 21 Nov 1980, *Hackwood Park, Hampshire* (oil on canvas, 39 1/2 x 49 1/4 ins / 100.2 x 125 cm) GBP 26,000. LONDON, 16 July 1981, *Romantic Landscape with Figures* (pen and watercolour, round, diam. 12 3/4 ins / 32.5 cm) GBP 800. LONDON, 16 July 1982, *Village in Oxfordshire* (oil on panel, 18 x 24 ins / 45.7 x 61 cm) GBP 1,500. LONDON, 29 March 1983, *Travellers' Rest* (1796, pencil, pen and wash, 11 3/4 x 13 3/4 ins / 30 x 35.2 cm) GBP 900. LONDON, 29 March 1983, *Reading Abbey Gate* (gouache/mounted paper/panel, 11 x 16 ins / 28.1 x 40.6 cm) GBP 10,000. LONDON, 14 March 1985, *Buildwas Abbey, Shropshire* (pencil and watercolour, 8 1/2 x 11 ins / 21.5 x 28 cm) GBP 1,300. LONDON, 21 Nov 1986, *The Vendage, Painshill, Surrey* (oil on canvas, 20 1/4 x 30 1/4 ins / 51.7 x 76.7 cm) GBP 22,000. LONDON, 25 Jan 1989, *Young Girl Standing with a Cat in her Arms* (pencil and ink, 5 1/2 x 2 3/4 ins / 14 x 7 cm) GBP 1,045. LONDON, 14 July 1989, *Vast Landscape with Figures in a Clearing near a Manor House* (oil on canvas, 32 1/4 x 44 ins / 82 x 112 cm) GBP 16,500. PARIS, 17 June 1994, *Windsor Castle from Datchet Lane* (black chalk, watercolour and gouache, 12 1/4 x 18 ins / 31.2 x 45.7 cm) FRF 155,000. LUDLOW, 29 Sept 1994, *View of Worcester in 1778* (hand-coloured aquatint, 14 1/4 x 21 1/4 ins / 36.5 x 54 cm) GBP 2,760. NEW YORK, 11 Jan 1996, *View of the Thames Estuary, Essex* (1807, oil on canvas, 25 1/2 x 40 1/2 ins / 64.8 x 102.9 cm) USD 43,125. LONDON, 13 Nov 1997, *View of Greece* (1779 and 1780, aquatint, set of twelve, each 1 1/4 x 2 ins / 3.3 x 5.1 cm) GBP 12,650. LONDON, 10 June 1999, *The North Terrace of Windsor Castle* (gouache on paper on panel, 18 x 24 ins / 46 x 61 cm) GBP 68,000. LONDON, 10 June 1999, *North Front of Windsor Castle from Datchet Lane* (pencil, gouache and wash, 15 x 22 ins / 38 x 55 cm) GBP 80,000. LONDON, 30 Nov 2000, *Eton College from the South West* (watercolour over pencil heightened with gouache, 12 x 19 ins / 31 x 47 cm) GBP 28,000. LONDON, 30 Nov 2000, *Town of Woolwich from the Conduit Hill, River Thames in the Distance* (watercolour over pencil heightened with gouache, 12 x 19 ins / 31 x 47 cm) GBP 35,000. LONDON, 21 Nov 2001, *Capriccio View of Italian Town. Travellers Approaching Fortified Bridge* (pencil, watercolour and gouache, a pair, 4 x 5 ins / 9 x 13 cm) GBP 7,000. LONDON, 6 June 2002, *Bayswater Road, Paddington* (pencil and gouache heightened with white, 12 x 18 ins / 30 x 45 cm) GBP 17,000. LONDON, 6 June 2002, *Middleham Castle, Yorkshire* (1788, pencil, pen, grey ink and watercolour, 14 x 19 ins / 35 x 48 cm) GBP 22,000. LONDON, 22 Jan 2003, *Woolwich from the Conduit Hill* (pencil, watercolour and gouache, 13 x 19 ins / 32 x 47 cm) GBP 24,000. LONDON, 15 May 2003, *Ross Castle, Killarney* (pencil and gouache, 25 x 35 ins / 63 x 89 cm) GBP 24,000. LONDON, 1 July 2004, *View of Windsor Castle and Part of the Town from the Spital Hill* (pen, grey ink and watercolour over pencil, laid on paper, 11 x 23 ins / 27 x 59 cm) GBP 20,000. LONDON, 23 Nov 2004, *Woolwich from the Conduit Hill* (1807, oil on canvas, 26 x 41 ins / 66 x 104 cm) GBP 38,000.

SANDBY, Pierre

British, 18th - 19th century.

Born 1732, in Nottingham; died 1808, in Woolwich.

Painter, engraver (etching/aquatint).

Pierre Sandby engraved landscapes, portraits and genre compositions.

SANDBY, Thomas

British, 18th century.

Born 1721, in Nottingham; died 24 June 1798, in Windsor.

Painter, watercolourist, draughtsman. Landscapes.

Thomas Sandby was the brother of the eminent watercolourist Paul Sandby and one of the leading architects of his time. He was a founder member of London's Royal Academy, and was also an accomplished draughtsman.

MUSEUMS AND GALLERIES:

EDINBURGH (Nat. Gal. of Scotland, Print Room): *Design for a Triumphal Bridge across the Thames* (watercolour and gouache) - LEEDS (City AG): watercolours - LONDON (Victoria and Albert Mus.): watercolours - MANCHESTER: watercolours - NOTTINGHAM (Castle Mus. & AG): watercolours - WINDSOR: watercolours.

AUCTION RECORDS:
LONDON, 8-18 July 1940, *Windsor Great Park* (drawing) GBP 115. LONDON, 14 March 1978, *Fruit-Seller under the Arcades near St Paul's Church, Covent Garden* (watercolour and pen, 25 x 19 ins / 63.5 x 48.2 cm) GBP 1,300. LONDON, 25 June 1981, *Snow-Clad Promontory, Windsor Great Park* (watercolour and pen, sketch, 12 1/2 x 19 ins / 32 x 48 cm) GBP 2,400. LONDON, 30 Nov 1983, *Perspective Design for a Bridge of Magnificence* (pencil, pen, wash and watercolour, 17 3/4 x 23 1/2 ins / 45 x 59.8 cm) GBP 2,400.

SANDBY, Thomas Paul
British, 18th - 19th century.
Painter. Landscapes.
Thomas Sandby was the son of Paul Sandby. He exhibited from 1791 to 1811.

SANDE, André van den
Belgian, 20th century.
Born 1910, in Antwerp.
Painter.
Poetic Reality.
André van den Sande studied at the higher institute of fine arts in Antwerp and went on to teach at the academy in Turnhout.

SANDE, Diego de, or Isande
Spanish, 18th century.
Active in Noya from 1712 to c. 1730.
Sculptor (wood/ivory).
Diego de Sande was Felipe de Castro's first teacher. He carved stone and ivory statues for churches in Santiago de Compostela.

SANDE, Jan van de
Flemish School, 17th century.
Born 17 February 1600, in Antwerp; died 1664 or 1665, in Antwerp.
Engraver (burin).
Jan van de Sande is known for an engraving of the *Conception of the Virgin*.

SANDE, Jan van de, or Sanden or Zande
Dutch, 17th century.
Active in Utrecht in 1616 and 1617.
Painter.

SANDE, Jan van de
Dutch, 17th century.
Active in Alkmaar in 1645.
Painter.

SANDE, Jan van de
Dutch, 17th century.
Painter.
Known for a *Vegetable Market* in the style of Hendrick Maartensz. Sorgh.

SANDE, Jean Baptiste
Flemish School, 17th - 18th century.
Active in Antwerp from 1675 to 1713.
Engraver (burin).
Jean Baptiste Sande was possibly the son of the engraver Jan van der Sande.

SANDE, Johann A.
German, 17th century.
Active in Nuremberg in 1618.
Engraver (burin), goldsmith.
Johann A. Sande engraved books on the goldsmith's trade.

SANDE, Michiel van de
Dutch, 17th century.
Born 1583 or 1584; died before 1643.
Painter.
Michiel van de Sande was active in Rotterdam, Venice and Amsterdam.

SANDE, René van de
Belgian, 20th century.
Born 1889, in Everberg; died 1964, in Anderlecht.
Painter, draughtsman. Landscapes, landscapes with figures, urban landscapes, architectural views.
René van de Sande studied at the fine arts academy in Brussels and was one of the driving forces behind the creation of the city's Broodhuis Museum. He was also responsible for designing Belgium's national emblem, *St Michael Slaying the Dragon*. During World War I, Van de Sande recorded the suffering experienced by his contemporaries. In 1918 he drew sites and public monuments in Brussels and its surroundings for incorporation into the first-ever illustrated guide to the Belgian capital.
AUCTION RECORDS:
BRUSSELS, 27 March 1990, *View of Dilbeek* (oil on canvas, 28 1/4 x 35 1/2 ins / 72 x 90 cm) BEF 140,000. LOKEREN, 10 Oct 1992, *Cattle near a Stream* (oil on canvas, 25 1/2 x 32 ins / 65 x 81 cm) BEF 70,000. LOKEREN, 4 Dec 1993, *Landscape with Pond* (oil on canvas, 21 1/4 x 25 1/2 ins / 54 x 65 cm) BEF 90,000; *Cattle near Water* (oil on canvas, 25 1/2 x 32 ins / 65 x 81 cm) BEF 55,000.

SANDE, Salomon van de
Dutch, 17th century.
Died before 1665.
Active in Amsterdam.
Painter. Flowers.

SANDE VAN DE BAKHUYZEN, Gerardina Jacoba, Hendrik, Julius Jacobus.
See **BAKHUYZEN**

SANDE-LACOSTE, Carel Eliza van der
Dutch, 19th century.
Born 1860, in Dordrecht; died 1894, in Dordrecht.
Portrait artist.
MUSEUMS AND GALLERIES:
DORDRECHT: two portraits.

SANDECKI, Vladyslav
Polish, 19th century.
Born 2 February 1869, in Warsaw; died 16 December 1889.
Painter.
The National Museum in Warsaw owns *Celebration of Pentecost* by Vladyslav Sandecki.

SANDEL, André
French, 20th - 21st century.
Born 3 November 1950, in Avignon.
Sculptor, designer of ornamental architectural features, illustrator.
André Sandel spent his formative years in a mason's yard fashioning marble. As an artist, he had to curb his imagination to ensure commercial success in order to support his family. He went on to participate as a stonemason/sculptor in the restoration of historic monuments, including The Louvre, the Invalides, the Place de la Concorde and the École Militaire in Paris, the façade of the Hôtel de Ville in Lyons; the Palais des Papes in Avignon; the Arsenal Portal in Toulon, and the fountain on the Place des Armes.

Working on his own account, he produces snow and ice sculptures for international symposia and festivals, together with wood carvings and pieces in bronze. His style varies with his chosen materials and reflects the broad sweep of modern French sculpture (Academism, Expressionism, Symbolism, and so forth).

SANDELLI, Daniele I
Italian, 16th century.

Active in Arco (Trento) during the second half of the 16th century.
Painter.
Daniele Sandelli I may have been the father of Marco Sandelli.

SANDELLI, Daniele II
Italian, 16th century.
Active in Arco (Trento) at the end of the 16th century.
Painter. Religious subjects.
Daniele Sandelli II was the son of Marco Sandelli and painted altar pieces.

SANDELLI, Lisandro
Italian, 16th century.
Active in Trento (Trentino-Alto Adige) in 1582.
Painter.

SANDELLI, Marco, called Marco Moretto
Italian, 16th century.
Died between 30 November 1596 and May 1602.
Painter.
Marco Sandelli was the father of Daniele Sandelli II. He worked in churches in Lomasso and Massone. He was identical with Marco Moretto, who painted frescoes in the church of S Giacomo, near Arco (Trentino-Alto Adige), and in SS Fabiano e Sebastiano church in Caneva, also near Arco.

SANDELS, Gösta, short for Adrian Gösta Fabian
Swedish, 20th century.
Born 25 April 1887, in Göteborg; died 14 August 1919, in Granada.
Painter. Portraits, urban landscapes, landscapes.
De Unga Group.
Gösta Sandels studied in Paris. He was influenced by the work of Van Gogh, Edvard Munch and the Fauves. His urban landscapes, frequently of Montmartre, have something of the freshness of a Maurice Utrillo. His portraits are striking to the extent that they exhibit deep insight into the sitter's psychological make-up.
BIBLIOGRAPHY:
Serner, Gertrud, *Gösta Sandels*, Stockholm, 1941. *Gösta Sandels*, exhibition catalogue, Konstmuseum, Göteborg, 1976.
MUSEUMS AND GALLERIES:
GÖTEBORG - OSLO - STOCKHOLM.
AUCTION RECORDS:
STOCKHOLM, 8 Dec 1987, *Working in the Fields* (1905, oil on canvas, 34 1/4 x 27 1/4 ins / 87 x 69 cm) SEK 103,000. LONDON, 29 March 1990, *Half-light* (1906, coloured chalks, 14 1/2 x 20 3/4 ins / 37 x 53 cm) GBP 1,650. STOCKHOLM, 5-6 Dec 1990, *Corner of Paris* (1907, oil on canvas, 25 1/2 x 22 ins / 65 x 55 cm) SEK 44,000. STOCKHOLM, 27 April 1999, *Woman by Spring* (1918, mixed media, 11 x 9 ins / 28 x 22 cm) SEK 14,000. STOCKHOLM, 22 Nov 1999, *On the Beach* (1918, oil on canvas, 49 x 45 ins / 125 x 115 cm) SEK 480,000. STOCKHOLM, 15 May 2000, *Landscape from Stufverod, Bohuslan* (1917, oil on canvas, 31 x 35 ins / 80 x 90 cm) SEK 355,000. STOCKHOLM, 27 Nov 2000, *Rider* (1918, oil on canvas, 23 x 26 ins / 58 x 65 cm) SEK 395,000. STOCKHOLM, 27 Nov 2001, *Brook* (1918, oil on canvas, 29 x 26 ins / 74 x 67 cm) SEK 650,000. STOCKHOLM, 23 April 2002, *Still-life with Fruit and Statuettes* (1912, oil on canvas, 24 x 19 ins / 61 x 48 cm) SEK 30,000. STOCKHOLM, 23 April 2002, *Olive Grove* (1919, oil on canvas, 20 x 24 ins / 50 x 60 cm) SEK 35,000. STOCKHOLM, 7 May 2003, *Girl under the Rowan Berry Tree* (1914, oil on canvas, 39 x 28 ins / 100 x 72 cm) SEK 160,000.

SANDEN, J. van
German, 18th century.
Engraver (burin).
J. van Sanden engraved the portrait of the elector of Cologne *Clement August of Bavaria*

SANDEN, Jan van de. See also **SANDE**

SANDER, Johann, pseudonym of Johann Jungblut
German, 19th - 20th century.
Born 16 April 1860, in Sarreburg (Trier); died 17 December 1912, in Düsseldorf.
Painter. Landscapes with figures, waterscapes, seascapes.
Johann Sander settled in Düsseldorf in 1885. A self-taught artist, he painted mainly Dutch landscapes, prompting the suggestion that he probably spent considerable time in the Netherlands. He also painted landscapes in Norway, notably in winter.
MUSEUMS AND GALLERIES:
MAINZ (Landesmus.): *Dutch Coast Landscape* - NEW YORK (Brooklyn): *Norwegian Winter Landscape*.
AUCTION RECORDS:
COLOGNE, 26 March 1971, *Winter in Holland*, DEM 3,600. COLOGNE, 13 Oct 1972, *Winter in Holland*, DEM 5,500. COLOGNE, 14 June 1976, *Winter Landscape* (oil on canvas, 32 x 47 1/4 ins / 81 x 120 cm) DEM 3,500. COLOGNE, 18 March 1977, *Winter Landscape* (oil on canvas, 32 x 47 1/4 ins / 81 x 120 cm) DEM 8,500. NEW YORK, 19 April 1977, *Mexican Summer* (oil on canvas, 29 1/2 x 39 ins / 75 x 99 cm) USD 1,300. COLOGNE, 30 March 1979, *Winter Evening* (oil on canvas, 26 x 37 ins / 66 x 94 cm) DEM 10,000. LONDON, 27 Nov 1981, *Winter Landscape with Figures* (oil on panel, 14 x 21 1/4 ins / 35.6 x 54 cm) GBP 2,800. COLOGNE, 9 May 1983, *Winter Landscape* (oil on canvas, 32 x 47 1/4 ins / 81 x 120 cm) DEM 18,000. COLOGNE, 19 Nov 1987, *Winter Landscape* (oil on canvas, 31 1/2 x 47 1/4 ins / 80 x 120 cm) DEM 9,000. COLOGNE, 15 Oct 1988, *Fishing for Eels with Hoop Nets in a Winter Landscape* (oil on canvas, 22 x 32 1/4 ins / 56 x 82 cm) DEM 2,000. STOCKHOLM, 15 Nov 1988, *Buildings and Figures in a Winter Landscape* (oil, 24 x 32 ins / 61 x 81 cm) SEK 33,000. AMSTERDAM, 16 Nov 1988, *Peasant Woman and her Child Walking on a Frozen Path in a Birch Forest* (oil on canvas, 31 1/2 x 47 1/4 ins / 80 x 120 cm) NLG 13,800. COLOGNE, 20 Oct 1989, *Winter Evening by a Dutch Canal* (oil on canvas, 31 1/2 x 47 1/4 ins / 80 x 120 cm) DEM 8,000. COLOGNE, 29 June 1990, *Winter Landscape* (oil on canvas, 31 1/2 x 23 3/4 ins / 80 x 60.5 cm) DEM 8,500. STOCKHOLM, 29 May 1991, *Winter Landscape with Children Playing on a Frozen Puddle* (oil on canvas, 31 1/2 x 47 1/4 ins / 80 x 120 cm) SEK 25,000. AMSTERDAM, 5-6 Nov 1991, *Fishermen Drawing Canal Water through a Hole in the Ice* (oil on canvas, 31 x 46 3/4 ins / 79 x 119 cm) NLG 16,100. AMSTERDAM, 14-15 April 1992, *Dutch Landscape in Winter* (oil on canvas, 31 x 48 ins / 79 x 121 cm) NLG 9,775. AMSTERDAM, 9 Nov 1993, *Winter in Holland* (oil on canvas, 30 3/4 x 23 ins / 78 x 58.5 cm) NLG 10,925. AMSTERDAM, 8 Nov 1994, *Dusk over a River Landscape in Winter* (oil on canvas, 35 x 15 3/4 ins / 88 x 40 cm) NLG 6,900. AMSTERDAM, 5 Nov 1996, *Two Women Carrying Baskets in a Vast River Landscape* (oil on canvas, 23 1/2 x 31 1/2 ins / 60 x 80 cm) NLG 4,956. MUNICH, 2 Dec 1997, *Autumn Landscape; Summer Landscape* (oils on wood, a pair, 12 x 16 1/4 ins / 30.5 x 41 cm) DEM 7,800. FRANKFURT, 3 March 2001, *River Landscape* (1887, oil on canvas, 26 x 37 ins / 66 x 94 cm) DEM 5,200.

SANDER, Johann Christian
German, 18th century.
Active in Breslau (now Wroclaw) in 1729.
Engraver (burin).
Johann Christian Sander is noted for his engraving *The Organs of Landshut*.

SANDER, Johann Heinrich
German, 19th century.

Born 12 March 1810, in Hamburg; died 21 January 1865, in Hamburg.
Active in Hamburg.
Painter (including gouache), lithographer. Portraits, urban landscapes, seascapes.

Johann Heinrich Sander studied in Hamburg, Munich and Paris.

AUCTION RECORDS:

HAMBURG, 24 June 1968, *The Painter and his Family Sitting in a Garden*, DEM 4,300. MUNICH, 12 June 1991, *Views of Hamburg* (gouache, set of four, each 7 1/2 x 11 ins / 19 x 27 cm) DEM 25,300.

SANDER, Karin

German, 20th - 21st century.
Born 1957, in Bensberg.
Installation artist.
Conceptual Art.

Karin Sander studied at the Akademie der Bildenden Künste in Stuttgart, and lives and works in Stuttgart, Berlin and New York. Her interventions - generally in places of passage and exteriors such as streets, doorways, courtyards and interiors such as galleries, corridors, windows and toilets - consist of reawakening viewers' perceptions of what makes up the places that she has selected for treatment. Usually, she whitens them in a neutral or grey context, sometimes polishing them or using other treatments appropriate to the precise circumstances.

She takes part in collective exhibitions. Her solo shows have included exhibitions at the Galerie Vera Engelhorn, New York (1988), the Galerie Ute Parduhn, Düsseldorf (1989), the Städtisches Museum Abteiberg, Mönchengladbach (1992), the Staatsgalerie, Stuttgart (2002).

BIBLIOGRAPHY:

Masséra, Jean-Charles, '*Karin Sander - polir aux passages*' in *Art Press* n° 179, periodical, Paris, April 1993. Schreier, Christoph, et al., *Karin Sander: Rubens-Föderpreis der Stadt Siegen*, exhibition catalogue, Städtische Gal. Haus Seel, Cantz, Ostfildern, 1994. Wäspe, Roland/Bitterli, Konrad, *Karin Sander*, exhibition catalogue, Kunstmuseum St. Gallen, Cantz, Ostfildern-Ruit, 1996 (text in German and English).

MUSEUMS AND GALLERIES:

METZ (FRAC Lorraine): *Wall Piece*.

SANDER, Ludwig

American, 20th century.
Born 1906, in New York; died 1975, in New York.
Painter.

Ludwig Sander graduated in the history of art from New York University and from 1925 he began to paint. He studied at the Art Students League of New York, in particular with Archipenko. He then travelled around Germany and Switzerland. In 1932 he was among a group of young American artists in Positano, Italy, who experimented with Abstraction, which was still in its infancy. Sander was later called up to serve in the American Army in World War II. Returning to New York, he was one of the founders of *The Club* and came into contact with the painters of the New York School, particularly Arshile Gorky, Willem De Kooning, Franz Kline and Ad Reinhardt. In 1961 he travelled via Paris to spend a year in Munich, where he attended painting courses with Hans Hofmann. He took part in many collective exhibitions, including: 1961 New York *American Abstract Expressionists and Imagists* at the Guggenheim Museum; 1962 New York *Geometric Abstraction in America* at the Whitney Museum; etc. His solo exhibitions included: 1952, 1959, 1961, 1962 New York. Massachusetts Institute of Technology awarded him Hallmark and Longview distinctions.

BIBLIOGRAPHY:

Morgan, Robert C., *Ludwig Sander: An Overview*, ACA Galleries, New York, 1991.

AUCTION RECORDS:

LOS ANGELES, 27 Feb 1974, *Scuppernong VII*, USD 1,500. NEW YORK, 9 Nov 1983, *Athabscam I* (1971, oil on canvas, 32 x 36 ins / 81 x 91.5 cm) USD 3,000. NEW YORK, 23 Feb 1985, *Untitled* (1963, oil on canvas, 54 x 60 ins / 137 x 152.5 cm) USD 7,000. NEW YORK, 7 May 1986, *Ranaqua I* (1972, oil on canvas, 22 x 20 ins / 56 x 50.5 cm) USD 4,800. NEW YORK, 29 Sept 1993, *Huron II* (1971, oil on canvas, 40 x 44 ins / 101.6 x 111.8 cm) USD 4,313. NEW YORK, 11 Nov 1993, *Huron I* (1968, acrylic/canvas, 60 x 66 ins / 152.4 x 167.6 cm) USD 4,025. NEW YORK, 14 June 1995, *Untitled* (1965, oil on canvas, 16 x 15 ins / 40.6 x 38.1 cm) USD 1,380. NORTH BETHESDA, 9 Feb 2002, *Chinook VII* (1969, oil on canvas, 32 x 36 ins / 81 x 91 cm) USD 3,000. OAK PARK, 3 March 2002, *Athabascan* (1974, oil on canvas, 22 x 40 ins / 56 x 102 cm) USD 3,500. CHICAGO, 1 June 2003, *Pensacola IV* (oil on canvas, 24 x 22 ins / 61 x 56 cm) USD 3,750. LAMBERTVILLE, 25 Oct 2003, *Genessee VII* (oil on canvas, 22 x 40 ins / 56 x 102 cm) USD 5,500. LAMBERTVILLE, 3 April 2004, *Chippewa V* (oil on canvas, 20 x 22 ins / 51 x 56 cm) USD 3,500. LAMBERTVILLE, 3 April 2004, *Untitled* (oil on canvas, 22 x 40 ins / 56 x 102 cm) USD 4,000.

SANDER, Theodor

German, 19th - 20th century.
Born 14 January 1858, in Flensburg.
Painter, engraver (etching).

SANDER, Wilhelm

German, 18th - 19th century.
Born c. 1766, in Breslau (now Wroclaw, Poland); died 22 August 1836, in Oels (now Olesnica, Poland).
Engraver (burin), lithographer.

SANDERAT, Étienne

French, 15th century.
Miniaturist, calligrapher.

In 1447 Jean de Chalon, Seigneur of Vitteou, commissioned from Étienne Sanderat 50 miniatures to illustrate a work entitled *The Properties of Things*.

SANDERCOCK, Henry Ardmare

British, 19th century.
Active in Moulsey.
Painter. Landscapes, seascapes.

Henry Sandercock exhibited in London from 1865 to 1883, showing principally Devon landscapes at the Royal Academy, the Suffolk Street Gallery and the Royal Institute of Painters in Water-Colours.

MUSEUMS AND GALLERIES:

MONTREAL: *Seascape*.

SANDERMAYR, Simon or Sigismund Thaddäus. See **SONDERMAYR**

SANDERS

French, 14th century.
Active in Tournai.
Sculptor.

Between 1361 and 1362 Sanders carved sculptures for the château of Louis de Male in Ghent.

SANDERS, Adam Achod

American, 20th century.
Born June 1889, in Sweden.
Sculptor. Statues, monuments.

Adam Achod Sanders studied at the Institute of Fine Arts in New York. He was a member of the Society of Independent Artists and of the American Arts Federation. He sculpted the *Commemorative monument to Abraham Lincoln* in Washington.

SANDERS, Alexander
German, 17th century.
Born 1624 (?), in Emden; died 1684, in Emden.
Painter.

Alexander Sanders was influenced by Frans Hals, B. van der Helst and Jan de Bray.

MUSEUMS AND GALLERIES:
BREMEN (Mus. im Roselius-Haus): *Male Portrait; Female Portrait.*

SANDERS, Christopher
British, 20th century.
Born 1905; died 1991.
Painter. Landscapes, flowers.

Christopher Sanders often painted in Provence.

AUCTION RECORDS:
LONDON, 12 Nov 1976, *Poppies and Irises* (oil on canvas, 32 x 32 ins / 81.5 x 81.5 cm) GBP 260. LONDON, 6 June 1991, *Farmhouse near Arles* (oil on canvas, 20 x 24 ins / 51 x 61 cm) GBP 2,035. LONDON, 14 May 1992, *Le Grau du Roi, South of France* (oil on canvas, 19 3/4 x 23 3/4 ins / 50 x 60.5 cm) GBP 1,320. LONDON, 25 Sept 1992, *Poppies Grew in the Walls* (oil on canvas, 20 x 24 ins / 51 x 61 cm) GBP 2,090. LONDON, 6 Dec 2000, *Seated Nude Adjusting Her Hair* (oil on canvas, 18 x 15 ins / 46 x 38 cm) GBP 1,700. ASHVILLE, 31 May 2003, *Sunlight, Shade and Irises* (oil on canvas, 32 x 32 ins / 81 x 81 cm) USD 5,800.

SANDERS, Edmond
Belgian, 20th century.
Died 1961.
Painter.

SANDERS, Frans, or Sandres
Flemish School, 16th century.
Died after 1542.
Active in Mechelen.
Painter.

Frans Sanders was a master in 1511. He painted a *Last Judgement* in 1526 for the Great Council Room of Mechelen and a *Madonna* for Infanta Marguerite of Austria.

SANDERS, George
British, 19th century.
Born 1810, in Exeter.
Engraver (mezzotint/steel).

George Sanders worked in Dublin from 1845 to 1858 and in London from 1861 to 1866. He engraved portraits and landscapes, mainly from foreign originals.

SANDERS, George Lethbridge.
See **SAUNDERS George**

SANDERS, Gerard
Dutch, 18th century.
Born 1707, in Wesel; died 17 March 1767, in Rotterdam.
Painter, watercolourist, draughtsman. Historical subjects, religious subjects, mythological subjects, portraits, landscapes, still-lifes, animals.

Gerard Sanders was a pupil of his brother-in-law Tobias van Nymegen, and of the latter's brother Elias van Nymegen. His wife, the engraver Johanna van Nymegen, died in 1734 or 1752.

MUSEUMS AND GALLERIES:
BRUSSELS: *Portrait of P. Rabus* - ROTTERDAM (Mus. Boijmans van Beuningen): *Macrèle* - ST-DIÉ-DES-VOSGES: *St Cecilia.*

AUCTION RECORDS:
PARIS, 1776, *Head of a Spaniel* (bistre wash, study) FRF 13. PARIS, 25 Feb 1937, *Diana at Rest,* FRF 820. PARIS, July 1946, *Wild Ducks and a Moorhen* (1753, watercolour) FRF 7,300. LONDON, 22 Oct 1982, *The Marriage of Alexander and Roxana; Queen Zenobia on Horseback* (1754, oil on panel, a pair, 19 1/2 x 15 ins / 49.5 x 38.1 cm) GBP 3,200. PARIS, 7 April 1995, *Flowers and Chestnuts on a Ledge* (1763, watercolour, 9 3/4 x 7 ins / 25 x 18 cm) FRF 8,000. MUNICH, 25 June 2004, *Venus and Bachus with a Little Cupid* (oil on canvas, 42 x 30 ins / 107 x 75 cm) EUR 7,500.

SANDERS, Helen. See **SAUNDERS**

SANDERS, Herkules or Hercules
Dutch, 17th century.
Born 1606, in Amsterdam; died after 1663, in Amsterdam.
Painter.

Herkules Sanders was active in Amsterdam from 1635. He is known for two portraits in Amsterdam and Hamburg, and a portrait of *Sir Robert Kerr, Count of Anerum* in Newbattle Abbey, Edinburgh.

H Sanders fe

MUSEUMS AND GALLERIES:
AMSTERDAM: *Portrait of a Woman* - HAMBURG: *Portrait of a Man.*

AUCTION RECORDS:
BELGIUM, 1900, *Portrait of a Distinguished Lady,* FRF 9,365; *Portrait of a Man* (the pendant of the preceding item) FRF 2,750. PARIS, 24 June 1968, *Portrait of a Noble Family,* FRF 10,500. NICE, 11 April 1973, *Portait of a Noble Family,* FRF 22,000.

SANDERS, Hugh
British, 20th - 21st century.
Born 1955, in London.
Sculptor (mixed media), engraver.

Hugh Sanders' sculptures, which are usually of considerable size despite being composed of wood, paper, paint and iron filings, reconstruct the metallic appearance of industrial machinery before the era of miniaturisation, machinery which is now obsolete and confined to rust on the scrap heap. He has taken part in various group exhibitions, including the second Normandy European Sculpture Biennale at the Centre d'Art Contemporain in Jouy-sur-Eure in 1984.

BIBLIOGRAPHY:
IIe Biennale européenne de sculpture de Normandie, exhibition catalogue, Centre d'Art contemporain, Jouy-sur-Eure, 1984.

SANDERS, Jan
Belgian, 20th century.
Born 1936, in Aalst.
Painter.

Jan Sanders studied at the fine arts academies in Aalst and Brussels.

SANDERS, John
British, 18th century.
Painter. History painting.

John Sanders exhibited at the Royal Academy with a *Saint Sebastian* in 1772 and a *Jael and Sisera.*

SANDERS, John
British, 18th - 19th century.
Painter.

John Sanders is in all probability the son of the historical painter John Sanders, but could be the son of another San(n)ders who died in Clifton in 1825. He exhibited at the Royal Academy from 1775 to 1820.

SANDERS, John (son), or Saunders or Sannders, also known as the Younger
British, 18th - 19th century.
Born c. 1750; died 1825, in Clifton.
Painter, engraver (burin). Portraits, landscapes, architectural views.

John Sanders was the father of John Arnold Sanders and, in all likelihood, the son of the portraitist and pastel painter John Saunders or San(n)ders. He studied at the Royal Academy Schools in 1769 and began exhibiting in 1771, when he was still identified in the catalogue as 'John Saunders or San(n)ders the Younger'. He is on record as having been in Norwich in 1778, but was later identified as living in Bath and calling himself 'Sanders'. He was not without merit as a portrait painter.
MUSEUMS AND GALLERIES:
LONDON (Foundling Mus.): *The Foundling Hospital Chapel looking West* (1773, watercolour); *The Girls' Dining Room of the Foundling Hospital* (1773, watercolour) - MANCHESTER: *Sunday Evening in Bagnigge Wells* (watercolour).
AUCTION RECORDS:
LONDON, 31 May 1946, *Pump Room in Bath*, GBP 115.

SANDERS, John. See also **SAUNDERS**

SANDERS, John Arnold
British, 19th century.
Born 1801, in Bath.
Painter, watercolourist, miniaturist, draughtsman.
Portraits, landscapes.
John Arnold Sanders was the son of the portraitist John Sanders of Bath. He was a cross-genre painter whose body of work includes pencil drawings heightened with watercolour, delightful miniatures and delectable watercolour landscapes. He started exhibiting in 1810 while still a child and his name features at London exhibitions until 1827. He broke off his painting career to write a novel. A problem involving one of his (female) students prompted him to emigrate to Canada around 1831; since then, all trace of him has been lost.
MUSEUMS AND GALLERIES:
BRISTOL (City Mus. & AG): *Interior of Bristol Cathedral*.

SANDERS, Joseph. See **SAUNDERS**

SANDERS, Katherine van or Catharina van. See **HEMESSEN**

SANDERS, Thomas. See **SANDARS**

SANDERS, Thomas Hale
British, 19th century.
Active 1874-1906.
Painter, watercolourist. Landscapes, historical subjects, seascapes.
Thomas Sanders painted the Thames and the docks in London in oils and watercolours. He lived in Balham in the London area and travelled to Holland and Scotland. He exhibited between 1855 and 1862 at the Royal Academy and at the British Institution, London.

SANDERS VAN HEMESSEN, Jan. See **HEMESSEN Jan Sanders, called Jan van**

SANDERSON, Charles Wesley
American, 19th century.
Born 1838, in Brandon; died 8 March 1905, in Boston.
Painter. Landscapes.
Charles Wesley Sanderson trained with S. Gerry at the Académie Julian in Paris, and with Mesdag in The Hague.

SANDERSON, Robert
British, 19th - 20th century.
Painter. Genre scenes.
Robert Sanderson was active from 1860 to 1905.
MUSEUMS AND GALLERIES:
GLASGOW: *Child without a Mother* (1895).
AUCTION RECORDS:
LONDON, 7 Feb 1910, *Waiting*, GBP 1. PERTH, 26 Aug 1991, *Race* (1894, oil on panel, 12 x 8 1/4 ins / 30.5 x 21 cm) GBP 1,430. EDINBURGH, 9 June 1994, *The Apple of his Eye, Cottage Interior with Couple and Baby* (1889, oil on canvas, 9 1/2 x 7 1/2 ins / 24.2 x 19 cm) GBP 1,610.

SANDERSON-WELLS, John Sanderson. See **WELLS**

SANDFELDT, Antonius, or Samfleet or Sambfliid, called Antonius Kontrefejer
Danish, 16th century.
Probably of German origin.
Active in Copenhagen 1567-1581.
Portrait artist.
MUSEUMS AND GALLERIES:
HILLERØD (Frederiksbörg Slot): *Portrait of Oluf Krognos and his Wife*.

SANDFORD, Francis
British, 17th century.
Born 1630, at Carnow Castle (Wicklow); died 17 January 1694, in London.
Engraver (burin), draughtsman.
Francis Sandford worked as an architect and heraldic designer. He served as a herald to King James II and, when the latter fled, moved to a new life in London, where he died in 1694 in the debtors' prison in Newgate. He left a remarkable work in the guise of a beautifully engraved and illustrated *Genealogy of the Kings of England*.

SANDHAAS, Josef
German, 18th - 19th century.
Born 1747 (?), in Haslach (Baden-Württemberg, Kinzig Valley); died 1828, in Darmstadt.
Painter, draughtsman. Architectural views.
Josef Sandhaas was the uncle of Karl Sandhaas and painter to the court of Darmstadt. He is noted for his *Views of Darmstadt*.

SANDHAAS, Karl
Austrian, 19th century.
Born 1801, in Hüfingen; died 12 April 1859, in Haslach.
Painter, engraver. Religious subjects.
Karl Sandhaas was a friend of Cornelius. He studied in Karlsruhe, Munich and Milan. He settled in Frankfurt in 1822 and concentrated almost exclusively on painting New Testament scenes. He engraved a series of plates for a work entitled *Träume und Schäume des Lebens* (*Life's Dreams and Illusions*) published in 1844.
MUSEUMS AND GALLERIES:
FRIBOURG (MAH): oil sketches - HASLACH (Heimathaus): 51 drawings and watercolours - MANNHEIM (Städtische Kunsthalle): *Portrait Head*.

SANDHAM, Henry John
Canadian, 19th - 20th century.
Born 24 May 1842, in Montreal; died 6 January 1910 or 1912, in London.
Painter, watercolourist, illustrator. Portraits, genre scenes.
Henry John Sandham worked in Boston.
MUSEUMS AND GALLERIES:
WASHINGTON DC (Smithsonian American AM): engravings, works of henry Wolf, copies after Henry Sandham.
AUCTION RECORDS:
TORONTO, 26 May 1981, *Indian Encampment, Canada* (1873, watercolour, 4 3/4 x 13 1/4 ins / 11.9 x 33.8 cm) CAD 2,600. TORONTO, 14 May 1984, *Two Fishermen in a Landscape with River* (1874, oil on canvas, 39 1/4 x 59 ins / 100 x 150 cm) CAD 28,000. MONTREAL, 30 April 1990, *Water Babies* (watercolour, 10 1/4 x 36 1/4 ins / 26 x 92 cm) CAD 990. MONTREAL, 6 Dec 1994, *Travellers in the Winter Blizzard* (1875, oil on canvas, 14 x 22 1/4 ins / 35.5 x 56.5 cm) CAD 5,200.

SANDHOLT, Marie
Danish, 19th - 20th century.

Born 22 March 1872, in Copenhagen.
Painter. Figures, landscapes.
Marie Sandholt studied at the Kunstakademi in Copenhagen and completed her artistic education in Paris.

SANDI, Andrea
Italian, 17th century.
Active in Feltre (Veneto), Italy.
Sculptor (wood).
A pupil of Francesco Terilli, Andrea Sandi is noted for a wooden *Crucifix* in the church of S Vittore in Feltre.

SANDI, Antonio
Italian, 18th - 19th century.
Born 9 October 1733, in Belluno (Veneto); died 4 September 1817, in Puos d'Alpage.
Engraver (burin).
The brother of Giuseppe, Antonio Sandi worked in Venice.

SANDI, Giuseppe
Italian, 18th century.
Born c. 1720, in Puos d'Alpage; died 16 May 1770, in Belluno.
Engraver (burin).
Giuseppe Sandi, like his brother Antonio, worked in Venice.

SANDIER, Pierre René, called du Verger
School of Lorraine, 18th century.
Active in Lunéville at the beginning of the 18th century.
Sculptor.
Sandier worked at Lunéville and Einville palaces.

SANDIG, Armin
German, 20th century.
Born 1929, in Hof an der Saale.
Painter, watercolourist, lithographer.
Armin Sandig was to all intents and purposes self-taught. He spent time in Munich from 1949 to 1951 before settling in Hamburg. As a young man he took the occasional lesson in painting from nature, but over time his work became progressively abstract. He elected to paint in smaller formats rather than on a large scale. His watercolours and lithographs are developed from permutations of lines and dots which combine to develop a semblance of form.

He showed his work in numerous group exhibitions, including the 1975 Young Artists' Biennale in Paris and the 1961 International Exhibition of Graphic Arts in Tokyo. Solo exhibitions of his work have been held on a frequent basis, starting with Munich (1951), followed by Hamburg (1953) and then Stuttgart, Düsseldorf, Brunswick, Lübeck, Wuppertal and other cities.

SANDINO, Santillo. See **SANNINO**

SANDKUHL, Hermann
German, 19th - 20th century.
Born 14 April 1872, in Bremen.
Painter. Portraits, genre scenes, landscapes.
Hermann Sandkuhl studied under Carl L. N. Bantzer at the fine arts academy in Dresden and under Stanislas or Karl de Kalckreuth at the academy in Stuttgart or Weimar. He also studied at the Académie Julian in Paris.

SANDLE, Michael
British, 20th century.
Born 18 May 1936, in Weymouth (Dorset).
Active in England until 1970, in Canada 1970-1972, in Germany from 1973.
Sculptor (metal and fibreglass), painter (gouache), watercolourist, engraver. Figures, military subjects.
Leicester Group.
Michael Sandle studied at the Douglas School of Art and Technology on the Isle of Man from 1951 to 1954, and at the Slade School of Fine Art in London under Anthony Gross, Lynton Lamb and Ceri Richards from 1956 to 1959. He was awarded an Abbey Minor travelling scholarship and a scholarship from the French government in 1959, which he used to go to Paris to work in lithography at the Atelier Patris. He taught at the Leicester College of Art from 1961 to 1963, during which time he formed the Leicester Group, and then at Coventry College of Art until 1968. From 1970 to 1972 he was visiting associate professor at the University of Calgary and then at the University of Victoria in Canada. He moved to Germany in 1973, becoming professor of sculpture at Pforzheim in 1977 and at the Akademie der Bildenden Künste in Karlsruhe in 1980.

Sandle's work concentrates on themes of war and contempt for the mass media, often with satirical overtones, as in his bronze medallion *Imperatrix: Impudens Belgrano Medallion* (1986) with an image of Death resembling the British prime minister Margaret Thatcher as a censure of British policy in the Falklands War. The highly polished surfaces of his large-scale sculptures suggest military efficiency and gleaming weapons, as in his bronze *Der Trommler* (*The Drummer*) (1985). Sandle's use of arches and tunnels in his work reflects his interest in Japanese art and architecture, and he has also been inspired by the Neo-Classical architect Karl Friedrich Schinkel, the engineer Isambard Kingdom Brunel and the Victorian sculptor Sir Alfred Gilbert. Sandle began to make small-scale bronzes in limited editions in the 1980s, such as *Shrouded Figure* (1981). His drawings and paintings show a high degree of precision and often continue his themes of war, conflict and death, as in *Taking Liberties/The New Jerusalem* (1987, charcoal, watercolour and chalk).

Sandle has exhibited at *British Art 1940-1980*, Hayward Gallery, London (1980); *Sculptors' Drawings*, British Council touring exhibition (1984); *Das Automobil in der Kunst 1886-1986* (*The Car in Art 1886-1986*), Haus der Kunst, Munich (1986); *Which Side of the Fence? Contemporary Art at the Imperial War Museum*, Imperial War Museum, London (1987); and *Comic Iconoclasm*, Institute of Contemporary Arts, London (1987). In 1986 he was awarded the Nobutaka Shikanai Prize at the First Rodin Grand Prize Exhibition, Utsukushi-ga-hara Open Air Museum, Japan. He has executed numerous commissions, including his first public monument *St George and the Dragon*, London (1987-1988, bronze), which combined traditional equestrian sculptural forms with Futurist movement; and the *Memorial for the Victims of a Helicopter Disaster*, Mannheim Airport (1985).

BIBLIOGRAPHY:
'*Vera Lindsay in Discussion with Michael Sandle*' in *Studio International*, vol 178, periodical, 1969. *Michae Sandle: Recent Drawings and Bronzes*, exhibition catalogue, Fischer Fine Art Ltd Gallery, London, 1981. Petherbridge, D., '*Disquieting Memorials: Drawings and Sculpture of Michael Sandle*' in *Architecture Review*, vol 169, periodical, June 1981. Morgan, Stuart, '*Michael Sandle*' in *Artforum*, periodical, November 1981. McEwan, John, '*Michael Sandle*' in *Artscribe*, periodical, October 1983. *Michael Sandle: Recent Drawings and Bronzes*, exhibition catalogue, Fischer Fine Art Ltd, London, 1985. *Michael Sandle: Memorials for the Twentieth Century*, exhibition catalogue, Tate Gallery, Liverpool, 1995. McEwan, John, *The Sculpture of Michael Sandle*, illustrated book, Henry Moore Foundation, Much Hadham, 2002.

MUSEUMS AND GALLERIES:
LINCOLN (Usher Gallery): *A Mighty Blow for Freedom - Fuck the Media* (1988, bronze sculpture) - LONDON (British Council): *U-Boat Bunker* (1974-1975, mixed media drawing); *Submarines in Glass* (1973, gouache and ink); *Memorial to a Pilot (Version IV)* (1982, watercolour); *Bunker Moonlight* (1979, etching and aquatint); *Mine Working Isle of Man Series* (1978, etching) - LONDON (Imperial War Mus.): *Imperatrix: Impudens Belgrano Medallion* (1986, bronze medallion) -

LONDON (Tate Collection): *Twentieth-Century Memorial* (1971-1978, bronze, brass and wood sculpture); *Sketches for 'A Twentieth-Century Memorial'* (1972-1976, mixed media on paper); *Untitled* (1976, lithograph); *Der Trommler* (*The Drummer*) (1985-1987, bronze sculpture) - MANCHESTER (AG): *Blue Lozenge* (aquatint and etching) - MANCHESTER (Whitworth Art Gall.): *Brennendes Denkmal (Burning Monuments) III* (1984, watercolour); *Falangist Endgame* (1976, etching and aquatint) - SOUTHAMPTON (AG): *Japanese Armour* (aquatint).
AUCTION RECORDS:
LONDON, 13 June 2002, *Proposal for Euston Road no. 2* (brown patinated bronze, h. 20 ins / 51 cm) GBP 1,200. LONDON, 4 Dec 2002, *Drummer* (dark brown patinated bronze, h. 13 ins / 32 cm) GBP 1,500.

SANDLY, Paul, Pierre and Thomas.
See **SANDBY**

SANDMANN, François Joseph or Franz Joseph
French, 19th century.
Born 15 December 1805, in Strasbourg; died 1852, in Vienna, Austria.
Watercolourist, lithographer. Landscapes.
MUSEUMS AND GALLERIES:
STRASBOURG: *Landscape* (watercolour).

SANDMANN, Johann Caspar.
See **SANDTMANN**

SANDNER, Georg Ernst
German, 18th - 19th century.
Born 1736; died 15 March 1811, in Gera.
Painter. Portraits, landscapes.
MUSEUMS AND GALLERIES:
GERA (Stadtmus.): *View of Gera.*

SANDOL, Ulysse. See **SANDOZ**

SANDOMIRSKAYA, Beatrisa Yurevna
Russian, 20th century.
Born 1894, in Moscow; died 1974.
Sculptor.
Beatrisa Sandomirskaya sculpted populist subjects such as *Cotton Gatherer* a wooden sculpture, remarkable for its qualities of strength and expression, she showed in Paris; it was later acquired by the Soviet Ministry of Culture. She featured in *L'Art Russe des Scythes à nos jours* (*Russian Art from the Scythians to Today*), Galeries Nationales du Grand Palais, Paris (1967).
BIBLIOGRAPHY:
L'Art russe des Scythes à nos jours, exhibition catalogue, Gal. nationales du Grand Palais, Paris, 1967.

SANDOMURI, Alexander
Russian, 19th century.
Of Greek origin.
Active during the first half of the 19th century.
Portrait artist, lithographer.
Alexander Sandomuri studied at the art academy in St Petersburg where he was active until around 1830.

SANDONA, Matteo
Italian, 20th century.
Born 15 April 1883, in Schio; died 1964
Active in the USA.
Painter, engraver. Portraits, genre scenes.
Matteo Sandona was a pupil of Napoleone Nani and Mosè di Giosuè Bianchi and the Accademia Cignaroli in Verona. He emigrated to the USA where he became a member of the American Federation of Arts. He was awarded a number of distinctions including a silver medal in Portland in 1905.

He painted portraits of many famous Americans of his time.
MUSEUMS AND GALLERIES:
SAN FRANCISCO (California Palace of the Legion of Honor): *Portrait of Roscoe F. Oakes* (1923, pastel and chalk); *Tropical Scene* (19th-20th century, etching).

SANDONI, Giovanni Battista
Italian, 18th century.
Died 28 November 1758.
Active in Bologna.
Painter.
Giovanni Sandoni was the pupil of St Orlandi.

SANDOR, Antal or Anton
Hungarian, 20th century.
Born 3 November 1884, in Nemet Palanca.
Painter. Genre scenes.
Antal Sandor trained in Budapest, Munich and Paris.
MUSEUMS AND GALLERIES:
BUDAPEST (Szépmuvészeti Múz.): *On the Way to Mass.*

SANDOR, Bela or Adalbert
Hungarian, 19th - 20th century.
Born 17 June 1872, in Gyor.
Painter.
Bela Sandor trained in Budapest and Munich. He lived in Budapest.
MUSEUMS AND GALLERIES:
BUDAPEST.

SANDOR, István
Hungarian, 20th century.
Born 23 February 1905, in Budapest; died 22 March 1927, in Paris.
Painter, engraver. Portraits, genre scenes.
István Sandor trained under István (or Stephen) Reti. He engraved etchings.

SANDOR, Joszef
Hungarian, 20th century.
Born 7 December 1887, in Gyömro.
Painter, engraver.
Joszef Sandor trained in Munich under Erwin Knirr and Christian Jank; he engraved etchings.
MUSEUMS AND GALLERIES:
BUDAPEST.

SANDOR, Mathias
Hungarian, 19th - 20th century.
Born 10 July 1857; died 3 November 1920, in New York.
Active in the USA.
Painter. Portraits, local scenes, landscapes.
Mathias Sandor trained in New York and Paris. He emigrated as a young man to the USA; he painted scenes of the life of the Hopi Indians.

SANDOR, Moric
Hungarian, 20th century.
Born 1885, in Felsöalap; died 7 April 1924, in Budapest.
Painter.
Moric Sandor trained in Budapest and Vienna.

SANDORFI, Istvan, later Étienne
French, 20th - 21st century.
Born 12 June 1948, in Budapest, Hungary.
Painter, lithographer. Figures, nudes, portraits, still-lifes.
Istvan Sandorfi fled Hungary as a child and lived with his family in Germany from 1956 to 1958, then moved again to France and settled in Paris in 1958. In around 1970, the work of Sandorfi was compared with American Hyperrealism. It is true to say, that his painting seeks to be as precise as possible. In his search for imitative renderings and out of a desire to make details legible, he deploys a technique close to Hyperrealism. He appears to exist only to paint. His cold, smooth and impersonal technique demands perfect equip-

ment, perfect materials and a dazzling range of colours, which he keeps in minute order. He paints with his curtains permanently closed, under artificial light. He composes each picture through the projection (simultaneous and juxtaposed or superimposed) of a number of slides. Once the composition has been finalised, the picture will require several months of work to complete.

In his early years, he painted portraits and self-portraits, often grimacing and with an accent on physical imperfection. He expressed anguish, tragedy and morbidity with an almost sadistic or masochistic complaisance. Later he turned away from self-portraits and began a series of portraits of his own daughter, transferring onto her his own slightly morbid narcissism. He also painted several brilliantly executed still-lifes. His world is above all made up of figures, often on foot, in a state more or less of undress or naked with the genitals shown in a provocative and openly sexual manner. The face, hands and feet either are not drawn or are simply non-existent, as if all tangled up in sheets. The figures stand motionless in closed interiors under pale lighting. They are haggard couples, women and anguished teenagers. They are emotionally bruised, with drama lurking beneath.

In 1973, he had his first solo exhibition, at the Musée d'Art Moderne de la Ville de Paris. Further solo exhibitions include: 1984 Paris, organised by the Galerie Isy Brachot at the Foire Internationale d'Art Contemporain (FIAC); 1989, Paris, presented by the Galerie Lavignes-Bastille at the FIAC; 1991, Paris, Galerie Prazan-Fitoussi. Further exhibitions include in 1988, the Armory Show in New York, a retrospective at the Abbaye des Cordeliers, Chateauroux, and a show at the Louise K. Meisel Gallery, New York; 1991, Galerie Prazan-Fitoussi; 1993, Maison des Princes in Pérouges, and Galerie Guénégaud in Paris and the Galerie Mann; 1994 and 1997, Jane Kahan Gallery, New York; 1999, Galerie Tempera, Brussells, and Galerihuset, Copenhagen; and 2001, l'Accademia d'Ungheria, Rome, and Galerie de l'Europe, Paris.

Auction records:

Paris, 6 March 1978, *Austere Self-portrait* (1970, acrylic/canvas, 63 1/2 x 51 1/4 ins / 161.5 x 130 cm) FRf 5,800. Paris, 27 Oct 1980, *Incident de parcours* (1973, acrylic/canvas, 69 x 69 ins / 175 x 175 cm) FRF 9,000. Paris, 25 Oct 1982, *Hallucination* (1972, acrylic/canvas, 21 1/4 x 25 1/2 ins / 54 x 65 cm) FRF 12,000. Paris, 26 Nov 1984, *Pigsty* (1979, oil on canvas, 76 3/4 x 110 1/4 ins / 195 x 280 cm) FRF 105,000. Paris, 6 June 1985, *Handmaid* (1976, acrylic/canvas, 59 x 59 ins / 150 x 150 cm) FRF 66,000. Paris, 28 Oct 1988, *D. vue à travers un soutien-gorge* (1978, acrylic/canvas, D: 31 1/2 ins / 80 cm) FRF 29,000. Paris, 14 Oct 1989, *No Man's Land* (1985-1987, oil on canvas, 57 1/2 x 45 ins / 146 x 114 cm) FRF 50,000. Paris, 13 Dec 1989, *L'Offrande de la culture* (oil on canvas, 86 1/2 x 59 ins / 220 x 150 cm) FRF 95,000. Paris, 18 Feb 1990, *Self-portrait in Front of a Landscape* (1972, oil on canvas, 45 3/4 x 28 3/4 ins / 116.5 x 73 cm) FRF 22,000. New York, 23 Feb 1990, *She: White Portrait* (1987, oil on canvas, 76 3/4 x 38 ins / 195 x 96.5 cm) USD 16,500. Paris, 8 April 1990, *Amendis, Black Painting* (1989, oil on canvas, 57 1/2 x 45 ins / 146 x 114 cm) FRF 95,000. Paris, 26 April 1990, *Catherine par temps d'orage* (oil on canvas, 31 1/2 x 35 1/2 ins / 80 x 90 cm) FRF 45,000. Paris, 3 May 1990, *That One's an Angel* (oil on canvas, 46 x 35 ins / 116 x 89 cm) FRF 75,000. Paris, 29 June 1990, *The Pardon* (oil on canvas, 45 x 63 3/4 ins / 114 x 162 cm) FRF 60,000. Paris, 25 June 1991, *Sock Story* (1977, acrylic/canvas, 45 x 63 3/4 ins / 114 x 162 cm) FRF 38,000. Paris, 6 July 1992, *Untitled* (lithograph, 43 1/4 x 30 3/4 ins / 110 x 78 cm) FRF 6,000. Paris, 24 Oct 1993, *Double Nude and Blue Socks* (1980, acrylic/canvas, 64 x 51 1/4 ins / 162.5 x 130 cm) FRF 35,000. Paris, 22 Nov 1995, *Figure Portrait* (1978, acrylic/canvas, 78 3/4 x 59 ins / 200 x 150 cm) FRF 30,000. Amsterdam, 18 June 1996, *Self-portrait in Pink of the Birth of Venus* (1978, oil on canvas, 95 x 67 1/4 ins / 241 x 170.5 cm) NLG 1,495. Paris, 17 Dec 1996, *Palette de la mémoire ou la Souillure des chromosomes* (1980, oil on canvas, 76 3/4 x 106 1/4 ins / 195 x 270 cm) FRF 115,000. Paris, 28 April 1997, *Photo Portrait No. II* (1975, oil on canvas, 76 3/4 x 45 ins / 195 x 114 cm) FRF 14,500.

SANDOZ, Adolf Karol

Polish, 19th - 20th century.
Born 1845, in Odessa, in 1848 in Trybusovka according to some sources.
Active in France.
Painter, illustrator. Portraits, genre scenes.
Orientalism.

Adolf Karol Sandoz trained in architecture in Paris at the École des Beaux-Arts. He studied painting with Puvis de Chavannes and Élie Delaunay.

He worked as an illustrator for a number of publishing houses including Hachette, Quantin and Delagrave. He contributed to the illustration of an edition of the *Complete Works* of Béranger. His illustrations were praised for their landscape scenery. He often portrayed monkeys in order to mock human behaviour. As a painter, he was essentially an Orientalist and his themes suggest that he made a trip to Algeria.

Bibliography:

Osterwalder, Marcus (ed.), *Dictionnaire des illustrateurs 1800-1914*, Ides et Calendes, Neuchâtel, 1989.

Museums and Galleries:

Lviv (Gallery of Paintings): *Inside a Hut in Biskra*; *Arab Woman*; *Portrait of the Sheik's Wife at the El-Kantara Oasis*; *Garden Art*.

Auction records:

London, 19 Nov 1993, *At the Oasis* (1879, oil on canvas, 16 1/4 x 24 1/2 ins / 41 x 62 cm) GBP 9,430. Paris, 8 March 1999, *Young Women in a Hammam* (oil on canvas, 13 x 16 ins / 33 x 41 cm) FRF 27,000. Paris, 8 Dec 2003, *Walking in the Gardens at the Mosque* (oil on canvas, 18 x 23 ins / 45 x 58 cm) EUR 3,500.

SANDOZ, Auguste

French, 18th century.
Painter, engraver, draughtsman.

Sandoz was active at the end of the 18th century. He exhibited portraits of Marat, Charlotte Corday and André Chénier at the Salon.

SANDOZ, Auguste

Swiss, 20th century.
Born 1901; died 1964.
Painter, draughtsman.

Auguste Sandoz painted from life, typically the human anatomy, but he 'decomposed' his subjects by resolutely breaking down their formal structure in a manner reminiscent of the Post-Cubist purism of Amédée Ozenfant and Jeanneret.

A-SANDOZ

Auction records:

Lucerne, 24 Nov 1990, *Woman* (1928, drawing/paper, 10 3/4 x 7 3/4 ins / 27.5 x 20 cm) CHF 2,000. Zurich, 17-18 June 1996, *Transparency* (1930, oil/plywood, 25 1/2 x 19 ins / 65 x 48.5 cm) CHF 6,000. Lucerne, 23 Nov 1996, *Cubist Faces* (1928, oil on paper, 18 x 11 3/4 ins / 46 x 30 cm) CHF 4,200.

SANDOZ, Claude

Swiss, 20th - 21st century.
Born 1946, in Zurich.
Painter.

Claude Sandoz was a pupil of Max Mühlenen, then worked in Rome and Amsterdam. In 1984, the museum in Solothurn put on a solo exhibition of his work.

SANDOZ, Edouard-Marcel
Swiss, 20th century.
Born 21 March 1881, in Basel; died 20 March 1971, in Lausanne.
Sculptor, potter. Figures, animals, cats. Busts, objets d'art, designs for ceramics.
Orientalism.

Edouard-Marcel Sandoz was an heir to the eponymous Swiss chemicals company dynasty. He trained as a chemist and physicist and has since been credited with a number of inventions, including black light. That said, he opted to be an artist and spent three years studying at the industrial art college in Geneva before moving to Paris in 1905 to study under Antonin Injalbert at the École des Beaux-Arts. He was made a Chevalier of the Légion d'Honneur.

Although he also painted and designed jewellery and numerous decorative objects, he was first and foremost a sculptor. He sculpted several portraits, chiefly in his early days, including a *Bust of a Man* (1904), a *Young Nude Girl Seated and Reading a Book* (1906), a *Woman Wearing a Wide-brimmed Hat* (1910) and a *Woman with an Egret* (1911). However, it is as an animal sculptor that he found his true vocation. He worked in bronze, stone, marble and, from 1924, in more exotic materials such as onyx, quartz, malachite, lapis-lazuli, aquamarine, garnet, topaz and tourmaline, to create a veritable bestiary of animal figures distinguished by their imaginative and decorative properties and, not least, by a subtle sense of humour.

Sandoz exhibited examples of his work at the National Fine Arts Exhibition in Lausanne in 1904. He would go on to exhibit in Paris, notably at the Salon de la Société Nationale des Beaux-Arts in 1906. He also exhibited in Brussels and Barcelona. Since his death, his work has been shown at various group exhibitions, most notably perhaps at *Haviland. L'Art et la Matière* (*Haviland: Art and Substance*), an exhibition held at the Musée des Arts Décoratifs in Bordeaux in 2003 to chart 160 years of the existence of the Haviland company.

Following his death in 1971, a number of retrospectives were held, among them several during the 1980s at the Cantonal Museum in Lausanne and at the Galerie Gismondi in Paris, together with *Images d'Atelier* (*Workshop Images*) at the Fondation Taylor in Paris (1991) and *De la Sculpture à la Porcelaine: Edouard-Marcel Sandoz* (*From Sculpture to Porcelain: Edouard-Marcel Sandoz*), an exhibition held in 1999 at the Musée National Adrien Dubouché in Limoges.

BIBLIOGRAPHY:
Genevoix, Maurice, *Le Bestiaire d'Édouard Marcel Sandoz*, La Bibliothèque des Arts, Lausanne, Paris, 1972. Marcilhac, Félix, *Édouard-Marcel Sandoz, sculpteur figuriste et animalier*, catalogue raisonné, Éd. de l'Amateur, Paris, 1993. *De la sculpture à la porcelaine: Édouard Marcel Sandoz*, exhibition catalogue, Musée national Adrien-Dubouché, Limoges, 1999.

MUSEUMS AND GALLERIES:
LAUSANNE (Cantonal MFA): *Great Dane* (1914, marble, in the round); *Head of a Panther* (1925-1930, lost-wax bronze, high relief); *Man in a Horse-box* (lost-wax bronze, in the round) - PARIS (Mus. d'Orsay): *Portrait Bust of A. Willette.*

AUCTION RECORDS:
NEW YORK, 2 May 1972, *Condor* (black marble) USD 7,750. GENEVA, 29 April 1974, *Large Fish* (bronze) CHF 7,000. PARIS, 24 March 1976, *Cat* (1927, brown-patinated bronze, h. 15 3/4 ins / 40 cm) FRF 5,000. ENGHIEN-LES-BAINS, 8 April 1979, *Cat* (1927, black-patinated bronze, h. 15 3/4 ins / 40 cm) FRF 12,200. MONTE CARLO, 19 April 1982, *Seated Monkey* (c. 1925, bronze, h. 11 ins / 28 cm) FRF 17,000. ENGHIEN-LES-BAINS, 11 Dec 1983, *Young Girl with Fennec* (bronze, h. 18 ins / 45.5 cm) FRF 45,000. PARIS, 18 Nov 1985, *Adam and Eve Represented by Two Monkeys* (bronze) FRF 41,100. PARIS, 3 Feb 1986, *Fennec* (patinated bronze medal, l. 11 3/4 ins / 30 cm) FRF 17,500. PARIS, 13 Dec 1989, *Woman with Egret* (1911, black-patinated bronze, h. 226 1/2 ins / 575 cm) FRF 170,000. GENEVA, 19 Jan 1990, *Pair of Fennecs* (bronze, 11 x 11 ins / 27 x 27 cm) CHF 32,000. PARIS, 26 Jan 1991, *Percheron* (lost-wax bronze, h. 13 1/4 ins / 33.5 cm) FRF 38,000. LILLE, 14 Dec 1992, *Hare* (bronze, h. 4 ins / 10 cm) FRF 16,500. PARIS, 9 March 1994, *Owl* (empty wooden pouch decorated with an owl) FRF 25,000. PARIS, 5 April 1995, *Cat Sitting* (1926, lost-wax bronze, h. 16 1/2 ins / 42 cm, l. 9 ins/23 cm, depth 8 1/2 ins/21.5 cm) FRF 68,000. PARIS, 23 June 1995, *Woman with a Wide-brimmed Hat* (1910, bronze, h. 22 ins / 56 cm) FRF 85,000. PARIS, 11 April 1996, *The Little Dog Dominique* (bronze, h. 6 1/2 ins / 16.7 cm) FRF 31,000. PARIS, 26-27 Nov 1996, *Fish* (bronze, h. 4 3/4 ins / 12.3 cm) FRF 11,500. PARIS, 27 Feb 1997, *Owl* (chromed bronze, h. 4 3/4 ins / 12 cm) FRF 6,200. PARIS, 11 June 1997, *Horseman* (black-patinated bronze, 6 1/2 x 4 3/4 ins / 16.5 x 12 cm) FRF 43,000. PARIS, 22 Nov 1999, *Carp in Water* (stone, h. 16 ins / 40 cm, w. 30 ins/75 cm) FRF 430,000. PARIS, 22 Nov 1999, *Condor* (black patinated bronze, h. 15 ins / 39 cm, w. 24 ins/60 cm) FRF 530,000. PONTOISE, 16 Dec 2000, *Magpie* (silver and bronze, h. 12 ins / 30 cm) FRF 108,000. PONTOISE, 16 Dec 2000, *Cockatoo, Head to the Right, Crest Raised* (brown-red patinated bronze, h. 17 ins / 42 cm) FRF 150,000. PARIS, 18 May 2001, *Group of Three Fennecs* (1938, brown patinated bronze, h. 9 ins / 23 cm) FRF 180,000. PARIS, 21 May 2001, *Head of a Smiling Faun* (red marble, 23 x 16x14 ins / 58 x 40x36 cm) FRF 730,000. CALAIS, 10 March 2002, *Perched Budgerigar with Head Turned* (green nephrite, 11 x 11x6 ins / 29 x 29x15 cm) EUR 23,000. PARIS, 11 Dec 2002, *Lily* (brown patinated bronze, 17 x 6x6 ins / 44 x 14x16 cm) EUR 26,500. PARIS, 19 May 2003, *Seated Fennec* (brown patinated bronze, h. 11 ins / 29 cm) EUR 8,500. PARIS, 24 Nov 2003, *Toad* (amethyst, 6 x 9x5 ins / 16 x 22x13 cm) EUR 25,000. PARIS, 29 June 2004, *Monkeys* (wood, 11 x 28x8 ins / 28 x 70x21 cm) EUR 15,000. PARIS, 1 Dec 2004, *Monkey with Fly* (1911, marble, 5 x 4x8 ins / 12 x 10x21 cm) EUR 23,000.

SANDOZ, Gérard
French, 20th century.
Born 1902, in Paris.
Painter, poster artist, worker in precious metals.
Jewels.

Gérard Sandoz's father kept a goldsmith's shop and his uncle, the decorative artist and architect Paul Follot, introduced him to modern design. He created remarkably restrained jewellery, often made of composite materials.

BIBLIOGRAPHY:
Paris-Moscou, 1900-1930, exhibition catalogue, Éd. du Centre Georges-Pompidou, Paris, 1979.

SANDOZ, Ulysse, or Sandol
Swiss, 19th century.
Born c. 1788, in La Chaux-de-Fonds; died 1815, in Paris.
Draughtsman. Portraits.

Ulysse Sandoz went to Paris in 1812 and joined David's studio. He died of consumption before he was able to realise his promise.

MUSEUMS AND GALLERIES:
NEUCHÂTEL: *Self-portrait* (black pencil).

SANDOZ-LASSIEUR, Bertha
Swiss, 20th century.
Born 1882, in Geneva; died 1919.
Painter.

Bertha Sandoz-Lassieur worked alongside Cuno Amiet and Giovanni Giacometti and, in Paris, with Paul Signac and Charles-Edmond Cross.

SANDOZ-ROLLIN, David Alphonse de (Baron)
Swiss, 18th century.

Born 1740; died 1809, in Neuchâtel.
Watercolourist, draughtsman. Landscapes.

MUSEUMS AND GALLERIES:
NEUCHÂTEL (MAH): watercolours; around 30 drawings.

SANDRART, Auguste von (Fra)
German, 19th century.
Active in Berlin.
Painter. Portraits, genre scenes.

Auguste von Sandrart exhibited in Berlin from 1856 to 1874. She is noted for a *Portrait of Emperor William I*, and for her *Child and Dog* at the Ravenet Gallery in Berlin.

SANDRART, Jakob von
German, 17th century.
Born 31 May 1630, in Frankfurt am Main; died 15 August 1708, in Nuremberg.
Draughtsman, engraver (burin).

Jakob von Sandrart was a child when he and his family, including his uncle Joachim von Sandrart I, had to flee religious persecution, moving to Hamburg and then to The Hague. He went to Amsterdam with his uncle around 1640, was a pupil of C. Danskerts and then of W. Hondjus in The Hague or Danzig (now Gdansk, Poland). He later lived in Regensburg and was an art dealer in Nuremberg. He engraved religious subjects and portraits. He may also have been a painter.

SANDRART, Jan or Johann von
German, 17th century.
Born c. 1588, in Frankfurt; died after 1679.
Painter, engraver (etching).

Jan von Sandrart lived for a long time in Rome, then in the Netherlands, and married Rachel Wurtz in Frankfurt in 1613. He is noted for his *Family Picture* (Neuville Collection in Frankfurt), *Annunciation, Christ Entering Jerusalem, Miracle of the Barley Loaves* (Idstein), and *Bohemian Encampment* (Schwerin). He is also noted for an engraving (a leaf with ornaments, arabesques and flowers).

SANDRART, Joachim von I
German, 17th century.
Born 12 May 1606, in Frankfurt am Main; died 14 October 1688, in Nuremberg.
Painter, engraver (etching), art writer.

Joachim von Sandrart I was born in Frankfurt to a family forced to seek refuge from religious persecution in Germany. His masters included Daniel Soréau in Hanau, Peter Isselburg in Nuremberg in 1620, and Aegidius Sadeler in Prague in 1622. In 1623 he returned to his parents' house in Frankfurt, but left shortly after for Utrecht and the home of Gerard Honthorst, whom he accompanied to London in 1627. He studied the collections of Charles I, the duke of Buckingham and the duke of Arundel.

He returned to Frankfurt for a short time before leaving for the Italian Tyrol, where he remained for eight years, striking up friendships with Nicolas Poussin and Claude Lorraine in Rome. He studied Titian and Veronese in Venice, then, forced to leave the city on account of the plague, he visited Bologna, Florence, Ferrara, Rome and Naples, where he was present during an eruption of Vesuvius. On his return to Rome he painted the *Portrait of Pope Urban VIII*, and Velázquez, who had just bought paintings by each of the 12 foremost masters of the period for the king of Spain, commissioned him to paint the *Death of Seneca* (Erfurt).

Von Sandrart returned to Frankfurt in 1635 via Florence, Milan and Switzerland, but the plague and the war forced him to move on. He went to Cologne and then to Amsterdam with his wife Johanna von Mickau of Stockau, whom he had married in 1637. Since his wife's property had been pillaged and destroyed by the French, he settled in Munich in 1647, then in Nuremberg in 1649. In that year he painted the *Peace Banquet*. Having been summoned to Vienna by Emperor Ferdinand III, Von Sandrart returned to Stockau and received visits from princes. He worked for Elector Prince Ferdinand Marie of Bavaria and in 1660 settled in Augsburg. In 1674 he remarried, this time to Esther Barbara Blomberg, daughter of a Nuremberg councillor, and settled in Nuremberg. He was very famous and received the highest honours from sovereigns from all over the world. He was also a collector and wrote numerous works on art, including the *Teutsche Akademie* published in 1675, which contains a good deal of first-hand information. M. Merian was his pupil around 1637.

MUSEUMS AND GALLERIES:
AMSTERDAM: *Company of Captain Cornelis Bicken Ready to Escort Marie de Medici in 1638; Pieter Corneliz Hoofs; Hendrick Bicker Eva Geclovinck; Jacob Bicker; Alida Bicker; Odysseus and Nausicaa* - AUGSBURG: *St Peter Casting the Net* - BAMBERG: *Beheading of St John; Mary Protecting the Ecclesiastical State and the Secular State* - BERGAMO (Accademia Carrara): *The Good Samaritan* - BERLIN (National Mus.): *Death of Seneca* - BRUNSWICK: *Fish-seller* - BUDAPEST: *Two Male Portraits* - ERFURT: *Death of Seneca* - FLORENCE: *Apollo Rejoicing at Having Killed the Serpent Python; The Artist* - GÖTEBORG: *Battle with Spears* - GRAZ (Landesmus. Joanneum): *Female Portrait* - MACERATA (Mus. e Pinacoteca Comunale): *Male Portrait* - MILAN (Pinacoteca di Brera): *The Samaritan Woman in the Gospel* - MOSCOW (Rumiantsev Mus.): *Moneylender* - MUNICH (Bayerisches Nationalmus.): *Portrait of Elector Adelheid Henrietta; Duke William of Pfalz-Neuburg; Portrait of a Prince* - MÜNSTER (Westfälisches Landesmus.): *Madonna with the Temple of Peace* - OBERSCHLEISSHEIM (Neues Schloss Schleissheim, Staatsgal.): *The Twelve Months* (12 paintings); *St Gaetan Healing the Plague-stricken; Jacob's Dream; Philip William of Neuburg, Later Elector Palatine* - RENNES: *Holy Family in a Landscape* - RIGA (MM): *Cavalryman* - SPEYER (Historisches Mus. der Pfalz): *Engagement of St Catherine; Portrait of Wolfgang Wilhelm of Pfalz-Neuburg* - VIENNA: *Night; Archimedes; Minerva and Saturn Protecting the Arts and Science; Marriage of St Catherine* - VIENNA (Liechtenstein Mus.): *Archimedes; Reception of the Austrian Envoy Schmidt by the Sultan* - WÜRZBURG: *Descent from the Cross.*

AUCTION RECORDS:
NEW YORK, 3 Feb 1938, *Female Portrait*, USD 370; *Portrait of a Gentleman*, USD 380. LONDON, 25-26 May 1941, *Female Portrait* (dated 1643, signed) GBP 54. LONDON, 27 April 1966, *St Paul*, Gns 720. LONDON, 10 July 1981, *Portrait of Samuel Coster* (oil on canvas, 47 x 41½ ins / 119.4 x 105.2 cm) GBP 4,500. VIENNA, 22 June 1983, *River and Mountain Landscape with Figures* (oil/copper, 5½ x 8¼ ins / 14 x 21 cm) ATS

65,000. HEIDELBERG, 12 Oct 2001, *Allegory of Miserliness* (oil on canvas, 30 x 24 ins / 76 x 61 cm) DEM 8,000. LONDON, 10 July 2002, *Virgin with the Christ Child Dictating the Gospel to St Luke* (black and red chalk, 6 x 4 ins / 15 x 11 cm) GBP 1,900.

SANDRART, Joachim von II
German, 17th century.
Born 26 July 1668, in Nuremberg; died 15 December 1691, in London.
Engraver (burin), draughtsman.

Joachim von Sandrart II was the son of Jakob von Sandrart and a pupil of Joachim von Sandrart I.

MUSEUMS AND GALLERIES:
BERLIN (Kupferstichkabinet): *Mythological Scene* (seven drawings).

SANDRART, Johann Jakob von
German, 17th century.
Born 1655, in Regensburg; died 24 March 1698, in Nuremberg.
Engraver, draughtsman.

Johann Jakob von Sandrart was the son and pupil of Jakob von Sandrart and the father of Lorenz von Sandrart. He produced burin engravings and etchings.

MUSEUMS AND GALLERIES:
BERLIN (Kupferstichkabinet): 13 drawings - NUREMBERG (Germanisches Nationalmus.): drawings.

AUCTION RECORDS:
NEW YORK, 20 Jan 1982, *Time Discovering Truth* (black chalk and wash heightened with white/grey paper, 15 x 14 1/4 ins / 38 x 36.5 cm) USD 1,050. LONDON, 3 April 1995, *Set of 15 Sketches of Illustrations for Ovid's Metamorphoses* (ink and wash, each 6 x 7 3/4 ins / 15.5 x 20 cm) GBP 2,300.

SANDRART, Lorenz von
German, 18th century.
Born c. 1682, in Nuremberg; died 13 January 1753, in Stuttgart.
Engraver (etching), enameller.

Lorenz von Sandrart was the son of Johann Jakob von Sandrart. He engraved a frontispiece for an edition of Ovid's *Metamorphoses* published in 1700.

SANDRART, Philipp von
German, 17th century.
Born 15 January 1615, in Frankfurt am Main.
Painter.

MUSEUMS AND GALLERIES:
NUREMBERG (Germanisches Nationalmus.): *Portrait of a Young Man* (1645).

SANDRART, Suzanne Maria von, later Frau Alt
German, 18th century.
Born 1707, in Nuremberg; died 1769.
Miniaturist, draughtswoman.

Suzanne Maria von Sandrart was undoubtedly a direct descendant of Philipp von Sandrart.

MUSEUMS AND GALLERIES:
BAMBERG (Staatsbibliothek): *Hare and Quail* (miniature).

SANDRART, Suzanne Marie de, or Suzanne Maria von, later Frau Auer, then Frau Endter
German, 17th - 18th century.
Born 10 August 1658, in Nuremberg; died 20 December 1716, in Nuremberg.
Painter, engraver, draughtswoman.

Suzanne Marie de Sandrart was the daughter and pupil of Jakob von Sandrart. She married the painter Hans Auer, then the bookseller W. M. Endter. She engraved portraits, religious subjects and genre scenes.

MUSEUMS AND GALLERIES:
NUREMBERG (Germanisches Nationalmus.): *Young Girl Lighting a Lamp.*

SANDRES, Frans. See **SANDERS**

SANDRES, Jean
Flemish School, 15th century.
Active in Tournai during the first half of the 15th century.
Sculptor.

In 1434 Jean Sandres carved a retable for the church of St-Nicolas in Tournai.

SANDRETIS, Stephanus de
15th century.
Active in the mid-15th century.
Illuminator, copyist.

The manuscript *Bartholomaci de Glanville de Rerum proprietatibus* in Amiens Library was copied and illuminated by Stephanus de Sandretis.

MUSEUMS AND GALLERIES:
AMIENS (Bibliothèque): *Bartholomaci de Glanville de Rerum proprietatibus.*

SANDREUTER, Hans
Swiss, 19th century.
Born 11 May 1850, in Basel; died 1 June 1901, in Riehen.
Painter, watercolourist, lithographer. Genre scenes, landscapes, landscapes with figures.
Art Nouveau.

Hans Sandreuter spent three years in Basel completing his apprenticeship in lithography. It would seem that he continued his studies in Würzburg and Verona. He was a pupil of Franz Xaver (?) Barth at the academy of fine arts in Munich and of Arnold Böcklin, whom he accompanied to Florence in 1874. Three years later he also worked in Paris. He returned to Italy and remained there from 1880 until 1884. In 1885 he settled in Basel.

Sandreuter's paintings reflect the strong influence of Böcklin. He later developed a more decorative style, the ornamental character of which is grounded in Art Nouveau.

The Kunstmuseum in Basel put on an exhibition of his work in 2001.

MUSEUMS AND GALLERIES:
BASEL: *Roman Sentinels*; *A Quadriga*; *Fountain of Youth*; *Forest of Chestnut Trees near Bignasco*; *Beech Forest with Woodcutters* (five watercolours) - BERN: *At the Gates of Paradise* - DRESDEN: *June Landscape in the Area around Basel* - GENEVA (MAH): *Banks of the Rhine*; *Seealp Lake* (two watercolours) - NEUCHÂTEL: *River Banks*; a watercolour.

AUCTION RECORDS:
ZURICH, 12 Nov 1976, *Children Fishing at the Edge of a Stream* (oil on canvas, 23 1/2 x 36 1/4 ins / 60 x 92 cm) CHF 2,000. ZURICH, 20 May 1977, *Children Playing in Undergrowth* (1880, oil on canvas, 28 1/4 x 45 1/4 ins / 72 x 115 cm) CHF 4,000. LUCERNE, 25 May 1982, *Scene from the Decameron* (1899, oil on canvas, 27 1/4 x 22 ins / 69 x 55 cm) CHF 15,000. MADRID, 12 June 1984, *Flower Meadow* (1878, oil on canvas, 35 x 51 1/4 ins / 89 x 130 cm) CHF 3,800. ZURICH, 4 June 1992, *Boats on Lake Maggiore* (watercolour and pencil/paper, 7 x 10 1/4 ins / 17.5 x 26 cm) CHF 1,356. ZURICH, 2 June 1994, *Evening on the Banks of the Doubs near Soubais in Switzerland* (1895, oil on canvas, 33 3/4 x 47 1/4 ins / 86 x 120 cm) CHF 5,520. ZURICH, 14 Sept 1999, *Waterfall near Tivoli* (oil on canvas, 45 x 28 ins / 115 x 70 cm) CHF 3,300.

SANDRI, Stefano
Italian, 18th century.
Born c. 1713, in Verona; died 14 October 1781, in Verona.
Painter. Religious subjects.

Stefano Sandri was taught by G.B. Tiepolo. He produced religious paintings for churches in Murano and Verona.

SANDRIN, Jean
French, 15th century.
Active in Rouen.
Painter.

Jean Sandrin painted 16 statues of the apostles and evangelists for the abbey church of Bec in 1433.

SANDRINO, Pietro
Italian, 16th - 17th century.
Active in Brescia.
Painter.

Pietro Sandrino was the brother of Tommaso Sandrino. He painted the frescoes on the ceiling of the church of S Caterina, in Brescia.

SANDRINO, Tommaso
Italian, 17th century.
Born 1575, in Brescia; died 1630.
Painter. History painting, architectural views.

The legacy of Tommaso Sandrino, the brother of Pietro Sandrino, includes the ceilings of the churches of S Faustino and S Domenico in Brescia, and that of the cathedral in the same city. He also worked on various public monuments in Milan and Ferrara.

SANDRO DI GUIDO, or Sandro Guidone
Italian, 13th century.
Active in Siena in 1296.
Illuminator.

SANDRO DI MARCO. See **FERRUCCI Sandro** or **Alessandro di Marco**

SANDRO, DI. See first name

SANDROCK, Christoph
Dutch, 19th - 20th century.
Born 23 January 1865, in Rotterdam.
Active in Berlin.
Painter. Portraits.

SANDROCK, Leonhard
German, 19th - 20th century.
Born 5 June 1867, in Neumarkt (Silesia); died 1945, in Berlin.
Painter, engraver. Scenes with figures, industrial landscapes.

Leonhard Sandrock studied under the seascape painter W. B. Hermann Heschke. His own work focused on themes drawn from the modern industrial age, such as factories, naval dockyards and railways.

Leonhard Sandrock

MUSEUMS AND GALLERIES:
ERFURT: *Naval Dockyard* - ESSEN: *Naval Dockyard* - HANOVER (Niedersächsisches Landesmus.): *Steamship under Construction* - WROCLAW: *Locomotive Shed*.

AUCTION RECORDS:
COLOGNE, 18 March 1989, *Martinswerk* (oil on card, 22½ x 17¾ ins / 57 x 45 cm) DEM 1,500. HAMBURG, 1 Sept 1999, *Shrimp Fishermen, Cuxhaven* (oil on canvas, 24 x 31 ins / 60 x 80 cm) DEM 6,500. COLOGNE, 28 Oct 1999, *Boat on a Canal in Amsterdam* (oil on canvas) DEM 9,000. HAMBURG, 19 Feb 2000, *Fishing Boats Returning to Harbour* (oil on canvas, 30 x 28 ins / 76 x 72 cm) DEM 10,500. KÖNIGSTEIN, 3 June 2000, *Steel Factory in the Evening* (oil on canvas, 29 x 35 ins / 73 x 90 cm) DEM 7,200. BERLIN, 30 June 2001, *On the Lower Elbe* (oil on board, 19 x 23 ins / 49 x 59 cm) DEM 4,000. COPENHAGEN, 3 Sept 2001, *Steamship in Hamburg Harbour* (oil on canvas, 18 x 22 ins / 45 x 56 cm) DKK 34,000. MUNICH, 4 Dec 2002, *Old Windmill on the Bank of a River with Small Harbour Town* (oil on canvas, 49 x 41 ins / 125 x 105 cm) EUR 2,200. HAMBURG, 5 Dec 2002, *Hamburg Harbour* (oil on board, 22 x 26 ins / 55 x 65 cm) EUR 6,500. FRANKFURT, 8 March 2003, *Winter Flood, Hamburg* (oil on canvas, 31 x 45 ins / 80 x 115 cm) EUR 2,600. HAMBURG, 6 Dec 2003, *View of St Katharein, Canal and Church* (oil on canvas, 30 x 28 ins / 76 x 72 cm) EUR 3,500. AHLDEN, 14 May 2004, *Harbour Fishermen, Hamburg* (oil on canvas, 19 x 26 ins / 49 x 66 cm) EUR 2,900.

SANDS, Antony. See **SANDYS Anthony Frederick Augustus**

SANDS, Ethel
American, 19th - 20th century.
Born 6 July 1873, in Newport (Rhode Island); died 19 March 1962, in London.
From 1900 active, then naturalised in England.
Painter. Interiors with figures, still-lifes.
London Group.

Ethel Sands moved with her family to England shortly after her birth. She became the pupil of Eugène Carrière in Paris from 1896-1900. In Paris she met her lifelong companion, Nan Hudson. She knew and worked with Walter Sickert and the Camden Town group of artists. From 1900-1920 she lived in Garsington, then moved to London and adopted British nationality. In 1913 she took part in founding the London Group. During World Wars I and II she served as a nurse.

Sands's work shows the influence of Vuillard, as in her *Spare Room*. She exhibited in Paris, from 1903 at the Salon d'Automne, of which she became a member in 1913. She had a number of solo exhibitions, the first in 1912.

BIBLIOGRAPHY:
Baron, Wendy, *Miss Ethel Sands and Her Circle*, Peter Owen, London, 1977.

MUSEUMS AND GALLERIES:
LONDON (National Portrait Gal.): *(Lloyd) Logan Pearsall Smith* (1932, oil on canvas) - LONDON (Tate Collection): *Chintz Divan* (1910); *The Chintz Couch* (1910, oil on millboard); *Tea with Sickert* (1911-1912, oil on canvas); *Flowers in a Jug* (1920s, oil on canvas).

AUCTION RECORDS:
LONDON, 8 June 1979, *Red Azalea* (oil on card, 22 x 25 ins / 56 x 63.5 cm) GBP 1,000. LONDON, 5 July 1983, *Sunny Interior, Auppegard Castle* (oil on canvas, 18 x 21½ ins / 46 x 54.5 cm) GBP 900. LONDON, 9 June 1988, *Oriental Teapot and Bowl of Fruit* (oil on canvas, 13¾ x 11¾ ins / 35 x 30 cm) GBP 7,700.

SANDS, James
British, 19th century.
Active in London from 1811 to 1841.
Engraver (burin), architect.

James Sands was an exhibitor at the Royal Academy from 1813 to 1841.

SANDS, Robert
British, 19th century.
Born 1792; died 1855.
Active in London.
Engraver (burin).

Robert Sands was possibly the brother of James Sands. He engraved architectural subjects and portraits.

SANDT, Christoph
German, 18th century.
Born 1695; died 1765.
Sculptor.

Christoph Sandt completed the stalls for Frauenburg Cathedral in East Prussia (now Frombork, Poland) in 1737.

SANDTMANN, Johann Caspar, or Sandmann
German, 17th century.
Born 17 May 1642, in Kassel; died 14 April 1695, in Leipzig.
Sculptor.

Johann Caspar Sandtmann worked for the churches and cemeteries in Leipzig.
MUSEUMS AND GALLERIES:
LEIPZIG (Stadtgeschichtliches Mus.): *God the Father and Christ; Apollo; Prince's Stall* (from the church of St Thomas).

SANDWITH, Noelle
South African, 20th century.
Born 31 July 1927, in Cape Town.
Painter. Local scenes.

Noelle Sandwith studied at the Art Schools in Kingston-on-Thames, Croydon and Heatherley in 1948. She participated in exhibitions at the Royal Academy, London, at the Starr Foundation Museum in Michigan, USA, and at the Royal Naval College in Greenwich. Her last solo exhibition took place at Foyles Art Gallery in 1960.

She travelled notably to Australia and specialised in ethnographical studies, painting scenes of life in the southern hemisphere. In Tonga she executed studies of Queen Salote and the royal family.

SANDY, Gyula or Julius
Hungarian, 19th century.
Born 1827, in Talya; died 1894, in Budapest.
Painter.

The Történeti Museum in Budapest owns *The Sculptor I. Ferenczy* by this artist, and the museum of Košice owns his *Peasants from Northern Hungary*.

SANDYS, Anthony, or Sands
British, 19th century.
Born 1806, in Norwich; died 9 February 1883, in Norwich.
Painter. Portraits, figures.

Anthony Sandys was the father of Emma and Anthony Frederick Sandys.
MUSEUMS AND GALLERIES:
LONDON (NG): *Frederick Sandys* (1848, oil/panel) - NORWICH (Castle Mus. and AG): *Portrait of Richard Roper Boardman; Triple Self-portrait.*

SANDYS, Anthony Frederick Augustus
British, 19th century.
Born 1 May 1829, in Norwich; died 25 June 1904, in London.
Painter, watercolourist, draughtsman, illustrator.
Allegorical subjects, portraits.
Symbolism.

Anthony Frederick Augustus Sandys was the son of the portraitist Anthony Sandys. He arrived in London at an early age and completed his studies by copying old masters in the National Gallery. In 1857, he met Dante Gabriel Rossetti; the two lived together in 1860. In 1851, Sandys began exhibiting at the Royal Academy; he would continue to do so until 1886.

As an illustrator, he started out working on publications with a regional bias, such as *Birds of Norfolk; Norfolk Antiquities.* On his move to London, however, and resulting from his friendship with Rossetti (who considered Sandys to be one of the best draughtsman of the day), he moved in Pre-Raphaelite circles and began receiving commissions from a whole range of periodicals, to which he contributed illustrations that were subsequently woodcut-engraved: *Once a Week; Cornhill Magazine; Good Words; Churchman's Family Magazine; Churchman's Shilling Magazine; English Illustrated Magazine* and so on. He also contributed illustrations to such diverse publications as *Bible Gallery; Hurst and Blackett's Standard Library; Idyllic Pictures; Touches of Nature* and the like, not forgetting Thornbury's *Legendary Ballads.* Around 1880, the publishing house MacMillan commissioned him to produce a series of pencil drawings of leading literary figures of the age; it was a task that took him several years to complete.

His earliest work comprised pencil portraits. He went on to use oils, particularly in his predominantly female portraits and his allegorical compositions. Although not, strictly speaking, a member of the Pre-Raphaelite group, he was nonetheless very much in tune with their approach and receptive to their ideas. The legendary themes and Symbolist overtones in his work presage the style that would come to be known as Art Nouveau.

The Royal Academy mounted a retrospective of his work in 1905 and a comprehensive exhibition of his paintings, drawings and illustrations was hosted by the Castle Museum and Art Gallery in his native Norwich in 2002.

BIBLIOGRAPHY:
Rose, Andrea, *Pre-Raphaelite Portraits,* Oxford Illustrated Press, Yeovil, Haynes Publications, Newbury Park, 1981.
Elzea, Betty (ed.), *Frederick Sandys 1829-1904,* catalogue raisonné, Antique collector's club, Woodbridge, 2001.
MUSEUMS AND GALLERIES:
BIRMINGHAM (Mus. and AG): *Autumn* (c. 1860-1862, oil/panel); *Morgan le Fay, Queen of Avalon; Medea* (oil/panel); *Portrait of Hermann Vezin* (pastel); *Mary Sandys* (c. 1871-1873, pastel) - MELBOURNE: *Pain* (drawing) - NORWICH (Castle Mus. and AG): *Autumn* (1860, oil on canvas); *Portrait of Lord Battersea (Cyril Flower)* (drawing); *Mary Magdalene* (1862, oil on canvas).
AUCTION RECORDS:
LONDON, 8 May 1925, *Morgan Le Fay,* GBP 388; *Medea,* GBP 525; *Viviane,* GBP 199. LONDON, 11 July 1969, *Female Head,* Gns 900. LONDON, 5 March 1971, *Young Girl holding a Chalice,* Gns 2,500. LONDON, 19 May 1978, *Whittlingham in Autumn* (1860, oil on canvas, 10 x 28 1/2 ins / 25.4 x 72.2 cm) GBP 7,500. LONDON, 2 Feb 1979, *Portrait of Mrs Susanna Rose, aged 67 Years* (1862, oil on panel, 13 x 10 1/2 ins / 33 x 26.7 cm) GBP 7,000. LONDON, 19 June 1979, *Pious Leuconolus* (1843, watercolour and pencil, 20 1/2 x 17 1/2 ins / 52 x 44.5 cm) GBP 450. LONDON, 1 Oct 1979, *Proud Maisie* (1903, red chalk, 14 1/4 x 11 ins / 36 x 27 cm) GBP 7,000. LONDON, 10 Nov 1981, *Morgan Le Fay* (ink/paper, 24 1/2 x 17 1/4 ins / 62 x 44 cm) GBP 12,500. LONDON, 19 July 1983, *Alcestis: Portrait of Lady Donaldson* (1877, black, white, red and green chalks heightened with white gouache/greenish-blue remounted paper/panel, 28 3/4 x 21 1/2 ins / 73 x 54.5 cm) GBP 5,000. LONDON, 19 June 1984, *Oriana* (1861, oil on panel, 10 x 7 3/4 ins / 25.5 x 20 cm) GBP 28,000. LONDON, 30 May 1985, *Herbert H. Roberts* (1874, colouring pencil, 24 3/4 x 17 ins / 63 x 43 cm) GBP 900. LONDON, 18 June 1985, *Portrait of Mrs Jane Lewis* (1864, oil on panel, 26 x 22 ins / 66 x 56 cm) GBP 14,000. LONDON, 2 Nov 1989, *A Beautiful Hand* (oil on card, 14 x 10 ins / 35.6 x 25.4 cm) GBP 4,400. LONDON, 12 Nov 1992, *Portrait of Cyril Flower (Lord Battersea)* (1872, coloured chalk, 24 3/4 x 20 ins / 63 x 51 cm) GBP 30,800. LONDON, 11 June 1993, *The White Lady of Avenel* (watercolour heightened with white and gold on pale blue paper, 12 3/4 x 10 ins / 32.7 x 25.4 cm) GBP 18,400. LONDON, 5 Nov 1993, *Portrait of Robert Browning* (1881, pencil and coloured chalk/greyish-green paper, 27 1/4 x 20 1/4 ins / 69.1 x 51.4 cm) GBP 14,950. NEW YORK, 1 Nov 1995, *King Pelle's Daughter holding the Chalice of the Holy Grail* (1861, ink/paper, 13 x 9 1/2 ins / 32.1 x 24.1 cm) USD 9,200. LONDON, 8 Nov 1996, *Miranda* (red and black chalks, 14 1/2 x 12 ins / 36.8 x 30.2 cm) GBP 3,000. LONDON, 6 June 1997, *Portrait of Julia Smith Caldwell* (oil on canvas, 44 x 29 1/2 ins / 112 x 75 cm) GBP 45, 500. LONDON, 5 Nov

1997, *Judith* (oil on panel, 15 3/4 x 11 3/4 ins / 40 x 30 cm) GBP 65,300. PONTOISE, 4 Dec 1999, *Water Duty* (1877, watercolour and gouache, 21 x 17 ins / 53 x 43 cm) FRF 17,000. IPSWICH, 9 Sept 2002, *Portrait of Mr Simms Reeve, Bust Length. Portrait of his Wife Anne* (black, white and red chalk, a pair, 21 x 17 ins / 53 x 42 cm) GBP 3,200. LONDON, 20 Feb 2003, *At Vespers* (oil on panel, 24 x 20 ins / 61 x 50 cm) GBP 28,000. LONDON, 20 Feb 2003, *Love's Shadow* (oil on panel, 16 x 13 ins / 41 x 32 cm) GBP 115,000.

SANDYS, Edwin
Irish, 17th - 18th century.
Died 1708, in Dublin.
Engraver, illustrator.

Edwin Sandys was an illustrator and cold-chisel engraver. He produced portraits and views to illustrate publications, including a portrait of *Sir William Petty*.

SANDYS, Emma
British, 19th century.
Born 1834; died 21 November 1877.
Painter, draughtswoman. Portraits, genre scenes.

Emma Sandys was the daughter of Anthony Sandys. She was active between 1867 and 1874.

MUSEUMS AND GALLERIES:

NORWICH (Castle Mus. and AG): *Portrait of a Lady in a Yellow Dress; Study of a Head.*

AUCTION RECORDS:

LONDON, 16 Nov 1976, *He Loves Me, He Loves Me Not...* (1876, oil on canvas, 20 x 17 ins / 51 x 43 cm) GBP 1,800. LONDON, 16 Oct 1981, *Portrait of a Little Girl* (oil on panel, 15 x 12 ins / 38 x 30.5 cm) GBP 2,500. LONDON, 15 June 1988, *Fiametta* (1876, oil on card, 12 x 10 ins / 30.5 x 25.5 cm) GBP 1,980. LONDON, 5 March 1993, *Fiametta* (1876, oil on card, 12 x 10 ins / 30.5 x 25.5 cm) GBP 3,680. LONDON, 3 June 1994, *Ann and Agnes Young* (1870, chalks/grey paper, 20 x 16 ins / 51 x 40.6 cm) GBP 1,265. LONDON, 7 June 1995, *Mirror* (1867, oil on canvas, 24 x 17 ins / 61 x 43 cm) GBP 1,265. LONDON, 29 March 1996, *Saxon Princess* (oil on canvas, 10 x 8 ins / 25.4 x 20.3 cm) GBP 1,955. NEW YORK, 18-19 July 1996, *Daydreaming* (oil on canvas, 20 x 16 ins / 50.8 x 40.6 cm) USD 6,900. LONDON, 22 June 1999, *Portrait of Woman in Gold Jacket, Earrings and Brooch* (oil on panel, 11 x 9 ins / 27 x 22 cm) GBP 3,200. NEWCASTLE, 13 March 2001, *Portrait of an Auburn Haired Young Woman in the pre-Raphaelite Manner* (1867, oil on panel, 13 x 11 ins / 33 x 27 cm) GBP 16,000. LONDON, 6 Sept 2001, *Medieval Beauty* (1866, oil on panel, 12 x 10 ins / 30 x 25 cm) GBP 3,500. LONDON, 20 Feb 2003, *Garland* (1870, oil on board, 17 x 13 ins / 43 x 33 cm) GBP 9,000. LONDON, 10 June 2003, *Preparing for the Ball* (1867, oil on canvas, 24 x 17 ins / 62 x 44 cm) GBP 4,500.

SANDYS, Winifred
British, 19th - 20th century.
Born 1875; died 1944.
Painter, watercolourist, pastellist, draughtswoman. Portraits.

The elder daughter and pupil of Anthony Frederick Augustus Sandys, Winifred Sandys was a recognised artist who exhibited pastels and watercolours.

AUCTION RECORDS:

LONDON, 5 June 1991, *Sprigs of Lavender* (1905, coloured chalks, 14 x 11 ins / 35.5 x 28 cm) GBP 715. LONDON, 29 March 1995, *Portrait of Percy Wood* (coloured chalks, 11 1/2 x 9 ins / 29.5 x 23 cm) GBP 1,035. LONDON, 5 June 2003, *Portrait of Percy Wood, in Indian Dress* (pencil and pastel, after Anthony Frederick Sandys, 11x9 ins / 28x23 cm) GBP 1,000.

SANDZEN, Birger, or Sven Birger
Swedish, 19th - 20th century.
Born 5 February 1871, in Bildsberg; died 1954.
Active in the USA from 1894.
Painter, engraver. Landscapes.

Birger Sandzen studied at the Artists' League in Stockholm under Anders Zorn, Carl Per Hasselberg and Sven Richard Bergh and, in Paris, under E. F. Aman-Jean.

MUSEUMS AND GALLERIES:

LONDON (British Mus.) - PARIS (BNF) - STOCKHOLM (Nationalmus.).

AUCTION RECORDS:

NEW YORK, 3 Feb 1978, *Landscape at Dusk* (oil on card, 16 x 12 ins / 40.5 x 30.5 cm) USD 1,500. STOCKHOLM, 13 Nov 1987, *Landscapes* (set of seven canvases, 73 1/4 x 18 1/2 ins / 186 x 47 cm) SEK 75,000. NEW YORK, 30 Sept 1988, *Sun Rising over the Coast* (1913, oil on canvas, 16 x 24 ins / 40.5 x 61 cm) USD 6,600. NEW YORK, 27 Sept 1990, *Poplars and Pines at Estes Park in Colorado* (oil on card, 19 1/2 x 23 3/4 ins / 49.5 x 60.4 cm) USD 7,150. NEW YORK, 30 Sept 1997, *'Autumn Glory', Rocky Mountain National Park, Colorado* (1946, oil on card, 21 3/4 x 27 3/4 ins / 55.3 x 70.5 cm) USD 20,700.

SANÉ, Jean François
French, 18th century.
Born c. 1732; died November 1779, in Paris.
Painter. History painting.

Sané exhibited at the Colisée in 1776. He worked in Rome.

MUSEUMS AND GALLERIES:

ANGERS: two genre scenes - DOUAI: *St Paul in Malta.*

AUCTION RECORDS:

PARIS, 1780, *Death of Socrates,* FRF 339; *Last Judgement* (after Michelangelo) FRF 500. LONDON, 20 April 2004, *Interior with a Soldier Greeting his Wife and Child* (oil on panel, 10 x 15 ins / 25 x 38 cm) GBP 2,800.

SANE, Pieter
Dutch, 17th century.
Painter, engraver.

Pieter Sane produced engraved portraits of four Amsterdam clerics.

SANEJOUAND, Jean-Michel
French, 20th century.
Born 1934, in Lyons.
Painter, sculptor, sculptor of assemblages, environmental artist, draughtsman.

In 1955 Jean-Michel Sanejouand obtained a law degree and a diploma from the Institute of Political Studies. In 1964 he was involved in setting up the *Poulet 20 NF* group. He lives and works in Vaulandry (Maine-et-Loire).

He began to paint while a university student and produced his first abstracts in 1958. In 1963 he gave up abstraction, then became a powerful force in the international avant-garde, and began the series *Charges-objets,* combinations of ordinary and unusual objects with little obvious connection or meaning. This in itself, however, represented a critique of contemporary art. Sanejouand, for example, critiqued New Realism or Pop Art with a washbasin stand supporting a glass balloon or an abstract geometrical shape, or else an assemblage of coloured ironing boards. In 1967 he began *Organisations of Space,* introducing contradictory elements into a pre-existing architectural context and thus making the viewer physically aware of voids. The first was a restructuring of the courtyard of the former École Polytechnique by means of an assemblage of small girders and the breaking up of space by metal grilles. He usually carried out these plans for restructuring space using industrial materials, especially metal tubes and grilles: *Diagram for the organisation of a wooded space, 'Homage to Le Nôtre'* of 1967. In 1968, with his *Organisation of Space* at the Musée Galliera, he demonstrated how the unassembled parts of a modern crane could be introduced into a museum built in an earlier architectural style. In 1970 he designed a plan for the building site then located where the former Gare Montparnasse stood, the future complex at the foot of Urbain Cassan's

Tour Montparnasse (Montparnasse Tower). In 1973 his plan for the organisation of the valley of the Seine from Le Havre to Paris took into account design, ecological and political considerations.

At the same time as the *Organisations of Space*, and from 1965, *Humorous Calligraphies* took him back to his first preoccupation with painting and drawing. These were sketches of figures, often elegant in line, often on a white background or covered with a flat coat of bright colour. He did not exhibit these until 1974, a moment when figuration was not popular with either artists or the public.

After the *Orientation Tables* of 1976, between 1978 and 1986 came *Spaces-Paintings*, a synthesis between his spatial experiments and his painting practice. They are sketchy landscapes, quite unrealistic, consisting of flat planes of bright colour, interspersed with roads on which silhouette figures with anonymous, mask-like faces wander, the whole punctuated by Abstract-Lyrical zigzags.

For more than five years from 1987, in *Black and White Paintings*, the masks of *Spaces-Paintings*, now black, become the main theme and are surrounded by landscape and equally black rocks, both masks and decorative elements appearing to be suspended over the white surface of the painting. At the same time he began to carve a series of small sculptures from stones chosen for their unusualness.

The series *Paintings-Colours* began in 1992. In them Sanejouand returns to colour and a more pictorial treatment than we find in the stones and trees that earlier accompanied the masks. Sometimes they include fish and birds that have more substance and are more realistic than the preceding human silhouettes.

Sanejouand's development may seem perplexing, swinging as it does between so many different forms of expression - from the concrete in real space to the imagined, from the tactile to the sign. This inconsistency is perhaps a mark of his indifference to the demands of figuration and abstraction as categories, a preparedness to explore the most contradictory routes to see where they will lead.

Group exhibitions in which Sanejouand has participated include: 1964, *Poulet 20 NF* group, Galerie Yvette Marin, Paris; 1976, Venice Biennale; 2002, *Les Années 70: l'art en cause* (*The 1970s: Art in Question*); 2003, *Un tableau dans le décor. Peintures 1970-2000* (*A Painting in the Décor: Paintings 1970-2000*), Château des Ducs de Bretagne, Nantes, *Esprit des lieux* (*The Spirit of Places*), contemporary work and its exhibition space, Palais des Papes, Avignon, and *L'état des choses* (*The State of Things*), an examination of the status of daily objects in contemporary art - these three exhibitions were part of *Trésors publics, 20 ans de création dans les Fonds régionaux d'art contemporain (FRAC)* (*Public Treasury, 20 Years of Creation in the Regional Collection of Contemporary Art*). He has held solo shows mainly in Paris and France: 1968, *Organisation d'espace* (*The Organisation of Space*), Musée Galliera, Paris; 1973, plan for the organisation of the valley of the Seine, Centre National d'Art Contemporain, Paris (CNAP); 1991, Musée d'Art Moderne, Villeneuve-d'Ascq; 1995, retrospective 1963-1995, MNAM Centre Georges-Pompidou, Paris; 2000, École Supérieure des Beaux-Arts, Tours; 2003, Transpalette, Bourges.

Bibliography:

Jean-Michel Sanejouand: peintures 1987-1989, Musée de l'Abbaye Sainte-Croix, Les Sables d'Olonne, 1989. Lamarche-Vadel, Bernard, *Jean-Michel Sanejouand, les Charges-Objets 1963-1967*, Fondation Fine Art of The Century, Éd. La Différence, Paris, 1990. Enrici, Michel/Pijaudier, Joëlle, *Jean-Michel Sanejouand: espaces-peintures 1978-1986*, exhibition catalogue, Musée d'Art moderne, Villeune-d'Ascq, La Différence, Paris, 1991. *Jean-Michel Sanejouand*, exhibition catalogue, Éd. du Centre Georges-Pompidou, Paris, 1995. *Jean-Michel Sanejouand: retrospective 1963-1995*, Éd. du Centre Georges-Pompidou, Paris, 1995. Goldberg, Itzhak, '*Jean-Michel Sanejouand*' in *Beaux-Arts Magazine* no. 137, periodical, Paris, September 1995. Ottinger, Didier, *-Jean-Michel Sanejouand ou l'éloge de l'irréductibilité*, exhibition catalogue, École supérieure des beaux-arts, Tours, 2000. Fréruchet, Maurice, et al., *Les Années soixante-dix: l'art en cause*, exhibition catalogue, Capc-Musée d'Art contemporain, Bordeaux, 2002. Zahm, Olivier (preface), et al., *Trésors publics, 20 ans de création dans les Fonds régionaux d'art contemporain*, Flammarion, Paris, 2003 (text in French and English).

Museums and Galleries:

Clermont-Ferrand (FRAC Auvergne): *Agreement between the Two 29/9 15/10 88* (1988); *Charge-objet* (1964) - Sélestat (FRAC Alsace): *Grilled Kayak* (1965).

Auction records:

Paris, 20 May 1992, *Untitled* (1981, oil and gouache/paper, 43 1/4 x 43 1/4 ins / 110 x 110 cm) FRF 9,500. Paris, 22 Dec 1995, *Landscape* (1978, acrylic/canvas, 34 3/4 x 46 ins / 88.5 x 116 cm) FRF 6,800.

SANESI, Niccolò or Nicola

Italian, 19th century.
Born 1818, in Florence; died 7 December 1889, in Florence.
Painter, engraver. Historical subjects, battles, genre scenes.

Museums and Galleries:

Prato (Mus. Civico): *The Execution of Margherite Pusterla*; *True Charity* (two paintings); *Soldiers in Medieval Costume* - Rome (Gal. Nazionale d'Arte Moderna): *Battle of San Martino*.

Auction records:

Milan, 7 Nov 1991, *Fortune-Telling* (1861, oil on canvas, 21 1/2 x 17 ins / 54.5 x 43 cm) ITL 5,400,000. London, 16 Sept 1999, *Seven Acts of Mercy* (oil on canvas, 42 x 57 ins / 107 x 146 cm) GBP 9,500.

SANFILIPPO, Antonio

Italian, 20th century.
Born 1923, in Partanna (Trapani); died 1980, in Rome.
Painter.
Forma 1 Group.

Antonio Sanfilippo was a student at the Accademia di Belle Arti in Florence. At the end of the World War II, he settled in Paris where he became friendly with Giulio Turcato, met up again with his fellow Sicilians Pietro Consagra and Ugo Attardi and married Carla Accardi. Together, they moved to Rome where they became close to Renato Guttuso, sharing his political ideas if not his ideas about painting. In 1947, Antonio Sanfilippo was, along with his friends, one of the cosignatories of the Forma 1 manifesto which put forward the group's position in relation to art - Marxist but abstract, in opposition to the prevailing socialist realism. He also wrote for the group's review of the same name.

His association with the Forma 1 group put him in the ranks of the second generation of abstract artists. He was opposed to all conformist realism, exploiting radically abstract forms which sought deliberately to avoid provoking intellectual or synesthetic associations with any kind of reality, feelings, or sensations. In his search for what was sometimes called at that time 'concrete' abstraction, Sanfilippo anticipated the asceticism of the future Minimalists. Although the division of the totality of an artist's work into different periods leads to somewhat arbitrary categories, in the case of Sanfilippo it is possible to discern two main groups of works. Those executed between 1947 and about 1950 are abstract paintings based on cut-out but not geometrical forms, very varied in shape and rich in coloration. After 1950, and particularly after 1960, abstract signs, dots, lines or blotches seem to emerge from the space of the canvas like particles emanating from the void. The energy of these elements draws them together in the centre, seeming to form a kind of star.

Sanfilippo took part in a number of collective exhibitions: in 1947 at the Art Club Gallery, Rome, with the Forma 1 group; Venice Biennale,1948, 1954; Rome Quadriennale 1948-1959. His first solo exhibition was held in Rome in 1951.

BIBLIOGRAPHY:

Dorazio, Piero/Collovini, Diego, *Forma 1 - 1947-1987*, group exhibition catalogue, Musée de Brou, Bourg-en-Bresse, Gal. municipale d'Art contemporain, St-Priest, 1987.

AUCTION RECORDS:

ROME, 19 June 1980, *Composition* (1967, acrylic/canvas, 27 1/2 x 35 1/2 ins / 70 x 90 cm) ITL 800,000. ROME, 22 May 1984, *Composition* (1944-1959, oil on canvas, 28 3/4 x 23 1/2 ins / 73 x 60 cm) ITL 2,000,000. MILAN, 14 Dec 1988, *Untitled* (1963, oil on canvas, 23 1/4 x 19 1/4 ins / 59 x 49 cm) ITL 3,200,000. ROME, 10 April 1990, *Work 7-60* (1960, oil on canvas, 28 3/4 x 21 1/4 ins / 73 x 54 cm) ITL 10,500,000. ROME, 30 Oct 1990, *Centuries After No. 1* (1955, oil on canvas, 23 1/2 x 19 3/4 ins / 60 x 50 cm) ITL 7,500,000. ROME, 19 April 1994, *Intimate Structure* (1959, oil on canvas, 28 3/4 x 39 1/4 ins / 73 x 100 cm) ITL 8,050,000. ROME, 14 Nov 1995, *Painting 12* (1958, oil on canvas, 22 x 16 1/4 ins / 55 x 41 cm) ITL 6,900,000. MILAN, 2 April 1996, *Untitled* (1962, oil on canvas, 38 x 57 1/4 ins / 96.5 x 145.5 cm) ITL 11,500,000. MILAN, 20 May 1996, *Composition* (1966, tempera/canvas, 77 1/4 x 57 ins / 196 x 145 cm) ITL 13,800,000. ROME, 25 Nov 1999, *Untitled* (1964, oil on canvas, 24 x 31 ins / 60 x 80 cm) ITL 5,500,000. FLORENCE, 19 Nov 2001, *Untitled* (1962, Indian ink and tempera, 20 x 28 ins / 50 x 70 cm) ITL 7,500,000. FLORENCE, 19 Nov 2001, *White Zone* (1961, oil on canvas, 57 x 35 ins / 146 x 89 cm) ITL 21,000,000. ROME, 18 April 2002, *Landscape* (1947, oil on canvas, 16 x 20 ins / 40 x 50 cm) EUR 7,400. VENICE, 8 June 2002, *Untitled* (1964, tempera on canvas, 35 x 50 ins / 88 x 128 cm) EUR 5,200. PRATO, 14 Nov 2003, *Untitled* (1956, hydropaint on canvas, 21 x 26 ins / 54 x 65 cm) EUR 8,500. FLORENCE, 26 Nov 2003, *Untitled* (1962, mixed media, 39 x 28 ins / 100 x 70 cm) EUR 2,600.

SANFORD, Edward Field

American, 20th century.
Born 6 April 1886, in New York; died 1934.
Sculptor. Figures.

Edward Sanford studied at the Academy of Fine Arts in New York, the academy of fine arts in Munich and at the Académie Julian in Paris.

AUCTION RECORDS:

NEW YORK, 29 Sept 1977, *Inspiration* (1929, green-patinated bronze, h. 18 3/4 ins / 47.6 cm) USD 800. NEW YORK, 22 May 1980, *Inspiration* (1929, gilded bronze, h. 18 3/4 ins / 47.9 cm) USD 2,600. NEW YORK, 23 March 1984, *Pegasus* (1914, bronze, h. 28 1/4 ins / 71.8 cm) USD 2,800. NEW YORK, 5 Dec 1986, *Pegasus* (1914, bronze, h. 28 1/4 ins / 71.8 cm) USD 3,500. NEW YORK, 9 Sept 1993, *Female Dancer* (bronze, h. 12 3/4 ins / 32.4 cm) USD 690.

SANFORD, Isaac

American, 18th - 19th century.
Active in Hartford (Connecticut) 1783-1822.
Miniaturist, engraver (burin).

SANFOURCHE, Jean-Joseph

French, 20th century.
Born 25 June 1929, in Rochefort.
Painter (including gouache), draughtsman, sculptor, mixed media.
Art Brut.

Jean-Joseph Sanfourche was born and lived as a child in Bordeaux and Rochefort, and during the war and occupation he was in Limoges. He appears to have then travelled quite extensively and spent some time at the abbey of Solignac, again near Limoges.

He paints on canvas, cloth, wood and tiles; since 1965 he has sculpted wood, scrap material, human bones, stone (granite or reject masonry and quarry stone), which he then paints. He also works in bronze and enamel.

Sanfourche has regularly exhibited in group exhibitions in Paris: 1960, the first Paris Biennale; 1965, 1966, the Salon des Réalités Nouvelles; until 1968, the Salon de la Jeune Peinture; until 1970 the Salon des Surindépendants; 1971, the Salon d'Art Sacré; regularly at the Musée des Arts Décoratifs, Compagnie de l'Art Brut, Paris, (directed by Jean Dubuffet); and 1972, Florence; 1985, Centre Culturel Jean-Gagnant, Limoges; 1985, 1986, Eymoutiers; 1984, Musée du Vieux Château, Laval; 1988, Museum of Modern Art, Amsterdam; 1989, Musée Ingres, Montauban; 1990, the Swiss Cultural Center, New York. He exhibited in a solo show for the first time with Fischer in 1950 at the Galerie François Miron, Paris, and subsequently during the 1970s in various Parisian galleries (Galeries Jacob, Camoin, Lauvin, François Miron); from 1980, regularly at the Fondation Pagani; 1980, the Museum of Modern Art, Milan; 1985, the Centre d'Art, Eymoutiers; 1987, the Musée des Art et Traditions Populaires, Guéret; 1992, the Espace Tecnic, Mulhouse; 2003 Galerie des Hospices, Limoges.

BIBLIOGRAPHY:

Rétrospective Jean-Joseph Sanfourche, exhibition catalogue, Gal. des Hospices, Limoges, 2003.

MUSEUMS AND GALLERIES:

BRUSSELS (Palais des Beaux-Arts) - CHARLEVILLE-MÉZIÈRES (Mus. Arthur-Rimbaud) - EYMOUTIERS (Collégiale) - LAUSANNE (Cantonal MFA) - LAVAL (Mus. d'Art naïf) - LES SABLES D'OLONNE (Musée de L'Abbaye Ste-Croix) - LIMOGES (FRAC Limousin) - LIMOGES (Mus. Municipal de L'Évêché) - LYONS (MBA) - PARIS (MNAM-CCI) - PARIS (Mus. des Arts décoratifs): painted stones - ROCHEFORT (MAH).

SÄNFTL, Franz

German, 18th century.
Born 1685, in Regen; died 1745, in Regen.
Painter.

Franz Sänftl was the father of Quirin Franz Sänftl.

SÄNFTL, Franz Joseph

German, 18th century.
Born 1709, in Regen; died 1763, in Regen.
Painter.

Franz Joseph Sänftl was the son of Franz Sänftl. He painted an altarpiece for the church of the Holy Spirit in Regen.

SÄNFTL, Quirin Franz

German, 18th century.
Born 1720, in Regen; died 1762, in Regen.
Painter.

Quirin Franz Sänftl was the brother of Franz Joseph Sänftl.

SANG, Frederic Jacques

French, 19th century.
Painter. Seascapes, architectural interiors.

He was active from 1840 to 1884.

MUSEUMS AND GALLERIES:

CARPENTRAS: *The Jersey Coast.*

AUCTION RECORDS:

PARIS, 11 Feb 1919, *Steamer Entering a Port,* FRF 100. LONDON, 19 May 1976, *View of the Trocadéro, Paris* (1876, oil on canvas, 12 1/2 x 17 3/4 ins / 32 x 45 cm) GBP 300. LONDON, 19 April 1978, *View of the Trocadéro* (1878, oil on canvas, 12 1/2 x 17 3/4 ins / 32 x 45 cm) GBP 900. LONDON, 17 Nov 1994, *Interior Views of the Conservative Club: the Entrance Hall and the Grand Staircase* (collection of 'trois crayons' and watercolours, approx. 13 1/2 x 15 1/4 ins / 34 x 39 cm) GBP 8,625.

AMSTERDAM, 3 Feb 2004, *View of the Trocadero and the Seine* (1878, oil on canvas, 13 x 18 ins / 32 x 46 cm) EUR 1,500.

SANG, Johann Georg
German, 18th century.
Born 30 October 1744, in Munich.
Painter.
Johann Georg Sang was a pupil of Gottfried Stuber. He executed paintings for churches in Freising and Munich.

SANGALLI, Baldassare or Carl Balthasar Innocentius
German, 18th - 19th century.
Born 3 September 1755, in Pavia; died 7 June 1818, in Stettin (now Szczecin, Poland).
Sculptor.
Baldassare Sangalli sculpted the altar and organ case for the church of Kremzow.

SANGALLO, Antonio da
Italian, 15th - 16th century.
Born 1455, in Florence; died 27 December 1534, in Florence.
Sculptor, architect.
Antonio da Sangallo was the son of Francesco (Giamberti) Sangallo, and the brother of Giuliano da Sangallo, who he worked with for many years. He sculpted statues and crucifixes.

SANGALLO, Francesco, called Giamberti
Italian, 15th century.
Born 1405; died 1480.
Sculptor (wood).
Francesco Sangallo was the father of Antonio and Giuliano da Sangallo.

SANGALLO, Francesco da, called Il Margotta
Italian, 16th century.
Born 1 March 1494; died 17 February 1576.
Sculptor, architect.
Francesco da Sangallo was the son of Giuliano da Sangallo, and brother of Sebastiano Sangallo. He was influenced by Michelangelo in Rome, and sculpted tombs in Rome, Florence, Monte Cassino and Naples.
BIBLIOGRAPHY:
Loukomski, G.K., *Les Sangallo*, Collection Les grands architectes, Paris, 1934.
MUSEUMS AND GALLERIES:
PRATO (Mus. Civico): *St John the Baptist* (bronze statue).

SANGALLO, Gian Giacomo da
Italian, 15th - 16th century.
Active from 1496 to 1517.
Sculptor.
Gian Giacomo da Sangallo worked in Milan Cathedral.

SANGALLO, Giuliano da
Italian, 15th - 16th century.
Born 1445, in Florence; died 20 October 1516, in Florence.
Active in Florence, Tuscany, Rome, Milan and Naples.
Sculptor, engineer, architect.
Giuliano da Sangallo was the son of Francesco (Giamberti) Sangallo, and the father of Francesco Margotta Sangallo and Sebastiano Sangallo. He was the spiritual successor to Brunelleschi.

SANGALLO, Sebastiano or Bastiano da, called Aristotile
Italian, 16th century.
Born 1481, in Florence; died 31 May 1551, in Florence.
Painter, decorative designer. History painting.
Sebastiano da Sangallo was the son of Giuliano da Sangallo, and brother of Francesco da Sangallo II. He was the pupil of Perugino. He was given the nickname Aristotile because of his knowledge of perspective and anatomy. He imitated the style of Michelangelo who employed him to prepare paintings for the Sistine Chapel.
Sebastiano da Sangallo later became a friend of Raphael, and built the Palazzo Pandolfini in Florence to Raphael's designs. As a painter Sebastiano da Sangallo seemed to have favoured works such as theatre decoration and house façades.

SANGAR, Thomas L.
British, 19th century.
Engraver.
Thomas Sangar was a cold-chisel engraver.

SANGARS. See **LA PEÑA Arnaldo de**

SANGEOT, Charles
French, 19th century.
Watercolourist. Landscapes.
MUSEUMS AND GALLERIES:
ROCHEFORT: a watercolour.

SÄNGER, Dominikus
German, 19th century.
Born 6 October 1845; died 6 March 1897.
Active in Munich.
Sculptor.

SANGER, John
British, 18th century.
Active in 1763.
Landscape artist.

SÄNGER, Philipp. See **SENGHER**

SÄNGER, Philipp Christian Bernhard
German, 18th century.
Painter. Religious subjects.
Philipp Christian Bernhard Sänger painted a *Holy Trinity* for the church of Untermassfeld in 1744.

SANGHER, Jan de
Flemish School, 17th century.
Sculptor (wood).
Jan de Sangher carved the confessionals in the church of St Anne in Bruges in 1699.

SANGIORGI, Nicolas
Italian, 19th century.
Engraver (burin).
He was working in Rome on 17 March 1844.

SANGIORGIO, Abbondio
Italian, 19th century.
Born 16 July 1798, in Milan; died 2 November 1879, in Milan.
Sculptor.
A pupil of Pacetti, he worked mainly in Milan and Turin.

SANGIOVANNI, Benedetto
Italian, 19th century.
Born 1781, in Laurino; died 13 April 1853, in Brighton, England.
Active in England from c. 1828.
Sculptor.
A self-taught sculptor, Sangiovanni settled in London in about 1828.

SANGLADA, Pedro, or Canglada
Spanish, 14th - 15th century.
Sculptor (wood).
Barcelona School.
Pedro Sanglada sculpted statues on a fountain in Barcelona and a statue of the Virgin in Monreale church, near Palermo, Sicily, in 1401.

SANGLER, Léa
French, 20th - 21st century.

Born 17 July 1957, in Paris.
Painter. Allegorical subjects, landscapes, flowers.
Léa Sangler exhibited at the Salon d'Automne in Paris in 1989.

SANGMOLEN, Martinus. See **SAAGMOLEN**

SANGNIER, Amédée
French, 19th - 20th century.
Born in Paris.
Painter. Landscapes.
Amédée Sangnier exhibited for the first time at the Salon de Paris in 1874.

SANGRONIZ, José, or Sangronis
Spanish, 16th century.
Died 1586, in Granada.
Sculptor.
José Sangroniz scupted the Fountain of the Lions in Granada town hall.

SANGSTER, Hendrik Alexander
Dutch, 19th century.
Born 25 September 1825, in Nijkerke; died 25 February 1901, in Amsterdam.
Portrait artist.
MUSEUMS AND GALLERIES:
AMSTERDAM: *Portrait of the Theatre Director Johan Eduard de Vries; Portrait of the Actress Maria Francisca Engelman-Bia, in the Role of Juffer Serklaas; Portrait of Johannes Hermanus Albregt, Actor.*

SANGSTER, Samuel
British, 19th century.
Born c. 1804; died 24 June 1872.
Engraver.
Samuel Sangster was a pupil of W. Finden. He engraved illustrations for yearbooks and periodicals.

SANGUESA, Miquel de
Spanish, 16th century.
Active in Castile.
Sculptor.
None of Miquel de Sanguesa's works survive. However, his contemporaries recognised his artistic skill, since he was chosen, with Miguel Ribas, to assess the retable of Pozuelo church, a work by Francisco Giralte.

SANGUIGNI, Battista di Biagio
Italian, 15th century.
Born 1392.
Active in Florence.
Illuminator.
Florentine School.
Battista di Biagio Sanguigni was influenced by Fra Angelico. He illuminated several antiphonaries for churches in Florence.

SANGUINETO, Rafael
Spanish, 17th century.
Died 15 June 1705.
Active in Madrid.
Painter.
Rafael Sanguineto was a friend of Alonso Cano. A member of the nobility, he painted only as an amateur.
AUCTION RECORDS:
LONDON, 7 July 1911, *Carolus Raepralius with Slaves in Chains,* GBP 41.

SANGUINETTI, Alessandro
Italian, 19th century.
Born 1816, in Carrara.
Sculptor.
Brother of Francesco Sanguinetti and pupil of Rauch, he settled in Florence in 1835.

SANGUINETTI, Carlo
Italian, 19th century.
Sculptor. Figures.
He was active in 1857.
MUSEUMS AND GALLERIES:
NANCY (MBA): *Young Neapolitan Fisherman.*

SANGUINETTI, Francesco
German, 19th century.
Born c. 1800, in Carrara; died 15 February 1870, in Munich.
Painter, sculptor. Landscapes.
Francesco Sanguinetti began by painting landscapes after completing part of his studies in Munich. He later devoted himself to sculpture, working in Milan, where his best works are to be found. Through almost squalid thrift he succeeded in amassing a substantial fortune and seems to have enjoyed an enviable lifestyle for a time, but his life was marked by great misfortune. His daughter, a young woman of remarkable beauty, was murdered through jealousy at the age of 19. Sanguinetti was tricked out of part of his fortune by a friend, and the important collections of works of art and paintings that he had put together were somehow purloined by unscrupulous dealers. He died destitute.

SANGUINETTI, Giovanni
Italian, 19th century.
Born 1789, in Mantua; died 7 September 1867, in Rome.
Painter, watercolourist. History painting.
Giovanni Sanguinetti worked and taught painting in Perugia for a number of years. His work shows the influence of Overbeck. His watercolours are highly regarded.

SANGUINETTI, Lazarus Maria
Austrian, 18th century.
Active in Nancy c. 1702.
Painter.
Lazarus Maria Sanguinetti was painter to Duke Leopold of Lorraine.

SANGYOAN. See **TANGEN**

SANH, Georges
French, 20th century.
Born 16 March 1909, in Hanoi, Indochina (now Vietnam).
Painter.
From 1935 Georges Sanh lived in Nice. He exhibited in group exhibitions in Nice, Cannes and Vence, and from 1949 in exhibitions of French painting held in the large cities of Sweden, Norway and Denmark.
AUCTION RECORDS:
NICE, 29-30 Dec 1954, *Still-life* (ceramic and flowers) FRF 16,000.

SANHES, Nicolas
Czech, 20th century.
Sculptor, engraver, draughtsman.
Nicholas Sanhes was of Ruthenian extraction. He exhibited at the Musée Denys-Puech, Rodez, France (1995).
MUSEUMS AND GALLERIES:
TOULOUSE (FRAC Midi-Pyrénées): *Untitled* (1994, four engravings).

SANI, Alessandro
Italian, 19th - 20th century.
Born in Florence.
Active 1879-1921.
Painter. Figures, genre scenes, interiors with figures.
The majority of Alessandro Sani's compositions depict cheerful scenes from rural and peasant life.

One of his works, an *Interior* bearing the signature Sani without a first name, is in the museum in Arras. It is thought

to be by Alessandro Sani but may possibly be by David Sani who painted similar subjects.
MUSEUMS AND GALLERIES:
ARRAS: *Interior* (attributed).
AUCTION RECORDS:
LONDON, 26 March 1929, *Interior of an Inn*, GBP 54. PARIS, 26 Feb 1947, *Two Greedy Monks*, FRF 15,000. LONDON, 12 May 1972, *Monks Drinking*, Gns 380. LONDON, 4 May 1973, *La Bonne Histoire*, Gns 500. LONDON, 15 March 1974, *Card Player*, Gns 500. LONDON, 9 May 1979, *Scene at the Inn* (oil on canvas, 19 1/2 x 14 1/4 ins / 49.5 x 36 cm) GBP 1,500. MILAN, 22 April 1982, *A Good Meal* (oil on canvas, 37 1/2 x 59 ins / 95.5 x 150 cm) ITL 7,500,000. NEW YORK, 24 Feb 1983, *A Cheerful Tune* (oil on canvas, 22 1/4 x 27 1/2 ins / 56.5 x 70 cm) USD 2,000. LONDON, 27 Feb 1985, *A Favourite Song* (oil on canvas, 23 1/2 x 18 1/2 ins / 59.5 x 47 cm) GBP 2,800. NEW YORK, 25 Feb 1988, *Tasting the Wine* (oil on canvas, 25 x 19 ins / 63.5 x 48 cm) USD 8,800. NEW YORK, 20 Jan 1993, *A Question of Taste* (oil on canvas, 12 x 15 3/4 ins / 30.5 x 40 cm) USD 2,300. NEW YORK, 17 Feb 1993, *The Family* (oil on canvas, 36 x 28 ins / 91.4 x 71.1 cm) USD 44,850. NEW YORK, 15 Oct 1993, *A Good Judge* (oil on canvas, 13 3/4 x 17 1/4 ins / 34.9 x 43.8 cm) USD 3,220. NEW YORK, 26 May 1994, *The Mishap* (oil on canvas, 20 x 25 ins / 50.8 x 63.5 cm) USD 5,750. LONDON, 16 Nov 1994, *The Love Letter* (oil on canvas, 15 x 11 1/2 ins / 38 x 29 cm) GBP 1,092. ROME, 5 Dec 1995, *17th-Century Scene* (oil on canvas, 23 1/2 x 19 3/4 ins / 60 x 50 cm) ITL 12,964,000. LONDON, 13 March 1996, *A Gift of Farm Produce* (oil on canvas, 15 3/4 x 22 ins / 40 x 56 cm) GBP 1,495. LONDON, 9 Oct 1997, *Reading: A Point in the Story* (oil on canvas, 24 x 19 1/2 ins / 61 x 49.5 cm) GBP 3,450. NEW YORK, 9 Feb 1999, *Welcome Repast* (oil on canvas, 30 x 41 ins / 75 x 103 cm) USD 39,000. NEW YORK, 7 Dec 1999, *Recital* (oil on canvas, 19 x 15 ins / 48 x 38 cm) USD 5,250. BILLINGSHURST, 24 July 2000, *Abbe Knows* (oil on canvas, 20 x 24 ins / 50 x 61 cm) GBP 5,000. TURIN, 4 Dec 2000, *Shopping Bill* (oil on canvas, 16 x 24 ins / 40 x 60 cm) ITL 13,000,000. GENOA, 7 June 2001, *Young Woman with Glass. Young Woman with Dead Game* (oil on canvas, a pair, 25 x 18 ins / 63 x 45 cm) ITL 15,400,000. NEW YORK, 3 Oct 2001, *Gourmet* (oil on canvas, 20 x 25 ins / 51 x 64 cm) USD 3,500. SAN FRANCISCO, 15 May 2002, *Sewing Lesson* (oil on canvas, 14 x 19 ins / 36 x 48 cm) USD 6,500. NEW YORK, 21 May 2002, *Monk and the Maiden* (oil on canvas, 19 x 15 ins / 48 x 38 cm) USD 3,500. LONDON, 17 June 2004, *Grandfather's Gift* (oil on canvas, 35 x 28 ins / 89 x 71 cm) GBP 17,000. LONDON, 23 Sept 2004, *Mannequin* (1901, oil on canvas, 24 x 34 ins / 62 x 87 cm) GBP 10,000.

SANI, David
Italian, 19th - 20th century.
Born in Florence.
Active 1864-1889.
Painter. Genre scenes.
He exhibited his work mainly in Florence.
AUCTION RECORDS:
VIENNA, 15 March 1977, *The Hand-Kissing* (oil on canvas, 23 1/2 x 15 3/4 ins / 60 x 40 cm) ATS 80,000. NEW YORK, 26 May 1992, *Blowing Soap Bubbles to Amuse the Baby* (1889, oil on canvas, 22 x 30 1/2 ins / 55.9 x 77.4 cm) USD 6,050. NEW YORK, 27 May 1993, *Love Letter* (oil on canvas, 25 x 20 ins / 63.5 x 50.8 cm) USD 9,200. NEW YORK, 28 May 1993, *Just Like Grandfather!* (oil on canvas, 24 x 30 1/4 ins / 61 x 76.7 cm) USD 6,325. NEW YORK, 20 July 1995, *Inquisitive Servant Girl* (oil on canvas, 16 x 13 ins / 40.6 x 33 cm) USD 4,312. LONDON, 25 March 1999, *Interior Scene* (oil on canvas, 26 x 20 ins / 65 x 51 cm) GBP 10,000. SAN FRANCISCO, 26 May 1999, *Peeping at My Lady's Letter* (oil on canvas, 43 x 33 ins / 109 x 83 cm) USD 16,000. LONDON, 5 Sept 2000, *Feeding Time* (oil on canvas, 33 x 24 ins / 85 x 60 cm) GBP 2,800. LONDON, 5 April 2001, *Ardent Suitor* (oil on canvas, 26 x 20 ins / 66 x 51 cm) GBP 8,000.

SANI, Domenico Maria, or Sanni
Spanish, 18th century.
Born 18 April 1690, in Cesena; died c. 1772.
Painter. History painting, genre scenes, figures.
Domenico Maria Sani settled in Spain in 1721 and was appointed court painter to Philip V and then Charles III of Spain.
MUSEUMS AND GALLERIES:
MADRID (Prado): *Madman*; *Beggar*; *The Village Charlatan*; *Beggars' Meeting*.

SANI, Ippolito
Italian, 17th century.
Active in Lucca at the beginning of the 17th century.
Painter.
Ippolito Sani was the first master of Pietro Ricchi.

SANIELEVICI, Salomon
Romanian, 20th century.
Born 1878, in Botosani.
Active in Germany.
Painter. Landscapes.
Salomon Sanielevici lived in Munich.
MUSEUMS AND GALLERIES:
BUCHAREST (Muz. National de Arta al României): *Sunny Landscape*.

SANIN, Piérart
Flemish School, 15th century.
Active in Tournai.
Sculptor.
Piérart Sanin worked for the church in St-Brice in 1447.

SANINI, Alemanno, or Sannini
Italian, 18th century.
Born possibly in 1690; died 1740.
Active in Pescia.
Painter.

SANJURJO, Antonio
Spanish, 19th century.
Born in Rábade; died 1830.
Active in Galicia.
Sculptor.
Antonio Sanjurjo was a pupil of J. Adan. He carved a group of angels in the great chapel of Lugo Cathedral and also worked for churches in Santiago de Compostela.

SANJUROPPO GAISHI. See **SAN'YO**

SANJUST, Luca
Italian, 20th - 21st century.
Born 1959, in Rome.
Painter, pastellist.
Luca Sanjust lives and works in Tuscany. His paintings consist of a few very simple abstract forms covered in flat tints of brilliant colour, sometimes completed by a figurative element with symbolic meaning.

His work has appeared in collective exhibitions, and in solo shows as follows: 1985, Milan and Rome; 1987, Accademia Tedesca, Rome; 1988, the Krief and Valence gallery in Paris; 1988, 1991, 1993, the studio Graffiti Now in Verona; 1989, the American Academy in Rome; 1990, Mantua; 1994, Mantua; and 1995, the Galerie Vidal-Saint Phalle in Paris.

SANLOT-BAGNINAULT, René
French, 19th century.
Born in Paris.
Painter. Landscapes.
He was a pupil of Thomas Couture. He exhibited at the Paris Salon, making his debut in 1865.

SANMARCHI, Marco. See **SAN MARTINO**

SANMARCO, Fabrizio
Italian, 17th century.

Died 12 August 1662, in Rocca.
Active in Rocca d'Evandro.
Painter.

SANMARTI Y AGUILO, Medardo
Spanish, 19th century.
Born in Barcelona; died 1891.
Sculptor. Busts, monuments.
Medardo Sanmarti y Aguilo was a pupil of Jeronimo Sunol. He carved busts and monuments in Madrid.
MUSEUMS AND GALLERIES:
MADRID (Mus. de Arte Moderno): *Bust of Don Manuel Becerra.*

SANMARTINO, Gennaro, or Sammartino
Italian, 18th - 19th century.
Modeller. Nativity figures.
The work of Gennaro Sanmartino, the brother and pupil of Giuseppe Sanmartino, is featured in almost every collection of nativity figures.
MUSEUMS AND GALLERIES:
MUNICH (Bayerisches Nationalmus.).

SANMARTINO, Giuseppe, or Sammartino or San Martino
Italian, 18th century.
Born 1720, in Naples; died 12 December 1793, in Naples.
Sculptor (including marble), modeller. Religious subjects. Nativity figures, groups.
Giuseppe Sanmartino was the brother of Gennaro Sanmartino and a pupil of F. (or Matteo) Bottiglieri. He was influenced by Bernini and is a typical exponent of 18th-century verism, specialising in nativity figures. His works can be found in the cathedral and churches of Naples. In 1753, in the former Sansevero chapel, which during the course of the 17th and 18th centuries became the church of Santa Maria di Pietà dei Sangro, he carved the subsequently famous figure of *Christo velato (Christ Veiled)*. This sculpture was for a long time attributed to Antonio Corradini (who was responsible for the allegorical statue of *Modesty* in the same location) and remained practically unknown as a result of its siting by Prince Raimondo di Sangro in a kind of subterranean crypt. Originally intended to be lit from above, it now occupies a position in the centre of the nave. The dead Christ is completely enveloped in a shroud, the countless folds of which were originally designed with unusual lighting conditions in mind and which reveal in a manner more theatrical than sorrowful the agonised body and emaciated face. In any case, the initially quite unique combination of circumstances led Sanmartino, in the mid-18th century, to create something much more in keeping with the Romanticism of the fantastic or even with the sophisticated charm of the New Style. During his period in Naples, Antonio Canova tried to acquire the work.
MUSEUMS AND GALLERIES:
MUNICH (Bayerisches Nationalmus.): crib figurines - NAPLES (Mus. di Capodimonte): crib figurines.
AUCTION RECORDS:
PARIS, 25 June 1970, *Children Symbolising the Seasons and the Elements* (marble, two groups) BEF 24,000.

SANMIGUEL, Manuel
Spanish, 19th century.
Born in Barcelona; died February 1903, in Mula.
Painter.
Manuel Sanmiguel executed decorative paintings in churches in Murcia.

SANMINIATELLI, Bino
Italian, 20th century.
Born 7 May 1896, in Florence; died 1984, in Chianti.
Draughtsman.
Sanminiatelli exhibited work at the Salon d'Automne and the Salon des Indépendants in Paris, as well as at the Société Léonard de Vinci.

SANN, Jacob
Norwegian, 19th - 20th century.
Born 1874, in Christiania (now Oslo).
Painter. Landscapes.
Jacob Sann was a pupil of Christian Krogh and, in Paris, of William Bouguereau.
MUSEUMS AND GALLERIES:
OSLO (Nasjonalgal.).

SANNA, Giovanni
Italian, 17th century.
Died 22 May 1622, in Rome.
Painter.

SANNA-PIU, Francesco
Italian, 18th century.
Active in Sassari (Sardinia), Italy during the first half of the 18th century.
Painter.
Francesco Sanna-Piu painted two *Scenes from the Passion* for the church in Galtelli in 1724.

SANNDERS, John (son). See **SANDERS John**

SANNE, Giovanni di Tommaso
Italian, 15th century.
Active at the end of the 15th century.
Sculptor.
Giovanni di Tommaso Sanne worked in Orvieto Cathedral in 1499.

SANNINO, Santillo, or Sandino
Italian, 17th century.
Died 1685.
Active in Naples.
Painter.
The pupil of M. Stanzioni, Santillo Sannino painted altarpieces for churches in Naples.

SANNOM, Charlotte Amalie
Danish, 19th - 20th century.
Born 29 September 1846, in Ryköbing; died 18 December 1923, in Nöddebo.
Painter.
Charlotte Amalie Sannom was a pupil of P. Vilhelm Kyhn.

SANNUTI, Giulio. See **SANUTO**

SANNYS, François de
French, 16th century.
Born 1559, in Antwerp.
Painter. Designs for tapestries.
François de Sannys worked in the porcelain factory of Fontainebleau from 1581.

SANO
Japanese, 20th century.
Painter. Figures, landscapes.
In 1952 Sano held a personal exhibition of his works which included figures painted in Japan together with broad Parisian landscapes. He was influenced by Western painting but owes his distinctive page set-up to the Japanese tradition.

SANO, E. B.
French, 19th century.
Born in Paris; died 1878, in Antwerp.
Active in Belgium.
Painter. Interiors, urban landscapes, architectural views, ruins.
This artist chiefly painted interiors, views of towns, and ruins.
MUSEUMS AND GALLERIES:
LIÈGE: *Interior of a Town.*

SANO DI ANDREA BATTILORI
Italian, 15th century.
Active in Siena in 1446.
Painter, illuminator.

SANO DI GIORGIO BERARDI. See **BERARDI**

SANO DI GIOVANNI
Italian, 14th century.
Active in Siena.
Sculptor.

Sano di Giovanni sculpted a low relief, a *Baptism of Christ,* in the church of the Congregation of Charity, in Citta di Castello (Umbria), in 1365.

SANO DI MATTEO, or Ansano
Italian, 15th century.
Died after 27 July 1434, probably in Perugia.
Sculptor, architect.
Sienese School.

Sano di Matteo worked for Siena and Orvieto Cathedrals, and later in Perugia.

SANO DI PIETRO, also known as Ansano di Pietro di Mencio
Italian, 15th century.
Born 1406, in Siena; died 1481, in Siena.
Painter, draughtsman. Religious subjects.
Sienese School.

It has been said that Sano di Pietro 'lived everything in God', and his enthusiasm for St Bernardine and his devotion to the Virgin provided him with two inexhaustible sources of inspiration. St Bernardine died in L'Aquila in 1444 and was canonised by Pope Nicholas V in 1450, during the Jubilee. This was a great event in Italy and throughout the Christian world, but even more so in Siena, where there was exceptional fervour.

Sano di Pietro produced many portraits of the saint, and scenes from the *Life of St Bernardine*. The monks of the Osservanza monastery asked him to produce the image of their founder. Elsewhere he decorated another church during Bernardine's lifetime, and perhaps under his direction.

St Catherine of Siena died in Rome in 1380 and was canonised by Pope Pius II in 1461. Sano di Pietro was asked to produce a painting of this new saint, the second patron of Siena. He decided that her image would be painted in one of the halls of the Palazzo Pubblico. He was able to depict the saint again, in the decoration of the city gate, Porta Romana.

However, Sano di Pietro was above all a painter of the Madonna. In this, his taste coincided with that of the public. Demand was such that he often simply reproduced the same types and compositions in a mechanical fashion. Nevertheless, his painting *Assumption*, which he produced at the age of 72, reveals that he retained all his vigour and creative power. His most interesting paintings of the Virgin are not those which emphasised celestial royalty, some are imprinted with an indefinably charming melancholy. An example is his triptych, *Virgin and Child,* whose central panel alone appears to have been by Sano di Pietro. The side panels and pediment suggest rather Lorenzo di Pietro, his brother, known as Il Vecchietta. This style may be seen in two paintings in the museum in Siena. In one, the look is expressive, combined with an anguished embrace which suggests a mysterious maternal sense of foreboding. The other, a work of exceptional purity, is painted in a range of light and sallow flesh tones. This was commissioned by a nun for her oratory 'for the soul of her father and mother'. The painter, inspired by this filial piety, produced a masterpiece.

BIBLIOGRAPHY:

Gaillard, Emile, *Un peintre siennois au XVe siècle. Sano di Pietro (1406-1481),* Dardel, 1923. Trübner, Jörg, *Die stilstische Entwicklung der Tafelbilder des Sano di Pietro (1405-1481),* Heitz, 1925.

MUSEUMS AND GALLERIES:

BORDEAUX: *Angel Gabriel* - CHANTILLY: *Mystical Marriage of St Francis of Assisi with Chastity, Poverty and Humility* - COLOGNE: *St Francis Receiving the Stigmata* - DRESDEN: three religious subjects - EDINBURGH (Nat. Gal. of Scotland): *The Coronation of the Virgin* (tempera and gold/panel, work of studio) - MOSCOW (Rumiantsev Mus.): *Holy Virgin* - NANTES: *St Francis of Assisi Receiving the Stigmata* - PARIS (Louvre): *Dream of St Jerome; St Jerome Kneeling in the Desert; Legend of St Jerome; Death of St Jerome; Appearance of St Jerome to Two People; Appearance of St Jerome and St John to St Augustine* - SIENA (Accademia): *St Catherine of Siena* (miniature); Madonnas - SIENA (Palazzo Pubblico): *St Catherine of Siena*.

AUCTION RECORDS:

PARIS, 11 May 1923, *Virgin and Infant Jesus,* FRF 65,000. LONDON, 8 Dec 1926, *Crucifixion,* GBP 220. PARIS, 25 Jan 1929, *Annunciation* (attributed) FRF 3,800. LONDON, 15 May 1929, *Virgin and Child,* GBP 580. LONDON, 12 June 1931, *Madonna and Child with Saints,* GBP 364. PARIS, 19 May 1933, *Virgin and Child* (triptych) FRF 71,500. LONDON, 20 April 1934, *Virgin and Child Surrounded by Saints,* GBP 273. LONDON, 22 April 1942, *Nativity Scene* (attributed) GBP 190. LONDON, 31 March 1944, *Virgin and Child,* GBP 735. NEW YORK, 21 Feb 1945, *St Sigismund,* USD 1,700. LONDON, 25 Oct 1946, *Virgin and Child,* GBP 126. LONDON, 18 Dec 1946, *Virgin and Child,* GBP 400. PARIS, 19 Dec 1949, *Madonna and Infant Jesus* (gilt ground) FRF 400,000. LONDON, 23 May 1951, *Creation of the World* (illumination) GBP 130. LONDON, 26 June 1964, *Birth of the Virgin,* Gns 11,000. LONDON, 23 June 1967, *St Donatus and the Dragon,* Gns 13,500. LONDON, 10 April 1970, *Virgin with Child,* Gns 13,000. LONDON, 1 Nov 1978, *Virgin and Child with Holy People and Angels* (oil on panel, gilt ground, with original frame, 26 1/2 x 18 1/2 ins / 67 x 47 cm) GBP 24,000. LONDON, 12 Dec 1980, *Virgin and Child with Holy People* (oil on panel, gilt ground, 24 3/4 x 17 3/4 ins / 62.8 x 45 cm) GBP 50,000. NEW YORK, 9 Jan 1981, *St Bernard of Siena Borne by Angels* (oil on panel, rounded at the top, 13 1/2 x 9 ins / 34.2 x 23 cm) USD 15,000. MILAN, 20 May 1982, *Resurrection* (tempera/panel, 29 1/4 x 26 3/4 ins / 74 x 68 cm) ITL 28,000,000. NEW YORK, 20 Jan 1983, *Virgin and Child* (tempera/panel, octagonal, diam. 9 ins / 23 cm) USD 8,000. LONDON, 6 July 1983, *Virgin and Child Surrounded by Angels* (oil on panel, gilt ground, 20 1/4 x 15 ins / 51.5 x 38 cm) GBP 32,000. LONDON, 10 July 1987, *Virgin and Child with St Francis of Assisi, Bernardine of Siena and Four Angels* (oil on panel, gilt ground, 25 1/2 x 17 ins / 64.5 x 43 cm) GBP 80,000. NEW YORK, 1 June 1989, *St Margaret of Antioch* (tempera with gilt ground/paper, ogival, 39 3/4 x 16 1/2 ins / 101 x 42 cm) USD 77,000. NEW YORK, 11 Jan 1991, *St Mary Magdalen* (tempera/panel with gilt ground, 8 1/4 x 10 ins / 20.8 x 25.2 cm) USD 52,800. LONDON, 10 July 1992, *Virgin and Child with St John the Baptist and St Leonard with Two Angels* (tempera/panel with gilt ground, 18 3/4 x 15 ins / 47.5 x 38 cm) GBP 27,500. NEW YORK, 20 May 1993, *Virgin with Child with St Catherine and St Dorothy and Four Angels* (tempera/panel with gilt ground, 25 1/4 x 17 1/2 ins / 64.1 x 44.5 cm) USD 167,500. LONDON, 10 Dec 1993, *Virgin with Child with St John the Baptist and St Leonard and Two Angels* (tempera/panel with gilt ground, 18 3/4 x 15 ins / 47.5 x 38 cm) GBP 89,500. MILAN, 4 April 1995, *Virgin with Child* (tempera/panel, 16 x 12 3/4 ins / 40.5 x 32.7 cm) ITL 172,500,000. NEW YORK, 16 May 1996, *Virgin with Child* (tempera/panel with gilt ground, 17 x 12 1/2 ins / 43.2 x 31.8 cm) USD 63,000. NEW YORK, 31 Jan 1997, *Nativity* (tempera with gilt ground/panel, 20 1/2 x 16 ins / 52.2 x 40.5 cm) USD 222,500. VENICE, 15 Dec 2001, *Christ between the Virgin and St John the Evangelist* (tempera on board, 8 x 30 ins / 21 x 77 cm) ITL 350,000,000. NEW YORK, 24

Jan 2002, *The Archangels Michael and Raphael. St Scholastica. Martyred Female Saint* (tempera on panel, four, 2 x 2 ins / 4 x 5 cm) USD 22,000. PARIS, 19 June 2002, *Madonna of Humility* (oil on panel, 19 x 15 ins / 48 x 37 cm) EUR 150,000. PARIS, 6 June 2003, *Virgin and Child Surrounded by Four Saints and Two Angels* (tempera on gold panel, 22 x 17 ins / 56 x 43 cm) EUR 97,000. MILAN, 29 Oct 2003, *Virgin* (tempera on board, 15 x 14 ins / 38 x 36 cm) EUR 37,000. LONDON, 7 July 2004, *Lady Perna Being Cured on Approaching St Bernardino's Body* (tempera on panel, 9 x 16 ins / 24 x 41 cm) GBP 120,000.

SANOGUEIRA, Rolando. See **SA-NOGUEIRA**

SANON

Haitian, 20th - 21st century.

Born 1957.

Painter.

Sanon's highly individual style has earned him the name 'Magician'.

AUCTION RECORDS:

PARIS, 24 Jan 1994, *Imaginary Harvest* (oil on canvas, 15 3/4 x 19 3/4 ins / 40 x 50 cm) FRF 5,000.

SANPOLO, Battista

Italian, 15th century.

Active in Bornato, at the end of the 15th century.

Sculptor, designer of ornamental architectural features.

Battista Sanpolo worked on the pediment of the town hall in Brescia from 1492 to 1493.

SANPOLO, Nicola. See **SAMPOLO**

SANQUIRICO, Alessandro, the Elder

Italian, 19th century.

Born 27 July 1777, in Milan, in 1780 according to some sources; died 12 March 1849, in Milan.

Painter, watercolourist, draughtsman. Historical subjects, architectural views. Stage sets.

Alessandro Sanquirico the Elder was a pupil of the theatre designer Giovanni Perego of Milan and worked chiefly for the La Scala theatre in Milan.

MUSEUMS AND GALLERIES:

MILAN (Gal. d'Arte Moderna): *Ceremony of the Keys of the City of Milan.*

AUCTION RECORDS:

NEW YORK, 11 Jan 1994, *The Great Ballroom in the Doge's Palace with Desdemona who Declares her Love for Othello before the Doge* (ink and wash, 11 1/2 x 15 ins / 28.9 x 38.3 cm) USD 2,070. PARIS, 22 Feb 1996, *View of an Egyptian Temple* (watercolour, 19 3/4 x 13 1/2 ins / 50 x 34 cm) FRF 11,000. LUCERNE, 13 Oct 1999, *Lake Como, Passengers on the Deck of the Steamship Lariano* (gouache, 7 x 10 ins / 18 x 25 cm) CHF 19,000. LONDON, 9 Dec 2002, *Stage Design for the Scala Theatre in Milan of the Interior of the Grande Sala de Ballo* (pen and ink wash, 11 x 15 ins / 29 x 38 cm) GBP 1,200. MILAN, 24 March 2004, *Remembrances* (oil on canvas, 9 x 14 ins / 24 x 35 cm) EUR 3,700.

SANQUIRICO, Alessandro, the Younger

Italian, 19th - 20th century.

Died 30 January 1926, in Milan.

Painter, art restorer.

The grandson of Alessandro Sanquirico the Elder and brother of Pio Sanquirico, he worked abroad after 1900.

SANQUIRICO, Paolo

Italian, 16th - 17th century.

Born 1565, in Villa de San Quirico; died 1630, in Rome.

Sculptor, medallist, architect.

Paolo Sanquirico was the pupil of C. Mariani and Giacomo Antonio Moro in Rome, and became director of the Papal mint.

SANQUIRICO, Pio

Italian, 19th century.

Born 20 October 1847, in Gudo Visconti; died 10 June 1900, in Milan.

Painter. History painting, portraits, genre scenes.

The grandson of Alessandro Sanquirico the Elder, Pio Sanquirico studied under G. Bertini at the Accademia di Belle Arti di Brera in Milan. He exhibited in Turn, Rome, Milan and Florence.

Sanquirico

MUSEUMS AND GALLERIES:

BUCHAREST (Muz. National de Arta al României): *Portrait of a Woman* - MILAN (Gal. d'Arte): *Flowers* - MILAN (Pinacoteca di Brera): *Giordano Bruno; Tommaso Campanella.*

AUCTION RECORDS:

MILAN, 5 Nov 1981, *Head of a Girl* (oil on canvas, 16 1/2 x 12 1/2 ins / 42 x 31.5 cm) ITL 2,200,000. PARIS, 1 Dec 1992, *Girl in Flowered Dress* (oil on canvas, 13 3/4 x 19 3/4 ins / 35 x 50 cm) FRF 10,000. MILAN, 8 June 1993, *Soap Bubble* (oil on canvas, 30 1/4 x 21 1/4 ins / 77 x 54 cm) ITL 7,000,000. ROME, 25 May 1999, *Portrait of a Peasant Girl* (oil on canvas, 20 x 13 ins / 50 x 33 cm) ITL 9,000,000. MILAN, 20 Oct 1999, *Lake Lecco* (oil on canvas, 30 x 24 ins / 75 x 60 cm) ITL 5,951,000. ROME, 21 Nov 2000, *Goose Girl* (oil on canvas, 59 x 39 ins / 150 x 100 cm) ITL 45,000,000. BERN, 5 Nov 2003, *Children Fishing for an Apple* (oil on canvas, 19 x 31 ins / 49 x 79 cm) CHF 4,000. VIENNA, 27 May 2004, *Children Fishing for an Apple* (oil on canvas, 19 x 31 ins / 49 x 79 cm) EUR 6,500.

SANRAKU, real name: Mitsuyori Kano, original name: Kimura, nicknames: Heizo, Shuri, pseudonym: Sanraku

Japanese, 16th - 17th century.

Born 1559, in Omi; died 1635.

Painter.

Kano School.

Sanraku was the son of the painter Kimura Nagamitsu and was adopted by his master Kano Eitoku (1543-1590, of whom he was the favourite disciple. After the death of Mitsunobu, the eldest son of Eitoku, in 1608 he worked with Sadanobu (1597-1623) at the head of the family studio. He was without doubt the artist who best illustrated the second part of the Momoyama period in Kyoto. He was the son of a warrior and served as a page to the shogun Hideyoshi, who noticed his talent and apprenticed him to Eitoku. Sankaru continued to benefit from the patronage of Hideyoshi, especially following the death of Eitoku, and in 1592 he was asked to carry out the decoration of Momoyama Castle. When the Kano family settled in Edo (now Tokyo), the new centre of power, Sanraku remained in Kyoto and the continuity of his studio in the name of Kyo-Kano, the Kano family of Kyoto, was assured by his descendents.

Quite a large number of works by Sanraku are extant, from cursive style washes to large brightly coloured decorative compositions, from delicate landscapes to Chinese historical scenes, demonstrating the great scope of his talent and the confidence of his technique. In the wall paintings executed around 1620 in two buildings of the Daitoku-ji monastery in Kyoto, the Kano tradition introduced by Motonobu (1476-1559) can be seen in the landscapes, pine trees with monochrome falcons with greater finesse of the brush stroke than that of Eitoku. His tendency to stylisation of line is pushed to the limit in the compositions in the Tenkyu-in sanctuary in the Myoshin-ji Zen temple in Kyoto executed by Sanraku and his adopted son Sansetsu (1590-1651) between 1631 and 1635, just before the death of this painter. The paintings have retained all their freshness, whether it be the tigers in the central room, the flowering bindweed on the bamboo fencing of the east room or the plum trees and birds of the west room. A large proportion of this collection is the work of Sansetsu, but the delicate sensitivity of Sanraku shows through in the skilfully calculated rhythm, the almost geometric aspect of the rocks and the twisted tree which approaches a static, even abstract beauty. His talent for drawing flows freely onto a screen, formerly in the old palace of the Kujos and now preserved in the Tokyo National Museum, showing a Japanese historical scene taken from *Romance of Genji: Kuruma-Arasoi*. The historical figures are drawn with all the detail of the Tosa School, a dynasty of court painters, but by introducing contemporary figures Sanraku brought considerable vivacity to the work.

BIBLIOGRAPHY:

Akiyama, Terukazu, *La Peinture japonaise*, Skira, Geneva, 1961.

MUSEUMS AND GALLERIES:

TOKYO (National Mus.): *Story of Genji: Kuruma-Arasoi* (screen).

SANREDAM. See **SAENREDAM**

SANREGRET, Anonyme

Canadian, 20th - 21st century.
Born c. 1960, in Montreal.
Painter, screen printer.

Anonyme Sanregret is involved in poetry and music as well as painting. He has participated in collective exhibitions since 1991 and also holds solo exhibitions, usually in alternative places, and often paints in public.

SANREINO, Matheus. See **SANREMO Matheus**

SANREMO, Matheus, or Sanreino

Spanish, 17th century.
Active in Valencia in 1602.
Miniaturist.

Matheus Sanremo was also a calligrapher.

SANS, Domingo

Spanish, 15th century.
Active in Catalonia during the second half of the 15th century.
Painter.

Domingo Sans was the father of Nicolás Sans, and worked at Lerida and Barcelona.

SANS, Eugène

French, 19th century.
Born in Montauban; died 1876.
Painter. History painting, portraits.

He was a pupil of Flandrin.

MUSEUMS AND GALLERIES:

BAGNÈRES: *Portrait of M Roques; The Virgin Mary, the Infant Jesus and St John; Portrait* (pastel).

SANS, Garcia

Spanish, 16th century.
Active during the first half of the 16th century.
Painter.

Garcia Sans worked in Palermo for the cathedral and a number of other churches. None of his works survive.

SANS, Klaas

Dutch, 20th century.
Born 1927, in Sappemeer (Groningen).
Painter.

Klaas Sans studied initially in Groningen, then at the Académie Ranson in Paris. He travelled in Canada and was a frequent visitor to Paris. He participated in group exhibitions, mostly in the Netherlands but also in Paris, notably at the Salon des Réalités Nouvelles in 1955.

SANS, Nicolás

Spanish, 16th century.
Active in Barcelona from 1506 to 1515.
Painter.

Nicolás Sans was the son of Domingo Sans.

SANS CORBELLA, Tomás

Spanish, 19th - 20th century.
Born 1869, in Barcelona; died 1911.
Painter. Genre scenes, landscapes.

Tomás Sans Corbella was a pupil of José Armet y Portanel.

SANS Y CABOT, Francisco

Spanish, 19th century.
Born 9 April 1828, in Barcelona; died 5 May 1881, in Madrid.
Painter. Religious subjects, figures.

Francisco Sans y Cabot was a pupil of Th. Couture.

MUSEUMS AND GALLERIES:

MADRID: *Head of St Paul; Don Wenceslas Ignals de Izco; St Luke the Evangelist; St Mark the Evangelist.*

SANSEBASTIANO, Michele

Italian, 19th - 20th century.
Born in Genoa.
Sculptor.

He exhibited work in Milan in 1881.

SANSETSU. See **KANO Sansetsu**

SANSHIRO. See **TOSHUN**

SANSOM, F.

Dutch, 18th century.
Born in London.
Painter, engraver. History painting, portraits.

F. Sansom was active in Rotterdam from 1788 to 1790; he produced engravings of contemporary figures and events.

SANSON, or Samson

French, 18th century.
Painter. Religious subjects.

Sanson was active in Paris in 1728. He produced five paintings for the church of St-André-des-Arts; they disappeared during the French Revolution.

SANSON, Antoine

French, 17th century.
Active 1660-1670.
Engraver.

SANSON, Charles Alexandre

French, 19th - 20th century.
Born in Maubeuge (Nord).
Sculptor.

Charles Alexandre Sanson exhibited in Paris at the Salon de la Société Nationale des Beaux-Arts.

SANSON, Jacques. See **SAMSON**

SANSON, Jules

French, 19th century.
Painter.

He showed his work at the Paris Salons of 1833 and 1836.

SANSON, Justin Chrysostôme

French, 19th - 20th century.
Born 8 August 1833, in Nemours; died 2 November 1910, in Paris.
Sculptor. Religious subjects, allegorical subjects, local figures, portraits, genre scenes. Statues.

Justin Chrysostôme Sanson entered the École des Beaux-Arts, Paris, on 12 October 1954 and became a pupil of Justin Marie Lequien and François Jouffroy. In 1859 he won the Second Prix de Rome and in 1861 the First Grand Prix. He first exhibited at the Salon de Paris in 1861, was awarded a medal in 1866, a third-class medal during the Exposition

Universelle of 1867, a second-class during the Exposition Universelle of 1878 and a bronze at the Exposition Universelle of 1889. He was made a Chevalier of the Légion d'Honneur in 1869. He carved *Commerce, Industry, St Martin, The Architect Herbault* for the Palais de Justice, Amiens.
MUSEUMS AND GALLERIES:
LE HAVRE (Mus. Malraux): *Pietà*.
AUCTION RECORDS:
COLOGNE, 15 June 1989, *Girls Dancing during a Bacchanalia* (bronze, h. 28 3/4 ins / 73 cm) DEM 2,800. PARIS, 21 March 1996, *Tambourine Player* (dark-patinated babbitt, h. 24 ins / 61 cm) FRF 13,000.

SANSON, Stella
French, 19th - 20th century.
Painter, watercolourist. Flowers.
AUCTION RECORDS:
PARIS, 4 Dec 1950, *Chrysanthemums* (watercolour) FRF 2,200.

SANSONE, Il. See **ALEOTTI Antonio**

SANSONE, Il. See also **MARCHESI Giuseppe**

SANSONE, Sebastiano
Italian, 17th century.
Active in Scandiano.
Painter.
Sebastiano Sansone was the pupil and assistant of Jean Boulanger in Modena.

SANSONE DI NICCOLÒ
Spanish, 15th century.
Active in Florence.
Painter.
The brother of Delle di Niccolò, Sansone di Niccolò worked in Seville in 1442 and painted the frescoes in the cloister of Avila Cathedral in 1465.

SANSONETTE, V. de
French, 19th century.
Born in Nancy; died 1861.
Watercolourist, draughtsman. Landscapes.
A pupil of Ingres, this artist exhibited at the Paris Salons of 1831 and 1835.
MUSEUMS AND GALLERIES:
BAGNÈRES-DE-BIGORRE: a drawing and a watercolour.

SANSONI, Guglielmo. See **TATO**

SANSONNET, Jacob
French, 17th century.
Active in Nancy.
Sculptor.

SANSOVINO, Andrea, or Andrea dal Monte San Savino, also known as Andrea Contucci, called Il Sansovino
Italian, 15th - 16th century.
Born c. 1460 or 1467, near Monte San Savino; died 1529, in the same area.
Sculptor, architect.
Florentine School.
It is probable that Andrea Sansovino studied sculpture in the studio of the Pollaiuolo brothers and architecture under Giuliano da Sangallo. After a period working in Florence, where he became a member of the guild in 1491, he went to Portugal where he entered the service of the king. He returned to Italy in 1500 and was kept very busy with commissions in Florence, Volterra, Rome and Loreto, specialising in reliefs for fonts and tombs.

Between 1502 and 1505, he carved a *Baptism of Christ* for the Baptistery in Florence. In 1502, he produced the font in Volterra and between 1505 and 1509 the tombs of Cardinals Ascanio Sforza and Girolamo della Rovere in the church of S Maria del Popolo in Rome. In 1513, he began a series of low reliefs portraying scenes from the *Life of the Virgin* for the Santa Casa in Loreto.

Sansovino's complex works display a mixture of Florentine and Roman styles and are richly decorated with niches and arches ornamented with grotesques. He had thoroughly assimilated the lessons of Antiquity and of the Renaissance and was capable of producing, particularly towards the end of his career, works whose restrained gravity highlights the skill with which they are executed.
MUSEUMS AND GALLERIES:
BERLIN (Bodemus.): *Portrait of Cardinal Antonio del Monte* (relief) - FLORENCE (Mus. Nazionale): *Virgin and Child* (terracotta).

SANSOVINO, Jacopo d'Antonio, pseudonym of Tatti
Italian, 16th century.
Born 1486, in Florence; died 1570, in Venice.
Sculptor, architect.
Florentine School, Venetian School.
A pupil of Contucci Andrea il Sansovino, whose name he took, Jacopo d'Antonio Sansovino also knew Giuliano di Sangallo. He was noticed by Bramante, and also by Popes Leo X and Clement VII. He started out as a sculptor and examples of his work can be seen in Florence where, in the Bargello, there is a *Bacchus* (1514), a low relief of *Christ* and a *St James the Greater* in the cathedral.

Between 1519 and 1527, Sansovino worked in Rome on reliefs for the funerary monuments of Cardinal Giovanni Michiel and Bishop Orso (1519) in the church of S Marcello. He also made a sculpture of the *Madonna del Parto* (1519-1521) for the church of S Agostino. While in Rome he also began to work as an architect, a career that became increasingly important in Venice from 1527, building the church of S Marcello and the Palazzo Niccolini and Palazzo Sante.

Moving to Venice after the sack of Rome, Sansovino devoted himself almost entirely to architecture and, in 1532, built the Palazzo Corner known as Ca' Grande in collaboration with F. Giorgi. Dating from 1534 is one of the rare sculptures of this period, the *Madonna and Child* from the Arsenale. Sansovino's energies were almost entirely taken up with work on the Biblioteca S Marco, a building combining elegance and restraint and a masterpiece of Venetian architecture that was to be highly influential on subsequent architects, but he received a term in prison in 1545 when one of the vaults of the building collapsed. Between 1537 and 1545, he was also working on the mint and, in 1540, the Loggetta and the base of the campanile (bell-tower) of St Mark's.

After the accident at the Biblioteca, Sansovino returned to sculptural work, particularly monuments. He also made the sacristy door, font and reliefs around the tribune of the choir in the basilica of S Marco and, in 1554, the statues of *Mars* and *Neptune* for the bottom of the Scala dei Giganti (Giants' Staircase) in the Doge's Palace. Two more architectural projects in Venice were the Palazzo Dolfin of 1562 and the oval church of the Incurabili but he was now being sought after elsewhere. In Padua, he designed the square courtyard of the university and in Livorno he built the church of the archbishopric in collaboration with Andrea Sansovino, his master. Other of his sculptures are *St James* in the church of S Maria in Monsorrat, *St Anthony* in the church of S Pietro in Bologna, low reliefs in the church of S Antonio in Padua, a *Virgin with Two Saints* in Verona and figures of *St John, St Bartholomew* and *St Mark* in Bergamo.
BIBLIOGRAPHY:
Lotz, W., '*The Roman Legacy in Sansovino's Venetian Buildings*' in *J. Soc. Archit. Hist, 22*, 1963. Garrard, M., *The Early Sculpture of Jacopo Sansovino: Florence and Rome*, dissertation, John Hopkins University, Baltimore, 1970. Garrard, M.,

'*Jacopo Sansovino's 'Madonna' in Sant'Agostino: An Antique Source Rediscovered*' in *J. Warb. & Court. Inst, 38,* 1975. Howard, D., *Jacopo Sansovino: Architecture and Patronage in Renaissance Venice,* Yale University Press, New Haven, 1975. Davis, C., '*Jacopo Sansovino's 'Loggetta di San Marco' and Two Problems of Iconography*' in *Mitt. Ksthist. Inst. Florenz, 29,* 1985. Huse, N./Wolters, W., *The Art of Renaissance Venice,* University of Chicago Press, Chicago, 1990. Boucher, B., *The Sculpture of Jacopo Sansovino (2 vols),* Yale University Press, New Haven, 1991. Davis, C., '*Jacopo Sansovino and the Engraved Memorials of the Cappella Badoer-Giustiniani in San Francesco dalla Vigna in Venice*' in *Münchn. Jb. Bild. Kst., 45,* 1994.

MUSEUMS AND GALLERIES:
FLORENCE (Mus. Nazionale del Bargello): *Bacchus* (1514); *Christ* (low relief).

AUCTION RECORDS:
NEW YORK, 1 Oct 1966, *Seated Athlete Leaning Forward with Twisted Torso* (bronze) USD 17,000. AMSTERDAM, 24 April 1968, *Neptune* (patinated bronze) NLG 39,000. LONDON, 2 July 1973, *Virgin and Child* (bronze) GBP 4,800.

SANT, E.
French, 19th century.
Painter. Flowers.

This artist took part in the exhibition at the Palais du Luxembourg in 1830, and exhibited at the Paris Salon of 1836.

SANT, Hans van
Dutch (?), 17th century.
Painter. Still-lifes.

Only three works by Hans van Sant are known, one dated 1620, another 1632. The scant details available for both Hans and V.S. van Sant seem to point to a common identity for both.

AUCTION RECORDS:
ZURICH, 25 May 1984, *Still-life* (1632, oil on panel, 15 3/4 x 23 ins / 40 x 58.5 cm) CHF 70,000. LONDON, 9 Dec 1994, *Still-life of a Rohmer Glass, a Small Overturned Bowl, a Fruit-cake, Bread and a Peeled Lemon in Pewter Dishes on a Table Draped with a White Cloth* (oil on canvas, 20 1/4 x 33 ins / 51.7 x 84 cm) GBP 19,550.

SANT, James
British, 19th - 20th century.
Born 23 April 1820, in Croydon; died 12 July 1916, in London.
Painter. Figures, portraits, genre scenes.

James Sant studied in London and exhibited there from 1840. He was an honorary member of the Royal Academy, London, in 1861, and was elected a Royal Academician in 1969. He appeared in exhibitions in Paris, and was awarded a bronze medal in 1889 (Exposition Universelle). He was painter to Queen Victoria in 1871.

MUSEUMS AND GALLERIES:
GLASGOW: *St Helena, the Last Phase* - HAMBURG: *Waiting* - LONDON (Wallace Collection): study - PRESTON: *Novice* - SYDNEY: *Lesbia.*

AUCTION RECORDS:
LONDON, 3 and 4 Feb 1898, *Fortune Teller,* FRF 1,625. LONDON, 15 July 1910, *Portrait of a Lady,* GBP 7. LONDON, 18 March 1911, *Small Island near the Coast,* GBP 21. LONDON, 11 July 1969, *Courage, Anxiety and Despair,* Gns 420. LONDON, 14 July 1972, *Ophelia,* Gns 600. LOS ANGELES, 27 May 1974, *Sisters,* USD 950. LONDON, 14 May 1976, *Contemplation* (oil on canvas, 30 x 25 ins / 76.2 x 63.5 cm) GBP 600. LONDON, 20 July 1979, *Love Letter* (oil on canvas, 49 1/2 x 39 1/4 ins / 125.8 x 99.7 cm) GBP 1,000. LONDON, 6 March 1981, *Turn Again Whittington* (oil on canvas, 30 3/4 x 24 1/2 ins / 78 x 62.2 cm) GBP 2,400. LONDON, 17 June 1983, *Portrait of a Lady* (oil on canvas, 93 x 53 ins / 236.1 x 134.6 cm) GBP 3,500. LONDON, 12 June 1985, *It is the Lark, the Herald of the Morn* (oil on canvas, rounded at the top, 84 1/4 x 47 1/4 ins / 214 x 120 cm) GBP 2,800. LONDON, 15 June 1988, *Portrait of the Russell Scott Sisters* (1853, oil on canvas, 36 x 29 ins / 91.5 x 73.5 cm) GBP 9,350. NEW YORK, 1 March 1990, *Portrait of the Russell Sisters* (1858, oil on canvas, oval, 36 1/4 x 29 ins / 92 x 73.9 cm) USD 33,000. LONDON, 13 June 1990, *Geraldine, the Daughter of Frederick Massey* (oil on canvas, sketch, 63 3/4 x 30 1/4 ins / 162 x 77 cm) GBP 15,400. GLASGOW, 22 Nov 1990, *Peaches* (oil on canvas, 45 x 32 1/2 ins / 114.3 x 82.8 cm) GBP 8,800. LONDON, 8 Feb 1991, *Portrait of a Lady, Bust Format* (oil on canvas, 30 x 25 ins / 76.2 x 63.5 cm) GBP 1,650. NEW YORK, 28 May 1992, *Waking Dream* (oil on canvas, 22 x 18 ins / 55.9 x 45.7 cm) USD 6,600. LONDON, 25 March 1994, *Music* (oil on canvas, diam. 36 ins / 91.4 cm) GBP 6,325. NEW YORK, 20 July 1995, *Two Small Daughters of Fishermen* (oil on canvas, 78 x 48 ins / 198.1 x 121.9 cm) USD 6,900. LONDON, 6 Nov 1995, *Children in the Woods* (oil on canvas, 27 x 45 ins / 68.5 x 114.5 cm) GBP 5,175. LONDON, 5 Nov 1997, *Motherhood* (oil on canvas, 36 x 36 ins / 91.5 x 91.5 cm) GBP 17,825.

SANT, V. S.
Dutch (?), 17th century.
Painter. Still-lifes.

See also Hans van Sant.

AUCTION RECORDS:
GENEVA, 6 May 1950, *Still-life with Cheese* (1630) CHF 1,500.

SANT, Vicente de
Spanish, 15th century.
Painter.

Probably the same person as Vicente de San Vincente, Vicente de Sant did some paintings in the Capilla Mayor in Valencia Cathedral in 1432.

SANT.... See also first name

SANT..., Master of. See **MASTERS**

SANT ACKER, F.
Dutch, 17th century.
Painter. Still-lifes.

MUSEUMS AND GALLERIES:
AMSTERDAM (Rijksmus.) - BERLIN (National Mus.): *Still-life with Partridge* - THE HAGUE (Bredius Mus.).

SANT'ANNA, Stefano
Italian, 16th century.
Painter. Religious subjects.

Stefano Sant'Anna painted a *St Denis* in the church dedicated to the saint in Messina in 1590.

SANT'ELIA, Antonio
Italian, 20th century.
Born 30 April 1888, in Como; died 10 October 1916, in Monte Zebio sul Carso.
Draughtsman, architect.
Futurism.

Antonio Sant'Elia settled in Milan and studied at the Academy of Fine Arts of the Brera from 1909 to 1911 after having received his diploma as an architect in 1905. Here he met Achille Funi, Mario Chiattone, Carlo Carrà. Romolo Romani and Leonardo Dudreville. He started an architectural practice in Milan in 1913 and was the co-founder of the group Nuove Tendenze. That same year, he was elected town councillor in Como where he had stood for the Socialist Party. In 1914 he published the manifesto *L'architettura futurista* (*Fu-*

turistic Architecture) in the review *Lacerba* and enrolled in 1915 in the Battaglione lombardo volontari ciclisti e automobilisti (Lombard Battalion of Voluntary Cyclists and Car Drivers), along with Marinetti, Bocciono and Russolo. He was sent to the front in 1916 and died in the war near to Monfalcone.

The fact that he left no important works of art is partly explained by his premature death but also by the fact that, like a number of French architects at the end of the 18th century - Étienne Louis Boullée, Claude Nicolas Ledoux and Jean-Jacques Lequeu - he was more interested in developing his vision of the ideal city of the future. He worked on many projects, leaving hundreds of designs in a variety of media.

Early projects for the central station in Milan and the Impegiati Company in Como show the influence of the flowery style of Art Nouveau.

Influenced by the industrial architecture of Wagner and de Loos, his main creations were drawings of a futuristic city, the *Città Nuova*. Here he showed boldness in a dynamic and functional vision of the architecture, conceived as a real futurist urban fabric. La Villa Olmo, at Como, has his drawings.

Sant'Elia's work was included in group exhibitions in 1914, *Mostra degli architetti lombardi* (*Exhibition of Lombard Architecture*), Famiglia Artistica, Milan; 1914, with the group Nuove Tendenze, Famiglia Artistica, Milan; and 2003, *Futurismo 1909-1926. La bellezza della velocità* (*Futurism 1909-1926: The Beauty of Speed*), Musée d'Ixelles, Brussels. A retrospective was held in 1991, *Antonio Sant'Elia: l'architettura disegnata* (*Antonio Sant'Elia: architectural designs*), at Ca' Pesaro, Venice.

BIBLIOGRAPHY:

Sartoris, Alberto/Ciucci, Carlo (introduction), *L'architetto Antonio Sant'Elia: manifesto dell'11 luglio 1914 di Antonio Sant'Elia*, Scheiwiller, Milan, 1930. Apollonio, Umbro/Mariani, Leonardo, *Antonio Sant'Elia*, Il Balcone, Milan, 1958. Caramel, Luciano/Longatti, Alberto, *Antonio Sant'Elia*, exhibition catalogue, Villa Comunale Dell'Olmo, Como, 1962. Longatti, Alberto, *Disegni di Sant'Elia*, exhibition catalogue, Stefanoni, Lecco, 1984. Ashton, Dora/Ballo, Guido, *Antonio Sant'Elia*, exhibition catalogue, The Cooper union for the advancement of science and art, New York, Mondatori, Milan, 1986. Caramel, Luciano/Longatti, Alberto, *Antonio Sant'Elia: l'opera completa*, exhibition catalogue, A. Mondadori, Milan, 1987 (text in Italian, English). *Antonio Sant'Elia: l'architettura disegnata*, exhibition catalogue, Cà Pesaro, Marsilio, Venice, 1991. Da Costa Meyer, Esther, *The work of Antonio Sant'Elia: retreat into the future*, exhibition catalogue, Yale University Press, New Haven [USA, CT], 1995. Masoero, Ada/Miracco, Renato (ed.), *Futurismo 1909-1926. La bellezza della velocità*, group exhibition catalogue, Musée d'Ixelles, Bruxelles, Mazzotta, Milan, 2003.

SANTA. See **SANT'**

SANTA, pseudonym of Santarelli, Claude

French, 20th century.

Born 6 March 1925, in Paris; died 10 March 1979.

Sculptor.

Santa studied sculpture at the École des Beaux-Arts, Paris. From 1951 he lived in St-Omer (Pas-de-Calais), and later moved to Tournan (Seine-et-Marne).

From 1958 he adopted a style taken from abstraction. Initially he worked with welded offcut metal, but in a later, more geometric period he contrasted vertical and horizontal elements. He then worked in more malleable brass sheets, baroquely folded and creased. Then, still using brass, but in thicker sheets, he returned to more extended forms with polished surfaces that he still contrasted with crinkles. About 1970, using the same technique, he created symbolic figures such as the *Sexy-Goddess* of 1968. He also worked in concrete and stainless steel when collaborating, as he did several times, with architects.

He exhibited in several group exhibitions including, in Paris, the Salon des Réalités Nouvelles and the Salon de Mai. In 1965 he was invited to the Montreal Symposium, and in 1983 was represented posthumously in the exhibition *Lyric + Geometrie* (*Lyric + Geometry*) held at the Treffpunkt Kunst gallery, Saarlouis.

AUCTION RECORDS:

PARIS, 1 June 1973, *Masculine-Feminine* (bronze) FRF 4,000.

SANTA. See also first name or name

SANTA, Catarina della

Italian, 18th century.

Painter. Still-lifes.

Catarina della Santa was active in Florence around 1786-1791.

AUCTION RECORDS:

MILAN, 14 Nov 1990, *Trompe l'Oeil with Frontispiece of the Series of Figures by Salvator Rosa, Pages of Incunabula, a Cameo and a Sestertius* (watercolour/paper heightened with pastels, 9 1/4 x 13 1/2in/23.5 x 34.5cm) ITL 15,000,000.

SANTA CAPPANINI

Italian, 19th century.

Born 1803; died 1860.

Painter.

A pupil of Agostino Ugolini, Santa Cappanini painted several works for the Dominican convent in Verona where she was a nun.

SANTA COLOMA, Emmanuel de

French, 19th century.

Born 1829, in Bordeaux or in Paris; died 1886, in Paris.

Sculptor, draughtsman. Animals. Groups.

He exhibited at the Salon between 1863 and 1870, and won a medal in 1864.

MUSEUMS AND GALLERIES:

BORDEAUX: *Spanish Cavalier* (statuette).

AUCTION RECORDS:

BORDEAUX, 1899, *The Avenue des Champs-Élysées* (Indian ink) FRF 13. ENGHIEN-LES-BAINS, 6 Oct 1985, *Runaway Horses* (1865, brown-patinated bronze, h. 22 3/4 ins / 58 cm) FRF 25,000. PARIS, 24 March 1995, *Two Children on a Horse* (bronze, 19 3/4 x 19 3/4 ins / 50 x 50 cm) FRF 23,000. PARIS, 8 Nov 1995, *Horse Resting* (bronze, h. 9 1/4 ins / 23.5 cm) FRF 26,500. NEW YORK, 28 June 2000, *Special Delivery, Bordeaux* (1886, oil on canvas, 79 x 63 ins / 200 x 161 cm) USD 6,000. PARIS, 30 Nov 2001, *Cobesse and Bellboy* (brown patinated bronze, 15 x 22 ins / 37 x 57 cm) FRF 35,000.

SANTA CROCE, Francesco di Simone da

Italian, 15th - 16th century.

Born between 1440 and 1445; died between 28 October and 4 November 1508, in Venice.

Painter. Religious subjects.

A pupil of Bellini, Francesco di Simone da Santa Croce became one of the leading followers of the Bellini School. He was the master of Francesco Santacroce di Rizzo, with whom he is often confused.

MUSEUMS AND GALLERIES:

CARRARA (Accademia di Belle Arti): *Annunciation*; *Christ between St John the Baptist and Alexander*.

AUCTION RECORDS:

NEW YORK, 2 June 1989, *Adoration of the Magi* (oil on panel, 29 1/2 x 46 ins / 75 x 117 cm) USD 38,500.

SANTA CRUZ, or Santos Cruz

Spanish, 15th century.

Active between 1475 and 1499.

Painter.

Santa Cruz worked with Pedro Berruguete on the altarpiece of the high altar of Avila Cathedral.

SANTA CRUZ, Antonio de
Spanish, 17th century.
Sculptor. Religious subjects. Statues.

Antonio de Santa Cruz carved altars and statues for churches in Seville. He worked in the city from 1618 to 1640 and was also an architect.

SANTA CRUZ, Francisco de
Spanish, 16th century.
Active in 1531.
Painter.

SANTA CRUZ, Francisco de
Spanish, 17th century.
Born c. 1586, in Barcelona; died 1658, in Barcelona.
Sculptor.

Francisco de Santa Cruz carved the *Holy Trinity* on the high altar of the church of La Trinidad Calzada in Barcelona and the statues of *St Francis Xavier* and *Young Jesus* in the Jesuit church, also in Barcelona.

SANTA CRUZ, Mariana (Countess).
See **WALDSTEIN Maria Anna von**

SANTA MARÍA, Andrés de
Colombian, 19th - 20th century.
Born 1860, in Bogotá; died 1945, in Brussels.
From 1869 active in France then Belgium.
Painter. Local figures, scenes with figures, landscapes, seascapes.

Andrés de Santa María was two years old when his diplomat father was posted to England. Here, later, Ruskin aroused the child's interest in art. The next posting was to Belgium, where the young Andrés was encouraged by James Ensor in Ostend. In 1878 Santa María senior was made chargé d'affaires to the Mac-Mahon government in Paris. The young man studied for some months with Fernand Humbert in 1882 and then with Gervex at the École des Beaux-Arts, where he got to know Zuloaga. He became friends with Manet and Monet, and may possibly have known Bourdelle. He married in St-Jean-de-Luz, and in 1893 returned to Colombia, where he received a teaching post at the art school in Bogotá. In 1901 he was back in Paris, and saw the retrospective *Van Gogh Exhibition* at the Bernheim gallery. He was made head of the Bogotá art school in 1904, and founded the School of Decorative and Industrial Art. In 1911 he left Colombia for good, taking his family to England, France and Holland, and then settling in Brussels.

He exhibited regularly at the Salon des Artistes Français in Paris, showing first of all his *Laundry Boat on the Seine*, and no doubt had shows in Colombia after his return there. Once settled in Brussels, he exhibited from time to time in Belgium, Paris and London. In Paris in 1985 the Musée Marmottan, home ground of Monet and Impressionism, hung some fifty of his paintings. Under the combined influence of Ensor, Manet and Monet, Santa María developed a style influenced on the one hand by the narrative impressionism of light touches, not unlike Caillebotte or James Tissot, and on the other, especially after his return from Colombia and his visit to the Van Gogh exhibition, by an Expressionism painted in strong brilliant touches of rich, thick colour.

As he spent most of his life in Europe, he had no direct influence on Colombian painting, but is held to be the greatest Colombian painter of the first half of the 20th century.

BIBLIOGRAPHY:

Santa María, Andrés de, *Nuevos testimonios, nueva visión: obras de las colecciones de Belgica*, Banco de la República, Biblioteca Luis-Ángel Arango, Bogotá, 1989.

AUCTION RECORDS:

NEW YORK, 19-20 Nov 1990, *The Spanish Woman* (1920, oil on card, 25 1/2 x 20 ins / 64.8 x 50.5 cm) USD 18,150. NEW YORK, 16 May 1996, *Two Women* (oil on canvas, 29 1/2 x 25 ins / 75 x 63.5 cm) USD 57,500. NEW YORK, 24-25 Nov 1997, *The Visitation* (c. 1933, oil on canvas, 23 1/2 x 28 3/4 ins / 60 x 73 cm) USD 85,000. LUCERNE, 24 May 2003, *Christ Walking on Water* (oil on panel, 16 x 20 ins / 41 x 52 cm) CHF 6,500. NEW YORK, 19 Nov 2003, *Christ Walking on Water* (oil on panel, 16 x 20 ins / 41 x 52 cm) USD 18,000.

SANTA MARÍA, Leopoldo Berthelemy
Spanish, 20th century.
Born 26 August 1887, in Obregon near Santander; died 22 October 1970, in L'Hay-les-Roses, France.
Also active in France from 1910.
Painter. Portraits, landscapes, flowers.

Leopoldo Santa María lived and studied in Cuba from 1900 to 1910 and divided his time between France and Spain from 1910 until his death in 1970. He studied at the École des Beaux-Arts in Paris from 1911 to 1913 and attended workshops by Cormon from 1915 to 1917. He lived and worked for many years at Auvers-sur-Oise. He stopped painting in 1965.

Santa María is remembered for landscapes of the Côte d'Azur which reminded him of his native Spain. He also painted landscapes around Auvers. He showed examples of his work at collective exhibitions of Spanish painters, including: Lyons (1943) and Galerie La Boétie, Paris (1952). The Centre Espagnol de Paris held a solo exhibition of his work in 1926.

BIBLIOGRAPHY:

Charmy, Roland, *Léopold Santa Maria*, exhibition catalogue, Gal. La Boétie, Paris, 1926.

AUCTION RECORDS:

PARIS, 13 Nov 1991, *Landscape near Auvers*, FRF 3,500. PARIS, 15 June 1994, *Painting* (oil on card) FRF 2,100.

SANTA MARÍA Y SEDANO, Marceliano
Spanish, 19th - 20th century.
Born 18 June 1866, in Burgos; died 12 October 1952, in Madrid.
Painter, sculptor. Religious subjects, allegorical subjects, portraits, genre scenes, landscapes. Murals.

Marceliano Santa María y Sedano studied initially under his father, then at the academy of art in Burgos and later at the college of fine arts in Madrid. He also took courses under Manuel Domínguez Sánchez. He visited Rome between 1891 and 1895 and was appointed principal of the college of arts and crafts in Barcelona.

He contributed to various periodicals: *Blanco y Negro* (*Black and White*), *La Ilustración Española y Americana* (*Spain and America Illustrated*) and *La Revista Moderna* (*Modern Review*). He painted a *Triumph of the Law over Evildoers* for the Courts of Justice in Madrid. Between 1939 and 1942, his best-known period, he demonstrated his mastery of composition and subtle use of colour in a number of luminous and spontaneously executed landscapes. Other examples of his work include *Pietà*, *Pontifical Mass*, *Vanquished; Shearing Time*, *Children Bathing* and *Village in Castile*. Santa María featured at various national and international exhibitions (Burgos, Barcelona, Madrid, Paris) and was awarded a bronze medal in 1890, a silver in 1892, an honourable mention in 1894, a further silver in 1895, a bronze at the 1900 Exposition Universelle in Paris and a medal of honour in 1934. From 1923, he exhibited solo on a number of occasions, notably in Madrid, Barcelona and Bilbao.

BIBLIOGRAPHY:

Azorin, '*La Cabeza de Castilla*' in *Col. Austral*, Espasa-Calpe, Madrid, 1980. *Catalogo del Museo Marceliano Santa Maria*,

Museo Marceliano Santa Maria, Burgos, 1981. Arnáiz, José Manuel/López Jiménez, Javier/Merchán Díaz, Manuel (ed.), '*Cien años de pintura en Espana y Portugal (1830-1930)*' in vol. X, Antiqvaria, Madrid, 1993.

MUSEUMS AND GALLERIES:

BARCELONA (MAM del Mus. Nacional d'Art de Catalunya): *A Case of Diptheria?* - BURGOS (Mus. Marceliano Santa Maria): *Triumph of the Holy Cross; Resurrecting the Dead* - CIUDAD REAL - MADRID (Prado): *To the Letter* - SANTIAGO.

AUCTION RECORDS:

MADRID, 24 Oct 1983, *Missive* (1904, oil on canvas, 14 1/4 x 19 ins / 36.5 x 48 cm) ESP 450,000. PARIS, 26 March 1998, *Oriental Woman with Tambourine* (1891, oil on canvas, 11 x 15 1/4 ins / 28 x 39 cm) FRF 17,000.

SANTA MARINA, Felipe de

Spanish, 17th century.

Active in Seville during the second half of the 17th century.

Sculptor.

Felipe de Santa Marina was at the Seville academy from 1660 to 1664.

SANTA MARINA, José María

Spanish, 19th - 20th century.

Painter. Still-lifes.

José María Santa Marina featured at the 1994 national fine arts exhibition in Barcelona.

AUCTION RECORDS:

LONDON, 14 Feb 1990, *Still-life* (1944, oil on canvas, 34 1/4 x 45 ins / 87 x 114 cm) GBP 4,620.

SANTA ROSA, Tomas

Brazilian, 20th century.

Born 1909; died 1956.

Painter, watercolourist.

The work of Tomas Santa Rosa combines a lyrical surrealism with fantasy and folklore and has been compared to that of Chagall.

AUCTION RECORDS:

RIO DE JANEIRO, 18 April 1983, *Standing Woman* (1954, oil on canvas, 27 1/2 x 17 1/2 ins / 70 x 44.5 cm) BRL 950,000.

SANTA-RITA, Guilherme de, or Santa-Rita Pintor

Portuguese, 20th century.

Born 1889 or 1890, in Lisbon; died 1918, in Lisbon.

Painter, collage artist, draughtsman. Figures, nudes. Futurism.

Guilherme de Santa-Rita studied at the college of fine arts in Lisbon and was awarded a scholarship in 1910 which enabled him to study in Paris until 1914. In Paris, he mixed with various Futurists, among them most notably Filippo Marinetti, whose *First Futurist Manifesto* had already appeared in the August 1909 issue of the *Azores Journal*. He returned to Portugal in 1914 and was actively involved in the artistic review *Orpheu* which was spearheaded by Fernando Pessoa and dedicated to a 'synthesis of all modern literary movements'. In the second (and last) issue of *Orpheu*, published in June 1915, a number of Santa-Rita's collages were reproduced (together with notification of several events that were destined never to take place). In November 1917, Santa-Rita arranged for the publication in Portuguese of the various Futurist Manifestos authored by Marinetti, together with texts by Guillaume Apollinaire and Blaise Cendrars and an article about Santa Rita himself; these appeared in the one and only issue of a review called *Portugal Futurista*, which was promptly confiscated by the police.

Santa-Rita produced a number of 'painting-collages', the titles of which are a clear indication in themselves of the provocative nature of his work and his unswerving adherence to the Futurist credo: *Head X-Ray + Ocular Apparatus + Superimposed Visual Dynamic + Reflections of the Ambient Environment and Light (Mechanical Sensitivity)* or *Dynamic Decomposition of a Table + Style of Movement (Plastic Intersection)*. On Santa-Rita's death - and at his specific request - virtually the entire corpus of his artistic output was destroyed. He was an exceptionally gifted artist who railed against the bourgeois conventions of early 20th century Lisbon, and an emblematic figure in Portugal's albeit brief flirtation with Futurism as an artistic movement dedicated to coming to terms with modernity.

BIBLIOGRAPHY:

Rivad, Philippe, *Fernando Pessoa. Poète pluriel*, La Différence, Paris, 1985. Arnáiz, José Manuel/López Jiménez, Javier/Merchán Díaz, Manuel (ed.), '*Cien años de pintura en Espana y Portugal (1830-1930)*' in vol. X, Antiqvaria, Madrid, 1993.

SANTACROCE, Agostino, called Pippo

Italian, 16th - 17th century.

Born in Genoa.

Sculptor (wood).

Agostino Santacroce was the son of Filippo Santacroce.

SANTACROCE, Filippo, or Croce, called Pippo

Italian, 16th century.

Born in Urbino; died 1609, in Genoa.

Sculptor. Religious subjects. Statues.

The father of Agostino, Giulio, Luca Antonio, Matteo and Scipione, Filippo Santacroce studied in Rome and then worked in the service of the Doria family in Genoa. He specialised in the sculpture of figurines and figures for Presepio (nativity) scenes, and made a number of crucifixes and statues for churches in Genoa.

SANTACROCE, Francesco

Italian, 17th century.

Sculptor (wood).

Francesco Santacroce was the son of Luca Antonio and the father of Poer Paolo Santacroce.

SANTACROCE, Francesco di Girolamo da, sometimes known as Francesco da Santacroce

Italian, 16th century.

Born 1516, in Venice; died 11 December 1584, in Venice.

Painter. Religious subjects, allegorical subjects.

Francesco di Girolamo da Santacroce was the son of Girolamo, whose work greatly influenced his own.

AUCTION RECORDS:

MILAN, 30 May 1991, *Nativity* (oil on panel, 26 1/2 x 36 1/2 ins / 67 x 93 cm) ITL 20,000,000. MILAN, 3 April 1996, *Allegory of Love* (oil on panel, 19 x 12 1/4 ins / 48 x 31 cm) ITL 8,050,000.

SANTACROCE, Francesco Rizzo da, real name: Francesco Bernardo de Vecchi or de Galizzi, called Rizzo da Santacroce

Italian, 16th century.

Born at the end of the 15th century, in Santa Croce; died probably after 1545.

Painter. Religious subjects.

When still young, Francesco Rizzo da Santacroce went to study in Venice, where he was a pupil of Francesco di Simone da Santacroce I. His active working career lasted from about 1505 to 1545. Two works bearing the dates 1529 and 1541 have been attributed to him, but the attribution of the latter, an altarpiece in a village near Mestre, has been questioned.

MUSEUMS AND GALLERIES:
VENICE: *Flagellation; Deposition with Saints; Resurrection.*
AUCTION RECORDS:
LONDON, 26 June 1936, *Annunciation*, GBP 105. LONDON, 21 April 1982, *Virgin and Child with Saints* (oil on panel, 33 x 49 1/4 ins / 84 x 125 cm) GBP 10,000. LONDON, 19 April 1996, *Virgin and Child with Saints* (oil on panel, 25 3/4 x 32 3/4 ins / 65.4 x 83.2 cm) GBP 13,800. ROME, 5 June 2000, *Mystic Marriage of St Catherine of Alexandria* (tempera on panel, 23 x 31 ins / 58 x 78 cm) ITL 75,000,000.

SANTACROCE, Giovanni Battista
Italian, 17th century.
Born in Genoa.
Sculptor (wood).
Giovanni Battista Santacroce produced sculptures for several churches in Genoa as well as carving organ chests.

SANTACROCE, Giovanni Battista, or Croce
Italian, 17th century.
Active in Savona c. 1670.
Painter.
A pupil of G.A. de Ferrari, Giovanni Battista Santacroce painted pictures of saints in the church of S Stefano in Savona.

SANTACROCE, Giovanni or Zuanne de' Vecchi or de' Galizzi
Italian, 16th century.
Died 11 June 1565, in Venice.
Painter. Religious subjects.
Giovanni de' Vecchi Santacroce was a cousin of Francesco Bernardo de' Vecchi or de' Galizzi, known as Francesco Rizzo da Santacroce. He painted a triptych including figures of martyred saints to which he has added the signature *Joanes de Galizis.*
MUSEUMS AND GALLERIES:
BERGAMO (Accademia Carrara, Pinacoteca d'Arte Antica): triptych.

SANTACROCE, Girolamo da, real name: Galizzi
Italian, 16th century.
Born soon after 1500, in Santa Croce; died after 9 July 1556.
Painter. Religious subjects, landscapes.
Believed to be related to Francesco Rizzo da Santacroce, Girolamo da Santacroce is thought to have acted as his assistant. He is likely to have been a pupil of Giovanni Bellini. His first dated work is an altarpiece of 1520 in the church of S Silvestro depicting *St Thomas* and *St John the Baptist*. In 1527, he painted the *Charity of St Martin* for the church at Luvigliano near Padua.

In 1532, Girolamo painted 14 frescoes (*Scenes from the Life of St Francis of Assisi*), now lost. Other works include *Christ Praying* and a *Martyrdom of St Lawrence*. His last known work, *The Last Supper* in the church of S Martino, was painted in 1549.

Girolamo's work has been said to lack originality but this is perhaps unfair; though not of the first order, his paintings have breadth of style and elevated emotion.
MUSEUMS AND GALLERIES:
BASEL: *Nativity; Resurrection* - BASSANO DEL GRAPPA: *Altarpiece* - BERLIN: *Nativity; Martyrdom of St Sebastian* - BUDAPEST: *Nativity* - DRESDEN: *Adoration of the Child; Martyrdom of St Lawrence* - LONDON (NG): *A Saint with a Fortress and a Banner* (1512-1525, oil/wood, attributed); *A Youthful Saint Reading* (1512-1525, oil/wood, attributed) - MILAN (Pinacoteca di Brera): *St Stephen Crowned by Angels* - PADUA: *Altarpiece* - VENICE: *St John the Evangelist; St Matthew; St Luke; St Mark; Mystic Marriage of St Catherine; St Gregory and St Augustine.*
AUCTION RECORDS:
LONDON, 6 July 1923, *Virgin and Child with Saints*, GBP 525. LONDON, 3 Dec 1924, *Landscape*, GBP 170. NEW YORK, 22 April 1932, *Virgin and Child with St Anthony and St Catherine*, USD 775. NEW YORK, 18 and 19 April 1934, *Nativity*, USD 400. LONDON, 10-14 July 1936, *Design for an Altar* (pen) GBP 50. NEW YORK, 6 May 1937, *Virgin and Child*, USD 325. PARIS, 27 June 1947, *Holy Family* (in the style of Santacroce) FRF 28,000. LONDON, 9 Dec 1959, *Christ Appearing to St Thomas*, GBP 800. LONDON, 22 June 1960, *Nativity*, GBP 600. LONDON, 28 May 1965, *Annunciation*, Gns 2,400. LONDON, 27 June 1969, *Annunciation*, Gns 4,000. LONDON, 10 July 1981, *Virgin and Child with St John the Baptist and St Catherine* (oil on panel, 27 1/4 x 46 ins / 69 x 117 cm) GBP 6,000. LONDON, 8 July 1988, *Virgin and Child with St John the Baptist and Saints Jerome, Benedict, Bernard and Francis* (oil on panel, 21 x 34 3/4 ins / 52.5 x 88.5 cm) GBP 28,600. LONDON, 7 July 1989, *Holy Family* (oil on canvas, 45 1/4 x 64 3/4 ins / 114.7 x 164.5 cm) GBP 16,500. NEW YORK, 13 Oct 1989, *Annunciation* (oil on panel, h. ma x . 10 ins / 25.5 cm, w. 13 1/4 ins/33.5 cm) USD 17,600. ROME, 8 March 1990, *Virgin and Child in a Landscape* (oil on panel, 23 1/2 x 16 1/2 ins / 60 x 42 cm) ITL 19,000,000. LONDON, 9 July 1993, *Virgin and Child with St John the Baptist, St George, St Jerome and St Roch* (oil on panel, 33 1/2 x 49 1/4 ins / 84.8 x 124.8 cm) GBP 23,000. NEW YORK, 19 May 1994, *Virgin and Child* (oil on panel, 22 1/2 x 19 ins / 57.2 x 48.3 cm) USD 20,700. LONDON, 19 April 1996, *Arrest of Christ in the Garden of Gethsemane* (oil on panel, 17 3/4 x 16 ins / 45.2 x 39.7 cm) GBP 20,700.

SANTACROCE, Girolamo da
Italian, 16th century.
Born c. 1502; died 1537.
Active in Naples.
Sculptor. Statues, monuments.
Much admired by Vasari, the sculptor Girolamo da Santacroce was in Carrara between 1520 and 1522. He was also an architect. He made many tombs, altars and statues of saints for the churches of Naples, and carried out some work in the church at Alcala de Henares in Spain.

SANTACROCE, Giulio, called Pippo
Italian, 16th - 17th century.
Born in Genoa.
Sculptor (wood).
The son of Filippo Santacroce, Giulio Santacroce carved the organ case in the church of S Lorenzo in Genoa in 1612-1613.

SANTACROCE, Liberale da
Italian, 15th century.
Active in 1462.
Painter.
Probably the elder brother of Francesco di Simone, Liberale da Santacroce worked in Padua.

SANTACROCE, Luca Antonio, called Pippo
Italian, 16th - 17th century.
Born in Genoa.
Sculptor (wood).
Luca Antonio Santacroce was the son of Filippo Santacroce and father of Francesco Santacroce IV.

SANTACROCE, Matteo, called Pippo
Italian, 16th - 17th century.
Born in Genoa.
Sculptor (wood).
Matteo Santacroce was the son of Filippo and father of Giovanni-Battista Santacroce.

SANTACROCE, Pier Paolo or Pietro Paolo
Italian, 17th century.
Died before 1620.
Painter. History painting.

Pier Paolo Santacroce was the son of Francesco de Santacroce, and probably worked in Padua.

MUSEUMS AND GALLERIES:
VENICE: *Jesus and the Samaritan Woman; Jesus at the House of the Two Marys.*

SANTACROCE, Scipione, called Pippo
Italian, 16th - 17th century.
Born in Genoa.
Sculptor (wood).

Scipione Santacroce was the son of Filippo Santacroce.

SANTACROCE, Vincenzo de' Vecchi or de' Galizzi
Italian, 16th century.
Died before 3 January 1531.
Painter.

Vincenzo de' Vecchi or de' Galizzi Santacroce was probably the brother and assistant of Francesco Santacroce II, known as Rizzo.

SANTAFEDE, Fabrizio
Italian, 16th - 17th century.
Born 1560; died 1634.
Painter. Religious subjects.

A pupil of F. Curia, Fabrizio Santafede continued his studies in Rome, Bologna, Modena, Parma and Venice with Tintoretto, Palma Giovane and Landro Bassano, and was influenced by the style of Caravaggio. He painted some 50 works, several of which have been lost.

MUSEUMS AND GALLERIES:
NAPLES (Mus. Nazionale): *Madonna with St Jerome and Pierre Cambacurta* - ROHRAU (Schlossmus., Graf Harrach'sche Familiensammlung): *Madonna with St Anne and St Gaetano.*

AUCTION RECORDS:
PARIS, 1776, *Death of a Saint; Another Subject; Study of Kneeling Figure of St Augustine* (Indian ink, red chalk and pen, collection) FRF 72. LONDON, 5 July 1967, *Virgin and Child in a Landscape,* GBP 500. LONDON, 10 April 1981, *Holy Family with St John the Baptist* (oil on canvas, 41 1/4 x 32 1/4 ins / 104.7 x 81.8 cm) GBP 4,200. ROME, 21 Nov 1985, *Adoration of the Shepherds* (oil on canvas, 70 x 53 1/4 ins / 178 x 135 cm) ITL 13,000,000. LONDON, 15 April 1992, *Dead Christ Supported by Angels* (oil on canvas, 52 x 42 ins / 132 x 106.7 cm) GBP 8,000. ROME, 22 Nov 1994, *Adoration of the Shepherds* (oil on panel, 72 3/4 x 56 3/4 ins / 185 x 144 cm) ITL 47,150,000. ROME, 17 Dec 2003, *Christ Captured* (oil on canvas, 93 x 72 ins / 235 x 183 cm) EUR 60,000.

SANTAFEDE, Francesco
Italian, 16th century.
Born c. 1519.
Painter. History painting.

The father of Fabrizio Santafede and a pupil of Andrea da Salerno, Francesco Santafede painted for the churches of Naples.

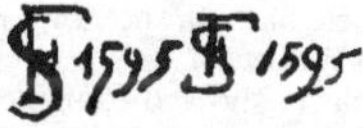

AUCTION RECORDS:
NEW YORK, 5 June 1986, *Annunciation* (oil/copper, 15 x 11 1/4 ins / 38 x 28.5 cm) USD 15,000.

SANTAFIORE, Michelangelo
Italian, 16th century.
Died 1586, in Rome.
Painter.

SANTAGATA, Antonio Giuseppe
Italian, 20th century.
Born 10 November 1888, in Genoa; died 1985.
Painter, sculptor, medallist. Portraits, genre scenes.

A student at the academy in Genoa, Antonio Santagata painted mainly portraits and genre scenes and a few landscapes. One of his best known works is his *Abduction of Andromeda.*

MUSEUMS AND GALLERIES:
GENOA (Gal. d'Arte Moderna): two paintings - ROME (Gal. Nazionale d'Arte Moderna) - UDINE.

SANTAGATI, Vincenzo
Italian, 17th century.
Active in Urbino during the second half of the 17th century.
Painter.

Vincenzo Santagati worked for the church of S Antonio in Urbino in 1664.

SANTAGOSTINO, Agostino
Italian, 17th century.
Born in Milan; died 1706, in Milan.
Painter, engraver (etching).

The son and probably also the pupil of Giacomo Antonio Santagostino, Agostino Santagostino frequently collaborated with his brother Giacinto, in particular at the church of S Fedele in Milan. In 1671, he published in Milan a treatise on painting entitled *L'Immortalità e gloria del Pennello.*

SANTAGOSTINO, Ambrogio
Italian, 16th century.
Active during the second half of the 16th century.
Sculptor (wood).

Ambrogio Santagostino carved the choir stalls in the church of S Vittorio al Corpo in Milan.

SANTAGOSTINO, Giacinto
Italian, 17th century.
Born in Milan.
Painter.

Giacinto was the son and probably also the pupil of Giacomo Santagostino. He collaborated frequently with his brother Agostino.

SANTAGOSTINO, Giacomo Antonio
Italian, 17th century.
Born c. 1588, in Milan; died 1648, in Milan.
Painter, engraver (burin). History painting.

This artist, the father of Agostino and Giacinto Santagostino, was the pupil of G. Cesare Procaccini. He worked for the churches of S Lorenzo Maggiore, S Maria del Lantasio and S Vittore in Milan.

SANTAGOSTINO, Giovanni Battista
Italian, 17th century.
Active in Milan.
Painter.

SANTAGUT, Guillem de, or Guillén
Spanish, 16th century.
Active in Valladolid.
Glass painter.

Guillem de Santagut made the stained glass windows for the church of Ciudad Rodrigo around 1556. The sculptor and architect Juan de Juni held him in high esteem and the two men often worked on joint projects.

SANTALINEA, Bartolomé, or Santolinea
Spanish, 15th century.
Active in Valencia during the first half of the 15th century.
Sculptor.

Bartolomé Santalinea carved a figure of *St Michael* in 1412, and in 1428 worked on the ceiling of the golden hall in the town hall of Valencia.

SANTALUS, Juan Bautista
Spanish, 17th century.
Painter.

Juan Bautista Santalus executed paintings in the chapel of the Imperial College in Madrid in 1641.

SANTAMARIA, Ricardo
Spanish, 20th century.
Born 1920, in Saragossa.
Also active in France from 1967.
Sculptor, painter, assemblage artist, mixed media.
Saragossa Group.

Ricardo Santamaria studied from 1940 at the colleges of arts and crafts in Saragossa and Barcelona; he spent 1956 travelling in Holland, France and Italy. He started out in around 1953 as a figurative painter but after his travels he began experimenting with various materials such as wood, cardboard and coloured sand and with new techniques. He operated by tearing, burning, glueing and assembling and produced low relief paintings and sculptures which drew on apparently contradictory components from which he aspired to construct a tactile and visually expressive synthesis of painting and sculpture.

In 1960 he participated in the revival of the Saragossa Group by showing his work in Saragossa (1961), Pamplona, Huesca, Lérida and Jaca (1963), Madrid and Barcelona (1964), Gulbenkian Foundation, Lisbon (1965), Beirut and Baghdad (1966), Galerie Creuze, Paris (1967), and at the Second European Sculpture Biennale, Contemporary Arts Centre, Jouy-sur-Eure in Normandy. Santamaria exhibited solo in Saragossa and Bilbao (1946), the Middle East (1966), Galerie du Haut-Pavé, Paris (1968), Galerie de France (1971), commemorative exhibition, Saragossa (1973) and Paris (1975).

BIBLIOGRAPHY:
IIe Biennale européenne de sculpture de Normandie, exhibition catalogue, Centre d'Art contemporain, Jouy-sur-Eure, 1984.

SANTANA, M. Raul
Venezuelan, 20th century.
Born 1893, in Caracas.
Painter, sculptor, caricaturist.

M. Raul Santana was a pupil of Herrera Toro in the Caracas Art School and of Francisco Labarta in Barcelona. In 1928 he won the sculpture prize at the Caracas School, and in 1931 and 1932 the first prize at the Humorists' Salon in Venezuela. He had many exhibitions and is well known in his own country.

SANTANDREU, Pedro Juan
Spanish, 19th century.
Born 1808, in Manacor; died 26 November 1838, in Palma (Majorca), Balearics.
Sculptor.

He was a pupil of J. Llado.

SANTANGELO, Ajacio
Italian, 16th century.
Active in Naples at the beginning of the 16th century.
Painter.

Ajacio Santangelo painted two altarpieces for the church of S Maria in Santa Caterina (Calabria).

SANTANTONIN, Ruben
Argentinian, 20th century.
Born 1919; died 1969.
Painter, sculptor, mixed media.

Ruben Santantonin was one of the earliest artists to work on projects at the Di Tella Institute in Buenos Aires which challenged the very status of art, questioning how it should be defined and practised and where it is going.

In 1965 he collaborated at the Institute with Marta Minujin on the creation of *La Menesunda*, a polymorphous piece of architecture offering internal passageways with sharply differentiated stages: a gallery of mirrors, streams of confetti, yielding floors, a giant female head, auto-transmission by closed circuit television, and so on. This can be seen as a cultural return to popular festivals.

SANTAOLARIA, Vicente
Spanish, 20th century.
Born 10 December 1886, in Cabanal (Valencia); died 1967.
Active in France from 1908.
Painter (gouache), watercolourist, sculptor, draughtsman, illustrator. Scenes with figures, portraits, genre scenes, still-lifes, landscapes, seascapes.

Vincente Santaolaria studied under Vicente Borras y Mompo and Antonio Caba y Casamitjana at the school of fine arts in Barcelona, then under Vicente Borras y Abella and Joaquin Sorolla y Bastida at the school of fine arts in Madrid. He was awarded a scholarship from the fine arts academy in Barcelona which enabled him to travel extensively in Castile and Andalusia before finally settling in Paris in 1908. He was an inveterate traveller and, as a relatively rich man, was able to finance visits to England, Switzerland, Belgium and Italy. He was a passionate admirer of African and Oriental art and was fluent in several languages and dialects, with a diploma in Oriental Studies. He did not mix in artistic circles and professed to paint only as a hobby. He was a close friend of Aurore Sand and a frequent visitor to Nohant and, between 1920 and 1940, to Sand's home in Antibes.

Santaolaria illustrated works by George Sand (*Berry, Elle et lui*) and Aurore Sand's *Guide to Nohant*. Although he never professed to be a sculptor, he nonetheless produced several busts, including one of *George Sand* to commemorate the fiftieth anniversary of her death, a piece fashioned from clay taken from Verneuil (close to Nohant itself). As a painter, he produced portraits of *Aurore Sand; María Blasco Ibáñez; Mademoiselle E. Adam* and the painters *Gaston Balande; Puig Perucho*, the sculptor *Martrus* and the poet *Maseras*.

Santaolaria's accomplished technique is demonstrated most convincingly in his portraits, but he also painted a broad variety of other subjects, figures and typical scenes often dismissed as set pieces in Spanish style. Among these, it is worth mentioning his *Lady of the Sierra; Spanish Woman with Fan; Lovers; Siesta in Seville; Nocturnal; Spanish Night*. He was more at home painting landscapes and seascapes from southern France and Spain; these exhibit a strong compositional sense and a powerfully expressive colour palette. His detailed and realistic street scenes and market views compare favourably with Constantin Guy's.

In 1904, Santaolaria showed examples of his work at the Exposición Nacional de Bellas Artes in Madrid, where he received an honourable mention. He went on to exhibit extensively in Paris, at the Salon des Artistes Français, Salon des Indépendants, Salon d'Automne, Salon de l'École Française, Salon des Peintres Orientalistes Français and the Winter Salon (of which he was a foreign member). During his travels, he also exhibited at the Royal Academy in London, the national exhibition in Madrid and the Brussels Salon. He was elevated to the rank of Chevalier of the Légion d'Honneur.

Bibliography:

Arnáiz, José Manuel/López Jiménez, Javier/Merchán Díaz, Manuel (ed.), '*Cien años de pintura en Espana y Portugal (1830*' in vol. X, Antiqvaria, Madrid, 1993.

Museums and Galleries:

Châteauroux (Hôtel de Ville) - Paris (Mus. Carnavalet).

Auction records:

Paris, 26 June 1992, *Spanish Dancers* (oil on canvas, 39 1/4 x 31 1/2 ins / 100 x 80 cm) FRF 20,000.

SANTARELLI, Andria

French, 20th century.
Born 25 March 1935, in Ajaccio (Corsica).
Painter.

Andria Santarelli, who studied at the École des Beaux-Arts, Paris, lives and works in Corsica. She takes fragmented images, found by chance, and inserts them in juxtaposed circles or octagons to form stars that she either treats as decorative elements, or paints again using fragments of landscape or architectural motifs. This multiplication, fragmentation and dispersal leads the viewer to read them as 'constellations' moving in space and time.

From 1961 she participated in group exhibitions in Paris, including the Salon d'Automne, the Salon des Artistes Français, and the Salon des Femmes Peintres et Sculpteurs. In 1983 she took part in the Salon Figuration Critique, and in 1985-1986 showed in San Francisco and Los Angeles. Since 1978 she has been represented in Paris and New York by the Galerie Liliane François, which organised a solo exhibition of her work in Paris in 1986.

Bibliography:

Di Savona, Ghjuvan, ''*LUMIÈRE, Lumières...*' in *Andria Santarelli*, exhibition catalogue, Gal. Liliane François, Paris, 1986.

SANTARELLI, Claude. See **SANTA**

SANTARELLI, Emilio

Italian, 19th century.
Born 1801, in Florence; died November 1886, in Florence.
Sculptor.

He was the son of Giovanni Antonio Santarelli and a pupil of Thorvaldsen in Rome.

Museums and Galleries:

Florence (Uffizi): *Michelangelo* (statue) - Montpellier: *A. L. J. P. Valedan* (bust); *Gache, Fabre's Executor* (bust).

SANTARELLI, Gaetano

Italian, 18th century.
Died at the beginning of the 18th century.
Painter.

Gaetano Santarelli was a pupil of O. Dandin and worked in Pescia.

SANTARELLI, Giovanni Antonio or Jean Antonio

Italian, 18th - 19th century.
Born 20 October 1758, in Manopello; died 30 May 1826, in Florence.
Sculptor, medallist, cameo engraver. Figures, historical figures. Busts.

The father of Emilio Santarelli, Giovanni Santarelli was a professor at the Accademia di Belle Arti in Florence.

Museums and Galleries:

London (British Mus.): *Head of the Young Hercules* (carved in onyx); *Portrait of Pius VI* (carved in onyx) - Montpellier: *F.X.P. Fabre (Founder of the Museum)* (marble bust finished by his son Emilio Santarelli).

SANTAS, Lamberto

Spanish, 18th century.
Active in Saragossa.
Sculptor.

Lamberto Santas was a pupil of J. Ramirez. He executed carvings on the high altar of the church of Sta Engracia in Saragossa.

SANTASUSAGNA SANTACREU, Ernesto

Spanish, 20th century.
Born 8 December 1900, in Barcelona; died 1964.
Painter, poster artist, decorative artist. Portraits, landscapes, still-lifes.

Ernesto Santasusagna Santacreu studied at the college of fine arts in Barcelona and went on to teach there from 1943. He is noted for *Waiting* and *Elegance in a Red Corsage*. He exhibited for the first time at the Sala Parès in Barcelona and later at the Barcelona Pinacoteca and in Madrid, Bilbao, San Sebastián, Italy, Egypt, Argentina and Brazil.

Bibliography:

Arnáiz, José Manuel/López Jiménez, Javier/Merchán Díaz, Manuel (ed.), '*Cien años de pintura en Espana y Portugal (1830-1930)*' in vol. X, Antiqvaria, Madrid, 1993.

Auction records:

Barcelona, 29 Jan 1981, *Nude* (1942, oil on canvas, 51 1/4 x 38 1/4 ins / 130 x 97 cm) ESP 170,000. Madrid, 22 June 1999, *Flowers* (oil on canvas, 39 x 31 ins / 100 x 80 cm) ESP 300,000. Madrid, 2 Dec 1999, *Gypsy Woman with Guitar* (1925, oil on canvas, 35 x 46 ins / 89 x 116 cm) ESP 550,000. Madrid, 8 May 2002, *Young Woman with Shawl and Fan* (oil on canvas, 29 x 24 ins / 74 x 62 cm) EUR 3,200.

SANTBERGEN, Jerry

Dutch, 20th century.
Born 1942, in Klundert.
Active in Canada from c. 1955.
Painter, sculptor.
Minimal Art.

Jerry Santbergen was hardly into his adolescence when he emigrated to Canada, where he lived in Regina, Saskatchewan, until 1966. He left for New York, but soon returned to Canada, settling in Toronto. Initially, he was influenced by the American Minimalists, producing large objects of vinyl or canvas stretched on frames, offering the viewer the primary sensations of coloured lines with no associative possibilities other than the immediate sensations. These coloured strips are very precisely arranged at breach points in the surrounding space, possibly so that the viewer's eye catches them all the more readily. He subsequently turned towards quasi-industrial manufacture of modules to be assembled.

He has participated in collective shows, notably *Canada: Art d'aujourd'hui* (*Canada: Art Today*) in Paris. He also took part in exhibitions in Rome, Lausanne, Brussels and at the 3rd American Biennale in Grabado, Chile. He won the Braniff International Award for Graphics and scholarships from the Canada Council.

Bibliography:

IIIe Salon international des Galeries Pilotes, exhibition catalogue, Musée cantonal, Lausanne, 1970.

SANTE. See **SANT'**

SANTE, followed by a second name. See second name

SANTE DA MARINO
Italian, 15th century.
Active in Perugia from 1471 to 1488.
Painter.

SANTE DI APOLLONIO DEL CELANDRO
Italian, 15th century.
Died 1486.
Active in Perugia.
Painter.
Sante di Apollonio del Celandro painted the tympanum of the altarpiece in the chapel of the town hall in Perugia.

SANTE MONACHESI. See **MONACHESI Sante**

SANTE NUCCI. See **NUCCI**

SANTEL, Alexander, or Sasa
Austrian, 20th century.
Born 15 March 1883, in Gorizia.
Painter, engraver. Landscapes.
Alexander Santel was the son of the painter Augusta Santel. He studied in Vienna and under Johann Brockhoff in Munich. He settled in Ljubljana and painted landscapes of Istria and Slovenia.

SANTEL, Augusta
Austrian, 19th - 20th century.
Born 1852, in Stainz; died 29 May 1935, in Ljubljana.
Painter, pastellist. Portraits.
Augusta Santel was the mother of Augusta, Henriette and Alexander Santel. She studied in Graz before settling in Ljubljana. She is noted for her crayon and pastel portraiture.

SANTEL, Augusta
Austrian, 19th - 20th century.
Born 21 July 1876, in Gorizia.
Painter. Landscapes, flowers.
Augusta Santel was the daughter of the painter Augusta Santel. She studied under Wilhelm von Debschitz in Munich and under Tina Blau in Vienna.

SANTEL, Henriette
Austrian, 19th - 20th century.
Born 28 August 1874, in Gorizia.
Painter.
Henriette Santel was the daughter of the painter Augusta Santel. She studied in Munich before settling in Ljubljana.
MUSEUMS AND GALLERIES:
LJUBLJANA (Narodna Gal.) - ZAGREB (Strossmayerova Galerija Starih Majstora Hrvatske Akademija Znanosti i Umjetnosti).

SANTELLI, Felice
Italian, 17th century.
Born c. 1601, in Rome; died 31 January 1656, in Rome.
Painter.
Felice Santelli worked with Baglioni on the church of S Maria in Campo Marzio.

SANTEN, Dirk Jansen van
Dutch, 17th century.
Born 1629; died 1699.
Active in Amsterdam and in Paris at the end of the 17th century.
Draughtsman, watercolourist. Landscapes, architectural views.
MUSEUMS AND GALLERIES:
LONDON (Conway Collection, Courtauld Institute): *Cupola Tower, Church of St Peter, Ghent* - VIENNA (Albertina Mus.): watercolours and drawings in chalk.

SANTEN, Gerrit van
Dutch, 17th century.
Died after 1650.
Painter. Battles.
Gerrit van Santen was a guild member in The Hague in 1629; he was active from 1637 to 1650, in the service of Prince Frederik Hendrik of Orange.
MUSEUMS AND GALLERIES:
AMSTERDAM - ANTWERP - BRUSSELS.
AUCTION RECORDS:
LONDON, 9 July 1976, *Battle Scene* (oil on canvas, 35½ x 54 ins / 90 x 137 cm) GBP 2,400.

SANTEN, Jan van. See **VASANZIO Giovanni**

SANTEN, N. van
Dutch, 18th century.
Active in the middle of the 18th century.
Painter.
MUSEUMS AND GALLERIES:
LEIDEN (Stedelijk Mus. De Lakenhal): *Portrait of Doctor C. Zumbach of Coesfelt.*

SANTER, Jakob Philipp
Austrian, 18th century.
Born 25 April 1756, in Bruneck; died 8 October 1809, in Bruneck.
Sculptor, architect.
Jakob Philipp Santer was the brother of Johann Peter Santer and a pupil of Georg Syli. He continued his studies in Augsburg and Stuttgart, then in Paris. He sculpted tombs and madonnas for churches in Brixen (now Bressanone, Italy), Bruneck and Innsbruck.

SANTER, Johann Peter
Austrian, 18th - 19th century.
Born 27 December 1759, in Bruneck; died 28 November 1823, in Vienna.
Sculptor.
Johann Peter Santer was the brother of Jakob Philipp Santer.

SANTER, Wilhelm. See **SANDER**

SANTERRE, Jean Baptiste
French, 17th - 18th century.
Born 23 March 1651, in Magny-en-Vexin (Val-d'Oise); died 21 November 1717, in Paris.
Painter, draughtsman. Religious subjects, portraits, genre scenes.
Santerre was the pupil of François Lemaire and Bon Boullogne. He became an Academician on 18 October 1704, and exhibited at the Salon in the same year. In Versailles he founded an academy for women, and designed a great many interesting models for their studies. Many of his works have been engraved.

Santerre was an interesting figure. He was a draughtsman, and the care he took to ensure the conservation of his works suggests considerable intelligence. Works by him are rare. He painted mainly portraits and genre subjects, well-drawn and attractively coloured.

Santerre often imbued his religious works with a sensual character which was not well received by his contemporaries. The most often quoted example of this is his *St Theresa*. This was inspired by Bernini's statue, yet caused a scandal. D'Argenville expressed his mistrust of the work with the following words: 'The heads are so beautiful and their expression and action so lifelike that this picture appears dangerous to scrupulous people.

Even ecclesiastics avoid celebrating the holy mysteries at the altar of this chapel.'

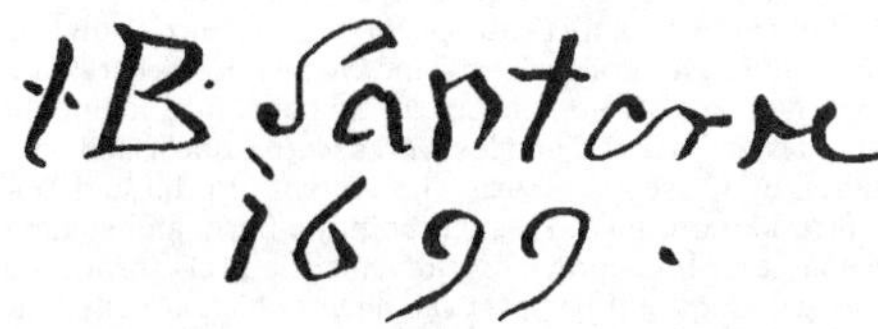

BIBLIOGRAPHY:

Tricentenaire du rattachement de Lille à la France. Au temps du Roi Soleil, les peintres de Louis XIV, exhibition catalogue, Palais des Beaux-Arts, Lille, 1968.

MUSEUMS AND GALLERIES:

BAYEUX (Mus. Baron-Gérard): *Young Woman* - CHAMBÉRY: *Young Smoker* - DUNKIRK: *P.M. Faulconnier and His Wife* - LE MANS: *Portrait of Madame Pelletier des Forts* - MOSCOW (Rumiantsev Mus.): *Music Lesson* - NANTES: *Cook Scraping a Carrot; Young Girl Asleep over Her Work* - ORLÉANS: *Painting; Curiosity* - PARIS (Louvre): *Susanna Bathing; Portrait of a Woman in Venetian Dress* - POZNAN (Muz. Mielzynskich): *Young Woman from Andalucia* - PRAGUE (Národní Gal.): *Portrait of a Young Sculptor* - PROVINS: *Portrait of a Woman* - PUY-EN-VELAY: *Young Girl at Her Window* - ROUEN: *Female Singer* - SAUMUR: *Duchess of Bourgogne* - ST PETERSBURG (Hermitage): *Portrait of a Young Woman; Dame Voilée (Veiled Lady)* - TOURS: *Geometry* - VERSAILLES (Château): *Duchess of Bourgogne; Regent and Madame de Parabère; Louise Adélaïde d'Orléans, Abbess of Chelles* (two paintings); *The Artist; Portrait of Nicolas Boileau.*

AUCTION RECORDS:

PARIS, 1767, *Pilgrim; Lady in a Ball Gown* (collection) FRF 1,301. PARIS, 1776, *Adam and Eve in Earthly Paradise,* FRF 12,400; *Woman Cutting Cabbage,* FRF 7,000. PARIS, 1888, *Religious Subject,* FRF 1,785. PARIS, 16 and 17 May 1892, *Lady Playing the Harp,* FRF 1,800. PARIS, 9 Feb 1905, *Portrait of the Marchioness of Rubel,* FRF 8,000; *Young Artist,* FRF 10,100. PARIS, 4 and 5 June 1905, *Portrait of a Young Woman,* FRF 1,400. PARIS, 5-10 June 1905, *Portrait of Philippe, Duke of Orléans,* FRF 1,730. PARIS, 3 and 4 Dec 1906, *Love Letter,* FRF 3,450. PARIS, 13 May 1907, *Portrait of a Woman,* FRF 2,250. PARIS, 16-18 May 1907, *Young Girl with a Budgerigar,* FRF 10,100; *Young Woman with a Letter,* FRF 3,800. NEW YORK, 12-14 April 1909, *Madame de Coislin,* USD 195; *Countess of Flavacourt,* USD 200. PARIS, 28 May 1909, *Portrait of a Woman,* FRF 1,400. PARIS, 17 June 1910, *Marchioness of Rubel,* FRF 7,000. NEW YORK, 4 March 1911, *Marquess of Rubel,* USD 1,900. NEW YORK, 6 and 7 April 1911, *Portrait of a Woman,* USD 575. LONDON, 12 April 1911, *Woman Plucking a Turkey,* GBP 8. PARIS, 13 March 1920, *Portrait of an Artist,* FRF 12,000. PARIS, 6 and 7 May 1920, *Portrait of a Young Woman,* FRF 12,700. PARIS, 27 April 1921, *Portrait of a Young Woman,* FRF 9,800. LONDON, 20 June 1924, *Swimming Pool,* GBP 168. PARIS, 29 Jan 1926, *Reading the Letter, Effect of Light,* FRF 800. PARIS, 13 Dec 1926, *Young Lady in Meditating Pose,* FRF 4,950. PARIS, 16 May 1927, *Susanna Bathing,* FRF 5,000. PARIS, 23 Nov 1927, *Portrait of a Painter* (pen and wash) FRF 230. LONDON, 22 Dec 1927, *Madame Catherine Marie Le Gendre,* GBP 546. LONDON, 31 Oct 1928, *Marchioness of Rubel,* GBP 105. PARIS, 19 Nov 1928, *Portrait of a Woman,* FRF 4,200. NEW YORK, 11 Dec 1930, *Marchioness of Épinay,* USD 375. PARIS, 14 May 1936, *Portrait of a Young Woman,* FRF 1,550. PARIS, 28 and 29 April 1941, *Portrait of a Young Woman Accompanied by a Black Boy Who is Giving Her a Dish* (school of Jean-Baptiste Santerre) FRF 10,000. PARIS, 4 Dec 1941, *Lady in a Mask* (school of Jean-Baptiste Santerre) FRF 7,300. PARIS, 8 May 1942, *Portrait of the Marchioness of Rubel,* FRF 1,200. PARIS, 30 Nov and 1 Dec 1942, *Portrait of a Young Girl,* FRF 8,900. PARIS, 21 Dec 1942, *Group of People* (attributed) FRF 19,100. PARIS, 14 May 1945, *Portrait of a Woman Wearing a Dress with Bare Shoulders, with Small Flowers in Her Hair* (attributed) FRF 8,200; *Portrait Presumed to be of Mademoiselle Favart* (attributed) FRF 5,000. PARIS, Oct 1945-July 1946, *Young Girl with a Budgerigar,* FRF 450,000. PARIS, 5 Feb 1947, *Half-length Portrait of Madame de Bonneval, Seated and Holding a Black Mask* (attributed) FRF 31,000. PARIS, 4 Dec 1950, *Lady in a Mask* (school of Jean-Baptiste Santerre) FRF 51,000. VERSAILLES, 1 March 1967, *Portrait of a Woman,* FRF 5,500. PARIS, 2 Feb 1976, *Woman Cutting Cabbage* (oil on canvas, 36 x 36 ins / 91.5 x 90.5 cm) FRF 2,250. BOURG-EN-BRESSE, 14 Oct 1979, *La Dormeuse (Sleeping Woman)* (oil on canvas, 31 1/2 x 24 1/2 ins / 80 x 62 cm) FRF 15,200. PARIS, 28 Nov 1984, *Virgin and Infant Jesus* (oil on canvas, 59 x 46 ins / 150 x 117 cm) FRF 170,000. NEW YORK, 13 March 1985, *Portrait of a Fashionable Lady in a Blue Dress Holding a Mask* (oil on canvas, 40 x 31 3/4 ins / 101.5 x 80.5 cm) USD 12,500. NEW YORK, 15 Jan 1986, *Portrait of an Artist* (oil on canvas, 51 1/4 x 38 3/4 ins / 130 x 98.5 cm) USD 28,000. PARIS, 24 June 1987, *Portrait of a Woman, Her Hand on a Letter* (1703, oil on canvas, 31 1/4 x 25 1/4 ins / 79.5 x 64 cm) FRF 200,000. PARIS, 14 April 1988, *Love Letter Delivered* (oil on canvas, 39 1/4 x 31 1/2 ins / 100 x 80 cm) FRF 140,000. NEW YORK, 11 Jan 1990, *Virgin with Child* (oil on canvas, 59 x 46 ins / 150 x 117 cm) GBP 27,500. NEW YORK, 1 June 1990, *Portrait of the Countess of Bersac* (oil on canvas, 40 x 31 3/4 ins / 101.5 x 80.5 cm) USD 18,700. MONACO, 21 June 1991, *Portrait of a Woman* (oil on canvas, 35 1/2 x 28 1/4 ins / 90 x 72 cm) FRF 33,300. NEW YORK, 12 Jan 1995, *Young Woman Warming Candle Wax to Seal an Envelope, Watched by a Putto* (oil on canvas, 27 1/4 x 37 ins / 69.2 x 94 cm) USD 39,100. PARIS, 13 Dec 1995, *Portrait of a Man in Hunting Clothes* (oil on canvas, 57 1/2 x 44 1/2 ins / 146 x 113 cm) FRF 85,000. NEW YORK, 29 Jan 1998, *Woman Being Helped by a Child to Seal a Letter by Candlelight* (oil on canvas, attributed to J.B. Santerre, 28 x 37 1/2 ins / 71 x 95.3 cm) USD 17,250. NEW YORK, 28 Jan 1999, *Philippe d'Orleans and Comtesse de Parabere as Adam and Eve* (oil on canvas, 40 x 32 ins / 101 x 81 cm) USD 35,000. LONDON, 3 July 2000, *Sleeping Girl Wearing Blue Velvet Bodice* (oil on canvas, 32 x 26 ins / 82 x 66 cm) GBP 1,600. NEW YORK, 26 Oct 2001, *Singer* (oil on canvas, 32 x 26 ins / 81 x 65 cm) USD 12,000. PARIS, 23 June 2004, *Young Woman with Love Letter* (oil on canvas, 36 x 29 ins / 91 x 73 cm) EUR 77,000.

SANTESA, Giovanni

Italian, 16th century.

Sculptor.

Giovanni Santesa carved the font in the church at Cerasola.

SANTESSON, Ninnan Gertrud Paulina

Swedish, 20th century.

Born 14 December 1891, in Fjäräs.

Sculptor. Statues, low reliefs.

Ninnan Gertrud Paulina Santesson studied under Sigrid Blomberg and at the fine arts academy in Stockholm.

MUSEUMS AND GALLERIES:

GÖTEBORG: *Fisherman* - STOCKHOLM (Nationalmus.): *Shepherd and Lamb.*

SANTFOORT. See **SANTVOORT**

SANTFORT MECHINENSIS, Antonio de. See **SANTVOORT Anthonie**

SANTHO, Milos or Nikolaus, pseudonyms: Chambertin or Chanteaux, Nicolas François

Hungarian, 19th - 20th century.

Born 6 June 1869, in Mocsonok.

Painter. Figures, nudes, portraits, interiors, landscapes. Milos Santho trained in Budapest and Munich. He worked in Waitzen.

AUCTION RECORDS:

AMSTERDAM, 24 April 1991, *Nude with a Mask* (1923, oil on canvas, 53 1/2 x 33 3/4 ins / 136 x 86 cm) NLG 7,475. VIENNA, 9 Feb 1999, *Female Nude Wearing Mask* (1923, oil on canvas, 54 x 34 ins / 136 x 86 cm) ATS 30,000.

SANTI. See also **SANTO**

SANTI, Andriolo di Pagano de

Italian, 14th century.
Died before 25 November 1375.
Active in Venice.
Sculptor.

Andriolo di Pagano de Santi carved tombs in churches in Padua and Venice. He also executed the tomb of Enrico Scrovegni in the Arena chapel in Padua.

SANTI, Antonio

Italian, 17th century.
Born c. 1670, possibly in Rimini; died c. 1700, in Venice.
Painter.

Santelli was a pupil of Cignani.

MUSEUMS AND GALLERIES:

VICENZA (Mus. Civico): *Lot and His Daughters*.

SANTI, Archimede

Italian, 20th century.
Born 6 March 1876, in Pergola; died 1947.
Painter, draughtsman. Landscapes, urban landscapes, still-lifes.

He studied art in Urbino, Parma and Bologna.

As well as producing paintings, Archimede Santi published a series of views of Pergola and the surrounding area.

AUCTION RECORDS:

ROME, 29 May 1990, *Still-lifes* (oil on canvas, a pair, each 16 3/4 x 23 1/2 ins / 42.5 x 59.5 cm) ITL 8,050,000.

SANTI, Bartolommeo de

Italian, 18th century.
Born c. 1700, in Lucca; died c. 1756.
Painter, decorative designer.

Bartolommeo de Santi studied in Bologna and worked in the theatre.

SANTI, Bruno

Italian, 20th century.
Born 26 April 1892, in Florence.
Painter, engraver. Wall decorations.

A pupil of Domenico Ferri at the Istituto di Belle Arti in Bologna, Bruno Santi painted decorative interiors in Palazzo Spada in Bologna and Palazzo Arioli in Milan.

SANTI, Carolina

Italian, 19th century.
Active during the first half of the 19th century.
Engraver (burin).

Carolina Santi produced engravings of architecture and funerary monuments.

SANTI, Ciro

Italian, 18th century.
Active in Bologna and in Siena until 1780.
Painter, engraver (burin).

Ciro Santi engraved landscapes, architectural views, Roman antiquities and ornamental works.

SANTI, Domenico, called Mingaccino, Mangazzino or Mengazzino

Italian, 17th century.
Born 1621, in Bologna; died 8 February 1694.
Painter, engraver (burin/etching), draughtsman (including charcoal), decorative designer. Mythological subjects, portraits, landscapes, perspectives.

The father of Giovanni Giuseppe Santi, Domenico Santi was one of the best pupils of Agostino Metelli. He decorated a large number of monuments in Bologna in addition to churches and palaces, and his works were embellished with figures by Giuseppe Metelli, Gio Antonio Burini and Domenico Maria Canuti. He used both the burin and etching techniques in his engravings. Domenico Santi also produced easel paintings and perspectival views, which are often attributed to his master.

AUCTION RECORDS:

PARIS, 1856, *Portrait of Agostino Carracci* (after Canuti) FRF 18. MILAN, 13 May 1993, *Hercules* (charcoal and chalk/paper, 16 3/4 x 11 3/4in/42.6 x 30cm) ITL 1,300,000.

SANTI, Domenico di

Italian, 16th century.
Mosaicist.

Domenico di Santi executed mosaics in the basilica of S Marco in Venice.

SANTI, Filippo de. See **FILIPPO DA VENEZIA**

SANTI, Francesco di Bartolomeo, called Il Papa

Italian, 15th century.
Active in Urbino during the second half of the 15th century.
Sculptor, designer of ornamental architectural features.

Francesco di Bartolomeo Santi collaborated with Antonio di Simone Francesco da Urbino.

SANTI, Giovanni

Italian, 14th century.
Died 7 August 1392.
Active in Venice.
Sculptor.

The son of Andriolo Santi, Giovanni Santi worked in the style of his father in Padua and Venice.

SANTI, Giovanni

Italian, 15th century.
Born c. 1435, in Castello di Collordalo, near Urbino; died 1 August 1494, in Urbino.
Painter, poet. Religious subjects.
Urbino School.

Known chiefly as the father of Raphael, Giovanni Santi was himself a talented artist. His *Virgin and Child* in the National Gallery in London makes it clear that not only was Raphael his son, but also inherited his feelings and sentiments. The works of father and son seem to stem from a similar ideal and conception, a certain tender gracefulness. It would be possible to take Giovanni's works for early Raphaels.

Giovanni was the son of a spice merchant and was expected to follow his father in that trade. He may have started out as a merchant but his inclination for painting began as a result of his friendship with Melozzo da Forlì and Piero della Francesca. His first known work was a pair of frescoes in the church of S Domenico in Cagli, the *Resurrection* and the *Virgin Enthroned with Saints*. Santi was a man of some means and in 1464 bought a house in Urbino in the Contrada del Monte. He married Maria Ciarla who gave birth, in March or April 1483, to Raffaello, known to us as Raphael. The young Raphael was used by his father as a model in, for example, Giovanni's *Christ and St John as Infants*. A fresco in Raphael's house in Urbino depicts a *Virgin and Child*, said to be a portrait of Maria Ciarla and her newborn baby. Giovanni, seeing the boy's obvious talent, encouraged his son to paint and was his first teacher.

Maria died in 1491 and in 1492 Giovanni took a second wife, Bernardina, the daughter of the jeweller Piero di Parte, but died two years later. Of his works, the most noteworthy are *Madonna with Saints* (1489) in the church of S Francesco in Urbino, *Virgin and Saints* in the convent of Monte Fiorentino near Urbino, *The Visitation* in the church of S Maria Nuova and a *Virgin and Saints* in the church of the Ospedale S Croce in Fano, *The Virgin Enthroned* dated 1492 in the Dominican church in Caglio and a *Martyrdom of St Sebastian* in the confraternity of St Sebastian in Urbino. Giovanni was also a poet; the manuscript of his epic poem *The Glorious Deeds of Duke Federigo of Urbino* is in the Vatican library.

MUSEUMS AND GALLERIES:

BERLIN: *Virgin and Child with Four Saints; Virgin and Child* - BUDAPEST: *Virgin and Saints* - FANO (Pinacoteca del Palazzo Malatestiano): *Madonna and Child with Saints* - FLORENCE (Gal. Corsini): *Clio; Polymnestus* (fragments) - LONDON (NG): *The Virgin and Child* (c. 1488, tempera and oil/wood) - MILAN (Pinacoteca di Brera): *Annunciation* - ROME (Gal. Colonna): *Portrait of a Child* - VATICAN (Mus. Vaticani): *St Jerome*.

AUCTION RECORDS:

LONDON, 11 May 1934, *Portrait of a Little Boy*, GBP 1,995. LONDON, 10-14 July 1936, *Study of a Flying Angel* (silverpoint) GBP 420.

SANTI, Giovanni
Italian, 18th century.
Active in Milan.
Sculptor.

Giovanni Santi sculpted a *Pietà* in the church of S Michele in Pavia.

SANTI, Giovanni Battista, called della Lavandara
Italian, 18th century.
Died 1732.
Active in Bologna.
Painter, decorative designer. Church decoration.

Giovanni Battista Santi was the pupil of Ercole Graziani. He produced works for churches and palaces in Bologna.

SANTI, Giovanni Giuseppe
Italian, 17th - 18th century.
Born 1644; died 1719.
Active in Bologna.
Painter, decorative designer.

The son of Domenico Santi, Giovanni Giuseppe Santi worked initially with his master, Domenico Maria Canuti, and subsequently produced paintings for palaces in Bologna, Milan, Udine and Verona.

SANTI, Giuseppe
Italian, 19th century.
Died 1825, in Ferrara.
Active in Bologna.
Painter.

A pupil of M. Gandoli, Giuseppe Santi settled in Ferrara in 1797, painting works for a number of churches and palazzi in that town and in Ravenna.

SANTI, Michele de
Italian, 17th century.
Active in Bologna c. 1660.
Painter.
Bolognese School.

Michele de Santi was probably taught by Guido Reni. He produced works for churches in Bologna.

SANTI, Orazio. See **SANTIS Orazio di**

SANTI, Pietro
Italian, 18th century.
Active in Rimini during the second half of the 18th century.
Engraver (burin).

SANTI, Raphaello, or Raphaeel, or Raffaello. See **RAPHAEL**

SANTI, Sebastiano
Italian, 19th century.
Born 6 August 1789, in Murano; died 18 April 1865, in Venice.
Painter, art restorer. Frescoes, church decoration.

Examples of Sebastiano Santi's work, particularly frescoes, can be found in the churches of Venice.

SANTI, Ziliberto I
Italian, 14th century.
Active in Venice.
Sculptor.

Ziliberto Santi I was the son of Pietro Santi.

SANTI, Ziliberto II
Italian, 14th century.
Active in Venice.
Sculptor.

The son of Mauro Santi, Ziliberto Santi II carved the tomb of Pietro di Dante in the cathedral library in Treviso.

SANTI DI TITO. See **TITO Santi di**

SANTI LEONCINI. See **LEONCINI Santi**

SANTI PACINI. See **PACINI Santi**

SANTIAGO, Juan de
Spanish, 16th century.
Active in Puebla del Dean during the second half of the 16th century.
Painter, sculptor.

Juan de Santiago executed frescoes in the church at Argalo and a *Christ* for the bridge at Padron.

SANTIAGO, Manuel
Brazilian, 20th century.
Born 1897.
Painter. Still-lifes.

Manuel Santiago was one of those who formed the 'Bernardelli Nucleus', created in 1931 in Buenos Aires, which was instrumental to opening up Brazilian art to modern ideas.

AUCTION RECORDS:

SÃO PAULO, 15 Sept 1982, *Still-life* (oil on canvas, 23 1/2 x 28 3/4 ins / 60 x 73 cm) BRL 1,200,000. RIO DE JANEIRO, 4 July 1983, *Kosmo* (1919, oil on canvas, 17 x 15 ins / 43 x 38 cm) BRL 2,400,000.

SANTIAGO, Simon de
Spanish, 16th century.
Illuminator.

Simon de Santiago decorated choir books for the monastery of S Lorenzo in 1584.

SANTIAGO CARDENAS ARROYO. See **CARDENAS Santiago**

SANTIAGO PALOMARES, Francisco Xavier de
Spanish, 18th century.
Born 5 March 1728, in Toledo; died 13 January 1796, in Madrid.
Painter, draughtsman. Portraits, landscapes.

Although Francisco de Santiago Palomares spent much of his life copying manuscripts for the royal libraries or in administrative or literary functions, he was also a painter of note. He painted portraits of a number of important figures of the period as well as landscapes. He was much sought after by authors and bookshops to draw frontispieces for their publications. Santiago Palomares was also an heraldist and calligrapher.

SANTIAGO WESTRETEN, Francisco and José. See **SANTIGOSA WESTRETEN**

SANTIFALLER, Anton
Austrian, 19th - 20th century.

Born 16 February 1853, in Gröden; died 2 February 1928, in Meran (now Merano, Italy).
Sculptor. Religious subjects. Statues.

Anton Santifaller sculpted numerous wood and stone statues for churches in South Tyrol.

SANTIFALLER, Franz
Austrian, 20th century.
Born 14 December 1894, in Meran (now Merano, Italy).
Active in Innsbruck.
Sculptor. Figures. Monuments, statues, groups, busts, low reliefs.

Franz Santifaller was presumably the son of either Anton or Vinzenz Santifaller. He studied under Anton von Kenner and Anton Hannak at the fine arts academy in Vienna and under Antoine Bourdelle in Paris. He sculpted statues, tombs and low reliefs in Innsbruck and other Austrian towns.

MUSEUMS AND GALLERIES:
MERANO: *Suffering; Bust of Hans Innerhofer* - VIENNA (Österreichische Gal. Belvedere): *Bust of an Architect* (bronze); *Mother and Child.*

SANTIFALLER, Vinzenz
Austrian, 19th - 20th century.
Born 1854, in Gröden; died 20 November 1929, in Meran (now Merano, Italy).
Sculptor.

Vinzenz Santifaller was the brother and assistant of Anton Santifaller.

SANTIGOSA WESTRETEN, Francisco
Spanish, 19th century.
Born 12 October 1835, in Tortosa.
Active in Valencia.
Sculptor, potter, medallist.

Francisco Santigosa Westreten studied under his brother José Santigosa Westreten. He carved statues and decorations for churches in Valencia.

SANTIGOSA WESTRETEN, José
Spanish, 19th century.
Sculptor.

José Santigosa Westreten was the brother and teacher of Francisco Santigosa Westreten.

SANTILLANA, Diego de
Spanish, 15th - 16th century.
Active in Burgos (Castilla y León).
Glass painter.

Diego de Santillana worked at Avila Cathedral in 1497, making four stained glass windows in collaboration with Juan de Valdivieso. One, representing *St John,* survives. He also made *Scenes from the Life of Christ* in stained glass for the library in the cloister.

SANTILLANA, Juan de
Spanish, 16th century.
Active in Valladolid.
Sculptor.

Juan de Santillana was called several times to advise on the price to be charged for major works.

SANTILLO, Alberto
Italian, 20th century.
Born 6 April 1882, in Santa Maria Capua Vetere (Campania).
Painter. Figures, portraits, genre scenes, landscapes with figures.

Alberto Santillo was a pupil of Vincenzo Volpe in Naples.

MUSEUMS AND GALLERIES:
NAPLES: *Sick Girl.*

AUCTION RECORDS:
PARIS, 2 May 1949, *Flood,* FRF 1,600; *Flock of Sheep,* FRF 500.

SANTILLO, Battista
Italian, 16th century.
Active in Naples during the second half of the 16th century.
Painter.

Battista Santillo painted some frescoes in the church of S Spirito in Naples in 1579.

SANTIN AICHEL. See **SANTINI Francesco, Giovanni** and **Johann**

SANTINE, Étienne
French, 16th century.
Active in Cambrai in 1588 and 1589.
Engraver. Coins.

SANTINI
Italian, 18th century.
Active in Lucca during the second half of the 18th century.
Painter.

In 1772, Santini painted 14 *Stations of the Cross* for the dormitory of the Carthusian monastery at Pavia.

SANTINI, Andrea
Italian, 18th century.
Cameo engraver.

SANTINI, Bernardino di Bartolommeo, the Elder
Italian, 17th century.
Born 1593, in Arezzo; died after 1652.
Painter, draughtsman.

Lanzi mentions a *St Catherine* by Santini the Elder in the monastery at Arezzo. Numerous frescoes and altarpieces in churches in Arezzo are also attributed to him.

MUSEUMS AND GALLERIES:
AREZZO: *Virgin Appearing to St Philip; Vision of Moses* - FLORENCE (Uffizi): drawings.

SANTINI, Bernardino di Bartolommeo, the Younger
Italian, 17th century.
Active in Arezzo during the first half of the 17th century.
Painter.

SANTINI, Francesco, real name: Franz Santin Aichel or Auchel or Eichel or Euchel
Austrian, 17th century.
Born 28 April 1680, in Prague; died 21 June 1709, in Prague.
Sculptor.

Francesco Santini was the son and pupil of Johann Santini. He worked initially with his brother Giovanni, and subsequently sculpted statues for churches and palaces in Prague, notably the statue of *St John Nepomuk,* which is at the foot of the steps of the town hall.

SANTINI, Francesco
Italian, 18th - 19th century.
Born 1763; died 1840.
Painter, designer of ornamental architectural features, architect. Architectural views.

A pupil of Serafino Barozzi, Francesco Santini worked in Bologna.

AUCTION RECORDS:
LONDON, 16-17 April 1997, *Design for a Temple (recto); Fragment of a Study for a Pedestal (verso)* (pen and brown ink and grey wash/black chalk, 11 1/2 x 8in/29.4 x 20.1cm) GBP 460.

SANTINI, Giovanni, pseudonym of Johann Blasius Santin Aichel or Auchel or Eichel or Euchel
Austrian, 17th - 18th century.
Born 1667, in Prague; died 7 December 1723, in Prague.
Painter, sculptor, architect.

Giovanni Santini was the son of Johann and brother of Francesco Santini. He was one of the masters of late Baroque in Bohemia. He trained in Italy and worked in Bohemia in the service of monasteries and the nobility. He was a notable architect and executed architectural paintings.

AUCTION RECORDS:
MILAN, 4 Dec 1986, *View of Florence from the Boboli Gardens* (pen and wash, 8¾ x 16¼ ins / 22.5 x 41 cm) ITL 3,600,000.

SANTINI, Imelda
Italian, 19th - 20th century.
Born 15 September 1857, in San Benedetto del Trono.
Painter. Religious subjects.

Imelda Santini painted two altarpieces for the church in Elice.

SANTINI, Johann, the Elder,
pseudonym of Santin Aichel or Auchel or Eichel or Euchel
Austrian, 17th century.
Born 23 October 1652, in Prague; died 27 November 1702, in Prague.
Sculptor. Decorative schemes.

Johann Santini was the father of Francesco and Giovanni Santini. He executed notably decorative sculpture for palaces and monasteries in Prague. In 1681 he executed the stucco for the grotto of the Neuhaus Palace. In 1690 he worked at the Czernin Palace in Prague.

SANTINI, Paolo
Italian, 20th century.
Born 1 April 1929, in Gimigliano.
Active from 1958 in France.
Sculptor (mixed media).

Paolo Santini studied at the art school in Turin and then spent eight years in Algeria. He worked for architectural and interior decoration companies. In 1958, he moved to Paris. He has taken part in a number of collective exhibitions including: sculptures in molten glass in 1967; Brussels, Hamburg and Lyons in 1970; *Sculptures and Forms in Aluminium* in Paris in 1971; Amsterdam.

His works have the appearance of totems decorated with monstrous anthropomorphic forms.

SANTINI, Pio
Italian, 20th century.
Born 1908, in Tivoli (Rome); died 1986.
Active in France c. 1933.
Painter. Figure compositions, figures, portraits, genre scenes, landscapes, waterscapes.

An early work by Pio Santi was a double full-length portrait of his parents, a painting full of restrained and serious tenderness. His rather conventional pictures of harlequins, gypsies and clowns appealed to a public that sought the reassurance of the familiar. His portraits of children are successful because of their transparent authenticity and his landscapes painted at Tivoli and on the banks of the river Loing in France are similarly sensitive.

He lived in Paris, in the 16th arondissement, for more than 50 years and a retrospective exhibition of his life's work was organised in 1992 by the council of this district. He was a professor at the Rome academy of fine art. He received a number of regional prizes and distinctions and was a member of a number of artistic groups including the Accademia dei 500 in Rome.

Santi participated in various collective exhibitions in Italy - at the Rome Quadriennale, for example - and France, particularly in Paris. These include: the Salons of the Société Nationale des Beaux-Arts, of the Tuileries and of the Indépendants. He was the secretary of the latter organisation.

SANTINI, Vincenzo
Italian, 19th century.
Born 2 July 1807, in Pietrasanta; died 1876.
Sculptor, art critic.

Vincenzo Santini studied in Rome with P. Tenerani. He was a professor at the art school in Pietrasanta.

SANTINO. See **SANTUCCI Santi**

SANTINO DI CHECCO DI PETRINCIONE
Italian, 16th century.
Sculptor.

A dealer in marble from Carrara, Santino di Checco di Petrincione worked in Palermo between 1504 and 1534. He carved the statues on the tribune of the church of S Cita and made the choir enclosure in Palermo Cathedral.

SANTIS, Amleto de
Italian, 20th century.
Born 1908, in Rome; died 1980.
Painter.

MUSEUMS AND GALLERIES:
ROME (Gal. Nazionale d'Arte Moderna).

SANTIS, Giovanni de
Italian, 17th century.
Active in Naples at the end of the 17th century.
Sculptor (wood).

In 1695, Giovanni de Santis was commissioned to produce a sculpture of the *Dead Christ*.

SANTIS, Orazio di, called d'Aquila or Aquilanho
Italian, 16th century.
Born probably in Aquila.
Active between 1568 and 1584.
Engraver (etching), print publisher.

According to Mariette, Orazio di Santis specialised in engravings after the work of Pompeo Dell'Aquila or Aquilano in Rome about 1572. Bartseli lists 70 of his plates. To this Nagler adds another 74 plates of antique statues in Rome, a series executed in collaboration with Cherubino Alberti and published in 1584.

SANTISTEBAN, Pedro de
Spanish, 16th century.
Active during the first half of the 16th century.
Sculptor.

In 1532, Pedro de Santisteban worked on the decoration of the vaults of the sacristy in the Capilla Real in Toledo Cathedral.

SANTLER, R.
British, 18th century.
Active in London in 1785.
Modeller (wax).

SANTLOFER, Jonathan
American, 20th - 21st century.
Born 1946, in New York.
Active in New York.
Painter, collage artist, sculptor, photographer.

Jonathan Santlofer studied at Boston University and at the Pratt Institute in Brooklyn. He supported his early painting career with several teaching jobs. He is also a writer of thrillers set in the New York art world, such as *Death Artist*

(Harper Collins, 2002) and *Color Blind* (William Morrow, 2004).

Santlofer's major concerns, complex space, velocity, illusionism, drama, and reality versus illusion, have remained constant throughout the evolution of his work. Long considered an abstract painter, he then began adding actual objects and photographic imagery to his work. This has moved his work into an area where the 'real' or representational world co-mingles with the abstract world; the result is a fascinating hybrid in which image and content integrate fully.

A turning point in Santlofer's development was a gallery fire in Chicago in 1989 in which five years of his work were destroyed. He retreated to Rome, where he spent time looking at Renaissance and Baroque art and drawing, and began to write fiction as a form of creative release. Almost five years after the fire, he returned to the art scene with figurative work including a series of 100 carved and painted relief portraits of famous artists (including Picasso and Henri Rousseau) against detailed replicas of each particular artist's famous work. Santlofer's style is a personal synthesis of Modernism, with echoes of Van Gogh, Matisse, Cubism, Futurism and Expressionism, and is distinguished by a vibrant, sensual, colourful palette. Works include *Romantic Criminal* (1984), *Andy Fights for Life, Blue Jackie, Calla Lily, Factory Snack, Gold Marilyn* and *Nave Nave Fenna* (2001).

His notable *Man Ray Series* consists of eight meticulous *trompe l'oeil* renditions of elements adapted from Man Ray's provocative Surrealist photographs. Combined with photographic self-portraits of Man Ray, these highly refined, sophisticated juxtapositions confound the viewer into accepting the illusion so convincingly presented. Santlofer's works are in the permanent holdings of many museums, as well as in numerous corporate and private collections.

He has shown work in over 100 solo and group exhibitions, including at the James Graham & Sons Gallery, the New Museum, and the Drawing Center, all in New York; the Institute of Contemporary Art in Tokyo; the Galleria Peccolo in Livorno; the Betsy Rosenfield and Klein Galleries in Chicago; and *The Man Ray Series* at the Montclair Museum in New Jersey (2003).

BIBLIOGRAPHY:

Stavitsky, Gail, *Jonathan Santlofer: The Man Ray Series*, exhibition catalogue, Montclair Art Museum, Montclair (NJ), 2003.

MUSEUMS AND GALLERIES:

CHICAGO (AI) - GRAND RAPIDS (Grand Rapids AM) - INDIANAPOLIS (MA) - NEW YORK (Metropolitan Mus. of Art) - NEW YORK (MoMA) - PASADENA (Norton Simon Mus.) - TOKYO (ICA).

SANTO. See also **SANT'**

SANTO (Fra), also known as Fra Fontana
Italian, 17th century.
Painter.

Santo, a Capuchin friar, was active in Venice at the beginning of the 17th century. He worked in Trento and in the monastery at Ala.

SANTO, followed by a second name. See second name

SANTO, Girolamo dal. See **SORDI Girolamo**

SANTO, Raimondo de
Italian, 15th century.
Active in the second half of the 15th century.
Painter.

Raimondo de Santo painted some works for ships in 1489.

SANTO CORBETTI. See **CORBETTI**

SANTO DOMINGO, Vincente de (Fray)
Spanish, 16th - 17th century.
Painter.

Vincente de Santo Domingo is chiefly remembered as the first to recognise the artistic talents of Navarrete 'el Mudo' and his first master. He encouraged Navarrete to go to Italy. Four paintings in the church at Estella, thought for many years to be by Santo Domingo, have been shown to have been painted by Navarrete in 1659. The grisaille work on the walls of the cloister is by Santo Domingo. Other works by him are in the convent of S Catalina in Talavera de la Reyna.

SANTO LUCA
Florentine School, 9th century.
Born in Florence.
Painter.

Santo Luca was a Florentine monk, and probably painted the pictures of *Virgin and the Infant Jesus* in the churches of Madonna di S Luca, Bologna, and S Maria Maggiore, Rome, formerly attributed to the evangelist St Luke, who was thought to have painted the Virgin when she was alive.

SANTO MAURITIO, Carlo di
French, 18th century.
Active c. 1793.
Engraver (etching).

Santo Mauritio was probably one and the same as Charles, Count of St-Morys.

SANTO PERANDA. See **PERANDA Sante,** or **Santo**

SANTO RINALDI, or Sante R., Santi R., called Il Tromba, or Tranba
Florentine School, 17th century.
Born c. 1620, in Florence; died c. 1676.
Painter. Battles, landscapes, architectural views.

Santo Rinaldi was the pupil of F. Furini.

SANTO ZAGO. See **ZAGO**

SANTOIRE DE VARENNE. See **VARENNE Dorothée Santoire de**

SANTOMASO, Giuseppe
Italian, 20th century.
Born 1907, in Venice; died 1990.
Painter (including gouache/mixed media), collage artist, lithographer, illustrator, potter. Murals.
Groups: Corrente, Fronte Nuovo delle Arti, Otto Pittori Italiani.

After studying at the academy of fine art in Venice, Giuseppe Santomaso travelled to Holland in 1937, where he discovered Van Gogh, and then to Paris where, particularly at the Exposition Internationale, he came into contact with many of the movements of the artistic avant-garde. He was much impressed by Picasso's *Guernica*, painted in just a few months for the Pavillion of the Spanish Republic. On the eve of World War II, he was, together with Birolli, Cassinari, Guttuso, Morlotti and Vedova, a member of the Corrente movement that opposed the purely nationalistic aspects of the work of the Italian artists associated with the Novecento movement set up during Mussolini's Fascist regime. In Milan in 1945, he published the collection of poetry by the French poet Éluard entitled *Grand Air* that he had illustrated with 27 drawings. In 1947, after the war, the Corrente group became the Fronte Nuovo delle Arti. Santomaso left the group to form, between 1950 and 1952, the Gruppo degli Otto Pittori Italiani (Group of Eight Italian Painters), the other seven being Birolli, Afro Basaldella, Corpora, Morlotti, Vedova, Turcato and Moreni. Between 1971 and 1974, he was a professor at the academy of fine art in Venice.

Santomaso's early work is heavily indebted to the Venetian tradition and the chromatic luminosity of Post-Impressionism as well as the Cubist construction of the post-Cézanne period. His works at this period were based on reality, often still-lifes, but a reality rearranged according to a system that he had evolved after studying the mosaics in St Mark's Basilica in Venice, where form is broken up into light and colour preserving and accentuating the poetic presence of the object. His work during this initial period shows the influence first of Pio Semeghini and then of the impressionist sculptor Medardo Rosso. Subsequent influences that were more constructive and very marked were those of Morandi and, particularly, Braque, who became a close friend. Ozenfant's Purism was also important.

From 1942, he moved increasingly towards International Abstraction. Initially, around 1950, his works were geometric in formulation but later, in the 1960s, they became more informal, with large undefined patches and splashes of rich colour subtly shading from one to another. The paint is applied with sensual brushstrokes or delicate transparency, fading into an undefined space. Energetic gestural strokes give a structure to the whole, co-ordinating the different patches of colour. During this period he worked on several versions of a *Homage to Cimabue's Crucifix* (1966-1969). This move towards Abstraction did not, however, cut him off from a reality that he saw as the basis of his poetic and emotional inspiration, a position characteristic of all eight of the Otto Pittori. He wrote:

I realise that none of the marks I make on paper have any connection with any objective representation or description, yet I also realise that, without this visual pretext, without this bruise, without this black post that scratches a line in the plaster, without the rolling of dice or the creaking of a wheel, these marks would not have come to be and would not have arranged themselves in an expressive order. We are in objects and with objects. There would be no imagination without objects.

As he distanced himself from the appearance of things, Santomaso moved increasingly towards 'abstract landscape-painting' or, perhaps a better description, 'poetic abstraction', the style of his greatest works. At the end of the 1970s, the strokes that formerly provided structure to the paintings become simpler and less evident, freeing up the surface to allow free rein to the interplay of patches of colour. His series of *Letters to Palladio* explores these possibilities.

Santomaso is considered one of the most important painters of the post-war period. With titles that often allude to memories of visual and/or aural sensations experienced in precise moments and places, often when travelling, (*Paso Doble*, 1960; *Green Memory*, 1953; *Reds and Greens of Harvest*, 1957; *Andalusian Song*, 1960) his works attempt to seize the fleeting moment and, as such, have direct links with Impressionism through his admiration of Medardo Rosso. Giuseppe Marchiori wrote with true understanding, on seeing the works of Santomaso, that he offers us 'a harmony in which music and painting truly become one'.

From 1928, he participated in many collective exhibitions devoted to contemporary Italian painting, including those at Documenta in Kassel and at the 1972 Venice Biennale. His solo exhibitions include one in 1937 in Amsterdam and one in 1939 in Paris, followed by many others in towns in Italy, Paris, London and in Germany and America. Retrospective exhibitions were held in 1960 in Amsterdam and Brussels and in 1982 in Venice.

Santomaso

BIBLIOGRAPHY:

Venturi, Lionello, *Otto pittori italiani*, De Luca Editore, Rome, 1952. Read, Herbert, *Santomaso*, Hanover Gall., London, 1953. Marchiori, Giuseppe, *Santomaso*, Alfieri, Venice, 1954. Venturi, Lionello, *Santomaso*, De Luca Editore, Rome, 1955. Apollonio, Umbro, *Santomaso*, Fischbacher, Paris, 1959. Santomaso, Giuseppe, *Santomaso Catalogo ragionato 1931-1974*, Alfieri, Venice, 1975. *Giuseppe Santomaso, opere 1939-1982*, exhibition catalogue, Palazzo reale, Electa, Milan, 1986.

MUSEUMS AND GALLERIES:

AMSTERDAM (Stedelijk Mus.): *Fire at S Maria del Mare* (1959) - FLORENCE (Gal. d'Arte Moderna): *Friuli Suite* (1963) - LA CHAUX-DE-FONDS: *Image No. 12* (1965) - RIO DE JANEIRO: *Hour of the Cicadas* (1953) - ROME (Gal. Nazionale d'Arte Moderna): *Interior* (1948); *Rural Rhythms* (1954) - SARREBRÜCKEN: *Ferment* (1962).

AUCTION RECORDS:

NEW YORK, 21 Oct 1964, *Suspended Night*, USD 900. COLOGNE, 9 Dec 1965, *Composition*, DEM 3,400. LONDON, 14 Dec 1967, *Homage to Cimabue's Crucifix*, GBP 350. MILAN, 25 May 1971, *Composition*, ITL 850,000. MILAN, 4 June 1974, *Green Memory*, ITL 6,000,000. NEW YORK, 28 May 1976, *Walls of Crakow* (1958, oil on canvas, 49 x 45 ins / 124.5 x 114.5 cm) USD 1,100. ROME, 16 Dec 1976, *Composition* (1958, gouache, 16 1/2 x 12 1/2 ins / 42 x 32 cm) ITL 380,000. ROME, 19 May 1977, *Rhythms in Grey* (1959, oil on canvas, 28 3/4 x 19 3/4 ins / 73 x 50 cm) ITL 1,200,000. MILAN, 26 April 1979, *Stones Like Meat* (1958, oil on canvas, 28 3/4 x 39 1/4 ins / 73 x 100 cm) ITL 2,600,000. ZURICH, 11 Nov 1981, *On the Borders of the Orient* (oil on canvas, 29 1/4 x 19 3/4 ins / 74 x 50 cm) CHF 9,000. MILAN, 5 April 1984, *Catalan Story* (1959, oil on canvas, 63 3/4 x 51 1/4 ins / 162 x 130 cm) ITL 9,500,000. MILAN, 26 March 1985, *Red Sign on White Field* (1969, mixed media/canvas remounted/panel, 36 1/2 x 28 3/4 ins / 93 x 73 cm) ITL 5,300,000. COLOGNE, 10 Dec 1986, *Aspect of the South No. 2* (1962, oil on canvas, 63 3/4 x 51 1/4 ins / 162 x 130 cm) DEM 44,000. BERN, 30 April 1988, *Landscape Seen from my Studio Window* (oil on canvas, 27 1/4 x 18 1/2 ins / 69 x 47 cm) CHF 4,000. MILAN, 14 Dec 1988, *Yellow (Lead Monoxide)* (1952, oil on canvas, 35 1/2 x 46 ins / 90 x 116 cm) ITL 40,000,000. MILAN, 20 March 1989, *Grill* (1948, oil on canvas, 23 1/2 x 29 3/4 ins / 60 x 75.5 cm) ITL 15,000,000. LONDON, 6 April 1989, *Venice* (1980, oil on canvas/synthetic resin, 57 x 45 ins / 145 x 114 cm) GBP 16,500. ROME, 8 June 1989, *Tension* (1973, oil and mixed media/canvas, 63 3/4 x 51 1/4 ins / 162 x 130 cm) ITL 38,000,000. LONDON, 26 Oct 1989, *Blue Memories* (1955, oil on paper/canvas, 39 1/4 x 26 1/2 ins / 100 x 67 cm) GBP 33,000; *The Office* (1953, oil on canvas, 45 1/4 x 35 1/4 ins / 115 x 89.5 cm) GBP 55,000. MILAN, 27 March 1990, *Untitled* (collage and oil on canvas, 12 1/4 x 19 ins / 31 x 48 cm) ITL 15,500,000. LONDON, 18 Oct 1990, *Untitled* (1961, oil on paper, 19 1/4 x 26 ins / 49 x 66 cm) GBP 19,800. MILAN, 24 Oct 1990, *Reaper* (1954, oil on canvas, 35 1/2 x 51 1/4 ins / 90 x 130 cm) ITL 125,000,000. NEW YORK, 6 Nov 1990, *Still-life* (1952, oil on canvas, 15 x 18 1/2 ins / 38.1 x 47.2 cm) USD 6, 820. ROME, 3 Dec 1990, *Red Sign on White Field* (1969, oil on canvas, 38 1/4 x 31 ins / 97 x 79 cm) ITL 46,000,000. AMSTERDAM, 12 Dec 1990, *View of the Doges' Palace in Venice* (oil on canvas, 25 1/2 x 31 1/2 ins / 65 x 80 cm) NLG 29,900. MILAN, 13 Dec 1990, *Narration No. 2* (1973, oil on canvas, 64 x 51 1/4 ins / 162.5 x 130 cm) ITL 66,000,000. ROME, 13 May 1991, *Untitled* (1983, mixed media and collage/paper, 21 1/4 x 22 3/4 ins / 54 x 58 cm) ITL 13,225,000. ZURICH, 16 Oct 1991, *Abstraction* (1986, mixed media and collage/paper, 24 x 18 ins / 61 x 45.5 cm) CHF 15,000. LONDON, 17 Oct 1991, *Open Space* (1961, oil on canvas, 29 x 22 ins / 73.5 x 55 cm) GBP 15,400. NEW YORK, 12 Nov 1991, *Untitled* (1983, chalks and coloured pencils, collage/paper, 18 x 14 ins / 45.7 x 35.6 cm) USD 3,080. ROME, 9 Dec 1991, *Nocturne* (1982, oil and collage/canvas, 39 1/4 x 32 ins / 100 x 81 cm) ITL 29,900,000. ZURICH, 29 April 1992, *Composition in Brown* (1977, mixed media/paper, 20 x 14 1/4 ins / 51 x 36 cm) CHF 13,000. ZURICH, 14-16 Oct 1992, *Archipelago* (1986, oil and collage/canvas, 24 x 19 3/4 ins / 61 x 50 cm) CHF 22,000. MILAN, 9 Nov 1992, *Untitled* (1946, gouache,

13 3/4 x 19 3/4 ins / 35 x 50 cm) ITL 1,700,000. MILAN, 9 Nov 1992, *Untitled* (1946, gouache, 13 3/4 x 19 3/4 ins / 35 x 50 cm) ITL 1,700,000. LONDON, 3 Dec 1992, *Aspect of the Sun* (1960, oil on canvas, 63 3/4 x 32 ins / 162 x 81 cm) GBP 30,800. ROME, 25 March 1993, *Untitled* (1948, oil on canvas, 23 1/2 x 29 1/2 ins / 60 x 75 cm) ITL 26,000,000. MILAN, 12 Oct 1993, *Lagoon* (1981, mixed media/canvas, 63 3/4 x 68 ins / 162 x 173 cm) ITL 41,400,000. AMSTERDAM, 31 May 1994, *Countryside* (1955, oil on canvas, 23 1/2 x 33 1/2 ins / 59.5 x 84.8 cm) NLG 42,550. ZURICH, 13 Oct 1994, *The Timbre of Colours* (mixed media/paper with collage/canvas, 27 3/4 x 20 1/2 ins / 70.5 x 52 cm) CHF 14,000. COPENHAGEN, 7 June 1995, *Composition* (1951, watercolour, 11 x 12 1/2 ins / 27 x 32 cm) DKK 10,000. ZURICH, 14 Nov 1995, *Composition No. 5* (1985, mixed media/lithograph, 21 1/4 x 23 ins / 54 x 57.5 cm) CHF 3,800. VENICE, 12 May 1996, *Tension* (1973, oil on canvas, 63 3/4 x 51 1/2 ins / 162 x 131 cm) ITL 52,000,000. MILAN, 25 Nov 1996, *Tension* (1976, oil on canvas, 51 1/4 x 63 3/4 ins / 130 x 162 cm) ITL 46,000,000. ROME, 8 April 1997, *Untitled* (1968, oil and sand/canvas, 20 x 15 1/4 ins / 51 x 38.5 cm) ITL 22,717,000. MILAN, 24 Nov 1997, *Card Game* (1984, oil and collage/canvas, 36 1/4 x 28 3/4 ins / 92 x 73 cm) ITL 36,800,000. COLOGNE, 28 May 1999, *Untitled* (1960, mixed media on canvas, 29 x 20 ins / 74 x 50 cm) DEM 28,000. MILAN, 17 Nov 1999, *Storm over the Farm* (1954, oil on canvas, 59 x 47 ins / 150 x 120 cm) ITL 105,000,000. MILAN, 30 May 2000, *Segui sul bianco* (1977, mixed media on canvas, 51 x 64 ins / 130 x 162 cm) ITL 48,000,000. LONDON, 6 Dec 2000, *Letter to Palladio no.2* (1977, oil on canvas, 64 x 51 ins / 162 x 130 cm) GBP 45,000. MILAN, 29 May 2001, *Nursery Garden* (1958, oil on canvas, 38 x 63 ins / 97 x 161 cm) ITL 88,000,000. MILAN, 30 May 2001, *Southern Ferments* (1960, oil on canvas, 46 x 35 ins / 116 x 89 cm) ITL 75,000,000. MILAN, 19 Nov 2002, *Red in Brown* (1969, mixed media on canvas, 36 x 29 ins / 92 x 73 cm) EUR 16,000. ROME, 18 Dec 2002, *Granary in Winter* (1952, oil on canvas, 47 x 31 ins / 120 x 80 cm) EUR 47,000. MILAN, 11 June 2003, *Sense of Time* (1961, oil on canvas, 31 x 31 ins / 80 x 80 cm) EUR 44,000. MILAN, 24 Nov 2003, *Night Song 2* (1960, oil on canvas, 64 x 51 ins / 162 x 130 cm) EUR 110,000. MILAN, 24 May 2004, *Tale* (1961, oil on canvas, 46 x 57 ins / 116 x 146 cm) EUR 175,000. MILAN, 25 May 2004, *Untitled* (1973, mixed media on canvas, 43 x 55 ins / 110 x 140 cm) EUR 25,000.

SANTONJA ROSALES, Eduardo

Spanish, 20th century.
Born 9 June 1899, in Madrid; died 4 January 1966, in Madrid.
Painter, illustrator, poster artist. Religious subjects, landscapes. Murals.

The grandson of Eduardo Rosales, Eduardo Santonja Rosales studied at the college of fine arts in Madrid. He ranks as an accomplished illustrator who also produced murals for a number of public buildings in Spain. His paintings include a notable *Virgin and Child*. He exhibited at the 1925 Exposition Internationale des Arts Décoratifs and, from 1931, at the national fine arts exhibitions in Madrid. He received various awards and distinctions, among them first prize in a cover illustration competition for *Blanco y Negro* (*White and Black*) in 1918 and 1935 and first prize in a 1926 poster competition under the auspices of the Madrid fine arts circle.

BIBLIOGRAPHY:

Arnáiz, José Manuel/López Jiménez, Javier/Merchán Díaz, Manuel (ed.), '*Cien años de pintura en Espana y Portugal (1830-1930)*' in vol. X, Antiqvaria, Madrid, 1993.

SANTORO, Francesco Raffaello

Italian, 19th - 20th century.
Born 1844, in Cosenza; died 1927, in Rome.
Painter. Genre scenes, landscapes.

The son of Giovanni Battista Santoro, he exhibited in Turin, Rome and Bologna.

AUCTION RECORDS:

LONDON, 7 March 1976, *Mountainous Landscape with Lake* (oil on canvas, 20 1/2 x 57 ins / 52 x 145 cm) GBP 800. MILAN, 23 March 1983, *Procession* (oil on canvas, 18 1/2 x 12 1/2 ins / 47 x 32 cm) ITL 4,000,000. ROME, 4 Dec 1990, *Roman Landscape* (attributed, oil on board, 12 1/4 x 9 ins / 31 x 22 cm) ITL 1,200,000. ROME, 11 Dec 1996, *Boy Playing a Pipe* (oil on panel, 14 1/4 x 9 1/4 ins / 36 x 23.5 cm) ITL 9,320; *Old Fountain in Viterbo* (oil on canvas, 14 1/4 x 9 1/4 ins / 36 x 23.5 cm) ITL 6,990. LONDON, 9 Oct 1997, *Fonti del Clitunno* (oil on canvas, 22 1/2 x 18 1/4 ins / 57.2 x 46.3 cm) GBP 1,610. AMSTERDAM, 7 July 1999, *Ponte Vecchio, Florence* (oil on canvas, 12 x 24 ins / 31 x 62 cm) NLG 8,000. LEYBURN, 25 Nov 1999, *Home from Play* (1875, oil on panel, 19 x 26 ins / 49 x 65 cm) GBP 2,700. CLEVELAND, 12 Oct 2000, *Capri, Italy* (oil on canvas, 10 x 16 ins / 25 x 41 cm) USD 4,000. PHILADELPHIA, 23 June 2002, *Courting Couple* (watercolour, 25 x 19 ins / 64 x 49 cm) USD 1,700. ROME, 11 June 2003, *Le fonti del Clitumno* (oil on canvas, 37 x 59 ins / 95 x 150 cm) EUR 4,200. TORONTO, 14 June 2004, *Tyrolean Street Scene* (1876, oil on panel, 8 x 17 ins / 20 x 44 cm) CAD 2,600.

SANTORO, Giovanni Antonio

Italian, 17th century.
Active in Naples at the beginning of the 17th century.
Painter.

In 1605, Giovanni Santoro painted a triptych depicting the *Visitation*, which can be found in the cathedral in Naples.

SANTORO, Giovanni Battista

Italian, 19th century.
Born 24 October 1809, in Fuscaldo; died c. 1895, in Naples.
Sculptor, lithographer.

The father of Francesco and Rubens Santoro, Giovanni Battista Santoro was a student at the Istituto di Belle Arti in Naples. He painted a *St Francis of Assisi* for the church at Petrarsa.

SANTORO, Rosalbino

Italian, 19th - 20th century.
Born 15 May 1857, in Fuscaldo.
Painter. History painting, portraits, genre scenes.

Rosalbino Santoro was a pupil of Filippo (?) Palizzi. He painted portraits of *King Umberto* and *Queen Margherita*.

SANTORO, Rubens

Italian, 19th - 20th century.
Born 25 October 1859, in Mongrassano; died 1942, in Naples.
Painter, watercolourist. Genre scenes, landscapes, waterscapes, urban landscapes, architectural views, seascapes.

The son of Giovanni Battista Santoro, Rubens Santoro was a pupil of Domenico Morelli at the academy of fine art in Naples. He exhibited in Naples, Turin, Venice, Rome and abroad including London and at the Salon des Artistes Français in Paris where he received an honourable mention in 1896.

He specialised almost exclusively in scenes of Venice with figures.

MUSEUMS AND GALLERIES:

CINCINNATI - REGGIO CALABRIA - TURIN.

AUCTION RECORDS:
PARIS, 16-17 May 1892, *Women at the Fountain*, FRF 500. NEW YORK, 7 May 1909, *Canal of SS Giovanni e Paolo in Venice*, USD 230. NEW YORK, 30 Jan 1930, *Venetian Canal*, USD 425. PARIS, 29 June 1951, *Canal in Venice*, FRF 16,000. LONDON, 22 Oct 1965, *The Traghetto, Venice*, Gns 420. LONDON, 7 Feb 1968, *View of Venice*, GBP 700. LONDON, 14 Nov 1973, *S Giorgio dei Greci*, GBP 4,200. NEW YORK, 17 April 1974, *View of Venice* (1902) USD 12,000. NEW YORK, 14 May 1976, *Canal in Venice* (oil on canvas, 19 x 14 1/4 ins / 48 x 36 cm) USD 6,250. PARIS, 5 Nov 1976, *Canal in Venice* (watercolour, 14 x 9 3/4 ins / 35.5 x 25 cm) FRF 2,900. MILAN, 15 March 1977, *Venice* (watercolour and tempera, 7 3/4 x 10 1/4 ins / 20 x 26 cm) ITL 1,100,000. NEW YORK, 7 Oct 1977, *People in a Gondola* (oil on canvas, 22 x 16 ins / 56 x 40.5 cm) USD 16,500. LONDON, 14 Feb 1979, *Gondolas in Venice* (oil on canvas, 19 1/4 x 14 ins / 49 x 35.5 cm) GBP 6,000. ROME, 18 Dec 1981, *Interior* (1889, oil on canvas, 29 1/2 x 39 3/4 ins / 75 x 101 cm) ITL 33,000,000. MILAN, 13 Dec 1984, *Figure in an Interior* (1889, oil on canvas, 33 3/4 x 39 3/4 ins / 86 x 101 cm) ITL 45,000,000. LONDON, 27 Nov 1985, *Canal Scene, Venice* (oil on canvas, 15 x 11 ins / 38 x 27 cm) GBP 8,500. ROME, 13 May 1986, *Ponte di Scafati at Torre Annunziata* (1918, oil on canvas, 50 1/2 x 37 3/4 ins / 128 x 96 cm) ITL 76,000,000. NEW YORK, 25 Feb 1987, *S Giorgio Maggiore* (oil on canvas, 15 1/4 x 20 ins / 39 x 51.1 cm) USD 27,000. MILAN, 23 March 1988, *View of a Canal in Venice* (oil on canvas, 15 1/4 x 16 1/4 ins / 38.5 x 41.5 cm) ITL 15,000,000. LONDON, 25 March 1988, *The Grand Canal in Venice* (oil on canvas, 19 1/2 x 14 ins / 49.5 x 35.5 cm) GBP 28,600. NEW YORK, 25 May 1988, *Canal in Venice* (oil on canvas, 15 x 7 3/4 ins / 37.2 x 19.7 cm) USD 14,300. MILAN, 1 June 1988, *Venice, Church of S Maria della Salute* (oil on canvas, 23 1/2 x 28 ins / 60 x 71 cm) ITL 55,000,000. LONDON, 24 June 1988, *Canal dei Greci in Venice* (oil on canvas, 20 x 14 3/4 ins / 50.7 x 37.5 cm) GBP 18,700. NEW YORK, 23 Feb 1989, *Grand Canal in Venice* (oil on panel, 12 3/4 x 16 1/4 ins / 32.4 x 41.3 cm) USD 35,200. MILAN, 14 March 1989, *Gondola on a Venetian Canal* (oil on canvas, 40 1/4 x 28 3/4 ins / 102 x 73 cm) ITL 80,000,000. LONDON, 5 May 1989, *Young Arabs* (oil on panel, 7 3/4 x 4 ins / 19.5 x 10 cm) GBP 2,420. LONDON, 24 Nov 1989, *Venetian Canal* (oil on canvas, 23 3/4 x 16 1/2 ins / 60.4 x 42 cm) GBP 19,800. MILAN, 8 March 1990, *Church of S Maria della Salute, Venice* (oil on canvas, 23 3/4 x 28 ins / 60.5 x 71 cm) ITL 65,000,000. MONACO, 21 April 1990, *Gondola on a Venetian Canal* (oil on canvas, 15 1/2 x 10 ins / 39.5 x 24.5 cm) FRF 155,400. NEW YORK, 22 May 1990, *Venetian Canal* (oil on canvas, 14 x 18 ins / 35.5 x 45.7 cm) USD 29,700. MILAN, 30 May 1990, *Boatmen on the Lagoon* (oil on panel, 9 x 6 ins / 22 x 15.5 cm) ITL 23,000,000. MILAN, 18 Oct 1990, *Courtyard with Figures Sitting under a Porch* (1880, oil on canvas, 20 3/4 x 12 ins / 53 x 30.5 cm) ITL 36,000,000. NEW YORK, 23 Oct 1990, *Canal Camello in Venice* (oil on canvas, 16 1/2 x 13 1/2 ins / 41.9 x 34.3 cm) USD 49,500. LONDON, 28 Nov 1990, *Venetian Canal in the Sun* (oil on canvas, 19 1/4 x 14 1/4 ins / 49 x 36 cm) GBP 39,600. LONDON, 15 Feb 1991, *Laundry Day in Venice* (oil on canvas, 16 1/2 x 11 1/2 ins / 42 x 29 cm) GBP 12,100. NEW YORK, 22 May 1991, *Minor Canal in Venice at Midday* (oil on canvas, 14 1/2 x 9 1/4 ins / 37.1 x 23.5 cm) USD 39,600. NEW YORK, 16 Oct 1991, *Grape Harvest* (1883, oil on panel, 20 x 15 1/2 ins / 50.8 x 39.4 cm) USD 66,000. LONDON, 18 March 1992, *Neapolitan Women in a Sunny Street* (1890, oil on canvas, 25 x 14 1/4 ins / 63.5 x 36.5 cm) GBP 27,500. MILAN, 16 June 1992, *Venetian Scene* (oil on panel, 13 x 9 1/4 ins / 33 x 23.5 cm) ITL 42,000,000. PARIS, 6 Nov 1992, *People in a Gondola in Venice* (oil on canvas, 18 x 12 1/4 ins / 46 x 31 cm) FRF 44,000. LUGANO, 8 May 1993, *Neapolitan Woman* (oil on canvas, 12 3/4 x 10 3/4 ins / 32.5 x 27.5 cm) CHF 6,000. LONDON, 19 Nov 1993, *S Geremia with Palazzo Labia, Venice* (oil on canvas, 19 3/4 x 14 1/2 ins / 50 x 37 cm) GBP 54,300. ROME, 29-30 Nov 1993, *Gondola on the Grand Canal* (oil on canvas, 23 1/4 x 14 3/4 ins / 59 x 37.5 cm) ITL 53,032,000. NEW YORK, 16 Feb 1994, *Gondoliers on a Canal* (oil on canvas, 14 1/4 x 19 1/4 ins / 36.2 x 48.9 cm) USD 85,000. LONDON, 17 March 1995, *Venetian Canal with the Campanile of the Church of the Frari in the Distance* (oil on canvas, 19 x 13 3/4 ins / 48.2 x 35 cm) GBP 49,900. LONDON, 15 March 1996, *Porch in the Sun* (oil on panel, 9 1/2 x 7 1/4 ins / 24 x 18.5 cm) GBP 80,700. MILAN, 26 March 1996, *Venetian Lagoon with a Fishing Boat in the Foreground and the Church of S Maria della Salute in the Background* (oil on canvas, 13 x 21 ins / 33 x 53.5 cm) ITL 41,400,000. ROME, 23 May 1996, *Gondolas in Venice* (oil on canvas, 18 x 12 1/4 ins / 46 x 31 cm) ITL 91,700,000. ROME, 28 Nov 1996, *Gondolas at S Barnaba* (oil on canvas, 13 x 9 3/4 ins / 33 x 25 cm) ITL 78,000,000. NEW YORK, 23 May 1997, *Venetian Canal* (oil on canvas, 13 x 9 1/2 ins / 33 x 24.1 cm) USD 37,950. LONDON, 19 Nov 1997, *Grand Canal, Venice* (oil on panel, 9 x 15 ins / 23 x 38 cm) GBP 38,900. LONDON, 21 Nov 1997, *The Traghetto, Venice* (oil on canvas, 15 3/4 x 11 3/4 ins / 40 x 29.8 cm) GBP 10,925. NEW ORLEANS, 5 June 1999, *Leaving Church in Venice* (oil on canvas, 19 x 14 ins / 48 x 36 cm) USD 57,500. NEW YORK, 1 Nov 1999, *Venetian Canal on a Sunny Afternoon* (1888, oil on canvas, 40 x 28 ins / 102 x 71 cm) USD 90,000. NEW YORK, 18 Oct 2000, *Venetian Canal with the Scuola Grande di S Marco and Campo S Giovanni, Venice* (oil on canvas, 19 x 15 ins / 48 x 37 cm) USD 72,000. NEW YORK, 31 Oct 2000, *Canals of Venice* (oil on canvas, 40 x 29 ins / 102 x 73 cm) USD 85,000. PADDINGTON, 27 Aug 2001, *Gondolas on the Grand Canal* (oil on canvas, 19 x 14 ins / 49 x 36 cm) AUD 175,000. NEW YORK, 1 Nov 2001, *Grand Canal, Looking towards S Maria della Salute, Venice* (oil on canvas, 20 x 15 ins / 50 x 37 cm) USD 110,000. LONDON, 19 Nov 2002, *S Maria della Salute, Venice* (oil on canvas, 19 x 14 ins / 49 x 36 cm) GBP 62,000. ROME, 26 Nov 2002, *Landscape in Sarno* (oil on canvas, 50 x 38 ins / 127 x 96 cm) EUR 54,000. LONDON, 18 March 2003, *Gondolas on a Venetian Backwater* (oil on canvas, 16 x 11 ins / 40 x 29 cm) GBP 48,000. NEW YORK, 29 Oct 2003, *Church of S Trovaso, a Venetian Backwater* (oil on panel, 16 x 13 ins / 41 x 32 cm) USD 80,000. NEW YORK, 23 April 2004, *Along the Canal* (oil on canvas, 19 x 15 ins / 49 x 37 cm) USD 52,500. NEW YORK, 23 April 2004, *On the Mediterranean Coast* (1887, oil on canvas, 15 x 25 ins / 38 x 64 cm) USD 80,000.

SANTOS, Ángeles
Spanish, 20th century.
Born 1912, in Gerona.
Painter. Portraits, genre scenes.
Symbolism.

Ángeles Santos showed examples of her work at the 1929 and 1930 Autumn Salon in Madrid.

BIBLIOGRAPHY:
Pagé, Suzanne/Winock, Michel/Michaud, Éric/Vidal, Aline, *Les Années trente en Europe. Le Temps menaçant*, exhibition catalogue, Musée d'Art moderne de la Ville de Paris, Paris musées, Flammarion, Paris, 1997.

MUSEUMS AND GALLERIES:
MADRID (Mus. Nacional Centro de Arte Reina Sofía): *World* (1929).

SANTOS, Antonio
French, 20th - 21st century.
Born 1955.
Sculptor.

AUCTION RECORDS:
PARIS, 5 Feb 1990, *Black Spanish Marble* (18 x 31 1/2 x 2 1/4 ins / 46 x 80 x 6 cm) FRF 20,000. PARIS, 3 June 1991, *Tribute to Everybody* (1989, Spanish marble, 25 1/2 x 18 1/2 x 6 ins / 65 x 47 x 15 cm) FRF 11,500. PARIS, 3 Feb 1992, *Circus Horsewoman* (1990, bronze, 9 3/4 x 7 3/4 ins / 25 x 20 cm) FRF 4,200.

SANTOS, Antonio Joaquim Dos
Portuguese, 18th century.

Died 1777, in Lisbon.
Painter.

SANTOS, Bartolomé
Spanish, 17th century.
Active in Valladolid in 1661.
Painter, sculptor (?).

SANTOS, Bartolomeu Cid dos
Portuguese, 20th century.
Born 1931, in Lisbon.
Engraver.

Bartolomeu Cid dos Santos studied between 1951 and 1955 at the college of fine arts in Lisbon before moving on to study under Anthony Gross at the Slade School of Art in London. He directed the Slade School's graphic arts department from 1960. Dos Santos initially engraved small-format items in dark tonalities. His body of work is a world of fantasy and dreams, full of labyrinthine cities and imaginary towns.

Dos Santos has featured at numerous collective exhibitions, including: *Young Contemporary Artists*, London (1957); *Contemporary Portuguese Engraving*, Madrid and Rome (1959); Colour Engraving Triennale in Grenchen (1961); Ljubliana Engraving Biennale (1865); International Engraving Biennale, Bradford (1968, 1970); International Engraving Biennale, Cracow (1972 and 1974); Florence Biennale (1974); *Contemporary Portuguese Engraving*, Gulbenkian Foundation, Paris (1975); Summer Exhibition, Royal Academy, London (1976); *Signatures of the Invisible*, Centre for Contemporary Art, Geneva (2002). He exhibited solo at the National Fine Arts Society, Lisbon (1959) and at various galleries in Oporto, Lisbon, London, Paris (Galerie Mazarine), Frankfurt and Tokyo. He was awarded the Gulbenkian Foundation Painting Prize in 1961.

BIBLIOGRAPHY:
Santos, Bartolomeu dos, *Bartolomeu Cid dos Santos. Exposição retrospectiva*, exhibition catalogue, Fundação Calouste Gulbenkian, Centro de Arte Moderna, Lisbon, 1989.

MUSEUMS AND GALLERIES:
BOSTON (MFA) - BRUSSELS (Bibliothèque royale Albert Ier) - CAMBRIDGE (Fitzwilliam Mus.) - COIMBRA (Mus. Nacional de Machado de Castro) - LISBON (Centro de Arte Moderna José de Azeredo Perdigão, Fundação Calouste Gulbenkian) - LISBON (Mus. do Chiado) - LIVERPOOL (Walker AG) - LONDON (British Mus.) - LONDON (Victoria and Albert Mus.).

SANTOS, Bernardo dos
Spanish, 18th century.
Active in 1730.
Engraver (burin).

SANTOS, Eder
Brazilian, 20th century.
Installation artist, video artist.

Work by Eder Santos has been included in collective exhibitions, for instance the 1996 Biennale in São Paulo.

BIBLIOGRAPHY:
Farias, Agnaldo, '*Brésil: petit manuel d'instructions*' in *Art Press* n° 221, periodical, Paris, February 1997.

SANTOS, followed by a second name. See second name

SANTOS, Francisco dos
Portuguese, 20th century.
Born 22 October 1878, in Rio de Mouro; died 27 April 1930.
Sculptor, painter. Figures.

Francisco dos Santos studied at Lisbon academy, then in Paris under Charles Verlet and later in Rome. He executed the *Ferryman at the Helm*, erected on the left bank of the Tagus River at Lisbon in 1915.

MUSEUMS AND GALLERIES:
LISBON (Mus. Mod.).

SANTOS, João José dos
Portuguese, 19th century.
Born 1806.
Active in Lisbon.
Engraver (etching).

João José dos Santos engraved illustrations for travel books. He was also an art writer.

SANTOS, Joao Maria dos
Brazilian, 20th century.
Born in Paris.
Painter. Genre scenes.

In 1946 Joao Maria dos Santos showed his canvas *Brazilian Dance* at the UNESCO exhibition in the Musée d'Art Moderne in Paris.

SANTOS, Juan
Spanish, 16th century.
Born c. 1516.
Active in Valladolid.
Sculptor (wood).

Juan Santos carved a processional throne for the church of St Julian in Valladolid in 1568.

SANTOS, Juan
Spanish, 17th century.
Active in Cádiz in 1662.
Fresco artist. Banners.

Juan Santos painted banners for the Spanish navy and small paintings for Andalusian ladies.

SANTOS, Juan
Spanish, 18th century.
Born c. 1770, in Lorca (Murcia).
Sculptor, engraver (burin).

Juan Santos carved a head of *St John the Baptist* for the church of S Mateo in Lorca.

SANTOS, Miguel dos
Brazilian, 20th century.
Born 1944, in Paraiba.
Painter.

The work of Miguel dos Santos is inspired by demonstrations of popular religious feeling.

SANTOS, Simão Francisco dos
Portuguese, 18th - 19th century.
Born 28 October 1758, in Lisbon; died 12 January 1830, in Lisbon.
Cameo engraver, medallist.

Simão Francisco dos Santos was a pupil of Jos Gaspar.

SANTOS CRUZ. See **SANTA CRUZ**

SANTOS DA CRUZ, Antonio dos
Portuguese, 18th century.
Born c. 1744, in Faro; died 1805.
Sculptor (wood).

Antonio dos Santos da Cruz was a pupil of M. Vieira.

SANTOS DE CARVALHO, Valentim dos
Portuguese, 18th century.
Born c. 1744; died 1806.
Active in Lisbon.
Sculptor.

Valentim Dos Santos de Carvalho carved a *St Sebastian* for the Pena church in Lisbon.

SANTOS DE TORRES, Juan
Spanish, 16th century.
Active at the end of the 16th century.
Sculptor.

Juan Santos de Torres worked at Orense in 1595.

SANTOS FERNANDEZ, Manuel. See **FERNÁNDEZ Manuel Santos**

SANTOS FREITAS, Manuel dos
Portuguese, 18th century.
Active in Lisbon during the second half of the 18th century.
Enameller.

SANTOS ROMO. See **ROMO Santos**

SANTOS TOROELLA, Ángeles
Spanish, 20th century.
Born 1912, in Portbou (Catalonia).
Painter. Genre scenes, figures, portraits.
Sister of the art historian and critic Rafael Santos Toroella, wife of the painter Emilio Grau Sala and mother of the painter Julian Grau Santos, Ángeles Santos Toroella studied under Cellino Perotti in Valladolid and settled in Paris in 1936. She was influenced by her husband's work but developed her own Impressionist technique, using small spots of colour to render her lyrical subject matter. Examples of her work include *World* and *Dead Child*.

Toroella has featured at various group and solo exhibitions, including the Athenaeum and Autumn Salon in Valladolid, where she showed around thirty items (an entire room having been given over to her work in 1930). She also exhibited in Paris (1931), at the Exhibition of Iberian Artists in Copenhagen (1932), in Barcelona (1935) and at the Venice Biennale (1936).

BIBLIOGRAPHY:
Arnáiz, José Manuel/López Jiménez, Javier/Merchán Díaz, Manuel (ed.), '*Cien años de pintura en Espana y Portugal (1830-1930)*' in vol. X, Antiqvaria, Madrid, 1993.

SANTRUCEK, Vaclav or Wenzel
Czech, 19th - 20th century.
Born 14 May 1866, in Elbeteinitz.
Sculptor, medallist.
Vaclav Santrucek trained under Josef Tautenhayn and Josef Vaclav Myslbek. He worked in Prague.

SANTUCCI, Santi, called Santino
Italian, 18th century.
Sculptor (wood), modeller (wax).
Santi Santucci worked in Pisa and Venice in the first half of the 18th century. He was also an engineer.

SANTURINI, Francesco
Italian, 17th century.
Born 1627, in Venice; died 1682, in Munich.
Painter, architect.
Francesco Santurini settled in Munich in 1654. He painted theatre sets and perspectives.

SANTVOERT, S. van. See **SANTVOORT Philipp or Jacob Philipp van**

SANTVOORT, Abraham Dircksz. van
Dutch, 17th century.
Born c. 1624; died 1669, in Chaam.
Engraver. History painting.
Abraham Dircksz. van Santvoort was doubtless the brother of the portrait-painter Dirck Dircksz. van Santvoort. He is recorded in Brussels in 1639, and in Amsterdam in 1644. He married Elizabeth de Kruyff in 1644, and was active in Breda from 1648 to 1653. He produced mostly prints of historical subjects, and was also a publisher.

SANTVOORT, Anthonie, or Santfoort, also known as Antonio de Santfort Mechinensis, called Groene Anthony, Antonio Verde, and Le Vert Antoine
Dutch, 16th century.
Died 1600, in Rome.
Active in Mechelen.
Painter, engraver.
Anthonie Santvoort lived in Italy with H. Speckaert and was a member of the Accademia di S Luca in Rome in 1577. In 1578 he was a beneficiary in the will of Cornelius Cort, and Hans van Achen and Joseph Heniz lived in his house. He engraved portraits and landscapes.

SANTVOORT, Dirck Dircksz. van, also known as Bontepaert
Dutch, 17th century.
Born 1610, in Amsterdam; buried in Amsterdam on 9 March 1680.
Painter. Religious subjects, portraits.
Son of the painter Dirck Pietersz. Bontepaert, Dirck Dircksz. van Santvoort was probably a pupil of Rembrandt. He was a master of the Amsterdam Guild of St Luke in 1636, and was active as its head in 1658. In 1641, he married the daughter of the painter Willem Jansz. Uyl. He remarried in 1657.

Santvoort painted religious scenes early in his career, but later became a celebrated society portrait painter. His subjects are depicted with great sobriety and restraint.

D.D. Santvoort. fe
1630
Santvoort fe 1644 1632·DVB.
D D Santvoort fe
1640
D.D. Santvoort fe
1630
Santvoort fe 1644

MUSEUMS AND GALLERIES:
AMSTERDAM (Rijksmus.): *Regentesses and Housemistresses of the Spinning House in Amsterdam* (1638); *Directors of the Serge Cloth Industry*; *The Burgomaster Dirck Bas Jacobsz. and his Family*; *Fredrick Dircksz. Alewyn*; *Clara Alewyn* - BASEL: *Fairground Singer, Accompanied by a Flute-player* - DARMSTADT: *Portrait of a Child* - EDINBURGH (Nat. Gal. of Scotland): *The Young Housekeeper* (oil/panel) - GLASGOW: *Portrait of a Young Girl* - HANOVER: *Portrait of a Young Woman* (uncertain attribution) - LONDON (NG): *Portrait of Geertruyt Spiegel with a Finch* (1639, oil/wood) - PARIS (Louvre): *Christ's Supper at Emmaüs* - ROTTERDAM: *Young Shepherd Playing the Flute* (1632); *Young Shepherdess* - THE HAGUE (Mauritshuis): *Portrait of a Man*; *Portrait of a Woman* (1640).

AUCTION RECORDS:
PARIS, 1898, *Portrait of a Woman*, FRF 420. PARIS, 9-11 April 1902, *Portrait of a Dutch Lady*, FRF 7,000. LONDON, 19 Nov 1926, *Young Girl in Yellow*, GBP 84. NEW YORK, 25-26 March 1931, *Portrait of a Woman*, USD 550. PARIS, 10 Feb 1943, *A Romelpot-player*, FRF 10,500. NEW YORK, 26 Oct 1946, *Two Little Dutch Boys*, USD 600. AMSTERDAM, 12 Dec 1950, *Family Portrait*, NLG 2,400. PARIS, 25 April 1951, *Portrait of a Young Woman*, FRF 100,000. LONDON, 23 June 1967, *Portrait of a Gentleman and his Wife*, Gns 1,600. PARIS, 12 June 1973, *Portrait of a Man*, FRF 20,000. PARIS, 10 June 1976, *Portrait of a Lady of Quality* (1636, oil on panel, 25 1/2 x 19 3/4 ins / 65 x 50 cm) FRF 20,500. LONDON, 14 April 1978, *Landscape with a Family Group* (oil on panel, 34 1/2 x 47 ins / 87.6 x 119.3 cm) GBP 4,000. PARIS, 22 March 1983, *Portrait of a Young Noblewoman* (1644, oil on panel, 24 1/2 x 16 3/4 ins / 62 x 42.5 cm) FRF 38,000. NEW YORK, 15 Jan 1985, *Two Young Boys, aged*

10 and 8 (1633, oil on canvas, 45½ x 35 ins / 115.5 x 88.9 cm) USD 18,000. London, 11 Dec 1987, *Portrait of Three Generations of a Family* (oil on canvas, 50¾ x 72¾ ins / 129 x 185 cm) GBP 28,000. New York, 12 Jan 1989, *Portrait of a Young Girl* (oil on panel, 27¾ x 22¾ ins / 70.5 x 58 cm) USD 19,000. New York, 10 Oct 1991, *Portrait of a Young Couple, Standing in an Interior* (oil on panel, 25¼ x 22 ins / 64.1 x 55.9 cm) USD 41,250. Stockholm, 19 May 1992, *Portrait of a Man* (oil on panel, 32¾ x 26½ ins / 83 x 67 cm) SEK 14,700. New York, 11 Jan 1995, *Portrait of a Young man Turning to the Right, Wearing a White Lace Collar* (oil on panel, 20¾ x 17½ ins / 52.7 x 44.2 cm) USD 10,925. London, 3 July 1996, *Portrait of a Couple and Their Daughter, in a Landscape* (oil on panel, 24 x 27½ ins / 61 x 70 cm) GBP 18,400.

SANTVOORT, Jan van
Dutch, 17th century.
Active during the second half of the 17th century.
Sculptor.

Jan van Santvoort established himself as a decorative sculptor in Edinburgh, in 1685.

SANTVOORT, Josse van
Flemish School, 16th century.
Active in Mechelen.
Sculptor.

Between 1536 and 1547 Josse van Santvoort worked principally for the abbey of Tongerloo.

SANTVOORT, Philipp or Jacob Philipp van
Flemish School, 18th century.
Painter. Genre scenes.

Philipp van Santvoort was a pupil of Gaspar van Opstal in Antwerp, where he was active from 1711 to 1722. He is probably identifiable as the artist S. van Santvoert, mentioned in Füssli.

Auction records:
Monaco, 2 Dec 1989, *Concert* (oil on canvas, 18¾ x 22 ins / 47.5 x 55 cm) FRF 72,150.

SANTVOORT, Pieter Dircksz. van, also known as Bontepaert
Dutch, 17th century.
Born 1603 or 1604, in Amsterdam; buried on 19 November 1653.
Painter. Winter landscapes, landscapes.

Pieter Dircksz. van Santvoort was the son of Dirksz. Pieter Bontepaert (the name refers to a sign hanging outside the family house, depicting a piebald horse). Bontepaert's sons all took the name Santvoort. In 1638, he married Marretje Coerten. A second, younger painter known as Pieter van Stanvoort of Haarlem, is recorded by some authors as having died on 10 October 1681; the latter is not, however, positively identifiable as a painter. Pieter Dircksz. van Santvoort was exclusively a landscape painter.

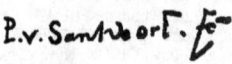

Museums and Galleries:
Berlin (Staatliche Mus.): *Landscape With a Farm* (1625) - Haarlem (Frans Halsmus.): *Winter Landscape.*

Auction records:
London, 10 April 1970, *Winter Landscape,* Gns 2,600. Amsterdam, 30 Nov 1976, *Village in Winter* (oil on panel, 12¼ x 20 ins / 31 x 50.5 cm) NLG 18,000. London, 12 July 1978, *Winter Landscape* (oil on panel, 15¾ x 20¾ ins / 40 x 53 cm) GBP 13,500. Amsterdam, 29 Oct 1979, *Wooded Landscape with a Bridge* (pen and wash, 8 x 6¼ ins / 20.2 x 15.7 cm) NLG 5,400. London, 8 July 1983, *Scene on the Seashore* (oil on panel, 13½ x 20½ ins / 34.6 x 51.8 cm) GBP 5,500. Amsterdam, 25 Nov 1991, *Wooded, Mountainous Landscape With a Bridge Over a River* (1623, black chalk and ink, 7 x 11 ins / 17.6 x 27.7 cm) NLG 12,650.

SANTWYCK, Françoys van
Dutch, 17th century.
Born c. 1637, in The Hague; died before 19 January 1685, in Amsterdam.
Painter.

Françoys van Santwyck joined the painters' guild in The Hague, in 1663.

Museums and Galleries:
The Hague (Bredius Mus.): *Musical gathering.*

SANTZ. See also **SANZ**

SÄNTZ, Gordian or Johann Gordian, or Sänz
German, 18th century.
Painter. Religious subjects.

Säntz executed altarpieces in churches in Passau and its surrounding areas about 1700.

SÄNTZ, Johann Georg and Johann Karl.
See **SANZ**

SANUTO, Giulio, or Sannutus
Italian, 16th century.
Active in Venice from 1540 to 1580.
Engraver (burin).

According to *Bryan's Dictionary* Giulio Sanuto was born about 1530 but it seems more likely he was born at least 10 years earlier, as one of his works, *Monstrous Child,* relates to an event that occurred in 1540 and the production of the print must have been that year or shortly afterwards. He engraved religious subjects, allegories and genre scenes after Titian, Raphael and his own drawings.

SANVITALE, Fortuniano
Italian, 16th - 17th century.
Born c. 1566, in Parma; died 29 December 1626, in Parma.
Painter, poet, writer.

Fortuniano Sanvitale painted scenes from the Passion and other religious subjects for churches in Parma and Vicenza.

SANVITALE, Giuseppina (Contessa)
Maiden name: Folcheri
Italian, 19th century.
Born April 1800, in Cuneo; died 1848, in Marseilles, France.
Painter.

Museums and Galleries:
Parma (Accademia Nazionale di Belle Arti): *Young Harpist* (pastel).

SANVITI, Stefano
Italian, 16th - 17th century.
Active in Mantua from 1587 to 1610.
Painter.

In the service of the Gonzaga family, Stefano Sanviti painted mythological and religious subjects.

SANWLAH
Hindu School, 16th - 17th century.
Active between 1556 and 1605.
Painter, illuminator.

Sanwlah collaborated on all the great works produced during the reign of Akbar the Great (1556-1605).

Museums and Galleries:
London (British Mus.): miniatures - London (Victoria and Albert Mus.): miniatures.

SANYAL, B. C.
Indian, 20th century.
Born 22 April 1902, in Dibrugarh; died 9 January 2003.
Sculptor, painter. Oils, watercolours, lithographs.
Sanyal was a student at the Government College of Arts and Crafts in Calcutta. He was subsequently professor at the Mayo School of Arts then set up the Lahore School of Fine Art in 1936. He settled in New Delhi where he co-founded the Delhi Shilpi Chakra in his studio and was head of the art department at the local Polytechnic. An associate member of the Lalit Kala Academy, he was secretary from 1960 to 1969. He has travelled to Europe and the USA.
Although personally never a follower of the new trends in contemporary art, Sanyal played a considerable role in the training of young Indian artists through his teaching activity.
MUSEUMS AND GALLERIES:
NEW DELHI (Lalit Kala Acad.) - NEW DELHI (NGMA).

SANYU, Yu. See **ZHANG YU**

SANZ, Alexander, or Sanzi
Italian, 18th century.
Active during the second half of the 18th century.
Sculptor.
Alexander Sanz sculpted statues of *St Andrew* and *St Matthew* for the cathedral in Bergamo.

SANZ, Antonio
Spanish, 18th century.
Born in Saragossa.
Active from 1791 to 1794.
Sculptor.
Antonio Sanz was a monk. He worked on the façade, portal and stalls of Huesca Cathedral.

SANZ, Bernhard Lukas
Italian, 17th - 18th century.
Born c. 1650; died after 1710.
Painter. Religious subjects.
The brother of Johann Georg and Johann Karl, Bernhard Lukas Sanz produced religious paintings for churches in Bergamo and Gandino.
AUCTION RECORDS:
NEW YORK, 22 May 1992, *Vast River Landscape with Travellers on a Mountain Path* (oil on canvas, 26½ x 36in/67.3 x 91.4cm) USD 6,600.

SANZ, Eduardo
Spanish, 20th century.
Born 1928, in Santander.
Painter (mixed media).
Eduardo Sanz studied at the college of fine arts in Madrid and travelled extensively in France, Switzerland and Italy. Around 1960, Eduardo Sanz developed a personal style that involved a mixture of techniques featuring strong rhythms and spatial volumes in black and white punctuated by radiating coloured spokes. He exhibited for the first time in 1954.

SANZ, Francisco
Spanish, 15th century.
Active in the first half of the 15th century.
Sculptor.
Francisco Sanz was commissioned with Pedro Balaguer to make a throne for the church of S Catalina in Valencia.

SANZ, Gordian, or Sanzi
Italian, 19th - 20th century.
Born 8 September 1856, in Bergamo.
Sculptor. Religious subjects. Statues.
The son and pupil of Alexander Sanz, he carved statues of saints.

SÄNZ, Gordian or Johann Gordian.
See **SÄNTZ**

SANZ, Inés Mercedes
Spanish, 19th - 20th century.
Born in Leina.
Painter.
Inés Mercedes Sanz showed examples of her work at the Salon des Artistes Français in Paris and received an honourable mention at the 1900 Exposition Universelle.

SANZ, Johann Anton, or Sanzi
Italian, 18th century.
Born 13 June 1702, in Bergamo; died 1787.
Sculptor (wood/marble).
Johann Anton Sanz, the son of Bernhard Lukas Sanz, was the pupil of Bartolomeo Guarina and subsequently of Giacomo Manni. He produced statues, stalls and confessionals for the cathedral and churches of Bergamo.

SANZ, Johann Georg, or Sanzi or Säntz
Italian, 18th century.
Born to a family originally from Passau, Germany.
Painter.
Johann Georg Sanz was the brother of Johann Karl and Bernhard Lukas Sanz. An imitator of J. Courtois, he worked in Bergamo around 1730.

SANZ, Johann Karl, or Sanzi or Säntz
Italian, 17th - 18th century.
Sculptor (wood).
Johann Karl Sanz was the brother of Johann Goerg and Bernhard Lukas Sanz. In 1696, he sculpted confessionals for the church of S Alessandro in Bergamo.

SANZ, José
Spanish, 18th century.
Active in Huesca from 1795 to 1797.
Sculptor.
José Sanz was the brother and assistant of Antonio Sanz and worked at Huesca Cathedral.

SANZ, Juan
Spanish, 17th century.
Active in Valladolid at the beginning of the 17th century.
Sculptor.
Juan Sanz executed part of the decorative sculpture at the church of S Pablo, the design of which was drawn up by Mora and the direction entrusted to Andrés de Nagera.

SANZ, Pedro
Spanish, 15th - 16th century.
Active from 1477 to 1519.
Painter.
Pedro Sanz painted some altarpieces for Valencia Cathedral.

SANZ, Ramón
Spanish, 17th century.
Sculptor.
Ramón Sanz executed sculptures for the abbey church of La Oliva in 1616.

SANZ, Roman
Spanish, 19th century.
Born 28 February 1829, in Sacedon, near Guadalajara (Castile-La Mancha).
Painter, watercolourist, sculptor, engraver, draughtsman, illustrator. Religious subjects, portraits, genre scenes, still-lifes, flowers.
Roman Sanz was a pupil of Juan Galvez, Antonio Brabo and F. Elias at the Academia de Bellas Artes in Madrid. He exhibited at various joint exhibitions, including the exhibitions of the national fine arts society of Madrid from 1860 to 1890, and at Guadalajara in 1876, where he was awarded a bronze medal. He also collaborated on various magazines, including *La Ilustración*.

Bibliography:
Arnáiz, José Manuel/López Jiménez, Javier/Merchán Díaz, Manuel (ed.), '*Cien años de pintura en Espana y Portugal (1830-1930)*' in vol. X, Antiqvaria, Madrid, 1993.
Museums and Galleries:
Madrid (Church of S Sebastian): paintings for the chapel of the Misericordia.

SANZ, Toribo
Portuguese, 19th - 20th century.
Born in Lenia.
Sculptor.
Toribo Sanz featured at the Salon des Artistes Français in Paris, where he was awarded a gold medal; he went on to be declared hors concours and serve on the jury at the 1900 Exposition Universelle.

SANZ ARIZMENDI, José
Spanish, 20th century.
Born 6 February 1885, in Seville; died 1929, in Bern or Zurich.
Painter, poster artist. Figures, portraits, genre scenes, landscapes.
A pupil of Gonzalo Bilbao and José Aranda, José Sanz Arizmendi moved to Zurich and studied architecture at the federal high school of technology (ETH), while working in the workshop run by Gustavo Gull.

In 1905, Sanz produced the official poster for the Semana Santa (Holy Week) and Feria (Festival) in Seville. He also collaborated in 1915 with the architect Gurruchaga on an urban development project in the Basque capital San Sebastián. Examples of his work include *Gypsy, Fortune-Teller, Coffee House Waiter, In the Wings* and *Granada*. José Sanz took part in various collective exhibitions including: International Exhibition, Düsseldorf (1903), shows in Granada, Málaga, Bern (1918) and Zurich. He was awarded a gold medal in 1903.
Bibliography:
Arnáiz, José Manuel/López Jiménez, Javier/Merchán Díaz, Manuel (ed.), '*Cien años de pintura en Espana y Portugal (1830-1930)*' in vol. X, Antiqvaria, Madrid, 1993.

SANZ CARTA, Valentin
Spanish, 19th century.
Born 1850; died 1898.
Active in Cuba from 1884.
Painter. Landscapes.
Valentin Sanz Carta was a Cuban of Spanish origin and was born in the Canary Islands. He left for Cuba in 1884 and was appointed to teach landscape art at the S Alejandro school in Havana on the recommendation of Miguel Melero. Under the influence of his Cuban wife, he espoused the separatist ideas of the period but had to emigrate to the USA and settled in New York. He died young due to illness.
Auction records:
New York, 16 Nov 1994, *Cuban Landscape* (oil on canvas, 30 x 20 ins / 76.2 x 50.8 cm) USD 5,462.

SANZ DE JÉRICA, Vicente
Spanish.
Sculptor.
Vicente Sanz de Jérica carved the altar of the Virgin in the former Charterhouse of Valldecristo.

SANZ DE LA LLOSA, Diego
Spanish, 17th century.
Born 17th century, in Valencia.
Painter.
Diego Sanz de la Llosa worked at the court of Parma in 1670.

SANZ DEL VALLE, Julián
Spanish, 19th century.
Born c. 1830, in Santa Fe.
Active in Granada.
Painter. Genre scenes.
Museums and Galleries:
Madrid (Prado): *Tavern* (two paintings); *Fruit Seller* (painting).

SANZ JIMENEZ, Luis
Spanish, 19th century.
Died at the beginning of the 19th century, in Granada.
Active in Granada.
Painter.
There are paintings by Luis Sanz Jimenez in Granada Cathedral and the Granada museum.

SANZEDO, Juan de, or Salzedo
Spanish, 16th - 17th century.
Painter.
Juan de Sanzedo worked on the decoration of the Alcazar for a number of years. He was still alive in 1600, when he appeared as a witness in an court case. He may be the same person as Juan de Salcedo.

SANZEL, Félix
French, 19th century.
Born 25 January 1829, in Paris; died December 1883, in Paris.
Sculptor.
He was a pupil of Fromange and Dumont. He debuted at the Paris Salon of 1849, and won a medal in 1868. His *Bust of Fénelon* can be seen at the École Normale Supérieure in Paris.
Museums and Galleries:
Orléans: *The Rogue*.

SANZI. See **SANZ Gordian**

SANZIANU, Michel
Romanian, 20th century.
Born 8 January 1944, in Bucharest.
Active in Switzerland from 1973.
Painter, draughtsman, illustrator.
Michel Sanzianu studied at the academy of fine art in Bucharest until 1965. In 1966, he began working as an illustrator for the Romanian press and for Romanian publishing houses. In 1969, he joined the union of Romanian artists. Between 1971 and 1973, he illustrated all four issues of the *Quadernos Hispanoamericanos* review. His most important drawings, which have the technical qualities of the best architectural drawings, develop from inextricable imbrications of constructed spaces, but according to the sort of surveyed perspectives pursued, in particular, by Albert Flocon. His paintings, with their fresh style and lively colours, are also generated from curved shapes and volumes, although they more often make reference to an abstraction inspired by Cubism. From 1969 to 1973, he took part in collective exhibitions in Bucharest. In 1974, he exhibited in Rome at the fourth annual *Incontri Europa* exhibition; in 1978 in Lausanne in *Rencontre avec* (*Meeting With*), held in the regional museum, and in Paris at the Salon de Mai and Salon des Grands et Jeunes d'Aujourd'hui; in 1979 in Paris in *Colle aux archéologues* (*Stick with Archaeologist*); in 1981 at the Salon de Québec, Bilan International de l'Art Contemporain, where he won a bronze medal. In 1971 in Belgrade, he had a solo exhibition of his drawings at the Yugoslav writers' cultural centre. In 1974 in Rome, he had a solo exhibition of his paintings and drawings at the Nuova Figurazione Gallery. Other solo exhibitions followed, in 1977 in Bern, in 1978 in Brussels, in 1980 in Lausanne at the Galerie Vallotton and in 1983-1984 in Lausanne at the Galerie Reymondin & Cie.
Bibliography:
Stern, Radu, *Sanzianu*, exhibition catalogue, Gal. Reymondin et Cie, Lausanne, 1983-1984.

SANZIO, Luca
Italian.

Painter. Seascapes.
MUSEUMS AND GALLERIES:
BERGAMO (Accademia Carrara): a work.

SANZIO, Raphael. See **RAPHAEL**

SÃO JOSÉ, Luiz de
Portuguese, 18th century.
Active in Lisbon c. 1700.
Draughtsman.
Luiz de São José was a member of the Cistercian Order. He drew views and illustrations for books.

SÃO JOSÉ, Simzo de
Portuguese, 16th century.
Active in Lisbon.
Illuminator.
Simzo de São José was a monk.

SAOZI
French, 20th century.
Born c. 1940, in Toulouse.
Painter, draughtsman. Scenes with figures. Designs for tapestries.
Saozi was a pupil at the École des Arts Décoratifs, Nice, and she continued her training in Paris, where she went to live.

Initially she painted still-lifes of fruit and flowers that were almost trompe-l'oeils. Later, she painted more complex pictures suggesting fights between indistinct horsemen, often barely sketched, almost abstract, consisting of an inextricable mingling of ovoid shapes that are themselves loaded with closely juxtaposed graphic signs.

She took part in a number of group exhibitions, including in Paris the Salon Comparaisons and the Salon de la Société nationale des Beaux-Arts, and in 1986 the exhibition of the group Réalité Seconde (Second Reality), held at the Galerie d'Art Contemporain, Chamalières. Her solo exhibitions include: 1964, Galerie Gérard Mourge; 1964, Galerie Paul Gilson; 1971, Galerie Bongers; 1974, Galerie Lambert; 1985, Galerie Ror Volmar; and 1975, the Alliance Française, Montevideo.
BIBLIOGRAPHY:
Réalité seconde, exhibition catalogue, Gal. d'Art contemporain, Chamalières, 1986.
MUSEUMS AND GALLERIES:
PARIS (MAMVP).

SAPALSKI, Feliks
Polish, 19th century.
Born in Warsaw; died 1844, near Piotrków.
Painter, miniaturist. Landscapes.
Feliks Sapalski studied with Kaiser, and later with the miniaturist Bechon. He painted landscapes, views of Lazienxi, Wilanóv and Gerniakov, and miniature portraits.

SAPATOV, Viktor
Ukrainian, 20th - 21st century.
Born 1952.
Painter.
Viktor Sapatov studied at the national institute of fine arts in Odessa. He became a member of the union of Soviet artists then of the artists' union of Ukraine. He says that in his pictures he is seeking for peace in his own soul. His brushstroke is rich and sophisticated. Pictures of Sapatov's are held in the Odessa Art Museum and in private collections in Ukraine and abroad. His work has been exhibited in Germany, Italy, Israel and the USA.
MUSEUMS AND GALLERIES:
KIEV (National Gallery of Art) - TOKYO (MMA).
AUCTION RECORDS:
PARIS, 4 Oct 1993, *King of the Waters* (oil on card, 40 x 41 ins / 101.5 x 104 cm) FRF 5,000.

SAPELLI, Carlo
Italian, 19th century.
Born in Cereseto.
Active during the first half of the 19th century.
Painter.
A student at the Accademia in Turin, he painted a *Prodigal Son* for the court in Turin.

SAPERE, Horacio
Argentinian, 20th - 21st century.
Born 1951, in Buenos Aires.
Active in Majorca (Balearic Islands).
Painter (mixed media), sculptor.
Sapere's work is either completely abstract or borrows elements from reality; it is reminiscent of Klee or Dubuffet. Since 1975, he has exhibited in galleries in Palma in Majorca, Madrid (at the Galeria Diart, 1986) and Vienna (at the Ariadne gallery, 1985-1991).
AUCTION RECORDS:
AMSTERDAM, 10 Dec 1992, *Ojo Comespacios* (*Space-consuming Eye*) (1988, mixed media/canvas, 36 1/2 x 32 ins / 93 x 81 cm) NLG 2,070.

SAPHARE, Jean
French, 17th century.
Died 10 October 1680.
Active in Orbec.
Sculptor (wood).
Jean Saphare sculpted and gilded the statue of *St James*, in Ste-Croix church in Bernay.

SAPHARE, Simon
French, 17th - 18th century.
Active in Orbec from 1654 to 1705.
Sculptor (wood).
Simon Saphare was the brother of Jean Saphare. He produced altarpieces for churches in Orbec.

SAPIA, Mariano
Argentinian, 20th - 21st century.
Born 1964, in Buenos Aires.
Painter.
Mariano Sapia studied painting and engraving with Ernesto Pesce and Carlos Gorriarena. He has exhibited regularly since 1982. The national arts fund awarded him a bursary in 1988 and the Antorchas foundation in 1990.
AUCTION RECORDS:
NEW YORK, 18 May 1994, *Saint* (1989, oil on canvas, 39 1/4 x 55 1/4 ins / 99.7 x 140.3 cm) USD 2,875. NEW YORK, 16 Nov 1994, *On No-Man's Land* (1990, oil on canvas, 61 1/2 x 74 3/4 ins / 155.9 x 189.9 cm) USD 4,485.

SAPIEHA, Anna de (Princesse Czartoryska)
French, 19th century.
Born 1798, in St-Germain-en-Laye (Yvelines); died 24 December 1864, in Montpellier.
Painter.
This artist was the daughter of Anna de Sapieha, née Zamoyska.

SAPIEHA, Anna von (Princess)
Maiden name: Zamoyska
Lithuanian, 18th - 19th century.
Born 1774; died 26 November 1859, in Paris.
Painter.
Anna Sapieha worked in Paris and Vilnius and painted flowers and miniatures.

SAPIENTIS. See **WITZ Konrad**

SAPIK, Vojteck or Adalbert
Polish, 20th century.
Born 8 April 1888, in Polska Ostrava; died 4 July 1916, on the front.
Sculptor, medallist.

Vojteck Sapik trained under Stanislav Sucharda at the school of fine art in Prague. The Národní Galerie in Prague houses a work by him for which he received the Narodni Listy Newspaper Prize.

MUSEUMS AND GALLERIES:
PRAGUE (Národní Gal.).

SAPOKHNIKOV, Andrei Petrovich, or Sapojnikov
Russian, 19th century.
Born 1795; died 29 March 1855, in St Petersburg.
Painter. Allegorical subjects, portraits.

Andrei Petrovich Sapokhnikov was a military officer. He painted portraits and allegories, members of the popular classes and Slav costumes.

MUSEUMS AND GALLERIES:
MOSCOW (State Tretyakov Gal.): *Love and Time*; *Bacchanalia*.

SAPOKHNIKOVA, Nadeshda
Russian, 19th century.
Lithographer.

Nadeshda Sapohnnikova was the daughter of Andrei Petrovitch Sapokhnikov.

SAPOKHNIKOVA, Vera
Russian, 19th century.
Lithographer.

Vera Sapokhnikova was the daughter of Andrei Petrovich Sapokhnikov.

SAPONARO, Salvatore
Italian, 20th century.
Born 30 March 1888, in San Cesario di Lecce (Puglia).
Sculptor. Monuments, low reliefs.

After training in Lecce Saponaro moved to Milan in 1921. He sculpted war memorials and low reliefs, examples of which can be found in Milan and Padua.

SAPORETTI, Edgardo
Italian, 19th - 20th century.
Born 13 February 1865, in Bagnacavallo; died 4 October 1909, in Bellaria.
Painter, sculptor. Portraits, genre scenes, landscapes.

The son and pupil of Pietro Saporetti, he exhibited in Rome, Bologna and Florence.

SAPORETTI, Pietro
Italian, 19th century.
Born 10 April 1832, in Bagnacavallo; died 17 September 1893, in Bassano.
Painter. History painting, genre scenes.

Pietro Saporetti was a pupil of Antonio Moni and then, in Venice, of Luigi Ferrari. He exhibited work at a number of different salons in Italy and abroad, including Vienna and Paris.

SAPORITI, Rinaldo
Italian, 19th - 20th century.
Born 27 April 1840, in Milan; died 29 March 1913, in Milan.
Painter. Genre scenes, landscapes, seascapes.

A pupil of Giuseppe Mazzola at the Accademia di Belle Arti di Brera in Milan, Rinaldo Saporiti exhibited in Parma, Turin and Milan.

SAPOVIUS, David or Johann or Christoph
German, 18th century.
Born to a family originally from Palatinat; died 1710, in Berlin.
Sculptor, goldsmith (?).

Sapovius was Schlüter's first teacher. He lived a long time in Danzig (now Gdansk, Poland) and settled in Berlin in 1702, where he worked at the royal palace.

SAPP, Allen
Canadian, 20th century.
Born 1929.
Painter. Genre scenes, local scenes.

Allen Sapp was born into a traditional Northern plains Cree family on the Red Pheasant reserve, in Saskatchewan. His interest in drawing was partly a result of childhood illness, but recognised by his great aunt, who named him Kiskayetum, meaning 'he perceives it' or 'he knows it'. His painting has a visionary quality although the subject-matter is taken from everyday life on the reservation. Sapp's talent was spotted in 1966 by Dr Allan Gonor, who subsequently became his patron and manager.

AUCTION RECORDS:
TORONTO, 15 May 1978, *Sam Thunderchild's Home* (1972, oil on canvas, 24 x 36 ins / 61 x 91.2 cm) CAD 1,800. TORONTO, 14 May 1979, *On Water Duty* (1972, acrylic/canvas, 23 1/2 x 29 1/2 ins / 60 x 75 cm) CAD 1,300. TORONTO, 2 March 1982, *Will Play Hockey Soon* (acrylic/canvas, 15 3/4 x 19 3/4 ins / 40 x 50 cm) CAD 2,200. TORONTO, 4 May 1983, *Coming Closer to my Home* (acrylic/canvas, 15 3/4 x 19 3/4 ins / 40 x 50 cm) CAD 2,600. MONTREAL, 25 April 1988, *Salaison de la viande de daim à Stoney Reserve* (oil on canvas, 30 x 48 ins / 76 x 122 cm) CAD 2,800. MONTREAL, 17 Oct 1988, *Baby Pointing at a Man* (1969, acrylic/canvas, 16 1/4 x 20 ins / 41 x 51 cm) CAD 1,200. CALGARY, 31 May 1999, *Untitled, Horses Feeding* (acrylic on canvas, 24 x 36 ins / 61 x 91 cm) CAD 5,000. TORONTO, 7 Dec 1999, *Dancing at Pow Wow* (oil on canvas, 24 x 35 ins / 60 x 90 cm) CAD 4,200. TORONTO, 15 Nov 2000, *It is a Cold Day. Building a House* (1971-1972, acrylic on canvas, two, 18 x 24 ins / 46 x 61 cm) CAD 3,000. TORONTO, 21 Nov 2000, *Almost Home* (oil on canvas, 24 x 35 ins / 60 x 90 cm) CAD 3,600. CALGARY, 17 Jan 2001, *House Needs Fixing* (acrylic on canvas, 18 x 24 ins / 46 x 60 cm) CAD 5,750. CALGARY, 19 Nov 2001, *Working Hard* (1978, acrylic on canvas, 16 x 20 ins / 41 x 51 cm) CAD 4,400. CALGARY, 25 Nov 2002, *Not So Cold Today for Working* (acrylic on canvas, 18 x 24 ins / 45 x 60 cm) CAD 3,500. CALGARY, 25 Nov 2002, *Log Hauling on a Crisp Winter Day* (acrylic on canvas, 30 x 47 ins / 75 x 120 cm) CAD 4,100. VANCOUVER, 15 May 2003, *Two Teams Went Together* (oil on canvas, 24 x 36 ins / 61 x 91 cm) CAD 5,000. VANCOUVER, 27 Nov 2003, *Some Kids Didn't Have Skates* (1976, acrylic on canvas, 30 x 48 ins / 76 x 121 cm) CAD 6,000. CALGARY, 18 April 2004, *Busy Cutting Wood* (acrylic on canvas, 24 x 36 ins / 61 x 91 cm) CAD 3,000. TORONTO, 1 June 2004, *Two Men Stooking* (acrylic on canvas, 18 x 24 ins / 45 x 60 cm) CAD 4,400.

SAPPA. See **MATTEO D'AMBROGIO**

SAPPER, Richard
German, 20th century.
Born 30 September 1891, in Coan, Guatemala, to German parents.
Active in Stuttgart.
Painter, illustrator. Landscapes.

Richard Sapper studied painting in Munich and Stuttgart.

SAPPEY, Pierre Victor
French, 19th century.
Born 11 February 1801, in Grenoble; died 1856, in Grenoble.
Sculptor, architect.

A pupil of Raggi and Ramey *fils*, Pierre Sappey entered the École des Beaux-Arts in Paris on 4 May 1825. His work was shown at the Salon of 1831. He won a competition to erect a monument at Chambéry in memory of General de Boigne.

Museums and Galleries:
Avignon: *Statue of Antoine Chantrou* - Grenoble (Mus. de Grenoble): *Death of Lucretia; The Isère* (allegorical figure); *The Drac* (allegorical figure).

SAPSER, Gregor
Austrian, 17th - 18th century.
Active in Tamsweg.
Sculptor (wood).
Sapser sculpted altarpieces and pulpits in churches in Tamsweg and the surrounding areas.

SAPUNOV, Nicolai Nicolaevich, or Sapunoff
Russian, 20th century.
Born 1880, in Moscow; died 15 June 1912, at Terioki in the Gulf of Finland, by drowning.
Painter. Still-lifes, flowers. Stage sets.
Symbolism.
Golubaya Roza (Blue Rose) group.
Nikolai Sapunov trained under Isaac Levitan at the institute of painting, sculpture and architecture in Moscow from 1893 to 1901, then under A. Kiselev at the academy of art in St Petersburg. He featured in collective exhibitions from 1907 onwards. He was also active as a performer and a free-lance designer in theatres in St Petersburg and Moscow.
Bibliography:
Halturin, Aleksandr/Hulten, Pontus/Gunar, Karl (ed.), *Paris-Moscou*, group exhibition catalogue, Éd. du Centre Georges-Pompidou, Paris, 1979.
Museums and Galleries:
Moscow (Cenral Theatre Mus.) - Moscow (Mus. of Western Art) - Moscow (State Tretyakov Gal.).

SAQUEREL, Jannin, or Sacarel or Saqueret
French, 15th century.
Active 1402-1416.
Glass painter.
Jannin Saquerel may have been the son of Pierre Saquerel. He was a master glazier in Lyons Cathedral and also worked for other churches.

SAQUEREL, Pierre, or Sacarel or Saqueret, also known as Péronnet
French, 14th - 15th century.
Active in Lyons 1378-1440.
Painter, glassmaker.
Pierre Saquerel was stained glass painter to the church of St-Étienne and Lyons Cathedral.

SAQUETI, Giovanni Battista.
See **SACCHETTI**

SARA, Carlo
Italian, 19th century.
Born 2 September 1844, in Pavia; died 23 January 1905, in Pavia.
Painter. History painting, genre scenes, landscapes.
He was a pupil of Giacomo Trecourt.
Museums and Galleries:
Pavia (Musei Civici del Castello Visconteo): paintings.

SARABAT. See **SARRABAT**

SARABIA, Andrés Ruiz de
Spanish, 16th - 17th century.
Active in Seville at the end of the 16th and at the beginning of the 17th century.
Painter.
School of Seville.
Andrés Ruiz de Sarabia was the father of Jose de Sarabia.

SARABIA, François de. See **ANTOLÍNEZ Y SARABIA Francisco**

SARABIA, José de
Spanish, 17th century.
Born 1608, in Seville; died 21 May 1669, in Cordova.
Painter. History painting, religious subjects.
Cordova School.
José de Sarabia studied under Agustin del Castillo until Castillo's death in 1626, when he continued his studies under Francisco Zurbarán. He lived mainly in Cordova and painted for a number of churches in the city. He has been criticised for taking a number of his subjects from engravings by Sadeler and Rubens and passing them off as his own creations.

J de Sarabia.

Museums and Galleries:
Cordova: *Adoration of the Shepherds* - Montpellier: *Virgin and Infant Jesus* (attributed).
Auction records:
Paris, 1852, *Virgin and Child*, FRF 2,605.

SARABIN, Louis Alexis
French, 19th - 20th century.
Born in Le Havre.
Painter. Landscapes with figures.
Louis Alexis Sarabin, a pupil of Charles Lhuiller at the École des Beaux-Arts, Le Havre, and of Isidore Pils in Paris, first exhibited at the Salon de Paris in 1875.
Auction records:
Paris, 25 May 1951, *Flock under Trees*, FRF 900.

SARACCO, Bartolomeo, or Saracho
Italian, 15th century.
Active in Venice from 1487 to 1492.
Painter.

SARACCO, Domenico di Jacopo, or Saracho
Italian, 15th - 16th century.
Active in Venice from 1467 to 1502.
Painter.
Venetian School.

SARACENI, Camillo
Italian, 17th century.
Active in Rome from 1626 to 1664.
Painter, gilder.
Camillo Saraceni worked at the Vatican and at the Palazzo Chigi in Rome.

SARACENI, Carlo, or Saracino or Sarucini, called Veneziano
Italian, 17th century.
Born between 1580 and 1585, in Venice; died 16 June 1620, in Venice.
Painter, engraver. Religious subjects, mythological subjects.
Carlo Saraceni arrived in Rome at the beginning of the 18th century during the pontificate of Clement VIII and frequented the studio of the Venetian sculptor Camillo Mariani. Six small mythological scenes suggest that he was also the pupil of the German painter Elsheimer, a supposition confirmed by the mannerism discernible in some of his later works.

In 1616-1617 Saraceni worked on the frescoes in the Sala Regia of the Palazzo del Quirinale alongside Tassi, Lanfranc, Spadarino and the two Caravaggesque painters Bassetti and Ottino, both of whom, like Saraceni, were born in Venetia. We know that he painted his pictures for the church of Santa Maria dell'Anima during that period, as they were paid for in 1618. In 1620 he was in Venice, collaborating with his friend Jean Le Clerc, a native of Lorraine, on a painting in the council chamber. Saraceni appears to have died before completing this project, which was finished by Le Clerc. It is, however, difficult to distinguish the work of these two artists during this period; for instance, the curious painting of the

Denial of St Peter in the Corsini gallery in Florence, which is wreathed in *ombres chinoises*, is impossible to attribute with certainty to either artist. Le Clerc was Saraceni's disciple before becoming his friend, and engraved a number of his works. The German artist Jan Lys was another of Saraceni's pupils.

The artist who exerted greatest influence over Saraceni was without doubt Caravaggio - from 1620, Saraceni was included in the list compiled by Mancini of the leading followers of Caravaggio - though it must be said that Saraceni's work has just an echo of Caravaggio's dramatic power. In his youthful works he attempted to combine luminarist research and use of the decorative landscape devices of Elsheimer and Domenico Feti with his early Caravaggesque influences. Some of his paintings on copper during this era may be attributed to Elsheimer. Subsequently, perhaps borrowing more from Caravaggio, he nevertheless transmuted the dramatic oppositions of light and shade in the latter's work to produce a measured, restrained chiaroscuro, designed above all to show the subject to best advantage. This reveals his Venetian origins, and led Longhi to attribute to him in 1951 the stylistic qualities of a florid Giorgione.

Works by Carlo Saraceni were featured in the collective exhibition on the theme of still-life in Italy, entitled *Stille Welt. Italienische Stilleben aus drei Jahrhunderten* (*Still World: Three Centuries of Italian Still-life Painting*), mounted at the Kunsthalle der Hypo-Kulturstiftung in Munich in 2003.

BIBLIOGRAPHY:

Caravaggio e caravaggeschi, exhibition catalogue, Palazzo reale, G. Macchiaroli, Naples, 1963. *Le Caravage et la Peinture italienne du XVIIe siècle*, exhibition catalogue, Musée du Louvre, Paris, 1965. Ottani Cavina, Anna, *Carlo Saraceni*, Spagnol, Milan, 1968. Gregori, Mina/Prinz, Johann Georg, *Stille Welt. Italienische Stilleben aus drei Jahrhunderten*, exhibition catalogue, Kunsthalle der Hypo-Kulturstiftung, Munich, 2003.

MUSEUMS AND GALLERIES:

AVIGNON: *Abraham, Hagar and Ishmael* - BASEL: *Annunciation to the Wife of Manoah* - BERLIN (National Mus.): *St Martin and the Beggar* - FRASCATI (Mus. de l'Ermitage des Camaldules): *Rest during the Flight into Egypt* - LILLE: *Flight into Egypt* - MUNICH: *St Jerome, St Anthony and St Mary Magdalene; Vision of St Francis* - NAPLES (Mus. di Capodimonte): six small mythological scenes - POMMERSFELDEN: *The Flood* - ROME (Church of S Maria in Trastevere): *Death of the Virgin* - ROME (Church of S Simone): *Virgin Enthroned* - ROME (Mus. Capitolini, Pinacoteca Capitolina): *Rich Man's Banquet; St Cecilia* - ROME (Mus. e Gal. Borghese): *Joseph Interprets the Dreams* - ROME (Palazzo del Quirinale): several frescoes - ROME (Palazzo Doria Pamphili): *Rest on the Flight into Egypt* - ROME (Palazzo Sciarra): *Death of St John the Baptist* - SIBIU: *Death of the Virgin* - STUTTGART (Staatsgal.): *Liberation of St Peter* - VENICE (Church of the Redentore): *St Francis in Ecstasy* - VENICE (Palazzo Manfredini): *Scene from the Flood* - VIENNA: *Judith*.

AUCTION RECORDS:

MILAN, 20 Nov 1963, *Judith with the Head of Holofernes*, ITL 2,800,000. LONDON, 10 Nov 1967, *Death of the Virgin*, Gns 1,800. NEW YORK, 6 June 1984, *Judith with the Head of Holofernes* (oil on canvas, 36 x 29in/91.3 x 73.5cm) USD 30,000. LONDON, 5 July 1989, *Virgin and Child with St Anne and Angels* (oil/copper, 11 1/2 x 14 1/4in/29.5 x 36.5cm) GBP 148,500. ROME, 13 April 1999, *Venus Bathing* (oil on canvas, 52 x 43 ins / 131 x 110 cm) ITL 70,000,000. PARIS, 6 Dec 2000, *The Flood* (oil on canvas, 45 x 38 ins / 115 x 96 cm) FRF 2,400,000.

SARACENI, Evangelista di Niccolo. See **EVANGELISTA DI NICCOLO SARACENI**

SARACENI, Francesco

Italian, 18th century.
Active in Naples from 1730 to 1745.
Draughtsman, engineer.

He may also have been known as Francesco Saracino. He designed the fireworks for the marriage of the Dauphin of France in 1745.

SARACENI, Francesco

Italian, 19th century.
Born 1798; died 1871.
Active in Ferrara.
Painter, copyist. History painting.

Saraceni specialised in making copies of paintings by other artists.

SARACHO. See **SARACCO**

SARACINO, Carlo. See **SARACENI**

SARACINO, Francesco

Italian, 18th century.
Active in Naples from 1700 to 1717.
Painter, decorative designer, architect, art restorer.

Probably the same as Francesco Saraceni. He carried out the restoration of the church of S Pietro a Majella in Naples.

SARAGOSSA. See **ZARAGOZA**

SARANKO, S. K.. See **SARYANKO Sergei Konstantinovich**

SARASIN. See also **SARAZIN, SARRASIN** and **SARRAZIN**

SARASIN, Betha

Swiss, 20th century.
Born 1930, in Aarau.
Active in Italy from 1962.
Sculptor, designer, illustrator.

Betha Sarasin studied in Basel and spent a decade working as a graphic designer and illustrator. She travelled extensively throughout Europe, the USA, the Soviet Union and Asia before settling in Venice in 1962. She worked in an architectural practice, designing furniture and everyday accessories. In tandem with her day-to-day occupation, she produced abstract and resolutely architectural sculptures based on geometrical forms.

Her work featured in numerous group exhibitions in Switzerland, Germany, the USA and Lebanon. Solo exhibitions include those in Switzerland, Italy and Germany.

SARASIN, Jacques. See **SARAZIN**

SARASIN, Régnault

Swiss, 20th century.
Born 9 August 1886, in Basel.
Active in Paris.
Painter, engraver. Landscapes.
Orientalism.

Régnault Sarasin studied under Victor Marec. He is remembered for his landscapes, notably those of France's overseas territories.

He took part in group exhibitions in Paris, notably at the Salon des Artistes Français (from 1909), securing an honourable mention in the engraving section in 1923, and at the Salon de la Société Nationale des Beaux-Arts (1924-1928). Other group exhibitions include those held in Lyons, Basel, Zurich, Geneva, Bordeaux and Liège, and the Exposition Coloniale in Paris in 1931, where his work was exceptionally well received.

SARATELLI, Alessandro, or Seratelli

Italian, 18th century.

Died 15 April 1722, in Rimini.
Painter. Architectural views.
Alessandro Saratelli painted the Teatro Fiera in Bologna in 1692 and 1702.

SARATELLI, Giulio
Italian, 18th century.
Active during the first half of the 18th century.
Sculptor (wood).
Giulio Saratelli carved stalls and reliquaries in the cathedral in Ferrara around 1713.

SARAUW, Laura Oline Adolphine
Danish, 19th - 20th century.
Born 29 June 1853, in Sorø; died 28 April 1912, in Cannet, France.
Painter, miniaturist. Portraits, flowers.
Laura Oline Adolphine Sarauw studied under Peter Vilhelm Kyhn and Holger K. Grönvold at the Kunstakademi in Copenhagen.

SARAVALL, Miguel
Spanish, 15th century.
Active in Valencia.
Sculptor.
Miguel Saravall worked at the royal palace in Valencia in 1459.

SARAVIA, Diego de
Spanish, 16th - 17th century.
Active in Seville from 1595 to 1604, and among other places at Vera Cruz.
Painter. Figurines.

SARAZANA, Il. See **FIASELLA Domenico**

SARAZIN, Jacques, or Sarasin or Sarrazin
French, 17th century.
Born 1588 or 1592, in Noyon (Oise); died 3 December 1660, in Paris.
Painter, sculptor.
Jacques Sarazin was the pupil of Guillain the Elder in Paris. He went to Italy, where he studied classical antiquity. Michelangelo was his real master, as evidenced by the decorations of the fountains at the Villa Frascati. It is thought that he spent around 18 years in Italy, then returned to Paris around 1629, where he married a relative of Simon Vouet. Sarazin was sculptor to the king, for which he received payment of 1,000 livres per year. He became an Academician on 1 February 1648, and first rector on 6 July 1655.

Between 1630 and 1632 Sarazin collaborated with Simon Vouet and Le Nôtre to produce the *Nymphaeum* in the park at Wideville. He produced the designs for the caryatids adorning the Pavillon de l'Horloge at the Louvre. He also produced decorative sculptures for the Château de Maisons, and funereal monuments for Cardinal de Bérulle and Henri de Bourbon, for whom he produced bronze bas-reliefs illustrating Petrarch's *Triumphs*.

MUSEUMS AND GALLERIES:
PARIS (Louvre): *Strength; Prudence; Justice; Temperance; La Douleur* (Pain); *St Peter; Mary Magdalene; Monument for Cardinal de Bérulle* - PARIS (Mus. des Monuments Français): *Michel Letellier; Lot and His Family Fleeing Sodom* (low relief) - VERSAILLES: *Flight to Egypt* (low relief).

AUCTION RECORDS:
VERSAILLES, 27 March 1977, *Louis XIV* (gilt bronze, h. with pedestal 29¼ ins / 74 cm) FRF 10,000.

SARAZIN, Jean
French, 17th century.
Died 17 January 1639, in Tours.
Active in Dijon.
Glass painter.
Jean Sarazin lived in Tours from 1612.

SARAZIN, Jean Baptiste. See **SARRAZIN**

SARAZIN, Jean Philippe
French, 18th century.
Born in Paris; died c. 1795.
Painter, engraver (etching). Landscapes.
Jean Philippe Sarazin engraved landscapes.

AUCTION RECORDS:
PARIS, 1846, *Landscape with Figures*, FRF 30; *Paysage, Chaumière* (*Landscape, Cottage*, FRF 34. PARIS, 7 and 8 May 1923, *Small Bridge; Sunken Lane* (two watercolours) FRF 1,600. PARIS, 8 May 1925, *Break at the Lakeside*, FRF 1,200. MONTE CARLO, 8 Feb 1981, *Village Street* (oil on panel, 13½ x 20½ ins / 34 x 52 cm) FRF 12,500. PARIS, 6 Dec 2002, *Italian Landscape with Waterfall* (1772, oil on panel, 11 x 14 ins / 29 x 35 cm) EUR 3,100.

SARAZIN, Pierre, or Sarrazin
French, 17th century.
Born 1601, in Noyon (Oise); died 7 April 1679, in Paris.
Painter.
Pierre Sarazin worked with his brother, Jacques Sarazin, and had a share in the latter's fame. He was sculptor to the king, and became an Academician on 6 June 1665.

SARAZIN, Pierre Jean. See **SARRAZIN**

SARAZIN DE BELMONT, Louise Joséphine
French, 19th century.
Born 14 February 1790, in Versailles; died 9 December 1870, in Paris.
Painter, lithographer. Landscapes, architectural views.
Her master was Valenciennes. She exhibited at the Salon between 1812 and 1867. She won a second-class medal in 1831 and a first-class medal in 1834.

MUSEUMS AND GALLERIES:
ANGERS: two landscapes - DRESDEN (Prints Collection): *Portrait of the Artist; Portrait of C Vogel von Vogelstein* - HANOVER (Kestner-Mus.): *Landscape* - MONTAUBAN: five landscapes - MUNICH: *In the Forest of Fontainebleau* - NANTES: *Interior of the Forest of Fontainebleau; View of Orvieto Cathedral* - PARIS (Louvre): *Landscape* - TOULOUSE: *San Miniato, Florence; Monte Mario, Rome; The Pausilippo, Naples; Paris Viewed from the Hills of Père-Lachaise; St-Saoni Convent and the Argelès Valley* - TOURS: *The Roman Forum, Morning; The Roman Forum, Evening*.

AUCTION RECORDS:
PARIS, 24 Feb 1943, *View of Rome* (1841) FRF 7,000. BERN, 23 Oct 1980, *Landscape in Brittany* (1837, oil on canvas remounted on board, 24½ x 35½ ins / 62.5 x 90 cm) CHF 6,000. LONDON, 25 June 1982, *View of the Île de la Cité in Paris* (1835, oil on canvas, 48½ x 64 ins / 123.2 x 162.5 cm) GBP 11,000. MONTE CARLO, 22 Feb 1986, *People Arriving in Sight of a Town* (1820, oil on canvas, 25½ x 32 ins / 65 x 81 cm) FRF 65,000. PARIS, 27 Nov 1989, *The Flute Examination* (oil on canvas, 40¼ x 47¼ ins / 102 x 120 cm) FRF 17,000. PARIS, 29 Nov 1995, *Bagnères de Luchon* (oil on canvas, 11½ x 19 ins / 29 x 48.5 cm) FRF 12,000. LONDON, 13 March 1997, *Classical Riverscape* (oil on canvas, 24 x 29 ins / 61 x 73.6 cm) GBP 2,530. PARIS, 25 Nov 1997, *View of Florence* (oil/card, 8 x 11 ins / 20.3 x 28 cm) FRF 46,000. PARIS, 27 Oct 1999, *Convent near Bibiena* (1849, oil on paper/card, 6 x 8 ins / 16 x 21 cm) FRF 21,000. PARIS, 20 Dec 1999, *View of the Château de Pierrefonds* (1837, oil on canvas, 28 x 42 ins / 71 x 107 cm) FRF 55,000. AMSTERDAM, 24 Oct 2000, *Panoramic View of Rome* (oil on canvas, 13 x 17 ins / 32 x 42 cm) NLG 16,000. PARIS, 17 Dec 2001, *View of a Waterfall in a Mountain Landscape* (oil on paper/card, 4 x 6 ins / 10 x 14 cm) FRF 12,500. PARIS, 19 Dec 2001, *View of a Canal* (oil on card, 6 x 7 ins / 14 x 19 cm) FRF 12,000. LYONS, 1 Dec 2002, *Italian Landscape* (oil on canvas, 19 x 24 ins / 48 x 61 cm) EUR 3,000. PARIS, 25 June 2003, *View*

of St-Jean de Luz (1830, oil on paper/card, 9 x 16 ins / 24 x 41 cm) EUR 9,500.

SARBACH, Jakob, called Labahürlin
Swiss, 15th century.
Died 1492.
Active in Basel.
Sculptor.

Jakob Sarbach carved the fountain of the fish market in Basel in 1467.

SARBOT. See **SAIRBOT**

SARBURGH, Bartholomäus or Bartholomé, or Sarburg, Sarbruck or Saarburck, called Treirsensio
German, 17th century.
Born c. 1590, in Trier.
Painter. Portraits.

Sarburgh worked in Basel between 1620 and 1628 and painted in the style of Van Dyck.

MUSEUMS AND GALLERIES:
BASEL: *Agrippa of Aubigné, Peter Ryff and his Wife, and Lutzelmann and his Wife in a Group* - BERLIN (Kupferstichkabinet): *Two Nudes* (charcoal) - MUNICH (Städtische Gal. im Lenbachhaus): *Frau Anna Heidelin with Her Grandson* - ZURICH (Schweizerisches Landesmus.): *Portrait of Frau Magdalena Nägelin*.

AUCTION RECORDS:
COLOGNE, 8 May 1969, *Old Woman and Child*, DEM 11,000. LONDON, 24 March 1971, *Portrait of a Gentleman; Portrait of a Lady of Quality* (two pendants) GBP 2,000. LONDON, 9 July 1982, *Young Peasant Playing the Flute* (1630, oil on panel, 26 1/4 x 20 ins / 66.7 x 50.8 cm) GBP 3,500. LONDON, 6 July 1990, *Bonifacius Iselin Dressed in Dark Colours with a White Ruff; Sara Mayer zu Pfeil in a Black Coat with a Fur Collar, White Ruff and Holding a Headdress* (1619, oil on canvas, two portraits, each 37 3/4 x 28 3/4 ins / 96 x 73 cm) GBP 13,200.

SARCERIUS, Cornelis
Dutch, 17th century.
Active in Utrecht in 1638 and 1642.
Painter.

SARCUS, Charles Marie de
French, 19th century.
Born 26 May 1821, in Dijon.
Painter, watercolourist, lithographer. Genre scenes, landscapes.

He was a pupil of Paul Delaroche and exhibited at the Salons of 1846 and 1848.

AUCTION RECORDS:
PARIS, 13 Dec 1937, *The Conservatory of Modern Dance* (two watercolour gouaches) FRF 110.

SARDA
French, 19th century.
Painter. Genre scenes.

MUSEUMS AND GALLERIES:
CHÂLONS-EN-CHAMPAGNE: *A Seigniorial Execution* (1876).

SARDAGNA, Lodovico
Italian, 17th century.
Born in Trento.
Draughtsman, architect, engraver.

Lodovico Sardagna designed several triumphal arches in Trento and engraved portraits of emperors in the Habsburg dynasty.

SARDELIC, Ante
Yugoslav, 20th - 21st century.
Born 3 February 1947, in Blato (Island of Korcula, now in Croatia).
Active in Canada from 1972, naturalised Canadian.
Painter, sculptor, engraver.
Nouvelle Figuration.

Ante Sardelic graduated from the school of fine arts in Split and later from the school of fine arts in Zagreb. In 1972, he left Yugoslavia for Canada, where he was granted Canadian nationality. His works are figurative and use strong colours, tending towards Expressionism and loaded anthropomorphic references. He draws his sources from the indigenous cultures of the Americas: from North American Indians, Mexican primitivism and folk art of the USA. He exhibited from 1969 in Yugoslavia, then in Canada and the USA. His work was featured in the first Biennale d'Arts Visuels in Lyons in 1979. The Centre Culturel Canadien in Paris organised a solo exhibition of his work in 1978. He won a first prize for sculpture in Toronto in 1971, the painting prize at the Lyons Biennale in 1979 and a first prize for engraving in Seoul (South Korea) in 1980.

SARDENT, Marie Geneviève
French, 19th - 20th century.
Born in Paris.
Painter, watercolourist. Portraits, genre scenes.

Marie Geneviève Sardent first exhibited in Paris at the Salon des Artistes Français in 1880.

SARDER, Philipp
German, 16th century.
Sculptor.

Philipp Sarder was the father of Wilhelm Sarder and a pupil of Jakob Murman in Augsburg. He carved the epitaph of Bishop Martin von Schaumburg in Eichstätt Cathedral.

SARDER, Wilhelm, or Sartor
German, 16th century.
Born in Augsburg.
Active during the second half of the 16th century.
Sculptor.

Wilhelm Sarder settled in Eichstätt in 1569 and carved many tombs in the city's cathedral and in the churches in the area.

SARDI, Gaetano, or Sarri
Italian, 18th century.
Probably born in Rome.
Active during the first half of the 18th century.
Painter.

Gaetano Sardi was the pupil of B. Luti and Pietro Bianchi.

SARDI, István or Stefan
Hungarian, 19th century.
Born 1846, in Eisenmarkt (now Hunedoara, Romania); died 1901, in Klausenburg (now Cluj-Napoca, Romania).
Painter, illustrator.

The national museum in Cluj owns works by Sardi.

SARDI, Jean
French, 20th - 21st century.
Born 1947.
Painter. Local figures, scenes with figures, landscapes, urban landscapes, seascapes.

Jean Sardi paints bustling Parisian street scenes.

AUCTION RECORDS:
VERSAILLES, 21 Jan 1990, *Market* (oil on canvas, 25 1/2 x 32 ins / 65 x 81 cm) FRF 10,000. NEUILLY, 27 March 1990, *Gypsies* (oil on canvas, 16 1/4 x 13 ins / 41 x 33 cm) FRF 4,000. VERSAILLES, 22 April 1990, *Boats at their Moorings* (oil on canvas, 25 1/2 x 32 ins / 65 x 81 cm) FRF 8,500. LA VARENNE-ST-HILAIRE, 16 June 1990, *Flea-Market* (oil on canvas, 25 1/4 x 22 ins / 64 x 55 cm) FRF 7,800. VERSAILLES, 8 July 1990, *Pedestrian Street* (oil on canvas, 28 3/4 x 36 1/4 ins / 73 x 92 cm) FRF 8,000. VERSAILLES, 23 Sept 1990, *Seascape* (oil on canvas, 23 1/2 x 28 3/4 ins / 60 x 73 cm) FRF 8,500. NEUILLY, 14 Nov 1990, *Paris Bridge* (oil on canvas, 39 1/4 x 32 ins / 100 x 81 cm) FRF 13,500. NEUILLY, 7 April 1991, *Rue St-Denis* (oil on canvas, 18 x 15 ins / 46 x 38 cm) FRF 5,000. NEUILLY, 11 June 1991, *Harvesting*

Olives in Provence (oil on canvas, 28¾ x 35¾ ins / 73 x 91 cm) FRF 7,000. NEUILLY, 19 March 1994, *Landscape with Cypresses* (oil on canvas, 25½ x 32 ins / 65 x 81 cm) FRF 9,000. PARIS, 21 March 1999, *Boats* (oil on canvas, 24 x 29 ins / 60 x 73 cm) FRF 18,500. PARIS, 31 May 1999, *Bathers in a Rocky Inlet, Cassis* (oil on canvas, 29 x 24 ins / 73 x 60 cm) FRF 18,000. PARIS, 12 March 2000, *Coteaux Varois* (oil on canvas, 21 x 26 ins / 54 x 65 cm) FRF 12,000. CALAIS, 11 March 2001, *Landscape and Villages in Provence* (oil on canvas, 26 x 32 ins / 65 x 81 cm) FRF 15,000. PARIS, 3 July 2002, *Southern Harbour* (oil on canvas, 18 x 22 ins / 46 x 55 cm) EUR 2,000. PARIS, 29 April 2003, *Cassis* (oil on canvas, 24 x 32 ins / 60 x 81 cm) EUR 2,400. MUNICH, 13 Nov 2003, *Still-life of Flowers* (oil on canvas, 29 x 35 ins / 73 x 89 cm) EUR 1,500.

SARDI, Pietro
Italian, 18th century.
Active in Venice.
Engraver (burin).
Pietro Sardi may have been the pupil of M. Pitteri. He engraved the portrait of *George IV of England*.

SARDI, Samuel
Hungarian, 18th century.
Active in Transylvania in the middle of the 18th century.
Engraver (burin), draughtsman.
The national museum in Cluj owns some book plates engraved by Samuel Sardi.

SARDI, Teresa
Maiden name: Giusti
Italian, 19th century.
Born 25 September 1795; died 28 April 1833, in Rome.
Painter.

SARDIN, Albert Edmond
French, 20th century.
Born 17 November 1878, in Arcis-sur-Aube.
Painter. Nudes, landscapes, waterscapes, still-lifes (flowers/fruit).
Albert Edmond Sardin was a great-grandnephew of Danton. He exhibited in Paris from 1902 at the Salon des Indépendants, and later at the Salon d'Automne and the Salon des Tuileries. His preferred subjects were peaceful river landscapes and he painted still-lifes of flowers and fruit with great accuracy.

SARDINA, Alonse de
Spanish, 17th century.
Active during the first half of the 17th century.
Sculptor.
Alonse de Sardina carved low reliefs on the façade and in the cloister of the church of S Esteban in Salamanca.

SARDINIER, T. P. W.
German, 18th century.
Active in Ottobeuren (Bavaria) at the beginning of the 18th century.
Draughtsman.
Sardinier designed architectural decorations.

SARDIORA
Austrian, 16th century.
Active during the first half of the 16th century.
Sculptor.
In 1520 Sardiora carved the fonts in the cemetery chapel of Schludens.

SARDOU, Honoré Charles
French, 19th century.
Born 15 October 1806, in Aix-en-Provence.
Painter, pastellist. Portraits.
His teacher was Louis Rioult. In 1857 he went to live in Marseilles. His work was included in the 1981 exhibition *Le portrait en Dauphiné au XIXe siècle* (*The Portrait in the Dauphiné Region in the 19th Century*), at the Fondation Hébert d'Uckermann in La Tronche (Rhône-Alpes).
MUSEUMS AND GALLERIES:
GRENOBLE (Mus. Dauphinois): *Portrait of a Bourgeois Woman* (1853).

SARDOU, Jean-Claude
French, 20th century.
Born 1904, in Nice; died 1967, in Le Revest-des-Brousses.
Painter. Figures, portraits, landscapes with figures, landscapes.
As a young man Jean-Claude Sardou received advice from Paul Signac, who several times asked him to come and work with him. It was at his suggestion that he travelled in Italy. He then went to live in the countryside near Nice. In 1930 he met Matisse, and he later worked in the Champagne and Brittany. He finally settled in Haute-Provence, leaving only once to visit North Africa.

He exhibited in Provence, Algeria and Paris, took part in the Menton Biennale and was active in the Association of the Friends of the Musée d'Art Moderne, Paris.

Signac's teaching led him to paint in the Post-Impressinist style, but during his stay in Italy he discovered the Primitives and he turned his back on pointillism. When in Nice he painted in dark colours, but with the move to Haute-Provence his palette lightened. His figures are always placed in landscapes.
MUSEUMS AND GALLERIES:
MONTPELLIER (Mus. Fabre): *Village in the Comtat Venaissin; Brittany at Low Tide*.

SARDOU, L.
French, 19th century.
Active in 1819.
Miniaturist. Portraits.

SARDOU, Victorien
French, 19th century.
Born 1831, in Paris; died 1908, in Paris.
Painter, draughtsman, dramatist.
Sardou was a playwright whose works include *Patrie, La Tosca* and *Madame Sans Gêne*. But he also enjoyed making sketches and watercolours of scenic parts of his native Paris - a place he loved dearly. He also drew strange landscapes, which he claimed to have seen on other planets in his dreams, and designed sets and costumes for the theatre.

SARDY, Brutus
Hungarian, 20th century.
Born 20 January 1892, in Parlasz.
Painter. Landscapes.
Brutus Sardy trained in Budapest.
MUSEUMS AND GALLERIES:
BUDAPEST (Fövárosi Képtár).

SARECZ, György or Georg
Hungarian, 18th century.
Active at the beginning of the 18th century.
Sculptor.
Gyorgy Sarecz sculpted the high altar of the church of St Matthew in Szeged.

SAREN, Quentin van der
Flemish School, 16th century.
Sculptor (wood).
In 1541-1542 Quentin van der Saren carved the stalls in the chapel of the hospital of Our Lady, Oudenaarde.

SARENCO, pseudonym of Mabellini, Isaia
Italian, 20th century.
Born 1945, in Vobarno (Brescia).
Action artist, performance artist.
Visual Poetry.

In about 1970 Sarenco embarked on his career as a multimedia artist, while he also organised international exhibitions and meetings and published books and magazines. In 1984 he started making films in collaboration with artists. His activities deal with the relationships between art and society, and do so in a violent and polemical way. For Sarenco his whole life is his work of art.

SARENT, J.
German, 19th century.
Active in 1833.
Miniaturist.

SARET, Alan
American, 20th century.
Born 1944, in New York.
Sculptor, sculptor of assemblages, draughtsman.

Alan Saret's works often seem at first sight to be characterised by their monumentality and their apparent disorganisation. In fact, they are wild constructions, made out of various objects such as sheet metal, wire netting, copper wire, cornices, windows and various objects from demolished buildings. As rudimentary shelters, these works are both sculptural and architectural. They are a little like Étienne-Martin's *Demeures* (*Residences*), although the intentions are very different. Saret's assemblages are only temporary states and are intrinsically unbalanced, while the structures seem unpredictable and almost anarchic. They are also the poetry of distant lands. Like the work of Eva Hesse, Keith Sonnier and even Richard Serra, Saret's work belongs to the mainly American movement which, probably as a reaction against the strict Constructivism of Minimal Art, exploited the resources of formlessness. In certain respects this closely resembles the almost contemporaneous Italian Arte Povera. In his later development, Saret made much smaller and more coherent works such as sculptural objects mainly made of plastic-coated or painted steel or copper wire and wire netting.

AUCTION RECORDS:
NEW YORK, 16 May 1980, *Untitled* (1969, wire and painted netting, 54 x 60 x 48 ins / 137 x 152.4 x 122 cm) USD 4,500. NEW YORK, 16 Feb 1984, *Untitled* (colouring pencil, 25 x 38 ins / 63.5 x 96.5 cm) USD 1,700. NEW YORK, 2 Nov 1984, *Red Dragon; Green Dragon* (1974, watercolour, a pair, 22 1/2 x 30 ins / 57 x 76 cm) USD 2,600. NEW YORK, 8 May 1990, *Shaped Pear* (galvanised steel wire, 60 x 48 x 36 ins / 152.4 x 121.9 x 91.4 cm) USD 14,300. NEW YORK, 2 May 1991, *Green and Scarlet Mountain Triumph* (1979, copper and steel wire, 40 1/2 x 30 x 22 ins / 102.8 x 76.2 x 55.8 cm) USD 8,800. NEW YORK, 13 Nov 1991, *Mind of an Idiot* (copper wire with coloured plastic casing, 36 x 27 x 22 ins / 91.4 x 68.6 x 55.9 cm) USD 7,700. NEW YORK, 22 Feb 1993, *Shoot of New Grass* (1988, colouring pencil and graphite/paper, 30 1/4 x 44 ins / 76.7 x 111.8 cm) USD 1,320. NEW YORK, 23 Feb 1994, *Green Wave of Air* (painted hexagonal mesh, 54 x 60 x 48 ins / 137 x 152.5 x 122 cm) USD 4,830. NEW YORK, 16 Nov 1995, *Beta Heliotis of Set VIII* (colouring pencil/paper, 26 1/2 x 40 ins / 67.3 x 101.6 cm) USD 1,265. NEW YORK, 7 May 1996, *Untitled* (aluminium wire, 50 x 24 x 20 ins / 127 x 61 x 50.8 cm) USD 1,955. NEW YORK, 19 Nov 1996, *Stun Bax Drunk* (1988, colouring pencil/paper, 31 1/2 x 35 3/4 ins / 80 x 90.8 cm) USD 575. NEW YORK, 12 Feb 2004, *Nest of Comets* (Wire, 42 x 28x19 ins / 107 x 71x48 cm) USD 14,000. LAMBERTVILLE, 24 April 2004, *Eight Drawings* (1983, colour pencil, eight, 4 x 5 ins / 9 x 12 cm) USD 8,000.

SARFATI, Albert
French, 20th century.
Born 3 August 1886, in Constantine, Algeria.
Painter.

Albert Sarfati exhibited in Paris at the Salon des Indépendants, the Salon d'Automne and the Salon des Tuileries.

AUCTION RECORDS:
PARIS, 18 Dec 1950, *The Tanagra*, FRF 750.

SARFF, Walter
American, 20th century.
Born in Illinois.
Painter.

Walter Sarff studied at the National Academy of Arts in Chicago and at the Grand Central School of Art.

SARG, Jörg or Georg. See **SORG**

SARG, Tony
American, 20th century.
Born 24 April 1880, in Coban, Guatemala; died 1942.
Painter, caricaturist, illustrator, sculptor. Wall decorations, marionettes.

Tony Sarg was active in New York, where he was a member of the Salmagundi Club. He produced murals for several hotels in New York and illustrated many books.

SARGANT, Francis W.
British, 19th - 20th century.
Born 10 January 1870, in London; died 11 January 1960, in Cambridge.
From 1899 to 1937 active in Italy.
Sculptor. Figures. Monuments, low reliefs.

Francis W. Sargant studied at New College Oxford and was apprenticed to the architect T.G. Jackson from 1891 to 1894. He attended the Slade School of Fine Art, London, from 1895 to 1896. He worked with Sir George James Frampton and Conrad Dressler. He lived in Florence from 1899 to 1937 (except during World War I) and trained under Adolf Hildebrand. He was a member of the Royal Society of British Sculptors. From 1919, he participated in exhibitions at the Royal Academy, London.

In 1913 he executed the monument in memory of Florence Nightingale in the church of Santa Croce in Florence. He also sculpted the low reliefs for the war memorial at Oakham School. He executed stone and bronze sculptures, producing work which seemed to have originated directly from the traditions of the Renaissance.

MUSEUMS AND GALLERIES:
LONDON (Tate Collection): *Carlino* (1902).

SARGEANT, Geneve Rixford
American, 19th - 20th century.
Born 14 July 1868, in San Francisco; died 1957.
Painter. Landscapes.

Geneve Rixford Sargeant was the pupil of Sören Emil Carlsen, William Merritt Chase, Julius Gari Melchers.

AUCTION RECORDS:
LOS ANGELES-SAN FRANCISCO, 12 July 1990, *Monterey Coast* (1961, oil on canvas, 17 x 24 ins / 43 x 61 cm) USD 825.

SARGEANT, H.
British, 19th century.
Painter. Seascapes.

H. Sargeant was a Royal Navy artist.

AUCTION RECORDS:
LONDON, 22 May 1991, *First Leg of The America's Cup passing Ryde Pier; Open Sea off Osborne* (oil on card, pair, each 11 x 15 ins / 28 x 38 cm) GBP 26,400.

SARGEANT, John, or Sarjeant
British, 19th century.
Active in London from 1824 to 1839.
Painter. Portraits, genre scenes, landscapes.

SARGENT, Alfred Louis
French, 19th century.
Born 11 May 1828, in Paris.
Engraver (wood).

He was the brother of Louis Sargent and the pupil of Tiennis. He made his Salon debut in 1855.

SARGENT, Frederick
British, 19th century.
Died 14 April 1899.
Painter. Portraits, genre scenes. Miniatures.
Frederick Sargent was a Royal Academy exhibitor between 1854 and 1874.
Museums and Galleries:
London (National Portrait Gal.): *George William Frederick Charles, 2nd Duke of Cambridge* (1870s, pencil); *Edward Cardwell, Viscount Cardwell* (1870s, pencil); *Frederick Thesiger, 1st Baron Chelmsford* (1870s, pencil); *John Hanmer, 1st Baron Hanmer* (1870s, pencil).

SARGENT, G. F.
British, 19th century.
Born 1811; died 1864.
Draughtsman, watercolourist, miniaturist. Landscapes.
Nottingham Museum houses 96 miniature drawings by G.F. Sargent that were destined to be reproduced as engravings. For the most part, they are illustrations to Peacock's *Polite Repository*.
Museums and Galleries:
Nottingham (Castle Mus. & AG): collection of 96 miniature drawings.

SARGENT, Giovanni. See **SARGENT John Singer**

SARGENT, Henry, or G. Henry
American, 18th - 19th century.
Born 25 November 1770, in Gloucester (Massachusetts); died 21 February 1845, in Boston.
Painter. History painting, genre scenes, portraits.
Henry Sargent was taught by John Singleton Copley and Benjamin West in London. He worked mainly in Boston.
Museums and Galleries:
Boston: *Tea Party*; *Portrait of Turner Sargent* - Boston (MFA): *Dinner Party* (c. 1821, oil on canvas).
Auction records:
London, 12 Dec 1910, *Young Boy*, GBP 21. New York, 14 Feb 1990, *Portrait of Nathaniel Amory* (oil on canvas, 30 x 25 1/4 ins / 76.5 x 64 cm) USD 2,200.

SARGENT, John Singer
American, 19th - 20th century.
Born 12 January 1856, in Florence, to American parents; died 15 April 1925, in London.
Active in France and England.
Painter (gouache), watercolourist, draughtsman. Figure compositions, religious subjects, genre scenes, figures, portraits, interiors with figures, landscapes, seascapes. Murals.
Grez-sur-Loing School (Colony).
John Singer Sargent came from an aristocratic, highly cultivated family, with several Governors of the State of Massachusetts figuring among their number. His father was a doctor. Sargent began his artistic studies in 1868, probably in Florence, under Carl Welsch, a German-American landscapist. He also had a taste for music and was a good pianist. From 1870 he studied at the academy of fine arts in Florence (some sources claim he studied for only a short period, in Rome). In 1874 he went to Paris with his family, where he was the pupil of the portrait painter Carolus Duran, through whom discovered the work of Frans Hals and Velázquez. In 1876 he made a short trip to the USA, which included a visit to the Centenary Exhibition in Philadelphia. Also in 1876 he visited the second Impressionist exhibition in Paris at the Galerie Durand-Ruel, where, in his own words, was simply 'bowled over'. He developed an interest in Courbet, the Impressionists (especially Degas and Whistler) and soon struck up a friendship with Monet, whose portrait he painted several times. The Sargent family travelled a good deal, spending their winters in southern Europe, returning to the north in summer. John Singer Sargent also travelled around Holland, Spain, North Africa. In Spain in 1879 he produced works in the style of Velàsquez, and the following year in Holland painted in the style of Frans Hals. In 1880-1882 he paid a visit to Venice. In 1884, Sargent left for London, disappointed that his submission to the Salon had caused a scandal. In London he was warmly welcomed by the writers Henry James, an American from the same social background as himself, and Robert Louis Stevenson, whose portrait he painted. Sargent worked in Whistler's studio and was temporarily influenced by him. In 1887 Sargent went again to the USA, staying in Boston for two years: the city's museum owns several of his most important paintings. He returned to Paris in 1889, met Monet again and stayed with him for a while at Giverny. He contributed to the fund established by a number of French museums to purchase Manet's work *Olympia*. He then returned to England where he settled, although he frequently returned to the USA, where he was commissioned to paint portraits and decorative murals.

In Paris he furthered his artistic training by painting landscapes in the French countryside, in 1875 at Barbizon, then at Grez-sur-Loing, where he renewed his contacts with the American artists Childe Hassam, Willard Metcalf, John Henry Twachtman. He also painted views of the Jardin du Luxembourg in Paris. In his first period he applied fluid brushstroke techniques that gave the appearance of being hatched: this was partly a response to his awareness of Monet's Impressionist work, and partly the influence of Velàsquez, which he had inherited from Carolus Duran. His technique soon changed, however, and he began to use broad, firm brushstrokes, as in *El Jaleo* of 1880, a horizontal composition, with chiaroscuro and lit by an artificial, almost theatrical light that evokes Spanish flamenco dance. The painting sharply contrasts areas of shadow and areas of light, thus creating a daring and jarring chromatism. Sargent's cross-hatching technique and the way he offsets patches of dark shadow against patches of light were features found in contemporary Impressionist painting. The same characteristics can be found in *The Daughters of Edward Darley Boit* which he submitted to the Salon in 1882. The subject-matter of this work gave Sargent greater freedom than he had enjoyed with his more official portraits, since it enabled him to catch the spontaneity of the girls' movements and attitudes, which brought him still closer to the concerns of the Impressionists. At the 1884 Salon Sargent exhibited his *Portrait of Madame Goutreau*, née Judith Avegno, who was from New Orleans in Louisiana, often known as *Portrait of Madame X*... He painted this work in 1882, though with some difficulty as the model refused to give him regular sittings. The subject is a woman famed for her beauty. She is shown standing; her long, dark dress is soberly cut, but her bust, arms, neck and head with its carefully coiffed hair, the face resolutely in profile, the contours firmly delineated, stand out clearly against the dark background, virtually without needing to be modelled; the influence of Manet's *Olympia* is clear. The painting brought outcry not on account of the boldness of the contrasts between the woman's strongly lit body and the ambient shadows, and the absence of modelling but because of the provocative stillness of the profile, the low-cut dress and the make-up, which was risqué for the time. Two years later, in London in 1886, Sargent exhibited his *Portrait of Miss Wicken* at the Royal Academy and the following year *The Vickers Children*. These two remarkable submissions helped establish his reputation as the portrait painter of choice in British society. This flattering acknowledgement and his consequent obligations as a society portrait painter undoubtedly prevented him from breaking new artistic ground. However, in 1888 he sought refuge in the English countryside, freely creating paintings that were closer to Impressionist techniques and to Monet. During his second stay in the USA he submitted *El Jaleo* to Boston and the *Daughters of Edward Darley Boit*, both warmly received. Boston Public Library then commissioned him to paint a series of murals on *History of Religion*. He began this task in 1890 but it was only in 1916 that he completed the work, which represented *Dogma and Redemption* and *Two Testaments*. The Boston Museum of Fine Arts in 1916, and the Widener Library at Harvard in 1921, also commissioned murals from Sargent.

Although historically he is still one of most outstanding American Impressionists, it must also be conceded that to a lesser extent than Whistler, Mary Cassatt or Prendergast, he was only an Impressionist intermittently, and in some ways more European than American. His public career was essentially devoted to portraiture, which encouraged some to regard him as the Van Dyck of the Edwardian era. Art historians are often perplexed when confronted with the dual aspects of Sargent's output - a relatively academic career as a quasi-official portraitist for the top social echelons, and an artist who painted for his own pleasure in Impressionist style. He was undoubtedly a very fine painter of chiaroscuro effects, following in the footsteps of Velàsquez and Manet. But, when he freed himself of the constraints of portraiture, he was also able to paint spontaneously out of doors, especially in watercolours. Closer to Manet than to Monet and the Impressionists, he claimed to be a master of dazzling facility - with just a few clean brushstrokes he could depict pomegranates hanging from their leafy boughs, undulations on the surface of water, rocks in swirling torrents, a fire on a mountain.

He made his Paris debut at the 1877 Salon with *Oyster Gatherers in Cancale* and continued to show works there regularly, primarily portraits and a few landscapes, winning many awards: in 1881 a second class medal; in 1889 he was made Chevalier of the Légion d'Honneur at the Universal Exposition; and at the Exposition Universelle of 1900 he was made Officier of the Légion d'Honneur. He was at the same time a member of the Société des Artistes Français. In 1890 he was a founder member of the Société Nationale des Beaux-Arts, where he continued to exhibit. He was a member of the Institut de France. In Britain he exhibited regularly from 1882 at the Royal Academy in London, notably in 1887 with *Carnation, Lily, Lily, Rose*; 1894 made associate member; 1897 elected full member of the Academy. He was also an honorary member of the Royal Scottish Academy; member of the Royal Institute of Watercolour Painters; honorary member of the Royal Institute of Oil Painters.

Beside his participation in various Salons in Paris and London, in 1885 the Galerie Georges Petit in Paris held a joint exhibition of work by Sargent and Monet. In 1886 he persuaded Durand-Ruel to organise a major Impressionist exhibition in New York. In 1887-1888, an exhibition of his works went on display in Boston. After his death in 1925, several retrospectives were organised in Boston in 1925, London 1926, at both the Royal Academy and the Tate Gallery. In 1963 the Centre Culturel Américain in Paris organised an exhibition entitled simply *John Singer Sargent*. In 1976, he was represented at the exhibition held by the Museum of Modern Art in New York, *Natural Paradise: Painting in America 1800-1950*. In Paris in 1982 he was represented at the *Impressionnistes Américains* (*American Impressionists*) exhibition at the Musée du Petit Palais; in 2001 in Giverny, as part of the exhibition *L'Héroïque et le quotidien: les artistes américains, 1820-1920* (*The Heroic and the Everyday: American Artists, 1820-1920*) at the Musée d'Art Américain; in 2002 in Lausanne at the exhibition *L'Impressionnisme américain 1880-1915* (*American Impressionism 1880-1915*) at the Fondation de l'Hermitage.

BIBLIOGRAPHY:

Downes, William Howe, *John S. Sargent: his Life and Work*, Little, Brown, Boston, 1925. *Memorial Exhibition of the Work of John Singer Sargent*, exhibition catalogue, Metropolitan Museum, New York, 1926. *John S. Sargent*, exhibition catalogue, Centre culturel américain, Paris, 1963. Ormond, Richard, *John Singer Sargent: Paintings, Drawings, Watercolors*, Harper and Row, New York, 1970. *Impressionnistes américains*, exhibition catalogue, Smithsonian Institution, Washington DC, musée du Petit Palais, Paris, 1982. Hills, Patricia, *John Singer Sargent*, exhibition catalogue, Whitney Museum of American Art, New York, Abrams, New York, 1986. Hélène Ahrweiler, Roger Mandle, D. Scott Atkinson, William H. Gerdts, Carole L. Shelby, Jochen Wierich, *Lasting Impressions: American Painters in France 1865-1915*, exhibition catalogue, Musée d'Art américain, Giverny, Terra Foundation for the Arts, Evanston (IL), 1992. C. Radcliff, *John S. Sargent*, Abbeville Press, London, 1997. Little, Carl/Skolnick, Arnold, *The Watercolors of John Singer Sargent*, University of California Press, Berkeley, 1998. Ormond, Richard/Kilmurray, Elaine, *John Singer Sargent: complete paintings*, Yale University Press, New Haven, 1998. Kilmurray, Elaine, *John Singer Sargent*, exhibition catalogue, Tate Gall., London, Princeton University Press, Princeton, 1998. Fairbrother, Trevor, *John Singer Sargent: the sensualist*, exhibition catalogue, Art Museum, Seattle, 2000. Cikovski, Nicolai/Hauptman, William, *L'Impressionisme américain 1880-1915*, exhibition catalogue, Fondation de l'Hermitage, Lausanne, 2002. Ormond, Richars/Kilmurray, Elaine, '*John Singer Sargent: Portraits of the 1890s. Complete Paintings*' in Vol. 2, catalogue raisonné, Paul Mellon Centre for Studies in British Art, New Haven, 2002. Ormond, Richard/Pixley, Mary, '*Sargent after Velazquez: the Prado studies*' in *The Burlington Magazine* vol. CXLV n° 1206, periodical, London, September 2003.

MUSEUMS AND GALLERIES:

BOSTON (Isabella Stewart Gardner Mus.): *El Jaleo* (1880); *Portrait of Isabella Stewart Gardner* - BOSTON (MFA): *Oyster Gatherers at Cancale* (1878); *Portrait of Young Boy*; *Artist's Studio*; *The Daughters of Edward Darley Boit* (*Daughters of Edward Darley Boit*) (1882, oil on canvas); *Master* - BOSTON (Public Library): *The Triumph of Religion (or Judaism and Christianity)* (*Triumph of Religion*) (wall paintings) - CHICAGO (Terra Museum of American Art): *Young Breton Girl with Basket* (1877, sketch for 'The Oyster Gatherers of Cancale'); *Young Girl on the Beach* (1877, sketch for 'The Oyster Gatherers of Cancale'); *Young Boy on the Beach* (1877, sketch for 'The Oyster Gatherers of Cancale'); *Young Paris Beggargirl* (c. 1880, oil on canvas); *Dennis Miller Bunker Painting at Calcot* (1888) - COLORADO SPRINGS (Fine Arts Center): *Portrait of Miss Elsie Palmer (or A Lady in White)* (*Portrait of Miss Elsie Palmer (or A Lady in White)*) (oil on canvas) - DENVER (AM): *Portrait of Lady Agnes Anstruther-Thompson*; *Portrait of Mrs George Lambton* - DUBLIN (NG of Ireland): *Portrait of President Woodrow Wilson* - EDINBURGH (Nat. Gal. of Scotland): *Gertrude, Lady Agnew of Lochnaw* (*Gertrude, Lady Agnew of Lochnaw*) (oil on canvas) - FLORENCE (Palazzo Pitti): *The Painter Ambrogio Raffaele* - FLORENCE (Uffizi): *Portrait of the Artist* - FORT WORTH (Amon Carter Mus.): *Portrait of Alice Vanderbilt Shepard* (*Portrait of Alice Vanderbilt Shepard*)

(1888, oil on canvas) - GLASGOW (AG and Mus.): *Sir David Richmond, Provost of Glasgow* - JOHANNESBURG (Art Gallery): *General Smuts* - KANSAS CITY (MISSOURI) (Nelson-Atkins Museum of Art): *Mrs. Cecil Wade (Mrs Cecil Wade)* (1886, oil on canvas) - LONDON (Imperial War Mus.): *Gassed Soldiers* - LONDON (National Portrait Gal.): *Coventry Patmore* (1894, oil on canvas); *Octavia Hill* (1898, oil on canvas); *Charles Russell, Baron Russell* (1900, oil on canvas, replica); *Henry James* (1913, oil on canvas); *General Officers of World War I* (1922, oil on canvas) - LONDON (NG): *Lord Ribblesdale* (1902, oil on canvas, portrait with subject standing) - LONDON (Tate Collection): *Study of Mme Gautreau* (c. 1884, oil on canvas); *Carnation, Lily, Lily, Rose* (1885-1886, oil on canvas); *Ellen Terry as Lady Macbeth* (1889, oil on canvas); *Claude Monet Painting by the Edge of a Wood* (1885?, oil on canvas, portraits of members of Wertheimer's family) - LONDON (Victoria and Albert Mus.): watercolour - MELBOURNE (Nat. Gal. of Victoria): *Hospital in Grenada*; *W. Brownlee* (sketch) - NEW YORK (Brooklyn Mus.): *Portrait of a Lady*; *Boats Out of the Water* (c. 1902-1909, watercolour); *Fire on the Mountain* (c. 1903-1908, watercolour); *In a Hayloft* (c. 1904-1907, watercolour); *Boboli* (1907, watercolour); *Port of Soller* (c. 1907-1908, watercolour); *Sleeping Violet* (c. 1907-1910, watercolour); *Pomegranates* (1908, watercolour); *White Boats* (1908, watercolour); *Simplon Bluff* (c. 1910, watercolour); *Aoste Valley, Rocks in a Torrent* (c. 1910); *Salmon River* (c. 1916, watercolour) - NEW YORK (Metropolitan Mus. of Art): *The Painter William A. Chase*; *Henry G. Marquand*; *Portrait of Madame Gautreau* (1883-1884); *The Wyndham Sisters*; *Two Ladies with parasols at Fladbury* (1889); *Miss Ch.L. Burkhardt*; *Mr and Mrs I.N. Phelps Stokes* (1897); *The Escutcheon of Charles V of Spain* (1912, watercolour) - PARIS (Mus. d'Orsay): *La Carmencita* (1890) - PORTLAND, ME (MA): *Mrs. Charles Pelham Curtis, née Ellen Sears Amory Anderson (Mrs Charles Pelham Curtis, née Ellen Sears Amory Anderson)* (1903, portrait) - RICHMOND (Virginia MFA): *Portrait of Mrs. Albert Vickers (Portrait of Mrs Albert Vickers)* (1884, oil on canvas); *The Sketchers (The Sketchers)* (c. 1913, oil on canvas) - ROME (Gal. Nazionale d'Arte Moderna): *The Painter Antonio Mancini* - THE HAGUE (Mesdag Museum): sketch - TOKYO (Museum of Fine Art): *The Poet Patmore* - WASHINGTON DC (Corcoran Gal. of Art): *Oyster Gatherers at Cancale* (1878) - WILLIAMSTOWN (Sterling and Francine Clark Art Institute): *Portrait of Carolus Duran* - WORCESTER (AM): *Venetian Water Carriers (Venetian Water Carriers)* (1880-1882, oil on canvas); *Muddy Alligators (Muddy Alligators)* (1917, watercolour).

AUCTION RECORDS:

LONDON, 30 April 1910, *Waiting*, GBP 504. PARIS, 23-24 June 1919, *Portrait of Madame G.*, FRF 14,200; *Moorish Woman* (watercolour) FRF 4,100. LONDON, 30 June 1922, *Church of Santa Maria della Salute, Venice* (drawing) GBP 399. PARIS, 13 June 1923, *Venice Under Grey Skies*, FRF 8,000. LONDON, 24-27 July 1925, *Florentine Palace* (drawing) GBP 210; *Pomegranate* (drawing) GBP 441; *Near Carrara* (drawing) GBP 1,050; *Women at Dawn* (drawing) GBP 861; *Isère Landscape* (drawing) GBP 892; *Villa Torlonia* (drawing) GBP 1,417; *A Venetian Canal* (drawing) GBP 4,830; *Javanese Dancer*, GBP 2,310; *Alpine Pond*, GBP 2,625; *Florence*, GBP 6,930; *Two Heads (Officers Meal)* (after Frans Hals) GBP 1,417; *Spinners* (after Velasquez) GBP 1,995; *Balthazar Carlos* (after Vélasquez) GBP 6,300. LONDON, 29 April 1927, *Loggia* (drawing) GBP 577; *Father Albera*, GBP 3,780; *Bohemian Encampment*, GBP 2,992. NEW YORK, 16 Nov 1933, *Laura Lister*, USD 15,600. PARIS, 18 Jan 1934, *Judith Gautier*, FRF 10,700; *Dunes at St Énogat*, FRF 18,000; *In the Garden* (watercolour) FRF 4,100. NEW YORK, 3 Dec 1936, *Storm over the Atlantic*, USD 1,350; *Madame Helleu*, GBP 4,700. NICE, 24 Feb 1949, *Woman in the Slate Blue Dressing Gown*, FRF 10,700. PARIS, 17 Dec 1954, *Spanish Dance* (Indian ink wash) FRF 42,000. NEW YORK, 11 Nov 1959, *Monet's Garden at Giverny*, USD 6,250. LONDON, 1 Dec 1961, *Javanese Dancer*, Gns 6,500. LONDON, 19 June 1964, *Santa Maria della Salute, Venice* (watercolour) Gns 800; *Temple in a Garden*, Gns 1,100. NEW YORK, 19 May 1965, *Portrait of a Lady*, USD 4,750. NEW YORK, 11 May 1966, *Game of Boules*, USD 12,500. LONDON, 13 Dec 1967, *Square of La Scuola San Rocco, Venice*, GBP 7,000. NEW YORK, 3 April 1968, *Claude Monet Painting in His Floating Studio*, USD 37,500. NEW YORK, 19 March 1969, *Portrait of Mrs Edward L. Davis and her Son, Sivingston Davis*, USD 72,500. PARIS, 6 Nov 1970, *Portrait of Judith Gautier* (watercolour) FRF 20,000. PARIS, 4 Dec 1970, *Dr Pozzi At Home*, FRF 420,000. LONDON, 27 June 1972, *Caroline de Bassano*, Gns 14,000. NEW YORK, 24 Jan 1973, *Woman LYING DOWN* (watercolour) USD 2,600. NEW YORK, 16 Oct 1974, *The Artist Dennis Bunker at Calcott* (1888) USD 60,000. LONDON, 5 March 1976, *View of Venice* (c. 1903-1904, watercolour, 20 x 14 ins / 51 x 35.5 cm) GBP 7,200. NEW YORK, 28 Oct 1976, *Patio* (1913, oil on canvas, 28 x 36 ins / 71.2 x 91.5 cm) USD 26,000. LONDON, 4 March 1977, *Eros and Psyche* (c. 1917, bronze, h. 12 ins / 30.5 cm) GBP 2,200. LONDON, 29 March 1977, *Mrs George Gribble* (1888, oil on canvas, 89 3/4 x 46 3/4 ins / 228 x 119 cm) GBP 5,500. NEW YORK, 22 March 1978, *Girgenti* (c. 1901, watercolour and pencil, 12 1/4 x 18 ins / 31 x 45.7 cm) USD 5,250. NEW YORK, 23 May 1979, *Cows Lying in the Field* (watercolour and gouache, 12 x 18 ins / 30.5 x 46 cm) USD 12,000. NEW YORK, 7 June 1979, *Ethel Barrymore* (pencil, 14 x 9 1/2 ins / 35.5 x 24.1 cm) USD 20,500. NEW YORK, 7 June 1979, *Portrait of Millicent, Duchess of Sutherland* (1904, oil on canvas, 100 x 57 1/2 ins / 254 x 146 cm) USD 210,000. NEW YORK, 25 Oct 1979, *Victory and Death in Combat* (c. 1922, patinated bronze, h. 12 1/4 ins / 31 cm) USD 19,000. LONDON, 25 May 1983, *Portrait of Mrs Gilbert Russell, née Maud Nelke* (1911, black chalk, 24 x 18 1/2 ins / 61 x 47 cm) GBP 2,600. NEW YORK, 3 June 1983, *Portrait of Mrs Ernest G. Raphael* (1905, oil on canvas, 64 1/2 x 44 3/4 ins / 163.8 x 113.7 cm) USD 300,000. NEW YORK, 21 Sept 1983, *Study of a Young Man* (1895, lithograph, 11 1/2 x 8 1/2 ins / 29.2 x 21.9 cm) USD 8,500. LONDON, 2 Nov 1983, *Palazzo Cavalli, Venice* (watercolour on pencil outlines heightened with gouache, 14 x 20 ins / 35.5 x 51 cm) GBP 85,000. LONDON, 15 May 1985, *Chess Game* (pen and wash, 10 x 15 ins / 25.5 x 38 cm) GBP 9,000. NEW YORK, 29 May 1986, *Mrs Cecil Wade* (1886, oil on canvas, 64 x 53 ins / 162.6 x 134.6 cm) USD 1,350,000. NEW YORK, 26 May 1988, *Portrait or Mrs Charles Stewart Carstairs, née Elizabeth Stebbins* (1914, charcoal/paper, 23 3/4 x 19 ins / 60.5 x 48 cm) USD 26,400. NEW YORK, 1 Dec 1988, *Karer See* (1914, watercolour and gouache/paper, 16 x 20 3/4 ins / 40.6 x 52.7 cm) USD 63,250. PARIS, 12 Dec 1988, *Miss Reubell Seated in Front of a Screen* (watercolour and gouache, 13 3/4 x 9 3/4 ins / 35 x 25 cm) FRF 675,000; *Boats Near La Salute, Venice* (drawing in lead pencil, 5 x 13 ins / 12.5 x 33 cm) FRF 24,500. NEW YORK, 24 Jan 1989, *Portrait of W.S. Gilbert* (pencil, 10 3/4 x 7 3/4 ins / 27.2 x 20 cm) USD 2,200. NEW YORK, 24 May 1989, *Carob Trees in Majorca* (oil on canvas, 22 1/2 x 28 1/2 ins / 57.1 x 72.4 cm) USD 55,000. NEW YORK, 30 Nov 1989, *Small Fruit Market* (1879, oil on card, 14 x 10 3/4 ins / 35.6 x 27.3 cm) USD 258,500. NEW YORK, 23 May 1990, *Portrait of Francis B. Chadwick* (1880, oil on panel, 13 3/4 x 9 3/4 ins / 35 x 25 cm) USD 143,000. NEW YORK, 24 May 1990, *Ena Wertheimer with Antonio Mancini* (1904, watercolour, gouache and pencil/card, 13 3/4 x 9 3/4 ins / 35 x 24.8 cm) USD 44,000. NEW YORK, 27 Sept 1990, *Portrait of Ramacho Ortigao* (1903, pencil/tinted paper, 15 x 10 ins / 38.3 x 25.3 cm) USD 23,100. NEW YORK, 29 Nov 1990, *Portrait of Marion Roller aged three* (1902, oil on canvas, 24 x 18 ins / 61 x 45.7 cm) USD 220,000. NEW YORK, 14 March 1991, *Coloured Paving Stones in Sicily* (watercolour/paper, 10 x 14 ins / 25.4 x 35.6 cm) USD 20,900. NEW YORK, 12 April 1991, *Pointy* (oil on panel, 10 3/4 x 8 1/2 ins / 27.3 x 21.6 cm) USD 34,100. NEW YORK, 5 Dec 1991, *Waiting*

- *Portrait of Frances Winifred Hill* (oil on canvas, 40 1/4 x 34 ins / 102.2 x 86.4 cm) USD 418,000. LONDON, 6 March 1992, *Reflections: Rocks and Water* (1908, watercolour and gouache, 9 3/4 x 11 3/4 ins / 25 x 30 cm) GBP 31,900. NEW YORK, 27 May 1992, *Male Model Resting* (oil on canvas, 22 x 28 ins / 55.9 x 71.1 cm) USD 66,000. LONDON, 5 June 1992, *Green Parasol* (pencil, watercolour and gouache, 18 3/4 x 13 3/4 ins / 47.5 x 35 cm) GBP 286,000. NEW YORK, 4 Dec 1992, *Portrait of Teresa Gosse* (oil on canvas, 24 x 20 ins / 61.2 x 51 cm) USD 242,000. NEW YORK, 26 May 1993, *Portrait of Major George Conrad Roller* (oil on canvas/card, 16 1/2 x 17 1/4 ins / 42 x 43.5 cm) USD 79,500. NEW YORK, 23 Sept 1993, *Portrait of Eleutherios Venizelos* (1924, charcoal/paper, 24 1/4 x 18 1/2 ins / 61.6 x 47 cm) USD 10,925. NEW YORK, 25 May 1994, *Spanish Dancer* (oil on canvas, 87 3/4 x 59 1/2 ins / 222.9 x 151.1 cm) USD 7,592,500. NEW YORK, 14 March 1996, *Storm over the Atlantic* (oil on canvas, 23 1/2 x 31 3/4 ins / 59.7 x 80.6 cm) USD 79,500. NEW YORK, 27 Sept 1996, *Mrs Asquith* (charcoal/paper, 21 1/4 x 14 3/4 ins / 54 x 37.3 cm) USD 17,250. PARIS, 22 Nov 1996, *Faust* (Indian ink wash heightened with gouache, 12 1/2 x 9 1/2 ins / 32 x 24 cm) FRF 68,000. NEW YORK, 5 Dec 1996, *Kashmir* (oil on canvas, 28 x 43 ins / 71.1 x 109.2 cm) USD 11,112,500. NEW YORK, 3 Dec 1997, *In the Garden, Corfu* (1909, oil on canvas, 36 x 28 ins / 91.4 x 71.1 cm) USD 8,362,500. NEW YORK, 21 May 1998, *Jerusalem* (oil on canvas, 28 x 22 ins / 71 x 56 cm) USD 550,000. NEW YORK, 2 Dec 1998, *Constellation - Rainy Day on Yacht* (1924, watercolour and pencil/paper/panel, 13 x 21 ins / 34 x 53 cm) USD 300,000. NEW YORK, 26 May 1999, *Moraine* (oil on canvas, 22 x 28 ins / 56 x 71 cm) USD 700,000. PARIS, 22 Nov 1999, *Edouard Pailleron Junior* (1879, oil on panel, 13 x 10 ins / 34 x 26 cm) FRF 2,950,000. NEW YORK, 29 Nov 2000, *Laurence Millet* (1887, oil on canvas, 30 x 20 ins / 77 x 51 cm) USD 950,000. NEW YORK, 29 Nov 2000, *Lady in the Alps Reading - the Cashmere shawl* (watercolour, 20 x 15 ins / 52 x 38 cm) USD 350,000. NEW YORK, 24 May 2001, *Portrait of Mrs Harry Vane Milbank* (1883, oil on canvas, 74 x 36 ins / 189 x 91 cm) USD 250,000. NEW YORK, 29 Nov 2001, *Portrait of Casper Goodrich* (oil on canvas, 26 x 19 ins / 66 x 49 cm) USD 1,400,000. NEW YORK, 22 May 2002, *Daisy, Princess of Pless* (charcoal, 24 x 19 ins / 61 x 48 cm) USD 75,000. NEW YORK, 4 Dec 2002, *Jacques Barenton* (1883, oil on canvas, 22 x 18 ins / 57 x 46 cm) USD 2,000,000. NEW YORK, 21 May 2003, *Vase Fountain, Pocantico* (watercolour and pencil, 21 x 16 ins / 53 x 40 cm) USD 270,000. LONDON, 11 June 2003, *Gassed* (1918-1919, oil on canvas, 11 x 27 ins / 27 x 69 cm) GBP 140,000. NEW YORK, 19 May 2004, *Robert Louis Stevenson and his Wife* (1885, oil on canvas, 20 x 24 ins / 51 x 61 cm) USD 7,850,000. NEW YORK, 1 Dec 2004, *Group with Parasols* (1905, oil on canvas, 22 x 28 ins / 55 x 71 cm) USD 21,000,000.

SARGENT, Louis
French, 19th century.
Born in Eu (Seine-Maritime).
Engraver (wood).

His brother was Alfred Louis Sargent. He exhibited at the Salon between 1863 and 1869.

SARGENT, Louis August
British, 20th century.
Born 14 October 1881; died 1965.
Painter. Landscapes, seascapes, still-lifes.

Louis August Sargent was active in London.

SARGENT, Walter
American, 19th - 20th century.
Born 7 May 1868, in Worcester (Massachusetts); died 19 September 1927, in North Scituate (Massachusetts).
Painter, illustrator. Landscapes.

Walter Sargent was the pupil of Léon Lhermitte and Paul-Louis Delance in Paris. He specialised in illustrating educational works.

SARGENTINO, Giuseppe
Italian, 19th century.
Died 1823, in Naples.
Active in Naples.
Painter.

SARGUES, Pierre de, or Salgues, called sometimes Pierre des Argues
French, 14th - 15th century.
Died 1417.
Active in Lyons.
Painter.

Pierre de Sargues was 'master painter' of Lyons Cathedral in 1362.

SARI, Arsène Étienne
French, 20th century.
Born 7 October 1895, in Marseilles.
Painter, sculptor. Landscapes.

Arsène Étienne Sari was a self-taught painter, but as a young man he had the good fortune to receive advice from Renoir, was a friend of Bourdelle, knew Albert André, and worked with Guillaumin. Reclusive by nature, he lived near Nice and the coast, and he exhibited rarely; though in 1920 he was represented in an exhibition that included works by Guillaumin, Lebourg, Luce, Maufra and Utrillo. The big Paris dealers exhibited his paintings in solo shows in 1960 and 1970, but he did not reach a wide public. He was much influenced by Renoir, Pissarro and Seyssaud, but he had a certain personal skill.

MUSEUMS AND GALLERIES:
MARSEILLES (Mus. Cantini): *Sunflowers* - PARIS (MAMVP).

AUCTION RECORDS:
NEUILLY, 12 Dec 1993, *Gemenos in a Storm* (oil on canvas, 35 1/2 x 46 ins / 90 x 116 cm) FRF 14,500.

SARIANKO. See **SARYANKO Sergei Konstantinovich**

SARIGA, Giuseppe
Italian, 18th century.
Born to a family originally from Tessin, Germany; died before 1782.
Painter.

Giuseppe Sariga was a court painter in Turin and produced works for the cathedral in Chieri.

SARIÑENA, Juan. See **ZARIÑENA Juan**

SARJEANT, John. See **SARGEANT**

SARJENT, Francis John
British, 18th - 19th century.
Active in London at the beginning of the 19th century.
Watercolourist. Landscapes.

Francis Sarjent was a Royal Academy exhibitor in 1802 and 1803.

MUSEUMS AND GALLERIES:
LONDON (Victoria and Albert Mus.): *View of London; Landscape.*

AUCTION RECORDS:
LONDON, 21 Nov 1985, *London from Greenwich Park* (watercolour, 21 1/2 x 30 1/2 ins / 54.5 x 77.5 cm) GBP 900.

SARJENT, G. R., or Serjent
British, 19th century.
Painter. Landscapes, architectural views, church interiors.

G. R. Sarjent exhibited at London's Royal Academy from 1811 to 1849, and produced numerous views of church interiors.

AUCTION RECORDS:
LONDON, 11 Oct 1996, *View of Constantinople* (oil on canvas, 10 x 14 1/4 ins / 25.5 x 36 cm) GBP 2,760.

SARJETZKIJ. See **SARZHETSKY**

SARKA, Charles Nicolas
American, 20th century.
Born 6 December 1879, in Chicago; died 1960.
Watercolourist, draughtsman, illustrator, poster artist.
Charles Nicolas Sarka travelled widely - Florida and southern California, the South Seas, Hawaii, Egypt, Morocco, the Caribbean and Europe - which provided the subject-matter for his artistic output.

SARKADI, Emil
Hungarian, 20th century.
Born 21 September 1881, in Vienna; died 24 June 1908, in Békéscsaba.
Painter, draughtsman, illustrator.
Emil Sarkadi studied in Budapest, Vienna and Munich and is noted for his ex-libris designs and his illustrations for satirical reviews such as *Le Rire* and *Simplicissimus*.

SARKANTYU, Simon
Hungarian, 20th century.
Born 1921.
Painter. History painting, landscapes, still-lifes.
Simon Sarkantyu was a student at the school of fine art in Budapest from 1941 to 1944 and at various private academies. He executed decorative murals at the Madach Theatre in Budapest and taught at the school of fine art in Budapest from 1960. Sarkantyu featured in collective exhibitions including: Paris (1959) and Venice Biennale (1966). He was awarded the Munkácsy Prize.
BIBLIOGRAPHY:
Hongrie 68, Pannonia, Budapest, 1968.

SARKANY, Gyula or Julius
Hungarian, 20th century.
Born 22 February 1887, in Szentek.
Painter.
Gyula Sarkany studied in Budapest, Munich and Paris. He lived in Budapest.
MUSEUMS AND GALLERIES:
BUDAPEST (Szépmuvészeti Múz.): *The Misanthropist*.

SARKER, Surita
Indian, 20th century.
Painter, draughtsman, illustrator.
Like a number of her compatriots, Surita Sarker has dealt with themes from the epic poem, the *Ramayana*.

SARKIS, pseudonym of Zabunyan, Sarkis
Armenian, 20th century.
Born 1938, in Istanbul.
Active in France from 1964.
Painter, watercolourist, sculptor of assemblages, installation artist. Multimedia.
Conceptual Art, Art Narratif.
After studying in Istanbul from 1957 to 1960, Sarkis began to paint. He worked in Paris from 1964 onwards and taught at the École des Arts Décoratifs in Strasbourg. Between 1960 and 1964, before his arrival in Paris, Sarkis' paintings expressed a revolutionary cry and he made references to Munch and Orozco. Until 1967 Sarkis belonged to the 'Nouvelle Figuration' movement in Paris, the European version of the return to reality inaugurated by the American Pop Artists, and shown at the Salon de la Jeune Peinture or at the *Figuration narrative* exhibition in 1965. He was painting at that time with traditional materials, often in stencilled series or producing collages.

The discovery of Joseph Beuys and Conceptual Art, not to mention Duchamp, led him to a period of reflection, at the end of which, having decided to take part in the conceptual movement then booming following the anti-establishment events of 1968, he featured in 1969 at the historic exhibition in Bern *When Attitudes Become Form* with Alain Jacquet. They were the only two artists living in France who had been invited. From this moment on, Sarkis' activity is difficult to pinpoint in the broadest conceptual context. He designed his exhibitions as selective, visual, sound and sensory stage sets, into which the spectator can and must enter, each set showing a moment in time in his mental development. He organized them according to the space at the location of the event, gallery, museum, church, disused building or factory. He unpacked, opened, assembled and installed a paraphernalia of accessories including neon lights for colour and wall projections for visual animation, atmospheric sound from a hoarse tape, familiar and even mythical objects, usually anonymous or unidentifiable. He added little icons he painted, memory trails, inextricable tangles of music tapes, unwound and finally silent. He wanted to cast doubt on their effectiveness as symbols of memory, these with the statuette of a blacksmith, a tiger's effigy and a fishing boat, were recurrent features identifying his operations. It should be pointed out that Sarkis did not completely abandon painting: for each installation he drew a plan first, which he coloured in watercolour, neatly explaining that 'the colour is diluted in water as light is in space'. An Eastern storyteller, through each object he produced with his own hands, he told stories and told himself tales, the titles of which he sometimes provided. At *Les Trésors du captain Sarkis*, Villeurbanne (1985) he showed wholly personal stories (*I Love My Lulu*), philosophical tales (*Rideau de la fin des siècles*), epic and sound stories (*Le Son du choc de Garuda avec la sculpture en fer coloré*). He never failed to put himself at the centre of the action as in *La Femme du peintre en bâtiment rêve les expositions de Sarkis* or *Le Forgeron et le Mineur en masques de Sarkis*.

In his strategy of juxtaposition of veiled/unveiled, familiar with military metaphors, Sarkis continued his series *Black-out* (1974 to 1978) which was taken over from 1976 by the series *Kriegsschatz* (*War treasure*). The black-out denoted camouflage, the act of hiding in order to reappear more effectively, the war treasure denoted the spoils of war, kidnapping, pillage and appropriation. He described himself as 'Captain Sarkis', claiming responsibility for his campaigns of conquests and plundering; a friendly, though totally egocentric character, he announced himself in the third person and found it easy to be authoritarian and actually triumphant, if only for his ability to impose his eclectic method of expression. Because of the eclectic nature of his assemblages and installations, some commentators consider Sarkis elusive as an artist. While the poverty of his materials prompted his assimilation into Arte Povera, Sarkis considered himself an Expressionist.

Sarkis took part in many collective exhibitions, including: Turkey (from 1961); *La Fête à la Joconde*, Paris 1965; *Figuration narrative*, Paris (1965); *Schèmes 66*, Musée d'Art Moderne, Paris (1966); Salon de la Jeune Peinture, Paris (1966 and 1967); *Le Monde en Question* (*The World in Question*), Musée d'Art Moderne, Paris (1967); Biennale des Jeunes Artistes, Paris; Mostra Premio Lissone, Milan; *When Attitudes Become Form*, Kunsthalle, Bern (1969); Institute of Contemporary Art, London (1969); Salon de Mai, Paris (from 1969); Krefeld museum (1970); *100 artistes dans la ville* (*100 Artists in the City*), Montpellier (1970); Documenta 7, Kassel (1982); *Electra*, Musée d'Art moderne de la Ville de Paris (1983); *Magiciens de la terre* (*Magicians of the Earth*), Centre Beaubourg, Paris (1989); *Les Années 70: l'art en cause* (*The 1970s: Art in Question*), Capc Musée d'Art Contemporain, Bordeaux (2002); *L'état des choses* (*The State of Things*), as part of *Trésors publics, 20 ans de création dans les Fonds régionaux d'art contemporain (FRAC)* (*Public Treasury, 20 Years of Creation in the Regional Collection of Contemporary Art (FRAC)*), Musée des Beaux-Arts, Nantes (2003) and exhibitions looking at the status of everyday objects in contemporary art.

Solo exhibitions, installations or events include: Istanbul (1960, 1963); Ankara (1962); Paris (1967, 1970); Musée d'Art moderne de la Ville de Paris with Boltanski. He also held solo exhibitions in galleries and art centres including: Galerie Sonnabend, Paris (1979); *Les Trésors du captain Sarkis* (*Captain Sarkis' Treasures*), Villeurbanne (1985); *Ma chambre de la rue Krutenau en satellite* (*My Room at Rue Krutenau by Satellite*) and *103 Watercolours*, La Vielle Douane, Strasbourg (1989); *Sarkis interpète le musée Constantin Meunier* (*Sarkis' version of the Musée Constantin Meunier*) and *Le Forgeron en masque de Sarkis, en rouge et vert, regarde l'atelier d'Antoine Wiertz* (*The Blacksmith as Sakis, in Red and Green, at Antoine Wiertz' Studio*), in the two venues mentioned in the titles, Brussels (1989); Galerie Éric Fabre, Paris (1990); *13 Ikônes en aquarelle et néon* (*13 Icons in Watercolour and Neon*), FIAC (Foire Internationale d'Art Contemporain); *Elle danse dans l'atelier de Sarkis avec le quatuor n° 15 de Dimitri Shostakovich* (*She Dances in Sarkis' Studio to the Quatuor n° 15 by Dimitri Shostakovich*), Galerie de Paris; *Scènes de nuit, scènes de jour* (*Night Scenes, Day Scenes*), Centre National d'Art Contemporain, Grenoble (1992); Musée des beaux-arts, Nantes (1997); Capc Museum of Contemporary Art, Bordeaux (2000); *Transflammation*, FRAC des Pays-de-la-Loire, Carquefou (2001); Musée d'Art Contemporain, Lyons (2002); *Trésor de Mnémosyne de Sarkis*, Musée de Frontignan (2003); *Sarkis, l'atterrisage adagio*, Musée Picasso, Antibes (2003).

Sarkis executed a State commissioned work in Sélestat. This was inaugurated in 1993. Through *Le Point de Rencontre: Le Rêve* he was able to adapt his usually selective, fleeting strategy to a real and lasting context, an organized activity around a river, its lock and a fortification rampart; he included in his design the surrounding site, street, quay, trees. The various components were placed in a meaningful context with red neon lights and enamelled plates with texts linked to the location. He also produced stained glass windows for the abbey in Silvacane.

BIBLIOGRAPHY:

Borgeaud, Bernard, '*Sarkis, Mécano + Goudron*' in *Opus international*, periodical, Paris, 1970. Clair, Jean, '*Expressionnisme 70*' in *Chroniques de l'Art Vivant*, periodical, Maeght, Paris, October 1970. Martin, J.H./Harding, A./Rossignol, C., *Trois mises en scène de Sarkis*, Éd. Lebeer Hossmann, Brussels, 1985. Touratier, J.-M., *Vie et légende du Captain Sarkis*, Pictura-Edelweiss, Toulouse, 1986. Zabunyan, Elvan, '*La Lampe du corps, c'est l'œil*' in *Sarkis - 103 aquarelles*, exhibition catalogue, Musées de Strasbourg, Strasbourg, 1989. Cousseau, Henry Claude, *42 heures du loup - Ici, la nuit est immense - Sarkis*, Musée des Beaux-Arts, Nantes, 1989. Lawless, Catherine, *Artistes et ateliers*, Éd. Jacqueline Chambon, Nîmes, 1990. Aubert, Jean/Ananth, Deepak/Köksal, Aykut/Allemand-Cosneau, Claude, *Au commencement le son de la lumière à l'arrivée, Sarkis*, exhibition catalogue, Musée des Beaux-Arts, Nantes, 1997. Cousseau, Henry Claude/Enrici, Michel/Fleckner, Uwe/Bullot, Erik, *Sarkis*, exhibition catalogue, Capc Musée d'Art contemporain, Bordeaux, 2000. Fréruchet, Maurice, et al., *Les Années soixante-dix: l'art en cause*, exhibition catalogue, Capc Musée d'Art contemporain, Bordeaux, 2002. Zahm, Olivier (preface), et al., *Trésors publics, 20 ans de création dans les Fonds régionaux d'art contemporain*, Flammarion, Paris, 2003 (text in French and English).

MUSEUMS AND GALLERIES:

BASEL (Kunstmus.) - CARQUEFOU (FRAC Pays de la Loire): *Froid au Dos* (1993, installation) - GENEVA (Mamco): *Travel Workshop* - LYONS (FRAC Rhône-Alpes): *Le forgeron dans le rôle de Kriegsschatz* (*Blacksmith in the Role of Kriegsschatz*) (1983) - MARSEILLES (Mus. Cantini): *The Twelve Kriegsschatz Flags* (1980, installation); *Flags, Miner, Blacksmith and Miner in Sarkis' Masks* (1980, watercolour) - NANTES (MBA) - PARIS (FRAC Île-de-France): *Gold Coast* (1984, installation) - PARIS (MAMVP) - PARIS (MNAM-CCI).

AUCTION RECORDS:

PARIS, 16 Oct 1988, *Study on a Musical Sculpture* (1984, watercolour and pencil, 28 x 36 1/2 ins / 71 x 93 cm) FRF 20,000. PARIS, 6 Dec 1993, *Made in Turkey 3* (1967, collage of photograph, 17 1/4 x 24 ins / 44 x 61 cm) FRF 5,000. PARIS, 3 April 1998, *Untitled* (1964, oil on paper and report photograph mounted on panel, 28 3/4 x 36 1/4 ins / 73 x 92 cm) FRF 6,500.

SARKISIAN, Paul

American, 20th century.
Born 1928, in Chicago.
Painter, collage artist.

Paul Sarkisian studied at the Chicago Institute of Art. During the 1950s he produced huge abstract, generally monochrome, canvases. He later returned to this format, but at the beginning of the sixties he began to work on a series of tiny collages. His work also oscillates between Surreal compositions and works with a more direct realism - sometimes with almost documentary overtones. Sarkisian does not, however, depict the aggressively showy side of American civilisation, as, it might be argued, is the case with Richard Estes, Don Eddy or John Salt. His drawings use monochrome black against a coloured background. Surreal fiction is never absent from Sarkisian's paintings; seeking to achieve a 'colour-less' status, hoping to make the 'painted picture' disappear, he attempts to render his illusions 'real' - an echo of photographic realism. Sarkisian's work has featured in many collective exhibitions since 1965, including the Documenta V in Kassel in 1972.

BIBLIOGRAPHY:

Sarkisian, Paul, *Paul Sarkisian: Paintings*, Arts Club of Chicago, Chicago, 1979.

MUSEUMS AND GALLERIES:

SAN FRANCISCO (MoMA): *Untitled (Waynesboro, PA)* (1969, acrylic on canvas).

AUCTION RECORDS:

NEW YORK, 4 May 1989, *Untitled 12* (acrylic/fabric, 46 x 48 ins / 116.8 x 122 cm) USD 19,800. LOS ANGELES, 2 May 2004, *Five Envelopes with Landscape* (1976, mixed media on paper, 28 x 36 ins / 71 x 91 cm) USD 3,500.

SARKISSIAN, Raffy

Lebanese, 20th century.
Born 1945, in Beirut.
Sculptor. Figures.

Raffy Sarkissian graduated from the École des Beaux-Arts, Paris, in 1975. He had a major exhibition in 1987 at the Galerie Bernier, Valence, including a number of bronzes.

SARKISSOFF, Maurice, called Sarki

Swiss, 20th century.
Born 3 January 1882, in Geneva; died 1946.
Sculptor. Nudes.

Maurice Sarkissoff was influenced by the work of A. von Niederhausen.

MUSEUMS AND GALLERIES:

GENEVA - SOLOTHURN.

AUCTION RECORDS:

LUCERNE, 15 May 1993, *Standing Female Nude* (1930, lost-wax bronze, h. 19 ins / 48 cm) CHF 2,600.

SARLIN, Robert

French, 20th century.
Born 1 April 1887, in Paris.
Sculptor. Portraits.

Robert Sarlin, a pupil of Hannaux, exhibited in Paris at the Salon des Artistes Français, of which he was a member from

1921. He was made a Chevalier of the Légion d'Honneur and awarded the Croix de Guerre.

SARLUIS, Léonard
Dutch, 19th - 20th century.
Born 21 October 1874, in The Hague; died 1949, in France.
Active then naturalised in France.
Painter, illustrator. Mythological subjects, portraits. Symbolism.

Léonard Sarluis arrived in Paris in 1894 when he was 20 years old and quickly became a well-known *boulevardier*. He travelled extensively, notably to Italy (Naples) and Russia. Oscar Wilde and Jean Lorrain sang his praises but, for all that, he remains something of a twilight figure, vacillating between Classicism and the still dubious affectations of the 'Modern Style'.

He is perhaps best remembered for his decorative illustrations for the refectory bar at the Paris daily *Le Journal*. He worked for years on a *Mystic Interpretation of the Bible*, the paintings for which featured in his London exhibition. These Symbolist compositions are astonishingly detailed and decorative, incorporating a welter of mythological elements. He also illustrated Gaston de Pavlowski's *Voyage to the Land of the Fourth Dimension* which, according to Jean Clair, was the inspiration behind Marcel Duchamp's *Large Glass*.

Sarluis exhibited his work at the Salon de la Rose Croix, the Salon des Artistes Français, a number of privately owned galleries in Paris and, in 1928, in London.

SARLUIS

SARLUIS

BIBLIOGRAPHY:
Halturin, Aleksandr/Hulten, Pontus/Gunar, Karl (ed.), *Paris-Moscou*, group exhibition catalogue, Éd. du Centre Georges-Pompidou, Paris, 1979.

AUCTION RECORDS:
PARIS, 24 Nov 1922, *Drunkenness of Apollo*, FRF 210. PARIS, 16 Feb 1927, *Russian Lady*, FRF 650. PARIS, 11 Dec 1946, *Heads of Women* (oils on canvas, two) FRF 6,000. PARIS, 7 March 1949, *Venus*, FRF 5,000. PARIS, 3 April 1973, *Mythological Themes* (oils on canvas, eight) FRF 16,500. PARIS, 25 Nov 1977, *The Gods* (1921, oil on canvas, 118 x 82 3/4 ins / 300 x 210 cm) FRF 12,500. ENGHIEN-LES-BAINS, 28 Oct 1979, *Mystic Scene* (gouache and watercolour, 16 1/4 x 13 ins / 41 x 33 cm) FRF 17,000. ENGHIEN-LES-BAINS, 28 Oct 1979, *Self-portrait* (1911, oil on panel, 17 1/4 x 11 1/4 ins / 44 x 28.5 cm) FRF 22,000. ENGHIEN-LES-BAINS, 24 May 1981, *David* (coloured pencil and red chalk, 7 x 5 1/4 ins / 18 x 13.3 cm) CHF 4,000. PARIS, 27 May 1982, *Allegorical Evocation* (1921, red chalk and Indian ink, 29 1/2 x 22 ins / 75 x 55 cm) FRF 18,000. PARIS, 29 June 1984, *Two Young People with the Back View of a Woman* (1921, oil on canvas, monochrome sepia paint, 101 1/4 x 61 1/4 ins / 257 x 155.5 cm) FRF 80,000. PARIS, 13 June 1986, *Young Wrestlers* (1937, paint/paper, 16 1/2 x 11 1/2 ins / 42 x 29 cm) FRF 41,000. PARIS, 3 Feb 1988, *Gorgon* (oil on canvas, 36 1/4 x 83 1/2 ins / 92 x 212 cm) FRF 70,000. PARIS, 26 Oct 1988, *Moses* (oil on canvas, 39 1/4 x 30 ins / 100 x 76 cm) FRF 14,000. LE TOUQUET, 8 June 1992, *Venus and Eros* (oil on canvas, 87 1/2 x 115 3/4 ins / 222 x 294 cm) FRF 69,500. NEW YORK, 30 June 1993, *Portrait of a Female Nude* (1931, oil on canvas, 40 x 29 3/4 ins / 101.6 x 75.6 cm) USD 2,300. PARIS, 29 April 1994, *Symbolist Scenes* (red chalk and Indian ink, a pair, 9 3/4 x 6 3/4 ins / 25 x 17 cm) FRF 5,000. PARIS, 16 Oct 1994, *Portrait of the Artist's Mother* (oil on panel, 25 1/2 x 18 1/2 ins / 65 x 47 cm) FRF 15,000.

SARMENTO, Julião
Portuguese, 20th - 21st century.
Born 1948.
Painter. Figure compositions.

Julião Sarmento gained a reputation through his photographic work during the 1970s, which earned him an association with conceptual and narrative art. Since the early 1980s, he has painted on surfaces divided into several rectangles made up of different materials. He paints each of these different compartments using a different technique. His work deals with images and tales taken from everyday life, films or fashion magazines, different subjects surrounding the central figure of man and the body such as eroticism or violence. The seduction of this painting lies in these chromatic pursuits and their elegant, skilful material effects. The formal purification increased in his work between 1989 and 1990, the use of white and black becoming more widespread, while the system of composition through juxtaposition leaves room for a more open, unresolved situation.

He held a solo exhibition in Paris in 1991.

BIBLIOGRAPHY:
Melo, Alexandre/Pinharanda, João, *Arte contemporânea portuguesa*, Grafispaço, Lisbon, 1986. '*Julia Sarmento*' in *Art Press* n° 157, periodical, Paris, April 1991.

AUCTION RECORDS:
AMSTERDAM, 9 Dec 1992, *The Scandalous Chronicle No. 679* (mixed media/paper, 25 1/2 x 19 3/4 ins / 64.5 x 50 cm) NLG 4,600. PARIS, 27 March 1996, *No. 408* (1985, oil on canvas, 70 3/4 x 53 1/4 ins / 180 x 135 cm) FRF 30,000. PARIS, 12 April 1999, *Untitled no. 578* (1987, mixed media on paper, 28 x 20 ins / 70 x 50 cm) FRF 25,000. NEW YORK, 17 Nov 1999, *Holding and Showing* (1995, graphite, 14 x 14 ins / 36 x 36 cm) USD 5,000. NEW YORK, 18 May 2000, *Foot and Mouth Disease* (acrylic on canvas, 76 x 60 ins / 193 x 152 cm) USD 35,000. NEW YORK, 17 Nov 2000, *Place Within us she Moves* (1997, graphite, 28 x 39 ins / 70 x 100 cm) USD 20,000. LONDON, 7 Feb 2003, *Savannah no. 442* (1985, acrylic and mixed media on canvas, 101 x 74 ins / 256 x 188 cm) GBP 34,000. LONDON, 27 June 2003, *Purloined Letter* (1989, mixed media on canvas, 74 x 83 ins / 189 x 210 cm) GBP 22,000. LONDON, 5 Feb 2004, *Emma 4* (1990-1991, acrylic, graphite and sand on canvas, 74 x 87 ins / 189 x 220 cm) GBP 42,000. NEW YORK, 13 May 2004, *Suffering, Despair and Ascent* (1997, oil on canvas, in three parts, 113 x 272 ins / 287 x 690 cm) USD 90,000.

SARMENTO GEORGIO (Viscount of Morses)
Portuguese, 20th century.
Born 1866; died 1922.
Painter, draughtsman. Portraits.

MUSEUMS AND GALLERIES:
LONDON (NG): *Marie Louise de la Ramée* (1904, red chalk).

SARMIENTO, Teresa (Duchess of Béjar)
Spanish, 17th century.
Painter. History painting.

Teresa Sarmiento worked for churches in Madrid.

SARNARI, Franco
Italian, 20th century.
Born 1933, in Rome.
Painter.

AUCTION RECORDS:
ROME, 18 May 1976, *About Love* (1968, oil on canvas, 83 x 45 1/4 ins / 211 x 115 cm) ITL 750,000. ROME, 15 Nov 1988, *Fragment* (1973, oil on shaped canvas, 39 1/4 x 37 1/2 ins / 100 x 95 cm) ITL 2,800,000. MILAN, 20 March 1989, *Fragment* (1974, oil on canvas, 22 1/2 x 23 1/2 ins / 57 x 60 cm) ITL 2,000,000. ROME, 17 April 1989, *Portrait of Pina* (1966, oil on canvas, 10 1/4 x 12 1/4 ins / 26 x 31 cm) ITL 1,600,000. MILAN, 14 April 1992, *Homage to Ingres* (oil on canvas, 37 x 37 1/2 ins / 94 x 95 cm) ITL 5,000,000. ROME, 14 June 1994, *Fragment 64* (1974, oil on shaped canvas, 39 1/4 x 37 1/2 ins / 100 x 95 cm)

ITL 3,450,000. ROME, 25 Nov 1999, *Large Fragment* (1977, oil on canvas, 51 x 53 ins / 130 x 135 cm) ITL 7,000,000. ROME, 13 May 2000, *Still-life with Wine Glass* (1998, oil on canvas, 18 x 20 ins / 46 x 52 cm) ITL 5,200,000. ROME, 21 May 2001, *Homage to Ingres* (1979, oil on canvas, 37 x 37 ins / 95 x 94 cm) ITL 10,000,000. ROME, 10 April 2003, *Still-life 2* (oil on canvas, 16 x 20 ins / 40 x 50 cm) EUR 2,100. ROME, 18 Nov 2003, *Perspective* (oil on canvas, 28 x 48 ins / 70 x 122 cm) EUR 2,850.

SARNECKI, Fabian
Polish, 19th century.
Born 1800, near Kalisz; died 1894, in Posen (now Poznan).
Painter, lithographer, copyist, art restorer. Genre scenes.
Fabian Sarnecki studied in Berlin and Paris, and settled in Posen, where he lost his sight. The Mielzynski museum in that town owns his *Woman with a Little Dog* and *Rinaldo on the Watch*.

SARNEEL, Ko
Dutch, 20th century.
Born 1926, in 's Hertogenbosch.
Painter. Scenes with figures, landscapes.
Ko Sarneel is best known for his landscapes, including those painted in winter, and a *View of Rome* painted on a trip in Italy.

SARNELLI, Antonio
Italian, 18th century.
Active in Naples from 1742 to 1793.
Painter.
Antonio Sarnelli was the brother of Gennaro and Giovanni Sarnelli and the pupil of Paolo de Matteis. He painted numerous frescoes and altarpieces for churches in Naples.
AUCTION RECORDS:
ROME, 28 May 1985, *Annunciation* (oil on canvas, 70 x 78¾in/178 x 200cm) ITL 3,000,000.

SARNELLI, Gennaro
Italian, 18th century.
Active in Naples during the second half of the 18th century.
Painter.
The brother of Antonio and Giovanni Sarnelli, Gennaro Sarnelli died young.

SARNELLI, Giovanni
Italian, 18th century.
Active in Naples from 1761 to 1781.
Painter.
The brother of Antonio and Gennaro Sarnelli and the pupil of Paolo de Matteis, Giovanni Sarnelli painted frescoes and altarpieces for churches in Naples, frequently in collaboration with his brother Antonio.
AUCTION RECORDS:
LONDON, 13 March 1963, *Portrait of a Musician,* GBP 400.

SARNEY
British, 18th century.
Active in London from 1766 to 1767.
Miniaturist.

SARNIGUET, Emilio J.
Argentinian, 20th century.
Born 1887, in Buenos Aires; died 1943, in Buenos Aires.
Sculptor.
Emilio J. Sarniguet obtained a grant which enabled him to visit Paris, where he exhibited at the Salon des Artistes Français from 1910 to 1913. His work as a whole displays a strong sense of drama.

SARNO, Giuseppe
Italian, 18th century.
Sculptor (wood), modeller.
Giuseppe Sarno worked for churches in Naples and the surrounding area, and is noted in particular for the figurines he made for nativity scenes.
MUSEUMS AND GALLERIES:
NAPLES (Mus. Civico): *Nativity Figurines*.

SAROFINI, Baldo de
Italian, 15th century.
Active in Perugia at the end of the 15th century.
Painter.
MUSEUMS AND GALLERIES:
URBINO (Gal. Nazionale Delle Marche): *Madonna and Child with Angels*.

SAROLO DA MURO
Italian, 12th - 13th century.
Active in Muro.
Sculptor, architect.
Brother of Ruggiero da Muro, with whom he built the porch of the church of S Maria di Perno, near S Fede, in 1190.

SARONI, Sergio
Italian, 20th century.
Born 1935 or 1938, in Turin; died 1990, in Turin.
Painter, engraver.
Sergio Saroni studied at the Turin academy of fine art and later became a professor at the Liceo Aristico in the same city. After 1957, he worked in a somewhat abstract expressionist style reminiscent of De Kooning but also related to the *art informel* in vogue in Italy in the 1950s thanks to the work of Wols, Mathieu and particularly Fautrier.

He took part in several collective exhibitions including: Venice Biennale 1956, 1958 and 1962; Pittsburgh International Exhibition put on by the Carnegie Foundation, 1958; São Paulo Biennale, 1959; the exhibition *Attraverso l'Immagine* (*Through the Image*) at the Centro culturale in Cremona. He was awarded many prizes including the Michetti in Francavilla al Mare in 1960; the Spiga in Milan in 1961; the La Spezia in Milan and the Manazzotti in Milan in 1963.

BIBLIOGRAPHY:
Attraverso l'immagine, exhibition catalogue, Centro culturale Santa Maria della Pietà, Cremona, 1995.
AUCTION RECORDS:
MILAN, 16 Oct 1973, *St Peter and the Thistle,* ITL 650,000. MILAN, 19 Dec 1978, *O.L.S.D. Selector* (1973, acrylic/canvas, 57 x 39¼ ins / 145 x 100 cm) ITL 1,100,000. MILAN, 14 Dec 1988, *Composition* (oil on canvas, 23½ x 19¾ ins / 60 x 50 cm) ITL 1,400,000. MILAN, 27 March 1990, *Scythe* (1977, acrylic/canvas, 32 x 25½ ins / 81 x 65 cm) ITL 1,000,000. MILAN, 14 April 1992, *Wounded Person* (oil on canvas, 59 x 47¼ ins / 150 x 120 cm) ITL 11,500,000. MILAN, 16 Nov 1993, *Impression, Study for the Allegory of the Heart* (1957, oil on canvas, 15¾ x 19¾ ins / 40 x 50 cm) ITL 4,600,000. MILAN, 14 Dec 1993, *Human Figure and Object* (1970, acrylic/canvas, 31½ x 31½ ins / 80 x 80 cm) ITL 1,495,000.

SAROUDNYĬ. See **SARUDNYI Ivan Petrovich**

SARP, Gerda Ploug
Danish, 20th century.
Born 8 December 1881, in Copenhagen.
Painter, illustrator. Portraits.
Gerda Ploug Sarp was the wife of the painter Otto Sörensen. She produced illustrations for Danish periodicals.

SARPEDON
3rd century BC.
Active c. 250 BC.
Sculptor.

Ancient Greek.
Sarpedon sculpted a *Statue of Dionysus* at Delos.

SARPENTIERO, Pietro Antonio
Italian, 18th century.
Born in Sagliano Micca, near Biella (Piedmont).
Active during the second half of the 18th century.
Sculptor (wood).
Sarpentiero sculpted numerous statues for churches in Piedmont in a realist and often grotesque style.

SARRA, Charles Léopold, called Desvarennes
French, 18th century.
Born 1702, in Nancy; died 15 July 1774, in Nancy.
Painter.
Sarra was painter to Duke Stanislaus.

SARRABAT, Daniel I
French, 17th century.
Born 1612; died 26 September 1669, in Paris.
Engraver, stonemason.
Daniel Sarrabat I was the uncle of Daniel Sarrabat II.

SARRABAT, Daniel II, or Sarabat
French, 17th - 18th century.
Born 1666, in Paris; died 21 June 1748, in Lyons.
Painter. History painting.
Daniel Sarrabat II won the second prize for painting in 1686, third prize in 1687 and first prize in 1688. He became an associate of the Académie in 1702, but did not become an Academician.
MUSEUMS AND GALLERIES:
PARIS (ENSBA): *Noah Leaving the Ark* - POMMERSFELDEN: *Moses and Jethro.*
AUCTION RECORDS:
PARIS, 10 Nov 1948, *Introduction of the Courtesan* (attributed) FRF 8,800.

SARRABAT, Isaac
French, 18th century.
Born c. 1680, in Les Andelys (Eure).
Engraver (mezzotint), print publisher.
Isaac Sarrabat was one of the first French artists to engrave in mezzotint, but did not demonstrate great skill. He depicted religious subjects, genre scenes and portraits.

SARRABEZOLLES, Charles or Carlo
French, 20th century.
Born 27 December 1888, in Toulouse; died 11 February 1971, in Paris.
Sculptor. Portraits. Monuments, groups.
Charles Sarrabezolles was a pupil of Antonin Mercié and Louis Marqueste. Although a large part of his work was religious sculpture, he also carved memorials and portraits. He was the inventor of the technique of cutting directly into concrete, which he used in the church of St-Louis, Marseilles, and the figures on the tower of the church of Villemomble (Seine-St-Denis). He also sculpted a bronze group, *The Elements*, on a wing of the Palais de Chaillot, Paris, and the *Spirit of the Sea* on the French Embassy in Belgrade.

Sarrabezolles exhibited regularly until 1932 at the Salon des Artistes Français, of which he was a member. He was awarded the Second Grand Prix de Rome in 1914, a silver medal in 1921, the Prix National in 1922, two gold medals at the Salon des Arts Décoratifs in 1925, the Grand Prix at the Exposition Universelle of 1937, and the Légion d'Honneur in 1932.
BIBLIOGRAPHY:
Lenormand-Romain, Antoinette/Bréon, Emmanuel, et al., *Sarrabezolles, sculpteur et statuaire*, Somogy, Paris, 2003.
AUCTION RECORDS:
PARIS, 8 Dec 1995, *Allegory of Victory* (bronze, h. 22 ins / 55 cm) FRF 4,000.

SARRACINO
Spanish, 10th century.
Active in the second half of the 10th century.
Miniaturist.
The Escorial Library has a *Codex Albeldensis* that Sarracino illuminated with miniatures.

SARRADE, Lucienne Marie Thérèse
French, 20th century.
Born 21 July 1903, in Air-sur-Adour (Landes); died 8 January 1987, in Air-sur-Adour.
Painter (including gouache), collage artist. Figures, still-lifes.
Lucienne Marie Thérèse Sarrade exhibited in Paris at the Salon d'Automne, the Salon des Indépendants and the Salon Populiste.

Her figurative work (largely visionary subjects such as the Dance Macabre, Faust, the Apocalypse, Walpurgis (is governed by circles and squares 'mathematically' organised into a learned grid.

SARRAGON, Joannes
Dutch, 17th century.
Active, probably in Middelburg, from 1621 to 1644.
Engraver (burin), painter.
Joannes Sarragon engraved portraits of *William I of Orange, Maurits* and *Frederik Hendrik of Orange.*

SARRASIN
French, 18th century.
Active at the end of the 18th century.
Painter.
MUSEUMS AND GALLERIES:
TOURS: *Landscape with Shepherds and Animals* (oval painting, two versions).

SARRAT, Vergé. See **VERGÉ-SARRAT Henri**

SARRAZIN (Mlle)
French, 18th century.
Painter. Landscapes.
Mlle Sarrazin was probably the daughter of Jean-Baptiste Sarrazin. She worked in Paris in 1789.

SARRAZIN
French, 19th century.
Painter. Genre scenes.
He worked in Nantes and exhibited at the Paris Salons of 1812 and 1814.

SARRAZIN. See also **SARASIN, SARAZIN** and **SARRASIN**

SARRAZIN, Bénigne
French, 17th century.
Born 14 January 1635, in Paris; died 3 August 1685, in Paris.
Painter.
Bénigne Sarrazin was the son and pupil of Jacques Sarazin. Louis XIV paid for him to complete his studies in Rome, and continued to allow his father to live at the Louvre. He worked in the chapel of the Hôtel de Ville (town hall) in Marseilles.

SARRAZIN, Jacques and Pierre.
See **SARAZIN**

SARRAZIN, Jean Baptiste, or Sarazin
French, 18th century.
Painter, watercolourist, draughtsman, decorative designer. Landscapes, seascapes.
Jean Baptiste Sarrazin was a teacher at the Académie de St-Luc. He exhibited at the Salon in 1791 and 1793, and at the exhibition at the Colisée in 1776. He was decorative painter in the court of Louis XIV.

AUCTION RECORDS:
PARIS, 21-22 Feb 1919, *Ruined Tower* (sepia) FRF 250. PARIS, 17 Nov 1924, *Landscape* (Indian ink wash) FRF 450. PARIS, 4 Nov 1927, *View of Abbeville* (watercolour) FRF 350. PARIS, 4 May 1928, *Seascape; Landscape with Castle* (two watercolours) FRF 1,150. PARIS, 16 and 17 May 1929, *Old Farmyard* (drawing) FRF 700. PARIS, 24 March 1947, *Park with Circular Monument; Chinese Temple* (1786, watercolour) FRF 1,500. NICE, 24 Feb 1949, *Old Castles on the River; Paysage Torrentueux (Landscape with Torrent)* (1781, matching pair) FRF 34,000. PARIS, 22 March 1950, *Stop; Ford* (black chalk, matching pair) FRF 7,000. PARIS, 6 Nov 1980, *View of Abbeville from the Pavilion de Bellevue in St-Gilles* (pen and watercolour, 10 3/4 x 15 1/4 ins / 27.5 x 39 cm) FRF 4,800. PARIS, 22 Nov 1988, *Dovecote and Fortified Castle by the Water's Edge* (1774, pen, grey wash heightened with blue chalk, 4 3/4 x 8 1/2 ins / 12 x 21.5 cm) FRF 6,000. PARIS, 16 Dec 1997, *Landscape with a Ruined Tower; River Scene with People Walking* (pair of oil/panel, 9 1/2 x 12 3/4 ins / 24 x 32.5 cm) FRF 7,000.

SARRAZIN, Michaud
French, 16th century.
Active in Cognac during the first half of the 16th century.
Sculptor, designer of ornamental architectural features.

Michaud Sarrazin was commissioned to make a tabernacle in 1533.

SARRAZIN, Pierre Jean, or Sarazin
Italian, 17th century.
Born 8 December 1633.
Painter.

Pierre Jean Sarrazin was the brother of Bénigne Sarrazin.

SARRAZIN DE BELMONT, Louise Joséphine. See **SARAZIN DE BELMONT**

SARRI, Corrado
Italian, 19th - 20th century.
Born 5 May 1866, in Florence; died 1944.
Painter, draughtsman, illustrator. Portraits.

Corrado Sarri was a pupil of Amos Cassioli and Pietro Saltini.

He worked as a court portrait artist and also illustrated many children's books including *Pinocchio, Story of an Alchemist* and *Don Quixote*.

BIBLIOGRAPHY:
Osterwalder, Marcus (ed.), *Dictionnaire des illustrateurs 1800-1914*, Ides et Calendes, Neuchâtel, 1989.

MUSEUMS AND GALLERIES:
FLORENCE (Palazzo Pitti): *Portrait of Amadeus of Savoy*.

SARRI, Egisto
Italian, 19th century.
Born 1837, in Figline (Valdarno); died 13 or 20 November 1901, in Florence.
Painter. History painting, portraits, genre scenes.

Egisto Sarri studied at the academy of fine art in Florence under Pollastrini and Bezzuoli. During these early years, he received a number of prizes, his success being crowned by his participation in the competition for a period of study in Rome in which he proved to be a worthy rival for the artist Raphael Sorbe. His painting of the *Apotheosis of the Virgin* was shown hors concours at the Alinari Competition Exhibition in 1900.

E Sarri

MUSEUMS AND GALLERIES:
FLORENCE (Uffizi): *Self-portrait; Portrait of the Artist E. de' Fabris* - PRATO (Mus. Civico): *Conrad of Swabia, a Prisoner in Naples, Listens Impassively to the Pronouncement of his Execution*.

AUCTION RECORDS:
LONDON, 20 Oct 1978, *Serenade* (1875, oil on canvas, 23 x 28 1/2 ins / 57.5 x 72.5 cm) GBP 750. LONDON, 20 April 1979, *Interrupted Dream* (1875, oil on canvas, 22 3/4 x 28 ins / 58 x 71.2 cm) GBP 950. NEW YORK, 16 Feb 1995, *First Steps* (1883, oil on canvas, 23 1/4 x 28 3/4 ins / 59.1 x 73 cm) USD 16,100. NEW YORK, 26 Feb 1997, *Appeasing the Tears* (1875, oil on canvas, 18 3/4 x 23 ins / 47.6 x 58.5 cm) USD 11,500.

SARRI, Gaetano. See **SARDI**

SARRIA, Garcia and Gonzalo. See **PÉREZ**

SARRINO, Agistino
Italian, 15th century.
Active in Messina c. 1400.
Painter.

Agistino Sarrino was commissioned to carry out the paintings in the choir of the church of S Stefano in Genoa.

SARROCCHI, Tito
Italian, 19th century.
Born 5 January 1824, in Siena; died 30 July 1900, in Siena.
Sculptor.

A pupil of L. Bartolini and Giovanni Dupré, Tito Sarrocchi was one of the best Italian sculptors of the 19th century. Numerous busts and monuments by him can be found in Siena and Florence.

MUSEUMS AND GALLERIES:
SIENA (Ospedale S Maria della Scala).

SARRON, Claudius or Johann Claudius
German, 18th century.
Born 22 October 1741, in Augsburg.
Draughtsman, engraver (burin).

Sarron was of French origin and worked in Augsburg from 1731 onwards, He engraved views of castles and cities.

SARRUT, Paul
French, 19th century.
Born 16 May 1822, in Grenoble.
Painter, engraver.

His masters were Bonnat and Luc-Olivier Merson. He began exhibiting at the Salon of the Société des Artistes Français in 1909 and won a medal for engraving in 1932.

SARSFIELD, John
Irish, 18th century.
Active in Dublin from 1765 to 1777.
Sculptor.

John Sarsfield was a pupil of Patrick Cunningham.

SARSON, Léonard
French, 16th century.
Active in Clermont during the second half of the 16th century.
Sculptor. Mythological figures.

MUSEUMS AND GALLERIES:
CLERMONT: *Athene* (1581, statue).

SART, Johann or Jan Gregor von der. See **SCHARDT**

SART, René
Belgian, 20th century.
Born 1927, in Spa.
Painter, art restorer, designer.

René Sart studied at the fine arts school in Spa in Belgium from 1941 to 1950 and went on to work as a restorer of objects fashioned from local wood ('bois de Spa').

SARTAIN, Emily
American, 19th - 20th century.

Born 17 March 1841, in Philadelphia; died 18 June 1927, in Philadelphia.
Painter, engraver (mezzotint). Portraits, genre scenes.
Emily Sartain was the daughter of John Sartain. She worked in Paris with Luminais, and after living for a while in Parma returned to the USA. She exhibited her work to great acclaim in 1876 and received an honourable mention in Buffalo in 1901.

SARTAIN, Harriet
American, 19th - 20th century.
Born 1873; died 1957.
Painter. Landscapes, flowers.
Harriet Sartain completed her artistic studies at the Philadelphia School of Design for Women and served as dean from 1920-1946. She painted in watercolour.

SARTAIN, Henry
American, 19th century.
Born 14 July 1833, in Philadelphia; died c. 1895, in Philadelphia.
Engraver (burin), printmaker.
Henry Sartain was the son of John Sartain.

SARTAIN, John
British, 19th century.
Born 24 October 1808, in London; died 25 October 1897, in Philadelphia.
Miniaturist, engraver (mezzotint).
John Sartain was the father of Emily, Henry, Samuel and William Sartain. He studied in London, then left for the USA in 1830. He acquired ownership of *Campbell's Magazine* in 1842 and subsequently founded *Sartain's Union Magazine*, a vehicle for the publication of his own work. He was held in esteem as a mezzotint engraver. He also produced numerous drawings and illustrations. He was a member of the Fine Arts Academy of Philadelphia.
MUSEUMS AND GALLERIES:
CHICAGO (Terra Foundation for American Art Collection): *Regional Election* (1854, coloured engraving).

SARTAIN, Samuel
American, 19th century.
Born 8 October 1830, in Philadelphia; died 20 December 1906, in Philadelphia.
Engraver, painter.
Samuel Sartain was the son and pupil of John Sartain.

SARTAIN, William
American, 19th - 20th century.
Born 21 November 1843, in Philadelphia; died 25 October 1924, in New York.
Painter, engraver. Genre scenes, local scenes, landscapes.
William Sartain studied at the Philadelphia Art School and then worked in Paris with Bonnat and Yvon. He lived for a while in Rome, in England, Algeria, Venice, Seville and Holland and completed many painted and drawn studies. He finally settled in New York, where he became a teacher. He won the bronze medal in Buffalo in 1901, silver medal in Charleston in 1902 and became a member of the National Academy in New York in 1880.
MUSEUMS AND GALLERIES:
NEW YORK (Metropolitan Mus. of Art): *A Chapter of the Koran* - WASHINGTON DC: *Street in Dinan* - WASHINGTON DC (National Portrait Gal.): mezzotint engravings - WASHINGTON DC (Smithsonian American AM): *Algerian Water Carrier* (after 1874, oil on canvas).
AUCTION RECORDS:
NEW YORK, 21-22 Jan 1900, *A Chapter of the Koran*, USD 1,300. NEW YORK, 1 May 1979, *Meadow Brook* (oil on canvas, 10 x 20 ins / 25.5 x 51 cm) USD 1,300. NEW YORK, 22 Sept 1993, *Landscape* (oil on canvas, 25 1/4 x 30 1/4 ins / 64.3 x 76.8 cm) USD 4,600. NEW YORK, 15 Nov 1993, *Trees* (oil on canvas, 16 x 20 ins / 40.6 x 50.8 cm) USD 805. NEW YORK, 21 May 1996, *Roman and Gothic Arch* (oil on canvas, 18 x 13 ins / 46 x 33 cm) USD 690.

SARTE, Marie Anne Élisabeth del
French, 19th century.
Born 9 March 1848, in Paris; died after 1883.
Sculptor, draughtswoman.
She was a pupil of T. Robert-Fleury. She made her Salon debut in 1868 with a plaster medallion and thereafter was a regular contributor to Salon exhibitions. Nothing is known about her activities after 1883.

SARTE, Marie Madeleine del. See **REAL DEL SARTE Marie Magdeleine**

SARTEEL, Léon
Belgian, 20th century.
Born 1882, in Ghent; died 1942.
Sculptor.
Léon Sarteel studied under Delvin at the academy in Ghent.
MUSEUMS AND GALLERIES:
ANTWERP.
AUCTION RECORDS:
LOKEREN, 23 April 1983, *The Good Judge* (before 1921, bronze, h. 23 1/4 ins / 59 cm) BEF 65,000. LOKEREN, 22 Feb 1986, *Bust of a Man* (bronze with dark brown patina, h. 9 ins / 22 cm) BEF 36,000. LOKEREN, 28 May 1988, *Summer* (bronze, h. 23 1/2 ins / 60 cm) BEF 170,000. LOKEREN, 21 March 1992, *Caress* (brown-patinated bronze, h. 19 ins / 48 cm, w. 12 3/4 ins/32.5 cm) BEF 70,000. LOKEREN, 23 May 1992, *Bather* (1934, beige-patinated plaster sculpture, h. 37 3/4 ins / 96 cm, w. 13 1/2 ins/34 cm) BEF 110,000. LOKEREN, 5 Dec 1992, *Optimism* (1935, black-patinated plaster, h. 12 1/2 ins / 32 cm, w. 7 3/4 ins/20 cm) BEF 30,000. LOKEREN, 15 May 1993, *Today and Tomorrow* (oak sculpture, h. 28 3/4 ins / 73 cm, w. 9 ins/23 cm) BEF 95,000. LOKEREN, 7 Dec 1996, *Eva* (before 1925, white marble, 18 1/2 x 6 ins / 47 x 15 cm) BEF 120,000. LOKEREN, 4 March 2000, *Bathing Woman Kneeling* (c. 1935, patinated plaster, h. 38 ins / 97 cm, w. 22 ins/56 cm) BEF 85,000. LOKEREN, 12 May 2001, *Grief* (c. 1936, green-brown patinated bronze, h. 20 ins / 52 cm, w. 19 ins/49 cm) BEF 160,000. BRUSSELS, 20 Nov 2001, *Family* (brown patinated bronze, h. 23 ins / 58 cm) BEF 90,000. BRUSSELS, 28 May 2002, *Lawyer* (patinated bronze, h. 20 ins / 52 cm) EUR 3,200.

SARTER, Armin
German, 19th century.
Born 1837, in Bonn.
Painter. Genre scenes, animals.
Armin Sarter trained in Düsseldorf, Munich and Paris, and settled in Düsseldorf.

SARTHOU, Claude
French, 20th century.
Painter, watercolourist, mixed media, draughtswoman.
Claude Sarthou lives and works in Montpellier and exhibits in group and solo exhibitions: 1973, Musée Ingres, Montauban; 1974, *Phases*, Van Elsem Museum, Brussels; 1979, National Fine Arts Society, Lisbon.

SARTHOU, Jean-Louis
French, 20th - 21st century.
Born 11 March 1947, in Paris.
Painter.
Jean-Louis Sarthou has been a member of the Lettrist Group since 1966. He works on various substrates to produce a mixture of signs and calligraphy together with everyday objects made of different materials. He also works as a theatre and variety compère.

SARTHOU, Maurice Élie
French, 20th century.

Born 15 January 1911, in Bayonne; died 11 June 1999.
Painter, lithographer, illustrator, watercolourist.
Portraits, genre scenes, landscapes, waterscapes, still-lifes. Murals, designs for stained glass.

Maurice Élie Sarthou was initially a pupil at the École des Beaux-Arts, Montpellier, and then won a scholarship that enabled him to study at the École des Beaux-Arts, Paris. He became an art teacher in 1934, first at the lycée of Bastia, then in Bordeaux in 1937, and finally in Paris from 1950. He was primarily a painter of the South of France, where he spent most of his time. In 1952 he renewed his links with the landscape of his childhood, dividing his time between Lasalle, in the Cévennes, and Sète, where he spent his summers.

He engraved a large number of lithographs and illustrated Paul Valéry's *Regards sur la mer* (*Glances at the Sea*) in 1965 and Rimbaud's *Le Bateau Ivre* in 1966-1967. He carried out mural decorations in Arcachon, Bordeaux and elsewhere, and also designed two windows for the church of Bouchevilliers in the Eure. His oils and watercolours depict typical scenes from the Camargue - herds of bulls, the marshes, the rock falls of the Val d'Enfer at Les Baux-en-Provence, the Mistral tugging at the sparse vegetation of the dunes, the peacefulness of mist over the lakes. His aim was to reconstitute nature in his art by noting its deeper structures, and he made small watercolour sketches from nature and worked from them in his studio. His works show that he knew and understood Francis Grüber, André Marchand and Édouard Pignon. He took his inspiration from natural phenomena - the sky, water, fire and wind. With *Fire in the Alpilles* he began a red period inspired by the fires that ravaged the region. After a journey to Greece and Iran he added blue to his palette.

Sarthou exhibited in group and solo exhibitions, including: 1945, in Paris, Salon des Artistes Français; Salon d'Automne; from 1949, Salon de Mai; 1955, Galerie Charpentier, Paris; regularly from 1955, Galerie Marcel Guiot, Paris; from 1956, Salon des Peintres Témoins de Leur Temps; 1959, exhibition of French art in Warsaw and Cracow; 1961, *Peintres contemporains de l'École de Paris* (*Contemporary Painters of the Paris School*) in Rabat, Casablanca; International *Black and White* Biennale, Lugano; 1963, *20th-century Portraiture* in the museums of Düsseldorf and Berlin; the Tokyo Biennale; 1965, Musée d'Art Moderne de la Ville de Paris; 1966, *Peintres français contemporains* (*Contemporary French Painters*) in Czechoslovakia, Hungary, Romania; 1968, retrospective exhibition, Musée Fabre, Montpellier; 1969, 1971, Houston; 1974, New York; 1981, Albi; 1985, Musée des Beaux-Arts, Dijon; 1986, Bourges; from 1987, Galerie Chardin, Paris. He was awarded a number of prizes, including the Prix de la Critique in 1955 and the Menton Biennale prize in 1957.

M.E-Sarthou

Bibliography:

Bay, André, *Sarthou*, Éd. Pierre Cailler, Geneva, 1968. Toesca, M., *Sarthou*, Éd. Martet, Dif. Wéber, 1977. Harambourg, Lydia, *L'École de Paris 1945-1965. Dictionnaire des peintres*, Ides et Calendes, Neuchâtel, 1993.

Museums and Galleries:

Bordeaux (MBA): *Woman Scaling Fish* - Cincinnati (AM): *Evening in the Camargue* (engraving); *Port of Sete* (engraving); *Camargue* (engraving) - Dijon (MBA) - Lyons (MBA) - Montpellier (Mus. Fabre) - Narbonne (MAH): *Beating Waves* - Paris (BNF) - Paris (FNAC) - Paris (MAMVP) - Paris (MNAM-CCI) - St-Étienne (Mus. d'Art et d'Industrie).

Auction records:

Paris, 1962, *A Port*, FRF 7,400. Geneva, 30 June 1976, *Horses in the Camargue* (oil on canvas, 23 1/2 x 32 ins / 60 x 81 cm) CHF 1,400. Versailles, 17 April 1988, *Landscape* (oil on canvas, 23 1/2 x 32 ins / 60 x 81 cm) FRF 4,600. Versailles, 29 Oct 1989, *Boats* (oil on canvas, 9 1/2 x 13 ins / 24 x 33 cm) FRF 9,500. Versailles, 10 Dec 1989, *Composition* (oil on canvas, 25 1/2 x 21 1/4 ins / 65 x 54 cm) FRF 9,000. Paris, 4 July 1990, *Blue Herd* (oil on canvas, 25 1/2 x 32 ins / 65 x 81 cm) FRF 6,800. Versailles, 23 Sept 1990, *Fire no.2* (oil on canvas, 23 1/2 x 32 ins / 60 x 81 cm) FRF 7,000. Paris, 17 Oct 1990, *South Wind* (1962, oil on canvas, 19 3/4 x 19 3/4 ins / 50 x 50 cm) FRF 9,500. Neuilly, 3 Feb 1991, *Blue Herd* (oil on canvas, 25 1/2 x 32 ins / 65 x 81 cm) FRF 9,000. Paris, 18 April 1991, *Bulls in the Evening* (1989, oil on canvas, 32 x 25 1/2 ins / 81 x 65 cm) FRF 30,000. Lucerne, 25 May 1991, *Boiling Sea* (acrylic/canvas, 31 1/2 x 31 1/2 ins / 80 x 80 cm) CHF 2,400. Neuilly, 20 Oct 1991, *Lava Ridges* (oil on canvas, 23 1/2 x 28 3/4 ins / 60 x 73 cm) FRF 4,300. Paris, 8 Nov 1991, *Landscape* (watercolour, 16 1/2 x 22 ins / 42 x 56 cm) FRF 3,800. Paris, 25 May 1994, *Trees on Fire* (oil on canvas, 31 1/2 x 31 1/2 ins / 80 x 80 cm) FRF 12,500. Paris, 19 Nov 1995, *The Val d'Enfer, les Baux* (1964, oil on canvas, 25 1/2 x 32 ins / 65 x 81 cm) FRF 7,000. North Bethesda, 9 Feb 2002, *Still-life with Suns* (1958, oil on canvas, 31 x 35 ins / 79 x 89 cm) USD 1,500.

SARTI, Alessandro

Italian, 17th century.
Sculptor.

Alessandro Sarti sculpted the marble tabernacle for the high altar in the church of S Silvestro in Capite in Rome between 1666 and 1667.

SARTI, Andrea

Italian, 16th century.
Died 1600.
Active in Carrara.
Sculptor.

Andrea Sarti worked in southern Italy, carving tombs, low reliefs, altars and fonts.

SARTI, Angelo

Italian, 18th century.
Active in Bologna in 1741.
Modeller (wax).

Museums and Galleries:

Berlin (Bodemus.): *Florentine Senator Reading.*

SARTI, Antonio

Italian, 17th century.
Active in Jesi, near Ancona, during the first half of the 17th century.
Painter. History painting.

Baldassani refers to a remarkable *Circumcision* by Antonio Sarti in the collegiate church of Massaccio.

Museums and Galleries:

Jesi (Pinacoteca Civica): *St Anne, the Virgin and Child.*

SARTI, Bartolomeo

Italian, 16th - 17th century.
Active in Carrara.
Sculptor.

Bartolomeo Sarti worked at Pisa Cathedral and for the church of S Maria di Monteoliveto in Naples.

SARTI, Carlo, called Rodellone

Italian, 18th century.
Born to a family originally from Bologna or Rimini; died 1771.
Sculptor. Religious subjects.

Carlo Sarti produced works for churches in Rimini and Faenza.

SARTI, Diego
Italian, 19th - 20th century.
Born 1860, in Bologna.
Sculptor. Busts.
Diego Sarti is mainly known for the busts he carved of his contemporaries in Bologna.

SARTI, Domenico
Italian, 17th century.
Active in Carrara in 1629.
Sculptor.

SARTI, Ercole, called Il Muto di Ficarolo
Italian, 17th century.
Born 23 December 1593, in Ficarolo; died c. 1639.
Painter. Religious subjects, portraits.
Ercole Sarti was born deaf and dumb. He appears not to have trained under a master. At the age of 16, he attracted attention by displaying an *Adoration of the Magi*, which he had painted secretly on the wall of his father's house, one feast day when there was a procession through the streets. He was then sent to study with Carlo Benoni of Ferrara, and frequently drew on the style of his contemporary Scarsellino for inspiration. One of his paintings can be found in the Benedictine church in Ficarolo.

SARTI, Ignazio
Italian, 19th century.
Born 1791, in Bologna; died 1854, in Ravenna.
Sculptor, painter, engraver (burin), architect.
The stepfather of Raffaele Sarti, Ignazio Sarti worked in Ravenna producing tombs and busts.

SARTI, Lorenzo, called Lorenzino del Mazza
Italian, 18th century.
Born in Bologna.
Sculptor, stucco artist.
A pupil of Giuseppe Mazza, Lorenzo Sarti worked in Bologna, Ferrara, Cento and Modena, and produced sculptures in the cathedrals of Bologna and Ferrara.

SARTI, Paolo
Italian, 19th century.
Born 1794.
Active in Florence.
Painter.
Paolo Sarti painted the fescoes in the choir of the collegiate church of Montesenario near Pratolino.

SARTI, Pier Angelo
Italian, 19th century.
Active in Vetriano during the first half of the 19th century.
Sculptor, poet.
He worked chiefly in London.

SARTI, Raffaele, born Martelli
Italian, 19th century.
Born 1814, in Bologna; died 12 January 1848, in Ravenna.
Sculptor, painter.
He was the stepson and pupil of Ignazio Sarti.

SARTI, Sebastiano, called Rodellone
Italian, 18th century.
Died c. 1740.
Active in Bologna.
Sculptor.
Sebastiano Sarti sculpted a *Pietà* in low relief in the sacristy of St Dominic's church in Bologna.

SARTINI, Giuseppe
Italian, 17th century.
Active in Venice in 1699.
Painter.

SARTO, Andrea del, real name Andrea d'Angiolo or d'Agnolo
Italian, 16th century.
Born 1487, in Florence, in 1486 according to some sources, in 1488 according to others; died 1530 or 1531, in Florence.
Painter, fresco artist. Religious subjects, portraits.
Florentine School.
Andrea acquired his nickname del Sarto ('of the tailor') from the occupation of his father, master tailor Angelo di Francesco. His talent for drawing became apparent early and he was apprenticed to a goldsmith to be taught engraving. A painter and sculptor, Giovanni Barile, seeing the young boy's drawings, persuaded Andrea's father to allow the boy to become his apprentice. After three years with Barile, Andrea entered the studio of Pietro di Cosimo. Here he studied the basics of technique, at the same time copying the frescoes of Masaccio and Ghirlandaio and the cartoons of Leonardo da Vinci and Michelangelo. From these masters he learned the draughtsmanship, breadth of vision and power of execution that later earned him the name *Sanza Errori* (without mistakes) from his fellow Florentines.

Early on Andrea del Sarto had become a close friend of Francesco Bigi, better known as Franciabigio. A few years older than Andrea, after working with Brancasci Chapel and Mariotto Albertinelli, Franciabigio was a talented portrait artist. Andrea left Pietro di Cosimo's studio and went to live with his friend, sharing a studio and collaborating on a number of paintings. Vasari, well placed to discuss del Sarto since he had been his pupil, does not tell us what these paintings were but it is likely that they would have earned a livelihood by painting portraits.

Andrea del Sarto established his reputation in 1509 with five frescoes in the church of SS Annunziata depicting *The Life of St Philip Benizi*. Associated with the cycle is a work often considered to be one of his masterpieces, the *Madonna del Sacco*. By 1511, when he was no more than 23, Andrea was sufficiently well-known to be awarded the commission to paint the decorations in the cloister of the Scalzi.

In 1518 or a little earlier, François I saw two paintings by Andrea in France and was so impressed that he summoned the artist to his court. Del Sarto was initially reluctant to go, for in 1512 he had married a very beautiful widow, Lucrezia del Fede, with whom he was passionately in love, but he eventually set off for Paris with his pupil Andrea Sguazzela at the end of May 1518. The king heaped him with presents, awarded him a generous allowance and paid a high price for the paintings that he produced. Until his arrival in France, Del Sarto, like most painters at that time, had not been well paid, but now he was in a position to make a fortune. A letter from his wife called him home and Andrea asked the king to release him. François was inclined to refuse but Andrea eventually persuaded him, and left in 1519, having sworn on the Bible that he would return in a few months and carrying a large sum of money entrusted to him by François with which to buy works of art. However, he squandered the money and so could not return to France. The many works he produced after this time must have paid badly, since he soon found himself destitute. Friends who had celebrated his return when he had money in his pocket fell away one by one, and his wife provoked him to extreme jealousy. The political revolution in Florence that had removed the Medici family from its position of power deprived him of his patrons and protectors. Finally, he was stricken by the plague that broke out in Florence after the town's surrender (12 August 1530). He died abandoned, even by the wife for whom he had sacrificed so much.

Andrea del Sarto's work for the Scalzi cloister depicts the story of St John the Baptist. The cartoons for the work are preserved in Palazzo Rinonuccini. While the *Baptism of*

Christ, the first to be executed, reveals the hand of a youthful artist under the influence of the great masters, particularly Dürer, the last two works to be painted (in 1526), *The Visitation* and *The Birth of St John the Baptist*, reveal a new personal voice. After this, he worked on the decoration of the monastery of S Salvi near Florence, including a very original *Last Supper*, for the church at San Gallo and for the great lords of Florence. Few works survive from his time in France apart from *Charity* (1518) in the Louvre. In addition to the work he did at the court itself, it appears that he also painted religious compositions for Semblançay, the *intendant* of Tours, and some works for the chateau of Marmoutier.

On his return to Florence, del Sarto completed the Scalzi series, to which Franciabigio had added two frescoes during his absence, but was no longer as sought after as in earlier years. Nevertheless, in addition to the works above, he produced a number of major works including the *Deposition* (1524 Palazzo Pitti, Florence), *The Madonna del Sacco* (1525) and *The Assumption* (1530 Palazzo Pitti). Four centuries after its disappearance from the Medici collections, the *Botti Madonna*, painted in about 1529 and thought to be a copy, was identified in 2001 by the American art historian John Shearman as an authentic Andrea del Sarto.

An anecdote by Vasari provides an example of del Sarto's technical ability. While passing through Florence, the Duke of Mantua, Federigo II, saw Raphael's portrait of Pope Clement VII and asked the Pope if he would give it to him. The Pope agreed and arranged for his nephew Ottavio de' Medici to have the painting conveyed to its destination. Ottavio, reluctant to hand it over, got Andrea del Sarto to copy it, sending the copy to Mantua. The copy was so perfect that Giulio Romano, then in the Duke of Mantua's service and who had been involved in the painting of the original, was deceived. He would not believe that he could be mistaken until Vasari, who had been present while Andrea del Sarto was working on the copy, showed him the artist's mark.

In some works, the *St John the Baptist* in the Palazzo Pitti for example, del Sarto shows himself to be a precursor of the realists. Yet, despite his technical brilliance, some critics have found his works rather bland. His work, with that of some of his contemporaries, prepared the way for the Academic art that was for centuries to define the theoretical rules of beauty. His pupils included Francesco Salviati, Giorgio Vasari, Giacomo da Pontormo, Il Nannoccio and Andrea Sguazella.

Del Sarto's work has often been exhibited, including: 1986, *Andrea del Sarto: dipinti e disegni a Firenze* (*Andrea del Sarto: paintings and drawings in Florence*) at the Palazzo Pitti in Florence; 1986, *Hommage à Andrea del Sarto* in the Cabinet des Dessins at the Louvre in Paris; 2001, *The Botti Madonna* at the Courtauld Institute in London, where this painting provided the central focus for the exhibition.

BIBLIOGRAPHY:

Jones, E., '*The Influence of Andrea del Sarto's Wife on his Art*' in *Applied Psycho-Analysis, 1*, 1913. Freeberg, Sydney Joseph, *Andrea del Sarto*, catalogue raisonné, Belknap Press of Harvard University Press, Cambridge (MA), 1963. Shearman, John, '*Andrea del Sarto*', *2 vol.*, Clarendon Press, Oxford, 1965. Borsook, Eve, *The Mural Painters of Tuscany: From Cimabue to Andrea del Sarto*, Oxford University Press, Oxford, 1980. *Hommage à Andrea del Sarto*, exhibition catalogue, Musée du Louvre, Cabinet des dessins, Paris, 1986. *Andrea del Sarto: 1486-1530: dipinti e disegni a Firenze*, exhibition catalogue, Palazzo Pitti, Florence, 1986. Natali, Antonio, *Andrea Del Sarto: maestro della maniera moderna*, Leonardo Arte, Milan, 1998. Goldner, G., '*Two New Drawings by Andrea del Sarto*' in *Master Drawings*, vol 36, no. 1, 1998. Natali, A., *Andrea del Sarto*, Abbeville Press, New York, 1999. Shearman, John, et al., *Andrea Del Sarto The Botti Madonna*, Courtauld Institute, London, 2001. Joannides, Paul, *Raphäel et son temps*, exhibition catalogue, Palais des Beaux Arts, Lille, 2002. Brown, B., *Andrea del Sarto Rediscovered*, Matthiesen Fine Art, London, 2002.

MUSEUMS AND GALLERIES:

BAYONNE (Mus. Bonnat): *Seated Man with Hands Resting on a Book* - BERLIN: *Portrait of a Young Woman*; *Virgin Enthroned with the Child and Saints* - BERN: *Holy Family* - BRUSSELS: *Jupiter and Leda* - CAEN: *St Sebastian Holding Two Arrows* - DRESDEN: *Mystic Marriage of St Catherine*; *Abraham Preparing to Sacrifice Isaac* - DUBLIN: *St Francis*; *St Lawrence*; *St Jerome and St Dominic*; *Adoration of the Magi*; *Pietà and Two Saints* (part of a predella) - FLORENCE (Palazzo Pitti): *Holy Family*; *Self-portrait*; *Annunciation to the Virgin Mary*; *Virgin and Four Saints*; *Portrait of the Artist and his Wife Lucrezia del Fede*; *Debate on the Trinity*; *Portrait*; *Holy Family*; *St John the Baptist* - FLORENCE (Uffizi): *Portrait of a woman in Blue*; *Virgin and Child with St John the Evangelist and St Francis*; *St James with Two Kneeling Children*; *Portrait of an Unknown Woman with a Basket of Spindles*; *Portrait of a Young Man in Black Suit and Hat*; *Self-portrait* - GENOA: *Cleopatra* - LILLE: *Virgin and Child with St John and Three Angels*; *Head* - LILLE (MBA, Wicar Collection): *Virgin and Child with St John the Baptist, St Elizabeth and St Anne* (c.1519, red chalk); *St Mark* (c. 1525, pen and ink); *Two Putti after Michelangelo* (1513, red chalk, recto); *Water Carrier after Antonio Pollaiuolo* (1513, red chalk, verso) - LONDON (NG): *The Madonna and Child with St Elizabeth and St John the Baptist* (c. 1513, oil/wood); *Portrait of a Young Man* (1517-1518, oil on canvas, formerly Portrait of a Sculptor) - LONDON (Wallace Collection): *Virgin and Child with St John the Baptist* - LYONS: *Sacrifice of Abraham* - MADRID (Prado): *Portrait of Lucrezia, the Artist's Wife* - MONTPELLIER: *Holy Family* - MOSCOW (Rumiantsev Mus.): *Head of Christ*; *Virgin and Child with St John the Baptist*; *Holy Family*; *Virgin and Child with St John the Baptist, St Elizabeth and an Angel* - NAPLES: *Pope Leo X* - PARIS (Louvre): *Charity*; *Holy Family* (two paintings); *Annunciation*; *Portrait of Andrea Fausti* - ROCHEFORT: *Nude Study* (drawing) - ROME (Mus. e Gal. Borghese): *Magdalene*; *Holy Family* - ROUEN: *St Romuald Preaching*; *Portrait* - ST-ÉTIENNE: *St Peter and St Paul Refusing to Sacrifice to the False Gods* - TOULON: *Self-portrait* - VIENNA: *Virgin and Child and the Infant St John the Bapist*; *Tobias Led by the Angel*; *Lamentation over the Dead Christ*.

AUCTION RECORDS:

PARIS, 1756, *Seated Virgin and Child with St Catherine and St Elizabeth who Presents the Infant St John to the Child Child*, FRF 6,300. PARIS, 1767, *St Peter Healing the Sick* (pen and bistre heightened with white) FRF 51. PARIS, 1787, *Holy Family* (pen drawing with bistre wash) FRF 100. PARIS, 1792, *Jupiter and Leda*, FRF 5,250. PARIS, 1797, *Hitory* (drawing in black chalk and stump) FRF 310; *Standing Figure of Christ with Outstretched Arms* (pen) FRF 150. LONDON, 1800, *Leda Caressed by Jupiter*, FRF 5,300. LONDON, March 1804, *Virgin and Child with St Joseph*, FRF 11,570. LONDON, 1806, *Madonna del Sacco*, FRF 15,740. LONDON, 1810, *Virgin and Child with St John*, FRF 30,190. LONDON, 1811, *Charity*, FRF 12,620. LONDON, 1820, *Holy Family*, FRF 10,210. LONDON, 1823, *St John Writing the Revelations on the Island of Patmos*, FRF 11,830. PARIS, 1825, *Virgin and Child with Saints*, FRF 45,100. PARIS, 1826, *Portrait of a Woman*, FRF 1,200; *Noah Helped by his Children Plants the Vine* (pen drawing, bistre wash heightened with white) FRF 326. PARIS, 1834, *Virgin and Child with Saints*, FRF 28,000. PARIS, 1850, *Holy Family*, FRF 175,000; *Virgin, St Anthony of Padua and Angel with Violin*,

FRF 63,000; *Head of a Child* (drawing in red chalk) FRF 514; *Assumption of the Virgin* (drawing) FRF 882; *Studies of Children in Various Attitudes* (drawing) FRF 714. PARIS, 1857, *Virgin and Child with Angel,* FRF 5,750. LONDON, 1860, *Charity Surrounded by a Group of Children,* FRF 13,120. PARIS, 1865, *Portrait of the Artist's Wife,* FRF 8,800. PARIS, 1868, *Scene from the Life of St John; Angel Approaching a Font* (drawing in pen and chalk with wash heightened with white) FRF 230. PARIS, 1870, *Virgin and Child with St John,* FRF 5,100. PARIS, 1878, *Pietà,* FRF 44,625. LONDON, 1892, *Pietà,* FRF 23,625; *Holy Family,* FRF 13,650. LONDON, 1899, *Portrait of the Artist,* FRF 23,350. PARIS, 26 May 1919, *Two Studies for St John* (red chalk) FRF 1,900. LONDON, 4 and 5 May 1922, *Virgin and Child with Infant St John* GBP 47. LONDON, 20 April 1923, *Gentleman in Red,* GBP 105. LONDON, 6 July 1923, *St Catherine,* GBP 420. LONDON, 4 July 1924, *Virgin and Child with St Elizabeth,* GBP 162. PARIS, 4 Feb 1925, *A Baptism* (red chalk) FRF 280. LONDON, 15 July 1927, *Altarpiece,* GBP 682. LONDON, 28-29 July 1927, *Countess Mattei,* GBP 420. LONDON, 8 June 1928, *Cardinal Altieri,* GBP 1,312. LONDON, 12 July 1929, *Virgin and Child with St John,* GBP 168. LONDON, 18 July 1930, *Pietà,* GBP 399. NEW YORK, 22 April 1932, *Holy Family with Saints,* USD 800. NEW YORK, 18-19 April 1934, *Portrait of a Man,* USD 850; *Virgin and Child,* USD 1,050. PARIS, 28 Nov 1934, *Standing Figure of a Man* (pen and reddish wash) FRF 800. LONDON, 5 April 1935, *Portrait of a Woman,* GBP 120. LONDON, 30 April 1937, *Jacopo Sannazaro,* GBP 11. LONDON, 2 July 1937, *Young Man in Black,* GBP 262. PARIS, 5 Dec 1941, *Head of a Man in Three-Quarters Profile Looking to Left* (red chalk, attributed) FRF 2,450. LONDON, 19 Dec 1941, *Self-portrait,* GBP 115. PARIS, 30 Oct 1942, *Holy Family, St Anne and St John* (School of Andrea del Sarto) FRF 5, 500. PARIS, 10 Feb 1943, *Virgin and Child with St Anne and the Infant St John* (School of Andrea del Sarto) FRF 16,000. PARIS, 14 May 1945, *Apostle* (black chalk and red chalk) FRF 7,500. LONDON, 31 May 1946, *Virgin and Child, Infant St John and Three Other Saints,* GBP 357. PARIS, 5 Feb 1947, *Virgin and Child with St John and St Joseph in a Landscape* (attributed) FRF 81,000. LONDON, 10 March 1950, *Pietà,* GBP 261. PARIS, 22 June 1950, *Holy Family* (School of Andrea del Sarto) FRF 13,500. PARIS, 8 Nov 1950, *Allegory of Charity* (black chalk) FRF 15,100. PARIS, 1 Dec 1950, *Holy Family with St John* (School of Andrea del Sarto) FRF 40,100. NEW YORK, 16 Jan 1957, *Portrait of a Cleric,* USD 8,250. LONDON, 26 June 1959, *Madonna and Child with the Infant St John,* GBP 2,730. LONDON, 23 June 1967, *Portrait of a Man,* Gns 38,000. COPENHAGEN, 30 April 1974, *Annunciation,* DKK 60,000. LONDON, 5 Dec 1977, *Head of a Child* (red chalk, 5 1/4 x 5 1/2 ins / 13.1 x 14.2 cm) GBP 6,000. BERN, 26 June 1981, *Man in Profile* (c. 1510, red chalk, 7 x 5 1/4 ins / 18 x 13.3 cm) CHF 4,000. NEW YORK, 14 Jan 1987, *Head of St John the Baptist* (black chalk/paper/remounted/panel, 12 3/4 x 9 1/4 ins / 32.5 x 23.3 cm) USD 150,000. NEW YORK, 31 Jan 1997, *Adoration of the Magi* (oil on panel, 25 1/4 x 30 1/2 ins / 64.2 x 77.2 cm) USD 398,500. NEW YORK, 28 Jan 1999, *St Matthew - Design for Embroidery* (black chalk/pen/brown ink wash) USD 45,000. NEW YORK, 28 Jan 2000, *Madonna and Child* (oil on panel, 33 x 24 ins / 85 x 62 cm) USD 1,000,000. BERN, 11 May 2000, *St John the Baptist* (oil on canvas, 36 x 26 ins / 92 x 67 cm) CHF 3,600. ZURICH, 30 March 2001, *Holy Family with Elizabeth and Infant St John* (oil on panel, 35 x 27 ins / 88 x 69 cm) CHF 28,000. NEW YORK, 22 Jan 2004, *Madonna and Child with Infant St John in Landscape* (oil on panel, 39 x 31 ins / 98 x 78 cm) USD 350,000.

SARTO, Domenico del
Italian, 16th century.
Sculptor.
Domenico del Sarto carved the throne in the church of S Andrea in Carrara in 1541 in collaboration with Nicodemo da Carrara.

SARTO, Jacqueline. See **SARTORIO**

SARTO, Johann or Jan Gregor von der. See **SCHARDT**

SARTONIS, Georges. See **SARTORIS**

SARTOR, Caspar
German, 17th century.
Active during the first half of the 17th century.
Sculptor.
Caspar Sartor was probably a member of the Sarder family of sculptors from Eichstätt. He worked in the abbey-church of Neresheim from 1610 to 1623.

SARTOR, Conrad or Johann Conrad
German, 18th century.
Active during the first half of the 18th century.
Miniaturist.
Conrad Sartor settled in London in 1715. He painted *Christ and the Repentant Sinner* in the style of Rubens.

SARTOR, Johann Jakob
German, 18th century.
Engraver (burin).
Johann Jakob Sartor engraved views and architectural views in Cologne. He lived in London from 1715 to 1719.

SARTOR, Michel
German, 18th century.
Active during the first half of the 18th century.
Miniaturist.
Michel Sartor was the brother of Conrad Sartor.

SARTOR, Wilhelm. See **SARDER**

SARTORE, Hugo
Uruguayan, 20th century.
Born 1934, in San José.
Painter (including mixed media).
Hugo Sartore first studied painting at the age of 12 in the studio of the city museum, and some years later he worked in the constructivist studio of Torres-Garcia. In 1956 he was given a grant to visit Europe. In Paris he joined a group of artists working with Poliakoff. He studied orphism and oriental art. In 1975 he went to Venezuela where he taught in the Aragua state school of fine art, then left to go to an archaeological research centre and for the next ten years studied the indigenous culture. He later moved to Newark in New Jersey.

Between 1959 and 1975 he divided his work between Montevideo and Buenos Aires, continuing his research into aspects of urban life. He understood the importance of geometry as the basis of his art, and produced compositions which have echoes of Orphism, Cubism and Conceptualism.

AUCTION RECORDS:
NEW YORK, 19(20 Nov 1990, *Construction and Assemblage in Polychrome Wood* (mixed media and timber, h. 19 1/2 ins / 49.5 cm) USD 6,600. NEW YORK, 16 Nov 1994, *Ourselves* (oil on canvas, 36 1/4 x 30 ins / 92.1 x 76.2 cm) USD 5,750. CARACAS, 1 Dec 2002, *Composition* (oil on canvas, 38 x 41 ins / 96 x 103 cm) USD 3,000. NEW YORK, 13 July 2004, *Construction* (painted wood, 34 x 13x3 ins / 87 x 34x8 cm) USD 2,400. MONTEVIDEO, 5 Oct 2004, *Composition in Colours* (oil on canvas, 36 x 19 ins / 92 x 48 cm) USD 1,800.

SARTORELLI, Carlo
Italian, 20th century.
Born 26 August 1896, in Venice; died 1956.
Painter, engraver. Landscapes.
He was the son and pupil of Francesco Sartorelli.
MUSEUMS AND GALLERIES:
LIMA - NAPLES.

SARTORELLI, Francesco
Italian, 19th - 20th century.

Born 14 September 1856, in Cornuda; died 1939, in Udine.
Painter. Landscapes, seascapes.

He owed his success to his views of Venice.

MUSEUMS AND GALLERIES:
PARIS (former Mus. du Luxembourg): *Venice, the Port.*

AUCTION RECORDS:
MILAN, 14 Nov 1974, *Landscape,* ITL 1,600,000. MILAN, 28 Oct 1976, *Road in the Suburbs* (oil on canvas, 35 1/2 x 59 ins / 90 x 150 cm) ITL 1,000,000. MILAN, 5 April 1979, *Landscape* (oil on canvas, 43 1/4 x 59 ins / 110 x 150 cm) ITL 950,000. MILAN, 16 Dec 1982, *Lagoon* (oil on canvas, 43 1/4 x 67 ins / 110 x 170 cm) ITL 4,400,000. LONDON, 23 March 1988, *Summer Pastures* (oil on canvas, 43 x 69 ins / 109 x 175 cm) GBP 1,650. MILAN, 17 Dec 1992, *Seascape* (oil on board, 8 1/4 x 11 1/2 ins / 21 x 29 cm) ITL 1,400,000. MILAN, 25 Oct 1994, *Landscape with Lake and Figures* (oil on canvas, 24 x 38 1/2 ins / 61 x 98 cm) ITL 4,600,000. MILAN, 19 Dec 1995, *Autumn* (oil on canvas, 21 x 31 1/2 ins / 53.5 x 80 cm) ITL 9,200,000. GRAVENHAGE, 6 Nov 2002, *Girls in a Sunny Garden* (oil on board, 27 x 39 ins / 68 x 98 cm) EUR 3,000. MILAN, 27 May 2003, *Sunset on the Rice Field* (oil on canvas, 29 x 59 ins / 74 x 150 cm) EUR 6,000. LUCERNE, 19 Nov 2003, *Peasant Woman Sitting in a Landscape, Lake beyond* (oil on canvas, 17 x 32 ins / 42 x 81 cm) CHF 3,200. MILAN, 25 May 2004, *Lake Landscape* (oil on canvas, 20 x 35 ins / 50 x 89 cm) EUR 2,300.

SARTORI. See also **SARTORY**

SARTORI, Angelo
Italian, 18th century.
Born 1740, in Verona; died 1794, in Verona.
Sculptor.

Angelo Sartori, who was probably the pupil of Giovanni Angelo Finali, sculpted numerous statues for the cathedral and churches of Verona and the surrounding area.

SARTORI, Augusto
Swiss, 20th century.
Born 14 May 1880, in Giubiasco.
Painter. Religious subjects, genre scenes, portraits.

Augusto Sartori studied at the Accademia di Belle Arti di Brera in Milan.

MUSEUMS AND GALLERIES:
LUGANO: *Annunciation* - ZURICH (Kunsthaus): *First Smile of Spring.*

SARTORI, C.
Dutch (?), 17th century.
Active during the second half of the 17th century.
Painter. Flowers.

C. Sartori is noted for a flower-painting in the F.T. Berg Collection, Stockholm.

SARTORI, Domenico
Italian, 18th century.
Active in Castione, near Mori (Trentino).
Sculptor, architect.

Domenico Sartori worked with his brother Giuseppe Antonio Sartori on the high altar of the cathedral in Trento, as well as other altars in churches in Trentino.

SARTORI, Emilio
Italian, 19th - 20th century.
Painter. Battles, landscapes.

He was a prolific artist.

SARTORI, Enrico
Italian, 19th century.
Born 4 February 1831, in Parma; died 25 October 1888.
Painter. Military subjects, genre scenes, landscapes.

He exhibited in Florence, Milan, Parma and Turin.

MUSEUMS AND GALLERIES:
PARMA: *Funeral of Vittorio Emmanuele in Parma Cathedral in 1878*; five paintings.

AUCTION RECORDS:
ROME, 24 Oct 1995, *Cavalry Encampment* (1881, oil on canvas, 15 1/4 x 27 1/4 ins / 39 x 69 cm) ITL 20,700,000.

SARTORI, Felicita, later Felicita Hoffmann
German, 18th century.
Born in Sacile; died 1760, in Dresden.
Painter, miniaturist, engraver.

Felicita Sartori received training from Rosalba Carriera in Venice, and became a very talented painter. After marrying a gentleman in the service of the king of Poland, the Elector of Saxony, she settled in Dresden, where she executed many works for the court.

MUSEUMS AND GALLERIES:
DRESDEN (Gemäldegal.): several works.

SARTORI, Giovanni Battista
Italian, 18th century.
Active in Castione, near Mori (Trentino), during the second half of the 18th century.
Sculptor.

Giovanni Battista Sartori sculpted two altars in the church in Garniga.

SARTORI, Girolamo. See **SARTORIO**

SARTORI, Giulio
Italian, 19th century.
Born c. 1840; died 1907.
Active in Verona.
Painter.

MUSEUMS AND GALLERIES:
VERONA: *Portrait of Domenico Scattola* (sometimes attributed to Giulio Aristide Sartorio).

SARTORI, Giuseppe
Italian, 19th century.
Born 1863, in Venice.
Painter. Historical subjects, genre scenes, architectural views, seascapes. Miniatures.

Giuseppe Sartori lived and worked in Milan. He exhibited work in Milan, Turin, Venice and Bologna.

SARTORI, Giuseppe Antonio or Joseph Anton
Italian, 18th century.
Born 1712, in Sacco, near Rovereto; died 16 August 1792, in Vienna.
Sculptor, architect.

Giuseppe Sartori was the brother of Domenico Sartori, with whom he sculpted the high altar and other altars of Trento Cathedral. He also executed sculptures in Sacco, Innsbruck and Rovereto.

SARTORI, Iginio
Italian, 20th century.
Born 1903, in Cremona; died 1980, in Cremona.
Painter. Figures, nudes, portraits, landscapes.

Iginio Sartori's paintings take their point of departure from a highly simplified drawing in broad sweeping lines in which the spaces and volumes are somewhat geometric. The colour range is restrained, each painting being based on a dominant colour that is developed almost like a cameo through gentle and discreet modulations rather than sudden leaps. The overall misty atmosphere of these paintings inspires feelings of dreamy melancholy. All these elements of his work show its close links with that of Balthus.

He took part in a number of collective exhibitions including *Attraverso l'Immagine* (*Through the Image*) held at the

Centro culturale in Cremona in 1995. He also showed his works at solo exhibitions.

BIBLIOGRAPHY:

Attraverso l'immagine, exhibition catalogue, Centro culturale Santa Maria della Pietà, Cremona, 1995.

SARTORI, J.C.

Italian, 17th century.

Painter, miniaturist.

The miniaturist J.C. Sartori painted two portraits of Cologne aristocrats in 1637.

SARTORI, Johann Siegmund

Austrian, 18th century.

Painter. Religious subjects, portraits.

Johann Sartori painted two portraits of prelates for St Florian's Abbey near Linz during the second half of the 18th century.

SARTORI, Martin

German, 18th century.

Sculptor.

Martin Sartori worked for the church of the Holy Cross in Dresden.

SARTORIO, Antoine

French, 20th century.

Born 27 January 1885, in Menton; died 18 February 1988, in Jouques (Bouches-du-Rhône).

Sculptor. Religious subjects. Monuments, groups, busts, low reliefs.

Antoine Sartorio, a pupil of Antoine Injalbert and Emmanuel Hannaux at the École des Beaux-Arts, Paris, did military service in the Vosges. He was awarded a travel scholarship in 1920.

He exhibited in a number of group exhibitions: from 1911, the Salon des Artistes Français, Paris; 1925, exhibition of decorative arts, Paris; 1931, Exposition Coloniale, Vincennes; 1937, Exposition Universelle, Paris. He was awarded a third and second-class medal in 1911, a silver medal in 1934, and a certificate of honour in 1937, and was made a Chevalier of the Légion d'Honneur in 1926.

From 1916 he carved various commemorative monuments and received commissions from the Municipality of Paris to decorate the façades of the Opéra and the Palais de Justice, and the outer walls of the Baumettes prison. In 1962 he worked on the restoration of the frieze of the Baptism of Clovis in Rheims Cathedral.

BIBLIOGRAPHY:

Ménard-Kiener, Violaine, *Antoine Sartorio. Sculpteur des corps et des âmes*, Privately printed, Le Tholonet, 1996.

AUCTION RECORDS:

LOKEREN, 12 March 1994, *Laurel Trees* (bronze, h. 14 1/4 ins / 36 cm, w. 2 3/4 ins/7 cm) BEF 28,000.

SARTORIO, Aristide or Giulio Aristide

Italian, 19th - 20th century.

Born 11 February 1860, in Rome; died 3 October 1932, in Rome.

Painter, pastellist, sculptor, medallist, engraver. Figure compositions, genre scenes, landscapes with figures.

A pupil of his father, Raffaello Sartorio, Aristide Sartorio's fame was based on the success of his vast compositions inspired by mythological subjects, not unlike the large works painted by the French academicians that regularly appeared at the salons in the last quarter of the 19th century. Taking his inspiration from the work of Dante Gabriel Rossetti, he was seen as one of the most important Italian painters of his generation. From time to time, Sartorio painted works in a rather different style, calm and harmonious with no sign of Impressionist influences. He illustrated Edmondo De Amici's children's book *Cuore*. He also worked as an architect and was a writer. Much has been written about his work, including a study by V. Picalini.

From 1891 he exhibited at the Salon des Artistes Français in Paris and then at the exhibitions in Munich and Berlin. He was awarded a gold medal at the Exposition Universelle of 1889.

G. A-SARTORIO

BIBLIOGRAPHY:

Osterwalder, Marcus (ed.), *Dictionnaire des illustrateurs 1800-1914*, Ides et Calendes, Neuchâtel, 1989.

MUSEUMS AND GALLERIES:

DIGNE-LES-BAINS: *Medal Commemorating the Expedition to the North Pole by Louis-Amédée of Savoy* - FLORENCE (Gal. d'Arte Moderna): *Hay Barn* - ROME (Gal. Nazionale d'Arte Moderna): *The Gorgon and the Hero*; *Diana of Ephesus and the Slaves* - TRIESTE (Civico Mus. Revoltella): *On the Sacred Island*; *The Victory at Ostia*.

AUCTION RECORDS:

ROME, 12 Feb 1974, *The Wounded Leg*, ITL 992,500. MILAN, 14 Dec 1976, *Child on the Beach* (1927, tempera, 11 3/4 x 23 1/2 ins / 30 x 60 cm) ITL 600,000. NEW YORK, 12 May 1978, *Albatrosses* (1924, oil on canvas remounted on board, 22 3/4 x 28 3/4 ins / 58 x 73 cm) USD 2,000. MILAN, 14 Dec 1978, *Children on the Beach* (tempera and pastel, 23 1/4 x 23 ins / 59 x 57.5 cm) ITL 1,900,000. LONDON, 10 May 1979, *Young Woman Reading by a Window* (1891, pastel, 25 3/4 x 11 1/2 ins / 65.5 x 29 cm) GBP 1,200. LONDON, 26 Nov 1980, *Albatross on a Pacific Island* (1924, oil on canvas remounted on board, 22 1/2 x 28 1/2 ins / 57 x 72.5 cm) GBP 600. MILAN, 22 April 1982, *Pontine Marches* (1908, oil on panel, 12 1/4 x 18 ins / 31 x 45.5 cm) ITL 4,000,000. ROME, 26 Oct 1983, *Gust of Wind* (1928, pastel, 12 1/4 x 31 ins / 31 x 79 cm) ITL 6,000,000. ROME, 26 Oct 1983, *Morning in Fregene* (1925, oil on canvas, 31 1/2 x 23 1/2 ins / 80 x 60 cm) ITL 22,000,000. ROME, 29 Oct 1985, *Catching Tuna* (oil on canvas, 113 x 228 1/4 ins / 287 x 580 cm) ITL 50,000,000. MILAN, 11 Dec 1986, *Allegory of Autumn* (oil on canvas, 98 1/2 x 141 3/4 ins / 250 x 360 cm) ITL 36,000,000. MILAN, 23 March 1988, *Monteleone from the Sea* (1920, oil on canvas, 22 x 28 1/4 ins / 56 x 71.5 cm) ITL 18,500,000. ROME, 25 May 1988, *River Landscape* (oil on canvas, 22 x 37 3/4 ins / 55 x 96 cm) ITL 7,000,000. ROME, 14 Dec 1988, *The Stele of Asarhaddon at Nahr el Kelb* (oil on canvas, 23 1/4 x 28 3/4 ins / 59 x 73 cm) ITL 19,000,000. NEW YORK, 23 Feb 1989, *Mexico, the Domes of El Carmel* (1924, oil on canvas mounted on board, 30 3/4 x 22 1/2 ins / 78.1 x 57.2 cm) USD 9,350. NEUILLY-SUR-SEINE, 16 March 1989, *The Tiber at Magliana* (1908, pastel, 11 x 22 1/2 ins / 28 x 57 cm) FRF 6,000. ROME, 12 Dec 1989, *The Valley of the Aniene* (pastel/paper, 9 1/4 x 22 1/2 ins / 23.5 x 57 cm) ITL 4,500,000. ROME, 14 Dec 1989, *Three Pigeons* (pastel, 11 x 14 1/4 ins / 28 x 36 cm) ITL 4,600,000. ROME, 31 May 1990, *Tierra del Fuego* (pastel/paper, 18 1/4 x 12 3/4 ins / 46.5 x 32.5 cm) ITL 6,500,000. ROME, 4 Dec 1990, *The Beach at Terracina* (oil on canvas, 18 1/2 x 22 1/4 ins / 47 x 56.5 cm) ITL 26,000,000. NEW YORK, 17 Oct 1991, *Allegory* (1892, oil on canvas, 19 3/4 x 24 1/2 ins / 50.2 x 62.2 cm) USD 7,700. ROME, 24 March 1992, *Young Leopard* (oil on canvas, 15 x 26 3/4 ins / 38 x 68 cm) ITL 18, 400,000. ROME, 9 June 1992, *Autumn* (pastel/paper, 17 1/4 x 9 3/4 ins / 44 x 25 cm) ITL 2,000,000. LONDON, 28 Oct 1992, *Penguins at Puntarenas in Chile* (pastel, gouache and gold paint, 11 x 22 ins / 28 x 55 cm) GBP 2,750. LONDON, 25 Nov 1992, *Shepherd and Flock in a Vast Landscape* (1896, oil on canvas mounted to board, 11 1/2 x 26 1/2 ins / 29.5 x 67 cm) GBP 7,150. ROME, 27 April 1993, *Swan on the Shore of a Lake* (pastel/paper, 11 x 14 3/4 ins / 27 x 37.5 cm) USD 3,941,000. MILAN, 9 Nov 1993, *Children on a Beach* (1927, oil on canvas, 78 3/4 x 36 1/4 ins / 200 x 92 cm) ITL 39,675,000. ROME, 8 March 1994, *Pine Trees at Castelfusano* (pastel/paper, 11 1/2 x 22 ins

/ 29 x 55 cm) ITL 11,500,000. LONDON, 16 March 1994, *Wooded Path* (1901, gouache and coloured chalks, 22 x 24 ins / 56 x 61 cm) GBP 2,185. NEW YORK, 20 July 1995, *Coastline near Arica* (oil on canvas board, 21 1/4 x 24 3/4 ins / 54 x 62.9 cm) USD 12,075. MILAN, 26 March 1996, *Flocks Grazing in the Roman Campagna* (1929, oil on canvas, 46 x 36 1/2 ins / 117 x 93 cm) ITL 30,475,000. MILAN, 25 March 1997, *Diana of Ephesis* (oil on canvas, 38 1/2 x 36 1/4 ins / 98 x 92 cm) ITL 20,970,000. ROME, 3 June 1999, *Campagna Romana, Colli Albani in the Background* (watercolour, 21 x 29 ins / 54 x 74 cm) ITL 13,000,000. LONDON, 21 Oct 1999, *Portrait of a Lady by an Urn* (oil on canvas, 79 x 35 ins / 200 x 89 cm) GBP 8,000. ROME, 4 June 2001, *Engine Room* (1929, mixed media on cardboard, 10 x 19 ins / 25 x 48 cm) ITL 7,500,000. ROME, 6 June 2001, *Square in Siena, Italy* (pastel, 10 x 14 ins / 26 x 36 cm) ITL 5,200,000. VENICE, 19 Oct 2002, *Anastasiella* (oil on canvas, 20 x 17 ins / 52 x 42 cm) EUR 4,000. MILAN, 10 Dec 2003, *Fregene Beach* (1927, oil on canvas/board, 31 x 22 ins / 79 x 57 cm) EUR 25,000. ROME, 11 Dec 2003, *Fishermen in Ardea* (1910, oil on canvas, 15 x 23 ins / 37 x 58 cm) EUR 32,000. MILAN, 12 Oct 2004, *Mount Leano from the Sea* (1920, oil on canvas, 22 x 28 ins / 56 x 71 cm) EUR 38,000.

SARTORIO, Girolamo, or Sartori
Italian, 19th century.
Active in Rome, from 1824 to 1830.
Sculptor.
He was the grandfather of Aristide Sartorio.
MUSEUMS AND GALLERIES:
MILAN (Biblioteca Ambrosiana): *Stag and Hunting Dog* (marble, group).

SARTORIO, Giuseppe
Italian, 19th century.
Born 1854, in Boccioleto.
Active in Turin.
Sculptor.
After studying with Antonino and then Tabacebi, Giuseppe Sartorio became a student at the Accademia di San Luca in Rome. In his later years, he devoted himself to carving funerary monuments, chiefly in Sardinia. He exhibited in Turin and Milan.

SARTORIO, Jacqueline, also known as Sarto
French, 20th century.
Sculptor.
Jacqueline Sartorio exhibited in Paris at the Salon des Artistes Français, of which she was a member and where she was awarded a bronze medal in 1943.

SARTORIO, Raffaele
Italian, 19th century.
Sculptor, painter.
He was the father of Aristide Sartorio.

SARTORIO, Xavier
Italian, 19th century.
Born 26 December 1846, in Calco Superiore.
Active in Geneva.
Modeller, sculptor, designer of ornamental architectural features.

SARTORIS, Alberto
Italian, 20th century.
Born 1901, in Turin; died 1998, in Cossonay-Ville (Lausanne).
Also active in Switzerland.
Painter (gouache), draughtsman, watercolourist, colourscreen printer, architect, art critic.
Futurism.
Alberto Sartoris studied at the School of Fine Arts in Geneva from 1916 to 1919, then at Turin from 1922 to 1926. He was one of the founders of the International Congress of Modern Architecture of Sarraz in 1928. In 1929 he organised the exhibition of Italian Futurist Artists; published in 1930 with Fillia the review *La Città Futurista* (*Futurist City*) and took part in 1932 in the exhibition of Italian Futurist Artists. In 1941, he signed the *Manifesto del Gruppo futurista primordiale Antonio Sant'Elia* and contributed from 1973 to the Spanish review *Nueva Forma*. He won the first grand prix of Architecture in Turin in 1927 and settled in Switzerland in 1930.

He met Marinetti and Prampolini at Geneva and also Theo van Doesburg in 1929, and developed at the heart of the European avant garde. He worked out a rationalist and functional work system, and drew numerous perspectives. He published many books, among which was a work of reference on modern architecture in 1932, *Gli elementi dell'architettura funzionale* (*The Elements of Functional Architecture*) and a work on *Sant'Elia e l'architettura futurista* (*Sant'Elia and Futuristic Architecture*). His house at Cossonay now contains his archive.

His work figured in the following group exhibitions: 1928, *First Italian Exhibition of Rationalist Architecture*, Rome; 1928, *First Exhibition of Futurist Architecture*, Turin; 1930, first Exhibition *Cercle et Carré*, Galerie 23, Paris; 1973, *Futurism 1909-1916*, Musée National D'Art Moderne, Paris; 1978, *Abstraction-Creation 1931-1936*, at Münster, and at the Musée d'Art Moderne de la Ville de Paris. His solo exhibitions included in 1972, Galleria d'Arte Martano, Turin; 1979, *Alberto Sartoris, un architetto razionalista* (*Alberto Sartoris, a rationalist architect*), National Gallery of Modern Art, Rome; 1980, Calouste Gulbenkian Foundation, Lisbon; 1986 Athenaeum School of Architecture, Lausanne; 1987, *Alberto Sartoris 1920-1985; mostra dell'opera grafica* (*Alberto Sartoris 1920-1985; exhibition of drawings*), Centro Culturale S. Agostino, Civic Museum, Crema; 1988, *Alberto Sartoris: l'immagine razionalista; 1917 - 1943* (*Alberto Sartoris: The Rationalist Image; 1917-1943*) Pinactoeca Civico, Como; 1995, Galerie Rivolta at Lausanne, Grenette at Sion and 2000, Centre Julio González, Valencian Institute of Modern Art, Valencia.
BIBLIOGRAPHY:
Rivadossi, Cristina, *L'integrazione delle arti ed il colore nel pensiero e nell'opera di Alberto Sartoris*, dissertation (Politecnico, Milan, 1994). Abriani, A., *Alberto Sartoris*, exhibition catalogue, Galleria d'Arte Martano, Turin, 1972. Fabre, Gladys C., *Abstraction-Création 1931-1936*, group exhibition catalogue, Westfälisches Landesmuseum für Kunst und Kulturgeschichte, Münster, Musée d'Art moderne de la Ville de Paris, Paris, 1978. Jeanneret, Marie-Louise, *Alberto Sartoris: dessins et aquarelles, projets d'architecture*, exhibition catalogue, Geneva, 1981. Krafft, Anthony/Gubler, Jacques (preface), *Alberto Sartoris, l'actualité du rationalisme*, exhibition catalogue, Bibliothèque des arts, Paris-Lausanne, 1986. Béguin, Martine/Felley, Jean-Paul, *Alberto Sartoris: en couleurs*, catalogue raisonné, Fondation Louis Moret, Martigny, 1992. Navarro, María Isabel/Casanova, Maria, et al., *Alberto Sartoris, 1901 - 1998: la concepción poética de la arquitectura*, exhibition catalogue, Centre Julio González, Instituto Valenciano de Arte Moderno, Valencia, 2000 (text in Spanish, English).

SARTORIS, Georges, or Sartonis
French, 19th century.
Born in La Roche-sur-Yon.
Painter. Historical subjects.
MUSEUMS AND GALLERIES:
LA ROCHE-SUR-YON: *Horse* (study) - POITIERS: *St Sebastian*.

SARTORIUS, C.. See **SARTORI**

SARTORIUS, C. J.
British, 19th century.
Active in London.

Painter. Seascapes.
C.J. Sartorius exhibited seascapes at the Royal Academy from 1810 to 1821.

SARTORIUS, C. J. Cl.

German, 18th century.
Active in Fritzlar in 1784.
Silhouettist (?).

C.J.Cl. Sartorius executed more than 700 silhouettes of his contemporaries.

SARTORIUS, Conrad

German, 16th century.
Born to a family originally from Monheim; died 1531.
Miniaturist, copyist.

Conrad Sartorius wrote and illuminated a psalter, now in the Bayerische Staatsbibliothek in Munich, in which the plants and animals are depicted with marvellous accuracy.

SARTORIUS, Francis, the Younger

British, 18th century.
Born c. 1777; died probably after 1808.
Painter. Seascapes.

Francis Sartorius the Younger was the son of the sports painter John Nott Sartorius.

MUSEUMS AND GALLERIES:
NORWICH (Castle Mus. and AG): *Stranded Vessel, Great Yarmouth; Saving a Crew at Anholt.*

AUCTION RECORDS:
LONDON, 9 Dec 1927, *Naval Battle,* GBP 60. BILLINGSHURST, 20 July 1999, *Shipping in Stormy Seas* (1808, oil on panel, a pair, 12 x 18 ins / 30 x 45 cm) GBP 1,800.

SARTORIUS, Francis, the Elder

British, 18th century.
Born 1734; died 5 March 1804, in London.
Active in London.
Painter. Hunting scenes, sporting subjects, horse racing scenes, landscapes, animals.

Francis Sartorius the Elder was the son of John and the father of John N. Sartorius. He exhibited sports compositions at the Society of Artists, the Free Society and the Royal Academy from 1773 to 1791. The success enjoyed at the end of the 18th century by both Francis and John N. Sartorius reflects not only the excellent quality of their respective animal portraiture but also the traditional Anglo-Saxon passion for sport in general and for horse-racing and hunting in particular.

AUCTION RECORDS:
LONDON, 22 July 1898, *Hunting Scene,* FRF 2,750. LONDON, 18 Dec 1909, *Landscape* (1767) GBP 16. LONDON, 12 March 1910, *Racing at Newmarket, April 20, 1767,* GBP 84; *Horse and Jockey* (1794) GBP 144. LONDON, 24 Feb 1922, *The Meet of Hounds,* GBP 262; *In Full Cry,* GBP 210; *Two Hunting Dogs,* GBP 99. LONDON, 31 March 1922, *Fox-Hunt* (four paintings) GBP 294. LONDON, 17 July 1925, *Colonel Foord Bowes,* GBP 241. LONDON, 20 Nov 1925, *Eclipse and Jockey,* GBP 157. LONDON, 21 June 1926, *Fox-Hunt,* GBP 115. LONDON, 5 July 1926, *Lord Bulkeley and Hunt,* GBP 168. LONDON, 4 March 1927, *Equestrian Event,* GBP 136. LONDON, 4 July 1927, *Horse-Race; Hunter* (collection) GBP 120. LONDON, 23 Nov 1928, *Racehorse; Racehorse 'Mist'* (both) GBP 231. LONDON, 15 March 1929, *Naval Battle,* GBP 273. LONDON, 12 April 1929, *Two Racehorses Competing,* GBP 357; *Jason beating Brillant to the Post,* GBP 325; *Race between a Grey and a Bay,* GBP 199. LONDON, 7 June 1929, *Fox-Hunt,* GBP 1,575. LONDON, 5 July 1929, *On the Way to the Meet,* GBP 136. LONDON, 29 Nov 1929, *Going to the Meet,* GBP 273. LONDON, 20 June 1930, *Richard Lambert and Hounds,* GBP 336. LONDON, 25 June 1930, *Hunting Scene,* GBP 340. LONDON, 18 June 1931, *The Hunt,* GBP 400. NEW YORK, 20 Nov 1931, *Horse Race,* USD 375. NEW YORK, 18 and 19 April 1934, *Racehorse 'Minister',* USD 450. LONDON, 13 Nov 1936, *C. Warre-Malet's Horses,* GBP 168. LONDON, 16 July 1937, *Fox-Hunt,* GBP 105. LONDON, 29 April 1938, *The Kill,* GBP 241. LONDON, 1 July 1938, *Hunters and Hounds,* GBP 131. LONDON, 27 July 1945, *In Full Cry,* GBP 357. LONDON, 3 July 1946, *The Meet,* GBP 290. LONDON, 5 Feb 1947, *Park with Horse and Hound,* GBP 100. NEW YORK, 26 and 27 Feb 1947, *Fox-Hunt* (four paintings) USD 540. LONDON, 6 Nov 1959, *Carousel,* GBP 273. LONDON, 24 Nov 1965, *Thoroughbred,* GBP 340. LONDON, 21 July 1967, *Landscape with Thoroughbred and Jockey,* Gns 1,200. LONDON, 27 Nov 1968, *Landscape with Hunter,* GBP 1,500. LONDON, 17 March 1971, *Two Gentlemen Riding in a Park,* GBP 780. LONDON, 19 July 1972, *Hunting Scene,* GBP 9,000. LONDON, 26 June 1974, *Master of Hounds,* GBP 10,000. LONDON, 18 June 1976, *Landscape with Six Hunters* (1774, oil on canvas, 34 1/2 x 48 ins / 87.6 x 122 cm) GBP 5,500. LONDON, 25 Nov 1977, *Bellario and Jockey* (oil on canvas, 9 1/2 x 13 1/2 ins / 24 x 34.2 cm) GBP 1,700. LONDON, 23 March 1979, *Hunting Scene* (oil on canvas, 32 x 59 ins / 81.2 x 149.8 cm) GBP 9,500. NEW ORLEANS, 26 June 1981, *Hunter with Horse and Hounds* (1776, oil on canvas, 25 x 30 ins / 63.5 x 76.2 cm) USD 25,000. NEW YORK, 6 June 1985, *Landscape with Thoroughbred* (oil on canvas, 24 x 29 1/4 ins / 61 x 74.5 cm) USD 10,500. NEW YORK, 6 June 1986, *Hunting Dogs in a Courtyard* (1787, oil on canvas, 33 1/4 x 47 1/4 ins / 84.3 x 120 cm) USD 42,000. LONDON, 15 July 1987, *John Beard holding Captain Bertie's 'Sportsman'* (1769, oil on canvas, 39 x 49 ins / 99 x 124.5 cm) GBP 36,000. LONDON, 9 Feb 1990, *Mares and Foals in a Meadow* (oil on canvas, 25 x 30 ins / 63.5 x 76.2 cm) GBP 1,760. LONDON, 14 March 1990, *Sailing in Heavy Seas* (1906, oil on panel, pair, each 11 1/2 x 17 3/4 ins / 29 x 45 cm) GBP 14,300. LONDON, 30 May 1990, *Vessel at Sea off Foreland* (1803, oil on panel, 12 x 18 ins / 30.5 x 46 cm) GBP 2,200. LONDON, 26 Oct 1990, *Landscape with Groom Riding a Hunter, accompanied by a Hound* (oil on canvas, 23 1/2 x 29 1/2 ins / 59.7 x 75 cm) GBP 1,980. LONDON, 22 May 1991, *Capture of Galleys Laden with Treasure off Cadiz, 1804* (oil on canvas, 25 x 34 ins / 63.5 x 86.5 cm) GBP 15,400. NEW YORK, 7 June 1991, *Gathering for the Hunt* (1780, oil on canvas, 37 x 57 ins / 94 x 144.8 cm) USD 28,600. LONDON, 10 July 1991, *The Honourable John Smith Barry and his Pack of Hounds* (oil on canvas, 20 1/2 x 39 1/4 ins / 52 x 100 cm) GBP 38,500. LONDON, 8 April 1992, *Start of the Hunt* (oil on canvas, 29 x 62 1/2 ins / 73.5 x 159 cm) GBP 18,700. LONDON, 10 April 1992, *Jockey Riding the Thoroughbred 'Goldfinger' with other Riders in the background* (oil on canvas, 25 x 30 ins / 63.5 x 76.2 cm) GBP 11,000. NEW YORK, 5 June 1992, *The Earl of Kingstone's 'Christophas'* (oil on canvas, 25 x 30 ins / 63.5 x 76.2 cm) USD 31,900. LONDON, 20 Nov 1992, *Thoroughbred 'Daniel' with Jockey and a Groom carrying a Horse-Blanket* (oil on canvas, 17 1/2 x 25 1/2 ins / 44.4 x 64.8 cm) GBP 13,200. MONACO, 2 July 1993, *Still-life with Fish* (1746, oil on canvas, 28 1/4 x 45 ins / 71.5 x 114 cm) FRF 33,300. NEW YORK, 3 June 1994, *Racehorse 'Minister'* (1774, oil on canvas, 40 1/4 x 50 1/2 ins / 102.2 x 128.3 cm) USD 46,000. LONDON, 13 July 1994, *'Bordeaux', a Thoroughbred Grey with Jockey* (1778, oil on canvas, 22 1/2 x 27 1/4 ins / 57 x 69.5 cm) GBP 3,450. NEW YORK, 9 June 1995, *Wooded Landscape with Pack of Hounds* (1785, oil on canvas, pair, each 33 1/2 x 39 ins / 85.1 x 99.1 cm) USD 48,875. LONDON, 13 Nov 1996, *Landscape with Small Dog* (1782, oil on canvas, 25 x 39 ins / 63.5 x 99 cm) GBP 5,750. NEW YORK, 11 April 1997, *Tortoise; Cardinal Puff; Pumpkin; Racehorse 'Snap'* (1766, oil on canvas, set of four, 10 x 14 ins / 25.4 x 35.6 cm and 9 1/4 x 13 ins/23.5 x 33 cm) USD 64,100. LONDON, 9 July 1997, *Groom leading the Bay 'Cullen'* (1772, oil on canvas, 25 x 30 ins / 63.5 x 76 cm) GBP 27,600. LONDON, 12 Nov 1997, *Landscape with Mares and Foals* (oil on canvas, 39 1/4 x 49 1/4 ins / 100 x 125 cm) GBP 23,000. LONDON, 12 Nov 1997, *Training at Newmarket* (oil on canvas, 41 3/4 x 56 ins / 106 x 142 cm) GBP 54,300. LONDON, 28 May 1999, *Hunt in Wooded Landscape with For-*

tified House and Church Beyond (1783, oil on canvas, 42 x 72 ins / 107 x 183 cm) GBP 27,000. LONDON, 14 July 1999, *Hunt in Full Cry, Breaking Cover* (oil on canvas, 36 x 60 ins / 91 x 152 cm) GBP 30,000. NEW YORK, 1 June 2001, *Two Pointers in a Landscape* (1787, oil on canvas, 25 x 30 ins / 63 x 76 cm) USD 6,000. LONDON, 4 July 2002, *Horseman on the Road to Bagshot. Horseman in a Landscape* (oil on canvas, a pair, 13 x 17 ins / 34 x 42 cm) GBP 6,200. LONDON, 27 Nov 2002, *Sir Patrick Blake's Sir Anthony held by a Groom in Landscape* (1770, oil on canvas, 24 x 29 ins / 61 x 74 cm) GBP 6,000. LONDON, 2 July 2003, *Goldfinger* (1770, oil on canvas, 24 x 29 ins / 61 x 73 cm) GBP 8,500. AMSTERDAM, 10 Dec 2003, *Laburnum, with Jockey Up* (1782, oil on canvas, 25 x 30 ins / 63 x 76 cm) EUR 28,000. LONDON, 21 May 2004, *Chaise Match Run on Newmarket Heath on Wednesday 29 August 1750* (oil on canvas, 20 x 30 ins / 51 x 77 cm) GBP 21,000. LONDON, 25 Nov 2004, *Race at Newmarket* (oil on canvas, 27 x 35 ins / 69 x 90 cm) GBP 20,000.

SARTORIUS, J. F. S.
British, 19th century.
Born c. 1775, in London; died c. 1830.
Painter. Sporting subjects, animals.

J.F.S. Sartorius was the eldest son of John N. Sartorius. He exhibited in London from 1793 to 1831 and at the Royal Academy between 1797 and 1829.

AUCTION RECORDS:

LONDON, 5 Dec 1928, *Hunter on Horseback with Two Hounds,* GBP 92. LONDON, 8 May 1936, *Fox Hunt* (four paintings) GBP 651. LONDON, 27 June 1945, *Gentleman with Groom and Hounds,* GBP 185. LONDON, 25 April 1969, *Landscape with Hunter and Three Hounds,* Gns 6,000. LONDON, 19 July 1972, *Hambletonian Horses; Eclipse* (two canvases) GBP 1,200. LONDON, 11 July 1984, *Hare* (oil on canvas, 14 1/2 x 17 3/4 ins / 37 x 45 cm) GBP 11,000. LONDON, 22 Nov 1985, *Neck-and-Neck* (1806, oil on canvas, 13 1/2 x 18 1/2 ins / 34.3 x 47 cm) GBP 6,500. NEW YORK, 5 June 1986, *Hunters and Hounds in a River Landscape* (oil on canvas, pair, 14 x 25 ins / 35.5 x 63.5 cm) USD 12,000. NEW YORK, 9 April 1999, *Rockingham and Whiskey, Racehorses* (1798, oil on copper, a pair, 5 x 6 ins / 12 x 16 cm) USD 6,000. NEW YORK, 9 April 1999, *Grey Diomed, Lurcher, Sir Thomas, Flying Childers* (oil on copper, set of four, 5 x 6 ins / 12 x 16 cm) USD 14,000. LONDON, 11 June 2002, *Going Out. Full Cry* (oil on canvas, a pair, 10 x 14 ins / 25 x 35 cm) GBP 4,500. LONDON, 3 June 2003, *Dead Game in an Interior - Woodcock, Snipe and Rabbit* (1862, oil on canvas, 20 x 24 ins / 50 x 60 cm) GBP 2,600. LONDON, 21 May 2004, *Dead Snipe Hanging from a Nail* (oil on canvas laid on panel, 13 x 12 ins / 34 x 30 cm) GBP 11,000.

SARTORIUS, Johann Christoph or Jakob Christopher, or Sartori
German, 17th - 18th century.
Painter, engraver. Portraits, still-lifes.

Johann Christoph or Jakob Christopher Sartorius worked in Nuremberg between 1680 and 1730. He engraved burin portraits and decorations for bookshops. He was himself a publisher.

AUCTION RECORDS:

STOCKHOLM, 10-12 May 1993, *Still-life of Flowers in an Urn Decorated with Putti* (oil/copper, 14 1/4 x 10 1/4 ins / 36 x 26 cm) SEK 80,000.

SARTORIUS, John
British, 18th century.
Born 1700, in Nuremberg; died c. 1780, in London.
Painter. Sporting subjects, horses.

John Sartorius was the father of Francis Sartorius the Elder. He exhibited at the Society of Artists and at the Free Society from 1768 to 1777 and specialised in horse portraits, with some hunting and racing scenes.

SARTORIUS, John Nott, or Nost
British, 18th - 19th century.
Born 26 May 1759, in London; died c. 1828.
Painter. Hunting scenes, sporting subjects, horse racing scenes, horses.

John Nott Sartorius was the son of Francis Sartorius the Elder. Probably the most prolific and technically competent member of this artist family, he exhibited at the Royal Academy from 1778 to 1824. A large number of his compositions were engraved in mezzotint by Walker, Webb and Peltro.

BIBLIOGRAPHY:

Coombs, David, '*The Englishman's art-sport and the countryside in English Painting 1650-1850*' in *Connoisseur, CXCVI/790*.

AUCTION RECORDS:

LONDON, 12 March 1910, *Coursing* (1821) GBP 37; *Death of the Fox,* GBP 231. LONDON, 23 Feb 1923, *Fox Hunt* (five paintings) GBP 283. LONDON, 23 May 1924, *In Full Cry,* GBP 336. PARIS, 14 Nov 1924, *Dandy on Horseback (Hunting Scene); The Hunt: Riders in Red Habits* (both) FRF 3,100. LONDON, 27 Feb 1925, *In Full Cry,* GBP 178. LONDON, 20 Nov 1925, *Hounds Harrying a Stag,* GBP 204; *Flushing Game; The Kill* (both) GBP 315. LONDON, 20 Nov 1925, *Mounted Gentleman,* GBP 210. LONDON, 12 Feb 1926, *Fox Hunt* (four paintings) GBP 252. LONDON, 12 March 1926, *Fox Hunt* (four paintings) GBP 525. LONDON, 19 May 1926, *Benjamin Aislabie,* GBP 136. LONDON, 30 June 1926, *Racehorse: 'Careless Cheery',* GBP 680. LONDON, 18 Nov 1927, *The Kill,* GBP 199. LONDON, 10 Feb 1928, *Smolensko Winning the Derby,* GBP 115. LONDON, 13 July 1928, *Thomas Oldaker in Hunting Dress,* GBP 4,935. LONDON, 27 July 1928, *Huntsmen and Hounds,* GBP 178. LONDON, 14 Dec 1928, *The Hunt* (pendants) GBP 3,255. LONDON, 22 Feb 1929, *Hunter Clearing a Hedge,* GBP 462. LONDON, 12 April 1929, *Fox Hunt,* GBP 609. LONDON, 28 June 1929, *Fox Hunt,* GBP 1,312. LONDON, 19 July 1929, *Duke of Beaufort's Hunt* (pair) GBP 3,045; *Horses and Groom,* GBP 252. LONDON, 21 Feb 1930, *Derby Day; Two Fighting Cocks,* GBP 168. LONDON, 26 Feb 1930, *Thomas Fenton,* GBP 199. LONDON, 20 June 1930, *Colonel Newport at the Hunt,* GBP 3,150. LONDON, 25 July 1930, *George III Hunting at Chalfont,* GBP 231. LONDON, 12 June 1931, *Pheasant Shoot.* LONDON, 16 April 1934, *Fox Hunt* (six paintings) GBP 924. LONDON, 22 Feb 1935, *Fox-Hunting at Braunston Hall,* GBP 420. LONDON, 20 Aug 1941, *The Meet; The Kill,* GBP 270. LONDON, 24 June 1942, *Racing at Ascot,* GBP 150; *Fox Hunt,* GBP 210. LONDON, 10 Dec 1943, *Racing at Newmarket,* GBP 262. LONDON, 3 Nov 1944, *Portrait of a Hunter,* GBP 220. LONDON, 26 Oct 1945, *In Full Cry,* GBP 315. LONDON, 31 May 1946, *Racing at Ascot,* GBP 220. LONDON, 25-26 Nov 1946, *Huntsman and Hounds,* GBP 420. LONDON, 10 Dec 1958, *Death of a Fox,* GBP 420. LONDON, 22 April 1959, *Death of a Fox,* GBP 320. NEW YORK, 20 Jan 1961, *Pack of Hounds,* USD 550. LONDON, 7 June 1961, *Race between Hambletonian and Diamond,* GBP 320. LONDON, 23 May 1962, *The 3,000 Guineas,* GBP 300. LONDON, 20 Nov 1963, *Hunting Party (The Quarry),* GBP 950. LONDON, 3 June 1964, *In Full Cry,* GBP 700. LONDON, 2 April 1965, *Stable Lads leading their Horses,* Gns 950. LONDON, 17 June 1966, *Hunt,* Gns 1,800. LONDON, 21 July 1967, *Horseman and Horsewoman in a Landscape,* Gns 3,200. LONDON, 12 March 1969, *Hunting Scenes* (four canvases, pendants) GBP 21,000. LONDON, 10 Dec 1971, *Landscape with Huntsman,* Gns 4,800. NEW YORK, 18 May 1972, *Landscape with Huntsman and Hound,* USD 10,500. LONDON, 21 June 1974, *Edward Parket on Horseback with his Son,* Gns 4,000. LONDON, 18 June 1976, *Hunting Scene* (1818, oil on canvas, 16 1/2 x 23 1/2 ins / 42 x 59.6 cm) GBP 1,500. LONDON, 25 Nov 1977, *Over the Jumps* (1788, oil on canvas, 9 1/2 x 11 1/2 ins / 24.2 x 29.2 cm) GBP 1,700. LONDON, 21 March 1979, *Three Horses in a Wooded Landscape* (1789, oil on canvas, 35 1/2 x 46 ins / 90 x 116 cm) GBP 8,000. LONDON, 18 March 1981, *Hambletonian beating Diamond at Craven Races* (1799, oil on canvas, 24 1/4 x 35 1/4 ins / 61.5 x 89.5 cm) GBP 12,500. NEW YORK, 11 April 1984, *Child Portrait T. Thornhill Esq. at the Hunt* (1789, oil on canvas, 25 x 30 1/4 ins / 63.5 x 77 cm) USD 21,000. NEW YORK, 7 June 1985, *Landscaper with Horseman* (1790, oil on canvas, 25 x 30 ins / 63.5 x 76.2 cm) USD 22,000. NEW YORK, 6 June 1986, *King David beating Surveyor in the Coronation Cup, Newcastle, July 5* (1815, oil on canvas, 24 1/4 x 30 ins / 61.6 x 76.5 cm) USD 85,000. LONDON, 15 July 1987, *The Old Surrey Stag Hounds...* (oil on canvas, 37 x 54 3/4 ins / 94 x 139 cm) GBP 40,000. LONDON, 15 July 1988, *Pair Tethered by the Stable* (oil on canvas, 28 x 34 1/4 ins / 71 x 86.7 cm) GBP 17,600. LONDON, 18 Nov 1988, *Landscape with the Bay Trotting Horse Samson* (1807, oil on canvas, 17 x 21 ins / 43.2 x 53.5 cm) GBP 3,300. NEW YORK, 24 May 1989, *The Kill* (1808, oil on canvas, 28 x 36 1/4 ins / 71.1 x 91.8 cm) USD 20,900. BRUSSELS, 19 Dec 1989, *Releasing the Pack* (1781, oil on canvas, 19 x 27 1/4 ins / 48 x 69 cm) BEF 110,000. NEW YORK, 1 March 1990, *Landscape with Coupé* (oil on canvas, 17 x 21 1/4 ins / 43.1 x 54 cm) USD 24,200. LONDON, 14 March 1990, *Jumping the Gate* (1814, oil on canvas, pair, each 17 1/2 x 27 1/2 ins / 44.5 x 70 cm) GBP 15,400. LONDON, 20 July 1990, *Clearing the Hedge* (oil on canvas, 17 x 21 ins / 43 x 53.5 cm) GBP 4,400. LONDON, 12 April 1991, *Pack Hound in a Mountain Landscape* (oil on canvas, 14 x 17 ins / 35.5 x 43 cm) GBP 4,950. NEW YORK, 7 June 1991, *Grey Hunter Saddled and Tethered to a Fence* (1791, oil on canvas, 25 x 29 3/4 ins / 63.5 x 75.6 cm) USD 8,800. LONDON, 12 July 1991, *Francis Drake-Brockman and his Pack* (1783, oil on canvas, 35 x 52 1/4 ins / 89 x 133 cm) GBP 19,800. LONDON, 8 April 1992, *Landscape with Huntsmen and Groom* (1789, oil on canvas, 36 x 46 ins / 90.5 x 116 cm) GBP 19,250. NEW YORK, 5 June 1992, *Calling a Halt; Pack on the Scent* (oil on canvas, pair, each 24 1/2 x 29 1/4 ins / 62.2 x 74.3 cm) USD 38,500. NEW YORK, 3 June 1994, *Landscape with Huntsman on a Chestnut Horse and Two Hounds* (1796, oil on canvas, 19 1/2 x 23 1/2 ins / 49.5 x 59.7 cm) USD 14,950. NEW YORK, 9 June 1995, *Hunt Entering the Woods* (1808, oil on canvas, 28 x 36 ins / 71.1 x 91.4 cm) USD 40,250. LONDON, 10 July 1996, *River Landscape with Huntsmen* (1787, oil on canvas, 27 x 35 ins / 68.5 x 89 cm) GBP 17,250. LONDON, 13 Nov 1996, *Lurcher ahead of Kitt Carr and Ormond, 1793* (oil on canvas, 29 1/4 x 41 ins / 74 x 104 cm) GBP 29,900. LONDON, 13 Nov 1997, *Epson Derby Sweepstakes; Ascot Oatlands Sweepstakes; Grey Diomed beating Travellers* (1790-1792, aquatint, three items) GBP 4,600. LONDON, 27 May 1999, *Colonel Newport and his Hounds in River Landscape* (1800, oil on canvas, 39 x 58 ins / 98 x 147 cm) GBP 81,000. LONDON, 28 May 1999, *Bay Hunter with Groom in Landscape. Saddled Bay Hunter Held by Groom* (1791, oil on canvas, a pair, 25 x 30 ins / 63 x 76 cm) GBP 32,000. LONDON, 4 July 2000, *Sophia Got by Buzzard, Bay Racehorse with Jockey Up on Newmarket Heath* (1811, oil on canvas, 28 x 36 ins / 71 x 91 cm) GBP 18,000. NEW YORK, 6 Dec 2000, *Waiting for Master. Waiting for Mistress* (oil on canvas, a pair, 14 x 17 ins / 36 x 44 cm) USD 23,000. NEW YORK, 7 June 2001, *Chestnut and Bay Hunter with Groom and Spaniel* (1783, oil on canvas, 28 x 36 ins / 70 x 91 cm) USD 35,000. NEW YORK, 7 June 2001, *Gentleman on a Bay Hunter with a Groom Leading a Black Hunter Outside a Stable* (1780, oil on canvas, 28 x 36 ins / 71 x 91 cm) USD 50,000. DORCHESTER, 28 Feb 2002, *Three Hunters in a Wooded Landscape with a Huntsman and a Groom* (1789, oil on canvas, 35 x 45 ins / 89 x 114 cm) GBP 22,000. LONDON, 28 Nov 2002, *Groom Holding a Lady and Gentleman's Hunters in a Landscape* (oil on canvas) GBP 14,000. SALISBURY, 1 Oct 2003, *Whipper-in with a Horse and Hounds* (oil on canvas, 13 x 17 ins / 34 x 43 cm) GBP 4,400. LEYBURN, 19 Nov 2003, *Racehorse Held by a Groom Beside a Building* (1772, oil on canvas, 24 x 29 ins / 62 x 74 cm) GBP 19,000. NEW YORK, 3 June 2004, *Run with Mr James Drake Brockham's Hounds at Beachborough, Kent. Hunting Scenes* (1792, oil on canvas, set of six, 20 x 24 ins / 51 x 62 cm) USD 90,000. LONDON, 25 Nov 2004, *Prince of Wales's Traveller Beating Lord Grosvenor's Meteor* (oil on canvas, 27 x 35 ins / 69 x 89 cm) GBP 24,000.

SARTORIUS, M. (Miss)
British, 19th century.
Painter. Still-lifes.

M. Sartorius exhibited examples of her work at the British Institution in London in 1813.

SARTORIUS, Paulus
Hungarian, 16th century.
Painter.

Paulus Sartorius painted an altarpiece for the church in Fiser in Romania in 1520.

SARTORIUS, Virginie de
Belgian, 19th century.
Born 1828, in Liège.
Painter. Genre scenes, still-lifes (flowers/fruit).

MUSEUMS AND GALLERIES:

LIÈGE.

AUCTION RECORDS:

PARIS, 25-26 June 1945, *Basket of Flowers and Fruit* (1852) FRF 3,500. NEW YORK, 24 May 1988, *Still-life with Fruit* (1855, oil on canvas, 30 1/4 x 26 1/4 ins / 76.8 x 66.7 cm) USD 22,000. AMSTERDAM, 19 Oct 1993, *Still-life with a Large Floral Composition Around a Marble Sculpture, Possibly a Bust of Marie-Louise d'Orléans, on a Table in Front of a Curtain* (1851, oil on canvas, 46 3/4 x 40 1/4 ins / 119 x 102 cm) NLG 19,550. NEW YORK, 23 Oct 1997, *Preparing a Bouquet* (oil on canvas, 31 1/2 x 23 1/2 ins / 80 x 59.7 cm) USD 21,850. BRUSSELS, 23 Nov 1999, *Still-life with Grapes and Peaches* (oil on canvas, 21 x 27 ins / 54 x 69 cm) BEF 70,000. AMSTERDAM, 5 Sept 2000, *Still-life of Fruit and Flowers on Marble Ledge* (oil on canvas, 22 x 27 ins / 55 x 68 cm) NLG 8,000. BRUSSELS, 21 March 2001, *Still-life with Fruit* (1869, oil on canvas, 22 x 28 ins / 57 x 71 cm) BEF 410,000. BRUSSELS, 19 March 2003, *Virgin Adoring the Child* (1863, oil on canvas, 35 x 28 ins / 90 x 70 cm) EUR 3,600. BRUSSELS, 18 June 2003, *Still-life with Flowers* (1875, oil on panel, 12 x 16 ins / 31 x 40 cm) EUR 1,800.

SARTORIUS, William G.
British, 18th century.
Painter. Portraits, animals, still-lifes (flowers/fruit/fish), insects.

William G. Sartorius exhibited animal portraits at the Free Society in London from 1773 to 1779.

AUCTION RECORDS:

LONDON, 11 July 1962, *Still-life with Lobster and Two Bottles of Wine*, GBP 800. LONDON, 23 June 1972, *Landscape with Horse*, Gns 800. LONDON, 27 June 1980, *Landscape with Spaniels, Terrier and Cat* (oil on canvas, 32 3/4 x 42 ins / 83.2 x 106.7 cm) GBP 7,000. LONDON, 9 July 1986, *Still-life with Fruit* (oil on canvas, 27 1/2 x 35 ins / 70 x 89 cm) GBP 10,000. AMSTERDAM, 28 Nov 1989, *Stlil-life with Autumnal Fruit on a Marble Slab* (oil on canvas, 18 1/4 x 25 ins / 46.5 x 62.6 cm) NLG 14,950. LONDON, 10 April 1991, *Still-life with Fruit on a Slab* (oil on canvas, pair, each 11 1/2 x 13 3/4 ins / 29 x 35 cm) GBP 3,960. LONDON, 12 July 1991, *Still-life with Mackerel, Gurnard and Other Fish with a Copper Stewpot and a Knife on a Stone Slab* (1754, oil on canvas, 23 x 34 1/2 ins / 58.5 x 87.5 cm) GBP 1,980. LONDON, 8 April 1992, *Still-life with Fruit, Birds and Insects in a Grotto* (oil on canvas, 23 1/4 x 26 ins / 59 x 66 cm) GBP 6,820. LONDON, 5 July 2000, *Still-life of Basket of Fruit on Stone Ledge* (oil on canvas laid on board, 12 x 14 ins / 30 x 35 cm) GBP 1,500.

SARTORJ, Federico
Italian, 18th century.

Active in 1769.
Cameo engraver.

SARTORY, Franz
Austrian, 18th - 19th century.
Born 1770, in Dürnholz; died 22 October 1846, in Vienna.
Painter (porcelain). Landscapes, ruins.

Franz Sartory trained at the academy in Vienna and was a painter at the Vienna Porcelain Factory. He painted the ruins of Austrian fortresses.

SARTORY, J. M.
Austrian, 18th century.
Active in Windischgrätz during the first half of the 18th century.
Painter.

J.M. Sartory painted religious subjects and still-lifes.

SARTORY, Josef August. See **SATORY**

SARU, Gheorghe
Romanian, 20th century.
Born 1 March 1920, in Checea, near Timisoara.
Collage artist. Designs for tapestries, designs for mosaics.

Gheorghe Saru trained at the school of fine art in Iasi from 1939 to 1944, then at the school of fine art in Bucharest from 1946 to 1948. He taught at the Nicolai Grigorescu Institute of Fine Art in Bucharest. He spent some time at Mexico City as well as in Italy, France and Portugal. Saru created very colourful, monumental works, notably mosaics and tapestries executed in various Romanian towns, including Iasi, Bucharest and Galati He also worked as an art critic and was editor in chief of the magazine *Art in the People's Republic of Romania*.

Saru featured in important exhibitions devoted to contemporary Romanian art including: Venice Biennale 1954, 1956, and 1960); Belgrade and Budapest (1959); Paris, Prague, Tel-Aviv and Moscow (1969); St Petersburg and Prague (1972); Washington and Chicago (1973); Berlin and Quebec (1974); Stockholm (1975); Madrid, Moscow and Shanghai (1977); New Orleans and Washington (1983). Solo exhibitions include: Bucharest (1956, 1960, 1970, 1977 and 1981); Moscow (1959); New Orleans (1983); Washington (1983 and 1987); New York from 1985).

MUSEUMS AND GALLERIES:
BUCHAREST (Muz. National de Arta al României) - PARIS (MAMVP) - ST PETERSBURG (Hermitage).

SARUCINI, Carlo. See **SARACENI**

SARUDNYI, Ivan Petrovich, or Zarudnyi
Russian, 18th century.
Sculptor.

Sarudnyi was active in Moscow during the first half of the 18th century. He also worked as an architect.

SARVIG, Edvard Joh
Danish, 20th century.
Born 6 June 1894, in Copenhagen.
Active in Kirke Värlöse.
Painter. Landscapes.

SARYAN, Martiros Sergeevich, or Sarian
Armenian, 20th century.
Born 28 February 1880, in Rostov-on-Don; died 1972, in Yerevan.
Painter (gouache). Scenes with figures, figures, portraits, still-lifes, flowers, landscapes. Stage sets. Symbolism.
Groups: Golubaya Roza (Blue Rose), Obshchestvo Khudoznikov 4 Iskusstva (Four Arts Society of Artists).

Martiros Saryan was interested from childhood in the history and traditions of Armenia, his family's region of origin. In 1896 he went to Moscow where he trained under Aleksei Korin, Leonid Pasternak and Abram Arkhipov, from 1897 to 1901, at the institute of painting, sculpture and architecture. He took his first trip to Armenia in 1901, then worked again in Moscow from 1903 to 1905 in the workshop of Valentin Serov and Konstantin Korovin. He belonged to the Golubaya Roza (Blue Rose) group which, with the Bubnovy Valet (Jack of Diamonds) group, arose from the Mir Izkusstva (World of Art) group which, in the last years of the 19th century, had started directing Russian art towards the concerns of Western painters and lasted until the Revolution. Saryan became a member of the Association of Russian Artists in about 1910-1911 and at the same time sold three of his works to the Tretyakov Gallery. He travelled to Turkey (1910), Egypt (1911) and Iran (1912). He joined wholeheartedly the Revolution in 1917 and a little later founded a Society of Artists in Rostov, his home-town. He left his region of origin in 1921 and, when invited by the authorities, returned to Yerevan, the capital of Armenia, where he settled. That same year, he was appointed director of the National Museum of Armenia. A member of the Four Arts Society of Artists from 1925 to 1929, he went on assignment to Paris in 1926 and stayed there for a year.

At the turn of the 20th century in Moscow, legends and fantasies dominated Saryan's production, and he was highly influenced by medieval miniatures. He gradually abandoned this Symbolism, letting go of the decorative refinements of colour for a more pithy style. He became acquainted with the work of French painters, the Impressionists in particular, but also Gauguin, by whom he was certainly inspired, and even Matisse, and directed his own pursuits along these lines. During his trips to Turkey, Egypt and Iran, he borrowed motifs and subjects from the life and culture of the countries of the Near East. He used them in his paintings and came close to Fauvism, with highly simplified, defined planes in bright, contrasting colours where the very harsh light contrasted sharply with shade. After the post-revolutionary enthusiasm, the political climate very quickly hardened and Saryan, true to his commitment, tackled subjects more compliant with the official directives. From 1921 onwards, having settled in Yerevan, he painted landscapes, the daily activities of the Armenian population of the time, and still-lifes. He also produced important work as a portrait artist, particularly from the 1930s onwards, with a treatment of the human face both simple and strong. Oddly enough, he sometimes juxtaposed several portraits of the same person at different ages on the same canvas. From then on, as an official figure and a painter, his method did not change and he persisted in a solid post-Cézanne construction, but protected himself against the Soviet cultural centralism by giving his work over to the celebration of Armenian identity. He is regarded as the founder of modern Armenian painting.

Saryan exhibited with a number of groups including Golubaya Roza (Blue Rose) (1907); Mir Izkusstva (World of Art), Association of Russian Artists, and Association of Moscow Painters (1910 to 1916). After the Revolution he took part in important exhibitions of Soviet art abroad including: Berlin (1922) and Venice Biennale (1924). He featured in *Paris-Moscow*, Centre Georges-Pompidou, Paris (1979). He held a solo exhibition in Paris at the conclusion of his stay there in 1926. An exhibition of all his work was organised in St Petersburg (1987) and at the Picasso Museum, Antibes (2003).

Saryan was awarded the title of People's Artist of Armenia in 1926 and of the USSR in 1960. He became a member of the Academy of Art of the USSR. in 1947 and of the Academy of Science of Armenia in 1956. He received real recognition on his 85th birthday in 1965 and a museum dedicated to his work was established in Yerevan in 1967. In addition to his honorary titles, he won many awards including: Grand Prix at the Exposition Universelle, Paris (1937); Stalin Prize

(1941); State Prize for the stage sets of A. A. Spendiarov's opera *Almast*; gold medal of the Exposition Internationale, Brussels (1958); Lenin Prize (1961); Armenian State Prize (1966).

BIBLIOGRAPHY:

Halturin, Aleksandr/Hulten, Pontus/Gunar, Karl (ed.), *Paris-Moscou*, group exhibition catalogue, Éd. du Centre Georges-Pompidou, Paris, 1979. *Martiros Sarian*, exhibition catalogue, St Petersburg, 1987. Andral, Jean-Louis, *Sarian: au pays du soleil levant*, exhibition catalogue, Musée Picasso, Antibes, 2003.

MUSEUMS AND GALLERIES:

KIROV (RM): *Blue Flowers* (1914) - MOSCOW (Mus. of Eastern Art): *Self-portrait with a Mask* (1933); *Southern Winter* (1934); *Ararat Valley* (1945) - MOSCOW (Mus. of the Revolution): *Gathering Peaches at the Kolkhoz* (1938) - MOSCOW (State Tretyakov Gal.): *Street in Constantinople: Noon* (1910); *Constantinople: Dogs* (1910); *Date Palm, Egypt* (1911, gouache); *Back Street in Cairo* (1911); *Persian Village* (1913); *Mountains* (1923); *Old Yerevan* (1928); *Grape Harvest in Achtarak* (1933) - ODESSA (Mus. of Eastern and Western Art): *Armenia* (1957) - ST PETERSBURG (Gosudarstvennyj Russkij Muz.): *Egyptian Women* (1912); *Old and New* (1929) - YEREVAN (Mus. of Literature and Yegisheh Charents Arts): *Alexander Tsaturian* (1915); *Portrait of the Poet Egishe Czarenz* (1923) - YEREVAN (musée Sarian): *Near the Sea* (1908, gouache); *Woman with Tiara* (1915) - YEREVAN (National Gallery of Armenia): *Panthers* (1907); *Mules Loaded with Hay* (1910); *Head* (1910); *Eastern Merchants* (1910); *Egyptian Masks* (1911); *Garegin Levonian* (1912); *Persian Still-life* (1913); *Light Still-life* (1913); *Flowers in Kalaki* (1914); *Armenia* (1923); *My Little Heart* (1923); *Caravan* (1926); *Portrait of C. Igumnov* (1934); *Portrait of A. Tamanian* (1933); *Portrait of Avetik Isaakian* (1940); *Self-portrait* (1942); *Portrait of I. Orbeli* (1943); *Cotton Harvest* (1949); *Ararat Valley seen from Dvin* (1952); *Karindj's Kolkhoz* (1952).

AUCTION RECORDS:

LONDON, 14 May 1980, *Portrait of Petrov-Vodkin* (1923, watercolour, 16 1/4 x 12 3/4 ins / 41 x 32.5 cm) GBP 1,800. LONDON, 23 Feb 1983, *View of Yerevan* (watercolour on pencil outlines, 12 1/4 x 17 3/4 ins / 31 x 45 cm) GBP 900. LONDON, 20 Feb 1985, *Still-life with Bananas and Jug* (1910, gouache, 18 3/4 x 13 1/4 ins / 47.5 x 33.5 cm) GBP 5,000. LONDON, 10 Oct 1990, *October Day* (1953, oil on canvas, 21 x 31 3/4 ins / 53.3 x 80.6 cm) GBP 6,380. PARIS, 23 Jan 1995, *Women* (1904, oil on canvas, 19 3/4 x 15 3/4 ins / 50 x 40 cm) FRF 50,000.

SARYANKO, Sergei Konstantinovich, or Zarianko

Russian, 19th century.

Born 24 September 1818, in the Mogilev region; died December 1870, in Moscow.

Painter. Portraits, perspectives.

Sergei Konstantinovich Saryanko studied at the art academy in St Petersburg and was taught by Venetsianov.

MUSEUMS AND GALLERIES:

MOSCOW (State Tretyakov Gal.): *View of the White Hall of the Winter Palace in St Petersburg*; nine portraits - ST PETERSBURG (Gosudarstvennyj Russkij Muz.): *Interior of the Nikolski Cathedral; Portrait of N.V. Sokurova; Portrait of the Singer O.A. Petrov*; and several more portraits.

SARZANA. See **SORMANO Leonardo**

SARZANA, Il. See **FIASELLA Domenico**

SARZETTI, Angiolo

Italian, 17th century.

Born 1656, in Rimini.

Active c. 1700.

Painter, engraver (burin).

Angiolo Sarzetti, who was the pupil of Cignani, produced oil paintings and frescoes for the church of the Angioli family in Rimini.

SARZHETSKY, Andrei Antonovich, or Zaretsky or Zaretskij

Russian, 19th - 20th century.

Born 1864.

Painter. Landscapes.

SARZILLO. See **ZARCILLO Y ALCARAZ**

SAS, Christian

German, 17th century.

Born 1648, in Nuremberg or in Rome.

Engraver (burin).

Sas engraved in the manner of J. Stella and A. Pomarancio.

SAS, Jan

Dutch, 17th century.

Active in the Netherlands, from 1640 to 1650.

Painter, draughtsman. Landscapes.

SAS, Marsal de. See **MARZAL DE SAX**

SAS, Steven

Dutch, 17th century.

Active during the second half of the 17th century.

Painter.

Steven Sas was active in Kampen and Amsterdam, in 1675.

SAS-BRUNNER, Ferenc or Franz

Hungarian, 20th century.

Born 25 June 1882, in Pécs.

Painter.

Ferenc Sas-Brunner trained in Budapest and worked in Nagykanizsa.

MUSEUMS AND GALLERIES:

BUDAPEST (Municipal Mus.).

SASAJIMA, Kihei

Japanese, 20th century.

Born 1906, in Tochigi Prefecture.

Engraver.

After working as a primary school teacher until 1945, Sasajima Kihei turned to wood engraving, learning the technical rudiments with Un'ichi Hiratsuka and then Shiko Munakata. Thereafter he began to take part in the activities of the national painting academy (Kokuga-kai), the Japanese engraving association and the ministry of education (Bunten). In 1952 he collaborated in the foundation of the Japanese engraving academy, which he left in 1960, as well as the association of the same name. He was a member of the national academy of painting.

In 1957 Sasajima's work appeared in the Contemporary Japanese Engraving Exhibition in Yugoslavia. From that date he appeared regularly at the International Print Biennales in Tokyo. He took part in the São Paulo Biennale in 1967. From 1959 he held a solo exhibition annually in Tokyo.

SASAKI, Shiro

Japanese, 20th century.

Born 1931, in Osaka.

Active since 1961 also in Germany.

Painter.

In 1956 Shiro Sasaki obtained his diploma from the department of Western painting of the Tokyo University of Fine Arts. In 1961 he settled in Germany where he spent two years at the school of fine arts in Munich. He continued his education at the Berlin school of fine arts from 1963. He lives in Germany.

His work has appeared in various group exhibitions: in 1963, the Exhibition of Young German Painters in Wortsburg; in 1965, *Berlin 65*, and the Exhibition of Japanese Painters Abroad at the National Museum of Modern Art in

Tokyo; in 1970 at the International Amnesty Exhibition in Berlin. From 1965 he also held several solo exhibitions in Berlin and Munich.

SASC, Julie de
Maiden name: Lisiewska
German, 18th century.
Born 1724, in Saxony; died 1794, in Berlin.
Painter.
Julie de Sasc was the daughter and pupil of Georg Lisiewski. She lived for some time in The Hague and was a member of the Pictura there in 1767.

SASKI, Karol
Polish, 19th century.
Born c. 1818, in Opoczno; died 1873, in Lugano, Switzerland.
Painter.
Karol Saski studied in Rome and in Switzerland. The National Museum in Warsaw owns his *Portrait of A. Mickiewicz.*
AUCTION RECORDS:
MILAN, 11 Dec 1986, *Garibaldi by the Wounded Luciano Manara* (oil on canvas, 36 1/2 x 43 ins / 93 x 109 cm) ITL 12,000,000.

SASKI, Sylwerjusz
Polish, 19th - 20th century.
Born 24 December 1864, in Nottingham.
Painter. Genre scenes, portraits.
Sylwerjusz Saski trained at the academy in Cracow with J. Matejko and at the academy in Munich with O. Seitz.
MUSEUMS AND GALLERIES:
CRACOW (Muz. Narodowe): *Female Model; Young Girl.*

SASMAYOUX, François
French, 20th century.
Born 1944, in Figeac (Lot).
Painter, pastellist. Figures, nudes, portraits, still-lifes, animals.
François Sasmayoux studied at the École des Beaux-Arts in Toulouse before moving to Paris in 1974. His work stands out for its accomplished technique coupled with an ability to convey sadness and sensuality via the expressive eyes and subtle body movements of portraits and nudes.

He showed examples of his work at the 1989 Salon des Artistes Français in Paris and has also exhibited at regional venues throughout the Midi-Pyrenées region as well as at numerous galleries in Paris, Toulouse, Lille, Nice and Marseilles and, not least, in Belgium and in Spain. He has received numerous awards and distinctions.

SASONOV, Vasili Kondratevich, or Sazonov
Russian, 19th century.
Born 1789, in Gomel; died 1870.
Painter. History painting, portraits.
Vasili Sasonov studied under Ogiumov at the art academy in St Petersburg.
MUSEUMS AND GALLERIES:
ST PETERSBURG (Gosudarstvennyj Russkij Muz.): *The Grand Duke Dimitri Donskoy after Kulikovo.*

SASS, Henrietta
British, 18th - 19th century.
Active in London from 1797 to 1813.
Painter. Landscapes, flowers.
Sister of Henry Sass.

SASS, Henry
British, 19th century.
Born 24 April 1788, in London; died 21 June 1844, in London.
Painter, engraver (etching), writer. History painting, portraits, genre scenes.
Henry Sass was the brother of Henrietta Sass and half-brother of the landscape painter Richard Sass. He began exhibiting in London in 1807, principally showing mythological subjects, and continued to exhibit until 1839, typically at the Royal Academy and the Suffolk Street Gallery. He spent time in Rome in 1816. Sass was a historian and occasional engraver, but devoted the majority of his time to teaching. He was the founder of Sass's Academy in Bloomsbury.

SASS, Michael
German, 18th century.
Born c. 1725; died 16 March 1789, in Bruchsal.
Sculptor.

SASS, Oswald von (Baron)
German, 19th century.
Born 27 May 1856, in Arensburg (island of Osel).
Painter. Genre scenes, portraits.
Oswald von Sass trained in Düsseldorf and Munich.
MUSEUMS AND GALLERIES:
RIGA (MM): *Watch.*

SASS, Richard. See **SASSE**

SASSE, Johan
Swedish, 17th century.
Draughtsman, engraver (burin). Historical subjects.
Sasse was in the military. He engraved a *View of Stockholm,* in addition to a number of historic ceremonies.

SASSE, Johann
German, 17th century.
Active in Attendorn during the second half of the 17th century.
Sculptor.
Johann Sasse sculpted an altar in the church at Fritzlar and a pulpit in the church of St Peter in Soest.

SASSE, Joost van
Dutch, 18th century.
Active in Amsterdam from 1716 to 1736.
Engraver (burin), cartographer. Architectural views.
Van Sasse, a cartographer, engraved city and architectural views.

SASSE, Richard, or Sass
British, 18th - 19th century.
Born 1774, in London; died 7 September 1849, in Paris.
Painter, watercolourist, engraver (etching). Landscapes.
Richard Sasse, of Baltic origin, was the half-brother of Henry Sass. In 1811 he was appointed tutor to Princess Charlotte and official landscape painter to the Prince Regent. He spent sometime in Ireland and published etchings of views of Ireland and Scotland in 1810. In 1815 he travelled in Europe and settled for a time in Paris (presumably where he added an 'e' to his original surname). Sasse exhibited numerous compositions in London between 1791 and 1813, notably at the Royal Academy and the Suffolk Street Gallery.
MUSEUMS AND GALLERIES:
HOVE (Hove Library) - LONDON (British Mus.) - LONDON (Victoria and Albert Mus.): two watercolours - NEWPORT (Newport Art Gallery) - SOUTHEND (Beecroft Art Gallery).
AUCTION RECORDS:
LONDON, 21 Nov 1946, *Ross Castle* (drawing) GBP 30. LONDON, 6 Nov 1973, *Ruins at Askeaton, Ireland* (watercolour) Gns 480. LONDON, 16 May 2002, *Waterscourt, near Dublin* (watercolour over pencil heightened with gouache, 23 x 30 ins / 59 x 77 cm) GBP 4,200. NEW YORK, 14 Nov 2002, *5502* (photograph mounted on plexiglas, 42 x 63 ins / 106 x 160 cm) USD 11,000.

SASSENBROUCK, Achiel van, or Achille
Belgian, 20th century.
Born 1886, in Bruges; died 1969.

Painter. Genre scenes, landscapes, seascapes, still-lifes. Achiel van Sassenbrouck studied under Frans Courtens and Frans van Leemputten at the fine arts academy in Antwerp and travelled extensively in Germany, Austria, France, the Netherlands and the USA. He was first and foremost a landscape painter whose compositions contained distinctive stylised elements.

Ach Van Sassenbrouck

Auction records:
Brussels, 24 March 1976, *Winter Landscape (Melting Snow)* (oil on canvas, 35½ x 31½ ins / 90 x 80 cm) BEF 36,000. Lokeren, 5 Nov 1977, *Flanders Landscape* (oil on panel, 23¼ x 24½ ins / 59 x 62 cm) BEF 70,000. Lokeren, 13 Oct 1979, *Church in Bruges* (oil on canvas, 32¼ x 54 ins / 82 x 137 cm) BEF 120,000. Lokeren, 17 Oct 1981, *Fishermen at Ostend* (1942, oil on canvas, 65 x 50½ ins / 165 x 128 cm) BEF 160,000. Brussels, 8 May 1985, *Skating Scene* (1921, oil on canvas, 52 x 53¼ ins / 132 x 135 cm) BEF 170,000. Lokeren, 28 May 1988, *Harvesting Potatoes* (oil on canvas, 61 x 65 ins / 155 x 165 cm) BEF 300,000. Amsterdam, 24 May 1989, *Christmas Eve: Winter Landscape with Skaters on a Frozen River* (1925, oil on canvas, 42½ x 51¼ ins / 108 x 130 cm) NLG 21,850. Brussels, 27 March 1990, *Sunny Landscape* (oil on canvas, 31½ x 35½ ins / 80 x 90 cm) BEF 170,000. Lokeren, 21 March 1992, *Snow-covered Landscape* (oil on panel, 13¼ x 17½ ins / 33.5 x 44.5 cm) BEF 33,000. Lokeren, 23 May 1992, *Landscape near Ternat* (oil on panel, 15 x 17¾ ins / 38 x 45 cm) BEF 36,000. Lokeren, 10 Oct 1992, *Winnowing* (oil on canvas, 31½ x 35½ ins / 80 x 90 cm) BEF 110,000. Lokeren, 20 March 1993, *Winter in Flanders* (oil on canvas, 48 x 59½ ins / 121 x 151 cm) BEF 190,000. Lokeren, 12 March 1994, *Winter in Flanders* (oil on canvas, 42¼ x 59 ins / 107 x 150 cm) BEF 120,000. Lokeren, 9 Dec 1995, *Winter in Brabant* (oil on canvas, 53¾ x 61¾ ins / 136.5 x 157 cm) BEF 300,000. Lokeren, 9 March 1996, *After Work* (oil on canvas, 31½ x 25¼ ins / 80 x 64 cm) BEF 130,000. Lokeren, 5 Oct 1996, *Fishing for Eels* (oil on panel, 14¾ x 17¼ ins / 37.5 x 44 cm) BEF 30,000. Lokeren, 6 Dec 1997, *Artist's Studio* (oil on canvas, 35½ x 31 ins / 90 x 79 cm) BEF 75,000. Brussels, 11 May 1999, *Busy Winter Landscape* (oil on canvas, 41 x 48 ins / 105 x 121 cm) BEF 105,000. Lokeren, 11 Dec 1999, *On a Winter Day* (oil on canvas, 31 x 35 ins / 80 x 90 cm) BEF 110,000. Lokeren, 4 March 2000, *Cows Resting* (oil on canvas, 39 x 43 ins / 100 x 110 cm) BEF 120,000. Antwerp, 30 May 2000, *Couple of Peasants before a Farm* (oil on canvas, 34 x 32 ins / 87 x 82 cm) BEF 100,000. Brussels, 12 Feb 2001, *Fishermen Repairing a Net* (oil on canvas) BEF 130,000. Lokeren, 8 Dec 2001, *Snow Scene with Willows* (oil on canvas, 39 x 43 ins / 100 x 110 cm) BEF 150,000. Lokeren, 9 March 2002, *Procession* (pastel and charcoal, 49 x 48 ins / 125 x 122 cm) EUR 1,700. Lokeren, 11 May 2002, *Snowy Landscape* (oil on canvas, 45 x 85 ins / 115 x 215 cm) EUR 4,700. Antwerp, 29 April 2003, *Still-life* (oil on canvas, 47 x 35 ins / 120 x 90 cm) EUR 1,600. Lokeren, 13 Dec 2003, *Mountain Pool* (oil on canvas, 31 x 35 ins / 80 x 90 cm) EUR 1,800. Lokeren, 15 May 2004, *Fishing Boats in the Harbour* (oil on canvas, 31 x 35 ins / 80 x 90 cm) EUR 1,600.

SASSETTA, IL, real name Stefano di Giovanni di Consolo, d'Asciano or da Cortone
Italian, 15th century.
Born 1392; died c. 1450 or 1451.
Painter. Religious subjects.
Sienese School.

The years 1260 (the birth of Duccio) and 1450, when Sassetta died, mark the beginning and end of the Sienese School of painting. Moving away from the rigid iconography of Byzantine painting with Duccio, it found its mature expression in the works of Simone Martini and the Lorenzetti brothers, and concluded with painters like Giovanni di Paolo, Sano di Pietro and Sassetta. All these artists were poets and mystics. Sienese painting was almost exclusively religious, a grandiose and delightful hymn of praise to the Virgin, protector of the city of Siena, which dedicated its cathedral to her.

The majority of Sassetta's works reveal his links with the older artist Simone Martini. In his *Ecstasy of St Francis* in Settignano, for example, the group of three angels in the upper section of the painting form a kind of halo above the figure of the saint. The angel on the left, dressed in white and holding a lily, comes from the same family as the angel by Simone Martini in the *Visitation* in the Uffizi in Florence. In the *Birth of the Virgin* in Asciano, are the same noble faces as in Martini's great *Maestà* in the Palazzo Pubblico in Siena, but rendered more human. Here the natural attitudes of the figures show a decisive break with the hieratic rigidity of Byzantine art. It can almost be seen as a genre scene, such is the degree of naturalism in the details, but it retains the poetic sweetness characteristic of Sienese art. In his *Mystic Marriage of St Francis* in the museum in Chantilly, it is again the figures that have pride of place. But now the landscape has become more important and we sense that real air surrounds the figures.

Sassetta's originality emerges most obviously in his *Procession of the Magi* and *Temptation of St Anthony*. A long line of migrating birds is flying above the winding procession of the Magi as it passes the walls of a sleeping town and through a wild landscape punctuated by leafless trees with curiously arranged branches. The same oddly fossilised trees appear in one of Sassetta's most ambitious landscapes, *Scene from the Life of St Anthony Abbot* in the Lehman collection in New York. Here the subject is a single figure, St Anthony clothed in heavy draperies and accompanied by a few tiny and imprecisely defined animals. The landscape, with its stony path bordered by stunted trees winding through the bleak hills, has become the main feature of the painting.

One of the last representatives of the Sienese School, Sassetta drew on the lessons of his predecessors. In his work can be found Simone Martini's angelic sweetness, Barna's realism and delight in the details of everyday life and the solemnity of Ambrogio Lorenzetti's processions. Sassetta's contribution was a new form of expression through austere and mysterious landscapes so much in advance of the conformism of his day.

Bibliography:
Langton-Douglas, R., '*A Forgotten Painter*' in *Burlington Magazine*, vol 3, 1903. Pope-Hennessy, John, *Sassetta*, Chatto and Windus, London, 1939. Brandi, Cesare, *Quattrocentisti senesi*, Hoepli, Milan, 1949. Zeri, F., '*Towards a Reconstruction of Sassetta's Arte della Lana Triptych*' in *Burlington Magazine*, vol 94, 1952. Carli, Enzo, '*Sassetta's Borgo S. Sepolcro Alterpiece*' in *Burlington Magazine*, periodical, London, May, 1952. Israels, M., '*New Documents for Sassetta and Sano di Pietro at the Porta Romana, Siena*' in *Burlington Magazine*, vol. 140, 1998.

Museums and Galleries:
Barnard Castle (Bowes Mus.): *The Miracle of the Holy Sacrament* (1423, tempera/panel, predella panel from the Arte della Lana altar) - Berlin (Bodemus.): *Virgin and Child; Virgin and Child with Two Saints; Mass of St Francis; Assumption; St Francis Appearing to a Cardinal in a Dream; Scene from the Life of St Anthony* - Bordeaux: *St Francis* - Boston: *Flagellation; Martyrdom of St Catherine; St Jerome in the Desert* - Budapest: *St Thomas Aquinas* - Chantilly (Mus. Condé): *Marriage of St Francis with Lady Poverty* - Dijon: *Dead Christ* - Gran (Gal. du Primat): *Assumption* - London (NG): *St Francis meets a knight poorer than himself and St*

Francis's vision of the founding of the Franciscan Order; Saint Francis renounces his Earthly Father; St Francis before the Pope: The Granting of the Indulgence of the Portiuncola; St Francis before the Sultan; The Wolf of Gubbio; The Stigmatisation of St Francis; The Funeral of St Francis and Verification of the Stigmata (1437-1444, tempera/wood, altarpiece from the San Sepolcro church, panels of the Life of St Francis) - MONTPELLIER: *Crucifixion* - NEW YORK (Metropolitan Mus. of Art): *Journey of the Magi* - NEW YORK (Metropolitan Mus. of Art, Robert Lehman Collection): *Scene from the Life of St Anthony Abbot* - SETTIGNANO: *Ecstasy of St Francis* - SIENA (Pinacoteca Nazionale): *Elijah; Elisha; Temptation of St Anthony; Last Supper; Four Saints; Four Fathers of the Church; Madonna and Child and Christ Blessing; Madonna and Child* - THE HAGUE: *Virgin and Child* - VATICAN (Mus. Vaticani): *Christ and St Thomas Aquinas.*

AUCTION RECORDS:

PARIS, 19 May 1933, *St Peter and the Angel,* FRF 11,000. AMSTERDAM, 11 July 1950, *Virgin and Child with Angels and Saints* (gold background) NLG 2,000.

SASSETTI, Francesco
Italian, 18th century.
Died 1712.
Active in Parma.
Painter.

The pupil of D. Sanz de la Lloza, Francesco Sassetti painted an *Elijah* for the church of S Frediano in Bologna.

SASSI. See also **SASSO**

SASSI, Francesco and Riccardo. See **SASSO**

SASSI, Giovanni Battista
Italian, 18th century.
Active in Milan from 1713 to 1747.
Painter, engraver (burin).

Giovanni Battista Sassi studied under Solimena in Naples. He painted a number of altarpieces in Milan and completed works that had been left unfinished by Pietro Gilandi (or Giraldi).

SASSI, Pietro, or Sasso
Italian, 17th century.
Died 1686.
Sculptor.

A stucco artist who was the pupil and assistant of Bernini, Pietro Sasso also worked at the Louvre in Paris and collaborated with Giovanni Rimbelli on works for the church of S Andrea at the Quirinale in Rome.

SASSI, Pietro
Italian, 19th century.
Born 18 July 1834, in Alessandria (Piedmont); died 30 December 1905, in Rome.
Painter. Landscapes, landscapes with figures, architectural views.

He exhibited in Turin, Milan, Rome and Venice.

MUSEUMS AND GALLERIES:

ROME (Gal. Nazionale d'Arte Moderna): *Summit of Monte Rosa.*

AUCTION RECORDS:

ROME, 1 June 1983, *Shepherd and Flock in a Landscape* (oil on canvas, 15¼ x 32¼ ins / 39 x 82 cm) ITL 2,600,000. LONDON, 17 March 1989, *The Roman Forum* (1904, watercolour, 16¼ x 22¾ ins / 41 x 58 cm) GBP 1,430. ROME, 31 May 1990, *View of Via della Pilotta; View of the Palace* (a pair of watercolours, 13½ x 19 ins / 34 x 48 cm) ITL 6,500,000. LONDON, 22 Nov 1990, *The Roman Forum* (watercolour, 22½ x 20½ ins / 57.4 x 52.1 cm) GBP 825. ROME, 11 Dec 1990, *Landscape with Small House* (1890, oil on panel, 9 x 4¾ ins / 22 x 12 cm) ITL 1,610,000. ROME, 14 Nov 1991, *Landscape with Flocks* (oil on panel, 4¼ x 7 ins / 11 x 18 cm) ITL 2,185,000. MILAN, 16 June 1992, *Girl with Turkeys* (oil on mounted paper, 12 x 18¼ ins / 30.5 x 46.5 cm) ITL 1,500,000. MILAN, 16 March 1993, *Olive Grove in Liguria* (oil on canvas, 17¾ x 24½ ins / 45 x 62 cm) ITL 5,500,000. ROME, 7 June 1995, *Autumn in Sabina* (oil on panel, 13 x 19 ins / 33 x 48 cm) ITL 3,220,000. ROME, 3 June 1999, *Genoa Port* (1871, oil on paper, 16 x 23 ins / 41 x 58 cm) ITL 8,000,000. ROME, 4 Dec 2002, *Crowd. Roman Countryside* (oil on board, a pair, 6 x 9 ins / 15 x 24 cm) EUR 6,000.

SASSNICK, Georg
German, 19th - 20th century.
Born 25 February 1858, in Berlin; died 26 January 1922, in Potsdam.
Painter, sculptor. Portraits, landscapes.

Georg Sassnick was a pupil of R. Schweinitz, Calandrelli and Max Michael.

SASSO. See the entry **ANGELUS**

SASSO. See also **SASSI**

SASSO, Domenico
Italian, 18th century.
Active during the second half of the 18th century.
Painter.

Domenico Sasso painted an *Ascension* for the cathedral in Mileto.

SASSO, Francesco, or Sassi
Italian, 18th century.
Died 1774.
Painter. Religious subjects.

Francesco Sasso painted a *St Pius V and St Vincent Ferrer Adoring the Holy Trinity* for the Oratorio del Suffragio in Genoa.

SASSO, Francesco
Italian, 19th century.
Born 1810, in Foligno (Umbria); died 6 April 1886, in Foligno.
Sculptor.

A pupil of D. Parodi, Francesco Sasso lived in Florence from 1840 to 1880. He worked mainly in wood.

SASSO, Giovanni Antonio
Italian, 19th century.
Active in Milan from 1809 to 1816.
Engraver.

SASSO, Giovanni Maria
Italian, 18th century.
Died 1803.
Active in Venice.
Painter, art restorer, art writer.

SASSO, Pietro. See **SASSI**

SASSO, Riccardo, or Sassi
Italian, 16th century.
Active in Bologna and in Rome from 1573 to 1599.
Painter.

Riccardo Sasso painted works for St Peter's in Rome and the Vatican.

SASSO, Silvestro del
Swiss, 16th century.
Active in Sonvico.
Painter.

Silvestro del Sasso worked for churches and on the façade of the town hall in Lugano.

SASSO DI PAOLO. See the entry **ANGELUS**

SASSOFERRATO, Il. See **SALVI Giovanni Battista**

SASSOLI, Fabiano di Stagio
Italian, 16th century.

Died c. 1513.

Painter. Designs for stained glass.

The father of Stagio di Fabiano Sassoli, Fabiano di Stagio Sassoli made stained glass windows for churches in Arezzo.

SASSOLI, Stagio di Fabiano

Italian, 16th century.

Glass painter.

The son of Fabiano di Stagio Sassoli, Stagio di Fabiano Sassoli collaborated with Guillaume de Marseille and Domenico Pecori in Arezzo between 1513 and 1529.

SASSONE, Antonio

Argentinian, 20th century.

Born 1906.

Sculptor.

Antonio Sassone studied at the Escuela de Bellas Artes in Buenos Aires. He exhibited regularly in the Buenos Aires Salon, and won the national prize in 1941.

SASSONE, Marco

Italian, 20th century.

Born 1942, in Florence.

Painter. Landscapes, waterscapes.

Marco Sassone studied at Milan art college under Silvio Loffredo. In 1968 he settled in California. He used vivid colours and a neo-Impressionist style to depict Florence and scenes in Italy as well as the city of San Francisco and seaports on the Californian coast. Water is a constant theme, its effects being carefully worked and rendered in brilliant tones.

He has had exhibitions in many galleries in the USA, and in Italy and New Zealand. In 1978 he was awarded a gold medal by the Italian academy of art, literature and science. In 1982 he was made a Cavaliere Ufficiale of the Italian Republic.

AUCTION RECORDS:

LOS ANGELES, 10 March 1976, *Windows, Venice* (1974, oil on canvas, 46 x 50 ins / 117 x 127 cm) USD 1,900. LOS ANGELES, 23-24 June 1980, *Harbour* (1978, oil on canvas, 18 1/2 x 22 3/4 ins / 47 x 58 cm) USD 1,700. LOS ANGELES, 29 June 1982, *Harbour Scene* (oil on canvas, 41 x 43 ins / 104 x 109 cm) USD 2,100.

SASSONIA, Mario Piero Francesco

Italian, 17th century.

Active in Padua in 1690.

Engraver.

Sassonia was primarily a scholar.

SASSU, Aligi

Italian, 20th century.

Born 1912, in Milan; died 2000.

Painter, watercolourist, sculptor, draughtsman.

Religious and allegorical subjects, genre scenes, animals, landscapes, flowers. Murals.

Corrente Group.

In the early years of his career Aligi Sassu's style remained linked to the impressionist tradition. When only 15 years old he briefly joined the Futurist movement, signing a manifesto with Munari celebrating the new world of machines. After 1932, he returned to an expressionist realism and was a member of the Corrente group between 1937 and 1940. He painted many murals, particularly in Liguria and Lombardy. He decorated the apse of Lodi Cathedral and that of the Carmelite church in Cagliari.

Sassu received a number of awards including one in 1951 at the Biennale del Mare in Genoa, the Modigliani Prize in Livorno in 1957 and the Prize for Sacred Art in Bergamo in 1964.He participated in many group exhibitions including the Venice Biennale in 1928, 1936, 1948, 1952 and 1954; Rome Quadriennale in 1951, 1955 and 1959; at the art gallery in Monza in 1965 and in Munich at the Staatsgalerie in 1987. His work has also appeared in thematic exhibitions including, in 2003, *De Chirico et la peinture italienne de l'entre-deux guerres* (*De Chirico and Italian Painting of the Interwar Period*) held at the museum in Lodève, France.

SASSU

BIBLIOGRAPHY:

Aligi Sassu, antologica 1927 - 1999, exhibition catalogue, Skira, Milan, 1999. Bonito Oliva, Achille/Iovane, Giovanni/Lista, Giovanni, et al., *De Chirico et la peinture italienne de l'entre-deux guerres*, exhibition catalogue, Musée de Lodève, 2003.

AUCTION RECORDS:

MILAN, 28 March 1962, *Last Supper*, ITL 700,000. MILAN, 27 Oct 1970, *Landscape*, ITL 3,500,000. MILAN, 28 Oct 1971, *Nudes* (watercolour) ITL 1,100,000. MILAN, 16 Oct 1973, *Wounded Horse*, ITL 4,800,000. MILAN, 5 March 1974, *Horse Riders*, ITL 7,000,000. MILAN, 6 April 1976, *Pink Nude* (1936, mixed media, 11 1/2 x 8 ins / 29.5 x 20.5 cm) ITL 1,300,000. MILAN, 8 June 1976, *The Acrobat's Family* (1936, oil on panel, 13 3/4 x 11 ins / 35 x 27 cm) ITL 2,400,000. MILAN, 7 June 1977, *Grey Horse* (1952?, oil on canvas, 22 x 27 1/4 ins / 55 x 69 cm) ITL 4,500,000. MILAN, 13 Dec 1978, *Alaior* (mixed media mounted on board, 12 1/2 x 19 ins / 32 x 48 cm) ITL 1,100,000. MILAN, 26 April 1979, *Horses in the Water* (oil on canvas, 31 1/2 x 39 1/4 ins / 80 x 100 cm) ITL 6,500,000. MILAN, 10 May 1979, *Mimi Guidi Bellentani* (1948, soft chalk and charcoal, 25 3/4 x 18 ins / 65.5 x 45.5 cm) ITL 1,200,000. MILAN, 25 Nov 1980, *Acrobats* (1938, pastel, 39 1/4 x 28 3/4 ins / 100 x 73 cm) ITL 9,000,000. ROME, 11 June 1981, *At the Café* (1958-1959, oil on canvas, 31 x 39 1/4 ins / 79 x 100 cm) ITL 19,000,000. MILAN, 9 Nov 1982, *The Toilette* (gouache on board, 17 3/4 x 25 1/2 ins / 45 x 65 cm) ITL 5,600,000. MILAN, 15 March 1983, *Lulu* (1958, pastel and oil on paper, 19 3/4 x 13 3/4 ins / 50 x 35 cm) ITL 4,000,000. MILAN, 14 June 1983, *El Picador Rosado* (1967, oil on canvas, 33 x 41 3/4 ins / 84 x 106 cm) ITL 15,500,000. MILAN, 15 Nov 1983, *Dioscuri and Horse* (1932, pen, 13 3/4 x 19 3/4 ins / 35 x 50 cm) ITL 2,300,000. MILAN, 5 Dec 1985, *Horse in a Landscape* (charcoal, 33 1/2 x 29 1/2 ins / 85 x 75 cm) ITL 4,000,000. MILAN, 9 Dec 1986, *Shepherds* (1931, oil on panel, 39 3/4 x 32 ins / 101 x 81 cm) ITL 56,000,000. PARIS, 4 May 1988, *White Rock* (1962, oil on board, 7 1/4 x 9 ins / 18.5 x 23 cm) FRF 18,000. ROME, 15 Nov 1988, *Don Quixote and the Donkey* (mixed media/paper/canvas, 14 1/2 x 20 ins / 37 x 51 cm) ITL 8,500,000; *Ariane* (1981, mixed media on board mounted on canvas, 19 3/4 x 25 1/2 ins / 50 x 65 cm) ITL 15,000,000. MILAN, 14 Dec 1988, *Bathers* (oil on canvas, 55 1/2 x 55 ins / 141 x 140 cm) ITL 135,000,000. LONDON, 22 Feb 1989, *Antique Horseman* (1961, oil on board, 19 1/4 x 25 ins / 48.7 x 63.8 cm) GBP 6,820. MILAN, 20 March 1989, *Horses* (1953, ceramic dish, diam. 12 1/2 ins / 32 cm) ITL 3,500,000; *Gossips in Albisola* (1948, oil/synthetic resin, 48 3/4 x 125 1/4 ins / 124 x 318 cm) ITL 115,000,000. ROME, 17 April 1989, *Pink horses* (oil on canvas, 4 x 6 1/4 ins / 10 x 16 cm) ITL 3,800,000. MILAN, 6 June 1989, *Melancholy* (1942, oil on canvas, 19 3/4 x 27 1/2 ins / 50 x 70 cm) ITL 64,000,000. ROME, 8 June 1989, *Black Horse* (1952, bronze, h. 18 ins / 46 cm) ITL 36,000,000. ROME, 28 Nov 1989, *Flowers in Red* (1933, oil on canvas, 30 1/4 x 23 1/2 ins / 77 x 60 cm) ITL 40,000,000. MILAN, 12 June 1990, *Horses Fighting* (1943, oil on canvas, 21 1/2 x 25 1/2 ins / 54.5 x 64.5 cm) ITL 55,000,000. ROME, 30 Oct 1990, *Horses on the Seashore* (oil on panel, 10 x 15 1/4 ins / 25.5 x 39 cm) ITL 28,000,000. MILAN, 19 Dec 1991, *Wanda* (1952, oil on canvas, 17 3/4 x 13 3/4 ins / 45 x 35 cm) ITL 34,000,000. MILAN, 14 April 1992, *Horses Startled by a Storm* (1946, oil on canvas, 23 1/2 x 37 1/2 ins / 60 x 95 cm) ITL 58,000,000. ROME, 27 May 1993, *Horses* (pastel and soft chalk/paper, 16 1/4 x 13 ins / 41 x 33 cm) ITL 6,000,000. ROME, 30 Nov 1993, *Jeanette and her Friends* (oil on canvas, 19 3/4 x 31 1/2 ins / 50 x 80 cm) ITL 52,900,000. MILAN, 27 April 1995, *Horse on the Beach* (oil/synthetic resin, 12 1/4 x 20 3/4 ins / 31 x 53 cm) ITL 12,075,000. MILAN, 26 Oct 1995, *Horse Riders* (1932, tempera/paper, 11 1/2 x 7 3/4 ins / 29 x 20 cm) ITL 13,800,000. MILAN, 23 May 1996, *Rider and Horses* (watercolour/mounted paper/Masonite, 9 1/4 x 16 1/4 ins / 23.5 x 41 cm) ITL 652,500,000. MILAN, 28 May 1996, *Alice* (oil on canvas, 19 3/4 x 23 1/4 ins / 50 x 59 cm) ITL 28,750,000. MILAN, 10 Dec 1996, *House of the Tellier Family* (1944, oil on artboard mounted to canvas, 14 3/4 x 12 ins / 37.5 x 30.5 cm) ITL 15,145,000. MILAN, 18 March 1997, *Horse at Dawn* (1959-1961, oil on canvas, 23 1/2 x 31 1/2 ins / 60 x 80 cm) ITL 47,765,000. MILAN, 24 Nov 1997, *Horses* (watercolour on artboard, 17 3/4 x 25 1/4 ins / 45 x 64 cm) ITL 5,175,000; *Diomedes* (1965, oil/plywood, 20 3/4 x 24 3/4 ins / 53 x 63 cm) ITL 39,100,000. VENICE, 25 April 1999, *Enchanted Garden* (pastel on board, 67 x 87 ins / 170 x 220 cm) ITL 10,000,000. MILAN, 22 June 1999, *Symposium* (1949, oil on board, 20 x 26 ins / 50 x 65 cm) ITL 36,000,000. MILAN, 11 April 2000, *Horse* (bronze, h. 15 ins / 37 cm) ITL 13,000,000. MILAN, 12 Dec 2000, *Garden of the Hesperides* (egg tempera on canvas, 106 x 118 ins / 270 x 300 cm) ITL 70,000,000. ROME, 21 May 2001, *Green-eyed Horse* (1985, mixed media on paper/canvas, 13 x 20 ins / 33 x 50 cm) ITL 14,500,000. PRATO, 26 May 2001, *Horse by the Sea* (oil on board, 60 x 38 ins / 152 x 97 cm) ITL 65,000,000. MILAN, 14 May 2002, *Faun and Knight* (1985, gouache on paper/canvas, 20 x 26 ins / 50 x 65 cm) EUR 8,500. MILAN, 19 Nov 2002, *Cyclops* (1987, oil on canvas, 20 x 28 ins / 50 x 70 cm) EUR 22,000. MILAN, 13 March 2003, *River Crossing* (1957, oil on canvas, 20 x 24 ins / 50 x 60 cm) EUR 28,000. MILAN, 26 May 2003, *Knights and Mephistopheles* (oil on canvas, 20 x 24 ins / 50 x 60 cm) EUR 23,000. VERCELLI, 13 March 2004, *The Dictator Osmin Aguirre* (1984, mixed media on paper/canvas, 20 x 26 ins / 50 x 65 cm) EUR 10,000. MILAN, 8 June 2004, *Lioness Downing a Horse* (1958, oil on canvas, 20 x 27 ins / 50 x 69 cm) EUR 20,000.

SASSU, Antonio
Italian, 20th - 21st century.
Born 6 July 1950, in Torreglia, near Padua.
Painter (mixed media), fresco artist. Allegorical subjects.

Antonio Sassu has created a number of mural paintings, using classical fresco themes and techniques. At the same time in his often very large easel paintings he opts for radical abstraction, although with the same gamut of tones. He places two or three rectangles vertically on the whole breadth of the canvas, and their colours mingle one by one where they meet, rather in the style of Rothko.

Work by Antonio Sassu has appeared in collective exhibitions, regularly since 1980 in Padua and in a travelling exhibition in Russia 1981-1982. His solo shows have mostly been in Italy: 1978, Padua and Treviso; 1979, Verona; 1980, Bologna and Verona.

SASSY, Attila, called Aiglon
Hungarian, 20th century.
Born 16 October 1880, in Miskolc.
Painter, engraver. Figure compositions.

After studying in Budapest, Munich and Paris, Attila Sassy went back to Budapest and settled there.

He treated religious and symbolic subjects in dark tones, and superimposed on them caricatures and fantastic figures twisting and turning like puppets.

MUSEUMS AND GALLERIES:
BUDAPEST (Szépmuvészeti Múz.): *Burial of Christ*; *Adam*.

AUCTION RECORDS:
PARIS, 25 March 1977, *Lust* (oil on canvas, 32 3/4 x 44 ins / 83 x 112 cm) FRF 4,800. BUDAPEST, 12 Oct 2001, *Nude in the City* (oil on cardboard, 26 x 24 ins / 65 x 60 cm) HUF 550,000. PARIS, 27 April 2004, *Lust* (1912, oil on canvas, 44 x 32 ins / 111 x 82 cm) EUR 2,800.

SASTRE, José
Spanish, 18th century.
Born 1720, in Palma (Majorca), Balearics; died 21 January 1797, in Palma (Majorca), Balearics.
Sculptor.

José Sastre carved altars and columns for the cathedral of Palma de Mallorca and for churches in the surrounding area.

SASTRE, Miguel, called el Pujol
Spanish, 17th century.
Active in Palma (Majorca).
Painter.

Miguel Sastre painted a portrait of Philip IV and some paintings of saints for the island's governor in 1657.

SATAKE SEII. See **HOHEI**

SATCHELL, Sarah
British, 19th century.
Born c. 1814; died 8 January 1894, in Sudbury.
Painter. Genre scenes.

SATCHWELL, R. W.
British, 18th - 19th century.
Miniaturist, painter. Portraits.

R.W. Satchwell was a Royal Academy exhibitor from 1793 to 1818.

MUSEUMS AND GALLERIES:
LONDON (Victoria and Albert Mus.): *Portrait of the Artist's Father*.

SATIÉ, Alain
French, 20th century.
Born 20 January 1944, in Toulouse.
Painter, sculptor, installation artist, draughtsman. Lettrism.

Alain Satié studied until 1963 at the École des Beaux-Arts in Toulouse, and aligned himself with the Lettrist Group exhibiting at the Paris Biennale of that year. He settled in Paris in 1967, visited Las Vegas in 1982 and has spent extended periods in New York. Between 1982 and 1986, Satié travelled in Turkey, Morocco and Eastern Europe.

Alain Satié authored a series of poems published in 1965 and, since then, he has concentrated his efforts on developing anthologies featuring the transcription and distortion of Latin calligraphy contained within a more or less precisely defined geometrical structure which also evokes a calligraphy base. As of 1970, he started to integrate into his work specific signs that combine to build various series of portraits and blow-ups of calligraphic sequences. Satié is passionate about book publishing and has worked alongside Roland Sabatier to produce some 120 Lettrist-based works.

Satié's style exhibits a touch of Orientalism. Like many other Lettrists, he has expanded his calligraphy into other fields, including furniture and even his own body (*Les Transparences* (*Transparencies*) 1983-1985). At the beginning of the 1980s, Satié produced a composition 14 metres high decorating the Berlin Wall. He has also produced similar compositions for the Acropolis site in Athens and for Stonehenge in England.

Examples of Alain Satié's work have been shown at various collective exhibitions: in 1965, at the Paris Biennale; in 1966 and 1972, at the Bibliothèque Nationale in Paris; in 1977, at the Schindler Gallery in Bern; in 1968 and 1970 at the Salon Comparaisons in Paris; in 1974, at the Manzoni Gallery in Milan; in 1977, at the Schindler Gallery in Bern; in 1979, at the Musée d'Orsay in Paris; in 1982, at the Musée National d'Art Moderne in Paris; in 1982, at a Lettrist exhibition held at the Centre Pompidou in Paris; in 1984, in Miami; in 1985, at *The Unknown: Lettrism and Hypergraphics* at the Franklin Furnace Gallery in New York; in 1985, 1986 and 1989, at the Galerie Michel Broomhead in Paris; in 1986, at

Écritures, Communication (*Calligraphy and Communication*), held at the Grand Palais in Paris; in 1987, at *Lettrisme: Les Débuts 1944-1966* (*Lettrism: The Early Years, 1944-1966*), hosted by the Galerie Rambert in Paris; in 1988, at *A Half-Century of Lettrism*, held at the 1900/2000 Gallery in Brussels; in 1989, at the Vivita Gallery in Florence and at the Investment and Placement Forum held at the Palais des Congrès in Paris; and, in 1990, at the Modern Art Gallery in Bologna and, that same year, at *Les Arts au Soleil* (*Arts of the Sun*), held within the framework of *La Caravane des Caravanes* (*The Caravan of Caravans*), a travelling exhibition organised under the auspices of the French Ministry of Culture and Communication.

Solo exhibitions by Alain Satié include those of 1965, at the Cultural Centre in Villengen; 1967, at the Galerie de l'Atelier in Toulouse; 1975, at the La Guilde Gallery in Paris; 1979, at a presentation of 'hypergraphic' furniture, held at the Musée du Luxembourg in Paris; 1985, in Berlin (Potzdamer Platz); 1986, at the Galerie Michel Broomhead in Paris; and 1988, at *Mise en relief* (*Alain Satié: Reliefs*), held in Paris at the Galerie Rambert.

Bibliography:

Isou, Isidore, *De l'impressionnisme au lettrisme*, Éd. Filipacchi, Paris, 1973. Isou, Isidore, *L'Art corporel lettriste, hypergraphique et esthapéïriste ou l'Art corporel ciselant, lettriste, hypergraphique, aphonique et esthapéïriste*, Publications PSI, Paris, 1977. *L'Art, la technique et les chefs-d'œuvre de Alain Satié*, Publications PSI, Paris, 1981. *Lettrisme: les débuts, 1944-1966. Isidore Isou, Gabriel Pomerand, Maurice Lemaître, Roland Sabatier, Alain Satié*, Gal. Rambert, Paris, 1987. Meunier, Jacques, *Alain Satié justement!*, exhibition catalogue, Gal. Rambert, Paris, 1988. Montbazet, Marie-Hélène, *Exposé sur les créations de Alain Satié*, Publications PSI, Paris, 1991.

Auction records:

Paris, 23 March 1987, *Relief on Wood* (1971, mixed media, Indian ink and oil on wood, 49 x 39 1/4 ins / 124.5 x 100 cm) FRF 10,000. Paris, 3 March 1989, *Lettrist Composition* (1978, oil on canvas, 13 3/4 x 11 ins / 35 x 27 cm) FRF 3,200. Paris, 14 June 1990, *Composition* (oil on canvas, 28 3/4 x 23 1/2 ins / 73 x 60 cm) FRF 20,000. Paris, 23 Oct 1990, *Words* (1986, oil/plastic/wood, 19 x 15 x 1 1/2 ins / 48 x 38 x 4 cm) FRF 8,000; *Transparencies* (1984, acrylic/canvas, 28 3/4 x 23 1/2 ins / 73 x 60 cm) FRF 18,000. Douai, 11 Nov 1990, *Lettrist Composition* (1966, ink, 19 1/2 x 12 1/2 ins / 49.5 x 32 cm) FRF 6,000. Paris, 15 April 1991, *Transparencies* (1984, acrylic/canvas, 28 3/4 x 23 1/2 ins / 73 x 60 cm) FRF 20,000.

SATLER. See **SATTLER**

SATO, Ado. See **ADO**

SATO, Hiromu

Japanese, 20th century.
Born 1923, in Mie, near Kyoto Prefecture.
Engraver.

Sato Hiromu studied at the municipal college of engineering in Nagoya in 1941, then subsequently turned to wood engraving and drawing. From 1955 he took part in exhibitions of the National Academy of Painting (Kokuga-kai) and the Japanese Engraving Association, the First Print Biennale in Tokyo in 1957, as well as various group exhibitions in Japan and overseas. In 1957 and 1959 he was awarded the Newcomer Prize by the National Academy of Painting, and in 1958 the Prize of Excellence from the Japanese Engraving Association. He was a member of the National Academy of Painting, the Japanese Engraving Association and the Graphic Art Club.

SATO, Kei, or Key

Japanese, 20th century.
Born 28 October 1906, in Oita; died 8 May 1978, in Beppu.
Also active in France.
Painter (including gouache/mixed media).
Shin-Seisaku Kyokai group.

Kei Sato was born in Oita City in the prefecture of Oita. He attended the Tokyo school of fine arts, working under the direction of Fujishima Takeji. He obtained his diploma in 1929. From 1930 to 1934 he stayed in Paris for the first time and was a pupil of the Colarrossi Academy in Paris. On his return to Japan in 1934 he became a founder member of the Artists' Association *Shin-Sensaku Kyokai* (new works), becoming a member of the committee in 1936. He was also a member of the committee of the Kamakura Museum of Modern Art. In 1952 he returned to settle in Paris where he remained other than returning to Japan for short periods. His son, the painter Ado, also joined him there. He then got into the Paris School and was part of the second wave of lyrical abstraction which asserted itself in the second half of the 1950s. He travelled to Greece, Italy, North Africa (Tunisia, Algeria, Morocco), Great Britain and the USA.

Kei Sato's work belonged in two very different periods, the figurative period followed by the abstract period. Indeed, after executing a few final figurative canvases which were enigmatic in their internalised poetic expression, he came to understand that he did not need to reproduce the external world in order to express his feelings or to give form to his thoughts on the subject of the universe. He was very drawn by the Cubist works of Picasso, and during his first sojourn in Paris he gravitated towards Abstraction. Although he was from the Far East, Kei Sato nonetheless had very little if anything to do with calligraphy, which is often viewed only too readily by westerners as the only specific plastic expression of Eastern countries. His paintings came to fruition very slowly, layer upon layer, and allowing a long time to dry, and his art is placed beyond time, the ephemeral and the gesture. He drew his inspiration from a kind of imaginary vision of the telluric world, the titles of his works being directly inspired by the geological universe: *The Rite of the Stone, Light in the Earth, History of Space, Axial Sun*. He himself wrote: 'I am attached to the navel of the world.' His models were minerals or geological stones collected on walks, as well as the roots thrown up as driftwood and branches, which were the objects of his future pictorial meditations and from which his palette would draw the dominant hues of black, white, brown and yellow ochre. The ceramics eroded from the dawn of time, the stones bearing the marks of their many journeys through the ages, the legacy of a rock charred by fire from a long extinct volcano, were for him the objects of his meditation.

Kei Sato took part in collective exhibitions: from 1926 to 1929 at the Tokyo National Salon, from 1931 to 1933 at the Salon d'Automne in Paris, in 1951 at the Carnegie Museum in New York; in 1952 and 1964 at the Carnegie International exhibition in Pittsburgh, from 1955 at the Salon de Mai in Paris; in 1957 at the International Exhibition in Carrara at which he was awarded the first prize for engraving; in 1958 *Artistes Japonais* (*Japanese Artists*) at the Galliera Museum in Paris; in 1960 at the 30th Biennale in Venice; in 1963 at *Japanese Avant-Garde Art* in Milan, the Tokyo and São Paulo Biennales and the First International Salon of the Experimental Galleries in Lausanne; in 1964 at the Menton Biennale, in which he won a prize, in 1965-1966 at the travelling exhibition *New Japanese Painting and Sculpture* at the Museum of Modern Art in New York and the major American museums, and from 1969 at the Salon des Réalités Nouvelles in Paris. He also displayed his works in solo exhibitions: in 1934, 1951 and 1954 in Tokyo; in 1954 in the Galerie Mirador in Paris; in 1959, 1960, 1961, 1964, 1968, 1970 and 1979 at the Galerie Jacques Massol in Paris; in 1964 at the Hamilton Gallery in London; in 1965 at the New York World House Gallery; in 1968 and 1971 at the Galerie Cavalero in Cannes; in 1970 in Esch-sur-Abrette, Luxembourg. He obtained various distinctions, among them the main prize of the Tokyo National Salon in 1932. He was selected for the Lissone prize in Milan.

BIBLIOGRAPHY:
Busse, Jacques, '*Un instantané de Key Sato ou la tommette*' in *Prisme des Arts* n° 19, periodical, Société Art et Industrie, Paris, February 1959. *Key Sato*, exhibition catalogue, Gal. Cavalero, Cannes, 1972. *Key Sato*, exhibition catalogue, Gal. Jacques Massol, Paris, 1973. Harambourg, Lydia, *L'École de Paris 1945-1965. Dictionnaire des peintres*, Ides et Calendes, Neuchâtel, 1993.

MUSEUMS AND GALLERIES:
KAMAKURA (MMA) - NANTES (MBA) - PARIS (BNF) - PARIS (MAMVP) - PARIS (MNAM-CCI) - STRASBOURG (Mus. d'Art Moderne et Contemporain) - TOKYO (National MMA).

AUCTION RECORDS:
PARIS, 24 April 1983, *Black Erosion* (1961, oil on canvas, 76 x 50 3/4 ins / 193 x 129 cm) FRF 26,000. PARIS, 20 March 1988, *White Night* (1957, oil on canvas, 25 1/2 x 32 ins / 65 x 81 cm) FRF 27,500. MILAN, 8 June 1988, *Shadow Reflection* (1955, oil on canvas, 18 x 25 1/2 ins / 46 x 65 cm) ITL 6,500,000. PARIS, 27 June 1988, *Composition* (1962, oil on canvas, 35 1/2 x 28 3/4 ins / 90 x 73 cm) FRF 36,000. PARIS, 18 Feb 1990, *Flame Stone* (1963, acrylic on canvas, 20 x 26 ins / 50.7 x 66 cm) FRF 56,000. PARIS, 15 April 1991, *Menton Bridge* (1956, oil on canvas, 18 x 15 ins / 46 x 38 cm) FRF 18,000. PARIS, 19 April 1991, *Untitled* (1971, mixed media on paper, 9 1/2 x 11 1/2 ins / 24 x 29 cm) FRF 11,500. PARIS, 21 March 1992, *Untitled* (1973, mixed media on rice paper, 9 3/4 x 12 1/4 ins / 25 x 31 cm) FRF 12,000. PARIS, 20 April 1994, *Shadow of Stones* (1963, oil on canvas/panel, 25 1/2 x 39 1/4 ins / 65 x 100 cm) FRF 14,000. NEW YORK, 27 April 1994, *History of Space (Black)* (1965, oil on canvas, 64 x 51 1/4 ins / 162.3 x 130.2 cm) USD 34,500. PARIS, 24 March 1996, *Double B Space* (1970, oil on canvas, 63 3/4 x 51 1/4 ins / 162 x 130 cm) FRF 24,000. PARIS, 28 June 1996, *Slumbering Stone* (1958, oil on canvas, 23 1/2 x 28 3/4 ins / 60 x 73 cm) FRF 8,500. PARIS, 23 Nov 1997, *Fossil of Fog* (1968, oil on canvas, 18 x 22 ins / 46 x 55 cm) FRF 11,000. NORWALK, 3 Oct 1999, *Abstract in Plum and White Texture* (1961, oil on canvas, 17 x 13 ins / 43 x 33 cm) USD 1,700. PARIS, 24 Nov 2002, *Sky Rust* (1962, oil on canvas, 29 x 24 ins / 73 x 60 cm) EUR 2,800. VERSAILLES, 15 Dec 2002, *Flame Stone* (1964, oil on canvas, 24 x 29 ins / 61 x 73 cm) EUR 2,200. PARIS, 26 Feb 2003, *Greetings Card* (1975, watercolour and ink, 7 x 11 ins / 18 x 28 cm) EUR 2,400. CALAIS, 18 May 2003, *Congealed Sea* (oil on canvas, 36 x 29 ins / 92 x 73 cm) EUR 3,000. PARIS, 3 March 2004, *Man Landscape* (1972, oil on canvas, 32 x 39 ins / 81 x 100 cm) EUR 2,200.

SATO, Kiyoto

Japanese, 20th century.
Born 1941.
Painter.

Sato Kiyoto was represented in various group exhibitions: from 1960 to 1968, Contemporary Japanese Art Exhibitions at the National Museum of Modern Art in Tokyo; from 1970, International Exhibitions of Young Artists in Tokyo; 1974, Exhibition of Japanese Art of Today at the Museum of Contemporary Art in Montreal. In 1968-1969 he won the prize of the Society of Modern Art, of which he became a member in 1972.

SATO, Satoru

Japanese, 20th century.
Born 14 November 1945, in Ishinomori (Miyagi).
Active in France since 1970.
Sculptor, painter, mixed media.

Satoru Sato won a diploma from the School of Fine Arts in Tokyo in 1969 and was made an assistant member. He left Japan for Paris where he enrolled for the School of Fine Arts, in the studio of Gustave Singier, up to 1974. He has created a great many monumental sculptures, for example: at Niigata, at the college of Minamikata, at the Museum of Outdoor Sculpture at Caracas, at the college of Bourg-en-Bresse, at the Kyoto Hotel, at the Jardin Public de Clermont Ferrand, at the Jardin des Ursulines at Mâcon. His works come into the category on the one hand, of geometric abstraction with an international consensus, and on the other hand, in the chance to invest public spaces with a modern look that has now become classical.

He has taken part in many group exhibitions and international fairs, including in Paris, at the Salons de la Jeune Sculpture, de Mai, des Réalités Nouvelles, and Grands et Jeunes d'Aujourd'hui, of which he has been a member of the Committee from 1986. Other group shows include in 1996, Symposium of Monumental Sculpture, Clermont Ferrand; 1998, Constructivist Group of Paris, Quito. He shows collections of his works in many solo exhibitions in Japan, in France and throughout the world. In 2000 he took the grand prix of the sculpture symposium of Korea.

BIBLIOGRAPHY:
Xuriguera, Gérard, *Satoru Sato*, FVW, Paris, 2001.

MUSEUMS AND GALLERIES:
DUNKIRK (MAC) - PARIS (BNF) - PARIS (FNAC).

AUCTION RECORDS:
DOUAI, 11 Nov 1990, *Composition* (1978, oil on canvas, 19 3/4 x 23 1/4 ins / 50 x 59 cm) FRF 12,800.

SATO, Shin'ichi

Japanese, 20th century.
Born 8 December 1915, in Aichi Prefecture.
Painter. Figure compositions, landscapes.

From 1923 Shin'ichi Sato educated himself in oil painting techniques under the instruction of Eiji Matsumoto. Although he began to paint at a very young age he nonetheless followed more advanced studies at the University of Kyoto from 1937, while continuing to paint with Kunitaro Suda. He was called up for the army during World War II from 1941 to 1946. In 1951 he settled in Tokyo. He left for Europe in 1958, where he travelled for one year. The influence of Fauvism is discernible in the landscapes of his figurative paintings, whilst the figures are reminiscent of Picasso in his blue period.

He began to exhibit his works in the Kansai region together with other painters in the Western style. Subsequently he presented his works in various collective exhibitions, including the Salons of the Nikatai group from 1947; exhibitions held by the Kodo Bijutsu Association, in which he won a prize in 1949, and of which association he became a member in 1952; in 1958 at the Salon de la Jeune Peinture in Paris, followed by the Mizue competition at the International Exhibition of Figurative Painting in Tokyo; at the Exhibition of Young Painters for the Yasui Prize, a travelling exhibition of contemporary Japanese works in China and in Russia and in 1965 at the *Senchu Generation* at the Museum of Modern Art in Kyoto. Since 1951 he has put on six-monthly personal exhibitions in Tokyo and in Osaka.

SATO, Tadashi

American, 20th century.
Born 1923, on Maui (Hawaii).
Painter.

Tadashi Sato studied at the School of Fine Arts in Honolulu. He arrived in New York in 1948 and enrolled at the Pratt Institute. He studied with Stuart Davis and John Ferren at the School of Art at Brooklyn Museum, where he later became an assistant. He won a John Hay Whitney scholarship in

1954 and went to work in Japan. He also received a bursary from a foundation in Honolulu in 1955. He lived in New York.

His paintings are abstract in style and have a geometric tendency, and rely on subtle colours. His forms, which he uses rarely, tend towards Brancusian simplification.

Bibliography:

Jenson, James, *Tadashi Sato: A Retrospective,* exhibition catalogue, The Contemporary Museum, Honolulu, 2002.

Museums and Galleries:

New York (Solomon R. Guggenheim Mus.).

Auction records:

New York, 12 March 1992, *Abstraction in Blue and Grey* (1948, oil on canvas, 18 x 23 ins / 46 x 58.5 cm) USD 1,320.

SATO, Tamotsu
Japanese, 20th century.
Born 1919, in Tokyo.
Painter.

Tamotsu Sato studied at the University of Fine Arts in Tokyo where he gained a diploma in 1941. He took part in many group exhibitions, including in 1960 the exhibition *Recent Developments in Painting in the Japanese Style* at the National Museum of Modern Art in Tokyo, in 1968 at the eighth exhibition of Contemporary Japanese Art, and from 1967 at JAFA (the Japanese Art Festival Association) in the USA.

SATO, Yasuo
Japanese, 20th century.
Born 1 January 1945, in Dairen, China, to Japanese parents.
Painter.

Yasuo Sato studied at the Tokyo School of Fine Arts. He took part in both collective and personal exhibitions: in 1970 with the group *Japan Arts Festival,* in 1974 *Figurative International* and in 1976 at the Takashimaya Gallery in Tokyo and the Galerie La Passerell St Louis in Paris.

SATOMI, Munetsugu
Japanese, 20th century.
Born 2 November 1900, in Osaka.
Painter, draughtsman, illustrator.

Munetsugu Satomi was a pupil of Fernand Cormon and Pierre Laurens. He collaborated on several magazines in Paris and in London. He took part in various collective and solo exhibitions in Paris including the Salon des Artistes Français and the Salon d'Automne, and, in 1932, the *Exposition de Publicité* at the Galerie de la Pléiade. He won a gold medal at the École des Beaux-Arts in Paris in 1926, and also at the 1932 international competition at the Foire de Paris.

SATORU, Sato. See **SATO Satoru**

SATORY, Josef August, or Sartory
Austrian, 19th century.
Active in Vienna during the first half of the 19th century.
Lithographer.

Satory engraved views, national costumes and flowers.

SATRAPITANUS. See **VOGTHERR Heinrich**

SATTERLÉE, Walter
American, 19th - 20th century.
Born 18 January 1844, in Brooklyn; died 28 May 1908, in New York.
Painter, engraver (etching), illustrator. Genre scenes.

Walter Satterlée studied at the National Academy of Design and with Edwin White in New York, with Bonnat in Paris and with Freeman in Rome. He later returned to America and settled there. He joined the National Academy in 1879 and was also a member of the American Watercolor Society.

Auction records:

New York, 19 April 1911, *Never Too Old to Dance,* USD 135.

SATTERTHWAITE, Thomas
British, 19th century.
Active in Ripon (Yorkshire) c. 1827.
Draughtsman. Portraits.

Museums and Galleries:

London (British Mus.): *Portrait of Francis Wilkinson.*

SATTLER, Caroline or Franziska.
See **TRIDON**

SATTLER, Claudia
American, 20th century.
Born 1940, in Akron (Ohio).
Draughtsman. Scenes with figures, figures.
Art Brut.

Claudia Sattler trained as a secretary, but began to draw from 1985, 'to free herself from the ghosts that haunted her'. Drawing her inspiration from literary and particularly poetic subjects (Baudelaire, Rimbaud), she drew in series of 12, using a biro, positioning her figures or imaginary personages head-to-foot as if to give her compositions a 'double meaning'. Her work featured in the 2001 exhibition *Noir sur Blanc. Mondes intérieurs* (*Black on White: Inner Worlds*) at the Halle St-Pierre in Paris.

Bibliography:

Gallien, Antoine/Lusardy, Martine/Pons, Louis, *Noir sur Blanc. Mondes intérieurs,* exhibition catalogue, La Halle Saint-Pierre, Paris, Travioles, Paris, 2001 (text in French and English).

SATTLER, Ernst, or Johann Ernst
German, 19th - 20th century.
Born 21 December 1840, in Schonungen, near Schweinfurt; died 29 September 1923, in Dresden-Hellerau.
Painter, engraver (etching). Genre scenes, landscapes, seascapes.

Ernst Sattler studied in Munich, Karlsruhe, Paris and Florence and went on to work as an assistant to Hans Thoma.

Museums and Galleries:

Munich (Stadtmus.): *Vintner's Cottage near Mainberg* - Szczecin (Mus. Stadt): *North German Port.*

SATTLER, Franz Joseph
Austrian, 18th century.
Active in Altstätten and in Vienna in 1744.
Sculptor.

SATTLER, Hans Martin
German, 17th century.
Active in Idstein during the second half of the 17th century.
Sculptor.

Hans Martin Sattler sculpted a pulpit and altar in the church of St Catherine in Frankfurt am Main.

SATTLER, Hubert
Austrian, 19th century.
Born 27 January 1817, in Vienna; died 3 April 1904, in Vienna.
Painter. History painting, landscapes, architectural views.
Orientalism.

Hubert Sattler was the son and pupil of Johann Michael Sattler. Although he trained in Vienna with J.J. Schindler, he is regarded as a Salzburg painter. It was in Salzburg that he exhibited for the first time. He brought back a number of landscapes from his travels in the Far East and Middle East between 1842 and 1846. He also visited North America and Central America in 1850.

Museums and Galleries:

Salzburg: *Temple of Ramses II; See of St John of Acre.*

Auction records:

Vienna, 9 June 1970, *Port of Piraeus,* ATS 38,000. Vienna, 22 May 1973, *Alpine Landscape,* ATS 22,000. Vienna, 17 Oct 1978, *View of the Château of Chillon* (oil on card, 6 3/4 x 9 ins

/ 17 x 22 cm) ATS 20,000. VIENNA, 14 Oct 1980, *View of Ragaz* (oil on card, 9 x 11 1/2 ins / 22 x 29.5 cm) ATS 21,000. VIENNA, 17 Nov 1981, *View of Constantinople* (oil on canvas, 29 1/2 x 40 ins / 75 x 101.5 cm) ATS 90,000. ZURICH, 30 Nov 1984, *View of the Port of Beirut* (1843, oil on canvas, 41 x 52 ins / 104 x 132 cm) CHF 125,000. NEW YORK, 24 May 1985, *Island of Philae with the Temple of Isis* (1861, oil on canvas, 41 1/2 x 52 1/2 ins / 105.4 x 133.4 cm) USD 12,000. LONDON, 17 March 1989, *Panorama of the Old Port of Genoa* (oil on canvas, 29 x 39 3/4 ins / 73.7 x 101 cm) GBP 34,100. LONDON, 5 Oct 1990, *Between Martigny and Sion in the Valais* (oil on canvas, 19 3/4 x 25 ins / 50.2 x 63.5 cm) GBP 4,400. NEW YORK, 22 May 1991, *View of Aleppo in Syria* (1848, oil on canvas, 16 1/4 x 26 3/4 ins / 41.3 x 67.9 cm) USD 20,900. MONACO, 18-19 June 1992, *View of the Old Port of Genoa* (oil on canvas, 28 1/4 x 39 ins / 72 x 99.3 cm) FRF 333,000. MUNICH, 22 June 1993, *View of Heidelberg Castle* (oil on canvas, 34 x 45 1/4 ins / 86.5 x 115 cm) DEM 19,550. MUNICH, 7 Dec 1993, *View of the Rosengarten in the Dolomites* (oil on canvas, 40 1/4 x 52 ins / 102 x 132 cm) DEM 15,525. LONDON, 15 Nov 1995, *English Felucca on the Nile near Abu-Simbel* (oil on canvas, 40 1/2 x 52 1/4 ins / 103 x 133 cm) GBP 12,650. LONDON, 13 March 1996, *View of Lake Mondsee* (1884, oil on canvas, 16 1/2 x 22 1/2 ins / 42 x 57 cm) GBP 2,990. LONDON, 9 Oct 1996, *View of Salzburg* (oil on canvas) GBP 80,700. LONDON, 13 Oct 1999, *Near Eastern Landscape, Probably the Lebanon* (1887, oil on canvas, 33 x 46 ins / 85 x 118 cm) GBP 15,000. LONDON, 24 Nov 1999, *View of London Bridge from the Thames* (1838, oil on canvas, 41 x 52 ins / 103 x 132 cm) GBP 45,000. VIENNA, 23 May 2000, *Midnight Sun* (oil on canvas, 19 x 29 ins / 47 x 74 cm) ATS 60,000. LONDON, 7 Dec 2000, *View of the Watzmann, near Salzburg* (oil on canvas, 24 x 34 ins / 61 x 87 cm) GBP 3,500. LONDON, 2 Oct 2001, *Medieval Procession, Bavaria* (oil on canvas, 39 x 29 ins / 100 x 74 cm) GBP 1,500. SION, 30 Nov 2001, *Alpine Landscape* (1883, oil on canvas, 24 x 29 ins / 60 x 73 cm) CHF 9,000. NUREMBERG, 20 June 2002, *The Entrance of Kaiser Maximilian I to Nuremberg* (oil on canvas, 38 x 28 ins / 97 x 71 cm) EUR 7,600. VIENNA, 28 Nov 2002, *View of Prague* (oil on canvas, 23 x 17 ins / 58 x 42 cm) EUR 5,000. VIENNA, 10 April 2003, *Jungfrau seen from Eisenflut* (oil on board, 9 x 13 ins / 24 x 32 cm) EUR 1,700. SALZBURG, 20 Nov 2003, *Swiss Mountain Valley* (oil on canvas, 17 x 21 ins / 42 x 53 cm) EUR 1,500. LONDON, 15 Jan 2004, *Midday Peace* (oil on canvas, 16 x 13 ins / 41 x 32 cm) GBP 1,800.

SATTLER, Jakob or Johann Jakob, or Sadler
Austrian, 18th century.
Born 27 February 1731, in St Florian, near Enns; died 23 October 1783, in St Florian, near Enns.
Sculptor.

Jakob Sattler was the son of Leonhard and brother of Johann Paul Sattler. He executed tombs, crucifixes and a fountain in the abbey of St Florian.

SATTLER, Johann Michael, or Satler
Austrian, 19th century.
Born 28 September 1786, in Neuberg, near Herzogenburg; died 28 September 1847, in Mattsee, near Salzburg.
Painter. Portraits, landscapes, panoramas.

Johann Michael Sattler was the father of Hubert Sattler. He trained at the academy in Vienna and settled in Salzburg. He exhibited in the main cities of Gemany.

MUSEUMS AND GALLERIES:
SALZBURG (Carolino Augusteum Mus.): *Portrait of Hubert Sattler; Portrait of Emperor Franz; Portrait of Marie Brandstätter; View over Maria Plain* - VIENNA (MM): two views of Vienna.

SATTLER, Johann Paul
Austrian, 18th century.
Active in St Florian from 1747 to 1753.
Sculptor (wood).

Johann Paul Sattler was the son of Leonhard and brother of Jakob Sattler. He executed statues and decorative sculpture for the abbey of St Florian.

SATTLER, Johannes
Swiss, 15th century.
Calligrapher, draughtsman.

In a German missal from the abbey of Einsielden, Johannes Sattler did drawings depicting the childhood and passion of Christ.

SATTLER, Josef Ignaz, or Sadler
Austrian, 18th century.
Born 17 February 1725, in Olmütz (now Olomouc, Czech Republic); died 1767.
Painter.

Josef Ignaz Sattler was the son of Philipp Sattler. He trained in Vienna and Rome. He painted frescoes and altarpieces in churches in Moravia.

SATTLER, Josef Ignaz
Austrian, 19th - 20th century.
Born 1 February 1852, in Linz; died 12 February 1927, in Linz.
Sculptor.

Josef Ignaz Sattler studied under Eugen Kolb in Munich and under C. Kundmann in Vienna. He sculpted statuary and cribs for churches in Upper Austria.

SATTLER, Joseph Kaspar
German, 19th - 20th century.
Born 26 July 1867, in Schrobenhausen; died 12 May 1931, in Munich.
Painter, watercolourist, engraver, draughtsman, illustrator, poster artist, graphic designer. Historical subjects. Ex-libris plates.
Jugendstil, Symbolism.

Joseph Kaspar Sattler was a pupil from 1886 to 1891 of the Academy of Munich in the studio of Nicolas Gysis. He was a teacher from 1891 in the School of Arts and Crafts in Strasbourg. He lived in Berlin from 1895 to 1904, then again in Strasbourg before settling in Munich in 1918. While at Strasbourg he became a member of an informal circle of artists, the 'St Leonard circle' united around the painter Charles Spindler and the patron Anselme Laugel. Joseph Sattler was an important artist in the history of the art of the book in Germany and particularly for illustration and the revival of the ex-libris at the turn of the century. He illustrated and often graphically conceived, several works, chiefly the *Legends of Alsace* by G. Spetz, *Der Schneider von Ulm* (*The Taylor From Ulm*) of Max Eyth, *Geschichte der Rheinischen Städtekultur* (*History of Rhineland City Culture*) (4 vols) by H. Boos, *Das deutsche drama der Gegenwart* (*German Drama of the Present*) by Rudolph Lothar, the works of Gottfried Keller, of Theodor Storm and of Will Vesper. He contributed to the magazines, *Simplicissimus* and *Pan*. His cover representing the god Pan for the magazine *Pan*, reprinted as a poster, is one of his best-known works. He designed a police letterpress, the Nibelungenschrift. His design style often took pictorial references from the German Renaissance. He appeared at the Salon des Artistes Français in Paris, winning an honourable mention in 1893.

BIBLIOGRAPHY:
Greiner, Daniel, '*Joseph Sattler und seiner Werke*' in *Deutsche Kunst und Dekoration*, 1903. Hollweck, Ludwig, *Joseph Kaspar Sattler: ein Wegbereiter des Jugendstils*, W. Ludwig, Pfaffenhoffen, 1988. Lotz, François, *Joseph Sattler: éléments biographiques, œuvre, ex-libris*, Musée de l'Imagerie peinte et populaire alsacienne, Pfaffenhoffen, 1988. Osterwalder, Marcus (ed.), *Dictionnaire des illustrateurs 1800-1914*, Ides et Calendes, Neuchâtel, 1989. Blum, Gernot, *Der Revolutionär*

des Exlibris um die Jahrhundertwende: Joseph Kaspar Sattler, catalogue raisonné, Blum, Mönchengladbach, 1999.
MUSEUMS AND GALLERIES:
SCHROBENHAUSEN (Sattlersammlung): graphic works - STRASBOURG: *Frontier*.

SATTLER, Leonhard
Austrian, 18th century.
Born in Altstätten; died 17 October 1744, in St Florian.
Sculptor (stone/wood/ivory).
Leonhard Sattler was the father of Johann Paul and Jakob Sattler. He settled in St Florian in 1711 where he executed many sculptures for the abbey of St Florian.

SATTLER, Maria Franziska
Austrian, 18th century.
Died 1792.
Active in St Florian.
Painter.
Maria Franziska Sattler was the wife of Jakob Sattler.

SATTLER, Maximilian
German, 17th century.
Born c. 1625, in Riedlingen; died 30 July 1691, in Kemnath.
Painter.
Maximilian Sattler executed paintings for the town hall and church in Kemnath.

SATTLER, Philipp, or Sadler
Austrian, 18th century.
Born c. 1696, in Wenns (Tyrol); died 21 May 1738, in Olmütz (now Olomouc, Czech Republic).
Sculptor, painter.
Philipp Sattler was the father of the painter Josef Ignaz Sattler. He executed a fountain, statues and an altar for the town and churches of Olmütz.

SATTLER, Thomas, called Gaudes
Austrian, 19th century.
Modeller.
MUSEUMS AND GALLERIES:
LAZNE KYNZVART (Zámek Kynzvart): statue, *Luna* (c. 1830, terracotta); statue, *Mars* (c. 1830, terracotta); *Bust of Metternich* (c. 1830).

SATTLER, Wilhelm or Julius Ferdinand Wilhelm
German, 19th century.
Born 17 February 1796, in Dresden; died 8 May 1866, in Dresden.
Portrait artist.
Wilhelm Sattler trained under C.A. Lindner and Pochmann at the academy in Dresden.

SATTMANN, Josef
Austrian, 19th century.
Died 26 June 1849, in Klagenfurt.
Active in Ferlach.
Painter.
Josef Sattmann painted altarpieces for churches in Ferlach and Maria Saal.

SATURNINUS
1st century.
Active during the first half of the 1st century.
Cameo engraver.
Ancient Roman.
Saturninus carved a cameo bearing the portrait of a woman.

SATYRIUS
3rd century BC.
Cameo engraver.
Ancient Greek.
Satyrius engraved the portrait of Arsinoe, the queen of Egypt, on crystal.

SATYRO. See **POELENBURGH Cornelis van**

SATYRUS I
4th century BC.
Born on Paros.
Sculptor. Statues, busts.
Ancient Greek.
Satyrus worked in the mid-4th century BC. He collaborated with Scopas and Bryaxis on the decoration of the Mausoleum at Halicarnassus and may have been involved in its construction with Pytheus. His sculptural work shows him as a kind of society portraitist, for he was commissioned to make statues of the members of the Hecatomnid dynasty.

His most remarkable portrait (if it is his) is that of Mausolus, a monumental statue with awe-inspiring presence and a very marked individuality. This attribution has been questioned, however, though it is known that he made statues of Mausolus' successors, Ada and Idreus, at Delphi around 345 BC.
MUSEUMS AND GALLERIES:
LONDON (British Mus.): *Mausoleum of Halicarnassus*.

SATYRUS II
4th century BC.
Sculptor.
Ancient Greek.
Satyrus made a statue at Larissa in about 300 BC.

SATZINGER, Karl
German, 19th - 20th century.
Born 6 July 1864, in Bubenheim.
Active in Grosshardern, near Munich.
Sculptor.
Karl Satzinger was a pupil of W. Ruemann.

SAUBER, Robert
British, 19th - 20th century.
Born 12 February 1868, in London; died 10 September 1936.
Painter, draughtsman, illustrator. Portraits, genre scenes.
Robert Sauber was the grandson of Charles Hancock, the painter of animals. He studied in Munich and at the Académie Julian in Paris. In 1890 he moved back to London and settled there. He was a member of the Society of British Artists, and vice-president of the Royal Miniature Society from 1896 to 1898. He exhibited in London from 1888, notably at the Royal Academy and Suffolk Street. He exhibited in Paris at the Salon des Artistes Français, and was awarded a third-class medal in 1907.

He worked for various magazines, including: *English Illustrated Magazine*, *Illustrated London News* and *Reading for Everyone*.
AUCTION RECORDS:
LONDON, 30 March 1994, *Constance Shepherd and Her Borzoi* (oil on canvas, 77 x 51 1/2 ins / 195.5 x 131 cm) GBP 45,500. LONDON, 16 Nov 1999, *Portrait of Elegant Lady in Evening Dress* (oil on canvas on board, 26 x 21 ins / 66 x 53 cm) GBP 1,050. NEW YORK, 8 March 2000, *Portrait of an Elegant Woman* (oil on canvas, oval, 35 x 27 ins / 90 x 69 cm) USD 10,000. LONDON, 4 April 2000, *Portrait of a Lady in Evening Dress* (oil on canvas, 29 x 24 ins / 73 x 60 cm) GBP 3,000. LONDON, 15 May 2001, *Portrait of Miss Kitty Wooliscroft, Artist's Niece* (oil on canvas, 22 x 19 ins / 57 x 47 cm) GBP 1,500.

SAUBERG, Johan, or Sauerberg or Saurberg
Swedish, 18th century.
Active during the first half of the 18th century.
Sculptor (wood).
Sauberg executed statues for churches in Ösmo and Denmark.

SAUBERGUE, John
British, 19th century.
Born 1803.
Active during the first half of the 19th century.
Painter. Figures, landscapes.
John Saubergue exhibited in London in 1829 and 1830.

SÄUBERLI, Peter
Swiss, 20th century.
Born 1930.
Painter, watercolourist.
MUSEUMS AND GALLERIES:
AARAU (Aargauer Kunsthaus): *Fossil* (1972); *Darkness* (1975).

SAUBÈS, Léon Daniel or Daniel
French, 19th - 20th century.
Born 6 March 1855, in Guiche (Pyrénées-Atlantiques); died 14 July 1922, in Paris.
Painter. History painting, genre scenes, figures, portraits.
Bayonne School.
Léon Daniel Saubès studied with Achille Zo at the École Municipale de Dessin et de Peinture, Bayonne, and with Léon Bonnat at the École des Beaux-Arts, Paris. He exhibited first at the Salon de Paris of 1880 with *The Dead Christ*, and subsequently at the Salon des Artistes Français, of which he became a member. He was awarded an honourable mention in 1880, a third-class medal in 1893, a second-class in 1895, a silver medal at the time of the Exposition Universelle of 1900, and became an out-of-competition, committee and jury member. He was made a Chevalier of the Légion d'Honneur in 1900. In 2001 the Bonnat Museum, Bayonne, organised an exhibition around a painting by Henri Achille Zo, *Léon Bonnat et ses élèves basques et béarnais* (*Léon Bonnat and his Basque and Béarnais Pupils*) (1914), which brought together the work of some of the artists who appear in this painting, including Léon Saubès.

He several times painted the features of subjects who were dead or on the point of death. As a pupil of Bonnat, he was one of the group of painters that Parisian critics of the period called the 'Bayonne School'.
MUSEUMS AND GALLERIES:
BAYONNE (Mus. Bonnat): *Head of the Dead Victor Hugo* (after Léon Bonnat) - CAHORS: *Sleeping Child (Dead?)*.
AUCTION RECORDS:
PARIS, July 1946, *Fishermen on a Quay, the upper part of their bodies lit by the rays of the setting sun,* FRF 4,000. PARIS, 9 July 1992, *Portrait of Madame de Castex and her son Léon* (oil on canvas, 85 x 49 1/4 ins / 215 x 125 cm) FRF 14,500.

SAUBIDET GACHE, Tito
Argentinian, 20th century.
Born 1891, in Buenos Aires.
Painter, poster artist.
In Paris Tito Saubidet Gache studied painting with Francisco Paolo Parisi, and also architecture. He showed work at the 1914 Salon des Humoristes in Paris, where he won first prize in the posters contest. He also received an honorary diploma at the *Exposition Internationale des Arts Décoratifs* (*International Exhibition of Decorative Art*) in Paris.
MUSEUMS AND GALLERIES:
PARIS (Mus. de l'Armée).

SAUCE, Jean Louis
French, 18th century.
Born c. 1730, in Paris; died 1788, in Paris.
Painter, draughtsman. Mythological subjects.
Sauce was a student at the Académie Royale in Paris.
AUCTION RECORDS:
NEW YORK, 10 Jan 1996, *Sacrifice to Priapus; Bacchanalian Dance by a Temple* (black chalk and ink, a pair, 11 1/2 x 18 1/2 ins / 29.2 x 47 cm) USD 7,820.

SAUCEDO, or Salcedo (?)
Spanish, 16th century.
Sculptor.
Saucedo carved the wooden Easter sepulchre in Seville Cathedral in 1561. He may have been one of the Salcedo family.

SAUCEDO. See also **SALCEDO**

SAUCKEN, Ernst von
German, 19th century.
Born 26 September 1856, in Tataren, near Tarputschen.
Painter. Hunting scenes, landscapes, animals.
Ernst von Saucken trained under Karl Steffeck and Christian Kröner.

SAUDAN, Olivier
Swiss, 20th century.
Sculptor, print artist.
MUSEUMS AND GALLERIES:
LAUSANNE (Cantonal MFA): *Execution of Major Davel* (1980).

SAUDE, Antonio
Portuguese, 20th century.
Born 2 July 1875, in Lisbon; died 1958.
Painter. Figures, genre scenes, landscapes, seascapes.
Antono Saude studied under Carlos Reis at the college of fine arts in Lisbon and was involved in the foundation of the Portuguese Artists' Group in 1945. He featured in collective exhibitions including: National Fine Arts Salon (of which he was a founder member), Lisbon (from 1901), international exhibition, Rio de Janeiro (1908 and 1923), Ibero-American Exhibition, Seville (1929). A posthumous retrospective was held in 1959. He received various awards and distinctions, including a bronze medal in 1901, silver medals in 1908 and 1923, gold in 1929 and 1936, and a medal of honour in 1950.
BIBLIOGRAPHY:
Arnáiz, José Manuel/López Jiménez, Javier/Merchán Díaz, Manuel (ed.), '*Cien años de pintura en Espana y Portugal (1830-1930)*' in vol. X, Antiqvaria, Madrid, 1993.
MUSEUMS AND GALLERIES:
LISBON (Centro de Arte Moderna José de Azeredo Perdigão, Fundação Calouste Gulbenkian): *Market Day*.
AUCTION RECORDS:
LISBON, 23-24 Oct 1973, *Seascape*, PTE 51,000.

SAUDEK, Rudolf
German, 20th century.
Born 20 October 1880, in Kolin.
Sculptor, engraver. Busts.
Rudolf Saudek studied at the academies of Leipzig, Prague and Florence.
MUSEUMS AND GALLERIES:
LEIPZIG (Mus. der Bildenden Künste): *Bust of Nietzsche* - LEIPZIG (Stadtgeschichtliches Mus.): *Bust of Albrecht Kurzwelly* - TRIBSCHEN: *Bust of Richard Wagner*.

SAUDEMONT, Émile
French, 20th century.
Born 14 October 1898, in Denain (Nord).
Painter. Urban landscapes, landscapes.
Émile Saudemont studied at the École des Beaux-Arts, Valenciennes, under Billotey and Lucien Jonas, and entered the École des Beaux-Arts, Paris, in 1914. He exhibited regularly at the Salon des Artistes Français, Paris, from 1946. He painted the well-known Parisian locations with charm and movement and decorated the town hall of Suresnes.
MUSEUMS AND GALLERIES:
DENAIN - NEW YORK - VALENCIENNES - ZURICH.
AUCTION RECORDS:
PARIS, 20 Oct 1997, *Montmartre* (1948, oil on canvas, 23 1/2 x 28 3/4 ins / 60 x 73 cm) FRF 8,000.

SAUDERAT, Étienne
French, 15th century.

Born in Auxerre.
Calligrapher, illuminator. Miniatures.

MUSEUMS AND GALLERIES:
AMIENS (Bibliothèque): *Book of the Properties of Things* (miniature).

SAUDNERS, Heinrich. See **DMOCHOWSKI**

SAUDUN, Auguste de
French, 19th century.
Painter. Genre scenes.

MUSEUMS AND GALLERIES:
BAYONNE (Mus. Bonnat): *The Fisherman's House*.

SAUER. See also **SAUR**

SAUER, Christian
German, 18th century.
Born 1731; died 1786, in Stuttgart.
Sculptor, stucco artist.
Christian Sauer executed sculptures in the Karlsruhe castle and at the Durlach Gate in Karlsruhe.

SAUER, E. L.
German, 19th century.
Active in Leipzig in 1829.
Draughtsman.

SAUER, Greta
Austrian, 20th century.
Born 1909, in Bregenz.
Active in France from 1937.
Painter (gouache), collage artist.
Greta Sauer worked as an abstract painter from 1939. Her range extends from graceful and delicate collages to sober and well-structured gouaches. She showed work in group exhibitions in Paris, notably at the Salon des Réalités Nouvelles in 1947, 1950, 1956 and 1957, and in Marseilles, Copenhagen, San Francisco and Turin, among other venues. Solo exhibitions of her work were held in Paris in 1948, 1950, 1951 and 1952.

SAUER, Heinrich
German, 19th century.
Painter. Flowers.
Heinrich Sauer was a pupil of Karl Röthig. He worked from 1824 to 1826 in Berlin. He also practised horticulture.

SAUER, Jacob
German, 18th century.
Sculptor (wood).
Jacob Sauer sculpted the altars of the Virgin and St Joseph in the church of Höpfingen between 1758 and 1760.

SAUER, Josef Eduard
German, 19th - 20th century.
Born 12 May 1868, in Buchelsdorf, near Neustadt; died 30 December 1909, in Pasing, near Munich.
Painter. Portraits, genre scenes, landscapes.
Josef Eduard Sauer was a pupil of Raupp.

SAUER, Mathias
Austrian, 19th century.
Born 1798; died 21 February 1862, in Vienna.
Painter. History painting.

SAUER, Michel
German, 20th century.
Active in Düsseldorf.
Sculptor.
Michel Sauer works in small formats and conventional materials such as plaster, bronze and zinc and his work has been described by one critic (Maïten Bouisset) as that of a 'sculptor/goldsmith'. He has exhibited at numerous group exhibitions and on a solo basis, including shows at the Schnela Gallery in Düsseldorf (1974, 1975, 1982, 1986), the Haus Lange Museum in Krefeld (1976), the fine arts gallery in Düsseldorf (1977), and the Galerie Philippe Casini in Paris (1985, 1986).

BIBLIOGRAPHY:
Bischoff, U., *Michel Sauer*, exhibition catalogue, Kunsthalle, Kiel, 1987.

SAUER, Walter Louis Émile
Belgian, 20th century.
Born 12 February 1889, in St-Gilles-lez-Bruxelles; died 6 September 1927, in Algiers.
Painter, pastellist, engraver, draughtsman, illustrator, lithographer. Figures, portraits.
Symbolism.
Walter Louis Émile Sauer studied under Montald, Jean Delville and Emile Fabry at the fine arts academy in Brussels and also took special courses in the art of Japanese printing. He painted female portraits that are both sensuous and withdrawn, a combination which imparts an uncommon inscrutability to his work. In 1921 he provided illustrations for Limbosch's *Symphonie Macabre*.

Walter Sauer

AUCTION RECORDS:
LONDON, 25 March 1980, *Young Girl with a Print Shawl* (coloured chalks and pencil, 13 1/4 x 11 1/4 ins / 33.5 x 28.5 cm) GBP 1,300. BRUSSELS, 10 Dec 1984, *Woman with Veil* (1917, drawing, 15 3/4 x 11 1/2 ins / 40 x 29 cm) BEF 55,000. BRUSSELS, 14 Oct 1985, *Portrait of Jean* (drawing, 33 1/2 x 18 3/4 ins / 85 x 47.5 cm) BEF 95,000. BRUSSELS, 3 Dec 1986, *Model* (1919, drawing, 20 x 17 3/4 ins / 51 x 45 cm) BEF 95,000. LOKEREN, 8 Oct 1988, *Young Woman* (black chalk and pastel, 13 1/2 x 9 1/2 ins / 34.5 x 24 cm) BEF 170,000. LONDON, 19 Oct 1988, *Bust of a Young Girl* (charcoal and pencil, 17 1/4 x 14 1/2 ins / 44 x 37 cm) GBP 3,300. AMSTERDAM, 10 April 1990, *Meditation* (1919, pencil/paper, 16 1/4 x 5 3/4 ins / 41.5 x 14.5 cm) NLG 10,925. LOKEREN, 21 March 1992, *Young Woman* (1919, pastel, 19 1/4 x 13 1/2 ins / 49 x 34 cm) BEF 95,000. AMSTERDAM, 9 Dec 1992, *Portrait of a Woman with a Veil over her Head* (1918, charcoal and pencil/paper, 11 1/2 x 10 3/4 ins / 29.5 x 27.5 cm) NLG 2,070. LOKEREN, 28 May 1994, *Woman Crocheting* (watercolour and pastel, 21 1/2 x 17 1/4 ins / 54.5 x 43.5 cm) BEF 145,000. AMSTERDAM, 7 Dec 1994, *Modesty* (1920, pencil, black chalk and coloured pencil/paper, 22 x 18 ins / 56 x 45.5 cm) NLG 12,650. LOKEREN, 11 March 1995, *Breton Girl* (1926, pastel, 36 1/2 x 26 3/4 ins / 92.5 x 68 cm) BEF 440,000. PARIS, 30 Nov 1995, *Woman with a Small Veil* (1922, pencil and charcoal heightened with pastel/Japanese paper, 24 1/2 x 18 1/2 ins / 62.5 x 47 cm) FRF 15,000. LOKEREN, 6 Dec 1997, *Pensive Young Woman* (c. 1919, pastel and pencil, 21 x 14 1/4 ins / 52.5 x 36 cm) BEF 330,000; *Draped Nude* (1918, red chalk and black chalk, 17 3/4 x 13 3/4 ins / 45 x 35 cm) BEF 200,000. LOKEREN, 9 Oct 1999, *Absinthe Drinker* (black chalk, 17 x 19 ins / 44 x 47 cm) BEF 300,000. BRUSSELS, 9 Nov 1999, *Oriental Woman Holding an Apple* (mixed media, 37 x 26 ins / 94 x 66 cm) BEF 280,000. BRUSSELS, 18 Jan 2000, *La Margo* (1923, charcoal and watercolour, 24 x 19 ins / 61 x 48 cm) BEF 134,000. LOKEREN, 7 Oct 2000, *Fisherwoman from the Island of Sein* (pastel, 26 x 33 ins / 65 x 85 cm) BEF 300,000. LOKEREN, 6 Oct 2001, *Hindu Goddess* (1919, pastel and black chalk, 21 x 6 ins / 53 x 14 cm) BEF 290,000. AMSTERDAM, 4 Dec 2001, *Woman* (1925, watercolour and colour crayon on card, 31 x 24 ins / 79 x 61 cm) NLG 25,000. BRUSSELS, 16 Sept 2002, *Young Girl with Grass Skirt* (1917, mixed media, 22 x 16 ins / 56 x 41 cm) EUR 6,400. BRUSSELS, 16 Sept 2002, *Young Girl in a Turban* (1919, mixed media, 19 x 6 ins / 48 x 15 cm) EUR 8,000. BRUSSELS, 15 April 2003, *Black Casket* (oil, silver leaf and colour crayon on canvas, 21 x 18 ins / 53 x 45 cm) EUR 19,000. AMSTERDAM, 2 Dec 2003, *Festival Scene* (1927, oil on

panel, 33 x 26 ins / 84 x 66 cm) EUR 8,000. LOKEREN, 15 May 2004, *Woman with Joined Hands* (1919, pastel and black chalk) EUR 4,800. ANTWERP, 13 Dec 2004, *Motherhood* (drawing, 23 x 17 ins / 58 x 44 cm) EUR 6,500.

SAUER, Wenzel
German, 18th century.
Born c. 1737; died 26 November 1787, in Proskau (now Proszków, Poland).
Modeller (glazed earthenware).
Sauer modelled many figurines for the Proskau Glazed Earthenware Factory.

SAUER, Wilhelm
German, 19th - 20th century.
Born 23 September 1865, in Odelshofen, near Kehl; died 20 March 1929, in Durlach.
Sculptor.
Wilhelm Sauer studied in Paris, Rome (under J. Knopf) and Karlsruhe. He sculpted statuary and fountains in Karlsruhe.

SAUER, Wilhelm
Austrian, 20th century.
Born 27 September 1892, in Vienna; died 10 December 1930.
Engraver, designer.
Wilhelm Sauer studied under O. Prutscher and R. von Larisch in Vienna and went on to specialise in ex-libris designs.

SAUERBERG, Johan. See **SAUBERG**

SAUERBREY, Jakob
German, 17th century.
Medallist.
Jakob Sauerbrey was the father of Jobst Friedrich Sauerbrey. He worked from 1688 to 1702 in Berlin.

SAUERBREY, Jobst Friedrich
German, 18th century.
Active from 1703 to 1718.
Medallist.
Jobst Sauerbrey was the son of Jakob Sauerbrey.

SAUERBREY, Nicolaus Friedrich
German, 18th century.
Died c. 1771, in Berlin.
Engraver. Cards, coats of arms.

SAUERBRUCH, Horst
German, 20th century.
Born 1941, in Rome, to German parents.
Painter (mixed media), watercolourist, sculptor, illustrator.
Horst Sauerbruch studied at the Akademie der Bildenden Künste in Munich from 1963 to 1969 and was appointed to the teaching staff there in 1972. From 1968, he produced monumental decorations, paintings, sculptures, mosaics and ceramics in churches, public buildings and private places. He illustrated several books, stories and tales. The diversity of his techniques produces a diversity of work. His paintings explore the plurality of currents of abstraction - lyrical, gestural, Tachist, Informel and Materist. His sculpted objects are in the quasi-humorist vein of Dada.

He took part in numerous collective exhibitions from 1965, mainly in Munich at the salons of the Haus der Kunst. He took part in the autumn shows there and also in the summer shows of other German towns, sometimes in a group with his pupils. He also took part in exhibitions in Cairo and Alexandria in 1988. He had numerous solo shows from 1996 in galleries in Munich, Frankfurt, Mainz and other German towns.
BIBLIOGRAPHY:
Horst Sauerbruch, exhibition catalogue, Gal. Karl und Faber, Munich, 1993 (good documentation).

SAUERHARD
German, 18th century.
Painter.
Sauerhard painted scenes from Biblical history for the church of the Holy Sepulchre in Deggendorf.

SAUERLAND, Philipp
German, 18th century.
Born 1677, in Danzig (now Gdansk, Poland); died 1750, 1760 or 1762, in Breslau (now Wroclaw, Poland).
Painter. Portraits, animals.
Philipp Sauerland was very well known as a painter of animals, but he also painted portraits. He lived a long time in Berlin, then settled in Breslau.
MUSEUMS AND GALLERIES:
BUDAPEST: *Peacocks* - WROCLAW: *Still-life*.
AUCTION RECORDS:
PARIS, 9 April 1951, *Stag Hunting*, FRF 11,000.

SAUERLÄNDER, Charles Jacques Antoine
Swiss, 19th century.
Born 8 October 1824, in Geneva; died 17 March 1866.
Miniaturist, enameller.
MUSEUMS AND GALLERIES:
GENEVA (MAH): several works.

SAUERLANDT, Leurentz
Dutch, 17th century.
Born 1640.
Active in Amsterdam.
Painter.

SAUERMAN, Conrad, or Sauerman von der Göltsch
German, 16th century.
Born in Breslau (now Wroclaw, Poland); died 1554.
Medallist.
Conrad Sauerman worked in the mints of Breslau and Prague.

SAUERMANN, Heinrich
German, 19th century.
Born 12 March 1842, in Flensburg; died 4 October 1904, in Flensburg.
Sculptor (wood).

SAUERMANN, Konrad
German, 17th century.
Active in Strössendorf during the first half of the 17th century.
Sculptor (wood).
Konrad Sauermann sculpted the organ case for the church of St Peter in Kulmbach.

SAUERSIK, Carl
Austrian, 19th century.
Active in Mies (now Stribro, Czech Republic).
Painter.
Sauersik painted altarpieces for churches in Bohemia.

SAUERWEID, Aleksandr Aleksandrovich, or Zauerveid
Russian, 19th century.
Painter. Seascapes.
This artist was the son of Aleksandr Ivanovich Sauerweid

SAUERWEID, Aleksandr Ivanovich, or Zauerveid
Lithuanian, 19th century.
Born 19 February 1783, in Kurland (now Kurzeme); died 25 October 1844, in St Petersburg.
Painter, watercolourist, draughtsman, engraver. Historical subjects, military subjects, battles, portraits, figures, landscapes with figures, animals.

Aleksandr Ivanovich Sauerweid studied at the art academy in Dresden. He spent many years living in France, but in 1814 received an invitation to work in St Petersburg from the Tsar Alexander I. He painted battle scenes in the style of Horace Vernet. He also produced etchings of military subjects, cavaliers, and skirmishes between cavaliers.

MUSEUMS AND GALLERIES:
MOSCOW (State Tretyakov Gal.): *Military Scene; Soldiers from the Guard of Nicholas I; Akhmetka, Nicholas I's Dwarf; Admiral Krusenstern's Voyage around the World* (two watercolours).
AUCTION RECORDS:
PARIS, 1823, *Battle Scene* (drawing in colour and watercolour) FRF 16. PARIS, 1880, *Tartar Cavaliers; Russian Cavaliers* (watercolour, watercolour and sepia, collection) FRF 75. PARIS, 20 March 1899, *Cossack Camp on the Champs-Elysees,* FRF 410. PARIS, 31 May 1928, *Hussar on Horseback* (wash) FRF 210. PARIS, 22 Nov 1948, *Tartar Cavaliers* (two pendants) FRF 13,000. PARIS, 5 Feb 1951, *Cossack Camp on the Champs-Elysees* (pencil, pen and wash) FRF 10,000. LONDON, 3 June 1983, *Portrait of the Tsar Alexander in his State Coach* (oil on canvas, 19 1/2 x 31 ins / 49.5 x 78.6 cm) GBP 4,200. LONDON, 20 June 1985, *Portrait of the General Thielmann; Portrait of an Officer of the Dragoons* (watercolour and pencil heightened with white, a pair, 15 3/4 x 13 3/4 ins / 40 x 35 cm) GBP 1,800. MONTE CARLO, 29 Nov 1986, *Cossack on Horseback* (watercolour and wash, 13 1/2 x 17 1/2 ins / 34 x 44.5 cm) FRF 20,000. NEW YORK, 13 Oct 1993, *Krasnow Kabak Avenue* (1813, ink and watercolour/paper, 23 1/2 x 36 1/2 ins / 59.4 x 93 cm) USD 13,800. LONDON, 14 Dec 1995, *Tsar Alexander I and his Coachman Ilya in a Cabriolet* (oil on canvas, 19 3/4 x 31 ins / 50 x 78.5 cm) GBP 12,650. LONDON, 19 Dec 1996, *Tsar Alexander I and his Coachman Ilya in a Cabriolet* (oil on canvas, 19 3/4 x 31 ins / 50 x 78.5 cm) GBP 11,500. PARIS, 12 April 1999, *Cossacks on the Champs Elysees* (Indian ink over black crayon, 15 x 39 ins / 37 x 98 cm) FRF 31,000. LONDON, 29 Nov 2000, *Prussian Hussars of the Guard* (watercolour over pencil heightened with bodycolour, 19 x 16 ins / 48 x 40 cm) GBP 1,400.

SAUERWEID, Nicolas Aleksandrovich, or Zauerveid
Russian, 19th century.
Born 1836, in St Petersburg; died 29 May 1866, in St Petersburg.
Painter. History painting, battles, portraits.

Nicolas Aleksandrovich Sauerweid was the son of Aleksandr Ivanovitch Sauerweid.
MUSEUMS AND GALLERIES:
MOSCOW (State Tretyakov Gal.): *Battle near Narva; Battle* (sketch).
AUCTION RECORDS:
LONDON, 15 Nov 1991, *The Battle of Waterloo with General Wellington on his Horse Copenhagen* (oil on canvas) GBP 7,150. LONDON, 29 Jan 2003, *Nicholas in a Horse-drawn Brichka* (watercolour, a pair, 7 x 9 ins / 17 x 24 cm) GBP 1,100.

SAUERWEIN, Barlaam
Austrian, 17th century.
Active during the second half of the 17th century.
Sculptor. Religious furnishings.

Barlaam Sauerwein sculpted an altar for the church in Bozen (now Bolzano, Italy) in 1682.

SAUERWEIN, Charlotte
German, 19th century.
Active in Berlin from 1814 to 1822.
Painter. Portraits, genre scenes.

SAUFFROIS. See **JOUFFROY**

SAUGER, Amélie
French, 20th century.
Painter, pastellist.

Amélie Sauger, a pupil of Marcel Baschet, exhibited in Paris at the Salon des Artistes Français, of which she was a member, at the Petit Palais group in 1918, and at the 'New Salon', perhaps the Salon des Surindépendants, in 1925 and 1926.

SAUGRAIN, Claude Marin
French, 18th century.
Born 1756, in Paris.
Engraver, draughtsman.

Claude Saugrain was the son of the bookseller Saugrain, whose establishment *Aux Écoles de Médecine* (*For The Schools of Medicine*) was in the Rue de la Bûcherie. He was the pupil of N. Cochin and entered the École de l'Académie Royale in September 1775.

SAUGRAIN, Élise
French, 18th century.
Born 1753, in Paris; died after 1783.
Reproductions engraver, draughtswoman.

Élise Saugrain was the pupil of Moreau the Younger. It is thought that she was the sister of the engraver Claude Marin Saugrain and daughter of the bookseller Saugrain, whose establishment was in the Rue de la Bûcherie. Her best-known works are her highly skilful reproductions of works by L.G. Moreau the Elder, particularly *Views of the Paris Area* (two plates), *View of Madrid Castle, View of Bagatelle Bridge, View of Vincennes Palace.* She also produced *View of Dresden*, after J.G. Wagner, engraved in 1783.
AUCTION RECORDS:
PARIS, 1897, *Landscape,* FRF 340.

SAUGY, Louis
French, 19th - 20th century.
Born 7 February 1863, in Paris.
Painter, draughtsman. Architectural views.
MUSEUMS AND GALLERIES:
BERN: *The Old Town, San Remo.*

SAÜL, Peter
American, 20th century.
Born 16 August 1934, in San Francisco.
Painter (including gouache), draughtsman, lithographer.
Pop Art, Nouvelle Figuration, Narrative Figuration, Citationism.

Peter Saül studied at Stanford University (California) and at the California School of Fine Arts in San Francisco from 1950-1952, then at Washington University in St Louis, Missouri, from 1949-1956. From 1952-1956 he worked with Fred Conway. He lived in Europe from 1956-1964, just as Pop Art was exploding in the USA. From 1956-1958 he lived in Holland; from 1958-1962 in Paris; from 1962-1964 in Rome, after which he returned to California before taking up a teaching post at the University of Texas in Austin. Thanks to his spending such a long time in Europe he was able to see American civilisation objectively, with the eyes of an outsider. In 1962 he was awarded the New Talent prize reserved for American art, as well as the Copley Foundation prize. He lives and works in Germantown (New York).

In the early part of his career, what Saül exploited from Pop Art was not what Pierre Restany called 'urban folklore' but the narrative of animated drawings in the style of Walt Disney (sorts of cartoons, which could be vulgar), with the aim of denouncing, if somewhat symbolically, the ridiculous nature of consumer society. It was this early period - full of bright colour, amusing drawings and dynamic - that influenced the appearance of a French Pop Art style, particularly in the work of Rancillac and Télémaque. Saül's social criticism then became more acerbic: in a style closer to caricature, with an exaggeration of physical details that sometimes had overtones of Otto Dix, he challenged financiers and politicians. Finally, with his deliberately monstrous designs, soft and visceral shapes created in a mix of oil paints and industrial paints (*Day-Glo*) and in shrill acidic colours, he took up the themes of Hippie protest, denouncing, not without a certain humour, the war in Vietnam and the crimes committed under American imperialist policy. From 1967 onwards, he inscribed the title of the work within the pictorial space itself. Saül also mocked the art world and in particular critics by creating the figure of *Clemunteena Gweenburg*, a parody of the celebrated American critic Clement Greenberg. From 1975 Saül parodied great masterpieces, such as Rembrandt's *Nightwatch* or Picasso's *Guernica*. In the 1980s he began depicting images of cowboys, including Ronald Reagan, and completed a number of self-portraits (including *Oedipus Junior*, 1983). In the 1990s he painted faces that looked as if they were made out of a rubber, in which huge mouths voraciously closed on all sorts of consumer products such as cigarettes or sweets, and occasionally disgorged them (*Mona Lisa Throws Up Pizza*, 1995). In 2002 he executed several lithographs.

Most of his early exhibitions were in Europe, beginning with the Salon de la Jeune Peinture in Paris in 1959, 1960. His work has been seen in a wide range of collective exhibitions: 1961, *International Selection*, Dayton Art Institute, Dayton, Ohio; 1962 to 1965, *Contemporary American Art Society*, Art Institute, Chicago; 1963, *New Directions* San Francisco Museum; 1963, *A New Realist Supplement*, Museum of the University of Michigan; 1963, 1er Salon International des Galeries Pilotes, Lausanne regional museum; 1963, *Thirteen Painters in Rome*, Rome; 1964, Art Institute, Chicago; 1964, *New Realism*, municipal museum, The Hague; 1964, 20th Century Museum, Vienna; 1964, *Mythologies Quotidiennes* (*Everyday Mythologies*), Musée d'Art Moderne de la Ville de Paris; 1965, Groupe *1/65*, Musée d'Art Moderne de la Ville de Paris; 1965, *La Figuration Narrative* (*Narrative Figuration*), Paris; 1966, *Painting and Sculpting Today*, Indianapolis Museum; 1967-1969, Salon de Mai, Paris; 1969, Salon Comparaisons, Paris; 1969, Musée Cantini, Marseilles; 1969-1971, Musée d'Art et d'Industrie, Saint-Étienne; 2001, *Eye Infection*, Stedelijk Museum, Amsterdam; 2003, with Rancillac and Boshier, *3 Pop Guys 40 Years After* at the Galerie du Centre, Paris.

He has also had many solo exhibitions of his paintings: regularly from 1961 to 1977, Allan Frumkin Gallery, Chicago; regularly from 1962 to 1987, Allan Frumkin Gallery, New York; regularly from 1962 to 1973, Galerie Breteau, Paris; 1963, La Tartaruga, Rome; 1963, Rolf Nelson Gallery, Los Angeles; 1964, Galleria Notizie, Turin; 1965, Galerie Anne Aebels, Cologne; 1980, retrospective, De Kalb, University of Northern Illinois; 1989 and from 1991 to 1995, Frumkin/Adams Gallery, New York; 1992, Musée de Maubeuge; 1996, Smart Art Museum, Chicago; 1997, 1998, George Adams Gallery, New York; 1999, touring exhibition seen at museums in Sables d'Olonne, Châteauroux, Dole and Mons (Belgium); 1999, Galerie Darthea Speyer, Paris; 2000, Galerie du Centre, Paris; 2002, Galerie Charlotte Moser, Geneva.

BIBLIOGRAPHY:

1/65, exhibition catalogue, Musée d'Art moderne de la Ville de Paris, Paris, 1965. Saül, Peter, *New Paintings and Works on Paper: Peter Saül*, Peter Saül, Allan Frumkin Gallery, New York, 1987. Carlozzi, Dimeo, *Peter Saül*, Aspen Art Museum, Aspen, 1989. Saül, Peter, *Peter Saül: Political Paintings 1965-1971*, Frumkin/Adams Gallery, New York, 1990. Storr, Robert, et al., *Peter Saül. Rétrospective*, exhibition catalogue, Somogy, Paris, 1999 (texts in French and English). Leydier, Richard, '*Peter Saul à l'envers*' in *Art Press 275*, periodical, Paris, January 2002.

MUSEUMS AND GALLERIES:

CHICAGO (AI) - DALLAS (MA) - LOS ANGELES (County MA) - MARSEILLES (Mus. Cantini): *San Francisco No. 2* (1966) - MONS (Musée des Beaux-Arts) - NEW YORK (Metropolitan Mus. of Art) - NEW YORK (MoMA) - NEW YORK (Whitney Mus. of American Art) - PARIS (MNAM-CCI) - PITTSBURGH (Carnegie MA) - SAN FRANCISCO (MoMA) - STOCKHOLM (Moderna Mus.).

AUCTION RECORDS:

LOS ANGELES, 27 Feb 1974, *Girl No. 3* (1962) USD 800. NEW YORK, 2 Nov 1984, *Highway of Social Justice* (1965, colouring pencil, felt pen and coloured ink/card, 40 x 56 ins / 101.5 x 142.2 cm) USD 3,800. NEW YORK, 2 Nov 1984, *De Kooning's Woman with Bicycle* (1976, acrylic/canvas, 100 1/2 x 75 1/2 ins / 255.2 x 191.7 cm) USD 14,000. NEW YORK, 23 Feb 1985, *Combat-Happy Joe* (1965, colouring pencil, felt pens, coloured inks and ball-point pen, 54 1/4 x 40 ins / 137.6 x 101.5 cm) USD 3,500. NEW YORK, 7 May 1986, *Untitled* (1960, gouache and pencil with collage, a pair, 21 1/4 x 28 1/2 ins / 54 x 72.4 cm and 34 1/2 x 25 1/2 ins/87.6 x 64.8 cm) USD 2,500. NEW YORK, 4 May 1989, *Study of Picasso's Guernica* (1976, acrylic and pencil/card, 20 x 44 ins / 50.8 x 111.7 cm) USD 12,100. NEW YORK, 8 Nov 1993, *Ice Box 6* (1963, oil on canvas, 74 3/4 x 63 ins / 189.8 x 160 cm) USD 13,800. NEW YORK, 14 June 1995, *Big Money* (1964, pencil and marker pen/paper, 27 1/2 x 31 1/2 ins / 69.9 x 80 cm) USD 1,955. PARIS, 22 Nov 1995, *Composition* (1964, gouache, watercolour, pastel and colouring pencil/paper, 26 1/2 x 33 1/2 ins / 67 x 85 cm) FRF 10,500. PARIS, 3 May 1996, *Untitled* (1970, acrylic/paper, 41 1/4 x 32 ins / 105 x 81 cm) FRF 8,500. LOKEREN, 15 May 1999, *Negro Art* (1970, watercolour and colour drawing, 42 x 35 ins / 106 x 89 cm) BEF 65,000. PARIS, 23 Nov 2000, *Hell* (acrylic on canvas, 43 x 35 ins / 110 x 90 cm) FRF 30,000. PARIS, 23 Nov 2000, *Napoleon on the Bridge of Arcole* (acrylic on canvas, 67 x 55 ins / 170 x 140 cm) FRF 40,000. NEW YORK, 13 Nov 2001, *Untitled - Upper Lower Class* (c. 1966, oil on canvas, 69 x 77 ins / 174 x 196 cm) USD 17,000. NEW YORK, 23 Sept 2003, *Untitled* (1964, crayon and ink on paper, 27 x 27 ins / 68 x 68 cm) USD 18,000.

SAULCY, Denis

French, 16th century.
Born in Ste-Menehould.
Active during the second half of the 16th century.
Painter.

Denis Saulcy painted the ceiling of the Salle Nouvelle in the ducal palace of Nancy in 1572.

SAULET, Arnaldo

Spanish, 14th century.
Active during the first half of the 14th century.
Sculptor.

MUSEUMS AND GALLERIES:

VIC (Mus. Episcopal): low relief in alabaster, from an altar (1341).

SAULI, Giuseppe

Italian, 19th century.
Active in Turin during the second half of the 19th century.
Painter. Genre scenes.

Perhaps the same person as Giuseppe Zauli, he exhibited in Turin, Rome and Livorno.

SAULINI, L.

British, 19th century.
Active from 1850 to 1860.
Cameo engraver, draughtsman. Portraits.

MUSEUMS AND GALLERIES:

NEW YORK (Metropolitan Mus. of Art): nine cameos.

SAULLES, George William de

British, 19th century.

Born 1862, in Birmingham; died 21 July 1903, in London.
Medallist.
George William de Saulles was principal engraver at the London Mint.

SAULMON. See **SALMON**

SAULMON, Michelet. See **SAUMON**

SAULNIER, Adam, called Adam-Saulnier
French, 20th century.
Born 24 August 1915, in Paris.
Painter.
Adam Saulnier's mother and father were both painters and art critics. He studied at the École des Arts Appliqués à l'Industrie and at seventeen began work as a draughtsman in advertising. He attended academies in Montparnasse, including La Chaumière. He took part in the main popular cultural movements and became a fine arts instructor, and then technical director, at the École des Métiers d'Art. He was successively a war correspondent and an art correspondent and critic for the French radio and television network. He first exhibited in Paris at the Salon des Indépendants of 1935.

After giving up advertising for painting, he received commissions to decorate churches and hospitals. Initially his work was figurative and highly realist, but he moved to a style in which a number of prevailing fantasies are apparent, partially hidden by the simplicity of forms and subjects.

SAULNIER, Emmanuel
French, 20th - 21st century.
Born 1952, in Paris.
Sculptor, watercolourist, draughtsman.
Emmanuel Saulnier spent 1985-1986 at the Villa Medici in Rome. He now lives and works in Paris.

Saulnier's outsize sculptures are fashioned from a permutation of glass, mirror glass and water and symbolise the transition from shade to light and from weight to lightness, exposing the viewer to prismatic and magnifying effects. His compositions are genuine 'inventions' developed with specialists rather than based on a juxtaposition of existing objects in use. Of his work, Saulnier has noted that 'it either contains or expands: when it contains, it goes vertical; when it expands, it develops horizontally'. Saulnier has produced a number of public commissions, including *Distant Figure*, commissioned by the City of Brest in 2003.

Saulnier's work has featured in group exhibitions: in 1979, at the Centre Pompidou in Paris; in 1990, at *Porcelaine* (*Porcelain*), an exhibition held in Limoges; and, in 1991, at *Sculpture*, held at the Musée-Château in Annecy. He has exhibited solo on a number of occasions: in 1978, at the Galerie Charley Chevallier in Paris; in 1986 and 1989, at the Galerie Montenay in Paris and at the Villa Medici in Rome; in 1987, at the Galerie Edouard Manet in Genevilliers; in 1988, at the Andata Ritorno Gallery; in 1991, at the Centre d'Art Contemporain at the Domaine de Kerguéhennec in Morbihan (Brittany); in 1994, at *Purgatoire* (*Purgatory*), where he showed sculptures and preparatory studies inspired by Dante's *Divine Comedy*; in 1996, at the Musée Zadkine Atelier in Paris; and, in 1998, at the La Chaufferie Art Centre in Strasbourg. He was awarded the Premier Grand Prix d'Art Contemporain in Flaine in 1992.

BIBLIOGRAPHY:
Perret, C./Dagognet, F./Collins, G., *Emmanuel Saulnier, sculptures*, exhibition catalogue, Centre d'Art contemporain du domaine de Kerguéhennec, Éd. du centre d'art, Locminé, 1991 (text in French and English). '*Emmanuel Saulnier*' in *Opus international* n° 126, periodical, Paris, autumn 1991. '*Emmanuel Saulnier*' in *Art Press* n° 190, periodical, Paris, April 1994. Greff, Jean-Pierre/Lang, Luc, *Emmanuel Saulnier, principe transparent*, La Chaufferie, Strasbourg, Éd. du Regard, Paris, 1999.

SAULNIER, Jeanne de
Belgian, 20th century.
Born 1888, in Dour.
Painter. Figures, portraits, landscapes, still-lifes.
Jeanne de Saulnier studied under Constant Montald at the fine arts academy in Brussels.

SAULNIER, Michel
Canadian, 20th - 21st century.
Born 1956, in Rimouski (Quebec).
Painter, sculptor, mixed media.
Michel Saulnier's works consist of two- and three- dimensional referential elements underlying and denoting an original approach to understanding space. In *Group of Seven*, 1983 (a collection of seven standardised houses with landscapes), the house, with an open or closed aspect, is drawn, painted, varnished, isolated and flattened against the wall. The formal image, with various changes, distorts the conventions of perception.

BIBLIOGRAPHY:
Les 20 ans du musée à travers sa collection, exhibition catalogue, Musée d'Art contemporain, Montreal, 1985.

MUSEUMS AND GALLERIES:
MONTREAL (MAC): *Diptych* (1983).

SAULO, Georges Ernest
French, 19th - 20th century.
Born 16 September 1865, in Angers.
Sculptor, medallist.
Georges Ernest Saulo, the father of Maurice Saulo, was a pupil of Pierre Jules Cavelier and Louis Auguste Roubaud. He exhibited in Paris at the Salon des Artistes Français, of which he became a member in 1888 and where he was awarded a third-class medal in 1889, a travel scholarship in 1891, and a silver medal at the time of the Exposition Universelle of 1889.

MUSEUMS AND GALLERIES:
ANGERS - BEAUFORT - BRIVES.

AUCTION RECORDS:
LONDON, 25 Sept 1981, *God and France!* (bronze and ivory, h. 12 1/2 ins / 32 cm) GBP 500. LOKEREN, 23 May 1992, *Bust of a Young Woman* (brown-patinated bronze, h. 10 1/4 ins / 26 cm, w. 12 1/2 ins/32 cm) BEF 50,000.

SAULO, Maurice
French, 20th century.
Born 14 December 1901, in Paris.
Sculptor.
Maurice Saulo was a pupil of his father, Georges Ernest Saulo, and Jules-Félix Coutan. His subject is often love and emotion. From 1919 he exhibited in Paris at the Salon des Artistes Français, of which he was a member and where he was awarded an honourable mention in 1921, a travel scholarship in 1925, a bronze medal in 1925, a silver in 1926, the Second Prix de Rome in 1927, and a gold medal in 1935.

MUSEUMS AND GALLERIES:
ANGERS: *Resignation* - PARIS (Mus. du Petit Palais): *Venetia*.

SAULTERRE, Georges
Italian, 20th century.
Born 1943, in Conegliano (Veneto).
Active and naturalised in France.
Painter, sculptor (including bronze), designer. Figures, animals, birds. Wall decorations.
Georges Saulterre studied at the École des Arts Appliqués in Paris. He worked both as a sculptor and a designer.

He began his career as a realist painter, then concentrated on sculpture. In 1975 he started making monumental sculptures of birds intended for the entrance halls of blocks of flats. From 1978 onwards he was involved in the creation of works of art for public places and was commissioned to produce works for motorways which were 'meant to be seen at 130 kph'. These included the gigantic *Grey Heron* on the Chartres-Orleans road, the giant crystal *Signal of the Alps* on the A51, the *Greenwich Meridian* on the Normandy road, *Cathedral Spires* on the Chartres-Orleans road and the *Viking Road* on the Paris-Normandy motorway. Similarly he has planned sculptures and mural decorations for nuclear installations at Cruas-Meysse (Drôme), Chooz (Aisne), Golfech (Gironde) and elsewhere. His simple and lofty structures, polished metal spires, discs, cylinders, and needles, soaring elegantly to a height of perhaps 70 feet (21 metres), unite dynamic form and a blaze of light in one single thrust, one equilibrium. He also makes smaller pieces in bronze, an assemblage of nails or clay, figures of silent warriors or naked women with clock-heads and chair-shaped bodies, strange and solitary creatures.

Bibliography:

Dichats, Emmanuel, *Le Geste de Saulterre*, Golfech. *La Route des vikings*, exhibition leaflet, Société de l'autoroute Paris-Normandie, Paris, 1990.

SAULX, Jean de. See **DESAULX Jean**

SAUM, Georg

German, 18th century.
Born 1736, in St Peter (Baden); died 1790, in Strasbourg.
Painter.

Georg Saum was a pupil of Franz Ludwig Hermann in Kempten. He worked in St Peter.

SAUMAREZ, Marion

British, 19th - 20th century.
Born 19th century, in London.
Painter.

Marion Saumarez appeared at exhibitions in Paris and received an honourable memtion in 1906.

SAUMON, Michelet, or Salemon or Salmon or Saulmon

French, 14th - 15th century.
Active 1375-1416.
Painter, miniaturist, sculptor, medallist.

Michelet Saumon worked in Paris and was court painter to the Duke de Berry from 1401 to 1416.

SAUNDERS. See also **SANDERS**

SAUNDERS, Charles L.

British, 19th century.
Died 1915.
Painter, watercolourist. Landscapes.

Charles L. Saunders worked in Conway, North Wales, and exhibited at the Royal Academy in London from 1881 to 1885.

Museums and Galleries:

Bootle: *Lancaster* (watercolour).

Auction records:

New York, 15 Oct 1991, *Dusk on a Devon Canal* (oil on canvas, 24 x 38 ins / 60.9 x 96.5 cm) USD 1,650. New York, 5 March 2003, *Punters on a River by a Cottage* (oil on canvas, 24 x 37 ins / 61 x 95 cm) USD 2,000.

SAUNDERS, Christina. See **ROBERTSON Christina**

SAUNDERS, George

British, 18th - 19th century.
Born 1762; died 1839, in London.
Architect, draughtsman.

George Saunders is noted for some remarkable drawings of bridges in Middlesex produced in 1825 and 1826, together with some interesting studies of churches in Verona.

Auction records:

London, 30 Nov 1983, *The British Museum* (1801, pencil, pen and watercolour, three drawings, 19 3/4 x 28 ins / 50 x 71 cm) GBP 7,500.

SAUNDERS, George, or Sanders

British, 18th - 19th century.
Born 1774, in Kinghorn; died 26 March 1846, in London.
Painter, miniaturist. Portraits.

George Saunders worked initially as a coachwork painter in Edinburgh before going on to teach and paint miniatures. He is also noted for a panorama of Edinburgh. George Saunders moved to London in 1807 and met with considerable success. Princess Charlotte, the Duke of Cumberland and Lord Byron all had their portraits done by Saunders. In or around 1812 he began to paint oil portraits; these were less successful. He travelled frequently to Europe and made drawings of compositions by the Old Masters, 26 of which are preserved in Edinburgh. Examples of his portraiture are to be seen at various locations throughout England.

Bibliography:

Wills, G., ' *A Forgotten Scottish Painter*' in *Country Life*, 8 October 1953. Beevers, R., ' *George Sanders and the Byronic Image*' in *Apollo*, Vol. 146, 427, London, 1997.

Museums and Galleries:

Edinburgh: 26 drawings copied from Old Masters - London (National Portrait Gal.): *Johann Baptist Cramer* (1827, watercolour and gouache/ivory); *Matthew Gregory Lewis* (c. 1800, watercolour/ivory).

Auction records:

London, 20 Sept 1909, *Portrait of Alexander Pope and Spouse* (two pendants) GBP 5. Paris, 24 April 1910, *Portrait of a Young Woman*, FRF 300.

SAUNDERS, Hébé, later Mrs Ph. Aug. Barnard

British, 19th century.
Miniaturist.

Hébé Saunders showed examples of her work in London from 1852 to 1857.

SAUNDERS, Helen

British, 20th century.
Born 4 April 1885, in Croydon (Surrey); died 1 January 1963, in Holborn, London.
Painter. Still-lifes. Murals.

Helen Saunders studied at the Slade School of Fine Art, London, from 1906 to 1907, and at the Central School of Art and Design, London. She signed the Vorticist manifesto as *H. Saunders*.

She worked on the design of the Eiffel Tower Restaurant with Wyndham Lewis. After 1920 her style became Naturalist.

She took part in various group exhibitions, including: 1912, 1913 and 1916, Allied Artists' Association; 1914, *20th-Century Art* at the Whitechapel Art Gallery; 1915, the *Vorticist* Exhibition; and 1916, with the London Group and Holborn Art Society.

Museums and Galleries:

London (Tate Collection): *Abstract Monochrome Composition* (1915); *Abstract Composition in Blue and Yellow* (1915); *Abstract Multicoloured Drawing* (1915).

SAUNDERS, John (son). See **SANDERS**

SAUNDERS, John, or Sanders

British, 18th century.
Painter, engraver (mezzotint).

Portrait engraver active around 1750; possibly the same artist as the portraitist and pastel painter John (?) Saunders.

SAUNDERS, John (?), or Sanders

British, 18th century.

Painter, pastellist. Portraits.
John Saunders was probably father of the painter of the same name; he was active from 1730 to 1765.
MUSEUMS AND GALLERIES:
OXFORD (Christ Church): *Portrait of Heny Aldrich*.

SAUNDERS, Joseph
British, 18th - 19th century.
Painter, miniaturist, engraver. Portraits.
Joseph Saunders was the publisher father of Robert Saunders and exhibitor from 1772 to 1808 at the Royal Academy, the Free Society and the British Institution. He painted predominantly female portraits, which were well thought of.
MUSEUMS AND GALLERIES:
LONDON (Victoria and Albert Mus.): *Portrait of the Painter William Beechey*.

SAUNDERS, Joseph, or Sanders
British, 18th - 19th century.
Born 1773, in London; died 1 January 1875, in Krzemieniec (now Kremenets, Ukraine).
Painter, engraver. Portraits, genre scenes.
Joseph Saunders was a pupil of Longhi. He settled in Poland and worked as an engraver between 1832 and 1836.

SAUNDERS, L. Pearl
American, 20th century.
Born in Tennessee.
Painter, draughtswoman, illustrator.
L. Pearl Saunders studied under Chase in Italy, and with Hawthorne and at the Art Students' League in New York. She was a member of the Société des Artistes Indépendants in Paris.

SAUNDERS, Raymond Jenning
American, 20th century.
Born 1934, in Pittsburgh.
Painter, draughtsman, collage artist, mixed media.
Raymond Jenning Saunders studied at the Carnegie Institute of Technology in Pittsburgh between 1950 and 1953. He then went to Pennsylvania Academy of Fine Arts from 1953 until 1957 and obtained a master's degree in Fine Arts at the College of Arts and Crafts in Oakland, California, in 1961. He won the Prix de Rome in 1964. He has regularly spent time in Mexico and France, and lives in Oakland in California.

Even though his energetic and visceral vocabulary of gestural marks places Saunders among the American Expressionists, he is very close in style to the generation of contemporaries of Rauschenberg that followed them. He continues to work in the tradition of collage, with memory playing as important a role for him as the creative act. References to Mexico and other cultures are evident in his work. His liking for balancing spontaneous pictorial elements with other more organised features goes some way towards explaining the profusion of checked patterns and geometric motifs taken from book illustrations and posters, as well as other such disparate elements as oriental calligraphy and children's drawings. An intuitive colourist, he makes black an active element in his colour palette, an element of composition that is full of formal and iconographic significance, which he punctuates with white reproductions of fruit or flowers, words and figures, which give the impression of being incised with chalk.

Saunders has taken part in collective exhibitions in the USA and abroad, including at the Carnegie Museum of Fine Arts in Pittsburgh, the Museum of Modern Art in San Francisco and the Pennsylvania Academy of Fine Arts in Philadelphia between 1952 and 1963; the Stedelijk Museum in Amsterdam, the Museum of Modern Art, the Whitney Museum of American Art and the Metropolitan Museum in New York, the American Academy in Rome, the Museum of Fine Art in Boston, and the Museum of Art in San Francisco between 1964 and 1974; ICA in London, the Stedelijk Museum in Amsterdam, the Musée des Arts Décoratifs in Lausanne, the Museum für Kunst und Gewerbe in Hamburg, the Palazzo delle Esposizione in Rome, the Art Museum of Philadelphia, the Museum of Modern Art in San Francisco, the Louisiana Museum, Humlebaeck, the Brooklyn Museum in New York, the Corcoran Gallery of Art in Washington, and the Cleveland Museum of Art between 1975 and 1985; and the Virginia Museum of Art in Richmond, the Albright-Knox Art Gallery in Buffalo and the Oakland Museum of Art in New Orleans between 1986 and 1990.

He has also shown his works in many private exhibitions since 1953, including: 1971 at the Museum of Modern Art, San Francisco; 1972 at the Museum of Art in Providence; 1974 at the Pennsylvania Academy of Fine Arts, Philadelphia; 1976 at the University Art Museum, Berkeley; regularly at the Stephen Wirtz Gallery in San Francisco since 1979; 1981 at the Art Museum in Seattle; and in 1990, 1993 and 1998 at the Galerie Resche in Paris.
BIBLIOGRAPHY:
Raymond Saunders, exhibition catalogue, Gal. Resche, Paris, 1991. Sanconie, Maïca, *'Noire Amérique'* in *Beaux-Arts Magazine* n° 105, periodical, Paris, October 1992. *Raymond Saunders*, exhibition catalogue, Stephen Wirtz Gallery, San Francisco, 1993. *Raymond Saunders: Recent Work*, exhibition catalogue, Oakland Museum, Oakland, 1994. Powell, Richard, *Black Art and Culture in the 20th century*, Thames and Hudson, London, 1997.
MUSEUMS AND GALLERIES:
NEW YORK (Metropolitan Mus. of Art) - NEW YORK (Whitney Mus. of American Art) - OAKLAND (Mus. of California) - PHILADELPHIA (Pennsylvania Academy of the Fine Arts Gal.) - PITTSBURGH (Carnegie MA): *Night Poetry* (1962, oil on canvas); *A Letter to Marie* (1978, paper, enamel, collage) - SAN FRANCISCO (FAM) - SAN FRANCISCO (MoMA): *Charlie Parker (formerly Bird)* (1977, enamel, masking tape, newsprint, paper, and ink/canvas) - SEATTLE (AM) - WASHINGTON DC (Corcoran Gal. of Art): *Red Star* (1970, mixed media).

SAUNDERS, Richard
British, 18th century.
Active in London in 1708.
Sculptor (wood).
Richard Saunders sculpted the statues of *Gog* and *Magog* for the east façade of London's Guildhall.

SAUNDERS, Robert
British, 18th - 19th century.
Active from 1790 to 1828.
Miniaturist.
Robert Saunders was the son of Joseph Saunders. He exhibited 31 miniatures at the Royal Academy between 1801 and 1828.

SAUNDERS, Wade
American, 20th - 21st century.
Born 1949, in Berkeley (California), USA.
Sculptor, draughtsman.
Wade Saunders studied from 1971 to 1974 at the Wesleyan University in Connecticut and subsequently graduated in art from the University of California in San Diego. He now teaches art and works as a critic. His art might best be described as midway between object and experiment. He works principally in wood and bronze.

Saunders has been involved in a number of group exhibitions: in 1983, at *Sculpture Now: Recent Figurative Works*, held at the Virginia Museum in Richmond and, in 1992, at *A Dialogue with Nature: Nine Contemporary Sculptors*, hosted by the Phillips Collection in Washington DC. He has exhibited solo on various occasions, including on a regular basis at Newspace in Los Angeles; in 1980 and subsequently at the Diane Brown Gallery in Washington DC; in 2000, at the Maison d'Art Contemporain (Chailloux, Fresnes); in 2001, at *Building Time*, at the Galerie Corinne Caminade in Paris; and, in 2003, at *Done and Undone*, also at the Gallery Corinne Caminade.

Museums and Galleries:

Baltimore (MA) - Chicago (MCA) - Göteborg (Konstmus.) - La Jolla (San Diego Mus. of Contemporary Art) - Loretto (Southern Alleghenies Mus. of Art) - New York (Metropolitan Mus. of Art) - Newark (Mus.) - Paris (Municipal Collection) - Sarasota (John and Mable Ringling MA) - Seattle (AM) - Washington DC (Corcoran Gal. of Art).

SAUNHAC, Marie Auguste de

French, 19th century.

Born in Tarbes (Hautes-Pyrenées).

Painter. History painting, genre scenes.

He was a pupil of Bonnat and debuted at the Salon in 1877.

SAUNIER, Charles

French, 19th century.

Born 17 September 1815, in Montlhéry (Seine-et-Oise); died 29 April 1889, in Paris.

Painter. Religious subjects, portraits. Designs for stained glass.

Saunier was a pupil of Ingres, and it was in his master's studio that he got to know Chassériau. Like so many artists, he travelled to Rome. On his return he was briefly influenced by Ary Scheffer, whose work inspired him to paint a large philosophical religious composition featuring Christ alongside the wise men of antiquity. However he did not achieve what he had hoped with this painting, and from that moment on he concentrated almost exclusively on portrait painting, travelling around France and working in Dôle, Rethel, Lyons, Vienne, St-Étienne, Orléans and Nantes.

He came back to Paris in around 1860, and exhibited at most of the Salons from 1862 until 1887. Among the portraits in oils and pastels that he showed at these exhibitions, the most memorable are: *Madame de Louvencourt* (1862); *Madame Bertillon* (1868); *Madame Goizet* (1869); *Madame Jacquin* (1873); *The Architect Pierre Chabot* (1878); and *Dr Robinet* (1887). He also sent in a self-portrait in 1870, and a portrait of his wife, who was also a painter, in 1878. In addition to these portraits, he painted a few religious pictures and some designs for stained glass windows.

Museums and Galleries:

Oisemont (church): stained glass window.

SAUNIER, Charlotte

French, 19th century.

Born in Orléans.

Painter. Portraits, genre scenes.

She was taught by her father, Charles Saunier. She exhibited at the Salon between 1866 and 1869.

SAUNIER, Hector

Argentinian, 20th century.

Born 1936, in Buenos Aires.

Engraver.

Hector Saunier studied architecture, composition and colour theory with H. Cartier; then he studied engraving with S.W. Hayter in Studio 17 in Paris. From 1963 to 1965 he went to England and now lives and works in Paris. He shows work in collective exhibitions, including the 1972 Biennale in Menton and the 2002 *Le Signe et la Marge* (*The Mark and the Margin*) in the Richard Anacréon Museum of Modern Art in Granville (Normandy, France).

SAUNIER, Marcel

French, 19th century.

Painter. Genre scenes, landscapes.

Orientalism.

He showed his work between 1839 and 1841.

SAUNIER, Noël

French, 19th century.

Born 28 September 1847, in Vienne (Isère); died 7 January 1890, in Paris.

Painter, watercolourist, illustrator. Portraits, genre scenes, landscapes.

Noël Saunier was the son of Charles Saunier and was taught by his father and by Isidore Pils at the École des Beaux-Arts in Paris. However, his studies were interrupted by the Franco-Prussian war. Once hostilities were over, he renounced academic instruction and began his artistic education anew, studying *plein air* painting and the human figure in nature. He first exhibited at the Paris Salon in 1870 and entered the competition for the Prix de Rome the same year. His next Salon exhibition was in 1872.

His best-known works include: *Gladiators Surrendering at the Circus*, *Bathers* and *In the Park*. This last painting in particular reveals the beginning of a quest for clarity that would characterise his later works: *Ophelia* (1874), *Marguerite* (1875), *Train Arriving* (1878), *In the Farmyard* and *Château de Dré* (1880). He followed these with a modernised revolutionary scene: *Here We Dance* (1881) and *Provincial Market* (1884). Successive trips to Saône-et-Loire, in Burgundy, kindled his interest in peasant life. He changed his style and painted the following works (in chronological order): *November Hay in Charolais*, *Pig Market in Aigueperse*, *The Village Drum*, *Loading Cattle into a Truck*, *A Turkey Market in Isère*. He also illustrated the first series of Jules Simon's *Memoirs of Other People* and created original watercolours to decorate the margins of a number of books published by the Libraire Conquet.

Noël Saunier - 1887-

Museums and Galleries:

Albi: *Provincial Market* - Nancy (MBA): *Pig Market in Aigueperse* - St-Malo: *Ferryboat*.

Auction records:

Paris, 1872, *Banks of the Seine at Samois* (watercolour) FRF 60. Paris, 1900, *Canal at Montargis* (watercolour) FRF 70. Paris, 4 Dec 1944, *Fairground Parade*, FRF 6,500. Paris, 12 May 1950, *Ophelia* (1874) FRF 4,000. Paris, 2 June 1950, *Public Ball during the Revolution*, FRF 35,000. Milan, 10 Dec 1980, *Biblical Scene* (oil on canvas, 32 x $27\frac{1}{2}$ ins / 81 x 70 cm) ITL 1,600,000. New York, 2 Dec 1986, *Young Married Couple* (1879, oil on canvas, $25\frac{3}{4}$ x $36\frac{1}{4}$ ins / 65.5 x 92 cm) USD 7,000. New York, 23 May 1989, *Reading in a Forest*; *The Picnic* (1871, oil on canvas, a pair, each $16\frac{1}{4}$ x $21\frac{3}{4}$ ins / 41.3 x 55.2 cm) USD 29,700. New York, 24 Oct 1990, *An Afternoon of Relaxation* (1872, oil on canvas, $16\frac{1}{4}$ x $21\frac{1}{4}$ ins / 41 x 54 cm) USD 11,000. Paris, 12 Dec 1990, *At Montmorency* (1885, oil on canvas, $10\frac{1}{4}$ x 22 ins / 26 x 55 cm) FRF 10,000. New York, 12 Oct 1993, *Quest after the Dance* (oil on canvas, $25\frac{3}{4}$ x $36\frac{1}{2}$ ins / 65.4 x 92.7 cm) USD 9,200. London, 17 Nov 1993, *The Lord's Pastime* (1876, oil on canvas, 33 x 53 ins / 84 x 134.5 cm) GBP 3,450. Paris, 3 Dec 1993, *A Visit to the Château* (oil on canvas, $12\frac{1}{2}$ x 10 ins / 32 x 24.5 cm) FRF 6,000. Paris, 13 June 1994, *On the Quay* (1873, oil on canvas, $25\frac{1}{4}$ x $36\frac{1}{4}$ ins / 64 x 92 cm) FRF 58,000. Paris, 30 April 1999, *Reading. Déjeuner sur l'Herbe* (1871, oil on canvas, a pair, 16 x 21 ins / 40 x 53 cm) FRF 215,000. Montreal, 21 Feb 2000, *Fête champêtre* (1877, oil on canvas, 32 x 22 ins / 81 x 55 cm) CAD 12,500. Boston, 10 Nov 2000, *Getting Ready for the Masked Ball* (oil on canvas, 24 x 17 ins / 60 x 44 cm) USD 2,000. Stockholm, 4 Dec 2001, *In the Green Grass* (1874, oil on canvas, 20 x 39 ins / 51 x 100 cm) SEK 88,000. London, 26 March 2002, *Blind Man's Buff* (1875, oil on canvas, 33 x 53 ins / 85 x 135 cm) GBP 5,000. Cherbourg, 19 April 2004, *Proces-*

sion of Caged Lions (oil on canvas, 22 x 32 ins / 55 x 82 cm) EUR 4,400.

SAUNIER, Octave Alfred
French, 19th century.
Born in Paris.
Painter. Landscapes.

A pupil of Ciceri, he was active from 1865 to 1882. He first showed his work at the Paris Salon in 1865, and in 1872 exhibited two landscapes: *Pond beneath the Beeches* and *Woods.*

AUCTION RECORDS:
PARIS, 17 Feb 1902, *The Hare and the Frogs,* FRF 430. PARIS, 6 June 1945, *Pheasants in the Woods* (1868, watercolour) FRF 200. LONDON, 6 Dec 1973, *Afternoon on the Riverbank,* GBP 1,100. PARIS, 7 Nov 1984, *Nymphs* (oil on canvas, 78 1/4 x 118 ins / 199 x 300 cm) FRF 68,000. PARIS, 16 March 1998, *Hunters at Marlotte; Forest of Fontainebleau* (two watercolour, the second dated 1868, 12 1/4 x 9 ins / 31 x 23 cm) FRF 4,900.

SAUNOIS, Nicolas
French, 18th century.
Born 23 February 1750, in Sampigny.
Painter.

Nicolas Saunois was the brother of Nicolas Charles Saunois. He studied in Rome, and painted *St Michael* in St-Mihiel abbey church.

SAUNOIS, Nicolas Charles
French, 18th century.
Born 1751.
Sculptor.

Nicolas Charles Saunois was the brother of Nicolas Saunois.

SAUPE, Louis
German, 19th century.
Active in Kassel and Dresden 1845 to 1847.
Painter, lithographer. Genre scenes.

SAUPIQUE, Georges Laurent
French, 20th century.
Born 17 May 1889, in Paris; died 8 May 1961, in Paris.
Sculptor.

Georges Laurent Saupique was a pupil of Jules-Félix Coutan, Hippolyte Lefebvre and Aristide Rousaud. He exhibited in group exhibitions in Paris, including: 1922, 1924, 1945, the Salon des Artistes Français; from 1923, the Salon d'Automne; 1925, the Salon des Arts Décoratifs; from 1926, the Salon des Tuileries, of which he became a member in 1930; and 1931, the Exposition Coloniale. He was awarded a bronze medal in 1922 and a Certificate of Honour at the Exposition Internationale of 1937. He was made a Chevalier of the Légion d'Honneur in 1938.

His bust of *The Fourth Republic* was chosen by the Municipality of Paris to be placed in town halls, and he carved the *Berlioz Listening to his Inspiration* that stands in the Place de Vintimille and replaces the bronze that was melted down during the German occupation.

MUSEUMS AND GALLERIES:
CAIRO: *Head of a Child* - PARIS (MAMVP): *Head of a Young Arab; Young Girl Nude* - TOUL: *Bust.*

AUCTION RECORDS:
PARIS, 19 Oct 1983, *Face of a Woman* (brown-patinated bronze, h. 21 1/4 ins / 54 cm) FRF 25,000.

SAUPPE, Johann Gottlob
German, 18th century.
Active during the second half of the 18th century.
Sculptor.

Sauppe sculpted capitals for the church of the Holy Cross in Dresden.

SAUR, Ferdinand Joseph
German, 18th century.
Active in Ehingen from 1734 to 1746.
Painter. Figures.

SAUR, Hans Michael
German, 18th century.
Born 29 September 1692, in Freiburg; died 6 January 1745, in Freiburg.
Painter.

Hans Michael executed paintings in churches in Freiburg, St Peter in the Black Forest and in Sölden.

SAUR, J. F.
German, 18th century.
Active in Augsburg.
Draughtsman, designer of ornamental architectural features. Urban views.

SAURA, Antonio
Spanish, 20th century.
Born 1930, in Huesca (Aragon); died 22 July 1998.
Also active in France from 1953.
Engraver, painter (gouache), watercolourist, lithographer, draughtsman. Religious subjects, portraits.
Nouvelle Figuration.
El Paso Group.

As a child, Antonio Saura was confined to bed for several years due to a serious illness, which curtailed his formal education. He began to paint at the age of seventeen but never received any formal artistic instruction. From 1947 he worked each summer in Cuenca. He moved to Paris in 1953 and remained there for three years. It is probable that during this period he was influenced by the work of the Surrealists, though their appeal would have been mitigated in his case by their attachment to and nostalgic view of the past. It is certain, however, that this time spent away from his native Spain nurtured in Saura a strong awareness of the Spanish socio-political situation. Accordingly, on his return to Madrid in 1957, Saura aligned himself with several other young Spanish artists (notably Millares, Canogar and Feito) to establish the El Paso group, whose credo was set out in an eponymous journal. The movement was dedicated to advocacy of modernism in Spanish painting as a reaction against 'official' Spanish art sanctioned by the reactionary Franco regime. Subsequently, Saura returned to Paris in 1967 and settled there. In 1968, in a fit of depression, he destroyed around a hundred of his paintings and, for the next ten years, he eschewed painting in favour of engraving, etching and working on paper. He also spent a year in Havana, Cuba.

As noted above, Saura was essentially self-taught. He started out between 1948 and 1950 with works entitled *Constellations, Rayogrammes* and *Landscapes* (the last-named being landscapes of the unconscious painted in the Surrealist manner). Some commentators date his preoccupation with Surrealism from 1954 and others suggest 1957, but the former date seems the more probable. His work from this period is little known; it features indeterminate, 'unreal' objects in the style of Yves Tanguy, but painted with due regard for compositional balance and perspective. In effect, Saura's involvement with Surrealism was short-lived. He quickly aligned himself with Abstract Expressionism as exemplified in the USA in the work of Willem de Kooning. In Saura's case, this represented an attempt to continue in the footsteps of the broad Spanish Expressionist movement which had constituted a vehement protest against social and historical injustice; it also testified to his great admiration for the works of El Greco, Velázquez, Ribera, Zurbarán, Goya and Picasso. In addition to this spiritual and social dimension, however, Antonio Saura was anxious to achieve a contextual violence not unlike that apparent at the time in the work of Jackson Pollock.

Prior to 1954, Saura worked in dense and muted colours and with a variety of materials, then, in 1954 and 1955, with colours that were brash and violent. From 1955, however, his technique proved remarkably consistent although his choice of subject matter changed continuously. In essence, the 'subject' covers the entire surface of the canvas; red and blue accents apart, he painted predominantly in blacks and whites with burnt sienna, earth shades, ochre and dark yellows. His subject matter revolves around the human figure, with different yet recurrent 'classical' themes (*Crucifixion, Temptation of St Anthony, St Theresa of Ávila* or *Priests*), together with innovative *Fantasy Portraits* or 'real' portraits such as those of *Ritva in his Favourite Chair, Goya, Silvia, Duchess of Alba, Brigitte Bardot* or *Philip II*. To create these portraits, he often had recourse to a ready-made image (an old master portrait or a fashion photograph). In each case, however, he succeeded in suffusing the image with something new and different, something abstract, or at times even distorting and monstrous. In other words, what mattered was the impact of the image. Other examples include Saura's tormented *Flayed*, his proud or shameful *Nudes*, and his *Mob Scenes* with people gathering to give vent to their anger.

This sense of violence and despair is also reflected in the lithographs which constitute a large part of Saura's work, not least the series of forty-two illustrating Francisco de Quevedo's *Three Visions* or the sixteen lithographs in his *Pintiquinestras* series of 1959. Saura returned to Quevedo in 1961, when he produced a series of etchings to illustrate the latter's *Dreams* and, in 1963, produced ten silk-screen colour illustrations for a series called *Diversaurio*. This was followed by a silk-screen series entitled *Cocktail Party*, an 'illustrated history' of the mindless social intercourse that is intrinsic to it. During the he time spent in Havana, Saura was also involved in murals. In addition to his paintings, he also built up an iconographic reference library culled from images cut out from various sources and produced graphics from postcards, magazine clippings and comic strips, which he combined to form collages complemented by annotations in oil and ink. In 1983, he designed the sets for his filmmaker brother Carlos Saura's production of Antonio Gadès' ballet *Carmen*.

Saura featured at a very large number of collective exhibitions including: First Salon International des Galeries Pilotes, Cantonal Museum, Lausanne (1953); São Paulo Biennale (1957); Venice (1958); École de Paris exhibition, Charpentier Gallery, Paris (1963); Documenta III, Kassel; *Figuration Narrative* (*Narrative Figuration*), Paris (1965); Salon de Mai, Paris (regularly); travelling exhibition to Geneva, Valencia, Madrid, Munich and Toulouse (1989-1990); Museo d'Arte Moderna, Lugano (1994); *Rainer/Saura*, a joint exhibition Nouveau Théâtre et Artothèque in Angers (2000); *Chronologie immédiate* (*Instant Chronology*) (an exhibition of eighty representations of the Crucifixion produced between the 1950s and the 1990s), Musée d'Art Moderne et Contemporain in Strasbourg (2002); *Antonio Saura. Portraits-autoportraits, estampes, livres* (*Antonio Saura: Portraits, Self-portraits, Etchings and Book Illustrations*), Musée de l'Hospice St-Roch, Issoudon (2002).

His work also featured in numerous solo exhibitions: Fine Arts Department, Madrid and Galerie Stadler, Paris (1956); Munich and Milan (1961); Pierre Matisse Gallery, New York (1961 and 1964); Paris, Palais des Beaux-Arts, Brussels, Municipal Museum, Eindhoven, Museum of Rotterdam, Modern Art Museum, Buenos Aires and the Museum of Modern Art, Rio de Janeiro (1963); Kunsthalle, Baden-Baden and the Museum of Göteborg (1964); Stedelijk Museum, Amsterdam (1964 and 1979); Americas House, Havana (1966); Munich and Frankfurt (1968); Paris (1970); Mexico, Madrid, Barcelona and Tokyo (1980); Majorca, Paris and Colombia (1981); Saragossa (1982); Paris, Madrid and Luxembourg (1983); Berlin, Barcelona and Munich (1984); Helsinki, Berlin, Geneva, Paris, Madrid and Vienna (1985); Galerie Stadler, Paris (1987); *Antonio Saura, peintures 1956-1985* (*Antonio Saura: Paintings 1956-1985*) retrospective, Madrid (1900); *Artcurial* a retrospective of his paintings between 1954 and 1964, Paris (1991); Galerie Lelong Paris (1997); retrospective of his paper works, Galerie Lelong, Paris (2000); *Estampes et livres illustrés* (*Engravings and Book Illustrations*), Musée des Beaux-Arts, Caen (2001).

Saura received various awards and distinctions, including the Guggenheim Prize in 1960, the Carnegie Prize in 1964, the Grand Prix at the 1966 *White and Black* exhibition in Lugano, and a first prize at the Menton Biennale.

Bibliography:

Arrabal, Fernando, *Saura*, exhibition catalogue, Gal. Stadler, Paris, 1969. *Écritures dans la peinture*, exhibition catalogue, Villa Arson-Centre national des Arts plastiques, Nice, 1984. Galfetti, Mariuccia/Frémon, Jean/Mason, Rainer Michael, *Antonio Saura, la obra gráfica, 1958-1984 (L'Œuvre gravé 1958-1984)*, catalogue raisonné, Ministerio de Cultura, Madrid, 1985 (text in French and Spanish). Scarpetta, G./Saura, A., *Élégia*, Éd. Cercle d'art, Paris, 1989. Bellido, Ramon Tio, '*Antonio Saura*' in *Artstudio* n° 14, periodical, Gal. Templon, Paris, autumn 1989. Mason, Rainer Michael/Cohen, Marcel/Lloren, Tomàs/Saura, Antonio, *Antonio Saura - peintures 1956-1985*, travelling exhibition catalogue, Musée d'Art et d'Histoire, Geneva, 1989. Harambourg, Lydia, *L'École de Paris 1945-1965. Dictionnaire des peintres*, Ides et Calendes, Neuchâtel, 1993. Ashton, Dore, '*Antonio Saura*' in *coll. Repères. Cahiers d'art contemporain* n° 92, exhibition catalogue, Gal. Lelong, Paris, 1997. Weber-Caflisch, Olivier/Kramer, Patrick/Cohen, Marcel, *Antonio Saura, l'œuvre imprimé*, catalogue raisonné, Gal. Patrick Cramer, Geneva, 2000 (text in French and Spanish).

Museums and Galleries:

Alicante (MAC) - Amsterdam (Stedelijk Mus.): *Infanta* - Antibes (Mus. Picasso) - Baltimore (MA) - Barcelona (MAM del Mus. Nacional d'Art de Catalunya): *Paula* - Brussels (MAM) - Buenos Aires (Instituto Torcuato Di Tella) - Buenos Aires (MAM) - Buffalo (Albright-Knox AG) - Canberra (Nat. Gal. of Australia) - Caracas (MAC Sofía Imber) - Caracas (MBA) - Cuenca (Mus. De Arte Abstracto Español, Fundación Juan March) - Eindhoven (Van Abbe Mus.) - Geneva (MAH) - Geneva (MAH, Prints Collection) - Göteborg (Konstmus.) - Havana (Casa de las Américas, Colleción Arte de Nuestra América Santamaría) - Helsinki (Ateneumin Taidemus.) - Huesca (MCA) - La Chaux-de-Fonds (MBA) - London (British Mus.) - London (Tate Collection): *Imaginary Portrait of Goya* (1966, oil on canvas) - Los Angeles (MMA) - Madrid (Biblioteca Nacional) - Madrid (Mus. Nacional Centro de Arte Reina Sofía) - Marseilles (Mus. Cantini): *Crucifixion*; *Ritva in his Favourite Chair* - Melbourne (Nat. Gal. of Victoria) - Mexico City (MMA) - Minneapolis (IA): *Maja* (1957, oil on canvas) - Munich (Neue Pinakothek) - New York (Brooklyn Mus.) - New York (MoMA) - New York (Solomon R. Guggenheim Mus.) - Nuremberg (Städtische Kunstsammlungen) - Ostend (Mus. voor Schone Kunsten) - Paris (BNF, Prints Collection) - Paris (FNAC) - Paris (MNAM-CCI): *Fantasy Portrait of Tintoretto*; *Goya's Dog*; *Diada* - Paris (Mus.-Gal. de la Seita) - Pittsburgh (Carnegie MA): *Imaginary Portrait of Goya* (1963, oil on canvas) - Rio de Janeiro (MAM) - Rotterdam (Mus. Boijmans Van Beuningen) - São Paulo (MAC, Universidade) - Saragossa (MCA) - Seville (Centro Andaluz de Arte Contemporáneo) - Stockholm (Moderna Mus.) - Vienna (Mus. Moderner Kunst Stiftung Ludwig) - Washington DC (Hirshhorn Mus. and Sculpture Garden): *Crucifixion*

(Triptych) (1959-1960, oil on canvas) - WROCLAW (Muz. Narodowe).

AUCTION RECORDS:

AMSTERDAM, 28 Nov 1967, *Fia*, NLG 4,000. NEW YORK, 2 Dec 1970, *Bambola*, USD 1,100. GÖTEBORG, 22 Nov 1973, *Figure* (gouache) SEK 4,800. PARIS, 9 April 1974, *Composition*, FRF 6,500. MADRID, 27 June 1974, *Portrait* (mixed media) ESP 90,000. LONDON, 30 June 1977, *Louise* (1960, oil on canvas, 51 1/4 x 38 1/4 ins / 130 x 97 cm) GBP 2,900. MADRID, 22 Nov 1977, *Crucifixion* (mixed media, 28 3/4 x 40 1/4 ins / 73 x 102 cm) ESP 130,000. LONDON, 3 July 1979, *Libia* (1958, oil on canvas, 51 1/4 x 38 1/4 ins / 130 x 97 cm) GBP 1,300. NEW YORK, 16 Oct 1981, *Amparo* (1960, oil on canvas, 51 x 38 ins / 129.5 x 96.5 cm) USD 2,100. NEW YORK, 5 May 1982, *Cocktail Party* (1962, mixed media and collage/paper, 27 x 38 1/2 ins / 68.5 x 98 cm) USD 1,400. LONDON, 6 Dec 1984, *Stima* (1959, oil on canvas, 63 3/4 x 51 ins / 162 x 129.8 cm) GBP 4,200. COLOGNE, 8 Dec 1984, *Composition* (1970, pen, 27 1/2 x 39 1/4 ins / 70 x 100 cm) DEM 2,000. HAMBURG, 8 June 1985, *Composition* (1961, gouache, 29 3/4 x 20 1/2 ins / 75.5 x 52 cm) DEM 2,600. LONDON, 28 May 1986, *Popea* (1959, oil on canvas, 51 1/2 x 38 1/4 ins / 130.5 x 97.2 cm) GBP 3,500. PARIS, 3 Dec 1987, *Don Quixote* (1974, ink and gouache/paper, 10 x 7 3/4 ins / 24.5 x 19.7 cm) FRF 9,000. PARIS, 22 Nov 1988, *Self-portrait* (1959, oil on canvas, 23 1/2 x 29 ins / 60 x 73.5 cm) FRF 195,000. AMSTERDAM, 8 Dec 1988, *Untitled* (ink/paper, 14 1/4 x 11 ins / 36 x 27 cm) NLG 1,955. PARIS, 16 Feb 1989, *Composition* (1984, Indian ink, 13 x 9 3/4 ins / 33 x 25 cm) FRF 19,000. LONDON, 23 Feb 1989, *Shroud 4* (1983, gouache and ink/card, 11 1/4 x 10 1/2 ins / 28.5 x 26.5 cm) GBP 2,420. LONDON, 25 May 1989, *Portrait of Brigitte Bardot No. 5* (1958, oil on canvas, 51 1/4 x 38 1/4 ins / 130 x 97 cm) GBP 35,200. PARIS, 19 June 1989, *Portrait* (1982, ink, 12 1/2 x 9 ins / 31.5 x 23 cm) FRF 33,000. NEW YORK, 21 Feb 1990, *Crucifixion* (1959, Indian ink/paper, 27 1/2 x 19 3/4 ins / 69.9 x 50.2 cm) USD 19,800. LONDON, 22 Feb 1990, *Untitled* (1960, oil on canvas, 18 x 21 ins / 45.7 x 52.4 cm) GBP 66,000. PARIS, 29 March 1990, *Crucifixion IV* (1959, oil on canvas, 50 x 63 ins / 127 x 160 cm) FRF 1, 450, 000. NEW YORK, 9 May 1990, *Portrait No. 66* (1959, oil on canvas, 23 1/2 x 28 3/4 ins / 60 x 73 cm) USD 96,250. COPENHAGEN, 30 May 1990, *Composition* (collage, 26 3/4 x 19 ins / 68 x 48 cm) DKK 75,000. LONDON, 28 June 1990, *Cat-Woman* (1959, oil on canvas, 64 x 51 ins / 162.5 x 129.5 cm) GBP 110,000. PARIS, 10 July 1990, *Cross* (1980, gouache and ink/paper, 27 1/2 x 39 1/4 ins / 70 x 100 cm) FRF 100,000. NEW YORK, 4 Oct 1990, *Untitled* (1966, ink and charcoal/paper, 24 1/2 x 19 3/4 ins / 62.5 x 50 cm) USD 14,300. LONDON, 18 Oct 1990, *Untitled* (acrylic, ink and gouache/card, 29 1/4 x 40 3/4 ins / 74.4 x 103.5 cm) GBP 22,000. NEW YORK, 7 Nov 1990, *Untitled* (oil on paper/canvas, 13 x 20 1/2 ins / 33 x 52 cm) USD 15,400. NEW YORK, 14 Nov 1990, *Fantasy Portrait of Philip II* (1967, oil on canvas, 18 x 15 ins / 45.7 x 38 cm) USD 44,000. PARIS, 27 Nov 1990, *Portrait* (1989, oil on canvas, 28 3/4 x 23 1/2 ins / 73 x 60 cm) FRF 320,000. LONDON, 6 Dec 1990, *Selo* (1957, oil on canvas, 51 1/4 x 38 1/4 ins / 130 x 97 cm) GBP 44,000; *Crucifixion* (1959, oil on canvas, triptych, side panels 77 x 38 ins / 195.5 x 96.5 cm, central panel 77 x 51 ins/195.5 x 129.5 cm) GBP 170,500. AMSTERDAM, 13 Dec 1990, *Untitled* (1975, ink/paper, 19 1/4 x 14 1/4 ins / 49 x 36.5 cm) NLG 17,250. MADRID, 13 Dec 1990, *Pisanella* (1963, oil on canvas, 51 1/4 x 38 1/4 ins / 130 x 97 cm) ESP 14,560,000. NEW YORK, 15 Feb 1991, *Untitled* (1962, gouache and ink/paper/paper, 20 1/4 x 27 1/2 ins / 51.5 x 70 cm) USD 16,500. LONDON, 21 March 1991, *Knife* (1956, oil on canvas, 63 3/4 x 51 1/4 ins / 162 x 130 cm) GBP 70,400. AMSTERDAM, 22 May 1991, *Untitled* (1980, ink/paper, 24 x 39 1/4 ins / 60.9 x 100 cm) NLG 16,100. NEW YORK, 13 Nov 1991, *Untitled* (oil on canvas, 63 x 51 ins / 160 x 129.5 cm) USD 79,200. PARIS, 30 Nov 1991, *Self-portrait* (1956, oil on canvas, 25 3/4 x 32 ins / 65.5 x 81 cm) FRF 260,000. LONDON, 29 May 1992, *Mademoiselle Tamara* (1967, oil on canvas, 63 1/4 x 51 ins / 160.7 x 129.5 cm) GBP 60,500. NEW YORK, 19 Nov 1992, *Amaplo* (1959, oil on canvas, 51 x 38 ins / 129.5 x 96.5 cm) USD 38,500. AMSTERDAM, 27-28 May 1993, *Untitled* (1980, oil, watercolour and ink/paper, 27 1/4 x 39 1/4 ins / 69.5 x 99.5 cm) USD 19,550. COPENHAGEN, 6 Sept 1993, *Face*. PARIS, 23 Nov 1993, *Fantasy Portrait of Philip II* (1988, oil on canvas, 51 1/4 x 38 1/4 ins / 130 x 97 cm) FRF 230,000. PARIS, 24 June 1994, *Crucifixion* (1980, oil and ink/paper, 15 x 19 1/4 ins / 38 x 49 cm) FRF 41,000. LONDON, 30 June 1994, *Sara* (1959, oil on canvas, 51 1/4 x 38 1/4 ins / 130 x 97 cm) GBP 45,500. LONDON, 28 June 1995, *Ursula* (oil on canvas, 63 3/4 x 51 1/4 ins / 162 x 130 cm) GBP 67,500. LONDON, 30 Nov 1995, *Crucifixion* (1960, ink/paper, 27 1/4 x 39 ins / 69 x 99 cm) GBP 8,280. PARIS, 7 Dec 1995, *Self-portrait* (1960, oil on canvas, 23 1/2 x 28 3/4 ins / 60 x 73 cm) FRF 150,000. AMSTERDAM, 5 June 1996, *Crucifixion* (1969, pencil and varnish/paper, 34 1/4 x 45 1/4 ins / 87 x 115 cm) NLG 36,800. LONDON, 27 June 1996, *Three Graces* (1959, oil on canvas, in three sections, each 76 3/4 x 38 ins / 195 x 96.5 cm) GBP 254,500. AMSTERDAM, 10 Dec 1996, *Untitled* (1979, black ink and oil on card, 8 1/4 x 11 1/2 ins / 21 x 29 cm) NLG 12,685. PARIS, 28 April 1997, *Crucifixion VI* (1959, oil on canvas, 50 x 63 ins / 127 x 160 cm) FRF 350,000. LONDON, 29 May 1997, *Nicolasa* (1962, oil on canvas, 63 3/4 x 51 ins / 162 x 129.8 cm) GBP 42,200. LONDON, 26 June 1997, *Self-portrait* (1960, oil on canvas, 23 1/2 x 28 1/2 ins / 59.7 x 72.4 cm) GBP 13,800. LONDON, 23 Oct 1997, *Portrait* (1962, oil on canvas, 23 1/2 x 28 3/4 ins / 60 x 73 cm) GBP 17,250. AMSTERDAM, 1 Dec 1997, *Crucifixion* (1967, watercolour, ink and pencil/card, 29 1/4 x 41 ins / 74 x 104 cm) NLG 33,040. LONDON, 30 April 1999, *La muerte y la nada* (*Death and Void*) (1984/1989, acrylic, ink and pencil on paper, 27 works, 11 x 18 ins / 29 x 45 cm) GBP 80,000. LONDON, 8 Dec 1999, *Foule* (*Crowd*) (1963, oil on panel, triptych, 64 x 154 ins / 162 x 391 cm) GBP 140,000. LONDON, 30 March 2000, *Prisca* (1960, oil on canvas, 63 x 51 ins / 161 x 130 cm) GBP 45,000. MADRID, 23 Oct 2000, *Multiple of 39 Images* (1974, mixed media on paper, 77 x 63 ins / 196 x 161 cm) ESP 13,000,000. LONDON, 8 Feb 2001, *Crucifixion* (1959, oil on canvas, triptych, 91 x 50 ins / 231 x 127 cm) GBP 440,000. LONDON, 25 June 2001, *Manola II* (1963, oil on canvas, 77 x 51 ins / 195 x 130 cm) GBP 110,000. LONDON, 6 Feb 2002, *Femme Chat* (*Catwoman*) (1959, oil on canvas, 64 x 51 ins / 162 x 130 cm) GBP 90,000. LONDON, 27 June 2002, *Portrait of the Duchess of Alba* (1959, oil on canvas, 64 x 51 ins / 162 x 130 cm) GBP 88,000. LONDON, 5 Feb 2003, *Pica* (1963, oil on canvas, 51 x 38 ins / 130 x 97 cm) GBP 60,000. LONDON, 6 Feb 2003, *Infanta* (oil on canvas, 64 x 51 ins / 162 x 130 cm) GBP 75,000. LONDON, 24 June 2004, *Hisha* (1958, oil on canvas, 64 x 50 ins / 162 x 128 cm) GBP 85,000. LONDON, 25 June 2004, *Fourteen Portraits* (oil on canvas, 28 x 119 ins / 71 x 301 cm) GBP 140,000.

SAURA, Domingo (Mosén)
Spanish, 17th - 18th century.
Born in Lucena (Cordova); died 17 October 1715, in Lucena (Cordova).
Painter.

Domingo Saura became a priest after the death of his wife and devoted himself to painting. He worked for churches in Lucena and Valencia.

SAURBERG, Johan. See **SAUBERG**

SAURBORN, Joseph
German, 19th century.
Active in Trier and in Koblenz from 1840 to 1847.
Lithographer.

SAURBORN, Wilhelm
German, 19th - 20th century.
Draughtsman.

Wilhelm Saurborn produced drawings of Koblenz and scenes from history.

SAUREL, Jean. See **TESTEVUIDE Jehan**

SAURER
German, 19th century.
Active in Freiburg.
Painter.
Saurer painted an altarpiece for the church in Hoppetenzell.

SAURÈS, E.
French (?), 20th century.
Painter. Allegorical subjects.
E. Saurès painted androgynous cupids and butterfly-women in the Art Nouveau style.
AUCTION RECORDS:
PARIS, 14 June 1976, *Nymph with a Pan Pipe* (oil on canvas, 32 x 21 1/2 ins / 81 x 54.5 cm) FRF 2,000.

SAURFELT, Léonard, or Saurfelz
French, 19th century.
Born in La Varenne-St-Maur.
Painter. Genre scenes, figures.
He exhibited at the Salon between 1864 and 1868.

L. Saurfelt.

MUSEUMS AND GALLERIES:
NICE: *The Place du Vieux Marché, in Rouen, during the Reign of Louis XVI.*
AUCTION RECORDS:
PARIS, 26-27 March 1920, *Parade*, FRF 500. PARIS, 16 June 1923, *Fairground Parade*, FRF 600. PARIS, 5 Nov 1928, *Market Scenes* (two canvases) FRF 2,240. PARIS, 26 Jan 1929, *Party in the Village*, FRF 2,300. PARIS, 18 March 1938, *Country Market*, FRF 520. PARIS, 1 March 1943, *Arriving at the Inn* (1873) FRF 4,500. PARIS, 17-18 Nov 1943, *Marketplace*, FRF 4,250. PARIS, 9 March 1944, *Vegetable Market* (1867) FRF 5,150. PARIS, 9 March 1944, *Vegetable Market* (1867) FRF 9,800. PARIS, 27 June 1945, *The Little Fish Seller* (1872) FRF 9,500; *Animated Landscape*, FRF 7,800. PARIS, July 1946, *Washerwomen on the Other Side of a Town* (1875) FRF 1,900. PARIS, 22 Nov 1946, *Circus Parade*, FRF 10,000. PARIS, 31 Jan 1949, *Market Day*, FRF 13,000. PARIS, 9 April 1951, *Market*, FRF 47,500. PARIS, 6 June 1951, *Fun Fair*, FRF 23,500. VERSAILLES, 13 June 1976, *Marketplace* (oil on canvas, 19 1/4 x 25 1/2 ins / 49 x 64.5 cm) FRF 5,500. COPENHAGEN, 2 Nov 1978, *Market Scene* (1876, oil on canvas, 18 x 15 ins / 46 x 38 cm) DKK 7,000. VERSAILLES, 1 June 1980, *Marketplace in a Town in the Nord* (1867, oil on panel, 12 1/2 x 16 1/4 ins / 32 x 41 cm) FRF 13,000. NEW YORK, 28 Oct 1981, *Commedia dell'Arte* (1876, oil on canvas, 13 x 9 3/4 ins / 33 x 25 cm) USD 2,500. NEW YORK, 29 June 1983, *Village Scene* (oil on canvas and oil on panel, a pair, 16 x 13 ins / 40.6 x 33 cm and 16 x 12 1/2 ins/40.6 x 31.7 cm) USD 3,250. NEW YORK, 15 Feb 1985, *Fun Fair* (1876, oil on card, 14 1/2 x 21 3/4 ins / 36.8 x 55.3 cm) USD 5,500. MONTE CARLO, 22 June 1986, *View of the Paris Opera from the Rue Auber* (oil on canvas, 19 1/4 x 35 3/4 ins / 49 x 91 cm) FRF 70,000. PARIS, 9 Dec 1988, *Proclamation* (oil on canvas, 18 x 15 ins / 46 x 38 cm) FRF 2,200. NEW YORK, 24 Oct 1989, *Arriving at the Hôtel de l'Ecu de France* (1889, oil on canvas, 19 x 30 1/2 ins / 48.2 x 77.7 cm) USD 7,150. PARIS, 12 June 1990, *The Little Fish Seller* (oil on canvas, 22 x 18 ins / 55 x 46 cm) FRF 30, 000. PARIS, 14 Dec 1990, *The Children and the Nest* (1867, oil on canvas, 12 3/4 x 18 ins / 32.5 x 46 cm) FRF 28,000. BRUSSELS, 7 Oct 1991, *Animated Landscape* (1883, oil on canvas, 26 x 19 3/4 ins / 66 x 50 cm) BEF 65,000. CALAIS, 13 Dec 1992, *Royal Proclamation* (1873, oil on canvas, 18 x 15 ins / 46 x 38 cm) FRF 20,000. PARIS, 27 May 1994, *Lisieux Market* (oil on canvas, 22 x 25 1/4 ins / 56 x 64 cm) FRF 11,200. PONTOISE, 5 June 1999, *Loading the Baskets* (oil on canvas, 21 x 26 ins / 54 x 65 cm) FRF 17,500. DOWNINGTON, 3 Dec 1999, *Market Scene* (1891, oil on canvas, 25 x 21 ins / 64 x 53 cm) USD 2,800. BOSTON, 12 May 2000, *Wash Day in Village* (1872, oil on canvas, 26 x 21 ins / 65 x 54 cm) USD 2,300. MELUN, 10 Dec 2000, *Market* (1873, oil on canvas, 18 x 15 ins / 46 x 38 cm) FRF 30,500. PARIS, 27 June 2001, *Country Meeting* (1894, oil on canvas, 26 x 21 ins / 65 x 54 cm) FRF 30,000. PARIS, 29 March 2002, *Setting off Hunting. Rest During the Hunt* (oil on panel, a pair, 10 x 16 ins / 25 x 40 cm) EUR 10,500. MELUN, 1 Dec 2002, *By Order of the King* (1884, oil on canvas, 37 x 29 ins / 93 x 73 cm) EUR 4,500. PARIS, 16 Nov 2003, *Washerwomen. Market in Rouen* (oil on panel, a pair, 16 x 12 ins / 41 x 31 cm) EUR 4,500. SAVANNAH, 7 June 2004, *Figures in a Landscape* (1892, oil on canvas, 22 x 31 ins / 56 x 79 cm) USD 2,900.

SAURI SIRES, Antonio
Spanish, 20th century.
Born 26 October 1871, in Barcelona.
Painter, engraver, draughtsman, illustrator, lithographer. Designs for mosaics.
Antonio Sauri Sires settled in Barcelona where he studied at the school of industry, the college of arts and crafts and, ultimately, the college of fine arts; he was one of the founder members of the Barcelona Salon. He is remembered for his views of Toledo, his stamp designs and his design for the sacred seal of Cardinal Reig. He also worked in mosaics, engraved commemorative plates (most notably for Barcelona and Toledo Cathedrals) and was active as a book illustrator.

He received several awards and distinctions, notably a medal at the Spanish Exhibition of Decorative Arts and Industry held in Mexico in 1910 to commemorate the centenary of Mexican independence, and a silver medal at the International Exhibition in Barcelona in 1911.
BIBLIOGRAPHY:
Arnáiz, José Manuel/López Jiménez, Javier/Merchán Díaz, Manuel (ed.), *'Cien años de pintura en Espana y Portugal (1830-1930)'* in vol. X, Antiqvaria, Madrid, 1993.
MUSEUMS AND GALLERIES:
BARCELONA (Municipal Mus.).

SAURIAS
Active in Samos.
Painter.
Ancient Greek.
Saurias is reputed to have invented the black-figure silhouette in profile.

SAURIN, Charles
French, 19th century.
Born in Toulon.
Painter. Landscapes.
He was a pupil of Cauvin, and he made his Salon debut in 1878.

SAURIN, Donatien Pierre
French, 19th - 20th century.
Born 30 June 1841, in Nantes.
Sculptor, medallist.
Donatien Pierre Saurin, a pupil of G. Grootaers and Roubaud, worked in Paris from 1880 to 1914.

SAURINA DE CORBERA
Spanish, 14th century.
Active in Pedralbes near Sarrià.
Painter.
Saurina de Corbera painted panels representing the 12 apostles.

SAURINES, Félix
French, 18th - 19th century.
Painter.
MUSEUMS AND GALLERIES:
AUCH: *Portrait of Louis XVIII; St John the Evangelist.*
AUCTION RECORDS:
PARIS, 6 Dec 1950, *Lady with Flowers* (1820) FRF 14,500.

SAURLAY, Jérôme. See **SORLAY**

SAURWEIN, Johann Lorenz
Austrian, 17th - 18th century.
Born c. 1665; died after 1729.
Active in Innsbruck.
Painter.
Saurwein painted landscapes and Biblical scenes.

SAUSENHOFER, Dominikus Christoph
German, 18th century.
Born c. 1727, in Vienna; died 1802, in Ludwigsburg.
Painter (including porcelain). Landscapes.
Sausenhofer worked in the Ludwigsburg Porcelain Factory from 1760 onwards.

SAUSGRUBER, Jakob
German, 18th century.
Active in Stadtamhof at the end of the 18th century.
Painter (porcelain).

SAUSSAT, Carlo
Italian, 18th century.
Born in Colorno (Emilia-Romagna); died 12 June 1796.
Engraver (burin).
A pupil at the academy in Parma, Saussat went on to produce works for the court of Parma.

SAUSSE, Honoré
French, 20th century.
Born 31 January 1891, in Toulon; died 1936.
Sculptor. Portraits. Monuments.
Honoré Sausse, a pupil of Jules-Félix Coutan, carved Memorials to the Dead for Toulon and Enghien and busts of *Mistral* and *Bokanowski*. He exhibited in Paris from 1911 at the Salon des Artistes Français, of which he was a member and where he was awarded a bronze medal in 1930, the A. Maignan prize in 1931, and a silver medal in 1932.

SAUSSOIS, Anne
French, 20th century.
Born 1945, in Paris.
Painter, draughtswoman. Landscapes. Murals, stage costumes and sets.
Anne Saussois has taught at the École des Beaux-Arts in Valenciennes (1985-1989), at the École des Beaux-Arts in Nancy (1994-1995) and at the l'École d'Architecture de Nantes. She is also noted for her costumes and theatre set designs for the Théâtre de l'Aquarium (1967-1971), the Théâtre du Petit Odéon (1975) and various venues in the USA (in collaboration with choreographer Beth Soll).

Anne Saussois' drawings and paintings are transcriptions of landscapes she has previously captured on photographs. She then proceeds to rework them in a bid to 'recreate space and breathe new life into areas she has visited in her travels, notably by the use of colour and light effects'. That said, her work has developed over time to the point where it has reduced to a lyrical monochrome based on lines and hatching.

Saussois has shown at various group exhibitions, among them: in 1981, at the Cité Internationale des Arts in Paris; in 1982, 1984 and 1986, at the Salon de Montrouge; in 1994, at the Galerie Romagny in Paris; and, in 1995, at the French Institute in Boston. Solo exhibitions by Saussois have included those held in 1980 at the Cité Internationale des Arts; in 1981 and 1983, at the Galerie Gabrielle Maubrie in Paris; in 1993, at the Galerie Anne Robin in Paris; and, in 1995, at the Galerie Romagny in Paris.

BIBLIOGRAPHY:
Le Bot, Marc, '*Anne Saussois*' in *Revue d'esthétique* n° 3, periodical, Paris, June 1982.

MUSEUMS AND GALLERIES:
PARIS (FNAC).

SAUSSURE, Horace de
Swiss, 19th - 20th century.
Born 15 May 1859, in Geneva; died 1926, in Geneva.
Painter (gouache), pastellist, engraver. Figures, portraits, landscapes.
Horace de Saussure was the son of the scholar Henri de Saussure and grandson of the scientist and explorer Horace Benedict de Saussure. He studied in Munich, Düsseldorf, Florence and Paris. He travelled extensively in North America before settling in Munich and, definitively, in Geneva. He is best known for his contribution to the ceiling decorations in the Stadttheater in Düsseldorf. He seldom exhibited, but some examples of his work were displayed at the Paris Salon during his stay in the French capital and he put in an occasional appearance at the Exposition Nationale in Geneva.

MUSEUMS AND GALLERIES:
GENEVA (MAH): *Young Lady with a Violin* - NEUCHÂTEL: *Farm in Savoy*.

SAUSSURE, Théodore de
Swiss, 19th century.
Born 3 July 1824, in Genthod, near Geneva; died 4 April 1903, in Genthod.
Painter, draughtsman. Genre scenes, portraits.
Théodore de Saussure was the grandson of the famous botanist and ascensionist Horace Benedict de Saussure. He studied law, dabbled in politics, then joined the Federal Army and achieved the rank of brigadier-colonel. But he tended to favour art, drawing and painting. He played an important role in the organisation of Geneva exhibitions and museums. He exhibited in Geneva in 1896.

A notable work by him is *Roughneck Soldier Recounting His Campaigns*. He also decorated his nephew's house with eight panels of family portraits.

SAUSSY, Hattie
American, 20th century.
Born 1890; died 1978.
Painter. Landscapes.
Hattie Saussy studied at the School of Decorative and Fine Arts in New York, and travelled in Europe before finally settling in Savannah in the 1920s. She was president of the Georgia Society of Artists in 1933-1934.

AUCTION RECORDS:
NEW YORK, 28 Sept 1989, *View from my Window* (1928, oil on card, 14 x 9 3/4 ins / 35.5 x 25 cm) USD 8,800.

SAUTAI, Paul Émile
French, 19th century.
Born 29 January 1842, in Amiens; died November 1901.
Painter. Religious subjects, figures, portraits, genre scenes, church interiors.
Paul Sautai's masters were Jules Lefebvre and Robert Fleury. He first exhibited at the Salon in 1868, and won a second-class medal in 1875, a third-class medal at the Exposition Universelle of 1878 and finally a gold medal at the Exposition Universelle of 1889. He was also made a Chevalier of the Légion d'Honneur. From 1865 to 1870 he lived in Italy. He was one of the founder members of the Société des Artistes Français.

P. Sautai

MUSEUMS AND GALLERIES:
AMIENS: *Fra Angelico; Capuchin Service; St Geoffrey, Bishop of Amiens, at La Grande Chartreuse* - BAYONNE: *Martyrdom of St Justine* - NANTES: *St Bonaventura* - PARIS (former Mus. du Luxembourg): *The Evening before a Capital Execution in Rome* - ROUEN: *Dante Sent into Exile*.

AUCTION RECORDS:
PARIS, 29 May 1926, *Italian Women Praying in a Church*, FRF 330. LONDON, 19 June 1985, *Nun in a Cloister* (oil on canvas, 61 x 44 1/2 ins / 154 x 113 cm) GBP 1,700. PARIS, 12 May 1995, *Woman Praying in a Church* (oil on canvas, 20 x 17 ins / 51 x 43 cm) FRF 11,000.

SAUTER
German, 18th century.
Active in Augsburg in 1750.
Engraver (burin).

SAUTER
Austrian, 19th century.
Active in Vienna at the beginning of the 19th century.
Miniaturist.
MUSEUMS AND GALLERIES:
CESKÁ LÍPA: *Portrait of a French Officer* (1810).

SAUTER. See also **SAUTTER**

SAUTER, Aloys
Belgian, 19th - 20th century.
Born 1875, in Stabroek, near Antwerp; died 1952, in Argentieres, France.
Painter. Interiors with figures, village scenes.
Some biographers describe Aloys Sauter as a French cabinet-maker who died at Montreuil near Paris, but he was in fact a Belgian antique dealer who had settled in Neuilly-sur-Seine. He is arguably of more interest as an occasional Surrealist than for his work as a Naive artist. Examples in that respect include his *Hymn to Universal Peace* and *Cabinet-maker's Workshop* (1931). Examples of his work featured at a major exhibition of the work of Naive painters held in Knokke-le-Zoute in 1958 and, in 2001, at *Die Naive: Aufbruch ins Verlorene Paradies* (*The Naïve Painters, Journey to a Lost Paradise*), an exhibition mounted at the fine arts gallery in Vienna to display some 200 works from the Charlotte Zander Museum private collection in Bönnigheim.
BIBLIOGRAPHY:
Bihalji-Merin, Oto, *Les Peintres naïfs*, Delpire, Paris, 1960. *Die Naive, aufbruch ins verlorene paradies*, exhibition catalogue, Kunsthaus, Vienna, 2001 (text in German and English).
MUSEUMS AND GALLERIES:
BÖNNIGHEIM (Mus. Charlotte Zander).
AUCTION RECORDS:
PARIS, 23 May 1984, *Village Street* (oil on canvas, 20 3/4 x 36 1/2 ins / 53 x 93 cm) FRF 22,000.

SAUTER, Carl Wilhelm
German, 19th century.
Born 1810, in Nuremberg.
Engraver (burin).
He trained in Munich from 1837 to 1845.

SAUTER, Georg
German, 19th - 20th century.
Born 20 April 1866, in Rettenbach; died 1937.
Painter, lithographer. Religious subjects, portraits, genre scenes, landscapes.
Georg Sauter spent time in London in 1897 before moving to Munich. He is noted for his *Portrait of the Political Agitator Carl Blind*. He exhibited in Berlin in 1896.
MUSEUMS AND GALLERIES:
BRUSSELS: *Music* - BUDAPEST: *Question and Hesitation* - CAPE TOWN: *Youth* - DUBLIN (Civic Mus.): *St Patrick Disembarking* - GHENT: *Bouquet* - LEEDS (City AG): *Spring Mood* (oil on canvas); *The Leeds Picture* (1908, oil on canvas); *Dispute* (1911, oil on canvas); *Memories of Love* (1911, oil on canvas); *Weisshorn* (1913, oil on canvas); *Outward Bound* (1912, oil on canvas) - LIVERPOOL: *Youth* - LONDON (Victoria and Albert Mus.): *Renunciation* - MUNICH: *Voice of Spring* - OTTAWA (NG. of Canada): *Word of God* - PARIS (Mus. d'Orsay): *Death of Abel* - ROME (Gal. Nazionale d'Arte Moderna): *Winter Evening*.
AUCTION RECORDS:
LONDON, 7 June 1985, *Figures in Mortimer Menpes' Studio* (oil on canvas, 27 1/4 x 21 ins / 69 x 53.5 cm) GBP 2,800. AMSTERDAM, 2 May 1990, *Misty Landscape with a Mountain River* (oil on canvas, 18 x 24 ins / 45.5 x 61 cm) NLG 1,840. LONDON, 4 Oct 1991, *Resurrection (The Call of Light and Life)* (1908, oil on canvas, 64 x 53 1/2 ins / 162.8 x 136 cm) GBP 2,750.

SAUTER, Heinrich
Swiss, 19th century.
Born 1827, in Zurich; died 1891.
Portrait artist.
Heinrich Sauter trained in Munich and Antwerp.
MUSEUMS AND GALLERIES:
BERN (Kunstmus.): *Portrait of a Woman*.

SAUTER, J. P.
German, 18th century.
Active c. 1730.
Painter.
J.P. Sauter painted *St Joachim and St Anne* for the church of Our Lady in Ehingen.

SAUTER, Jakob. See **SAUTTER**

SAUTER, Johann Georg
German, 19th century.
Born 20 April 1782, in Aulendorf; died 21 October 1856, in Aulendorf.
Painter, engraver. Portraits, genre scenes, landscapes.
Johann Georg Sauter trained at the academy in Vienna and was the father of Karoline Sauter.
MUSEUMS AND GALLERIES:
DONAUESCHINGEN: *View from Waldburg over Lake Constance*; *Landscape with Farm*.
AUCTION RECORDS:
MUNICH, 17 Sept 1986, *Country Fair Scene* (1836, oil on canvas, 27 1/2 x 34 ins / 70 x 85.5 cm) DEM 80,000.

SAUTER, Johann Georg I, or Sautter
Swiss, 18th century.
Born 16 March 1712, in Arbon; died 2 August 1801, in Arbon.
Engraver, draughtsman. Portraits.
MUSEUMS AND GALLERIES:
ARBON (Historisches Mus.): *Portrait of the Artist's Fiancée*; *Portrait of the Artist's Parents*; *Portrait of the Artist's Parents-in-Law*; *Self-portrait*.

SAUTER, Johann Georg II, or Sautter
Swiss, 18th - 19th century.
Born 24 May 1758, in Arbon; died 9 June 1840.
Draughtsman. Landscapes.
Johann George Sauter II was the son of Johann Georg Sauter I.

SAUTER, Johann Thaddäus
German, 18th century.
Died 1759, in Eichstätt.
Active in Eichstätt.
Painter.
Johann Thaddäus Sauter executed altarpieces for churches in Eichstätt and Röttenbach.

SAUTER, Jonathan, or Sautter
German, 16th - 17th century.
Born 1549; died 1612.
Active in Stuttgart, and in Ulm from 1587.
Engraver (etching), calligrapher. Portraits, urban views.
Jonathan Sauter was in the service of the duke of Württemberg.

Museums and Galleries:
Stuttgart (Gal. der Stadt): *View of Stuttgart* - Vienna (Kunsthistorisches Mus.): a volume with the seals of the princes of Württemberg.

SAUTER, Judas Thaddäus
German, 18th century.
Active in Buch and in Rome in 1730.
Painter.

SAUTER, Karoline
German, 19th century.
Draughtswoman. Landscapes.
Karoline Sauter was the daughter of Johann Georg Sauter.

SAUTER, Martin
Austrian, 17th century.
Active in Bruneck in 1691.
Sculptor.

SAUTER, Thaddäus
German, 18th century.
Born 1675; died 1726, in Augsburg.
Active in Augsburg.
Painter. Portraits.

SAUTER, Thomas
German, 18th century.
Active in Constance.
Painter.
Thomas Sauter painted two altarpieces for the church of St Stephen in Augsburg.

SAUTER, Willy de
Belgian, 20th century.
Born 13 November 1938, in Dudzele, near Bruges.
Painter, engraver.
Willy de Sauter studied at the St Luke's Institute in Ghent from 1956 to 1963. His sober abstracts were shown in Belgium on a regular basis at solo exhibitions from 1960, most notably in 1979 at the Veranneman Foundation in Kruishoutem.

SAUTEREAU, René Georges Fernand
French, 19th - 20th century.
Born 12 September 1862, in Paris.
Painter.
René Georges Fernand Sautereau, a pupil of Cartier and Ernest Marché, exhibited in Paris from 1911 at the Salon des Artistes Français, of which he was a member.

SAUTERLEUTE, Joseph or Franz Joseph
German, 19th century.
Born 1796, in Weingarten; died 21 March 1843, in Nuremberg.
Glass painter.
Sauterleute trained under Isoppi. He began his career at Ludwigsburg Porcelain Factory. In 1812, he went to Nuremberg to increase his knowledge of glass painting. He was very successful there. In 1837, he painted 12 windows for the prince of Thurn and Taxis in Regensburg. About the same era he painted the stained glass windows for Landsberg Castle in Meiningen, working with Vortel from Munich. He notably reproduced *Scenes from the Virgin's Life*, in the style of Albrecht Dürer, in stained glass windows.

SAUTIN, René
French, 20th century.
Born 12 October 1881, in Montfort-sur-Risle; died 23 July 1968, in Les Andelys.
Painter, watercolourist. Landscapes, waterscapes, still-lifes, flowers.
School of Normandy.
René Sautin was a pupil of Zacharie at the École des Beaux-Arts, Rouen, and then attended the Ferrier studio in Paris, where he met Lebourg. He was also an architect and lived in Les Andelys.

He exhibited in Paris at the Salon des Indépendants from 1920, and also at the Salon des Tuileries. In 2003 he was represented in the group exhibition *Autour de l'Impressionisme: dix-neuf peintres de l'école normande (Around Impressionism: Nineteen Painters from the School of Normandy)*, held at the Maison des Arts, Antony.

He painted landscapes of his native area that favoured colour over light and were inspired by the Impressionist brushstroke and Fauvist experiments, which he reduced to restrained and veiled tints.

R Sautin

Bibliography:
Autour de l'Impressionnisme: dix-neuf peintres de l'école normande, exhibition catalogue, La Maison des Arts, Antony, 2003.

Auction records:
Paris, 22 May 1942, *Cockerel* (1934) FRF 300; *Les Andelys in Snow* (1935) FRF 1,050. Zurich, 8 Nov 1980, *The Seine at Les Andelys* (1931, oil on canvas, 11 3/4 x 23 1/2 ins / 30 x 60 cm) CHF 2,200. Versailles, 21 Feb 1988, *Summer on the Risle* (oil on card, 14 3/4 x 22 ins / 37.5 x 55 cm) FRF 10,000; *Entrance to a Village* (oil on card, 18 x 23 3/4 ins / 46 x 60.5 cm) FRF 14,000; *Bridge on the Eure and Chartres Cathedral* (oil on card, 18 x 24 ins / 46 x 61 cm) FRF 19,000; *The Seine at Les Andelys in Autumn* (oil on card, 18 x 24 ins / 46 x 61 cm) FRF 13,800. Versailles, 23 Oct 1988, *Sailing Boat* (oil on canvas, 18 x 24 ins / 46 x 61 cm) FRF 13,000. Paris, 18 June 1989, *Tug on the Seine* (oil on card, 14 3/4 x 22 ins / 37.5 x 55 cm) FRF 23,000. Versailles, 24 Sept 1989, *Jug of Flowers* (oil on card, 23 3/4 x 18 ins / 60.5 x 45.5 cm) FRF 12,200. Versailles, 26 Nov 1989, *The Seine at Les Andelys* (oil on card, 15 x 22 ins / 38 x 55 cm) FRF 16,000. Versailles, 21 Jan 1990, *The Coast in Snow* (oil on canvas, 21 1/4 x 25 1/2 ins / 54 x 64.5 cm) FRF 20,500. Paris, 31 Jan 1990, *Bouquet of Flowers* (oil on canvas, 24 1/2 x 18 ins / 62 x 46 cm) FRF 13,500. Versailles, 25 March 1990, *Paris, Montmartre and the Sacré-Coeur* (oil on canvas, 13 3/4 x 11 ins / 35 x 27 cm) FRF 14,000. Paris, 26 Oct 1990, *The Seine at La Vacherie* (1930, oil on canvas, 21 1/4 x 28 3/4 ins / 54 x 73 cm) FRF 28,000. Paris, 4 March 1992, *Snow on the Risle, Pont-Audemer* (1930, oil on canvas, 25 1/2 x 36 1/4 ins / 65 x 92 cm) FRF 13,500. Calais, 13 Dec 1992, *The Seine at Les Andelys* (oil on panel, 15 x 22 ins / 38 x 55 cm) FRF 9,500. Le Touquet, 30 May 1993, *Hortensias* (oil on panel, 22 x 15 ins / 55 x 38 cm) FRF 5,000. Paris, 2 June 1993, *The Current of the Blavet* (oil on card, 14 3/4 x 21 1/2 ins / 37.5 x 54.5 cm) FRF 11,600; *Bouquet of Flowers* (oil on panel, 22 x 18 ins / 55 x 46 cm) FRF 9,000. Paris, 22 March 1994, *Riverbank* (watercolour, 11 x 17 1/4 ins / 27 x 43.5 cm) FRF 4,000. Madrid, 9 March 1999, *Seascape* (oil on board, 18 x 24 ins / 46 x 61 cm) ESP 600,000. Calais, 7 Nov 1999, *Boat on the Seine* (oil on panel, 18 x 20 ins / 46 x 51 cm) FRF 17,000. Paris, 14 Dec 2001, *Barge and Steamboat on the Seine* (1932, oil on canvas, 13 x 22 ins / 33 x 55 cm) FRF 16,000. Paris, 24 March 2003, *Autumn at the Seine* (oil on canvas, 15 x 18 ins / 38 x 46 cm) EUR 1,600. Le Havre, 11 Nov 2003, *Risle a Montfort* (oil on cardboard, 15 x 22 ins / 38 x 55 cm) EUR 1,650. Le Havre, 7 March 2004, *The Dam at Audemer Bridge* (1930, oil on cardboard, 21 x 29 ins / 54 x 73 cm) EUR 3,400.

SAUTNER, Johann
Austrian, 18th - 19th century.
Born 27 October 1747, in Breitenbrunn; died 28 November 1823, in Vienna.
Sculptor. Statues.
Johann Sautner trained at the academy in Vienna.

MUSEUMS AND GALLERIES:
VIENNA (Schloss Schönbrunn): statues.

SAUTNER, Joseph. See **SUTTER**

SAUTNER, Lipot or Leopold
Hungarian, 20th century.
Born 18 October 1889, in Budapest.
Painter. Figures, landscapes.
Lipot Sautner trained under M. Liebermann.

SAUTRAY, Charles Guillaume or Guillaume
French, 18th century.
Active 1751-1780.
Sculptor.
Sautray became a member of the Académie de St-Luc and exhibited at the academy's exhibitions in 1752.

SAUTS, T.
Dutch, 17th century.
Active in The Hague.
Painter. Seascapes, still-lifes.
AUCTION RECORDS:
PARIS, 26 Sept 1984, *Still-life with Lemon* (oil on canvas, 39 x 29 ins / 99 x 73.5 cm) FRF 75,000.

SAUTTER. See also **SAUTER** and **SUTTER**

SAUTTER, Adolf or Franz Adolf, or Sautner
German, 19th - 20th century.
Born 30 October 1872, in Pforzheim.
Active 1890-1915.
Sculptor. Mythological subjects.
AUCTION RECORDS:
NEW YORK, 26 May 1994, *Ganymede and the Eagle* (bronze, h. 15 3/4 ins / 40 cm) USD 2,875.

SAUTTER, Hans
German, 19th - 20th century.
Born 1877, in Munich.
Sculptor. Religious subjects. Statuettes.
MUSEUMS AND GALLERIES:
ESSEN (Folkwang Mus.): *Madonna* (statuette).

SAUTTER, Jakob, or Sauter
German, 18th century.
Active during the second half of the 18th century.
Sculptor (wood).
Jakob Sautter sculpted the pulpit in the church of Oberstadion in 1773.

SAUTTER, Jo. or Johann
Swiss, 18th century.
Painter.
A notable work by Sautter is *Portrait of the family of Karl von Büren*, which was painted in 1745. He can be compared with Johann Georg Sauter, Johann Suter and with Joseph Sutter.

SAUTTER, Johann Georg. See **SAUTER**

SAUTTER, Jonathan. See **SAUTER**

SAUTTER, Joseph. See also **SUTTER**

SAUTTER, Joseph, or Sautner
German, 18th century.
Active in Landau (River Isar) from 1729 to 1741.
Painter. Figures.
Joseph Sautter painted a *St Roch* and *St Sebastian* for the church in Landau-on-the-Isar in 1734.

SAUTTER, Walter
Swiss, 20th century.
Born 1911, in Zurich; died 1991, in Zumikon.
Painter. Portraits, landscapes.
Walter Sautter showed his work at exhibitions mounted by the Swiss Society of Painters and Sculptors.
AUCTION RECORDS:
ZURICH, 5 May 1976, *Portrait of Cuno Amiet* (1960, oil on canvas, 32 x 25 1/2 ins / 81.5 x 65 cm) CHF 4,600. ZURICH, 5 June 1996, *Port of Hamburg* (1972, oil on canvas, 43 1/4 x 59 ins / 110 x 150 cm) CHF 10,925. ST GALL, 10 May 2000, *Moonlit Night* (1978, oil on board, 24 x 20 ins / 61 x 50 cm) CHF 2,800. ST GALL, 10 May 2000, *Winter Scene before a School* (1940, oil on canvas, 26 x 31 ins / 65 x 80 cm) CHF 3,500. ST GALL, 8 May 2001, *Extensive Landscape in the Evening* (1956, oil on canvas, 37 x 51 ins / 95 x 130 cm) CHF 5,000. ZURICH, 18 March 2002, *Winter Evening* (1958, oil on canvas, 28 x 45 ins / 70 x 115 cm) CHF 5,300.

SAUVAGE, Alfred Léon
French, 20th century.
Born 22 February 1892, in Condé-sur-Escaut (Nord); died 26 November 1974, in Clichy-la-Garenne.
Painter, designer.
Alfred Léon Sauvage was a pupil of Joseph-Fortuné Layraud in Valenciennes and then of Fernand Cormon at the École des Beaux-Arts, Paris. He served in the army during World War I and took up his studies again after the war.
In 1929 he founded a company that developed a wall covering that was used in many public and private commissions, including: the liner Normandie, the Museum of Oceanography, Biarritz, and the chapel of Asperren (Pyrénées-Atlantiques).

SAUVAGE, Antoine. See **LEMIRE Antoine Sauvage**

SAUVAGE, Antoon
Flemish School, 17th century.
Born 28 August 1626, in Ghent; died 13 May 1677.
Sculptor.
Antoon Sauvage was the son and pupil of Jacob Sauvage, whose work he copied. He carved pulpits for the parish churches of Saffelaere and Wachtbeke.

SAUVAGE, Antoon
Flemish School, 17th - 18th century.
Born December 1653; died between 1729 and 1733.
Sculptor.
Antoon Sauvage carved figures of angels for the church of St Nicholas in Ghent.

SAUVAGE, Arsène Symphorien
French, 19th century.
Born in Rosière-devant-Barre (Meuse).
Painter. Portraits, still-lifes, fruit.
He was a pupil of Gérôme; he debuted at the Salon in 1868.
AUCTION RECORDS:
PARIS, 27 June 1997, *Still-life Trompe l'Oeil with Bird Shooting Trophy*; *Still-life Trompe l'Oeil with Rabbit Hunting Trophy* (panel, a pair, each 17 3/4 x 13 ins / 45 x 33 cm) FRF 21,100. NEW YORK, 5 Oct 1999, *The Soldier's Letter* (oil on panel, 10 x 13 ins / 26 x 33 cm) USD 2,600. PARIS, 19 June 2000, *Hunting Trophies* (oil on panel, a pair, 18 x 13 ins / 46 x 32 cm) FRF 16,000.

SAUVAGE, Charles Gabriel. See **LEMIRE**

SAUVAGE, Frans Jacob
Flemish School, 17th century.
Born 17 January 1662.
Active in Ghent.
Sculptor.
Frans Jacob Sauvage was the son of Norbert Sauvage I, and brother of Norbert Sauvage II. He worked at the Byloke Hospital in Ghent.

SAUVAGE, Georges or Auguste Albert Georges, called Georges Sauvage
French, 19th century.
Born in Caen.

Painter, engraver (etching), lithographer. History painting, portraits, genre scenes.

George Sauvage was a pupil of P. Mauron, Gérôme and Lecomte du Nouy. He exhibited at the Paris Salon from 1874 to 1913 and was made a life member in 1883. He won medals for painting in 1879 and 1900 (at the Exposition Universelle) and for engraving in 1896, 1898 and 1900 (a silver medal at the Exposition Universelle).

MUSEUMS AND GALLERIES:

CAEN: *Death of Gaudry, Archbishop of Laon* - LE HAVRE: *François Villon Suffering the Ordeal by Water in 1457*.

AUCTION RECORDS:

NEW YORK, 23-24 May 1996, *Arab Guard Smoking a Pipe* (1878, oil on canvas, 18 x 14 ins / 45.7 x 35.6 cm) USD 19,550. LONDON, 21 March 1997, *Arab Guard Smoking a Pipe* (1878, oil on canvas, 18 x 13 1/2 ins / 45.7 x 34.2 cm) GBP 43,300.

SAUVAGE, Guy de

Belgian, 20th century.
Born 1921, in Brussels.
Painter, watercolourist, collage artist, potter.

Guy de Sauvage's work is essentially governed by a geometrical approach.

SAUVAGE, Henri Charles

French, 19th century.
Born 1853, in Blois; died 1895 or 1912.
Painter, sculptor, potter, engraver, illustrator.
Mythological subjects, portraits, genre scenes, interiors with figures, still-lifes.

Henri Sauvage was a pupil of Charles Busson in Montoire-sur-le-Loir, central France, then studied in Paris with Léon Bonnat and Fernand Humbert. His work was shown at the Paris Salon from 1877 onward and he was granted an honourable mention in 1885. A posthumous exhibition of his work was held at the Château de Blois in 1977.

MUSEUMS AND GALLERIES:

BLOIS: *Interior of the Church of St-Nicolas* - CHÂTEAUROUX: *Old Abandoned Cloister at Vienne-les-Blois* - LISIEUX: *Portrait of Mr Paul Banaston*.

AUCTION RECORDS:

PARIS, 20 Nov 1942, *The Kitchen in the Lavardin Presbytery*, FRF 9,500.

SAUVAGE, Jacob, or Savaige or Savayge or Sauvaige or Souvaige or Sauvagie or Souasie

Flemish School, 17th century.
Sculptor (wood).

Jacob Sauvage was active in Ghent. He was possibly the father of Norbert Sauvage I, and hence the founder of the Sauvage family of sculptors (his seniority would explain the large number of variant spellings of his family name). He carved pulpits, choir-stalls and altars for churches in Assenede and Watervliet.

SAUVAGE, Jean

French, 17th century.
Active during the second half of the 17th century.
Sculptor (wood).

In 1660, Jean Sauvage was commissioned to produce an altar and a retable for the Chapelle des Échevins in Poitiers.

SAUVAGE, Jean Baptiste

French, 18th century.
Born in Lunéville (Meurthe-et-Moselle).
Painter.

Jean Baptiste Sauvage has been incorrectly credited with *Portrait of Jean-Baptiste Rousseau*, in Valenciennes Museum, by some biographers. It was actually painted by Piat Joseph Sauvage.

SAUVAGE, Jean Pierre

Flemish School, 18th century.
Born 1699, in Lunéville (?); died 27 September 1780, in Brussels.
Painter.

Jean Pierre Sauvage was a painter at the court of Charles of Lorraine and Maria Theresa of Austria.

MUSEUMS AND GALLERIES:

BRUSSELS (Mus. royaux d'Art et d'Histoire): *Portrait of the Emperor Frans I; Portrait of the Empress Maria Theresa* - OSTEND (Mus. voor Schone Kunsten): *Portrait of Maria Theresa*.

SAUVAGE, Joseph Grégoire

Flemish School, 18th century.
Born 1733, in Flanders; died after 1787, in the Hôpital St-Pierre in Brussels.
Miniaturist, enameller.

Joseph Grégoire Sauvage was the son of Jean Pierre Sauvage. He spent 17 years as a court painter to Charles of Lorraine, and returned penniless to his home country upon the latter's death.

SAUVAGE, N.

French.
Active in Châlons-sur-Marne, France.
Painter. Landscapes.

MUSEUMS AND GALLERIES:

CHÂLONS-EN-CHAMPAGNE: *Chalk Quarry at Soulange*.

SAUVAGE, Napoléon

French, 19th century.
Born in Gorron (Mayenne).
Engraver.

A student of E Aubert, he exhibited at the Salon of 1847.

SAUVAGE, Nicolas

French, 18th century.
Painter. Religious subjects.

Nicolas Sauvage decorated the Jesuit church in Nancy, between 1725 and 1779.

SAUVAGE, Norbert I

Flemish School, 17th century.
Born 14 July 1631; died 1702, in Ghent.
Sculptor.

Norbert Sauvage I was the father of Frans Jacob and Norbert Sauvage II. He was a also a sculptor in stone.

MUSEUMS AND GALLERIES:

GHENT (Bijlokemus.): firesplaces from the town hall; woodcarvings from the Byloke Hospital, Ghent - GHENT (Church of St-Niklaas): pulpit, choir-stalls.

SAUVAGE, Norbert II

Flemish School, 17th century.
Born 3 October 1668, in Ghent.
Painter, engraver. Anatomical subjects.

Son of Norbert Sauvage I, and brother of Frans Jacob. He produced engravings of anatomical subjects and coats of arms.

SAUVAGE, Philippe François

French, 19th century.
Born in Villiers-le-Bel (Seine-et-Oise).
Painter. Genre scenes.

He was a student of Edouard Frère, A Dupuis and L Dansaert. He made his Salon debut in 1863.

AUCTION RECORDS:

COLOGNE, 17 March 1978, *Laundry Day* (oil on panel, 15 x 12 3/4 ins / 38 x 32.5 cm) DEM 5,000. NEW YORK, 11 Feb 1981, *Picture Book* (oil on panel, 10 x 7 1/2 ins / 25.5 x 19 cm) USD 4,500. NEW YORK, 1 March 1984, *Children Feeding a Donkey* (oil on canvas, 19 3/4 x 25 ins / 50.2 x 63.5 cm) USD 2,600. CHESTER, 4 Oct 1985, *Brother and Sister* (oil on panel, 13 x 9 1/2 ins / 33 x 24 cm) GBP 4,000. LONDON, 9 Oct 1997, *Mother and Child in a Kitchen Interior* (oil on panel, 11 1/4 x 8 3/4 ins / 28.6 x 22.2 cm) GBP 1,265. LONDON, 29 March 2001, *Broken*

Pot of Cherries (oil on panel, 11 x 9 ins / 27 x 22 cm) GBP 5,000. ZOFINGEN, 30 Nov 2001, *Two Little Cooks* (oil on panel, 14 x 10 ins / 35 x 26 cm) CHF 5,000. PARIS, 11 March 2002, *Little Girls in the Kitchen* (oil on panel, 14 x 11 ins / 36 x 27 cm) EUR 4,200. LONDON, 8 Oct 2003, *Playmates at the Kitchen Window* (oil on panel, 13 x 9 ins / 33 x 22 cm) GBP 1,200.

SAUVAGE, Pierre
French, 17th century.
Active in Nancy c. 1697.
Painter.

SAUVAGE, Pierre or Jean-Pierre Armand
French, 19th century.
Born 11 April 1821, in Abbeville; died 20 June 1883, in Vichy (Allier).
Sculptor, medallist. Mythological subjects, figures. Busts.

MUSEUMS AND GALLERIES:
ABBEVILLE: three busts in plaster; a bronze medallion.

AUCTION RECORDS:
LONDON, 17 March 1983, *The Nymph Amanthea with a Goat* (c. 1870, brown-patinated bronze, h. 25 1/4 ins / 64 cm) GBP 1,500.

SAUVAGE, Pieter-Joseph or Pierre or Piat
Belgian, 18th - 19th century.
Born 1744, in Tournai; died 11 June 1818, in Tournai.
Painter (gouache), painter (enamel/porcelain), miniaturist, sculptor, draughtsman. Allegorical subjects, genre scenes, portraits, still-lifes, flowers.

Pieter-Joseph Sauvage was the father of Charles Gabriel Sauvage. He was a pupil of J. Geraerts and G. van Spaendonk in Antwerp. Shortly before 1774, he settled in Paris, where he subsequently enjoyed considerable renown, becoming a member of the Academie Française on 29 March 1783 and, later, a member of the Academy of Toulouse. He returned to his native Tournai in 1810, and was appointed to a professorship at the city's art academy. He became a member of the Academy of St Luke, where he exhibited in 1774; he also exhibited regularly with the Académie Royale, from 1781. He exhibited at the Salon de la Correspondance in 1783, and the Paris Salon of 1804. Sauvage was chiefly a portrait painter, but also produced remarkable trompe-l'œil work, imitating marble and old terracotta.

MUSEUMS AND GALLERIES:
AMIENS (Mus. de Picardie): *The First Consul* - ANGERS: gouache - ARRAS: *Bonaparte, First Consul* - BORDEAUX (MBA): imitation marble low relief in grisaille - CHANTILLY: portrait miniatures of Louis XVI and Marie-Antoinette - COMPIÈGNE (Mus. national du Château): several lunettes, in grisaille - LA ROCHELLE: *La Marchande d'Amours* (grisaille/blue ground); *Wealth Distributing Crowns to a Group of Genii* - LILLE: *Painting and Sculpture under the Protection of Minerva* (grisailles) - MONTAUBAN: *Cupids* (grisaille) - MONTPELLIER: *Infant Bacchanale* - ORLÉANS: *Three Angels Hanging a Bronze Medal of Christ From a Palm-tree, Using Garlands of Flowers; Three Angels Hanging a Bronze Medal of the Virgin From a Palm-tree, Using Garlands of Flowers; Cupid, With a Basket of Flowers* - PARIS (Mus. Marmottan-Monet): *Bonaparte, First Consul* - SEMUR-EN-AUXOIS: *Cupids Threshing Wheat* (grisaille) - SÈTE: *Cupids* - TOULOUSE: *Bacchic Procession* (low relief in grisaille) - TOURNAI: *Self-portrait; Triumph of Bacchus* (grisaille); *The French Revolution* - VALENCIENNES: *J.-B. Rousseau*.

AUCTION RECORDS:
PARIS, 1808, *Two Subjects in Low relief* (paintings on porcelain) FRF 470. PARIS, 12 May 1898, *Profile Portrait of the Duchess of Angoulême* (miniature in grisaille) FRF 540. PARIS, 1900, *Groups of Children, Painted in Grisaille* (three lunettes) FRF 1,255. NEW YORK, 4-5 March 1909, *Kitchen Scene*, USD 55. PARIS, 6-8 Dec 1920, *Triumph of Bacchus* (sepia) FRF 1,550. PARIS, 29 June 1927, *Childrens' Games* (grisaille) FRF 3,000. PARIS, 21 April 1937, *Children's Games* (series of three compositions in grisaille) FRF 1,450. PARIS, 26-27 May 1941, *Battle of the Tritons* (grisaille) FRF 2,000. PARIS, 23 March 1949, *Bacchanale* (grisaille) FRF 10,100. PARIS, 24 May 1950, *Dancing Cupids*, FRF 17,000. LONDON, 12 Nov 1969, *Putti* (grisaille) GBP 380. PARIS, 7 March 1970, *Cupids Leading a Ram in Procession* (monochrome painting) FRF 6,300. PARIS, 28 Feb 1973, *Music, Sculpture, Geography, Science* (four canvases in grisaille) FRF 14,100. PARIS, 4 March 1976, *Cupids and Animals at Play* (oil on canvas two pendants, 35 1/2 x 51 1/4 ins / 90 x 130 cm) FRF 6,600. NEW YORK, 6 Dec 1980, *Putti in a Field of Wheat* (oil on canvas, in grisaille, 26 3/4 x 49 1/2 ins / 68 x 126 cm) USD 3,400. NEW YORK, 11 June 1981, *Allegories of the Arts, Science and Justice* (oil on canvas, three paintings in grisaille, 55 1/4 x 64 ins / 140.5 x 162.5 cm) USD 10,000. LONDON, 12 Dec 1984, *Allegory of Music; Allegory of Painting* (oil on canvas, a pair, 23 1/4 x 48 ins / 59 x 121 cm) GBP 16,000. NEW YORK, 7 April 1989, *Putti Playing With a Goat* (oil on canvas in grisaille, 37 x 44 1/2 ins / 94 x 113 cm) USD 12,100. BRUSSELS, 7 Oct 1991, *Interior With a Child and Cat* (oil on canvas, 12 3/4 x 9 1/4 ins / 32.5 x 23.5 cm) BEF 80,000. PARIS, 16 June 1993, *Venus Shooting an Arrow at Cupid* (oil/white marble, grisaille in imitation of bronze. LONDON, 8 Dec 1993, *Trompe l'Oeil With Putti and Animals* (oil on canvas, a pair, each 18 3/4 x 32 1/4 ins / 47.5 x 82 cm) GBP 28,750. PARIS, 31 March 1995, *Trompe l'Oeil with Female Fauns* (oil/copper, 9 1/4 x 11 1/2 ins / 23.5 x 29.5 cm) FRF 35,000. AMSTERDAM, 15 Nov 1995, *Hercules and Antaeus* (black and white chalk/blue paper, 20 x 17 ins / 51 x 43 cm) NLG 4,720. NEW YORK, 17 Jan 1996, *Infant Bacchus With Two Putti* (oil on panel in grisaille, 6 3/4 x 9 3/4 ins / 17.1 x 24.8 cm) USD 4,887. LONDON, 16-17 April 1997, *Putti With Musical Instruments* (1769, pen with black and brown ink/black chalk, 5 3/4 x 9 ins / 14.7 x 22 cm) GBP 517. NEW YORK, 21 Oct 1997, *Trompe l'Oeil: the Triumph of Bacchus* (oil on panel, grisaille, 12 1/4 x 32 ins / 31.3 x 81 cm) USD 27,600. NEW YORK, 16 June 1999, *Procession of Putti* (1785, oil on canvas with trompe l'oeil ivory, 2 x 6 ins / 5 x 16 cm) USD 7,500. LONDON, 11 July 2000, *Three Putti at Play with Fruit* (grisaille, miniature) GBP 1,500. PARIS, 19 June 2001, *Trompe-l'oeil Portrait of Napoleon I as First Consul* (oil on canvas) FRF 70,000. NEW YORK, 24 Jan 2002, *Trompe l'oeil of Putti Playing with a Goat* (oil on canvas, grisaille, 13 x 22 ins / 32 x 55 cm) USD 40,000. PARIS, 28 June 2002, *Children's Bacchanale* (oil on panel, 12 x 33 ins / 31 x 84 cm) EUR 22,500. PARIS, 21 May 2003, *Madame Royale* (grisaille, miniature) EUR 2,100. LONDON, 22 May 2003, *Gentleman in Profile* (grisaille, miniature, cicular, h. 1 1/2 ins / 4 cm) GBP 1,100. LONDON, 25 May 2004, *Jugate Profiles of King Louis XVI, Queen Marie Antoinette and the Dauphin* (grisaille, miniature) GBP 4,500.

SAUVAGE, Sylvain
French, 20th century.
Born 8 May 1888, in Beaume-les-Messieurs; died January 1948, in Paris.
Painter, draughtsman, illustrator. Mythological subjects, landscapes.

Sylvain Sauvage, a book designer, was director of the École Estienne (École du Livre), where he was the successor of the academician Georges Lecomte. He exhibited in Paris at the Salon des Artistes Décorateurs and was awarded a silver medal in 1930.

He illustrated G. d'Annunzio's *Triomphe de la Mort* (*Triumph of Death*), Balzac's *La Fille aux yeux d'or* (*Girl with the Golden Eyes*), Casanova's *Memoirs*, Diderot's *Les Bijoux indiscrets* (*Indiscreet Jewels*), Anatole France's *Les sept femmes de Barbe Bleue* (*Bluebeard's Seven Wives*), the *Pastorals* of Longus, *Les Chansons de Bilitis* (*Songs of Bilitis*) of Pierre Louÿs, Henri de Régnier's *Le mariage de minuit* (*Midnight Marriage*), the Marquis de Sade's *Ernestine*, A. Samain's *Tales*, Voltaire's *Candide*, R. Boysleve's *La Leçon d'amour dans un parc* (*Love Lesson in a Park*), de Laclos' *Liaisons Dangereuses* and *Manon Lescaut* by the Abbé Prévost.

AUCTION RECORDS:

ENGHIEN-LES-BAINS, 28 Oct 1979, *Leda and the Swan* (Indian ink, wash and colouring pencil, 37 x 28 ins / 94 x 71 cm) FRF 6,500. METZ, 14 Oct 1990, *Village* (oil on panel, 10 1/2 x 18 1/4 ins / 26.5 x 46.2 cm) FRF 4,200.

SAUVAGE, Zette
French, 20th century.
Born in Nancy.
Sculptor.

Zette Sauvage exhibited in Paris at the Salon d'Automne, of which she was a member.

SAUVAGEAU, Louis
French, 19th century.
Born 22 July 1822, in Paris; died c. 1874.
Sculptor, medallist. Religious subjects, mythological subjects, figures, genre scenes, animals. Busts, low reliefs.

Louis Sauvageau's masters were Alexandre Lequien and Armand Toussaint. He exhibited at the Paris Salon from 1848 to 1874.

He sculpted a large number of works in terracotta. He is particularly well known for the monumental fountain in the Place aux Gueldres, St-Denis (Paris), entitled *Ascension of the Virgin*. In 1861 he made another, of equally monumental dimensions, in the Val d'Oise, which was sent to Brazil in 1878. Since then it has been dismantled and replaced several times.

AUCTION RECORDS:

LONDON, 8 Dec 1976, *Young Woman and Child* (bronze, h. 32 3/4 ins / 83 cm) GBP 880. VERSAILLES, 27 March 1977, *Cavalier Hunting Tiger* (bronze, h. 24 3/4 ins / 63 cm and w. 38 1/2 ins/98 cm) FRF 8,100.

SAUVAGEON, H.
French, 19th century.
Died c. 1870, in Visan (Vaucluse).
Painter. Landscapes.

MUSEUMS AND GALLERIES:

AVIGNON (Mus. Calvet): *Memory of the Banks of the Lison.*

SAUVAGEOT (Mme). See **GALIOT Désirée-Charlotte**

SAUVAGEOT, Charles Théodore
French, 19th century.
Born 22 February 1826, in Paris; died 15 February 1883, in Fontainebleau.
Painter, watercolourist. Genre scenes, landscapes, waterscapes.

He was a pupil of Isabey. His first Salon exhibition was in 1863.

CH-SAUVAGEOT

MUSEUMS AND GALLERIES:

ROCHEFORT: *The Artist's Studio, Cour de Rohan.*

AUCTION RECORDS:

PARIS, 1880, *Peasant Woman Talking* (watercolour) FRF 58. PARIS, 15 Feb 1907, *The Blacksmith,* FRF 250. PARIS, 30 March 1925, *Farmyard in Barbizon,* FRF 80. ORLÉANS, 26 Nov 1983, *Townhouses* (oil on panel, 16 1/2 x 10 1/4 ins / 42 x 26 cm) FRF 11,500. NEUILLY, 17 June 1992, *Riverbank* (oil on panel, 9 x 11 ins / 22 x 27 cm) FRF 5,000. NEW YORK, 16 Feb 1993, *Shepherd and His Flock Surrounded by Fields* (oil on canvas, 35 1/4 x 57 ins / 89.5 x 145 cm) USD 3,520. FONTAINEBLEAU, 5 Dec 1999, *Banks of the Loing Seen from Montigny* (oil on panel, 11 x 16 ins / 27 x 41 cm) FRF 14,500.

SAUVAGEOT, Claude
French, 19th century.
Born 1832, in Santenay; died 1885.
Engraver, draughtsman, architect. Architectural views. Ornaments.

A pupil of Gaucherel, he made his Salon debut in 1855. He was made a Chevalier of the Légion d'Honneur in 1885.

SAUVAGEOT, Denis François
French, 19th century.
Born 2 September 1793, in Paris.
Painter, draughtsman. Landscapes, architectural views.

He was married to Désirée Charlotte Sauvageot. His master was G Bourgeois, and he exhibited at the Salon between 1822 and 1831.

MUSEUMS AND GALLERIES:

SOISSONS: *Portrait of a Child.*

AUCTION RECORDS:

PARIS, 10 March 1986, *View of the Roman Countryside* (pencil and wash, two drawing, 14 3/4 x 24 1/2 ins / 37.5 x 62 cm) FRF 38,000.

SAUVAGIE, Jacob. See **SAUVAGE**

SAUVAGNAC, Jean
French, 19th century.
Born in Paris.
Painter. Genre scenes, still-lifes.

His teachers were Tabar, Menard, Ange Tissier and Rivet. He made his debut at the Salon in 1863.

SAUVAIGE, Louis Paul
French, 19th century.
Born 5 April 1827, in Lille; died 31 July 1885, in Trouville.
Painter. Landscapes, seascapes.

Louis Sauvaige was the father of Marcel Louis Sauvaige. He is incorrectly listed as 'Sauvaigne' in *Bryan's Dictionary*. He was taught by both Corot and Daubigny, then went to work in Lille. He exhibited at the Paris Salon for the first time in 1873 and won a third-class medal in 1881.

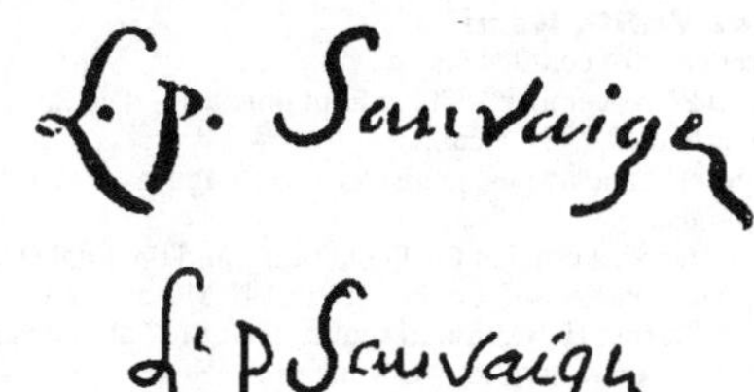

MUSEUMS AND GALLERIES:

COUTANCES: *Calm* - LILLE: *Seascape.*

SAUVAIGE, Marcel Louis
French, 20th century.
Born in Lille; died December 1927.
Painter. Seascapes.

Marcel Louis Sauvaige, a pupil of his father, Louis Paul Sauvaige, and Lansyer, exhibited in Paris at the Salon des Artistes Français, of which he was a member from 1884 and where he was awarded an honourable mention in 1903 and a third-class medal in 1906. The honourable mention was for *Port of Camaret,* which is now in the museum of Dieppe.

AUCTION RECORDS:

PARIS, 14 April 1943, *Breton Nocturne* (pastel) FRF 450.

SAUVAIGNE, Louis Paul. See **SAUVAIGE**

SAUVAN, Gabrielle
French, 18th century.
Painter.

Gabrielle Sauvan was the daughter of Philippe Sauvan.

SAUVAN, Honoré
French, 17th century.
Painter.
Honoré Sauvan was the father of Philippe Sauvan, and worked in Arles.

SAUVAN, Philippe
French, 18th century.
Born 1698, in Arles; died 8 January 1789, in Avignon.
Painter, engraver, draughtsman. Religious subjects, portraits.
Philippe Sauvan was the pupil of his father, Honoré Sauvan, and of Parrocel. He settled in Avignon in 1729 and painted altarpieces and portraits in Arles, Aix and Avignon. He also produced etchings.
MUSEUMS AND GALLERIES:
AVIGNON: *City of Avignon Restored to the Supreme Pontiff; St Margaret; Sovereignty; Le Génie Consulaire (Consular Spirit); Winged Spirit; Esprit Calvet (Calvet Spirit); Portraits of Joaquim Leviuex de la Verne, Joseph-François de Salvador and Simon Reboulet, Famous People from Avignon*; sketch - CARPENTRAS: *St Ursula*.
AUCTION RECORDS:
PARIS, 26 Nov 1919, *Voltaire* (à trois crayons) FRF 145. PARIS, 29-30 March 1943, *Assumption* (Indian ink heightened with gouache, attributed) FRF 420. PARIS, 11 March 1988, *Virgin in Glory* (black chalk, pen and ink, 7 3/4 x 5 ins / 19.8 x 13 cm) FRF 2,200.

SAUVAN, Pierre
French, 18th century.
Born 1722, in Avignon; died 1799, in Bilbao, Spain.
Painter. Religious subjects.
Pierre Sauvan was the son and pupil of Philippe Sauvan.
AUCTION RECORDS:
PARIS, 18 April 1991, *A King Converted by St Bruno* (oil on canvas, 14 3/4 x 11 ins / 37.5 x 28 cm) FRF 17,000. PARIS, 27 June 1991, *Saint Adoring the Virgin of the Assumption* (oil on canvas, arched, 14 x 9 ins / 35.5 x 23 cm) FRF 8,500.

SAUVARD, Henri
French, 20th century.
Born 25 November 1880, in Fontainebleau; died 23 March 1973, in Noiseau.
Painter. Landscapes, landscapes with figures, flowers, animals.
Henri Sauvard, a pupil at the École Boule and the École Germain Pilon, Paris, set up his studio in Moret-sur-Loing, Seine-et-Marne. He exhibited regularly at the Salon des Indépendants, of which he was a member. He painted many views of the Île-de-France, his favourite subjects being the forest of Fontainebleau and the woods of Meudon and Vincennes. He called himself the 'Man of the Woods'.

SAUVAT, Jean-Louis
French, 20th - 21st century.
Born 1947.
Sculptor (cardboard/plaster/resin/bronze), draughtsman (charcoal). Figures, animals, horses.
Born into a family of artists, Jean-Louis Sauvat trained at the École des Métiers d'Art, and was then taught by Robert Couturier at the École des Beaux-Arts. He became Professor of Sculpture at the École Nationale des Arts Appliqués et Métiers d'Art in Paris. He lives and works in Illiers-Combay (Eure-et-Loir).

He has created numerous public works of art for schools and colleges. He has illustrated *Propos sur des croquis équestres* (*Talking about Sketching Horses*) with the rider Nuno Oliveira (Éditions Belin, Paris), a book by Dominique Barbier and three books by Major A. de Padirac. He collaborated on the show *Triptych* by Bartabas. Sauvat specialises in equestrian sculpture, and is himself a dedicated rider. Not surprisingly, the subject-matter of his drawings and sculptures is the horse in motion. This is a difficult branch of art with a long tradition, but one in which he is singularly accomplished. He uses pieces of cardboard to make sculptures that capture the essence of his subject.

He has participated in group exhibitions: Salon Jeune Sculpture, Paris, 1970; Salon de Mai, Paris, 1975 and 1976; Muséum d'Histoire Naturelle, Paris, 1997. He has shown his work in solo exhibitions: Musée d'Étampes, 1984; Château de Duras, 1986; Galerie L'Orme, Paris, 2000; *Sculptures et dessins*, Conservatoire de l'Agriculture, Chartres, 2002.
BIBLIOGRAPHY:
Providence, Jean-Marc (ed.)/Bonnebas, Mireille, et al., *Sauvat. Sculptures et dessins*, exhibition catalogue, Conservatoire de l'agriculture, Chartres, 2002.

SAUVAT, Patrick
French, 20th century.
Born 1943.
Also active in Germany.
Engraver.
Patrick Sauvat studied graphics and engraving and went on to exhibit on a regular basis in Switzerland, Germany and France.

SAUVAYRE, Maurice
French, 20th century.
Born 17 March 1889, in Paris.
Painter, illustrator. Landscapes.
Maurice Sauvayre exhibited in Paris at the Salon des Independents, of which he was a member, the Salon des Tuileries and the Salon des Humoristes. He illustrated Henri Béraud's *La Gerbe d'Or* (*The Golden Wreath*) for the society 'Les Annales'.
AUCTION RECORDS:
PARIS, 27 Dec 1926, *Landscape*, FRF 300. PARIS, 15 Feb 1930, *Landscape*, FRF 100.

SAUVÉ, Christian
French, 20th century.
Born 12 July 1943.
Painter. Figures, nudes, landscapes, animals, still-lifes.
Christian Sauvé studied at the École des Beaux-Arts in Rouen then at the École des Beaux-Arts in Paris (1967). In 1968, he travelled through Italy, Belgium Holland and England. He was awarded the Casa Velázquez Grand Prix in 1969, following which he visited Spain and Portugal in 1970, including the Canary Islands, where he was fascinated by the volcanic terrain of Lanzarote. He spent time in Africa in 1971 before returning to teach painting and composition on a regular basis in Rouen as of 1974.

Sauvé's paintings include landscapes where trees and earth are stripped back to their raw and, at times, brutal natural state. He also paints more conventional compositions which feature figures rendered in oils or wash, together with still-lifes. His technique is fluid and dynamic.
BIBLIOGRAPHY:
Christian Sauvé, exhibition catalogue, Gal. Rollin, Rouen, 1991.
MUSEUMS AND GALLERIES:
NEUCHÂTEL-EN-BRAY (Musée Mathon-Durand) - ROUEN (MBA).

SAUVÉ, Jean
French, 17th century.
Born in Senlis (Oise).
Active in Paris 1660-1691.
Engraver (burin), print publisher.
Jean Sauvé also worked in Bologna and Munich.

SAUVÉ, Jean Jacques Théodore or Théodore
French, 19th century.

Born 25 August 1792, in Paris; died January 1869, in Paris.
Engraver (burin), lithographer.

A student of David, he entered the École des Beaux-Arts on 14 December 1813. His work was shown at the Salon of 1831. He is chiefly remembered for some lithographs of heads, inspired by Raphael's frescoes in the Vatican.

SAUVÉ, Joachim

French, 19th century.
Born in Coisy (Somme).
Painter.

His master was C. Crauk. He made his Salon debut in 1880.

SAUVÉ, Sébastien

French, 17th century.
Born 1668, in Senlis (Oise).
Draughtsman, engraver (burin).

MUSEUMS AND GALLERIES:
LONDON (British Mus.): *Portrait of a Group.*

SAUVEGRAIN

French, 20th century.
Painter. Scenes with figures.

Sauvegrain exhibited in Paris at the Salon d'Automne in 1952. Among his works is *Fourteenth of July.*

SAUVENIÈRE, Jules

Belgian, 19th - 20th century.
Born 1855; died 1920.
Painter. Landscapes.

Jules Sauvenière exhibited at the Cercle des Beaux-Arts from 1893 to 1909.

MUSEUMS AND GALLERIES:
LIÈGE (Mus. de l'Art wallon): *Road; Undergrowth.*

SAUVESTRE, Stéphen or Eugène Stéphen

French, 19th century.
Born 26 December 1847, in Bonnétable (Sarthe).
Painter, watercolourist, architect. Landscapes, architectural views.

SAUX, Jules de (Mme), called Henriette Browne

Maiden name: Henriette Sophie de Bouteillier
French, 19th century.
Born 1829, in Paris; died 1901.
Painter, engraver, draughtswoman. Genre scenes, local scenes (harems).

A pupil of Chaplin, she was equally successful as a painter and an engraver. She debuted at the Paris Salon in 1853. She won third-class medals in 1855 and 1857; a second-class medal for painting in 1861; and a medal for engraving in 1863. She is generally known by her pseudonym, Henriette Brown. She is perhaps best remembered for her many paintings on subjects drawn from the lives of the Arabs of North Africa.

AUCTION RECORDS:
PARIS, 1865, *Catechism,* FRF 16,000. LONDON, 1881, *Sisters of Charity,* FRF 12,975. LONDON, 1886, *Visit to a Harem,* FRF 32,810. LONDON, 1888, *Jewish School in Cairo,* FRF 18,235. LONDON, 7 Dec 1907, *More Fear than Evil* (drawing) GBP 3. LONDON, 29 June 1908, *In the Harem,* GBP 21; *An Oriental School* (drawing) GBP 78. LONDON, 26 April 1909, *Alsace,* GBP 2. LONDON, 24 June 1909, *The Toilette,* GBP 52. LONDON, 27 May 1910, *Fairytale,* GBP 54. LONDON, 27 Jan 1922, *An Oriental Beauty* (1861) GBP 17; *Reading the Bible* (1857) GBP 16. LONDON, 13 May 1927, *In the Harem,* GBP 13. LONDON, 25 April 1930, *A Turkish School* (1870) GBP 10. LONDON, 21 Dec 1933, *A Turkish School* (1870) GBP 5. LONDON, 15 Feb 1935, *Village School,* GBP 14. NEW YORK, 29 Oct 1981, *Young Student* (1865, oil on canvas, 39 1/4 x 24 3/4 ins / 100 x 63 cm) USD 7,000. LONDON, 25 June 1982, *Nubian Children* (1870, oil on canvas, 35 x 46 ins / 89 x 117 cm) GBP 4,000. LONDON, 22 June 1983, *Harem Scene* (oil on canvas, 33 3/4 x 44 3/4 ins / 86 x 113.5 cm) GBP 4,000. TORONTO, 29 May 1986, *The Ducat* (1876, oil on canvas, 45 1/2 x 35 ins / 115.5 x 89 cm) CAD 7,500. NEW YORK, 28 Feb 1990, *An Oriental Beauty* (1861, oil on canvas, 58 x 45 ins / 147.3 x 114.3 cm) USD 15,400. NEW YORK, 16 July 1992, *Sisters of Charity* (oil on canvas, 40 x 31 ins / 101.6 x 78.7 cm) USD 2,200.

SAUZAY, Adrien Jacques

French, 19th - 20th century.
Born 1841, in Paris; died 24 November 1928.
Painter. Landscapes with figures, landscapes, waterscapes.

Adrien Jacques Sauzay, a pupil of Audre and Alberto Pasini, exhibited at the Salon de Paris from 1863, then at the Salon des Artistes Français, of which he was an out-of-competition member from 1883. He was awarded a third-class medal in 1881, a second-class in 1883, a bronze at the Exposition Universelle of 1889, and another at the Exposition Universelle of 1900. He was made a Chevalier of the Légion d'Honneur in 1906.

A. Sauzay

MUSEUMS AND GALLERIES:
ARRAS: *Neufchâteau* - BREST (MBA): *Pond near Paris; Lock of Notre-Dame de la Garenne* - CARPENTRAS: *Felled Trees in the Forest of Bondy* - GLASGOW: *Patoral Landscape* - GUÉRET: *Les Dalles, Côtes de Normandie* - LE HAVRE: *Meadows near Pont-de-l'Arche* - LOUVIERS (Mus. municipal): *Les Viornes, Road to Comelles; Port Pinché; The Legendre House, Port-Joie; Le Giboxin, Rangiport* - MONT-DE-MARSAN: *Under the Pine Trees, Capbreton.*

AUCTION RECORDS:
PARIS, 17 March 1904, *Landscape,* FRF 110. NEW YORK, 16-17 Feb 1911, *Riverbank,* USD 220. PARIS, 6 June 1924, *Village of Montmacq (Oise),* FRF 860. PARIS, 30 Nov 1944, *Landscape,* FRF 3,100. PARIS, 10 March 1949, *Pond,* FRF 4,500. LONDON, 6 Dec 1974, *Beach,* Gns 480. PARIS, 6 April 1976, *Washerwomen* (oil on panel, 13 x 26 1/2 ins / 33 x 67 cm) FRF 4,200. ZURICH, 29 Nov 1978, *Washerwoman by a River* (oil on panel, 13 x 24 1/4 ins / 33 x 61.5 cm) CHF 7,000. VERSAILLES, 19 Oct 1980, *Peaceful River* (oil on panel, 13 1/2 x 24 1/2 ins / 34 x 62 cm) FRF 37,500. PARIS, 24 June 1981, *Hamlet by a Pond* (oil on panel, 13 x 23 1/2 ins / 33 x 60 cm) FRF 23,000. NEW YORK, 24 May 1984, *Hamlet by a Pond* (oil on panel, 13 1/4 x 24 1/2 ins / 33.5 x 62 cm) USD 8,000. HONFLEUR, 1 Jan 1985, *Village by a River* (oil on canvas, 24 x 15 ins / 61 x 38 cm) FRF 37,000. PARIS, 7 Dec 1987, *View of St-Denis* (oil on panel, 14 1/4 x 7 3/4 ins / 36 x 20 cm) FRF 11,000. NEUILLY, 9 March 1988, *Moor in Brittany* (oil on panel, 13 x 24 1/2 ins / 33 x 62 cm) FRF 18,000. PARIS, 19 Dec 1988, *Riverbank* (oil on canvas, 18 x 24 ins / 46 x 61 cm) FRF 12,000. VERSAILLES, 5 March 1989, *Riverbank* (oil on panel, 9 1/4 x 13 3/4 ins / 23.2 x 34.8 cm) FRF 10,500. PARIS, 17 April 1989, *Landscape* (oil on panel, 12 1/4 x 18 1/2 ins / 31 x 47 cm) FRF 26,000. VERSAILLES, 19 Nov 1989, *Marshy Fields* (oil on canvas, 13 3/4 x 24 1/2 ins / 35 x 62 cm) FRF 20,000. NEW YORK, 23 May 1990, *Hamlet by a Pond* (oil on panel, 12 3/4 x 24 ins / 32.3 x 61 cm) USD 6,600. PARIS, 12 Oct 1990, *Pond* (oil on canvas, 25 1/4 x 19 1/4 ins / 64 x 49 cm) FRF 14,500. PARIS, 24 May 1991, *By a Pond* (oil on canvas, 26 3/4 x 36 1/4 ins / 68 x 92 cm) FRF 24,000. LE TOUQUET, 8 June 1992, *Boat by a Riverbank* (oil on panel, 11 x 17 ins / 28 x 43 cm) FRF 10,000. PARIS, 10 Feb 1993, *Washerwomen* (oil on canvas, 14 1/4 x 24 1/2 ins / 36 x 62 cm) FRF 13,000. PARIS, 10 July 1995, *Washerwomen on the Edge of a Village* (oil on panel, 13 1/4 x 24 1/2 ins / 33.5 x 62.5 cm) FRF 17,000. NEW YORK, 10 Feb 1998, *Washing Day* (1878, oil on panel, 13 x 24 1/4 ins / 33 x 61.5 cm) USD 16,100.

SAUZAY, J. de
French, 19th century.
Painter, miniaturist. Portraits.
He exhibited at the Paris Salon between 1835 and 1839.
AUCTION RECORDS:
PARIS, 10 May 1950, *Portrait of a Young Girl; Portrait of a Young Woman; Portrait of a Man* (three miniatures in the same frame) FRF 10,800.

SAUZAY, Louis Charles Valentin
French, 19th century.
Born in Paris.
Painter. History painting.
He studied art with Périn, Amaury-Duval, Ingres and Boulanger. He made his Salon debut in 1870.

SAUZAY, Pierre, or Sauzée
French, 17th century.
Active in Baugé 1654-1673.
Painter, glassmaker.
Sauzay produced an *Annunciation* in the church in Linières-Bouton.

SAUZEDO. See **SALCEDO**

SAUZET, Claude
French, 20th century.
Born 1941, in La Grand-Combe (Gard).
Painter, draughtsman, lithographer. Figure compositions, figures, nudes, landscapes, landscapes with figures, urban landscapes, still-lifes.
Symbolism.
Claude Sauzet studied at the École des Beaux-Arts in Nîmes. Sauzet's technique is resolutely academic. As a watercolorist, he paints predominantly female figures, lively street scenes, café terraces, landscapes of the Midi region of France and of Italy. He showed his work at various group exhibitions, notably in Paris at the Salon des Artistes Français, the Salon d'Automne and the Salon de la Société Nationale des Beaux-Arts (of which he is a member). He has also exhibited solo both in France and abroad, not least at one-man shows held at the Galerie Le Jardin des Arts in Paris in 1998 and 2000. Sauzet was awarded the Prix de la Jeune Peinture at the 1978 Paris Salon d'Automne.
AUCTION RECORDS:
AUBAGNE, 24 June 1990, *Erotic Nude* (oil on canvas, 31 1/2 x 39 1/4 ins / 80 x 100 cm) FRF 41,000.

SAVADOV, Arseni Vladimirovich
Ukrainian, 20th - 21st century.
Born 1962, in Kiev.
Painter. Allegorical subjects, figure compositions.
Arseni Savadov studied at the Kiev institute of art, graduating in 1986. His compositions are designed in large format, with allegorical figures and legendary animals or monsters depicted in desert-type landscapes. His work has been seen in several exhibition, including solo exhibitions in 1987 in Paris and Madrid.
BIBLIOGRAPHY:
Art soviétique contemporain, exhibition catalogue, Gal. de France, Paris, 1987.

SAVAGE, Augusta Christine
Maiden name: Fells
American, 20th century.
Born 29 February 1892, in Green Cove Springs (Florida); died 26 March 1962, in New York.
Sculptor (clay/plaster/bronze). Portraits. Busts.
Harlem Renaissance.
306 Group.
After experiencing difficulty in establishing herself as a sculptor in the South, Augusta Savage moved to New York in 1921, settling in Harlem. She studied at Cooper Union (1924-1926), and at the Académie de la Grande Chaumière in Paris (1929-1931) on a Julius Rosenwald Fellowship. In 1932, she opened a studio in Harlem, the Uptown Laboratory, which was later renamed the Savage Studio of Arts and Crafts. There, she began a long teaching career in the black community, acting as guide and mentor to numerous young African-American artists then condemned to isolation because of laws and other practices that perpetuated racial segregation. In 1937, she became director of the Harlem Community Art Center, New York, which had been founded by the Work Progress Administration (a programme established by President Roosevelt in 1934 that included the Federal Arts Project, which enabled artists to work and teach). She also helped with the establishment of the Harlem Arts Guild (1935-1941), an independent artist group working on the socio-political aspects of their profession. She was also a member of the 306 Group. In 1939, she opened a gallery, the Salon of Contemporary Negro Art, in Harlem, but it soon closed. After 1945, she concentrated on her teaching career and retired to the Saugerties, New York. She was also a poet.

Savage sculpted famous and not-so famous African-Americans. Among her celebrity portraits are those of W.E.B. DuBois (1868-1963, the sociologist who became one of the leaders of the National Association for the Advancement of Colored People), Marcus Garvey (1887-1940, the Pan-Africanist nationalist and founder of the Universal Negro Improvement Association), and Frederick Douglass (1818-1895, the former slave and abolitionist). She worked mainly in clay, bronze being too expensive during the years of the Great Depression. Two of her best-known works are *Gamin (Child)* (1930), the bust of her nephew, with its deep yet disabused expression, and *The Harp* (1939), which was commissioned in 1937 by the Board of Design for the 1939-1940 New York World's Fair. This work, with its traditional academic style, is far from the African claims of the period. Inspired by James Weldon Johnson's hymn *Lift Every Voice and Sing*, the piece features a choir of some ten black singers who take the place of the harpstrings, with a kneeling youth in front who holds a bar of notes. Savage played a key role in the Harlem Renaissance, which sought to bring together African-American artists within their own community to defend their rights and ideals.

Augusta Savage took part in a variety of group shows: the Sesqui-Centennial, Philadelphia (1926); the Société des artistes français, the Salon d'automne, and the Exposition coloniale (Colonial Exhibition), Paris (1929); at the Metropolitan Museum of Art, New York (1934); the *American Negro Exhibition*, Chicago (1940). After she died, her work was included in such thematic group shows as *Three Generations of African-American Women Sculptors: a Study in Paradox*, The Equitable Gallery, New York (1996); and *Narratives of African-American Art and Identity*, High Museum of Art, Atlanta (2000). In 1988, a retrospective, *Augusta Savage and the Art Schools of Harlem*, was held of her work at the Schomburg Center for Research in Black Culture, New York Public Library, New York.
BIBLIOGRAPHY:
Locke, Alain, *The Art of the American Negro (1851-1940)*, group exhibition catalogue, Chicago, 1940. *Augusta Savage and the Art Schools of Harlem*, exhibition catalogue, Schomburg Center for Research in Black Culture, New York Public Library, New York, 1988. *Three Generations of African-American Women Sculptors: a Study in Paradox*, group exhibition catalogue, The Equitable Gall., New York, 1996.
MUSEUMS AND GALLERIES:
NEW YORK (Public Library): Schomburg Collection.

SAVAGE, Donald Percival
Australian, 20th century.
Born 12 October 1926, in Brisbane.
Painter, sculptor.
Groups: Miya, Half-dozen.

Donald Percival Savage initially trained as a sculptor and then attended painting lessons at the Technical College in Brisbane. There he joined the Miya group, reserved for all artists under the age of 21 involved in painting, literature or the theatre. He also joined the Half-dozen group, who were at the forefront of fine arts in Brisbane.

In 1947 he continued his art training in Sydney, where he became a member of the Royal Art Society of New South Wales. In 1949 he moved to Paris. He exhibited frequently and quickly caught the attention of the press.

SAVAGE, Edward
American, 18th - 19th century.
Born 26 November 1761, in Princeton (Massachusetts); died 6 July 1817, in Princeton.
Painter, engraver (burin). Portraits.

Edward Savage was a pupil of Benjamin West.

MUSEUMS AND GALLERIES:
WORCESTER, MA (AM): *Self-portrait.*

AUCTION RECORDS:
LONDON, 30 June 1924, *The Washington Family,* GBP 42. NEW YORK, 27 Jan 1938, *Penn Treaty with the Indians,* GBP 310. NEW YORK, 21 Jan 1984, *Portrait of George Washington with his Wife, Son and Daughter* (oil on canvas, 28 1/2 x 35 1/2 ins / 72.5 x 90 cm) USD 1,500. NEW YORK, 1 Dec 1999, *Portrait of George Washington* (oil on canvas, 30 x 25 ins / 76 x 63 cm) USD 1,000,000. NEW YORK, 30 Nov 2000, *Stedman Bust Portrait of George Washington* (oil on canvas, 30 x 25 ins / 76 x 63 cm) USD 650,000.

SAVAGE, Eugene Francis
American, 20th century.
Born 29 March 1883, in Covington (Indiana); died 1978.
Painter. History painting, genre scenes. Murals.

Eugene Savage studied at the Corcoran School in Washington, the Chicago Academy and under Groeber in Munich. He was an alumni member of the American Academy in Rome. He received many awards, including a gold medal in New York in 1921.

Savage mainly painted genre scenes, but also produced some works depicting events in history. He also painted mural panels and easel paintings in the art deco style of the 1920s.

MUSEUMS AND GALLERIES:
CHICAGO (AI) - ST LOUIS (AM).

AUCTION RECORDS:
NEW YORK, 29 April 1976, *The Orchid Trail* (1935, oil on canvas, 23 x 21 ins / 58.5 x 53.3 cm) USD 1,100. NEW YORK, 26 Sept 1990, *Pastoral* (tempera and gold-leaf/panel, 28 x 28 ins / 71.1 x 71.1 cm) USD 44,000. NEW YORK, 12 April 1991, *Mid-Westchester* (1947, oil on canvas, 29 1/4 x 34 1/2 ins / 74.3 x 87.6 cm) USD 4,400. NEW YORK, 28 Sept 1995, *Last Port* (1946, oil on canvas, 18 1/2 x 25 1/4 ins / 47 x 64.1 cm) USD 4,312. NEW YORK, 27 May 1999, *Pastoral* (c. 1913, tempera and gold leaf on cradled panel, 28 x 28 ins / 71 x 71 cm) USD 65,000. OAK PARK, 19 March 2000, *Faith Hope and Charity* (1948, oil on canvas, 17 x 17 ins / 43 x 43 cm) USD 2,600. SAN FRANCISCO, 9 June 2002, *Expulsion from Eden* (tempera on panel, 22 x 19 ins / 55 x 49 cm) USD 6,500. NEW YORK, 30 Oct 2003, *Bathers* (oil on canvas, 29 x 28 ins / 74 x 71 cm) USD 17,000. PASADENA, 15 June 2004, *Figure in Tropical Landscape* (1953, oil on canvasboard, 11 x 15 ins / 28 x 38 cm) USD 4,500.

SAVAGE, James Henry
British, 19th century.
Born 1813, in London.
Painter. History painting, genre scenes.

James Henry Savage studied at the Academy in London. He also travelled extensively in Italy and spent some time in Munich.

SAVAGE, John
Irish, 14th century.
Active in Dublin in 1344.
Sculptor (wood).

SAVAGE, John
British, 17th - 18th century.
Active in London from 1680 to 1700.
Engraver.

John Savage appears to have been a popular engraver in his day. He is noted for his portrayals of notorious criminals, but also engraved likenesses of leading public figures and contributed illustration to Tempest's *Town Cries of London.*

SAVAGE, Marguerite D.
American, 20th century.
Painter, illustrator.

Marguerite Savage studied under Edmund Messer and Morse in Washington, and Richard Miller in Paris, and exhibited in Cleveland, New York and Washington. She also produced illustrations for magazines.

SAVAGE, William
British, 18th - 19th century.
Born 1770, in Howden; died 25 July 1843, in London.
Painter, engraver.

William Savage studied at the Royal Academy Schools and went on to make a name for himself as a decorative artist and wrote *Practical Hints on Decorative Painting,* with woodcut colour illustrations, published in 1822 by the Type Press.

SAVAIGE, Jacob. See **SAUVAGE**

SAVAJOLS-CARLE, Odile
French, 20th century.
Born 1923, in Marseilles.
Painter, draughtswoman. Landscapes.

Odile Savajols-Carle studied philosophy and then took up painting. She held solo exhibitions in Marseilles and was awarded the Prix de la Ville de Cassis in 1959 and the Prix de l'Association France-Israël in 1961.

Her landscapes, fluidly painted in suggestive half-tones, are taken from nature and tend towards a bareness that in 1956 became almost abstraction. Later she drew in the open-air, using diluted acrylic with pastel heightening, and sometimes adding text. She also contributed to the illustration of books.

BIBLIOGRAPHY:
Cantini 69. Naissance d'une collection, exhibition catalogue, Musée Cantini, Marseilles, 1969. *L'Art moderne à Marseille. La Collection du Musée Cantini,* Musée Cantini, Marseilles, 1988.

MUSEUMS AND GALLERIES:
MARSEILLES (Mus. Cantini): *The Sea* (1957).

SAVALO. See **SAWALO**

SAVANNI, Francesco, or Savani
Italian, 18th century.
Born 1723, in Brescia; died 4 May 1772, in Brescia.
Painter.

The pupil of Angelo Paglia and Francesco Monti, Francesco Savanni painted altarpieces for several churches in and around Brescia.

SAVARD, Jean
French, 19th century.
Painter. Portraits.

He exhibited at the Salon between 1831 and 1848.

SAVART, Pierre
French, 18th century.
Born 1737, in St-Pierre-de-Thimer (Eure-et-Loir); died after 1780.
Draughtsman, engraver (burin), print publisher.

Savart was a remarkable artist who mainly engraved portraits after the French masters of the 17th and 18th centuries. His style recalls that of Ficquet. According to *Bryan's Dictionary*, he was born in Paris in 1750.

SAVARUEV, Konstantin Yakovlevich, or
Zavartsev or Zavaruev
Russian, 19th century.
Born 17 May 1804.
Portrait artist.

Konstantin Yakovlevich Savaruev studied at the art academy in St Petersburg.

SAVARY. See also **SAVERY**

SAVARY, A. (Mlle)
French, 19th century.
Painter. Portraits.

She showed her work at the Salons of 1833 and 1834.

SAVARY, Adolphe Auguste
French, 19th century.
Born in Lille.
Painter. Landscapes.

A pupil of Moral, he first exhibited at the Salon in 1880.

SAVARY, Auguste
French, 19th century.
Born 15 April 1799, in Nantes.
Painter. Landscapes.

He was a pupil of Boissier. He entered the École des Beaux-Arts in Paris on 27 May 1819, and exhibited at the Salon between 1824 and 1859.

AUCTION RECORDS:
PARIS, 7-8 Dec 1923, *Animated Landscapes* (two canvases) FRF 500. PARIS, 1 July 1924, *View of Switzerland*, FRF 180.

SAVARY, Charles de. See **DESAVARY Charles Paul**

SAVARY, Claude
French, 17th century.
Active in Lyons during the first half of the 17th century.
Engraver (burin), painter, print publisher. Historical subjects.

Savary engraved historical subjects.

AUCTION RECORDS:
PARIS, 26 Feb 1979, *Walk to Calvary* (1672, oil/copper, 27 1/2 x 35 ins / 70 x 88 cm) FRF 5,500.

SAVARY, Gilles
Flemish School, 15th century.
Painter.

Gilles Savary painted an altarpiece for the church of St Peter in Roye in 1492.

SAVARY, Jacob. See **SAVERY**

SAVARY, Maurice Robert
French, 20th century.
Born 20 April 1920, in Paris; died 2000.
Painter, watercolourist, lithographer, illustrator. Figures, nudes, portraits, interiors, landscapes, landscapes with figures, urban landscapes, gardens, waterscapes, seascapes, still-lifes, flowers. Decorative panels, designs for stained glass.

Maurice Robert Savary was a pupil of Nicolas Untersteller and Maurice Brianchon at the École des Beaux-Arts, Paris, from 1940 to 1949. He spent time in Madrid from 1948 to 1949, then went to Italy, returning with the Prix de Rome. He was then appointed a professor at the École des Beaux-Arts, Rouen. From 1957 he lived in Paris and passed most of his summers in Collioure. He won a number of awards, including: 1950, the First Grand Prix de Rome; 1948, the Casa Velázquez prize, Madrid; 1957, the international prize at the Menton Biennale; 1975, gold medal at the Salon des artistes Français, Paris; 1982, medal at the Academie des Beaux-Arts Institut de France; 1985, silver medal at the Salon de la Marine, Paris, and a gold medal two years later.

He exhibited at the Paris salons and other group exhibitions: from 1946, the Salon de Mai, the Salon des Tuileries; from 1949, the Salon des Independents, the Salon des Moins de Trente ans; 1952, the 2nd São Paulo Biennale; 1955, Galerie Drouant-David and Galerie Guiot, Paris; 1960, Musée Galliéra, Paris; from 1960, Salon Comparaisons; 1962, 1976 Galerie Guiot, Paris; and the Salon des Artistes Français, the Salon d'Automne, of which he was a member, and the Salon de la Société Nationale des Beaux-Arts.

He held solo shows in various French and foreign towns, including Düsseldorf in 1986. In 2002 the Chisseaux Rive Gauche Galerie, Paris, organised a homage to him with a group of works taken from various collections and studios.

Initially, influenced by Spanish painting, his palette veered to browns and greys and his vision of the world was organised on the architectural principles of Cézanne. We can also detect the influence of Edouard Pignon. However, he soon discovered his own style, as he interpreted landscapes he was moved by when out walking. He painted large-format works depicting Normandy and the South of France; and views of Paris from the Butte de Montmartre (one of his favourite subjects) to Notre Dame, famous buildings or crowded scenes of the popular quarters. He also painted decorative panels in: 1956, the Palais des Consuls, Rouen; 1960, the École Nationale de la Marine Marchande, Nantes; 1961, the Halles aux Toiles, Rouen; 1967, the Lycée Claude Monet, Le Havre; 1970, the lycée of Cherbourg; 1980, the sculpture lecture room of the lycée of Fécamp; and, 1982, the school of Neubourg. He illustrated St-Exupéry's *Vol de Nuit* (*Night Flight*), Eugène Dabit's *Les Faubourgs de Paris* (*The Suburbs of Paris*), and Jean Giono's *Colline* (*Hill*).

He was a poet of colour, inviting us to share his joie de vivre and his passionate love of nature. Raymond Cogniat writes of him, '... white becomes for him, as it did for Bonnard, a colour in itself, rich in subtleties; it is a way of heightening the whole range of colours and linking them with light and freshness...'.

Savary

BIBLIOGRAPHY:
Savary, exhibition catalogue, Gal. Guiot, Paris, 1976. Lespinasse, François, *Savary*, Imprimerie S.I.C., Lagny-sur-Marne, 1990. Harambourg, Lydia, *L'École de Paris 1945-1965. Dictionnaire des peintres*, Ides et Calendes, Neuchâtel, 1993.

MUSEUMS AND GALLERIES:
PARIS (MAMVP) - PARIS (MNAM-CCI) - ROUEN (MBA).

AUCTION RECORDS:
VERSAILLES, 16 Nov 1980, *Walkers in a Wood* (oil on canvas, 32 x 46 ins / 81 x 116 cm) FRF 4,300. VERSAILLES, 25 Sept 1988, *Garden in Magagnosc* (oil on canvas, 25 1/2 x 32 ins / 65 x 81 cm) FRF 8,000. NEUILLY, 27 March 1990, *Collioure* (oil on canvas, 23 1/2 x 29 1/4 ins / 60 x 74 cm) FRF 15,500. PARIS, 6 June 1990, *Blue Flowers* (1951, oil on panel, 29 x 13 ins / 73.5 x 33 cm) FRF 7,200. PARIS, 18 July 1990, *Summer in Cabris* (oil on canvas, 23 1/2 x 28 3/4 ins / 60 x 73 cm) FRF 7,500. PARIS, 17 Oct 1990, *Port* (oil on canvas, 23 1/2 x 28 3/4 ins / 60 x 73 cm) FRF 5,500. CALAIS, 9 Dec 1990, *Regatta in La Baule* (1957, oil on canvas, 21 1/4 x 25 1/2 ins / 54 x 65 cm) FRF 12,000. PARIS, 6 Feb 1991, *Gardens on the Estérel* (oil on canvas, 28 3/4 x 36 1/4 ins / 73 x 92 cm) FRF 8,000. NEUILLY, 11 June 1991, *Façade in Montmartre* (oil on canvas, 39 1/4 x 28 3/4 ins / 100 x 73 cm) FRF 9,600. PARIS, 20 Nov 1991, *Notre Dame, Paris* (oil on canvas, 28 3/4 x 23 1/2 ins / 73 x 60 cm) FRF 10,000. PARIS, 25 March 1993, *Public Park* (oil on canvas, 23 3/4 x 28 3/4 ins / 60.5 x 73 cm) FRF 6,000. ZURICH, 21 April 1993, *Quay on the Île St-*

Denis (oil on canvas, 21 1/4 x 32 ins / 54 x 81 cm) CHF 950. PARIS, 7 June 1995, *Mediterranean Beach* (oil on canvas, 29 1/4 x 35 1/2 ins / 74 x 90 cm) FRF 7,100. PARIS, 25 Feb 1996, *Street in Grasse* (oil on canvas, 36 1/4 x 23 1/2 ins / 92 x 60 cm) FRF 10,000. CALAIS, 15 Dec 1996, *Orchestra of the Paris Conservatoire* (oil on canvas, 19 3/4 x 25 1/4 ins / 50 x 64 cm) FRF 7,000. PARIS, 25 Feb 1997, *Afternoon in Cannes, the Croisette* (1950, oil on canvas, 23 1/2 x 29 1/2 ins / 60 x 75 cm) FRF 6,000. PARIS, 20 March 1998, *Paris, the Sacré Coeur* (1968, oil on canvas, 28 1/4 x 23 1/2 ins / 72 x 60 cm) FRF 5,000. PARIS, 5 May 1999, *Provence in May* (1966, oil on canvas, 35 x 46 ins / 89 x 116 cm) FRF 12,000. VERSAILLES, 10 June 2001, *View of Sacré-Coeur* (oil on canvas, 36 x 29 ins / 92 x 73 cm) FRF 18,000. PARIS, 27 Oct 2001, *Landscape* (oil on canvas, 29 x 36 ins / 73 x 92 cm) FRF 13,000. PARIS, 14 May 2003, *Beach* (oil on canvas, 32 x 39 ins / 81 x 100 cm) EUR 2,250. CALAIS, 9 Nov 2003, *Spring at Grasse* (1969, oil on canvas, 57 x 45 ins / 146 x 114 cm) EUR 1,900.

SAVARY DE PAYERNE, Lily. See **KÖNIG**

SAVAYGE, Jacob. See **SAUVAGE**

SAVAZZI, Vittorino

Italian, 18th century.

Born in Viadana (Lombardy); died 17 September 1792.

Sculptor (wood).

This artist carved the organ chest and tribune in St Peter's church in Viadana.

SAVAZZINI, Antonio

Italian, 18th - 19th century.

Born 14 July 1766, in Parma; died 3 June 1822, in Parma.

Painter.

Having studied in Parma, Antonio Savazzini painted religious subjects and portraits.

SAVE, Gaston Gilbert Daniel

French, 19th century.

Born 22 August 1844, in St-Dié (Vosges); died 20 July 1901, in St-Dié.

Painter, draughtsman, lithographer.

This artist was a pupil of Gleyre. He worked in Strasbourg, Nancy and St-Dié, eastern France. He painted religious pictures and designed theatre sets.

SAVE, Philippe de

Flemish School, 16th century.

Sculptor (wood).

Philippe de Save carved a statue of St Romuald for Mechelen Cathedral.

SAVEL, Ilja

Czechoslovak, 20th - 21st century.

Born 9 February 1951.

Painter. Interiors, still-lifes.

Ilja Savel studied at the school of fine arts in Prague and with F. Jiroudek. He has exhibited in Czechoslovakia, Sweden, Russia, Russia, Italy, Germany and Cuba.

SAVEL, Vladimir (Jr.)

Czechoslovak, 20th - 21st century.

Born 8 November 1949.

Painter. Genre scenes, still-lifes.

Vladimir Savel was the pupil of Z. Sykora and K. Linhart. His work has featured in many exhibitions abroad, including: 1984, Utrecht; 1987, Rotterdam; 1988, Frederikshavn (Denmark); 1989, Damme (Belgium); 1990, Vilnius (Lithuania); 1991, Avesta (Sweden), Munich and Turin; 1992, Rome and Barcelona.

MUSEUMS AND GALLERIES:

FREDERIKSHAVN (Kunstmuseum) - PESCARA (Museo Civico Basilio Cascella) - VILNIUS (Library).

AUCTION RECORDS:

PARIS, 31 Jan 1993, *Still-life with Edelweiss* (oil on panel, 23 1/2 x 20 1/2 ins / 60 x 52 cm) FRF 3,000.

SAVELBERGEN, G. H.

Dutch, 17th century.

Active c. 1620.

Draughtsman.

SAVELBERGEN VAN

Dutch, 17th century.

Active in Amsterdam in 1619.

Glass painter.

SAVELEV, Dmitri Savelevich

Russian, 19th century.

Born 1807; died 1843.

Sculptor.

Dmitri Savelevich Savelev studied at the art academy in St Petersburg. He sculpted busts.

SAVELIEV, Fiodor

Russian, 20th century.

Born 1917, near Vitebsk.

Painter. Landscapes.

Fiodor Saveliev studied at the school of fine art in Vitebsk. He was a member of the Association of Artists of the U.S.S.R.

SAVELIEV, Slava

Russian, 20th century.

Born 1944, in Moscow.

Active in France from 1982.

Painter, watercolourist. Figure compositions, religious subjects, landscapes with figures.

Art Cloche.

Slava Saveliev studied at the school of fine arts in Moscow. He settled in France in 1982, where he is president of the Association des Artistes Russes de Paris and a member of the non-conformist Art Cloche collective. In Moscow, from 1972 to 1982, he belonged to the Group of 20. He has taken part in several Paris salons, such as the Salon d'Automne in 1983, the Salon d'Art Sacré in 1984, the Salon de Mai in 1985 and Salon des Artistes Français in 1988. He also exhibited in Madrid and Brussels in 1990. In 1963, he had his first solo exhibition, in Moscow.

BIBLIOGRAPHY:

Art cloche. Élément pour une rétrospective. Squatt artistique, auction catalogue, Maître Pierre Cornette de Saint-Cyr, Paris, 30 January 1989. *L'École de Léningrad*, auction catalogue, Drouot, Paris, 19 November 1990.

MUSEUMS AND GALLERIES:

GENEVA (Petit Palais) - PARIS (Mus. d'Art Russe Contemp.).

AUCTION RECORDS:

PARIS, 27 Nov 1989, *Clown* (1989, watercolour/paper, 24 x 19 ins / 61 x 48 cm) FRF 8,600; *Musicians* (watercolour/paper, 28 x 26 1/2 ins / 71 x 67 cm) FRF 5,000. PARIS, 11 June 1990, *Musicians* (watercolour/paper, 23 1/2 x 28 1/4 ins / 60 x 72 cm) FRF 4,500. PARIS, 19 Nov 1990, *Eternal Wanderer* (watercolour/paper, 22 x 29 1/4 ins / 55 x 74 cm) FRF 4,000.

SAVELIEVA, Valentina

Russian, 20th century.

Born 1938, in Leningrad (now St Petersburg).

Painter. Nudes, still-lifes.

Valentina Savelieva trained at the Ilya Repin Institute where she was V. M. Oreshnikov's student. She became a member of the Association of Leningrad Painters.

Museums and Galleries:
Kiev (Museum of Russian Art) - Krasnodar (MFA) - Moscow (Ministry of Culture) - Omsk (MCA) - St Petersburg (Gosudarstvennyj Muz. Istorii) - St Petersburg (Gosudarstvennyj Russkij Muz.).
Auction records:
Paris, 26 April 1991, *Nude Seated* (oil on canvas, 31 1/4 x 23 1/2 ins / 79.2 x 59.6 cm) FRF 11,000. Paris, 24 Sept 1991, *Latest News* (oil on canvas, 48 x 28 3/4 ins / 122 x 73 cm) FRF 6,500. Paris, 5 April 1992, *Flowers of the Fields* (oil on canvas, 24 1/4 x 31 3/4 ins / 61.5 x 80.5 cm) FRF 4,000. Paris, 23 Nov 1992, *Still-life* (oil on canvas, 23 1/2 x 30 3/4 ins / 59.4 x 78.4 cm) FRF 8,500. Paris, 25 Jan 1993, *Still-life with Apples* (oil on canvas, 28 1/4 x 39 1/4 ins / 72 x 100 cm) FRF 4,000. Paris, 13 Dec 1993, *Table of Fruit* (oil on canvas, 25 1/4 x 27 1/4 ins / 64 x 69.5 cm) FRF 5,000. Paris, 3 Oct 1994, *Still-life with Fruit* (oil on canvas, 25 1/2 x 27 1/4 ins / 64.5 x 69.5 cm) FRF 10,100. Paris, 9 Oct 1995, *Still-life with Fruit* (oil on canvas, 25 1/2 x 31 1/2 ins / 65 x 80 cm) FRF 4,100.

SAVELLI. See **SPERANDIO Savelli**

SAVELLI, Angelo
Italian, 20th century.
Born 30 October 1911, in Pizzo Calabro (Catanzaro); died 1995.
Also active in the USA.
Painter, engraver.

Angelo Savelli studied at the Liceo Artistico in Rome. He won a national fresco competition in 1935 and in 1948 he was awarded a bursary to study in Paris. In 1954, he went to live in the USA where he taught painting at the New School for Social Research in New York and at Pennsylvania University. Although his work developed into a non-figurative style, he remained faithful to the expressive energy of his first Italian period and the Abstract Expressionists. He also made prints, sometimes combining a relief impression without ink with the pale tones characteristic of colour lithography. He sought rather to enrich the whiteness of the paper than to create explosive forms.

Savelli's work has featured in various collective exhibitions including the Rome Quadriennale in 1943. 1948 and 1959; Venice Biennale in 1950, 1952 and 1954; in Paris, Helsinki, Göteborg, Oslo and Copenhagen in 1951 and in exhibitions of Italian art in Austria. He has also exhibited in Cairo, Alexandria, Buenos Aires, Washington, New York and Switzerland.
Auction records:
Rome, 17 April 1989, *Friends* (1941, oil on canvas, 19 x 21 1/4 ins / 48 x 54 cm) ITL 4,000,000. Milan, 20 May 1996, *Irregular Shape* (1975, Liquitex/canvas, 19 3/4 x 23 1/4 ins / 50 x 59 cm) ITL 3,220,000. Lambertville, 24 April 2004, *Paradise VI* (1969, acrylic and rope on wood, 5 x 4 ins / 12 x 10 cm) USD 1,800.

SAVELLI, Cosimo
Italian, 17th century.
Active in Rome in 1632.
Painter.

SAVELLI, Giovanni Battista
Italian, 18th century.
Painter.

Giovanni Battista Savelli painted a *Transfiguration of St Dominic* on the ceiling of the church of S Domenico in Atri.

SAVELLY (Mme)
French, 19th century.
Born c. 1780, in Nantes.
Portrait painter.

SAVERIJS, Albert and Jan. See **SAVERYS**

SAVEROT, Alain
French, 20th - 21st century.
Born 25 March 1947, in Sousse, Tunisia.
Painter (including mixed media). Murals.

Alain Saverot studied at the École des Beaux-Arts in Dijon from 1964 to 1967.

In 1982, he was involved in the painting of a 325 feet (100 metre) long fresco in colour and in relief on the Berlin Wall. His work is distinguished as a whole by a strong graphic content and by bursts of strong colour.

He has shown his work at group exhibitions and one-man shows: in 1973, at the École des Beaux-Arts in Paris; in 1975-1976, at the Paris Salon des Artistes Français (of which he remained a member until 1983); in 1987, 1991 and 1992, in Tokyo; in 1987-1988, in Bern, Brussels, London, Madrid and Rome; in 1988, in Sydney; in 1990, at the Galerie Ariane in Paris; and, on several occasions, at art fairs in Tokyo, Taipei, Hong Kong and Singapore.
Museums and Galleries:
Melun (Hôtel de la Préfecture).

SAVERY. See also **XAVERY**

SAVERY, Butler Frederic
French, 19th century.
Born in Paris.
Painter. Seascapes.

He was a pupil of Kessier and Deisseldorf. He debuted at the Salon in 1863.

SAVERY, Claude. See **SAVARY**

SAVERY, Jacob I or Jacques
Flemish School, 16th century.
Born c. 1545, in Courtrai; died 1602, in Amsterdam, of the plague.
Active in Holland.
Miniaturist, draughtsman, painter (gouache), engraver (etching). History painting, genre scenes, landscapes, flowers, animals.

Jacob Savery I was the father of Jacob Savery the Younger and may have been the brother or father of Roeland Savery. He was a pupil of Hans Bol and became a burgher of Amsterdam in 1591. Frans Pietersz. Grebber was a pupil of his. His pen drawings are very similar to those of Pieter Bruegel the Elder.

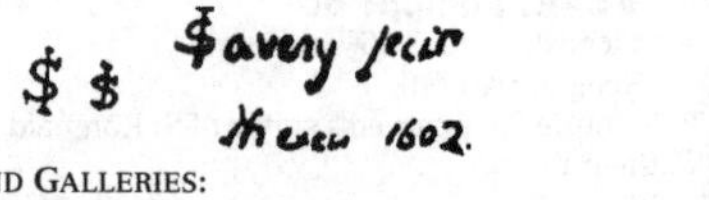

Museums and Galleries:
Amsterdam (Rijksmus.): *The Daughter of Jephtha Greeting her Father* (miniature) - Berlin (Kupferstichkabinet) - London (Victoria and Albert Mus.).
Auction records:
Paris, 24 March 1953, *Harvest in the Village; Approach to the Village* (two pendants) FRF 480,000. London, 29 June 1960, *Spring Flowers*, GBP 520. London, 13 Dec 1973, *Cavalry Charge* (gouache) GBP 2,000. Amsterdam, 27 Nov 1979, *Orpheus Playing his Harp among the Animals* (oil on panel, 18 1/4 x 36 1/2 ins / 46.5 x 92.5 cm) NLG 60,000. New York, 21 Jan 1982, *Village Fair* (oil on panel, 10 x 14 3/4 ins / 25.5 x 37.5 cm) USD 125,00. London, 10 Dec 1993, *Town in Winter with a Marriage Procession and Woodcutters in the Foreground* (oil on panel, 16 1/4 x 26 1/2 ins / 41 x 67.2 cm) GBP 166,500. Amsterdam, 15 Nov 1995, *Landscape with a Village around the Church* (ink, 4 x 8 ins / 10 x 20.1 cm) NLG 16,520. London, 8 Dec 1995, *Vast Landscape with a Hunting Party* (oil on panel, 14 1/4 x 21 1/2 ins / 36.2 x 54.6 cm) GBP 29,900. Amsterdam, 11 Nov 1997, *View of a Mountain River with a Small Fortress and Arch on the Right and a Town in the Distance* (pen and brown ink/traces of black chalk, 9 1/4 x 13 ins / 23.3 x 33 cm)

NLG 177,000. BERLIN, 13 May 2004, *Deer Hunt* (etching copperplate, 8 x 12 ins / 20 x 30 cm) EUR 4,500. BERLIN, 13 May 2004, *Deer Hunt by Water, Chapel and Tower* (etching copperplate, 7 x 11 ins / 19 x 29 cm) EUR 5,300.

SAVERY, Jacob II, the Younger

Dutch, 17th century.

Born c. 1593, in Amsterdam; died after October 1627.

Painter, engraver (etching). Landscapes, village scenes, local scenes (kermesses).

Jacob Savery II was the son of Jacob Savery I; he was married in Amsterdam in 1622.

MUSEUMS AND GALLERIES:

AMSTERDAM: *Wheatfield* - THE HAGUE: *Fête on St Sebastian's Day* - VIENNA: *Church Fête*.

AUCTION RECORDS:

PARIS, 20 Dec 1944, *Village Fête* (attributed) FRF 230,000. LONDON, 21 March 1962, *Adam and Eve Beneath a Tree Surrounded by Animals*, GBP 700. LONDON, 5 July 1985, *The Animals Entering Noah's Ark* (oil on panel, 16 1/2 x 28 1/2 ins / 42 x 72.5 cm) GBP 35,000. LONDON, 10 Dec 1986, *Village Fête on the Outskirts of a Town* (oil on panel, 10 x 14 1/4 ins / 25.5 x 36.5 cm) GBP 46,000. VIENNA, 7 June 2000, *After the Fall of Men* (oil on copper, 7 x 11 ins / 17 x 27 cm) ATS 140,000.

SAVERY, Jacob III

Dutch, 17th century.

Born 1617, in Amsterdam; died 1666; buried on 23 September in Amsterdam.

Engraver (burin), publisher.

Jacob Savery III was the son of Salomon Savery. He was married in Amsterdam in 1643 and 1652, and lived in Delft from 1657 to 1665. The date of his death is disputed.

SAVERY, Jan or Hans

Dutch, 17th century.

Born 1597, in Courtrai; died 1654, in Utrecht.

Painter, engraver, draughtsman. Animals.

Jan or Hans Savery was a pupil of his uncle Roeland. He painted a picture for the Hospital of Job in Utrecht, in 1629. In 1638, he married Wellempgen van Angeren, and he seems to have worked in London around 1651. He also produced etchings.

MUSEUMS AND GALLERIES:

OXFORD: *Ruins on the Banks of a River*.

AUCTION RECORDS:

LONDON, 30 Oct 1985, *Landscape with Wildfowl* (oil on panel, 24 3/4 x 42 1/4 ins / 63 x 107 cm) GBP 7,800. LONDON, 2 July 1990, *A Lion Attacking a Horse, With a Monkey Looking on From a Tree* (black chalk heightened with white and touches of yellow/blue paper, 11 1/4 x 13 3/4 ins / 28.8 x 35 cm) GBP 3,850.

SAVERY, Pieter

Dutch, 17th century.

Died after December 1637.

Active in Haarlem.

Painter. Naval battles.

Pieter Savery was a guild member in 1593.

AUCTION RECORDS:

LONDON, 22 July 1983, *Naval Battle* (oil on panel, 12 1/2 x 17 ins / 32 x 43 cm) GBP 6,000.

SAVERY, Roeland or Roetlandt or Roland or Roelant Jacobsz

Dutch, 17th century.

Born 1576, in Courtrai; died 25 February 1639, in Utrecht.

Painter, engraver (etching). Landscapes, animals, flowers.

Prague School.

Roeland Savery was a pupil of Jacob Savery, his brother or father, and Hans Bol, in Amsterdam around 1591. He was summoned to the court of Henri IV in Paris, and in 1604 to the court of the Holy Roman Emperor Rudolph II, in Prague. At the Emperor's request, he spent two years painting 'wonders' in the Tyrol, and executed numerous works for Rudolph's new gallery at Prague Castle, designed by Giovannia Gargiolli and built between 1587 and 1596. Following Rudolph's death in 1612, he became court painter to the Emperor Matthias before returning to Amsterdam in 1616; he is recorded as a member of the Utrecht painters' guild in 1619. Savery was a renowned artist during his lifetime, but Houbraken states that he died in poverty and insane. His pupils included W. van Nieuwla, Gillis Houdecoeter (in 1594), A. van Everdingen and Isak Major.

His choice of themes in his early work shows the influence of his Flemish compatriot Pieter Breughel the Elder, another favourite of Rudolph II (*Tower of Babel, Country Dance*). Later, his travels in the Tyrol inspired romantic alpine landscapes similar to those of G. van Coninxloo. Human figures in his paintings were gradually replaced by animals; compositions depicting variations on the theme of *Orpheus Taming the Wild Beasts* feature stylised animals and vegetation, reminiscent of arabesque motifs. Savery's compositions characteristically feature strong contrasts between the dark brown and gold tones of the foreground, and a more luminous background painted in silvery greys. His neutral palette is enlivened by touches of bright red. His *Landscape with Birds* (1622) typifies his work as a painter of 'animalist landscapes'. His flower paintings date chiefly from his return to Holland. The *Bouquet* of 1624 synthesises the genre's pictorial traditions, featuring a luminous composition of flowers of every variety, together with insects, lizards and butterflies.

In common with other artists at the court of Rudolph II, such as Joris Hoefnagel, Savery's work reflects an emerging Naturalism and a lively interest in the realistic depiction of everyday 'low' life. His paintings have featured in a number of thematic exhibitions, including *Praga Magica. L'Art à Prague au temps de Rodolphe II* (*Praga Magica. Art in Prague under Rudolph II*) (Musée Magnin, Dijon, 2002). Retrospectives of his work have also been held at the Ghent Fine Arts Museum (1954), and the Wallraf-Richartz-Museum, Cologne (*Roelant Savery in seiner Zeit (1576-1639)* (*Roelant Savery in his time: 1576-1639*), in 1985).

BIBLIOGRAPHY:

Laes, A., '*Le Peintre courtraisien R. Savery*' in *Revue belge d'Archéologie et d'Histoire de l'Art* n° 4, periodical, Académie royale d'archéologie de Belgique, Brussels, 1931. *Roelant Savery in seiner Zeit (1576-1639)*, exhibition catalogue, Wallraf-Richartz-Museum, Cologne, 1985. DaCosta Kaufmann, Thomas, *L'École de Prague*, Flammarion, Paris, 1985. Hairs, Marie-Louise, *Les Peintres de fleurs flamands au XVIIe siècle*, Lefebvre et Gillet, Brussels, 1985. Müllenmeister, Kurt J., *Roelant Savery. Die Gemälde mit kritischem Œuvrekatalog*, Luca Verlag, Freren, 1988.

MUSEUMS AND GALLERIES:

AMSTERDAM: *Deer-hunt in a Rocky Landscape; The Poet's Coronation at the Feast of the Animals; Elijah Fed by the Ravens; The Fable of the Stag Among Bulls; Interior of a Stable; Village Inn* - AVIGNON: two landscapes - BERGAMO (Accademia Carrara): two landscapes - BERLIN (National Mus.): *Paradise* - BRUNSWICK: *Landscape with Bulls; Mountain Landscape* - BRUSSELS: *Landscape with Birds* - COPENHAGEN (Statens Mus. for Kunst): *Bouquet of Flowers* - DRESDEN: *Boar-hunt; Fortress in a Forest; Ruined Towers Near the Lake of Birds; The Animal Kingdom Assembled Before Noah's Ark; Forest Landscape With Animals From the Garden of Eden; Mountain Stream Flowing Between Rocks and Pine Trees; The Animals after the Flood* - FLORENCE: *Landscape with Figures* - FRANKFURT AM MAIN: *Orpheus Among the Wild Beasts* - GENEVA (Mus. Ariana): *Bulls Attacked by a Hyena* - HAMBURG: *Virgin Forest After a Violent Storm* - HANOVER: *Paradise; Mountain Landscapes* - LILLE: *Bouquet of Flowers* - MAINZ: *Landscape with Animals* - MOSCOW (Rumiantsev Mus.): *Courtyard of a Rustic House* - MUNICH: *Boar in a Wood; Paradise* - OBERSCHLEISSHEIM (Neues Schloss Schleissheim, Staatsgal.): *Forest of Oak Trees; Landscape with Animals; Landscape with Ruins and a Cascade* - ORLÉANS: *Landscape* - OSLO: *Landscape with Animals* - RHEIMS: *The Flood; Noah Thanking God for Saving Creation* (c. 1625) - ROTTERDAM: *Hen* - SCHWERIN: *Flowers* - ST PETERSBURG (Hermitage): *Orpheus Taming the Wild Beasts* - THE HAGUE: *Orpheus Taming the Wild Beasts* - TURIN: *Landscape with Wild Animals* - UTRECHT: *The Animals Listening to Orpheus; Flowers* - VALENCIENNES: *Earthly Paradise* - VIENNA: *Orpheus in the Underworld; Paradise* (two landscapes with animals); *Rocky Landscapes; Bouquet in a Vase; Mountain Landscape; Landscape with Animals; Landscape; Landscape with Hunters; Landscape with Orpheus Taming the Wild Beasts* - WARSAW: *Noah's Ark* - WASHINGTON DC (Georgetown University): *Hunting Scene* (c. 1610, oil on canvas).

AUCTION RECORDS:

PARIS, 1705, *Landscape with a Wood-cutter,* FRF 520. AMSTERDAM, 31 March 1706, *Beasts, Birds, Ruins,* FRF 165. PARIS, 1750, *Landscape with Cows, Goats and Ewes,* FRF 460; *Earthly Paradise,* FRF 290. PARIS, 1777, *The Entry of the Animals into Noah's Ark* (gouache) FRF 110. PARIS, 1845, *Wilderness,* FRF 282. PARIS, 1862, *Orpheus Taming the Wild Beasts,* FRF 165. PARIS, 10-12 May 1900, *Seascape,* FRF 130. NEW YORK, 7 May 1909, *St Cecilia,* USD 80. AMSTERDAM, 23 June 1910, *Landscape,* NLG 220. LONDON, 12 April 1911, *Landscape with Figures,* GBP 12. PARIS, 8-10 June 1920, *Seascapes* (two pen drawings) FRF 1,205. PARIS, 29 Dec 1920, *Landscape in the Broglie,* FRF 2,500. LONDON, 28 April 1922, *Fantastic Landscape,* GBP 34. LONDON, 24 Nov 1922, *Gardens of Eden,* GBP 33. PARIS, 14 June 1923, *Paradise,* FRF 1,120. PARIS, 2 Feb 1927, *Orpheus,* FRF 1,100. LONDON, 9 Dec 1927, *Flowers in a Vase, with Reptiles,* GBP 241. PARIS, 23 Jan 1928, *Goatherd and Flock,* FRF 1,600. LONDON, 29 June 1928, *River Scene,* GBP 115. PARIS, 28 Nov 1928, *Houses Beside a Stretch of Water,* FRF 850. LONDON, 22 March 1929, *Tyrolean Landscape,* GBP 504. NEW YORK, 27-28 March 1930, *Virgin Forest,* USD 700. PARIS, 22 Nov 1935, *Landscape with Figures and Animals,* FRF 6,260. LONDON, 10-14 July 1936, *View of Prague* (watercolour) GBP 105. LONDON, 24 July 1936, *River Scene,* GBP 162. PARIS, 10 June 1938, *Mountain Landscape Traversed by a Stream* (gouache) FRF 2,300. PARIS, 7 Dec 1942, *Animals in Paradise* (attributed) FRF 8,000. PARIS, 17-18 Dec 1942, *Orpheus Taming the Wild Beasts* (attributed) FRF 41,000. LONDON, 17 Nov 1944, *Singerie: Barbers,* GBP 273. PARIS, 20 Dec 1944, *Animals at Pasture Among Rocks,* FRF 110,000. PARIS, July 1946, *Earthly Paradise* (attributed) FRF 30,000. LONDON, 10-12 Feb 1947, *Young Artist at Work in a Forest* (black chalk) GBP 70. PARIS, 15 June 1949, *Animals in the Earthly Paradise* (attributed) FRF 25,000. LONDON, 8 Nov 1950, *Wooded Landscape with Christ and Two Apostles in the Foreground,* GBP 340. PARIS, 5 Dec 1950, *Riders on the Edge of a Wood,* FRF 37,000. PARIS, 7 Dec 1950, *Earthly Paradise,* FRF 660,000. BRUSSELS, 12 March 1951, *Animals in Paradise,* BEF 13,000. PARIS, 1 June 1951, *Ruined Palace on the Seashore,* FRF 75,000. PARIS, 6 June 1951, *Rocky Landscape With a Stone Bridge Over a River (recto); Castle (verso)* (pen and wash, heightened with blue) FRF 4,900. PARIS, 2-3 Dec 1952, *Landscape with Birds,* FRF 550,000. PARIS, 29 June 1959, *Earthly Paradise,* FRF 750,000. LONDON, 9 Dec 1959, *Wooded Landscape,* GBP 650. LONDON, 23 March 1960, *Orpheus Taming the Wild Beasts,* GBP 1,150. LONDON, 25 Jan 1961, *Wooded Landscape With Cattle and a Stag in the Background,* GBP 260. LONDON, 12 July 1963, *Wooded Landscape with Figures and Camels,* Gns 1,000. PARIS, 20 March 1964, *Wooded Landscape,* FRF 9,000. LONDON, 24 March 1965, *Bouquet of Flowers,* GBP 8,000. LONDON, 7 July 1966, *Landscape with a Wooden Bridge* (watercolour) GBP 1,120. LONDON, 19 April 1967, *Wooded Landscape with Birds and Animals,* GBP 5,000. COLOGNE, 25 April 1968, *Landscape with Diana the Huntress,* DEM 20,000. COLOGNE, 28 March 1969, *Mountain Landscape,* DEM 70,000. LONDON, 8 Dec 1972, *Riverscape,* Gns 9,500. AMSTERDAM, 26 April 1976, *Village Wedding* (1615, oil on panel, 18 1/2 x 24 ins / 47 x 61 cm) NLG 340,000. AMSTERDAM, 31 Oct 1977, *Hunter with Dogs in a Wooded Landscape* (oil/copper, 4 1/2 x 6 1/4 ins / 11.4 x 15.8 cm) NLG 70,000. NEW YORK, 12 Jan 1979, *Fantastic Landscape* (1613, oil on panel, 7 x 11 ins / 17.5 x 27 cm) USD 130,000. LONDON, 24 June 1980, *Thatched Cottages Reflected in a Pond (recto); Study of Roots (verso)* (pen and colour wash heightened with white/greyish-brown paper, 6 1/4 x 8 ins / 15.9 x 20.2 cm) GBP 6,000. AMSTERDAM, 15 Nov 1983, *Riverscape with a Cascade* (black chalk and red wash, 12 1/2 x 16 ins / 31.6 x 40.8 cm) NLG 228,000. LONDON, 6 July 1984, *Gardens of Eden, with the Temptation of Adam by Eve* (1620, oil on panel, 33 1/4 x 55 ins / 84.4 x 139.8 cm) GBP 110,000. LONDON, 3 April 1985, *Old Man Seated in a Forest* (oil on panel, 16 1/4 x 11 ins / 41 x 28 cm) GBP 100,000. LONDON, 30 June 1986, *Study of a Peasant, Seen From the Back (verso); Peasant Carrying a Bundle of Sharpened Sticks (verso)* (pen and wash, 6 1/4 x 4 ins / 16 x 10.1 cm) GBP 6,800. LONDON, 8 July 1987, *Adam and Eve* (1618, oil on panel, 31 1/2 x 54 ins / 80 x 137 cm) GBP 155,000. LONDON, 22 April 1988, *Orpheus Taming the Wild Beasts* (1621, oil on panel, 20 x 35 3/4 ins / 50.8 x 91 cm) GBP 52,800. NEW YORK, 1 June 1990, *Forest Landscape With a Stag, a Boar, Dogs and Birds* (oil on canvas, 26 1/4 x 30 3/4 ins / 66.5 x 78 cm) USD 49,500. NEW YORK, 11 Oct 1990, *Still-life With a Large Floral Composition in a Niche, With a Lizard and Frog* (oil on panel, 15 x 11 ins / 38 x 28 cm) USD 35,200. PARIS, 3 Dec 1990, *Animals Leaving Noah's Ark* (1610, oil on panel, 22 x 39 3/4 ins / 56 x 101 cm) FRF 4,700,000. NEW YORK, 31 May 1991, *Landscape with Hunters and a River Flowing Between Wooded Banks* (oil on panel, 23 1/2 x 18 1/4 ins / 59.7 x 46.4 cm) USD 99,000. LONDON, 3 July 1991, *Shepherds and Their Flocks in a Cave* (1613, oil on panel, 6 1/2 x 9 1/4 ins / 16.5 x 23.3 cm) GBP 35,200. LONDON, 1 Nov 1991, *Fishermen Unloading Their Catch on a Rocky Coast Under Stormy Skies Pierced by the Sun's Rays* (oil on panel). LONDON, 11 Dec 1992, *Street Battle 15 February 1611 on Petikostelni Square, in Prague* (oil on panel, 9 1/2 ins / 24 cm, 2 1/4 x 13 3/4 ins/6 x 35 cm, 3/4 ins/2 cm) GBP 38,500. NEW YORK, 19 May 1993, *Extensive Wooded Landscape with Tower, Ruins and Other Buildings near a Waterfall* (oil on panel, 11 1/2 x 19 1/4 ins / 29.2 x 49.2 cm) USD 40,250. PARIS, 29 March 1994, *Exploitation of a Stone Quarry at the Foot of an Abbey* (oil on oak panel, 7 x 11 ins / 17.5 x 27 cm) FRF 1,800,000. AMSTERDAM, 17 Nov 1994, *Orpheus Taming the Wild Beasts* (oil on panel, 11 3/4 x 16 1/4 ins / 30 x 41.2 cm) NLG

299,000. LONDON, 9 Dec 1994, *Mountain Landscape With Peasants on a Footpath* (1607, oil/two copper plates, 6 1/2 x 8 1/2 ins / 16.7 x 21.5 cm) GBP 40,000. PARIS, 12 Dec 1995, *Deer-hunting* (oil on panel, 20 x 30 1/4 ins / 51 x 77 cm) FRF 600,000. NEW YORK, 12 Jan 1996, *Large Floral Composition With Irises, Tulips, Forget-me-nots, Narcissi and Other Flowers in a Jug on a Wooden Table* (10 1/4 x 7 1/4 ins / 26 x 18.3 cm) USD 112,500. LONDON, 3 July 1996, *Rocky Landscape With the Entrance to a Mine* (oil on birch panel, 7 x 10 3/4 ins / 18 x 27.5 cm) GBP 56,500. PARIS, 18 Dec 1996, *Paradise of the Birds* (1637, oil on panel, 11 x 13 3/4 ins / 27 x 35 cm) FRF 180,000. LONDON, 30 Oct 1997, *Two Bulls and a Fox Fighting in a Rocky Landscape with a Stream and Other Animals in the Distance* (1620, oil on canvas, 24 x 33 1/2 ins / 61 x 85 cm) GBP 10,350. LONDON, 16 Dec 1999, *Rocky Wooded Landscape with Cattle* (1626, oil on copper, 8 x 13 ins / 21 x 33 cm) GBP 62,000. LONDON, 6 July 2000, *Coastal Scene under a Glowering Sky, with Goats and Other Animals and Peasants among Ruins* (oil on panel, 15 x 21 ins / 38 x 53 cm) GBP 32,000. LONDON, 6 July 2000, *Orpheus Charming the Animals* (oil on panel, 22 x 39 ins / 56 x 100 cm) GBP 220,000. NEW YORK, 23 Jan 2001, *Peasant Man and Peasant Woman with Basket on her Back. Peasant Man and Woman* (coloured ink over graphite, double-sided, 4 x 6 ins / 10 x 14 cm) USD 32,000. LONDON, 12 July 2001, *Still-life of Iris, Tulip, Rose, and Other Flowers Flanked by Lizard* (1612, oil on copper, 7 x 5 ins / 17 x 13 cm) GBP 1,600,000. NEW YORK, 25 Jan 2002, *Forested Mountain Landscape with Pilgrims on a Road to the Left and a Distant Hilltop Castle* (black chalk and colour wash, 7 x 11 ins / 19 x 27 cm) USD 28,000. VIENNA, 2 Oct 2002, *Landscape with Cows, Stags and Water Flow by Waterfall* (1623, oil on panel, 18 x 25 ins / 45 x 64 cm) EUR 80,000. AMSTERDAM, 14 May 2003, *Wooded River Landscape with Deer, Goats and Lizards by a Waterfall and Cattle* (oil on panel, 22 x 34 ins / 56 x 86 cm) EUR 85,000. LONDON, 10 Dec 2003, *Stag, Deer, Heron and Other Animals in a Forest* (oil on canvas, 30 x 43 ins / 76 x 109 cm) GBP 130,000. NEW YORK, 17 June 2004, *Wooded Landscape with Cow, Birds and Other Animals by a Lake* (oil on panel, 25 x 36 ins / 63 x 92 cm) USD 58,000. PARIS, 29 June 2004, *Animals Coming Out of the Ark* (1619, oil on panel, 22 x 41 ins / 56 x 105 cm) EUR 650,000.

SAVERY, Salomon, or by error Sebastian

Dutch, 17th century.

Born 1594; died after 6 November 1665, in Amsterdam. Active in Amsterdam.

Engraver (burin/etching), painter (?).

Salomon Savery was the nephew of Roelandt Savery. He was active by the age of 16, in 1610. In 1616, he married Mayken Pantens and travelled to England. In 1664, he was a member of the booksellers' guild in Amsterdam. He executed or published copies of Rembrandt's etchings of the *Old Man Seen From the Front, Ecce Homo, Good Samaritan* and *Rat-poison Peddler*.

AUCTION RECORDS:

PARIS, 26 June 1950, *A Fool* (black chalk and wash, attributed) FRF 1,300.

SAVERYS, Albert, or Saverijs

Belgian, 20th century.

Born 12 May 1886, in Deinze (East Flanders); died 29 April 1964, in Deinze.

Painter, designer. Landscapes, landscapes with figures, waterscapes, still-lifes, flowers.

Albert Saverys studied drawing and composition in his native Deinze and did not receive a formal artistic education until 1922, when he enrolled at the fine arts academy in Ghent and studied under Georges Minne. He quickly made a name for himself but continued to develop his creative talent, not least during a sojourn in Moret-sur-Loing in France in 1943. He exhibited at numerous Salons and taught at the fine arts institute in Antwerp from 1935. He was accepted into membership of the Royal Belgian Academy of Sciences, Arts and Letters and was the recipient of numerous awards and distinctions.

Saverys was influenced by Claus and by Luminism, the Belgian style similar to Impressionism. The River Lys emerges as the dominant motif in his landscape work. He was particularly attracted to river landscapes and painted memorable compositions featuring riverbanks and fishing boats while visiting Moret-sur-Loing and Sannois-sur-Seine in 1943. He also painted still-lifes and floral compositions in a style that was pleasing if somewhat disjointed. According to one commentator (Paul Haesarts), Saverys' principal delight as a painter was to 'capture a sense of movement in water, clouds and trees and to render the stillness of fruit, flowers and game'. Saverys was something of an individualist to the extent that he did not mingle with painters of the Laethem School and appears to have been influenced only sporadically by Expressionism.

BIBLIOGRAPHY:

Corbet, A., *Albert Saverys*, De Sikkel, Antwerp, 1950.

MUSEUMS AND GALLERIES:

ANTWERP - BRUGES - BRUSSELS (MBA) - BUDAPEST - EINDHOVEN - FLORENCE - GHENT - GRENOBLE - IXELLES - LA LOUVIÈRE - LIÈGE - LISBON - MECHELEN - MOSCOW - NEW ZEALAND - PARIS - PITTSBURGH - PRAGUE - PRETORIA - RIGA - ROME - TOURNAI - VENICE.

AUCTION RECORDS:

BRUSSELS, 2 Dec 1950, *River Lys in Winter*, BEF 10,000. ANTWERP, 5 Oct 1965, *River Lys at Springtime*, BEF 50,000. ANTWERP, 1-2 Oct 1968, *Still-life with Fish and Oysters*, BEF 360,000. ANTWERP, 22 Oct 1974, *Fair in Mechelen* (1920) BEF 660,000. ANTWERP, 19 Oct 1976, *Village in Winter* (1930, oil on canvas, 23 1/4 x 30 3/4 ins / 59 x 78 cm) BEF 270,000. BRUSSELS, 23 March 1977, *Thaw on the River Lys* (oil on canvas, 35 1/2 x 47 1/4 ins / 90 x 120 cm) BEF 260,000. BREDA, 26 April 1977, *Villefranche* (watercolour, 18 x 26 1/2 ins / 46 x 67 cm) NLG 6,000. BRUSSELS, 24 Oct 1979, *Winter Landscape at Deinze* (oil on canvas, 31 1/2 x 39 1/4 ins / 80 x 100 cm) BEF 600,000. ANTWERP, 22 April 1980, *Landscape with Mill* (watercolour, 13 1/2 x 19 3/4 ins / 34 x 50 cm) BEF 45,000. BRUSSELS, 17 Dec 1981, *Winter Landscape* (oil on canvas, 41 1/4 x 41 1/4 ins / 105 x 105 cm) BEF 375,000. ANTWERP, 26 April 1983, *First Snow* (c. 1924, oil on canvas, 45 1/4 x 48 ins / 115 x 122 cm) BEF 600,000. LOKEREN, 26 May 1984, *Landscape* (watercolour, 19 x 26 1/2 ins / 48 x 67 cm) BEF 160,000. LOKEREN, 19 Oct 1985, *Castle in Flanders* (oil on canvas, 52 x 57 ins / 132 x 145 cm) BEF 330,000. LOKEREN, 18 Oct 1986, *Still-life with Fish* (1962-1963, oil on panel, 31 1/4 x 47 1/4 ins / 79.5 x 120 cm) BEF 650,000. LOKEREN, 28 May 1988, *Winter Landscape* (1942, oil on panel, 39 1/4 x 47 1/4 ins / 100 x 120 cm) BEF 550,000. LOKEREN, 8 Oct 1988, *Meadow with Cattle in the Deinze Region* (oil on canvas, 25 3/4 x 28 ins / 65.5 x 71 cm) BEF 600,000. AMSTERDAM, 24 May 1989, *Village in Winter* (oil on card, 16 x 19 3/4 ins / 40.5 x 50 cm) NLG 31,050. AMSTERDAM, 22 May 1990, *Stand of Willows* (oil on card, 24 x 31 1/2 ins / 61 x 80 cm) NLG 34,500. BRUSSELS, 9 Oct 1990, *Landscape with Watercourse* (watercolour, 19 x 26 3/4 ins / 48 x 68 cm) BEF 85,000. AMSTERDAM, 12 Dec 1990, *Harbour* (ink/paper, 19 1/4 x 27 ins / 49 x 68.5 cm) NLG 4,600. AMSTERDAM, 13 Dec 1990, *River Landscape* (oil on canvas, 34 1/4 x 46 3/4 ins / 87 x 119 cm) NLG 51,750. LOKEREN, 21 March 1992, *Still-life in an Interior with Ivory Walls* (oil on canvas, 49 1/2 x 53 1/2 ins / 126 x 136 cm) BEF 800,000. LOKEREN, 23 May 1992, *Banks of the*

Lys (oil on canvas, 31 1/2 x 39 1/4 ins / 80 x 100 cm) BEF 500,000. LOKEREN, 15 May 1993, *Orchard with Farmhouse in the Background* (1913, oil on canvas, 39 1/4 x 49 1/4 ins / 100 x 125 cm) BEF 600,000. AMSTERDAM, 27-28 May 1993, *Cattle Returning to the Foreshore* (1941, oil on panel, 31 1/2 x 23 1/2 ins / 80 x 60 cm) NLG 20,700; *Snow-covered Landscape* (1916, oil on canvas, 21 1/4 x 27 1/4 ins / 54 x 69.5 cm) NLG 32,200. LOKEREN, 9 Oct 1993, *Still-life with Ducks* (oil on canvas, 39 1/4 x 55 ins / 100 x 140 cm) BEF 700,000. AMSTERDAM, 8 Dec 1993, *River Lys* (gouache/paper, 19 1/2 x 23 1/2 ins / 49.5 x 59.5 cm) NLG 8,050. LOKEREN, 8 Oct 1994, *Still-life with Dead Ducks* (oil on canvas, 39 1/4 x 55 ins / 100 x 140 cm) BEF 550,000. LONDON, 26 Oct 1994, *Landscape with Trees and a Lake* (oil on canvas, 31 1/2 x 39 ins / 80 x 99 cm) GBP 9,200. AMSTERDAM, 6 Dec 1995, *River Landscape in Summer* (oil on card, 15 3/4 x 19 3/4 ins / 40 x 50 cm) NLG 12,650. LOKEREN, 9 March 1996, *Vase of Flowers* (oil on panel, 31 1/2 x 23 1/2 ins / 80 x 60 cm) BEF 360,000. LOKEREN, 18 May 1996, *Procession* (1921, oil on canvas, 35 1/2 x 39 1/4 ins / 90 x 100 cm) BEF 440,000; *Lys River in Winter* (oil on panel, 19 3/4 x 23 1/2 ins / 50 x 60 cm) BEF 280,000. LOKEREN, 5 Oct 1996, *Port of Trouville* (1961, watercolour, 18 x 26 1/2 ins / 46 x 67.5 cm) BEF 110,000. AMSTERDAM, 2-3 June 1997, *River Lys* (1959, oil on canvas, 23 1/2 x 34 1/4 ins / 60 x 87 cm) NLG 29,500. LOKEREN, 11 Oct 1997, *Lys River in Winter* (oil on canvas, 23 1/2 x 31 1/2 ins / 60 x 80 cm) BEF 620,000; *Orchard in Winter* (c. 1955, oil on canvas, 31 3/4 x 39 1/4 ins / 80.5 x 100 cm) BEF 550,000. AMSTERDAM, 2 Dec 1997, *Winter Landscape* (oil on canvas, 39 1/4 x 47 1/4 ins / 100 x 120 cm) NLG 27,676. AMSTERDAM, 12 Oct 1999, *Winter Landscape* (c. 1924, oil on canvas, 47 x 52 ins / 120 x 133 cm) NLG 80,000. AMSTERDAM, 25 Oct 1999, *Wintry Landscape* (oil on canvas, 31 x 39 ins / 80 x 100 cm) NLG 35,000. BRUSSELS, 14 Feb 2000, *Winter at Deinze* (oil on canvas, 39 x 47 ins / 100 x 120 cm) BEF 800,000. ANTWERP, 24 Oct 2000, *Meander of the Lys in Winter* (oil on canvas, 53 x 49 ins / 135 x 125 cm) BEF 1,350,000. AMSTERDAM, 4 Dec 2001, *Trees in a Field* (1916, oil on canvas, 27 x 18 ins / 69 x 45 cm) NLG 55,000. BRUSSELS, 10 Dec 2001, *Winter Landscape at Laethem Saint Martin* (oil on canvas, 35 x 39 ins / 90 x 100 cm) BEF 820,000. BRUSSELS, 28 May 2002, *Bouquet of Arum Lilies in a Vase* (oil on canvas, 39 x 31 ins / 100 x 80 cm) EUR 15,000. BRUSSELS, 26 Nov 2002, *Winter Sun over the Lys* (oil on canvas, 35 x 39 ins / 90 x 100 cm) EUR 18,000. BRUSSELS, 17 June 2003, *Houses by the Lys* (oil on canvas, 33 x 39 ins / 85 x 100 cm) EUR 16,000. AMSTERDAM, 2 Dec 2003, *Landscape* (oil on panel, 31 x 39 ins / 80 x 100 cm) EUR 16,000. AMSTERDAM, 8 June 2004, *Stille Avonden* (1915, oil on canvas, 59 x 49 ins / 151 x 125 cm) EUR 80,000. LOKEREN, 11 Dec 2004, *Blue Avenue with Crop Farm* (oil on canvas, 28 x 39 ins / 70 x 99 cm) EUR 15,000.

SAVERYS, Jan, or Jean
Belgian, 20th century.
Born 1924, in Petegem, near Deinze (East Flanders).
Painter (including gouache), watercolourist, pastellist.
Groupe Art Abstrait.

Jan Saverys was the son of Albert Saverys. He studied at the fine arts academy in Ghent from 1943 to 1946 and at the Académies Libres in Paris from 1946 to 1948. His first abstract works date from 1949 and are reminiscent of the lyrical calligraphy espoused by Hans Hartung or compositions by Huguette-Aimée Bertrand. He was part of the Belgian Art Abstrait (Abstract Art) group and participated in group exhibitions, notably in Belgium (Brussels, Knokke, Antwerp, Charleroi and elsewhere), Norway (Bergen), the United Kingdom (Edinburgh) and Paris (at the Salon des Réalités Nouvelles in 1953 and 1954).

Jan Saverys

BIBLIOGRAPHY:
Seuphor, Michel/Bilcke, Maurits/Sosset, Léon-Louis/Walrens, Jan, *La Peinture abstraite dans les Flandres*, Éd. Arcade, Brussels, 1963.

AUCTION RECORDS:
ANTWERP, 19 Oct 1976, *View at Lerzeke* (pastel, 19 x 26 3/4 ins / 48 x 68 cm) BEF 75,000. LUCERNE, 24 Nov 1990, *Composition* (1953, gouache/paper, 19 1/4 x 23 1/2 ins / 49 x 60 cm) CHF 4,600. LOKEREN, 4 Dec 1993, *Composition* (1951, watercolour, 17 1/4 x 21 3/4 ins / 43.5 x 55.5 cm) BEF 28,000. MUNICH, 25 May 2004, *Abstract Composition* (charcoal and chalks, 23 x 19 ins / 58 x 49 cm) EUR 1,700.

SAVI, Giovanni
Italian, 17th century.
Engraver (etching).

SAVI, Paolo. See **SAVIN**

SAVIGNAC, Alfred de
French, 19th century.
Born 1827, in Niort (Deux-Sèvres); died 1855.
Painter. History painting, religious subjects.

MUSEUMS AND GALLERIES:
NIORT: *Descent from the Cross* (unfinished).

SAVIGNAC, Camille de
French, 19th century.
Painter. Portraits, genre scenes, interiors with figures.

He exhibited at the Paris Salon in 1841 and 1849.

SAVIGNAC, Claude Edme Charles de Lioux de. See **LIOUX DE SAVIGNAC**

SAVIGNAC, Louis de
French, 18th century.
Born 1734.
Painter (porcelain). Landscapes.

Savignac worked in Sèvres from 1752 to 1759.

SAVIGNAC, Raymond
French, 20th century.
Born 6 April 1886, in St-Étienne.
Painter. Landscapes.

Raymond Savignac, a self-taught painter, travelled extensively in tropical countries - Africa, the Americas, the East... He exhibited in Paris in group exhibitions (1929, the Salon d'Automne and later the Salon des Tuileries) and held a solo show there in 1932. He painted many pictures, such as *Sunset in Tahiti*, that were the fruit of his travels. F. Vanderpil called him the `exploring colourist' and M. Gauthier praises his `decorative cadences'.

MUSEUMS AND GALLERIES:
PARIS (Mus. des Arts d'Afrique et d'Océanie).

SAVIGNAC, Raymond
French, 20th century.
Born 6 November 1907, in Paris; died 30 October 2002, in Trouville.
Painter (gouache), draughtsman, poster artist, graphic designer.

While working with various firms, Raymond Savignac from the age of fifteen taught himself the art of graphic design. He published his first poster in 1933 and between 1935 and 1938 he collaborated with Cassandre. In 1948-1949 he and a friend, the graphic designer Bernard Villemot, decided to show their works, including rejected designs, in a gallery in the Rue des Beaux-Arts, Paris. Among them was Savignac's poster *Monsavon with Milk* (1949), in which the cow's udders lead directly into the bar of soap being advertised. This had been turned down by the advertisers, but was reconsidered as a result of the exhibition and eventually used. It was this poster that launched Savignac's career. From 1972 he lived and worked in Trouville and in 2000 a prize bearing his name was set up.

His work was exhibited in several exhibitions and retrospectives: 1971, *Défense d'afficher* (*No Bill-sticking*), Galerie Delpire, Paris; 1982-1983, travelling exhibition in Fréjus, Munich, Honfleur, Trouville; 1996, 2000, La Rampe, Échirolles, as part of the Graphic Design Month; 1998, Carré Ste-Anne, Montpellier; 2001, Bibliothèque Forney, Paris.

After World War II there was an expansion of poster design and advertising, and Savignac was certainly the most popular of the French artists involved. He designed dozens of advertisements for companies such as *Air-Wick, Perrier, Cinzano, Verigoud, Gitanes, Frigeco, Olivetti, Dunlop* 1953, *Life*... In 1969 he designed the sets and costumes for a production of Molière's *L'Avare* (*The Miser*) at the Comédie Française, in 1978 the poster advertising the Poster Museum (later the Advertisement Museum), and in 1996 the poster for the Football World Cup, held that year in France.

In the interests of direct, clear and effective communication, he used a very French style of advertisement, humorous and poetic rather than purely graphic, his taste for jokes growing out of his enthusiasm for the work of Chaplin. In the 1970s, when there was a drop-off in commissions, he created with the support of the gallery owner Delpire `anti-posters'. These are less well-known, but illustrate a vision of society that protests against pollution and subservience to television, and they demonstrate, if it were necessary, the independence of a true artist.

BIBLIOGRAPHY:

Savignac, Raymond/Weil, Alain, *Savignac, l'affiche de A à Z*, Éd. Hoëbeke, Paris, 1987. Lelieur, Anne-Claude/Bachollet, Raymond, *Savignac, affichiste*, exhibition catalogue, catalogue raisonné, Bibliothèque Forney, Paris bibliothèques, Paris, 2001. Jover, Manuel, '*Savignac le sourire de l'affiche*' in *L'Œil* n° 543, periodical, Paris, January 2003.

MUSEUMS AND GALLERIES:

PARIS (Mus. de la Publicité) - TROUVILLE-SUR-MER (Mus. de Trouville villa Montebello): permanent exhibition space.

AUCTION RECORDS:

PARIS, 16 Oct 1982, *Instant Aspro* (gouache and tempera/card, design for a poster, 23 1/2 x 59 ins / 60 x 150 cm) FRF 45,000. PARIS, 24 June 1994, *Extra-Stretch Braces* (gouache, design for a poster, 14 x 20 3/4 ins / 35.5 x 53 cm) FRF 6,000.

SAVIGNAC DE MONTAMY, Achille de

French, 19th century.
Born 1785, in Niort (Deux-Sèvres); died 1857.
Painter. Genre scenes, landscapes.

MUSEUMS AND GALLERIES:

NIORT: *The Rocher du Moulin at Salboeuf*; *Young Shepherd and His Dog*.

AUCTION RECORDS:

PARIS, 20 March 1901, *Landscape with River*; *Mountainous Landscape*, FRF 120.

SAVIGNARD, Dominique

French, 20th - 21st century.
Born 1953.
Painter.

Dominique Savignard studied at the École des Beaux-Arts in Paris and has exhibited solo in Paris from 1988. Marguerite Yourcenar's *Hadrian's Memoirs* (published in 1951) has exerted a strong influence on his painting.

SAVIGNON

French, 20th century.
Painter. Landscapes.

SAVIGNY, Jean-Paul

French, 20th century.
Born 17 June 1933, in Pont-Aven.
Painter, engraver. Portraits, landscapes, waterscapes, still-lifes.

Jean-Paul Savigny studied in Quimper under Robert Villard between 1948 and 1949, at the École Paul Collin from 1950 to 1952, and at the Académie Julian from 1953 to 1954. He exhibited at a group exhibition in St-Servan-sur-Oust and held solo shows that have included: 1970, Quimper; 1971, Pont-l'Abbé; 1972, Paris; 1980, 1984, 1986, 1989, Pont-Aven; 1996, 1997, 1998, Scaër.

Among his works is *The Port of Kerdruc*. His painting makes use of the principle of the prismatic break-down of light and he effectively uses only three colours - blue, yellow and red.

MUSEUMS AND GALLERIES:

BREST: *Snow in Kernéant* - VATICAN (Mus. Vaticani): *Still-life with Carnations*.

SAVII, Tommaso di

Italian, 16th century.
Active in Venice at the end of the 16th century.
Medallist.

MUSEUMS AND GALLERIES:

BERLIN (Bodemus.): *Madonna with St Mark and the Kneeling Doge* (bronze, plaquette).

SAVILL

British, 17th century.
Painter, miniaturist. Portraits.

Savill is noted for *Portrait Miniatures of Samuel Pepys and Spouse* painted in London in or around 1660 at the time of the Restoration of Charles II.

SAVILL, Bruce Wilder, or Saville

American, 20th century.
Born 16 March 1893, in Quincy (Massachusetts); died 1938.
Sculptor.

Bruce Savill studied at the School of Fine Arts in Boston under the direction of Cyrus Dallin and Henry Kitson, and was a member of the American Federation of Arts. He sculpted many commemorative monuments.

SAVILL, Edith

British, 19th century.
Active in London.
Painter. Portraits.

Edith Savill showed examples of her work at the Royal Academy and the Suffolk Street Gallery in London from 1880 to 1883.

SAVILLE, Dorothea

British, 17th century.
Painter. Portraits.

Dorothea Saville worked in London from 1650 to 1660; Mollar and Thomas Cross produced engravings from Dorothea Saville originals.

SAVILLE, Jenny

British, 20th - 21st century.
Born 1970, in Cambridge.
Painter, photographer. Female nudes, portraits.

Jenny Saville graduated from the Glasgow School of Art in 1992 and went on to teach figure painting at the Slade School of Fine Art in London, where she lives and works. Saville experienced immediate success, selling every work she had produced for the graduate exhibition in 1992. She was propelled to fame when British collector Charles Saatchi approached her with an 18-month contract, which culminated in an exhibition, *Young British Artists III*, at the Saatchi Gallery in London in 1994. Her self-portrait *Plan* became the signature piece of the exhibition. The painting shows a nude woman, like a mountain of flesh that rises above the viewer, the woman's tiny face peering from the top of the canvas. Contour lines trace the shapes of the woman's body like lines on a map or lines drawn by a plastic surgeon. Based on the feminist ideas of scholars such as

Luce Irigaray, Saville's work reveals an ambiguity towards the female body and its representation. In 1995 and 1996, Saville collaborated with the photographer Glen Luchford producing a series of works, *Closed Contact #12*, depicting a female model pressed against a sheet of glass. The impression is of a distorted female body, which nevertheless engages the viewer to contemplate its identity, sexuality, and purpose. Saville has participated in a number of group exhibitions including *Jenny Saville/Glen Luchford: A Collaboration*, Pace McGill Gallery, New York in 1996; *Sensation: Young British Artists from the Saatchi Collection*, The Royal Academy of Arts in 1997; *The Nude in Contemporary Art* at Aldrich Museum of Art, Ridgefield, Connecticut in 1999; and *Ant Noises* at the Saatchi Gallery in 2000. Gagosian Gallery in New York hosted *Territories*, a solo exhibition, in 1998.

BIBLIOGRAPHY:

Kent, S., *Young British Artists III*, exhibition catalogue, Saatchi Gallery, London, 1994. Brittain, D., *'Jenny Saville'* in *Creative Camera, 334*, periodical, June-July 1995 (interview with artist). LaGrace Volcano/Weintraub, D. and B. M., *Territories*, exhibition catalogue, Gagosian Gallery, New York, 1999. Kuspit, Donald, *'Jenny Saville at Gagosian'* in *Artforum*, periodical, December 1999. Nochlin, L., *'Floating on Gender Nirvana'* in *Art in America*, vol 33, no. 3, periodical, March 2000. Darwent, Charles, *'Big Really Does Mean Beautiful'* in *Independent on Sunday*, 16 April 2000. Murphy, Anna, *'An Obsession with Bodily Extremes'* in *The Sunday Telegraph*, 3 September 2000.

AUCTION RECORDS:

LONDON, 8 Dec 1999, *Branded* (oil on canvas, 24 x 20 ins / 61 x 51 cm) GBP 32,000. NEW YORK, 17 May 2001, *Interfacing* (oil on canvas, 48 x 40 ins / 122 x 102 cm) USD 175,000. LONDON, 27 June 2001, *Branded* (1992, oil on canvas, 84 x 72 ins / 213 x 183 cm) GBP 300,000. NEW YORK, 14 May 2002, *Figure 11.23* (1997, oil on canvas, 60 x 60 ins / 152 x 152 cm) USD 480,000. LONDON, 25 June 2003, *Untitled* (c. 1990, oil on canvas, 80 x 72 ins / 204 x 183 cm) GBP 280,000. LONDON, 24 June 2004, *Knead* (1995-1996, oil on canvas, 54 x 62 ins / 137 x 157 cm) GBP 180,000. NEW YORK, 9 Nov 2004, *Factor 8* (1992, oil on canvas, 51 x 39 ins / 129 x 98 cm) USD 350,000.

SAVIN, Bashen

Russian, 17th century.
Active in the middle of the 17th century.
Icon painter.

Bashen Savin produced the paintings in the Uspenski Cathedral in Moscow.

SAVIN, Christophe

French, 18th century.
Painter, engraver.

Christophe Savin engraved the portrait of the president, Claude Expilly, for the biography published in 1803 by the abbot J.-C. Martin. The portrait is signed *Savin*. There may be a connection between Christophe, Jacob and Jacques Christophe Savin.

SAVIN, Fedor

Russian, 17th century.
Active c. 1600.
Icon painter.

Fedor Savin executed the paintings in the Solivchegodsk Cathedral in Moscow.

SAVIN, Istoma

Russian, 17th century.
Active c. 1600.
Icon painter.

Istoma Savin worked for the Stroganov family and the Tsar. He was appointed 'Head of the Tsar's Workshop'. His works include a *Virgin of Bogoliubsk*.

MUSEUMS AND GALLERIES:

MOSCOW (State Tretyakov Gal.): *Triptych of Metropolitan Petr*.

SAVIN, Jacob

German, 19th century.
Engraver (burin).

There is perhaps a link between Christophe, Jacob and Jacques Christophe Savin. He was active in Leipzig around 1800.

SAVIN, Jacques Christophe

German, 18th - 19th century.
Painter, engraver, draughtsman. Landscapes.

There is perhaps a link between Christophe, Jacob and Jacques Christophe Savin. He engraved views of Rome and its surrounding areas; Münster and the castle of Wilhelmshöhe near Kassel.

SAVIN, Maurice Louis, pseudonym: Jimmy Savin

French, 20th century.
Born 17 October 1894, in Moras-en-Valloire (Drôme); died 17 March 1973, in Paris.
Painter (gouache), sculptor, medallist, potter, engraver, draughtsman, illustrator, lithographer. Nudes, portraits, genre scenes, still-lifes, landscapes. Designs for tapestries.

After studying at the École Nationale des Arts Décoratifs in 1913, Maurice Louis Savin's artistic career was interrupted by World War I. He was invalided out of the army and awarded the Croix de Guerre, and then studied pottery for several months at the Sèvres factory. He became a friend of the Spanish potter Artigas. He was intensely active during World War II, when, while continuing to paint and pot, he began to work in high-warp tapestry. He visited the Netherlands in 1948, Cairo in 1948, where he taught French tapestry at the school of fine art, and Italy in 1952.

He exhibited regularly at a number of group exhibitions in Paris: regularly at the Salon d'Automne, of which he was a member; 1919-1920, Salon des Humoristes et Caricaturistes; from 1932, the Salon des Tuileries; 1936, Galerie Drouet; 1937, Exposition Universelle; from 1949, Salon de la Société des Peintres Graveurs Français at the Bibliothèque Nationale; 1953, Salon des Peintres de Leur Temps; 1954, the exhibition *École de Paris* (*The Paris School*), Galerie Charpentier; and abroad in Switzerland, Germany and Japan. In 1980 two of his works were exhibited in the exhibition *150 ans de peinture dauphinoise* (*150 Years of Painting from the Dauphiné Region*), Château de la Condamine, Corenc Town Hall. He also held solo shows: 1954, Galerie Drouant-David, Paris; 1958, Galerie Vendôme, Paris; 1962, 1964, 1967, Galerie Drouant, Paris; 1969-1970, Palais de la Méditerranée, Nice. Posthumous retrospectives were held in 1979 at the Musée d'Art Moderne, Paris, and in 1994 at the Château des Adhémar, Montélimar.

He contributed to humorous reviews under the name Jimmy Savin (He exhibited in Paris at the Salon des Humoristes in 1919, and at the Salon des Caricaturistes. He contributed to the reviews *Le Rire*, *Le Sourire* and *La Baïonnette*.). His palette was restrained, making extensive use of browns, reddish-browns, ochre and sienna; and, whether painting fruit or the female body, he aimed to recapture something of the fullness and richness of Rubens. He began to work in ceramics early in his career: a ceiling of porcelain tiles for the Sèvres pavilion at the Exposition Universelle of 1937; a ceramic fountain for the *La Coupole* brasserie, Montparnasse; mural decorations for the town hall of Montélimar, 1938, and, 1939, for the Sanatorium des Étudiants, St-Hilaire. He designed many tapestries, including: *Work and Recreation in the Countryside*, 1942; *The Months of the Year*, twelve tapestries, 1946-1950; *Kermis*, 1945; *Salamander*, 1945. He illustrated A. Spire's *Refuges*, 1927; O. de Serres' *Ecrits sur le Vin*

(*Writings on Wine*), 1946; Maupassant's *Country Tales*, 1948. He also designed medals that were published by the Paris Mint.

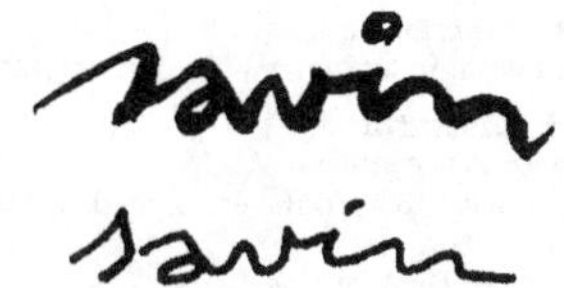

BIBLIOGRAPHY:

Lanoux, Armand, *Savin*, Éd. Pierre Cailler, Geneva, 1967. Wantellet, Maurice, *Deux siècles et plus de peinture dauphinoise*, M. Wantellet, Grenoble, 1987. Harambourg, Lydia, *L'École de Paris 1945-1965. Dictionnaire des peintres*, Ides et Calendes, Neuchâtel, 1993.

MUSEUMS AND GALLERIES:

ALGIERS: *Still-life with Tomatoes*; *Still-life with Drawings*; *Egyptian Negress* - CAIRO: *Hunt* (tapestry) - ÉPINAL (Mus. départemental d'Art ancien et contemporain): *Nude* (1928, on loan from the Musée National d'Art Moderne, Paris) - FAENZA: *Gossip* (faience) - GRENOBLE: *Reclining Nude*; *Still-life*; *Parisian Landscape*; *White Hen* (faience); *Bust of a Faun* (faience) - LAUSANNE: *Thrushes* (tapestry) - LONDON (Victoria and Albert Mus.): tapestry - ORLÉANS: *Woman Weaving a Tapestry* - OSLO: engravings - PARIS (MAMVP): *Nude with Curtain* (1929); , 1944); faience (1945) - PARIS (MNAM-CCI) - PARIS (Mus. du Petit Palais): *Provencal Landscape* (1936); *Standing Nude* (1946); several statuettes in faience (1937) - ROMANS-SUR-ISÈRE: prints - SÈVRES: *Bust of the Artist's Wife* (1940, faience) - ST-ÉTIENNE (Mus. d'Art et d'Industrie): engravings - ST-TROPEZ: *Landscape woth Olive Trees* - STOCKHOLM: *Bust of Mme Rosa Granoff* (faience) - TUNIS: *Open Window* - VALENCIA: *Butcher's Shop*; *Woman in an Interior*; *Landscape* - WARSAW: *A Hamlet*.

AUCTION RECORDS:

PARIS, 22 Oct 1920, *Dance Hall*, FRF 155. PARIS, 14 Nov 1927, *Woman Ironing*, FRF 600. PARIS, 20 June 1944, *Woman Sewing*, FRF 10,000. PARIS, 12 Dec 1946, *Landscape*, FRF 15,500. PARIS, 29 Nov 1954, *Nude*, FRF 28,100. LONDON, 30 Oct 1970, *Violinist*, GBP 280. ZURICH, 16 May 1974, *Beach Scene* (gouache) CHF 4,000. VERSAILLES, 15 June 1976, *Reapers* (oil on canvas, 25 1/2 x 36 1/4 ins / 65 x 92 cm) FRF 20,000. VERSAILLES, 26 Sept 1976, *Provencal Landscape* (watercolour, 12 1/2 x 18 1/4 ins / 31.5 x 46.5 cm) FRF 2,500. VERSAILLES, 4 Dec 1977, *The Three Graces* (oil on canvas, 31 3/4 x 25 1/2 ins / 80.5 x 65 cm) FRF 8,000. VERSAILLES, 13 June 1979, *Reapers Resting* (oil on canvas, 28 3/4 x 39 1/4 ins / 73 x 100 cm) FRF 21,500. VERSAILLES, 29 Nov 1981, *Harvest* (oil on canvas, 44 1/2 x 74 3/4 ins / 113 x 190 cm) FRF 30,000. PARIS, 10 July 1983, *Lunch in the Open Air* (1961, oil on panel, 25 1/2 x 35 3/4 ins / 65 x 91 cm) FRF 31,000. PARIS, 15 March 1985, *Grape-Pickers* (1965, oil on canvas, 21 1/4 x 28 3/4 ins / 54 x 73 cm) FRF 19,000. VERSAILLES, 7 Dec 1986, *Couple in the Country* (1963, oil on canvas, 23 1/2 x 28 3/4 ins / 60 x 73 cm) FRF 53,000. PARIS, 9 Dec 1987, *Rest* (1957, oil on canvas, 25 1/2 x 36 1/4 ins / 65 x 92 cm) FRF 51,000. VERSAILLES, 13 Dec 1987, *Still-life* (1957, oil on canvas, 18 x 22 ins / 46 x 55 cm) FRF 32,000. VERSAILLES, 20 March 1988, *Nude* (1924, oil on canvas, 28 3/4 x 23 1/2 ins / 73 x 60 cm) FRF 11,500; *Still-life with Atlas* (1936, oil on canvas, 21 1/4 x 28 3/4 ins / 54 x 73 cm) FRF 14,000. PARIS, 21 April 1988, *Valleyed Landscape* (oil on canvas, 15 x 18 ins / 38 x 46 cm) FRF 7,500; *Provencal Landscape* (oil on canvas, 15 x 18 ins / 38 x 46 cm) FRF 8,300. PARIS, 12 Dec 1988, *Still-life with Guitar* (1922, oil on canvas, 24 x 15 ins / 61 x 38 cm) FRF 7,000. PARIS, 14 Dec 1988, *Dressing* (1945, oil on canvas, 32 x 26 ins / 81.5 x 66 cm) FRF 40,000. PARIS, 12 Feb 1989, *Landcape in Cassis* (oil on canvas, 21 1/4 x 28 3/4 ins / 54 x 73 cm) FRF 14,000. PARIS, 22 March 1989, *Three Women Bathing* (1967, oil on canvas, 36 1/4 x 25 1/2 ins / 92 x 65 cm) FRF 70,000. PARIS, 4 April 1989, *Two Women Bathing* (1962, oil on canvas, 25 1/2 x 36 1/4 ins / 65 x 92 cm) FRF 56,000. PARIS, 21 June 1989, *Women Bathing, with Dog* (oil on canvas, 28 3/4 x 36 1/4 ins / 73 x 92 cm) FRF 70,000. LE TOUQUET, 12 Nov 1989, *Wooded Walk near the Porte de Vanves* (oil on canvas, 15 x 18 ins / 38 x 46 cm) FRF 20,000. PARIS, 26 Jan 1990, *Hunting* (oil on paper, 33 1/2 x 61 1/2 ins / 85 x 156 cm) FRF 10,000. CALAIS, 4 March 1990, *Young Woman on a Terrace* (oil on canvas, 15 x 18 ins / 38 x 46 cm) FRF 21,000. PARIS, 26 April 1990, *Market Scene* (oil on canvas) FRF 125,000. PARIS, 6 July 1990, *Woman Wearing a Hat* (oil on canvas) FRF 12,000. FONTAINEBLEAU, 18 Nov 1990, *Nude with Mirror* (1936, oil on canvas, 46 x 32 ins / 116 x 81 cm) FRF 47,500. PARIS, 20 Jan 1991, *A Secret* (1949, oil on canvas, 21 1/4 x 28 1/2 ins / 54 x 72.5 cm) FRF 56,000. PARIS, 14 June 1991, *Success* (oil on canvas, 46 x 35 ins / 116 x 89 cm) FRF 82,000. PARIS, 6 Dec 1991, *Regulars in a Bar* (1963, oil on canvas, 36 1/4 x 25 1/2 ins / 92 x 65 cm) FRF 85,000. LOKEREN, 21 March 1992, *Meadow in Normandy* (1939, oil on panel, 15 x 22 ins / 38 x 55 cm) BEF 65,000. PARIS, 23 March 1992, *Woman Wearing a Red Dress* (oil on canvas, 22 x 18 ins / 55 x 46 cm) FRF 20,000. LE TOUQUET, 8 Nov 1992, *Reclining Nude* (oil on canvas, 19 3/4 x 24 ins / 50 x 61 cm) FRF 20,000. PARIS, 3 Dec 1993, *Seated Woman Bathing* (1960, oil on canvas, 28 3/4 x 21 1/4 ins / 73 x 54 cm) FRF 19,000. PARIS, 8 Dec 1994, *Red Oxen* (1944, oil on canvas, 55 x 74 3/4 ins / 140 x 190 cm) FRF 125,000. CALAIS, 24 March 1996, *Sleeping Nude* (1941, oil on canvas, 21 1/4 x 28 3/4 ins / 54 x 73 cm) FRF 17,000. PARIS, 16 Oct 1996, *Two Women Bathing* (oil on canvas, 22 3/4 x 18 1/2 ins / 58 x 47 cm) FRF 11,000. PARIS, 8 Dec 1996, *Boat Trip* (1965, oil on canvas, 21 1/4 x 28 3/4 ins / 54 x 73 cm) FRF 13,500. PARIS, 20 March 1998, *Field* (oil on canvas, 21 1/4 x 29 1/4 ins / 54 x 74 cm) FRF 3,600. PARIS, 19 March 1999, *The Meal* (1966, oil on canvas, 26 x 36 ins / 65 x 92 cm) FRF 29,500. CALAIS, 7 Nov 1999, *After the Bath* (oil on canvas, 36 x 26 ins / 92 x 65 cm) FRF 32,000. CALAIS, 12 March 2000, *Two Bathers* (oil on canvas, 18 x 22 ins / 46 x 55 cm) FRF 28,000. PARIS, 29 May 2000, *Siesta* (oil on canvas, 21 x 29 ins / 54 x 73 cm) FRF 37,000. VERSAILLES, 18 March 2001, *Greenness* (1946, oil on paper, 66 x 78 ins / 168 x 198 cm) FRF 27,100. VERSAILLES, 18 March 2001, *Hunting Wild Boar* (1947, oil on paper, 65 x 114 ins / 166 x 290 cm) FRF 30,000. BERN, 1 May 2002, *Summer* (1929, oil on canvas, 51 x 77 ins / 130 x 195 cm) CHF 115,000. CALAIS, 10 Nov 2002, *Summer* (1929, oil on canvas, 51 x 77 ins / 130 x 195 cm) EUR 18,000. PARIS, 14 May 2003, *Table on the Terrace infront of Vines* (1960, oil on canvas, 18 x 22 ins / 46 x 55 cm) EUR 1,800. BERN, 5 Nov 2003, *Venus* (oil on canvas, 36 x 29 ins / 92 x 73 cm) CHF 2,600. PARIS, 26 March 2004, *Harvester's* (1966, oil on canvas, 21 x 28 ins / 53 x 72 cm) EUR 2,100. CALAIS, 30 May 2004, *Venus* (oil on canvas, 36 x 29 ins / 92 x 73 cm) EUR 7,500.

SAVIN, Nazari

Russian, 17th century.

Icon painter.

Nazari Savin was the son of Istoma Savin. He worked for the court in Moscow in 1621.

SAVIN, Nikofor, or Istomin

Russian, 17th century.

Active in Moscow.

Icon painter.

He was the brother of Istoma Savin. He was one of best representatives of the Stroganov school.

MUSEUMS AND GALLERIES:

MOSCOW (State Tretyakov Gal.) - ST PETERSBURG (Gosudarstvennyj Russkij Muz.).

SAVIN, Paolo
Italian, 15th - 16th century.
Active in Venice from 1497 to 1516 (?).
Sculptor.
Venetian School.
Paolo Savin made numerous sculptures for churches in Venice.

SAVINA, Jean
French, 16th century.
Active in Riez.
Sculptor.
Jean Savina worked in Marseilles in 1503 and may be the same person as the sculptor Jean Brissonet, called Savine, who worked in Troyes from 1505 to 1521.

SAVINE, Léopold Pierre Antoine
French, 19th - 20th century.
Born 6 March 1861, in Paris.
Sculptor. Religious subjects, mythological subjects.
Léopold Pierre Antoine Savine, a pupil of Antoine Injalbert, was a member of the Salon des Artistes Français, Paris, from 1888 and exhibited there until 1920. He was awarded an honourable mention in 1892 and a bronze medal at the Exposition Universelle of 1900.
MUSEUMS AND GALLERIES:
LYONS (MBA): *St Jerome*.
AUCTION RECORDS:
PARIS, 3 Dec 1984, *Lake Nymph* (gilded bronze, h. 19 3/4 ins / 50 cm) FRF 15,000.

SAVINI, Alfonso
Italian, 19th - 20th century.
Born 1836, in Bologna; died March 1908, in Bologna.
Painter, watercolourist. Portraits, genre scenes, still-lifes, flowers.
The father of Alfredo Savini, Alfonso Savini exhibited in Turin, Florence, Venice and Bologna.
MUSEUMS AND GALLERIES:
BOLOGNA (Pinacoteca Nazionale).
AUCTION RECORDS:
LONDON, 10 June 1910, *The Musician,* GBP 16. LONDON, 29 Oct 1976, *Dreaming Violinist* (oil on panel, 15 x 12 1/2 ins / 38 x 32 cm) GBP 1,200. COLOGNE, 11 June 1979, *Flirtation* (oil on panel, 7 3/4 x 9 1/4 ins / 20 x 23.2 cm) DEM 7,000. COLOGNE, 22 Oct 1982, *Music Hour* (oil on panel, 9 1/2 x 7 ins / 24 x 18 cm) DEM 5,000. NEW YORK, 19 July 1990, *Quarrel* (oil on canvas, 31 1/2 x 23 1/2 ins / 80.1 x 59.7 cm) USD 6,050. AMSTERDAM, 30 Oct 1991, *Stolen Kiss* (oil on panel, 13 x 17 1/4 ins / 33 x 43.5 cm) NLG 11,500. LONDON, 16 March 1994, *Prelude to the Night* (watercolour, 12 1/2 x 19 1/4 ins / 32 x 49 cm) GBP 1,955. SAN FRANCISCO, 26 May 1999, *Lover's Dispute* (oil on canvas/board, 32 x 24 ins / 81 x 60 cm) USD 20,000. NEW YORK, 1 Nov 1999, *Lovers' Farewell* (oil on canvas, 32 x 24 ins / 81 x 60 cm) USD 22,000. SEVENOAKS, 18 July 2000, *Musical Moment* (1874, oil on panel, 12 x 18 ins / 30 x 45 cm) GBP 6,500. LONDON, 21 Nov 2002, *Ardent Suitor* (oil on panel, 6 x 5 ins / 15 x 12 cm) GBP 2,500. MANCHESTER, 16 Sept 2003, *Classical Female Holding a Yarn Winder in an Interior* (1874, oil on canvas, 18 x 13 ins / 46 x 33 cm) GBP 1,150. LONDON, 26 Aug 2004, *Fragrance Maker* (oil on canvas, 19 x 13 ins / 47 x 32 cm) GBP 2,500.

SAVINI, Alfredo
Italian, 19th - 20th century.
Born 3 April 1868, in Bologna; died 28 October 1924, in Verona.
Painter. Figures, portraits.
He was the son and pupil of Alfonso Savini.
MUSEUMS AND GALLERIES:
VERONA.

SAVINI, Enrico
Italian, 19th century.
Active during the second half of the 19th century.
Painter.
MUSEUMS AND GALLERIES:
CHEMNITZ (Kunstsammlungen): *White Slaves* (1862).

SAVINI, Gaetano
Italian, 19th - 20th century.
Born 10 January 1850, in Ravenna; died 13 March 1917, in Pesaro.
Painter, writer. Decorative schemes.

SAVINI, Giovanori Paolo, or Savino
Italian, 17th century.
Active probably in Casteldurante c. 1600.
Painter (majolica).
Giovanori Paolo Savini was the assistant of Diomede Durante in Rome.

SAVINI, Pompeo
Italian, 18th century.
Active in Rome from 1769 to 1780.
Mosaicist, marquetry worker.
Pompeo Savini produced urban and architectural views.

SAVINI, Salvio
Italian, 17th century.
Active in Florence at the beginning of the 17th century.
Painter.
Salvio Savini worked in Città della Pieve and painted an altarpiece for the church of S Ubaldo in Gubbio in 1608.
AUCTION RECORDS:
LONDON, 6 April 1984, *Banquet of Esther and Ahasuerus* (oil on canvas, 90 1/2 x 116in/229.7 x 294.5cm) GBP 10,000.

SAVINIO, Alberto, pseudonym of Chirico, Andrea de
Italian, 20th century.
Born 1891, in Athens, to Italian parents; died 1952, in Rome.
Also active in France.
Painter, draughtsman, illustrator. Scenes with figures. Stage sets.
Pittura Metafisica (Metaphysical Painting), Futurism.
Les Artistes Italiens de Paris group.
The brother of Giorgio de Chirico, Alberto Savinio studied music at the conservatoire in Athens, winning first prize for composition when he was 13 years old. He continued his studies in Munich with Max Reger. (It was in a magazine at Reger's house that Giorgio, who used to accompany his brother to his music lessons, first encountered Arnold Böcklin's gloomy landscapes.) Alberto Savinio arrived in Paris in 1911 with his mother and his brother. The two boys soon got to know Apollinaire, Breton, Picasso, Cendrars and Cocteau. In 1917, he was in Ferrara with his brother on the occasion of the setting up of the group identifying itself with *pittura metafisica* (metaphysical painting). In 1922, with artists including Giorgio de Chirico, Morandi and Carlo Carra, he founded the Novecento group. He returned to stay in Paris between 1927 and 1933, holding a solo exhibition in Paris in 1927.A multi-talented artist, Savinio was a writer and a musician before becoming a painter. Having taken a pseudonym soon after his arrival in Paris he agreed, in 1914, to collaborate with Apollinaire on the review *Soirées de Paris.* That same year he published his first collection of poetry, *Le Chant de la Mi-Mort*, a kind of lyrical commentary on the artistic world he shared with Giorgio where we already find the themes central to metaphysical art, female figures and enigmatic figurines rising out of never-ending perspectives, standing in deserted squares, or sitting in abandoned armchairs in the shadows of rows of arcades. Although mainly known as a writer and novelist with publications including a

collection of his writings entitled *Hermaphrodite* in 1918 and *Toute la Vie*, he was active in many other art forms. He designed the stage sets for his play, of which he was the author and director, *Alceste de Samuel*, and also put on a production of Stravinsky's *Firebird*. He wrote many pieces on art theory for the reviews *La Voce*, *La Ronda* and *Valori Plastici*, the 1919 edition of the latter containing a famous essay on the aesthetics of metaphysical painting. Nor did he neglect his music, composing ballets and operas that were performed by the Metropolitan Opera in New York and at La Scala in Milan. They include *Perseus*, *The Death of Niobe* and *Carmela*.By 1926, Savinio was coming to the conclusion that painting was a medium better suited than words to express his poetic ideas. His work as a painter conformed to the law of Surrealist art - the most faithful and realistic representation of a random group of objects was required in order to make it comprehensible. Savinio insists on this requirement, saying, 'The more immaterial the concept, the more realistic must be the representation of it.' Only something apparently possible can be summarily suggested, something that the understanding can complete easily.

As a painter, Savinio gave form to the creations of his writings. We find in his paintings a metaphysical world not dissimilar to that of Giorgio de Chirico with the same jointed mannequins, frozen statues, tall goddesses with the heads of birds and landscapes that stretch away into infinity. Between 1927 and 1940, Alberto Savinio painted in rich oil paints, later preferring the drier gouache and pastel. His technique is more supple and flowing than his brother's geometricism. Both in his writing and his painting he remained faithful to his original inspiration where objects throw off the restraints of everyday life and create an effect of instability that upsets the order of a too peaceful universe. The figures are shadows and the unending perspectives give us the measure of time.

Judged the work of a mere dilettante, a 'Jack of all trades and master of none', Savinio's paintings were long ignored by a public that found a safer guarantee in the work of the serious and more consistent De Chirico. Today, however, there is a new interest in Savinio's paintings, in the series of toys in faded forests entitled *Battle of the Centaurs* that fascinate us 'with their mutant and blind creatures, their nightmarish skies and their disconcerting and grotesque landscapes'. André Breton thought Savinio's paintings equal to those of De Chirico, writing: 'All modern mythology, still in the process of evolution, can be seen as resting on the almost indistinguishable work of Alberto Savinio and his brother Giorgio de Chirico'.

Some of his work featured in the collective exhibition held in 2003 at the museum in Lodève (France), *De Chirico et la peinture italienne de l'entre-deux guerres* (*De Chirico and Italian Painting of the Interwar Period*). Several important retrospective exhibitions devoted to his work were held after his death: at the Galleria d'Arte Moderna in Rome, 1952 and 1967; Venice Biennale, 1954; Palais des Beaux-Arts, Brussels, 1976; Rome, 1978; Munich at the Städtische Galerie im Lenbachhaus und Kunstbau, 2002, the exhibition being entitled *Die Andere Moderne De Chirico, Savinio.*

Savinio

BIBLIOGRAPHY:

Carra, M./Waldberg, P./Rathke, E., *Metafisica*, Gabriele Mazzotta, Milan, 1968. Russoli, Franco/Rognoni, Luigi, *Alberto Savinio*, exhibition catalogue, Palazzo Reale, Milan, 1976. *Alberto Savinio 1891-1952*, exhibition catalogue, Palais des Beaux-Arts, Brussels, 1976. Fagiolo dell'Arco, Maurizio/Fonti, Daniela/Vivarelli, Pia, *Alberto Savinio*, exhibition catalogue, Palazzo delle Esposizioni, Éd. De Luca, Rome, 1978. Semin, D./Fauchereau, S., '*Alberto Savinio. Dessins*' in *Cahiers de l'abbaye Sainte-Croix* n° 59, periodical, Musée de l'abbaye Sainte-Croix, Les Sables d'Olonne, 1987. *Savinio, gli anni di Parigi, dipinti 1927-1932*, exhibition catalogue, Palazzo Forti, Vérone, Electa, Milan, 1990. '*Alberto Savinio*' in *Opus international* n° 123-124, periodical, Paris, April-May 1991. Briganti, Giuliano/Sciascia, Leonardo, *Alberto Savinio. Peinture et littérature*, FMR, Paris, 1992. Vivarelli, Pia, *Alberto Savinio, catalogo generale*, catalogue raisonné, Electa, Milan, 1996. Baldacci, Paolo/Fagiolo dell'Arco, Maurizio/Friedel, Helmut/Vivarelli, Pia/Groos, Gerd, *Die Andere Moderne. De Chirico, Savinio [The Other Modernism. Savinio, De Chirico]*, exhibition catalogue, Städtische Gal. im Lenbachhaus und Kunstbaus, München, Hatje Cantz Verlag, Stuttgart, 2001. Bonito Oliva, Achille/Iovane, Giovanni/Lista, Giovanni, et al., *De Chirico et la peinture italienne de l'entre-deux guerres*, exhibition catalogue, Musée de Lodève, 2003.

MUSEUMS AND GALLERIES:

MILAN (Gal. d'Arte Moderna) - ROME (Gal. Nazionale d'Arte Moderna) - TURIN (Gal. Civica d'Arte Moderna e Contemporanea).

AUCTION RECORDS:

PARIS, 12 April 1930, *Annunciation*, FRF 280. PARIS, 20 June 1941, *Lost Ship*, FRF 1,400; *Marriage of the Cock*, FRF 1,650. PARIS, July 1946, *Migrants* (1929) FRF 3,000; *The Dial of Hope* (1928) FRF 2,800. PARIS, 29 Oct 1948, *Abandoned Objects in the Forest* (1928) FRF 6,000. PARIS, 4 May 1955, *Lost Ship*, FRF 19,500. MILAN, 27 March 1962, *The Angel Mediterranean*, ITL 900,000. MILAN, 1 Dec 1964, *Head with Bunch of Grapes*, ITL 1,200,000. MILAN, 29 Nov 1966, *Portrait of a Woman*, ITL 2,400,000. PARIS, 5 Dec 1969, *Abandoned Objects in a Forest*, FRF 62,000. MILAN, 29 May 1973, *Siesta*, ITL 15,000,000. ROME, 20 May 1974, *Marine Procession*, ITL 21,000,000. ROME, 19 May 1977, *Nudes in the Mountains* (1929, oil on canvas, 23 1/2 x 28 3/4 ins / 60 x 73 cm) ITL 24,000,000. ROME, 6 Dec 1978, *Monument to God* (tempera, 15 1/4 x 11 1/2 ins / 39 x 29 cm) ITL 5,500,000. ROME, 24 May 1979, *Study for Life of Man* (charcoal heightened with white, set design, 19 1/4 x 23 1/4 ins / 49 x 59 cm) ITL 4,000,000. MILAN, 26 June 1979, *Tunis* (1929, oil on canvas, 25 1/2 x 31 1/2 ins / 65 x 80 cm) ITL 28,000,000. MILAN, 25 Nov 1980, *Antique Figures* (1927, mixed media, 18 x 24 ins / 46 x 61 cm) ITL 9,000,000. MILAN, 26 Feb 1981, *The Astrologer Meridian* (1929, oil on canvas, 32 x 25 1/2 ins / 81 x 65 cm) ITL 56,000,000. MILAN, 24 Oct 1983, *Apollo* (1936, tempera/canvas, 50 1/4 x 29 1/4 ins / 127.5 x 74.5 cm) ITL 70,000,000. MILAN, 15 Nov 1983, *Apollinaire* (pen, 19 x 15 3/4 ins / 48 x 40 cm) ITL 15,500,000. ROME, 5 Dec 1983, *Annunciation* (1929, oil on canvas, 31 1/2 x 25 1/2 ins / 80 x 65 cm) ITL 110,000,000. MILAN, 19 Dec 1985, *Family Group* (1927, oil on canvas, 17 1/4 x 21 1/4 ins / 44 x 54 cm) ITL 65,000,000. MILAN, 28 Oct 1986, *Migrants* (1929, oil on canvas, 32 x 39 1/4 ins / 81 x 100 cm) ITL 260,000,000. MILAN, 19 May 1987, *Dreams* (1943, pen and ink, 15 3/4 x 11 3/4 ins / 40 x 30 cm) ITL 20,500,000. MILAN, 26 May 1987, *Reception Day* (1930, oil on canvas, 36 1/4 x 28 3/4 ins / 92 x 73 cm) ITL 300,000,000. PARIS, 3 Dec 1987, *Marine Idyll* (oil on canvas, 28 3/4 x 23 1/2 ins / 73 x 60 cm) FRF 800,000. ROME, 7 April 1988, *Red Silk Door* (1950, mixed media/paper, study for a stage set, 11 x 8 1/2 ins / 27 x 21.5 cm) ITL 14,000,000. ROME, 15 Nov 1988, *Flowers* (1930, oil on canvas, 28 1/2 x 23 1/2 ins / 72.5 x 60 cm) ITL 240,000,000. MILAN, 20 March 1989, *Family* (1930, oil on canvas, 28 1/2 x 23 1/2 ins / 72.5 x 60 cm) ITL 650,000,000. ROME, 9 April 1991, *Face of a Woman* (oil on canvas, 14 1/2 x 11 ins / 37 x 28 cm) ITL 50,000,000. ROME, 13 May 1991, *Dancers* (1927, oil on canvas, 28 1/2 x 36 1/4 ins / 72.5 x 92 cm) ITL 402,500,000. NEW YORK, 12 May 1992, *Schoolboys* (1929, oil on canvas, 25 1/2 x 21 1/4 ins / 64.8 x 54 cm) USD 275,000. MILAN, 21 May 1992, *Ancestor* (1948, pencil, 9 3/4 x 7 ins / 25 x 17.5 cm) ITL 5,600,000. PARIS, 29 March 1993, *Ascension* (1929, oil on canvas, 39 1/4 x 32 ins /

100 x 81 cm) FRF 2,450,000. Milan, 12 Oct 1993, *Cyclops Playing a Flute* (1948, pencil, 13 x 9 1/2 ins / 33 x 24 cm) ITL 16,100,000. Milan, 22 Nov 1993, *Fighting Angels* (1930, oil on canvas, 28 3/4 x 36 1/4 ins / 73 x 92 cm) ITL 341,765,000. Milan, 24 May 1994, *Treasure Island* (1929, oil on canvas, 22 x 18 ins / 55 x 46 cm) ITL 306,400,000. Milan, 27 April 1995, *Untitled* (1927, oil on canvas, 22 3/4 x 32 ins / 58 x 81 cm) ITL 356,500,000. Paris, 22 June 1995, *Wedding March* (1931, oil on canvas, 51 1/4 x 28 ins / 130 x 71 cm) FRF 1,800,000. Milan, 19 March 1996, *Composition with Statue and Puppet* (oil on canvas, 22 x 18 ins / 55 x 46 cm) ITL 402,500,000. Milan, 20-23 May 1996, *Penelope* (1944-1945, tempera/panel, 13 3/4 x 9 3/4 ins / 35 x 25 cm) ITL 114,300,000; *Memory of my Childhood* (1947, pencil/paper, 13 x 9 1/4 ins / 33 x 23.5 cm) ITL 23,000,000. Milan, 10 Dec 1996, *Cosmic Tree* (c. 1941, pencil/paper, 11 1/2 x 7 3/4 ins / 29.5 x 20 cm) ITL 17,475,000. Milan, 22 June 1999, *Nocturnal Figures* (1950, tempera on panel, 20 x 16 ins / 50 x 40 cm) ITL 60,000,000. Milan, 9 Nov 1999, *Occhi di ricambio* (*New Eyes for Old*) (c. 1942, ink, 9 x 7 ins / 24 x 17 cm) ITL 13,500,000. Paris, 29 March 2000, *Kite* (oil on canvas, 14 x 11 ins / 35 x 27 cm) FRF 520,000. Prato, 25 Nov 2000, *Figures in a Room* (charcoal on paper/canvas, 18 x 25 ins / 45 x 64 cm) ITL 37,000,000. Milan, 29 May 2001, *Hercules Three Times* (ink and pencil, 13 x 9 ins / 32 x 23 cm) ITL 22,000,000. Prato, 1 Dec 2001, *Tempest* (1927, oil on canvas, 28 x 21 ins / 72 x 53 cm) ITL 410,000,000. Milan, 14 May 2002, *Dreams* (1943, ink, 20 x 16 ins / 50 x 40 cm) EUR 17,500. Prato, 25 May 2002, *Fish* (1927-1928, oil on canvas, 20 x 26 ins / 50 x 65 cm) EUR 120,000. Milan, 24 Nov 2003, *Town of Promises* (1928, oil on canvas, 38 x 57 ins / 97 x 146 cm) EUR 600,000. Prato, 29 Nov 2003, *Ulysses and Polyphemus* (1932, tempera on canvas, 20 x 26 ins / 50 x 65 cm) EUR 300,000. Prato, 29 May 2004, *Untitled* (1948-1950, tempera on cardboard, 13 x 10 ins / 32 x 26 cm) EUR 80,000.

SAVINIO, Ruggero
Italian, 20th century.
Born 1934, in Turin.
Painter. Figures, landscapes.

Auction records:
Rome, 28 Nov 1989, *Embrace* (1962, oil and distemper/canvas, 49 1/2 x 56 1/4 ins / 126 x 143 cm) ITL 8,000,000. Milan, 20 June 1991, *Distance of a Landscape* (1971, oil on canvas, 35 1/2 x 39 1/4 ins / 90 x 100 cm) ITL 4,000,000. Rome, 12 May 1992, *Distance of a Landscape* (1973, oil on panel, 19 3/4 x 15 3/4 ins / 50 x 40 cm) ITL 2,600,000. Milan, 15 Dec 1992, *Cuma Conversation* (1984, oil on canvas, 59 3/4 x 54 1/4 ins / 152 x 138 cm) ITL 8,000,000. Milan, 6 April 1993, *Distance of a Landscape* (1972, oil on canvas, 35 1/2 x 39 1/4 ins / 90 x 100 cm) ITL 5,000,000. Milan, 5 May 1994, *Park* (1985, oil on canvas, 72 1/2 x 56 ins / 184 x 142 cm) ITL 16,100,000. Milan, 22 June 1995, *Figure in a Landscape* (1974, oil/synthetic resin, 39 1/4 x 35 1/2 ins / 100 x 90 cm) ITL 5,750,000. Milan, 22 June 1999, *The Golden Age* (1982, oil on canvas, 79 x 79 ins / 200 x 200 cm) ITL 10,000,000. Milan, 16 Dec 1999, *The Golden Age* (1977, oil on paper/canvas, 77 x 67 ins / 195 x 170 cm) ITL 7,000,000. Milan, 15 Nov 2000, *Obscure Life* (oil on canvas, 31 x 39 ins / 80 x 100 cm) ITL 5,000,000.

SAVINKOV, Aleksandr Dmitrievich
Russian, 18th century.
Born 1769.
Engraver (burin).
Aleksandr Dmitrievich Savinkov engraved portraits, vignettes and book illustrations.

SAVINO, Giovanni Paolo. See **SAVINI Giovanori Paolo**

SAVINOV, Gleb
Russian, 20th century.
Born 1915.
Painter. Scenes with figures, genre scenes, interiors with figures, landscapes, urban landscapes, gardens.
Gleb Savinov attended the Ilya Repin Institute in Leningrad (now St Petersburg) and was taught by Aleksandr Osmerkin and Aleksandr Savinov. He featured from 1940 onwards in collective exhibitions in Moscow and Leningrad. His work was recognised abroad from 1958, notably in Brussels where he was awarded second prize at the *Contemporary Art of the USSR* exhibition (1958) and also in Paris, Tokyo, London, Osaka, Montreal and Madrid. Three solo exhibitions were devoted to him in Leningrad (1981, 1982 and 1988). Gleb Savinov was a member of the Association of Soviet Artists, was a People's Artist and taught at the academy of fine art in Leningrad

Bibliography:
L'École de Léningrad, auction catalogue, Drouot, Paris, 19 November 1990.

Museums and Galleries:
Bratislava (Slovenská Národná Gal.) - Dresden (Gemäldegal.) - Irkutsk (MFA) - Manchester (MFA) - Moscow (Ministry of Culture) - Moscow (State Tretyakov Gal.) - Osaka (Gal. of Soviet Art) - St Petersburg (Gosudarstvennyj Muz. Istorii) - St Petersburg (Gosudarstvennyj Russkij Muz.) - Tambov (MFA) - Tbilisi (MFA) - Tokyo (Gal. of Contemporary Art).

Auction records:
Paris, 11 June 1990, *Conversation on the Telephone* (1953, oil on canvas, 24 x 21 1/4 ins / 61 x 54 cm) FRF 33,500. Paris, 19 Nov 1990, *Old St Petersburg* (1948, oil on canvas, 23 1/4 x 31 ins / 59 x 79 cm) FRF 29,000. Paris, 25 March 1991, *Young Pianist* (1956, oil on canvas, 27 1/2 x 23 1/2 ins / 70 x 60 cm) FRF 52,500. Paris, 15 May 1991, *Marina* (1958, oil on canvas, 9 3/4 x 19 1/4 ins / 25 x 49 cm) FRF 10,500. Paris, 25 Nov 1991, *Garden in Bloom* (1957, oil on canvas, 31 x 24 ins / 79 x 61 cm) FRF 11,200. Paris, 23 March 1992, *Verandah* (oil on canvas, 39 x 37 ins / 99 x 94 cm) FRF 10,000. Paris, 20 May 1992, *Vatslav Square* (1957, oil on canvas, 27 1/4 x 33 1/2 ins / 69 x 85 cm) FRF 11,500.

SAVINSKY, Vasili Evmenevich
Russian, 19th - 20th century.
Born 24 March 1859; died 1937.
Painter, draughtsman.

Museums and Galleries:
Moscow (State Tretyakov Gal.): *Portrait of the Painter P. P. Chistyakov* (drawing); *Self-portrait* (oil on canvas).

SAVINUS
Italian, 15th century.
Active in Faenza during the second half of the 15th century.
Miniaturist.
Savinus worked on the illumination of the psalters of Cesena Cathedral in 1486.

SAVIO, Francisco or Franz de. See **SAIVE Franz de**

SAVIO, Pietro
Italian, 16th century.
Active in Vercelli at the end of the 16th century.
Sculptor (wood).
Pietro Savio carved a section of the choir stalls at Vercelli Cathedral in 1590.

SAVIOTTI, Pasquale
Italian, 19th century.
Born 17 July 1792, in Faenza; died 18 August 1855, in Florence.
Painter, engraver, lithographer, stucco artist.

A pupil of Giuseppe Zauli, Pasquale Saviotti executed paintings for Faenza Cathedral and painted some façades of palazzi in Florence.

SAVIRON Y ESTEBAN, Paulino
Spanish, 19th century.
Born 2 September 1827, in Alustante.
Active in Saragossa.
Painter, engraver.
Paulino Saviron y Esteban was a pupil of A. Ferran and J. Masferrer. He painted portraits and a painting of *St Lucy* for the high altar of the church of Monreal del Campe.

SAVITRY, Émile
French, 20th century.
Born 1903; died 1967.
Painter, photographer, poet. Landscapes.
A friend of Robert Desnos and Jacques Prévert, Émile Savitry is better known as a photographer and for having introduced Django Reinhart to Jazz in 1931.

SAVITSKY, Konstantin Apollonovich
Russian, 19th century.
Born 1841, or 1844; died 1905.
Painter. Genre scenes, landscapes.
Peredvizhniki (Wanderers) group.
In 1876, Konstantin Apollonovich Savitsky visited the Auvergne region of France, where he produced several paintings, two of which are in the Russian museum in St Petersburg. His *Travellers in the Auvergne* was originally in the personal art collection of Tsar Nicholas II.
MUSEUMS AND GALLERIES:
MOSCOW (State Tretyakov Gal.): *Seascape; Fire in a Village* (sepia); as well as other works - ST PETERSBURG (Gosudarstvennyj Russkij Muz.): *War Scene; Travellers in the Auvergne*.
AUCTION RECORDS:
LONDON, 17 July 1996, *Auvergne* (oil on card, 8 3/4 x 13 1/2 ins / 22.5 x 34 cm) GBP 3,220.

SAVOIA, Achille
Italian, 19th century.
Born 1842, in Pavia; died 3 October 1886, in Pavia.
Painter, sculptor. Equestrian portraits. Statues.
Achille Savoia was a pupil of Cesare Ferreri.
MUSEUMS AND GALLERIES:
PAVIA (Musei Civici del Castello Visconteo): *Equestrian Statue of Benedetto Cairoli*.

SAVOIE. See also **SAVOYE**

SAVOIE, Louise de
French, 15th century.
Art patron.
Louise de Savoie was the daughter of Philippe II, Duke of Savoy, the wife of Charles, Duke of Angoulême, and the mother of François I and Marguerite d'Alençon. She was one of the earliest supporters of the developing Renaissance in France. In seeking actively to extend the library of Cognac, which she had inherited, she often employed the copyist Jean Michel and the illuminator Robinet Testar. Among the manuscripts that date from this period are the following: *Le Triomphe de la Force de la Prudence* (*The Triumph of the Power of Prudence*) in the Hermitage, St Petersburg; *Les Heures de Louise de Savoie* (*The Hours of Louise de Savoie*) in the British Museum; *Commentaire sur le Livre des Échecs Amoureux* (*Commentary on the Book of the Amorous Game of Chess*), *Le Triomphe des Vertus* (*The Triumph of the Virtues*), *Les Chants Royaux du Puy d'Amiens* (*The Royal Songs of Puy d'Amiens*), and *La Messe de Sainte Anne* (*The Mass of St Anne*) in the Bibliothèque Nationale in Paris; *Le Miroir des Dames* (*The Ladies' Mirror*); *Fleur de Vertu* (*Flower of Virtue*); *Instruction de la Religion Chrétienne pour les Enfants* (*Instruction in the Christian Religion for Children*); and a book of hours that was in the possession of the duchess of Berry. Several of these manuscripts contain superb miniatures and they are decorated with the coats of arms of France and Savoy or the houses of Orléans and Milan.

SAVOIE, Robert
Canadian, 20th century.
Born 1939, in Quebec.
Painter, engraver, draughtsman.
Robert Savoie studied at the École des Beaux-Arts and the Institut des Arts Graphiques in Montreal. He then took a course at the Chelsea School of Art in London. Having been granted a scholarship by the Arts Council of Canada he went to study in Paris and then also received a grant from the French government to study in eastern Europe and Mexico. He stayed in Japan on several occasions.

Savoie is influenced by Japanese art, particularly in his engravings, which are produced in strong relief and close to Abstract Expressionism. He turned towards kinetic art at the beginning of the 1970s, then returned to engraving, producing informal works. He has taken part in group exhibitions, including the Biennale de Menton in 1972 and at the Musée d'Art Contemporain in Montreal in 1985.
BIBLIOGRAPHY:
Les 20 ans du Musée à travers sa collection, exhibition catalogue, Musée d'Art contemporain, Montreal, 1985.
MUSEUMS AND GALLERIES:
MONTREAL (MAC): *North Coast* (1964); *Scarabs* (1965); *M-8* (1971, silk screen print and electric motor); *Yakusa* (1976, etching); *Yamashiro* (1978, etching) - OTTAWA (Carleton University Art Gallery).

SAVOLDO, Giovanni Girolamo, sometimes called Girolamo da Brescia
Italian, 16th century.
Born between 1480 and 1485, in Brescia; died after 1548.
Painter. History painting, portraits.
Brescia School.
Giovanni Girolamo Savoldo seems to have begun his apprenticeship in his hometown, and was a member of the guild of painters in Florence in 1508. He is thought to have moved to Venice in about 1521, where he stayed for many years. He must have gone to Verona, where he painted the altarpiece in the church of S Maria in Organo (1533), and Milan between 1529 and 1535. In a letter written in Venice dated December 1548, Aretino mentions Savoldo, describing him as a great but now ageing artist whose talent was in decline.

Savoldo was inevitably influenced by Giorgione and Titian, and many hallmarks of the Venetian School - an excellent grasp of form, penetrating insights - are present in his paintings. Nevertheless, Savoldo's own personality combined with a sense of colour that is more akin to the Brescia School. Like Giorgione and Titian, he delighted in painting landscape and the effects of light. One of his most important works is the altarpiece for the Dominican church in Pesaro, now in the Brera in Milan. Others include an altarpiece in the church of S Niccolò in Treviso; an *Adoration of the Shepherds* in an impressive landscape in Turin; and a *Holy Family*, a replica of which signed *Savoldo da Brescia facebat 1527* is at Hampton Court outside London. The latter work has a particularly beautiful Madonna. The church of S Giobbe in Venice houses a remarkable *Adoration of the Shepherds*. A portrait by Savoldo in the Louvre in Paris shows that he was talented in this genre as well.

Apart from the favourable remarks of Aretino and Vasari, if we are to judge by the number of replicas of his own works painted by Savoldo, he seems to have been very successful during his lifetime. Unusual among Venetian painters in preferring to paint on a small scale, he shows an interest in contrasting effects of bright light and dense shade, and in the rendering of precious materials in a style that appears at first sight to be objective but which tends towards the lyrical.

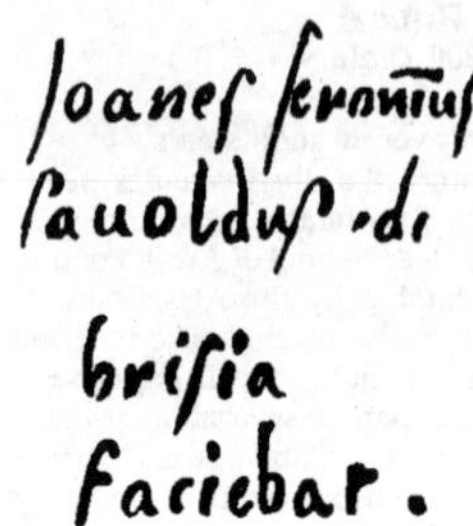

BIBLIOGRAPHY:
Venturi, Lionello, *La Renaissance italienne*, Skira, Geneva, 1951.

MUSEUMS AND GALLERIES:
BERLIN: *Venetian Woman; Lamentation over the Dead Christ* - BONN (Rheinisches Landesmus.): *Lamentation over the Dead Christ* - BUDAPEST: *Virgin, St James and St John the Evangelist; Entombment* - FLORENCE: *Transfiguration* - LONDON (NG): *Mary Magdalene* (c. 1530, oil on canvas); *St Jerome* (1527?, oil on canvas) - LOS ANGELES (Getty Mus.): *Mary Magdalene at the Sepulchre* (1530-1539, oil on canvas) - MILAN (Pinacoteca di Brera): *Jesus and the Virgin with Sts Peter, Dominic, Paul and Jerome* - PARIS (Louvre): *Portrait thought to be of Gaston de Foix* - ROME (Mus. e Gal. Borghese): *Head of a Young Man* - TURIN (Gal. Sabauda): *Adoration of the Shepherds* - VENICE: *St Anthony Abbot and St Paul the Hermit; A Dominican Monk* - VENICE (S Giobbe): *Adoration of the Shepherds* - VIENNA: *Lamentation over the Dead Christ; Aristotle* (uncertain).

AUCTION RECORDS:
PARIS, 15 March 1909, *Portrait of a Man*, FRF 1,750. PARIS, 20 Oct 1920, *Judith with the Head of Holofernes*, FRF 260. PARIS, 6 May 1925, *Portrait of a Man in a Dark Green Cap* (attributed) FRF 5,500. LONDON, 22 March 1929, *Boy Playing a Flute*, GBP 441. NEW YORK, 15 Jan 1937, *Gentleman*, USD 775. LONDON, 20 Nov 1958, *Head of a Bearded Man Inclined to the Right* (charcoal) GBP 892. LONDON, 21 June 1968, *Mary Magdalene*, Gns 8,000. LONDON, 24 June 1970, *Portrait of a Bearded Man*, GBP 3,000. NEW YORK, 13 Jan 1994, *Portrait of a Young Man with a Flute* (oil on canvas, 29 1/4 x 39 1/2 ins / 74.3 x 100.3 cm) USD 1,542,500. VENICE, 14 Dec 2003, *St Dominique. St Veneranda. St Anthony. St Vincent* (oil on canvas, four, 59 x 39 ins / 150 x 98 cm) EUR 690,000.

SAVOLINI, Cristoforo

Italian, 17th century.
Born in Cesena; died after 1680.
Painter.

Cristoforo Savolini was the pupil of Cristoforo Serra. One of his works, the *Martyrdom of St Columba*, can be found in the cathedral of S Colomba in Rimini.

SAVONANZI, Emilio

Italian, 17th century.
Born 1580, in Bologna; died 1660, in Camerino.
Painter. Religious subjects.

Born into a noble family, Emilio Savonanzi devoted himself to painting. His masters included Ludovico Carracci, Guido Reni, Guernino and the sculptor Algardi. He lived in Ancona and Camerino.

MUSEUMS AND GALLERIES:
BOLOGNA (Pinacoteca Nazionale): *Deposition* - CAMERINO: *Mystical Marriage of St Catherine* - FLORENCE (NG): *Deposition; Holy Family* - PARMA: *Adoration of the Shepherds.*

AUCTION RECORDS:
PARIS, 20 May 1992, *Sacrifice of Isaac* (oil on canvas, 60 1/4 x 46 1/2in/153 x 118cm) FRF 700,000.

SAVORELLI, Gaetano

Italian, 18th century.
Died July 1791, in Rome.
Painter, draughtsman.

Gaetano Savorelli is noted for having supplied the engraver Giovanni Ottaviani with drawings of the grotesques of Giovanni da Udine in the Vatican.

SAVORELLI, Pietro

Italian, 18th century.
Born c. 1765.
Active in Rome.
Painter, engraver (burin).

Pietro Savorelli was probably the son of Gaetano Savorelli.

SAVORELLI, Sebastiano

Italian, 17th century.
Active in Forlì c. 1690.
Painter. History painting.

Sebastiano Savorelli, a priest, was the pupil of Cignani. He produced works for churches in and around Forlì.

SAVORNIN, Claude, or Savournin

French, 18th century.
Sculptor, decorative designer.

Claude Savornin was active in Avignon, working in 1705. He sculpted tabernacles and frames.

SAVORNIN, Jean François

French, 20th century.
Born 22 October 1943, in Toulouse.
Painter. Animals. Stage sets.

Jean François Savornin was educated at the École des Beaux-Arts in Toulon, where he studied painting and ceramics under Tamary and Baboulène. His work is deliberately non-realist, tending towards an occasionally confused caricature of the external world. Above all, his work is distinguished by his sense of colour.

He has exhibited solo in Monte Carlo, Cannes and Avignon and has also designed numerous theatre sets.

SAVORY, Eva

British, 20th century.
Born in Weybridge (Surrey).
Active in the 1920s.
Painter.

Eva Savory exhibited in Paris at the Salon des Artistes Français from 1926.

SAVOSTIANOV, Fiodor

Russian, 20th century.
Born 1924.
Painter. Scenes with figures, portraits, landscapes.
Socialist Realism.

Fiodor Savostianov trained under Boris Ioganson at the Ilya Repin Institute in Leningrad (now St Petersburg). He complied with the requirements of Socialist Realism, and adopted a Post-Impressionist technique to describe scenes of everyday life in which children frequently featured. He took part in collective exhibitions from 1951 onwards including: Spring Salon, Leningrad (1951 and 1990); *40 Years of Communist Youth*, Moscow (1958); *Art of Leningrad*, Tokyo (1960 to 1964); *Art of Leningrad* in Helsinki (1978); *Leningrad School*, Montreal (1986); *Leningrad Painters*, Tokyo (1988). Solo exhibitions include: Leningrad (from 1981 to 1983 and 1987). He was a member of the Association of Leningrad Painters.

MUSEUMS AND GALLERIES:
CHADRINSK (MFA) - MOSCOW (Ministry of Culture) - NOVGOROD (MFA) - ROSTOV-ON-DON (Gal. of Russian Art) -

St Petersburg (Gosudarstvennyj Muz. Istorii) - St Petersburg (Mus. of the October Revolution).

Auction records:

Paris, 25 March 1991, *Children and Birds* (1957, oil on canvas, 15¾ x 23½ ins / 40 x 60 cm) FRF 16,500. Paris, 6 Dec 1991, *Fishing Party* (oil on canvas, 15¾ x 27½ ins / 40 x 70 cm) FRF 4,000. Paris, 13 March 1992, *Summer in the Country* (oil on canvas, 27¼ x 35¼ ins / 69.5 x 89.5 cm) FRF 7,500. Paris, 23 March 1992, *Conversation* (oil on canvas, 31½ x 39¼ ins / 80 x 100 cm) FRF 11,500. Paris, 17 June 1992, *Summer Holidays* (oil on canvas, 43 x 33 ins / 109 x 84 cm) FRF 19,000. Paris, 7 April 1993, *Boat Ride* (oil on canvas, 35 x 40½ ins / 88 x 103 cm) FRF 16,000. Paris, 27 March 1994, *Young Girls Near the Stream* (oil on canvas, 27¼ x 37 ins / 69.5 x 94 cm) FRF 7,000.

SAVOURÉ, E.

French, 19th century.
Active in Saumur (Maine-et-Loire).
Painter. History painting.

He showed his work at the Salon between 1837 and 1845.

SAVOURNIN

French, 18th century.
Active in 1767.
Painter.

Savournin painted a *Death of St Joseph* for the church of St-Jean de Malte in Aix-en-Provence.

SAVOURNIN, Pierre

French, 17th century.
Painter.

Pierre Savournin was the master of François Faure in Grenoble, in 1673 and 1675, and master of François the son of Jacques Douric, in 1677.

SAVOY, Carel van, or Savoye or Savoyen

Dutch, 17th century.
Born c. 1621, in Antwerp; died 1665; buried on 24 January in Amsterdam.
Painter. History painting.

Carel van Savoy was a pupil of Jan Coessiers in Antwerp, in 1635. He married Catharina Wandelman in Amsterdam in 1649, and became a burger of the city in 1649.

C.V. S.

Museums and Galleries:

Bordeaux: *Venus and Cupid Riding on a Dolphin* - Darmstadt (Hessisches Landesmus.): *Christ at Emmaüs; Presentation in the Temple.*

Auction records:

Paris, 1703, *Two Small Landscapes,* FRF 125; *Venus and Cupid,* FRF 65. London, 16 April 1982, *Portrait of Mary of Orange* (1653, oil on canvas, 49¾ x 39 ins / 126.3 x 99 cm) GBP 6,500.

SAVOY, Philipp or Filips van

Flemish School, 17th century.
Born c. 1630, in Antwerp; died 1664; buried in August in Amsterdam.
Painter.

Philipp Savoy was the brother of Crael van Savoyen. He was married in Amsterdam in 1661.

SAVOYE, Anaïs

French, 19th century.
Painter. Portraits.

She exhibited at the Salons of 1835 and 1838.

SAVOYE, Catherine

French, 20th century.
Born 1942, in Algiers, to French parents.
Painter (gouache). Scenes with figures, landscapes.

Catherine Savoye's work is tightly structured and pared down, achieving enigmatic and mysterious effects.

She has shown examples of her work at various group exhibitions in Paris, including the Salon d'Automne and the Salon des Artistes Indépendants. She has also exhibited solo on a regular basis in Ibiza from 1981, in Paris from 1982, and, in 1982-1983, at the Galerie d'Art Municipale in Levallois-Perret.

SAVOYE, César

French, 17th century.
Born in Grenoble; died before 1670.
Painter. History painting, portraits.

César Savoye was the son of the master carpenter Louis Savoye and married Dorothée Meynard on 6 December 1648. He founded a painting academy in Grenoble with several of his colleagues. He produced two full-length portraits of the Frère presidents.

Bibliography:

Wantellet, Maurice, *Deux siècles et plus de peinture dauphinoise,* M. Wantellet, Grenoble, 1987.

SAVOYE, Daniel

Austrian, 18th century.
Painter.

Daniel Savoye was active in Ljubljana from 1725 to 1730. He painted portraits.

SAVOYE, Daniel de

French, 17th - 18th century.
Born 20 September 1654, in Grenoble; died 16 March 1716, in Erlangen (Bavaria), Germany.
Painter. History painting, portraits.

Daniel de Savoye was the son of the painter César Savoye. He made his will on 5 May 1670, before leaving for Paris, where he wanted to study painting. His master was Sébastien Bourdon. He is believed to have produced etchings of soldiers and of the clothing of Louis XIII's period, which were probably copies.

Museums and Galleries:

Darmstadt: *Portrait of a Man* - Dresden (Gemäldegal.): *Wife of the Artist* - Frankfurt am Main: *Portrait of a Family* - Munich (Bayerisches Nationalmus.): *Portrait of a General.*

SAVOYEN, Carel van. See **SAVOY**

SAVRASOV, Aleksei Kondratevich, or Savrassov

Russian, 19th century.
Born 1830; died 1897.
Painter. Genre scenes, landscapes.
Peredvizhniki (Wanderers) group.

Museums and Galleries:

Moscow (State Tretyakov Gal.): *Landscape; View of Oranienbaum; The Moose Island at Sokolniky; Forest Road at Sokolniky; The Petehersh Monastery in Nizny Novgorod; Portrait of A. Kunzevo* - St Petersburg (Gosudarstvennyj Russkij Muz.): *The Volga Bursting its Banks.*

Auction records:

Paris, 13 May 1974, *Volga Boatmen,* FRF 5,600. New York, 22-23 July 1993, *Landscape* (oil on canvas, 19 x 32 ins / 48.3 x 81.3 cm) USD 3,163. London, 17 Dec 1999, *Threatening Clouds over an Icy River* (1868, oil on canvas, 31 x 53 ins / 79 x 134 cm) GBP 32,000.

SAVREUX, Henri Eugène

French, 19th century.
Born in Paris.
Sculptor.

His masters were Léon Cogniet, Cornu and Jouffroy. He first exhibited at the Salon in 1869.

SAVREUX, Maurice

French, 20th century.

Born 27 May 1884, in Lille; died 30 December 1970.

Painter, watercolourist. Landscapes, still-lifes, flowers. Maurice Savreux, who was seriously wounded in World War I, was the curator of the ceramics museum of Sèvres and an honorary director of the factory.

He first exhibited in Paris at the Salon des Artistes Français in 1906, then later at the Salon d'Automne, the Salon des Indépendants and the Salon des Tuileries. He was a committee member of the Salons d'Automne and des Tuileries, and an out-of-competition and jury member of the Exposition Internationale of 1937. In 1950 the Musée des Beaux-Arts of Lille, his native city, organised a large exhibition of his work. He was made a Chevalier of the Légion d'Honneur, and then an Officier in 1947.

There is in his painting none of Cormon's cold academicism. He was a skilful painter who responded warmly to his subjects and produced balanced and sensitive landscapes, still-lifes and bouquets of flowers.

MUSEUMS AND GALLERIES:
GRENOBLE: *Morning in Provence* - LA ROCHELLE: *Bouquet of White Roses* - LYONS: *Bouquet* - PARIS (MAMVP): *Roses and Casket on a Louis XIV Commode; Vase of Flowers; Wheelbarrow; Provençal Landscape; Fireside* - ROUEN: *Landscape near Toulon.*

AUCTION RECORDS:
PARIS, 24 Nov 1928, *Flowers in a Blue Vase,* FRF 4,500. PARIS, 31 Jan 1944, *Vase of Flowers,* FRF 10,100. PARIS, July 1946, *Winter,* FRF 20,000. PARIS, 5 July 1948, *Flowers,* FRF 25,000. PARIS, 9 June 1950, *Bouquet,* FRF 25,000. PARIS, June 1953, *Flowers,* FRF 65,000. PARIS, 3 Feb 1961, *Provencal Landscape,* FRF 1,400. PARIS, 13 June 1974, *Three Vases of Flowers* (watercolour) FRF 5,600. VERSAILLES, 30 Nov 1980, *Bouquet of Flowers* (oil on canvas, 21 1/2 x 14 3/4 ins / 54.5 x 37.5 cm) FRF 6,500. PARIS, 23 June 1988, *Bouquet of Flowers against a Woodwork Background* (c. 1930, oil on canvas, 32 x 25 1/2 ins / 81 x 65 cm) FRF 60,000. LE TOUQUET, 12 Nov 1989, *Still-life with Peaches* (oil on canvas, 32 x 25 1/2 ins / 81 x 65 cm) FRF 36,000. NEUILLY, 5 Dec 1989, *Bouquet of Flowers* (oil on canvas, 18 x 13 ins / 46 x 33 cm) FRF 13,500. PARIS, 12 June 1991, *House in Snow* (oil on canvas, 18 x 22 ins / 46 x 55 cm) FRF 11,000. PARIS, 8 Feb 1995, *Provencal Fruit* (oil on canvas, 65 3/4 x 78 1/4 ins / 167 x 199 cm) FRF 5,000. PARIS, 12 Dec 1996, *Vase of Roses on a Table in front of a Window* (oil on canvas, 32 x 25 1/2 ins / 81 x 65 cm) FRF 15,000. PARIS, 27 Oct 1997, *Bouquet* (oil on panel, 13 x 9 1/4 ins / 33 x 23.5 cm) FRF 3,000. PARIS, 11 June 1999, *Large Bouquet of Flowers* (c. 1950, oil on panel, 32 x 26 ins / 81 x 65 cm) FRF 23,000. PARIS, 10 July 2003, *Landscape at Midday* (oil on board, 20 x 26 ins / 50 x 65 cm) EUR 1,600.

SAVRY. See also **SAVERY**

SAVRY, Hendrick, or Savrij
Dutch, 19th - 20th century.
Born 4 November 1823, in Haarlem; died 13 March 1907, in Haarlem.
Painter. Landscapes with figures, landscapes, animals.

Hendrick Savry was a pupil of Martinus Savry.

MUSEUMS AND GALLERIES:
MONTREAL: *Landscape with Livestock* - THE HAGUE (Gemeentemus.): *Cattle in a Meadow.*

AUCTION RECORDS:
LONDON, 4 May 1973, *Landscape with Livestock,* Gns 450. NEW YORK, 15 Oct 1976, *Landscape with Livestock* (1868, oil on canvas, 33 x 49 1/4 ins / 84 x 125 cm) USD 2,000. LONDON, 4 May 1977, *Livestock at a Drinking Place* (oil on canvas, 45 x 73 ins / 114.5 x 185.5 cm) GBP 550. NEW YORK, 26 Jan 1979, *Landscape with Livestock* (oil on canvas, 24 x 42 1/2 ins / 61 x 108 cm) USD 3,250. NEW YORK, 18 June 1982, *Livestock Returning* (oil on canvas, 33 1/4 x 52 ins / 84.5 x 132 cm) USD 4,300. AMSTERDAM, 25 April 1990, *River Landscape with Figures and Livestock* (oil on canvas, 17 1/4 x 27 1/4 ins / 43.5 x 69 cm) NLG 5,290. NEW YORK, 18 Feb 1993, *Young Shepherdess in a Vast Rural Landscape* (oil on canvas, 33 1/4 x 51 1/2 ins / 84.5 x 130.9 cm) USD 12,650. NEW YORK, 19 Jan 1994, *Livestock in a Meadow* (oil on canvas, 24 1/4 x 42 1/2 ins / 61.9 x 108 cm) USD 6,325. AMSTERDAM, 14 June 1994, *Cattle Grazing in a River Landscape* (oil on canvas, 23 3/4 x 42 1/4 ins / 60.5 x 107 cm) NLG 4,140. AMSTERDAM, 11 April 1995, *Farmer Tending his Livestock* (oil on canvas, 23 1/2 x 41 1/2 ins / 59.5 x 105.5 cm) NLG 9,204.

SAVRY, Henri M.
Dutch, 19th - 20th century.
Born 1871 or 1872, in Haarlem; died 1942.
Painter. Landscapes.

Henri M. Savry was the son of the painter Hendrick Savry.

AUCTION RECORDS:
AMSTERDAM, 11 Sept 1990, *Polder Landscape with Farm* (1893, oil on canvas, 13 1/2 x 21 3/4 ins / 34.5 x 55.5 cm) NLG 1,380.

SAVRY, Martinus
Dutch, 19th century.
Painter.

Martinus Savry was active in Haarlem in the first half of the 18th century. He was the father and teacher of Hendrick Savry.

SAVRY, Salomon. See **SAVERY**

SAVSKI, Andrej. See **IRWIN group**

SAVTCHEKO, Valentin
Russian, 20th - 21st century.
Born 2 March 1955, in Rostov.
Active in France from 1990.
Painter (mixed media).
Symbolism.

Valentin Savtcheko left Grekov School in Rostov in 1971 and six years later graduated from the Repin Institute in Petrograd (St Petersburg). He paints large-format compositions dominated by strong colours. He mixes abstraction and figuration into graphic works that have a symbolic content and, he says, 'attempt to orchestrate the sphere of spiritual communication between the human being and the universe'. His best-known works are: *Energy of the Intelligence of the 3rd Millenium, Saving the Soul* and *Origin of the World.* He calls his style Sens-Art. He has shown his work frequently in Russia and overseas: Paris (notably at the Galerie de Nesle, 1991), Barcelona, Oslo and San Diego, as well as Germany, Britain, Sweden and Belgium.

AUCTION RECORDS:
PARIS, 1 March 1993, *The sleeping Horse* (1989, oil on canvas, 25 1/2 x 36 1/4 ins / 65 x 92 cm) FRF 3,500.

SAVTCHENKOVA, Maria
Russian, 20th century.
Born 1917.
Painter. Scenes with figures, portraits, landscapes.

Maria Savtchenkova trained at the V. Surikov school of fine art in Moscow and worked under Sergei Gerasimov. She was a member of the Association of Moscow Painters, and was nominated U.S.S.R. Painter Emeritus.

MUSEUMS AND GALLERIES:

MOSCOW (Ministry of Culture) - MOSCOW (Pushkin MFA) - MOSCOW (State Tretyakov Gal.) - ST PETERSBURG (Gosudarstvennyj Russkij Muz.).

AUCTION RECORDS:

PARIS, 25 Nov 1991, *In the Garden* (1949, oil on canvas, 39 1/4 x 27 1/2 ins / 100 x 70 cm) FRF 7,500.

SAVY, Max

French, 20th century.

Born 1918, in Albi.

Painter. Landscapes.

Before he devoted himself full-time to painting Max Savy was an art teacher in Carcassone. He exhibited in Paris at the Salon d'Automne, the Salon Peintres de Leurs Temps, the Salon Comparaisons, and the Salon de la Société Nationale des Beaux-Arts. He has held solo shows in France and abroad: Brussels, Zurich, Geneva, London and New York, including one in 2003 at the Centre National et Musée Jean Jaurès, Castres.

He painted landscapes of the South of France and Egypt, especially the Nile.

MUSEUMS AND GALLERIES:

NARBONNE (MAH): *The Garrigue on Fire* (1984).

AUCTION RECORDS:

ST-JEAN-CAP-FERRAT, 16 March 1993, *The Nile* (oil on canvas, 44 1/2 x 57 1/2 ins / 113 x 146 cm) FRF 20,000; *Feluccas on the Nile* (oil on canvas, 28 3/4 x 36 1/4 ins / 73 x 92 cm) FRF 12,000.

SAVY, Yo. See **SERMAYER**

SAVYALOV, Fedor Semenovich, or Zavialov

Russian, 19th century.

Born 21 October 1810; died 15 June 1856.

Painter. History painting, portraits.

Fedor Semenovich Savyalov studied and later taught at the art academy in St Petersburg.

SAWADA, Masahiro

Japanese, 20th century.

Born 1894, in Shizuoka (Kyuchu Island).

Painter, sculptor. Religious subjects.

Sawada Masahiro obtained a diploma from the department of sculpture at the University of Fine Arts in Tokyo. He specialised in Buddhist sculpture working mainly for the temples. From 1921 his work appeared in many group and individual exhibitions in Tokyo.

SAWALO, or Sawalon

Flemish School, 12th century.

Illuminator.

Sawalo illustrated a Bible in five volumes, each of which is decorated with a miniature. He is thought to be the same person as the illuminator of the same period called Sawalon, who was a monk in the abbey of Amand-en-Pevèle in 1143.

SAWICZEWSKI, Stanislav

Polish, 19th - 20th century.

Born 31 March 1866, in Cracow.

Painter, illustrator. Portraits, architectural views.

Stanislav Sawiczewski trained in Cracow, Munich, Vienna and Breslau (now Wocrlaw). He lived and worked in Warsaw.

MUSEUMS AND GALLERIES:

LVIV (Art Gallery) - WARSAW (Muz. Narodowe).

SAWIN, Nazaire. See **SAVIN Nazari**

SAWIN, Nicéphore. See **SAVIN Nikofor**

SAWIN, Ustoma. See **SAVIN Istoma**

SAWKA, Jan

Polish, 20th - 21st century.

Born 10 December 1946, in Zabrze.

Active in the USA from 1977.

Painter (including mixed media), illustrator, engraver, sculptor. Scenes with figures, figures, landscapes. Posters, stage sets.

Jan Sawka studied architecture before enrolling in the school of fine arts in Wroclaw from 1969 to 1972. In 1976, fleeing Poland, he lived for a while in Paris as a resident artist at the Centre Georges Pompidou, then moved to New York, where he set up a graphic art company. As well as designing posters, he also paints, mixing media that favour a strongly coloured register, with warm tones, in a suggestive style. He works from fragments of images which he combines in special ways, drawing his inspiration from the reality of his subjects, in particular from the omnipresent human in his canvases. He has been showing his works in solo exhibitions since 1971. In 1976 and 1980 he showed at the poster museum, Warsaw; in 1977 at the Galerie Noire, Paris; in 1978 at the Musée d'Art Moderne de Paris; in 1991 at the Galerie Lefor-Openo, Paris, and at the Polish national museum in Gdansk; in 1992 at the Queens Museum of Art at the Bulova Corporate Center, at the universal exhibition in Seville, at the museum of art and science in Prague and at the national museum in Gdansk.

BIBLIOGRAPHY:

Cuba, L. Stanley, *Jan Sawka, a Selected Rétrospective*, travelling exhibition catalogue, Center for the Arts and Humanities, Arvada (CO), 1990. Souchaud, Pierre, '*Jan Sawka, une fabuleuse exubérance imagée*' in *Artension*, periodical, Rouen, autumn 1991. Rostworowski, Marek/Chruscicki, Tadeusz/Simons, Thomas W., *Jan Sawka, powroty [Jan Sawka, The Returns]*, travelling exhibition catalogue, Muzeum Narodowe, Cracow, 1991 (text in Polish and English).

MUSEUMS AND GALLERIES:

AMSTERDAM (Stedelijk Mus.) - BRNO (Moravská Gal.) - BRUSSELS (Bibliothèque royale Albert Ier) - CAGNES-SUR-MER (Mus.-Château) - COPENHAGEN (Kunstindustrimus.) - COTTBUS (Brandenburgische Kunstsammlungen) - CRACOW (Muz. Narodowe) - ESSEN (Mus.) - FORT COLLINS (AM) - JERUSALEM (Israel Mus.) - LAHTI (Lahden taidemuseo) - NEW YORK (MoMA) - PARIS (Bibliothèque Forney) - PARIS (MNAM-CCI) - PARIS (Mus. de la Publicité) - POZNAN (Muz. Narodowe) - PRAGUE (Art and Science Mus.) - TOYAMA (MMA) - WASHINGTON DC (Library of Congress) - WROCLAW (Muz. Narodowe).

SAWREY, Hugh David, or Saurey

Australian, 20th century.

Born 1923; died 1999.

Painter. Scenes with figures, local scenes, landscapes.

Hugh David Sawrey speciaised in the representation of the Australian way of life, notably cattle breeders, and scenes with a Western mood such as *Train Hold-up*.

AUCTION RECORDS:

ROSEBERY, 7 Sept 1976, *The Opal Gougers Camp* (oil on canvas, 19 1/4 x 23 1/4 ins / 49 x 59 cm) AUD 1,600. ROSEBERY, 21 June 1977, *Picaninny Dawn* (oil on canvas, 23 1/2 x 29 1/2 ins / 60 x 75 cm) AUD 950. SYDNEY, 30 June 1980, *The Discussion by the Saddle Room* (oil on canvas, 29 1/2 x 39 1/4 ins / 75 x 100 cm) AUD 2,900. SYDNEY, 21 Sept 1981, *The Scandal Monger* (oil on canvas, 20 x 23 1/2 ins / 51 x 60 cm) AUD 1,800. SYDNEY, 14 March 1983, *Packing the Nags, Western Queensland* (oil on card, 29 1/2 x 39 1/4 ins / 75 x 100 cm) AUD 2,000. SYDNEY, 25 March 1985, *Robbing the Bendigo Mail* (oil on canvas, 29 1/2 x 39 1/4 ins / 75 x 100 cm) AUD 3,000. SYDNEY, 4 July 1988, *Yellow Bobber* (oil on card, 19 3/4 x 23 1/2 ins / 50 x 60 cm) AUD 1,100. SYDNEY, 21 Nov 1988, *Train Hold-up* (oil on card, 29 1/2 x 39 1/4 ins / 75 x 100 cm) AUD 1,600; *Crowd Movement* (oil on card, 20 x 24 ins / 51 x 61 cm) AUD 3,000.

SYDNEY, 20 March 1989, *Arrival of the Grazcos Sheep Shearers* (oil on card, 19 3/4 x 23 1/2 ins / 50 x 60 cm) AUD 2,600. SYDNEY, 3 July 1989, *Small Church in Warwick* (oil on canvas, 30 x 40 1/4 ins / 76 x 102 cm) AUD 6,000. LONDON, 30 Nov 1989, *Steadying the Leaders, Western Queensland* (oil on canvas, 20 x 24 ins / 50.8 x 60.9 cm) GBP 3,300. SYDNEY, 26 March 1990, *Camp of the Seasonal Workers* (oil on card, 11 3/4 x 14 1/4 ins / 30 x 36 cm) AUD 4,600; *Dinner in the Camp along the Warrigo* (oil on canvas, 19 3/4 x 23 1/2 ins / 50 x 60 cm) AUD 6,000. SYDNEY, 2 July 1990, *Herd of Wild Cattle in Motion* (oil on canvas, 28 1/4 x 40 1/4 ins / 72 x 102 cm) AUD 11,000. SYDNEY, 15 Oct 1990, *Warriors of the Pinturi* (oil on canvas, 30 x 39 3/4 ins / 76 x 101 cm) AUD 7,500. SYDNEY, 2 Dec 1991, *Hold-up* (oil on canvas, 30 x 39 3/4 ins / 76 x 101 cm) AUD 10,500. SYDNEY, 29-30 March 1992, *Cattlemen by Heifer Creek* (oil on canvas, 30 x 40 1/4 ins / 76 x 102 cm) AUD 9,000. SYDNEY, 3 Aug 1999, *Quinn's Farm, Darling Downs, Queensland* (oil on canvas, 30 x 39 ins / 75 x 100 cm) AUD 9,500. SYDNEY, 26 Oct 1999, *The Urger* (oil on canvas, 30 x 39 ins / 75 x 100 cm) AUD 15,000. MELBOURNE, 27 Nov 2000, *Travelling Mob along the Barcoo River, West Queensland* (oil on canvas, 29 x 39 ins / 74 x 99 cm) AUD 11,000. MELBOURNE, 29 Nov 2000, *Harry Peacock and his Family - Packing Up at the Guv'mint Bore, West Queensland* (oil on composition board, 20 x 24 ins / 50 x 60 cm) AUD 11,000. MELBOURNE, 9 May 2001, *Territory Trooper on Patrol with His Black Boy at Number 10 Bore, NT* (oil on canvas, 30 x 39 ins / 75 x 100 cm) AUD 12,000. PADDINGTON, 27 Aug 2001, *Argyle Station Cattleman, Kimberley Region, WA* (oil on canvas, 36 x 48 ins / 91 x 122 cm) AUD 13,000. PADDINGTON, 25 Aug 2002, *Camp by the Broncho Yard, Dimantina Lakes Station* (oil on canvas, 29 x 39 ins / 74 x 99 cm) AUD 13,000. SYDNEY, 21 Oct 2002, *Plainsman, NW Queensland* (oil on canvas, 30 x 40 ins / 77 x 102 cm) AUD 13,000. SYDNEY, 29 Oct 2003, *When Smithy Rung the Shed* (oil on canvas, 29 x 39 ins / 74 x 100 cm) AUD 19,000. SYDNEY, 29 Oct 2003, *Cockatoo* (oil on board, 29 x 39 ins / 74 x 98 cm) AUD 19,000. MELBOURNE, 10 March 2004, *When Quigley Won the Boulia Cup* (oil on canvas, 30 x 40 ins / 76 x 102 cm) AUD 26,000. MELBOURNE, 10 March 2004, *Moriaty's Shout* (oil on canvas, 30 x 39 ins / 75 x 100 cm) AUD 26,000.

SAWYER, Edward Warren
American, 20th century.
Born 17 March 1876, in Chicago; died 1932, in Clos Vert la Palasse (Toulon), France.
Sculptor, engraver, medallist.

Edward Sawyer studied under Jean Paul Laurens, Jean Antoine Injalbert, Charles Raoul Verlet, Emmanuel Fremiet and Auguste Rodin in Paris. He received several awards including a mention at the Salon des Artistes Français in Paris in 1914.

MUSEUMS AND GALLERIES:
NEW YORK - PARIS (MAMVP) - WASHINGTON DC.

SAWYER, F.
British, 19th century.
Painter.

F. Sawyer was awarded a prize in 1841.

SAWYER, Helen Alton, Mrs Jerry Farnsworth
American, 20th century.
Born 1900; died 1999.
Painter.

Helen Sawyer took part in international exhibitions at the Carnegie Foundation in Pittsburgh.

SAWYER, Philippe Ayer
American, 20th century.
Born 18 June 1877, in Chicago; died 1949.
Painter, engraver.

Philippe Sawyer studied under Léon Bonnat at the École des Beaux-Arts in Paris and at the Art Institute in Chicago. He founded the Salon of Independent Artists in Detroit and was secretary at the American Academy in Rome, and was also an art critic. He produced etchings.

Sawyer exhibited in Paris at the Salon d'Automne, the Salon de la Société Nationale des Beaux-Arts and the Salon des Indépendants, and also in Detroit and Honolulu.

MUSEUMS AND GALLERIES:
NEW YORK (American Library): etchings.

SAWYER, R.
British, 19th century.
Active from 1820 to 1830.
Engraver (etching/stippling). Portraits.

R. Sawyer engraved portraits of leading public figures of his day.

SAWYER, Wells Moses
American, 19th - 20th century.
Born 31 January 1861, in Iowa; died 1961.
Painter, illustrator. Landscapes, architectural views.

Wells Sawyer studied at the Art Institute in Chicago, the Art Students' League in New York, the Corcoran School of Art in Washington and under Howard Helmick. He was a member of the Salmagundi Club.

SAX
German, 18th century.
Active in Mosbach in 1774.
Painter (glazed earthenware).

Sax painted a watchcase which can be found at Karlsruhe castle.

SAX, Jaap
Dutch, 20th century.
Born 1899; died 1982.
Painter. Landscapes, animals.

Jaap Sax painted scenes of country life.

AUCTION RECORDS:
AMSTERDAM, 24 May 1989, *Chickens in front of a Farmhouse* (oil on panel, 19 3/4 x 27 1/2 ins / 50 x 70 cm) NLG 1,035. AMSTERDAM, 8 Dec 1994, *Farm* (oil on panel, 19 3/4 x 27 1/2 ins / 50 x 70 cm) NLG 1,725. AMSTERDAM, 18 June 1996, *Mountain Outcrop* (oil on panel, 11 x 11 1/2 ins / 28 x 29 cm) NLG 1,610.

SAX, Marçal de. See **MARZAL DE SAX**

SAXE, Henry
Canadian, 20th century.
Born 24 September 1937, in Montreal.
Painter, engraver, collage artist, sculptor.
Minimal Art.

Henry Saxe studied in Albert Dumouchal's studio at the École des Beaux-Arts in Montreal from 1956 until 1961. He has visited the USA several times, and lives and works in Tamworth (Ontario).

Saxe's first pictures were Expressionist in style, colourful and exuberant. In 1964 and 1965 he created works in which clearly coloured shapes with sharply defined contours intersected with and were superimposed on each other. Then he began to work with irregularly shaped panels of wood onto which he painted geometric shapes. More recently he has turned to sculpture, having linear forms produced in a factory, which can then be assembled in different ways. He has orientated his work towards the Minimal Art inspired by America, exploiting primary structures, or simple modules, in order to create sensitivity to the perception of space, volume or colour, most importantly without any mental effort being required to achieve this.

Saxe has taken part in many collective exhibitions at the Musée des Beaux-Arts and the Galerie Nationale du Canada in Montreal, and also in the Biennale des Jeunes de Paris in 1967; in *Canada art d'aujourd'hui* (*Art of Today in Canada*) in

Paris, Lausanne, Rome and Brussels at the same time; the third Salon International des Galeries Pilotes at the Musée Cantonal in Lausanne and the Musée d'Art Moderne de la Ville de Paris in 1970; the Musée d'Art Contemporain in Montreal in 1973; *Les Vingt Ans du Musée à travers sa Collection (Twenty Years On: the Museum through its Collections)* at the Musée d'Art Contemporain in Montreal in 1985. He has shown his works regularly in private exhibitions in Montreal since 1962, including at the Musée des Beaux-Arts in 1967, and also in Toronto in 1968 and 1970, and London, Ontario, in 1969.

BIBLIOGRAPHY:

IIIe Salon international des Galeries Pilotes, exhibition catalogue, Musée cantonal, Lausanne, 1970. *Les 20 ans du Musée à travers sa collection*, exhibition catalogue, Musée d'Art contemporain, Montreal, 1985. *METAlogic: Sculpture from the Collection of the Robert McLaughlin Gallery*, exhibition catalogue, Robert McLaughlin Gallery, Oshawa, 2001.

MUSEUMS AND GALLERIES:

MONTREAL (MAC): *The Time Machine* (etching); *Black Strap* (1963, lithograph); *Doubleview* (1965, laminated wood); *Parrylaxis* (1968); *Untitled* (1963, acrylic/paper); *For Three Blacks* (1976, steel plaques) - OSHAWA (Robert McLaughlin Gal.) - OTTAWA (NG. of Canada) - WATERLOO (University of Waterloo AG).

SAXELIN, Into

Finnish, 20th century.
Born 1883; died 26 May 1926, in Paris.
Sculptor. Statuettes.

MUSEUMS AND GALLERIES:

HELSINKI (Ateneumin Taidemus.): three statuettes.

SAXESEN, Wilhelm or Friedrich Wilhelm Reisig

German, 19th century.
Born 1792, in Oehe; died 1850, in Kiel.
Painter, engraver. Portraits, landscapes.

Saxesen trained in Dresden. He engraved and produced lithographs of landscapes in the Harz.

MUSEUMS AND GALLERIES:

KIEL (Stadtmus.): *Eisenach and the Castle of Wartburg.*

AUCTION RECORDS:

COLOGNE, 26 March 1976, *Mountainscape* (1834, oil on canvas, 20½ x 26½ ins / 52 x 67.5 cm) DEM 5,200.

SÄXINGER, Johann Jakob

German, 18th century.
Active in Pfeffenhausen in 1770.
Sculptor (wood).

Säxinger sculpted the side altars in the church of Mirskofen near Landshut.

SAXOD, Pierre

Swiss, 20th century.
Born 1958, in Geneva; died 1990, in Paris.
Active in France.
Painter, pastellist. Scenes with figures, urban landscapes, still-lifes.

In 1988, Pierre Saxod participated in the creation of the literary review *Le Serpent à Plumes (Quilled Serpent)*, several issues of which he illustrated. He took part in collective exhibitions at Montrouge (1982), at the city hall in Paris (1983), at the Musée des Beaux-Arts, Tours, and at the Musée des Arts Décoratifs, Paris (1984). He had solo shows at the Galerie Karl Flinker, Paris (1983), at the Musée des Beaux-Arts, Belfort (1984), at the Galerie des Bastions, Geneva (1985, 1987) and at the Galerie Blondel, Paris (1986).

BIBLIOGRAPHY:

Le Serpent à plumes n° 7, periodical, Paris, 1990.

MUSEUMS AND GALLERIES:

BORDEAUX (FRAC Aquitaine) - CLERMONT-FERRAND (FRAC Auvergne).

SAXON, James

British, 19th century.
Born in Manchester; died after 1828, in London.
Painter. Portraits.

James Saxon exhibited at the Royal Academy from 1795 to 1817. It appears that he travelled extensively: he is known to have lived in Edinburgh and to have left for London in 1805, after which he spent several years in St Petersburg before spending a period in Glasgow, then settling on a permanent basis in London.

MUSEUMS AND GALLERIES:

EDINBURGH (Scottish National Portrait Gal.): *Portrait of John Clerk of Eldin* - LONDON (National Portrait Gal.): *Sir Richard Phillips* (1806, oil on canvas).

SAXON, John Gordon. See SAXTON

SAXON MASTER, or Meister Sächsicher

German, 16th century.
Active c. 1550.
Painter, engraver (wood).

The museum in Cologne has several works by the Saxon Master.

SAXONI, Charles

French, 19th century.
Painter. Architectural views, landscapes.

He exhibited in Paris, at the Salon, in 1835 and 1839, and in London in 1846.

SAXTON, Christopher

British, 16th century.
Born between 1542 and 1544, in Yorkshire.
Engraver.

Christopher Saxton worked in the service of Thomas Seckford, Master of Requests. He made a series of maps of the counties of England and Wales, some of which he engraved with the assistance of R. Hogenberg, Auguste Ryllier and others. The collection appeared in 1579 and was dedicated to Queen Elizabeth I.

MUSEUMS AND GALLERIES:

GLASGOW (University Library, Special Collections): *Atlas of the Countries of England and Wales* (c. 1579, map).

SAXTON, John Gordon, or Saxon

American, 19th - 20th century.
Born 1860, in Troy (New York).
Painter. Landscapes.

John Saxton studied under Jules Lefèvre, Luc-Olivier Merson and Robert Fleury in Paris. He received several awards including an honourable mention at the Exposition Universelle (Universal Exhibition) in Paris in 1900, a mention in Buffalo in 1901 and a bronze medal in Saint Louis in 1904.

SAY, Frederick Richard

British, 19th century.
Born 1827; died probably 1860.
Painter, engraver. Portraits.

Frederick Richard Say was the son of the engraver William Say. Between 1825 and 1954 he exhibited numerous works in London, notably at the Royal Academy and, on occasion, at the British Institution. For a time Say's work was very much in vogue and a number of his portrait originals were subsequently engraved by Samuel Cousins. His work is sometimes mistaken for early examples of compositions by Sir Thomas Lawrence.

MUSEUMS AND GALLERIES:

LONDON (National Portrait Gal.): *Edward Law, 1st Earl of Ellenborough* (c. 1845, oil on canvas); *Edward Stanley, 14th Earl of Derby* (1844, oil on canvas); *Henry Clinton, 5th Duke of Newcastle* (1848, oil on canvas); portraits commissioned by Sir Robert Peel for his 'Statesmen's Gallery'.

AUCTION RECORDS:

LONDON, 9 Oct 1928, *Jane Edwardes, Lady Dering*, GBP 388. NEW YORK, 2 April 1931, *Miss Gray*, USD 225. NEW YORK, 29 April 1965, *Portrait of a Young Girl and herTwo Brothers*, USD 2,750. NEW YORK, 17 Jan 1985, *Landscape with a Group Portrait of Three Children* (oil on canvas, 42 1/2 x 35 ins / 108 x 89 cm) USD 7,000. LONDON, 18 April 1986, *Portrait of Robert Robertson, his Wife and their Two Daughters* (oil on canvas, 64 1/4 x 50 1/2 ins / 163 x 128.3 cm) GBP 9,000. LONDON, 14 July 1989, *Portrait of Robert Robertson, standing next to his wife Bridget and their two daughters Bridget and Amelia* (oil on canvas, 64 1/4 x 50 1/2 ins / 163 x 128.3 cm) GBP 30,800.

SAY, Geza
Hungarian, 20th century.
Born 16 June 1892, in Székesfehérvár.
Painter. Portraits, landscapes.

Geza Say studied in Budapest.

MUSEUMS AND GALLERIES:

BUDAPEST (Fővárosi Képtár).

SAY, Thekla von, Married name Kurelec
Hungarian, 20th century.
Born 1887, in Székesfehérvár.
Painter. Figures, landscapes.

Thekla von Say trained in Budapest where she lived and worked, and in Paris.

SAY, William
British, 18th - 19th century.
Born 1768, in Lakenham, near Norwich; died 24 August 1834, in London.
Painter, engraver (mezzotint).

William Say was the father of Frederick Say. He did not take up art until he moved to London after the age of 21 and following his marriage. He studied under James Ward and rapidly made a name for himself as an engraver. In 1807 he was retained as an engraver by the Duke of Gloucester. William Say is credited with around 300 engravings, notably from originals by contemporaries such as Turner.

Stamp of sale

AUCTION RECORDS:

LONDON, 1895, *Lady Mildmay*, FRF 1,825. LONDON, 2 May 1922, *The Alps* (drawing) GBP 12; *Ten Plagues of Egypt* (drawing) GBP 10.

SAYCE, John
British, 19th century.
Active c. 1800.
Engraver.

John Sayce was a portrait engraver who favoured a scraper technique.

SAYED, Khalifa. See **KHALIFA Sayed**

SAYER, Franz Joseph
German, 19th century.
Born 22 February 1816, in Rottweil; died 8 September 1891, in Rottweil.
Painter.

Franz Joseph Sayer executed paintings for churches in Bochingen, Gösslingen, Mulfingen and Neufra.

SAYER, George
British, 19th century.
Active in London.
Painter. Portraits.

George Sayer was an exhibitor at the Royal Academy from 1843 to 1848.

SAYER, James, or Sayers
British, 18th - 19th century.
Born August 1748, in Yarmouth; died 20 April 1823, in London.
Caricaturist, engraver (etching/mezzotint).

James Sayer worked originally as a prosecuting attorney's clerk. He moved to London in 1780, however, and began to produce caricatures. His support for Pitt in his political battle against Charles Fox led to lucrative commissions.

SAYER, Paul
German, 19th century.
Born 13 June 1832, in St Märgen; died 2 October 1890, in Munich.
Sculptor.

Paul Sayer trained under Max von Widnmann. He sculpted statues and tombs for churches in Munich, Sewen and Strasbourg.

SAYER, Reuben Thomas William.
See **SAYERS**

SAYERS, James. See **SAYER**

SAYERS, Reuben Thomas William, or Sayer
British, 19th century.
Born 1815; died 18 October 1888.
Painter. Genre scenes, portraits.

Reuben Sayers exhibited between 1841 and 1867 at London's Royal Academy, the British Institution and the Society of British Artists.

MUSEUMS AND GALLERIES:

SALFORD (Museum and AG): *A Bride*.

AUCTION RECORDS:

LONDON, 21 July 1978, *Alexander and Diogenes* (1861, oil on canvas, after Sir Edwin Landseer, 43 1/2 x 56 1/4 ins / 110.5 x 142.8 cm) GBP 900. LONDON, 10 Feb 2004, *Portrait of a Young Girl Holding a Rabbit* (oil on canvas, oval, 36 x 28 ins / 91 x 71 cm) GBP 1,200.

SAYGIN, Hasan
Turkish, 20th - 21st century.
Born 1958.
Painter. Figures, nudes.

Hasan Saygin integrates representations of the body copied from Raphael, Michelangelo, Caravaggio, Ingres and Canova with abstract compositions. Since 2000, he has painted in a representational style, producing hyperrealist still-lifes on coloured foundations evoking stone with nudes curled up in front of windows that open on to cloudy skies. He has shown his works in solo exhibitions, including in 1992 in Paris and in 2003 at the Galerie Vendôme in Paris.

SAYLER, Ulrich
German, 15th century.
Active in Augsburg.
Sculptor (wood).

Ulrich Sayler carved the woodwork in a room in the monastery of St Ulrich and St Afra, Augsburg.

SAYRE, Fred Grayson
American, 20th century.
Born 1879; died 1938.
Painter. Landscapes.

AUCTION RECORDS:

NEW YORK, 30 May 1986, *Great Silence* (oil on canvas, 50 x 60 ins / 127.3 x 152.5 cm) USD 10,000. NEW YORK, 31 March 1993, *Californian Landscape* (oil/synthetic resin, 11 3/4 x 14 3/4 ins / 29.8 x 37.5 cm) USD 1,725. PASADENA, 16 Feb 1999, *Wasteland, Panoramic Landscape* (oil on canvas, 40 x 50 ins / 102 x 127 cm) USD 9,500. CINCINNATI, 23 May 1999, *Trapped*

(c. 1925, oil on canvas, 36 x 28 ins / 91 x 71 cm) USD 8,000. LOS ANGELES, 24 Oct 2000, *Verbena Clad Dunes* (oil on canvas, 28 x 36 ins / 71 x 91 cm) USD 22,000. PASADENA, 14 Nov 2000, *Cottonwood Rancho* (oil on canvas, 20 x 24 ins / 51 x 61 cm) USD 3,750. PASADENA, 13 Feb 2001, *Coastal Landscape* (oil on canvas on masonite, 13 x 16 ins / 33 x 41 cm) USD 1,800. PASADENA, 13 Feb 2001, *Landscape* (oil on canvas, 16 x 20 ins / 41 x 51 cm) USD 2,000. WASHINGTON, 27 April 2002, *Tropical Landscape with Figures Along River* (oil on canvas on masonite, 30 x 25 ins / 76 x 63 cm) USD 1,800. SAN FRANCISCO, 19 Nov 2002, *Lure of Desert Trails* (oil on canvas, 20 x 24 ins / 51 x 62 cm) USD 4,000. LOS ANGELES, 16 May 2004, *Desert Landscape* (oil on canvas, 20 x 24 ins / 51 x 61 cm) USD 5,000. PASADENA, 15 June 2004, *Pool in a Mountain Eucalyptus Landscape* (oil on canvas, 30 x 36 ins / 76 x 91 cm) USD 3,000.

SAYTER, Daniel or Joseph Daniel.
See **SEITER**

SAYTOUR, Patrick

French, 20th century.
Born 1935, in Nice.
Painter, draughtsman, sculptor, mixed media, installation artist.
Groupe Supports-Surfaces, 1968-1971.

Patrick Saytour studied first at the École des Arts Décoratifs, Nice, and then at the École Camondo, Paris. Initially he was involved in theatre and set design. He is a professor at the École des Beaux-Arts, Montpellier, and lives and works in Aubais.

He has exhibited in many group exhibitions, in the 1970s especially those of the Groupe Support-Surfaces: 1967, 1969, Paris Biennale; 1968, Menton Biennale; 1969, dispersal of works made from materials found in the village of Coaraze, *La peinture en question* (*Painting in Question*) at the Museum of Le Havre, Salon de Mai; 1970, *Été 70* (*Summer 70*), various works on the beach, on grass, in a forest, a creek, a gallery, on the village square (...); 1970, 1977, 1983, ARC at the Musée d'Art Moderne, Paris; 1970, 1980 FIAC (Foire Internationale d'Art Contemporain), Paris; 1971, Musée Galliera, Paris; 1974, *Nouvelle Peinture en France* (*New Painting in France*), the Musée d'Art et d'Industrie, St-Étienne, the museums of Chambéry, Lucerne, Aix-la-Chapelle; 1980, Museum of Arles, Musée d'Art et d'Industrie, St-Étienne; 1982, *Leçons de chose*, Kunsthalle, Bern, the Museum of Toulon, the Musée Savoisien, Chambéry nd the Maison de la Culture, Châlon-sur Saône, then the ARC, Paris, under the title *Truc et Troc*; 1983, Menton Biennale; 1984, ELAC (Espace Lyonnais d'Art Contemporain), Lyons, Galerie d'Art Contemporain des Musées de Nice; 1984, 1985, Musée Ziem, Martigues; 1986, 1988, Centre d'Art Contemporain at the abbey of St-André, Meymac; 1991, Lyons Biennale; 1992, Ludwig Museum, Koblenz; 1994, Salon of Montrouge; 1994, Central Artists' House, Moscow; 1995, Musée d'Art Moderne, Villeneuve-d;Ascq; 1996, Salon of Montrouge, Museum of Nice; 2002, *Les Années 70: l'art en cause* (*The 1970s: Art in Question*), CAPC-Musée d'Art Comtemporain, Bordeaux; 2003, *L'état des chose* (*The State of Things*), a look at the status of everyday objects in contemporary art, an exhibition held as part of *Trésors publics, 20 ans de création dans les Fonds régionaux d'art comtemporain (FRAC)* (*Public Treasury, 20 Years of Creation in the Regional Collection of Contemporary Art*), Musée des Beaux-Arts, Nantes.

He held no solo exhibitions while the Groupe Supports-Surfaces was in existence, but showed alone in: 1975, 1976, 1978, 1979, 1981, Galerie Éric Fabre, Paris; 1976, ADDA, Marseilles; 1980, Galerie Errata, Montpellier; 1981, Musée Savoisien, Chambéry; 1982, Musée d'Art et d'Industrie, St-Étienne; 1983, Rotterdam; 1984, Tokyo; 1986, Musée Ingres, Montauban; 1987, École des Beaux-Arts, Paris; 1987, 1993, 1996, Galerie de Paris, Paris; 1988, Galerie d'En Haut, Villeneuve d'Ascq; 1989, CNAP (Centre National des Arts Plastiques), Paris; 1990, Calder Studio, Saché; 1993, 1996, Galerie de Paris, Paris; 1994, FRAC Languedoc-Roussillon, Château de Castellnou; 1996, Maison de la Culture, Bourges; 2003, Centre d'Art Contemporain Le Quartier, Quimper.

The public commissions he has carried out have been mainly sculptures: 1987, for Vitrolles, 1988, for the prefecture of Nevers, and a fountain consisting of five statues for the Place victor Hugo, Hirson (Aisne).

He was one of the members of the Groupe Supports-Surfaces, which questioned painting materials and challenged those traditionally used. In the 1970s he exhibited canvases up to 30 metres long and deployed them freely in nature to underline their material qualities. He uses this ordinary material in a piece or strips - a classic painting material freed from its frame. Using manufacturing techniques, he modifies the material by folding (which implies unfolding), rolling up (which implies unrolling), burning (by fire), fading (by the sun), and in the series *Tuilages* by stretching and dipping (in tar, glue or road-marking paint)... The material changes, successively printed (flag), solidified (waxed canvas, balata), woven (tapestry), then increased in volume and bunched.

Continuing to make use of everyday odd-and-ends, he introduced the three-dimensional in the form of furniture and household elements (especially in the series of tents), ironically changing their function: anchor chains found in the shipyards of St-Nazaire used to make umbrella designs or foliage; owners of garments associated with their reproduction in painting (*Chronicles* of 1990). Drawing on popular imagery, his assemblages of disparate objects become less restrained and have a tendency to kitsch - imitation materials, false marble and gilt, waxcloth, imitation leather, synthetic textiles; but also objects such as plastic flowers, unfashionable furniture (from the 50s) such as rocking chairs on spiral bases, plastic luggage cases, pieces of ironwork, neon lamps. At the end of the 1980s he returned to more traditional techniques and genres, such as drawing from models, still-lifes, nudes, portraits, plaster casts. He works on the stereotype, borrows from history and gives birth to effigies of Pétain in gilded resin.

Starting from an ordinary object or image, Saytour makes us aware of the gesture, the manipulation that gives rise to a work of art: `Not the tearing of objects or things from their ordinary condition, but the understanding of how this uprooting changes them, turns them into cult objects' (Saytour).

BIBLIOGRAPHY:

Bioulès, Vincent/Viallat, Claude/Valensi/Saytour/Devade, Marc/Dezeuze, Daniel, *Supports-Surfaces*, exhibition catalogue, ARC musée d'Art moderne de la Ville de Paris, Paris, 1970. G., D., '*Supports-Surfaces*' in *Chroniques de l'Art Vivant* n° 14, periodical, Maeght, Paris, October 1970. *Saytour*, exhibition catalogue, Musée Savoisien, Chambéry, 1981. *Saytour 1967-1974-1980*, exhibition catalogue, Musée d'Art et d'Industrie, St-Étienne, 1983. Poinsot, Jean-Marc, '*Supports-Surfaces*' in *coll. Mise au point sur l'Art actuel*, Limage 2, Paris, 1983. Descendre, Nadine, '*De l'apparence à l'idée: Patrick Saytour symboliste*' in *Artstudio* n° 5, periodical, Gal. Templon, Paris, summer 1987. Carrein, Catherine, *Supports/Surfaces: 1966-1974*, exhibition catalogue, Musée d'Art moderne, St-Étienne, 1991. *Saytour - Peur-Senex*, exhibition leaflet, Château de Castellnou, Castellnou, 1994. *Saytour*, exhibition catalogue, Maison de la Culture, Bourges, 1996. Fréruchet, Maurice, et al., *Les Années soixante-dix: l'art en cause*, exhibition catalogue, Capc musée d'Art contemporain, Bordeaux, 2002. Zahm, Olivier (preface), et al., *Trésors publics, 20 ans de création dans les Fonds régionaux d'art contemporain*, Flammarion, Paris, 2003 (text in French and English).

MUSEUMS AND GALLERIES:
DÔLE (FRAC Franche-Comté): *Juxtaposition III* (1984) - MARSEILLES (Mus. Cantini): *Balance of Terror* (1981) - PARIS (FNAC): *Hall no. 5* (1982, sculpture) - PARIS (MNAM-CCI): *Untitled* (1968); *Untitled* (1974); *Tuilage* (1977) - ST-ÉTIENNE (MAM): *Untitled* (1967) - TOULOUSE (FRAC Midi-Pyrénées) - VILLEURBANNE (FRAC Rhône-Alpes).

SAYU, nickname: Katsura
Japanese, 18th century.
Active in the Osaka region c. 1760.
Painter, illustrator.

SAYVE. See **SAIVE**

SAZONOFF. See **SASONOV Vasili Kondratevich**

SAZONOV. See **SASONOV Vasili Kondratevich**

SAZYEPIN, Nikolai Konstantinovich, or Zatsepin
Russian, 19th century.
Born 1818; died 10 May 1855, in Sebastopol, at the front.
Painter. Genre scenes, portraits.
Nikolai Konstantinovich Sazyepin was a military engineer and studied painting under Bryullov. His painting *Nun in the Choir of a Church*, dated 1853, brought him great success.

SBARBI, Antonio
Italian, 17th - 18th century.
Born 1661; died before 1750, in Milan.
Painter. Landscapes, animals.
Having studied in Bologna with Lorenzo Pasinelli, Antonio Sbarbi worked for Ranuccio Farnese in Piacenza, and in Cremona and Milan.

SBISA, Carlo
Italian, 20th century.
Born 1899, in Trieste; died 1964.
Painter.
MUSEUMS AND GALLERIES:
TRIESTE (Civico Mus. Revoltella).

SBISCO DE TROTINA. See **TROTINA Zbisco** or **Zbyseen** or **Zbysek von**

SBRAVATI, Giuseppe
Italian, 18th - 19th century.
Born 1743, in Parma; died 30 October 1818, in Parma.
Sculptor.
The pupil of J.B. Boudard and a professor at the school of painting in Parma, Giuseppe Sbravati sculpted numerous statues in marble and wood for the churches and chapels of Parma.

SBRICOLI, Silvio
Italian, 19th century.
Born 1864, in Rome; died 30 November 1903, in Rome, in 1911 according to some sources.
Sculptor.
A pupil of P. d'Épinay, Silvio Sbricoli exhibited in Turin, Venice and Bologna.
AUCTION RECORDS:
MILAN, 11 Dec 1986, *Allegory of Vanity* (terracotta, h. 15 3/4 ins / 40 cm) ITL 1,100,000.

SBRINGA, Alessandro
Italian, 17th century.
Died 1687, in Rome.
Active in Ascoli.
Sculptor, painter.
Alessandro Sbringa was a member of the Congregazione dei Virtuosi in 1653.

SBRUEV, Aleksei Alekseevich, or Sbronev or Zbruev
Russian, 19th century.
Born 1799; died 1832, in Moscow.
Painter, engraver. Genre scenes.
Aleksei Alekseevich Sburev studied at the art academy of St Petersburg.
MUSEUMS AND GALLERIES:
MOSCOW (State Tretyakov Gal.): *Grandmother and Grandson* (pen drawing heightened with watercolour).

SCABARI, Nicolo
Italian, 18th century.
Born 1735, in Vicenza; died 1802, in Vicenza.
Painter.
Nicolo Scabari imitated the style of the Bassano family of artists. His works can be found in churches in Vicenza, Padua and Verona.

SCABINA DE ROSSA, Balthasar, or Scabino
Italian, 18th century.
Active in Vienna at the beginning of the 18th century.
Painter.
Balthasar Scabina de Rossa painted a picture of the *Flight into Egypt* for the high altar of the church of the Mater Dolorosa in Vienna.

SCACCERI, Giovanni Antonio. See **SCACCIERA**

SCACCHO, Cristoforo. See **SCACCO**

SCACCIANI, Camillo, called Carbone
Italian, 18th century.
Born in Pesaro; died 1749.
Active at the end of the 18th century.
Painter. History painting.
Camillo Scacciani is noted for a *Death of S Andrea Avellino* in the cathedral in Pesaro.

SCACCIATI
Italian, 18th century.
Painter, engraver. Religious subjects.
There is a reference to Scacciati by C. Le Blanc around 1775. His legacy includes a *Last Supper* after Palma and an engraving of *Our Lady of the Rosary* from a drawing by Cirro Ferri. He used the aquatint method. Despite the discrepancy in the dates, he may have been the same as Andrea Scacciati the Younger.

SCACCIATI, Andrea, the Elder
Italian, 17th century.
Born 1642, in Florence; died 6 June 1704, in Florence.
Painter. Still-lifes (flowers), birds, animals.
Andrea Scacciati the Elder was the pupil of Mario Balassi, Pietro Dandini and Lorenzo Lippi.
MUSEUMS AND GALLERIES:
WROCLAW: *Still-life with Fruit*.
AUCTION RECORDS:
NEW YORK, 22 Jan 1969, *Still-life with Flowers*, USD 3,750. LONDON, 4 March 1970, *Still-lifes* (two canvases) GBP 1,100. MILAN, 21 Nov 1974, *Still-lifes with Flowers* (two canvases) ITL 4,000,000. MILAN, 27 April 1978, *Still-life with Flowers* (oil on canvas, 34 1/4 x 46in/87 x 116cm) ITL 2,800,000. ROME, 18 Dec 1981, *Still-life with Flowers* (oil on canvas, 26 1/2 x 30 3/4in/67 x 78cm) ITL 6,000,000. NEW YORK, 19 Jan 1984, *Still-life with Flowers* (1679, oil on canvas, 48 1/4 x 70 1/4in/122.5 x 178.5cm) USD 10,000. LONDON, 2 July 1986, *Still-lifes with Flowers and Dog* (1683, oil on canvas, a pair, 17 3/4 x 34 3/4in/45 x 88.2cm) GBP 13,500. PARIS, 28 June 1988, *Vase of Flowers on an Entablature* (oil on canvas, 24 3/4 x 30in/63 x 76cm) FRF 60,000. MILAN, 4 April 1989, *Still-life with Flowers, Fruit and Mushrooms; Still-life with Flowers, Fruit and Thistles* (oil on canvas, a pair, each 19 3/4 x

41 1/4in/50 x 105cm) ITL 100,000,000. PARIS, 18 Dec 1991, *Basket of Flowers and Hazelnuts on an Entablature; Basket of Flowers and Carob Nuts on an Entablature* (oil on panel, diam. 17in/43cm) FRF 95,000. PARIS, 10 April 1992, *Still-life with Parrots and Chinese Vase* (oil on canvas, 34 x 45 1/2in/85.5 x 115.5cm) FRF 160,000. MILAN, 19 Oct 1993, *Still-life with Flowers* (oil on canvas, 42 1/4 x 33in/107 x 84cm) ITL 27,025,000. LONDON, 8 July 1994, *Floral Composition in a Sculpted Urn* (oil on canvas, 46 x 35in/116.9 x 89cm) GBP 25,300. LONDON, 3-4 Dec 1997, *Still-life of Flowers in a Pinchbeck Vase* (1682, oil on canvas, 27 1/2 x 22 1/2in/70 x 57cm) GBP 23,000. MADRID, 8 May 2000, *Still-life with Flowers* (1683, oil on canvas, 18 x 26 ins / 46 x 67 cm) ESP 3,500,000. LONDON, 12 Dec 2003, *Flowers in an Urn on a Marble Ledge* (oil on canvas, 26 x 21 ins / 66 x 53 cm) GBP 9,200.

SCACCIATI, Andrea, the Younger
Italian, 18th century.
Born 1725; died 1771.
Draughtsman, engraver.

Andrea Scacciati the Younger was the pupil of Schweickhard in Florence. He engraved religious subjects and genre scenes using the burin technique. He is noted in particular for a series of aquatint reproductions of drawings from the Uffizi museum, on which he collaborated with Stefano Mulmari.

SCACCIERA, Giovanni Antonio, or Scacceri or Scaccierare, called Il Frate (the Friar)
Italian, 16th century.
Active in Modena, from 1506 to 1524.
Painter, sculptor.

Giovanni Antonio Scacciera painted frescoes in the churches in the area around Modena.

MUSEUMS AND GALLERIES:
MODENA (Gal. Estense): altar.

SCACCIONI, Achille
Italian, 19th century.
Active in Rome.
Painter.

A pupil of Tommaso Minardi, Achille Scaccioni painted frescoes in the basilica of S Paolo fuori le Mura in Rome.

SCACCO, Cristoforo, or Scaccho
Italian, 15th - 16th century.
Born in Verona.
Painter. Religious subjects.

Cristoforo Scacco seems to have studied first in the regions of Veneto and Lombardy between 1485 and 1490 and was also taught by Melozzo da Forlì. His work shows the influence of Antoniazzo Romano.

In 1493, Scacco painted the Pente polyptych now in Naples and, in 1500, the polyptych in the museum at Capua. In about 1500, he was working in southern Italy. The church of the Annunziata in Nola has an *Annunciation* by him, and S Pietro in Vincoli in Salerno has a *St Michael*. Triptychs by Scacco are in the Duomo in Fondi, in S Giovanni Battista in Monte San Biagio and at the Capodimonte museum in Naples.

His early works, such as *St John the Baptist* (Avignon, Musée du Petit Palais), show the influence of Bramante's geometric style and an acquaintance with the works of Mantegna. Although Scacco always worked in the provinces, he shows an awareness of the artistic tendencies of the day, spreading from Flanders to Spain by way of France.

MUSEUMS AND GALLERIES:
AVIGNON (Mus. du Petit Palais): *St John the Baptist* - CAPUA: polyptych - NAPLES (Mus. di Capodimonte): *Virgin and Child*; Pente polyptych; *Coronation of the Virgin* (triptych, uncertain).

AUCTION RECORDS:
LONDON, 2 July 1965, *St John the Baptist*, Gns 10,000. MILAN, 24 Oct 1989, *Pietà* (oil on panel with gold background, 15 x 26 1/2 ins / 38 x 67 cm) ITL 19,000,000.

SCACHAR, Pedro. See **STAQUAR**

SCADA, Guillermo, or Escada or Scoda
Spanish, 15th century.
Active in Valencia from 1403 to 1421.
Painter.

SCADDON, R.
British, 18th century.
Draughtsman.

Scaddon drew the portrait *Dorothy Jeffery*.

SCAELDEKEN. See **ROMBAUTS Jan I**

SCAFFAI, Luigi
Italian, 19th century.
Born 18 August 1837, in Livorno; died 1899.
Painter. Genre scenes, interiors with figures.

Scaffai studied at the Accademia di Belle Arti in Florence.

AUCTION RECORDS:
PARIS, 6 July 1951, *Family Scene*, FRF 42,000. LONDON, 4 July 1972, *Peasants in an Interior*, Gns 550. LONDON, 19 April 1978, *Noisy Children in a Peasant Interior* (oil on canvas, 15 3/4 x 22 ins / 40 x 55 cm) GBP 1,300. NEW YORK, 25 Jan 1980, *Grandmother's Helper* (oil on canvas, 13 1/2 x 17 1/2 ins / 34 x 44.5 cm) USD 1,800. MILAN, 17 June 1982, *Frugal Meal* (oil on canvas, 46 x 35 ins / 116 x 89 cm) ITL 3,600,000. MILAN, 8 Nov 1983, *Woman Weaving* (oil on panel, 17 1/4 x 13 1/2 ins / 44 x 34 cm) ITL 17,000,000. NEW YORK, 17 Jan 1990, *Reading* (oil on canvas, 14 1/2 x 18 1/2 ins / 37 x 46.8 cm) USD 3,850. NORWALK, 3 Jan 1999, *Maid and Gentleman* (oil on panel, 17 x 12 ins / 43 x 30 cm) USD 3,200.

SCAGLIA, Bruno
Italian, 20th century.
Born 1921, in Pontevico near Brescia.
Painter.

As can be seen from the titles of his works, for example *The Red Tree* (1990), *Autumn* (1993) or *Landscape and Rider* (1994), Bruno Scaglia's inspiration comes from the natural world. But here nature is transformed into abstract compositions animated by whirlwinds, fragmented planes and superimposed volumes. Through a technique derived from Divisionism he sets up a kaleidoscopic rhythm that gives a prominent role to the dynamic power of colour.

Scaglia took part in a number of collective exhibitions in Italy, Vienna and elsewhere. He has held several solo exhibitions of his work in locations including Brescia, Milan and Livorno.

BIBLIOGRAPHY:
Il Paesaggio inquieto di Bruno Scaglia, exhibition catalogue, Biblioteca communale, Pontevico, 1994.

SCAGLIA, Girolamo, sometimes called Il Parmigianino
Italian, 17th century.
Born in Lucca; died 9 May 1686, in Lucca.
Painter.

The pupil of P. Paolini, Girolamo Scaglia imitated Pietro da Cortona. He worked in Pisa in 1672 and produced two paintings for the cathedral in that city.

SCAGLIA, Giuseppe
Italian, 17th century.

Born c. 1650, in Perugia; died c. 1700.
Sculptor.
The son and pupil of Leonardo Scaglia, Giuseppe Scaglia sculpted an altar and statues for the church of St Domenico in Perugia.

SCAGLIA, Leonardo
Italian, 17th century.
Of French origin.
Sculptor.
From 1640 to 1650, Leonardo Scaglia sculpted statues and crucifixes in the cathedral in Perugia and for the church of S Medardo in Ancona.

SCAGLIONE, Carlos
Argentinian, 20th century.
Born 1942.
Painter.
AUCTION RECORDS:
NEW YORK, 1 May 1990, *Grey Afternoon* (1988, oil on canvas, 11 3/4 x 39 1/4 ins / 30 x 100 cm) USD 2,860.

SCAIARO, Giovanni
Italian, 18th century.
Active in Venice during the second half of the 18th century.
Fresco artist.
Giovanni Scaiaro, a pupil of Zugno, produced paintings for the church of S Simone Il Profeta in Venice.

SCAICHIS. See **SCHAYCK**

SCAILLIET, Emile Philippe
French, 19th - 20th century.
Born 1846, in Paris; died 1911.
Sculptor.
Emile Philippe Scailliet, a pupil of Henri Lehmann, François Jouffroy and Augustin Moreau-Vautier, first exhibited in Paris in 1906 at the Salon des Artistes Français, of which he became a member in 1908 and where he was awarded an honourable mention in 1907.

SCAJARO. See also **BASSANO**

SCALA, Alessandro
Italian, 16th century.
Active in Carona at the beginning of the 16th century.
Sculptor.
Alessandro Scala carved statues and low reliefs in Genoa and Tirano.

SCALA, Armando
Italian, 20th century.
Born 12 February 1883, in Naples.
Painter. Figures.

SCALA, Bernardino
Italian, 15th century.
Active in Carona and in Sinigaglia in 1496.
Sculptor.

SCALA, Cesare
Italian, 17th century.
Active in Cento and in Ferrara c. 1690.
Painter. Still-lifes.

SCALA, Francesco
Italian, 17th century.
Active in Faenza in 1614.
Sculptor.

SCALA, Francesco
Italian, 17th century.
Born c. 1643, in Ádria, near Ferrara; died 21 December 1698, in Ferrara.
Painter, decorative designer. Church decoration, ornaments.
Francesco Scala was the pupil of F. Ferrari and C. Pronti. He produced paintings in the churches and palaces of Ferrara and Romagna.

SCALA, Gaspare della
Italian, 15th century.
Died before 1504.
Active in Carona.
Sculptor.
Gaspare della Scala carved the portals of Palazzo Cattaneo and Palazzo Sauli in Genoa.

SCALA, Giorgio
Italian, 16th century.
Active in Carona during the second half of the 16th century.
Sculptor.
Giorgio Scala carried out some work for the church of S Agostino at La Spezia in 1579.

SCALA, Giovanni Battista
Italian, 17th century.
Active in Naples during the second half of the 17th century.
Sculptor.
Giovanni Battista Scala collaborated on the tomb of Gaspar Roomer in the church of S Maria della Vita in Naples.

SCALA, Giuseppe
Italian, 18th century.
Died c. 1740.
Active in Naples.
Painter.
Giuseppe Scala was the pupil of Paolo de Matteis.

SCALA, Pietro Angelo della
Italian, 16th century.
Active in Carona during the first half of the 16th century.
Sculptor.
Pietro Angelo della Scala worked in Genoa in association with the Aprile family.

SCALA, Pietro della
Italian, 16th century.
Active in Genoa in 1503.
Sculptor.

SCALA, Sante or Santino della
Italian, 17th century.
Sculptor.
Sante Scala produced the diagonal ribs on the southern side of the church of S Antonio in Padua during the first half of the 17th century.

SCALA, Vincenzo
Italian, 19th century.
Born in Naples.
Painter. Genre scenes, landscapes with figures.
A student at the Accademia di Belle Arti in Naples, Vincenzo Scala exhibited in Milan, Turin and abroad (most importantly Paris, Vienna and Berlin) in the second half of the 19th century.
AUCTION RECORDS:
MILAN, 20 Dec 1977, *Horses and Cart* (oil on canvas, 20 x 41 ins / 51 x 104 cm) ITL 1,200,000. ROME, 11 Dec 1990, *Landscape with Peasants* (oil on panel, 7 1/2 x 12 1/2 ins / 19 x 32 cm) ITL 1,725,000. NEW YORK, 16 Feb 1993, *Peasant by a Stream in the Woods* (oil on canvas, 39 1/2 x 65 ins / 100.3 x 165.1 cm) USD 6,050. ROME, 29-30 Nov 1993, *Shepherdess and Flock* (oil on canvas, 27 1/2 x 35 1/2 ins / 70 x 90 cm) ITL 3,300,000. ROME, 2 June 1994, *Walk in the Woods* (oil on canvas, 19 x 15 ins / 48 x 38 cm) ITL 4,140,000. MILAN, 8 June 1994, *Peasant Girl with a Bunch of Grasses* (oil on canvas, 20 x 14 ins / 50.5 x 35.5 cm) ITL 6,900,000.

SCALABRIN, Jeremias or Hieronymus, or Scalabrino, Scällebrin or Scalberino
Austrian, 16th - 17th century.
Painter. Animals.

Jeremias Scalabrin painted pictures at the Tiergarten in Innsbruck in 1591.

SCALABRIN, Thomas
Austrian, 16th century.
Sculptor.

Thomas Scalabrin worked for the castle of Ambras, near Innsbruck, and for the court church.

SCALABRINO. See **ANSELMI Michelangelo**

SCALABRINO. See **VOLPONI Giovanni Battista**

SCALABRINO, Marco Antonio
Italian, 16th century.
Active in Verona c. 1565.
Painter.

Marco Antonio Scalabrino painted several works for the church of S Zeno in Verona.

SCALAMANZO, Leonardo
Italian, 15th century.
Died before 1500.
Active in Venice from 1459.
Sculptor (wood).

Leonardo Scalamanzo initially worked with Alvise Bastiani. In 1488, he carved the choir stalls in the church of S Stefano in Venice.

SCALAMANZO, Niccolò di Demetrio
Italian, 15th century.
Active in Venice from 1444 to 1476.
Sculptor (wood).
Venetian School.

Niccolò di Demetrio Scalamanzo was commissioned to make the organ case in the church of S Giovanni-Battista in Venice.

SCALAMANZO, Pietro
Italian, 16th century.
Active in Venice in 1522.
Sculptor (wood).

Pietro Scalamanzo may have been the son of Niccolò di Demetrio Scalamanzo.

SCALANI, Jacopo
Italian, 17th century.
Active c. 1600.
Painter.

Jacopo Scalani painted altarpieces for churches in Pavia.

SCALATELLI, Gino
Italian, 19th - 20th century.
Painter, watercolourist. Landscapes.

Gino Scalatelli painted many views of London.

AUCTION RECORDS:
MILAN, 21 Nov 1990, *Westminster Abbey* (1924, watercolour/paper, 19 x 26 1/2 ins / 48 x 67 cm) ITL 1,800,000. MILAN, 21 Nov 1990, *Piccadilly Circus, London* (watercolour/paper, 18 1/2 x 26 1/2 ins / 47 x 67 cm) ITL 1,000,000. MILAN, 29 March 1995, *Cathedral, London* (1897, watercolour/paper, 20 x 27 1/4 ins / 51 x 69 cm) ITL 2,300,000. MILAN, 27 May 2003, *View of the Thames with Boats* (watercolour, 28 x 39 ins / 70 x 100 cm) EUR 1,700.

SCALBERGE, Frédéric
Flemish School, 17th century.
Born in Flanders.
Also active in Italy and in France.
Painter, engraver.

Frédéric Scalberge was the brother of Pierre Scalberghe. He specialised in etchings. He was active in Rome from 1623 to 1627, and in Paris in 1636, under Vouet.

SCALBERGE, Pierre, or Scalberg or Scalle Berge or Schallberge
French, 17th century.
Born c. 1592, in Sedan (Ardennes), of Dutch origin; died 1640, in Paris.
Painter, engraver (etching). Mythological subjects, allegorical subjects.

Scalberge stayed in Italy from 1618 to 1622. He engraved mythological subjects, often after his own drawings. In particular, he produced a series of engravings, *School of Love*, published in Paris in 1638, representing Cupid becoming freed from Venus - an allegory of the birth of the passions of love. Nothing is known about his paintings, but he and his brother had a painting studio at the Louvre.

The *School of Love* appeared in the group exhibition *Les Mystérieux du XVIIe Siècle. Une Enquête au Cabinet d'Art Graphique* (*Mysteries of the 17th century: An Exploration of the Graphic Art Collection*) in 2002. This exhibition at the Musée des Beaux-Arts in Nancy featured forgotten artists from the 17th century, whose works are known only from engravings.

BIBLIOGRAPHY:
Paul, Céline/Harent, Sophie, *'Les Mystérieux du XVIIe siècle. Une enquête au cabinet d'art graphique'* in *coll. Lire en filigrane*, Musée des Beaux-Arts, Nancy, 2002.

AUCTION RECORDS:
NEW YORK, 8 Jan 1981, *Roman Charity* (1631, oil/metal, 22 x 16 1/2 ins / 56 x 42 cm) USD 8,000. NEW YORK, 15 Jan 1985, *Roman Charity* (1631, oil/copper, 22 1/4 x 16 ins / 56.5 x 40.6 cm) USD 4,800.

SCALBERINO, Jeremias or Hieronymus. See **SCALABRIN**

SCALBERT, Jules
French, 19th - 20th century.
Born 9 August 1851, in Douai.
Painter, pastellist. Allegorical subjects, figures, genre scenes, flowers.

Jules Scalbert, a pupil of Isidore Pils and Henri Lehmann, exhibited at the Salon de Paris from 1876, and later at the Salon des Artistes Français, of which he became a member in 1883. He was awarded an honourable mention in 1889 and third-class medals in 1891 and 1901.

AUCTION RECORDS:
PARIS, 29 March 1893, *Rest*, FRF 240. LONDON, 25 July 1947, *A Fine Bottle*, GBP 78. NICE, 15-16 July 1954, *Psyche; After Bathing* (two pastels) FRF 8,000. LONDON, 18 Oct 1978, *A Good Vintage* (oil on panel, 18 x 22 ins / 45.5 x 55 cm) GBP 1,500. LONDON, 19 March 1980, *Women Bathing on a Beach* (oil on canvas, 28 1/4 x 43 1/4 ins / 72 x 110 cm) GBP 3,400. NEW YORK, 26 Feb 1986, *Women Bathing* (pastel, 18 x 12 3/4 ins / 45.8 x 32.5 cm) USD 2,000. NEW YORK, 25 Feb 1988, *Women Bathing* (oil on canvas, 18 1/4 x 15 ins / 46.4 x 38.1 cm) USD 7,700. NEW YORK, 17 Oct 1991, *Homage to Louis Pasteur* (oil

on canvas, 50 1/2 x 65 1/2 ins / 128.3 x 166.4 cm) USD 19,800. NEW YORK, 28 May 1992, *Women Bathing* (oil on canvas, 28 1/4 x 39 1/2 ins / 71.8 x 100.3 cm) USD 16,500. AMSTERDAM, 2 Nov 1992, *Young woman Bathing* (pastel, 12 1/4 x 16 ins / 31 x 40.5 cm) NLG 3,450. PARIS, 4 May 1994, *Young Girl with her Dog* (oil on panel, 15 3/4 x 12 1/2 ins / 40 x 31.5 cm) FRF 14,000. LONDON, 22 Feb 1995, *Self-portrait* (oil on panel, 16 1/4 x 11 1/2 ins / 41 x 29 cm) GBP 3,680. NEW YORK, 1 Nov 1995, *Nymphs and Satyr* (oil on canvas) USD 79,500. NEW YORK, 9 Jan 1997, *Women Bathing on a Beach* (oil on canvas, 18 x 22 ins / 45.7 x 55.9 cm) USD 9,200. PARIS, 2 April 1997, *Reclining Nude* (pastel, 14 1/2 x 23 1/4 ins / 37 x 59 cm) FRF 9,000. NEW YORK, 15 June 1999, *Gentle Breezes* (pastel on paper, 24 x 19 ins / 61 x 48 cm) USD 3,200. HOUSTON, 18 Sept 1999, *Flower Maidens in the Park* (oil on canvas, 32 x 25 ins / 81 x 64 cm) USD 12,000. PARIS, 30 Oct 2000, *Portrait of a Woman* (pastel) FRF 26,000. LONDON, 3 Dec 2002, *Three Graces Dancing with a Faun* (oil on canvas, 26 x 32 ins / 65 x 81 cm) GBP 6,200. NEW YORK, 22 April 2004, *Crown of Roses* (oil on canvas, 51 x 38 ins / 130 x 97 cm) USD 18,000. LONDON, 13 Oct 2004, *Nude Back* (pastel, 14 x 23 ins / 36 x 59 cm) GBP 1,500.

SCALCAGNA, Michele di Niccolò dello
Italian, 15th century.
Sculptor.
Florentine School.

Michele di Niccolò dello Scalcagna was Ghiberti's assistant for the doors of the Battistero (Baptistery) in Florence.

SCALDAFERRI, Carlo
Italian, 20th century.
Born 11 September 1924, in Salvador (Bahia), Brazil, to Italian parents.
Painter. Landscapes, seascapes.

Carlo Scaldaferri spent his childhood in Brazil, then lived and worked in Italy in Trecchina in Basilicata. He took part in many collective exhibitions in Italy and had a number of solo exhibitions in Paris and, on a regular basis, in Florence. He was awarded a gold medal at the Lutèce International Competition in Paris.

His works present a romantic vision of nature, titles including *Working at Sea, Peaceful Countryside* and *Burnt Horizon*.

SCALÉ, Bernard
Irish, 18th century.
Active in Dublin, from 1756 to 1780.
Draughtsman. Maps.

SCALES, Edith Marion
American, 20th century.
Born in Newark.
Painter.

Edith Scales exhibited her work at the Salon des Artistes Français in Paris from 1924.

SCALES, James
British, 19th century.
Painter. Architectural views.

James Scales exhibited in London from 1808 to 1826.

SCALETA, Sebastiano
Italian, 18th century.
Born in Cagliari.
Painter, fresco artist. Religious subjects.

Sebastiano Scaleta painted frescoes in the cupola and altarpieces in churches in Cagliari.

SCALETTI, Alitichieo or Altichiero
Italian, 15th century.
Active in Faenza from 1451 to 1473.
Painter.

The son of Cristoforo Scaletti, Alitichieo Scaletti specialised in painting *cassoni* (chests) for weddings.

SCALETTI, Cristoforo
Italian, 15th century.
Died before 30 May 1451.
Active in Faenza.
Painter.

Cristoforo Scaletti was the father of Alitichieo Scalleti.

SCALETTI, Gaspare
Italian, 15th - 16th century.
Active in Faenza from 1477 to 1529.
Painter.

Gaspare Scaletti, son of Leonardo Scaletti I, ran a workshop producing painted wedding chests or *cassoni*.

SCALETTI, Leonardo I
Italian, 15th century.
Died before 14 February 1487.
Active in Faenza.
Painter.

The father of Gaspare Scaletti, Leonardo Scaletti I was one of the most important painters in Faenza.

MUSEUMS AND GALLERIES:
EDINBURGH (Nat. Gal. of Scotland): *Virgin and Child with St Francis and St Jerome* - FAENZA (Pinacoteca Comunale d'Arte Antica e Moderna): *Virgin with St John the Baptist and Angels*.

SCALETTI, Leonardo II
Italian, 16th century.
Active in Faenza during the first half of the 16th century.
Painter.

The son of Gaspare Scaletti, Leonardo Scaletti II was assistant to Sebastiano Scaletti and Lattanzio Mengari.

SCALETTI, Luca
Italian, 16th century.
Died probably before 1554.
Active in Faenza.
Painter.

The son of Sebastiano Scaletti, Luca Scaletti is probably identical with Luca da Faenza, who worked with Giulio Romano in Mantua.

SCALETTI, Sebastiano
Italian, 16th century.
Active in Faenza from 1503 to 1559.
Painter.

Father of Luca Scaletti, Sebastiano Scaletti worked for the Dominicans in Faenza and the surrounding areas.

SCALI, Madeleine
French, 20th century.
Born 4 August 1911, in Oran, Algeria.
Painter. Figures, landscapes, still-lifes.

Madeleine Scali trained first at the École des Beaux-Arts, Oran, and then, until 1939, at the École Nationale Supérieure des Beaux-Arts, Paris. In 1936 she became a member of the Salon des Artistes Français. She returned to Oran, where she worked as a teacher and held a number of solo shows, but finally settled in Paris in 1957. She exhibited regularly at the Salon des Artistes Français (1957, 1958, 1962 and 1988), presented her work at the Musée de Gemmail, Tours from 1972 to 1980, and became a member of the Salon d'Automne, the Salon des Indépendants and the Salon de la Société Nationale des Beaux-Arts. She was awarded the Grand Prix of the Municipality of Oran in 1946, the Grand Prix d'Oranie in 1951, and in the same year was short-listed at the 1st Menton Biennale.

She painted mainly still-lifes, compositions of great simplicity in which the treatment of colour and light is reminiscent of Cézanne.

MUSEUMS AND GALLERIES:
PARIS (MNAM-CCI).

SCALI, Vincent
French, 20th - 21st century.
Born 26 November 1956, in Paris.
Sculptor, painter, draughtsman, pastellist, mixed media.
Vincent Scali lives and works in Paris. He produces bronzes which rework Catholic lithurgy.

He has been involved in various group exhibitions, among them: in 1980, 1982 and 1983, at the Salon de Montrouge; in 1989, at the Centre d'Art Contemporain in Vassivières; at the FIAC (Foire Internationale d'Art Contemporain) on a regular basis since 1989; in 1990, at TAC 90 in the Salla Parpallo in Valencia; in 1991, at the Frankfurt and Brussels Art Fair and at the Sculpture Biennale in St-Raphaël; in 1992, at the Salon Découvertes in Paris; in 1993, at the Centre d'Art Contemporain in Angers; and, in 1994, at the Chicago Fair.

Solo exhibitions by Vincent Scali have been held in 1983 and 1986 at the Galleria Flaviana in Locarno; as of 1986 on a regular basis at the Galerie Michel Vidal in Paris; in 1989, at Cadaquès; in 1991, at the Centre d'Art Contemporain in Vassivières; and, in 1992, at the Centre d'Art Contemporain in Riberac.

AUCTION RECORDS:
PARIS, 7 March 1990, *Untitled* (1989, bronze, 20 1/2 x 26 x 5 ins / 52 x 66 x 13 cm) FRF 11,000. PARIS, 30 June 1992, *Composition* (1991, oil on paper/canvas, 75 1/2 x 67 1/4 ins / 192 x 171 cm) FRF 16,000. PARIS, 17 Sept 1995, *Wall Sculpture* (1988, bronze, triptych, 65 x 31 ins / 165 x 78.5 cm) FRF 6,800; *Bronze* (1991, green-patinated bronze, 47 1/4 x 17 3/4 x 17 3/4 ins / 120 x 45 x 45 cm) FRF 10,500.

SCALIGERI, Bartolo or Bartolommeo, or Scaligero
Italian, 17th century.
Born 1630, in Venice.
Painter, engineer.
Bartolo Scaligeri was the pupil of Alessandro Varotari and the uncle of Luca Scaligeri. He spent most of his life in Venice and produced works for churches there. A painting in the church of Corpus Domini is considered his best work.

SCALIGERI, Lucia, or Scaligera
Italian, 17th century.
Born 1637, in Venice; died 1700.
Painter.
Lucia was the niece of Bartolo Scaligeri and the pupil of Chiara Varotari. As well as producing works for Venetian churches, she was a woman of letters and a musician.

SCALINGER, Nicola. See **SKALINGER**

SCALINO, Marcello. See **SCALZINI**

SCALLE BERGE. See **SCALBERGE**

SCÄLLEBRIN, Jeremias or Hieronymus. See **SCALABRIN**

SCALLO. See **ALBERT Schallo**

SCALOBRINO. See **ANSELMI Michelangelo**

SCALVATI, Antonio
Italian, 16th - 17th century.
Born 1557 or 1559, in Bologna; died 1622, in Rome.
Painter. History painting, portraits.
Antonio Scalvati worked in the Sala di Costantino in Rome in collaboration with his master Tommaso Laureti, and Pope Sixtus V employed him in the Biblioteca Vaticana. He painted a portrait of *Clement VIII*.

SCALVE, Agostino de, or Scalvino
Italian, 17th century.
Active in Brescia c. 1625.
Painter.

SCALVE, Giuseppe da, or Scalvini
Italian, 16th century.
Born 1538, in Brescia; died after 1588, in Brescia.
Sculptor (stone/wood), architect, marquetry worker.
Giuseppe da Scalve was responsible for the balustrade of the town hall on Brescia and the choir stalls in S Maria del Monte near Cesena.

SCALVINI, Pietro, or Scalvino
Italian, 18th century.
Born 1718, in Brescia; died 1792, in Brescia.
Painter.
The pupil of Ferdinando del Cairo, Pietro Scalvini worked for churches in Brescia, Berzo Inferiore and Darfo.

SCALVINONE, Giovanni Battista
Italian, 18th (?) century.
Engraver.

SCALVO, Luca
Italian, 15th - 16th century.
Born possibly in Castel Leon.
Active from 1450 to 1500.
From 1450 to 1500.

SCALZA, Alessandro
Italian, 17th century.
Active in 1603 in Todi.
Sculptor.
Alessandro was the brother of Ippolito Scalza.

SCALZA, Francesco
Italian, 16th - 17th century.
Active in Orvieto from 1580 to 1620.
Mosaicist, architect.
Possibly the brother of Ippolito and Lodovico Scalza, Francesco Scalza made the mosaic of the *Baptism of Christ* above the left portal of Orvieto Cathedral.

SCALZA, Giulio. See **BORGIANI Giulio**

SCALZA, Ippolito, or Scalzi
Italian, 16th - 17th century.
Born 1532; died 22 December 1617.
Sculptor, stucco artist, architect.
From 1554, Ippolito Scalza worked at Orvieto Cathedral, making several statues and a wooden throne. He executed two tombs in Amelia Cathedral. He may have been the brother of Francesco and Lodovico Scalza.

SCALZA, Lodovico, or Scalzi
Italian, 16th century.
Born in Orvieto.
Active from 1548 to 1599.
Sculptor, draughtsman, stucco artist. Ornaments.
Perhaps the brother of Francesco and Ippolito Scalza, Lodovico Scalza worked at the cathedrals of Orvieto and Perugia.

SCALZI. See also **SCALZA**

SCALZI, Alessandro. See **PADUANO Alexander**

SCALZINI, Marcello, or Scalzino or Scalino, called Il Camerino
Italian, 16th century.
Born 1556, in Camerino.
Draughtsman, calligrapher.
Marcello Scalzini published several books on calligraphy, illustrating them with his own examples.

SCAMBELLA. See **CIAMBELLA DI FRANCESCO Giovanni**

SCAMINOSSI, Raffaello. See **SCHIAMINOSSI**

SCAMOZZI, Muzio
Italian, 18th century.
Active during the second half of the 18th century.
Sculptor, architect.

SCANARDI, Giorgio
Italian, 15th century.
Active in Bergamo during the second half of the 15th century.
Painter.

Giorgio Scanardi was the father of Giacomo Scannardi of Averara.

SCANARDI, Scipione
Italian, 16th century.
Painter.

In 1529, Scipione Scanardi painted a *Virgin and Child Seated in the Clouds* for S Pancrazio in Bergamo.

SCANARDI D'AVERARA, Giacomo.
See **SCANNARDI D'AVERARA**

SCANAVINI, Maurelio. See **SCANNAVINI**

SCANAVINO, Emilio
Italian, 20th century.
Born 28 February 1922, in Genoa; died 1986, in Milan.
Painter (including gouache), sculptor, mixed media.
Figures.

Emilio Scanavino was a pupil at the Liceo Artistico in Genoa until 1942 after which he studied architecture for a year. He met Francis Bacon while on a visit to London in 1951, although this encounter seems not to have had any lasting influence on his work.

In the period following World War II, Scanavino's paintings showed both the influence of Picasso and Expressionist tendencies. He was a member of the group associated with *spazialismo*, the Italian version of a Europe-wide movement experimenting with 'lyrical abstraction', as opposed to geometric abstraction and other gestural, calligraphic and informal abstractions. From 1953 he began to develop his own very idiosyncratic language, his work soon being instantly recognisable among the multitude of styles co-existing in the avant-garde art of the time. He executed whitish backgrounds, often divided into a succession of boxes, the squares of an alphabet or a board game, covered with signs suggesting the birth of a new vocabulary of ideograms. These signs appear to be ordered in some way, as with a language where the syntax will begin to emerge naturally from its morphology. Alternatively abstract signs, reminiscent of those of MacLaren, appear like the successive frames of an animated cartoon and initiate the subsequent movement and action. In these 1950s works, Scanavino showed the impenetrable traces of his inner torment or, in Appollonio's words, 'the inevitable and insidious anxiety of a state of suffering, expressed through appropriate figurative exponents'. Later, Scanavino frequently abandoned the grid-like arrangement in favour of canvases with a single image. In these, the background is no longer necessarily white but often black, blue or red and covered with a network of scratched marks from which emerge evocations of as yet unborn forms.

Scanavino took part in several exhibitions including: Venice Biennale (1950, 1954, 1958 receiving the Prampolini prize and 1966 receiving the Grand Prix); Documenta, Kassel (1959); Rome Quadriennale (1960 receiving the Rome City Council prize and 1973); International Exhibition, Carnegie Institute, Pittsburgh (1964); Tokyo Biennale, (1966); Prospekt, Kunsthalle, Düsseldorf (1968); Menton Biennale (1970); Museum of Modern Art, Mexico (1971). His work has also been the subject of many solo exhibitions including: Genoa (since 1948); London (1951); Venice (1953); Galleria del Naviglio, Milan (1955, 1959, 1961, 1963, 1967, 1969 and 1973); Rome (1957); Galerie des Beaux-Arts, Brussels (1960); Galerie Internationale d'Art Contemporain, Paris (1960 and 1962); Kunsthalle, Darmstadt and Palazzo Grassi, Venice (1973). Awards include: Graziano prize, Milan (1956); Lissone prize, Milan (1958); city of Palermo prize and Spoleto prize (1960).

BIBLIOGRAPHY:

Jouffroy, Alain, *La Question S.*, Phantomas, Brussels, 1962.
Jouffroy, Alain, '*Scanavino l'insaisissable*' in *Opus international* n° 38, periodical, Paris, November 1972.

AUCTION RECORDS:

ROME, 18 May 1976, *Presumptuous Image* (1969, acrylic/hardboard, 39 1/4 x 39 1/4 ins / 100 x 100 cm) ITL 2,200,000. MILAN, 7 June 1977, *Above and Below* (oil on canvas, 39 1/4 x 39 1/4 ins / 100 x 100 cm) ITL 3,200,000. MILAN, 18 Dec 1979, *Moment No. 8* (1965, oil on canvas, 10 1/4 x 14 1/4 ins / 26 x 36 cm) ITL 750,000. MILAN, 22 May 1980, *Composition* (1957, mixed media, 19 1/4 x 27 1/4 ins / 49 x 69 cm) ITL 800,000. MILAN, 16 June 1981, *Two Parts* (oil on canvas, 39 1/4 x 39 1/4 ins / 100 x 100 cm) ITL 2,800,000. MILAN, 15 March 1983, *Birth* (acrylic/canvas, 39 1/4 x 39 1/4 ins / 100 x 100 cm) ITL 2,300,000. ROME, 6 May 1986, *Inferno* (1976, oil on canvas, 78 3/4 x 55 ins / 200 x 140 cm) ITL 11,500,000. MILAN, 8 June 1988, *Morphology* (1970, oil on panel, 25 1/2 x 32 ins / 65 x 81 cm) ITL 3,000,000; *Ball* (1963, oil on canvas, 32 x 39 1/4 ins / 81 x 100 cm) ITL 10,500,000. LONDON, 30 June 1988, *Untitled* (1959, oil on canvas, 18 x 25 1/2 ins / 45.8 x 65 cm) GBP 3,520. ROME, 15 Nov 1988, *Untitled* (1963, mixed media /paper/canvas, 13 x 17 1/4 ins / 33 x 44 cm) ITL 1,400 000. AMSTERDAM, 9 Dec 1988, *Composition* (wax crayon and oil on paper, 11 1/4 x 13 3/4 ins / 28.5 x 35 cm) NLG 1,092. MILAN, 14 Dec 1988, *Red Linked with Black* (acrylic/paper, 26 1/2 x 37 1/2 ins / 67 x 95 cm) ITL 3,200,000. PARIS, 12 Feb 1989, *Form in Evolution no. 3* (1961, 20 x 28 3/4 ins / 51 x 73 cm) FRF 14,000. MILAN, 20 March 1989, *Larva* (1967, oil on canvas, 59 x 39 ins / 150 x 99 cm) ITL 9,000,000; *Mirror* (1964, bronze, 17 3/4 x 26 3/4 x 7 1/2 ins / 45 x 68 x 19 cm) ITL 14,500,000. MILAN, 8 Nov 1989, *Composition* (1957, oil on canvas, 22 x 29 3/4 ins / 55 x 75.5 cm) ITL 19,000,000. ROME, 6 Dec 1989, *Composition* (1975, acrylic/paper/synthetic resin, 27 1/2 x 19 3/4 ins / 70 x 50 cm) ITL 4,025,000. MILAN, 19 Dec 1989, *Composition* (mixed media/board, 39 1/4 x 51 1/4 ins / 100 x 130 cm) ITL 10,500,000. MILAN, 27 March 1990, *Homage to my Town* (1958, oil on canvas, 61 x 85 ins / 155 x 215 cm) ITL 52,000,000. MILAN, 24 Oct 1990, *Endless Alphabet* (oil on canvas/panel, 38 1/4 x 51 1/4 ins / 97 x 130 cm) ITL 20,500,000. MILAN, 26 March 1991, *Image* (1963, oil on canvas, 46 x 34 3/4 ins / 116 x 88.5 cm) ITL 30,000,000. ROME, 3 Dec 1991, *Plot* (1975, oil on canvas, 23 1/2 x 23 1/2 ins / 60 x 60 cm) ITL 10,500,000. MILAN, 14 April 1992, *Composition* (1957, oil on canvas, 19 3/4 x 27 1/2 ins / 50 x 70 cm) ITL 11,500,000. MILAN, 9 Nov 1992, *Ligurian Hinterland* (1956, oil on canvas, 18 x 34 ins / 46 x 85.5 cm) ITL 10,000,000. AMSTERDAM, 9 Dec 1992, *Untitled* (wax crayons and pencil/paper, 13 1/2 x 19 1/4 ins / 34.5 x 49 cm) NLG 1,150. MILAN, 6 April 1993, *Web* (1974, oil on canvas, 59 x 59 ins / 150 x 150 cm) ITL 21,500,000. LONDON, 23 June 1993, *Figures* (oil on canvas, 60 x 69 ins / 152.4 x 175.1 cm) GBP 8,000. MILAN, 12 Dec 1995, *Germination* (1959, oil on canvas, 36 1/4 x 28 3/4 ins / 92 x 73 cm) ITL 17,250,000. MILAN, 20 May 1996, *Unititled* (1962, pencil, ink and gouache/paper, 19 3/4 x 17 ins / 50 x 43 cm) ITL 4,830,000. MILAN, 23 May 1996, *Untitled* (mixed media/mounted paper, 13 1/2 x 19 3/4 ins / 34 x 50 cm) ITL 2,070,000. MILAN, 10 Dec 1996, *From Above* (1972, oil on canvas, 31 1/2 x 31 1/2 ins / 80 x 80 cm) ITL 9,320,000. COPENHAGEN, 29 Jan 1997, *Immediately* (1958, oil on canvas, 28 3/4 x 23 1/2 ins / 73 x 60 cm) DKK 31,000. COPENHAGEN, 22-24 Oct 1997, *Immediately Afterwards* (1958, oil on canvas, 28 3/4 x 23 1/2 ins / 73 x 60 cm) DKK 28,000. MILAN, 9 Nov 1999, *Form in Evolution* (1969, oil on board, 29 x 39 ins / 73 x 100 cm) ITL 17,000,000. MILAN, 9 Nov 1999, *Quadro (Painting)* (1971, oil on canvas, 39 x 39 ins / 100 x 100 cm) ITL 18,000,000. PRATO, 24 Nov 2000, *Homage to the Master* (1962, oil on canvas, 59 x 51 ins / 150 x 130 cm) ITL 48,000,000. MILAN, 12 Dec 2000, *Homage to my Town* (oil on canvas, 61 x 85 ins / 155 x 215 cm) ITL 54,000,000. VERCELLI, 20 Oct 2001, *Endless Alphabet* (oil on canvas, 44 x 57 ins / 112 x 146 cm) ITL 40,000,000. PRATO, 30 Nov 2001, *Little Moon* (1966, oil on canvas, 79 x 79 ins / 200 x 200 cm) ITL 44,000,000. PRATO, 24 May 2002, *Reminder* (1962, oil on canvas, 77 x 77 ins / 195 x 195 cm) EUR 25,000. VERCELLI, 23 Nov 2002, *Plot with Circle* (1975, oil on canvas, 39 x 39 ins / 100 x 100 cm) EUR 20,000. VERCELLI, 4 Jan 2003, *Endless Alphabet* (1980, oil on canvas, 44 x 57 ins / 112 x 146 cm) EUR 22,000. VERCELLI, 6 Sept 2003, *Endless Alphabet* (1982, oil on canvas, 32 x 39 ins / 81 x 100 cm) EUR 16,000. VERCELLI, 13 March 2004, *I Built a White Triangle* (1966, oil on canvas, 59 x 59 ins / 150 x 150 cm) EUR 22,000. VERCELLI, 30 May 2004, *Curved Image* (1968, oil on canvas, 39 x 39 ins / 100 x 100 cm) EUR 21,000.

SCANCIO
Italian, 14th century.
Sculptor.
Scancio carved a statue of *The Virgin and Child* for the Torre San Giovanni in Chieti.

SCANDELLARI, Filippo, or Scandellara
Italian, 18th century.
Born 1717; died 1801.
Sculptor.
The pupil of Giacomo Scandellari and Angelo Pio, Filippo Scandellari worked for churches in Bologna and other towns in Romagna.

SCANDELLARI, Giacomo Antonio, or Scandellara
Italian, 18th century.
Sculptor. Religious subjects.
Giacomo Scandellari, the father of Filippo Scandellari, was the pupil of Giovanni Viani. He sculpted a *Pietà* and a *Resurrection* in the Carthusian monastery in Bologna around 1750.

SCANDELLARI, Giulio, or Scandellara
Italian, 18th century.
Painter.
Giulio Scandellari was active in Bologna during the second half of the 18th century.

SCANDELLARI, Giuseppe, or Scandellara
Italian, 18th century.
Painter. Architectural views.
Giuseppe Scandellari decorated the atrium of the church of San Biagio in Bologna around 1750.

SCANDELLARI, Pietro, or Scandellara
Italian, 18th century.
Born 1711, in Bologna; died 1789.
Painter. Religious subjects. Decorative schemes.
Pietro Scandellari was the pupil of Ferdinando Galli Bibiena. He painted works for churches in Bologna.

AUCTION RECORDS:
ROME, 8 March 1990, *View of Lake with Figures, Bridge and Chapel; View of Lake with Monks* (tempera, a pair, 11¾ x 15¾in/30 x 40cm) ITL 16,000,000.

SCANDRETT, Thomas
British, 19th century.
Born 1799/1800, in Worcester; died 1870.
Painter, draughtsman. Architectural views, portraits.
Thomas Scandrett exhibited from 1824 to 1870 at the Royal Academy, the British Institution and the Suffolk Street Gallery. He is noted for his views of churches.

AUCTION RECORDS:
PARIS, 20 Nov 1981, *Interior of Saint Bavon Cathedral, Ghent* (watercolour and gouache, 36¼ x 24¾ ins / 92 x 63 cm) FRF 8,000. PARIS, 26 Jan 1983, *Interior of St-Bavon Cathedral, Ghent* (watercolour and gouache, 36¼ x 24¾ ins / 92 x 63 cm) FRF 7,500.

SCANES, Mrs. See **GOODMAN Maud** or **Maude**

SCANFERLA, Maria Domenica
Italian, 18th century.
Born 14 December 1729, in Padua; died 18 June 1763, in Padua.
Painter, embroiderer. Portraits, religious subjects.
Maria Scanferla painted a *St Teresa* and a portrait in pastels of Pope *Clement XIII*.

SCANGA, Italo
Italian, 20th century.
Born 6 June 1932, in Lago (Calabria); died 2001.
Active from 1947 in the USA.
Sculptor, draughtsman, installation artist.
Italo Scanga's work has appeared in many collective exhibitions including: Institute of Arts, Detroit (1957); First International Festival of Contemporary Art, Pittsburgh (1959); Institute of Contemporary Art, Boston (1966); Whitney Museum of American Art, New York (1970); Museum of Modern Art in New York, Museum of Contemporary Art, Chicago and Corcoran Art Gallery, Washington (1971); Fogg Museum, Cambridge, Mass. (1973). He has also held solo exhibitions including: University of Valparaíso (1959); Art Center, Milwaukee, Wisconsin (1964); Rhode Island School of Design, Providence (1970); University of Rochester, New York and University of Massachusetts, Amherst (1971); Tyler School of Art, Rome, Whitney Museum, New York, Academy of Fine Arts, Philadelphia and Museum of Contemporary Art, Chicago (1972).

MUSEUMS AND GALLERIES:
CAMBRIDGE, MA (Fogg AM, Harvard University) - MILWAUKEE (Art Center) - NEW YORK (Metropolitan Mus. of Art) - PHILADELPHIA (MA) - PHILADELPHIA (Pennsylvania Academy of the Fine Arts Gal.) - PROVIDENCE (Rhode Island School of Design).

AUCTION RECORDS:
NEW YORK, 8 Oct 1986, *Untitled* (painted wood, machete and spade, assemblage, 71 x 22 x 3 ins / 179.5 x 56 x 7.8 cm) USD 4,250. NEW YORK, 20 Feb 1988, *Untitled* (mixed media, 82 x 15 x 37¾ ins / 208.2 x 38.1 x 95.7 cm) USD 4,400. NEW YORK, 10 Nov 1988, *Fear of Aging* (1980, mixed media, 68½ x 8½ x 8½ ins / 174 x 21.6 x 21.6 cm) USD 3,080. NEW YORK, 14 Feb 1989, *Nude with Two Skulls* (1984, charcoal/paper, 46¾ x 36¾ ins / 118.7 x 93.3 cm) USD 1,760. NEW YORK, 5 Oct 1989, *Untitled* (1983, painted wood, h. 89 ins / 226 cm) USD 11,000. NEW YORK, 8 May 1990, *Untitled* (1983, sculpture and oil on wood, 107¼ x 60 x 23¼ ins / 272.4 x 152.1 x 59 cm) USD 11,000. NEW YORK, 7 May 1991, *Moonlight* (1981, oil on wood, 77¼ x 14 x 9¼ ins / 195.9 x 35.8 x 23.2 cm) USD 2,200.

SCANLAN, Joe
American, 20th century.
Installation artist.
Joe Scanlan lives and works in Chicago. He displays rubbish, dust, eggshells and other left-overs as fetishes.

Scanlan took part in the exhibitions *I, myself and others* at the Magasin, Centre National d'Art Contemporain in Grenoble in 1992, and *Présence de l'objet* (*Presence of the Object*), at Grand-Hornu Images, Hornu, in 2001. He shows his works in private exhibitions, for example at the Galerie Ghislaine Hussenot, Paris, in 1995, and D'Amelio Terras, New York, in 1999.

MUSEUMS AND GALLERIES:
MARSEILLES (FRAC Provence-Alpes-Côte d'Azur): *Mirrors* (1994, two mirrors, aluminium sheets, glass, wooden frame).

SCANLAN, Robert Richard
Irish, 19th century.
Died perhaps c. 1876.
Painter. Portraits, genre scenes, animals.
Robert Richard Scanlan worked in Dublin and in London.
AUCTION RECORDS:
LONDON, 19 July 1983, *Screwdriver Dealer* (watercolour and pen heightened with white, 10 3/4 x 15 1/2 ins / 27.5 x 39.5 cm) GBP 1,800. NEW YORK, 20 Feb 1992, *Donnybrooke Fair* (oil on canvas, 40 1/2 x 56 ins / 102.9 x 142.2 cm) USD 10,450. LONDON, 16 May 1996, *Famine* (1852, brown wash and pencil, 20 1/2 x 35 1/4 ins / 52 x 89.5 cm) GBP 3,220. DUBLIN, 31 March 2004, *Musicians, Playing a Fiddle, a Flute, a Guitar and a Box Organ* (1833, watercolour, set of four, 9 x 6 ins / 22 x 16 cm) EUR 2,000.

SCANNABECCHI, Dalmasio, also known as Lippo di Dalmasio or Lippo della Madona or Maso da Bologna
Italian, 14th - 15th century.
Born c. 1352; died before 1421.
Painter.
Bolognese School.
One of the first masters of the Bolognese School, Dalmasio Scannabecchi is believed to have been a pupil of Vitale da Bologna and to have worked between 1376 and 1410, the year in which he made his will. The elegance of his line suggests that he had come into contact with Florentine art. His works are very rare.
MUSEUMS AND GALLERIES:
BOLOGNA (Church of S Maria della Misericordia): *Madonna* (1397, attributed) - BOLOGNA (Pinacoteca Nazionale): *Coronation of the Virgin* (attributed) - LONDON (NG): *The Madonna of Humility* (1390-1400, tempera/canvas).

SCANNAPIECO, Onofrio
Italian, 15th century.
Glass painter.
Onofrio Scannapieco made windows for Naples Cathedral in 1499.

SCANNARDI. See also **SCANARDI**

SCANNARDI D'AVERARA, Giacomo, called Oloferne
Italian, 15th - 16th century.
Born c. 1452, in Averara; died between 1519 and 1529.
Active in Bergamo.
Painter.
Lombard School.
The son of Giorgio Scanardi, Giacomo Scannardi d'Averara worked in Bergamo in 1447 with Troso da Monza. Crowe and Cavalcaseele attribute the fragments of fresco removed from the remains of the church of S Maria delle Grazie, now in the bishops' palace, to these two artists.

SCANNATELLA
Italian, 17th century.
Painter.
Scannatella produced paintings in the cathedral in Mazzara, Sicily in 1696.

SCANNAVINI, Maurelio, or Scannavino or Scannavesi or Scanavini
Italian, 17th century.
Born 7 May 1655, in Ferrara; died 1 June 1698, in Ferrara.
Painter. History painting, portraits.
Maurelio Scannavini worked initially in his native city with Francesco Ferrari. He then went to Bologna, where he was taught by Carlo Cignani, becoming one of his master's best pupils. Scannavini was mainly active in Ferrara and is noted for a number of works in ecclesiastical buildings there, in particular 14 paintings depicting the *Life of St Dominic* in the refectory of the Dominican friary. Mention is also made of an *Annunciation* in San Stefano, a *St Thomas of Villanova Distributing Alms to Augustinian Monks* and a *St Bridget* in the church of Santa Maria della Grazie.

SCANNAVINO, Francesco
Italian, 17th century.
Born c. 1641, in Ferrara; died 1688.
Painter.
Scannavino was a pupil of Carlo Cignani.

SCANNO, Geremia di. See **DISCANNO Geremia**

SCANREIGH, pseudonym of Petit Jean-Marie
French, 20th - 21st century.
Born 1950, in Marrakech, Morocco.
Painter, sculptor.
Scanreigh lives and works in Lyons. His work featured in *De Bonnard à Baselitz - Dix Ans d'enrichissements du cabinet des estampes 1978-1988* (*From Bonnard to Baselitz: A Decade of Acquisitions by the Prints Collection 1978-1988*), an exhibition held in 1993 at the Bibliothèque Nationale in Paris.
MUSEUMS AND GALLERIES:
PARIS (BNF): *An End to Life: His Real Successor* (seven-plate set of lithographs).

SCANREIGH, Jean Marc
French, 20th - 21st century.
Born 1950, in Alsace.
Painter, collage artist, engraver, sculptor, mixed media.
Jean Marc Scanreigh adopts a minimalist approach to painting, working in geometrical monochrome blocks or with felt-pen lines that gradually peter out. The influence of the Support/Surfaces Group is evident in his approach to compositions that incorporate different techniques (engraving, painting, collage and camouflage). He has also emerged as a book illustrator and as an inventive engraver of wood, copper and linoleum.

Jean Marc Scanreigh has shown his work at group exhibitions, including: in 1984, at FRAC Alsace in Sélestat; in 1986, at the European Engraving Biennale in Mulhouse; in 1988, at the Musée de l'Estampe Originale (Original Prints Museum) in Gravelines; in 1991, at the Espace Cordeliers in Lyons; and, in 2000, at the St'Art Contemporary Arts Fair in Strasbourg (under the auspices of the Lucien Schweitzer Gallery in Luxembourg). Solo exhibitions by Scanreigh include those of 1983 in Nancy; 1985, in Châteauroux; 1986, in Lyons and at the Musée de l'Estampe Originale in Gravelines; in 1988, at the Municipal Library in Caen; and, in 1991, at the Galerie Claudine Lustmann in Paris and the Jean Gagnant Cultural Centre in Limoges.
BIBLIOGRAPHY:
Rocher, Jean-Louis/Lontin, Annick, *Scanreigh. Estampes, sérigraphies, eaux-fortes, gravures sur linoléum, gravures sur bois, lithographies de 1973 à 1974, de 1983 à 1988*, exhibition catalogue, Bibliothèque municipale, Lyons, 1988. Terrail, Jean/Scanreigh, Jean-Marc, *Jean-Marc Scanreigh. Peintures, estampes, livres d'artistes*, exhibition catalogue, Gal. du Théâtre de Saint-Quentin-en-Yvelines, St-Quentin-en-Yvelines, 1988. Michaud, Éric, *Le Grimaçant des choses. Peintures de Jean-Marc Scanreigh*, Éd. M. Chomarat, Lyons, 1990. '*L'Archipel Scanreigh: portrait kaléïdoscope de Jean-Marc Scanreigh*' in *Art et Métiers du Livre* n° 182 p. 2-8, periodical, Paris, 1993.

SCANZI, Allegrino
Italian, 16th century.

Active in Soncino, at the beginning of the 16th century.
Painter.

Allegrino Scanzi was the father of Ermete and Francesco Scanzi.

SCANZI, Ermete
Italian, 16th century.
Active in Soncino at the beginning of the 16th century.
Painter.

Ermete Scanzi was the son of Allegrino Scanzi.

SCANZI, Francesco
Italian, 16th century.
Active in Soncino, at the beginning of the 16th century.
Painter.

Francesco Sanzi was the son of Allegrino Scanzi.

SCAPARRA, Pedro
Italian, 15th century.
Active in Syracuse, and also in Puigcerdà in 1446.
Painter.

SCAPIN, Carlo
Italian, 18th century.
Painter.

Carlo Scapin painted two pictures for the chancel in the church of St Gaetano in Padua.

SCAPIN, Jacopo
Italian, 16th century.
Sculptor.

Jacopo Scapin executed the door in Doric style on the north side of the church of S Antonio in Padua.

SCAPPETTA, Pietro, or Scopetta
Italian, 19th - 20th century.
Born 15 February 1863, in Amalfi; died 9 February 1920, in Naples.
Painter, watercolourist, draughtsman, illustrator.
Figures, portraits, genre scenes, landscapes.

Pietro Scappetta studied at the Istituto di Belle Arti in Naples and with Giacomo di Chirico in the same town. He made his debut in 1880 and exhibited in Naples, Venice and Milan (1918). He was also a poet.

MUSEUMS AND GALLERIES:
NAPLES (Biblioteca Nazionale Vittorio Emanuele III).
AUCTION RECORDS:
VIENNA, 31 May 1951, *Amalfi in Summer*, ATS 2,000. MILAN, 10 April 1969, *Portrait of a Woman*, ITL 700,000. FLORENCE, 15 April 1972, *The Parisienne*, ITL 600,000. LONDON, 23 Oct 1974, *View of Amalfi*, GBP 650. LONDON, 29 Sept 1976, *View of Amalfi* (oil on canvas, 17 1/2 x 27 1/2 ins / 44.5 x 70 cm) GBP 2,200. LONDON, 20 July 1977, *View of Amalfi* (oil on canvas, 17 1/2 x 27 1/2 ins / 44.5 x 70 cm) GBP 1,000. MILAN, 10 June 1981, *Street in Paris* (oil on canvas, 18 1/2 x 24 ins / 47 x 61 cm) ITL 5,500,000. MILAN, 30 Oct 1984, *View of Amalfi* (1892, oil on canvas, 8 3/4 x 15 ins / 22.5 x 38 cm) ITL 1,400,000. LONDON, 28 Nov 1985, *Street in Paris* (watercolour and pastel, 9 1/2 x 13 1/2 ins / 24 x 34 cm) GBP 1,400. MILAN, 11 Dec 1986, *Portrait of a Fashionable Woman* (oil on canvas, 63 x 37 1/2 ins / 160 x 95 cm) ITL 12,500,000. ROME, 25 May 1988, *Portrait of Marchesa Valdambrini* (charcoal/paper, 13 1/2 x 17 1/4 ins / 34 x 43.5 cm) ITL 3,000,000. MILAN, 19 Oct 1989, *Amalfi Coast* (oil on canvas, 13 3/4 x 23 1/2 ins / 35 x 60 cm) ITL 42,000,000. MILAN, 6 Dec 1989, *Lady in a Hat* (oil on board, 20 x 17 3/4 ins / 51 x 45 cm) ITL 13,500,000. ROME, 14 Dec 1989, *Garden in Bloom* (oil on panel, 11 x 6 3/4 ins / 28 x 17 cm) ITL 12,650,000. MONACO, 21 April 1990, *Portrait of an Elegant Young Woman* (oil on panel, 9 x 6 1/4 ins / 22 x 16 cm) FRF 55,500. MILAN, 30 May 1990, *Young Woman Reading* (oil on board, 11 x 8 1/4 ins / 28 x 21 cm) ITL 15,500,000. NEW YORK, 23 Oct 1990, *Window Shopping* (oil on board, 13 3/4 x 98 1/2 ins / 34.9 x 250.3 cm) USD 13,200. ROME, 4 Dec 1990, *Head of a Woman* (oil on board, 4 x 3 1/4 ins / 10 x 8 cm) ITL 3,200,000. ROME, 11 Dec 1990, *Algerian Pavillion at the 1889 Exposition Universelle* (oil on panel, 7 1/2 x 10 ins / 19 x 24.5 cm) ITL 13,800,000. MILAN, 12 March 1991, *The Parisienne* (oil on canvas, 14 1/4 x 9 3/4 ins / 36 x 25 cm) ITL 21,000,000. MILAN, 6 June 1991, *The Seine in Paris* (oil on board, 5 1/2 x 7 3/4 ins / 14 x 20 cm) ITL 16,500,000. LONDON, 19 June 1991, *Coastal Landscape* (oil on board, 18 1/2 x 23 1/4 ins / 47 x 59 cm) GBP 3,300. NEW YORK, 17 Oct 1991, *Arc du Carrousel and the Louvre* (oil on board, 5 1/2 x 8 ins / 14 x 20.3 cm) USD 13,750. ROME, 14 Nov 1991, *Seated Woman* (pencil, 15 1/4 x 11 1/4 ins / 39 x 28.5 cm) ITL 1,380,000. MILAN, 17 Dec 1992, *Coast at Naples* (oil on canvas, 12 1/4 x 24 1/2 ins / 31 x 62.5 cm) ITL 34,000,000. MILAN, 22 Nov 1993, *Amalfi* (1892, oil on canvas, 9 x 15 ins / 22 x 38 cm) ITL 34,176,000. NEW YORK, 17 Feb 1994, *Parisian Women* (oil on strengthened canvas, 17 x 13 1/4 ins / 43 x 33.5 cm) USD 9,200. ROME, 31 May 1994, *Small Children and Nannies in Paris* (oil on panel, 7 1/4 x 16 1/4 ins / 18.5 x 41 cm) ITL 30,641,000. ROME, 6 Dec 1994, *White Lace* (oil on canvas, 7 x 5 ins / 18 x 13 cm) ITL 5,657,000. MILAN, 25 Oct 1995, *Portrait of Signora Carrara* (oil on board, 18 x 14 1/2 ins / 46 x 37 cm) ITL 11,500,000. NEW YORK, 1 Nov 1995, *Naples* (oil on canvas mounted on board, 17 x 22 3/4 ins / 43.2 x 57.8 cm) USD 161,000. ROME, 23 May 1996, *Place de la Concorde* (oil on canvas, 7 3/4 x 11 3/4 ins / 20 x 30 cm) ITL 10,350,000. ROME, 4 June 1996, *The Art of Seduction* (watercolour/paper, diam. 7 3/4 ins / 20 cm) ITL 3,680,000. LONDON, 12 June 1996, *Fishermen at Amalfi* (oil on canvas, 17 3/4 x 13 3/4 ins / 45 x 35 cm) GBP 5,980. LONDON, 14 June 1996, *Joie de Vivre* (oil on board, 18 1/4 x 15 ins / 46.4 x 38.2 cm) GBP 5,750. ROME, 28 Nov 1996, *Elegant Woman in an Interior* (pastel on board, 26 3/4 x 19 ins / 68 x 48 cm) ITL 30,000,000. ROME, 2 Dec 1997, *Outskirts of Paris* (oil on canvas, 18 x 11 ins / 45.5 x 28 cm) ITL 10,350,000.

SCAPPI, Alessandro
Italian, 17th century.
Active in Sinigaglia at the end of the 17th century.
Sculptor (wood).

From 1692, Alessandro Scappi collaborated with Domenico Antonio Colicci and others on the stalls in the church in Monte Cassino.

SCAPPINI, Giovanni
Italian, 17th - 18th century.
Born 1655, in Venice; died 1733.
Painter, art restorer. Figures, landscapes.

SCAPRE-PIERRET, Jeanne
French, 19th century.
Born in Versailles.
Painter. Portraits.

She was a pupil of Madame Blot and Perrault, and made her Salon debut in 1872.

SCAPUZZI, Andrea
Italian, 18th century.
Active in Gaeta (Lazio), Italy during the second half of the 18th century.
Painter.

Andrea Scapuzzi studied in Rome.
MUSEUMS AND GALLERIES:
ROME (Gal. dell'Accademia Nazionale di S Luca): *Achilles Sees Iris*.

SCARABELLI, Anastasio, called L'Abate Scarabelli
Italian, 18th century.
Died 1763 or 1764.
Painter.

Scarabelli worked on churches and public buildings in Bologna as well as in Spain.

SCARABELLI, Orazio
Italian, 16th century.
Active in Florence c. 1589.
Engraver (burin). Scenes with figures.
Orazio Scarabelli produced engravings depicting the festivities of the marriage between Grand Duke Ferdinand I of Tuscany and Christine of Lorraine.
MUSEUMS AND GALLERIES:
LONDON (British Mus.): *Marriage of Grand Duke Ferdinand I of Tuscany and Christine of Lorraine* (10 plates).

SCARABELLO, Angelo
Italian, 18th century.
Born 1711, in Este; died 1795.
Engraver, goldsmith, draughtsman, founder.
Angelo Scarabello worked in Padua, where he made the doors of the church of S Antonio.

SCARABELOTTO, G.
Italian, 19th century.
Painter.
MUSEUMS AND GALLERIES:
TRIESTE (Civico Mus. Revoltella): *Countryside outside Rome; Moonlight; Cemetery.*

SCARAMANZO, Girolamo
Italian, 16th century.
Active in Venice at the beginning of the 16th century.
Sculptor, designer of ornamental architectural features.
Girolamo Scaramanzo was commissioned to provide the floral decorations on the ceiling of the church of S Maria delle Grazie in Udine.

SCARAMUCCI, Domenico, or Scaramuccia
Italian, 18th century.
Active in Rome during the first half of the 18th century.
Sculptor.
Domenico Scaramucci sculpted the statue of *St John the Evangelist* on the façade of the basilica of San Giovanni in Laterano in Rome.

SCARAMUCCIA, Giovanni Antonio
Italian, 17th century.
Born 1580, in Monte Colognola; died 16 March 1633, in Perugia.
Active in Perugia.
Painter.
The pupil of Roncalli and imitator of the Carracci brothers, Giovanni Scaramuccia worked for churches in Perugia and for the Capuchin monastery. He is criticised for his excessively sombre colouring.
AUCTION RECORDS:
NEW YORK, 16 Jan 1985, *Head of a Child* (black and red chalk, 9 x 9 1/2in/22 x 24.1cm) USD 6,200.

SCARAMUCCIA, Luigi Pellegrini, or
Scaramuzza or Scaramuzzi, called Il Perugino
Italian, 17th century.
Born 3 December 1616, in Perugia; died 3 August 1680, in Milan.
Painter, engraver (etching), art writer.
The pupil of his father Giovanni Antonio Scaramuccia, Guido Reni and Guercino, Luigi Scaramuccia produced works for various buildings in Perugia, Bologna and Milan. He is noted in particular for his *Coronation of Charles V of Spain* in the Palazzo Pubblico in Bologna and his *St Barbara* in the church of S Marco in Milan. He engraved religious subjects.

SCARAMUZZA, Camillo
Italian, 19th - 20th century.
Born 23 May 1842, in Parma; died 1915?, in Milan.
Painter, decorative designer. Figures, landscapes, architectural views.
MUSEUMS AND GALLERIES:
PARMA (GA): *View of the Alps.*

SCARAMUZZA, Francesco
Italian, 19th century.
Born 15 July 1803, in Sissa, near Parma; died 10 October 1886, in Parma.
Painter, draughtsman.
Francesco Scaramuzza studied first in Parma where he was much inspired by the works of Correggio. He went to Rome where he worked chiefly as an illustrator. He made a series of drawings to illustrate Dante's *Divine Comedy* very similar to Gustave Doré's, whose work he has been accused of copying.
MUSEUMS AND GALLERIES:
PARMA (GA): *St John the Baptist; Cupid and Psyche; Aminta and Silvia; Wetnurse.*
AUCTION RECORDS:
MILAN, 30 Nov 1933, *Anger of Saul,* ITL 1,400.

SCARAMUZZA, Giovanni
Italian, 19th century.
Born 1 February 1818, in Rivolta (Lombardy); died in Rome.
Painter.
Giovanni Scaramuzza was a student at the Accademia di Belle Arti di Brera, Milan.
MUSEUMS AND GALLERIES:
BERGAMO (Accademia Carrara): *Self-portrait.*

SCARANI, Giulio Cesare
Italian, 17th - 18th century.
Active in Bologna from 1680 to 1730.
Painter, engraver (etching).
Giulio Cesare Scarani was the pupil of Domenico Viani.

SCARANO, Giovanni Battista
Italian, 16th century.
Active at the end of the 16th century.
Sculptor.
Giovanni Battista Scarano executed a door in multicoloured marble for the church of S Maria del Carmine Maggiore in Naples.

SCARATI, Bernardino de'
Italian, 16th century.
Active in Gandino, in 1525.
Sculptor (wood).
Bernardino de' Scarati worked with his nephew Valerio Scarati on the choir stalls in S Maria Maggiore in Bergamo.

SCARATI, Valerio
Italian, 16th century.
Active in 1525.
Sculptor (wood).
Valerio Scarati worked with his uncle Bernardino de' Scarati on the choir stalls in S Maria Maggiore in Bergamo.

SCARBE. See **SCHARBE**

SCARBINA
French, 19th century.
Painter. Genre scenes.
Scarbina is mentioned by Mireur.
AUCTION RECORDS:
PARIS, 28 Feb 1898, *Herring Seller,* FRF 200.

SCARBO, J. F.
German, 18th century.
Active in Berlin in 1793.
Painter.

SCARBOROUGH, Frank William, or Frederick William, or Scarbrough
British, 19th - 20th century.
Painter (gouache), watercolourist. Waterscapes, urban landscapes.

Frank William Scarborough and Frederick William Scarborough, both mentioned in the sales catalogues, are probably one and the same painter. He specialised in views of London, notably the Thames and the Port of London.

AUCTION RECORDS:

LONDON, 21 June 1983, *On the Thames* (watercolour heightened with white, 9 1/2 x 23 1/2 ins / 24 x 60 cm) GBP 750. CHESTER, 4 Oct 1985, *Blackwall Reach, London* (watercolour heightened with gouache, 9 1/2 x 13 1/2 ins / 24 x 34 cm) GBP 1,000. LONDON, 16 Dec 1986, *Pool of London with Tower Bridge, London* (watercolour heightened with white, 13 3/4 x 21 ins / 35.2 x 53.5 cm) GBP 3,200. LONDON, 3 June 1987, *View of the Port of London* (watercolour heightened with white, a pair, 20 1/2 x 13 1/2 ins / 52 x 34 cm) GBP 3,400. LONDON, 25 Jan 1988, *London Bridge* (watercolour, 20 x 13 1/2 ins / 51 x 34 cm) GBP 1,650. LONDON, 31 Jan 1990, *Daybreak over the Port of London* (watercolour and gouache, 13 x 20 1/2 ins / 33 x 52 cm) GBP 2,420. LONDON, 22 May 1991, *Navigation on the Thames* (watercolour heightened with white, a pair, each 9 x 20 ins / 23 x 51 cm) GBP 3,080. LONDON, 14 June 1991, *Navigation of the Thames* (pencil and watercolour, 9 3/4 x 13 3/4 ins / 24.8 x 34.9 cm) GBP 1,595. LONDON, 7 Oct 1992, *Dusk over London Docks* (watercolour, 6 3/4 x 10 ins / 17 x 24.5 cm) GBP 1,430. LONDON, 16 July 1993, *Port of London at Dusk* (watercolour heightened with white, 13 x 20 1/4 ins / 33 x 51.5 cm) GBP 2,070. LONDON, 11 Oct 1995, *Fishing Boats and Yachts in a Port* (watercolour, 14 1/4 x 10 1/2 ins / 36.5 x 26.5 cm) GBP 667. AMSTERDAM, 9 March 1999, *Pool of London with Tower Bridge. Limehouse, London* (watercolour, a pair, 9 x 13 ins / 23 x 34 cm) NLG 8,500. TORONTO, 1 June 1999, *Off Rotherithe, Port of London* (oil on canvas, 15 x 23 ins / 39 x 59 cm) CAD 10,000. BILLINGSHURST, 25 May 2000, *Pool of London* (oil on canvas, 15 x 24 ins / 39 x 60 cm) GBP 3,000. LEYBURN, 14 July 2000, *Lower Pool, London* (watercolour and gouache, 14 x 20 ins / 35 x 52 cm) GBP 3,800. LONDON, 5 Sept 2001, *Tower Bridge London* (watercolour heightened with white, 13 x 29 ins / 34 x 74 cm) GBP 11,000. LONDON, 5 Nov 2001, *Sunset, Pool of London* (watercolour heightened with white, 9 x 13 ins / 24 x 34 cm) GBP 3,700. LONDON, 15 Aug 2002, *Unloading Lowestoft Trawlers. Misty Morning Whitby* (watercolour heightened with white, a pair, 17 x 11 ins / 42 x 29 cm) GBP 4,000. LONDON, 16 Dec 2002, *Lower Pool, London* (watercolour, 13 x 20 ins / 34 x 52 cm) GBP 5,400. LONDON, 16 Sept 2003, *Sunset on the Thames London* (watercolour heightened with white, 9 x 13 ins / 23 x 33 cm) GBP 3,200. LONDON, 16 Sept 2003, *London Bridge. Early Morning, Blackwall Reach, London* (watercolour heightened with white, a pair, 9 x 13 ins / 24 x 34 cm) GBP 6,000. LONDON, 14 Sept 2004, *Blackwall Reach* (watercolour heightened with white, 6 x 9 ins / 16 x 24 cm) GBP 2,600. LONDON, 14 Sept 2004, *Off Wapping, London* (watercolour heightened with white, 13 x 9 ins / 33 x 23 cm) GBP 3,200.

SCARBOROUGH, John
American, 19th century.
Active in Charleston during the early 19th century.
Painter, miniaturist. Portraits.

SCARBOROUGH, William Harrison
American, 19th century.
Born 7 November 1812, in Dover; died 16 August 1871, in Columbia.
Painter, miniaturist.

William Harrison Scarborough studied in Cincinnati and worked in Charleston, Darlington and Columbia.

MUSEUMS AND GALLERIES:

COLUMBIA, SC (MA): *Crossing a Ford* (oil on canvas, after Thomas Gainsborough); *Falls on the Reedy River*.

SCARCELLA, Ippolito, or Scarsella or Scarcellini or Scarcellino
Italian, 16th - 17th century.
Born 1551, in Ferrara; died 27 October 1620, in Ferrara.
Painter, fresco artist, engraver, draughtsman. Religious subjects, mythological subjects, portraits. Miniatures.
Ferrara School.

Ippolito Scarcella's father Sigismondo Scarcella was his first master, then he went to Venice to study with Giacomo Bassano. After a period in Parma, he returned to Ferrara where he executed many commissions. He also made engravings of religious subjects.

MUSEUMS AND GALLERIES:

BERGAMO (Accademia Carrara): *Martyrdom of a Saint*; Small triptych - BOLOGNA (Pinacoteca Nazionale): *Adoration of the Magi* - BUDAPEST: *Mystical Marriage of St Catherine* - CARPI (Mus. Civico G. Ferrari): *Annunciation* - CHAMBÉRY (MBA): *Augustus and the Sibyl* - DARMSTADT: *Flight into Egypt* (attributed) - DRESDEN: *Holy Family in the Carpenter's Workshop*; *Holy Family, St Barbara and St Charles Borromeo*; *Virgin and Child with St Clare and St Catherine* - ERFURT (Angermus.): *Guardian Angel and Satan* - FERRARA (Benedictine Convent): *Adoration of the Magi* - FERRARA (Church of S Benedetto): *Assumption* - FERRARA (Church of S Maria Nuova): *Annunciation*; *Visitation*; *Assumption*; *Marriage at Cana* - FERRARA (Church of S Paolo): frescoes - FLORENCE (NG): *Judgement of Paris*; *Holy Family* - FLORENCE (Palazzo Pitti): *Birth of a Child* - HANOVER: *Joseph and his Brothers*; *Eight Scenes from the Life of Job*; *Children's Room in Venice* - KARLSRUHE: *Virgin and Child* - MADRID: *Virgin and Child* - MILAN (Pinacoteca di Brera): *Virgin and Child with the Doctors of the Church* - ROME (Gal. Colonna): *Priest Receiving the Scapular* - ROME (Mus. e Gal. Borghese): *Venus Crowned by Cupid*; *St Mary Magdalene and Jesus at the House of Simon the Pharisee*; *Venus and Cupid*; *Massacre of the Innocents*; *Diana and Endymion*; *Venus Mourning the Dead Adonis*; *Holy Family*; *Venus Bathing*; *A King with a Courtier and a Slave*; *Christ and his Disciples on the Road to Emmaus* - ST PETERSBURG (Hermitage): *Holy Family* - STOCKHOLM: *Holy Family and St Catherine of Alexandria*.

AUCTION RECORDS:

PARIS, 1814, *Adoration of the Magi*, FRF 62. PARIS, 1815, *The Woman Taken in Adultery*, FRF 34. PARIS, 12 and 13 June 1933, *Flight into Egypt*, FRF 2,100. MILAN, 24 Nov 1965, *Virgin and Redeemer Appearing to Sts Jerome, Dominic and Francis*, ITL 750,000. LONDON, 6 Dec 1967, *Venus and Adonis*, GBP 5,500. LONDON, 5 Dec 1969, *Sacra Conversazione*, Gns 800. LONDON, 15 July 1970, *Eleven Nymphs Bathing*, GBP 2,100. NEW YORK, 4 June 1980, *Virgin and Child with Two Saints* (oil on canvas, 74 x 52 ins / 188 x 132 cm) USD 7,500. LONDON, 23 April 1982, *Holy Family with the Infant St John the Baptist in a Landscape* (oil on panel, 12 3/4 x 18 1/4 ins / 32.4 x 46.2 cm) GBP 4,800. NEW YORK, 22 March 1984, *St Margaret of Antioch in a Landscape* (oil on canvas, 22 x 16 3/4 ins / 55 x 42.5 cm) USD 10,500. LONDON, 19 Dec 1985, *Flight into Egypt* (oil on panel, 25 1/4 x 16 1/4 ins / 64 x 41 cm) GBP 19,500. PARIS, 30 May 1988, *Jesus and the Woman Taken in Adultery* (oil on canvas, 36 1/4 x 48 ins / 92 x 122 cm) FRF 160,000. MILAN, 12 June 1989, *Virgin Adoring the Child* (oil on canvas, 29 1/2 x 22 1/2 ins / 75 x 57 cm) ITL 22,000,000. LONDON, 11 April 1990, *Mystic Marriage of St Catherine* (oil on panel, 14 3/4 x 10 1/2 ins / 37.5 x 26.5 cm) GBP 29,700. PARIS, 30 Jan 1991, *Visitation* (oil on canvas, 60 1/4 x 46 1/2 ins / 153 x 118 cm) FRF 48,000. NEW YORK, 11 April 1991, *Virgin and Child with a Franciscan Saint in a Landscape* (oil on panel, 12 3/4 x 8 3/4 ins / 32.5 x 22.5 cm) USD 44,000. MILAN, 30 May 1991,

Mystic Marriage of St Catherine (oil on panel, 19 x 22 1/2 ins / 48 x 57 cm) ITL 28,000,000. LONDON, 8 July 1992, *Mars and Venus* (oil on canvas, 19 1/4 x 15 3/4 ins / 49 x 40 cm) GBP 11,000. PARIS, 29 March 1993, *Entombment* (oil on canvas, 19 x 13 1/2 ins / 48 x 34 cm) FRF 85,000. NEW YORK, 20 May 1993, *Deposition* (oil on canvas, 86 x 55 ins / 218.4 x 139.7 cm) USD 123,500. LONDON, 16 April 1997, *Angel with the Three Marys at the Tomb* (oil on canvas, 16 x 13 3/4 ins / 40.8 x 35 cm) GBP 7,130.

SCARCELLA, Sigismondo, or Scarsella, called Mondino
Italian, 16th - 17th century.
Born 1530, in Ferrara; died 1614, in Ferrara.
Painter.

Sigismondo Scarcella, father of Ippolito Scarcella, was the pupil of Paolo Veronese for three years and worked in a similar style. He executed decorative paintings in several public buildings in Ferrara and also worked as an architect.

MUSEUMS AND GALLERIES:
CHAMBÉRY (MBA): *Portrait of a Man* - FERRARA (Pinacoteca Nazionale): *Entombment*.

AUCTION RECORDS:
PARIS, 1793, *Jesus and the Disciples in Emmaus*, FRF 2,500.

SCARCELLINO, Ippolito. See **SCARCELLA**

SCARDON, Guillelmo. See **SCARSERDON Guillelmo**

SCARELLA
Italian, 19th century.
Miniaturist.

Scarella is known for an ivory miniature with a *Portrait of a Man*.

SCARFAGLIA, Lucrezia
Italian, 17th century.
Active in Bologna c. 1677.
Painter.

Lucrezia Scarfaglia was the pupil of Elisabetta Sirani and D.M. Canuti. She produced works for the churches and palaces of Bologna.

SCARFI, Giovanni
Italian, 19th century.
Born 11 November 1852, in Fano Superiore, near Messina.
Sculptor.

A pupil of Monteverde and Massini in Rome, Giovanni Scarfi executed many statues and busts now in Messina and Catania.

SCARIGLIA, Antonio
Italian, 15th century.
Active in Naples in 1492.
Miniaturist.

SCARLET, James
British, 18th century.
Active during the second half of the 18th century.
Painter. Genre scenes.

James Scarlet studied under J. Stuart and went on to exhibit in London from 1768 to 1770.

SCARLETT, C.
British, 18th century.
Active in London from 1740 to 1743.
Draughtsman, engraver (burin).

SCARLETT, Rolph
Canadian, 20th century.
Born 1889; died 1984.
Painter (mixed media/gouache), designer, jeweller.
Stage sets.

Rolph Scarlett was drawn to abstract painting at the beginning of his career. His association with Salomon R. Guggenheim and Hilla Rebay in the 1930s and 40s was the decisive factor in determining the direction that his career was to take. They were very taken with his work and promoted it at the museum of non-objective painting, eventually called the Salomon R. Guggenheim Museum. He was a speaker there, his job being to publicise the works of Kandinsky and Rudolph Bauer and raise awareness of them in the USA. He became the most fervent defender of Modernist theories in the US.

After Guggenheim's death Scarlett settled in Woodstock and continued to paint in an abstract style. The Musée des Beaux-Arts in Montreal presented a retrospective of his work in 2003.

BIBLIOGRAPHY:
Nasby, Judy, *Rolph Scarlett: Painter, Designer, Jeweller*, McGill-Queens University Press, Kingston, 2004.

MUSEUMS AND GALLERIES:
LINCOLN (Sheldon Memorial AG, University of Nebraska): *Untitled no. 49* (c. 1940, gouache and graphite).

AUCTION RECORDS:
NEW YORK, 27 March 1985, *Untitled* (gouache, a pair, 8 x 28 1/4 ins / 20.6 x 71.8 cm and 10 1/4 x 9 ins/26 x 22.8 cm) USD 1,200. NEW YORK, 28 Sept 1989, *Geometric Abstraction* (oil on canvas, 33 1/2 x 50 ins / 85.1 x 127 cm) USD 22,000. NEW YORK, 24 Jan 1990, *Abstract Landscape* (oil and pastel/paper, 18 x 24 ins / 45.5 x 61 cm) USD 4,950. NEW YORK, 16 March 1990, *Allegretto in Brown* (oil on canvas, 59 x 71 1/4 ins / 149.8 x 181 cm) USD 19,800. NEW YORK, 23 May 1990, *Fanfare in Black* (oil on canvas, 68 x 49 3/4 ins / 173 x 126.5 cm) USD 16,500. NEW YORK, 30 May 1990, *Abstraction* (acrylic, ink and pencil/card, 32 x 25 ins / 81.4 x 63.5 cm) USD 2,750. NEW YORK, 17 Dec 1990, *Untitled* (mixed media/paper, 17 x 17 ins / 43.3 x 43.3 cm) USD 3,575. NEW YORK, 18 Dec 1991, *Abstract Composition* (gouache, ink and graphite/paper, 17 3/4 x 18 ins / 45.1 x 45.7 cm) USD 2,420. NEW YORK, 12 March 1992, *Geometric Abstraction* (oil on canvas, 40 1/4 x 48 ins / 102 x 121 cm) USD 4,950. NEW YORK, 25 Sept 1992, *Largo* (oil on canvas, 48 x 56 ins / 121.9 x 142.2 cm) USD 8,800. NEW YORK, 28 Nov 1995, *Cat and Plant* (oil on canvas, 20 x 16 1/4 ins / 51 x 41 cm) USD 4,830. NEW YORK, 26 Sept 1999, *Abstract Composition* (oil on canvas, 53 x 70 ins / 135 x 178 cm) USD 2,600. SAN FRANCISCO, 26 Oct 1999, *Untitled* (oil on canvas, 36 x 48 ins / 91 x 122 cm) USD 26,000. NEW YORK, 23 Jan 2000, *Abstract Composition* (oil on canvas on masonite, 42 x 48 ins / 107 x 122 cm) USD 2,000. PITTSFIELD, 8 Sept 2001, *Non Objective, Red, White, Black. Non Objective, Multicolour Composition* (gouache and pencil, a pair, 9 x 9 ins / 23 x 23 cm) USD 1,500. NEW YORK, 13 Feb 2002, *Abstraction* (c. 1950, oil and pencil on canvas, 44 x 39 ins / 112 x 99 cm) USD 3,500. SAN FRANCISCO, 19 Nov 2002, *Untitled, Geometric Abstract* (oil on canvas, 40 x 52 ins / 102 x 132 cm) USD 18,000. NEW YORK, 21 May 2003, *Abstraction* (c. 1940, oil on canvas, 52 x 39 ins / 132 x 99 cm) USD 20,000. CHICAGO, 9 Nov 2003, *Untitled* (gouache, 8 x 8 ins / 20 x 20 cm) USD 2,900. NEW YORK, 8 Feb 2004, *Abstract* (watercolour and gouache, 15 x 11 ins / 38 x 28 cm) USD 2,500. CHICAGO, 16 May 2004, *Untitled* (oil on canvas, 9 x 9 ins / 23 x 23 cm) USD 2,100.

SCARLETT, Samuel
American, 18th - 19th century.
Born 1775, in Staffordshire, England.
Active during the first half of the 19th century.
Painter, art restorer. Landscapes.

Samuel Scarlett was a pupil of Nathan T. Fielding in London around 1795. He worked in Bath (Avon), England until 1817, then emigrated to the USA and went to work in Philadelphia. He exhibited at the Pennsylvania Academy of the Fine Arts and was a curator there from 1829 to 1846. He also exhibited at the Boston Athenaeum.

SCARLOT, H.
French.
Watercolourist. Waterscapes, architectural views.
MUSEUMS AND GALLERIES:
PERPIGNAN: *Chateau by a River* (drawing).
AUCTION RECORDS:
PARIS, 5 April 1943, *Riverscape* (watercolour) FRF 35.

SCARMEUSE, Jean
Flemish School, 17th century.
Sculptor.
Jean Scarmeuse worked on the fountain at Oudenaarde in 1676 and 1677.

SCARNATI, Marina
Italian, 20th century.
Born 25 October 1943, in Rome.
Painter.
Lettrism.
Marina Scarnati joined the Lettrist group in 1966.

SCARNATI, Sandra
French, 20th century.
Born 1937, in Paris.
Painter.
Lettrism.
From 1970 Sandra Scarnati was a member of the Lettrist Group. To traditional alphabets she added an invented alphabet based diagrams of choreographical positions. She also used in her compositions a variety of objects that she often aligned as if on a music stave.

SCARON, Alexandre Joseph
Belgian, 19th century.
Born 1788, in Brussels; died 1850, in Ixelles.
Painter. Flowers, fruit.
MUSEUMS AND GALLERIES:
BRUSSELS: *Flowers*.
AUCTION RECORDS:
BRUSSELS, 20 March 1973, *Basket of Flowers and Eggs*, BEF 90,000.

SCARONI, Annibale
Italian, 20th century.
Born 1891, in Brescia.
Painter. Landscapes.
AUCTION RECORDS:
ROME, 11 Dec 1990, *Canal in Chioggia* (1925, oil on canvas, 33 3/4 x 46 ins / 86 x 117 cm) ITL 5,750,000. MILAN, 21 Dec 1993, *Canal dei Mendicanti in Venice* (1937, oil on canvas, 25 1/2 x 31 1/2 ins / 65 x 80 cm) ITL 2,990,000.

SCARPA, Gino
Italian, 20th century.
Born 1924, in Venice.
Active in Denmark.
Painter, sculptor.
After studying architecture, Gino Scarpa decided to become a painter in about 1945. He taught history of art in Bressanone between 1953 and 1957. Scarpa's works explore complex combinations of materials, usually cement and copper. His abstractions are often inspired by his study of ancient Scandinavian rune stones.

His work has appeared in a number of major collective exhibitions since 1956, at the Venice Biennale in 1948 and the Rome Quadriennale in 1948 and 1959.
MUSEUMS AND GALLERIES:
BOLZANO - CHARLOTTENBURG - COPENHAGEN - TRENTO - VENICE - VIENNA.
AUCTION RECORDS:
ROME, 4 April 1974, *Sol Lilja* (wood, plaster, aluminium) ITL 700,000. PARIS, 24 March 1988, *Dancing Couple* (two bronzes, h. 8 ins / 205 cm and h. 9 ins/23 cm) FRF 11,000. COPENHAGEN, 4 March 1992, *Dance on the River* (oil on canvas, 39 1/4 x 31 1/2 ins / 100 x 80 cm) DKK 4,100. OSLO, 16 Dec 1999, *Adam and Eve* (oil on canvas, 43 x 39 ins / 110 x 100 cm) NOK 24,000. OSLO, 30 Aug 2001, *Landscape from Froya* (oil on canvas, 39 x 31 ins / 100 x 80 cm) NOK 18,500. PARIS, 3 July 2002, *Female Bust* (bronze, h. 67 ins / 170 cm) EUR 8,300. PARIS, 3 July 2002, *Wave* (bronze, h. 72 ins / 183 cm) EUR 10,800.

SCARPA, Michel
French, 20th century.
Born 1942, in Paris.
Collage artist.
Michel Scarpa moved to London in 1958 and studied at the Chelsea School of Art. He uses crumpled pages torn from magazines to impart bulk to his collages. His work is resolutely abstract but nonetheless evokes a richly-coloured world of words and figures.

He has exhibited solo on various occasions, including: in 1988, at the Galerie Pierre Lescot in Paris; in 1989, in Zurich and Basel; in 1990, in Cannes, Seattle and Liège; and, in 1991, in Marseilles, St-Paul-de-Vence, Lyons, St Rémy-de-Provence, Vence and Cannes. He also represented the Galerie Eterso in Cannes at the 1992 Salon Découvertes in Paris.
BIBLIOGRAPHY:
Scarpa, exhibition catalogue, Gal. Eterso, Cannes, 1992.

SCARPAGNI, Antonio, called Lo Scapargnino
Italian, 16th century.
Died 1558, in Venice.
Sculptor.
Antonio Scarpagni worked in Venice, particularly at the churches of S Giovanni and S Sebastiano. With P. Lombardo, he completed the sculptures on the east façade of the Doge's Palace.

SCARPARIO, Giovanni, called Popossio
Italian, 14th century.
Active in Udine in 1352.
Painter. Coats of arms.

SCARPATIO, Vittore. See **CARPACCIO**

SCARPETTA, Antonio. See **MARA Antonio**

SCARPINATO, Francesco
Italian, 19th century.
Born in Sicily.
Painter. Landscapes.
Francesco Scarpinato exhibited in Venice, Turin, Rome and Livorno.

SCARPITTA, Salvatore
American, 20th century.
Born 1919, in New York.
Active from 1936 in Italy.
Painter, sculptor.
Salvatore Scarpitta spend his childhood in America, but went to Italy in 1936 and settled there. He staged his first exhibition in Rome in 1949 and exhibited there again in 1951, 1955 and 1956. He exhibited in New York for the first time in 1959.

Scarpitta talks of the 1950s as a time of transition, of awakening. He described his first pictures as torn up paintings - he literally tore up the canvas. He explained that the canvas became so hostile to him, that in order to find any kind of peace with himself he had to tear it up, and he made his paintings out of these pieces. And, indeed, his paintings from that time are like informal patchworks: there are seams, knots and weaving, revealing neutral material, since they are either monochrome or made of subtle variations of beige, ecru and raw canvas, but they are also sensually loaded and exhibitionist.

A visit to New York in 1959 helped Scarpitta to focus his work. The grime of New York fascinated him as the most fitting expression of American civilisation. Without resorting to graffiti like Tàpies he restricted himself to using pieces of unpainted canvas in his assemblages, but fixed or paralysed them by coating them in plastic, rendering them inert, trapping them like ingrained dirt, focusing the attention on the canvas. Pursuing this idea of inertia in texture he then replaced the canvas with elastic bands, which were also suddenly immobilised in plastic, but were still able to evoke the idea of tension. He also introduced colour, in monochrome, but a definite single colour.

Around 1965 X-shaped compositions of diagonals inside a cardboard box or a wooden construction appeared like an interlude in Scarpitta's work. He then created some *Pictures of Straps and Cuts*. However, in 1964 his work took on a new direction, scrutinising the past, trying to capture memories. Wanting to rediscover the universe of his childhood and the things that fascinated him, he began to construct old racing cars, made out of odds and ends at first, then reproduced increasingly faithfully. This exploration of a whole mythology of memories was not unusual in the art world at the end of the 1960s, and his racing cars can be compared with the aeroplanes built by the young Belgian, Panamarenko.

AUCTION RECORDS:
MILAN, 4 June 1974, *Secret Marriage*, ITL 7,000,000. ROME, 10 April 1990, *Composition* (1956, tempera/paper, 27 1/2 x 19 3/4 ins / 70 x 50 cm) ITL 4,000,000. NEW YORK, 31 May 1990, *Pinnacle* (1928, bronze, h. 18 1/4 ins / 46.4 cm) USD 880. ROME, 9 April 1991, *Untitled* (oil on canvas, 23 1/2 x 31 1/2 ins / 60 x 80 cm) ITL 12,000,000. ROME, 30 Nov 1993, *Still-life of Bottles* (oil on canvas, 19 3/4 x 23 1/2 ins / 50 x 60 cm) ITL 2,875,000. NEW YORK, 23 Feb 1994, *Red Freight* (oil and fibreglass/canvas, 75 x 61 ins / 190.5 x 154.9 cm) USD 26,450. MILAN, 2 April 1996, *Demonstration in New York* (1954, oil on canvas, 25 1/2 x 31 1/2 ins / 65 x 80 cm) ITL 9,775,000. MILAN, 20 May 1996, *Secret Marriage* (1962, painting/canvas, 63 3/4 x 51 1/4 ins / 162 x 130 cm) ITL 41,400,000. ROME, 25 Nov 1999, *A per Adulterio* (*A for Adultery*) (1956, oil on canvas, 32 x 39 ins / 81 x 100 cm) ITL 22,000,000. LONDON, 25 Oct 2000, *Flying Dutchman* (1959, mixed media on paper, 55 x 70 ins / 140 x 178 cm) GBP 34,000. NEW YORK, 7 Nov 2000, *Conveyor* (oil on canvas with ladder and crumpled newspaper, 46 x 142 ins / 118 x 360 cm) USD 10,000. NEW YORK, 20 Feb 2001, *X-Frame* (1961, resin over canvas on panel, 72 x 56 ins / 183 x 143 cm) USD 10,000. NEW YORK, 15 May 2001, *Cairn Sled* (1975, wood, canvas, wax and resin, 106 x 20x34 ins / 270 x 51x86 cm) USD 11,000. ROME, 21 Nov 2002, *Remembering Harlem* (1955, oil on canvas, 28 x 35 ins / 70 x 90 cm) EUR 11,000. NEW YORK, 14 May 2003, *Sal's Red Hauler Special* (1967, racing car, 44 x 108x48 ins / 112 x 274x123 cm) USD 37,500. PRATO, 30 May 2003, *Composition* (1956, tempera on paper laid on canvas, 39 x 28 ins / 100 x 71 cm) EUR 9,000.

SCARPITTA, Salvatore Cartaino
Italian, 20th century.
Born 28 February 1887, in Palermo; died 1948.
Active in the USA.
Sculptor. Portraits. Busts.
Salvatore Scarpitta studied in Palermo and Rome. He made portrait busts of *Sergey Rachmaninov*, *Marlene Dietrich* and *Mussolini*.
AUCTION RECORDS:
NEW YORK, 24 April 1981, *Child with Goose* (bronze, fountain, h. 31 ins / 79 cm) USD 2,800.

SCARRATA, Francesco
Italian, 17th century.
Painter.
Francesco Scarrata painted the *Madonna of Itria* in the church of S Stefano Medio in Messina, Sicily.

SCARSELL, Jessie E.
Australian, 19th century.
Painter. Seascapes.
MUSEUMS AND GALLERIES:
SYDNEY: *Deserted River Bank*.

SCARSELLA, Ippolito. See **SCARCELLA**

SCARSELLA, Sigismondo. See **SCARCELLA**

SCARSELLI, Adolfo
Italian, 19th - 20th century.
Born 1866, in Florence; died 1945.
Painter. Genre scenes.
Adolfo Scarselli studied at the Accademia di Belle Arti in Florence and with Giovanni Fattori. He exhibited mainly in Florence.
MUSEUMS AND GALLERIES:
ROME (Gal. Nazionale d'Arte Moderna): *Flower of Melancholy*.

SCARSELLI, Alessandro
Italian, 18th century.
Born 1684; died 1773.
Miniaturist, copyist, engraver (burin/wood).
The husband of Maria Catarina Scarselli, Alessandro Scarselli worked in Bologna.

SCARSELLI, Giovanni Pietro
Italian, 17th century.
Active in Bologna c. 1680.
Painter, decorative designer.
Giovanni Scarselli painted biblical scenes in the chapel of the Crucifix in the church of San Giacomo Maggiore in Bologna.

SCARSELLI, Girolamo, or Scarsello
Italian, 17th century.
Active in Bologna c. 1670.
Painter, engraver (etching).
The pupil of Fr Gessi, Girolamo Scarselli worked in Bologna, Milan and Turin.

SCARSELLI, Maria Catarina. See **CANOSSA-SCARSELLI**

SCARSELLINO, Ippolito. See **SCARCELLA**

SCARSERDON, Guillelmo
Spanish, 14th century.
Painter.
Probably the same artist as Guillelmo Scardon, in 1328 he carried out some work in Palma Cathedral, Majorca.

SCARTEZZINI, Giovanni Battista Antonio, or Scartezini
Italian, 18th century.
Born in Civezzano, near Trieste; died 9 December 1726, in Mais, near Merano.
Painter, embroiderer. Landscapes, flowers.
MUSEUMS AND GALLERIES:
BERLIN (Kunstgewerbemus.): several works.

SCARTEZZINI, Giuseppe
Swiss, 20th century.
Born 1895; died 1967.
Painter, watercolourist.
MUSEUMS AND GALLERIES:
AARAU (Aargauer Kunsthaus): *Carpet-weaver* (watercolour).

SCARVELLI, Spyridon or Spiridon
Italian, 19th - 20th century.
Born 1868; died 1942.
Painter, watercolourist, draughtsman. Landscapes. Orientalism.
AUCTION RECORDS:
LONDON, 30 March 1990, *Corfu* (pencil and watercolour, 11 3/4 x 18 ins / 30 x 46 cm) GBP 4,180. BOLOGNA, 8-9 June 1992, *Oriental Lane* (watercolour, 13 3/4 x 10 ins / 35 x 24.5

cm) ITL 1,840,000. London, 18 June 1993, *On the Nile* (watercolour/paper, 9 1/2 x 15 1/4 ins / 24 x 39 cm) GBP 2,300. London, 17 Nov 1993, *Fishermen on the Shore in Corfu* (watercolour, 11 x 24 ins / 28 x 61 cm) GBP 5,980. London, 16 March 1994, *Views of Corfu* (watercolour, a pair, each 8 3/4 x 17 1/4 ins / 22.5 x 44 cm) GBP 4,140. Rome, 13 Dec 1995, *Corfu and Greek Village by the Sea* (watercolour/paper, a pair, 11 x 18 1/2 ins / 27 x 47 cm) ITL 6,670,000. London, 12 June 1996, *Views of the Corfu Coast* (watercolour, a pair, each 11 x 19 ins / 28 x 48 cm) GBP 4,370. New York, 18-19 July 1996, *On the Nile* (watercolour/paper, 11 3/4 x 20 3/4 ins / 29.8 x 53 cm) USD 2,070.

SCATIZZI, Sergio
Italian, 20th century.
Born 1918, in Lucca.
Painter, mixed media. Landscapes, flowers.

Auction records:
Milan, 6 April 1976, *Land* (1962, mixed media/canvas, 15 3/4 x 19 3/4 ins / 40 x 50 cm) ITL 330,000. Milan, 14 Dec 1988, *Vase of Flowers* (oil on canvas, 23 3/4 x 19 3/4 ins / 60.5 x 50 cm) ITL 1,400,000. Milan, 20 March 1989, *Landscape* (oil on board, 28 x 20 ins / 71 x 50.5 cm) ITL 1,700,000. Milan, 7 June 1989, *Near Valdinievole* (1949, oil on board, 28 1/4 x 20 ins / 72 x 51 cm) ITL 4,000,000. Milan, 7 Nov 1989, *Landscape* (1983, oil on canvas, 219 3/4 x 22 ins / 558 x 55 cm) ITL 2,400,000. Milan, 27 Sept 1990, *Landscape* (oil on board, 18 3/4 x 13 1/2 ins / 47.5 x 34 cm) ITL 700,000. Milan, 14 April 1992, *Landscape* (oil on board, 28 x 22 ins / 71 x 55 cm) ITL 2,500,000. Florence, 5 June 2000, *Still-life* (oil on canvas, 19 x 24 ins / 49 x 60 cm) ITL 3,100,000. Prato, 30 March 2001, *Landscapes* (1956, oil on board, a pair, 27 x 20 ins / 69 x 50 cm) ITL 5,000,000. Prato, 8 June 2001, *Landscape* (oil on canvas, 24 x 31 ins / 60 x 80 cm) ITL 5,500,000. Florence, 22 May 2004, *Lagoon* (oil on board, 20 x 28 ins / 51 x 72 cm) EUR 2,000. Milan, 8 June 2004, *Valdarno, Tuscany* (1964, oil on canvas, 20 x 24 ins / 50 x 60 cm) EUR 2,200.

SCATTAGLIA, Pietro
Italian, 18th century.
Active in Venice during the second half of the 18th century.
Engraver (burin), print publisher.
Pietro Scattaglia collaborated with Innocenzo Alessandri.

Museums and Galleries:
Padua (Musei Civici): several engraved sheets.

SCATTER, Francis
British, 16th century.
Active during the second half of the 16th century.
Engraver (burin). Maps.

SCATTOLA, Domenico
Italian, 19th century.
Born 1814, in Verona; died 8 June 1876, in Milan.
Painter. Genre scenes.

Museums and Galleries:
Bergamo (Accademia Carrara): paintings - Verona (Pinacoteca): paintings.

Auction records:
Milan, 7 Nov 1985, *Medieval Scene* (oil on canvas, 46 x 37 3/4 ins / 116 x 96 cm) ITL 4,000,000.

SCATTOLA, Ferruccio
Italian, 19th - 20th century.
Born 15 September 1873, in Venice; died 1950, in Rome.
Painter. Landscapes, seascapes.
A self-taught artist, Feruccio Scattola's work shows the influence of the French Impressionists.

Museums and Galleries:
Milan (Gal. d'Arte Moderna): *End of March* - Paris (former Mus. du Luxembourg): *Night Scene, San Gimignano* - Rome (Gal. Nazionale d'Arte Moderna): *Market in Assisi; Blacksmith; Chalk Cliffs near Volterra* - Trieste (Civico Mus. Revoltella) - Udine (Gal. d'Arte Moderna).

Auction records:
Milan, 30 Oct 1984, *Inner Courtyard* (oil on canvas, 30 1/4 x 35 3/4 ins / 77 x 91 cm) ITL 2,800,000. Rome, 25 May 1988, *Village Square* (oil on panel, 5 1/4 x 7 3/4 ins / 13.5 x 19.5 cm) ITL 1,100,000. Rome, 14 Dec 1988, *Seascape* (oil on canvas, 9 3/4 x 12 3/4 ins / 25 x 32.5 cm) ITL 750,000. Milan, 14 June 1989, *Rainy Day in Cadore* (oil on panel, 7 3/4 x 11 ins / 20 x 28 cm) ITL 1,400,000. Rome, 29 May 1990, *By a Canal in Venice* (oil on board, 13 3/4 x 19 1/4 ins / 35 x 49 cm) ITL 2,070,000. Rome, 29-30 Nov 1993, *Horses* (oil on board, 9 1/2 x 13 3/4 ins / 24 x 35 cm) ITL 1,179,000. Milan, 22 March 1994, *Huts* (oil on board, 10 x 13 1/4 ins / 24.5 x 33.5 cm) ITL 2,990,000. Rome, 23 May 1996, *Boat in Venice* (oil on paper, 19 3/4 x 19 3/4 ins / 50 x 50 cm) ITL 1,265,000. Venice, 22 Sept 2002, *Rialto* (oil on board, 9 x 13 ins / 24 x 34 cm) EUR 2,520. Milan, 18 March 2003, *St Mark's* (oil on canvas, 11 x 16 ins / 27 x 40 cm) EUR 2,300. Milan, 10 Dec 2003, *Figures on the Beach* (oil on canvas, 25 x 33 ins / 64 x 85 cm) EUR 5,000. Turin, 8 June 2004, *Venice* (oil on board, 9 x 13 ins / 23 x 34 cm) EUR 1,500. Milan, 8 June 2004, *Procession* (oil on board, 10 x 8 ins / 25 x 20 cm) EUR 3,000.

SCAUFLAIRE, Edgard
Belgian, 20th century.
Born 1893, in Liège; died 1960.
Painter, watercolourist, pastellist, draughtsman, illustrator. Genre scenes, interiors with figures, figures, nudes, portraits, animals, still-lifes. Murals, designs for tapestries, designs for mosaics.
Edgard Scauflaire studied under Adrien de Witte, Emile Berchmans and Auguste Donnay at the fine arts academy in Liège. He worked initially as a journalist and chaired the Atelier Libre group. His paintings were the product of his own fertile imagination. He was influenced by Picasso and Braque but also by painters of the Laethem Group and by Gustave de Smet. He also produced decorative compositions for public schools in Liège. He exhibited in 1948 at the Salon d'Art Moderne et Contemporain in Liège and, from 1923 to 1944, at the Cercle des Beaux-Arts in Brussels.

ed. Scauflaire

Museums and Galleries:
Basel - Brussels - La Louvière - Liège (Drawings and Prints Collection): *Le Nu Sage* - Liège (Mus. de l'Art wallon): *Self-portrait* (1952) - Verviers.

Auction records:
Brussels, 23 March 1977, *Portrait of a Woman* (1921, heightened drawing, 17 x 13 1/2 ins / 43 x 34 cm) BEF 12,000. Breda, 26 April 1977, *Reclining Nudes* (pastel, 19 x 24 3/4 ins / 48 x 63 cm) NLG 2,800. Antwerp, 17 Oct 1978, *Fisherman and Lode Star* (1929, oil on canvas, 27 1/2 x 18 ins / 70 x 46 cm) BEF 55,000. Antwerp, 8 May 1979, *Birds* (1957, gouache) BEF 26,000. Antwerp, 23 Oct 1979, *Still-life with Green Bottle* (oil on canvas, 18 x 27 1/2 ins / 46 x 70 cm) BEF 38,000. Brussels, 12 Dec 1979, *Wanderers* (1928, coloured drawing, 19 x 24 3/4 ins / 48 x 63 cm) BEF 40,000. Brussels, 27 March 1990, *Reclining Nudes* (1925, drawing, 16 1/2 x 27 1/2 ins / 42 x 70 cm) BEF 75,000. Amsterdam, 23 May 1991, *Untitled* (1925, gilded glass, 15 3/4 x 19 1/2 ins / 40 x 49.5 cm) NLG 9,200. Liège, 11 Dec 1991, *The Three Graces* (oil on panel, 27 1/2 x 18 ins / 70 x 45.5 cm) BEF 120,000. Lokeren, 21 March 1992, *Fairground Folk* (1928, pastel, 18 3/4 x 24 3/4 ins / 47.5 x 63 cm) BEF 120,000. Lokeren, 23 May 1992, *Girls in a Window* (watercolour and pastel, 19 x 25 1/2 ins / 48 x 65 cm) BEF 260,000. Lokeren, 10 Oct 1992, *Still-life* (1952, oil on panel, 28 3/4 x 35 ins / 73 x 89 cm) BEF 120,000. Lokeren, 4 Dec 1993, *Woman with a Bouquet of Flowers* (gilded glass, 22 1/2 x 17 1/4 ins / 57 x 44 cm) BEF 190,000. Amster-

DAM, 7 Dec 1994, *Birds* (oil on card, 17 1/4 x 35 1/4 ins / 43.5 x 89.5 cm) GBP 2,300. LOKEREN, 20 May 1995, *Red Men* (1920, oil on canvas, 39 1/4 x 30 ins / 100 x 76 cm) BEF 330,000. LOKEREN, 8 March 1997, *Seated Man* (charcoal, 13 3/4 x 10 1/2 ins / 35 x 26.5 cm) BEF 15,000. BRUSSELS, 28 Sept 1999, *Panoramic Town View with Harlequin* (1936, oil on cardboard, 20 x 26 ins / 51 x 65 cm) BEF 160,000. BRUSSELS, 6 Oct 1999, *Still-life with Bust* (1947, oil on canvas, 30 x 39 ins / 77 x 100 cm) BEF 125,000. BRUSSELS, 4 April 2000, *Panoramic Town View with Harlequin* (1936, oil on canvas, 20 x 26 ins / 51 x 65 cm) BEF 140,000. BRUSSELS, 9 Oct 2000, *Young Female Nude. Nude and Harlequin. Nude Family. Nudes on the Beach* (drawings, four, 14 x 10 ins / 35 x 26 cm) BEF 72,000. BRUSSELS, 21 May 2001, *Family* (oil on cardboard, 21 x 26 ins / 54 x 66 cm) BEF 130,000. BRUSSELS, 12 Nov 2001, *Pierrot* (1929, mixed media, 27 x 20 ins / 69 x 50 cm) BEF 145,000. BRUSSELS, 12 June 2002, *Adolescence* (paint on glass, 21 x 17 ins / 54 x 42 cm) EUR 2,200. LOKEREN, 7 Dec 2002, *Matelot* (1928, pastel, 19 x 24 ins / 47 x 62 cm) EUR 3,300. BRUSSELS, 19 March 2003, *Portrait of the Artist's Wife with Bare Breasts* (1925, pastel, 26 x 18 ins / 67 x 46 cm) EUR 6,000. BRUSSELS, 13 May 2003, *Landscape with Fields and Farms* (1943, oil on panel, 36 x 42 ins / 91 x 107 cm) EUR 3,400. BRUSSELS, 13 Oct 2004, *Still-life with Bouquet* (oil on panel, 30 x 27 ins / 75 x 69 cm) EUR 3,400. BRUSSELS, 13 Oct 2004, *Family* (1933, mixed media, 27 x 22 ins / 68 x 55 cm) EUR 3,800.

SCAVENIUS, Roger, or Fergus Roger
Danish, 20th century.
Born 24 October 1880, in Klinthom.
Active in Hellerup, near Copenhagen.
Painter. Religious subjects.
Roger Scavenius was a pupil of Frede Vermegren, John Rohde and Jens Ferdinand Willumsen. He is noted for a *Christ on the Cross* in the church at Hellun.

SCAVERY, Pieter or P. R.
Dutch, 17th century.
Active in Utrecht c. 1672.
Sculptor. Scenes with figures.
MUSEUMS AND GALLERIES:
AMSTERDAM: *Two Madmen Taunting One Another.*

SCAWEN
British, 18th century.
Active c. 1770.
Engraver.
Scawen was an engraver who used the scraper technique and was noted for a portrait engraving of *George Lord Pigot.*

SCAYCHIS. See **SCHAYCK**

SCAZERI, Giovanni Antonio. See **SCACCIERA**

SCAZZOLA, Paolo Antonio de, or Scazzoli or Scazoli
Italian, 15th - 16th century.
Painter. Religious subjects.
Lombard School.
Paolo Antonio de Scazzola was the son of the engineer Simonino Scazoli mentioned in the mid-15th century in the town archives of Milan and Cremona. De Scazzola was active in Cremona between 1475 and 1506, painting works for the church of S Abbondio. Documents record that he took part in a number of other projects in the town including decorative work for the cathedral and the Torrazzo ('big tower'), where he painted the clock.
MUSEUMS AND GALLERIES:
LONDON (Wallace Collection): *Annunciation.*
AUCTION RECORDS:
MILAN, 21 April 1988, *Mother and Child with Angels and Two Saints* (tempera/wood, 45 x 18 3/4 ins / 114.5 x 47.5 cm) ITL 150,000,000.

SCEEMACKER
French, 18th century.
Sculptor, architect.
Sceemacker was a member of the Académie de St-Luc. He exhibited at the academy's exhibitions between 1756 and 1764.

SCEIBEL, Johann Joseph, the Elder. See **SCHEUBEL**

SCELLES, Jean
French, 18th century.
Active in Caen 1728-1730.
Painter.
Scelles was commissioned to paint an altarpiece for the church of St-Gilles in Caen.

SCELLIER, Madeleine
French, 20th century.
Born 1928, in St-Denis.
Painter, illustrator, watercolourist. Figures.
Madeleine Scellier, a pupil of Georges d'Espagnat at the École des Beaux-Arts, Paris, where she lived and worked, exhibited at the Salon des Moins de Trente Ans and the Salon des Femmes Peintres, of which she was a member.
She illustrated with graceful silhouettes *Poèmes interdits* (*Forbidden Poems*) and *Moments* by Simone Michel Azias and engraved sixteen lithographs for Zola's *Contes à Ninon* (*Tales for Ninon*).
MUSEUMS AND GALLERIES:
PARIS (BNF): *Nude with Flower* (lithograph).

SCELLINC, Heinric
Flemish School, 15th century.
Active in Ghent in 1426.
Painter.

SCELZA, Italo
Italian, 20th century.
Born 1939, in Avellino (Campania).
Painter. Urban landscapes.
Nouvelle Figuration.
Italo Scelza's works are in the Nouvelle Figuration style. His subjects are urban life, buildings and industrial landscapes, their geometrical relationships rendered schematically and economically. These deserted, silent and inhuman places appeared illuminated not by natural sunlight but by cinema lights or floodlights. Scelza has exhibited mainly in Italy, in Rome (1962, 1973), Naples (1964) and Florence (1973).

SCENES, Master of the. See **MASTERS**

SCEPENS, Elisabeth. See **SCHEPERS**

SCERANO. See **SCHERANO**

SCERMIER, Cornelis. See **SCHERMIER**

SCERRIER, Michael or Michel, or Schernier
Belgian, 16th century.
Active in Bruges.
Sculptor.
In 1551, in collaboration with Lancelot Blondeel, Michael Scerrier carved the tomb of Archduchess Marguerite of Austria in the church of the Annunciation in Bruges.

SCETI, Gaudenzio
Swiss, 17th century.
Died 1698.
Active in Campertogno.
Sculptor, engraver (wood).
Sceti sculpted the altar in the church of St Martin in Rocca Pietra.

SCETO, Jean
Italian, 19th century.

Born in Riva.
Sculptor.
A student at the École des Beaux-Arts in Lyons and of Carpeaux, Jean Sceto made his debut at the Salon of 1869.

SCEUTRE, Jean
French, 14th - 15th century.
Active in Lille.
Sculptor.
Jean Sceutre carved the gable of the town hall in Lille and the city arms for the cemetery of the church of St-Étienne.

SCEVENELS, Auguste
Belgian, 20th century.
Born 1922, in Liège.
Painter.
Auguste Scevenels was self-taught.

SCEVOLA, Victor Luçien Guirand de. See **GUIRAND DE SCÉVOLA**

SCHAACK, Abraham
Dutch, 18th century.
Born 1707; died 1752.
Active in Amsterdam.
Miniaturist.
Abraham Schaack painted a number of portraits of himself and his family.

SCHAACK, Jean
Luxembourg, 20th century.
Born 1895, in Walferdange; died 1959, in Luxembourg.
Painter. Religious subjects, portraits, landscapes.
Jean Schaack studied at the trades college in Luxembourg before enrolling at the school of decorative arts in Strasbourg and then Munich. He went on to work in the Munich studio of Walter Thor and August Hoffmann before enrolling at the fine arts academy in Munich, where he studied from 1917 to 1920. He was one of the founder members of the first Salon de la Sécession held in Luxembourg in 1927.
BIBLIOGRAPHY:
Cent cinquante ans d'Art luxembourgeois, exhibition catalogue, Musée national d'Histoire et d'Art, Luxembourg, 1989.
MUSEUMS AND GALLERIES:
LUXEMBOURG (Mus. national d'histoire et d'art): *Landscape* (1916); *Self-portrait* (1919); *St Sebastian* (1926).

SCHAACK, Jeremias van. See **VAN SCHAAK Jeremias**

SCHAAF, Anton
American, 19th - 20th century.
Born 22 February 1869, in Milwaukee (Wisconsin); died 1943.
Sculptor.
Anton Schaaf studied under Shirley Cox, James Carroll Beckwith and Augustus St-Gaudens, and at the National Academy of Art in New York. He was a member of the American Federation of Arts. He created commemorative monuments and statues of several American generals.

SCHAAG
German, 18th century.
Sculptor.
Schaag sculpted two monuments in about 1723 in the cemetery of the Kassel Altstadt.

SCHAAK, B. or C. and P.
Dutch, 17th century.
Active in Rotterdam.
Painter. Genre scenes, still-lifes.

B Schaak f

MUSEUMS AND GALLERIES:
AMSTERDAM: *Vanitas*.

SCHAAK, J. S. C.
British, 18th century.
Painter. Historical subjects, portraits, genre scenes.
J.S.C. Schaak lived and worked in Westminister from 1761 to 1769.
MUSEUMS AND GALLERIES:
LONDON (National Portrait Gal.): *Charles Churchill* (c. 1763-1764, oil on canvas); *James Wolfe* (c. 1767, oil on canvas, attributed).
AUCTION RECORDS:
LONDON, 9 Dec 1927, *General Wolfe Directing Operations in Quebec*, GBP 630. LONDON, 25 Feb 1938, *General Wolfe*, GBP 183.

SCHAAK, J. van
Dutch, 18th century.
Active in The Hague during the first half of the 18th century.
Medallist.
J. van Schaak executed portrait medals of *J. Fr. Helvetius* and *Bombardus Sandijk*.

SCHAAK, Willem
Dutch, 18th century.
Active c. 1700.
Draughtsman, engraver.
Willem Schaak favoured the scraper technique.

SCHAAK, Willem
Dutch, 18th century.
Active in Alkmaar in 1720.
Painter.

SCHAAL, Louis Jacques Nicolas
French, 19th century.
Born 13 February 1800, in Paris; died after 1859.
Painter, engraver (burin), art writer.
Louis Schaal's masters were Daguerre and Léthière. He entered the École des Beaux-Arts on 6 November 1816 and regularly exhibited his work at the Salon from 1825 to 1853. He seems to have concentrated on the decorative arts, and he also wrote several books: most notably a *Treatise on Landscape*, which was accompanied by 24 lithographs and *Regeneration of the Western Empires by the Fine Arts*.

SCHAAL, Solange
French, 20th century.
Born 29 July 1899, in St-Germain-en-Laye.
Painter. Figures, nudes, portraits, landscapes, still-lifes.
Solange Schaal exhibited in Paris at the Salon d'Automne from 1926.

She painted landscapes of France, particularly the south-west, Spain, Italy, Germany, Sweden, Norway, Denmark, Switzerland and North Africa. Critics have often noted the influence of Derain's seriousness on a painter who, nevertheless, preserved her own spontaneity. G. Turpin speaks of `realism tempered by a poetry full of charm'. Among her works are: *Egyptian Dancer - Sleeping Woman - Still-life with Soup Tureen - Basket of Fruit on an Open Window - Dordogne Landscape - Woman Wearing a Mantilla*.

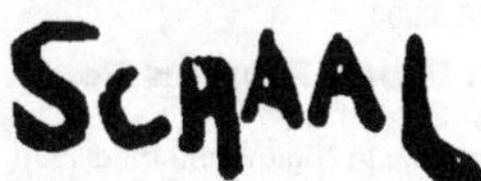

MUSEUMS AND GALLERIES:
CAHORS: *Cahors Landscape* (1928).

SCHAALER, Hans. See **SCHALLER**

SCHAALJE, C. J.
Dutch, 18th - 19th century.

Painter. Still-lifes (flowers).

C.J. Schaalje was active in Leiden from 1790 to 1806.

MUSEUMS AND GALLERIES:

SPEYER (Historisches Mus. der Pfalz): two still-lifes.

AUCTION RECORDS:

NEW YORK, 11 Jan 1996, *Still-life With Roses, Convulvus, Tulips, Iris and Other Flowers in a Vase on a Table-top* (1806, oil on panel, 17 x 13 ins / 43.2 x 33 cm) USD 17,250.

SCHAAN, Paul

French, 19th - 20th century.

Born in St Petersburg, to French parents.

Painter. Genre scenes, architectural views.

Paul Schaan exhibited in Paris at the Salon des Artistes Français, of which he was a member and where he was awarded an honourable mention in 1892. He quite often painted genre scenes depicting the clergy indulging in simple worldly pleasures.

P. Schaan

AUCTION RECORDS:

NEW YORK, 2 Feb 1906, *Set Free,* USD 290. PARIS, 11 Feb 1919, *Game of Cards,* FRF 11,000. PARIS, 14 Nov 1924, *Two Gourmets,* FRF 1,750. PARIS, 23 Jan 1950, *Musketeer Scene: End of the Meal,* FRF 15,100. LONDON, 27 Feb 1973, *Onlooker,* GBP 650. PARIS, 4 Dec 1974, *Cardinals Waking Up* (1924) FRF 5,800. NEW YORK, 28 Oct 1981, *Clergyman Feeding a Parrot* (1907, oil on panel, 18 x 14 3/4 ins / 45.7 x 37.5 cm) USD 3,000. NEW YORK, 16 Dec 1983, *Game of Tricktrack* (1911, oil on panel, 25 1/2 x 21 ins / 65 x 53.4 cm) USD 3,600. PARIS, 4 May 1988, *Serenade* (oil on panel, 18 1/2 x 15 1/4 ins / 47 x 39 cm) FRF 16,000. VERSAILLES, 5 March 1989, *Still-life with Goblet and Fruit* (oil on panel, 8 3/4 x 12 1/4 ins / 22.5 x 31 cm) FRF 6,800. PARIS, 20 Feb 1990, *Monseigneur's Secretary* (oil on panel, 22 x 18 ins / 55 x 46 cm) FRF 22,000. PARIS, 22 March 1990, *Market Gardeners* (oil on panel, 13 1/2 x 10 1/4 ins / 34 x 26 cm) FRF 11,000. NEW YORK, 16 Feb 1993, *Napoleon* (1912, oil on panel, 13 3/4 x 10 1/2 ins / 34.8 x 26.8 cm) USD 1,870. LONDON, 17 March 1993, *Just a Drop* (oil on panel, 21 1/4 x 25 1/2 ins / 54 x 65 cm) GBP 7,475. PARIS, 27 May 1994, *Champagne* (oil on canvas, 21 1/4 x 25 1/4 ins / 54 x 64 cm) FRF 17,000. NEW YORK, 19 Jan 1995, *A Good Bottle* (oil on canvas, 21 1/2 x 26 ins / 54.6 x 66 cm) USD 7,475. LONDON, 9 Oct 1997, *A Tasty Little Pleasure* (oil on panel, 16 x 12 1/2 ins / 40.6 x 31.8 cm) GBP 4,370. PARIS, 14 April 1999, *The Taste* (oil on canvas, 20 x 24 ins / 50 x 61 cm) FRF 30,000. NORTH BETHESDA, 3 June 2000, *Neo-classical Friezes* (oil on canvas, a pair, 24 x 54 ins / 60 x 136 cm) USD 5,500. NEW ORLEANS, 17 Nov 2000, *One Little Sweet* (1918, oil on canvas, 18 x 15 ins / 46 x 38 cm) USD 7,500. LONDON, 5 April 2001, *Good Liqueur* (watercolour, 18 x 15 ins / 45 x 38 cm) GBP 2,000. NEW YORK, 22 May 2001, *Without Appetite* (oil on canvas) USD 9,000. WASHINGTON, 24 April 2004, *Portrait of Napoleon Bonaparte in his Library* (1914, oil on panel, 22 x 16 ins / 56 x 41 cm) USD 8,500. PARIS, 28 June 2004, *A Sweet Knowledge* (oil on panel, 18 x 15 ins / 46 x 37 cm) EUR 3,000.

SCHAAP, Egbert Rubertus Derk

Dutch, 19th - 20th century.

Born 4 July 1862, in Niglevecht; died 1939.

Painter. Scenes with figures, landscapes.

Egbert Rubertus Derk Schaap worked also as an art critic and historian.

MUSEUMS AND GALLERIES:

AMSTERDAM (Rijksmus.) - AMSTERDAM (Stedelijk Mus.): *Apple Blossom.*

AUCTION RECORDS:

VIENNA, 14 Sept 1983, *Spring Landscape* (oil on canvas, 13 1/2 x 19 3/4 ins / 34 x 50 cm) ATS 25,000. AMSTERDAM, 2 May 1990, *Dazzling Spring* (oil on canvas, 23 1/4 x 36 1/2 ins / 59 x 93 cm) NLG 4,830. AMSTERDAM, 5-6 Feb 1991, *Peasant and Cart on a Village Street in Autumn* (oil on canvas, 24 1/2 x 36 ins / 62 x 90.5 cm) NLG 1,840. AMSTERDAM, 14 Sept 1993, *Spring* (oil on canvas, 22 3/4 x 36 1/4 ins / 58 x 92 cm) NLG 1,380. AMSTERDAM, 19 Oct 1993, *Villa Nova in Bosch* (oil on canvas, 15 x 23 1/2 ins / 38 x 59.5 cm) NLG 1,150. AMSTERDAM, 20 March 2001, *Interior of the Artist's Studio, Villa Nova* (oil on canvas, 34 x 47 ins / 86 x 120 cm) NLG 7,500.

SCHAAP, H. W. J.

Maiden name: Van der Pek

Dutch, 20th century.

Painter.

H. W. J. Schaap was the wife of Egbert Rubertus Derk Schaap.

SCHAAP, Hendrik

Dutch, 19th - 20th century.

Born 1878; died 1955.

Painter. Seascapes.

AUCTION RECORDS:

AMSTERDAM, 7 Nov 1995, *View of a Port* (oil on canvas, 12 1/4 x 16 ins / 31 x 40.5 cm) NLG 1,770. ROTTERDAM, 5 May 2001, *View of the Delft to Rotterdam Waterway with Figures* (oil on canvas, 19 x 27 ins / 48 x 68 cm) NLG 3,600. THE HAGUE, 5 Nov 2003, *City View of Rotterdam near Het Steiger* (1956, oil on canvas, 27 x 19 ins / 68 x 48 cm) EUR 1,700. THE HAGUE, 3 Nov 2004, *Market Scene* (oil on canvas, 15 x 19 ins / 38 x 49 cm) EUR 5,400.

SCHAAP, Henri

Dutch, 19th century.

Born 1778; died 1850?.

Painter. Seascapes.

MUSEUMS AND GALLERIES:

BRUSSELS: four watercolours.

AUCTION RECORDS:

COLOGNE, 27 June 1974, *Warship,* DEM 8,500.

SCHAAP, W.

Dutch, 19th century.

Painter. Seascapes.

W. Schaap was active in Utrecht from 1806 to 1820, when he settled in Amsterdam.

SCHAAR, Erzsebet or Elisabeth

Hungarian, 20th century.

Born 27 July 1908, in Promontor; died 1975, in Budapest.

Sculptor.

Erzsebet Schaar trained under Sigmund Kisfaludi Strobl at the academy of fine art in Budapest where she lived and worked. Then she travelled to Paris, Munich and Vienna. She started out under the influence of a sensualism that was still Impressionist. Surrealist motifs were introduced into her figurative style. In the following period, her sculptures were the material expression of portions of space. *Interior* (1967), *Between the Doors* (1967), *Between the Walls* (1968), *Vaults* (1969), *Between the Houses* portray the link between humanity and architecture. Continuing her searches for internal space (which would be the very opposite of a vacuum), her forms strive for the greatest purity.

Erzsebet Schaar took part in collective exhibitions from 1926 including: Budapest, Vienna, Italy, 9th Middelheim Biennale; Norway; and *Small Bronze International Exhibition,* Madrid (1970). Solo exhibitions include: Budapest (1960 and 1966). She was awarded many prizes including: Young Szinyei Prize, Munkácsy Prize, First Prize at the Statuettes Biennale, Pécs (1969).

Bibliography:
Csorba, Géza, *Art hongrois contemporain*, exhibition catalogue, Musée Galliera, Paris, 1970.

SCHAAR, Monique
Belgian, 20th century.
Born 1939, in Brussels.
Painter.
Monique Schaar specialised in the decorative arts.

SCHAAR, Pierre
Belgian, 19th - 20th century.
Born 30 July 1872, in Brussels.
Sculptor, medallist. Animals.
Pierre Schaar studied at the fine arts academy in Brussels. He is noted for his dog sculptures.

SCHAAR, Pinchas. See **SHAAR**

SCHAAR, Sipke van der
Dutch, 19th - 20th century.
Born 1879; died 1961.
Painter. Scenes with figures.
Auction records:
Amsterdam, 5-6 Nov 1991, *Figures in an Oasis* (oil on canvas, 37 x 55 ins / 94 x 140 cm) NLG 3,450.

SCHAARDT, Carl
German, 18th century.
Born 1722, in Berlin; died after 1786.
Painter, engraver (etching).

SCHAARDT, Franz Philipp
German, 18th century.
Born 1763, in Berlin.
Painter, decorative designer.
Franz Philipp Schaardt was the son of Carl Schaardt. He was a painter in Schwedt in 1783.

SCHAARSCHMIDT, Friedrich
German, 19th century.
Born 4 February 1863, in Bonn; died 13 June 1902, in Böblingen.
Painter, art writer. Historical subjects, landscapes.
Friedrich Schaarschmidt trained under Wilhelm Sohn at the academy in Düsseldorf. He painted landscapes, which were often inspired by Italian locations. He was an art writer and curator at the academy in Düsseldorf. He exhibited in Berlin from 1891 onwards.

SCHAARSCHMIDT, Johann Gotthilf
German, 19th century.
Born 27 December 1823, in Streckewalde, near Wolkenstein; died 1850, in Dresden.
Sculptor.
Johann Gotthilf Schaarschmidt was trained by Fr Funk and E. Rietschel. He sculpted notably busts. He was deaf and mute.

SCHAASBERG, Adriaen
Dutch, 18th century.
Active in The Hague in 1733.
Painter, medallist (?).
Adriaen Schaasberg was the father of Simon Schaasberg.

SCHAASBERG, Simon
Dutch, 18th century.
Died after 1794.
Active in The Hague.
Painter, miniaturist, silhouettist. Portraits, landscapes.
Simon Schaasberg was the son of Adriaen Schaasberg. He was a guild member in The Hague in 1779.

SCHAB, Oskar von
German, 20th century.
Born 1 August 1901, near Parma, Italy, to German parents.
Active in Berlin.
Painter.
Oskar von Schab studied at the fine arts academy in Munich.

SCHABARD, Thomas
Austrian, 18th century.
Painter.
Thomas Schabard painted altarpieces for the church in Saar (Moravia) in 1705.

SCHABATKA, Ferenc or Franz
Hungarian, 19th century.
Active in Temesvár (now Timisoara, Romania) and in Pest during the first half of the 19th century.
Painter, draughtsman. Animals.
Ferenc Schabatka produced zoological drawings for the Magyar Nemzeti Galéria in Budapest.

SCHABEL, August
German, 19th - 20th century.
Born 26 May 1845, in Schwäbisch-Gmünd; died August 1920, in Munich.
Sculptor, medallist.
August Schabel was a pupil of August von Kreling.

SCHABELITZ, Rudolph Frederick
American, 20th century.
Born 10 June 1884, in Stapleton (New York State); died 1959.
Painter, illustrator.
Rudolph Schabelitz studied under Carl Marr in Munich. He was a member of the Salmagundi Club.
Auction records:
New York, 27 Jan 1984, *Second Avenue* (oil on canvas, 22 x 20 ins / 55.9 x 50.8 cm) USD 1,800. New York, 11 May 2002, *Egyptian King Presents Necklace to his Princess* (oil on canvas, 22 x 25 ins / 56 x 64 cm) USD 6,000.

SCHABENHENGST, Sigmund
German, 16th century.
Active in Munich 1533-1544.
Sculptor.
Munich School.

SCHABERG, Laura
German, 19th - 20th century.
Born 5 May 1866, in Münster.
Active in Halberstadt.
Painter, engraver.
Laura Schaberg was a pupil of Max Uth.

SCHABERSCHUL, Max
German, 19th - 20th century.
Born 20 August 1875, in Dresden.
Active in Langebrück.
Painter, illustrator.
Max Schaberschul was a pupil of Gotthardt Kühl.

SCHABERT, Eduard Anton
German, 19th century.
Born 7 April 1826, in Mitau (now Jelgava, Latvia); died 7 September 1854, in Mitau.
Lithographer.
Eduard Anton Schabert was the son of Ernst David Schabert.

SCHABERT, Ernst David
German, 19th century.
Born 17 February 1796, in Mitau (now Jelgava, Latvia); died 24 February 1853, in Mitau.
Miniaturist, lithographer.
Schabert was a pupil of K.A. Senff.

SCHABERT, Melchior
German, 16th century.
Active in Donauwörth.

Sculptor (wood).
Melchior Schabert carved the stalls in the church of Auhausen in 1520.

SCHABET, Fidelis
German, 19th century.
Born 21 June 1813, in Wurzach.
Active in Munich.
Painter. History painting, portraits.
Schabet trained under von Cornelius. He painted many altarpieces for churches in Bavaria.
MUSEUMS AND GALLERIES:
MUNICH (Bayerisches Nationalmus.): *Scenes from Bavaria History* (three frescoes).

SCHABINGER VON SCHOWINGEN, Julius Thomas
German, 19th - 20th century.
Born 4 March 1871, in Michefeld; died 9 August 1920, in Munich.
Painter. Portraits.
Julius Thomas Schabinger von Schowingen studied at the academy in Karlsruhe and went on to paint portraits of Italian jurists for the law courts in San Marino.

SCHABLIK, Karoly or Karl
Hungarian, 20th century.
Born 10 March 1876, in Alsósajó; died 21 July 1909, in Rožnava.
Painter. Landscapes.
Karoly Schablik studied in Budapest.

SCHÄBLIN, Margaretha
Austrian, 17th - 18th century.
Active in Salzburg, from 1698 to 1705.
Painter.
Schäblin painted the altarpiece for the church of St George in the citadel of Salzburg in 1698.

SCHABRACQ, Alexander, or Schabraque
Dutch, 20th - 21st century.
Born 1957 or 1963.
Assemblage artist.
Alexander Schabracq lives and works in Amsterdam, where he exhibits his work in solo shows. He uses polychrome materials, or more recently bronze, to produce quasi-Surrealist works, opening the way to the most unexpected associations from the starting point of found or decorative objects.
BIBLIOGRAPHY:
Jourdan, Annie, '*Alexander Schabracq*' in *Art Press* n° 170, periodical, Paris, June 1992.
AUCTION RECORDS:
AMSTERDAM, 22 May 1990, *Untitled* (relief in painted welded iron, 23 1/2 x 31 1/2 ins / 60 x 80 cm) NLG 1,840. AMSTERDAM, 10 Dec 1992, *Untitled* (1988, neon, bark, lead, crystal beads and plywood, 31 1/2 x 23 1/2 x 7 3/4 ins / 80 x 60 x 20 cm) NLG 2,070.

SCHABRACQ, Emanuel
German, 18th century.
Active at the end of the 18th century.
Miniaturist.
Schabracq produced some notable miniature portraits.

SCHABUNIN, Nikolai Avenirovich. See **CHABUNIN**

SCHACH, Lienhard. See **SCHACHT**

SCHACH-DUC, Yvonne
French, 20th century.
Born 1933, in Vitry-aux-Loges.
Draughtswoman, engraver (burin). .
Yvonne Schach-Duc was represented in the exhibition *De Bonnard à Baselitz - Dix Ans d'enrichissements du cabinet des estampes 1978-1988* (*From Bonnard to Baselitz: A Decade of Acquisitions by the Prints Collection 1978-1988*) held at the Bibliothèque Nationale, Paris, in 1992.
MUSEUMS AND GALLERIES:
PARIS (BNF): *Ampedus cinnibarinus; Pyrochroa coccinea* (1982, two engravings).

SCHACHER, C.
British, 19th century.
Active in Edinburgh.
Lithographer.
C. Schacher engraved portraits of *Albert, Prince Consort, Thomas Charmers* and *Jonathan Otley*.

SCHACHER, Eugen
German, 19th - 20th century.
Born 29 April 1861, in Breslau (now Wroclaw, Poland).
Active in Berlin.
Painter. Portraits.

SCHACHINGER, Gabriel
German, 19th - 20th century.
Born 31 March 1850, in Munich; died 9 May 1912, in Egfing.
Painter. Figures, portraits, landscapes, flowers.
Gabriel Schachinger studied at the academy in Munich and under Carl Theodor Piloty. He visited Italy before settling in Munich.
MUSEUMS AND GALLERIES:
HAMBURG (Kunsthalle): *Self-portrait; Portrait of the Artist's Father* - MUNICH (Pinakothek): *Young Female Nude on the Grass; Portrait of the Painter B. Grönvold.*
AUCTION RECORDS:
LONDON, 1894, *In the Garden*, FRF 1,310. NEW YORK, 23 Feb 1983, *Portrait of a Young Woman in a Striped Dress* (pastel/brown paper, 33 x 30 1/4 ins / 83.8 x 76.8 cm) USD 4,000. NEW YORK, 26 Oct 1983, *Child Presenting a Bouquet of Flowers* (1880, oil on canvas, 64 x 42 ins / 162.5 x 106.5 cm) USD 6,250. AMSTERDAM, 21 April 1994, *Unhappy Love Affair* (oil on canvas, 27 3/4 x 39 3/4 ins / 70.5 x 101 cm) NLG 40,250. LONDON, 17 June 1994, *Vase of Peonies on a Table* (oil on canvas, 35 1/2 x 27 1/2 ins / 90.2 x 69.8 cm) GBP 24,150.

SCHACHINGER, Hans
Austrian, 20th century.
Born 20 May 1888, in Vienna.
Active in Vienna.
Painter. Portraits.
Hans Schachinger studied at the fine arts academy in Vienna.

SCHACHMANN, Karl Adolph Gottlieb von, or Carl Gottlob, or Gottfried (Baron)
German, 18th century.
Born 28 November 1725, in Hermsdorf Castle (Saxony); died 28 January 1789, in Königshayn.
Painter, engraver (etching). Landscapes.
Schachmann travelled throughout Norway and Sweden. His works are in Saxony.
MUSEUMS AND GALLERIES:
GÖRLITZ (Städtische Kunstsammlungen): etchings.

SCHACHNER, Thérèse
Austrian, 19th - 20th century.
Born 29 May 1869, in Vienna; died 1950.
Painter. Portraits, landscapes, flowers.
Thérèse Schachner was a pupil of Hugo Darnaut and Albin Egger-Lienz. She also composed music.

T. Schachner.

AUCTION RECORDS:
VIENNA, 12 Nov 1980, *Summer Day* (oil on canvas, 20 1/2 x 26 3/4 ins / 52 x 68 cm) ATS 25,000. VIENNA, 15 May 1984, *Farmyard* (oil on card, 15 x 10 ins / 38 x 25.5 cm) ATS 25,000. NEW YORK, 19 Jan 1994, *Landscape with a Field of Oats and Wild Flowers* (oil on canvas, 26 x 31 ins / 66 x 78.7 cm) USD 6,038. VIENNA, 15 June 1999, *Large Autumnal Still-life* (oil on canvas, 43 x 35 ins / 110 x 90 cm) ATS 50,000.

SCHACHOMAIR, Georg
German, 16th century.
Active in Kempten.
Painter. Maps.

SCHACHOVSKOJ, Nicolaï Pavlovitch.
See **CHAKHOVSKY Nikolai Pavlovich**

SCHACHT, Daniel, the Elder
German, 16th century.
Born c. 1532; died before 1592.
Active in Danzig (now Gdansk).
Painter. Portraits.

SCHACHT, Daniel, the Younger
German, 16th - 17th century.
Born c. 1560, in Danzig (now Gdansk, Poland); died after 23 July 1615, in Danzig.
Painter.
Danzig School.
Daniel Schacht the Younger was the son of Daniel Schacht the Elder and painted portraits of Boris Godunov and his son.

SCHACHT, Lienhard, or Schach
German, 16th century.
Active in Nuremberg 1580-1585.
Sculptor.
Between 1576 and 1582 Lienhard Schacht carved the figures for the fountain of Kronberg.

SCHACHT, Rudolf
German, 20th century.
Born 1910, in Munich; died 1974, in Freiburg (Baden-Württemberg).
Painter.
AUCTION RECORDS:
COLOGNE, 26 March 1982, *Halt at an Inn* (oil on canvas, 35 1/2 x 45 1/4 ins / 90 x 115 cm) DEM 6,000. COLOGNE, 15 Oct 1988, *Unexpected Visitor* (oil on canvas, 39 1/4 x 33 3/4 ins / 100 x 86 cm) DEM 6,500. NEW YORK, 18-19 July 1996, *Horses at Pasture* (oil on canvas, 19 1/4 x 27 ins / 48.9 x 68.6 cm) USD 632. NUREMBERG, 23 Nov 2000, *Town Hall in Rothenburg* (oil on canvas, 36 x 45 ins / 92 x 115 cm) DEM 4,800. NUREMBERG, 7 Feb 2002, *Run Down Building in Taubertal* (1918, oil on canvas, drawing, a pair, 7 x 10 ins / 19 x 25 cm) EUR 2,300. AMSTERDAM, 2 Sept 2003, *Midnight Mail* (oil on canvas, 28 x 31 ins / 70 x 80 cm) EUR 1,600. NUREMBERG, 20 Nov 2003, *Horse and Cart beneath Medieval Stone Arch* (1919, oil on canvas, 28 x 24 ins / 71 x 61 cm) EUR 2,000. NUREMBERG, 16 Sept 2004, *Horse-drawn Cart* (1943, oil on canvas, 15 x 19 ins / 39 x 49 cm) EUR 3,300. NUREMBERG, 25 Nov 2004, *Haymaking* (oil on canvas, 35 x 52 ins / 90 x 133 cm) EUR 3,000.

SCHACHT, Wilhelm
German, 19th - 20th century.
Born 6 December 1872, in Leipzig.
Painter. Landscapes.
Wilhelm Schacht studied at the fine arts academies of Leipzig and Munich and went on to live and work in Rothenburg as a painter and lithographer.
AUCTION RECORDS:
COLOGNE, 18 March 1983, *Landscape at Sunset with Figures* (oil on canvas, 30 1/4 x 40 1/4 ins / 77 x 102 cm) DEM 5,000. COLOGNE, 23 March 1990, *Spring in Rothenburg* (oil on canvas, 15 3/4 x 19 3/4 ins / 40 x 50 cm) DEM 4,500. FÜRTH, 2 Feb 2001, *Farmhouses and Trees* (oil on panel, 15 x 19 ins / 39 x 48 cm) EUR 1,940. WARSAW, 30 March 2003, *Ducks in an Orchard* (c. 1900, oil on canvas, 24 x 31 ins / 60 x 80 cm) PLN 7,000.

SCHACHTEL, Augustin Paul, or Schachtl
Austrian, 16th century.
Born in Kemnath; died 30 November 1605, in Vienna.
Painter.
Augustin Paul Schachtel was a monk and worked for the monastery of the Premonstrants in Klosterbruck, Moravia.

SCHACK, or Schaek
German, 18th century.
Painter. Landscapes.
Schack painted two landscapes of the banks of the Rhine in 1773.

SCHACK, Albert, or Schagk
German, 16th century.
Active in Königsberg (now Kaliningrad, Russia) 1562-1581.
Painter. Portraits.

SCHACK, Franziska
German, 19th century.
Born 1 December 1788, in Regensburg.
Active in Munich.
Painter. Landscapes.
Franziska Schack was a pupil of G. von Dillis.

SCHACK, Heinrich Franz, or Schalck or Schalk or Schaek
German, 19th century.
Born 1791; died 15 October 1832, in Karlsruhe.
Painter. Portraits, genre scenes, landscapes.
Schack was the son of Johann Peter Joseph Schalck. He worked in Mainz, Frankfurt and Karlsruhe.
MUSEUMS AND GALLERIES:
MAINZ: *Market Square with Cathedral in 1820 and Important Figures of Mainz*; series of nine portraits (watercolour).

SCHACK, Juliane
German, 20th century.
Born 1927, in Düsseldorf.
Active in Ramatuelle (Var), France.
Painter, engraver.
Juliane Schack featured in *De Bonnard à Baselitz: Dix Ans d'Enrichissements du Cabinet des Estampes 1978-1988* (*From Bonnard to Baselitz: A Decade of Acquisitions by the Prints Collection 1978-1988*), an exhibition held at the Bibliothèque Nationale in Paris in 1992.
MUSEUMS AND GALLERIES:
PARIS (BNF): *Water and Land* (1981, lithograph).

SCHACK, Sophus Peter Lassenius
Danish, 19th century.
Born 21 January 1811, in Copenhagen; died 21 April 1864, in Copenhagen.
Painter, illustrator. Figures, portraits, genre scenes.
Schack studied at the Kunstakademi in Copenhagen and with Christopher Wilhelm Eckersberg. He was also a writer.
MUSEUMS AND GALLERIES:
COPENHAGEN (Nationalmus.) - HILLERØD (Frederiksborg Slot): *Portrait of B. Thorvaldsen*.
AUCTION RECORDS:
COPENHAGEN, 19 Aug 1981, *Family Portrait in a Pram* (1853, oil on canvas, 49 1/4 x 36 1/2 ins / 125 x 93 cm) DKK 29,000. COPENHAGEN, 21 Feb 1990, *Fristelsen* (1853, oil on canvas, 32 x 24 ins / 81 x 61 cm) DKK 5,000. COPENHAGEN, 1 May 1991, *Artist and His Wife in the Studio* (1863, oil on canvas, 39 1/4 x 30 ins / 100 x 76 cm) DKK 20,000. COPENHAGEN, 26 May 2003, *Merry Soldiers, Episode from 1864* (oil on canvas, 19 x 25 ins / 47 x 63 cm) DKK 20,000.

SCHACKT, Thomas. See **SACX**

SCHAD, Aquilin

German, 19th century.
Born 1815, in Stainach.
Active in Munich.
Engraver (burin).

Aquilin Schad trained under S. Amsler and A. Reindel.

SCHAD, Christian

German, 20th century.
Born 21 August 1894, in Miesbach (Bavaria); died 1982, in Stuttgart.
Painter, draughtsman, engraver. Figures, nudes, portraits, landscapes.
Dadaism, Neue Sachlichkeit (New Objectivity).
Zurich Dadaist Group.

Christian Schad studied for a time in 1913 under Heinrich J. Zügel at the fine arts academy in Munich. Between 1915 and 1920 he frequented a group of writers and artists in Zurich and Geneva, among them Franz Masereel, Alexander Archipenko, Romain Rolland, Hans Arp, Hugo Ball, Emmy Hennings, and other members of the Dadaist circle. In 1920 he moved to Rome and remained there for several years, making friends with Giulio Evola and Enrico Prampolini. He was forced to flee Germany at the advent of the Nazis in the mid-1930s and settled successively in Zurich, Geneva and Italy.

Between 1913 and 1917, Schad published woodcut engravings in various periodicals. He made the acquaintance of Walter Serner at precisely the time when the latter was in the process of setting up the review to be known as *Sirius*, and Schad was promptly invited to contribute illustrations.

Schad started out as an Expressionist, but Cubist elements soon crept into his work, followed by Futurist overtones, which were at their most pronounced in his *Traumatism* (1917) and *Transmission* (1919). In Zurich in 1918, Schad devised a process he elected to term 'Schadography', which combined collage with the direct imprint of objects applied to emulsified paper and exposed to the light before being 'fixed' like a conventional photograph; it was essentially the process Man Ray would later use for his 'Rayogrammes'.

In 1919-1920 Schad started to produce abstract reliefs made of scraps and planks painted in lurid colours, a violent counterpoint to the gentle curves peculiar to Hans Arp. He distanced himself from the Dada movement from around 1920 and turned again to a figurative approach as he became increasingly preoccupied with portraiture (not least following his exposure to Raphael and Ingres while visiting Italy in the mid-1920s). Eventually - not unlike the route followed by Otto Dix - Schad's portraits took on the pessimistic photographic qualities of the Neue Sachlichkeit (New Objectivity) movement which dominated the arts, literature and cinema in the Germany of the 1920s. His 'portraits' are drawn from every social stratum, from streetwalkers to popes, and the subjects are scrutinised in inexorable detail to reveal them at their most primitive and base. He thus contrived to produce a glacial galaxy of folly and perversion, with a deliberate and lingering focus on erotic practices and a clinical eye for anatomical minutiae.

Schad took part in a large number of group exhibitions, including at the following: the Salon Neri in Geneva (1916); the Kunstverein (Artists' Union) in Munich (1921); the Kunstverein in Düsseldorf (1928); the Stedelijk Museum in Amsterdam (1929); the Museum of Modern Art in New York (1936); the Kunstverein in Berlin (1940, 1942); the Kunsthalle in Baden-Baden (1969); the Kunstverein in Stuttgart (1971); and the Galleria Civica d'Arte Moderna in Turin (1973). He exhibited solo for the first time in Frankfurt in 1921, and then on numerous occasions, notably at the following: the Wurthler Gallery in Vienna (1927); Berlin (1928, 1929, 1930, 1961); the Kunstverein in Frankfurt (1956, 1959); the Städtisches Museum in Brunswick (1960); the Städtische Galerie in Würzburg (1962); the Kunstverein in Wuppertal (1967); Milan and Rome (1970); the Staatliche Kunsthalle in Berlin (1980); the Goethe Institute in Paris (1982); the Kunsthaus in Zurich (1997); and the Fondation Dina Vierny-Musée Maillol in Paris (2002).

SCHAD

SCHAD

BIBLIOGRAPHY:

Dorival, Bernard/Hoog, Michel, *Dada*, exhibition catalogue, Musée national d'Art moderne, Paris, 1966. *C. Schad*, exhibition catalogue, Staatliche Kunsthalle, Berlin, 1980. *Christian Schad: Etchings, Woodcuts, Schadographs. 1 December-19 December 1981*, Leinster Fine Art, London, 1981. Hülsewig-Johnen, Jutta, *Neue Sachlichkeit, magischer Realismu*, exhibition catalogue, Kunsthalle, Bielefeld, 1991. Dachy, Marc, *'La Nouvelle Objectivité mise à nu'* in *Beaux-Arts Magazine*, periodical, Paris, April 1991. Cobry, Yves, *'Autour d'une œuvre: Autoportrait au modèle par Christian Schad'* in *Beaux-Arts Magazine*, no. 160, periodical, Paris, September 1997. Lloyd, Jill/Peppiatt, Michael, *Christian Schad, 1894-1982*, exhibition catalogue, Réunion des musées nationaux, Paris, 2002.

MUSEUMS AND GALLERIES:

BERLIN (Berlinische Gal.): *Portrait of the Writer Ludwig Bäumer* (1927) - HANOVER (Niedersächsisches Landesmus.) - LUGANO (Thyssen-Bornemisza Collection): *Maria and Annunziata* (1923); *Portrait of Dr Haustein* (1928) - MUNICH (Städtische Gal. im Lenbachhaus): *Operation* (1929) - VIENNA (Mus. Moderner Kunst Stiftung Ludwig) - WUPPERTAL (Von der Heydt Mus.).

AUCTION RECORDS:

HAMBURG, 8 June 1974, *Teatro Rossini* (1921) DEM 16,500. MUNICH, 29 Nov 1977, *Teatro Rossini* (1921, oil on canvas, 30 3/4 x 23 1/2 ins / 78 x 60 cm) DEM 8,000. MUNICH, 29 May 1979, *Theatre Box* (1920, oil on canvas, 29 3/4 x 21 3/4 ins / 75.5 x 55.2 cm) DEM 18,000. HAMBURG, 6 June 1980, *Young Girl Seated* (pen, 6 x 4 1/4 ins / 15.3 x 10.5 cm) DEM 1,800. MUNICH, 31 May 1983, *Portrait of Grosa Vescu* (pencil, 27 1/2 x 19 3/4 ins / 70 x 50 cm) DEM 2,400. LONDON, 4 Dec 1985, *Portrait of Elisabeth Epstein* (1918, oil and collage/canvas, 23 1/4 x 19 ins / 59 x 48 cm) GBP 15,000. LONDON, 5 Dec 1985, *Rascha, the Black Dove* (1929, charcoal, 15 1/4 x 14 1/4 ins / 39 x 36 cm) GBP 6,500. HAMBURG, 10 June 1986, *Couple Dancing* (c. 1926-1927, pen, 5 3/4 x 3 1/4 ins / 14.6 x 8.5 cm) DEM 8,500. HAMBURG, 13 June 1987, *Girl Friends* (1929, pen and coloured chalks, 13 1/2 x 11 3/4 ins / 34.5 x 29.9 cm) DEM 15,000. LONDON, 29 Nov 1989, *Portrait of Hermine Lisa Benkö* (1925, oil on canvas, 39 1/4 x 27 1/2 ins / 100 x 70 cm) GBP 93,500. MUNICH, 13 Dec 1989, *Crouching Nude* (oil on canvas, 23 1/4 x 17 3/4 ins / 59 x 45 cm) DEM 93,500. LONDON, 30 June 1992, *Bust of a Female Nude* (1930, lead pencil and colour/paper, 12 x 8 3/4 ins / 30.5 x 22.3 cm) GBP 8,800. MUNICH, 1-2 Dec 1992, *Traitress* (1917, woodcut, 7 x 4 1/2 ins / 17.5 x 11.5 cm) DEM 3,105. LONDON, 23 June 1993, *Crouching Nude* (1919, oil on canvas, 23 1/4 x 17 3/4 ins / 59 x 45 cm) GBP 20,700. LONDON, 18 Oct 2000, *Narcissus* (1927, watercolour, wash, pen, ink and pencil, 7 x 5 ins / 18 x 13 cm) GBP 6,000. HAMBURG, 25 Nov 2000, *Male Nude with Boy* (1931, pencil, 12 x 9 ins / 31 x 23 cm) DEM 6,800. LONDON, 10 Oct 2001, *Girl Friends* (1930, oil on canvas, 12 x 9 ins / 31 x 23 cm) GBP 140,000. MILAN, 14 May 2002, *Disfiguration* (1927, Indian ink, 8 x 6 ins / 21 x 15 cm) EUR 5,800. COLOGNE, 26 Nov 2003, *Parisian House: Father Cafard* (pencil, 11 x 7 ins / 27 x 18 cm) EUR

6,000. COLOGNE, 26 Nov 2003, *Farewell* (1929, Indian ink, 11 x 7 ins / 27 x 18 cm) EUR 8,000. PARIS, 19 March 2004, *Profile Portrait of a Woman* (1935, oil on canvas, 9 x 6 ins / 23 x 15 cm) EUR 55,000. COLOGNE, 4 Dec 2004, *Paris, Church of St Eustache* (pencil, 11 x 7 ins / 27 x 18 cm) EUR 6,000.

SCHAD, Christoph Friedrich Thedosius von
German, 18th century.
Born 1 May 1769, in Ansbach.
Active in Nuremberg.
Draughtsman, engraver (burin).
Christoph Schad was trained by J.C. Berndt and J.E. Ihle.

SCHAD, Joseph, or Schatt
Austrian, 16th century.
Painter.
Joseph Schad painted the pictures on the Krems Door in Eggenburg and did paintings for the town hall of the same city.

SCHAD-ROSSA, Paul
German, 19th - 20th century.
Born 1 January 1862, in Nuremberg; died 1916, in Berlin.
Painter. Portraits, landscapes.
Paul Schad-Rossa was a pupil of Ludwig Löfftz. and Franz von Defregger.

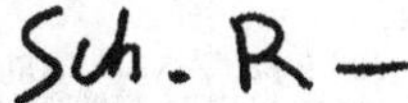

MUSEUMS AND GALLERIES:
GRAZ (Landesmus. Joanneum, Neue Gal.): *Towards Evening* - HALLE (MM): *The Damned* - KLAGENFURT (Landesmus. Kärnten): *Small Village* - MUNICH (Pinakothek): *Portrait of Luitpold of Bavaria.*
AUCTION RECORDS:
NEW YORK, 24 Jan 1980, *Grandfather's Favourite* (1888, oil on canvas, 40 x 32 ins / 101.6 x 81.3 cm) USD 5,000.

SCHADE, E.
German, 19th century.
Born 1840, in Munich.
Painter (porcelain).

SCHADE, Johannes
Dutch, 18th century.
Sculptor.
Johannes Schade produced decorative carvings for the organ lofts in the parish church at Berlikum, and the Mennonite church in Leiden, in 1780.

SCHADE, Julius
German, 17th century.
Active in Zellerfeld during the second half of the 17th century.
Sculptor.
Julius Schade sculpted the pulpit in the church of Stapelburg in 1685.

SCHADE, Karl Martin
Austrian, 19th - 20th century.
Born 17 January 1862, in Rokytzan (Bohemia).
Painter. Landscapes.
Karl Martin Schade was a pupil of Ludwig Minnigrode.
MUSEUMS AND GALLERIES:
BRNO (Muz. Mesta) - PRAGUE (Národní Gal.).
AUCTION RECORDS:
PARIS, 30-31 Dec 1946, *Landscape*, FRF 300.

SCHADE, Rudolph Christian
German, 18th - 19th century.
Born c. 1760, in Hamburg; died 16 May 1811, in Hamburg.
Portrait artist, draughtsman.
Rudolph Schade was trained by Tischbein, Ehrenreich, and Juel in Copenhagen. He worked in Berlin, Dresden and Hamburg.
MUSEUMS AND GALLERIES:
HAMBURG (Kunsthalle): *Portrait of Nicolaus Gottlieb Lütkens.*

SCHADE, Wilhelm
German, 19th century.
Born 21 May 1859, in Niedergrund-on-the-Elbe.
Active in Dresden.
Painter, illustrator. Genre scenes.
Wilhelm Schade was trained by G. von Hackl and O. Seitz.
AUCTION RECORDS:
LONDON, 20 June 1980, *Liebesfrühling* (1881, oil on panel, 13 x 17¼ ins / 33 x 44 cm) GBP 1,700.

SCHADE, Willi Ernst
German, 20th century.
Born 31 December 1892, in Berlin.
Sculptor, potter.
Willi Ernst Schade produced decorative sculptures for buildings in Berlin.

SCHADELAND, Jürgen
German, 17th century.
Died 1679.
Sculptor (wood).
Schadeland executed the sculptures for the panels of the stalls in Lübeck Cathedral.

SCHADELOCK
German, 18th century.
Sculptor.
Schadelock sculpted the altar for the church of St James in Rostock from 1781 to 1783.

SCHADEN, Adolph von, or Johann Nepomuk Adolph
German, 19th century.
Born 18 May 1791, in Oberdorf, near Hindelang; died 30 March 1840, in Munich.
Painter, writer.

SCHADEN, Heinrich
Swiss, 17th century.
Active in Porrentruy (Bernese Jura) at the beginning of the 17th century.
Sculptor (wood).
Heinrich Schaden was commissioned to produce 23 stalls for the old collegiate church in Porrentruy in 1606.

SCHADET, B.
French, 19th - 20th century.
Born in Dunkirk; died 1907.
Sculptor. Figures. Busts.
MUSEUMS AND GALLERIES:
DUNKIRK: *Plaster Bust of François Tixier.*

SCHADL, János
Hungarian, 20th century.
Born 1892; died 1944.
Painter, draughtsman. Nudes, landscapes.
János Schadl studied in Budapest. He was initially influenced by Expressionism, Cubism and Futurism, then moved towards Naturalism.
BIBLIOGRAPHY:
Passuth, Krisztina/Szabó, Júlia, *L'Art en Hongrie 1905-1930. Art et révolution*, exhibition catalogue, Musée d'Art et d'Industrie, Saint-Étienne, Musée d'Art moderne de la ville de Paris, Paris, 1980.
MUSEUMS AND GALLERIES:
BUDAPEST (Magyar Nemzeti Gal.): *St Sebastian* (1918, Indian ink) - PÉCS (Janus Pannonius Mus.): *Back of Male Nude* (1918, Indian ink); *Town* (1919, oil on canvas).

SCHÄDLER, August
German, 19th - 20th century.
Born 22 June 1862, in Ratzenried; died 28 September 1925.
Sculptor, potter.
August Schädler was a pupil of Max Widnmann. He sculpted a portrait of *A. von Gegenbaur* in Wangen.

SCHÄDLER, Johann Georg. See **SCHEDLER**

SCHADOW, Albert Dietrich
German, 19th century.
Born 2 May 1797, in Potsdam; died 5 September 1869, in Berlin.
Painter, architect.
Albert Schadow trained in Berlin and travelled to Italy in 1838 and 1839. He became blind in 1862.

SCHADOW, C. L.
German, 19th century.
Active in Neuruppin at the beginning of the 19th century.
Painter (porcelain).

SCHADOW, Félix
German, 19th century.
Born 21 June 1819, in Berlin; died 25 June 1861, in Berlin.
Painter. History painting, portraits, genre scenes.
Félix Schadow was the son of Gottfried Schadow and brother of Rudolf and Wilhelm Schadow. He settled in Dresden in 1840 and trained under Bendemann at the academy in Dresden. On returning to Berlin, he worked with his family and exhibited *Christ at the Home of Martha and Mary* in 1834, and *Children Flying a Kite* in 1836.

AUCTION RECORDS:
MUNICH, 25 June 1996, *Young Italian Woman* (1855, oil on canvas, 24 3/4 x 20 3/4 ins / 63 x 53 cm) DEM 7,800.

SCHADOW, Gottfried or Johann Gottfried
German, 18th - 19th century.
Born 20 May 1764, in Berlin; died 27 January 1850, in Berlin.
Sculptor, engraver, draughtsman. Monuments.
Gottfried Schadow was a pupil of P. Tassaerts. He went to Rome in 1785 and worked there under the supervision of Trippels. In 1787, on returning to Berlin, he was the secretary of the academy. In 1816 he became its principal.

He worked with the architects who created the new Berlin, including Langhans, the creator of the Brandenburg Gate. Assisted by his pupils, Schadow decorated the Gate with low reliefs and the famously large quadriga. He was the creator of the tomb of the count of La Mark in the Dorotheenkirche, of the group of the princesses *Louise and Frederica of Prussia*. He etched portraits and genre scenes.

He advocated the study of nature to his pupils at the academy. He is regarded as one of the creators of the German Modern School. In 2003, his work was included in a collective exhibition entitled *L'esprit créateur de Pigalle à Canova. Terres cuites européennes 1740-1840* (*The Creative Spirit from Pigalle to Canova. European Terracotta 1740-1840*) at the Louvre Museum in Paris.

BIBLIOGRAPHY:
Mackowsky, Hans, *Schadows Graphik*, Deutscher Verein für Kunstwissenschaft, Berlin, 1936. Draper, James David/Scherf, Guilhem, et al., *L'esprit créateur de Pigalle à Canova. Terres cuites européennes 1740-1840*, exhibition catalogue, Musée du Louvre, Paris, 2003.

MUSEUMS AND GALLERIES:
BERLIN: *Bust of Goethe; Bust of Princess Lichtenant; Bust of Crown Princess Luise; Bust of King Frederick III; Bust of Queen Luise; Bust of Salomon Veit; Bust of the Artist; Bust of His First Wife; Frederick the Great and Two Greyhounds - Rough Shape of the Monument of the Prince Leopold of Dessau - Rough Shape of the Monument of the Ziethen Monument - Four Roman Reliefs; Head of Blücher; Archer* (two); *Eros Resting; Woman* (three); *Triumphal Race; Fight; Adam and Eve; Young Girl Sleeping; Young Girl Kneeling - 13 Sketches; Achilles* (sketch); *Self-portrait* - BERLIN (Friedrichswerder Church): *Doppelstandbild der Prinzessinnen Luise und Friederike von Preussen* (*Double portrait of the princesses Luise and Friederike von Preussen*) (1795) - BERLIN (Nationalgal.): *Young Woman Draped* (c. 1811-1817, terracotta); *Young Man at Altar* (c. 1811-1817, terracotta); *Achilles* (1786-1787, terracotta) - DRESDEN (Albertinum): *Count Hoyn* - HAMBURG: *Frederick the Great and the Hounds Statuette; Crown Princess Luise; Frederick William III, then Crown Prince; Self-portrait; His First Wife; Salomon Veit; Young Satyr; Young Priest; Young Man at Table; Young Man before Altar; Crown Princess Luise and Her Sister, Princess von Preussen, Later Queen of the House of Hanover; Goddess; Young Man with Horn of Plenty; Nature; Young Greek; Female Dancer; Young Girl Resting; Young Girl Sleeping; Princess Luise von Preussen; Crown Princess Luise - Rough Shape of the Monument to Queen Luise; Leopold of Dessau - model of the Commemorative Monument; Goethe; Four Roman Banner Bearers; Adam and Eve; Gentleman; Traveller; Archer; Archer; Academies* - MUNICH (Neue Pinakothek): *Iffland* - ROSTOCK: *Blücher* (1819) - WITTENBERG: *Luther* (1821).

AUCTION RECORDS:
MUNICH, 26 Nov 1981, *Expert Adviser on Rudolf Schadow's Accounts* (1824, lithograph) DEM 2,500. NEW YORK, 22 May 1991, *Frederick the Great* (brown-patinated bronze, h. 35 ins / 88.9 cm) USD 8,250. BERLIN, 4 June 1999, *Portrait of Rudolf Schadow* (1824, lithograph, 11 x 7 ins / 28 x 17 cm) DEM 10,000. MUNICH, 23 June 1999, *Bust of Goethe* (1923, brown patinated bronze, h. 19 ins / 48 cm) DEM 3,000. COLOGNE, 20 Oct 2000, *Schadow's Brother, Rudolf Schadow* (chalk lithograph, 11 x 7 ins / 28 x 17 cm) DEM 16,000. BERLIN, 30 Nov 2001, *Preliminary Study for Fireplace Sketch* (pencil and brush, 7 x 9 ins / 17 x 23 cm) DEM 4,200. BERLIN, 30 Nov 2001, *Fireplace Sketch* (pen and wash, 7 x 9 ins / 18 x 23 cm) DEM 7,500.

SCHADOW, Hans
German, 19th - 20th century.
Born 8 January 1862, in Berlin; died 16 October 1924, in Bad Driburg.
Painter.
Hans Schadow studied in Berlin, in Munich under Johann Caspar Herterich and Paul Nauen, and in Paris under Tony Robert-Fleury.

MUSEUMS AND GALLERIES:
BRUNSWICK (Herzog Anton Ulrich-Mus.): *Portrait of Prince Albert of Prussia; Portrait of O. Finsch* - VATICAN (Mus. Vaticani): *Portrait of Pope Leo XIII.*

SCHADOW, Rudolf or Karl Zeno Rudolf, called Ridolfo
German, 19th century.
Born 9 July 1786, in Rome; died 31 January 1822, in Rome.
Sculptor.
Rudolf Schadow was the son of Gottfried Schadow and pupil of Thorvaldsen in Rome.

MUSEUMS AND GALLERIES:
BERLIN (Deutsches Historisches Mus.): *Bust of Friedrik Unger* - BERLIN (Nationalgal.): *Deluge* - MUNICH (Neue Pinakothek): *Young Girl Tying Her Sandal; Bust of Vittoria Caldoni.*

AUCTION RECORDS:
LONDON, 12 June 1986, *Young Girl Tying Her Sandal* (c. 1819, white marble, h. 46 ins / 117 cm) GBP 16,000.

SCHADOW, Wilhelm or Friedrich Wilhelm
German, 19th century.
Born 6 September 1788, in Berlin, in 1786 according to some sources; died 19 March 1862, in Düsseldorf.
Painter. Religious subjects, portraits.
Nazarenes group. School of Düsseldorf.
Wilhelm Schadow was the second son of Gottfried Schadow. He went to Rome with his brother Rudolf in 1810, where he shared the ideas of the 'Nazarenes' Group, which had gathered around Overbeck. On his return, he became a member of the academy in Berlin, in 1819, and later a member of the Institute of France. In 1826, he succeeded Cornelius as principal of Düsseldorf academy, followed by his pupils J. Hubner, Hildebrondt, John and Karl F. Lesinsi. He re-organised this artistic establishment, and in 1829 founded the Westphalia Association of Arts. In 1836, his strong preference for religious painting - he had been a Catholic since 1814 - earned him violent attacks. In 1840, he returned to Rome, and in 1859, he gave up his post as principal of the academy. In 1843 he had been conferred a title of nobility. He was also a writer. He died blind.
His portraits are regarded as his best works.

MUSEUMS AND GALLERIES:
ANTWERP: *Charity* - BERLIN: *Portrait of a Woman; Portraits of Thorvaldsen; William and Rudolf Schadow* (group); *Jacob's Complaint; Joseph in Prison; The Late Queen Luise; Adoration of the Shepherds; The Pilgrims of Emmaus; Self-portrait* - DÜSSELDORF: *Portrait of a Roman Woman; The Poet Immermann* (painting) - FRANKFURT AM MAIN: *Parable of the Wise and Foolish Virgins* (painting) - HAMBURG (Kunsthalle): *Portrait of Agnès d'Alton* - MUNICH: *Holy Family* - MUNICH (Neue Pinakothek): *Portrait of Fanny Ebers* - MUNICH (Residenzmus.): *Young Girl* - POZNAN: *Portrait of a Knight Templar; Salome with the Head of St John the Baptist.*
AUCTION RECORDS:
COLOGNE, 15 Nov 1972, *Self-portrait*, DEM 8,000. COLOGNE, 19 Nov 1981, *St Barbara* (oil on canvas, 45 1/4 x 32 3/4 ins / 115 x 83 cm) DEM 11,000. COLOGNE, 26 Oct 1984, *Portrait of a Young Girl* (oil on canvas, 19 x 15 1/2 ins / 48 x 39.5 cm) DEM 15,000. MUNICH, 7 Dec 1993, *Double Portrait of Paul and Max von Mila in the Garden of Bellevue Castle* (oil on canvas, 25 3/4 x 24 1/2 ins / 65.5 x 62.5 cm) DEM 103,300. MUNICH, 27 June 1995, *Portrait of the Children of the Painter* (watercolour/card, diam. 6 1/4 ins / 16 cm) DEM 8,625. COLOGNE, 19 May 2001, *Male Nude from Behind* (pencil, 13 x 8 ins / 32 x 20 cm) DEM 4,400. COLOGNE, 24 Nov 2001, *Bearded Knight Templar* (oil on canvas, 24 x 20 ins / 62 x 50 cm) DEM 40,000. MUNICH, 20 March 2002, *Portrait of Bearded Man* (oil on canvas, 19 x 15 ins / 47 x 38 cm) EUR 3,300. BERLIN, 27 Nov 2003, *Mignon* (watercolour heightened with gold, 8 x 6 ins / 20 x 15 cm) EUR 11,000. BREMEN, 26 March 2004, *Mourning of Christ* (oil on board, 16 x 13 ins / 40 x 32 cm) EUR 2,100. ZURICH, 22 Sept 2004, *Portrait of a Young Woman* (pencil, 11 x 9 ins / 27 x 23 cm) CHF 4,200.

SCHADTZ, E.
American, 19th century.
Born in Leipzig, Germany, to American parents.
Engraver.
E. Schadtz exhibited in Paris and won a silver medal in 1900 at the Exposition Universelle.

SCHAECK, Andries Andriesz.
Dutch, 17th century.
Died before 26 June 1682.
Active in Rotterdam.
Painter.
Schaeck was active in Amsterdam.

SCHAECK, Andries Jacobsz.
Flemish School, 17th century.
Painter.
Andries Jacobsz. Schaeck was the father of Andries Andriesz. and Jacob Andriesz. Schaeck. He was active in Rotterdam from 1608 to 1627.

SCHAECK, Cornelis
Flemish School, 17th century.
Painter.
Cornelis Schaeck was active in Rotterdam in 1663. He may perhaps be identifiable with Schaak B. or C.

SCHAECK, Jacob Andriesz.
Flemish School, 17th century.
Died 1657.
Painter.
Jacob Andriesz was the son of Andries Jacobsz. Schaeck; he was active in Rotterdam.

SCHAECK, Willem. See **SCHAAK**

SCHAEDLER, Johann Georg. See **SCHEDLER**

SCHAEF, Catharina
Dutch, 17th century.
Active in The Hague during the first half of the 17th century.
Painter.
The city library in Riga has a *Parrot* in watercolour by Catharina Schaef.

SCHAEFELS, Hendrik Frans, or Henri François
Belgian, 19th - 20th century.
Born 2 December 1827, in Antwerp; died 9 June 1904, in Antwerp.
Painter, engraver. History painting, landscapes with figures, seascapes.
Hendrik Frans Schaefels studied under Jacobs Jakob and inherited the latter's taste for broad-scale romantic compositions, as may be seen in his *Battle of 'The Avenger'* sent to the Paris Salon in 1849. That said, Schaefels was not above painting more modest views of the Scheldt and the canals and old port of Antwerp. He may safely be said to have made a significant contribution to the rebirth of etching in Antwerp.

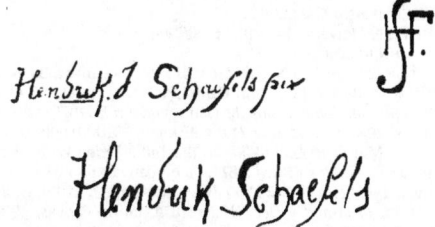

MUSEUMS AND GALLERIES:
ANTWERP: *'The Ageseras' at the Battle of Trafalgar; Siege of Vlissingen by an English Boat Squadron in 1809*; 13 sketches - BRUSSELS: *View of Antwerp* - COURTRAI: *Festival of St Job in Antwerp.*

AUCTION RECORDS:
LONDON, 16 April 1910, *Ports of Antwerp*, GBP 8. LONDON, 21 June 1926, *Antwerp Fair in the 16th Century*, GBP 120. ANTWERP, 14-16 Feb 1938, *Antwerp Fair*, BEF 5,200. BRUSSELS, 15 April 1939, *Visit*, BEF 5,000. PARIS, 16 April 1945, *Dutch Landscape* (graphite) FRF 260. LONDON, 27 July 1973, *Figures in the Market Square in Antwerp*, Gns 1,360. PARIS, 16 March 1976, *Sailing Boats on the Scheldt* (1886, oil on canvas, 11 x 15¼ ins / 28 x 38.5 cm) FRF 6,000. NEW YORK, 7 Oct 1977, *Wreck of 'The Avenger'* (1854, oil on canvas, 42½ x 62½ ins / 108 x 159 cm) USD 9,000. NEW YORK, 4 May 1979, *Royal Boat* (1870, oil on canvas, 43 x 64¼ ins / 109 x 163 cm) USD 10,000. NEW YORK, 26 Feb 1982, *In a Town Square* (1880, oil on panel, 24¾ x 20 ins / 62.9 x 50.9 cm) USD 2,800. SAN FRANCISCO, 20 June 1985, *Embarkation* (1873, oil on canvas, 28 x 43 ins / 71 x 109 cm) USD 4,500. NEW YORK, 22 May 1986, *Fête in the Garden of a Palace* (1850, oil on canvas, 19 x 26½ ins / 48.2 x 67.4 cm) USD 5,000. NEW YORK, 13 Oct 1993, *Wreck of 'The Avenger'* (1854, oil on canvas, 44 x 65 ins / 111.8 x 165.1 cm) USD 29,900. LOKEREN, 28 May 1994, *Family* (1884, oil on panel, 27½ x 21¼ ins / 70 x 54 cm) BEF 300,000. AMSTERDAM, 9 Nov 1994, *Coastal View* (1881, oil on panel, 10¼ x 14¾ ins / 26 x 37.5 cm) NLG 3,910. LOKEREN, 20 May 1995, *Annual Fair* (1860, oil on panel, 30¾ x 25½ ins / 78 x 65 cm) BEF 360,000. AMSTERDAM, 7 Nov 1995, *Happy Moments* (1854, oil on canvas, 25¼ x 20 ins / 64 x 51 cm) NLG 6,372.

SCHAEFELS, Hendrik Raphaël
Belgian, 19th century.
Born 1785, in Antwerp; died 15 February 1857, in Antwerp.
Painter, decorative designer.
Hendrik Schaefels was the father of Hendrik Frans and Lucas Schaefels.

SCHAEFELS, Lucas
Belgian, 19th century.
Born 6 April 1824, in Antwerp; died 17 September 1885, in Antwerp.
Painter, engraver. Still-lifes (including flowers).
Decorative painting.
Lucas Schaefels was the son and pupil of Hendrik Raphaël Schaefels, and brother of Hendrik Frans. He was a professor at the Antwerp academy of art, and produced engravings for frontispieces.

Luc·Schaefels fecit

Luc Schaefels

MUSEUMS AND GALLERIES:
ANTWERP: *Flowers* - MONTREAL: *Still-life*.
AUCTION RECORDS:
LONDON, 20 April 1979, *Still-life* (1874, oil on canvas, 35¼ x 52¼ ins / 89.4 x 132.7 cm) GBP 1,500. NEW YORK, 19 Oct 1984, *Still-life With Goldfish, Game and Fruit* (1870, oil on canvas, 28¼ x 36½ ins / 71.8 x 92.8 cm) USD 10,000. NEW YORK, 1 March 1990, *Still-life With a Table Laden With Victuals, and a Goldfish Bowl* (1871, oil on canvas, 63 x 78¼ ins / 160 x 198.8 cm) USD 33,000. NEW YORK, 15 Oct 1991, *Still-life With Fruit and a Dead Hare* (1871, oil on canvas, 49 x 33½ ins / 124.5 x 85 cm) USD 3,850. AMSTERDAM, 16 April 1996, *Still-life With Flowers on a Table* (1885, oil on canvas, 35½ x 47¼ ins / 90 x 120 cm) NLG 59,000. LONDON, 21 March 1997, *Still-life With Flowers on a Table* (1885, oil on canvas, 35½ x 47¼ ins / 90.2 x 120 cm) GBP 23,000. ANTWERP, 15 March 1999, *Still-life with Poultry and Fruit* (1877, oil on canvas, 28 x 39 ins / 72 x 98 cm) BEF 120,000. CREWKERNE, 15 May 2003, *Still-life of Fruit and a Goblet upon a Draped Stone Ledge* (oil on canvas, 31 x 50 ins / 79 x 128 cm) GBP 5,000.

SCHAEFER. See also **SCHÄFER**

SCHAEFER, Anne
German, 20th century.
Born 21 June 1888, in Magdeburg.
Painter.
Anne Schaefer was a pupil of Lovis Corinth.

SCHAEFER, Edmund
German, 19th - 20th century.
Born 9 June 1880, in Bremen.
Active in Berlin.
Painter, engraver, illustrator.
Edmund Schaefer studied under Ferdinand Keller. He is noted for eight drawings (*Under the Banner of War*) and assorted book illustrations.

SCHAEFER, Hans
Austrian, 19th - 20th century.
Born 13 February 1875, in Sternberg (Moravia).
Active in Chicago from 1919.
Sculptor. Busts, statues.
MUSEUMS AND GALLERIES:
BUCHAREST (Muz. National de Arta al României): *Statue of King Karl I* - VIENNA (NM): *Bust of Archduke Ferdinand Charles; Bust of Archduke Rainier; Bust of the Wife of Archduke Rainier.*

SCHAEFER, Henry Thomas. See **SCHAFER**

SCHAEFER, Maria. See **SCHÄFER**

SCHAEFER, Victor
French, 20th century.
Born 1908, in North Vietnam, to French parents.
Painter, watercolourist. Figures, landscapes, seascapes.
Victor Schaefer has exhibited in Paris since 1975 at the Salon des Artistes Français and the Salon de la Marine, and has held solo shows there. He specialises in painting Chinese landscape and civilisation. Among his works is *Junk in Dry Dock, Haiphong*.
MUSEUMS AND GALLERIES:
TULLE (Mus. du Cloître): thirteen watercolours.

SCHAEFER-MINERBE, Liliane
French, 20th century.
Born 1934, in Rouen.
Engraver, draughtswoman.
Liliane Schaeffer-Minerbe was represented in the exhibition *De Bonnard à Baselitz - Dix Ans d'enrichissements du cabinet des estampes 1978-1988* (*From Bonnard to Baselitz: A Decade of Acquisitions by the Prints Collection 1978-1988*) held at the Bibliothèque Nationale, Paris, in 1992.
MUSEUMS AND GALLERIES:
PARIS (BNF): *Ibexes* (1979, aquatint and dry-point).

SCHAEFF, Cornelis Hermansz.
Dutch, 17th century.
Sculptor.
Cornelis Schaeff was active at the church of St Stephen in Nijmegen from 1632 to 1652.

SCHAEFFER
French, 19th century.
Painter, miniaturist. Portraits.
He exhibited at the Salons of 1808 and 1814.

SCHAEFFER. See also **SCHÄFFER**

SCHAEFFER, August
Austrian, 19th - 20th century.

Born 30 April 1833, in Vienna; died 29 November 1916, in Vienna.
Painter, watercolourist, engraver (etching), lithographer, art writer. Landscapes.
August Schaeffer studied under Franz Steinfeld at the academy in Vienna and went on to work variously in the city's central library, the academy art gallery and the Imperial Museum (of which he was made principal in 1892).
MUSEUMS AND GALLERIES:
BUFFALO: *St Wolfgang Lake* - TBILISI: *Caucasus Landscapes* (ten) - VIENNA (Liechtenstein Mus.): *A March Day in the Viennese Forest* - VIENNA (Österreichische Gal. Belvedere): *On the Way to the Vienna Exhibition of 1873; At the Vienna Zoo; Near Caroline Lock; Gothic Bridge at Laxenburg; Views of Laxenburg* (14).
AUCTION RECORDS:
LONDON, 14 June 1972, *Landscape*, GBP 500. VIENNA, 3 Dec 1974, *Landscape* (1858) ATS 120,000. NEW YORK, 12 Oct 1978, *Walking along a Coastal Cliff* (1897, oil on canvas, 27 1/4 x 38 ins / 69 x 96.5 cm) USD 2,200. VIENNA, 16 Jan 1979, *Salzburg Landscape* (1860, oil on paper, 11 x 18 ins / 27 x 46 cm) ATS 30,000. MUNICH, 30 June 1983, *Riders in a Wooded Landscape* (1869, oil on card, 16 1/4 x 22 ins / 41.5 x 56 cm) DEM 7,000.

SCHAEFFER, Augusta, later Mrs von Kendler
Austrian, 20th century.
Died 1924.
Painter. Still-lifes.
Augusta Schaeffer was the daughter of the painter August Schaeffer.

SCHAEFFER, C.
German, 19th century.
Architectural draughtsman.
C. Schaeffer drew *Views of the Castle of Wilhelmshöhe near Kassel*, where he worked around 1800.

SCHAEFFER, Carl
Austrian, 19th century.
Active in Vienna during the first half of the 19th century.
Painter, engraver (etching).
Carl Schaeffer is perhaps one and the same as Karl Albert Eugen Schaeffer.
MUSEUMS AND GALLERIES:
HANOVER (Niedersächsisches Landesmus.): *Italian Landscape*.

SCHAEFFER, Carl Fellman
Canadian, 20th century.
Born 1903, in Hanover (Ontario); died 1995.
Watercolourist.
Carl Fellman Schaeffer studied at the Ontario College of Art in Toronto (1921-1924) under J.E.H. MacDonald, Arthur Lismer, G.A. Reid and Robert Holmes. He taught at the Central Technical School in Toronto in 1930, and later taught at the Ontario College of Art (1948-1970). Schaeffer was associated with the Group of Seven and exhibited with them, and was a founder member of the Canadian Group of Painters. He was awarded the Order of Canada.
MUSEUMS AND GALLERIES:
OTTAWA (NG. of Canada): *Spring in Norwich, Vermont* (1941) - TORONTO (AG of Ontario): *Cattle Ramp* (1942, graphite and watercolour); *Pears* (1934, watercolour); *Storm over the Fields* (1937, oil on canvas).

SCHAEFFER, Christian
German, 17th century.
Active during the second half of the 17th century.
Painter. Portraits.
Christian Schaeffer executed the paintings of the dukes of Saxony-Weissenfels and Saxony-Zeitz.

SCHAEFFER, Eugen Eduard, or Schäffer or Scheffer
German, 19th century.
Born 30 March 1802, in Frankfurt am Main; died 7 January 1871, in Frankfurt am Main.
Engraver (burin), draughtsman, lithographer.
Eugen Eduard Schaeffer began his training at the Städel Institute, with Ulmer, then worked in Düsseldorf with Cornelius. In 1826 he went to Munich, where he remained until he was appointed a teacher at the Städel Institute. In 1844 he was reportedly in Florence, engraving the *Madone della Sedia* by Raphael. From 1852 to 1856 he lived in Rome. He engraved religious subjects, portraits and allegories in the style of Raphael and Cornelius.
MUSEUMS AND GALLERIES:
FRANKFURT AM MAIN (Städel): *Portrait of BG Niebuhr*.

SCHAEFFER, Francis Jean
French, 19th century.
Born 1808; died 1874.
Painter. Landscapes, waterscapes.
MUSEUMS AND GALLERIES:
LONDON: *Banks of a River*.
AUCTION RECORDS:
PARIS, 2 March 1951, *People in the Roman Countryside*, FRF 9,000. BERN, 22 Oct 1976, *Summer Landscape* (oil on canvas, 19 1/4 x 32 1/4 ins / 49 x 82 cm) CHF 1,600.

SCHAEFFER, Heinrich
German, 19th century.
Painter. Portraits.
Heinrich Schaeffer exhibited in Berlin from 1839 to 1860.
AUCTION RECORDS:
LOS ANGELES, 23 June 1980, *Market Scene in Antwerp; View of Chartres* (1890, oil on canvas, a pair, 16 x 12 ins / 40.6 x 30.5 cm) USD 5,000.

SCHAEFFER, Heinrich or Henri, or Schäfer
German, 19th century.
Born 1818, in Trier; died 5 September 1873, in Rome.
Sculptor. Figures. Busts.
MUSEUMS AND GALLERIES:
NICE: *Bust of Augustus Carlone*.

SCHAEFFER, Henri Alexis
French, 20th century.
Born 9 August 1900, in Paris; died 1975.
Painter. Religious subjects, urban landscapes.
Henri Alexis Schaeffer, a pupil of Cormon at the École des Beaux-Arts, Paris, exhibited in Paris at the Salon des Artistes Français, of which he was a member, from 1934. He painted mainly religious pictures (in the church of St-François-de Sales, Paris, the church of Argenteuil, in St-Pierre d'Entremont (Savoy) and views of Paris.
AUCTION RECORDS:
BREST, 16 Dec 1984, *Paris Boulevards* (oil on canvas, 17 3/4 x 22 ins / 45 x 55 cm) FRF 10,500. LOS ANGELES, 9 June 1988, *The Grand-Hôtel, Paris* (oil on canvas, 18 x 22 ins / 46 x 55 cm) USD 6,050. PARIS, 14 Dec 1988, *Autumn Evening on the Paris Boulevards* (oil on canvas, 17 1/4 x 22 ins / 44 x 55 cm) FRF 18,000; *Circus* (oil on canvas, 26 3/4 x 23 1/4 ins / 68 x 59 cm) FRF 48,500. DOUAI, 23 April 1989, *Place Vendôme* (oil on canvas, 11 x 13 3/4 ins / 27 x 35 cm) FRF 20,800. PARIS, 11 July 1989, *Place Vendôme* (oil on canvas, 11 x 13 3/4 ins / 27 x 35 cm) FRF 20,000. LE TOUQUET, 12 Nov 1989, *Paris, the Boulevards* (oil on canvas, 15 x 18 ins / 38 x 46 cm) FRF 18,000. CALAIS, 25 June 1995, *The Paris Boulevards* (oil on canvas, 18 x 22 ins / 46 x 56 cm) FRF 4,000. TORONTO, 7 Dec 2000, *The Louvre, Caroussel Bridge* (oil on canvas, 19 x 27 ins / 48 x 69

cm) CAD 2,300. SANDBACH, 14 March 2001, *Breville Cathedral* (oil on canvas, 16 x 12 ins / 41 x 30 cm) GBP 1,400. PARIS, 14 June 2004, *La Madeleine* (oil on canvas, 18 x 22 ins / 46 x 55 cm) EUR 1,500.

SCHAEFFER, Johannes David
German, 17th century.
Active in Tübingen in 1631.
Silhouettist.

SCHAEFFER, Karl Albert Eugen
German, 19th century.
Born 29 May 1780, in Pless; died 3 June 1866, in Leobschütz.
Painter, engraver (etching).
Karl Schaeffer trained at the academy in Berlin. He executed historical scenes and landscapes.

SCHAEFFER, Mead
American, 20th century.
Born 15 July 1898, in Freedom Plains (New York); died 1980.
Painter, illustrator. Religious subjects.
Mead Schaeffer studied under Dean Cornwell. He was a member of the New York Society of Illustrators, and illustrated many books, including *Les Misérables* by Victor Hugo and *Sans Famille* by Hector Malot.
AUCTION RECORDS:
NEW YORK, 21 Oct 1982, *Mutinous Pirate* (oil on canvas, 32 x 22 3/4 ins / 81 x 58 cm) USD 1,900. NEW YORK, 2 Dec 1992, *Paradise Poachers* (oil on canvas, 30 x 42 1/4 ins / 76.2 x 107.3 cm) USD 2,200. NEW YORK, 6 Nov 1999, *Struggle on Beach* (oil on canvas, 25 x 38 ins / 64 x 97 cm) USD 7,500. NEW YORK, 6 May 2000, *Young Woman, Governess and Dog Snub Man at Fountain* (oil on canvas, illustration, 24 x 42 ins / 61 x 107 cm) USD 17,000. NEW YORK, 4 Nov 2000, *Armed Confrontation on Horseback* (oil on canvas, 15 x 24 ins / 38 x 61 cm) USD 2,900. NEW YORK, 5 May 2001, *Group of Cavaliers Around a Table* (oil on canvas, 25 x 38 ins / 64 x 97 cm) USD 26,000. NEW YORK, 11 May 2002, *Woman with Rifle Confronts Three Men* (c. 1938, oil on canvas, 24 x 32 ins / 61 x 81 cm) USD 13,000. NEW YORK, 15 Nov 2003, *Colonial Troops with Indian Guides* (1921, oil on canvas, 25 x 34 ins / 64 x 86 cm) USD 20,000. NEW YORK, 15 May 2004, *Three Musketeers* (oil on canvas, 32 x 26 ins / 81 x 66 cm) USD 30,000.

SCHAEFFER VON WIENWALD, Augusta
Maiden name: Wahrmund
Austrian, 19th - 20th century.
Born 25 April 1862, in Vienna.
Miniaturist, painter (enamel).
Augusta Schaeffer von Wienwald was the wife of the painter August Schaeffer. She was also an author.

SCHAEFFER-BERGER, Francisque Jean
French, 19th century.
Born 13 February 1808, in Paris; died 1874.
Painter. Landscapes.
He was taught painting by Bertin and Ingres. He showed his work at the Salon between 1836 and 1868, and won a third-class medal in 1844.
MUSEUMS AND GALLERIES:
BAGNEUX - BAYEUX - LANGRES.

SCHAEFFLER. See also **SCHÄFFLER** or **SCHEFFLER**

SCHAEFFLER, Franz Mathias, or Matheus. See **SCHEFFLER**

SCHAEFFLER, Thomas Christian. See **SCHEFFLER, Christoph**

SCHAEFLER, Fritz
German, 20th century.
Born 31 December 1888, in Eschau; died 1954.
Active in Cologne.
Painter, engraver.
AUCTION RECORDS:
MUNICH, 29 May 1984, *Wooded Landscape* (1919, oil on canvas, 29 3/4 x 24 1/2 ins / 75.5 x 62 cm) DEM 8,500. COLOGNE, 7 June 2000, *Bathers in a Woodland Stream* (1949, oil on board, 17 x 12 ins / 43 x 30 cm) DEM 3,400. HEIDELBERG, 13 Oct 2000, *Gorge* (watercolour over pencil, 24 x 19 ins / 60 x 47 cm) DEM 4,800. MUNICH, 17 May 2001, *Bathing Huts* (watercolour over pencil, 14 x 10 ins / 35 x 25 cm) DEM 3,200. MUNICH, 19 May 2001, *Cutters* (watercolour over pencil, 19 x 22 ins / 49 x 57 cm) DEM 5,000. HAMBURG, 23 March 2002, *Waterfall* (watercolour over pencil, 24 x 20 ins / 62 x 50 cm) EUR 1,800. MUNICH, 6 Dec 2002, *Female Nude* (c. 1923, watercolour over pencil, 22 x 20 ins / 55 x 50 cm) EUR 2,100. MUNICH, 30 Nov 2004, *Children in Wood* (watercolour over pencil, double-sided, 22 x 16 ins / 56 x 40 cm) EUR 2,000.

SCHAEK. See **SCHAAK** or **SCHACK**

SCHAEKEN, Wilhelmus or Guillaume
Belgian, 18th - 19th century.
Born 1754, in Weert; died 28 December 1830, in Antwerp.
Painter. History painting.
Wilhelmus Schaeken was a pupil of J. Borrekens in Antwerp. His own pupils later included M. J. van Bree. He spent two years in Italy, and 12 years in Antwerp.

SCHAENBORGH, P. van
Dutch, 17th century.
Painter. Still-lifes.
P. van Schaenborgh was known for a painting of *Fish* (sold by Wermal Dahl in Amsterdam, in 1905).

SCHAEP, Arnoldus
Dutch, 17th century.
Arnoldus Schaep is known for a series of six landscapes.

SCHAEP, Henri Adolphe
Dutch, 19th century.
Born 1826; died 1870.
Painter, engraver. Genre scenes, seascapes.

MUSEUMS AND GALLERIES:
ANTWERP: *Shipwreck*.
AUCTION RECORDS:
PARIS, 28-29 Nov 1923, *Seascape*, FRF 530. PARIS, 18 Oct 1934, *Galley and Small Boats; Maritime Landscape* (a pair) FRF 520. BRUSSELS, 11 Dec 1937, *Village Fête*, FRF 1,300. VIENNA, 22 Sept 1964, *Arrival of the Sailing-ship*, ATS 50,000. VIENNA, 18 June 1968, *Fishermen's Festivities*, ATS 55,000. NEW YORK, 14 May 1976, *Shipwreck off the Coast* (oil on canvas, 11 3/4 x 15 ins / 30 x 38 cm) USD 800. NEW YORK, 12 May 1978, *Fishing-boat in Calm Seas* (1860, oil on panel, 10 1/4 x 13 ins / 26 x 33 cm) USD 1,800. LONDON, 5 Oct 1979, *Riverscape with Fishing-boat* (1841, oil on canvas, 13 x 18 1/4 ins / 33 x 46.5 cm) GBP 600. LONDON, 26 March 1982, *Boats off the Dutch Coast* (1861, oil on canvas, 37 1/4 x 55 1/4 ins / 94.6 x 140.3 cm) GBP 2,400. COLOGNE, 22 March 1985, *Medieval Town on the Seashore* (1860, oil on canvas, 23 1/2 x 34 ins / 59.5 x 86.5 cm) DEM 12,000. AMSTERDAM, 23 April 1991, *Figures in a Boat on a River Beside the Walls of a Town* (oil on panel, 19 3/4 x 24 3/4 ins / 50 x 63 cm) NLG 12,075. LONDON, 16 Nov 1994, *Harbour Scene with Figures* (oil on panel, 19 1/4 x 29 1/4 ins / 49 x 74 cm) GBP 4,600. NEW YORK, 16 Feb 1995, *Shipwreck* (1862, oil on canvas, 24 x 29 3/4 ins / 61 x 75.6 cm) USD 8,050. AMSTERDAM, 7 Nov 1995, *Riverscape With Figures in a Boat Near a Town Wall*

(oil on panel, 19 3/4 x 24 3/4 ins / 50 x 63 cm) NLG 13,570. LONDON, 2 Dec 1999, *Fire on Shore in Moonlight* (1856, oil on canvas, 19 x 27 ins / 47 x 69 cm) GBP 5,500. PARIS, 19 April 2000, *Embarcation Scene in a Dutch Port* (oil on panel, 21 x 28 ins / 54 x 70 cm) FRF 350,000. STUTTGART, 22 Sept 2000, *Sailing Ships on the High Seas* (1854, oil on canvas, 26 x 35 ins / 66 x 88 cm) DEM 36,000. LONDON, 21 Nov 2002, *Gathering Outside a Dutch Hostelry* (1847, oil on panel, 18 x 21 ins / 45 x 54 cm) GBP 4,000. BRUSSELS, 9 Dec 2002, *Departure of a Three-master under Escort, with a Town in the Background* (1853, oil on canvas, 24 x 32 ins / 62 x 82 cm) EUR 20,000. AHLDEN, 19 Sept 2003, *Ships in Stormy Seas* (oil on canvas, 28 x 41 ins / 72 x 105 cm) EUR 5,500. AMSTERDAM, 21 Oct 2003, *Shipping in Choppy Seas* (1850, oil on canvas, 26 x 35 ins / 67 x 88 cm) EUR 15,000. LONDON, 23 March 2004, *Elegant Figures Seated by a Fountain, a Harbour Beyond* (1852, oil on panel, 20 x 30 ins / 52 x 75 cm) GBP 5,000.

SCHAEP, M.
Dutch, 17th century.
Active in the middle of the 17th century.
Engraver (etching).

SCHAEP, M. S.
17th century.
Engraver.
M.S. Schaep is mentioned by Le Blanc as having engraved six prints after Cornelis Bega.

SCHAEPELINCK, François
Flemish School, 17th century.
Sculptor (wood).
Schaepelinck carved the choir-stalls at the churches of St Anne and Notre-Dame in Bruges.

SCHAEPHERDERS, Jaak
Belgian, 20th century.
Born 1890, in Mechelen; died 1964.
Painter. Landscapes, seascapes, still-lifes, flowers.

SCHAEPHERDERS, Rik
Belgian, 19th - 20th century.
Born 1862, in Bruges; died 1949, in Mechelen.
Painter. Landscapes, still-lifes.

SCHAEPKENS, Alexander
Dutch, 19th century.
Born in Maastricht; died 1 September 1899, in Maastricht.
Painter, engraver (etching). Landscapes.
Alexander Schaepkens was the brother of Arnaud and Théodor Schaepkens, and a pupil at the academies of Antwerp and Brussels. He engraved landscapes and genre scenes.
MUSEUMS AND GALLERIES:
YPRES (Mus.): *The Children of Bethlehem.*

SCHAEPKENS, Arnaud or Jean Antoine Arnaud or Arnold
Dutch, 19th century.
Born 31 October 1816, in Maastricht; died 7 June 1904, in Brussels.
Painter, engraver (etching).
Arnaud Schaepkens was the brother of Alexander Schaepkens, and a pupil of Erin Corr. He engraved religious subjects, landscapes and genre scenes.

SCHAEPKENS, Théodor
German, 19th century.
Born 27 January 1810, in Maastricht; died 18 December 1883, in St Joost-ten-Noode.
Painter, engraver (etching).
Théodor Schaepkens was the brother of Alexander and Arnaud Schaepkens. He was trained by Van Bree. He engraved religious subjects and genre scenes.

Ch. S Th. S.

MUSEUMS AND GALLERIES:
AACHEN: *Death of a Cavalryman.*

SCHAER-KRAUSE, Ida
German, 19th - 20th century.
Born 13 February 1877, in Berlin.
Active in Zug, Switzerland.
Sculptor.
Ida Schaer-Krause was a pupil of Hermann Kolkowsky and Adolf Brütt.

SCHAERER, H. L.
Engraver.
H.L. Schaerer produced a number of small prints, usually copies of Herman Sachleven or Pieter Jansz. Saenredam.

SCHAERER, Hans
Swiss, 20th century.
Born 1927.
Painter, collage artist.
AUCTION RECORDS:
LUCERNE, 24 Nov 1990, *Untitled* (1960, collage and mixed media, 11 3/4 x 19 3/4 ins / 30 x 50 cm) CHF 2,000. LUCERNE, 23 May 1992, *Raspberry Madonna* (1972, spatula-applied mixture, oil and synthetic resin, 44 1/2 x 35 ins / 113 x 89 cm) CHF 24,000. LUCERNE, 21 Nov 1992, *Untitled* (1982, mixed media/paper, 26 3/4 x 39 1/4 ins / 68 x 100 cm) CHF 3,700.

SCHAERF, Eran
Israeli, 20th - 21st century.
Born 1962, in Tel Aviv.
Active in Belgium and Germany.
Assemblage artist, installation artist.
Eran Schaerf lives and works in Berlin and Brussels. He takes the component parts of his work, objects, publicity images, words, from everyday life and combines them according to their internal logic. He is interested in cross-cultural issues and the idea of world identity. His installation *Recasting*, which he exhibited at the FRAC Champagne-Ardenne, addressed these concerns through fashion. No matter what his colour or origins, man yields to designer clothes in every corner of the world.

He has taken part in a large number of group exhibitions, including: 1987, 1990 Künstlerhaus Bethanien, Berlin; 1989 Kunstverein Hamburg; 1990 Karl Ernst Osthaus Museum, Hagen; 1992 Corcoran Art Gallery, Washington, Documenta 9, Kassel; 1993 *Parcours européen III Allemagne - Qui, quoi? où? (A trip through Europe III: Germany - Who? What? Where?*, Museum of Modern Art, Paris. He has also exhibited at one-man shows in Berlin (regularly since 1988) and 1997, FRAC Champagne-Ardenne; 2002, Bonner Kunstverein, Bonn.
BIBLIOGRAPHY:
Bossé, Laurence/Obrist, Hans-Ulrich, *Parcours européen III Allemagne - Qui, quoi? où? - Un regard sur l'Allemagne en 1992*, exhibition catalogue, Musée d'Art moderne de la ville de Paris, Paris, 1993. *Eran Schaerf, Peter Wüthrich, Nedko Solakov, Anders Widoff, Nathalie Tison*, exhibition catalogue, Shedhalle, Zurich, 1993 (text in German and English). Jarton, Cyril, '*Eran Schaerf*' in *Art Press* n° 230, periodical, Paris, December 1997.

SCHAERFF, Johann Wendelin
German, 19th century.
Born 1811, in Alzey.
Active in Munich.
Painter. Figures, portraits.

SCHAERLAECKEN, P. J.
Flemish School, 18th century.
Sculptor.
P.J. Schaerlaecken collaborated on the pulpit of the church of Notre-Dame in Bruges in 1743.

SCHAETZEL, Jean Baptiste, or Schaetzell
French, 18th century.
Born 1763, in Colmar.
Painter.
Schaetzel studied in Paris under P.G. Doyen, and worked in Strasbourg from 1790 to 1800.
MUSEUMS AND GALLERIES:
STRASBOURG (Prints and Drawings Collection): *Shepherds with Flock.*

SCHAEYENBORGH, Pieter van, or Schayenborgh or Schaffenburg
Dutch, 17th century.
Painter. Still-lifes, animals.
Pieter van Schaeyenborgh was a guild member in Alkmaar in 1635. J. Th. Blankerhoff was his pupil.
MUSEUMS AND GALLERIES:
ALKMAAR (Stedelijk Mus.): *Freshwater and Saltwater Fish* (two still-lifes).

SCHÄFER
German, 18th century.
Sculptor. Religious subjects.
Schäfer was active in Karlstadt, where he worked in 1747. He sculpted the altars and pulpit of the church in Retzbach.

SCHÄFER. See also **SCHAEFER**

SCHÄFER, Adam Joseph
German, 19th century.
Born 6 March 1798, in Kronach; died 30 December 1871, in Bamberg.
Sculptor.
Adam Joseph Schäfer was trained by Georg Hoffmann in Bamberg and at the academy in Munich. He sculpted fountains, altars and tombs, notably in Bamberg.

SCHÄFER, Albert Quirin
German, 19th - 20th century.
Born 10 October 1877, in Karlsruhe.
Landscape artist.

SCHÄFER, Alexander
German, 19th century.
Miniaturist, engraver.
Alexander Schäfer trained under W. Reuter at the academy in Berlin. He worked in Berlin during the first half of the 19th century.

SCHÄFER, Anton
German, 18th century.
Born 1722, in Düsseldorf; died 1799, in Mannheim.
Medallist.
Anton Schäfer was the son of Wiegand Schäfer.

SCHÄFER, Bruno Otto
German, 20th century.
Born 5 September 1883, in Leipzig.
Active in Frankfurt am Main.
Sculptor.

SCHAFER, Dirk
Dutch, 19th - 20th century.
Born 12 February 1864, in The Hague; died 1941.
Painter, engraver (etching).
Dirk Schafer studied under Franz Becker.
MUSEUMS AND GALLERIES:
THE HAGUE: *Carrying the Cross* (1911).
AUCTION RECORDS:
AMSTERDAM, 30 Aug 1988, *Still-life with Drum, Sword and Helmet on a Cloth-covered Table* (oil on canvas, 26 1/2 x 42 1/4 ins / 67.5 x 107 cm) NLG 1,725. AMSTERDAM, 3 Nov 1992, *Concert* (oil on panel, 13 1/2 x 20 ins / 34.5 x 51 cm) NLG 1,380.

SCHÄFER, Emil
Swiss, 19th - 20th century.
Born 4 February 1870, in Basel.
Painter. Designs for stained glass.
Emil Schäfer was deaf and mute. He studied under Fritz Schider and Eugen Enslen.

SCHAFER, Florian
Austrian, 18th - 19th century.
Born 1749; died 1828.
Active in Reichenberg (now Liberec, Czech Republic).
Painter. Cribs.
Florian Schafer taught Jak. Ginzel.

SCHAFER, Frederick Ferdinand
American, 19th - 20th century.
Born 1839 or 1841; died 1917 or 1927.
Painter. Landscapes with figures, mountainscapes, landscapes.
AUCTION RECORDS:
LOS ANGELES, 15 Oct 1979, *Two Indians in a Desert Landscape* (oil on canvas, 20 x 35 3/4 ins / 50.5 x 91 cm) USD 2,600. SAN FRANCISCO, 18 June 1980, *Fishermen in High Sierras* (oil on canvas, 22 x 36 ins / 56 x 91.5 cm) USD 4,750. SAN FRANCISCO, 24 June 1981, *Olympic Mountains* (oil on canvas, 20 x 36 1/4 ins / 51 x 92 cm) USD 3,000. NEW YORK, 17 March 1988, *North Heads Point on the Pacific Coast of California* (oil on canvas, 29 1/2 x 49 1/4 ins / 75 x 125 cm) USD 1,320. LOS ANGELES-SAN FRANCISCO, 12 July 1990, *Yosemite Landscape* (oil on canvas, 30 x 50 ins / 76 x 127 cm) USD 1,100; *Black Hill with Shasta in the Distance seen from Sissons* (oil on canvas, 20 x 30 ins / 51 x 76 cm) USD 1,320. NEW YORK, 31 March 1993, *Bear Lake and the Wasatch Mountains in Utah* (oil on canvas, 30 x 50 ins / 76.2 x 127 cm) USD 4,888.

SCHÄFER, Friedrich
German, 18th century.
Born 1725, in Düsseldorf; died 1776, in Eisenach.
Medallist.
Friedrich Schäfer was the son of Wiegand Schäfer.

SCHÄFER, Friedrich, the Elder, or Schäferle or Schäfferle or Schöfferli
Swiss, 18th century.
Born c. 1709, in the Tyrol; died 11 December 1786, in Lucerne.
Sculptor. Religious subjects. Monuments.
Friedrich Schäfer the Elder sculpted crucifixes, fountains and statues.

SCHÄFER, Friedrich, the Younger
Swiss, 18th - 19th century.
Active in Lucerne.
Sculptor.
Friedrich Schäfer the Younger was the son and assistant of Friedrich Schäfer the Elder.

SCHÄFER, Friedrich or Carl Friedrich. See **SCHÄFFER**

SCHÄFER, Friedrich Wilhelm
German, 18th century.
Born c. 1763, in Frankfurt am Main; died 1807, in Frankfurt am Main.
Painter, engraver (etching).
Friedrich Wilhelm Schäfer was trained by J.A.B. Nothnagel. He painted several allegorical scenes in Frankfurt town hall.
MUSEUMS AND GALLERIES:
BERLIN (Kupferstichkabinet): three drawings (Indian ink).

SCHÄFER, Georg
German, 18th century.
Sculptor.
Georg Schäfer sculpted altars in churches in Karlstadt and the surrounding areas.

SCHÄFER, Georg
German, 18th century.
Active in Oggersheim in 1786.
Painter.
Georg Schäfer painted *The Divine Lamb with Angels* in Godramstein.

SCHÄFER, Georg
German, 19th century.
Active in Karlstadt in 1819.
Sculptor.
Georg Schäfer sculpted the high altar for the church of St Michael in Ettleben.

SCHÄFER, Georg Christoph
German, 18th century.
Active in Hannoverisch-Münden in 1789.
Painter (porcelain).

SCHÄFER, Georg Joseph Bernhard
German, 19th - 20th century.
Born 20 August 1855, in Karlstadt; died 26 November 1912, in Munich.
Active in Munich.
Painter. Portraits, genre scenes, interiors.

MUSEUMS AND GALLERIES:
MUNICH (Pinakothek): *Allotria Artists' Tavern prior to its Demolition* - SPEYER (Historisches Mus. der Pfalz): *Portrait of the Poet Martin Greif.*

SCHÄFER, Gertrud
Belgian, 19th - 20th century.
Born 1 February 1880, in Loth, near Brussels.
Active in Dresden.
Painter, lithographer.

SCHAFER, Heinrich or Hermann
German, 19th century.
Born c. 1815, in Halberstadt.
Painter, watercolourist. Landscapes.
Heinrich Schafer trained at the academy in Düsseldorf under C.F. Sohn.

AUCTION RECORDS:
LONDON, 11 Feb 1976, *Bamberg, Bavaria* (1881, oil on canvas, 19 1/4 x 29 1/2 ins / 49 x 75 cm) GBP 600. NEW YORK, 7 Jan 1981, *St-Ouen, Rouen* (watercolour, 23 1/4 x 17 1/2 ins / 59 x 44.5 cm) USD 1,500. LONDON, 15 March 1982, *Figures in front of the Cathedral, Freiburg, Baden* (1885, oil on canvas, 28 x 20 ins / 71 x 51 cm) GBP 1,350. LONDON, 5 Oct 1983, *View of Antwerp* (1887, oil on canvas, 31 1/4 x 26 ins / 79.5 x 66 cm) GBP 1,700. NEW YORK, 19 Oct 1983, *Interior of Milan Cathedral* (watercolour, gouache and pencil, 24 1/2 x 18 1/2 ins / 62.3 x 47 cm) USD 1,600. PARIS, 28 March 1985, *Morning Read* (oil on canvas, 12 1/4 x 18 3/4 ins / 31 x 47.5 cm) FRF 25,000. BRUSSELS, 18 Nov 2003, *Bustling Alleyway below the Cathedral* (1874, oil on canvas, 16 x 12 ins / 40 x 31 cm) EUR 2,000.

SCHAFER, Henry Thomas, or Schaffer
British, 19th - 20th century.
Born 1854; died after 1915.
Painter, watercolourist, draughtsman. Figures, scenes with figures, genre scenes, church interiors, landscapes, waterscapes, urban landscapes, architectural views.
Henry Thomas Schafer was active from 1873 to 1915. He was a member of the Royal Society of British Artists. He exhibited *The Writer* at the Royal Academy and Suffolk Street in London, and at the Royal Scottish Academy in 1911.

MUSEUMS AND GALLERIES:
HULL (Ferens Art Gallery): *Needle and Thread* (oil on canvas).

AUCTION RECORDS:
LONDON, 5 March 1910, *Symphony* (1844) GBP 26. LONDON, 24 May 1910, *Poetry* (1888) GBP 19. LONDON, 23 Oct 1974, *View of Limoges,* GBP 420. LONDON, 7 May 1976, *View of Metz* (oil on canvas, 16 x 12 1/4 ins / 40.5 x 31 cm) GBP 520. LONDON, 20 July 1977, *View of Bruges* (1890, oil on canvas, 15 x 11 1/2 ins / 38 x 29 cm) GBP 700. LONDON, 15 May 1979, *Rose Time* (1877, oil on canvas, 28 x 35 ins / 71 x 89 cm) GBP 1,600. LONDON, 23 March 1981, *Divinely Fair* (1893, oil on canvas, 63 x 35 1/2 ins / 160 x 90 cm) USD 5,200. LONDON, 19 Oct 1983, *Rest* (1881, oil on canvas, 19 x 31 ins / 48 x 79 cm) GBP 2,000. LONDON, 26 Feb 1988, *City on the Continent* (1878, oil on canvas, 14 x 12 ins / 35.5 x 30.5 cm) GBP 682. AMSTERDAM, 30 Aug 1988, *Market Square in Louvain, Belgium, with Numerous Villagers* (watercolour and ink/paper, 17 1/4 x 13 1/2 ins / 44 x 34 cm) NLG 1,092. BERN, 26 Oct 1988, *Riverscape with Poplars and a Monastery Church* (oil on canvas, 9 1/2 x 13 1/2 ins / 24 x 34 cm) CHF 800. NEW YORK, 17 Jan 1990, *St Vandrue in Mons, Belgium* (oil on canvas, 26 1/4 x 21 1/2 ins / 66.7 x 54.6 cm) USD 3,575. MONTREAL, 30 April 1990, *Ste-Madeleine, Troyes* (oil on canvas, 12 1/4 x 9 3/4 ins / 31 x 25 cm) CAD 935. LONDON, 15 June 1990, *Abbeville and Caudebec, Normandy* (oil on canvas, a pair, 18 x 14 ins / 45.7 x 35.6 cm) GBP 2,640. LONDON, 26 Sept 1990, *Unloading the Fish* (oil on canvas, 25 1/4 x 22 ins / 64 x 55 cm) GBP 1,320. LONDON, 22 Nov 1990, *Street of a Continental City with Figures* (oil on canvas, 12 x 9 3/4 ins / 30.4 x 24.8 cm) GBP 550. NEW YORK, 21 May 1991, *Going to Church* (oil on canvas, 27 x 35 1/2 ins / 68.6 x 90.2 cm) USD 4,400. NEW YORK, 21 May 1991, *Church of St-Vincent in Rouen, Normandy* (oil on canvas, 18 1/4 x 14 1/4 ins / 46.4 x 36.2 cm) USD 4,620. NEW YORK, 16 Feb 1993, *North Transept of the Toledo Cathedral* (watercolour and ink heightened with gouache, 43 1/4 x 29 1/2 ins / 110 x 75 cm) USD 3,300. LONDON, 11 June 1993, *Antwerp; Romerberg in Frankfurt am Main* (1889, oil on canvas, a pair, each 16 x 12 ins / 40.6 x 30.5 cm) GBP 3,450. NEW YORK, 15 Oct 1993, *Toledo Cathedral, Spain* (watercolour and pencil/reinforced paper, 18 1/4 x 12 1/4 ins / 46.4 x 31.1 cm) USD 920. LONDON, 5 Nov 1993, *Divinely Beautiful* (1893, oil on canvas, 35 x 63 ins / 89.2 x 160.3 cm) GBP 10,120. LONDON, 30 March 1994, *Old House in Rouen; Market Square, Nuremberg* (oil on canvas, a pair, each 16 x 12 ins / 40.5 x 30.5 cm) GBP 2,415. NEW YORK, 20 July 1994, *St-Wulfran in Abbeville, Normandy* (1889, oil on canvas, 15 3/4 x 12 ins / 40 x 30.5 cm) USD 920. LONDON, 7 June 1995, *Distributing the Grain for the Pigeons; By the Docks* (1889, oil on panel, a pair, each 23 1/2 x 12 1/4 ins / 60 x 31 cm) GBP 3,220. LONDON, 9 May 1996, *Rouen, Normandy; Utrecht, Holland* (1888, oil on canvas, a pair, each 9 3/4 x 8 ins / 25 x 20.5 cm) GBP 1,782. LONDON, 9 Oct 1996, *Morlaix, Brittany; Place-de-la-Croix in St-Pierre, Normandy* (oil on canvas, a pair, 15 3/4 x 12 1/4 ins / 40 x 31 cm) GBP 3,450. LONDON, 13 March 1997, *St-Pierre, Caen; Koblenz, Germany* (oil on canvas, a pair, 16 x 12 ins / 40.7 x 30.4 cm) GBP 3,200. BILLINGSHURST, 18 May 1999, *Market Scene, Bamber, Bavaria. Morlaix, Brittany* (oil on canvas, a pair, 15 x 11 ins / 39 x 29 cm) GBP 4,500. JERSEY, 29 Sept 1999, *Frankfurt, Germany. Strasbourg, Alsace* (oil on canvas, a pair, 18 x 14 ins / 46 x 35 cm) GBP 4,800. LONDON, 21 June 2000, *Rue de Louviers, Bruges, Belgium. Antwerp* (oil on canvas, a pair, 16 x 12 ins / 40 x 30 cm) GBP 3,400. CHICAGO, 16 Sept 2000, *Caen and Rouen* (1883, oil on canvas, a pair, 16 x 12 ins / 41 x 30 cm) USD 4,400. NEW YORK, 2 May 2001, *Spring Blossoms* (1876, oil on canvas, 30 x 22 ins / 76 x 56 cm) USD 12,000. LONDON, 20 Sept 2001, *Buying Fruit by a Canal. Bustling Continental Street* (oil on canvas, a pair, 16 x 12 ins / 41 x 30 cm) GBP 2,500. LONDON, 1 May 2002, *Cologne Cathedral* (oil on canvas, 40 x 30 ins / 102 x 76 cm) GBP 3,600. LONDON, 30 May

2002, *Luys Near Morlaix, Britanny. Eveux, Normandy* (1882, oil on canvas, two, 20 x 16 ins / 51 x 41 cm) GBP 3,200. MADRID, 18 Feb 2003, *Burgos Cathedral* (oil on canvas, 44 x 34 ins / 112 x 86 cm) EUR 6,500. LONDON, 19 Nov 2003, *Peacock Fan* (1879, oil on canvas, 19 x 31 ins / 48 x 79 cm) GBP 6,800. LONDON, 4 March 2004, *Strasbourg, Alsace. St Pierre, Caen, Normandy* (oil on canvas, a pair, 16 x 12 ins / 41 x 30 cm) GBP 2,000.

SCHÄFER, Hermann, or Schäfer-Kirchberg
German, 19th - 20th century.
Born 2 February 1880, in Kirchberg am Jagst.
Active in Jena.
Painter.
Hermann Schäfer was a pupil of Emil Doepler the Younger.
MUSEUMS AND GALLERIES:
BERLIN (Staatliche Mus.): *Visit to the Big City.*
AUCTION RECORDS:
LONDON, 24 June 1981, *Views of Morlaix and Bamberg* (oils on canvas, a pair, 15 1/2 x 11 3/4 ins / 39.5 x 30 cm) GBP 1,200.

SCHÄFER, J. F.
German, 17th century.
Sculptor.
J.F. Schäfer sculpted the organ case in the church of Eschwege from 1676 to 1678.

SCHÄFER, Jakob
German, 18th century.
Active in Karlstadt.
Sculptor.
Jakob Schäfer sculpted the altar of the church in Erlenbach in 1747.

SCHÄFER, Johann Michael, or Schäffer
German, 18th century.
Painter.
Johann Michael Schäfer painted the altarpieces in several churches of Bavaria.

SCHÄFER, Johannes
German, 19th century.
Born 8 May 1830, in Kalkobes, near Hersfeld; died 24 October 1862, in Welheiden, near Kassel.
Sculptor.

SCHÄFER, Joseph
German, 18th century.
Born 1731, in Düsseldorf; died 1766, in Mannheim.
Medallist.
Joseph Schäfer was the son of Wiegand Schäfer.

SCHÄFER, Karl
German, 20th century.
Born 30 June 1888, in Geislingen an der Steige.
Painter, sculptor. Figures.
Karl Schäfer studied at the fine arts academies of Stuttgart and Munich. He is noted for decorative sculptures in Berlin, Cologne and Ulm.
MUSEUMS AND GALLERIES:
STUTTGART (Staatsgal.): *Southern Plant; Lady in Red* - ULM (Ulmer Mus.): *Little Jörg; Crucified.*

SCHÄFER, Karl. See also **SCHÄFFER**

SCHÄFER, Kurt
German, 20th century.
Born c. 1886; died 13 September 1915.
Active in Berlin.
Painter, engraver (woodcut).
Kurt Schäfer was a pupil of Ludwig Hofmann and Moritz Melzer.

SCHÄFER, Laurenz
German, 19th century.
Born 5 July 1840, in Lüftelberg; died 14 October 1904.
Painter. Portraits.
Laurenz Schäfer was trained by Bendemann and C. Shon in Düsseldorf.
MUSEUMS AND GALLERIES:
COLOGNE: *Portrait of the Theologian Jos. Mooren.*

SCHÄFER, Ludwig
German, 19th - 20th century.
Born 9 December 1879, in Berlin; died 6 March 1915.
Engraver (etching).
Ludwig Schäfer was a pupil of Hans Meyer and also studied in Rome.

SCHÄFER, Maria
German, 19th century.
Born 18 June 1854, in Dresden.
Active in Darmstadt.
Painter.
Maria Schäfer was trained by B. Budde, A. Baur and A. Eisenmenger. She painted altarpieces for churches in Biedenkopf, Darmstadt and Nierstein.

SCHÄFER, Mattheus. See **SCHEFFER**

SCHÄFER, Maximilian
German, 19th - 20th century.
Born 19 June 1851, in Berlin; died 21 July 1916, in Berlin.
Painter, illustrator. Portraits, genre scenes.
Maximilian Schäfer studied at the fine arts academy in Berlin and went on to teach both there and at the fine arts academy in Weimar. He exhibited in Berlin from 1877.

SCHÄFER, Paul
German, 20th century.
Born 10 August 1886, in Tholey.
Active in Bonn.
Painter.
Paul Schäfer studied under Angelo Jank, Heinrich von Zügel and Adolf Münzer.

SCHÄFER, Philipp Otto
German, 19th - 20th century.
Born 28 April 1868, in Darmstadt.
Painter (including gouache), sculptor. Murals.
Philipp Otto Schäfer was a pupil of Ferdinand Keller, Ludwig von Loefftz and Franck Kirchbach. He was first and foremost a fresco painter.
MUSEUMS AND GALLERIES:
DARMSTADT (Hessisches Landesmus.): *Bacchic Scene* (gouache).

SCHÄFER, Rudolf Siegfried Otto
German, 19th - 20th century.
Born 16 September 1878, in Altona.
Painter, engraver, illustrator. Religious subjects.
Rudolf Siegfried Otto Schäfer studied at the fine arts academies in Munich and Düsseldorf. He painted religious compositions for numerous churches in northern Germany and produced book illustrations.

SCHAFER, Theresia. See also **FRANK**

SCHÄFER, Ulrich
German, 18th century.
Active in Neumarkt during the first half of the 18th century.
Sculptor (wood).
Ulrich Schäfer sculpted the high altar of the church of the Visitation in Seligporten in 1728.

SCHÄFER, Wiegand or Vigand, or Schäffer
German, 18th century.
Born 1689, in Copenhagen; died 1758, in Mannheim.
Medallist.

Wiegand Schäfer was the father of Anton, Friedrich and Joseph Schäfer. He was an engraver at the courts of Mainz and Heidelberg.

SCHÄFER, Wilhelm
German, 19th century.
Born 8 March 1839, in Berlin.
Watercolourist, illustrator.

SCHÄFERLE, Friedrich. See **SCHÄFER**

SCHAFF. See also **SAFF** or **SCHAEFF**

SCHAFF, Vojtech Eduard. See **SAFF Vojtech Edward**

SCHAFFENBURG, Pieter van. See **SCHAEYENBORGH**

SCHAFFENHÄUSER, Elie
German, 18th century.
Engraver.
Schaffenhäuser is mentioned by Ris-Paquot in Augsburg in about 1700.

SCHÄFFER. See also **SCHÄFER** and **SCHAEFFER**

SCHÄFFER, Adalbert or Béla
Hungarian, 19th century.
Born 1815, in Gross-Karóly; died 1 March 1871, in Düsseldorf.
Painter. Portraits, genre scenes, still-lifes.
Adalbert Schäffer studied in Pest and Vienna.
MUSEUMS AND GALLERIES:
SIBIU: *Portrait of Kraus, a Street Singer.*
AUCTION RECORDS:
LUCERNE, 17 July 1950, *Still-life of a Laden Table* (1854) CHF 1,200. NEW YORK, 14 Jan 1977, *Still-life of Flowers and Fruit* (1870, card, 12 x 14 1/4 ins / 30.5 x 36 cm) USD 1,100. NEW YORK, 26 Feb 1986, *Still-life of Fruit* (1858, oil on canvas, 17 3/4 x 21 ins / 45 x 53.6 cm) USD 6,000. MUNICH, 25 June 1992, *Still-life of Grapes and Peaches by a Silver Jug and a Glass of Wine* (oil on panel, 19 3/4 x 17 1/4 ins / 50 x 44 cm) DEM 4,520. CONNECTICUT, 9 Aug 1999, *Fruit and Tankards* (oil on panel, 36x30 ins / 91x76 cm) USD 8,250. NEW YORK, 13 Sept 2000, *Still-life with Grapes, Pomegranate and Nautilus Cup* (1853, oil on panel, 19x15 ins / 47x37 cm) USD 3,200. COLOGNE, 4 July 2002, *Still-life with Fruit and Trophy* (1857, oil on panel, 22x16 ins / 55x40 cm) EUR 2,200. MUNICH, 4 Dec 2002, *Still-life with Roses in a Delft Vase and Coin-covered Tankard* (oil on panel, 14x11 ins / 36x29 cm) EUR 1,900. MUNICH, 5 Nov 2003, *Still-life with Flowers and Fruit* (1857, oil on board, 24x28 ins / 60x70 cm) EUR 6,000.

SCHÄFFER, Amand, or Scheffer or Schöffer
German, 15th - 16th century.
Born c. 1454, in Strasbourg; died 27 June 1534, in Salem.
Miniaturist.
Amand Schäffer was a Cistercian monk.

SCHAFFER, Amélie
Austrian, 19th century.
Active in Vienna c. 1840.
Miniaturist.
Amélie Schaffer painted and drew portraits and groups.

SCHÄFFER, Anton
German, 17th century.
Active in Munich in 1649.
Painter.

SCHÄFFER, August. See **SCHAEFFER**

SCHÄFFER, Eugen Eduard. See **SCHAEFFER**

SCHÄFFER, Friedrich or Carl Friedrich, or Schäfer
German, 18th century.
Died at the end of September 1781, in Rome.
Sculptor.
Friedrich or Carl Friedrich Schäffer trained under Gottfried Knöfler in Dresden. He was a sculptor at the court in Dresden and also worked for Meissen Porcelain Factory.

SCHAFFER, Gustav Adolf
German, 20th century.
Born 14 November 1881, in Niederhäslich.
Active in Chemnitz.
Painter, engraver.
Gustav Adolf Schaffer studied at the Dresden college of decorative arts.
MUSEUMS AND GALLERIES:
CHEMNITZ - DRESDEN - MAGDEBURG.

SCHAFFER, Hans
German, 17th century.
Sculptor (wood).
MUSEUMS AND GALLERIES:
DRESDEN: three richly decorated spoons.

SCHÄFFER, Hans Jacob, or Schöffer
German, 17th century.
Died 20 August 1662, in Frankfurt am Main.
Active in Ettersheim.
Painter.

SCHAFFER, Hinrich
German, 18th century.
Sculptor. Statues.
Hinrich Schaffer was active in Berlin. He also carved the wooden statues for the church of Our Lady in Rostock in 1720.

SCHÄFFER, J. G.
German, 18th century.
Sculptor (wood).
J. G. Schäffer carved the louver for the pulpit of the church of St Nicholas in Rostock in 1755.

SCHAFFER, J. Melchior
German, 18th century.
Active in Neustadt-on-the-Saale during the second half of the 18th century.
Painter.
J. Melchior Schaffer painted the altarpiece for the church in Mallrichstadt. It depicts the *Death of St Kilian* and is dated 1772.

SCHÄFFER, Johann Michael. See **SCHÄFER**

SCHÄFFER, Johannes David
German, 17th century.
Active in Tübingen in 1631.
Silhouettist.

SCHÄFFER, Jósef
Hungarian, 19th century.
Painter.
The father of Adalbert Schäffer, Jósef Schäffer painted two altarpieces in the church in Vál in 1824.

SCHAFFER, Joseph
Austrian, 18th - 19th century.
Active in Vienna from 1780 to 1810.
Draughtsman, engraver (burin).
Joseph Schaffer was the brother of Peter Schaffer, with whom he engraved views and genre scenes.

AUCTION RECORDS:
LONDON, 6 June 1983, *View of Innsbruck, the Capital of the Tyrol* (1786, coloured etching, after Peter Schaffer, 13 x 18 ins / 33.3 x 45.7 cm) GBP 600.

SCHÄFFER, Karl, or Schäfer
German, 19th century.
Born 20 April 1821, in Frankfurt am Main; died 20 May 1902, in Kronberg.
Watercolourist, engraver (etching). Landscapes.
Karl Schäffer was trained by J. Becker.
AUCTION RECORDS:
MUNICH, 26 Nov 1981, *Mountainscape with a Mill* (watercolour, 7 x 8 1/2 ins / 18 x 21.5 cm) DEM 3,000.

SCHÄFFER, Ludwig
German, 19th century.
Painter. Genre scenes.
Ludwig Schäffer exhibited in Karlsruhe in 1861.
MUSEUMS AND GALLERIES:
KARLSRUHE: *Rural Scene.*

SCHÄFFER, Magdalena Margrethe.
See **BAERENS Magdalene Margrethe**

SCHÄFFER, Mattheus. See **SCHEFFER**

SCHAFFER, Peter
Austrian, 18th - 19th century.
Active in Vienna from 1780 to 1810.
Draughtsman, engraver (burin).
Peter Schaffer was the brother of Joseph Schaffer with whom he worked.

SCHÄFFER, Wiegand or Vigand.
See **SCHÄFER**

SCHÄFFER, Wilhelm
German, 20th century.
Born 19 February 1891, in Neckargartach.
Active in Heilbronn.
Painter, sculptor.
Wilhelm Schäffer was a pupil of Heinrich Altherr.
MUSEUMS AND GALLERIES:
STUTTGART.

SCHAFFGOTSCH, Franz (Graf)
German, 20th century.
Painter.
Franz Schaffgotsch died in a concentration camp during World War II but examples of his work survived; some were featured at *Verfemt. Vergessen. Wiederentdeckt. Schicksale expressiver Bildkunst im 20. Jahrhundert* (*Condemned. Forgotten. Rediscovered. The Fate of Expressive Art in the 20th Century*), an exhibition held in 2001 at the Cultural and Historical Museum in Osnabrück to 'rediscover' a generation of German and Austrian artists of the 1920s and 1930s whose work was consigned to oblivion in the wake of cultural and political oppression by the Nazi regime.
BIBLIOGRAPHY:
Verfemt. Vergessen. Wiederentdeckt. Schicksale expressiver Bildkunst im 20. Jahrhundert. Sammlung Gerhard Schneider, exhibition catalogue, Kulturgeschichtiches Museum, Osnabrück, 2001.

SCHAFFHAUSER, Elias, or Schafhauser
German, 18th century.
Born c. 1684; died 1738, in Augsburg.
Engraver (burin).
Schaffhauser worked initially in Augsburg, then, from 1720 onwards, in Vienna. He engraved portraits, views and illustrations for books.

SCHAFFHIRT, Johann Michael
German, 18th century.
Active in Stolberg during the second half of the 18th century.
Painter.
Schaffhirt painted the altar of the church in Vatterode in 1761.

SCHÄFFLER, Johann Christoph
German, 18th century.
Painter.
Schäffler worked at Meissen Porcelain Factory in 1712.

SCHÄFFLER, Johann Engelhard.
See **SCHÄFLER**

SCHÄFFLER, Mathias
German, 18th century.
Sculptor (wood).
Schäffler carved altars for the churches in Bertoldshofen, Buch-am-Erlbach and Oberostendorf.

SCHAFFNABURGENSIS, Matthaus
German, 16th century.
Active in Wittenberg during the first half of the 16th century.
Engraver (wood).
Wittenberg School.
Matthaus Schaffnaburgensis made woodcuts for a bible published in Wilhelmberg in 1545. His woodcuts carry the monogram: M. S. Some authors believe that he is the same person as Matthias Grünewald.

M. MS. MS.

SCHAFFNER, Ambrosius
German, 16th century.
Died before 1559.
Active in Ulm 1538-1544.
Painter.
Ambrosius Schaffner was the son of Martin Schaffner.

SCHAFFNER, Franz
German, 19th - 20th century.
Born 3 August 1876, in Hamburg.
Painter. Seascapes.
Franz Schaffner studied at the fine arts academy in Düsseldorf.

SCHAFFNER, Marcel
Swiss, 20th century.
Born 1931.
Painter (including gouache).
AUCTION RECORDS:
LUCERNE, 24 Nov 1990, *Outside Town* (oil/synthetic resin, 55 x 48 ins / 140 x 122 cm) CHF 15,000. LUCERNE, 23 May 1992, *Drawing* (1985, gouache and chalk/paper, 27 1/2 x 39 1/4 ins / 70 x 100 cm) CHF 4,000. LUCERNE, 8 June 1996, *Untitled* (1965, gouache/paper, 20 3/4 x 17 3/4 ins / 53 x 45 cm) CHF 1,500. ZURICH, 23 March 1999, *Number 3* (1961, gouache, 15 x 19 ins / 38 x 49 cm) CHF 2,400. LUCERNE, 22 Nov 2003, *Composition* (1953, oil on canvas, 21 x 17 ins / 53 x 43 cm) CHF 3,000.

SCHAFFNER, Martin or Martino
German, 15th - 16th century.
Born 1478 or 1479, in Ulm; died between 9 August 1546 and 6 February 1549, in Ulm.
Painter, engraver (wood), medallist. Religious subjects, portraits, vanitas.
Ulm School.
Martin Schaffner was the father of Ambrosius Schaffner. His monogram is a superimposed M and S, though it sometimes consists of the letters MM. S. M. Z. V., which translate as 'Martin Schaffer Malher zu Ulm' (Martin Schaffer Painter in Ulm). The archives for 1496 show that he was in Ennetach

as a collaborator with Jörg Stocker, but there is no further trace of him until 1508, when he appears in the register of the burghers of Ulm.

Painting at the start of the 16th century, Schaffner was prolific. His works are signed and dated and include: a series of Old Testament scenes between 1510 and 1519, now in the Staatsgalerie, Stuttgart; scenes from the *Passion* in the Städtische Kunstsammlungen in Augsburg; an *Adoration of the Magi* in the Germanisches Nationalmuseum in Nuremberg, which is part of a lost retable for which the agreed date is 1512; four scenes from the *Life of the Virgin* that were also part of a retable, this time in Wettenhausen, painted in 1523-1524; and the retable for the high altar of Ulm, known as the *Hutz Altar* after the name of the family that donated it.

Schaffner was not only a painter of religious pictures, but one of the rare portraitists of his time. This point underlines the link between his works and those of Holbein the Elder, who certainly influenced him. The influence has recently been established by the discovery in the museum of Béziers of a *Virgin* carrying Schaffner's monogram. He also appears to have been influenced by his Ulm compatriot Zeitblon, and by Dürer's disciple Schäuffelein. His most important portraits are *Count Wolfgang of Öttingen* of 1508 and *Eitel Hans Besserer I von Schnürpflingen* painted around 1533, both in the Alte Pinakothek in Munich. This gallery thus has the most important collection of Schaffner's work. The museum of Berlin has a *Portrait of a Man* by him that contains a *vanitas*; a skull that symbolises the central and only certain outcome of human life. The portrait of *Eitel Besserer* already mentioned depicts an undisguisedly old man with a bushy beard and a fur cap saying his rosary, his face wrinkled by the years; a man meditating on his own death.

Museums and Galleries:
AUGSBURG (Schaezler-Palais, Staatsgal.): eight panels from an altarpiece representing the Passion - BERLIN: two altar side panels - BERLIN (National Mus.): *Six Saints in a Garden; Portrait of a Man with a Skull* - DIJON: *Annunciation; Adoration of the Child Jesus* - HANOVER: *Portrait of a Man with Blond Curls* - KARLSRUHE: *St Peter the Apostle; St Paul the Apostle* - KASSEL: plate painted with allegories, astrology and other things - MUNICH (Alte Pinakothek): *Annunciation; Presentation in the Temple; Holy Spirit; Death of the Virgin; Count Wolfgang I of Öttingen; Eitel Hans Besserer I von Schnürpflingen* - MUNICH (Bayerisches Nationalmus.): *Jesus Taking Leave of his Mother* - NUREMBERG: *Adoration of the Magi; The Apostle Philip; The Apostle James the Younger* - OBERSCHLEISSHEIM (Neues Schloss Schleissheim, Staatsgal.): *Scene from the Passion* - STUTTGART: *Entombment; Descent from the Cross; Resurrection of Christ; Holy Spirit; Epitaph for the Amoyl Family; Ludwig von Freyberg and his Wife; Wendelin, the Holy Shepherd; Nicholas of Bari in Bishop's Vestments.*

Auction records:
LONDON, 16 July 1930, *Marriage of the Virgin*, GBP 125. LONDON, 21 June 1968, *Jesus Appearing to the Virgin and the Apostles in the Garden*, Gns 8,000. MUNICH, 29 Sept 1999, *Death of Mary* (oil on panel, 11 x 44 ins / 28 x 111 cm) DEM 32,000.

SCHAFFOLT, Hans
German, 17th century.
Active in Altdorf in the first half of the 17th century.
Painter.
Hans Schaffolt executed the paintings in the chapels of Blitzenreute and Staig.

SCHAFFRAN, Emmerich
Austrian, 20th century.
Born 29 May 1883, in Vienna.
Painter, engraver. Landscapes. Murals.
Emmerich Schaffran studied under Aviov Hlavacek and Hans Lietzmann. He was an art critic who also painted frescoes for villas, hotels and sanatoria. He also produced landscapes, primarily of mountainous regions.

Museums and Galleries:
HANOVER - TURIN - VIENNA.

SCHAFFROTH, Johannes Stanislaus
German, 18th - 19th century.
Born 1765; died 20 September 1851, in Baden-Baden.
Painter.
Schaffroth was trained by Philipp Jakob Becker in Karlsruhe. He painted altarpieces.

Museums and Galleries:
FREIBURG (MAH): *Portrait of Grand Duke Karl Friedrich of Baden.*

SCHAFFSTOR, Heinrich
German, 17th century.
Active at the beginning of the 17th century.
Draughtsman.

Museums and Galleries:
BERLIN (Kupferstichkabinet): *Body of the Dead Christ.*

SCHAFHAUSER, Elias. See SCHAFFHAUSER

SCHÄFLER. See also SCHEFFLER

SCHÄFLER, Georg
German, 18th century.
Active in Munich in 1727.
Painter.

SCHÄFLER, Johann Engelhard, or Schäffler or Schöfler
German, 17th century.
Active in Kassel.
Painter.

Museums and Galleries:
HILLERØD (Frederiksbörg Slot): *Portrait of Hedwig Sophie of Hesse-Kassel.*

SCHAFLER, Joseph
Austrian, 18th century.
Active in Karlsbad (now Karlovy Vary, Czech Republic) at the end of the 18th century.
Lithographer.
A notable work by Joseph Schafler is *Schiller Mounted on a Donkey* and *View of Petschau.*

SCHAFT, Dominicus
Dutch, 17th century.
Painter.
Dominicus Schaft was known by the nickname Weltvreden, during his time in Rome.

SCHÄFTLMAYR, Carl, or Scheftlmayr
German, 19th century.
Born 10 August 1808, in Munich; died 13 July 1842, in Munich.
Engraver (etching). Landscapes.

SCHAGEN, Adriaen Eeuwoutsz. van
Dutch, 17th century.
Died 1663.
Active in Middelburg.
Portrait artist.
Adriaen Schagen was a pupil of Karel Slabbaert in 1654. He became a guild master in 1657. His career flourished during the period 1650 to 1658.

SCHAGEN, G. van
Dutch, 17th century.
Painter.
G. van Schagen painted a landscape in the town hall at Texel.

SCHAGEN, Gerbrand Fredrik van
Dutch, 19th - 20th century.
Born 1880, in The Hague; died 1968, in Laren.
Painter. Scenes with figures, landscapes.
AUCTION RECORDS:
COLOGNE, 29 June 1990, *Peasant House* (1938, oil on canvas, 15 3/4 x 19 3/4 ins / 40 x 50 cm) DEM 1,400. AMSTERDAM, 30 Oct 1991, *River Landscape with a Swing Bridge* (oil on canvas, 19 3/4 x 27 1/2 ins / 50 x 70 cm) NLG 3,450. AMSTERDAM, 28 Oct 1992, *Polder Landscape with Peasants in a Boat* (1941, oil on canvas, 23 1/2 x 38 1/2 ins / 60 x 98 cm) NLG 2,300. AMSTERDAM, 21 April 1994, *Figures Walking on a Snow-covered Quay* (1940, oil on canvas, 19 3/4 x 27 1/2 ins / 50 x 70 cm) NLG 4,600. AMSTERDAM, 18 June 1996, *View of Amsterdam with St Nicholas Church and the Scheyerstoren* (1942, oil on canvas, 18 x 24 ins / 46 x 61 cm) NLG 3,450. AMSTERDAM, 5 Nov 1996, *Figures in a Boat near a Bridge* (oil on canvas, 27 1/2 x 39 1/4 ins / 70 x 100 cm) NLG 3,776. AMSTERDAM, 19 Jan 1999, *Polder Landscape with Farm* (1945, oil on canvas, 22 x 43 ins / 55 x 110 cm) NLG 4,000. AMSTERDAM, 30 Jan 2001, *Blossoming Orchard* (1939, oil on canvas, 23 x 31 ins / 59 x 79 cm) NLG 4,200. AMSTERDAM, 23 April 2001, *Winter Landscape with Moored Boats in a Canal* (oil on panel, 9 x 12 ins / 24 x 31 cm) NLG 5,500. AMSTERDAM, 19 April 2004, *Sailing Boats for Hire at the Loosdrechtse Lake* (1934, oil on canvas, 27 x 39 ins / 68 x 98 cm) EUR 9,500.

SCHAGEN, Gerrit Lucasz. van
Dutch, 17th century.
Born 1642.
Engraver (burin), picture dealer.
Gerrit Lucasz. van Schagen was married in Amsterdam in 1677, and produced engravings after Van Ostade and Berghem.

SCHAGEN, Gillis van
Dutch, 17th century.
Born 24 June 1616, in Alkmaar; died 18 April 1668, in Alkmaar.
Painter, engraver. History painting, portraits, still-lifes.
Gillis van Schagen was a pupil of Salomon van Ravesteyn and P. Verbeeck. He visited Danzig (now Gdansk, Poland) in 1637, and painted the portrait of King Stanislas of Poland. In 1639, he visited Dieppe, Paris and Orléans. He is known for a number of prints, including a copy of a painting by Michelangelo for the lord of Yvry, and a Christ by Rubens for the lord of Toylière. He travelled to England, and was a spectator during Admiral Tromp's attack on the Spanish fleet. He later returned to Brabant, and visited Liège and Cologne in 1651. He was highly decorated upon his return to Alkmaar.
AUCTION RECORDS:
PARIS, 1870, *The Luncheon*, FRF 700. PARIS, 14 Dec 1989, *Still-life with Monkeys and Parrots* (oil on canvas, 43 1/4 x 62 3/4 ins / 110 x 159.5 cm) FRF 39,000.

SCHAGEN, Jan
Dutch, 17th century.
Painter.
Jan Schagen taught Salomon van Ravesteyn in Alkmaar in 1636.

SCHAGERL, Josef
Austrian, 20th century.
Born 1923.
Sculptor.
AUCTION RECORDS:
VIENNA, 19 March 1985, *Untitled* (patinated metal, 30 x 39 1/4 ins / 76 x 100 cm) ATS 38,000. PARIS, 21 March 1996, *Mecca* (bronze and silver-plated brass, h. 14 1/4 ins / 36 cm) FRF 7,200.

SCHAGK, Albert. See **SCHACK**

SCHÄGOTNIG, Joseph. See **SCHOKOTNIGG**

SCHAIBEL, Johann Joseph. See **SCHEUBEL**

SCHAIDER, Alexander
Austrian, 18th century.
Sculptor.
Schaider sculpted an altar in the church of St Augustine in Rattenberg at the start of the 18th century.

SCHAIDER, Heinrich
German, 15th - 16th century.
Glass painter.
Heinrich Schaider carried out work in the church of St James in Straubing between 1486 and 1503.

SCHAIDER, Niklas
German, 15th century.
Glass painter.
Niklas Schaider worked for the church of St Peter in Straubing in 1486.

SCHAIDER, Ruepp
Austrian, 17th - 18th century.
Active in Salzburg from 1686 to 1708.
Sculptor (wood).
Schaider carved the altars in the churches of Maxglan and Mülln near Salzburg.

SCHAIDHAUF, Johann, or Schaidtauf or Scheidhauf or Scheithauf
German, 19th century.
Active during the second half of the 19th century.
Sculptor (wood).
Schaidhauf worked in Munich.

SCHAIDHAUF, Thomas, or Schaidtauf or Scheidhauf or Scheithauf
German, 18th century.
Born 12 December 1735, in Raisting; died 17 March 1807, in Neresheim.
Sculptor, stucco artist.
Although Schaidhauf was initially influenced by Rococo, he became one of the most important artists at the start of Classicism in Bavaria. He worked in Stuttgart and notably for the monastery in Neresheim.

SCHAIK, Hugo van
Dutch, 19th - 20th century.
Born 1872; died 1946.
Painter. Seascapes.
AUCTION RECORDS:
AMSTERDAM, 24 Sept 1992, *Fishermen in a Boat and Sailing Boats on a Canal near a Church* (oil on canvas, 35 x 49 1/2 ins / 88 x 126 cm) NLG 3,450.

SCHÄKEL, Theodor Wilhelm
German, 19th - 20th century.
Born 1 January 1870, in Hamburg.
Active in Berlin.
Painter.
Theodor Wilhelm Schäkel studied at the fine arts academy in Berlin.
MUSEUMS AND GALLERIES:
BERLIN.

SCHAKEWITS, Jozef
German, 19th - 20th century.
Born 1848; died 1913.
Painter. Scenes with figures, landscapes, seascapes, still-lifes.

AUCTION RECORDS:
BRUSSELS, 5 Oct 1976, *Seascape: Fishermen's Return* (two oils on canvas, forming a pair, 11 3/4 x 20 1/2 ins / 30 x 52 cm) BEF 20,000. LOKEREN, 13 Oct 1979, *Fishermen in Harbour* (oil on canvas, 9 3/4 x 15 ins / 25 x 38 cm) BEF 28,000. LOKEREN, 28 May 1988, *In an Orchard* (oil on canvas, 11 3/4 x 20 1/2 ins / 30 x 52 cm) BEF 44,000. BRUSSELS, 9 Oct 1990, *Boats Run Aground* (oil on canvas, 16 1/4 x 16 1/2 ins / 41 x 42 cm) BEF 40,000. LOKEREN, 20 March 1993, *Still-life with a Duck* (1881, oil on canvas, 20 x 35 1/2 ins / 50.5 x 90 cm) BEF 55,000. LOKEREN, 15 May 1993, *Noah's Curse on Shem* (1876, oil on canvas, 43 3/4 x 55 1/2 ins / 111 x 141 cm) BEF 60,000. LOKEREN, 9 Oct 1993, *Blessing the Boats in Oldenburg* (1875, oil on canvas, 43 1/4 x 33 1/2 ins / 110 x 85 cm) BEF 70,000. NEW YORK, 15 Feb 1994, *Noah Cursing Shem* (1876, oil on canvas, 43 1/4 x 55 ins / 109.8 x 139.7 cm) USD 9,200. LOKEREN, 8 Oct 1994, *Beached Sailing Boats* (oil on canvas, 35 x 55 ins / 89 x 140 cm) BEF 110,000.

SCHALBER, Johann
German, 18th century.
Died 1796.
Active in Betzisried.
Painter.
Schalber worked notably for the monastery in Ottobeuren.

SCHALBURG, Jean Hakon
Danish, 20th century.
Born 27 August 1885, in Vedbaek, near Copenhagen.
Painter.
Jean Hakon Schalburg was a pupil of Henri Matisse in Paris.

SCHALCH
Dutch, 18th century.
Active in The Hague in 1763.
Painter. Landscapes.

SCHALCH, Elias
Swiss, 18th century.
Active in Vienna.
Engraver.

SCHALCH, Johann Friedrich
Swiss, 19th century.
Born 5 January 1814, in Schaffhausen.
Draughtsman, engraver (burin), painter (porcelain).
Schalch emigrated to America in 1850.

SCHALCH, Johann Heinrich
Swiss, 17th century.
Born 9 January 1623, in Schaffhausen; died after 1704.
Modeller (wax).
MUSEUMS AND GALLERIES:
SCHAFFHAUSEN (Mus. zu Allerheiligen): *Head of a Man with a Beard*.

SCHALCH, Johann Jacob or Johann Adolf
Swiss, 18th century.
Born 23 January 1723, in Schaffhausen; died 21 August 1789, in Schaffhausen.
Painter, watercolourist, engraver. Genre scenes, animals, landscapes, landscapes with figures, still-lifes.
Johann Jacob Schalch was trained by Schnatzler and C.-W. Hamilton in Augsburg. He visited Holland and England. He produced notably etchings.
MUSEUMS AND GALLERIES:
BERLIN (Kupferstichkabinet): *Rhine Falls near Schaffhausen* - GENEVA (Mus. Ariana): *Peasants Going to Market* - SIBIU: *Peasants with Livestock; Landscape with Sailing Boat* - VIENNA (Albertina Mus.): *Cavalryman near the Fountain; Beggar; Baptism of Eunuch*.
AUCTION RECORDS:
LONDON, 14 March 1947, *Far-off View of the Church in Langhton*, GBP 115. LUCERNE, 21 June 1974, *Riverscapes* (two panels) CHF 7,200. MUNICH, 30 May 1979, *Flock* (watercolour, 13 3/4 x 20 ins / 35 x 51 cm) DEM 1,800. LONDON, 20 June 1979, *Peasant and Three Horses in a Landscape* (oil on card, 19 x 25 1/4 ins / 48 x 64 cm) GBP 1,000. LONDON, 5 July 1993, *Landscape with Sheep and Cattle* (oil on canvas, a pair, 9 1/4 ins / 23.5 cm and 9 x 10 ins/22 x 24.5 cm) GBP 2,300. NEW YORK, 12 Jan 1995, *Still-life of Birds and Insects in the Undergrowth at the Foot of a Tree* (oil on panel, a pair, each 21 1/2 x 15 ins / 54.6 x 38.4 cm) USD 23,000. BERN, 9 Nov 2001, *Cloudy Landscape with Shepherd, Cows and Sheep* (oil on canvas, 19 x 25 ins / 47 x 64 cm) CHF 6,000. BERN, 14 May 2004, *Summer Landscape with Cows* (1770, oil on panel, 15 x 18 ins / 38 x 45 cm) CHF 6,000.

SCHÄLCHLI, Walter
Swiss, 20th century.
Born 1907, in Bern; died 1984.
Painter.
Walter Schälchli was a pupil of Max von Mühlenen.

SCHALCK, Ernst or Adam Ernst
German, 19th century.
Born 8 March 1827, in Frankfurt am Main; died 23 August 1865, in Frankfurt am Main.
Painter, draughtsman. Genre scenes.
Ernst Schalck was the son of Heinrich Franz Schalck and trained at the Städel Institute in Frankfurt am Main.
MUSEUMS AND GALLERIES:
FRANKFURT AM MAIN (Städel): *Grandfather and Grandson*.
AUCTION RECORDS:
LUCERNE, 19 May 1983, *Midday Rest* (oil on canvas, 31 3/4 x 40 3/4 ins / 80.5 x 103.5 cm) CHF 4,800. FRANKFURT, 17 Nov 2001, *Peasant Family and Herder Resting by Field* (oil on canvas, 38 x 65 ins / 97 x 165 cm) DEM 9,000. LONDON, 18 June 2003, *At the Picture Gallery* (1863, oil on canvas, 24 x 30 ins / 61 x 76 cm) GBP 1,500.

SCHALCK, Heinrich
German, 19th century.
Born 15 April 1825, in Frankfurt am Main; died 1 August 1846, in Frankfurt am Main.
Portrait artist.
Heinrich Schalck was the brother of Ernst Schalck and trained at the Städel Institute in Frankfurt.

SCHALCK, Heinrich Franz. See **SCHACK**

SCHALCK, Johann Peter Joseph, or Schalk
German, 18th century.
Died 3 September 1801, in Frankfurt am Main.
Painter.
Johann Schalck was the father of Heinrich Franz Schack.
MUSEUMS AND GALLERIES:
FRANKFURT AM MAIN (Historisches Mus.): *View of the City of Frankfurt* (1783).

SCHALCKE, Cornelis Symonsz. van der
Dutch, 17th century.
Born in Haarlem, baptised 15 February 1611; died 1671, in Haarlem, buried 5 March.
Painter, draughtsman. Genre scenes, landscapes, landscapes with figures.
Cornelis Symonsz. van der Schalke was the sacristan of the church of St Bavo from 1638 to 1670, and a sergeant with the arquebusiers of St George in 1639. He was married in 1640, and is known to have been active as an artist from 1640 to 1664. His *View of Bloemendael* was kept in the sacristy at St Bavo's until 1870. His paintings show the influence of Adriaen van Ostade, Pieter Molijn and, later, Van Goyen, Van Ruisdael and Rembrandt, to the extent that they have often been overlooked and mistaken for the work of other artists. A *Landscape* in the Louvre was for many years attributed to

Bouwer, for example. Van der Schalke's subjects are often given a highly contrasted chiaroscuro treatment.

C S·V Schalcke 1645

MUSEUMS AND GALLERIES:
BERLIN (Staatliche Mus.): *Dune Landscape* (1652) - CASTRES: *Evening* - HAARLEM: *Landscape with Shepherds* - PARIS (Louvre): *Landscape* - ROTTERDAM (Mus. Boijmans van Beuningen): *Cabin Beneath the Trees* - THE HAGUE (Mauritshuis): *Pig Being Skinned by Moonlight*.

AUCTION RECORDS:
LONDON, 16 April 1969, *The Beach at Scheveningen*, GBP 1,350. LONDON, 15 July 1970, *Landscape with Figures*, GBP 2,800. NEW YORK, 11 Jan 1979, *Travellers in a Wooded Landscape* (1645, oil on panel, 14 3/4 x 22 3/4 ins / 37.5 x 58 cm) USD 24,000. NEW YORK, 3 June 1980, *Peasants in Front of an Inn* (black chalk, 6 3/4 x 10 3/4 ins / 17.1 x 27.6 cm) USD 1,200. AMSTERDAM, 13 Nov 1990, *Travellers Conversing on a Sandy Track, With a Village in the Background* (oil on panel, 15 1/2 x 24 ins / 39.5 x 61 cm) NLG 25,300. AMSTERDAM, 16 Nov 1993, *Fishermen Selling their Catch on the Shore* (1649, oil on panel, 9 1/4 x 12 3/4 ins / 23.5 x 32.5 cm) NLG 43,700. AMSTERDAM, 10 Nov 1997, *Brigands Around a Fire on a Riverbank Beneath the Walls of a Fortified Town, at Night* (oil on canvas, 10 x 12 3/4 ins / 25.1 x 32.7 cm) NLG 11,532. AMSTERDAM, 9 Nov 1999, *Hilly Landscape with Artist Sketching* (black chalk and grey wash, 7 x 11 ins / 17 x 27 cm) NLG 9,000. LONDON, 16 Dec 1999, *River Landscape with Men in Rowing Boat and Cattle on Shore* (1649, oil on canvas, 16 x 24 ins / 40 x 60 cm) GBP 60,000. COLOGNE, 17 Nov 2001, *Wide River Landscape* (oil on panel, 15 x 24 ins / 38 x 61 cm) DEM 20,000.

SCHALCKEN, Godfried or Godfridus, or Schalken
Dutch, 17th century.
Born 1643, in Made, near Dordrecht; died 13 or 16 November 1706, in The Hague.
Painter, draughtsman, engraver. Religious subjects, mythological subjects, figures, portraits, genre scenes, interiors with figures.

Godfried Schalcken studied with Samuel van Hoogstraten in Dordrecht in 1656 and Gerrit Dou in Leiden. He returned to Dordrecht in 1665, where he was a standard-bearer with the arquebusiers. In 1679 he married Françoise van Dimen, of Breda, with whom he had seven children, six of whom died young. He was a guild member in The Hague in 1691, before leaving to spend several years in London, attracted by the success of his fellow-countryman Kneller.

Schalken seems to have made his fortune in England, although some biographers dispute his popularity with the English public. He returned to The Hague in 1698 and was made a burger of the city the following year. In 1703 he was active at the court of Düsseldorf. His pupils included his sister Maria, his nephew Jacobus, Karel de Moor, A. van Boonen, A. Vreem, R. Moris, S. Germyn and Jan van Bentum.

Schalken sought to replicate the 'finished', highly polished, somewhat precious style of Gerrit Dou. He painted small pictures featuring striking effects of light, especially candlelight, for which he is reported to have used a camera obscura. For a brief period he attempted to adopt Rembrandt's bolder handling, but was clearly dissatisfied with the results and quickly returned to his earlier style. His portraits are particularly interesting, and show a certain sensitivity.

G Schalcken, 1699

G S G S G Schalken

MUSEUMS AND GALLERIES:
AMSTERDAM: *William III, Prince of Orange and King of England; 'Each to his Own'; A Difference of Taste; Fire and Light; The Smoker; Josina Clara van Citters; Miss van Gool; Josina Parduyn; Charlotte Elisabeth van Bleyenburgh; Lemon; Woman Selling Herrings* - ANGERS: *The Two Ages* - AUGSBURG: *Palatine Princess; Flagellation of Christ* - BAYEUX (Mus. Baron-Gérard): *Child by Candlelight* (attributed) - BERLIN: *Boy Preaching* - BOURGES: *Ceres Bearing a Flaming Torch* - BREMEN: *Portrait of a Woman* - BRUNSWICK: *Man with a Feathered Hat; Young Man Playing With a Mouse; Young Girl Blowing on the Embers of a Fire* - BRUSSELS: *Game With Melted Wax* - CHÂTEAUROUX: *Woman Blowing on a Stove* - COLOGNE: *Portrait of a Man* - COPENHAGEN (Statens Mus. for Kunst): *Woman Concealing a Letter* - DARMSTADT: *William III* - DORDRECHT: *Portrait of a Woman* - DRESDEN: *Young Girl Reading a Letter; Woman with a Candle; Old Man; Young Man with Earrings; Young Girl Holding a Egg Before a Lamp* - DUBLIN: *Lost Girl's Return* - ÉPINAL: *Woman Visiting a Prisoner* - FLORENCE: *The Artist; Sculptor in his Studio; Young Girl Protecting a Burning Candle; Woman Playing a Trumpet; Young Woman Sewing by Candlelight; Pietà* - FRANKFURT AM MAIN: *Holy Family; Young Girl with a Lighted Candle; Portrait of the Artist* - GENEVA (Mus. Ariana): *Night Scene* - GLASGOW: *Extinguishing the Light* - GRAZ: *Proserpina and Pluto* - HAMBURG: *Child with an Omelette* - KARLSRUHE: *Two Bathers; Soldier Bathing; Musician* - KASSEL: *Woman Selling Waffles; Penitant Magdalene*; two works; *Toilette of Venus, or an Effect of Daylight; Venus Holding Out a Burning Arrow to Cupid, or an Effect of Artificial Light; Old Man in Profile* - LE MANS: *Portrait* - LE PUY-EN-VELAY: *Judith Bearing the Head of Holofernes* - LEIDEN: *Pierre de la Court* - LILLE: *Effect of Light* - LONDON (NG): *An Old Woman scouring a Pot* (1660s, oil/wood); *A Woman Singing and a Man with a Cittern* (c. 1665-1670, oil/wood); *A Candlelight Scene: A Man offering a Gold Chain and Coins to a Girl seated on a Bed* (c. 1665-1670, oil/copper); *Allegory of Virtue and Riches* (c. 1667, oil/copper) - LONDON (Wallace Collection): *Girl Threading a Needle by Candlelight* (late 1670s, oil/panel) - LYONS: *Smoker* - MADRID: *Man Reading by Candlelight* - MUNICH: *Wise and Foolish Virgins; Virgin and Child* - NANTES: *Pygmalion and his Statue* - OBERSCHLEISSHEIM (Neues Schloss Schleissheim, Staatsgal.): *Rest on the Flight into Egypt; Princess Maria-Anna-Louise* - PARIS (Louvre): *Holy Family; Two Women by the Light of a Candle; Old Man Answering a Letter* - ROHRAU (Schlossmus., Graf Harrach'sche Familiensammlung): *St Peter Recognised in the Home of the High Priest* - SCHWERIN: *Little Girl and Boy* - ST PETERSBURG (Hermitage): *Barber* - STOCKHOLM: *Bunch of Grapes* - STUTTGART: *Hermit in his Cave* - THE HAGUE: *William III; Young Woman Fixing an Earring; Pointless Moral; Empirical Doctor; Woman With Two Doves* - TURIN: *The Artist; Latona Turning the Peasants into Frogs* - VIENNA: *Old Man Reading* - VIENNA (Czernin'sche Gemäldegal.): *Young Girl Sleeping, by Candlelight* - VIENNA (Liechtenstein Mus.): *Portrait of a Man and a Woman* - VIENNA (Schönborn-Buckheim): *Joyful Conversation by Candlelight* - YPRES: *Concert: An Effect of the Light*.

AUCTION RECORDS:
DORDRECHT, 2 May 1708, *Bathsheba*, FRF 245. PARIS, 1742, *Halberdier*, FRF 450. PARIS, 1762, *La Belle Suivante*, FRF 1,312. PARIS, 1767, *Tobacco Shop*, FRF 2,410. PARIS, 1773, *Pretty Woman Seated at a Table Threading a Needle by the Light of a Candle*, FRF 1,650. PARIS, 1793, *Pork-butcher's Wife*, FRF 2,001. PARIS, 1801, *Judas Receiving the Price of his Betrayal*, FRF 5,000. LONDON, 1803, *King Stripped Bare*, FRF

10,230. LONDON, 1807, *Family Concert*, FRF 6,040. PARIS, 1807, *Interior of a Tobacco Shop*, FRF 4,800. PARIS, 1837, *Interior of a Dutch Kitchen*, FRF 4,000. PARIS, 1843, *Scene with Soldiers*, FRF 3,500. PARIS, 1861, *Penitant Magdalene*, FRF 2,350. PARIS, 1868, *Surprise*, FRF 3,100. PARIS, 6-9 March 1872, *Eve of Battle*, FRF 4,000. PARIS, 15-17 May 1898, *Flower-girl*, FRF 2,000. PARIS, 1899, *Allegorical Figure* (drawing) FRF 300. MUNICH, 1899, *Young Shepherd and Shepherdess*, FRF 4,363; *Landscape by Moonlight*, FRF 2,875. PARIS, 20 March 1900, *Flirtatious Scene*, FRF 3,125. PARIS, 29 June 1903, *Diana and Nymphs*, FRF 1,210. PARIS, 4-7 Dec 1907, *Woman Looking for Fleas*, FRF 1,250. LONDON, 21 Feb 1910, *Portrait of Cholière and Jean Miel, with Children's Heads*, GBP 13. BERLIN, 3 May 1910, *Portrait of a Man*, FRF 1,120. LONDON, 12 May 1910, *Interior: Light Effect*, GBP 81. LONDON, 13 March 1911, *Sick Woman*, GBP 17. LONDON, 11-12 May 1911, *Boys and Girls with Fruit*, GBP 12. PARIS, 31 May-1 June 1920, *Hermit in Meditation*, FRF 11,200; *Young Woman Working at Cross-stitch*, FRF 1,750. PARIS, 15 Feb 1923, *Portrait of a Woman in a Blue Coat*, FRF 700. PARIS, 22 Nov 1923, *Portrait of a Young Woman as Diana*, FRF 5,000. LONDON, 5 Dec 1923, *Old Woman Reading*, GBP 38. PARIS, 5 June 1924, *Young Woman at her Window*, FRF 4,500. PARIS, 17 June 1924, *Young Woman Beside a Fountain*, FRF 14,000. PARIS, 12-13 June 1925, *Housewife Counting her Gold*, FRF 2,100. LONDON, 16 April 1926, *Vertumnus and Pomona*, GBP 99. PARIS, 20-24 Oct 1927, *Soap Bubbles*, FRF 5,000. PARIS, 23 Nov 1927, *Young Woman at her Window*, FRF 4,200. PARIS, 8 Nov 1928, *Venus and Cupid*, FRF 1,100. LONDON, 3 May 1929, *Satyr and Sleeping Nymph*, GBP 99. PARIS, 15 May 1931, *Portrait of a Woman*, FRF 1,250. PARIS, 16 Nov 1932, *Portrait of a Woman Leaning on her Elbow, Against a Background of Drapery and Parkland*, FRF 630. PARIS, 28 Nov 1934, *Portrait Bust of a Young Woman* (ink wash) FRF 600. LONDON, 9 April 1935, *Woman Selling Cherries*, GBP 126. PARIS, 11 Feb 1943, *Woman Playing the Lute*; *Woman Playing a Piccolo* (two pendants, attributed) FRF 5,600. PARIS, 12 April 1943, *Reading by Candlelight* (attributed) FRF 3,600. LONDON, 16 July 1943, *Young Girl*, GBP 105. PARIS, 18 Dec 1946, *Figures Conversing by Candlelight* (attributed) FRF 1,300. LONDON, 14 March 1947, *Pawnbroker*, GBP 231; *Favourite Parrot*, GBP 178. PARIS, 18 Feb 1949, *Woman Eating Waffles* (attributed) FRF 7,300. PARIS, 8 July 1949, *Serving Girl, Courted* (school of G. S.) FRF 5,800. PARIS, 15 Dec 1949, *Young Boy, Smoking* (school of G. S.) FRF 14,800. PARIS, 19 Dec 1949, *Young Musicians* (1684) FRF 126,000. PARIS, 23 Dec 1949, *Old Woman by Candlelight* (attributed) FRF 53,000. PARIS, 8 Nov 1950, *Drowsy Serving-girl*, FRF 110,000. PARIS, 9 March 1951, *Lines of the Hand*, FRF 28,100. PARIS, 13 June 1952, *Flower-girl*, FRF 320,000. LONDON, 1 May 1964, *Visit to the Doctor*, Gns 800. BERLIN, 3 July 1969, *Narcissus*, DEM 4,800. VIENNA, 22 Sept 1970, *Pipe-smoker*, ATS 32,000. LONDON, 26 March 1971, *Man with a Pipe, by Candlelight*, Gns 3,500. AMSTERDAM, 20 Nov 1973, *Sleeping Woman, Surprised*, NLG 29,000. COLOGNE, 14 Nov 1974, *The Surprise*, DEM 29,000. AMSTERDAM, 30 Nov 1976, *Portrait of a Young Woman by Candlelight* (oil on panel, 17 x 12 1/2 ins / 43 x 32 cm) NLG 20,000. LONDON, 6 April 1977, *Cabaret Scene* (oil on panel, 15 x 12 ins / 38 x 30.5 cm) GBP 35,000. LONDON, 30 March 1979, *Portrait of a Child* (oil on panel, oval, 6 1/4 x 4 3/4 ins / 16 x 12 cm) GBP 14,000. LONDON, 30 Nov 1983, *Salome* (oil on canvas, 45 x 32 3/4 ins / 114 x 83 cm) GBP 34,000. LONDON, 19 April 1985, *Annunciation* (oil on panel, 10 1/4 x 8 ins / 26 x 20.2 cm) GBP 85,000. LONDON, 12 Dec 1986, *Old Woman Feeding a Parrot* (oil on panel, 11 x 8 1/4 ins / 27 x 21 cm) GBP 14,000. LONDON, 15 April 1988, *Seated Three-quarter Profile Portrait of John Acton* (oil on canvas, 49 x 39 1/4 ins / 124.7 x 99.7 cm) GBP 9,900. BERN, 26 Oct 1988, *Young Boy with a Lighted Candle* (oil on canvas, 16 1/4 x 11 3/4 ins / 41 x 30 cm) CHF 2,200. NEW YORK, 11 Jan 1989, *Man Writing by Candlelight* (oil on canvas, 32 1/2 x 26 ins / 82.5 x 66 cm) USD 16,500. STOCKHOLM, 15 Nov 1989, *Figures Around a Table by Candlelight* (oil, 17 1/4 x 14 1/4 ins / 44 x 36 cm) SEK 8,000. MONACO, 2 Dec 1989, *Young Boy Offering a Basket of Grapes to a Woman* (oil on panel, 14 1/4 x 11 ins / 36 x 27 cm) FRF 721,500. STOCKHOLM, 14 Nov 1990, *Face of a Young Woman by Candlelight* (oil on canvas, 24 1/2 x 17 1/4 ins / 62 x 44 cm) SEK 9,700. LONDON, 24 May 1991, *Portrait of a Young Man Offering an Orange to his Lover, While Cupid Draws an Arrow* (oil/silver-plated copper, 7 x 6 ins / 17.9 x 14.4 cm) USD 16,500. STOCKHOLM, 29 May 1991, *Face of a Young Woman by Candlelight* (oil on canvas, 24 1/2 x 17 1/4 ins / 62 x 44 cm) SEK 8,000. LONDON, 3 July 1991, *Portia* (oil on canvas, 40 1/2 x 51 1/2 ins / 103 x 130.5 cm) GBP 25,300. PARIS, 26 June 1992, *Allegorical Portrait* (copper, oval, 7 x 6 ins / 18 x 15 cm) FRF 40,000. LONDON, 10 July 1992, *Narcissus* (oil on canvas, 16 3/4 x 13 1/2 ins / 42.5 x 34.3 cm) GBP 13,200. LONDON, 23 April 1993, *Young Boy Offering a Basket of Grapes to a Woman Sitting on a Terrace* (oil on panel, 14 1/4 x 10 1/2 ins / 36 x 26.7 cm) GBP 78,500. LONDON, 8 Dec 1993, *Young Serving-girl Cooking by Candllelight* (oil on panel, 6 1/4 x 5 3/4 ins / 16 x 14.5 cm) GBP 26,450. LONDON, 17 April 1996, *Woman at her Toilette in Front of a Mirror in a Wooded Landscape* (oil on panel, 14 1/2 x 11 1/4 ins / 37 x 28.8 cm) GBP 309,500. LONDON, 11 Dec 1996, *Young Girl in a Feathered Hat Playing the Guitar by the Light of a Candle* (oil on canvas, 30 x 25 ins / 76.5 x 63.8 cm) GBP 62,000. LONDON, 13 Dec 1996, *Gentleman Offering a Ring to a Woman in a Bedroom Lit by Candlelight* (oil on panel, 15 x 11 1/2 ins / 37.2 x 29.2 cm) GBP 111,500. LONDON, 18 April 1997, *Portrait Bust of a Seated Woman Wearing a Dressing-gown and a Wig, Feeding a Parrot* (oil on canvas, 31 x 25 1/2 ins / 78.7 x 64.5 cm) GBP 128,000. LONDON, 3 July 1997, *Venus and Cupid* (c. 1695, oil/copper, 8 x 6 ins / 20.4 x 15 cm) GBP 32,200. NEW YORK, 29 Jan 1999, *Lady Admiring an Earring by Candlelight* (oil on canvas, 25 x 30 ins / 63 x 77 cm) USD 115,000. VIENNA, 24 March 1999, *Young Girl Playing with Doll by Candlelight* (oil on panel, 10 x 8 ins / 26 x 21 cm) ATS 220,000. NEW YORK, 28 Jan 2000, *Lady Gazing at a Mirror Beneath a Canopy in a Wooded Landscape* (oil on panel, 15 x 11 ins / 37 x 29 cm) USD 775,000. LONDON, 14 Dec 2000, *Boy Playing the Cittern* (oil on panel, 8 x 6 ins / 20 x 15 cm) GBP 130,000. CREWKERNE, 26 April 2001, *Still-life of Peaches, Grapes and a Melon with Butterfly on a Stone Ledge* (oil on panel, 16 x 14 ins / 40 x 35 cm) GBP 9,200. LONDON, 13 Dec 2001, *Young Woman as an Allegorical Figure* (oil on canvas, 13 x 11 ins / 34 x 27 cm) GBP 80,000. ANTWERP, 27 May 2002, *Woman in a Window with a Candle* (oil on panel, 9 x 7 ins / 22 x 18 cm) EUR 2,800. AMSTERDAM, 5 Nov 2002, *Portrait of Matthijs Pompe* (oil on panel, 9 x 7 ins / 24 x 19 cm) EUR 5,000. ZURICH, 19 Sept 2003, *Still-life with Peaches, Grapes and Melons with Butterfly* (oil on panel, 16 x 14 ins / 40 x 35 cm) CHF 18,000. STUTTGART, 11 Dec 2003, *Portrait of a Woman on a Balcony* (oil on copper, 17 x 13 ins / 42 x 34 cm) EUR 6,000. NEW YORK, 21 Jan 2004, *Lovers* (oil on canvas, 30 x 25 ins / 76 x 63 cm) USD 480,000. NEW YORK, 22 Jan 2004, *Woman Weaving Garland* (oil on panel, 11 x 8 ins / 27 x 20 cm) USD 375,000.

SCHALCKEN, Jacob

Dutch, 18th century.

Born 1683 or 1686, in Over-Maasche; died February 1733, in Amsterdam.

Painter. Portraits, genre scenes.

Jacob Schalcken was the pupil of his uncle, Godfried, and a guild master in The Hague, in 1717. Jacob's works are often attributed to Godfried.

AUCTION RECORDS:

MONTE CARLO, 5 March 1984, *Portrait of William IV, Prince of Orange Nassau-Dietz* (oil on canvas, 13 1/2 x 9 3/4 ins / 34 x 25 cm) FRF 45,000.

SCHALCKEN, Maria
Dutch, 17th century.
Painter. Genre scenes.
Maria Schalcken was the sister and pupil of Godfried Schalcken.

SCHALCKH, J. C.
German, 18th century.
Draughtsman.
Schalckh drew 171 plates in the style of J. Bosch.

SCHÄLER, F. A.
German, 18th century.
Portrait artist.

SCHALER, Hans. See **SCHALLER**

SCHALER, Jakob or Philipp Hans Jakob. See **SCHALLER**

SCHALER, Michael. See **SCHALLER**

SCHALHAIMER, Davis
German, 16th century.
Active at the end of the 16th century.
Engraver, designer of ornamental architectural features. Designs (jewellery).
Davis Schalhaimer engraved decorations for rings in 1592.

SCHALHAS, Carl Philipp. See **SCHALLHAS**

SCHALK. See also **SCHALCK**

SCHALK, Ada van der
Italian, 20th century.
Born 31 December 1883, in Milan.
Painter.
Ada van der Schalk studied in Munich with Angelo Jank as well as in Paris and the Netherlands.

SCHALK, Christoph
German, 17th century.
Active in Neuburg at the end of the 17th century.
Painter.
Christoph Schalk was a painter at the court of Neuburg.

SCHALK, Josefine
German, 19th - 20th century.
Born 6 November 1850, in Trier.
Painter. Portraits.
Josefine Schalk studied in Frankfurt under Johann H. Haselhorst and went on to work both in Frankfurt and in Kronberg.

SCHALL, G.
German, 17th century.
Active during the first half of the 17th century.
Painter.
G. Schall painted two altarpieces in the abbey-church of Roggenburg.

SCHALL, J. C.
German, 19th century.
Lithographer, painter.
J.C. Schall trained at the academy in Berlin. He exhibited portraits and religious subjects in Berlin from 1828 to 1860.

SCHALL, Jean Fréderic or Frédéric Jean, or Challe, Chall
French, 18th - 19th century.
Born 14 March 1752, in Strasbourg; died 24 March 1825, in Paris.
Painter. History painting, portraits, genre scenes.
Schall went to Paris at a very young age. In June 1772 he entered the École des Élèves Protégés of the Académie Royale under the patronage of Brenet. He stayed there completing his studies until 1777. Around that time he produced his first works, *Offering to Love*, in 1776, and *Morning* and *Afternoon*, which were engraved in colour by Louis-Marin Bonnet in 1778. Works from that period reveal his signature at that time to have been Challe ('Challe fecit parisiis'), no doubt trying to benefit from the public's infatuation with the Academician Michel-Ange Challe. He later signed his works *F. Schall*.

After leaving the school, Schall immediately found himself launched into the world of frivolous and romantic high society which enlivened Paris during the Ancien Régime. It was a world in which actresses from the Comédie Française, dancers and fashionable women rubbed shoulders with the financiers and princes of whom they were the mistresses. Schall quickly became the beloved painter of this world. While not achieving the importance of Fragonard, his depiction of lesser and often risqué subjects made him one of the most exquisite witnesses to the era of a gentle way of life, a chronicler of 'fêtes galantes', idealised romantic scenes, and a historian of young mistresses.

Schall was at first in the service of Duke Christian IV of Deux-Ponts, and painted the very daring works *Fidèle Indiscret, Finissez!* and *Slipper* for the duke's secret museum. These works were to the taste of German gentlemen in the duke's entourage, and were engraved by Gabriel Marchand or Nerbé. His patrons or protectors included the Érard family, famous manufacturers of pianos, who purchased *Impromptu Bouquet* from him, and the rich marine controller, Godefroy, for whom he produced two famous paintings, *Modesty* and *Coquetry*. These were engraved several times, the latter with the title *Multiple Charms* by Antoine-François Dennel.

From then on, sustained by increasing success and aware of his vocation, Schall continued to produce works in the same vein and style until the end of his career. He called himself a history painter, which should be interpreted as painter of stories and of amorous anecdotes. Sometimes his works playfully depicted a selected scene from the romantic life of his patrons, such as De Beaujon in *While Marriage Sleeps, Love Awakens*, or Abbé de Ventadour in *Romantic Meeting*. At other times his works recounted easy virtues, composing genre scenes in a realistic and at the same time imaginary background, in which he introduced fashionable beauties with satirical intent.

Thus he depicted Madame du Barry in Versailles Park, with her black attendant, the young boy Zamore, and her dog Mirza. He also depicted her at home, surrounded by her familiar objects including the precious Dresden china chamberpot. Madame de Genlis is depicted at the home of the princes of Orléans, initiating the young Louis-Philippe in the mysteries of love, in *Walk of the Favourite Woman, Hour of Pleasure* and *Unofficial Maid*. He also produced works with other themes, equally to the public taste, in the same spirit, such as *Broken Fan, Arranged Model, Comparison* and *La Fleur Consultée*, most of which were immediately reproduced in engravings - often in colour - by Augustin Legrand, Louis-Marin Bonnet, Alexandre Chaponnier and Charles-Melchior Descourtis, among others.

As well as a painter of romantic scenes, Schall was one of the most delicate portraitists of actresses and dancers of his time, bequeathing pictures of Dugazon, Sophie Arnaud, Joseph Dazincourt and Louise Contat from the Comédie Française. He also produced numerous delightful scenic portraits of dancers, often accompanied with variations on their lines, which were destined to decorate the offices of their rich protectors, or the salons of the romantic 'societies' of which they were members. As a painter of ballets, Schall knew better than anyone how to imprint a fleeting movement onto canvas with ineffable grace, as did Watteau, whom he copied.

Schall also worked in a different mode in producing many illustrations for literary works, providing material for engravers. The works *Paul et Virginie* (*Paul and Virginia*), *Para-*

dise Lost and *The Loves of Psyche* and, especially, Rousseau's *Confessions*, provided themes to inspire him. He produced an important series for *Confessions*, comprising *Kiss Given, Kiss Received, Madame de Warens Initiated into Love, Gentle Resistance, Stream* and *Cherries*, which were loose paraphrases of romantic and sentimental scenes narrated by the philosopher. Schall met Jean-Jacques Rousseau at the Marquess of Girardin's home in Ermenonville, and drew the well-known and much copied portrait of him, called *Natural Man*.

At the time of the French Revolution, when spartan behaviour became all-important, he turned briefly to depicting patriotic themes and narrative compositions, such as *Allegory of Liberty* or *General Lacombe-St-Michel Delivering the French from Tunis*, painted in 1797. As soon as he was able, however, he returned to his former, preferred subjects, idylls and tender conversations, such as *Lover Surprised, Rogues*, now in the Louvre, *Engaged Couple* and *Married Couple*. The titles themselves reveal that his later works echoed the lightheartedness of those produced in his youth, and that his public remained faithful to him.

Schall reflected his times, and was both frivolous and important, in the same way as the gentle way of life and the refinements of luxury were both frivolous and important to society. The old painter, whose success had not faded, continued to work hard during the Consulate and the Empire, near his wife and children, in the Louvre, on the chapel staircase, and in the 'Childebert' phalanstery of artists near St-Germain-des-Prés abbey. Records reveal that he exhibited at the Salons of 1793, 1798 and 1806, where the Jury of Arts awarded a prize to his work *False Appearance*. Schall was faithfully depicted as he appeared at that time in Boilly's work *Meeting of Artists in Isabey's Studio*, produced in 1798, now in the Louvre.

Schall's paintings have nearly all been catalogued, accompanied by detailed and sometimes confused pedigrees. Some works were attributed to Fragonard or Callet during the 19th century, and others were even auctioned as works by Jean-Baptiste Huet (*Broken Fan* and *Lover Being Listened To*, attributed to J.-B. Huet at Muhlbacher auction house in 1899).

Bibliography:

Girodie, André, *Un peintre de fêtes galantes: Jean-Frédéric Schall*, Kahn, Strasbourg, 1927. Girodie, André, *Jean-Frédéric Schall*, catalogue raisonné, Hôtel Jean Charpentier, Paris, 1929.

Museums and Galleries:

Château-Thierry: *Portrait of a Young Girl* - Nantes: *Dancer in a Louis XVI Costume; Allegory of Liberty* - Paris (Louvre): *Rogues* - Strasbourg: *Heroism of William Tell.*

Auction records:

Paris, 1862, *Comparison*, FRF 350. Paris, 1870, *Lovers' Nest*, FRF 8,600; *Les Ruches aux Amours* (*Lovers Beehive*, FRF 8,000. Paris, 1873, *Young Girl Tormented by Lovers*, FRF 2,350. Paris, 1873, *Return from Market*, FRF 1,300; *Market Girl*, FRF 1,450. Paris, 1883, *Walk in the Park* (gouache) FRF 3,665. Paris, 1889, *Lady Walking*, FRF 1,560. London, 1898, *Swarm of Lovers; Lovers' Food* (matching pair) FRF 10,500. Paris, 1899, *Woman Lying*, FRF 2,700. Paris, 1899, *Portrait of the Countess of Barry* (drawing) FRF 1,000. Paris, 10-25 March 1901, *Rogues*, FRF 3,000. Paris, 13 Apr-15 May 1907, *Engaged Couple*, FRF 6,300; *Married Couple*, FRF 6,300. Paris, 14 Dec 1908, *Arranged Model*, FRF 1,830. Paris, 28 May 1909, *Dancer wearing Flowers*, FRF 12,500; *Dancer Wearing Mauve; Dancer Wearing Pink*, FRF 28,000. Paris, 17 June 1910, *Young Girl Holding a Rose*, FRF 10,100. Paris, 27 June 1919, *Nest of Lovers*, FRF 3,650. Paris, 12 March 1920, *Stop!*, FRF 30,500. Paris, 6-7 May 1920, *Young Woman in a Park*, FRF 18,500. Paris, 10-11 May 1920, *Feigned Resistance*, FRF 162,000; *Le Coucher; Le Lever* (both) FRF 174,000; *Pretty Visitor*, FRF 153,000. Paris, 6-8 Dec 1920, *Blind Man's Buff*, FRF 13,700. Paris, 15 Dec 1920, *Young Woman in a Park*, FRF 29,700; *Fais le Beau* (*Do the Good Thing*, FRF 30,500. London, 4-5 May 1922, *Woman and Her Children* (sepia wash) GBP 105. London, 20 April 1923, *Cowgirl; Flower Seller* (both) GBP 105. Paris, 22 Nov 1923, *Message of Love*, FRF 10,000. Paris, 25 Nov 1924, *Dancer*, FRF 75, 100. London, 22 May 1925, *Mademoiselle Camargo; Mademoiselle Parizot* (both) GBP 1,207. Paris, 10-11 June 1925, *Dancer*, FRF 45,000. London, 26 June 1925, *Mademoiselle Guimard*, GBP 504. Paris, 27-28 May 1926, *Scenes from The Marriage of Figaro*, FRF 38,000. Paris, 22-24 June 1927, *Dear Portrait*, FRF 240,000. Paris, 24-25 May 1928, *Young Girl Wearing Pink*, FRF 75,000. Paris, 1 June 1928, *Young Musician*, FRF 87,000. Paris, 22 April 1929, *Favourite Dove*, FRF 185,000. Paris, 2-3 July 1929, *Arranged Model*, FRF 51,000. New York, 11 Dec 1930, *Woman Playing the Viol*, USD 1,500; *Pastoral*, USD 450; *Mademoiselle de They*, USD 3,400. Paris, 15 May 1931, *Dancer*, FRF 195,000; *Dancer*, FRF 95,000; *Dancer*, FRF 77,000; *Dancer*, FRF 63,000. Paris, 3 June 1931, *Dancer*, FRF 76,000; *Kiss Given*, FRF 291,000; *Favourite Dog*, FRF 65,000; *Dancer*, FRF 79,000; *Forgiveness*, FRF 132,000; *Interrupted Reading*, FRF 91,000; *Walk in the Park*, FRF 48,500. Paris, 1-2 Dec 1932, *Portrait of a Young Woman*, FRF 39,000. Paris, 20-21 May 1935, *Feigned Resistance*, FRF 85,000; *Le Coucher; Le Lever* (matching pair) FRF 160,000. London, 27-29 May 1935, *Seated Woman* (drawing) GBP 21. Paris, 26 May 1937, *Unofficial Maid*, FRF 100,000. Paris, 9 June 1937, *Stop! or Dangerous Familiarity; Slipper* (gouache, collection) FRF 15,000. London, 22 July 1937, *The Example To Follow; Declaration* (collection) GBP 260. London, 6 May 1939, *Woman Dancing* (matching pair) GBP 462. Paris, 4 April 1941, *Pretty Musician and Her Suitors* (attributed) FRF 10,500. Paris, 20 Nov 1941, *Young Woman in a Park*, FRF 160,000; *Dancers* (matching pair) FRF 360,000. Paris, 28 Nov 1941, *Young Woman with Bichon*, FRF 120,000. Paris, 6 March 1942, *Romantic Scene in a Park* (attributed) FRF 30,000. Paris, 24 Dec 1942, *Lot and His Daughters* (attributed) FRF 50,000. New York, 7-9 Jan 1943, *Favourite Dove*, USD 3,600; *Useless Resistance*, USD 3,300; *Two Friends*, USD 2,500; *Dancer*, USD 4,400. Paris, 18 Jan 1943, *Dancer* (attributed) FRF 220,000. Paris, 7 April 1943, *Love Letter* (attributed) FRF 46,500. Paris, 15 March 1944, *Nest*, FRF 250,000. New York, 24-25 Nov 1944, *Young Woman in a Park*, USD 1,500; *Pretty Visitor*, USD 2,500. London, 27 Sept 1946, *Flirt*, GBP 315. Paris, 25 Nov 1946, *Unlaced Shoe* (attributed) FRF 14,100. Paris, 20 Dec 1946, *Interrupted Sleep* (in the style of F.J. Schall) FRF 68,000. London, 25 June 1947, *Flight*, GBP 260. Paris, 19 May 1950, *Dancer*, FRF 410,000. Paris, 23 May 1950, *Feigned Resistance*, FRF 930,000. London, 21 Dec 1950, *Love; Charity* (matching pair) GBP 609. Paris, 27 April 1951, *Pleasant Meeting*, FRF 250,000. Paris, 23 May 1951, *Dancer*, FRF 820,000. Paris, 9 March 1954, *Unofficial Maid*, FRF 2,140,000. New York, 23 May 1959, *Dancer*, USD 3,000. Paris, 9 Dec 1960, *Bathers or The Comparison*, FRF 10,500. Paris, 14 June 1961, *Lovers*, FRF 14,000. Lausanne, 30 Oct-2 Nov 1962, *Feast of Bacchus*, CHF 35,000. London, 26 June 1963, *Love Letter*, GBP 1,600. Paris, 9 June 1964, *Broken Fan*, FRF 60,000. London, 1 April 1966, *Declaration*, Gns 4,500. London, 10 July 1968, *Young Woman Sitting by a Window*, GBP 2,700. Basel, 24 Jan 1970, *Jeune Danseuse en Costume de Fête Galante* (*Young Dancer Dressed for a Romantic Meeting*) (gouache) CHF 15,500. New York, 8 May 1971, *Dancer (Mademoiselle Colombe)*, USD 8,000. New York, 18 May 1972, *Pretty Visitor*, USD 8,000. Paris, 7 Feb 1973, *Pretty Visitor*, FRF 20,000. London, 13 July 1977, *Young Woman with a Dog* (oil on canvas, 11 3/4 x 9 ins / 30 x 22 cm) GBP 9,000. London, 18 April 1980, *Feigned Resistance* (oil on canvas, 13 1/2 x 17 1/2 ins / 34.2 x 44.5 cm) GBP 22,000. Monte Carlo, 26 Oct 1981, *Seller of Geese in Strasbourg* (oil on canvas, 12 1/2 x 9 ins / 31.5 x 23 cm) FRF 70,000. Monte Carlo, 5 March 1984, *Lovers' Trap* (oil on canvas, 58 1/4 x 37 1/2 ins / 148 x 95 cm) FRF 260,000. Monte

CARLO, 22 June 1985, *Couple in a Landscape* (oil on canvas, 14½ x 11½ ins / 37 x 29.5 cm) FRF 70,000. LONDON, 2 July 1986, *Young Woman with a Dog in a Park* (oil on panel, 10 x 13 ins / 25.5 x 33 cm) GBP 15,500. PARIS, 1 July 1988, *Romantic Scene by a Fountain* (oil on canvas, 17 x 14½ ins / 43 x 37 cm) FRF 45,000. NEW YORK, 28 Oct 1988, *Useless Resistance* (oil on panel, 12¾ x 9½ ins / 32.5 x 24 cm) USD 77,000. PARIS, 9 Dec 1988, *Young Amorous Couples* (two oils on canvas mounted/panel, matching pairs, 5½ x 4½ ins / 14 x 11.5 cm) FRF 20,000. NEW YORK, 7 April 1989, *Portrait of a Young Woman Wearing Country Dress* (oil on panel, 13 x 9 ins / 33 x 23 cm) USD 9,350. LONDON, 21 April 1989, *Interior Scene with a Servant Attracting the Attention of Her Master While a Lover Steals a Kiss from His Wife* (oil on canvas, 31¾ x 29¾ ins / 80.5 x 75.5 cm) GBP 20,900. MONACO, 16 June 1989, *Young Woman Wearing a Green Dress, Sitting in a Boudoir, Holding a Letter on Her Knees* (oil on panel, 17½ x 14½ ins / 44.5 x 37 cm) FRF 99,900. NEW YORK, 11 Jan 1990, *Dancer* (oil on panel, 12½ x 9½ ins / 32 x 24 cm) USD 148,500. PARIS, 25 April 1990, *Young Woman Holding a Dove* (oil on canvas, 13 x 9½ ins / 33 x 24 cm) FRF 75,000. MONACO, 5-6 Dec 1991, *Romantic Scene in a Park* (oil on canvas, 14½ x 11¾ ins / 37 x 30 cm) FRF 77,700. PARIS, 27 March 1992, *Dancer* (pen and wash). NEW YORK, 22 May 1992, *Lover Being Listened To* (oil/copper, 10 x 8¾ ins / 25.4 x 22.5 cm) USD 52,250. MONACO, 18-19 June 1992, *Awakening of Psyche* (oil on canvas, 30½ x 48½ ins / 77.5 x 123 cm) FRF 199,800. LONDON, 21 April 1993, *Don Quixote Tied to a Window by Maritones' Mischievousness* (oil on canvas, 11 x 15 ins / 28 x 38 cm) GBP 3,680. PARIS, 30 June 1993, *Romantic Scene in a Park* (oil on canvas, 12½ x 9½ ins / 32 x 24 cm) FRF 20,000. PARIS, 27 March 1995, *Young Woman Lying on a Sofa* (oil on canvas, 12¾ x 16 ins / 32.5 x 40.5 cm) FRF 35,000. LONDON, 30 Oct 1996, *Portrait of Marie-Thérèse of Savoy, Countess of Artois* (oil on panel, 17½ x 14¾ ins / 44.5 x 37.4 cm) GBP 6,900. NEW YORK, 30 Jan 1997, *Ladies at Market Buying Poultry* (oil on canvas, 15¾ x 13 ins / 40 x 32.1 cm) USD 10,350. LONDON, 18 April 1997, *Louis XIV Declaring His Love to Louise de la Vallière; Louis XIV with Louise de la Vallière in Bois de Vincennes* (oil on canvas, a pair, 14 x 19¼ ins / 35.5 x 49.2 cm) GBP 32,200. PARIS, 14 May 1997, *Portrait of Marie-Antoinette Playing the Harp* (oil on canvas, 17 x 13½ ins / 43 x 34 cm) FRF 128,000. PARIS, 11 June 1997, *Fais le Beau! (Do the Good Thing!)* (oil on panel, 12¾ x 10 ins / 32.5 x 24.5 cm) FRF 85,000. NEW YORK, 16 Oct 1997, *Young Woman Sitting by a Dressing Table by an Empty Bird Cage and a Bird's Nest with Broken Eggs, and in the Background a Young Boy Behind a Curtain Secretly Watching Her* (oil on panel, 11¼ x 9¾ ins / 28.6 x 24.7 cm) USD 10,350. PARIS, 17 Dec 1997, *Arranged Model* (canvas, 16¼ x 12¾ ins / 41.5 x 32.5 cm) FRF 65,000. NEW YORK, 30 Jan 1998, *Young Woman before a Laid Table with Her Dog* (oil on panel, 13 x 10 ins / 32.1 x 24.5 cm) USD 51,750. PARIS, 30 March 1998, *Young Dancer Before a Park with a Waterfall* (oil on panel, 12½ x 9½ ins / 31.5 x 24 cm) FRF 65,000. NEW YORK, 28 Jan 1999, *Young Lady in Garden Holding Flower Garland* (oil on canvas, 17 x 13 ins / 43 x 33 cm) USD 30,000. NEW YORK, 29 Jan 1999, *Mademoiselle de La Valliere in the Couvent de Chaillot* (oil on canvas, 13 x 19 ins / 34 x 47 cm) USD 22,000. NEW YORK, 18 Oct 2000, *Amorous Couple in an Interior* (oil on paper laid on canvas, 15 x 12 ins / 39 x 30 cm) USD 3,500. LONDON, 12 July 2001, *Young Girl Adorning a Term of Venus with a Garland of Flowers* (oil on canvas, 13 x 10 ins / 32 x 25 cm) GBP 7,500. NEW YORK, 26 Oct 2001, *Lady at her Toilet* (oil on canvas, oval, 11 x 9 ins / 28 x 23 cm) USD 32,000. PARIS, 2 Dec 2003, *Ladies Running in the Fields* (oil on panel, a pair, 9 x 7 ins / 23 x 19 cm) EUR 14,000. NEW YORK, 23 Jan 2004, *Dancing Lady in a Landscape* (oil on panel, 11 x 7 ins / 28 x 19 cm) USD 12,000. NEW YORK, 4 Feb 2004, *Seated Young Woman by her Dressing Table* (oil on panel, 11 x 9 ins / 27 x 23 cm) USD 5,000.

SCHALL, Joseph Friedrich August
German, 19th century.
Born 3 March 1785, in Glatz (now Klodzko, Poland); died 19 October 1867, in Breslau (now Wroclaw, Poland).
Draughtsman, miniaturist, lithographer, engraver (burin).

Joseph Schall produced pen-and-(Indian) ink drawings.

MUSEUMS AND GALLERIES:
WROCLAW (Muz. Narodowe): *Self-portrait; Landscapes* (drawings).

SCHALL, Marie
German, 19th century.
Active in Berlin.
Portrait artist.

Marie Schall is probably the wife of J.C. Schall. She exhibited in Berlin in 1856 and 1860.

SCHALL, Raphael Joseph Albert
German, 19th century.
Born 27 December 1814, in Breslau (now Wroclaw, Poland); died 18 August 1859, in Breslau.
Painter. History painting.

Raphael Schall was the son of Joseph Friedrich August Schall. He was trained by Carl Sohn in Düsseldorf. He exhibited in Berlin in 1842 and 1844, and in Frankfurt and Leipzig in 1841 and 1854. He painted religious subjects for churches in Breslau.

MUSEUMS AND GALLERIES:
WROCLAW (Muz. Narodowe): *Fiancée of the Artist; Still-life; Self-portrait*; drawings.

SCHALLA, Johann Peter
German, 18th century.
Born 5 October 1720, in Hamburg; died 8 September 1796, in Hamburg.
Painter. Landscapes, still-lifes.

Schalla was an art teacher in Hamburg.

SCHALLBERG, Adolph von
Austrian, 19th century.
Active in Vienna.
Painter. Portraits.

Schallberg exhibited in Vienna from 1837 to 1839, in 1842 and in 1864. He worked for many churches.

SCHALLBERGE, Frédéric and **Pierre**.
See **SCALBERGE**

SCHALLEHN, Christian Gottlieb
German, 18th - 19th century.
Born 8 November 1753, in Berlin; died 23 February 1835, in Hamburg.
Painter, draughtsman. Landscapes, flowers.

SCHALLENBERG, Johann Georg
Swiss, 19th century.
Born 1810, in Zug.
Painter. Portraits, figures.

Schallenberg trained in Zurich under J.C. Schinz and in Düsseldorf under C. Sohn. He worked in Bonn.

SCHALLER, Anton
Austrian, 18th - 19th century.
Born 1773, in Vienna; died 26 September 1844, in Vienna.
Miniaturist, painter (porcelain), draughtsman. Portraits.

Anton Schaller was the brother of Johann Nepomuk and father of Eduard and Ludwig Schaller. He worked at the Vienna Porcelain Factory, and taught anatomy at the academy in Vienna.

MUSEUMS AND GALLERIES:
VIENNA (Albertina Mus.): drawings.

SCHALLER, Charlotte (Mme). See **SCHALLER-MOUILLOT**

SCHALLER, Cyprian
Austrian, 17th century.
Active from 1607 to 1615.
Engraver. Seals.

SCHALLER, Cyprian
German, 17th century.
Active in Coldberg in 1682.
Painter.

SCHALLER, Eduard
Austrian, 19th century.
Born 1802, in Vienna; died 2 February 1848, in Vienna.
Painter.
Eduard Schaller was the son of Anton Schaller. He trained at the academy in Vienna. He travelled a great deal. He painted altarpieces for several churches in Bohemia.

SCHALLER, Eleazar
Austrian, 16th century.
Active in Vienna at the end of the 16th century.
Painter.
Viennese School.
Eleazar Schaller was a burgher of Vienna in 1599.

SCHALLER, Ernst Johannes
German, 19th century.
Born 1847, in Wasungen; died 25 June 1887, in Coburg.
Painter. Animals.
Ernst Johannes Schaller trained under Preller in Weimar. Then he increased his knowledge in Berlin and Dresden, where he studied in the zoological gardens. Upon returning to Weimar he trained under Pauwel. He finally settled in Berlin and became a teacher at Berlin's school of fine art.
MUSEUMS AND GALLERIES:
WROCLAW (Muz. Narodowe): three watercolours.

SCHALLER, Frederic de
German, 19th - 20th century.
Born 19 December 1853, in Augsburg.
Active in Switzerland.
Painter. Portraits, landscapes.
Frederic de Schaller studied in Augsburg, Munich and Paris before settling in Fribourg in Switzerland.

SCHALLER, Friedrich
German, 19th century.
Born 1812; died 23 January 1899, in Berlin.
Painter. History painting, portraits, genre scenes.
Friedrich Schaller trained under A. von Klöber. He was in Rome from 1854 to 1855.

SCHALLER, Georg Ludwig
German, 17th century.
Died 1616.
Painter.
Georg Ludwig Schaller was the father of Ludwig (or Jörg Ludwig) Schaller. He worked in Ulm.

SCHALLER, Hans, or Schaler or Schaaler
German, 16th century.
Born c. 1540, in Ulm; died 1594, in Ulm.
Sculptor.
Ulm School.
Hans Schaller was the son of Michael Schaller I and the father of Jakob and Michael Schaller II. He carved many tombs and low reliefs for churches in southern Germany.

SCHALLER, Isak
German, 17th century.
Born 1590.
Sculptor.
Isak Schaller was the son of Michael Schaller II. He sculpted tombs in Ulm Cathedral and in other churches in the surrounding areas of Ulm.

SCHALLER, Jakob or Philipp Hans Jakob, or Schaler
German, 16th century.
Born 1568, in Ulm.
Sculptor.
Jakob Schaller was the son of Hans Schaller and carved tombs in the church of St George in Nördlingen.

SCHALLER, Johann Michael
German, 18th century.
Active in Velburg during the first half of the 18th century.
Sculptor.
Johann Michael Schaller sculpted the altars in the churches of Eutenhofen, Günching and Velburg from 1728 to 1730.

SCHALLER, Johann Nepomuk
Austrian, 19th century.
Born 30 March 1777, in Vienna; died 15 or 16 February 1842, in Vienna.
Sculptor, engraver (etching).
Johann Nepomuk Schaller was the brother of Anton Schaller and a modeller at the Vienna Porcelain Factory.
MUSEUMS AND GALLERIES:
INNSBRUCK (Tiroler Landesmus. Ferdinandeum): *Busts of Emperors Ferdinand I and Franz I* - LINZ: *Bust of Emperor Franz I* - NUREMBERG (Germanisches Nationalmus.): *Bust of Emperor Franz I* - OPAVA: *Bust of an Unknown Person; Bust of Emperor Franz I* - VIENNA (MM): *Bust of Emperor Franz I; Bust of Hammer; Purgstall* - VIENNA (Österreichische Gal. Belvedere): *Venus Shows Mars Her Wounded Hand; Bust of Emperor Franz I and Empress Maria Ludovica; Bellerophon Fighting the Chimera; Bust of the Painter Jos. Rebell; Cupid with the Features of a Young Man.*

SCHALLER, Jonas
Swiss, 16th - 17th century.
Active in Lucerne 1597-1607.
Glass painter.

SCHALLER, Ludwig
German, 19th century.
Born 10 October 1804, in Vienna; died 29 April 1865, in Munich.
Sculptor, draughtsman.
Ludwig Schaller was the son of Anton Schaller and trained at the academies in Vienna and Munich. He sculpted many statues in Vienna, Munich and Weimar.
MUSEUMS AND GALLERIES:
BUDAPEST (Magyar Nemzeti Múz.): six statues - MUNICH (Stadtmus.): three drawings.

SCHALLER, Ludwig or Jörg Ludwig
German, 17th century.
Born 1588.
Active in Ulm.
Painter.
Ludwig Schaller was the son of Michael Schaller II. He worked for the town hall of Ulm.

SCHALLER, Michael I, or Schaler
German, 16th century.
Born 1510, possibly in Hall; died 1576, in Ulm.
Sculptor.
Michael Schaller I was the father of Hans Schaller and carved statues and tombs.

SCHALLER, Michael II
German, 16th century.
Born 1564, in Ulm; died probably c. 1605.
Sculptor.

Michael Schaller II was the son of Hans Schaller and carved many tombs, statues and low reliefs.

SCHALLER, Michael III
German, 17th century.
Born 1600, in Ulm.
Painter.
Michael Schaller III was the son of Michael Schaller II. He worked at the town hall of Ulm in 1625.

SCHALLER, Romain de
Swiss, 19th century.
Born 8 December 1838, in Freiburg.
Watercolourist, architect. Landscapes.
Romain de Schaller was the husband of Thérèse de Schaller. He trained in Vienna at the home of Th. Hansen.
MUSEUMS AND GALLERIES:
FRIBOURG (MAH): watercolours.

SCHALLER, Stephan or István
Hungarian, 18th century.
Born in Raab.
Active from 1757 to 1778.
Painter.
Stephan Schaller painted altarpieces and frescoes in churches in Western Hungary.

SCHALLER, Thérèse de
Maiden name: de Maillardoz de Rue
Swiss, 19th century.
Born 15 August 1858, in Mâcon, France; died 2 March 1908, in Freiburg.
Painter.
Thérèse de Schaller was the wife of Romain de Schaller.

SCHALLER-HÄRLIN, Käte
German, 19th - 20th century.
Born 19 October 1877, in Mangalore, India, to German parents.
Active in Stuttgart.
Painter. Religious subjects. Murals.
Käte Schaller-Härlin was a pupil of Adolf Hölzel and Angelo Jank. She produced frescoes and paintings on glass for Protestant churches.
MUSEUMS AND GALLERIES:
STUTTGART (Staatsgal.).

SCHALLER-MOUILLOT, Charlotte (Mme)
Swiss, 20th century.
Born in Bern.
Painter.
Charlotte Schaller-Mouillot exhibited in Paris from 1910 at the Salon des Indépendants and at the Salon d'Automne, of which she was a member.

SCHALLHAS, Carl Philipp, or Schalhaas
Slovak, 18th century.
Born 1767, in Pressburg (now Bratislava); died 21 September 1797, in Vienna.
Painter, engraver (etching).
Carl Philipp Schallhas was a student at the Akademie der Bildenden Künste in Vienna, and was appointed a teacher there in 1792. He engraved landscapes and genre scenes. The Magyar Nemzeti Galéria in Budapest owns 12 landscapes and a portrait by him.

RC. Schallhas. ft.1794.
C. Schallhas ft.793

AUCTION RECORDS:
VIENNA, 10 June 1980, *Wooded Landscape with Figures* (oil/metal, 11 x 15 1/2 ins / 28 x 39.5 cm) ATS 75,000. VIENNA, 5 June 2002, *Landscape with Shepherdess and Flock* (1792, gouache on paper/metal, 7x11 ins / 19x28 cm) EUR 2,200.

SCHALLO. See **ALBERT**

SCHALLUD, Franz
Slovak, 19th - 20th century.
Born 26 November 1861, in Pressburg (now Bratislava).
Active in Austria.
Painter. Stage sets.
Franz Schallud lived and worked in Vienna.

SCHALTEGGER, Emanuel
German, 19th - 20th century.
Born 2 September 1857, in Altersweiler; died 4 January 1909, in Munich.
Painter. Portraits, landscapes.
Emanuel Schaltegger studied in Vienna and Munich.

SCHALTENDORFER, Hans
Swiss, 15th century.
Died 1493, in Basel.
Active in Nuremberg.
Painter.
Hans Schaltendorfer settled in Basel in 1479 and painted a *Madonna* and a *St Sebastian* for the city's Charterhouse in 1486.

SCHALTZ, Daniel
German, 17th century.
Born in Danzig (now Gdansk, Poland); died 1686.
Painter, engraver. Portraits, animals.
See also Daniel Scholtz.

SCHAM, Kaspar
German, 16th century.
Died 12 December 1597, in Ottobeuren (Bavaria).
Sculptor.
Kaspar Scham worked in the abbey of Ottobeuren from 1558.

SCHAMBACHER, Wilhelm
German, 19th century.
Active in Berlin from 1844 to 1846.
Portrait artist, lithographer.
Schambacher was trained by E. Meyer.

SCHAMBERG, Morton Livingston
American, 20th century.
Born 15 October 1881, in Philadelphia; died 13 October 1918.
Painter, collage artist, assemblage artist, watercolourist.
Morton Schamberg studied architecture at the University of Pennsylvania, then painting with Merrit Chase at the Pennsylvania Academy of Fine Arts. In 1909 he discovered the modern movement in Paris with Sheeler and was strongly influenced by Matisse, Cubism and then Robert Delaunay from 1910 until 1912. In 1915 he abandoned the plastic development of planes of abstract colours in favour of a more linear and analytical experimentation with forms. This led him to his final phase in 1916, when he allied himself with Dada and the Precisionists.

Schamberg was the first American artist to follow the teachings of Marcel Duchamp and Picabia in his final watercolours, oils and assemblages. His knowledge of architecture and experience in photography prepared him for this, which can clearly be seen in *Machine* of 1916. His career was cut short by the influenza epidemic of 1918.

Schamberg exhibited in New York with the Independent Artists in 1910 and at the Armory Show in 1913. He was one of A. Stieglitz's associates at Gallery 291 and took part in the development of the Society of Independent Artists.

Museums and Galleries:
Fort Worth (Amon Carter Mus.): *Figure* (1913, oil on canvas) - Philadelphia (MA): *Mechanical Abstraction* (1916); *God* (c. 1918).
Auction records:
Washington DC, 8 March 1986, *Untitled* (1915, oil on panel, a pair, 14 x 10 ins / 35.5 x 25.3 cm) USD 116,000. New York, 1 Dec 1988, *Landscape* (1913, oil on panel, 10 x 14 ins / 25.4 x 35.6 cm) USD 66,000. New York, 25 May 1989, *Composition* (1916, pastel and pencil/paper, 7 1/2 x 5 1/2 ins / 19.1 x 14.2 cm) USD 8,800. New York, 30 Nov 1989, *Abstract Landscape* (1913, oil on panel, 7 3/4 x 9 3/4 ins / 19.7 x 24.8 cm) USD 33,000. New York, 23 May 1990, *Untitled - Landscape with Bridge* (1914, oil on canvas, 26 1/4 x 32 ins / 66.5 x 81 cm) USD 308,000. New York, 28 May 1992, *Composition* (pastel and pencil/paper, 9 x 6 1/2 ins / 22.8 x 16.8 cm) USD 14,300. New York, 26 May 1999, *Abstraction* (oil on canvas, 7 x 11 ins / 19 x 27 cm) USD 26,000. New York, 26 May 1999, *Nude* (oil on panel, 11 x 8 ins / 27 x 20 cm) USD 38,000. New York, 29 Nov 2000, *Composition I* (pastel on panel, 10 x 16 ins / 26 x 41 cm) USD 75,000. New York, 5 March 2003, *Composition* (c. 1916, pastel, 6 x 9 ins / 14 x 22 cm) USD 25,000. New York, 21 May 2003, *Abstraction* (oil on panel, 7 x 11 ins / 19 x 27 cm) USD 32,500.

SCHAMBERGER, Nikolaus or Johann Nikolaus
German, 18th - 19th century.
Born 1771; died 1 September 1841, in Erlangen.
Sculptor, gilder.
Schamberger sculpted statues, tombs, crucifixes and baptismal fonts for various different churches in Erlangen and the surrounding areas of Erlangen.

SCHAMMERT, Friedrich or August Friedrich
German, 19th century.
Born 6 December 1817, in Coswig.
Draughtsman. Portraits.
Schammert trained at the academy in Dresden.

SCHAMPHELEER, Edmond de
Belgian, 19th century.
Born 21 July 1824, in Brussels; died 12 March 1899, in St Joost-ten-Noode.
Painter, engraver. Landscapes, landscapes with figures, waterscapes.
Barbizon School.
Edmond de Schampheleer was a pupil of Edmond de Block. He was active for a number of years in Munich, and subsequently settled in Barbizon. His early work included landscapes and original etchings; during his Barbizon period, his paintings evolved to embrace realistic natural scenes, painted out of doors. His work featured in numerous group exhibitions, earning him several awards, including gold medals in Munich (1864), Brussels (1866), Berlin (1872) and Paris (1877).

EDS. E DE Schampheleer 1878

Museums and Galleries:
Antwerp: *Memory of Gouda; Harvest; Memory of the Zuiderzee* - Brussels (MBA): *The Old Rhine near Gouda* - Courtrai: *Countryside around Dordrecht* - Liège: *Storm, Countryside around Amsterdam*.
Auction records:
Paris, 1886, *The Sluipwyck Marshes*, FRF 270. London, 27 May 1910, *Riverbank with Animals*, GBP 4. London, 25 April 1924, *Countryside Around Loosdrecht*, GBP 21. Brussels, 28 March 1938, *Landscape*, BEF 1,350. Paris, 28 Dec 1949, *Harvest* (1853) FRF 1,300. Brussels, 15 June 1976, *The Kralingen Dyke near Rotterdam* (1892, oil on canvas, 21 1/4 x 39 1/4 ins / 54 x 100 cm) BEF 80,000. Brussels, 23 March 1977, *Coastal Landscape* (1869, oil on canvas, 32 3/4 x 55 ins / 83 x 140 cm) BEF 36,000. Brussels, 21 May 1980, *Marshy Landscape at Dusk* (oil on canvas, 26 x 43 1/4 ins / 66 x 110 cm) BEF 100,000. Brussels, 25 Feb 1981, *Marshy Landscape* (oil on canvas, 33 1/2 x 49 1/4 ins / 85 x 125 cm) BEF 130,000. Paris, 18 April 1989, *Cows Drinking* (1877, oil on canvas, 21 1/4 x 39 1/4 ins / 54 x 100 cm) FRF 18,000. Le Touquet, 12 Nov 1989, *The Banks of the River Scheldt* (1866, oil on canvas, 24 x 39 1/4 ins / 61 x 100 cm) FRF 33,500. Lokeren, 21 March 1992, *The North Sea Coast in the Netherlands* (1890, oil on canvas, 33 x 55 ins / 84 x 140 cm) BEF 220,000. Amsterdam, 24 Sept 1992, *Polder Landscape with Cows* (oil on panel, 10 3/4 x 18 ins / 27.5 x 45.5 cm) NLG 2,070. Lokeren, 9 March 1996, *Peat Bog* (oil on canvas, 20 1/4 x 28 ins / 51.5 x 71 cm) BEF 85,000. Glasgow, 25 Feb 1999, *Between Middelbourg and Rotterdam* (1877, oil on canvas, 21 x 39 ins / 54 x 100 cm) GBP 2,800. London, 2 Dec 1999, *Shipping off Dutch Town* (1883, oil on canvas, 33 x 55 ins / 84 x 140 cm) GBP 7,000. Lokeren, 4 March 2000, *In the Polders* (1881, oil on canvas, 33 x 55 ins / 85 x 140 cm) BEF 520,000. Brussels, 17 April 2000, *Riverbank* (1871, oil on canvas, 30 x 40 ins / 75 x 101 cm) BEF 320,000. Calais, 11 March 2001, *Windmills by an Estuary near Rotterdam* (1870, oil on canvas, 25 x 40 ins / 63 x 101 cm) FRF 25,500. Amsterdam, 4 Sept 2001, *Storm Approaching, Cows Fording a Stream in a Landscape* (1890, oil on panel, 18 x 30 ins / 45 x 75 cm) EUR 8,500. Amsterdam, 3 Sept 2002, *View of Dordrecht* (1872, oil on canvas, 19 x 40 ins / 49 x 101 cm) EUR 3,500. Melun, 1 Dec 2002, *Near Dordrecht* (1885, oil on panel, 11 x 19 ins / 29 x 48 cm) EUR 3,000. Brussels, 18 March 2003, *Cowherd and Cattle Returning to the Village* (1856, oil on canvas, 25 x 35 ins / 64 x 90 cm) EUR 2,600.

SCHAMS, Franz
Austrian, 19th century.
Born 22 March 1823, in Vienna; died 22 March 1883, in Vienna.
Painter, engraver. History painting, portraits, genre scenes.
Schams trained at the school of fine art in Vienna. He also produced lithographs.
Museums and Galleries:
Vienna: *Duke Frederick IV is Acknowledged by the Tyrolians; Portrait of Waldmüller*.
Auction records:
London, 16 June 1993, *Thief* (1882, oil on panel, 15 3/4 x 12 ins / 40 x 30.5 cm) GBP 4,025. New York, 7 Dec 1999, *Madonna and Child* (1854, oil on canvas, oval, 36 x 30 ins / 91 x 76 cm) USD 2,200.

SCHAMSCHIN. See **SHAMCHIN**

SCHAMSCHULA, Eric
Czechoslovak, 20th century.
Born 1925, in Prague.
Active in France.
Sculptor.
Eric Schamschula exhibited in Paris, at the Musée du Verre Contemporain, Rouen (1985) and in Brussels. He produced sculptures in decorative sintered glass.

SCHAN, Lukas
German, 16th century.
Active in Strasbourg 1526-1555.
Watercolourist.
Lukas Schan painted designs for woodcuts, and illustrated the famous ornithological work *Historiae Animalium Lib. III qui est Avium Natura* (Zurich, 1555) by the Swiss physician Conrad Gesner.
Bibliography:
Galimard Flavigny, Bertrand, '*Des ailes aux feuilles, les livres d'ornithologie*' in *La Gazette de l'Hôtel-Drouot* n° 2 p. 99, periodical, Paris, 2002.

SCHANART, Antoine, or Schanaert
French, 17th century.
Born in Brussels.
Active in Grenoble in 1616.
Painter.

Antoine Schanart belonged to the Reformed Church. His wife was Jeanne Avenier. In 1608 and 1609 he received payments for portraits and paintings commissioned by Marshal Lesdiguières who appears to have been his main client. On 4 July 1609 Schanart started on the altarpiece representing the *Holy Trinity* for the church of the Frères Prêcheurs, and on 10 September 1610 began a painting representing the *Conception of the Blessed Virgin* for the high altar of the church of the Pères Récollets. On 11 December 1611 he undertook the execution of eight paintings based on the designs of the engineer Jean de Beins, which were to fit in the eight frames in the gallery of Lesdiguières' Château de Vizille: *Pontecharra Encounter* (1592); *Molettes Encounter* (1597); *Siege and Capture of Grenoble* (1590); *Capture of Fort Barraux* (1598); *Fortress of Exilles in the Savoy; Don Rodrigo Defeated at Salabertrand* (1595); *Capture of Chamousse Fort* (1597); and *Defeat of Allemagne-en-Provence*. A fire destroyed six of these paintings in 1825. The remaining two, which were being restored in Grenoble, escaped destruction.

MUSEUMS AND GALLERIES:
VIZILLE (Mus. de la Révolution Française): two battle scenes.

SCHANCHE, Hermann Garman
Norwegian, 19th century.
Born 7 September 1828, in Bergen; died 21 December 1884, in Düsseldorf.
Landscape artist.

Schanche was a pupil at the Kunstakademi in Düsseldorf. He made numerous study trips to Germany and Portugal. Upon his return to Norway, he tried to convey in his work the atmosphere of nature in the Norwegian fjords and mountains.

MUSEUMS AND GALLERIES:
BERGEN: *Landscape* - STOCKHOLM: *Landscape*.

AUCTION RECORDS:
LONDON, 14 April 1924, *Norwegian Landscape,* GBP 35.

SCHANDORFF, Johannes
Danish, 18th - 19th century.
Born 1766 or 1767, in Copenhagen; died 9 July 1826, in Copenhagen.
Painter, silhouettist.

Schandorff worked at the royal porcelain factory in Copenhagen from 1791 until 1797.

SCHANDORFF, Peter
Danish, 18th - 19th century.
Active in Copenhagen from 1796 to 1800.
Painter (porcelain).

SCHANENTHALLER, Hans. See **SCHWANTHALER**

SCHANKER, Louis
American, 20th century.
Born 1903, in New York; died 1981.
Painter, engraver.
The Ten Group.

Louis Schanker studied at the art schools in New York. He lived in Europe, in France and Spain, from 1931 until 1933. He taught wood engraving at the New School for Social Research in New York from 1943 and in 1944 he published a collection of coloured woodcuts.

Schanker held his first solo exhibition in New York in 1934, followed by many others, always in New York, after 1944.

AUCTION RECORDS:
NEW YORK, 24 April 1981, *Still-life* (1937, oil on canvas, 28 1/2 x 35 3/4 ins / 72.7 x 91.1 cm) USD 2,800. NEW YORK, 23 June 1983, *Abstract Composition* (1939, oil on canvas, 36 x 44 1/2 ins / 91.5 x 113 cm) USD 3,300. NEW YORK, 23 June 1983, *Football* (1936, painted wood, low relief, 13 1/2 x 26 ins / 34.3 x 66 cm) USD 1,700. NEW YORK, 1 June 1984, *Mural Project for the 1939 New York World Fair* (1938, tempera, brush, black ink and pencil, 14 1/2 x 30 ins / 37 x 76.1 cm) USD 1,200. NEW YORK, 23 May 1990, *Three Men on a Beach* (oil on canvas, 19 3/4 x 23 3/4 ins / 50.3 x 60.5 cm) USD 13,200. NEW YORK, 15 May 1991, *Untitled - Abstract Composition* (1938, oil on sacking, 27 1/2 x 23 1/4 ins / 69.9 x 59.1 cm) USD 3,025. NEW YORK, 31 March 1993, *North Wall* (1938, gouache and pencil/card, 9 1/4 x 20 ins / 23.2 x 50.5 cm) USD 2,645. NEW YORK, 4 May 1993, *Study of a Mural for W.Y.N.C.* (1937, watercolour and ink/card, 6 3/4 x 23 ins / 17 x 58.3 cm) USD 4,370. NEW YORK, 31 March 1994, *Man in Action* (oil on canvas, 35 x 43 1/2 ins / 88.9 x 110.5 cm) USD 5,463. SAN FRANCISCO, 26 Oct 1999, *Nude with Cello* (oil and sand on canvas, 54 x 36 ins / 137 x 91 cm) USD 18,000. NORTH BETHESDA, 19 May 2002, *Forms* (1944, oil on canvas, 19 x 24 ins / 49 x 60 cm) USD 1,600. NORTH BETHESDA, 19 May 2002, *Untitled, Forms* (1944, oil on canvas, 28 x 35 ins / 71 x 90 cm) USD 1,700. NEW YORK, 19 Dec 2003, *Football* (1938, colour crayon, black ink and pencil, 14 x 17 ins / 35 x 42 cm) USD 2,250.

SCHANN, Alexandre
French, 19th century.
Born in Paris; died in Paris.
Painter. Portraits.

Alexandre Schann was depicted in a famous novel by Henri Murger, entitled *Scenes of Bohemian Life*. It was a fairly honest portrayal of his true nature, and the author originally gave him the name Schannard. However, a misprint accidentally transformed the name of the character from Schannard to Schaunard, and this was how it remained. Schann was the son of a toy manufacturer from the Marais district of Paris and, although he liked to pretend that his youth was more reckless than it actually was, he continued the family business after his father's death. He would often leave the factory to go and compose music or paint, but would almost always leave the composition unfinished, despite starting each project with great enthusiasm. There is a portrait of Schann by Léon Delaine in the Musée Carnavalet in Paris.

SCHANNTZ, Peter
German, 15th century.
Active in Worms at the end of the 15th century.
Sculptor (wood).

Peter Schanntz carved the stalls in the chapel of Büdingen Castle between 1497 and 1499.

SCHANTA, Friedrich. See **SCHAUTA**

SCHANTZ, C. A.
Austrian, 18th century.
Active in Prague from 1755 to 1760.
Engraver (burin).

SCHANTZ, Philip von
Swedish, 20th century.
Born 1928.
Painter, watercolourist. Still-lifes.

AUCTION RECORDS:
STOCKHOLM, 29 Nov 1983, *Still-life* (1975, oil on canvas, 25 1/2 x 32 1/4 ins / 65 x 82 cm) SEK 29,000. STOCKHOLM, 20 April 1985, *Composition* (1977, watercolour, 22 1/2 x 15 3/4 ins / 57 x 40 cm) SEK 13,500. STOCKHOLM, 9 Dec 1986, *Still-life with Turnips* (1983, oil on canvas, 28 3/4 x 36 1/4 ins / 73 x 92 cm) SEK 64,000. STOCKHOLM, 30 May 1991, *Shadows on a Window Blind* (oil on canvas, 24 x 22 ins / 61 x 55 cm) SEK 7,200. STOCKHOLM, 21 May 1992, *Chirico's Green Sky* (oil on canvas, 23 1/2 x 28 3/4 ins / 60 x 73 cm) SEK 22,000. STOCKHOLM, 10-12 May 1993, *Pail Filled with Cassis* (1979, watercolour, 21 1/4 x 15 1/4 ins / 54 x 39 cm) SEK 25,000. STOCKHOLM, 22

Nov 1999, *Still-life with Fennel* (1984, watercolour, 13 x 17 ins / 32 x 42 cm) SEK 21,000. STOCKHOLM, 22 Nov 1999, *Still-life with Apples* (1987, oil on canvas, 20 x 26 ins / 50 x 65 cm) SEK 70,000. UPPSALA, 10 Dec 2000, *Reindeer Soap* (oil on canvas, 39 x 32 ins / 100 x 81 cm) SEK 120,000. STOCKHOLM, 21 May 2001, *Urns* (1990, watercolour, 22 x 29 ins / 57 x 73 cm) SEK 26,000. STOCKHOLM, 21 May 2001, *Wooden Crate with Turnips* (1983, oil on canvas, 39 x 32 ins / 100 x 81 cm) SEK 150,000. STOCKHOLM, 5 Nov 2002, *Bowl Full of Blueberries* (1976, oil on canvas, 29 x 24 ins / 73 x 60 cm) SEK 220,000. STOCKHOLM, 6 Nov 2002, *Vaado Canal* (1990, gouache, 22 x 30 ins / 57 x 75 cm) SEK 35,000. STOCKHOLM, 5 Nov 2003, *Silver Birch Trunks* (1978, oil on canvas, 18 x 22 ins / 46 x 55 cm) SEK 52,000. STOCKHOLM, 5 Nov 2003, *Plums* (1997, mixed media, 15 x 15 ins / 39 x 37 cm) SEK 56,000. STOCKHOLM, 2 Nov 2004, *Redcurrants* (1980, watercolour, 12 x 16 ins / 30 x 40 cm) SEK 31,000. STOCKHOLM, 2 Nov 2004, *Near Vaddo Canal* (1988, oil on canvas, 47 x 59 ins / 120 x 150 cm) SEK 130,000.

SCHANZ, Heinz
German, 20th century.
Born 1927, in Genkingen bei Reutlingen.
Painter.

Heinz Schanz studied under Grieshaber at the fine arts academy in Karlsruhe and went on to live and work in that city. Schanz produces lyrical compositions that are full of movement, employing blocks of colour to create an illusion of depth and transparency.

Examples of his paintings have featured at group exhibitions, most recently in 2002 at *Neue Figurationen Karlsruhe* (*New Figurations: Karlsruhe*), an exhibition held at the Schlichtenmaier Gallery in Grafenau. Schanz also exhibited solo, notably in 1983 in Reutlingen (*Heinz Schanz: Paintings and Drawings*) and in 1994 at the Degeler Gallery in Bad Dürkheim

BIBLIOGRAPHY:
Bardon, A./Gallwitz, K./Schanz, H./Thimme, J., *Heinz Schanz. Malerei und Graphik*, exhibition catalogue, Kunstmuseum, Reutlingen, 1983. Forstbauer, Nikolai B., *Neue Figurationen Karlsruhe*, exhibition catalogue, Gal. Schlichtenmaier, Schloss Dätzingen, Grafenau, 2002.

SCHANZE, Clemens Oskar
German, 20th century.
Born 8 February 1884, in Dresden.
Painter. Figures, landscapes.

Clemens Oskar Schanze studied at the fine arts academy in Dresden.

MUSEUMS AND GALLERIES:
CHEMNITZ - DRESDEN.

SCHANZI, Giacomo. See **SCIANZI**

SCHAPER, Christian
German, 19th century.
Active in Hanover.
Painter, decorative designer.

Christian Schaper was the father of Hermann Schapar.

SCHAPER, Dorothea
German, 20th century.
Born 5 May 1897, in Berlin.
Sculptor. Allegorical subjects. Busts.

Dorothea Schaper was the daughter of the sculptor Fritz Schaper. She studied at the school of decorative arts in Berlin and went on to sculpt portrait busts and allegorical figures.

SCHAPER, Friedrich, or Fritz
German, 19th - 20th century.
Born 13 November 1869, in Brunswick; died 1956.
Active in Hamburg.
Painter, engraver. Figures, portraits, genre scenes, interiors with figures, animals, landscapes.

MUSEUMS AND GALLERIES:
HAMBURG: *Portrait of the Artist's Parents; Farm Interior on the Island of Finkenwärder; Rainy Day in Duhnen; Finkenwärder* - KIEL (Stadtmus.): *In the Suburbs.*

AUCTION RECORDS:
BREMEN, 31 Oct 1981, *Old Woman Sitting in her Doorway* (1905, oil on canvas, 37 3/4 x 28 1/2 ins / 96 x 72.5 cm) DEM 10,500. HAMBURG, 7 Dec 2000, *Wooded Landscape* (1920, oil on canvas, 16 x 20 ins / 41 x 50 cm) DEM 4,800. VEJLE, 13 Nov 2001, *Hamburg Harbour with Fishing Boats* (oil on canvas, 31 x 39 ins / 80 x 100 cm) DKK 40,000. HAMBURG, 28 Sept 2002, *Landscape* (1925, oil on board, 13 x 16 ins / 32 x 41 cm) EUR 2,000. HAMBURG, 11 Oct 2003, *Farmer's Wife with Cows* (1920, oil on canvas, double-sided, 16 x 20 ins / 40 x 50 cm) EUR 2,600. HAMBURG, 19 June 2004, *Village Pond in Langenhorn near Hamburg* (1945, oil on cardboard, 12 x 16 ins / 31 x 40 cm) EUR 2,600. HAMBURG, 1 Sept 2004, *Landscape near Duhnen, Cuxhaven* (oil on canvas, 24 x 28 ins / 62 x 70 cm) EUR 3,400.

SCHAPER, Fritz
German, 19th - 20th century.
Born 31 July 1841; died 28 November 1919, in Berlin.
Sculptor. Figures, nudes. Busts, monuments.

Fritz Schaper was the father of Dorothea and Wolfgang Schaper. He studied at the fine arts academy in Berlin and went on to sculpt monuments to famous people for various towns and cities in Germany.

MUSEUMS AND GALLERIES:
BERLIN (Nationalgal.): *Young Nude Girl Reclining; Bust of General A. von Goeben; Bust of Friedrich Althoff.*

SCHAPER, G.
German, 18th - 19th century.
Born 1776, in Hamburg.
Painter, watercolourist. Genre scenes, landscapes with figures.

G. Schaper exhibited in Hamburg from 1790 to 1791.

AUCTION RECORDS:
PARIS, 21 Feb 1924, *Landscapes with Ruins, River, Figures and Animals* (two watercolours) FRF 900.

SCHAPER, Gottfried Dietrich Christoph
Danish, 19th century.
Born 2 December 1775, in Hamburg; died 21 November 1851, in Copenhagen.
Sculptor. Monuments.

Schaper sculpted the tomb of J.C. Tode in Copenhagen in 1811. He was also an architect.

SCHAPER, Hermann
German, 19th - 20th century.
Born 13 October 1853, in Hanover; died 12 June 1911, in Hanover.
Painter, draughtsman, designer, art restorer. Figures, portraits.

Hermann Schaper was the son of the painter Christian Schaper. He studied at the fine arts academy in Munich and also trained as an architect. He was instrumental in the restoration of the interior of Aachen Cathedral and provided numerous frescoes and mosaics for other churches in Germany.

AUCTION RECORDS:
VIENNA, 11 March 1980, *Street Scene in Spain* (1868, oil on canvas, 16 1/4 x 11 3/4 ins / 41 x 30 cm) ATS 25,000.

SCHAPER, Johann, or Schapper or Shaper
German, 17th century.
Baptised 10 May 1621 in Hamburg; died 2 or 3 February 1670, in Nuremberg.

Glass painter, painter (glazed earthenware). Battles, landscapes.

Johann Schaper went to Nuremberg and settled there in 1640. He mainly painted on glass, decorating goblets and bottles with small landscape scenes and battle scenes, which were executed with meticulous care.

MUSEUMS AND GALLERIES:

MUNICH (Bayerisches Nationalmus.): *Series of Stained-Glass Windows* - NUREMBERG (Germanisches Nationalmus.): *Two Window Panes decorated with Coats of Arms* - STUTTGART (Württembergisches Landesmus.): *Portrait on Glass of the River Danube*.

SCHAPER, Wolfgang

German, 20th century.

Born 23 January 1895, in Berlin; died 1930, in Berlin.

Sculptor, engraver. Figures, sporting subjects, landscapes.

Wolfgang Schaper was the son of the sculptor Fritz Schaper. He studied under Erich Wolfsfeld and Gerhard Adolf Janensch and went on to produce sculptures of children and sports personalities.

SCHAPF, J.

German, 18th century.

Active in 1784.

Painter.

Schapf painted portraits of important persons in the town hall of Landsberg.

SCHAPIRO, Miriam

Canadian, 20th century.

Born 15 November 1923, in Toronto.

Active in the USA.

Painter, watercolourist, draughtswoman.

Miriam Schapiro graduated from the University of Iowa. She is married to the painter Paul Brach. Her early works were marked by the influence of the Surrealist Arshile Gorky. She then evolved into Lyrical Abstraction.

Schapiro regularly takes part in collective exhibitions in New York, for example: Brooklyn Museum in 1947, several times at the Whitney Museum of American Art (1969 and 1971 Whitney Annuals, 1969 *New Acquisitions*, 1971 *Women in Whitney Collection*), Stable Gallery in 1952, several times at the Museum of Modern Art (1957 *New Talent*, 1962 *Abstract Drawings and Watercolours*, 1965 *New Prints*). She also exhibited at the Walker Art Center in Minneapolis in 1972; Carnegie International in Pittsburgh in 1958; the Museum of Modern Art in Long Beach in 1972; and the Harbor Art Museum in Newport in 1974, among others.

She has shown her work in solo exhibitions, at the University of Missouri in 1950; the Wesleyan University of Illinois in 1951; and in New York in 1958, 1960 and 1961.

MUSEUMS AND GALLERIES:

NEW YORK (MoMA) - NEW YORK (Whitney Mus. of American Art) - ST LOUIS (AM) - WASHINGTON DC (National Mus. of Women in the Arts): *Shrine* (1966, lithograph).

AUCTION RECORDS:

LONDON, 2 Dec 1980, *Fan* (1979, collage and acrylic/canvas, 48 x 96 ins / 122 x 244 cm) GBP 3,500. NEW YORK, 2 Nov 1984, *Maria Cosway - Vestiture Series No 5* (1979, acrylic and collage of fabric/canvas, 60 x 50 ins / 152.5 x 127 cm) USD 2,200.

SCHÄPLER, Hans

German, 17th century.

Active at the beginning of the 17th century.

Painter.

Schäpler painted a *St Francis* for the church of the Capuchins in Landshut in 1614.

SCHAPOCHNIKOFF, Lev or Leon. See **SHAPOSHNIKOV**

SCHAPPER, Friedrich

German, 19th century.

Born c. 1810, in Allendorf.

Draughtsman, lithographer.

Friedrich Schapper trained in Munich and worked in Wiesbaden.

SCHAPPER, Georg

Austrian, 18th century.

Sculptor (wood).

Georg Schapper carved the stalls in the cathedral of St Stephen in Vienna in 1722.

SCHAPPER, Johann. See **SCHAPER**

SCHÄPPLI, Sophie

Swiss, 19th - 20th century.

Born 21 July 1852, in Winterthur; died 1921, in Zurich.

Painter, illustrator.

Sophie Schäppli studied in Munich and Paris.

MUSEUMS AND GALLERIES:

ZURICH (Kunsthaus): *Head Study*.

SCHAR, Valentin

German, 16th century.

Active in Speyer in the second half of the 16th century.

Painter.

Valentin Schar was a burgher of Frankfurt am Main in 1578.

SCHARASONE, Bartolomé

Italian, 17th century.

Painter.

Bartolomé Scharasone was the pupil of T. Verhacht in Antwerp in 1605.

SCHARBE, Johann Friedrich

German, 18th century.

Painter.

Johann Friedrich Scharbe was a painter at the court of Dresden before 1727.

SCHARBE, Johann Michael

German, 18th century.

Active in Dresden in 1728.

Painter.

SCHARBE, Michael

German, 17th - 18th century.

Born 1650, in Cottbus; died 1723, in Lübben.

Painter.

Michael Scharbe decorated the altars of the churches in Baruth and Frankena with paintings.

SCHARBE, Michael Friedrich

German, 18th century.

Active in Dresden in 1740.

Painter.

SCHARDNER, Roger

French, 20th century.

Born 2 May 1898, in Paris; died 1981, in Paris.

Painter, draughtsman, engraver, illustrator. Portraits, landscapes.

Roger Schardner studied in Paris and at the École des Beaux-Arts, Angers. He exhibited in Paris at the Salon d'Automne, the Salon des Artistes Français, the Salon des Humoristes, and the Salon des Indépendants, of which he was a member. He also held solo shows in New York, Milan and Brussels. He was awarded an honourable mention at the Salon des Artistes Français in 1929. He was represented in the exhibition *De Bonnard à Baselitz - Dix Ans d'enrichissements du cabinet des estampes 1978-1988* (*From Bonnard to Baselitz: A Decade of Acquisitions by the Prints Collection 1978-1988*) held at the Bibliothèque Nationale, Paris, in 1992. He was made a Chevalier des Arts et Lettres in 1958 and awarded the Arts, Lettres et Sciences crimson medal.

He used a wide variety of techniques, including lithography, illustrated Baudelaire's *Les Fleurs du Mal* (1945), Renan's *La Vie de Jésus* (*Life of Jesus*) (1946), and Géraldy's *Toi et Moi* (*You and Me*) (1945), and did a great deal of typographical and calligraphic work.
Museums and Galleries:
Paris (BNF): *The Seine and the Alexandre III Bridge, Paris* (1928, lithograph).

SCHARDT, Caspar
German, 17th century.
Active in Würzburg at the beginning of the 17th century.
Sculptor (wood).
Schardt carved the pulpit of the church in Himmelspforten.

SCHARDT, Johann or Jan Gregor von der, or Sart or Sarto or Zar
German, 16th century.
Born c. 1530, in Nijmegen; died after 1581.
Active in Nuremberg.
Sculptor.
Johann von der Schardt travelled to Rome and Florence. He made terracottas and was also a metal caster.
Museums and Galleries:
Berlin (National Mus.): *Bust of Frederick II, King of Denmark; Man with a Beard* (a medallion).
Auction records:
London, 24 June 1982, *Minerva* (c. 1570-1575, patinated bronze, h. 20 3/4 ins / 53 cm) GBP 90,000.

SCHARENBERG
German, 19th century.
Active in Berlin from 1805 to 1839.
Portrait artist.

SCHÄRER, H. L.
German, 16th century.
Engraver (burin).
H. L. Schärer engraved plates after J. Saenredam.

SCHÄRER, Hans
Swiss, 20th century.
Born 1927, in Bern.
Painter, watercolourist, draughtsman, mixed media.
Figures.
Nouvelle Figuration.
Hans Schärer lived in Paris from 1949 to 1956 and subsequently moved to Lucerne. He used a deliberately rudimentary calligraphy and thickly applied, strongly pigmented colours to achieve an effect comparable to the Art Brut style as defined by Jean Dubuffet. His subject matter typically comprises female portrait busts against monochrome backgrounds. As a rule, his busts are in the form of a spiral - reminiscent of Père Ubu - and are on occasion complemented by a coarse necklace. The breasts are rarely highlighted other than perhaps as a pair of shallow nipples. The face is framed by straight black hair (or, on occasion, blonde and wavy hair). There is no more than a most cursory suggestion of a nose. The eyes protrude or are heavily accentuated, the cheeks are two round splashes of colour, and the mouth is half-open to expose a double row of carnivorous teeth. Generally speaking, Schärer identified his creatures as *Madonna* or endowed them with a specific first name. A vengeful treatment of his subject is the rule rather than the exception.

His work was shown in group exhibitions in Lucerne, notably in *Art Jeune* (*Young Art*) at the fine arts museum in 1956, and in *Climat de l'Écart* (*Climate of Disparity*) at the same venue in 1969.
Bibliography:
Kneubühler, Theo, *Kunst: 28 Schweizer*, exhibition catalogue, Gal. Raeber, Lucerne, 1972.
Museums and Galleries:
Aarau (Aargauer Kunsthaus): *Madonna; Three Figures; Spring.*
Auction records:
Lucerne, 20 Nov 1993, *Untitled* (1978, 39 1/4 x 27 1/2 ins / 100 x 70 cm) CHF 4,600. Lucerne, 4 June 1994, *Untitled* (1979, ink and watercolour/paper, 6 1/2 x 5 ins / 16.5 x 13 cm) CHF 850. Lucerne, 26 Nov 1994, *Untitled* (1960, mixed media, oil and mortar/canvas, 37 1/2 x 46 ins / 95 x 116 cm) CHF 2,500. Lucerne, 20 May 1995, *Madonna* (1970, oil, mortar, stone and glass/synthetic resin, 35 1/2 x 27 1/2 ins / 90 x 70 cm) CHF 13,000. Lucerne, 8 June 1996, *Untitled* (1961, mixed media/canvas, 59 x 47 1/4 ins / 150 x 120 cm) CHF 3,900. Lucerne, 23 Nov 1996, *Untitled* (1962, mixed media, mortar and oil on canvas, 39 1/4 x 31 1/2 ins / 100 x 80 cm) CHF 2,800. Lucerne, 7 June 1997, *Night Transfigured* (1961, mixed media/canvas, 35 1/2 x 45 1/4 ins / 90 x 115 cm) CHF 4,400. Lucerne, 29 May 1999, *Madonna* (1969, oil, ceramic and snail shells on board, 35 x 24 ins / 89 x 60 cm) CHF 12,000. Lucerne, 20 Nov 1999, *Two Women in Whipping Game* (1971, watercolour and gouache over pen, 15 x 19 ins / 39 x 48 cm) CHF 3,200. Lucerne, 27 Nov 1999, *Untitled* (1968, oil, putty, stone and wood, 8 x 6x2 ins / 21 x 15x5 cm) CHF 2,900. Lucerne, 27 Nov 1999, *Woman in Interior* (1956, oil on canvas, 59 x 37 ins / 150 x 94 cm) CHF 15,000. Bern, 12 May 2000, *Master and Dog Wearing Masks* (1978, oil on cardboard, 11 x 8 ins / 28 x 21 cm) CHF 2,700. Lucerne, 27 May 2000, *Untitled 1986* (1986, oil and paste on canvas, 9 x 6 ins / 24 x 16 cm) CHF 2,500. Lucerne, 26 May 2001, *Night* (1961, mixed media and oil, 35 x 45 ins / 90 x 115 cm) CHF 4,300. Lucerne, 26 May 2001, *Madonna* (1983, mixed media, oil, stones and glass on pavatex, 39 x 34x2 ins / 99 x 87x5 cm) CHF 19,000. Lucerne, 23 Nov 2002, *Small Madonna* (1974, oil, mortar and collage on panel, 29 x 17 ins / 73 x 42 cm) CHF 4,800. Lucerne, 24 May 2003, *Untitled* (1990, oil on canvas, 26 x 21 ins / 65 x 54 cm) CHF 4,000. Zurich, 24 June 2003, *Two Small Madonnas* (1972, oil, mortar, stone, glass and string on pavatex, 28 x 24x2 ins / 70 x 61x5 cm) CHF 4,200. Zurich, 8 June 2004, *Mister X* (1988, oil on paper, 26 x 18 ins / 65 x 45 cm) CHF 2,400.

SCHÄRER, Hans Felix
Swiss, 17th century.
Born February 1586; died 9 November 1636.
Active in Zurich.
Glass painter.

SCHÄRER, Johann Kaspar
Swiss, 18th century.
Born 31 May 1739, in Schaffhausen; died 17 November 1806, in Brunswick.
Painter.

SCHÄRER, Johann or Hans Jakob, or Scherrer
Swiss, 18th century.
Born 9 May 1676, in Schaffhausen; died 9 October 1746, in Schaffhausen.
Painter, architect. Portraits.
Johann Schärer painted portraits for the town hall in Schaffhausen.

SCHARF. See also **SCHARFF** and **SCHARPF**

SCHARF, George, the Younger (Sir)
British, 19th century.
Born 16 December 1820, in London; died 19 April 1895, in London.
Painter, draughtsman, engraver (etching), archaeologist.
George Scharf was the son of a father of the same name. He studied at the Royal Academy Schools in 1838 and immediately started giving lessons in drawing and composition. In 1840 he accompanied Fellow to Asia Minor and in 1843, was

retained as official artist to the British government expedition to Lycia (Anatolia). In 1845 and 1846 Scharf exhibited at the Royal Academy and the British Institution. Scharf was first and foremost an illustrator and, as such, his output was prodigious. He was admitted to membership of the Society of Antiquaries in 1852 and to the National Portrait Gallery Foundation in 1857, going on to serve the foundation as its Secretary and, as of 1882, Principal; he resigned the latter post in 1895. George Scarf was knighted by Queen Victoria.

BIBLIOGRAPHY:

Gray, Donald J., *'Views and sketches of London in the nineteenth century'* in *Victorian Artists and the City: a collection of critical essays*, Pergamon, New York, 1980. Jackson, Peter, *George Scharf's London: Sketches and Watercolours of a Changing City, 1820-1850*, John Murray, London, 1987. Jackson, Peter, *Drawings of Westminster by Sir George Scharf*, London Topgraphical Society, London, 1994.

SCHARF, George or Georg, the Elder

German, 19th century.
Born 1788, in Mainburg, near Munich; died 11 November 1860, in London.
Painter, watercolourist, engraver, draughtsman.
Military subjects, landscapes, urban landscapes.

George or Georg Scharf trained in Paris and Antwerp. In 1815 he was attached to the English army during the campaign against France. He went to London in 1816 and was employed to do drawings by the Geological Society there. He underwent several journeys to France and Belgium, which provided him with subjects for paintings and drawings. In 1834, he became a member of the Institute of Painters in Watercolours. He introduced lithography to England.

MUSEUMS AND GALLERIES:

DUBLIN: *View of Woolwich Hospital in 1824* - LONDON (British Mus.): *Views of Old London* - LONDON (Victoria and Albert Mus.): *Interior of the Premises of the Geological Society* (1816).

AUCTION RECORDS:

LONDON, 10 July 1984, *Buildings of Crooked Lane Removed for Approaches to New London Bridge* (1831, pen and grey wash, 9 1/4 x 26 ins / 23.5 x 66 cm) GBP 900.

SCHARF, Johann

Austrian, 18th century.
Born 31 December 1765, in Vienna; died 6 October 1794, in Vienna.
Painter, draughtsman. Natural history (botanical subjects).

Johann Scharf was initially employed by a wallpaper manufacturer. When his drawings attracted the attention of the botanist Jacquin, the latter employed him as a painter and draughtsman of plants and flowers. He demonstrated an impressive skill for this kind of artwork.

SCHARF, Kenny

American, 20th - 21st century.
Born 23 November 1958, in Los Angeles.
Active in New York City.
Painter (mixed media), sculptor.
Neo-Pop Art.

Kenny Scharf studied at the School of Visual Arts, New York, obtaining a BFA in 1980. At college he met artists Keith Haring and Jean-Michel Basquiat, whose work in the graffiti art movement influenced Scharf, as seen by the graffitied wall in his painting *When Worlds Collide* (1984). He was artist in residence at PS1 in New York in 1981-1982. Scharf believes that the artist has a social responsibility to go beyond the elitist boundaries of fine art and to bring the creative process into everyday life. Fascinated by 1960s television's vision of the future, he cites the children's television shows The Flintstones and The Jetsons as major influences on his work.

Scharf has incorporated pop iconography into his work, such as Felix the Cat and images of Jackie Kennedy Onassis, or washing powder boxes as in *Supersudsil* (1998). His work is often highly stylised and garishly coloured, as in *Absolut Vodka* (1987) or *Tikitotemoniki* (2000). Scharf has painted and exhibited his 'cels', painted frames as part of a series of designs for The Universals, an animated television special on the Cartoon Network. He has also designed a tape dispenser for the Museum of Modern Art, New York, which is sold in their museum shop.

Scharf's exhibitions include at the Whitney Museum of American Art, New York (1983, 1985, 1988, 1991, 1995); *Space Invaders*, PS1, New York (1982); at the Montreal Museum of Contemporary Art (1984); a solo show at the Salvador Dalí Museum, St Petersburg, FL (1997); at the Musée du Louvre, Paris (1992); *Pop Surrealism*, Aldrich Museum of Contemporary Art, Ridgefield, CT (1998); *Closet #16*, Nexus Contemporary Art Center, Atlanta (1998); *Fashion at the Beach*, Bass Museum, Miami (1998); *Kenny Scharf: New Sculpture*, Portland Institute for Contemporary Art (1999); *Splat, Boom, Pow*, Contemporary Arts Museum, Houston; *Sea of Forking Paths*, Appleton Museum of Art, Florida State University, Tallahassee (2001); *Quest*, Vincent van Gogh Museum, Amsterdam (2003); and *Kenny Scharf: California Grown*, Pasadena Museum of California Art (2004).

BIBLIOGRAPHY:

Marzorati, G., *'Kenny Scharf's Fun House Big Bang'* in *ARTnews*, vol. 34, Journal article, September 1985. *Kenny Scharf: New Paintings*, exhibition catalogue, Akira Ikeda Gallkery, Tokyo, 1986. *Kenny Scharf*, exhibition catalogue, Tony Shafrazi Gallery, New York, 1987. *Kenny Scharf: The Master's Choice, Art as Freedom*, Video, Visual Studies, San Francisco, 1990?. Laurent, Rachel, *'Kenny Scharf'* in *Art Press*, periodical, Paris, autumn 1990. *Kenny Scharf*, exhibition catalogue, Tony Shafrazi Gallery, New York, 1998. Blinderman, Barry, et al., *Kenny Scharf*, exhibition catalogue, University Galleries, Illinois State University, Normal (IL), 1998.

MUSEUMS AND GALLERIES:

AMSTERDAM (Stedelijk Mus.): *Supersudsil* (1998) - GRONINGEN (Groninger Mus.) - LOS ANGELES (MCA): *The Light* (1985, acrylic) - NEW YORK (Guggenheim Mus.) - NEW YORK (Whitney Mus. of American Art): *When Worlds Collide* (1984, oil, enamel, spraypaint) - RIO DE JANEIRO (MAM) - SAN DIEGO (MCA): *Resurrection on Bedrock Beach* (1982) - TALLAHASSEE (Appleton Mus.): *Felix on a Pedestal* (1998, silk screen); *The Three Faces of Jackie* (1998, silk screen).

AUCTION RECORDS:

NEW YORK, 6 Nov 1985, *The Idea Falls into Place in Space* (1984, acrylic and spray paint/canvas, 96 x 108 ins / 244 x 274.5 cm) USD 28,000. NEW YORK, 7 Nov 1985, *Fred, William and Friend* (1983, felt pen and coloured inks, 30 x 46 ins / 76 x 117 cm) USD 1,000. NEW YORK, 7 May 1986, *Love* (1982, acrylic/canvas, 60 x 72 ins / 152.4 x 182.9 cm) USD 19,000. NEW YORK, 13 Nov 1986, *Television Set* (c. 1981, acrylic, coloured glass, paper strips and toy/television, 14 1/4 x 10 x 12 ins / 36.5 x 25.4 x 30.5 cm) USD 1,000. NEW YORK, 8 Oct 1988, *Chat* (1982, acrylic/synthetic resin, 38 1/4 x 25 1/2 ins / 97.2 x 64.7 cm) USD 6,050. NEW YORK, 10 Nov 1988, *Untitled (Elroys)_* (1981, acrylic/plastic, 58 x 60 ins / 147.5 x 152.5 cm) USD 5,720. NEW YORK, 4 May 1989, *L'idée tombe à sa place dans l'espace* (1984, acrylic and spray paint/canvas, 96 x 108 ins / 244 x 274.5 cm) USD 49,500. NEW YORK, 23 Feb 1990, *Forever Now* (1984, oil and varnish on spray/canvas in a wood and plaster frame, 55 1/4 x 79 ins / 140.3 x 200.7 cm) USD 93,500. NEW YORK, 9 May 1990, *Travel Time* (1984, acrylic and spray paint/canvas, 72 x 96 ins / 182.9 x 243.9 cm) USD 71,500. NEW YORK, 14 Feb 1991, *Fredopus Realizes* (1982, acrylic and spray paint/canvas, 60 x 94 ins / 152.4 x 238.7 cm) USD 38,500. NEW YORK, 3 Oct 1991, *Pikki Taki*

Chop (acrylic, spray paint and oil on canvas, 87 1/2 x 72 ins / 222.5 x 183 cm) USD 30,250. NEW YORK, 27 Feb 1992, *Elroy and Leroy* (1982, acrylic/canvas, 60 x 96 ins / 152.4 x 243.8 cm) USD 35,200. PARIS, 14 April 1992, *'Je ne sais pas'* (1984, ink/paper, wood, plaster) FRF 12,000. NEW YORK, 6 May 1992, *Major Blast* (1984, acrylic and lacquer spray/canvas, 96 x 96 ins / 243.9 x 243.9 cm) USD 33,000. PARIS, 14 May 1992, *Sculpture montgolfière* (oil/polyester resin, h. 39 1/4 ins / 100 cm, diam. 39 1/4 ins/100 cm) FRF 32,000. NEW YORK, 19 Nov 1992, *Tangello purple tempeto* (1985, acrylic and oil on canvas, 48 x 49 1/4 ins / 122 x 125 cm) USD 26,400. LONDON, 25 March 1993, *New Frontier* (1984, acrylic and spray paint/canvas, 85 1/2 x 87 ins / 217.2 x 221 cm) GBP 8,625. NEW YORK, 11 Nov 1993, *The Days of Our Lives* (1984, acrylic/canvas in a wooden frame by the artist, 115 x 103 ins / 292.1 x 261.6 cm) USD 41,400. PARIS, 16 March 1995, *Ob Glob No. 4* (1989, acrylic/canvas, 40 1/4 x 48 ins / 102 x 122 cm) FRF 27,000. NEW YORK, 22 Feb 1996, *Bali Roma* (acrylic spray paint, plastic collage and oil on canvas, 101 x 126 ins / 256.4 x 320 cm) USD 15,525. PARIS, 11 March 1998, *Why* (1990, acrylic/canvas and frame in Sky green, 55 1/2 x 43 1/4 ins / 141 x 110 cm) FRF 37,000. NEW YORK, 20 May 1999, *Shape Flow* (1984, acrylic and spray enamel on canvas, 84 x 74 ins / 213 x 189 cm) USD 22,000. NEW YORK, 17 Nov 1999, *Hot Dickety Devil* (1985, acrylic, spray paint and oil on canvas, 43 x 38 ins / 108 x 96 cm) USD 6,000. NEW YORK, 17 Nov 2000, *Check Array* (1988, oil and acrylic on canvas, 81 x 81 ins / 206 x 206 cm) USD 18,000. NEW YORK, 17 Nov 2000, *Fertility* (1983, oil and spray paint on canvas, 48 x 72 ins / 122 x 183 cm) USD 68,000. PITTSFIELD, 12 May 2001, *Forever Now* (1984, oil, acrylic and enamel spray paint on canvas, 48 x 72 ins / 122 x 183 cm) USD 17,500. NEW YORK, 18 May 2001, *Agua Polination* (1983, oil and enamel on canvas, 90 x 104 ins / 228 x 264 cm) USD 32,000. NEW YORK, 16 May 2002, *Monumental Structures* (1996, acrylic, oil and mixed media on canvas, 43 x 48 ins / 108 x 121 cm) USD 8,000. NEW YORK, 13 Nov 2002, *Past Is New* (1990, acrylic, oil, silk screen and ink on canvas, 59 x 50 ins / 151 x 126 cm) USD 8,000. NEW YORK, 7 Oct 2003, *Lick Tickles* (1984, gouache, 26 x 38 ins / 66 x 96 cm) USD 2,250. NEW YORK, 13 Nov 2003, *Admire an Admiral* (1988, oil, acrylic and gemstone on canvas, 63 x 63 ins / 161 x 160 cm) USD 25,000. NEW YORK, 13 May 2004, *Green Waves* (1983, oil and spray paint on shaped canvas, 58 x 88 ins / 147 x 223 cm) USD 34,000. NEW YORK, 29 Sept 2004, *News Now* (1988, acrylic, oil and marker on canvas, 106 x 56 ins / 270 x 143 cm) USD 22,000.

SCHARF, Viktor
Austrian, 19th - 20th century.
Born 1872, in Vienna.
Painter. Portraits, genre scenes.

Viktor Scharf studied under J. Herterich, E. Carrière and J. Whistler and went on to exhibit portraits at the Salon de la Société Nationale des Beaux-Arts in Paris.

MUSEUMS AND GALLERIES:
VATICAN (Mus. Vaticani): *Portrait of Pope Pius XI.*

AUCTION RECORDS:
NEW YORK, 24 May 1988, *Preparing a Basket of Fruit* (oil on canvas, 21 1/4 x 25 1/2 ins / 54 x 65 cm) USD 12,100.

SCHARFENBERCH, Jürgen
German, 16th century.
Painter.

Jürgen Scharfenberch painted the coats of arms of the city of Lübeck in the second half of the 16th century.

SCHARFENBERG, Georges van
Dutch, 16th century.
Engraver (wood).

Georges van Scharfenberg is mentioned by Ris-Paquot.

SCHARFENBERG, Wilhelm von
German, 19th - 20th century.
Born 19 July 1879, in Bonn.
Active in Wanfried.
Sculptor.

Wilhelm von Scharfenberg studied in Brussels under Charles van der Stappen and in Paris under Jean Lefèvre and Charles Raoul Verlet.

SCHARFF
German, 19th century.
Miniaturist.

Scharff worked in Mannheim in 1810.

SCHARFF, Anton
Austrian, 19th century.
Born 10 June 1845, in Vienna; died 5 July 1903, in Brünn-am-Gebirge.
Sculptor, medallist.

Anton Scharff trained at the academy in Vienna. His work appeared in Paris exhibitions, including the 'Grand Prix' at the 1900 Exposition Universelle.

SCHARFF, Cäsar
German, 19th century.
Born 22 December 1864, in Hamburg; died 21 October 1902, in Alt-Rahlstedt.
Sculptor.

SCHARFF, Edwin, or Erwin
German, 20th century.
Born 1887, in Neu Ulm; died 1955, in Hamburg.
Sculptor, painter, engraver. Figures, nudes, portraits, scenes with figures, animals. Busts, monuments.

Edwin Scharff initially studied painting under Gabriel von Hackly and one of the Herterich brothers at the school of fine arts in Munich from 1904 to 1907, and it was not until he moved to France that he started training in sculpture (1911-1913). 1913 saw him become one of the founder members of the New Secession in Munich. He served in World War I and, following it, went on to teach at the school of fine arts in Berlin from 1923. He was removed from his post in 1933 when the Nazis came to power. Although he was subsequently hired by the academy in Düsseldorf, he was again dismissed (1937) and this time prohibited from working elsewhere as a teacher. Some 40 of his canvases were confiscated and destroyed. He was appointed to a teaching post at the academy in Hamburg in 1946 and taught there until his death in 1955.

Throughout his career, Scharff returned time and again to a cluster of favourite themes: riders, grooms, men in boats, and full-length studies of women, more often than not with their arms crossed behind their backs. Although he worked in the classical tradition, there are modern touches in his work which echo those of a Lehmbruck or a Maillol, notably with regards to his generous treatment of volumes. Scharff left a substantial number of portraits of his contemporaries, not least those of Heinrich Mann, Heinrich Wölfflin, Max Liebermann, Lovis Corinth and Emil Nolde. He also produced a number of major public monuments, including the *Neu Ulm Monument* (1929-1932), a seven-metre high *Groom* (1936-1939) for the grounds of the Exhibition Centre in Düsseldorf, and a 10 feet (3 metre) high *Mother and Child* low relief for the new public health monument in Hamburg.

Scharff exhibited for the first time in 1913 in Munich and also exhibited in Paris in 1929. Several retrospectives were held, including in Berlin in 1930 and posthumously at the Kunsthalle in Hamburg in 1956.

MUSEUMS AND GALLERIES:

BERLIN (Nationalgal.): *Couple of Lovers* - GDANSK (Muz. Historyczne): *Head of the Artist's Late Brother, a Casualty of War* - HAMBURG (Kunsthalle): *Bust of the Actress Helene Rischer* - KALININGRAD (MM): *Bust of Lovis Corinth* - MANNHEIM (Städtische Kunsthalle): *Head of the Actress Annie Mewes; Athlete; Horses at the Trough* - MUNICH (NG): *Bust of Annie Mewes; Busts of A. L. Mayer and Heinrich Wölfflin* - ULM (Ulmer Mus.): *Coast near Douarnenez; Two Female Busts; Bust of Burgomaster Schwammberger.*

AUCTION RECORDS:

HAMBURG, 10 June 1972, *Kneeling Woman* (patinated bronze) DEM 5,400. COLOGNE, 17 May 1980, *Head of a Woman with a Beret* (bronze, h. 15 1/4 ins / 39 cm) DEM 1,600. MUNICH, 2 June 1981, *Seated Nude* (patinated bronze, 8 x 4 1/4 x 7 3/4 ins / 20.5 x 11 x 19.5 cm) DEM 3,400. MUNICH, 29 Nov 1983, *Bust of a Woman* (1918, patinated bronze, 14 1/2 x 7 3/4 x 10 3/4 ins / 37 x 19.5 x 27.5 cm) DEM 6,000. HAMBURG, 5 Dec 1985, *Horse* (1919, bronze, 7 1/2 x 6 3/4 x 3 1/4 ins / 19 x 17 x 8.5 cm) DEM 6,400. HEIDELBERG, 11 April 1992, *Reclining Female Nude* (bronze relief, 9 x 14 3/4 ins / 23 x 37.4 cm) DEM 2,000. BERLIN, 1 Dec 2001, *Sitting: Torso* (black-brown patinated bronze, 6 x 6x4 ins / 16 x 15x10 cm) DEM 4,500. HAMBURG, 15 June 2002, *Horse* (bronze, 7 x 7x4 ins / 19 x 18x9 cm) EUR 6,300. HAMBURG, 14 June 2003, *Youth Fighting with Swordfish* (bronze, 8 x 8x3 ins / 20 x 20x7 cm) EUR 4,000. COLOGNE, 4 Dec 2003, *Bather* (1914, bronze, 17 x 6x7 ins / 44 x 16x18 cm) EUR 6,000.

SCHARFF, Hermann

German, 19th century.

Born 1817, in Frankfurt am Main.

Painter. Genre scenes, portraits.

Hermann Scharff trained at the academy in Munich.

SCHARFF, Johann Andreas

German, 18th century.

Active in Coburg, from 1760 to 1785.

Draughtsman, engraver, goldsmith.

Johann Andreas Scharff drew the illustrations for a manual on the goldsmith's and silversmith's trade.

SCHARFF, Johann Michael

Austrian, 19th century.

Born 11 November 1806, in Vienna; died 22 May 1855, in Vienna.

Cameo engraver, medallist.

Johann Michael Scharff engraved many medals for his contempories, and cameos bearing the effigies of the Archdukes Joseph and Charles (Vienna Museum)

MUSEUMS AND GALLERIES:

VIENNA (Kunsthistorisches Mus.): cameos.

SCHARFF, William, or Niels William

Danish, 20th century.

Born 30 October 1886, in Copenhagen; died 1959, in Tisvilde.

Painter. Landscapes.

William Scharff studied under P.H. Kristian Zahrtmann and Johann Rohde at the Kunstakademi in Copenhagen. He travelled extensively in Italy, France and Germany. He initially painted in a resolutely Realist style but was influenced by the works of Cézanne and Vincent van Gogh and, latterly, Picasso and, above all, Wassily Kandinsky. He now ranks as one of the most accomplished Danish Cubists. He drew inspiration from the vast tracts of forest in the Scandinavian region, but also produced a number of views of the Tuscan township of San Gimignano.

AUCTION RECORDS:

COPENHAGEN, 22 Feb 1951, *Fir Trees* (1944) DKK 3,450. COPENHAGEN, 15-16 May 1963, *Wooded Landscape*, DKK 14,000. COPENHAGEN, 13 May 1970, *Composition*, DKK 22,000. COPENHAGEN, 25 Oct 1972, *San Gimignano*, DKK 12,000. COPENHAGEN, 28 Nov 1974, *Fir Forest*, DKK 23,500. COPENHAGEN, 21 Oct 1976, *Portrait of the Artist's Sister* (1914, oil on canvas, 54 x 36 1/4 ins / 137 x 92 cm) DKK 7,500. COPENHAGEN, 6 Oct 1977, *Flautist* (1942, oil on canvas, 30 1/4 x 41 1/4 ins / 77 x 105 cm) DKK 10,500. COPENHAGEN, 23 Jan 1979, *Wooded Landscape* (oil on canvas, 43 x 63 ins / 109 x 160 cm) DKK 16,500. COPENHAGEN, 26 Nov 1981, *White Foal* (1925, oil on canvas, 33 x 23 1/4 ins / 84 x 59 cm) DKK 12,500. COPENHAGEN, 25 Sept 1985, *Wooded Landscape* (1920, oil on canvas, 34 1/4 x 43 1/4 ins / 87 x 110 cm) DKK 20,000. COPENHAGEN, 10 May 1989, *Standing Model* (oil on canvas, 40 1/2 x 32 1/4 ins / 103 x 82 cm) DKK 5,000. COPENHAGEN, 20 Sept 1989, *Fir Forest at Tibirke* (oil on canvas, 31 1/2 x 39 1/4 ins / 80 x 100 cm) DKK 21,000. COPENHAGEN, 21-22 March 1990, *Nordic Landscape* (1926, oil on canvas, 39 1/4 x 35 ins / 100 x 89 cm) DKK 8,000. COPENHAGEN, 9 May 1990, *Fir Forest* (oil on canvas, 31 1/2 x 39 1/4 ins / 80 x 100 cm) DKK 19,000. COPENHAGEN, 31 Oct 1990, *Forest* (oil on canvas, 25 1/4 x 31 ins / 64 x 79 cm) DKK 6,000. COPENHAGEN, 2 April 1992, *Exhibition Poster* (watercolour and gouache, design, 25 1/2 x 19 3/4 ins / 65 x 50 cm) DKK 30,000. COPENHAGEN, 21 Oct 1992, *Fir Forest* (oil on canvas, 19 3/4 x 27 1/2 ins / 50 x 70 cm) DKK 8,000. COPENHAGEN, 21 April 1993, *Fir Forest* (1940, oil on canvas, 31 1/2 x 39 1/4 ins / 80 x 100 cm) DKK 19,000. COPENHAGEN, 19 Oct 1994, *Hens among Fir Trees* (1946, oil on canvas, 38 1/2 x 68 1/2 ins / 98 x 174 cm) DKK 35,000. VEJLE, 17 March 1999, *Summer Day on the Beach at Tisvilde* (1929, oil on canvas, 28 x 35 ins / 71 x 88 cm) DKK 12,000. COPENHAGEN, 6 Oct 1999, *Pine Forest* (1937, oil on canvas, 63 x 89 ins / 160 x 225 cm) DKK 19,000. COPENHAGEN, 25 April 2001, *The Mirror* (1917, oil on canvas, 47 x 33 ins / 120 x 84 cm) DKK 75,000. COPENHAGEN, 30 May 2001, *Pine Forest* (1922, watercolour, 26 x 33 ins / 67 x 83 cm) DKK 13,000. COPENHAGEN, 20 Feb 2002, *Pine Forest* (1934-1937, oil on canvas, 46 x 39 ins / 117 x 100 cm) DKK 34,000. COPENHAGEN, 10 April 2002, *Pine Forest with Blue Sky in the Background* (oil on canvas, 33 x 49 ins / 85 x 125 cm) DKK 28,000. COPENHAGEN, 1 April 2003, *Study of Pines* (1912, oil on canvas, 49 x 43 ins / 125 x 110 cm) DKK 50,000. COPENHAGEN, 7 Oct 2003, *Poultry among Ill Weeds That Grow Apace: Cubist Composition* (1917, oil on paper on canvas, 53 x 33 ins / 135 x 84 cm) DKK 140,000. COPENHAGEN, 25 Feb 2004, *The Artist's Sister Johanne Sewing. Cubist Composition* (oil on canvas, double-sided, 39 x 32 ins / 99 x 81 cm) DKK 24,000. COPENHAGEN, 29 March 2004, *Seated Female Model, possibly the Artist's Wife* (1917, oil on canvas, 49 x 32 ins / 125 x 81 cm) DKK 38,000.

SCHARFFEN, I. A.

Polish, 17th - 18th century.

Engraver. Portraits.

Scharffen engraved portraits of *Copernicus, Luther, A.C. Zaluski* and *S. Dabski.*

SCHARFFENSTEIN, Georg Friedrich

German, 18th - 19th century.

Born 13 December 1760, in Montbéliard; died 1817, in Ulm.

Miniaturist.

Scharffenstein trained at the Karlsschule in Stuttgart and was a friend of Schiller, whose portrait he painted in miniature. He was an officer.

SCHARL, Arthur, or Artur

Austrian, 19th - 20th century.

Born 1870, in Vienna; died 4 October 1918, in Budapest.

Watercolourist.

SCHARL, Josef
German, 20th century.
Born 9 December 1896, in Munich; died 1954, in New York.
Painter. Figures, portraits, still-lifes.
Josef Scharl studied at the fine arts academy in Munich.
BIBLIOGRAPHY:
Grimms' Fairy Tales, Routledge & Kegan Paul, London, 1948 (with 212 illustrations by Josef Scharl). Firmenich, Andrea, et al., *Josef Scharl, Monographie und Werkverzeichnis*, exhibition catalogue, catalogue raisonné, Kunsthalle, Emden, Wienand, Cologne, 1999.
MUSEUMS AND GALLERIES:
MUNICH (NG): *Mother and Child* - MUNICH (Städtische Gal. im Lenbachhaus): *Portrait of the Artist* - NUREMBERG (Municipal Gal.): *Portrait of A. Einstein.*
AUCTION RECORDS:
MUNICH, 23 Nov 1973, *Still-life*, DEM 3,000. HAMBURG, 3 June 1978, *Woman at her Embroidery* (1923, oil on canvas, 32 1/2 x 17 1/2 ins / 82.8 x 44.7 cm) DEM 5,500. MUNICH, 28 Nov 1980, *Couple* (1932, watercolour, 13 1/2 x 17 1/2 ins / 34 x 44.5 cm) DEM 1,600. MUNICH, 2 Dec 1980, *Priest* (1928, oil on canvas, 31 1/2 x 25 1/2 ins / 80 x 65 cm) DEM 7,400. MUNICH, 30 June 1981, *Three Trees* (1932, pen, 17 x 15 1/4 ins / 43 x 38.5 cm) DEM 3,800. COLOGNE, 1 Dec 1982, *War Grave* (1929, oil on canvas, 19 3/4 x 24 1/2 ins / 50 x 62 cm) DEM 8,500. MUNICH, 31 May 1983, *Street Scene: Berlin by Night* (1932, watercolour, 13 1/4 x 17 1/2 ins / 33.5 x 44.5 cm) DEM 7,500. MUNICH, 29 Nov 1983, *Still-life with Flowers* (1937, oil on canvas, 16 3/4 x 12 3/4 ins / 42.5 x 32.5 cm) DEM 9,200. HAMBURG, 8 June 1985, *Park* (1947, oil on canvas, 19 x 27 1/2 ins / 48 x 70 cm) DEM 14,500. MUNICH, 3 June 1987, *Setting Sun* (1943, gouache, 15 1/4 x 22 ins / 38.5 x 56 cm) DEM 3,500. MUNICH, 8 June 1988, *Public Auction* (pencil, 11 x 14 ins / 28 x 35.5 cm) DEM 8,800. LONDON, 29 Nov 1988, *Battered Prostitute* (1931, oil on canvas, 35 1/4 x 22 1/2 ins / 89.6 x 57.2 cm) GBP 8,800. NEW YORK, 5 Oct 1989, *Man Reading* (1933, oil on canvas, 38 1/2 x 31 3/4 ins / 97.8 x 80.7 cm) USD 20,900. MUNICH, 26-27 Nov 1991, *Portrait of a Man* (1948, ink, 20 x 14 ins / 51 x 35.5 cm) DEM 2,300. MUNICH, 26 May 1992, *Landscape* (1936, gouache, 15 x 19 1/2 ins / 38 x 49.5 cm) DEM 3,450. MUNICH, 1-2 Dec 1992, *Composition* (1936, ink, 11 1/2 x 14 3/4 ins / 29.5 x 37.5 cm) DEM 4,255. HEIDELBERG, 15-16 Oct 1993, *Nude* (1952, brown ink, 17 3/4 x 23 1/2 ins / 45.3 x 59.8 cm) DEM 1,650. HAMBURG, 12 June 1999, *Southern Garden* (1937, gouache on board, 13 x 18 ins / 32 x 45 cm) DEM 3,800. MUNICH, 20 Nov 1999, *Worker's Portrait II* (1933, oil on canvas, 25 x 20 ins / 63 x 51 cm) DEM 30,000. MUNICH, 6 June 2000, *Don Quijote de la Mancha* (1936, oil on canvas, 31 x 26 ins / 79 x 65 cm) DEM 66,000. LONDON, 18 Oct 2000, *Soup Eater* (1932, oil on canvas, 45 x 36 ins / 115 x 92 cm) GBP 40,000. COLOGNE, 1 June 2001, *Man Clothed in Lace* (1930, oil on canvas, 31 x 26 ins / 80 x 65 cm) DEM 50,000. HAMBURG, 7 Dec 2001, *Retreat into Confusion* (1946, tempera, colour chalk and gouache on canvas, 19 x 24 ins / 47 x 62 cm) DEM 6,000. HAMBURG, 23 March 2002, *Path* (1936, gouache, 12 x 17 ins / 30 x 43 cm) EUR 1,900. HAMBURG, 23 March 2002, *Portrait of Woman* (1939, gouache, 20 x 16 ins / 51 x 41 cm) EUR 2,600. BERLIN, 31 May 2003, *Boy* (1930, oil on canvas, 25 x 19 ins / 63 x 49 cm) EUR 12,000. COLOGNE, 26 Nov 2003, *Still-life with Fruit* (1945, tempera on canvas, 11 x 15 ins / 29 x 38 cm) EUR 2,600. MUNICH, 25 May 2004, *Tiger Lilies in Red Vase* (tempera on canvas, 11 x 11 ins / 27 x 29 cm) EUR 1,700. MUNICH, 25 May 2004, *Thunderstorm at Cape Cod* (1954, tempera on canvas, 14 x 19 ins / 35 x 49 cm) EUR 2,100.

SCHARLACH, Eduard
German, 19th century.
Born 1811, in Hanover-Münden; died before 1891, in Hanover.
Painter. Military subjects, portraits, animals.
Scharlach was a painter of military subjects; he trained at the academy in Düsseldorf under Th. Hildebrandt around 1836.
MUSEUMS AND GALLERIES:
HANOVER: *Mare and Foal* (1847); *Don Quixote's Stallion*; *The Queen's Hussars*; *Battle Horse under the Yoke*; *Hanoverians.*

SCHARLOW, G. C.
German, 19th century.
Active in Riga from 1820 to 1840.
Draughtsman, lithographer.
Scharlow drew and engraved views of Riga and portraits.

SCHÄRMER, Augustin, or Schermer
Austrian, 19th century.
Born 1800, in Wildermieming (Tyrol); died 26 September 1886, in the same area.
Sculptor (wood).
Nazarenes group (related to).
Augustin Schärmer was self-taught and influenced by the Nazarenes. He worked for churches in the Tyrol.

SCHARMER, Johann Martin, or Schermer
Austrian, 19th century.
Born 21 November 1785, in Nassereith (Tyrol); died 10 January 1868, in Vienna.
Painter, miniaturist, draughtsman. Portraits.
Johann Scharmer trained at the academy of fine art in Vienna.
MUSEUMS AND GALLERIES:
INNSBRUCK (Tiroler Landesmus. Ferdinandeum).

SCHARNAGEL, Franz Sebastian
German, 19th century.
Born 4 May 1791, in Bamberg; died 13 April 1837, in Bamberg.
Painter, lithographer. History painting.
Scharnagel trained under Joseph Dorn. He attended the academy in Munich in 1811 and returned to Bamberg in 1815. A notable work by him is a *Martyrdom of St Bartholomew.*

SCHARNER, C.
German, 19th century.
Miniaturist, painter. Religious subjects.
MUSEUMS AND GALLERIES:
MUNICH (Residenzmus.): *St Mary Magdalene.*

SCHARNER, Michael
German, 17th century.
Active in Munich from 1666 to 1676.
Painter, miniaturist. Portraits.
The Residenzmuseum in Munich houses several portraits by Michael Scharner of the Bavarian princely family.
MUSEUMS AND GALLERIES:
MUNICH (Residenzmus.).

SCHARNER, Thomas Mathias
Austrian, 17th century.
Active in Vienna in 1691.
Miniaturist. Portraits.

SCHARNHORST, H.
Swedish, 18th century.
Active at the beginning of the 18th century.
Portrait artist.

SCHAROLD, Carl
German, 19th century.
Born 1811, in Würzburg; died c. 1865, in Würzburg.
Painter. Architectural views, landscapes.
MUSEUMS AND GALLERIES:
MUNICH (Stadtmus.): *Interior of the Cathedral of Brienne*; *Interior of Ulm Cathedral*; *View of Verona.*

SCHARPF, Erasmus or Asmus
German, 16th century.
Active in Nördlingen 1543-1575.
Painter, engraver. Maps.
Erasmus Scharpf was the son of Franz Scharpf.

SCHARPF, Franz, called Tausendschön
German, 16th century.
Active in Nördlingen 1522-1543.
Painter, engraver. Maps.
Franz Scharpf was the father of Erasmus Scharpf.

SCHARRATH, Karl
German, 19th - 20th century.
Born 10 August 1870, in Bielefeld; died March 1907, in Stuttgart.
Active in Stuttgart.
Sculptor.
Karl Scharrath studied at the fine arts academy in Düsseldorf.

SCHARRER, Oskar Wolfgang
German, 19th - 20th century.
Born 15 December 1879, in Mühldorf am Inn.
Painter, engraver, illustrator. Figures, landscapes.
Oskar Wolfgang Scharrer was a pupil of Heinrich Knirr and Moritz Heymann. He was a contributor to the periodicals *Fliegende Blätter* and *Meggendorfer Blätter*.

SCHARSIG, Carl Friedrich
German, 18th - 19th century.
Born 1766; died 22 October 1808, in Dresden.
Painter (porcelain). Landscapes.
Scharsig exhibited in Dresden in 1777, and worked in Dresden as a porcelain painter after 1799.

SCHART, Georg, the Younger
German, 17th - 18th century.
Born in Danzig (now Gdansk, Poland); died 21 December 1712, in Breslau (now Wroclaw, Poland).
Painter.
Georg Schart was a teacher in Breslau in 1687.

SCHART, Georg or Jürgen, the Elder
German, 17th century.
Born c. 1630.
Painter.
Georg or Jürgen Schart was accepted as a teacher in Danzig (now Gdansk, Poland) in 1655.

SCHART, Johann or Jan Gregor von der.
See **SCHARDT**

SCHART, Nathanaël
German, 17th century.
Died 1683.
Active in Danzig (now Gdansk, Poland).
Painter.
Nathanaël Schart is perhaps the son of Georg Schart the Elder.

SCHARTMANN, Emil Adalbert
German, 19th century.
Born 1809, in Berlin.
Painter. Flowers.
Schartmann trained at the academy in Berlin under Herbig, then in Düsseldorf under Sohn. He worked in Berlin.

SCHARTOW, Marianne
German, 19th century.
Born 27 October 1856, in Frankfurt am Main.
Active in Berlin.
Painter. Landscapes.

SCHARUCHIN, Dimitri Yacovlevich
Russian, 19th century.
Born 9 October 1813; died 1901.
Painter. History painting, portraits.
Dimitri Scharuchin studied at the St Petersburg academy.
MUSEUMS AND GALLERIES:
VIATKA (Mus.): paintings.

SCHARVOGEL, Johann Jakob Julius
German, 19th - 20th century.
Born 3 April 1854, in Mainz; died 27 February 1938, in Munich.
Ceramicist.
Darmstadt Artists' Colony. Jugendstil.
Johann Scharvogel was destined for a career in business but preferred to study ceramics which he did first in London then in Paris. He worked for fifteen years for the faïence factory Villeroy & Boch at Mettlach, and was responsible for the design studio. He was the co-founder in 1897 of the Vereinigte Werkstätten für Kunst im Handwerk (United Studios for Art in the Craft Industry) in Munich, the city where he fixed his studio. These studios of the applied arts that gave order to artists and then sold and exhibited their works allowed the Munich Jugendstil to develop rapidly. In 1900 he worked with artists such as the painter Walter Magnussen, the designer Paul Haustein and decorator of porcelain, Theo Schmuz-Baudiss. He was given an order in 1904 by the Grand-Duke Ernst Ludwig von Hessen for the manufacture of ceramics by the artists' colony of Mathildenhöhe at Darmstadt, up to 1913, when he returned to Munich. He was among the co-founders of the German Werkbund an association founded in 1907 by architects, designers and industrialists who suggested the use of simple, solid shapes applied as much to architecture as to consumer goods. He gave courses from 1915 to 1925 at the Technical High School of Munich.

He is recognised as being the first to have created in Germany, ceramics in decorated sandstone, and developed the art of the 'flambé' glaze which had only been done by Françaís Carriès, Ernest Chaplet, Dalpayrat. His work was from the beginning totally decorative then became utilitarian. He also worked from 1915 in creating ceramic tiles for architecture and construction, and was adviser in the development of a ceramics industry in Turkey.

In 1899 he exhibited his stoneware at the Glass Palace in Munich. He won the gold medal at the Exposition universelle in Paris in 1900. He also exhibited at Turin in 1902, at St Louis in 1904, with the Darmstadt factory during the Brussels Exhibition in 1913.
BIBLIOGRAPHY:
Umelecka Kolonie Darmstadt, 1899-1914, exhibition catalogue, Narodni Galerie, Prague, 1989. ZurMegede, H. D./Ulmer, R., *Jakob Julius Scharvogel. Keramiker des Jugendstils*, exhibition catalogue, Museum Künstlerkolonie, Stuttgart, Arnoldsche Art Publishers, Stuttgart, 1995.
MUSEUMS AND GALLERIES:
BERLIN (Kunstgewerbemus.): *Vase* (1904, earthenware); *Plate* (1900, earthenware) - DARMSTADT (Hessisches Landesmuseum, 1899): *Vase* - HAMBURG (Mus. für Kunst und Gewerbe): *Vase* (1899, ceramic).

SCHARWIN, Jakof Vassiliévitch.
See **SHARVIN Jakov Vasilievich**

SCHARY, Saul
American, 20th century.
Born 1904; died 1978.
Painter.
AUCTION RECORDS:
NEW YORK, 28 May 1992, *Pierrot* (1929, oil on canvas, 57¾ x 45 ins / 146.8 x 114.3 cm) USD 19,800. NEW YORK, 23 Sept 1992, *Portrait of Arshile Gorky* (oil on canvas, 28 x 22 ins / 71 x 56 cm) USD 2,750. SAN FRANCISCO, 12 Dec 2001, *Autumn Wild Flowers, No 8* (oil on canvas, 28 x 20 ins / 71 x 51 cm) USD 1,800.

SCHATEN, Hubert
Danish, 17th century.
Active in Copenhagen from 1675 to 1696.
Engraver (burin).
Schaten was an engraver, who worked almost exclusively on portraits.

SCHATT, Joseph. See **SCHAD**

SCHATT, Michaële-Andréa
French, 20th - 21st century.
Born 1958.
Painter.
Michaële-Andréa Schatt studied at the École Nationale des Beaux-Arts in Paris and showed her work there at a group exhibition held in 1995. Her compositions are based on layers of transparent sheets carrying superimposed signs and symbols. The overall effect is akin to that of a Rorschach Test. She works in series (*Pandora's Boxes; Finite and Infinite Games; In Praise of Folds*).

She has shown examples of her work at solo exhibitions held on a regular basis at the Galerie Zürcher in Paris and at CRAC Alsace in Altkirch and the Maison des Associations in Bart.

BIBLIOGRAPHY:
Suchère, Éric, '*Les Mille-feuilles de Michaële-Andréa Schatt*' in *Beaux-Arts Magazine* n° 144, periodical, Paris, April 1996.
Suchère, Éric, '*Michaële-Andréa Schatt*' in *Art Press* n° 227, periodical, Paris, 1997.

MUSEUMS AND GALLERIES:
PARIS (FNAC): *Vanity* (1994, print).

AUCTION RECORDS:
PARIS, 30 Jan 1989, *Composition* (1987, mixed media, 51 1/4 x 38 1/4 ins / 130 x 97 cm) FRF 9,000. COPENHAGEN, 22-24 Oct 1997, *Red Tree* (1988, oil on canvas, 57 1/2 x 44 ins / 146 x 112 cm) DKK 9,000.

SCHATTANEK, Karl
Austrian, 20th century.
Born 28 March 1890, in Vienna.
Active in Innsbruck.
Painter, engraver (woodcut).

SCHATTENHOFER, Amalia von
Maiden name: Baader
German, 18th - 19th century.
Born 1763, in Erding; died c. 1840.
Painter, engraver (burin).
Schattenhofer was trained by J. Dorner in Munich. She engraved portraits and copies of Rembrandt and the Italian Masters.

SCHATTENSTEIN, Nikol or Nicolaus
Lithuanian, 20th century.
Born 1877, in Poniemon, near Kaunas; died 1954.
Active in the USA.
Painter.
Nikol Schattenstein studied at the academy of fine art in Vienna and Rome. He was awarded two gold medals at the International Exhibition in Vienna and an honourable mention at the Salon de Paris.

MUSEUMS AND GALLERIES:
CRACOW (Muz. Narodowe).

AUCTION RECORDS:
NEW YORK, 28 May 1982, *Reading* (oil on canvas, 27 1/4 x 39 1/4 ins / 69.2 x 99.7 cm) USD 2,600. NEW YORK, 29 April 1988, *Woman's Portrait* (oil on canvas, 78 3/4 x 48 1/2 ins / 200 x 123.2 cm) USD 11,550. LONDON, 12 June 1996, *Portrait of Mrs Rosenfeld* (1907, oil on canvas, 62 1/2 x 51 1/4 ins / 159 x 130 cm) GBP 2,300. NEW YORK, 18 March 2003, *Portrait of a Woman. Portrait of a Gentleman* (oil on canvas, a pair, 46 x 35 ins / 117 x 89 cm) USD 2,400.

SCHATZ, Bezalel
Israeli, 20th century.
Born 1912, in Jerusalem; died 1983
Painter.
The son of Boris Schatz, Bezalel Schatz studied in Paris and New York. His work consists of a calligraphic, lyrical form of Abstraction which he exhibited at shows in Israel, the US, London and Paris.

SCHATZ, Boris
Russian, 19th - 20th century.
Born 23 December 1867, in Vorno; died 23 March 1932, in Denver.
Active in Bulgaria and in Israel.
Sculptor, designer.
Of Jewish extraction, Boris Schatz went to Bulgaria after 1878 and studied in Warsaw and Paris. He taught at the academy of fine art that opened in Sofia after liberation from the Turks. Having then arrived in the state of Israel, he founded the first academy of fine art. Schatz is regarded as the founder of the Bulgarian school of sculpture. He was also an art critic.

MUSEUMS AND GALLERIES:
SOFIA (Nacionalna chudozestvena galerija/National Gallery of Art): *Mother of Moses*.

SCHATZ, David
German, 16th - 17th century.
Active in Colditz 1599-1612.
Sculptor (wood).
David Schatz carved the Renaissance pulpit in the church of St Nicholas in Döbeln.

SCHATZ, Felix
Austrian, 19th century.
Born 1847, in Thaur; died 26 January 1905, in Innsbruck.
Painter, illustrator.
Felix Schatz trained in Innsbruck and Munich. He worked notably as a draughtsman of cartoons for stained glass windows.

SCHATZ, Louise
Israeli, 20th century.
Born 1916.
Active from 1950 in the USA.
Painter, watercolourist.
Louise Schatz studied in California. Her works initially showed the influence of Paul Klee, but then evolved towards a more pronounced form of Abstraction. She has shown in various public exhibitions, including a series dedicated to Israeli art held in the US, London and Paris. She was awarded a silver medal at the Milan Triennial in 1954.

SCHATZ, M.
German, 17th century.
Active during the second half of the 17th century.
Painter.
Schatz painted a *Descent from the Cross* in the church of Our Lady in Lübeck.

SCHATZ, Otto Rudolf
Austrian, 20th century.
Born 1900, in Vienna; died 1961, in Vienna.
Painter, watercolourist, engraver (wood). Portraits, landscapes.
Otto Rudolf Schatz studied at the school of applied arts in Vienna. He spent time in the USA in 1936 and in 1938 was obliged to emigrate to the then Czechoslovakia, where he was interned in a work camp until 1944. He was awarded the City of Vienna Engraving Prize in 1947. He produced numer-

ous woodcut engravings devoted to the theme of work and the workplace. With the advent of the Nazi regime, however, he turned to landscapes and portraiture.

Examples of his work featured in *Phantom der Lust. Visionen des Machochismus in der Kunst* (*Phantom of Desire. Visions of Masochism in Art*), an exhibition devoted to the life and works of Leopold von Sacher-Masoch, held in 2003 at the Neue Galerie am Landesmuseum in Graz.

BIBLIOGRAPHY:

Pagé, Suzanne/Winock, Michel/Michaud, Éric/Vidal, Aline, *Les Années trente en Europe. Le Temps menaçant*, exhibition catalogue, Musée d'Art moderne de la Ville de Paris, Paris musées, Flammarion, Paris, 1997. Weibel, Peter (ed.), '*Phantom der Lust. Visionen des Masochismus in der Kunst*' in *2 vols*, exhibition catalogue, Neue Galerie am Landesmuseum, Graz, Belleville Verlag, Munich, 2003.

AUCTION RECORDS:

VIENNA, 4 Dec 1984, *New York* (watercolour, 18 1/4 x 16 ins / 46.5 x 40.5 cm) ATS 25,000. VIENNA, 3 Dec 1986, *New York* (watercolour, 21 x 15 1/4 ins / 52.5 x 39 cm) ATS 28,000. VIENNA, 27 May 1999, *Play* (1930, oil on canvas, 76 x 67 ins / 193 x 171 cm) ATS 3,200,000. VIENNA, 11 Oct 1999, *Altstaedter Ring and Teyn Church in Prague* (oil on canvas, 21 x 26 ins / 54 x 67 cm) ATS 120,000. VIENNA, 15 May 2000, *Rockefeller Centre, New York* (watercolour, 17 x 22 ins / 43 x 57 cm) ATS 60,000. VIENNA, 15 May 2000, *New York in the Evening* (oil on canvas, 31 x 39 ins / 80 x 100 cm) ATS 320,000. VIENNA, 15 May 2001, *Female Nudes* (oil on canvas, 32 x 42 ins / 81 x 106 cm) ATS 450,000. VIENNA, 27 Nov 2001, *Girls' Room* (1924, watercolour and Indian ink, 23 x 16 ins / 58 x 41 cm) ATS 28,000. VIENNA, 25 Nov 2002, *Standing Female Nude* (charcoal, colour pen and oil, 18 x 11 ins / 45 x 29 cm) EUR 5,500. VIENNA, 25 Nov 2002, *New York, Wall Street* (oil on canvas, 33 x 26 ins / 83 x 65 cm) EUR 14,000. VIENNA, 27 May 2003, *Still-life with Flowers* (watercolour, 17 x 22 ins / 42 x 56 cm) EUR 3,500. MUNICH, 13 Nov 2003, *Studio Scene in new York* (oil on canvas, 22 x 26 ins / 55 x 65 cm) EUR 7,000. VIENNA, 27 Jan 2004, *Paris* (oil on paper on board, 13 x 17 ins / 32 x 44 cm) EUR 8,000. VIENNA, 27 May 2004, *Female Nude seen from Behind* (1922, black chalk, oil and gouache on paper, 16 x 13 ins / 41 x 34 cm) EUR 4,600.

SCHATZBERGER, Michael

German, 19th century.
Active c. 1820.
Lithographer.

SCHÄTZIG, Adolph

German, 19th century.
Active in Berlin in 1836.
Engraver.

SCHATZLE, Kristof

Belgian, 20th century.
Painter.

Kristof Schatzle exhibits in Belgium.

SCHAUB, J. Friedrich Wilhelm

German, 18th century.
Active in Berlin from 1776 to 1788.
Painter, engraver (etching), draughtsman. Landscapes.

MUSEUMS AND GALLERIES:

BERLIN (Kupferstichkabinet).

SCHAUBERG, Dorothea. See **MENN**

SCHAUBERGER, Johann Georg

Austrian, 18th century.
Died 14 December 1744, in Brunn (now Brno, Czech Republic).
Sculptor, stucco artist.

Schauberger worked in Olmütz (now Olomouc, Czech Republic) and Brno where he sculpted tabernacles, baptismal fonts, altars and pulpits.

SCHAUBROECK. See **SCHOUBROECK Pieter**

SCHAUDT, Johann Emil

German, 20th century.
Born 14 August 1871, in Stuttgart; died 6 April 1957, in Berlin.
Architect, draughtsman, designer. Furniture.

Johann Emil Schaudt trained in architecture at the technical school in Stuttgart then in Vienna and was a pupil of von Neckelmann, Ernst von Ihne, and Paul Wallot. He renovated and erected annexes to the building at the commercial centre Kaufhaus des Westens (1906-1907) in Berlin, known at that time for being one of the most luxurious in the world and for which Peter Behrens designed the lighting. This building was in part destroyed during World War II then reconstructed. He worked for the Dresden Studios created in 1899 (Dresdener Werkstätten für Handwerkskunst) whose object was to create furniture and domestic utensils of quality in a sober, elegant style. The furniture that he created is of the Jugendstil type. He left a drawing for competition for the Alexanderplatz in Berlin.

BIBLIOGRAPHY:

Osborn, Max/Schache Wolfgang (presentation), *Johann Emil Schaudt*, Mann, Berlin, 1996 (reprinted from a work from 1930).

MUSEUMS AND GALLERIES:

BERLIN (Berlinische Gal.).

SCHAUE, Hanns Georg

German, 18th century.
Active in Fürth c. 1700.
Painter.

Schaue executed paintings in the church of Berg in Bavaria.

SCHAUER. See also **SCHAUR**

SCHAUER, Franz, or Schaur

German, 18th century.
Died before 1730.
Active in Munich.
Painter.

Schauer worked for the court as well as for churches and monasteries in Munich.

SCHAUER, Franz, or Schaur

German, 19th century.
Active in Munich in 1842.
Painter.

SCHAUER, Franz Sebastian, or Schaur or Schaurd

Austrian, 18th century.
Active in Salzburg.
Engraver (burin).

Franz Schauer engraved ex libris, allegories and calendars.

SCHAUER, Friedrich

German, 19th century.
Active in Berlin.
Draughtsman, engraver. Portraits.

Friedrich Schauer exhibited in Berlin in 1840 and in 1842. He engraved several portraits on steel.

SCHAUER, Gustav

German, 19th century.
Born 24 June 1826, in Beeskow; died 8 January 1902, in Berlin.
Painter. History painting.

Gustav Schauer was trained by Piloty.

SCHAUER, Hans Jörg

German, 17th century.
Painter. Religious subjects.

Hans Schauer was active in Neustift and worked on the altar of the chancel of Freising Cathedral in 1624.

SCHAUER, Johann Georg, or Schaur
German, 17th century.
Painter, engraver. Portraits.
Johann Schauer worked in Augsburg at the end of the 17th century. He engraved portraits of monks and Church Fathers. He favoured the scraper technique.

SCHAUER, Josef
Austrian, 19th century.
Active in Seekirchen at the beginning of the 19th century.
Painter.
Josef Schauer painted a *Way of the Cross* in Kirchberg in 1808.

SCHAUER, Joseph Anton
Austrian, 18th century.
Active in Olmütz (now Olomouc, Czech Republic).
Engraver (mezzotint). Portraits.

SCHAUER, Joseph Christian
German, 18th century.
Active in 1749.
Painter.
Joseph Christian Schauer executed an altarpiece for the church of the Holy Spirit in Ingolstadt.

SCHAUER, Leopold
Austrian, 19th century.
Born 2 May 1841, in Mileschau, Bohemia (now Germany).
Watercolourist.
Leopold Schauer trained at the academies in Prague, Dresden and Vienna. He settled in Vienna.

SCHAUER, Mathias
Austrian, 18th - 19th century.
Active in Seekirchen.
Painter.
Mathias Schauer painted *Ways of the Cross*.

SCHAUER, Nicolaus, or Schaur
German, 17th century.
Active in Schleusingen c. 1680.
Portrait artist.

SCHAUER, Otto
German, 20th century.
Born 1923, in Stuttgart; died 1985.
Active in France from 1950.
Painter. Figures, landscapes, still-lifes.
Otto Schauer received informal instruction from Anton Kolig and Willi Baumeister. The work of Willi Baumeister exerted a particularly strong early influence on him. Subsequently, his still-lifes, landscapes and figures evolved in the direction of Lyrical Abstraction, on occasion to a point where some compositions, while not in fact Surrealist, were 'unusual' enough to find favour with such painters as Hélion and Balthus. He exhibited solo in Paris in 1952 and 1963, at the House of Arts and Leisure in Laon in 1971, and at the Centre National d'Art Contemporain in Paris in 1972.
BIBLIOGRAPHY:
Otto Schauer, exhibition catalogue, Centre national d'Art contemporain, Paris, 1972.
AUCTION RECORDS:
PARIS, 27 Feb 1996, *Heart of Linas* (1955, oil on canvas, 18 x 22 ins / 46 x 55 cm) FRF 18,000. PARIS, 15 Nov 2002, *Lamp in the Garden* (1960, oil on canvas, 46 x 35 ins / 116 x 89 cm) EUR 3,500. PARIS, 2 Dec 2003, *Still-life* (1963, oil on canvas, 26 x 21 ins / 65 x 54 cm) EUR 1,500.

SCHAUERTE, Hermann, or Sutoris
German, 17th century.
Active in Winkhausen.
Sculptor.
Schauerte worked in Attendorn, Berghausen and Dorlar.

SCHÄUFEL, Joseph Ignaz. See **SCHEUFEL**

SCHAUFELBERGER, Johann Jakob
Swiss, 18th century.
Born 21 May 1702, in Zurich; died 1763, in Zurich.
Painter, engraver. Landscapes.
Schaufelberger engraved in burin a work entitled *Italian Peasants*. It is dated 1742.

SCHAUFELEIN, Hans Léonard or Leonhard.
See **SCHÄUFFELIN**

SCHAUFF, Johann Nepomuk, or Schauf
Austrian, 18th - 19th century.
Born 16 May 1757, in Hermanmestec (Bohemia); died 31 May 1827, in Varazdin.
Painter, engraver. Historical subjects, architectural views.
Schauff was also a writer and publisher.

SCHÄUFFELEN, Konrad Balder
German, 20th century.
Born 1929, in Ulm (Baden-Württemberg).
Active in Munich.
Sculptor of assemblages, installation artist, mixed media. Artists' books.
Visual Poetry.
Konrad Balder Schäuffelen studied philosophy and medicine before following courses at the fine arts academy in Munich in 1957. He exercised his profession as a psychiatrist/psychoanalyst in tandem with a career in the arts. He also produced 'concrete' and 'visual' poetry.

Schäuffelen's work featured in group exhibitions, including Documenta 6 in Kassel in 1977 and *De Bonnard à Baselitz: Dix Ans d'Enrichissements du Cabinet des Estampes 1978-1988* (*From Bonnard to Baselitz: A Decade of Acquisitions by the Prints Collection 1978-1988*) at the Bibliothèque Nationale in Paris in 1992.
MUSEUMS AND GALLERIES:
PARIS (BNF): *Needle Book* (1975).

SCHÄUFFELIN, Hans, the Younger, or Schaufelein or Schuffelin or Sciffelin
German, 16th century.
Born after 1515, in Nördlingen; died c. 1582, in Fribourg, Switzerland.
Active in Fribourg.
Painter, draughtsman.
Hans Schäuffelin the Younger was the son of Hans Léonard Schäuffelin and worked for the monastery of Einsiedeln. Some biographers give 1542 as the date of his birth, but this would mean that he was born two years after his father's death.

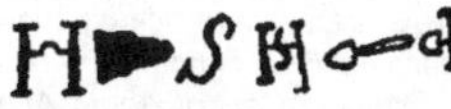

SCHÄUFFELIN, Hans Léonard or Leonhard, or Schauffele, Schäufelein, Schäuffelein, Scheifelin, Schenfelein, Schenflein or Schoyffelin
German, 15th - 16th century.
Born c. 1480, in Nuremberg; died between 1538 and 1540, in Nördlingen, or in Nuremberg according to some sources.
Painter, engraver, draughtsman, illustrator. Religious subjects, battles, portraits.
Hans Léonard Schäuffelin was a pupil of Albrecht Dürer and, until 1505, one of his assistants. His first known work is

the painting of the retable of Ober-Sankt-Veit, the design of which was by Dürer. Around 1509 he was in the Tyrol and Augsburg. In 1515 he became a burgher of Nördlingen, the result of which seems to have been that the magistrates of his native town barred him from going back there.

Among his paintings are the following: *Siege of Bethulia*; a *Story of Judith*; the *Ziegler Retable*; *Last Supper*; *Dead Christ*; and a *Descent from the Cross*. Schäuffelein did little engraving, and the majority of his works in this medium were woodcuts. He illustrated most of the romance of the *Theuerdank*.

He was both imaginative and technically skilful and produced works of much interest.

BIBLIOGRAPHY:

Winkler, Fr., *Die Zeichnungen Hans Süss von Kulmbachs und Hans Leonhard Schäufeleins,* Deutscher Verein für Kunstwissenschaft, Berlin, 1942. Schreyl, Karl Heinz, *Hans Schaüffelein: the Graphic Work,* Alan Wofsy Fine Arts, San Francisco, 1990.

MUSEUMS AND GALLERIES:

AACHEN: *Six Scenes from the Passion* - AUGSBURG (Schaezler-Palais, Staatsgal.): *St Ulrich Enters the Monastery of St Gallen; St Ulrich Promoted to Bishop* - AUHAUSEN (Church): *Coronation of the Virgin* (16 panels) - BAMBERG (Neue Residenz, Staatsgal.): *Crown of Thorns* - BASEL: *Portrait of a Man; Virgin and Child with St John* - BERLIN: *St Jerome; Adoration of the Lamb; Holy Communion* - BESANÇON: *Portrait of a Man* - BONN: *St Jerome* - FLORENCE: *St Peter Walking on the Water; Martyrdom of St Paul; St Peter Delivered from Prison by the Angel; St Peter and St Paul Being Led to Prison; St Peter Preaching* - GRAN: *Adoration and Circumcision* - HALLE: *Chist Takes his Leave of the Holy Women* - HAMBURG (Kunsthalle): *Nativity* - INNSBRUCK (Tiroler Landesmus. Ferdinandeum): *Adoration of the Magi* - KARLSRUHE (Staatliche Kunsthalle): *Crucifixion* - LEIPZIG: *Flagellation of Christ* - MAINZ: *Stoning of St Stephen* - MUNICH: *Death of the Virgin; Nailing to the Cross; Coronation of the Virgin; Christ Falling under the Weight of the Cross; Christ Saving St Peter from the Waves; Crown of Thorns and Blasphemy* (two); *The Virgin Receiving a Palm from an Angel; Flight into Egypt; Burial of the Virgin; St Peter Bringing the Dead Back to Life; Freeing of St Peter; Christ before Pilate; Christ on the Mount of Olives* - MUNICH (Alte Pinakothek): *Crucifixion of St Peter; Ecce Homo; Christ Meeting his Mother and St John; Erection of the Cross; Head of Christ; St Ulrich Curing the Sick* - NÖRDLINGEN: *Story of Judith; Ziegler Retable* - NÖRDLINGEN (Rathaus): *Siege of Bethulia* (fresco) - NUREMBERG: *Christ on the Cross; St Brigitte; St Onuphrius* (two); *St Jerome; Deliverance of St Peter; Virgin and the Apostles; Pope St Martin; St Lawrence; Ecce Homo; Portrait of an Old Man* - NUREMBERG (Cathedral): *Dead Christ* - NUREMBERG (Church of St George): *Descent from the Cross* - OBERSCHLEISSHEIM (Neues Schloss Schleissheim, Staatsgal.): *Flagellation; Christ on the Banks of the Cedron; Ecce Homo; Portrait of Abbot Alexander Hummel von Deggingen* - PRAGUE (Rudolfinum Gal.): *St Jerome* - STUTTGART: *Susanna and the Elders; Adoration of the Magi* (fragment) - ULM (Münster): *Last Supper* - VIENNA: *Portraits of a Man and Woman; Altar with Three Wings* - VIENNA (Liechtenstein Mus.): *Visitation* - WARSAW (Muz. Narodowe): *Portrait of a Man* - WIESBADEN: *Portrait of a Man.*

AUCTION RECORDS:

COLOGNE, 1862, *Christ Seated in the Forecourt of Pilate's Palace,* FRF 225; *Mary and Joseph Going to Meet Elizabeth,* FRF 191; *Adoration of the Magi,* FRF 105. PARIS, 1882, *Group of People* (pen) FRF 95. PARIS, 1892, *Ecce Homo* FRF 1,410. PARIS, 1898, *Burial of Christ* (pen drawing) FRF 51. AMSTERDAM, 15-18 June 1908, *A Pope Receiving from a Bishop the Written Rules of a New Religious Order,* FRF 3,360. LONDON, 20 May 1927, *Crucifixion,* GBP 94. LONDON, 7 May 1937, *Simon de Montfort,* GBP 409. LONDON, 19 Dec 1941, *Portrait of a Woman,* GBP 315. NEW YORK, 5 Nov 1942, *Assumption of the Virgin,* USD 475. LONDON, 12 July 1946, *Emperor Maximilian,* GBP 336. PARIS, 20 March 1953, *Circumcision,* FRF 160,000. LONDON, 14 May 1958, *Resurrection,* GBP 1,100. LONDON, 2 July 1965, *Virgin and St John,* Gns 1,800. LONDON, 26 June 1970, *Adoration of the Magi (recto); Flagellation of Christ (verso),* Gns 10,000. LONDON, 9 April 1981, *Christ Taking Leave of his Mother* (1510, pen, 10 3/4 x 8 1/4 ins / 27.4 x 21 cm) GBP 42,000. LONDON, 14 May 1981, *Battle of Pavia* (engraving/wood, 30 x 47 ins / 76 x 119.3 cm) GBP 1,800. LONDON, 30 June 1986, *Self-portrait* (black chalk and wash, 7 x 5 ins / 17.7 x 12.7 cm) GBP 120,000. AMSTERDAM, 22 May 1990, *Portrait of a Lady* (oil on panel, 17 3/4 x 11 3/4 ins / 45 x 30 cm) NLG 207,000. NEW YORK, 24 Jan 2001, *St Catherine Leaning on a Sword* (1514, pen/brown ink, 11 x 5 ins / 27 x 13 cm) USD 60,000. NEW YORK, 23 Jan 2002, *Portrait of Man, Bust-length, Wearing Hat* (1515, chalk, 7 x 7 ins / 19 x 18 cm) USD 240,000.

SCHAUFUSS, Heinrich Gotthelf

German, 18th - 19th century.

Born 20 October 1760, in Chemnitz; died 19 May 1838, in Meissen.

Miniaturist, engraver (burin).

Schaufuss was trained by J.E. Schoenau. He engraved in the style of Van Dyck, Mengs and Solimena.

SCHAUM, Bernhard

German, 19th - 20th century.

Born c. 1880; died 26 October 1916.

Active in Berlin.

Painter, illustrator.

SCHAUM, Johann Valentin

German, 18th century.

Born 16 April 1714, in Fulda; died 15 December 1771, in Fulda.

Sculptor, modeller (porcelain).

Schaum worked for Fulda Cathedral and Fulda Porcelain Factory.

SCHAUMAN, Sigrid

Finnish, 19th - 20th century.

Born 1877; died 1979.

Painter. Landscapes.

AUCTION RECORDS:

LONDON, 16 March 1989, *Fir Trees on a Hill* (oil on card, 12 1/4 x 8 1/2 ins / 31 x 21.5 cm) GBP 8,250. HELSINKI, 25 April 1999, *Landscape from Borga* (oil on canvas, 18 x 15 ins / 46 x 38 cm) FIM 29,000. HELSINKI, 11 Dec 1999, *Park* (oil on canvas, 19 x 15 ins / 47 x 38 cm) FIM 31,000. HELSINKI, 13 May 2000, *Park* (oil on board, 16 x 13 ins / 41 x 33 cm) FIM 44,000. HELSINKI, 13 May 2000, *Landscape* (oil on board, 9 x 13 ins / 24 x 32 cm) FIM 48,000. HELSINKI, 12 May 2001, *Villa Aurelia, Rome* (oil on board, 12 x 14 ins / 30 x 35 cm) FIM 58,000. HELSINKI, 2 Dec 2001, *From Borga* (1934, oil on board, 13 x 16 ins / 33 x 41 cm) FIM 31,000. HELSINKI, 27 April 2002, *Houses* (oil on canvas on board, 15 x 18 ins / 38 x 46 cm) EUR 8,200. HELSINKI, 1 Dec 2002, *Villa Aurelia* (oil on board, 13 x 17 ins / 34 x 44 cm) EUR 11,000. HELSINKI, 17 May 2003, *Aagatan in Borgaa, Street Scene* (oil on canvas, 18 x 15 ins / 46 x 38 cm) EUR 9,600. HELSINKI, 29 Nov 2003, *View from a Park* (oil on canvas, 18 x 15 ins / 46 x 38 cm) EUR 5,800. HELSINKI, 8 May 2004, *View from Brunnsparken* (1945, oil on board, 11 x 13 ins / 27 x 32 cm) EUR 7,000. HELSINKI, 15 May 2004, *Landscape from Tolo* (oil on board, 16 x 13 ins / 41 x 33 cm) EUR 6,200.

SCHAUMANN, Christoph
Swiss, 16th century.
Active in Mindelheim 1503-1522.
Painter.

SCHAUMANN, Ernst
German, 20th century.
Born 7 February 1890, in Königsberg (now Kaliningrad, Russia).
Painter. Military subjects, landscapes, animals.
Ernst Schaumann was a pupil of Paul Friedrich Meyerheim, Otto Heichert and Ludwig Dettmann.

SCHAUMANN, Heinrich or Wilhelm Heinrich
German, 19th century.
Born 2 February 1841, in Tübingen; died 6 July 1893, in Stuttgart.
Painter. Genre scenes, animals.
Heinrich Schaumann was trained by Funk, Nener and Rustige at the school of fine art in Stuttgart. He settled in Munich.
MUSEUMS AND GALLERIES:
MUNICH: *Monkey Playing with a Dog* - STUTTGART: *Popular Fête in Cannstatt.*
AUCTION RECORDS:
COLOGNE, 26 March 1982, *Village Musicians* (oil on canvas, 24 3/4 x 26 1/2 ins / 63 x 67 cm) DEM 10,000. STUTTGART, 25 June 1999, *Apes as Art Critics - Parody and Mirror of Human Society* (oil on panel, 10 x 23 ins / 26 x 58 cm) DEM 8,000.

SCHAUMANN, Johann Carl
German, 18th century.
Born 12 July 1721, in Nuremberg; died 1787 or 1795.
Modeller (wax).
Johann Carl Schaumann modelled portraits, animals and fruit in wax.

SCHAUMANN, Johann Christoph
German, 18th century.
Active in Nuremberg c. 1725.
Painter. Portraits.

SCHAUMANN, Ruth
German, 20th century.
Born 24 August 1899, in Hamburg.
Active in Munich.
Sculptor, engraver.
Ruth Schaumann was a pupil of Joseph Wackerle. In addition to writing poetry, she carved religious statuary and crucifixes, notably in lime wood.
MUSEUMS AND GALLERIES:
MUNICH (Städtische Gal. im Lenbachhaus).

SCHAUMBERGER, Cajetan
Austrian, 18th century.
Born in Graz.
Active during the second half of the 18th century.
Painter, architect. Decorative schemes.
Cajetan Schaumberger settled in Brno and worked for the theatre and Diet in Brno.

SCHAUMBERGER, Johann Martin
Austrian, 18th century.
Died 1712.
Active in Salzburg.
Painter.
Johann Schaumberger executed many altarpieces for churches in Salzburg and the surrounding areas.

SCHAUMBURG, Jules or Julius
Belgian, 19th century.
Born in Antwerp.
Painter, engraver. Seascapes.
Jules Schaumburg was a pupil of Schaefels; he was active around 1861, producing etchings and engravings.
AUCTION RECORDS:
AMSTERDAM, 25 April 1990, *Seascape* (1860, oil on canvas, 20 1/2 x 26 ins / 52 x 66 cm) NLG 8,050. NEW YORK, 24 Feb 1999, *Shipping off Coast* (1861, oil on canvas, 19 x 26 ins / 48 x 66 cm) USD 1,800. LONDON, 21 Sept 2000, *Shipping off the Port of Calcutta* (1870, pencil, watercolour and gum arabic heightened with white, 11 x 20 ins / 29 x 52 cm) GBP 2,200. LONDON, 27 April 2004, *Shipping in the Hoogly River, Calcutta* (1874, watercolour, a pair, 18 x 26 ins / 46 x 66 cm) GBP 4,600. LONDON, 14 July 2004, *Shipping off Calcultta* (1869, oil on canvas, 31 x 46 ins / 78 x 116 cm) GBP 16,000.

SCHAUMEYER, Carl Gottfried
German, 19th century.
Born 1778, in Nuremberg; died 1811, in Nuremberg.
Painter, draughtsman, engraver (etching), decorative designer. Landscapes.
Schaumeyer trained in Dresden and Stuttgart and worked in Nuremberg.

SCHAUMPFEFFER, Hans
German, 16th century.
Sculptor.
Hans Schaumpfeffer worked for the town hall of Andernach from 1572 to 1577.

SCHAUPP, Johann Christoph
German, 18th century.
Born 1 September 1685, in Biberach; died 20 November 1757, in Biberach.
Medallist, cameo engraver.
Schaupp engraved a series of 197 heads of Roman emperors and his portrait in cornaline.

SCHAUPP, Richard
Swiss, 19th - 20th century.
Born 17 November 1871, in St Gall.
Active in Munich.
Painter, engraver, illustrator.
Richard Schaupp studied under Karl Raupp, Wilhelm von Lindenschmit and Wilhelm von Diez.

SCHAUR. See also **SCHAUER**

SCHAUR, Georg
German, 18th century.
Active in Rottenburg at the beginning of the 18th century.
Painter.
Georg Schaur worked in Schatzhofen in 1710.

SCHAUR, Hanns
German, 15th - 16th century.
Active in Cracow, Munich and Augsburg 1465-1520.
Painter, illustrator.
MUSEUMS AND GALLERIES:
LONDON (British Mus.): confession book with illustrations - NUREMBERG (Germanisches Nationalmus.): *Rosary* (illustrated).

SCHAUR, Johann Adam
German, 18th century.
Died 1797, in Augsburg.
Fresco artist.
Johann Adam Schaur worked in Harthausen. He produced notably external frescoes.

SCHAUR, Johann Georg
German, 17th century.
Painter.
Johann Georg Schaur worked in Weihmichl and Rottenburg.

SCHAUROTH, Lina von
German, 19th - 20th century.
Born 9 December 1875, in Frankfurt am Main.
Stained glass painter, engraver.
Lina von Schauroth was a pupil of Wilhelm Trübner and Ludwig Hohlwein.

SCHAUSS, Ferdinand
German, 19th - 20th century.
Born 27 October 1832, in Berlin; died 20 October 1916, in Berlin.
Painter. Religious subjects, nudes, portraits, genre scenes.
Ferdinand Schauss studied under Steffeck in Berlin and under L. Cogniet in Paris. He visited England, the Netherlands, Italy and Spain before going on to teach at the school of fine arts in Weimar from 1874 to 1876 and then moving to Berlin, where he exhibited from 1866.
MUSEUMS AND GALLERIES:
OLDENBURG (Landesmus. für Kunst und Kulturgeschichte): *Female Nude in the Open Air.*
AUCTION RECORDS:
NEW YORK, 14 Jan 1977, *Bathing in a River* (oil on canvas, 15¾ x 19¾ ins / 40 x 50 cm) USD 1,700. COLOGNE, 18 March 1983, *Rustic Meal* (oil on canvas, 32¾ x 40¾ ins / 83.5 x 103.5 cm) DEM 14,500. LONDON, 1 Dec 1989, *Calm after the Storm* (oil on canvas, 43 x 77 ins / 109 x 195.5 cm) GBP 6,050. NEW YORK, 28 May 1992, *St John the Baptist as a Child* (oil on canvas, 62 x 49½ ins / 157.5 x 125.7 cm) USD 22,000. PARIS, 16 June 1997, *Meditation* (oil on canvas, 13¾ x 10 ins / 35 x 25.5 cm) FRF 32,000.

SCHAUSS, Martin
German, 19th - 20th century.
Born 25 September 1867, in Berlin; died January 1927, in Berlin.
Sculptor, medallist. Figures. Busts.
Martin Schauss studied at the fine arts academies of Berlin and Rome.
MUSEUMS AND GALLERIES:
BERLIN (Nationalgal.): *Boy with Cockerel* - BRUNSWICK: *Siesta* - DRESDEN (Albertinum): *Bust of Hermann Prell* - DÜSSELDORF (Kunstmus.): *Flora.*

SCHAUTA, Friedrich, also known as Moos
Austrian, 19th century.
Born 6 January 1822, in Vienna; died 10 September 1895, in Bades, near Vienna.
Painter. Flowers, fruit, animals.
Friedrich Schauta is sometimes wrongly called Friedrich Schanta. He was trained by J. Höger and F. Steinfeld. He lived and worked entirely in Vienna.

SCHAVENIUS, Johann Nicolai
Norwegian, 18th century.
Active in Drontheim.
Painter. Religious subjects, portraits.
Schavenius painted a *Crucifixion,* which is now situated in a church in Drontheim.

SCHAVIJE, Louiza. See **STAPLEAUX Louiza Schavije**

SCHAW, William
British, 16th century.
Born 1550, in Scotland; died April 1602, in Edinburgh.
Architect, draughtsman.
William Schaw was 'works superintendent' to the Scottish King James VI and carried out works in Holyrood and repairs in Dunfermline. He accompanied James to Denmark, where he was warmly welcomed by Queen Anne. Some of his drawings are preserved in Fredensborg Castle and a number of drawings in Holyrood are attributed to him. The queen of Denmark appointed him her chamberlain and erected a monument to him in the abbey of Dunfermline.

SCHAWBERG, Johann Heinrich or Jean Henri van
Flemish School, 18th century.
Born 18 November 1717, in Antwerp; died 1760.
Engraver (burin).
Johann Heinrich Schawberg was the son of Peter Joseph Schawberg. He was active mainly in Cologne, where he produced engravings of religious subjects.

SCHAWBERG, Peter Joseph
German, 18th century.
Died after 1722.
Engraver (burin).
Peter Joseph Schawberg was the father of Johann Heinrich Schawberg. He engraved a *Genealogical Tree of Christ* and a *Portrait of Pope Benedict XIII*

SCHAWINSKY, Xanti
Swiss, 20th century.
Born 1904, in Basel; died 1979, in Locarno.
Active in the USA from 1936.
Painter. Landscapes. Stage sets.
Xanti Schawinsky trained as an architect before studying at the Bauhaus from 1924 to 1929, following various disciplines (painting, design, photography, graphics and, above all, theatre). He worked as a decorator/set designer in Magdeburg (1929-1933) and in Italy (1933-1936). At the urging of Josef Albers, Schawinsky emigrated to the USA in 1936 and taught painting at Black Mountain College in North Carolina while continuing to hone his own personal style and technique. From 1938 he devoted himself entirely to painting and from 1961 divided his time between the USA and Switzerland, where he painted mountain landscapes and completed his series entitled *Eclipse.*

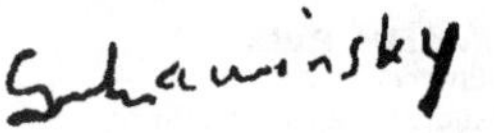

BIBLIOGRAPHY:
Leymarie, Jean/Herzogenrath, Wulf/Grote, Ludwig/Gropius, Walter, *Le Bauhaus,* exhibition catalogue, Württembergischer Kunsteverein, Stuttgart, Musée national d'Art moderne, Paris, 1969. *Xanti Schawinsky,* exhibition catalogue, Grafis, Bologna, 1975.
AUCTION RECORDS:
ROME, 21 March 1989, *Skyline* (1954, oil on canvas, 12 x 12 ins / 30.5 x 30.5 cm) ITL 2,000,000. MILAN, 8 Nov 1989, *Double Eclipse* (oil on canvas/tulle, 58½ x 80 ins / 148.5 x 203 cm) ITL 6,500,000. LUCERNE, 24 Nov 1990, *Untitled* (1975, oil and mixed media/paper, 20 x 16¼ ins / 51 x 41 cm) CHF 4,000. LUCERNE, 23 May 1992, *Composition* (1961, oil on canvas, 11¾ x 11¾ ins / 30 x 30 cm) CHF 6,600. MILAN, 23 June 1992, *Composition* (1974, painted television set, 27½ x 23½ ins / 70 x 60 cm) ITL 3,000,000. NEW YORK, 29 Sept 1993, *The Finney Family* (1960, oil/synthetic resin, 47½ x 48 ins / 120.7 x 121.9 cm) USD 2,415. AMSTERDAM, 31 May 1995, *Reclining Woman* (1914, watercolour and ink/paper/card, 16¾ x 37 ins / 42.5 x 94 cm) NLG 2,124.

SCHAWR, Hans. See **SCHAUR Hanns**

SCHAXEL, Blasius
German, 18th century.
Active in Herbolzheim.
Sculptor (wood).
Schaxel carved the altar and organ case of the church of Allmannsweier in 1783.

SCHAYCK, Adriaan Jansz. van
Dutch, 17th century.
Active in Utrecht in 1635.
Glass painter.

SCHAYCK, Cornelis
Dutch, 16th century.
Active in Utrecht 1558-1576.
Painter.
Utrecht School.
Cornelis Schayck was the brother of Ernst Schayck II and the son of Joachim Schayck. He was a member of the guild in 1569.

SCHAYCK, Ernst I
Dutch, 15th century.
Died before 1509.
Painter. Religious subjects.
Ernst Schayck I was the father of Jan Schayck and painted an altarpiece for the high altar of Utrecht Cathedral in 1496.

SCHAYCK, Ernst II
Flemish School, 16th century.
Active in Utrecht 1558-1569.
Painter. Religious subjects.
Ernst Schayck II was the son of Joachim and the father of Ernst Schayck III. A *Stoning of St Stephen* is attributed to him.
MUSEUMS AND GALLERIES:
AMSTERDAM (Rijksmus.): *Stoning of St Stephen.*

SCHAYCK, Ernst III
Dutch, 16th - 17th century.
Active in Italy 1567-1626.
Painter, draughtsman. Religious subjects, mythological subjects.
Ernst Schayck III was the son of Ernst Schayck II. He painted altarpieces for the churches of Appignano, Camerano, Castelfidardo, Filottrano, Lugo, Recanati and Sanseverino.
MUSEUMS AND GALLERIES:
DARMSTADT (Prints Collection): *Hercules* (drawing) - UTRECHT (Centraal Mus.): *St Sebastian and St Roch.*

SCHAYCK, Evert
Dutch, 16th century.
Active in Utrecht 1515-1574.
Painter.
MUSEUMS AND GALLERIES:
UTRECHT (Centraal Mus.): *Plan of the City of Utrecht.*

SCHAYCK, Govert
Dutch, 16th century.
Active in Utrecht from the beginning of 1582.
Painter.
Govert Schayck painted a *View of the Basilica of St Peter in Rome.*

SCHAYCK, Jan
Flemish School, 16th century.
Died before 1531.
Active in Utrecht 1500-1512.
Sculptor (wood).

SCHAYCK, Joachim
Dutch, 16th century.
Active in Utrecht during the first half of the 16th century.
Painter.
Joachim Schayck was the father of Ernst Schayck II and Cornelis Schayck.

SCHAYENBORGH, Pieter van. See **SCHAEYENBORGH**

SCHEBANOFF. See **CHIBANOV Mikhail**

SCHEBEK, Ferdinand
Austrian, 19th - 20th century.
Born 23 February 1875, in Vienna.
Active in Germany.
Painter, engraver. Animals.
Ferdinand Schebek studied at the fine arts academy in Vienna.
AUCTION RECORDS:
COLOGNE, 23 March 1990, *Ducks on the Edge of a Pond* (1942, oil on canvas, 31 1/2 x 46 3/4 ins / 80 x 119 cm) DEM 2,200. VIENNA, 24 Feb 2004, *Birds in Reeds* (oil on canvas, 22 x 26 ins / 55 x 66 cm) EUR 2,000. VIENNA, 21 June 2004, *Ducks by the Water* (oil on canvas, 22 x 26 ins / 55 x 66 cm) EUR 2,000.

SCHEBEN, Gerhard
German, 16th - 17th century.
Born c. 1545; died 27 March 1610, in Cologne.
Sculptor.
Gerhard Scheben carved the tomb of Duke William the Rich of Julich-Cleve-Berg in the church of St Lambert, Düsseldorf.

SCHEBESTA, Franz Anton. See **SEBASTINI**

SCHEBOTAREV, Piotr Ivanovich
Russian, 19th century.
Born 1818; died 1888.
Painter. Portraits.

SCHEBOUYEFF, Vassilyi Kousmitch. See **SHEBUEV Vasili Kuz'mich**

SCHECK, Bernhard or Johann Bernhard
German, 18th century.
Active in Straubing from 1752 to 1795.
Painter.
Bernhard Scheck executed several paintings in the church of St James in Straubing.

SCHECK, Ferdinand, the Elder
Austrian, 19th century.
Painter.
Ferdinand Schuck the Elder was the father of Ferdinand Schuck the Younger. He worked in Linz from 1820 to 1824.
BIBLIOGRAPHY:
Fuchs, Heinrich, *Die Österreichchischen Maler des 19. Jahrhunderts*, Selbstverlag, Vienna, 1972-1974.
AUCTION RECORDS:
VIENNA, 22 Sept 1964, *Bouquet of Flowers*, ATS 70,000. LONDON, 16 March 1994, *Composition of Flowers and Fruit with Hazelnuts and Butterflies* (1816, oil on canvas, 27 x 20 1/2 ins / 68.5 x 52 cm) GBP 12,075.

SCHECK, Ferdinand, the Younger
Austrian, 19th century.
Painter.
Ferdinand Scheck the Younger was the son of Ferdinand Scheck the Elder. He worked in Linz from 1856 to 1869.

SCHECK, Gottlieb
German, 19th century.
Born 15 March 1844, in Rutesheim.
Active in Stuttgart.
Sculptor.
Gottlieb Scheck was trained by Th. Wagner and Fr. Jouffroy in Paris. He sculpted tombs and medals of portraits.

SCHECK, Martin
German, 17th century.
Active in Risstissen.
Draughtsman, engraver (burin).
Martin Scheck drew architectural views.

SCHECKS, Kaspar, or Schegs or Scheck
German, 17th century.

Died 18 August 1665, in Augsburg.
Engraver (burin), painter (?).

SCHECROUN, Jean Pierre
French, 20th century.
Painter.

Jean Pierre Schecroun, a pupil of Fernand Léger, held his first solo exhibition in Paris in 1964.

By the mid-60s we no longer find in his work the misleading influences to which he sometimes gave way; his painting is characterised by a certain dynamism of abstract forms. Jacques Damase describes it as `Half-moon, quarter moon, quarter circle - these signs are a sort of puzzle that the artist refuses to knit together'.

SCHEDEL, Martin, or Schedl or Schödle
Austrian, 18th century.
Born 1677, in Tannheim (Tyrol); died 1748.
Engraver.

Martin Schedel was trained by A. Birkhart, anf continued his training in Venice and Rome. He worked in Prague and Salzburg. He engraved using a burin.

SCHEDEL, Sebastian
German, 18th century.
Active in Aub during the first half of the 18th century.
Painter.

Sebastian Schedel executed the paintings on the altars of the churches in Berolzheim, Mergentheim and Sonderhofen.

SCHEDEL HARTMAN
Polish, 15th - 16th century.
Born 1440; died 1514.
Painter, engraver.

Schedel Hartman is known to have engraved *Cracow and its Castle*.

SCHEDLER, Johann Georg, or Schaedler, Schädler, Schödler
Swiss, 19th century.
Born 27 April 1777, in Constance; died 20 November 1866, in Innsbruck.
Painter, miniaturist, engraver (etching), lithographer.

Schedler worked notably in Innsbruck. He painted landscapes and portraits with gouache.

MUSEUMS AND GALLERIES:
INNSBRUCK (Tiroler Landesmus. Ferdinandeum): *Portrait of Andreas Hofer* (several).

SCHEDONI, Bartolomeo, or Schedone, Schidone
Italian, 17th century.
Born 23 January 1578, in Modena; died 23 December 1615, in Parma.
Painter, watercolourist, engraver. Religious subjects, portraits, genre scenes.

Although biographical details are scarce, a study of this artist is merited by the sheer number of his works in European museums. According to some critics he was a pupil of the Carracci brothers, but there is no evidence to support this. He worked for the ducal palace of Modena between 1602 and 1606, then entered the service of Duke Ranuccio of Parma from 1607 to 1615 as first painter to the court, where he was highly favoured.

Careful examination of his works shows that he studied the paintings of Correggio and that he had an even greater affinity with Caravaggio. He loved to use light to simplify and delineate volumes very clearly in an almost schematic fashion. The effect of such harsh illumination is to produce not only pronounced chiaroscuro but also a marked contrast between vibrant colours. Schedoni is known to have been a keen gambler, and he died relatively young, having incurred a significant gambling debt in a single night that he was unable to pay.

MUSEUMS AND GALLERIES:
AMIENS: *Mary Magdalene* - BAYONNE: *St Sebastian* - BERGAMO (Accademia Carrara): *Virgin and the Infant Jesus; Holy Family* - BESANÇON: *Adoration of the Shepherds* - CHÂTEAUROUX: *St Jerome* - CHERBOURG: *Martyrdom of St Sebastian* - COPENHAGEN: *Charity* - CREMONA: *Madonna with Child* - DRESDEN: *Holy Family in a Landscape; Death of St Francis* - FLORENCE (NG): *Virgin, Jesus and St John; Virgin with Jesus in Her Arms; Holy Family* - FLORENCE (Palazzo Pitti): *Holy Family; Virgin and the Infant Jesus; St Paul* - GLASGOW: *Cupid with an Hourglass* - HELSINKI: *Young Boy* - KARLSRUHE: *Lot and His Daughters* - LYONS: *Jesus in the Garden of Gethsemane* - MAINZ: *St John in the Desert* - MILAN (Pinacoteca di Brera): *Virgin, Infant Jesus, St John and St Francis* - MODENA: *St Jerome; St John the Baptist; Supper at the House of Simon; Madonna with Child* (twice); *Holy Family* - MODENA (Mus. Civico d'Arte): *Harmony; Exploits of Coriolanus* - MODENA (Mus. Civico d'Arte, Campori Collection): *Madonna with Child* - MONTAUBAN: *Hope* - MONTPELLIER: *Holy Family* - MOSCOW (Rumiantsev Mus.): *Virgin, Infant Jesus and St Charles Borromeo* - MUNICH: *Mary Magdalene in a Grotto; Lot and His Daughters; Mary Magdalene, Penitent* - NANCY: *Virgin and the Infant Jesus; Mary Magdalene, Penitent* - NANTES: *Good Rich Man* (watercolour, sketch) - NAPLES: *Portrait of a Shoemaker; Erminia with the Shepherds; St Eustace before the Stag; Portrait of Vincenzo Grassi; Infatuation; Holy Family with Angel; Holy Family with St John; St Jerome; Charity; St Sebastian Tended by Holy Women; Annunciation of the Massacre of the Innocents; Holy Family Surrounded by Saints; St John the Baptist; St Sebastian Tied to the Pillar; St Peter; St Paul* - NAPLES (Mus. di Palazzo Reale): *Alms; Holy Family* - NARBONNE: *Holy Family with St John* - NICE: *Pietà* - OLDENBURG: *Mary Magdalene* - PARIS (Louvre): *Holy Family; Christ Carried to the Tomb; Entombment* - PARMA: *St Francis; Adoration of the Shepherds; Madonna with Child; Entombment; Mary before the Tomb; Last Supper* - PONTOISE: *Education of the Infant Jesus; Jesus in the Garden of Gethsemane* - ROHRAU (Schlossmus., Graf Harrach'sche Familiensammlung): *Holy Family; Head of a Womn* - ROME (Gal. Nazionale d'Arte Antica di Palazzo Barberini): *Holy Family* - ROME (Mus. e Gal. Borghese): *Portrait; Virgin and the Infant Jesus* - ROME (Palazzo Doria Pamphili): *St Roch with an Angel* - ST PETERSBURG (Hermitage): *St John the Baptist; Virgin and the Infant Jesus; Virgin, Infant Jesus and Saints; Cupid; Holy Family; Diana and Actaeon* (these latter two not certain) - VALENCIENNES: *Mystical Marriage of St Catherine* - VENICE (Gal. dell'Accademia): *Jesus Carried to the Sepulchre* - VIENNA: *Virgin and the Infant Jesus* - VIENNA (Akademie der Bildenden Künste): *St Sebastian; Infant St John* - VIENNA (Czernin'sche Gemäldegal.): *St John the Baptist; Small Boy with Clasped Hands.*

AUCTION RECORDS:
PARIS, 1742, *Descent from the Cross,* FRF 4,015. PARIS, 1756, *Holy Family* (bistre drawing) FRF 200. PARIS, 1776, *Sketch for 'Alms'* (bistre, heightened with white) FRF 580; *Virgin Holding the Infant Jesus* (pen and bistre) FRF 500. PARIS, 1777, *Virgin and the Infant Jesus, St Joseph and St John,* FRF 5,001. PARIS, 1795, *Holy Family,* FRF 5,001. LONDON, 1804, *Virgin and the Infant Jesus, St Joseph and St John,* FRF 17,860. PARIS, 1810, *St John in the Wilderness, Revealing the Saviour,* FRF 2,600. PARIS, 1832, *Holy Family and St John the Baptist,* FRF 4,000. PARIS, 1849, *Young Girl Learning Her Prayers,* FRF 19,685. PARIS, 1850, *Mary Magdalene,* FRF 2,700. PARIS, 1859, *Young Girl Learning the Alphabet,* FRF 10,530. LONDON, 1884, *Virgin Teaching the Infant Jesus,* FRF 7,346. PARIS, 29 and 30 April 1920, *Cherubim on Clouds Presenting the Instruments of the Passion of Christ,* FRF 2,400. PARIS, 10 June 1925, *Holy Family,* FRF 1,350. PARIS, 21-23 Nov 1927, *Virgin and the Infant Jesus,* FRF 950. PARIS, 6-7 May 1929, *Holy Family and St John* (attributed) FRF 15,500.

LONDON, 12 July 1929, *Holy Family*, GBP 252. BRUSSELS, 6 Dec 1937, *Holy Family*, BEF 3,200. PARIS, 11 April 1945, *Ceres* (attributed) FRF 5,100. MILAN, 28 Feb 1951, *Bacchus and Ariadne; Triumph of Venus* (two pendants) ITL 400,000. PARIS, 7 March 1951, *Holy Family* (school of Bartolomeo Schedoni) FRF 11,100. PARIS, 18 Feb 1981, *Head of a Woman* (red chalk heightened with white, 9 1/4 x 7 3/4in/23.6 x 20cm) FRF 6,800. MILAN, 20 May 1982, *Virgin and Child* (oil on panel, 13 1/2 x 17 3/4in/34 x 45cm) ITL 8,000,000. LONDON, 2 July 1984, *Head of an Old Bearded Man Looking Upwards* (black and white chalk/blue paper, 14 1/2 x 9 1/2in/36.7 x 24.1cm) GBP 3,300. NEW YORK, 31 May 1991, *Mary Magdalene, Penitent* (oil on panel, 37 1/4 x 28 3/4in/94.6 x 73.3cm) USD 97,900. PARIS, 7 April 1995, *Study of Three Figures* (black chalk and brown wash, 7 3/4 x 5 1/2in/19.8 x 14cm) FRF 8,500. NEW YORK, 30 Jan 1997, *Holy Family with an Angel* (oil on panel, 20 x 16in/50.8 x 40.6cm) USD 1,432,500. LONDON, 3 Dec 1997, *St John the Baptist in the Wilderness* (c. 1611, oil on canvas, 53 1/2 x 36 1/2in/136 x 93cm) GBP 89,500. NEW YORK, 28 Jan 1999, *Rest on the Flight into Egypt in Moonlit Landscape* (oil on panel, 12 x 15 ins / 30 x 39 cm) USD 700,000. NEW YORK, 29 Jan 1999, *Holy Family with Infant St John the Baptist and St Elizabeth* (oil on panel, 19 x 27 ins / 48 x 68 cm) USD 130,000. LONDON, 14 Dec 2000, *Holy Family with St Francis Adoring the Christ Child* (oil on canvas, 34 x 28 ins / 87 x 72 cm) GBP 13,000. MILAN, 25 Feb 2004, *St John the Baptist in the Desert* (oil on canvas, 54 x 36 ins / 136 x 92 cm) EUR 353,000.

SCHEDRIN. See **SHCHEDRIN**

SCHEE, Jan
Flemish School, 18th century.
Painter.

Jan Schee was apprenticed to Thomas Gaal, in Middelburg in 1776.

SCHEEKMACKERS. See **SCHEEMAECKERS**

SCHEEL, Albert
German, 19th century.
Active during the first half of the 19th century.
Painter. Genre scenes, portraits.

Albert Scheel trained at the academy in Berlin from 1839 to 1840.

SCHEEL, Benedix
German, 18th century.
Died 8 May 1745.
Active in Hamburg.
Painter.

Benedix Scheel was a teacher of the Gilde in 1707.

SCHEEL, Ernst
German, 19th - 20th century.
Born 15 February 1861, in Potsdam.
Painter, sculptor, engraver, designer. Genre scenes.

Ernst Scheel studied at the fine arts academy in Berlin and under Otto Knille.

AUCTION RECORDS:
LONDON, 18 March 1994, *In a Lost World* (1896, oil on canvas, 22 1/2 x 26 1/2 ins / 57 x 67 cm) GBP 8,280.

SCHEEL, Georg Friedrich
German, 18th century.
Active during the second half of the 18th century.
Painter.

Georg Friedrich Scheel entered the guild in Frankfurt am Main in 1778.

SCHEEL, Johann Daniel
German, 18th - 19th century.
Born 15 March 1773, in Frankfurt am Main; died 28 January 1833, in Frankfurt am Main.
Painter, engraver (etching).

Johann Daniel Scheel trained in Düsseldorf.

MUSEUMS AND GALLERIES:
FRANKFURT AM MAIN (MM): watercolours.

SCHEEL, Joseph
German, 19th - 20th century.
Born 7 February 1853, in Wäschenbeuren; died August 1923, in Munich.
Sculptor.

Joseph Scheel was a pupil of Sirius Eberle.

SCHEEL, Max
German, 19th - 20th century.
Born 2 January 1866, in Berlin.
Painter.

Max Scheel studied under Caspar Ritter, Gustav Schönleber, Max Thedy and Max Koner. He is noted for compositions painted in the new town hall building in Dessau in 1901.

SCHEEL, Sebastian, or Schel, Schell or Schöll
Austrian, 15th - 16th century.
Born c. 1479; died 1554, in Innsbruck.
Painter. Religious subjects, landscapes.
Tyrolean School.

Sebastian Scheel worked for the court of Innsbruck, painting religious subjects, coats of arms and shields.

MUSEUMS AND GALLERIES:
INNSBRUCK (Tiroler Landesmus. Ferdinandeum): altar of Annaberg; *Raising of Lazarus*; several fragments of altar paintings.

AUCTION RECORDS:
MONACO, 17 June 1988, *Landscape with Boat* (oil on panel, 6 x 10 ins / 15.5 x 25.5 cm) FRF 13,320.

SCHEEL, Signe
Norwegian, 19th - 20th century.
Born 1860, in Hamar.
Painter. Figures, portraits, landscapes.

Signe Scheel studied variously under Christian Krogh, Erik Werenskiold and Eilif Peterssen in Oslo, under Karl Gussow in Berlin and under Puvic de Chavannes in Paris.

MUSEUMS AND GALLERIES:
GÖTEBORG: *Old Woman in a Rocking Chair* - OSLO (Nasjonalgal.): *Rothenburg Motif*; *Portraits of the Artist's Two Sisters*.

SCHEELE, Karl Axel Adam
Swedish, 19th century.
Born 12 April 1797, in Prinsnäs, near Jönköping; died 29 August 1873, in Stockholm.
Lithographer.

Scheele was a pupil of Senefelder in Munich. He engraved *Memories of the Life of Napoleon*.

SCHEELE, Kurt
German, 20th century.
Born 1905, in Frankfurt am Main.
Painter, engraver (woodcut).

Kurt Scheele studied under Rud Koch in Offenbach and under Delevilla in Frankfurt.

SCHEEMAECKERS, Hendrik, or Scheekmackers or Scheemakers
Flemish School, 18th century.
Born in Antwerp; died 18 July 1748, in Paris.
Sculptor.

Hendrik Scheemaeckers was the pupil of his father, Peeter Scheemaeckers I. He studied in Copenhagen with J.C. Sturmberg and travelled to France and England before settling in Paris.

SCHEEMAECKERS, Peeter I
Flemish School, 17th - 18th century.
Born 1640, in Antwerp; died 1714, in Arendonk.
Sculptor.

Peeter Scheemaeckers I was a pupil of Pieter Verbruggen I. He was a guild member in Antwerp in 1675. His works include the *Van Delft family monument* in Antwerp Cathedral, a relief in the church of St James, the tomb marker of the *Marquess Delpico* in the city's Citadel church in het Zuidkasteel, which was demolished in 1876, and the *Tomb of Count Karel de Lalaing*, at the church of St Catherine in Hoogstraten.

MUSEUMS AND GALLERIES:
MUNICH (Bayerisches Nationalmus.): *Cupids at Play* (four high reliefs in ivory).

AUCTION RECORDS:
LONDON, 11 Dec 1986, *Virgin and Child with the Infant St John* (wood, h. 11 1/2 ins / 29.2 cm) GBP 22,000.

SCHEEMAECKERS, Peeter II or Peeter Gaspar
Flemish School, 18th century.
Born 16 January 1691, in Antwerp; died 12 September 1781, in Antwerp.
Sculptor.

Peeter Scheemaeckers II was the pupil of his father Peeter Scheemaeckers I. He returned to Antwerp in 1771 after travelling to Italy, Copenhagen and London. He was especially active in London, where he carved 14 tombs for the abbey of Westminster.

AUCTION RECORDS:
LONDON, 13 April 1978, *Flora* (1732, ivory, h. 10 1/4 ins / 26 cm) GBP 3,200.

SCHEEMAECKERS, Peeter III, or Scheemackers or Scheemakers
French, 18th century.
Died 19 October 1765, in Paris.
Sculptor, draughtsman, engraver, architect, designer of ornamental architectural features.

Peeter Scheemaeckers III was the son of Hendrik Scheemaeckers. He was a member of the Académie de St-Luc in 1755. He engraved a series of *Antique Vases* and *Antique Clocks*.

SCHEEMAECKERS, Thomas, or Scheemakers
British, 18th century.
Born 1740; died 15 July 1808, in London.
Sculptor.

Son and successor to Peter Scheemaeckers II, Thomas Scheemaeckers exhibited in London from 1765 to 1804.

SCHEER
19th century.
Painter. Genre scenes.

Scheer was mentioned in Art Prices Current.

AUCTION RECORDS:
LONDON, 7 March 1910, *Hotel Interior* (1856; *Soldiers Playing* (1857, two pendants) GBP 8.

SCHEER, Dmitri, or Cher
Russian, 19th century.
Active during the first half of the 19th century.
Sculptor (ivory).

MUSEUMS AND GALLERIES:
ST PETERSBURG (Hermitage): *Annunciation* (low relief).

SCHEERBART, Paul
German, 19th - 20th century.
Born 8 January 1863, in Danzig (now Gdansk, Poland); died 15 October 1915, in Berlin.
Draughtsman, illustrator.

Paul Scheerbart illustrated and decorated with motifs several of his own poems.

SCHEERER, F.
German, 19th century.
Miniaturist.

SCHEERES, Hendricus Johannes
Dutch, 19th century.
Born 3 August 1829, in The Hague; died 12 January 1864, in The Hague.
Painter. Genre scenes, figures.

Hendricus Scheeres' work featured in the 1849 Exposition, held at The Hague.

MUSEUMS AND GALLERIES:
THE HAGUE (Gemeentemus.): *Before the Oven*.

AUCTION RECORDS:
COLOGNE, 25 June 1976, *At the Antique Dealer's Shop* (1856, oil on panel, 7 x 9 ins / 17.5 x 23 cm) DEM 3,300. LONDON, 23 Feb 1977, *A Game of Chess* (1856, oil on panel, 8 1/4 x 7 ins / 21 x 17.8 cm) GBP 1,000. AMSTERDAM, 24 April 1979, *Blacksmith* (1854, oil on panel, 8 x 10 1/2 ins / 20.5 x 26.5 cm) NLG 5,600. LONDON, 5 Oct 1983, *Interior* (oil on panel, 8 1/4 x 6 1/4 ins / 21 x 16 cm) GBP 950. COLOGNE, 29 June 1990, *A Game of Chess* (oil on panel, 15 3/4 x 20 1/2 ins / 40 x 52 cm) DEM 3,800. AMSTERDAM, 11 Sept 1990, *'Prepared to Burn his Souvenirs'* (1855, oil on panel, 7 3/4 x 6 ins / 20 x 15 cm) NLG 2,990. STOCKHOLM, 19 May 1992, *Man Resting Beside the Hearth* (oil on panel, 8 1/4 x 6 3/4 ins / 21 x 17 cm) SEK 12,000. AMSTERDAM, 2-3 Nov 1992, *The Awning* (oil on panel, 6 1/2 x 5 ins / 16.5 x 12.5 cm) NLG 1,725. AMSTERDAM, 30 Oct 1996, *A Game of Cards* (oil on panel, 17 x 22 ins / 43 x 55 cm) NLG 10,995. AMSTERDAM, 27 Oct 1997, *The House-maid* (oil on panel, 10 1/4 x 7 3/4 ins / 26 x 20 cm) NLG 11,800. TORONTO, 26 Nov 2001, *In a Kitchen Cellar* (oil on panel, 8 x 6 ins / 20 x 15 cm) CAD 2,800. LOKEREN, 8 Dec 2001, *The Armourer* (1859-1860, oil on panel, two, 7 x 6 ins / 19 x 14 cm) BEF 120,000. LOKEREN, 9 March 2002, *Rembrandt in Studio* (oil on panel, 7 x 6 ins / 18 x 14 cm) EUR 1,800. LONDON, 20 March 2003, *Cavalier Writing a Letter. Young Girl Reading a Letter* (oil on panel, a pair, 11 x 9 ins / 28 x 23 cm) GBP 2,500. PARIS, 19 Dec 2003, *Young Woman Holding Glass* (1853, oil on panel, 8 x 6 ins / 20 x 15 cm) EUR 1,600.

SCHEERRE, Herman, or Scheere
German, 15th century.
Active in England 1400-1416.
Miniaturist, illuminator.

Herman Scheerre worked in London in 1407 and signed works with his name or with: *Si quis amat non laborat quod Hermannus*. He painted series of miniatures for both secular and religious manuscripts, such as the *Breviary of Archbishop Chichele*, the *Psalter of the Duke of Bedford*, the *Book of Hours of the Duke of Bedford*, the *Bible of Richard II*, and the *Book of Offices and Prayers*. The *Beaufort Book of Hours*, illuminated between 1401 and 1410, has the Annuciation as its theme, and includes portraits of Jean de Beaufort and his wife Margaret de Holand.

MUSEUMS AND GALLERIES:
LONDON (British Mus.): *Psalter of the Duke of Bedford; Book of Hours of the Duke of Bedford; Beaufort Book of Hours*.

SCHEFER, Émile André
French, 20th century.
Born 14 February 1896, in Paris; died 15 March 1942, in Paris.
Painter, draughtsman.

Émile André Schefer's favourite subject was railways.

SCHEFFAUER, Philipp Jakob
German, 18th century.
Born 7 May 1756, in Stuttgart; died 13 November 1808, in Stuttgart.
Sculptor.

Scheffauer was a sculptor at the court in Stuttgart. In 2003, his work was included in a collective exhibition entitled *L'esprit créateur de Pigalle à Canova. Terres cuites européennes 1740-1840* (*The Creative Spirit from Pigalle to Canova. European Terracotta 1740-1840*) at the Louvre Museum in Paris.

BIBLIOGRAPHY:

Draper, James David/Scherf, Guilhem, et al., *L'esprit créateur de Pigalle à Canova. Terres cuites européennes 1740-1840*, exhibition catalogue, Musée du Louvre, Paris, 2003.

MUSEUMS AND GALLERIES:

STUTTGART (Staatsgal.): *Bust of Stuber, a Counsellor in Calw; Spirit of Death; Jacob Wrestling with the Angel; Portrait in Medallion Form of the Banker Ch. Heigelin* - TOULOUSE (MBA, Mus. des Augustins): *Méléagre* (c. 1785-1789, terracotta).

SCHEFFEL, Johan Henrik

Swedish, 18th century.
Born 9 April 1690, in Wismar; died 21 December 1781, in Västerås.
Painter, miniaturist, draughtsman.

Scheffel studied in Germany and France, and in Stockholm with David von Krafft. He lived in Stockholm from 1723 until 1765. He became a member of the drawing academy in 1735, and its director in 1763. He lived in Västerås from 1765 onwards, and taught Per Krafft the Elder. He is known to have produced 175 paintings, most of which are unsigned. The best among them were produced between 1730 and 1740.

MUSEUMS AND GALLERIES:

GÖTEBORG: *Unknown Lady of the Liewen Family; Professor Lars Laurel; Portrait of the Artist by Himself* - HELSINKI: *Colonel Kristoffer* - MARIEFRED (Gripsholms Slott): *Marquis Filip Sack; Count Fredrik Ulrik Höpken; Twenty Portraits of Officers* - STOCKHOLM: *Major Malkolm Sinclair; Marquis Korut Gustav Sparre; Marquis Abraham Leijonhufoud; Anna Margareta Walcker; The Deputy Erik Ersson.*

AUCTION RECORDS:

STOCKHOLM, 21 April 1982, *Portrait of Gustaf Fredrik von Rosen* (oil on canvas, 31½ x 25¼ ins / 80 x 64 cm) SEK 16,500. STOCKHOLM, 30 Oct 1984, *Portrait of Augustin Ehrensvard* (oil on canvas, 30¼ x 24½ ins / 77 x 62 cm) SEK 36,000. STOCKHOLM, 15 Nov 1988, *Portrait of Kristina Charlotta Vult von Steijern* (oil, 31 x 25¼ ins / 79 x 64 cm) SEK 14,000. STOCKHOLM, 15 Nov 1989, *Portrait of Jakobina Henrietta Hildebrand* (oil on canvas, 30¾ x 22½ ins / 78 x 57 cm) SEK 9,700. STOCKHOLM, 16 May 1990, *Portrait of a Man* (oil on canvas, 26¾ x 20½ ins / 68 x 52 cm) SEK 15,500. STOCKHOLM, 14 Nov 1990, *Bust Portrait of Merchant Pehr Reimers* (oil on canvas, 30 x 24½ ins / 76 x 62 cm) SEK 8,000. STOCKHOLM, 29 May 1991, *Portrait of General Eberhard Bildstein in Armour* (1727, oil on canvas, 52¾ x 43¼ ins / 134 x 110 cm) SEK 37,000. STOCKHOLM, 19 May 1992, *Portrait of Margareta Katarina Ugla as a Child* (oil on canvas, 19¾ x 15¾ ins / 50 x 40 cm) SEK 14,000. STOCKHOLM, 10-12 May 1993, *Bust Portrait of a Man* (oil on canvas, 30¾ x 24¾ ins / 78 x 63 cm) SEK 17,500. STOCKHOLM, 26 May 1999, *Portraits of Lars Stierneldh and his Wife Sara Catharina Hacker* (oil on canvas, a pair, 31 x 25 ins / 80 x 63 cm) SEK 74,000. STOCKHOLM, 16 May 2000, *Portrait of Young Lady* (oil on canvas, 28 x 22 ins / 71 x 57 cm) SEK 21,000. STOCKHOLM, 29 May 2001, *Portrait of Ulrica Eleonora Gerner* (oil on canvas, 31 x 24 ins / 78 x 62 cm) SEK 31,000. STOCKHOLM, 29 May 2001, *Portrait of Jacob Gerner* (oil on canvas, 31 x 25 ins / 78 x 63 cm) SEK 32,500. STOCKHOLM, 26 May 2003, *Portrait of Man, Possibly Georg Wilhelm von Scheven* (oil on canvas, 30 x 25 ins / 77 x 64 cm) SEK 24,000.

SCHEFFEL, Martin

Swedish, 18th century.
Born 1729, in Sigtuna; died 19 February 1783, in Stockholm.
Miniaturist.

This artist was the son of Johan Henrik Scheffel. He painted several miniatures that were attributed either to his father, or to his sister Margaretha. The Nasjonalgaleriet in Stockholm has one of his miniatures, *The Judgement of Paris*.

SCHEFFELHUBER, Franz.

See **SCHÖFFTLHUBER**

SCHEFFER. See also **SCHÄFFER**

SCHEFFER, Amand. See **SCHÄFFER**

SCHEFFER, Ambrosius

German, 16th century.
Active in Würzburg.
Painter.

Ambrosius Scheffer does not appear to be the same artist as Ambrosius Schaffner.

SCHEFFER, Arnold

French, 19th century.
Born 1839, in Paris; died 1873, in Venice.
Painter (gouache). History painting, portraits.

He was taught by his father, Henry Scheffer, and by Picot. He exhibited at the Salon between 1859 and 1870.

MUSEUMS AND GALLERIES:

BESANÇON: *League Members Demonstrating outside the Guise Chapel* - MAYENNE: *Venetian Women in Prayer.*

AUCTION RECORDS:

PARIS, 30 Dec 1922, *Henri III and His Court in Chartres Cathedral,* FRF 400. PARIS, 7 Feb 1923, *Young Girl* (gouache) FRF 1,450. PARIS, 24 Nov 1995, *Portrait of a Young Man* (1860, oil on canvas, 21¾ x 18¾ ins / 55.5 x 47.5 cm) FRF 5,000.

SCHEFFER, Ary

Dutch, 19th century.
Born 10 February 1795, in Dordrecht; died 15 June 1858, in Argenteuil.
Active in France from 1812.
Painter, sculptor, engraver. History painting, portraits, genre scenes.

Ary Scheffer was the son of the German painter Johann-Baptist Scheffer, who had settled in Holland and married the Dordrecht artist Cornelia Lamme. Growing up in an artistic household, Ary developed his markedly confident style and painterly expression at an early age. Following the death of his father (a painter at the court of Napoleon's brother, King Louis Napoleon), Scheffer's mother travelled to Paris and enrolled her son in the studio of the painter Guérin, in August 1811. Guérin taught drawing to the children of the Duke of Orléans; following the latter's accession to the throne in 1830, Ary was appointed court painter.

Scheffer exhibited his first painting at the age of 10. He quickly earned popularity with the bourgeois public, who appreciated his 'romantic' genre paintings, with their evocative titles: *The Soldier's Widow, The Mariner's Family, The Sister of Charity, The Orphans at the Cemetery.* Following the accession of Louis-Philippe, he was commissioned to paint many of the large pictures destined for the historical galleries at the palace of Versailles. In addition to these official commissions, he also painted a large number of private portraits. His paintings reflect the cultural events of his day (*The Death of Géricault*), and scenes from history or the lives of the saints, particularly the Versailles commissions: *Charlemagne Subduing the Saxons* (1837), or *St Augustine and St Monica* (1855). He also painted portraits of Dante, Goethe, Byron and Walter Scott. His highly distinctive, polished technique, bordering on grisaille, earned him a remarkable reputation with the general public.

In 1810 he submitted a painting to a public exhibition in Amsterdam, and he was a regular exhibitor at the Paris Salon from 1812 until 1855. In 1816 his painting *Abraham and the Three Angels* won an award in Antwerp; he was awarded another medal in 1817, and made a Chevalier of the Légion d'Honneur in 1828 (he was promoted to Officier in 1835). In 2003, his work featured in the exhibition *De blijvende verlokking: Nederlandse kunstenaars in Italië, 1806-1940* (*Lasting Attraction: Dutch Artists in Italy, 1806-1940*), at the Kunsthal in Rotterdam, showcasing the importance of the Italian Grand Tour for the work of Dutch artists.

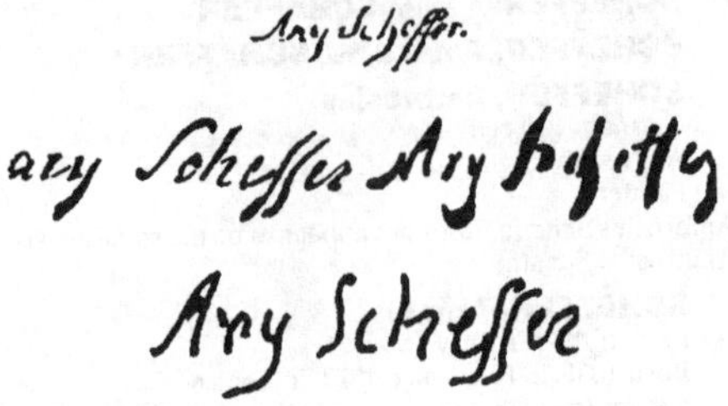

BIBLIOGRAPHY:

Ary Scheffer, exhibition catalogue, Musée de la Vie romantique, Paris, 1996. *De blijvende verlokking: Nederlandse kunstenaars in Italië, 1806-1940*, exhibition catalogue, Kunsthal, Rotterdam, 2003.

MUSEUMS AND GALLERIES:

ALENÇON: *Ch. Ph. Lasteyrie* - AMSTERDAM (Fodor Mus.): *Christ the Consoler* - AMSTERDAM (Stedelijk Mus.): *Mary Magdalene at the Foot of the Cross; Blessed are the Pure of Heart* - ANGERS: *Las Cases* - ARENENBERG (Napoleon Mus.): *Hortense Beauharnais* - AUTUN: *General Changarnier* - BESANÇON: *Mme Marjolin, the Artist's Daughter; M. H. E. Baudrand* - BOSTON: *Eberhard de Wurtemberg before the Body of his Son; Dante and Beatrice* - CAEN: *Doctor Duval* - CALAIS: *Faust; Marguerite* - CHANTILLY: *Prince Talleyrand; Duke of Orléans; Louis Philippe; Queen Marie-Amélie* - DORDRECHT (Dordrechts Mus., Ary Sheffer's room): *The Brothers Henry, Ary and Arnold Scheffer, in a Landscape; Th. d'Aquin Preaching Upon the Sea; 'Allons Enfants de la Patrie'; Botzaris; The Artist's Mother, on her Death-bed; Mignon; Ecce Homo; Prodigal Son; Two Self-portraits; Marble Bust of the Artist's Mother; The Artist's Mother on her Death-bed* - ÉVREUX: *Dupont as a Child; J. Ch. Dupont de l'Eure* - FLORENCE: *Portrait of Giuseppe Fontanelli* - FRANKFURT AM MAIN (Goethe Mus.): *Goethe; Schiller* - FRANKFURT AM MAIN (Städel): *Ruth and Naomi* - GRAZ: *Monks in a Boat* - GRENOBLE: *The Painter Hersent* - HAMBURG: *Blessed are the Suffering* - KALININGRAD: *Afflicted Mother and her Two Children* - LE MANS: *David d'Angers* - LILLE: *The Dead Travel Fast* - LONDON (National Portrait Gal.): *Charles Dickens* (1855, oil on canvas) - LONDON (NG): *Mrs Robert Hollond* (1851, oil on canvas); *Sts Augustine and Monica* (1854, oil on canvas) - LONDON (Wallace Collection): *Margaret at the Fountain* (1858, oil on canvas); *Portrait of a Child* (in collaboration with Eugène Isabey); *Francesca da Rimini* (1835, oil on canvas); *The Return of the Prodigal Son* (1857, oil/panel); *The Sister of Mercy* (1829, oil/canvas/panel); *Mother and Child* (c. 1825-1830, water and bodycolour/paper) - MARSEILLES: *Mary Magdalene* - MELBOURNE: *Temptation of Christ* - MONTPELLIER: *Professor Lallemand; Philosopher* - NANTES: *Child Prodigy* - PARIS (Bibliothèque-Mus. de l'Opéra): *A. Tamburini* - PARIS (Louvre): *Death of Géricault* (1824); *Les Femmes Souliotes; Temptation of Christ; St Augustin and his Mother St Monica* (1855); *Christ with a Reed; Villemain; Lamennais; Mlle de Fauveau; Paolo and Francesca; Eberhard der Greiner; Ecce Homo; Fr. Arago* - PARIS (Mus. Carnavalet): *Béranger* - PARIS (Mus. du Petit Palais): *Mme Caillard* - PAU: *Henri IV* - PONTOISE: *Watercolour* - POZNAN: *Alms* - ROTTERDAM: *Count Eberhard Pursuing his Son Ulrich; Count Eberhard Beside the Body of his Son; Two Sketches* - ROUEN: *Armand Carrel, in Death; General La Fayette in Civilian Dress* - TOLEDO, OH: *Mary Magdalene* - UTRECHT (Centraal Mus.): *Christus Remunerator* (c. 1846, oil on canvas) - VENICE (Mus. Correr): *Daniele Manin; The Same, on his Death-bed; Emilia Manin on his Death-bed* - VERSAILLES (Mus. d'Histoire de France): *Battle of Zulpich; Entry of Philippe Auguste into Paris after the Battle of Bouvines; St Louis Conferring Royal Powers Upon the Queen Mother Before his Departure for the Crusade; Entry of Charles VII into Rheims; Entry of Louis XII into Genoa; Equestrian Portrait of Louis Philippe with his Sons; Maréchal Mouton; Baron de Barante and his Wife; M. E. Baudrand; Paul Louis Courier; Gounod; H. Lamartine; Horace Vernet; Maria Taglioni; Chopin; Duke of Orléans Receiving the First Regiment of the Hussars, Under the Command of the Duke of Chartres, at the Barrière du Trône; Same Subject; Battle of Tolbiac; Charlemagne Accepting the Surrender of Wittekind at Paderborn* (1837); *Henri IV; Hoche; Death of Gaston de Foix at Ravenna; Charlemagne Presenting his First Capitularies at the Assembly of the Franks in 779; Olivier de Clisson; Marie Joseph La Fayette; Lobau* - WARSAW (Krasinski Mus.): *Count Krasinki* - WASHINGTON DC (Corcoran Gal. of Art): *Commodore Ch. Morris* - WEIMAR (Liszt Haus): *Liszt.*

AUCTION RECORDS:

PARIS, 1834, *Subject Taken From the Modern Greek Wars,* FRF 4,500. PARIS, 1850, *The Three Magi,* FRF 12,428. PARIS, 1852, *Francesca da Rimini,* FRF 43,600; *The Giaour,* FRF 23,500; *Christ the Consoler,* FRF 52,500; *Medora,* FRF 19,500. PARIS, 1860, *Sister of Charity,* FRF 12,600. LONDON, 1862, *Leonora* (watercolour) FRF 2,600. PARIS, 1863, *Leonora,* FRF 5,500; *Martha and Margaret,* FRF 4,100. LIÈGE, 1863, *The Holy Women at the Tomb of Christ,* FRF 13,650. PARIS, 1865, *Young Mother,* FRF 6,500. PARIS, 1870, *Francesca da Rimini,* FRF 100,000. PARIS, 1872, *Margaret at the Well,* FRF 56,000; *Convalescent Mother,* FRF 7,600. PARIS, 1872, *Margaret Leaving the Church,* FRF 53,000; *Margaret at the Church,* FRF 40,000. PARIS, 1876, *Young Girl's Complaints,* FRF 17,000. PARIS, 1876, *Dante and Beatrice,* FRF 40,000. LONDON, 1887, *Mary Magdalene,* FRF 16,275; *St John the Apostle,* FRF 15,215. LONDON, 1894, *Dante and Beatrice,* FRF 50,000. LONDON, 1900, *Hebe,* FRF 2,625. PARIS, 21 Jan 1901, *Faust and Marguerite,* FRF 1,200. PARIS, 26-29 April 1904, *Mother,* FRF 1,650. LONDON, 15 May 1911, *Visit to Grandmother* (1884) GBP 81. PARIS, 5 June 1911, *Portrait of Louis Philippe,* FRF 565. PARIS, 21 June 1919, *Motherly Remonstrances,* FRF 810. PARIS, 17 March 1923, *Sick Mother Walking to Church, Leaning on Her Two Children,* FRF 2,020. PARIS, 12 May 1923, *St Augustine and St Margaret,* FRF 1,500. LONDON, 23 Nov 1923, *Hebe,* GBP 60. PARIS, 6 May 1925, *Romeo and Juliet,* FRF 1,700. PARIS, 20 May 1925, *Portrait of a Young Boy,* FRF 750. PARIS, 17 and 18 June 1927, *King of Thulé,* FRF 1,000. PARIS, 26 April 1928, *King Louis Philippe taking the Oath Before the Chambers,* FRF 1,480. PARIS, 30 May 1929, *Abduction* (drawing) FRF 950. PARIS, 26 June 1933, *Pastor's Sermon,* FRF 420. PARIS, 5 May 1937, *Portrait of a Man in Black,* FRF 400. PARIS, 8 Dec 1941, *Young Blonde Girl,* FRF 4,500. PARIS, 19 and 20 Jan 1942, *Soldier's Widow,* FRF 5,700. PARIS, 27 Jan 1943, *Young Blonde Girl,* FRF 10,000. PARIS, 8 March 1943, *Marguerite Leaving the Church* (graphite, study) FRF 1,000. PARIS, 10 Nov 1943, *Children Dancing in a Ring* (1831) FRF 14,100; *Study,* FRF 2,100. PARIS, 20 March 1944, *Shipwreck,* FRF 10,000. PARIS, 24 Nov 1944, *Portrait, Thought to be Princess Marie of Orléans,* FRF 7,800. PARIS, July 1946, *Portrait of an Old Man,* FRF 5,000; *Portrait, Thought to be Walter Scott,* FRF 5,000. PARIS, 20 Nov 1946, *Scene from 'Faust',* FRF 8,000; *Scene from 'Faust',* FRF 10,000. PARIS, 24 Nov 1948, *Arrest of Charlotte Corday,* FRF 8,500. PARIS, 5 May 1949, *Young Spinster,* FRF 10,000. PARIS, 28 June 1950, *Portrait of a Man; Woman and Child* (two pendants) FRF 29,000. PARIS, 7 Feb 1951, *Nun Visiting a Sick Patient* (watercolour) FRF 1,600. PARIS, 25 June 1951, *Return from the Falcon-hunt* (watercolour) FRF 4,100. PARIS, 23 Feb 1954, *Recreation* (1831) FRF 6,600. PARIS, 15 June 1954, *Young Mother,* FRF 35,000. LONDON, 10 Oct 1969, *Self-portrait,* Gns 300. PARIS, 4 Dec 1972, *Portrait of a Young Boy,*

FRF 15,000. VERSAILLES, 18 July 1976, *His Royal Highness Ferdinand-Philippe* (oil on canvas, 87 x 48 ins / 221 x 122 cm) FRF 6,500. LONDON, 30 Nov 1977, *Portrait of a Woman* (1847, oil on canvas, 46 1/2 x 28 3/4 ins / 118 x 73 cm) GBP 5, 800. LONDON, 5 Oct 1979, *Paolo and Francesca* (1851, oil on canvas, 9 1/2 x 12 3/4 ins / 24.2 x 32.3 cm) GBP 3,200. LONDON, 2 Oct 1981, *Portrait of a Young Noblewoman* (1841, oil on canvas, 25 x 16 1/2 ins / 63.5 x 42 cm) GBP 1,800. PARIS, 10 Dec 1984, *Ecstasy, or Conjugal Felicity* (watercolour, 15 1/4 x 11 3/4 ins / 39 x 30 cm) FRF 20,000. PARIS, 10 Dec 1984, *Portrait of a Young Girl* (oil on canvas, 28 3/4 x 23 1/2 ins / 73 x 60 cm) FRF 20,000. PARIS, 9 Dec 1985, *Portrait of Maréchal Mouton, Count Lobau* (1836, oil on canvas, 25 1/2 x 16 1/4 ins / 65 x 41 cm) FRF 26,000. PARIS, 23 April 1986, *Profile Portrait of a Child* (oil on panel, 14 1/4 x 11 ins / 36 x 28 cm) FRF 32,000. PARIS, 20 April 1988, *Hunting with Hounds* (oil on panel, 21 1/4 x 25 1/2 ins / 54 x 64.5 cm) FRF 150,000. PARIS, 23 June 1988, *Portrait of Alphonsine de Saint Amand, Aged 10 Months* (oil on canvas, 14 x 10 3/4 ins / 35.5 x 27.3 cm) FRF 27,000. PARIS, 17 March 1989, *Portrait of Madame Le Beau* (lead pencil, 7 3/4 x 6 ins / 20 x 15.5 cm) FRF 8,000. MONACO, 17 June 1989, *Emperor's Siesta* (oil on canvas, 12 x 16 1/2 ins / 30.5 x 42 cm) FRF 24,420. MONACO, 3 Dec 1989, *Paolo and Francesca* (oil on paper/canvas, 20 3/4 x 25 1/4 ins / 53 x 64 cm) FRF 99,900. LONDON, 30 March 1990, *Paolo and Francesca* (1851, oil on canvas, 68 x 94 ins / 172.7 x 238.8 cm) GBP 143,000. PARIS, 6 July 1990, *Portrait of a Young Girl with Her Hair Undone* (oil on canvas, 18 x 15 ins / 46 x 38 cm) FRF 7,000. AMSTERDAM, 24 April 1991, *Crowd of the Faithful* (1841, oil on canvas, 39 1/4 x 23 1/2 ins / 100 x 60 cm) NLG 40,250. PARIS, 22 May 1991, *Battle of Tolbiac* (ink and white gouache) FRF 9,000. NEW YORK, 23 May 1991, *Ariadne* (oil on canvas, 38 3/4 x 27 ins / 98.4 x 68.6 cm) USD 13,200. LONDON, 21 June 1991, *Faust and Marguerite in the Garden* (1846, oil on canvas/panel, 85 3/4 x 53 ins / 217.8 x 134.6 cm) GBP 126,500. PARIS, 26 June 1991, *The Shades of Francesca da Rimini and her Lover Appear to Dante and Virgil* (oil on canvas, 94 1/2 x 122 ins / 240 x 310 cm) FRF 275,000. PARIS, 21 Feb 1992, *St John the Baptist Preaching in the Wilderness* (black chalk, 11 x 9 1/2 ins / 27 x 24 cm) FRF 4,400. PARIS, 26 June 1992, *Marguerite at the Spinning Wheel* (oil on canvas, 48 x 35 1/2 ins / 121 x 90 cm) FRF 38,000. LONDON, 27 Oct 1993, *The Three Marys* (oil on panel, 18 x 12 ins / 46 x 30.5 cm) GBP 1,380. PARIS, 31 March 1995, *Apparition of the Virgin to a Female Saint* (1849, oil on canvas, rounded at the top edge, 51 1/2 x 28 3/4 ins / 131 x 73 cm) FRF 125,000. ROUEN, 29 Oct 1995, *Portrait, Thought to be of the Duchess of Saxe Coburg-Gotha, Princess of Orléans* (1844, oil on canvas, 52 1/4 x 32 1/4 ins / 133 x 82 cm) FRF 230,000. NEW YORK, 12 Feb 1997, *Dante and Virgil Encounter the shadows of Francesca and Paolo da Rimini in Hell* (oil on canvas, 9 3/4 x 13 ins / 24.8 x 33 cm) USD 74,000. LONDON, 11 June 1997, *Dante and Beatrice* (watercolour, 14 1/4 x 7 3/4 ins / 36 x 19.5 cm) GBP 19,550. PARIS, 15 Dec 1997, *Soldier's Widow* (1823, oil on canvas, 16 1/4 x 12 3/4 ins / 41.5 x 32.5 cm) FRF 18,000. NEW YORK, 5 May 1999, *Paolo and Francesca* (oil on panel, 13 x 18 ins / 33 x 45 cm) USD 50,000. PARIS, 13 Dec 1999, *Christ and St John or The Last Supper, The Kiss of Judas* (1857, oil on panel, pair, 24 x 20 ins / 61 x 50 cm) FRF 86,000. NEW YORK, 25 Oct 2000, *Medora* (oil on canvas, 9 x 7 ins / 24 x 19 cm) USD 8,000. NEW YORK, 3 Oct 2001, *Portrait of General Lafayette in Great Coat over Stripped Waistcoat* (oil on canvas, 93 x 51 ins / 235 x 130 cm) USD 40,000. PARIS, 19 April 2002, *Greece on the Ruins of Missolonghi* (1822, oil on canvas, 13 x 9 ins / 32 x 24 cm) EUR 14,000. LONDON, 3 Dec 2003, *Paolo and Francesca* (oil on panel, 13 x 18 ins / 33 x 46 cm) GBP 40,000. PARIS, 26 March 2004, *The Battle of Tolbiac* (oil and pencil, 19 x 22 ins / 49 x 56 cm) EUR 4,600.

SCHEFFER, August
German, 19th century.
Born 3 July 1785.
Painter.

August Scheffer trained and was a teacher at the school of fine art in Berlin, and was an art teacher at the school of fine art in Brunswick.

MUSEUMS AND GALLERIES:
BRUNSWICK (Städtisches Mus.): a painting.

SCHEFFER, Cornelia
Maiden name: Lamme
Dutch, 18th - 19th century.
Born 23 April 1769, in Dordrecht; died 4 July 1839, in Paris.
Miniaturist.

Cornelia Scheffer was the wife of J.-B. Scheffer and mother of Ary and Henry Scheffer. The Ary Scheffer Museum in Dordrecht has a portrait of the poet *Jens Baggesen* by her, together with several other pictures of her relatives and sons, and five portraits of Cornelia by her son Ary.

SCHEFFER, Cornelia, later Mme Marjolin
French, 19th century.
Born 29 July 1830, in Paris; died 20 December 1899, in Paris.
Sculptor, painter, draughtswoman. Figures. Busts.

She was the daughter of Ary Scheffer.

MUSEUMS AND GALLERIES:
DORDRECHT (Dordrechts Mus., Ary Sheffer's room): *Goethe* (bust); *Ary Scheffer* (1846,, bust); *Ary Scheffer on His Death Bed* (drawing) - ROTTERDAM (Mus. Boijmans Van Beuningen): *Ary Scheffer* (bust).

SCHEFFER, Eugen Eduard. See **SCHAEFFER**

SCHEFFER, Henry
French, 19th century.
Born 25 September 1798, in The Hague; died 15 March 1862, in Paris.
Painter. Religious subjects, genre scenes, portraits.

The son of Jean-Baptiste Scheffer and Cornelia Lamme, Henry Scheffer was the younger brother of Ary Scheffer. He came to Paris in 1811 with his mother, who had been recently widowed. He entered the studio of Paulin-Guérin at the same time as his brother, in 1813. Henry benefited from his brother's fame and quickly acquired his own clientele. He also taught painting, and Puvis de Chavannes was one of his pupils.

He exhibited at the Paris Salon from 1824 to 1859. He won a second-class medal in 1824 and first-class medals in 1831 and 1855. He was made a Chevalier of the Légion d'Honneur in 1837.

He appears to have painted more portraits than his elder brother, and he was never short of commissions. His most famous work is a painting of *Christ* in the church of St-Roch in Versailles. He is also known for the following works: *Christ in the Lap of the Virgin, Young Girl Nursing Her Sick Mother, The Day After the Burial, Parents Mourning the Death of Their Child.*

henry Scheffer.

henry Scheffer

henry Scheffer

MUSEUMS AND GALLERIES:
AMIENS (Mus. de Picardie): *Vision of Charles IX* - ANGERS: *Guillaume Bodinier; Las Cases* - BESANÇON: *Dr Marjolin* - BREST: *Charlotte Corday being Arrested* - DORDRECHT (Dordrechts Mus., Ary Sheffer's room): *Exhortation; Portrait of Népomucène Lemercier; Karel Arnoldus Scheffer* - KALININGRAD: *Unfortunate Family* - LONS-LE-SAUNIER: *Nicolas Jousserandot* - MAISONS-LAFFITTE: *Jacques Laffitte* - MONTPELLIER (Mus. Fabre): *M Collt* - PÉRIGUEUX: *The Virgin and the Infant Jesus* - ROTTERDAM: *First Born* - ROUEN (MBA): *Woman Praying* - VERSAILLES: *Battle of Cassel; Joan of Arc Entering Orleans; Casimir Delavigne; Philippe de Mornay du Plessis-Marly; Montfort l'Amaury; Claude Beauvoir; La Palice; Montluc (Blaise de Montesquiou); Jean Toiras.*
AUCTION RECORDS:
PARIS, 1862, *Young Mother and Her Children,* FRF 640. PARIS, 1867, *Reading the Bible,* FRF 940. PARIS, 6 June 1924, *Portrait of Jacques Laffitte* (1832) FRF 1,920; *Death of Joan of Arc,* FRF 6,000. PARIS, 7 Feb 1945, *Charlotte Corday being Arrested,* FRF 2,800. PARIS, 5 Dec 1978, *Portrait of a Young Girl* (oil on canvas, 18 1/2 x 16 1/4 ins / 47 x 41 cm) FRF 5,500. MONACO, 14-15 Dec 1996, *Portrait of HRH the Duke of Orleans, Painted from Memory* (1842, oil on canvas, 50 1/2 x 32 3/4 ins / 128.5 x 83 cm) FRF 44,460. PARIS, 29 March 2000, *Lady with a Fan Dressed in Ermine* (oil on canvas, 52 x 32 ins / 132 x 82 cm) FRF 55,000.

SCHEFFER, Jean Baptiste
German, 18th century.
Born 1765, in Hamburg, in 1773 in Kassel according to some sources; died 30 June 1809, in Amsterdam.
Painter, engraver.

Jean Baptiste Scheffer was trained by J Fr Aug Tischbein. He went to Holland at a very young age. He married Cornelia Lamme and they had two sons, the painters Henry and Ary Scheffer. He painted many historical paintings and portraits, notably that of *Louis Bonaparte, King of Holland.*
MUSEUMS AND GALLERIES:
AMSTERDAM: *Joanna Cornelia Ziesenis* - DARMSTADT: *Pétion, Mayor of Paris; Emperor Joseph II* - DORDRECHT (Dordrechts Mus., Ary Sheffer's room): *Eight Portraits and an Interior* - KARLSRUHE: *Teaching Writing by Candlelight* - NIMEGEN: *Henri Hoogers* - THE HAGUE (Gemeentemus.): *Portrait of a Lady* - UTRECHT: *Portrait of Hinlopen.*

SCHEFFER, Jean Gabriel
Swiss, 19th century.
Born 12 December 1797, in Geneva; died 25 September 1876, in Geneva.
Painter, lithographer. Portraits, genre scenes.

Jean Gabriel Scheffer went to Paris at a very young age and trained under Regnault. He then went to Italy and struck up friendships with Corot, Aligny and Léopold Robert. He exhibited at the Salon in Paris from 1822 to 1846. He also produced many humorous lithographs. Some are signed with the initials J.S., such as *Are You Bored with Me?* and *Who Do You Belong to, Sir?* (1824), while others are signed J.G.S., such as *Monologue of the Paisley(-Pattern) in the Silhouette* and *Griseltiana.* On returning to Geneva, he devoted his life to his work. He also worked with pastels. The Ariana Museum in Geneva houses a watercolour entitled *Young Italian Woman,* signed J. Scheffer, which is believed to be by him.
MUSEUMS AND GALLERIES:
GENEVA (Mus. Ariana): *Young Italian Woman* (watercolour).
AUCTION RECORDS:
BERN, 25 Oct 1979, *Little Musician* (oil on canvas, 29 1/4 x 35 1/2 ins / 74 x 90 cm) CHF 2,900.

SCHEFFER, Mattheus, or Schäffer or Schäfer
German, 17th century.
Born c. 1575, in Münnerstadt; died 22 May 1614, in Coburg.
Painter.

Mattheus Scheffer is mentioned as being at the court in Coburg.

SCHEFFER, Paolo. See **SCHEPHEN**

SCHEFFER, Paul
German, 20th century.
Born 20 April 1877, in Kassel; died April 1916, in Kassel.
Painter, fresco artist. Landscapes.

Paul Scheffer was a pupil of Victor Weishaupt.
MUSEUMS AND GALLERIES:
KASSEL (Town Hall): frescoes.

SCHEFFER, Robert
Austrian, 19th century.
Born 6 May 1859, in Vienna.
Painter. Genre scenes.

Robert Scheffer was trained by Griepeukerl, Wurzinger, Leopold Muller and Ferdinand Keller.
MUSEUMS AND GALLERIES:
VIENNA (MM): *Franz-Joseph Barracks in Vienna.*
AUCTION RECORDS:
MUNICH, 6 Nov 1981, *Amorous Tyrolian* (1891, oil on canvas, 28 x 22 ins / 71 x 56 cm) DEM 5,200. LONDON, 28 Nov 1990, *Picnic in the Garden* (1895, oil on canvas, 27 3/4 x 35 1/2 ins / 70.5 x 90 cm) GBP 5,500. NEW YORK, 22 May 1991, *Thoughts Tending towards an Absent One* (1920, oil on canvas, 36 1/4 x 28 ins / 92.1 x 71.1 cm) USD 6,600. LONDON, 15 June 1994, *Contemplation* (1927, oil on canvas, 31 x 22 ins / 79 x 56 cm) GBP 3,910. VIENNA, 8 Feb 2000, *This Year* (oil on canvas, triptych, 8 x 63 ins / 20 x 160 cm) ATS 32,000. NEW YORK, 28 March 2000, *Courtship* (1888, oil on canvas, 37 x 28 ins / 95 x 72 cm) USD 5,500.

SCHEFFER VON LEONHARDSHOFF, Johann Baptist, or Scheffer von Leonhartshoff
Austrian, 19th century.
Born 30 October 1795 or 1796, in Vienna; died 12 January 1822, in Vienna.
Painter, engraver, draughtsman. Religious subjects, portraits.
Nazarenes group.

Johann Baptist Scheffer von Leonhardshoff was trained at the academy of fine art in Vienna. His patron was the count of Salm Reifferscheid, a prince and bishop of Gurk who funded his studies in Italy. He went notably to Rome where he joined the brotherhood of St Luke. He was then made a knight of the Order of Christ by Pope Pius VII. Afterwards, he returned to Vienna and was given many commissions.

Although he was a member of the Nazarenes group, he was able to shake off conventional 'Raphaelism' and remain original. During his first stay in Rome, in 1817, he produced the *Portrait of Pius VII,* then, during his second stay there, around 1820, he painted his masterpiece entitled *St Cecilia Dying.*
MUSEUMS AND GALLERIES:
BERLIN (Nationalgal.): *Holy Family; Education of Holy Mary* - BUDAPEST: *Drawing for an Altarpiece* - ESSEN (Folkwang Mus.): *St George and the Dragon* (1815) - VIENNA: *St Cecilia Dying; Madonna and the Child Jesus* - VIENNA (Albertina Mus.): *Portrait of Grillparger* - VIENNA (Österreichische Gal. Belvedere): *Self-portrait in front of Gothic Architecture; Self-portrait Drawing in a Forest; Count Lamberg; Cardinal Salm; Portrait of Jul. Schnorr von Carolsfeld.*
AUCTION RECORDS:
MUNICH, 28 Nov 1979, *Virgin with Child* (1817, pen/pencil outlines, 9 3/4 x 7 3/4 ins / 25 x 20 cm) DEM 3,200.

SCHEFFERS, N.
Dutch, 18th century.
Born to a family originally from Utrecht.
Active c. 1700.
Painter. History painting.
N. Scheffers worked under the direction of the Italian artist Verrio in London, and subsequently worked in Utrecht.

SCHEFFLER. See also **SCHÄFFLER**

SCHEFFLER, Caspar
German, 18th century.
Active in Oberfinning.
Painter.
Caspar Scheffler painted notably subjects of religious inspiration.

SCHEFFLER, Christoph, or sometimes Christian, Thomas, or Schaeffler, Schaefler
German, 18th century.
Born 1699 or 1700, in Munich; died 25 January 1756, in Augsburg.
Painter, draughtsman. Religious subjects. Frescoes.
Christoph Scheffler received his first artistic training from his father, Johann Wolfgang Scheffler. After having left the Jesuit Order, he lived notably in Freising and Augsburg. He devoted himself to frescoes, with which he decorated the Jesuit colleges in Dilligen and Landsberg. In the paintings in the nave of St Paul in Trier, which are dedicated to the *Triumph of the Cross*, he surrounded the main scene with tortured blocks of rocks, with the sun's rays beating down through the faults in these rocks. The consequent relief and density of the rocks seem to transform them into sculpted motifs of Baroque stucco ornamentation. Here, as in all the ornamentation from the Germanic Baroque era, there is fusion between architecture, sculpture and painting, symbolising the final fusion of heaven and earth.

SCHEFFLER, Félix Anton
German, 18th century.
Born 29 August 1701, in Munich; died 10 January 1760, in Prague.
Painter.
Félix Scheffler received his first artistic training from his father, Johann Wolfgang. He lived in Prague, Augsburg, and Bavaria. He was particularly notable as a painter of frescoes in artistic circles in Bavaria, Silesia, Moravia and Bohemia.

SCHEFFLER, Franz Benedikt and Georg (brothers)
German, 18th century.
Active in Augsburg.
Sculptors.
The stucco statues of *St Stephen, St Laurence* and the two of *St John* at the high altar of St Martin in Schwyz-Dorf are attributed to Franz Benedikt and Georg Scheffler.

SCHEFFLER, Franz Mathias, or Matheus
German, 18th century.
Died 19 September 1757, in Munich.
Miniaturist. Religious subjects.
MUSEUMS AND GALLERIES:
MUNICH (Residenzmus.): *Adoration of the Virgin by Prince Max Emmanuel of Bavaria.*

SCHEFFLER, Friedrich Johann, or Schöffler
German, 18th century.
Died 8 April 1750.
Active in Munich from 1724.
Painter.

SCHEFFLER, Hermann
German, 20th century.
Born 14 June 1879, in Berlin.
Painter, engraver.
Hermann Scheffler was the painter of portraits of President Hindenburg.
MUSEUMS AND GALLERIES:
MALBORK: *Portrait of Hindenburg.*

SCHEFFLER, Johann Carl
German, 18th century.
Active in Berlin.
Sculptor (wood).
Johann Carl Scheffler executed all the ornaments of Rheinsberg Castle from 1737 to 1740. He also decorated the castles/palaces of Frederick II. He is probably the creator of the desk in the library of Sans-Souci.

SCHEFFLER, Margarete, or Scheffer
German, 19th - 20th century.
Born 25 July 1871, in Berlin.
Painter. Still-lifes.
Margarete Scheffler was the pupil of Robert Müller called Warthmüller and Walter Leistikow at Frankfurt am Main. She worked in Frankfurt am Main.
AUCTION RECORDS:
AMSTERDAM, 5 June 1990, *Mimosa and Lemons on the Table* (oil on canvas, 20 x 31 1/2 ins / 50.5 x 80 cm) NLG 2,070.

SCHEFFLER, Rudolf
German, 20th century.
Born 5 December 1884, in Zwickau; died 1973.
Active in the USA.
Painter, engraver. Portraits, landscapes. Designs for mosaics.
Old Lyme Artists' Colony, Valley Cottage Artists' Colony.
Rudolf Scheffler was a pupil at the academy of fine arts in Dresden, studying under Otto Guzmann and Hermann Prell. He travelled in England and France, then went to Florence, Venice and Holland before being attracted to the USA by a commission for a mosaic in the cathedral of St Louis. He later settled in Brooklyn, where he soon opened a studio and became a friend of Robert Laurent, Yasuo Kuniyoshi, Marsden Hartley and Jules Pascin. He obtained the Prix de Rome and numerous gold and silver medals awarded by the American government and also by the royal academy of Dresden.

Towards the end of the 1920s he discovered the group of artists of Old Lyme in Connecticut. He shared his time between this group and that of Valley Cottage in New York. By then he had acquired his personal style, which was imbued with Impressionism. Nevertheless, he was tempted by Seurat's theories on pointillism of which his portrait of *Max Schleming* is an example.
MUSEUMS AND GALLERIES:
ZWICKAU (Städtisches Mus.).
AUCTION RECORDS:
NEW YORK, 24 Jan 1990, *A Street near Williamsburg Bridge in New York* (1928, watercolour and pencil/paper, 24 1/2 x 19 ins / 62.2 x 48.2 cm) USD 1,430. NEW YORK, 16 March 1990, *Sunflowers near a Hangar at Lyme in Connecticut* (oil on canvas, 35 3/4 x 2 x 39 1/4 ins / 91 x 5 x 99.8 cm) USD 31,900. NEW YORK, 3 Dec 1992, *Max Schmeling* (1929, oil on canvas, 84 x 66 ins / 213.4 x 167.6 cm) USD 19,800. NEW YORK, 23 April 1997, *Autumn Harvest* (1942, oil on canvas, 39 x 36 ins / 99 x 91.5 cm) USD 4,600.

SCHEFFNER, Johann Gottfried
German, 18th - 19th century.
Born 1765, in Mitau (now Jelgava, Latvia); died 18 December 1825, in Mitau.
Engraver (burin).
Scheffner was a pupil of S. Kutner, and trained in Jena, Wittenberg and Halle. He was an art teacher in Cologne and at the high school in Berlin from 1795 to 1797. In 1797 he taught at the University of Leipzig, and from 1806 to 1817, at

the School in Libau (now Liepaja, Latvia). From 1817 onwards, he worked in Mitau. He engraved portraits of *Clementi (Beethoven),, Wölfl, Guyton, Baron de Morveau* and *Scheele.*

SCHEFFNER, Karl Heinrich Ferdinand
Baltic School, 19th century.
Born 7 April 1805, in Libau (now Liepaja in Latvia); died June 1865, in Riga.
Painter.
Karl Scheffner was the son of Johann Gonfried, and studied under Senff.

SCHEFFOLT, Hans
German, 17th century.
Active in Altdorf near Ravensburg.
Painter.

SCHEFFSTOSS, Christoph
German, 17th century.
Painter.
Scheffstoss executed two paintings depicting *St Peter* and *St Paul* at the church in Dilligen.

SCHEFOLD, Johannes
German, 18th - 19th century.
Born 26 December 1719, in Markdorf; died 10 July 1809, in Biberach.
Painter.
Schefold worked from 1780 in Buchau and from 1803 in Biberach, where he taught J.B. Pflug.

SCHEFSTOS, Dominikus
17th century.
Painter.
A painting by Schefstos, dated 1658, was found in the monastery at Seitenstetten.

SCHEFTLHUBER, Dominikus. See **SCHÖFFTLHUBER**

SCHEFTLMAYR, Carl. See **SCHÄFTLMAYR**

SCHEGA, Franz Andreas
German, 18th century.
Born 16 November 1711, in Rudolfswert, Yugoslavia; died 6 December 1787, in Munich.
Painter, engraver, medallist.
Franz Schega, the son of a box-maker, initially pursued the same profession as his father, but it was noticed that he showed great talent for engraving his guns. He also engraved medals and portraits in relief, and is regarded as the best 18th-century German medallist. He lived notably in Munich. Towards the end of his career, he produced pastel portraits, and engraved some of them. He became blind in 1780. His brother Johann Anton left medallions of emperor *Charles IV* and his wife to the Bavarian National Museum in Munich.
MUSEUMS AND GALLERIES:
AUGSBURG: *Portrait of Georg de Marées and His Wife* - MUNICH (Bayerisches Nationalmus.): *Self-portrait.*

SCHEGGIA, Giovanni. See **GIOVANNI DI SER GIOVANNI**

SCHEGGINI DA LARCIANO, Giovanni di Michele. See **GRAFFIONE DI MICHELE SCHEGGINI DA LARCIANO**

SCHEGLOV, Valerian
Russian, 20th century.
Born 1901, in Kaluga; died 1984.
Draughtsman, illustrator.
Valerian Scheglov was a student of V. Levandovski. From 1920 he designed posters and book illustration and was from 1927 sought after by the major magazines and publishing houses. He illustrated A. Tolstoy's *Bread*. He became a member of the Association of Artists of the U.S.S.R. in 1933. His first solo exhibition took place in 1934.
BIBLIOGRAPHY:
Catalogue raisonné de l'œuvre de Valerian Scheglov.
AUCTION RECORDS:
PARIS, 29 Nov 1990, *Cellist* (1920, pencil/paper, 6 1/4 x 6 3/4 ins / 16 x 17 cm) FRF 3,800.

SCHEGS, Kaspar. See **SCHECKS**

SCHEI, Peter
Flemish School, 17th - 18th century.
Active c. 1678.
Painter. Landscapes.
A painter called Peter Schei was a pupil of Jan Fierens in Middelburg in 1706.

SCHEIB, Christian Friedrich
German, 18th - 19th century.
Born 1737, in Worms; died 1810, in Hamburg.
Painter, watercolourist.
Scheib was a pupil and imitator of Seekatz. He visited France and settled in Hamburg. He died in the reformatory in Hamburg. He painted landscapes with ruins and waterfalls.
MUSEUMS AND GALLERIES:
HAMBURG (Kunsthalle): *Fire* (two paintings).

SCHEIB, Johann Daniel
German, 17th - 18th century.
Born 22 May 1670, in Thuringia; died 6 December 1727, in Bayreuth.
Engraver (stone/glass).

SCHEIBE, Richard
German, 20th century.
Born 19 April 1879, in Chemnitz; died 1964, in Chemnitz.
Sculptor. Figures, animals.
Richard Scheibe studied painting in Dresden and Munich, and at the age of 20 he went to Rome to study sculpture. He worked in Frankfurt am Main as a teacher at the school of fine arts and in Berlin from 1935 as a teacher at the academy. He is the creator of the monument raised to Höchst to commemorate the liberation of the Saar in 1935.
AUCTION RECORDS:
MUNICH, 1-2 Dec 1992, *Sitting Orangutan* (bronze, h. 7 3/4 ins / 20 cm) DEM 5,750. NEW YORK, 29 Sept 1993, *Woman standing* (bronze, 13 1/2 ins / 34.3 cm) USD 2,875. MUNICH, 27 Feb 1999, *Seated Girl* (1937, gold-patinated bronze, h. 17 ins / 43 cm, w. 11 ins/27 cm) DEM 6,000. AHLDEN, 5 May 2001, *Liberation* (brown patinated bronze, h. 28 ins / 71 cm) DEM 10,600. COLOGNE, 4 Dec 2001, *Grieving Soldier* (green-brown patinated bronze, h. 14 ins / 36 cm) DEM 6,500. BERLIN, 8 June 2002, *Nymph* (1937, green patinated bronze, h. 16 ins / 40 cm) EUR 8,200. BERLIN, 30 Nov 2002, *Memorial for Oranierkirche, Biebrich am Rhein* (brown patinated bronze, h. 14 ins / 36 cm) EUR 4,000. STUTTGART, 2 April 2003, *Standing Boy* (1928, brown patinated bronze, h. 13 ins / 34 cm) EUR 5,000. HAMBURG, 14 June 2003, *Seated Girl - Nymph* (bronze, 13 x 10x10 ins / 32 x 25x25 cm) EUR 8,000. HAMBURG, 10 June 2004, *Standing Monkey* (bronze, 8 x 4x3 ins / 20 x 9x7 cm) EUR 4,800. HAMBURG, 4 Dec 2004, *Horse* (bronze, 13 x 11x3 ins / 32 x 29x7 cm) EUR 4,500.

SCHEIBEL, Johann Joseph. See **SCHEUBEL**

SCHEIBER, Christian
Austrian, 17th century.
Active in Wörth c. 1600.
Painter.

SCHEIBER, Franz Paul
Austrian, 20th century.
Born 23 March 1875, in Umhausen.
Sculptor. Religious subjects.

Franz Paul Scheiber was a pupil of Wilhelm von Rümann and Balthasar Schmidt. He sculpted *The Virgin and the Child Jesus* and the *St John* in the city hall at Charlottenburg, and also *The Sheaf Binder*.

MUSEUMS AND GALLERIES:

INNSBRUCK (Tiroler Landesmus. Ferdinandeum): *The Sheaf Binder*.

SCHEIBER, Hugo

Hungarian, 19th - 20th century.

Born 1873, in Budapest; died 1950, in Budapest.

Painter (gouache), pastellist, illustrator. Scenes with figures, figures, portraits.

Hugo Schreiber trained at the school of decorative art in Budapest. From 1920 onwards, he was involved with the gallery and magazine Der Sturm in Berlin and the Italian Futurists, who invited him to Rome in 1933. His works changed from a magical Expressionism reminiscent of Chagall to a temperate, lively, decorative Post-Cubist stylisation. Collective exhibitions include: Budapest (with Belar Kadar - 1921) and Catherine Dreier's Société Anonyme, New York (between the wars). A posthumous exhibition was dedicated to him in Budapest (1964). His work was featured in *L'Art en Hongrie 1905-1930. Art et révolution* (*Art in Hungary 1905-1930. Art and Revolution*), Musée de l'Art et de l'Industrie, St Étienne and the Musée d'Art Moderne de la Ville de Paris (1980), in *L'Avant-Garde en Hongrie 1910-1930* (*The Avant-Garde in Hungary, 1910-1930*), Galerie Franka Berndt, Paris (1984) and in *Beöthy et L'Avant-Garde Hongroise* (*Beöthy and the Hungarian Avant-Garde*), Galerie Franka Berndt, Paris and (1985-1986).

BIBLIOGRAPHY:

Passuth, Krisztina/Szabó, Júlia, *L'Art en Hongrie 1905-1930. Art et révolution*, exhibition catalogue, Musée d'Art et d'Industrie, Saint-Étienne, Musée d'Art moderne de la ville de Paris, Paris, 1980. Passuth, Krisztina, *L'Avant-garde en Hongrie 1910-1930*, exhibition catalogue, Gal. Franka Berndt, Paris, 1984. *Beöthy et L'Avant-Garde Hongroise*, exhibition catalogue, Gal. Franka Berndt, Paris, 1985-1986.

AUCTION RECORDS:

NEW YORK, 3 Nov 1978, *Figure Walking* (c. 1925, gouache, 26 x 19 1/2 ins / 66 x 49.5 cm) USD 2,700. NEW YORK, 6 Nov 1979, *Man's Portrait* (c. 1920-1925, gouache, 20 x 17 ins / 51 x 43 cm) USD 1,500. NEW YORK, 19 May 1981, *Village Scene* (gouache/mounted paper/card, 23 1/2 x 19 1/4 ins / 59.5 x 49 cm) USD 3,800. LONDON, 22 March 1983, *Can-Can* (coloured chalks and charcoal, 26 x 20 1/2 ins / 66 x 52 cm) GBP 1,200. LYONS, 23 Oct 1984, *Women Sitting at Table* (gouache, 24 x 19 ins / 61 x 48 cm) FRF 43,000. ZURICH, 10 Nov 1984, *Cubist Nude* (oil on card, 26 1/2 x 20 3/4 ins / 67 x 53 cm) CHF 5,500. LONDON, 3 Dec 1985, *Clowns* (graphite and colouring pencil, 20 x 19 ins / 51 x 48 cm) GBP 1,000. LONDON, 2 Dec 1986, *Harbour* (oil on card, 28 x 40 1/4 ins / 71 x 102 cm) GBP 7,000. NEW YORK, 18 Feb 1988, *Woman Reading* (gouache/paper, 34 x 25 1/2 ins / 85.5 x 65 cm) USD 5,280. LONDON, 24 Feb 1988, *Woman With a Cigarette* (watercolour gouache/kraft paper, 23 x 17 ins / 58.5 x 43 cm) GBP 2,530. TEL AVIV, 26 May 1988, *Venice* (watercolour and gouache, 24 3/4 x 19 ins / 63 x 48 cm) USD 4,950. LONDON, 19 Oct 1988, *Clown* (pastel and watercolour, 26 1/2 x 19 ins / 67.5 x 48 cm) GBP 2,640. LONDON, 24 May 1989, *Saxophonists* (gouache and pastel /paper, 17 1/4 x 24 ins / 43.6 x 61 cm) GBP 2,750. TEL AVIV, 30 May 1989, *Fiacre At night* (gouache and pencil/paper, 13 1/2 x 9 1/4 ins / 34 x 23.5 cm) USD 3,960. AMSTERDAM, 13 Dec 1989, *Dancing Couple* (gouache/paper, 19 1/4 x 13 1/2 ins / 49 x 34.5 cm) NLG 3,450. TEL AVIV, 3 Jan 1990, *Man Seated* (pastel and gouache, 23 1/2 x 19 1/4 ins / 59.5 x 49 cm) USD 2,420. PARIS, 24 Jan 1990, *Town at Night* (gouache and pastel, 17 3/4 x 24 1/2 ins / 45 x 62 cm) FRF 45,000. NEW YORK, 21 Feb 1990, *Woman's Portrait* (mixed media/paper, 26 1/2 x 19 ins / 67.4 x 48.1 cm) USD 4,125. PARIS, 8 April 1990, *Music Hall Dancer* (gouache and pastel, 25 1/4 x 19 ins / 64 x 48 cm) FRF 75,000. PARIS, 26 April 1990, *Circus* (oil on canvas, 27 1/4 x 23 1/4 ins / 69 x 59 cm) FRF 120,000. BERN, 12 May 1990, *Spanish Dancer* (mixed media, 27 1/4 x 21 1/2 ins / 69.5 x 54.5 cm) CHF 3,800. AMSTERDAM, 22 May 1990, *Reaper* (gouache/paper, 26 1/2 x 19 ins / 67.5 x 48.5 cm) NLG 10,350. TEL AVIV, 19 June 1990, *Industrial Landscape* (oil on card, 19 1/4 x 26 1/2 ins / 49 x 67 cm) USD 5,060. PARIS, 25 June 1990, *Musician* (gouache, 23 x 16 1/2 ins / 58.5 x 42 cm) FRF 26,500. NEW YORK, 10 Oct 1990, *Woman's Portrait* (oil on paper/card, 24 3/4 x 18 1/2 ins / 62.9 x 46.8 cm) USD 2,200. LUCERNE, 24 Nov 1990, *Woman's Portrait* (mixed media/paper, 20 1/2 x 15 ins / 52 x 38 cm) CHF 10,000. AMSTERDAM, 12 Dec 1990, *Woman Seated (Ülo Nö)* (1940, colouring pencil/paper, 23 1/2 x 17 1/4 ins / 60 x 44 cm) NLG 1,955. TEL AVIV, 1 Jan 1991, *Landscape* (pastel and charcoal, 33 1/2 x 24 1/4 ins / 85 x 61.5 cm) USD 2,200. PARIS, 14 April 1991, *Jazz Musician* (gouache/card, 24 3/4 x 19 1/4 ins / 63 x 49 cm) FRF 47,000. ROME, 13 May 1991, *Figures With a Glass* (1920, oil on canvas, 23 1/2 x 15 3/4 ins / 60 x 40 cm) ITL 39,100,000. ROME, 9 Dec 1991, *Woman* (mixed media/paper, 19 3/4 x 17 3/4 ins / 50 x 45 cm) ITL 6,900,000. AMSTERDAM, 12 Dec 1991, *Village* (gouache/paper, 17 1/4 x 14 1/4 ins / 44 x 36 cm) NLG 6,210. TEL AVIV, 6 Jan 1992, *Nude Among the Trees* (oil and gouache/paper, 16 1/4 x 11 ins / 41.5 x 28 cm) USD 1,210. ZURICH, 29 April 1992, *Man's Portrait* (gouache/card, 24 3/4 x 18 3/4 ins / 62.9 x 47.8 cm) CHF 1,800. NEW YORK, 9 May 1992, *Village Path* (coloured chalk/buff-coloured paper/paper, 22 1/4 x 16 3/4 ins / 56.8 x 42.5 cm) USD 1,760. PARIS, 27 Oct 1992, *Street With Figures* (1925, pastel and graphite/paper, 26 3/4 x 19 ins / 68 x 48 cm) FRF 52,500. NEW YORK, 10 Nov 1992, *Man On a Bench In a Park* (gouache and watercolour/buff-coloured paper, 20 3/4 x 19 1/2 ins / 52.7 x 49.8 cm) USD 2,090. PARIS, 12 May 1993, *Portrait of Madame B.* (1929, pastel/paper, 14 1/2 x 14 1/4 ins / 37 x 36 cm) FRF 31,500. ROME, 3 June 1993, *Landscape With Trees and Houses With Red Roofs* (1930, mixed media/paper, 29 1/2 x 25 1/2 ins / 75 x 65 cm) ITL 12,000,000. PARIS, 25 March 1994, *Mephisto* (gouache, 20 x 26 1/2 ins / 51 x 67 cm) FRF 4,000. AMSTERDAM, 31 May 1994, *Can-Can Dancer* (charcoal and pastel/paper, 26 x 19 3/4 ins / 66 x 50 cm) NLG 5,175. NEW YORK, 9 June 1994, *Man Smoking a Cigarette* (watercolour and pastel/orange paper/card, 27 1/2 x 19 1/4 ins / 69.9 x 48.9 cm) USD 1,150. PARIS, 16 Dec 1994, *Figures in a Park* (gouache, pastel and ink/paper, 24 x 17 3/4 ins / 61 x 45 cm) FRF 5,600. NEW YORK, 24 Feb 1995, *Street Lamps* (gouache/paper, 22 1/2 x 18 ins / 57.2 x 45.7 cm) USD 2,070. TEL AVIV, 22 April 1995, *Urban Landscape* (oil and gouache/card, 19 x 26 1/4 ins / 48 x 66.5 cm) USD 4,600. LONDON, 23 Oct 1996, *Cannes* (oil on canvas, 23 1/2 x 18 1/2 ins / 60 x 47 cm) GBP 2,990. PARIS, 13 Dec 1996, *Man Seated* (1917, gouache and pastel/paper, 24 1/4 x 18 1/4 ins / 61.7 x 46.3 cm) FRF 15,000. PARIS, 20 March 1998, *Dance* (oil on canvas, 14 1/4 x 10 ins / 36 x 25.5 cm) FRF 10,000. LONDON, 18 Oct 2000, *Anxiety, Self Portrait* (c. 1920-1922, oil on cardboard, 19 x 19 ins / 48 x 48 cm) GBP 12,000. STUTTGART, 20 Oct 2000, *Path in Park* (oil on board on masonite, 28 x 19 ins / 70 x 49 cm) DEM 22,000. BUDAPEST, 12 Oct 2001, *Lady in the Bar* (mixed media, 23 x 17 ins / 59 x 43 cm) HUF 2,400,000. BUDAPEST, 7 Dec 2001, *Carnival* (oil on cardboard, 28 x 40 ins / 70 x 102 cm) HUF 6,500,000. BUDAPEST, 9 Dec 2002, *Boats under the Bridge* (pastel, 26 x 33 ins / 65 x 85 cm) HUF 2,800,000. BUDAPEST, 9 Dec 2002, *Three Dancers* (mixed media, 20 x 26 ins / 52 x 66 cm) HUF 3,000,000. BUDAPEST, 16 May 2003, *Athletic Championship* (oil on canvas, 31 x

37 ins / 78 x 95 cm) HUF 10,000,000. BUDAPEST, 4 Oct 2003, *Street Carnival* (oil on canvas, 22 x 28 ins / 56 x 72 cm) HUF 5,000,000. BUDAPEST, 12 Oct 2004, *In the Park* (pastel, 23 x 16 ins / 58 x 40 cm) HUF 2,200,000. BUDAPEST, 12 Oct 2004, *Park* (oil on cardboard, 28 x 39 ins / 71 x 100 cm) HUF 5,500,000.

SCHEIBER, Moritz
Austrian, 17th century.
Active in Innsbruck.
Sculptor.

SCHEIBER, Paul
Austrian, 18th century.
Born in Perfuchs near Landeck,.
Painter. Religious subjects.

Paul Scheiber painted three altarpieces around 1750 for the church of St Anne in Bludenz.

SCHEIBER, Reichart or Richard
Austrian, 17th century.
Born c. 1615; died 15 April 1673.
Active in Salzburg.
Painter.

Reichart Scheiber decorated a triumphal gate around 1665 for the entry of Emperor Leopold I into Salzburg.

SCHEIBL, Hubert
Austrian, 20th - 21st century.
Born 1952, in Gmunden.
Painter.

Hubert Schiebl is a fervent believer in the intensity of colour, which he uses to generate light in his series or large-format diptychs. His abstract works are made up of several successive layers of colour worked with a spatula. He pierces the paint by rubbing or scratching it to create an effect in which colours disappear and show through.

He has participated in group events, including *Austria Vision* at the Fundación La Caixa, Barcelona, and the Fundación Caja de Pensiones, Madrid (1995). He took part in the salon at Montrouge (1998), and in *Museum auf Abruf: Des Eisbergs Spitze* (*Museum on Tap: The Tip of the Iceberg*) at the Kunsthalle Vienna (1998). He had solo shows at the Galerie Thaddaeus Ropac, Paris (1998, 2001), at the Museum Moderner Kunst, Sammlung Ludwig, Vienna (1998). His show *Paintings 1986-2001* was held at the Rhenish Centre of Contemporary Art, Altkirch.

BIBLIOGRAPHY:

Garimorth, Julia/Buci-Glucksmann, Christine/Altoé, Jean-Claude, *Hubert Scheibl: liquids minds*, Centre rhénan d'Art contemporain, Altkirch, 2001 (text in French, German and English).

AUCTION RECORDS:

NEW YORK, 20 Feb 1988, *Tired Warrior* (1983, oil on canvas, 78¾ x 98½ ins / 200.3 x 250.5 cm) USD 1,320. NEW YORK, 8 Oct 1992, *Untitled* (oil on canvas, 59 x 59¼ ins / 149.8 x 150.5 cm) USD 7,150. LONDON, 23-24 March 1994, *Untitled* (1986, oil on canvas, 78¾ x 86¼ ins / 200 x 219 cm) GBP 5,750. VIENNA, 9 March 1999, *Untitled* (1985, oil on canvas, 31 x 40 ins / 79 x 102 cm) ATS 65,000. VIENNA, 19 May 1999, *Untitled Composition* (1986, oil on canvas, 31 x 43 ins / 78 x 108 cm) ATS 40,000. VIENNA, 11 April 2000, *X R 6 Diptychon* (1991, oil on canvas on panel, diptych, 59 x 8 ins / 149 x 21 cm) ATS 50,000. VIENNA, 29 Nov 2000, *Soul* (1986, oil on canvas, 79 x 69 ins / 200 x 175 cm) ATS 100,000. VIENNA, 23 April 2002, *Chochin 6* (watercolour, 24 x 18 ins / 61 x 46 cm) EUR 2,000. VIENNA, 14 May 2002, *Joy Knots* (1987, oil on canvas, 98 x 79 ins / 250 x 200 cm) EUR 6,500. VIENNA, 28 Nov 2003, *W CU* (1994, oil on canvas, 31 x 20 ins / 80 x 50 cm) EUR 2,000. VIENNA, 12 Oct 2004, *Untitled* (1982, oil on canvas, 79 x 61 ins / 200 x 155 cm) EUR 7,500. BERLIN, 27 Nov 2004, *Wittgenstein's Journey: The Chair II* (1985, oil on canvas, 99 x 52 ins / 252 x 132 cm) EUR 4,400.

SCHEIBLBRANDER, Karl
German, 20th century.
Born 24 December 1884, in Radstadt.
Painter. Landscapes.

Karl Scheiblbrander was from 1925 to 1932 a teacher in the school of industrial arts in Innsbruck.

SCHEIBLER, Carl Friedrich Heinrich
German, 19th century.
Active in Berlin at the beginning of the 19th century.
Sculptor.

Scheibler was a pupil of Em. Bardou. He sent works to the academy from 1800 to 1838.

SCHEIBLICH, Otto
German, 19th century.
Born 1830, in Niederfähre; died 1873, in Meissen.
Painter.

Scheiblich worked at Meissen Porcelain Factory.

MUSEUMS AND GALLERIES:

MEISSEN (Town Hall): *Butchers' Door in Meissen* (painting).

SCHEIBMAIER, Anton Wilhelm
German, 19th century.
Born 22 March 1818, in Munich; died 7 December 1893, in Munich.
Painter.

Scheibmaier produced many altarpieces for Bavarian churches.

SCHEIBNER, Johann Heinrich
German, 18th century.
Born 1759, in Laubegast, near Dresden; died c. 1807.
Draughtsman, engraver (burin).

Scheibner was a pupil of Giuseppe Canale. Portraits and city panoramas are attributed to him.

SCHEIBOLT, Johann Joseph.
See **SCHEUBEL**

SCHEICHER, Franz, or Scheucher
Austrian, 18th century.
Born c. 1756, near Imst (Tyrol); died 10 January 1803, in Freising.
Sculptor (wood).

MUSEUMS AND GALLERIES:

NUREMBERG (Germanisches Nationalmus.): *Emperor Charles VII Dressed as a Roman Emperor* (statue).

SCHEICKER, Gottfried
German, 17th century.
Active probably in Stolpen.
Painter.

Scheicker lived in Saxony Switzerland and painted altarpieces.

SCHEICKHARDT, Hendrik Willem or Heinrich Wilhelm. See **SCHWEICKARDT**

SCHEICZLICH, Hans. See **SCHENCK**

SCHEID, Johann Baptist. See **SCHEITH**

SCHEID, Lore
Austrian, 20th century.
Born 1889, in Pforzheim; died 1946, in Wels.
Painter. Landscapes.

AUCTION RECORDS:

MUNICH, 7 Dec 1993, *Lake Hallstätter* (1921, oil on canvas, 37½ x 47½ ins / 95 x 120.5 cm) DEM 8,050. NEW YORK, 17 Jan 1996, *Lake Hallstätter* (1921, oil on canvas, 37¾ x 47¾ ins / 95.9 x 121.6 cm) USD 5,175.

SCHEIDAM, Ph.
German, 17th century.
Active in Hamburg c. 1623.
Painter.

SCHEIDECKER, Paul Frank
French, 19th century.
Born in Manchester, England, to French parents.
Painter (gouache), watercolourist. Genre scenes, landscapes.
His teachers were his father, Lehmann and Luc-Olivier Merson. He first exhibited at the Salon in 1879.
AUCTION RECORDS:
PARIS, 6 Nov 1935, *The Seine* (watercolour and gouache) FRF 22.

SCHEIDEGGER, Johann
Swiss, 19th century.
Born 1777, in Trachselwald; died 3 February 1858.
Painter. Landscapes.

SCHEIDEL, Franz Anton von, or Scheidl
Austrian, 18th century.
Born 1731; died 14 January 1801, in Vienna.
Painter, watercolourist, draughtsman. Flowers, animals.
Scheidel painted notably botanical plates and specialised in depicting animals.
AUCTION RECORDS:
NEW YORK, 3 June 1981, *Shellfish* (watercolour/outline in black chalk, 20 1/4 x 14 1/4 ins / 51.3 x 36 cm) USD 10,000. NEW YORK, 22 June 1983, *Twenty-Seven Shellfish* (watercolour/outlines in black chalk, 20 1/4 x 14 1/4 ins / 51.5 x 36.2 cm) USD 4,750. LONDON, 5 Nov 1987, *Flowers, Plants and Fruit* (1765-1770, watercolour, volume of 161 pages, 20 x 14 1/4 ins / 50.8 x 36 cm) GBP 155,000. NEW YORK, 12 Jan 1990, *Lazy One on a Branch* (watercolour/black chalk, 12 1/2 x 18 1/2 ins / 32 x 47 cm) USD 3,300. NEW YORK, 9 Jan 1991, *White Ferret; Young Anteater* (black chalk and watercolour, 14 x 19 1/4 ins / 35.6 x 48.8 cm and 14 x 19 3/4 ins/35.6 x 50.2 cm) USD 2,420. PARIS, 20 June 1991, *Three Plates of Shellfish, Black Stone* (pen and watercolour, 19 1/2 x 13 1/2 ins / 49.5 x 34 cm) FRF 51,000. NEW YORK, 10 Jan 1995, *Study of Four Snakes: Muraena Coeca and Coluber Atropos* (ink and watercolour/black chalk, 14 x 20 ins / 35.6 x 50.8 cm) USD 690. LONDON, 16-17 April 1997, *Lion* (watercolour/traces of black chalk, 13 x 20 ins / 33 x 51 cm) GBP 1,955. NEW YORK, 27 Jan 1999, *Study of Shells* (colour ink and watercolour, a pair, 20 x 14 ins / 51 x 36 cm) USD 13,000. AMSTERDAM, 10 Nov 1999, *Tamandua tetradactyla* (black lead and watercolour, 14 x 20 ins / 35 x 52 cm) NLG 14,000. LONDON, 9 July 2001, *Coiled Serpent* (pencil heightened with gum arabic, 14 x 20 ins / 36 x 50 cm) GBP 6,000. PARIS, 21 March 2002, *Studies of Apes* (chalk, pen and ink wash, 14 x 20 ins / 36 x 50 cm) EUR 6,500.

SCHEIDHAUER, Rudolf
Hungarian, 19th century.
Active in Hungary from 1836 to 1860.
Painter. Portraits.

SCHEIDHAUF. See **SCHAIDHAUF**

SCHEIDL, Johann
Austrian, 19th century.
Active in Salzburg.
Sculptor.
Johann Scheidl worked notably for the churches in his region.

SCHEIDL, Jordan
Austrian, 18th century.
Born 1728; died 4 November 1780, in Vienna.
Painter. History painting.

SCHEIDL, Karl, or Seidl
Austrian, 18th century.
Painter.
Karl Scheidl is particularly well-known for his paintings of faces on porcelain which he executed at Vienna Porcelain Factory.

SCHEIDL, Roman
Austrian, 20th - 21st century.
Born 1949, in Leopoldsdorf.
Painter, engraver.
Roman Scheidl lives and works in Vienna. He is a line-engraver. In 1992 he was represented in the exhibition *De Bonnard à Baselitz: Dix ans d'enrichissements du cabinet des estampes 1978-1988* (*From Bonnard to Baselitz: A Decade of Acquisitions by the Prints Collection 1978-1988*) at the Bibliothèque Nationale in Paris.

SCHEIDLER, Anton
German, 18th century.
Died after 1775.
Painter.
Anton Scheidler was Th. Chr. Wink's first teacher.

SCHEIDLER, Johann
Austrian, 18th century.
Born 1764; died 21 November 1799, in Vienna.
Painter. History painting.

SCHEIDNAGEL, Ruppert
German, 19th century.
Active in Regensburg.
Painter.
Scheidnagel trained at the academy in Munich in 1823.

SCHEIDT, Carl von
German, 19th century.
Active at the beginning of the 19th century.
Glass painter.
Scheidt worked with Samuel and Gottlob Mohn in Dresden, then alone in Berlin. He depicted views of Dresden, Berlin and Vienna on glass and on porcelain cups.

SCHEIDT, Johann Baptist. See **SCHEITH**

SCHEIDTS, Andreas or Matthias. See **SCHEITS**

SCHEIFEL, Joseph Ignaz. See **SCHEUFEL**

SCHEIFELIN, Hans Léonard or Leonhard. See **SCHÄUFFELIN**

SCHEIFELIN, Leonhard, or Scheufele
German, 17th century.
Born 30 August 1645, in Ulm.
Draughtsman.
Scheifelin worked in Ulm and Vienna.
MUSEUMS AND GALLERIES:
NUREMBERG (Town Hall): *Portrait of Emperor Leopold I* - REGENSBURG (Town Hall): *Portrait of Emperor Leopold I.*

SCHEIFFARTZ VON MEIRROEDE, Margarete, or Merode
German, 15th century.
Born to a family originally from Bornheim.
Miniaturist.
The Magyar Nemzeti Galéria in Budapest owns a *Self-portrait* by this artist.

SCHEIFFEL. See **SCHEUFEL**

SCHEIFFELE, Johann Thomas
German, 19th century.
Born 21 December 1806, in Stuttgart; died before December 1845.
Lithographer.
Scheiffele notably produced views of Stuttgart.

SCHEIMANN, Aleksei Fedorovich, or Cheiman
Russian, 20th century.

Born 21 January 1867, in Wjasmino.
Engraver.
Aleksei Scheimann was Pojalostin's student. He practised engraving.

SCHEIN, Françoise
Belgian, 20th century.
Active from 1977 to 1987 in the USA then active in France.
Sculptor, mixed media.
Françoise Schein lived in the USA from 1977 to 1987, studying architecture and design at Columbia University, then settled in Paris. She exhibited her works in private exhibitions, including the 1991 Espace Electra in Paris. She won a competition in urban sculpture for Soho in 1985. She worked on the city and its identity, which she presented in boxes, introducing sources of information on a place (statements about topography, plants, fragments of soil, but also fuller texts). She worked on the city of Paris, compiling a register of American cities with the same name and presenting assemblages, created from characteristic elements of each stage, in showcases, for example, lights for Paris-Pennsylvania, cotton fields for Paris-Mississippi.
BIBLIOGRAPHY:
Debecque-Michel, Laurence, '*De la connaissance scientifique à l'utopie poétique: Françoise Schein*' in *Opus international no.125*, periodical, Paris, summer 1991. Francblin, Catherine, '*Les Paris/Paris de Françoise Schein*' in *Art Press no.164*, periodical, Paris, December 1991.

SCHEIN, Henri F. R.
French, 20th century.
Painter.
Henri F.R. Schein exhibited regularly in Paris at the Salon des Artistes Français, of which he was a member and where he was awarded a silver medal in 1936.

SCHEIN, Medard
Bavarian School, 17th century.
Cabinet maker.

SCHEINER, Jakob
German, 19th - 20th century.
Born 1821, in Sohlbach, near Geisweid; died 1911, in Potsdam.
Watercolourist. Landscapes.
AUCTION RECORDS:
COLOGNE, 21 Nov 1985, *The Crypt of St Gideon in Cologne* (watercolour, 16 1/2 x 18 3/4 ins / 42 x 47.5 cm) DEM 4,600.

SCHEINER, Wilhelm
German, 19th - 20th century.
Born 1852, in Siegen; died 1922, in Cologne.
Painter. Landscapes.
Wilhelm Scheiner was the son of Jakob Scheiner
.
MUSEUMS AND GALLERIES:
SIEGEN.

SCHEINERT, Karl Samuel
German, 19th century.
Born 12 January 1791, in Dresden; died 20 January 1868, in Meissen.
Draughtsman, glass painter.
Scheinert trained at the academy in Dresden. He was a teacher at the school for painting on porcelain in Meissen.

SCHEINHAMMER, Otto
German, 20th century.
Born 6 January 1897, in Munich.
Painter.
Otto Scheinhammer was a pupil of Carl J. Becker-Gundahl and of Franz Klemmer.

SCHEINHUTTE, Michael Hubert Aloys Joseph
German, 19th century.
Born 1796, in Cologne; died 8 September 1856, in Cologne.
Painter, lithographer. Portraits.

SCHEINIG, Kaspar
German, 15th century.
Sculptor (wood).

SCHEINS, Karl Ludwig
German, 19th century.
Born 15 September 1808, in Aachen; died 23 October 1879, in Düsseldorf.
Painter. Hunting scenes, landscapes with figures.
Scheins was trained by Scheiner.
MUSEUMS AND GALLERIES:
DÜSSELDORF: *Winter Landscape*.
AUCTION RECORDS:
MUNICH, 28 Nov 1974, *Wooded Landscape in the Rain,* DEM 12,500. COLOGNE, 22 Nov 1979, *Winter Landscape* (oil on canvas, 48 3/4 x 39 ins / 124 x 99 cm) DEM 11,000. COLOGNE, 25 Nov 1983, *Winter Landscape* (oil on canvas, 13 1/2 x 19 1/4 ins / 34 x 49 cm) DEM 12,000. LONDON, 13 Oct 1994, *Hunter and His Dogs in an Undulating Landscape* (1838, oil on canvas, 21 3/4 x 30 3/4 ins / 55.2 x 78.2 cm) GBP 2,530. RADOLFZELL, 20 March 1999, *Schloss Petersberg* (oil on canvas/panel, 20 x 37 ins / 52 x 95 cm) DEM 4,800. COPENHAGEN, 29 Feb 2000, *Faggot Gatherers in Mountainous Winter Landscape* (oil on canvas, 48 x 41 ins / 121 x 103 cm) DKK 38,000. RADOLFZELL, 21 Oct 2000, *Wooded Landscape* (oil on canvas, 35 x 45 ins / 90 x 115 cm) DEM 4,500. LONDON, 20 March 2003, *Winter's Walk* (oil on canvas, 35 x 48 ins / 88 x 122 cm) GBP 2,500. COLOGNE, 10 April 2003, *Winter Wooded Landscape* (oil on canvas, 15 x 21 ins / 39 x 53 cm) EUR 1,500.

SCHEIRING
German, 18th century.
Born to a family originally from Saint-Martin.
Active at the end of the 18th century.
Sculptor.

SCHEIRING, Leopold
German, 20th century.
Born 4 December 1884, in Nassereith (Tyrol), Austria; died 1927.
Painter. Landscapes.
Leopold Scheiring lived and worked in Innsbruck. He painted pictures of high mountain scenery.
MUSEUMS AND GALLERIES:
INNSBRUCK (Tiroler Landesmus. Ferdinandeum).
AUCTION RECORDS:
VIENNA, 18 Sept 1974, *Alpine Landscape* (1920) ATS 16,000. VIENNA, 16 Feb 1979, *Mountainous Landscape* (1918, oil on card, 27 1/2 x 39 1/4 ins / 70 x 100 cm) ATS 13,000. VIENNA, 6 March 2001, *Mountain Landscape* (oil on canvas, 22 x 29 ins / 57 x 73 cm) ATS 32,000. VIENNA, 15 May 2001, *Mountain Landscape* (1921, oil on canvas, 30 x 39 ins / 75 x 99 cm) ATS 65,000.

SCHEITERBERG, Adrian
German, 19th - 20th century.
Born c. 1864; died September 1910, in Diessen.
Painter. Landscapes.

SCHEITH, Johann Baptist, or Scheid, Scheidt
Austrian, 18th century.
Died 20 April 1755.
Active in Graz.
Painter.
Several altarpieces attributable to Scheith are distributed between several churches in Styria.

SCHEITHAUF. See **SCHAIDHAUF**

SCHEITLIN, Othmar
Swiss, 17th century.
Born 1631, in St Gall.
Painter.

Scheitlin worked in Rudolstadt and Schleiz.

SCHEITS, Andreas, or Scheidts or Scheutz
German, 17th - 18th century.
Born c. 1665, in Hamburg; died 1735, in Hanover.
Painter, engraver (etching). Genre scenes.

Andreas Scheits was trained by his father, Matthias Scheits. He lived in Holland and was a painter at the court of Hanover. He painted notably portraits.

MUSEUMS AND GALLERIES:
FLORENCE: *Portrait of Leibnitz* - HAMBURG: *Portrait of a Rabbi; Still-life* - HANOVER (Niedersächsisches Landesmus.): *Portrait of a Young Man; Portrait of an Aged Scholar.*

SCHEITS, Hendrik, or Scheutz
German, 17th century.
Active in Hamburg.
Painter.

SCHEITS, Matthias, or Scheidts or Scheitz or Scheutz
German, 17th century.
Born c. 1630 or 1640, in Hamburg; died c. 1700, in Hamburg.
Painter, engraver (etching). Genre scenes.

Matthias Scheits was trained by Philips Wouwerman in Haarlem. Initially he painted in the style of his teacher, then imitated Teniers. He engraved genre subjects and landscapes. He painted with originality and a rich sense of colour.

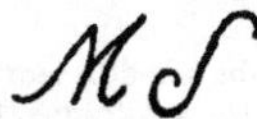

MUSEUMS AND GALLERIES:
ASCHAFFENBURG: *Family of Peasants Having a Meal* - BRUNSWICK: *Portrait of a Woman* - GÖTTINGEN: *Cavalry Fight* - HAMBURG: *Musician* - KASSEL: *Bust of an Old Man; Jew; Biblical Scene; Presentation of the Sacrament; Image of Life; Life of Village People; Baptism; Adam and Eve; Wine, Women and Song; Walk; Child and Nest; Two Peasants; Two Village People; Rebecca and Eliezer at the Well; Musical Entertainment* - OBERSCHLEISSHEIM (Neues Schloss Schleissheim, Staatsgal.): *Peasants Drinking* - SCHWERIN: *Cavalry Fight.*

AUCTION RECORDS:
PARIS, 26-27 June 1941, *Two Drawings Enhanced with White* (attributed) FRF 440. HAMBURG, 7 June 1979, *Biblical Scenes* (c. 1670, pen drawing and wash, series of 40, 9 1/2 x 7 1/2 ins / 24.3 x 19.2 cm) DEM 8,200. HEIDELBERG, 10 April 1981, *Jesus Healing the Ill Man* (c. 1670, pen and wash, 10 x 7 3/4 ins / 24.5 x 19.5 cm) DEM 1,600. VIENNA, 24 March 1999, *Attack* (oil on panel, 22 x 22 ins / 57 x 56 cm) ATS 45,000. ZURICH, 15 March 2000, *Rider on White Horse with Apple-seller at Roadside* (oil on panel, 5 x 7 ins / 12 x 18 cm) CHF 12,000. LINDAU, 30 June 2001, *Musketeer Dining* (oil on canvas, 39 x 29 ins / 98 x 74 cm) DEM 4,200.

SCHEIWE, Walter
German, 20th century.
Born 7 June 1892, in Posen (now Poznan, Poland).
Painter, engraver. Landscapes.

Walter Scheiwe lived and worked in Düsseldorf.

SCHEIWILLER, Silvano
Italian, 20th century.
Born 1937, in Milan; died 1986, in Milan.
Engraver (etching). Figures, landscapes.

Scheiwiller participated in a number of collective exhibitions including *Attraverso l'Immagine* (*Through the Image*) held in 1995 at the Centro Culturale in Cremona. He made etchings that he sometimes expanded into large watercolours.

BIBLIOGRAPHY:
Scheiwiller - Incisioni: 1957-1979, All'insegna del pesce d'oro, Milan, 1979. *Attraverso l'immagine*, exhibition catalogue, Centro culturale Santa Maria della Pietà, Cremona, 1995.

SCHEIWL, Josef. See **SEIWL**

SCHEKEV, Fedor Ivanovich
Russian, 18th - 19th century.
Born 17 February 1774.
Painter. Portraits.

Fedor Schekev studied at the St Petersburg academy.

SCHEL, David Joachim, or Schell
German, 17th century.
Medallist.

Schel engraved medals bearing the effigy of *William III* and the archbishop of Cologne *Joseph Clement.*

SCHEL, Sebastian. See **SCHEEL**

SCHELBERG, Ernst Ferdinand
German, 17th century.
Born c. 1645, of Liégeois origin; died 2 November 1669, in Rome.
Painter.

SCHELCHER, Johann Friedrich Adolph
German, 18th - 19th century.
Born 17 September 1762, in Dresden; died 13 May 1813, in Dresden.
Painter.

Schelcher was a pupil of Klengel, and became an art teacher in Dresden. He painted landscapes, portraits and battles.

SCHELCHER, Mathilde Elisabeth
German, 19th century.
Born 1795; died 24 November 1867.
Active in Dresden.
Painter. Genre scenes, portraits.

Schelcher was trained by Friedrich Rensch. She exhibited in Dresden from 1822 onwards.

SCHELCK, Maurice
Belgian, 20th century.
Born 1906 or 1907, in Alost; died 1978.
Painter. Figures, portraits, landscapes, still-lifes.

Maurice Schelck studied at the academy of fine arts in Alost, and in Brussels, Rome and Paris. He exhibited in Belgium, Holland, Paris, London, Milan and South Africa, and in 1931 he received the Godecharle Prize. After painting for some time, he stopped doing so for many years. When he began again, he turned towards the abstract. But this abstract period was temporary and he abandoned non-figurative art with the striking *Goodbye to the Abstract.* Returning to the Neo-Expressionism of his youth, he used lavish colour and a rich subject matter, which idealised the Flemish landscape and its inhabitants. Declining to use the distortions common in Expressionism, he adopted a synthetic construction, often depicting massive shapes evoking Gromaire. Essentially a landscape painter, he was also interested in faces, which he caught in moments of fixed expression as if they were in the process of speaking.

AUCTION RECORDS:
LONDON, 12 Nov 1970, *View of a Village,* GBP 420. ANTWERP, 12 Oct 1971, *Flowers,* BEF 65,000. ANTWERP, 18 April 1972, *Woman with a Coffee Grinder,* BEF 55,000. ANTWERP, 3 April 1973, *Iris on a Winter Evening,* BEF 70,000. ANTWERP, 2 April 1974, *Stormy Sky,* BEF 110,000. LOKEREN, 6 Nov 1976, *Snowy Landscape* (oil on panel, 35 x 49¼ ins / 88 x 125 cm) BEF 110,000. LOKEREN, 5 Nov 1977, *Still-life* (oil on panel, 35½ x 47¼ ins / 90 x 120 cm) BEF 100,000. ANTWERP, 8 May 1979, *Last Sheaves* (oil on panel, 23½ x 31½ ins / 60 x 80 cm) BEF 100,000. ANTWERP, 27 Oct 1981, *Summer Landscape* (1942, oil on canvas, 31½ x 39¼ ins / 80 x 100 cm) BEF 120,000. ANTWERP, 25 Oct 1983, *Still-life* (oil on panel, 24 x 33 ins / 61 x 84 cm) BEF 70,000. LOKEREN, 20 April 1985, *Still-life with Potatoes* (oil on canvas remounted/panel, 31 x 39¼ ins / 79 x 100 cm) BEF 150,000. LOKEREN, 28 May 1988, *Young Villagers* (oil on panel, 23½ x 30¼ ins / 60 x 77 cm) BEF 40,000. LOKEREN, 21 March 1992, *Winter Landscape with Setting Sun* (1971, oil on canvas/panel, 31½ x 39¼ ins / 80 x 100 cm) BEF 240,000. LOKEREN, 23 May 1992, *The Fervour of Tenacity* (oil on canvas, 59 x 32 ins / 150 x 81 cm) BEF 90,000. LOKEREN, 5 Dec 1992, *Iris in Winter* (oil on canvas/panel, 31½ x 39¼ ins / 80 x 100 cm) BEF 220,000. LOKEREN, 15 May 1993, *Snow on the Banks of the Lys* (oil on panel, 19¾ x 27½ ins / 50 x 70 cm) BEF 100,000. LOKEREN, 4 Dec 1993, *Nude* (black chalk, 28¼ x 21¼ ins / 72 x 54 cm) BEF 40,000; *Still-life in My Garden* (oil on canvas/panel, 39¼ x 31½ ins / 100 x 80 cm) BEF 150,000. LOKEREN, 12 March 1994, *Summer at Latem* (1978, oil on canvas, 19¾ x 23½ ins / 50 x 60 cm) BEF 100,000. AMSTERDAM, 31 May 1994, *An Imposing Brain* (oil on canvas, 39 x 31 ins / 99 x 79 cm) NLG 4,600. LOKEREN, 20 May 1995, *Landscape with a Farm* (oil on panel, 35½ x 47¼ ins / 90 x 120 cm) BEF 240,000. AMSTERDAM, 31 May 1995, *Still-life with Apples* (1964, synthetic resin and oil on paper/card, 19¾ x 27½ ins / 50 x 70 cm) NLG 4,248. LOKEREN, 9 March 1996, *Clown* (oil on panel, 48 x 35½ ins / 122 x 90 cm) BEF 280,000. LOKEREN, 6 Dec 1997, *Bunch of Flowers* (oil on panel, 19¾ x 15¾ ins / 50 x 40 cm) BEF 75,000. LOKEREN, 6 March 1999, *People of My Village* (oil on panel, 39 x 48 ins / 100 x 122 cm) BEF 400,000. LOKEREN, 15 May 1999, *Dreamer* (oil on panel, 39 x 47 ins / 100 x 120 cm) BEF 160,000. LOKEREN, 13 May 2000, *Winter Sun at Latem* (oil on panel, 39 x 47 ins / 100 x 120 cm) BEF 260,000. LOKEREN, 7 Oct 2000, *Summer with Red Light* (oil on panel, 31 x 39 ins / 80 x 100 cm) BEF 330,000. LOKEREN, 10 March 2001, *Harvest* (oil on panel, 31 x 39 ins / 80 x 100 cm) BEF 260,000. LOKEREN, 12 May 2001, *Still-life with Flowers* (oil on panel, 31 x 24 ins / 80 x 62 cm) BEF 180,000. LOKEREN, 5 Oct 2002, *Landscape with Red Light* (oil on panel, 31 x 39 ins / 80 x 100 cm) EUR 3,300. ANTWERP, 21 Oct 2003, *Winter Landscape* (oil on panel, 24 x 31 ins / 60 x 80 cm) EUR 2,000. ANTWERP, 9 Dec 2003, *Lys in Winter* (oil on panel, 31 x 39 ins / 80 x 100 cm) EUR 2,200. ANTWERP, 27 April 2004, *Still-life with Flowers* (oil on canvas, 34 x 28 ins / 87 x 70 cm) EUR 1,600. ANTWERP, 26 Oct 2004, *Landscape* (oil on panel, 24 x 35 ins / 60 x 90 cm) EUR 2,800.

SCHELDE
Flemish School, 17th century.
Born 1586, in Friesland; died in Antwerp.
Engraver. Portraits, landscapes, historical subjects.

Schelde was a pupil of Rubens and produced numerous copies after his master. He is mentioned by Ris-Paquot.

SCHELDE, Cornelis van der
Flemish School, 16th - 17th century.
Active in Ghent in 1575 and in Middelburg 1587-1602.
Painter.

SCHELDEN, Baudouin van der. See the entry **SCHELDEN Paul** or **Pauwels van der**

SCHELDEN, Hendrik van der
Flemish School, 16th century.
Engraver (wood).

SCHELDEN, Lievin van der
Flemish School, 16th century.
Active in Ghent 1556-1587.
Miniaturist.

SCHELDEN, Paul or Pauwels van der
Flemish School, 16th century.
Sculptor.

Paul van der Schelden was the son of the architectural decorator Jan van der Schelden. He carved the entrance to the Magistrates' Room in the town hall of Audenarde between 1531 and 1534. His son, Baudouin van der Schelde, is referred to between 1553 and 1570.

SCHELDERLE, Moyses
German, 18th century.
Active in Rottenburg.
Sculptor.

SCHELER, Friedrich
German, 19th century.
Born 5 May 1818, in Coburg; died 20 October 1851, in Coburg.
Painter (including porcelain). Portraits, genre scenes.

Friedrich Scheler was the father of Heinrich Scheler.

SCHELER, Heinrich Christ. Friedrich
German, 19th century.
Born 6 May 1843, in Coburg; died 1 March 1900, in Coburg.
Sculptor.

Heinrich Scheler was the son of Friedrich and the father of the architect Eduard. He was trained by Th. Von Wagner and was a sculptor at the court. The gigantic bust of *Fr. Buckert* is attributed to him, for the former's monument in Neuses, and the Coburg and Themar war memorials.

SCHELER, Lucie, sometimes Thomas Lucie
French, 20th century.
Born in Paris.
Sculptor.

Lucie Scheler exhibited in Paris at the Salon de Mai of 1998. Her sculptures sometimes have the dynamism of the work of Raymond Duchamp-Villon.

SCHELFHOUT, Andreas
Dutch, 19th century.
Born 16 February 1787, in The Hague; died 19 April 1870, in The Hague.
Painter, watercolourist, engraver (etching), draughtsman. Animals, landscapes with figures, seascapes.

Andreas Schelfhout was the son of a picture-framer in The Hague. A pupil of J. Brekenheimer, he also studied at the academies of Amsterdam, Brussels and Ghent, becoming a renowned teacher whose own pupils included C. Leickert and J.B. Jongkind. Together with B.C. Koekkoek and F.M. Kruseman, Schelfhout was one of the three great Dutch landscape painters of the 19th century, with a confident, assured technique. He excelled in the depiction of winter scenes.

BIBLIOGRAPHY:

Laanstra, Willem, *Andreas Schelfhout*, Rokin Art Press, Amsterdam, 1995 (Dutch/English parallel text). Voigt, Verena, '*Andreas Schelfout: ein Meister der holländischen Landschaft*' in *Weltkunst*, no. 66, periodical, Munich, 1996.

MUSEUMS AND GALLERIES:

AMSTERDAM: *Winter*; *Landscape*; *Winter Panorama in Holland*; *Banks of the Meuse in Winter* - HAMBURG: *Winter Landscape* - KALININGRAD: *Skaters* - LONDON (Wallace Collection): *Winter in Holland* - MUNICH: *River-bank*; *Winter Landscape* - ROTTERDAM: *Beach View* - THE HAGUE (Gemeentemus.): a watercolour; *Three Landscapes*; *A Wood in Winter*; *Seascape*; *Landscape with Ruins*.

AUCTION RECORDS:

PARIS, 1842, *Winter Landscape: Fishermen Spreading their Nets on the Ice*, FRF 2,500. PARIS, 1844, *View of the Normandy Coast (Seascape)*, FRF 4,550; *Landscape*, FRF 2,0250. PARIS, 1849, *Landscape: Environs of Haarlem*, FRF 1,550. GHENT, 1856, *Landscape with Figures*, FRF 1,650. PARIS, 1869, *View of Haarlem in Winter*, FRF 3,400. PARIS, 1871, *Winter in Holland*, FRF 6,704. AMSTERDAM, 1881, *Winter View*, FRF 6,510. AMSTERDAM, 1881, *Winter*, FRF 2,310. VIENNA, 1881, *Scheveningen Coast*, FRF 2,415. PARIS, 1889, *Winter in Holland*, FRF 3,000; *Scheveningen Beach*, FRF 1,050. PARIS, 18 Feb 1898, *Winter*, FRF 1,260. LONDON, 4 Dec 1909, *Low Tide*; *Seashore* (two pendants) GBP 12. LONDON, 24 May 1910, *Frozen River and Skaters*, GBP 7. LONDON, 3 Dec 1910, *Fishing Village*, GBP 11. PARIS, 15 Nov 1912, *Winter in Holland*; *Skaters* (collection) FRF 400. PARIS, 18 March 1920, *Winter in Holland*, FRF 1,320. PARIS, 28 Nov 1923, *Winter in Holland*, FRF 1,250; *Summer Landscape*, FRF 700. PARIS, 16 May 1925, *Figures by a Beach* (watercolour) FRF 200. PARIS, 17-18 March 1927, *Ferry* (black chalk and wash) FRF 180. PARIS, 14 Nov 1927, *Snowy Landscape* (watercolour) FRF 350. PARIS, 18 March 1929, *Returning from Market*, FRF 590. LONDON, 18 March 1932, *View of Dordrecht*, GBP 84. PARIS, 22 Jan 1934, *Sharecropping Farm*, FRF 1,000. PARIS, 22 Jan 1943, *Landscape*, FRF 7,900. PARIS, 11 June 1945, *Winter Pastimes* (attributed) FRF 16,500. PARIS, 25 June 1945, *Sailing Boats in an Estuary*, FRF 3,100. PARIS, 4 April 1949, *Winter Scene* (1852) FRF 1,200. AMSTERDAM, 3 April 1950, *Winter Landscape*, NLG 3,400. AMSTERDAM, 20 June 1950, *Winter Landscape by a Harbour*, NLG 720. PARIS, 6 July 1950, *Winter Pleasures*, FRF 10,100. AMSTERDAM, 19 Sept 1950, *Panoramic Landscape* (1849) NLG 1,900; *Winter Landscape*, NLG 1,050. AMSTERDAM, 13 March 1951, *Entertainment on the Ice in the Polder*, NLG 1,100; *Winter Landscape*, NLG 475. VIENNA, 15 March 1951, *Winter Landscape* (1843) ATS 9,000. AMSTERDAM, 1 May 1951, *Seashore: Storm*, NLG 1,000. VIENNA, 31 May 1951, *Landscape in the Coutryside around Dordrecht, with Skaters*, ATS 4,500. PARIS, 25 June 1951, *Snowy Landscape* (watercolour) FRF 450. AMSTERDAM, 3 July 1951, *Panoramic Landscape in the Gelderland*, NLG 950. PARIS, 17 Dec 1954, *Frozen River with a Sled and Skaters*, FRF 105,000. LONDON, 8 April 1960, *Canal Scene in Winter*, GBP 472. LONDON, 18 Dec 1963, *Winter Landscape*, GBP 310. AMSTERDAM, 29-30 Sept 1965, *Winter Landscape*, NLG 14,000. LONDON, 3 Feb 1967, *Winter Landscape*, Gns 1,100. AMSTERDAM, 21 May 1968, *Skaters on a Canal*, NLG 19,000. LONDON, 14 March 1969, *Winter Landscape*, Gns 7,500. LONDON, 2 May 1972, *Falconry* (in collaboration with Josephus Jodocus Moerenhout) Gns 20,000. LONDON, 6 Oct 1972, *Seashore*, Gns 3,500. LONDON, 4 May 1973, *Landscape with Frozen River and Figures*, Gns 24,000. LONDON, 6 March 1974, *Winter Landscape with Skaters* (1828) GBP 18,000. AMSTERDAM, 27 April 1976, *Beach Scene* (1836, oil on panel, 9 1/2 x 12 ins / 24 x 30.5 cm) NLG 39,000. AMSTERDAM, 26 April 1977, *Riverscape with Mill* (1840, oil on panel, 16 1/4 x 21 1/4 ins / 41.5 x 54 cm) NLG 36,000. AMSTERDAM, 29 Oct 1979, *Figures on a Frozen River near a Bridge* (pen and wash/black chalk, 7 1/2 x 9 1/2 ins / 18.8 x 23.9 cm) NLG 6,800. LONDON, 28 Nov 1979, *Frozen River* (oil on panel, 20 x 31 1/2 ins / 51 x 80 cm) GBP 40,000. AMSTERDAM, 19 May 1981, *Winter Landscape with Skaters* (1867, oil on panel, 7 3/4 x 11 1/4 ins / 20 x 28.5 cm) NLG 36,000. AMSTERDAM, 15 March 1983, *Skaters and Sleds on a Frozen River* (1839, oil on panel, 22 3/4 x 30 1/2 ins / 58 x 77.5 cm) NLG 78,000. AMSTERDAM, 25 April 1983, *Landscape with a Watermill and Figures* (pencil and wash, 10 x 14 1/2 ins / 25.5 x 36.9 cm) NLG 3,600. LONDON, 21 June 1984, *Winter Landscape* (watercolour heightened with white, 8 x 11 1/4 ins / 20.2 x 28.5 cm) GBP 2,400. AMSTERDAM, 19 Nov 1985, *Sled in a Winter Landscape* (watercolour and pen, 9 x 12 1/4 ins / 23 x 31 cm) NLG 3,800. AMSTERDAM, 14 April 1986, *Anglers in a Wooded Landscape* (oil on canvas, 38 1/4 x 51 ins / 97 x 129.5 cm) NLG 48,000. AMSTERDAM, 10 Feb 1988, *Landscape with a River with Wooded Banks, a Cutter at Anchor and Two Fishermen in a Boat* (1859, oil on panel, 6 x 7 1/4 ins / 15 x 18.5 cm) NLG 14,950. AMSTERDAM, 16 Nov 1988, *Anglers on a Wooden Bridge in a Wooded Landscape* (oil on panel, 14 1/2 x 17 ins / 37 x 43 cm) NLG 23,000. AMSTERDAM, 28 Feb 1989, *Rocky Coastline with a Two-master at Sea in Stormy Conditions* (1851, oil on panel, 11 1/4 x 15 3/4 ins / 28.5 x 40 cm) NLG 17,250. LONDON, 21 June 1989, *Winter Landscape* (1855, oil on canvas, 21 1/4 x 27 1/4 ins / 54 x 69 cm) GBP 38,500. AMSTERDAM, 10 April 1990, *Wooded Winter Landscape with Skaters* (ink and wash, 11 x 13 1/2 ins / 27 x 34 cm) NLG 6,900. AMSTERDAM, 2 May 1990, *Vast Dutch Winter Landscape with Skaters and a Horse-drawn Sleigh on a Frozen River* (1839, oil on panel, 23 1/2 x 30 1/4 ins / 59.5 x 77 cm) NLG 483,000. AMSTERDAM, 6 Nov 1990, *Country Scene on a Frozen River at the Foot of a Windmill* (1857, oil on panel, 13 3/4 x 18 ins / 35 x 46 cm) NLG 184,000. STOCKHOLM, 14 Nov 1990, *Winter Landscape with Skaters* (oil on panel, 9 1/2 x 11 3/4 ins / 24 x 30 cm) SEK 25,000. AMSTERDAM, 5-6 Feb 1991, *Wooded River Landscape with Shepherds Praying near a Chapel* (oil on panel, 12 3/4 x 10 1/4 ins / 32.5 x 26 cm) NLG 6,900. AMSTERDAM, 5-6 Feb 1991, *Polder Landscape with Cows in a Meadow* (1851, oil on panel, 7 3/4 x 9 1/2 ins / 19.5 x 24 cm) NLG 5,175. LONDON, 21 June 1991, *Skaters near a Hamlet* (1850, oil on panel, 22 x 29 1/4 ins / 55 x 74.5 cm) GBP 71,500. AMSTERDAM, 30 Oct 1991, *Winter Landscape with a Woman and her Child Pushing a Sled on a Frozen Canal, with Dordrecht in the Distance* (1846, oil on panel, 19 x 26 ins / 48.5 x 66 cm) NLG 207,000. NEW YORK, 19 Feb 1992, *Skaters in a Winter Landscape* (oil on canvas, 14 1/4 x 22 3/4 ins / 36.5 x 57.8 cm) USD 19,800. AMSTERDAM, 22 April 1992, *Winter Landscape with Peasants near a Copse and Skaters on a Canal near a Mill* (1857, oil on panel, 22 3/4 x 31 ins / 58 x 78.5 cm) NLG 431,250. AMSTERDAM, 28 Oct 1992, *Beached Fishing Boats, with Elegant Figures Going for a Walk* (ink and watercolour/paper, 11 x 17 1/4 ins / 28 x 44 cm) NLG 19,550. NEW YORK, 29 Oct 1992, *Beached Fishing Boats* (oil on panel, 12 1/4 x 16 ins / 31.1 x 40.6 cm) USD 27,500. AMSTERDAM, 2-3 Nov 1992, *Vast Panorama with a City in the Distance, Probably Delft* (1853, oil on panel, 11 x 14 1/2 ins / 28 x 37 cm) NLG 55,200. PARIS, 15 Dec 1992, *Canal in Winter* (1945, oil on panel, 19 x 26 ins / 48 x 66 cm) FRF 500,000. AMSTERDAM, 20 April 1993, *Figures and Horses Pulling a Boat onto a Beach* (1859, oil on panel, 12 1/2 x 17 1/4 ins / 32 x 43.5 cm) NLG 94,300. LONDON, 16 March 1994, *Winter Landscape with Skaters* (1833, oil on panel, 26 3/4 x 34 ins / 68 x 86.5 cm) GBP 31,050. AMSTERDAM, 21 April 1994, *Winter Landscape with Skaters on a Canal* (ink, watercolour and gouache/paper, 9 x 11 3/4 ins / 22 x 30 cm) NLG 13,800. AMSTERDAM, 8 Nov 1994, *Winter Landscape with Figures on a Frozen Pond* (1849, oil on panel, 11 1/4 x 15 3/4 ins / 28.5 x 40 cm) NLG 138,000. LOKEREN, 11 March 1995, *Winter Landscape with a Frozen Canal* (oil on panel, 20 x 23 1/2 ins / 51 x 59.5 cm) BEF 330,000. TOURS, 20 Nov 1995, *Winter Landscape*; *Rural Landscape* (oil on panel, a pair, each 13 1/2 x 17 1/4 ins / 34 x 44 cm) FRF 309,000. AMSTERDAM, 16 April 1996, *Winter Landscape with Peasants near a Farm* (oil on panel, 15 3/4 x 19 3/4 ins / 40 x 50 cm) NLG 29,500. AMSTERDAM, 5 Nov 1996, *Cows Drinking near Ruins* (pen and wax, 5 3/4 x 7 3/4 ins / 14.5

x 20 cm) NLG 3,068; *Couple Resting in a Vast Landscape, with a Town in the Distance* (1868, oil on panel, 10 3/4 x 15 ins / 27.5 x 38 cm) NLG 35,400. LONDON, 20 Nov 1996, *Windmill near a Frozen River* (oil on canvas, 34 1/4 x 43 3/4 ins / 87 x 111 cm) GBP 331,500. AMSTERDAM, 22 April 1997, *Winter Landscape with Skaters on a Frozen River; Summer Landscape with a Shepherd on a Path* (1827, oil on panel, a pair, each 16 1/2 x 21 1/4 ins / 42 x 54 cm) NLG 177,000. NEW YORK, 23 May 1997, *Frozen Thoroughfare* (1845, oil on panel, 18 1/4 x 26 ins / 46.4 x 66 cm) USD 151,000. AMSTERDAM, 27 Oct 1997, *Summer Landscape with a Shepherd on a Path* (pen and grey wash, 11 x 14 3/4 ins / 28 x 37.5 cm) NLG 10,030. LONDON, 19 Nov 1997, *Figures Skating in a Winter Landscape* (1843, oil on panel, 8 1/2 x 11 ins / 21.5 x 28 cm) GBP 31,050. LONDON, 21 Nov 1997, *Winter Landscape with Figures on a Frozen River* (oil on panel, 6 3/4 x 9 1/2 ins / 17.2 x 24.2 cm) GBP 24,150. AMSTERDAM, 21 Jan 1998, *Elegant Figures Greeting the Fleet on Scheveningen Beach* (oil on panel, 7 1/4 x 9 ins / 18.5 x 23 cm) NLG 69,192. LONDON, 25 March 1999, *Winter Landscape* (1839, oil on canvas, 34 x 43 ins / 87 x 109 cm) GBP 170,000. NEW YORK, 3 Nov 1999, *Frozen Winter Landscape* (oil on panel, 23 x 29 ins / 59 x 73 cm) USD 440,000. PARIS, 21 June 2000, *Winter Landscape with Sleigh* (oil on panel, 16 x 22 ins / 40 x 56 cm) FRF 1,500,000. LONDON, 27 Oct 2000, *Shipping in Stormy Water* (1844, oil on panel, 23 x 28 ins / 59 x 72 cm) GBP 88,000. AMSTERDAM, 23 April 2001, *Boats on the Merwede near Dordrecht* (1843, oil on panel, 19 x 24 ins / 49 x 62 cm) NLG 310,000. COLOGNE, 28 June 2001, *On the Ice* (oil on panel, 11 x 16 ins / 29 x 40 cm) DEM 130,000. AMSTERDAM, 24 April 2002, *Outskirts of a Dutch Town on a Summer's Day* (1835, oil on panel, 13 x 17 ins / 34 x 43 cm) EUR 58,000. GRAVENHAGE, 24 April 2002, *Beach Scene with Elegant Couple near a Wooden Boat* (1832, oil on panel, 6 x 13 ins / 16 x 32 cm) EUR 84,000. AMSTERDAM, 29 April 2003, *Summer in Holland - Panoramic View of a Village in the Dunes* (1842, oil on panel, 15 x 20 ins / 38 x 51 cm) EUR 155,000. AMSTERDAM, 28 Oct 2003, *Sunlit Winter Landscape with Huntsman Conversing with Villagers on the Ice* (1834, oil on canvas, 25 x 32 ins / 64 x 81 cm) EUR 105,000. AMSTERDAM, 20 April 2004, *Skaters on a Frozen River near a Koek en Zopie* (1857, oil on panel, 10 x 15 ins / 26 x 38 cm) EUR 180,000. AMSTERDAM, 21 April 2004, *Shepherdess with Flock and Travellers in a Summer Landscape* (1849, oil on canvas, 44 x 57 ins / 111 x 146 cm) EUR 270,000.

SCHELFHOUT, Lodewijk

Dutch, 20th century.

Born 1881, in The Hague; died 1943.

Painter, engraver, draughtsman. Landscapes, still-lifes.

Lodewijk Schelfhout was the uncle of Andreas Schelfhout and a pupil of Théophile de Bock. He was in Paris from 1903 to 1913, where he met the majority of Dutch painters as they passed through. He shared his accommodation with Mondrian after the latter had come to Paris in 1911. In Paris, he came under the influence of Cézanne and Van Gogh, and was the first Dutch artist to take up Cubism. In 1913 Schelfhout settled in Hilversum.

MUSEUMS AND GALLERIES:

BERLIN (Nationalgal.): *The Dream* - THE HAGUE (Gemeentemus.): *Portrait of the Author/Painter by Himself; Portrait of Jan Toorop; Still-life.*

AUCTION RECORDS:

AMSTERDAM, 12 Dec 1990, *Still-life with Flowers in a Vase and Fruits on an Entablature* (1909, oil on card, 29 1/4 x 24 ins / 74 x 61 cm) NLG 13,800. AMSTERDAM, 22 May 1991, *The Village 'The English'* (1910, oil on canvas, 32 x 35 1/2 ins / 81 x 90 cm) NLG 55,200. AMSTERDAM, 14 Sept 1993, *Pierrot* (black chalk and pastel/paper, 38 1/2 x 25 1/4 ins / 98 x 64 cm) NLG 2,185. AMSTERDAM, 8 Dec 1993, *Still-life with a Pike, an Earthenware Jug and Fruits on a Table* (oil on canvas, 15 3/4 x 23 1/2 ins / 40 x 60 cm) NLG 1,380. AMSTERDAM, 1 Dec 2004, *Village in Provence, Les Angles* (1912, oil on canvas, 27 x 20 ins / 68 x 51 cm) EUR 32,000.

SCHELHAMMER, Johann Melchior. See **SCHÖLLHAMMER**

SCHELHAS, Abraham

German, 17th century.

Active in Augsburg.

Painter.

Schelhas painted portraits before 1600.

SCHELHASSE, Heinrich

German, 20th century.

Born 3 October 1896, in Lippspringe.

Painter, engraver. Religious subjects. Designs for stained glass, designs for mosaics.

Heinrich Schelhasse was a pupil of the academy of fine arts in Kassel. He lived and worked in Berlin.

SCHELHAUER, Franciscus

German, 17th century.

Engraver (burin).

SCHELHORN. See **SCHELLHORN**

SCHELKOVNIKOFF, Andrei Michailovitch. See **SHELKOVNIKOV Andrei Mikhailovich**

SCHELL

French, 18th century.

Painter. History painting, landscapes.

Schell exhibited at Place Dauphine in 1788 and at the Académie Royale in 1793.

SCHELL, Caspar

Swiss, 17th century.

Active in Zug.

Sculptor (wood).

Caspar Schell carved the pulpit for the church of St Wolfgang.

SCHELL, David Joachim. See **SCHEL**

SCHELL, F. B.

American, 19th century.

Born in the USA; died c. 1905, in Chicago.

Painter, watercolourist. Landscapes.

F.B. Schell visited Australia to research a book he was illustrating, in collaboration with other artists, called *Picturesque Atlas*. While he was there he drew numerous views of Australia, Tasmania and New Zealand. He died after accidentally falling from a window.

MUSEUMS AND GALLERIES:

SYDNEY: *High Tide, Bondi*; numerous drawings.

SCHELL, Francis H.

American, 19th century.

Born 1834, in Germantown; died 31 March 1909, in Philadelphia.

Painter, draughtsman. Military subjects.

SCHELL, Frank Cresson

American, 19th century.

Born 3 May 1857, in Philadelphia; died 1942.

Active in Philadelphia.

Illustrator.

Frank Cresson Schell was a pupil of Eakins and Anschutz.

SCHELL, Jacob

Austrian, 19th century.

Born 1809, in Vienna.

Painter. History painting, portraits.

Jacob Schell trained at the academy and worked in Munich from 1836 to 1840. He then returned to Vienna where he remained until 1852.

SCHELL, Johannes

Swiss, 17th century.

Active in Salem at the beginning of the 17th century.
Painter.

SCHELL, Joseph
Austrian, 18th century.
Painter.
Joseph Schell trained at the academy in Vienna where he was awarded first prize in 1740.

SCHELL, Karl
Swiss, 17th century.
Active in Zug.
Sculptor (wood).
Karl Schell carved a statue of the *Virgin* in 1686 for the fountain of Our Lady in Einsiedeln.

SCHELL, Sebastian. See **SCHEEL**

SCHELLAUF, Andreas
Austrian, 18th century.
Died 13 September 1742, in Wiener Neustadt.
Active in Wiener Neustadt.
Engraver.
The statues of the high altar of the church of the New Monastery in Wiener Neustadt are attributed to Schellauf.

SCHELLBACH, Karl Hermann
German, 19th - 20th century.
Born 27 February 1850, in Berlin; died 21 December 1921, in Berlin.
Painter. Portraits, genre scenes.
Karl Hermann Schellbach was a pupil of Karl Gussow.
MUSEUMS AND GALLERIES:
KALININGRAD (Castle).
AUCTION RECORDS:
LONDON, 18 Dec 1997, *First Love* (oil on canvas, 20 x 14 3/4 ins / 50.8 x 37.5 cm) GBP 575.

SCHELLBACH, Siegfried
German, 19th - 20th century.
Born 14 August 1866, in Berlin.
Sculptor.
Siegfried Schellbach lived and worked in Mustin (Lauenbourg).

SCHELLE, Franz Joseph
German, 19th century.
Born in Landsberg; died 20 May 1888, in Landsberg.
Painter.
Franz Joseph Schelle worked in Munich. An altarpiece at the church of the Trinity in Landsberg is attributed to him.

SCHELLEIN, Karl
Austrian, 19th century.
Born 11 June 1820, in Bamberg (Bavaria), Germany; died 9 April 1888, in Vienna.
Painter, art restorer.
Schellein trained at the academy in Munich.
AUCTION RECORDS:
VIENNA, 22 May 1973, *Despair,* ATS 45,000. NEW YORK, 7 Dec 1999, *Floral Still Life on a Ledge with Peaches and Grapes* (1853, oil on canvas, 19 x 15 ins / 48 x 38 cm) USD 4,500. LONDON, 17 Jan 2002, *Joseph and the Angel* (oil on canvas, after Raphael Mengs, 44 x 34 ins / 113 x 87 cm) GBP 1,600.

SCHELLEMANS, Franz. See **SCHILLEMANS**

SCHELLENBERG, Christian Friedrich, the Elder
German, 18th century.
Born 1710; died 30 December 1749.
Active in Leipzig.
Sculptor.

SCHELLENBERG, Christian Friedrich, the Younger
German, 18th century.
Born 1748, in Leipzig.
Sculptor.
Christian Friedrich Schellenberg the Younger was the son of Christian Friedrich Schellenberg the Elder.

SCHELLENBERG, Daniel Friedrich
German, 18th - 19th century.
Born 1763; died 1813.
Active in Leipzig.
Sculptor.

SCHELLENBERG, Johann Rudolph
German, 18th century.
Born 4 January 1740, in Basel; died 6 August 1806, in Töss.
Painter, engraver (etching/burin), poet.
Johann Rudolph Schellenberg was the son of Johann Ulrich Schellenberg. He engraved portraits, genre scenes and landscapes. He produced etchings, notably for Lavater, and engravings in the style of Chodowiecki. He also provided portraits for the *Life of Painters* by Fuessli. Several of his caricatures were shown at the exhibition of *Karikaturen von Hogarth bis Daumier* (*Caricatures from Hogarth to Daumier*) at the Kunsthaus in Zurich in 2001.

SCHELLENBERG, Johann Ulrich
German, 18th century.
Born 8 November 1709, in Winterthur; died 1 November 1795, in Winterthur.
Engraver (burin). Landscapes.
Johann Ulrich Schellenberg was the father of Johann Rudolf. He worked in Basel, Bern and Winterthur.
MUSEUMS AND GALLERIES:
BERN: *Portrait of the Sturler Family*; portraits of two patrician children; a seascape - WINTERTHUR: *Portrait of Dr Salomon Hegner* - WINTERTHUR (Stadtbibliothek): drawings and watercolours - ZURICH (ETH Graphics Collection): drawings and watercolours.
AUCTION RECORDS:
ZURICH, 15 Nov 1983, *View of the Town of Winthertur* (1752, coloured etching, 10 3/4 x 22 3/4 ins / 27.2 x 57.6 cm) CHF 4,400.

SCHELLENBERGER, Johann Jacob
German, 17th century.
Active c. 1660, 1674.
Engraver.
Johann Jacob Schellenberger executed the plates for the *History of Emperor Leopold* by Priorato.

SCHELLER, F. Augustin
German, 18th century.
Born c. 1719, in Augsburg; died 1790, in Augsburg.
Engraver (burin), draughtsman.

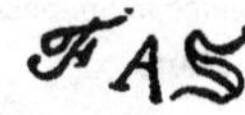

SCHELLER, Hans Walter
Swiss, 20th century.
Born 1896, in Bern; died 1964, in Zurich.
Painter. Interiors with figures.
AUCTION RECORDS:
LUCERNE, 30 Sept 1988, *Parisian Cafe* (1934, oil on canvas, 20 x 20 ins / 51 x 51 cm) CHF 2,800.

SCHELLER, Hermann
German, 17th century.
Born 13 May 1637, in Brunswick; died 27 May 1679, in Brunswick.
Sculptor.

SCHELLER, Jörg
German, 16th century.
Active in Magdeburg.
Sculptor (wood).
Jörg Scheller carved portraits of Martin Luther and his wife.

SCHELLER, Theophil Arsatius
Swiss, 19th century.
Born 7 September 1817, in Wädenswil; died 13 December 1878, in San Francisco.
Painter.

SCHELLHAMMER, Hans Jakob
German, 17th century.
Died 1613.
Active in Breslau (now Wroclaw).
Sculptor.

SCHELLHORN, C. van
Dutch, 19th century.
Active at the beginning of the 19th century.
Painter, engraver.
C. van Schellhorn is mentioned by Ris-Paquot.

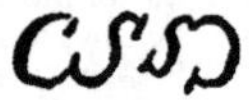

SCHELLHORN, Carl
German, 19th century.
Born c. 1840.
Sculptor (wood).
Carl Schellhorn was in charge of the technical college for wood sculpture in Gmund in Carinthia from 1873 to 1878, and in charge of the one in Villach from 1878 to 1884.

SCHELLHORN, Christoph
German, 19th century.
Active in Munich c. 1820.
Engraver.

SCHELLHORN, Christoph Veit
German, 19th century.
Born 1800, in Nuremberg; died 1850, in Nuremberg.
Engraver (burin).
Christoph Veit Schellhorn trained at the academy in Nuremberg from 1816 to 1823.

SCHELLHORN, Franz Wilhelm
German, 18th - 19th century.
Born 5 March 1750, in Weimar; died 12 January 1836.
Miniaturist. Portraits.
MUSEUMS AND GALLERIES:
WEIMAR: *Portraits of the Duke and Duchesses Anna, Amelie and Louise of Saxony Weimar.*

SCHELLHORN, Friedrich Paul
German, 19th century.
Active in Sonneberg in Thuringia.
Painter.
Friedrich Schellhorn trained in Sonneberg and Munich.

SCHELLHORN, Hans
German, 20th century.
Born 11 November 1879, in Kiel.
Sculptor. Groups, monuments.
Hans Schellhorn was a pupil at the academy of fine arts in Berlin. He created the groups of Tritons in the Berlin-Weissensee Park and the regimental monument to the Emperor Alexander in the church of the Garrison in Berlin.

SCHELLHORN, Paul
Austrian, 19th century.
Active c. 1820.
Painter. Portraits.

SCHELLING, Heinrich
Swiss, 19th - 20th century.
Born 22 August 1867, in St Gall.
Draughtsman.
Heinrich Schelling was a pupil of Jakob Stauffacher.

SCHELLING, Henrik
Belgian, 15th century.
Active in Louvain c. 1455.
Painter.

SCHELLINKS, Daniel, or Schellincks
Dutch, 17th century.
Born c. 1627, in Amsterdam; died 23 September 1701.
Painter, draughtsman. Landscapes, seascapes.
Daniel Schellinks was the brother of Willem Schellinks. He seems to have enjoyed a certain reputation during his lifetime. His drawings are remarkable and highly sought-after.

DS.

MUSEUMS AND GALLERIES:
TURIN: *Path between Two Hills* - VIENNA (Albertina Mus.): several drawings - VIENNA (Liechtenstein Mus.): *Landscape.*

SCHELLINKS, Willem
Dutch, 17th century.
Born 2 February 1627, in Amsterdam; died 12 October 1678, in Amsterdam.
Painter, draughtsman, engraver. History painting, landscapes with figures, landscapes, seascapes.
Willem Schellinks was probably a pupil of Karel du Jardin; several of his pictures recall the latter's style, notably his animal studies and effects of sunlight. Some biographers state that he studied under Lingelbach. He may have studied with both masters upon their respective returns from Italy (Lingelbach in 1652, Karel du Jardin in 1655). From 1661 to 1665 Schellinks travelled to England, France, Italy (particularly Sicily), Malta, Germany and Switzerland. He returned to Amsterdam in 1667, where he married Maria Neus. His most renowned works include *Charles II Embarking for England Following his Restoration* painted for the Witsen family, and the *Burning of the English Fleet near Chatham.* Schellinks was a gifted landscape and seascape artist, and an accomplished painter of figures, particularly groups. As such, he was often called upon to paint staffage figures for Wynants and Heusch. He was also a poet.

MUSEUMS AND GALLERIES:
AMSTERDAM: *Charles II Embarking for England Following his Restoration* (drawing); *Procession to Chatham* - AMSTERDAM (Stedelijk Mus.): *Country House of the Burgomaster Pancras; Navigation School* - AUGSBURG: *Port of Livorno* - BUDAPEST: *Fountain* (attributed) - BUENOS AIRES: *Horseman at a Fountain* - CAEN: *Scene with Soldiers* - COPENHAGEN (Statens Mus. for Kunst): *Landscape with Ancient Ruins* - FLORENCE (Palazzo Pitti): *Two Landscapes* - FRANKFURT AM MAIN: *Southern Landscape* - GENEVA: *Procession to Chatham* - GLASGOW (AG and Mus.): *Landscape with a Hunting Party* - KIEV (Chanenko Mus.): *Inn* - NAPLES (Mus. Nazionale): *Falconry* - PHILADELPHIA: *Italian Landscape* - ST PETERSBURG (Hermitage): *Landscape* - TISTAD: *Charles II Leaving Holland for London* - VIENNA (Akademie der Bildenden Künste): *Italian Cemetery.*
AUCTION RECORDS:
PARIS, 1773, *Departure of the Prince of Orange for England* (drawing in pen and Indian ink) FRF 240. PARIS, 1776, *Two Ruins and Several Groups of Figures and Animals* (drawing in pen and bistre) FRF 235. PARIS, 1831, *Landscape,* FRF 206. PARIS, 1831, *Interior,* FRF 180. PARIS, 1842, *View of a Park,*

FRF 720. LONDON, 19 Feb 1910, *Wooded Landscape* (in collaboration with Hagen) GBP 24. LONDON, 14 May 1911, *Departure of Charles II from the Dutch Coast,* GBP 105. PARIS, 25 March 1925, *Village with a Mill by a River and Figures* (pen with Indian ink wash) FRF 800. PARIS, 17 and 18 March 1927, *Temple of Portunus in Rome* (brush and Indian ink) FRF 190. LONDON, 25 July 1947, *Frozen River Scene,* GBP 78. VIENNA, 23 March 1965, *Women Bathing,* ATS 25,000. PARIS, 19 March 1966, *Returning from the Hunt,* FRF 12,000. LONDON, 21 March 1973, *River Landscape,* GBP 1,200. LONDON, 6 July 1976, *Landscape with Castle* (black chalk and wash, 7h x 11 ins / 17.7 x 28.1 cm) GBP 1,400. ZURICH, 12 Nov 1976, *Winter Landscape with Figures* (oil on canvas, 19 3/4 x 26 ins / 50 x 66 cm) CHF 26,000. VERSAILLES, 13 Feb 1977, *Falconers Setting Out for the Hunt* (oil on wood, 15 x 20 1/2 ins / 38 x 52 cm) FRF 27,000. VERSAILLES, 24 Feb 1980, *Horsemen and Villagers by a Lake* (oil on canvas, 16 x 20 3/4 ins / 40.5 x 53 cm) FRF 30,000. AMSTERDAM, 18 Nov 1980, *View of a Town at the Foot of a Mountain* (black chalk and grey wash, 8 x 16 ins / 20.5 x 39.7 cm) NLG 2,800. LONDON, 8 July 1981, *The Great Moghul Hunting* (oil on canvas, 20 x 24 1/4 ins / 51 x 61.5 cm) GBP 12,500. LONDON, 5 July 1984, *Turkish Sultan Watching Dancing Girls* (oil on canvas, 19 1/2 x 23 1/2 ins / 49.5 x 59.5 cm) GBP 8,200. LONDON, 22 May 1985, *Travellers in a Wooded Landscape* (oil on canvas, 26 1/2 x 31 1/4 ins / 67.4 x 79.3 cm) GBP 5,200. AMSTERDAM, 18 Nov 1985, *View of Geneva* (black chalk and grey wash with touches of ink, 10 x 14 1/2 ins / 25.4 x 36.7 cm) NLG 8,200. NEW YORK, 14 Jan 1994, *Rocky Landscape with a Cowherd Watering his Animals in a Stream* (oil on canvas, 20 x 26 3/4 ins / 50.5 x 67.9 cm) USD 9,200. NEW YORK, 11 Jan 1996, *Boats at Anchor in a Southern Italian Port* (oil on canvas, 16 x 19 ins / 40.6 x 48.3 cm) USD 20,700. NEW YORK, 4 Oct 1996, *Travellers Resting on a Path in a Mountain Landscape with a River* (oil on panel, 14 x 19 1/4 ins / 35.5 x 48.9 cm) USD 2,990. LONDON, 1 Nov 1996, *Angel Appearing to the Shepherds* (oil on canvas, 16 1/4 x 16 3/4 ins / 41.3 x 42.8 cm) GBP 2,875. AMSTERDAM, 11 Nov 1997, *Western View of Chatham* (black chalk and wax, 8 1/2 x 14 ins / 21.9 x 35.3 cm) NLG 21,240. LONDON, 13 April 1999, *Sportsmen in a Wooded River Landscape* (oil on canvas, 48 x 71 ins / 123 x 180 cm) GBP 11,000. VIENNA, 6 Oct 1999, *Southern Mountain River Landscape with Ruined Monastery* (oil on panel, 16 x 22 ins / 40 x 55 cm) ATS 100,000. LONDON, 5 July 2000, *Winter Landscape with Woodmen before a Cottage* (oil on canvas, 35 x 48 ins / 90 x 121 cm) GBP 5,500. BREMEN, 8 Dec 2000, *Landscape with Tavern and Travellers* (oil on panel, 29 x 42 ins / 73 x 106 cm) DEM 15,000. LONDON, 14 June 2002, *Study Interior with a Philosopher at a Table by a Window* (oil on canvas, 20 x 18 ins / 51 x 46 cm) GBP 20,000. LONDON, 10 April 2003, *Landscape with Figures and Animals Crossing a River by Ferry* (oil on canvas, 39 x 61 ins / 100 x 154 cm) GBP 16,000. MUNICH, 19 Sept 2003, *Wooded Landscape with Mounted Falconer, Falcon Hunters and Dogs* (oil on panel, 20 x 26 ins / 52 x 67 cm) EUR 15,000. MUNICH, 26 March 2004, *Forest Landscape with Rider, Falcon and Dogs* (oil on panel, 20 x 26 ins / 52 x 67 cm) EUR 7,000.

SCHELNAKOV, Nikita

Russian, 18th century.

Born 1734.

Engraver. Portraits, landscapes.

Nikita Schelnakov was the pupil of Georg Friedrich Schmidt.

SCHELSKI, Joseph, or Schelzki, Schelzehi

German, 18th century.

Painter. Religious subjects.

Schelski was active in Botzen (now Bolzano, Italy) and painted religious subjects.

SCHELTEMA, Jan Hendrik

Dutch, 19th - 20th century.

Born 7 August 1876 or 1861, in Nes; died 1938.

Painter. Landscapes, animals.

Jan Hendrik Sheltema spent some time in Australia.

MUSEUMS AND GALLERIES:

MELBOURNE (Nat. Gal. of Victoria): *Going out to Pasture at Sunrise.*

AUCTION RECORDS:

MELBOURNE, 14 March 1974, *Herd/Flock in a Landscape,* AUD 1,000. LONDON, 19 May 1976, *Herd/Flock in a Landscape* (oil on canvas, 31 1/2 x 49 1/4 ins / 80 x 125 cm) GBP 1,200. MELBOURNE, 20 March 1978, *Horses out at Pasture* (oil on canvas, 19 x 28 3/4 ins / 48 x 73 cm) AUD 4,800. SYDNEY, 10 March 1980, *Mount Riddell, Healsville* (oil on canvas, 26 3/4 x 20 3/4 ins / 68 x 53 cm) AUD 4,200. SYDNEY, 2 March 1981, *Shepherdess and Flock* (oil on canvas, 19 3/4 x 29 1/2 ins / 50 x 75 cm) AUD 7,500. ARMADALE (AUSTRALIA), 12 April 1984, *Drinking at the Ford* (oil on canvas, 22 1/2 x 38 1/2 ins / 57 x 97.5 cm) AUD 14,000. LONDON, 20 Nov 1986, *Hazy Evening* (oil on canvas, 24 x 41 ins / 60.9 x 104.2 cm) GBP 6,500. SYDNEY, 29-30 March 1992, *Closure of Post and the Station* (oil on card, 11 1/2 x 13 3/4 ins / 29 x 35 cm) AUD 1,600. MELBOURNE, 29 April 1997, *Horses Grazing* (oil on canvas, 19 1/2 x 30 ins / 49.5 x 76 cm) AUD 5,750. VICTORIA, 20 April 1999, *Cattle Grazing* (oil on canvas, 16 x 22 ins / 40 x 55 cm) AUD 6,000. SYDNEY, 17 Aug 1999, *Cattle in the Early Morning* (oil on canvas, 15 x 22 ins / 39 x 55 cm) AUD 6,500. VICTORIA, 4 April 2000, *Droving the Sheep to Drink* (oil on canvas, 25 x 17 ins / 64 x 44 cm) AUD 10,000. VICTORIA, 14 Nov 2000, *Brumbies* (oil on canvas, 22 x 35 ins / 57 x 90 cm) AUD 10,000. PADDINGTON, 3 June 2001, *Kitchen Interior with Woman and Children* (oil on canvas, 15 x 24 ins / 39 x 60 cm) AUD 10,000. SYDNEY, 28 Aug 2001, *Cows* (oil on canvas, 30 x 36 ins / 77 x 92 cm) AUD 10,000. PADDINGTON, 25 Aug 2002, *Bullock Team in the Forest of Canungra, Queensland* (oil on canvas, 28 x 41 ins / 70 x 105 cm) AUD 14,000. SYDNEY, 18 Nov 2002, *Morley's Track, Fernshaw* (oil on canvas, 39 x 59 ins / 100 x 150 cm) AUD 120,000. MELBOURNE, 2 April 2003, *Cattle Grazing in a Summer Pastoral* (oil on canvas, 28 x 39 ins / 70 x 100 cm) AUD 20,000. VICTORIA, 13 Oct 2003, *At the End of the Day* (oil on canvas, 17 x 29 ins / 42 x 74 cm) AUD 11,500. MELBOURNE, 3 May 2004, *Hunter's Reward* (oil on canvas, 19 x 30 ins / 49 x 75 cm) AUD 20,000. PADDINGTON, 24 Aug 2004, *Droving Sheep* (oil on canvas, 28 x 40 ins / 71 x 101 cm) AUD 23,000.

SCHELTEMA, Taco I

Dutch, 18th - 19th century.

Born c. 1760; died 7 September 1837.

Painter. Portraits, landscapes.

Taco Scheltema I studied under Antony van Dyck and travelled to Germany, visiting Düsseldorf and Saxony, where he painted a number of portraits. Upon his return to the Netherlands, he married Jaconima van Nymegen in Rotterdam and settled in Velp, near Arnhem. He was a frequent visitor to Amsterdam and Rotterdam, and a prolific portrait painter.

AUCTION RECORDS:

PARIS, 1876, *Gentleman Looking at a Portrait in a Case,* FRF 1,120. PARIS, 1880, *Gentleman Looking at a Portrait in a Case,* FRF 2,310.

SCHELTEMA, Taco II

Dutch, 19th century.

Born 2 April 1831, in Arnhem; died 14 October 1867, in The Hague.

Painter. History painting, portraits, genre scenes.

Taco Scheltema II was the son of Taco Scheltema I and a pupil of J. E. J. van de Berg. His work shows the influence of Ary Scheffer.

MUSEUMS AND GALLERIES:

AMSTERDAM (Stedelijk Mus.): *Gentleman Inspecting an Engraving.*

SCHELVER, August Franz
German, 19th century.
Born 1805, in Osnabrück; died October 1844, in Munich.
Painter. Battles, genre scenes.

Schelver was initially trained by Neslmeyer, but then found patrons who provided him with the means to go and continue his training in Munich. In 1833 he painted *Battle near Hanau* which received great success. He produced hunting scenes and horse market scenes.

MUSEUMS AND GALLERIES:
KALININGRAD: *Battle near Hanau* - MUNICH: *Coach on a Mountain Road; Battle Painting.*

AUCTION RECORDS:
PARIS, 7 April 1896, *River banks,* FRF 600. LONDON, 27 Nov 1981, *Travellers and Horses in a Landscape* (oil on canvas, 22 x 29¼ ins / 55.8 x 74.2 cm) GBP 2,400. MUNICH, 27 Feb 1999, *Exchange of Horses* (1837, oil on canvas, 24 x 33 ins / 62 x 84 cm) DEM 13,000. LUCERNE, 19 May 1999, *Horse Market in Partenkirchen* (1837, oil on canvas, 26 x 34 ins / 65 x 87 cm) CHF 20,000. LONDON, 5 July 2001, *Military Encampment* (1840, oil on canvas, 43 x 61 ins / 109 x 155 cm) GBP 6,500. LONDON, 5 July 2001, *Battle Scene* (1839, oil on canvas, 41 x 57 ins / 103 x 146 cm) GBP 22,000.

SCHEMBERA, Josef. See **SEMBERA**

SCHEMBERGER, Johann Jakob, or Schenperger
Austrian, 18th century.
Born c. 1710, in Mattsee; died 13 April 1786, in Hallein.
Active in Hallein (Salzburg).
Painter.

Schemberger painted religious subjects.

SCHEMIAKIN, Michail Feodorovitch.
See **SHEMYAKIN Mikhail Fedorovich**

SCHEMMER, Jakob
Bavarian School, 18th century.
Active in Kelheim.
Painter.

SCHEN, Johann
German, 17th century.
Active at the beginning of the 17th century.
Draughtsman.

SCHENACH, Johann Georg.
See **SCHENNACH**

SCHENAU, or Scheneau, Schönau, real name: Johann Eleazar Zeizig, or Zeisig
German, 18th century.
Born c. 1737, in Gross Schönau, near Zittau; died 1806, in Dresden.
Painter, watercolourist, engraver, draughtsman.
Religious subjects, allegorical subjects, portraits, genre scenes.

J.G. Wille gave some interesting and very complete details on Schenau in his *Memoirs*. Schenau's father was a manufacturer of damask and refused to let his son become an artist. Schenau, therefore, ran away from his paternal home at a very young age to go and train in Dresden. He was brought back to his father's house, but ran away again shortly afterwards. This time, however, he managed to hide from those seeking him, and began to make a living by making copies for the legal profession. Saxony was at war at the time, and the Prussians, who were occupying Dresden, attempted to press-gang him into their army. He managed to avoid them and reach Paris thanks to his patron, Louis de Silvestre (the third son and pupil of Israel Silvestre, the then principal of the academy in Dresden), who was returning to France after a long stay in Saxony. He arrived there in 1756. He went to see Wille who became his patron, gave him advice and bought paintings from him, as well as encouraging him to sell paintings to others. In 1769, Wille bought seven paintings from him at approximately 40 francs each, including *Little Schoolgirl* which Wille later engraved. In 1770, Schenau was summoned to Dresden by the elector of Saxony, who granted him an allowance of 1,600 livres. He left Paris on 11 March. In 1772, he was appointed an art teacher at Meissen Porcelain Factory. In 1774, he was appointed a teacher at the academy, and in 1777, together with Casamorra, he became the principal of this establishment.

He executed a painting in Dresden in about 1771-1772 depicting the *Family of the Elector of Saxony*. It comprised 17 figures and was very successfully received. Wille was commissioned to make an engraving of it. Schenau also produced an allegory on the recovery of the princess who was the wife of the elector. In 1790 he produced a *Crucifixion* for the Kreuzkirche in Dresden. He exhibited at the Colysée in 1776.

He aroused interest by his links with the 18th-century French School. Many of his small paintings have been reproduced by engravers and his etchings are sought after on account of their decorative nature.

MUSEUMS AND GALLERIES:
AVIGNON: *Young Girl Kissing the Hand of a Lady* - DESSAU: *Boy with Mousetrap* - DRESDEN: *Little Schoolgirl; Family of the Prince Elector of Saxony* - DRESDEN (Academy): *Priam Requests Achilles for the Body of Hector* - GÖRLITZ: *Family Portrait* - SCHWERIN (Staatliches Mus.): *Reading from the Bible* - WEIMAR: *Young Girl in front of the Mirror.*

AUCTION RECORDS:
PARIS, 1862, *Fishmonger,* FRF 249. PARIS, 1862, *Wigmaker's Shop under Louis XIV,* FRF 108. PARIS, 1883, *Getting Ready* (Indian ink wash and watercolour) FRF 230. PARIS, 1895, *Two Young Elegantly Dressed Women and Three Men Gathered Together in a Salon Playing Cards* (unfinished watercolour) FRF 305. PARIS, 1896, *Chamber Concert* (drawing) FRF 995. PARIS, 1898, *Broken Clog* (Indian ink wash and watercolour) FRF 250. PARIS, 9 May 1898, *Freed Slave* (Indian ink drawing) FRF 300. PARIS, 5 Dec 1900, *The Letter* (watercolour) FRF 405. PARIS, 21-22 June 1920, *Gothic Arch* (drawing) FRF 1,450. PARIS, 9 Dec 1920, *Happy Mother,* FRF 1,010. PARIS, 22 Nov 1923, *Reading the Newspaper,* FRF 13,600. PARIS, 12 Dec 1924, *Visit of the Jeweller,* FRF 1,150. PARIS, 28 June 1926, *Art Lesson; Letter* (two) FRF 7,100. PARIS, 16 May 1927, *Preparations for Motherhood; Washing the Newborn Babe* (two drawings in wash and watercolours) FRF 15,500. PARIS, 5 Dec 1927, *Flirt* (lead pencil heighlights) FRF 1,350. PARIS, 22 Dec 1930, *Young Mother* (pen and Indian ink wash) FRF 520. PARIS, 5 May 1933, *Amusing Bad Side,* FRF 855. PARIS, 16 Dec 1933, *Good Housekeeping; Bad Housekeeping* (two watercolours) FRF 4,100. PARIS, 15 Feb 1936, *Greedy Abbot and Curious Abbot,* FRF 7,800. PARIS, 14 Dec 1936, *Beautiful Schemer* (red chalk, study) FRF 3,000. PARIS, 21 May 1941, *Preparations for Motherhood; Washing the Newborn Babe* (two drawings in pen and watercolour wash, pendants) FRF 9,000; *Sacrifice of the Rooster,* FRF 27,000. PARIS, 17 July 1941, *Beautiful Schemer* (red chalk, study for the main figure in the Intrigues amoureuses paintings) FRF 7,200. PARIS, 20 March 1942, *Market Scene* (pen and wash) FRF 500. PARIS, 6 July 1942, *Reading the Newspaper,* FRF 39,100. PARIS, 25-26 Jan 1943, *Still-life with Basket of Peaches* (1758) FRF 13,000. PARIS, 31 March 1943, *Cupids Playing with Garlands around Two Initials* (graphite and sepia wash) FRF 850. PARIS, 25 Nov 1946, *Portrait of an Officer* (watercolour, attributed) FRF 1,100. PARIS, 17 March 1947, *Gallant Presentation* (attributed) FRF 20,000. PARIS, 22 March

1950, *Departure of the Volunteer; Return of the Volunteer* (two pendants) FRF 7,500. PARIS, 5 Dec 1950, *Card Game* (attributed) FRF 47,000. PARIS, 9 March 1951, *Cup of Chocolate* (attributed) FRF 35,000. PARIS, 14 June 1951, *Judgement of the Cat* (attributed) FRF 26,000. COLOGNE, 5 May 1966, *Painter and His Family,* DEM 4,000. MUNICH, 27 May 1974, *Interior Scene* (watercolour) DEM 2,700. VERSAILLES, 1 Dec 1974, *Young Shepherdess and Her Cavalier,* FRF 14,000. VERSAILLES, 26 Feb 1978, *Broken Bottle; Baby's Tea Party* (two oils on canvas, one dated 1767, 18 1/2 x 14 1/2 ins / 47 x 37 cm) FRF 21,000. LONDON, 11 July 1979, *Letter; Art Lesson* (two oils paintings on panel, 15 x 11 1/2 ins / 38 x 29 cm) GBP 2,800. PARIS, 22 Oct 1982, *Happy Piece of News* (1770, pen and wash heightened with watercolour and white gouache, 12 3/4 x 9 ins / 32.5 x 22.8 cm) FRF 19,000. MUNICH, 21 Sept 1983, *Happy Family; Unhappy Family* (1767, oil on canvas, a pair, 19 x 15 ins / 48.5 x 38 cm) DEM 18,000. PARIS, 19 June 1986, *Maternal Surprise* (1760, oil/copper, 14 x 11 1/4 ins / 35.3 x 28.7 cm) FRF 165,000. PARIS, 14 Dec 1989, *Happy Father of the Family* (oil on panel, 10 x 7 1/4 ins / 24.5 x 18.5 cm) FRF 68,000. PARIS, 9 April 1990, *Jealous Husband; Fortune-teller* (oil on canvas, a pair, 23 1/2 x 20 1/4 ins / 60 x 51.5 cm) FRF 550,000. PARIS, 22 March 1991, *Woman Holding a Young Child on Her Knees* (pen and grey wash, 13 x 9 1/4 ins / 33 x 23.5 cm) FRF 5,500. PARIS, 3 July 1991, *'She-loves-Me, She-Loves-me-Not'* (oil on canvas, 17 1/4 x 15 ins / 44 x 38 cm) FRF 55,000. NEW YORK, 14 Oct 1992, *Three Girls Watching a Small Boy Playing with a Small Windmill* (oil on canvas, 12 x 9 ins / 30.5 x 22.9 cm) USD 6,600. PARIS, 1 Dec 1992, *Young Peasant Carrying a Board on Her Head Accompanied by a Child* (pen and grey wash, 10 x 6 3/4 ins / 24.5 x 17 cm) FRF 3,500. PARIS, 28 June 1993, *Concert in a Salon* (oil on canvas, 33 1/2 x 26 3/4 ins / 85 x 68 cm) FRF 180,000. PARIS, 17 June 1994, *Married Happiness and the Dispute* (pen and watercolour, a pair, 12 1/2 x 9 3/4 ins / 32 x 25 cm) FRF 42,000. PARIS, 25 Nov 1997, *Beautiful Schemer* (red chalk, 13 1/4 x 10 1/2 ins / 33.5 x 26.5 cm) FRF 24,000. PARIS, 15 Dec 1997, *Sultaness Resting* (oil on canvas, 13 1/2 x 10 1/4 ins / 34.5 x 26 cm) FRF 30,000. HAMBURG, 8 May 1999, *Antiochus and Stratonike, present from Napoleon for Count Esterhazy* (1805, oil on canvas, 60 x 81 ins / 153 x 206 cm) DEM 40,000. LONDON, 16 Dec 1999, *Vulcan's Forge* (en brunaille, oil on canvas, 27 x 33 ins / 68 x 83 cm) GBP 16,000. MUNICH, 21 March 2001, *Music Lesson* (oil on canvas, 21 x 17 ins / 54 x 44 cm) DEM 36,000. PARIS, 29 March 2001, *Sacrifice of the Rooster* (oil on canvas, 18 x 22 ins / 46 x 55 cm) FRF 85,000. NEW YORK, 4 June 2003, *Apollo and Hyacinthus* (1803, oil on canvas, 92 x 56 ins / 234 x 142 cm) USD 15,000.

SCHENCK. See also **SCHENK**

SCHENCK, August Friedrich Albrecht

Danish, 19th century.

Born 23 April 1828, in Glückstadt (Duchy of Holstein); died 1 January 1901, in Écouen.

Active in France.

Painter. Landscapes, landscapes with figures, mountainscapes, animals.

Schenck studied with Leon Cogniet at the École des Beaux-Arts de Paris. He made several trips to England and Portugal and finally settled in Écouen, where he ended his career. He exhibited at the Salon de Paris from 1857 onwards and received a medal in 1865. In 1885, he was made a Chevalier of the Légion d'Honneur.

Schenck painted many winter landscapes, focusing especially on snow, and its effects on horses, dogs and sheep.

Schenck

Schenck

MUSEUMS AND GALLERIES:

BREMEN: *Sheep in Pasture in Brittany* - LILLE: *Snow Effect* - MELBOURNE: *Anxiety* - PÉRIGUEUX: *Sheep Attacked by Eagles* - RHEIMS (MBA): *At the Seashore* - SHEFFIELD: *A Mule Surprised by a Wolf.*

AUCTION RECORDS:

PARIS, 1868, *The Deer,* FRF 2,550; *The Goats of Mont-Dore,* FRF 3,000. PARIS, 1873, *The Surprise,* FRF 800. PARIS, 6 April 1877, *Herd of Sheep and Cattle Surprised by a Flurry of Snow,* FRF 720. NEW YORK, 2 Feb 1906, *Sheep in a Snowstorm,* USD 700. PARIS, 20 Nov 1925, *Livestock in the Heather,* FRF 1,050. NEW YORK, 20 Feb 1930, *The Storm in the Mountains,* USD 375. PARIS, 21 Jan 1943, *Sheep,* FRF 20,000. PARIS, July 1946, *Shepherd and His Sheep,* FRF 4,200. PARIS, 22 Nov 1950, *Sheep in a Snowstorm,* FRF 12,500. PARIS, 30 March 1955, *The Shepherd,* FRF 15,000. MUNICH, 28 Nov 1974, *Livestock in a Snowstorm,* DEM 1,450. NEW YORK, 14 May 1976, *Flock of Sheep in a Landscape* (oil on canvas, 35 1/2 x 55 ins / 90 x 140 cm) USD 1,000. NEW YORK, 25 Oct 1977, *Shepherd and Flock in a Landscape* (oil on canvas, 23 x 35 ins / 58.5 x 89 cm) USD 1,300. NEW YORK, 25 Jan 1980, *Sheep in a Snowstorm* (oil on canvas, 15 1/4 x 18 1/2 ins / 39 x 47 cm) USD 2,000. LOS ANGELES, 22 June 1981, *Shepherdess and Her Flock* (1872, oil on panel, 17 x 25 ins / 43 x 63.5 cm) USD 3,500. NEW YORK, 29 June 1983, *Sheep in a Snowstorm* (oil on canvas, 24 x 36 ins / 61 x 91.5 cm) USD 1,500. LONDON, 16 March 1989, *Shepherdess and Flock in a Snowy Hillside Landscape* (oil on canvas, 29 x 36 1/2 ins / 73.5 x 92.8 cm) GBP 2,750. VERSAILLES, 19 Nov 1989, *Shepherd and His Flock on the Moor* (oil on canvas, 15 3/4 x 23 1/2 ins / 40 x 60 cm) FRF 10,000. VERSAILLES, 18 March 1990, *Livestock on the Moor* (oil on canvas, 16 x 23 3/4 ins / 40.5 x 60.5 cm) FRF 10,000. PARIS, 6 July 1990, *Shepherd and Flock of Sheep* (oil on canvas, 13 3/4 x 19 3/4 ins / 35 x 50 cm) FRF 6,700. PARIS, 24 May 1991, *The Sheepfold* (oil on canvas, 86 1/2 x 70 3/4 ins / 220 x 180 cm) FRF 100,000. PARIS, 30 March 1992, *Flock of Sheep in the Snow* (oil on canvas, 13 3/4 x 19 3/4 ins / 35 x 50 cm) FRF 10,000. NEW YORK, 16 July 1992, *In the Snowstorm* (oil on canvas, 34 1/2 x 48 ins / 87.6 x 121.9 cm) USD 3,025. PARIS, 6 April 1993, *The Flock of Sheep* (oil on panel, 13 1/2 x 23 ins / 34 x 57.5 cm) FRF 5,500. PARIS, 30 April 1999, *Flock of Sheep Alarmed by Snow Storm* (oil on canvas, 35 x 58 ins / 90 x 147 cm) FRF 48,000. LONDON, 16 Sept 1999, *Playing in Snow* (oil on canvas, 24 x 35 ins / 60 x 90 cm) GBP 6,500. LUCERNE, 11 Nov 2000, *Sheep and Donkey Resting* (oil on canvas, 16 x 24 ins / 40 x 60 cm) CHF 3,800. PARIS, 29 Nov 2000, *Livestock in a Storm* (oil on canvas, 16 x 24 ins / 40 x 60 cm) FRF 24,000. COPENHAGEN, 5 March 2001, *Landscape with Small Shepherd Boy* (oil on canvas, 20 x 35 ins / 50 x 88 cm) DKK 25,000. PORTSMOUTH, 3 Nov 2001, *Sheep on a Snowy Mountainside* (oil on canvas, 16 x 11 ins / 41 x 28 cm) USD 1,500. ASHVILLE, 5 Jan 2002, *Shepherd and Sheep* (oil on canvas, 35 x 55 ins / 89 x 140 cm) USD 4,600.

SCHENCK, Christoph Daniel, or Schenk

German, 17th century.

Died 1691, in Constance.

Sculptor. Religious subjects.

Schenck, whose work had certain similarities with Baroque, was inspired by the traditions of mannerism, which prevailed in the region of Lake Constance. Particularly notable is the powerful musculature of his figures carved in wood.

MUSEUMS AND GALLERIES:

BERLIN (Deutsches Historisches Mus.): *Christ on the Cross between Mary and John* - MUNICH (Bayerisches Nationalmus.): *Martyrdom of St Ernest of Zwiefalten.*

SCHENCK, Christoph Hans

German, 17th century.

Painter, engraver. Religious subjects.

Christoph Hans Schenck sculpted a large crucifix for the central arch of the chancel of Constance Cathedral.

SCHENCK, Franklin Lewis
American, 19th - 20th century.
Born 1855, in New York; died February 1926.
Painter. Portraits, landscapes.
Franklin Schenck studied under Thomas Eakins.
MUSEUMS AND GALLERIES:
NEW YORK (Brooklyn Chamber of Commerce) - PHILADELPHIA (MA): *Portrait of Eakins.*

SCHENCK, Hans, or Schenk, also known as Scheuszlich, Scheutzlich or Scheiczlich
German, 16th century.
Born c. 1500, in Schneeberg (Saxony).
Sculptor, medallist.
Berlin School.
Between 1526 and 1528 Hans Schenck worked at the court of Prince Albert of Prussia in Königsberg. In 1543 he became a citizen of Berlin and worked until his death for the court of Joachim II. He carved several epitaphs in the north German Baroque style.

SCHENCK, Hans, or Schenk
German, 17th century.
Active in Constance.
Sculptor (wood). Portraits.
Hans Schenck carved notably religious figures.

SCHENCK, Jean Claude
French, 20th century.
Born 1 July 1928, in Paris.
Painter.
Jean Claude Schenk, who studied at the École des Arts Décoratifs, Paris, exhibited at the Salon d'Automne, the Salon des Jeunes Peintres and the Salon de Mai. He was short-listed for various painting prizes in 1952 and 1953, and showed in solo exhibitions at the Galerie Jean Castel, Paris.

SCHENCK, Johann Caspar, or Schenk, Schenckh
Austrian, 17th century.
Died 1674, in Vienna.
Sculptor, engraver.
The ivory reliefs by Johann Caspar Schenck at the imperial court in Vienna were executed with meticulous care, but were no match for the works of his contemporary Maucher.

SCHENCK, Philipp
German, 17th century.
Active in Constance.
Sculptor (wood). Portraits.

SCHENCK, Simon, or Schenckh, Schent, Schönckh
German, 17th century.
Born to a family originally from Mindelheim; died 20 April 1655, in Munich.
Active in Munich.
Sculptor.
Simon Schenck executed the new organ for the church of St Peter in Munich in 1647.

SCHENCKBECHER, Charles François
French, 20th century.
Born 5 August 1887, in Niederehnheim.
Painter. Landscapes, flowers.
Charles François Schenkbecher was a member of the Groupe de Mai.
MUSEUMS AND GALLERIES:
STRASBOURG.

SCHENCKEL, Lampert. See **SCHENKEL**

SCHENCKEL, Peter
German, 16th century.
Active in Leipzig, c. 1599.
Miniaturist.

SCHENCKENHOFER, Christoph
German, 19th century.
Born 1830, in Augsburg.
Painter, sculptor.
Christoph Schenckenhofer was trained by Piloty. He worked in Aarau from 1871 to 1875, and then in Munich.

SCHENCKER, Nicolas. See **SCHENKER**

SCHENCKH, Rudolf
Slav, 17th century.
Sculptor.

SCHENDEL, Anna van, or Schyndel
Dutch, 18th century.
Painter. Genre scenes.
Anna van Schendel was a member of the Haarlem guild in 1709.

AUCTION RECORDS:
BERN, 26 Oct 1988, *Evening at the Market* (oil on canvas, 23 1/4 x 19 ins / 59 x 48 cm) CHF 750.

SCHENDEL, Bernardus van, or Scheyndel, Schyndel
Dutch, 17th century.
Born 1649, in Weesp, baptised 19 December 1647 according to some sources; died 26 May 1709, in Haarlem.
Painter. Portraits, genre scenes, village scenes, landscapes with figures.
Bernardus van Schendel is thought to have been a pupil of Hendrik Mommers. He was a guild member in Haarlem in 1696, but little else is known about him. He may have married Lysbet Sanderins in 1677. Some accounts state that he was a native of Louvain and taught Jelle Sybrants and Regnier Brakenburg. *Bryan's Dictionary* gives 1634 as his date of birth, and, incorrectly, 1693 as the year of his death.

MUSEUMS AND GALLERIES:
AMSTERDAM: *Woman Making Pastries; Schoolmaster* - KIEV (Chanenko Mus.): *Group of Musicians* - LIÈGE: *Group of Musicians.*
AUCTION RECORDS:
PARIS, 1844, *View of a Frozen River,* FRF 320. MARSEILLES, 1864, *Landscape with Skaters on a Frozen Canal,* FRF 150. PARIS, 1869, *Fish Market in The Hague,* FRF 6,100. PARIS, 1872, *New Market of Amsterdam,* FRF 6,920; *Fair at Night,* FRF 6,950. BRUSSELS, 1873, *Fish Market,* FRF 4,100. PARIS, 2 June 1954, *Feast of the Kings,* FRF 40,000. LONDON, 5 July 1991, *Fishermen Sharing Out their Catch on the Shore* (oil on canvas, 12 1/2 x 15 3/4 ins / 31.8 x 40 cm) GBP 3,080. NEW YORK, 12 Jan 1996, *Peasants Gathered Around a Travelling Salesman in a Village Square* (1704, oil on panel, 11 1/4 x 14 ins / 28.3 x 35.5 cm) USD 9,200. PARIS, 17 July 1996, *Village Fête* (1704, oil on panel, 10 3/4 x 14 ins / 27.5 x 35.5 cm) FRF 45,000. VIENNA, 24 March 1999, *Christmas Carol Singing* (oil on canvas, 19 x 25 ins / 48 x 63 cm) ATS 150,000. LONDON, 26 Oct 1999, *Daifilo and Granida* (oil on canvas, 26 x 26 ins / 65 x 67 cm) GBP 1,450. LONDON, 14 Dec 2000, *Interiors with Figures Conversing and Drinking* (oil on panel, a pair, 11 x 10 ins / 29 x 25 cm) GBP 4,500. PARIS, 27 March 2002, *Daughters of Cecrops Discovering Erichthonius* (oil on canvas, a pair, 32 x 27 ins / 81 x 68 cm) EUR 10,000. LONDON, 8 July 2003, *Interior*

with Marriage Scene (oil on canvas, 23 x 27 ins / 58 x 69 cm) GBP 1,800.

SCHENDEL, C. L. van. See **SCHYNDEL**

SCHENDEL, Gillis van. See **SCHEYNDEL**

SCHENDEL, Gysbert van

Dutch, 17th century.

Active in Utrecht and in Amsterdam in 1633.

Painter.

SCHENDEL, J. van, or Scheyndel, Schijndel, Schyndel

Dutch, 17th century.

Painter. Landscapes.

MUSEUMS AND GALLERIES:

BUDAPEST (Mus.): *Italian Landscape.*

SCHENDEL, Johann Wolfgang. See **SCHINDEL**

SCHENDEL, Mira

Swiss, 20th century.

Born 1919, in Zurich; died 1988.

From 1949 active in Brazil.

Painter.

Mira Schendel was born in Zurich to a Jewish Czech father and an Italian Catholic mother, and she spent her childhood in Milan, where she studied art and philosophy. In 1946 she emigrated to Brazil, settling first in Porto Allegre and in 1953 in São Paulo.

After the 1960s, and while continuing her work in oils and tempera on canvas, she experimented with Indian ink, ecoline, watercolour, pastels and also gold and silver on paper. She made monotype prints on rice paper and, uniting the substance of the image or writing with that of the fragile paper, created works at the very edge of sculpture, sometimes hanging from nylon thread (*Draguilhas*), and she examined transparency, using drawings made on sheets of translucid paper held between two pieces of suspended plexiglas (*Linhas, Escritas*). In the late 1970s and the 1980s she used geometric shapes, introducing letters and words, as in neo-concrete art. In the *Sarrafos* she included tempera, acrylic and plaster in this way and added slabs of wood, thus establishing a dialogue between the second and third dimensions. Her work was included in collective exhibitions: Biennale in São Paulo (1951, 1954), where she showed representational and then abstract paintings; the Venice Biennale (1968); *Modernidade: art brésilien du XXe siècle* (*Modernity: Brazilian Art in the 20th Century*) at the Musée d'Art Moderne in Paris (1987-1988). In 1954 the Museu de Arte Moderna in São Paulo hosted her first solo exhibition. In 1996 São Paulo Museum organised her first large retrospective, followed in 2001 by an exhibition at the Galerie Nationale du Jeu de Paume in Paris which showed 79 of her works together for the first time in France.

BIBLIOGRAPHY:

Souza Dias, Geraldo de, *Mira Schendel*, exhibition catalogue, Gal. nationale du Jeu de Paume, Réunion des musées nationaux, Paris, 2001.

SCHENDEL, Petrus van

Belgian, 19th century.

Born 21 April 1806, in Terheyde, near Breda; died 28 December 1870, in Brussels.

Painter. History painting, genre scenes, market scenes.

Petrus van Schendel was a pupil of J. van Bree in Antwerp. He subsequently travelled to the Netherlands and was active in Amsterdam, Rotterdam and The Hague, chiefly as a portrait painter. He finally settled in Brussels in 1845 or 1850. He painted market scenes, often with striking light effects.

PVS:

MUSEUMS AND GALLERIES:

AMIENS: *St Mary Magdalene* - AMSTERDAM: *Market Square in a Friesland Town; Adriana Johanna van Wyck* - BRNO: *Dutch Fruit Market at Evening* - COURTRAI: *Moonlight* - HANOVER: *Fish Market at Evening* - LEIPZIG: *Returning from the Hunt; Fish Market* - MELBOURNE: *Woman Selling Poultry* - MONTREAL: *St Joseph and the Virgin; Market Scene in Antwerp by Moonlight; Market Scene* - MUNICH: *Market Square in Antwerp* - NICE: *Woman Selling Fruit* - STUTTGART: *Woman Selling Vegetables* - YPRES: *Woman Selling Fish: Light Effect.*

AUCTION RECORDS:

PARIS, 1850, *Fish Market,* FRF 2,750. BRUSSELS, 1875, *Light Effect,* FRF 1,500. PARIS, 1881, paintings, studies and sketches, a total of around 50 paintings) FRF 10,800. ROTTERDAM, 1891, *Man Selling Fruit and Vegetables,* FRF 625; *Fish Market Hall in The Hague,* FRF 750; *Market,* FRF 550; *Woman Selling Fish at Scheveningen,* FRF 710. LONDON, 2 April 1910, *Woman on a Market Stall: Light Effect,* GBP 21. PARIS, 6 June 1923, *Market Scene,* FRF 2,000. LONDON, 20 July 1923, *Night Festivities in Brussels,* GBP 33. LONDON, 21 Dec 1923, *Vegetable Market,* GBP 63. LONDON, 4 June 1928, *Vegetable Stall,* GBP 73. PARIS, 26 Jan 1942, *Young Cook by Candlelight,* FRF 2,400. PARIS, 24 May 1944, *Woman Selling Fish,* FRF 2,000. PARIS, 25 June 1945, *Peasant Woman Sitting with her Child,* FRF 850. PARIS, Oct 1945-July 1946, *Open-air Bonfire,* FRF 2,100. LONDON, 11 Nov 1949, *Market Scene,* GBP 178. AMSTERDAM, 13 March 1951, *Market Square in Brussels* (1847) NLG 3,600. AMSTERDAM, 1 May 1951, *Winter fête by moonlight* (1845) FRF 38,000. AMSTERDAM, 5-18 Oct 1965, *Market Scene,* NLG 7,700. LONDON, 21 Jan 1966, *Market Scene,* Gns 1,100. LONDON, 15 Oct 1969, *Preparations for the Ball,* GBP 1,900. LONDON, 14 June 1972, *Market Scene by Candlelight,* GBP 3,500. LONDON, 4 May 1973, *Fishmonger,* Gns 11,000. AMSTERDAM, 20 May 1974, *Woman Selling Fish* (1851) NLG 90,000. LONDON, 11 Feb 1977, *Market Scene at Night in Amsterdam* (oil on panel, 30 1/2 x 44 ins / 77.5 x 112 cm) GBP 4,800. AMSTERDAM, 30 Oct 1979, *Market Scene at Night* (1866, oil on panel, 29 x 40 1/2 ins / 73.5 x 103 cm) NLG 108,000. NEW YORK, 29 May 1981, *Reverie* (oil on panel, 6 1/2 x 4 ins / 16.5 x 10 cm) USD 4,000. AMSTERDAM, 29 Oct 1984, *Market Scene at Evening* (oil on panel, 34 1/2 x 47 ins / 87.5 x 119.5 cm) NLG 120,000. NEW YORK, 15 Feb 1985, *Night Market at Antwerp* (oil on panel, 30 3/4 x 24 ins / 78.1 x 61.2 cm) USD 36,000. NEW YORK, 28 Oct 1986, *Avondmarkt* (1868, oil on panel, 28 1/4 x 21 1/4 ins / 71.8 x 54 cm) USD 30,000. LONDON, 24 June 1987, *Woman Selling Eggs* (oil on canvas, 26 x 20 1/4 ins / 66 x 51.5 cm) GBP 20,000. NEW YORK, 24 Oct 1996, *Vegetable Market at Night* (1846, oil on panel, 29 x 22 3/4 ins / 73.7 x 57.8 cm) USD 109,750. LONDON, 21 Nov 1996, *Woman Selling Apples* (1863, oil on panel, 9 1/4 x 12 ins / 23.5 x 30.5 cm) GBP 15,525. PARIS, 16 Dec 1996, *Bust of a Young Woman* (1850, oil on canvas, 19 1/4 x 14 1/2 ins / 49 x 37 cm) FRF 15,000. NEW YORK, 23 Oct 1997, *Dress-maker Working by the Light of an Oil Lamp* (1851, oil on panel, 10 3/4 x 8 3/4 ins / 27.3 x 22.2 cm) USD 39,100. LONDON, 19 Nov 1997, *Market Stall Displaying Game* (oil on panel, 15 1/4 x 12 1/2 ins / 39 x 32 cm) GBP 18,975. LONDON, 21 Nov 1997, *Vegetable Market by Candlelight* (oil on panel, 39 1/2 x 30 1/2 ins / 100.3 x 77.2 cm) GBP 188,500. NEW YORK, 18 March 1998, *Market at Night* (oil on panel, 11 x 10 ins / 27.9 x 25.4 cm) USD 51,750. LONDON, 30 Nov 1999, *Figures in a Moonlit Market* (1841, oil on panel, 30 x 25 ins / 75 x 63 cm) GBP 82,000. LONDON, 1 Dec 1999, *Moonlit Marketplace* (1842, oil on panel, 35 x 45 ins / 89 x 114 cm) GBP 195,000. NEW YORK, 1 May 2000, *Evening Serenade* (oil on panel, 33 x 26 ins / 83 x 67 cm) USD 95,000. LONDON, 27 Oct 2000, *Apple Seller* (oil on panel, 21 x 17 ins / 53 x 43 cm) GBP 88,000. NEW YORK, 1 Nov 2001, *Moonlit Vegetable Market* (oil on panel, 26 x 19 ins / 65 x 49 cm) USD 165,000. LONDON, 9 Nov 2001, *Night Market in Antwerp* (1861, oil on canvas, 49 x 40 ins / 124 x 102 cm) GBP 100,000. NEW YORK, 30 Oct 2002,

Night Market (oil on panel, 27 x 20 ins / 69 x 52 cm) USD 170,000. LONDON, 19 Nov 2002, *Moonlit Market* (oil on panel, 22 x 17 ins / 57 x 42 cm) GBP 95,000. BOSTON, 12 Sept 2003, *Market at Night* (oil on board, 28 x 23 ins / 71 x 58 cm) USD 140,000. AMSTERDAM, 28 Oct 2003, *Girl Selling Vegetables at the Night-market with the Dam Palace beyond* (oil on panel, 26 x 20 ins / 65 x 50 cm) EUR 145,000. AMSTERDAM, 20 April 2004, *Accusation* (oil on panel, 29 x 24 ins / 74 x 61 cm) EUR 25,000. NEW YORK, 27 Oct 2004, *Family in a Candlelit Interior* (c. 1845, oil on panel, 22 x 17 ins / 55 x 44 cm) USD 52,000.

SCHENEBERG, Leonhard
Swiss, 16th century.
Engraver.
Leonhard Scheneberg worked for the Basel mint.

SCHÉNER, Mihaly
Hungarian, 20th century.
Born 1923.
Painter.
Although he did not subscribe to the general trends in western European art, Mihaly Schener was nevertheless drawn to those modern forms of expression that developed in the whole of Europe during the first half of the 20th century.
BIBLIOGRAPHY:
Nemeth, Lajos, *Moderne ungarische Kunst*, Corvina Kiadó, Budapest, 1969.

SCHENFELD, Johann Henrich.
See **SCHÖNFELDT**

SCHENFFELIN, Hans Léonard or Leonhard.
See **SCHÄUFFELIN**

SCHENING, Curd and Ludekin
German, 15th century.
Active in Hamburg.
Glass painters.

SCHENING, Martin. See **SCHONINCK**

SCHENK
17th century.
Sculptor.

SCHENK. See also **SCHENCK**

SCHENK, Albert
Swiss, 20th century.
Born 18 October 1876, in Schaffhausen.
Painter.
Albert Schenk studied at the academy of fine arts in Karlsruhe, and in Paris with Louis Olivier Merson and Henri Biva. From 1909 he worked as a picture restorer at Mannheim.

SCHENK, Albrecht Ludwig Emanuel
Swiss, 19th century.
Born 1778, in Bern; died 28 October 1818, in Bern.
Medallist, engraver. Coins.

SCHENK, Alois Georg
German, 20th century.
Born 4 February 1888, in Schwäbisch-Gmünd.
Painter. Religious subjects.
Alois Georg Schenk was a pupil of Robert Poetzelberger, Christian A. Landenberger and Joseph Hölzel.

SCHENK, Daniel, or Schenck
German, 18th century.
Stucco artist.
From 1715 onwards, Daniel Schenk was in the service of the bishop of Bamberg and the prince elector of Mainz, Lothar Franz von Schönborn. He lived notably in Mainz and was one of the masters of German decoration in the Regency style. He decorated the House of the German Order in Sachsenhausen, near Frankfurt.

SCHENK, Friedrich
German, 19th century.
Born 1811, in Marburg.
Lithographer, painter.
Friedrich Schenk worked in Munich.

SCHENK, Georg
Swiss, 17th century.
Active in St Gall between 1606 and 1652.
Painter.

SCHENK, Georg
German, 17th century.
Active in Mindelheim.
Sculptor.

SCHENK, Jan
Dutch, 18th century.
Active in Amsterdam 1731-1746.
Engraver (burin).

SCHENK, Johann
German, 18th century.
Painter.
Johann Schenk worked at the court of the prince elector, Clement Augustus, in Cologne around 1740.

SCHENK, Johann Georg
German, 18th century.
Died 1785.
Active in Jena.
Painter, draughtsman, engraver.
Johann Georg Schenk painted portraits and engraved views of Jena, Weimar and the surrounding areas.

SCHENK, Karl
Swiss, 20th century.
Born 1905, in Bern; died 1973.
Painter.
Karl Schenk was also an architect.

K·Schenk

AUCTION RECORDS:
BERN, 12 May 1984, *Young Woman and Horses at the Drinking Trough* (oil on panel, 32 3/4 x 43 3/4 ins / 83 x 111 cm) CHF 4,300. BERN, 30 April 1988, *Young Peasant Woman with a Horse Drinking at the Fountain* (1972, oil on canvas, 39 1/4 x 50 3/4 ins / 100 x 129 cm) CHF 8,000. BERN, 5 Nov 1999, *Young Woman in a Blue Dress with a Flower in an Extensive Hilly Landscape* (oil on board, 55 x 48 ins / 140 x 122 cm) CHF 10,000. BERN, 5 Nov 1999, *Young Man with Three Women, Judgement of Paris* (oil on canvas, 81 x 108 ins / 205 x 275 cm) CHF 11,000. BERN, 3 Nov 2000, *Girl Holding Flower* (oil on canvas, 16 x 13 ins / 41 x 33 cm) CHF 3,900. BERN, 3 Nov 2000, *Children Nibbling* (oil on board, 35 x 29 ins / 90 x 73 cm) CHF 4,500. BERN, 11 May 2001, *Girls Picking Flowers* (oil on panel, 30 x 31 ins / 75 x 79 cm) CHF 3,300. BERN, 9 Nov 2001, *Two Young Girls with a Doll in a Garden* (oil on panel, 24 x 28 ins / 60 x 72 cm) CHF 4,000. BERN, 8 Nov 2002, *Girl with a Doll in a Doll's Pram* (oil on panel, 16 x 20 ins / 40 x 52 cm) CHF 3,600. BERN, 8 Nov 2002, *Two Boys with Paper Hats* (oil on panel, 30 x 27 ins / 76 x 68 cm) CHF 4,000. BERN, 9 May 2003, *Girl with White Paper Bag* (oil on panel, 19 x 16 ins / 49 x 40 cm) CHF 2,300. BERN, 14 May 2004, *Young Shepherdess* (oil on panel, 30 x 45 ins / 77 x 115 cm) CHF 3,600. BERN, 12 Nov 2004, *Young Shepherdess Carrying a Lamb* (oil on panel, 43 x 32 ins / 109 x 81 cm) CHF 4,200.

SCHENK, Karl Wilhelm
German, 19th century.
Born 1780, in Leipzig; died 1827, in Brunswick.
Engraver (burin), miniaturist.

Karl Wilhelm Schenk trained at the academy in Leipzig from 1802 to 1804. He engraved for the almanacs of the era.

SCHENK, Leonardus, or Schenck
Dutch, 18th century.
Active in Amsterdam 1720-1746.
Engraver.

Leonardus Schenk is known for his *Hunt of Atalanta* after Charles Le Brun, *Jupiter and Semele* after S. Cleef, *Jean Lourd, The Young Louis XV,* and 21 plates for the *Chronicle of Alkmaar* by C. van de Woude.

SCHENK, Pieter I, or Schenck
Dutch, 17th - 18th century.
Born 1660, in Elberfeld; died 1718 or 1719, in Amsterdam.
Painter, engraver, draughtsman. Portraits.

Pieter Schenk I travelled to Holland as a young man and studied drawing and engraving in Amsterdam. His first works were topographical prints, produced in collaboration with the publisher Gérard Valcke, whose daughter Agatha he married in 1687. He was appointed court engraver by King Augustus II of Poland, Elector of Saxony. He completed over 600 works, including several in collaboration with other engravers, and a number of mezzotint portraits.

AUCTION RECORDS:
LONDON, 14 June 1984, *Young Woman Seated; Man Standing* (mezzotints, a pair, 10 x 7 ins / 25.1 x 17.7 cm) USD 1,300. NEW YORK, 7 April 1988, *Trompe-l'oeil: An Engraving, an Almanach and a Comb Nailed to a Plank of Wood* (oil on canvas, 26¼ x 23 ins / 66.5 x 58.5 cm) USD 3,300.

SCHENK, Pieter II, the Younger
Dutch, 18th century.
Painter, engraver. Genre scenes.

Pieter Schenk the Younger is noted for his *Entertainment on the Ice* and *Chinese Landscapes.*

SCHENK, Stefan
German, 18th century.
Painter. Stage sets.

Stefan Schenk was in the service of Mannheim theatre in 1749.

SCHENKE, Max
German, 20th century.
Born 21 August 1891, in Arnstadt.
Painter, engraver.

Max Schenke was a pupil at the academy of fine arts in Dresden, under the direction of Richard Müller, Carl Bantzer and Robert Sterl.

SCHENKEL, Friedrich
German, 20th century.
Born 25 December 1877, in Kirchheim.
Sculptor, medallist.

Friedrich Schenkel lived and worked in Berlin.

SCHENKEL, Jan Jacob
Dutch, 19th century.
Born 7 February 1829, in Amsterdam; died 16 July 1900, in Amsterdam.
Painter. Figures, church interiors, architectural views.

MUSEUMS AND GALLERIES:
AMSTERDAM (Stedelijk Mus.): *Nieuwe Kerk in Amsterdam.*

AUCTION RECORDS:
ROTTERDAM, 1891, *Haarlem Cathedral,* FRF 300; *Interior of the Church of Alkmaar,* FRF 160. NEW YORK, 14-17 March 1911, *Church Interior,* USD 100. LONDON, 16 Oct 1968, *Cathedral Interior,* GBP 400. LONDON, 4 May 1973, *Church Interior,* Gns 650. ZURICH, 20 May 1977, *Gothic Church Interior* (oil on panel, 24½ x 19 ins / 62.5 x 48 cm) CHF 3,500. ZURICH, 16 May 1980, *Church Interior* (oil on panel, 24½ x 19 ins / 62.5 x 48 cm) CHF 3,400. AMSTERDAM, 5 June 1990, *Church Interiors with figures at Prayer* (oil on panel, 15¾ x 11¼ ins / 40 x 28.5 cm) NLG 1,725. AMSTERDAM, 30 Oct 1991, *Interior of Delft Cathedral with the Tomb of William of Orange* (1858, oil on panel, 26¾ x 20 ins / 68 x 50.5 cm) NLG 7,475. AMSTERDAM, 18 April 2000, *Church Interior* (oil on canvas, 26 x 19 ins / 66 x 49 cm) NLG 17,000. AMSTERDAM, 23 April 2001, *View of the Portuguese Israelite Synagoge, Amsterdam* (oil on panel, 23 x 19 ins / 59 x 49 cm) NLG 38,000. AMSTERDAM, 24 April 2001, *Interior of the Bakenesse Church, Haarlem* (pencil, pen, ink, watercolour and gouache, 10 x 14 ins / 25 x 36 cm) NLG 17,000. AMSTERDAM, 22 Jan 2002, *Interior of the St Bavo, Haarlem* (pencil and watercolour heightened with white, 16 x 13 ins / 41 x 33 cm) EUR 5,000. MICHIGAN, 18 Sept 2002, *Cathedral Interiors with figures* (oil on panel, 20 x 15 ins / 51 x 38 cm) USD 4,000. AMSTERDAM, 19 April 2004, *Church Interiors with figures* (oil on panel, 20 x 16 ins / 52 x 40 cm) EUR 2,200.

SCHENKEL, Lampert, or Schenckel
Dutch, 16th century.
Draughtsman.

SCHENKER, Hans
Swiss, 16th century.
Fresco artist.

SCHENKER, Jacques Matthias
Swiss, 19th - 20th century.
Born 24 February 1854, in Lucerne; died 1927, in Vitznau.
Active in Germany.
Painter. Landscapes.

Jacques Matthias Schenker studied from 1870 to 1876 at the academy of fine arts in Düsseldorf and at the school of fine arts in Weimar. From 1876 to 1907 he worked in Dresden, where he founded in 1879 a school for women. From 1907 he lived at Vitznau. He painted landscapes of Normandy.

MUSEUMS AND GALLERIES:
DRESDEN: *Low Tide at Dieppe; Spring on the Banks of the Channel* - ST GALL: *Beach on the Coast of Normandy* - WEIMAR: *Beside a Stream.*

AUCTION RECORDS:
COPENHAGEN, 24 April 1979, *View of a Little Town in Normandy* (oil on canvas, 19¼ x 27½ ins / 49 x 70 cm) DKK 36,000. COLOGNE, 23 March 1990, *Alpine Lake* (oil on canvas, 22¾ x 35½ ins / 58 x 90 cm) DEM 2,400. LONDON, 31 Oct 1996, *Street Scene in Turkey* (oil on canvas, 17¼ x 30 ins / 44 x 76 cm) GBP 6,325.

SCHENKER, Nicolas, or Schencker
Swiss, 18th - 19th century.
Born c. 1760, in Paris; died 17 February 1848, in Geneva.
Engraver.

Previous biographers have incorrectly stated that Schenker was born in Geneva, and that he died in 1822. In fact, he died in 1848, and moved to Geneva when very young. He belonged to a family who originally came from Transylvania. He began his art training in Geneva, then went to Paris and worked with St-Ours and Macret. He produced many graceful subjects, working in France and England for Bartolozzi He also engraved in the style of Schall, Carl Vernet, Bosio, Le Barbier the Elder, Lemire, Laffitte and in the style of his brother-in-law Firmin Massot. His works are generally stippled. He is mentioned as being in Paris in 1779. In 1788 he returned to Geneva, and in 1794 he married Jeanne Pernette Massot, a distinguished painter. He became a citizen of Geneva in 1817, and that same year was appointed principal of a school of engraving.

SCHENKL, Joseph, or Schenckl
Austrian, 19th century.
Born 1794, in Vienna.
Painter. Landscapes, still-lifes.

SCHENNACH, Johann Georg, or Schenach
Austrian, 18th century.
Born in Lermoos; died 23 July 1777, in Innsbruck.
Sculptor.
The majority of Schennach's works were destined for churches in Innsbruck.

SCHENNICH, Martin
Austrian, 17th century.
Active in Ried (Tyrol) during the second half of the 17th century.
Cabinet maker, sculptor.

SCHENNIS, Hans Friedrich Emanuel van
German, 20th century.
Born 17 June 1852, in Elberfeld; died 4 April 1918, in Berlin.
Painter, engraver. Landscapes.
Hans Schennis was a pupil at the school of fine arts in Weimar and of Theodor J. Hagen. He travelled in Italy and in France.
MUSEUMS AND GALLERIES:
BERLIN: *Park of Versailles* - DÜSSELDORF: *Twilight*.
AUCTION RECORDS:
LONDON, 18 Jan 1980, *Reverie* (oil on canvas, 18½ x 23½ ins / 47 x 59.7 cm) GBP 600. COLOGNE, 15 Oct 1988, *Ship Near the Isle of Rugen* (oil on canvas, 12½ x 15¾ ins / 32 x 40 cm) DEM 1,300.

SCHENPERGER, Johann Jakob.
See **SCHEMBERGER**

SCHENPUECHER, Bernhard
Austrian, 16th century.
Fresco artist.
Bernhard Schenpuecher decorated the church of Traiskirchen.

SCHENSON, Hilda Maria Helena
Swedish, 19th century.
Born 31 July 1847, in Uppsala.
Painter.
Schenson studied at the Kungliga Akademi för de Fria Konsterna in Stockholm, and with Charles-Auguste-Emile Durand and Jean-Jacques Henner in Paris.

SCHENSTRØM, Christian Vilhelm
Danish, 19th century.
Born 12 February 1828, in Assens; died 21 April 1876, in Copenhagen.
Painter.
Schenstrøm was a pupil at the Kunstakademi in Copenhagen.

SCHENT, Simon. See **SCHENCK**

SCHEPELERN, Frederik Anton
Danish, 19th century.
Born 24 December 1796, in Fredericia; died 29 April 1883, in Nykøbing.
Draughtsman, lithographer.

SCHEPENS, Louis
Flemish School, 19th century.
Born c. 1816; died 17 February 1884, in Ghent.
Painter.
Louis Schepens was a pupil of A. Ottevaere.

L. Schepens

SCHEPER, Hinnerk
German, 20th century.
Born 1897, in Badbergen, near Osnabrück; died 1957, in Berlin.
Painter. Murals.
Hinnerk Scheper was first a pupil of mural painting in the school of applied arts, then at the academy of fine arts, in Düsseldorf. He also studied at the school of applied arts in Bremen. From 1919 to 1922 he was a pupil of the Bauhaus (then in Weimar), returning to the school from 1925 (in Dessau) up to 1933 (Berlin) as Director of the studio of mural painting. He took leave from 1929-1930, having been called to Moscow as Director of the Consultative Committee on Architectural Decoration, no doubt by Hannes Meyer, who had probably himself just left the Bauhaus directorship to be a director in the USSR. From 1945 he was an adviser and instructor on colour in architecture in Berlin.
BIBLIOGRAPHY:
Leymarie, Jean/Herzogenrath, Wulf/Grote, Ludwig/Gropius, Walter, *Le Bauhaus*, exhibition catalogue, Württembergischer Kunsteverein, Stuttgart, Musée national d'Art moderne, Paris, 1969.

SCHEPERS
Spanish, 18th century.
Painters (porcelain).

SCHEPERS, Elisabeth, or Scepens, Scepins
Flemish School, 15th century.
Active in Bruges.
Miniaturist.
Bruges School.
Elisabeth Schepers was a member of the painters' guild from 1476 to 1489.

SCHEPERS, Jan, or Schepper, called Giovanni Fiammingo
Flemish, 16th century.
Active in Antwerp.
Painter.
In 1579, Jan Schepers became a citizen of Perugia. He was the prior of the confraternity of the Ultramontanes between 1583 and 1585.
MUSEUMS AND GALLERIES:
PERUGIA (Town Hall): *Landscapes* (four frescoes).

SCHEPERS, Jan or Hans. See **SCHEPPERS**

SCHEPERS, Petrus
Dutch, 20th century.
Born 1908, in Aarle-Rixtel.
Painter. Scenes with figures.
Petrus Schepers was a carpenter who dedicated his free time to painting meticulous, but clumsy, pictures of places that featured in his daily life.
BIBLIOGRAPHY:
Gans, Louis, *Meesters der Europese naïven, Centraal Museum Utrecht, 2. april-31 mei 1970*, exhibition catalogue, Centraal Museum, Utrecht, 1970.

SCHEPHEN, Paolo, or Scheffer, Schepers
Dutch, 16th century.
Active in Naples during the second half of the 16th century.
Painter.
Paolo Schephen painted frescoes in the dome of the church of SS Severino e Sossio in Naples.

SCHEPP, Auguste
German, 19th century.
Born 3 April 1846, in Wiesbaden; died 12 April 1905, in Freiburg im Breisgau.
Painter. Figures, genre scenes, interiors, still-lifes.

Schepp was a pupil of Neurenther and K. Sohn. He continued his artistic training in Vienna and Paris. He worked in Munich and Freiburg.
AUCTION RECORDS:
LONDON, 4 May 1973, *An Artist,* Gns 680. LUCERNE, 12 April 2000, *Still-life with China, Glass, Pocket Watch and Pipe* (oil on canvas, 31 x 23 ins / 78 x 58 cm) CHF 4,800.

SCHEPPELEN
British, 18th century.
Active in London in 1768.
Painter. Portraits.

SCHEPPELIN, Jakob Andreas, or Scheppem
Swiss, 18th century.
Painter. Portraits.
Scheppelin worked in Frankfurt am Main from 1762 to 1763.
MUSEUMS AND GALLERIES:
FRANKFURT AM MAIN (Goethe Mus.): *Bust of Johann Wolfgang Textor, the Grandfather of Goethe.*

SCHEPPERE, Louis Benoît Ferdinand de
Dutch, 18th - 19th century.
Born 1748; died c. 1811.
Painter, engraver (etching).
Louis Benoît Ferdinand de Scheppere was a pupil of Sauveur Legros.

SCHEPPERS, Jan or Hans, or Schepers, Schepper
Belgian, 17th century.
Active in Antwerp.
Painter.
Jan Scheppers was a pupil of Jan van Delft in 1622 and 1623.

SCHEPPERS, Marguerite
Flemish School, 16th century.
Illuminator.
Marguerite Scheppers had Cornelia van Wulfskerke as a pupil. She illuminated a missal for the convent of Our Lady of Sion, Bruges, in 1503.

SCHEPS. See **SCHÖPS Augustin**

SCHER, Hans
German, 16th century.
Active in Freiburg im Brisgau.
Engraver.

SCHER, Jacob
German, 16th century.
Active in Danzig (now Gdansk).
Painter.
Jacob Scher was a pupil of Daniel von Block.

SCHER, Julia
American, 20th - 21st century.
Born 1954, in Hollywood.
Mixed media artist, installation artist. Web art, performances.
Julia Scher came of age artistically in the mid-1970s, the heyday of information-oriented video and media art. As a painting student at the University of California in Los Angeles, she couldn't take the film production classes she wanted to. She was, however, exposed to performance, installation and video art by the likes of the Kipper Kids, Paul McCarthy, Vito Acconci and the video subject-object manipulator Bruce Nauman.

It took until the mid-1980s for Scher to find her way. After receiving an MFA from the University of Minnesota in 1984, she started a cleaning service that prompted *Hardly Feel It Going In* (1985), her first surveillance camera piece, which was surreptitiously shot while she cleaned a gym. A year later she produced *Softly Tapping the Wires* (1986) with tools and hardware treated in a fetishistic way. That year she also moved to New York and began to offer security services for women. She was certainly not the first artist to merge art and business; *Safe & Secure Productions* was an actual business springing primarily from economic necessity.

Sher lectures extensively on the topic of security, often with a feminist slant, and in that capacity visited Harvard University, the Massachusetts Institute of Technology, Princeton University and Rutgers University.

Her work focuses on the subjects of surveillance, insecurity and the cyber-sphere. Aiming at the exposure of dangers and ideologies of monitoring systems, she creates temporary and transitory web/installation/performance works that explore issues of power, control and seduction. For years she has been making complex installations with surveillance cameras, revealing the mechanisms and menace present in technological developments in this field. She has also made photoworks and works for the web. In Sher's installations, the apparatus of surveillance becomes both object, in a sculptural sense, and subject of the artist's project; she also uses sound and language with texts appearing on screen and monitors. Sher is true to her definition of herself: 'I am Big Brother's Little Sister.' Her works include *Superdesk Surveillance Desk, Security by Julia, Surveillance Sex Bed, Security by Julia II, Securityland* (1996) and *Washroom Male, Washroom Female* (1997).

Her work has been shown both on the web and regularly in the US and in Europe, especially after 1998. In 2000, seven of her internet artworks were included in the Whitney Biennial.

SCHERACK, Eduard
Austrian, 19th century.
Born 1812, in Tulleschitz.
Engraver (stone/ivory).
Scherack started his training at the academy in Vienna in 1833.

SCHERANO, or Scerano or Sciarano, also known as Alessandro or Sandro di Giovanni Fancelli, called Il Scherano
Italian, 16th century.
Active in Settignano.
Sculptor.
Scherano made some of the statues decorating the Villa Medici in Rome.

SCHERAUF. See **SCHERHAUFF**

SCHERBECK, Jean
French, 20th century.
Painter.
Jean Scherbeck exhibited in Paris at the Salon des Artistes Français, of which he was a member and where he was awarded an honourable mention in 1934.

SCHERBER, Johann Friedrich
18th century.
Active in Ansbach from 1764 to 1766.
Modeller (porcelain).

SCHERBRING, Karl
German, 19th century.
Born 7 October 1859, in Memel (now Klaipeda, Lithuania); died 18 December 1899, in Munich.
Painter. Landscapes.
Scherbring was trained by Heinz Heim and G. Schönleber. He started working in Munich in 1890.
AUCTION RECORDS:
HEIDELBERG, 15 Oct 1994, *Start of Spring* (oil on canvas, 17 3/4 x 28 3/4 ins / 45 x 73 cm) DEM 1,500. VIENNA, 16 June 2003, *Spring Idyll* (1897, oil on canvas, 23 x 29 ins / 59 x 73 cm) EUR 3,200.

SCHERELL, Christian Friedrich
German, 18th - 19th century.
Draughtsman, painter (?).
Scherell was an art teacher in Leipzig where he lived from 1770 to 1825.

SCHEREMETIEFF, Vassili Vassilievitch.
See **SHEREMETEV Vasili Vasilievich de**

SCHERENBERG, Hermann
German, 19th century.
Born 20 January 1826, in Swinemünde (now Swinoujscie, Poland); died 21 August 1897, in Gross-Lichterfelde.
Painter, draughtsman. Portraits, genre scenes.
After having been a pupil at the academy in Berlin, Scherenberg trained with Theodor Hildebrandt in Düsseldorf and made several trips to Antwerp. He also worked in the Couture studio in Paris. He went and settled in Berlin where he worked notably with Burger on the decoration of the town hall. He made a great reputation for himself as an illustrator.

SCHEREPANOV, Nikifor Jevstafevich
Russian, 18th - 19th century.
Born 1762; died 13 August 1823.
Draughtsman. Portraits.

SCHERER
German, 18th century.
Sculptor.

SCHERER. See also **SCHÄRER**

SCHERER, Alois
German, 19th century.
Born 7 December 1818, in Ettelried; died 27 May 1887, in Ettelried.
Painter.
Alois Scherer was the brother of Joseph and Sebastian Scherer. He trained at the academy in Munich and painted genre paintings and religious subjects.

SCHERER, Baptist
American, 19th - 20th century.
Born 15 March 1869, in Altona; died 22 January 1910, in Kassel.
Painter, pastellist. Portraits, landscapes.
Baptist Scherer studied at the Académie Julian in Paris, under Jacques Doucet and Gabriel Ferrier, and at the academy of fine arts in Munich with Paul Hoecker.

SCHERER, Fritz
German, 20th century.
Born 7 November 1877, in Freiburg im Breisgau; died 11 February 1929, in Munich.
Painter.
Fritz Scherer was a pupil of Franz Wilhelm Voigt in Munich from 1909 to 1918.

SCHERER, Giorgio
Italian, 19th century.
Born 6 March 1831, in Parma; died 1896.
Painter. History painting, genre scenes.
A pupil of F. Scaramuzza, Giorgio Scherer was later a professor at the Accademia di Belle Arti in Parma. He exhibited in Parma, Florence and Turin.
MUSEUMS AND GALLERIES:
PARMA (Gal. Nazionale): *Abdolomiro King of Sidon; The Last Moments of Niccolò de Lapis; Alcibiades Attacking.*

SCHERER, Hans
German, 17th century.
Sculptor (wood).

SCHERER, Hermann, or Scherrer
Swiss, 20th century.
Born 8 February 1893, in Rümmigen; died 13 May 1927, in Basel.
Sculptor, painter, engraver, draughtsman. Religious subjects, figures, landscapes.
Hermann Scherer was a pupil of Otto Roos and was influenced by Ernst Kirchner.
MUSEUMS AND GALLERIES:
AARAU (Aargauer Kunsthaus): *Mother and Child; Portrait of Werner Neuhaus.*
AUCTION RECORDS:
BERN, 21 June 1980, *Tessin Landscape with Self-portrait* (c. 1925, pastel, 17 1/4 x 22 3/4 ins / 43.7 x 57.8 cm) CHF 2,300. BERN, 25 June 1981, *Tessin Landscape* (1925-1926, charcoal, 16 3/4 x 22 1/2 ins / 42.8 x 57 cm) CHF 1,500. ZURICH, 11 Nov 1981, *Tessin Landscape* (oil on canvas, 45 1/4 x 39 1/4 ins / 115 x 100 cm) CHF 20,000. BERN, 26 June 1982, *Portrait of Camenisch* (c. 1925, two woodcuts, 23 1/2 x 15 1/4 ins / 59.8 x 38.7 cm and 23 1/2 x 15 1/4 ins/60 x 39 cm) DEM 1,100. ZURICH, 4 June 1992, *Pieta* (plaster, 43 1/4 x 24 x 28 ins / 110 x 61 x 71 cm) CHF 7,345. LUCERNE, 20 May 1995, *Tessin Landscape* (1925, coloured wax crayon/canvas, 45 1/4 x 59 ins / 115 x 150 cm) CHF 190,000. BERN, 20-21 June 1996, *The Acceptance* (c. 1925, woodcut, 13 x 10 3/4 ins / 33.3 x 27.5 cm) CHF 2,200. LUCERNE, 23 Nov 1996, *Portrait of Werner Neuhaus* (1925, oil on canvas, 27 1/2 x 31 1/2 ins / 70 x 80 cm) CHF 115,000.

SCHERER, Jakob
Austrian, 16th century.
Engraver, medallist.
Jakob Scherer was a pupil of Abondino. He worked in the mint of Vienna.

SCHERER, Johann
German, 19th century.
Born 12 December 1779, in Dinkelscherben; died 6 September 1857, in Ettelried.
Painter.

SCHERER, Johann
German, 19th - 20th century.
Born 13 September 1858, in Ettelried; died January 1934, in Ettelried.
Painter, fresco artist. Religious subjects, portraits, genre scenes.
Johann Scherer was a pupil of his uncle, Joseph Scherer, and attended the school of fine arts in Munich with August Spiess. He painted frescoes in churches in the Ettelried region.

SCHERER, Johann Friedrich
Swiss, 18th - 19th century.
Born 1741, in Schaffhausen; died c. 1810.
Painter, engraver (burin). Landscapes, flowers.
Johann Friedrich Scherer was an art teacher at the University of Helmstedt. In 1791 he became a painter at the court in Brunswick.

SCHERER, Joseph
German, 19th century.
Born 1 November 1814, in Ettelried; died 25 March 1891, in Ettelried.
Painter. Mythological subjects, figures, genre scenes, landscapes.
Joseph Scherer was the son of Johann Scherer I. He trained at the school of fine art in Augsburg with L. Hundertpfund and J. Geyer, at the academy in Munich with J. Schlotthauer and H. Hess, and with the glass painter Wilhelm Vörtl. From 1842 to 1844 he went on a study trip to Asia, Constantinople, Malta, Sicily, Italy and Switzerland. He worked in Stuttgart from 1847 to 1853, in Munich from 1853 to 1879, and in Ettelried from 1879 onwards.

The frescoes in the residential palace in Athens are attributed to him. They depict the battle of Patras, the welcome for

King Otto after his landing in Greece; landscapes and mythological scenes. Many of his works, however, can be found scattered among various different churches in Germany.
AUCTION RECORDS:
LONDON, 25 March 1988, *Greek Shepherd* (oil on paper, 15 3/4 x 11 3/4 ins / 40 x 30 cm) GBP 4,400. LONDON, 19 Nov 1993, *Young Greek* (1844, oil on paper, 113 1/2 x 8 ins / 288.5 x 20.5 cm) GBP 4,370.

SCHERER, Leo
German, 19th century.
Born 21 January 1827, in Ettelried; died 29 April 1876, in Munich.
Painter.
Leo Scherer was the brother of Joseph, Sebastian and Alois Scherer.

SCHERER, Max von
Austrian, 19th - 20th century.
Born 17 July 1866.
Engraver. Urban landscapes.
Max von Scherer lived and worked in Vienna and made engravings of urban views.

SCHERER, Rosa
Austrian, 19th - 20th century.
Born 21 June 1868, in Wagrein.
Painter. Flowers.
Rosa Scherer was a pupil of Peter Paul Müller in Munich and of Olga Wisinger-Florian in Vienna. She worked in Linz.
MUSEUMS AND GALLERIES:
LINZ: *Flowers*.

SCHERER, Sebastian
German, 19th century.
Born 1823; died 20 August 1873, in Munich.
Painter.
Sebastian Scherer was the brother of Alois and Leo Scherer.

SCHERERSCHEVSKI, Vladimir
Polish, 19th - 20th century.
Born September 1863, in Brest-Litovsk.
Painter. Landscapes.
Vladimir Schererschevski was active in Munich from 1882.
MUSEUMS AND GALLERIES:
VENICE (Mus. d'Arte Moderna): *Holding Prison in Siberia*.

SCHERF, Christian Gottlob, or Scherff
German, 19th century.
Born 31 May 1793, in Werdau (Saxony).
Engraver (burin).
Scherf worked in Dresden until 1847. He trained at the academy in Dresden with Toscani and C.G. Schultze. He engraved notably the portraits of contemporary princely key figures.

SCHERFIG, Hans
Danish, 20th century.
Born 1905, in Osterbro, Copenhagen; died 1979.
Painter. Animals.
Hans Scherfig has sometimes been considered a follower of Douanier Rousseau. He is best known for his work as a writer but he began his career as a painter. In 1925 he travelled to Vienna where he met his wife Elisabeth Karlinsky, who was part of the Austrian Futurist movement. He debuted as an artist at the Copenhagen Student Society in 1928. In the same year he took part in Kunstnernes Efterårsudstilling (Autumn Exhibition) and had a solo exhibition in 1929. In 1929 he also made a trip to New York City, where he stayed for seven months. Unable to make a living as a painter Scherfig devoted himself to his writings, for which he won a reputation as one of the most important Danish writers of the 20th century.
AUCTION RECORDS:
COPENHAGEN, 7 April 1976, *Elephant in the Virgin Forest* (oil on canvas, 17 3/4 x 16 1/4 ins / 45 x 41 cm) DKK 4,100. COPENHAGEN, 12 May 1977, *Tiger in the Virgin Forest* (1947, oil on canvas, 44 x 48 ins / 112 x 122 cm) DKK 12,500. COPENHAGEN, 24 April 1979, *Animals in the Savannah* (oil on canvas, 32 x 48 ins / 81 x 122 cm) DKK 5,500. COPENHAGEN, 15 Oct 1985, *Giraffes and Zebras in the Savannah* (1950, oil on canvas, 24 1/2 x 48 ins / 62 x 122 cm) SEK 50,000. COPENHAGEN, 30 Nov 1988, *Animals in the Savannah near the River* (1958, oil on canvas, 33 1/2 x 43 1/4 ins / 85 x 110 cm) DKK 48,000. COPENHAGEN, 10 May 1989, *Monkeys in the Jungle* (paint/synthetic resin, 11 x 4 3/4 ins / 28 x 12 cm) DKK 8,500. COPENHAGEN, 22 Nov 1989, *In the Jungle* (oil on canvas, 9 1/2 x 11 1/2 ins / 24 x 29 cm) DKK 8,000. COPENHAGEN, 21-22 March 1990, *Flying Fish* (1970, oil on canvas, 20 x 35 ins / 51 x 88 cm) DKK 16,000. COPENHAGEN, 14-15 Nov 1990, *Lions and the Flute PLayer in the Savannnah* (1937, tempera, 39 1/4 x 41 ins / 100 x 104 cm) DKK 16,000. COPENHAGEN, 13-14 Feb 1991, *Woman and Elephants in the Savannah* (oil on canvas, 30 x 22 ins / 76 x 56 cm) DKK 17,000. COPENHAGEN, 4 Dec 1991, *Elephants in the Jungle* (1938, tempera, 26 1/2 x 30 ins / 67 x 76 cm) DKK 17,000. COPENHAGEN, 21 April 1993, *Giraffes and Zebras in the Savannah* (1944, oil/synthetic resin, 15 3/4 x 23 1/2 ins / 40 x 60 cm) DKK 19,000. COPENHAGEN, 20 Oct 1993, *Pelicans and Monkeys near a Lake in the Forest* (1964, paint/synthetic resin, 14 1/2 x 7 1/2 ins / 37 x 19 cm) DKK 11,000. COPENHAGEN, 27 April 1995, *Elephants in the Jungle* (paint/synthetic resin, 10 1/4 x 19 3/4 ins / 26 x 50 cm) DKK 17,000. COPENHAGEN, 17 April 1997, *The Sirens, The Odyssey* (1954, oil/Masonite, 17 x 35 1/2 ins / 43 x 90 cm) DKK 15,000. COPENHAGEN, 23 March 1999, *Elephant Running among Trees* (c. 1935, oil on canvas, 16 x 20 ins / 40 x 51 cm) DKK 23,000. COPENHAGEN, 22 June 1999, *Animals in the Jungle* (1967, oil on panel, 6 x 6 ins / 14 x 14 cm) DKK 15,500. COPENHAGEN, 28 March 2000, *Four Elephants* (1957, oil on panel, 33 x 48 ins / 85 x 122 cm) DKK 160,000. VEJLE, 25 Sept 2000, *Landscape with Women and a Man Bathing* (1943, watercolour and pen, 8 x 13 ins / 21 x 34 cm) DKK 14,500. COPENHAGEN, 2 April 2001, *Wandering Elephants* (1957, oil on panel, 33 x 48 ins / 85 x 122 cm) DKK 120,000. COPENHAGEN, 2 Oct 2001, *Two Tapirs in the Jungle* (1949, tempera on panel, 12 x 20 ins / 31 x 50 cm) DKK 52,000. COPENHAGEN, 10 April 2002, *Mother and Baby: Elephant and Young in the Jungle* (1977, oil on panel, 12 x 15 ins / 30 x 39 cm) DKK 34,000. COPENHAGEN, 10 April 2002, *Blue Elephant in the Jungle* (c. 1940, tempera on cardboard, 15 x 18 ins / 38 x 45 cm) DKK 52,000. COPENHAGEN, 26 Feb 2003, *Jungle Picture with Elephants* (1958, oil on panel, 17 x 24 ins / 43 x 60 cm) DKK 74,000. COPENHAGEN, 17 Sept 2003, *Jungle Picture* (oil on board, 22 x 27 ins / 57 x 69 cm) DKK 50,000. COPENHAGEN, 29 March 2004, *Jungle Picture with Rhino, Monkey and Birds* (oil on panel, 16 x 30 ins / 40 x 75 cm) DKK 55,000. COPENHAGEN, 5 Oct 2004, *Savannah with Wild Animals* (1950, oil on canvas, 24 x 48 ins / 61 x 122 cm) DKK 150,000.

SCHERFLING, Otto
German, 19th century.
Born 1828, in Berlin; died 1881, in Wahren, near Brixen, South Tyrol (now Bressanone, Italy).
Active in Berlin.
Watercolourist, draughtsman. Landscapes.
MUSEUMS AND GALLERIES:
BERLIN (Nationalgal.): 16 drawings and watercolours.

SCHERHAUFF, Leonhard, or Scherauf
Austrian, 15th century.
Painter. Religious subjects.
Leonhard Scherhauff painted pictures for the presbytery of Blixen.

SCHERICH, Joseph Franz Raimund.
See **SCHERRICH**

SCHERINO, Antonio
Italian, 17th century.
Active c. 1635.
Sculptor (wood).
Antonio Scherino collaborated with Simone Berti.

SCHERKASOV, Mikihail Matveevich
Russian, 19th century.
Born 1793.
Miniaturist.
Mikhail Scherkasov studied at the St Petersburg academy.

SCHERKASOV, Pavel Alekseevich
Russian, 19th century.
Born 1834, in St Petersburg; died 29 February 1900, in St Petersburg.
Painter. Landscapes.
Pavel Scherkasov studied at the St Petersburg academy.

SCHERLENSKI, E. J.
Dutch, 18th century.
Draughtsman.

SCHERM, Lorenz, or Laurens
Dutch, 18th century.
Born c. 1690, in the Rhine Provinces.
Active in Amsterdam 1720-1735.
Draughtsman, engraver (burin).
Lorenz Scherm was a pupil of R. de Hooge. He engraved landscapes and architectural views.

SCHERMAN, Tony
Canadian, 20th - 21st century.
Born 1950, in Toronto.
Painter. Mythological subjects, figures, portraits, landscapes, landscapes with figures, animals.
Tony Scherman lived in Paris from 1955 to 1959, and then went to London where he studied at the Bryan Shaw School of Painting and Drawing from 1968 to 1971. He graduated with a Master of Arts from the Royal College of Art in London in 1974 and settled in Toronto when he returned to Canada in 1976. Scherman uses the wax technique in his paintings, which resemble travel books in the simplicity of their themes and the way they deal with images taken from life or translated from documents. Through portraits of historical characters such as *Bonaparte Dreaming of Napoleon*, 1998-1999, he tries to capture souls of departed beings. Solo exhibitions include: Penny Rubenstein Gallery, New York, 1991; Galerie Karl Pfefferle, Munich, 1993 and 2001; Galerie Daniel Templon, Paris, 1995; *Banquo's Funeral*, Leonard & Bina Ellen Art Gallery, Montreal, 1996; *About 1789*, Galerie Daniel Templon, Paris, 1997; Galerie Haas & Fuchs, Berlin, 1997, 2000 and 2001.
BIBLIOGRAPHY:
Förschl, Eve/Crone, Rainer, *Tony Scherman. 'Callisto': ein Zyklus aus Ovids Metamorphosen*, exhibition catalogue, Gal. Karl Pfefferle, Munich, 1993. Scherman, Tony, *Banquo's funeral*, exhibition catalogue, Leonard & Bina Ellen Art Gall., Montreal, 1996 (text in English and French). Henric, Jacques, *Tony Scherman. About 1789*, exhibition catalogue, Gal. Templon, Paris, 1997. Henric, Jacques, *Napoléon dévisagé*, Catleya, Paris, 1999 (includes conversation with the artist).
MUSEUMS AND GALLERIES:
CHATTANOOGA (Hunter Mus. of American Art).
AUCTION RECORDS:
NEW YORK, 1 Nov 1994, *Dog* (1989, oil and encaustic/canvas, 60 x 54 1/4 ins / 152.4 x 137.8 cm) USD 11,500. NEW YORK, 22 Feb 1995, *Midnight Bath* (1989, encaustic and oil on canvas, 70 x 60 ins / 177.8 x 152.4 cm) USD 17,250. NEW YORK, 6 May 1997, *Rape of Callisto: Jupiter* (1993, encaustic/canvas, 60 x 54 ins / 152.2 x 137 cm) USD 9,200. NEW YORK, 20 May 1999, *Banquo's Funeral - Peonies* (1995, encaustic, 32 x 36 ins / 81 x 91 cm) USD 12,000. VANCOUVER, 27 May 1999, *Still-life* (1997, encaustic on paper, 20 x 28 ins / 51 x 71 cm) CAD 4,800. NEW YORK, 1 June 2000, *Blue Highway* (encaustic on canvas) USD 3,520. LONDON, 26 Oct 2000, *Unsolved Mysteries* (1989, encaustic on canvas, 70 x 62 ins / 178 x 158 cm) GBP 6,800. TORONTO, 10 Sept 2001, *Kirkman* (1983, charcoal and encaustic on paper, 26 x 20 ins / 66 x 51 cm) CAD 2,750. VANCOUVER, 8 Nov 2001, *Flying Down to Rio* (1981, encaustic on paper, 36 x 60 ins / 91 x 152 cm) CAD 13,000. VANCOUVER, 14 Nov 2002, *Wolf Child* (1982, mixed media on paper, 39 x 28 ins / 99 x 70 cm) CAD 3,500. VANCOUVER, 15 May 2003, *Untitled - Comforts of Food* (1988, on paper, 30 x 60 ins / 76 x 152 cm) CAD 14,000. VANCOUVER, 27 Nov 2003, *The Death of Echo* (1993-1994, encaustic on canvas, 48 x 42 ins / 121 x 106 cm) CAD 18,000. TORONTO, 31 May 2004, *Lena's Daughter. Cupid* (1986 and 1995, works on paper, pair, 26 x 20 ins / 65 x 51 cm) CAD 6,500. TORONTO, 1 June 2004, *Otherside of Tuscany II* (encaustic on paper, 59 x 71 ins / 150 x 180 cm) CAD 12,000.

SCHERMAUL, Jenny
Austrian, 19th century.
Born 1828, in Liblin, near Kraklowitz.
Active in Prague.
Painter. Flowers.

SCHERMER, Augustin. See **SCHÄRMER**

SCHERMER, Cornelis Albertus Johannes
Dutch, 19th - 20th century.
Born 12 June 1824, in The Hague; died 4 January 1915, in The Hague.
Painter, watercolourist, engraver. Sporting subjects, landscapes, animals.
Cornelis Schermer lived from 1875 at Bouvignes near Dinant. He was above all a painter of horses, like Mœrenhoudt and Boubled, with whom he studied under Van der Bergh. He also painted landscapes. He exhibited for the first time in 1847 at The Hague.

C Schermer

MUSEUMS AND GALLERIES:
AMSTERDAM: *Horse Market on the Maliebaan at The Hague* - THE HAGUE (Gemeentemus.): *Horses*; *Hunt Meeting near Namur*.
AUCTION RECORDS:
DORDRECHT, 12 Dec 1972, *Snowy Landscape with Peasants and Horses*, NLG 3,600. AMSTERDAM, 9 March 1978, *At the Races* (watercolour, 15 3/4 x 27 1/2 ins / 40 x 70 cm) NLG 4,600. ZURICH, 6 June 1984, *?* (1861, oil on panel, 13 1/4 x 18 1/2 ins / 33.5 x 47 cm) CHF 9,500. AMSTERDAM, 10 Feb 1988, *Young Horseman and his Horse* (oil on panel, 5 1/4 x 7 1/4 ins / 13.5 x 18.5 cm) NLG 3,450. LONDON, 5 Oct 1990, *Horse Fair* (1874, oil on canvas, 17 1/4 x 31 1/2 ins / 44 x 80 cm) GBP 3,080. AMSTERDAM, 17 Sept 1991, *Horse Market* (oil on canvas, 24 1/2 x 38 1/4 ins / 62.5 x 97 cm) NLG 9,775. AMSTERDAM, 21 Jan 1998, *Peasant with Horses by a River* (oil on panel, 7 1/2 x 10 ins / 19 x 24.5 cm) NLG 1,960.

SCHERMER, Johann Martin. See **SCHARMER**

SCHERMIER
16th century.
Painter.
Schermier was accused of heresy, together with Bernard d'Orley, in 1527.

SCHERMIER, Cornelis, or Scermier, Schernier
Flemish School, 16th century.
Active in Brussels.
Painter.
According to Dr Wurzbach, Cornelis Schermier may be the same artist as Cornelis van Coninxloo (see entry).

SCHERMINI, Bartolomeo
Italian, 19th century.
Born 26 March 1841, in Brescia; died 25 November 1896, in Brescia.
Painter. Genre scenes.

Bartolomeo Schermini studied at the Accademia di Belle Arti di Brera in Milan under Bertini, went to Paris on a study trip and worked in Florence and Brescia. He exhibited in Milan and Rome.

MUSEUMS AND GALLERIES:
BRESCIA (Pinacoteca Tosio-Martinengo): painting.

SCHERNBERG, David von
Austrian, 18th century.
Died 1725, in Klagenfurt.
Active in Klagenfurt.
Painter.

Two *Virgins*, two *Ecce Homo* and one head of *Gertrude* have survived.

SCHERNIER, Michael or Michel.
See **SCERRIER**

SCHERPE, Johann
Austrian, 19th - 20th century.
Born 15 December 1855, in Vienna.
Sculptor. Busts.

Johann Scherpe was a pupil of Carl Kundmann. He left a *Dying Warrior* to the Akademie der Bildenden Künste in Vienna, and busts of the chemists *Berzelius, Fr. Wöhler* and *Hlasiwets* to the polytechnic school of Vienna.

SCHERPEREEL, Koen
Belgian, 20th - 21st century.
Born 1961, in Bruges.
Painter. Scenes with figures, figures.

Koen Scherpereel paints people, breaking up their shape in various ways - for example, introducing alien shapes on their bodies such as the head of a dog, a face or a landscape. The deformations and overlays that make monsters of these beings evoke a troubled universe with a hint of anguish.

AUCTION RECORDS:
LOKEREN, 23 May 1992, *Figures* (1989, oil on canvas, 59 x 59 ins / 150 x 150 cm) BEF 70,000. LOKEREN, 6 Oct 2001, *Composition* (1988, oil on canvas, 47 x 47 ins / 120 x 120 cm) BEF 90,000.

SCHERRE, Theoderich
German, 16th century.
Active in Duisburg, and in Xanten 1532-1557.
Painter.

SCHERRER. See also **SCHÄRER** and **SCHERER**

SCHERRER, Cécile
French, 20th century.
Born 1899, in Clermont-Ferrand.
Painter, watercolourist. Nudes, portraits, landscapes, interiors. Designs for tapestries.

Cécile Scherrer, a pupil of Othon Friesz and Dufy, exhibited in Paris regularly from 1929 at the Salon d'Automne, the Salon des Tuileries, the Salon des Indépendants and the Salon de la Société Nationale des Beaux-Arts. She took part in the Paris Exposition Internationale of 1937, and held solo exhibitions in Paris, Strasbourg, Aix-en-Provence, Alès and Milan.

A lover of nature, she painted it in the Impressionist style, and travelled extensively in Spain, Italy, Algeria and Portugal. She also painted the Cevennes, the Dordogne and the Île-de-France (*Rue de Montmartre* 1927 - *Grez-sur-Loing* 1942 - *Fields of the Yonne* 1944). Among the tapestries she designed were: *Amphytrite* 1945 and *Sonata* 1946.

MUSEUMS AND GALLERIES:
BOULOGNE-SUR-MER: *Nude at the Boat Races* - MOULINS: *Portrait of Mme Chabaneix*.

AUCTION RECORDS:
PARIS, 15 Feb 1950, *Bathing Pool, Le Perreux* (1932) FRF 3,000. PARIS, 21 April 1950, *Balcony; Cannes* (both) FRF 5,500.

SCHERRER, Hedwig
Swiss, 20th century.
Born 11 March 1878, in Bad Sulgen.
Painter, illustrator. Portraits, landscapes.

Hedwig Scherrer was a pupil of Becker Gundahl and of Schuster-Woldan and lived and worked at St Gall.

SCHERRER, Jean Jacques
French, 19th century.
Born in Lutterbach.
Painter. History painting, figures, portraits, genre scenes, still-lifes.

Jean Jacques Scherrer's masters were Cabanel, Barrias and Cavelier. He debuted at the Paris Salon in 1877. He became a life member of the Société des Artistes Français in 1884 and was granted a travel bursary in 1881. He received an honourable mention in 1884 and won a third-class medal in 1887, a second-class medal in 1892 and a bronze medal in 1900 at the Exposition Universelle. He was made a Chevalier of the Légion d'Honneur in 1901.

MUSEUMS AND GALLERIES:
MULHOUSE: *Raising of the Widow's Son of Nain; Robespierre, Marat and Danton at the Inn on Rue Paon; Youth of Frederick the Great; Still-life; Portraits of Isaac Schlumberger and Daniel Dollfus-Ausset*.

AUCTION RECORDS:
PARIS, 1890, *Horses Sheltering*, FRF 3,400. PARIS, 3 Feb 1928, *The Violoncellist*, FRF 300. ROME, 24 March 1992, *The Sermon* (oil on canvas, 69¼ x 52 ins / 176 x 132 cm) ITL 13,800,000.

SCHERRER, Johann or Hans Jakob.
See **SCHÄRER**

SCHERRES, Alfred
German, 20th century.
Born 21 September 1864, in Danzig (now Gdansk, Poland); died 1924.
Painter. Landscapes.

Alfred Scherres was a pupil at the academy of fine arts of Berlin from 1885 to 1886. He worked at Königsberg (now Kaliningrad, Russia) from 1886 to 1889, and at Karlsruhe from 1889 to 1892 with Hermann Baisch and Gustav Schönleber.

SCHERRES, Carl
German, 19th - 20th century.
Born 31 March 1833; died 21 April 1923, in Berlin.
Painter. Landscapes.

Carl Scherres studied first at the academy of fine arts in his native city of Danzig (now Gdansk, Poland) then travelled for purposes of study on the banks of the Rhine, in Switzerland and in northern Italy. Returning to his own country he perfected his skills working in the Danzig region for several years. In 1868 he was appointed a teacher in Berlin, at the school of drawing, where he specialised in painting the landscapes of eastern Prussia.

MUSEUMS AND GALLERIES:
BERLIN: *Flooding in East Prussia* - KALININGRAD: *Sunset in a Hut in the Forest; Lonely Cabin in the Marshes* - WROCLAW: *Rainy Day near the River Havel*.

Auction records:
Cologne, 23 Nov 1978, *Winter Landscape* (oil on canvas, 30 x 42¼ ins / 76.3 x 107 cm) DEM 3,600.

SCHERREWITZ, Johann Frederik Cornelis
Dutch, 19th - 20th century.
Born 1868, in Hilversum; died 1951.
Active in England.
Painter. Genre scenes, animals, landscapes, landscapes with figures, seascapes.

Johann Scherrewitz took part in 1907 in the exhibition at the Royal Academy, in 1916 in the exhibition at the Scottish Royal Academy. He also exhibited in 1909 at Liverpool. He specialised in depicting agricultural scenes, including views of ploughing and the care of the animals.

Auction records:
New York, 21 March 1907, *The Return of the Herd*, USD 170. New York, 1 April 1909, *Ploughing in Holland*, USD 325. New York, 12-14 April 1909, *Return at Twilight*, USD 225. London, 22 June 1923, *The Herd*, GBP 136. London, 13 May 1927, *New Pastures*, GBP 126. London, 10 Oct 1969, *Landscape*, Gns 400. London, 12 June 1974, *The Mudlark*, GBP 1,800. Amsterdam, 7 Sept 1976, *Cattle Beside a Pond* (oil on canvas, 30½ x 38¼ ins / 77.5 x 97 cm) NLG 5,200. New York, 7 Oct 1977, *Fishermen on the Shore at Low Tide* (oil on panel, 12½ x 16¼ ins / 32 x 41 cm) USD 4,250. Amsterdam, 31 Oct 1979, *Man and Horses on the Shore* (oil on canvas, 27¼ x 39¼ ins / 69.2 x 99.5 cm) NLG 11,500. San Francisco, 3 Oct 1981, *Return of the Fishing Fleet* (oil on canvas, 36 x 32 ins / 91.5 x 81 cm) USD 7,000. London, 18 April 1983, *Return of the Fishing Fleet* (oil on canvas, 18¼ x 26½ ins / 46.5 x 67 cm) GBP 3,500. London, 30 May 1986, *The Hay Cart* (oil on canvas, 14½ x 22 ins / 37 x 56 cm) GBP 3,000. Amsterdam, 26 March 1988, *Wood Gatherer Loading his Cart in the Dunes* (oil on canvas, 15¾ x 23½ ins / 40 x 60 cm) NLG 6,325. Toronto, 30 Nov 1988, *Shell Gatherers* (oil on canvas, 20 x 26 ins / 50.5 x 66 cm) CAD 11,500. New York, 24 Oct 1989, *Collecting Seaweed* (oil on canvas, 35½ x 31¾ ins / 90.2 x 80.7 cm) USD 7,700. Amsterdam, 25 April 1990, *Raking the Shells* (oil on canvas, 15¼ x 27¼ ins / 38.5 x 69 cm) NLG 16,100. New York, 19 July 1990, *Ploughing in Holland* (oil on canvas, 21¾ x 39½ ins / 55.2 x 100.4 cm) USD 4,675. New York, 24 Oct 1990, *Fishermen Working on the Shore* (oil on canvas, 26 x 22 ins / 66 x 55.9 cm) USD 13,200. Amsterdam, 5-6 Feb 1991, *Farmers Working in a Field* (oil on canvas, 10 x 18 ins / 25.5 x 46 cm) NLG 3,450. London, 15 Feb 1991, *Herdsman and his Beasts on a Plain* (oil on canvas, 27¾ x 39¾ ins / 70.5 x 101 cm) GBP 2,420. Amsterdam, 23 April 1991, *Fishing for Shells* (oil on canvas, 19¾ x 35¾ ins / 50 x 91 cm) NLG 14,375. New York, 21 May 1991, *Cart on a Forest Path* (oil on canvas, 30 x 20 ins / 76.1 x 50.8 cm) USD 2,640. Montreal, 4 June 1991, *End of the Day* (oil on canvas, 26 x 33 ins / 66 x 83.8 cm) CAD 3,200. Amsterdam, 17 Sept 1991, *Peasant Woman Collecting Wood at the Edge of the Forest* (oil on canvas, 16 x 22 ins / 40.5 x 55 cm) NLG 4,370. Amsterdam, 30 Oct 1991, *Peasant Loading a Cart* (oil on canvas, 20 x 36 ins / 51 x 91.5 cm) NLG 14,950. Amsterdam, 18 Feb 1992, *Landscape of Wooded Dunes with a Peasant Driving a Cart* (oil on canvas, 17¾ x 22 ins / 45 x 55 cm) NLG 5,520. Amsterdam, 22 April 1992, *Peasant and his Cows in the Farmyard at Heeze* (oil on canvas, 12½ x 20½ ins / 32 x 52 cm) NLG 6,325. New York, 13 Oct 1993, *The Day's Harvest* (oil on canvas, 21½ x 37¾ ins / 54.6 x 95.9 cm) USD 13,800. Amsterdam, 9 Nov 1993, *Collector of Firewood with a Horse and Cart* (oil on canvas, 19¾ x 29½ ins / 50 x 75 cm) NLG 16,100. London, 11 Feb 1994, *Peasants with a Horse and Cart in the Dunes* (oil on canvas, 28 x 39¼ ins / 70.2 x 100 cm) GBP 7,475. Montreal, 21 June 1994, *Clam Gatherers* (oil on canvas, 20 x 30 ins / 50.8 x 76.2 cm) CAD 9,500. New York, 20 July 1994, *Sand Quarry in Holland* (oil on canvas, 16 x 27½ ins / 40.6 x 69.9 cm) USD 5,750. Amsterdam, 7 Nov 1995, *Sailing Boat in a Port* (oil on panel, 7 x 10 ins / 18 x 24.5 cm) NLG 1,770. Amsterdam, 5 Nov 1996, *Fishing for Mussels* (oil on canvas, 15¾ x 27¾ ins / 40 x 70.5 cm) NLG 15,340. Edinburgh, 27 Nov 1996, *Unloading the Haycart* (oil on canvas, 23½ x 43¼ ins / 59.7 x 110 cm) GBP 9,775. London, 13 March 1997, *Fishermen on the Shore* (oil on panel, 12 x 16 ins / 30.5 x 40.6 cm) GBP 8,625. Amsterdam, 22 April 1997, *Milking Time* (oil on panel, 10 x 18 ins / 25.5 x 46 cm) NLG 8,850. Amsterdam, 27 Oct 1997, *Boat on the Shore* (oil on panel, 7 x 9 ins / 17.5 x 23 cm) NLG 24,780. New York, 10 Feb 1998, *The Clam Gatherer* (oil on panel, 12½ x 16½ ins / 31.7 x 42 cm) USD 8,050. Amsterdam, 26 Oct 1999, *Cows on Riverbank with Peasant at Gate* (oil on canvas, 26 x 22 ins / 65 x 56 cm) NLG 17,000. Toronto, 2 Dec 1999, *On the Beach, Scheveningen* (oil on canvas, 17 x 23 ins / 43 x 58 cm) CAD 52,000. London, 22 June 2000, *On the Beach* (oil on canvas, 18 x 30 ins / 46 x 76 cm) GBP 12,000. Amsterdam, 24 Oct 2000, *Shellfisher* (oil on canvas, 22 x 39 ins / 56 x 100 cm) NLG 78,000. Amsterdam, 24 April 2001, *Shellfisher in the Breakers* (oil on canvas, 21 x 39 ins / 54 x 99 cm) NLG 160,000. Toronto, 28 May 2001, *Unloading the Day's Catch* (oil on canvas, 16 x 28 ins / 41 x 70 cm) CAD 34,000. Amsterdam, 22 Jan 2002, *Horses and a Cart on a Heath* (oil on canvas, 16 x 28 ins / 40 x 70 cm) EUR 10,000. Amsterdam, 22 Oct 2002, *Shellfisher on the Beach, Noordwijk* (oil on canvas, 14 x 24 ins / 35 x 60 cm) EUR 11,000. Amsterdam, 15 April 2003, *Unloading the Catch* (oil on canvas, 12 x 19 ins / 31 x 49 cm) EUR 19,000. Amsterdam, 29 April 2003, *Gathering Nets* (oil on plywood, 13 x 17 ins / 32 x 42 cm) EUR 36,000. Amsterdam, 19 Oct 2004, *Shellfisher on Scheveningen Beach* (oil on canvas, 24 x 20 ins / 60 x 51 cm) EUR 28,000. Amsterdam, 26 Oct 2004, *Sheelfishers on a Windswept Beach* (oil on canvas, 38 x 30 ins / 96 x 76 cm) EUR 35,000.

SCHERRICH, Joseph Franz Raimund, or Scherich
German, 17th century.
Painter. Religious subjects.

Joseph Scherrich worked in Landshut in Bavaria, producing exclusively paintings for churches.

SCHERS, Leonhart
German, 17th century.
Active in Lüneburg.
Draughtsman.

SCHERSCHMID, Balthasar
German, 16th - 17th century.
Painter.

Balthasar Scherschmid worked in the court of Brieg (now Brzeg, Poland) between 1568 and 1600.

SCHERTEL, Johann Heinrich
German, 18th century.
Born 1685; died 1733, in Bayreuth.
Painter.

Johann Schertel was a painter at the court in Bayreuth.

SCHERTEL, Josef
German, 19th century.
Born 10 January 1810, in Augsburg; died 8 March 1869, in Munich.
Painter. Landscapes.

Josef Schertel trained under Chr. Morgenstern.

Auction records:
London, 12 Oct 1984, *Wooded Landscape with View of a Castle in the Background* (oil on canvas, 27¼ x 42 ins / 69.2 x 106.6 cm) USD 6,000. Paris, 12 Oct 1988, *Landscape with*

Fishermen (1852, oil on canvas, 23 1/4 x 29 1/2 ins / 59 x 75 cm) FRF 48,000.

SCHERTLE, Valentin
German, 19th century.
Born 31 January 1809, in Villingen; died 24 February 1885, in Frankfurt am Main.
Lithographer.

Schertle trained under F. Hanfstängl in Munich. He then worked in St Petersburg, Warsaw, and, from 1846 onwards, in Frankfurt am Main. He produced many reproductions of Delaroche, Domenichino, Raphael and Guido Reni.

SCHERVITZ, Mathias or Matyis, or Seravits, Schibiz, Xeravich
Bohemian School, 18th century.
Born 1701, in Ofen (now Buda); died 12 March 1771, in Ofen.
Painter.

Mathias Schrvitz painted altarpieces.

SCHERZ, Ernst Bruno
German, 20th century.
Born 12 December 1889, in Berlin.
Painter.

Ernst Bruno Scherz was a pupil of Bruno Paul. He was also an architect.

SCHERZER, Alexander
German, 19th century.
Born 4 September 1835, in Hamburg; died 11 July 1871, in Hamburg.
Painter, engraver, lithographer. Seascapes.

AUCTION RECORDS:
MUNICH, 6 Dec 1994, *Moat of the Citadel of Nuremberg on a Rainy Day* (oil on canvas, 29 3/4 x 24 ins / 75.5 x 61 cm) DEM 7,820.

SCHERZER, Conrad
German, 20th century.
Born 9 January 1893, in Nuremberg.
Painter, engraver.

SCHERZHAUSER, Mathias
Austrian, 17th century.
Born 1630.
Painter (glazed earthenware).

Scherzhauser worked in his brother-in-law's studio in Salzburg.

SCHERZI, Agostino
Italian, 18th century.
Died 1721, in Rome.
Active in Pistoia, Italy.
Painter.

Agostino was the father of Lodovico Scherzi.

SCHERZI, Lodovico
Italian, 18th century.
Died before 1721, in Rome.
Painter.

Lodovico was the son of Agostino Scherzi.

SCHESCHENIN. See **CHECHENIN**

SCHESTAUBER, Gustav
Austrian, 19th century.
Born 27 April 1847, in Vienna.
Painter. Architectural views.

Schestauber trained under Th. Alphons. Watercolours by him are housed at the Kunsthistorisches Museum in Vienna.

SCHETH, Georg
Austrian, 19th century.
Born 1808, in Vienna.
Painter, lithographer. Genre scenes, landscapes, architectural views.

Scheth started training at the academy in Vienna in 1828, and exhibited there from 1832 to 1839.

SCHETKY, John Alexander
British, 19th century.
Born 1785, in Edinburgh; died 1824, in Cape Coast Castle (Cape Colony).
Draughtsman, watercolourist. Military subjects, landscapes.

John Alexander Schetky was the brother of seascape painter John Christian Schetky. As an army surgeon attached to the Third Dragoon Guards, Schetky served under Lord Dalhousie in the Peninsula War. In his free time he drew from nature, focusing notably on views of the Pyrenées. After the war he specialised in scientific or medicine-related drawings and worked in part for James MacGregor's Pathological Museum. He was appointed to the post of medical inspector-general in Africa and served out his career there. Schetky exhibited watercolour landscapes at the Society of Painters in Watercolours in 1816 and 1817.

AUCTION RECORDS:
LONDON, 25 May 1928, *American Vessels under Attack by Five English Vessels* (drawing) GBP 60.

SCHETKY, John Christian
British, 19th century.
Born 11 August 1778, in Edinburgh; died 28 January 1874, in London.
Painter, watercolourist. Seascapes.

John Christian Schetky was the older brother of John Alexander Schetky. He studied under Masmyth and went on to specialise in seascapes inspired by 17th-century Dutch masters, in particular Willem van de Velde. Schetky taught drawing and composition at the Royal Military College in Great Marlowe, at the Royal Naval College in Portsmouth and at the East India College in Addiscombie.

John Christian Schetky's body of work is characterised by his meticulous attention to detail and his intimate knowledge of naval architecture. A seascape painter listed in Royal Academy catalogues of 1805 to 1825 by the initials 'J.T.' is also shown to have lived in Oxford - as did John Christian Schetky. It is possible that this 'J.T.' was related to John Christian Schetky and even that the two painters are one and the same.

Schetky exhibited his work in London between 1808 and 1872, typically at the Royal Academy, the British Institution, the Suffolk Street Gallery and the Society of Painters in Watercolours.

BIBLIOGRAPHY:
Greenway, Winifred, '*The Marine Man, J.C. Schetky*' in *Turner Studies, VII*, 1987.

MUSEUMS AND GALLERIES:
NORWICH (Castle Mus. and AG): *HMS Amelia Chasing the French Frigate 'Aréthuse'*; *HMS Amelia and the French Frigate 'Aréthuse' in Action.*

AUCTION RECORDS:
LONDON, 16 Feb 1922, *Harbour in the Shetland Isles* (watercolour) GBP 12. LONDON, 17 Nov 1967, *Sailing Vessels off the Scottish Coast,* Gns 400. LONDON, 9 May 1969, *La Valetta Harbour, Malta,* Gns 420. LONDON, 23 Nov 1973, *Bombardment of Algiers, August 27, 1816,* Gns 3,800. LONDON, 15 March 1978, *Naval Engagement* (1840, oil on canvas, 24 1/2 x 35 1/2 ins / 62 x 90 cm) GBP 2,200. LONDON, 21 March 1979, *Frigate 'Andromeda' in Heavy Seas; Frigate 'Andromeda' Demasted* (two oils on canvas, 14 1/4 x 19 1/2 ins / 36.5 x 49.5 cm) GBP 1,300. LONDON, 27 March 1981, *Bombardment of Algiers, August 27, 1816* (1841, oil on canvas, 36 x 66 ins / 91.5 x 167.6 cm) GBP 3,200. LONDON, 28 Jan 1983, *Sailing Vessels at Sea off Whitby* (1841, oil on card, 10 1/4 x 14 1/4 ins / 26 x 36.3 cm) GBP 1,500. LONDON, 5 June 1985, *Squadron at Sea off Tantallon Castle* (oil on canvas, 17 3/4 x 30 ins / 45 x

76.5 cm) GBP 3,800. LONDON, 16 Dec 1986, *HMS Pique coming off the Rocks on the Labrador Coast, October 23, 1830* (1830, oil on canvas, 44 1/2 x 72 ins / 113 x 183 cm) GBP 23,500. LONDON, 15 June 1990, *Schooner under Full Sail, two Royal Navy Vessels, a US Merchantman and assorted Vessels* (1857, oil on canvas, 18 x 30 ins / 45.7 x 76.2 cm) GBP 9,350. LONDON, 18 Nov 1992, *The Frigate 'Aigle' (Eagle) off the Coast of Cephalonia* (1843, oil on canvas, 19 x 28 1/4 ins / 48 x 71.5 cm) GBP 4,400. EDINBURGH, 15 May 1997, *The Flagship 'Queen' and Numerous Other Vessels Riding at Anchor in a Calm Sea* (oil on canvas, 24 x 36 ins / 61 x 91.5 cm) GBP 25,300. LONDON, 8 June 1999, *Capture of 'Guillaume Tell'. Last of the Wooden Walls* (1864, pencil, colour ink and colour wash, two, sold with two similar works, 10 x 15 ins / 26 x 37 cm) GBP 2,400. NEW ORLEANS, 4 Dec 1999, *The 'Constitution' and the 'Guerrière' 19 Aug 1812* (watercolour, 10 x 16 ins / 25 x 41 cm) USD 1,600. LONDON, 11 May 2000, *Guillaume Tell in Action with HMS Penelope* (1834, oil on canvas, 33 x 58 ins / 84 x 147 cm) GBP 25,000. LONDON, 11 May 2000, *Lord Belfast's Yacht Emily Hove-to for Owner to Board, off Belem Tower, Lisbon* (oil on canvas, 30 x 45 ins / 75 x 114 cm) GBP 42,000. LONDON, 24 May 2001, *Island Queen off Cowes* (oil on canvas, 21 x 34 ins / 53 x 86 cm) GBP 2,500. LONDON, 15 Aug 2002, *Bombardment of Algiers, 27th August 1816* (1841, oil on canvas, 36 x 66 ins / 91 x 168 cm) GBP 86,000. LONDON, 18 June 2003, *Khedive's Disaster, a Troop Ship in Distress being Rescued by the Royal Yacht Squadron* (oil on canvas, 21 x 31 ins / 54 x 79 cm) GBP 1,800. VANCOUVER, 9 Dec 2003, *Fresh Breeze off the Dutch Coast* (oil on panel, 16 x 24 ins / 41 x 61 cm) CAD 2,500. BOSTON, 24 Jan 2004, *Portrait of HMS Talbout in Action at the Battle of Navarino* (oil on canvas, 24 x 34 ins / 61 x 86 cm) USD 2,200. NEW YORK, 17 June 2004, *Squall off the Dutch Coast* (oil on panel, 10 x 14 ins / 25 x 36 cm) USD 7,500.

SCHETTINO, Tommaso
Italian, 18th century.
Active in Naples.
Sculptor.

Tommaso Schettino produced terracotta nativity figures, animals in particular.

SCHETZLI, H.
German, 17th century.
Painter.

MUSEUMS AND GALLERIES:
SCHONGAU (Stadtmus.): *Tree of Jesse.*

SCHEU, Heinrich
Austrian, 19th century.
Born 19 October 1845, in Vienna.
Engraver (wood).

Scheu was trained by R. von Waldheim. From 1885 to 1891 he was a teacher of the decorative arts in Florence. He started working in Zurich in 1893.

SCHEU, Leo
Austrian, 20th century.
Born 28 March 1886, in Olmütz (now Olomouc, Czech Republic); died 1958, in Graz.
Painter. Portraits, still-lifes.

Leo Scheu worked in Vienna from 1907 to 1908, and at the academy of Prague with Franz Thiele from 1912. He lived and worked in Graz.

MUSEUMS AND GALLERIES:
GRAZ (Episcopal Palace): *Bishop Pavlikovski; Fifteen Portraits of Rectors of the University* - GRAZ (Landesmus. Joanneum): *Portrait of a Young Girl.*

AUCTION RECORDS:
MUNICH, 25 June 1996, *Still-life with Oranges and Lilac* (1955, oil/synthetic fibres, 34 1/4 x 26 3/4 ins / 87 x 68 cm) DEM 3,450.

SCHEUBEL, Johann Joseph, the Elder, or Sceibel, Schaibel, Scheilbel, Scheibelt, Scheubeld, Schweigel, Schweipel
German, 17th - 18th century.
Born in Regensburg; died 4 June 1721, in Regensburg.
Painter. History painting.

Johann Scheubel married in Bamberg in 1686. His patron was the prince-bishop of Regensburg. The latter appointed him a painter at his court and provided him with the means to go and train in Venice for a time. Upon his return, Scheubel the Elder notably painted a *Stoning of St Stephen* for the church of St Stephen in Bamberg, a *Descent from the Cross*, an altarpiece for the church of Jacob and a ceiling for the church in Gandolf.

SCHEUBEL, Johann Joseph, the Younger
German, 18th century.
Born 27 October 1686, in Bamberg; died 2 February 1769, in Bamberg.
Painter.

Johann Joseph Scheubel the Younger was the son of Johann Joseph Scheubel the Elder. He was sent by the prince elector of Bamberg to Vienna, where he attended the academy in Vienna and became influenced by P. von Strudel. From Vienna he went to Venice, Bologna and Rome. After returning to Germany, and being a court painter, he became the most highly esteemed painter in Bamberg. He was notably an eclectic painter who was influenced by the Italian Baroque.

MUSEUMS AND GALLERIES:
BAMBERG: *Busts of the Apostles Peter and Paul; Charity with Children and Spirits* - BAYREUTH (Neues Schloss): *Peter's Repentance and Mary Magdalene's Atonement* - MEMMELSDORF (Schloss Seehof): *The Four Seasons* - POMMERSFELDEN: *Cimon and Pero.*

SCHEUBEL, Johann Joseph, the Younger
German, 18th century.
Born 1733, in Bamberg; died 9 April 1801, in Bamberg.
Painter. History painting, genre scenes.

Johann Joseph Scheubel the Younger was trained in Munich by the Swedish painter Georg de Marées. The bishop of Bamberg provided him with the means to travel to France and Italy. Upon his return, the bishop appointed him a painter at his court. In 1776, Scheubel was sent to Paris by his patron. He lived there for two years and notably painted four allegorical subjects at the town hall. An excellent portrait of the bishop of Seinsheim has survived.

AUCTION RECORDS:
LUCERNE, 19 June 1971, *Portrait of a Prelate*, CHF 17,000.

SCHEUBER, Peter
Swiss, 18th century.
Active in Bamberg (Bavaria), Germany.
Sculptor.

Peter Scheuber worked in Längendorf, near Soleure.

SCHEUBLIN, Georg
Swiss, 16th - 17th century.
Died 14 January 1624.
Painter.

From 1580 Georg Scheublin was a monk in the monastery of Muri, which still has some of his paintings and drawings.

SCHEUCH, Ludwig
German, 18th century.
Painter.

In 1729 Ludwig Scheuch painted a *St Norbert* and *St Augustine* for the Weissenau cloister.

SCHEUCHER, Franz. See **SCHEICHER**

SCHEUCHZER, August Heinrich
Swiss, 19th century.
Born 1812; died c. 1876, in Zurich.

Active in Zurich.
Painter.

SCHEUCHZER, Caspar
Swiss, 19th century.
Born 1808, in Zurich; died 1874.
Painter, lithographer.
Caspar Scheuchzer was the brother of Wilhelm Scheuchzer. He was a painter of wood and plaster cast.

SCHEUCHZER, David
Swiss, 18th century.
Born 1704, in Zurich; died 1739, in Thalwil.
Engraver.
There are four drawings attributed to David Scheuchzer.

SCHEUCHZER, Wilhelm
Swiss, 19th century.
Born 24 March 1803, in Zurich; died 28 March 1866, in Munich.
Painter. Landscapes.
Wilhelm Scheuchzer was trained by Heinrich Maurer. He worked in Switzerland, the Black Forest, Karlsruhe and Munich, and was employed by the prince of Fürstenberg from 1826 to 1829. The freshness of his colours is greatly appreciated.
MUSEUMS AND GALLERIES:
MUNICH (Pinakothek): *By the Lake at Zurich.*
AUCTION RECORDS:
LUCERNE, 19 Nov 1976, *View of Interlaken* (oil on canvas, 30 x 42 ins / 76 x 106.5 cm) CHF 14,000. VIENNA, 5 Dec 1984, *Fishermen in the Moonlight* (1844, oil on canvas, 12 3/4 x 17 3/4 ins / 32.5 x 45 cm) ATS 28,000. PARIS, 22 June 1988, *Mountainscape along the Edge of a River with Figures* (1848, oil on canvas) FRF 110,000. KEMPTEN, 14 Jan 2000, *Ruins in Alpine Landscape* (1847, oil on board, 8 x 9 ins / 20 x 23 cm) DEM 12,000. LUCERNE, 8 Nov 2000, *Blacksmith in Forge* (oil on canvas, 11 x 13 ins / 27 x 32 cm) CHF 2,600. LONDON, 11 July 2001, *Cowherd Leading his Livestock on a Mountain Path. Peasant Droving his Livestock* (oil on canvas, a pair, 25 x 19 ins / 63 x 48 cm) GBP 2,400. ZURICH, 3 Dec 2001, *Schloss Kyburg* (1847, oil on panel, 11 x 13 ins / 27 x 34 cm) CHF 21,000. MUNICH, 18 April 2002, *Fussen* (grisaille, 9 x 13 ins / 24 x 33 cm) EUR 2,800. MUNICH, 21 June 2002, *The Au near Munich* (1840, oil on canvas, 13 x 18 ins / 34 x 45 cm) EUR 32,000. ZURICH, 28 March 2003, *Glarnerland - Mollis against Glarnisch* (oil on canvas, 31 x 42 ins / 78 x 107 cm) CHF 9,000. MILAN, 25 May 2004, *Villa Pliniana on Lake Como* (1825, oil on board, 7 x 9 ins / 19 x 22 cm) EUR 2,700.

SCHEUER, Otto
German, 19th - 20th century.
Born 8 October 1865, in Frankfurt am Main; died 17 November 1921, in Frankfurt am Main.
Painter. Religious subjects.
Otto Scheuer studied at the Städel Institute in Frankfurt. He made altar paintings for churches around Frankfurt.

SCHEUER, Salomon. See **SCHEURER**

SCHEUERER, Franz. See **SCHEYERER**

SCHEUERER, Julius, or Scheurer
German, 19th - 20th century.
Born 30 January 1859, in Munich; died 11 April 1913, in Planegg.
Painter. Hunting scenes, animals, birds, farmyard scenes, landscapes.
Julius Scheuerer specialised in painting poultry.

MUSEUMS AND GALLERIES:
BUCHAREST (Muz. National de Arta al României): *Poultry.*
AUCTION RECORDS:
LONDON, 13 Dec 1909, *Poultry*, GBP 3. PARIS, 10 Nov 1949, *Farmyard*, FRF 2,600. COLOGNE, 19 Oct 1973, *The Farmyard*, DEM 3,500. COLOGNE, 21 June 1974, *Hunting Dogs*, DEM 2,400. NEW YORK, 2 April 1976, *Farm Scenes* (two oils on panel, 5 1/2 x 7 ins / 14 x 18 cm) USD 3,700. NEW YORK, 7 Oct 1977, *The Farmyard* (oil on canvas, 12 1/2 x 20 3/4 ins / 32 x 53 cm) USD 2,100. COLOGNE, 19 Oct 1979, *Two Hunting Dogs and a Stag* (oil on panel, 6 1/2 x 15 1/4 ins / 16.5 x 38.5 cm) DEM 6,500. NEW YORK, 28 May 1981, *Fowls in a Landscape* (oil on panel, a pair, 4 x 7 1/2 ins / 10 x 19 cm) USD 9,000. NEW YORK, 24 Feb 1983, *Fowls in a Farmyard* (oil on panel, 6 x 15 3/4 ins / 15 x 40 cm) USD 6,250. MUNICH, 26 June 1985, *Ducks, Geese and Peacocks at the Edge of the Pond* (oil on panel, 14 1/4 x 11 ins / 36 x 27 cm) DEM 21,000. CHESTER, 10 July 1986, *Hens and Chickens at the Fountain* (oil on canvas, 14 x 22 ins / 35.5 x 56 cm) GBP 3,800. LONDON, 26 Feb 1988, *A Stag in a Landscape* (oil on canvas, 23 1/2 x 18 ins / 60 x 46 cm) GBP 1,100. COLOGNE, 15 Oct 1988, *Turkey Quarrelling with a Couple of Ducks* (oil on panel, 6 1/4 x 8 ins / 16 x 20.5 cm) DEM 4,300. STOCKHOLM, 15 Nov 1988, *Hen and Cock Turkeys in a Pasture* (oil on canvas, 4 1/4 x 5 1/4 ins / 11 x 13.5 cm) SEK 10,000. COLOGNE, 20 Oct 1989, *Farm Yard Animals on a Prairie* (oil on canvas, 16 1/4 x 20 1/2 ins / 41 x 52 cm) DEM 7,500. NEW YORK, 22 May 1990, *Ducks at the Edge of a Pond* (oil on canvas, 15 3/4 x 12 1/2 ins / 40 x 31.7 cm) USD 12,100. NEW YORK, 21 May 1991, *Cock, Hens and Ducks* (oil on panel, 10 x 7 1/2 ins / 25.4 x 19 cm) USD 2,750. MUNICH, 25 June 1992, *Poultry in a Farmyard* (oil on canvas, 7 x 16 1/4 ins / 17.5 x 41 cm) DEM 5,650. NEW YORK, 29 Oct 1992, *Fowls Pecking; Ducks Near a Stream* (oil on panel, a pair, each 2 3/4 x 7 ins / 7 x 17.8 cm) USD 4,400. NEW YORK, 17 Jan 1996, *Hens and Turkeys Near a Lake* (oil on panel, a pair, each 3 x 8 1/4 ins / 7.9 x 21 cm) USD 4,887. MUNICH, 23 June 1997, *Farmyard* (oil on wood, 6 1/4 x 15 3/4 ins / 16 x 40 cm) DEM 10,800. NEW YORK, 10 Feb 1998, *Cocks, Hens and Ducks at the Farm* (oil on panel, 5 1/2 x 9 ins / 14 x 22.9 cm) USD 4,025.

SCHEUERER, Otto, or Scheurer
German, 19th - 20th century.
Born 31 October 1862, in Munich; died 5 December 1934, in Munich.
Painter. Animals, birds, farmyard scenes.
Otto Scheuerer was the brother of Julius Scheuerer and was a pupil of Karl Raupp at the academy of fine arts in Munich. He painted mainly birds and game.

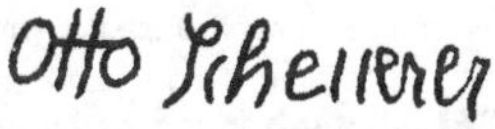

AUCTION RECORDS:
COLOGNE, 14 June 1976, *In the Woods* (oil on card, 8 1/4 x 11 ins / 21 x 27 cm) DEM 1,400. HEIDELBERG, 21 Oct 1977, *The Farmyard* (oil on canvas, 11 1/2 x 13 1/2 ins / 29.5 x 34.5 cm) DEM 3,800. HANOVER, 7 June 1980, *The Farmyard* (oil on card, 12 1/2 x 17 ins / 31.5 x 43 cm) DEM 6,000. LONDON, 30 Jan 1981, *Capercaillie in a Wooded Landscape* (oil on card, 9 x 13 ins / 22.9 x 33 cm) GBP 1,100. LONDON, 22 June 1983, *Farmyard* (oil on panel, 5 x 8 1/4 ins / 12.5 x 21 cm) GBP 1,200. LUCERNE, 7 Nov 1985, *The Love Display of Capercaillies* (oil on canvas, 12 3/4 x 16 ins / 32.5 x 40.5 cm) CHF 8,500. STOCKHOLM, 19 April 1989, *The Farmyard* (oil on panel, 7 x 9 1/2 ins / 18 x 24 cm) SEK 13,000. COLOGNE, 20 Oct 1989, *The Chicken House* (oil on panel, 6 1/4 x 12 1/2 ins / 16 x 32 cm) DEM 1,800. COLOGNE, 23 March 1990, *Peacock and Farmyard Animals in a Meadow* (oil on paper, 8 1/2 x 10 1/2 ins / 21.5 x 26.5 cm) DEM 5,000. NEW YORK, 28 May 1993, *Brood of Ducklings at the Edge of a Pond; Chicks Pecking* (oil on panel, a pair, 4 1/2 x 6 1/4 ins / 11.6 x 15.8 cm) USD 5,750. AMSTERDAM, 21 April

1994, *A Peacock, Chickens and Ducks* (oil on panel, 4 x 5 ins / 10 x 13 cm) NLG 1,840. LONDON, 14 Oct 1999, *Farmyard Chickens* (oil on panel, 7 x 9 ins / 18 x 24 cm) GBP 1,200. COLOGNE, 6 April 2000, *Hens and Roosters. Hens and Roosters before Coop* (oil on cardboard, a pair, 7 x 9 ins / 17 x 22 cm) DEM 4,400. AHLDEN, 20 May 2000, *Landscape with Ducks by a Pond* (oil on canvas, 24 x 31 ins / 60 x 80 cm) DEM 5,000. AHLDEN, 28 Sept 2001, *Poultry Yard* (oil on board, 14 x 18 ins / 35 x 46 cm) DEM 5,500. LONDON, 21 June 2002, *Farmyard Animals* (oil on canvas, 10 x 12 ins / 25 x 31 cm) GBP 1,200. MUNICH, 2 July 2003, *Poultry outside Barn* (oil on board, 10 x 15 ins / 26 x 37 cm) EUR 2,200. COLOGNE, 20 Nov 2003, *Poultry Yard* (oil on board, a pair, 6 x 8 ins / 16 x 21 cm) EUR 1,800. ERLANGEN, 19 June 2004, *Poultry at the Railway Station* (oil on canvas on panel, 20 x 28 ins / 50 x 70 cm) EUR 2,000.

SCHEUERMANN, Carl Georg
Danish, 19th century.
Born 3 November 1803, in Copenhagen; died 5 May 1859, in Copenhagen.
Painter. Landscapes.

Scheuermann was a pupil at the Kunstakademi in Copenhagen. Three of his paintings are in the Johann Hansen collection in Copenhagen.

SCHEUERMANN, Emanuel or Jakob Samuel Johann. See **SCHEURMANN**

SCHEUERMANN, Julia Virginia
German, 20th century.
Born 1 April 1878, in Frankfurt am Main.
Sculptor.

Julia Scheuermann was a pupil of Gustav H. Eberlein.

SCHEUERMANN, Ludwig
German, 19th - 20th century.
Born 18 October 1859, in Burghersdorp; died 1 September 1911, in Herrsching.
Painter, engraver. Landscapes.

Ludwig Scheuermann was a pupil at the academy of fine arts in Munich with Gyulia Benczur, Alexander Straehuber and Ludwig Löffitz, and at the Julian Academy in Paris. He lived in Munich.

AUCTION RECORDS:

SAN FRANCISCO, 4 May 1980, *The Carpet Sellers* (1888, oil on canvas, 39 x 29 1/4 ins / 99 x 74 cm) USD 7,500.

SCHEUERMANN, Viktor
German, 19th - 20th century.
Born c. 1859; died March 1919, in Munich.
Painter.

Viktor Scheuermann was a pupil of the academy of fine arts in Karlsruhe from 1884 to 1892.

SCHEUFEL, Joseph Ignaz, or Schäufel, Scheifel, Scheufele
German, 18th - 19th century.
Born 5 March 1733, in Passau (Bavaria); died 11 May 1812, in Munich.
Medallist.

Scheufel trained with J.K. Hedlinger in Schwyz. He was a medallist at the court in Munich and engraved several portraits, notably those of *Karl Theodor, Elisabeth Augusta, Frobenius* and *Forster*.

SCHEUFELE, Leonhard. See **SCHEIFELIN**

SCHEUFELEIN, Hans Léonard or Leonhard. See **SCHÄUFFELIN**

SCHEUFEN, Walter
German, 20th century.
Born 14 July 1881, in Düsseldorf; died 1917, in Flanders.
Sculptor.

Walter Scheufen was a pupil of Karl Janssen.

AUCTION RECORDS:

BERLIN, 30 May 1991, *Absalom* (1914, bronze, h. 15 3/4 ins / 40 cm) DEM 3,885.

SCHEULT. See **SEHEULT**

SCHEUMANN, Friedrich Philipp
German, 17th century.
Died 27 April 1704, in Oschatz (Saxony).
Sculptor.

Scheumann worked for the town hall.

SCHEUNER, Rudolf
German, 19th century.
Born 20 March 1846, in Wingendorf; died 26 November 1903, in Görlitz.
Watercolourist.

SCHEURECK, Friedrich August
German, 18th century.
Active in Leipzig.
Engraver.

MUSEUMS AND GALLERIES:

LEIPZIG: *View of the City* (several).

SCHEUREN, Caspar Johann Nepomuk
German, 19th century.
Born 22 August 1810, in Aachen; died 12 June 1887, in Düsseldorf.
Painter, watercolourist, engraver, draughtsman. Genre scenes, landscapes, landscapes with figures.

Caspar Scheuren was the son of Johann Peter Scheuren. He trained at the academy in Düsseldorf with Lessing and Schirmer, and was appointed a teacher at the academy in 1855. His engravings notably featured Rhine landscapes.

AUCTION RECORDS:

HAMBURG, 6 June 1969, *Landscape*, DEM 6,000. COLOGNE, 24 Nov 1971, *Family of the Fisherman on the Beach*, DEM 4,400. COLOGNE, 7 June 1972, *Fisherman's Family*, DEM 6,500. MUNICH, 29 May 1976, *Landscape with Mill* (1866, watercolour/pen strokes, 18 1/4 x 24 ins / 46.5 x 60.8 cm) DEM 5,200. COLOGNE, 14 June 1976, *View of Eltz Castle* (oil on canvas, 17 1/4 x 19 1/2 ins / 44 x 49.5 cm) DEM 2,600. VIENNA, 14 March 1978, *Mountainscape* (1844, oil on canvas, 7 3/4 x 9 1/2 ins / 20 x 24 cm) ATS 45,000. COLOGNE, 13 June 1980, *Interior of a Stable* (oil on canvas, 7 x 7 1/4 ins / 17.5 x 18.5 cm) DEM 2,400. LONDON, 22 March 1984, *Hofgarten, Düsseldorf* (1838, watercolour heightened with white, 6 x 8 1/4 ins / 15 x 21 cm) GBP 2,600. LONDON, 23 March 1984, *The Artist with His Pupils in a Boat on the Rhine* (oil on canvas, 9 x 11 3/4 ins / 23 x 30 cm) GBP 10,000. COLOGNE, 20 May 1985, *Landscape with Mill* (oil on canvas, 21 1/2 x 30 3/4 ins / 54.5 x 78 cm) DEM 12,000. STOCKHOLM, 23 April 1986, *Mountainscape* (1849, oil on canvas, 37 x 30 3/4 ins / 94 x 78 cm) SEK 54,000. BRUSSELS, 27 March 1990, *Landscape with Figures* (1839, oil on canvas, 16 1/2 x 22 1/2 ins / 42 x 57 cm) BEF 80,000. LONDON, 15 Feb 1991, *Farm on the Edge of a Lake Surrounded by Trees* (1849, oil on canvas, 10 x 13 1/2 ins / 25.5 x 34 cm) GBP 6,380. MUNICH, 1-2 Dec 1992, *Ruins of a Church* (pencil and watercolour, 5 1/2 x 8 ins / 14 x 20.5 cm) DEM 1,955. BERN, 17 May 1999, *View of Castle by River in Wooded Landscape* (1879, ink and watercolour, 18 x 24 ins / 46 x 60 cm) CHF 5,500. COLOGNE, 28 Oct 1999, *Village with Windmill in Extensive River Landscape* (1844, oil on canvas, 17 x 25 ins / 43 x 64 cm) DEM 30,000. DÜSSELDORF, 26 Feb 2000, *Hauling in the Nets* (1839, oil on canvas, 14 x 19 ins / 36 x 48 cm) DEM 18,000. COLOGNE, 21 Sept 2001, *Pictures of Stolzenfels* (watercolour, pen, Indian ink and brush, album of 50 works, 5 x 8 ins / 12 x 21 cm) DEM 165,000. AHLDEN, 30 Nov 2001, *Lower Rhine Landscape with Approaching Storm* (1846, oil on canvas, 21 x 32 ins / 54 x 81 cm) DEM 10,000. FRANKFURT, 1 June 2002, *Cargo Boat, Fishing Boat and Skiff at the Coast* (oil on canvas, 14 x 20 ins

/ 36 x 52 cm) EUR 3,300. ZURICH, 9 Dec 2002, *Returning to the Monastery* (1867, watercolour and Indian ink, 19 x 25 ins / 49 x 63 cm) CHF 3,000. COLOGNE, 10 April 2003, *Soldiers Sheltering in Tower in Winter Landscape* (1839, oil on canvas, 14 x 11 ins / 36 x 28 cm) EUR 3,000. COLOGNE, 3 July 2003, *Koblenz* (watercolour, 10 x 14 ins / 26 x 35 cm) EUR 3,500. BERN, 17 June 2004, *Salzburg Fortress* (watercolour over bistre pen, 6 x 9 ins / 14 x 24 cm) CHF 4,000.

SCHEUREN, Johann Peter
German, 18th - 19th century.
Born 27 March 1774, in Aachen; died 7 June 1844, in Aachen.
Miniaturist, draughtsman.

Johann Peter Scheuren was the father of Caspar Scheuren. He painted portraits and panoramas of towns and cities.

MUSEUMS AND GALLERIES:
AACHEN (Couven Mus.): *Portrait of Bishop Berdolet.*

SCHEURENBERG, Joseph
German, 19th - 20th century.
Born 7 September 1846, in Düsseldorf; died 4 May 1914, in Berlin.
Painter. History painting, genre scenes.

Joseph Scheurenberg was a pupil of Carl Sohn at the academy in Düsseldorf. In 1868 he worked in Paris. He became a teacher in 1879 at the school of fine arts in Kassel, and in 1891 at the school of fine arts in Berlin. He exhibited at the Royal Academy in London in 1878.

MUSEUMS AND GALLERIES:
BERLIN: *The Day of the Saviour; Professor Zeller; General von Steinmetz; Legend; Country Fair in the 18th Century* - COLOGNE: *Guitar Player in Old-Fashioned Costume.*

AUCTION RECORDS:
LONDON, 4 Feb 1911, *Song of the Old Times* (1869) GBP 22. NEW YORK, 10 Oct 1944, *The Novel,* USD 310. COLOGNE, 21 May 1970, *The Amusing Read,* DEM 2,700. COLOGNE, 13 Oct 1972, *Nymph,* DEM 3,300. NEW YORK, 27 Oct 1982, *Reading* (1878, oil on canvas, 18 1/4 x 12 1/4 ins / 46.6 x 31.1 cm) USD 2,300.

SCHEURER
German, 19th century.
Died 1819.
Painter.

Scheurer was an amateur painter and a lieutenant in Hessen. He died during a duel.

SCHEURER, Franz. See **SCHEYERER**

SCHEURER, Jean
Swiss, 20th century.
Sculptor.

Jean Scheurer created sculptures from Plexiglas, lamps, plastic and cable wire.

MUSEUMS AND GALLERIES:
LAUSANNE (Mus. Cantonal des Beaux Arts): *Aquarium and Filaments III; Multiple.*

SCHEURER, Salomon, or Scheuer, Scheyer, Scheyher
Austrian, 17th century.
Died 2 November 1620.
Painter.

Scheurer was a painter at the court in Graz.

SCHEURICH, Paul
American, 20th century.
Born 24 October 1883, in New York; died 18 November 1945, in Brandenburg.
Painter, engraver, draughtsman, decorative designer. Figures. Designs for ceramics, stage sets.
Jugendstil, Art Deco.

Paul Scheurich studied at the arts academy in Berlin from 1902 to 1904. In 1912, on the recommendation of Max Adolf, he worked for the Schwarzburger Werkstätten für Porzellankunst (Schwarzburg Porcelain Art Studios). In 1913, he worked as a graphic artist for *Simplicissimus,* the satirical magazine, and as an instructor at the Meissen porcelain works and the arts academy in Dresden. In about 1923, he worked on animated films and in the theatre with Max Reinhardt.

Scheurich's highly decorative, almost Neo-Rococo designs were mainly figures which he made for the Schwarzburg, Nymphenburg, Meissen and Karlsruhe porcelain factories. He is known for his figures of dancers, including that of *Vaslav Nijinsky* of Diaghilev's Ballets Russes.

In 1999, Scheurich was included in the exhibition *Traumwelten. Porzellanfiguren zwischen Jugendstil und Art deco (Dreamworlds: German Porcelain Figures from Jugendstil to Art Deco)* held at the Huelsmann Museum, Bielefeld.

BIBLIOGRAPHY:
Rafael, Johannes, *Paul Scheurich 1883-1945: Porzellan für die Meissener Manufaktur,* exhibition catalogue, Staatliche Porzellan-Manufaktur, Meissen, 1995. *Porzellan. Kunst und Design 1889 bis 1939 vom Jugendstil zum Funktionalismus,* exhibition catalogue, Bröhan-Museum, Berlin, 1996.

MUSEUMS AND GALLERIES:
BERLIN (Bröhan-Mus.) - KARLSRUHE (Badisches Landesmus.): two statuettes (1914, porcelain).

SCHEURING, Petra
German, 20th century.
Born 21 May 1942, in Ulm.
Active in France from 1968.
Painter.

Petra Scheuring became known initially in fashion, active first in Germany, then in France, where she lived from 1968. From 1972, she went over entirely to painting after attending courses at various private academies and studios. She has exhibited in Paris and Germany. Her meeting with the painter Christian Zeimert was a determining event in the assertion of her personality. She became aware of her identity and expresses it forcefully in an Expressionist style.

SCHEURITZEL, Anton
German, 19th - 20th century.
Born 23 March 1874, in Quellendorf.
Painter, engraver.

Anton Scheuritzel was a pupil of Wernicke at Dessau, then a painter of theatre scenery there and in Berlin.

SCHEURLE, Paul
German, 20th century.
Born 18 June 1892, in Rechberghausen.
Sculptor.

Paul Scherle lived and worked in Munich.

SCHEURLEER, H.
Dutch, 18th century.
Active in The Hague 1750-1760.
Painter, draughtsman, engraver. Panoramas.

SCHEURMANN, Emanuel, or Scheuermann
Swiss, 19th century.
Born 25 June 1807, in Aarau; died 13 August 1862, in Zurich.
Engraver (burin).

Scheurmann was the son of and worked with Jakob S.J. Scheurmann.

SCHEURMANN, Jakob Samuel Johann, or Scheuermann
Swiss, 18th - 19th century.
Born 20 April 1770, in Bern; died 27 January 1844, in Aarau.

Engraver (burin).

Scheurmann engraved cards and panoramic views of Switzerland.

SCHEUSS, Johannes. See **SCHIESS Johannes**

SCHEUSSLICH. See **SCHENCK Hans**

SCHEUTZ, Andreas and Matthias. See **SCHEITS**

SCHEUTZE, Jost or Joost. See **SCHUTZE**

SCHEUTZLICH, Hans. See **SCHENCK**

SCHEVCHENKO, Alexander
Russian, 20th century.
Born 1883; died 1943.
Painter. Still-lifes.

AUCTION RECORDS:
COPENHAGEN, 21 April 1993, *Still-life* (1931, oil/synthetic resin, 16 1/2 x 18 1/2 ins / 42 x 47 cm) DKK 12,000.

SCHEVE, Sophie von
German, 19th - 20th century.
Born 1869, in Mecklenburg.
Painter. Religious subjects.

Sophie Scheve was a pupil of Karl Franz Edouard von Gebhardt and worked in Munich.

MUSEUMS AND GALLERIES:
SCHWERIN: *St Cecilia*.

SCHEVE-KOSBOTH, Luise von
German, 19th - 20th century.
Born 30 August 1859, in Neisse (now Nysa, Poland).
Painter. Portraits, genre scenes.

Luise von Scheve-Kosboth was a pupil of Wilhelm Durr and Carl von Marr at the academy of fine arts in Munich, where she lived and worked.

SCHEVELINCK, Cornelis Claesz. van. See **SCHEVENINCK**

SCHEVEN, Günther von
German, 20th century.
Born 17 April 1908, in Krefeld.
Sculptor.

Günther von Scheven followed courses in the schools of Berlin. By 1930 he had discovered his own personal style.

SCHEVENHUIZEN, Antoine
Dutch, 17th century.
Active c. 1695.
Engraver (burin).

SCHEVENINCK, Cornelis Claesz. van, or Schevelinck, Schevelinge
Dutch, 16th century.
Active in The Hague 1538-1571.
Painter.

Cornelis Claesz. van Scheveninck was the father of David Cornelisz.

SCHEVILL, William Valentine, or Schwill
American, 19th - 20th century.
Born 2 March 1864, in Cincinnati (Ohio); died 1951.
Painter. Portraits, genre scenes.

William Schevill studied with Nikolaus Gysis, Ludwig Löfftz, Wilhelm von Lindenschmidt and Carl Marr in Munich between 1884 and 1891.

MUSEUMS AND GALLERIES:
INDIANAPOLIS (MA): *Portrait of Prince Henry of Prussia* - LEIPZIG: *Portrait of Alfred Thieme*.

SCHEWEN, Bernhard
German, 19th - 20th century.
Born 1874, in Münster; died 7 May 1907, in Neuss.
Sculptor.

Bernhard Schewen was a pupil at the academy of fine arts in Düsseldorf.

MUSEUMS AND GALLERIES:
STEINHAGEN: war memorial monument.

SCHEWTSCHENKO, Tarass Grigorievitch. See **SHEVTCHENKO Jaras Grigorievich**

SCHEX, Joseph
German, 19th century.
Born 1819, in Wesel; died 13 April 1894, in Düsseldorf.
Painter. History painting, genre scenes.

Wesel town hall houses a work by Schex entitled *The Spaniards being Driven out of Wesel.*

MUSEUMS AND GALLERIES:
BRUNSWICK: *Salvation* - LIVERPOOL: *Cromwell Refusing the Crown.*

SCHEY, Jean
French, 19th century.
Born 23 April 1791, in Paris; died 1843.
Sculptor.

A pupil of Lemot and Regnault, he entered the École des Beaux-Arts on 26 November 1813. He exhibited at the Salons of 1839 and 1840 and won a third-class medal in 1840.

SCHEY, Philip
Flemish School, 17th century.
Active during the first half of the 17th century.
Painter. Scenes with figures.

PHIL: SCHEI:
IN: ET FE:
Ao 1626

MUSEUMS AND GALLERIES:
AMSTERDAM: *Festivities by the Water* (painted on the lid of a spinet).

SCHEYER, Salomon. See **SCHEURER**

SCHEYERER, Franz, or Scheuerer, Scheurer, Scheyrer
Austrian, 18th - 19th century.
Born 1770, in Prague; died 11 June 1839, in Vienna.
Painter. Landscapes.

Scheyerer trained at the academy in Prague.

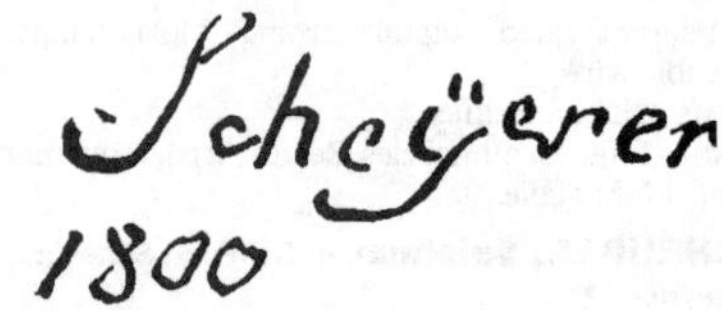

MUSEUMS AND GALLERIES:
PRAGUE (Národní Gal.): *Evening Landscape; Morning Landscape; Italian Landscape* - VIENNA: *View of the Schneeberg.*

AUCTION RECORDS:
NEW YORK, 19 May 1993, *Huge Landscape with Travellers Resting by the Side of the Road; Huge Riverscape with Fishermen on the Bank* (oil on canvas, a pair, each 22 1/2 x 29 ins / 57.1 x 73.7 cm) USD 20,700. NEW YORK, 7 Oct 1993, *Huge Mountainscape with Figures* (oil on canvas, 23 1/2 x 30 1/2 ins / 59.6 x 77.5 cm) USD 6,325. VIENNA, 2 Oct 2002, *Italian Landscape by Moonlight* (1803, oil on canvas, 23 x 29 ins / 58 x 73 cm) EUR 6,500. VIENNA, 2 Oct 2002, *Ruin of Weitenegg Castle*

and Weitenbache, Lower Austria (oil on canvas, 41 x 55 ins / 103 x 140 cm) EUR 28,000.

SCHEYERN, Conrad von. See **CONRAD VON SCHEYERN**

SCHEYFFELIN, Hans Léonard or Leonhard. See **SCHÄUFFELIN**

SCHEYHER, Salomon. See **SCHEURER**

SCHEYNBURG, Pieter
Dutch, 17th century.
Active in Amsterdam.
Painter.
Pieter Scheynburg was the teacher of Jan Tennisz. Blankhof.

SCHEYNDEL, Bernardus van. See **SCHENDEL**

SCHEYNDEL, Gilles or Georg van, or Scheindel, Schendel
Dutch (?), 17th century.
Died c. 1662, in Haarlem.
Painter, draughtsman, engraver. Genre scenes, landscapes, landscapes with figures.
Gilles Scheyndel produced etchings in the style of Callot, featuring charming landscapes with spiritedly drawn figures, and excellent genre scenes.

SCHEYNDEL, Gillis van, or Scheindel, Schendel
Dutch, 17th century.
Born 1635, in Abkoude; died December 1678, in Amsterdam.
Painter, watercolourist, draughtsman. Genre scenes.
Gillis van Scheyndel became a burgher of Amsterdam on 13 June 1676.
AUCTION RECORDS:
PARIS, 22 March 1995, *Travelling Fair on a Village Square* (brown ink and watercolour, 4 x 5 3/4 ins / 10 x 14.5 cm) FRF 6,000.

SCHEYNDEL, J. van. See **SCHENDEL**

SCHEYNMEYTZLER. See **SZEYMECLER**

SCHEYREN, Conrad von. See **CONRAD VON SCHEYERN**

SCHEYRER, Franz. See **SCHEYERER**

SCHEYSLER, Georg
Dutch, 17th century.
Sculptor (wood).

SCHEYTEN
Painter. History painting.
MUSEUMS AND GALLERIES:
YPRES: *The Children of Bethlehem.*

SCHGOER, Julius
German, 19th century.
Born 1847, in Salzburg; died 21 September 1885, in Hallein.
Painter. Genre scenes.
Schgoer was trained by W. von Diez in Munich, where he worked.
AUCTION RECORDS:
LONDON, 4 April 1910, *Return Home,* GBP 9. MUNICH, 30 Nov 1978, *Young Peasant Woman Offering a Cool Drink to a Rider* (oil on panel, 6 1/4 x 10 ins / 16 x 24.5 cm) DEM 3,000. VIENNA, 14 June 2000, *Landscape with Two Women and Horseman* (1890, oil on board, 8 x 12 ins / 20 x 30 cm) ATS 25,000. VIENNA, 24 Nov 2003, *Deer Hunt* (oil on canvas, 39 x 71 ins / 99 x 180 cm) EUR 4,500.

SCHIAFFINO, Antonio
Italian, 20th century.
Born 14 March 1879, in Camogli (Liguria); died 1968.
Painter. Scenes with figures.
Schiaffino was a pupil of Cesare Viazzi and Tullio Quinzio at the academy of fine art in Genoa and of Giuseppe Pennasilico.
MUSEUMS AND GALLERIES:
ROME (Gal. Nazionale d'Arte Moderna): *Children in a Field of Poppies.*

SCHIAFFINO, Bernardo
Italian, 18th century.
Born 1678, in Genoa; died 6 May 1725, in Genoa.
Sculptor.
The brother and master of Francesco Schiaffino, Bernardo was the pupil of Domenico Parodi and the friend of the painters of the Piola family.
MUSEUMS AND GALLERIES:
GENOA: *Bust of the Doge Francesco Brignole Sale* (marble).

SCHIAFFINO, Eduardo
Argentinian, 19th century.
Born in Buenos Aires.
Painter.
Eduardo Schiaffino showed work in exhibitions in Paris and won a bronze medal at the 1889 Exposition Universelle.

SCHIAFFINO, Francesco
Italian, 18th century.
Born 1691, in Genoa; died 3 January 1765.
Sculptor.
The brother and pupil of Bernardo Schiaffino, Francesco inherited his brother's studio, became very famous and received commissions from numerous churches in Liguria and even from Portugal. The Duke of Richelieu, who was in command of the French troops in Genoa in 1747, commissioned a marble bust of himself; it served as a model for the statue in the ducal palace, which was destroyed by fire in 1777. Schiaffino's works also include an *Abduction of Proserpina* in the royal palace in Genoa and two busts at the Palazzo Sopranis.
AUCTION RECORDS:
LONDON, 19 March 1970, *Busts of a Gentleman and His Wife* (two sculptures in marble) Gns 4,200.

SCHIALVINO, Gianfranco
Italian, 20th - 21st century.
Born 1948.
Engraver.
Work by Gianfranco Schialvino was included in the exhibition *Contemporary Relief Engravings* at the Musée du Dessin et l'Estampe Originale in Gravelines in 1987.

SCHIAMINOSSI, Raffaello, or Scaminossi, Scaminozzi, Sciaminossi
Italian, 16th - 17th century.
Born c. 1529; died 1622.
Active in Borgo San Sepolcro (Arezzo).
Painter, engraver (burin).
A pupil of Raffaello dal Colle, Raffaello Schiaminossi's technique as an engraver is skilled, if his drawing leaves something to be desired. He made engravings of religious subjects, historical scenes and allegories.

SCHIANCHI, Federico
Italian, 19th - 20th century.
Born 1858, in Modena; died 1919, in Rome.
Painter, watercolourist. Urban landscapes, architectural views.
Federico Schianchi specialised in painting picturesque views of Rome.

AUCTION RECORDS:
ROME, 14 Dec 1988, *Fountain at the Villa Medici* (distemper/paper, 13 x 20 1/2 ins / 33 x 52 cm) ITL 3,000,000. ROME, 31 May 1990, *Pontine Marshes* (watercolour/paper, 12 3/4 x 20 1/4 ins / 32.2 x 51.5 cm) ITL 3,000,000. ROME, 10 Dec 1991, *Tiber below Castel Sant'Angelo* (oil on panel, 7 1/4 x 9 3/4 ins / 18.5 x 25 cm) ITL 3,000,000; *Roman Forum and Via della Consolazione* (oil on canvas, 29 1/4 x 38 3/4 ins / 74 x 98.5 cm) ITL 20,000,000. ROME, 26 May 1993, *Castel Sant'Angelo* (oil on panel, 7 1/2 x 15 1/4 ins / 19 x 39 cm) ITL 3,000,000. ROME, 13 Dec 1995, *St Peter; Fountain at the Villa Medici* (watercolour/paper, 11 3/4 x 6 ins / 30 x 15 cm and 6 3/4 x 14 ins/17 x 35.5 cm) ITL 3,450,000. ROME, 4 June 1996, *View of Rome* (watercolour/paper, 10 1/4 x 29 1/2 ins / 26 x 75 cm) ITL 3,450,000. LONDON, 17 July 2001, *Forum, Rome. Castel Sant'Angelo* (watercolour, a pair, 6 x 11 ins / 14 x 29 cm) GBP 1,100. FORMIGINE, 30 March 2003, *Bay of Naples* (watercolour, 14 x 21 ins / 35 x 54 cm) EUR 2,000. ROME, 24 June 2003, *The Appia* (watercolour, 13 x 21 ins / 34 x 53 cm) EUR 1,600. ROME, 10 June 2004, *View of the Colosseum* (watercolour on card, 14 x 21 ins / 35 x 54 cm) EUR 2,000.

SCHIANION, Raphaël, or Schianon
Painter.
Schianion is mentioned in Ris-Paquot.

SCHIANO, Evangelista, or Schiani
Italian, 18th century.
Active in Naples.
Painter.

SCHIANO, Salvatore
Italian, 18th century.
Active in Naples.
Painter.
Salvatore Schiano worked at the porcelain factory in Naples from 1773 to 1803, painting landscapes, flowers and figures in national costume.

SCHIANTESCHI, Domenico
Italian, 18th century.
Active in Borgo San Sepolcro.
Painter. Architectural views.
Domenico Schianteschi was the pupil of Bibiena. He painted decorative perspectival views for various palaces in Borgo San Sepolcro.

SCHIAPAPIETRA, Sebastião Clemente
Portuguese, 18th - 19th century.
Active in Lisbon at the end of the 18th century and the beginning of the 19th century.
Painter.
From 1763 to 1784 Sebastião Clemente Schiapapietra was a pupil of J. F. del Cusco and J. Pillement.

SCHIASSI, Antonio
Italian, 18th century.
Born 1722, in Bologna; died 26 March 1777, in Bologna.
Sculptor.
Antonio Schiassi was the pupil of Angelo Mazza, D. Pio and F. Monti. He devoted himself primarily to the reproduction of religious figures and scenes.

SCHIASSI, Antonio
Italian, 19th century.
Born 1807, in Faenza; died 28 February 1877, in Rome.
Engraver (burin).
A pupil of P. Toschi, Antonio Schiassi was appointed professor at the Accademia di Belle Arti in Florence in 1873. His works include: *Scene from the Beatification of Pope Eugene III; Portrait of Queen Maria Cristina of Naples; The School of Athens* and other works by Raphael.

SCHIATESSI, Antonio. See **GENTILESCHI Artemisia**

SCHIATTINO, Gerolamo
Italian, 19th century.
Born in Santa Margherita (Liguria); died 2 December 1875, in Florence.
Painter.
Gerolamo Schiattino studied at the academy in Genoa and with Bezzuoli.

SCHIAVETTA, Beppe
Italian, 20th - 21st century.
Born 1949, in Savona.
Painter.
In 1993 at the Salon Découvertes in Paris, Beppe Schiavetta exhibited work shown by the Orti Sauli gallery of Genoa. He creates a poetic universe, enhanced by signs and scratch-marks.

SCHIAVI, Elena
French, 20th century.
Painter.
A strictly figurative artist, Elena Schiavi depicted in encaustic small versions of the objects usually found in still-lifes. They stand out against dark backgrounds in the Pompeian style.

BIBLIOGRAPHY:
Courthion, Pierre, *Art indépendant*, Albin Michel, Paris, 1958.

SCHIAVI, Giuseppe Antonio
Italian, 18th century.
Born 1686; died after 1758.
Active in Verona.
Sculptor.
Giuseppe Schiavi was the son of the architect Prospero Schiavi. He was the father of the painter Prospero Schiavi and the architect Francesco Schiavi. The pupil of A. Marchesini and D. Negri, he is known for the statues in the Palazzo Canossa in Verona.

SCHIAVI, Prospero
Italian, 18th century.
Born 1730; died 11 May 1803.
Active in Verona.
Painter.
Prospero Schiavi was the son of Giuseppe Antonio Schiavi and the pupil of Giambattista Cignaroli. He mostly painted saints for churches in Verona.

SCHIAVO, Marco. See the entry **SCHIAVO Paolo**

SCHIAVO, Paolo, also known as Paolo di Stefano Badaloni
Italian, 15th century.
Born 1397, in Florence; died 1478, in Pisa.
Painter. History painting.
Paolo Schiavo lived in Pisa for many years. According to Vasari, he was much influenced by Masolino, whose pupil he is said to have been. Later he studied with Castagno. His son Marco was also a painter.

MUSEUMS AND GALLERIES:
ALTENBURG: *Mystic Marriage of St Catherine* - BERLIN: *Assumption of the Virgin; Last Judgement* (miniature) - BONN: *St Jerome and St Lawrence* - CAMBRIDGE (Fitzwilliam Mus.): *The Virgin of Humility* (c. 1440, tempera with gold/panel, tabernacle) - COLOGNE (Wallraf-Richartz Mus.): *Madonna* - PISA: *Raising of Lazarus*.

AUCTION RECORDS:
PARIS, 31 May 1988, *Achilles and Polyxena* (tempera/panel, 17¾ x 14½ ins / 45 x 37 cm) FRF 120,000. NEW YORK, 21 May 1992, *Reclining Venus Offering a Garland of Flowers to a Cherub in a Landscape with a River* (tempera/panel, panel from a chest, 20 x 67 ins / 50.8 x 170.2 cm) USD 77,000. LONDON, 22 April 1994, *Virgin and Child Enthroned with St Anthony and St Francis* (tempera/panel with gold background, pointed top, 40¼ x 22¼ ins / 102.5 x 56.5 cm) GBP 36,700.

SCHIAVO, Vincenzo
Italian, 20th century.
Born 19 July 1888, in Gorla di Velezo (Lombardy).
Painter. Landscapes.
Vincenzo Schiavo was a pupil of Baldassare Longoni.

SCHIAVOCAMPO, Paolo
Italian, 20th century.
Born 1924.
Painter.
AUCTION RECORDS:
MILAN, 19 June 1991, *Black Factory* (1958, oil on canvas, 27½ x 39¼ ins / 70 x 100 cm) ITL 1,800,000.

SCHIAVON, Vittorio
Dutch, 20th century.
Born c. 1900.
Painter. Landscapes.
AUCTION RECORDS:
AMSTERDAM, 11 April 1995, *View of Prinsengracht with the Westerkerk* (oil on canvas, 74½ x 37½ ins / 189 x 95 cm) NLG 2,832.

SCHIAVONE, Battista. See **BATTISTA DA SAN DANIELE**

SCHIAVONE, Giacomo di Giorgio
Italian, 15th century.
Sculptor.

SCHIAVONE, Giorgio Chiulinovitch or Chiulinovic, also known as Giorgio di Tomaso
Croat, 15th century.
Born 1434, in Scardone (Dalmatia), at the end of 1436 according to some sources, at the beginning of 1437 according to others; died 6 December 1504, in Sebenico (now Sibenik, Croatia).
Painter.
Little is known about the training received by Giorgio Chiulinovitch Schiavone although his early *Madonnas* show the influence of Filippo Lippi. He started working in the studio of Squarcione in Padua and was to retain the rather unusual aspect of his master's work in his complex paintings such as the two works depicting the *Virgin and Child* in Turin and London. In 1462, he was in Zara (now Zadar, Croatia) and then in Sebenico.

Schiavone's style is complex and this is accentuated by elaborate surrounds of coloured marbles, cameos and foliage.

MUSEUMS AND GALLERIES:
LONDON (NG): *The Virgin and Child* (c. 1456-1460, tempera/wood); *The Virgin and Child enthroned* (central panel); *Saints Bernardino, Anthony of Padua, Peter Martyr and John the Baptist* (from left to right); *Pietà* (upper part, central panel); *Saints Jerome, Catherine, Sebastian and a female saint* (upper part, from left to right); polyptych of the Virgin and Child Surrounded by Saints (1458-1460, tempera/wood) - TURIN: *Virgin and Child.*
AUCTION RECORDS:
NEW YORK, Jan 1998, *Imago Pietatis* (tempera/panel, 23¼ x 14 ins / 59.1 x 35.6 cm) USD 118,000.

SCHIAVONE, Giovanni. See **CARSO Giovanni dal**

SCHIAVONE, Luca. See **LUCA SCHIAVONE**

SCHIAVONE, Michele or Michelangelo
Italian, 18th century.
Active in Dalmatia.
Painter, engraver (burin).

SCHIAVONE, Niccolo. See **NICCOLO DE BARI**

SCHIAVONE, Sebastiano (Fra), also known as Fra Bastiano da Silena or Fra Bastian Virgola, called Sebastiano da Rovigno, or Zoppo
Italian, 15th century.
Born c. 1420, in Rovigno (Istria); died 11 September 1505, in Venice.
Engraver (wood).
Sebastiano Schiavone spent time in many different monasteries. He carved town views on the choir stalls in the monastery of S Elena.

SCHIAVONE, IL, pseudonym of Meldolla or Medulla Andrea
Croat, 16th century.
Born 1522, in Sibenik (Dalmatia); died 1 December 1563 or 1582, in Venice.
Painter, engraver, draughtsman. Religious subjects, mythological subjects, portraits, landscapes.
Venetian School.
Andrea Schiavone was an important member of the school of Giorgione and Titian, whose work he greatly admired. Their influence is clear in his earlier works. Later he was to adopt the elegant and rather insipid forms of Parmigiano, who was probably his master. Although Schiavone lived obscurely and received few commissions, Titan thought enough of his work to arrange for the painting of the Biblioteca San Marco in Venice to be entrusted to him.

Schiavone generally chose profane subjects but also produced a number of important religious works. His paintings merit close attention, for they were often attributed to more important painters of the Venetian School. They are never banal and his style is full of unaffected elegance. The paint is applied with great freedom, with fine use of colour and transparency of tone.

Schiavone lived a life of poverty, shabbily dressed and only visiting those artists who gave him work or the dealers who paid him tiny sums to paint coffers, chests and boxes. He was extremely modest, thinking little of his talents. Like many artists of the time, he painted many external frescoes, now lost. To his numerous paintings can be added his engravings, of which Bartsch has identified 134. Despite a productive life, he died at the age of 60 leaving no money to pay for his burial.
MUSEUMS AND GALLERIES:
BERLIN (Bodemus.): *Wooded Landscape with Fabulous Beings; Wooded Landscape with Diana and Hunting Scenes; Parables* - BERLIN (Palace): *Christ at Emmaus* - BUDAPEST: *Christ on the Road to Golgotha* - CHAMBÉRY (MBA): *Neptune and Amphitrite* - CHATSWORTH: *Venus and Cupid* - DRESDEN: *Pietà; Madonna and Child with Saints; Self-portrait* - DUBLIN: *Two Mythological Scenes* - FLORENCE (Palazzo Pitti): *Samson Slaying a Philistine, or Death of Abel; Portrait of a Man; Portrait of a Man in a Franciscan Habit* - FLORENCE (Uffizi): *Adoration of*

the Shepherds - GENOA: *David Slaying Goliath* - GENOA (Palazzo Reale): *Birth of a King* - GLASGOW: *Salome with the Head of St John the Baptist* - KARLOVY VARY: *Three Fragments from an Entombment* - KASSEL: *Psyche* - LILLE: *Lapidation of St Stephen* - LONDON (Bridgewater Gal.): *Mystic Marriage of St Catherine* - LONDON (NG): *Two Mythological Figures* (1548-1550, oil on canvas); *A Mythological Figure* (1548-1550, oil on canvas, formerly Apollo Slaying the Python, attributed) - LONDON (Royal Collection): *The Holy Family with Sts John and Catherine; The Judgement of Midas; The Blessing of Jacob; The Meeting of Jacob and Rachel; The Meeting of Jacob and Esau; The Departure of Briseis; Christ before Pilate; The Adoration of the Kings; Figures in a Landscape* (three paintings) - MILAN: *Allegory of Faith* - NAPLES: *Christ before Herod* - PARIS (Louvre): *Holy Family; Head and Shoulders of St John the Baptist* - PHILADELPHIA (MA, Johnson Collection): *Shepherd with his Flock* - SIBIU: *Mystic Marriage of St Catherine* - ST PETERSBURG (Hermitage): *Jupiter and Io* - STUTTGART: *Venus and Anchises; Aeneus and Dido* - TURIN: *Greek Sacrifices in Aulis; Judgement of Paris; Capture of Troy; Rape of Helen* - VENICE (Biblioteca Marciana): *Three Oval Paintings from the Ceiling of the Great Hall and Portraits of Philosophers* - VENICE (Gal. dell'Accademia): *Presentation in the Temple; Christ before Pilate; Deucalion and Pyrrha; Judgement of Midas; Psyche* - VERONA: *Judgement of Solomon; A Hero Making a Prayer of Thanksgiving after his Victory over the Enemy; The Ark of the Covenant; Belshazzar's Feast; Drunkeness of Noah* - VICENZA: *Madonna and Child* - VIENNA (Kunsthistorisches Mus.): *Christ before Pilate; Portrait of a Man; Curius Dentatus; Holy Family with St Catherine and St John; Birth of Jupiter; Jupiter Captured by Amaltheus; Scipio Africanus; Alexander the Great and the Family of Darius; Apollo and Daphne; Apollo and Cupid; Adoration of the Shepherds; Tobias and the Angel; Kneeling Woman with Boys; Apparition of St Mark; Count Paul Esterhazy; Narcissus; Ernst Schwarz; Rape of a Group of Women.*

AUCTION RECORDS:

PARIS, 13 Dec 1954, *Boar Hunt* (pen) FRF 53,000. LONDON, 27 June 1958, *Marriage of Cupid and Psyche,* GBP 4,725. LONDON, 3 July 1963, *Ecce Homo,* GBP 900. LONDON, 28 May 1965, *Venus and Adonis,* Gns 1,800. PRATOLINO, 21 April 1969, *Prisoners,* ITL 4,800,000. LONDON, 28 April 1976, *Mystic Marriage of St Catherine with Doge Francesco Donati* (pen and wash, 10 3/4 x 12 1/2 ins / 27.2 x 31.7 cm) GBP 25,000. LONDON, 8 Dec 1976, *Infant Bacchus among the Nymphs* (oil on canvas, 24 1/4 x 38 1/2 ins / 61.5 x 98 cm) GBP 9,000. MILAN, 27 May 1980, *Prophets and Sibyls* (black chalk and red chalk, 7 1/4 x 10 ins / 18.5 x 25.4 cm) ITL 1,800,000. LONDON, 10 April 1981, *Diana the Huntress* (oil on panel, 13 x 50 1/4 ins / 33 x 127.5 cm) GBP 6,500. PARIS, 27 April 1984, *Study of a Seated Man* (1560, black chalk and red chalk heightened with white chalk, 8 1/4 x 11 ins / 21 x 27 cm) FRF 32,000. LONDON, 5 Dec 1985, *Minerva and the Muses* (etching, 9 1/4 x 7 ins / 23.2 x 16.9 cm) GBP 3,800. NEW YORK, 27 March 1987, *Battle between Centaurs and Lapiths* (oil on canvas, 12 x 22 ins / 30.5 x 56 cm) USD 15,000. ROME, 23 May 1989, *Christ Presented to the People* (oil on canvas, 38 3/4 x 45 1/4 ins / 98.5 x 115 cm) ITL 27,000,000. NEW YORK, 1 June 1989, *Christ in the house of Jairus* (oil on canvas, 42 1/4 x 69 ins / 107.5 x 175.3 cm) USD 55,000. NEW YORK, 11 Jan 1990, *Battle of Centaurs and Lapiths* (oil on canvas, 12 x 22 ins / 30.5 x 56 cm) USD 18,700. LONDON, 2 July 1990, *Mystic Marriage of St Catherine with St Francis, St Mark and a Doge, probably Francesco Donato* (ink and wash heightened with white, 10 3/4 x 12 1/2 ins / 27.2 x 31.7 cm) GBP 110,000. LONDON, 1 April 1992, *Virgin and Child with St John and St Anne* (oil on canvas, 38 1/2 x 44 ins / 97.5 x 111.5 cm) GBP 18,150. NEW YORK, 20 May 1993, *Perseus Rescuing Andromeda* (oil and tempera/panel, 11 x 19 1/2 ins / 27.9 x 49.5 cm) USD 23,000. MILAN, 2 Dec 1993, *Shipwreck* (oil on panel, 11 1/4 x 50 ins / 28.5 x 127 cm) ITL 27,600,000. NEW YORK, 7 Oct 1994, *Peace Personified as a Woman* (oil on canvas, 9 1/4 x 5 3/4 ins / 23.5 x 14.9 cm) USD 5,175. LONDON, 3-4 Dec 1997, *Nymphs in a Landscape* (oil on panel, 10 x 46 1/2 ins / 25.1 x 118.1 cm) GBP 19,550.

SCHIAVONETTI, Luigi or Lewis

Italian, 18th - 19th century.
Born 1 April 1765, in Bassano; died 7 June 1810, in London.
Draughtsman, engraver (etching/stippling). Historical subjects.

Luigi Schiavonetti was the son of a bookseller. He showed an inclination towards drawing from an early age, studying first with Giulio Golini. At the age of 16 he began studying engraving. He went to London and entered Bartolozzi's studio as a pupil, assisting him in the execution of a number of works. At that time, the works of Bartolozzi were extremely popular, and Schiavonetti imitated some of these. He eventually became established in his own right in the English capital and enjoyed considerable success. His numerous plates include two in the series *Cries of London* by Francis Wheatley and four portraying Louis XVI during the Revolution, copied from drawings by Benazech.

AUCTION RECORDS:

LONDON, 13 Nov 1997, *Parting of Louis XVI from his Family; Final Meeting between Louis XVI and his Inconsolable Family; Calm and Composure of Louis XVI Leaving his Confessor, Edgeworth; Memorable Speech by Louis XVI at the Bar of the National Convention; The Dauphin Taken from his Mother; Royal Family of France; Louis XVI Bidding his Inconsolable Family Farewell; Robespierre, Marat and Others* (1793, 1794, 1795 and 1796, dry-point engraving, series of 18 works) GBP 3,450.

SCHIAVONETTI, Nicoló

Italian, 19th century.
Born in Bassano (Veneto); died 1813, in London.
Engraver.

The younger brother of Luigi Schiavonetti, Nicoló Schiavonetti was his collaborator and imitator. He produced a number of works in his own right, mainly religious subjects, portraits and historical scenes. He engraved a plate of the *London Cries* after Wheatley.

SCHIAVONI, Felice

Italian, 19th century.
Born 19 March 1803, in Trieste; died 30 January 1881, in Venice.
Painter. Religious subjects, mythological subjects, portraits, genre scenes.

The pupil of his father Natale Schiavoni, Felice Schiavoni went with him to Vienna and Milan. He was in Venice in 1821.

MUSEUMS AND GALLERIES:

MILAN (Pinacoteca di Brera): *Cupid* - PADUA: *Portrait* (three works) - TRIESTE (Civico Mus. Revoltella): *Child.*

AUCTION RECORDS:

NEW YORK, 11 Dec 1930, *Virgin and Child with the Infant St John,* USD 700. LONDON, 24 Nov 1976, *Portrait of a Russian Princess* (1841, oil on canvas, 41 x 37 ins / 104 x 94 cm) GBP 1,500. MILAN, 1 June 1988, *Portrait of a Young Woman in Oriental Costume* (oil on canvas, 32 x 26 ins / 81 x 66 cm) ITL 9,000,000. AMSTERDAM, 2 May 1990, *After the Carnival* (oil on canvas, 18 1/2 x 15 1/4 ins / 47 x 38.5 cm) NLG 4,370. MILAN, 18 Oct 1995, *Venus and Cupid* (1831, oil on canvas, 78 x 59 ins / 198 x 150 cm) ITL 104,650,000.

SCHIAVONI, Giovanni

Italian, 19th century.
Born July 1804, in Trieste; died 7 September 1848, in Venice.
Painter, miniaturist, engraver (burin).

Giovanni Schiavoni was the son of Natale and brother of Felice Schiavoni. He worked in Hungary, Iasi (Romania), Odessa, St Petersburg and Venice. He painted in oils and executed frescoes.

Museums and Galleries:

Eger (Cathedral): *Dying Christ* - Verona (Church of S Luca Evangelista): *St Luke; St Sylvester.*

Auction records:

London, 16 Feb 1979, *View of Venice* (oil on canvas, 18 x 24¼ ins / 45.7 x 61.6 cm) GBP 1,200. Vienna, 27 March 2003, *Sleeping Child* (1843, oil on canvas, 31 x 40 ins / 80 x 101 cm) EUR 10,000.

SCHIAVONI, Natale

Italian, 19th century.

Born 25 April 1777, in Chioggia (Veneto); died 16 April 1858, in Venice.

Painter, engraver. History painting, portraits.

Natale Schiavoni studied engraving in Florence with Raphael Morghen. In 1797, he went to Venice to work under Maggioto. He seems to have started out as a painter of miniatures. His first important work is a *St Francis* painted for the church of S Francesco in Chioggia. Between 1802 and 1816, he lived in Trieste. Amongst other works produced at this time, he painted the portraits of the Emperor and Empress of Austria. In 1825 he moved to Milan, where he painted an important altarpiece for the church of S Antonio in 1841. In 1840, he was appointed professor at the Accademia di Belle Arti in Venice.

He enjoyed a considerable reputation as an engraver, and executed some fine reproductions of works of Titian.

Museums and Galleries:

Brescia: *Venus* - Frankfurt am Main: *Bacchante* - Milan (Ambrosiana): *Ronchetti* - Milan (Gal. d'Arte Moderna): *Melancholy* - Trieste: *Sadness; Jealousy; Sleep; Odalisque* - Turin: *Portrait of a Man* - Vienna: *Mary Magdalene.*

Auction records:

Paris, 1 June 1931, *Woman Asleep,* FRF 1,900. Paris, 5 May 1949, *Odalisque Reclining* (1842) FRF 8,000. Milan, 18 May 1971, *Portrait of a woman,* ITL 1,200,000. Lindau, 8 Oct 1980, *Odalisque* (oil on canvas, 31 x 24¾ ins / 78.5 x 63 cm) DEM 8,800. Milan, 21 April 1986, *Venus and Cupid* (oil on canvas, 30 x 24½ ins / 76 x 62 cm) ITL 6,000,000. Rome, 22 March 1988, *Woman Bathing* (oil on canvas) ITL 3,000,000. Monaco, 6 Dec 1991, *Venus with a Looking Glass* (1843, oil on canvas, 46 x 59½ ins / 117 x 151 cm) FRF 122,100. New York, 29 Oct 1992, *Shepherds and Baby Jesus* (oil on canvas, 150 x 111 ins / 381 x 281.9 cm) USD 28,600. Milan, 8 June 1995, *Adam and Eve* (oil on canvas, 32¼ x 41¼ ins / 82 x 105 cm) ITL 14,950,000. London, 31 Oct 1996, *Mary Magdalene* (1854, oil on canvas, 41¾ x 35 ins / 106 x 89 cm) GBP 3,450. Neuilly, 23 Oct 1999, *Melancholy Young Woman* (oil on canvas, 35 x 27 ins / 88 x 69 cm) FRF 27,000. Lindau, 3 Dec 1999, *Madonna with Sleeping Infant Jesus* (oil on canvas, 26 x 21 ins / 66 x 53 cm) DEM 12,000. Venice, 14 Dec 2000, *Portrait of Young Woman* (oil on canvas, 24 x 20 ins / 62 x 50 cm) ITL 4,400,000. London, 19 April 2001, *Lost in Thought* (oil on canvas laid on panel, 14 x 12 ins / 35 x 31 cm) GBP 2,000. Bern, 1 May 2002, *Portrait of Oriental Woman* (1842, oil on canvas, 32 x 25 ins / 82 x 64 cm) CHF 13,000. Detroit, 11 April 2003, *Girl Playing Lute* (oil on canvas, 32 x 26 ins / 81 x 66 cm) USD 6,000. Stuttgart, 11 Dec 2003, *Holy Family Resting on the Flight into Egypt* (oil on canvas, 20 x 24 ins / 51 x 61 cm) EUR 5,500.

SCHIBIG, Philippe

Swiss, 20th century.

Born 1940.

Draughtsman, collage artist.

Museums and Galleries:

Aarau (Aargauer Kunsthaus): *For L.* (ball-point pen).

Auction records:

Lucerne, 24 Nov 1990, *Composition* (1983, ball-point pen, colouring pencil and collage/paper, 15¾ x 11¾ ins / 40 x 30 cm) CHF 5,500. Lucerne, 25 May 1991, *Untitled* (1969, ball-point pen/paper, 5½ x 6¾ ins / 14 x 17 cm) CHF 900. Lucerne, 15 May 1993, *Landscape in a Box of Sand* (1979, ball-point pen, colouring pencil and tempera/paper, 12 x 10 ins / 30.5 x 24.5 cm) CHF 2,400. Lucerne, 20 May 1995, *Engelberg* (1993, mixed media and collage/paper, 19¾ x 27½ ins / 50 x 70 cm) CHF 8,000. Lucerne, 22 Nov 2003, *Termite City* (1980, mixed media collage, 15 x 12 ins / 39 x 30 cm) CHF 2,600.

SCHIBIZ, Mathias or Matyis.
See **SCHERVITZ**

SCHIBLI, Joseph

Swiss, 20th century.

Born 1925, in Lachen.

Active from 1948 in Sweden.

Painter, engraver.

Joseph Schibli lived and worked at Norrköping. He took part in 1992 in the exhibition *De Bonnard à Baselitz - Dix ans d'enrichissements du cabinet des estampes 1978-1988* (*From Bonnard to Baselitz: A Decade of Acquisitions by the Prints Collection 1978-1988*) at the Bibliothèque Nationale in Paris.

Museums and Galleries:

Paris (BNF): (etching and aquatint).

SCHICHE, Martin

Austrian, 14th century.

Active in Augsburg.

Sculptor, architect.

Martin Schiche worked on the choir of Augsburg Cathedral before moving to Bozen (now Bolzano, Italy).

SCHICHINSKY, Leonid

Ukrainian, 20th century.

Born 3 January 1896, in Kiev.

Painter, draughtsman.

Leonid Schichinski was a student between 1912 and 1918 in the faculty of art and architecture in Kiev, and then from 1919 to 1922 at the academy of art in Kiev. From 1922 to 1926, he studied at the academy of art in Leningrad, in the studio of Mitrochin and Konachevitch. Work by him was exhibited in 1950 in Leningrad, and in Prague and Brno in 1957, 1958 and 1959. In 1962, he came to Paris for a study trip. Schichinski's painting is realist and inspired by popular Russian tales. From 1928, he also produced illustrations.

SCHICHKO, Sergeï

Russian, 20th century.

Born 1911.

Painter. Still-lifes, flowers.

Auction records:

Paris, 23 Nov 1990, *Vase of Flowers and White Cup* (1988, oil on canvas, 25½ x 29½ ins / 65 x 75 cm) FRF 21,000. Paris, 25 March 1991, *Vase of Roses* (1979, oil on canvas, 23¾ x 25 ins / 60.5 x 63.5 cm) FRF 32,000.

SCHICHTI, Xaver August

German, 19th - 20th century.

Born 20 April 1849, in Munich; died 22 October 1925, in Hanover.

Sculptor.

Xaver August Schichti sculpted figures, mainly dolls.

SCHICHTMEYER, Johannes

German, 19th - 20th century.

Born 2 May 1861, in Danzig (now Gdansk, Poland).

Sculptor.

Johannes Schichtmeyer was a pupil of Fritz Schaper. He exhibited in Paris, notably in 1900 at the Exposition Universelle where he received an honourable mention.

SCHICK, Gottlieb Christian
German, 19th century.
Born 15 August 1776, in Stuttgart; died 11 April 1812, in Stuttgart.
Painter. History painting, portraits, landscapes with figures, landscapes.

Schick was trained by Philipp Friedrich Hetsch, then by Dannecker at the school of fine art in Stuttgart. He continued his training in Jacques-Louis David's studio in Paris from 1798 onwards. In 1802, he returned to Stuttgart, but left again for Rome in the same year. In 1811, he returned to Germany an ill man and died soon afterwards. He was one of the founders of the German Modern School, and produced some notably outstanding portraits, which revealed both the influence of the classics and the Nazarenes. He occasionally introduced mythological figures into his landscapes.

MUSEUMS AND GALLERIES:
BERLIN (Nationalgal.): *Portrait of Heinrike Dennecker* - COLOGNE (Wallraf-Richartz Mus.): *Eve and the Serpent* - MAGDEBURG (Kulturhistorisches Mus.): *Narziss* - MANNHEIM: *Birth of the Red Rose* - STUTTGART (Staatsgal.): *David spielt vor Saul* (1803); *Noah's Sacrifice*; *Apollo among Shepherds*; *Bacchus and Ariadne*; *Portraits of Dannecker and His Wife*.

AUCTION RECORDS:
BERLIN, 5 Nov 1970, *Portrait of a Lady of Quality*, DEM 9,500. MUNICH, 29 Nov 1984, *Noah Thanking the Heavens* (c. 1804, pen/pencil outlines, 16¼ x 20¼ ins / 41 x 51.5 cm) DEM 5,200. NEW YORK, 3 May 2000, *Allegory of the Divine Beauty of Nature* (oil on canvas, 50 x 67 ins / 127 x 170 cm) USD 120,000. BATH, 2 Dec 2002, *Rhineland Landscape* (oil on panel, 8 x 11 ins / 20 x 29 cm) GBP 1,100.

SCHICK, Jakob
German, 15th - 16th century.
Active in Kempten at the end of the 15th and the beginning of the 16th century.
Painter.

Jakob Schick carved altars.

MUSEUMS AND GALLERIES:
AUGSBURG (Maximilianmus.): altar - MUNICH (Bayerisches Nationalmus.): altar.

AUCTION RECORDS:
BERLIN, 20 Sept 1930, *Mary and the Child*; *St Anthony*; *St Augustine* (triptych) DEM 4,100.

SCHICK, Karl Friedrich
German, 19th century.
Born 17 April 1826, in Hilgertsau; died 26 June 1875, in Tretenhof.
Painter. History painting.

Schick trained at the academies in Dresden and Düsseldorf.

MUSEUMS AND GALLERIES:
DRESDEN: *Suzanne Bathing* - KARLSRUHE: *Dead Child*.

SCHICK, Pieter, or Schik
German, 17th century.
Painter. Portraits.

Schick painted the double portrait of a brother and sister in the style of Nicolas Maes.

SCHICK, Rudolf
German, 19th century.
Born 8 August 1840, in Berlin; died 26 February 1887, in Berlin.
Painter. Portraits, genre scenes, landscapes.

Rudolf Schick was trained by Schirmer in Berlin, then went to Rome to improve. On his return to Germany, he took part in many exhibitions.

MUSEUMS AND GALLERIES:
BERLIN: *Near Schlanders in the Tyrol*; *Amalfi*; *Mountain Road*; studies - COLOGNE: study - SIBIU: *Young Girl from Villanders*; *Peasant from Carrara*.

SCHICK, Seraphia Maria Susanna Magdalena von. See **LÖWENFINCK**

SCHICK, Thomas
German, 16th century.
Active in Kirkheim 1513-1544.
Painter. Religious subjects.

Thomas Schick married the daughter of the goldsmith Heinrich Zobel in Basel. He painted a *Last Judgement* in the parish church of Weilheim and worked with Teck in Kirkheim.

SCHICKARD, Hans, or Schickhardt
German, 16th century.
Born 1512, in Herrenberg; died 17 October 1585, in Tübingen.
Painter.

SCHICKART
Austrian, 17th century.
Active in Bamberg (Bavaria), Germany.
Cabinet maker.

SCHICKDANZ, Albert
Hungarian, 19th - 20th century.
Born 14 October 1846, in Biala, Galicia (now in Poland); died 11 July 1915, in Budapest.
Painter.

Albert Schickdanz worked initially at the architecture school in Karlsruhe, then went to Vienna and Budapest. From 1880 to 1902, he was professor at the fine arts school in Budapest.

MUSEUMS AND GALLERIES:
BUDAPEST.

SCHICKER, Christian Gottfried Emanuel
German, 19th century.
Active in Meissen c. 1811.
Painter (porcelain).

SCHICKH, Frans, or Schikh
Austrian, 18th century.
Active in Vienna between 1721 and 1740.
Sculptor.

SCHICKH, Georg
German, 17th century.
Active in Krum.
Sculptor.

SCHICKHARDT, Heinrich, the Elder
German, 15th - 16th century.
Born 1464, in Siegen; died 23 August 1540, in Herrenberg.
Sculptor (wood).

Heinrich Schickhardt the Elder carved the choir stalls of the church of Herrenberg. It is uncertain whether or not he was responsible for the monument of Henri de Montbéliard that is in the gilded room of Urach Castle.

SCHICKHARDT, Karl
German, 19th - 20th century.
Born 7 July 1866, in Esslingen; died February 1933, in Stuttgart.
Painter. Landscapes.

Karl Schickhardt was a pupil of Jakob Grünenwald and of Albert Kappis at the school of fine arts in Stuttgart.

MUSEUMS AND GALLERIES:
STUTTGART: *Laucher Valley, Evening*.

SCHICKHARDT, Lucas, the Elder
German, 16th century.
Born 1511, in Herrenberg; died after 1560, in Herrenberg.
Sculptor (wood).

SCHICKHARDT, Lucas, the Younger
German, 16th century.
Born 1560, in Herrenberg; died 7 September 1602.
Sculptor (wood).

SCHICKHARDT, Wilhelm
German, 17th century.
Born 22 April 1592, in Herrenberg; died 23 October 1635, in Tübingen.
Painter, engraver (wood/burin).
Orientalism.

Schickhardt was a mathematician and teacher at the University of Tübingen.

SCHICKHLER, Franz
German, 18th century.
Active in Passau.
Painter.

SCHICKLER, J.
German, 17th century.
Active in Nuremberg.
Engraver (wood).

In 1869 Schickler engraved the illustrations for an edition of Ovid's *Metamorphoses*.

SCHICKRATT, Hans Georg
German, 17th century.
Draughtsman.

SCHIDER, Fritz
Austrian, 19th - 20th century.
Born 13 February 1846, in Salzburg; died 15 March 1907, in Basel.
Painter, draughtsman, engraver. Portraits, landscapes, still-lifes.

Fritz Schider attended the academy in Vienna then was a pupil of F. Wagner and of Ramberg at Munich. He settled in Basel in 1876 and became a teacher at the school of arts and crafts there. He obtained an honourable mention at the University of Basel for his anatomy drawings.

MUSEUMS AND GALLERIES:
BASEL: *The Chinese Tower in Munich; Still-life; The Woman Painter; The Chief Cook; The Dentist; Supermarket Trolley; Portrait of the Artist by Himself* - BERLIN (Nationalgal.): *Baptism of a Child* - COLOGNE (Wallraf-Richartz Mus.): *Woman in Grey with a Child* - DARMSTADT: *Interior at Twilight* - DÜSSELDORF (Kunstmus.): *The Chinese Tower; Portrait of Mme Birsinger* - HANOVER (Niedersächsisches Landesmus.): *Christmas in the Leibl Family* - SOLOTHURN: *Fruits* (watercolour).

AUCTION RECORDS:
MUNICH, 20 Oct 1983, *Little Girl Cutting Flowers* (oil on canvas, 12 1/4 x 18 ins / 31 x 45.5 cm) DEM 9,500. LONDON, 17 March 1989, *The English Garden at Munich* (oil on panel, 17 x 12 1/4 ins / 43 x 31 cm) GBP 3,300. ZURICH, 4 June 1992, *Peach Tree Branch* (watercolour/paper, 8 x 11 ins / 20.5 x 28 cm) CHF 1,356; *Still-life with a Bouquet and a Fan* (watercolour/paper, 18 1/4 x 24 1/2 ins / 46.5 x 62.5 cm) CHF 3,955.

SCHIDLER, Heinrich
Austrian, 19th century.
Born in Waidhofen-an-der-Thaya.
Painter. Genre scenes, portraits.

Schidler trained at the academy in Vienna from 1836 to 1843.

SCHIDONE, Baldassare
Italian, 17th century.
Painter. Religious subjects.

In 1629, Schidone painted a *Death of St Francis of Assisi* for the oratory of St Francis of the Merchants in Messina.

SCHIDONE, Bartolomeo. See **SCHEDONI**

SCHIEBEL, Carl Christian, or Schiebell
German, 19th century.
Born 22 April 1784, in Niederjahna; died 25 December 1838, in Meissen.
Painter (porcelain).

Schiebel trained at the art school in Meissen until 1804, then became a painter at Meissen Porcelain Factory.

SCHIEBLE, Erhard. See **ERHARD**

SCHIEBLING, Christian
German, 17th century.
Born 2 March 1603; died 22 February 1663.
Active in Dresden.
Painter.

Christian Schiebling was trained by his brother-in-law, Chilian Fabritius. He travelled to Italy, visiting Rome and Naples. He was appointed a painter at the court in Dresden and completed Fabritius' paintings at Dresden palace. He painted notably portraits, landscapes and animals.

SCHIEBLING, Christian Ehrenfried
German, 17th century.
Died 1687, in Dresden.
Active in Dresden.
Painter.

From 1674 to 1676, Christian Ehrenfried Schiebling decorated the new book of privileges for the City of Dresden.

SCHIEBLIUS, J. G.
Dutch, 17th century.
Painter. Landscapes.

MUSEUMS AND GALLERIES:
AMSTERDAM: *Italian Landscape*.

SCHIEDBACH, Johann Samuel
German, 18th century.
Painter.

Schiedbach worked on glazed earthenware at Dorotheenthal Factory from 1718 to 1735.

SCHIEDER, Josef
German, 19th - 20th century.
Born 1873, in Castelruth.
Active in Clausen.
Sculptor.

SCHIEDGES, Peter Paul, or Petrus Paulus
Dutch, 19th century.
Born 7 June 1812, in The Hague; died 1 December 1876, in The Hague.
Painter. Landscapes with figures, landscapes, seascapes.

Peter Paul Schiedges was a pupil of Louis Meyer.

MUSEUMS AND GALLERIES:
THE HAGUE (Gemeentemus.): *View of a River at Sunset*.

AUCTION RECORDS:
LONDON, 13 June 1974, *Seascape* (1858) Gns 380. AMSTERDAM, 22 Nov 1974, *Livestock in a Landscape* (watercolour) NLG 2,600. AMSTERDAM, 27 April 1976, *Scheveningen Beach* (1862, oil on panel, 7 x 11 ins / 18 x 27 cm) NLG 9,000. NEW YORK, 28 May 1980, *Landscape with Mill* (oil on canvas mounted on board, 16 1/4 x 24 1/4 ins / 41 x 61.5 cm) USD 1,500. COLOGNE, 21 May 1981, *Seascape* (1858, oil on panel, 10 x 13 1/2 ins / 24.5 x 34 cm) DEM 4,400. AMSTERDAM, 15 May 1984, *Landscape with Mill* (oil on canvas, 39 1/4 x 28 1/4 ins / 100 x 72 cm) NLG 5,200. AMSTERDAM, 10 Feb 1988, *Estuary with a Fisherman in his Boat and Other Vessels* (oil on panel, 9 1/2 x 13 1/2 ins / 24 x 34 cm) NLG 1,092. AMSTERDAM, 3 Sept 1988, *Farmer Turning the Soil beside a Horse-drawn Cart* (oil on canvas, 20 x 29 ins / 50.5 x 73.5 cm) NLG 1,725. AMSTERDAM, 16 Nov 1988, *Polder Land-*

scape with a Peasant in a Boat near a Mill (1889, oil on canvas, 23 1/2 x 31 1/2 ins / 60 x 80 cm) NLG 3,220. LONDON, 5 May 1989, *Boat Pulled Up on a Beach* (1857, oil on panel, 10 x 13 1/2 ins / 24.5 x 34.5 cm) GBP 1,980. AMSTERDAM, 2 May 1990, *Dutch Boat at Sea in Changeable Weather* (1870, oil on panel, 10 x 12 3/4 ins / 24.5 x 32.5 cm) NLG 5,750. AMSTERDAM, 5-6 Feb 1991, *Lake Bordered by Willow Trees* (oil on canvas, 13 3/4 x 18 1/2 ins / 35 x 47 cm) NLG 3,220. AMSTERDAM, 24 April 1991, *Dinghy Approaching Merchant Vessels in a Stormy Sea* (1859, oil on canvas, 38 1/2 x 52 3/4 ins / 98 x 134 cm) NLG 17,250. LONDON, 22 Nov 1991, *Beached Fishing Boats* (1869, oil on panel, 8 1/4 x 11 ins / 20.9 x 27.9 cm) GBP 1,045. AMSTERDAM, 14-15 April 1992, *Sailors in a Boat Towing a Fishing Boat* (1856, oil on panel, 13 1/2 x 19 3/4 ins / 34 x 50 cm) NLG 17,250. AMSTERDAM, 3 Nov 1992, *Sailing Boats in an Estuary* (1852, oil on panel, 8 3/4 x 12 ins / 22.5 x 30.5 cm) NLG 4,830. LONDON, 17 June 1994, *Sailing Ships off the Coast of a Town* (1859, oil on panel, 9 1/2 x 13 ins / 24.1 x 33.2 cm) GBP 3,680. AMSTERDAM, 11 April 1995, *Fishermen at Work on a Shore* (1857, oil on panel, 6 x 7 3/4 ins / 15 x 19.5 cm) NLG 6,844. AMSTERDAM, 26 Oct 1999, *Rowing Boat Approaching a Fishing Smack* (1856, oil on panel, 13 x 19 ins / 32 x 48 cm) NLG 38,000. AMSTERDAM, 26 Oct 1999, *Zwartewaalse Gaffelaar Leaving Port, Frigates beyond* (oil on panel, 18 x 23 ins / 45 x 58 cm) NLG 55,000. AMSTERDAM, 24 Oct 2000, *Shipping in the Harbour of Batavia* (1856, oil on canvas, 15 x 29 ins / 38 x 74 cm) NLG 10,000. GRAVENHAGE, 31 Oct 2000, *Sheep Grazing near Laren* (oil on canvas, 57 x 39 ins / 146 x 99 cm) NLG 17,000. GRAVENHAGE, 25 April 2001, *Figures and Boat on the Beach at Scheveningen* (1855, oil on canvas, 29 x 39 ins / 74 x 100 cm) NLG 48,000. AMSTERDAM, 22 Oct 2001, *Sailing Ship in Sunny Weather* (1860, oil on panel, 9 x 13 ins / 24 x 34 cm) NLG 9,500. AMSTERDAM, 3 Sept 2002, *Windmill in a Polder Landscape* (pencil and watercolour heightened with white, 18 x 27 ins / 46 x 68 cm) EUR 1,900. AMSTERDAM, 22 Oct 2002, *Figures on Scheveningen Beach* (1858, oil on panel, 11 x 17 ins / 28 x 43 cm) EUR 28,000. AMSTERDAM, 29 Sept 2003, *Shepherd with Flock* (oil on canvas, 31 x 47 ins / 80 x 120 cm) EUR 6,000. AMSTERDAM, 28 Oct 2003, *Shipping off the Coast of the Molukken* (1853, oil on panel, 14 x 19 ins / 36 x 48 cm) EUR 5,500. LONDON, 10 March 2004, *Barges off the Coast* (oil on board, 9 x 9 ins / 24 x 22 cm) GBP 4,800. AMSTERDAM, 17 March 2004, *Fisherman in Rowing Boat* (oil on canvas, 44 x 61 ins / 111 x 154 cm) EUR 6,200.

SCHIEDGES, Petrus Paulus
Dutch, 19th - 20th century.
Born 1860, in The Hague; died 1922, in Amersfoort.
Painter. Landscapes with figures, landscapes.

AUCTION RECORDS:
AMSTERDAM, 18 Feb 1992, *Shepherdess and Her Flock* (oil on canvas, 18 3/4 x 26 ins / 47.5 x 66 cm) NLG 1,955. AMSTERDAM, 24 Sept 1992, *Walkers in a Village in Grey Weather* (oil on canvas, 19 x 14 3/4 ins / 48.5 x 37.5 cm) NLG 2,530. AMSTERDAM, 21 April 1994, *Shepherd and His Flock* (oil on canvas, 34 x 23 3/4 ins / 85.5 x 60.5 cm) NLG 8,050. AMSTERDAM, 5 Nov 1996, *House at the Edge of the Water* (oil on canvas, 24 3/4 x 19 ins / 63 x 48 cm) NLG 2,596. LONDON, 19 June 2001, *Sheep Grazing near Laren* (oil on canvas, 39 x 58 ins / 99 x 148 cm) GBP 8,000.

SCHIEFERDECKER, Christian Karl August
German, 19th century.
Born 1823; died 1878.
Active in Leipzig.
Painter, lithographer.

Schieferdecker was a pupil of Neher the Younger. A large collection of works by him is to be found in the Leipzig Museum.

SCHIEFFER, Joseph, or Schiffer
German, 19th century.
Born c. 1808.
Painter, sculptor.

Joseph Schieffer was active in Cologne until 1860.

SCHIEFFER, Peter
German, 19th century.
Born c. 1811; died 15 December 1869, in Cologne.
Active in Cologne.
Lithographer.

Peter Schieffer drew panoramic views of towns.

SCHIEHEL, Wolf Caspar
Austrian, 17th century.
Active in Enns.
Painter.

In 1625, Schiehel worked for the monastery of St Florian.

SCHIEL, Jacob Gotthelf, or Schiele
German, 18th century.
Active in Leipzig between 1755 and 1774.
Painter.

SCHIEL, Johann Niklaus
German, 18th century.
Born 1751; died 7 March 1803, in Bern.
Active in Frankfurt am Main.
Draughtsman, engraver. Urban landscapes.

Johann Niklaus Schiel settled in Bern in 1783.

SCHIEL, Nikolaus
Austrian, 17th century.
Active in Brixen, South Tyrol (now Bressanone, Italy).
Painter.

Nikolaus Schiel painted the seven wonders of the world in the monastery of Neustift in 1670. He is also known for a portrait of *Karl Kempter*.

SCHIELDERUP, Leys Georgia Elise
Norwegian, 19th - 20th century.
Born 12 April 1856, in Christiansand; died 10 July 1933, in Roskilde.
Painter. Portraits, genre scenes.

Leys Georgia Schielderup was a pupil of Félix Joseph Barrias, Charles Chaplin and E. Hébert in Paris. From 1886 she stayed in Denmark.

MUSEUMS AND GALLERIES:
BERGEN: *Edvard Grieg*.

SCHIELE, Egon
Austrian, 20th century.
Born 12 June 1890, in Tulln (Danube); died 31 October 1918, in Vienna.
Painter (gouache), watercolourist, draughtsman, engraver. Figures, nudes, portraits, interiors with figures, landscapes.
Neukunstgruppe.

Egon Schiele's father was the stationmaster of Tulln. Egon Schiele was born in the station, which has now become his memorial birthplace. He was a pupil of the Akademie der Bildenden Künste in Vienna from 1906 to 1909, where he came into conflict with his teacher Christian Griepenkerl and with classical tradition. In 1909, with several young painters, he founded the Neukunstgruppe (New Art Group) He later settled at Krummau then at Neulenbach, where in 1912 he was imprisoned for three months because of the indecency of his drawings and watercolours. Following this, he returned to Vienna where he took courses in engraving in 1914. In 1915 he separated from his companion and model, Wally Neuzil to marry Edith Harms. A short time afterwards he was recruited into the army at Prague, then at Vienna, where he collaborated on the review *Der Anbruch*. The following year, the Expressionist review *Action* devoted an issue to him. He died prematurely of Spanish flu.

From the beginning his paintings were influenced by the style of the Secession and, in particular, by Gustav Klimt, whom he knew and admired. In 1909, of the four paintings that he sent to the Secession's Art Exhibition, one, a landscape, gave full expression to the connection between the clarity of tones of Impressionism and the decorative, arabesque stylisation of the Secession. However, it was mainly to portraits and to the human body that Egon Schiele dedicated his work. Alongside his paintings, he produced a great many drawings and watercolours, in which a quicker and lighter touch allowed him a greater spontaneity both of inspiration and of creation. The personalities delineated are all drawn with a feverish, tortured stroke, and are visibly haunted characters. Their outlines are enclosed in meandering rings around which concentric lines are focused, depicting the facial features. This gives a result that is graphic to the point of abstraction. The figures are set on chalky backgrounds broken, in the style of Klimt, into decorative motifs and have a very elaborate ornamental and highly coloured design - as if to accentuate the morbidity of the faces. Apart from the feminine figures, maternal or erotic images, he painted those close to him (Klimt, Erwin Dominik Osen, Heinrich and Otto Benesch), heterosexual couples or ordinary people.

He also produced a great many self portraits. He was obsessed by his own face, as if searching for his own identity. Always stressing the anguish of being, he chooses often to represent himself as being older than his real age. With humanity, he presents life and death, joy and suffering, uniting these in *Pregnant Woman and Death* - adopting a theme dear to the Symbolists in retaining the morbid aspect. Around 1912 it seems he experienced the influence of Hodler, in more balanced, calmer compositions. The *Sunrise* of the same period also shows the influence of Hodler. While in the army he continued to paint nudes of men and of women, and the eroticism of some of them caused a scandal. He painted landscapes of imaginary towns, decorative patchworks of coloured surfaces, landscapes with trees in fanciful rhythms, and affecting scenes between mother and child (*Mother and Two Children, The Family*). His works become less aggressive and gain in realism, a melancholy realism freed from the tormented vision of the previous years.

He took part in numerous public exhibitions in his lifetime: 1909, International Art Show and Exhibition of the Neukunstgruppe (New Art Group); 1911, Salon Miethke; 1914, Kunstsalon and Salon Pisko; 1918, an event of the Secession group. Also: 1908, Kaisersaal, Klosterneuburg; 1912, event of the Secession group at Munich; 1914, Kunsthalle, Bremen; 1917, Liejevalche Konsthall, Stockholm. After his death he was represented particularly in exhibitions devoted to fin-de-siécle Vienna: 1948, Venice Biennale; 1981, Kunsthalle, Hamburg; 1985, Künstlerhaus, Vienna; 1986, Historisches Museum der Stadt at Vienna and *Vienna 1880-1938 - The Joyous Apocalypse*, Centre Georges-Pompidou, Paris; 1994, exhibition of *Chefs-d'œuvre du Belvédère de Vienne* (*Masterpieces from the Belvedere in Vienna*), Musée Marmottan, Paris; 2004, ***Klimt Schiele Klee - Wotruba an de avant-garde*** (***Klimt, Schiele, Klee, Wotruba and the Avant-Garde***), Gemeentemuseum, The Hague. The Secession Association gave him an entire room. Numerous private posthumous exhibitions have been shown: 1923, 1928, 1948, Neue Galerie de Vienna; 1960, Institute of Contemporary Arts of Boston, Carnegie Institute of Pittsburgh and Institute of Arts of Minneapolis; 1964, 1969, Marlborough Fine Art of London; 1965, with Klimt at the Solomon R. Guggenheim Museum of New York; 1968, 1981, 1990, Historisches Museum der Stadt in Vienna; 1968, Osterreichische Galerie inVienna; 1971, Art Centre of Des Moines; 1989, Kunsthaus of Zurish, Kunstforum of Vienna, Kunsthalle der Hypo-Kulturstiftung of Munich; 1990, Albertina of Vienna, County Museum of Nassau; 1991, Royal Academy of London; 1992, Museum-Gallery of la Seita in Paris; 1995 Kunsthalle of Tübingen, Kunstsammlung Nordrhein-Westfalen de Düsseldorf, Kunsthalle of Hamburg, Fondation Pierre Gianadda at Martigny; 1998, Minoritenkloster, Schielemuseum and Schielegeburtshaus at Tulln, for the eightieth anniversary of his death; 2001, *The Naked Truth*, fondation Dina Vierny-musée Maillol. In 1990 the Egon Schiele Museum was created in his native city for the hundredth anniversary of his birth.

BIBLIOGRAPHY:

Egon Schiele, exhibition catalogue, Institute of Contemporary Art, Boston, 1960. Kallir-Nirenstein, Otto, *Egon Schiele. Das druckgraphische Werk*, Paul Zsolnay, Wels, 1970. Leopold, Rudolf, *Egon Schiele Gemälde, Aquarelle, Zeichnungen*, catalogue raisonné, Phaidon, London, Residenz Verlag, Salzburg, 1973. Comini, Alessandra, *Egon Schiele's portraits*, University of California Press, Berkeley, 1974. Comini, Alessandra, *Egon Schiele*, Éd. du Seuil, Paris, 1976. *Egon Schiele*, exhibition catalogue, Gal. Octave Negru, Paris, 1976. Nebehay, Christian Michael, *Egon Schiele 1890-1918: Leben, Briefe, Gedichte*, Residenz Verlag, Salzburg, Vienna, 1979. Whitford, Frank, *Egon Schiele*, Thames & Hudson, London, 1981, 1990. Whitford, F., *Egon schiele*, London, 1981. Mitsch, Erwin, *The Art of Egon Schiele (2nd ed.)*, Oxford, 1988. Schroder, Klaus Albrecht/Szeeman, Harald, et al., *Egon Schiele and His Contemporaries: Austrian Painting and Drawing from 1900 to 1930 from the Leopold Collection, Vienna*, Munich, 1989. Sabarsky, Serge, *Egon Schiele. 1890-1918. A Centennial Retrospective*, County Museum of Art, Nassau, 1990. Kallir, Jane, et al., *Egon Schiele. Œuvres complètes*, catalogue raisonné, Abrams, New York, Gallimard, Paris, 1990 (new revised and expanded edition, 1998 and 2001). *Egon Schiele*, exhibition catalogue, Graphische Sammlung Albertina, Vienna, 1990. *Egon Schiele*, exhibition catalogue, Historisches Museum der Stadt, Vienna, 1990. Comini, Alessandra, *Egon Schiele's Portraits*, University of California Press, Berkeley, 1990. *Egon Schiele*, exhibition catalogue, Musée-galerie de la Seita, Paris, 1992. Dufour, Philippe, *Schiele: œuvres sur papier*, André Sauret, Paris, 1993. Mitsch, Erwin, *Egon Schiele 1890-1918*, Phaidon, London, 1993. Kallir, Jane, *Egon Schiele*, Abrams, New York, 1994. *Egon Schiele*, exhibition catalogue, Fondation Pierre Gianadda, Martigny, 1995. Leopold, Rudolf, *Egon Schiele: Leopold Collection Vienna*, DuMont, Cologne, October 1997. Hutton, Andrew/Marlow, Tim, *Schiele*, video, Seventh Art for Channel Five, London, c. 2003.

MUSEUMS AND GALLERIES:

CAMBRIDGE, MA (Fogg AM, Harvard University): *Study for the Double Portrait of Heinrich and Otto Benesch* (1913) - DARMSTADT (Hessisches Landesmus.): *Tree in Autumn and Fuchsias* (1909) - GRAZ (Landesmus. Joanneum, Neue Gal.): *Sailing Boats in Choppy Water* (1907); *Suburb* (1917-1918); *Nude Stretched Out* (1918) - LINZ (Neue Gal. der Stadt): *Ancient Alley in Klosterneuburg* (1907); *Krumau Landscape* (1916) - MINNEAPOLIS (IA): *Gerti Schiele in a Plaid Garment* (c.

1908-1909, charcoal and tempera/paper); *Portrait of Paris von Gütersloh* (1918, oil on canvas) - MUNICH (Neue Pinakothek): *Agony* (1912) - MUNICH (Staatliche Graphische Sammlung): *Young Woman with Black Hair* (1914) - NEW YORK (MoMA): *Portrait of Gerti Schiele* (1909); *Nude with a Raised Arm* (1910); *Young Girls with Black Hair* (1911) - OBERLIN (Allen Memorial AM): *Young Black Girl* (1911) - OBERSCHLEISSHEIM (Neues Schloss Schleissheim, Staatsgal.) - PARIS (BNF): *Secession 49, Austellung* (1918, lithograph) - PRAGUE (Národní Gal.): *Pregnant Woman and Death* (1911); *Seated Woman with Left Leg Bent* (1917); *Nude* (1917) - STOCKHOLM (Nationalmus.): *Self-portrait* (1913) - STUTTGART (Staatsgal.): *Der Prophet (Doppelselbstbildnis) (The Prophet (Double Self-portrait))* (1911) - THE HAGUE (Gemeentemus.): *The Artist's Wife* (1915) - TULLN (Egon Schiele Mus.) - VIENNA (Albertina Mus.): *Max Oppenheimer* (1910); *Prison Drawing* (1912); *Self-portrait* (1916); *Edith Schiele* (1917); *Paris von Gutersloh* (1918) - VIENNA (Kunsthistorisches Mus.): *Arthur Roessler* (1910); *Self-portrait with Fingers Spread Out* (1911); *Franz Blei* (1918) - VIENNA (Leopold Mus.) - VIENNA (Österreichische Gal. Belvedere): *Otto Wagner* (1910); *Nude* (1912); *Anatomy* (1912); *Trees* (1917); *Family* (1918); *Portrait of Viktor Ritter Bauer* (1918) - ZURICH (Kunsthaus): *Dead City IV* (1912) - ZURICH (Prints Collection): *The Virgin* (1913).

AUCTION RECORDS:

BERN, 25 May 1962, *Moa, Nude Lying Down* (watercolour) CHF 11,500. VIENNA, 18 March 1964, *Woman in Black Hat,* ATS 380,000. VIENNA, 24 March 1965, *Portrait of Silvia Koller* (watercolour) ATS 90,000. LONDON, 30 March 1966, *Self-portrait* (bronze) GBP 800. NEW YORK, 18 Sept 1968, *Self-portrait* (patinated bronze) USD 2,100. LONDON, 2-3 Dec 1970, *Friends Seated Around a Table,* GBP 39,500. VIENNA, 7 June 1972, *Farmyard,* ATS 26,000. LOS ANGELES, 25 Feb 1974, *Naked Man Seen From Behind,* USD 8,750. NEW YORK, 18 March 1976, *Opera Singer* (1911, gouache, watercolour and pencil/paper, 17 1/2 x 11 3/4 ins / 44.6 x 30 cm) USD 31,000. HAMBURG, 4 June 1976, *Standing Nude* (1917, chalk, 16 1/4 x 6 ins / 41.5 x 15.5 cm) DEM 15,000. BERN, 10 June 1976, *Young Woman* (1918, lithograph) CHF 6,600. VIENNA, 18 March 1977, *Houses by the Water* (1908, oil on canvas, 10 1/4 x 10 1/4 ins / 26 x 26 cm) ATS 150,000. BERN, 9 June 1977, *Kuumernis* (1914, dry-point printed in dark green/yellowish-vellum) CHF 5,600. LONDON, 6 Dec 1977, *Woman in Striped Stockings, Leaning, Seen From Behind* (1910, watercolour and black chalk/beige paper, 11 1/2 x 16 ins / 29.3 x 40.5 cm) GBP 12,000. BERN, 8 June 1978, *Self-portrait (Nude)* (1912, lithograph) CHF 5,600. NEW YORK, 2 Nov 1978, *Intertwined Couple* (1913, watercolour, tempera and pencil, 12 1/2 x 19 ins / 32 x 48.2 cm) USD 120,000. VIENNA, 15 Dec 1978, *Dead City* (1912, oil on panel, 14 1/2 x 11 1/2 ins / 36.7 x 29.5 cm) ATS 1,400,000. NEW YORK, 16 May 1979, *Self-portrait I* (1912, lithograph, 18 x 15 3/4 ins / 44.8 x 40 cm) USD 5,750. NEW YORK, 16 May 1979, *Woman in Yellow* (1914, tempera and pencil/paper, 19 x 12 1/4 ins / 48.2 x 31.1 cm) USD 62,500. LONDON, 5 July 1979, *Woman Lying Down* (c. 1910, pencil and watercolour, 12 1/2 x 17 1/4 ins / 32 x 44 cm) GBP 15,500. BERN, 25 June 1982, *Nude Lying Down* (1917, watercolour and gouache/outlines in black chalk, 11 1/4 x 18 ins / 28.8 x 45.9 cm) CHF 188,000. LONDON, 2 Dec 1982, *Chewing* (1914, dry-point, 20 3/4 x 14 1/2 ins / 52.6 x 36.6 cm) GBP 17,000. NEW YORK, 5 May 1983, *Secession 49, Exhibition* (1918, coloured lithograph, 26 3/4 x 21 ins / 67.8 x 53.2 cm) USD 5,500. NEW YORK, 16 Nov 1983, *Portrait of a Woman* (1918, black chalk, 18 1/2 x 11 3/4 ins / 47 x 30 cm) USD 22,000. LONDON, 7 Dec 1983, *Kniender Akt* (1915, watercolour and gouache on pencil outlines, 13 x 19 1/2 ins / 33 x 49.8 cm) GBP 95,000. LONDON, 26 June 1984, *Self-portrait* (bronze, after a clay original from 1917-1918, h. 10 1/2 ins / 26.7 cm) GBP 50,000. LONDON, 4 Dec 1984, *Married Couple (Man and Wife 1)* (1914, oil on canvas, 46 3/4 x 54 3/4 ins / 119 x 139 cm) GBP 2,900,000. VIENNA, 10 Dec 1985, *Nude* (1914, pencil and gouache, 19 x 12 1/2 ins / 48.2 x 31.8 cm) ATS 2,800,000. LONDON, 28 May 1986, *Self-portrait* (1917-1918, cement, h. 10 1/2 ins / 26.7 cm) GBP 6,000. LONDON, 8 Oct 1986, *Cathedral of the Convent of Klosterneuburg at Night* (1908, oil and gold paint/canvas, 39 1/4 x 39 1/4 ins / 100 x 100 cm) GBP 70,000. LONDON, 31 March 1987, *Portrait of the Painter Anton Peschka* (1909, oil on canvas, 43 1/4 x 39 1/4 ins / 110 x 100 cm) GBP 1,600,000. LONDON, 10 Feb 1988, *Russian Countryman* (1915, pencil, 17 x 12 1/4 ins / 43 x 31 cm) GBP 28,600; *Study of Characters* (lead and coloured pencil, 2 3/4 x 3 1/2 ins / 7 x 9 cm) GBP 1,045. LONDON, 19 Oct 1988, *Nude Study* (1911, pencil, 20 x 13 1/2 ins / 51 x 34.5 cm) GBP 6,600. NEW YORK, 12 Nov 1988, *Sunflowers* (1918, gouache and pencil/paper, 17 3/4 x 11 1/2 ins / 45 x 29.2 cm) USD 341,000; *Portrait of a Woman (Serena Lederer)* (1917, pencil/paper, 17 1/2 x 11 1/2 ins / 44.5 x 29.5 cm) USD 165,000. LONDON, 29 Nov 1988, *Landscape* (1907, oil/primer, 9 x 10 3/4 ins / 22.9 x 27.3 cm) GBP 24,200. PARIS, 7 March 1989, *Study of Woman in Stockings* (1918, black chalk/paper, 17 3/4 x 11 1/2 ins / 45 x 29.5 cm) FRF 255,000. NEW YORK, 10 May 1989, *Summer Landscape* (1917, oil on canvas, 43 1/2 x 54 3/4 ins / 110.5 x 139 cm) USD 5,940,000. PARIS, 21 June 1989, *Squatting Nude* (1916, graphite, 11 x 7 1/2 ins / 28 x 19 cm) FRF 52,000. NEW YORK, 13 Nov 1989, *Standing Nude* (1911, gouache and pencil/paper, 21 3/4 x 12 3/4 ins / 55.2 x 32.3 cm) USD 880,000. NEW YORK, 14 Nov 1989, *Sister of the Artist: Melanie*. LONDON, 3 April 1990, *Nude* (1913, pencil/paper, 17 1/4 x 10 1/4 ins / 44 x 26 cm) GBP 46,200. LONDON, 4 April 1990, *Flowery Garden* (1907, oil on card, 13 3/4 x 10 ins / 35 x 24.5 cm) GBP 55,000; *Head of Young Girl* (coloured chalk, 12 1/2 x 11 1/4 ins / 31.7 x 28.7 cm) GBP 35,200. NEW YORK, 16 May 1990, *Girl in Black Stockings, Seated* (1911, gouache, watercolour and pencil/tinted paper, 20 x 12 1/2 ins / 51 x 32 cm) USD 440,000. PARIS, 13 June 1990, *Village in the Mountains* (1907, oil on canvas, 9 x 11 ins / 22 x 28 cm) FRF 255,000. LONDON, 4 Dec 1990, *Portrait of Madame Tony Rieger* (1917, pencil and gouache/tinted paper, 17 1/2 x 11 1/2 ins / 44.5 x 29.5 cm) GBP 220,000. NEW YORK, 14 Feb 1991, *Austrian Landscape* (1907, oil on card, 7 x 9 ins / 17.8 x 22.9 cm) USD 37,400. NEW YORK, 8 May 1991, *Female Nude Standing* (1912, pencil/paper, 19 x 12 1/2 ins / 48 x 31.5 cm) USD 41,250. LONDON, 26 June 1991, *Little Girl with Striped Apron* (1911, watercolour and pencil, 19 x 12 1/2 ins / 48.5 x 31.5 cm) GBP 137,500. NEW YORK, 6 Nov 1991, *Seated Nude (recto), Portrait (verso)* (watercolour and lead pencil/paper). LONDON, 2 Dec 1991, *Two Young Hooligans* (1910, gouache and watercolour/pencil, 15 1/2 x 13 ins / 39.1 x 32.1 cm) GBP 154,000. NEW YORK, 12 May 1992, *Standing Man, Self-portrait* (1911, watercolour and gouache/paper, 17 1/2 x 12 1/4 ins / 44.5 x 30.8 cm) USD 242,000. MILAN, 21 May 1992, *Female Nude* (1917, wax crayon, 11 1/2 x 18 ins / 29.5 x 46 cm) ITL 45,000,000. LONDON, 30 June 1992, *Portrait of Edith Schiele Seated* (1915, pencil and gouache, 20 x 15 3/4 ins / 51 x 40.1 cm) GBP 572,000. NEW YORK, 11 Nov 1992, *Portrait of a Little Girl* (1913, pencil/paper, 18 x 10 ins / 45.7 x 25.1 cm) USD 71,500. LONDON, 1 Dec 1992, *Young Boy in Sailor's Costume* (1914, gouache, watercolour, lead pencil and colour, 18 3/4 x 12 1/4 ins / 47.8 x 31.2 cm) GBP 429,000. LONDON, 2 Dec 1992, *Russian Prisoner of War in a Fur Hat* (1915, pencil, 17 x 12 1/4 ins / 43 x 31 cm) GBP 68,200. LONDON, 22 June 1993, *Adolescent Stretched Out, Paul Erdmann* (1917, watercolour, gouache and lead pencil, 11 1/2 x 18 ins / 29.4 x 45.7 cm) GBP 199,500. NEW YORK, 3 Nov 1993, *Couple in Bed (Man and Woman I)* (oil on canvas, 47 x 54 3/4 ins / 119.1 x 139.1 cm) USD 4,677,500. NEW YORK, 11 May 1994, *Nude Couple* (1911, gouache, watercolour and pencil/paper, 14 1/4 x 20 1/2 ins / 36.5 x 52.1 cm) USD 134,500. LONDON, 29 June 1994, *Erich Lederer Applauding* (pencil, 19 x 12 1/2 ins / 48 x 32 cm) GBP 54,300. PARIS, 28 Nov 1994, *Young Woman Seated* (1913, pencil heightened with gouache and watercolour, 18 1/4 x 11 3/4 ins / 46.5 x 30 cm) FRF 510,000.

LONDON, 29 Nov 1994, *Woman in Black Apron Draped in a Checkered Blanket* (gouache, watercolour and charcoal, 17 3/4 x 11 3/4 ins / 45.1 x 29.9 cm) GBP 342,500. NEW YORK, 8 May 1995, *Nude Study* (1908, oil on card, 9 1/2 x 7 1/4 ins / 24.4 x 18.1 cm) USD 200,500. PARIS, 24 May 1995, *Woman in Black Stockings* (lead pencil and watercolour, 19 x 12 1/2 ins / 48 x 31.5 cm) FRF 440,000. LONDON, 27 June 1995, *Field of Flowers* (1910, gouache, watercolour and gold paint/paper, 17 1/2 x 12 ins / 44.4 x 30.6 cm) GBP 463,500. NEW YORK, 7 Nov 1995, *Self-portrait with Elbow Lifted to Put On a Leather Garment* (1914, gouache, black chalk and pencil/paper, 19 x 12 1/4 ins / 48 x 31 cm) USD 1,872,500. LONDON, 27 Nov 1995, *Embrace* (1913, gouache, watercolour and pencil/paper, 12 1/2 x 19 ins / 32 x 48 cm) GBP 518,500. NEW YORK, 1 May 1996, *Self-portrait Kneeling* (1912, watercolour and gouache/paper, 17 1/4 x 11 3/4 ins / 43.8 x 29.8 cm) USD 827,500; *Woman in Black Hat (Gerturde Schiele)* (1909, gold and silver paint and oil on canvas, 39 1/4 x 39 1/4 ins / 100 x 99.7 cm) USD 2,972,500. LONDON, 25 June 1996, *Seated Nude Seen from Behind* (1910, watercolour and black chalk, 17 3/4 x 9 3/4 ins / 45 x 24.8 cm) GBP 210,500. NEW YORK, 12 Nov 1996, *Young Woman with Black Stockings* (1911, gouache, watercolour and pencil, 18 3/4 x 15 ins / 47.6 x 38.1 cm) USD 464,500. NEW YORK, 14 Nov 1996, *Female Nude on her Knees* (1917, pastel/paper, 18 x 11 3/4 ins / 46 x 29.9 cm) USD 129,000. LONDON, 3 Dec 1996, *Anton Faistauer with Hands Folded* (pencil and pen/paper, 12 1/4 x 12 ins / 31.4 x 30.5 cm) GBP 40,000; *Seated Child, Anton Pechka Jnr* (1917, gouache and pencil/paper, 18 x 11 1/2 ins / 46 x 29.5 cm) GBP 155,500. NEW YORK, 13 May 1997, *Conversion* (1912, oil on canvas, 28 x 32 ins / 71.1 x 81 cm) USD 3,412,500. LONDON, 24 June 1997, *Embrace* (1913, gouache, watercolour and black chalk/paper, 18 1/2 x 12 1/4 ins / 47.3 x 31.1 cm) GBP 331,500. LONDON, 25 June 1997, *Self-portrait* (1912, watercolour and pencil/paper, 19 x 12 1/2 ins / 48.1 x 31.6 cm) GBP 84,000. NEW YORK, 12 Nov 1997, *Seated Nude* (1914, pencil/paper, 19 x 12 1/2 ins / 48.2 x 31.8 cm) USD 55,200. NEW YORK, 11 May 1999, *Seated Male Nude with Outstretched Right Hand* (1910, watercolour, black crayon and charcoal, 17 x 12 ins / 44 x 30 cm) USD 375,000. NEW YORK, 11 May 1999, *Reclining Boy with Upright Torso, Paul Erdmann* (1917, watercolour, gouache and black crayon, 12 x 18 ins / 30 x 45 cm) USD 420,000. LONDON, 18 Oct 2000, *Portrait of the Art Dealer Guido Arnot* (1918, oil on canvas, 56 x 43 ins / 141 x 109 cm) GBP 6,500,000. NEW YORK, 8 Nov 2000, *Woman in Green Blouse with Muff* (1915, gouache and pencil on paper on card, 19 x 12 ins / 49 x 30 cm) USD 1,250,000. LONDON, 5 Feb 2001, *Portrait of the Painter Anton Peschka* (1909, oil, silver, gold, bronze and paint on canvas, 43 x 39 ins / 110 x 100 cm) GBP 7,000,000. NEW YORK, 5 Nov 2001, *House with Washing Hung Out* (1917, oil on canvas, 43 x 55 ins / 110 x 140 cm) USD 9,000,000. LONDON, 9 April 2002, *Kneeling Woman* (1912, gouache, watercolour and pencil, 12 x 19 ins / 31 x 48 cm) GBP 220,000. NEW YORK, 4 Nov 2002, *Nude* (1913, watercolour and black crayon, 16 x 11 ins / 41 x 29 cm) USD 300,000. LONDON, 23 June 2003, *Krumau Landscape, Town and River* (1916, oil, tempera and coloured chalk on canvas, 43 x 56 ins / 110 x 141 cm) GBP 11,300,000. COLOGNE, 26 Nov 2003, *Two Women* (1911, watercolour and gouache over pencil, 22 x 14 ins / 55 x 36 cm) EUR 670,000. LONDON, 3 Feb 2004, *Girl with a Green Pinafore* (1910, watercolour and black crayon, 18 x 9 ins / 45 x 22 cm) GBP 1,350,000. LONDON, 21 June 2004, *Lovers* (1913, gouache, watercolour and pencil, 19 x 13 ins / 48 x 32 cm) GBP 1,700,000.

SCHIELE, Marjorie
American, 20th century.
Born 30 March 1913, in Cincinnati (Ohio).
Painter.

Marjorie Schiele studied under and assisted Amédée Ozenfant in his art school in New York.

Schiele took part in collective exhibitions, including *The Women*, a travelling exhibition organised by Peggy Guggenheim in 1944; at the San Francisco Museum of Modern Art in 1945; the Biennale in Menton in 1961; and at the Art Institute in Dayton in 1965 and 1966. She also showed her works in private exhibitions, in London in 1939, New York in 1945, and Vence, Vallauris and Biot in 1958 and 1959.

SCHIELIN, Hans. See **SCHÜCHLIN**

SCHIELLE, Sebastian
School of Alsace, 17th century.
Died 1649, in Landau.
Active in Strasbourg.
Painter.

SCHIELTVED, Carl Oluf Angelo
Danish, 19th century.
Born 5 June 1829, in Copenhagen; died 10 June 1891, in Copenhagen.
Sculptor, potter.

Schieltved studied at the Kunstakademi in Copenhagen and with Gustav Friedrich Hetsch. From 1853 until 1891, he worked at the royal porcelain factory in Copenhagen.

SCHIEMER, Friedrich
German, 19th century.
Born 1810, in Mergentheim.
Active in Mergentheim.
Painter.

Schiemer studied at the academy in Munich.

SCHIEMER, Johann-Baptist
German, 19th - 20th century.
Born 5 December 1853, in Nocherthurn; died 3 April 1912, in Nuremberg.
Sculptor.

Johann-Baptist Schiemer was a pupil of Johann N. Meintel from 1868 to 1873, at Meintel's studio of Christian art at Horb (Wurtemberg). He also attended the school of fine arts in Nuremberg. Several of his works can be seen in Nuremberg.

SCHIER, Franz
German, 19th - 20th century.
Born 5 July 1852, in Neuwel Harrachsdorf; died January 1922, in Munich.
Painter. Genre scenes.

Franz Schier also painted on porcelain.

AUCTION RECORDS:
NEW YORK, 15 Oct 1991, *A Suitor* (oil on canvas, 44 x 37 1/2 ins / 111.9 x 95.3 cm) USD 3,850.

SCHIERBECK, Christian Peter
Danish, 19th century.
Born 31 March 1835, in Copenhagen; died 8 October 1865, in Rome.
Sculptor.

Schierbeck was a pupil of P. Petersen and Herman-Vilhelm Bissen at the Kunstakademi in Copenhagen. He worked in Rome from 1863 to 1865.

MUSEUMS AND GALLERIES:
AALBORG - COPENHAGEN.

SCHIERBECK, F.
Danish, 19th century.
Sculptor.

Schierbeck's marble sculpture, *Young Boys at the Bath*, is in the Copenhagen Museum.

CI⊃

SCHIERBECK, J.C., or Shierbeck
Danish, 18th - 19th century.
Painter.

From 1790 until 1803, J.C. Schierbeck was a porcelain painter at the royal porcelain factory in Copenhagen.

SCHIERECKE, Jan Frederik
Dutch, 19th century.
Active in Middelburg c.1800.
Draughtsman, watercolourist.
Jan Frederik Schierecke was a pupil of Krahe in Düsseldorf.

SCHIERFBERK, Helena Sofia, or Helene.
See **SCHJERFBECK**

SCHIERHOLZ, C.
German, 19th century.
Active in Clausthal, in the Harz, c. 1840.
Painter (porcelain).
A number of cups signed C. Schierholz are in the Brunswick Museum.
MUSEUMS AND GALLERIES:
BRUNSWICK: cups.

SCHIERHOLZ, Friedrich Johann Georg
German, 19th century.
Born 27 April 1840, in Frankfurt am Main; died 2 February 1894, in Frankfurt am Main.
Sculptor.
Friedrich Schierholz studied at the Städel Institute in Frankfurt and with Widnmann. His monument to *Schopenhauer* of 1895 can be seen in Frankfurt. There are also busts by him of *Schopenhauer* and *Geiger* in the city library, a statue of *Mozart* at the opera house and statues of *Gideon, David* and *Melchisedech* in the cathedral.

SCHIERHOLZ, Karoline
German, 19th century.
Born 29 July 1831, in Frankfurt am Main.
Painter.
Karoline Schierholz was a pupil of J. Becker.

SCHIERING, Kurt
German, 20th century.
Born 5 November 1885, in Markranstadt, near Leipzig; died 14 March 1918, in Banos del Toro, near Coquimbo (Chile).
Active from 1913 in Argentina and Chile.
Painter. Landscapes.
Kurt Schiering was a pupil at the academy of fine arts in Leipzig. From 1913 he spent time in South America, in Argentina and Chile. In 1929 the Museum of Ethnography of Leipzig organised a posthumous exhibition of his works entitled *Tropical Landscapes.*

SCHIERITZ, Johann Gottlob
German, 18th century.
Born 1692; died 31 July 1738.
Active in Dresden.
Painter.

SCHIERL, Josef
German, 19th century.
Painter, engraver. Portraits, genre scenes.
Schierl was active in Munich around 1835.
AUCTION RECORDS:
LONDON, 28 March 1996, *The Music Lesson* (1832, oil on panel, 10 x 12 1/2 ins / 25.3 x 31.7 cm) GBP 1,840. MUNICH, 3 Dec 2003, *Sleeping Girl. Girl Crying over a Letter* (1845, oil on canvas, a pair, 16 x 13 ins / 41 x 34 cm) EUR 4,500.

SCHIERTZ, August Ferdinand
German, 19th century.
Born 1804, in Leipzig; died 10 September 1878, in Niederfähre, near Meissen.
Painter. Religious subjects, portraits, genre scenes, still-lifes.
August Schiertz started out as a merchant, then became an actor. He worked as a painter from 1830, frequently as a restorer of old paintings.
MUSEUMS AND GALLERIES:
LEIPZIG: *Still-life; Portrait of an Old Man* - ROSENSTADT (Church): *The Adoration of the Magi.*
AUCTION RECORDS:
NEW YORK, 16 July 1992, *Carabinieri Stopping Three Travellers on a Road* (1839, oil on panel, 13 3/4 x 18 1/2 ins / 34.9 x 47 cm) USD 3,300.

SCHIERTZ, Franz Wilhelm
German, 19th century.
Born 1813, in Leipzig; died 1887, in Bakstrand.
Painter, watercolourist, illustrator. Hunting scenes, landscapes, seascapes, architectural views.
Franz Wilhelm was the younger brother of August Ferdinand Schiertz. He studied with Dahl in Dresden, and then visited Sweden and Norway, where he painted a large number of landscapes. He illustrated a work by Dahl on Norwegian architecture with drawings heightened with watercolour.
MUSEUMS AND GALLERIES:
OSLO: 15 drawings.
AUCTION RECORDS:
LONDON, 14 June 1974, *Whale-hunting in an Arctic Landscape,* Gns 1,500. LUCERNE, 26 June 1976, *Antarctic Landscape at Dusk* (1881, oil on canvas, 14 1/4 x 21 1/4 ins / 36 x 54 cm) CHF 3,200. COLOGNE, 11 May 1977, *The Bear Hunt* (1880, oil on canvas, 14 1/4 x 21 1/4 ins / 36.5 x 54 cm) DEM 3,000. NEW YORK, 21 Jan 1978, *Seal Hunters on an Ice Floe* (1882, oil on canvas, 29 1/2 x 45 1/2 ins / 75 x 115.5 cm) USD 5,250. LONDON, 21 March 1980, *Estuary at Dusk* (oil on canvas, 23 1/4 x 33 1/4 ins / 59 x 84.5 cm) GBP 3,500. LONDON, 19 June 1981, *Icebergs off the Coast of Greenland* (1880, oil on canvas, 18 1/4 x 28 ins / 46.4 x 71.1 cm) GBP 1,700. NEW YORK, 16 Dec 1983, *Glaciers and Fishing Fleet off the Greenland Coast* (1878, oil on canvas, 18 1/4 x 28 ins / 46.4 x 71.1 cm) USD 8,500. LONDON, 11 Oct 1995, *View of a Norwegian Fjord* (1873, watercolour, 12 1/2 x 17 3/4 ins / 32 x 45 cm) GBP 1,035. OSLO, 26 Jan 1999, *Mountain Landscape* (oil on paper, 11 x 15 ins / 28 x 38 cm) NOK 18,000. OSLO, 7 Feb 2000, *Up towards Boya Glacier in Fjaerland* (1886, oil on canvas, 8 x 12 ins / 20 x 30 cm) NOK 16,000. COPENHAGEN, 4 Dec 2000, *Midnight by the Island Starck, Spitzbergen with Family of Polar Bears* (1881, oil on canvas, 14 x 21 ins / 35 x 53 cm) DKK 27,000. STUTTGART, 20 Sept 2001, *Seal Hunters in Arctic Landscape* (1882, oil on canvas, 30 x 45 ins / 76 x 114 cm) DEM 10,000. OSLO, 10 Dec 2001, *Fishing Village in Finnmark* (1883, oil on canvas, 19 x 28 ins / 47 x 72 cm) NOK 54,000. OSLO, 17 Dec 2002, *Sailing Vessel and Pilot Boat by Lindesnes* (1844, oil on canvas, 15 x 21 ins / 37 x 53 cm) NOK 20,000. HAMBURG, 4 June 2003, *Fjord Beach in Norway* (oil on canvas, 31 x 46 ins / 79 x 118 cm) EUR 4,500.

SCHIERTZ, Leo
German, 19th century.
Born 9 March 1840, in Leipzig; died 3 October 1881, in West Newton (Massachusetts).
Active in the USA.
Painter, lithographer.
Leo Schiertz was active in West Newton from 1868.

SCHIES, Hermann
German, 19th century.
Born 29 July 1836, in Eltville-on-Rhine; died 19 February 1899, in Wiesbaden.
Sculptor.
Schies studied with Hopfgarten and Drake in Berlin, and later taught at the school of fine arts in Wiesbaden. He sculpted the war memorials in Eisenach, Hagen, Kastrop and Wiesbaden.

SCHIESCHNECK, Ernst

Austrian, 19th century.

Born 7 July 1844, in Vienna.

Painter, engraver (burin). Portraits, landscapes.

Schieschneck studied with C. Mayer, Wurzinger and Engerth and worked in Prague.

SCHIESL, Ferdinand

German, 19th century.

Born 1775, in Munich; died 1820.

Painter, watercolourist, engraver, draughtsman, caricaturist.

Schiesl was a pupil of Mettenleiter. He engraved vignettes.

SCHIESS, Adrian

Swiss, 20th - 21st century.

Born 1959, in Zurich.

Active in France.

Watercolourist, installation artist.

Adrian Schiess started out by scattering fragments or debris of boxes smeared with paint over the floor of the exhibition venue. Later, he used pieces of painted wood. From 1986-1987 he moved on from the random to the orderly, while at the same time producing watercolours on paper placed directly on the wall. He arranged plates of prefabricated monochrome aluminium on the floor to make fields of horizontal colour that pick up the reflections of the surroundings and the public.

He has been represented in collective exhibitions at the Verein Kunsthalle, St Gall, and Shedhalle, Zurich (1986), in Zurich, Graz, Zagreb and Vienna (1987), in Bordeaux and Cologne and in *La Couleur Seule: L'Expérience du Monochrome* (*Colour Alone: The Experience of Monochrome*) at the Musée St-Pierre in Lyons (1988), in Winterthur, Frankfurt, and Perugia and at the Kunstverein, Cologne (1989), at the Venice Biennale and at St Gall (1990), at the Ancienne Douane, Strasbourg, and in London and Chicago (1991), in Vienna and at Documenta 9, Kassel (1992), at the Centre d'Art Contemporain, Kerguehennec (1993) and in *Painting on the Move*, an exhibition of a century of contemporary painting held simultaneously at the Kunstmuseum, the Kunsthalle and the Museum für Gegenwartskunst in Basel in 2002.

He has had solo shows in Winterthur (1984), St Gall (1988), Cologne (1989), at the Aargauer Kunsthaus, Aarau (1990), at the Villa Arson, Nice (1991), in Cologne, in Bern and at the Galerie Ghislaine Hussenot, Paris (1992), at the Musée d'Art Moderne de la Ville de Paris and in Berlin (1993) and at the Kunsthalle, Zurich, and in London and St Gall (1994).

BIBLIOGRAPHY:

Jouannais, Jean-Yves, '*Adrian Schiess, l'harmonie du chaos*' in *Art Press* n° 169, periodical, Paris, May 1992. *Adrian Schiess*, exhibition catalogue, Musée d'Art moderne de la Ville de Paris, Paris, 1993-1994 (good documentation). Damianovic, Maia, '*La Peinture au risque du dilemme*' in *Art Press* n° 211, periodical, Paris, March 1996. Bürgi, Bernhard Mendes, et al., *Painting on the Move*, exhibition catalogue, Kunstmuseum, Kunsthalle, Museum für Gegenwartskunst, Basel, 2002 (texts in German and English).

MUSEUMS AND GALLERIES:

CARQUEFOU (FRAC Pays de la Loire): *Untitled* (1993) - PARIS (FNAC): *Works on the Flat* (1995, set of 10 plates) - RHEIMS (FRAC Champagne-Ardenne).

SCHIESS, Ernest Traugott or Ernesto

Swiss, 19th - 20th century.

Born 17 September 1872, in Basel; died November 1919, in Valence.

Active from 1908 in France.

Painter. Local scenes, landscapes, landscapes with figures.

Ernest Traugott Schiess was a pupil of Eugen Bracht. He settled in Paris from 1908, and travelled in Corsica, Spain, Algeria and the Middle East. He was also an orientalist.

MUSEUMS AND GALLERIES:

AARAU (Aargauer Kunsthaus): *Algerian Women* (c. 1917-1919); *Street in Algiers* (c. 1917-1919) - BERN: *Sea Shore; Garden in the South; A Couple in a Forest Landscape; Landscape in the Balearics*.

AUCTION RECORDS:

BERN, 7 May 1976, *View of Majorca* (oil on card, 13 3/4 x 19 ins / 35 x 48 cm) CHF 1,500. BERN, 10 June 1978, *Shepherd and Flock* (oil on card, 19 3/4 x 13 1/2 ins / 50 x 34 cm) CHF 3,400. LUCERNE, 23 May 1992, *Three Arab Women* (oil on card, 16 1/2 x 20 1/2 ins / 42 x 52 cm) CHF 3,700. LUCERNE, 15 May 1993, *Corte Corsica* (1912, oil on card, 16 1/2 x 22 3/4 ins / 42 x 58 cm) CHF 1,800. ZURICH, 12 June 1995, *Reichenbach Falls near Meiringen; Richisau (Glärnisch)* (oil on paper and oil on canvas, two paintings, each 9 1/2 x 13 3/4 ins / 24 x 35 cm) CHF 2,300. LUCERNE, 2 May 2001, *Hay Harvest* (oil on paper on board, 10 x 13 ins / 25 x 33 cm) CHF 3,800. LUCERNE, 14 Nov 2001, *Interior* (1919, oil on canvas, 14 x 20 ins / 36 x 50 cm) CHF 3,000.

SCHIESS, Hans Rudolf

Swiss, 20th century.

Born 24 December 1904, in Atzenbach, near Basel; died 1978.

Painter.

Hans Schiess lived in Basel and in 1923 and 1924 was a pupil at the school of applied arts of Basel. In 1927 he became a pupil of Ernst L. Kirchner at the Bauhaus in Dessau and in 1928 he spent some time in Berlin. His paintings are difficult to classify. After touching on surrealism very effectively, almost photographically, his forms appear abstract, not geometric in the full sense but architectural, creating depths in the canvas, alternating light and dark patches, suggesting buildings in construction.

From 1931 to 1936 he took part in the group and exhibitions in Paris of Abstraction-Creation, joining with Arp, Sophie Taüber, Chériane, Ernst, L. Frague, Herbin, Seligmann; in 1932 at Basel he exhibited with Arp, Brigori and Seligmann at the Kunsthalle; in 1936 in Zurich he took part in the exhibition *The Problem of Time in Swiss Painting and Sculpture*; in 1938 in Basel he exhibited in *Art Nouveau in Switzerland* at the Kunsthalle; in 1957-1958 in Neuenberg he exhibited in *Fantasy Painting in Basel* at the Kunstmuseum. In 1977 the Kunsthalle of Basel organised a private exhibition of the whole of his work.

BIBLIOGRAPHY:

Hans Schiess, exhibition catalogue, Kunsthalle, Basel, 1977. Fabre, Gladys C., *Abstraction-Création 1931-1936*, exhibition catalogue, Westfälisches Landesmuseum für Kunst und Kulturgeschichte, Münster, Musée d'Art moderne de la ville de Paris, Paris, 1978. Gasser, Bruno, *H. R. Schiess*, Reinhardt, Basel, 1988.

AUCTION RECORDS:

LUCERNE, 24 Nov 1990, *Untitled* (1972, oil on canvas, 21 3/4 x 43 1/2 ins / 55.5 x 110.5 cm) CHF 8,500; *Untitled* (1974, oil on canvas, 25 1/4 x 16 ins / 64 x 40.5 cm) CHF 5,600. LUCERNE, 25 May 1991, *Palette* (oil on wood, 17 x 14 1/4 ins / 43 x 36 cm) CHF 1,400. BERN, 7 May 1999, *Composition with Geometric Elements* (oil on canvas, 34 x 18 ins / 86 x 46 cm) CHF 3,300. COLOGNE, 29 May 1999, *Mountain Landscape near Davos - Clavadel* (1927, oil on canvas, 40 x 47 ins / 101 x 120 cm) DEM 36,000. ZURICH, 21 Nov 2000, *Composition* (oil on canvas, 26 x 22 ins / 65 x 55 cm) CHF 4,000. ZURICH, 26 May 2003, *Composition* (oil on canvas, 36 x 29 ins / 92 x 73 cm) CHF 3,200. ZURICH, 7 June 2004, *Spring Morning* (1928, oil on canvas, 47 x 59 ins / 120 x 150 cm) CHF 15,000.

SCHIESS, Heinrich
Swiss, 17th century.
Active in Rapperswil.
Painter.

SCHIESS, Johannes, or Scheuss
Swiss, 19th century.
Born 28 February 1799, in Herisau (Appenzell); died 28 February 1844, in St Gall.
Watercolourist, draughtsman, engraver. Landscapes.
Johannes Schiess studied with Tanner and Lory. He worked in Bern, Neuenburg, Basel, Schaffhausen and St Gall.

SCHIESS, Klaus
Swiss, 16th century.
Active in Rapperswil 1567-1582.
Painter.

SCHIESS, Traugott
Swiss, 19th century.
Born 9 February 1834, in St Gall; died 14 November 1869, in Munich.
Painter. Landscapes with figures, landscapes.
Traugott Schiess studied in Basel, then became a pupil of J.G. Steffan in Munich and Rudolf Koller in Zurich. He was also influenced by Böcklin.
MUSEUMS AND GALLERIES:
BASEL: *Waterfall.*
AUCTION RECORDS:
LUCERNE, 11 June 1951, *Shepherd and Flock* (1859) CHF 1,900. LUCERNE, 15 Nov 1974, *Mountainous Landscape,* CHF 2,200. COLOGNE, 18 Nov 1982, *Swiss Landscape* (oil on canvas, 17 3/4 x 23 1/2 ins / 45 x 60 cm) DEM 4,000. VIENNA, 5 Oct 1999, *Chamois High in Mountains* (1861, oil on canvas, 36 x 54 ins / 92 x 136 cm) ATS 120,000. ZURICH, 8 Dec 1999, *River Inn near St Moritzersee with Piz Margna* (oil on canvas, 19 x 25 ins / 48 x 63 cm) CHF 10,000. ZURICH, 21 March 2000, *Rhine Valley at Dusk* (oil on board, 8 x 11 ins / 21 x 27 cm) CHF 3,200. MUNICH, 27 Sept 2000, *Goats on Rocky Plateau in Mountains* (oil on canvas, 35 x 52 ins / 90 x 133 cm) DEM 4,000. BERN, 3 May 2002, *Young Shepherd* (1863, oil on canvas, 17 x 14 ins / 43 x 35 cm) CHF 2,500.

SCHIESSL, Johann Karl
Austrian, 19th century.
Died 1828.
Active in Baden near Vienna, Austria.
Painter.
MUSEUMS AND GALLERIES:
VIENNA (Historisches Mus.): *The New Redoutensaal in the Hofburg.*

SCHIESTL, Heintich or Heinz
German, 19th - 20th century.
Born 23 February 1864, in Würzburg.
Sculptor. Religious subjects. Low reliefs.
Heintich Schiestl was a pupil of Syrius Eberle at the academy of fine arts in Munich. He worked in Würzburg, where he created bas-reliefs for altars in Franciscan churches.

SCHIESTL, Matthäus, the Elder
German, 19th - 20th century.
Born 1834; died 1915.
Engraver.
Matthäus Schiestl the Elder was the father of Heinrich, Matthäus the Younger and Rudolf Schiestl. He worked in Salzburg and, from 1863, in Würzburg.

SCHIESTL, Matthäus, the Younger
German, 19th - 20th century.
Born 27 March 1869, in Gingl, near Salzburg; died 1939.
Painter, engraver. Religious subjects, landscapes with figures.
Matthäus Schiestl was the son of Matthäus Schiestl the Elder and brother of Heinrich and Rudolf. He was a pupil of Wilhelm von Diez and Ludwig von Löfftz at the academy of fine arts in Munich. He made paintings for altars in an antique style for the churches of Sankta-Elisabeth in Bonn, and Sankta-Maria in Kaiserslautern.
AUCTION RECORDS:
COLOGNE, 20 March 1981, *Christmas Night* (mixed media/panel, 19 3/4 x 15 1/2 ins / 50 x 39.5 cm) DEM 6,500. VIENNA, 29-30 Oct 1996, *Chapel in the Mountains with Figures* (1922, oil on panel, 23 1/2 x 15 1/2 ins / 59.7 x 39.2 cm) ATS 126,500. KEMPTEN, 4 April 2002, *Stream in an Autumn Landscape* (oil on board, 19 x 26 ins / 49 x 66 cm) EUR 2,500.

SCHIESTL, Rudolf
German, 20th century.
Born 8 August 1878, in Würzburg; died 30 January 1931, in Nuremberg.
Painter, engraver, illustrator. Local scenes, genre scenes.
Rudolf Schiestl was the son of Matthäus Schiestl the Elder, and brother of Heinrich and Matthäus the Younger. He was a pupil of Gabriel von Hackl and Franz von Stuck at the academy of fine arts in Munich. He continued his studies in Innsbruck in 1899 and later in Italy. In 1916 he married the writer Margarete Bentlage, and in 1917-1918 he illustrated the Journal de guerre de Lille. From 1908 he was a teacher at the school of fine arts in Nuremberg, where he settled. He mainly painted and engraved scenes of peasant life.

SCHIESZL, Ferdinand
Austrian, 18th century.
Born 1721, in Vienna.
Painter.
From 1753, Schieszl was active in Temesvár (now Timisoara, Romania), and from 1761 he lived in Arad. He painted the main altarpiece in the Franciscan church in Timisoara.

SCHIETERE, Theodor de
Belgian, 19th century.
Born 1807, in Brussels.
Active in Rome 1838-1858.
Painter.

SCHIETTINI, Giuseppe
Italian, 17th century.
Active in Castello di Villore.
Painter.
Schiettini worked in Florence.
MUSEUMS AND GALLERIES:
PISTOIA (Church of S Francesco): *Nativity.*

SCHIETZOLD, August Robert Rudolf
German, 19th - 20th century.
Born 4 July 1842, in Dresden; died 6 September 1908, in Munich.
Painter. Waterscapes, seascapes, landscapes.
August Schietzold was a pupil of Ludwig Richter at the academy of fine arts in Dresden, and of Adolf Lier and Eduard Schleich at the Academy of Munich.
MUSEUMS AND GALLERIES:
DRESDEN: *Lake Sternberg; Isle of Capri* - LEIPZIG: *Lake Sternberg.*

SCHIEVELBEINE, Hermann Friedrich Anton
German, 19th century.
Born 18 November 1817, in Berlin; died 6 August 1867, in Berlin.
Sculptor, architect.
Schievelbeine originally studied painting at the academy in Berlin, winning a major prize. However, he became attracted to sculpture, which he studied with Widemann, and subsequently devoted himself mainly to sculpture and architecture. He is best known for his statues of *Luther* and

Melanchthon in Kaliningrad (formerly Königsberg) and for *Pallas Athena Teaching the Young Man the Use of Weapons*, *The Burying of Pompeii*, *Pegasus* and the tomb of Baron von Stein in Berlin. His fame was such that he was summoned to St Petersburg, where he worked on the rebuilding of the Winter Palace. He is also known for two important paintings: *Winter Evening* and *Summer Evening*.

SCHIEVELKAMP, Helmuth

German, 19th century.
Born 15 April 1849, in Berlin.
Active in Berlin.
Sculptor.

Schievelkamp is remembered for the Bismarck fountain in Flensburg.

SCHIFALDO, Gerardo

Italian, 17th century.
Painter.

In 1620, Schifaldo was the pupil of Pietro Antonio Novelli in Monreale.

SCHIFANO, Mario

Italian, 20th century.
Born 1934, in Al Khums near Tripoli (Libya); died 26 January 1998, in Rome.
Pastellist, painter (mixed media), collage artist.

Mario Schifano lived and worked in Rome. He worked with his archaeologist father on the restoration of works from the in the Villa Giulia Etruscan Museum. A self-taught artist, he took up painting in the late 1950s.

Schifano worked in many different techniques, often using them in combination. He was particularly interested in experimenting with the mechanical graphic possibilities of advertising and neon lighting. Initially, around 1960, his work showed the influence of American Pop Art in his monochrome panels depicting the archetypes of contemporary society through elements of urban landscape with its markings and signals. After a visit to the USA, where he was much impressed by the work of Franz Kline, he began in 1962-1964 to exploit the possibilities of printed letters and advertising logos such as Esso and Coca-Cola. He did not use them to make any sociological point but as objects, as primary structures of pure perception.

Around 1965, following the tendency in the trans-avant-garde, he began to introduce into his paintings references to, and quotations from, avant-garde artists of earlier periods such as Van Gogh, Monet and the Futurists. It was at this same period that he also began to investigate ways of conveying time and movement in space through a static medium like painting, by making use of polaroids. After 1980, he adopted a highly gestural technique involving the accumulation of several different sketches on the same canvas as in his *Botanical Gardens* (1982) and *Landscapes* (1988-1989). The results have a delightful spontaneity in both the graphics and the use of colour.

In the early years of his career, the intervention of colour merely hinted at obscure borrowings from reality but later, purely for the pleasure of painting 'things', he introduced a number of stereotypical figures: a horse and rider, a fish, a bicycle, a dancer. With time, Schifano's painting began to obey two rules. The first was that of a rigid frontality with no depth. The second was that the surface of the canvas should represent space and the colour, applied over sectors of space on the canvas, should represent time - the time taken by the artist in applying it and the time taken by the viewer contemplating it.

Mario Schifano took part in many collective exhibitions including: São Paulo Biennale (1965); exhibition of contemporary Italian art, Museum of Modern Art, Tokyo (1967); *Aspects of Italy*, Vienna and Innsbruck (1969); 3rd International Salon of the Galeries Pilotes, cantonal museum, Lausanne (1970); Nouvelle Biennale, Paris (1985). He took part in the Apollinaire and Marzotto Prize exhibitions.

His solo exhibitions include: Paris (1963), Rome (1963, 1964 and 1965), Milan (1965, 1967 and 1968), Calcografia Nazionale, Rome (1980); Galleria Communale, Cesena (1980); Galleria De' Foscherari, Bologna (1981); Galleria Emilio Mazzoli, Modena (1982); Pinacoteca Communale, Ravenna (1982); Galleria Tucci Russo, Turin (1982); Sala di Rappresentanza, Messina (1983); Galleria Bergamini, Milan (1983); Annina Nosei Gallery, New York (1983); Galleria Emilio Mazzoli, Modena (1984); Piombi Gallery, Venice (1984); Musée St-Pierre d'Art Contemporain, Lyons (1985); Paris (1988); Centre d'Art Contemporain, St-Priest (1992-1993).

BIBLIOGRAPHY:

IIe Salon international des Galeries Pilotes, exhibition catalogue, Musée cantonal, Lausanne, 1970. *Mario Schifano*, Ed. La Nazionale, Parma, 1974. Bonito Oliva, Achille, *'Mario Schifano'* in *Nouvelle Biennale de Paris*, exhibition catalogue, Electa, Le Moniteur, Paris, 1985. *Mario Schifano: vert physique*, exhibition catalogue, Tour Fromage, Aosta, 1988 (good documentation).

AUCTION RECORDS:

MILAN, 9 April 1970, *True Love*, ITL 700,000. MILAN, 9 March 1972, *Composition*, ITL 1,000,000. MILAN, 5 March 1974, *Detail of a Desert*, ITL 750,000. ROME, 18 May 1976, *Coca-Cola* (1962, enamel on board, 27 1/2 x 20 3/4 ins / 70 x 53 cm) ITL 800,000. MILAN, 16 Nov 1976, *Poor Hearts No. 5* (pastel and collage, 39 1/4 x 27 1/2 ins / 100 x 70 cm) ITL 330,000. ROME, 19 May 1977, *A La Balla* (1965, oil on canvas, 59 x 37 3/4 ins / 150 x 96 cm) ITL 2,400,000. LONDON, 2 Dec 1980, *Baci Perugina* (1967-1968, mixed media/canvas, 78 3/4 x 39 1/4 ins / 200 x 100 cm) GBP 2,200. ROME, 11 June 1981, *Grey 402* (1961, oil on canvas, 43 x 58 1/4 ins / 109 x 148 cm) ITL 7,500,000. MILAN, 14 June 1983, *Sign 7E 8E* (1961, oil on canvas mounted to board, 43 1/4 x 59 ins / 110 x 150 cm) ITL 11,000,000. ROME, 23 April 1985, *Untitled* (1963, pencil, 27 1/2 x 39 1/4 ins / 70 x 100 cm) ITL 2,400,000. ROME, 18 March 1986, *For the Construction of an Oasis* (steel, multiple, h 96 1/2 ins / 245 cm) ITL 1,800,000. MILAN, 9 Dec 1986, *En Plein Air after New York* (1964, oil and varnish/mounted paper/canvas, 49 1/2 x 100 ins / 126 x 254 cm) ITL 20,500,000. ROME, 7 April 1988, *Field of Corn* (1984, varnish/mounted paper/canvas, 63 x 74 3/4 ins / 160 x 190 cm) ITL 10,000,000. MILAN, 8 June 1988, *Untitled* (1962, varnish/canvas, 29 1/4 x 21 ins / 74.5 x 52.5 cm) ITL 2,400,000. ROME, 15 Nov 1988, *Direct from the Moon* (mixed media/canvas, 19 3/4 x 23 1/2 ins / 50 x 60 cm) ITL 950,000. ROME, 15 Nov 1988, *Large High Corner* (1960, acrylic/canvas, 31 1/2 x 51 1/4 ins / 80 x 130 cm) ITL 13,000,000. MILAN, 14 Dec 1988, *Coca Cola* (1962, varnish/paper/panel, 39 1/4 x 27 1/4 ins / 100 x 69 cm) ITL 13,500,000. MILAN, 20 March 1989, *Esso* (1964, felt/paper, 55 x 35 1/2 ins / 140 x 90 cm) ITL 15,000,000. ROME, 17 April 1989, *December 1883, Dresden* (1970, neon, felt and acrylic/treated canvas, 78 3/4 x 137 3/4 ins / 200 x 350 cm) ITL 45,000,000. PARIS, 29 Sept 1989, *Information* (1985-1986, oil on canvas, 19 3/4 x 19 3/4 ins / 50 x 50 cm) FRF 8,000. PARIS, 8 Oct 1989, *Via delle Mantellate* (1988, acrylic/paper, 39 1/4 x 27 1/2 ins / 100 x 70 cm) FRF 28,000. ROME, 6 Dec 1989, *Energy* (1961, oil on paper/canvas, 47 1/4 x 39 1/4 ins / 120 x 100 cm) ITL 28,750,000. PARIS, 18 Feb 1990, *Sun* (1974, acrylic/canvas, 47 1/4 x 47 1/4 ins / 120 x 120 cm) FRF 35,000. MILAN, 27 March 1990, *Blue Monochrome* (felt on mounted paper, 43 1/4 x 43 1/4 ins / 110 x 110 cm) ITL 23,500,000. MILAN, 13 June 1990, *Elements of a Landscape* (oil on canvas, 46 x 35 ins / 116 x 89 cm) ITL 27,000,000. ROME, 30 Oct 1990, *Sign No. 2* (1961, felt/paper/canvas, 51 1/4 x 47 1/4 ins / 130 x 120 cm) ITL 29,000,000. PARIS, 8 Nov 1990, *Botanical Garden* (1982, acrylic/canvas, 80 x 118 ins / 203 x 300 cm) FRF 50,000. LUCERNE,

24 Nov 1990, *Bicycle* (acrylic/canvas, 39 1/4 x 39 1/4 ins / 100 x 100 cm) CHF 3,300. ROME, 9 April 1991, *Acronym of Energy - Esso* (1964, varnish/paper/canvas, 55 x 35 1/2 ins / 140 x 90 cm) ITL 25,000,000. ZURICH, 16 Oct 1991, *Landscape* (1989, oil on canvas, 17 3/4 x 17 3/4 ins / 45 x 45 cm) CHF 1,600. MILAN, 14 Nov 1991, *Water Lily* (1985, oil and varnish/canvas, 32 x 43 3/4 ins / 81 x 111 cm) ITL 3,000,000. ROME, 3 Dec 1991, *Venus de Milo* (1964, acrylic/panel, 35 1/2 x 29 1/4 ins / 90 x 74 cm) ITL 16,000,000. MILAN, 14 April 1992, *Romazzano - the Alighiero House* (1988, varnish and acrylic/canvas, 102 1/4 x 78 3/4 ins / 260 x 200 cm) ITL 8,000,000. ROME, 12 May 1992, *Figure in Motion* (1965, felt/paper/canvas, 63 x 51 1/4 ins / 160 x 130 cm) ITL 11,000,000. MILAN, 23 June 1992, *Detail of a Landscape* (1969, varnish and collage/mounted paper, 60 x 39 ins / 151.5 x 99 cm) ITL 5,200,000. MILAN, 9 Nov 1992, *Coca-Cola* (1962, mixed media/paper, 27 1/2 x 39 1/4 ins / 70 x 100 cm) ITL 6,500,000. MUNICH, 1-2 Dec 1992, *Field of Wheat* (acrylic/canvas, 27 1/4 x 39 1/4 ins / 69.5 x 99.5 cm) DEM 2,415. MILAN, 15 Dec 1992, *All the Stars* (oil on canvas/Plexiglas, 69 1/4 x 62 1/2 ins / 176 x 159 cm) ITL 14,500,000. LUCERNE, 15 May 1993, *Untitled* (acrylic/canvas, 27 1/2 x 19 3/4 ins / 70 x 50 cm) CHF 2,350. ROME, 27 May 1993, *Body in Motion and in Equilibrium* (1964, oil on canvas, three panels, 78 3/4 x 118 ins / 200 x 300 cm) ITL 38,000,000. ROME, 30 Nov 1993, *Fountains* (varnish/paper/canvas, 63 x 74 3/4 ins / 160 x 190 cm) ITL 10,350,000. MILAN, 9 March 1995, *All Starry* (acrylic/canvas, 47 1/4 x 47 1/4 ins / 120 x 120 cm) ITL 2,070,000. ROME, 28 March 1995, *No. 1 from the Archives of Futurism* (1965, oil on canvas, 63 x 45 1/4 ins / 160 x 115 cm) ITL 29,900,000. MILAN, 20 May 1996, *Esso* (varnish/mounted paper/canvas, 47 1/4 x 70 3/4 ins / 120 x 180 cm) ITL 8,050,000; *Landscape* (collage and mixed media/paper, 39 1/4 x 27 1/2 ins / 100 x 70 cm) ITL 1,150,000. MILAN, 28 May 1996, *Door* (acrylic and varnish/canvas, 47 1/4 x 47 1/4 ins / 120 x 120 cm) ITL 11,500,000. MILAN, 25 Nov 1996, *Bitter* (varnish/canvas, 31 1/2 x 39 1/4 ins / 80 x 100 cm) ITL 2,415,000. MILAN, 10 Dec 1996, *Large Green* (1960, varnish/canvas, 59 x 59 ins / 150 x 150 cm) ITL 25,047,000. MILAN, 24 Nov 1997, *Water Lily (to Me and You)* (acrylic/canvas, 37 1/2 x 81 3/4 ins / 95 x 207.5 cm) ITL 13,800,000. ROME, 27 April 1999, *Segnaletico no. 2* (1961, enamel on paper laid on canvas, 51 x 47 ins / 130 x 120 cm) ITL 50,000,000. ROME, 25 Nov 1999, *Numbers 90 and 100* (1960, enamel on paper laid on canvas, two joined panels, 34 x 49 ins / 87 x 125 cm) ITL 107,000,000. MILAN, 28 Nov 2000, *Palinurus* (1961, enamel on paper laid on canvas, 51 x 39 ins / 130 x 100 cm) ITL 108,000,000. LONDON, 6 Dec 2000, *Anaemic Landscape III* (1965, acrylic on two canvases, 87 x 79 ins / 220 x 200 cm) GBP 60,000. ROME, 12 April 2001, *Homage to Balla* (1964, enamel on paper laid on canvas, 99 x 50 ins / 252 x 126 cm) ITL 134,000,000. MILAN, 29 May 2001, *Indication* (1961, enamel on paper laid on canvas, 55 x 63 ins / 140 x 160 cm) ITL 140,000,000. MILAN, 21 May 2002, *Untitled* (1967-1969, pencil and enamel on paper laid on canvas, 59 x 71 ins / 150 x 180 cm) EUR 40,000. PRATO, 29 Nov 2002, *Anaemic Landscape* (enamel on paper, 79 x 126 ins / 200 x 320 cm) EUR 29,000. ROME, 10 April 2003, *Landscape* (enamel, 79 x 118 ins / 200 x 300 cm) EUR 55,000. MILAN, 27 May 2003, *Untitled* (1964, enamel, pastel and collage on paper laid on canvas, 50 x 99 ins / 127 x 251 cm) EUR 72,000. MILAN, 24 May 2004, *Totem Maze from Freud's Point of View* (1970, acrylic and enamel, 88 x 130 ins / 224 x 330 cm) EUR 40,000. LONDON, 19 Oct 2004, *Big Initial* (1962, enamel on paper laid on canvas, 91 x 59 ins / 230 x 150 cm) GBP 150,000.

SCHIFERT
Italian, 17th century.
Probably active during the 17th century.
Painter.

Schifert's *Holy Family* in the Sabauda gallery in Turin reveals the influence of the Bologna School.

SCHIFF, Jeanne Henriette (Mme).
See **DUBERTRAND SCHIFF Jeanne**

SCHIFF, Mathias
French, 19th century.
Born 1862, in Rethel-lès-Sierck (Moselle); died 1886, in Nancy.
Sculptor, painter. Mythological subjects, figures, historical figures. Monuments, statues, equestrian statues.

He was the pupil of Charles Pétre, Émile (?) Thomas and Alexandre Falguière.

Despite his early death, he left behind some substantial works, which are now in the Musée des Beaux-Arts in Nancy (Lorraine), France.

M Schiff 1885

MUSEUMS AND GALLERIES:
NANCY (MBA): *Portrait of the Artist at the Age of Twenty-three* (painting); *Study for the Equestrian Statue of Duke René II*; *Equestrian Statue of Duke René II*; *General Henaion*; *Victor Poirel*; *Daphnis and Chloe*.

SCHIFF, Robert
Austrian, 19th - 20th century.
Born 17 January 1869, in Vienna.
Painter.

Robert Schiff was a pupil at the academy of fine arts in Berlin and continued his training in Munich and Paris with Benjamin-Constant and Jean-Paul Laurens. From 1905 to 1907 he worked in London. He finally settled in Vienna.

AUCTION RECORDS:
VERSAILLES, 5 March 1989, *The Model in the Studio* (1904, oil on panel, 16 1/4 x 22 ins / 41 x 55 cm) FRF 30,000. PARIS, 24 April 2002, *Nude with Virginia Creeper* (oil on panel, 16 x 13 ins / 41 x 32 cm) EUR 3,000. VIENNA, 27 Nov 2002, *Portrait of a Little Girl* (1912, oil on canvas, 60 x 34 ins / 153 x 86 cm) EUR 3,400.

SCHIFFAUER, Johann
Austrian, 18th - 19th century.
Painter. Flowers.

Schiffauer is best known for his paintings of flowers on porcelain for the Vienna factory where he worked from 1778 to 1829.

SCHIFFELERS, Grégoire
Belgian, 17th century.
Active in Venloo.
Sculptor.

Grégoire Schiffelers completed work on the altar in Liège Cathedral in 1634. He may have been the same person as Gregorius Schyseler.

SCHIFFER, Anton
Austrian, 19th century.
Born 18 August 1811, in Graz; died 13 June 1876, in Vienna.
Painter. Landscapes with figures, mountainscapes, waterscapes.

Anton Schiffer was the grandson of Matthias Schiffer and studied at the academy in Vienna.

MUSEUMS AND GALLERIES:
GRAZ: *Lake* - VIENNA: *The Schneeberg and the Hollental with the Kaiserbrunnen*.

AUCTION RECORDS:
VIENNA, 14 Nov 1950, *Alpine Landscape* (1846) ATS 2,500. VIENNA, 14 June 1966, *View of Ischl*, ATS 30,000. VIENNA, 16 Sept 1969, *View of Heiligenblut*, ATS 30,000. VIENNA, 22 Sept 1970, *Mountian Landscape with Lake*, ATS 32,000. VIENNA, 27 May 1974, *Mountainous Landscape* (1844) ATS 110,000. COLOGNE, 26 March 1976, *Alpine Landscape* (1872, oil on canvas, 13 3/4 x

16½ ins / 35 x 42 cm) DEM 3,500. VIENNA, 15 March 1977, *View of Fusch* (1868, oil on card, 11 x 14¾ ins / 28 x 37.5 cm) ATS 100,000. VIENNA, 14 June 1977, *View of Berchtesgaden* (1842, watercolour, 10¼ x 13 ins / 26 x 33 cm) ATS 32,000. VIENNA, 19 June 1979, *Alpine Landscape* (oil on canvas, 20 x 25 ins / 50.5 x 63.5 cm) ATS 45,000. VIENNA, 19 May 1981, *Tyrolean Landscape* (1868, oil on canvas, 12¼ x 15¾ ins / 31 x 40 cm) ATS 70,000. LONDON, 8 June 1983, *View of a Town by an Alpine Lake* (1868, oil on card, 16 x 21¼ ins / 40.5 x 54 cm) GBP 3,400. NEW YORK, 29 Oct 1986, *View of Ischl* (1865, oil on panel, 15¼ x 19 ins / 38.5 x 48.2 cm) USD 7,500. HEIDELBERG, 14 Oct 1988, *Traveller by a Mountain Lake* (oil on panel, 13½ x 16½ ins / 34 x 42 cm) DEM 1,900. COLOGNE, 15 Oct 1988, *View of Lake Traun* (oil on canvas, 13¾ x 19 ins / 35 x 48 cm) DEM 4,000. MUNICH, 7 Dec 1993, *Castle in Austria* (1864, oil on card, 19¼ x 25¼ ins / 49 x 64 cm) DEM 23,000. NEW YORK, 17 Jan 1996, *Outside the Palace Gates* (1864, oil on card, 19½ x 25 ins / 49.5 x 63.8 cm) USD 9,775. VIENNA, 29-30 Oct 1996, *Berchtesgaden with the Watzmann Mountains in the Distance* (1869, oil on canvas, 38 x 49½ ins / 96.5 x 126 cm) ATS 333,500. DÜSSELDORF, 31 Jan 2000, *Altausee with Dachstein* (August 1847, oil on paper/canvas, 11 x 15 ins / 29 x 39 cm) DEM 28,000. DÜSSELDORF, 31 Jan 2000, *Grundelsee* (1859, oil on board, 10 x 12 ins / 26 x 31 cm) DEM 28,000. VIENNA, 28 May 2001, *Entrance to Wimbach* (1 September 1848, oil on paper/canvas, 12 x 15 ins / 30 x 39 cm) ATS 160,000. VIENNA, 22 May 2003, *View of Orts Church in Ramsau, Berchtesgaden* (oil on board, 8 x 10 ins / 20 x 26 cm) EUR 8,500.

SCHIFFER, Arthur
Hungarian, 20th century.
Born 18 January 1885, in Esseg (now Osijek Croatia).
Painter. Portraits, landscapes.
Arthur Schiffer studied in Budapest and Paris, where he settled.

SCHIFFER, Ethel Bennett
American, 20th century.
Born 10 March 1879, in Brooklyn (New York City).
Painter, engraver.
Ethel Schiffer studied at the Art Students' League in New York. She was a member of the Society of Independent Artists, the American Artists Professional League and the American Federation of Arts.

SCHIFFER, Franz Josef
Austrian, 19th century.
Active in Graz.
Painter.
Franz Josef Schiffer was the son of Matthias Schiffer. He was a scene painter at the theatres in Klagenfurt and Bruck.

SCHIFFER, Joseph. See **SCHIEFFER**

SCHIFFER, Matthias
Austrian, 18th - 19th century.
Born 1744, in Weiz (Styria); died 1827, in Graz.
Painter, fresco artist. Church interiors.
Matthias Schiffer painted a large number of frescoes and pictures for churches in Styria. He was the last representative of the Baroque style in that region.
AUCTION RECORDS:
BERN, 26 Oct 1988, *Interior of a Gothic Cathedral* (oil on canvas, 24 x 30¼ ins / 61 x 77 cm) CHF 6,500.

SCHIFFERDECKER, Heinz
German, 20th century.
Born 13 July 1889, in Ludwigshafen; died 21 January 1924, in Mannheim.
Painter.

SCHIFFERL, Josef
Slav, 18th century.
Painter.

SCHIFFERLE, Franz
German, 17th century.
Active in Lauingen in 1692.
Sculptor.

SCHIFFERLE, Klaudia
Swiss, 20th - 21st century.
Born 1955.
Painter (gouache), draughtswoman. Figures, still-lifes.
MUSEUMS AND GALLERIES:
LAUSANNE (Cantonal MFA): *Untitled* (1988, mixed media in the round).
AUCTION RECORDS:
LUCERNE, 24 Nov 1990, *Untitled* (gouache/paper, 16¼ x 23¼ ins / 41 x 59 cm) CHF 4,400. LUCERNE, 26 Nov 1994, *Woman with a Mask* (pencil/paper, 16½ x 11¾ ins / 42 x 30 cm) CHF 2,000. LUCERNE, 20 May 1995, *Untitled: Composition with Cups* (gouache and gold paint/paper, 9½ x 13¼ ins / 24 x 33.6 cm) CHF 840. LUCERNE, 8 June 1996, *Untitled* (1983, chalk/paper, 18 x 24½ ins / 46 x 62 cm) CHF 1,450. LUCERNE, 5 June 1999, *Praying Plant* (1985, oil on canvas, 59 x 24 ins / 150 x 60 cm) CHF 5,000. ZURICH, 15 May 2001, *Dinner* (1986, oil on canvas, 24 x 20 ins / 60 x 50 cm) CHF 3,600. ZURICH, 4 June 2002, *Still-life* (1982, acrylic and varnish on canvas, 64 x 62 ins / 163 x 158 cm) CHF 5,000. ZURICH, 24 June 2003, *Untitled* (1982, varnish on tin, 38 x 17 ins / 97 x 44 cm) CHF 3,000. LUCERNE, 22 Nov 2003, *Beggar with Tourist* (1984, gouache, 16 x 23 ins / 41 x 58 cm) CHF 2,300.

SCHIFFI, Ezio
Italian, 19th - 20th century.
Born 15 September 1859, in Valenza (Piedmont); died 1940.
Painter, sculptor.
Orientalism.
A self-taught artist, Ezio Schiffi worked in Munich, in Paris in 1892, in Istanbul and in Rome.
MUSEUMS AND GALLERIES:
LYONS (MBA): *Foundling*.

SCHIFFLIN, Georg Heinrich
German, 17th - 18th century.
Born 1666; died 1745.
Active in Augsburg.
Engraver (burin).
Schifflin worked almost exclusively for the publisher Jeremias Wolff. He engraved mainly views of Augsburg and portraits of bishops.

SCHIFFMANN, Johann Jost
Swiss, 18th century.
Died 9 December 1723, in Hergiswald, near Lucerne.
Painter. Armorials.

SCHIFFMANN, Jost Joseph Niklaus
Swiss, 19th century.
Born 30 August 1822, in Lucerne; died 11 May 1883, in Munich.
Painter. Genre scenes, landscapes, architectural views.
Around 1850, Schiffmann settled in Munich, where he studied with Eduard Gerhardt.
MUSEUMS AND GALLERIES:
ST GALL: *Tyrolean Landscape* - WINTERTHUR (Kunstmus.): *Seashore with Ruins*; *View of Rigi*.
AUCTION RECORDS:
VIENNA, 15 March 1977, *Sunday in the Prater* (oil on canvas, 29 x 39¼ ins / 73.5 x 99.5 cm) ATS 28,000. LUCERNE, 7 Nov 1980, *Landscape in the Bernese Oberland* (oil on card/remounted panel, 12 x 15½ ins / 30.5 x 39.5 cm) CHF 5,000. VIENNA, 17 Feb 1981, *Woodland Avenue* (oil on canvas, 29 x 39¼ ins / 73.5 x 100 cm) ATS 14,000. ZURICH, 24 Nov 1993, *City Square by Night* (1860, oil on panel, 17¾ x 12¾ ins / 45 x 32.5 cm) CHF 6,900. ZURICH, 2 June 1994, *Musician by*

Moonlight (1854, oil on panel, 22 3/4 x 15 ins / 58 x 38 cm) CHF 7,475. WARSAW, 9 March 2000, *Clifftop Castle* (1854, oil on canvas, 39 x 28 ins / 98 x 71 cm) PLN 27,000. ZURICH, 5 Dec 2000, *Lake Landscape, Lake Lucerne* (oil on canvas, 30 x 27 ins / 77 x 68 cm) CHF 6,500.

SCHIFFNER, Anton
Austrian, 19th century.
Born 1811, in Graz; died 1876.
Painter. Landscapes.
Schiffner studied at the academy in Vienna and became quite famous during his lifetime.

SCHIFFNER, Gottlieb
French, 18th century.
Born 1755, in Groszschönau; died 1795, in Dresden.
Painter.
Gottlieb Schiffner studied at the academy of Dresden with Schenau. From 1782 to 1787 he was working in Warsaw. He was a member of the academy of St Petersburg in 1787 and returned to Dresden in 1788. He painted landscapes and portraits, and made copies of works by J. Vernet, Krafft and Bacciarelli.
MUSEUMS AND GALLERIES:
JELGAVA: *Duke Pierre de Courlande; Pastor E. D. Werth; E. C. von der Recke, née Von Kupffer; King Stanislas Augustus of Poland; Young Jewess* - ZITTAU: *Landscape*.

SCHIFFNER, Johannes
German, 20th century.
Born 24 June 1886, in Hamburg.
Sculptor.
Johannes Schiffner worked in Berlin.
AUCTION RECORDS:
COLOGNE, 7 Dec 1983, *Dancer* (dark brown patinated bronze, h. 22 1/2 ins / 57 cm) DEM 2,500.

SCHIJNDEL, J. van. See **SCHENDEL**

SCHIK, Pieter. See **SCHICK**

SCHIKANEDER, Jakub or Jacob
Czech, 19th - 20th century.
Born 27 February 1855, in Prague; died 15 November 1924, in Prague.
Painter, pastellist. Genre scenes, scenes with figures, urban landscapes, landscapes with figures.
Jakub Schikaneder was a descendant of the librettist of Mozart's opera *The Magic Flute* (*Zauberflöte*) in Vienna, Emanuel Schikaneder. From 1891 to 1923, he was professor at the fine arts school in Prague.

In line with the realist trend that preceded the generation of Impressionist artists in Europe in the 19th century, Schikaneder initially depicted social subjects, using a suitable and relatively academic technique: a country woman collecting dead wood, an old woman all alone, the various ceremonials associated with death, and sordid crimes arising from squalour. In the last years of the century, he began to paint a few more intimist subjects - couples in love, a woman at a door open to the new spring. These subjects marked not just Schickaneder's moving away from moralising themes, but also his moving towards a technique that was noticeably influenced by the passing of Impressionism, even though the atmospheres of his work remained those of misty autumn dusks and snowy winter nights. Apart from cityscapes lit by the dim light of street lamps or the weak and watery light of the moon, Schikaneder produced some relatively unusual canvases of interiors at night-time, poorly lit by candlelight. In order to depict the trembling gleam of his misty and blurry subjects, Schikaneder developed a technique based on small, discreet brushstrokes, perhaps inspired by the Neo-Impressionist approach, as is sometimes found in works by Whistler. Such a desire to depict shadow in general, whether outdoors or in interiors, indicates a poetic choice on the part of Schikaneder, and the deeply nostalgic atmosphere in Schikaneder's painting is reminiscent of fin de siècle Symbolism.

Schikaneder's work remained unknown to the public in Czechoslovakia during the course of the 20th century, probably because Cubist and Surrealist art had totally monopolised interest and attention. Thanks to a retrospective exhibition at the Národní galerie in Prague in 1998-1999, Schikaneder's work was rediscovered.
BIBLIOGRAPHY:
Vlcek, Tomas, *Jakub Schikaneder 1855-1924 - Prague Painter of the Turn of the Century*, exhibition catalogue, Národní galerie, Prague, 1998-1999.
MUSEUMS AND GALLERIES:
PRAGUE (Národní Muz.).
AUCTION RECORDS:
LONDON, 6 June 1990, *The Christmas Market in Prague* (oil on canvas, 23 1/4 x 17 1/4 ins / 59 x 43.5 cm) GBP 1,980. PRAGUE, 27 May 2000, *Prague Corners in Night* (coloured crayon, 25 x 20 ins / 64 x 52 cm) CZK 300,000. LONDON, 15 June 2004, *Interior* (oil on canvas, 36 x 30 ins / 91 x 77 cm) GBP 15,000.

SCHIKANEDER, Konrad
German, 20th century.
Born 24 January 1888, in Kitzingen.
Painter, engraver.
Konrad Schikaneder was active in Munich.

SCHIKH, Franz. See **SCHICKH Frans**

SCHILBACH, Christian, or Schildbach
German, 18th century.
Died 1742.
Painter.
Christian Schilbach was active in Vienna and, in 1714, in Bamberg, where he painted three portraits of the Elector Franz von Schönborn. In 1727, while working at the court of Gotha, he painted the portrait of an Arabian prince.
MUSEUMS AND GALLERIES:
GOTHA (Bibliothek): *Portrait of Ernst Salomon Cyprian*.

SCHILBACH, Heinrich Christian Friedrich
German, 18th - 19th century.
Active in Altenburg.
Painter.

SCHILBACH, J. D.
German, 18th century.
Active in Gotha c. 1727.
Draughtsman.

SCHILBACH, Johann Christian
German, 18th century.
Died c. 1760.
Active in Gotha.
Painter.
Johann Christian Schilbach painted the portrait of Duchess Magdalena Augusta of Saxe-Gotha.
AUCTION RECORDS:
LONDON, 7 Dec 1962, *The Forum*, Gns 420.

SCHILBACH, Johann Heinrich
German, 19th century.
Born 1798, in Barchfeld; died 9 May 1851, in Darmstadt.
Painter, engraver.
Johann Heinrich Schilbach studied with Primavesi. In 1828, he was appointed painter to the court in Darmstadt. He engraved views of Athens, and produced a large number of engravings. Works by Schilbach were included in the 2001 exhibition *Un Paese incantato. Italia dipinta da Thomas Jones a Corot* (*An Enchanted Country: Depictions of Italy from Thomas Jones to Corot*) at the Centro Internazionale d'Arte e di Cultura di Palazzo Tè in Mantua.

Bibliography:

Bergsträsser, Gisela, *Johann Heinrich Schilbach: ein Darmstædter Maler der Romantik,* Darmstadt, 1959. Märker, Peter/Pohl, Klaus-D., *Der Traum vom Süden. Johann Heinrich Schilbach (1798-1851): Zeichnungen, Aquarelle, ölstudien und Gemälde,* exhibition catalogue, Hessisches Landesmuseum, Darmstadt, Kehrer, Heidelberg, 2000. Ottani Cavina, Anna (ed.), *Un Paese incantato. Italia dipinta da Thomas Jones a Corot,* exhibition catalogue, Electa, Milan, 2001.

Museums and Galleries:

Berlin (Nationalgal.): *Landscape* - Copenhagen (Thorvaldsens Mus.): *View of the Roman Campagna* (two studies) - Darmstadt (Hessisches Landesmus.): *Castel Gandolfo* (oil on paper); *Cloud over a Distant Landscape* (oil/card); *The Coast Near Sorrento* (watercolour); *Reefs off Capri* (watercolour); *Buildings with Cupolas* (oil on paper).

Auction records:

Paris, 3 Nov 1944, *Landscapes* (two paintings) FRF 3,050. London, 12 Oct 1967, *The Forum seen from the Arch of Trajan,* Gns 850. London, 28 Nov 1985, *A Steep Woodland Path* (pencil and pen, 14 x 10¾ ins / 35.7 x 27.6 cm) GBP 1,600. Zurich, 8 June 1999, *Village on River in Mountainous Landscape* (oil on canvas, 19 x 24 ins / 47 x 60 cm) CHF 35,000. Hamburg, 7 June 2000, *Olevano* (oil on paper, 8 x 11 ins / 21 x 29 cm) DEM 16,000. Cologne, 25 Nov 2000, *Schloss Schonberg on Mountain Road* (1838, oil on canvas, 16 x 21 ins / 40 x 54 cm) DEM 90,000. Cologne, 17 Nov 2001, *Rhein Landscape with Oberwesel* (oil on canvas, 31 x 44 ins / 80 x 111 cm) DEM 80,000. Cologne, 16 Nov 2002, *Mountain Landscape near Berchtesgaden* (1847, oil on canvas, 18 x 23 ins / 45 x 59 cm) EUR 30,000.

SCHILCHER

German, 18th century.
Active in Eggenburg.
Sculptor.

SCHILCHER, Anton von

German, 19th century.
Born 1795, in Mindelheim; died 4 March 1827, in Paros, Greece.
Painter, engraver. Military subjects.

Anton von Schilcher studied in Munich. He joined the Bavarian army and accompanied General Heydegger to Greece.

SCHILCHER, Friedrich

Austrian, 19th century.
Born 1811, in Vienna; died 6 May 1881, in Vienna.
Painter, decorative designer. Portraits, genre scenes.

Friedrich Schilcher studied at the academy in Vienna.

Museums and Galleries:

Brno: *Cherub* - Riga: *Portrait of a Man; A Slovak* - Vienna: *Satyr* - Vienna (Akademie der Bildenden Künste): *Girl; Portrait of a Child* - Vienna (Kunsthistorisches Mus.): *Portrait of Ferdinand Raimund.*

Auction records:

London, 22 June 1983, *Girl with a Garland of Flowers (Thought to be a Portrait of Fanny Elssler)* (1853, oil on canvas, 40½ x 31¾ ins / 103 x 80.5 cm) GBP 1,200. Vienna, 18 April 2000, *Kaiser Franz Joseph I von Osterreich* (c. 1860, oil on canvas, 48 x 37 ins / 123 x 95 cm) ATS 100,000. Stuttgart, 22 March 2001, *Young Women with Tamburine* (oil on canvas, 52 x 40 ins / 132 x 102 cm) DEM 13,000.

SCHILCHER, Jacob

Austrian, 18th - 19th century.
Born 14 March 1763, in Ammergau; died 31 March 1827, in Vienna.
Active in Vienna.
Painter.

SCHILD, Bartholomäus Franz

German, 18th century.
Born 1749, in Bonn.
Painter. History painting, flowers, fruit.

SCHILD, Carl

Austrian, 19th century.
Born 1831, in Vienna; died 22 July 1906, in Vienna.
Sculptor, painter.

Carl Schild studied with Franz Dobiaschofsky, Franz Bauer, Josef Kässmann and Hanns Gasser at the academy of fine arts in Vienna.

Museums and Galleries:

Vienna (Rathaus): *Portrait of Bürgermeister Dr Andreas Zelinska.*

SCHILD, Charlotte Rebekka, later Frau Damiset

German, 18th century.
Born 1734, in Frankfurt am Main.
Engraver.

Charlotte Rebekka Schild was the daughter of Christian Lebrecht Schild. She worked as an engraver of armorials in Hanau and Paris.

SCHILD, Christian Lebrecht

German, 18th century.
Born 1711, in Harburg (Bavaria); died 3 October 1751, in Frankfurt am Main.
Engraver.

From 1733, Christian Lebrecht Schild worked in Frankfurt am Main as a gem engraver and medallist.

SCHILD, Eduard

Swiss, 20th century.
Born 18 January 1878, in Brienz (Bern); died 1944.
Painter. Landscapes.

Eduard Schild mainly worked in Brienz.

Ed-Schild

Auction records:

Paris, 19 March 1990, *Square at Hyères* (1931, oil on canvas, 21¼ x 25½ ins / 54 x 65 cm) FRF 7,500. Bern, 12 May 1990, *Peasant's House* (oil on canvas, 17¼ x 20½ ins / 44 x 52 cm) CHF 900.

SCHILD, H. D.

Dutch, 19th - 20th century.
Born 1 September 1872, in The Hague.
Painter.

H.D.Schild was a pupil at the royal academy of fine arts at The Hague.

SCHILD, Johann Erich

German, 17th century.
Active in Hanover between 1678 and 1695.
Engraver. Coins.

SCHILD, Johann Matthias

German, 18th century.
Born 23 October 1701, in Düsseldorf; died 28 November 1775, in Bonn.
Painter. Portraits, animals.

Johann Matthias Schild was a court painter to the princes Clemens August and Max Friedrich of Cologne.

SCHILD, Maria Helena Florentina

German, 18th - 19th century.
Born 1745, in Bonn; died 1827, in Bonn.
Painter. History painting.

Maria Schild was taught by her father Johann Matthias. She was a member of the academy in Düsseldorf.

SCHILD, Mathäus
Swiss, 19th - 20th century.
Born 22 October 1872, in Brienz (Bern).
Painter. Landscapes.
Mathäus Schild was a relative of Eduard Schild.

SCHILD, Peter
Swiss, 19th century.
Born 23 October 1852, in Brienz (Bern); died 9 February 1878, in Brienz (Bern).
Engraver (wood).

SCHILDBACH, Christian. See **SCHILBACH**

SCHILDE, Emil August
German, 19th - 20th century.
Born 23 August 1869, in Breitenbach.
Painter, engraver.
Emil Schilde studied in Munich and was a pupil of Léon Pohle and Ferdinand Pauwels at the academy of fine arts at Dresden. He based himself up Dresden.

SCHILDER, Andrei Nicolaievitch, or Childer
Russian, 19th - 20th century.
Born 1861, in Torna; died 1919.
Painter, draughtsman. Waterscapes, landscapes.
Andrei Schilder was a student of Ian Schichkin. He became a member of the academy in 1903.
MUSEUMS AND GALLERIES:
MOSCOW (State Tretyakov Gal.): *Escarpment above the River; Pine Forest near the Sea*; a sheet of studies.
AUCTION RECORDS:
LONDON, 20 Feb 1985, *Winter Landscape at Dusk* (1915, oil on canvas, 31 x 46 ins / 79 x 117 cm) GBP 6,000. LONDON, 13 Feb 1986, *Summer Landscape* (oil on canvas, 27 3/4 x 41 1/2 ins / 70.5 x 105.5 cm) GBP 3,000. NEW YORK, 24 May 1989, *Thatched Cottages by a River* (oil on canvas, 28 1/2 x 42 ins / 72.4 x 106.9 cm) USD 6,050. LONDON, 5 Oct 1989, *Stream in a Forest* (1886, oil on card, 37 x 24 3/4 ins / 94 x 63 cm) GBP 6,050. LONDON, 14 Dec 1995, *Clouded Mountains* (oil on panel, 12 1/2 x 18 1/4 ins / 32 x 46.5 cm) GBP 2,070.

SCHILDER, Nikolai Gustavovich, or Childer
Russian, 19th century.
Born 1828; died 1898.
Painter. Battles, genre scenes.
Nikolai Gustavovich Schilder studied at the art academy in St Petersburg, and became member of the academy in 1861.
MUSEUMS AND GALLERIES:
MOSCOW (State Tretyakov Gal.): *The Seduction.*

SCHILDER VON BABINBERG, Johann
German, 14th century.
Born in Oppenheim.
Painter.
Johann Schilder von Babinberg was a German Primitive. He painted an altarpiece for the high altar of Frankfurt Cathedral in 1382.

SCHILDGE, Marc
French, 20th - 21st century.
Born 1953, in Paris.
Painter.
In 1981, Marc Schildge was awarded a scholarship by the Paris-based Fondation Nationale des Arts Graphiques et Plastiques. He initially painted panel comprising many vividly coloured elements which combine to produce a pleasingly decorative overall effect.

He has shown his work at group exhibitions: in 1980, at the Galerie Peinture Fraîche in Paris; in 1984 and 1985, at the Salon de Montrouge; in 1985, at the Salon de la Jeune Sculpture in Paris; in 1985, at *Travaux sur Papier* (*Working with Paper*), an exhibition held in Villeparisis, and in 1987 at *Carte Blanche à l'Association des Amis du Centre Georges Pompidou* (*Carte Blanche for the Association of Friends of the Georges Pompidou Centre*) at the Centre Pompidou in Paris. He exhibited solo at the Galerie Le Roman in Paris in 1985.

SCHILDKNECHT, Georg
German, 19th - 20th century.
Born 30 April 1850, in Fürth.
Painter. Figures, portraits, genre scenes.
Georg Schildknecht worked in Munich, Leipzig, Nuremberg and Paris, where he exhibited at the Salon des Artistes Français and received an honourable mention in 1909.
MUSEUMS AND GALLERIES:
MUNICH (Pinakothek): *Head of Old Woman of Dachau.*

SCHILDKNECHT, Hans, or Schiltknecht
German, 15th century.
Active in Hamburg in 1481.
Painter.

SCHILDKNECHT, Hans
German, 19th - 20th century.
Born 1 January 1871, in Fürth.
Painter.
Hans Schildknecht was related to Georg Schildknecht, and studied with Nicolas Gysis and Wilhelm von Diez at the academy of fine arts in Munich.

SCHILDKNECHT, Johann Reinhold
German, 17th century.
Active in Leipzig between 1649 and 1673.
Engraver (burin).
Schildknecht engraved portraits.

SCHILDT, Carl
German, 19th - 20th century.
Born 5 December 1851, in Elmshorn; died 1 March 1920, in Hamburg.
Painter, engraver. Figures, landscapes.
Carl Schildt was a pupil of Franz T. Grosse at the academy of fine arts in Dresden, and of Karl Gussow at the academy of fine arts in Berlin. He was based in Hamburg.

SCHILDT, Johan Henrik, or Schildte
Swedish, 18th century.
Born 1678, in Copenhagen; died 20 August 1732, in Bispmotala.
Painter. History painting, portraits. Miniatures.
Schildt was a pupil of David Klöcker von Ehrenstrahl, of David von Krafft, and of the draughtsman Christoffer Klöcker.
MUSEUMS AND GALLERIES:
STOCKHOLM (Historiska Mus.): *Portrait of Duchess Hedwig Sophia von Holstein* - UPPSALA (Universitet Konstsamling): *The Coronation of King Frederik I; The Coronation of Queen Ulrika Eleonora* (watercolour/parchment).

SCHILDT, Martinus
Dutch, 19th - 20th century.
Born 29 August 1867, in Rotterdam.
Painter. Figures, genre scenes, interiors, still-lifes.
Martinus Schildt exhibited in Paris, obtaining a silver medal in 1900 for the Exposition Universelle. He was an exponent of the Dutch tradition, painting genre scenes and scenes of interiors.
MUSEUMS AND GALLERIES:
MUNICH: *Laundry* - ROTTERDAM: *Still-life; Peasant's House* - THE HAGUE (Gemeentemus.): *Milkmaid.*
AUCTION RECORDS:
DORDRECHT, 12 Dec 1972, *Interior Scene*, NLG 8,000.

SCHILER, Michelangelo di Giuseppe and **Pietro Antonio**. See **SCHILLES**

SCHILGEN, Philipp Anton
German, 19th century.

Born 1792, in Osnabrück; died 1857, in Munich.
Painter. History painting.
Schilgen worked under Cornelius in Düsseldorf and accompanied his master to Munich in 1825. Most notably, he painted a number of works for the royal palace, on subjects from the tragedies of Aeschylus after drawings by Schwanthaler. He is also known for a painting of the *Abduction of Helen* after a cartoon by Cornelius.
MUSEUMS AND GALLERIES:
MUNICH (Neue Pinakothek): *Abduction of Helen*.

SCHILHABL, Franz
Bohemian School, 19th century.
Born 19 March 1824, in Elbogen; died 30 December 1902, in Elbogen.
Painter. Landscapes, waterscapes.
He worked in Eger from 1855 to 1885.
MUSEUMS AND GALLERIES:
EGER: *Twelve Landscapes* (twelve landscapes) - ELBOGEN: *Six Landscapes* (six landscapes).
AUCTION RECORDS:
COLOGNE, 25 Nov 1976, *Landscape with a River* (oil on card, 12 x 15 3/4 ins / 30.5 x 40 cm) DEM 1,300.

SCHILHER, Plato Mathias
German, 16th century.
Born c. 1560, in Nuremberg.
Active in Hamburg.
Draughtsman.
Plato Mathias Schilher was also a doctor.

SCHILISS, Jacob. See **SCHILLES**

SCHILIZOFF, Pavel Sawitch. See **CHILTSOV Pavel Savvich**

SCHILKING, Heinrich
German, 19th century.
Born 25 November 1815, in Warendorf; died 3 October 1895, in Oldenburg.
Painter. Landscapes.
Schilking studied at the academy in Düsseldorf. He visited France, Belgium and Holland and worked in Brunswick, Oldenburg and Düsseldorf.
MUSEUMS AND GALLERIES:
BREMEN (Kunsthalle): *Ruins in a Winter Landscape*.

SCHILL, Emil
Swiss, 20th century.
Born 3 February 1879, in Basel; died 1958, in Kerns.
Painter, engraver, lithographer. Genre scenes, landscapes, landscapes with figures.
Emil Schill was a pupil of Caspar Ritter at the academy of fine arts in Karlsruhe, of Paul Hocker at the academy of fine arts in Munich, and of Jules Lefebvre and Robert Fleury in Paris. He was also an engraver on wood.
MUSEUMS AND GALLERIES:
BASEL: *View on the Bilstein near Langenbruck*.
AUCTION RECORDS:
BERN, 30 April 1988, *Landscape at Langenbruck* (1947, oil on canvas, 12 1/2 x 15 ins / 32 x 38 cm) CHF 2,700. LUCERNE, 30 Sept 1988, *The Peaks Widderfeld and Nünalphorn* (oil on wood, 12 1/2 x 15 ins / 32 x 38 cm) CHF 1,600. AMSTERDAM, 25 April 1990, *Shepherd and His Son Feeding a Dog* (oil on panel, 22 x 17 3/4 ins / 56 x 45 cm) NLG 5,750. ZOFINGEN, 28 May 1999, *Inner Swiss Mountain Landscape with Lake and Cloud Formations* (1927, oil on canvas, 24 x 28 ins / 60 x 70 cm) CHF 3,100. ZURICH, 2 May 2001, *Schontal* (oil on canvas, 30 x 32 ins / 75 x 82 cm) CHF 4,000. ZOFINGEN, 13 June 2003, *Nut Tree* (1912, oil on canvas, 30 x 37 ins / 76 x 94 cm) CHF 5,500. ZOFINGEN, 28 Nov 2003, *Kilchzimmer near Langenbruck* (1908, 20 x 24 ins / 52 x 60 cm) CHF 3,500. BERN, 14 May 2004, *Swiss Autumn Landscape with Trees* (1943, oil on canvas, 30 x 37 ins / 75 x 93 cm) CHF 4,200.

SCHILLE, Johann
Austrian, 17th century.
Active in Vienna.
Sculptor (wood).
Schille carved two altars for the Holy Cross Monastery.

SCHILLE, Tobias
Bohemian School, 17th century.
Active in Prague c. 1670.
Engraver.

SCHILLEMANS, Corneille
Flemish School, 17th century.
Born 9 September 1618, in Mechelen; died 6 November 1689.
Sculptor.

SCHILLEMANS, Franz, or Schellemans
Dutch, 16th - 17th century.
Born 1575, in Middelburg.
Draughtsman, engraver.
Franz Schillemans worked for a number of booksellers and engraved mostly portraits.

SCHILLEMANS, Gaspar
Flemish School, 17th century.
Died 1670, in Mechelen.
Active in Mechelen.
Painter, designer, sculptor.
Gaspar Schillemans was a guild member in Mechelen in 1608.

SCHILLER, Benedikt
German, 18th century.
Active in Rottau c. 1799.
Painter.
An altar panel by Benedikt Schiller representing *St Nicholas* is to be found in the church in Rottersham.

SCHILLER, Carl
British, 19th century.
Active in London.
Miniaturist.
Carl Schiller is cited in 1843 as a mentor of George Sala. He exhibited in his own right in London between 1844 and 1867, showing two miniatures at the Royal Academy and two further miniatures at the Suffolk Street Gallery.

SCHILLER, Christophine. See **REINWALD**

SCHILLER, Franz Bernhard, or Schuller
German, 19th century.
Born 28 October 1815, in Ostritz (Saxony); died 13 May 1857, in Hamburg.
Sculptor.
Frantz Schiller studied with Joseph Gareis in Ostritz, Schwanthaler in Munich and Rietschel in Dresden. He was active in Hamburg from 1842. He carved a marble bust of Mayor Bartels, which is kept in the library of Hamburg University.

SCHILLER, Ida
Hungarian, 19th - 20th century.
Born 1856, in Torna, Russia.
Painter. Portraits, landscapes.
Ida Schiller was active in Budapest.

SCHILLER, Iris Sara
Israeli, 20th - 21st century.
Born 1955.
Sculptor, draughtsman, installation artist.
Iris Schiller's works strive to express the origins of mankind and the creation of the world, as reflected in the titles such as *Adam* or *Original Sin*. Her installations are composed of wood or plaster shapes and allude to elements such as the human body, a budding branch or an egg, and have an organic unity that derives from their simplicity.

In 1994 she exhibited at Credac/Galerie Fernand in Léger d'Ivry-sur-Seine, and at the Languedoc-Roussillon FRAC (Fond Régional d'Art Contemporain) in Montpelier. In 2003 she had a solo exhibition at Grimaldi Castle in Antibes.

BIBLIOGRAPHY:

Ardenne, Paul, *'Iris Sara Schiller'* in *Art Press* n° 192, periodical, Paris, June 1994. Bernadac, Marie-Laure, *Iris Sara Schiller: une fille est une fille est une fille d'une fille*, exhibition catalogue, Hazan, Paris, 2003.

MUSEUMS AND GALLERIES:

PARIS (FNAC): *Funeral Rites* (1995, sculpture).

SCHILLER, Johann Felix von
German, 19th century.
Born 1805, in Breslau (now Wroclaw, Poland); died 31 January 1853, in Munich.
Painter. Landscapes.

Johann von Schiller studied law before devoting himself to painting. After training in Munich, he took nature as his guide and was particularly inspired by the scenery of the Bavarian Alps.

MUSEUMS AND GALLERIES:

WROCLAW: *Lake Chiem*.

SCHILLER, Julius
Austrian, 16th century.
Draughtsman.

SCHILLER, Leonardus
Dutch, 18th century.
Active in The Hague c. 1729.
Painter.

SCHILLER, Michael
Austrian, 16th century.
Born to a family originally from Breslau (now Wroclaw).
Painter.

Michael Schiller painted the ceiling in the parish church of Merani.

SCHILLER, Michelangelo di Giuseppe and **Pietro Antonio**. See **SCHILLES**

SCHILLES, Jacob, or Schillis, Schilisz, Schiliss
German, 18th century.
Painter.

Schilles worked at the Hanau pottery factory between 1706 and 1718.

SCHILLES, Michelangelo di Giuseppe, or Schiler, Schiller
Flemish School, 18th century.
Active in Naples.
Painter, engraver. Genre scenes, animals, still-lifes.

Michelangelo di Giuseppe Schilles decorated a room in the home of Prince di S Nicandro in Naples. His only surviving painting is a *Holy Trinity with St Francis of Assisi* at the church of St Bernard and St Margaret in Naples.

SCHILLES, Pietro Antonio, or Schiler or Schiller
Italian, 17th century.
Born c. 1679; died 1707, in Naples.
Painter.

Pietro Antonio Schilles was the brother of Michelangelo Schilles and the pupil of F. Solimena. His legacy includes frescoes in the church of Jesus and the church of the Holy Apostles in Naples.

SCHILLI, Anton
German, 18th century.
Sculptor.

Schilli decorated the church in Aklshausen.

SCHILLIG, Joséphine
Swiss, 19th - 20th century.
Born 19 July 1846, in Altdorf.
Painter. Portraits, flowers.

Joséphine Schillig was a pupil of Xaver Schwegler, probably at Lucerne. From 1894 she lived at Ebikon.

SCHILLIGER, Felix Joseph, or Schillinger
Swiss, 18th century.
Born 1743; died 5 October 1798.
Active in Stans.
Sculptor (wood).

Schilliger decorated the interior of St Martin's church in the village of Schwyz and the carved the choir screen for the monastery of Stans.

SCHILLIGER, Joseph Anton
Swiss, 16th - 17th century.
Died 29 April 1644, in Lucerne.
Active in Lucerne from 1595.
Glass painter, goldsmith.

Joseph Anton Schilliger was a mediocre glass painter.

SCHILLINCK, Emmerich
German, 16th century.
Sculptor.

MUSEUMS AND GALLERIES:

PARIS (Louvre): *Funerary Monument of Precentor von Lansteyn*.

SCHILLING, Adam
German, 16th - 17th century.
Active in Grossenhain.
Painter.

Adam Schilling worked in Freiberg, Saxony, where he became a master in 1594. He was in the service of the court of Saxony from 1605 to 1618.

SCHILLING, Albrecht
German, 20th century.
Born 1929, in Bremen.
Painter.

Albrecht Schilling was active in Bremen. From 1946 he began painting without having had any training. In 1951 he travelled in Italy and in Switzerland, and in 1952 in Paris. In 1955 he appeared at the Salon des Réalités Nouvelles in Paris. After a period influenced by Post-Cubism from 1950, he turned to pure abstraction, particularly Geometric Abstraction.

SCHILLING, Alexander, or Shilling
American, 19th - 20th century.
Born 1859, in Chicago; died 1937.
Active in New York.
Painter, engraver. Landscapes.

Alexander Schilling took part in collective exhibitions and was awarded a gold medal in Philadelphia in 1901 and a silver medal in Saint Louis in 1904.

SCHILLING, Alfons
Austrian, 20th century.
Born in Vienna.
Active in the USA.
Performance artist, painter.
Aktionismus group.

Alfons Schilling worked in New York. In the Viennese Aktionismus group, he created ritualised productions: in 1963 watering the public with the blood of a dead lamb, throwing eggs against the walls, then chewing a rose. Later, he created in a similar fashion paintings in the style of Hyperrealism.

SCHILLING, Carl Friedrich Bernhard
German, 19th century.
Born 1815, in Weimar; died 12 September 1880.
Painter. Stage sets.

Carl Schilling was active in Mainz from 1855. He was the father of Carl Halfdan Schilling.

SCHILLING, Carl Halfdan
Norwegian, 19th century.
Born 1835, in Christiania (now Oslo); died 2 January 1907, in Mouseron.
Active in Belgium.
Painter. Genre scenes, landscapes.
Schilling received his training in Düsseldorf. He became a Barnabite monk in a Belgian cloister.

SCHILLING, Christian
German, 17th century.
Painter.
Christian Schilling was the son of Adam Schilling.

SCHILLING, Clotilde
German, 19th - 20th century.
Born 1856, in Altenberg.
Painter. Landscapes.
Clotilde Schilling worked in Dresden.

SCHILLING, Felix Nepomuk
German, 18th century.
Born 16 April 1742; died 1808.
Active in Munich.
Painter.
Felix Nepomuk Schilling was the son of Ignaz Joseph Schilling. He decorated the theatres in Amberg and Seefeld.

SCHILLING, Frede
Danish, 20th century.
Born 1928.
Painter (mixed media), collage artist.
Frede Schilling can be seen at the Galise Petersen gallery in Thonon-les-Bains. He practised an elegant abstract style, reconciling a structural construction with informal Matterist intrusions. He worked in sober harmonies of grey and brown tints.

SCHILLING, Friedrich Christian Hermann
German, 19th - 20th century.
Born 11 January 1845, in Weimar; died 5 December 1917, in Mainz-Bretzenheim.
Painter. Stage sets.
Friedrich Schilling was active in Mainz.
MUSEUMS AND GALLERIES:
MAINZ (Stadtarchiv Mainz): sketches of stages sets.

SCHILLING, Georg Johann or Johann Georg
German, 19th century.
Born 1797, in Unterthingau (Bavaria); died 1839, in Unterthingau.
Painter, watercolourist. Landscapes with figures.
Georg Johann Schilling is best known for 10 landscapes with figures on subjects taken from Greek life, after watercolours by Rottmann, painted for the royal palace in Munich.

SCHILLING, Heinrich
German, 18th century.
Painter. Religious subjects.
Heinrich Schilling was active in Villingen, and in 1728 and 1736, he worked for the Catholic church in Donaueschingen.

SCHILLING, Heinrich
German, 20th century.
Born 1898.
Painter. Urban landscapes.
Heinrich Schilling lived in Essen in the Ruhr. He was a wheelwright at the Krupp factories in Essen but, although he was without any training, he turned to painting. Unlike the minute detailing that characterises most naive painters, Schilling made rough sketches, similar to Mathieu-Verdilhan. He represented the landscape of his country poetically - a landscape that was naturally beautiful but disfigured by intensive industrialisation.

BIBLIOGRAPHY:
Bihalji-Merin, Oto, *Les Peintres naïfs*, Delpire, Paris, 1960.

SCHILLING, Ignaz Balthasar
German, 18th century.
Born 29 December 1739, in Munich; died 30 June 1808, in Munich.
Painter. Stage sets.
Ignaz Balthasar was the son of Ignaz Joseph Schilling. He was a painter at the theatre and the court of Munich.

SCHILLING, Ignaz Joseph or Joseph Ignaz
German, 18th century.
Born 1702, in Villingen; died 2 April 1773, in Munich.
Painter. Religious subjects.
Ignaz Joseph Schilling was the son of the painter Johann Heinrich Schilling and the father of Ignaz Balthasar and Felix Nepomuk. From 1726, he was a pupil of Johann Georg Sang in Munich and became a master painter in 1730. He worked for the churches of Villingen and Munich.

SCHILLING, Johannes
German, 19th - 20th century.
Born 23 June 1828, in Mittweida; died 21 March 1910, in Klotzsch, near Dresden.
Sculptor. Mythological subjects, allegorical subjects.
Johannes Schilling studied from 1842 at the academy of fine arts in Dresden. He continued his training until 1850, then after a period of study in Berlin he went to Italy, where he spent three years analysing the works of the old masters. On his return to Dresden in 1868 he became a teacher at the academy. He was considered one of the chief artists of the idealist school of sculpture at Dresden.
MUSEUMS AND GALLERIES:
HAMBURG: *Jupiter and Ganymede; Spring* - LEIPZIG: *Phidias; Young Centaur; Female Centaur* - WEIMAR: *Night With Sleep and Dream.*

SCHILLING, Karoline
Maiden name: Senff
Estonian, 19th century.
Born 1801, in Tartu, Estonia; died 20 May 1840, in Schwaneburg.
Painter. Flowers.
Karoline Schilling was the daughter of the burin engraver Karl August Senff.

SCHILLING, Lorenz
German, 17th century.
Born c. 1575, in Nieder Wesel; died 19 November 1637, in Frankfurt am Main.
Medallist, engraver. Coins.

SCHILLING, Matthes
German, 16th century.
Medallist, engraver. Coins.
Matthes Schilling was a descendant of an Alsatian family that emigrated to southern Germany. He lived in Cracow, Danzig (now Gdansk), and later Vilna (now Vilnius).

SCHILLING, Sebastian Johann
Swiss, 18th century.
Born 21 January 1722, in Villingen; died 22 January 1773, in Villingen.
Painter.
In 1753, Sebastian Johann Schilling painted pictures for the church in Villingen and frescoes for the church in Breitnau.

SCHILLING VON TORDA, Oskar or Oszkar
Hungarian, 20th century.
Born 23 October 1880, in Kolozsvár (now Cluj-Napoca, Romania).
Painter, engraver.
Oskar Schilling von Torda was active in Budapest.

SCHILLINGER, Felix Joseph.
See **SCHILLIGER**

SCHILLINGER, Johann Jakob
German, 18th - 19th century.
Born 1750, in Öhringen (Württemberg); died 1829, in Öhringen.
Painter.
Schillinger studied with Scotti and Guibal in Stuttgart and spent three years in Italy. Most of his works are lost.

SCHILLINGER, Julius or Gyula
Hungarian, 20th century.
Born 20 February 1888, in Budapest; died 5 April 1930, in Davos, Switzerland.
Sculptor, illustrator. Animals.
Julius Schillinger was awarded the Prix de Rome in 1913.
MUSEUMS AND GALLERIES:
BUDAPEST: several statuettes of animals.

SCHILLINGOVSKI, Pawel Alexandrovitch.
See **SHILLINGOVSKY Pavel Aleksandrovich**

SCHILLMARK, Nils, or Schillmarck
Finnish, 18th century.
Born 1745; died 1804.
Active in Loviisa.
Painter. Portraits, landscapes.
He is considered to be the most productive Finnish portrait artist. His works, of which there are about a hundred, are mainly located in Finland and Sweden.

SCHILOFF, Ivan Anfimovich. See **CHILOV**

SCHILPEROORT, Adriaen Coenen van
Dutch, 16th century.
Active in Scheveningen (southern Holland), the Netherlands, from 1574.
Draughtsman.
Adriaen Coenen van Schilperoort was the father of Koenraad Schilperoort.

SCHILPEROORT, Bergwardus Joachimsz. van
Dutch, 17th century.
Active in Amsterdam 1633-1680.
Engraver (burin).

SCHILPEROORT, Koenraad Adriaensz. van
Dutch, 16th - 17th century.
Born 1577; died 1635, in Leiden.
Active in Leiden.
Landscape painter.
Koenraad Adriaensz. van Schilperoort was the son of Adriaen Schilperoort. He was a founding member of the Leiden guild in 1610. Van Goyen was his pupil.

SCHILPLI, Simon, or Schulple, Schulpli
Swiss, 16th - 17th century.
Active in Brugg 1595-1623.
Glass painter.

SCHILSKY
German, 18th century.
Active in Berlin during the second half of the 18th century.
Draughtsman.
Schilsky drew mainly landscapes.

SCHILT, Louis Pierre
French, 19th century.
Born 11 September 1790, in Paris; died 13 September 1859, in Sèvres.
Painter (porcelain).
One of the most famous painters from the Sèvres porcelain manufactory in Paris. He started out as a pupil of the ceramic painter Constant, then went on to study with Lefebvre. In 1822 he entered the Sèvres porcelain manufactory, where he worked until his death. In 1850 he was decorated with the Légion d'Honneur, on the recommendation of Paul Delaroche. He produced several series of lithographs, including: *The Months*; *Flowers and Fruit*; and *The Porcelain Decorator*.

SCHILT, Otto Henrich
Swiss, 20th century.
Born 1888, in Frauenfeld.
Sculptor.
Otto Schilt was a pupil of James Vibert at the school of fine arts in Geneva and was active in Geneva.

SCHILTER, Joseph
Swiss, 19th - 20th century.
Born 18 May 1871, in Steinen.
Painter.
Jospeh Schilter studied at Munich and at Düsseldorf.

SCHILTER, Ulrich
German, 15th century.
Active in Munich.
Painter.
Ulrich Schilter was a member of the guild from 1426. He painted for the town hall a *Last Judgement* that was destroyed in the fire of 1429.

SCHILTKNECHT, Hans.
See **SCHILDKNECHT**

SCHIMANSKY, Hanns
German, 20th - 21st century.
Born 1949, in Bitterfeld.
Draughtsman.
Hanns Schimansky grew up in the former East Germany, in Stralsund and Rostock. He worked as an engineer, while also producing the drawings that won him the title 'Meisterschüler' at the Akademie der Künste in Berlin. He became a professor at the Kunsthochschule Berlin-Weissensee in 1998. He works exclusively in Indian ink and coloured pencils, using the technique of folding. He develops Abstract forms that are highly reminiscent of Expressionism or Constructivism, but in a Surrealist atmosphere. His graphic work is sometimes associated with music. His solo exhibitions include one at the Neue Nationalgalerie in Berlin in 1990, and an exhibition covering 15 years of his work at the Musée d'Art et d'Histoire in Neuchâtel in 2000.
BIBLIOGRAPHY:
Blume, Eugen, *Soixante-quatorze dessins*, Musée d'Art et d'Histoire, Neuchâtel, 2000.

SCHIMECK, Ludwig, or Simek
Bohemian School, 19th century.
Born 19 February 1837, in Prague; died 25 January 1886, in Prague.
Sculptor.
Ludwig Schimeck studied at the Prague academy. He worked for Joseph Max for several years, and then worked in Munich with Windmann, and in Rome from 1864 to 1870. The old Rudolfinum in Prague owns a statue of *Johann von Weert* by him.

SCHIMITSCH, Pavao or Paul. See **SIMIC**

SCHIMKOWITZ, Herbert
Austrian, 20th century.
Born 6 February 1898, in Vienna.
Painter, engraver.
Herbert Schimkowitz was the son of Othmar Schimkowitz. From 1921 to 1925 he studied at the Akademie der Bildenden Künste in Vienna. He painted portraits of personalities of his time, including *Professor Karl R. von Ettmaier*, *Cardinal Archbishop Innitzer* and the poet *Joseph Weinhaber*.

SCHIMKOWITZ, Othmar
German, 19th - 20th century.
Born 2 October 1864, in Tarts, Hungary, to German parents.
Active in Austria.
Sculptor.
Othmar Schimkowitz was a pupil of Edmund von Hellmer and Karl Kundmann at the Akademie der Bildenden Künste in Vienna. From 1892 to 1895 he worked in New York at the studio of Karl T.F. Bitter, and from 1895 he had his own studio in Vienna. From 1898 he was a member of the Viennese Secession, becoming its president in 1929-1930.
MUSEUMS AND GALLERIES:
LINZ: *Project for a Monument to the Memory of the Poet and Miniaturist Adalbert Stifter* (engraving).

SCHIMMEL, Gerrit
Dutch, 17th century.
Died 1684, in Amsterdam.
Painter.

SCHIMMEL, Hugo
German, 18th century.
Born 9 September 1689, in Chemnitz.
Active in Munich.
Painter.
Hugo Schimmel studied with Bantzer in Dresden and Morisset in Paris. Six pictures by this artist are on show in the foyer of the theatre in Neustrelitz.

SCHIMMEL, Johann Andreas
German, 18th century.
Born 1705; died 25 November 1772, in Bayreuth.
Active in Bayreuth.
Painter.

SCHIMMEL, Johann Ludwig
German, 17th century.
Died 1637, in Frankfurt am Main.
Active in Frankfurt am Main.
Painter.

SCHIMMELPENNING, Jochen
German, 20th - 21st century.
Born 10 July 1948, in Oldenburg.
Painter.
Jochen Schimmelpenning trained at the academy in Salzburg under the direction of Molderan and Syskovic, then from 1968 to 1974 at the Akademie der Bildenden Künste in Munich. She won the international Monaco Prize in 1983.

SCHIMON, Ferdinand
Hungarian, 19th century.
Born 6 April 1797, in Budapest; died 29 August 1852, in Munich.
Painter. Portraits, genre scenes.
Ferdinand Schimon was a singer and actor before becoming a successful portrait painter. He worked on the painting of the loggias of the Alte Pinakothek in Munich, after designs by Cornelius.
MUSEUMS AND GALLERIES:
BERN: *Maternal Sollicitude* - BUDAPEST: *Portrait of a Lady*.
AUCTION RECORDS:
VIENNA, 29-30 Oct 1996, *Woman playing a Lute* (1838, oil on canvas, 29 x 30 ins / 73.5 x 76 cm) ATS 149,500. BREMEN, 20 Oct 2000, *Young Italian Woman with Tambourine* (1843, oil on canvas, 28 x 22 ins / 70 x 56 cm) DEM 3,500.

SCHIMON, Maximilian
Hungarian, 19th century.
Born 1705, in Pest; died 13 June 1859, in Vienna.
Painter.
Maximilian Schimon was the brother of Ferdinand and a pupil of Marastoni.

SCHIMONY, Joseph
Austrian, 19th century.
Born 1775; died 10 July 1815, in Vienna.
Landscape artist.

SCHIMPF, Andreas
Swiss, 19th century.
Born 1809, in Alsace.
Painter. Military subjects, portraits.
Schimpf was active in Basel.

SCHIMPFERMANN, Carl G.
German, 18th - 19th century.
Born 1768, in Schulpforta (Thuringia); died 28 April 1833, in Zittau.
Painter, engraver. Portraits, urban landscapes. Stage sets.

SCHIMSER, Anton
Austrian, 19th century.
Died 1836.
Sculptor.
Schimser studied at the academy in Vienna. He worked in Paris and Lemberg (now Lvov, Ukraine) after 1812. He was influenced by Canova. There are a number of memorials by him in Lvov.

SCHINAGEL, Emil, or Szinagel
Polish, 20th century.
Born 6 January 1899, in Drohojow.
Painter.
Emil Schinagel was a doctor of medicine. He studied painting with Theodor Axentowicz at the fine arts academy in Cracow and, in 1930, was a student of Henri van Haelen at the Brussels academy. He founded the artists' association Zwornik.
MUSEUMS AND GALLERIES:
CRACOW (Muzeum Narodowe/National Gallery).

SCHINAGL, Franz
Austrian, 18th century.
Born 1739; died 25 May 1773, in Vienna.
Painter. Landscapes.

SCHINAGL, Maximilien Joseph, or Schinnagel, Schinnagl
German, 18th century.
Born 28 April 1697, in Burghausen (Bavaria); died 22 March 1762, in Vienna.
Painter. Hunting scenes, harbour views, landscapes with figures, landscapes, seascapes.
Maximilien Schinagl was a pupil of his father-in-law, Joseph Kammarloher. Janneck and Aagen often painted the figures in his landscapes.
MUSEUMS AND GALLERIES:
BUDAPEST: *Landscape with Church*; *The Village* - GRAZ: *Landscape* - VIENNA: *Forest Landscape* (four works) - WROCLAW: *Mountain Stream* (two versions); *Rocky Valley* (two works); *Forest Landscape* (two works); *Mountains in Germany* (two works); *Romantic Valley* (two works).
AUCTION RECORDS:
PARIS, 1869, *Ways into the Woods, with Figures* (two pendants) FRF 200. MONTE CARLO, 8 Dec 1984, *Panoramic Landscape with a Market Scene* (oil/copper, 11 3/4 x 16 1/4 ins / 30 x 41.5 cm) FRF 100,000. LONDON, 9 April 1986, *Harbour Scene*; *Coastal Scene in Stormy Weather* (oil on canvas, a pair, 6 3/4 x 9 1/4 ins / 17 x 23.5 cm) GBP 6,000.

SCHINARDO, Giovanni
Italian, 17th century.
Active in Bologna c. 1600.
Painter.
Schinardo was the pupil of G. Ferrantini.

SCHINCHINELLI, Europa.
See **ANGUISCIOLA**

SCHINDEL, Johann Wolfgang, or Schendel
German, 18th century.
Born 1691, in Solnhofen; died 1774, in Augsburg.
Sculptor.
Schindel was a pupil of Abraham Danbeckh in Augsburg. He produced mainly fountains.

SCHINDELAAR, Hendrick Petrus
Dutch, 18th century.
Active in The Hague c. 1770.
Painter. Flowers, fruit. Ornaments.

SCHINDELE, Joseph
Austrian, 18th century.
Painter (porcelain).
Schindele worked at the Vienna porcelain factory from 1762 to 1784.

SCHINDELER, Wolf
German, 17th century.
Active c. 1630-1650.
Glass painter.

SCHINDELIN, Johann Christian
German, 17th century.
Engraver (burin).

SCHINDELMEYER, Karl Robert, or Schindelmayer
Austrian, 18th - 19th century.
Born c. 1769; died 1839.
Active in Vienna.
Engraver (burin).
Schindelmeyer engraved illustrations for the works of Gerstenberg, Klopstock and Ovid.

SCHINDLAUER, Leopold
Austrian, 18th century.
Sculptor.

SCHINDLER
German, 17th century.
Draughtsman.

SCHINDLER, Albert
Austrian, 19th century.
Born 19 August 1805, in Engelsberg, in 1806 according to some sources; died 3 May 1861, in Vienna, in 1871 according to some sources.
Painter, watercolourist, engraver. Figures, self-portraits, genre scenes, interiors with figures.
Albert Schindler studied with Peter Fendl at the academy of fine arts in Vienna. He became quite successful.
MUSEUMS AND GALLERIES:
VIENNA: *A Wounded Officer; The Bedroom;* two watercolours.
AUCTION RECORDS:
VIENNA, 13 Jan 1976, *The Hunter's Departure* (oil on panel, 15 1/4 x 18 1/4 ins / 38.5 x 46.5 cm) ATS 20,000. VIENNA, 23 Feb 1989, *Self-portrait Painting His Niece in His Studio* (oil on panel, 7 x 9 1/2 ins / 18 x 24 cm) ATS 330,000. NEW YORK, 19 Jan 1994, *Nursery Games* (oil on panel, 9 x 7 ins / 22.9 x 17.8 cm) USD 5,175. VIENNA, 2 Dec 1999, *Portrait of Young Girl with Landscape Background* (oil on canvas, oval) ATS 40,000. STUTTGART, 22 Sept 2000, *Extensive Landscape with Ruin* (1830, oil on canvas, 10 x 13 ins / 26 x 32 cm) DEM 4,150. LONDON, 4 Dec 2003, *Peek-a-boo* (oil on panel, 13 x 11 ins / 34 x 28 cm) GBP 6,500.

SCHINDLER, Andreas
Bohemian School, 18th century.
Painter.

SCHINDLER, Anna Margareta
Austrian, 20th century.
Born 26 October 1893, in Kennelbach; died 14 June 1929, in Vienna.
Sculptor.
Anna Margareta Schindler studied at the school of fine arts in Geneva, and with Josef Müllner at the Akademie der Bildenden Künste in Vienna. She continued her training in Rome.

SCHINDLER, Anton Joseph
Austrian, 18th century.
Active in Olmütz (now Olomouc, Czech Republic).
Engraver (burin).

SCHINDLER, D.
Swiss, 17th century.
Active c. 1600.
Possibly a painter.
Mentioned by Lügt.

SCHINDLER, Emil Jacob or Jacob Emil
Austrian, 19th century.
Born 27 April 1842, in Vienna; died 9 August 1892, in Westerland auf Sylt.
Painter, decorative designer. Figures, genre scenes, landscapes, waterscapes.
Emil Jacob Schindler studied at the academy of fine arts in Vienna in the studio of Albert Zimmermann. His study of nature led him to embrace the ideas of the masters of the French school of 1830 and his works were influenced by the painters of the Barbizon school, such as Théodore Rousseau, Camille Corot, Charles Daubigny and Jules Dupré. He was appointed a member of the academy in Vienna, where Carl Moll was among his students.

His paintings of various landscapes on the Mediterranean coast show a particular attention to effects of light. He was also responsible for the decoration of a number of buildings.
MUSEUMS AND GALLERIES:
BERLIN: *View of the Prater in Vienna, near the old Hunting Lodge* - LEIPZIG: *The Valley of Peace* - MUNICH: *In March; Sawmill in Upper Austria* - VIENNA: *On the Dalmatian Coast; Pax; Beech Forest at Plankenberg* - VIENNA (Österreichische Gal. Belvedere): *Mill at Goisern; Steamer stop at Kaisermühlen on the Danube* - WROCLAW: *Rain Effect.*
AUCTION RECORDS:
LONDON, 9 June 1911, *River Bank with Mill* (1878) GBP 141. NEW YORK, 17 Feb 1944, *Duck Pond,* USD 600. PARIS, July 1946, *River Bank,* FRF 10,500. VIENNA, 13 March 1962, *Garden in Flower at Weissenkirchen on the Danube,* ATS 100,000. VIENNA, 12 Sept 1967, *Landscape with a Watermill,* ATS 130,000. VIENNA, 21 March 1972, *Landscape with a Church,* ATS 110,000. VIENNA, 27 May 1974, *Landscape* (1874) ATS 75,000. VIENNA, 2 Nov 1976, *Farm Entrance* (oil on panel, 5 x 8 1/2 ins / 12.7 x 21.7 cm) ATS 75,000. VIENNA, 15 March 1977, *View of Ragusa* (1890, oil on canvas, 55 x 70 3/4 ins / 140 x 180 cm) ATS 300,000. VIENNA, 18 Sept 1979, *Banks of the Danube* (c. 1878, oil on panel, 14 1/2 x 22 3/4 ins / 37 x 58 cm) ATS 300,000. VIENNA, 17 March 1981, *Woman gathering Firewood* (oil on panel, 5 1/4 x 8 1/2 ins / 13.5 x 21.5 cm) ATS 220,000. VIENNA, 16 Nov 1983, *View of the River Eger* (1882, oil on panel, 15 3/4 x 23 1/2 ins / 40 x 60 cm) ATS 350,000. LONDON, 26 Nov 1985, *Landscape with a Wooden Bridge* (1881 and 1885, oil on canvas, 38 1/4 x 33 1/4 ins / 97 x 84.5 cm) GBP 75,000. LONDON, 10 Oct 1986, *Wooded River Landscape* (oil on panel, 8 1/2 x 5 ins / 21.5 x 12.5 cm) GBP 3,000. NEW YORK, 28 Feb 1990, *Meadow full of Wild Flowers* (oil on canvas, 14 1/4 x 11 ins / 36.2 x 28.2 cm) USD 29,700. NEW YORK, 23 May 1991, *Women Bathing* (oil on panel, 12 x 12 3/4 ins / 30.5 x 32.4 cm) USD 6,600. NEW YORK, 30 Oct 1992, *View of Ragusa (recto); Rocky Slope by Moonlight (verso)* (1887, oil on panel, 10 1/4 x 13 1/4 ins / 26 x 33.7 cm)

USD 7,150. LONDON, 13 Oct 1994, *Washerwomen by a River* (oil on card/canvas, 12¾ x 16½ ins / 32.7 x 42 cm) GBP 11,500. PARIS, 14 March 1997, *River Bank* (oil on panel, 8¼ x 12¾ ins / 21 x 32.5 cm) FRF 75,000. LONDON, 9 Oct 1997, *The Stream at Goisern* (oil on panel, 22¼ x 15¼ ins / 56.5 x 39 cm) GBP 44,400. VIENNA, 20 April 1999, *View of Praterauen* (oil on panel, 5 x 8 ins / 13 x 21 cm) ATS 150,000. LONDON, 8 July 1999, *View from Plankenberg* (oil on panel, 24 x 37 ins / 60 x 95 cm) GBP 48,000. VIENNA, 23 May 2000, *The Kiss in the Forest* (oil on panel, 10 x 8 ins / 26 x 20 cm) ATS 120,000. VIENNA, 3 Oct 2000, *Storm over Landscape* (colour wash/ink heightened with white, 7 x 9 ins / 17 x 24 cm) ATS 28,000. VIENNA, 28 May 2001, *On the Wehr* (oil on panel, 8 x 5 ins / 21 x 12 cm) ATS 40,000. LONDON, 9 April 2002, *Bauernhof bei Haslau an der Donau - Farmhouse near Haslau on the Danube* (c. 1880, oil on panel, 18 x 22 ins / 45 x 56 cm) GBP 21,000. VIENNA, 16 May 2002, *Seine on Autumn Evening* (oil on panel, 3 x 8 ins / 8 x 21 cm) EUR 7,000. VIENNA, 28 Oct 2003, *Dutch Landscape* (oil on canvas, 13 x 18 ins / 33 x 46 cm) EUR 18,000. VIENNA, 28 Oct 2003, *Ragusa* (oil on canvas, 21 x 19 ins / 54 x 48 cm) EUR 20,000. NEW YORK, 30 March 2004, *Boats at Dock along the Riverbank* (oil on canvas, 13 x 18 ins / 33 x 46 cm) USD 5,000. VIENNA, 28 April 2004, *Probably Salzburg* (oil on panel, 9 x 16 ins / 23 x 41 cm) EUR 25,000.

SCHINDLER, Ferdinand Hieronymus
German, 19th century.
Died before 1867.
Active in Berlin.
Sculptor.

Ferdinand Schindler studied with Schievelbein. He worked in Rome from 1858 to 1859.

SCHINDLER, Franz Johann Alois
German, 19th century.
Born 1808, in Urmitz, near Koblenz; died 12 December 1856, in Rome.
Sculptor.

Franz Schindler settled in Rome in 1840.

SCHINDLER, Jakob
Swiss, 17th century.
Died 5 January 1654.
Active in Lucerne.
Painter, engraver (burin).

SCHINDLER, Johann
Swiss, 18th century.
Born 1698, to a family originally from Zug; died 1736.
Painter.

In 1736, Schindler painted four lateral altars for the church of the Discalced Carmelites in Lucerne.

SCHINDLER, Johann
Austrian, 19th century.
Born 15 May 1822, in Taschendorf (Silesia); died 1893, in Vienna.
Sculptor.

SCHINDLER, Johann Josef, or Josef
Austrian, 19th century.
Born 28 July 1777, in St Pölten; died 22 July 1836, in Vienna.
Painter, engraver, lithographer. Genre scenes.

Johann Josef Schindler studied at the academy in Vienna and became a member in 1818. He was professor of drawing at the École Normale de St Anne in Vienna. He painted an altarpiece for St Michael's Church in Vienna.

MUSEUMS AND GALLERIES:
VIENNA: *Coming Home from the Fireworks*; *Walk in the Forest.*

AUCTION RECORDS:
VIENNA, 14 May 1881, *In April,* FRF 1,942; *On the Banks of the Traun,* FRF 2,310. FRANKFURT AM MAIN, 12 Dec 1892, *Landscape,* FRF 1,575.

SCHINDLER, Johann Melchior
Swiss, 17th century.
Born 1638, in Lucerne; died 4 April 1704, in Lucerne.
Engraver (burin).

SCHINDLER, Joseph
Austrian, 19th century.
Painter. Flowers.

Joseph Schindler is best known as a painter of flowers on porcelain for the Vienna factory where he worked from 1801 to 1863.

SCHINDLER, Joseph
Austrian, 19th century.
Born 1823; died 7 January 1853, in Vienna.
Sculptor.

SCHINDLER, Karl
Austrian, 19th century.
Born 23 October 1821, in Vienna; died 22 August 1842, in Laab.
Painter, lithographer. Portraits, genre scenes.

Karl Schindler was first taught by his father Johann Josef, then continued his studies at the academy in Vienna with Gsellhofer and Fendi. He published a series of lithographs entitled *War and its Sculptural Representation.* He was also influenced by the French artists Bellangé, Charlet, Eugène Lami and Raffet.

MUSEUMS AND GALLERIES:
NUREMBERG: *The Conscript* - VIENNA: *The Sentry; The Recruitment.*

AUCTION RECORDS:
VIENNA, 3-6 Dec 1963, *The Gallant Lieutenant,* ATS 50,000. VIENNA, 2 June 1964, *Head of an Old Man* (watercolour) ATS 25,000. LONDON, 21 March 1984, *Study of a Girl* (oil on paper, 9 x 7 ins / 23 x 18 cm) GBP 3,400. BERN, 22 June 1984, *Zriny's Sortie from Szigeth; Medieval Cavalry Battle* (c. 1840, pen, two drawings, 3½ x 4½ ins / 9 x 11.2 cm and 3 x 5 ins/7.6 x 11.8 cm) CHF 4,000. VIENNA, 11 Sept 1986, *Death of Wallenstein* (c. 1838-1839, watercolour, 3¾ x 5 ins / 9.5 x 12.5 cm) ATS 280,000. MUNICH, 12 June 1991, *The Conscript* (oil on card, 5 x 7 ins / 13 x 18 cm) DEM 6,600. MUNICH, 2 Dec 1997, *Recto: Soldier before Karlskirche; Verso: Small Child with a Dog* (two watercolours/paper, 7½ x 9 ins / 19 x 23 cm) DEM 20,400. VIENNA, 26 March 2004, *Military Funeral* (watercolour on paper/board, 4 x 6 ins / 10 x 14 cm) EUR 2,000.

SCHINDLER, Osmar
German, 19th - 20th century.
Born 22 December 1869, in Burkhardtscharf, near Chemnitz; died 19 June 1927, in Wachwitz, near Dresden.
Painter, pastellist, poster artist. Religious subjects.
Jugendstil.

Osmar Schindler was a pupil of Ferdinand W. Pauwels and Leon Pohle at the Academy of Fine Arts at Dresden, where he himself became a teacher. He contributed to the review *Die Jugend.* He produced several paintings for churches, for example, a fresco for Die Jahnsbacher Church at Thum and an altar painting entitled *Ich bin der Heiland für alle, kommet zu mir! (I am the Saviour for all, Come to Me)* for the Lutheran parish church in Chemnitz as well as works for the Christuskirche at Klotzsche-Königswald and the church at Bischofswerda.

BIBLIOGRAPHY:
Kern, Andrea, et al., *Jugendstil in Dresden, Aufbruch in die Moderne,* exhibition catalogue, Staatliche Kunstsammlungen, Dresden, 1999.

Museums and Galleries:
Dresden (Gemäldegalerie Neue Meister, Kupferstich Kabinett): *Internationale Kunstausstellung, Dresden* (1897).

SCHINDLER, Philipp Ernst

German, 18th century.
Born 1695, in Dresden; died 14 July 1765, in Meissen.
Painter (porcelain).

From 1725, Philipp Ernst Schindler worked at the Meissen factory.

SCHINDLER, Philipp Ernst

German, 18th century.
Born 1723, in Dresden; died 14 August 1793, in Vienna.
Painter (porcelain).

Philipp Ernst Schindler worked at the Vienna porcelain factory from 1750. His father, also called Philipp Ernst Schindler, was a porcelain painter in Meissen.

Museums and Galleries:
Vienna (Österreichisches Mus. für Angewandte Kunst): several cups.

SCHINDLER, Rosina Elisabeth

Maiden name: Kärner
German, 18th century.
Active in Leipzig.
Medallist, engraver.

Rosina Schindler was active in Berlin around 1705.

SCHINDLER, Theodor

German, 19th - 20th century.
Born 1 April 1870, in Malsch, near Ettlingen.
Painter. Figures, portraits, landscapes, waterscapes.

Theodor Schindler was a pupil of Ludwig Schmid-Reutte at the academy of fine arts in Karlsruhe. He also worked with Friedrich, Julius or Konrad Fehr.

Museums and Galleries:
Karlsruhe: *Portrait of Woman* - Mannheim: *Peasant in the Open Air; Summer Landscape; Houses on the Banks of a Stream; Banks of the Rhine* - Wuppertal: *Peasant Woman.*

SCHINKEL, Augustin

Czech, 20th century.
Born 1905, in Prague; died 1983, in Cologne.
Also active in Germany and in Austria.
Painter, engraver, illustrator, draughtsman. Figures, scenes with figures.
Gruppe Progressiver Künstler (Progressive Art Group).

Augustin Schinkel studied at the school of applied arts in Prague from 1921 to 1924. He associated with Franz Seiwert in Cologne and became a member of the Progressive Art Group, then worked in Vienna where he met Gerd Amtz.

A committed artist, he painted modern society and the world of work in particular and the conflict it caused. His texts and engravings appeared in various magazines, *The Capitalist* of 1933, *The Strike* and *Man and Machine*, both 1935, are examples.

Bibliography:
Pagé, Suzanne/Winock, Michel/Michaud, Éric/Vidal, Aline, *Les Années trente en Europe. Le Temps menaçant*, exhibition catalogue, Musée d'Art moderne de la Ville de Paris, Paris musées, Flammarion, Paris, 1997.

SCHINKEL, Karl Friedrich

German, 19th century.
Born 13 March 1781, in Neuruppin
(Brandenburg); died 9 October 1841, in Vienna.
Painter (gouache), watercolourist, copyist, engraver, draughtsman, illustrator, lithographer, decorative designer. Portraits, landscapes, architectural views.

Schinkel began his studies at the academy of architecture in Berlin, then devoted himself mainly to painting. He visited Italy in 1803, and after returning to Germany he had a brilliant career as both a painter and an architect. In 1810, he was advised by Caspar David Friedrich in Berlin. Schinkel obtained the post of set-painter at the Königsberg (now Kaliningrad) theatre for the romantic painter Carl Blechen. A number of Schinkel's works, formerly kept in the Berlin Museum, were destroyed in 1945.

During his stay in Italy, Schinkel painted landscapes, copied old masters, drew costumes and ancient monuments, and even invented vast cathedrals. He painted six large landscapes, *Six Hours of the Day*, for the silk manufacturer Humbert, and a famous picture, *Glimpse of Greece's Golden Age*, which was given to Princess Louise by the city of Berlin on the occasion of her marriage to Prince Frederick of the Netherlands. His paintings show that he paid particular attention to the effects of light, something he learned from Friedrich. He was very active as an architect, and was responsible for many neo-classical buildings in Berlin between 1816 and 1824. He provided the designs for the decoration of the entrance hall of the British Museum in London. As a theatrical scene-painter, this many-sided artist created sets in the style of classical antiquity for Mozart's *Magic Flute*. By contrast, he gave his imagination free rein when it came to designing sets for plays by authors of the 'Sturm und Drang' period, for instance a Gothic palace in the perpendicular style for Schiller's *Maid of Orleans* and a Mexican temple for Spontini's *Fernand Cortez*. He also produced lithographs and etchings, as well as drawing the illustrations for works on architecture.

An exhibition devoted to Schinkel's links with the theatre, bringing together about a hundred of his drawings and prints, was held at the Art Institute of Chicago in 1984.

Bibliography:
Karl Friedrich Schinkel, collected architectural designs, Academy Editions, London, St. Martin's Press, New York, 1982. Krieger, Peter, *Gemälde der deutschen Romantik in der Nationalgalerie Berlin Staatliche Museen Preussischer Kulturbesitz: Caspar David Friedrich, Karl Friedrich Schinkel, Carl Blechen*, exhibition catalogue, Staatliche Museen Preussischer Kulturbesitz, Berlin, 1985. Zukowsky, John/Forster, Kurt W., *Karl Friedrich Schinkel, 1781-1841: the drama of architecture*, exhibition catalogue, Art Institute of Chicago, Chicago, Tübingen, Berlin, E. Wasmuth, Chicago, 1994 (text in English and German). *'Schinkel'* in *Beaux-Arts Magazine* n° 128, periodical, Paris, November 1994. Ohff, Heinz, *Karl Friedrich Schinkel oder die Schönheit in Preussen*, Piper, Munich, 2000. Trempler, Jörg, *Das Wandbildprogramm von Karl Friedrich Schinkel: Altes Museum Berlin*, dissertation, Mann, Berlin, 2001 (University, Erlangen, Nuremberg, 1998). Abri, Martina/Ibbeken, Hillert, *Karl Friedrich Schinkel. Das architektonische Werk heute*, Mengès, Stuttgart, 2001. Haus, Andreas, *Karl Friedrich Schinkel als Künstler: Annäherung und Kommentar*, Kunstverlag, Munich, 2001. Peik, Susan M., *Karl Friedrich Schinkel: aspects of his work*, Mengès, Stuttgart, London, 2001 (text in English and German). Zadow, Mario, *Karl Friedrich Schinkel. Ein Sohn der Spätauklärung. Die Grundlagen seiner Erziehung und Bildung*, Axel Mengès, Stuttgart, London, 2001.

Museums and Galleries:
Amsterdam (Rijksmus.): *Der Traunsee bei Gmunden* (lithograph) - Berlin: *Gothic Cathedral; La Porte de Rocher* (1818); *Tomb of Queen Louise* - Berlin (Schloss Charlottenburg, Gal. der Romantik): *Mittelalterliche Stadt an einem Fluss* (1815).

Auction Records:
Munich, 4 June 1981, *Gothic Church* (1810, lithograph heightened with white) DEM 25,000. Bern, 23 June 1983, *Der Traunsee bei Gmunden* (after 1811, lithograph, 20 x 24¼ ins / 50.6 x 61.7 cm) CHF 46,000. London, 21 June 1984, *Draft of the title page for Italienische Märchen (Italian Fairy Tales) by Clemens von Brentano* (1815, gouache and

pen, 7 x 4 3/4 ins / 18 x 12 cm) GBP 19,000. MUNICH, 21 June 1994, *Marie, Susanne and Karl, the artist's children* (oil on canvas/card in three panels, oval, 29 1/4 x 17 1/4 ins / 74.5 x 43.5 cm and 23 3/4 x 16 1/4 ins/60.5 x 41 cm) DEM 227,600. LONDON, 11 Oct 1995, *Gothic Cathedral behind the Trees* (1814-1815, pencil, ink and watercolour/paper, 9 1/2 x 8 3/4 ins / 24.3 x 22.5 cm) GBP 95,000; *Vast Italian Landscape (recto); Sketch of a Gothic Window (verso)* (watercolour/paper and pencil/paper, 7 x 11 ins / 17.8 x 28.2 cm) GBP 67,500. BERLIN, 4 June 1999, *Berlin, Unter den Linden with View of Opera House Square* (pencil, 9 x 14 ins / 22 x 35 cm) DEM 4,500. BERLIN, 4 June 1999, *Sketch of Castle Babelsberg near Potsdam* (c. 1826, pencil, 8 x 13 ins / 21 x 33 cm) DEM 5,500. BERLIN, 26 May 2000, *Schloss Prediama in Crein XII Stund, Triest* (lithograph, 16 x 12 ins / 40 x 31 cm) DEM 18,000. COLOGNE, 20 Oct 2000, *Gothic Church with Churchyard with Oak Tree* (pen/lithograph, 20 x 14 ins / 50 x 35 cm) DEM 80,000. BERLIN, 30 Nov 2001, *Notes and Sketches for Architectural Detail for Tegel Castle,* DEM 4,400. NEW YORK, 23 Jan 2002, *Design for a New Stairwell for North Facade of the Schloss at Stettin* (pencil/pen/ink/watercolour, 8 x 11 ins / 21 x 29 cm) USD 65,000. BERLIN, 29 Nov 2002, *Gothic Church in Oak Grove* (lithograph, 19 x 13 ins / 49 x 34 cm) EUR 63,000. NEW YORK, 22 Jan 2003, *Pediment of Doric Building. Study* (1836, chalk/watercolour, two, 14 x 11 ins / 36 x 27 cm) USD 42,000. BERLIN, 27 Nov 2003, *Gothic Church Behind Trees* (pen/lithograph heightened with white, 19 x 13 ins / 48 x 34 cm) EUR 17,000.

SCHINKEL, Theodor
German, 19th - 20th century.
Born 9 November 1871, in Gross-Strehlitz.
Painter, lithographer. Landscapes. Stage sets.
Theodor Schinkel was a pupil of Eugen F.P. Brachet at the high school in Berlin.

SCHINN, Julius
German, 19th century.
Born 1817, in Coburg.
Painter.

SCHINNAGL, Franz Ignaz
German, 17th century.
Born 7 September 1655; died 29 September 1701.
Active in Burghausen.
Painter.
Franz Ignaz Schinnagl was the son of Tobias and father of Maximilian Joseph Schinnagl. He painted altarpieces.

SCHINNAGL, Leopold
Austrian, 18th century.
Born 1727; died 14 April 1762, in Vienna.
Painter. History painting.

SCHINNAGL, Max
Austrian, 18th century.
Born 1732; died 25 December 1800, in Vienna.
Painter. Landscapes.

SCHINNAGL, Maximilien Joseph.
See **SCHINAGL**

SCHINNAGL, Tobias
German, 17th century.
Died 17 January 1702.
Active in Burghausen.
Painter.
Tobias Schinnagl was the father of Franz Schinnagl and painted only altarpieces.

SCHINNERER, Adolf Ferdinand
German, 20th century.
Born 25 September 1876, in Schwarzenbach; died 1949.
Painter, engraver. Genre scenes.
Adolf Schinnerer was a pupil of Ludwig Schmid-Reutte, Walter Conz and Wilhelm Trübner at the academy of fine arts in Karlsruhe. He won the Prix de Rome and stayed in Rome during 1909-1910. In 1929 in Paris, he was represented at the exhibition of German painter-engravers at the Bibliothèque Nationale.
MUSEUMS AND GALLERIES:
COLOGNE (Wallraf-Richartz Mus.): *Mountain Festival* - FREIBURG IM BREISGAU: *Goodbyes* - MUNICH: *Dogs Fighting; Summer House; Apparition.*
AUCTION RECORDS:
MUNICH, 26 May 1977, *Forte dei Marmi* (1910, oil on canvas, 19 1/4 x 31 ins / 49 x 79 cm) DEM 3,600. MUNICH, 3 June 1980, *Nude Lying Down with Child* (1912, oil on canvas, 36 x 47 1/4 ins / 90.5 x 120 cm) DEM 2,400. MUNICH, 27 Nov 1981, *Tulip Bulbs* (1933, oil on canvas, 26 x 32 1/4 ins / 66 x 82 cm) DEM 20,000. MUNICH, 6 June 1986, *Bathers on the Banks of the Rhine at Cologne* (1934, oil on canvas, 35 3/4 x 30 3/4 ins / 91 x 78 cm) DEM 18,000.

SCHINSECK, Johann
German, 17th century.
Active in Munich.
Engraver (burin).

SCHINTONE, Daniel, for André Daniel
French, 20th century.
Born 4 February 1927, in Bort-les-Orgues.
Painter, illustrator. Figures, nudes, landscapes, flowers.
From 1941 to 1947 Daniel Schintone was a pupil at the École des Beaux-Arts, Toulouse, where he eventually became a professor. He was also influenced by the art of the Far East. He exhibits in Toulouse groups, in Paris at the Salon des Artistes Français, the Salon d'Automne, and the Salon des Peintres Témoins de Leur Temps, and has held solo shows at galleries in Toulouse and Paris.

His paintings use broad areas of colour in a decorative, mural style. He is greatly interested in military history and the history of costume. In 1991 he published *Silhouettes of Toulouse.*
MUSEUMS AND GALLERIES:
NARBONNE (MAH): *Nude with Curtain* - TOULOUSE (MBA, Mus. des Augustins).

SCHINZ, Caspar
Swiss, 19th century.
Born 1804, in Zurich; died 1848.
Lithographer.
Caspar Schinz was active in Bern and Fribourg.

SCHINZ, Johann Georg
Swiss, 19th century.
Born 13 March 1794, in Zurich; died 1845.
Painter. Landscapes, animals.
Johann Georg Schinz was a pupil of J.K. Gessner. He painted views of Switzerland.
MUSEUMS AND GALLERIES:
ZURICH (Kunsthaus): *Stormy Landscape.*

SCHINZ, Johann Heinrich
Swiss, 18th century.
Born c. 1740, in Zurich.
Painter.

SCHINZ, Johann Kaspar
Swiss, 19th century.
Born 16 April 1797, in Zurich; died 9 August 1832, in Zurich.
Painter.
Johann Kaspar Schinz studied at the Zurich school of fine arts. He lived much of his life in Italy, where he painted most of his works. In Rome he became friendly with Overkeck. He painted mainly religious and biblical scenes and episodes from Swiss political history.

SCHIØDT, Sigvard
Danish, 19th century.
Born 9 September 1781, in Trondheim; died 11 December 1865, in Horsens.
Painter (including porcelain), miniaturist. Landscapes.
Schiødt studied the art of the miniature first in Hamburg, in 1823, and then in Berlin. He devoted himself to painting on porcelain. From 1833 until 1843, he worked in Berlin and Copenhagen.

SCHIÖDTE, Harald Valdemar Immanuel, or Schiötte
Danish, 19th - 20th century.
Born 14 December 1852, in Copenhagen; died 18 July 1924, in Copenhagen.
Painter. Figures, scenes with figures, genre scenes.
Harald Schiödte was the pupil of Christian Vilhelm Nielsen and of the Kongelige Danske Kunstakademi in Copenhagen.
AUCTION RECORDS:
NEW YORK, 23 May 1989, *The Suitors* (1882, oil on canvas, 26¾ x 30 ins / 67.9 x 76.2 cm) USD 7,700. NEW YORK, 26 May 1994, *The Bridge of a Steamer on the Rhine* (oil on canvas, 39 x 61 ins / 99.1 x 154.9 cm) USD 12,650.

SCHIÖLBERG, Guido
Norwegian, 20th century.
Born 30 May 1886, in Kragerø.
Painter, engraver.
Guido Schiölberg was a pupil of Christian Krogh at Halvdan Ström. In Paris, he worked under the direction of Othon Friesz and Raoul Dufy. From 1920 to 1922 he travelled iin Spain and later settled in Oslo.

SCHIÖLDBORG, Frida
Norwegian, 20th century.
Born 23 June 1885; died 19 April 1926, in Oslo.
Painter.

SCHIÖLER, Inge
Swedish, 20th century.
Born 1908, in Strömstad; died 1971.
Painter (gouache), watercolourist. Figures, portraits, flowers, landscapes, waterscapes, seascapes.
Inge Schiöler was a pupil of Tor Bjurström at the School of Fine Arts of Valand, at Göteborg. In 1930 she travelled in Spain and in France. After 1933, struck by a mental illness, she had to stop painting for some time, resuming in 1944. In 1932 and 1933 she exhibited works of her first productive period at Stockholm. In these works the drawing of shapes is deliberately kept uncertain while colour is emphasised. The use of colour is in the tradition of Bonnard, directed towards strong expression.

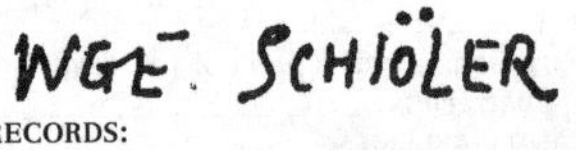

AUCTION RECORDS:
STOCKHOLM, 31 Jan 1947, *Spanish Landscape,* SEK 2,680. STOCKHOLM, 24 April 1947, *Standing Model,* SEK 3,400; *Shore of a Lake,* SEK 2,225. STOCKHOLM, 19 April 1972, *Summer Landscape,* SEK 8,400. GÖTEBORG, 29 March 1973, *Summer Landscape,* SEK 16,800. GÖTEBORG, 23 Nov 1973, *Landscape* (watercolour) SEK 4,800. GÖTEBORG, 7 Nov 1979, *Still-life* (oil on canvas, 15¾ x 19¼ ins / 40 x 49 cm) SEK 12,500. STOCKHOLM, 26 Nov 1981, *Edge of the Sea* (1967, oil on canvas, 25½ x 28¾ ins / 65 x 73 cm) SEK 18,000. STOCKHOLM, 29 Nov 1983, *Edge of the Sea* (oil on canvas, 28¾ x 31½ ins / 73 x 80 cm) SEK 77,000. GÖTEBORG, 7 Nov 1984, *Boats at Mooring* (1961, pastel, 14½ x 17¾ ins / 37 x 45 cm) SEK 21,000. STOCKHOLM, 20 April 1985, *Summer Landscape* (1965, oil on canvas, 23½ x 21¼ ins / 60 x 54 cm) SEK 103,000. GÖTEBORG, 27 Nov 1985, *Hav, kobbar och skär* (1971, silk screen print, portofolio with six works) SEK 14,500. STOCKHOLM, 27 May 1986, *Landscape at the Edge of the Sea* (1964, oil on canvas, 17¾ x 15 ins / 45 x 38 cm) SEK 65,000. COPENHAGEN, 4 May 1988, *Geranium* (1948, gouache, 29¼ x 23¼ ins / 74 x 59 cm) DKK 28,000. STOCKHOLM, 6 June 1988, *Clump of Marigolds* (1957, oil, 5¾ x 6¾ ins / 14.5 x 17 cm) SEK 32,000. GÖTEBORG, 18 May 1989, *Sea* (oil on canvas, 7¾ x 9½ ins / 20 x 24 cm) SEK 33,000. STOCKHOLM, 5-6 Dec 1990, *A Park* (oil on canvas, 19¼ x 25¼ ins / 49 x 64 cm) SEK 50,000. STOCKHOLM, 30 May 1991, *Sandy Beach at Koster* (oil on canvas, 14½ x 16½ ins / 37 x 42 cm) SEK 45,000. STOCKHOLM, 21 May 1992, *Rocky Coastline* (1960, oil on canvas, 17 x 16½ ins / 43 x 42 cm) SEK 44,000. STOCKHOLM, 10-12 May 1993, *Flowery Meadow near a Lake* (oil on canvas, 24 x 26¾ ins / 61 x 68 cm) SEK 150,000. STOCKHOLM, 30 Nov 1993, *Little Boats Anchored near the Open Sea* (oil on canvas, 28¼ x 28¼ ins / 72 x 72 cm) SEK 162,000. STOCKHOLM, 27 April 1999, *Sunset, Koster* (1959, oil on canvas, 26 x 31 ins / 65 x 80 cm) SEK 350,000. STOCKHOLM, 26 Oct 1999, *Summer by Koster Fjord* (1956, oil on canvas, 29 x 32 ins / 74 x 81 cm) SEK 500,000. STOCKHOLM, 2 May 2000, *Rocky Shore, North Koster* (1965, oil on canvas, 33 x 36 ins / 84 x 92 cm) SEK 420,000. STOCKHOLM, 15 May 2000, *Landscape, North Koster* (oil on canvas, 21 x 24 ins / 54 x 61 cm) SEK 370,000. STOCKHOLM, 2 May 2001, *Lagoon, Koster* (1968, oil on canvas, 20 x 22 ins / 50 x 55 cm) SEK 205,000. STOCKHOLM, 6 Nov 2001, *Fishing Village on the West Coast* (1964, oil on canvas, 21 x 24 ins / 54 x 60 cm) SEK 200,000. STOCKHOLM, 24 April 2002, *Fishing Boats in Harbour* (1959, oil on canvas, 29 x 32 ins / 74 x 82 cm) SEK 230,000. STOCKHOLM, 6 Nov 2002, *Autumn Day in Sydkoster* (1965, oil on canvas, 26 x 29 ins / 66 x 73 cm) SEK 230,000. STOCKHOLM, 7 May 2003, *Punts at Anchor, Langestrand, Koster* (1959, oil on canvas, 28 x 28 ins / 72 x 72 cm) SEK 275,000. STOCKHOLM, 4 Nov 2003, *Fishing Hut and Boat, Koster* (1966, oil on canvas, 26 x 29 ins / 66 x 73 cm) SEK 280,000. STOCKHOLM, 26 April 2004, *Aspen Forest by a Meadow, Koster* (1966, oil on canvas, 32 x 29 ins / 81 x 73 cm) SEK 195,000. STOCKHOLM, 26 April 2004, *Beach on a Windy Day* (oil on canvas, 26 x 29 ins / 66 x 73 cm) SEK 200,000.

SCHIOLL, Marianne Martha Wilhelmina
Maiden name: Glaser
German, 20th century.
Born 23 June 1922, in Plauen.
Naturalised in Norway through marriage, active in Hong Kong from 1953.
Painter, pastellist.
Marianne Schioll's husband's duties took her to Hong Kong, where she followed a course in Chinese painting. She exhibited there in 1954, 1955, 1956, 1959, 1966 and 1976 in private areas, hotels, the narthex of the cathedral, the Alliance Française and galleries. She also exhibited at Hamburg, Stockholm and, in 1957, in Oslo.

SCHIÖLLER, Johannes Caspar.
See **SCHØLLER**

SCHIOPETTA, Domingos Antonio, or Schiopeta or Scopeta
Portuguese, 19th century.
Active in Lisbon between 1810 and 1826.
Painter, lithographer, architect.
Domingos Antonio Schiopetta was a pupil of V. Mazzoneschi. He was the painter of the St Charles theatre in Lisbon.

SCHIOPPI. See **ALABARDI Giuseppe**

SCHIØTT, August Heinrich Georg
Danish, 19th century.
Born 17 December 1823, in Helsingør; died 25 June 1895, in Hellebæk.
Painter. Figures, portraits, landscapes, architectural views.

August Schiøtt was the father of the landscapist Elisabeth Schiøtt, who was born on 12 February 1856, in Copenhagen. He was a pupil at the Kunstakademi in Copenhagen. He travelled extensively, visiting Paris, England and Italy from 1850 to 1852, and Egypt, Greece and Palestine from 1872 until 1873.

MUSEUMS AND GALLERIES:

COPENHAGEN: *The Painter Lund; Self-portrait.*

AUCTION RECORDS:

COPENHAGEN, 19 Feb 1970, *Interior with Old Man and Child,* DKK 5,700. COPENHAGEN, 27 Sept 1983, *Portrait of Ida Trepke* (1850, oil on canvas, 35 x 22 ins / 89 x 55 cm) DKK 17,000. COPENHAGEN, 20 Aug 1986, *Repairing the Nets* (oil on canvas, 27 1/2 x 38 1/2 ins / 70 x 98 cm) DKK 37,000. LONDON, 26 Feb 1988, *River in a Wood* (1884, oil on canvas, 26 3/4 x 39 1/4 ins / 68.2 x 99.6 cm) GBP 825. LONDON, 16 March 1989, *Portrait of a Standing Woman in a White Dress* (oil on canvas, 50 1/2 x 37 3/4 ins / 128.2 x 96 cm) GBP 14,300. LONDON, 17 March 1989, *In the Caravanserai (Caravan Inn)* (1876, oil on canvas, 34 x 49 ins / 86.4 x 124.5 cm) GBP 26,400. LONDON, 5 Oct 1990, *A Father Presenting a Demand in Marriage for His Son* (oil on canvas, 38 x 51 ins / 96.5 x 129.5 cm) GBP 11,000. COPENHAGEN, 6 May 1992, *Little Girl Frightened by a Turkey* (1868, oil on canvas, 20 3/4 x 17 ins / 53 x 43 cm) DKK 8,500. LONDON, 25 Nov 1992, *Group of Young Boys on the Beach at Aalsgaarde* (oil on canvas, 67 3/4 x 78 3/4 ins / 172 x 200 cm) GBP 7,150. COPENHAGEN, 5 May 1993, *Portrait of Benedicte Treschow* (1861, oil on canvas, oval, 27 1/4 x 22 ins / 69 x 55 cm) DKK 5,000. COPENHAGEN, 15 Nov 1993, *Portrait of Frederik VII* (oil on canvas, 25 1/4 x 22 ins / 64 x 55 cm) DKK 5,000. LONDON, 20 Nov 1996, *Riot Scene in a Street* (1875, oil on canvas, 34 1/4 x 49 1/4 ins / 87 x 125 cm) GBP 10,350. COPENHAGEN, 23 Feb 1999, *Portraits of Georg V Drechsel and his Wife Elisabeth* (1849, oil on canvas, a pair, 22 x 18 ins / 57 x 46 cm) DKK 28,000. COPENHAGEN, 1 June 1999, *Portraits of M. E. Gron and his Wife Caroline* (oil on canvas, oval, a pair, 27 x 22 ins / 68 x 56 cm) DKK 19,000. COPENHAGEN, 30 May 2000, *Portrait of the Young Mr and Mrs Gottschalk* (1859, oil on canvas, a pair, oval, 27 x 22 ins / 68 x 55 cm) DKK 27,000. VEJLE, 14 Nov 2000, *Boys Bathing One Summer's Day at Aalsgaarde in North Sjælland* (1884, oil on canvas, 69 x 93 ins / 175 x 235 cm) DKK 460,000. COPENHAGEN, 3 Sept 2001, *From an Egyptian Carpet Seller's* (oil on canvas, 13 x 19 ins / 33 x 47 cm) DKK 18,000. VEJLE, 22 Sept 2003, *View of Cairo* (oil on canvas, 15 x 24 ins / 38 x 62 cm) DKK 13,500. COPENHAGEN, 9 Dec 2003, *The Artist's Fiancée Miss Oline Mathilde Lund* (1847, oil on canvas, 16 x 13 ins / 41 x 32 cm) DKK 14,000. VEJLE, 15 March 2004, *Portrait of Ida Comtesse Marie Bille Brahe* (1854, oil on canvas, 27 x 22 ins / 69 x 55 cm) DKK 13,000. PARIS, 15 June 2004, *Study of Young man Standing* (oil on canvas, 37 x 22 ins / 93 x 56 cm) EUR 3,000.

SCHIØTT, Søren

Danish, 19th century.

Born 1795, in Copenhagen; died 14 September 1868.

Engraver (burin).

SCHIÖTTE, Harald Valdemar Immanuel.

See **SCHIÖDTE**

SCHIÖTTZ-JENSEN, Ida Marie Juliane

Maiden name: Nielsen

Danish, 19th - 20th century.

Born 25 November 1861, in Horsens (Jutland); died 5 February 1932, in Roskilde.

Painter. Portraits, scenes with figures, genre scenes, interiors, landscapes.

Ida Schiöttz-Jensen was a pupil of Peter Vilhelm Kyhn, Laurits Tuxen and Kristian Zahrtmann.

AUCTION RECORDS:

COPENHAGEN, 16 Sept 1969, *Fisherman Repairing his Net,* DKK 5,700.

SCHIÖTTZ-JENSEN, Niels Frederik

Danish, 19th - 20th century.

Born 5 February 1855, in Vordingborg; died 1941.

Painter. Figures, scenes with figures, genre scenes, landscapes, seascapes.

Niels Schiöttz-Jensen was a pupil of Niels Simonsen at the Kongelige Danske Kunstakademi in Copenhagen, and of Frederick Vermehren, Johan Exner and Jørgen Roed. In 1882 and 1883 he was a pupil of the Academy Colarossi in Paris. He worked a great deal in Italy and, in 1900, in Tunis.

AUCTION RECORDS:

COPENHAGEN, 30 Aug 1977, *The Water Carrier, Capri* (oil on canvas, 30 1/4 x 20 1/2 ins / 77 x 52 cm) DKK 11,000. COPENHAGEN, 30 May 1979, *Seaside, Capri* (1908, oil on canvas, 20 x 30 1/4 ins / 51 x 77 cm) DKK 6,200. COPENHAGEN, 7 Oct 1981, *Peasant Woman in a Landscape* (1889, oil on canvas, 19 x 28 3/4 ins / 48 x 73 cm) DKK 13,000. LONDON, 28 Nov 1984, *Return of the Reapers* (1885, oil on canvas, 19 3/4 x 33 ins / 50 x 84 cm) GBP 5,000. NEW YORK, 30 Oct 1985, *The Reapers* (1885, oil on canvas, 20 1/2 x 33 1/2 ins / 52.1 x 85.1 cm) USD 9,500. STOCKHOLM, 15 Nov 1988, *The Coastline with Wrecked Boats on the Beach seen from Skagen* (oil on canvas, 11 x 16 1/4 ins / 27 x 41.5 cm) SEK 13,000. COPENHAGEN, 5 April 1989, *Port at the Mouth of a River* (1905, oil on canvas, 17 1/4 x 27 1/4 ins / 44 x 69 cm) DKK 8,500. LONDON, 5 May 1989, *Capri* (1908, oil on canvas, 23 1/4 x 36 ins / 59 x 91.5 cm) GBP 1,760. LONDON, 4 Oct 1989, *Child Gleaning* (1890, oil on canvas, 38 1/2 x 26 1/2 ins / 97.5 x 67 cm) GBP 3,740. COPENHAGEN, 25 Oct 1989, *The Olive Harvest in Italy* (oil on canvas, 26 1/2 x 35 ins / 67 x 88 cm) DKK 29,000. COPENHAGEN, 21 Feb 1990, *Man Rolling a Wheelbarrow at the Edge of the Sea* (1902, oil on canvas, 18 x 13 3/4 ins / 46 x 35 cm) DKK 7,000. LONDON, 27-28 March 1990, *Fishing with a Rod on a Rainy Day* (oil on canvas, 18 x 25 1/2 ins / 46 x 65 cm) GBP 3,520. LONDON, 29 March 1990, *A Moment of Reverie* (1888, oil on canvas, 30 1/2 x 22 1/4 ins / 77.5 x 56.5 cm) GBP 15,400. COPENHAGEN, 25-26 April 1990, *Young Italian Woman in a Loggia* (1921, oil on canvas, 20 x 15 ins / 51 x 38 cm) DKK 5,000. COPENHAGEN, 1 May 1991, *Italian Woman of Capri* (oil on canvas, 20 1/2 x 13 ins / 52 x 33 cm) DKK 5,500. LONDON, 17 May 1991, *On a Terrace in Capri* (1880, oil on canvas, 19 3/4 x 27 ins / 50 x 68.5 cm) GBP 1,650. COPENHAGEN, 6 May 1992, *Italian with an Ox Cart* (1914, oil on canvas, 19 3/4 x 31 1/2 ins / 50 x 80 cm) DKK 10,500. LONDON, 11 Feb 1994, *Fishermen on the Shore* (1909, oil on canvas, 16 x 23 3/4 ins / 39.7 x 60.3 cm) GBP 1,840. COPENHAGEN, 7 Sept 1994, *Hunter and his Dog in a Forest Path* (1897, oil on canvas) DKK 11,000.

SCHIPMANS, Gauthier, or Sciepmans

Belgian, 16th century.

Sculptor.

SCHIPPER, Urbanus

Romanian, 17th century.

Born 1587, in Cluj.

Painter, cabinet maker.

Urbanus Schipper was a Jesuit.

SCHIPPER-SCHRAMM, Erna

Dutch, 20th century.

Born 1908, in Amstelveen.

Painter. Landscapes.

Erna Schipper-Schramm was a housewife, who started painting by herself. She painted the countryside around the town in a naive style.

BIBLIOGRAPHY:

Gans, Louis, *Meesters der Europese naïven, Centraal Museum Utrecht, 2. april-31 mei 1970*, exhibition catalogue, Centraal Museum, Utrecht, 1970.

SCHIPPERS, Charles Joseph

Belgian, 19th century.

Born 24 October 1813, in Antwerp; died 19 February 1874, in Antwerp.

Painter. History painting, portraits, genre scenes.

Charles Joseph Schippers was a pupil of Van Bree.

SCHIPPERS, Joseph

Belgian, 20th century.

Born 1868, in Antwerp; died 1950.

Painter, draughtsman. Figures, portraits, scenes with figures, landscapes, seascapes, animals.

Joseph Schippers was the grandson of Charles Schippers. He studied with Piet Van Havermaet, Frans Lauwers, Jan-Willem Rosier and Léon Brunin at the academy of fine arts in Antwerp, and with Frans Van Leemputten at the Nationaal Hoger Instituut voor Schone Kunsten. He often painted monkeys, putting them in scenes of human life.

AUCTION RECORDS:

ANTWERP, 4 Dec 1984, *With The Family* (oil on canvas, 19 3/4 x 23 1/2 ins / 50 x 60 cm) BEF 80,000. ANTWERP, 21 May 1985, *The Last Counsel* (oil on canvas, 28 x 20 3/4 ins / 71 x 53 cm) BEF 500,000. LONDON, 14 Feb 1990, *Lazy Cats* (oil on panel, 13 3/4 x 17 ins / 35 x 43 cm) GBP 2,750. LONDON, 16 July 1991, *Sleeping Kittens* (oil on panel, oval, 14 3/4 x 18 3/4 ins / 37.4 x 47.7 cm) GBP 2,420. AMSTERDAM, 3 Sept 1996, *Monkeys Making Music* (1931, oil on canvas, 24 1/2 x 32 3/4 ins / 62 x 83 cm) NLG 20,757. LOKEREN, 9 Oct 1999, *At Consultation* (1924, oil on canvas, 26 x 31 ins / 65 x 80 cm) BEF 700,000. ANTWERP, 30 Nov 1999, *Monkey* (ink, 10 x 9 ins / 26 x 24 cm) BEF 75,000. ANTWERP, 16 Oct 2000, *At Consultation* (oil on canvas, 21 x 28 ins / 54 x 70 cm) BEF 960,000. ANTWERP, 5 Dec 2000, *Suzanna Bathing* (1928, oil on canvas, 28 x 35 ins / 71 x 88 cm) BEF 510,000. ANTWERP, 4 Dec 2001, *Portrait of a Little Monkey* (1935, oil on panel, 10 x 8 ins / 25 x 20 cm) BEF 120,000. ANTWERP, 17 Dec 2001, *Bibliophiles* (oil on mahogany panel, 8 x 11 ins / 21 x 28 cm) BEF 100,000. ANTWERP, 22 April 2002, *Monkey Head* (1947, oil on copper, 10 x 8 ins / 25 x 20 cm) EUR 3,800. ANTWERP, 14 Oct 2002, *Chimpanzee* (oil on panel, 14 x 10 ins / 35 x 25 cm) EUR 4,500. ANTWERP, 2 Dec 2003, *Two Little Monkeys* (1907, oil on panel, 15 x 18 ins / 38 x 46 cm) EUR 18,000. LOKEREN, 13 Dec 2003, *Chemist* (1943, oil on canvas, 22 x 28 ins / 55 x 70 cm) EUR 28,000. ANTWERP, 30 March 2004, *Suzanna Bathing* (pastel, 12 x 9 ins / 31 x 23 cm) EUR 1,500. ANTWERP, 30 March 2004, *Banker* (1926, oil on canvas, 20 x 24 ins / 50 x 60 cm) EUR 29,000.

SCHIPPERS, Pierre Joseph

Belgian, 19th century.

Born 10 October 1799, in Antwerp; died 21 April 1827.

Painter. Genre scenes, portraits.

Pierre Joseph Schippers was a pupil of M. I. van Bree. His works are to be found in Ghent.

AUCTION RECORDS:

GHENT, 1856, *Fortune-teller*, FRF 80. ANTWERP, 31 Jan 1938, *Plea*, BEF 5,000. ANTWERP, 14-16 Feb 1938, *Susanna Bathing*, BEF 3,400; *Cats*, BEF 3,200. PARIS, 25 June 1951, *Monkey*, FRF 2,500. ANTWERP, 20-22 May 1968, *Art Lover*, BEF 42,000.

SCHIPPERS, Stella, married name: Mackers

Belgian, 20th century.

Born 1912, in Turin, to Belgian parents.

Painter. Portraits, scenes with figures, still-lifes, animals.

Stella Schippers was a descendant of the family of Belgian artists of the same name. She was a student at Turin for four years at the art school, then for four more years at the Accademia Albertina, studying painting. She qualified as a teacher of drawing and taught in Turin. In 1941 she returned to Belgium, settled in Brussels and taught drawing in Bruges from 1941 to 1971. First in Italy, then in Belgium, she took part in public exhibitions, winning several distinctions. She also showed collections of her work in private exhibitions, mainly in Bruges and Brussels.

SCHIPPERS, Willem Theodor

Dutch, 20th century.

Born 1942, in Groningen.

Draughtsman, painter (gouache), sculptor.

Willem Schippers studied at the institute of arts and crafts in Amsterdam, where he lives and works. He is best known for the *Groten Stoel* (Big Seat) set up in Parc Vondel in Amsterdam.

AUCTION RECORDS:

AMSTERDAM, 10 Dec 1996, *A Good Many Flowers* (1961, collage/paper, 13 3/4 x 13 3/4 ins / 35 x 35 cm) NLG 7,495.

SCHIPPERUS, Pieter Adrianus

Dutch, 19th - 20th century.

Born 6 March 1840, in Rotterdam; died 1929, in The Hague.

Painter (gouache), watercolourist. History painting, portraits, landscapes with figures, landscapes, seascapes.

MUSEUMS AND GALLERIES:

ROTTERDAM: *Landscape at Sunset.*

AUCTION RECORDS:

NEW YORK, 12-17 March 1911, *Quay at Rotterdam*, USD 80. NEW YORK, 16 June 1923, *Edge of the Village*; *Hamlet by the Water* (both) FRF 400. AMSTERDAM, 27 Nov 1974, *Horseman on a Road* (watercolour) NLG 2,800. AMSTERDAM, 20 Oct 1976, *Landscape with Stormy Sky* (1913, oil on card, 18 x 27 3/4 ins / 45.5 x 70.5 cm) NLG 7,000. AMSTERDAM, 28 Feb 1989, *Peasant Chatting with a Child on a Canal Path* (watercolour and gouache/paper, 13 1/4 x 20 ins / 33.5 x 51 cm) NLG 2,990. AMSTERDAM, 2 Nov 1992, *People in a Creek near Kralingen* (watercolour, 17 3/4 x 30 1/2 ins / 45 x 77.5 cm) NLG 1,668. AMSTERDAM, 19 April 1994, *Wood Gatherers in the Forest* (watercolour, 4 3/4 x 7 3/4 ins / 12 x 19.5 cm) NLG 1,955. PARIS, 2 Dec 1994, *Princess Emma of Waldeck-Pyrmont, Second Wife of King WIlliam III of the Lowlands* (oil on canvas, 19 x 13 3/4 ins / 48 x 35 cm) FRF 15,500. AMSTERDAM, 7 Nov 1995, *River Landscape with Boats Aground in Winter* (1922, oil on canvas/card, 14 3/4 x 20 1/2 ins / 37.5 x 52 cm) NLG 1,770. AMSTERDAM, 2 Sept 1997, *A Farm in a Polder Landscape* (oil on panel, 14 1/4 x 17 1/2 ins / 36 x 44.5 cm) NLG 2,306.

SCHIRCK, Éliane

French, 20th - 21st century.

Born 17 July 1947, in Mulhouse.

Painter, watercolourist, pastellist, engraver. Figures, nudes.

Éliane Schirck studied at the École des Beaux-Arts in Paris, where she graduated with a degree in painting in 1979. Since 1982, she has painted exclusively in tempera on Japanese rice paper. Her work betrays two principal sources of inspiration: until 1985, she worked on a series called *Dolls* and, as of 1989, she has been engaged on a series entitled *Venice*. She has worked as an engraver since 1976 and devotes most of her time to etching, aquatint, dry-point and ex libris engravings.

Schirck's techniques involves transposing and recomposing Venetian landscapes and figures. Her technique is simple yet effective, using egg tempera and gold dust to develop a surface texture to her work to achieve effects best described as 'transparent watercolour' or 'mother-of-pearl pastel'. This lends an intrinsically lyrical aspect to her work. Her paintings are timeless, dream-like compositions featuring landscapes and figures, with technique subordinated to an overall impression of elegance and beauty.

She showed examples of her work at various group exhibitions, among them: in 1970, 1971, 1972 and 1973, at the Salon des Indépendants and, in 1975 and 1976, at the Salon d'Automne in Paris; in 1977, in Versailles; in 1977 and 1978, at the Salon des Artistes Français in Paris; in 1980, at the Bilan de l'Art Contemporain in Quebec; in 1982 and 1983, at the Contemporary Art Exhibition in New York; in 1991 and 1994, at the 3rd Prints Biennale in Chamalières; and, in 1996, at the European Graphic Arts Biennale in Bruges. She has also exhibited solo, including in 1982 and 1985, at the Musée Bartholdi in Colmar and, in 1984, 1986 and 1989, at the Galerie Jean Camion in Paris. Schirck has been the recipient of various awards and distinctions, among them a bronze medal in 1982.

MUSEUMS AND GALLERIES:
CARLA-BAYLE (Musée Pierre-Bayle) - CHAMALIÈRES (MAC) - ROTTERDAM.

SCHIRL, Friedrich
Austrian, 18th century.
Active in Saaz.
Sculptor.

SCHIRM, Karl
German, 19th - 20th century.
Born 24 November 1852, in Wiesbaden; died 3 April 1928, in Amelinghausen.
Painter. Landscapes, seascapes.

Karl Schirm was a pupil of Hans Gude at the academy of fine arts in Karlsruhe. Afterwards he travelled all over Germany making a particular study of the Black Forest region. In 1880 he travelled to Syria and visited the banks of the Caspian Sea and the Sinaï Peninsula.

MUSEUMS AND GALLERIES:
BERLIN (Nationalgal.): *Landscapes of Palestine* - WROCLAW: *Evening Landscape*.

AUCTION RECORDS:
HANOVER, 17 March 1979, *Winter Evening in the Forest* (1879, oil on panel, 6 x 4 1/4 ins / 15 x 10.5 cm) DEM 2,200. COLOGNE, 21 May 1981, *Landscape* (oil on canvas, 27 1/2 x 37 ins / 70 x 94 cm) DEM 4,200.

SCHIRMER, Achille
French, 19th century.
Born 9 July 1826, in Commercy (Meuse); died 29 March 1888, in Prunuit.
Draughtsman, caricaturist, modeller.

SCHIRMER, Andreas
German, 17th century.
Active in Tharandt.
Sculptor.

SCHIRMER, August
German, 19th - 20th century.
Born 26 July 1860, in Schlottstall.
Draughtsman. Landscapes, architectural views.

August Schirmer was a pupil of Albert Kappis and Friedrich von Keller at the school of fine arts in Stuttgart. From 1901 he taught drawing there.

SCHIRMER, Christian
German, 17th century.
Active in Danzig (now Gdansk, Poland) and in Königsberg (now Kaliningrad, Russia) in Prussia.
Engraver. Coins.

SCHIRMER, Friedrich
German, 19th century.
Active in Aachen.
Draughtsman. Scenes with figures.

MUSEUMS AND GALLERIES:
AACHEN (Burg Frankenberg): *Celebration outside the Town Hall in Aachen*.

SCHIRMER, G.
German, 19th century.
Born 1804, in Berlin; died 1866, in Berlin.
Painter, decorative designer. Landscapes.

Schirmer studied at the academy in Berlin. He concentrated mainly on decoration and painted a large number of frescoes. It seems likely that he visited Italy, as some of his landscapes represent views of that country. He is best known for the decoration of the palace of Prince Albert of Prussia and of the Berlin Museum. He became a professor at the academy in Berlin.

MUSEUMS AND GALLERIES:
BERLIN: *View of Sorrento* (oil on canvas); *View of the Palace of Sans-Souci* (oil on canvas).

SCHIRMER, Georg
German, 19th century.
Born 1816; died 1880.
Active in Kassel.
Painter.

Georg Schirmer painted *Napoleon III* and members of the Hessian aristocracy.

SCHIRMER, Johann Heinrich
German, 18th century.
Born c. 1708; died 1743, in Bayreuth.
Painter.

Johann Heinrich Schirmer was an earthenware maker at the factory at St Georgen in the Black Forest.

SCHIRMER, Johann Wilhelm
German, 19th century.
Born 5 September 1807, in Jülich; died 11 September 1863, in Karlsruhe.
Painter, watercolourist, engraver, lithographer, draughtsman. Landscapes.
Düsseldorf School.

After first working as a bookbinder, Johann Schirmer became a student at the academy in Düsseldorf in 1826 and joined Schadow's studio in 1827. After extensive study tours in Europe, he was appointed professor at the academy in Düsseldorf. In 1853, he became the director of the school of fine arts in Karlsruhe. The 26 charcoal drawings known as his 'Biblical Landscapes' date from this time. He became a member of the Berlin academy in 1833 and an honorary member of the Dresden academy in 1851. Johann Schirmer founded a new school of landscape painting and taught a large number of pupils.

Collective thematic exhibitions: 2001, *Un Paese incantato. Italia dipinta da Thomas Jones a Corot* (*An Enchanted Country. Italy Depicted by Artists from Thomas Jones to Corot*), Centro Internazionale d'Arte e Cultura di Palazzo Tè, Mantua; 2003, *Das Irdische Paradies. Sammlung Volmer* (*An Earthly Paradise: the Volmer Collection*), an exhibition on the Düsseldorf School between 1819 and 1918, Von der Heydtmuseum, Wuppertal. Solo exhibitions: 1982, Stadthalle, Jülich; 2002, *Johann Wilhelm Schirmer in seiner Zeit: Landschaft im 19. Jahrhundert zwischen Wirklichkeit und Ideal* (*Johann Wilhem Schirmer and his Times: Landscape in the 19th Century between Reality and the Ideal*), Staatliche Kunsthalle, Karlsruhe.

BIBLIOGRAPHY:

Theilmann, Rudi, *Johann Wilhelm Schirmers Karlsruher Schule*, dissertation, Universität, Heidelberg, 1971. Berthold, Ettrich, *Parktraum - Traumpark: A. J. W. Schirmer, Aquarelle und Zeichnungen zu Pücklers Andeutungen über Landschaftgärtnerei*, exhibition catalogue, Niederlausitzer Landesmuseum, Cottbus, 1993. Franzke, Andreas, *Johann Wilhelm Schirmer (1807-1863). Studien nach der Natur*, exhibition catalogue, Badenwerk, Karlsruhe, 1994. Ottani Cavina, Anna (ed.), *Un Paese incantato. Italia dipinta da Thomas Jones a Corot*, exhibition catalogue, Electa, Milan, 2001. *Johann Wilhelm Schirmer in seiner Zeit: Landschaft im 19. Jahrhundert zwischen Wirklichkeit und Ideal*, exhibition catalogue, Staatliche Kunsthalle Karlsruhe, Karlsruhe, 2002.

MUSEUMS AND GALLERIES:

BERLIN (Nationalgal.): *Mountain Landscape; Abraham's Entry into the Promised Land; Abraham Praying for Sodom and Gomorrah; Deliverance and Promise; The Sacrifice of Isaac; Eliezer and Rebecca at the Well* - COLOGNE: *Italian Landscape; Landscape; Chapel in the Woods* (six sketches of biblical landscapes) - DARMSTADT: *Evening Landscape* - DÜSSELDORF (Kunstmus.): *Landscape on the Lower Rhine; Landscape; Landscape in the Rhön Hills; Forest Landscape* (26 biblical landscapes); *Castle near Altenahr; The Watterhorn* (16 studies in oils); *Cypresses at the Villa d'Este* (oil on canvas) - FRANKFURT AM MAIN: *Landscape* (two works); *The Good Samaritan (Landscape)* - HAMBURG: *Forest Path* - HANOVER: *Avalanche; Storm; Autumn Landscape; At Terni; Mountainous Landscape* - KALININGRAD: *Evening Rest* - KARLSRUHE: *Landscape; Surprise Attack; Storm Building up in the Countryside; Landscapes* (78 oil studies) - KARLSRUHE (Staatliche Akademie der Bildenden Künste): *Raphael's Villa in Rome* (oil on paper) - KARLSRUHE (Staatliche Kunsthalle): *In the Roman Campagna* (oil/card) - LEIPZIG: *Egeria's Grotto; Landscape* (three works) - MUNICH: *Wooded Landscape* - STUTTGART: *Biblical Landscape* - SZCZECIN: *Landscape near Sorrento*.

AUCTION RECORDS:

PARIS, 1898, *Landscape*, FRF 1,225. COLOGNE, 12 Dec 1934, *Wooded Landscape*, DEM 680. PARIS, 27 April 1950, *The Roman Campagna*, FRF 5,800. MUNICH, 4-6 Oct 1961, *Klostervorhalle*, DEM 5,200. MUNICH, 6-8 Nov 1963, *Landscape in Stormy Weather* (watercolour) DEM 4,200. MUNICH, 11 Dec 1968, *Wooded Landscape*, DEM 5,200. MUNICH, 17 Nov 1971, *Wooded Landscape*, DEM 6,200. ZURICH, 24 Oct 1979, *Wooded Landscape with a Stream* (oil on canvas, 29 1/2 x 41 3/4 ins / 75 x 106 cm) CHF 19,000. MUNICH, 28 Nov 1979, *St Mary Magdalene in a Landscape* (chalk heightened with white, 11 x 16 1/2 ins / 27 x 42 cm) DEM 2,800. MUNICH, 28 Nov 1979, *Italian Landscape* (watercolour, 9 x 18 3/4 ins / 23 x 47.5 cm) DEM 15,000. COLOGNE, 21 May 1981, *Wooded Landscape* (oil on canvas, 35 1/2 x 55 1/2 ins / 90 x 141 cm) DEM 60,000. COLOGNE, 24 May 1982, *Shepherd and Flock in a Stormy Landscape* (gouache and watercolour, 11 3/4 x 17 ins / 30 x 43 cm) DEM 14,000. COLOGNE, 21 May 1984, *Landscape with Ruins and Figures* (oil on canvas, 10 3/4 x 17 1/4 ins / 27.5 x 43.5 cm) DEM 9,000. LONDON, 9 Oct 1997, *Travellers in a Wooded and Rocky Landscape* (oil on canvas, 37 1/2 x 27 ins / 95.3 x 68.5 cm) GBP 2,990. MUNICH, 27 Feb 1999, *Forest Landscape with Gnarled Oak and Two Brushwood Collectors* (oil on canvas, 29 x 44 ins / 74 x 113 cm) DEM 26,000. COLOGNE, 15 May 1999, *Swiss Alpine Landscape with View of Jungfrau* (oil on canvas, 27 x 34 ins / 69 x 87 cm) DEM 60,000. DÜSSELDORF, 31 Jan 2000, *Countryside near Castle* (oil on canvas, 15 x 22 ins / 39 x 55 cm) DEM 16,000. MUNICH, 22 March 2000, *Mountain Stream Cascading between Rocks* (oil on canvas, 34 x 26 ins / 86 x 67 cm) DEM 10,000. FRANKFURT, 3 March 2001, *River Landscape* (oil on canvas, 35 x 51 ins / 88 x 129 cm) DEM 52,000. COLOGNE, 19 May 2001, *Southern Italian Landscape with Herders* (oil on canvas, 46 x 65 ins / 116 x 165 cm) DEM 140,000. MUNICH, 26 June 2002, *Mountain Landscape with the Prophet Elias by Waterfall* (oil on canvas, 19 x 15 ins / 47 x 39 cm) EUR 5,000. LONDON, 4 Dec 2002, *View of Civitella, Italy* (oil on paper, 12 x 20 ins / 30 x 51 cm) GBP 22,000. COLOGNE, 17 May 2003, *Swiss Alpine Landscape with Jungfrau* (oil on canvas, 27 x 34 ins / 69 x 87 cm) EUR 65,000. COLOGNE, 15 Nov 2003, *Alpine Landscape with Wild River* (oil on canvas, 16 x 23 ins / 41 x 59 cm) EUR 13,500. MUNICH, 17 March 2004, *Extensive River Valley in the Mountains* (oil on canvas, 17 x 22 ins / 44 x 57 cm) EUR 11,000. STAUFEN, 25 March 2004, *Sunny Woodland* (oil on board, 23 x 28 ins / 58 x 71 cm) EUR 2,200.

SCHIRMER, Karl Josef

Austrian, 19th century.

Born 16 February 1838, in Graz; died 26 March 1893, in Puchbach, near Köflach.

Painter.

Karl Josef Schirmer studied at the academies of Munich, Dresden, Berlin and Stuttgart.

SCHIRMER, Karl Michael

German, 19th century.

Born 1 June 1808, in Greifswald; died 1 May 1876, in Dresden.

Painter.

Karl Michael Schirmer studied in Copenhagen and Dresden.

SCHIRMER, Oswald

Austrian, 17th century.

Born in Steyr; died 20 May 1613, in Kulmbach.

Painter.

SCHIRMER, Robert

German, 19th - 20th century.

Born 11 July 1850, in Berlin; died 23 September 1923, in Berlin.

Sculptor.

SCHIRMER, Simprecht

Austrian, 16th century.

Born to a family originally from Graz.

Painter.

SCHIRMER, Wilhelm August Ferdinand

German, 19th century.

Born 6 May 1802, in Berlin; died 8 June 1866, in Nyon or in Vevey.

Painter, engraver. Landscapes, architectural views, flowers, fruit.

Wilhelm Schirmer began by painting flowers for the Berlin factory. Between 1827 and 1830, he travelled in Italy and was one of the founders of the artistic association of Rome. He became a member of the academy in Berlin in 1835. He was influenced by Schinkel.

MUSEUMS AND GALLERIES:

BADEN-BADEN (Schloss): *Marine Landscape* - BERLIN: *Terracina; On Lake Como; View of Ancient Rome; The Valley of Narvi; Evening; The Roman Campagna; Fisherman near Sorrento* - ERFURT: *Coast at Naples* - GDANSK: *View of Naples with Queen Joanna's Palace* - HALLE: *The Villa Borghese*.

AUCTION RECORDS:

HELSINKI, 11 Dec 1999, *Die Ruhelose* (1854, oil on canvas, 42 x 59 ins / 107 x 149 cm) FIM 95,000. BERLIN, 31 May 2002, *Heroic Landscape* (oil on canvas/board, 9 x 12 ins / 22 x 30 cm) EUR 2,800.

SCHIRMER, Wilhelm August Ferdinand

Austrian, 19th century.

Born 1807, in Jülich; died 1863, in Karlsruhe.

Painter. Landscapes, landscapes with figures, mountainscapes, architectural views.

Emperor Frederick William IV commissioned Schirmer to put together an album of views of various castles.

AUCTION RECORDS:
MUNICH, 10 May 1989, *After the Storm* (oil on canvas, 40 1/2 x 57 ins / 103 x 145 cm) DEM 66,000. MUNICH, 29 Nov 1989, *Shepherd in a Mountain Landscape* (oil on canvas, 13 1/2 x 19 ins / 34 x 48.5 cm) DEM 22,000. HEIDELBERG, 11 April 1992, *Clouds on the Mountains and the Wetterhorn* (watercolour and ink, 19 1/2 x 16 1/4 ins / 49.7 x 41.3 cm) DEM 5,800. MUNICH, 10 Dec 1992, *Italian Landscape with Nymphs Bathing in a Lake* (1847, oil on canvas, 55 x 85 ins / 140 x 216 cm) DEM 79,100. LONDON, 19 Nov 1993, *Arcadian Landscape* (pencil and watercolour/paper, 8 1/2 x 15 1/4 ins / 21.9 x 38.8 cm) GBP 3,220. MUNICH, 21 June 1994, *Egiria's Grotto* (oil on canvas, 22 3/4 x 34 1/2 ins / 58 x 87.5 cm) DEM 74,750. HEIDELBERG, 15 Oct 1994, *Bathers in a Pond* (oil on canvas, 15 x 20 3/4 ins / 38 x 53 cm) DEM 16,000. MUNICH, 27 June 1995, *View of Tivoli* (1838, pencil/paper, 12 1/4 x 15 1/4 ins / 31 x 38.5 cm) DEM 1,725. VIENNA, 29-30 Oct 1996, *Castle on the Heights; Castle in a Forest* (oil on canvas, a pair, 7 1/2 x 6 ins / 19 x 15 cm) ATS 161,000.

SCHIRMES, Albert
German, 19th century.
Born 18 February 1838, in Leipzig; died 23 July 1899, in Wettin.
Painter. Architectural views, landscapes.

Schirmes was a pupil of Adolf Eltzner.

SCHIRMPÖCK, Hans, or Schirnbeck
German, 17th century.
Active in Nuremberg.
Painter.

SCHIRNBÖCK, Ferdinand
Austrian, 19th - 20th century.
Born 27 August 1859, in Oberhollabrunn; died 16 September 1930, in Perltholdsdorf, near Vienna.
Engraver.

Ferdinand Schirnböck was a pupil of Ferdinand Laufberger from 1878 to 1888 at the school of arts and crafts in Vienna. From 1880 to 1886 he was a pupil of Ludwig Jacoby and Johannes Sonnenleiter at the special school for engraving at the Akademie der Bildenden Künste in Vienna. He specialised in engraving bank notes and postage stamps.

SCHIRREN, Ferdinand
Belgian, 19th - 20th century.
Born 8 November 1872, in Antwerp; died 1944, in Molenbeek-St-Jean.
Painter, watercolourist, sculptor. Figures, portraits, landscapes, still-lifes.
Brabant Fauvism.

Ferdinand Schirren was a pupil of J.-B. de Keyser and Joseph Stallaert at the academy of fine arts in Brussels, where he trained mainly as a sculptor, and of the studio of Jef Lambeaux. In 1898 he founded the group Labeur (Labour) with August Oleffe, Willem Paerels and Louis Thévenet, and was also a member of the group Le Sillon (The Furrow). Schirren was a friend of Rik Wouters. He stayed in Paris from 1919 to 1922.

About 1900 he abandoned sculpture to devote himself exclusively to painting. At first, he came under the influence of Impressionists such as Van Rijsselberghe and Claus; then he evolved his own style to become one of the first exponents of 'Brabant Fauvism', using clear, intense colours that prevailed over the design. Today, Ferdinand Schirren is best known for his watercolours.

F. Schirren

BIBLIOGRAPHY:
Van de Voorde, Urbain, *Ferdinand Schirren*, Meddens, Brussels, 1963.

MUSEUMS AND GALLERIES:
BRUSSELS (MBA): *Woman in Blue*.

AUCTION RECORDS:
ANTWERP, 23 April 1969, *Maternity* (watercolour) BEF 65,000. ANTWERP, 13 Oct 1970, *Woman in Blue in an Interior*, BEF 400,000. BRUSSELS, 24 Oct 1972, *Couple in Bed* (watercolour) BEF 60,000. ANTWERP, 7 April 1976, *Woman in front of a Mirror* (watercolour, 22 x 17 1/4 ins / 55 x 44 cm) BEF 46,000. LOKEREN, 12 March 1977, *Nude with Flowers* (1920, watercolour, 23 1/2 x 19 ins / 60 x 48 cm) BEF 55,000. BREDA, 26 April 1977, *The Street Pedlar* (bronze, h. 19 3/4 ins / 50 cm) NLG 2,000. LOKEREN, 16 Feb 1980, *Young Girl* (1904, bronze, h. 13 3/4 ins / 35 cm) BEF 45,000. BRUSSELS, 19 March 1980, *Landscape* (watercolour, 17 x 21 1/4 ins / 43 x 54 cm) BEF 100,000. ANTWERP, 27 April 1982, *The Gardener* (watercolour, 15 3/4 x 20 ins / 40 x 51 cm) BEF 110,000. ANTWERP, 26 Oct 1982, *Mother, Child and Doll* (drawing, 41 1/4 x 29 1/4 ins / 105 x 74 cm) BEF 65,000. ANTWERP, 26 April 1983, *Flowers and Fruits* (watercolour, 20 3/4 x 24 ins / 53 x 61 cm) BEF 100,000. BRUSSELS, 15 June 1983, *View from the Port* (oil on panel, 25 1/4 x 26 3/4 ins / 64 x 68 cm) BEF 95,000. LOKEREN, 15 Oct 1983, *The Pedlar* (bronze, h. 19 1/4 ins / 49 cm) BEF 55,000. ANTWERP, 3 April 1984, *Seated Nude* (drawing, 35 3/4 x 19 1/4 ins / 91 x 49 cm) BEF 40,000. LOKEREN, 16 Feb 1985, *Nude in a Landscape* (watercolour, 20 1/2 x 13 1/2 ins / 52 x 34 cm) BEF 190,000. LOKEREN, 28 May 1988, *Vase of Flowers* (oil on card, 17 3/4 x 14 1/4 ins / 45 x 36.5 cm) BEF 140,000. LOKEREN, 8 Oct 1988, *Still-life with Flowers and a Statuette of the Buddha* (watercolour and pencil, 13 3/4 x 12 1/2 ins / 35 x 32 cm) BEF 95,000. LOKEREN, 23 May 1992, *Maternity* (black chalk, 19 x 13 3/4 ins / 48 x 35 cm) BEF 90,000. LOKEREN, 15 May 1993, *Dune Landscape* (1913, watercolour, 11 x 14 1/4 ins / 27 x 36 cm) BEF 130,000. AMSTERDAM, 26 May 1993, *Garden Terrace* (watercolour/paper, 9 1/2 x 12 1/4 ins / 24 x 31 cm) NLG 1,840. LOKEREN, 12 March 1994, *Dune Landscape* (1913, watercolour, 11 x 14 1/4 ins / 27 x 36 cm) BEF 140,000. LOKEREN, 8 Oct 1994, *Biting Cold* (plaster, h. 19 ins / 48.3 cm) BEF 80,000. LOKEREN, 10 Dec 1994, *Young Man* (bronze, h. 18 1/2 ins / 47 cm, l. 12 1/2 ins/32 cm) BEF 220,000. LOKEREN, 11 March 1995, *Seated Nude* (watercolour and pencil, 13 x 14 1/4 ins / 33 x 36 cm) BEF 180,000. AMSTERDAM, 1 Dec 1997, *At the Breast* (pastel and ink/paper, 27 1/4 x 20 1/2 ins / 69 x 52 cm) NLG 16,520. LOKEREN, 9 Oct 1999, *Seated Nude* (c. 1917, oil on cardboard on panel, 30 x 25 ins / 75 x 63 cm) BEF 650,000. AMSTERDAM, 12 Oct 1999, *Still-life* (1912, oil on board on panel, 35 x 29 ins / 90 x 73 cm) NLG 20,000. LOKEREN, 4 March 2000, *Still-life with Flowers and Naked Figure* (c. 1935, oil on canvas, 26 x 21 ins / 65 x 54 cm) BEF 160,000. ANTWERP, 4 April 2000, *Vase with Chrysanthemums* (mixed media, 29 x 26 ins / 74 x 65 cm) BEF 230,000. LOKEREN, 6 Oct 2001, *Still-life with Pitcher* (c. 1920, watercolour, 22 x 26 ins / 55 x 67 cm) BEF 310,000. LOKEREN, 6 Oct 2001, *Woman Sitting at Table* (c. 1914, oil on canvas, 13 x 16 ins / 32 x 40 cm) BEF 360,000. LOKEREN, 9 March 2002, *Still-life with Flowers* (watercolour, 23 x 20 ins / 59 x 50 cm) EUR 4,800. LOKEREN, 11 May 2002, *Still-life* (watercolour, 25 x 30 ins / 64 x 75 cm) EUR 8,000. LOKEREN, 13 March 2004, *Seated Nude in an Interior* (1925, oil on canvas, 45 x 35 ins / 115 x 90 cm) EUR 22,000. ANTWERP, 7 Dec 2004, *Young Woman* (oil on canvas) EUR 15,000. LOKEREN, 11 Dec 2004, *After the Bath* (watercolour, 24 x 20 ins / 60 x 50 cm) EUR 5,000. LOKEREN, 11 Dec 2004, *View of a Garden* (watercolour, 26 x 32 ins / 66 x 81 cm) EUR 6,000.

SCHIRRER, Albert
French, 19th - 20th century.
Born in Menton.
Sculptor.

Albert Schirrer exhibited in Paris at the Salon des Artistes Français, where he was awarded an honourable mention at the time of the Exposition Universelle of 1889 and a third-class medal in 1901.

SCHISANO, Nicola
Italian, 17th century.
Active in Naples.
Sculptor (wood).

SCHISCHELOV, Nikolai Ivanovich
Russian, 19th century.
Born 15 January 1857, in Moscow.
Painter. History painting.
Nikolai Schischelov studied at the St Petersburg academy.

SCHISCHKIN, Ivan Ivanovich.
See **CHICHKIN**

SCHISCHKOV, Matvei Andreevich.
See **CHICHKOV**

SCHISHOV, Matvei Afanassevich
Russian, 19th century.
Born 10 November 1838, in Pudowo.
Sculptor.
Matvei Schishov studied at the St Petersburg academy. He sculpted busts and statues of infants and genre figures.
MUSEUMS AND GALLERIES:
MOSCOW (Rumiantsev Mus.): *Fire* - ST PETERSBURG (Gosudarstvennyj Russkij Muz.): *Bust of J. K. Rivasovsky; Bust of A. Bogoliubov; Game of Blind Man's Buff.*

SCHISI, Mario
Italian, 17th century.
Active in Ferrara.
Painter, designer of ornamental architectural features.

SCHISSLER, Gregorius
Austrian, 17th century.
Sculptor.

SCHISSLER, Hans
German, 18th century.
Cabinet maker.

SCHISSLER, Stephan
Austrian, 18th century.
Painter.
Stephan Schissler painted on porcelain at the Vienna factory between 1742 and 1750.

SCHIT, Nicolaus
German, 16th century.
Active c. 1500.
Painter.
Nicolaus Schit left few paintings, but those we have are notable for the quality of their colours. He may have painted the *Niedererlenbach Altar* that dates from 1497, and a *Nativity* now in the museum of Aschaffenburg.
MUSEUMS AND GALLERIES:
ASCHAFFENBURG: *Nativity.*
AUCTION RECORDS:
MUNICH, 16-18 March 1966, *Scenes from the Life of St Blaisius* (two pendants) DEM 22,000. LONDON, 21 June 1968, *Christ Wearing the Crown of Thorns,* Gns 1,900.

SCHITERBERG, Anton
Swiss, 16th century.
Died 1588.
Active in Lucerne.
Painter. Religious subjects.

SCHITTENHELM. See **SCHUTTENHELM**

SCHITTIG
German, 18th century.
Born to a family originally from Obernburg, Germany.
Sculptor (wood).

SCHITZ, J.
Austrian, 18th century.
Painter. Architectural views, landscapes.
J. Schitz may have been confused with Albert Gustav Schivert.

SCHITZ, Jules Nicolas
French, 19th century.
Born 9 February 1817, in Paris; died 29 April 1871, in Troyes.
Painter. Architectural views, landscapes.
He was a pupil of Joseph Rémond. He began exhibiting at the Paris Salon in 1840, and won a third-class medal that very first year. He was appointed Director of the École Municipale de Dessin in Troyes.
MUSEUMS AND GALLERIES:
TROYES: *Interior of the Church of St-André; The Jube of St Mary Magdalene; Grésivaudan Valley; View from Troyes; Environs of Grenoble*; two studies.

SCHIVERT, Albert Gustav
Austrian, 19th century.
Born 9 April 1826, in Hermannstadt (now Sibiu, Romania); died 18 June 1881, in Graz.
Painter.
Albert Schivert was the father of Viktor Schivert. He studied with the portrait painter Johann Agotha and also at the academy of fine arts in Vienna.
MUSEUMS AND GALLERIES:
SIBIU: *Portrait of Baron Josef von Bruckenthal; Portrait of Baron Karl von Bruckenthal; Portrait of Baron Hermann von Bruckenthal.*

SCHIVERT, Viktor
Romanian, 19th - 20th century.
Born 8 May 1863, in Iasi.
Active in Germany.
Painter, illustrator. Portraits, genre scenes.
Viktor Schivert was the son of Albert Schivert, and a student of Aloïs Gabl and Otto Seitz.
AUCTION RECORDS:
COLOGNE, 7 June 1972, *Invitation to the Dance,* DEM 9,500. NEW YORK, 7 Oct 1977, *Tavern Scene* (1891, oil on canvas, 20½ x 16 ins / 52 x 40.5 cm) USD 5,000. LONDON, 28 Nov 1980, *The Conversation* (oil on canvas, 25¼ x 20½ ins / 64.2 x 52 cm) GBP 1,500. COLOGNE, 29 June 1984, *Tavern Scene* (oil on canvas, 30¼ x 36½ ins / 77 x 93 cm) DEM 4,000. WARSAW, 5 Dec 1999, *Encounter* (oil on panel, 16 x 12 ins / 41 x 31 cm) PLN 6,800. MUNICH, 21 March 2001, *Girl Being Entertained by Three Men* (oil on panel, 20 x 15 ins / 50 x 39 cm) DEM 6,000. MUNICH, 20 Sept 2002, *Two Female Nudes on Shore* (oil on canvas, 28 x 44 ins / 71 x 112 cm) EUR 2,500. MUNICH, 4 Dec 2002, *Tavern with Cavalier and Young Woman at a Table* (oil on canvas on canvas, 21 x 25 ins / 53 x 63 cm) EUR 2,600. KEMPTEN, 10 July 2003, *The Last Trip - Executioner with Nude Woman* (oil on canvas, 56 x 44 ins / 141 x 111 cm) EUR 2,000. ERLANGEN, 19 June 2004, *Small Figure* (oil on canvas, 37 x 30 ins / 93 x 77 cm) EUR 1,800.

SCHIVILOV, Mikhail Nikandrovich
Russian, 19th century.
Born 1837, in the Kostroma region; died 27 February 1861, in Dresden.
Painter. History painting.
Mikhail Schivilov studied at the St Petersburg academy.
MUSEUMS AND GALLERIES:
ST PETERSBURG (Mus. of AFA): *Self-portrait.*

SCHIZ, Mathias. See **SCHÜTZ**

SCHJELDERUP, Leis
Norwegian, 19th - 20th century.
Painter. Genre scenes.

Leis Schjelderup and Leys Georgia Elise Schjelderup are thought to be the same person. Lei Schjelderup appeared in exhibitions of the Salon des Artistes Français in Paris and received a bronze medal for the Exposition Universelle.

AUCTION RECORDS:

NEW YORK, 19 Feb 1992, *Game of See-saw at the Seaside* (oil on canvas, 45 1/2 x 62 ins / 115.6 x 157.5 cm) USD 14,300.

SCHJERFBECK, Helena Sofia, or Helene, or Schjerberk, Schierfberk
Finnish, 19th - 20th century.
Born 10 July 1862, in Helsingfors (Helsinki); died 23 January 1946.
Painter (including gouache), watercolourist, draughtsman, lithographer. Genre scenes, figures, portraits, landscapes.
Symbolism.

Helena Schjerfbeck suffered from poor health since childhood, but she was completely absorbed by her art. When she was 11, she began her studies at the school of the Finnish Association of the Arts in Helsinki. By the time she was 18, she was painting noteworthy portraits of children and of genre scenes. After having passed through various studios in the school she left Finland for Paris in 1880. She took part in the Salon des Artistes Français (she continued to contribute to it afater she left Paris), winning a bronze medal for the Exposition Universelle of 1900. In the 1880s she lived in St Ives and was a member of the artists community

The 1888 version of *The Little Convalescent* shows a wonderful mastery of traditional technique. Later she became interested in esotericism, an interest that was reinforced during her travels, between 1892 and 1894. From 1892 to 1894 she travelled to St Petersburg, Vienna and Florence, before returning to Finland, she then spent the last two years of her life in Sweden, near Stockholm. In France she met the artists of Concarneau and Pont-Aven, where she painted landscapes in the open air, in the style of Gauguin and the Nabis. Later, she considered this collection of landscapes as 'an impersonal and inexpressive period' in her work. In about 1882 she began studies on the theme of dancing shoes. She pursued this theme in a lithograph in 1938. One of the characteristics of her work is the repetition of several themes, which continued throughout her life. One of these themes was the series of self portraits that from 1910 became an obsession with her. The development of these these themes display the evolution of her technique and its pictorial conception, which tended towards an ever more radical emancipation the well-mannered painting in the Scandinavian countries. In 1888 she was painting still in the spirit and technique of the nineteenth-century post-Romantic tradition, but by 1890 she came under the influence of the Symbolists. The earlier treatment - exact and detailed - was refined and replaced by a style that progressively reflected the painters of Pont-Aven.

Schjerfbeck is considered one of the greatest Finnish painters of the turn of the nineteenth century, and is best known most for *The Little Convalescent*. After the first version of 1888, she took up the theme again in 1927, using different techniques, and then again in still different ways in 1938-1939, using drawings, watercolours and lithographs. The 1927 version shows a tighter composition with insignificant details of the décor eliminated, than in the first painting of 1888. The creation is direct, spontaneous and syntheticist, but the pigmentary matter is still smooth and sensuous. In *Portrait of Gösta* of 1933, vivid paint textures in places, give shape and life to a face created with large, flat, syntheticist strokes, and with firm, simple strokes marking the eyebrows, eyes, nose, and mouth.

During the last two years of her life in Sweden she was still working on the last version of *The Little Convalescent*. All the simplifications of stroke, surface, volume, detail and décor climax here. Apart from the contrast between the black jersey and the clear ochres of the face, hands and bed linen, there are almost no colours - only pink and yellow ochres. No more vivid paint surfaces, just a sparse flatness. The drawing, reduced to the minimum of information, is placed on top of the flatness. The deprivation of technique and form is overwhelming, as if the painter is telling us of the suffering that had been with her since childhood and of her constant dialogue with death.

She is represented in several public or thematic exhibitions, among which were: 1987, *Lumières du Nord: La Peinture Scandinave 1885-1905* (*Northern Lights: Scandinavian Painting 1885-1905*) at the musée du Petit Palais, Paris; 1998, *Visions du Nord* (*Visions of the North*), Musée d'Art moderne de la Ville de Paris; 2002 *Les Mondes intérieurs. Le Symbolisme finlandais* (*Inner Worlds: Finnish Symbolism*), Musée d'Ixelles at Bruxelles.

BIBLIOGRAPHY:

Ahtela, H., *Hélène Schierfbeck*, Helsinki, 1953. Holger, Lena, *Helena Schjerfberk: liv och konstnärskap*, Raster, Stockholm, 1987. Sinisalo, Soili/Sarajas-Korte, Salme/Konttinen, Riitta, *Helene Schjerfbeck*, exhibition catalogue, The Finnish National Gall. Ateneum, Helsinki, 1992 (text in English). Holger, Lena, *Helene Schjerfbeck, Kvinder, mandsporttræг, selvsportrætter, Landskaber, stilleben*, exhibition catalogue, Nordjyllands Kunstmuseum, Aalborg, 1997 (text in Danish). Pagé, Suzanne/Andral, Jean-Louis/Burluraux, Odile, *Visions du Nord*, exhibition catalogue, Musée d'Art moderne de la Ville de Paris, Paris musées, Paris, 1998.

MUSEUMS AND GALLERIES:

HELSINKI (Ateneumin Taidemus.): *Wounded Finnish Warrior Stretched out on the Snow*; *Young Boy Feeding his Little Sister*; *The Convalescent* (1888, oil on canvas); *Self-portrait with Dark Background* (1915); *The Convalescent* (1938-1939, lithograph); *Self-portrait with Red Spot* (1944) - HELSINKI (Villa Gyllenberg Taidemus.): *Last Self-portrait* (1945) - STOCKHOLM (Moderna Mus.): *Self-portrait with a Palette* (1937) - TURKU (Turun Taidemus.): *Self-portrait with a Silver Background* (1915, study); *Self-portrait with Black Mouth* (1939); *Self-portrait* (1944-1945).

AUCTION RECORDS:

COPENHAGEN, 13 Oct 1967, *Portrait of Old Woman*, DKK 12,000. COPENHAGEN, 13 June 1968, *Landscape with Bench, Pont-Aven*, DKK 74,000. COPENHAGEN, 20 Oct 1971, *Portrait of Young Blonde Girl*, DKK 26,000. COPENHAGEN, 21 Oct 1972, *Portrait of Man*, DKK 17,000. STOCKHOLM, 23 April 1980, *Head of Young Girl* (watercolour and pastel, 14 x 16 1/2 ins / 35.5 x 42 cm) SEK 35,000. GÖTEBORG, 8 May 1980, *Convalescent* (coloured lithograph, 13 3/4 x 19 ins / 35 x 48 cm) SEK 6,200. STOCKHOLM, 23 April 1981, *Young Girl on a Sofa* (1882, oil on canvas, 14 1/2 x 17 3/4 ins / 37 x 45 cm) SEK 71,000. STOCKHOLM, 31 Oct 1984, *Head of Man in Profile*

(1928, oil on canvas, 19 x 15 ins / 48 x 38 cm) SEK 700,000. STOCKHOLM, 10 April 1985, *The Convalescent* (1927, oil on canvas, 22 x 29 1/2 ins / 56 x 75 cm) SEK 1,700,000. STOCKHOLM, 23 April 1986, *Portrait of Young Girl* (1920-1925, oil on canvas, 18 x 15 1/4 ins / 46 x 39 cm) SEK 280,000. STOCKHOLM, 19 Oct 1987, *Young Girl Seated on a Bench* (1925, oil on canvas, 24 x 14 1/4 ins / 61 x 36 cm) SEK 950,000. STOCKHOLM, 21 Oct 1987, *The Convalescent* (coloured lithograph, 19 1/4 x 27 1/4 ins / 49 x 69 cm) SEK 60,000. LONDON, 24 March 1988, *Ballet Shoes* (1883, oil on canvas, 7 3/4 x 10 ins / 20 x 25.5 cm) GBP 209,000; *Plums in an Upturned Bucket* (watercolour heightened with white, 11 x 14 1/2 ins / 27 x 37 cm) GBP 29,600; *Self-portrait* (oil on paper, 11 3/4 x 9 3/4 ins / 30 x 25 cm) GBP 198,000. LONDON, 16 March 1989, *The Convalescent* (1945, black chalk, watercolour and gouache, 16 1/4 x 20 ins / 41.5 x 51 cm) GBP 308,000; *Portrait of Göta* (1933, oil on canvas/card, 13 x 11 1/2 ins / 33 x 29 cm) GBP 88,000. STOCKHOLM, 15 Nov 1989, *Portrait of Young Girl: Hjördis* (oil on canvas, 20 3/4 x 17 3/4 ins / 53 x 45 cm) SEK 2,700,000. LONDON, 27-28 March 1990, *Ballet Shoes* (oil on canvas, 24 1/2 x 26 3/4 ins / 62 x 68 cm) GBP 1,100,000. LONDON, 29 Nov 1990, *Self-portrait with Eyes Closed* (1945, charcoal/paper, 13 x 16 1/4 ins / 33 x 41 cm) GBP 60,500. STOCKHOLM, 10-12 May 1993, *At the Cafe* (watercolour and charcoal, 25 1/4 x 22 1/2 ins / 64 x 57 cm) SEK 200,000. STOCKHOLM, 18 May 1999, *Martha Dancing. Sketch of Town Beauty* (1917, charcoal, watercolour and gouache, double-sided, 26 x 20 ins / 67 x 50 cm) SEK 1,825,000. STOCKHOLM, 24 Nov 1999, *Little Girl's Neck* (oil on canvas, 9 x 13 ins / 22 x 32 cm) SEK 2,400,000. HELSINKI, 6 May 2000, *Broken Chord* (oil on canvas, 28 x 24 ins / 70 x 61 cm) FIM 2,600,000. LONDON, 27 June 2000, *Mans Schjerfbeck* (1929, oil on canvas, 18 x 15 ins / 45 x 37 cm) GBP 80,000. LONDON, 6 June 2001, *Nurse. Kaija. Lahtinen* (1943, watercolour and charcoal, three, 17 x 14 ins / 43 x 36 cm) GBP 145,000. HELSINKI, 2 Dec 2001, *My Mother* (1909, oil on canvas, 32 x 33 ins / 81 x 83 cm) FIM 5,200,000. STOCKHOLM, 29 May 2002, *Lady from California* (1934, watercolour, 16 x 12 ins / 40 x 30 cm) SEK 2,100,000. HELSINKI, 1 Dec 2002, *Hjordis* (oil on canvas, 19 x 15 ins / 47 x 37 cm) EUR 500,000. LONDON, 3 Feb 2003, *Alarm* (1935, oil on canvas, 29 x 24 ins / 74 x 62 cm) GBP 600,000. LONDON, 4 Feb 2003, *Mother from the Alarm* (1935, watercolour and charcoal, 14 x 11 ins / 35 x 29 cm) GBP 95,000. LONDON, 3 Feb 2004, *Girl Reading* (c. 1910, charcoal and gouache, 11 x 8 ins / 27 x 21 cm) GBP 45,000. LONDON, 3 Feb 2004, *Shadow on the Wall* (1883, oil on canvas on panel, 18 x 15 ins / 45 x 38 cm) GBP 280,000.

SCHKOLNYK, Laurent

French, 20th - 21st century.
Born 24 May 1953, in Paris.
Engraver (mezzotint). Landscapes, still-lifes, flowers, birds.

Laurent Schkolnyk attended evening courses at the École des Beaux-Arts in Nantes, where he studied engraving. He engraves in mezzotint and in colour. His themes are predominantly drawn from nature, typically flowers and birds. The mezzotint technique enables him to celebrate bursts of vivid colour, notably bright yellows, vermilions and carmine reds, which he sets off against violets, blues and dark greens.

He has been involved in various group exhibitions, notably in Nantes, Colmar, Limoges and, in 1985, in Paris, where he showed examples of his work at the Salon de la Jeune Gravure Contemporaine. He has exhibited solo since 1985, notably in Lyons, Cannes, Paris, Tokyo, Nantes, Osaka, and St-Brieuc and his work is now on permanent show in Paris - at the Breheret and Vanuxem Galleries - and at the Michael Gallery in Beverly Hills.

BIBLIOGRAPHY:
'Laurent Schkolnyk: éloge de la manière noire en couleur' in *Art et Métiers du Livre* n° 188, periodical, Paris, 1994.
MUSEUMS AND GALLERIES:
LOS ANGELES (County MA) - PARIS (BNF, Prints Collection) - SAN FRANCISCO (California Palace of the Legion of Honor): *Telephone* (1983, mezzotint).

SCHKUHR, Christian

German, 18th - 19th century.
Born 1741, in Regau; died 1811, in Wittenberg.
Draughtsman, engraver.

Schkuhr drew and engraved the plates for a work on botany, which he published.

SCHLABITZ, Adolf

German, 19th - 20th century.
Born 7 June 1854, in Gross-Wartenberg.
Painter. Genre scenes, figures, landscapes.

Adolf Schlabitz was a pupil of the academy of fine arts in Paris, then of Jules Lefebvre and Gustave Boulanger at the École des Beaux-Arts in Paris.
MUSEUMS AND GALLERIES:
BERLIN (Nationalgal.): *The Green Demoiselle* - BREMEN: *Waiting* - WROCLAW: *Court Session.*
AUCTION RECORDS:
LONDON, 21 July 1976, *Autumn Landscape* (1918, oil on canvas, 32 3/4 x 32 3/4 ins / 83 x 83 cm) GBP 550. AMSTERDAM, 18 June 1997, *Red Curtain* (oil on canvas, 27 1/4 x 36 ins / 69.5 x 90.5 cm) NLG 10,378.

SCHLACHTER, Hans

German, 17th century.
Died before 1614, in Kulmbach.
Active in Kulmbach.
Sculptor.

SCHLACHTER, J. Anton

Austrian, 18th - 19th century.
Active in Prague.
Painter. Battles.

AUCTION RECORDS:
LONDON, 21 June 1991, *The Battle of Dresden* (1815, oil on canvas, 37 1/4 x 54 1/4 ins / 94.5 x 137.5 cm) GBP 12,100.

SCHLADERMUNDT, Herman T.

American, 19th - 20th century.
Born 4 October 1863, in Milwaukee; died 1937, in Kent (Connecticut).
Painter, decorative designer.

Herman Schladermundt was active in Bronxville, New York.

SCHLADITZ, Ernst

German, 19th - 20th century.
Born 1862, in Leipzig.
Active in the USA.
Painter, engraver.

Ernst Schladitz was active in New York and was a painter and engraver on wood.

SCHLAFHORST, Marie

German, 19th - 20th century.
Born 12 April 1865, in Mönchengladbach; died 15 January 1925, in Mönchengladbach.
Sculptor. Busts.

Marie Schlafhorst was a pupil of Henrich Waderé, most probably in Munich. She sculpted for the city of Augsburg busts of *King Maximilian II*, of the *Prince Regent Leopold.*

SCHLÄFLI, Eugen

Swiss, 19th - 20th century.
Born 7 March 1855, in Burgdorf.
Painter. Landscapes.

Eugen Schläfli was a pupil of Johann Joseph Geisser in Lausanne, of Paul Volmar in Bern and of Louis Émile Dardoize in Paris.

SCHLAG, Jakob
Austrian, 17th century.
Active in Vienna.
Stucco artist.

SCHLAGETER, Arthur Charles
Swiss, 20th century.
Born 11 December 1883, in Clarens; died 1963.
Sculptor.
Arthur Schlageter studied with Armand Cacheux, Pierre Narcisse Jacques, Albert Carl-Angst and Barthélemy Caniez at the school of industrial arts in Geneva. He sculpted decorative figures on the façade of the Museum of Geneva, the Hôtel de Ville at Roubaix and the Theatre at Denain. He worked on the restoration of Lausanne cathedral.
MUSEUMS AND GALLERIES:
BERN: *Women of the Bush* - LAUSANNE (Mus. Cantonal des Beaux Arts): *Shivering Woman* (1950, stone in the round); *Head of Woman* (1952, bronze in the round); *Bust of Young Woman* (1952, plaster in the round); *Simone, Bust Portrait of Young Woman* (1952, plaster low relief); *Snake* (1952, marble high-relief); *Nude Man* (1952, marble in the round) - LE LOCLE: *Child with Shellfish*.
AUCTION RECORDS:
ZURICH, 13 Nov 1976, *Swimmers* (1955, stone, h. 7 3/4 ins / 20 cm, Long. 23 1/2 ins/60 cm) CHF 900.

SCHLAGETER, Eduardo
Venezuelan, 20th century.
Born 1893, in Caracas.
Painter.
Eduardo Schlageter was probably of Swiss parentage. He worked in Switzerland and Paris.

SCHLAGETER, Karl
Swiss, 20th century.
Born 13 July 1894, in Lucerne; died 1978 or 1990, in Zurich.
Painter. Portraits, landscapes, waterscapes, seascapes.
Karl Schlageter was a pupil of Angelo Janck at the academy of fine arts in Munich.
MUSEUMS AND GALLERIES:
BERN: *Self-portrait* - BIEL: *Mother* - LUCERNE: *The Föhn*.
AUCTION RECORDS:
ZURICH, 5 May 1976, *The Fishing Port* (oil on canvas, 27 1/2 x 59 ins / 70 x 150 cm) CHF 1,900. HEIDELBERG, 14 Oct 1988, *Reeds Bordering the Lake* (1920, oil on card, 19 3/4 x 27 1/2 ins / 50 x 70 cm) DEM 1,900. ZURICH, 7-8 Dec 1990, *Mount Mythen Reflected in the Lake* (1921, oil on canvas, 19 3/4 x 27 1/2 ins / 50 x 70 cm) CHF 2,000. ZURICH, 16 Oct 1991, *Composition* (oil on canvas, 30 1/4 x 25 1/2 ins / 77 x 65 cm) CHF 1,500. ZURICH, 24 Nov 1993, *Port* (1957, oil/synthetic resin, 26 3/4 x 37 1/2 ins / 68 x 95 cm) CHF 1,725. BERN, 7 May 1999, *Female Nude and Women Washing at Lake Shore* (1927, oil on panel, 55 x 47 ins / 140 x 120 cm) CHF 5,000. BERN, 9 Nov 2000, *Landscape* (1916, oil on canvas, 24 x 39 ins / 62 x 100 cm) CHF 6,500.

SCHLAIKJER, Jes William
American, 20th century.
Born 22 September 1897, in New York; died 1982, in Washington DC.
Painter, illustrator.
Jes Schlaikjer studied under Elmer A. Forsberg, Dean, Dunn and Harvey Cornwell. He was a member of the Salmagundi Club and the American Federation of Arts.

SCHLANDERER, Josef
Austrian, 18th century.
Painter.
Schlanderer was active in Salzburg from 1797 to 1798.

MUSEUMS AND GALLERIES:
SALZBURG (Carolino Augusteum Mus.): *Portrait of Count Leopold Lodron*.

SCHLANGENHAUSEN, Emma
German, 20th century.
Born 9 March 1882, in Halle.
Active in Austria.
Painter, engraver. Religious subjects.
Emma Schlangenhausen was a pupil of Ludwig Michalek, Kolo Moser and Alfred Roller, probably at the school of applied arts in Vienna, and of Cuno Arniet. She spent 1909-1914 in Paris. In 1934 she painted *The Life of St Francis of Assisi* at the monastery of Salzburg and, for the House of Missions on the Mönchesberg, a large painting for the altar and the Stations of the Cross.

SCHLANK, Ignaz
Austrian, 19th century.
Active in Grafenberg c. 1801.
Painter.

SCHLANTZ, Adam
Bavarian School, 15th century.
Painter.
Adam Schlantz was chamberlain to the prince abbot of Kempten in the 15th century. The Diocesan Museum of Freiberg, Bavaria, has a panel by him depicting *Scenes from the Passion*.

SCHLÄPFER, Konrad
Swiss, 19th - 20th century.
Born 18 June 1871, in Appenzell; died 3 December 1913, in Fribourg.
Painter.
Konrad Schläpfer studied under Hans Wildermuth and Léon Petua at the technical school in Winterthur. He also studied in Paris at the École des Arts Décoratifs and the Académie Julian. From 1896 he was a teacher at the industrial school in Fribourg.

SCHLAPP, Franz and Jeremias (brothers)
Swiss, 18th century.
Born to a family originally from the Vorarlberg.
Sculptors.
From 1770 to 1772, the Schlapp brothers worked on St Ursus Cathedral in Solothurn.

SCHLAPPAL, Jodocus
German, 19th century.
Born 1793; died 2 October 1837, in Cologne.
Lithographer.
In 1822, Schlappal became the owner of a lithographic workshop.

SCHLAPPRITZI, Kaspar
Swiss, 19th century.
Born 1790, in St Gall; died 1835, in St Gall.
Painter.
Schlappritzi was a pupil of J.H. Kunkler. He later studied with J. B. Seele in Stuttgart and at the academy in Vienna.

SCHLATER, Alexander Georg Fedorovitch, or Chliater
German, 19th century.
Born 1834, in Tartu, Estonia; died 12 June 1879, in Düsseldorf.
Landscape artist.
Schlater came from a German family, and was first taught by his father, Friedrich. He studied at the academy in St Petersburg from 1853 to 1856, and settled in Düsseldorf in 1872.

SCHLATER, Friedrich Georg Fridrikovich, or Chliater
Lithuanian, 19th century.

Born 1804, in Tilsit (now Sovetsk in Lithuania); died 14 April 1870, in Tartu.
Painter, lithographer. Landscapes.
Friedrich Georg Fridrikovich Schlater was the father of Alexander Schlater.

SCHLATT, Franz
Swiss, 18th - 19th century.
Born 16 September 1765, in Lucerne; died 28 December 1843, in Lucerne.
Sculptor.
Schlatt carved busts for the façade of the municipal theatre in Lucerne.

SCHLATTER, Ernst Emil
Swiss, 20th century.
Born 27 November 1883, in Zurich.
Painter, lithographer. Landscapes.
Ernst Schlatter studied at the school of fine arts in Stuttgart and from 1915 was a teacher at the school of fine arts in Zurich. He settled and worked at Uttwil.

SCHLATTER, Louise
Swiss, 19th century.
Born 5 February 1825, in St Gall; died 17 May 1880, in St Gall.
Painter. Flowers.

SCHLATTMANN, Julius
German, 19th - 20th century.
Born 7 April 1857, in Borken (Westphalia).
Painter, humorist artist.
Julius Schlattmann studied under Albert Baur in Düsseldorf, and Friedrich Geselschap in Berlin.

SCHLAWING, Adolf
German, 20th century.
Born 4 September 1888, in Gross-Lunau.
Painter, sculptor. Figures, portraits, landscapes.
Adolf Schlawing was a pupil of Ernst Wilhelm Müller-Schonefeld and settled at Vietze-am-Elbe. In 1921 he created the Monument to the Dead of Vietze-am-Elbe.

SCHLAYER, Heinrich, or Schleyer
German, 19th century.
Born 1782, in Würzburg.
Active in Friesenhausen.
Painter.
Schlayer was a pupil of G. de Marées. He became a member of the academy in Munich in 1770 and worked at the court of the prince bishop of Würzburg.

SCHLECHT, Benedikt Franz
German, 18th century.
Engraver.
Benedikt Schlecht was court painter in Würzburg. The choir stalls in Würzburg cathedral are by him.

SCHLECHT, Charles
German, 19th century.
Born 1843, in Stuttgart; died after 1905.
From 1852 active in the USA.
Engraver. Banknotes.
Charles Schlecht was a pupil of the Scottish-American Charles Burt and the banknote engraver Alfred Jones. He also specialised in the engraving of banknotes.

SCHLECHT, Johann Ernst
German, 18th century.
Sculptor.

SCHLECHTA, Adalbert
Bohemian School, 18th century.
Active in Chrudim and c. 1789 in Luze.
Painter. Portraits.

SCHLECHTE, Friedrich Wilhelm
German, 19th century.
Born 1812; died 1869, in Meissen.
Painter (porcelain).
Schlechte worked at the Meissen porcelain factory until 1858.

SCHLECHTER, Anton, or Schletter
German, 18th century.
Engraver.
Schlechter studied with Geyser in Leipzig. He mainly engraved reproductions.

SCHLEDER, Martin Johann. See **SCHLÖDER**

SCHLEDERER, Jakob Christoph. See **SCHLETTERER**

SCHLEE, C.
Swiss, 19th century.
Died 1843.
Active in Bern.
Sculptor, medallist.

SCHLEE, Kaspar Johann Michael
Swiss, 19th century.
Born 14 June 1799, in Beromünster; died 12 December 1874, in Bern.
Sculptor.
Schlee studied with Franz Schlatt.
MUSEUMS AND GALLERIES:
BERN (Kunstmus.): *Bust of the Painter Lory* (clay); *Bust of Karl Ricidi* (clay); *Bust of Mayor E.F. von Fischer* (clay).

SCHLEEDORN, Hans Georg or Jörg. See **SCHLEHENDORN**

SCHLEEHAUF, Johann Konrad, or Schlehauf
German, 18th century.
Born 1739, in Heslach, near Stuttgart; died 12 August 1785, in Stuttgart.
Painter.
Schleehauf was painter to the court of Wurtemberg. In 1771, he became professor of painting and drawing at the Akademie Schloss Solitude in Stuttgart.

SCHLEER, Sem or Simon. See **SCHLÖR**

SCHLEGEL
German, 17th century.
Painter. Religious subjects.
Active in Landshut around 1664, Schlegel painted an altarpiece of *St Sebastian*, which was originally intended for the church of the Holy Spirit.

SCHLEGEL
German, 18th century.
Cabinet maker.
Schlegel was responsible for the choir stalls in the church of Our Lady in Bruchsal.

SCHLEGEL, Anton Georg
Swiss, 18th century.
Active in Lucerne between 1730 and 1771.
Sculptor, stucco artist.
In 1744, Schlegel carved the altar of St Sebastian for St Peter's Chapel in Lucerne.

SCHLEGEL, Cornelius. See **SZLEGEL Korneli** or **Cornelius**

SCHLEGEL, Eva
Austrian, 20th century.
Painter, installation artist.
Eva Schlegel took part in 1995 in the Venice Biennale and, in Paris. She also participated in the FIAC (Foire Internationale

d'Art Contemporain) put on at the Galerie Krinzinger in Vienna.

SCHLEGEL, Félix and Franz Anton.
See **TRINER**

SCHLEGEL, Franz
Austrian, 19th - 20th century.
Born 15 January 1851, in Pravali; died 1920, in Vienna.
Illustrator.
Franz Schlegel was a pupil of Hermann von Königsbrunn at the academy of fine arts in Graz.

SCHLEGEL, Friedrich Abraham
German, 18th century.
Painter (porcelain).
Between 1751 and 1756, Friedrich Abraham Schlegel worked at the Meissen porcelain factory, and in 1776 at the Copenhagen factory. He was still living in 1796.

SCHLEGEL, Friedrich August
German, 19th century.
Born 18 March 1828, in Heidersdorf; died in Dresden.
Painter, watercolourist. Portraits, landscapes, still-lifes.
Friedrich August Schlegel painted portrait miniatures in oils and landscapes in watercolour.
AUCTION RECORDS:
LONDON, 16 Oct 1974, *Still-life with Mask* (1846) GBP 1,000. AMELIA, 18 May 1990, *Still-life with Fruits* (oil on canvas, 15 x 39 ins / 38 x 99 cm) ITL 1,900,000. LONDON, 17 Nov 1993, *Still-life with a Mask, a Flask, a Glass of Wine and a Pipe* (1846, oil on canvas, 20½ x 17¾ ins / 52 x 45 cm) GBP 4,830.

SCHLEGEL, Friedrich or Moritz Friedrich
Czech, 19th - 20th century.
Born 27 December 1865, in Prague.
Painter, illustrator. Murals.
Friedrich Schlegel was a student of Christian Griepenkerl and Josef von Trenkwald at the Akademie der Bildenden Künste in Vienna.
MUSEUMS AND GALLERIES:
VIENNA (Church of St John): four ceilings.

SCHLEGEL, Friedrich Samuel or Samuel Friedrich
German, 18th century.
Born 1732, in Gromsdorf, near Weimar; died 5 February 1799, in Leipzig.
Sculptor.
Friedrich Samuel Schlegel sent his first entry, *Hercules at the Crossroads* to the Dresden exhibition in 1767. He carved a memorial to Gellert for St John's Church in Leipzig.

SCHLEGEL, Herbert Rolf
German, 20th century.
Born 26 August 1889, in Breslau (now Wroclaw, Poland).
Active in Austria.
Painter, engraver. Genre scenes, landscapes.
Herbert Schlegel was a pupil of Hans Olde at the academy of fine arts in Weimar. He settled in Schöndorf.
AUCTION RECORDS:
LONDON, 23 March 1988, *Young Woman and her Servant* (oil on canvas, 38½ x 35 ins / 98 x 88 cm) GBP 2,860. COLOGNE, 15 Oct 1988, *Autumn Day* (oil on canvas, 35½ x 39¼ ins / 90 x 100 cm) DEM 1,800. LONDON, 5 May 1989, *Railway by Night* (1919, oil on canvas, 30¾ x 35 ins / 78 x 88 cm) GBP 1,870. TOESTORF, 13 Nov 2004, *Young Girls by the Ammersee Chatting, Bathing and Picking Flowers* (oil on canvas, 39 x 47 ins / 100 x 120 cm) EUR 2,400.

SCHLEGEL, Hermann
German, 19th - 20th century.
Born 1 June 1860, in Coburg; died 5 December 1917, in Darmstadt.
Painter, watercolourist. Landscapes. Stage sets.
From 1882 Hermann Schlegel was a scene painter at the Theatre of the Court in Darmstadt.
MUSEUMS AND GALLERIES:
DARMSTADT: *Landscape* (watercolour).

SCHLEGEL, Hugo Johann
German, 18th century.
Born 1679, in Frankfurt am Main; died 26 December 1737, in Frankfurt am Main.
Painter.
Hugo Schlegel taught Justus Junker, Christian Georg Schuz and Johann Georg Trautmann.

SCHLEGEL, Johann Caspar
German, 18th century.
Born c. 1689; died January 1777.
Painter.

SCHLEGEL, Johann Georg, or Schlögl
Hungarian, 18th - 19th century.
Born 1754; died 8 July 1811, in Tata.
Ceramicist.
Johann Schlegel became the director of the ceramic factory in Tata in 1785.
MUSEUMS AND GALLERIES:
BUDAPEST (Iparmüvészeti Múz.).

SCHLEGEL, Johann Heinrich
Austrian, 18th century.
Born 2 December 1697, in Bensen; died 28 December 1741, in Prague.
Painter.
Johann Heinrich Schlegel was a pupil and imitator of Peter Johann Brandel.
MUSEUMS AND GALLERIES:
BENSEN (Church): *St Francis Xavier*.

SCHLEGEL, Julius
German, 19th century.
Active in Potsdam and from the beginning of 1870 in Berlin.
Painter. Landscapes, architectural views.
Julius Schlegel trained in Rome between 1847 and 1855. He became court painter to Prince William of Prussia and sent paintings to the Berlin academy exhibitions from 1846 to 1874.

SCHLEGEL, Léopold Eugénie
Maiden name: Lalouette
French, 19th century.
Painter. Portraits, genre scenes.
He exhibited at the Salon between 1840 and 1849.

SCHLEGEL, Rudolf
Bohemian School, 19th century.
Active in Haida.
Glass painter.

SCHLEGELL, Gustav von
American, 20th century.
Born 16 September 1877, in St Louis; died 1950, in White Plains (New York).
Painter. Landscapes.
Schlegell began his studies in Minneapolis, and also studied under Karl von Marr at the academy of fine arts in Munich and Jean-Paul Laurens in Paris.
MUSEUMS AND GALLERIES:
ST LOUIS (AM).

SCHLEGELL, Martha von
Maiden name: Schulz
Austrian, 19th - 20th century.

Born 12 January 1861, in Johanngeorgenstadt.
Sculptor, painter. Landscapes.
Martha von Schlegell studied with Anton Klamroth.

SCHLEGLE, Jean Georges
French, 18th century.
Painter.
Jean Georges Schlegle was admitted into the Académie de St-Luc on 17 October 1753.

SCHLEH, Anna
German, 19th century.
Born 1833, in Berlin; died 7 September 1879.
Painter.
Anna Schleh was a pupil of Julius Schrader.

SCHLEHAHN, Albin
German, 19th - 20th century.
Born 1 July 1870, in Eichigt.
Painter. Landscapes, flowers.
Albin Schlehahn was active in Plauen.

SCHLEHAUF, Johann Konrad.
See **SCHLEEHAUF**

SCHLEHENDORN, Hans Georg or Jörg, or Schleedorn
German, 17th century.
Born 1616, in Rudolstadt; died 2 January 1672, in Kulmbach.
Sculptor.
Hans Georg Schlehendorn was the son of the cabinet maker Hans Schlehendorn. He was married in Coburg in 1644 and became a freeman of Kulmbach in 1654. He worked for many years with the sculptor Johann Brenk on the decoration of the churches in Kulmbach.

SCHLEHENRIED, Johann Sigismund
German, 17th century.
Active in Heilbronn.
Draughtsman.

SCHLEIBNER, Kaspar
German, 19th - 20th century.
Born 23 February 1863, in Hallstadt; died 27 January 1931, in Munich.
Painter.
Kaspar Schleibner studied with Gabriel von Hackl, Ludwig von Herterich and Wilhelm von Lindenschmit the Younger at the academy of fine arts in Munich. In 1895 and in 1904 he worked in Rome. In 1900 he married the daughter of the sculptor Guido Entres.

SCHLEICH, Adrien
German, 19th century.
Born 7 December 1812, in Munich; died 28 November 1894, in Munich.
Engraver, draughtsman.
Adrien Schleich was a pupil of Amsler. He produced a large number of illustrations by steel engraving.

SCHLEICH, Anton
German, 19th century.
Born 1809, in Munich; died 1851, in Munich.
Painter, engraver. Landscapes.

SCHLEICH, August
German, 19th century.
Born 1814, in Munich; died 26 December 1865, in Munich.
Painter, engraver. Animals.

MUSEUMS AND GALLERIES:
MUNICH (Pinakothek): *Dead Birds.*

SCHLEICH, Carl, the Younger
German, 19th century.
Born 1788, in Augsburg; died 1840, in Munich.
Engraver (burin), lithographer.
Carl Schleich the Younger was the son of Johann Carl and father of Carl Peter. He was an inspector of the Offices of Military Topography in Munich.

SCHLEICH, Carl Peter
German, 19th century.
Born 1823, in Munich.
Engraver.
Carl Peter Schleich engraved panoramas and topographical views of cities.

SCHLEICH, Eduard, the Elder
German, 19th century.
Born 12 October 1812, in Haarbach; died 8 January 1874, in Munich.
Painter. Landscapes with figures, waterscapes, mountainscapes.
Eduard Schleich the elder studied at the academy in Munich. He visited Northern Italy, France and the Netherlands. He was appointed professor at the Munich academy in 1868.

He drew his inspiration mainly from the old masters and from nature. The mountains of Bavaria provided his favourite subjects.

MUSEUMS AND GALLERIES:
BERLIN: *Evening Landscape* - BREMEN: *Landscape of the Isar* - DARMSTADT: *Landscape* - DRESDEN: *Flock in the Water* - HAMBURG: *The Allgäu Alps* - KALININGRAD: *Bavarian Landscape; The Plain of the Isar near Munich* - LEIPZIG: *The Surroundings of Munich; Landscape of Upper Bavaria; Landscape, Lake Chiem* - MUNICH: *The River Isar at Munich; By the Ammersee; Storm Breaking; The Castle of Pommersfelden; Castle and Church; Dachau; Group of Trees; On the Riverbank; Cowherd's Hut in the High Mountains; At Braunenberg*; a sketch - STUTTGART: *Landscape; Cottage in a Wood* - WROCLAW: *Landscape with Church.*

AUCTION RECORDS:
FRANKFURT AM MAIN, 1894, *Landscape Motif near Munich,* FRF 3,500. PARIS, 3 Feb 1919, *Women in the Fields,* FRF 250; *Small Houses in a Green Landscape,* FRF 270. FRANKFURT AM MAIN, 11-13 May 1930, *Landscape,* DEM 3,550. COLOGNE, 30 Oct 1937, *Dutch Landscapes,* DEM 4,000. LUCERNE, 17 June 1950, *Landscape with Cows,* CHF 2,100. COLOGNE, 14 Nov 1963, *Alpine Landscape,* DEM 22,000. MUNICH, 28-30 June 1967, *The Picnic,* DEM 10,000. MUNICH, 20 March 1968, *Alpine Landscape,* DEM 15,000. MUNICH, 19-20 March 1969, *Landscape with Lake,* DEM 31,000. COLOGNE, 27 May 1971, *Cows in a Landscape,* DEM 23,000. LONDON, 14 June 1972, *Landscape with Figures,* GBP 7,500. LONDON, 4 May 1973, *Landscape with Lake,* Gns 4,800. LONDON, 15 March 1974, *Flock by the Sea,* Gns 2,500. MUNICH, 25 Nov 1977, *Girl Praying in a Landscape* (oil on canvas, 23 1/2 x 29 1/2 ins / 60 x 75 cm) DEM 5,200. LOS ANGELES, 23 June 1980, *Flock Passing through a Village* (oil on canvas, 37 x 44 1/2 ins / 94 x 113 cm) USD 51,000. MUNICH, 4 June 1981, *View of the Roman Campagna with the Claudian Aqueduct* (c. 1871, oil on panel, 14 1/4 x 33 3/4 ins / 36 x 86 cm) DEM 60,000. NEW YORK, 24 Feb 1983, *The Farm Pond* (oil on canvas, 23 1/2 x 37 1/2 ins / 60 x 95 cm) USD 23,000. MUNICH, 29 Nov 1984, *Mountainous Landscape with Lake* (watercolour/pencil outlines, 6 1/4 x 10 ins / 16 x 24.5 cm) DEM 2,800. MUNICH, 23 Oct 1985, *Landscape with Rainbow* (oil on canvas, 21 1/4 x 32 1/4 ins / 54 x 82 cm) DEM 75,000. MUNICH, 10 May 1989, *Young Boy Resting in a Landscape* (1833, oil on canvas, 14 x 18 1/2 ins / 35.5 x 47 cm) DEM 143,000. MUNICH, 12 June 1991, *Cattle Drinking at the Edge of a Lake* (oil on panel, 18 1/2 x 8 3/4 ins / 47 x 22.5 cm) DEM 68,200. MUNICH, 22 June 1993, *Landscape with Ruins* (oil on panel, 5 1/2 x 17

ins / 14 x 43 cm) DEM 20,700. MUNICH, 21 June 1994, *Storm Arriving over Lake Starnberg* (oil on panel, 5 1/2 x 16 1/4 ins / 14 x 41.5 cm) DEM 39,100. MUNICH, 27 June 1995, *River Landscape with Cows*. VIENNA, 29-30 Oct 1996, *The Ammersee near Hersching* (oil on canvas, 9 3/4 x 15 1/4 ins / 25 x 39 cm) ATS 253,000. MUNICH, 27 Feb 1999, *Upper Bavarian Bogland with Pond* (oil on canvas, 32 x 53 ins / 82 x 135 cm) DEM 26,000. MUNICH, 27 Feb 1999, *Ripe Cornfield in Front of Mountain Landscape* (oil on canvas, 15 x 13 ins / 38 x 32 cm) DEM 31,000. DÜSSELDORF, 31 Jan 2000, *Harvesters in Landscape with Watering Cattle* (1873, oil on panel, 8 x 22 ins / 20 x 57 cm) DEM 25,000. MUNICH, 22 March 2000, *Children Playing in Garden before Farmstead* (oil on canvas, 12 x 25 ins / 31 x 63 cm) DEM 24,000. MUNICH, 27 June 2001, *Moonlit Dachstein* (oil on canvas, 29 x 57 ins / 73 x 146 cm) DEM 26,000. HEIDELBERG, 12 Oct 2001, *Cows Drinking in Dachau Moos* (oil on canvas, 12 x 22 ins / 31 x 56 cm) DEM 5,500. MUNICH, 20 March 2002, *Moonlit Landscape* (oil on canvas, 19 x 27 ins / 49 x 68 cm) EUR 4,800. MUNICH, 4 Dec 2002, *Dutch Landscape at Dusk with Windmill near Water* (oil on canvas, 7 x 17 ins / 19 x 42 cm) EUR 3,200. MUNICH, 2 July 2003, *Cows Watering in Pond* (oil on panel, 11 x 19 ins / 27 x 47 cm) EUR 9,500. MUNICH, 10 Dec 2003, *Isar Landscape* (oil on canvas, 7 x 12 ins / 19 x 30 cm) EUR 6,000. FONTAINEBLEAU, 6 June 2004, *Herd by the Sea* (oil on paper/canvas, 14 x 12 ins / 36 x 31 cm) EUR 5,200. MUNICH, 30 June 2004, *Starnberger See* (oil on panel, 15 x 34 ins / 37 x 87 cm) EUR 7,000.

SCHLEICH, Eduard, the Younger
German, 19th century.
Born 15 February 1853, in Munich; died 28 October 1893.
Painter. Landscapes with figures, mountainscapes.

MUSEUMS AND GALLERIES:
MUNICH (Pinakothek): *In Autumn*; *Landscape with Flock*.

AUCTION RECORDS:
NEW YORK, 28 April 1977, *Bavarian Landscape* (oil on canvas, 23 x 29 1/2 ins / 58.5 x 75 cm) USD 1,800. MUNICH, 5 Dec 1979, *Landscape* (oil on canvas, 19 x 29 1/4 ins / 48.5 x 74 cm) DEM 3,700. NEW YORK, 24 Feb 1983, *Farm by an Alpine Stream* (oil on canvas, 15 x 22 3/4 ins / 38 x 58 cm) USD 6,250. MUNICH, 8 May 1985, *Cart on a Country Lane* (oil on canvas remounted on board, 7 3/4 x 11 1/2 ins / 20 x 29 cm) DEM 5,000. VIENNA, 29-30 Oct 1996, *Wooded Mountain Landscape with a Castle at the Summit* (oil on canvas, 48 x 59 ins / 121 x 150 cm) ATS 161,000. DÜSSELDORF, 31 Jan 2000, *Moonlit Landscape* (oil on canvas, 24 x 20 ins / 62 x 50 cm) DEM 4,500. MUNICH, 7 Nov 2001, *Landscape with Oak Trees and Figures* (oil on board, 10 x 11 ins / 25 x 27 cm) DEM 7,500. MUNICH, 25 Sept 2002, *Horse Drawn Cart on Country Track* (oil on canvas/board, 8 x 11 ins / 20 x 29 cm) EUR 2,100. ERLANGEN, 7 Dec 2002, *Extensive Isar Landscape with Boat and Figures* (1886, oil on canvas, 9 x 13 ins / 24 x 34 cm) EUR 2,900. MUNICH, 5 Nov 2003, *Landscape with Stream* (oil on canvas, 11 x 17 ins / 28 x 42 cm) EUR 2,200. COLOGNE, 13 Dec 2003, *Riverside Village with Peasants Returning Home* (oil on canvas, 12 x 18 ins / 30 x 45 cm) EUR 3,000. STUTTGART, 24 June 2004, *Pre-alpine Landscape beneath Cloudy Skies* (oil on canvas, 12 x 25 ins / 30 x 63 cm) EUR 4,000.

SCHLEICH, Hans
German, 19th - 20th century.
Born 24 June 1834, in Stettin (now Szczecin, Poland); died 10 June 1912, in Berlin.
Painter. Landscapes, seascapes.

SCHLEICH, Johann Carl
German, 18th - 19th century.
Born 1759, in Augsburg; died 1842, in Munich.
Engraver, reproductions engraver.

Johann Carl Schleich was the father of Anton, August, Carl and Joseph Schleich. He was a pupil of F.X. Jungwirth and J. Mettenleiter.

SCHLEICH, Joseph
German, 19th century.
Born 1791, in Augsburg.
Draughtsman, engraver (burin).

Joseph Schleich was the son of Johann Carl Schleich.

SCHLEICH, Matheis
German, 16th - 17th century.
Active in Augsburg.
Cabinet maker.

SCHLEICH, Peter Johann
German, 17th century.
Active in Nuremberg.
Painter.

SCHLEICH, Robert
German, 19th - 20th century.
Born 13 July 1845, in Munich; died 14 October 1934, in Munich.
Painter. Landscapes with figures, landscapes.

Robert Schleich was the son of the engraver Adrien Schleich and studied with Wilhelm von Diez at the academy of fine arts in Munich. He is best known for work scenes in the countryside.

Rob Schleich

MUSEUMS AND GALLERIES:
AUGSBURG: *Haymaking in Bavaria* - HEIDELBERG: *Haymaking* - MUNICH (Pinakothek): *On the Road*; *Haymaking in Upper Bavaria*; *Octoberfest* - WUPPERTAL: *Landscape with Labourers*.

AUCTION RECORDS:
MUNICH, 29-30 Sept 1965, *Livestock Fair*, DEM 6,000. MUNICH, 17 Nov 1971, *Landscape with Pond*, DEM 5,200. NEW YORK, 21 Jan 1978, *Winter Landscape with Skaters* (1885, oil on panel, 9 x 12 3/4 ins / 23 x 32.5 cm) USD 14,500. LOS ANGELES, 17 March 1980, *Harvest Scene* (oil on canvas, 4 3/4 x 5 ins / 12 x 13 cm) USD 9,500. NEW YORK, 27 Feb 1982, *Travellers' Halt* (pen, watercolour and pencil, 2 3/4 x 4 1/2 ins / 7.3 x 11.2 cm) USD 1,600. ZURICH, 12 Nov 1982, *Rest at Midday* (oil on canvas, 24 3/4 x 41 1/2 ins / 63 x 105.5 cm) CHF 41,000. MUNICH, 15 March 1984, *Harvest* (oil on canvas, 30 x 39 3/4 ins / 76.5 x 101 cm) DEM 27,000. LONDON, 21 June 1985, *Harvesters* (oil on panel, 4 1/2 x 9 ins / 11.2 x 22.8 cm) GBP 7,000. NEW YORK, 28 Oct 1986, *Harvesters* (1900, oil on panel, 8 x 15 1/4 ins / 20.3 x 38.6 cm) USD 15,000. LONDON, 23 March 1988, *Peasant Watering his Livestock at a Waterhole, near the Village* (1875, oil on canvas, 20 1/2 x 34 1/4 ins / 52 x 87 cm) GBP 8,250. MUNICH, 18 May 1988, *Pause for Refreshment* (oil on card, 1 1/2 x 2 1/4 ins / 4 x 5.5 cm) DEM 4,840. NEW YORK, 28 May 1992, *Haystacks* (oil on canvas, 9 1/4 x 15 1/2 ins / 23.5 x 39.4 cm) USD 22,000. MUNICH, 25 June 1992, *Peasant and his Cattle by a Stream* (oil on wood, 3 3/4 x 7 3/4 ins / 9.5 x 19.5 cm) DEM 8,814. MUNICH, 10 Dec 1992, *Haymaking with an Approaching Storm* (oil on canvas, 4 3/4 x 5 ins / 12 x 13 cm) DEM 14,690. NEW YORK, 26 May 1993, *Horse Market* (oil on panel, 4 1/2 x 6 1/2 ins / 11.4 x 16.5 cm) USD 4,888. MUNICH, 22 June 1993, *Peasants Loading a Haycart* (oil on panel, 4 1/4 x 8 1/2 ins / 11 x 21.5 cm) DEM 14,950. NEW YORK, 19 Jan 1994, *Peasants with Sheep* (oil on card, 2 x 2 1/2 ins / 5.1 x 6.4 cm) USD 4,140. MUNICH, 21 June 1994, *Cattle Drinking in a Landscape with a Mill* (oil on panel, 8 1/4 x 14 3/4 ins / 21 x 37.5 cm) DEM 4,370. VIENNA, 29-30 Oct 1996, *Fishermen Lifting their Nets at Dawn* (1871, oil on canvas, 16 1/4 x 35 ins / 41.5 x 88 cm) ATS 207,000.

SCHLEICHER
German, 18th century.
Active in Nuremberg.
Engraver.
Schleicher is known for a reproduction of St Catherine's Church in Nuremberg, which is kept in the Nuremberg City Library.

SCHLEICHER, Adolphe C.
German, 20th century.
Born 25 September 1887, in Cologne.
Painter. Genre scenes, landscapes.
Adolphe C. Schleiger was a pupil of Wilhelm Ekstein and settled at Icking.
MUSEUMS AND GALLERIES:
DORTMUND - DÜREN - DÜSSELDORF - ELBERFELD - STUTTGART.
AUCTION RECORDS:
PARIS, 4 May 1994, *Tavern Scene* (oil on canvas, 12 1/2 x 11 ins / 32 x 27 cm) FRF 5,500.

SCHLEICHER, Franz
German, 19th century.
Active in Munich c. 1820-1840.
Lithographer.
MUSEUMS AND GALLERIES:
MUNICH (Staatliche Graphische Sammlung): 14 drawings.

SCHLEIDEN, Eduard
German, 19th century.
Born 1809, in Pyrmont; died after 1883.
Painter. Portraits, genre scenes, landscapes.
Eduard Schleiden worked in Munich from 1837 to 1845. He was a pupil of Kaulbach.

SCHLEIDEN, Ludwig
German, 19th century.
Born 1802, in Aachen; died 1862, in Aachen.
Painter. History painting, portraits.
MUSEUMS AND GALLERIES:
AACHEN (Burg Frankenberg): *Self-portrait* - AACHEN (Suermondt-Ludwig Mus.): *St Gertrude's Night in Aachen in 1278; Frankenburg near Aachen.*

SCHLEIDEN, Peter von der
German, 17th century.
Active in Cologne.
Glass painter.

SCHLEIDT, Cornelius
German, 19th century.
Born 20 February 1814, in Mainz; died 31 March 1868, in Mainz.
Sculptor, modeller.
Schleidt taught drawing in Mainz.

SCHLEIFF, Heinrich or Hendrich or Henri
19th century.
Died 18th December 1869, in Valenciennes.
Sculptor.
Schleiff was probably of German origin.

SCHLEIFF, Pierre, or Schlief, Sclief
French, 17th century.
Born in Valenciennes; died 14 August 1641, in Valenciennes.
Sculptor, architect.
Pierre Schleiff executed the porch of the church of the Carmelite monks in Valenciennes and worked for the church of the monastery of Vicoigne in 1631.
MUSEUMS AND GALLERIES:
VALENCIENNES: *Bust of Simon Leboucq.*

SCHLEIFFENBERGER, Daniel
German, 17th century.
Active in Leipzig 1670-1677.
Painter, draughtsman.

SCHLEIN, Eduard
German, 19th - 20th century.
Born 30 January 1863, in Friedland.
Painter.
Eduard Schlein was a pupil of Johann Caspar Herterich at the academy of fine arts in Munich. He established himself in Nuremburg.

SCHLEINING, Johann
German, 18th century.
Active in Alsfeld.
Sculptor (wood).

SCHLEISNER, Christian Andreas
Danish, 19th century.
Born 2 November 1810 or 1820, in Lyngby; died 14 July 1882, in Copenhagen.
Painter. Portraits, genre scenes, interiors, landscapes.
Schleisner was a pupil at the Kunstakademi in Copenhagen. He also worked in Munich. He made numerous study trips from 1840 to 1842, aided by a grant from the Kunstakademi of Copenhagen. Ten years later, he became a professor in, and a member of, that institution.
MUSEUMS AND GALLERIES:
COPENHAGEN (Statens Mus. for Kunst): *En scene i værtshuset Brokkensbod (Sailors in a Cabaret)* (1847) - MUNICH: *The Poultry Seller; A Boilermaker.*
AUCTION RECORDS:
COPENHAGEN, 6 Oct 1950, *Young Girl at the Tinker's,* DKK 2,500. COPENHAGEN, 23 Jan 1951, *The Siesta,* DKK 3,500. COPENHAGEN, 1 and 13 May 1964, *Fishing Boats,* DKK 16,000. COPENHAGEN, 19 Feb 1970, *The Young Violinist,* DKK 7,200. COPENHAGEN, 4 April 1974, *The Game of Cards* (1858) DKK 14,000. COPENHAGEN, 31 Aug 1976, *The Tasting Cups* (oil on canvas, 17 1/4 x 14 1/2 ins / 44 x 37 cm) DKK 8,000. COPENHAGEN, 7 Dec 1977, *Peasant Couple on a Road* (1869, oil on canvas, 17 3/4 x 22 ins / 45 x 55 cm) DKK 10,000. COPENHAGEN, 29 Aug 1978, *Interior with Fishermen Playing Dice* (1882, oil on canvas, 13 3/4 x 17 3/4 ins / 35 x 45 cm) DKK 8,000. COPENHAGEN, 18 March 1980, *Grandfather and Grandson* (oil on canvas, 15 3/4 x 12 1/2 ins / 40 x 32 cm) DKK 8,700. COPENHAGEN, 16 April 1985, *Tavern Scene* (1869, oil on canvas, 17 3/4 x 22 ins / 45 x 55 cm) DKK 50,000. COPENHAGEN, 23 March 1988, *Cloister in Italy with Two Monks* (oil on canvas, 16 1/2 x 13 1/2 ins / 42 x 34 cm) DKK 7,500. COPENHAGEN, 1 May 1991, *The First Pipe* (1882, oil on canvas, 13 3/4 x 11 ins / 35 x 28 cm) DKK 23,000. COPENHAGEN, 6 May 1992, *Grandmother Teaching Her Grandchildren to Read* (1872, oil on canvas, 15 3/4 x 11 3/4 ins / 40 x 30 cm) DKK 9,000. COPENHAGEN, 16 May 1994, *The Post Office in Copenhagen* (oil on canvas, 23 1/4 x 35 1/2 ins / 59 x 90 cm) DKK 15,000. COPENHAGEN, 16 Nov 1994, *Portrait of the Young Frederik Holm Standing* (1839, oil on canvas, 15 1/4 x 11 ins / 39 x 28 cm) DKK 8,000. COPENHAGEN, 17 May 1995, *Interior with Sleeping Peasant Woman and Little Girl with a Cat* (1856, oil on canvas, 16 1/2 x 12 1/4 ins / 42 x 31 cm) DKK 17,500. COPENHAGEN, 30 Nov 1999, *Interior Scene with Fisherman's Family at Table* (1857, oil on canvas, 17 x 20 ins / 42 x 52 cm) DKK 35,000. ANTWERP, 13 Dec 1999, *Farmhouse Interior with Girl Sewing her Brother's Jacket* (1873, oil on canvas, 17 x 14 ins / 42 x 35 cm) BEF 160,000. VEJLE, 19 Jan 2000, *Interior Scene with Family around Table, Dog and Chickens in Foreground* (1857, oil on canvas, 17 x 20 ins / 42 x 52 cm) DKK 19,000. AHLDEN, 22 Sept 2000, *Fishing Family* (1874, oil on canvas, 21 x 25 ins / 53 x 64 cm) DEM 6,000. VEJLE, 14 March 2001, *Exterior with Figures by House, Cows in Background* (1836, oil on canvas, 27 x 21 ins / 68 x 53 cm) DKK 30,000. LONDON, 5 April 2001, *Family in an Interior* (oil on canvas, 17 x 20 ins / 43 x 52 cm) GBP 3,500. MUNICH, 26 June 2002, *Tyrolean Boy* (1843, oil on canvas, 13 x 9 ins / 32 x 24 cm) EUR 2,800. COPENHAGEN, 27 Aug 2002, *Interior*

Scene with Fisherman's Family - Grandparents Watching Children Playing Skittles (1854, oil on canvas, 20 x 27 ins / 50 x 69 cm) DKK 26,000. VEJLE, 12 Jan 2004, *Old Fisherman Holding Basket Looking out to Sea* (1863, oil on canvas, 37 x 30 ins / 94 x 76 cm) DKK 21,500.

SCHLEISS, Franz
Austrian, 20th century.
Born 1 October 1884, in Gmunden.
Potter.

Franz Schleiss studied at the technical school in Teplitz-Schönau (now Teplice, Czech Republic), at the school of industrial arts in Vienna and at the Académie Ranson in Paris. He married Émilie Simandl and they established themselves in Gmunden.

MUSEUMS AND GALLERIES:
STUTTGART (Württembergisches Landesmus.) - VIENNA (Österreichisches Mus. für Angewandte Kunst).

SCHLEISS-SIMANDL, Émilie
Maiden name: Simandl
German, 20th century.
Born 27 January 1880, in Rothenburg.
Active in Austria.
Sculptor, potter. Busts.

Émilie Simandl-Schleiss was the wife of Franz Schleiss and was established in Gmunden.

SCHLEITH, Ernst
German, 19th - 20th century.
Born 23 May 1871.
Painter, draughtsman.

Ernst Schleith was a pupil of Robert Pötzelberger, and of Carlos Grethe at the academy of fine arts in Stuttgart. He also studied under Karl or Stanislas Kalckreuth (most probably at the academy of Weimar), and Hans Thoma (possibly at the academy of Karlsruhe). He settled in Wiesleth, near Lörrach.

SCHLEMMER, Ferdinand Louis
American, 20th century.
Born 26 September 1893, in Crawfordsville; died 1947.
Painter.

Ferdinand Schlemmer studied under Charles Hawthorne and Harry Mills Walcott.

SCHLEMMER, Leonhard
German, 18th - 19th century.
Born 1772, in Hammer, near Laufenholz.
Active in Nuremberg.
Engraver (burin).

SCHLEMMER, Oskar
German, 20th century.
Born 4 September 1888, in Stuttgart; died 1943, in Baden-Baden.
Sculptor (mixed media), painter, watercolourist, engraver, lithographer. Figures, landscapes. Stage sets.

Oskar Schlemmer was an apprentice from 1903 to 1905 in a studio of marquetry. From 1905 to 1909 he studied at the academy of fine arts in Stuttgart, where he was a fellow student of Willy Baumeister and of the Swiss Otto Meyer-Amden, who would remain his close friend and for whom he always had great admiration. From 1910 to 1912, he stayed in Berlin, where he had some contact with French painting, particularly Cézanne and Seurat. From 1912 to 1914, he was a pupil of Christian Landenberger, and especially of Adolf Hölzel, at the academy in Stuttgart. After 1915, he served in the army. He returned to Stuttgart in 1919, where he attempted to influence the direction of the academy. In 1920 he was invited by Walter Gropius to be a teacher of the Bauhaus. From 1920 to 1929 Schlemmer held several posts at the Bauhaus in Weimar, then at Dessau, first as director of the studio on stone carving, and then as director of the studio on metal. From 1929 to 1932 he was a teacher of perspective at the national schools of art in Berlin. In 1933 he was dismissed from his post by the official arrival of Nazi power, accused of promoting degenerate art.

During his period in Berlin from 1910 to 1912 he was inspired by post-Impressionism and neo-Impressionism. On his return to the academy in Stuttgart in 1912 he was influenced by the mysticism of the work of his teacher Adolf Hölzel and by Hans von Marées. In 1914, under the direction of Hölzel and in collaboration with Baumeister, he carried out three wall paintings for the exhibition of the Association of Werkbund in Cologne.

In the years preceding 1915, he emphasised geometric shapes; when applied to human figures, this resulted in a sort of mannequin composed of an equal play of curves and counter curves. In 1919 his doctrine of the idiosyncratic man materialises in his geometric personnages. Of these sculptures and reliefs only thirteen remain, of which eleven are reliefs. His very important decoration of the Bauhaus at Weimar, consisting of a cycle of reliefs in tinted cement, rhythmic with curved lines, was destroyed around 1928 - five years after its construction - by the Nazis within hours of the departure of the Bauhaus, which was obliged to leave under the Weimar threat on Dessau.

While carrying out these reliefs (whose plastic function was to give rhythm and create awareness of the space) he continued to emphasise the animation of space through the creation of ballet shows, setting the scenes and dancing in them himself. In taking his place beside the creators of the Ballets Russes (*Parade* dated 1917) - the direction German, the staging British - Schlemmer was attempting to synthesise the arts, where the human being remained the universal medium, in spite of being depersonalised as part of the scenery. For him the scenic space was a living organism, from the characters, whose costumes suggested general rhythmic movement, to the elements of the décor or the use of lighting.

His experimentations in the domain of ballet came to a head in his *Triad Ballet* (1923), with music by Paul Hindemith, which absorbed a large part of his activity for several years. In 1925 he published his reflections project in *The Stage in the Bauhaus*. Other ballets followed, among them *The Dance of the Lances* of 1927, *The Dance of the Metals* of 1928. From 1928 to 1930 he did wall paintings for the Folkwang Museum of Essen, which were also destroyed by the Nazis. In 1931, he created a construction of iron filings, still on the human theme, for the house of Dr Rabe, built by Adolf Rading at Zwenkau. Around 1930-1932 Schlemmer added diagonals to his work which brought a dynamism to his materialisations of space, particularly in *Bauhaus Staircase*. The oblique line, the most familiar since the futurists and forbidden by Mondrian, conflicted with the immobility of the horizontals and verticals.

His painting evolved uring his period of retreat at Sheringen-Bade. With the death of his great friend Otto Meyer-Amden in 1933, which coincided with his own exile, his painting certainly lost something of its rigour. The forms became more fluid, the handling of the brush regained an Impressionist touch, the colours darkened and, above all the mystical content of his works, instead of being hidden appeared more insistently evident. In 1936 under the generic title of *Symbolics*, he painted a series of abstract works, like skilful scaffolding of coloured planes. In 1942, with the series of *Windows*, he returned once more to representing human forms, blurred and seen through windows, as if in process of dissolving.

His work in public and private exhibitions, mainly posthumously: 1961 Zurich, *Oskar Schlemmer and the Abstract Scene*, Kunstegewerbemuseum; 1962 Berlin, *Comprehensive Collection of the Work of Oskar Schlemmer*, academy of fine arts; 1968, Stuttgart, *Schlemmer*, Staatsgalerie; 1969 Paris, *Bauhaus*, Musée Nationale d'Art Moderne and Musée d'Art Moderne de la Ville; 1977, Paris, *Aspects Historiques du Constructivisme et de l'Art Concret* (*Historical Aspects of Constructivism and Concrete Art*), Musée d'Art Moderne de la Ville; 1999, Marseilles *Oskar Schlemmer*.

BIBLIOGRAPHY:

Man and Mask: Oskar Schlemmer and the Bauhaus stage, video, Peasemarch, London (a Bavaria Atelier GMBH production). Schlemmer, Oskar, *'Mensch un Kunstfigur: Die Bühne im Bauhaus'* in *Bauhausbücher 4*, Munich, 1925 (English translation 1961). Schlemmer, Oskar, *Otto Meyer-Amden, aus Leben, Werk and Briefen*, Zurich, 1934. Schlemmer, Tut, *Oskar Schlemmer: Briefe und Tagebücher*, Munich, 1950 (English translation 1972). Hildebrandt, Hans, *Oskar Schlemmer*, Prestel, Munich, 1952. *Oskar Schlemmer: Winter 1954-55*, Stedelijk Museum, Amsterdam, 1954. *Oskar Schlemmer und die abstrakte Bühne*, exhibition catalogue, Kunstgewerbemuseum, Zurich, 1961. Gropius, Walter, *The Theatre of the Bauhaus*, Wesleyan University Press, Middletown (CT), 1961. Killy, Herta Elisabeth, *Oskar Schlemmer*, exhibition catalogue, Akademie der Künste, Berlin, 1963. Grohmann, Will/Schlemmer, Tut, *Oskar Schlemmer*, Gerd Hatje, Stuttgart, 1965. *Schlemmer: Ausstellung zum 80. Geburtstag. Zeichnungen, Aquarelle und Pastelle*, exhibition catalogue, Staatsgalerie, Stuttgart, 1968. Leymarie, Jean/Herzogenrath, Wulf/Grote, Ludwig/Gropius, Walter, *Le Bauhaus*, exhibition catalogue, Württembergischer Kunsteverein, Stuttgart, Musée national d'Art moderne, Paris, 1969. *Man: Teaching notes from the Bauhaus*, Lund Humphries, London, 1971. Maur, Karin von, *Oskar Schlemmer*, Thames and Hudson, London, 1972. Herzogenrath, Wulf, *Oskar Schlemmer: die Wandgestaltung der neuen Architektur*, Prestel, Munich, 1973. Maur, Karin von, *Oskar Schlemmer. Monographien. Oeuvrekatalog der Gemälde, Aquarelle, Pastelle und Plastiken*, Prestel, Munich, 1979. Maur, Karin von, *Oskar Schlemmer*, Prestel, Munich, 1982. Eberle, Matthias, *World War I and the Weimar Artists: Dix, Grosz, Beckman, Schlemmer*, Yale University Press, New Haven, 1985. *Oskar Schlemmer*, exhibition catalogue, Baltimore museum of art, Baltimore, 1986. *Oskar Schlemmer*, Baltimore Museum of Art, Baltimore, c. 1986. *Oskar Schlemmer: San Diego Museum of Art, 6 September-12 October 1986*, IBM Corporation, 1986. *Oskar Schlemmer, Aquarelle*, exhibition catalogue, Staatsgalerie, Cantz, Stuttgart, 1988. Louis, Eleonora/Stooss, Toni, *Oskar Schlemmer. Tanz, Theater, Bühne*, exhibition catalogue, Sprengel Museum, Hanover, Hatje, Stuttgart, 1994. *Oskar Schlemmer*, exhibition catalogue, Musées de Marseille, Réunion des musées nationaux, Paris, 1999.

MUSEUMS AND GALLERIES:

BASEL (Kunstmus.): *Römisches* (1925) - BERLIN (Nationalgal.) - COLOGNE (Wallraf-Richartz Mus.): *Group of Fourteen Persons in an Imaginary Architecture* (1930) - ESSEN (Folkwang Mus.) - FRANKFURT AM MAIN (Städel) - MUNICH (Neue Pinakothek) - NEW YORK (MoMA): *The Bauhaus Staircase* (1932) - STUTTGART (Staatsgal.): *Vorübergehender (Passant)* (1924, watercolour); *Concentric Group* (1925); *Entrance to the Stadium* (1930) - VIENNA (Mus. Moderner Kunst Stiftung Ludwig): *Abstract Figure* (1921, sculpture).

AUCTION RECORDS:

STUTTGART, 3-4 May 1962, *Four Heads* (watercolour) DEM 26,000; *Group of Four*, DEM 45,000. BERN, 11 June 1966, *Woman's Profile* (watercolour) CHF 16,500. BERN, 15 June 1968, *Group*, CHF 21,000. HAMBURG, 25 June 1968, *Four Profiles* (watercolour) DEM 32,000. MUNICH, 20 May 1969, *Conversation*, DEM 66,000. PARIS, 29 May 1972, *Three Figures Half Way Down* (watercolour) FRF 26,500. NEW YORK, 4 May 1973, *Ornamental Sculpture*, USD 7,500. HAMBURG, 16 June 1973, *Two Heads* (watercolour and Indian ink) DEM 24,500. HAMBURG, 8 June 1974, *Head in Profile to the Left* (watercolour and Indian ink) DEM 28,000. NEW YORK, 18 March 1976, *Rehung* (1929, watercolour and pencil, 22 x 13 3/4 ins / 55 x 35 cm) USD 29,000. MUNICH, 26 Nov 1976, *Grotesque* (sculpture in gilded silver, h. 22 ins / 55 cm) DEM 32,000. MUNICH, 26 Nov 1977, *Grotesque* (1923, sculpture in gilded silver) DEM 34,000. MUNICH, 23 May 1978, *Black figure* (c. 1924, watercolour heightened with white, 9 1/4 x 3 3/4 ins / 23.8 x 9.7 cm) DEM 10,500. NEW YORK, 31 Oct 1978, *Head with Illuminated Forehead* (1937, oil on paper, 16 1/2 x 9 ins / 42 x 22 cm) USD 19,000. MUNICH, 27 Nov 1979, *Three Women Seen from the Back* (1932, watercolour and pencil, 5 3/4 x 5 3/4 ins / 14.5 x 14.5 cm) DEM 31,000. HAMBURG, 6 June 1980, *Three Figures* (1935, pen, 11 x 5 ins / 27.8 x 12.5 cm) DEM 10,000. NEW YORK, 14 Nov 1980, *Abstract Figure, to the Left* (1923, etching, 12 1/2 x 9 1/4 ins / 31.5 x 23.8 cm) USD 5,500. NEW YORK, 18 May 1981, *Grotesque, Abstract Figure* (1923, gilded silver, h. 21 1/2 ins / 54.3 cm) USD 32,000. NEW YORK, 19 May 1981, *Blue-Red-Yellow* (c. 1931, watercolour and pencil, 21 x 17 ins / 53.5 x 43 cm) USD 100,000. COLOGNE, 30 May 1981, *Head of Young Girl* (1936, pen and watercolour, 9 x 9 1/2 ins / 22 x 24 cm) DEM 26,000. NEW YORK, 17 Feb 1982, *Person Seen from the Side* (1922, lithograph, 14 x 9 1/2 ins / 35.7 x 24 cm) USD 2,500. LONDON, 2 Dec 1982, *Relief II* (1919, aluminium, 25 3/4 x 10 1/2 ins / 65.4 x 26.5 cm) GBP 6,500. MUNICH, 31 May 1983, *Two Women at Table* (1923, colouring pencil, 7 1/4 x 5 3/4 ins / 18.5 x 14.8 cm) DEM 9,700. HAMBURG, 10 June 1983, *Figure Plan* (1919-1920, lithograph) DEM 3,200. COLOGNE, 7 Dec 1983, *Vase of Flowers* (1925, oil on canvas, 25 3/4 x 19 1/4 ins / 65.4 x 48.8 cm) DEM 14,000. NEW YORK, 15 Nov 1984, *Meeting in Space* (1928, watercolour and pencil/mounted paper/card, 34 x 20 1/4 ins / 86.5 x 51.7 cm) USD 100,000. HAMBURG, 8 June 1985, *Figure Plan* (1919-1920, lithograph) DEM 4,200. COLOGNE, 4 Dec 1985, *Six Persons in an Interior (recto)* (tempera and oil/pencil outlines); *Study of Nude Standing (verso)* (after 1937, oil and tempera, 17 x 36 1/4 ins / 43 x 92 cm) DEM 290,000. HAMBURG, 10 June 1986, *Head of Woman in Profile to Left* (1935, oil on paper, 11 3/4 x 8 1/4 ins / 29.7 x 21 cm) DEM 60,000. HAMBURG, 13 June 1987, *Group of Seven People* (1931, lead pencil and colour, 5 3/4 x 4 3/4 ins / 14.6 x 12.1 cm) DEM 66,000. HAMBURG, 13 June 1987, *The Last Tableau* (1921, watercolour, 6 3/4 x 10 3/4 ins / 17.1 x 27.2 cm) DEM 30,000. BERLIN, 30 May 1991, *Two Heads and Two Nudes, Silvered Hair IV* (1931, oil and tempera/canvas, 13 x 21 1/2 ins / 33 x 54.5 cm) DEM 521,700. LONDON, 3 Dec 1991, *HK* (1926, watercolour and pencil/paper, 21 3/4 x 16 ins / 55.3 x 40.4 cm) GBP 143,000. HEIDELBERG, 11 April 1992, *Silhouettes* (lithograph, 13 x 8 1/2 ins / 32.8 x 21.5 cm) DEM 9,800. MUNICH, 26 May 1992, *Concentric Group of Figures K1* (1921, lithograph, 19 1/4 x 13 1/2 ins / 49 x 34 cm) DEM 20,125. BERLIN, 27 Nov 1992, *Grotesque* (cast silver, h. 22 ins / 56 cm) DEM 84,750. LONDON, 13 Oct 1994, *Woman from Left Profile* (1932, oil on rough canvas/panel, 8 x 12 1/2 ins / 20.5 x 31.6 cm) GBP 84,000. AMSTERDAM, 8 Dec 1994, *Happy Hand* (1930, pencil/black paper, 13 1/4 x 19 1/4 ins / 33.7 x 48.7 cm) NLG 46,000. BERN, 20-21 June 1996, *Head in Left Profile* (1927, pencil, 13 x 10 3/4 ins / 33 x 27.5 cm) CHF 25,500. HEIDELBERG, 11-12 April 1997, *Head in Profile with Black Surround* (1920-1921, lithograph, 7 3/4 x 5 1/2 ins / 19.7 x 14 cm) DEM 8,000. LONDON, 9 Oct 1997, *Plait Seen from Back* (1932, oil and pencil/panel, 12 1/2 x 6 ins / 31.5 x 15 cm) GBP 155,500. LONDON, 6 Oct 1999, *Woman Climbing Stairs* (1936, oil and pencil on paper laid on card, 26 x 6 ins / 66 x 14 cm) GBP 140,000. LONDON, 7 Oct 1999, *Four Heads for Folkwang Study III* (1928, oil and tempera on canvas, 18 x 12 ins / 45 x 30 cm) GBP 250,000. LONDON, 18 Oct 2000, *Group of Grey Boys* (1930, oil and tempera on board, 29 x 16 ins / 74 x 41 cm) GBP 410,000. MUNICH, 2 Dec 2000, *Instruction* (watercolour and pencil on paper on linen, 11 x 9 ins / 28 x 22 cm) DEM 205,000. New York, 5 Nov 2001, *Grotesque* (1923, gold-plated silver, h. 21 ins / 54 cm) USD 85,000. New York, 5 Nov 2001, *Meeting in a Room* (1932, watercolour on paper on board, 34 x 20 ins / 86 x 51 cm) USD 420,000. London, 8 Oct 2002, *Concentric Group of Girls* (1928, watercolour, gouache and pencil, 22 x 17 ins / 55 x 44 cm) EUR 380,000. London, 8 Oct 2002, *Blue Steps* (1966, oil on canvas, 26 x 19 ins / 65 x 48 cm) EUR 400,000. Berlin, 30 May 2003, *Head in Profile* (tempera on canvas on board, 6 x 2 ins / 14 x 5 cm) EUR 34,000. Berlin, 28 Nov 2003, *Woman Holding Up Her Hand, Small Painting II* (1932, pencil and nettle on board, 10 x 6 ins / 26 x 16 cm) EUR 70,000. Hamburg, 10 June 2004, *Relief H* (aluminium, 26 x 11 ins / 65 x 27 cm) EUR 30,000. London, 21 June 2004, *Against One Another* (1928, oil, caparol and spray paint on linen on board, 20 x 28 ins / 50 x 70 cm) GBP 180,000.

SCHLENK, Georg
German, 16th century.
Died at the end of September 1557.
Active in Nuremberg.
Painter.

Georg Schlenk was a pupil and assistant of Dürer. He may be the artist who painted a diptych depicting *Hans Schaub and his Wife*, which is in the Germanisches Nationalmuseum in Nuremberg.

SCHLENKER, Kathinka. See **OCHS**

SCHLEPKAU, Jacob
German, 17th century.
Died 29 December 1636.
Active in Hamburg.
Painter.

In 1622, Schlepkau painted the prophets and the apostles in St Peter's church.

SCHLEPPE, Simon
German, 17th century.
Active in Klagenfurt c. 1634.
Painter.

SCHLERTH, F. A. von
German, 19th century.
Active c. 1818.
Lithographer.

SCHLESIER, Niklas. See **SCHLESITZER**

SCHLESINGER, Adam Johann
German, 18th - 19th century.
Born 1759, in Ebertsheim (Rhineland Palatinate); died 1829, in Grünstadt.
Painter. Portraits, still-lifes, animals.

Adam Schlesinger was taught by his grandfather Trutenbach. He studied in Berlin and spent a number of years in Worms.

Museums and Galleries:
Berlin (Nationalgal.): *Redcurrants; Bird's Nest; Strawberry Plant and Snail; Butterfly* - Speyer (Historisches Mus. der Pfalz): *Portrait of Councillor Franz Georg Sperl; Portrait of Eva Josephe Sperl.*

Auction records:
Paris, 15 Nov 1976, *Vase of Flowers and Bird's Nest* (1824, oil on wood, 13 3/4 x 11 1/2 ins / 35 x 29 cm) FRF 3,500. London, 16 June 1993, *Still-life of a Branch of Cherry Tree with two Birds and a Snail; Redcurrants with a Lizard* (a pair, oil on panel, each 9 3/4 ins / 25.. cm 2 x 7 1/2 ins/5 x 19 cm) GBP 12,075.

SCHLESINGER, Adolf
German, 19th century.
Born 1817, in Mainz; died 1870, in Cologne.
Painter. Genre scenes, portraits.

Adolf Schlesinger was the son of Johann Georg Schlesinger. He was a pupil of J.W. Schirmer in 1814.

SCHLESINGER, Eugène
French, 19th - 20th century.
Born in Paris.
Painter. Landscapes.

Eugène Schlesinger, a pupil of Émile Lambinet and Léon Mellé, first exhibited at the Salon de Paris in 1877.

SCHLESINGER, Felix
German, 19th - 20th century.
Born 9 October 1833, in Hamburg; died 1910, in Hamburg.
Painter. Genre scenes, interiors with figures, landscapes with figures, landscapes.

Felix Schlesinger, who, like Rudolf Jordan, was a pupil at the fine arts academy in Düsseldorf, worked for a time in Paris and settled in Munich. A painter of genre scenes, he was fond of scenes depicting children, particularly those in which children are playing with rabbits.

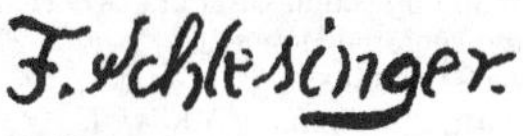

Museums and Galleries:
Bremen: *The Tuba Player.*

Auction records:
New York, 26 Jan 1906, *Preparations of the Rôtisseur*, USD 300. London, 12 Feb 1910, *Youth* (1870) GBP 17. Paris, 30 Oct 1925, *Woman and Child before a Mirror*, FRF 4,400. London, 20 April 1951, *Waters at Baden-Baden* (1860) GBP 110. Cologne, 15 Nov 1972, *Children Playing with Rabbits*, DEM 15,000. London, 13 June 1973, *Honest and Dishonest Flower Sellers* (two pendants) GBP 4,000. Cologne, 14 Nov 1974, *Interior Scene*, DEM 22,000. New York, 7 Oct 1977, *Feeding the Rabbits* (oil on panel, 12 3/4 x 16 ins / 32.5 x 40.5 cm) USD 32,000. New York, 4 May 1979, *First Snowfall* (oil on canvas, 20 3/4 x 24 ins / 53 x 61 cm) USD 36,000. Vienna, 14 Sept 1983, *Beim Dorfbader* (oil on panel, 18 1/2 x 24 3/4 ins / 47 x 63 cm) ATS 550,000. Zurich, 21 June 1985, *Three Children in a Farmyard* (oil on canvas, 15 1/4 x 19 1/4 ins / 39 x 49 cm) CHF 70,000. Munich, 17 Sept 1986, *Alms* (oil on canvas, 26 1/2 x 31 1/2 ins / 67 x 80 cm) DEM 75,000. Cologne, 18 March 1989, *Fisherman's Family outside his House* (1856, oil on canvas, 15 1/4 x 12 1/2 ins / 39 x 32 cm) DEM 14,000. Cologne, 20 Oct 1989, *Rustic Idyll with Small Girl and her Rabbits* (oil on panel, 8 1/4 x 11 ins / 21 x 27 cm) DEM 56,000. New York, 25 Oct 1989, *Two Children Playing with Rabbits* (oil on panel, 14 1/2 x 16 ins / 36.9 x 40.7 cm) USD 28,600. New York, 23 Oct 1990, *Asking the Way* (oil on panel, 11 1/2 x 14 1/2 ins / 29.2 x 36.8 cm) USD 23,100. London, 21 June 1991, *Returning Home for Tea* (oil on panel, 23 1/2 x 31 ins / 60 x 78.8 cm) GBP 33,000. New York, 17 Oct 1991, *Small Girl with her Rabbits* (oil on canvas, 12 x 8 1/2 ins / 30.5 x 21.6 cm) USD 20,900. London, 29 Nov 1991, *Leaving for America* (1859, oil on canvas, 32 1/2 x 43 1/4 ins / 82.5 x 109.9 cm) GBP 22,000. Munich, 10 Dec 1991, *Small Girl with Rabbits* (oil on canvas, 13 x 11 ins / 33 x 28 cm) DEM 46,000. New York, 27 May 1992, *Visiting Grandfather* (oil on canvas, 16 x 19 ins / 40.6 x 48.3 cm) USD 9,900. London, 12 Feb 1993, *The Grapes of Wrath* (oil on canvas, 33 1/2 x 62 3/4 ins / 85.1 x 159.4 cm) GBP 7,150. New York, 16 Feb 1994, *Games Room* (oil on panel, 9 1/2 x 13 ins / 24.1 x 33 cm) USD 31,050. London, 16 Nov 1994, *Young Mother* (oil on panel, 20 x 16 1/4 ins / 51 x 41 cm) GBP 27,600. London, 17 Nov 1995, *Children Giving Food to Rabbits* (oil on canvas, 14 1/4 x 16 3/4 ins / 36 x 42.7 cm) GBP 23,000. New York, 23-24 May 1996, *Eating Cherries* (oil on panel, 25 x 18 ins / 63.5 x 45.7 cm) USD 63,000. London, 21 Nov 1996, *Teasing* (oil on canvas, 14 x 16 ins / 35.5 x 40.6 cm) GBP 20,700. New York,

23 May 1997, *Old and Young* (oil on panel, 20 x 27 ins / 50.8 x 68.6 cm) USD 46,000.

SCHLESINGER, Georg

German, 19th century.
Born in Grünstadt.
Active in Frankfurt 1816-1827.
Painter. History painting, portraits.

SCHLESINGER, Henri Guillaume or Heinrich Wilhelm

German, 19th century.
Born 6 August 1814, in Frankfurt am Main; died 21 February 1893, in Neuilly-sur-Seine (Hauts-de-Seine), France.
Active then naturalised in France.
Painter, watercolourist, miniaturist. Portraits, genre scenes, still-lifes.

Schlesinger was a student at the academy in Vienna, then continued his studies in Paris. He exhibited at the Paris Salon from 1840 to 1889, then at the Salon des Artistes Français, of which he wasa member. He won a third class medal in 1840 and a second class in 1847. He was made a Chevalier of the Légion d'Honneur.

MUSEUMS AND GALLERIES:
VERSAILLES: *Portrait of Mahmoud Khan II* - VIENNA: *At the Dressing Table.*

AUCTION RECORDS:
PARIS, 1861, *Woman Washing Herself,* FRF 126. PARIS, 1870, *The Little Sister,* FRF 5,100; *Portrait of a Child,* FRF 5,000; *Speaking Portrait,* FRF 5,000. LONDON, 31 July 1947, *Broken Vase of Flowers,* GBP 150. LONDON, 19 March 1950, *Ce n'est pas moi* (1872) GBP 330. PARIS, 30 June 1950, *The Young Coquette* (1857) FRF 81,000. LONDON, 12 May 1972, *Couple in a Cab,* Gns 300. PARIS, 15 March 1976, *Children's Chatter* (oil on canvas, 29 1/4 x 27 1/4 ins / 74 x 69 cm) FRF 5,700. LONDON, 4 May 1977, *Girl with a Bunch of Grapes* (1847, oil on canvas, 31 1/2 x 25 1/4 ins / 80 x 64 cm) GBP 1,300. LONDON, 5 Oct 1979, *Girl with a Flower* (1871, oil on canvas, oval, 30 x 25 1/4 ins / 76.2 x 64 cm) GBP 800. LONDON, 24 June 1981, *Girl with a Bunch of Grapes* (1847, oil on canvas, 31 1/2 x 25 1/4 ins / 80 x 64 cm) GBP 1,400. LYONS, 1 June 1983, *Girl with Dogs in a Park* (1842 or 1862, oil on canvas, 32 x 25 1/2 ins / 81 x 65 cm) FRF 30,000. LONDON, 27 Nov 1985, *Monkey Wearing His Mistress's Bonnet* (1879, oil on canvas, 51 x 39 ins / 129.5 x 99 cm) GBP 7,000. LONDON, 5 May 1989, *The Letter* (1877, oil on canvas, 46 x 35 1/2 ins / 117 x 90 cm) GBP 4,180. LONDON, 6 Oct 1989, *Ce n'est pas moi!* (1872, oil on canvas, 32 x 39 1/2 ins / 81 x 100.5 cm) GBP 13,200. NEW YORK, 21 May 1991, *Young Lady with her Dog* (1865, oil on canvas/panel, 30 1/2 x 25 1/4 ins / 77.5 x 64 cm) USD 5,500. LONDON, 19 June 1991, *Interior of a Harem* (1846, oil on canvas, 28 3/4 x 35 3/4 ins / 73 x 91 cm) GBP 27,500. STOCKHOLM, 19 May 1992, *Girl with her Goat* (oil on canvas, 35 3/4 x 28 ins / 91 x 71 cm) SEK 17,000. LONDON, 17 June 1992, *Ce n'est pas moi!* (oil on canvas, 32 x 39 1/2 ins / 81 x 100.5 cm) GBP 18,700. LONDON, 16 March 1994, *Blind Man's Buff* (1844, oil on canvas, 28 x 35 1/2 ins / 71 x 90 cm) GBP 32,200. NEW YORK, 20 July 1994, *The Two Sisters* (oil on canvas, 61 x 46 ins / 154 x 115.9 cm) USD 9,200. LUDLOW (SHROPSHIRE), 29 Sept 1994, *A Moment of Reflection* (1868, oil on canvas, 28 1/4 x 22 3/4 ins / 72 x 58 cm) GBP 8,625. NEW YORK, 24 May 1995, *Young Woman and Baby* (1878, oil on canvas, 32 x 26 ins / 81.3 x 66 cm) USD 14,950. PARIS, 11 Dec 1995, *The Fox and the Grapes* (oil on canvas, 88 1/4 x 128 ins / 224 x 325 cm) FRF 320,000.

SCHLESINGER, Jacob

German, 19th century.
Born 13 January 1792, in Worms; died 12 May 1855, in Berlin.
Painter, lithographer, copyist, art restorer. Portraits, still-lifes, landscapes.

Jacob Schlesinger studied first with his father, the painter Johann Schlesinger, then in Mannheim and Munich. In 1822, he was appointed a professor in Berlin. Although he is best known as a skilful copyist and restorer of paintings, he also left some portraits and paintings of fruits. He was curator of the Berlin Museum.

MUSEUMS AND GALLERIES:
BERLIN (Nationalgal.): *Portrait of the Philosopher Hegel* - FRANKENTHAL: *Portrait of the Painter Christian Köster* - HEIDELBERG: *Portrait of the Lawyer Welcker and his Wife* - KALININGRAD: *Portrait of G.H.L. Nicolovius* - MANNHEIM: *Portrait of Johann Adam Schusslier* - SPEYER: *Portrait of Dr Hoffmann; Still-life.*

AUCTION RECORDS:
HEIDELBERG, 13 Oct 1979, *Portrait of a Nobleman* (1813, oil on canvas, 16 1/4 x 13 ins / 41 x 33 cm) DEM 3,700. HEIDELBERG, 15 Oct 1999, *Portrait of Old Man* (oil on tin, 13 x 10 ins / 32 x 26 cm) DEM 5,300.

SCHLESINGER, Johann

German, 18th - 19th century.
Born 1768, in Ebertsheim; died 18 January 1840, in Sausenheim.
Active in Mannheim.
Painter. Portraits, still-lifes.

MUSEUMS AND GALLERIES:
MAINZ: *Portrait of Herr Schmutz as a Young Man.*

SCHLESINGER, Johann Georg

German, 19th century.
Born 1775; died 8 November 1841, in Cologne.
Painter.

Johann Georg Schlesinger was the father of Adolf Schlesinger.

SCHLESINGER, Karl or Carl

Swiss, 19th century.
Born 23 March 1825, in Lausanne; died 12 June 1893, in Düsseldorf.
Painter. History painting, genre scenes, landscapes.

Karl Schlesinger studied first in Prague, then with Dyckman in Antwerp. In 1852, he settled in Düsseldorf. He is best known for a series of paintings on subjects from the Reformation, but he also painted some landscapes of the banks of the Moselle.

G. Schlesinger

MUSEUMS AND GALLERIES:
HAMBURG - HANOVER.

AUCTION RECORDS:
COLOGNE, 14 June 1976, *Shepherd with His Flock* (1870, oil on canvas, 25 1/2 x 22 1/2 ins / 65 x 57 cm) DEM 10,000. VIENNA, 15 March 1977, *Woodcutters at Rest* (1863, oil on canvas, 21 1/4 x 26 3/4 ins / 54 x 68 cm) ATS 110,000. ZURICH, 28 Oct 1981, *People beside Lake Lucerne* (1884, oil on canvas, 24 x 40 ins / 61 x 101.5 cm) CHF 10,000. NEW YORK, 15 Feb 1985, *A Young Beauty* (oil on canvas, 36 1/2 x 28 1/2 ins / 92.7 x 72.4 cm) USD 4,800. COLOGNE, 20 Oct 1989, *Baptismal Procession Leaving the Church* (1873, oil on canvas, 37 x 62 ins / 94 x 157.5 cm) DEM 35,000. COPENHAGEN, 25-26 April 1990, *Two Fishermen's Children near a Boat* (1859, oil on canvas, 17 1/4 x 20 3/4 ins / 44 x 53 cm) DKK 9,000. MUNICH, 6 Dec 1994, *Children Bathing* (1865, oil on canvas, 15 1/4 x 18 1/4 ins / 38.5 x 46.5 cm) DEM 11,270. MUNICH, 29 Sept 1999, *Feeding the Rabbit* (oil on canvas, 17 x 24 ins / 44 x 60 cm) DEM 85,000. COLOGNE, 28 Oct 1999, *Peasant Couple Returning with Harvest* (oil on canvas, 31 x 49 ins / 80 x 125 cm) DEM 10,000. AHLDEN, 28 Sept 2001, *Italian Peasant Girl* (1866, oil on canvas, oval, 29 x 24 ins / 74 x 60 cm) DEM 7,300. LUCERNE, 15 May 2002, *Woman with Child Peeling*

Apple (1858, oil on canvas, 17 x 22 ins / 44 x 55 cm) CHF 4,000. UPPSALA, 25 May 2003, *Landscape with Women Resting* (1864, oil on canvas, 13 x 16 ins / 33 x 40 cm) SEK 18,000. FLORIDA, 17 Aug 2003, *Family Group in a Hilly Landscape Praying before a Meal* (oil on canvas/board, 25 x 33 ins / 64 x 84 cm) USD 4,000. LONDON, 16 June 2004, *Homeward Bound* (1860, oil on canvas, 30 x 44 ins / 77 x 112 cm) GBP 4,000.

SCHLESINGER, Niklas. See **SCHLESITZER**

SCHLESINGER, S.
German, 18th - 19th century.
Active in Berlin 1791-1804.
Painter, watercolourist. Architectural views, landscapes.

SCHLESITZER, Niklas, or Schlesier or Schlesinger or Schlessinger
German, 15th - 16th century.
Active in Munich 1482-1517.
Painter.
Munich School.

SCHLETT, Johann Georg
German, 18th century.
Sculptor.
Schlett was a pupil of Oeser in Leipzig.

SCHLETTER, Anton. See **SCHLECHTER**

SCHLETTER, Salomon Gottlob
German, 18th century.
Died 1807.
Active in Leipzig.
Engraver.

SCHLETTERER, Jakob Christoph, or Schlederer, Schletter
Austrian, 18th century.
Born 22 July 1699, in Wenns (Tyrol); died 19 May 1774, in Vienna.
Sculptor.
Schletterer was a student of Stanetti in Vienna and at the academy, winning a silver medal in 1732 and a gold in 1735. In 1726, he worked with Donner in Salzburg on the Mirabell Castle. His most important works are *Leda and the Swan* in the Benedictine monastery in Altenburg, a large altar in the Carmelites' church in Vienna, two apostles on the altar of the Virgin in the Court Church in Vienna, four statues in the Theresianum, also in Vienna, *Minerva Triumphing over Envy* in the Vienna Museum of the Baroque, and the statue of *Artemis* in the garden of Schönbrunn Palace.

SCHLEUEN, J. F. W.
German, 18th century.
Engraver.
J. F. W. Schleuen was probably the son of the engraver Johann Friedrich Schleuen. He engraved small portraits of *Frederick II* and *Peter the Great* and illustrated the German translation of Cuvier's *Elementary Table of the Natural History of Animals*.

SCHLEUEN, J. G.
German, 18th century.
Engraver.
J.G. Schleuen was the brother of Johann David and Johann Friedrich Schleuen. He engraved portraits after the manner of Rembrandt.

SCHLEUEN, J. W.
German, 18th century.
Engraver.
J.W. Schleuen worked as an engraver for the Berlin Society of Naturalists.

SCHLEUEN, Johann David, the Elder
German, 18th century.
Engraver.
Johann David Schleuen the Elder engraved vignettes for Frederick II's *General Principles of Warfare* in 1753 and plates for the works of Basedow.

SCHLEUEN, Johann David, the Younger
German, 18th century.
Engraver.
Johann David Schleuen the Younger was the son of Johann David Schleuen the Elder.

SCHLEUEN, Johann Friedrich
German, 18th century.
Engraver.
Johann Friedrich Schleuen was the elder brother of Johann David Schleuen. He engraved a large number of portraits for the Allgemeine Deutsche Bibliothek.

SCHLEUNIG, Johann Georg
German, 18th century.
Born c. 1715, in Pottenstein.
Sculptor (wood), decorative designer.
Johann Georg Schleunig was the son of Johann Konrad Schleunig, and lived in Bayreuth from 1741. He worked on the decoration of the Ermitage near Bayreuth. He moved to Potsdam in 1763.

SCHLEUNIG, Johann Konrad
German, 18th century.
Born 1669; died 26 November 1739.
Active in Pottenstein.
Sculptor, painter.

SCHLEUSNER, Thea
German, 20th century.
Born 30 April 1879, in Wittenberg.
Painter. Portraits, genre scenes.
Thea Schleusner was a pupil at the Académie Colarossi and the Académie Carrière in Paris, and was taught by Franz Skarbina, Reinhold Lepsius and Curt Stoeving in Berlin.
MUSEUMS AND GALLERIES:
BERLIN (Akademie der Wissenschaften): *Portrait of Dr Albrecht Weber* - BERLIN (City Collection): *Self-portrait by the Artist; Mass at St Mark's Basilica in Venice.*

SCHLEY, Bruno
German, 20th century.
Born 6 October 1895, in Rastatt.
Active in Freiburg im Brisgau.
Painter, engraver.

SCHLEY, Jakob van der, or van
Dutch, 18th century.
Born 1715, in Amsterdam; died 1779, in Amsterdam.
Draughtsman, engraver.
Jakob van der Schley was a pupil of B. Picart, whose style he copied. Following Picart's death, Van der Schley completed several of his unfinished plates. He engraved a large number of portraits, together with illustrations for *The Life of Marianne*, published in The Hague (1735-1747), and works by Brantôme.

AUCTION RECORDS:
PARIS, 1885, *Vignettes* (drawing) FRF 340. PARIS, 5 Dec 1900, *Fame and Cupids* (drawing, frontispiece) FRF 220.

SCHLEY, Paul
German, 19th - 20th century.
Born 22 July 1854, in Berlin.
Sculptor, designer of ornamental architectural features.

Paul Schley was the pupil of his father, Carl Schley. He sculpted in wood, and also studied at the school of fine arts in Berlin. From 1870 to 1875, he worked for the studio of H. Naack in Berlin, and from 1876 onwards for A. Waagen in Vienna.

SCHLEY, Philippus van der
Dutch, 18th - 19th century.
Born 1724, in Amsterdam; died 1817, in Amsterdam.
Draughtsman, engraver.

Philippus van der Schley was a pupil of his brother Jakob van der Schley. He became a drawing teacher and art dealer.

SCHLEYER, Erhard
Austrian, 19th century.
Born 1821, in Vienna; died 9 September 1842, in Vienna.
Engraver (burin). Landscapes.

SCHLEYER, Heinrich. See **SCHLAYER**

SCHLEYER, Sem or Simon. See **SCHLÖR**

SCHLEYSER, J. H.
German, 18th century.
Painter.

SCHLICHT, Abel
German, 18th - 19th century.
Born 1754, in Mannheim; died c. 1826.
Painter, engraver, architect. Genre scenes, portraits, landscapes. Stage sets.

Schlicht was a pupil of L. Quaglia. He engraved portraits, genre scenes and landscapes. He was a professor at the academy in Düsseldorf.

SCHLICHT, Carl von
German, 19th - 20th century.
Born 1 June 1833, in Gutenpaaren; died 1912.
Painter. Landscapes, seascapes.

Carl von Schlicht was the pupil of Andreas Achenbach and Hans Fredrik Gude at the fine arts academy in Düsseldorf, and of Stanislas de Kalckreuth at the fine arts academy in Weimar. He was active in Weimar, Kreuznach, Düsseldorf and later also in Potsdam. He appears to have been an architect and to have built Catholic churches.

AUCTION RECORDS:
COLOGNE, 21 March 1980, *Alpine Lake at Sunset* (1860, oil on canvas, 24 x 36 1/4 ins / 61 x 92 cm) DEM 5,500.

SCHLICHTEGROLL, Carl Felix von
German, 19th - 20th century.
Born 13 January 1862, in Gross-Behnkenhagen.
Painter, illustrator.

Carl Felix von Schlichtegroll was the pupil of Ernst Albert Fischer-Corlin. He was taught by Max Michael at the academy of fine arts in Berlin, by Carl Heinrich Hoff the Elder at the Karlsruhe academy, and by Claudius von Schraudolph the Younger at the Stuttgart fine arts school. He was active in Leipzig.

SCHLICHTEN, Jan Philipp van
Dutch, 18th century.
Born 1681, in the Netherlands; died 1745, in Mannheim.
Painter. Genre scenes.

Jan Philipp van Schlichten was a pupil of Adriaen van der Werff, whose style he copied. In 1720 he entered the service of Charles Philip, Elector Palatine of the Rhine, in Mannheim. His works are to be found in Munich, Schleissheim and at the Liechtenstein Museum in Vienna.

MUSEUMS AND GALLERIES:
BRUSSELS: *Portrait of Johan Wilhelm, Elector Palatine of the Rhine and Count Palatine of Neuberg* - ERLANGEN: *Village Musician* - GENEVA (Mus. Ariana): *Still-life* - MANNHEIM: *Portrait of Charles Philip, Elector Palatine of the Rhine* - MUNICH (Bayerisches Nationalmus.): *Portrait of Princess Anna Christina of Sulzbach* - NUREMBERG: *Portrait of a Court Fool* - ORANIENBAUM: *Interior of a Glass Factory during Working Hours* - SPEYER: *Christian III, Count of Birkenfeld-Bischweiler* - VIENNA (Liechtenstein Mus.): *Man Smoking; Boy with a Dog; Young Man with a Cat.*

AUCTION RECORDS:
COLOGNE, 1862, *Young Lord Gambling Together with Ladies*, FRF 262.

SCHLICHTEN, Johann Franz von der
German, 18th century.
Born 1725, in Mannheim; died 1795, in Mannheim.
Painter. Genre scenes.

Schlichten was the son, and probably also the pupil of Jan Philipp van Schlichten. He completed his training with a stay in Italy, where he studied with Torelli and Conca. After returning to Germany, he painted small genre scenes after the manner of Metsu and Netscher. He also painted imitations of low reliefs. He was the director of the Mannheim museum.

Von der Schlichten. f. 1731.
V.D.S. V.S.

MUSEUMS AND GALLERIES:
MANNHEIM: *Portrait of a Painter* - SPEYER: *Woman Playing the Lute.*

SCHLICHTER, Rudolf
German, 20th century.
Born 6 December 1890, in Calw; died 1955, in Munich.
Painter (gouache), watercolourist, engraver, lithographer, draughtsman, illustrator, sculptor. Scenes with figures, figures, portraits, landscapes.
Dadaism, Neue Sachlichkeit (New Objectivity).
Groups: Rihgruppe, Novembergruppe, Berlin Dadaist, Rote Gruppe (Red Group).

Rudolf Schlichter was initially apprenticed as a painter and enameller in a factory in Pforzheim. From 1907 to 1910 he was a pupil at the school of arts and crafts in Stuttgart, then studied as the pupil of Wilhelm Trübner and Hans Thoma at the fine arts academy in Karlsruhe until 1916. After serving during World War I, he returned to Karlsruhe, where he was one of the founders of the Rihgruppe. In 1919 he settled in Berlin, where he became a member of the Novembergruppe (November Group) and joined the Dada group. During a Dada demonstration, he is said to have shown great courage in redeeming a situation that had become critical for his friends.

In 1924, together with Heartfield and George Grosz, Schlichter created the Rote Gruppe (Red Group), and in 1928 was involved in the ASSO, an association of revolutionary artists. In 1932, apparently abandoning political activity, he left Berlin for Rottenburg, then moved to Stuttgart in 1935. In 1937, 17 of his works were confiscated by the Nazis and a number of others were shown in the exhibition *Entartete Kunst* (*Degenerate Art*). In 1939, he went to Munich, where he was assimilated in the conservative Catholic circles associated with Ernst Jünger.

On joining the Dada group, Schlichter wrote that he had only become involved in the activities of the group because his brother Max ran a restaurant where the group's leading members - George Grosz, Raoul Hausmann and Richard Huelsenbeck - used to congregate, an interpretation of the facts which belies the true nature of his involvement in the movement. The drawings of Rudolf Schlichter published in the satirical journals *Der Gegner* (*The Opponent*), *Der Knüppel* (*The Cudgel*)) and *Die rote Fahne* (*The Red Flag*), although different in character, less caricatural and less acerbic than those of Grosz, are nevertheless clearly combative in nature, offering a particularly critical view of the post-war German capital.

In 1920, Schlichter collaborated with Heartfield in Berlin on the sculpture *Prussian Archangel*, which entered the annals of Dadaism and which 'graced' the platform of the first major international Dadaist fair. Covered in verdigris, this mannequin depicted a German officer with the head of a pig, wearing a peaked cap and with a sign round his neck bearing the words 'hung by the revolution'. This sculpture was central to the legal proceedings brought by the German state against the Berlin Dadaists. One of Schlichter's watercolours from the 'New Objectivity' period, *Hausvogteiplatz*, dating from around 1926, depicts a mixed crowd of haggard-looking proletarians, depraved middle-class individuals and women of the demi-monde in their finery. The scene, dominated by a gallows whose noose tightens with the waxing of the moon, is made up of motifs and symbols which would have been worthy of Grosz and Otto Dix at that time, but which are still in keeping with some of Schlichter's Dadaist initiatives, such as the *Prussian Archangel* of 1920.

As a painter, Schlichter is best known for the portraits he painted of his friends. His subjects were chosen from both ends of the political spectrum, including Bertold Brecht, Alfred Döblin, Erich Kästner and others.

Rudolf Schlichter's personality was complex. Anti-establishment, Dadaist, involved in *Neue Sachlichkeit* and extreme left-wing politics, he was a genuinely religious Roman Catholic. Though not abandoning the drawings devoted to social satire, he nurtured a fantastic vein in his work and exploited this in his illustrations of adventures recounted by Fenimore Cooper and Karl May. The figures in his painted compositions of around 1925, which are less pessimistic and also less sombre, bear some resemblance to the mannequins of De Chirico's 'metaphysical painting'. This aspect of his art, which closely approaches Surrealist fantasy, also manifested itself in his illustrations of crimes of passion and in his erotic drawings.

Schlichter took part in a number of collective exhibitions, including several of those mounted from 1919 onwards in Berlin by the Novembergruppe as well as the exhibition *Neue Sachlichkeit* (New Objectivity) at the Kunsthalle in Mannheim in 1925. He was represented at the collective exhibition *Phantom der Lust. Visionen des Masochismus in der Kunst* (*Phantom of Desire. Visions of Masochism in Art*) dedicated to Baron Sacher-Masoch, who first described masochism, and mounted in the Neue Galerie of the regional museum in Graz in 2003. In 1984, the national art gallery in Berlin, the Staatliche Kunsthalle, mounted a posthumous exhibition of the works of this artist under the title *Rudolf Schlichter*.

BIBLIOGRAPHY:

Dorival, Bernard/Hoog, Michel, *Dada*, exhibition catalogue, Musée national d'Art moderne, Paris, 1966. *Rudolf Schlichter*, exhibition catalogue, Staatliche Kunsthalle, Berlin, 1984. Hülsewig-Johnen, Jutta, *Neue Sachlichkeit, magischer Realismus*, exhibition catalogue, Kunsthalle, Bielefeld, 1991. Dachy, Marc, *'La Nouvelle Objectivité mise à nu'* in *Beaux-Arts Magazine*, periodical, Paris, April 1991. Weibel, Peter (ed.), *'Phantom der Lust. Visionen des Masochismus in der Kunst'*, *2 vol.*, exhibition catalogue, Neue Galerie am Landesmuseum, Graz, Belleville Verlag, Munich, 2003.

MUSEUMS AND GALLERIES:

BERLIN (Berlinische Gal.): *Studio on the Roof* (c. 1920); *Jenny Seated* (c. 1922-1923); *Blind Power* (1937) - BERLIN (Märkisches Mus.): *Portrait of Margot* (1924) - MANNHEIM (Städtische Kunsthalle): *Portrait of E. Erwin Kisch* (c. 1928); *Self-portrait* - MUNICH (Städtische Gal. im Lenbachhaus): *Portrait of Bertolt Brecht*.

AUCTION RECORDS:

HAMBURG, 27 Nov 1965, *Tingel-Tangel* (gouache) DEM 4,400. HAMBURG, 8 June 1974, *Blackjack* (watercolour) DEM 2,500. MUNICH, 30 Nov 1976, *Königsee* (watercolour and Indian ink, 23 1/2 x 19 ins / 60 x 48.5 cm) DEM 950. HAMBURG, 4 June 1977, *Tingel-Tangel* (watercolour, 21 x 18 ins / 53.4 x 45.9 cm) DEM 17,500. MUNICH, 30 Nov 1979, *Three Young Girls (recto)* (c. 1925, pencil heightened with chalk); *Lavender Fields (verso)* (pencil, 15 x 9 ins / 38 x 23 cm) DEM 2,100. COLOGNE, 5 Dec 1979, *The Nagold* (1931, watercolour/pen outline, 23 1/2 x 18 1/2 ins / 60 x 46.8 cm) DEM 4,800. MUNICH, 30 May 1980, *Portrait of a Young Woman in a Landscape* (1934, oil on canvas, 24 3/4 x 19 1/4 ins / 63 x 49 cm) DEM 14,000. MUNICH, 8 June 1982, *Brothel* (c. 1918, pencil, 19 1/2 x 14 ins / 49.5 x 35.8 cm) DEM 8,500. MUNICH, 8 June 1982, *Speedy Seated* (1937, watercolour and pencil, 30 x 21 3/4 ins / 76 x 55.5 cm) DEM 15,000. ROME, 22 May 1984, *Cabaret Scene (late 1920s)* (pen, 19 1/2 x 25 ins / 49.5 x 63.4 cm) ITL 2,800,000. MUNICH, 6 June 1984, *Nightmare* (1952, oil/card, 32 1/4 x 20 1/2 ins / 82 x 52 cm) DEM 5,200. MUNICH, 11 June 1985, *Lebendes sprengt Totes* (1940, oil on card, 39 1/4 x 29 1/4 ins / 99.5 x 74.6 cm) DEM 6,000. LONDON, 5 Dec 1985, *Portrait of Dr Sternberg* (c. 1927, charcoal, 23 1/2 x 19 3/4 ins / 59.5 x 50 cm) GBP 1,800. LONDON, 28 May 1986, *Lebendes sprengt Totes* (1940, oil on card, 39 1/4 x 29 1/4 ins / 100 x 74.5 cm) GBP 3,000. MUNICH, 8 June 1988, *Drunkards* (charcoal, 19 3/4 x 18 ins / 50 x 46 cm) DEM 12,100. ROME, 21 March 1989, *Speedy Standing Up* (1934, oil on canvas, 75 x 33 1/4 ins / 190.5 x 84.5 cm) ITL 85,000,000. ROME, 6 Dec 1989, *Speedy* (1937, watercolour/paper, 30 x 22 ins / 76 x 56 cm) ITL 28,750,000. ZURICH, 16 Oct 1991, *Dupe* (1927, pencil drawing, 25 1/2 x 18 3/4 ins / 64.7 x 47.5 cm) CHF 4,800. MUNICH, 26 May 1992, *Old Farm in the Jura* (1934, ink, 19 3/4 x 25 1/2 ins / 50 x 65 cm) DEM 2,300. HEIDELBERG, 9 Oct 1992, *Californian Bar* (lithograph, 15 1/2 x 16 1/4 ins / 39.5 x 41 cm) DEM 1,300. BERLIN, 27 Nov 1992, *Explosion* (ink and watercolour on pencil/vellum, 14 x 7 3/4 ins / 35.5 x 20 cm) DEM 21,470. MUNICH, 1-2 Dec 1992, *Apocalyptic Landscape with Coloured Creatures* (oil and watercolour, 10 x 6 3/4 ins / 24.5 x 17 cm) DEM 21,850. LONDON, 9 Oct 1997, *At the Café* (1924, pencil, 23 1/4 x 18 ins / 59.3 x 45.9 cm) GBP 2,530. BERLIN, 4 June 1999, *Heliogabal* (c. 1922, watercolour over pencil on vellum and paper, 27 x 20 ins / 68 x 50 cm) DEM 40,000. BERLIN, 5 June 1999, *In Cafe. Seated Woman in Hat* (1922, ink and watercolour, double-sided, 23 x 17 ins / 59 x 42 cm) DEM 11,000. BERLIN, 27 May 2000, *Death of the Anarchist Moro* (watercolour over pencil, 20 x 22 ins / 50 x 56 cm) DEM 40,000. LONDON, 18 Oct 2000, *Portrait of Richard Masseck. Study for Portrait of Richard Masseck* (oil on canvas, double-sided, 30 x 21 ins / 76 x 54 cm) GBP 30,000. LONDON, 11 Oct 2001, *Speedy, the Artist's Wife* (1929, watercolour and pencil, 29 x 22 ins / 73 x 55 cm) GBP 9,000. BERLIN, 1 Dec 2001, *Dadaist Experiment* (1919-1920, watercolour over pencil, 16 x 14 ins / 41 x 35 cm) DEM 49,000. BERLIN, 7 June 2002, *On the Underground Train* (Indian ink, 25 x 20 ins / 64 x 50 cm) EUR 7,000. COLOGNE, 4 Dec 2002, *Maid* (1929, watercolour and pencil, 30 x 22 ins / 77 x 56 cm) EUR 9,000. BERLIN, 25 Oct 2003, *Indian and General* (watercolour and Indian ink, 20 x 25 ins / 50 x 64 cm) EUR 12,000.

SCHLICHTING, Christian Ludwig

German, 18th century.

Active in Havelberg 1702-1723.

Painter.

SCHLICHTING, Ernst Hermann

German, 19th century.

Born 5 May 1812, in Reval (now Tallinn, Estonia); died 8 May 1890, in Dresden.

Painter, lithographer. Genre scenes.

Ernst Schlichting was the brother of Wilhelmine Schlichting. He studied with the engraver K.A. Senff in Dorpat (now Tartu), and also with Hildebrandt at the academy in Düsseldorf.

MUSEUMS AND GALLERIES:

RIGA: *Birthday Table; The Emigrant* - TALLINN: *The Old Sustern Gate in Reval.*

SCHLICHTING, Max

German, 19th - 20th century.

Born 16 June 1866, in Sagan (Silesia); died 1937.

Painter, lithographer, illustrator. Scenes with figures, landscapes, urban landscapes, seascapes, flowers.

Max Schlichting was the pupil of Waldemar Friedrich, Franz Skarbina and Eugen Bracht at the fine arts academy in Berlin and of Jules Lefebvre and Gabriel Ferrier at the Académie Julian in Paris. He was active in Berlin and worked during his travels, in particular in Paris and Venice.

A significant part of his work is devoted to Parisian views and scenes with figures.

M schlichting

MUSEUMS AND GALLERIES:

BERLIN (City Collection): *In the Port of Venice; On the Grand Canal; Cars at a Halt; Friedrich-August-Brücke in Dresden* - BERLIN (Prussian National Collection): *Beneath the Stars; Ball at the Opéra; On the Boulevards in Paris; Pavot in Bloom; Paris Seen from Montmartre* - DÜSSELDORF: *View of Paris.*

AUCTION RECORDS:

LOKEREN, 15 Oct 1983, *Promenade Albert I in Ostend* (1912, oil on canvas, 39 1/4 x 45 1/4 ins / 100 x 115 cm) BEF 190,000. LONDON, 3 Dec 1985, *Beach Scene* (oil on canvas, 23 3/4 x 39 1/4 ins / 60.5 x 100 cm) GBP 2,500. STOCKHOLM, 16 May 1990, *Breakers on a Sandy Beach* (oil on canvas, 20 x 24 ins / 51 x 61 cm) SEK 5,000. AMSTERDAM, 19 Oct 1993, *People Walking on the Champs-Élysées* (1898, oil on card, 5 3/4 x 8 3/4 ins / 14.5 x 22.5 cm) NLG 2,300. LONDON, 27 Oct 1993, *Rue du Faubourg-Montmartre in Paris* (oil on canvas, 34 1/4 x 18 1/2 ins / 87 x 47 cm) GBP 5,980.

SCHLICHTING, T.

German, 18th century.

Sculptor.

Schlichting was a sculptor at the court of the Bishop of Eutin, near Lübeck.

SCHLICHTING, Wilhelmine

19th century.

Died 1888, in Dresden.

Painter.

Wilhelmine was the sister of the painter Ernst Hermann Schlichting.

SCHLICHTING-CARLSEN, Karl Peter August

Danish, 19th century.

Born 16 October 1853, in Flensburg (then in Denmark, now in Schleswig-Holstein, Germany), in 1852 according to some sources; died 16 October 1903; in 1893 according to some sources.

Painter. Scenes with figures, landscapes, still-lifes.

From 1874 to 1878, he was a pupil at the Kunstakademi in Copenhagen. He exhibited in Paris, at the Salon des Artistes Français during the Exposition Universelle in 1900. He received an honourable mention.

He attempted a still-life in 1873, but then turned to landscape painting. He painted Danish subjects, notably the outskirts of Hillerød, but he also painted views of Italy and Switzerland, and of the Midi region in France.

MUSEUMS AND GALLERIES:

STOCKHOLM: *Lake in the Sjælland Forest in Summer.*

AUCTION RECORDS:

STOCKHOLM, 21 April 1982, *The Croquet Players* (oil on canvas, 29 1/2 x 47 1/4 ins / 75 x 120 cm) SEK 15,100. COPENHAGEN, 22 Aug 1985, *An Old Pergola in Capri* (1884, oil on canvas, 49 1/4 x 38 1/2 ins / 125 x 98 cm) DKK 22,000. STOCKHOLM, 15 Nov 1988, *Hillside Landscape* (oil on canvas, 13 3/4 x 24 ins / 35 x 61 cm) SEK 9,000. LONDON, 7 June 1989, *The Croquet Game* (oil on canvas, 29 1/4 x 47 1/4 ins / 74 x 120 cm) GBP 9,350. STOCKHOLM, 15 Nov 1989, *Summer in a Beech Wood* (1883, oil, 16 1/4 x 24 1/2 ins / 41 x 62 cm) SEK 4,200. COPENHAGEN, 27 May 2002, *Spring Day by Woodland Lake* (oil on canvas, 15 x 23 ins / 39 x 58 cm) DKK 30,000.

SCHLICHTKRULL, Johann Christopher

Danish, 19th - 20th century.

Born 28 February 1866, in Copenhagen.

Painter. Portraits, genre scenes, landscapes.

Johann Schlichtkrull was the pupil of Holger Grønvold, Karl Heinrich Bloch, J Frederick Vermehren and Peter Severin Krøyer at the school of fine arts in Copenhagen. He exhibited in Paris at the Salon des Artistes Français for the 1900 World's Fair and received a commendation.

MUSEUMS AND GALLERIES:

COPENHAGEN: *At Sunset; Portrait.*

SCHLICK, Alexander

German, 19th century.

Born 1834, in Dresden.

Painter.

SCHLICK, Benjamin

French (?), 19th - 20th century.

Watercolourist. Landscapes, urban landscapes, architectural views.

Benjamin Schlick, who worked in Italy, is known only from auction records.

AUCTION RECORDS:

PARIS, 16 Oct 1950, *Italian Views* (6 watercolours, collection) FRF 5,000. PARIS, 7 March 1951, *The City of Florence* (watercolour) FRF 5,000.

SCHLICK, Gustav Friedrich

German, 19th century.

Born 1804, in Leipzig; died 6 September 1869, in Loschwitz near Dresden.

Painter, illustrator, lithographer. Portraits, genre scenes.

Gustav Schlick studied at the academy in Leipzig with Hans Schnorr von Karolsfeld. He went on study tours to Berlin and Paris.

MUSEUMS AND GALLERIES:

LEIPZIG (Stadtgeschichtliches Mus.): six portraits.

SCHLICKUM, Carl

German, 19th century.

Active in Berlin.

Painter. Landscapes.

Schlickum was a pupil of Wilhelm Schirmer.

BIBLIOGRAPHY:

Kunze, Andreas, *Romantisches Westfalen: Bilder aus vergangener Zeit. Der Maler Carl Schlickum und die deutsche Geschichte*, Lesezeichen, Hagen, 1996.

SCHLIEBEN, A. von

German, 18th century.

Active in Berlin.

Draughtswoman.

In 1793, A. von Schlieben exhibited two of her drawings on parchment at the academy in Berlin: *The Death of General Wolfe* and *Death of Clorinda.*

SCHLIEBEN, Caroline von, later Frau Lose
German, 19th century.
Born in Dresden.
Draughtswoman, engraver.
Caroline von Schlieben was a pupil of Retzscke. In collaboration with her husband, Friedrich Lose, and on his instigation, she engraved views of Milan and the most important cities of Italy.

SCHLIEBEN, Hedwig von
Maiden name: Warnow
German, 20th century.
Born 7 January 1882, in Haguenau.
Painter.
Hedwig von Schlieben was active in Munich. She married the painter Ludwig von Schlieben.

SCHLIEBEN, Ludwig von
German, 20th century.
Born 20 February 1875, in Krossenhein.
Painter. Portraits, landscapes.
Ludwig von Schlieben was the pupil of Peter Jansen and Fritz von Uhde, probably at the fine arts academy in Berlin. He was active in Munich and married Hedwig von Schlieben.

SCHLIECKER, August Eduard
German, 19th - 20th century.
Born 12 September 1833, in Hamburg; died 31 March 1911, in Lauenburg.
Painter, lithographer. Landscapes, seascapes, urban landscapes.
August Schliecker was the pupil of Eduard Ritter and Martin Gensler in Hamburg and of Oswald Achenbach and Hans Fredrik Gude at the academy of fine arts in Düsseldorf.
MUSEUMS AND GALLERIES:
LÜBECK: *At the Port of Dieppe* - ROSTOCK: *Halberstadt Motif.*
AUCTION RECORDS:
LONDON, 27 Feb 1985, *Rustic Scene* (oil on canvas, 23 3/4 x 37 ins / 60.5 x 94 cm) GBP 4,200.

SCHLIEF, Pierre. See **SCHLEIFF**

SCHLIEPHACKE, Walter
German, 20th century.
Born 12 October 1877, in Ilsenburg.
Painter, sculptor.
Walter Schliephacke was a pupil at the school of industrial arts in Hanover and at the fine arts academy in Munich. He was active in Kassel.
MUSEUMS AND GALLERIES:
KASSEL - MARBURG.

SCHLIEPSTEIN, Gerhard
German, 20th century.
Born 21 October 1886, in Brunswick.
Sculptor. Genre scenes.
Gerhard Schliepstein executed models for the Rosenthal and Berlin porcelain works.

SCHLIER, Daniel
French, 20th - 21st century.
Born 1960, in Dannemarie (Haut-Rhin).
Painter (including mixed media), assemblage artist.
Daniel Schlier lives and works in Strasbourg. He uses various techniques, including painting under glass or working in tempera on a cork or glass fibre substrate. His work is eclectic and somewhat Surrealist, combining real objects, such as shoes, stones, animal figures, bridges, boats and the like, with fantastical elements and allusions to images drawn from art history.

He has been involved in a number of group exhibitions, notably in 2000, at *Offre Publique d'Échange (O.P.E.)* (*Share Exchange Offer*) held by the FRAC Collection in Poitou-Charentes and at the Voûtes du Port Municipal Gallery in Royan, in 2002, at *Le Portrait s'envisage...* (*Portraiture Looks Inward*), held at the Château de Tanlay (Yonne); in 2002, as a guest of Richard Fauguet, at the Musée de l'Abbaye Ste-Croix in Les Sables d'Olonne; and, in 2003, at *Esprit des lieux* (*The Spirit of Places*), an exhibition held within the framework of *Trésors publics, 20 ans de création dans les Fonds régionaux d'art contemporain (FRAC)* (*Public Treasury, 20 Years of Creation in the Regional Collection of Contemporary Art*), an event held at the Papal Palace in Avignon.

Schlier has also exhibited solo, notably in 1994, at the Galerie Jean-François Dumont in Bordeaux; in 1996, at the Büchsenhausen Exhibition Halls in Innsbruck; in 1997, at the École Régionale des Beaux-Arts in Nantes; in 1997, at the La Ferme du Buisson Centre d'Art Contemporain in Noisel (Marne-la-Vallée); in 1997, at the Le Channel Gallery in Calais; in 2002, at the Galerie Art-Concept in Paris; in 2002, at Decimus Magnus Art Gallery in Bordeaux; in 2002, at *Richard Fauguet et Daniel Schlier: œuvres à quatre mains* (*Richard Fauguet and Daniel Schlier: The Work of Four Hands*), held at the Regional Centre d'Art Contemporain in Montbéliard; in 2003, at the Le Quartier Centre d'Art Contemporain in Quimper; and, in 2003, at the Musée d'Art Moderne et Contemporain in Strasbourg.
BIBLIOGRAPHY:
Besson, Christian, *Les Jours maigres, les jours gras*, exhibition catalogue, Centre d'Art contemporain La Ferme du Buisson, Marne-la-Vallée, 1997 (text in French and English).
Arnaudet, Didier, "*Daniel Schlier. Des images entre deux eaux*' in *Art Press* n° 227, periodical, Paris, September 1997.
Hergott, Fabrice/Brugerolles, Marie de/Guignon, Emmanuel, *Daniel Schlier*, exhibition catalogue, Musées de Strasbourg, Strasbourg, 2003.
MUSEUMS AND GALLERIES:
ANGOULÊME (FRAC Poitou-Charentes): *Blowers* (1995); *Landscape (Inverted France)* - PARIS (FNAC): *Untitled* (1988, drawing with watercolour) - SÉLESTAT (FRAC Alsace): *Head Admixture with Bird* (1992).

SCHLIER, Michael
German, 18th century.
Born 1744, in Königstein (Hesse); died 23 July 1807.
Painter. Architectural views, church interiors.
Schlier was a pupil of Christian Stöcklin.
MUSEUMS AND GALLERIES:
FRANKFURT AM MAIN (Historisches Mus.): *Ancient Ruins; Market Place in Antwerp* (on wood).
AUCTION RECORDS:
LONDON, 8 July 1992, *Church Interior* (1789, oil on panel, 9 3/4 x 11 1/2 ins / 24.8 x 29.4 cm) GBP 2,200. LONDON, 9 July 1993, *Architectural Capriccio of the Interior of a Magnificent Baroque Church Decorated with the Arms of Clement XII* (oil on panel, 17 3/4 x 22 1/4 ins / 45 x 56.8 cm) GBP 4,600.

SCHLIESSER, Thomas
German, 20th century.
Painter, installation artist, mixed media.
Having been both a mime artist and a clown, Thomas Schliesser chose to become a 'shadow painter'. In each of his works he used a different specific material, such as industrial oil, fragments of aluminium, carbon paper, peat or graphite mixed with paint.
AUCTION RECORDS:
PARIS, 8 Oct 1989, *Bridge* (1987, oil/aluminium/canvas, 59 x 78 3/4 ins / 150 x 200 cm) FRF 30,000.

SCHLIESSLER, Otto
German, 20th century.
Born 18 October 1885, in Forbach.
Sculptor, engraver.

Otto Schliesser was the pupil of Hermann Volz in Karlsruhe and continued his training in Rome and Florence.
Museums and Galleries:
Karlsruhe - Mannheim - Nuremberg - Wiesbaden - Worms.

SCHLIESSMANN, Hans
German, 19th - 20th century.
Born 6 February 1852, in Mainz; died 14 February 1920, in Vienna.
Active in Austria.
Watercolourist, illustrator, newspaper cartoonist, humorist, lithographer. Genre scenes.
Hans Schliessmann was initially apprenticed in a xylographic (wood engraving) studio in Vienna, where he soon settled. He collaborated on a number of satirical periodicals, in particular *Humoristische Blätter* from 1874 and the revue *Kikeriki* from 1880 onwards, and others including *Fliegende Blätter* and *Wiener Luft*. He contributed to the albums *Wien und Niederösterreich* (*Vienna and Lower Austria*) and *Österreichische Monarchie in Wort und Bild* (*Austrian Monarchy in Words and Pictures*). Schliessmann also published a number of his own albums, including the 1889 *Schliessmann Album*, followed by *Wiener Schattenbilder* (*Viennese Shadow Pictures*) in 1892, *Dirigenten von Gestern und Heute* (*Conductors of Yesterday and Today*) in 1928 and *Konzertierende Frauen* (*Women Concert Performers*) in 1930.

In all his activities Hans Schliessmann was an illustrator of contemporary popular Viennese culture. His humour was often caustic, as in the *Engravings of Original Fashions for Gigolos or Those Disposed to Become Gigolos*.
Bibliography:
Osterwalder, Marcus (ed.), *Dictionnaire des illustrateurs 1800-1914*, Ides et Calendes, Neuchâtel, 1989.

SCHLIETER, L. W.
German, 19th century.
Miniaturist.

SCHLIMARSKI, Heinrich Hans
Austrian, 19th - 20th century.
Born 5 October 1859, in Olmütz (now Olomouc, Czech Republic).
Painter. Portraits, genre scenes.
Heinrich Schlimarski, who was a pupil of Hans Makart at the fine arts academy in Vienna, also studied in Munich and in Italy.
Museums and Galleries:
Baden-Baden (Schloss): *Shakespeare at the Court of Elizabeth.*
Auction records:
Vienna, 19 June 1979, *Portrait of a Young Girl* (oil on canvas, 27½ x 22¾ ins / 70 x 58 cm) ATS 28,000. London, 18 Feb 1983, *Oriental Dancer* (oil on canvas remounted/panel, 58½ x 32¾ ins / 148.5 x 83.2 cm) GBP 3,800. London, 28 March 1990, *Oriental Beauty Offering a Bowl of Fruit* (oil on canvas, 48¾ x 34½ ins / 124 x 87.5 cm) GBP 9,900.

SCHLIMPERT, Johann Gottlob
German, 18th century.
Active in Meissen.
Painter (porcelain).

SCHLINTZING, Liborius
German, 18th century.
Engraver (burin), painter. Monograms.
Schlintzing engraved *Pêche étrange* and *Caiaphas Judging Jesus*.

SCHLIPF, Ernst
German, 20th century.
Born 3 December 1883; died 1915.
Painter, engraver. Landscapes.
Ernst Schlipf was taught, presumably at the fine arts academy in Stuttgart, by Robert Pötzelberger, Karl de Kalckreuth, Carlos Grethe and Adolf Hölzel. He was killed on the Eastern Front.

SCHLIPF, Eugen
German, 19th - 20th century.
Born 10 March 1869, in Buchau (Württemberg).
Sculptor, painter. Busts, medals.
Eugen Schlipf was the pupil of the sculptors Adolf Donndorf at the fine arts academy in Stuttgart and Wilhelm von Rümann at the Munich academy.
Museums and Galleries:
Biberach: *Bust of Emperor Wilhelm II; Wilhelm II* (plaquette); *Franz-Josef I* (plaquette); *The Tuba Player.*

SCHLIPPENBACH, Andreas
German, 18th century.
Born 1705, in Trondheim; died 1770, in Trondheim.
Painter.
Schlippenbach painted a portrait of a child in 1747.

SCHLIPPENBACH, Paul von (Baron)
German, 19th - 20th century.
Born 20 March 1869, in Olai, near Mitau (now Jelgava, Latvia); died 9 October 1933, in Berlin.
Painter, engraver. Portraits, landscapes, urban landscapes.
Paul von Schlippenbach was the pupil of Jean-Paul Laurens at the Académie Julian in Paris, where he was also a frequent visitor to Whistler's studio. He engraved a series of portraits of German theatrical artists in Berlin.
Auction records:
London, 8 Feb 1984, *View of Venice* (1909, oil on canvas, 36½ x 42½ ins / 92.4 x 108 cm) GBP 1,400. London, 21 Oct 1988, *Piazetta in Venice Seen from the Lagoon* (1909, oil on canvas, 36¼ x 43¼ ins / 92 x 110 cm) GBP 6,050.

SCHLITT, Heinrich
German, 19th - 20th century.
Born 21 August 1849, in Biebrich-Mosbach; died 1923, in Munich.
Painter, illustrator. Genre scenes.
Heinrich Schlitt was a pupil of Wilhelm von Lindenschmit at the fine arts academy in Munich, where he settled. He specialised in magical scenes peopled with gnomes.

Schlitt

Heinrich Schlitt

Museums and Galleries:
Wiesbaden: *Gnome as a Painter.*
Auction records:
London, 25 Nov 1981, *David Teniers in his Studio* (1881, oil on canvas, 24½ x 34 ins / 62 x 86.5 cm) GBP 4,200. Cologne, 15 Oct 1988, *Fairy Landscape with a Gnome by the Edge of a Pond where a Boat made of Shells is Floating, Pulled by a Toad* (1924, oil on panel, 10¼ x 13¾ ins / 26 x 35 cm) DEM 9,200. London, 28 Oct 1992, *Gnome Carrying a Poisonous Mushroom with a Snail* (oil on panel, 10¼ x 8¼ ins / 26 x 21 cm) GBP 1,540. New York, 19 Jan 1994, *Pose for a Portrait* (1880, oil on panel, 13 x 17¼ ins / 32.1 x 43.8 cm) USD 5,463. Munich, 3 Dec 1996, *Knife-Grinder* (1883, oil on canvas, 23½ x 17¾ ins / 59.5 x 45 cm) DEM 12,000.

SCHLITTE, Friedrich
German, 19th century.
Born 14 October 1820, in Magdeburg.
Active in Leipzig.
Engraver (wood).

SCHLITTER, Johann Georg.
See **SCHLUTTER**

SCHLITTERLAU, Friedrich Gottlob
German, 18th century.
Born 1730, in Dresden; died 22 April 1782, in Dresden.
Engraver (burin).
Schlitterlau engraved portraits.

SCHLITTGEN, Hermann
German, 19th - 20th century.
Born 23 June 1859, in Roitzsch; died 9 June 1930, in Wasserburg.
Painter, engraver, illustrator, caricaturist.
Hermann Schlittgen was a pupil at the fine arts academies in Leipzig and Munich, and was taught by Theodor Hagen at the fine arts school in Weimar and by Jules Lefebvre at the Académie Julian in Paris. In addition to collaborating on *Fliegende Blätter*, Schlittgen illustrated *Humoristische Gechichten* and Hackländer's *Der letzte Bombardier* (*The Last Bombardier*). He illustrated scenes of daily life using a simple but effective style of draughtsmanship and in a spirit of sociological enquiry rather than caustic satire.

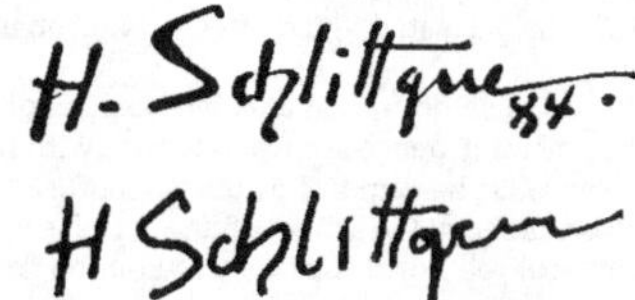

BIBLIOGRAPHY:
Osterwalder, Marcus (ed.), *Dictionnaire des illustrateurs 1800-1914*, Ides et Calendes, Neuchâtel, 1989.
MUSEUMS AND GALLERIES:
LEIPZIG: *Woman at the Piano* - WEIMAR: *Self-portrait.*
AUCTION RECORDS:
STUTTGART, 9 May 1981, *At the Theatre* (pastel, 24 x 20 ins / 61 x 51 cm) DEM 5,800. MUNICH, 18 May 1988, *The Apprentice Jockey* (oil on canvas, 53 1/4 x 35 ins / 135 x 88 cm) DEM 5,720.

SCHLITZ, Emil Friedrich Franz Maximilian von (Count), called von Görtz
German, 19th - 20th century.
Born 15 February 1851, in Berlin; died 9 October 1914, in Frankfurt am Main.
Sculptor.
Emil von Schlitz was the pupil of Josef Echteler in Munich and was director of the school of fine arts in Weimar from 1885 to 1901. Sculptures by Schlitz in Berlin include the *Monument to Ludwig the Roman* in the Siegesallee, the *Monument to Admiral Coligny* at the Schloss and the *Angel of the Resurrection* at the cathedral.

SCHLITZOR, Erhard
French, 16th century.
Active in Strasbourg.
Painter.

SCHLOBACH, Willy
Belgian, 19th - 20th century.
Born 27 August 1864, in Brussels; died 1951, in Nonnenhorn (Bavaria).
Painter, watercolourist. Portraits, landscapes, architectural views, still-lifes.
Groupe des Vingt (XX).
Willy Schlobach was a pupil at the fine arts academies in Brussels and Ghent. During a stay in England from 1884 to 1887, he was very impressed by Turner and by Pre-Raphaelite Symbolism. On his return to Belgium, he struck up a friendship with Théo van Rysselberghe and subsequently settled at Nonnenhorn on Lake Constance.

In Brussels, Willy Schlobach took part in the exhibitions of the Groupe des XX, of which he was a founder member, as well as those of La Libre Esthétique (Free Aesthetics) from 1902 onwards.

Schlobach practised the Divisionism of the Neo-Impressionists, but abandoned this technique around 1890 to ally himself more closely to the Pre-Raphaelites, as his output became more literary in character. He subsequently renounced this false Pre-Raphaelitism, returning to the effects of light and mists which were the legacy of Turner.
MUSEUMS AND GALLERIES:
BRUSSELS (Bibliothèque royale Albert Ier): *La Morte* (*Dead Woman*) (pastel) - TOURNAI: *Landscape.*
AUCTION RECORDS:
PARIS, 23 May 1975, *Riverside* (oil on canvas, 24 x 27 1/2 ins / 61 x 70 cm) FRF 950. LONDON, 19 Oct 1989, *Cliffs in Cornwall* (oil on canvas, 23 3/4 x 31 1/2 ins / 60.4 x 80 cm) GBP 6,600.

SCHLÖDER, Martin Johann, or Schleder
German, 17th century.
Born 5 June 1646, in Frankfurt am Main; died 1703, in Frankfurt am Main.
Painter.
In 1680, Schlöder painted angels' heads in St Catherine's church in Frankfurt.

SCHLOEM, SCHLOEP, SCHLOES.
See **SCHLOM, SCHLOP, SCHLOS** for the names starting with these letters

SCHLOESSER, Carl Bernhard.
See **SCHLÖSSER**

SCHLOETH, Lukas Ferdinand. See **SCHLÖTH**

SCHLÖGL, Anton
Austrian, 19th century.
Active in Vienna c. 1850.
Lithographer.

SCHLÖGL, Johann
Austrian, 19th century.
Born 29 November 1794; died 24 December 1856, in Vienna.
Painter. Flowers. Stage sets.
MUSEUMS AND GALLERIES:
VIENNA (Opera Museum): stage set for Verdi's 'Attila' (sketches).

SCHLÖGL, Johann Georg. See **SCHLEGEL**

SCHLÖGL, Josef von
Austrian, 19th - 20th century.
Born 31 March 1851, in Vienna.
Painter. Mountainscapes, waterscapes, landscapes.
Josef von Schlögl lived in Merano.
MUSEUMS AND GALLERIES:
BAUTZEN: *Autumn Day by a Lakeside.*
AUCTION RECORDS:
MUNICH, 19 Sept 1979, *View of Lake Maggiore* (oil on panel, 15 3/4 x 24 ins / 40 x 61 cm) DEM 6,500. VIENNA, 17 March 1981, *Mountain Landscape* (oil on panel, 18 x 14 3/4 ins / 46 x 37.5 cm) ATS 30,000. MUNICH, 22 June 1993, *Obersee with the Devil's Horns; Lake Garda* (1900, oil on panel, a pair, each 8 1/4 x 11 1/2 ins / 21 x 29 cm) DEM 8,050. MUNICH, 21 June 1994, *By the Glacier* (1903, oil on panel, 12 3/4 x 17 1/4 ins / 32.5 x 43.5 cm) DEM 9,200.

SCHLÖGL, Rupert Egidius
German, 17th - 18th century.
Active in Landshut between 1690 and 1720.
Painter.

SCHLÖLER, Juge. See **SCHIÖLER Inge**

SCHLOMACH, Melchior
German, 17th century.

Born 16 May 1607; died after 1678.
Draughtsman.
Schlomach was an army general.

SCHLÖMANN, Eduard
German, 20th century.
Born 25 June 1888, in Düsseldorf.
Painter. Landscapes, seascapes.
Eduard Schlömann studied in Düsseldorf and was the pupil of Gustav Schönleber at the school of fine arts in Karlsruhe. He travelled in Tierra del Fuego and Patagonia.
MUSEUMS AND GALLERIES:
DÜSSELDORF: *Patagonian Landscape* - KARLSRUHE: *Port.*

SCHLOMKA, Alfred
Hungarian, 19th - 20th century.
Born in Pest (now Budapest).
Painter. Landscapes.
Alfred Schlomka worked in France and exhibited in Paris, at the Salon des Artistes Français where he was awarded an honourable mention in 1886, and at the Exposition Universelle where he was awarded a silver medal in 1889.
AUCTION RECORDS:
PARIS, 29 Jan 1951, *Antibes,* FRF 2,800. PARIS, 12 May 2000, *On the Heights of Algiers* (1888, oil on canvas, 26 x 21 ins / 65 x 53 cm) FRF 30,000. VERSAILLES, 12 Nov 2000, *The Joys of Childhood* (oil on canvas, 29 x 21 ins / 73 x 54 cm) FRF 12,000. NEW YORK, 3 Oct 2001, *Playful Kittens* (1915, oil on canvas, 29 x 24 ins / 74 x 61 cm) USD 3,500.

SCHLÖPKE, Theodor
German, 19th century.
Born 6 March 1812, in Schwerin; died 13 January 1878, in Schwerin.
Painter, illustrator. Historical subjects, portraits.
Schlöpke went on many study tours. In 1853, he became painter to the court of the Grand Duke Frederick Francis II of Mecklenburg. From 1855 to 1857, he lived in Paris, where he worked under the direction of Horace Vernet.

Among the pictures he painted for the Grand Duke Frederick Francis II of Mecklenburg are several on subjects from the Schleswig-Holstein War. During his stay in Paris, he painted his major work *The Death of Niclot.*
MUSEUMS AND GALLERIES:
SCHWERIN: a large collection of works.
AUCTION RECORDS:
COLOGNE, 21 Oct 1977, *The Pillaging of a Farm* (oil on canvas, 18 1/2 x 23 1/2 ins / 47 x 60 cm) DEM 5,500. AMSTERDAM, 24 March 1999, *Equestrian Portrait of Frederick Francis II* (oil on canvas, 39 x 31 ins / 98 x 80 cm) NLG 6,500.

SCHLÖR, Hans
German, 17th century.
Active in Lübeck between 1626 and 1640.
Painter.

SCHLÖR, Sem or Simon, or Schleer or Schleyer
German, 16th century.
Born c. 1530, in Lautenbach; died 1597 or 1598, in Schwäbisch Hall.
Sculptor.

SCHLORCH, Johann Christoph.
See **SCHLURCH**

SCHLOS, Johann, or Schloss
German, 18th century.
Born 17 September 1684, in Hadamar; died 16 July 1760, in Cologne.
Cabinet maker.

SCHLOSS, Gerard van, known as Du Château
Flemish School, 17th century.
Active in Brussels.
Painter. Portraits.
Gerard van Schloss was court painter to Habsburg Emperor Leopold I, of whom he made several portraits. Leopold sent him to Spain to paint the portrait of his fiancée, the Infanta Margarita Teresa.

SCHLÖSSER, Bernhard
German, 19th century.
Born 4 March 1802, in Darmstadt; died 8 September 1859, in Frankfurt am Main.
Painter, lithographer. Portraits, genre scenes. Miniatures.
Bernhard Schlösser studied with Franz Herbert Müller in Darmstadt. He also trained in Paris.
MUSEUMS AND GALLERIES:
GDANSK (Municipal Library): *Portrait of Schopenhauer* (lithograph).
AUCTION RECORDS:
LONDON, 17 June 1992, *Prayer for the Sick Child* (1839, oil on canvas, 20 1/2 x 19 ins / 52 x 48 cm) GBP 3,300. BERN, 6 Nov 2002, *Young Bird Lover* (1891, oil on canvas, 43 x 26 ins / 109 x 66 cm) CHF 4,600.

SCHLÖSSER, Carl Bernhard
German, 19th - 20th century.
Born 1832, in Darmstadt; died after 1914, probably in London.
Painter, pastellist, draughtsman (charcoal), engraver. Figures, portraits, genre scenes, interiors with figures.
Carl Schlösser was the pupil of Thomas Couture in Paris, where he also studied at the school of fine arts. He was a frequent exhibitor at the Royal Academy in London from 1858 onwards.
MUSEUMS AND GALLERIES:
DARMSTADT: *Portrait of Miss Ethel* - LIVERPOOL: *Village Lawyer.*
AUCTION RECORDS:
NEW YORK, 16 Nov 1910, *Reading the News,* USD 70. PARIS, 13-14 Jan 1926, *Schoolmaster,* FRF 520. PHILADELPHIA, 30-31 March 1932, *Mozart Playing 'Don Juan' to his Wife,* USD 390. PARIS, 4 April 1946, *Visiting Grandfather* (1867) FRF 32,000. LONDON, 21 Jan 1966, *Young Austrian Peasant,* Gns 300. LUCERNE, 25 Nov 1972, *Interior,* CHF 9,000. MUNICH, 21 Sept 1978, *Forbidden Fruit* (1863, oil on canvas, 26 x 42 1/2 ins / 66 x 108 cm) DEM 36,000. NEW YORK, 2 May 1979, *An Interesting Story* (oil on canvas, 22 3/4 x 35 ins / 58 x 89 cm) USD 5,200. NEW YORK, 25 Feb 1982, *Reading an Edict* (1867, oil on canvas, 23 x 28 3/4 ins / 58.5 x 73 cm) USD 1,800. LONDON, 21 June 1984, *Young Girl with a Vase of Flowers* (1913, pastel and charcoal, oval, 21 1/4 x 13 1/2 ins / 54 x 34 cm) GBP 750. LONDON, 16 July 1985, *Three Generations* (1865, oil on canvas, 23 1/2 x 18 1/2 ins / 60 x 47 cm) GBP 2,400. LONDON, 21 March 1986, *Cart with Broken Wheel* (1878, oil on canvas, 23 x 45 ins / 58.4 x 114.2 cm) GBP 7,000. NEW YORK, 25 Feb 1988, *The New Pupil* (1862, oil on canvas, 28 3/4 x 24 ins / 73 x 61 cm) USD 11,000. LONDON, 11 Oct 1995, *Young Boy with Cane* (1878, oil on panel, 9 x 3 1/2 ins / 22 x 9 cm) GBP 862. LONDON, 9 Oct 1997, *The Newcomer (Birth)* (1859, oil on canvas, 23 x 26 1/2 ins / 58.4 x 67.3 cm) GBP 3,680.

SCHLOSSER, Ernest
German, 19th - 20th century.
Born in Wiesbaden.
Also active in France.
Sculptor.
Ernest Schlosser was active in Paris, where he was the pupil of Antoine Injalbert. He exhibited at the Salon des Artistes Français in Paris, where he received a commendation in 1909.

SCHLOSSER, Gérard
French, 20th century.
Born 1931, in Lille.

Painter. Figure compositions, landscapes, seascapes. Nouvelle Figuration, Figuration Narrative.

Gérard Schlosser has lived in Paris since 1947. He first worked as a sculptor and goldsmith and did not devote himself to painting until 1953.

Since the 1960s he has exhibited in Paris: from 1965 to 1972 at the Salon de la Jeune Peinture; 1966, *Le Nouveau Paysage* (*The New Landscape*); 1967, *Salle rouge pour le Viet-Nam* (*Red Room for Vietnam*) at the Salon de la Jeune Peinture; 1969, Paris Biennale, Musée Galliéra; 1970, *Aspects de racisme* (*Aspects of Racism*); 1977, *Mythologies quotidiennes* (*Everyday Mythologies*), ARC II (Art, Recherche, Confrontation), Musée d'Art Moderne de la Ville de Paris; 1979, *Tendance de l'Art en France 68-79* (*Trends in French Art 68-79*), ARC II; 1980, *Accrochages IV* (*Hangings IV*), Centre Beaubourg; and: 1971, *Intox*, Maison de la Culture, Grenoble; 1972, Palazzo dei Diamanti, Ferrara; 1981, *L'Arbre* (*The Tree*), Centre Culturel, Boulogne-Billancourt; and elsewhere.

He held solo shows in: 1966, Paris, Galerie du Fleuve; 1972, Genoa and Turin; 1973, Paris, ARC, Musée d'Art Moderne; 1977, Paris, FIAC (Foire Internationale d'Art Contemporain), at the Galerie Beaubourg; 1978, Modena, Galleria Mutina; 1979, Paris, FIAC, Galerie Beaubourg, and Mâcon, Centre d'Action Culturelle; 1980, Château de Ratilly; 1981, Châteauroux, Centre Régional d'Art Contemporain; and elsewhere.

The elements that were to characterise his style were present from the start of his career: a sound acrylic painting technique, the paint often applied over a layer of sand that he used for various purposes at different times; highly realistic figuration, almost photographic; unusual framing that acts as a screen between the eye of the viewer and, on some occasions, the receding planes of the picture; wide fragmented planes that fill entirely the foreground of the canvas - planes of detail so enlarged as to be hardly interpretable. The overall continuity of his work is, however, subject to limited variations from time to time. In the pre-1970s paintings Schlosser uses large planes that concentrate on a body part - often a leg or a forearm - that describes a curve against a usually neutral background. Later, this approach to the human body, which is nearly always at rest, is made in terms of flat surfaces, unmodulated in volume, that are placed next to each other like cut-outs; indeed, in 1968, for example in *Card Players*, he used silhouettes cut out and stuck to an already painted background; and when the background was figurative - for example, a beach - he replaced it with sand attached to the canvas. These juxtapositions of surfaces, painted or otherwise, posed the question of the relationship between surface and image.

However, Schlosser was never tempted to explore this problem in a radical way by giving the surface, the plastic consideration, priority.

On the contrary, in his next period he chose to explore the image and established an almost invariable way of constructing the picture. In the front plane a knee, an arm, a leg, the bottom of a dress or a pair of trousers, takes up half, or more, of the canvas; in the second main plane there is an object, also cut off, social, not neutral in its suggestions - a bag, a shoe, a book, a radio, the wing of a car, a wheel, a camping stool; between these two planes, forming a logical and plastic link between them, he places grass or sand; sometimes, at the back, there is a distant view of a landscape or the sky. When he paints skin or textiles he uses the sand not as such, but to convey the grain of the skin or the silkiness of the material.

In the 1980s his work underwent a radical change of direction. He painted landscapes and seascapes, the sea often extending the land without any interruption. Here it is more tempting to speak of realism, in the style of Courbet or Denis Rivière, than of hyperrealism, with which, however badly defined, these landscapes have nothing in common. In the 1990s, no doubt to bring together his preceding periods, he reintroduced his earlier anecdotes into the recent natural landscapes.

Auction records:

Paris, 2 Dec 1974, *Cat* (1966) FRF 5,800. Paris, 21 April 1975, *Entr'acte* (1966) FRF 7,200. Paris, 2 Dec 1976, *You are coming with me* (1973, acrylic and sand, 39 1/4 x 39 1/4 ins / 100 x 100 cm) FRF 7,000. Paris, 8 March 1977, *Still 10 minutes* (1970, acrylic/canvas, 59 x 59 ins / 150 x 150 cm) FRF 7,200. Paris, 19 March 1979, *There's no one here* (1973, acrylic, 51 1/4 x 51 1/4 ins / 130 x 130 cm) FRF 10,000. Paris, 26 April 1982, *The wine was good* (1973, acrylic/canvas, 51 1/4 x 51 1/4 ins / 130 x 130 cm) FRF 20,000. Paris, 26 Nov 1984, *Oh, it's lovely here!* (1973, oil on canvas, 74 3/4 x 74 3/4 ins / 190 x 190 cm) FRF 48,000. Paris, 6 June 1985, *The sun's nice* (1974, acrylic/canvas) FRF 26,000. Paris, 3 Dec 1987, *We still haven't had news of them* (oil on canvas, 74 3/4 x 74 3/4 ins / 190 x 190 cm) FRF 24,000. Paris, 20 March 1988, *It's better without* (1986, acrylic/canvas, 63 3/4 x 51 1/4 ins / 162 x 130 cm) FRF 25,000. Paris, 16 Oct 1988, *You've got a mark on your dress* (1973, acrylic/sanded canvas, 50 3/4 x 38 1/4 ins / 129 x 97 cm) FRF 18,000; *Place des Fêtes, on the left* (1981, acrylic/sanded canvas, 39 1/4 x 39 1/4 ins / 100 x 100 cm) FRF 25,000. Paris, 21 June 1990, *Study for a Painting* (1989, collage of photos and manuscript/paper, 11 3/4 x 15 3/4 ins / 30 x 40 cm) FRF 4,000. Paris, 26 Oct 1990, *You've got a mark on your dress* (1973, acrylic/canvas, 51 1/4 x 38 1/4 ins / 130 x 97 cm) FRF 44,000. Paris, 23 March 1992, *Untitled* (1964, acrylic/canvas, 31 3/4 x 39 1/4 ins / 80.5 x 100 cm) FRF 10,000. Paris, 21 May 1992, *His face fell* (1985, acrylic/canvas, 59 x 59 ins / 150 x 150 cm) FRF 32,000. Paris, 14 March 1993, *Untitled* (1979, acrylic/canvas, 70 x 112 1/4 ins / 178 x 285 cm) FRF 45,000. Paris, 25 March 1994, *I'd live there all the year round* (1974, acrylic/canvas, 59 x 59 ins / 150 x 150 cm) FRF 29,000. Paris, 29-30 June 1995, *Shipwreck* (1966, acrylic/canvas, 51 1/4 x 63 3/4 ins / 130 x 162 cm) FRF 34,500. Paris, 1 July 1996, *Because of the red light* (1985, acrylic on sanded canvas, 39 1/4 x 39 1/4 ins / 100 x 100 cm) FRF 17,000. Paris, 11 Dec 1997, *Phew I* (1966, acrylic/canvas, 63 3/4 x 51 1/4 ins / 162 x 130 cm) FRF 49,000. Paris, 11 March 1998, *That's better* (1976, acrylic/sanded canvas, 39 1/4 x 39 1/4 ins / 100 x 100 cm) FRF 87,000. Paris, 17 June 1999, *J'en ai gardé quelques unes* (1989, oil on canvas, 51 x 51 ins / 130 x 130 cm) FRF 65,000. Paris, 11 Dec 1999, *La séance de 16h* (acrylic on grained canvas, 51 x 51 ins / 130 x 130 cm) FRF 43,000. Paris, 19 April 2000, *11H35* (acrylic on sanded canvas, 45 x 57 ins / 114 x 146 cm) FRF 68,000. Paris, 7 June 2000, *Trois Beaks* (1972, acrylic on sanded canvas, 39 x 39 ins / 100 x 100 cm) FRF 68,000. Lille, 7 April 2001, *One Would Not Believe It* (acrylic on sanded canvas, 39 x 39 ins / 100 x 100 cm) FRF 65,000. Lille, 27 Oct 2001, *Apres ce qui s'est passe* (*After This Which Has Happened*) (acrylic, 79 x 67 ins / 200 x 170 cm) FRF 165,000. Paris, 4 Feb 2002, *Ils ne le diront pas* (*They Will Not Say It*) (1990, acrylic on sanded canvas, 79 x 79 ins / 200 x 200 cm) EUR 23,000. Paris, 18 March 2002, *In How Much Time?* (acrylic, 79 x 79 ins / 200 x 200 cm) EUR 16,500. Paris, 29 April 2003, *Il ne vient pas* (*It Is Not Coming*) (1970, acrylic, 44 x 57 ins / 113 x 145 cm) EUR 25,000. Paris, 2 July 2003, *You Come* (1966, acrylic, 51 x 63 ins / 130 x 161 cm) EUR 22,500. Paris, 29 March 2004, *You Know that Josette is going to Marry?* (1970, acrylic on sanded canvas, 79 x 79 ins / 200 x 200 cm) EUR 37,000. Paris, 27 May 2004, *You are Sending the Social Security Papers* (1972, oil on canvas, 64 x 51 ins / 163 x 130 cm) EUR 25,000.

SCHLÖSSER, Hermann Julius

German, 19th century.

Born 21 December 1832, in Elberfeld; died 21 June 1894, in Rome.
Painter, sculptor. Mythological subjects, figures, portraits.

Hermann Schlösser studied in Düsseldorf with Carl Sohn and then, between 1855 and 1858, in Rome and Paris.

MUSEUMS AND GALLERIES:
GÖRLITZ (Städtische Kunstsammlungen): *Pandora before Prometheus* - HAMBURG: *Thetis Surprised by Peleus* - WUPPERTAL: *The Hero Triumphant in Death; Amymone Rescued by Poseidon; Hercules Delivering Hesione.*

AUCTION RECORDS:
PARIS, 18 Oct 1995, *The Birth of Venus* (1870, oil on canvas, 102 x 79½ ins / 259 x 202 cm) FRF 300,000. LONDON, 29 Nov 2001, *Diana and her Nymphs* (oil on canvas, 53 x 73 ins / 134 x 186 cm) GBP 18,000.

SCHLOSSER, Johann Georg
German, 18th - 19th century.
Born 1749, in Ludwigsburg; died 5 January 1816, in Nymphenburg.
Painter (porcelain). Landscapes.

Schlosser worked at the Nymphenburg porcelain factory.

SCHLOSSER, Johann Ludwig
German, 18th century.
Active in Nassau-Saarbrücken c. 1787.
Painter (porcelain).

SCHLÖSSER, Leopold Ludwig, or Schlosser
German, 19th century.
Born to a family originally from Berlin; died 1 April 1836, in Düsseldorf.
Landscape artist.

In 1828 and 1829, Leopold Schlösser travelled to Rome and Naples with his master, Carl Blechen. From 1832 to 1835, he studied at the academy in Düsseldorf with Schadow and Schirmer.

SCHLÖSSER, Richard
German, 20th century.
Born 21 March 1879, in Hanover.
Painter.

Richard Schlösser was the pupil of both Carl Bantzer and Hermann Prell at the fine arts academy in Dresden. He was himself a professor and an art critic.

MUSEUMS AND GALLERIES:
BERLIN (Nationalgal.).

SCHLOT, Georg
German, 16th century.
Active in Frankfurt am Main c. 1515.
Painter.

SCHLOTERMANN, Heinrich
German, 19th - 20th century.
Born 24 July 1859, in Ruhland (Thuringia).
Painter. Landscapes.

Heinrich Schlotermann was the pupil of Eugen Bracht at the Hochschule für Kunst in Berlin.

SCHLÖTH, Achilles
Swiss, 19th - 20th century.
Born 7 November 1858, in Basel; died 5 July 1904, in Basel.
Sculptor.

Achilles Schlöth was the nephew and pupil of Lukas Ferdinand Schlöth.

SCHLÖTH, Lukas Ferdinand, or Schloth
Swiss, 19th century.
Born 25 January 1818, in Basel; died 2 August 1891, in Thal.
Sculptor.

Schlöth was one of the masters of Swiss sculpture. He studied in Basel, Munich, and mainly in Rome. He produced a large number of works.

MUSEUMS AND GALLERIES:
BASEL: *Adam and Eve; Psyche; Jason and the Golden Fleece; Head of Christ*; Roman vase with medallion; vase with Bacchus, Love and Apollo - NEUCHÂTEL: *Maximilien de Meuron.*

SCHLOTHEIM, Ernst Friedrich von (Baron)
German, 18th - 19th century.
Born 2 April 1764, in Almenhausen; died 28 March 1832, in Gotha.
Draughtsman. Natural history.

Ernst von Schlotheim illustrated books on natural history.

SCHLOTHEIM, Hartmann von
German, 18th - 19th century.
Born in Gotha.
Draughtsman.

Hartmann von Schlotheim was a Prussian officer until 1805, then he trained in Potsdam, where he was a pupil of Wilhelm Reuter.

SCHLOTT, Franz Anton
German, 18th century.
Born 1697, in Würzburg; died 14 December 1736, in Bamberg.
Sculptor. Religious subjects.

Franz Anton Schlott was a son of the painter Joachim David Schlott. He worked as a sculptor in wood and stone for the churches in Bamberg and the surrounding area.

SCHLOTT, Franz Joachim
Austrian, 18th century.
Born 1696, in Würzburg; died 4 October 1775, in Bamberg.
Sculptor, stucco artist.

Franz Joachim Schlott was the brother of Franz Anton. He carved the high altar, organ chest and confessionals for the church of the Salesian Sisters in Amberg.

SCHLOTT, Joachim David
German, 17th century.
Born 1644; died 21 January 1707, in Würzburg.
Painter.

SCHLOTTER, Eberhard
German, 20th century.
Born 1921, in Hildesheim.
Painter. Local scenes, landscapes, urban landscapes, still-lifes.

Eberhard Schlotter was a pupil at the fine arts academy in Munich. At the end of World War II he settled in Darmstadt, and subsequently went to work in Altea in Spain from 1956 to 1960.

After 1950, Schlotter, who remained a resolutely figurative artist, executed a number of decorative murals on public buildings in Darmstadt. During his stay in Spain he painted folklore scenes, while in his usual environment in Germany he seems to have been affected in the longer term by the desolate landscapes of war. Using a spectrum of greys, heightened in a cold manner with particular shades of pink and violet, he painted towns which had been destroyed, with stretches of crumbling wall and deserted beaches, seemingly devoid of human presence since time immemorial, and still-lifes, the origins of which appear to be rooted in a distant, timeless landscape.

Schlotter took part in a number of collective exhibitions, including the Exposition Internationale in Brussels in 1958, the exhibition at Grenchen in Switzerland in 1961, the Triennale d'Art Graphique en Couleur and others. He showed collections of his work in solo exhibitions, the first of which was mounted in Darmstadt in 1949. In 1954 he was awarded a prize by the federal league of German industry to encourage artists and in 1959, he was awarded the Stroeher prize.

AUCTION RECORDS:

HEIDELBERG, 14 Oct 1988, *Fiesta Campera* (1963, watercolour, 14 1/4 x 18 3/4 ins / 36.5 x 47.5 cm) DEM 1,400. KEMPTEN, 11 Jan 2002, *Fishermen on Beach* (1946, oil on canvas, 25 x 31 ins / 63 x 80 cm) EUR 1,750. MUNICH, 13 Nov 2003, *The Big Shadow* (1954, mixed media, 27 x 17 ins / 69 x 44 cm) EUR 1,500. STUTTGART, 30 April 2004, *Southern Town Landscape in Midday Heat* (mixed media, oil and sand, 28 x 34 ins / 71 x 86 cm) EUR 2,200.

SCHLOTTER, Georg
German, 20th century.
Born 23 February 1889, in Hildesheim; died 5 December 1915, in Göttingen.
Painter. Figures, flowers.

Georg Schlotter was the brother of Heinrich Schlotter and was possibly also related to Eberhard Schlotter. In 1920, the museum in Hildesheim organised a posthumous exhibition of his works.

SCHLOTTER, Heinrich
German, 20th century.
Born 16 June 1886, in Hildesheim.
Sculptor.

Heinrich Schlotter was the younger brother of Georg Schlotter and may have been related to Eberhard Schlotter. He studied under Walter Schmarje and Wilhelm Haverkamp in Berlin.

SCHLOTTERBECK, Christian Jakob
German, 18th - 19th century.
Born 27 July 1757, in Böblingen; died 1811; in 1820 according to some sources.
Painter, engraver.

Christian Schlotterbeck was the son of a stonemason. He studied medicine, then devoted himself to art. He studied at the Karlsakademie in Wurtemberg in 1784, then with Tischbein and J.G. von Müller. In 1785, he was appointed engraver to the court of Wurtemberg. He painted portraits of Duke Charles and King Frederick, but his artistic talents were mainly employed in engraving.

SCHLOTTERBECK, Wilhelm Friedrich
Swiss, 19th century.
Born 23 February 1777, near Basel; died 6 April 1819, in Vienna.
Draughtsman, engraver (aquatint).

Wilhelm Schlotterbeck studied with Christian Mechel in Basel. He settled in Vienna in 1801 and in 1803, he travelled to Salzburg. Between 1803 and 1812, he engraved a *Collection of Views of Switzerland,* 60 views of Salzburg and Berchtesgaden, and some views of Vienna, Austria and Styria.

SCHLOTTHAUER, Josef
German, 19th century.
Born 14 March 1789, in Munich; died 5 June 1869, in Munich.
Painter, lithographer.

Josef Schlotthauer started out as a carpenter. His talent for drawing led him to join the academy in Munich as a student. He abandoned his studies for a time towards the end of the Napoleonic Wars, in order to enlist as a volunteer. On returning to Munich, he joined Cornelius' studio in 1819, and painted a number of frescoes after the cartoons drawn by his master. In 1838, he painted a number of altars for Bamberg cathedral. A visit to Pompeii in 1845 led him to discover a new technique for painting frescoes known as stereochromy. He is also known for a series of 53 lithographs he produced in 1832 after Holbein's *Dance of Death.*

MUSEUMS AND GALLERIES:

MUNICH (Pinakothek): *Head of Christ.*

SCHLOTTHAUER, Karl
German, 19th century.
Born 1803, in Munich.
Painter. Landscapes, architectural views.

Karl Schlotthauer was taught by his uncle, Josef Schlotthauer. He taught at the school of fine arts in Lindau. He often painted views of the Bavarian Alps.

SCHLÖZER, Caroline Friederike von
Maiden name: Röderer
German, 18th century.
Born 1753, in Göttingen (Lower Saxony); died May 1808, in Göttingen.
Engraver, painter. Portraits, landscapes.

On 5 November 1769, she married the historian August Ludwig von Schlözer.

SCHLUBECK, Arthur
German, 20th century.
Born 25 August 1875, in Stettin (now Szczecin, Poland).
Painter. Portraits, local scenes, landscapes.

Arthur Schlubeck lived in Berlin and was a pupil at the fine arts academy there. As well as portraits, local scenes and landscapes he also painted oriental subjects.

SCHLUMBERGER, Camille Gabriel
French, 19th - 20th century.
Born 11 November 1864, in Strasbourg.
Draughtsman.

Camille Gabriel Schlumberger, a grandson of Henri Hofer, was a pupil of J.L. Gérôme, Aimé Morot, Eugène Grasset and Luc-Olivier Merson at the École des Beaux-Arts, Paris. He later worked in Ribeauvillé.

SCHLUMBERGER, Eugène Jacques
French, 20th century.
Born 9 March 1879, in Mulhouse; died 1960.
Painter. Landscapes, flowers.

From 1913 Eugène Jacques Schlumberger exhibited mainly in Paris at the Salon des Artistes Français, where he was awarded a silver medal in 1930, a silver at the time of the Exposition Universelle of 1937, and a gold, out-of-competition, in 1938. He also exhibited in many provincial towns and in Copenhagen.

MUSEUMS AND GALLERIES:

CLERMONT-FERRAND - ROTTERDAM.

AUCTION RECORDS:

PARIS, 15 March 1950, *Flowered Doorway,* FRF 5,100. ENGHIEN-LES-BAINS, 23 June 1985, *Breton Women by the Sea* (oil on canvas, 27 x 30 ins / 68.5 x 76.5 cm) FRF 15,000. LONDON, 20 Oct 1999, *Girl in Boat Reading* (oil on canvas, 24 x 29 ins / 60 x 73 cm) GBP 2,000.

SCHLUMBERGER, Georg
French, 19th century.
Born 1807, in Mulhouse; died 1862, in Zurich.
Draughtsman, painter. Flowers.

SCHLUMPP, Hans, or Schlump
German, 16th century.
Died 1514.
Active in Ulm.
Painter. Monograms.

SCHLUMPRECHT, Heinrich
German, 19th - 20th century.
Born 4 January 1859, in Munich; died 17 December 1908, in Munich.
Engraver, reproductions engraver.

Heinrich Schlumprecht was the brother of Rupert Schlumprecht.

SCHLUMPRECHT, Rupert
German, 19th - 20th century.

Born 24 March 1854, in Munich; died 7 August 1904, in Munich.
Engraver, reproductions engraver.
The brother of Heinrich Schlumprecht, Rupert Schlumprecht was a wood engraver.

SCHLUP, Elisabeth
Swiss, 19th - 20th century.
Born 4 October 1860, in Balm.
Painter. Figures, portraits, genre scenes, landscapes, still-lifes.
Elisabeth Schlup was the pupil of Caspar Ritter at the fine arts school in Karlsruhe. She also studied in Paris and Munich.
MUSEUMS AND GALLERIES:
BERN: *The Little Artist.*

SCHLUPF, Johann
German, 18th century.
Active in Augsburg.
Sculptor.
Johann Schlupf was the master who taught Goetzl.

SCHLUPF, Sebastian Vitus
German, 18th century.
Active in Augsburg.
Sculptor.
In 1793, Sebastian Schlupf was the first professor of drawing at the Hamburg Society for the Advancement of the Arts.

SCHLUPF, Wilhelm
German, 18th century.
Active in Augsburg.
Sculptor.

SCHLURCH, Johann Christoph, or Schlurk or Schlorch or Schlork
German, 18th century.
Active in Berlin between 1704 and 1737.
Engraver (glass).

SCHLUSSELFELD, Hans von (Master).
See **RODLEIN Hans**

SCHLUTER, Andreas
German, 17th - 18th century.
Born c. 1660 or 1664, probably in Danzig (now Gdansk) or in Hamburg; died 1714, in St Petersburg.
Sculptor, architect.
The beginnings of Schluter's career are unknown, but when he arrived in Berlin in 1694, he showed a knowledge of Italian and French sculpture, especially Coysevox, Desjardins and Girardon, that would make it appear he had travelled in France before settling in Germany. As soon as he arrived in Berlin in 1696, he began work on the equestrian memorial statue, originally intended for Frederick III, but which in the end became a monument to the Grand Elector, erected in 1703. This work still shows the influence of Girardon, but Schluter imbued it with a totally different kind of passion. In 1698, he was commissioned to oversee the building of the new palace in Berlin, for which he created Baroque interior decorations inspired by Bernini. In the same year, he also oversaw the work on the Arsenal, which had already been started in 1695, before he arrived. However, he was relieved of this post in 1699, perhaps as a result of a series of complications due to too heavy an attic being placed on the entablature. The masks of dying warriors that he carved for the decoration of the Arsenal have an amazing expressionist quality. As an architect he was not very lucky, as the Coin Tower (Münzturm) he built had to be pulled down in 1706. As he had received no more commissions, he left for St Petersburg in 1714. The manner of his death is unknown. His best-known works are a statue of *Frederick III* in Königsberg (Kaliningrad), a bust of *Frederick II of Hessen-Homburg* in Homburg Castle and the tomb of a royal couple in Berlin cathedral.
MUSEUMS AND GALLERIES:
HAMBURG (Kunsthalle): *Memorial of the Grand Elector* (model) - WEIMAR: *Two Masks of Dead Warriors.*
AUCTION RECORDS:
AMSTERDAM, 24 April 1968, *Horses* (two patinated bronzes) NLG 85,000.

SCHLÜTER, August
German, 19th - 20th century.
Born 22 January 1858, in Münster; died 19 December 1928, in Düsseldorf.
Painter, watercolourist, lithographer. Landscapes.
August Schlüter was the pupil of Eugen Dücker at the fine arts academy in Düsseldorf.
MUSEUMS AND GALLERIES:
BRUSSELS (Gal. of Duc d'Arenberg).
AUCTION RECORDS:
COLOGNE, 30 March 1984, *Woman Collecting Faggots with Children beside a Pond* (1887, oil on canvas, 51½ x 38½ ins / 131 x 98 cm) DEM 9,000. COLOGNE, 18 March 1989, *Italian Coast in Summer* (oil on canvas, 23¼ x 42¼ ins / 59 x 107 cm) DEM 1,400.

SCHLUTER, Carl
German, 19th century.
Died 6 March 1844, in Hanover.
Engraver. Coins.

SCHLUTER, Christoph Heinrich
German, 17th century.
Medallist.
Christoph Schluter worked first for the town of Goslar and then for the Prince of Lippe.

SCHLUTER, Henning
German, 17th century.
Died 1672.
Active in Goslar.
Medallist.
Henning Schluter engraved many medals and pictures for Duke Frederick Ulrich and Duke Augustus of Brunswick-Luneburg.

SCHLUTER, Karl H. W.
German, 19th century.
Born 24 October 1846, in Pinneberg; died 25 or 26 October 1884, in Dresden.
Sculptor. Nudes, portraits. Statues, busts.
Karl Schluter was a pupil of Johannes Schilling at the academy of fine art in Dresden. He travelled to Rome.
MUSEUMS AND GALLERIES:
BERLIN (Nationalgal.): *Bust of a Young Woman; Young Roman Pastor* - DRESDEN: *Frau Bierling; Bust of the Artist's Wife; Nude Girl* - LEIPZIG: *Girl Going to Fetch Water from the Well* - SCHLESWIG (Thaulow-Mus.): *Bust of Professor Thaulow.*

SCHLUTER, Matthias, or Schlutter
German, 17th century.
Active in Lübeck.
Painter.

SCHLUTTER, Johann Georg, or Schlitter
German, 18th century.
Painter. Portraits.
Schlutter was active in Leipzig around 1750 and in Thorn in 1751.

SCHLUTTER, Vasco Laurent
German, 19th - 20th century.
Born 12 August 1841, in Zella (Thuringia).

From 1870 active in Switzerland.
Medallist, engraver.
Vasco Schlutter settled in Geneva.

SCHLUYMER, M.
Dutch, 18th century.
Draughtsman.

SCHMÄCK, Emilie, or Schmück
Austrian, 19th century.
Painter.
Emilie Schmäck worked in London between 1837 and 1845, in Venice and Vienna between 1850 and 1855 and in Graz from 1857.

SCHMACKE, Claudia
German, 20th century.
Sculptor of assemblages, installation artist.
In 1993, Claudia Schmacke exhibited at the Patricia Dorfmann gallery in Paris with Renate Koch, the two women having met and struck up a friendship during a stay in Bratislava in 1992.

Both artists are attuned to the atmosphere and to the sound waves generated in it, to the healing sounds of running water, and to the elements which are most natural and essential for life; these are exploited and celebrated in assemblages and installations, and their pollution by the world of reckless consumption is questioned from a clear ecological point of view. For her part, Claudia Schmacke gives material form to various aspects of water, in particular suggesting its absence by casts of washbasins, boxes of taps and images of fish captured in transparent wax.

SCHMAEDEL, Max von
German, 19th - 20th century.
Born 14 May 1856, in Augsburg.
Painter. Portraits, genre scenes.
Max von Schmaedel was the pupil of Max Adamo, Karl von Piloty and Alexander von Wagner at the fine arts academy in Munich, where he had settled.
AUCTION RECORDS:
LONDON, 20 June 1980, *Pierrot with Broken Guitar* (oil on canvas, 14 1/2 x 11 3/4 ins / 37 x 29.7 cm) GBP 2,000. LONDON, 12 Feb 1993, *The Grapes of Wrath* (oil on canvas, 33 1/2 x 62 3/4 ins / 85.1 x 159.4 cm) GBP 7,150. LONDON, 21 Nov 1997, *The Grapes of Wrath* (oil on canvas, 33 1/2 x 62 3/4 ins / 85 x 159.5 cm) GBP 6,325.

SCHMAEDL, Franz Xaver, or Schmädel, Schmadl
German, 18th century.
Born 1 November 1705, in Oberstdorf; died 16 July 1777, in Weilheim.
Sculptor. Religious subjects.
Schmaedl carved a large number of not very original pieces for churches in the area.

SCHMAHEL, Johann
German, 19th century.
Born 1786.
Active in Breslau (now Wroclaw).
Architectural draughtsman.

SCHMAHL, Hans
German, 17th century.
Painter.

SCHMAHL, J. Matthaeus
German, 18th century.
Possibly active in Augsburg c. 1765.
Draughtsman, engraver.

SCHMAHLFELD, Frederik Georg Ludwig, or Schmallfeldt
Danish, 19th - 20th century.
Born 13 March 1829, in Stade; died 28 March 1907, in Copenhagen.
Medallist, metal worker, engraver.
Frederik Schmahlfeld was the pupil of his father, the goldsmith Carl Georg Ferdinand Schmahlfeld, before going on to study at the technical university in Hanover. He produced numerous engraved cups.
MUSEUMS AND GALLERIES:
COPENHAGEN (Kunstindustrimus.): chiselled cup.

SCHMAIS, Friedrich von
German, 19th - 20th century.
Born 1855; died 4 April 1918, in Berlin.
Painter, engraver.

SCHMAKOFF, Mickhaïl Alexandrovitch.
See **SHMAKOV Mickail Aleksandrovich**

SCHMAL, Carl
Austrian, 18th - 19th century.
Born 6 May 1769, in Graz; died 29 February 1836, in Vienna.
Engraver.

SCHMAL, Josef
Austrian, 19th century.
Painter.
Schmal sketched the design for the decoration of the Knights' Hall in Graz.

SCHMALE, H., or Smale
Dutch, 18th century.
Painter. Portraits.
MUSEUMS AND GALLERIES:
ALKMAAR (Stedelijk Mus.): *Portrait of Daniel Ras*; *Portrait of Cornelia Catharina von Arssea, Wife of Daniel Ras*.

SCHMALER, Jakob
German, 17th century.
Born to a family originally from Landsberg.
Sculptor.
Schmaler settled in Überlingen in 1609.

SCHMALFUSS, Friedrich August
German, 19th century.
Born 1792, in Altdöbern.
Painter.
Schmalfuss studied at the academy in Dresden with Toscani and Matthäi. He remained in Dresden until 1827.

SCHMALHAUSEN, Otto
German, 20th century.
Born 30 January 1890, in Antwerp, of German origin.
Painter, sculptor.
Dadaism.
Otto Schmalhausen was the brother-in-law of George Grosz. A member of the Berlin Dada group, he acquired the nickname 'Dada-Oz' and founded a kind of Dada Institute in 1920. In this same year, he participated in the first great international Dada fair in Berlin, where he showed a bust of Beethoven sporting a large moustache and a squint.
BIBLIOGRAPHY:
Dorival, Bernard/Hoog, Michel, *Dada*, exhibition catalogue, Musée national d'Art moderne, Paris, 1966.

SCHMALHOFER, Leopold
Austrian, 18th century.
Engraver.

SCHMÄLING, Johann Heinrich and Friedrich (father and son), or Schmeeling, Schmidling
German, 18th - 19th century.
Painters (glazed earthenware).
The Schmälings worked at the Hanau factory between 1780 and 1801.

SCHMALIX, Hubert
Austrian, 20th - 21st century.
Born 1952, in Graz.
Painter, watercolourist.
Hubert Schmalix trained at the Akademie der Bildenden Künste in Vienna from 1971 to 1976. His style of painting is decorative, with elements of reality and fantasy integrated in compositions tending towards abstraction. From 1972, he was represented in numerous collective exhibitions in Austria, Germany, England, Spain, Italy, the USA and Australia. From 1976, he had solo shows in several countries, notably in Los Angeles in 1988.

BIBLIOGRAPHY:
Hubert Schmalix: All About, exhibition catalogue, Turske and Whitney Gall., Los Angeles, 1988.
AUCTION RECORDS:
VIENNA, 11 Sept 1984, *Head* (1979, oil on canvas, 59 x 51 1/4 ins / 150 x 130 cm) ATS 35,000. VIENNA, 10 Sept 1985, *Untitled* (1982, gouache, 35 1/2 x 49 1/4 ins / 90 x 125 cm) ATS 25,000. NEW YORK, 13 May 1988, *Krishna* (oil on canvas, 78 3/4 x 78 3/4 ins / 200 x 200 cm) USD 4,620. LOKEREN, 21 March 1992, *Confused Ideas* (1982, oil on canvas, 78 3/4 x 78 3/4 ins / 200 x 200 cm) BEF 240,000. PARIS, 24 June 1994, *Untitled* (1984, oil on canvas, 90 1/2 x 33 3/4 ins / 230 x 86 cm) FRF 5,500. LUCERNE, 26 Nov 1994, *Untitled* (oil on canvas, 90 1/2 x 33 3/4 ins / 230 x 86 cm) CHF 3,100. AMSTERDAM, 6 Dec 1995, *Green Grass* (1988, oil on canvas, 63 x 48 ins / 160 x 121 cm) NLG 5,750. VIENNA, 20 April 1999, *Untitled: Green, Black and Yellow Head in Profile, Orange Ground* (1987, gouache, pastel and crayon, 13 x 9 ins / 32 x 24 cm) ATS 55,000. VIENNA, 1 Dec 1999, *Night* (oil on canvas, 79 x 67 ins / 200 x 170 cm) ATS 140,000. VIENNA, 11 April 2000, *Cypress Park VI* (1991, oil on canvas, 69 x 53 ins / 175 x 134 cm) ATS 130,000. VIENNA, 11 April 2000, *Untitled* (1991, oil on canvas, 69 x 41 ins / 175 x 104 cm) ATS 250,000. VIENNA, 26 Sept 2001, *Untitled* (1982, oil on canvas, 62 x 60 ins / 157 x 152 cm) ATS 100,000. VIENNA, 26 Sept 2001, *Untitled: Venetian Water with Three Balls* (oil on canvas, 89 x 98 ins / 225 x 250 cm) ATS 110,000. VIENNA, 23 April 2002, *Untitled* (1987, gouache on wallpaper, 7 x 28 ins / 19 x 70 cm) EUR 1,700. VIENNA, 23 April 2002, *Melancholy* (oil on canvas, 55 x 55 ins / 140 x 140 cm) EUR 13,000. VIENNA, 20 May 2003, *North Wind, South Wind* (oil on canvas, 114 x 154 ins / 290 x 390 cm) EUR 13,000. VIENNA, 28 Nov 2003, *Untitled* (1983, gouache, 40 x 32 ins / 102 x 82 cm) EUR 3,500. VIENNA, 28 April 2004, *Hector Berlioz* (oil on canvas, 79 x 79 ins / 200 x 200 cm) EUR 11,000. VIENNA, 25 May 2004, *Untitled* (2002, mixed media, 30 x 22 ins / 75 x 56 cm) EUR 3,200.

SCHMALKALDER, Samson
German, 17th century.
Born 22 March 1667, in Dimmeringen (Lorraine).
Draughtsman.
Schmalkalder left two sketchbooks.

SCHMALLFELDT, Frederik Georg Ludwig.
See **SCHMAHLFELD**

SCHMALZ
French, 18th century.
Active in Deux-Ponts c. 1760.
Painter.
Schmalz was the brother-in-law of the painter Jacob Frédéric Leclerc.

SCHMALZ, Anton
Swiss, 17th century.
Died November 1638, in Bern.
Painter.
Anton Schmalz was at first a monk in a monastery in Fribourg, but then converted to Protestantism. He painted masks and costumes, which are housed in the Historisches Museum in Bern.

SCHMALZ, David
Swiss, 16th century.
Born 30 January 1540; died 1577.
Active in Bern from 1568.
Glass painter.
David Schmalz was the son of Niklaus Schmalz.

SCHMALZ, Heinrich P., or Schmaltz
German, 19th century.
Painter. Still-lifes (flowers).
Heinrich Schmalz was a pupil of G.W. Völcker and worked in Berlin.
MUSEUMS AND GALLERIES:
SZCZECIN.
AUCTION RECORDS:
HAMBURG, 7 June 1979, *Still-life with Flowers* (1838, oil on canvas, 18 1/2 x 15 ins / 47.3 x 38 cm) DEM 14,000.

SCHMALZ, Herbert Gustave
British, 19th - 20th century.
Born 1856 or 1857, in London; died 1935.
Painter. Religious subjects, mythological subjects, figures, portraits, genre scenes.
He took part in the exhibitions at the Royal Academy, London, from 1879 to 1918.
MUSEUMS AND GALLERIES:
BRISTOL: *Inspiration*.
AUCTION RECORDS:
LONDON, 18 June 1974, *Morning of the Resurrection*, GBP 300. LONDON, 30 March 1976, *Clorinda* (1900, oil on panel, 12 x 15 1/4 ins / 30.5 x 39 cm) GBP 250. LONDON, 5 July 1978, *Young Girl with a Floppy Hat* (1886, oil on panel, 12 x 10 ins / 30.5 x 25.5 cm) GBP 700. LONDON, 24 March 1981, *Young Girl Picking Flowers* (1900, oil on panel, 20 3/4 x 14 1/4 ins / 53 x 36 cm) GBP 2,600. LONDON, 13 June 1984, *Denise* (1885, oil on canvas, 17 3/4 x 12 ins / 45.4 x 30.5 cm) GBP 3,000. LONDON, 11 June 1986, *Eve in Exile* (oil on canvas, 74 x 40 ins / 188 x 101.5 cm) GBP 5,000. LONDON, 15 June 1990, *Love Awakening..* (1894, oil on canvas, 43 1/4 x 58 1/4 ins / 110 x 148 cm) GBP 17,050. GLASGOW, 22 Nov 1990, *Ninon, Ninon, What Are You Doing with Your Life? (Alfred de Musset)* (1900, oil on panel, tondo, diam. 11 ins / 27.9 cm) GBP 5,280. LONDON, 8 Feb 1991, *Bethany* (1890, oil on canvas, 17 x 24 ins / 43 x 61 cm) GBP 1,100. LONDON, 19 June 1991, *The Daughters of Juda in Babylon* (oil on canvas, 62 x 32 ins / 157.5 x 81 cm) GBP 23,100. LONDON, 11 Oct 1991, *Iphigenia* (oil on panel, 14 x 9 1/4 ins / 35.5 x 23.5 cm) GBP 1,760. NEW YORK, 18-19 July 1996, *Forsaken Love Letters* (oil on canvas, 44 x 56 ins / 111.8 x 142.2 cm) USD 2,760. LONDON, 7 Nov 1997, *When Life is Wonderful* (oil on canvas, variation of the Virgin and Child, 16 1/2 x 15 ins / 42 x 38 cm) GBP 5,175.

SCHMALZ, Niklaus
Swiss, 16th century.
Died 1556.
Active in Bern.
Glass painter.
Niklaus Schmalz was a pupil of Hans Funk and painted windows for the churches of Bern.

SCHMALZHAVER, Thomas
Austrian, 18th century.
Active in Mondsee.
Painter.

SCHMALZIGAUG, Friedrich Ferdinand
German, 19th century.
Born 15 February 1847, in Friedrichshafen; died 5 July 1902.
Painter. Animals.

Schmalzigaug studied first in Stuttgart, then with Piloty in Munich.

MUSEUMS AND GALLERIES:

COLOGNE: *Cows in a Yard.*

AUCTION RECORDS:

COLOGNE, 16 June 1978, *The Duckpond* (oil on canvas, 16 1/4 x 26 ins / 41 x 66 cm) DEM 11,000. VIENNA, 12 Feb 1980, *Sheep in a Landscape* (oil on canvas, 33 1/2 x 54 1/4 ins / 85 x 138 cm) ATS 100,000. NEW YORK, 29 Oct 1986, *Sheep at the Watering Hole* (1882, oil on canvas, 29 3/4 x 51 1/2 ins / 75.5 x 130.8 cm) USD 8,500.

SCHMALZIGAUG, Jules

Belgian, 20th century.

Born 26 September 1886, in Antwerp; died 12 May 1917, in The Hague.

Painter (gouache), pastellist, draughtsman. Portraits, landscapes.

Futurism.

Jules Schmalzigaug was the pupil of Isidore Verheyden at the fine arts academy in Brussels and of Lucien Simon and Émile René Ménard in Paris. He also studied at the Karsruhe academy during the course of a stay in Germany before travelling to Italy, where in Rome in 1905 he was the correspondent for the publication *L'Art Contemporain.* He subsequently returned to Venice, living there from 1912 to 1914, and settled in Holland during World War I. His death at the age of 30 robbed Belgium of one of its major artistic prospects.

Schmalzigaug featured in the exhibition *De blijvende verlokking: Nederlandse kunstenaars in Italië, 1806-1940* (*Lasting Attraction: Dutch Artists in Italy, 1806-1940*) mounted at the Kunsthal in Rotterdam in 2003, which showed how Dutch artists had benefited from travelling in Italy. In the same year, he was represented in the exhibition *Aux origines de l'abstraction (1800-1914)* (*The Origins of Abstraction, 1800-1914*) at the Musée d'Orsay in Paris. A retrospective posthumous exhibition was devoted to this artist at the Musée d'Art Moderne in Brussels.

Schmalzigaug published an essay entitled *La Panchromie* (*Panchromatism*). Influenced early in his career by Expressionism, a movement which was traditionally present in Belgium, Schmalzigaug was subsequently influenced by Futurism during a stay in Venice, as is shown by his canvas entitled *Dynamic Expression of a Car at Speed,* before turning to Abstraction from 1914 onwards. Practically unknown by his contemporaries, he ranks as one of the very first Belgian painters to have embraced Abstraction, together with Lempereur-Haut, Victor Servranckx and especially Joseph Lacasse.

SCHMALZIGAUG

BIBLIOGRAPHY:

De blijvende verlokking: Nederlandse kunstenaars in Italië, 1806-1940, exhibition catalogue, Kunsthal, Rotterdam, 2003.

Lemoine, Serge/Rousseau, Pascal, et al., *Aux origines de l'abstraction (1800-1914),* exhibition catalogue, Musée d'Orsay, Paris, 2003.

MUSEUMS AND GALLERIES:

BRUSSELS: *Portrait of Baron Francis Delbeke.*

AUCTION RECORDS:

LOKEREN, 15 Oct 1983, *View of Delft* (pastel, 10 x 15 1/2 ins / 25.5 x 39.5 cm) BEF 60,000. LOKEREN, 10 Oct 1987, *Wooded Landscape* (1915-1917, pastel and watercolour, 13 x 19 ins / 33 x 48 cm) BEF 170,000. LOKEREN, 5 March 1988, *Composition* (gouache, pencil, Indian ink, 14 1/4 x 19 1/2 ins / 36.5 x 49.5 cm) BEF 80,000. LOKEREN, 28 May 1988, *Mrs Nelly Hurzelbrinck* (1917, pencil, 24 x 17 1/4 ins / 61 x 43.5 cm) BEF 138,000. LONDON, 27 June 1989, *Het Dynamische van de Dans* (*Dynamics of the Dance*) (1913, oil on canvas, 39 1/4 x 51 ins / 100 x 129.6 cm) GBP 132,000. LONDON, 19 Oct 1989, *Dynamics of the Dance* (1914, oil on canvas, 37 1/2 x 41 1/4 ins / 95 x 105 cm) GBP 154,000. PARIS, 26 Feb 1990, *Composition* (oil on canvas, 31 1/2 x 39 1/4 ins / 80 x 100 cm) FRF 360,000. LOKEREN, 21 March 1992, *Woman Seated* (red chalk, 13 3/4 x 11 ins / 35 x 27 cm) BEF 36,000. LOKEREN, 10 Dec 1994, *Gendarme* (watercolour and charcoal, 6 x 3 3/4 ins / 15 x 9.5 cm) BEF 28,000. LOKEREN, 20 May 1995, *View of Delft* (1917, pastel, 15 1/2 x 9 1/2 ins / 39.5 x 24 cm) BEF 260,000. AMSTERDAM, 5 June 1996, *Dynamics of the Dance* (oil on canvas, 39 1/4 x 51 ins / 100 x 129.6 cm) NLG 172,500. LOKEREN, 9 Oct 1999, *Doge's Palace, Venice* (oil on panel, 9 x 11 ins / 23 x 28 cm) BEF 95,000. LOKEREN, 9 Oct 1999, *Motion of a Spiral* (watercolour and crayon, 17 x 12 ins / 42 x 31 cm) BEF 280,000. ANTWERP, 22 Oct 2001, *View of Venice* (oil on panel, 11 x 8 ins / 27 x 21 cm) BEF 80,000. ANTWERP, 23 April 2002, *Firework* (watercolour, 16 x 20 ins / 41 x 51 cm) EUR 4,600. LOKEREN, 13 Dec 2003, *View of Beach in Scheveningen* (pastel, 12 x 15 ins / 30 x 39 cm) EUR 2,800.

SCHMALZL, Max

German, 19th - 20th century.

Born 7 July 1850, in Falkenstein; died 7 January 1930, in Gars am Kamp, Austria.

Painter, illustrator. Murals.

In 1870-1871, Max Schmalzl was the pupil of Theodor Spiess in Munich. He painted the chapel of the Redemptorists in Vilsbiburg.

SCHMALZL, Rudolf

German, 20th century.

Born 4 April 1890, in Falkenstein; died 27 April 1932, in Munich.

Painter.

Rudolf Schmalzl, the nephew of Max Schmalzl, was the pupil of Martin Feuerstein at the fine arts academy in Munich.

SCHMAND, J. Philipp

American, 19th - 20th century.

Born 24 February 1871, in Germania (Pennsylvania); died 1942.

Painter.

J. Philipp Schmand studied under Lucius W. Hitchcock and Henry Siddons Mowbray. He was a member of the Salmagundi Club and the American Federation of Arts. He painted portraits of famous Americans of his time.

SCHMARJE, Walter

German, 19th - 20th century.

Born 16 August 1872, in Flensburg; died 6 November 1921, in Berlin.

Sculptor. Mythological subjects.

Walter Schmarje was the pupil of Reinhold Begas at the fine arts academy in Berlin. His works, in addition to funeral monuments, include the fountain in the market square in Dantzig-Langfuhr.

MUSEUMS AND GALLERIES:

BRUNSWICK: *Young Satyr.*

SCHMAROFF, Pavel Dimitrevich.

See **SHMAROV Paul**

SCHMAUK, Karl

German, 19th - 20th century.

Born 12 January 1868, in Untertürkheim, near Stuttgart.

Painter, illustrator. Interiors, landscapes.

Karl Schmauk was the pupil of Jakob Grünenwald and Claudius von Schraudolph the Younger at the fine arts school in Stuttgart. He was also active in Stuttgart-Untertürkheim.

SCHMAUNZ, Matthias, or Schmauz
German, 19th century.
Painter.

SCHMAUSER, Karl
German, 20th century.
Born 20 October 1883, in Berlin.
Painter. Landscapes.
Karl Schmauser was the pupil of Heinrich Harder in Berlin. He was active in Hamburg.

SCHMAUSS, Karl
German, 19th century.
Born 1804; died 6 May 1879, in Nymphenburg.
Modeller.
Schmauss worked at the Nymphenburg porcelain factory from 1825.

SCHMAUT, Lucas. See **SMONT**

SCHMEDDES, Heinrich
German, 17th century.
Born to a family originally from Koesfeld.
Sculptor.
Schmeddes provided the ornamentation for the fountain in the park at Raesfeld Castle.

SCHMEDINGEN, Alfred
German, 19th - 20th century.
Born 14 August 1871, in Mehrin, near Frankfurt an der Oder.
Painter. Portraits, still-lifes.
Alfred Schmedingen was a pupil at the fine arts academy in Berlin and at the Académie Julian in Paris. He was active in Munich until 1919, then settled in Bamberg.

SCHMEDLA, Ignac
Bohemian School, 19th century.
Born 1802, in Prague.
Active in Prague.
Painter. Portraits.
Ignac Schmedla was a student at the art academy in Prague in 1815.

SCHMEDTGEN, William Hermann
American, 19th - 20th century.
Born 18 May 1862, in Chicago; died 1936.
Painter, illustrator.
William Schmedtgen was the director of the arts section of the Chicago *Herald* from 1866 until 1901. During the Spanish campaign he was sent to Santiago as a war artist. He illustrated many books on art.

SCHMEELING, Johann Heinrich and Friedrich (father and son). See **SCHMÄLING**

SCHMEHRFELD, Johanna Elisabeth von. See **SCHMERFELD**

SCHMEIDLER, Carl Gottlob
German, 18th - 19th century.
Born 8 December 1772, in Nimptsch; died 2 September 1838, in Breslau (now Wroclaw, Poland).
Painter. Portraits, landscapes.
Schmeidler studied theology, and became a portrait painter because he had no other means of earning a living. After training at the academy in Dresden, he settled in Wroclaw. Among his best-known works are several portraits of princes of the Prussian royal family.

SCHMELING, Bruno, or Schmielingh
German, 17th century.
Active in Cologne.
Glass painter.
Schmeling became a member of the guild in 1612 and created a number of stained glass windows for the Minorites' monastery in Cologne in 1620 and 1621.

SCHMELKOFF, Piotr Michailovitch. See **SHMELKOV Petr Mikhailovich**

SCHMELLER, Johann Joseph
German, 19th century.
Born 12 July 1796, in Gross-Obringen, near Weimar; died 1 October 1841, in Weimar.
Painter, draughtsman. Portraits.
Schmeller was a pupil of Jagermann. In 1820, he received a pension from the Grand Duke enabling him to go to Antwerp and continue his studies with Van Bree. On his return, he was appointed master of the art school in Weimar. He was also a protégé of Goethe, whose portrait he painted twice. He also drew a large number of pencil portraits of notable persons for the famous poet, which were collected in an album. Anyone who is aware of Goethe's talents as a draughtsman will realise that this constitutes the highest possible praise of Schmeller's skill.
MUSEUMS AND GALLERIES:
NANTES (MBA): a drawing.

SCHMELTZ, Bruno
French, 20th century.
Born 1943.
Painter. Figures, portraits.
Bruno Schmeltz studied at the École des Beaux-Arts in Paris from 1962. He uses a detailed hyper-realist technique to explore themes drawn from nature and from country life. He is also noted for his portraits of figures, accompanied without exception by a dog.

He has shown examples of his work at group exhibitions, notably at the Salon Grands et Jeunes d'Aujourd'hui in Paris in 1972, 1973, 1974 and 1975. His solo exhibitions have included those in Paris in 1974, in 1991 at the Galerie Alain Blondel, and 2003 at the Espace Pierre Cardin.
AUCTION RECORDS:
PARIS, 24 April 1988, *Self-portrait* (oil on canvas, 63 3/4 x 38 1/4 ins / 162 x 97 cm) FRF 16,000. PARIS, 28 May 1993, *Man Standing Stripped to the Waist and Carrying a Wounded Young Man* (oil on canvas, 69 x 45 ins / 175 x 114 cm) FRF 36,000. PARIS, 8 April 2002, *Female Nude* (1986, acrylic on canvas, 39 x 39 ins / 100 x 100 cm) EUR 2,000. PARIS, 19 March 2004, *Dali* (oil on canvas, 31 x 47 ins / 80 x 120 cm) EUR 4,000. VENDÔME, 18 April 2004, *Two Men and a Woman* (1985, oil on canvas, 69 x 45 ins / 175 x 114 cm) EUR 1,900.

SCHMELTZING. See **SMELTZING**

SCHMELZ, Carl Simon Wilhelm
German, 19th century.
Born 1787, in Hessen-Kasselschen.
Engraver (burin). Natural history.
Carl Schmelz was active in Paris as an illustrator of works on natural history.

SCHMELZ, G.
German, 18th century.
Active in Stuttgart c. 1737.
Medallist.
Schmelz engraved a medal on the occasion of the death of Duke Charles Alexander of Wurtemberg.

SCHMELZ, Johann Christoph, or Schmölz
German, 18th century.
Born 1726, to a family originally from Biberach; died 1770.
Engraver (precious stones), medallist.
Johann Schmelz was the father of the goldsmith Georg Adolf Schmelz, who was born in 1757 and died in 1793 in the Tyrol.

SCHMELZEISEN, Gustav Klemens
German, 20th century.

Born 1900, in Düsseldorf.
Painter.
A doctor of law and a professor of legal history, Gustav Schmelzeisen did not begin experimenting with abstract painting until after World War II.

SCHMELZER, Bernhard Johann
German, 19th century.
Born 1833, in Annaberg.
Painter. Genre scenes.
Bernhard Schmelzer was a pupil of Julius Hubner in Dresden.

SCHMELZER, Josef
Austrian, 19th century.
Sculptor.
Josef Schmelzer was active in Budapest around 1809 and in Vienna from 1820 to 1824.

SCHMERFELD, Johann Daniel von
19th century.
Born 21st April 1774, in Kassel; died 1811, in Kharkov, Russia.
Painter, draughtsman.
Johann Daniel von Schmerfeld was the son of Johanna Elisabeth von Schmerfeld.

SCHMERFELD, Johanna Elisabeth von, or Schmehrfeld
Maiden name: Schwarzenberg
German, 18th century.
Born in Kassel; died 12 April 1803, in Kassel.
Painter. Landscapes.
Johanna von Schmerfeld was a pupil of Johann Heinrich Tischbein the Elder.

SCHMERLIN, Hans
German, 17th century.
Active in Augsburg.
Cabinet maker.

SCHMERLING, Pauline von (Baroness). See **KOUDELKA Pauline von Schmerling von**

SCHMETTERER, Franz Anton
German, 19th century.
Active in Regensburg c. 1810.
Painter (porcelain).

SCHMETTERLING, Christiane Josefa
German, 19th century.
Born 19 December 1796, in Amsterdam; died 18 March 1840, in Amsterdam.
Painter. Flowers.
Christiane Schmetterling was a daughter of Joseph Adolf Schmetterling.

SCHMETTERLING, Elisabeth Barbara
German, 19th century.
Born 30 November 1804, in Amsterdam.
Miniaturist, engraver (burin).
Elisabeth Schmetterling was a daughter of Joseph Adolf Schmetterling.

SCHMETTERLING, Joseph Adolph
German, 18th - 19th century.
Born c. 1751, in Vienna; died 1828, in Amsterdam.
Miniaturist, silhouettist.
Joseph Adolf Schmetterling settled in Amsterdam and became a successful miniature painter. He was the father of Christiane Josefa and Elisabeth Barbara Schmetterling.
AUCTION RECORDS:
PARIS, 20 and 21 Feb 1929, *The Meal* (drawing) FRF 2,800.

SCHMETZ, Betty
Belgian, 20th century.
Born 1915, in Haaltert.
Painter, engraver, draughtswoman. Designs for tapestries.
Betty Schmetz was the pupil of Jean Donnay and Georges Comhaire at the fine arts academy in Liège. She exhibited mostly in Belgium, but also took part in collective exhibitions in France, Holland and Austria and showed her work at the São Paulo Biennale and the Ljubljana Biennale.

As an engraver, Schmetz used a large number of different techniques, including etching, burin, aquatint and soft-ground etching. Her painting, consisting of lines and dashes, is abstract, almost informal, a product of the artist's spontaneity.
MUSEUMS AND GALLERIES:
AALST - ANTWERP (Prentenkabinet) - BRUSSELS (Bibliothèque royale Albert Ier, Prints Collection) - SAN FRANCISCO (Academy of Art College) - SKOPJE - VERVIERS.

SCHMETZ, Johann Jacob. See **SCHMITZ**

SCHMETZ, Wilhelm
German, 20th century.
Born 14 March 1890, in Düsseldorf.
Painter, engraver. Landscapes.
Wilhelm Schmetz was active in Laurensberg, near Aachen.
MUSEUMS AND GALLERIES:
DÜSSELDORF: *Dutch Landscape*.

SCHMEYKAL, Thaddäus
Bohemian School, 18th century.
Active c. 1778.
Painter.

SCHMIALEK, Bruno
German, 20th century.
Born 5 October 1888, in Lazisk (Silesia); died 1963.
Painter, engraver, draughtsman.
Bruno Schmialek, a pupil at the fine arts academy in Breslau (now Wroclaw, Poland), was active in Beuthen. The town of his birth became Polish after 1918, and a great deal of his work was destroyed during the 1939-1945 war. In 1988, his collected engravings were exhibited at the Centre Universitaire of the Grand Palais in Paris.

Schmialek was above all a wood engraver, a crude technique which suited his subject matter. He engraved a number of highly expressive heads and was conscious of the misery in the world; he is sometimes linked with the Expressionist artists of the group Die Brücke in Dresden.

SCHMICHT, Georg Friedrich. See **SCHMIEG**

SCHMID
Swiss, 18th century.
Active in Lucerne c. 1783.
Painter.

SCHMID
French, 19th century.
Painter.
He exhibited at the Salon between 1834 and 1839. He is best remembered for his rustic interiors and depictions of life in Brittany.

SCHMID. See also **SCHMIDT**

SCHMID, Adolf
German, 19th - 20th century.
Born 15 July 1867, in Stuttgart.
Sculptor, medallist, metal worker.
Adolf Schmid basically worked in bronze and produced statuettes including those of *Prince Charles of Baden*, *Franz Liszt* and *J.P. Hebel*.
AUCTION RECORDS:
MONTREAL, 7 Dec 1995, *Child with Cats* (bronze, h. 11 1/2 ins / 29 cm) CAD 1,200.

SCHMID, Albert. See **SCHMIDT Albert**

SCHMID, Albrecht
German, 17th - 18th century.
Born c. 1667, in Ulm; died 1774, in Augsburg.
Painter. Monograms.

Albrecht Schmid was a pupil of Schulte in Ulm. He was active in Augsburg from 1694.

SCHMID, Aldo
Italian, 20th century.
Born 1935, in Trento.
Painter.

Since 1963, Alto Schmid has been involved in exploring colour contrasts, producing pictures of a very simple formal structure - often no more than simple bands of colour - but where the passage from one colour to the next is resolved in an original way.

He has taken part in a number of collective exhibitions including, in 1972, the Venice Biennale and the Rome Quadriennale. His solo exhibitions include: Riva (1957); Venice (1959, 1963, 1965 and 1967); and Florence (1962, 1965 and 1973), as well as Bologna and Milan.

SCHMID, Alexander
Swiss, 19th century.
Born 29 November 1802, in Olten; died 1876.
Painter.

Alexander Schmid was a Capuchin monk.

SCHMID, Alexander
German, 19th century.
Born 14 February 1833, in Sonneberg; died 7 March 1901, in Coburg.
Sculptor, decorative artist. Monuments, statues.

In 1858, Alexander Schmid founded a school of drawing in Sonneberg. He lived in Coburg from 1884. He created a monument to Victory and a statue of Germania in Meissen.

SCHMID, Alois Joseph
German, 18th century.
Active in Lechbruck.
Cabinet maker.

SCHMID, Andreas
German, 18th century.
Sculptor.

Andreas Schmid carved choir stalls and two confessionals for the church in Mickhausen.

SCHMID, Antoine
Swiss, 20th century.
Born 8 January 1891, in Fribourg; died 1920, in Montana.
Painter. Landscapes.

Antoine Schmid completed his training in Paris.

SCHMID, August
Swiss, 20th century.
Born 30 July 1877, in Diessenhofen.
Painter, watercolourist, draughtsman.

August Schmid was a pupil at the school of fine arts in Zurich and the school of decorative arts in Paris, and was taught by Johann Caspar or Ludwig Herterich at the fine arts academy in Munich.

MUSEUMS AND GALLERIES:
SCHAFFHAUSEN (Town Collection): a painting, several watercolours.

SCHMID, Augustin
Swiss, 18th - 19th century.
Born 21 January 1770, in Schussenried; died 2 April 1837, in Lucerne.
Painter.

Augustin Schmid was a teacher of drawing in Lucerne from 1770.

MUSEUMS AND GALLERIES:
ALTDORF (Historisches Mus. Uri): watercolours - LUCERNE (Bibliothèque Municipale): *Panorama of Lucerne* (large watercolour) - LUCERNE (Kunstmus.): watercolours.

SCHMID, Balthasar, or Schmidt
Swiss.
Active in Rheinau.
Cabinet maker.

SCHMID, Carl Friedrich Ludwig, or Schmidt
German, 19th century.
Born 1799, in Stettin (now Szczecin, Poland); died after 1850.
Painter. History painting, portraits, genre scenes.

Carl Schmid was the son of Peter and the brother of Wilhelm Schmid. He studied in Berlin and Paris and worked in Aachen. Between 1831 and 1833, he went on study tours to Rome, and from 1834 to 1835 and again in 1842 he went to study in London. He exhibited portraits of *Schleiermacher*, *Colonel von Schepeler*, the painter *Franz Nadorp in Rome* and the *Duke of Sussex* at the Royal Academy in London.

MUSEUMS AND GALLERIES:
BERLIN (Mus. Hohenzollern): *William I*; *Schinkel* - BERLIN (Nationalgal.): *Schinkel* - FLORENCE (Uffizi): *Self-portrait*.

AUCTION RECORDS:
PARIS, 28 April 1993, *Three-quarter Portrait of an Officer in the Prussian Army* (oil on canvas, 46 1/2 x 37 1/2 ins / 118 x 95 cm) FRF 18,000.

SCHMID, Daniel
Swiss, 18th century.
Active in Basel.
Engraver.

SCHMID, David Alois
Swiss, 19th century.
Born 9 February 1791, in Schwyz; died 2 April 1861, in Schwyz.
Watercolourist, engraver (burin/etching), draughtsman (including ink). Panoramas, village views, urban landscapes.

David Schmid was the brother of Martin and Franz Schmid. He studied with Hauser and Johann Heinrich Meyer. He drew a large number of panoramic views.

MUSEUMS AND GALLERIES:
ZURICH (Prints Collection): twelve drawings.

AUCTION RECORDS:
BERN, 26 June 1981, *View of the Village and Castle of Oberhofen* (c. 1820, watercolour/pen outlines, 6 1/2 x 9 1/2 ins / 16.3 x 24.3 cm) CHF 5,800. BERN, 24 June 1983, *View of the City of Lucerne as Seen from the Allerwinden Countryside* (c. 1825, coloured etching, 15 x 19 ins / 38 x 48.4 cm) CHF 10,500. ZURICH, 12 June 1995, *The Baths of Schinznach in the Canton of Aargau* (ink and watercolour/paper, 7 3/4 x 13 1/4 ins / 20 x 33.5 cm) CHF 3,680. BERN, 5 Nov 1999, *View of Lensburg in Canton Aargau* (watercolour, 9 x 14 ins / 24 x 36 cm) CHF 6,000. BERN, 11 May 2000, *Brunnen am Vierwaldstattersee* (watercolour over pencil, 9 x 13 ins / 23 x 33 cm) CHF 16,000. ST GALL, 15 Nov 2000, *View of Trogen* (pen, 9 x 15 ins / 24 x 37 cm) CHF 3,800. LUCERNE, 16 June 2004, *House Belonging to Niklaus von der Flue* (c. 1833, watercolour/pencil, 4 x 6 ins / 11 x 14 cm) CHF 3,000.

SCHMID, Emil
Swiss, 20th century.
Born 17 July 1891.
Painter, engraver. Portraits, landscapes.

Emil Schmid was the pupil of the engraver Peter Halm at the fine arts academy in Munich. He was active in Heiden.

MUSEUMS AND GALLERIES:
ST GALL: *Portrait of a Peasant Woman*.

SCHMID, Erich
Austrian, 20th century.
Born 14 October 1908, in Vienna; died 30 December 1984, in Paris.
Active from 1940 in France.
Painter. Landscapes, still-lifes.
Erich Schmid was a pupil at the school of applied arts in Vienna from 1930 to 1934. In 1939, he left Austria and stayed for a while in Belgium before settling in Paris, where he took part in one of the very first Salons des Réalités Nouvelles. He showed collections of his paintings in numerous solo exhibitions in the USA, France and Belgium, including those mounted at the Michel Grandier gallery in Paris in 1951, the St-Georges gallery in Lyons in 1960, 1969 and 1991, the Mendel Art Gallery in Saskatoon, Canada in 1965, the Kriegel gallery in Paris in 1972, 1975 and 1977, the Claude Hemery gallery in Paris in 1984, the Guénégaud gallery in Paris in 1995 and the La Capitale gallery in Paris in 2001.

During the 1940s, Erich Schmid was attracted by Abstraction, which he saw as 'the only way open to painters'. Following his participation in the abstract Salon des Réalités Nouvelles, and convinced of his own insincerity, he renounced his former creed and returned to Figuration, finding himself once again completely at home. Broadly inspired by street landscapes in Brussels, Paris and Vienna, he evoked these places of eternal wandering in which anonymous figures stroll between the façades of houses beneath darkening skies. The paint, generously applied, sensuous and tortured, plays a fundamental role, while the contrasts of light and shade create an atmosphere which is often tragic.

SCHMID, Eugen Julius
German, 20th century.
Born 1890, in Munich.
Draughtsman.
Eugen Schmid was active in Munich.

SCHMID, Franz, or Schmidt
Austrian, 18th century.
Born in Munich.
Painter. History painting, portraits. Miniatures.
Franz Schmid worked in Vienna, where he became a member of the academy in 1755.

SCHMID, Franz
Swiss, 19th century.
Born 4 October 1796, in Schwyz; died 1 September 1851, in Ried-ob-Schwyz.
Painter, watercolourist, draughtsman, engraver (etching). Landscapes, urban landscapes, urban views, architectural views.
Franz Schmid was taught by his father, David Alois Schmid and also by F.W. Moritz in Neuchâtel. In 1828, he worked in Paris and in 1842 in Italy. He drew panoramic views of Schwyz, Zurich, Paris, Vienna, Salzburg, Karlsruhe and Freiburg im Breisgau.
MUSEUMS AND GALLERIES:
ZURICH (Prints Collection): drawings.
AUCTION RECORDS:
BERN, 30 Nov 1976, *View of Bern* (watercolour, 7 3/4 x 11 1/4 ins / 19.6 x 28.4 cm) CHF 5,900. LONDON, 22 May 1984, *View of the Lower Part of the City of Bern* (1830, hand-coloured etching, 10 x 19 ins / 25.5 x 48.5 cm) GBP 2,200. LONDON, 20 June 1985, *View of Bern* (watercolour and pencil, 7 1/2 x 11 ins / 19 x 28 cm) GBP 7,500. ZURICH, 2 June 1994, *Peasant Woman's House from the Canton of Obwalden* (watercolour/paper, 7 1/2 x 11 ins / 19 x 28 cm) CHF 4,370.

SCHMID, Franz Ignaz
Swiss, 18th century.
Active in Sarnen.
Sculptor.
Franz Ignaz Schmid was the brother of Karl Anton Schmid.

SCHMID, Franz Xaver or Xaver Franz
German, 19th century.
Born to a family originally from Dischingen (Württemberg); died 1822, in Maihingen.
Miniaturist.
Franz Xaver Schmid studied with Martin Knoller in Ettal and Neresheim from 1796 to 1775. Four of his miniatures were exhibited in Lemberg (now Lvov) in 1812.

SCHMID, Fritz
Swiss, 20th century.
Born 1898, in Basel.
Active in England.
Painter.
Fritz Schmid settled in London, where he was the pupil of Philip Wilson Steer at the Slade School of Art.

SCHMID, Georg
Swiss, 16th - 17th century.
Active in Überlingen at the end of the 16th and the beginning of the 17th century.
Sculptor.

SCHMID, Georg Matthäus
German, 18th - 19th century.
Born 21 May 1771, in Lorch.
Active in Lorch.
Sculptor.
Georg Matthäus Schmid settled in Stuttgart in 1812. He is known for a statue of King William I of Wurtemberg, which was housed in Ludwigsburg Castle until 1918.

SCHMID, Hans
German, 15th century.
Died between 1503 and 1504, in Schaffhausen.
Glass painter.
Hans Schmid was the father of Thomas Schmid.

SCHMID, Hans, or Szmid
German, 16th century.
Died before 1524.
Painter.
Breslau School.
Hans Schmid was a master and burgher of Breslau (now Wroclaw) around 1505.

SCHMID, Hans, or Schmidt
Austrian, 16th century.
Died between 1 September 1603 and 8 November 1604.
Painter.
Tyrolean School.
Hans Schmid was court painter in Innsbruck in the service of Archbishop Ferdinand, for whom he worked for 15 years. At the end of his life he became painter to Cardinal Andreas in Blixen. Several of his works can be seen in the Hofburg, Innsbruck.

SCHMID, Hans. See also **FLANDEREISEN**

SCHMID, Hans Johann B.
German, 19th - 20th century.
Born 16 January 1871, in Teuschnitz.
Painter. Religious subjects.
Hans Schmid was the pupil of Ludwig Schmid-Reutte at the fine arts academy in Karlsruhe, of Gabriel von Hackl, Karl Raupp and Rudolf von Saitz at the Munich academy and of Ludwig von Seitz in Rome. He was also a writer.

Following the example of Ludwig von Seitz, Schmid produced most of his paintings for churches.

SCHMID, Hans Sebastian
German, 19th - 20th century.

Born 22 June 1862, in Munich; died probably in 1926.
Painter, sculptor. Portraits, genre scenes.

Hans Sebastian Schmid was the pupil of Max von Widnmann at the fine arts academy in Munich. He was also an art critic and writer.

SCHMID, Hans Toder or Theodor
Swiss, 16th century.
Born 1508.
Active in Zurich.
Glass painter.

Hans Toder Schmid is known to have been still working in 1578.

SCHMID, Heinrich. See **SCHMIDT**

SCHMID, Henri
Swiss, 20th century.
Born 1924, in Winterthur.
Painter. Landscapes with figures, landscapes.

AUCTION RECORDS:

ZURICH, 10 Nov 1984, *Paris Stock Exchange* (1968, oil on canvas, 30¼ x 32 ins / 77 x 81 cm) CHF 3,800. ZURICH, 12 June 1995, *Landscape in the Uesslingen Region* (1969, oil on canvas, 28¾ x 43¼ ins / 73 x 110 cm) CHF 5,750. ZURICH, 30 Nov 1995, *Horseman in a Winter Landscape* (1970, oil on canvas, 30¼ x 32 ins / 77 x 81 cm) CHF 5,750. ZURICH, 5 June 1996, *Landscape* (1967, oil on canvas, 27½ x 24 ins / 70 x 61 cm) CHF 3,220. ZURICH, 14 March 2000, *Zurichsee by Dawn* (oil on canvas, 37 x 29 ins / 93 x 73 cm) CHF 3,300. ZURICH, 4 Nov 2000, *Still-life with Nectarines* (1987, oil on canvas, 20 x 20 ins / 50 x 51 cm) CHF 2,600. ZURICH, 24 June 2003, *The Circus has Arrived* (1970, oil on canvas, 29 x 45 ins / 73 x 115 cm) CHF 3,000.

SCHMID, Henry
French, 19th - 20th century.
Born in Paris.
Sculptor.

Henry Schmid, a pupil of Émile Thomas, exhibited in Paris at the Salon des Artistes Français, of which he became a member in 1893 and where he was awarded an honourable mention in 1896, a second-class medal in 1897, and an honourable mention and third-class medal at the time of the Exposition Universelle of 1900.

SCHMID, Hermann
Austrian, 19th - 20th century.
Born 18 February 1870, in Steyr.
Painter. Landscapes, architectural views.

Hermann Schmid was the pupil of H. Vincenz Havliceck in Vienna, where he was active.

MUSEUMS AND GALLERIES:

LINZ (Oberösterreichisches Landesmus.) - VIENNA (MM).

SCHMID, Joachim
German, 18th century.
Sculptor.

Joachim Schmid worked on St Peter's Church in the Black Forest.

SCHMID, Johann
Swiss, 19th century.
Lithographer, engraver.

Johann Schmid was active in Budapest from 1808 to 1835.

SCHMID, Johann. See also **SCHMIDT**

SCHMID, Johann Christian. See **SCHMIDT**

SCHMID, Johann Franz
German, 18th century.
Painter.

Johann Franz Schmid painted an altarpiece for Petershausen, a suburb of Constance.

SCHMID, Johann Georg. See **SCHMIDT**

SCHMID, Johann Jakob
Swiss, 18th century.
Born 9 November 1759, in Schaffhausen; died 1798, in Rome.
Sculptor.

Johann Jakob Schmid studied at the Kunstakademi in Copenhagen. There is a statuette of *Prometheus* by him in the Copenhagen Museum.

SCHMID, Johann Kaspar
German, 18th century.
Stucco artist.

SCHMID, Johann Michael
German, 18th century.
Stonemason.

Johann Michael Schmid became a freeman of Mainz in 1701. In 1720, he was commissioned to carve two altars for Trier cathedral, and in 1742 he carved all the sculptures for the palace of Kesselstadt in Trier.

SCHMID, Johann Rudolf (Baron von Schwarzenhorn)
Swiss, 17th century.
Born April 1590, in Stein on the Rhine; died 12 April 1667, in Vienna.
Draughtsman.

Johann Rudolf Schmid was ambassador to Constantinople. He drew views of the city and its surroundings.

SCHMID, Johannes
German, 18th century.
Active in Ulm.
Engraver.

In 1717, Johannes Schmid struck a medal in honour of Luther.

SCHMID, Joseph
German, 16th century.
Born in Urach; died 1555.
Sculptor.

Joseph Schmid lived for some time in Heidelberg and specialised in the carving of tombs.

SCHMID, Joseph
German, 17th century.
Stucco artist.

SCHMID, Joseph
Austrian, 19th - 20th century.
Born 2 August 1842, in Botzen (now Bolzano, Italy); died 23 February 1914, in Innsbruck.
Sculptor, draughtsman. Church decoration.

Joseph Schmid, a pupil at the fine arts academy in Munich from 1864 to 1866, decorated church interiors in the Tyrol.

SCHMID, Joseph Anton
German, 18th century.
Active in Augsburg.
Engraver (burin).

SCHMID, Julius
Austrian, 19th - 20th century.
Born 3 February 1854, in Vienna; died 1 February 1935.
Painter. Historical subjects, portraits, scenes with figures, interiors with figures.

Julius Schmid was a pupil of August Eisenmenger at the academy of fine arts in Vienna. He was awarded the Prix de Rome in 1878. He spent some time in Italy before settling in Vienna on his return to Austria. He exhibited at the Salon des Artistes Français in Paris and in 1900 won a bronze medal at the World's Fair.

MUSEUMS AND GALLERIES:

VIENNA (Kunsthistorisches Mus.): *Marie von Ebner Eschenbach; Beethoven; Haydn Quartet; Evening Devoted to Schu-*

bert in a House of the Viennese Bourgeoisie - VIENNA (Rathaus): *Emperor Franz-Josef; Burgomaster Prix.*
AUCTION RECORDS:
NEW YORK, 18 March 1998, *Beethoven in Meditation* (oil on canvas, 36 x 56 ins / 91.4 x 142.2 cm) USD 8,625.

SCHMID, Karl, or Schmidt, Schmitt
Austrian, 18th - 19th century.
Born 3 October 1763, in Seytingen; died 2 April 1831, in Vienna.
Medallist, painter. Portraits. Miniatures.
MUSEUMS AND GALLERIES:
GRAZ (Landesmus. Joanneum): several portrait miniatures - VIENNA (Österreichisches Mus. für Angewandte Kunst): several portrait miniatures.

SCHMID, Karl
Austrian, 19th century.
Born 1837; died 1871.
Active in Vienna.
Landscape artist.
Karl Schmid was a pupil of Anton Hansch.

SCHMID, Karl Anton
German, 18th century.
Born 1697; died 1754.
Active in Sarnen.
Painter.
Karl Anton Schmid was the brother of Franz Ignaz Schmid. He painted an *Assumption of the Virgin* for the church in Sarnen.

SCHMID, Karl August
German, 19th century.
Born 1807, in Neuburg; died 1834, in Munich.
Watercolourist, draughtsman. Landscapes, natural history.
Karl August Schmid studied at the academy in Munich from 1822 to 1825. After that date he studied from nature, travelling extensively in the Tyrol, Germany and Upper Italy. In 1831, he painted a series of watercolours relating to his travels. He produced a large number of natural history drawings.
MUSEUMS AND GALLERIES:
BESANÇON: *Morning by a Lake; Sunset over a Lake.*

SCHMID, Karl Emil
Swiss, 20th century.
Born 1 August 1888, in Bern; died 6 March 1915, in Winterthur.
Painter, draughtsman.

SCHMID, Konrad
Swiss, 20th century.
Born 10 July 1899, in Zurich; died 1958 or 1979, in Zollikon.
Painter.
Konrad Schmid was a pupil at the school of fine arts in Zurich.
MUSEUMS AND GALLERIES:
AARAU (Aargauer Kunsthaus): *Woman Painter* (c. 1940) - ZURICH.
AUCTION RECORDS:
BERN, 25 Oct 1979, *Fishermen on the Beach* (1924, oil on canvas, 19 x 24 ins / 48.5 x 61 cm) CHF 1,600. ZURICH, 8 Dec 1994, *Woman in a Garden* (1921, oil on canvas, 12 1/4 x 13 3/4 ins / 31 x 35 cm) CHF 4,600.

SCHMID, Leberecht
Austrian, 18th - 19th century.
Born 1751; died 2 April 1831, in Vienna.
Painter. Portraits.

SCHMID, Lorenz
German, 18th century.
Born 1743, in Augsburg; died 6 December 1799, in Bern.
Stucco artist.
Lorenz Schmid carried out the stucco decoration of the ceiling and the new hall of the Bern Library.

SCHMID, Martin Joseph
Swiss, 19th century.
Born 26 May 1786, in Schwyz; died 30 October 1842, in Ried.
Painter, watercolourist, miniaturist. Portraits.
Martin Joseph Schmid was the brother of David Alois and Franz Schmid. He studied with J.A. Janser and J.V. Sonnenschein.
AUCTION RECORDS:
PARIS, 11 Feb 1921, *Schaffhausen; Entlibuch* (watercolour, a pair) FRF 260. BERN, 26 June 1981, *St Gallen* (c. 1830, colour etching, 5 x 6 3/4 ins / 12.5 x 17.2 cm) CHF 1,500.

SCHMID, Matthias
Austrian, 19th - 20th century.
Born 14 November 1835, in the Tyrol; died 22 January 1923, in Munich.
Painter, illustrator. Historical subjects, figures, genre scenes, interiors with figures, landscapes, urban landscapes, seascapes.
Matthias Schmid was the pupil of Johann Hiltensperger, Johann Schraudolph and Karl von Piloty at the fine arts academy in Munich. He was the father of Rosa Schmid-Göringer.

BIBLIOGRAPHY:
Luger, Petra R., *Mathias Schmid*, Tyrolia-Verlag, Innsbruck, 1999.
MUSEUMS AND GALLERIES:
BAUTZEN: *Tyrolean Singer* - BUDAPEST: *Dream of the Hermit* - INNSBRUCK (Tiroler Landesmus. Ferdinandeum): *Inner Joy* - MUNICH (Pinakothek): *View of Feldkirch* - MUNICH (Städtische Gal. im Lenbachhaus): *Peasant Bedchamber.*
AUCTION RECORDS:
LONDON, 22 July 1927, *Dignity of Labour,* GBP 199. PARIS, 30 Nov-1 Dec 1942, *Seascape,* FRF 5,100. VIENNA, 1-4 Dec 1964, *Two Young Peasant Women before the Door of a Monastery,* ATS 35,000. VIENNA, 10 Feb 1976, *Man Carrying a Woman in a Mountain Landscape* (oil on canvas, 63 1/2 x 41 3/4 ins / 161 x 106 cm) ATS 38,000. MUNICH, 28 June 1983, *The Good Gift* (oil on canvas, 22 1/4 x 19 1/4 ins / 56.5 x 49 cm) DEM 4,800. COLOGNE, 20 May 1985, *The Refugees* (oil on canvas, 35 x 46 ins / 89 x 117 cm) DEM 38,000.

SCHMID, Melchior, or Schmidt
German, 17th century.
Born in Obersonthofen (Allgäu); died 1634, in Heilbronn.
Sculptor. Monuments.
Melchior Schmid carved a number of tombs.

SCHMID, Nikolaus, or Smed
German, 15th century.
Died before 1487.
Active in Breslau (now Wroclaw, Poland) in 1451 and 1469.
Painter.
In 1469 Nikolaus Schmid painted frescoes in the imperial chapel of Breslau.

SCHMID, Paul. See **SCHMIDT**

SCHMID, Peter
German, 16th century.
Died 9 December 1608, in Ulm.
Active in Ulm.
Sculptor.
Peter Schmid carved tombs and coats of arms.

SCHMID, Peter
German, 18th - 19th century.
Born 1769, in Trier; died 22 November 1853, in Ehrenbreitstein.
Painter.
Peter Schmid worked in Szczecin, Berlin and Frankfurt, following a system of his own invention, based on the study of nature. In 1834, he became a teacher of drawing in Berlin. He published a number of works, in which he developed his theories.

SCHMID, Peter or Petrus
Austrian, 18th century.
Born to a family originally from Fügen (Tyrol); died 6 March 1787.
Sculptor.
Peter Schmid worked mainly on religious subjects.

SCHMID, Richard Alan, or Richard Schmid
American, 20th - 21st century.
Born 1934, in Chicago.
Painter. Landscapes, portraits, nudes.
Richard Schmid showed an interest in the arts early in life, enrolling at the Famous Artists Course when he was 12 years old. He went on to study at the American Academy of Art under the instruction of William Mosby in 1952-1955. His works include portraits, nudes and landscapes, often depicting snow, painted in an impressionistic style.

Schmid has taken part in numerous group exhibitions, including: the Invitational Drawing Exhibition, 1966; the 33rd Annual Exhibition at the Butler Institute of American Art, 1968; and the 23rd American Drawing Biennial, 1969. Schmid has also had many solo shows.

In 1967 Schmid received the Jane Peterson Prize, and in 1971 and in 1972 he received the Gold Medal of Honour at the AWCS Exhibition.

AUCTION RECORDS:
HAYDEN, 31 July 1999, *Fort Collins' Winter* (oil on canvas, 18 x 24 ins / 46 x 61 cm) USD 22,500. HAYDEN, 31 July 1999, *Exeter Cottage* (oil on canvas, 24 x 40 ins / 61 x 102 cm) USD 45,000. NEW ORLEANS, 29 July 2000, *Sarah's Cow, a Still-life* (1965, oil on canvas, 20 x 30 ins / 51 x 76 cm) USD 1,750. HAYDEN, 29 July 2000, *Nancy and the Swans* (oil on canvas, 36 x 24 ins / 91 x 61 cm) USD 120,000. HAYDEN, 28 July 2001, *Irish Ducks* (oil on board, 8 x 12 ins / 20 x 30 cm) USD 17,000. HAYDEN, 28 July 2001, *Coronado Sundown* (oil on canvas, 9 x 14 ins / 24 x 36 cm) USD 25,000. HAYDEN, 27 July 2002, *Dogwood* (oil on canvas, 20 x 30 ins / 51 x 76 cm) USD 19,000. CEDAR FALLS, 23 Nov 2002, *Nude* (1965, oil on canvas, 18 x 12 ins / 46 x 30 cm) USD 7,500. SANTA FE, 23 May 2003, *Buckhorn Steam* (oil on board, 10 x 16 ins / 25 x 41 cm) USD 15,000. SANTA FE, 1 Nov 2003, *Michelle* (oil on canvas, 24 x 36 ins / 61 x 91 cm) USD 24,000. SANTA FE, 15 May 2004, *Manhattan Street near Penn Station* (oil on board, 12 x 20 ins / 30 x 51 cm) USD 10,000. SANTA FE, 23 Oct 2004, *Lilies and Carnations* (1992, oil on canvas, 24 x 30 ins / 61 x 76 cm) USD 27,000.

SCHMID, Samantha
French, 20th century.
Sculptor, glassmaker.
Samantha Schmid was awarded the Cognac municipal prize in 1990 and the Grand Prix des Métiers d'Art in 1997. She regularly exhibits at exhibitions devoted to glass-work, including the international festival that is held in Palau del Vidre, Catalonia. She held a solo exhibition at the Galerie La Capitale in 2001. She assembles strips of pale green, bluish and dark glass and adds inscription or small figures to the labyrinthine shapes she constructs.

SCHMID, Thomas, called Glaser
Swiss, 16th century.
Died between 1550 and 1560, in Schaffhausen.
Active in Schaffhausen.
Painter. Religious subjects.
Several of Thomas Schmid's paintings are preserved in the collections (Fürstlich Hohenzollernsche Sammlungen) in Sigmaringen Castle.

AUCTION RECORDS:
BERN, 5 Dec 1964, *Massacre of the Innocents; St Bartholomew*, CHF 12,000.

SCHMID, Ulrich
Swiss, 16th century.
Sculptor.
Ulrich Schmid carved the ceilings of several churches in the canton of Zurich.

SCHMID, Walter
Swiss, 20th century.
Born 1925.
Painter, watercolourist. Animals.

MUSEUMS AND GALLERIES:
AARAU (Aargauer Kunsthaus): *Wild Swan*.

SCHMID, Wilhelm
German, 19th century.
Painter. Portraits.
Wilhelm Schmid was the son of Peter Schmid and the brother of Carl Friedrich Ludwig Schmid. He exhibited in Berlin between 1834 and 1840 and settled in Trier in 1840.

SCHMID, Wilhelm
Swiss, 20th century.
Born 1892, in Remigen (Zurich); died 1971, in Bré, near Lugano.
Painter, watercolourist, draughtsman. Genre scenes, scenes with figures, figures, landscapes, village views, still-lifes (flowers/fruit).

W SCHMID

MUSEUMS AND GALLERIES:
AARAU (Aargauer Kunsthaus): *Castle at Villeneuve-les-Avignon* (1913, drawing); *Walpurgisnacht* (c. 1917-1918, watercolour); *Luna* (c. 1919-1920); *Italian Landscape* (c. 1920, watercolour); *Maize in flower* (c. 1923); *Billiard Players* (c. 1924-1931); *St-Gervais, Paris* (c. 1924-1931, watercolour); *Flowers* (c. 1925); *Flowers in a Pot* (c. 1925); *Summer Sun* (1930); *Lemons* (c. 1930); *Algerian Woman* (c. 1930); *Red Onions in a Green Bowl* (c. 1930); *Still-life with Cups* (c. 1930, watercolour); *Stiegüferli* (c. 1932); *Southern Landscape* (after 1937, watercolour); *Bré with the House of the Painter* (after 1937); *Ticino Landscape* (after 1937); *Butcher's Shop in Aarau* (1940); *Butcher's Shop in Aarau* (c. 1940); *Still-life with Drum* (1942); *Moonlit Night* (c. 1945); *Cureglia near Lugano* (c. 1945); *Woman Seated* (c. 1945); *Woman Viewed from the Rear* (1946); *Bré in May* (c. 1950); *Bré in an Early Spring* (1954); *Bré in May* (1956) - ESSEN (Folkwang

Mus.): two drawings - SZCZECIN: *Young Girl with Cat; Woman Crouching* (watercolour); *Ticino Landscape* (watercolour).

AUCTION RECORDS:

VERSAILLES, 22 April 1990, *Two Friends* (oil on card, 28 3/4 x 19 1/2 ins / 73 x 49.5 cm) FRF 4,800. LUCERNE, 23 May 1992, *Duel* (oil on canvas, 13 x 16 1/4 ins / 33 x 41 cm) CHF 7,400. ZURICH, 4 June 1992, *Still-life with a Vase of Flowers* (oil on canvas, 20 3/4 x 16 3/4 ins / 53 x 42.5 cm) CHF 2,825. PARIS, 27 Jan 1993, *Blue House* (oil on canvas, 25 1/2 x 32 ins / 65 x 81 cm) FRF 4,000. LUCERNE, 4 June 1994, *Town in the South of France* (oil on canvas, 19 3/4 x 25 1/2 ins / 50 x 65 cm) CHF 5,600. ZURICH, 12 June 1995, *Still-life with Apples and Pears* (oil on panel, 15 x 21 1/4 ins / 38 x 54 cm) CHF 2,530. ZURICH, 8 April 1997, *Villa in Bré* (gouache and oil on paper, 12 1/4 x 16 ins / 31 x 40.5 cm) CHF 1,800. ZURICH, 18 Nov 1997, *Sausages* (oil on wood, 21 1/4 x 28 3/4 ins / 54 x 73 cm) CHF 4,400. ZURICH, 9 June 1999, *Pierrot* (1929-1962, oil on board, 22 x 15 ins / 55 x 38 cm) CHF 4,500. ST GALL, 2 Nov 1999, *Village of Bré in Early Spring* (oil on board, 24 x 32 ins / 60 x 81 cm) CHF 6,400. ZURICH, 7 Dec 2000, *Vase of Flowers* (oil on panel, 24 x 19 ins / 61 x 48 cm) CHF 8,500. ZURICH, 7 Dec 2000, *Snooker Players* (oil on canvas, 28 x 35 ins / 71 x 90 cm) CHF 13,000. ZOFINGEN, 30 Nov 2001, *Flowers* (oil on canvas, 22 x 19 ins / 57 x 48 cm) CHF 2,700. ZOFINGEN, 30 Nov 2001, *Still-life of Flowers* (oil on canvas, 18 x 20 ins / 45 x 51 cm) CHF 3,100. PARIS, 13 March 2002, *The Card Players* (oil on panel, 14 x 19 ins / 36 x 47 cm) EUR 8,200. ST GALL, 6 Nov 2002, *Landscape with Pruned Trees* (oil on board, 24 x 32 ins / 60 x 81 cm) CHF 6,000. ZURICH, 8 Dec 2003, *Southern Landscape with Small Town* (oil on canvas, 21 x 26 ins / 54 x 65 cm) CHF 9,800.

SCHMID, Willy

German, 20th century.
Born 23 October 1890, in Munich.
Painter.

Willy Schmid was the pupil of Angelo Janck and Julius Diez. He was active in Obermenzing, near Munich.

MUSEUMS AND GALLERIES:

BOCHUM - MUNICH (Städtische Gal. im Lenbachhaus) - MUNICH (State Collection): *Self-portrait*; other works - WUPPERTAL (Ruhmeshalle).

SCHMID-BREITENBACH, Franz Xaver

German, 19th - 20th century.
Born 17 August 1857, in Munich; died 3 January 1927, in Munich.
Painter. Genre scenes.

Franz Schmid-Breitenbach was the pupil of Alexander Strähuber, Michaël Echter, Gyula Benczur and Ludwig von Löfftz at the academy of fine arts in Munich.

MUSEUMS AND GALLERIES:

MUNICH (Pinakothek): *Magical Illusion*.

AUCTION RECORDS:

MUNICH, 21 June 1994, *Die hohe Zeche* (*The Hefty Bill*) (oil on panel, 19 3/4 x 15 3/4 ins / 50 x 40 cm) DEM 2,070.

SCHMID-DIETENHEIM, Nikolaus

German, 20th century.
Born 24 February 1878, in Dietenheim; died 7 March 1915, in France, at the front.
Painter, engraver. Landscapes.

SCHMID-FICHTELBERG, Josef Anton

German, 20th century.
Born 8 February 1877, in Munich.
Painter. Portraits, landscapes.

SCHMID-GOERTZ, Gustav

German, 20th century.
Born 15 November 1889.
Painter.

Gustav Schmid-Goertz was the pupil of Fritz Mackensen and Julius Gari Melchers. He was active in Hamburg.

SCHMID-GÖRINGER, Rosa

Austrian, 19th - 20th century.
Born 21 April 1868, in Salzburg.
Also active in Germany.
Painter. Portraits, still-lifes.

Rosa Schmid-Göringer was the daughter and pupil of Matthias Schmid.

SCHMID-REUTTE, Ludwig

Austrian, 19th - 20th century.
Born 13 January 1863, in Lech-Aschau (Tyrol); died 13 November 1909, in Illenau.
Also active in Germany.
Painter. History painting, portraits.

Ludwig Schmid-Reutte was the pupil of Ludwig von Löfftz at the fine arts academy in Munich. He seems to have had a teaching post in Munich around 1890, and was a professor at the academy of fine arts in Karlsruhe from 1899 onwards.

MUSEUMS AND GALLERIES:

KARLSRUHE: *Consumatum est* - MANNHEIM: *Portrait of the Artist's Mother* - STUTTGART: *Fugitives at Rest*.

SCHMIDELY, Daniel, or Schmitteli

Austrian, 18th century.
Born 1710; died c. 1780, in Presburg, now Bratislava.
Active in Presburg.
Painter. Portraits.

Schmidely studied with Kamauf and, from 1728, at the academy in Vienna.

SCHMIDGRUBER, Anton

Austrian, 19th - 20th century.
Born 26 March 1837, in Vienna; died 18 April 1909, in Vienna.
Sculptor.

Anton Schmidgruber was the pupil of Franz Bauer at the fine arts academy in Vienna. He followed Bauer's example by going to work in Rome in 1868.

SCHMIDHAMMER, Arpad

German, 19th - 20th century.
Born 12 February 1857, in St Joachimsthal (Bohemia), Czech Republic; died 13 May 1921, in Munich.
Painter, illustrator. Still-lifes (flowers/fruit).

Arpad Schmidhammer studied in Graz and Vienna and was the pupil of Ludwig von Löfftz, Gabriel von Hackl, Johann Caspar Herterich and Hugo Diez at the fine arts academy in Munich.

From 1896 onwards he collaborated on the review *Jugend*, as well as on other publications including the *Berliner illustrierte Zeitung, Jungbrunnenhefte, Knecht Ruprecht, Jugendland*, etc. He produced drawings for children's books and illustrated numerous works, chiefly fairy tales, including Musäus' *Rübezahl und das Hirschberger Schneiderlein* in 1902, Ganghofer's *Märchen von Karfunkelstein, Hänsel und Gretel, Tischlein deck dich* by the Brothers Grimm in 1906, and *Wieviel sind's* by Holst in 1926. He was the author and illustrator of works including *Mucki*, 1905, *Der verlorene Pfennig*, 1908, *Nordpolspass*, 1910, *Drei Helden, Heinzelmännchen, Heiteres Spiel* and *Guck hinein* in 1911 and the *Geschichte von General Hindenburg* in 1915. Although his style of drawing was on the whole caricature-like, it was nevertheless highly effective.

BIBLIOGRAPHY:

Osterwalder, Marcus (ed.), *Dictionnaire des illustrateurs 1800-1914*, Ides et Calendes, Neuchâtel, 1989.

AUCTION RECORDS:

NEW YORK, 19 Jan 1995, *Still-life with an Urn, Flowers and Fruit* (oil on canvas, 57 x 29 3/4 ins / 144.8 x 75.6 cm) USD 6,900.

SCHMIDHAMMER, Franz
Austrian, 18th century.
Born in Vienna; died 1796, in Kaschau (now Košice, Slovakia).
Painter.
Schmidhammer studied at the Kunstakademie in Vienna from 1767.

SCHMIDHAUSER, Janos Johann, or Schmidhausen
Austrian, 18th century.
Born c. 1730, in Kremnitz (now Kremnica, Slovakia); died 25 April 1800, in Kremnitz.
Medallist.
Schmidhauser studied at the academy in Vienna.

SCHMIDL
Bohemian School, 18th century.
Active in Bechlín in 1746.
Painter.
Schmidl painted an altarpiece for the church in Petrovice.

SCHMIDL, Heinrich
German, 19th century.
Active c. 1803.
Engraver.
Schmidl engraved mainly reproductions.

SCHMIDLIN, Adolf
German, 19th - 20th century.
Born 20 May 1868, in Lahr.
Painter. Figures, portraits, landscapes.
Adolf Schmidlin was the pupil of Ernst Schurth, Theodor Poeckh, Kaspar Ritter and Ferdinand Keller at the fine arts academy in Karlsruhe. He continued his artistic training in Munich, at the Académie Julian in Paris and in Rome and was active in Freiburg im Brisgau.

SCHMIDLIN, David
German, 17th century.
Active in Freiburg im Breisgau c. 1626.
Painter.

SCHMIDMANN, Laszlo or Ladislaus
Hungarian, 20th century.
Born 23 June 1888, in Székesfehérvár.
Sculptor.
Laszlo Schmidmann studied in Munich and Budapest, where he settled.

SCHMIDS, Charles
French, 19th century.
Portrait painter.
His work was shown at the Salons of 1839 and 1850.

SCHMIDT
German, 18th century.
Born to a family originally from Dresden.
Active at the end of the 18th century.
Sculptor (wood).
Schmidt worked at the academy in St Petersburg.

SCHMIDT
German, 18th century.
Active in Nordheim c. 1788.
Cabinet maker.
Schmidt carved altars in Harrbach.

SCHMIDT, Adalbert
German, 19th century.
Born 1804, in Ansbach.
Painter.
Adalbert Schmidt studied at the academy in Munich.

SCHMIDT, Adam
German, 19th century.
Born to a family originally from Crailsheim.
Painter (porcelain).
Adam Schmidt was active in Ludwigsburg around 1810.

SCHMIDT, Adolf
German, 19th century.
Active c. 1803.
Draughtsman. Portraits.
Adolf Schmidt drew the portrait of Friedrich Friesen, the adjutant of Lutzow.

SCHMIDT, Adolf
German, 19th century.
Born 1804, in Berlin.
Painter. Genre scenes, portraits.
Adolf Schmidt studied in Düsseldorf with W. Wach, and in Berlin.
MUSEUMS AND GALLERIES:
HANOVER (Niedersächsisches Landesmus.): a genre scene.
AUCTION RECORDS:
COLOGNE, 14 March 1986, *Genre Scene* (oil on canvas, 28 1/2 x 30 1/4 ins / 72.5 x 77 cm) DEM 14,000.

SCHMIDT, Adolf
German, 19th century.
Born 17 May 1827, in Dresden; died 21 June 1888, in Munich.
Painter. Genre scenes, landscapes with figures, landscapes, animals.
Adolf Schmidt worked in Dresden, Berlin and Munich.
MUSEUMS AND GALLERIES:
DRESDEN: *Horses at Rest; Winter Landscape* - MAINZ: *Strolling Players in a Winter Landscape*.
AUCTION RECORDS:
COLOGNE, 23 Nov 1977, *Street Scene with a Large Number of Figures, by the Bay of Sorrento* (oil on canvas, 13 1/4 x 18 1/2 ins / 33.5 x 47 cm) DEM 8,500. MUNICH, 2 May 1979, *Wooded Landscape* (oil on canvas, 9 1/2 x 13 1/2 ins / 24 x 34 cm) DEM 3,500. COLOGNE, 22 Oct 1982, *Sledge in a Winter Landscape* (oil on panel, 11 1/4 x 16 ins / 28.5 x 40.5 cm) DEM 5,000. VIENNA, 9 Oct 1985, *Stopping outside the Inn* (oil/paper remounted on board, 10 1/4 x 13 3/4 ins / 26 x 35 cm) ATS 45,000. COLOGNE, 20 Oct 1989, *Two Horsemen in a Bavarian Village* (oil on canvas, 10 x 14 1/4 ins / 25.5 x 36 cm) DEM 6,500. COLOGNE, 23 March 1990, *The Dangerous Road* (oil on panel, 11 1/4 x 16 ins / 28.5 x 40.5 cm) DEM 4,600.

SCHMIDT, Albert
Swiss, 20th century.
Born 1 September 1883, in Geneva; died 1970, in Geneva.
Painter, watercolourist, draughtsman, engraver, lithographer. Figures, nudes, portraits, landscapes. Symbolism.
Albert Schmidt was a pupil at the school of decorative arts and the school of fine arts in Geneva, and subsequently received guidance from Ferdinand Hodler and Eugène Gilliard. He took part in a very large number of collective exhibitions between 1904 and 1951, in particular at the Swiss Salon de la Société Nationale des Beaux-Arts and the Salon d'Automne; he showed his work in solo exhibitions with similar frequency. In around 1920 he was regarded as a leading disciple of Hodler and a prominent contemporary of Cuno Amiet.

A. Schmidt

BIBLIOGRAPHY:
Albert H. Schmidt, exhibition leaflet, Museum of New Mexico Press, Santa Fe (NM), 1958. *Albert Schmidt*, Éd. Perret-Gentil, Geneva, 1974.
MUSEUMS AND GALLERIES:
GENEVA (MAH): *Cherry Tree in Blossom*.

AUCTION RECORDS:
LUCERNE, 30 Sept 1988, *Female Nude in a Park* (oil on paper, 24 3/4 x 17 1/4 ins / 63 x 44 cm) CHF 1,400. BERN, 26 Oct 1988, *Landscape in the Salève Region* (1916, oil on canvas, 21 1/4 x 25 1/2 ins / 54 x 65 cm) CHF 1,500. BERN, 12 May 1990, *Plantation of Trees* (1915, watercolour and pencil, 11 1/4 x 16 1/2 ins / 28.5 x 42 cm) CHF 3,300. LUCERNE, 15 May 1993, *Female Nude, Standing* (1915, oil on canvas, 35 1/2 x 16 1/4 ins / 90 x 41 cm) CHF 1,200. ZURICH, 12 June 1995, *Rocks* (oil on card, 17 x 22 1/2 ins / 43 x 57 cm) CHF 2,645. BERN, 7 May 1999, *Apple Tree in Garden* (oil on canvas, 20 x 24 ins / 50 x 61 cm) CHF 2,800. ZURICH, 15 June 1999, *Woman in Lilac* (oil on canvas, 24 x 20 ins / 62 x 51 cm) CHF 3,200. BERN, 9 Nov 2000, *Two Sailing Boats at Jetty* (1916, oil on canvas, 40 x 40 ins / 101 x 101 cm) CHF 6,500. BERN, 7 Nov 2003, *Three Standing Female Nudes* (oil on canvas, 26 x 21 ins / 65 x 54 cm) CHF 3,800. BERN, 14 May 2004, *Winter in the Mountains* (oil on panel, 19 x 2 ins / 48 x 5 cm) CHF 3,000.

SCHMIDT, Albrecht Elvinus, or Schmid
Danish, 19th - 20th century.
Born 9 April 1870, in Copenhagen.
Painter. Interiors, landscapes.
Albrecht Schmidt was the pupil of Kristian Zahrtmann and of the stage set painters Valdemar Gyllich and Carl Christian Lund. He was active in Copenhagen as a writer and actor as well as an artist.
MUSEUMS AND GALLERIES:
SKAGEN (Skagens Mus.).

SCHMIDT, Alfred
German, 19th - 20th century.
Born 29 April 1867, in Dresden.
Painter, engraver, lithographer.
Alfred Schmidt was the pupil of August Eduard Nicolaus Meyer in Karlsruhe. He studied at the Académie Julian in Paris. From 1900 onwards he was active in Stuttgart, where he was the director of a school of painting.

SCHMIDT, Alfred Michael Roedsted
Danish, 19th - 20th century.
Born 3 May 1858, in Horsens (Jutland).
Painter, illustrator, draughtsman, caricaturist.
Alfred Michael Roedsted Schmidt was the pupil of Frederik Helsted, Jørgen Roed and Christian Thomsen at the academy of fine arts in Copenhagen. He collaborated on a number of humorous publications.

SCHMIDT, Allan
Danish, 20th century.
Painter. Landscapes with figures.
AUCTION RECORDS:
COPENHAGEN, 12 March 1996, *Red Figure in a Landscape* (1964, oil on canvas, 51 1/4 x 63 3/4 ins / 130 x 162 cm) DKK 6,000.

SCHMIDT, Alois
German, 19th - 20th century.
Born 15 August 1855, in Raiersdorf.
Sculptor.
Alois Schmidt, who sculpted in wood, settled in Bad Landeck in 1876.

SCHMIDT, Andreas
German, 17th century.
Sculptor (wood).

SCHMIDT, Andreas
Austrian, 18th century.
Died 22 February 1757, in Rein, near Graz.
Painter.
Andreas Schmidt was in holy orders and worked at the monastery of Rein, near Graz.

SCHMIDT, Andreas
German, 18th century.
Born 1726, in Rössel (Prussia); died 1789 or 1790, in Königsberg (now Kaliningrad, Russia).
Sculptor.
Andreas Schmidt spent the last part of his life in Königsberg and carved the high altar for the city's Catholic church.

SCHMIDT, Antal or Anton
Austrian, 18th century.
Active in Kremnitz (now Kremnica, Slovakia).
Painter.
Antal Schmidt was a pupil of J.L. Kracker.

SCHMIDT, Anton Karl
Austrian, 20th century.
Born 18 April 1887, in Vienna.
Painter, watercolourist. Portraits, landscapes, still-lifes.
Anton Schmidt was a pupil at the academy of fine arts in Vienna, where he settled.
MUSEUMS AND GALLERIES:
VIENNA (Albertina Mus.): two watercolours.

SCHMIDT, August
German, 19th century.
Born 1811; died 24 January 1886, in Augsburg.
Sculptor.
August Schmidt studied at the academy in Munich and worked in Munich and Augsburg.

SCHMIDT, Augusta
German, 18th - 19th century.
Born at the end of the 18th century, in Berlin.
Painter. Portraits, genre scenes.
Augusta Schmidt studied in Paris with J. B. Mauzaisse and exhibited there in 1827.

SCHMIDT, Balthasar
German, 17th century.
Engraver.
Balthasar Schmidt was active in Augsburg in the first half of the 17th century as an engraver of armorials and coins.

SCHMIDT, Bastian
Austrian, 19th century.
Active c. 1857.
Engraver (burin).

SCHMIDT, Bernhard
Austrian, 18th century.
Born 1712; died 1782.
Active in Gmunden.
Painter.
Bernhard Schmidt painted altarpieces.

SCHMIDT, Bernhard
German, 19th century.
Born 21 March 1820, in Zettemin, near Stavenhagen; died 4 December 1870, in Niesky, near Rothenburg.
Painter, draughtsman. Landscapes, waterscapes, architectural views.
Bernhard Schmidt studied in Berlin with Wilhelm Schirmer, and in Düsseldorf and Munich. He spent some time in Berlin.
MUSEUMS AND GALLERIES:
SCHWERIN: *On the Banks of Lake Neukwal, near Schwerin.*

SCHMIDT, C.
German, 17th century.
Medallist.

SCHMIDT, Carl
German, 18th - 19th century.
Born 1770; died 11 September 1850, in Altenburg.
Painter (including porcelain). Figures, flowers.

Carl Schmidt was a professor of drawing and also a writer. He worked with Christian Scheilz and Johann Georg Gabel at the porcelain factory in Gotha, painting figures and flowers on porcelain.

SCHMIDT, Carl
German, 19th century.
Active in Berlin.
Painter. Genre scenes.
Carl Schmidt was a pupil of Wilhelm Herbig. He worked in Rome between 1831 and 1832.

SCHMIDT, Carl
American, 20th century.
Born 1885; died 1969.
Painter. Landscapes.
AUCTION RECORDS:
LOS ANGELES-SAN FRANCISCO, 10 Oct 1990, *Irvine Ranch at Laguna Beach* (oil on canvas, 30 1/2 x 36 ins / 77.5 x 91.5 cm) USD 9,900. DETROIT, 8 Jan 1999, *Hill Top Riders, Cowboys on Horses* (oil on board, 30 x 36 ins / 76 x 91 cm) USD 1,700. CINCINNATI, 23 May 1999, *Hilltop Riders* (c. 1930, oil on canvas, 30 x 36 ins / 76 x 91 cm) USD 1,800. OAK PARK, 22 Oct 2000, *Waiting for the Herder* (oil on canvas, 40 x 50 ins / 102 x 127 cm) USD 5,500. OAK PARK, 8 Dec 2002, *High Sierras* (c. 1930, oil on canvas, 30 x 36 ins / 76 x 91 cm) USD 3,750. CINCINNATI, 7 June 2003, *Covered Wagon* (c. 1930, oil on canvasboard, 6 x 8 ins / 16 x 20 cm) USD 2,500.

SCHMIDT, Carl Christian
German, 19th - 20th century.
Born 18 December 1868, in Rostock.
Active in Stettin (now Szczecin, Poland).
Painter.

SCHMIDT, Carl Friedrich Wilhelm
German, 19th century.
Born 1812, in Berlin.
Painter, lithographer. Flowers.
Schmidt was a pupil of K. Röthig, and in 1835 he studied at the academy in Munich.

SCHMIDT, Carl Heinrich Frantz
Danish, 19th - 20th century.
Born 27 April 1858, in Horsens (Jutland); died 27 September 1923, in Copenhagen.
Painter, illustrator.

SCHMIDT, Carl Heinrich Wilhelm
German, 19th century.
Born 31 May 1790, in Dresden; died 22 January 1865, in Dresden.
Painter.
Carl Heinrich Wilhelm Schmidt was the son of the court painter Johann Heinrich Schmidt, the brother of Heinrich Friedrich Thomas and the father of Julius Schmidt, born 1826, Adolf, born 1827, and Theodor. He studied at the academy in Dresden and worked in Rome from 1823 to 1824. He painted his own portrait and that of the father of Ludwig Richter.

SCHMIDT, Carsten
Austrian, 16th century.
Active in Greifswald.
Painter. Religious subjects. Murals.
Carsten Schmidt worked for the church of St James in Greifswald.

SCHMIDT, Christian
German, 19th - 20th century.
Born 11 June 1869.
Sculptor.
Christian Schmidt, a pupil at the academy of fine arts in Dresden, was based in Halle.
MUSEUMS AND GALLERIES:
HALLE (Zoological Garden): *Archer.*

SCHMIDT, Christian Andreas
German, 18th century.
Born to a family originally from Goslar; died 1775, in Amsterdam.
Engraver (burin).
Christian Andreas Schmidt was active in Göttingen between 1745 and 1748, the year in which he moved to Amsterdam.

SCHMIDT, Christian Bernhard
German, 18th century.
Born 1734, in Rössel (Prussia); died 1784, in Rössel (Prussia).
Sculptor.
Christian Bernhard Schmidt is known to have carved the altars in the Catholic churches of Bischofstein and Peterswald.

SCHMIDT, Christian Elias. See **SCHMIDT Georg Matthias** and **Christian Elias**

SCHMIDT, Christoph
German, 17th century.
Born 1632, in Nuremberg.
Engraver (burin).
Christoph Schmidt was active in Augsburg and was married there in 1654.

SCHMIDT, Christoph
German, 17th century.
Born probably in Dresden; died beginning August 1688, in Dresden.
Painter.
Christoph Schmidt was the son of Georg Schmidt.

SCHMIDT, Christoph J.
German, 19th century.
Active in Offenbach am Main (Hesse).
Lithographer, engraver (burin).

SCHMIDT, Christoph Lorenz
German, 17th century.
Born in Wunsiedel.
Sculptor.
Christophe Lorenz Schmidt was married in Wunsiedel in 1689. He was active in Bayreuth in 1694.

SCHMIDT, Eduard
German, 19th century.
Born 1806, in Berlin; died 1862.
Painter. Landscapes, seascapes.
Eduard Schmidt studied with Carl Blechen at the academy of fine arts in Berlin. He painted the coasts of Heligoland, England and Sweden.
MUSEUMS AND GALLERIES:
SCHWERIN: *Rough Sea* - TRIESTE (Civico Mus. Revoltella): *Ramsgate.*
AUCTION RECORDS:
COLOGNE, 21 June 1974, *Fishing Boats off the English Coast,* DEM 4,200. NEW YORK, 14 Jan 1977, *Fishing Boats at Sea* (oil on canvas, 27 x 37 3/4 ins / 68.5 x 96 cm) USD 4,000. NEW YORK, 30 May 1980, *Fishing Boat in a High Sea* (oil on canvas, 14 x 21 ins / 35.6 x 53.3 cm) USD 1,900. LONDON, 22 June 1983, *Estuary in Winter* (oil on canvas, 15 x 19 ins / 38 x 48 cm) GBP 850. LONDON, 7 June 1989, *Small Boats at Sea* (oil on canvas, 27 1/4 x 37 ins / 69 x 94 cm) GBP 4,620. NEW YORK, 18-19 July 1996, *The Forge* (oil on panel, 8 x 10 ins / 19.4 x 25.1 cm) USD 15,525. BERN, 9 Nov 2000, *Fishing Boats in Storm* (oil on canvas, 31 x 42 ins / 78 x 107 cm) CHF 3,500. BERN, 9 Nov 2000, *Landscape in Helgoland* (oil on canvas, 17 x 24 ins / 42 x 60 cm) CHF 4,300. LONDON, 17 Jan 2001, *Dutch Fishing Boats Leaving a Breakwater, Paddle Steamer Beyond* (oil on canvas, 26 x 37 ins / 67 x 94 cm) GBP 4,000. BREMEN, 12 Oct 2001, *Northern Tip of Helgoland* (oil on canvas, 26 x 38 ins /

67 x 96 cm) DEM 8,000. AHLDEN, 20 Sept 2002, *Harbour in Morning Light* (oil on canvas, 23 x 17 ins / 59 x 42 cm) EUR 5,800. AMSTERDAM, 15 April 2003, *Windmill in a Winter Landscape* (oil on canvas, 18 x 22 ins / 45 x 57 cm) EUR 4,800. NEW YORK, 3 Dec 2003, *Coastal City* (oil on canvas, 27 x 38 ins / 69 x 96 cm) USD 5,000.

SCHMIDT, Eduard
German, 19th century.
Born 1809, in Schweinfurt.
Painter.
Eduard Schmidt studied at the academy of fine arts in Munich from 1826 to 1829, and with Ludwig Doell in Altenburg in 1831. He settled in Bamberg in 1839.

SCHMIDT, Eduard
German, 20th century.
Born 16 October 1885, in Offenbach am Main (Hesse).
Painter.
Eduard Schmidt was the pupil of Robert Pötzelberger and Christian Landenberger, almost certainly at the fine arts academy in Stuttgart. He was based in Alsbach, on the Bargstrasse.

SCHMIDT, Elias
German, 17th century.
Born in Freiberg; died 18 August 1639, in Meissen.
Sculptor.
Elias Schmidt was probably a pupil of Balthasar Barthel. He married in Meissen in 1623, and became a freeman of the city in 1627.
MUSEUMS AND GALLERIES:
NEUSTADT (Church): several low reliefs.

SCHMIDT, Elisabeth
German, 19th - 20th century.
Born 12 February 1862, in Gadebusch.
Painter. Genre scenes, interiors.
Elisabeth Schmidt was the pupil of Karl Gussow andd Karl Stauffer-Bern at the academy of fine arts in Berlin. She was also taught by Friedrich Fehr and Ludwig Schmid-Reutte at the Karlsruhe academy (or at the Munich academy, according to some sources) and studied at the Académie Julian in Paris.
MUSEUMS AND GALLERIES:
ROSTOCK: *Interior* (two works).

SCHMIDT, Elisabeth
German, 20th century.
Born 18 February 1882, in Sophienberg, near Posmahlen (East Prussia).
Painter. Portraits, landscapes, flowers.

SCHMIDT, Ernst Christian
German, 19th century.
Born 1809, in Eisenach.
Engraver (burin), draughtsman.
Ernst Christian Schmidt studied in Munich.

SCHMIDT, Esaias
German, 17th century.
Died 30 June 1639, in Freiburg (Saxony).
Active in Freiburg (Saxony).
Sculptor. Portraits.

SCHMIDT, Felix
German, 19th - 20th century.
Born 6 June 1857, in Lübeck.
Painter, watercolourist, lithographer. Scenes with figures, landscapes, animals.
Felix Schmidt was the pupil of Gyula Benczur, Georg Raab and Ludwig von Löfftz at the fine arts academy in Munich.
AUCTION RECORDS:
COLOGNE, 30 March 1984, *Cowboy Shooting at an Indian* (watercolour, 6 x 9 ins / 15.5 x 23 cm) DEM 4,000.

SCHMIDT, Franz
Austrian, 18th century.
Of Viennese origin.
Painter.

SCHMIDT, Franz
German, 18th century.
Born c. 1767.
Painter.
Franz Schmidt was active in Rome from 1787 to 1788.

SCHMIDT, Franz
German, 19th century.
Painter.
Franz Schmidt was the son of Wilhelm Ludwig and the brother of Gottfried Schmidt. He worked in Heidelberg and Stuttgart. He painted a portrait of Queen Catherine of Wurtemberg.

SCHMIDT, Franz. See also **SCHMID**

SCHMIDT, Franz Michael
Austrian, 18th century.
Born in Grafenwörth, near Krems; died before 1800, probably in Vienna.
Landscape artist.
Franz Michael Schmidt was the younger brother of the stonemason Martin Johann Schmidt.

SCHMIDT, Franz Willibald
Austrian, 18th century.
Born 1764, in Planá, Bohemia; died 2 February 1796.
Painter. Flowers.
Franz Willibald Schmidt was a botanist and painted flowers.

SCHMIDT, Franz Xaver
Austrian, 19th - 20th century.
Died March 1917, in Vienna.
Painter. Landscapes.
MUSEUMS AND GALLERIES:
VIENNA (Julian Brück Collection).

SCHMIDT, Frédéric Albert
French, 19th - 20th century.
Born 9 December 1846, in Sundhouse; died 24 January 1916, in Weimar.
Also active in Germany.
Painter. Figures, genre scenes, interiors with figures, landscapes, seascapes, architectural views.
Frédéric Albert Schmidt, a pupil of Eugène Lavieille, fist exhibited at the Paris Salon in 1876. In his landscapes he shows that he was very aware of hourly and seasonal changes in light.
MUSEUMS AND GALLERIES:
MULHOUSE: *Reading*; *The Sea in Capri* - WEIMAR: *Twighlight*; *Alder Forest in Autumn*; *Fishing Boat near Dieppe*; *Beech Trees in Spring*.
AUCTION RECORDS:
NEW YORK, 28 Oct 1981, *Water Mill* (oil on panel, 6 x 4 1/4 ins / 15.2 x 10.8 cm) USD 1,800.

SCHMIDT, Friedrich
German, 17th century.
Born in Buttstädt; died 9 May 1670, in Buttstädt.
Painter.
In 1642, Friedrich Schmidt decorated the church of St Lawrence in Hof.

SCHMIDT, Friedrich
Austrian, 17th century.
Born 27 February 1663, in Grins (Tyrol).
Sculptor (stone).

SCHMIDT, Friedrich
German, 19th century.

Born 1808, in Augsburg.
Painter. Portraits.
Friedrich Schmidt studied at the academy in Munich.

SCHMIDT, Friedrich
German, 19th century.
Painter. Portraits.
Friedrich Schmidt was a student at the academy of fine art in Munich in 1829. He was active in Breslau (now Wroclaw, Poland).

SCHMIDT, Friedrich August
German, 19th century.
Born 1796, in Gera; died 5 January 1866, in Hanover.
Painter (including porcelain). Portraits.
Friedrich August Schmidt studied at the academy in Dresden. He worked in Halberstadt from 1823 to 1824, then in Göttingen, Luneburg, Hamburg, Salzwedel, Stade, Bremen and Frankfurt. From 1834 he settled in Hanover. He painted *King George V*, when he was heir to the throne, and Queen *Friederike*. He also painted miniature portraits.
MUSEUMS AND GALLERIES:
HANOVER (Niedersächsisches Landesmus.): *Portrait of Colonel August Reinecke.*

SCHMIDT, Friedrich August
German, 19th century.
Painter, engraver (burin), lithographer. Landscapes, architectural views.
Friedrich August Schmidt studied in Dresden from 1814 to 1816. From 1824, he worked in Berlin, and exhibited at the academy in Berlin from 1824 to 1848. He visited Italy in 1831 and 1832.

SCHMIDT, Friedrich Wilhelm
German, 18th century.
Active in Berlin during the second half of the 18th century.
Engraver. Vignettes.
Friedrich Wilhelm Schmidt was the son of Johann Gottlieb Schmidt.

SCHMIDT, Friedrich Wilhelm
German, 19th century.
Born 1787, in Eckartsberga, near Weimar.
Draughtsman.
Friedrich Wilhelm Schmidt studied at the Weimar Art School from 1806 to 1808.

SCHMIDT, Friedrich Wilhelm Christian
German, 18th century.
Died 7 April 1772.
Active in Brunswick.
Engraver. Armorials.

SCHMIDT, Fritz
German, 20th century.
Born 3 February 1876, in Munich; died 21 February 1935, in Munich.
Sculptor, worker in precious metals.
Fritz Schmidt was a pupil at the school of industrial arts in Munich, where he later became a professor.

SCHMIDT, Fritz Philipp
German, 19th - 20th century.
Born 11 April 1869, in Dresden.
Painter, illustrator. Historical subjects, genre scenes.
The son of Theodor Gustav Ernst Schmidt, Fritz Philipp Schmidt was the pupil of Leon Pohle and Hermann Prell at the fine arts academy in Dresden and of Ludwig von Löfftz and Paul Höcker at the Munich academy. He exhibited in Paris at the Salon des Artistes Français, where he received a commendation in 1897.
MUSEUMS AND GALLERIES:
LEIPZIG: *Foreman of the Jury.*

SCHMIDT, G. D.
British, 17th century.
Active c. 1680.
Engraver.

SCHMIDT, Georg
German, 16th century.
Painter. Monograms.

SCHMIDT, Georg
German, 17th century.
Born 1615, in Bamberg; died 4 July 1686, in Bamberg.
Painter.

SCHMIDT, Georg
German, 17th century.
Born 1653, in Somsdorf.
Active in Dresden.
Painter.
Georg Schmidt was the father of the painter Christoph Schmidt.

SCHMIDT, Georg Christoph
German, 18th - 19th century.
Born 1740, in Gattenhofen; died 29 July 1811, in Jena.
Engraver.
Georg Christoph Schmidt engraved portraits and maps.
MUSEUMS AND GALLERIES:
JENA (Stadtmus.).

SCHMIDT, Georg Friedrich
German, 18th century.
Born 24 January 1712, in Berlin; died 25 January 1775, in Berlin.
Draughtsman, engraver, pastellist.
Georg Friedrich Schmidt first studied drawing and engraving with G.P. Busch at the academy in Berlin. He then went to Paris, where he studied with Nicolas Larmessin. He acquired a sound technique, but some critics consider his work to be lacking in warmth. He was accepted into the royal academy of Paris in 1742, and presented a remarkable portrait of Pierre Mignard as his reception piece. He exhibited at the Salon in Paris in 1742 and 1743. J. G. Wille discusses him at length in his memoirs. What he says about Schmidt's change of attitude after his admission to the academy does not indicate a very noble character. In 1744, Schmidt returned to Berlin, where he was appointed engraver to the king of Prussia. In 1757, he was summoned to St Petersburg by the Empress Elizabeth, having engraved a portrait of her after Tocqué. In St Petersburg, he organised a school of engraving for the reproduction of portraits of the emperors of Russia. He returned to Berlin in 1862.

Schmidt produced a considerable body of work, consisting of almost 200 pieces, mostly portraits. At the end of his career, he produced a few etchings after the style of Rembrandt.

Stamp of sale

SCHMIDT, Georg Matthias and Christian Elias
German, 18th century.
Active in Erfurt.
Painters (porcelain).

AUCTION RECORDS:
PARIS, 21 Nov 2001, *Portrait of Man* (1743, crayon heightened with red chalk, 12 x 9 ins / 31 x 24 cm) FRF 12,000.

SCHMIDT, George Adam
Dutch, 19th century.
Born 17 May 1791, in Dordrecht; died 22 March 1844, in Dordrecht.
Painter.
George Adam Schmidt was a pupil of Hofman.

MUSEUMS AND GALLERIES:
AMSTERDAM: *Reading the Bible* - HAMBURG: *Grandfather and Granddaughter*.
AUCTION RECORDS:
AMSTERDAM, 24 April 1979, *Interior with Peasants Playing Draughts* (oil on panel, 19 1/2 x 24 3/4 ins / 49.5 x 63 cm) NLG 8,800. AMSTERDAM, 17 May 2004, *Farm Interior* (oil on panel, 28 x 37 ins / 70 x 93 cm) EUR 7,500.

SCHMIDT, Gerhard Michael
German, 20th century.
Born 1922, in Lesten (Silesia).
Painter.
Initially an office worker in Berlin, Gerhard Schmidt did not start painting until the end of World War II. He attended courses at the studio of Willy Breest at the school of fine arts in Hamburg from 1948 to 1952. He took part in collective exhibitions in Germany after 1952 and made several visits to Paris, where he mounted a solo exhibition in 1952 and a joint exhibition with two friends in 1955. His painting technique is abstract, typical of the international movement in the 1950s.

SCHMIDT, Gerhardt or Erhardt
German, 16th century.
Born to a family originally from Rotenburg (Hanover).
Sculptor, stucco artist.
Gerhardt Schmidt worked in Nolfenbuttel, Königsberg, Heidenheim and Freudenstadt. He was responsible for the stucco work in the great hall of Weikersheim Castle and in Hellenstein Castle, Heidenheim.

SCHMIDT, Gottfried
German, 18th century.
Active in Leipzig c. 1740-1750.
Painter. Portraits.

SCHMIDT, Gottfried
Austrian, 18th - 19th century.
Painter.
Gottfried Schmidt painted on porcelain at the Vienna factory between 1775 and 1827.

SCHMIDT, Gottfried
German, 19th century.
Active in Heidelberg c. 1820.
Painter, miniaturist. Portraits.
Gottfried Schmidt was the son of Wilhelm Ludwig and the brother of Franz Schmidt.

SCHMIDT, Gustav
German, 19th century.
Painter. Portraits.
Gustav Schmidt was a student at the academy in Berlin in 1824.
MUSEUMS AND GALLERIES:
GÖTTINGEN: *Portrait of the Historian Karl Friedrich Eichhorn*.

SCHMIDT, Gustav Adolf
German, 19th century.
Born 13 May 1807, in Altenburg; died 5 July 1836, in Rome.
Painter. Genre scenes, portraits.
Gustav Adolf Schmidt was the son of Carl Schmidt. He was a pupil of Fr L. Doell.

SCHMIDT, Gustav Heinrich
German, 19th century.
Born 1803, in Königsberg (now Kaliningrad, Russia); died between 1846 and 1849.
Sculptor.
Gustav Heinrich Schmidt was the son of Johann Heinrich Schmidt. He studied with L. W. Wichmann in Berlin from 1822 to 1826, at the academy in Vienna in 1827, and with K. Eberhard at the academy in Munich from 1828 to 1829.

SCHMIDT, H. A.
German, 18th century.
Born December 1733, in Brunswick.
Engraver (including burin). Natural history.
H. A. Schmidt was active in Offenbach am Main between 1782 and 1799. He engraved illustrations for works on natural history, as well as a page showing *The Aeronaut Pierre Blanchard's Attempt at Balloon Flight on 3 October 1785*.

SCHMIDT, H. W.
German, 18th century.
Active in Nuremberg.
Engraver (glass).

SCHMIDT, Hans
German, 17th century.
Active in Tondern 1615-1629.
Painter.

SCHMIDT, Hans
German, 17th century.
Born in Lübeck; died March 1645, in Dresden.
Painter.

SCHMIDT, Hans. See also **SCHMID**

SCHMIDT, Hans. See also **SCHMIDT Johann**

SCHMIDT, Hans David. See **SCHMIED**

SCHMIDT, Hans Georg
Austrian, 17th century.
Born in Röctendorf.
Painter.
From 1667, Hans Georg Schmidt was in the service of the bishop of Breslau (now Wroclaw). In 1673, he painted his masterpiece, the *Birth of Christ*. He abandoned his wife and fled to Danzig (now Gdansk) in 1686.

SCHMIDT, Hans W.
German, 19th - 20th century.
Born 6 October 1859, in Hamburg.
Painter, engraver, illustrator. History painting, genre scenes, portraits.
Hans Schmidt was the pupil of Albert Brendel at the school of fine arts in Weimar, where he was active.
MUSEUMS AND GALLERIES:
IENA (New University): *Karl August of Saxe-Weimar with Goethe* - WEIMAR: *Grand Duke Wilhelm Ernst of Saxe-Weimar Seizing Power*.
AUCTION RECORDS:
NEW YORK, 18 Feb 1993, *The Kill* (1896, oil on canvas, 47 1/2 x 65 ins / 120.7 x 165.1 cm) USD 17,050. NEW YORK, 15 Feb 1994, *Refreshments for All* (1883, oil on canvas, 24 1/2 x 39 ins / 62.2 x 99 cm) USD 10,350. NEW YORK, 23 April 2003, *Happy Couple* (1909, oil on canvas, 28 x 20 ins / 70 x 50 cm) USD 12,000.

SCHMIDT, Hanson, or Smidt
Danish, 18th century.

Born in Denmark; died 1746, in Danzig (now Gdansk, Poland).

Painter. History painting, portraits.

Schmidt worked in Danzig in 1840. He executed a portrait of the abbot Grandius Schmidt, which was engraved by Bernigeroth in 1744.

SCHMIDT, Harold von

American, 20th century.

Born 19 May 1893, in Alameda (California); died 1982.

Painter, illustrator. Western scenes, scenes with figures, war scenes, genre scenes.

Harold von Schmidt studied at the California School of Art in Berkeley. He acted as a model for Maynard Dixon in return for instruction, and in 1924 studied under Harvey Dunn at the Grand Central Art School in New York. Von Schmidt also studied with Worth Ryder. He sold his first painting in 1913, and worked as an illustrator for more than 30 major magazines including *Liberty, Colliers, Cosmopolitan, Saturday Evening Post* and *Sunset*, preferring not to do covers, but to produce interior illustrations. Some of his illustrations were painted in a large format to allow bold and energetic brushstrokes. He also illustrated books, such as Willa Cather's *December Night: A Scene from Death Comes for the Archbishop*.

Von Schmidt was particularly known for his realistic depictions of Western subjects, stemming from summers spent in Taos in New Mexico, such as *Fight by Firelight* (1947), or *The Getaway*. From 1944 Von Schmidt was an artist-correspondent in World War II, flying on bombing runs and being present at the occupation of Japan, producing works such as *National Guard Patrol over Oahu, Hawaii*. He also painted war posters during both world wars, such as *They Stake their Lives on your Ordnance* (1942). Von Schmidt was a member of the USA Olympic rugby team in 1920; a life trustee of the Artists Guild, New York; president of the Society of Illustrators (1938-1941); president of Westport Artists (1950-1951); a member of the American Indian Defense Association; and a founding member of the Famous Artists Schools, where he also taught. He was elected to the Hall of Fame of the Society of Illustrators in 1959, and was awarded the first Gold Medal from the National Cowboy Hall of Fame in 1968. His work has been shown at *Westport Waters*, Westport Art Center, Connecticut (2003).

BIBLIOGRAPHY:

Reed, Walt, *Harold von Schmidt Draws and Paints the Old West*, illustrated book, Northland Press, Flagstaff, 1972. Carroll, John M., *Von Schmidt: the Complete Illustrator*, illustrated book, Old Army Press, Fort Collins, Colorado, 1973. Reed, Walt (ed.), *The Western Art of Harold von Schmidt*, illustrated book, Peacock Press, New York, 1976.

MUSEUMS AND GALLERIES:

MINNEAPOLIS (Public Library): *They Stake their Lives on your Ordnance* (1942, poster) - OKLAHOMA CITY (National Cowboy and Western Heritage Mus.) - PRINCETON (Princeton University Library): 12 pen and ink illustrations - WASHINGTON DC (United States Air Force Art Collection): *Aerial Battle in World War I; First Solo Pacific Flight; National Guard Patrol over Oahu, Hawaii; Sanno Shrine, Tokyo; B-62s over North Korea; Air to Air - North Korea, April 1953*.

AUCTION RECORDS:

NEW YORK, 22 Oct 1981, *Indian Scouting Party* (1948, oil on canvas, 30 x 50 ins / 76.2 x 127 cm) USD 42,000. NEW YORK, 31 May 1984, *Cowgirl with Horses* (1928, oil on canvas, 30 x 40 ins / 76.2 x 101.6 cm) USD 9,000. NEW YORK, 5 Dec 1985, *Race with Death* (1947, oil on canvas, 27 x 43 ins / 68.6 x 109.2 cm) USD 19,000. NEW YORK, 29 May 1986, *The Sutler's Daughter* (1950, oil on canvas, 30 x 30 ins / 76.3 x 76.3 cm) USD 5,000. NEW YORK, 24 May 1989, *Attack on the Camp by the Glimmer of the Firelight* (1947, oil on canvas, 25 x 46 ins / 63.5 x 116.9 cm) USD 22,000. NEW YORK, 25 May 1989, *In the heat of combat* (1951, oil on canvas, 26 3/4 x 42 ins / 68.2 x 106.6 cm) USD 14,300. NEW YORK, 16 March 1990, *Rixe in the saloon* (1956, oil on canvas, 21 x 48 ins / 53.3 x 122 cm) USD 33,000. NEW YORK, 26 Sept 1990, *Ambush at the waterhole* (1951, oil on canvas, 30 x 50 ins / 76.2 x 127 cm) USD 15,400. NEW YORK, 12 April 1991, *Double Hold-up* (1951, oil on canvas, 30 x 40 ins / 76.2 x 101.6 cm) USD 11,000. NEW YORK, 5 Dec 1991, *Herders* (1931, oil on panel, 24 x 50 ins / 61 x 127 cm) USD 18,700. NEW YORK, 27 May 1992, *A phantom column* (1932, oil on canvas, 30 x 30 ins / 76.2 x 76.2 cm) USD 8,250. NEW YORK, 10 March 1993, *Tugboat `Annie' in action* (1934, oil on canvas, 30 x 50 ins / 76.2 x 127 cm) USD 5,750. HILTON HEAD ISLAND, 20 Nov 1999, *Surprise* (oil on canvas, 16 x 40 ins / 41 x 102 cm) USD 15,000. LOS ANGELES, 9 Dec 1999, *Hays, You Palmed Them Three Ten Spots* (1930, gouache, 19 x 31 ins / 47 x 79 cm) USD 2,750. PASADENA, 15 Feb 2000, *Night Riders* (1924, gouache on board, 14 x 22 ins / 36 x 56 cm) USD 4,250. NEW YORK, 6 May 2000, *Cavalry Charge* (illustration, 30 x 50 ins / 76 x 127 cm) USD 18,000. BOSTON, 11 May 2001, *Cavalry Officer Battles a Bear* (1945, oil on canvas, 27 x 35 ins / 68 x 88 cm) USD 15,000. NEW YORK, 10 Nov 2001, *Frontierswoman Surrounded by Indians* (c. 1931, oil on canvas, 24 x 50 ins / 61 x 127 cm) USD 12,000. CHEYENNE, 15 March 2002, *Untitled* (oil on canvas, 24 x 50 ins / 61 x 127 cm) USD 4,750. SANTA FE, 1 Nov 2003, *Celebration, West Townsend* (oil on canvas, 28 x 32 ins / 71 x 81 cm) USD 2,200. NEW YORK, 15 May 2004, *Man and Gorilla Confronting Each Other* (oil on canvas, 35 x 28 ins / 89 x 71 cm) USD 2,600. SANTA FE, 23 Oct 2004, *Fighting for Footing* (1945, oil on canvas, 24 x 32 ins / 61 x 81 cm) USD 10,000.

SCHMIDT, Heinrich

German, 15th - 16th century.

Born c. 1470.

Active in Leipzig.

Painter. Religious subjects.

SCHMIDT, Heinrich

German, 18th - 19th century.

Born 1740 or 1760, in Saarbrücken; died May 1821, in Darmstadt.

Painter. History painting, portraits, landscapes.

Heinrich Schmidt worked for a long time in Naples and was painter to the court of Hesse-Darmstadt.

MUSEUMS AND GALLERIES:

DARMSTADT (Hessisches Landesmus.): *Adam and Eve; Artemis; Diana and Callisto; The Roneiglione Region* - DARMSTADT (MM): *Self-portrait* - DARMSTADT (Schlossmus.): *The Bergstrasse near Eberstadt; The Encampment at Gross Gerau; Queen Louise of Prussia; Ludwig I, Grand Duke of Hesse; Grand Duchess Louise of Hesse; Grand Duchess Caroline Friederike Louise of Mecklenburg Strelitz; The Countess Palatine Augusta of Zweibrücken; Ludwig I, Grand Duke of Hesse*.

AUCTION RECORDS:

NEW YORK, 14 Jan 1994, *Portrait of a Nobleman in a Park with Venice in the Background* (1815, oil on panel, 34 1/4 x 30 3/4 ins / 87 x 78.1 cm) USD 23,000.

SCHMIDT, Heinrich

German, 19th century.

Born 1788, in Thangelstedt, near Weimar.

Painter, draughtsman.

Heinrich Schmidt worked in the Blankenhain porcelain factory. Later he was a pupil of Franz Kotta in Rudolstadt. From 1813 to 1815, he studied at the Weimar art school.

SCHMIDT, Heinrich

German, 19th century.

Born 1780, in Dresden.

Engraver (burin).

Heinrich Schmidt trained in Dresden, then in Leipzig and, from 1819 to 1821, in Rome.

SCHMIDT, Heinrich
Swiss, 19th century.
Born 1808, in Neftenbach.
Painter. Portraits, landscapes.
Until 1829, Heinrich Schmidt was a student at the academy of fine art in Munich.

SCHMIDT, Heinrich, or Schmid
German, 19th century.
Born c. 1810.
Painter. Portraits, genre scenes.
In 1830, Heinrich Schmidt was a pupil of the professor of drawing Peter Schmid. He worked in Berlin.

SCHMIDT, Heinrich
German, 20th century.
Born 1895, in Berlin.
Painter. Urban landscapes, landscapes, architectural views.
Living off a private income, Heinrich Schmidt turned to painting as a self-taught artist, depicting in minute detail the sites and monuments of the surrounding region, such as the tea pavilion in the park at Charlottenburg.
BIBLIOGRAPHY:
Gans, Louis, *Meesters der Europese naïven*, exhibition catalogue, Centraal Museum, Utrecht, 1970.

SCHMIDT, Heinrich. See also **SCHMITZ**

SCHMIDT, Heinrich Friedrich Thomas
German, 19th century.
Born 1780, in Berlin.
Painter, engraver. Portraits.
Heinrich Schmidt did burin engravings of portraits, notably those of *Schiller* and Tsar *Alexander I*. He was active in Leipzig and Weimar.

SCHMIDT, Heinrich or Genrich, Genrichovitch
Russian, 19th - 20th century.
Born 1861.
Painter.
Heinrich Schmidt was a student at the St Petersburg Academy from 1886 to 1894.

SCHMIDT, Heinrich Wilhelm
German, 18th century.
Born c. 1767, in Altenburg.
Painter, architect.
Heinrich Wilhelm Schmidt stayed in Rome in 1798 and 1799.

SCHMIDT, Henri I
German, 19th century.
Born 1802, in Pfalzburg; died 1877, in Haguenau.
Painter, draughtsman. Portraits.

SCHMIDT, Henri II
German, 19th century.
Born 1837; died 1895, in Haguenau.
Painter, draughtsman. Landscapes.
Son of Henri Schmidt I.

SCHMIDT, Henrichs
German, 17th century.
Active c. 1661.
Painter. Portraits.

SCHMIDT, Henry
British, 19th century.
Painter. Portraits.
MUSEUMS AND GALLERIES:
LONDON (Royal Society): *Portrait of the Naturalist William Clift* (1833).

SCHMIDT, Herman
Austrian, 17th century.
Born 1605; died 15 August 1655, in Vienna.
Sculptor. Religious subjects.
Herman Schmidt married in Vienna in 1645. He did a great deal of work for the abbey church of Göttweig.

SCHMIDT, Hermann
German, 19th century.
Born 1819, in Magdeburg; died 29 September 1903, in Berlin.
Painter. Landscapes.
AUCTION RECORDS:
AMSTERDAM, 30 Oct 1990, *German Village by a River with a Castle on a Hill in the Background* (oil on canvas, 7½ x 9¾ ins / 19 x 25 cm) NLG 2,760.

SCHMIDT, Hermann
German, 19th century.
Born 12 February 1833, in Hamburg; died 5 October 1889, in Hamburg.
Painter, decorative designer, draughtsman. Landscapes.
Hermann Schmidt had his own studio for decorative painting whose speciality was Neo-Gothic. He won a gold medal at the Exhibition of Trades and Industry in Hamburg in 1889. He has decorated the churches of St Peter in Altona, a district of Hamburg, and St Gertrude in Hamburg. He was also an art critic.
BIBLIOGRAPHY:
Europäischer Jugendstil, exhibition catalogue, Museum für Kunst und Gewerbe, Hamburg, 1991 (exhibition, Muzeum Narodowe, Cracow, trilingual edition in Polish, German and English).
MUSEUMS AND GALLERIES:
HAMBURG (Mus. für Kunst und Gewerbe): several drawings.

SCHMIDT, Hermine
German, 19th - 20th century.
Born 13 November 1873, in Oldenburg.
Painter, engraver.
Hermine Schmidt studied in Berlin and became established in Oldenburg. She practised the burin engraving technique.

SCHMIDT, Hermione von. See **PREUSCHEN**

SCHMIDT, Hugo Carl
Swiss, 19th - 20th century.
Born 10 August 1856, in Geneva.
Painter, lithographer, caricaturist. Genre scenes, interiors, landscapes.
Hugo Schmidt was the pupil of Jean-Paul Laurens in Paris.

SCHMIDT, Hugo Ernst, pseudonym: Robert Richter
German, 19th century.
Born 1863, in Breslau (now Wroclaw, Poland); died 24 August 1899, in Berlin.
Painter. Figures, landscapes.

SCHMIDT, Ignaz
German, 19th century.
Born 1804, in Mainz; died 1880.
Painter. Portraits, genre scenes.
Ignaz Schmidt was active in Mainz and Rome.
MUSEUMS AND GALLERIES:
MAINZ: *Italian Woman Praying*.

SCHMIDT, Izaak
Dutch, 18th - 19th century.
Born 11 June or July 1740, in Amsterdam; died 17 May 1818, in Amsterdam.
Painter, engraver (etching). Portraits, landscapes.

Isaak Schmidt was a pupil of his father and of Jan van Huysum and J. M. Quinkhart. He was employed at a tapestry workshop, and was also a playwright and a writer on art. Initially a portrait painter, he was disappointed by his own limitations in the genre and subsequently turned to landscapes. His works are rare. He is best known for a *Life of Rubens*.
MUSEUMS AND GALLERIES:
AMSTERDAM: *Portrait of a Woman* (pastel).
AUCTION RECORDS:
PARIS, 27 and 28 June 1927, *Landscapes* (two watercolours) FRF 300.

SCHMIDT, Izaak Riewert
Dutch, 19th century.
Died 26 January 1826, in Delft.
Active in Amsterdam.
Painter. Portraits.
Izaak Riewert Schmidt was a pupil of his father Izaak Schmidt and of A. de Lelie. He was a teacher at the school of artillery and engineering in Delft.

SCHMIDT, Jakob
Austrian, 19th century.
Born 1776.
Active in Vienna.
Medallist.

SCHMIDT, Jakob Friedrich Carl
German, 18th century.
Died 1805.
Painter.
Jakob Friedrich Karl Schmidt was a pupil of Wilhelm Ludwig Schmidt. He was professor of drawing at Heidelberg University from 1799.

SCHMIDT, Jean Charles. See **SCHMIDT Johann Martin Karl** or **Jean Charles**

SCHMIDT, Jean Joseph
French, 18th century.
Born in Paris.
Painter.
Jean Joseph Schmidt studied under Lantara and Casanova. He took part in the Expositions de la Jeunesse at Place Dauphine in 1783 and in the Salons from 1783 to 1800. He painted landscapes.

SCHMIDT, Jean Philippe
French, 19th century.
Born 13 March 1790, in Paris.
Engraver, lithographer.
Jean Schmidt exhibited at the Salon between 1824 and 1833. He wrote two books: an *Ornamental Design Course for Use in Schools of Industrial Art and Design*; and a *New Comprehensive Manual for the Ornamental Decorative Artist, Engraver and Painter, in Letters, Text and Atlas* (published in Paris in 1848).

SCHMIDT, Johann, or Schmitt
German, 17th century.
Born 26 December 1629, in Rössel (Prussia); died 1701, in Rössel.
Sculptor.

SCHMIDT, Johann
Austrian, 18th century.
Born end 1688 or beginning 1689; died 28 June 1761, in Mautern.
Sculptor.
Johann Schmidt was responsible for all the exterior and interior decoration of the church in Durnstein.

SCHMIDT, Johann
Austrian, 18th century.
Active c. 1796.
Draughtsman.

SCHMIDT, Johann, or Schmid
German, 19th century.
Born 1806, in Aschaffenburg.
Lithographer.
Johann Schmidt studied in Munich.

SCHMIDT, Johann Andreas
German, 18th century.
Active in Planá, Bohemia.
Painter.

SCHMIDT, Johann Baptist
German, 18th - 19th century.
Born 7 March 1774, in Würzburg.
Active in Amberg.
Painter. Landscapes.
Johann Baptist Schmidt painted a *View of Amberg*, which was engraved by Laminit.

SCHMIDT, Johann Baptist
German, 19th century.
Born 1811, in Oberdorf.
Sculptor.
Johann Baptist Schmidt studied in Munich from 1831 to 1840.

SCHMIDT, Johann Christian
German, 17th century.
Active in Merseburg.
Painter.

SCHMIDT, Johann Christian, or Schmid or Schmitt
German, 18th century.
Born 1701; died 1759, in Rössel (Prussia).
Sculptor.

SCHMIDT, Johann Christian Lebrecht
German, 18th century.
Painter.
Johann Christian Lebrecht Schmidt appears not to be the same artist as Lebrecht Schmid. He was a porcelain painter at the Volkstedt factory around 1786.

SCHMIDT, Johann Christoph
German, 17th century.
Active c. 1693.
Painter.

SCHMIDT, Johann Ernst
German, 19th century.
Born 5 June 1809, in Eisenach; died 20 November 1868, in Dresden.
Engraver, reproductions engraver.

SCHMIDT, Johann Friedrich
German, 17th century.
Active c. 1679.
Sculptor.
Johann Friedrich Schmidt carved the Samaritan fountain in Zittau in Saxony.

SCHMIDT, Johann Friedrich
German, 18th century.
Engraver (burin).
Johann Friedrich Schmidt was active in Rothenburg and also, between 1730 and 1785, in Nuremberg. He engraved the illustrations for Georg Wolfgang Knorr's book *Deliciae Naturae Selectae*, Nuremberg, 1766-1767.

SCHMIDT, Johann Friedrich
German, 18th century.
Born to a family originally from Niederau.
Painter (porcelain).

Johann Friedrich Schmidt was an apprentice in Meissen from 1742.

SCHMIDT, Johann Georg
German, 18th century.
Born c. 1675, in Kloster Wasserburg (Bavaria); died 29 November 1720, in Amberg.
Stucco artist.
Johann Georg Schmidt probably decorated St George's church in Amberg.

SCHMIDT, Johann Georg, or Schmid
Austrian, 18th century.
Born 1694, in Planá, Bohemia; died 1 September 1765, in Prague.
Painter.
Johann Georg Schmidt was the son of Kaspar and the brother of Paul and Wenzel Schmidt. His entire output of works of a religious nature can be found in Wroclaw cathedral and churches in Bavaria.

SCHMIDT, Johann Georg, called Wienerschmidt
German, 18th century.
Born 23 August 1694, in Augsburg; died 1767, in Brunswick.
Painter, engraver. Religious subjects, portraits.
Johann Georg Schmidt made burin engravings of portraits of royalty.
AUCTION RECORDS:
NEW YORK, 3 June 1988, *The Martyrdom of a Saint, Possibly Pope Stephen I* (oil on canvas, 11 1/2 x 8 ins / 29 x 20.5 cm) USD 6,600.

SCHMIDT, Johann Georg
German, 18th century.
Born to a family originally from Schweinfurt.
Engraver.

SCHMIDT, Johann Georg
German, 18th century.
Painter.
Johann Georg Schmidt went on a study tour to Rome with Johann Jakob Mestenleiter in 1776.

SCHMIDT, Johann Georg, or Schmid
Danish, 18th century.
Active between 1768 and 1781.
Engraver. Architectural views. Cards.

SCHMIDT, Johann Georg
German, 19th century.
Active in Leipzig c. 1802.
Engraver (burin).

SCHMIDT, Johann Gottfried
German, 18th century.
Active in Hanover.
Sculptor.
Johann Gottfried Schmidt made three busts of Leibnitz between 1787 and 1789.

SCHMIDT, Johann Gottfried
German, 18th century.
Born 22 June 1764, in Dresden; died 7 July 1803, in Paris.
Engraver (burin).
Johann Gottfried Schmidt studied with Rasp. He moved to Dresden and then, in 1802, to Paris. He is known for a series of 50 portraits of theologians, statesmen and military leaders.
MUSEUMS AND GALLERIES:
DRESDEN (Prints Collection): many engravings - LEIPZIG (Stadtbibliothek): many engravings.

SCHMIDT, Johann Gottlieb
German, 18th century.
Born c. 1742; died 14 February 1800, in Berlin.
Engraver. Portraits. Vignettes.
Johann Gottlieb Schmidt was the father of the engraver Friedrich Wilhelm Schmidt.

SCHMIDT, Johann Gottlieb
German, 19th century.
Born 1801, in Johanngeorgenstadt.
Painter. History painting, portraits, genre scenes.
Johann Gottlieb Schmidt studied in Dresden and was active in Berlin and Hanover around 1842.

SCHMIDT, Johann Heinrich
German, 18th century.
Sculptor (wood).

SCHMIDT, Johann Heinrich
German, 18th - 19th century.
Born c. 1741, in Derenthal; died 1 December 1821, in Ludwigsburg.
Sculptor.
Johann Heinrich Schmidt was the father of the porcelain manufacturer Johann Jakob Schmidt.
MUSEUMS AND GALLERIES:
STUTTGART (Schloss Mus.): three vases.

SCHMIDT, Johann Heinrich
German, 18th - 19th century.
Born 1749; died 1829.
Pastellist.
Johann Heinrich Schmidt is mentioned in the records of public auctions. He was a court painter and the father of Carl Heinrich Wilhelm and Heinrich F.R. Thomas Schmidt.
AUCTION RECORDS:
PARIS, 10-11 Dec 1928, *Portrait of a Woman* (pastel) FRF 4,100. PARIS, 4 April 2001, *Young Woman Dressed in a Silk Ivory-coloured Dress* (miniature, 4 x 4 ins / 11 x 9 cm) FRF 32,000.

SCHMIDT, Johann Heinrich
German, 19th century.
Born 1777, in Berlin.
Sculptor.
Johann Heinrich Schmidt was active in Königsberg (now Kaliningrad) from 1798. He was the father of Gustav Heinrich Schmidt.

SCHMIDT, Johann Jacob
German, 18th century.
Painter.
Johann Jakob Schmidt was an earthenware maker at the Ansbach factory between 1724 and 1749. The National Museum in Munich has a dish by him, decorated with a Chinese landscape.
MUSEUMS AND GALLERIES:
MUNICH (Bayerisches Nationalmus.): a plate.

SCHMIDT, Johann Jakob
Swiss, 19th century.
Born 4 November 1808, in Schlattingen; died 1844, in Florence.
Painter.
Johann Jakob Schmidt was active in Rome from 1837 to 1839.

SCHMIDT, Johann Jakob August
German, 19th century.
Active in Dresden c. 1810.
Watercolourist, engraver (burin). Landscapes.
Johann Jakob August Schmidt was a pupil of Christian Gottlieb Hammer.

SCHMIDT, Johann Martin Karl or Jean Charles
Austrian, 18th century.
Born 22 August 1769, in Stein.
Engraver.

Johann Martin Karl Schmidt was an amateur artist, the son of Martin Johann Schmidt. He engraved *Socrates and Alcibiades* and *Tarquin and Lucretia*.

SCHMIDT, Johann Matthäus, or Schmied
Austrian, 18th century.
Born 1702, in Planá, Bohemia; died 23 October 1754, in Prague.
Painter.

Johann Matthäus Schmidt was the father of Karl Anton Schmidt.

SCHMIDT, Johann Nepomuk
German, 19th century.
Born 1775.
Active in Eichstätt.
Painter. History painting, portraits.

SCHMIDT, Johann Philipp
German, 18th century.
Painter (porcelain).

In 1747, Johann Philipp Schmidt joined the earthenware factory in Frankfurt am Main.

SCHMIDT, Johann Thomas
Danish, 18th century.
Died 1790, in Hildburghausen.
Painter. Portraits, animals.

Schmidt was the father of Johann Heinrich Schmidt. He was associated with the Hildburghausen court. He executed a portrait of *Ernst Friedrich Carl, Duke of Saxony-Hilburgh* which is now at the Frederiksborgmuseet.

SCHMIDT, Johann Wolfgang
German, 18th century.
Born to a family originally from Vorchheim.
Miniaturist.

From 1736, Johann Wolfgang Schmidt worked in Würzburg. He painted fruits and flowers.

SCHMIDT, Johann Zacharias
German, 18th century.
Active in Leipzig c. 1779.
Draughtsman, engraver.

SCHMIDT, Johannes
Flemish School, 18th century.
Active c. 1700.
Engraver.

Johannes Schmidt made engravings after works by A. Bloemaert, F. Bol and Rubens. (See also Johannes Schmid.)

SCHMIDT, Joost
German, 20th century.
Born 1893, in Wimstorf (Hanover); died 1948, in Nuremberg.
Sculptor, graphic designer.

Joost Schmidt was a pupil at the fine arts academy in Weimar from 1911 to 1914. After World War I, from 1919 onwards, he was a student at the Bauhaus, and in 1925, he became a teacher at the Dessau Bauhaus, where he remained until 1932, having been made responsible for the publicity department after 1928. In 1935, he was appointed professor at the Reimann school of arts in Berlin, and continued to teach in Berlin after 1945. Originally a sculptor, Schmidt collaborated on the decorations for the Sommerfeld house in Berlin, which was built by Walter Gropius. He worked on the reliefs on the door at the entrance in particular, as well as those in the entrance hall and the stairwell. From 1922 onwards, he was preoccupied with typographical works, especially notices, including the notice advertising the first major Bauhaus exhibition in Weimar. He subsequently designed many others for the company Ykomobil. Joost Schmidt, who also worked with Hugo Häring on a *History of Perspective*, is regarded as one of the creators of modern typography.

BIBLIOGRAPHY:
Leymarie, Jean/Herzogenrath, Wulf/Grote, Ludwig/Gropius, Walter, *Le Bauhaus*, exhibition catalogue, Württembergischer Kunsteverein, Stuttgart, Musée national d'Art moderne, Paris, 1969.

SCHMIDT, Josef
Austrian, 18th century.
Active in Salzburg.
Stucco artist.

SCHMIDT, Josef
German, 18th century.
Born 1731, in Rössel.
Sculptor.

SCHMIDT, Joseph
German, 18th century.
Active in Augsburg.
Painter.

SCHMIDT, Joseph
German, 18th century.
Born 1711.
Painter.

Joseph Schmidt stayed in Munich from 1734.

SCHMIDT, Joseph
Austrian, 18th - 19th century.
Born 22 May 1750, in Gross Meierhöfen (now Velké Dvorce); died 29 June 1816, in Prague.
Engraver (burin).

SCHMIDT, Joseph
German, 18th - 19th century.
Born 1767; died 1824, in Frankfurt am Main.
Painter.

The Frankfurt am Main Historical Museum has a view of the city by this artist.

SCHMIDT, Joseph Michael
German, 18th century.
Active in Voitsberg.
Painter.

SCHMIDT, Jozsef, or Schmitt
Hungarian, 19th century.
Born 1810, in Pest.
Active in Pest until 1833.
Painter. History painting, portraits. Miniatures.

Jozsef Schmidt was a student at the Akademie der Bildenden Künste in Vienna. He painted classical subjects and scenes from Hungarian history.

SCHMIDT, Julius
German, 19th century.
Born 6 February 1826, in Dresden; died 6 March 1886, in Munich.
Sculptor.

Julius Schmidt was the son of Carl Heinrich Wilhelm and the brother of Adolf, born 1827, and Theodor Schmidt. He worked in Frankfurt, Wiesbaden, Hamburg, and finally Munich. He carved some figures on the façade of the old Rudolphinum in Prague.

SCHMIDT, Karl
Austrian, 18th - 19th century.
Born c. 1800, in Vienna.
Painter (porcelain). Landscapes.

Karl Schmidt worked at the Vienna porcelain factory.

SCHMIDT, Karl
German, 19th century.
Born 1790, in Saalfeld; died 5 August 1874, in Bamberg.
Painter (porcelain).

Karl Schmidt founded a school for painting on porcelain in Coburg in 1818, which he transferred to Bamberg in 1833.

SCHMIDT, Karl
German, 19th - 20th century.
Born 1873, in Leipzig; died 1948.
Painter, designer. Furniture.

Karl Schmidt first trained as a carpenter, then was a pupil at the Academy of Fine Arts in Leipzig and Berlin and later at the Académie Julian in Paris. He also spent time in England and put into practice what he learned from William Morris and the Arts and Crafts Movement. In 1898 he founded the Dresdener Werkstätten für Handwerkskunst (Dresden Studios) which he merged in 1907 with the Munich Werkstätten für Wohnungeinrichtung of Karl Bertsch, to create the Deutsche Werkstätten at Dresden-Hellerau. Karl Schmidt was seeking to expand and so in 1909 he bought a piece of land at Dresden Hellerau, and it was his idea to construct a city-garden that included his factory, the Deutsche Werkstätten für Handwerkskunst and a collection of homes for his workers. He called on the renowned Jugendstil architects, Richard Riemerschmid and Heinrich Tessenow, the latter giving a hallmark to the Cultural Centre (House of Festivals). The production of these studios was marked by the social ideal to give priority to the masses. With this in mind, he launched a series of 'Maschinenmöbel' (furniture made in series by a machine) that he also called 'Typenmöbel'. These were made with standardised parts associating craftwork and industrial arts. His Dresden Studios were a very important centre for the creation of applied art in the artistic milieu at the beginning of the century. Richard Riemerschmid said of Richard Schmidt that he was the father of the Deutscher Werkbund founded in 1907.

SCHMIDT, Karl
American, 20th century.
Born 11 January 1890, in Worcester (Massachusetts); died 1962.
Painter. Landscapes.

Karl Schmidt was a self-taught painter. He was a member of the Salmagundi Club.

AUCTION RECORDS:
LOS ANGELES-SAN FRANCISCO, 12 July 1990, *Rocky Coast* (oil on canvas, 24 1/4 x 48 1/4 ins / 61.5 x 122.5 cm) USD 3,850; *Sunny Afternoon* (1921, oil on panel, 24 x 48 ins / 61 x 122 cm) USD 3,575. LOS ANGELES-SAN FRANCISCO, 10 Oct 1990, *House Surrounded by Eucalyptus at Nightfall* (oil on panel, 30 x 72 ins / 76 x 183 cm) USD 8,250. PASADENA, 19 June 2001, *Landscape, Oak Trees and Poppies* (oil on board, 3 x 5 ins / 7 x 12 cm) USD 11,000. SAN FRANCISCO, 12 Dec 2001, *Landscape* (oil on panel on board, triptych, 16 x 32 ins / 41 x 81 cm) USD 6,000. PASADENA, 17 June 2003, *Eucalyptus Landscape, California* (1934, oil on canvas, 26 x 38 ins / 66 x 97 cm) USD 6,750. SAN FRANCISCO, 10 Dec 2003, *Dramatic California Sunset* (1928, oil on board, triptych, 9 x 18 ins / 22 x 45 cm) USD 12,000.

SCHMIDT, Karl. See also **SCHMID, SCHMIDT Anton Karl, SCHMIDT-ROTTLUFF**

SCHMIDT, Karl Christian
German, 19th century.
Died 1892, in Stuttgart.
Active in Stuttgart in 1808.
Painter. History painting.

Karl Christian Schmidt studied with Müller in Stuttgart, Cornelius in Munich and Ingres in Paris.

MUSEUMS AND GALLERIES:
STUTTGART: *Christ before Pilate* - SYDNEY: *Psyche.*

SCHMIDT, Kaspar
German, 16th century.
Active in Leipzig.
Painter.

SCHMIDT, Kaspar
Austrian, 17th century.
Born in Planá, Bohemia; died in Prague.
Active during the second half of the 17th century.
Painter.

SCHMIDT, Käthe. See **KOLLWITZ Käthe Schmidt**

SCHMIDT, Katherine, later Mrs Irvine J. Shubert and Kuniyoshi Kath. Schmidt
American, 20th century.
Born 15 August 1898, in Xenia (Ohio); died 1978.
Painter. Still-lifes (flowers/fruit).

Katherine Schmidt studied under Kenneth Hayes Miller. She was active in New York. She was a member of the Society of Independent Artists.

AUCTION RECORDS:
NEW YORK, 24 June 1988, *Still-life with Cucumbers* (1932, oil on canvas, 25 1/2 x 17 3/4 ins / 65 x 45 cm) USD 4,950. NEW YORK, 9 Sept 1993, *Rose* (1939, oil on canvas, 13 x 15 ins / 33 x 38.1 cm) USD 920.

SCHMIDT, Konrad
German, 17th century.
Born 1599; died 1617.
Sculptor.

SCHMIDT, Konstantin. See **SCHMITT**

SCHMIDT, Leonhard
German, 20th century.
Born 19 January 1892, in Backnang.
Painter. Figures, portraits, genre scenes, landscapes.

Leonhard Schmidt was the pupil of Heinrich Altherr. He was active in Stuttgart.

MUSEUMS AND GALLERIES:
BERLIN (Nationalgal.): *Young Peasant Woman* - STUTTGART: *All Saints' Day in Moravia; The Red House; Portrait of a Young Girl; Winter Landscape; Woman Busy Writing.*

AUCTION RECORDS:
MUNICH, 26 Nov 1985, *Avenue Lined with Trees* (1928, oil and pencil/card, 37 3/4 x 31 1/2 ins / 96.2 x 80 cm) DEM 11,000. STUTTGART, 23 Oct 1999, *Portrait of Charlotte Scheef* (oil on panel, 22 x 15 ins / 55 x 38 cm) DEM 4,400. STUTTGART, 2 April 2003, *Winter Landscape* (1958, oil on canvas, 22 x 29 ins / 55 x 73 cm) EUR 5,500.

SCHMIDT, Leopold
Austrian, 19th century.
Born 16 November 1824, in Prague.
Engraver.

Leopold Schmidt was a pupil of Döbler. He engraved mainly reproductions.

SCHMIDT, Louise
German, 19th - 20th century.
Born 20 November 1855, in Elmenhorst; died 24 May 1924, in Schwerin.
Painter.

In 1872-1873, Louise Schmidt was the pupil of David Simonson in Dresden and of Gottlieb Biermann and Franz Skarbina in Berlin, and was taught in Paris from 1881 to 1885 by Henner, Carolus Duran and Benjamin-Constant. She was a portraitist, and painted well-known contemporary figures in Schwerin.

MUSEUMS AND GALLERIES:
SCHWERIN: *Councillor Klicfoth; Councillor Hermann von Buchka; Councillor Karl von Bülow; Minister Alexander von Bülow; Councillor Georg Wilhelm Wetzell; Councillor Adolf von Pressentin; Minister Count von Bassewitz-Levetzow; Professor Schlil.*

SCHMIDT, Louise
German, 19th - 20th century.
Born 2 April 1874, in Frankfurt am Main.
Sculptor.
Louise Schmidt was the pupil of Friedrich Karl Hausmann at the academy of drawing in Hanau and of Denis Puech in Paris. She executed the *Monument to Prince Wallram of Nassau* in Usingen and the *Monument to His Excellency von Chappuis* in Eppstein.

SCHMIDT, Lucien Louis Jean Baptiste, or Schmith or Smith
French, 19th century.
Born 22 August 1825, in Miellin; died 1891.
Painter. Genre scenes, still-lifes.
He was a student of Frédéric Grobon, Bonnefond and the Flandrin brothers. He made his Salon debut in 1857.
MUSEUMS AND GALLERIES:
LANGRES: *Cakes* - ST-BRIEUC: *Ready to Go Ploughing* - ST-ÉTIENNE: *Bust of an Old Blind Man.*

SCHMIDT, Ludwig
German, 19th century.
Painter (glass).
Ludwig Schmidt worked in Munich and, from 1848, in Cologne.

SCHMIDT, Ludwig. See also **SCHMID Carl Friedrich Ludwig**

SCHMIDT, Ludwig Carl or Carl Ludwig
German, 18th century.
Engraver.
Ludwig Carl Schmidt was an engraver of maps in Berlin around 1787.

SCHMIDT, Ludwig or Louis
German, 19th century.
Born 2 February 1816, in Nebra; died 8 April 1906, in Gotha.
Painter, miniaturist, draughtsman. Portraits.
Ludwig Schmidt was both a teacher of drawing and an architect.

SCHMIDT, Lukas
German, 18th century.
Born 4 April 1690, in Neustadt; died in the monastery at Himmelspforten, near Würzburg.
Draughtsman.

SCHMIDT, Maggie
Canadian, 20th century.
Active at the beginning of the 20th century.
Painter. Genre scenes, figures.
AUCTION RECORDS:
MONTREAL, 17 Oct 1988, *Young Girl in Red* (oil on paper, 30 x 22 ins / 76 x 56 cm) CAD 700. AMSTERDAM, 28 Oct 1992, *Fisherman Smoking His Pipe while His Wife Arranges a Bouquet of Flowers, in an Interior in Volendam* (1919, oil on canvas, 25 3/4 x 18 3/4 ins / 65.5 x 47.5 cm) NLG 2,530. CALGARY, 14 April 2002, *Untitled, Chicken Lady* (1978, oil on board, 48 x 32 ins / 121 x 81 cm) CAD 1,050.

SCHMIDT, Martin
German, 15th - 16th century.
Sculptor.

SCHMIDT, Martin
German, 20th century.
Born 1886, in Gerlachsheim (Baden-Württemberg); died 1914, in Roblemont, at the front.
Painter. Landscapes, seascapes.
MUSEUMS AND GALLERIES:
GÖRLITZ: *Port of Antwerp.*

SCHMIDT, Martin Joachim or Johann, called Kremser Schmidt
German, 18th century.
Born 25 September 1718, in Grafenwörth, near Krems; died 28 June 1801, in Stein, near Krems.
Painter, engraver, draughtsman. Religious subjects.
After being taught the basics by his father, Martin Joachim Schmidt became a pupil of Gottlieb Starmayr. He also applied himself to the study of the old masters. He became a member of the academy in Vienna in 1768. He settled in Stein, near Krems, where he ended his career. He owes his nickname to the fame of his decoration of the parish church of Krems, which he carried out in 1787. As an engraver he is particularly known for religious subjects. He made altarpieces after the style of Rembrandt and Castiglione.
MUSEUMS AND GALLERIES:
GRAZ: *Jason and the Golden Fleece; Mars with the Furies of War, Appeased by Venus; Holy Family; The Massacre of the Innocents; The Titans Attacking Olympus; The Martyrdom of St Vitus; Baptism of Christ; The Battle of the Centaurs and Lapiths* - VIENNA: *Crucifixion; Christ and the Samaritan Woman; Christ Healing the Blind Man.*
AUCTION RECORDS:
VIENNA, 2 Dec 1969, *Adoration of the Shepherds,* ATS 25,000. VIENNA, 28 Nov 1972, *The Satyr's Family,* ATS 500,000. VIENNA, 16 March 1976, *The Holy Family* (c. 1775, oil on canvas, 27 3/4 x 21 3/4 ins / 70.5 x 55.5 cm) ATS 160,000. VIENNA, 15 March 1977, *St Thomas* (oil on canvas, 39 x 49 1/4 ins / 99 x 125 cm) ATS 1,000,000. BERLIN, 23 April 1980, *The Archangel Michael Fighting the Devil* (pen/outline in black chalk, 11 1/2 x 7 1/2 ins / 29.1 x 19.1 cm) DEM 3,600. VIENNA, 16 Sept 1980, *Crucifixion* (1784, oil/copper, 32 x 20 3/4 ins / 81 x 53 cm) ATS 380,000. NEW YORK, 8 Jan 1991, *St Matthew and St Mark (recto), the Baptism of Christ (verso)* (ink, 12 1/2 x 7 1/4 ins / 31.6 x 18.2 cm) USD 3,850. MUNICH, 26 May 1992, *An Angel Celebrating the Eucharist, Surrounded by Cherubs* (ink and black chalk, 11 1/2 x 7 1/2 ins / 29 x 19.3 cm) DEM 5,290. NEW YORK, 12 Jan 1995, *The Trinity* (oil on canvas, 22 x 17 1/2 ins / 55.9 x 44.5 cm) USD 18,400. NEW YORK, 10 Jan 1996, *Nymphs Dancing* (lead pencil and ink, 5 3/4 x 3 1/2 ins / 14.6 x 9.2 cm) USD 863.

SCHMIDT, Martin Johann. See **SCHMIDT Martin Joachim** and the entry **SCHMIDT Franz Michael**

SCHMIDT, Martin Karl Gustav
German, 19th - 20th century.
Born 15 May 1863, in Hamburg; died 14 March 1930, in Hamburg.
Sculptor.
Martin Schmidt was the pupil of Ernst Pfeifer and Wilhelm von Rümann at the fine arts academy in Munich.

SCHMIDT, Mathias
German, 18th - 19th century.
Born 1749, in Mannheim; died 1823, in Munich.
Painter, engraver.
Mathias Schmidt painted landscapes and copied plates from Karel Dujardin, Adriaen Van de Velde and Jan Fyt. Le Blanc also mentions his series of prints after original pen drawings by F. Kobell, Rembrandt, Salviati.

SCHMIDT, Matthias
German, 18th century.
Died c. 1803, in Augsburg.
Active in Augsburg.
Painter, engraver.
Matthias Schmidt was a painter and engraver of genre scenes, animals and landscapes.

SCHMIDT, Max
German, 19th century.

Born 23 August 1818, in Berlin; died 8 January 1901, in Königsberg (now Kaliningrad, Russia).
Painter, watercolourist, draughtsman. Genre scenes, landscapes, architectural views. Murals.

Max Schmidt studied with Karl Joseph Begas, Karl Kruger, Wilhelm Schirmer, and also at the academy of fine art in Berlin. Between 1861 and 1870, he travelled to Turkey, Palestine, Egypt, the Ionian Islands, Italy and England. In 1868, he was appointed professor at the Weimar school of art, and in 1872, he was summoned to teach at the academy of fine arts in Königsberg, and later became its director. He took part in exhibitions in Vienna and Berlin, winning numerous medals. He painted mainly landscapes and architectural subjects.

MUSEUMS AND GALLERIES:

COLOGNE: *Summer Day* - KALININGRAD: *Isolation; The Forest of Teuteburg; Dune on the Baltic Coast* (watercolour).

AUCTION RECORDS:

LONDON, 12 June 1974, *View of the Roman Campagna*, GBP 550. LONDON, 22 July 1977, *Winter Landscape with Figures* (oil on canvas, 21 1/2 x 30 1/2 ins / 54.6 x 77.3 cm) GBP 3,800. LONDON, 25 Nov 1982, *View of Beirut* (watercolour and pencil heightened with white, 9 1/2 x 13 3/4 ins / 24.2 x 35 cm) GBP 3,200. LONDON, 21 June 1984, *The Temple of Minerva in Athens* (watercolour and pencil, 15 1/2 x 21 ins / 39.5 x 53.5 cm) GBP 900. COLOGNE, 20 May 1985, *View of Constantinople* (oil on canvas, 28 3/4 x 39 1/4 ins / 73 x 100 cm) DEM 23,000. AMSTERDAM, 28 Oct 1992, *View of a Bay* (oil on card, 10 1/2 x 17 3/4 ins / 26.5 x 45 cm) NLG 1,150. LONDON, 17 Nov 1994, *The Dome of the Rock, Seen from the North of Jerusalem* (pencil and watercolour/paper, 11 1/2 x 17 1/2 ins / 29 x 44.5 cm) GBP 8,970. LONDON, 11 April 1995, *View of Beirut* (oil on panel, 11 x 19 ins / 28 x 48 cm) GBP 9,775. MUNICH, 25 June 1996, *Girl Guarding Cows by a River* (oil on canvas, 37 x 49 1/2 ins / 94 x 126 cm) DEM 19,000. MUNICH, 1 Dec 1999, *Waterfall in Mountain Landscape* (oil on canvas, 25 x 19 ins / 63 x 47 cm) DEM 3,500. BERLIN, 26 May 2000, *Sunny Rocky Devonshire Coast* (oil on canvas, 43 x 66 ins / 108 x 167 cm) DEM 7,500. AHLDEN, 3 May 2002, *Landscape with Pond and Cows* (1869, oil on canvas, 29 x 40 ins / 73 x 102 cm) EUR 11,000. BREMEN, 26 Sept 2003, *Italian Mountain Landscape with Cow Herder* (oil on canvas, 28 x 37 ins / 70 x 94 cm) EUR 3,000. AMSTERDAM, 10 Dec 2003, *Looking Out Over the Ostsee* (oil on canvas, 33 x 46 ins / 84 x 116 cm) EUR 3,000.

SCHMIDT, Max

German, 19th - 20th century.
Born 21 October 1868, in Stettin (now Szczecin, Poland).
Painter. Portraits, sporting subjects.

Max Schmidt was the pupil of Emil Neide, Georg D.S. Knorr, Johannes Heydeck, Max Schmidt (to whom he may have been related) and Carl Steffeck at the fine arts academy in Königsberg (now Kaliningrad, Russia). He was active in Berlin.

SCHMIDT, Max Walter

German, 19th - 20th century.
Born 31 July 1870, in Dresden; died 8 May 1915, in Ypres, at the front.
Painter, engraver. Landscapes.

SCHMIDT, Maximilian

German, 18th - 19th century.
Born 1758, in Lissa (now Leszno, Poland); died 1826, in Königsberg (now Kaliningrad, Russia).
Sculptor.

SCHMIDT, Michael

German, 19th century.
Died 1825, in Munich.
Lithographer.

SCHMIDT, Michael

German, 19th century.
Born 1814, in Lauingen.
Painter.

Michael Schmidt studied at the academy in Munich until 1836.

SCHMIDT, Nicolaï Outzen

Danish, 19th - 20th century.
Born 2 March 1844, in Ribe; died 18 March 1910, in Copenhagen.
Sculptor. Mythological subjects.

Nicolaï Schmidt was a pupil at the Kongelige Danske Kunstakademi in Copenhagen. He was active in Rome from 1874 to 1877.

MUSEUMS AND GALLERIES:

RIBE: *Polyphemus* (statue).

SCHMIDT, Ole Jørgen, or Smith

Danish, 19th century.
Born 13 July 1793, in Copenhagen; died 27 February 1848, in Hamburg.
Draughtsman, architect.

Schmidt studied at the Kunstakademi in Copenhagen for three years, with great success. He then left for Italy, where he undertook a meticulous study of the ruins of the Herculaneum and of Pompeii. In 1830, he published a large collection reproducing the paintings and decorations that he discovered in those cities.

SCHMIDT, Oskar Friedrich

German, 19th century.
Born 3 October 1825, in Weissenfels; died 28 January 1871, in Leipzig.
Engraver (wood).

Oskar Schmidt studied with H. Barkner. He engraved mainly reproductions.

AUCTION RECORDS:

NEW YORK, 24 Jan 1980, *The Scientist's Imaginings* (oil on canvas, 23 1/4 x 31 1/2 ins / 59 x 80 cm) USD 950.

SCHMIDT, Paul, or Schmid, Schmied, Schmiedt

Austrian, 18th century.
Born in Planá, Bohemia.
Painter. Flowers, fruit.

Paul Schmidt was the son of Kaspar and the brother of Johann Georg and Wenzel Schmidt.

AUCTION RECORDS:

PARIS, 27-28 Dec 1928, *The Watermill*, FRF 145.

SCHMIDT, Peter

German, 17th century.
Born c. 1585, in Lichtenberg.
Painter.

Peter Schmidt became a master painter in Breslau (now Wroclaw) in 1613. In 1614, he painted the frescoes in the aisle of the church of Our Lady on the Sands in Breslau and several panels for St Bernard's Church in the same city.

SCHMIDT, Peter Paul

Austrian, 18th century.
Active in Vienna.
Painter, decorative designer.

Peter Paul Schmidt worked for the Viennese Court in 1750.

SCHMIDT, Philipp

German, 19th century.
Active in Munich.
Painter. Portraits.

Philipp Schmidt studied at the academy in Munich around 1814.

SCHMIDT, Philipp. See also **SCHMITT Georg Philipp**

SCHMIDT, Reinhold
German, 17th century.
Born in Putzig; died 1698.
Painter. History painting, portraits.

SCHMIDT, Reinhold
German, 19th - 20th century.
Born 14 July 1861, in Flein, near Heilbronn.
Painter. Landscapes with figures, animals.
Reinhold Schmidt was the pupil of Karl von Häberlin and Claudius von Schraudolph the Younger at the fine arts school in Stuttgart, the city in which he settled. He specialised in painting horses, either in their own right or to add interest to a landscape.

R.Schmidt

AUCTION RECORDS:
LONDON, 22 Feb 1995, *Horses Drinking Beside a River* (oil on canvas, 30 x 37 3/4 ins / 76 x 96 cm) GBP 1,725.

SCHMIDT, Robert
German, 19th - 20th century.
Born 3 June 1863, in Nuremberg.
Painter. Genre scenes.
Robert Schmidt was the pupil of Hugo Diez at the fine arts academy in Munich, where he was active.

SCHMIDT, Robert G.
French, 20th century.
Born 5 June 1923, in Paris.
Painter. Figure compositions, figures, landscapes, urban landscapes, seascapes, still-lifes, flowers.
In 1936, at a competition between the Paris schools organised by Art Vivant, Robert G. Schmidt won the prize for drawing. Though he began to draw and paint, he earned his living as a bookbinder for over twenty years from 1941. Between 1961 and 1963 he studied drawing and painting again.

He exhibited in Paris at: from 1969, the Salon de la Société Nationale des Beaux-Arts, the Salon des Indépendants, the Salon d'Automne, of which he was a member, and the Salon Terres Latines; from 1970, the Salon Comparaisons, of which he was a committee member; in 1972, the Salon des Peintres Témoins de Leur Temps, the Salon de la Marine and the Salon Populiste. He also exhibited in regional groups, where he won a number of awards. He was short-listed for the Paris Prix de la Critique in 1969.

He held his first solo show at the Galerie Vendôme, Paris, in 1969, and this was followed by others in 1972, 1975, 1978 on the theme of *Coffee Pots*, 1983 and 1987. The Galerie St-Roch, Paris, showed collections of his work in 1992 and 1996, and other shows were held in Aubonne in 1970 and Gargilesse in 1971.

He painted his first pictures in the Touraine in 1947. Later, he painted compositions with figures, Paris landscapes, and the villages of the South of France, using bright colours and an impetuous brushstroke. He moved indiscriminately from Post-Cubist figuration to Post-Fauvist Expressionism to decorative semi-abstraction.

BIBLIOGRAPHY:
Bouillot, Roger, *Robert G. Schmidt*, Tarbes, 1923. *Robert G. Schmidt*, exhibition catalogue, Gal. Vendôme, Paris, 1987 (good documentation).

MUSEUMS AND GALLERIES:
NARBONNE (MAH): *Boat with a Red Sail* (1971-72).

AUCTION RECORDS:
VIENNA, 21 March 1972, *Philatelists*, ATS 22,000. PARIS, 27 Oct 1988, *Village of Le Cap* (oil on canvas, 24 x 19 3/4 ins / 61 x 50 cm) FRF 4,200. VERSAILLES, 22 April 1990, *Violin with Chinese Pot* (oil on canvas, 21 x 25 1/2 ins / 53.5 x 65 cm) FRF 11,000. PARIS, 5 Feb 1992, *Fishermen's Quay* (oil on canvas, 24 3/4 x 36 1/2 ins / 63 x 92.5 cm) FRF 14,000. LES ANDELYS, 18 Dec 1994, *The Café des Marches* (oil on canvas, 21 1/4 x 28 3/4 ins / 54 x 73 cm) FRF 24,500. SCEAUX, 9 April 1995, *Entrance to a Château* (oil on canvas, 17 3/4 x 20 3/4 ins / 45 x 53 cm) FRF 5,200.

SCHMIDT, Rudolf
Austrian, 20th century.
Born 8 December 1873, in Vienna; died 1963.
Painter, watercolourist. Scenes with figures, urban landscapes, landscapes with figures. Stage sets.
Rudolf Schmidt was active in Vienna. He worked in the theatrical décor studio of Burckhardt, Johann Kautsky and Carlo Brioschi. He was a member of the Albrecht Dürer association.

MUSEUMS AND GALLERIES:
VIENNA: *View of Vienna* (several works).

AUCTION RECORDS:
VIENNA, 16 March 1976, *Hackney Carriages* (watercolour, 11 x 16 1/4 ins / 27 x 41 cm) ATS 6,000. VIENNA, 11 March 1980, *Freyung* (watercolour and gouache, 5 1/2 x 6 ins / 14 x 15 cm) ATS 13,000. NEW YORK, 17 Jan 1990, *Flower Market in a Square* (watercolour/paper, 3 3/4 x 4 1/4 ins / 9.5 x 11 cm) USD 1,760. VIENNA, 1 Oct 2002, *Market Day in Freyung* (watercolour, 5 x 6 ins / 12 x 16 cm) EUR 2,000.

SCHMIDT, Rudolf
Austrian, 20th century.
Born 19 April 1894, in Vienna.
Sculptor, medallist. Busts.
Rudolf Schmidt was the pupil of Otto Hofner and studied at the fine arts academy in Vienna. He was active in Rodaun, near Vienna, where he executed a bronze bust of *Hugo von Hoffmansthal*.

MUSEUMS AND GALLERIES:
VIENNA (Kunsthistorisches Mus.): several medals.

SCHMIDT, Sigmund
German, 17th century.
Active in Freiberg in Saxony.
Sculptor (wood).

SCHMIDT, Simone
Belgian, 20th century.
Born 1912, in Brussels.
Painter, watercolourist, draughtsman.
Simone Schmidt was the pupil of Jef de Pauw, Leon Navez and Albert Crommelynck.

SCHMIDT, Theodor
German, 19th - 20th century.
Born 1855, in Stuttgart.
Painter. Genre scenes.
Theodor Schmidt was the pupil of Karl von Häberlin at the fine arts school in Stuttgart. In 1875, he travelled to Venice and then Switzerland, becoming the pupil of Wilhelm von Lindenschmit the Younger at the Munich academy on his return.

MUSEUMS AND GALLERIES:
STUTTGART: *Postal Mission*.

AUCTION RECORDS:
LONDON, 22 Nov 1990, *At the Window* (1893, oil on panel, 6 x 5 ins / 15.3 x 12.7 cm) GBP 2,200.

SCHMIDT, Theodor Gustav Ernst
German, 19th century.
Born 9 November 1828, in Dresden; died 25 May 1904, in Dresden.
Painter.
Theodor Schmidt was the son of Carl Heinrich Wilhelm and the father of Philipp Schmidt. He studied with Richter, Schnorr and Bendemann at the academy in Dresden. He devoted himself mainly to restoring pictures.

SCHMIDT, Thomas
German, 18th century.
Died 2 November 1790, in Meiningen.
Portrait artist.

SCHMIDT, Wenzel Samuel Theodor
Austrian, 18th century.
Born in Planá, Bohemia; died 1756, in Plan.
Painter.
Wenzel Schmidt was the son of Kaspar and the brother of Johann Georg and Paul Schmidt. He painted almost exclusively religious subjects.

SCHMIDT, Werner
German, 20th century.
Born 5 July 1888, in Nauendorf, near Gotha.
Painter, illustrator.
Werner Schmidt was active in Munich.

SCHMIDT, Wilhelm
German, 19th - 20th century.
Born 27 March 1842, in Assamstadt (Baden); died 1922, in Reutlingen.
Sculptor.
Wilhelm Schmidt was the pupil of the professor of drawing and architecture, Ludwig or Louis Schmidt. He was active in Reutlingen.

SCHMIDT, Wilhelm Ludwig
German, 18th century.
Born in Baden.
Painter, engraver. Portraits.
Wilhelm Ludwig Schmidt learned his trade from Joseph Melleng in Strasbourg, then spent three years in Stuttgart, from where he moved on to Heidelberg. He painted portraits of the Margrave *Carl Friedrich* and *Louise Caroline of Baden*.
MUSEUMS AND GALLERIES:
HEIDELBERG.

SCHMIDT, Wilhelm or Wilm
German, 16th - 17th century.
Active in Schleswig.
Sculptor (wood), designer of ornamental architectural features.
Wilhelm Schmidt worked from 1597 to 1635 in Gottorf.

SCHMIDT, Willem Hendrik
Dutch, 19th century.
Born 12 April 1809, in Rotterdam; died 1849; buried 1 June in Delft.
Painter. Portraits, genre scenes.
Willem Hendrik Schmidt was a pupil of G. Gillis and Meijer. In 1842 he was a professor at the academy in Delft.
MUSEUMS AND GALLERIES:
AMSTERDAM (Fodor Mus.): *Gustave Adolphe and his Little Daughter Christine; Oldenbarneveld Dying* - AMSTERDAM (Rijksmus.): *Self-portrait; Raising of Jairus' Daughter* - COLOGNE (Wallraf-Richartz Mus.): *Prayer beside the Body of a Dead Man* - MUNICH: *Dutch Schoolroom* - ROTTERDAM (Mus. Boijmans Van Beuningen): *Emilie of Nassau; Monks at Prayer* - STUTTGART: *Message.*
AUCTION RECORDS:
LONDON, 23 April 1910, *Michelangelo in his Studio* (1891) GBP 43; *Philosopher,* GBP 91. LONDON, 13 June 1910, *Alchemist* (1878) GBP 31. LONDON, 4 Feb 1911, *Old Student,* GBP 28. LONDON, 22 Oct 1971, *Amsterdam Bourgeois,* Gns 600. AMSTERDAM, 26 March 1980, *Pity the Poor* (1842, oil on panel, 12 1/2 x 11 ins / 31.5 x 27 cm) NLG 2,700. STOCKHOLM, 27 April 1983, *Visiting a Sick Woman* (1840, oil on canvas, 37 1/2 x 45 ins / 95 x 114 cm) SEK 60,000. AMSTERDAM, 5-6 Nov 1991, *Invitation* (1840, oil on panel, 14 3/4 x 13 1/2 ins / 37.5 x 34.5 cm) NLG 2,875. ANTWERP, 7 Dec 1999, *Treason* (1843, oil on canvas, 55 x 67 ins / 140 x 170 cm) BEF 240,000.

SCHMIDT-CARLSON, Friedrich Heinrich Karl
German, 19th century.
Born 12 September 1806, in Lübeck; died 2 April 1887, in Lübeck.
Painter.
Schmidt-Carlson studied with Danckwardt in Lübeck, with Gröger and Aldenrath in Hamburg, and in Dresden and Berlin. He is known for a portrait of the merchant *Gottfried Carl Buskist,* painted in 1855.

SCHMIDT-CASSELLA, Otto
German, 19th - 20th century.
Born 10 September 1876, in Wiesbaden.
Painter, draughtsman. Landscapes, architectural views.
Otto Schmidt-Cassella was the pupil of Ludwig von Herterich or his brother Johann Caspar at the academy of fine arts in Munich, of Ludwig Schmid-Reutte at the Karlsruhe academy and of Eugen Bracht at the university in Berlin. He was active in Berlin.

SCHMIDT-CRANS, Johannes Marinus.
See **CRANS Johannes Marinus Schmidt**

SCHMIDT-GLINZ, Franz
German, 19th - 20th century.
Born 2 June 1860, in Priestäblich; died 26 February 1929, in Leipzig.
Painter, watercolourist, lithographer. Landscapes.
Franz Schmidt-Glinz was active in Leipzig.
MUSEUMS AND GALLERIES:
LEIPZIG: four drawings and watercolours.

SCHMIDT-HELMBRECHTS, Carl
German, 20th century.
Born 1872, in Helmbrechts; died 1936, in Nuremberg.
Painter. Urban landscapes.
AUCTION RECORDS:
MUNICH, 6 Dec 1994, *By the Beautiful Fountain in Nuremberg* (oil on card, 24 x 17 3/4 ins / 61 x 45 cm) DEM 5,175.

SCHMIDT-HERBOTH, Eugen
German, 19th - 20th century.
Born 11 July 1864, in Berlin.
Painter. Portraits, landscapes.
Eugen Schmidt-Herboth studied at the academy of fine arts in Berlin, where he was probably the pupil of Carl Gustaf Hellqvist, Hugo Vogel and Eduard Meyerheim. He was active in Berlin.

SCHMIDT-HILD, Wilhelm
German, 20th century.
Born 30 January 1880, in Hildesheim.
Painter, illustrator. Landscapes, animals.
Wilhem Schmidt-Hild specialised in paintings of birds.
MUSEUMS AND GALLERIES:
BRUNSWICK: *Colibri; Woodcock* - SZCZECIN: *Sea Eagle.*

SCHMIDT-HUNGERER, Alicia
Maiden name: Hungerer
German, 20th - 21st century.
Born 18 November 1955, in Baden-Baden.
Active in Italy.
Painter, draughtswoman, engraver, environmental artist, video installation artist, photographer, writer.
Alicia Schmidt-Hungerer studied sculpture and art education at the Kunsthochschule in Münster and Berlin from 1973 to 1979. She taught at the university of Giessen from 1981 to 1983.

She has created urban environments, such as *Pavement Scars* in the centre of Paris in 2003, in which she used chemical processes to reveal the marks of repairs or holes in the pavements, left either by the laying of new surfaces or by holes dug to lay various pipes. She pursues this work on perception in her videos such as *Lockung* (*Enticement*), in which she projects, on several screens simultaneously, the faces of people listening to pieces of music, the rain, the sound of the sea, the laughter of children in a playground, a television series in black and white. Her drawings and engravings deal with the same sensory problems, with the colour yellow playing a minor role in effects of transparency. The subject of the drawing thus appears to escape from an overall vision, only appearing in successive fragments until the eye of the viewer restores it to its entire shape, which is then immediately revealed. Schmidt-Hungerer is also a poet and the author of two novels, one of which, *Die Warten* (*Viewpoints*), was published in 1999.

Group exhibitions in which she has participated include: Documenta in Kassel (1980); at the Cultural Center in Chicago (1986); and at the Galerie Resche in Paris (1992). Solo exhibitions include one on her drawings and engravings at the California College of Arts and Crafts in Oakland in California in 1995, and another at the Galleria del Carmine in Lucca in 2002.

BIBLIOGRAPHY:

Woolf, Pansy, *Alicia Hungerer-Schmidt: l'impossible détour*, exhibition catalogue, Galleria del Carmine, Lucques (ITA), Quidam Editeur, Meudon, 2002 (text in Italian, English and French).

MUSEUMS AND GALLERIES:

AACHEN (Ludwig Forum für Internationale Kunst): *For David* (1999) - BONN: *Rain* (1990, engraving) - REGENSBURG (Ostdeutsche Mus.): *Agreed*.

AUCTION RECORDS:

COLOGNE, 7 Dec 1984, *Wind* (1982, ink/paper, 36¼ x 27¼ ins / 92 x 69 cm) DEM 1,000. ROME, 28 March 1995, *Disturbing Curves*.

SCHMIDT-KESTNER, Erich

German, 20th century.
Born 15 January 1877, in Berlin.
Sculptor.

Erich Schmidt-Kestner was active in Königsberg (now Kaliningrad, Russia).

AUCTION RECORDS:

NICE, 28 June 1977, *Amazon Woman on her Rearing Horse* (bronze, 22½ x 13 x 7½ ins / 57 x 33 x 19 cm) FRF 3,500. LUCERNE, 8 Nov 2000, *Nude Female Figure* (white marble, h. 24 ins / 60 cm) CHF 4,200. STUTTGART, 8 Dec 2000, *Female Nude and Horse* (brown patinated bronze, h. 15 ins / 37 cm) DEM 5,000. COLOGNE, 11 April 2002, *The Farewell* (bronze, h. 16 ins / 41 cm) EUR 1,900. RUDOLSTADT, 30 May 2003, *Farewell Scene* (brown bronze, h. 18 ins / 46 cm) EUR 1,600. LONDON, 21 April 2004, *Amazon with a Horse* (brown patinated bronze, h. 13 ins / 32 cm) GBP 3,500.

SCHMIDT-MICHELSEN, Alexandre

German, 19th - 20th century.
Born 5 November 1859, in Leipzig; died 20 November 1908, in Berlin.
Painter. Scenes with figures, interiors with figures, landscapes, urban landscapes, architectural views.

Alexandre Schmidt-Michelsen studied in Munich and was the pupil of William Bouguereau and Tony Robert-Fleury in Paris. He lived in Berlin from 1892 onwards.

MUSEUMS AND GALLERIES:

FRANKFURT AM MAIN (Städel): *Obelisk at Rheinsberg* - LEIPZIG: *Market in Leipzig; In the Artist's Studio; Baker's Shop; Cherry Tree in Bloom; Market at Furnes; Grisaille; Orvieto* - STRASBOURG: *Town Gate at Dinkelsbühl*.

SCHMIDT-PECHT, Elisabeth

Maiden name: Sachs
German, 19th - 20th century.
Born 1857, in St Blasien; died 1940, in Constance.
Painter, ceramicist. Designs (ceramic).

Elisabeth Schmidt-Pecht was trained as a painter. From 1894 to 1914 she carried out decorative designs for a firm of ceramic producers, Zeller at Zell am Harmersbach. She became a member of the Vereinigte Werkstätten für Kunst im Handwerk (United Studios for Art in the Craft Industry) in Munich. This organisation, very important for the development of the Jugendstil of Munich, passed orders to the artists and sold and exhibited their work. With her husband, Heinrich Schmidt-Pecht, she founded her own pottery business.

BIBLIOGRAPHY:

Franzke, Irmela, *Jugendstil. Glas, Graphik, Keramik, Metall, Möbel, Skulpturen und Textilien von 1880 bis 1915*, exhibition catalogue, Badisches Landesmuseum, Karlsruhe, 1987.

MUSEUMS AND GALLERIES:

KARLSRUHE (Badisches Landesmus.).

SCHMIDT-PECHT, Heinrich

German, 19th - 20th century.
Born 9 January 1854, in Constance; died 1948, in Constance.
Painter, draughtsman. Landscapes. Designs for ceramics.

Heinrich Schmidt-Pecht was the pupil of Ferdinand Keller at the fine arts school in Karlsruhe. His ceramics were featured at the World's Fairs in Chicago, Paris and St Louis. He founded his own business with his wife, Elisabeth Schmidt-Pecht, and was curator of the Wessenberg art gallery in Constance from 1889 to 1945.

BIBLIOGRAPHY:

Jugendstil bis 1950er Jahre, exhibition catalogue, Keramikzentrum, Konstanz, 1997.

SCHMIDT-POLEX, Rudolf Heinrich, called Polex

German, 19th - 20th century.
Born 3 February 1865, in Frankfurt am Main.
Painter. Portraits, landscapes.

Rudolf Schmidt-Polex was the pupil of William Bouguereau and Gabriel Ferrier in Paris.

SCHMIDT-PRISELDECK, Carl

Danish, 19th - 20th century.
Born 24 November 1853, in Flensburg; died 15 April 1917, in Sorø.
Painter.

Carl Schmidt-Priseldeck exhibited in Paris at the Salon des Artistes Français and obtained a commendation at the 1989 Exposition Universelle.

SCHMIDT-ROTTLUFF, Karl

German, 20th century.
Born 1 December 1884, in Rottluff, near Chemnitz (Saxony); died August 1976, in Berlin.
Painter, watercolourist, draughtsman, engraver, lithographer, sculptor. Figure compositions, figures, nudes, portraits, landscapes, urban landscapes, still-lifes, flowers.
Die Brücke group.

Karl Schmidt-Rottluff was the son of a miller in Rottluff. In 1902, he met Erich Heckel while at college in Chemnitz, where both men belonged to the literary circle Vulkan. Just before 1905, having completed his studies in Chemnitz and obtained his university entrance qualifications, he settled in Dresden and studied architecture at the Hochschule für Bildende Kunst there. He became close to three of his fellow students who already shared the same interests, namely Ernst Ludwig Kirchner, Fritz Bleyl and Erich Heckel. From 1902 onwards, Kirchner had communicated his own passion for drawing and painting to Bleyl, and then in 1904 to Heckel.

In 1905, the four decided to found a group uniting various avant-garde artistic movements. It was at this point that Karl Schmidt adopted the name of his native town as part of his surname. As a symbol of this determination to establish alliances, and perhaps in a reference to Nietzsche's Zarathustra, for whom man is a bridge, a gradual development, the group was called Die Brücke (The Bridge). It attracted other artists, including Emil Nolde, whom Schmidt-Rottluff accompanied in 1906 to his home in Als, then Max Pechstein, Van Dongen and Otto Mueller. During the early years of the group, its four founder members practically lived together, working together with a shared conviction, to the point that it is extremely difficult to distinguish between their works in that era. In 1908, Paul and Martha Rauert, who lived near Hamburg, began what was to become the largest private collection of Schmidt-Rottluff's work. In 1909, the *Die Brücke Album* was devoted entirely to Schmidt-Rottluff.

From 1910 to 1912, during the winter months, Schmidt-Rottluff worked in a studio in Hamburg, spending the summer of 1911 in Norway, then finally left Dresden for Berlin, where he collaborated on the revue *Der Sturm* (*The Storm*) and struck up friendships with Otto Mueller and Lyonel Feininger. It was decided to disband the group in 1913 when it became clear that there were inevitable divergences in the views of its members.

Nevertheless, the works produced by Die Brüke had defined in concrete terms a fundamental aspect of what was to be labelled 'German Expressionism'. However, Die Brüke is not to be confused with Expressionism as a whole. The group had kept itself very much to itself in Dresden. Other very prominent Expressionists, such as August Macke and Franz Marc, were to regroup in the much wider contexts of the Neue Künstlervereinigung München (New Munich Artists' Association) in Munich and then in Kandinsky's Blaue Reiter (Blue Rider) group.

In 1913, Schmidt-Rottluff, having returned to Berlin, collaborated on the revue *Das neue Pathos*, and in 1914 on the revue *Die Aktion*. In June 1914, he stayed on the Baltic coast and spent World War I on the Eastern Front before settling permanently in Berlin in 1919. He travelled extensively, visiting Italy in 1923, Paris in 1924, Ticino in 1928 and 1929, and Jershäft, a port in Pomerania, every summer from 1928 to 1932.

In 1931, Karl Schmidt-Rottluff was elected a member of the fine arts academy in Berlin, but was excluded from the academy when the Nazis came to power in 1933. In 1937, 608 of his works were confiscated in Germany as examples of 'degenerate art', including 51 which were exhibited initially in Munich, and later in other German towns, as part of the propaganda exhibition *Entartete Kunst* (*Degenerate Art*). In 1941, like Nolde and others, Schmidt-Rottluff received notification that he was forbidden to paint and would be placed under police surveillance. Following the destruction of his studio in a bombardment in 1944, he returned to Chemnitz until 1947. In 1946, he was appointed professor at the school of fine arts in Berlin, and in 1967, as the last surviving member of the German Expressionist group, he helped found the Brücke-Museum in Berlin.

In the early years of the century, when the Brücke group was created in Dresden in 1905, Schmidt-Rottluff and his friends, though in principle opposed to the *Jugendstil*, nevertheless retained certain of its characteristics, in particular the curvilinear drawings, the fondness for arabesque and the passion for colour of artists such as Klimt. In the early days of the group, their quest for a specifically German character led them from 1905 onwards to practise the art of wood engraving, popular in medieval Germany; the simplified, synthetic graphic quality of these engravings manifested itself in the case of Schmidt-Rottluff in rough, thick black rings. In 1906, pursuing the aim of simplifying curvilinear drawing and arabesques, he initiated his friends in the art of lithography. Of the artists in the group, Schmidt-Rottluff is closest to the Fauves; his work is characterised by greater elegance in the structure of the compositions using arabesques, less aggression in the expressive distortions and a more structurally balanced approach to the use of colour.

After World War I, in 1917-1918, Schmidt-Rottluff again worked on a series of wood engravings, with large black flat tints, on Old Testament subjects such as *Christ and the Woman Taken in Adultery*, 1918, and *The Prophetess*, 1919. In the 1920s, he devoted a considerable amount of energy to graphic works, watercolours, wood engravings, lithographs and etchings.

Karl Schmidt-Rottluff participated in a number of collective exhibitions, for the first time in 1905 at the Sächsischer Kunstverein. The first and second exhibitions by the Die Brücke group were mounted in Dresden-Löbtau in 1906, followed by others in Dresden, in 1909 at the Kunstsalon Emil Richter and in 1910 at the Galerie Arnold. During this period, he was taking part in the exhibitions of the New Secession in Berlin. In 1912, he exhibited with the Sonderbund in Cologne and was invited to exhibit with the Blaue Reiter group in Munich; he also exhibited for the first time with Die Brücke in Berlin. After World War II, a number of exhibitions throughout the world provided increased awareness of the significance of German Expressionism and its originality, including *Paula Modersohn and the Painters of Die Brücke* at the Kunsthalle in Bern in 1948, the major *Die Brücke* exhibition at the 1950 Venice Biennale, and *Le Fauvisme français et les débuts de l'Expressionnisme allemand* (*French Fauvism and the Beginnings of German Expressionism*) shown at the national museum of modern art in Paris and the Kunsthaus in Munich in 1966.

After his death, works by Schmidt-Rottluff continued to be shown in collective thematic exhibitions devoted to German Expressionism, including *Figure du moderne 1905-1914 - L'Expressionnisme en Allemagne* (*The Face of Modernity 1905-1914: Expressionism in Germany*) at the modern art museum in Paris in 1993, *Die Brücke in Dresden, 1905-1911* at the Staatliche Kunstsammlungen in Dresden in 2001, and *Le Fauvisme en noir et blanc. De Gauguin à Vlaminck, l'estampe des fauves et son environnement* (*Fauvism in Black and White. From Gauguin to Vlaminck, Fauvist Engraving and its Setting*) at the modern art museum in Villeneuve d'Ascq, also in 2001.

Works by Schmidt-Rottluff were also shown in a number of solo exhibitions, in 1910 at the Galerie Commeter, Hamburg; at the Fritz Gurlitt gallery in Berlin and the Folkwang Museum, Hagen, in 1914; and at the Kunstverein in Leipzig in 1915. In 1917, while he was on military service, his works were exhibited at the Goltz gallery, Munich, and in the exhibition *Schmidt-Rotluff: 250 Graphic Works after 1905* at the Kunsthalle in Hamburg. A number of solo exhibitions followed in the inter-war years: at the Arnold gallery in Dresden in 1927; *Schmidt-Rottluff, Oil Paintings, Watercolours* at the Kunsthütte in Chemnitz in 1929; at the Provinz Museum in Hanover in 1930; in Berlin again in 1935, despite the rise of the Nazis, and in New York in 1936. After World War II, he exhibited at the Schlossberg Museum in Chemnitz in 1946; at the premises of the Kestner Gesellschaft in Hanover in 1952 (*Schmidt-Rottluff. Oil Paintings, Watercolours, Wood Engravings, Sculptures*); at the Kunstverein in Hanover in 1963-1964; at the Folkwang Museum in Essen (the retrospective *Karl Schmidt-Rottluff. Paintings, Watercolours, Graphic Works*); at the Staatsgalerie, Stuttgart (*Karl Schmidt-Rottluff on his 90th Birthday*) and at the Altonaer Museum in Hamburg (*Karl Schmidt-Rottluff Paintings*) in 1974; and in 1974-1975 in Stuttgart (*Karl Schmidt-*

Rottluff. The Black Engravings), at the Städtisches Museum in Chemnitz, at the Neue Meister art gallery in Dresden and the national gallery in Berlin.

A number of posthumous exhibitions were also mounted: at the Brücke-Museum in Berlin in 1984; *Karl Schmidt-Rottluff for his Centenary* at the Landesmuseum in Schleswig, also in 1984; *The Wood Engraving as a Work of Art - The Wood Engravings of Karl Schmidt-Rottluff from 1905 to 1930* at the Brücke-Museum in Berlin in 1985; at the Los Angeles County Museum of Art, also in 1985; at the Kunsthalle in Bremen in 1989; *Karl Schmidt-Rottluff* at the Musée Matisse in Nice in 1995; *Karl Schmidt-Rottluff* at the Brücke Museum in Berlin in 1997; at the Kunsthalle der Hypo-Kulturstiftung in Munich, also in 1997; and *Karl Schmidt-Rottluff: ein Maler des 20. Jahrhunderts; Gemälde, Aquarelle und Zeichnungen von 1905 bis 1972* (*Karl Schmidt-Rottluff, a Painter of the 20th Century: Paintings, Watercolours and Drawings, 1905-1972*) at the museum on the Ostwall in Dortmund in 2001.

Schmidt-Rotluff was undoubtedly one of the most important representatives of German Expressionism of his century. Still painting landscapes characterised by large areas of vibrant colour during his latter years, this artist, who had played a decisive role in defining the objectives of Die Brücke, remained faithful to its precepts throughout the era of Nazi persecution and to the very end of his long life.

Rottluff

KARL Schmidt Rottluff

S-R

BIBLIOGRAPHY:

Grohmann, Will, '*Karl Schmidt-Rottluff*' in *Allegemeines Lexikon der bildenden Künstler von der Antike bis zur Gegenwart..., herausgegeben von Dr. Ulrich Thieme und Dr. Felix Becker*, vol. XXX, E. A. Seemann, Leipzig, 1936. *Karl Schmidt-Rottluff*, exhibition catalogue, Städtische Kunstsammlungen, Chemnitz, 1946. *Karl Schmidt-Rottluff: an exhibition of graphic works and stone carvings*, Leicester Museum and Art Gallery, Leicester, 1953. Grohmann, Will, *Karl Schmidt-Rottluff*, W. Kohlhammer, Stuttgart, 1956. Thiem, Gunther, *Karl Schmidt-Rottluff: Aquarelle und Zeichnungen*, F. Bruckmann, Munich, 1963. Shapiro, Rosa/Rathenau, Ernest, *Karl Schmidt-Rottluff, das graphische Werk seit 1923*, Ernest Rathenau, New York, 1964. Cichy, Bodo, *Moderne Malerei, Beginn und Entwicklung*, E. E. Thoma, Munich, 1965. Wietek, Gerhard, *Schmidt-Rottluff Graphisme*, Thiemig, Munich, 1971. Brix, Karl, *Karl Schmidt-Rottluff*, E. A. Seemann, Leipzig, 1972. Rathenau, Ernest, *Das graphische Werk seit 1923*, Rathenau, New York, 1976. *Karl Schmidt-Rottluff, aquarelles des années 50*, exhibition catalogue, Goethe-Institut, Paris, 1976. Wietek, Gerhard, *Karl Schmidt-Rottluff im Hamburg und Schleswig-Holstein*, K. Wachholtz, Neumünster, 1984. Schapire, Rosa, *Karl Schmidt-Rottluff. Das graphische werk bis 1923*, Euphorion, Berlin, Ernest Rathenau, New York, 1984-1987. *Prints by Erich Heckel and Karl Schmidt-Rottluff: a centenary celebration*, Los Angeles County Museum of Art, Los Angeles, 1985. *Karl Schmidt-Rottluff*, exhibition catalogue, Musée Matisse, Nice, 1995. Moeller, Magdalena M., *Karl Schmidt-Rottluff*, exhibition catalogue, Brücke-Museum, Berlin, 1997. *Karl Schmidt-Rottluff*, exhibition catalogue, Kunsthalle der Hypo-Kulturstiftung, Munich, 1997. Moeller, Magdalena M., *Karl Schmidt-Rottluff: ein Maler des 20. Jahrhunderts*, travelling exhibition catalogue, Museum am Ostwall, Dortmund, 2001. *Die Brücke in Dresden 1905-1911*, exhibition catalogue, Staatliche Kunstsammlungen Dresden, Gal. Neue Meister, Dresden, 2001.

MUSEUMS AND GALLERIES:

AMSTERDAM (Stedelijk Mus.) - BERLIN (Berlinische Gal.) - BERLIN (Brücke Mus.): *Young Man Asleep* (1905, woodcut); *From a Mountain Village* (1905, woodcut); *Portrait of Rosa Shapiro* (1911); *Port* (1912, woodcuts); *Woman Kneeling* (1914, woodcuts); *The Walk* (1923, approx. 60 works) - BERLIN (Nationalgal.): *Self-portrait with Monocle* (1910); *Pine Trees in Front of the White House* (1911); *Houses by Night* (1912); *Houses on the Banks of the Canal* (1912); *Three Nudes* (1913) - BERLIN (Neue Nationalgal.): *Estate at Dangast* (1910); *Self-portrait* (1950) - BONN (Städtische Kunstsammlungen): *Still-life with White Vase* (1921) - BREMEN (Kunsthalle): *Self-portrait* (1908, etching); *Three at a Table* (1914, woodcut) - CHEMNITZ: *Sick Child* - COLOGNE (Mus. Ludwig): *Still-life with Negro Sculpture* (1913) - COLOGNE (Wallraf-Richartz Mus.): *Spurs at the Window* (c. 1922) - DORTMUND (Mus. am Ostwall): *Early Spring* (1911) - DRESDEN (Gemäldegal. Neue Meister): *After the Bath* (1912); *Landscape with Trees* - DUISBURG (Wilhelm Lehmbruck Mus.): *Landscape with Fields* (1911) - DÜSSELDORF (Kunstmus.): *Woman Crouching* (1913, ink and watercolour); *Moon over the Village* (1924, watercolour) - ESSEN (Folkwang Mus.): *Seated Nude* (1909, woodcut) - FRANKFURT AM MAIN (Städel): *African Cup* - HALLE: *Portrait of the Artist* - HAMBURG (Altonaer Mus.): *Sunset over the Sea* (1910, woodcut) - HAMBURG (Kunsthalle): *Resting in the Studio* (1910); *Houses I* (1910, lithograph); *Lofthus* (1911); *Lane with Trees* (1911, woodcut); *Forest* (1921) - HANOVER (Niedersächsisches Landesmus.): *Summer, Nudes in the Open Air* (1913) - KIEL: *Two Women* (1910, woodcut) - LEICESTER: *Port at Low Tide* (1907, lithograph); *Young Girl with Outstretched Arm* (1911, woodcut) - LONDON (Tate Collection): *Woman with a Bag* (1915, oil on canvas); *Male Head* (1917, wood); *Dr Rosa Schapire* (1919, oil on canvas) - LUGANO (Thyssen-Bornemisza Collection): *Little House* (1906) - MANNHEIM (Städtische Kunsthalle): *Town with a Tower* (1912); *Window in Summer* (1937) - NEW YORK (MoMA): *The Pharisees* (1912) - OLDENBURG (Landesmus. für Kunst und Kulturgeschichte): *Autumn* (1909, woodcut); *Young Girl Leaning on her Arm* (1913, woodcut); *Woman in the Dunes* (1914) - SCHLESWIG (Landesmus. für Kunst und Kulturgeschichte): *Three Bathers (Nudes in the Open Air)* (1913); *Landing Stage on the River* (1959) - SEEBÜLL (Nolde Institute): *Self-portrait* (1906) - STUTTGART (Staatsgal.): *House with Tower* (1909, woodcut); *Factory* (1910, woodcut); *Seated Female Nude* (1911, pencil drawing); *House with Tower* (1911, woodcut); *Two Female Nudes on the Beach* (1913, ink and colour wash); *In the Studio* (1913, woodcut); *Woman Wearing a Necklace* (1914, woodcut); *Young Girl in front of the Mirror* (1914, woodcut) - THE HAGUE (Gemeentemus.): *Two Women* (1914) - VIENNA (Mus. Moderner Kunst Stiftung Ludwig): *At the Station* (1908).

AUCTION RECORDS:

FRANKFURT AM MAIN, 22 April 1950, *Trees and Houses*, DEM 2,900. COLOGNE, 28 April 1958, *Woman in a Red Gown*, DEM 18,000. STUTTGART, 3-4 May 1962, *The Little House*, DEM 47,000. MUNICH, 12 Dec 1968, *Summer's Day*, DEM 62,000. NEW YORK, 9 April 1969, *Landscape with Birches* (watercolour) USD 4,250; *Lavender Fields by the Sea*, USD 35,000. GENEVA, 12 June 1970, *Village of Dangast* (watercolour) CHF 65,000. BERN, 12 June 1971, *Village in Ticino* (watercolour) CHF 33,000. HAMBURG, 16 June 1973, *Trees in Blossom*, DEM 410,000. BERN, 15 June 1974, *Landscape* (1914) CHF 225,000. MUNICH, 25 May 1976, *Vase of Flowers against a Blue Background* (1954, watercolour, 26 x

19 ins / 66 x 48 cm) DEM 25,000. LONDON, 29 June 1976, *Friends* (1914, oil on canvas, 34 1/2 x 40 ins / 87.5 x 101.5 cm) GBP 26,000. COLOGNE, 3 Dec 1976, *Peasant Woman with a Cow* (1922, woodcut, 19 3/4 x 15 1/2 ins / 50 x 39.5 cm) DEM 6,000. MUNICH, 26 May 1977, *Mountain Village with Bridge 279* (1927, lithograph) DEM 9,400. HAMBURG, 4 June 1977, *Vase of Flowers* (c. 1969, chalk and Indian ink, 21 1/4 x 15 3/4 ins / 54 x 39.9 cm) DEM 8,200. HAMBURG, 4 June 1977, *Houses by the Seashore* (c. 1924, watercolour, 15 3/4 x 21 1/4 ins / 40.1 x 54 cm) DEM 18,600. HAMBURG, 4 June 1977, *Dahlias* (1919, oil on canvas, 26 1/2 x 19 ins / 67.5 x 48.5 cm) DEM 65,000. MUNICH, 24 Nov 1978, *Young Girl Seated* (1913, woodcut) DEM 7,000. HAMBURG, 9 June 1979, *Reclining Model* (1911, woodcut heightened with colour) DEM 40,000. HAMBURG, 9 June 1979, *Seated Nude* (1913, Indian ink, 19 1/4 x 24 1/2 ins / 49.2 x 62.2 cm) DEM 18,000. HAMBURG, 9 June 1979, *Still-life with Bottles* (1952, oil on canvas, 35 1/2 x 30 ins / 90 x 76 cm) DEM 42,000. MUNICH, 27 Nov 1979, *Street Lined with Trees* (1955, watercolour, 19 3/4 x 27 3/4 ins / 50 x 70.3 cm) DEM 32,000. LONDON, 31 March 1982, *Woman in the Field* (1919, oil on canvas, 35 x 29 1/2 ins / 89 x 75 cm) GBP 30,000. MUNICH, 29 June 1983, *Lily* (1971, coloured chalk and Indian ink, 21 1/4 x 15 3/4 ins / 54 x 40 cm) DEM 17,500. NEW YORK, 16 Nov 1983, *Woman with her Hair Undone* (1913, woodcut, 14 x 11 1/2 ins / 35.5 x 29 cm, 2 ins/5 cm) USD 14,000. HAMBURG, 9 June 1984, *Landscape at Dangast* (1909, watercolour, 14 x 20 1/2 ins / 35.4 x 52.2 cm) DEM 220,000. NEW YORK, 14 Nov 1984, *Still-life with Vase* (1921, oil on canvas, 26 x 28 3/4 ins / 65.2 x 73 cm) USD 70,000. MUNICH, 23 Oct 1985, *Dark Gloxinia* (1964, Indian ink and chalk, 19 3/4 x 27 1/2 ins / 50 x 70 cm) DEM 24,000. LONDON, 23 June 1986, *Fire Lilies* (1921, oil on canvas, 35 1/2 x 30 1/4 ins / 90.2 x 76.8 cm) GBP 80,000. LONDON, 29 March 1988, *Still-life with Blue Flowers* (1924-1925, watercolour/paper, 26 3/4 x 19 ins / 68 x 48.3 cm) GBP 26,400; *Two Nudes* (1953, oil on canvas, 30 x 39 3/4 ins / 76 x 101 cm) GBP 68,200. MUNICH, 8 June 1988, *Still-life* (watercolour and ink, 27 3/4 x 19 3/4 ins / 70.5 x 50 cm) DEM 44,000; *Street in Winter* (ink, 19 3/4 x 27 1/2 ins / 50 x 70 cm) DEM 18,700. MUNICH, 26 Oct 1988, *Village in Snow* (oil on canvas, 35 1/2 x 30 ins / 90 x 76 cm) DEM 308,000. MUNICH, 7 June 1989, *Still-life with Peony* (1951, oil on canvas, 25 1/2 x 29 ins / 65 x 73.5 cm) DEM 187,000. LONDON, 27 June 1989, *Two Nudes in the Fields* (1913, oil on canvas, 25 3/4 x 29 ins / 65.4 x 73.5 cm) GBP 242,000. LONDON, 20 Oct 1989, *Thistles* (watercolour/paper, 19 1/2 x 27 1/2 ins / 49.5 x 70 cm) GBP 12,100. NEW YORK, 16 Nov 1989, *Houses in Erzgeburg* (1936, oil on canvas, 30 x 44 ins / 76.2 x 112 cm) USD 115,500. MUNICH, 13 Dec 1989, *Trees by a Stream* (ink and colouring pencil, 19 3/4 x 27 1/2 ins / 50 x 70 cm) DEM 19,800. NEW YORK, 16 May 1990, *Avenue in a Park* (1921, oil on canvas, 40 x 34 1/4 ins / 101.9 x 87 cm) USD 396,000. MUNICH, 31 May 1990, *Autumn Landscape* (1911, oil on canvas, 30 1/4 x 33 1/4 ins / 77 x 84.5 cm) DEM 616,000. NEW YORK, 14 Nov 1990, *Garden* (1906, oil on card, 33 x 25 1/2 ins / 84 x 65 cm) USD 440,000. COPENHAGEN, 13-14 Feb 1991, *Landscape* (1911, oil on canvas, 26 1/2 x 38 1/2 ins / 67 x 98 cm) DKK 180,000. NEW YORK, 14 Feb 1991, *Landscape* (watercolour ink and wash/paper/card, 19 1/2 x 27 ins / 49.7 x 68.6 cm) GBP 7,700. BERLIN, 30 May 1991, *Bowl of Red and Yellow Dahlias* (watercolour, 19 3/4 x 27 1/2 ins / 50 x 70 cm) DEM 36,630. MUNICH, 26-27 Nov 1991, *Portrait of Woman in a Reverie* (pencil and soft chalk, 3 1/2 x 5 1/2 ins / 9 x 14 cm) DEM 17,250. LONDON, 2 Dec 1991, *Still-life with Apples and a Bottle* (oil on card, 20 x 28 ins / 51 x 71 cm) GBP 132,000. MUNICH, 26 May 1992, *Village with Trees at the Foot of a Mountain* (1925, woodcut, 23 1/2 x 19 1/2 ins / 60 x 49.5 cm) DEM 16,100. BERLIN, 29 May 1992, *Still-life with Peonies* (watercolour and ink/vellum, 19 1/2 x 27 1/4 ins / 49.8 x 69 cm) DEM 106,220. BERLIN, 27 Nov 1992, *Glass Utensils* (1969, ink and watercolour, 19 1/2 x 27 1/2 ins / 49.5 x 70 cm) DEM 31,640. MUNICH, 1-2 Dec 1992, *Autumn Foliage* (watercolour and ink, 27 1/4 x 19 3/4 ins / 69.5 x 50 cm) DEM 51,750. LONDON, 20 May 1993, *The Magi* (1917, woodcut, 19 3/4 x 15 1/4 ins / 50.3 x 38.9 cm) GBP 9,200; *Kappellenberg* (watercolour/paper, 19 1/4 x 26 ins / 49 x 66 cm) GBP 18,400. LONDON, 13 Oct 1994, *Avenue at the Entrance* (1910, oil on canvas, 30 1/4 x 33 1/2 ins / 77 x 85 cm) GBP 958,500; *House at the end of the Lane* (1922, watercolour/paper, 18 1/4 x 23 ins / 46.5 x 58.4 cm) GBP 63,100. NEW YORK, 24 Feb 1995, *Still-life with Fruit* (watercolour/paper, 13 3/4 x 20 ins / 35.2 x 50.8 cm) USD 14,950. LUCERNE, 20 May 1995, *Head of a Woman* (woodcut, 69 3/4 x 9 1/2 ins / 177.2 x 24.1 cm) CHF 1,600. LONDON, 11 Oct 1995, *Lighthouse* (1913, oil on canvas, 25 3/4 x 31 ins / 65.5 x 79 cm) GBP 430,500. ZURICH, 26 March 1996, *View over the Gulf* (pencil and ink, 15 1/4 x 20 1/2 ins / 39 x 52 cm) CHF 15,000. LONDON, 9 Oct 1996, *Still-life with Thistles* (pen, ink and watercolour/paper, 19 1/2 x 27 1/2 ins / 49.4 x 70 cm) GBP 13,800. LONDON, 3 Dec 1996, *House with Red Roof* (pastel, brush and black ink/paper, 15 3/4 x 21 1/4 ins / 40 x 54 cm) GBP 13,800. LONDON, 4 Dec 1996, *Covered Bridge* (1959, watercolour/paper, 19 1/2 x 27 1/4 ins / 49.5 x 69.3 cm) GBP 9,200. NEW YORK, 19 Feb 1997, *Portrait of a Woman* (1913, watercolour and wash ink/paper, 20 x 15 3/4 ins / 50.5 x 40.3 cm) USD 24,150. LONDON, 9 Oct 1997, *Park at Dangast* (1910, oil on canvas, 30 x 33 1/4 ins / 76.2 x 84.5 cm) GBP 925,000. BERLIN, 4 June 1999, *Nude* (1914, oil on canvas, 35 x 30 ins / 90 x 76 cm) DEM 1,300,000. LONDON, 7 Oct 1999, *Red Roses* (1922, oil on canvas, 26 x 29 ins / 65 x 73 cm) GBP 210,000. NEW YORK, 5 Nov 2001, *The Farm* (1914, oil on canvas, 30 x 36 ins / 77 x 91 cm) USD 950,000. NEW YORK, 5 Nov 2001, *The Reader* (1911, oil on canvas, 30 x 33 ins / 77 x 85 cm) USD 3,600,000. BERLIN, 7 June 2002, *Hay Harvest* (1924, watercolour on card, 23 x 19 ins / 58 x 49 cm) EUR 105,000. BERLIN, 7 June 2002, *Approaching Thunderstorm* (c. 1919-1920, oil on canvas, 39 x 44 ins / 98 x 112 cm) EUR 720,000. MUNICH, 5 May 2003, *Model* (colour woodcut, 11 x 17 ins / 29 x 43 cm) EUR 110,000. COLOGNE, 4 Dec 2003, *Water Lilies II* (1946, watercolour, 19 x 25 ins / 48 x 64 cm) EUR 56,000. NEW YORK, 6 May 2004, *Landscape with Seated Figure* (watercolour, 20 x 27 ins / 50 x 69 cm) USD 85,000. BERLIN, 11 June 2004, *Landscape with Poplar* (oil on masonite, 30 x 48 ins / 77 x 123 cm) EUR 85,000.

SCHMIDT-WOLFRATSHAUSEN, Karl
German, 20th century.
Born 12 January 1891, in Wolfratshausen.
Painter, engraver.

Karl Schmidt-Wolfratshausen was active in Nabburg.

SCHMIDTBAUER, Paul
Croat, 20th century.
Born 7 July 1892, in Lividraga.
Painter, engraver, lithographer. Self-portraits.

Paul Schmidtbauer was self-taught as an artist, and was active in Graz.

MUSEUMS AND GALLERIES:
GRAZ: *Portrait of the Artist by Himself*; other works.

SCHMIDTBAUER, Wolfgang
German, 18th century.
Born c. 1740, in Bamberg; died c. 1790, in Bamberg.
Miniaturist, painter. Genre scenes.

Schmidtbauer studied for five years at the academy in Vienna. His most notable work is a portrait of Emperor Joseph II.

SCHMIDTCASSEL, Gustav
German, 19th - 20th century.
Born 2 November 1867, in Kassel.
Sculptor.

Schmidtcassel was the pupil of Ernst Gustav Herter at the academy of fine arts in Berlin, where he settled. He sculpted a *Statue of Peter the Great* for the city of Riga and a *Statue of the Emperor Frederick* for the city of Graz.

SCHMIDTGARTNER, Matthias
German, 18th century.
Stucco artist.
Schmidtgartner worked on the decoration of the church of the Holy Spirit in Munich between 1724 and 1730.

SCHMIDTHAMMER. See **SCHMIDHAMMER**

SCHMIDTHANS
Bohemian School, 18th century.
Painter.
Schmidthanns painted three crucifixes and several scenes from the *Life of St Bernard*, for the church in Waldsassen in about 1725.

SCHMIDTLEITH, Andreas
German, 17th century.
Active in Frankfurt am Main.
Sculptor.

SCHMIDTMAYER, Franz
Austrian, 19th century.
Born 26 March 1813, in Prachatitz; died 25 June 1873, in Vienna.
Painter.

SCHMIDTNER, Johann Georg Melchior. See **SCHMITTNER**

SCHMIDTS, Heinrich. See **SMIDTS Heinrich** or **Hendrick**

SCHMIECHEN, Hermann
German, 19th - 20th century.
Born 22 July 1855, in Neumarkt (Silesia).
Painter. Portraits, local figures, genre scenes.
Hermann Schmiechen was the pupil of K.F. Eduard von Gebhardt at the fine arts academy in Berlin and studied at the Académie Julian in Paris.
AUCTION RECORDS:
LONDON, 28 Nov 1984, *Mother and Child before the Fireplace* (oil on canvas, 39 3/4 x 48 1/2 ins / 101 x 123 cm) GBP 6,200. COLOGNE, 18 March 1989, *Portrait of a Young Woman* (1880, oil on canvas, 9 1/2 x 7 ins / 24 x 18 cm) DEM 3,500. LONDON, 5 May 1989, *Fruit Seller* (1876, oil on canvas/panel, 9 x 6 ins / 22 x 15 cm) GBP 770. PARIS, 13 Feb 1995, *Portrait of a Woman* (oil on panel, 23 x 17 ins / 57.5 x 43 cm) FRF 11,000.

SCHMIED, Florian
German.
Born to a family originally from Krems.
Painter.

SCHMIED, François-Louis
Swiss, 20th century.
Born 8 November 1873, in Geneva; died 19 January 1941, in Tahanaout or Tahahaouf (Morocco).
Also active in France.
Painter (gouache), engraver, illustrator, binder. Genre scenes, local scenes, landscapes.
Orientalism.
Originally destined for a career in commerce, François-Louis Schmied attended drawing lessons every morning before going to work at his father's business. Persuaded of the quality of his drawings, his family allowed him to go to the school of industrial arts in Geneva as an apprentice wood engraver, where he was first the pupil of Alfred Martin and was subsequently taught by Barthélemy Menn. It was there that he made the acquaintance of Jean Dunand, a lifelong friend with whom he also collaborated on the production of a number of extraordinary books. In 1895, he arrived in Paris, where he was soon joined by Dunand, and where in 1897 he met Dampt. In 1933, he embarked on a voyage to the Antilles, Guyana and Venezuela, and from 1934 onwards he made frequent visits to Morocco.

François-Louis Schmied exhibited at the Société Nationale des Beaux-Arts in Paris from 1904 to 1914. His first work with wood engravings, *Sous la tente* (*Under the Tent*) by Edouard Maury, appeared in 1911, and was followed by coloured wood engravings after Jouve to illustrate Rudyard Kipling's *Jungle Book*. Begun after the war, this book was not finished until 1919. Schmied's success persuaded him to publish his own work, and between 1922 and 1941 over 35 publications appeared in which he was by turns typographer, illustrator, model maker and book-binder. Some of these were quite exquisite, in particular *Les Climats* by the Comtesse de Noailles and Alfred de Vigny's *Daphné*; his most curious book is undoubtedly the *Song of Songs* of 1925. Other notable works include Flaubert's *Salammbô* (1923), Oscar Wilde's *Two Tales* (1926), the numerous transcriptions of Egyptian, Arabic and Semitic texts of Dr Mardrus, Suetonius' *Twelve Caesars* (1927), La Fontaine's *Fables* (1929), Loti's *Le Pélerin d'Angkor* (1930), the *Odyssey* (1934) and *Faust* (1938).

Apart from his various activities in the sphere of books, Schmied travelled and painted, frequently linking the two activities, for example in a series of tempera paintings based on Moroccan landscapes and subjects taken from Moroccan life. The colours in these pictures are vibrant, with an iridescent Mannerist quality evoking a mirage suddenly frozen in time.
BIBLIOGRAPHY:
Monod, Luc, *Manuel de l'amateur de livres illustrés modernes 1875-1975*, Ides et Calendes, Neuchâtel, 1992.
AUCTION RECORDS:
PARIS, 30 April 1975, *The Kasbah in Asni* (1936) FRF 18,500; *Marabout at Safi*, FRF 10,500. PARIS, 14 June 1976, *Bearer (Martinique)* (tempera/hardboard, 35 1/2 x 24 1/2 ins / 90 x 62 cm) FRF 4,000. PARIS, 29 Oct 1979, *In the Tropics* (1933, gouache and tempera/hardboard panel, 39 1/4 x 25 1/4 ins / 100 x 64 cm) FRF 4,800. PARIS, 18 Feb 1980, *Miracle of Dar Kaid el Ouriki* (1935, tempera/panel, 37 x 22 3/4 ins / 94 x 58 cm) FRF 17,000. PARIS, 22 Nov 1984, *Narcissus* (oil on panel, 15 plaques in polychrome chased enamel, 50 1/2 x 71 ins / 128 x 179.5 cm) FRF 300,000. LONDON, 20 June 1985, *Ruth and Boaz* (woodcut in colour and gold, 28 items) GBP 1,500. NEW YORK, 13 Dec 1986, *Norman Knight* (c. 1932, gouache, 25 1/2 x 16 1/2 ins / 64.8 x 42 cm) USD 2,600. PARIS, 27 March 1987, *Safi* (1936, gouache, Indian ink and tempera, 22 3/4 x 33 3/4 ins / 58 x 86 cm) FRF 28,500. PARIS, 25 March 1988, *Tahanaout* (tempera/paper, 25 1/2 x 37 1/2 ins / 65 x 95 cm) FRF 41,000. PARIS, 22 June 1990, *Lovers* (oil on panel, 17 x 23 ins / 43 x 57.5 cm) FRF 32,000. PARIS, 17 Dec 1999, *Fields of Wheat* (1905, oil on canvas, 19 x 28 ins / 48 x 70 cm) FRF 25,000. PARIS, 23 May 2000, *Self-portrait* (1904, graphite, 11 x 8 ins / 27 x 21 cm) FRF 22,000. PARIS, 29 June 2001, *Profile of a Woman* (polychrome and wood relief, 17 x 12 ins / 42 x 30 cm) FRF 27,000. PARIS, 30 Nov 2001, *View of the Kasbah in Asni, Morocco* (1938, oil on panel, 20 x 24 ins / 50 x 60 cm) EUR 9,755.

SCHMIED, Friedrich or Frédéric
Swiss, 20th century.
Born 26 July 1893, in Zurich.
Sculptor. Figures, nudes. Busts.
Friedrich Schmied was the pupil of James Vibert at the school of fine arts in Geneva, where he became established.
MUSEUMS AND GALLERIES:
GENEVA: *Male Torso* (marble) - LA CHAUX-DE-FONDS: *Dawn* (bronze) - LAUSANNE (Cantonal MFA): *Female Torso* (1925, marble in the round) - LUGANO: *Bust of the Painter Estappey* (bronze) - OLTEN: *Bust of a Female Worker*.

SCHMIED, Hans David, or Schmidt, Schmiedt
Austrian, 17th century.
Active in Elbogen.
Sculptor (wood).
Schmied became a master sculptor in 1674.

SCHMIED, Johann Chr
German, 18th century.
Painter.

SCHMIED, Johann Matthäus. See **SCHMIDT**

SCHMIED, Joseph
Austrian, 19th century.
Born 1816, in Vienna.
Landscape artist.
Joseph Schmied was a student at the royal academy in Vienna.

SCHMIED, Théo
French, 20th century.
Born 1901, in Paris.
Engraver.
Théo Schmied, the son of François Louis Schmied, collaborated with his father in the publishing of fine books and engraved his father's illustrations.
BIBLIOGRAPHY:
'Théo Schmied, le successeur' in *Art et Métiers du Livre* n° 177 p. 31-35, periodical, Paris, 1993.

SCHMIED, Wolf. See **SICHELSCHMIED**

SCHMIEDEBERG, Ludwig
German, 19th century.
Born c. 1796; died 26 March 1845, in Grandenz.
Draughtsman, lithographer.

SCHMIEDEBERG-BLUME, Else von
German, 20th century.
Born 10 April 1876, in Worbis.
Painter. Portraits, landscapes.
Else von Schmiedeberg-Blume studied at the fine arts academy in Leipzig and was the pupil of Lucien Simon at the school of fine arts in Paris.

SCHMIEDECKE, Friedrich August
German, 19th century.
Born 1784, in Leipzig.
Painter.
Schmiedecke studied with J.E. Schenaus and H.V. Schnorr of Karolsfeld.

SCHMIEDEL, Michael
German, 16th century.
Born between 1535 and 1540, in Geithain; died 11 February 1591, in Geithain.
Painter.
The parish church of Geithain has three paintings by Michael Schmiedel: *Christ in the Garden of Gethsemane*, *Ascension of Elijah* and *Resurrection of the Dead*.

SCHMIEDER, Konrad
German, 19th century.
Born 12 November 1859, in Ubelbach; died 5 July 1898, in Mannheim.
Painter. Religious subjects. Murals.
Konrad Schmieder was active in Karlsruhe, where he painted three scenes from the life of St John the Baptist in the church in Donaueschingen.

SCHMIEDER, Samuel Friedrich
German, 18th century.
Painter.
Four oil paintings by Samuel Schmieder of views of Regensburg are now owned by the city.

SCHMIEDHUBER, Mathias
Austrian, 18th century.
Active between 1768 and 1785.
Sculptor.

SCHMIEDT, Hans David. See **SCHMIED**

SCHMIEDT, Paul. See **SCHMIDT**

SCHMIEG, Georg Friedrich, or Schmicht, Schmigd, Schmitt
German, 18th century.
Active in Amorbach.
Sculptor, engraver (wood).

SCHMIEGELOW, Pedro Ernst Johann
German, 19th - 20th century.
Born 17 July 1863, in Hamburg.
Painter. Portraits, urban landscapes, landscapes.
Pedro Schmiegelow was active in Fulda.
MUSEUMS AND GALLERIES:
LEIPZIG (Stadtgeschichtliches Mus.): *Butchers' Market Square in Leipzig* - WÜRZBURG (Martin-von-Wagner-Mus., Universität): ten small landscapes.

SCHMIEL, Ernst
German, 19th century.
Painter (porcelain).
Ernst Schmiel was active in Berlin around 1832.

SCHMIEL, Julius
German, 19th century.
Active in Berlin.
Painter. Portraits, genre scenes, flowers.
Julius Schmiel exhibited from 1838 to 1842.

SCHMIELINGH, Bruno. See **SCHMELING**

SCHMIETH, Bertha
German, 19th - 20th century.
Born 1 February 1860, in Schleswig.
Painter.
Bertha Schmieth spent her youth in Itzehoe, in Holstein, and at the age of 27 went to train as a painter in France before settling in Schwerin in 1896.

SCHMIGAÜS. See **SMICHÄUS**

SCHMIGD, Georg Friedrich. See **SCHMIEG**

SCHMILIPÄUS, Georg Felix
Bohemian School, 17th century.
Active in Chrudim in 1641.
Painter.
Some of the paintings by Georg Schmilipäus, in the style of Albert Dürer, have survived.

SCHMIRGUELA, Nicolas
Bulgarian, 20th century.
Born in Bulgaria.
Sculptor.

SCHMISCHEK. See **SMISEK**

SCHMISCHKE, Julius
German, 20th century.
Born 20 September 1890, in Parösken (Eylau).
Active from 1921 in Brazil.
Painter. Portraits, landscapes.
Julius Schmischke was a pupil at the fine arts academy in Königsberg (now Kaliningrad, Russia). In 1921, he left Königsberg and settled in São Paulo.

SCHMIT, Alvarus
Austrian, 18th century.
Painter.
An altarpiece by Schmit depicting *St Thomas Aquinas* can be seen in the church in Tautendorf.

SCHMIT, Paul
French, 17th century.
Active in Paris c. 1650.
Draughtsman, goldsmith.

SCHMITGEN, Georg
German, 19th century.
Born 1856, in Bernkastel (Moselland); died 8 June 1903, in Potsdam.
Painter. Landscapes, seascapes.

Schmitgen studied at both the Munich and Berlin Academies. He painted the landscape of Brandenburg and seascapes of the Baltic and Norwegian coasts.

SCHMITH, Lucien Louis Jean Baptiste. See **SCHMIDT**

SCHMITHALS, Hans
German, 20th century.
Born 23 March 1878, in Bad Kreuznach; died 1964, in Munich.
Painter, pastellist, draughtsman, designer, interior designer. Murals, furniture, carpets, jewellery.
Jugendstil.

Hans Schmithals was a pupil in Munich of the Debschitz-Schule co-founded by Obrist where he later taught the painting of wallpaper. Between 1909 and 1911 he studied in Paris. With Franz von Stuck, Richard Riemerschmid, Fritz Endell and, his tutor Obrist, he contributed to the elaboration of Jugendstil. Shcmithals' output was lost after World War I or was destroyed during World War II. He had several projects in furniture, did some interior decorations in Berlin, Munich and in Switzerland and, with Wolfgang von Wersin, founded a exhibition group called 'Austellungsverband für Raumkunst' where he showed carpets for which he drew the sketches. Schmithals encouraged the endless growth of the arabesque for its own sake, to the point that his first landscapes are reduced to pieces of the circle. Reaching the point of abstraction, it is possible to see a relationship between the first graphic abstract art of Franz Kupka and the personal version that Schmithals had given to the Jugendstil. It is that aspect that brought him out of anonymity.

BIBLIOGRAPHY:
Hans Schmithals. L'avanguardia Jugendstil, exhibition catalogue, Galleria del Levante, Milan, 1965. Bloom Hiesinger, Kathryn, *Art nouveau in Munich. Masters of Jugendstil*, exhibition catalogue, Museum of Art, Philadelphia, 1989.

MUSEUMS AND GALLERIES:
MUNICH (Bayerische Staatsgemäldesammlung): *Composition in Blue* (1902) - MUNICH (Stadtmus.): *North Star and Draco* (1902).

AUCTION RECORDS:
NEW YORK, 18 March 1976, *Fire* (1903, gouache and charcoal, 17 x 13 ins / 43 x 33 cm) USD 2,100.

SCHMITHS, Heinrich. See **SCHMITZ**

SCHMITSON, Teutwart
German, 19th century.
Born 18 April 1830, in Frankfurt am Main; died 2 September 1863, in Vienna.
Painter. Military subjects, animals.

Schmitson first studied architecture, and taught himself to paint before 1854. He worked in Düsseldorf and Karlsruhe in 1856, in Berlin from 1858 to 1860, in Italy in 1861, and in Vienna from 1861.

MUSEUMS AND GALLERIES:
BERLIN (Nationalgal.): *Transporting Marble in Carrara; Horses in the Puszta; Grazing* - HAMBURG: *Capturing Wild Horses in Hungary; The Rich Man's Cow; The Poor Man's Cow; Team of Oxen Bolting* - KARLSRUHE: *Hungarian Horses Frightened by an Overturned Cart* - LIBEREC: *Nude and Animal Studies* - VIENNA (Österreichische Gal. Belvedere): *Horse Trough.*

AUCTION RECORDS:
PARIS, 1889, *Tartar Horses*, FRF 1,800. VIENNA, 29-30 Oct 1996, *Artillery Manoeuvre* (oil on canvas, 22 x 38 1/2 ins / 56 x 97.5 cm) ATS 48,300. PONTOISE, 5 June 1999, *Hare Hunt* (oil on canvas, 20 x 32 ins / 51 x 81 cm) FRF 16,000. MUNICH, 4 Dec 2002, *Winter Forest with Cart Filled with Wood and Two Farm Hands Driving Oxen and Cows* (oil on canvas, 39 x 63 ins / 100 x 160 cm) EUR 2,700. AHLDEN, 9 May 2003, *Horse Dip* (oil on canvas, 18 x 25 ins / 46 x 64 cm) EUR 2,500.

SCHMITT
German, 18th century.
Painter. Portraits.

Schmitt painted the portrait of Prince *Dietrich of Anhalt Dessau* in the castle of Oranienbaum, near Dessau.

SCHMITT. See also **SCHMIDT**

SCHMITT, Albert Felix
American, 19th - 20th century.
Born 14 June 1873, in Boston.
Active in Biarritz, France.
Painter. Mythological subjects, figures, landscapes.

Albert Schmitt studied at the Boston Art School and also continued his education abroad. He was a member of the Academic Association of International History.

MUSEUMS AND GALLERIES:
BOSTON: *On the River Bank* - PARIS (Mus. d'Orsay): *Young Blonde Girl; Dancing Nymph* - PROVIDENCE (Rhode Island School of Design) - ST LOUIS (AM).

SCHMITT, André
French, 20th century.
Born 21 November 1888, in Strasbourg.
Painter.

André Schmitt studied in Munich and Paris.

MUSEUMS AND GALLERIES:
STRASBOURG.

SCHMITT, August Ludwig
German, 20th century.
Born 10 June 1882, in Appenmühle, near Karlsruhe.
Painter.

August Schmitt was the pupil of Ludwig Dill and Adolf Hölzel, probably in the latter's private school or at the fine arts academy in Stuttgart, in connection with which his name is mentioned at a later stage. He was active in Möhringen.

MUSEUMS AND GALLERIES:
STUTTGART: *Self-portrait of the Artist.*

SCHMITT, Balthasar
German, 19th - 20th century.
Born 29 May 1858, in Aschach.
Sculptor, painter. Religious subjects, allegorical subjects. Statues, groups, monuments.

Balthasar Schmitt was the pupil of Michaël Arnold at the school of drawing in Kissingen and of Syrius Eberle at the fine arts academy in Munich. He also studied in Nuremberg and, from 1889 to 1892, in Rome. He was active in Solln and was a professor at the Munich academy from 1906 onwards. In Munich, he created a colossal statue of the Romantic painter Moritz Ludwig von Schwind, as well as a *Crucifixion with Mary at Prayer* and a group depicting *Justice*, and created the *Kilian Fountain* in Würzburg.

SCHMITT, Bartolomeus
German, 19th century.
Born in Amberg.
Painter. Landscapes.

Bartolomeus Schmitt was active in Munich from 1814.

SCHMITT, Carl
American, 20th century.

Born 6 May 1889, in Trumbull; died 1989.
Painter, engraver.
Carl Schmitt was active in Norwalk, Connecticut.

SCHMITT, Émile
French, 19th - 20th century.
Born in Mulhouse.
Painter. Landscapes.
Émile Schmitt first exhibited in 1879 at the Salon de Paris, which became the Salon des Artistes Français in 1881.

SCHMITT, François
French, 20th - 21st century.
Born 11 April 1959, in Neuilly-sur-Seine.
Painter, performance artist.
Neo-Constructivism.
François Schmitt graduated from high school in 1977 and went on to study at the École des Beaux-Arts in Paris (1983-1985) and the École des Beaux-Arts in Nîmes. In 1987, Schmitt mounted a solo 'performance' at the Place du Marché in Nîmes and, in 1989, he assisted Claude Viallat at an 'installation' also held in Nîmes, and Daniel Buren, at a further installation presented at the Musée d'Art Moderne de la Ville de Paris. His work is based on simple geometric figures with flatly-applied colours. His paintings are exhibited by reference to the available exhibition space. Thus, in the case of his polyptychs, the interval of wall between the individual panels is regarded as an integral part of the overall work.

He has been involved in various group exhibitions: in 1985, at the Monnaie Gallery in Paris and in Nîmes; in 1986, in Nîmes; in 1990, at the Kunstpalast in Düsseldorf; in 1992, at *GS-Art - Jeune Création* at the École des Beaux-Arts in Paris; and so on. Solo exhibitions have included one in 1990, at the Espace Confluence in Paris, and another of 1996 at the Galerie Lahumière, also in Paris.

SCHMITT, Franz
German, 19th century.
Born 26 September 1816, in Wolfstein, near Kaiserslautern; died 7 July 1891, in Frankenthal.
Painter.
Franz Schmitt was taught by his father Georg Philipp and also studied at the Munich academy. He devoted himself to restoring paintings and became a teacher at the industrial school in Frankenthal.
MUSEUMS AND GALLERIES:
FRANKENTHAL: *Pewter Plate with Apricots and Grapes* - HEIDELBERG: *Strawberries and Raspberries; Study of Fruits; The Garden of Heidelberg Castle* - KARLSRUHE: *Erlenbach on the Rhine* - MANNHEIM: *Self-portrait in a Forest; Pumpkins and Tomatoes* - MUNICH: *Fruits.*

SCHMITT, Georg
German, 19th century.
Born 12 January 1840, in Offenbach; died 21 April 1898, in Offenbach.
Lithographer.

SCHMITT, Georg Friedrich. See **SCHMIEG**

SCHMITT, Georg Philipp
German, 19th century.
Born 1808, in Spesbach; died 1873, in Heidelberg.
Painter.
The brother of Franz and father of Guido and Nathanael, Georg Schmitt studied at Heidelberg with Christian Xeller, then from 1825 to 1829 at the academy in Munich with P.Cornelius and J.Schnorr von Carosfeld. His career was spent in Heidelberg.
MUSEUMS AND GALLERIES:
DÜSSELDORF: *Self-portrait* - HEIDELBERG: *Engagement of the Young Tobias; Young Mendicant; Myrtle; Branch of Cherry Tree in Blossom; Apple Trees in Blossom; Wood Pigeon; St John, the Virgin and Mary Magdalene*; watercolour; *View of the Main Bank of Heidelberg; Elisabeth door at Heidelberg Castle; The Young Schmitt Painting* - KARLSRUHE: *Branch of Cherry Tree in Blossom; Noli me Tangere; Portrait of Child; Leiningen Castle; Heidelberg Castle.*

SCHMITT, Georgette
French, 19th - 20th century.
Born in Paris.
Painter, watercolourist. Flowers.
Georgette Schmitt first exhibited in 1880 at the Salon de Paris, which became the Salon des Artistes Français in 1881.

SCHMITT, Gilberte
French, 20th century.
Born 16 June 1907, in Bordeaux.
Painter.
Gilberte Schmitt, who studied at the École des Arts Décoratifs, Paris, exhibited annually at the Salon de la Société Nationale des Beaux-Arts, of which she was a member.

SCHMITT, Guido Philipp
German, 19th - 20th century.
Born 1834, in Heidelberg; died 8 August 1922, in Miltenberg.
Active in England from 1859 to 1896.
Painter, watercolourist. Figures, portraits, landscapes.
Guido Schmitt, the son of Georg Philipp Schmitt and brother of Nathanael Schmitt, was taught by his father. He settled in London, where from 1859 to 1896 he was held in high esteem as a portraitist, before retiring to Heidelberg.
MUSEUMS AND GALLERIES:
HEIDELBERG: *Young Girl at the Fountain; Sevenoaks in the County of Kent; Garden of the Artist in Heidelberg; Master Mason Kaspar Moog with his Child; Apple* (watercolour); *Young Girl Reading* (watercolour).
AUCTION RECORDS:
LONDON, 20 Feb 1976, *Wayside Cross* (1867, oil on canvas, 17 1/2 x 22 ins / 44.5 x 56 cm) GBP 2,600. VIENNA, 18 Sept 1979, *The Young Artist* (oil on canvas, 24 x 18 ins / 61 x 46 cm) ATS 100,000. LONDON, 12 May 1993, *Portrait of a Young Child* (oil on canvas, 16 1/2 x 13 1/2 ins / 42 x 34.5 cm) GBP 1,495.

SCHMITT, Hans
German, 17th century.
Active c. 1600.
Sculptor.
Hans Schmitt sculpted the statues of *St Michael* and *St Barbara* in clay for the church in Munnerstadt.

SCHMITT, Heinrich
German, 19th - 20th century.
Born 5 July 1860, in Mainz; died 1 May 1921, in Buffalo.
Active in the USA.
Sculptor.

SCHMITT, Heinrich Nikolaus
German, 19th century.
Born 1 July 1796, in Bamberg.
Engraver, lithographer.
Heinrich Schmitt worked in Garmisch and was the brother of Joseph.

SCHMITT, Jakob Ludwig
German, 20th century.
Born 11 October 1891, in Mainz.
Sculptor. Religious subjects, figures, genre scenes.
Jakob Schmitt was active in Mainz. Having been wounded during the war, he became blind in 1914. His works include the *The Duck Catcher* on the rag market fountain in Mainz, the *Bowls Player* in Essen and a *Statue of St Teresa* in the cathedral in Frankfurt am Main.

SCHMITT, Johann. See **SCHMIDT**

SCHMITT, Johann Baptist
German, 18th - 19th century.
Born 1768, in Mannheim; died 6 December 1819, in Hamburg.
Painter. Landscapes, architectural views. Decorative schemes.
MUSEUMS AND GALLERIES:
HAMBURG (Mus. für Hamburgische Geschichte): *View of Poppenbuttel* (watercolour).

SCHMITT, Johann Christian. See **SCHMIDT**

SCHMITT, Johann Philipp
German, 19th century.
Born 1815, in Colmar.
Painter.
Johann Schmitt attended the academy in Munich until 1838.

SCHMITT, Josef
Austrian, 19th century.
Born 17 April 1781, in Vienna; died 10 August 1866, in Vienna.
Engraver. Coins.
In 1810 Josef Schmitt struck a medal commemorating the *Marriage of Napoléon and Marie-Louise*.

SCHMITT, Joseph
German, 18th century.
Active in Würzburg from 1770-1790.
Miniaturist.

SCHMITT, Joseph
German, 19th century.
Born 21 March 1790, in Bamberg.
Engraver.
The brother of Nikolaus, Joseph Schmitt was active in Burgpreppach.

SCHMITT, Jozsef. See **SCHMIDT**

SCHMITT, Karl. See **SCHMID**

SCHMITT, Karl J.J.
German, 20th century.
Born 24 July 1880, in Worms.
Active in Worms.
Painter. Landscapes.
MUSEUMS AND GALLERIES:
WORMS.

SCHMITT, Konstantin, or Schmidt
German, 19th century.
Born 13 July 1817, in Mainz.
Active in Darmstadt.
Landscape artist.
Konstantin Schmitt worked from 1837 to 1841 at the academy in Düsseldorf with E.W. Pose, from 1842 to 1843 in Rome, then in Darmstadt and from 1845 to 1854 in Pamelfort, near Düsseldorf.
MUSEUMS AND GALLERIES:
KALININGRAD (Castle): *Forest Landscape*.

SCHMITT, Louis
French, 19th century.
Born 7 February 1807, in Geneva, Switzerland; died 28 July 1890, in Lyons.
Medallist.
He was a pupil of Pradier.

SCHMITT, Nathanael
German, 19th - 20th century.
Born 1847, in Heidelberg; died 1918, in Karlsruhe.
Painter. Portraits, landscapes, architectural views, still-lifes, flowers.
Nathanael Schmitt was the son of Georg Philipp Schmitt, by whom he was taught, and the brother of Guido. He worked in Rome from 1872 to 1880 and in Saarbrücken from 1881 to 1886, subsequently settling in Karlsruhe.
MUSEUMS AND GALLERIES:
KARLSRUHE: *Magnolias*.
AUCTION RECORDS:
HEILBRONN, 3 Dec 1977, *Portrait of a Young Woman* (oil on canvas, 23 1/2 x 19 1/4 ins / 60 x 49 cm) DEM 4,500. NEW YORK, 25 Oct 1989, *Woman Giving Alms* (1874, oil on canvas, 31 x 23 1/4 ins / 78.7 x 59 cm) USD 24,200.

SCHMITT, Noémie
French, 19th - 20th century.
Born in Sceaux.
Painter. Mythological subjects.
Noémie Schmitt, who first exhibited in Paris at the Salon de Paris in 1879, worked mainly on fans. She may be the same artist as the Noémie Schmitt who painted miniatures.

SCHMITT, Noémie
French, 19th - 20th century.
Born in Paris.
Miniaturist.
Noémie Schmitt was a pupil of Paul L.F. Schmitt, to whom she may have been related, and of Gustave Surand and Louis Bèroud. She exhibited regularly in Paris at the Salon des Artistes Français, of which she became a member in 1896 and where she was awarded an honourable mention and a third-class medal in 1895 and a bronze medal at the time of the Exposition Universelle of 1900. She was perhaps the same Noémie Schmitt who painted mythological subjects.

SCHMITT, Otto Michael
German, 20th century.
Born 1 January 1904, in Laufen.
Painter. Religious subjects. Murals.
Otto Schmitt was the pupil of Robert Engels at the school of arts and crafts in Munich from 1924 to 1926 and of Franz Klemmer at the fine arts academy from 1926 to 1932 before settling in Augsburg. He worked primarily as a decorator of churches.
MUSEUMS AND GALLERIES:
AUGSBURG (Municipal Collection).

SCHMITT, Paul Léon Félix
French, 19th century.
Born 1856, in Paris; died November 1902, in Paris.
Painter. Landscapes, waterscapes, architectural views, animals.
His master was Antoine Guillemet. He exhibited first at the Paris Salon, from 1879 onward, then at the Salon of the Société des Artistes Français. He won a third-class medal in 1888 and a bronze medal at the Exposition Universelle of 1889.

He chiefly painted views of the banks of the River Oise and of Paris.
MUSEUMS AND GALLERIES:
AMIENS (Mus. de Picardie): *Ladies Bathing at Dammarie-les-Lys* - GRAY: *Notre-Dame de Paris* - PARIS (Mus. du Petit Palais).
AUCTION RECORDS:
PARIS, 20-21 Nov 1941, *View of the Louvre and St-Gervais*, FRF 880. PARIS, 13 July 1942, *Village*, FRF 360. PARIS, 18 April 1951, *Street in Quimperlé*, FRF 4,600; *Banks of the Oise*, FRF 3,800; *Church*, FRF 1,000. ENGHIEN-LES-BAINS, 9 Dec 1979, *River Crossing the Forest* (oil on canvas, 39 3/4 x 29 1/4 ins / 101 x 74 cm) FRF 6,300. PARIS, 3 July 1981, *The Edge of the Hamlet* (1881, oil on canvas, 14 3/4 x 21 3/4 ins / 37.5 x 55.5 cm) FRF 10,000. RHEIMS, 17 June 1990, *Haymaking* (oil on canvas, 15 x 22 ins / 38 x 55 cm) FRF 8,000. PARIS, 28 Oct 1990, *Landscape* (oil on canvas) FRF 9,000. LE TOUQUET, 10 Nov 1991, *Horse and Young Foal* (oil on canvas, 196 3/4 x 24 ins / 500 x 61 cm) FRF 14,000. PARIS, 15 Dec 1999, *Paris, Porte*

de Chatillon (oil on canvas, 9 x 13 ins / 24 x 32 cm) FRF 20,000. COPENHAGEN, 30 May 2000, *Street Scene, Neuilly* (oil on canvas, 10 x 13 ins / 25 x 32 cm) DKK 20,000. BUENOS AIRES, 9 Aug 2000, *Landscape Near a Village* (oil on canvas, 21 x 29 ins / 54 x 73 cm) USD 5,500.

SCHMITT, Stephan Wilhelm Josef
German, 19th - 20th century.
Born 23 April 1872, in Mainz; died 29 November 1924, in Mainz.
Painter.

MUSEUMS AND GALLERIES:
MAINZ (Stadtarchiv).

SCHMITT, Wilhelm
German, 19th century.
Born 1831; died 25 March 1891, in Karlsruhe.
Painter. Landscapes with figures, animals.

AUCTION RECORDS:
MUNICH, 21 June 1994, *Herd of Livestock Waiting to be Ferried across Lake Constance* (1883, oil on canvas, 27 1/2 x 43 1/4 ins / 70 x 109.6 cm) DEM 20,700.

SCHMITT-SPAHN, Karl Friedrich
German, 20th century.
Born 14 October 1877, in Mannheim.
Painter.

Karl Schmitt-Spahn was the pupil of Ludwig Schmid-Reutte and Wilhelm Trübner at the fine arts academy in Karlsruhe.

SCHMITTELI, Daniel. See **SCHMIDELY**

SCHMITTER, Hans Melchior. See **HUG**

SCHMITTNER, Franz Leopold, or Schmitner
Austrian, 18th century.
Born 1703, in Vienna; died 25 March 1761, in Vienna.
Engraver.

The pupil of Andreas Schmutzer, Franz Schmitter engraved the portraits of the empress *Maria Theresa*, the emperor *Franz I* count *Michael Althan* and *Heinrich Auersperg*.

SCHMITTNER, Johann Georg Melchior, or Schmidtner, Schmitner, Schmittmer, Schmiedtmer
German, 17th century.
Born 1625; died 1705, in Augsburg.
Painter. Religious subjects.

Johann Schmitter completed his apprenticeship in Italy and evolved under the influence of Kager, Sandrart and Schönfeld.

SCHMITZ
German, 19th century.
Painter. Portraits.

Active around 1800, Schmitz' repertoire included miniatures.

MUSEUMS AND GALLERIES:
STOCKHOLM: *Portrait of General K.M. Klingstrom.*

SCHMITZ, Adolf Heinrich Gustav, also known as Schmitz-Crolenburgh
German, 19th century.
Born 4 June 1825, in Darmstadt; died 18 March 1894, in Düsseldorf.
Painter, illustrator. Landscapes.

After studying under E. Rauch, Adolf Schmitz continued his artistic training at the academy in Düsseldorf, then Antwerp and from 1851 at Frankfurt am Main, where he completed his major canvas *Canossa.*

From 1860 he lived in Düssldorf. His best-known picture *Feldberg im Taunus* was destroyed in a fire in 1932 in Munich.

SCHMITZ, Antoine Guillaume
French, 19th century.
Born 24 May 1788, in Paris.
Painter. Genre scenes, portraits.

A pupil of Gros, he entered the École des Beaux-Arts in Paris on 26 November 1813. He exhibited at the Palais du Luxembourg in 1830.

SCHMITZ, Anton
German, 19th - 20th century.
Born 2 July 1855, in Grimlinghausen (Rhineland-Palatinate).
Painter. Animals.

In 1876, Anton Schmitz was the pupil of the animal painter Karl Dietrich Deiker in Düsseldorf, where he settled.

AUCTION RECORDS:
LONDON, 11 Feb 1994, *Wild Boar* (1889, oil on canvas, 10 3/4 x 8 1/4 ins / 27.3 x 21 cm) GBP 3,910.

SCHMITZ, C. L.
German, 19th - 20th century.
Painter. Waterscapes.

C.L. Schmitz was active in Düsseldorf.

AUCTION RECORDS:
COLOGNE, 15 Oct 1988, *River Landscape with a Village* (oil on canvas, 22 x 32 1/4 ins / 55 x 82 cm) DEM 1,800. COLOGNE, 20 Oct 1989, *Lake in Switzerland* (oil on canvas, 18 1/2 x 29 1/4 ins / 47 x 74 cm) DEM 3,300. HEIDELBERG, 11-12 April 1997, *Mountain Lake as Thunderstorm Approaches* (oil on canvas, 25 1/2 x 37 3/4 ins / 65 x 96 cm) DEM 4,600.

SCHMITZ, Carl Ludwig
American, 20th century.
Born 1900; died 1967.
Sculptor.

AUCTION RECORDS:
NEW YORK, 25 Sept 1992, *Dancer* (black-patinated bronze, h. 41 ins / 104.1 cm) USD 4,675.

SCHMITZ, D. A.
Dutch, 18th century.
Active in the 18th century.
Painter.

SCHMITZ, Ernst
German, 19th - 20th century.
Born 27 February 1859, in Düsseldorf; died February 1917, in Munich.
Painter. Portraits, genre scenes, interiors, landscapes.

Ernst Schmitz was the pupil of Franz Keller in Düsseldorf, at the fine arts academy in that city. He was active in Karlsruhe, Freiburg im Brisgau, Stuttgart and Munich.

AUCTION RECORDS:
LONDON, 14 Nov 1969, *Riverbanks,* Gns 390. VIENNA, 19 May 1981, *A Little Drop* (oil on panel, 7 1/2 x 5 1/2 ins / 19 x 14 cm) ATS 130,000. NEW YORK, 20 Feb 1992, *In the Studio* (oil on canvas, 27 1/4 x 37 1/2 ins / 69.2 x 95.3 cm) USD 18,700. NEW YORK, 19 Jan 1995, *Portraits of Bavarians* (1908-1912, oil on panel, a pair, 8 1/2 x 6 1/4 ins / 21.6 x 15.9 cm and 7 1/4 x 5 1/2 ins/18.1 x 14 cm) USD 6,325.

SCHMITZ, F.
Dutch, 18th century.
Painter.

SCHMITZ, Ferdinand Josef
German, 18th century.
Painter.

Ferdinand Schmitz' key work is the portrait of *Everhard Melchior zum Putz* in the Cologne Rathaus.

SCHMITZ, Franz Hieronymus
German, 18th century.
Painter.

Franz Schmitz was the son of Johann Jacob.

SCHMITZ, Georg
German, 19th - 20th century.
Born 6 May 1851, in Düsseldorf.
Painter. Landscapes, seascapes.

Georg Schmitz was a pupil at the fine arts academy in Düsseldorf from 1866 to 1870. He spent a period of time in Berlin before settling in Hamburg.
MUSEUMS AND GALLERIES:
KREFELD.
AUCTION RECORDS:
LONDON, 25 March 1981, *Frozen River at Dusk* (1903, oil on canvas, 28 3/4 x 38 1/2 ins / 73 x 98 cm) GBP 1,200. LONDON, 18 June 1993, *Port of Hamburg* (1890, oil on canvas, 8 x 9 3/4 ins / 19.4 x 24.8 cm) GBP 1,610.

SCHMITZ, Heinrich, or Schmidt, Schmiths, Smiths
German, 18th century.
Born 1758, in Kaiserswerth; died 23 July 1787, in Düsseldorf.
Engraver.
From 1773 to 1775 Heinrich Schmitz attended the academy in Düsseldorf, then he spent four years in Wille's workshop in Paris. In 1782 he was appointed court engraver in Düsseldorf and engraved plates for the *Picturesque Journey through Switzerland*.

SCHMITZ, Hermann
German, 19th century.
Born 1812, in Düsseldorf.
Painter. Genre scenes, portraits.
The pupil of Hilderbrandt, Hermann Schmitz was active in Düsseldorf until 1870.

SCHMITZ, J. H.
German, 18th century.
Painter.
Four of J. H. Schmitz' views of old Elberfeld, dated 1684, 1687, 1696 and 1741 are in the museum in Wuppertal.

SCHMITZ, Jean
Swiss, 17th century.
Active in Geneva in 1695.
Sculptor (wood).

SCHMITZ, Jean
French, 18th century.
Active in Paris.
Cabinet maker.
Jean Schmitz was probably the same person as Joseph Schmitz.

SCHMITZ, Johann Jacob
German, 18th - 19th century.
Born 1724, in Cologne; died 21 August 1810, in Cologne.
Painter.
Johann Schmitz belonged to the painters' guild of Cologne on 23 March 1759.
MUSEUMS AND GALLERIES:
COLOGNE (Wallraf-Richartz Mus.): *Portrait of the Artist's Wife; Portrait of Leopold I.*

SCHMITZ, Johann Josef
German, 19th century.
Born 19 April 1784, in Hanover.
Painter. Landscapes.
The pupil of Wolff in Amsterdam, Johann Schmitz went to Java in 1816.

SCHMITZ, Josef
German, 18th century.
Active in Cologne in 1772.
Painter.

SCHMITZ, Joseph
French, 18th century.
Died before 1782.
Active in Paris.
Cabinet maker.
Joseph Schmitz became a master craftsman in 1761. He was probably the same person as Jean Schmitz.

SCHMITZ, Jules Léonard
French, 19th century.
Painter. Hunting scenes, animals.
He exhibited at the Paris Salon between 1824 and 1850.
AUCTION RECORDS:
PARIS, 9 May 1994, *Racehorse with Jockey* (oil on canvas, 19 1/4 x 22 3/4 ins / 49 x 58 cm) FRF 17,200.

SCHMITZ, Michael Hubert
German, 19th century.
Born 1831, in Aachen; died 14 January 1898, in Aachen.
Painter (glass).
MUSEUMS AND GALLERIES:
VATICAN (Biblioteca Vaticana): *Portrait of Pius IX.*

SCHMITZ, Paul
Belgian, 20th century.
Born 1910, in Ypres; died 1974, in Spa.
Painter. Scenes with figures.
Paul Schmitz, who was a self-taught artist, illustrated the life of peasants and painted the landscapes of his native Ypres.

SCHMITZ, Peter Augustin
German, 17th - 18th century.
Born to a family originally from Antwerp.
Painter. Religious subjects.
The father of Johann Jacob, Peter Schmitz became a member of the guild on 15 November 1719.
MUSEUMS AND GALLERIES:
COLOGNE (Churches).

SCHMITZ, Peter Joseph
German, 18th century.
Active from 1759-1770.
Painter.
Peter Schmitz was a painter at the court of Prince-Electors in Cologne - Clemens August and Max Friedrich. His reproduction of a cycle of eight pictures in the Carthusian monasatery of Cologne, *The Life of St Bruno,* was inspired by the cycle of Eustace Le Sueur in the Louvre.

SCHMITZ, Philipp
German, 19th century.
Born 1824; died 1887.
Active in Düsseldorf.
Painter. Portraits, genre scenes.
Philipp Schmitz specialised in portraits of manufacturers and traders.
AUCTION RECORDS:
COLOGNE, 30 March 1979, *Father's Birthday* (oil on canvas, 33 1/2 x 27 1/4 ins / 85 x 69 cm) DEM 10,000. VIENNA, 20 May 1999, *The Lottery Ticket Seller, Interior Scene* (1856, oil on canvas, 31 x 30 ins / 80 x 75 cm) ATS 90,000.

SCHMITZ, Richard Ferdinand
German, 20th century.
Born 24 October 1876, in Gonzenheim (Hesse).
Painter. Landscapes.
Richard Schmitz was the pupil of the landscape painter Richard Kaiser in Munich, where he settled.

SCHMITZ-CROLENBURGH. See **SCHMITZ Adolf Heinrich Gustav**

SCHMITZBERGER, Hans
Austrian, 17th century.
Stonemason.

SCHMITZBERGER, Josef
German, 19th - 20th century.
Born 28 January 1851, in Munich.
Painter. Animals, hunting scenes, landscapes with figures, winter landscapes.

Museums and Galleries:
Munich (Pinakothek): *Solitude in the Mountains.*
Auction records:
Cologne, 22 Oct 1965, *Hinds*, DEM 3,300. New York, 7 Oct 1977, *Puppies* (oil on canvas, 17 1/4 x 23 1/4 ins / 44 x 59 cm) USD 3,250. San Francisco, 24 June 1981, *Cats and Kittens* (oil on canvas, 29 1/2 x 40 1/4 ins / 75 x 102 cm) USD 5,500. Vienna, 16 May 1984, *Stag in a Snowy Landscape* (oil on canvas, 59 x 51 1/4 ins / 150 x 130 cm) ATS 60,000. London, 25 March 1988, *The Inseparables* (oil on canvas, 17 1/4 x 21 ins / 44 x 53.5 cm) GBP 6,600. New York, 15 Feb 1994, *Spaniel Fetching a Duck* (oil on canvas, 24 3/4 x 34 1/2 ins / 62.9 x 87.6 cm) USD 8,050. Munich, 21 June 1994, *Stag in a Snowy Glade* (oil on canvas, 50 1/2 x 41 1/4 ins / 128.5 x 105 cm) DEM 4,025. London, 21 Nov 1997, *Chamois in a Mountain Landscape in Winter* (oil on canvas, 42 x 55 1/4 ins / 106.4 x 140.3 cm) GBP 5,175.

SCHMOL, Johann
German, 16th century.
Painter. Portraits.
Johann Schmol's name appears with this spelling in an auction annual.
Auction records:
Hamburg, 29 March 1951, *Bust Portrait of Frederick the Wise*, DEM 2,500.

SCHMOLL, Georg Friedrich, or Schmohl
German, 18th century.
Born to a family originally from Ludwigsburg; died 24 April 1785, in Urdorf, near Zurich.
Draughtsman, miniaturist, engraver. Portraits.
Georg Schmoll accompanied Lavater in 1774 to Ems, marrying his sister in 1776. He executed numerous drawings for Lavater's *Physiognomy* and drew several portraits of *Goethe* and his parents.

SCHMOLL VON EISENWERTH, Fritz
Austrian, 20th century.
Born 25 August 1883, in Vienna; died 17 July 1963, in Munich.
Active in Germany.
Interior designer, sculptor, medallist. Designs (decorative arts/fabrics/jewellery/precious metals).
Fritz Schmoll von Eisenwerth grew up in Darmstadt and studied at the Kunstgewerbeschule of Karlsruhe. He became from 1906 an interior designer and taught at Munich at the Obrist-Debschitz school, a famous private school that taught the applied arts with a modern viewpoint. After the war, he trained as a sculptor with a stonecutter and created medals, tombs and funerary monuments; this part of his work has recently been rediscovered. His textile work was shown in 2004 at the exhibition *Schönheit der Formen. Textilien des Münchner Jugendstils* (*Beauty of Form. Textiles of the Munich Jugendstil*) at the Villa Stuck in Munich.
Bibliography:
Ottomeyer, Hans (ed.)/Brandlhuber, Margot, *Wege in die Moderne. Jugendstil in München 1896 bis 1914*, Klinkhardt & Biermann, Munich, Berlin, 1997. Küppers, Barbara, *Fritz Schmoll genannt Eisenwerth (1883-1963)*, Vdg-Verlag, Weimar, 2003.
Museums and Galleries:
Bremen (Kunsthalle): medal*Grenzschutz in den Vogesen* (1918, bronze); medal*Herkules kämpft gegen die Hydra* (1918, bronze); medal*Bergsteiger* (1929, bronze).

SCHMOLL VON EISENWERTH, Karl
Austrian, 20th century.
Born 18 May 1879, in Vienna; died 1947, in Stuttgart.
Active in Germany.
Painter, draughtsman, illustrator, poster artist, graphic designer. Figures, genre scenes.
Art Nouveau.
A member of the Künstlerkolonie (Artists' Colony) in Darmstadt, Karl Schmoll von Eisenwerth initially received guidance from Richard Hölscher. In 1898, he was the pupil of Paul Höcker and then of Ludwig von Herterich at the Munich fine arts academy. In 1902, he pursued his artistic training in Rome, in the company of Paul Klee, and subsequently stayed in Paris. Having married the daughter of the painter Emil Reynier, he taught in Munich from 1905 to 1907, then settled in Stuttgart, becoming a professor at the Technische Hochschule, of which he was director from 1927 to 1929.

Karl Schmoll von Eisenwerth collaborated on a number of publications, including *Ver Sacrum* and *Zeitung der 10. Arlee in Litauen*. He illustrated Dauthendy's *Seasons* and drew *ex libris* plates, calendars and advertisements, in particular for *Jacobi* cognac, and posters, notably for an artists' festival in Munich. As a painter, he was influenced by the floral, Symbolist variety of Jugendstil, of which Franz von Stuck was a proponent.
Bibliography:
Osterwalder, Marcus (ed.), *Dictionnaire des illustrateurs 1800-1914*, Ides et Calendes, Neuchâtel, 1989.
Museums and Galleries:
Darmstadt: *Italian Woman* - Mannheim: *The Walk* - Stuttgart: *At the Old Woman's House.*

SCHMÖLZ, Johann Christoph. See **SCHMELZ**

SCHMOLZE, Karl Hermann, or Schmolzé
Franco-German, 19th century.
Born 1823, in Zwei-Brücken, Germany; died 1861, in Philadelphia, USA.
From 1848 active in the USA.
Painter, engraver, illustrator. Genre scenes.
He trained as an artist for three years in Metz, eastern France. In 1841 he went to Munich, then in 1848 went to Paris, London, and finally America.

During his time in Munich he contributed to the comic magazine *Fliegende Blätter (The Flying Leaves)*. He was also a poet.
Auction records:
Munich, 15 March 1984, *Rustic Interior with Puppet Theatre* (1842, oil on canvas, 23 1/2 x 26 1/2 ins / 60 x 67 cm) DEM 5,500.

SCHMON, Johann Baptist, or Schmonn
German, 18th century.
Active in Augsburg.
Painter.
Johann Schmon handled religious subjects and specialised in glass painting.

SCHMOZER. See **SCHMUTZER**

SCHMÜCK, Emilie. See **SCHMÄCK**

SCHMUCKER, Andreas, or Schmuker
Swiss, 17th century.
Born c. 1575, in Stein on the Rhine; died 23 November 1650, in Stein on the Rhine.
Painter.
Andreas Schmucker was the pupil of the glassmaker Marx Grimm in Schaffhousen from 1589 to 1592. In 1615 he painted a Noah's Ark on the façade of the *Red Ox* in Stein.

SCHMUCKER, Augustin
German, 16th century.
Died 1539.
Active in Augsburg.
Painter.

SCHMUCKER, Felix
German, 17th century.
Died before August 1620, in Augsburg.
Active in Augsburg.
Engraver (burin).

SCHMUCKER, Joseph
Swiss, 17th century.
Died 26 August 1623.
Active in Stein on the Rhine.
Glass painter.

SCHMUD, Tomas. See **SCHMUTH Tomas Valentin**

SCHMURR, Wilhelm
German, 20th century.
Born 1 March 1878, in Hagen (North Rhine-Westphalia); died 1959.
Painter. Figures, portraits, landscapes, still-lifes.
Wilhelm Schmurr was the pupil of K.F. Eduard von Gebhardt and Claus Meyr at the fine arts academy in Düsseldorf. He was active in Düsseldorf and was a professor at the academy there from 1927 onwards.

MUSEUMS AND GALLERIES:
DORTMUND: two works - DÜSSELDORF: four works.
AUCTION RECORDS:
COLOGNE, 17 March 1978, *Still-life with Potatoes* (oil on card, 25 1/4 x 39 ins / 64 x 99 cm) DEM 4,000. COLOGNE, 16 June 1978, *Motherhood* (pastel, 63 3/4 x 43 3/4 ins / 162 x 111 cm) DEM 4,500. COLOGNE, 28 Oct 1999, *Figures by Farmhouse in Hungarian Landscape* (oil on panel, 39 x 34 ins / 100 x 86 cm) DEM 5,300.

SCHMUTH, Anton
Czech, 18th century.
Died 7 March 1795.
Painter.
Anton Schmuth worked at the court in Prague.

SCHMUTH, Tomas Valentin, or Schmud, Smuth
Austrian, 18th century.
Died 29 June 1749.
Painter.
Tomas Schmuth worked in Prague.

SCHMUTZ, Franz
Austrian, 18th century.
Born 1729; died 15 September 1795, in Vienna.
Active in Vienna.
Sculptor.

SCHMUTZ, Gustave
German.
Born in Colmar.
Painter. Religious subjects, flowers.
MUSEUMS AND GALLERIES:
COLMAR: *Peonies*; *The Holy Family* (after Andrea del Sarto).

SCHMUTZ, J. Johann Rudolph
Swiss, 17th - 18th century.
Born 2 January 1670, in Regensburg; died 1715, in London.
Also active in Great Britain.
Painter. History painting, portraits.
A pupil of Mathias Fuessli, he initially carried out historical paintings, subsequently devoting himself to portrait painting. He was in London when Godfrey Kneller was at his peak and imitated the style of this leading portraitist.
MUSEUMS AND GALLERIES:
ZURICH: *Portrait of A Moor.*

SCHMUTZER
Swiss, 18th century.
Painter. Portraits.
MUSEUMS AND GALLERIES:
ST GALL (City Library): *Portrait of the Burgomaster Zublin.*

SCHMUTZER, Adam Johann, or Schmuzer
Austrian, 18th century.
Born 1680, in Vienna; died 1739.
Engraver.
Adam Schmutzer collaborated with Andreas and Joseph Schmutzer, predominantly on the reproduction of engravings.

SCHMUTZER, Andreas, or Schmuzer
Austrian, 18th century.
Born 1700, in Vienna; died 1740.
Engraver.
The father of Jakob Schmutzer the Younger, Andreas Schmutzer collaborated with Adam Johann and Joseph Schmutzer. He specialised in the reproduction of engravings.

SCHMUTZER, Anton Christoph, or Schmozer
Austrian, 18th century.
Born 11 June 1756, in Innsbruck.
Painter, engraver (burin).
Anton Schmutzer decorated the churches of Stams and Villnös.

SCHMUTZER, Carl
Austrian, 18th century.
Active in Eggenburg.
Sculptor.
Carl Schmutzer worked in Znaim (now Znojmo, Czech Republic) in 1778.

SCHMUTZER, Ferdinand, the Elder
Austrian, 19th - 20th century.
Born 1833, in Vienna; died April 1915, in Vienna.
Sculptor. Animals.
The son of the sculptor Vincent Schmutzer, Ferdinand Schmutzer was himself the father of Ferdinand Schmutzer the Younger. In 1849-1850, he was the pupil of Franz Bauer at the academy of fine arts in Vienna.

SCHMUTZER, Ferdinand, the Younger
Austrian, 19th - 20th century.
Born 1870, in Vienna; died 1928, in Vienna.
Painter, engraver. Genre scenes.
Ferdinand Schmutzer the Younger was the pupil of the engraver William Unger at the academy of fine arts in Vienna. In 1894, he was awarded the Prix National. He spent two years perfecting his technique in Holland before returning to settle in Vienna. He produced approximately three hundred engravings over the course of his career.
AUCTION RECORDS:
HEIDELBERG, 13 Oct 1979, *View of Rothenburg with the Double Bridge* (pen and wash, 27 1/4 x 35 1/2 ins / 69 x 90 cm) DEM 2,700. VIENNA, 16 Nov 1983, *Motherly Advice* (1894, oil on panel, 38 1/2 x 29 1/2 ins / 98 x 75 cm) ATS 60,000. LONDON, 25 June 1985, *Sigmund Freud* (1926, black chalk, heightened with white/grey paper, 15 3/4 x 11 1/2 ins / 40.2 x 29.3 cm) GBP 1,100. LONDON, 8 Oct 1986, *View of the Fortress of Dürnstein on the Danube* (oil on canvas, 23 1/2 x 32 1/4 ins / 60 x 82 cm) GBP 3,800.

SCHMUTZER, Jakob Christoph, or Schmozer
Austrian, 18th century.
Born 23 July 1761, in Innsbruck; died 1 June 1805, in Innsbruck.
Painter.

SCHMUTZER, Jakob Mathias, the Younger, or Schmuzer
Austrian, 18th - 19th century.
Born 1733, in Vienna; died 1811, in Vienna.

Painter, engraver, draughtsman. Mythological subjects, religious subjects, portraits, genre scenes.

Jakob Schmutzer was the son of Andreas Schmutzer. After having worked with Donner in Vienna, he studied under Wille in Paris. In Vienna he was Director of the academy founded by Maria Theresa.

AUCTION RECORDS:

PARIS, 21-23 Nov 1927, *Landscape near Fesendorf* (wash) FRF 160. PARIS, 24 June 1929, *Man's Head* (drawing) FRF 80. MUNICH, 29 Oct 1985, *Portrait of a Man* (red chalk, 22 x 15 3/4 ins / 56 x 40 cm) DEM 2,200. NEW YORK, 11 Jan 1989, *Young Man Sitting Asleep on Rocks* (red chalk, 17 1/4 x 22 1/4 ins / 43.6 x 56.7 cm) USD 4,400. NEW YORK, 9 Jan 1996, *Portrait of a Man, Presumably Joseph Haydn* (black chalk, 9 1/2 x 7 1/2 ins / 24.1 x 19.1 cm) USD 2,300. MUNICH, 1 Dec 1999, *Peasant Family by River in Mountain Landscape* (1809, pen and ink, brush, sepia and pencil, 19 x 25 ins / 47 x 63 cm) DEM 3,800.

SCHMUTZER, Jakob Philipp, or Schmozer
Austrian, 18th century.
Active in Augsburg.
Stucco artist.

SCHMUTZER, Johann
Austrian, 19th century.
Born 1783; died 30 May 1845, in Vienna.
Sculptor.

SCHMUTZER, Johann Georg.
See **SCHMUZER**

SCHMUTZER, Johann Michael, or Schmozer
Austrian, 18th century.
Born 11 June 1764, in Innsbruck.
Active in Innsbruck.
Painter.

SCHMUTZER, Josef I, or Schmozer
Austrian, 18th century.
Born 4 December 1714, in Innsbruck; died 5 June 1770, in Innsbruck.
Painter.

SCHMUTZER, Josef II, or Schmozer
Austrian, 18th century.
Born 1749, in Innsbruck; died 10 November 1808, in Innsbruck.
Painter.

Josef Schmutzer II was the son of Joseph I.

MUSEUMS AND GALLERIES:

VORARLBERG (Provincial Mus.): *Portrait of Peter Leone and his Wife; Portrait of Anna Atzger.*

SCHMUTZER, Josef Michael, or Schmozer
Austrian, 18th century.
Painter.

SCHMUTZER, Joseph, or Schmuzer
Austrian, 18th century.
Born 1683, in Vienna; died 1740.
Engraver.

Joseph Schmutzer collaborated with Adam Johann and Andreas Schmutzer and, most importantly, did engravings of reproductions.

SCHMUTZER, Joseph
Austrian, 19th century.
Born 1806, in Vienna; died 1837.
Painter, lithographer.

Joseph Schmutzer attended the academy in Vienna and engraved lithographs after the old German masters.

SCHMUTZER, Matthias
Austrian, 18th century.
Active in Vienna.
Miniaturist.

SCHMUTZER, Matthias
Austrian, 18th - 19th century.
Born 11 May 1752, in Vienna; died 19 June 1824, in Vienna.
Painter. Botanical subjects.

A distinguished botanist, Matthiass Schmutzer taught drawing at the Viennese court.

SCHMUTZER, Sigmund Ignaz, or Schmozer
Austrian, 18th century.
Born 5 July 1712, in Innsbruck; died 25 February 1768, in Innsbruck.
Painter.

SCHMUTZLER, Leopold
Austrian, 19th - 20th century.
Born 28 March 1864, in Mies (now Stribro, Czech Republic); died 1941, in Munich.
Active in Germany.
Painter. History painting, genre scenes, figures, portraits.

Leopold Schmutzler trained at the Viennese art academy and under Otto Seitz at the Munich academy. He worked in Rome, Paris, and New York, and settled in Munich, where he supported the Nazi regime in the 1930s.

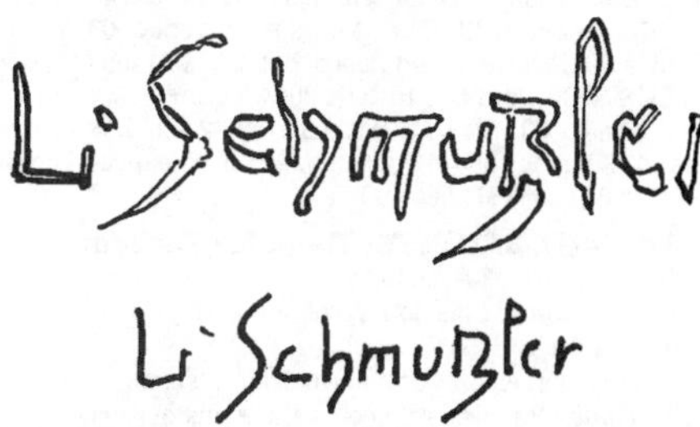

BIBLIOGRAPHY:

Pagé, Suzanne/Winock, Michel/Michaud, Éric/Vidal, Aline, *Les Années trente en Europe. Le Temps menaçant*, exhibition catalogue, Musée d'Art moderne de la Ville de Paris, Paris musées, Flammarion, Paris, 1997.

MUSEUMS AND GALLERIES:

BUDAPEST: *Salome* - NUREMBERG: *Portrait of a Lady.*

AUCTION RECORDS:

NEW YORK, 12 March 1908, *Return from the Baptism*, USD 950. LONDON, 29 April 1911, *A Welcome Visitor* (1890) GBP 44. COLOGNE, 15 March 1968, *Portrait of a Young Girl*, DEM 4,000. VIENNA, 15 Nov 1972, *Portrait of a Woman*, ATS 15,000. COLOGNE, 12 Nov 1976, *Gypsy Playing the Guitar* (oil on canvas, 36 1/4 x 28 1/4 ins / 92 x 72 cm) DEM 3,500. MUNICH, 26 Oct 1978, *Guitar Player* (oil on card, 35 3/4 x 26 3/4 ins / 91 x 68 cm) DEM 5,000. LONDON, 7 May 1980, *Portrait of a Bohemian* (oil on canvas, 34 1/2 x 25 3/4 ins / 87.5 x 65.5 cm) GBP 1,200. MUNICH, 6 Nov 1981, *Who is the most Beautiful?* (oil on panel, 42 1/4 x 30 ins / 107 x 76 cm) DEM 5,500. BREMEN, 22 Oct 1983, *Flower Seller* (oil on canvas, 37 1/2 x 26 ins / 95 x 66 cm) DEM 6,000. NEW YORK, 30 Oct 1985, *Newborn Baby* (oil on canvas, 25 x 32 1/4 ins / 63.5 x 82.2 cm) USD 13,000. NEW YORK, 26 Feb 1986, *The Interrupted Marriage Proposal* (1889, oil on canvas, 27 1/4 x 36 ins / 69.2 x 91.4 cm) USD 18,000. NEW YORK, 25 May 1988, *Liberty* (oil on card, 38 1/4 x 30 ins / 97.2 x 76.2 cm) USD 4,950. COLOGNE, 20 Oct 1989, *Portrait of a Young Girl and her Doll* (oil on canvas, 39 x 28 3/4 ins / 99 x 73 cm) DEM 4,800. NEW YORK, 23 Oct 1990, *Compliments to the Baby* (oil on canvas, 32 1/2 x 27 1/2 ins / 82.6 x 69.9 cm) USD 11,000. LONDON, 17 May 1991, *Venetian Beauty* (oil on card, 35 x 24 1/4 ins / 88.8 x 61.3 cm) GBP 3,300. MUNICH, 12 June 1991, *Venetian Beauty* (oil on canvas, 39 x 28 3/4 ins / 99 x 73 cm) DEM 6,600. NEW YORK, 19 Feb 1992, *Woman Carrying*

Water (oil on canvas, 37 1/2 x 27 1/4 ins / 95.5 x 69.5 cm) USD 6,600. New York, 20 Feb 1992, *Domestic Bliss* (oil on canvas, 30 1/4 x 37 ins / 76.8 x 94 cm) USD 27,500. Munich, 22 June 1993, *Young Woman Reading a Note* (oil on canvas, 31 x 22 1/2 ins / 79 x 57 cm) DEM 5,750. London, 11 Feb 1994, *Carmen* (oil on canvas, 38 3/4 x 29 1/4 ins / 98.6 x 74.5 cm) GBP 6,325. London, 31 Oct 1996, *Young Woman Playing a Lyre* (oil on card, 38 1/2 x 30 3/4 ins / 98 x 78 cm) GBP 2,875. London, 11 June 1997, *Flamenco Dancer* (oil on canvas, 70 1/2 x 42 1/4 ins / 179 x 107 cm) GBP 11,500. Munich, 20 May 1999, *Gypsy Girl with Fruit Basket* (oil on canvas, 38 x 29 ins / 97 x 74 cm) DEM 9,000. Cologne, 26 June 1999, *Portrait of a Young Lady* (oil on panel, 33 x 22 ins / 85 x 57 cm) DEM 8,500. Detroit, 14 Jan 2000, *Interior with Lady and Three Gentlemen* (oil on canvas, 21 x 25 ins / 53 x 64 cm) USD 5,000. Warsaw, 19 March 2000, *Portrait of a Young Woman* (oil on canvas, 31 x 22 ins / 79 x 57 cm) PLN 27,000. New York, 1 May 2000, *Nude on the Beach* (oil on board, 39 x 59 ins / 99 x 150 cm) USD 40,000. Amsterdam, 24 April 2001, *Flora* (oil on board, 39 x 28 ins / 100 x 72 cm) NLG 14,000. Zurich, 3 Oct 2002, *Amazon with Spear* (oil on board, 33 x 28 ins / 84 x 72 cm) CHF 11,000. Ahlden, 29 Nov 2002, *Female Musician* (oil on canvas, 37 x 28 ins / 94 x 70 cm) EUR 3,800. Munich, 19 March 2003, *Young Woman with Lyre* (oil on canvas, 38 x 30 ins / 97 x 75 cm) EUR 3,200. Munich, 19 Sept 2003, *Young Girl by a Stone Vase* (oil on board, oval, 39 x 31 ins / 98 x 78 cm) EUR 2,600. London, 16 June 2004, *Divine Reflection* (oil on canvas, 45 x 37 ins / 115 x 93 cm) GBP 2,500. London, 16 June 2004, *Bathers at a Woodland Pool* (oil on canvas, 26 x 34 ins / 66 x 86 cm) GBP 2,500.

SCHMUZ-BAUDISS, Theo, for Theodor

German, 19th - 20th century.

Born 4 August 1859, in Herrnhut (Saxony); died 1942, in Garmisch.

Painter (porcelain), ceramicist, draughtsman, illustrator.

Theo Schmuz-Baudiss studied at the Kunstgewerbeschule (1879-1882) then at the Art Academy (1882-1890) of Munich. Although successful as a painter he was directed towards ceramics after his meeting with Treffler and learned the technique in a pottery studio at Diessen am Ammersee. He was employed from 1902 by the Royal Porcelain Manufacture (KPM) of Berlin to paint designs in the form of landscapes and city views. He became artistic director of the factory from 1908 to 1926. He was trained in the technique of porcelain with Swaine and Co at Huttensteinach in Thuringia. He is known for his vases painted in relief with floral or animal motifs. His work in ceramics is distinguished by the brightness of its colours. Little by little his pieces became very sculptural. He also painted landscapes on glass mounts. In the field of the graphic arts he did illustrations for *Die Jugend*, the important Munich review defending the Jugendstil.

He showed his first creations in ceramics in 1897 at the exhibition at the Glass Palace of Munich and was an immediate success. In 1898, he became a member of the Vereinigte Werkstätten für Kunst im Handwerk (United Studios for Art in the Craft Industry) in Munich. He appeared at the Exposition universelle de Paris in 1900.

Bibliography:

Berliner Porzellan von Jugendstil zum Funktionalismus 1889-1939, Bröhan-Museum, Berlin. Siemen, Wilhelm (ed.), *Theodor Hermann Schmuz-Baudiss, 1859-1942. Ein Jugendstilkünstler ersten Ranges. Gemälde, Keramik, Möbel, Porzellan*, exhibition catalogue, Museum der Deutschen Porzellanindustrie, Hohenberg an der Eger, 1989. Ottomeyer, Hans (ed.)/Brandlhuber, Margot, *Wege in die Moderne. Jugendstil in München 1896 bis 1914*, Klinkhardt & Biermann, Munich, Berlin, 1997.

Museums and Galleries:

Berlin (Berlin-Porzellansammlung Belvedere): *Soup Dish* (1913, porcelain, produced by the Königliche Porzellan-Manufaktur KPM) - Berlin (Schloss Charlottenburg): archives of the KPM - Düsseldorf (Hetjens-Museum Deutsches Keramikmuseum) - Karlsruhe (Badisches Landesmus.): *Vase* - Nuremberg (Gewerbemuseum): *Jug* (1897); *Vase* (1897).

SCHMUZER, Adam, Johann, Andreas, Jakob, Joseph, Mathias. See **SCHMUTZER**

SCHMUZER, Johann Georg

Austrian, 19th century.

Sculptor.

SCHNAAR, Heinrich Wilhelm

German, 19th - 20th century.

Born 23 April 1820, in Elberfeld; died 1 February 1914, in Urdenbach.

Painter. Landscapes.

SCHNAARS, Alfred

German, 20th century.

Born 19 March 1875, in Hamburg; died 1926, probably in Frankfurt am Main.

Painter.

Alfred Schnaars was trained by Weishaupt, Thoma and Trubner.

SCHNABEL, Andreas

German, 19th century.

Died c. 1815, in Starnberg.

Active in Munich.

Painter.

Andreas Schnabel painted religious subjects, portraits and popular scenes.

SCHNABEL, Daisy, known as Day

Maiden name: Talberg

Austrian, 20th century.

Born 1898, in Vienna; died 6 March 1991, in Paris.

Active in the USA and France.

Sculptor.

Daisy Schnabel studied painting at the art academy in Vienna between 1915 and 1918, and later continued her studies in Berlin and Florence. Following her marriage to Oscar Schnabel she lived in Holland for three years, and studied architecture with Barend Jordaens, focusing particularly on sculpture. After moving to Paris in 1932, she continued sculpting in the studios of Gimond, Malfray and Zadkine. Living in the USA during World War II, she became friends with Lipchitz, Jackson Pollock and Lassow. She returned to France in 1946 where she moved in a circle of artists including Schneider, Soulages, Gilioli, Schöfer and Brancusi.

Her work featured in group exhibitions in Paris, notably, in the Salon de Mai, the Salon des Réalités Nouvelles from 1956, the Salon de la Jeune Sculpture and the Salons de Sculpture Contemporaine at the Musée Rodin. The celebrated New York gallery owner Betty Parsons organised three solo exhibitions of her work in 1946, 1951 and 1957. She also exhibited at the Palais des Beaux-Arts in Brussels in 1963, and at the Centre Culturel Américain (Centre of American Culture) in Paris in 1968.

Her works combined the Abstract and figurative styles, and featured both organic and geometric shapes. In 1942 she sculpted a strongly stylised *Man's Head*, then a series of small rounded sculptures in organic shapes with a rough finish. After 1953 she produced some expressive baroque reliefs made from scrap metal and old car bodies. In 1964 and 1965 she reverted to a more organised concept of space based on orthogonal or curved pieces, each one fitting harmoniously into the other. Her *Labyrinths* of 1963 accentuated this return to constructivism, symbolic lines and measured proportions, which were evocative of human presence. In the 1980s, her figurative style came to the fore again.

AUCTION RECORDS:

PARIS, 10 May 1994, *Eternal Mother* (1942, bronze, 11 x 6 ins / 28 x 15 cm) FRF 30,000; *Pagoda* (1957, bronze, 11 1/2 x 7 3/4 x 5 ins / 29 x 20 x 12.5 cm) FRF 15,000; *The Fly* (1948, bronze, 11 3/4 x 9 1/2 x 4 1/4 ins / 30 x 24 x 11 cm) FRF 10,500.

SCHNABEL, Heinrich
German, 19th - 20th century.
Painter.

Heinrich Schnabel was instrumental in founding the Neue Künstlervereinigung München (NKVM: the New Artists' Association Munich), with Marianne von Werfkind, Wassily Kandinsky, Alexej von Jawlensky, Alexander Kanoldt, Adolf Erslöh, Alfred Kubin and Gabriele Münter.

SCHNABEL, Johann, the Elder
German, 17th century.
Born 5 August 1603, in Coburg; died 27 November 1679, in Coburg.
Painter.

SCHNABEL, Johann Franz, or Schnabl
German, 17th - 18th century.
Died 30 October 1724, in Munich.
Active in Munich c. 1694.
Draughtsman, miniaturist.

SCHNABEL, Johann Hans, the Younger
German, 17th century.
Born 15 October 1642, in Coburg; died 27 February 1709, in Coburg.
Painter, engraver.

Active in Coburg in 1688, Johann Schnabel engraved numerous medals and was also an architect.

SCHNABEL, Julian
American, 20th - 21st century.
Born 1951, in New York.
Painter. Figures, portraits, landscapes, landscapes with figures, still-lifes.
Bad Painting, Citationism.

Julian Schnabel settled in Texas with his family in 1965. He studied at the University of Houston from 1969 to 1972 and then joined an Independent Study Programme at the Whitney Museum of American Art in New York from 1973 to 1974. He was a friend of Ross Bleckner and David Diao. In 1976, he settled in New York and visited Europe for the first time. He lived in Italy in 1977 and made another visit to Europe in 1978, to Spain in particular. Hailed as a rising star of painting in 1980, Schnabel has achieved international renown.

Drawn by the temporal and symbolic permanence of the past and the history of its associated artistic forms, Schnabel brought paintings dominated by quotations back from his trips to Europe. Quotations became a fundamental characteristic of his technique and for several years, a special style of painting. In Barcelona he discovered Gaudi's baroque architecture with its use of tiles and mosaics. Schnabel sticks broken crockery and pots onto wooden panels and then sometimes paints over them copiously and with a steady hand draws figures with chaotic contours on this relief, such as *Blue Nude with Sword*, 1979-1980. He is interested in using the most varied materials and supports. It is not unusual to find antlers in his work, or objects in cast bronze, fur, velvet, blankets, rubbish, canvas sheeting, modelling clay and plaster. In a style that could easily be classified as eclectic, his art brings in all manner of objects: crucifixions, figures painted back to front, saints, pictures from magazines, many pictorial quotations (Baselitz, Polke, Gaudi, Beuys, Munch, Beckmann, Blinky Palermo, Caravaggio) and just as many literary references (Ignatius Loyola, Curé d'Ars, Dostoyevsky, Baudelaire, Artaud, Kafka), abstract signs, areas of flat colour and eclectic styles (Antiquity, Classicism, Baroque, Symbolism, Bad Painting, Abstract Expressionism). The phallic figures on the 1984-1985 canvases are inspired by primitivism, as is the 'Mexican' series of 1986. In 1983, meanwhile, he began tackling sculpture, and produced monumental pieces in bronze such as *Balzac*, 1983. Around 1987-1988 Schnabel's work underwent a kind of 'unloading' and as a result the signs and text became lighter. In these works Schnabel portrays less than he recalls or thinks (*I Hate to Think*, 1988) even in tributes in which he handles the symbolism of words or hints which cross each other, sometimes rather like ideograms, as in his tribute to William Gaddis (*Reconocimientos*, a series shown at the Cuartel del Carmen in Seville).

Along with David Salle and Eric Fischl, Julian Schnabel is one of the Americans reviving the style of painting characteristic of the 1980s. Contrary to the Modernist Formalism and Conceptualism that so heavily influenced the 1960s and 1970s, especially in the USA, Schnabel's large-format paintings in the Abstract Expressionist tradition forcefully affirm the vitality of a style of painting that an analytical art technique would call moribund if not dead. Schnabel's sudden appearance in the art world and his statement that he paints 'feelings that spurt out', soon provoked criticism and many debates in an era imbued with Post-Modernist ideology. 'I am my memory. I transpose what happens to me into my work,' emphasises Schnabel, who applies this principle to the letter and without restraint. Schnabel appears to have adopted the traditional approach of an artist who is witness of a fragmented world as in the present case, and of a creative artist, whose idealism is challenged by an entire modern saga.

Schnabel has participated in numerous collective exhibitions since 1971, including: *Tendances actuelles de l'art américain* (*Contemporary Trends in American Art*), Galerie Templon, Paris, 1980; Venice Biennale, 1980; Whitney Biennial, New York, 1981, 1983; *Issues: New Allegory*, Institute of Contemporary Arts, Boston, 1982; *'60'80 Attitudes/Concepts/Images*, Stedelijk Museum, Amsterdam, 1982; *The New Art*, Tate Gallery, London; *New Image, Pattern and Decoration*, Kalamazoo Institute of the Arts, Los Angeles, 1983; *Légendes*, CAPC Musée d'Art Contemporain, Bordeaux, 1984; Nouvelle Biennale de Paris, 1985; *Carnegie International 85*, Museum of Art, Carnegie Institute, Pittsburg, 1985; *Post-Abstract Abstraction*, the Aldrich Museum of Contemporary Art, Ridgefield, 1987; *American Art in the 20th Century: Painting and Sculpture*, Martin-Gropius-Bau, Berlin, and Royal Academy of Arts, London, 1993. His first solo exhibition was at the Contemporary Arts Museum, Houston, in 1976, and many others followed, including: Galerie Dezember, Düsseldorf, 1978; Mary Boone Gallery, New York, 1979, 1982; Galerie Bruno Bischofberger, Zurich, 1980, 1982, 1983, 1984 and 1985; Mary Boone-Leo Castellies, New York, 1981; Kunsthalle, Basel, 1981; Stedelijk Museum, Amsterdam, 1982; Tate Gallery, London, 1982; Leo Castelli, New York, 1983; Daniel Templon, Paris, 1983, 1995; Waddington Galleries, London, 1983, 1985, 1988; The Pace Gallery, New York, 1984, 1986; Galeries Contemporaines, Musées National d'Art Moderne, Paris, 1987; Galerie Yvon Lambert, Paris, 1987, 1988; *Julian Schnabel: Paintings 1975-1986*, a travelling exhibition at the Whitechapel Art Gallery, London, followed by Paris, Düsseldorf, New York, San Francisco, Houston, 1986-1988; *Works on Paper 1975-1988*, a travelling exhibition at the Museum für Gegenwarstkunst, Basel, and then in Nîmes, Munich, Brussels, Edinburgh and Chicago, 1989-1990; Cuartel del Carmen, Seville, 1988; CAPC Musée d'Art Contemporain, Bordeaux, 1989;

Chenonceau Castle, France, 1996; *Malerie 1978-2003 Julian Schnabel*, Schirn Kunsthalle, Frankfurt, 2004.

BIBLIOGRAPHY:

Kuspit, Donald, '*The Rhetoric of Rawness: Its Effects on Meaning in Julian Schnabel's Painting*' in *Art Magazine lix/7*, periodical, 1975. Schiff, G., *Julian Schnabel*, exhibition catalogue, Pace Gallery, New York, 1984. *Nouvelle Biennale de Paris*, exhibition catalogue, Electa, Le Moniteur, Paris, 1985. McEvilley, T., *Julian Schnabel: Paintings, 1975-1986*, exhibition catalogue, Whitechapel Art Gallery, Pompidou Centre, London Paris, 1986 (with interview and writings by the artist). *Schnabel*, exhibition catalogue, Capc musée d'Art contemporain, Bordeaux, 1989. Zutter, Jörg, *Julian Schnabel. Works on Paper 1975-1988*, Prestel, Munich, 1990. *The Conversion of St Paolo, Malfi/Julian Schnabel*, exhibition catalogue, PaceWildenstein, New York, 1996. *Julian Schnabel: Portrait Paintings*, exhibition catalogue, PaceWildenstein, New York, 1997. *Julian Schnabel*, Harry N. Abrams, New York, 2003 (illustrated book).

MUSEUMS AND GALLERIES:

AACHEN (Suermondt-Ludwig Mus.) - AMSTERDAM (Stedelijk Mus.) - LOS ANGELES (MMA) - MARSEILLES (Mus. Cantini): *Painting on Palstic-coated Cardboard* (1988) - NEW YORK (Whitney Mus. of American Art) - PARIS (MNAM-CCI).

AUCTION RECORDS:

NEW YORK, 20 May 1983, *Notre Dame* (1979, oil, wax and plates/panel, 90 x 108 x 12 ins / 228.6 x 274.3 x 30.5 cm) USD 85,000. NEW YORK, 16 Feb 1984, *Bob Williams & Crist in Zihuatenejo* (1980, watercolour, 38 x 25 ins / 96.5 x 63.5 cm) USD 4,500. NEW YORK, 2 Nov 1984, *Untitled* (1981, black ink and graphite, 43 x 31 ins / 109.2 x 78.7 cm) USD 3,800. NEW YORK, 1 Oct 1985, *The Death of the Dry Fart* (1979, red chalk and plaster/paper, 30 x 40 ins / 76.3 x 101.6 cm) USD 5,000. NEW YORK, 12 Nov 1986, *Tower of Babel (for A. A.)* (1976-1978, oil and wood/canvas, 72 x 119 ins / 182.9 x 302.2 cm) USD 110,000. NEW YORK, 3 May 1988, *Helen of Troy* (bronze, 26 3/4 x 35 3/4 x 35 3/4 ins / 68 x 91 x 91 cm) USD 165,000. NEW YORK, 9 Nov 1988, *You Must Only be Close to a Few People* (1979, encaustic/canvas, 102 1/4 x 60 1/4 ins / 259.5 x 152.8 cm) USD 154,000. NEW YORK, 10 Nov 1988, *Untitled* (1979, pencil and oil on paper, 27 3/4 x 39 1/4 ins / 70.5 x 99.9 cm) USD 7,150. NEW YORK, 4 May 1989, *Lola* (1984, etching/velvet, 108 x 60 ins / 274.3 x 152.4 cm) USD 30,800. LONDON, 5 Oct 1989, *Untitled* (1975, wax crayon and oil on paper, 15 x 22 1/4 ins / 38 x 56.5 cm) GBP 11,000. NEW YORK, 23 Feb 1990, *Brennero* (1983, gouache/mounted map, 20 x 15 ins / 51 x 38 cm) USD 20,900. LONDON, 5 April 1990, *Going Downhill Psychologically with a Skier* (pencil and oil/photograph, 49 1/4 x 37 3/4 ins / 125.4 x 96.2 cm) GBP 6,600. NEW YORK, 8 May 1990, *Portrait of David McDermott* (1987, mixed media and oil on wood, 60 x 48 x 8 ins / 152.3 x 122 x 20.3 cm) USD 242,000. PARIS, 9 Dec 1990, *Malette: Memory of the Crucifixion* (1982, oil on canvas, 100 1/2 x 74 3/4 ins / 255 x 190 cm) FRF 580,000. NEW YORK, 30 April 1991, *Bay of Tangiers* (1985, fibreglass and oil/lino, 100 x 96 ins / 254 x 243.8 cm) USD 66,000. NEW YORK, 1 May 1991, *Ethnic 4* (1984, animal hair, modelling clay and oil/velvet, 108 x 120 ins / 274.4 x 304.8 cm) USD 242,000. LONDON, 27 June 1991, *Fox Farm* (1989, oil, gesso and marker pen/velvet, 96 x 72 ins / 244 x 183 cm) GBP 115,500. NEW YORK, 3 Oct 1991, *Journey of the Lost Tooth* (1982, tempera/map, 50 1/2 x 30 ins / 128 x 76.5 cm) USD 14,300. NEW YORK, 13 Nov 1991, *Forms of Rubbish* (1989, collage of sacking, paper and oil on canvas, 99 3/4 x 80 ins / 253.3 x 203.2 cm) USD 66,000. NEW YORK, 25-26 Feb 1992, *Sad Vase* (1983, oil/velvet, 108 x 84 ins / 274.3 x 213.4 cm) USD 126,500. NEW YORK, 6 May 1992, *Bob's Worlds* (wax, bits a pottery, horns and oil on canvas and wood, 97 1/2 x 146 x 12 ins / 247.7 x 371 x 30.5 cm) USD 319,000. PARIS, 30 June 1992, *Portrait of Jean Cocteau* (1989, ink/paper, 12 1/2 x 9 1/2 ins / 32 x 24 cm) FRF 27,500. NEW YORK, 17 Nov 1992, *Untitled* (1983, oil/velvet, 108 x 84 ins / 274.3 x 213.4 cm) USD 187,000. NEW YORK, 19 Nov 1992, *Untitled* (1985, oil, ceramic and bondo/wood, 59 3/4 x 48 x 8 ins / 151.8 x 122 x 20.4 cm) USD 71,500. LONDON, 3 Dec 1992, *Untitled (Underwater Painting)* (oil/velvet, 108 x 84 ins / 274.3 x 213.4 cm) GBP 55,000. PARIS, 4 Dec 1992, *Bingo* (1989, oil on canvas, 49 1/2 x 45 1/2 ins / 125.5 x 115.5 cm) FRF 225,000. NEW YORK, 4 May 1993, *Taste of Surf* (sculpture of plates, mixture and oil on wood, 108 x 228 x 24 ins / 274.3 x 579.1 x 61 cm) USD 140,000. NEW YORK, 9 Nov 1993, *Portrait of Jacqueline* (1984, ceramic, coating and oil on wood, 60 x 48 ins / 152.4 x 122 cm) USD 123,500. NEW YORK, 2 Nov 1994, *Private School in California* (1984, modelling clay and oil/velvet, 120 x 108 ins / 304.8 x 274.4 cm) USD 195,000. NEW YORK, 3 May 1995, *Domodossola* (1983, oil/map of Italy, 20 x 13 1/2 ins / 50.8 x 34.3 cm) USD 5,462. LONDON, 30 Nov 1995, *Bingo II* (1989, acrylic/bare canvas, 49 1/4 x 45 1/4 ins / 125 x 115 cm) GBP 10,925. NEW YORK, 9 Nov 1996, *Lola* (1984, aquatint, 108 x 60 1/4 ins / 274.5 x 153 cm) USD 3,450. NEW YORK, 21 Nov 1996, *Portrait of Joe Glasco* (c. 1984, oil/velvet, 69 x 120 ins / 174.4 x 304.8 cm) USD 48,300. NEW YORK, 6-7 May 1997, *Malabristas* (1993, gesso, map and oil on canvas, 87 x 71 ins / 221 x 180.3 cm) USD 51,750. NEW YORK, 8 May 1997, *Portrait of Eva Ferraro and her Two Sons* (1983, oil, ceramic plates and bondo/panel, 108 x 96 ins / 274.3 x 243.8 cm) USD 32,200. LONDON, 29 May 1997, *Bill* (1988, oil/tarpaulin, 102 1/4 x 94 1/2 ins / 260 x 240 cm) GBP 23,000. LONDON, 27 June 1997, *Portrait of Brian* (1983, oil, plates and bondo/wood, 47 3/4 x 45 ins / 121.5 x 114.5 cm) GBP 34,500. NEW YORK, 19 Nov 1997, *What Once Was Chaos* (oil, ceramic plates). NEW YORK, 17 Nov 1999, *Maria Callas No. 4* (oil on velvet, 108 x 122 ins / 274 x 310 cm) USD 290,000. NEW YORK, 18 Nov 1999, *Portrait of a Girl* (oil plates bondo on wood, two parts, 96 x 84 ins / 244 x 213 cm) USD 325,000. NEW YORK, 17 May 2000, *L'amour - Carmen Iris Rivera* (oil on tempera on muslin, 143 x 130 ins / 363 x 330 cm) USD 120,000. NEW YORK, 17 Nov 2000, *Indecipherable Narratives* (tempera on muslin Kabuki, 130 x 176 ins / 330 x 447 cm) USD 140,000. NEW YORK, 14 Nov 2001, *Mimi* (oil on linoleum on wood panel with horns, 144 x 107x17 ins / 366 x 273x44 cm) USD 270,000. NEW YORK, 16 Nov 2001, *Egyptische Helena* (oil and tempura on muslin kabuki, 189 x 150 ins / 480 x 381 cm) USD 220,000. NEW YORK, 14 May 2002, *Adieu Batista* (1985, oil on canvas, 95 x 166 ins / 241 x 422 cm) USD 320,000. NEW YORK, 16 May 2002, *View of Dawn in the Tropics* (1993, oil, resin and collage on dropcloth, 96 x 120 ins / 244 x 305 cm) USD 220,000. LONDON, 21 Oct 2003, *Holy Night* (1984, oil and modelling paste on velvet, 120 x 108 ins / 305 x 274 cm) GBP 110,000. NEW YORK, 12 Nov 2003, *Untitled - Albondigas* (1992, oil, modeling paste and suede on dropcloth, 96 x 120 ins / 244 x 305 cm) USD 150,000. MADRID, 30 March 2004, *Monjas de Calle* (1993, oil on canvas) EUR 98,000. PARIS, 18 July 2004, *Self-portrait in White T-shirt* (collage and plates on wood, 60 x 47 ins / 152 x 119 cm) EUR 110,000.

SCHNABEL, Michael

German, 17th century.

Born 24 December 1627, in Coburg; died 19 January 1664, in Coburg.

Painter.

Michael Schnabel was the father of Moritz Schnabel.

SCHNABEL, Moritz

German, 17th - 18th century.

Born January 1661, in Coburg; died 31 May 1720, in Coburg.

Painter.

Moritz Schnabel was the son of Michael Schnabel.

SCHNABL, Johann Franz. See **SCHNABEL**

SCHNABL, Johann Jakob

German, 18th century.

Active in Burghausen.

Sculptor.

MUSEUMS AND GALLERIES:
HEILIGENSTATT (Church): two apostles; six angels.

SCHNACKENBERG, Walter
German, 20th century.
Born 1880, in Leuterberg; died 1961, in Munich.
Painter. Portraits, genre scenes.

Schnackenberg worked at the art academy in Munich for one year and made frequent trips to Holland, Belgium, France and Morocco. He lived and worked in Munich. In 1911 he became a member of the Luitpold group.

AUCTION RECORDS:
LUCERNE, 3 Dec 1988, *Dancer with Tiara* (mixed media/paper, 11 x 8 1/4 ins / 27 x 21 cm) CHF 950. MUNICH, 26-27 Nov 1991, *Young Woman with a Cactus* (ink and watercolour, 19 x 14 1/4 ins / 48.5 x 36.5 cm) DEM 1,495. MUNICH, 6 Dec 2002, *German Theatre - Mainly Munich Variety* (c. 1920, colour lithograph, 25, 46 x 33 ins / 117 x 85 cm) EUR 9,000. NEW YORK, 14 Nov 2003, *Untitled* (1990, oil on canvas, 79 x 98 ins / 201 x 250 cm) USD 39,000.

SCHNAIDER, Amable Louis.
See **SCHNEIDER**

SCHNAITMANN, Thomas
Austrian, 19th century.
Born 1796, in Hellbach, near Stuttgart; died 30 September 1821, in Vienna.
Painter, engraver, lithographer. History painting, portraits.

Thomas Schnaitmann attended the academy in Vienna from 1816.

SCHNAITTER, Andrea
Austrian, 18th century.
Died 1783.
Active in Zirl.
Painter.

Andrea Schnaitter painted religious subjects, flowers and landscapes.

SCHNAKENBERG, Henry Ernest
American, 20th century.
Born 14 September 1892, in Brighton (New York State); died 1970.
Painter, engraver.

Henry Schnakenberg studied under Kenneth Hayes Miller. He was a member of the Society of Independent Artists, and regularly exhibited at the Carnegie Foundation in Pittsburgh. He is represented at the Pennsylvania Academy of Fine Arts.

MUSEUMS AND GALLERIES:
SAN FRANCISCO (California Palace of the Legion of Honor): *Little Mushrooms* (1949, watercolour) - SAN FRANCISCO (De Young Mus.): *The Mullen Plant* (oil on canvas).

AUCTION RECORDS:
NEW YORK, 26 June 1981, *Still-life of Plums* (1924, oil on canvas, 16 x 20 ins / 40.6 x 50.8 cm) USD 1,100. NEW YORK, 31 May 1984, *Cat and Kittens* (1930, oil on canvas, 45 x 30 ins / 114.3 x 76.2 cm) USD 4,500. NEW YORK, 20 June 1985, *Place to Swim* (oil on canvas, 45 x 66 ins / 114.3 x 167.7 cm) USD 3,000. NEW YORK, 21 May 1991, *Claus Jensen* (oil on canvas, 30 x 24 ins / 76.2 x 61 cm) USD 1,100. NEW YORK, 31 March 1993, *Place to Swim* (oil on canvas, 45 x 66 ins / 114.3 x 167.6 cm) USD 1,150. NEW YORK, 31 March 1994, *Copa d'oro* (1965, watercolour/card, 15 x 22 ins / 38.1 x 55.9 cm) USD 633. NEW YORK, 28 Sept 1995, *Beside the Gorges* (oil on canvas, 30 x 30 ins / 76.2 x 76.2 cm) USD 1,035.

SCHNAPHAN, Abraham de. See **SNAPHAEN**

SCHNAPPER, J. J.
German, 18th century.
Active in Offenbach.
Engraver (burin).

J.J. Schnapper engraved satirical plates commemorating the victory of Catherine II over the Turks.

SCHNARRENBERGER, Wilhelm
German, 20th century.
Born 30 June 1892, in Buchen; died 1966.
Painter. Figures, portraits, landscapes.

Schnarrenberger trained at the industrial art college in Munich.

BIBLIOGRAPHY:
Nedo, Ingrid, *Wilhelm Schnarrenberger 1892-1966*, Eberhard-Karls-Universität, Tübingen, 1982.

MUSEUMS AND GALLERIES:
NUREMBERG: *Woman by the Sea* - STUTTGART (Gal. der Stadt): *Large Family Portrait* (1925).

AUCTION RECORDS:
MUNICH, 27 Nov 1974, *Still-life*, DEM 5,000. STUTTGART, 24 April 1999, *Still-life with Glasses and Cutlery on a Table* (1959, oil on canvas, 16 x 19 ins / 40 x 48 cm) DEM 11,000. BERLIN, 5 June 1999, *Still-life with Flowers in Vases and Glasses* (1952, oil on canvas, 18 x 22 ins / 46 x 57 cm) DEM 9,500. HEIDELBERG, 13 Oct 2000, *Dusk* (1937, oil on canvas, 20 x 16 ins / 50 x 40 cm) DEM 5,500. HEIDELBERG, 13 Oct 2000, *Berlin Avenue in the Fog* (1936, oil on canvas, 30 x 37 ins / 75 x 95 cm) DEM 10,000. MUNICH, 29 May 2001, *Still-life with Laden Table* (oil on canvas, 24 x 17 ins / 62 x 42 cm) DEM 17,000. STUTTGART, 27 Sept 2001, *Shops at Night* (1956, oil on canvas, 35 x 24 ins / 89 x 62 cm) DEM 10,000.

SCHNARS-ALQUIST, Hugo
German, 19th century.
Born 29 October 1855, in Hamburg.
Active in Hamburg.
Painter. Seascapes.

The son of a family of Hamburg wholesalers, Hugo Schnars-Alquist travelled extensively worldwide. A large altar painting signed by him *By Way of the Cross to the Light* is in the garrison church in Wilhelmshaven.

MUSEUMS AND GALLERIES:
ELBLAG: *Undertow* - ST LOUIS: *Equinox*.

AUCTION RECORDS:
BREMEN, 22 Oct 1983, *Steamer at Sea under Stormy Sky* (1932, oil on canvas, 28 x 42 1/4 ins / 71 x 107.5 cm) DEM 6,000. COLOGNE, 22 March 1985, *Alte und neue Zeit* (oil on canvas, 43 x 69 ins / 109 x 175 cm) DEM 13,000. BREMEN, 11 Dec 1999, *Choppy Lake Waters* (oil on panel, 27 x 39 ins / 69 x 99 cm) DEM 4,900. HAMBURG, 25 April 2001, *Ship on Heavy Sea* (1913, oil on canvas, 27 x 41 ins / 68 x 104 cm) DEM 4,800. HAMBURG, 8 Dec 2001, *Many Ships and Boats around Niederelbe in Moonlight* (oil on canvas, 16 x 26 ins / 40 x 65 cm) DEM 7,700. BREMEN, 29 Nov 2002, *Full-rigged Ship at Sea Near Einbruch in the Night* (1921, oil on canvas, 31 x 47 ins / 80 x 120 cm) EUR 3,300. HAMBURG, 11 Oct 2003, *Elb Panorama with Ships* (1922, oil on canvas, 45 x 72 ins / 114 x 182 cm) EUR 15,000. HAMBURG, 26 March 2004, *Steamer and Other Ships off Santa Cruz, Tenerife* (oil on canvas, 12 x 17 ins / 30 x 44 cm) EUR 5,000.

SCHNATTERPECK, Hans
Austrian, 15th century.
Probably of Swabian origin.
Painter.
Tyrolean School.

Hans Schnatterpeck became a member of the municipal council of Meran (now Merano, Italy) in 1499, probably after having emigrated to the Tyrol from Swabia.

SCHNÄTZLER, Ulrich Johann.
See **SCHNETZLER**

SCHNAUDER, Erwin
German, 19th - 20th century.

Born 1 February 1863, in Waldheim; died 1 November 1925, in Dresden.
Painter. Portraits.
Erwin Schnauder was the brother of Reinhard Schnauder, and studied at the art academy in Dresden from 1878 to 1883.

SCHNAUDER, Reinhard
German, 19th - 20th century.
Born 9 December 1856, in Plauen; died 14 October 1923, in Dresden.
Sculptor.
Reinhard Schnauder was the son of draughtsman Franz Julius, and trained at the art academy in Dresden and later in Hähnel's studio. He worked on the decoration of the Görlitz Memorial Hall.

SCHNAUDER, Richard Georg
German, 20th century.
Born 12 January 1886, in Dresden.
Sculptor.
Richard Georg Schnauder studied at industrial art colleges in Dresden and Paris.

SCHNEBACH, Christoph, or Schneebach
German, 16th century.
Sculptor. Religious subjects.
Würzburg School.
Christoph Schnebach worked in Würzburg but his works are to be found in churches all over Bavaria.

SCHNEBBEFER, Johann Ulrich.
See **SCHNETZLER Ulrich Johann**

SCHNEBBELIE, Jacob C.
British, 18th century.
Born 30 August 1760, in London; died 21 February 1792, in London.
Draughtsman, engraver, watercolourist.
Jacob C. Schnebbelie was a pupil of Paul Sandby and official illustrator of the Society of Antiquaries. He also illustrated numerous archaeological works.
MUSEUMS AND GALLERIES:
LONDON (Victoria and Albert Mus.): several watercolours.

SCHNEBBLIE, Robert Bremmel
British, 19th century.
Died c. 1849.
Active during the first half of the 19th century.
Draughtsman, watercolourist, illustrator. Urban landscapes, urban views, architectural views.
Robert Bremmel Schnebblie exhibited views of public monuments at the Royal Academy from 1803 to 1821 and worked as a contributor to the *Gentleman's Magazine*. It is believed that he starved to death.
MUSEUMS AND GALLERIES:
LONDON (Victoria and Albert Mus.): two watercolours.
AUCTION RECORDS:
LONDON, 5 and 6 Nov 1924, *Cheapside and Newgate* (watercolour) GBP 13. LONDON, 17 Nov 1983, *River Thames at Hammersmith* (1838, watercolour, 14 1/2 x 22 ins / 37 x 56 cm) GBP 10,000. LONDON, 9 July 1985, *View of London* (1805, watercolour pen and pencil, four items, 3 1/2 x 6 1/4 ins / 9 x 16 cm) GBP 2,300.

SCHNECK, Franz
Austrian, 18th - 19th century.
Born 1773, in Vienna; died 14 February 1857, in Vienna.
Portrait artist.

SCHNECK, Johann. See **SCHNEGG**

SCHNECK, Johann
Austrian, 18th century.
Born 1759; died 28 May 1794, in Vienna.
Miniaturist. Portraits. Miniatures.
AUCTION RECORDS:
PARIS, 4-5 Feb 1925, *Half-length Portrait of Woman, Dressed in White* (miniature) FRF 1,000.

SCHNECK, Johann Andreas
German, 18th century.
Born c. 1749; died 10 March 1792, in Ulm.
Active in Ulm.
Painter, engraver. History painting, portraits, landscapes.
Johann Schneck's master was Karl Schneider.
MUSEUMS AND GALLERIES:
ULM (Ulm Mus.): five paintings, two on wood.

SCHNECK, Karl
Austrian, 19th century.
Active in Vienna in 1817.
Miniaturist.
Karl Schneck attended the academy, exhibiting there in 1839.

SCHNECK, Mathias
Austrian, 18th - 19th century.
Born 1750; died 3 March 1812, in Vienna.
Miniaturist.

SCHNECK, Peter
German, 18th century.
Active in Munich.
Engraver (burin).

SCHNECKENDORF, Josef Emil
Romanian, 19th - 20th century.
Born 29 December 1865, in Brasov; died 11 July 1949, in Munich.
Active in Germany.
Sculptor, glassmaker.
Darmstadt Artists' Colony. Jugenstil.
Josef Schneckendorf trained in sculpture at Bucharest, Budapest and Vienna then got into the Munich Academy of Fine Art in 1890. Trained in glass-blowing he produced lamps in glass. Between 1907 and 1911 he was director of a glass factory, the Grossherzoglichen Edelglasmanufaktur at Darmstadt, and a member from 1906 of the famous colony of artists, Mathildenhöhe, at Darmstadt directed by Joseph Maria Olbrich. He later worked at Starnberg and Munich. His work appeared in the exhibition *Reassembled: Glass 1860-1960 One Hundred Years of Design* at MAK in Vienna in 2001.
BIBLIOGRAPHY:
Franzke, Irmela, *Jugendstil. Glas, Graphik, Keramik, Metall, Möbel, Skulpturen und Textilien von 1880 bis 1915*, exhibition catalogue, Badisches Landesmuseum, Karlsruhe, 1987. *Umelecka Kolonie Darmstadt, 1899-1914*, exhibition catalogue, Narodni Galerie, Prague, 1989.
MUSEUMS AND GALLERIES:
DARMSTADT (Schlossmus.).

SCHNEE, Herman
German, 19th - 20th century.
Born 5 September 1840, in Treuenbrietzen; died 24 February 1926, in Berlin.
Painter (gouache). Genre scenes, landscapes, mountainscapes.
Herman Schnee studied under Gude in Düsseldorf. He worked in Karlsruhe for a short time and in 1867 founded an art school in Berlin.

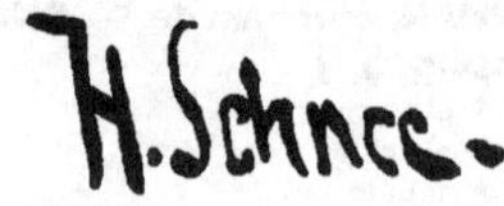

MUSEUMS AND GALLERIES:
BERLIN: *Stolberg in the Harz.*
AUCTION RECORDS:
COLOGNE, 22 Nov 1979, *Mountain Landscape* (oil on canvas, 29½ x 38½ ins / 75 x 98 cm) DEM 6,000. COLOGNE, 18 March 1989, *Leaving Church after the Baptism* (oil on canvas, 29½ x 38½ ins / 75 x 97.5 cm) DEM 11,000. NEW YORK, 20 July 1995, *Mountain Village Surroundings* (gouache/card, 14½ x 21 ins / 36.8 x 53.3 cm) USD 2,185. VIENNA, 29-30 Oct 1996, *Midday near a Stream in the Forest* (1869, oil on panel, 23¾ x 29½ ins / 60.5 x 75 cm) ATS 43,700.

SCHNEEBACH, Christoph. See **SCHNEBACH**

SCHNEEBELI, William
Swiss, 20th century.
Born 10 October 1874, in St Gall.
Painter. Landscapes, animals.
William Schneebeli lived and worked in St Gall.

SCHNEEBERGER, Hans Jakob
German, 16th century.
Active in Amberg.
Glass painter.

SCHNEEBERGER, Jacob Ernst
German, 19th century.
Active in Darmstadt.
Painter.

SCHNEEBRUEGEL. See the entry **MOLANUS Mattheus**

SCHNEELI, Gustav
Swiss, 20th century.
Born 12 November 1872, in Zurich.
Painter, art critic.
Schneeli was also a diplomat. He was influenced by Hodler and Puvis de Chavannes. He painted portraits of *Queen Maria of Naples*, the Austrian actor *Alexander Moissi* and the pianist *Vladimir Cernikoff*.

SCHNEEMANN, Carolee
American, 20th - 21st century.
Born 12 October 1939, in Fox Chase (Pennsylvania).
Performance artist, assemblage artist, installation artist, video artist. Multimedia.
Neo-Dadaism, Feminist Art, Body Art.
Carolee Schneemann received a BA from Bard College, Annandale-on-Hudson, and an MFA from the University of Illinois. She also studied at Columbia University School of Painting and Sculpture, New York; the New School for Social Research; and Universidad de Puebla, Mexico. She has taught at the University of Illinois (1961-1962); Dartington College, Totnes, Devon (1972); the Art Institute of Chicago; the Universities of Colorado, Ohio and California; and the Pratt Institute, New York. Schneemann was artist in residence at Colby College, Waterville, Maine (1968). She was founder-director of Kinetic Theater movement and design workshops in New York (1963-1968), and was a founder member of International-Local Group, New York (1976). Schneemann has received National Endowment for the Arts grants (1974, 1977, 1978, 1983); a Creative Artists Public Service Grant (1978); an Individual Artist Grant, Gottlieb Foundation (1987); a Guggenheim Fellowship (1993); Pollack-Krasner Foundation Grants (1997, 1998); an Art Pace International Artist Residency, San Antonio, Texas (1999); a Lifetime Achievement Award, Chicago Caucus for Women in the Arts (2000); a Distinguished Artist Award for Lifetime Achievement, College Art Association (2001); a Rockefeller Foundation Fellowship (2001); and an Honorary Doctorate of Fine Arts, Maine College of Art, Portland.

Schneemann painted in an expressionistic style before 1962, and moved to painted collages and boxed constructions during the mid-1960s, such as *Native Beauties* (1962-1964), a collaged and constructed diptych showing an image of a Senegalese woman next to Schneemann on a beach towel. Schneemann is best known for her performance art, which examines issues of body, sexuality and gender. She has used her own body in pioneering works of experimental film and Body Art, such as her breakthrough work *Eye Body* (1963), a film recording the naked, body-painted Schneemann interacting with paint, glue, fur, feathers, and garden snakes. In *Meat Joy* (1964), she and scantily-clad performers roll about with chicken carcasses. By the mid-1970s Schneemann moved from large-scale performance to mixed media works, such as *Fresh Blood - A Dream Morphology* (1981-1987) which combined live performance with slide images to explore the symbology of menstruation; or *Mortal Coils* (1994), an installation involving projected images of dead friends with slithering motorised ropes representing the 'mortal coils' of life.

Schneemann has been involved with the following exhibitions: a solo, University of California Art Museum, Berkeley (1974); *Sound Art*, Sculpture Center, New York (1984); Contemporary Arts Center, Cincinnati (1990); Venice Biennale (1990); San Francisco Museum of Modern Art (1991); Georges Pompidou Centre, Paris (1994-1996); *Neo-Dada: Redefining Art*, Milwaukee Art Museum (1995, tour); a solo, Kunstraum, Vienna (1995); *L'Âme au Corps - Le Corps Exposé de Man Ray à Nos Jours* (*Body Art: The Exposed Body from Man Ray to the Present*), Musée d'Art Contemporain, Marseilles (1996); New Museum of Contemporary Art, New York (1997, 1996 retrospective); the Museum of Contemporary Art, Los Angeles (1998); *Coming to Life, The Figure in American Art 1955-1965*, Henry Art Gallery, University of Washington, Seattle (1999); *Les Années 70: l'Art en Cause* (*The 1970s: Art in Question*), Capc-Musée d'Art Contemporain, Bordeaux (2002); *Up To and Including her Limits*, Block Museum, Northwestern University, Evanston (2003).

BIBLIOGRAPHY:
Schneemann, Carolee, *Cézanne, She Was A Great Painter: Essays on History, Sexuality and Naming, Unbroken Words to Women*, Trespuss Press, New Paltz, New York, 1975. *Carolee Schneemann: I. early work, 1960/1970*, exhibition catalogue, Max Hutchinson Gall., New York, 1982. *Carolee Schneemann*, video, Bennington College, Bennington, Vermont, 1983. Beatty, Maria, *Imaging her Erotics: Carolee Schneemann*, video, Vesper Video, New York, 1993. Birringer, Johannes, '*Imprints and Re-Visions: Carolee Schneemann's Visual Archaeology*' in *Performance Art Journal*, June 1993. Cameron, Dan/Stiles, Kristine/Levis Strauss, David, *Carolee Schneemann: up to and including her limits*, exhibition catalogue, New Museum of Contemporary Art, New York, 1996. McPherson, Bruce R., *More than meat joy: performance works & selected writings*, McPherson & Co., Kingston (NY), 1997. Morgan, Robert C., '*Jacques Roch - Carolee Schneemann*' in *Art Press no 221*, periodical, Paris, February 1997. Fréruchet, Maurice, et al., *Les Années soixante-dix: l'art en cause*, exhibition catalogue, Capc Musée d'Art contemporain, Bordeaux, 2002.
MUSEUMS AND GALLERIES:
CHICAGO (MCA) - LONDON (ICA) - LONDON (Tate Collection): *Interior Scroll* (1975, screenprint) - NEW YORK (MoMA) - PHILADELPHIA (MMA) - SAN FRANCISCO (MoMA): *Infinity Kisses* (1981-1987, installation).

SCHNEET, Carl Ludwig. See **SCHNOEDT**

SCHNEEWEIS, Karl
Austrian, 18th - 19th century.
Born 15 April 1745, in Salzburg; died 30 April 1826, in Salzburg.
Active in Salzburg.
Draughtsman.

Karl Schneeweis studied under Schmutzer at the academy in Vienna.
MUSEUMS AND GALLERIES:
SALZBURG (Carolino Augusteum Mus.): *Three Roses.*

SCHNEGG, Alfons
Austrian, 20th century.
Born 2 November 1895, in Mühlau, near Innsbruck; died 10 April 1932, in Mühlau.
Painter.

SCHNEGG, Gaston
French, 20th century.
Born 1866 in Bordeaux; died 1953.
Painter, sculptor. Religious subjects, landscapes.
Gaston Schnegg exhibited from 1896 at the Salon de la Société Nationale des Beaux-Arts, of which he later became a member. During the Paris Exposition Universelle he was awarded a bronze medal for sculpture at the Salon des Artistes Français. In 2001 he was represented in the exhibition *Autour de Barye et de Pompon. Sculptures animalières des XIXe et XXe siècles* (*Around Barye and Pompon. Animal Sculptures of the 19th and 20th Centuries*), held at the Musée des Arts Décoratifs, Bordeaux.
BIBLIOGRAPHY:
Gaston Schnegg (1866-1953), exhibition catalogue, Gal. des Beaux-Arts, Bordeaux, 1986. *Autour de Barye et de Pompon. Sculptures animalières des XIXe et XXe siècles*, exhibition catalogue, Musée des Arts décoratifs, Bordeaux, Réunion des musées nationaux, Paris, 2001.
MUSEUMS AND GALLERIES:
BORDEAUX (MBA): *Hen; Cockerel.*

SCHNEGG, Hugo Ernst
German, 20th century.
Born 8 August 1876, in Ansbach.
Painter. Figures, portraits, landscapes with figures.
Hugo Ernst Schnegg studied in Munich from 1901 to 1903 and from 1904 to 1907. He lived and worked in Altona Blankenese.
MUSEUMS AND GALLERIES:
AUGSBURG: *Mountain Landscape before the Storm* - HAMBURG: *Young Girl Lying Down* - WUPPERTAL: *Industrial Landscape; Needlework.*

SCHNEGG, Johann, or Schneck
Austrian, 18th century.
Born 27 May 1724, in Imsterberg (Tyrol); died 19 November 1784.
Sculptor.
Johann Schnegg was taught by J. Jois in Imst and Kölle in Fendels. His repertoire included groups of river gods in the Schloss Hermitage in Bayreuth as well as several sculptural groups in Potsdam.

SCHNEGG, Lucien
French, 19th - 20th century.
Born 19 April 1864, in Bordeaux; died 22 December 1909.
Sculptor.
After studies in decorative art in Bordeaux, Lucien Schnegg worked in the studio of Alexandre Falguière at the École des Beaux-Arts, Paris.
He exhibited in Paris from 1887 at the Salon des Artistes Français, where he was awarded a gold medal during the Exposition Universelle of 1900, and from 1892 at the Salon de la Société Nationale de Beaux-Arts, of which he became a member. He also exhibited at the Salon des Indépendants from 1905.
With Rodin and other sculptors of his time such as Bourdelle, Despiau and Pompon, he promoted a new approach to sculpture, and worked towards the end of his life at the simplification of masses and the giving of priority to line. In 1894 he received a commission to carve a fountain in Toul, and he also decorated several private residences.
MUSEUMS AND GALLERIES:
PARIS (MNAM-CCI): *Bust of a Young Girl* - PARIS (Mus. du Petit Palais): *Aphrodite; Young Man* (bronze, statuettes).
AUCTION RECORDS:
PARIS, 17 Dec 1979, *Woman Dressing* (black-patinated bronze, h. 16 1/4 ins / 41 cm) FRF 4,300.

SCHNEID, Otto
Czech, 20th century.
Born 1900, in Jablunkova.
Active from 1939 in Israel.
Painter, sculptor, illustrator.
Otto Schneid studied in Vienna and Paris and was the author of several books on prehistoric, Greek, Chinese and Jewish art. From 1936 to 1938, he worked at the Jewish Art Museum in Vilan. In 1939, he settled in Israel, and from 1947 to 1960, taught history of art in Haifa. He then abandoned his teaching commitments in order to concentrate exclusively on painting. Schneid's work is symbolic in character, treading a path between the fantastical and the naive. There have been several solo exhibitions of his work in the USA and Canada.
AUCTION RECORDS:
NEW YORK, 9 Jan 1964, *Still-life with Fruit*, USD 1,000.

SCHNEIDAU, Christian von
American, 20th century.
Born 1893; died 1976.
Painter. Figures, landscapes.
BIBLIOGRAPHY:
Dominick, Janet B., *Christian von Schneidau*, Petersen Publishing Co., Los Angeles, 1986.
AUCTION RECORDS:
NEW YORK, 24 June 1988, *Early Spring on Lake Mary in Yellowstone Park* (22 x 17 3/4 ins / 55 x 45 cm) USD 1,650. LOS ANGELES-SAN FRANCISCO, 10 Oct 1990, *Evelyn* (oil on canvas, 30 x 36 ins / 76 x 91.5 cm) USD 2,750; *Young Country Girl* (1920, oil on card, 24 x 18 ins / 61 x 46 cm) USD 4,125. NEW YORK, 27 Sept 1996, *Californian Coast* (oil on canvas, 20 x 28 ins / 50.8 x 71.1 cm) USD 690. PASADENA, 16 Feb 1999, *The Old Fish Hole, Lobster Creek, Oregon* (oil on canvas, 18 x 24 ins / 46 x 61 cm) USD 2,000. LOS ANGELES, 9 Dec 1999, *Chinese Parasol* (oil on canvas, 46 x 40 ins / 117 x 102 cm) USD 8,000. PASADENA, 12 Feb 2002, *Fish Pool* (oil on board, 8 x 10 ins / 20 x 25 cm) USD 2,500. PASADENA, 11 June 2002, *Road to Laguna Canyon* (oil on canvas, 30 x 36 ins / 76 x 91 cm) USD 5,000. FLORIDA, 22 June 2003, *Interior Scene with Young Woman Playing an Organ* (c. 1925, oil on canvas, 22 x 31 ins / 56 x 79 cm) USD 3,500.

SCHNEIDER
French, 20th century.
Medallist.
Schneider, a pupil of Dropsy, was awarded the Second Grand Prix de Rome in 1945.

SCHNEIDER, Abraham
German, 16th century.
Active in Wasserburg.
Glass painter.

SCHNEIDER, Adolphe Charles
French, 19th century.
Born in Paris.
Painter. Landscapes.
He debuted at the Paris Salon in 1864.

SCHNEIDER, Alexander, or Chneider
Russian, 20th century.
Born 21 September 1870, in St Petersburg; died 18 August 1927.
Painter, engraver.

Alexander Schneider was a student at the fine arts academy in Dresden from 1889 to 1892. He was professor at the fine arts school in Weimar from 1904 to 1908, and then spent time in Florence and Dresden. Schneider's work was influenced by Titian, Cornelius, Klinger and Böcklin. He painted a fresco entitled *The Triumph of the Cross throughout the History of the World* for the Church of St John in Meissen.

MUSEUMS AND GALLERIES:
DRESDEN: *Judas Iscariot* - ERFURT: *Gratitude* - MAGDEBURG: *Christ and Judas.*

AUCTION RECORDS:
LINDAU, 7 May 1980, *Swinemünde (Swinoujscie)* (oil on canvas, 10 3/4 x 9 ins / 27.5 x 22 cm) DEM 4,500. MUNICH, 12 Dec 1990, *The Judgement of Paris* (oil on canvas, 49 1/2 x 70 1/4 ins / 125.5 x 178.5 cm) DEM 16,500. BERLIN, 30 Nov 2002, *Standing Naked Boy Holding Garland* (watercolour over pencil, 35 x 19 ins / 90 x 47 cm) EUR 4,000.

SCHNEIDER, Amable Louis, or Schnaider
French, 19th century.
Born 18 October 1824, in Paris; died 1884.
Painter, engraver.

His teachers were Drolling and Fournier. He exhibited at the Paris Salon for the first time in 1861, and won a third-class medal the same year. His engravings include the *Coronation of Mary*, a portrait of *Louis Napoleon* and a *St Francis of Assisi*.

SCHNEIDER, Andreas
Norwegian, 19th - 20th century.
Born 29 July 1861, in Naes Jernverk; died 4 January 1931, in Vestre Aker.
Painter, potter. Designs for tapestries and stained glass windows.

Andreas Schneider also drew designs for furniture and vases.

SCHNEIDER, Anne-Marie
French, 20th - 21st century.
Born 1962, in Chauny (Aisne).
Draughtswoman, watercolourist, pastellist, sculptor, film producer, photographer.

Anne-Marie Schneider lives and works in Paris.

She has exhibited in group exhibitions, including: 1997, Documenta, Kassel; 1998, charcoal drawings, *Tu parles - J'écoute* (*You Talk - I Listen*), organised by the Galerie Anne de Villepoix, Paris, the Jet Lag K. Society, Malakoff, Taipei Fine Arts Museum, Taipei; 1999, *Ainsi de suite* (*So next*), Centre Régional d'Art Contemporain Languedoc-Roussillon, Sète. Her solo shows include: 1999, *L'Autre sommeil* (*The Other Sleep*), Musée d'Art moderne, Paris; 2000, *Petites familles* (*Small Families*), Galerie Nelson, Paris; 2003, *Anne-Marie Schneider. Fragile Incassable* (*Anne-Marie Schneider. Fragile Unbreakable*), Musée d'Art Moderne, Paris.

Her drawings, most often in ink or gouache, are either allegories that make use of objects or sentient beings, or visual poems, or social and political criticism, or, most recently, explorations of the egg as a symbol. Her films are similar in pictorial style and combine documentary images with animated drawings.

BIBLIOGRAPHY:
Chevrier, Jean-François, *Anne-Marie Schneider*, exhibition catalogue, Fonds régional d'Art contemporain de Picardie, Amiens, 1997. Bossé, Laurence (preface), Chevrier, Jean-François, et al., *Anne-Marie Schneider. Fragile Incassable*, exhibition catalogue, Musée d'Art Moderne de la Ville de Paris, Paris, 2003.

SCHNEIDER, August
German, 19th - 20th century.
Born 7 April 1866, in Görlitz.
Sculptor.

August Schneider lived and worked in Görlitz.

SCHNEIDER, August Adolf
German, 18th - 19th century.
Active in Leipzig at the end of the 18th and at the beginning of the 19th century.
Sculptor.

August Schneider carried out sculptural modifications to the Nikolaikirche in Leipzig.

SCHNEIDER, August Friedrich Christian
German, 19th century.
Born 1812, in Demmin.
Painter. Genre scenes, landscapes.

August Schneider went to Munich in 1836.

SCHNEIDER, August Gerhard
Norwegian, 19th century.
Born 1842, in Flekkefjord; died 1872, in Antwerp.
Painter, illustrator.

Schneider studied at the Eckersberg school in Christiania (now Oslo), before studying at the academies in Copenhagen, from 1868 to 1870, and in Antwerp, from 1870 to 1872. He illustrated the popular tales of Asbjørnsen.

SCHNEIDER, Bernhard
German, 19th century.
Active in Blasewitz near Dresden.
Painter. Landscapes.

Bernhard Schneider exhibited from 1878 to 1887.

SCHNEIDER, C.
German, 18th century.
Active c. 1770.
Painter. Portraits, landscapes.

C. Schneider left a portrait of a man as well as portraits of his wife, son and daughter.

SCHNEIDER, Caspar Johann or Johann Caspar
German, 18th - 19th century.
Born 19 April 1753, in Mainz; died 24 February 1839, in Mainz.
Painter. Portraits, landscapes.

Caspar Schneider was the brother of Georg and pupil of Heideloff the Younger.

MUSEUMS AND GALLERIES:
ASCHAFFENBURG: *View of Aschaffenburg* - COLOGNE (Wallraf-Richartz Mus.): *Nocturnal Landscape* - DARMSTADT: *Moonlight* - FRANKFURT AM MAIN (Städel): *Landscape of Plain* - MAINZ: *View of Hattenberg-am-Taunus; Two Landscapes; Two River Landscapes; Landscape of the Lower Rhine; From Lorch to Trechtinghausen; From Lorch to Bacharach; Caub bei Pfalz; Portrait of Canon of Mainz; Portrait of Frau Apollonia Pfaff; Portrait of Frau Elisa Stöhr; Portrait of Schmutz; Portrait of the Historian Schaab; Portrait of Graf Franz von Kesselstadt* - MUNICH: *Landscape of the Rhine.*

AUCTION RECORDS:
PARIS, 15 May 1936, *Rhineland landscapes*, FRF 650. COLOGNE, 11 June 1979, *Rhineland landscape* (oil on panel, 6 1/2 x 8 3/4 ins / 16.5 x 22.5 cm) DEM 5,000. LONDON, 7 July 1982, *Banks of the Rhine* (1790, oil on panel, a pair, 15 3/4 x 22 1/2 ins / 40 x 57 cm) GBP 8,000. STUTTGART, 22 Sept 2000, *Ideal River Landscape* (oil on panel, 20 x 26 ins / 52 x 67 cm) DEM 16,000. FRANKFURT, 3 March 2001, *Extensive Landscape* (oil on canvas, 24 x 37 ins / 60 x 95 cm) DEM 50,000. COLOGNE, 5 April 2001, *River Landscape* (oil on copper, 21 x 27 ins / 53 x 69 cm) DEM 20,000. MU-

NICH, 4 Dec 2002, *Resting Farm Family on Slope of Meadow and Castle on Hilltop* (1825, oil on copper, 19 x 24 ins / 48 x 61 cm) EUR 6,500. MUNICH, 4 Dec 2002, *Farm Families Bathing at Stream Edge with Timber Buildings and Castle* (1825, oil on copper, 19 x 24 ins / 48 x 61 cm) EUR 6,500.

SCHNEIDER, Charles
French, 20th century.
Born 23 February 1881, in Château-Thierry.
Sculptor, engraver.

Charles Schneider, a pupil of Chaplain, exhibited from 1906 at the Salon des Artistes Français, of which he became a member and where he won a silver medal in 1926. He was awarded the Légion d'Honneur in 1925.

SCHNEIDER, Christian
German, 16th century.
Born in Pappenheim.
Sculptor (wood).

SCHNEIDER, Christian
French, 20th century.
Born 27 June 1917, in Paris.
Painter. Landscapes with figures, urban landscapes, landscapes.

Christian Schneider graduated at the Académie Daroux in 1938. In 1955 he met Sebire in Spain and in 1968 he won a prize at the Salon Populiste, Paris.

He exhibits in Paris in group exhibitions and is a member of the Salon des Indépendants, the Salon d'Automne, the Salon des Artistes Français, the Salon de l'Art Libre, the Salon Populiste and the Salon des Terres Latines. He held solo shows in 1959; 1963, Galerie des Capucines, Paris; 1979, 1982, 1985, 1991, Galerie Ror Volmar, Paris; 1990, Deuil-La-Barre.

He paints landscapes and urban landscapes with a heavy brushstroke that is sometimes reminiscent of Utrillo or Vlaminck.

SCHNEIDER, Christian Heinrich
German, 19th century.
Born 1793; died 12 November 1854.
Active in Hamburg.
Painter. Portraits.

SCHNEIDER, Daniel
German, 17th century.
Active in Breslau (now Wroclaw).
Glass painter.

SCHNEIDER, Daniel
German, 17th century.
Painter. Portraits, landscapes.

MUSEUMS AND GALLERIES:
WITTENBERG (Church of St Marien): *Portrait of Superintendent Abraham Calov.*

SCHNEIDER, Émil
German, 20th century.
Born 20 January 1873, in Illkirch-Graffenstaden (near Strasbourg).
Painter. Portraits, genre scenes.

Emil Schneider was active in Strasbourg.

MUSEUMS AND GALLERIES:
STRASBOURG: *Roman (Study of Head); The Old Fireman; Self-portrait; Seascape* - STRASBOURG (Mus. Historique): *Portrait of General Hirschauer.*

AUCTION RECORDS:
STRASBOURG, 29 Nov 1989, *Musicians* (1898, watercolour, 7 1/4 x 11 ins / 18.5 x 27 cm) FRF 8,000.

SCHNEIDER, Ernst Friedrich
German, 17th century.
Medallist.

SCHNEIDER, F. A.
German, 18th century.
Active in Dresden c. 1750.
Painter. Portraits.

SCHNEIDER, Félicie
Maiden name: Fournier
French, 19th century.
Born 28 December 1831, in St-Cloud; died 1888.
Painter, pastellist. Genre scenes, portraits, flowers, fruit.

She was taught by her father and by Léon Cogniet. She debuted at the Paris Salon in 1849.

MUSEUMS AND GALLERIES:
PÉRIGUEUX: *Alone.*

AUCTION RECORDS:
NEW YORK, 16 Feb 1995, *Sleeping Boy* (oil on canvas, diam. 17 ins / 43.2 cm) USD 5,750. PARIS, 12 June 2001, *Portrait of Jeanne d'Osmond, Duchesse de Maille* (oil on canvas, 45 x 34 ins / 114 x 87 cm) FRF 65,000.

SCHNEIDER, Friedrich August
German, 19th century.
Born 22 April 1799, in Freiberg; died 2 July 1855, in Berthelsdorf, near Freiberg.
Painter. Military subjects, battles.

Friedrich Schneider was an artillery officer and painted war scenes.

MUSEUMS AND GALLERIES:
DRESDEN: *Scene from the Battle of Dresden on 27 August 1813.*

SCHNEIDER, Friedrich Wilhelm
German or Austrian, 19th century.
Active c. 1837.
Miniaturist. Portraits.

SCHNEIDER, Fritz
German, 19th century.
Born 15 November 1848, in Munich; died 12 December 1885, in Heilbronn.
Painter. Genre scenes.

The brother of Hermann, Fritz Schneider was taught by Piloty and completed his artistic education in Düsseldorf.

SCHNEIDER, Georg
German, 18th - 19th century.
Born 16 July 1759, in Mainz; died 24 April 1842, in Mainz.
Painter (gouache), watercolourist. History painting, landscapes, urban landscapes, architectural views.

Georg Schneider mostly painted events and landscapes in the surroundings of Mainz and the Rhine valley.

MUSEUMS AND GALLERIES:
MAINZ: *View of Mainz and Pastel at the end of the XVIIIth Century; Kostheim during the Siege of Mainz* (1793); *Fire in the Cathedral during the Siege; Two Views of Kostheim and Hochheim; Bingen and View in the Nahe Valley; View of Rhine from Niederwald; View of Mainz in 1791* (watercolour); *Interior of the Church of Our Lady in Mainz* (watercolour).

AUCTION RECORDS:
COLOGNE, 23 May 1985, *View of the Rhine at St Goar* (1822, oil on panel, 11 3/4 x 17 ins / 30 x 43 cm) DEM 8,000. LINDAU, 4 Oct 2000, *River Landscape* (oil on panel, 9 x 12 ins / 22 x 30 cm) DEM 4,180. FRANKFURT, 9 June 2001, *Extensive Landscape* (oil on canvas, 20 x 28 ins / 51 x 71 cm) DEM 4,600.

SCHNEIDER, Georg Jakob
German, 18th century.
Died 19 November 1721.
Active in Nuremberg.
Engraver (burin).

SCHNEIDER, Georg Michael
German, 19th century.
Born 1813; died after 1850.
Painter. Portraits.

Georg Schneider worked in Geneva from 1843 to 1845 and after that in Munich.

SCHNEIDER, Gérard Ernest
Swiss, 20th century.
Born 28 April 1896, in Ste-Croix; died 8 July 1986, in Paris.
Active in France from 1922 then naturalised in 1948.
Painter (including gouache/mixed media), watercolourist, pastellist, lithographer.

Gérard Ernest Schneider attended secondary school in Neuchâtel, Switzerland. At the beginning of World War I he went to Paris, where from 1916 he studied at the École des Arts Décoratifs (School of Decorative Arts) under Paul Renouard, before entering Cormon's studio in 1918. He finished his studies in 1919. He settled in France from 1922, and his training in traditional craftsmanship and the influence of his father, an established cabinetmaker and antique dealer, enabled him to earn his living restoring antique paintings. In 1930 he met Picasso. Between 1941 and 1943 he taught Gurjieff. He worked in Bouligny-sur-Essonne for several years. Gérard Schneider illustrated several works, including Robert Ganzo's *Language* in 1949, Eugenio Montale's *Poems* in 1964, and Eugène Ionesco's *Gérard Schneider: Killed in Flight*.

Writers have given differing descriptions of Schneider's works from the inter-war period. According to Schneider himself, 'After an initial period of classical studies and a Post-Impressionist palette until 1925, I began research on transposed, and then imaginary figurative art in 1930. Then came a Surrealist period (1937), then the creation of monumental forms (1939), followed by lyrical and abstract art (1943). I then moved on to research of a mural nature, involving juxtaposing shapes in 1947, then Expressionism from 1956.' In 1939 and 1940, his forms, until then dramatic, took on an architectural appearance. In 1948, he returned to this architectural sense of shape. In this period, Schneider's abstraction consisted of shapes, deliberate, clearly outlined, gracefully alternating straights and curves, all without stiffness, delineated as with Matisse, in blocks of plain colours, fitting ingeniously one into the other, like arabesques. However it was not until 1956 that his visual language settled into definitive rules.

After World War II, Gérard Schneider moved on from the diversity of his earlier work, and assumed, with Hartung and Soulages, an important place in the second generation of Abstract artists (who practised lyrical Abstraction rather than geometric Abstraction). Most of the first generation of abstract artists, in particular those associated with Bauhaus, the various movements of Russian constructivists, and the De Stijl group, believed abstraction to be inseparable from visual communication, which in turn was inseparable from a controlled, geometric formulation. In contrast, Schneider dedicated himself to the radical denial of any association between painting and reality. His painting is nothing more than painting. It is not even concerned with attaching titles, apart from allusions to the language of music, to which he likened painting.

He participated in many group exhibitions, including: 1926, and regularly from 1969, the Salon d'Automne, Paris; between 1936 and 1938, and from 1945, the Salon des Surindépendants, Paris; 1946, Galerie Denise René, Paris; 1946-1949 and 1956-1958, the Salon des Réalités Nouvelles; 1947, *Abstract Paintings*, galerie Denise René, Paris; from 1947, the Salon de Mai, of which he was a committee member between 1949 and 1956; 1948, Galerie Breteau, Paris; 1948, 1964, 1966, Venice Biennale; 1949, Colette Allendy, Paris; 1951, 1953, 1961, São Paulo Biennale; 1952, *The New Paris School*, Galerie de Babylone, Paris, exhibition organised by Charles Estienne; 1954, *Divergences-Nouvelle Situation*, Galerie Arnaud, Paris, exhibition organised by R. van Gindertaël; 1955, Documenta I, Kassel; 1955 9th Premio Lissone, Milan; 1955, 1957, 1959, International Exhibition of Comtemporary Engraving, Ljubljana; 1956, *The Adventure of Abstract Art*, Galerie Arnaud, Paris, exhibition presented by M. Ragon; 1956, the *Paris School* exhibition held at the Palais des Beaux-Arts in Lille; the 10th Premio Lissone, Milan in 1957, the Carnegie International in Pittsburgh in 1958, the Documenta II in Kassel in 1959, the IIe Salon International des Galeries Pilotes in Lausanne in 1966, *Ten Years of Modern Art* at the Fondation Maeght, St-Paul-de-Vence in 1967; the 1970 Menton Biennale, the 1977 exhibition of *20th Century Art* held at the Palais des Beaux-Arts in Paris, the Paris exhibition Hommage du Salon d'Automne in 1979, the *Paris-Paris* exhibition at the Georges Pompidou Centre in Paris in 1981, and an exhibition in 1999 at the Carcassonne art gallery.

He showed his works in numerous solo exhibitions and retrospectives, including: 1920 at the Galerie Léopold Robert, Neuchâtel; 1947, 1948 and 1950 at the Galerie Lydia Conti, Paris; 1951, at the Galerie de Beaune, Paris; 1953, at the Palais des Beaux-Arts, Brussels; 1954, at the Galerie Galanis, Paris; 1954, 1956, 1957, 1959, at the Koots Gallery, New York; 1961, at the Galerie Arditi, Paris; two retrospectives at the Düsseldorf Kunstverein and the Palais des Beaux-Arts in Brussels in 1962; the Musée des Beaux-Arts in Verviers in 1965; in 1965, 1967, 1968 and 1970 at the Galerie Arnaud in Paris; retrospectives in 1970 at Turin's Galleria Civica d'Arte Moderna and the exhibition hall in Montreal; a touring exhibition from 1974-1975 in the French Institutes in the Latin American capitals; Galerie Beaubourg in Paris in 1975; retrospectives in 1983 at the Musée d'Art et d'Histoire in Neuchâtel, then the Musée d'Art Contemporain in Dunkirk; Galerie Patrice Trigano in Paris in 1986; Musée Pierre von Allmen, Closel Bourbon Thielle-Wavre in Switzerland from 1989-1990; *Gérard Schneider. Les années 50* (*Gérard Schneider. The Fifties*) exhibition at the Musée Henri-Martin in Cahors in 2001; a retrospective in 2001 at the museums in Cour d'or and Metz.

He received many prizes and distinctions, including the main prize for abstract painting at the International Premio Lissone in Milan in 1957, the Tokyo prize at the 1959 international art exhibition, the French Grand Prix National des Arts in 1975, and the Médaille de Vermeil in Paris in 1983.

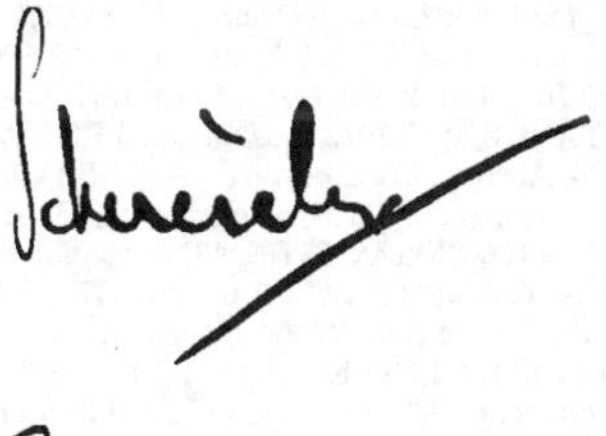

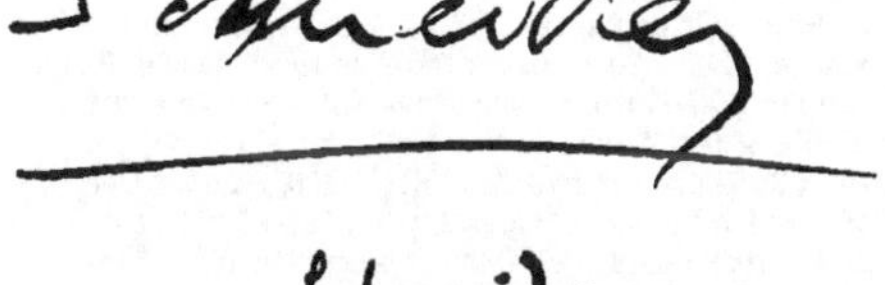

Schneider

BIBLIOGRAPHY:

Schneider, Gérard, *'Pour et contre l'art abstrait'* in *Arts*, periodical, Paris, 10 December 1948. Pobé, Marcel, *'Schneider'* in *coll. Musée de poche*, Georges Fall, Paris, 1959. Pobé, Marcel, *Schneider*, Gal. Lorenzelli, Milan, 1961. Ragon, Michel, *Gérard Schneider*, Bodensee-Verlag, Amriswil (CHE), 1961. Brion, Marcel/Gindertael, R.V., *Schneider*, Alfieri, Venice, 1967. Kaisserlian, Giorgio, *Gérard Schneider*, exhibition catalogue, Gal. San Fedele, Milan, 1968. Ionesco, Eugène, *Gérard Schneider - Construction et devenir*, exhibition catalogue, Gall. Civica d'Arte Moderna, Turin, 1970. Dunoyer, Jean-Marie, *Schneider*, Musée des Beaux-Arts, Neuchâtel, 1983. Orizet, Jean, *Schneider: peintures*, L'Autre musée, La Différence, Paris, 1984. Frederik, Loïs, *Gérard Schneider. Œuvres de 1916 à 1986*, exhibition catalogue, Château royal, Fondation Saint-Louis, Amboise, Expressions contemporaines, Angers, 1991 (text in French and English). Ragon, Michel, *Schneider*, Expressions contemporaines, Angers, 1998.

MUSEUMS AND GALLERIES:

BERGAMO (Lorenzelli Gal.): *Opus 53 I* (1967) - BRUSSELS (MAM) - BUFFALO (Albright-Knox AG) - CEDAR FALLS (Iowa State College) - COLOGNE (Wallraf-Richartz Mus.) - COLORADO SPRINGS (Fine Arts Center): *Painting II* (1954, oil on canvas) - DUNKIRK (MAC) - EXETER, NH, USA (Lamont Gallery, Philipps Exeter Academy) - GRENOBLE: two paintings - HØVIKODDEN (Henie Onstad Kunstsenter) - LIÈGE (Mus. of Modern and Contemporary Art) - LISSONE (Civica Gal. d'Arte Contemporanea) - LOS ANGELES (UCLA) - MINNEAPOLIS (Walker Art Center) - MONTREAL (MBA) - NANTES (MBA) - NEUCHÂTEL (MAH) - NEW YORK (MoMA) - PARIS (MAMVP): *Opus 12 F* (1961) - PARIS (MNAM-CCI): *Composition* (1944); *Opus 95 E* (1961) - PHOENIX (AM): *Peinture 67c* (*Painting 67c*) (1957, oil on canvas) - PRINCETON (AM, Princeton University) - RIO DE JANEIRO (MAM) - ROME (Gal. Nazionale d'Arte Moderna) - ST LOUIS (GA, Washington University): *10-D* (1958, oil on canvas) - TOULOUSE (MBA, Mus. des Augustins) - TURIN (Gal. Civica d'Arte Moderna e Contemporanea) - VERVIERS (Mus. communal des Beaux-Arts et de la Céramique) - WASHINGTON DC (Phillips Collection) - WORCESTER, MA (AM): *Sans titre* (*Untitled*) (1956, oil on canvas) - ZURICH (Kunsthaus).

AUCTION RECORDS:

MILAN, 28 March 1962, *Compositions*, ITL 550,000. MILAN, 1 Dec 1964, *Reference 42 E*, ITL 1,800,000. PARIS, 3 March 1970, *Compostion 70 E*, FRF 9,500. PARIS, 1 Dec 1972, *Composition*, FRF 8,500. PARIS, 8 April 1973, *Abstraction*, FRF 10,100. PARIS, 12 June 1974, *Abstract Compostion* (1974) FRF 13,000. MILAN, 9 Nov 1976, *Composition* (1961, oil on canvas, 9 3/4 x 13 ins / 25 x 33 cm) ITL 440,000. MILAN, 13 Dec 1977, *Painting 32-E* (1960, oil on canvas, 32 x 39 1/4 ins / 81 x 100 cm) ITL 1,500,000. MILAN, 26 June 1979, *Opus 81 I* (1969, oil on canvas, 36 1/4 x 28 3/4 ins / 92 x 73 cm) ITL 1,600,000. PARIS, 25 Jan 1982, *Composition* (1978, gouache, 29 1/2 x 42 1/2 ins / 75 x 108 cm) FRF 8,000. PARIS, 24 April 1983, *Red and Green Composition* (1971, gouache, 20 1/2 x 29 1/4 ins / 52 x 74 cm) FRF 11,500. PARIS, 22 June 1984, *59 E* (1960, oil on canvas, 45 x 57 1/2 ins / 114 x 146 cm) FRF 52,000. PARIS, 27 Nov 1985, *Composition* (1955, gouache, 14 1/2 x 20 1/2 ins / 37 x 52 cm) FRF 13,000. PARIS, 6 Dec 1986, *60-L* (1976, acrylic/canvas, 32 x 39 1/4 ins / 81 x 100 cm) FRF 56,000. PARIS, 27 Nov 1987, *Untitled* (1964, gouache, 20 1/2 x 29 1/4 ins / 52 x 74 cm) FRF 25,100. PARIS, 3 Dec 1987, *Composition* (gouache/paper, 20 3/4 x 29 1/4 ins / 53 x 74 cm) FRF 17,000. PARIS, 17 Feb 1988, *Composition* (oil on canvas, 24 x 19 3/4 ins / 61 x 50 cm) FRF 45,000. LONDON, 25 Feb 1988, *Untitled* (1959, mixed media, 20 x 28 3/4 ins / 51 x 73 cm) GBP 2,750. PARIS, 20 March 1988, *Composition* (1972, gouache, 14 1/2 x 21 1/4 ins / 37 x 54 cm) FRF 12,500. PARIS, 9 May 1988, *Red and Green Composition* (1974, oil on canvas, 13 1/4 x 16 1/4 ins / 33.5 x 41 cm) FRF 225,000. PARIS, 26 Oct 1988, *Opus 479* (1951, oil on canvas, 29 1/4 x 36 1/4 ins / 74 x 92 cm) FRF 245,000. PARIS, 28 Oct 1988, *Composition* (1969, acrylic and oil on canvas, 9 1/2 x 13 1/2 ins / 24 x 34 cm) FRF 28,000. PARIS, 12 Feb 1989, *Composition* (1977, acrylic/paper, 19 3/4 x 25 1/2 ins / 50 x 65 cm) FRF 32,000. PARIS, 12 Feb 1989, *Composition* (1960, oil on canvas, 38 1/4 x 51 1/4 ins / 97 x 130 cm) FRF 425,000. PARIS, 23 March 1989, *Opus 75 F* (1963, oil on canvas, 39 1/4 x 32 ins / 100 x 81 cm) FRF 380,000. PARIS, 12 April 1989, *Composition* (1967, acrylic/paper, 19 3/4 x 25 1/2 ins / 50 x 65 cm) FRF 90,000. AMSTERDAM, 24 May 1989, *Abstract Composition* (1972, oil on canvas, 27 3/4 x 27 3/4 ins / 70.5 x 70.5 cm) NLG 6,325. PARIS, 5 June 1989, *Composition* (1978, gouache/paper, 19 3/4 x 25 1/4 ins / 50 x 64 cm) FRF 60,000. MILAN, 6 June 1989, *Untitled* (1965, oil on canvas, 21 1/2 x 25 1/2 ins / 54.5 x 65 cm) ITL 36,000,000. LONDON, 29 June 1989, *Painting no. 19* (1962, oil on canvas, 28 3/4 x 36 1/4 ins / 73 x 92 cm) GBP 33,000. PARIS, 29 Sept 1989, *Composition* (1976, gouache/paper, 6 1/4 x 8 1/4 ins / 16 x 21 cm) FRF 12,500. PARIS, 8 Oct 1989, *Composition* (1964, oil on canvas, 38 1/4 x 51 1/4 ins / 97 x 130 cm) FRF 450,000. PARIS, 9 Oct 1989, *Composition* (1959, oil on canvas, 45 1/4 x 57 1/2 ins / 115 x 146 cm) FRF 900,000. PARIS, 26 Nov 1989, *Composition 55 K* (acrylic/canvas, 38 1/4 x 51 1/4 ins / 97 x 130 cm) FRF 350,000. PARIS, 18 Feb 1990, *Composition* (1960, oil on canvas, 45 x 57 3/4 ins / 114 x 147 cm) FRF 1,150,000. LONDON, 22 Feb 1990, *Untitled* (1974, oil on canvas, 18 x 21 3/4 ins / 45.7 x 55.2 cm) GBP 20,900. RAMBOUILLET, 4 March 1990, *After the Storm* (acrylic/paper/canvas, 57 3/4 x 41 3/4 ins / 147 x 106 cm) FRF 850,000. MILAN, 27 March 1990, *Untitled* (1970, oil on canvas, 28 3/4 x 36 1/4 ins / 73 x 92 cm) ITL 82,000,000. PARIS, 8 April 1990, *Composition* (1957, oil on canvas, 35 x 46 ins / 89 x 116 cm) FRF 500,000. PARIS, 3 May 1990, *Composition* (1982, pastel and watercolour/paper, 7 3/4 x 10 1/4 ins / 20 x 26 cm) FRF 18,000. NEUILLY, 10 May 1990, *53 E* (1960, oil on canvas, 39 1/4 x 32 ins / 100 x 81 cm) FRF 780,000. PARIS, 30 May 1990, *Composition* (oil on canvas, 23 1/2 x 31 1/2 ins / 60 x 80 cm) FRF 275,000. PARIS, 10 June 1990, *Untitled* (1956, oil on canvas, 51 1/4 x 63 1/2 ins / 130 x 161 cm) FRF 1,010,000. MILAN, 13 June 1990, *Opus 40 D* (1959, oil on canvas, 45 x 57 1/2 ins / 114 x 146 cm) ITL 120,000,000. PARIS, 18 June 1990, *Composition* (1971, oil on canvas, 28 1/4 x 46 1/2 ins / 71.5 x 118 cm) FRF 270,000. PARIS, 27 Nov 1990, *Composition with Red and Blue Background* (1984, gouache and collage/paper, 19 3/4 x 25 1/2 ins / 50 x 65 cm) FRF 30,000. ROME, 3 Dec 1990, *Untitled* (1955, mixed media/paper/canvas, 14 3/4 x 21 ins / 37.5 x 52.5 cm) ITL 12,650,000. LONDON, 6 Dec 1990, *88 B* (1955, oil on canvas, 51 1/4 x 63 1/2 ins / 130 x 161 cm) GBP 37,400. MILAN, 26 March 1991, *Opus 105 Y* (1969, oil on mounted paper, 9 1/2 x 12 3/4 ins / 24 x 32.5 cm) ITL 14,000,000. MILAN, 20 June 1991, *Untitled* (1962, gouache/mounted card, 20 3/4 x 29 1/4 ins / 53 x 74.5 cm) ITL 20,000,000. LONDON, 27 June 1991, *Opus 85-D* (1960, oil on canvas, 57 1/2 x 45 ins / 146 x 114 cm) GBP 50,600. PARIS, 3 July 1991, *Great Sign* (acrylic and pastel/card, 8 3/4 x 9 ins / 22.5 x 22 cm) FRF 5,500. ROME, 9 Dec 1991, *Composition* (mixed media/paper/canvas, 9 x 12 ins / 23 x 30.5 cm) ITL 4,025,000. PARIS, 16 Feb 1992, *Untitled* (1957, oil on canvas, 38 1/4 x 50 3/4 ins / 97 x 129 cm) FRF 165,000. LOKEREN, 23 May 1992, *Composition* (1973, gouache, 29 x 41 3/4 ins / 73.5 x 106 cm) BEF 330,000. PARIS, 1 Oct 1992, *Opus 54 L* (1976, acrylic/canvas, 35 x 46 ins / 89 x 116 cm) FRF 105,000. MILAN, 9 Nov 1992, *Opus 21 H* (1965, oil on canvas, 18 x 22 ins / 46 x 55 cm) ITL 14,000,000. LONDON, 24-25 March 1993, *Opus 42 C* (oil on canvas, 35 x 45 1/2 ins / 89 x 115.5 cm) GBP 17,250. ZURICH, 21 April 1993, *Composition* (1974, acrylic/canvas, 22 x 18 ins / 56 x 46 cm) CHF 7,000. PARIS, 14 June 1993, *Composition* (1957, oil on canvas, 28 3/4 x 36 1/4 ins / 73 x 92 cm) FRF 98,000. PARIS, 6 Feb 1994, *Composition* (1977, gouache, 14 1/2 x 22 1/4 ins / 37 x 56.3 cm) FRF 19,000. LOKEREN, 12 March 1994, *Composition* (1952, oil on canvas, 25 1/2 x 32 ins / 65 x 81 cm) BEF 400,000. PARIS, 22 June 1994, *Untitled* (1964, oil on canvas, 32 x 39 1/4 ins / 81 x 100 cm) FRF 70,000. PARIS, 24 Nov 1995, *Composition 93 C* (1958, oil on canvas, 38 1/4 x 51 1/4 ins / 97 x 130 cm) FRF 110,000. LONDON, 30 Nov 1995, *Opus 13-C* (1956, oil on canvas, 64 1/4 x 52 ins / 163 x 132 cm) GBP 16,100. ZURICH, 26 March 1996, *Composition* (1960, acrylic/paper, 29 1/2 x 39 3/4 ins / 75 x 100.9 cm) CHF 5,000. PARIS, 11 July 1996, *Composition* (acrylic/paper, 14 3/4 x 21 1/4 ins / 37.5 x 54 cm) FRF 7,800. PARIS, 5 Oct 1996, *Composition* (1948, pastel and charcoal/paper, 19 3/4 x 25 1/2 ins / 50 x 65 cm) FRF 25,500. LONDON, 5 Dec 1996, *Opus XXII F* (1962, oil on canvas, 59 x 78 3/4 ins / 150 x 200 cm) USD 13,225. PARIS, 16 March 1997, *Untitled* (1972, acrylic/paper, 42 1/4 x 29 1/4 ins / 107 x 74 cm) FRF 18,000. PARIS, 18 June 1997, *Untitled, Brown Background* (1953, oil on canvas, 23 1/2 x 28 3/4 ins / 60 x 73 cm) FRF 44,000. LONDON, 23 Oct 1997, *Opus 15-D* (1958, oil on canvas, 45 x 57 1/2 ins / 114 x 146 cm) GBP 12,650. PARIS, 23 Nov 1997, *Untitled* (1971, acrylic/canvas, 15 1/4 x 19 ins / 39 x 48 cm) FRF 13,500. PARIS, 1 April 1998, *Opus 7K* (1971, oil on canvas, 51 1/4 x 38 1/4 ins / 130 x 97 cm) FRF 65,000. VERSAILLES, 11 April 1999, *Opus 33C* (1957, oil on canvas, 38 x 51 ins / 97 x 130 cm) FRF 134,000. PARIS, 1 Dec 1999, *Composition* (1950, oil on canvas, 32 x 26 ins / 81 x 65 cm) FRF 130,000. PARIS, 14 April 2000, *Abstract Composition* (1950, oil on canvas, 31 x 39 ins / 80 x 99 cm) FRF 120,000. PARIS, 7 June 2000, *Opus 18 K* (1972, oil on canvas, 35 x 46 ins / 89 x 116 cm) FRF 95,000. PARIS, 21 June 2000, *Opus 28 D* (1958, oil on canvas, 38 x 51 ins / 96 x 130 cm) FRF 145,000. PRATO, 25 May 2001, *Composition* (1977, acrylic on canvas, 45 x 57 ins / 114 x 146 cm) ITL 36,000,000. PARIS, 16 Aug 2001, *Untitled* (oil on canvas, 36 x 29 ins / 92 x 73 cm) FRF 140,000. MILAN, 19 Nov 2002, *95J* (1971, oil on canvas, 58 x 45 ins / 147 x 114 cm) EUR 22,000. PARIS, 24 Nov 2002, *475* (1951, oil on canvas, 30 x 37 ins / 76 x 95 cm) EUR 23,000. PRATO, 29 Nov 2002, *Untitled* (1983, miixed media, 58 x 41 ins / 147 x 105 cm) EUR 15,500. VERSAILLES, 29 June 2003, *Composition C59* (1957, oil on canvas, 51 x 38 ins / 130 x 97 cm) EUR 39,000. VERSAILLES, 14 Dec 2003, *Opus 95D* (1960, oil on canvas, 51 x 64 ins / 130 x 162 cm) EUR 48,000. VERCELLI, 13 March 2004, *Untitled* (mixed media on cardboard, 59 x 41 ins / 149 x 105 cm) EUR 11,000. VERSAILLES, 25 April 2004, *Opus 42B* (1953, oil on canvas, 34 x 46 ins / 86 x 116 cm) EUR 36,000.

SCHNEIDER, Hans
German, 17th century.
Sculptor.

Hans Schneider was in Kitzingen from 1695 to 1696.

SCHNEIDER, Heinrich Justus
German, 19th century.
Born 20 July 1811, in Coburg; died 26 July 1884, in Gotha.
Painter. History painting, portraits.

After studying under Schnorr in Munich, Heinrich Schneider spent some time in Belgium, visiting Rome in 1843 and settling in Gotha in 1849. In the Gotha museum is his *Portrait of the Astronomer Hansen*. It is also likely that he was responsible for the painting *The Landgravine Marguerite and her Children*, catalogued in the museum of Hanover bearing the initials JF.

SCHNEIDER, Henriette
German, 18th - 19th century.
Born 1747, in Neuwied; died 1812, in Munich.
Painter, miniaturist. Portraits.

Henriette Schneider was the daughter and pupil of Ludwig Schneider and also worked in enamel.

MUSEUMS AND GALLERIES:

MUNICH (Bayerisches Nationalmus.): *Charles Theodor, Kürfurst von der Pfalz; Portrait of his Wife Elisabeth Maria* (two miniatures).

SCHNEIDER, Herman or Hermann
German, 19th - 20th century.
Born 15 June 1847, in Munich; died 24 July 1918, in Munich.
Painter, illustrator.

Herman Schneider studied under H. Dyk, Moritz von Schwind and Piloty, and became the artistic director of the *Fliegende Blätter* journal in 1871. In 1884 he finished a Bacchus cycle in twelve parts for one of the rooms in the Drachenburg near Königswinter.

AUCTION RECORDS:

PARIS, 2 Dec 1976, *Composition* (1969, oil on canvas, 22 x 18 ins / 55 x 46 cm) FRF 9,000. NEW YORK, 31 Oct 1985, *Two Women on a Terrace* (oil on canvas, 32 1/2 x 40 3/4 ins / 82.5 x 103.5 cm) USD 3,000.

SCHNEIDER, J. A.
German, 19th century.
Born 1814, in Coburg; died 3 November 1862, in Prague.
Watercolourist.

J.A. Schneider worked in Dresden and from 1842 in Prague.

SCHNEIDER, Jean-Pierre
French, 20th - 21st century.
Born 1946, in Paris.
Painter.

Jean-Pierre Schneider studied at the École des Beaux-Arts in Lille. He coats the surface of his canvas with various pigments mixed with powdered marble, then scores and scratches the textured surface. He is noted for a number of series, including *Urns, Men and Sheep, Swimmers* and *Marat* (based on the painting by David). Typically, Schneider employs a vast monochrome surface in green and light and dark ochre tones, where an elliptic tracing in blue pigment suggests a swimmer's arm emerging from the water. Using such simple and economic detail, he succeeds in evoking a specific place, a sense of space and the subject matter in question. His work has been succinctly described as 'modest but persistent, a quiet dream world with overtones of ballet'.

He has shown his work at group exhibitions: from 1987 to 1997, at the Salon des Réalités Nouvelles in Paris; in 1988, 1989 and 1990, at FRAC Haute-Normandie in Sotteville-lès-Rouen; in 2000, at the Galerie Sabine Puget in Paris; in 2000, at Linéart in Ghent (presented by the Patrick Gauthier Gallery); in 2001, at the March Salon in Geneva; and, in 2001, at *Œuvres d'Arbres* (*Jean-Pierre Schneider: Trees*), held at the Musée des Beaux-Arts in Pau.

To date, Schneider has exhibited solo in 1992, 1994 and 1995, at the Galerie Anne Bourdier in Rouen; in 1992, 1994 and 1996, at the Galerie Lise et Henri de Menthon in Paris; and, in 1999 and 2002, at the Galerie Sabine Puget in Paris.

BIBLIOGRAPHY:

Puget, Sabine/Schneider, Jean-Pierre, *Jean-Pierre Schneider, l'estran, peintures 1990-1996*, exhibition catalogue, Gal. de Menthon-Noulens, Paris, 1996. Chambaz, Bernard/Dieuzaide, Michel, *La déposition, Jean-Michel Schneider*, Le Temps qu'il fait, Cognac, 2003.

MUSEUMS AND GALLERIES:

SOTTEVILLE-LÈS-ROUEN (FRAC Haute-Normandie).

SCHNEIDER, Johann
Austrian, 18th century.
Active in Schwaz.
Sculptor.

SCHNEIDER, Johann Georg
German, 18th century.
Born 20 September 1713, in Ilminau; died 1759, probably in Eisenach.
Sculptor.

Johann Schneider worked until 1752 in Ilmenau, then in Eisenach. In 1756 he was appointed Court Sculptor in Weimar.

SCHNEIDER, Johann Jakob
Swiss, 19th century.
Born 1822, in Diegten; died 1889, in Basel.
Watercolourist, draughtsman.

A selection of Johann Schneider's works appeared in 1880 under the title *Old Basel*.

SCHNEIDER, Johann Josef
German, 18th century.
Died before 1737.
Painter. Portraits.

Johann Schneider was a court painter in Munich.

SCHNEIDER, Johann Ludwig
Danish, 19th century.
Born 6 February 1809, in Copenhagen; died 30 December 1870, in Copenhagen.
Painter, actor. Landscapes.

SCHNEIDER, Josef
German, 20th century.
Born 25 April 1876, in Eslohe (Westphalia).
Sculptor. Memorials.

Josef Schneider lived and worked in Düsseldorf. He sculpted several war memorials.

SCHNEIDER, Julius
German, 19th century.
Born 1824, in the Giants' Mountains; died 1870, in Breslau (now Wroclaw, Poland).
Painter.

First and foremost a portrait painter, he also composed altar paintings for churches in the environs of Breslau.

SCHNEIDER, Jürgen
German, 20th century.
Born 1941.
Active in Belgium.
Painter, engraver.

Jürgen Schneider studied in Düsseldorf and won the graphic arts prize in eastern Flanders.

SCHNEIDER, Karl
German, 18th century.
Active in Augsburg.
Painter.

SCHNEIDER, Karl
Swiss, 20th century.
Born 20 September 1872, in Basel.
Painter.

Karl Schneider was trained by Raupp, Windmann and Rudolf von Seitz. He painted the ceiling of Stuttgart's Apollo Theatre.

SCHNEIDER, Karoly or Karl
Hungarian, 19th - 20th century.
Born 1860, in Budapest.
Painter. Landscapes, still-lifes.

Karoly Schneider lived and worked in Budapest.

AUCTION RECORDS:
LONDON, 26 Nov 1986, *Swan Lake* (oil on canvas, 60 1/4 x 83 3/4 ins / 153 x 213 cm) GBP 17,000.

SCHNEIDER, Kaspar
German, 18th century.
Active in Cologne in 1797.
Painter.

SCHNEIDER, Leonhard
German, 18th century.
Born 1716, in Geislingen-an-der-Steige; died in Schwabach.
Painter. History painting, portraits.

MUSEUMS AND GALLERIES:
ULM: *Portrait of Veronika von Krafft.*

AUCTION RECORDS:
MUNICH, 13 Sept 1984, *Portrait of Johan Jakob Laemmermann* (1758, oil on canvas, 36 1/2 x 30 1/4 ins / 92.5 x 77 cm) DEM 5,500.

SCHNEIDER, Ludwig
Austrian, 18th century.
Born 1712, in Gotha; died 16 November 1789, in Vienna.
Miniaturist, pastellist.

The father of Henriette, Ludwig Schneider studied at the academy in Vienna and was court painter at Darmstadt from 1739 to 1744.

SCHNEIDER, Nicolaus
German, 16th century.
Born to a family originally from Dippoldiswald; died 1583, in Dresden.
Painter.

SCHNEIDER, Ottilie
Czech, 20th century.
Born 1875, in Prague.
Painter.

Ottilie Schneider lived and worked in Prague.

SCHNEIDER, Otto
German, 19th century.
Born to a family originally from Nauen.
Painter. Portraits, genre scenes.

Otto Schneider was the pupil of F.W. Herbig in Berlin from 1839 to 1842.

SCHNEIDER, Otto J.
American, 20th century.
Born 1875, in Atlanta; died 1946.
Painter, engraver, illustrator.

SCHNEIDER, Otto Ludwig
German, 19th century.
Born 25 September 1858, in Dresden.
Painter. Landscapes.

Otto Schneider lived and worked in Dresden.

SCHNEIDER, Robert
German, 19th century.
Born 25 February 1809, in Dresden; died 21 October 1885, in Hamburg.
Portrait artist.

Robert Schneider attended the academy in Dresden and subsequently crossed Europe, settling in Hamburg around 1843.

MUSEUMS AND GALLERIES:
DRESDEN: *Ludwig Tieck* - HAMBURG: *Peter Simon Brödermann; Frau Brödermann; Self-portrait; Director of the Gurlitt Gymnasium* - LÜBECK: *Em. Geibel.*

SCHNEIDER, Sascha, for Rudolph Karl Alexander
German, 19th - 20th century.
Born 1870; died 1927.
Painter, sculptor, illustrator.
Jugendstil, Symbolism.

Sascha Schneider was a close friend of the writer Karl May, many of whose works he had illustrated. He represented figures in an extreme academic style and his many male nudes derive from the symbolism of the Jugendstil. He was also responsible for the interior design in the hall of the book market (Buchhandlerhaus) in Leipzig.

BIBLIOGRAPHY:
Mees, Heinz, *Sascha Schneider und Karl May: eine Künstlerfreundschaft*, exhibition catalogue, Hamburg, 1992. Röder, Hans-Gerd, *Sascha Schneider, ein Maler für Karl May: Ju-*

biläumsausgabe zum 125. Geburtstag des Malers, exhibition catalogue, Karl-May-Verlag, Bamberg, 1995. Kern, Andrea, et al., *Jugendstil in Dresden, Aufbruch in di Moderne,* exhibition catalogue, Staatliche Kunstsammlungen, Dresden, 1999. Range, Annelotte, *Zwischen Max Klinger und Karl May: Studien zum zeichnerischen und malerischen Werk von Sascha Schneider (1870 - 1927),* exhibition catalogue, Karl-May-Verlag, Bamberg, 1999.

MUSEUMS AND GALLERIES:

DRESDEN (Skulpturensammlung): *Gürtelbinder* (1913) - RADEBEUL (Karl-May Mus.) - WEIMAR (Kunstsammlungen): *Ikarus* (1901, oil on canvas); *Figure* (bronze).

AUCTION RECORDS:

LONDON, 20 May 1993, *Dependence on the Physical* (oil on canvas, 98 3/4 x 65 1/4 ins / 250.7 x 165.8 cm) GBP 17,250.

SCHNEIDER, Simon
German, 16th century.
Born 21 January 1560.
Active in Celle.
Painter.

SCHNEIDER, Susan Hayward
American, 20th century.
Born 1876, in Pana (Illinois).
Painter.

Susan Schneider studied under Henry Rittenberg and Carl Leopold Vass in Munich. She was a member of the American Federation of Arts.

SCHNEIDER, Theophile
American, 20th century.
Born 5 December 1872, in Freiburg (Baden), Germany; died c. 1960.
Active in the USA.
Painter.

Theophile Schneider studied under Monks, Noyes and Dadol. He was a member of the Salmagundi Club.

SCHNEIDER, Wilhelm Heinrich
German, 19th century.
Born 14 January 1821, in Neukirchen, near Chemnitz; died 5 August 1900, near Dresden.
Painter. Landscapes, architectural views.

The pupil of Ludwig Richter, Wilhelm Schneider was admitted to the academy in Dresden in 1841.

MUSEUMS AND GALLERIES:

CHEMNITZ (Kunstsammlungen): a painting.

AUCTION RECORDS:

LONDON, 15 Oct 1970, *Farm at River's Edge,* GBP 380.

SCHNEIDER, William G.
American, 19th - 20th century.
Born 1863, in Monroe; died 6 November 1915, in New York.
Watercolourist.

William Schneider studied in Paris.

SCHNEIDER, Wolfgang, or Schnider
Swiss, 16th century.
Active in Zurich.
Sculptor.

Wolfgang Schneider became a burgher of Zurich in 1519.

SCHNEIDER-BLUMBERG, Bernhard
German, 20th century.
Born 17 May 1881, in Blumberg (Baden).
Painter. Figure compositions, figures, portraits, landscapes.

Bernhard Schneider-Blumberg trained at the art academy in Karlsruhe. He lived on the island of Reichenau on Lake Constance.

MUSEUMS AND GALLERIES:

DONAUESCHINGEN: *The Veteran of 1870; Bust of Emile Wagner* - FREIBURG IM BREISGAU: *Village Elders* - MAINZ (Römisch-Germanisches Zentralmus.): *The Hohentwiel.*

SCHNEIDER-BORDACHAR, Denys
French, 20th century.
Painter.

Denys Schneider-Bordachar exhibited regularly in Paris at the Salon des Artistes Français, where he was awarded an honourable mention in 1937.

SCHNEIDER-DIDAM, Wilhelm
German, 19th - 20th century.
Born 14 May 1869, in Altenhunden (Westphalia); died 5 April 1923, in Düsseldorf.
Painter. Portraits.

Wilhelm Schneider-Didam trained at the art academy in Düsseldorf under P. Jansen, Roeting and Crola.

MUSEUMS AND GALLERIES:

DÜSSELDORF: several works.

SCHNEIDER-KAINER, Lene
Austrian, 20th century.
Born 16 May 1885, in Vienna; died 15 June 1971, in Cochabamba, Bolivia.
Painter, draughtsman, engraver, lithographer, illustrator. Nudes, landscapes, urban landscapes.

Born into a Jewish family, Lene Schneider-Kainer studied in Vienna, Munich, Paris and Holland from 1914 to 1916. She married the painter Ludwig Kainer in 1910, but they separated in 1926. The same year she went to Asia, accompanied by the poet Bernhard Kellerman, and travelled across Persia, Tibet, the Indies, Siam and China. She was living in Berlin by the end of the 1920s. In 1931 she received the Villa Massimo prize. She fled from the political regime in 1932, first to the Balearic island of Ibiza, then in 1938 to the USA where she illustrated works; in 1954 she moved to Bolivia. She held an exhibition of her work in Berlin in 1917 at the Gurlitt gallery and regularly exhibited in the USA. In 2001 she was represented in the Los Angeles County Museum of Art exhibition *Women and Modernity: In and Around German Expressionism.* She painted landscapes and towns that she visited throughout her life, including Amsterdam, to which she devoted an album of lithographs. An artist who has been unjustifiably forgotten, her style combines the French Impressionist style with Expressionism. She also produced erotic engravings.

BIBLIOGRAPHY:

Dahmen, Sabine, *Leben und Werk der jüdischen Künstlerin Lene Schneider-Kainer im Berlin der zwanziger Jahre,* Ebersbach, Dortmund, 1999.

SCHNEIDERFRANKEN, Joseph, called Boyin Ra
German, 20th century.
Born 25 November 1876, in Aschaffenburg.
Painter, writer. Landscapes.

Joseph Schneiderfranken studied in Venice, in Munich under Gino Parin and at the Académie Julian in Paris under Tony Robert-Fleury and Jules Joseph Lefebvre. He lived and worked in Lugano. In 1920 he founded the Jacob Böhme Association.

He painted landscapes of Greece, Sweden and the natural park area of Spessart in Bavaria.

SCHNEIDERHAN, Maximilian
German, 19th - 20th century.
Born 19 May 1844, in Rexingen, near Horb; died 24 November 1923, in St Louis.
Sculptor.

Maximilian Schneiderhan studied under J.N. Meindel and with J. Knabl at the academy in Munich from 1866 until 1870.

He settled in America in 1870, living in Louisville, Washington and St Louis. He created a statue of the *Virgin* for the great altar in Lyons cathedral, and statues for the cathedral in Belleville and many churches in St Louis.

SCHNEIDERS, Carl
German, 20th century.
Born 19 February 1905, in Aachen.
Painter. Portraits, landscapes.
Carl Schneiders studied at the art schools in Weimar and Berlin. He was trained by Ulrich Hubner and Ernst Pfannschmidt. In 1935 he was awarded a prize by the academy of fine art for a *Self-portrait*.
MUSEUMS AND GALLERIES:
AACHEN: *Landscape*.

SCHNEIDERS VAN GREIJFFENSWERT, Bonifacius Cornelis
Dutch, 19th century.
Born 21 October 1804, in Gierikzee; died 1873.
Painter. Landscapes.
Bonifacius Cornelis Schneiders van Greijffenswert was a professional lawyer and studied painting with A. J. Couwenberg. He travelled and studied in Belgium and Germany before settling in Arnhem.
AUCTION RECORDS:
LOS ANGELES, 15 Oct 1979, *Still-life with Game* (1836, oil on card, 34 1/4 x 29 1/2 ins / 87 x 75 cm) USD 2,400. AMSTERDAM, 14 April 1986, *Wooded Landscape with Figures and Livestock* (oil on canvas, 49 1/4 x 44 ins / 125 x 112 cm) NLG 19,000.

SCHNEIDT, Max
German, 20th century.
Born 27 April 1858, in Geisenfeld; died 1937.
Active in the Netherlands.
Painter. Genre scenes.
Max Schneidt trained under Benezur, Lindenschmidt and Löfftz.

M Schneidt

SCHNEIT, Achille Hubert
French, 19th century.
Born in Paris.
Painter. History painting.
He was a pupil of Couder and Picot. He exhibited at the Paris Salon from 1843 to 1861.

SCHNELL, Bernard
Canadian, 20th - 21st century.
Born 1954, in Ottawa.
Active in Belgium.
Engraver, illustrator.
Bernard Schnell studied at the Cologne, Berlin, La Cambre and Watermael-Boitsfort academies. He uses the various techniques of engraving, mezzotint and etching.

SCHNELL, Elfriede
German, 19th - 20th century.
Born 8 April 1897, in Landsberg (Prussia); died 16 June 1930, in Königsberg (now Kaliningrad, Russia).
Painter.
Elfriede Schnell studied at the royal academy of fine arts in Königsberg from 1915 to 1918.

SCHNELL, Emanuel
German, 17th century.
Active during the second half of the 17th century in Augsburg and Lindau.
Painter.
Emanuel Schnell painted a number of portraits.

SCHNELL, Ferdinand or Franz
German, 18th century.
Born 1707, in Wessobrunn-Haid; died 30 October 1776, in Dorfen.
Stucco artist.

SCHNELL, Johann
Swiss, 17th - 18th century.
Born 28 April 1672, in Basel; died 24 November 1714, in Bristol (England).
Painter.

SCHNELL, Johann
German, 18th century.
Stucco artist.

SCHNELL, Johann Konrad (father and son)
German, 17th century.
Born respectively in 1646 and 1675
the father died in 1704, the son in 1726.
Painters.
The Schnells were father and son, both painters. The father did numerous portraits on enamel.

SCHNELL, Johann Michael
German, 18th century.
Born 1700, in Ansbach; died 2 October 1763, in Bayreuth.
Painter (porcelain/glazed earthenware).

SCHNELL, Ludwig Friedrich
German, 19th century.
Born c. 1790, in Darmstadt; died 14 June 1834, in Karlsruhe.
Painter, engraver, draughtsman.
Ludwig Schnell was the pupil and son-in-law of Chr. Haldenwang whom he succeeded as Court Engraver. He carried out line engravings of views of Heidelberg, Mannheim, Fribourg and Strasbourg. Among his key works is an engraving *The Cathedral of Strasbourg* after a drawing by August von Bayer.

SCHNELL, Martin
German, 18th century.
Died before 1740, probably in Warsaw.
Painter.
Martin Schnell worked around 1717 at the porcelain factory in Meissen. In about 1727 he was court painter at Dresden and later worked in Warsaw.

SCHNELL, Michael
Swiss, 17th century.
Stucco artist.
Michael Schnell worked in Obermarchtal and in the cloister of Rheinau.

SCHNELL, Michael
German, 18th century.
Born 1721, in Bartenbach; died 1785, in Augsburg.
Draughtsman, engraver (burin).
The pupil of Jakob Haid and son-in-law of Gottlieb Heiss, Michael Schnell engraved portraits, figures of saints and mythological subjects.

SCHNELL, Sebastian
German, 17th century.
Active in Freiburg.
Glass painter.

SCHNELL, Theodor
German, 19th century.
Born 18 May 1870, in Ravensburg.
Active in Ravensburg.
Sculptor, architect.
Theodor Schnell sculpted numerous altars for Catholic churches.

SCHNELLAWEG. See **MANG Hans**

SCHNELLBOLZ, Gabriel
German, 16th century.
Born c. 1536, in Wittenberg.
Engraver (wood).
Gabriel Schnellbolz is referred to by Ris-Paquot.

SCHNELLBOLZ, Hans
German, 16th century.
Active in Berlin c. 1576.
Illuminator.

SCHNELLENBUHEL, Gertraud von
German, 19th - 20th century.
Born 1878, in Jena; died 1959, in Dresden.
Draughtswoman. Designs (metalwork, jewellery, silverware).
Jugendstil.
Gertraud von Schnellenbuhel trained as a painter in Munich. She was later one of the first students at the school of art, Obrist unde Debschitz Lehr und Versuch-Ateliers für Angewandte und Freie Kunst, in Munich. She worked in the studio dedicated to metal. Influenced by August Endell and Hermann Obrist, she had a very linear version of Jugendstil decoration. Biographical information about her is lacking after World War I. Her best work is a candelabra with 24 branches, which was acquired by Obrist.
BIBLIOGRAPHY:
Bloom Hiesinger, Kathryn, *Art nouveau in Munich. Masters of Jugendstil,* exhibition catalogue, Museum of Art, Philadelphia, 1989.
MUSEUMS AND GALLERIES:
KARLSRUHE (Badisches Landesmus.): *Embroidery* (attributed) - MUNICH (Stadtmus.): *24- Branch Candelabra* (1910-1913, brass, silverplate).

SCHNELLER, Johannes
Austrian, 16th century.
Active in Carinthia in 1573.
Painter.

SCHNERB, Jacques Félix Simon
French, 19th - 20th century.
Born 15 September 1879, in Avignon; died 23 May 1915, near Ablain St-Nazaire.
Painter, engraver, art critic. Interiors, landscapes.
Initially Jacques Félix Simon Schnerb was an engraver and it was only later he turned to painting. He died in battle. From 1908 he exhibited landscapes of the South of France and Brittany in Paris at the Salon des Indépendants and the Salon d'Automne.
AUCTION RECORDS:
PARIS, 29 Nov 1948, *Interior,* FRF 2,000.

SCHNERR, Johann Christian
German, 18th century.
Born c. 1724; died 1795, in Dresden.
Painter.
Johann Schnerr worked in the porcelain factory in Meissen.

SCHNETOLER, Johann Ulrich.
See **SCHNETZLER Ulrich Johann**

SCHNETZ, Jean George
German, 18th - 19th century.
Born 1755, in Frankfurt am Main; died 1815.
Painter, engraver (etching).
Johann Schnetz engraved genre subjects and portraits.

SCHNETZ, Jean Victor
French, 19th century.
Born 14 April 1787, in Versailles; died 16 March 1870, in Paris.
Painter, watercolourist, pastellist, engraver. Religious subjects, portraits, genre scenes.
Jean Victor Schnetz studied with David, Regnault and Gros. He exhibited at the Salon between 1812 and 1867 and won first-class medals in 1819 and in 1855 at the Exposition Universelle. He made several trips to Italy and was appointed director of the Villa Medici in 1840. He worked in Paris for the churches of Notre Dame de Lorette and St-Séverin. He also made lithographs.

Some of his works portray popular scenes of Italian life, viewed from a grotesque perspective, which Baudelaire described as 'crude Italian paintings'. However, he also produced some small-scale compositions which are imbued with real vitality.

MUSEUMS AND GALLERIES:
AMIENS: *Episode from the Sack of Aquila by Attila; Monk Praying at the Bedside of a Sick Child* - ARRAS: *Esther and Mordecai* - BAGNÈRES-DE-BIGORRE: *Young Girl from Albano* - DOUAI: *Death of General Auguste Colbert* - NANTES: *Funeral of a Young Martyr in the Catacombs in Rome* - PARIS (Louvre): *Vow to the Madonna; Youth of Sixtus V;* antique ceramic ceiling; *Charlemagne Surrounded by His Chief Officers, Receiving Alcuin, Who is Presenting Him with Manuscripts Produced by His Monks;* Voussures; *Medallions of Pietro of Pisa, Roland, St Benedict of Aniane, Angilbert, and Geniuses of Science, Music, the Arts, War, and Civil and Religious Legislation* - RHEIMS: *Mazarin Bringing Colbert before Louis XIV* - ROUEN: *The Flood* - SEMUR-EN-AUXOIS: study - STRASBOURG: *Flight of Italian Peasants during the War* - TOULOUSE: *Boetius the Consul Bidding His Family Farewell* - VALENCIENNES: *Monk Supporting a Woman with a Wounded Foot* - VERSAILLES: *Count Eudes Defending Paris against the Normans; Henri Harcourt, Grand Equerry of France; Anne-Pierre Harcourt; J-A Mailly; Matignon; Battle of Rocroi; Fabert; Battle of Ascalon; Battle of Ceresole; Crusaders Arriving outside the Gates of Jerusalem; Procession of the Crusaders outside Jerusalem.*
AUCTION RECORDS:
PARIS, 24 March 1884, *Maria Grazia, Wife of a Brigand of the Roman State,* FRF 4,600. PARIS, 9 Nov 1938, *Trooper Plucking a Goose,* FRF 560. PARIS, 26 June 1950, *Portrait of Pope Pius VII* (pastel and watercolour, copied after David) FRF 1,600. VERSAILLES, 7 April 1974, *Death of a General,* FRF 4,200. PARIS, 27 Feb 1984, *Scene from History* (sepia, heightened with white, 9 x 9 ins / 22 x 22 cm) FRF 7,900. NEW YORK, 29 Oct 1986, *The Wounded Warrior* (black chalk and wash heightened with white/brown paper, 9 1/4 x 7 1/4 ins / 23.2 x 18.2 cm) USD 2,200. PARIS, 18 March 1987, *The Great Condé at the Battle of Rocroi* (pen and brown wash heightened with white gouache/pencil sketch, 11 1/2 x 17 1/4 ins / 29 x 44 cm) FRF 28,000. PARIS, 15 April 1988, *Roman Swordsman* (panel/canvas, 31 1/2 x 43 1/4 ins / 80 x 110 cm) FRF 12,000. NEW YORK, 26 Oct 1990, *Study of a Person Sleeping* (coloured chalks/paper, 8 1/2 x 9 3/4 ins / 21.6 x 24.8 cm) USD 4,400. PARIS, 11 June 2004, *Portrait of Monsieur Destouches* (1818, oil on canvas, 29 x 24 ins / 74 x 61 cm) EUR 6,500.

SCHNETZLER, Leonhard
Swiss, 18th century.
Born 19 May 1714, in Schaffhausen; died April 1772, in Oxford.
Painter, stucco artist.
Leonhard Schnetzler came to London in 1743 and ended his career in England.

SCHNETZLER, Ulrich Johann, or Schnätzler, Schnebbefer, Schnetoler
Swiss, 18th century.
Born 27 August 1704, in Schaffhausen; died 25 or 30 May 1763, in Schaffhausen.
Painter, stucco artist. Portraits.
After studying under J.J. Schärer, Ulrich Schnetzler studied for six years at the academy in Vienna. Between 1735 and 1739 he taught Em. Handmann in Schaffhausen. From 1747 to 1750 he worked in Bonn as a portraitist. Two of his portraits are in the Rathaus in Schaffhausen. He also executed a few pictures of historical subjects including *Pyramus and Thisbe* at the Kunstmuseum in Bern. In 1750 he returned to Schaffhausen where he ended his career. A house in the town shows two fresco cycles by him: *The Story of Joseph* and *Isaac and Jacob*.
MUSEUMS AND GALLERIES:
BERN (Kunstmus.): *Pyramus and Thisbe*.

SCHNEUER, David
Israeli, 20th century.
Born 1905, in Poland (formerly Austro-Hungaria); died 1988, in Tel Aviv.
Painter, lithographer, poster artist. Scenes with figures, figures. Stage sets, murals.
BIBLIOGRAPHY:
David Schneuer: graphic works: Munich and Tel Aviv, exhibition catalogue, The Israel Museum, Jerusalem, 1984 (text in English and Hebrew). "*David Schneuer*" in *Art et Métiers du Livre* n° 215, p. 90, periodical, Paris, 1999.
MUSEUMS AND GALLERIES:
BOSTON (Fine Art Mus.) - JERUSALEM (Israel Mus.) - MUNICH (Stadtmus.) - OSTEND (Mus. voor Moderne Kunst) - SALZBURG (Rupertinum) - TEL AVIV (MA).

SCHNEY, Fr. van
Flemish School, 17th century.
Active in 1610.
Painter. Still-lifes.
MUSEUMS AND GALLERIES:
BRUNSWICK: *Still-life* - CAMBRIDGE: *Still-life* - OSLO: *Still-life*.

SCHNEYDER, Anton
German, 18th century.
Active in Dresden c. 1763.
Painter. Portraits.

SCHNIDER. See also **SCHNEIDER**

SCHNIDER, Adolf
Swiss, 20th century.
Born 24 October 1890, in Basel.
Active in Germany.
Painter, engraver.
Adolf Schnider was trained by C. Bräger and Hugo Pfendsack. He worked in Paris from 1909 to 1911. In 1912 he travelled to Italy on a study tour, primarily to Florence, returning at the end of 1912 to the academy of fine art in Munich where he worked with H. Gröber and C. Bercker-Gundahl until the war. He lived and worked in Turbenthal near Winterthur.

SCHNIDER, Claus
German, 17th century.
Born 10 July 1633, in Meldorf; died 16 January 1685, in Meldorf.
Painter.

SCHNIDER, Wolfgang. See **SCHNEIDER**

SCHNIDTMANN, Anton
German, 18th century.
Died 1725.
Active in Neustadt.
Sculptor (wood).
Anton Schnidtmann was the father of Balthasar and worked mostly for local churches.

SCHNIDTMANN, Balthasar
German, 18th century.
Sculptor (wood).
Balthasar Schnidtmann was the son of Anton.

SCHNIRCH, Bohuslav
Bohemian School, 19th century.
Born 10 August 1845, in Prague; died 30 September 1901, in Prague.
Sculptor.
He studied under P. Grein, Fr. Bauer and M. von Widmann. He travelled in Italy from 1871 to 1873. He worked for the Rudolphinum and the museum of Bohemia in Prague.

SCHNITKER, Arp
German, 17th - 18th century.
Active from 1670 to 1700.
Sculptor (wood).

SCHNITKER, Jakob
German, 17th century.
Active in Katharinenheerd from 1614-1631.
Sculptor.

SCHNITKER, Johann
German, 17th century.
Active in Stedesand.
Sculptor.
Johann Schnitker can be compared to Johann von Groningen.

SCHNITKER, Lambrecht
German, 17th century.
Born 1591; died 1654.
Active in Tetenbull.
Sculptor.

SCHNITKER, Peter, or Sniker
German, 16th century.
Active in Flensburg c. 1577.
Sculptor.

SCHNITKER, Peter, called Peter Petersen, or Sniker
Danish, 17th century.
Died after 1697.
Sculptor.
Schnitker was the father of Peter Petersen. He worked in Tondern in Denmark.

SCHNITT, Conrad
Swiss, 16th century.
Born in Constance; died November 1541, in Basel.
Painter, draughtsman.

SCHNITTER, Johann
German, 17th century.
Active in Zittau.
Sculptor.
Johann Schnitter was a sculptor. In the church of Our Lady in Zittau is a *Christ on the Cross* and statues representing *Faith, Love* and *Hope*.

SCHNITTSPAHN, Ernst August
German, 19th century.

Born 17 April 1795, in Darmstadt; died 22 May 1882, in Darmstadt.
Painter, draughtsman.
Ernst Schnittspahn was a court painter and also did out stage-sets. He conjured up the past of old Darmstadt in a series of 40 watercolours belonging to the Grand Duke of Hessen.

SCHNITZ, Johann Josef. See **SCHMITZ**

SCHNITZER, Andras
Austrian, 16th century.
Active in Salzburg.
Sculptor.

SCHNITZER, Balzer
German, 16th century.
Sculptor.

SCHNITZER, Johann
German, 15th century.
Active in Arnhem c. 1486.
Engraver (wood).
Among the works of Johann Schnitzer, a Primitive, are the wood engravings for a volume published in Ulm in 1486. There is a map of the world in it which is decorated and the winds are represented by ten heads. It carries the words: *Insculptum est per Johannem Schnitzer de Arnhem.*

SCHNITZER, Johann
German, 20th century.
Born 25 March 1886, in Elmen.
Sculptor.
Johann Schnitzer lived and worked in Elmen.

SCHNITZER, Joseph Joachim von, or Schnizer
German, 19th century.
Born 19 March 1792, in Weingarten; died 30 April 1870, in Stuttgart.
Painter. Battles, portraits.
After attending the academy in Munich, Joseph Schnitzer fought in campaigns from 1813 to 1815 and was later appointed court painter at Würzburg.
MUSEUMS AND GALLERIES:
STUTTGART (Staatsgal.): *Portrait of A Child; Portrait of A Head; Line of Infantry in Action.*

SCHNITZER, Lukas
German, 17th century.
Active in Nuremberg between 1633 and 1671.
Painter, engraver. Urban landscapes.
This Lukas Schnitzer could be close to Lukas Schnitzer, active in Ulm around 1634.

SCHNITZER, Lukas
German, 17th century.
Active in Ulm c. 1634.
Engraver (burin).
He mainly engraved portraits and could be close to Lukas Schnitzer, active in Nuremberg between 1633 and 1671.

SCHNITZER, Sigmund
German, 16th century.
Died 1518, in Munich.
Painter. Portraits.
Sigmund Schnitzer was court painter and painted portraits of Duke Wilhelm IV of Bavaria and his brother Ludwig.

SCHNITZER, Theodor
German, 19th - 20th century.
Born 5 December 1866, in Stuttgart.
Painter, engraver.
Theodor Schnitzer trained under Jakob von Grunenwald and Friedrich von Keller.

SCHNITZLER, Christa von
German, 20th century.
Born 1922, in Cologne.
Sculptor.
Christa von Schnitzler studied at the art academy in Munich. She lived and worked in Frankfurt.

She exhibited with Munich's Neue Gruppe (New Group), and her work featured in group exhibitions, including *Der Andere Blick: Künstlerinnen des 20. Jahrhunderts (A Different Perspective: Women Artists of the 20th Century)* at the Diözesanmuseum in Trier. She has shown her work in solo exhibitions, including at Cologne's Kunstverein in 1958, the Günther Franke gallery in Munich in 1959 and 1963, at Wiesbaden's Landesmuseum in 1967, at the Von Laar gallery in Munich in 1979, and in 1990 at the Appel und Fertsch gallery in Frankfurt am Main.

Christa von Schnitzler produces full-size sculptures in bronze or wood in a very pure form. Her style of Abstraction is sober and she employs a sensitive, non-geometric line, subtly removing the emphasis on shape, and working on the substance.
BIBLIOGRAPHY:
Der andere Blick: Künstlerinnen des 20. Jahrhunderts, exhibition catalogue, Diözesanmuseum, Trier, 1998.

SCHNITZLER, Franz Xaver
German, 19th century.
Born to a family originally from Neuburg.
Painter.
Franz Schnitzler did two lateral altar paintings in the old church of Pfersee, near Augsburg.

SCHNITZLER, Leonhard
Austrian, 19th century.
Died 1907.
Glass painter.
Leonhard Schnitzler established glass painting at Dornbirn. There are several works by him in the museum in Bergenz.

SCHNITZLER, Michael Johann
German, 19th century.
Born 24 September 1782, in Neustadt (Oberpfalz); died 1 October 1861, in Munich.
Painter. Still-lifes, birds.
The son of a painter, Michael Schnitzler worked in Munich, Stuttgart, Augsburg and Ulm. As a painter of stage-sets, he was inspired by Hondekoeter.

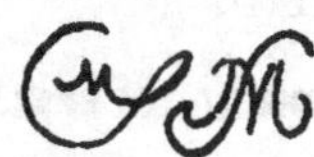

MUSEUMS AND GALLERIES:
MUNICH (Pinakothek): *Bird of Prey with Booty*; Dead birds, three paintings.

SCHNITZSPAHN, Christian
German, 19th century.
Born 6 December 1829, in Darmstadt; died 15 July 1877, in Darmstadt.
Medallist.
Christian Schnitzspahn did his artistic training at the academies in Munich, Berlin and London and was appointed Medallist at Darmstadt Court. He also became an honorary member of the academies in Vienna and St Petersburg.

SCHNOBEL, Johann
German, 17th century.
Active in Strakonitz c. 1652.
Painter.

SCHNOEDT, Carl Ludwig, or Schneet
German, 17th century.
Painter. Portraits.

Carl Schnoedt was in the service of the prince of Anhalt-Köthen in the 17th century and painted the portrait of Prince Karl Georg Lebrecht or his father August Ludwig.

SCHNÖLLER, Josef Anton
German, 19th century.
Born in Stockach.
Active in Munich from 1848 to 1877.
Sculptor.

SCHNOPS, Tomasz
Polish, 17th century.
Active in Vilna (now Vilnius, Lithuania).
Engraver (burin).

Tomasz Schnops painted the portraits of the bishop *Alex. Sapieha* and of the military governor *P.J. Sapieha.*

SCHNORR, Franz
German, 19th century.
Born 28 July 1794, in Schweinau, near Nuremberg; died 1859.
Painter, lithographer.

Franz Schnorr worked in Stuttgart from 1828 to 1845.

AUCTION RECORDS:
STUTTGART, 29 April 1974, *Königstrasse, Stuttgart,* DEM 22,000.

SCHNORR, Johann Daniel
German, 18th century.
Born 4 April 1717, in Frankfurt am Main; died 23 February 1784, in Frankfurt am Main.
Sculptor.

Johann Schnorr sculpted four angel musicians for the organ of the old church of St Peter in Frankfurt am Main.

SCHNORR, Peter
German, 19th - 20th century.
Born 26 April 1862, in Stuttgart; died 1 June 1912, in Stuttgart.
Painter, watercolourist, draughtsman, illustrator, writer. Posters.

Peter Schnorr produced watercolour illustrations for Wieland's *Oberon* and books by Karl May, including *Durch die Wüste.*

BIBLIOGRAPHY:
Osterwalder, Marcus (ed.), *Dictionnaire des illustrateurs 1800-1914,* Ides et Calendes, Neuchâtel, 1989.

MUSEUMS AND GALLERIES:
BIBERACH: watercolours.

SCHNORR VON CAROLSFELD, Hans Veit Friedrich
German, 18th - 19th century.
Born 11 May 1764, in Schneeberg; died 30 April 1841, in Leipzig.
Painter, engraver, draughtsman. Religious subjects, portraits.

Hans Schnorr von Carolsfeld studied law until 1789, when he became the pupil of Oeser in Leipzig. When his father died, he transferred to Königsberg (now Kaliningrad, Russia) where he focused exclusively on painting. In 1802 he visited Paris and Vienna and in 1803 he was appointed Professor of Drawing at the academy in Leipzig where he became Director in 1816.

He engraved portraits, genre scenes and mythological subjects, in particular, the illustrations to the works of Wieland and Klopstock. His three sons: Eduard, who died in 1819, Ludwig and Julius and his one daughter Ottilie were all painters.

MUSEUMS AND GALLERIES:
LEIPZIG: *St Peter Healing the Cripple; Portrait of Superintendent Dr. Tzschirner.*

SCHNORR VON CAROLSFELD, Julius Veit Hans
German, 19th century.
Born 26 March 1794, in Holzschnitt; died 24 May 1872, in Leipzig.
Painter, draughtsman. History painting.
Nazarenes group.

Julius Schnorr von Carolsfeld was the pupil of Hans Veit Schnorr. In 1811, he took up a teaching post at the academy in Vienna, leaving in 1812 for Italy. In Rome he was in close contact with Cornelius, Overbeck, Veit and Koch, sharing many of the ideas of this group of painters known as the Nazarenes.

When they obtained a significant commission for the decoration of the Villa Massimi in Rome, Schnorr von Carolsfeld was allocated the hall of Ariosto that he worked on from 1820 to 1825. He dedicated other frescoes to the Niebelunglied (German legend of the Niebelung).

His most romantic subjects convey an Italianate softness, which he probably learned from his close association with the Nazarenes - they were German pseudo-Pre-Raphaelites. However, the shading of the facial expressions of his characters is reminiscent of Dürer's drawings.

In 1825 he was summoned to teach at the academy in Munich, but took up the post in 1827, after visiting Sicily. In 1846 he became Professor at the Dresdner Akademie and Director of the picture gallery there. In 1851 he went to London where he received the commission for his famous Bible. He was also responsible for the cartoons on windows of St Paul's Cathedral.

Schnorr von Carolsfeld had a number of pupils and was a member of the academies in Berlin, Dresden and Munich. In 1871 he lost his sight.

MUSEUMS AND GALLERIES:
BASEL: *Chriemhild's Complaints; Domine, Quo Vadis?* - BERLIN: *Annunciation* - BREMEN: *Cavalry Combat; The Six Contests on the Island of Lipadusa* - COLOGNE: *The Virgin* - DRESDEN: *The Family of St John the Baptist with the Holy Family; View of Salzburg; Ananias Visiting Paul* - FRANKFURT AM MAIN: *The Good Samaritan;* 10 cartoons, subjects taken from Arioste's poem Roland The Furious - MUNICH: *Scene from the 'Niebelungenlied'* - STUTTGART: *Siegfried's Victorious Return Home.*

AUCTION RECORDS:
STUTTGART, 29 Nov 1957, *Italian Landscape* (pen) DEM 5,300. MUNICH, 24 Nov 1973, *Virgin and Child,* DEM 17,000. MUNICH, 28 Nov 1974, *Scene from the 'Niebelungenlied'* (1840) DEM 5,500. MUNICH, 30 May 1979, *St Elisabeth Helping to Build a Hospital* (watercolour/pencil outlines, 13 1/2 x 9 ins / 34 x 23 cm) DEM 2,600. MUNICH, 28 Nov 1979, *Mounted Horseman Arriving* (1819, pen/pencil outlines, 6 1/4 x 9 1/2 ins / 16 x 24 cm) DEM 97,000. COLOGNE, 21 May 1981, *Naked Child* (pencil and chalk, 7 1/4 x 5 1/2 ins / 18.5 x 14 cm) DEM 2,000. LONDON, 23 June 1983, *Noah Leaving the Ark* (1826, pen and brown ink/traces of pencil, 8 1/2 x 10 1/4 ins / 21.5 x 26 cm) GBP 2,800. LONDON, 27 Nov 1986, *Rebecca and Eliezer Meeting Isaac* (1842, pen and grey ink, 10 1/2 x 9 ins / 26.5 x 22 cm) GBP 10,500. LONDON, 24 June 1987, *Moses Slaying the Egyptian* (1828, pen and brown ink, 8 1/2 x 10 ins / 21.5 x 25.5

cm) GBP 7,500. HEIDELBERG, 14 Oct 1988, *St John the Baptist Preaching in the Wilderness* (1853, ink, 10 x 10 3/4 ins / 24.5 x 27.5 cm) DEM 7,800. LONDON, 30 Nov 1990, *Virgin and Child* (1855, oil on canvas, 27 1/4 x 18 1/2 ins / 69.2 x 47 cm) GBP 16,500. NEW YORK, 22-23 July 1993, *Two Male Nudes* (1815, ink and pencil/paper heightened with white, 24 1/4 x 16 1/2 ins / 61.3 x 41.9 cm) USD 4,025. LONDON, 11 Feb 1994, *Aristides in his Study* (1842, pencil and watercolour/paper, 10 1/4 x 9 ins / 26 x 23 cm) GBP 9,200. HEIDELBERG, 5-13 April 1994, *Recumbent Male Nude* (1833, pencil, 10 3/4 x 17 1/4 ins / 27.2 x 43.5 cm) DEM 6,800. LONDON, 11 Oct 1995, *The End of the 'Niebelungenlied' - Death of Kriemhilde* (1845, ink and wash/paper/canvas, 22 1/4 x 25 ins / 56.5 x 63.5 cm) GBP 6,900. NEW YORK, 24 Oct 1996, *Ruth Gleaning in the Field of Boaz* (1828, oil on canvas, 23 1/4 x 27 1/2 ins / 59.1 x 69.8 cm) USD 228,000. HAMBURG, 7 June 2000, *The Flood* (1851, pen, 9 x 10 ins / 22 x 26 cm) DEM 8,500. LONDON, 29 June 2000, *Besiegung Wittekind bei Burberg* (1835, pencil, red chalk and wash, 22 x 26 ins / 55 x 65 cm) GBP 36,000. NEW YORK, 24 Jan 2001, *Nude Male in Profile* (pen and brown ink, 16 x 11 ins / 41 x 28 cm) USD 18,000. BERLIN, 18 May 2001, *Abraham Surveys the Promised Land* (pen, 9 x 10 ins / 23 x 26 cm) DEM 13,000. BERLIN, 31 May 2002, *Return of Heyden* (1839, pen over pencil, 6 x 8 ins / 16 x 20 cm) EUR 2,000. HAMBURG, 7 Dec 2002, *Pavias Conquest* (1840, pen over pencil, ochre and sepia wash, 18 x 26 ins / 46 x 65 cm) EUR 68,000. NEW YORK, 22 Jan 2003, *Crucifixion* (1843, chalk and wash, 27 x 24 ins / 69 x 60 cm) USD 35,000. HEIDELBERG, 11 April 2003, *David and Bathsheba Mourning their Son* (pen over pencil, 8 x 10 ins / 21 x 26 cm) EUR 4,400. HAMBURG, 11 June 2004, *Julius Macabeer Conquering the Enemy and Cleaning out the Temple* (pen over pencil, 8 x 10 ins / 21 x 26 cm) EUR 6,000. BERLIN, 19 June 2004, *Three Figures from the Nibelungen* (oil on canvas, 17 x 21 ins / 43 x 53 cm) EUR 3,400.

SCHNORR VON CAROLSFELD, Ludwig Ferdinand

German, 19th century.

Born 11 October 1788, in Leipzig; died 13 April 1853, in Vienna.

Painter, engraver, draughtsman. Religious subjects, portraits.

The son of Hans and brother of Julius and Eduard Schnorr, Ludwig was initially his father's pupil and after that worked in the academy in Vienna. He adopted Fuger's style and engraved a few etchings.

MUSEUMS AND GALLERIES:

BERLIN: *Portrait of Johannes Leth; Madonna* - DRESDEN: *Portrait of Old Man; Small Half-length Portrait* - INNSBRUCK (Tiroler Landesmus. Ferdinandeum): *Tyrolean Peasants Revolt by Andreas Hofer* - LINZ: *St Cecilia* - LUTZSCHENA: *Portrait of a Man; Götz von Berlichingen* - MUNICH: *King of the Alders* - VIENNA (Erzbischöfliches Dom- und Diözesanmus.): *St Peter in Prison* - VIENNA (Österreichische Gal. Belvedere): *The Large Pine Tree of Mödling; Temptation of the Lord; Faust, Prison Scene; Return of the Horseman; Horseman Leaving; Hermit* - WASHINGTON DC (Georgetown University): *Three Marys at the Tomb of Christ* (c. 1835, oil on canvas) - WROCLAW: *Holy Family*.

AUCTION RECORDS:

BERLIN, 1 -2 April 1966, *Rest on the Flight into Egypt*, DEM 4,800. MUNICH, 11 June 1970, *Marriage of Ondine*, DEM 3,400. COLOGNE, 15 June 1973, *Christopher Columbus on the Saint Mary*, DEM 8,500. LONDON, 24 March 1988, *Romeo and Juliet* (1820, pencil, charcoal and white gouache, 11 x 7 3/4 ins / 27 x 19.5 cm) GBP 825. MUNICH, 27 Feb 1999, *Archduke Ferdinand Meets his Bride Philippine Welser* (oil on canvas, 33 x 27 ins / 84 x 68 cm) DEM 40,000. DÜSSELDORF, 31 Jan 2000, *Christ Risen from the Dead* (1837, oil on canvas, 23 x 15 ins / 59 x 38 cm) DEM 22,000. DÜSSELDORF, 31 Jan 2000, *Return of the Prodigal Son* (1838, oil on canvas, 31 x 36 ins / 80 x 91 cm) DEM 65,000.

SCHNUG, Leo

French, 20th century.

Born 17 February 1878, in Strasbourg; died 18 December 1933.

Painter, engraver. History painting.

Leo Schnug was a pupil at the École des Beaux-Arts, Strasbourg, and the Gysis, Munich. He painted murals in the girls' school of Lõwenbrau and the Kammerzell House, Strasbourg.

MUSEUMS AND GALLERIES:

STRASBOURG: *The Banner of Strasbourg at the Battle of Hansbergen*.

SCHNUPP, R.

German, 19th century.

Lithographer.

R. Schnupp's lithographs conjure up the past of Hessen.

SCHNUPP-PFAFF, Gerhard

German, 20th century.

Born 22 February 1899, in Alzey.

Painter. Landscapes.

Gerhard Schnupp-Pfaff lived and worked in Goldentraum near Greifenberg (Silesia). The Hessian state and the towns of Darmstadt and Giessen have several of his works.

SCHNUR, Marie

German, 19th - 20th century.

Born 19 February 1869.

Painter. Portraits, genre scenes, still-lifes.

Marie Schnur studied in Berlin under G. Fehr, and in Munich under Schmid-Reutte and W. Durr.

SCHNURER, Johann Georg

German, 18th century.

Born 1678; died 9 February 1745, in Bayreuth.

Painter.

Johann Schnurer's widow Marguerite and his daughters were involved in the decoration of the chapel of the hospital at Bayreuth and his son Matthias Heinrich painted a number of portraits kept in Bayreuth's castles.

SCHNYDER, Albert

Swiss, 20th century.

Born 1898, in Delsberg; died 1989, in Delsberg.

Painter (gouache), draughtsman. Landscapes, landscapes with figures, mountainscapes.

Albert Schnyder was a member of the Swiss Society of Painters and Sculptors. He mainly painted landscapes of the Jura and the Doubs region of France.

MUSEUMS AND GALLERIES:

AARAU (Aargauer Kunsthaus): *Der Nadelberg Basel* (1960).

AUCTION RECORDS:

ZURICH, 12 Nov 1976, *Jura Landscape* (1964, oil on canvas, 23 1/2 x 28 3/4 ins / 60 x 73 cm) CHF 12,000. BERN, 9 June 1977, *Rustic Swing* (1956, oil on canvas, 23 1/2 x 32 ins / 60 x 81 cm) CHF 15,000. BERN, 26 Oct 1979, *Policeman's House* (1944, pencil, 14 3/4 x 21 1/4 ins / 37.7 x 54.2 cm) CHF 1,900. ZURICH, 22 May 1980, *Stream* (1978, oil on canvas, 21 1/2 x 25 1/2 ins / 54.5 x 65 cm) CHF 24,000. ZURICH, 11 Nov 1981, *Crossroads* (1966, oil on canvas, 19 x 42 1/2 ins / 48.5 x 108 cm) CHF 29,000. ZURICH, 10 Nov 1984, *Farm on the Roadside* (1964, oil on canvas, 14 1/4 x 46 ins / 36.5 x 116 cm) CHF 30,000. BERN, 26 Oct 1985, *Six Farms* (1966, oil on canvas, 19 3/4 x 39 1/4 ins / 50 x 100 cm) CHF 28,000. BERN, 20 June 1986, *Farmhouse in Büre* (1943, oil on canvas, 23 3/4 x 29 1/4 ins / 60.5 x 74 cm) CHF 14,000. BERN, 12 May 1990, *Two Farms in Jura* (1956, gouache, 12 3/4 x 18 ins / 32.5 x 45.5 cm) CHF 7,000. ZURICH, 4 June 1992, *House in the Gorges* (1961, oil on canvas, 28 3/4 x 36 ins / 73 x 91.5 cm) CHF 14,690. ZURICH, 24 June 1993, *Horses near Cerlatez* (oil on panel, 9 1/2 x 51 1/2 ins / 24 x 131 cm) CHF 19,000. ZURICH, 24 Nov 1993, *Field Landscape in Doubs* (1964, oil on canvas, 29 1/4 x 36 1/2 ins / 74 x 93 cm) CHF 20,700. ZURICH, 5 June 1996, *Boys by the Side of a Stream* (1939-1940, oil on canvas, 26 1/2 x 30 1/2 ins / 67.5 x 77.5 cm) CHF 28,750. BERN, 20-21 June 1996, *The Bridge of St-Ursanne* (c. 1930, oil on canvas, 16 1/4 x 21 3/4 ins / 41 x 55.5 cm) CHF 12,500. ZURICH, 18 Nov 1997, *Farm in the Freibergen* (1949-1950, oil on canvas, 9 1/4 x 51 3/4 ins / 23.5 x 131.5 cm) CHF 17,000. BERN, 7 May 1999, *Village* (oil on canvas, 20 x 39 ins / 50 x 100 cm) CHF 17,000. ZURICH, 8 June 1999, *Village Edge* (1962, oil on canvas, 26 x 39 ins / 65 x 100 cm) CHF 27,000. ZURICH, 29 May 2000, *Summer Landscape* (oil on canvas, 24 x 29 ins / 60 x 73 cm) CHF 15,000. BERN, 3 Nov 2000, *In the Gorges* (1961, oil on board, 24 x 29 ins / 61 x 73 cm) CHF 21,000. ST GALL, 8 May 2001, *River Landscape* (oil on canvas, 21 x 26 ins / 54 x 65 cm) CHF 15,000. BERN, 11 May 2001, *Fir Forest* (oil on canvas, 24 x 43 ins / 61 x 108 cm) CHF 24,000. ST GALL, 22 May 2002, *Landscape with Grey Clouds* (1967, oil on canvas, 26 x 36 ins / 66 x 92 cm) CHF 20,000. BERN, 8 Nov 2002, *Rocks at Vicques* (oil on panel, 29 x 36 ins / 73 x 92 cm) CHF 15,000. BERN, 9 May 2003, *Les Franches-Montages* (1978, oil on canvas, 20 x 39 ins / 50 x 100 cm) CHF 13,000. BERN, 7 Nov 2003, *Hamlet* (oil on canvas, 23 x 57 ins / 59 x 146 cm) CHF 13,000. BERN, 14 May 2004, *In Ajoie* (oil on canvas, 29 x 36 ins / 73 x 92 cm) CHF 16,000. BERN, 14 May 2004, *Summer Landscape* (oil on canvas, 29 x 58 ins / 73 x 147 cm) CHF 19,000.

SCHNYDER, Anton
Swiss, 19th century.
Born 30 May 1823, in Lucerne; died 17 January 1897, in Lucerne.
Sculptor, medallist, goldsmith.

SCHNYDER, Heinrich
Swiss, 17th century.
Died c. 1615, in Schaffhausen.
Active in Schaffhausen.
Glass painter.

He set himself up as a master in Schaffhausen.

SCHNYDER, Heinrich
Swiss, 17th century.
Died 8 August 1616, in Rapperswil.
Active in Rapperswil.
Glass painter.

He was the pupil of the glass painter Franz Fallenter in Lucerne.

MUSEUMS AND GALLERIES:
ZURICH (Schweizerisches Landesmus.): *The Good Samaritan*.

SCHNYDER, Jean-Frédéric
Swiss, 20th century.
Born 1945, in Basel.
Painter, sculptor of assemblages, installation artist.
Nudes, landscapes, still-lifes.
Conceptual Art.

Jean Frédéric Schnyder settled in Bern, where he teaches photography. From 1967 he worked in a Pop Art or Neo-Realist style. Shortly before 1970 he created conceptually inspired objects rather like those the Surrealists produced, involving the participation of the spectator and entailing mirrors, fur and other materials which appeal to the physical senses of sight, touch and smell and make the viewer aware of his own perceptions. Since 1970 he has resorted to painting, to create parodies of three major genres - the nude, landscapes and still-lifes. He has been represented in collective exhibitions including *Environnements* (*Surroundings*) at the Kunsthalle, Bern (1968), at the Paris Biennale in 1971 and at the Nouvelle Biennale in 1975.

BIBLIOGRAPHY:
Kneubühler, Theo, *Kunst: 28 Schweizer*, exhibition catalogue, Gal. Raeber, Lucerne, 1972. *Nouvelle Biennale de Paris*, exhibition catalogue, Electa, Le Moniteur, Paris, 1985.

AUCTION RECORDS:
FRANKFURT AM MAIN, 14 June 1994, *Snowman No. 449* (1987, oil on canvas, 16 1/2 x 11 3/4 ins / 42 x 30 cm) DEM 8,000. LUCERNE, 8 June 1996, *Habkern* (1989, oil on canvas, 8 1/4 x 11 3/4 ins / 21 x 30 cm) CHF 3,200.

SCHNYDER, Walter
Swiss, 20th century.
Born 9 September 1873, in Grenchen (Solothurn).
Painter. Landscapes.

In 1893 Walter Schnyder settled in Onsingen.

SCHNYDER VON WARTENSEE, Jost
Swiss, 19th century.
Born 16 June 1822, in Lucerne; died 11 July 1894, in Lucerne.
Painter. Figures, landscapes with figures, landscapes, mountainscapes.

Jost Schnyder von Wartensee was taught by R. Zund and J. Schwegler.

AUCTION RECORDS:
LUCERNE, 8 Nov 1984, *Goat girl in Alpine Landscape* (1860, oil on panel, 18 x 14 1/2 ins / 46 x 37 cm) CHF 7,500.

SCHNYDER VON WARTENSEE, Ludwig
Swiss, 19th century.
Born 25 February 1858, in Lucerne.
Active in Lucerne.
Decorative artist.

A pupil and then teacher at the art school in Lucerne, Ludwig Schnyder travelled to Munich and Salzburg to study. His brother, who was born on 26 October 1859 in Lucerne and died there on 7 September 1894, worked with him.

SCHOBBENS, Alexander Franciscus
Flemish School, 18th century.
Born 9 October 1720, in Antwerp; died 15 November 1781, in Antwerp.
Sculptor.

Alexander Franciscus Schobbens was a pupil of Alex van Papenhoven and also studied at the Académie Royale in Paris. A master in the guild of Antwerp from October 1751, he was also director of the academy of Antwerp from 1752 to 1780. He executed a number of tombs, including the Borsbeke family monument in the church of St Walpurgis in Antwerp. Other works include a *Virgin* for the parish church of Verdun, and two marble figures, *Hope* and *Charity*, for the church of St Michael in Ghent.

SCHÖBEL
German, 18th century.
Active in Weilitzken in East Prussia c. 1700.
Sculptor.

SCHÖBEL, Georg
German, 19th - 20th century.
Born 10 December 1860 or 1858, in Berlin.
Painter, illustrator. History painting, genre scenes.

In 1884 Georg Schöbel was a pupil at the art academy in Berlin and was influenced by Meyerheim and Adolf Menzel.

He mainly painted scenes from the life of Frederick II, and from 1914 onwards depicted World War I scenes on the Western front.

AUCTION RECORDS:
PARIS, 18 May 1897, *Christmas Eve in Berlin*, FRF 250. LONDON, 28 Nov 1985, *Christmas Day* (watercolour, 12 1/4 x 19 1/4 ins / 31 x 49 cm) GBP 2,800. MUNICH, 22 March 2000, *Once I Had a Friend and Comrade* (oil on canvas, 29 x 22 ins / 73 x 55

cm) DEM 4,250. KÖNIGSTEIN, 25 May 2001, *Frederick II Speaking to Voltaire* (oil on canvas, 33 x 26 ins / 85 x 66 cm) DEM 7,000.

SCHÖBEL, Karl Friedrich
German, 19th century.
Born to a family originally from Ludwigslust.
Painter. Landscapes, architectural views.
In 1835 Karl Schöbel studied under Blechen.

SCHOBELT, Paul
German, 19th century.
Born 9 March 1838, in Magdeburg; died 3 May 1893, in Breslau (now Wroclaw, Poland).
Painter. Mythological subjects, genre scenes, portraits.
Paul Schobelt attended the academies of Düsseldorf and Berlin and studied under Gleyre in Paris. The Prussian government awarded him a scholarship that enabled him to continue his studies in Italy. He settled in Breslau where he taught. Among his works are *The Rape of Proserpine* and *The Triumph of Genius*.
AUCTION RECORDS:
MUNICH, 10 May 1989, *Two Little Girls with Cherries* (1892, oil on canvas, 37 1/2 x 28 1/4 ins / 95.5 x 72 cm) DEM 9,900.

SCHOBER
German, 18th century.
Active in Helchenbach.
Engraver. Portraits.

SCHOBER, Franz von
Swedish, 19th century.
Born 17 May 1796, near Malmö; died 13 August 1882, in Dresden.
Poet, writer, draughtsman, lithographer.
Schober lived in Weimar from 1843 to 1853. There he befriended Liszt, and often travelled to Dresden. He is known for his design of Schubert's tomb in the Währing cemetery.

SCHOBER, Hans Wilhelm
German, 16th century.
Painter.
There is reference to Hans Wilhelm Schober working in the court of Dresden.

SCHOBER, Hermann
Austrian, 18th - 19th century.
Painter.
Hermann Schober is mainly known for his floral compositions on porcelain made at the porcelain factory in Vienna from 1795 to 1836.

SCHOBER, Joseph
Austrian, 19th century.
Active c. 1802.
Miniaturist.

SCHOBER, Peter Jakob
German, 20th century.
Born 13 December 1897, in Gschmend (Franconia).
Painter, engraver. Genre scenes, landscapes with figures, flowers.
Peter Jakob Schober was a pupil of Poetzelberger, Landenberger, Altherr and Eckner. In 1932 he became an assistant lecturer at the Stuttgart academy. He lived and worked in Stuttgart.
MUSEUMS AND GALLERIES:
STUTTGART (Staatsgal.): *Picnic; Hyacinths* - ULM: *Lake Constance Landscape*.
AUCTION RECORDS:
MUNICH, 31 May 1983, *Spring Landscape* (1948, oil on canvas, 20 x 24 ins / 50.5 x 61 cm) DEM 3,400. STUTTGART, 18 Sept 2003, *Fishing Boats in Venice Harbour* (1924, oil on board, 20 x 24 ins / 50 x 60 cm) EUR 1,600. STUTTGART, 30 April 2004, *Southern Landscape with Buildings and Figures* (oil on canvas, 25 x 30 ins / 64 x 76 cm) EUR 2,400. STUTTGART, 30 April 2004, *Still-life with Flowers* (oil on canvas, 32 x 26 ins / 81 x 65 cm) EUR 2,800.

SCHOBINGER, Karl Friedrich
Swiss, 20th century.
Born 14 December 1879, in Lucerne; died 1951, in Lucerne.
Painter. Allegorical subjects, figures.
Karl Friedrich Schobinger studied in Lucerne, then in Geneva in 1904. From 1911 to 1914 he was a professor at the Art School in Breslau, Silesia (now Wroclaw, Poland).

K. F. Schobinger

MUSEUMS AND GALLERIES:
ZURICH: *The Sin of Mankind*.
AUCTION RECORDS:
LUCERNE, 19 May 1983, *Swiss Soldiers* (1935, gouache, 22 3/4 x 44 1/4 ins / 58 x 112.5 cm) CHF 15,000. LUCERNE, 30 Sept 1988, *Swiss Guard* (distemper, 17 1/4 x 11 ins / 44 x 27 cm) CHF 2,000. BERN, 5 Nov 1999, *Wooded Hilltop under Cloudy Sky* (oil on canvas, 23 x 26 ins / 59 x 67 cm) CHF 3,000. LUCERNE, 15 May 2002, *Country Boys* (tempera and goldleaf on canvas, 23 x 44 ins / 58 x 111 cm) CHF 5,000. LUCERNE, 9 Nov 2002, *De Saulipuur* (*Old Man in Rustic Interior*) (1916, oil on canvas, 40 x 35 ins / 102 x 90 cm) CHF 8,000.

SCHOBINGER, Leo
German, 20th century.
Born 22 July 1897, in Hemigkofen (Baden-Württemberg).
Painter. Genre scenes, landscapes with figures.
Leo Schobinger was trained by Waldschmidt, Landenberger and Altherr.
MUSEUMS AND GALLERIES:
STUTTGART: *Coffee in the Castle Garden; Landscape*.

SCHOBIUS, Christian or Christjern
Danish, 19th century.
Born 5 October 1872, in Aalborg; died 7 June 1900, in Copenhagen.
Painter. Figures, landscapes.
Schobius was a pupil of Kristian Zahrtmann.
MUSEUMS AND GALLERIES:
COPENHAGEN (Statens Mus. for Kunst): *Tilhørere i en landsbykirke* (*In the Village Church*) (1894); *Pige, der læser et brev* (*Young Girl Reading*) (1898).

SCHOCH, Abraham
German, 18th century.
Born 1724; died 1772.
Active in Augsburg.
Painter, engraver (burin). Portraits.
Abraham Schoch engraved a portrait of *Stanislaw August*, King of Poland.

SCHOCH, Karl
German, 19th century.
Born 8 September 1848, in Burgdorf; died 23 March 1903, in Munich.
Painter (porcelain). Landscapes.
Karl Schoch was a pupil of Lips. He worked in Thur and Munich.

SCHOCHER, Jozsef
18th century.
Active in Grosswardein (now Oradea, Romania).
Painter.

SCHÖCHLIN-RÖMER, Bertha
Maiden name: Römer
Swiss, 19th - 20th century.

Born 22 September 1860, in Biel (Bern).
Painter. Landscapes, still-lifes, flowers.
Bertha Schöchlin-Römer trained under Auguste Bachelin, Paul Volmar and Wilhelm Benteli. She travelled to Panama and Chilli, later settling in Biel. She was a drawing teacher.

In 1890 she won prizes at the Santiago and Valparaíso exhibitions.

SCHOCK, Michael
Austrian, 19th century.
Born to a family originally from Ried.
Active c. 1818.
Painter.

SCHOCKEN, Wilhelm
German, 20th century.
Born 1874, in Pleschen (now Pleszew, Poland).
Painter, engraver.
Wilhelm Schocken was also a doctor of philosophy. He lived and worked in Berlin.

He composed a series of seventeen wood engravings for the *Lamentations of Jeremiah*.

SCHOCKHATNIG, Joseph.
See **SCHOKOTNIGG**

SCHOCKHOLZ, Kaspar
German, 15th century.
Active c. 1446.
Sculptor (wood).

SCHÖDL, Heinrich
Austrian, 19th century.
Born 1777, in Tachau; died 1838, in Prague.
Miniaturist. Portraits.
Heinrich Schödl attended the academy in Prague.

SCHÖDL, Martin. See **SCHEDEL Martin**

SCHÖDLBERGER, Johann Nepomuk, or Schödelberger
Austrian, 19th century.
Born 1779, in Vienna; died 26 January 1853, in Vienna.
Painter, engraver (etching). Church interiors, landscapes with figures, landscapes, architectural views.
Johann Schödlberger engraved etchings of landscapes. After travelling a great deal to study, he settled in Vienna where he became a member of the academy in 1835.

MUSEUMS AND GALLERIES:
GRAZ: *Arcadian Landscape* - INNSBRUCK: *Southern Landscape* - VIENNA: *Interior of Italian Church; Burial Vault; The Traun Fall at Gmunden; Ideal Landscape; The Cascade at Tivoli.*

AUCTION RECORDS:
PARIS, 30 May 1973, *Arcadian Landscape,* FRF 11,000. VIENNA, 19 Sept 1978, *Shepherds in Italian Landscape* (oil on canvas, $24\frac{1}{2}$ x $34\frac{1}{2}$ ins / 62 x 87.5 cm) ATS 90,000. VIENNA, 18 Sept 1979, *Merry Gathering in Mountainous Landscape* (1833, oil on canvas, $13\frac{1}{2}$ x $16\frac{1}{2}$ ins / 34 x 42 cm) ATS 45,000. LONDON, 21 June 1983, *Arcadian Landscape* (1810, oil on canvas, $61\frac{1}{2}$ x $83\frac{3}{4}$ ins / 156 x 213 cm) GBP 11,000. LONDON, 10 Oct 1984, *Card-players in a landscape* (oil on canvas, $35\frac{1}{2}$ x 49 ins / 90 x 124.5 cm) GBP 1,500. LUCERNE, 23 May 1985, *Wooded Landscape with Figures* (1815, oil on canvas, 30 x $37\frac{1}{4}$ ins / 76 x 94.5 cm) CHF 27,000. VIENNA, 29-30 Oct 1996, *Classical Landscape with Peasants on Path and Temple and Village in Distance* (oil on canvas, $26\frac{3}{4}$ x 37 ins / 68 x 94 cm) ATS 195,500. VIENNA, 20 May 1999, *View of Hallstadt, Lake Landscape, Logs Floating at Shore* (1834, oil on board, 19 x 25 ins / 49 x 63 cm) ATS 30,000. VIENNA, 3 Oct 2001, *Idyllic Landscape with Ruins* (oil on canvas, one of a pair, 28 x 35 ins / 71 x 88 cm) ATS 180,000. VIENNA, 28 Nov 2002, *Extensive Landscape at Dusk* (1816, oil on canvas, 20 x 26 ins / 50 x 65 cm) EUR 7,000. VIENNA, 24 Nov 2003, *Evening Prayer in the Mountains* (1826, oil on canvas, 14 x 17 ins / 35 x 42 cm) EUR 3,300.

SCHÖDLER, Johann Georg. See **SCHEDLER**

SCHODT, J. Sigmund. See **SCHOTT**

SCHOEBROECK, Pieter.
See **SCHOUBROECK**

SCHOECK, Alfred
Swiss, 19th century.
Born 4 December 1841, in Basel.
Active in Brunnen.
Painter. Landscapes.
Alfred Schoeck studied in Basel with F. Horner and in Paris with Fr. Diday. After that, he travelled in Norway, Hungary, the Balkans and Canada.

SCHOEDDER, Paul Hermann
German, 20th century.
Born 17 November 1887, in Iserlohn (North Rhine-Westphalia).
Painter, engraver. Portraits, landscapes.
Paul Hermann Schoedder lived and worked in Munich. He was a pupil of Alois Rolf, Tentsch and Becker-Gundahl.

AUCTION RECORDS:
COLOGNE, 21 March 1980, *Bouquet of Flowers* (1939, oil on panel, $39\frac{1}{4}$ x 30 ins / 100 x 76 cm) DEM 2,000. LONDON, 12 June 1997, *Poppies, Daisies, Irises, Sweet Williams and Peonies in a Vase* (1930, oil on panel, $41\frac{1}{2}$ x $34\frac{1}{4}$ ins / 105.5 x 87 cm) GBP 3,220.

SCHOEDL, Max, or Schödl
Austrian, 19th - 20th century.
Born 1834, in Vienna; died March 1921.
Painter. Still-lifes.
Max Schoedl was a pupil of Friedrich Friedlander von Malheim at the Viennese Art Academy. He worked in Vienna, Paris, London and Italy. He was awarded a medal in Sydney in 1879.

MUSEUMS AND GALLERIES:
MUNICH - SYDNEY - VIENNA.

AUCTION RECORDS:
NEW YORK, 21 and 22 Jan 1909, *Still-life,* USD 200. VIENNA, 21 Sept 1971, *Objets d'art from the Far East,* ATS 32,000. LONDON, 13 June 1973, *Still-life of Books,* GBP 600. VIENNA, 16

March 1976, *Still-life* (1878, oil on panel, 7½ x 5½ ins / 19 x 14 cm) ATS 30,000. LONDON, 4 May 1977, *Still-life* (oil on panel, 11 x 9½ ins / 28 x 24 cm) GBP 1,050. LOS ANGELES, 22 June 1981, *Still-life of Fruit and Champagne* (1887, oil on panel, 7¾ x 5½ ins / 19.5 x 14 cm) USD 5,250. ROME, 10 Dec 1991, *Still-life with a Helmet* (oil on panel, 19 x 12½ ins / 48 x 31.5 cm) ITL 4,600,000. LONDON, 16 June 1993, *The Artist's Studio* (1906, oil on panel, 12½ x 9½ ins / 32 x 24 cm) GBP 3,105. MUNICH, 21 June 1994, *Still-life* (1881, oil on panel, 13½ x 10 ins / 34 x 25.5 cm) DEM 4,600. NEW YORK, 17 Jan 1996, *Still-life with a Champagne Flute* (oil on panel, 12¾ x 9½ ins / 32.4 x 24.1 cm) USD 920.

SCHOEFF, Jean, or Schooff
Flemish School, 16th century.
Born c. 1475, in Mechelen; died after 1533, probably in Mechelen.
Painter.
Mechelen School.

Jean Schoeff was a Primitive and is first mentioned in the public accounts of Mechelen for 1504-1505. In the following year his name occurs in the registers with the official title of city painter. He was engaged in various decorative works, the restoration of paintings, the gilding and painting of statues, and decorations for processions. In 1514-1515 the city commissioned a painting for the Treasury Room that was to depict the judicial court at the time of its foundation and to include portraits of those present at the occasion. Before World War I this painting was preserved in the city's archives. According to the research of A. J. Wauters, upon whose work this biography largely depends, the painting, its signature and date partly defaced, was attributed by the catalogue of the museum in Mechelen (1869 edition) to Jehan Cossaet and dated 1561, and attributed by Henri Hymons in his *Van Mouder* to Jehan Gossaert (16th century). However, according to the most authoritative critics, the work is by Schoeff. The museum in Brussels has a smaller version of the Mechelen painting that Wauters believes is a model or a subsequent reduced replica painted by the artist himself. In the judicial court of Vienna there are three other representations of the judicial court of Mechelen: the first presided over by Charles the Rash in 1474; the second by Maximilian, with his young son Philip at his side, in 1478; the third by Philip the Fair in 1503. There are still small copies of these paintings in the Mechelen archives.

MUSEUMS AND GALLERIES:
BRUSSELS: *Judicial Court of Mechelen* (model or replica).

SCHOEFF, Johannes Pietersz., or Pieterszoon
Dutch, 17th century.
Born 1608, probably in The Hague; died after 1666, in Bergen op Zoom.
Active in The Hague 1638-1660.
Painter. Mountain landscapes, seascapes, landscapes.
The Hague School.

Johannes Pietersz. Schoeff's work was strongly influenced by Jan van Goyen. His widow was still living in The Hague in 1681. Few of his pictures have survived.

MUSEUMS AND GALLERIES:
AMSTERDAM: *Landscape* - THE HAGUE: *Landscape* (attributed) - THE HAGUE (Gemeentemus.): *Mountain Landscape*.

AUCTION RECORDS:
LUCERNE, 22 June 1963, *River-bank with Fishing Boats*, CHF 7,500. LONDON, 12 Nov 1969, *Two Warships at Sea*, GBP 580. AMSTERDAM, 26 May 1970, *Warships*, NLG 10,000. ZURICH, 17 Nov 1972, *Riverscape*, CHF 29,000. ZURICH, 12 Nov 1976, *Fishermen in their Boats Pulling In their Nets* (1643, oil on panel, 19 x 25¼ ins / 48.2 x 64 cm) CHF 40,000. AMSTERDAM, 23 April 1979, *Fishermen on a River* (oil on panel, 16¼ x 13¼ ins / 41 x 33.5 cm) NLG 7,600. GENEVA, 4 May 1981, *River with Fishermen Placing their Nets* (oil on panel, round) CHF 17,500. VIENNA, 16 Nov 1983, *Fishermen Pulling In their Nets* (1645, oil on wood, 15¼ x 24 ins / 39 x 61 cm) ATS 320,000. PARIS, 25 April 1985, *Leaving for the Hunt* (oil on panel, 15¾ x 23 ins / 40 x 57.5 cm) FRF 32,500. LONDON, 11 Dec 1986, *Fishermen in an Estuary; Wooded River Landscape with Peasants on a Wooden Bridge* (1645, oil on panel, a pair, 11¼ x 14¾ ins / 28.6 x 37.5 cm) GBP 6,000. AMSTERDAM, 16 Nov 1993, *Travellers Crossing the Dunes* (1655, oil on panel, 11¾ x 18¼ ins / 30 x 46.5 cm) NLG 39,100. AMSTERDAM, 4 Nov 2003, *Extensive Landscape with Church and Trees* (pen, brown ink and blue wash, 7 x 12 ins / 18 x 31 cm) EUR 2,000. LONDON, 11 Dec 2003, *River Landscape with Peasants Netting Fish from Boats* (1647, oil on canvas, 23 x 31 ins / 59 x 80 cm) GBP 30,000. AMSTERDAM, 17 May 2004, *Extensive Wooded Landscape with Herdsman Resting Cattle* (oil on panel, 23 x 27 ins / 58 x 69 cm) EUR 5,000.

SCHŒFFER, Francisque Jean
French, 19th century.
Born 13 February 1808, in Paris; died 1874.
Landscape painter.

He was a student of both Bertin and Ingres.

MUSEUMS AND GALLERIES:
BAYEUX: a work.

AUCTION RECORDS:
PARIS, 1 Feb 1950, *Views of Villages* (1848, two pendants) FRF 4,600.

SCHOEFFER, Jean
16th century.
Painter.

Jean Schoeffer is mentioned in Ris-Paquot.

SCHOEFFER, Nicolas. See **SCHÖFFER**

SCHOEFFT, August Theodor
Hungarian, 19th century.
Born 1809, in Pest; died 1888, in London.
Painter. Portraits, genre scenes, local scenes.

August Schoefft was the son of Jósef August. He studied in Vienna and in Rome from 1844 to 1846. He travelled widely in Europe and Asia, and painted a large number of portraits.

AUCTION RECORDS:
LONDON, 19 March 1980, *The Presentation of the Bride* (oil on canvas, 56 x 42½ ins / 142 x 108 cm) GBP 700. PARIS, 21 May 1992, *Noblewoman in an Indian Shawl* (1837, oil on canvas, 43¼ x 36¼ ins / 110 x 92 cm) FRF 5,200. NEW YORK, 11 March 1999, *Six Kickapoo Indians, Chief and Family* (c. 1860, oil on canvas, 31x41 ins / 80x103 cm) USD 50,000. MADRID, 20 March 2000, *British Soldier in the War of Independence* (1830, oil on canvas, 46x39 ins / 118x98 cm) ESP 650,000. PARIS, 12 Dec 2003, *Duke St Simeon* (oil on canvas, 30x26 ins / 76x66 cm) EUR 4,000.

SCHOEFFT, Barbara
Hungarian, 19th century.
Painter.

Barbara Schoefft was the daughter of Jósef August. She painted landscapes around 1840.

SCHOEFFT, Jósef
Hungarian, 18th century.
Born c. 1745, in Doberschau; died after 1803, in Pest.
Painter.

SCHOEFFT, Jósef August
Romanian, 19th century.

Born 1778, in Pest; died 1860, in Pest.
Painter.
He lived and worked in Bucharest. He painted portraits.

SCHOEFTMAYER, Eberhard and Martin
German, 16th century.
Active in Munich.
Painters.

SCHOEL, Hendrik van, or Schöl
Dutch, 16th century.
Engraver.
Hendrik van Schoel had a printing works and bookshop in Rome. His engravings are mainly of religious subjects taken from the Italian masters.

SCHOELL, Johann Abraham
German, 18th century.
Born 29 May 1733, in Frankfurt am Main; died 24 August 1791.
Miniaturist.

SCHOELLER, Johann Christian
French, 19th century.
Born 1782, in Ribeauvillé; died 10 November 1851, in Vienna.
Painter, draughtsman.
Johann Schoeller started out as a merchant in Augsburg (Bavaria), Germany, before becoming a pupil of Klotz at the Munich academy. He travelled around Switzerland and France. In 1812 he worked in Paris, then went to Provence. He went to work in Vienna (Venice), Italy, in 1815. His most famous work is his contribution to the *Galerie de scènes intéressantes et comiques des théâtres de Vienne* (*Gallery of Comic and Interesting Scenes from the Theatres of Vienna*) and his *Galerie d'images du théâtre* (*Gallery of Images from the Theatre*).
AUCTION RECORDS:
PARIS, 14 Feb 1951, *Napoleon I* (miniature) FRF 22,000.

SCHOELLER, R.
German, 19th century.
Active c. 1815.
Miniaturist.

SCHOELLHORN, Hans Karl
Swiss, 20th century.
Born 10 February 1892; died 1983.
Painter, lithographer, illustrator. Figures, portraits, urban landscapes, seascapes.
Hans Karl Schoellhorn studied at the Winterthur technical college, then from 1911 to 1912 at the Geneva art school. From 1912 to 1913 he worked with Gröber in Munich, Dresden and Leipzig, and until the war in Paris. He returned to Geneva in 1917, and worked in Zurich and Winterthur. He went on study trips to Spain and North Africa.
MUSEUMS AND GALLERIES:
AARAU (Aargauer Kunsthaus): *Weiblicher Akt* (*Female Act*) - WINTERTHUR: *Portrait of the Artist in French Uniform*; *The Model*.
AUCTION RECORDS:
ZURICH, 12 May 1977, *Young Woman in Black Stockings* (1917, oil on canvas, 25 1/2 x 25 1/4 ins / 65 x 64 cm) CHF 2,500. BERN, 3 May 1979, *Seated Woman in a Blue Dress* (1918, oil on canvas, 22 x 18 ins / 55 x 46 cm) CHF 3,200. PARIS, 26 April 1990, *The Old Port of Marseilles* (1926, oil on canvas, 18 x 22 ins / 46 x 55 cm) FRF 20,000. PARIS, 19 Nov 1991, *Street Corner in Geneva* (1930, oil on canvas, 22 x 18 ins / 55 x 46 cm) FRF 6,500. ST GALL, 10 May 2000, *Young Woman on a Chair* (1917, oil on canvas, 29 x 21 ins / 73 x 54 cm) CHF 4,000. LONDON, 18 Oct 2000, *Nightly Noise* (1919, oil on canvas, 22 x 20 ins / 57 x 51 cm) GBP 180,000. LONDON, 10 Oct 2001, *Exotic Princess* (1919, oil and gold leaf on panel, 27 x 23 ins / 69 x 59 cm) GBP 80,000. BERLIN, 1 Dec 2001, *Industrial Peasants* (lithograph, 10 x 14 ins / 26 x 36 cm) DEM 6,000. LONDON, 9 Oct 2002, *Lovers* (1920, oil and leaf on panel, 19 x 20 ins / 49 x 51 cm) GBP 100,000. NEW YORK, 5 Nov 2003, *Von Kommenden Dingen* (1922, oil on board, 30 x 38 ins / 75 x 97 cm) USD 510,000.

SCHŒLMACKER, Jakob or Jacobus, or Schœmaker-Doyer
Dutch, 19th century.
Born 24 June 1792, in Krefeld; died 9 June 1867, in Zutphen.
Painter.
Jakob Schœlmacker was taken to Amsterdam as a child by his father, who enrolled him as a pupil of J. Adriaensz. He also worked in Antwerp with Van Bree. Upon his return to the Netherlands, he produced portraits, genre scenes and, occasionally, history paintings, dividing his time between Zwolle and Amsterdam.
MUSEUMS AND GALLERIES:
AMSTERDAM: *Payday*; *Van Speiyk Lighting the Powder*; *Van Speiyk Hesitating before Blowing Up his Ship*.

SCHOEMAKER, Andreis, or Schomacher
Dutch, 17th - 18th century.
Born 9 October 1660, in Amsterdam; died 23 December 1735, in Amsterdam.
Painter, draughtsman.
The Bergen Museum in Norway has one painting by Andreis Schoemaker: *Man Leaning Out of a Window Cutting Up a Herring*.

SCHOEMBS, Friedrich
German, 19th century.
Born 26 October 1832, in Offenbach; died 11 September 1879, in Offenbach.
Lithographer.
Friedrich Schoembs was the son of Philipp Peter.

SCHOEMBS, Hermann
German, 19th century.
Born 10 March 1858, in Offenbach; died 20 January 1888, in Offenbach.
Lithographer.
Hermann Schoembs was the son of Friedrich.

SCHOEMBS, Philipp Peter
German, 19th century.
Born 26 September 1806, in Friesenheim; died 2 August 1882, in Offenbach.
Lithographer.

SCHOEN, Daniel Albert
French, 20th century.
Born 13 December 1873, in Mulhouse.
Painter. Portraits, landscapes.
From 1897 to 1904 Daniel Albert Schoen was head of Émile Gallé's studio in Nancy, and from 1919 a professor at the École des Arts Industriels, Strasbourg.

He exhibited in Paris from 1905 at the Salon des Artistes Français, the Salon de la Société Nationale des Beaux-Arts, the Salon des Indépendants, and also at the Salon d'Automne.

SCHOEN, Erhard, or Schön
German, 16th century.
Born c. 1491; died 1542.

Painter, draughtsman, engraver, illustrator. Portraits. Nuremberg School.

Erhard Schoen lived in Nuremberg, but it is not known whether he was born there. His woodcuts appear in books published in Nuremberg or Lyons by Koberger. These include the *Hortulus Animœ* (editions of 1517, 1518 and 1520), and bibles published in Lyons in 1519, 1520 and 1521. There is also mention of him working on a bible published in Nuremberg by Payrus in 1524. These illustrations are mixed with those of Springinklee. He also designed a pack of cards. He is said to have cut the frontispiece of a bible printed in Prague in 1529. He was an imitator of Dürer and may even have been a pupil of his.

Museums and Galleries:
Douai: *Adoration of the Magi*.

Auction records:
Paris, 1864, *Adoration of the Magi* (pen and Indian ink wash) FRF 35. Bern, 20 June 1980, *Portrait of Albrecht Dürer* (engraving/coloured wood) CHF 11,000. Bern, 26 June 1981, *Turkish Dignitary in a Chariot* (1532, pen and bistre ink, 9 3/4 x 14 1/2 ins / 24.7 x 36.8 cm) CHF 800. Paris, 22 May 1996, *David and Bathsheba* (1531, pen, 7 1/2 x 6 ins / 18.8 x 15.3 cm) FRF 172,000.

SCHOEN, Eugen
German, 20th century.
Born 18 October 1863, in Stuttgart; died 10 October 1908, in Constance.
Painter.

Eugen Schoen studied at the art school and academy in Stuttgart with Schraudolph, at the Munich Art Academy with Frank Kirchbach and in Paris and Italy.

He decorated the house of Melanchthon at Bretten in Baden.

SCHOEN, Fritz
German, 20th century.
Born 23 April 1871, in Darkehnen (Prussia).
Painter, caricaturist, architect.

Fritz Schoen studied in Berlin and Paris.

SCHOEN, Karl
Austrian, 19th century.
Born c. 1788, in Prague; died 1824, in Prague.
Painter.

Karl Schoen attended the royal academy from 1803 to 1808.

SCHOENBECK, Albert
German, 19th century.
Active in Potsdam.
Landscape artist.

He exhibited in Berlin from 1834 to 1860.

SCHOENBECK, Richard
German, 19th - 20th century.
Born 20 May 1840, in Potsdam; died 31 March 1919, in Berlin.
Painter. Horses.

Richard Schoenbeck was an officer.

SCHOENBERG, Arnold. See **SCHÖNBERG**

SCHOENDORFF, Max
French, 20th century.
Born 1934, in Lyons.
Painter, engraver, illustrator.
Phases group.

Max Schoendorff lives and works in Lyons. In 2000 he was represented in the exhibition *Le Movement Phases de 1952 à l'horizon 2001* (*The Phases Movement from 1952 to the New Millennium*), held at the Kiosque Centre Culturel, Mayenne, and the Centre Noroit, Arras.

Initially he painted abstract, ample, 'matterist' works, similar to those of his friend Modesto Cuixart. Later, inspired by religious history (descents from the Cross, the Holy Face, Crucifixions) or mythology (Venus, bacchanalia), his painting became figurative, fantastic, sometimes erotic, flayed. In dissecting myths, breaking them open in a gloomy and luxuriant celebration, he confused the line that separates anguish from orgasm. He illustrated Jacques Neyme's collection of poems *À vif, à peine, un mot*.

Bibliography:
Lambert, Jean-Clarence, *Schoendorff*, exhibition catalogue, Ville de Lyon, 1980. *Max Schoendorff: peinture-théâtre*, exhibition catalogue, Toulouse, 1988.

SCHŒNECKERN, Regina Catherine. See **QUARRY**

SCHOENEMANN, Friedrich
German, 18th century.
Active in Leipzig and in Hamburg 1745-1760.
Engraver (burin).

Friedrich Schoenemann painted portraits and views of Hamburg.

SCHOENEMANN, Johann Christoph
German, 18th century.
Born 18 November 1765, in Dresden.
Engraver (burin). Portraits.

Museums and Galleries:
Leipzig (Stadtgeschichtliches Mus.): engraved portraits.

SCHOENENBERGHE. See **SCOENENBERGHE**

SCHOENER
German, 16th century.
Born c. 1532, in Mainz.
Painter. Portraits.

Schoener is referred to by Ris-Paquot.

SCHŒNEWERK, Alexandre, or Schoenewerck
French, 19th century.
Born 18 February 1820, in Paris; died 22 July 1885, in Paris.
Sculptor. Religious subjects. Monuments, statues, busts.

Alexandre Schœnewerk was a pupil of David of Angers, Jollivet and Triqueti. He debuted at the Paris Salon in 1842 and was awarded a third-class medal in 1845, and first-class medals in 1861, 1863 and 1878 at the Exposition Universelle. He was made a Chevalier of the Légion d'Honneur in 1863, and was also an honorary member of the Munich academy.

Schœnewerk was very much in favour during the Second Empire and enjoyed the protection of Princess Mathilde. In 1885 the Salon refused his *Salomé* and he became so dejected that he threw himself out of a window on the third floor of his house in rue Vavin. He died the following day.

Museums and Galleries:
Amiens: *Morning* - Angers: *David of Angers* - Caen: *Young Fisherman with a Turtle* - Geneva: *Henri the Lion; Otto the Child*; monument of the Duke of Brunswick - La Rochelle: *Hesitation; Young Girl at a Fountain* - Lyons: *Dawn* - Paris (Bibliothèque-Mus. de l'Opéra): *Lulli* (marble statue) - Paris (Church of St-Augustin): *Two Angels* - Paris (Church of Ste-Marguerite): *St Elizabeth of Hungary* - Paris (Façade of the Sorbonne): *St Thomas Aquinas* (statue) - Paris (Government

Collection): *Lulli* (statue) - PARIS (Louvre): *Young Girl at a Fountain; Bust of Bouchardon; Galatea.*

AUCTION RECORDS:

LONDON, 10 Nov 1983, *Young Woman Picking Flowers* (c. 1850, dark-brown patinated bronze, h. $16\frac{1}{4}$ ins / 41 cm) GBP 800. NEW YORK, 17 Jan 1996, *Andromeda* (bronze, h. 22 ins / 55.9 cm) USD 2,645. LONDON, 13 Dec 2000, *The Bather* (white marble, h. 26 ins / 66 cm) GBP 2,600. BRUSSELS, 19 Dec 2000, *Pan's Flute* (brown patinated bronze, h. 21 ins / 54 cm) BEF 110,000. MICHIGAN, 3 April 2001, *Bacant* (bronze, h. 23 ins / 58 cm) USD 2,000. LONDON, 27 April 2001, *Andromeda* (brown patinated bronze, h. 22 ins / 56 cm) GBP 3,000. OLYMPIA, 25 April 2002, *Sappho* (gilt bronze, h. 19 ins / 47 cm) GBP 2,000. PARIS, 26 April 2002, *Woman by the River* (gold and silver patinated bronze, 2 x 2x2 ins / 5 x 5x5 cm) EUR 2,600.

SCHOENFELD, Friedrich
German, 19th century.
Active in Potsdam 1802-1816.
Pastellist, miniaturist.

SCHOENFELD, Johann Heinrich.
See **SCHÖNFELDT**

SCHOENFELD, Richard
German, 20th century.
Born 13 July 1884, in Achserleben.
Painter. Portraits, landscapes.

Richard Schoenfeld studied at art schools in Breslau (now Wroclaw, Poland) and Weimar, and at the art academy in Munich. He went on study tours to Italy, Paris and Norway. He lived and worked in Bad Soden, near Frankfurt am Main.

MUSEUMS AND GALLERIES:

FRANKFURT AM MAIN (Historisches Mus.) - FRANKFURT AM MAIN (Städel).

SCHOENGRUN, Alice
French, 19th - 20th century.
Born 26 May 1869, in Lille.
Painter.

Alice Schoengrun, a pupil of Baschet and Jules Adler, exhibited in Paris from 1914 at the Salon des Artistes Français, of which she became a member and where she was awarded a silver medal in 1927.

SCHOENHAUPT, Louis
French, 19th century.
Born 28 February 1822, in Mulhouse; died 27 February 1895.
Painter. Genre scenes.

This artist won a medal in 1867 (at the Exposition Universelle). In 1883 he illustrated a *Golden Book of Mulhouse*, and an *Armorial of Alsatian Outbuildings*.

MUSEUMS AND GALLERIES:

MULHOUSE: *Album of the Christian Faith* (20 miniature drawings).

SCHOENINGER, Leo
German, 19th century.
Born 21 January 1811, in Weil der Stadt; died 20 December 1879, in Munich.
Painter, engraver. Portraits, genre scenes.

Leo Schoeninger engraved religious subjects, portraits and genre scenes and perfected the galvanoplastic technique, invented by Franz von Kobell (1803-1882), replacing colour with chemical chalk.

SCHOENJANS, Jan. See **SCHOONJANS**

SCHOENMAECKERS, Egidius Gilles, or Schoenmakers, Schoonmaeckers
Dutch, 18th century.
Born to a family originally from Antwerp; died 24 November 1736, in The Hague.
Sculptor.

Egidius Gilles Schoenmaeckers became a guild member in The Hague in 1716, and produced some 40 portrait medals.

SCHOENMAKER, Johannes Pietersz., or Schoenmackers
Dutch, 18th - 19th century.
Born 1 November 1755, in Dordrecht; died 4 June 1842.
Painter. Landscapes, urban landscapes, waterscapes.

Johannes Pietersz. Schoenmaker was a pupil of Jakob van Stry. He produced a small number of prints and vignettes. He was a talented painter, chiefly of city views in the manner of Van der Heyden. His work is highly sought-after by collectors in his native Holland.

MUSEUMS AND GALLERIES:

AMSTERDAM: *View of a Town* (figures by J. C. Schotel).

AUCTION RECORDS:

AMSTERDAM, 6 May 1996, *Landscape with a Canal near a Village* (oil on panel, $14\frac{1}{4}$ x $20\frac{1}{4}$ ins / 36 x 51.5 cm) NLG 12,980.

SCHOENMAKERS, P.
Dutch, 18th century.
Active c. 1784.
Draughtsman.

SCHOEPFER, Françoise, or Schopfer Franziska
German, 18th - 19th century.
Born 1763, in Mannheim; died 12 June 1836, in Munich.
Painter, miniaturist, engraver, lithographer. Religious subjects, portraits, landscapes.

A pupil at the academy in Mannheim with J.W. Hoffnas, Françoise Schoepfer worked at Mannheim and Munich where she was court oainter before transferring to Bamberg. She engraved religious subjects and portraits.

AUCTION RECORDS:

LONDON, 19 March 1981, *Bavarian Landscapes* (1831, watercolour and pencil, a pair, each 4 x 5 ins / 10.2 x 12.8 cm) GBP 950.

SCHOERMAN, John. See **SCHURMAN**

SCHOESETTERS, Jan Baptist
Belgian, 19th century.
Born c. 1804, in Antwerp; died 10 June 1870, in Antwerp.
Lithographer.

Jan Baptist Schoesetters travelled to Germany in 1826.

SCHOEVAERDTS, Frans
Flemish School, 18th century.
Painter. Genre scenes.

Frans Schoevaerdts was the brother of Mathys Schoevaerdts. He was a guild master in Brussels in 1704.

SCHOEVAERDTS, Mathys or Mathieu, or Schovaerts
Flemish School, 17th century.
Born c. 1665, in Brussels; died 1694 or 1723.
Painter, engraver. Genre scenes, village scenes, landscapes, landscapes with figures, seascapes.

Mathys Schoevaerdts was a pupil of A.F. Boudewyns in 1682, master of the Brussels guild in 1690 and dean from 1692 to 1694. He produced paintings and prints of village fêtes and festive gatherings.

MUSEUMS AND GALLERIES:

ANTWERP: *View of Antwerp from the River Scheldt* - BERLIN: *Fête at a Village Church* - BRUSSELS: *Parading the Fattened Bull; Fishing Port; Fish Market; Landscape* - FLORENCE: *Small Landscape* - LA FÈRE - LE HAVRE: *Fair* - MONTPELLIER: *Landscape* - PARIS (Louvre): *Landscapes* (two) - RENNES: *Land-*

scape with Figures and Animals - STOCKHOLM: *Fruit Market by a River; Fish Market.*

AUCTION RECORDS:

PARIS, 1834, *Landscape with Ruins, Figures and Animals,* FRF 110. PARIS, 1844, *View of a Village in Flanders,* FRF 240. PARIS, 1868, *Main Thoroughfare,* FRF 351; *Winter,* FRF 800. PARIS, 4 June 1878, *Market Day in Antwerp,* FRF 500. BRUSSELS, 30 May 1899, *Landscape with Figures,* FRF 880. PARIS, 29 June 1900, *Village on a River,* FRF 200. PARIS, 9-10 April 1902, *Park,* FRF 420. LONDON, 27 March 1910, *Landscapes* (two) GBP 9. LONDON, 25-26 May 1911, *Horseman on a Mountain Path,* GBP 25. PARIS, 22-23 April 1921, *Main Road,* FRF 910. PARIS, 10 March 1924, *View of a Port with Numerous Figures,* FRF 310. PARIS, 19 Dec 1928, *Village under Snow; Washerwomen* (two) FRF 12,100. PARIS, 23 May 1932, *Entrance to a Village,* FRF 1,300. BRUSSELS, 21 March 1938, *Riverscape,* BEF 3,500. ANTWERP, 4 and 5 April 1938, *Landscape,* BEF 4,500. PARIS, 3 Dec 1941, *Fishermen Hauling In their Nets at the Foot of a Ruined Palace,* FRF 18,500. PARIS, 24 June 1942, *Forest Walk,* FRF 4,500. PARIS, 5 Nov 1942, *Fortified Castle with Figures,* FRF 16,100. PARIS, 17 March 1943, *Fair in a Town Square,* FRF 145,000. PARIS, 29-30 March 1943, *Harbours* (two pendants) FRF 22,000. PARIS, 21 April 1944, *Market by the Water* (school of Mathys Schoevaerdts) FRF 14,000. PARIS, 27 Feb 1950, *Village Scene,* FRF 27,500. BRUSSELS, 2-4 June 1965, *Landscape with Watercourse,* BEF 115,000. PARIS, 6 Dec 1966, *Outskirts of a Village,* FRF 10,500. LONDON, 26 March 1971, *Landscape with a Mill and Numerous Figures,* Gns 3,200. VIENNA, 21 March 1972, *Outskirts of a Village with Numerous Figures,* ATS 180,000. COLOGNE, 6 June 1973, *Village Street,* DEM 18,000. AMSTERDAM, 26 Nov 1974, *Banks of the Rhine,* NLG 20,000. COLOGNE, 14 June 1976, *Village Scene* (oil on panel, 11 x 17 1/4 ins / 27 x 44 cm) DEM 23,000. NEW YORK, 11 March 1977, *Wooded Landscape with Numerous Figures* (oil on panel, 12 x 16 1/4 ins / 30.5 x 41 cm) USD 22,000. VIENNA, 20 Sept 1977, *Village Festivities* (oil on canvas, 13 1/4 x 17 1/4 ins / 33.5 x 43.5 cm) ATS 120,000. LONDON, 28 March 1979, *Castle with Numerous Figures* (oil on panel, 12 1/2 x 17 1/2 ins / 32 x 44.5 cm) GBP 10,000. PARIS, 7 Dec 1981, *Square with an Obelisk and Figures* (oil on wood, 12 1/4 x 17 1/4 ins / 31 x 43.5 cm) FRF 48,000. LONDON, 5 July 1984, *Fish Market in a River Landscape* (oil/copper, 12 x 16 3/4 ins / 30.5 x 42.5 cm) GBP 21,500. LONDON, 11 Dec 1985, *Village Fête* (oil on panel, 11 x 17 1/4 ins / 27 x 44 cm) GBP 19,500. LONDON, 17 July 1986, *Wooded Landscapes with Travellers and Fruit-sellers* (oil on panel, a pair, 10 x 14 1/4 ins / 25.7 x 36.2 cm) GBP 13,000. LONDON, 13 May 1988, *Rustic Italian Landscape; River with Fishermen, Farm Buildings and Peasants Driving Horses and Cattle* (oil on panel, a pair, each 9 x 11 3/4 ins / 22 x 30 cm) GBP 10,120. LONDON, 17 June 1988, *River in a Wooded Landscape with Figures* (oil on panel, 10 x 13 ins / 24.5 x 33 cm) GBP 7,150. PARIS, 1 July 1988, *Return from Fishing* (oil on panel, 7 x 10 ins / 18 x 24.5 cm) FRF 65,000. GÖTEBORG, 18 May 1989, *Landscape with Figures by a Church* (oil on panel, 12 1/2 x 16 1/2 ins / 32 x 42 cm) SEK 17,000. LONDON, 19 May 1989, *River Quays with Travellers, Merchants, Peasants and Townspeople* (oil on canvas, a pair, each 16 x 23 ins / 40.7 x 58.4 cm) GBP 35,200. LONDON, 7 July 1989, *Village Kermesse* (oil on panel, 10 1/4 x 15 ins / 26 x 37.2 cm) GBP 30,800. AMSTERDAM, 28 Nov 1989, *Wooded Landscape with Numerous Figures near a Village* (oil on panel, 10 1/2 x 14 1/2 ins / 26.7 x 36.8 cm) NLG 48,300. MONACO, 2 Dec 1989, *Returning from Market* (oil on panel, 11 1/4 x 16 1/4 ins / 28.5 x 41.5 cm) FRF 333,000. ROME, 8 May 1990, *View of an Eastern Port with Figures* (oil on canvas, 42 1/2 x 41 1/2 ins / 108 x 105.5 cm) ITL 15,000,000. PARIS, 22 June 1990, *Walkers in a Forest; Landscape with Livestock Crossing a Ford* (pair of oak panels, 11 1/2 x 16 1/2 ins / 29 x 42 cm) FRF 260,000. LONDON, 20 July 1990, *Mediterranean Port with Merchants and Townspeople on a Quayside* (oil on canvas, 16 1/4 x 23 1/4 ins / 41 x 59 cm) GBP 4,400. LONDON, 31 Oct 1990, *Landscape with Figures, Classical Ruins and a Lake* (oil on canvas, 14 1/4 x 20 ins / 36.5 x 50.5 cm) GBP 5,500. PARIS, 5 April 1991, *Vast Landscape with a Gathering of Figures* (oil on oak panel, in two parts, 11 x 16 1/4 ins / 28 x 41 cm) FRF 78,000. LONDON, 1 Nov 1991, *Classical Ruins with Pilgrims and Travellers Stopping by a Spring to Water their Horses* (oil on panel, 11 1/2 x 16 1/4 ins / 29.2 x 41.3 cm) GBP 6,380. LONDON, 11 Dec 1992, *Mediterranean Port with Merchants and Townspeople on a Quayside Watching Sailors Unloading Merchandise, with a Two-master Anchored out at Sea* (oil on canvas, 16 1/4 x 23 ins / 41 x 58.5 cm) GBP 4,950. PARIS, 14 Dec 1992, *Peasants before a Farm* (oil on panel, 11 x 17 1/4 ins / 27 x 44 cm) FRF 135,000. LONDON, 21 April 1993, *Falconers in a Vast River Landscape* (oil/copper, 19 3/4 x 26 1/2 ins / 50.2 x 67.3 cm) GBP 25,300. AMSTERDAM, 17 Nov 1994, *Vast Landscape with Travellers Resting by a Stream* (oil on panel, 13 1/2 x 20 ins / 34 x 50.5 cm) NLG 126,500. NEW YORK, 11 Jan 1995, *Italian Landscape with a Troop of Actors Performing to a Large Crowd; Italian Landscape with Bathers in a Pond near Classical Ruins and a Bridge* (oil on canvas, a pair, 13 1/2 x 18 1/4 ins / 34.3 x 46.3 cm and 13 1/4 x 18 ins/33.6 x 45.7 cm) USD 40,250. CHAMBÉRY, 24 Sept 1995, *Coastal Landscape with a Tower, a Crowd of Figures and Sailing Ships in the Distance* (oil on canvas, 20 3/4 x 26 3/4 ins / 53 x 68 cm) FRF 122,000. AMSTERDAM, 7 May 1996, *Coastal Landscape with Women Selling Fish; Villagers on the Banks of a River* (oil on canvas, a pair, 11 1/4 x 16 ins / 28.3 x 40.8 cm) NLG 40,250. LONDON, 1 Nov 1996, *Riverscape with Merchants and Travellers.* PARIS, 10 Dec 1996, *Landscape with Figures* (oil on panel, 11 1/2 x 14 ins / 29 x 35.5 cm) FRF 72,000. PARIS, 14 May 1997, *Landscape with Mill; Landscape with Boats and a Church* (oil on canvas, a pair, each 16 1/4 x 24 ins / 41 x 61 cm) FRF 220,000. LONDON, 31 Oct 1997, *Villagers outside a Church with a Landscape and Castle in the Distance* (oil on canvas, 14 3/4 x 20 1/4 ins / 37.5 x 51.7 cm) GBP 5,750. PARIS, 4 Nov 1997, *Mediterranean Sea Port* (panel, 5 1/4 x 7 3/4 ins / 13.5 x 20 cm) FRF 128,000; *Ferry Crossing* (copper, 11 1/2 x 14 1/4 ins / 29 x 36 cm) FRF 180,000. PARIS, 6 March 1998, *Village Square* (oil on canvas, 14 3/4 x 20 1/2 ins / 37.5 x 52 cm) FRF 80,000. MADRID, 12 Jan 1999, *Meal Time at the Cathedral Door* (oil on canvas, 15 x 20 ins / 37 x 51 cm) ESP 3,250,000. LONDON, 14 April 1999, *River Landscape with Travellers Conversing by a Fountain* (oil on copper, 7 x 8 ins / 18 x 20 cm) GBP 6,500. NEW YORK, 27 Jan 2000, *Coastal Scene with Drovers and Herds. Estuary with Peasants in Boats and other Shipping* (oil on panel, a pair, 19 x 26 ins / 47 x 65 cm) USD 270,000. PARIS, 30 June 2000, *Ancient Ruins near the Shore with Sailors and Turkish Merchants* (oil on panel, 11 x 16 ins / 29 x 40 cm) FRF 240,000. PARIS, 29 March 2001, *Market Scene in a Ruined Landscape* (oil on copper, 20 x 26 ins / 50 x 65 cm) FRF 270,000. LONDON, 13 Dec 2001, *Harbour Scene with Orientals on a Quay* (oil on canvas, 13 x 19 ins / 33 x 48 cm) GBP 14,000. PARIS, 6 March 2002, *Stop by a Mill* (oil on panel, 11 x 14 ins / 27 x 36 cm) EUR 15,000. LONDON, 11 Dec 2002, *Tower of Babel* (oil on canvas, 37 x 30 ins / 93 x 76 cm) GBP 82,000. LILLE, 23 March 2003, *Return from Market* (oil on panel, 12 x 17 ins / 31 x 44 cm) EUR 42,000. LONDON, 10 July 2003, *River Landscape with Orientals and Locals Conversing before Ruins* (oil on canvas, 21 x 27 ins / 54 x 68 cm) GBP 16,000. LONDON, 21 April 2004, *Coastal Landscape with Merchants and Peasants. Coastal Landscape with Fishermen Loading the Catch* (oil on panel, a pair, 5 x 7 ins / 13 x 18 cm) GBP 13,000. LONDON, 9 July 2004, *River Landscape with Figures* (oil on canvas, 17 x 24 ins / 43 x 60 cm) GBP 20,000.

SCHOEVAERDTS, Pieter, or Schovaerts
Flemish School, 18th century.
Active in Brussels.
Painter.

Pieter Schoevaerdts was the nephew of Mathys Schoevaerdts. A master in the guild of Brussels in 1731, he is best known for his *Emperor Frans I (or Charles VI) at Furnes.*

SCHOFF, Otto
German, 20th century.
Born 24 May 1888, in Bremen.
Painter, engraver.

Otto Schoff studied in Paris, and under Emil Orlik in Berlin.

SCHOFF, Steffen Alonso
American, 19th century.
Born 1818, in Danville; died 1905, in Brandon.
Engraver.

Steffen Alonso Schoff engraved genre scenes and portraits. He studied in Boston with O. Pelton and J. Andrews, and in Paris with Paul Delaroche. He engraved a portrait of *Emerson*, and *Sailors among the Ruins of Carthage* after Vanderlyn.

SCHÖFFELHUBER, Dominikus.
See **SCHÖFFTLHUBER**

SCHÖFFELHUEBER, Matthias, or Schöfflhueber
German, 17th century.
Died 1671.
Active in Weilheim.
Painter.

SCHOFFENIELS, Ernest
Belgian, 20th century.
Born 1927, in Liège.
Painter, engraver.
Op Art.

SCHÖFFER, Hans Jacob. See **SCHÄFFER**

SCHÖFFER, Nicolas, or Schoeffer
Hungarian, 20th century.
Born 6 September 1912, in Kalocsa; died 8 January 1992.
Active from 1936 then naturalised in France.
Painter, sculptor.
Kinetic Art, Cyber Art.

Nicolas Schöffer initially received a completely classical training, at the fine arts school in Budapest. He then went to live in Paris, in 1936, and continued his training from 1937 to 1939 at the École des Beaux-Arts, where he was a student of Sabatté. From 1969 to 1971, he taught at the École des Beaux-Arts. Schöffer started out as a painter. It is difficult to glean information about his early works, and he had eclectic tastes: he admired the *Victory of Samothrace* and Vermeer, but hated Picasso. Schöffer's art, like that of other acolytes of Optical and Kinetic Art, was barely influenced by 20th-century art, unless by the Russian constructivists, Bauhaus and Mondrian - the most authoritarian manifestations of functionalism. Dada is only an influence in so far as he foresaw the advent of 'positive constructors'.

Schöffer's first sculptures were unrestrained tributes to Mondrian, embodying a three-dimensional version of Neo-Plasticism; this makes them rather like the sculptures of Jean Gorin. Reading *Cybernetics and Society* by Norbert Wiener, the creator of cybernetics, gave Schöffer's work a new focus. Schöffer was moved to define what he termed 'spatiodynamism' as 'the constructive and dynamic integration of space in the fine arts'; although expressed in a somewhat intimidating manner, this was perhaps not entirely new. In about 1950, he presented his first kinetic sculptures at an exhibition. Instead of trusting in the viewer's ability to read any space that is delimited by segments and which be deciphered progressively, and to appreciate the balance of thrusts in the various elements of his scaffolding constructions, Schöffer chose to make certain elements of his work mobile, thus making the time factor in the reading of his works explicit. At the same time, he collaborated with the engineer Henri Perlstein to produce an electric spatiodynamic clock. Around 1954, he was in a position to construct a spatiodynamic and cybernetic sound tower, in the Par de Saint-Cloud in Paris, for the Salon des Travaux Publics. In 1956, on Poetry Night at the Théâtre Sarah-Bernhardt, he presented his first cybernetic sculpture, *CYSP I*, which he had just finished in collaboration with an engineer; in the same year, Maurice Béjart worked this sculpture into a work of choreography.

In 1957, he defined 'lumino-dynamism': basically, he added the elements of light and colour to his cybernetic constructions; this was achieved by means of a simple system of three moving light beams in the primary colours, modified by various filters and projected onto a screen, composing, decomposing and recomposing an infinity of effects, like an automatic kaleidoscope. In 1960, his work moved further down this path of development, and Schöffer presented his *Musiscope*, a sort of modern version of older research into colour keyboards. In 1961, he constructed a 650 feet (200-metre) high pivoting music and light cybernetic tower in front of the Palais des Congrès in Liège. In 1962, directing his vision of Utopia towards the city, Schöffer exhibited a *Light Wall* at the *Object* exhibition at the Musée des Arts Décoratifs. In 1967, he conceived a plan for a mobile tower for the new quarter of La Défense. The tower was to be almost 1000 feet (307 metres) high, to transmit huge quantities of information and signals via computer, and to consist, among other things (recorded in minute detail worthy of a book by Raymond Roussel or even Jules Verne, whom Schöffer greatly admired), of 2,250 projectors, 2,085 electronic flashlights, and 363 turning mirrors. In conjunction with an electronics firm with an international presence, Schöffer produced various machines, all based on the principle of coloured and moving light beams, including the *Luminodynamic Brick*, the *Teleluminoscope*, and the *Luminorelaxe*, which were brought out in limited editions.

While working on his more multi-disciplinary works, Schöffer collaborated with avant-garde musicians such as Henry Pousseur, Pierre Boulez and Pierre Henry, with theatre directors such as Roger Planchon and Jean-Louis Barrault, with choreographers such as Maurice Béjart, and with architects and engineers. In fact, Schöffer's conception of artistic creativity is totalising and collectivist. Schöffer was a lively man, ready for any project, and an eloquent defender of his own works. He did tend to generalise and claim that his conception of art was the only one valid for the age, however he was not aggressive towards other modes of expression, as the adherents of Optical Art would be.

There is a museum dedicated to Schöffer in Hungary. Work by him was shown at group exhibitions, including the Salon d'Automne and the Salon des Tuileries (1937); the UNESCO international exhibition (1946); and at the Salon des Réalités Nouvelles and the Salon de Mai (1948 onwards). From 1950, he stopped exhibiting paintings and began exhibiting sculptures. His work has of course featured at the largest international exhibitions given over to Kinetic Art and Lumino-Kinetic Art. There have also been solo exhibitions of his work, including several at the Galerie Denise René in Paris; at the Washington Gallery of Modern Art (1966); and at the Centre Culturel Noroît in Arras (1994). In 1968, he was awarded the Grand Prix at the Venice Biennale.

Bibliography:
Habasque, G./Cassou, J., *Nicolas Schöffer*, Éd. du Griffon, Neuchâtel, 1963. Seuphor, Michel, *Le Style et le Cri*, Éd. du Seuil, Paris, 1965. Hahn, Otto, '*Nicolas Schöffer, sculpteur de la lumière*' in *L'Express*, periodical, Paris, 9 May 1966. '*L'Express va plus loin avec Nicolas Schöffer*' in *L'Express*, periodical, Paris, 1969. Popper, Frank, *L'Art cinétique*, Gauthier-Villars, Paris, 1970.
Museums and Galleries:
New York (Jewish Mus.) - Paris (MAMVP) - Paris (MNAM-CCI) - Rome (Gal. Nazionale d'Arte Moderna).
Auction records:
New York, 28 May 1976, *Lux 11* (stainless steel, h. 24 ins / 61 cm) USD 1,000. London, 4 Dec 1979, *Lux 13* (aluminium and Plexiglas, h. 22 1/2 ins / 57 cm, w. 15 3/4 ins/40 cm) GBP 550. Stockholm, 17 May 1984, *Lux XIII* (chromium metal, h. 33 ins / 84 cm) SEK 10,000. Paris, 20 June 1988, *Lux 13* (chromium metal sculpture, 23 1/2 x 15 3/4 x 7 3/4 ins / 60 x 40 x 20 cm) FRF 14,500. Paris, 21 Sept 1989, *Abstract Composition* (oil on emery canvas, 12 1/2 x 7 3/4 ins / 32 x 20 cm) FRF 6,500. Paris, 1 April 1996, *Spatio-dynamic Composition* (oil and collage of objects on panel, 24 1/2 x 20 ins / 62 x 50.8 cm) FRF 29,000.

SCHÖFFERLI, Friedrich or Carl Friedrich.
See **SCHÄFFER**

SCHÖFFHUEBER, Franz.
See **SCHÖFFTLHUBER**

SCHÖFFLER, Friedrich Johann.
See **SCHEFFLER**

SCHÖFFTLHUBER, Dominikus, or Schöffelhuber
German, 18th century.
Born 16 November 1728, in Munich.
Painter.
Dominikus Schöfftlhuber became a master in Munich in 1766 and worked on the decoration of the Residenz there.

SCHÖFFTLHUBER, Franz, or Schöffhueber
Austrian, 17th century.
Active in Vienna.
Painter.
In 1658 Franz Schöfftlhuber painted the gate of honour built to mark the arrival of King Leopold I into Vienna.

SCHOFIELD, Flora
American, 20th century.
Born in Chicago.
Painter.
Flora Schofield exhibited at the Salon d'Automne and the Salon des Indépendants.

SCHOFIELD, John William
British, 19th - 20th century.
Born 1865, in Halifax; died 23 October 1944, in London.
Painter (including wash). Portraits, landscapes.
John William Schofield trained at the Westminster School of Art, London, under Fred Brown and in Paris with Bouguereau and Lefebvre. He lived in Halifax until 1890, then in North Devon, settling eventually in London.

Schofield is noted for his moonlit scenes, such as (*Cattle Grazing by Moonlight*) and for his portraits (*Portrait of a Boy with a Book*). He was a member of the Royal British Colonial Society, of the Royal Institute of Painters and Watercolour Artists (from 1917) and of the Royal Society of British Artist (from 1903). He exhibited at the Royal Academy from 1888 and at the Paris Salon between 1889 and 1925.
Museums and Galleries:
Cardiff (National Museum and Galleries of Wales): *Caerphilly Castle*.

SCHOFIELD, Walter Elmer
American, 19th - 20th century.
Born 9 September 1869, in Philadelphia, or in 1867 according to some sources; died 1944.
Painter. Landscapes.
Walter Elmer Schofield began his artistic studies in his home town, then went to work in Paris with Bouguereau, Ferrier, Doucet and Aman-Jean. He was awarded honourable mentions in Paris in 1900 at the Exposition Universelle and in Pittsburgh. He also won silver medals in Buffalo in 1901 and St Louis in 1904. He was a member of the Salmagundi Club in New York and the Chelsea Arts Club in London. He became an associate of the National Academy of Design in New York in 1902 and was admitted as a member in 1907.
Museums and Galleries:
Buffalo: *Autumn in Brittany* - Indianapolis (MA): *The Old Mills on the Somme* - New York: *Sand Dunes near Lebant*.
Auction records:
New York, 12-17 March 1911, *Winter Landscape*, USD 150. New York, 14 Oct 1943, *At a Crossroads*, USD 400. New York, 27 Oct 1977, *Farm in Picardy* (oil on canvas, 37 3/4 x 48 ins / 96 x 121.9 cm) USD 5,500. New York, 23 May 1979, *Cornish Village* (oil on canvas, 38 1/4 x 48 ins / 97 x 122 cm) USD 6,500. New York, 31 May 1984, *Winter Stream* (c. 1925, oil on canvas, 26 x 30 ins / 66 x 76.2 cm) USD 9,000. New York, 5 Dec 1985, *Autumn in Cornwall* (1925, oil on canvas, 40 1/4 x 48 ins / 102.2 x 121.9 cm) USD 31,000. New York, 3 Dec 1987, *Tohegan River* (oil on canvas, 50 x 60 ins / 127 x 152.4 cm) USD 50,000. New York, 1 Dec 1988, *Winter's End* (1903, oil on canvas, 38 1/4 x 48 1/4 ins / 97.1 x 122.5 cm) USD 30,800. New York, 24 Jan 1989, *Landscape at Dawn* (oil on canvas, 23 1/2 x 29 1/2 ins / 60 x 75 cm) USD 5,500. New York, 25 May 1989, *August Afternoon* (1922, oil on canvas, 26 x 30 ins / 66 x 76.2 cm) USD 13,200. New York, 18 Oct 1989, *North Cliffs* (oil on canvas, 26 x 30 ins / 66 x 76.2 cm) USD 12,100. New York, 16 March 1990, *Icy Morning* (1913, oil on canvas, 26 x 30 ins / 66 x 76.5 cm) USD 33,000. New York, 23 May 1990, *Summer Afternoon* (oil on canvas, 36 1/4 x 40 1/4 ins / 92 x 102.2 cm) USD 26,400. New York, 27 May 1992, *Cliffs* (oil on canvas, 30 x 36 ins / 76.2 x 91.4 cm) USD 8,250. New York, 4 Dec 1992, *McLegrenow Farm* (1920, oil on canvas, 30 x 35 3/4 ins / 76.5 x 90.8 cm) USD 36,300. New York, 31 March 1994, *Port of White Sand* (oil on reinforced canvas, 12 x 13 3/4 ins / 30.5 x 35.2 cm) USD 4,313. New York, 25 May 1995, *Maine Coast* (oil on canvas, 29 3/4 x 36 ins / 75.6 x 91.4 cm) USD 34,500. New York, 22 May 1996, *Coastal Landscape* (oil on canvas, 30 x 36 ins / 76.2 x 91.4 cm) USD 23,000.

SCHOFIELD, William Bacon. See **SCOFIELD**

SCHÖFLER, Johann Engelhard.
See **SCHÄFLER**

SCHOFSTAIN
German, 16th century.
Active in Elbing (now Elblag, Poland).
Sculptor.
Schofstain carved an altar in the church of the Three Kings, Elbing.

SCHOGGOTTNIGG, Marx or Marcus.
See **SCHOKOTNIGG**

SCHOGLOKOV, Mikhail Ivanovich
Russian, 17th - 18th century.
Active 1678-1702.
Icon painter.
Mikhail Schoglokov was the pupil of Besmin. He worked in Moscow, producing painted murals and icons.

SCHOHN, René
French, 20th century.

Born 19 January 1909, in Paris; died 1 November 1995, in Paris.
Sculptor. Monuments, busts, statues.

Trained in Paris at the École Nationale Supérieur des Arts Décoratifs and the École des Beaux-Arts, René Schohn exhibited several times at the Salon des Artistes Français, the Salon d'Automne and the Galerie Bernheim-Jeune. He carved monuments, fountains, busts (including Henri de Montherlant, Paul Valéry and Hervé Bazin), and life-size statues of dancers. He was president of the Association des Peintres et Sculpteurs de Danse, and a board member of the Comité National de la Danse.

SCHOKATNIK. See **SCHOKOTNIGG**

SCHOKOTNIGG, Joseph, or Schockhatnig, Schägotnig
Austrian, 18th century.
Born 1700, in Graz; died 1755, in Graz.
Active in Graz.
Sculptor.

Joseph Schokotnigg's most significant work was the high altar of the Mariahilfer-Kirche in Graz.

SCHOKOTNIGG, Marx or Marcus, or Schoggottnigg, Schokatnik, Sokhätnukh, Sokotnik
Austrian, 17th - 18th century.
Born 1661; died 1731, in Graz.
Active in Graz.
Sculptor.

The father of Joseph, Marx Schokotnigg worked in Italy from 1682 to 1691. Afterwards he lived in Graz, after he was summoned there by Fischer von Erlach to decorate a mausoleum to Ferdinand II.

SCHÖL, Hendrik van. See **SCHOEL**

SCHOLANDER, E. W.
Painter, draughtsman.

MUSEUMS AND GALLERIES:
HELSINKI: *The Saga of King Svegder* (pen drawing).

SCHOLANDER, Fredrik Vilhelm
Swedish, 19th century.
Born 23 June 1816, in Stockholm; died 9 May 1881, in Stockholm.
Painter, watercolourist.

Two watercolours by Scholander, *Moorish Fountain in Palermo* and *Oberwesel Street on the Banks of the Rhine*, are in the museum in Oslo. He worked in Stockholm from 1831 to 1836, in Paris, with Lebas, from 1841 to 1848, and in Rome from 1844 to 1845. He became a member of the Kungliga Akademi för de Fria Konsterna in Stockholm. From 1847 he was a professor there, and he became director between 1851 and 1853.

SCHOLD, Julius
German, 20th century.
Born 1 January 1881, in Hamburg.
Painter.

Julius Schold studied at the art academy in Karlsruhe under Schmidt-Reutte, Weishaupt and Trubner. He lived and worked in Karlsruhe.

SCHOLDER, Fritz
American, 20th - 21st century.
Born 6 October 1937, in Breckenridge (Minnesota); died 10 February 2005, in Scottsdale, Arizona.
Active in Sacramento from 1957 to 1961, in New Mexico and Arizona from 1961.
Painter, sculptor, lithographer, etcher. Figures, landscapes, Native American scenes.

Fritz Scholder was a member of the Luiseño tribe of Mission Indians. Although he did not consider himself an American Indian, he was regarded by many as a leader of the New American Indian Art movement. He was first introduced to art by Oscar Howe, a noted Sioux painter, while in high school in Pierre, South Dakota. In 1957, Scholder moved to Sacramento where he was first exposed to Abstract Expressionism and Pop Art by Wayne Thiebaud at Sacramento City College. Thiebaud invited Scholder to join him in creating a co-operative gallery in Sacramento and helped arrange his first solo exhibition. He exhibited throughout the region including at the Crocker Art Museum in Sacramento and the Palace of Legion of Honor in San Francisco.

In 1961, Scholder was granted a full scholarship to the Southwestern Indian Art Project at the University of Arizona. After graduating with a Master's of Fine Arts degree in 1964, Scholder became an instructor in Advanced Painting and Contemporary Art History at the newly formed Institute of American Indian Arts (IAIA) in Santa Fe, New Mexico. In 1967, his new series depicting the 'real Indian' caused an immediate controversy. Using Pop Art ideas, he attempted to break the long-held and loaded American Indian clichés. Scholder resigned from the IAIA after five years of teaching.

Beginning in the late 1960s, Scholder was a guest artist or artist-in-residence at American University, Idyllwild School of Music and the Arts, Oklahoma Arts Institute, Santa Fe Institute of Fine Arts and Dartmouth College. In 1970, Tamarind Institute moved from Los Angeles to Albuquerque, and Scholder was invited to do his first major project, a suite of lithographs, *Indian Forever*. In 1972, Adelyn Breeskin of the America Museum of Art at the Smithsonian Institution organised a highly-acclaimed two-person show of the work of Scholder and T.C. Cannon, one of his former students. The show travelled to Romania, Yugoslavia, Berlin and London. His first exhibition of photographs was shown at the Heard Museum in 1978, and the Tucson Museum of Art held a retrospective of his work in 1981. Scholder was named life-time Societaire of the Salon d'Automne and exhibited at the Grand Palais in Paris in 1984. In 1994, Scholder returned to Arizona and established his private press, Apocrypha. In 1995, two major shows opened: *The Private Work of Fritz Scholder* at the Phoenix Art Museum and *Fritz Scholder: Icons & Apparitions* at the Scottsdale Center for the Arts in Arizona. In 2000, Scholder worked in London, Paris and Budapest on the *Millennium* series and held a major exhibition in October 2001 of paintings and sculpture, *Last Portraits*, at the Tweed Museum of Art, University of Minnesota in Duluth. In March 2002, Chiaroscuro Galleries in Scottsdale opened a major show entitled *Orchids and Other Flowers*, Scholder's reaction to the September 11th attacks.

BIBLIOGRAPHY:
Taylor, J. and others, *Two American Painters: Fritz Scholder and T.C. Cannon*, exhibition catalogue, National Museum of American Art, Washington DC, 1972. Adams, Clinton, *Fritz Scholder: Lithographs*, New York Graphic Society, Boston, 1975. *Indian Kitsch: The Use and Misuse of Indian Images*, exhibition catalogue, Heard Museum, Phoenix (AZ), 1979. Broder, Patricia Janis, *Leading the West, the Modern Vision*, New York Graphic Society, Boston, 1984. *Fritz Scholder: Mystery Women and Other Recent Works*, exhibition catalogue, Sena Galleries West, 1987. Wilmerding, John/Strick, Jeremy/Newlin, Richard, *Fritz Scholder, Paintings and Monotypes*, Twin Palms Publishers, 1988. *Fritz Scholder: Paintings and Monotypes*, exhibition catalogue, Alexander Gallery, 1991. Rushing, W. Jackson, *'Authenticity and Subjectivity in Post-war Painting: Concerning Herrer, Scholder and Cannon'* in *Shared Visions: Native American Painters and Sculptors in the Twentieth Century (Archuleta, Margaret/Strickland, Rennard, eds.)*, exhibition catalogue, The Heard Museum, Phoenix (AZ), 1991. Lucie-Smith, Edward, *A Survey of Paintings, 1970-1993*, 1993.

MUSEUMS AND GALLERIES:
BELOIT (Wright MA, Beloit College): *Strawberry Fields II* (oil on canvas) - CODY, WYOMING (Whitney Gallery of Western Art, Buffalo Bill Historical Center): paintings - NORMAN, OKLAHOMA (Fred Jones Jr. Museum of Art, University of Oklahoma): *Indian with Tear* (acrylic on canvas) - POMONA, CALIFORNIA (Pomona College Museum of Art): lithographs - TAOS, NEW MEXICO CITY (Harwood Museum of Art): *Indian with Pigeon* (1975) - TULSA, OK (Philbrook Mus. of Art): *The End of the Trail* (oil on canvas).
AUCTION RECORDS:
NEW YORK, 2 Oct 1980, *Dartmouth portrait No. 4* (1973, oil on canvas, 40 x 30 ins / 101.5 x 76.2 cm) USD 4,250. NEW YORK, 10 Nov 1982, *Indian from the Plains* (1974, oil on canvas, 68 x 54 ins / 172.8 x 137 cm) USD 8,250. NEW YORK, 1 Nov 1984, *Diseased Indian with Bird* (1975, acrylic/canvas, 68 x 54 ins / 172.7 x 137.2 cm) USD 7,000. NEW YORK, 1 Oct 1985, *Indian Portrait with Blood* (1975, acrylic/canvas, 80 x 68 ins / 203.2 x 172.7 cm) USD 13,500. NEW YORK, 22 Feb 1986, *Indian with Aura* (1977, oil on canvas, 80 x 68 ins / 203.2 x 172.7 cm) USD 16,000. NEW YORK, 4 May 1988, *Eagle Dancer* (acrylic/canvas, 68 x 54 ins / 172.8 x 137.2 cm) USD 24,200. NEW YORK, 10 Nov 1988, *American Portrait with Earth Vibration* (1975, acrylic/canvas, 800 1/2 x 68 1/4 ins / 2033 x 173.1 cm) USD 33,000. NEW YORK, 7 May 1991, *NYC 5/13/82* (1982, oil on canvas, 40 x 30 ins / 101.6 x 76.2 cm) USD 7,150. NEW YORK, 17 Nov 1992, *Monster Love Number 10* (1986, acrylic/canvas, 50 x 40 ins / 127 x 101.6 cm) USD 8,800. NEW YORK, 4 May 1993, *Hollywood Indian 5* (1973, acrylic/canvas, 80 x 68 ins / 203.2 x 172.7 cm) USD 14,375. NEW YORK, 2 Dec 1993, *Custer* (oil and acrylic/canvas, 40 x 30 ins / 101.6 x 76.2 cm) USD 18,400. NEW YORK, 25-26 Feb 1994, *Portrait in New York 2* (oil on canvas, 40 x 30 ins / 101.6 x 76.2 cm) USD 5,463. NEW YORK, 13 Nov 2001, *American Portrait* (1982, oil on canvas, 40 x 30 ins / 102 x 76 cm) USD 3,600. ST LOUIS, 19 April 2002, *American Portrait No. 43* (c. 1982, oil on canvas, 80 x 68 ins / 203 x 173 cm) USD 9,500. WASHINGTON, 27 April 2002, *Woman with Green Mask* (brown patinated bronze, h. 24 ins / 61 cm) USD 2,800. DALLAS, 13 May 2004, *Near the Opera* (oil on canvas) USD 10,000.

SCHOLDERER, Otto

German, 19th century.
Born 25 January 1834, in Frankfurt am Main; died 25 January 1902, in Frankfurt am Main.
Also active in England.
Painter. Portraits, genre scenes, landscapes, landscapes with figures, still-lifes.

Otto Scholderer trained at the Städelschen Kunstinstitut in Frankfurt under Johann David Passavant and Jakob Becker. He was in Paris from 1857 to 1859 where he met Victor Müller who had a great influence on him, and later became his brother in law, as well as Fantin-Latour, Manet, Courbet and Legros. He spent the period from 1859 to 1865 in Frankfurt, Kronberg and in the Black Forest. From 1866 to 1868, he was in Düsseldorf where he met Hans Thoma; he went back with him to Paris in 1868. Back in Germany at the outbreak of the war in 1870, he joined the circle around F. Leibl in Munich. In 1871 he was in London where he met Whistler, Millais and Burne-Jones; by 1899 he was back in Frankfurt. He married Luise Sternwaldt in Roehampton in 1872.

Scholderer achieved recognition as a painter during his lifetime for his still-lifes and his portraits, which often have an introspective, romantic mood. He was influenced by contemporary French painting, especially Fantin-Latour, Manet and Courbet.

BIBLIOGRAPHY:
Kropmanns, Peter, '*Otto Scholderer (1834-1902), la collection La Caze et Chardin*' in *Revue du Louvre* n° 1 p. 76, periodical, Paris, February 2003.

MUSEUMS AND GALLERIES:
DÜSSELDORF: *Kitchen with Young Woman* - FRANKFURT AM MAIN (Heyman Mus.): *Little Court at Cronberg; Still-life; Frau Scholderer at the Breakfast Table* - FRANKFURT AM MAIN (Städel): *Violin-player at the Window; Portrait of the Child Karl Stiebel* - GDANSK: *Nook in the Taunus* - HAMBURG: *Self-portrait; Portrait of Oswald Sickert; Gladioli in Vase* - KARLSRUHE: *Dead Hare and Woodcocks; Peaches in Silver Basket; Mill in the Black Forest* - SHEFFIELD: *Man and Hares* - WIESBADEN: *Dead Hare* - WUPPERTAL: *Ham.*
AUCTION RECORDS:
LUCERNE, 27 Nov 1964, *Young Italian Woman in Popular Dress,* CHF 4,000. COLOGNE, 6 June 1973, *Portrait of Girl,* DEM 3,800. LONDON, 26 June 1978, *Still-life* (c. 1880, oil on panel, 8 1/4 x 12 ins / 21 x 30.5 cm) GBP 12,000. COLOGNE, 21 May 1981, *Still-life with Apples* (oil on canvas, 14 1/4 x 18 ins / 36 x 46 cm) DEM 8,000. COLOGNE, 22 Nov 1984, *Still-life with Apples* (oil on canvas, 14 1/4 x 18 ins / 36 x 46 cm) DEM 12,000. LONDON, 7 Feb 1986, *Tavern Scene* (oil on canvas, 26 1/2 x 30 1/2 ins / 67.3 x 77.5 cm) GBP 4,800. AMSTERDAM, 10 Feb 1988, *Stags in Alpine Forest* (oil on canvas, two pendants, each 11 3/4 x 15 3/4 ins / 30 x 40 cm) NLG 3,450. COLOGNE, 29 June 1990, *Poachers* (oil on canvas, 9 x 7 ins / 22 x 18 cm) DEM 3,500. LONDON, 16 Nov 1994, *Still-life of Overturned Basket of Peaches and Bouquet of White Flowers on Marble Mantelshelf* (oil on canvas, 11 3/4 x 16 1/4 ins / 30 x 41 cm) GBP 63,100. VIENNA, 29-30 Oct 1996, *Young Woman Arranging Flowers* (1900, 45 1/4 x 37 1/4 ins / 115 x 94.5 cm) ATS 2,775,000. STUTTGART, 19 March 1999, *Hunting Still-life with Game and Poultry* (1865, oil on canvas, 30 x 25 ins / 76 x 64 cm) DEM 5,500. MUNICH, 1 Dec 1999, *Return from Harvest, Farmer and Two Maids Carrying Baskets* (1881, oil on canvas, 41 x 52 ins / 103 x 131 cm) DEM 38,000. DÜSSELDORF, 31 Jan 2000, *Still-life with Fish and Oysters* (oil on canvas, 19 x 9 ins / 48 x 23 cm) DEM 9,000. LONDON, 29 March 2001, *Return from the Harvest* (1881, oil on canvas, 47 x 52 ins / 119 x 131 cm) GBP 50,000. AHLDEN, 12 May 2001, *Still-life of Fruits in a Wooden Box* (oil on canvas, 16 x 20 ins / 40 x 50 cm) DEM 10,000. HEIDELBERG, 19 April 2002, *Girl's Portrait* (oil on panel, 11 x 9 ins / 28 x 22 cm) EUR 1,800. FRANKFURT, 23 Nov 2002, *Summer Landscape with River and Cows* (1899, oil on board, 17 x 22 ins / 44 x 57 cm) EUR 3,600. STUTTGART, 25 Sept 2003, *Woman's Portrait* (1866, oil on canvas, 28 x 24 ins / 72 x 62 cm) EUR 3,000. STUTTGART, 25 Sept 2003, *Self-portrait* (oil on canvas, 24 x 20 ins / 60 x 50 cm) EUR 9,000. HEIDELBERG, 2 April 2004, *Young Woman* (oil on canvas, 28 x 24 ins / 72 x 62 cm) EUR 3,400.

SCHOLE

Austrian, 19th century.
Died December 1866, in Prague.
Active in Prague.
Painter. Flowers.

Schole lived for some time as a political refugee in Serbia.

SCHÖLE, Joachim, or Scholle

German, 16th century.
Painter.

SCHOLER, Jakob

20th century.
Born 1910.
Draughtsman.

MUSEUMS AND GALLERIES:
AARAU (Aargauer Kunsthaus): *Floral ornament; State flower garden and fishpond.*

SCHÖLER, Johann Jósef

Bohemian School, 18th century.
Active in Reichenberg (now Liberec, Czech Republic).
Painter.

SCHØLER, Peter Christian
Danish, 19th century.
Born 13 July 1803, in Hammel; died 16 November 1867.
Engraver (burin).
Schøler was a pupil of Johan Ludwig Lund.

SCHOLEUS, Hieronymus
Swedish, 16th century.
Draughtsman.
Hieronymus Scholeus drew views of Stockholm and Bergen.

SCHOLIJ, J. C.
German, 17th century.
Draughtsman.

SCHOLKMANN, Wilhelm Ludwig
German, 19th - 20th century.
Born 25 December 1867, in Berlin.
Painter, engraver.
Worpswede Artists' Colony.
Wilhelm Ludwig Scholkmann worked in Munich, and for a time at the Munich art academy with Herterich and Raab. He lived and worked in Ostendorf, near Worpswede.

SCHOLL
German, 18th century.
Painter, engraver. Religious subjects, portraits.
He worked in Otterbach and carried out sculptures in the Protestant church in Jugenheim.

SCHOLL, Anton Friedrich
German, 19th century.
Born 27 September 1839, in Mainz; died 7 April 1892, in Mainz.
Sculptor. Figures. Busts.
After studying under Bläser, Anton Scholl went to Paris, England and Italy.
MUSEUMS AND GALLERIES:
MAINZ: *The painter Philipp Veit* (bust); *The Painter Ph. Janz* (bust); *The Painter L. Lindenschmit* (bust).

SCHÖLL, Georg Christof
German, 18th century.
Born 1720; died 7 August 1805, in Ansbach.
Sculptor.
A court painter, Georg Schöll worked mainly for the castle at Ansbach.

SCHOLL, Hermann
German, 20th century.
Born 27 March 1875, in Darmstadt.
Sculptor.
Hermann Scholl was trained by his father Karl and uncle Anton Friedrich. He undertook a study trip to Berlin from 1896 to 1900 and subsequently lived in Darmstadt. He sculpted a memorial erected in Heppenheim in memory of the councillor *Ludwig*.

SCHOLL, Johann
German, 18th century.
Active in Bonn.
Sculptor.

SCHOLL, Johann
German, 18th century.
Born 1 March 1728, in Munich; died 19 July 1799, in Munich.
Painter, miniaturist. Portraits.
Johann Scholl was the pupil of G. de Marées.

SCHOLL, Johann Adam
German, 18th century.
Born 1733, in Obereuerheim; died in Trier.
Sculptor.
After studying in Hamburg, he settled in Trier.

SCHOLL, Johann Baptist, the Elder
German, 19th century.
Born 1784, in Bamberg; died 6 July 1854, in Darmstadt.
Sculptor.
Johann Scholl was the son of Johann W. Wurzer. Grand Duke Ludwig I of Hessen appointed him court painter at Darmstadt. There he collaborated regularly with Georg Moller and sculpted several busts in a classical style.

SCHOLL, Johann Baptist, the Younger
French, 19th century.
Born 6 April 1818, in Mainz, Germany; died 26 September 1881, in Limburg, Netherlands.
Painter, sculptor, engraver.
Johann Scholl was the son and pupil of the sculptor Johann Baptist Scholl. He worked at the Munich academy from 1832 to 1840. From 1840 to 1875 he lived in Frankfurt, Rodelheim (near Frankfurt) and Darmstadt. He spent his final years in Limbourg, north-east Belgium. He created the monuments to *Schiller* in Mainz (central Germany) and Wiesbaden (southern Germany). He also painted the ceilings in the Darmstadt theatre.
MUSEUMS AND GALLERIES:
DARMSTADT: *Mother* (painting) - FRANKFURT AM MAIN: *Comedy and Tragedy* (canvas).

SCHOLL, Johann Georg
German, 18th - 19th century.
Born 1763, in Bamberg; died 22 October 1820, in Mainz.
Sculptor.
A pupil and later collaborator of Johann Bernhard Kamm, Johann Scholl was the assistant of Pfaff in Mainz from 1787 to 1794. He was responsible for the monument to the *Graf von Wolkenstein* in Mainz and four allegorical figures of the castle at Schönbusch, near Aschaffenburg.

SCHOLL, Johann Valentin
German, 18th century.
Born 1730, in Obereuerheim; died 3 November 1799, in Bamberg.
Sculptor.

SCHOLL, Joseph Franz
German, 19th century.
Born 4 December 1796, in Mainz; died 7 April 1842, in Mainz.
Sculptor, art restorer. Portraits.
Joseph Scholl was the pupil of his father Johann Georg, in Rome he frequented the Overbeck circle in 1829-1830. He was the most sought-after sculptor in Mainz in the first third of the 19th century and was responsible for the restoration of the pulpit in its cathedral.
MUSEUMS AND GALLERIES:
MANNHEIM: *Portrait of Professor Lehne.*

SCHOLL, Karl
German, 19th - 20th century.
Born 11 July 1840, in Munich; died 12 January 1912, in Darmstadt (Hesse).
Sculptor.
Karl Scholl was trained by his father Johann Baptist Scholl the Younger and at the art school at Frankfurt am Main. He left two marble statues of the Grand Dukes *Louis I* and *Louis III* at the theatre in Darmstadt.

SCHOLL, Peter Ignaz
German, 19th century.
Born 1780, in Bamberg; died 1825, in Bremen.
Sculptor.

SCHOLL, Philipp Johann Joseph, called Johannes
German, 19th century.

Born 1805, in Bremen; died 7 October 1861, in Copenhagen.
Sculptor.
Philipp Scholl was the son of a sculptor. His masters were his uncle J.-B. Scholl, K. Eberhard in Munich and Schwanthaler and Thorvaldsen in Rome. He worked in Copenhagen and Bremen.
MUSEUMS AND GALLERIES:
BREMEN (Kunsthalle): *Suffer the Little Children to Come unto me.*

SCHÖLL, Sebastian. See **SCHEEL**

SCHOLLA, Pierre
French, 20th century.
Born 5 August 1928, in Pavillons-sous-Bois.
Painter, draughtsman, screen printer. Landscapes with figures.
Poetic Reality.
In Paris Pierre Scholla attended the Académie de la Grande Chaumière in Montparnasse and the Académie Samson-Vilcot. He was a pupil of Armand Nakache. He went to New York, where he became acquainted with American abstraction. He was a friend of Lorjou and is president of the Société d'Art of Corbeil-Essones.

He has exhibited in group exhibitions and solo shows, including: 1967, Galerie Jean Campion, Paris; 1972, Centre d'Art Contemporain, Corbeil; 1981, Pflaster's Gallery, Dallas; 1991, Galerie Josette Meyer, Paris; 1992, Town Hall, Propriano; 1992, Galerie Stopin, Juvisy; 1995, Orangerie du Parc de Villeroy, Mennecy; 1995, Ste-Geneviève-des-Bois; 1997, Commanderie St-Jean, Corbeil; 2001, *Une fenêtre sur le monde* (*A Window on the World*), Huis-Clos, Paris; 2001 *Pierre Scholla Insolite* (*Unusual Pierre Scholla*), Galerie d'Art, Corbeil-Essones; 2002, Musée de la Tour Carrée, Ste-Maxime; 2003, Espace Culturel Paul Bedu, Milly-la-Forêt (Essones).

Initially Pierre Scholla painted clowns, mimes and harlequins in the post-war expressionist and miserabilist style. He then moved to an extreme simplification of drawing. His landscapes of the South of France and Corsica are painted in a stylised abstraction, restrained and refined, that uses planes and flat areas of contrasted colours.

SCHOLLAERT, Adriaen
Belgian, 15th - 16th century.
Active in Alost.
Painter.
In 1494 and 1515 Adriaen Schollaert painted decorations for the town procession in Alost.

SCHOLLE, Joachim. See **SCHÖLE**

SCHOLLENBERGER, Johann Jakob
German, 17th century.
Active in Nuremberg c. 1675.
Painter, engraver (burin).
Johann Schollenberger was primarily a portrait artist.

SCHOLLER, Hanns
German, 15th - 16th century.
Born to a family originally from Nuremberg.
Active at the end of the 15th and the beginning of the 16th century.
Engraver. Portraits.
From 1490 to 1517 Hanns Scholler was in the service of King Ladislas of Bohemia and Hungary.

SCHØLLER, Johannes Caspar, or Schiöller
Danish, 18th century.
Born in Denmark.
Painter. Portraits, landscapes.
Schøller was a pupil at the Kunstakademi in Copenhagen from 1759 until 1762. He reproduced landscapes and executed the portrait of *Christian VII* at the Leinstranden church.

SCHOLLER, Matthias
German, 17th century.
Born to a family originally from Mewe.
Sculptor (wood).

SCHOLLER, Rezsö or Rudolf
Hungarian, 20th century.
Born 28 June 1882, in Neumarkt (now Tîrgu Mures).
Painter. Landscapes.
Scholler lived and worked in Budapest.

SCHOLLER, Severin, or Scholer
German, 17th century.
Active in Trier 1650-1666.
Sculptor.

SCHÖLLER, Thomas
German, 18th century.
Active c. 1758.
Painter.
Thomas Schöller painted the portrait of *Franz Wenzl* who was a rector at the Jesuit college in Breslau (now Wroclaw, Poland) from 1726 to 1736.

SCHÖLLGEN, Hubert
German, 20th century.
Born 23 February 1897, in Düsseldorf.
Painter, engraver.
Hubert Schöllgen was a pupil at the royal academy with Emil Orlik and Thorn-Prikker.

SCHÖLLHAMMER, Johann Melchior, or Schelhammer
German, 18th - 19th century.
Born 1745; died 15 April 1816.
Painter (porcelain).
Johann Schöllhammer worked at the porcelain factory at Ansbach Bruckberg, where he became Director.

SCHOLTE, Dirck and Lauwerus
Dutch, 17th century.
Active in The Hague.
Painters.
Two artists by the name of Scholte appear in the guild register of painters in The Hague: Dirck (1677) and Lauwerus (1690).

SCHOLTE, Rob
Dutch, 20th - 21st century.
Born 1958.
Painter. Figure compositions, figures.
Rob Scholte studied audio-visual techniques at the Minerva Academy in Groningen (1975-1976), then at the Gerrit Rietveld Academie in Amsterdam (1977-1982). As a painter, he is self-taught. He lives and works in Amsterdam. Early on, he acquired a certain notoriety. Often linked with Pop Art, his paintings are full of quotations and distorted images, presenting a realist iconography that clashes. Technically, he retouches his paintings after an initial silkscreen print. He conveys, with a sharp edge, a criticism of the standardisation of the world of art and culture.

He has taken part in collective exhibitions such as Prospect 86, Frankfurt (1986), Documenta 8, Kassel (1987), *Aperto*, Venice Biennale (1988), and the Venice Biennale again in 1990. Solo shows have been in Amsterdam (Living Room, 1984), Musée St-Pierre, Lyons (1987), Boymans Van Beuningen Museum, Rotterdam (1988), Galerie Charles Cartwright, Paris (1989), Musée d'Art et d'Histoire, Luxembourg (1994) and the Abbaye Ste-Andrée, Meymac (1994).

Museums and Galleries:
Amsterdam (Stedelijk Mus.) - Lyons (MBA): *The Theory of Dominoes* - Rotterdam (Mus. Boijmans Van Beuningen).
Auction records:
Amsterdam, 11 Dec 1991, *The Fall of the Pole Star* (acrylic/canvas, 47 1/4 x 59 ins / 120 x 150 cm) NLG 8,050. Amsterdam, 31 May 1995, *Platitude* (1986, acrylic/canvas, 69 x 69 ins / 175 x 175 cm) NLG 29,500. Amsterdam, 2-3 June 1997, *Zaak IIIA, IIIB, IIIC* (1979, acrylic/canvas, triptych, each 13 1/2 x 13 1/4 ins / 34.3 x 33.6 cm) NLG 18,880. Amsterdam, 4 June 1997, *Overspel* (1986, oil on canvas, 78 3/4 x 61 1/4 ins / 200 x 155.5 cm) NLG 74,958. Amsterdam, 9 June 2004, *Mondrian Revisited: Grey and Red Composition* (1998, oil on canvas, 51 x 51 ins / 130 x 130 cm) EUR 2,600.

SCHOLTEN, Hendrik Jacobus

Dutch, 19th century.
Born 11 July 1824, in Amsterdam; died 29 May 1907, in Heemstede.
Painter, engraver, draughtsman. Historical subjects, figures, genre scenes, interiors with figures.

Hendrik Jacobus Scholten was a pupil of Petrus Jacobus Greive and L. J. Hansen. He later became curator of the Tyler Museum in Amsterdam.
Museums and Galleries:
Amsterdam: *Sunday Morning; Gerrit Honthorst Showing the Drawings of his Pupil Louise of Bohemia to Amalia van Sohns*; drawings - Amsterdam (Stedelijk Mus.): *Morning Stroll; Vossius and Vondel's Farewell; Rose; Morning Reading.*
Auction records:
Paris, 1873, *Tric-trac Players,* FRF 2,000. Amsterdam, 1884, a painting, subject unspecified) FRF 2,217. Rotterdam, 1891, *Duo,* FRF 830; *Women Musicians,* FRF 325. London, 8 March 1926, *Departure* (drawing) GBP 21. London, 23 May 1962, *Writing a Letter,* GBP 700. London, 3 Feb 1967, *Letter,* Gns 400. Bern, 7 May 1971, *Studio Visit,* CHF 10,000. London, 16 June 1978, *Galileo* (oil on panel, 13 1/4 x 11 3/4 ins / 33.5 x 30 cm) GBP 800. Los Angeles, 16 March 1981, *Man with a Mandolin* (oil on canvas, 22 x 19 ins / 56 x 48.5 cm) USD 2,100. Amsterdam, 29 Oct 1984, *Bad News* (1855, oil on panel, 16 1/4 x 19 ins / 41 x 48.5 cm) NLG 5,800. New York, 15 Feb 1985, *Young Woman with a Bouquet of Flowers* (oil on canvas, 30 3/4 x 23 ins / 78.1 x 57.5 cm) USD 3,800. Amsterdam, 25 April 1990, *In a Rose Garden* (1887, oil on panel, 7 3/4 x 6 1/4 ins / 20 x 16 cm) NLG 5,750. Amsterdam, 11 Sept 1990, *Sad News* (1855, oil on panel, 16 1/4 x 19 3/4 ins / 41.5 x 50 cm) NLG 4,600. Amsterdam, 14-15 April 1992, *Maternal Happiness* (1895, oil on panel, 15 x 20 ins / 38 x 51 cm) NLG 7,820. Amsterdam, 20 April 1993, *Woman Carrying Roses in her Apron, Accompanied by a Dog* (1887, oil on panel, 17 1/4 x 13 3/4 ins / 44 x 35 cm) NLG 3,450. Amsterdam, 21 April 1994, *Rose Season* (1887, oil on panel, 17 3/4 x 12 3/4 ins / 45 x 32.5 cm) NLG 5,175. London, 17 June 1994, *Some Good Advice* (oil on panel, 15 x 19 1/2 ins / 38 x 49.5 cm) GBP 6,325. Amsterdam, 8 Nov 1994, *Two Young Women Playing Music* (oil on panel, 19 1/4 x 15 1/4 ins / 49 x 39 cm) NLG 29,900. Amsterdam, 7 Nov 1995, *Declaration* (oil on panel, 21 1/4 x 19 1/2 ins / 54 x 49.5 cm) NLG 14,160. London, 11 June 2002, *Sunday Morning* (oil on panel, 32 x 24 ins / 82 x 60 cm) GBP 15,000. London, 21 Nov 2002, *Letter* (oil on canvas, 30 x 22 ins / 77 x 57 cm) GBP 7,500. Lokeren, 13 March 2004, *Mother by the Cradle* (oil on panel, 15 x 12 ins / 38 x 30 cm) EUR 3,800.

SCHOLTEN, Petrus Nicolas

Dutch, 19th century.
Born 19 July 1805, in The Hague.
Painter. Still-lifes.

Petrus Nicolas Scholten was a pupil of Westenberg. He was also an innkeeper in Amsterdam.

SCHOLTZ, Christoph

German, 18th century.
Active in Warmbrunn 1713-1721.
Engraver.

Christoph Scholtz was an engraver of glass and crystal.

SCHOLTZ, Daniel, or Scholtze

German, 17th century.
Born 1657; died 19 July 1686, in Breslau (now Wroclaw, Poland).
Engraver. Armorials.

Daniel Scholtz was the son of Johann Gottfried. See also Daniel Schaltz.

SCHOLTZ, Elias

German, 18th century.
Stucco artist.

Elias Scholtz did out the stucco decoration at the castle of Wandsbeck, near Hamburg.

SCHOLTZ, Georg, the Elder

German, 17th century.
Born 1588; died 12 February 1647, in Breslau (now Wroclaw, Poland).
Painter.

A master in Breslau from 1616 onwards, Georg Scholtz painted the portrait of *Chr. Cholerus* in the church of St Elisabeth there.

SCHOLTZ, Georg, the Younger

German, 17th century.
Born 4 April 1622; died 20 April 1677, in Breslau (now Wroclaw, Poland).
Painter.

Georg Scholtz was a prolific painter and the son of Georg Scholtz the Elder.

SCHOLTZ, Heinrich

Austrian, 17th century.
Active in Brieg (now Brzeg, Poland) during the second half of the 17th century.
Engraver, silhouettist.

SCHOLTZ, Johann Gottfried

German, 17th century.
Born 1619; died 30 August 1666.
Painter, miniaturist. Portraits.

Johann Scholtz was the son of Georg and the brother of Daniel. From 1647 he was a master in Breslau (now Wroclaw, Poland). Two of his miniature portraits are in the municipal museum in Leipzig.

SCHOLTZ, Julius

German, 19th century.
Born 12 February 1825, in Breslau (now Wroclaw, Poland); died 2 June 1893, in Dresden.
Painter. History painting, portraits, genre scenes.

Julius Scholtz attended the academy in Dresden and was taught by Julius Hubner. After spending time in Belgium and France, he became, in 1863, a member of the academy in Dresden and in 1874 a member of the academy in Berlin. On 1st November 1874 he was appointed Professor at the academy in Dresden. In 1866 he received the gold medal in Berlin.
Museums and Galleries:
Bautzen: *Portrait of the Elder Thielau* - Berlin (Nationalgal.): *Banquet of the Generals of Wallenstein* - Chemnitz: *Portrait of Countess Einsiedel* - Dresden (Gemäldegal. Neue Meister): *Portrait of Frau Köpping, the Artist's Mother-in-law; Consul Mahs; Portrait of Frau Mahs; Study for the Painting of the Volunteers of Breslau; The Venice Lido; Sleeping Herdsman; In the Grossiedlitz Park; Visit; Peasants Going Home* - Dresden (Stadtmus.): *Combat on the Dresden Barricades in May 1849; Saxon Troup Returning to Dresden 11 July, under*

the Leadership of Prince Albert; King Johannes and Queen Amalie in the Catholic Church of the Court at Dresden - KARLSRUHE: *Banquet of the Generals of Wallenstein* - MUNICH: *The Officer's Widow* - WROCLAW: *Volunteers of 1813 before King Friedrich Wilhelm III in Breslau.*

AUCTION RECORDS:

VIENNA, 16 March 1976, *Hermann Dorothea* (1886, oil on canvas, 51 1/2 x 33 1/2 ins / 131 x 85 cm) ATS 32,000. COLOGNE, 12 June 1980, *Interior of Church* (1856, oil on card, 11 1/4 x 9 ins / 28.5 x 23 cm) DEM 2,200. COLOGNE, 1 July 2004, *Shepherd Boy Sleeping in a Mountainous Landscape* (1874, oil on board, 10 x 12 ins / 26 x 31 cm) EUR 6,000.

SCHOLTZ, Robert Friedrich Karl

German, 20th century.
Born 14 April 1877, in Dresden.
Painter, engraver. Landscapes.

Robert Friedrich Karl Scholtz was the son of the musician Hermann Scholtz, who died in 1918. He studied under his uncle Robert Nadler in Budapest for seventeen years. He studied at the art academy in Dresden under L. Pohle, and from 1900 at the Munich art academy under Karl Marr. In spring 1901 he travelled to Paris. In 1903 he settled in Breslau (now Wroclaw, Poland). He undertook many more journeys, including in 1907 to Morocco and Spain, in 1908 to England, Ireland and Paris, in 1989 to Rome, and in 1910 to Egypt and Italy. From 1907 he lived in Berlin, where he joined the leaders of the Berliner Secession: Corinth, Spiro and Leo von König.

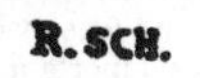

Stamp of sale

MUSEUMS AND GALLERIES:

BERLIN (Nationalgal.): *Millenium Lime in the March; The Klobich Lake.*

SCHOLTZ, Walther

German, 19th - 20th century.
Born 20 February 1861, in Dresden; died 2 August 1910, in Meersbury.
Painter. Portraits, genre scenes, landscapes.

Walther Scholtz was the son of history painter Julius Scholtz, studied at the art academy in Dresden and worked in the studio of Pauwels. He continued his artistic training in Munich where he spent several years, before returning to settle in Dresden. He was awarded a silver medal in Dresden in 1886.

MUSEUMS AND GALLERIES:

DRESDEN: *Dresden Women Nursing Injured French Soldiers during the Battle of Dresden; View from the Terrace in Bruhl.*

SCHOLTZ, Wilhelm

German, 19th century.
Born 23 January 1824, in Berlin; died 20 June 1893, in Berlin.
Painter, draughtsman.

Wilhelm Scholtz's master was Wilhelm Wach. He abandoned painting early on to dedicate himself to drawing. From 1848 he was employed by Adolf Hoffmann to illustrate the *Kladderadatch*, a satirical magazine which was not long established. He was best-known for his caricatures of Bismarck and Napoleon.

SCHOLTZE, Johannes

German, 17th century.
Active in Bautzen.
Painter.

Johannes Scholtze's works show the influence of Netherlandish engravings.

MUSEUMS AND GALLERIES:

BAUTZEN (Stadtmus.): *Last Judgement; Resurrection.*

SCHOLZ, August

German, 18th - 19th century.
Born c. 1771; died 14 March 1838, in Breslau (now Wroclaw, Poland).
Painter, engraver. Landscapes, architectural views, flowers, insects.

SCHOLZ, Augustin

German, 18th century.
Active in Olmütz (now Olomouc, Czech Republic) 1744-1751.
Sculptor.

SCHOLZ, E.

German, 19th century.
Active in Breslau (now Wroclaw) c. 1840.
Painter (porcelain).

SCHOLZ, Eduard

German, 19th century.
Born 1808.
Painter. Genre scenes, portraits.

SCHOLZ, Georg

German, 20th century.
Born 10 October 1890, in Wolfenbüttel; died 1945, in Karlsruhe.
Painter, engraver, draughtsman, lithographer. Genre scenes, landscapes, landscapes with figures.
Neue Sachlichkeit (New Objectivity).

Georg Scholz studied at the art academy in Karlsruhe between 1908 and 1912 under Caspar Ritter, Ludwig Dill and Wilhelm Trübner, and in Berlin under Lovis Corinth. From 1919 he was a member of the Novembergruppe (November Group). He became friends with Otto Dix and taught at the art school in Karlsruhe. He decorated the church of St Urbain in Freiburg.

His work shows his Dadaist influence, and he portrayed, with biting irony, the petit-bourgeois morals of Weimar Society. He painted mostly urban and industrial landscapes between 1923 and 1927, and later painted some portraits. His style was realist, and approached the aesthetics of die Neue Sachlichkeit.

MUSEUMS AND GALLERIES:

DÜSSELDORF: *Guard House* - KARLSRUHE: *View from the Kitchen Window* - MANNHEIM: *Grötzingen.*

AUCTION RECORDS:

MUNICH, 2 Dec 1980, *Masters of the World* (1925?, lithograph, 11 1/2 x 15 3/4 ins / 29.5 x 40 cm) DEM 1,600.

SCHOLZ, Heinrich Karl

Austrian, 20th century.
Born 16 October 1880, in Mildenau, Bohemia (now Saxony-Anhalt, Germany).
Sculptor.

MUSEUMS AND GALLERIES:

VIENNA (Kunsthistorisches Mus.): medals.

AUCTION RECORDS:

NEW YORK, 1 March 1980, *Pierrot and Pierrette* (1919, patinated bronze, h. 14 ins / 35.5 cm) USD 1,200.

SCHOLZ, Karl

Austrian, 20th century.
Born 9 October 1879, in Horn.
Painter.

Karl Scholz studied at the art academy in Vienna.

SCHOLZ, Leopold

Austrian, 19th - 20th century.
Born 6 December 1874, in Vienna.
Active in Athens.
Sculptor.

Leopold Scholz was a pupil of Anton Brenek, E. von Hellmer and C. Kundmann.

SCHOLZ, Max

German, 19th - 20th century.
Born 1855, in Neiss; died 1906.
Painter. Genre scenes.

Max Scholz trained under Anton Brenek, E. von Hellmer and C. Kundmann. He lived and worked in Munich.

AUCTION RECORDS:

LONDON, 3 Oct 1979, *Monk Studying* (1883, oil on canvas, 25 1/2 x 17 1/4 ins / 65 x 44 cm) GBP 2,000. VIENNA, 17 Nov 1981, *Entertaining Newspaper* (oil on panel, 12 1/2 x 15 3/4 ins / 32 x 40 cm) ATS 65,000. NEW YORK, 25 May 1984, *A Good Vintage* (oil on canvas, 19 3/4 x 24 1/4 ins / 50.2 x 61.6 cm) USD 3,800. NEW YORK, 30 Oct 1985, *Monk with a Tankard of Ale; Monk with a Glass of Wine* (oil on panel, a pair, 15 3/4 x 12 3/4 ins / 40 x 32.5 cm) USD 8,500. MUNICH, 29 Nov 1989, *A Lake in Bavaria* (oil on canvas, 16 1/2 x 39 ins / 42 x 99 cm) DEM 19,800. NEW YORK, 17 Feb 1994, *Cardinal Reading in his Office* (oil on panel, 12 1/2 x 16 1/4 ins / 32 x 41 cm) USD 4,830. NEW YORK, 26 Feb 1997, *A Clergyman and some Monks round a Table* (oil on canvas, 29 1/4 x 34 1/2 ins / 74.2 x 87.6 cm) USD 3,680.

SCHOLZ, Paul

Austrian, 19th - 20th century.
Born 1 October 1859, in Vienna.
Painter.

Paul Scholz was a pupil of Georg Sturm, Ferdinand Laufberger, Rudolph Hölzel, Bernhard Buttersack and Henry Luyten. He taught at the Graz Art School from 1884 to 1915. He lived and worked in Graz.

His principal work was the decoration of the university and Scottish church in Vienna, the Llyod palace in Triest, and the Post and Telegraph Office in Graz.

SCHOLZ, Peter

German, 20th century.
Painter.

Peter Scholz produced very detailed paintings of imaginary ruins.

SCHOLZ, Richard

German, 19th - 20th century.
Born 29 December 1860, in Hanover; died 3 August 1939.
Painter. Figures, portraits, genre scenes.

Richard Scholz was the son of choirmaster Bernhard Scholz. In 1877 he entered the Karlsruhe art school, where he was a pupil of Ernst Hildebrand. In 1880 he went to Berlin. He lived in Dresden, and later, from 1903 until his death, in Munich.

He was influenced by C. Gusvow. From 1889 to 1895 he lived in Frankfurt, where he painted mostly portraits.

MUSEUMS AND GALLERIES:

MAINZ: *Portrait of a Young Lady* - WROCLAW: *Marigolds; Meeting of the Town Council.*

SCHOLZ, Richard

German, 20th century.
Born 19 March 1872, in Berlin.
Painter, illustrator.

Richard Scholz studied in Berlin and Munich and worked in Dresden.

SCHOLZ, Siegmund

German, 18th century.
Medallist.

SCHOLZ, Werner

German, 20th century.
Born 1898, in Berlin; died 1982, in Alpbach.
Painter, pastellist. Figure compositions, figures, landscapes.

Werner Scholz entered art school in Berlin in 1916, but interrupted his studies to serve in the army. At the age of 18, during World War I, his left forearm was amputated. From 1919 to 1921 he returned to his studies in Berlin.

In 1930 he met Emil Nolde. Their acquaintance was his only direct contact with Expressionism. In 1937 the Nazi party declared his art 'degenerate', along with that of Grosz, Dix, Beckmann, and in particular, Nolde. All his works were removed from museums, and he was banned from exhibiting in Germany. In 1939 he fled to Tyrol, where he remained permanently. His studio in Berlin, which housed several of his paintings, was destroyed in 1944 by bombing, and much of his other work has disappeared.

He painted his first triptychs in the 1930s. From 1948 to 1951 he created a series of pastels on the themes of the *Old* and *New Testaments*. The 48 pastels on the *Apocalypse* were bought by the Albertina Museum in Vienna. Several works from c. 1952 were also inspired by ancient mythology. This marked a period of relative calm in the artist's life and art; he was commissioned to produce a triptych on the *World of Steel* (1954), and from 1957 began painting landscapes. Before this, most of his work had been a reflection of his sombre life and social anxiety. In common with other German expressionists of the 1930s, he was preoccupied with the political evolution of his country.

His paintings featured pathetic characters, lacking a distinct identity, but tending to represent a general type. The faces of these characters are painted with sweeping strokes, shadowed with black, often with a fleeting impression of a single eye. Religion often rubs shoulders with abject misery. His sympathy for mankind was evident in his depiction of poor children. Black was important in his work, and served to form outlines, but also to darken his colours, at least in his earlier work. From around 1930, under Nolde's influence, he learned to contrast bright colours with black.

His work remained tragic even after he fled to Tyrol, but he was gradually drawn to its mountainous landscapes, and his first landscapes date from this period. They were initially disturbing, inhuman, inhospitable, and empty of people. His approach softened in the 1960s, and although still aware of the contradictions and evils of society, he expressed them with less pathos, and sometimes allowed an element of humour to appear, as in the work *Amsterdam II*.

He first exhibited at the Nierendorf Gallery in Berlin in 1930, then in 1932 at Essen's Museum Folkwang, at the Kunstverein in Cologne in 1934, in Constance in 1946, at the Museum of Art in Santa Barbara (USA) in 1950 and at the Musée des Beaux-Arts in Lyons in 1970.

BIBLIOGRAPHY:

Behme, Adolf, *Werner Scholz*, E. Stichnote, Potsdam, 1948. Myers, Bernard Samuel, *Die Malerei des Expressionismus: eine Generation im Aufbrucht*, DuMont, Cologne, 1957. Forter, O.H., *Werner Scholz*, Essen, 1958. Myers, Bernard Samuel, *The German Expressionists, a Generation in Revolt*, McGraw-Hill, New York, 1963. Gadamer, H.G., *Werner Scholz*, A. Bongers, Recklinghausen, 1968. Fricker, Jacques, *Werner Scholz*, exhibition catalogue, Musée des Beaux-Arts, Lyon, Recklinghausen, 1970. Zemter, Wolfgang, *Werner Scholz: zum 100 Geburtstag*, exhibition catalogue, Bönen, Kettler, 1998.

Museums and Galleries:
Berlin (Nationalgal.) - Cologne (Wallraf-Richartz Mus.): *Tyrolean Madonna* (1933) - Detroit - Duisburg - Essen (Folkwang Mus.) - Hamburg (Kunsthalle) - Innsbruck - Mannheim (Städtische Kunsthalle) - Moscow - Munich - Nuremberg - St Petersburg (Hermitage) - Stavanger - Stuttgart (Staatsgal.) - Vienna (Albertina Mus.) - Vienna (Historisches Mus.) - Vienna (Kunstmus.) - Witten (Märkisches Mus.).
Auction records:
Cologne, 3 Dec 1977, *Yellow Tulips* (hardboard, 28¼ x 22¼ ins / 72 x 56.5 cm) DEM 4,400. Cologne, 19 May 1979, *Still-life with Flowers* (coloured chalk, 19 x 22¾ ins / 48.2 x 58 cm) DEM 1,800. Munich, 30 Nov 1979, *Portrait of a Woman* (1971, oil on paper, 19 x 15¾ ins / 48 x 40 cm) DEM 1,800. Munich, 30 May 1980, *The Dancer* (1950, pastel, 20½ x 11¾ ins / 52 x 30 cm) DEM 2,400. Munich, 29 May 1984, *Girl at Prayer* (1937, oil on card, 46½ x 32¼ ins / 118 x 82 cm) DEM 5,000. Cologne, 8 Dec 1984, *Cardinal* (1945, pastel, 24¾ x 19 ins / 63 x 48 cm) DEM 2,500. Munich, 1-2 Dec 1992, *Embrace* (1931, oil on paper, 40½ x 28¼ ins / 103 x 72 cm) DEM 54,050. Berlin, 5 June 1999, *Mother and Child* (1930, oil on card, 31 x 23 ins / 79 x 59 cm) DEM 24,000. Berlin, 5 June 1999, *Birthday* (1927, oil on card, 25 x 20 ins / 64 x 50 cm) DEM 24,000. Munich, 2 Dec 2000, *Butterflies* (pastel, 21 x 15 ins / 53 x 37 cm) DEM 3,800. Munich, 2 Dec 2000, *Schlern* (1959, oil on board, 15 x 31 ins / 39 x 80 cm) DEM 16,000. Munich, 19 May 2001, *The Monstranz* (1933, oil on board, double-sided triptych, 47 x 33 ins / 120 x 83 cm) DEM 25,000. Cologne, 4 Dec 2001, *In Appenin* (oil on panel, 30 x 30 ins / 75 x 75 cm) DEM 16,000. Berlin, 27 April 2002, *Engadine II* (oil on panel, 24 x 42 ins / 60 x 106 cm) EUR 3,000. Berlin, 31 May 2003, *Dschott* (oil on panel, 24 x 28 ins / 60 x 70 cm) EUR 4,500. Hamburg, 4 June 2003, *Five Finger Peaks* (oil on masonite, 30 x 26 ins / 76 x 67 cm) EUR 6,500. Berlin, 11 June 2004, *In the Park. Dead Child* (1927, oil on cardboard, double-sided, 29 x 29 ins / 74 x 74 cm) EUR 19,000. Berlin, 11 June 2004, *The Afflicted* (1930, oil on cardboard, 29 x 29 ins / 74 x 74 cm) EUR 60,000.

SCHOLZE, J. G.
German, 19th century.
Born to a family originally from Kamenz.
Active c. 1818.
Painter.
Museums and Galleries:
Lenz bei Grossenhain (Church of St-Peter): *Portrait of the Pastor Johann Gottlieb Werther.*

SCHOLZE, Nikolai Henrikh Karlovich, or Choltse
Russian, 19th century.
Born 10 January 1827; died 22 December 1883, in Rome.
Painter.
Nikolai Henrikh Karlovich Scholze studied at the art academy in St Petersburg, and settled in Rome in 1851.

SCHOMACHER, Andries. See **SCHOEMAKER Andreis**

SCHOMAKER, Albert. See **SCHUHMACHER**

SCHOMANN
German, 19th century.
Active in Rostock c. 1800.
Painter. Portraits.

SCHOMANN, Willi
German, 20th century.
Born 16 January 1881, in Parchim (Mecklenburg); died September 1917, in Ypres, Belgium, on the front.
Painter, designer. Murals.
Willi Schomann studied at the art museum school in Berlin under Max Koch and Richard Böhland, and at the art academy under Wald. Friedrich, Joseph Scheurenberg and Raffael Schuster-Woldan. He went on study trips with Oswald Kuhl.

He decorated several churches in Mecklenburg.

SCHOMBERG, César de
French, 19th century.
Born in Strasbourg (Bas Rhin).
Painter. Military subjects.
He made his debut at the Paris Salon in 1869.
Auction records:
Paris, 30 April 1951, *Military Quarters* (1877) FRF 550.

SCHÖMBERG, Christian Gotthelf. See **SCHÖNBERG**

SCHOMBURG, Christoph
German, 18th century.
Died 1753, in Copenhagen.
Active in Ratzeburg.
Painter. Portraits.
After working in Rome from 1732 to 1742, Christoph Schomburg was active in Brussels, Vienna and Copenhagen, where he was Inspector in its art gallery.

SCHOMBURG, Johann Georg
German, 18th century.
Active in Dresden 1716-1734.
Medallist.

SCHOMMER, François
French, 19th - 20th century.
Born 20 November 1850, in Paris; died 1935.
Painter, engraver, watercolourist, draughtsman, illustrator, designer. Religious subjects, portraits, genre scenes, landscapes with figures, landscapes. Murals.
François Schommer, a pupil of Isidore Pils, Henri Lehmann and Jean Éloi Malenfant, won the Premier Prix de Rome in 1878.

He exhibited at the Salon de Paris from 1870, and then at the Salon des Artistes Français, of which he became a member in 1884. He was awarded a second-class medal in 1884, a silver at the Exposition Universelle of 1889, and another at the Exposition of 1900. He was made a Chevalier of the Légion d'Honneur in 1890 and later promoted to Officier, and held an important position as a professor at the École des Beaux-Arts, Paris.

He painted the ceilings of the new Sorbonne, Paris, of the Town Hall of Tours and the École des Beaux-Arts, Paris.

Museums and Galleries:
Besançon: *Mary Magdalene* - Paris (Mus. d'Orsay): *Gondoliers Resting* - Valenciennes: *An Aide de Camp*; *The Poet Albert Méral.*
Auction records:
Paris, 1895, *Oriental Woman* (drawing) FRF 32. Paris, 29 April 1899, *Cavalry Charge,* FRF 230. Paris, 18-21 Dec 1918, *Old Street in Italy* (watercolour) FRF 105. Paris, 19 Nov 1924, *Officer of the First Empire Guard,* FRF 105. Paris, 4 April 1936, *Bonaparte in Italy,* FRF 255. Paris, 5 Nov 1946, *Portrait of a Woman,* FRF 7,850. Paris, 18 Dec 1946, *Young Woman Seated on a Sofa,* FRF 5,800. Paris, 16 March 1976, *Sentinel* (oil on canvas, 12¼ x 9¼ ins / 31 x 23.5 cm) FRF 2,100. Versailles, 4 Oct 1981, *Fantasia* (oil on canvas, 22 x 18¼ ins / 55 x 46.5 cm) FRF 20,100. Le Touquet, 11 Nov 1990, *Corner of a*

Park with Figures (oil on canvas, 13 1/2 x 9 3/4 ins / 34 x 25 cm) FRF 80,000.

SCHOMMER, J. G.
Bohemian School, 18th century.
Active c. 1707.
Draughtsman. Portraits.

SCHOMPER, J. J.
Flemish School, 19th century.
Active c. 1840.
Painter. Portraits.

SCHÖN, Alois
German, 19th century.
Active at the beginning of the 19th century.
Draughtsman, engraver (burin).
Alois Schön worked with his brother Johann and was the pupil of Johann Carl Schleich in Munich. He engraved portraits, landscapes and in 1800 *Germany Served*.
AUCTION RECORDS:
VIENNA, 15 March 1977, *Portrait of A Young Oriental Woman* (oil on canvas, 15 3/4 x 12 1/2 ins / 40 x 32 cm) ATS 22,000.

SCHÖN, Andreas
German, 20th - 21st century.
Born 1955, in Kassel.
Painter. Landscapes, architectural views.
Neo-Conceptual Art.
Andreas Schön lives and works in Düsseldorf. He worked as Gerhard Richter's assistant. He does aerial views of real or fictional ancient Aegean sites in a range of greens and browns. His works raise the problem of the perception of reality somewhere between photographic appearance and pictorial representation. He had solo shows in New York, Geneva (Galerie Faust, 1990), Paris (Galerie Xeno Rippas, 1996), and elsewhere.
BIBLIOGRAPHY:
Damianovic, Maia, '*La Peinture au risque du dilemme*' in *Art Press* n° 211, periodical, Paris, March 1996.
AUCTION RECORDS:
NEW YORK, 23-25 Feb 1993, *Benevento* (1989, oil on canvas, 55 x 78 3/4 ins / 139.7 x 200 cm) USD 5,750. NEW YORK, 4 May 1993, *Dover* (1989, oil on canvas, 78 1/2 x 98 1/2 ins / 199.4 x 250.2 cm) USD 11,500. LONDON, 24 Oct 1996, *Dover II* (1989, oil on canvas, 78 3/4 x 118 ins / 200 x 300 cm) GBP 11,500. NEW YORK, 17 Nov 1999, *Umland I* (1988, oil on canvas, 30 x 55 ins / 77 x 140 cm) USD 5,000. MUNICH, 26 Nov 2000, *Flowers* (oil on canvas, 47 x 55 ins / 120 x 140 cm) DEM 12,000. LONDON, 27 June 2002, *Umland I* (1988, acrylic on canvas, 31 x 55 ins / 80 x 140 cm) GBP 5,000.

SCHÖN, Arthur
Belgian, 20th century.
Born 1887, in Schaerbeek (Brussels); died 1940.
Painter, engraver. Portraits, landscapes.

SCHÖN, Barthel. See **SCHONGAUER**

SCHÖN, Bernhard Johann
French, 19th century.
Born 19 February 1854, in Mulhouse.
Painter. Portraits.
From 1873 onward he worked in Walterswill.

SCHÖN, Caspar
Swiss, 16th century.
Died 1585, in Zurich.
Engraver (wood), architect.

SCHÖN, Erhard. See **SCHOEN**

SCHÖN, Ferenc or Franz
Austrian, 19th century.
Active in Presburg 1807-1820.
Painter.

SCHÖN, Franz Wilhelm
German, 19th century.
Born 1784, in Cologne; died 5 November 1871, in Lons-le-Saunier (Jura), France.
Painter. History painting, portraits, landscapes.
Franz Schön was a pupil of J.A. Gros.
MUSEUMS AND GALLERIES:
LONS-LE-SAUNIER: *Hunting Trophies*.

SCHÖN, Friedrich Wilhelm
German, 19th century.
Born 1816, in Worms; died 16 January 1868, in Munich.
Painter, lithographer. Genre scenes.
Friedrich Schön worked in Darmstadt In 1826. From 1830 to 1831 he was in Karlsruhe and from 1831 in Munich, attending the academy there from 1832.
MUSEUMS AND GALLERIES:
DRESDEN (Gemäldegal. Neue Meister): *Sunday Morning*.

SCHÖN, Hans, or Schon, called Schönhanns
German, 15th century.
Active in Munich.
Painter.

SCHÖN, Johann Daniel Friedrich, or Schöne
German, 18th - 19th century.
Born probably in 1767; died 11 June 1836, in Breslau (now Wroclaw, Poland).
Painter. History painting, portraits, landscapes.

SCHÖN, Johann Gottlieb
German, 18th century.
Born c. 1720, in Thuringia.
Painter. Landscapes.
A pupil of J.A. Thiele, Johann Schön painted landscapes of Thuringia and a few of Italy.

SCHÖN, Josef
Austrian, 19th century.
Born 15 August 1809, in Vienna; died 5 March 1843, in Vienna.
Medallist, engraver. Coins.
Josef Schön attended the academy in Vienna.

SCHÖN, Karl
German, 19th - 20th century.
Born 7 September 1868, in Berlin.
Painter. Seascapes.
Karl Schön trained under Saltzmann.

SCHÖN, Konrad
German, 15th century.
Died 5 January 1479, in Nuremberg.
Active in Nuremberg.
Painter.
Konrad Schön was probably the brother of Marx Schön I.

SCHÖN, L. A.
19th century.
Painter. Figures, mythological figures, portraits.
MUSEUMS AND GALLERIES:
COPENHAGEN: *Portrait of A.F.Z. Verlin; Centaur; Study of Young Girl*.

SCHÖN, Lorenz
Austrian, 19th century.
Born 1817, in Budapest.
Painter, engraver (etching), lithographer. Landscapes.
Franz Schön attended the academy in Vienna from 1838 and exhibited there from 1847 to 1850.

SCHÖN, Luise
Austrian, 19th century.
Born 24 January 1848, in Vienna.
Active in Vienna.
Painter. Portraits, still-lifes, flowers.

Luise Schön was taught by Fr. and Karoline Pönninger and Geyling.

SCHÖN, Martin. See **SCHONGAUER**

SCHÖN, Marx I
German, 15th century.
Died between 1467 and 1470.
Active in Nuremberg in the latter half of the 15th century.
Painter.
Marx Schön I was perhaps also a stained glass painter.

SCHÖN, Marx II
German, 16th century.
Died between 13 December 1510 and March 1511.
Active in Nuremberg.
Painter.
Nuremberg School.
Marx Schön II was the son of Marx Schön I and the father of Erhard.

SCHÖN, Otto
German, 20th century.
Born 26 March 1893, in Suhl (Thuringia).
Painter, engraver. Interiors with figures.
A pupil at the school of applied arts in Munich, Otto Schön subsequently worked in the town, and his work is displayed in the Bavarian State collections.
MUSEUMS AND GALLERIES:
MUNICH (Staatsgal.).
AUCTION RECORDS:
COLOGNE, 21 Oct 1977, *The Artist's Wife Arranging Flowers in the Studio* (1932, oil on canvas, 43 3/4 x 39 ins / 111 x 99 cm) DEM 6,500.

SCHON, P. H.
19th century.
Painter. Self-portraits.
MUSEUMS AND GALLERIES:
COPENHAGEN: *Self-portrait*.

SCHÖN, Seraphin
Swiss, 17th century.
Died 1644.
Active in Menzingen (canton of Lugano).
Painter.
Seraphin Schön was a Franciscan friar. He did an altar painting *The Baptism of Christ* for the church at Menzingen and the *Holy Family at Table* for the refectory of the Franciscan sanctuary at Trsat.

SCHÖNAU. See **SCHENAU**

SCHÖNAU, Carl
German, 19th century.
Active in Berlin.
Painter. Genre scenes, portraits.
Carl Schönau exhibited from 1840 to 1846.

SCHÖNAU, Hermann
German, 19th century.
Born 20 April 1861, in Bollstedt (Thüringen); died 7 July 1900, in Nuremberg.
Sculptor.
Hermann Schönau attended the art school in Nuremberg and later the academy in Dresden. After further study in Berlin, he went to Italy and was in Rome from 1890 to 1892 before settling in Nuremberg.
MUSEUMS AND GALLERIES:
NUREMBERG: *Sicilian Man; Girl*.

SCHÖNAUER, Jacob Heinrich
Swiss, 18th century.
Active in Basel c. 1700.
Engraver (burin).
Jacob Schönauer engraved the portraits of the reformer *Joh. Ocolampadius* and the theologian of Basel *Jakob Grynaeus*.

SCHÖNAUER, Joseph
German, 19th century.
Active in Landshut.
Painter.
Joseph Schönauer worked at the academy in Munich around 1814, and after that returned to Landshut.

SCHÖNAUER, Philipp
Austrian, 18th century.
Active in Poysdorf.
Sculptor.

SCHÖNBÄCHLER, Franz Xaver
Swiss, 18th century.
Born 1719, in Einsiedeln (Zug).
Active in Einsiedeln.
Engraver (burin).
Franz Schönbächler engraved views of Einsiedeln.

SCHÖNBÄCHLER, Meinrad Anton
Swiss, 19th century.
Born 1825, in Einsiedeln (Zug); died 1879.
Sculptor (wood).

SCHÖNBAUER, Henry or Henrik, or Schoenbauer
Hungarian, 20th century.
Born 1 March 1894, in Güns (now Koszeg).
Sculptor.
Henry Schöbauer was a student at the fine arts academies in Munich, Vienna and Budapest.
AUCTION RECORDS:
NEW YORK, 9 Sept 1993, *Male Nude Lying Down* (bronze, l. 24 ins / 61 cm) USD 2,300.

SCHÖNBERG, Adolf
Austrian, 19th century.
Born 1813; died 1868.
Engraver, lithographer.
Adolf Schönberg was the son of Johann and was taught by Franz Stöber.

SCHÖNBERG, Alexander von
German, 19th century.
Born 1792, in Dresden; died 4 January 1838.
Painter. Landscapes.
Alexander von Schönberg's masters were Hans Veit Schnorr von Carolsfeld in Leipzig, Reinhart in Rome and Peter Hess in Munich. He was an officer.

SCHÖNBERG, Arnold, or Schoenberg
Austrian, 19th - 20th century.
Born 13 September 1874, in Vienna; died 13 July 1951, in Los Angeles, USA.
Active from 1933 and naturalised in the USA.
Painter. Portraits.
Der Blaue Reiter group.
Arnold Schönberg was better known as a composer and conductor. He was also a painter, and was largely self-taught, although he learnt a few rudimentary techniques from Richard Gerstl. A Jew, Schönberg converted to Protestantism for a time to fit in with Viennese society, only to return, in a courageous act of defiance, to Judaism with the arrival of Nazi power in Germany. In 1933 he left Europe via Spain and France, before settling in California, becoming a US citizen in 1941.

In 1910 Hugo Heller's bookshop-gallery in Vienna held an exhibition of his works, of which the musician Gustav Mahler bought three. Admired by Kandinsky, the two artists worked together in the projection of the work of total art, and Kandinsky invited Schönberg to participate in the first

Blaue Reiter exhibition in Munich in the winter of 1911. They also worked together on the *Blue Rider Almanac*, and until the war broke out, they corresponded regularly, exchanging ideas.

He painted mainly between 1908 and 1911, after the suicide of Richard Gerstl and until the death of Gustav Mahler. He produced 65 oil paintings in total, including *The Burial of Gustav Mahler* in 1911, some watercolours and some drawings. Several hypotheses have been put forward to try to explain his short-lived painting career; it could have been the disappointment caused by the lack of public comprehension of his music, or the confusion caused bt learning that his wife Mathilde had been having an affair with the young Gerstl. This dramatic personal episode coincided, in 1909, with the composition of *Erwartung* (*Expectation*), which is the story a woman looking for her lover in the forest, ended with her finding him dead.

His artistic activity started with a series of hallucinatory self-portraits. Then he offered to paint portraits of patrons, aristocrats or the Viennese bourgeoisie. In the event, he painted mostly portraits of relations and friends, his wife Mathilde, Alban Berg, and Gustav Mahler.

Apart from the self-portraits and portraits, his work included some landscapes and evocations of mental states, in a style that could be termed abstract. In most cases, but particularly in the series of self-portraits and imaginary faces, *Red Glance, Hatred, Vision,* he focuses on the expression in the eyes: 'I have never seen faces, but since I've been looking people in the eyes, I have seen nothing but their glances. A true painter can capture an entire man in a single glance. I myself can only capture his soul.'

In 2003 his work featured in a group exhibition *Aux origines de l'abstraction (1800-1914)* (*The Origins of Abstraction, 1800-1914*) at the Musée d'Orsay, Paris. In 1995, during a Schönberg festival at the Opéra du Châtelet in Paris, the Musée de l'Art Moderne in Paris put on an exhibition entitled *Arnold Schönberg Regards*. In 2002, the Schirn Kunsthalle in Frankfurt showed 150 of his Expressionist works for an exhibition entitled *The Visions of Arnold Schönberg*.

BIBLIOGRAPHY:

Kallir, Jane, *Arnold Schönberg's Vienna,* exhibition catalogue, Gal. St. Etienne, Rizzoli, New York, 1984. Vallier, Dora, *La Rencontre Kandinsky-Schönberg,* L'Échoppe, Caen, 1987. Hollein, Max, *Die Visionen des Arnold Schönberg (Arbeitstitel),* Hatje Cantz, Ostfildern, 2002.

SCHÖNBERG, Christian Gotthelf, or Schömberg
German, 18th century.
Born 1760, in Dresden; died in Leipzig.
Engraver (burin).

In 1787 Christian Schönberg went to work for a few years in St Petersburg. He engraved landscapes for *Travels across Saxony* by Leske and did the illustrations for a theoretical manual of horticulture by Hirschfeld (1779-1785) in five volumes.

SCHÖNBERG, Johann
Austrian, 19th century.
Born 1780, in Sopron; died 1863, in Vienna.
Engraver (burin).

Johann Schönberg was the pupil of Jakob Schmutzer.

SCHÖNBERG, Johann Nepomuk
Austrian, 19th century.
Born 1844.
Painter, illustrator.

The son of Adolf, Johann Schönberg spent two years at the academy in Vienna before going to Munich. He contributed to the *Monde Illustré*, the *Journal Illustré* and *Daheim*. He also provided some of the illustrations to Patuzzi's *History of the Popes* and Alvenslaeben's the *World History*.

AUCTION RECORDS:

VIENNA, 19 June 1979, *Sailing Ship at Sea* (1912, oil on canvas, 21 x 14 1/2 ins / 53.5 x 37 cm) ATS 15,000.

SCHÖNBERG, Rodolphe
Belgian, 20th century.
Born 1901, in Brussels; died May 1944.
Draughtsman, engraver.

Rodolphe Schönberg studied at the art academy in Brussels, and later under Kurt Peiser and Gérard Jacobs. He was shot by the Germans for acts of resistance.

SCHONBERG, Torsten Johan
Swedish, 20th century.
Born 21 July 1882, in Stockholm.
Painter, draughtsman, engraver.

Torsten Johann Schonberg studied at the technical college and art academy in Stockholm. He produced several series of caricatures and lithographs of twelve historical portraits.

SCHÖNBERG, Xaver Maria Cäsar von, or Schönberg-Rothschönberg
German, 18th - 19th century.
Born 20 February 1768, in Paris; died 19 September 1853, in Dresden.
Painter, engraver, draughtsman. Portraits.

Xaver Schönberg joined the French army, where he rose to the rank of lieutenant-colonel. From 1793 he lived in Saxony, settling in Dresden in 1846 where he followed Klengel's teaching as an amateur.

MUSEUMS AND GALLERIES:

WEIMAR (Goethe-Nationalmus.): *Goethe* (drawing).

SCHÖNBERGER, Alfred Karl Julius Otto von
German, 19th century.
Born 9 October 1845, in Graz; died 1880, in Frankfurt.
Painter. Landscapes, mountainscapes.

After studying in Munich with A. Lier and K. Millner, Alfred Schönberger went to Europe, the East and Africa to study. From 1880 he lived in Frankfurt.

AUCTION RECORDS:

VIENNA, 14 Sept 1976, *Mountain Lake* (oil on canvas, 18 x 15 ins / 46 x 38 cm) ATS 20,000. MUNICH, 21 June 1994, *Alpine Landscape* (oil on panel, a pair, each 8 x 11 ins / 20.5 x 27 cm) DEM 5,980. BERN, 9 May 2001, *Rowing Boats on Alpine Lake* (oil on board, 7 x 9 ins / 18 x 24 cm) CHF 3,000. MUNICH, 27 June 2001, *Mountain Lake with Fishermen in Boat* (oil on canvas, 26 x 37 ins / 66 x 95 cm) DEM 4,800. FRANKFURT, 23 Nov 2002, *Landscape with Pond* (oil on canvas, 22 x 30 ins / 55 x 75 cm) EUR 3,300.

SCHÖNBERGER, Armand
Hungarian, 20th century.
Born 2 April 1885, in Galgoc or in Freistadt; died 1974, in Budapest.
Painter, sculptor, art critic. Figures, portraits, still-lifes.

Armand Schönberger studied in Budapest, Munich and Nagybanya. He was a founder member of the KUT movement. Schönberger's painting is characterised by rigorously harmonised muted tones, and is reminiscent of Cézanne's early period.

Work by him was exhibited at the Belvedere in Vienna (1927); at the Tamas Gallery in Budapest (1930); at the Mücsarnok in Budapest (1958); and at the exhibition *Beöthy et l'avant-garde hongroise* (*Beöthy and the Hungarian Avant-Garde*) at the Galerie Franka Berndt, Paris (1985-1986). There was a retrospective of his work in 1972 in Budapest.

Schönberger

BIBLIOGRAPHY:
Szij, B., *Schönberger Arman Kiállístása*, exhibition catalogue, Gal. Magyar Nemzeti, Budapest, 1970. Muveszet Kiskonyvtara, A., *Armand Schönberger*, Éd. Andras, 1984.
AUCTION RECORDS:
LONDON, 24 Feb 1988, *Bathers* (gouache and oil on paper, 23 1/2 x 16 3/4 ins / 59.5 x 42.5 cm) GBP 1,540. PARIS, 12 May 1993, *Still-life* (ink/paper, 6 x 7 ins / 15 x 17.5 cm) FRF 6,000. BUDAPEST, 27 April 2001, *Railway Station* (oil on canvas, 37 x 27 ins / 94 x 69 cm) HUF 2,000,000. BUDAPEST, 12 Oct 2001, *Still-life* (1954, oil on cardboard, 31 x 23 ins / 80 x 58 cm) HUF 1,400,000. BRATISLAVA, 1 Oct 2002, *Cafe Interior* (oil on canvas, 31 x 28 ins / 80 x 70 cm) SL.K 825,000. BUDAPEST, 9 Dec 2002, *Concert in the Coffee House* (1928, oil on canvas, 39 x 31 ins / 99 x 80 cm) HUF 16,000,000. BUDAPEST, 11 April 2003, *Woman Reading in Studio* (oil on board, 20 x 15 ins / 51 x 37 cm) HUF 1,400,000. BUDAPEST, 12 Dec 2003, *Town - Houses in Buda* (oil on canvas, 24 x 24 ins / 60 x 60 cm) HUF 1,900,000. BUDAPEST, 28 April 2004, *Company by Table* (1920, oil on paper, 18 x 17 ins / 45 x 43 cm) HUF 6,500,000. BUDAPEST, 12 Oct 2004, *Cabaret* (oil on canvas, 43 x 29 ins / 108 x 73 cm) HUF 30,000,000.

SCHÖNBERGER, Artur
Hungarian, 19th century.
Born 1838, in Szeged.
Lithographer.
Artur Schönberger studied in Budapest and Vienna.

SCHÖNBERGER, Karl
Bohemian School, 19th century.
Active in Falkenau in Bohemia c. 1805.
Glass painter.

SCHÖNBERGER, Lorenz Adolf
German, 18th - 19th century.
Born 1768, in Vöslau; died 1847, in Mainz.
Painter, engraver (etching).
Lorenz Schönberger attended the academy in Vienna and was taught by M. Wuttky. He travelled to Central Europe, Paris (1804), Frankfurt am Main, Italy, Rome from 1817 to 1825 and to the nordic countries in 1826 and England in 1840. He engraved landscapes and is believed to be the same artist as the painter Schönberger who exhibited Italian views in Paris and *The Falls of the Rhine* in the Salon in 1804.
MUSEUMS AND GALLERIES:
BRUNSWICK: *The Gulf of Livorno* - DARMSTADT: *Sunset* - ERLANGEN: *Landscape with Ulysses* - OBERSCHLEISSHEIM (Neues Schloss Schleissheim, Staatsgal.): *The Falls of the Rhine at Schaffhausen* - PRAGUE (Národní Gal.): *Moonlit Landscape* - SPEYER: *Ideal Landscape* - VIENNA: *Landscape with Waterfall; Golfe de Baia at Sunset* - WILHELMSHOHE: *Landscape*.

SCHÖNBERGER, Martin
Swiss, 19th - 20th century.
Born 28 February 1864, in Munich, to Swiss parents.
Painter, pastellist. Portraits, genre scenes.
Martin Schönberger studied under Kanlbach at the Munich art academy from 1882 to 1888. In 1893 and 1894 he worked in Paris, and from 1894 to 1895 lived in Florence. He settled in Zurich in 1898.

He took part in various exhibitions in Switzerland, Munich and Paris, receiving a commendation at the Exposition Universelle in Paris in 1900. He produced mainly pastel portraits.

SCHONBOE, Henrik
Danish.
Landscape artist.
MUSEUMS AND GALLERIES:
COPENHAGEN: *The Month of April*.

SCHONBORN, Anton
German, 19th century.
Died 1871.
Painter, watercolourist.
Anton Schonborn was a topographical painter who focused, above all, on the forts of western America during the 1859-1871 period, including Fetterman, Fred. Steele, Kearney and Laramie.
MUSEUMS AND GALLERIES:
FORT WORTH (Amon Carter Mus.): portfolio including views of eleven forts.
AUCTION RECORDS:
NEW YORK, 12 April 1991, *Four Forts of Western America: Kearney, Laramie, Fred. Steele and Sanders* (watercolour, collection of ovals, 4 1/4 x 7 1/2 ins / 10.8 x 19.2 cm) USD 22,000.

SCHÖNBROD, Peter
German, 20th century.
Born 21 May 1889, in Colmar; died 31 October 1914, near Zandwoorde.
Sculptor (wood).
Peter Schönbrod studied in Strasbourg and Munich under Wadere and Kurz. He died at the front.

SCHÖNBRUNNER, Franz Xaver
Austrian, 19th century.
Born 1846, in Vienna; died 22 April 1903, in Molz, near Kirchberg.
Painter, decorative designer.

SCHÖNBRUNNER, Ignaz
Austrian, 19th - 20th century.
Born 1 May 1835, in Vienna; died 1921.
Painter.
Ignaz Schönbrunner was trained by Fürich and Rahl. His brothers Josef and Karl were also painters.
AUCTION RECORDS:
LONDON, 7 April 1993, *Still-life of a Pot of Flowers and a Tea Set on a Table* (oil on canvas, 15 3/4 x 20 ins / 40 x 51 cm) GBP 1,610.

SCHÖNBRUNNER, Josef Edler von
Austrian, 19th century.
Born 14 February 1831, in Vienna; died 2 December 1905, in Vienna.
Painter, draughtsman.
The brother of Karl and Ignaz, Joseph Schönbrunner was taught by Joseph von Fuhrich and became Director of the Albertina in Vienna.

SCHÖNBRUNNER, Karl
Austrian, 19th century.
Born 4 October 1832, in Vienna; died 21 February 1877, in Hirschstetten, near Vienna.
Painter.
After attending the academy at Vienna with Rahl and Führich, Karl Schönbrunner went to Venice and Rome. He painted a *Resurrection of the Dead* and 14 Stations of the Cross, after Overbeck's cartoons, under the arcades of the German cemetery in Rome.

SCHÖNCHE, Gottfried. See **SCHÖNICHE**

SCHÖNCHEN, Beatrice
Maiden name: Frederickson
German, 19th - 20th century.
Born 16 March 1865, near Alexandria (Egypt).
Painter, pastellist, watercolourist. Portraits.
Beatrice Schönchen was the wife of Leopold Schönchen.

SCHÖNCHEN, Heinrich
German, 19th - 20th century.
Born 11 April 1861, in Munich; died 8 May 1933.
Painter. Portraits.
Heinrich Schönchen trained at the art academy in Munich under Gysis and Löfftz.

SCHÖNCHEN, Léopold
German, 19th - 20th century.
Born 1 February 1855, in Augsburg; died 19 January 1935, in Munich.
Painter. Seascapes.
Leopold Schönchen was the husband of Beatrice Schönchen. He studied at the art academy in Munich under Anton Baisch, and at the Karlsruhe art academy under Schönleber. He worked in Munich, Holland, Belgium, England and Scandinavia. Some of his paintings are in the Staatl. Galerie in Munich. He received a commendation at the 1886 Jubilee Art Exhibition at the academy of arts in Berlin.
MUSEUMS AND GALLERIES:
MUNICH.
AUCTION RECORDS:
LONDON, 4 May 1977, *Return of the Fishermen* (oil on panel, 14 x 11 ins / 35.5 x 27 cm) GBP 1,000.

SCHÖNCKH, Simon. See **SCHENCK**

SCHONDEL, Otto Ludwig Sofus
Danish, 19th century.
Born 8 July 1837, in Middelfart; died 10 April 1905, in Copenhagen.
Painter, decorative artist. Flowers.
Schondel was a pupil of Georg Hilker. He worked in Italy from 1870 to 1872. He became a professor at the Kunstakademi in Copenhagen, and also decorated the St Paul church in Copenhagen.

SCHÖNEBECK, Eugen
German, 20th century.
Born 1936, in Heidenau.
Painter, draughtsman.
Eugen Schönebeck started his artistic training in 1954 in what was then East Berlin, before moving to West Berlin the following year to continue his studies at the Hochschule für Bildende Kunst. He met Georg Baselitz in 1957, and worked with him on his first and second 'Pandemonium' manifestos in 1961 and 1962. Although they no longer worked together after this date, Schönebeck's work closely paralleled that of Baselitz until 1966, when he chose to stop painting at the age of thirty. Over the course of his short but active career he completed over two dozen oil paintings and hundreds of drawings. Since then, Schönebeck has become well-known in Germany, where he is seen as a precursor of German post-war painting.

He held a solo exhibition in Berlin in 1965. In 1992 he was awarded the Fred Thiele Prize for painting. In 2003 his work featured at the *Berlin-Moscow/Moscow-Berlin 1950-2000* exhibition held at the Martin Gropius building in Berlin and Moscow's Tretyakov Gallery. This was a follow-up to the 1900-1950 exhibition, which highlighted 50 years of artistic and cultural German-Russian relations.

After having been tempted by abstract art at the start of the sixties, he tended towards an expressive style, which he himself defined ironically as 'Socialist Realism', a kind of Anglo-Saxon pop art. His art derives from various pictorial styles.
BIBLIOGRAPHY:
'Berlin-Moskau/Moskau-Berlin 1950-2000', 2 vol., exhibition catalogue, Martin-Gropius-Bau, Berlin, 2003 (text in German).
MUSEUMS AND GALLERIES:
BERLIN (Berlinische Gal.): *The Crucifixion* (1964).

SCHÖNECKER, Regina Catherine. See **QUARRY**

SCHÖNECKER, Toni
Czech, 20th century.
Born 1 November 1893, in Falkenau an der Eger (now Sokolov).
Painter, engraver, sculptor, fresco artist.
Toni Schönecker studied in Vienna in 1910, and at the Akademie der Bildenden Künste in Munich from 1910 to 1924. He painted frescoes.

SCHÖNELE, Balthasar
German, 17th century.
Stucco artist.

SCHÖNENBERGER, Josef
Swiss, 20th century.
Born 17 November 1882, in Appenzell.
Painter, sculptor. Landscapes.
Josef Schönenberger lived and worked in Basel. He studied under Rosenthal and Knirr in Munich.

SCHÖNER, Anton
German, 19th - 20th century.
Born 14 March 1866, in Nuremberg; died 15 April 1930, in Berchtesgaden.
Painter, illustrator, art critic. Portraits.
Anton Schöner started his career as a lithographer before studying at the art academy in Munich. He worked in Berlin from 1891, and then settled in Munich.
MUSEUMS AND GALLERIES:
ALTENBURG: *Franciscan Brewmaster* - MERANO: *Portrait of Menzl; Portrait of Lenbach; Portrait of Begas* - NUREMBERG: *Portrait of Begas; Portrait of Tovote.*

SCHÖNER, Daniel
German, 17th century.
Active in Nuremberg.
Painter.

SCHÖNER, Georg Friedrich Adolf
German, 18th - 19th century.
Born 24 December 1774, in Mannsbach, near Hersfeld; died 10 March 1841, in Bremen.
Painter, lithographer. Portraits.
The nephew and pupil of Conrad Geiger, Georg Schöner studied with Anton Graf in Dresden from 1795 to 1796.
MUSEUMS AND GALLERIES:
BERLIN (Bodemus.): *Buchhorn the Painter* - BERLIN (Nationalgal.): *Half-length Portrait of Joh. Heinrich Dräseke.*

SCHÖNESEIFFER, Peter Joseph
German, 19th - 20th century.
Born 1856; died 26 February 1922, in Marburg.
Sculptor.
Peter Joseph Schöneseiffer sculpted two figures for the church of St Elisabeth in Marburg, as well as sculptures on the portal of the cathedral at Frankfurt am Main.

SCHÖNEVELDT, Johann Stephan von
German, 18th century.
Painter.

SCHÖNEWITZ, Georg Benjamin
German, 18th century.
Died between 1746 and 1747, in Potsdam.
Sculptor.
Georg Schönewitz was responsible for part of the external decoration at the palace of Sanssouci in Potsdam.

SCHONFELD, Eduard
German, 19th century.
Born 24 April 1839, in Düsseldorf; died 27 November 1885, in Düsseldorf.
Landscape artist.
MUSEUMS AND GALLERIES:
DÜSSELDORF (Stadtmus.): *Landscape of High Mountains.*

SCHÖNFELD, Heinrich
German, 19th century.
Born 1809, in Dresden; died 5 May 1845, in Munich.
Painter, lithographer. Urban landscapes, scenes with figures.

Heinrich Schönfeld attended the academy in Munich and did a number of engravings of the most important German towns.

Museums and Galleries:

Munich (Neue Pinakothek): *The Quai des Bouchers in Strasbourg* - Riga: *Market in Basel.*

SCHÖNFELD, Paul Ludwig

German, 20th century.

Born 13 February 1882, in Leipzig.

Painter, engraver. Portraits.

Paul Ludwig Schönfeld worked at the art school and the academy in Dresden from 1911 to 1914 under Gotthardt Kuehl and C. Banzer. He undertook a study trip to Florence and Rome. He lived and worked in Dresden.

Museums and Galleries:

Dresden (Albertinum): *Portrait of Georg Treu.*

Auction records:

London, 18 June 1986, *Schoolboys Playing Chess* (oil on canvas, 33 1/2 x 39 ins / 85 x 99 cm) GBP 4,200.

SCHONFELDT, Joachim

South African, 20th - 21st century.

Born 1958, in Pretoria.

Performance artist, video artist, draughtsman, writer.

Joachim Schonfeldt took part in *Un Art Contemporain d'Afrique du Sud* (*Contemporary Art of South Africa*) at the Galerie de l'Esplanade in La Défense in Paris in 1994.

SCHÖNFELDT, Johann Heinrich, or Schönfeld or Schoenfeld or Schenfeld

German, 17th century.

Born 1609, in Biberach; died c. 1682, in Augsburg.

Painter, engraver. Religious subjects, battles, figures, landscapes.

The pupil of Johann Sichelbein, Johann Schönfeldt worked in Germany's major towns before visiting Italy. In Rome he did works in the church of Sta Elisabetta di Fornari and in Palazzo Orsini. On his return to Germany, he was employed in Vienna, Munich and Salzburg, among other cities. He was responsible for a few prints of landscapes and subjects known as 'epic pastorals' in Italy.

Museums and Galleries:

Augsburg (Kreuzkirche): *Christ On His Walk to Calvary; Deposition* - Augsburg (Senate Palace) - Besançon: *Two Battles* - Biberach: *Rebecca at the Well* - Dresden: *Shepherds' Feast; Giants Fighting; Musical Gathering* - Graz: *Martydom of St Catherine* - Sibiu: *Allegory of the Past; Arcadian Landscape with Women Bathing; Arcadian Landscape with the Nine Muses* - Stuttgart: *Jacob and Rachel at the Well* - Ulm: *Ecce Homo* (attributed) - Vienna: *Jacob and Esau* (two paintings); *Sacrifice; Gideon Testing his Army in Jordan.*

Auction records:

Paris, 16 Oct 1940, *St James,* FRF 1,700. London, 27 June 1969, *Calvary,* Gns 4,000. London, 6 April 1977, *The Triumph of David* (oil on canvas, 50 x 81 ins / 127 x 206 cm) GBP 3,000. London, 18 April 1978, *Philosopher Musing on the Human Condition* (etching, 6 1/4 x 5 1/4 ins / 16 x 13.1 cm) GBP 850. London, 16 May 1984, *David with the head of Goliath* (oil on canvas, oval, 42 1/4 x 30 1/2 ins / 107.5 x 77.5 cm) GBP 2,000. Milan, 26 Nov 1985, *Contest between Apollo and Marsyas* (oil on canvas, 26 3/4 x 38 1/2 ins / 68 x 97.5 cm) ITL 36,000,000. London, 11 Dec 1992, *A King Watching the Resurrection of one of his Ancestors in the Presence of Seer* (oil on canvas, 37 1/4 x 52 1/4 ins / 94.9 x 132.7 cm) GBP 5,500. London, 7 July 1993, *Battle Scene* (oil on canvas, 37 1/4 x 51 1/2 ins / 94.5 x 131 cm) GBP 13,800.

SCHÖNFELT, Jacob

Swedish, 18th century.

Born c. 1707, in Göteborg; died after 1766.

Painter.

Schönfelt was the son of the painter Christian Schonfelt. He executed still-lifes and allegorical compositions.

SCHONGAUER, Barthel, or Schön

German, 15th century.

Active in Ulm c. 1479.

Engraver.

Some biographers claim, wrongly, that Barthel Schongauer was the brother of Martin Schongauer, whose style he imitated and whose works he copied. At the present time nothing can be definitively claimed about his life or even his name. He signed his works with a B. and an S. separated by a cross. A dozen prints are known to be by him, most of them in the British Museum, London.

SCHONGAUER, Ludwig, the Elder

German, 15th century.

Born before 1440, in Augsburg; died after 1493, in Colmar.

Painter, engraver.

Ludwig Schongauer the Elder was the son of the jeweller Caspar Schongauer the Elder and the brother of Martin Schongauer. He engraved religious subjects and animals. His talent was in no way comparable with that of his brother, whose workshop he took over in 1491. It was there that in 1492 he entertained the young Dürer. In 1493 he became a member of the Confraternity of the Rosary in Colmar.

Auction records:

London, 24 March 1965, *Christ before Pontius Pilate; Resurrection,* GBP 4,000.

SCHONGAUER, Martin, called Schön, Hipsch Martin or Le Joli Martin

German, 15th century.

Born between 1430 and 1450, in Colmar (Upper Rhine); died 2 February 1491, in Brisach.

Painter, engraver, draughtsman. Religious subjects, portraits.

Martin Schongauer came from a patrician Augsburg family. His father, the jeweller Caspar Schongauer, moved to Colmar around 1440 and was a citizen of the town in 1445. Caspar had five sons: Ludwig, Caspar, Georg, Paul and Martin. Ludwig was also a painter. Martin Schongauer received a good education. In 1465 he was a student at the university of Leipzig. It is probable that he studied in Colmar in the workshop of Isenmann, who was a great admirer of Van Eyck and Roger van der Weyden. He completed his training in Flanders with pupils of Van der Weyden. According to information given to Vasari by Lambert Lombard, he was a pupil of Van der Weyden himself.

Early attributions include the *Stauffenberg Altarpiece* (c.1455-1460) and the *Bergheim Predella* (both in Museum Unterlinden, Colmar). The latter work, however, has recently been attributed to Jost Haller, a Strasbourg artist active in the mid-15th century.

Schongauer's first exposure to Netherlandish painting was on a trip to Cologne where he saw the *St Columba Triptych* by Van der Weyden (c.1455, Alte Pinakothek, Munich). The influence of this work can be seen in Schongauer's *Orlier Alterpiece* (Museum Unterlinden, Colmar) painted around 1465-1470. In Schongauer's early work it is also possible to see the influence of Jost Haller's work, especially in the oval facial shape of his depictions of the Virgin.

By 1469 Schongauer had a house in Colmar and in 1477 he bought another building. In 1488 he endowed a mass for himself and his family in the church of St Martin, probably as a farewell to his native city, because the following year he appears as a citizen of Brisach. Frescoes painted by Schongauer in Brisach Cathedral just before he died have recently been discovered. It is believed that in 1483 he painted a self-portrait, now lost, of which Burkmair later made a copy that is now in the Munich Pinakothek. Burkmair, a German painter who worked in Germany, was one of Schongauer's pupils and a master of the Augsburg School.

Schongauer was a goldsmith before he was an engraver and an engraver before he was a painter. He played an important role in the development of engraving as an art and as a technique. His goldsmith's training influenced his work as an engraver with assured hand movements allowing him a dynamic yet elegant style. All of his engravings bear the monogram *M+S*. Among the 116 engravings attributed to him, the *Virgin in the Courtyard* stands out with its expression of maternal feeling, its combination of a sense of divinity with ornamental detail, its representation of material (in the astonishing folds of the dress), and its schematisation of the décor, modern in its treatment. Of Schongauer's *Virgin of the Rose Bush*, T. de Wyzéwa wrote: 'It is one of those almost impersonal works, the attraction of which is felt more strongly than can be accounted for, and which forces the most restless art critic to interrupt for a moment his little comparisons and theories in order to enjoy its pure beauty in silence.' This painting (formerly in the collegiate church of St Martin, now in the Dominican Church, Colmar) is the only dated work by Schongauer. The date, 1473, is therefore an important reference point in his career. The monumental effect which so impresses the spectator is emphasised by the size of the work (6ft 6ins x 6ft 10ins/2m x 2.1m). The Virgin faces the viewer holding the baby in her arms while two angels hold a crown above her head. The bony and slightly rough features and the precision of the details are characteristic of the Flemish School. The face of the Virgin and those of the angels holding up the crown are reminiscent of the *Last Judgement* in the hospice of Beaune.

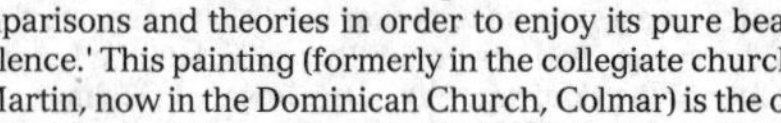

BIBLIOGRAPHY:

Shestack, A., *The Complete Engravings of Martin Schongauer*, New York, 1969. Minott, C. I., *Martin Schongauer*, New York, 1971. Hutchison, J. C. (ed.), *'Early German Artists'* in *The Illustrated Bartsch, 8*, Abaris Books, New York, 1980. Bernhard, Marianne, *Martin Schongauer und sein Kreis*, Südwest Verlag, Munich, 1980. Heck, Christian, *Martin Schongauer*, SAEP, Ingersheim, 1985. *Martin Schongauer: maître de la gravure rhenane*, exhibition catalogue, Musée du Petit Palais, Paris, 1991. *'Martin Schongauer and his school'* in *Iconclass Indexes: Early German Prints: An Iconographic Asselle to All German Prints Described by Adam von Bartsch, Fritz Laupichler, Roelof Van Straten*, vol 1, Davaco, Doornspijk, 1995. Nicolaisen, Jan, *Martin Schongauer: die Entwicklung des Kupferstichs zur eigenständigen Kunstgattung*, dissertation, Universität, Freiburg im Breisgau, 1995. Koreny, P., *'Martin Schongauer as a Draftsman: A Reassessment'* in *Master Drawings, xxxiv/2*, Summer 1996. Schmitt, Lothar/Stogdon, Nicolas, *'Ludwig Schongauer to Martin Schongauer'* in *Hollstein's German Engravings, Etchings and Woodcuts 1400-1700*, vol 49, Van Gendt, Amsterdam, 1999 (edited by Fedja Anzelewski).

MUSEUMS AND GALLERIES:

BERLIN: *Nativity; Carrying of the Cross; Crucifixion; Entombment; Resurrection of Christ* (altar paintings) - BRUSSELS: *Jesus Presented to the People* - COLMAR: *Virgin of the Rose Bush; Annunciation; Virgin Adoring Christ; Isenheim Retable; St Anthony* - FRANKFURT AM MAIN: *Virgin and the Child Jesus* - MUNICH: *Nativity* - VIENNA: *Holy Family*.

AUCTION RECORDS:

PARIS, 1850, *Death of the Virgin*, FRF 6,135. PARIS, 1864, *St Margaret* (pen drawing and indigo wash heightened with white) FRF 400. PARIS, 1872, *Coronation of Mary*, FRF 10,500. PARIS, 1877, *Adoration of the Angels* (pen and ink drawing) FRF 120; *Portrait of a Man* (pen and ink drawing) FRF 150. LONDON, 1896, *Annunciation*, FRF 12,620. LONDON, 11 March 1911, *Three Saints in a Garden*, GBP 1,680. PARIS, 25 Feb 1924, *Wise Virgin and Study for St Ursula* (pen, two figures) FRF 6,500. PARIS, 11 April 1924, *Un Clerc* (pen) FRF 1,500. LONDON, 9 July 1924, *St Ursula* (pen) GBP 39. LONDON, 8 July 1925, *Nativity*, GBP 75. PARIS, 10 and 11 May 1926, *Wise Virgin and Study for St Ursula* (pen, two figures) FRF 8,500. LONDON, 27 Jan 1928, *Group of Five Ladies and Gentlemen* (pen) GBP 262. PARIS, 28 Nov 1928, *Virgin and Study for St Ursula* (drawing) FRF 20,000. LONDON, 19 July 1929, *Nativity*, GBP 241. LONDON, 10-14 July 1936, *Head of a Bearded Man* (pen) GBP 220. LONDON, 26 June 1970, *Portrait of a Young Girl*, Gns 40,000. MUNICH, 25 Nov 1976, *Death of the Virgin* (copper) DEM 16,500. MUNICH, 24 Nov 1977, *Flight into Egypt* (engraved copper) DEM 92,000. LONDON, 27 June 1979, *St Sebastian* (engraved copper, 6 1/4 x 4 1/4 ins / 15.7 x 11.1 cm) GBP 1,650. MUNICH, 25 Nov 1982, *Birth of Jesus* (engraving/copper) DEM 16,000. LONDON, 21 April 1983, *Christ on the Cross with Four Angels* (engraving/copper, 11 1/2 x 7 3/4 ins / 29.1 x 19.8 cm) GBP 17,000. MUNICH, 13 June 1985, *The Twelve Apostles* (engraving/copper, complete set of 12) DEM 225,000. LONDON, 29 June 1987, *Censer* (engraving/copper, 10 1/4 x 8 1/4 ins / 26.2 x 20.9 cm) GBP 56,000. MUNICH, 26-27 Nov 1991, *Adoration of the Magi* (1482, engraved copper) DEM 5,290. MUNICH, 26 May 1992, *Flight into Egypt* (engraved copper) DEM 13,800. STOCKHOLM, 10-12 May 1993, *Crucifixion* (oil on canvas, 38 1/2 x 31 1/2 ins / 98 x 80 cm) SEK 40,000. BERLIN, 4 June 1999, *Christ Blesses the Virgin Mary* (oil on copper engraving, 6 x 6 ins / 16 x 15 cm) DEM 18,000. LONDON, 22 June 1999, *Christ Carrying the Cross* (c. 1475-80, engraving, 11 x 17 ins / 29 x 43 cm) GBP 7,500. BERLIN, 26 May 2000, *Christ on the Cross with Four Angels* (copperplate, 11 x 7 ins / 29 x 19 cm) DEM 30,000. LONDON, 5 Dec 2000, *Christ Carrying the Cross* (engraving, 11 x 17 ins / 28 x 43 cm) GBP 11,000. BERN, 22 June 2001, *Madonna with Apple* (copperplate) CHF 95,000. NEW YORK, 1 May 2002, *Shield with a Unicorn, Held by a Woman* (c. 1480-90, engraving) USD 13,000. LONDON, 10 Oct 2002, *Christ before Pilate* (c. 1475-80, engraving, 6 x 4 ins / 16 x 11 cm) GBP 12,000. NEW YORK, 6 Nov 2002, *Flight into Egypt* (c. 1470-75, engraving, 10 x 6 ins / 25 x 16 cm) USD 24,000. BERLIN, 27 Nov 2003, *Madonna on Crescent Moon* (copperplate, 7 x 4 ins / 17 x 11 cm) EUR 4,500. BERLIN, 27 Nov 2003, *Capture of Christ* (copperplate, 7 x 5 ins / 17 x 12 cm) EUR 20,000. HAMBURG, 26 March 2004, *St Anthony Tempted by Demons* (oil on copperplate, 12 x 9 ins / 31 x 23 cm) EUR 43,000. NEW YORK, 6 May 2004, *Christ Appearing to Mary Magdalene* (c. 1480-90, engraving, 6 x 6 ins / 15 x 15 cm) USD 24,000.

SCHÖNGE, Gottfried. See **SCHÖNICHE**

SCHONGER, Caspar
German, 18th century.
Active in Botzen (now Bolzano, Italy).
Sculptor.

SCHONGER, Konrad
German, 18th century.
Draughtsman.

SCHÖNHAMMER, Philipp
German, 19th century.
Born 1793, in Biberach.
Landscape painter.
Philipp Schönhammer was a landscape painter. He was also an officer who went with Heydeck to Greece, where he fought for the liberation of the country.

SCHÖNHANNS. See **SCHÖN Hans**

SCHONHARDT, Henry
American, 20th century.
Born 24 April 1877, in Providence (Rhode Island).
Sculptor, painter.
Henry Schonhardt studied under Puech, Dubois and Verlet at the Académie Julian, and David and Chevignard at the École des Arts Décoratifs in Paris. He taught at the art school on Rhode Island.

Schonhardt took part in the Salon des Artistes Français in Paris, where he received an honourable mention in 1908. He sculpted the monument to *H.H. Young* in Providence and the monument to the dead in Bristol.

SCHÖNHEIM, Johann
German, 17th century.
Active in Schweidnitz.
Sculptor.

SCHÖNHEIT, Carl Simon or Johann C. S.
German, 18th century.
Born 1764, in Colditz; died 1798, in Dresden.
Draughtsman, architect.
Carl Schönheit attended the academy in Dresden from 1779 to 1784 and did views of castles in Saxony.

SCHÖNHEIT, Johann Carl
German, 18th century.
Born 1730, probably in Dresden; died 1805, in Meissen.
Sculptor.
From 1745 Johann Schönheit worked at the factory in Meissen. He sculpted several groups after the drawings of Johann Eleazar Schenau as well as a number of unglazed porcelain sculptures, notably the busts of Mars, Apollo, Jupiter, Bacchus and Neptune.

SCHÖNHERR, Anton
German, 19th century.
Active in Munich.
Painter.
In 1820 Anton Schönherr painted the ceilings of the Neue Schloss (New Castle) at Pappenheim.

SCHÖNHERR, Josef
Austrian, 19th century.
Born 7 February 1809, in Botzen (now Bolzano, Italy); died 12 June 1833, in Innsbruck.
Painter, engraver (burin).
The pupil of J.G. Schädler, Josef Schönherr painted views of the Tyrol and especially Innsbruck.

SCHÖNHERR, Karl Gottlob
German, 19th century.
Born 15 August 1824, in Lengefeld; died 9 July 1906, in Dresden.
Painter.
After attending the academy in Dresden with J.Hubner, Karl Schönherr went to Italy from 1852 to 1854, staying in Rome in particular. From 1857 to 1900 he taught at the academy in Dresden.

SCHÖNHEYDER, Anna Hartmann
Norwegian, 20th century.
Born 22 August 1877; died 11 April 1927.
Painter.
Anna Hartmann Schönheyder trained under Johann Nordhagen. She painted church interiors.

SCHÖNHOFER, Sebald
German, 14th century.
Active in Nuremberg.
Sculptor.
Sebald Schönhofer may have worked at Shönbrunn Palace and in the church of Our Lady in Nuremberg.

SCHÖNHOFER, Sebastian
Austrian, 18th century.
Active in Schärding.
Painter.
Sebastian Schönhofer painted a *St Martin* for the high altar in the parish church of Diersbach.

SCHÖNI, Stephan
Swiss, 16th century.
Active in Solothurn.
Sculptor.

SCHÖNIAN, Alfred
German, 19th - 20th century.
Born 16 March 1856, in Frankfurt an der Oder; died c. 1936, in Munich.
Painter, illustrator. Animals, birds, farmyard scenes.
Schönian studied in Leipzig under the sculptor Melchior Zur Strassen and in Munich under Benczur and L. Raab.

He specialised in painting birds.

AUCTION RECORDS:
LONDON, 20 Oct 1978, *Farmyard* (oil on canvas, 5 1/2 x 11 1/4 ins / 14 x 28.5 cm) GBP 650. COLOGNE, 24 May 1982, *Farmyard* (oil on panel, 7 x 11 ins / 18 x 28 cm) DEM 4,800. VIENNA, 20 March 1985, *Fowl in a Farmyard* (oil on panel, 6 1/4 x 9 1/2 ins / 16 x 24 cm) ATS 35,000. COLOGNE, 28 June 1991, *Cock and Hens next to a Wooden Fence* (oil on panel, 4 3/4 x 6 1/4 ins / 12 x 16 cm) DEM 4,400.

SCHÖNICHE, Gottfried, or Schönche or Schönchen or Schönge
German, 18th - 19th century.
Born 4 October 1740, in Arnhem (Holland); died 1816 or 1820, in Munich.
Painter, pastellist. Portraits.
Gottfried Schöniche was primarily a pastellist and a musician. From 1763 to 1772 he was Music Master at the Court at Mannheim and from 1779 at the Court at Munich.

MUSEUMS AND GALLERIES:
MANNHEIM: *Portrait of Joh. Goswin Widder* - MUNICH (Residenzmus.): *Young Lady*.

SCHÖNIGER, Johann Jakob, or Schönig or Schöninger
German, 17th century.
Active in Bayreuth.
Stucco artist.

SCHONINCK, Martin, or Schening or Schöning
German, 16th century.
Died probably c. 1560.
Active in Danzig (now Gdansk) 1536-1539.
Painter.

SCHÖNING, Franz
German, 19th century.
Lithographer, engraver.

SCHÖNINGER, Christoph
German, 17th century.
Active in Leipzig.
Painter.

SCHÖNINGER, Jakob
German, 18th century.
Active in Weil der Stadt.
Cabinet maker.

SCHÖNINGER, Johann Jakob.
See **SCHÖNIGER**

SCHÖNITZER, Sepp
Austrian, 20th century.
Born 23 February 1896, in Graz.
Painter. Seascapes, still-lifes.

Sepp Schönitzer was a pupil of Alfred Zoff and Daniel Pauluzzi.

SCHÖNLAUB, Christoph
Austrian, 18th century.
Of Viennese origin.
Sculptor.

The pupil of R. Donner, Christoph Schönlaub did a few figures in lead, attributed to Franz Kohl, which are now in Schloss Schönbrunn.

SCHÖNLAUB, Fidelius Johann
Austrian, 19th century.
Born 24 April 1805, in Vienna; died 20 December 1883, in Munich.
Sculptor. Religious subjects. Statues.

Fidelius Schönlaub studied with his brother Franz, then attended the academy in Vienna in 1819 with Klieber. From 1830 he worked with L. Schwanthaler at the academy in Munich

MUSEUMS AND GALLERIES:
BAMBERG (Cathedral): *The Virgin and Mary Magdalene*; 22 stone statues - REGENSBURG (Church): several statues.

SCHÖNLAUB, Franz
Austrian, 18th - 19th century.
Born 1765; died 27 September 1832, in Vienna.
Sculptor.

Franz Schönlaub was a sculptor at the Viennese Court.

SCHÖNLEBER, Elisabeth
German, 20th century.
Born 3 March 1877, in Zwickau.
Painter. Landscapes.

Elisabeth Schönleber was trained by Otto Altenkirch and her father Gustav Schönleber. She lived and worked in Krontal.

SCHÖNLEBER, Gustav or Gustave
German, 19th - 20th century.
Born 3 December 1851, in Bietigheim-am-Neckar; died 1 February 1917, in Karlsruhe.
Painter. Urban landscapes, landscapes, waterscapes, seascapes, architectural views.

Gustave Schönleber was the son of a woollen cloth manufacturer whose factory was situated on the banks of a river. It was in this river that Schönleber learnt to swim and fish for crayfish. His love of nature, light and movement made him a master of painting rural scenes.

He was self-taught, and later said that he did not know how he had become a painter. He went to Munich to work, and in 1881 became a teacher at the art school in Karlsruhe. He travelled to the Italian riviera, but disliked the clear skies. In 1893 he travelled down the Rhine to Holland, where he found more inspiration in the Dutch than the Italian school. His Dutch landscapes were a great success.

In 1891 he was nominated as a member of the art academy in Berlin. He was awarded medals in Berlin in 1880 and 1889, in Munich in 1888, Chicago in 1893 and a silver medal in Paris at the Exposition Universelle in 1900.

Schönleber belonged to the Bavarian school. He was strongly influenced by the French Impressionist painters, in particular by Monet, and painted water using techniques borrowed from the French master, drawing on his light palette, the authority of his touch and his sharpness of observation, even though this ran counter to the approach of the Munich school, which tended more towards strong expression. Schönleber specialised in a delicate touch, and liked portraying the tenderness of nature. He made much use of the colour blue in his paintings, as was the fashion in the late 19th century.

G Schönleber

MUSEUMS AND GALLERIES:
BERLIN: *Autumn Storm, Rapallo*; *Enzwehr near Bietigheim* - COLOGNE: *Dutch Coast* - CONSTANCE: watercolour - DARMSTADT: *Seascape* - DRESDEN: *Low Tide*; *Cliff* - DÜSSELDORF: *First Greenery* - FRANKFURT AM MAIN: *Old Essengen* - HAMBURG: *Lagunas near Venice* - LEIPZIG: *Fishing Boat in Venetian Lagunas* - MAINZ: *Cathedral and Canal in Dordrecht* - MUNICH: *Village in Holland*; *Punta della Madonetta* - STUTTGART: *Canal in Dordrecht*; *Spring* - WROCLAW: *Morning in the Laguna at Venice*; *Dyke on the Neckar near Bietigheim*.

AUCTION RECORDS:
FRANKFURT AM MAIN, 12 Dec 1892, *Low Tide at Antwerp*, DEM 11,250. LONDON, 20 March 1925, *Boats on the Laguna at Venice*, GBP 183. LONDON, 13 Dec 1937, *Small Boats at Anchor*, GBP 100. PARIS, 2 Feb 1949, *Houses by the Sea*, FRF 7,000. COLOGNE, 28 April 1965, *The Mediterranean Coast*, DEM 8,050. COLOGNE, 5 May 1966, *The Coast at Scheveningen*, DEM 16,000. COLOGNE, 15 Nov 1967, *Street Scene (Genoa)*, DEM 9,000. NEW YORK, 10 Oct 1973, *Harbour Scene*, USD 20,000. COLOGNE, 12 Nov 1976, *Capri* (1902, oil on canvas, 39 1/4 x 51 1/2 ins / 100 x 131 cm) DEM 5,000. COLOGNE, 23 Nov 1977, *Italian Landscape* (oil on card, 13 1/2 x 23 ins / 34.5 x 58.5 cm) DEM 3,400. COLOGNE, 17 March 1978, *View of Biesigheim* (1899, oil on canvas, 14 1/2 x 28 1/4 ins / 37 x 72 cm) DEM 5,600. MUNICH, 29 Nov 1979, *Dunes at La Panne* (1901, oil on canvas remounted on board, 11 x 16 1/4 ins / 27 x 41.5 cm) DEM 2,600. COLOGNE, 30 March 1984, *Small Fishing Boat in Harbour* (1875, oil on canvas, 13 x 10 ins / 33 x 25.5 cm) DEM 9,500. MUNICH, 18 Sept 1985, *Fishing Boats off the Dutch Coast* (1885, oil on canvas, 59 3/4 x 34 1/4 ins / 152 x 87 cm) DEM 6,000. LONDON, 26 Nov 1986, *Bogliasco* (1886, oil on canvas, 32 3/4 x 26 3/4 ins / 83 x 68 cm) GBP 18,000. NEW YORK, 28 Oct 1987, *View of a Town* (black chalks and colour/mounted paper/panel, 30 3/4 x 59 1/2 ins / 78 x 151 cm) USD 3,200. MUNICH, 18 May 1988, *Cliff by the Sea* (oil on canvas, 19 1/4 x 23 1/4 ins / 49 x 59 cm) DEM 7,700. NEW YORK, 1 March 1990, *View of the Church at Overschie* (1882, oil on card, 20 x 9 1/4 ins / 51.1 x 23.5 cm) USD 4,950. LONDON, 19 Nov 1993, *Fishing Boat on Calm Seas* (1894, oil on canvas/panel, 11 x 14 1/4 ins / 27.8 x 36 cm) GBP 3,450. MUNICH, 7 Dec 1993, *Cap Lungo* (1886, oil on canvas/panel, 17 1/4 x 22 ins / 43.5 x 56 cm) DEM 40,250. MUNICH, 21 June 1994, *Houses by the Water* (oil on canvas, 19 3/4 x 16 1/4 ins / 50 x 41.5 cm) DEM 8,280. VIENNA, 29-30 Oct 1996, *Dutch Canal* (1891, oil on canvas/card, 16 1/4 x 18 ins / 41.5 x 46 cm) ATS 115,000. NEW YORK, 12 Feb 1997, *Quinto al Mare, Riviera* (1888, oil on canvas, 71 x 103 ins / 180.3 x 261.6 cm) USD 49, 450. MUNICH, 23 June 1997, *Re-*

turn of the Fishing Boats (1900, oil on canvas, 22 1/2 x 40 1/2 ins / 57 x 103 cm) DEM 20,400.

SCHÖNLEBER, Hans Otto
German, 19th - 20th century.
Born 12 November 1889, in Karlsruhe; died end June 1930, in Stuttgart.
Engraver.

Hans Otto Schönleber was an engraver and carver. He was also a doctor of medicine.

SCHÖNMANN, Joseph
Austrian, 19th century.
Born 19 April 1799, in Vienna; died 26 May 1879, in Vienna.
Painter. History painting.

Joseph Schönmann studied under Joseph Mössner. He went to Naples in 1834 and to Sicily in 1835. In 1848 he became a member of the academy in Vienna.

MUSEUMS AND GALLERIES:
GRAZ: *Portrait of Count Von Saurau* - VIENNA (Österreichische Gal. Belvedere): *Holy Family*.

AUCTION RECORDS:
LONDON, 17 Nov 1993, *David and Abigail* (oil on canvas, 52 1/4 x 67 ins / 133 x 170 cm) GBP 16,100.

SCHÖNN, Alois
Austrian, 19th century.
Born 11 March 1826, in Vienna; died 16 September 1897, in Krumpendorf.
Painter, engraver, draughtsman. Portraits, landscapes.

Alois Schönn was taught by Führiclo and L. Russ in Vienna and from 1850 to 1851 by Horace Vernet in Paris. After a trip to Italy in 1848, he spent time in Paris. He also visited the East and Hungary. In 1875 he received the gold medal in Berlin, in 1878 he was made Chevalier of the Légion d'Honneur and in 1882 and 1883 he received the Order of François-Joseph. He participated in various exhibitions, settling in Vienna where he enjoyed considerable success as a portrait artist and painter of genre scenes, often borrowed from popular Jewish-German references.

MUSEUMS AND GALLERIES:
BADEN-BADEN: *Fish Market at Chioggia* - GRAZ: *Piazza of the Porticus of Octavia, Rome* - INNSBRUCK: *Tyrolean Students Leaving their Classes* - OPAVA: *Wedding Procession in Egypt* - VIENNA: *Attck on the Entrenched Camp of Lodrome on 22 May 1848; On the Genoese Shore; Artist; Roman Wine Grower* (a watercolour); *Market in Cracow* - VIENNA (Akademie der Bildenden Künste): *Feast at Lazia in Carinthia; Turkish Bazaar* - VIENNA (Kunsthistorisches Mus.): *Marriage Request in Vienna; Markt am Schanzl; Entry of the Mollnary Infantry Regiment into Vienna; Ruines of Taormina* - WROCLAW: *Linseed Oil Courtyard in Palermo*.

AUCTION RECORDS:
LONDON, 19 April 1978, *The Ball* (oil on canvas, 68 x 52 ins / 172.5 x 132 cm) GBP 2,300. LONDON, 15 June 1979, *Fish Market, Venice* (1869, oil on canvas, concave corners, 72 3/4 x 54 3/4 ins / 185 x 139 cm) GBP 1,800. VIENNA, 15 Sept 1982, *Painter's Studio* (1887, oil on canvas, 33 1/2 x 51 1/2 ins / 85 x 131 cm) ATS 80,000. VIENNA, 22 June 1983, *Market Scene near Port in Vienna* (1895, oil on card, 24 1/2 x 36 ins / 62.5 x 91.5 cm) ATS 220,000. VIENNA, 11 Sept 1985, *Farm Scene* (oil on canvas, 22 3/4 x 31 1/2 ins / 58 x 80 cm) ATS 32,000. PARIS, 18-19 Nov 1991, *Meal in the Shade* (1871, oil on canvas, 42 1/4 x 64 1/4 ins / 107 x 163 cm) FRF 455,000. PARIS, 16 Nov 1992, *Moorish Café* (1861, oil on canvas, 25 1/2 x 33 ins / 65 x 84 cm) FRF 400,000. LONDON, 21 March 1997, *Return from Vineyard* (oil on canvas, 53 x 89 1/4 ins / 134.7 x 227 cm) GBP 177,500. LONDON, 19 Nov 1997, *Cabbage Market, Vienna* (1895, oil on canvas, 29 1/2 x 22 3/4 ins / 75 x 58 cm) GBP 26,450. VIENNA, 29 April 1999, *Market Day* (watercolour heightened with white over pencil, 9 x 14 ins / 22 x 36 cm) ATS 40,000. MONTREAL, 14 June 1999, *Scene in Cracow* (oil on canvas, 29 x 21 ins / 73 x 54 cm) CAD 5,500. PARIS, 3 April 2000, *Relaxing on a Terrace in Constantinople* (oil on canvas, 17 x 29 ins / 42 x 73 cm) FRF 90,000. STUTTGART, 8 Dec 2000, *Shepherds Resting* (oil on canvas, 11 x 17 ins / 28 x 43 cm) DEM 3,600. VIENNA, 28 May 2001, *Gathering of Oriental Men* (oil on canvas, 29 x 39 ins / 74 x 100 cm) ATS 800,000. LONDON, 17 Oct 2001, *River Traders* (1881, oil on canvas, 31 x 49 ins / 79 x 125 cm) GBP 20,000. VIENNA, 13 June 2002, *Going Up to Alpine Pastures* (oil on canvas, 20 x 15 ins / 52 x 39 cm) EUR 1,800.

SCHÖNN, Ricka
Austrian, 19th - 20th century.
Born 8 December 1867, in Vienna.
Painter. Portraits, interiors.

Ricka Schönn was taught by her father, Alois Schönn.

SCHÖNNENBECK, Adolf
German, 19th - 20th century.
Born 10 May 1869, in Senkenberg, Westphalia.
Painter, watercolourist, lithographer. Portraits, genre scenes.

From 1886 to 1894, Adolf Schönnenbeck was a pupil at the art academy in Düsseldorf under Peter Janssen. In 1902 he received a scholarship to travel to Italy. He lived and worked in Senkenberg in Westphalia.

MUSEUMS AND GALLERIES:
COLOGNE (Wallraf-Richartz Mus.): a watercolour - DÜSSELDORF - MUHLHEIM - WUPPERTAL.

SCHÖNPFLUG, Fritz
Austrian, 20th century.
Born 15 June 1873, in Vienna; died 18 February 1951, in Vienna.
Painter, caricaturist, illustrator.

Mainly self-taught and a remarkable painter of horses, Fritz Schönpflug also specialised in military caricatures and the portrayal of Viennese people. He founded the wartime journal *Die Muskete* (*The Musket*) and collaborated on the *Figaro* in Vienna and London's *Sketch*.

AUCTION RECORDS:
VIENNA, 12 Feb 1985, *The Violin Players* (1945, watercolour, 9 1/2 x 13 1/2 ins / 24 x 34 cm) ATS 18,000. VIENNA, 15 May 2001, *Scenes in Vienna* (watercolour, six, 12 x 14 ins / 31 x 36 cm) ATS 70,000. VIENNA, 15 Oct 2002, *Dining Room with Diners and Musicians* (Indian ink and watercolour, 17 x 28 ins / 43 x 71 cm) EUR 1,600.

SCHÖNREITHER, Georg
Austrian, 19th century.
Born in Vienna; died 1883.
Painter. Landscapes.

From 1861 to 1862 Georg Schönreiter attended the academy in Vienna, where he exhibited from 1868 to 1883.

AUCTION RECORDS:
VIENNA, 7 April 1981, *View of Klostenburg* (oil on canvas, 16 1/2 x 23 ins / 42 x 58.5 cm) ATS 35,000.

SCHÖNROCK, Julius
German, 19th century.
Born 1835, in Danzig (now Gdansk, Poland).
Painter. Portraits, landscapes.

Julius Schönrock attended academies in Königsberg (now Kaliningrad, Russia) and Berlin and lived in Berlin until 1878.

AUCTION RECORDS:
COLOGNE, 28 June 1991, *Rustic Scene with Cottage near Cascade* (oil on panel, 7 3/4 x 16 1/4 ins / 20 x 41 cm) DEM 2,200. NEW YORK, 28 March 2000, *Evening River Landscape* (oil on canvas, 24 x 40 ins / 60 x 101 cm) USD 3,000. HAMBURG, 6 Oct 2001, *Evening Lake with Figures* (oil on canvas, 25 x 35 ins /

63 x 89 cm) DEM 3,600. MUNICH, 20 Sept 2002, *Walk in the Rain* (oil on canvas, 22 x 32 ins / 56 x 82 cm) EUR 1,800.

SCHÖNSCHUTZ, Joseph
Austrian, 19th century.
Born 1788, in Vienna; died 29 June 1844, in Klausenburg (now Cluj-Napoca, Romania).
Painter, lithographer. Portraits.

Joseph Schönschutz accompanied the army of occupation in France as a lithographer and officer, exhibiting in 1820 at the academy in Vienna. His portrait, painted by Goebel in 1820, is in the museum in Graz.

SCHÖNTHALER, Franz
Austrian, 19th century.
Born 21 January 1821, in Neusiedl; died 26 December 1904, in Gutenstein.
Sculptor, decorative designer, architect.

Franz Schönthaler worked in the studios of Fourdinois and Lafrance in Paris. He contributed to the decoration of a number of palaces in Vienna as well as the Arsenal (Military Museum), the Börse and the Opera in this city.

SCHÖNWERTH, Christoph
German, 18th - 19th century.
Born 28 January 1728, in Amberg; died after 1810.
Painter.

SCHÖNWERTH, Joseph
German, 19th century.
Born 29 March 1783, in Amberg.
Painter, miniaturist. Portraits.

Joseph Schönwerth was the son of Christoph.

SCHONZEIT, Ben
American, 20th century.
Born 1942, in Brooklyn (New York City).
Painter.

Ben Schonzeit studied at Cooper Union and visited Europe in 1964 and 1965. Although generally likened to Hyperrealism, his painting differs significantly from it both in the freedom of its layout and in its detached view of reality. Furthermore, he did not appear in the Hyperrealism exhibitions responsible for the success of the movement, apart from Documenta V in Kassel in 1972. In some respects, moreover, Schonzeit's painting resembles Rosenquist as much as Richard Estes. Like Rosenquist, he sometimes looks for the unusual in the juxtaposition of images. Thus in the picture *Buffalo Bill,* he portrays this character in the middle of a collection of key rings and pill-boxes. To reinforce the distance between image and a reality he considers illusory, Schonzeit uses a fuzziness that makes acid colours shine and thus accentuates the 'kitsch' and the mysterious. Schonzeit exhibited for the first time in 1970 in New York, then in Aachen, Berlin and Paris. Collective exhibitions include: *Hypermental,* an exhibition on the unreal, the transreal and the reconstruction of reality, at the Kunsthalle in Hamburg in 2001 and *Hyperréalismes USA 1965-75* at the Musée d'Art Moderne et Contemporain in Strasbourg in 2003.

BIBLIOGRAPHY:
Lebensztejn, Jean-Claude, et al., *Hyperréalismes USA 1965-75,* group exhibition catalogue, Musée d'Art moderne et contemporain, Strasbourg, Hazan, Paris, 2003.

AUCTION RECORDS:
PARIS, 12 April 1973, *Come with Me A. E.,* FRF 8,500. PARIS, 30 Nov 1974, *Sugar* (1972) FRF 19,000. NEW YORK, 8 Nov 1979, *Canada Dry Ice* (1973, oil on canvas, 84 x 84 ins / 213.4 x 213.4 cm) USD 5,000. NEW YORK, 13 May 1981, *Buffalo Bill* (1970, oil on canvas, 72 x 72 ins / 183 x 183 cm) USD 15,000. NEW YORK, 21 May 1983, *Feathers and Peanut Brittle* (1970, acrylic/canvas, 48 x 72 ins / 122 x 183 cm) USD 1,500. NEW YORK, 7 Nov 1985, *Cupcakes (Moon)* (1970, acrylic/canvas, 72 x 72 ins / 182.8 x 182.8 cm) USD 4,000. NEW YORK, 7 May 1986, *A. Brooklyn Bridge* (1980, oil on panel, four panels, 84 x 144 ins / 213.4 x 366 cm) USD 10,000. STOCKHOLM, 23 April 2002, *The Music Room III* (1978, mixed media on paper, 96 x 72 ins / 244 x 183 cm) SEK 70,000.

SCHOOCK, Hendrik, or Schook
Flemish School, 17th century.
Born 1630; died 1707.
Active in Utrecht 1669-1696.
Painter. Still-lifes (flowers/fruit).
Utrecht School.

Hendrik Schoock was the son of the Bommel painter Gysbert Schook. He was a pupil of A. Boemaer, J. Lievensz. and D. de Heem. With Hoet he co-founded the school of design in Utrecht.

MUSEUMS AND GALLERIES:
BOURGES - MEININGEN: *Fruit.*

AUCTION RECORDS:
PARIS, 1888, *Flowers,* FRF 285. PARIS, 16 Oct 1940, *Fruit,* FRF 310. PARIS, 16 Dec 1942, *Still-life with Fruit,* FRF 2,900. LONDON, 13 July 1962, *Still-life with Pink Tulips and Poppies,* Gns 1,600. LONDON, 16 March 1966, *Vase of Flowers,* GBP 3,000. LONDON, 25 June 1969, *Bouquet of Flowers,* GBP 2,800. AMSTERDAM, 3 Dec 1985, *Still-life with a Basket of Fruit* (oil on canvas, 45 x 35¾ ins / 114.5 x 91 cm) NLG 55,000. STOCKHOLM, 30 Nov 1993, *Still-life with an Arrangement of Fruit in a Niche* (oil on canvas, 26¾ x 22 ins / 68 x 55 cm) SEK 20,000. MONACO, 4 Dec 1993, *Still-life of a Large Arrangement of Fruit with Oranges, Pomegranates, Grapes, Lemons, Walnuts and a Knife on a Table Covered with a Blue Cloth* (1657, oil on canvas, 23 x 30 ins / 58.5 x 76.2 cm) FRF 122,100. AMSTERDAM, 8 Nov 1999, *Basket of Grapes and other Fruit on a Stone Ledge* (oil on canvas, 45 x 36 ins / 114 x 91 cm) NLG 100,000. LONDON, 11 July 2002, *Still-life with Tulips, Roses and other Flowers in a Glass Vase on a Stone Ledge* (oil on panel, 20 x 15 ins / 50 x 38 cm) GBP 25,000. SAN FRANCISCO, 18 May 2004, *Still-life with Tulips, Roses, Blackberries and other Flowers in a Glass Vase on a Ledge* (oil on panel, 21 x 17 ins / 54 x 43 cm) USD 92,000.

SCHOOF, Gerard I, or Schooff
Flemish School, 16th century.
Died before 13 October 1586.
Painter, sculptor. Religious subjects.
Mechelen School, Antwerp School.

In 1516 Gerard Schooff I became a member of the guild in Mechelen and in 1518 joined the guild in Antwerp as a sculptor. From 1542 to 1571 he was the official painter of the city of Mechelen. He frequently farmed out to other workshops the orders he received for retables and concentrated on his career as a painter.

SCHOOF, Gerard II
Flemish School, 17th century.
Died 1624, in Antwerp.
Active mainly in Mechelen.
Painter. Religious subjects.

Gerard Schoof II was the grandson of Gerrit Schoof I and the father of Rudolf Schoof. In 1612 he presented a *Deposition* to the parish church at Hoboken.

SCHOOF, Guliam
Flemish School, 17th century.
Painter.

Guliam Schoof became a master of the Antwerp guild in 1614, and was married in Amsterdam in 1636.

SCHOOF, Rudolf
Flemish School, 17th century.
Painter.

Rudolf Schoof was the son of Gerrit Schoof II. He settled in Paris around 1615 as court painter to Louis XIII. A. de Bie was his pupil.

SCHOOFF, Jacques
Flemish School, 16th century.
Born in Mechelen; died 1591.
Active c. 1551.
Painter.

Jacques Schooff was the son of Gerard Schooff the Elder.

SCHOOFF, Jean. See **SCHOEFF**

SCHOOFF, Johannes Pietersz.. See **SCHOEFF**

SCHOOFF, Philip
Flemish School, 16th - 17th century.
Active in Ghent.
Painter.

Philip Schooff was a pupil of P. Pieters in 1599 and became a guild master in 1601.

SCHOOFS, Henri
Belgian, 19th century.
Died 1862, in Brussels.
Painter (?), writer.

Henri Schoofs was a pupil of P. Lauters.

SCHOOFS, Rudolph
German (?), 20th century.
Born 1920.
Engraver.

Between 1954 and 1962 works by Rudolf Schoofs were shown at the Salon des Réalités Nouvelles in Paris. He also exhibited in Munich.

He was linked to the Germanic movement of Geometric Abstraction without austerity, which grew around the Bauhaus school.

AUCTION RECORDS:

COLOGNE, 30 May 1981, *Landscape* (1972, pencil, 19 1/2 x 27 1/4 ins / 49.7 x 69.5 cm) DEM 2,000. COLOGNE, 28 May 1999, *Male Torso* (1964, green patinated bronze, h. 11 ins / 28 cm) DEM 4,800. HAMBURG, 14 June 2002, *Untitled* (oil on canvas, 63 x 79 ins / 160 x 200 cm) EUR 4,200. COLOGNE, 24 May 2003, *Utopian Architecture* (1970, mixed media on board, 35 x 39 ins / 90 x 100 cm) EUR 1,600. COLOGNE, 28 May 2003, *Untitled* (1990, oil on canvas, 37 x 53 ins / 95 x 135 cm) EUR 2,000.

SCHOONBECK, Adrian
Dutch, 17th century.
Active c. 1690.
Engraver (etching).

Adrian Schoonbeck is noted for an etching of *Flight of James II of England*.

SCHOONBEEK, Johannes Nicolas
Dutch, 18th - 19th century.
Born 6 December 1778, in Groningen.
Painter. Portraits, landscapes.

Johannes Nicolas Schoonbeek was a pupil of H. and G. Wieringa, and of David in Paris from 1802 to 1806. Eelkema was his pupil.

SCHOONBERGEN, Henri van
Belgian, 16th century.
Active in Louvain.
Glass painter.

SCHOONE, A. G. van
Dutch, 19th century.
Active in Amsterdam 1823-1840.
Painter. Landscapes.

SCHOONEBEECK, Adriaan
Dutch, 17th century.
Born c. 1658; died 1705, in Moscow.
Painter, engraver, draughtsman. Religious subjects, portraits.

Adriaan Schoonebeeck was a pupil of Romeyn de Hooghe. He was married in Amsterdam in 1685. He engraved portraits and illustrations and a large number of frontispieces. He was also a publisher and is best known for two volumes on the customs of the various European religious orders.

A.S / A S.B f

AUCTION RECORDS:

AMSTERDAM, 10 May 1994, *The Sons of Aaron: Nasab and Abihu Struck Down by the Wrath of Jehovah* (ink and wash/blue paper, 6 3/4 x 11 1/2 ins / 17.3 x 29.2 cm) NLG 4,600.

SCHOONEVLIET, Hubert van
Belgian, 15th century.
Active in Brussels.
Painter.

Hubert van Schoonevliet painted the framework of a tabernacle on the altar of the Holy Sacrament in Louvain Cathedral.

SCHOONHOVE, Jan Cornelisz.
Dutch, 17th century.
Active in Delft c.1613.
Painter.

SCHOONHOVEN, Johannes Jacobus, called Jan
Dutch, 20th century.
Born 1914, in Delft; died 1994.
Painter, sculptor, draughtsman.
Neo-Constructivism, Op Art.
Nul Group.

Johannes Jacobus Schoonhoven began his career as an industrial designer and studied at the art academy in the Hague from 1930 to 1934. From 1946 to 1979 he worked for the Dutch postal service.

In 1957 he founded, with Armando, Henk Peters, Jan Hendrikse and Kees Van Bohemen, the Dutch 'informel' Group, and in 1960, the Nul Group.

He participated in many exhibitions, including: the 1962 exhibition of the Zero Group at Amsterdam's Stedelijk Museum; *Anti-Painting* in Antwerp in 1962; the 1977 exhibition *Aspects historiques du constructivisme et de l'art concret* (*Historical Aspects of Constructivism and Concrete Art*) at the Musée d'Art Moderne de la Ville de Paris; *Un tableau dans le décor, Peintures 1970-2000* (*A Painting in the Décor: Paintings 1970-2000*), an exhibition held in 2003 to commemorate the 20th anniversary of FRAC at the Château des Ducs de Bretagne, Nantes. His first solo exhibition was at the Galerie Wulfengasse in Klagenfurt, Germany in 1965, and in 1988 he held his first solo exhibition in France at the Institut Néederlandais (Dutch Institute), an exhibition which was then presented at the Musée de Peinture et de Sculpture de Grenoble later that year.

Initially Schoonhoven painted in an Expressionist style, but then moved towards non-figuration, specifically, informal landscapes and then tachisme. He was little-known until 1956, when he created some painted reliefs in papier mâché, some of which were on the borderline between optical and informal art. In the early 1960s he produced white monochromes in leaves of card and paper; a direct development from the research of the kinetic group Zero in Germany (founded in Düsseldorf in 1957), where only the shadows of shapes could be seen in the square pattern and repeating relief, whilst the perception of the picture changed according to the position of the viewer. He subsequently developed this aspect of his work, notably in his black and white drawings or in his reliefs with small pieces sloped like a roof. He catalogued his works by date, coding them R (relief) or T (tekening - drawing). In the context of his optical art, he produced some luminous objects.

BIBLIOGRAPHY:

Popper, Frank, *L'Art cinétique*, Gauthier-Villars, Paris, 1970. F. Bool, et al., *Jan Schoonhoven: Retrospectief*, exhibition catalogue, Gemeentemus, The Hague, 1984. Lemoine, S., *Jan Schoonhoven: Rétrospective*, exhibition catalogue, Fond. Custodia, Institut Néerlandais, Paris, 1988.

MUSEUMS AND GALLERIES:

AMSTERDAM (Stedelijk Mus.) - DIJON (FRAC Bourgogne): *R 72-46* (1972) - GRENOBLE (Mus. de Grenoble) - THE HAGUE (Gemeentemus.).

AUCTION RECORDS:

AMSTERDAM, 24 Oct 1983, *R69-9* (mixed media, 41 x 41 ins / 104 x 104 cm) NLG 14,000. AMSTERDAM, 5 June 1984, *Spider's Web* (1964, plastic in relief, 40 1/4 x 31 3/4 ins / 102 x 80.5 cm) NLG 12,500. AMSTERDAM, 10 April 1989, *Rectangular Composition in Relief* (1963, white paint/papier maché, 11 x 6 3/4 ins / 27 x 17 cm) NLG 13,800. AMSTERDAM, 13 Dec 1989, *Oblique Reliefs Towards the Centre* (1967, white paint/papier maché in relief, 15 x 12 1/2 ins / 38 x 32 cm) NLG 25,300. AMSTERDAM, 10 April 1990, *144 Squares* (1965, oil on papier maché, 39 1/4 x 39 1/4 ins / 100 x 100 cm) NLG 86,250. AMSTERDAM, 22 May 1990, *No title* (1965, white paint on papier maché relief, 30 1/4 x 23 1/2 ins / 77 x 60 cm) NLG 69,000. AMSTERDAM, 13 Dec 1990, *No Title* (1937, oil/glass, 9 x 7 ins / 23 x 18 cm) NLG 2,300. AMSTERDAM, 22 May 1991, *R74-14* (1974, white paint on papier maché relief, 24 3/4 x 24 3/4 ins / 63 x 63 cm) NLG 63,250. AMSTERDAM, 11 Dec 1991, *R61-4* (white paint on papier maché relief, 35 1/2 x 29 1/2 ins / 90 x 75 cm) NLG 63,250. AMSTERDAM, 21 May 1992, *R72-15* (1972, white paint on papier maché relief, 17 x 13 3/4 ins / 43 x 35 cm) NLG 23,000. AMSTERDAM, 10 Dec 1992, *R-77-15* (1977, white paint on papier maché relief, 37 1/2 x 31 1/2 ins / 95 x 80 cm) NLG 43,700. AMSTERDAM, 26 May 1993, *Scrap Iron and Vegetation* (1955, gouache/paper, 26 1/2 x 18 ins / 67 x 46 cm) NLG 8,050. LONDON, 24 June 1993, *R60-27* (1960, papier mâché/wood and paint, relief, 28 3/4 x 19 x 1 3/4 ins / 73 x 48.5 x 4.5 cm) GBP 17,250. AMSTERDAM, 8 Dec 1993, *R-73-19* (white papier mâché, relief, 23 1/2 x 19 3/4 ins / 60 x 50 cm) NLG 25,300. AMSTERDAM, 31 May 1995, *R 85 3* (1985, whitewash/card/panel, relief, 48 x 26 ins / 122 x 66 cm) NLG 41,300. AMSTERDAM, 5 June 1996, *Relief* (1963, white papier mâché relief, 19 3/4 x 9 ins / 50 x 22 cm) NLG 43,700. AMSTERDAM, 10 June 1996, *R. 60-10* (papier mâché, relief, 25 1/2 x 5 1/2 ins / 64.5 x 14 cm) NLG 7,495. AMSTERDAM, 17-18 Dec 1996, *Relief* (1968, wash/papier mâché, 26 x 19 3/4 ins / 66 x 50 cm) NLG 50,740. AMSTERDAM, 2-3 June 1997, *R 72-33* (1972, white distemper/card, 17 x 17 ins / 43 x 43 cm) NLG 61,360. AMSTERDAM, 1 Dec 1997, *R72-12* (1972, white wash/card, relief, 17 x 13 3/4 ins / 43 x 35 cm) NLG 54,280. AMSTERDAM, 10 June 1999, *R72 - 16* (1972, painted papier mache relief, 17 x 14 ins / 43 x 35 cm) NLG 38,000. AMSTERDAM, 1 Dec 1999, *R 69-40* (1969, painted papier mache relief, 41 x 41 ins / 104 x 104 cm) NLG 140,000. AMSTERDAM, 8 June 2000, *5 Zeichnungen - Edition Hake, Published by Walterake and Text by Henk Peters* (1965, pen and ink, 10 x 10 ins / 25 x 25 cm) NLG 15,000. AMSTERDAM, 13 June 2001, *R73-10* (papier mache relief, 12 x 10 ins / 30 x 25 cm) NLG 75,000. AMSTERDAM, 3 Dec 2001, *The Circle* (1967, white painted paper mache/board) NLG 300,000. AMSTERDAM, 28 May 2002, *R72-28* (1972, white painted relief, 14 x 14 ins / 35 x 35 cm) EUR 32,000. AMSTERDAM, 26 Nov 2002, *32 Small schuine vlakjes* (1966, white painted paper-mache relief, 17 x 7 ins / 42 x 19 cm) EUR 38,000. AMSTERDAM, 27 May 2003, *R72-73-M-13* (1973, white painted papier mache) EUR 50,000. AMSTERDAM, 2 Dec 2003, *Quadraten* (1969, white painted papier mache/wood) EUR 75,000. AMSTERDAM, 8 June 2004, *Series of Nine White Reliefs* (1964, white painted paper-maché/wood) EUR 110,000. AMSTERDAM, 30 Nov 2004, *R72-41* (1972, white painted cardboard relief) EUR 44,000.

SCHOONJANS, Anton, or Anthoni, known as Parhasius or Parrhasios
Flemish School, 17th - 18th century.
Born c. 1655, in Antwerp; died 1726, in Vienna.
Painter. History painting, figures, portraits.

Anton Schoonjans was a pupil of Erasmus Quellinus in 1668. He travelled to Rome around 1674, where he decorated several churches, and was subsequently called to the court of Emperor Leopold in Vienna. His sudden departure from that city, after marrying a singer, is unexplained, but he seems to have spent time in Berlin (1702) and The Hague (1704) before settling in Amsterdam. He was also active in Düsseldorf at the court of the Count Palatine Johann Wilhelm. He later returned to Vienna as an imperial court painter, and probably also worked in London.

An t Schoonjans
P 1710. AAS

MUSEUMS AND GALLERIES:

AUGSBURG: *Job Tormented by his Wife* - BERLIN (Imperial Collection): *King Frederik Wilhelm Aged 14* - BUDAPEST: *Mandolin Player* - FLORENCE: *Self-portrait* - HANOVER: *Doctor; Little Girl* - MANNHEIM: *Baptism of Christ* - NUREMBERG: *St Sebastian; St Jerome* - OBERSCHLEISSHEIM (Neues Schloss Schleissheim, Staatsgal.): *Princess Palatine Maria-Anna Luisa Aloisia de' Medici; Self-portrait; Little Girl with Bird*; two paintings of old women - SIBIU: *Self-portrait* - SPEYER: *Self-portrait*.

AUCTION RECORDS:

VIENNA, 16 March 1976, *Diogenes* (oil on canvas, 48 x 35 3/4 ins / 121 x 91 cm) ATS 50,000. PARIS, 18 March 2002, *Self-portrait* (oil on canvas, 27 x 22 ins / 68 x 56 cm) EUR 25,000.

SCHOONJANS, Jan, or Schoenjans or van der Stene
Flemish School, 15th century.
Active in Mechelen 1441-1447.
Painter.

SCHOONMAECKERS, Egidius Gilles.
See **SCHOENMAECKERS**

SCHOONOVER, Frank Earle
American, 20th century.
Born 1877; died 1972.
Painter. Figures, scenes with figures, genre scenes.

Frank Schoonover often painted fight scenes.

Frank E. Schoonover

BIBLIOGRAPHY:

Frank E. Schoonover: Illustrator, exhibition catalogue, Brandywine Conservancy, Chadds Ford, 1979.

AUCTION RECORDS:

NEW YORK, 27 Oct 1977, *Lone Hand* (1927, oil on canvas, 33 x 30 ins / 83.8 x 76.2 cm) USD 6,500. NEW YORK, 24 Oct 1979, *Francis Drake at Nova Albion* (1941, oil on canvas, 30 x 42 1/4 ins / 76.5 x 107 cm) USD 5,000. NEW YORK, 19 June 1981, *Indians Wrestling* (1923, oil on canvas, 36 x 30 ins / 91.5 x 76.2 cm) USD 14,000. NEW YORK, 26 Oct 1984, *Mexico* (1906, oil on canvas remounted on board, 35 x 23 1/2 ins / 88.9 x 59.7 cm) USD 3,500. NEW YORK, 4 Dec 1986, *Indians* (1919, oil on canvas, in grisaille, 32 x 44 ins / 81.3 x 111.8 cm) USD

26,000. NEW YORK, 24 June 1988, *Man from the North* (1920, oil on canvas, 27 1/2 x 35 1/2 ins / 70 x 90 cm) USD 7,700. NEW YORK, 30 Nov 1990, *Pirate* (1911, oil on canvas, 22 x 33 ins / 56 x 83.8 cm) USD 30,800. NEW YORK, 14 March 1991, *Masked Indian Dancer* (oil on canvas, 27 x 38 ins / 68.5 x 96.5 cm) USD 12,100. NEW YORK, 22 May 1991, *Wagon Train* (1936, oil on canvas, 50 1/4 x 54 1/4 ins / 127.5 x 137.5 cm) USD 38,500. NEW YORK, 18 Dec 1991, *Adventurous Lion* (oil on canvas in grisaille, 30 x 40 ins / 76.2 x 101.6 cm) USD 880. NEW YORK, 4 Dec 1992, *Trooper Shifted Both Hands* (1926, oil on canvas, 30 x 38 ins / 76.2 x 95.6 cm) USD 14,300. NEW YORK, 23 Sept 1993, *'Forward! Forward!' He Cried* (1921, oil on canvas, 36 x 30 ins / 91.4 x 76.2 cm) USD 6,900. NEW YORK, 17 March 1994, *Contact* (1918, oil on canvas, 36 x 27 1/4 ins / 91.4 x 69.2 cm) USD 24,150. NEW YORK, 23 May 1996, *Deerstalker* (1919, oil on canvas, 39 1/4 x 30 ins / 99.7 x 76.2 cm) USD 43,700. NEW YORK, 3 Dec 1996, *She Had No Weapons* (1919, oil on canvas, 34 x 25 ins / 86.4 x 63.5 cm) USD 4,830. LOS ANGELES, 9 Dec 1999, *Astride Saddle Sat Three-year-old Boy* (pencil and gouache, 13 x 11 ins / 32 x 27 cm) USD 7,500. NEW YORK, 24 May 2000, *The Vision* (1921, oil on canvas, 40 x 20 ins / 102 x 51 cm) USD 55,000. NEW YORK, 29 Nov 2000, *Northern Mist* (1916, oil on canvas, 31 x 36 ins / 79 x 92 cm) USD 250,000. NEW YORK, 5 May 2001, *Man with Torch Discovering Treasure Vault* (1933, oil on canvas, 30 x 21 ins / 76 x 53 cm) USD 19,000. HAYDEN, 28 July 2001, *Open Range* (oil on canvas, 26 x 36 ins / 66 x 91 cm) USD 22,500.

SCHOOP, Ulrich, called Uli
German, 20th century.
Born 17 October 1903, in Cologne.
Sculptor. Animals.

Ulrich Schoop exhibited in Paris at the Salons des Indépendants and the Salon d'Automne from 1928, and also in Zurich.

MUSEUMS AND GALLERIES:
AARAU (Aargauer Kunsthaus): *Cats* (1950); *Panther* (1972).

SCHOOR, Abraham van der
Flemish School, 17th century.
Active in Amsterdam 1643-1650.
Painter. Portraits, genre scenes, still-lifes.

MUSEUMS AND GALLERIES:
AMSTERDAM: *Vanitas; Man with a Red Beard* - LEEUWARDEN: *Portrait.*

AUCTION RECORDS:
AMSTERDAM, 12 May 1992, *Esther and Mordecai* (1643, oil on canvas, 55 3/4 x 67 3/4 ins / 141.5 x 172.3 cm) NLG 74,750. AMSTERDAM, 16 Nov 1993, *Fish on a Shore* (1658, oil on panel, 4 1/4 x 22 ins / 11 x 56 cm) NLG 41,400. NEW YORK, 23 May 1997, *Interior with Tricksters Cheating at Cards* (1656, oil on canvas, 40 1/4 x 54 ins / 102 x 137 cm) USD 65,200.

SCHOOR, Gillis van, or Verschoren
Flemish School, 17th century.
Born 18 July 1596, in Antwerp.
Engraver.

Gillis van Schoor was a pupil of Theodor Galle in 1613. He became a guild master in 1617.

SCHOOR, Guilliam van, or Schoore, Schore
Flemish School, 17th century.
Painter. Urban landscapes.

Guilliam van Schoor was master of the Brussels guild from 1653 to 1676.

MUSEUMS AND GALLERIES:
BRUSSELS (Mus. royaux des Beaux-Arts de Belgique): *Hôtel de Nassau in Brussels.*

SCHOOR, Jacobus van, or Schoore
Flemish School, 17th century.
Engraver. Portraits.

Jacobus van Schoor was a pupil of T. van Merlen in the Antwerp guild in 1633.

SCHOOR, Jan Jansz. van der
Flemish School, 16th - 17th century.
Active in Antwerp.
Painter.

Jan Jansz. van der Schoor was a pupil of the painter Hans van Haecht and in 1612 was mayor of Delft.

SCHOOR, Lucas van
Flemish School, 16th - 17th century.
Born c. 1566, in Antwerp; died c. 1610, probably in Italy.
Painter.

Lucas van Schoor painted a *Crucifixion* in the church of S Maria Maggiore in Bergamo.

SCHOOR, Ludwig van, or Nicolas, Nicolaes
Flemish School, 17th century.
Born c. 1666, possibly in Antwerp; died in Antwerp.
Painter.

Ludwig van Schoor produced history paintings and portraits, but also lighter subjects of considerable charm, and flowers. He made designs for the tapestry workshops in Brussels. Kramm refers to him as Nicolaes van Schoor.

MUSEUMS AND GALLERIES:
BRUCHSAL: *Alexander* - GHENT: *Charles II of Spain at 18 Years of Age* - KARLSRUHE: *Birth of Venus.*

SCHOOR, Matheus van
Flemish School, 17th century.
Active in Amsterdam in 1631 and in Louvain.
Painter.

SCHOORE, Stephanus van. See **SCHORE**

SCHOOREEL, Jan van. See **SCOREL**

SCHOORMAN
German, 17th century.
Active in Ulm.
Painter. Portraits.

MUSEUMS AND GALLERIES:
COLOGNE: *Portrait of Lady.*

SCHOORMAN. See also **SCHORMAN**

SCHOORMAN, Jan, or Schuermans
Flemish School, 16th century.
Active in Ghent 1567-1585.
Sculptor.

Jan Schoorman was the son-in-law of the sculptor Jan van Heere I and the brother-in-law of Jan van Heere II.

SCHOOT, Jacob
Dutch, 17th century.
Active in Haarlem c. 1647.
Painter.

SCHOOTEN, Abraham van
Dutch, 17th century.
Active in Amsterdam.
Painter.

SCHOOTEN, Arent van
Dutch, 17th century.
Died 1662.

Active in Leiden.
Painter.
Arent van Schooten was the son of Joris van Schooten.

SCHOOTEN, Floris Gerritsz. van, or Schoten, Verschoten
Flemish School, 17th century.
Born 1587; died c. 1665.
Active 1605-1655.
Painter. Still-lifes (including fruit/fish).

Floris Gerritsz. van Schooten was married in Haarlem in 1612. His works feature in numerous museum collections. His still-lifes eschew facile visual appeal in favour of a high degree of artistic rigour. As such, his work ushers in the flowering of still-life painting in the Netherlands in the 17th century. His carefully calculated compositions integrate the spaces between objects into a geometrically and rhythmically structured whole. Van Schooten's palette favours neutral ochres and bistre tones against dark backgrounds, enlivened by the inclusion of red fruits which provide touches of bright colour.

MUSEUMS AND GALLERIES:

ATHENS (Ethnikí Pinakothíki): *Butter, cheeses and Herring* (oil/panel) - CAMBRIDGE (Fitzwilliam Mus.): *Kitchen Utensils, Meat and Vegetables* (oil on canvas).

AUCTION RECORDS:

PARIS, 12 Dec 1935, *Still-life: Lunch* (attributed) FRF 5,200. PARIS, 2 April 1941, *Chicken, Bread and Glass; Ham, Cakes, Bread and Goblet* (two pendants, attributed) FRF 12,000. PARIS, 20 March 1950, *Still-life with Fruit* (attributed) FRF 10,500. AMSTERDAM, 4 April 1951, *Still-life with Fruit and Cooking Pots*, NLG 1,750. PARIS, 25 April 1951, *Still-life with a Table Set for a Meal*, FRF 600,000. LONDON, 30 March 1962, *Still-life with Fruit*, Gns 900. AMSTERDAM, 18 May 1965, *Still-life with a Table Set for a Meal*, NLG 13,000. MILAN, 31 May 1966, *Still-life*, ITL 1,900,000. AMSTERDAM, 20 May 1969, *Still-life*, NLG 19,000. COPENHAGEN, 9 May 1972, *Still-life*, DKK 70,000. STOCKHOLM, 4 April 1973, *Still-life*, SEK 111,000. LONDON, 10 July 1974, *Still-life with Fruit*, GBP 4,000. COLOGNE, 14 June 1976, *Still-life with Fruit* (oil on panel, 18 3/4 x 31 ins / 47.5 x 79 cm) DEM 28,000. AMSTERDAM, 24 May 1977, *Still-life* (oil on panel, 15 1/4 x 22 ins / 39 x 55 cm) NLG 66,000. LONDON, 12 Dec 1979, *Still-life* (oil on panel, 20 1/4 x 33 ins / 51.5 x 84 cm) GBP 20,000. NEW YORK, 11 June 1981, *Still-life with Fruit* (oil on panel, 12 3/4 x 22 ins / 32.5 x 55 cm) USD 47,500. LONDON, 8 July 1983, *Still-life with Fruit* (oil on panel, 20 x 32 3/4 ins / 50.8 x 83.2 cm) GBP 14,000. MADRID, 27 Feb 1985, *Still-life with Fruit* (oil on panel, 18 x 25 1/4 ins / 46 x 64 cm) ESP 1,207,500. LONDON, 9 April 1986, *Still-life with Ham and Fish* (oil on canvas, 20 1/2 x 25 1/2 ins / 52 x 65 cm) GBP 7,000. LONDON, 9 Dec 1987, *Still-life with Fruit and Pewter Dishes* (oil on panel, 15 3/4 x 22 ins / 40 x 56 cm) GBP 82,000. NEW YORK, 3 June 1988, *Still-life with Fruit in Porcelain Bowls* (oil on panel, 15 1/4 x 17 3/4 ins / 39 x 45 cm) USD 66,000. LONDON, 21 April 1989, *Display of Fruit and Vegetables, with Children Choosing Fruit* (oil on panel, 23 3/4 x 31 1/2 ins / 60.3 x 80.3 cm) GBP 19,800. NEW YORK, 13 Oct 1989, *Still-life with Grapes, Apples and Other Fruit in a Pottery Bowl on a Table Covered with a Cloth* (oil on panel, 20 1/4 x 28 ins / 51.5 x 71 cm) USD 33,000. LONDON, 1 Nov 1991, *Display of Fruit in a Village Street in Holland* (oil on panel, 23 x 25 ins / 58.5 x 63.5 cm) GBP 3,300. LONDON, 10 July 1992, *Still-life with an Engraved Silver Cup and a Spoon, a Loaf of Bread, Blackcurrants, Gooseberries and Strawberries in Pewter Plates on a Draped Entablature* (oil on panel, 15 3/4 x 21 3/4 ins / 40 x 55.5 cm) GBP 23,100. NEW YORK, 15 Jan 1993, *Still-life with Wild Strawberries, Currants, Grapes and a Peeled Lemon in Pewter Tableware with a Cup on a Table* (oil on panel, 16 x 22 ins / 39.7 x 55.9 cm) USD 33,350. LONDON, 21 April 1993, *Still-life with a Platter of Fruit and Vegetables on a Table Laid by Two Serving Women* (oil on canvas, 43 x 59 ins / 108.3 x 149.8 cm) GBP 40,000. LONDON, 7 July 1993, *Still-life of a Table Laid with Strawberries, Ham, Cheese and Biscuits on Plates, with Bread and a Glass of Beer* (oil on panel, 20 1/4 x 32 3/4 ins / 51.4 x 83.3 cm) GBP 20,700. BOURG-EN-BRESSE, 12 Dec 1993, *Still-life with Fruit* (oil on panel, 15 1/4 x 21 3/4 ins / 39 x 55.5 cm) FRF 405,000. PARIS, 5 March 1994, *Dishes of Fruit on an Entablature* (oil on panel, 22 1/2 x 38 1/4 ins / 57 x 97 cm) FRF 290,000. AMSTERDAM, 16 Nov 1994, *Serving Woman by a Kitchen Table Laden with Fruit, Vegetables and Victuals* (oil on canvas, 40 x 60 3/4 ins / 101.5 x 154.5 cm) NLG 18,400. MILAN, 4 April 1995, *Kitchen Interior* (1620, oil on canvas, 40 1/2 x 60 1/4 ins / 103 x 153 cm) ITL 85,100,000. PARIS, 28 Oct 1996, *Young Woman Preparing Hares* (oil on panel, 35 3/4 x 32 1/4 ins / 91 x 82 cm) FRF 60,000. LONDON, 11 Dec 1996, *Still-life of a Market Stall with Hazelnuts, Walnuts, Cherries, Bread, Pretzels, Waffles, Two Little Girls and Two Little Boys* (oil on panel, 30 x 35 ins / 76.5 x 89 cm) GBP 67,500. NEW YORK, 17 Oct 1997, *Still-life with a Plate of Biscuits, Butter, a Silver Beaker and Grapes on a Draped Entablature* (oil on panel, 14 1/2 x 20 3/4 ins / 36.8 x 52.7 cm) USD 43,700. PARIS, 9 Dec 1999, *Larder in a Dutch Interior* (1620, oil on panel, 36 x 62 ins / 92 x 157 cm) FRF 290,000. WARSAW, 16 Dec 1999, *Still-life with Hawk and Jay on a Perch with Dead Game on a Ledge* (oil on canvas, 33 x 53 ins / 85 x 134 cm) PLN 220,000. NEW YORK, 27 Jan 2000, *Grapes, Plums, Medlars, other Fruit and Peas on a Draped Table* (oil on panel, 14 x 23 ins / 35 x 59 cm) USD 45,000. VIENNA, 7 June 2000, *Still-life with Shrimps, Olives, Pewter Plates and a Glass of Wine and Beer* (oil on panel, 20 x 29 ins / 52 x 74 cm) ATS 450,000. AMSTERDAM, 9 May 2001, *Pewter Jug, Berkemeyer, Fruit, Butter, Leg of Ham and Bun on a Table* (oil on panel, 24 x 39 ins / 60 x 100 cm) NLG 145,000. LONDON, 12 Dec 2001, *Grapes in a Basket with Pears, Plums, Cheese and Butter in a Porcelain Dish* (oil on panel, 20 x 33 ins / 52 x 84 cm) GBP 24,000. LONDON, 9 July 2003, *Apples, Plums and other Fruit on a Draped Ledge* (oil on panel, 14 x 20 ins / 36 x 50 cm) GBP 20,000. LONDON, 11 Dec 2003, *Still-life with Cheese, Food and Objects on a Draped Table* (oil on oak panel, 15 x 22 ins / 39 x 55 cm) GBP 30,000. MILAN, 25 Feb 2004, *Still-life with fruit and bread* (oil on board, 16 x 22 ins / 40 x 56 cm) EUR 33,000. AMSTERDAM, 17 May 2004, *Pewter Plates with Oysters, Fish, Tobacco and Objects on a Table* (oil on panel, 14 x 19 ins / 36 x 49 cm) EUR 138,000.

SCHOOTEN, Franciscus van, or Schoten
Dutch, 17th century.
Born 1581; died 1646, in Leiden.
Draughtsman, engraver.

Franciscus van Schooten was the brother of Joris van Schooten.

SCHOOTEN, Jacob Pouwelsz. van der, or Schoten
Dutch, 17th century.
Active in Leiden.
Painter.

SCHOOTEN, Joris van, or Verschooten
Dutch, 17th century.
Born 1587, in Leiden; died 1651, in Leiden.
Painter. History painting, portraits, group portraits.

Joris van Schooten was a pupil of Kryns van der Maes in 1604 (or, according to some authors, of E. Conrad van der Maes). His reputation as an accomplished portrait painter was established by the age of 20. He was a founder member of the Leiden painters' guild. He excelled at group portraits and was frequently commissioned by the city's guilds and corporations, notably the arquebusiers. He married in

Leiden in 1617. His pupils included Jan Lievens, Rembrandt and A. van den Tempel.

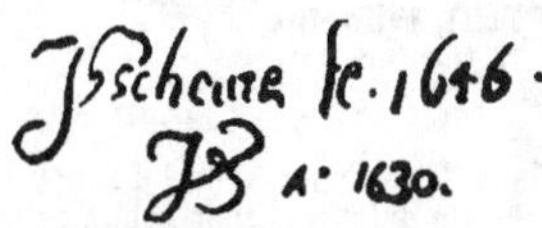

Museums and Galleries:
Amsterdam (Rijksmus.): *Portrait of Jacob Gerrit van der Mij*; *Adoration of the Magi* - Braunfels (Schloss): *Portrait of a Woman* - Leiden (Stedelijk Mus. de Lakenhal): *Allegory of the Siege of Leiden*; *Tabula Cebetio*; six paintings of arquebusiers - Philadelphia (Pennsylvania Academy of Fine Arts): *Portrait of Anthon Thysuis* - St Petersburg: *Portrait of a Woman*.

SCHOOTEN, Willem
Dutch, 17th century.
Painter.
Willem Schooten was a pupil of Jakob van der Heyden.

SCHOPENHAUER, Adèle Louise
German, 19th century.
Born 12 June 1797, in Hamburg; died 25 August 1849, in Bonn.
Painter, engraver, poet.
The sister of the philosopher Arthur Schopenhauer, Adèle Schopenhauer painted landscapes and genre scenes which were appreciated by Goethe.
Museums and Galleries:
Weimar (Goethe-Nationalmus.): several works.

SCHÖPF, Albert Johann
German, 18th century.
Active in Munich.
Painter.
Albert Schöpf worked mainly for the theatre.

SCHÖPF, Eberhard Wolfgang
German, 17th century.
Active in Munich.
Painter.

SCHÖPF, Jakob
German, 18th century.
Active in Straubing.
Engraver.

SCHÖPF, Johann Adam
German, 18th century.
Born 1702; died 10 January 1772, in Egenburg.
Painter, engraver.
The father of Johann Nepomuk, Johann Schöpf chiefly handled religious subjects. He lived mainly in Munich from 1742.

SCHÖPF, Johann Nepomuk, or von Schöpf
German, 18th century.
Born c. 1735, in Prague; died after 1785.
Painter, engraver.
The son and pupil of Johann Adam, Johann Nepomuk became, in 1770, a member of the academy in Munich. Most of his works are in Bavarian churches.

SCHÖPF, Josef
Austrian, 18th - 19th century.
Born 2 February 1745, in Telf (Tyrol); died 15 September 1822, in Innsbruck.
Painter.
After studying under Haller in Innsbruck from 1756 to 1758, Josef Schöpf went to Vienna, Passau and Salzburg. He mostly handled historical and religious subjects, initially in the manner of the Meng School and then in the style of J.J. David. Later he devoted himself to fresco painting on church ceilings.

SCHÖPF, Joseph
German, 18th century.
Sculptor.

SCHÖPF, Lorenz
German, 19th century.
Born 1793, in Munich; died 31 October 1881, in Munich.
Draughtsman.
Lorenz Schöpf was the son of Peter Paul Schöpf.

SCHÖPF, Peter
German, 19th century.
Born 1804, in Munich; died 13 September 1875, in Rome.
Sculptor.
The brother of Lorenz, Peter Schöpf attended the academy of Munich and in 1832 went with Schwanthaler to Rome where he completed his artistic training in Thorvaldsen's studio. He returned to Munich in autumn 1838, leaving again for Rome in 1841 where he lived until his death.

SCHÖPF, Peter Paul
German, 18th - 19th century.
Born 1757, in Imst (Tyrol); died 27 April 1841, in Munich.
Sculptor.
After working for 12 years in J.A. Renn's studio, Peter Schöpf went to Munich in 1788 where he became a master in 1790. He then went to Augsburg, returning to Munich in 1793. He sculpted crucifixes, religious statuettes and numerous crib figurines.

SCHÖPFER, Abraham
German, 16th century.
Active in Munich in 1533.
Painter.
Abraham Schöpfer was a pupil of Wolfgang Huber. The only painting signed by him, *Mucius Scaevola before Porsena*, is in the museum of Stockholm.
Museums and Galleries:
Basel: *Resurrection of Christ* - St Petersburg (Hermitage): *God the Father with Jesus and Mary Kneeling*.

SCHÖPFER, Anton
German, 17th century.
Died 17 May 1660.
Active in Munich.
Painter. Armorials.
Anton Schöpfer was the son of Wilhelm and became a master in 1635.
Auction records:
London, 26 June 1985, *St Sebastian* (etching/filigree paper, 9 1/2 x 5 1/4 ins / 24.2 x 13.6 cm) GBP 1,700.

SCHÖPFER, Friedrich Anton Otto
Austrian, 19th century.
Born 14 January 1825, in Botzen (now Bolzano, Italy); died 26 February 1903, in Graz.
Draughtsman.
A lawyer by profession, Friedrich Schöpfer was, nonetheless, one of the most original draughtsmen of the 19th century. His handling of biblical and mythological subjects has been described as sarcastic.

SCHÖPFER, Hans I, the Elder
German, 16th century.
Active from 1520 until after 1567.
Painter. Mythological subjects, portraits.

Museums and Galleries:
Nuremberg (Mus.): *Portrait of Margrave Philibert of Baden* - Stockholm: *Judgement of Paris.*
Auction records:
London, 23 March 1990, *Portrait of a Lady Wearing a White Headdress, Dressed in Black, with a Collar and Gold Chain and Holding Gloves* (oil on panel, 20 1/4 x 15 1/2 ins / 51.4 x 39.5 cm) GBP 5,500. New York, 30 Jan 1998, *Portrait of a Man Identified as Baron von Maxlrain* (c. 1542, oil on panel, 25 1/2 x 19 1/2 ins / 64.8 x 49.5 cm) USD 13,800.

SCHÖPFER, Hans II, the Younger
German, 17th century.
Born in Munich; died 1610.
Painter. Religious subjects, portraits.
Hans Schöpfer did several altar paintings, in particular one at the chapel of the Pilgrims at Ramersdorf, near Munich, though he seems mainly to have been a portrait artist. His works have often been often attributed to Dürer and Hans Schaufelin. He signed his works with his initials followed by a roughly drawn spoon.
Museums and Galleries:
Munich (Bayerisches Nationalmus.): four portraits de dame, eleven portraits de membres de la famille d'Albert V - Nuremberg: *Hans Kaspar van Pienzenan; Gräfin Von Furstenberg; Mrs Nothaft, née Lose; Mrs von Annaberg, née Kainin; Sophia von Reindorf; Johanna, Gräfin Sulz; Elisabeth von Königsegg; Jakoba Rosenbusch.*
Auction records:
New York, 24 May 1944, *Portrait of A Woman,* USD 2,100.

SCHÖPFER, Heinrich Herm. Ignaz
Austrian, 19th century.
Born 29 July 1821, in Botzen (now Bolzano, Italy); died 16 October 1899, in Botzen.
Draughtsman.
The brother of Friedrich, Heinrich Schöpfer was friendly with Canon, Schwind and Führich and was influenced by Genell and Schwind. He primarily handled historical, religious and mythological subjects such as *Ariadne and Bacchus, The Gods of Greece, Numa Pompilius, The Golden Calf* and *Emperor Barbarossa.*

SCHÖPFER, Hieronymus
German, 16th - 17th century.
Active at the end of the 16th and the beginning of the 17th century.
Painter.
School of Alsace.
In 1597 Hieronymus Schöpfer was a pupil of Hans Werle in Munich. He became a burgher of Rouffach in Alsace and painted mainly flowers.

SCHOPFER, Pierre
Swiss, 20th century.
Born 1943.
Engraver (etching/wood), illustrator. Artists' books, banknotes.
Pierre Schopfer originally came from La Chaux. He was a pupil of Yersin. He has engraved banknotes and postage stamps. He produced woodcuts and etchings to illustrate *Vignes pour un Miroir* (*Vines for a Mirror*), which were accompanied by poems by S. Corinna Bille. This book, which won a silver medal at the international competition in Leipzig, was presented to the Bibliothèque de la Riponne in Lausanne in 2000. Schopfer donated around 100 engravings to the Musée Alexis Forel, a museum specialising in engravings in Morges. As a result of this, he featured in the exhibition presenting the museum's collection and successive new additions at the Cabinet Cantonal des Estampes in the Musée Jenisch in Vevey in 2003. The Galerie L'Entracte in Lausanne has staged several exhibitions of his work.
Museums and Galleries:
Morges (Musée Alexis Forel).

SCHÖPFER, Wilhelm
German, 17th century.
Died 1634.
Painter.
The son of Hans the Younger, Wilhelm Schöpfer became a master in 1608. He did a few altar paintings and is documented at the court in Munich in 1627.

SCHÖPFFELL, Hans Jacob
German, 17th century.
Active in Heidelberg 1673-1680.
Painter.

SCHÖPFLER, Felix Anton
German, 18th century.
Born 1701, in Munich; died 1760, in Prague.
Painter.
Felix Schöpfler studied under C.D. Asam and then Ch. Grooth in Stuttgart. He painted the staircase of the episcopal palace in Worms and a Way of the Cross in Prague.

SCHÖPFLIN, August Friedrich
German, 18th - 19th century.
Born 1771, in Weitenau.
Engraver (burin).
The pupil of Johann Gotth. Muller, August Schöpflin taught drawing at the Universities of Charkow in about 1804 and Wüzburg about 1806.

SCHOPIN, Eugène Louis
French, 19th century.
Born in Paris.
Painter. Landscapes.
He was taught by his father, Frédéric Schopin. His first Salon exhibition was in 1865.

SCHOPIN, Frédéric Henri
French, 19th century.
Born 12 June 1804, in Lübeck (Schleswig-Holstein), Germany, to French parents; died 26 October 1880, in Montigny-sur-Loing (Seine-et-Marne).
Painter. Religious subjects, genre scenes.
Contrary to what some sources claim, this artist was not the brother of the musician Frédéric Chopin, nor was he related to him in any way. He was a pupil of the history painter Baron Gros. He came second in the Prix de Rome in 1830, and won it in 1831 with *Xanthus Pursuing Achilles.* Legend has it that Raffet was so disappointed not to have won the first prize that he abandoned painting and took up lithography instead. Schopin exhibited at the Paris Salon between 1835 and 1879. During a trip to St Petersburg he was made a member of the Russian imperial academy.

He was an academically trained, Neoclassical painter, but also enjoyed moderate success as a genre painter, particularly with *Paul and Virginie* (after the novel by Bernardin de St-Pierre) and *Don Quixote and the Inn Girls.* Furthermore, a significant number of his paintings were engraved by Paul Jazet and various other artists who worked in a similar style.
Museums and Galleries:
Douai: *Final Moments of the Cenci Family* - London (Wallace Collection): *The Divorce of the Empress Josephine* (1846, oil on canvas) - Metz: *Battle of Hohenlinden* - Toulouse: *Jacob at the House of Laban* - Versailles: *Battle beneath the Walls of Antioch, 1098; Cl Fr Olsfeldt; Régis de Cambacérès; Battle of Hohenlinden.*
Auction records:
Paris, 1865, *Roman Soldiers Setting a Young Woman Free,* FRF 250; *Sleeping Nymph,* FRF 310; *Divorce of the Emperor Napoleon and Empress Josephine,* FRF 2,350. Paris, 1 Dec 1891, *Odalisque,* FRF 110. Paris, 3 May 1928, *Amazons Symbolising the Four Corners of the World,* FRF 9,700. Par-

IS, 18 May 1934, *Arrival and Presentation of the New Sultana*, FRF 800. PARIS, 27 June 1951, *Paul and Virginie: Their Prayer; The Oath* (1841-1842, two pendants) FRF 152,000. PARIS, 23 June 1978, *The Chariot of Bacchus* (oil on canvas, 45 x 74 1/2 ins / 114 x 189 cm) FRF 31,100. LONDON, 26 Nov 1980, *At the Seraglio* (1868, oil on canvas, 22 1/4 x 35 1/2 ins / 56.5 x 90 cm) GBP 4,800. LONDON, 30 Nov 1984, *Arrival of the Harem* (1842, oil on canvas, 32 1/4 x 25 1/2 ins / 82 x 65 cm) GBP 5,000. PARIS, 11 Dec 1987, *Paul and Virginie* (oil on canvas, 28 3/4 x 21 1/4 ins / 73 x 54 cm) FRF 30,000. NEW YORK, 24 Oct 1989, *Slave Market* (oil on canvas, 24 x 19 3/4 ins / 61 x 50 cm) USD 126,500. LONDON, 28 March 1990, *Boaz Welcoming Ruth* (1842, oil on canvas, 31 1/2 x 25 1/4 ins / 80 x 64 cm) GBP 4,400. PARIS, 7 Nov 1990, *Child Wearing a Boater* (1837, oil on canvas, 9 x 7 1/2 ins / 22 x 19 cm) FRF 12,000. PARIS, 19 June 1992, *Meleager Taking up Arms again at His Wife's Request* (oil on canvas, 44 x 57 ins / 112 x 145 cm) FRF 90,000. PARIS, 6 July 1993, *Two Children in Profile* (1867, oil on canvas, 13 x 10 ins / 33 x 24.5 cm) FRF 5,800. PARIS, 27 April 1994, *Portrait of Angélique and Blanche Potocka* (oil on canvas, 12 3/4 x 10 ins / 32.5 x 24.5 cm) FRF 7,500. PARIS, 21 Nov 1995, *Young Girl Playing with a Rabbit* (oil on canvas, 21 1/4 x 26 ins / 54 x 66 cm) FRF 28,000. PARIS, 30 June 1999, *Penitent Mary Magdalene* (oil on metal, 26 x 22 ins / 66 x 55 cm) FRF 13,500. MUNICH, 21 March 2001, *Arab Family Surprised by Lions* (oil on canvas, 18 x 23 ins / 45 x 58 cm) DEM 8,000. LONDON, 17 Oct 2001, *Lion Attacking an Arab Family* (oil on canvas, 18 x 23 ins / 46 x 59 cm) GBP 3,500. PARIS, 19 April 2002, *Penitent Mary Magdalene* (oil on copper, 26 x 23 ins / 67 x 58 cm) EUR 2,600. PARIS, 26 June 2002, *Mohammed's Paradise* (oil on canvas, 30 x 46 ins / 77 x 116 cm) EUR 10,200.

SCHOPIN, Georges
French, 19th century.
Born in Paris.
Painter. Landscapes.

He was taught by his father, Frédéric Schopin. He first exhibited at the Salon in 1859.

SCHOPPE, Julius, the Elder
German, 19th century.
Born 27 January 1795, in Berlin; died 30 March 1868, in Berlin.
Painter, miniaturist, lithographer. History painting, portraits, landscapes.

Julius Schoppe attended the academy in Berlin, worked in Vienna and visited Switzerland and Italy where he studied, in particular, the works of Raphael, Correggio and Titian. In 1825 he became a member of the academy in Berlin and in 1836 taught there. He decorated Prince Charles' Residenz at Ghenicke near Potsdam. His output includes numerous oil paintings in miniature, which are generally more highly regarded than his large-scale works.

MUSEUMS AND GALLERIES:

BERLIN (Märkisches Mus.): *Portrait of the Jeweller J.H. Schoppe, his Uncle, the Painter and his Wife; Mme Lampson; Evening at the Dönhoffplatz* - BERLIN (Nationalgal.): *Portrait of Lady with Dog*.

AUCTION RECORDS:

BERLIN, 4 and 5 April 1968, *The Two Sisters*, DEM 5,000. COLOGNE, 18 Nov 1982, *Portrait of Young Lady* (oil on canvas, 26 x 21 1/4 ins / 66 x 54 cm) DEM 13,000. STAUFEN, 23 May 2003, *Portrait of A. Schadow, Aged 17* (1814, oil on canvas, 20 x 16 ins / 52 x 41 cm) EUR 3,900.

SCHOPPE, Julius, the Younger
German, 19th century.
Born 3 August 1832, in Berlin; died 4 February 1898, in Berlin.
Painter.

The pupil of his uncle Julius Schoppe the Elder, Julius Schoppe exhibited mainly landscapes at the academy in Berlin.

SCHÖPS, Augustin, or Schepe, Scheps, Szeps
German, 18th century.
Active in Posen (now Poznan, Poland) 1758-1767.
Sculptor.

SCHOR, Andreas, or Schorer
German, 17th century.
Born to a family originally from Augsburg; died 1635, in Sangerhausen.
Painter.

SCHOR, Bonaventura
Austrian, 17th century.
Born 1624, in Innsbruck; died January 1692, in Innsbruck.
Painter.

The son of Hans and brother of Johann Paul and Egid, Bonaventura Schor worked in the cloister of Stams where he painted two mural frescoes representing the *Miracle of St Bernard of Clairvaux*.

SCHOR, Christoph
Austrian, 17th century.
Born 1655, in Rome; died 2 July 1701, in Rome.
Engraver (burin), architect.

Christoph Schor was the son of Johann Paul and the brother of Philipp. He was employed for a while by the Viceroy of Naples, Marchese del Carpio. He then went to Spain where he was architect to Charles II, King of Spain.

SCHOR, Diana
Romanian, 20th century.
Born 17 March 1926, in Galati.
Active since 1980 in the USA.
Painter, ceramicist. Designs for tapestries.

Diana Schor studied under Lola Schmirer-Roth in Galati, and subsequently from 1945 to 1950 at the fine arts academy, and the N. Grigorescu Art Institute in Bucharest, in the studio of the painter Camil Ressu. She also studied violin at the Lira conservatory in Bucharest between 1947 and 1950. From 1968 to 1970, she worked in Paris. She left Romania for the USA in 1980, and settled in San Francisco.

Schor's work reflects her passion for music. Hers works of Lyrical Abstraction seem to pulsate with the harmony of their colours and the undulations of their rhythms. Some of her works are inspired directly by music, such as her tapestry *Bach*, others are landscapes, including aerial views and cycles of figures - *Dolls*, *Ballerinas* and *Infantas*.

Work by her has been shown at several group exhibitions in Romania and abroad. There have also been solo exhibitions, includings ones in Bucharest (at the N. Cristea Gallery, 1952, 1954, 1958, 1960, 1963, 1966, 1967, 1968); at the Hertzlia Museum, Israel (1968, 1972, 1975); at the Galerie Sipaora, Paris (1976); at 19 Grammersi Park, New York (1978); and in San Francisco (1981 at the Petit Trianon, 1982, 1983). She was awarded the Prix Jolliot-Curie at the Festival Mondial de la Jeunesse in 1953. Other awards followed: at the international ceramics exhibition in Faenza (1962), at the Erfurt decorative arts Quadriennale (1974), and at the tapestry triennale in Lódz (1975).

BIBLIOGRAPHY:

Ionel Jianou, *Romanian Artists and the West*, American Romanian Academy of Arts and Sciences, Los Angeles, 1986.

SCHOR, Egid
Austrian, 17th century.
Born 1627, in Innsbruck; died 2 July 1701, in Innsbruck.
Painter.

Egid Schor was the son and pupil of Hans, brother of Bonaventura and Johann Paul and the father of Johann-Baptist. He worked on the decoration of the Montecucculi Palace in Vienna and was responsible for introducing the Baroque style into painting in the Tyrol, as seen in a number of churches around Innsbruck.

SCHOR, Hans, or Socher
Austrian, 17th century.
Died 1674, in Innsbruck.
Painter. Religious subjects.

The father of Johann Paul and Egid, Hans Schor was the oldest member of the Schor family, German in origin, which produced a number of painters in the Tyrol. As court painter he was employed by Maximilian III, Leopold V and Archduchess Claudia. He handled mainly religious subjects.

SCHOR, Heinrich van
Dutch, 16th century.
Active in Roermond, Amsterdam and Basel.
Cabinet maker.

SCHOR, Johann Baptist Ferdinand
Austrian, 18th century.
Born 1686, in Innsbruck; died 4 January 1767, in Prague.
Painter, engineer.

The son of Egid, Johann Baptist Schor worked, after the death of his brother, with Josef Waldmann. In 1705 he went to Rome where he trained as an architectural draughtsman. From 1713 he worked as a painter and also did decoration in Prague, where he taught at the College for Specialised Training.

SCHOR, Johann Paul, called Giovanni Paolo Tedesco
Austrian, 17th century.
Born 1615, in Innsbruck; died 1674, in Rome.
Painter, decorative designer.

Johann Paul Schor was the son of Hans, brother of Bonaventura and Egid and the father of Philipp and Christoph. From 1640 onwards he lived in Rome, where he became a member of the Academy of St Luke in 1654. He painted scenes of towns, stage-sets and gala carriages as well as decorating churches in Rome, Vatican rooms and the Borghese and Colonna Palaces in an exuberant Baroque style.

SCHOR, Philipp
Austrian, 17th century.
Born 1646, in Rome.
Painter, architect.

The son of Johann Paul and the brother of Christoph, Philipp Schor did portraits of *Charles X* and *Innocent XI*.

SCHORB, Jakob
German, 19th century.
Born 2 February 1809, in Koblenz; died 21 March 1858, in Koblenz.
Sculptor.

Jakob Schorb went to Paris and worked with David d'Angers from 1842 to 1844. He continued his studies in Rome and Florence from 1845 to 1847.

MUSEUMS AND GALLERIES:
KOBLENZ (Church of Our Lady): *Crucifix* - KOBLENZ (Town Collection): *The Physician Joh. Muller* (bust); *Josef Görres* (bust).

SCHORE, Guilliam van. See **SCHOOR**

SCHORE, Stephanus van, or Schoore, Schorre
Flemish School, 17th century.
Active in Brussels 1619-1626.
Sculptor.

SCHOREEL, Jan van. See **SCOREL**

SCHORENDORFF, Konrad, or Schorndorf
German, 15th - 16th century.
Active in Ulm 1499-1507.
Sculptor.

SCHORER, Andreas. See **SCHOR**

SCHORER, Carl Johann. See **SCHORER Joseph**

SCHORER, Hans Friedrich. See **SCHRORER**

SCHORER, Joseph
German, 18th century.
Died 1754, in Eichstätt.
Active in Nassenbeuren near Mindelheim.
Sculptor.

SCHORER, Leonard
German, 18th century.
Born 1715, in Königsberg (now Kaliningrad, Russia); died 1777, in Litau (now Jelgava, Latvia).
Painter.

Leonard Schorer worked in Königsberg from 1734 to 1744 and Dresden from 1736 to 1737.

MUSEUMS AND GALLERIES:
JELGAVA: *Duke Charles de Courlande; Von Offenberg; Von Ziegenhorn; Voigt* - LEIPZIG (Universität Leipzig): *Portrait of Gottsched; Portrait of Mme Gottsched* - RIGA: *J.D. Brederlo.*

SCHORER, Maria. See **SLAVONA**

SCHORIGUS, Georg Wilhelm, the Elder, or Schurrius or Schorse
German, 17th century.
Died 25 February 1661.
Active in Brunswick.
Sculptor.

SCHORIGUS, Wilhelm, the Younger
German, 17th century.
Born 1 April 1635; died 1 September 1687, in Brunswick.
Active in Brunswick.
Sculptor.

SCHÖRK, Hans
Austrian, 19th century.
Born 6 December 1849, in Vienna.
Active in Vienna.
Sculptor. Portraits.

Hans Schörk was a pupil at the academy in Vienna.

SCHORKENS, Juan. See **SCHORQUENS**

SCHORLER, Vicke
German, 17th century.
Died 1625, in Rostock.
Active in Rostock.
Draughtsman.

SCHORMAN, Jacob
Dutch, 17th century.
Painter. Portraits.

SCHORN, Carl
German, 19th century.
Born 16 October 1803, in Düsseldorf; died 7 October 1850, in Munich.
Painter. History painting, genre scenes.

Carl Schorn studied in Munich with Cornelius. From 1824 to 1825 he was taught by Gros and Ingres in Paris. In 1832 he went to Berlin and spent time in Wach's studio. While he was there he produced various historical paintings. After various trips to Italy, he settled in Munich and in 1847 was appointed Professor at the academy there.

MUSEUMS AND GALLERIES:
BERLIN (Nationalgal.): *Paul III in front of the Portrait of Luther; The Anabaptists in front of the Episcopal Palace in Munster* - KALININGRAD: *Cromwell in the Dunbar Encampment* - MUNICH: *The Deluge; Young Monk Entering the Orders* - WÜRZBURG (Martin-von-Wagner-Mus., Universität): *John Knox.*

SCHORN, J.
German, 19th century.
Active c. 1800.
Miniaturist. Portraits.

AUCTION RECORDS:
PARIS, 4 Feb 1925, *Half-length Portrait of Woman, in Green Low-cut Corsage* (large miniature) FRF 1,120.

SCHORN, Theobald
German, 19th - 20th century.
Born 1865, in Munich.
Painter. Genre scenes, landscapes.

AUCTION RECORDS:
LONDON, 18 Feb 1983, *Arab Encampment* (oil on panel, 11 1/2 x 18 ins / 29.2 x 46 cm) GBP 1,600.

SCHORN, Villy Sophus Maximilian
Danish, 19th - 20th century.
Born 6 December 1834, in Copenhagen; died 25 March 1912, in Copenhagen.
Painter, writer. Genre scenes.

SCHORNBÖCK, Alois
Austrian, 19th - 20th century.
Born 29 May 1863, in Vienna.
Painter.
Alois Schornböck studied under Ludwig von Löttz, and lived and worked in Vienna.

SCHÖRNDL, Johannes
German, 15th century.
Painter.
Johannes Schörndl was a Benedictine monk.

SCHORNDORF, Konrad. See also **SCHORENDORFF**

SCHORNDORF, Konrad von
German, 15th - 16th century.
Born to a family originally from Lucerne.
Active in Lucerne 1473-1524.
Glass painter.

SCHORNICK, Paul
German, 20th century.
Born 28 February 1874, in Quedlinburg.
Painter.
Paul Schornick lived and worked in Berlin.

SCHORNO, Johann Franz
Swiss, 18th century.
Born to a family originally from Schwyz, Switzerland.
Painter.
Johann Schorno painted mural panels in the chapel of St Antony in Ibach showing scenes from the *Life of St Anthony*.

SCHORNO, Thomas
Swiss, 17th century.
Active in Schwyz.
Painter.
Thomas Schorno painted solely altar paintings.

SCHORPP, Michael
German, 15th century.
Active in Ulm at the end of the 15th century.
Painter, engraver.
Michael Schorpp was a member of the guild from 1495 to 1499. Among his works are 12 engravings depicting scenes from *The Legend of St Catherine of Alexandria*.

SCHORQUENS, Juan, or Schorkens
Dutch, 17th century.
Active in Madrid 1618-1630.
Engraver, draughtsman.
Juan Schorquens' works are occasionally signed *J. van Schorquens, fecit, in Madrid*. He worked for numerous booksellers and is noted for his remarkable frontispieces.

SCHORRER, Paul
German, 17th century.
Painter.
Paul Schorrer did two altar paintings for an altar dedicated to St Adalbert in Aachen.

SCHORSE, Georg Wilhelm. See **SCHORIGUS Georg Wilhelm**

SCHORSE, Johann Christian
German, 18th century.
Died 8 December 1768, in Brunswick.
Active in Brunswick.
Sculptor. Portraits.

SCHORSTEIN, Lucien de
French, 19th - 20th century.
Born in Paris.
Painter. Portraits, interiors, urban landscapes.
Lucien de Schorstein studied at the École des Beaux-Arts, Paris, under Lefebvre, Tony Robert-Fleury, Luc Olivier Merson and Raphaël Collin. He was a member of the Association of *Peintres de la Femme* (*Painters of Woman*), and exhibited in 1911 and 1913 at the Salon de la Société Nationale des Beaux-Arts, and at the Salon des Tuileries from 1924. He also took part in various provincial exhibitions and was awarded an honourable mention at Versailles in 1912.

There are many of his paintings in collections in Paris, St Petersburg, Moscow, and Albany in the USA.

SCHOSCHKIN, Ivan. See **CHOCHKIN**

SCHOSSBERGER, Klara (Baroness)
Hungarian, 20th century.
Born in Budapest.
Painter. Portraits, still-lifes.
Klara Schossberger lived and worked in Budapest.

SCHOSSEL, Andras
Hungarian, 19th century.
Born in Dubnica nad Vahóm; died 1874.
Sculptor.

SCHOT, Conrad
Dutch, 16th century.
Painter. Portraits.
Conrad Schot was a pupil of Antonis Mor around 1549.

AUCTION RECORDS:
PARIS, 16 April 1917, *Portrait of a Gentleman*, FRF 730. PARIS, 27 April 1928, *Bust Portrait of a Woman* (attributed) FRF 5,000.

SCHOT, Francina Louise (Mej.)
Dutch, 19th century.
Born 1816; died 1894.
Active in Rotterdam c. 1840.
Painter. Still-lifes (flowers).

AUCTION RECORDS:
COLOGNE, 22 March 1985, *Still-life* (oil on canvas, 35 1/4 x 29 1/4 ins / 89.5 x 74 cm) DEM 30,000. AMSTERDAM, 16 Nov 1988, *Still-life with Roses, Poppies, Lilac and Jasmine beside a Silver Needle-case and a Book on a Carved Dresser* (oil on canvas, 41 1/4 x 33 1/2 ins / 105 x 85 cm) NLG 20,700. GRAVENHAGE, 2 Nov 1999, *Still-life with Grapes* (oil on board, 14 x 20 ins / 35 x 51 cm) NLG 4,000. AMSTERDAM, 24 Oct 2000, *Rosebush with Butterflies and Dragonfly* (oil on panel, 31 x 26 ins / 80 x 66 cm) NLG 55,000.

SCHOTANUS, Petrus
Dutch, 17th century.
Active in Leeuwarden.
Painter. Portraits, landscapes, still-lifes.

Petrus Schotanus painted mostly still-lifes.

MUSEUMS AND GALLERIES:

ST PETERSBURG (Hermitage): *Portrait of Henri l'Oiseleur.*

AUCTION RECORDS:

LONDON, 13 May 1970, *Still-life* (trompe-l'oeil painting) GBP 920. COLOGNE, 14 June 1976, *Still-life* (oil on panel, 23 1/2 x 32 3/4 ins / 60 x 83 cm) DEM 11,000. LONDON, 6 July 1983, *Still-life* (oil on panel, 25 1/4 x 18 1/2 ins / 64 x 47 cm) GBP 4,000. AMSTERDAM, 20 June 1989, *Vanitas with a Globe of the Heavens, Books, an Hourglass and Dead Birds on an Entablature* (oil on panel, 32 1/2 x 23 ins / 82.7 x 58.7 cm) NLG 41,400. NEW YORK, 15 Jan 1993, *Farmyard Animals* (oil on panel, 23 x 31 ins / 58.4 x 78.7 cm) USD 5,175. AMSTERDAM, 6 May 1993, *Woodcocks and Other Game Birds with a Basket of Vegetables on a Table* (oil on panel, 17 3/4 x 15 1/2 ins / 45.4 x 39.5 cm) NLG 5,980. LONDON, 12 July 2001, *Still-life with Globe, Candlestick, Birds and Hourglass on a Wooden Table* (oil on canvas, 16 x 21 ins / 40 x 54 cm) GBP 1,800. VIENNA, 21 March 2002, *Vanitas Still-life with Gospel, Globe and Dead Game Birds* (oil on panel, 23 x 32 ins / 59 x 81 cm) EUR 6,500.

SCHOTANUS, Piter
Flemish School, 17th century.
Active in Louvain.
Painter. Genre scenes, landscapes, still-lifes.

Piter Schotanus is possibly identifiable as the Leiden artist Pauwels van Schoten, who was a burgher of Delft in 1640 and still active in the city as late as 1667. Schotanus is thought to have painted mostly as an amateur.

SCHOTANUS VAN STERRINGA, Bernard, or Schotanus à Sterringa
Dutch, 18th century.
Active in Friesland.
Draughtsman.

Bernard Schotanus van Sterringa collaborated on the atlas published by Dr Matheus Broverius van Niedek.

SCHOTEL, Anthonie Pieter
Dutch, 20th century.
Born 5 September 1890, in Dordrecht; died 24 September 1958, in Laren.
Painter (including gouache). Seascapes, harbour scenes.

Anthonie Pieter Schotel was self-taught, and began painting in 1915. He made several visits to France - to Brittany and Normandy. In 1929 he settled in Laren. His palette was sombre.

AP Schotel

AUCTION RECORDS:

ZURICH, 7 Nov 1981, *River Landscape, Amsterdam* (oil on canvas, 31 1/2 x 39 1/4 ins / 80 x 100 cm) CHF 4,800. AMSTERDAM, 30 Aug 1988, *Harbour at Huizen* (oil on canvas, 15 3/4 x 15 3/4 ins / 40 x 40 cm) NLG 1,495. AMSTERDAM, 6 Nov 1990, *The Volendam 27 with Marken in the Background* (oil on canvas, 31 x 27 ins / 78.5 x 68.5 cm) NLG 8,050. AMSTERDAM, 23 April 1991, *Fishing Boats at Volendam* (oil on canvas, 30 1/2 x 38 1/2 ins / 77.5 x 98 cm) NLG 5,980. AMSTERDAM, 24 Sept 1992, *Sailing into a Harbour at Dusk* (1929, oil on sacking, 19 1/4 x 26 ins / 49 x 66 cm) NLG 1,955. AMSTERDAM, 21 April 1993, *Grey Weather* (oil on canvas, 26 1/2 x 36 ins / 67 x 91.5 cm) NLG 3,450; *Boats in the Harbour at Dordrecht* (1923, oil on canvas, 32 x 39 1/2 ins / 81 x 100.5 cm) NLG 4,600. AMSTERDAM, 19 April 1994, *Harbour Scene* (oil on canvas/panel, 15 1/4 x 11 1/2 ins / 39 x 29 cm) NLG 1,725. AMSTERDAM, 21 April 1994, *Boats Moored in the Harbour at Stellendam* (1920, oil on canvas, 59 1/2 x 56 ins / 151 x 142 cm) NLG 13,800. AMSTERDAM, 16 April 1996, *Sailing on the Zuiderzee* (oil on canvas, 12 1/4 x 16 1/4 ins / 31 x 41 cm) NLG 1,298. AMSTERDAM, 19-20 Feb 1997, *Fishermen Having a Break in the Harbour at Volendam* (oil on canvas, 24 x 27 3/4 ins / 61 x 70.5 cm) NLG 8,649. AMSTERDAM, 2-3 June 1997, *Platbodem op de wal bij muiden* (gouache/paper, 15 1/4 x 15 1/4 ins / 39 x 39 cm) NLG 3,776.

SCHOTEL, Christina Petronella
Dutch, 19th century.
Born 26 February 1818, in Dordrecht; died 7 July 1854, in Aardenberg.
Painter. Still-lifes.

Christina Petronella Schotel was a pupil of her father Jan Christianus Schotel.

AUCTION RECORDS:

AMSTERDAM, 20 April 1993, *Still-life with Game* (oil on canvas, 28 3/4 x 23 1/2 ins / 73 x 60 cm) NLG 1,150.

SCHOTEL, Johan, or Johannes, Jan Christianus
Dutch, 19th century.
Born 11 November 1787, in Dordrecht; died 21 December 1838, in Dordrecht.
Painter, watercolourist, engraver. Landscapes, seascapes.

Johan Schotel was a soldier and, later, a pupil of A. Meulemans and M. Schonman. His atmospheric, conscientiously executed seascapes were highly prized during his lifetime.

MUSEUMS AND GALLERIES:

AMSTERDAM: *Stormy Sea; Calm Sea; Rough Sea; View of a Beach* - HANOVER: *Katwig* - MUNICH: *Seascape* - NANCY: *Short-master* - ROTTERDAM: *View of the River Moerdyk* - STUTTGART: *Storm at Sea near the Coast.*

AUCTION RECORDS:

PARIS, 1838, *Ships Sailing on the High Sea,* FRF 1,025. PARIS, 1844, *Storm with Vessels in Distress,* FRF 4,150. PARIS, 1849, *Seascape,* FRF 2,550. PARIS, 1850, *Seascape,* FRF 3,250; *Seascape,* FRF 3,250. GHENT, 1856, *Seascape: Stormy Sea with Numerous Ships,* FRF 4,000. PARIS, 1860, *View of Flessingen,* FRF 2,804; *Seascape* (drawing) FRF 323. PARIS, 1871, *Harbour Entrance with Stormy Sea,* FRF 1,187. BRUSSELS, 1873, *Seascape,* FRF 3,600. PARIS, 1873, *Seascape,* FRF 2,050. PARIS, 1876, *Seascape: Dutch Coastline,* FRF 1,620. THE HAGUE, 1889, *Het Bossche Veld,* FRF 430. PARIS, 21 June 1900, *Tugboat,* FRF 105. PARIS, 20 Feb 1929, *Fishing Port at Low Tide* (drawing) FRF 1,050; *Fishing Boats* (drawing) FRF 400. PARIS, 12 March 1943, *River-bank with Boats* (watercolour) FRF 1,200. PARIS, 1 March 1950, *Seascape: Stormy Sea* (pen and wash) FRF 9,500. AMSTERDAM, 13 March 1951, *Fishing Boats,* NLG 1,150. AMSTERDAM, 8 Feb 1966, *Seashore,* NLG 4,200. DORDRECHT, 25 Nov 1969, *Harbour Scene,* NLG 12,000. DORDRECHT, 15 June 1971, *Seascape,* NLG 15,000. LONDON, 27 July 1973, *Estuary Scene,* Gns 1,800. LONDON, 12 June 1974, *Boats off the Coast,* GBP 4,500. AMSTERDAM, 27 April 1976, *Departure of the Fishermen* (oil on panel, 25 1/2 x 32 3/4 ins / 65 x 83 cm) NLG 37,000. AMSTERDAM, 26 May 1976, *Sailing Ships off the Coast* (watercolour, 10 x 16 1/4 ins / 24.5 x 41 cm) NLG 4,200. AMSTERDAM, 27 Nov 1979, *Seascape* (oil on panel, 25 1/2 x 34 1/4 ins / 65 x 87 cm) NLG 26,000. AMSTERDAM, 14 March 1983, *Seaside Scene* (oil on panel, 14 3/4 x 20 ins / 37.5 x 50.7 cm) NLG 20,000. AMSTERDAM, 19 Nov 1985, *Fishing Boats in High Seas* (oil on canvas, 28 x 36 3/4 ins / 71 x 93.5 cm) NLG 22,000. AMSTERDAM, 14 April 1986, *Sailing Boats off a Jetty* (oil on panel, 15 x 21 ins / 38 x 52.5 cm) NLG 16,000. AMSTERDAM, 16 Nov 1988, *Frigate Drawing In its Sails near a Jetty* (ink and watercolour/paper, 23 3/4 x 30 1/4 ins / 60.5 x 77 cm) NLG 4,370. AMSTERDAM, 28 Feb 1989, *Two-master in*

Distress off a Jetty (1826, ink and watercolour/paper, 24 3/4 x 37 3/4 ins / 63 x 96 cm) NLG 1,495. AMSTERDAM, 2 May 1990, *Fishermen Hauling their Boat onto Shore* (oil on panel, 19 x 25 1/4 ins / 47.4 x 63.9 cm) NLG 36,800. AMSTERDAM, 30 Oct 1990, *Coastline with Boats at Anchor and Fishermen on the Shore* (oil on panel, 15 1/4 x 20 1/4 ins / 38.5 x 51.5 cm) NLG 25,300. LONDON, 21 June 1991, *Coastal Landscape with Sailing Ships Approaching Land* (oil on canvas, 25 1/2 x 33 3/4 ins / 64.5 x 86 cm) GBP 13,200. AMSTERDAM, 17 Sept 1991, *Transport Boat Approaching a Two-master in Rough Sea* (oil on canvas, 18 1/4 x 24 1/4 ins / 46.5 x 61.5 cm) NLG 8,050. AMSTERDAM, 30 Oct 1991, *The Galliot Johanna Sailing in Rough Seas off a Jetty with Other Vessels in the Distance* (oil on canvas, 33 1/2 x 49 1/2 ins / 85 x 126 cm) NLG 34,500. HEIDELBERG, 3 April 1993, *Harbour Scene with Sailing Ships* (sepia wash, 7 1/4 x 12 ins / 18.1 x 30.2 cm) DEM 1,000. AMSTERDAM, 20 April 1993, *Vessels on the Merwede near Dordrecht* (oil on canvas, 27 3/4 x 36 1/2 ins / 70.5 x 93 cm) NLG 98,900. LONDON, 19 Nov 1993, *Sailing Ships Anchored by a Jetty on an Estuary with Frigates off the Coast in Calm Seas* (oil on canvas, 49 x 65 ins / 124.5 x 165.4 cm) GBP 74,100. AMSTERDAM, 7 Nov 1995, *Sailing in an Estuary* (oil on canvas, 32 x 43 1/4 ins / 81.5 x 110 cm) NLG 103,840. NEW YORK, 10 Jan 1996, *Naval Battle between Dutch and English Warships* (ink and wash heightened with white, 17 1/2 x 25 ins / 44.5 x 63.5 cm) USD 2,760. AMSTERDAM, 27 Oct 1997, *Coastal Scene with Boats at Anchor* (oil on panel, 15 x 20 1/4 ins / 38 x 51.5 cm) NLG 21,240. LONDON, 26 March 1999, *Figures at Shore* (oil on panel, 13 x 17 ins / 32 x 44 cm) GBP 17,000. PARIS, 22 June 1999, *Fishing Boats by the Shore* (oil on panel, 27 x 33 ins / 69 x 85 cm) FRF 360,000. PARIS, 31 March 2000, *Seascape with Cannon Shot on Amsterdam Harbour* (1820, pen, pencil and wash, 14 x 20 ins / 35 x 52 cm) FRF 165,000. LONDON, 7 April 2000, *The Rescue* (oil on canvas, 44 x 58 ins / 113 x 148 cm) GBP 22,350. GRAVENHAGE, 25 April 2001, *Boats on a Calm Sea* (oil on canvas, 29 x 39 ins / 74 x 98 cm) NLG 27,000. STUTTGART, 6 Dec 2001, *Stormy Sea* (oil on canvas, 37 x 46 ins / 95 x 117 cm) DEM 75,000. GRAVENHAGE, 24 April 2002, *Four Day Sea Battle with the English 'Swift Shore' and Dutch 'Reiger'* (oil on canvas, 18 x 25 ins / 46 x 63 cm) EUR 24,000. COLOGNE, 15 May 2002, *Seascape* (watercolour over pencil, 5 x 8 ins / 12 x 20 cm) EUR 4,400. PARIS, 24 March 2003, *Boats at Shore* (pen, Indian ink and wash, 10 x 14 ins / 26 x 35 cm) EUR 3,000. PARIS, 2 Dec 2003, *Marine Landscape* (oil on panel, 15 x 20 ins / 39 x 51 cm) EUR 22,000. PARIS, 9 April 2004, *Boats in a Storm* (oil on canvas, 28 x 37 ins / 71 x 93 cm) EUR 30,000.

SCHOTEL, Petrus Jan, or Johannes
Dutch, 19th century.
Born 19 August 1808, in Dordrecht; died 23 July 1865, in Dresden.
Painter, engraver, lithographer.

Petrus Jan Schotel was a pupil and imitator of his father Johan Schotel. He taught at the school of navigation in Medemblik and settled in Düsseldorf in 1856. He exhibited at the Paris Salon and was highly commended in 1863.

P J Schotel

MUSEUMS AND GALLERIES:
AMSTERDAM: *Choppy waters; Choppy Waters; Squadron under the Command of Prince Hendrik of the Netherlands in Flessingen Harbour; Squadron of Prince Hendrik of The Netherlands* - ANTWERP: *Seascape* - HANOVER: *Shipwreck* - KALININGRAD: *Shipwreck of a Merchant Vessel* - MAINZ: *Stormy Sea*.

AUCTION RECORDS:
PARIS, 20 June 1924, *Seascape* (Indian ink) FRF 240. PARIS, 10 June 1926, *Squall at Sea* (pen and wash) FRF 720. PARIS, 6 June 1947, *Seascape*, FRF 3,500. DORDRECHT, 6 June 1967, *Sailing Ships at Anchor in Port*, NLG 4,600. LONDON, 15 Nov 1968, *Fishing Boats in High Seas*, Gns 500. LONDON, 14 June 1972, *Seascape*, GBP 700. AMSTERDAM, 29 Oct 1979, *Sailing Ships at Sea* (black chalk and wash, 12 x 19 1/2 ins / 30.4 x 49.6 cm) NLG 5,000. BREMEN, 28 March 1981, *Frigates and Sailing Ships in High Seas* (oil on canvas, 36 3/4 x 48 ins / 93.5 x 122 cm) DEM 18,000. PARIS, 1 July 1987, *Naval Battles* (pen and wash, two drawings, each 8 3/4 x 14 1/4 ins / 22.2 x 36 cm) FRF 17,500. AMSTERDAM, 10 Feb 1988, *Fishermen in a Rowing Boat with Other Vessels in Calm Summer Weather* (oil on panel, 4 x 5 1/4 ins / 10 x 13.5 cm) NLG 4,830. BERN, 26 Oct 1988, *Rocky Coast with Heavy Seas* (oil on canvas, 31 x 39 1/4 ins / 79 x 100 cm) CHF 7,000. AMSTERDAM, 23 April 1991, *Fishermen on a Beach* (oil on canvas, 13 3/4 x 19 1/4 ins / 35 x 49 cm) NLG 9,200. AMSTERDAM, 14-15 April 1992, *Sailing Ships on the Zuiderzee* (oil on panel, 10 1/2 x 14 1/4 ins / 26.5 x 36 cm) NLG 8,050. LONDON, 17 March 1993, *Rescue at Sea* (oil on canvas, 30 3/4 x 39 ins / 78 x 99 cm) GBP 6,900. AMSTERDAM, 20 April 1993, *Riverscape by Moonlight* (1860, oil on canvas, 7 1/2 x 10 ins / 19 x 25.5 cm) NLG 4,140. AMSTERDAM, 19 Oct 1993, *Mariner Putting a Boat to Sea, with a Saling Ship off the Coast* (1857, oil on canvas, 26 1/2 x 34 1/4 ins / 67 x 87 cm) NLG 27,600. AMSTERDAM, 12 Nov 1996, *Sailing Ships on a Choppy Sea* (pencil, black ink and brown wash/black chalk, 10 1/2 x 13 3/4 ins / 26.5 x 35.2 cm) NLG 4,720. LONDON, 19 Nov 1997, *Boats and Frigates in an Estuary* (oil on canvas, 27 1/4 x 34 1/4 ins / 69 x 87 cm) GBP 18,975. STOCKHOLM, 27 May 1999, *Seascape* (oil on canvas, 23 x 31 ins / 59 x 80 cm) SEK 37,000. LONDON, 21 Oct 1999, *Battle of Kamperduin, 1799* (oil on canvas, 19 x 25 ins / 48 x 64 cm) GBP 19,500. HAMBURG, 7 June 2000, *Entering Harbour in a Storm* (oil on canvas, 19 x 25 ins / 47 x 64 cm) DEM 16,000. AMSTERDAM, 8 Nov 2000, *Estuary Scene with Boats in a Strong Wind* (pen, grey and brown ink, watercolour and black chalk, 13 x 17 ins / 33 x 44 cm) NLG 10,000. AMSTERDAM, 14 April 2003, *Prince of Orange Greeting the English Fleet before Dutch Coast* (oil on panel, 29 x 39 ins / 74 x 98 cm) EUR 40,000. NEW YORK, 29 May 2003, *Sailing Vessels in Rough Seas* (oil on canvas, 45 x 59 ins / 115 x 150 cm) USD 37,500. AMSTERDAM, 20 April 2004, *Sailing Vessels on the Zuiderzee* (oil on panel, 18 x 24 ins / 46 x 62 cm) EUR 15,000. COLOGNE, 22 May 2004, *Fishing Boats in Harbour* (pen and wash, 13 x 17 ins / 33 x 44 cm) EUR 3,600.

SCHOTEN, Floris Gerritsz. van. See **SCHOOTEN**

SCHOTEN, Franciscus van. See **SCHOOTEN**

SCHOTEN, Pauwels van. See the entry **SCHOTANUS Piter**

SCHOTIS, Gottardo de. See **SCOTTI**

SCHOTIS, Melchiorre de. See **SCOTTI**

SCHOTO. See **SCOTO**

SCHOTSMA, G.
Dutch, 18th century.
Sculptor (wood).

SCHOTT
Hungarian, 17th century.
Reproductions engraver.

Schott worked in Tyrnau (now Trnava, Slovakia) around 1692.

SCHOTT, Albert
Austrian, 19th century.
Born 1833, in Köflach.
Active in Graz.
Landscape artist.

SCHOTT, August Ludwig Friedrich
German, 19th century.
Born 16 March 1811, in Giessen; died 19 February 1843.
Painter, draughtsman, engraver, lithographer.
Historical subjects, religious subjects.

August Schott initially worked with Ducorée, later attending the Städelsches Kunstinstitut in Frankfurt and the academy in Munich. In his style he is indebted to Overbeck and Steinle, reproducing several of their works as lithographs.

AUCTION RECORDS:
BERN, 25 Oct 1979, *St Elisabeth Distributing Bread to the Poor* (1835, oil on canvas, 26 1/2 x 19 3/4 ins / 67.5 x 50 cm) CHF 7,000.

SCHOTT, Bernard
German, 18th century.
Active in Mainz c. 1780.
Engraver.

SCHOTT, Creszentia von
German, 18th century.
Active in Mannheim.
Painter, engraver.

Creszentia von Schott was the pupil of Ferdinand Kobell around 1790.

SCHOTT, Erhard
German, 19th century.
Born 1810, in Kiechlingsbergen.
Lithographer.

In 1836 Erhard Schott was studying in Munich.

SCHOTT, Ferdinand
Swiss, 20th century.
Born 23 August 1887, in Delsberg (Jura).
Painter, engraver. Landscapes, animals.

Ferdinand Schott studied in Munich with Gröber and Von Hayek, and in Paris with H. Martin.

SCHOTT, J. Sigmund, or Schodt
German, 17th century.
Active 1690-1697.
Engraver.

SCHOTT, Johann, or Schot
German, 17th century.
Active in Frieberg-on-Hesse.
Painter.

In 1632 Johann Schott was a master in Cologne.

SCHOTT, Karl Albert von
German, 19th - 20th century.
Born 1840, in Stuttgart; died 21 February 1911, in Stuttgart.
Painter. Battles, landscapes.

Karl Albert von Schott was an officer who fought in the campaigns of 1866 and 1870. He did not take up painting until 1888.

MUSEUMS AND GALLERIES:
STUTTGART: *Battle of Villiers.*

SCHOTT, Max
19th century.
Active at the end of the 19th century.
Painter. Figures.

AUCTION RECORDS:
NEW YORK, 22 and 23 Feb 1907, *Ideal Face,* USD 210. PARIS, 28 May 1923, *Head of a Woman,* FRF 150. PARIS, 29 May 1926, *Souvenirs,* FRF 285. PARIS, 29 Oct 1948, *Bust of a WBuste de femmoman* (1904) FRF 5,000. NEW YORK, 24 Jan 1980, *Temptress* (1907, oil on canvas, 21 x 16 3/4 ins / 53.5 x 42.5 cm) USD 1,500.

SCHOTT, Philippe Charles
Belgian, 20th century.
Born 1886; died 19 June 1964.
Painter, engraver. Landscapes, interiors, still-lifes.

SCHOTT, Rolf
German, 20th century.
Born 1892, in Mainz.
Engraver, lithographer, writer.

SCHOTT, Walter
German, 19th - 20th century.
Born 18 September 1861, in Ilserburg; died October 1938, in Berlin.
Painter, sculptor. Genre scenes.

Walter Schott studied under Carl Dopmeyer in Hanover from 1878 to 1879, and under Fritz Schaper at the art academy in Berlin.

He took part in exhibitions in Paris and was awarded a gold medal in 1900 at the Exposition Universelle. He lived and worked in Berlin, where much of his work remains, including a statue of *Frederick William I* at the castle, a statue of *William II* at the art academy, a monument in memory of William of Orange, and his major work *Woman Playing Bowls.*

MUSEUMS AND GALLERIES:
BERLIN (Nationalgal.): *Woman Playing Bowls* - DÜSSELDORF: *Woman Playing Bowls.*

SCHOTTENBERGER, Michael
Austrian, 18th century.
Active in Freistadt.
Painter.

SCHÖTTLI, Emanuel
Swiss, 19th - 20th century.
Born 22 October 1895, in Schaffhausen; died 7 August 1926, in Basel.
Painter. Portraits, landscapes.

SCHOTZ, Benno
Estonian, 20th century.
Born 1891, in Arensburg; died 1984.
Sculptor. Figures, portraits.

Benno Schotz travelled to Glasgow in Scotland at the age of 20 to pursue a career as a sculptor. His first work, a bust of *Tolstoy,* dates from 1917. He is best known for his portraits of Scots personalities, and was quickly hailed as a leading figure in contemporary art. Schotz headed the sculpture department at Glasgow School of Art from 1938-1961, and was appointed Sculptor Ordinary to the Queen in 1963. His talent for portraiture drew favourable critical attention, and his work has been compared with that of Jacob Epstein. Drawing on diverse materials - wood, terracotta, plaster, bronze, cement - Schotz's vocabulary recalls that of Maillol or Rodin. Later works evolved towards semi-abstraction inspired by the natural forms of trees and rocks.

His work featured in a number of group exhibitions, notably with the Royal Scottish Academy, from 1918 until his death. Schotz also held one-man shows in London, Jerusalem, Haïfa, Edinburgh, Glasgow and Philadelphia.

BIBLIOGRAPHY:
Benno Schotz Retrospective Exhibition, exhibition catalogue, Diploma Galleries, Royal Scottish Academy, 1971. Schotz, Benno, *Bronze in my Blood: The Memoirs of Benno Schotz,* G. Wright Publishers, Edinburgh, 1981. *Fonds d'atelier de Benno Schotz,* auction catalogue, Christie's Scotland, Glasgow, September 24, 1997.

AUCTION RECORDS:
LONDON, 11 June 1976, *Seated Nude* (1929, bronze, h. 11 ins / 28 cm) GBP 380. LONDON, 23 Nov 1982, *The Boy Bather* (1924-1925, bronze, h. 20 ins / 50.5 cm) GBP 700. EDINBURGH, 30 April 1986, *The Artist's Daughter, Cherna Schotz, Aged 2* (1932, bronze, h. 8 1/2 ins / 21.6 cm) GBP 1,100. LONDON, 24 May 1990, *Woman Resting* (1929, bronze, h. 11 1/2 ins / 29 cm) GBP 2,090. GLASGOW, 24 Sept 1997, *Portrait of Francis George*

Scott (1947, green and bronze patinated plaster, h. 13¾ ins / 35 cm) GBP 1,265; *Acrobats* (1965, bronze welded with manganese, h. 62½ ins / 158.8 cm) GBP 9,200; *Requiem* (1966, welded bronze, h. 70 ins / 177.8 cm) GBP 3,220; *Moses the Sculptor* (1949, earthenware, h. 84¼ ins / 213.7 cm) GBP 17,250. BILLINGSHURST, 24 July 2000, *Bather, Woman Bending Over Drying Herself with a Towel* (brown patinated bronze, h. 15 ins / 39 cm) GBP 1,300. EDINBURGH, 25 May 2001, *Generations* (green patinated bronze, h. 14 ins / 36 cm) GBP 1,700. EDINBURGH, 7 Dec 2001, *Kunle* (lignum vitae, h. 13 ins / 32 cm) GBP 2,000. LONDON, 16 April 2002, *Boy Bather* (1926, dark green patinated bronze, 20 x 11 ins / 50 x 28 cm) GBP 2,800. EDINBURGH, 21 Aug 2003, *Woman with Towel* (bronze, h. 15 ins / 39 cm) GBP 2,000. EDINBURGH, 21 Aug 2003, *Unde Undressing* (1929, bronze, h. 17 ins / 42 cm) GBP 2,500.

SCHOU, Karl Holger Jacob
Danish, 20th century.
Born 9 March 1870, in Copenhagen; died 8 March 1938, in Charlottenlund.
Painter. Figures, portraits, interiors, landscapes, still-lifes.

Karl Holger Jacob Schou trained under Malthe Engelsted and Kristian Zahrtmann. He lived and worked in Charlottenlund.

AUCTION RECORDS:
COPENHAGEN, 5 April 1989, *Red House in the Snow* (oil on canvas, 15¾ x 22¾ ins / 40 x 58 cm) DKK 5,000. COPENHAGEN, 21 Feb 1990, *Landscape with a Stream under the Trees* (oil on canvas, 18½ x 25½ ins / 47 x 65 cm) DKK 5,500. COPENHAGEN, 25-26 April 1990, *Near St Paul's Ramparts* (1913, oil on canvas, 23½ x 29¼ ins / 60 x 74 cm) DKK 6,000.

SCHOU, Ludvig Abelin
Danish, 19th century.
Born 11 January 1838, in Slagelse; died 30 September 1867, in Florence.
Painter. Figures, nudes, portraits.

Schou was the brother of Peter Alfred. He was a pupil of both Niels Simonsen and Wilhelm Marstrand. He worked in Rome from 1864 to 1867.

MUSEUMS AND GALLERIES:
COPENHAGEN.

AUCTION RECORDS:
COPENHAGEN, 21 Feb 1990, *Standing Nude From Behind, With Knee on a Bench* (oil on canvas, 37½ x 24½ ins / 95 x 62 cm) DKK 42,000. COPENHAGEN, 23 May 1996, *Portrait of a Young Girl Seated* (1863, oil on canvas, 11¾ x 9¾ ins / 30 x 25 cm) DKK 6,600. VEJLE, 22 Jan 1999, *Nude Female Seen from Behind by Boxes with Green Cloth* (oil on canvas, 37 x 24 ins / 94 x 62 cm) DKK 20,000. VEJLE, 22 Jan 1999, *Nude Female seen from Behind by Boxes with Red Cloth* (oil on canvas, 35 x 27 ins / 88 x 68 cm) DKK 20,000. COPENHAGEN, 29 Feb 2000, *Reclining Female Model* (oil on canvas, 17 x 20 ins / 42 x 51 cm) DKK 125,000. ARHUS, 8 May 2000, *Study of Nude Female* (oil on canvas, 37 x 25 ins / 95 x 63 cm) DKK 30,000. VEJLE, 16 Jan 2001, *Summer Landscape from Hornsherred* (1859, oil on canvas, 6 x 7 ins / 14 x 19 cm) DKK 19,500. VEJLE, 4 Aug 2003, *Portrait of Nude Woman Seen from the Side, Seated on Stone in Wood* (oil on canvas, 27 x 20 ins / 68 x 50 cm) DKK 46,000.

SCHOU, Peter Alfred
Danish, 19th - 20th century.
Born 8 October 1844, in Copenhagen; died 21 November 1914, in Copenhagen.
Painter. Figures, portraits, interiors, still-lifes.

The brother of Danish artist Ludvig Abelin, Peter Alfred Schou trained at the art academy in Dresden from 1873 to 1874, and under T. Chartran and L. Bonnat in Paris between 1875 and 1880.

MUSEUMS AND GALLERIES:
COPENHAGEN (Kunstakademi): *The Painter; Serious Moment*; 17 paintings - COPENHAGEN (Statens Mus. for Kunst).

SCHOU, Peter Johan
Danish, 19th - 20th century.
Born 25 April 1863, in Copenhagen; died 29 October 1934, in Copenhagen.
Painter, designer. Landscapes.

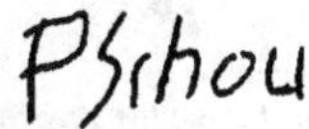

SCHOU, Sigund Sölver
Danish, 20th century.
Born 30 July 1875; died 1944.
Painter, designer. Landscapes.

Sigund Sölver Schou trained under brothers Gustave and Sophus Vermehren. He lived and worked in Lynäs.

MUSEUMS AND GALLERIES:
COPENHAGEN - RIBE.

AUCTION RECORDS:
LONDON, 29 March 1990, *Summer Idyll* (1916, oil on canvas, 33 x 22¼ ins / 83.8 x 56.6 cm) GBP 4,400. COPENHAGEN, 29 Aug 1991, *Play of Light on a Fjord near Lynaes* (oil on canvas, 14¼ x 18 ins / 36 x 46 cm) DKK 5,000.

SCHOU, Sven Holger
Danish, 20th century.
Born 10 June 1877, in Copenhagen; died 11 March 1961, in Hadsund.
Painter. Landscapes, animals.

Sven Holger Schou lived and worked in Havnö Enge near Hadsund in Jutland.

SCHOUBERG, Johannes Petrus
Dutch, 19th century.
Born 10 January 1798, in The Hague; died 6 January 1864, in Utrecht.
Medallist, engraver.

SCHOUBOE, Henrik August
Danish, 20th century.
Born 16 June 1876, in Ringsted; died 31 October 1949, in Frederiksberg.
Painter. Figures, portraits, interiors, landscapes.

Henrik August Schouboe lived and worked in Copenhagen.

MUSEUMS AND GALLERIES:
COPENHAGEN (Statens Mus. for Kunst): *April. Et ungt par i et landskab (April)* (1908).

SCHOUBOE, Pablo
Danish, 19th - 20th century.
Born 1874, in Ringsted; died 1941, in Copenhagen.
Painter. Landscapes.

Pablo Schouboe lived in Chile and Brazil during the 1920s.

AUCTION RECORDS:
COLOGNE, 23 March 1990, *Walk in the Brazilian Savannah* (oil on canvas, 26¾ x 20¾ ins / 68 x 53 cm) DEM 2,200. LONDON, 29 March 1990, *Garden Path* (1920, oil on canvas, 40 x 50 ins / 101.6 x 127 cm) GBP 4,180.

SCHOUBROECK, Pieter, or Schaubroeck, Schoebroeck, Schubruck, Schaubruck
Flemish School, 16th century.
Born c. 1570, in Hessheim, near Frankenthal; died 1607, in Frankenthal.
Painter. History painting, mythological subjects, landscapes with figures, landscapes.
Frankenthal School.

Pieter Schoubroek was a son of the Protestant minister Niklas Schoubruck, who fled to Frankenthal to escape religious persecution. Pieter was a pupil of Gilles Coninxloo in

Frankenthal, worked in Nuremberg in 1597, and married in Frankenthal in 1598. He taught Elsenheimer landscape painting.

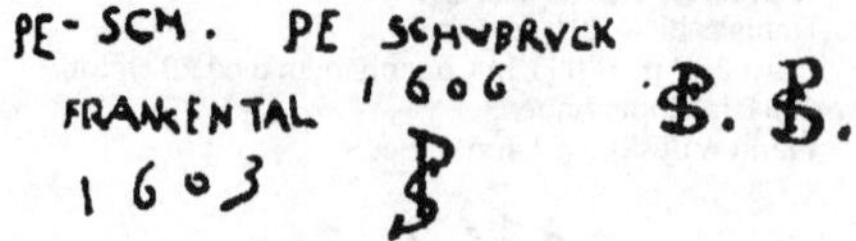

Museums and Galleries:
BRUNSWICK: *St John the Baptist Preaching* - COPENHAGEN (Statens Mus. for Kunst): *Landscape* - DRESDEN: *Battle of the Amazons; Siege of a Fortress; Sodom and Gomorrha* - KASSEL: *Destruction of Troy; Temptation of St Anthony* - ROHRAU (Schlossmus., Graf Harrach'sche Familiensammlung): *Landscape with Citadel* - VIENNA: *Troy in Flames.*
Auction records:
LONDON, 4-5 May 1922, *Destruction of Troy,* GBP 44. PARIS, 12 Dec 1934, *Attack on a Fortified Town,* FRF 4,200. AMSTERDAM, 21 Oct 1949, *Dido and Aeneas,* NLG 2,900. COPENHAGEN, 22 March 1966, *Winter Landscape with Skaters,* DKK 37,000. NEW YORK, 17 May 1972, *Town in Winter,* USD 90,000. LONDON, 12 Dec 1979, *Summer. Autumn* (two oils/copper, 8 x 11 ins / 20.5 x 28 cm) GBP 66,000. LONDON, 23 June 1982, *Fire of Troy* (1605, oil/copper, 7 x 10 ins / 18 x 25.5 cm) GBP 7,500. LONDON, 9 March 1983, *Numerous Figures Fleeing the Burning City of Troy* (oil/copper, 10 1/4 x 11 3/4 ins / 26 x 30 cm) GBP 3,800. NEW YORK, 6 June 1985, *Landscape with Numerous Figures* (oil/copper, 18 x 30 3/4 ins / 46 x 78 cm) USD 49,000. LONDON, 10 July 1987, *Diana and Actaeon in a Wooded Landscape* (oil/copper, 12 3/4 x 21 1/2 ins / 32.4 x 54.3 cm) GBP 18,000. MONACO, 16 June 1989, *Flight from Troy* (oil/copper, 9 1/4 x 11 3/4 ins / 23.3 x 29.7 cm) FRF 333,000. NEW YORK, 31 Jan 1997, *Mountain Landscape with Travellers Talking on a Road* (oil/copper, 7 x 10 1/2 ins / 17.5 x 26.4 cm) USD 19,550. PARIS, 27 April 2000, *Flight from Troy* (oil on copper, 7 x 10 ins / 18 x 26 cm) FRF 70,000. PARIS, 25 June 2002, *St John Preaching* (oil on copper, 11 x 16 ins / 28 x 40 cm) EUR 51,000.

SCHOUK, Cornelis
Dutch, 17th century.
Died 1675.
Active in Rotterdam.
Painter. Genre scenes.

SCHOUKHAEFF, Basil. See **CHUKAEV Stepan Grigorievich**

SCHOUKOVSKY, P. V.. See **JOUKOVSKI Pavel Vassiliévitch von**

SCHOULER, Willard C.
American, 19th century.
Born 6 September 1852, in Arlington (Massachusetts); died 1934.
Active in Arlington.
Painter.
Willard C. Schouler was a pupil of Day and Rimmer.
Museums and Galleries:
BOSTON: *Arizona Indians.*

SCHOULTZ, Emma von. See **SCHULZ**

SCHOUMAN, Aert
Dutch, 18th century.
Born 4 March 1710, in Dordrecht; died 7 May 1792, in The Hague.
Painter, draughtsman, engraver. History painting, portraits, animals, landscapes with figures.
Aert Schouman was a pupil of Adrien van den Burg for eight years. Schouman became a guild master in The Hague in 1748 and divided his time between Dordrecht and The Hague before settling in the latter in 1753. His pupils included Wouter Dam, Wouter Uiterlimming and Martinus Schouman. He painted mainly pictures of birds, in the style of Hondekoeter and Weeninx, as well as a number of scenes from Ovid's *Metamorphoses*. He also made a number of mezzotints.

Museums and Galleries:
'S HERTOGENBOSCH (Stadhuis): *Love's Idyll* - AMSTERDAM (Rijksmus.): *Pheasants in a Field; Hen-house; Self-portrait* - DORDRECHT: two self-portraits - DORDRECHT (Mus. Simon Van Gijn): *Wisdom in the Temple of Charity with Two Orphans*; two decorative panels with birds - EDAM (Church of St Nicholas): *Portrait of J. Munnekemolen* - GLASGOW: *Hens and Falcon* - MIDDELBURG: *Huis van Bewaring; Self-portrait* - PARIS (Mus. des Arts décoratifs): *Duck* - ST PETERSBURG (Hermitage): *Interior with a Young Woman Having her Feet Measured for Shoes* - THE HAGUE: *Portraits of Jan Hudde Dedel; T. Hoog; J. van der Heim and Maria Aroudina Gevaerts; Allegory: Love of the Arts Spares Not the Need for Application* - UTRECHT: *Still-life with a Calf's Head.*
Auction records:
PARIS, 1776, *Landscape with Figures and Animals* (drawing) FRF 128. PARIS, 1823, *Family of Peasants and Shepherd with his Livestock in a Large Forest* (bistre drawing) FRF 20. PARIS, 7 Dec 1858, *Young Woman in front of a Mirror* (watercolour) FRF 18. LONDON, 11 Feb 1911, *Peacock and Ducks,* GBP 3. PARIS, 5 and 6 March 1920, *Duck, Pigeon, Pheasant and Monkey,* FRF 3,700. PARIS, 4 Dec 1925, *Two Birds Perched on a Branch* (watercolour) FRF 400. PARIS, 3 March 1926, *Study of a Duck* (watercolour) FRF 650. PARIS, 26 Feb 1927, *Garden Walk; Departure of the Coach* (two gouaches) FRF 2,700. PARIS, 4 May 1928, *Music Lesson,* FRF 1,750. PARIS, 14 April 1937, *Three Greyhounds* (watercolour) FRF 350. PARIS, 26 and 27 May 1941, *Magpie* (gouache) FRF 950. PARIS, 13 April 1942, *Golden Pheasant, Guinea-fowl and Parrot,* FRF 10,500. PARIS, 18 Oct 1946, *Nymph and Satyr in a Landscape* (watercolour) FRF 2,300. PARIS, 7 Dec 1967, *Birds in a Landscape,* FRF 13,000. LONDON, 23 June 1970, *Birds* (gouache) Gns 320. LONDON, 21 March 1973, *View of Dordrecht* (watercolour) GBP 1,500. AMSTERDAM, 18 Nov 1980, *Three Birds on a Branch* (watercolour, 9 3/4 x 7 ins / 24.8 x 16.9 cm) NLG 4,200. AMSTERDAM, 16 Nov 1981, *Bird with Blue Plumage* (1756, watercolour, 14 1/2 x 10 ins / 36.7 x 25.2 cm) NLG 5,000. AMSTERDAM, 28 Nov 1985, *Birds in a Landscape* (watercolour, 5 1/4 x 7 1/4 ins / 13.4 x 18.6 cm) NLG 6,600. PARIS, 6 March 1986, *Parrots* (watercolour, 14 1/4 x 10 ins / 36 x 25.5 cm) FRF 38,000. PARIS, 24 Feb 1987, *Two Birds on a Branch* (1738, watercolour and gouache, 10 3/4 x 7 1/2 ins / 27.5 x 19 cm) FRF 13,000. PARIS, 9 March 1988, *Parrot and Bird of Paradise on a Branch* (watercolour and gouache, 14 1/4 x 10 ins / 36.5 x 25.5 cm) FRF 28,000. AMSTERDAM, 14 Nov 1988, *Three Birds on a Branch* (1779, black chalk, 14 1/2 x 10 1/4 ins / 36.8 x 26.2 cm) NLG 1,955; *Couple Seated in an Interior, the Man Holding a Cat and the Woman Holding a Greyhound* (1742, oil/copper, 7 1/2 x 5 3/4 ins / 19 x 14.5 cm) NLG 24,150. NEW YORK, 2 June 1989, *Parrot and Other Exotic Birds in a Landscape* (oil on canvas, 52 1/2 x 55 1/2 ins / 133.5 x 141 cm) USD 77,000. PARIS, 26 June 1989, *Ornamental Birds around a Statue in a Park* (watercolour, 11 1/4 x 6 3/4 ins / 28.8 x 17 cm) FRF 38,000. AMSTERDAM, 25 Nov 1991, *Currant Bush in a*

Landscape (watercolour, 14 1/4 x 9 3/4 ins / 36 x 24.6 cm) NLG 5,750. AMSTERDAM, 11 Nov 1992, *Juno Ordering Argos to Watch Over Io* (1738, oil on canvas/card, 34 1/4 x 33 ins / 87 x 84 cm) NLG 14,950. AMSTERDAM, 25 Nov 1992, *Woman Spinning* (pencil, watercolour and ink, 8 x 7 ins / 20.2 x 16.9 cm) NLG 8,625. PARIS, 16 Nov 1993, *Two Parrots from the East Indies* (watercolour and gouache, 13 1/2 x 9 3/4 ins / 34 x 25 cm) FRF 17,000. AMSTERDAM, 17 Nov 1993, *Goldfinch, Long-tailed Tit and Nuthatch on a Branch with Dordrecht in the Distance* (watercolour and black chalk, 9 1/2 x 6 1/2 ins / 24.3 x 16.8 cm) NLG 8,280. PARIS, 29 April 1994, *Amazonian Parrot* (1755, watercolour, 9 x 6 1/2 ins / 23.1 x 16.4 cm) FRF 29,000. NEW YORK, 19 May 1994, *Ibis with Pheasants and a Crow in a Landscape* (oil on canvas, 31 x 24 3/4 ins / 78.7 x 62.9 cm) USD 16,100. AMSTERDAM, 15 Nov 1995, *Ring Ouzel and Canary on a Branch* (watercolour, 16 1/2 x 10 1/2 ins / 41.8 x 26.7 cm) NLG 4,720. LONDON, 3 July 1996, *Yellow-crested Cockatoos in a Tropical Landscape* (watercolour/black chalk, 13 3/4 x 10 ins / 35.2 x 24.5 cm) GBP 8,280. AMSTERDAM, 9 Nov 1999, *Children Making Pancakes* (1771, watercolour, 11 x 9 ins / 27 x 23 cm) NLG 6,000. NEW YORK, 27 Jan 2000, *Peacock, Pheasant, Cockerel and other Birds in a Landscape* (1746, oil on canvas, 48 x 39 ins / 123 x 100 cm) USD 38,000. AMSTERDAM, 8 Nov 2000, *Eider Ducks by a Pond* (black chalk and watercolour, 14 x 10 ins / 36 x 25 cm) NLG 9,000. NEW YORK, 25 Jan 2001, *Study of Three Birds and a Butterfly* (watercolour, 14 x 10 ins / 36 x 25 cm) USD 5,200. PARIS, 30 Sept 2003, *Thistle in a Landscape* (graphite and watercolour, 16 x 11 ins / 41 x 27 cm) EUR 4,000. AMSTERDAM, 4 Nov 2003, *Duck* (watercolour and gouache, 14 x 11 ins / 36 x 27 cm) EUR 4,500. AMSTERDAM, 17 May 2004, *Portrait of a Family, said to be Yoan van Wageningen and Children* (1749, oil on panel, 23 x 20 ins / 58 x 50 cm) EUR 8,500. AMSTERDAM, 19 May 2004, *Bergamot Plant* (1753, watercolour, 17 x 11 ins / 43 x 28 cm) EUR 32,000.

SCHOUMAN, Cornelis

Dutch, 18th century.
Born in Dordrecht; died before 15 July 1749.
Active in Middelburg.
Painter.

Cornelis Schouman was a guild master in Middelburg in 1729. He was the brother of Aert Schouman.

SCHOUMAN, Isaak

Dutch, 19th century.
Born 1798 or 1801, in Dordrecht.
Painter. Military subjects, landscapes, seascapes.

Isaak Schouman was the son of Martinus Schouman. He taught at the military academy in Breda in 1836.

AUCTION RECORDS:
AMSTERDAM, 17 Sept 1991, *Full-length Portrait of a Woman in a Blue Dress with a White Lace Bodice, Holding a Rose, with Ships on the River Dordrecht in the Background* (1852, oil on canvas/card, 41 3/4 x 33 1/4 ins / 106 x 84.5 cm) NLG 3,450. PARIS, 1 Feb 1996, *Three-master in High Seas* (oil on panel, 13 3/4 x 17 1/4 ins / 35 x 44 cm) FRF 17,000. AMSTERDAM, 20 April 1999, *Young Jacobus* (pen and watercolour, 16 x 24 ins / 40 x 60 cm) NLG 3,800. AMSTERDAM, 14 April 2003, *Portrait of Adrianus Vos. Portrait of Heilje Joanna von Buul, Wife of Adrianus Vos* (1829, oil on canvas, a pair, 37 x 31 ins / 94 x 80 cm) EUR 1,500.

SCHOUMAN, Martinus

Dutch, 18th - 19th century.
Born 29 January 1770, in Dordrecht; died 30 October 1848, in Breda.
Painter. Military subjects, seascapes.

Martinus Schouman was a pupil of M. Versteeg and his uncle Aert Schouman. His pictures demonstrate a remarkable knowledge of ships and the sea in all its aspects.

MUSEUMS AND GALLERIES:
AMSTERDAM: *Gunboat No. 2 Blown Up before the City of Antwerp; Surrender of the Dutch Fleet at Boulogne in 1809; Bombardment of Algiers* (1816); *Expedition of Palembourg* (1821).

AUCTION RECORDS:
PARIS, 1857, *Rough Sea with Vessels and Sailing Boats* (watercolour) FRF 14. PARIS, 1858, *Seascape* (drawing in pen and bistre with ink wash) FRF 10. PARIS, 19 May 1927, *Shipwreck* (watercolour) FRF 300. LONDON, 14 June 1974, *Riverscape with Boats*, Gns 3,400. AMSTERDAM, 24 April 1979, *Sailing Ships off the Coast of Dordrecht* (oil on panel, 26 3/4 x 33 ins / 68 x 84 cm) NLG 34,000. AMSTERDAM, 29 Oct 1979, *Ships at Sea* (1793, watercolour and pen, 9 x 11 1/4 ins / 22 x 28.6 cm) NLG 7,200. LONDON, 26 Nov 1982, *Sailing Ships at Sea* (oil on panel, 13 x 20 ins / 33 x 50.5 cm) GBP 1,100. NEW YORK, 21 Oct 1988, *Sailing Ships in High Seas* (oil on canvas, 28 1/4 x 37 1/2 ins / 71.7 x 95 cm) USD 11,000. AMSTERDAM, 16 Nov 1988, *The Frigate Dankbaarheid* (oil on canvas, 19 1/4 x 24 3/4 ins / 49 x 63 cm) NLG 14,950. AMSTERDAM, 10 April 1990, *Dutch Two-master and Another Vessel in Stormy Seas* (ink and watercolour/paper) NLG 3,105. AMSTERDAM, 20 April 1993, *Seascape* (oil on canvas/panel, 11 1/2 x 15 ins / 29 x 38 cm) NLG 3,450. AMSTERDAM, 19 Oct 1993, *Dutch Boat with a Square Sail and Other Vessels off the Coast in Stormy Seas* (oil on canvas, 28 1/4 x 36 1/4 ins / 72 x 92 cm) NLG 8,625. LONDON, 18 March 1999, *Shipping off a Jetty* (oil on canvas, 20 x 27 ins / 50 x 68 cm) GBP 8,500. AMSTERDAM, 7 March 2000, *Dutch Brig Coming to the Aid of a Frigate in Distress* (oil on panel, 20 x 27 ins / 50 x 69 cm) NLG 8,000. ANTWERP, 22 May 2000, *Sailing Boats in the Harbour* (wash, 12 x 18 ins / 30 x 46 cm) BEF 170,000. LONDON, 24 May 2001, *Flushing State Yacht Running Past the Scheldt Estuary* (oil on canvas, 59 x 81 ins / 151 x 206 cm) GBP 17,000. COLOGNE, 24 Nov 2001, *Sailing Boats in Stormy Seas* (oil on canvas, 28 x 37 ins / 71 x 93 cm) DEM 11,000. AMSTERDAM, 12 March 2002, *Threemasters in Distress off the Coast* (oil on panel, 13 x 19 ins / 32 x 47 cm) EUR 3,000. LONDON, 11 April 2002, *Bedchamber with a Woman Eating in Bed and a Nurse Feeding Her Baby* (1789, watercolour, 9 x 11 ins / 22 x 29 cm) GBP 1,300. LONDON, 21 May 2003, *Dutch Shipping in a Heavy Swell* (1811, oil on panel, 13 x 17 ins / 32 x 43 cm) GBP 2,000. AMSTERDAM, 2 Sept 2003, *Stiff Breeze* (oil on canvas, 28 x 36 ins / 70 x 92 cm) EUR 4,000. AMSTERDAM, 3 Feb 2004, *Threemaster Louisa Prinses der Nederlanden in Full Sail* (oil on canvas, 28 x 37 ins / 72 x 94 cm) EUR 6,500. NEW YORK, 10 Feb 2004, *English Flagship Venerable Engaging the Dutch Flagship Vrijheid* (oil on canvas, 32 x 46 ins / 81 x 118 cm) USD 38,000.

SCHOUPPÉ, Alfred von

Polish, 19th century.
Born 23 December 1812, in Grabownica; died 17 April 1899, in Szczawnica.
Painter. Landscapes, ruins.

Alfred von Schouppé founded a society for the patronage of fine arts in Warsaw.

MUSEUMS AND GALLERIES:
CRACOW: *The Pier at Gaeta; The Ruins at Rabstine; Two Landscapes* - LVIV: *Ten Landscapes* - WARSAW: *Smugglers.*

SCHOUTE, Gilbert or Gysbert J. G., or Schouten

Dutch, 18th century.
Active in Amsterdam.
Draughtsman, engraver.

Gilbert Schoute was an engraver, apparently working mostly for booksellers.

SCHOUTE, Hubert, or Schouten
Dutch, 18th century.
Active in Amsterdam 1747-1775.
Draughtsman, engraver. Landscapes.

SCHOUTE, Jan
Dutch, 18th century.
Active in Amsterdam in the middle of the 18th century.
Draughtsman, engraver (burin).

SCHOUTEN, Gerrit Jan
Dutch, 19th century.
Born 8 October 1815, in Amsterdam.
Painter. Landscapes.

Gerrit Jan Schouten was a pupil of L. Meyer. He travelled extensively before settling in Amsterdam in 1838.

SCHOUTEN, Henri
Belgian, 19th - 20th century.
Born 1864, in Indonesia; died 1927, in Ghent.
Painter. Landscapes, animals.

AUCTION RECORDS:
BRUSSELS, 15 June 1976, *Farmyard* (oil on canvas, 26 3/4 x 39 1/4 ins / 68 x 100 cm) BEF 26,000. BRUSSELS, 27 Sept 1979, *Cattle Grazing* (oil on canvas, 26 x 39 1/4 ins / 66 x 100 cm) BEF 44,000. VIENNA, 16 Nov 1983, *Young Shepherdess* (oil on canvas, 30 x 22 3/4 ins / 76 x 58 cm) ATS 50,000. AMSTERDAM, 6 June 1984, *Ducks by a Pond* (oil on canvas, 29 x 38 1/4 ins / 73.5 x 97 cm) NLG 4,000. LONDON, 9 Oct 1985, *Three Dogs* (oil on canvas remounted/panel, 34 x 28 ins / 86.5 x 71 cm) GBP 2,000. COLOGNE, 15 Oct 1988, *Hens at the Edge of a Wood* (oil on canvas, 37 3/4 x 52 ins / 96 x 132 cm) DEM 5,000. CHESTER, 20 July 1989, *Old Friends* (oil on canvas, 19 1/2 x 29 1/4 ins / 49.5 x 74 cm) GBP 1,650. AMSTERDAM, 19 Sept 1989, *Peasant Woman Leading Two Oxen along a Path* (oil on canvas, 23 3/4 x 35 1/2 ins / 60.5 x 90 cm) NLG 4,830. AMSTERDAM, 2 May 1990, *Cows Drinking by a River* (oil on canvas, 24 1/4 x 35 3/4 ins / 61.5 x 91 cm) NLG 6,900. BRUSSELS, 12 June 1990, *Horses and Cows at a Drinking Trough* (oil on canvas, a pair, each 19 3/4 x 29 1/2 ins / 50 x 75 cm) BEF 90,000. LONDON, 15 Jan 1991, *Hunter with his English and Gordon Setters; Hunter with his English and Irish Setters* (oil on canvas, a pair, each 32 x 25 ins / 81.2 x 63.5 cm) GBP 2,860. BRUSSELS, 7 Oct 1991, *Cows by a River* (oil on canvas, 28 3/4 x 39 1/4 ins / 73 x 100 cm) BEF 70,000. AMSTERDAM, 5-6 Nov 1991, *Hunter* (oil on canvas, 31 1/2 x 23 1/2 ins / 80 x 60 cm) NLG 5,980. CALAIS, 2 Feb 1992, *Empty-handed; The Game Will Have to be Bought* (oil on panel, 17 x 20 3/4 ins / 43 x 53 cm) FRF 26,000. AMSTERDAM, 18 Feb 1992, *Sheep and Lambs in a Landscape* (oil on canvas, 24 3/4 x 19 ins / 63 x 48.5 cm) NLG 2,300. AMSTERDAM, 22 April 1992, *Memory of Scotland: Shetland Ponies and Sheep in a Landscape* (1892, oil on canvas, 39 3/4 x 59 1/2 ins / 101 x 151 cm) NLG 10,350. LOKEREN, 10 Oct 1992, *Rural Landscape* (oil on canvas, 31 1/2 x 47 1/4 ins / 80 x 120 cm) BEF 110,000. LONDON, 25 Nov 1992, *Group of Arabian Riders* (1899, oil on canvas, 27 1/4 x 39 ins / 69 x 99 cm) GBP 8,800. PARIS, 2 April 1993, *Returning from Ploughing* (oil on canvas, 31 1/2 x 39 1/4 ins / 80 x 100 cm) FRF 6,500. LOKEREN, 4 Dec 1993, *Polder Landscape with some Cows* (oil on canvas). NEW YORK, 16 Feb 1994, *Cobblers* (1895, oil on canvas, 26 x 22 ins / 66 x 55.9 cm) USD 3,450. LOKEREN, 10 Dec 1994, *Cows in a Polder Landscape* (oil on canvas, 25 1/2 x 33 1/4 ins / 65 x 84.5 cm) BEF 40,000. LOKEREN, 11 March 1995, *Cows Going to Drink* (oil on canvas, 35 x 49 1/4 ins / 89 x 125 cm) BEF 85,000. LONDON, 11 April 1995, *Old Friends* (oil on canvas, 23 1/4 x 28 1/4 ins / 59 x 72 cm) GBP 4,140. AMSTERDAM, 7 Nov 1995, *Bull in a Landscape* (1911, oil on canvas, 38 3/4 x 59 ins / 98.5 x 149 cm) NLG 3,068. AMSTERDAM, 16 April 1996, *The Four Seasons* (four oils on canvas, collection of ovals, each 32 x 26 1/4 ins / 81 x 66.5 cm) NLG 24,780. NEW YORK, 11 April 1997, *Three Setters* (oil on canvas, 31 1/2 x 23 1/2 ins / 80 x 59.7 cm) USD 4,830.

SCHOUTEN, Henry M.
Dutch, 19th century.
Born 1791; died 1835.
Active c. 1815.
Painter, engraver. Genre scenes, landscapes.

Henry M. Schouten produced mostly engravings.

AUCTION RECORDS:
NEW YORK, 17 Jan 1996, *Sheepfold* (oil on canvas, 20 x 31 1/4 ins / 50.8 x 79.4 cm) USD 3,737.

SCHOUTEN, Hubert. See **SCHOUTE**

SCHOUTEN, Hubert Pieter, or Shoute
Dutch, 18th - 19th century.
Born 1747, in Amsterdam; died 1822, in Haarlem.
Painter.

Hubert Pieter Schouten was the son of the engraver Hubert Schouten and a pupil of Paul van Liender and Ploos van Amstel. He collaborated with his father and produced drawings of city views in the manner of Jan van der Heyden.

AUCTION RECORDS:
PARIS, 26 June 1891, *Donkeys on a Beach,* FRF 260. LONDON, 14 Dec 1938, *Dutch Town Scene* (drawing) GBP 90. PARIS, 18 April 1951, *Church in Sunlight* (watercolour, attributed) FRF 4,300. AMSTERDAM, 3 April 1978, *View of Haarlem* (watercolour and pen, 5 3/4 x 7 3/4 ins / 14.5 x 20 cm) NLG 4,200.

SCHOUTETTEN, Louis, or Schouttetten
French, 19th century.
Born 1833, in Lille; died 1907.
Painter. Genre scenes, landscapes, flowers.

He made his Salon debut in 1864. His painting *Dusk* earned him an honourable mention in 1882.

MUSEUMS AND GALLERIES:
DUNKIRK: *Dusk.*

SCHOUW, Andreas
Danish, 19th century.
Born 21 July 1791, in Copenhagen; died 12 September 1829, in Copenhagen.
Painter.

SCHOUWENBERGH, Johann Heinrich or Jean Henri van. See **SCHAWBERG**

SCHOVAERTS, Mathys or Mathieu and Pieter. See **SCHOEVAERDTS**

SCHOVELIN, Axel Thorsen
Danish, 19th century.
Born 22 March 1827, in Copenhagen; died 18 December 1893, in Copenhagen.
Painter. Landscapes with figures, landscapes, waterscapes.

Schovelin was a pupil at the Kunstakademi in Copenhagen.

MUSEUMS AND GALLERIES:
AALBORG.

AUCTION RECORDS:
COPENHAGEN, 21 Sept 1950, *Wooded Landscape* (1860) DKK 2,500. LONDON, 13 June 1974, *River Landscape,* Gns 280. COPENHAGEN, 16 March 1976, *Summer Landscape* (1889, oil on canvas, 39 1/4 x 52 1/4 ins / 100 x 133 cm) DKK 3,200. LONDON, 12 Oct 1984, *Wooded Landscape with Stream* (oil on canvas, 34 1/4 x 47 3/4 ins / 87 x 121.2 cm) GBP

1,400. Copenhagen, 18 April 1985, *Landscape* (1873, oil on canvas, 35 3/4 x 52 3/4 ins / 91 x 134 cm) DKK 26,000. London, 24 March 1988, *Wooded Landscape with Figures Along a River* (1855, oil on canvas, 38 1/2 x 49 1/4 ins / 98 x 125 cm) GBP 7,700. Stockholm, 15 Nov 1988, *Park with Buildings* (oil, 13 1/2 x 20 1/2 ins / 34 x 52 cm) SEK 12,000. London, 16 March 1989, *Wooded Landscape with a Stag by a Lake* (oil on canvas, 39 x 49 1/2 ins / 99 x 126 cm) GBP 4,950. Stockholm, 19 April 1989, *Park with a Herd of Stags* (1869, oil on canvas, 22 1/2 x 31 1/2 ins / 57 x 80 cm) SEK 7,500. London, 16 Feb 1990, *Wooded Landscape* (oil on canvas, 26 1/2 x 37 ins / 67 x 94 cm) GBP 1,980. Copenhagen, 21 Feb 1990, *View of Heidelberg* (oil on canvas, 34 1/4 x 49 1/4 ins / 87 x 125 cm) DKK 24,000. Stockholm, 16 May 1990, *Dyrehaven Park* (oil on canvas, 22 1/2 x 31 1/2 ins / 57 x 80 cm) SEK 8,500. London, 27 Oct 1993, *Vast Wooded Landscape* (oil on canvas, 23 3/4 x 35 1/2 ins / 60.5 x 90 cm) GBP 1,725. London, 11 Oct 1995, *Vast Landscape with Stag* (1877, oil on canvas, 24 1/2 x 37 ins / 62 x 94 cm) GBP 1,495. London, 13 March 1997, *Heidelberg Castle and its Gardens* (oil on canvas, 31 1/2 x 46 3/4 ins / 80 x 118.8 cm) GBP 2,300. Denmark, 28 June 1999, *View of Tasinge towards Fyn* (oil on canvas, 33 x 51 ins / 85 x 130 cm) DKK 20,000. Copenhagen, 2 Sept 1999, *Anglers in Lake Landscape, Autumn* (oil on canvas, 22 x 29 ins / 56 x 74 cm) DKK 17,000. Copenhagen, 29 Feb 2000, *Autumn Landscape, Jægersborg Dyrehave* (1865, oil on canvas, 31 x 45 ins / 80 x 114 cm) DKK 18,000. Vejle, 18 May 2000, *Summer Landscape with Houses and View of Sea* (oil on canvas, 33 x 52 ins / 85 x 133 cm) DKK 20,000. Copenhagen, 3 Sept 2001, *Autumn Landscape near Jægersborg Dyrehave* (1869, oil on canvas, 31 x 44 ins / 80 x 111 cm) DKK 40,000. Copenhagen, 27 Nov 2001, *Fishing Village near Wood with Fisherman about to Dry his Nets* (1872, oil on canvas, 42 x 60 ins / 107 x 153 cm) DKK 90,000. Copenhagen, 3 June 2002, *Landscape View from Himmelbjerget* (oil on canvas, 34 x 50 ins / 87 x 127 cm) DKK 24,000. Copenhagen, 2 Sept 2003, *Stags by Large Trees in Dyrehagen* (oil on canvas, 46 x 53 ins / 116 x 135 cm) DKK 28,000. Copenhagen, 9 Dec 2003, *From the Village Kragholm at Faareveile Manor, Langeland* (oil on canvas, 28 x 37 ins / 71 x 95 cm) DKK 140,000. Vejle, 10 May 2004, *Landscape from Gudebæk* (oil on canvas, 23 x 36 ins / 58 x 92 cm) DKK 16,000.

SCHOVITZ, C. A.
Bohemian School, 18th century.
Active c. 1758.
Engraver (burin).

SCHOW, Joachim Godske
Danish, 19th century.
Born 1776, in Copenhagen; died 25 August 1857, in Copenhagen.
Landscape artist.

SCHOXEN, Carl
Norwegian, 19th century.
Born 1841, in Norway; died 1 January 1876.
Painter.

Schoxen was a young artist who died before being able to fulfil his artistic potential. His *Beach on the Edge of the Oslo Fjord* is in the museum in Oslo.

SCHOY, Johann Jacob, or Shoy
Austrian, 18th century.
Born 1686, in Marburg; died 1733, in Graz.
Active in Graz.
Sculptor.

Johann Schoy was the best-known sculptor of Styria in the first third of the 18th century. After a formative Italian period, he developed his own individual style. His work is mainly religious in its inspiration. A number of churches in Graz have works by him.

SCHØYEN, Carl
Norwegian, 19th century.
Born 1848, in Odalen; died 1875.
Painter. Seascapes.

Schøyen was a pupil of Hans Gude. One of his works is in the Nasjonalgaleriet in Oslo.

SCHOYERER, Josef
German, 19th - 20th century.
Born 7 March 1844, in Berching; died 12 July 1923, in Munich.
Painter. Landscapes.

Josef Schoyerer was a pupil of Charles Miller.

Auction records:
Munich, 24 May 1974, *River Landscape*, DEM 4,000. New York, 7 Oct 1977, *Wiesbachhorn, Tyrol* (1883, oil on canvas, 29 3/4 x 39 3/4 ins / 75.5 x 101 cm) USD 1,900. Zurich, 16 May 1980, *View of Lauterbrunnen and the Jungfrau Massif* (oil on canvas, 27 1/2 x 21 1/4 ins / 70 x 54 cm) CHF 15,500. Vienna, 19 June 1985, *Tyrolean Landscape* (oil on canvas, 17 x 24 ins / 43 x 61 cm) ATS 40,000. Munich, 31 May 1990, *Mountain Landscape with Peasants and a Chalet* (1874, oil on canvas, 47 1/4 x 30 ins / 120 x 76 cm) DEM 24,200. Munich, 26-27 Nov 1991, *Landscape in the Glonntal Area near Grafing* (oil on canvas, 19 1/2 x 28 1/2 ins / 49.5 x 72.5 cm) DEM 6,440. Amsterdam, 19 Oct 1993, *Torrent in a Mountain Landscape* (1875, oil on canvas, 24 1/2 x 29 ins / 62.5 x 73.5 cm) NLG 7,130.

SCHRADER, Antonio
German, 19th century.
Active in Berlin 1811-1836.
Painter. Landscapes, seascapes.

Antonio Schrader was the father of Julius.

SCHRADER, Bertha
German, 19th - 20th century.
Born 11 June 1845, in Memel (now Klaipeda, Lithuania); died 11 May 1920, in Dresden.
Painter, engraver (wood), lithographer. Interiors, landscapes.

Bertha Schrader was trained by Paul Graeb and Paul Baum. She engraved on wood.

SCHRADER, C.
German, 19th century.
Active in Hanover c. 1840.
Lithographer.

SCHRADER, C. A.
German, 18th century.
Painter.

Museums and Galleries:
Oranienbaum (Mus. Schloss): *Portrait of Juliana Sibylle Charlotte, Wife of Duke Ferdinand von Wurtemberg* - Wernigerode (Schloss): *Portrait of Ludwig Gunther Martini.*

SCHRADER, C.F.
Danish, 18th century.
Active in Copenhagen.
Miniaturist, enameller.

Museums and Galleries:
Copenhagen (Statens Mus. for Kunst): *Portrait of Christian VII of Denmark* (miniature).

SCHRADER, Hans Jacob
Danish, 18th century.
Active in Copenhagen between 1751 and 1769.
Painter (enamel), goldsmith.

In 1751 and 1752, Schrader painted several portraits on enamel of *Frederik V of Denmark.* He worked at the Louis Fournier factory in Denmark from 1760 to 1765. Several of his works are in the museum in Brunswick: a bust of Weimar, one of *Frederik V of Denmark,* and an *Adoration of the Shepherds.*

SCHRADER, Heinrich
German, 20th century.
Born 8 February 1876, in Eldagsen.
Painter. Portraits, landscapes.
Heinrich Schrader lived and worked in Hanover.

SCHRADER, J. C.
German, 18th century.
Died c. 1758.
Active in Göttingen.
Engraver (burin).
J. C. Schrader engraved portraits.

SCHRADER, Julius Friedrich Anton
German, 19th century.
Born 16 June 1815, in Berlin; died 16 February 1900, in Berlin.
Painter, engraver. History painting, portraits, genre scenes.
The son of Antonio Schrader, Julius Schrader attended the academy in Berlin and was then taught by Schadow in Düsseldorf. He visited France and the Netherlands and was in Italy in 1844. On his return to Berlin, he was appointed a member of the academy in 1847 and taught there the following year. In Berlin he received a gold medal in 1850 and 1853. He was also awarded gold medals in Vienna in 1873 and in Paris. He received a first-class medal in 1855 at the Exposition Universelle.
MUSEUMS AND GALLERIES:
BERLIN (Akademie der Künste): *Portrait of the Painter Herbig* - BERLIN (Nationalgal.): *The Consul Wagener; Obeisance of the Towns of Berlin and Cologne in 1415; Leopold von Ranke; The Surrender of Calais; Charles I and his Family Leaving; Esther before Ahasuerus; Portrait of Leopold von Ranke* - BERN: *Abdication of Henry IV of Germany in 1105* - COLOGNE (Wallraf-Richartz Mus.): *Cromwell at his Daughter's Bedside; Portraits of Wittgenstein, P. von Cornelius and Chr. Matzerath; The Artist; D. Fisher; Oppenheim* - HANOVER: *In the Church* - KALININGRAD: *Jephthah's Daughter with her playmates* - LEIPZIG: *Frederick II after the Battle of Kollin* - NEW YORK (Metropolitan Mus. of Art): *Baron Alexander von Humboldt* (1859, oil on canvas) - SCHWERIN: *The Virgin* - STUTTGART: *The Young Shakespeare Accused of Poaching before the Justice of the Peace.*
AUCTION RECORDS:
COLOGNE, 21 April 1967, *Portrait of Alexander von Humboldt,* DEM 6,000. LONDON, 21 July 1976, *Philippina Welser Receiving Charles V* (1862, oil on canvas, 41 x 51 ins / 104 x 129.5 cm) GBP 3,000. NEW YORK, 29 May 1980, *Queen Elizabeth and her Chancellor* (1870, oil on canvas, 62 x 48½ ins / 157.5 x 123 cm) USD 7,750. LUCERNE, 7 Nov 1985, *The Virgin and Sleeping Child* (1858, oil on canvas, 43¼ x 30¾ ins / 110 x 78 cm) CHF 9,000.

SCHRADER, Jurgen Gerhard
German, 17th - 18th century.
Sculptor. Monuments.
Jurgen Schrader sculpted several tombs in the cemetery of St Andrew in Hanover from 1689-1725.

SCHRADER, Lorenz
German, 18th century.
Died c. 1760.
Painter.
In 1730, Lorenz Schrader worked for Baron Stosch in Rome.

SCHRADER, Osias
German, 16th century.
Active in Osterwick, and in Regensburg 1586-1594.
Glass painter.

SCHRADER, Romanus
German, 18th century.
Active in Zerbst.
Painter.

SCHRADER, Rudolf
German, 19th century.
Born 2 December 1853, in Paddeim.
Painter. Figures, portraits, landscapes.
Rudolf Schrader worked in Charlottenburg.
AUCTION RECORDS:
NEW YORK, 19 Jan 1995, *Needlework by the Window* (oil on canvas, 17½ x 21¼ ins / 44.5 x 54 cm) USD 1,725.

SCHRADER-VELGEN, Carl Hans
German, 20th century.
Born 8 March 1876, in Hanover; died 1945.
Painter. Nudes, still-lifes.
Carl Hans Schrader-Velgen was a pupil of P. Höcker and Ludwig Herterich. He lived and worked in Munich.
MUSEUMS AND GALLERIES:
MUNICH (Neue Pinakothek): several nudes.
AUCTION RECORDS:
LONDON, 26 Oct 1977, *Path through the Undergrowth* (oil on canvas, 33¾ x 24¾ ins / 86 x 63 cm) GBP 800. HEILBRONN, 4 April 1981, *Return of the Herd* (oil on canvas, 27½ x 36¼ ins / 70 x 92 cm) DEM 11,000. COLOGNE, 20 Oct 1989, *Still-life with a Floral Arrangement in a Vase* (oil on canvas, 27½ x 22¾ ins / 70 x 58 cm) DEM 4,400. MUNICH, 11 Nov 1999, *Reclining Female Nude in a Park Landscape* (oil on board, 19 x 26 ins / 49 x 65 cm) DEM 7,000. MUNICH, 27 Sept 2000, *Winter Landscape with Trees by a Snowy Stream* (oil on canvas, 25 x 33 ins / 64 x 84 cm) DEM 8,000. COLOGNE, 20 Nov 2003, *Still-life with Flowers including Gladioli and Dahlias* (oil on canvas, 28 x 23 ins / 70 x 58 cm) EUR 3,300. STAUFEN, 25 March 2004, *Avenue in Haimhausen in August* (1922, oil on canvas, double-sided, 30 x 37 ins / 77 x 94 cm) EUR 1,500. STAUFEN, 25 March 2004, *Three Female Nudes by Water* (oil on canvas, 29 x 35 ins / 74 x 89 cm) EUR 3,800.

SCHRADRE
French, 18th century.
Died 1785.
Painter.
Schradre produced mostly landscapes and birds for the Sèvres porcelain manufactory in 1773.

SCHRAEBELIN, J.
German, 19th century.
Active in Frankfurt am Main c. 1800.
Engraver.
J. Schraebelin was the pupil of J.A.B. Nothnagel.

SCHRAEGLE, Gustav Peter Franz
German, 19th century.
Born in Burgel, near Offenbach; died 29 March 1867.
Active in Frankfurt am Main.
Painter.
Gustav Schraegle was taught by J. Grunewald, Fr. Keller and G. Igler.
MUSEUMS AND GALLERIES:
FRANKFURT AM MAIN (Städel): several works.

SCHRAG, Julius
German, 19th - 20th century.
Born 27 July 1864, in Nuremberg; died 1948.
Painter, engraver.
Julius Schrag was a pupil of Johann Leonhard Raab, Wilhelm von Diez, W. von Lindenschmit and Heinrich Zugel.

AUCTION RECORDS:
MUNICH, 30 May 1979, *Road in Stralsund* (1919, oil on canvas, 20 x 25 1/4 ins / 51 x 64 cm) DEM 4,800.

SCHRAG, Karl
German, 20th century.
Born 1912, in Karlsruhe; died 1995.
Active in the USA.
Painter, engraver.

Karl Schrag studied painting in Geneva and Paris, where he worked with Roger Bissière. He moved to New York in 1938 and studied engraving at the Art Students' League. He established his reputation as an engraver with S. W. Hayter's *Studio 17*, and became the director of the studio in 1950. He taught at Brooklyn College and the Cooper Union.

He held his first solo exhibition at the Smithsonian Institution. A retrospective exhibition of his work was held by the American Federation of Arts.

Initially focusing on reality in nature, Schrag developed his subjects in the tachiste style. His drawing is both Oriental in its sobriety and Expressionist in its energy. Combined with a vivid palette, his calligraphy reflects a turbulent and optimistic vision of nature.

AUCTION RECORDS:
NEW YORK, 26 June 1985, *Red Sky* (watercolour, pastel and gouache, 26 1/4 x 39 ins / 66.6 x 98.2 cm) USD 1,900.

SCHRAG, Martha
German, 20th century.
Born 29 August 1870, in Borna, near Leipzig.
Painter, engraver.

Martha Schrag was a pupil of Weiszgerber and Adolf Höfer. She lived and worked in Borna.

SCHRAGE, Jakob, or Schragen or Schrager
German, 17th century.
Active in Danzig (now Gdansk, Poland).
Painter.

SCHRAID, Georg Adam
German, 18th century.
Born 1729, in Darmstadt; died September 1786, in Frankfurt am Main.
Painter.

Georg Schraid's master was Joh. Chr. Fiedler. The *Römer* of Frankfurt am Main holds his *Allegory of Spring* (1776).

SCHRAID, Wilhelm
German, 19th century.
Active in Kassel c. 1828.
Painter.

MUSEUMS AND GALLERIES:
KASSEL (Gemäldegal. Alte Meister): several works.

SCHRAM, Alois Hans, or Schramm
Austrian, 19th - 20th century.
Born 20 August 1864, in Vienna; died 8 April 1919, in Vienna.
Painter, sculptor. Historical subjects, figures, nudes, portraits, scenes with figures, genre scenes, local scenes, interiors with figures, landscapes with figures, urban landscapes, waterscapes, seascapes. Wall decorations.

Alois Hans Schram studied at the art academy in Vienna and was awarded a silver medal in Vienna in 1892. He decorated the Fränkel palace with Leopold Burger, and also produced the *Benefits of Peace* on the stairway at the Viennese Parliament, and an *Apotheosis of the House of Habsburg* at the new Hofburg.

MUSEUMS AND GALLERIES:
VIENNA (MM): *Children Paying Homage at the Castle Gate.*

AUCTION RECORDS:
COLOGNE, 25 Nov 1976, *Young Woman in a Feathered Hat* (oil on canvas remounted on board, 21 1/4 x 17 1/4 ins / 54 x 44 cm) DEM 1,700. LONDON, 18 June 1980, *Playing Cards on a Terrace* (1897, oil on canvas, 36 3/4 x 54 1/4 ins / 93.5 x 138 cm) GBP 3,500. VIENNA, 17 Feb 1981, *Chamber Music* (oil on canvas, 39 1/4 x 23 1/2 ins / 100 x 60 cm) ATS 45,000. LONDON, 23 Feb 1983, *Japanese Placing Flowers at the Shrine to the Buddha* (oil on canvas, 33 x 38 3/4 ins / 84 x 98.5 cm) GBP 2,000. LONDON, 20 March 1985, *Beach Scene* (oil on canvas, 17 1/4 x 32 1/4 ins / 44 x 82 cm) GBP 9,200. LONDON, 26 Nov 1986, *Pedlars in Palermo with View of Monte Pellegrino* (1890, oil on canvas, 55 x 43 1/2 ins / 140 x 110.5 cm) GBP 9,000. LONDON, 30 March 1990, *A Difficult Decision* (1893, oil on canvas, 39 1/4 x 39 1/4 ins / 99.6 x 99.6 cm) GBP 14,300. LONDON, 19 June 1991, *Melancholy Moment Beside a Lake* (1904, oil on canvas, 23 1/4 x 15 1/4 ins / 59 x 38.5 cm) GBP 7,700. NEW YORK, 29 Sept 1993, *Nude* (oil on panel, 15 1/4 x 11 1/2 ins / 38.7 x 29.2 cm) USD 2,070. NEW YORK, 23 May 1997, *Dutch Shooting Competition* (1887, oil on canvas, 25 1/4 x 40 ins / 64.1 x 101.6 cm) USD 27,600. LONDON, 11 June 1997, *Rural Scene* (1905, oil on canvas, 42 1/2 x 49 1/4 ins / 108 x 125 cm) GBP 10,120.

SCHRAM, Anton. See **HANNOTIN**

SCHRAM, Georg
German, 18th century.
Born 4 April 1679, in Mährenk; died 13 June 1720, in Regensburg.
Cabinet maker.

Georg Schram did the furnishings in the church of St Paul at Regensburg.

SCHRAM, Gustav
Austrian, 19th century.
Born 1851, in Vienna.
Active in Clausen.
Landscape artist.

SCHRAM, Konrad
Bavarian School, 17th century.
Active c. 1683.
Engraver (wood).

SCHRAMANN, Burkhard, or Schrammann
Austrian, 17th century.
Active in Salzburg 1636-1674.
Painter, draughtsman.

Burkhard Schramann worked mainly for the Benedictine monastery of St Peter.

SCHRAMEK, Anton Nikodemus
Austrian, 18th century.
Active in Polna (Bohemia) c. 1769.
Painter.

SCHRAML, Ignaz, or Schrammel
Austrian, 18th - 19th century.
Born 1762, in Wallern; died 1846, in Wallern.
Sculptor, painter.

SCHRAMM, Alexander
German, 19th century.
Born 1814; died 1864.
Painter. Portraits, genre scenes.

Alexander Schramm worked in Berlin and Stuttgart from 1834 to 1848.

MUSEUMS AND GALLERIES:
ADELAIDE (AG of South Australia): *Scene in Southern Australia* (1850) - BERLIN (Märkisches Mus.): *Musical Company on the Banks of the Spree.*

Auction records:
Paris, 8 Nov 1993, *Woman with Hookah* (oil on canvas, 55 x 32 ins / 140 x 81 cm) FRF 70,000.

SCHRAMM, Carl Christian
German, 18th century.
Engraver (burin) (?), draughtsman.
Carl Schramm was active around 1730 in Dresden.

SCHRAMM, Friedrich
German, 15th - 16th century.
Active in Regensburg 1480-1515.
Sculptor.
Regensburg School.
The facts about Friedrich Schramm and the works attributed to him are matters of considerable dispute.

SCHRAMM, J. Mat.
Austrian, 18th century.
Active c. 1762.
Painter.

SCHRAMM, Johann Michael
German, 18th - 19th century.
Born 8 December 1772, in Sulzbach; died 6 January 1835, in Munich.
Miniaturist, engraver, lithographer.
In 1793 Johann Schramm went to Munich where he produced engravings and miniatures. From 1801 to 1804 he completed his studies at the academy in Vienna and then returned to Munich.

SCHRAMM, Johann or Johannes Heinrich
Austrian, 19th century.
Born 21 May 1810, in Teschen; died 1865, in Vienna.
Painter. Portraits.
Johann Schramm held a doctorate. He did portraits in crayon of *Thorvaldsen, Mendelssohn, Grimm* among others.

SCHRAMM, Jósef
Bohemian School, 18th century.
Born to a family originally from Saaz.
Painter.

SCHRAMM, Lukas von
German, 18th century.
Active in Styria.
Painter.
Lukas Schramm did frescoes in the church of Mariatrost, near Graz.

SCHRAMM, Peter
Dutch.
Active in Amsterdam.
Painter.

SCHRAMM, Viktor
Romanian, 19th - 20th century.
Born 19 May 1865; died 18 November 1929.
Painter, illustrator.
Viktor Schramm studied at the Akademie der Bildenden Künste in Munich. He lived and worked in Poplet, near Orsova, Romania.
Museums and Galleries:
Budapest (Hadtörténeti Múz.): 26 portraits of Hungarian Officer Generals - Vienna (Heeresgeschichtliches Mus.): *Portrait of Pfanzer-Baltin.*
Auction records:
Amsterdam, 28 Feb 1989, *Young Woman Sitting near her Dog in a Middle-Class Interior, Holding Flowers* (oil on canvas, 27 1/4 x 37 ins / 69 x 94 cm) NLG 2,070. New York, 22 May 1991, *Portrait of a Young Girl* (oil on canvas, 48 1/2 x 37 1/4 ins / 123.2 x 94.9 cm) USD 5,500. Paris, 16 Dec 2002, *War Scene Between Turks and Hungarians* (1896, oil on canvas, 64 x 96 ins / 162 x 244 cm) EUR 15,000.

SCHRAMM-ZITTAU, Max Rudolph or Rudolf
German, 20th century.
Born 1 March 1874, in Zittau (Saxony); died November 1950, in Kronstadt near St Petersburg, Russia.
Painter. Waterscapes, animals, farmyard scenes.
Max Rudolph Schramm-Zittau worked in Dresden, Karlsruhe and Munich. His work featured in exhibitions in Paris, and he was awarded a bronze medal at the Exposition Universelle in Paris in 1900.

RUDOLF SCHRAMM-ZITTAU

Museums and Galleries:
Boston: *Farmyard* - Dresden: *Poultry in the Henhouse* - Mainz: *Fishermen* - Munich: *Turkey.*
Auction records:
Vienna, 17 June 1977, *Spring Landscape* (oil on canvas, 23 1/2 x 31 1/2 ins / 60 x 80 cm) ATS 20,000. London, 20 April 1979, *Farmyard* (oil on panel, 6 1/2 x 13 1/2 ins / 16.5 x 34.2 cm) GBP 950. Munich, 4 June 1981, *The Woman Painter* (c. 1900, oil on canvas, 13 1/2 x 23 1/2 ins / 34.5 x 59.5 cm) DEM 5,600. Cologne, 26 Oct 1984, *Street Scene, Dresden* (oil on canvas, 23 1/2 x 31 1/2 ins / 60 x 80 cm) DEM 13,000. London, 27 Feb 1985, *Ducks in an Estuary* (oil on canvas, 10 x 13 1/2 ins / 25.5 x 34 cm) GBP 1,700. Cologne, 15 Oct 1988, *People in the Royal Gardens in Dresden* (oil on canvas, 31 1/2 x 43 1/4 ins / 80 x 110 cm) DEM 7,000. Cologne, 15 June 1989, *Ducks Coming out of the Water* (1943, oil on paper, 5 3/4 x 9 1/2 ins / 14.5 x 24 cm) DEM 1,600. London, 16 Feb 1990, *Ducks on a River* (oil on canvas, 39 1/2 x 24 ins / 100.5 x 61 cm) GBP 3,520. Munich, 1-2 Dec 1992, *Henhouse* (oil on canvas, 23 1/2 x 39 1/4 ins / 60 x 100 cm) DEM 3,450. Munich, 22 June 1993, *Pack in the Kennels* (oil on canvas, 22 3/4 x 31 ins / 58 x 79 cm) DEM 7,475. Amsterdam, 9 Nov 1993, *Ducks near a Pond* (oil on card, 6 3/4 x 10 ins / 17 x 25.5 cm) NLG 1,610. Düsseldorf, 4 March 1999, *Hens* (oil on canvas, 18 x 31 ins / 45 x 79 cm) DEM 3,800. Munich, 30 Nov 1999, *Munich Octoberfest* (oil on canvas, 24 x 31 ins / 60 x 80 cm) DEM 14,000. Düsseldorf, 26 Feb 2000, *City Scene* (oil on canvas) DEM 17,000. Dresden, 17 June 2000, *Ducks in the Sun* (oil on canvas, 14 x 24 ins / 35 x 60 cm) DEM 3,800. Copenhagen, 28 May 2001, *Deer in Forest* (oil on canvas, 45 x 30 ins / 115 x 75 cm) DKK 20,000. Munich, 3 Nov 2001, *Market Square* (oil on canvas, 24 x 31 ins / 60 x 80 cm) EUR 1,740. Switzerland, 31 May 2002, *Sunday Outing in the Park - People Walking in a Landscape* (oil on canvas, 31 x 43 ins / 80 x 110 cm) CHF 8,500. Graz, 5 Dec 2002, *Chinese Tower - Munich* (1933, pastel and chalk, 19 x 23 ins / 47 x 58 cm) EUR 1,600. Bern, 5 Nov 2003, *Fox in Winter* (oil on canvas on panel, 13 x 23 ins / 34 x 59 cm) CHF 3,500. Munich, 3 Dec 2003, *Ducks Swimming in a Pond* (oil on canvas, 14 x 24 ins / 35 x 60 cm) EUR 2,800. Munich, 24 March 2004, *Ehrwald in Tyrol with Zugspitze* (1945, oil on canvas, 28 x 39 ins / 70 x 100 cm) EUR 2,000. Munich, 16 June 2004, *Hens in a Garden* (oil on cardboard, 20 x 28 ins / 50 x 70 cm) EUR 2,800.

SCHRÄMMEL, Erhard, or Schremmel
German, 15th century.
Active in Ingolstadt, and in Nuremberg 1481-1490.
Painter.
Nuremberg School.

SCHRAMMEL, Ignaz. See **SCHRAML**

SCHRANDTER, Johann Paulus
German, 17th century.
Painter.

SCHRANIL, Wenzel or Vaclav
Austrian, 19th century.
Born 1821, in Prague.
Painter. Figures, portraits.

SCHRANK, Franz von Paula
German, 18th - 19th century.
Born 21 August 1747, in Varnbach, near Schärding; died 12 December 1835, in Munich.
Painter, draughtsman. Genre scenes, interiors with figures.

Franz Schrank belonged to the Society of Jesus.

MUSEUMS AND GALLERIES:

COLOGNE (Wallraf-Richartz Mus.): *Interior with Family.*

SCHRANZ, Anton
German, 19th century.
Born 1769; died 1839.
Painter, watercolourist, draughtsman. Seascapes, landscapes.

Like his son Jean, Anton Schranz specialised in landscapes and seascapes, notably of Valetta.

AUCTION RECORDS:

LONDON, 20 Feb 1976, *The Bridge of Malta* (oil on canvas, 14 1/2 x 22 ins / 37 x 56 cm) GBP 480. LONDON, 11 April 1980, *Nelson's Fleet Leaving Malta* (oil on canvas, 21 1/2 x 32 3/4 ins / 54.6 x 83.2 cm) GBP 5,500. LONDON, 26 June 1981, *English Battleships Anchored at Port Mahon, Minorca* (oil on canvas, 15 3/4 x 24 3/4 ins / 40 x 62.8 cm) GBP 3,000. LONDON, 14 March 1984, *Views of the Environs of Port Mahon; Minorca* (c. 1800, oil on canvas, a pair, 18 1/4 x 34 1/2 ins / 46.5 x 87.5 cm) GBP 10,000. LONDON, 20 April 1990, *Port Mahon at Minorca and English Two-decker at Anchor* (oil on canvas, 17 1/2 x 35 3/4 ins / 44.5 x 90.8 cm) GBP 24,200. LONDON, 30 May 1990, *The Port of Valetta in Malta* (oil on canvas, 11 x 18 ins / 28 x 46 cm) GBP 8,250. LONDON, 10 April 1991, *The Seringapatam at Anchor in the Port of Valetta in Malta* (oil on canvas, 13 1/2 x 20 3/4 ins / 34 x 53 cm) GBP 13,750. LONDON, 8 April 1992, *Entry of the Vessel Hastings with Queen Douairière Adélaïde on Board in the Port of Valetta in 1838* (oil on canvas, 22 3/4 x 33 ins / 58 x 84 cm) GBP 28,600. LONDON, 9 Nov 1994, *View of Port Mahon, Minorca* (oil on canvas, 19 1/4 x 58 1/4 ins / 49 x 148 cm) GBP 10,925. VIENNA, 29 April 1999, *Minerva Temple* (watercolour over pencil, three works, 16 x 22 ins / 40 x 56 cm) ATS 30,000. LONDON, 13 May 1999, *Royal Navy First Rate Entering Harbour at Port Mahon, Minorca* (oil on canvas, 16 x 25 ins / 41 x 63 cm) GBP 17,000. LONDON, 16 June 2000, *HMS Caledonia Clearing Port Mahon. View of Port Mahon with Naval Shipping* (oil on canvas, a pair, 15 x 24 ins / 39 x 60 cm) GBP 21,000. LONDON, 30 Nov 2000, *View of the Grand Harbour at Valetta* (oil on canvas, 27 x 41 ins / 68 x 103 cm) GBP 40,000. PARIS, 3 June 2004, *Greek Subjects* (watercolour and crayon, ten works, 10 x 7 ins / 25 x 18 cm) EUR 4,500.

SCHRANZ, Jean or Giovanni or Johann or John
German, 19th century.
Born 1794, in Minorca; died 1882, in Malta.
Painter, watercolourist, draughtsman. Seascapes, landscapes.

With his father Anton, Jean Schranz specialised in landscapes and seascapes.

AUCTION RECORDS:

LONDON, 23 March 1976, *View of the Port of Malta* (watercolour and pencil, 14 3/4 x 21 1/4 ins / 37.6 x 53.7 cm) GBP 220. LONDON, 13 March 1980, *View of Corfu* (watercolour and pencil, 14 1/4 x 12 1/2 ins / 36.3 x 31.7 cm) GBP 600. LONDON, 17 March 1982, *Frigate Entering the Port of Valetta, Malta* (oil on canvas, 22 x 37 1/4 ins / 56 x 94.5 cm) GBP 1,700. LONDON, 11 July 1984, *Arrival of Queen Adélaïde in Malta in 1838* (oil on canvas, 22 x 32 3/4 ins / 56 x 83 cm) GBP 8,500. LONDON, 4 Nov 1987, *View of Valetta* (after 1839, watercolour/pencil outlines, 11 1/2 x 16 1/4 ins / 29.5 x 41 cm) GBP 1,700. LONDON, 24 June 1988, *Southern View of Corfu* (watercolour, 10 1/4 x 18 1/4 ins / 26 x 46.4 cm) GBP 3,520. LONDON, 17 Nov 1989, *Frigate Entering the Port of Valetta, Malta* (oil on canvas, 16 3/4 x 25 1/2 ins / 42.7 x 64.8 cm) GBP 15,400. LONDON, 9 Feb 1990, *Frigate Entering the Port of Valetta with Fishermen in Foreground* (oil on canvas, 9 x 12 3/4 ins / 23 x 32.2 cm) GBP 3,300. LONDON, 14 March 1990, *Warship Entering Port of Valetta* (1866, oil on canvas, 17 x 26 3/4 ins / 43 x 68 cm) GBP 15,400. LONDON, 30 March 1990, *Corfu* (pencil and watercolour, 7 1/2 x 10 1/2 ins / 19.1 x 26.7 cm) GBP 2,200. LONDON, 4 Oct 1991, *Bay of Galitsa towards Palaion Frourion in Corfu* (watercolour/paper, 5 x 7 3/4 ins / 12.8 x 19.6 cm) GBP 1,430. LONDON, 22 Nov 1991, *English Warship and other Boats Caught in Wind off Valetta, Malta* (1866, oil on canvas, 17 1/4 x 28 ins / 43.7 x 71.1 cm) GBP 19,800. LONDON, 18 June 1993, *Citadel at Corfu* (watercolour/paper, 7 1/2 x 13 1/2 ins / 19 x 34.3 cm) GBP 1,495. LONDON, 13 July 1994, *Frigate and other Boats in the Port of Valetta* (oil on canvas, a pair, each 15 1/4 x 24 ins / 39 x 61 cm) GBP 35,600. PARIS, 11 April 1995, *English Warships in the Port of Valetta* (oil on canvas, 17 3/4 x 26 1/2 ins / 45 x 67.5 cm) FRF 95,000. LONDON, 15 March 1996, *Three-masted Ship in the Port of Valetta, Malta* (oil on canvas, 18 1/4 x 28 1/4 ins / 46.5 x 71.7 cm) GBP 26,450. LONDON, 30 May 1996, *The Port of Valetta in Malta and Warship Flying British Flag* (oil on canvas, 15 1/4 x 23 1/4 ins / 39 x 59 cm) GBP 19,550. LONDON, 26 March 1997, *English Fleet in the Port of Valetta, Malta* (oil on canvas, 18 x 28 1/4 ins / 46 x 72 cm) GBP 24,150.

SCHRANZ, Josef
Austrian, 18th century.
Draughtsman, watercolourist.
Orientalism.

Josef Schranz was active in St Johann de Pongau, near Salzburg.

AUCTION RECORDS:

LONDON, 20 June 1985, *View of the Bay of Corsica* (watercolour and pencil, 11 1/4 x 17 1/4 ins / 28.5 x 44 cm) GBP 1,200. LONDON, 27 Nov 1986, *The Golden Horn, Constantinople* (watercolour and pen, 13 3/4 x 24 1/2 ins / 35 x 62.5 cm) GBP 5,500. LONDON, 27 Nov 1987, *Views of Corsica* (watercolour and pencil, a pair, 7 x 10 1/2 ins / 17.7 x 26.6 cm) GBP 2,200. MUNICH, 30 Nov 1999, *Southern Lake Landscape* (watercolour over pencil, 7 x 9 ins / 17 x 22 cm) DEM 3,400. LONDON, 15 Oct 2002, *Golden Horn, Constantinople* (watercolour over pencil, 15 x 21 ins / 37 x 54 cm) GBP 3,000. LONDON, 15 Oct 2002, *View of Zante* (pen, ink, watercolour over pencil, 10 x 16 ins / 25 x 41 cm) GBP 3,000.

SCHRANZHOFER, Josef Anton
Austrian, 18th century.
Born in the Tyrol, to parents from Innicheu; died c. 1770.
Sculptor.

SCHRATT, Ferdinand
German, 18th century.
Sculptor.

Ferdinand Schratt sculpted the statues of *Jupiter* and *Mercury* for the fountain in Constance.

SCHRATTENBACH, Ludwig, the Elder
Austrian, 19th century.
Active in Vienna 1820-1832.
Painter. Animals.

SCHRATTENBACH, Ludwig, the Younger
Austrian, 19th century.
Born 1821; died 21 November 1845.
Painter. Landscapes with figures, waterscapes.

Ludwig Schrattenbach was active in Vienna.

AUCTION RECORDS:

VIENNA, 10 Feb 1976, *Resting by Riverside* (1844, oil on canvas, 20 3/4 x 26 ins / 53 x 66 cm) ATS 10,000.

SCHRATTENBACH, Max
Austrian, 19th century.

Active in Vienna c. 1848.
Landscape artist.

SCHRATZENSTALLER, Georg Jacob, or Schrazenstaller
German, 18th century.
Born 8 July 1767, in Nuremberg; died 6 November 1795, in Nuremberg.
Watercolourist, engraver (burin).
Georg Schratzenstaller was taught by J.G. Sturm and J.E. Ihle.

SCHRAUDOLPH, Claudius von, the Elder
German, 19th century.
Born 1813, in Oberstdorf; died 13 November 1891, in Oberstdorf.
Painter, draughtsman, lithographer. Historical subjects. Frescoes.
The younger brother of Johann von Schraudolph, Claudius von Schraudolph attended the academy in Munich. He visited Europe and Greece as well as studying the art of fresco painting in Italy. Examples of his frescoes are in the Benedictine convent in Deggendorf, Bavaria.

SCHRAUDOLPH, Claudius von, the Younger
German, 19th century.
Born 4 February 1843, in Munich; died 1891, in Stuttgart.
Painter, illustrator. History painting, genre scenes.
The pupil of his father Johann von Schraudolph, Claudius von Schraudolph studied under Anschutz and Hiltensperger at the academy in Munich. He visited Italy and France and became director of the arts academy in Stuttgart. In 1884 he painted frescoes for the Nuremberg exhibition.
MUSEUMS AND GALLERIES:
MUNICH (Stadtmus.): several watercolours.

SCHRAUDOLPH, Johann von
German, 19th century.
Born 13 June 1808, in Oberstdorf; died 31 May 1879, in Munich.
Painter, engraver. History painting.
Johann von Schraudolph studied under Schotthauer and Cornelius at the academy in Munich where he taught on his return from Rome. His decoration of the cathedral at Spire is considered to be his best work.
MUSEUMS AND GALLERIES:
BASEL: *Annunciation; Two Angels Hovering Aloft* - MUNICH: *The Virgin, Christ and St John; St Agnes; Christ Healing the Sick; St Peter Casting his Net; The Virgin, Mary Magdalene and St John at Golgotha; St Agnes* (two paintings); *The Virgin and Christ Child; The Ascension of Christ.*
AUCTION RECORDS:
BERN, 4 May 1985, *Nativity* (oil on card, 8¾ x 11 ins / 22.5 x 28 cm) CHF 7,000. MUNICH, 27 Feb 1999, *Christ and Mary Magdalene* (1860, oil on canvas, 16 x 13 ins / 41 x 33 cm) DEM 4,300. COPENHAGEN, 30 Nov 1999, *Mary's Coronation in Heaven* (1862, oil on canvas, 47 x 28 ins / 120 x 72 cm) DKK 26,000.

SCHRAUDOLPH, Matthias
German, 19th century.
Born 24 February 1817, in Oberstdorf; died 17 January 1863, in Metten.
Painter. History painting.
The pupil of his brother Johann, Mathias Schraudolph entered the Benedictine monastery in Metten.
MUSEUMS AND GALLERIES:
METTEN (Abbey church): *The Way of the Cross* (with fourteen stations).

SCHRAUDOLPH, Robert
German, 20th century.
Born 1 August 1887, in Sonthofen.
Painter. Figures, portraits, landscapes.
Robert Schraudolph was a pupil of Gabriel von Hackl and Carl von Marr.

SCHRAUTH, Johannes
German, 18th century.
Sculptor (wood).

SCHRAYHAUEN
German, 18th century.
Born to a family originally from Leipzig.
Painter.
MUSEUMS AND GALLERIES:
ARNSTADT (Schlossmus.): *Still-life.*

SCHRAZENSTALLER, Georg Jacob. See **SCHRATZENSTALLER**

SCHRECK, Carl Friedrich
German, 19th century.
Active in Berlin.
Painter. Genre scenes, portraits.
Carl Schreck studied under W. Hensel in 1836.

SCHRECK, Joseph von
German, 18th century.
Active in Laufen.
Painter.
The Germanisches Nationalmuseum at Nuremberg has a portrait of *Joh. Martin L. B. v. Voelderndorff* by Joseph Schreck.

SCHRECK, Konrad or Kurt
German, 16th century.
Died 1580, in Berlin.
Active in Berlin.
Painter, goldsmith, medallist.
Konrad Schreck worked for Prince Elector Joachim II.

SCHRECK, Michael. See **SCHRÖCK**

SCHRECKENFUCHS, Wolfgang
Austrian, 16th century.
Born to a family originally from Salzburg; died 1603, in Willenberg.
Engraver, sculptor. Portraits.
Wolfgang Schreckenfuchs worked for the Saxon castles of Annaburg, Torgau and Grimma.

SCHREDER, Marianne
Austrian, 20th century.
Born 27 May 1871, in Baden, near Vienna.
Painter, engraver.

SCHREFL, Anna Edle von
Austrian, 18th century.
Born 1768.
Active in Ofen.
Engraver (burin).
Anna von Schrefl was the pupil of J. Schmutzer.

SCHREGARDUS, Adrianus
Dutch, 18th century.
Born to a family originally from Amsterdam.
Active in Naarden in 1776.
Painter, engraver (etching?). Portraits.
Adrianus Schregardus was a pupil of J.M. Quinckhard in The Hague in 1767.

SCHREGEL, Bernard or Bernardus Petrus
Dutch, 20th century.
Born 17 May 1870, in The Hague; died 1956.
Painter. Landscapes.
Bernard Schregel trained under F. Jansen and Jan Vrolijk. Several of his paintings are owned by Beatrix, Queen of the Netherlands.

MUSEUMS AND GALLERIES:
THE HAGUE (Mus. Mesdag).
AUCTION RECORDS:
AMSTERDAM, 30 Aug 1988, *Peasant with a Loaded Wheelbarrow next to a Barn* (oil on canvas, 39 1/4 x 23 1/2 ins / 100 x 60 cm) NLG 2,070. AMSTERDAM, 5 June 1990, *Clogs in front of the Farmhouse Door* (oil on canvas, 17 3/4 x 23 1/2 ins / 45 x 60 cm) NLG 1,265. AMSTERDAM, 11 Sept 1990, *A Goat in a Farmyard in Summer* (oil on canvas, 27 x 20 ins / 68.5 x 51 cm) NLG 1,150. AMSTERDAM, 3 Nov 1992, *Peasant and his Cows in a Polder* (oil on canvas, 8 3/4 x 13 1/2 ins / 22.5 x 34 cm) NLG 2,070. AMSTERDAM, 20 April 1993, *Woman and Child on a Path* (oil on card, 7 1/2 x 11 ins / 19 x 28 cm) NLG 1,150.

SCHREGEN, Hans
German, 15th century.
Active in Ulm c. 1498.
Glass painter.

SCHREIB, Werner
German, 20th century.
Born 1925, in Berlin; died 1969.
Engraver, painter.

Werner Schreib trained at various schools of industrial arts and crafts, and later under S. W. Hayter at his *Atelier 17* in Paris.

In 1959 he won first prize at the International Exhibition of Graphic Art at the first Paris Biennale des Jeunes (Biennale Exhibition of Young Artists), and that same year took part in Documenta II in Kassel. In 1960 his work featured in the Biennale Exhibition in Venice and the Second International Biennale Exhibition of Graphic Art in Tokyo. He also held several solo exhibitions.

His descriptive style of drawing, reminiscent of Wols, was minutely detailed, bordering on the obsessive. He simplified reality into a system of signs, coining the semantic term 'natural signs'. He adhered to visual and graphic theories similar to those of the Italian Luciano Lattanzi, with whom he exhibited from 1960. He made his name with his *Macabre Drawings of the Astonishing Mr Schreib* in 1958.
AUCTION RECORDS:
ZURICH, 18 Nov 1976, *Astronautic Landscape III* (mixed media/hardboard, 29 1/2 x 35 1/2 ins / 75 x 90 cm) CHF 4,400.

SCHREIBER
Swiss, 17th century.
Born in Hochdorf (Lucerne).
Active at the end of the 17th century.
Sculptor (ivory), engraver (copper).

Schreiber was active in Lucerne from 1690 to 1700. He was the uncle and teacher of Jak. Frey the Elder.

SCHREIBER, family of artists
German, 17th - 18th century.
Painters (glazed earthenware).

The Schreiber family lived and worked in Hanau. Worthy of mention are the following: Johann Heinrich, who died on 22 April 1727 at the age of 74, Jesaias, who was active 1702-1732, and Johann Nikolaus, active 1704-1724.

SCHREIBER
German, 18th century.
Painter. Genre scenes, landscapes.

Schreiber was the pupil of JS Beck in Erfurt.

SCHREIBER, Alfred
Austrian, 19th century.
Born in Vienna.
Sculptor.

From 1853 to 1854, Alfred Schreiber attended the academy in Vienna, where he exhibited in 1860 and 1861.

SCHREIBER, C.
German, 19th century.
Active c. 1820.
Lithographer.

SCHREIBER, Charles Baptiste
French, 19th century.
Born in Paris; died 1903.
Painter. Figures, portraits, genre scenes, interiors.

He was a pupil of Bonnat and Brandon. He first exhibited at the Paris Salon in 1868, and was accorded an honourable mention there in 1901.
MUSEUMS AND GALLERIES:
RHEIMS: *Young Italian Woman Knitting.*
AUCTION RECORDS:
PARIS, 14-15 May 1902, *Cardinal,* FRF 240. NEW YORK, 18-20 April 1906, *Dominicans,* USD 215. NEW YORK, 21-22 Jan 1909, *Music Lesson,* USD 185. LONDON, 2 April 1910, *Rehearsal,* GBP 17. LONDON, 18 Feb 1911, *Parrot; Violinist,* GBP 38. PARIS, 17-19 Nov 1919, *Abbot Playing the Violin,* FRF 400. LONDON, 12 May 1922, *Nice Medicine,* GBP 38; *An Important Letter,* GBP 45. PARIS, 7 March 1924, *Monk Reading,* FRF 680. LONDON, 14 Nov 1924, *Game of Chess,* GBP 48. PARIS, 6 May 1925, *Little Italian Girl with a Jug,* FRF 300. PARIS, Oct 1945-July 1946, *Hand of Cards,* FRF 8,000. PARIS, 7 Nov 1946, *Italian Spinner* (1876) FRF 4,300. PARIS, 25 Oct 1948, *Odalisque,* FRF 1,900. PARIS, 17 Oct 1949, *Interior,* FRF 600. PARIS, 1 June 1950, *Wool Carders* (1875) FRF 9,000. LONDON, 12 Feb 1969, *The Pose,* GBP 780. LONDON, 24 Nov 1976, *Abbé à son chevalet* (oil on panel, 9 x 6 1/2 ins / 22 x 16.5 cm) GBP 800. LONDON, 20 April 1978, *Duet* (oil on canvas, 14 1/2 x 17 3/4 ins / 37 x 45 cm) GBP 1,300. PARIS, 27 June 1979, *Draughts Players in Algiers* (1884, oil on canvas, 19 3/4 x 25 1/2 ins / 50 x 65 cm) FRF 10,000. LOS ANGELES, 22 June 1981, *Young Girl at a Fountain* (oil on panel, 11 x 7 ins / 28 x 17.5 cm) USD 1,800. VIENNA, 14 Sept 1983, *Curate and His Dog* (oil on panel, 9 x 6 3/4 ins / 23 x 17 cm) ATS 45,000. NEW YORK, 30 Oct 1985, *Young Musician; Young Seamstress* (oil on panel, a pair, 5 3/4 x 3 1/2 ins / 14.6 x 8.9 cm) USD 2,000. NEW YORK, 17 Jan 1990, *Vegetable Market in Rome* (1874, oil on canvas, 32 1/4 x 39 1/2 ins / 82 x 100.4 cm) USD 8,800. PARIS, 12 Oct 1990, *Interior Scene: by the Hearth* (oil on canvas, 13 3/4 x 11 ins / 35 x 27 cm) FRF 35,000. AMSTERDAM, 24 April 1991, *International Affairs* (oil on panel, 8 1/2 x 6 1/4 ins / 21.5 x 16 cm) NLG 3,450. LONDON, 7 April 1993, *Priest Smoking His Pipe* (oil on panel, 9 x 6 3/4 ins / 23 x 17 cm) GBP 977. RHEIMS, 19 Dec 1993, *Portrait of a Young Woman with a Fan* (oil on panel, 9 1/2 x 7 1/4 ins / 24 x 18.5 cm) FRF 8,000. NEW YORK, 19 Jan 1995, *Young Girl at a Fountain* (oil on panel, 10 3/4 x 7 ins / 27.3 x 17.8 cm) USD 4,887.

SCHREIBER, Christian
German, 17th century.
Painter.

Christian Schreiber was the pupil of Georg Christoph the Elder in Regensburg.

SCHREIBER, Conrad Peter
German, 19th century.
Born 11 August 1816, in Fürth; died 19 February 1894, in Nuremberg.
Painter, engraver. Landscapes.

After studying under Schirmer in Berlin, Conrad Schreiber completed his artistic training in Munich and Italy.
AUCTION RECORDS:
ZURICH, 25 Nov 1977, *View of Capri* (oil on canvas, 25 1/2 x 56 3/4 ins / 65 x 144 cm) CHF 4,500. ZURICH, 8 Nov 1980, *Italian Landscape* (1841, gouache, 17 3/4 x 23 1/4 ins / 45 x 59 cm) CHF 1,800. LONDON, 19 June 1992, *Lake Averno and Vesuvius* (1856, oil on canvas/card, 16 x 20 1/2 ins / 40.7 x 52.1 cm) GBP 3,850. NUREMBERG, 16 Sept 1999, *Italian Fantasy Landscape* (works on paper, 23 x 19 ins / 58 x 47 cm) DEM 5,000. NUREMBERG, 16 Sept 1999, *Italian Coastal Landscape with*

Figures and Architecture (gouache, 22 x 18 ins / 57 x 46 cm) DEM 5,000. MUNICH, 27 June 2003, *Naples* (gouache on board, 23 x 20 ins / 58 x 50 cm) EUR 2,200. AMSTERDAM, 1 July 2003, *Mediterranean Landscape with Travellers on a Patch* (1847, oil on canvas, 30 x 23 ins / 76 x 58 cm) EUR 2,000.

SCHREIBER, Friedrich
Romanian, 20th century.
Born 26 January 1936, in Brasov.
Active since 1980 in Germany.
Painter. Scenes with figures. Murals, stage sets.

Friedrich Schreiber was a student at the N. Grigorescu Art Institute in Bucharest, where he specialised in monumental painting. From 1963 to 1978, he was professor of drawing at the University of Timisoara. From 1980, he lived and worked in Regensburg. Using symbolic images with Surrealist associations, Schreiber generally produced large-scale works that probe the human condition and the place of man in the universe. He places scenes in desolate architectural landscapes, generally painted in a uniform manner in dark colours, with an occasional flash of light illuminating the darkness; they include *The Ship of Fools* and *The Inhabitants of the Earth*.

In 1971, he won the painting prize awarded by the State Committee for Culture and the Arts in Romania. Work by him was shown at group exhibitions in Europe, as well as in solo exhibitions, at Timisoara (from 1968 to 1975); Resita (1977); at the Ostdeutsche Galerie, Regensburg (1986). He painted figurative compositions at the 1 May Station in Timisoara (1966), and at the Cultural Centre in San Nicolaul Mare (1971).

BIBLIOGRAPHY:
Ionel Jianou, *Romanian Artists and the West*, American Romanian Academy of Arts and Sciences, Los Angeles, 1986.

SCHREIBER, Friedrich Gottlob
German, 19th century.
Born 19 March 1809, in Mittweida; died 21 July 1888, in Chemnitz.
Painter. Genre scenes, portraits, landscapes, flowers.

Friedrich Schreiber studied at the academy in Dresden from 1841-1844.

MUSEUMS AND GALLERIES:
CHEMNITZ (Kunstsammlungen): *Portrait of the Rector Pomsel; Portrait of Unknown Man* - CHEMNITZ (Rathaus): *Portrait of the Burgomaster Christian Friedr. Wehner; Portrait of Johann Friedrich Muller; Portrait of the Chairman of the Town Council Ang. Rewitzer.*

SCHREIBER, Friedrich Julius
German, 19th century.
Born 9 April 1837, in Mittweida; died 11 May 1890, in Chemnitz.
Painter.

The pupil of his uncle Friedrich Gottlob, Friedrich Schreiber also attended the academy in Dresden from 1852 to 1858. He was influenced by L. Richter.

SCHREIBER, Gabriel
German, 16th century.
Active in Lauda-Königshofen.
Sculptor. Portraits.

SCHREIBER, Georges
Belgian, 20th century.
Born 1904, in Brussels; died 1977.
Active in the USA.
Painter. Portraits, genre scenes, landscapes with figures, seascapes.

Georges Schreiber studied at the school of industrial arts and crafts in Erbelfeld in Germany. He later settled in the USA.

He exhibited at the Salon des Indépendants in Paris, and later in the USA at the Carnegie Foundation in Pittsburgh.

He painted with a vigorous, energetic technique reminiscent of Expressionism, translating the forces of nature into symbols.

AUCTION RECORDS:
NEW YORK, 20 April 1944, *Return to the House*, USD 850. PARIS, 17-18 Jan 1945, *End of the Day* (drawing) USD 1,300. PARIS, 12 Dec 1974, *Circus*, USD 1,300. LOS ANGELES, 15 Oct 1979, *Traffic Jam at the Theatre* (1945, watercolour, 22 x 29 3/4 ins / 56 x 75.5 cm) USD 1,700. NEW YORK, 18 Dec 1991, *Landscape with a Village* (1928, oil on canvas, 25 3/4 x 31 ins / 65.4 x 78.7 cm) USD 1,980. NEW YORK, 31 March 1994, *Portrait of Tom Benton* (1945, oil on canvas, 24 1/2 x 30 ins / 62.2 x 76.2 cm) USD 11,500. NEW YORK, 30 Sept 1997, *Boy in a Field of Maize* (1942, gouache and watercolour/card, 13 x 17 1/2 ins / 32.1 x 44.5 cm) USD 3,162.

SCHREIBER, Georges L.
French, 19th - 20th century.
Born 1866; died 1943.
Also active in the USA.
Painter. Genre scenes, landscapes.

Georges L. Schreiber is best known in the USA, where he lived for a long period.

AUCTION RECORDS:
VIENNA, 17 March 1981, *Resting by a Roadside* (1891, oil on canvas, 25 1/4 x 36 ins / 64 x 90.5 cm) ATS 28,000. NEW YORK, 15 June 1984, *Still-life with Self-portrait* (1944, oil on canvas, 19 3/4 x 24 1/2 ins / 50.4 x 62.3 cm) USD 2,300. NEW YORK, 30 Sept 1988, *Sheltering from Bombardment* (1942, oil on canvas, 28 x 33 ins / 71.1 x 83.8 cm) USD 6,600.

SCHREIBER, Grégoire
Ukrainian, 20th century.
Born 1 June 1889, in Odessa; died 26 January 1953, in Paris.
Active from 1922 then naturalised in France.
Painter, watercolourist.

Grégoire Schreiber studied watercolour painting with Michel Papiche, and produced solely watercolours from that point on. He mainly painted landscapes of the Île-de-France with great sensitivity. Work by him was shown at the Salon d'Automne, the Salon de l'École Française, and the Salon d'Hiver.

SCHREIBER, Guido
German, 19th century.
Born in Bad Dürrheim (Black Forest); died 13 May 1886.
Active in Villingen.
Painter, illustrator.

Guido Schreiber was self-taught.

MUSEUMS AND GALLERIES:
DONAUESCHINGEN (Fürstlich Fürstenbergisches Sammlungen): two paintings.

SCHREIBER, Gustav Adolf
German, 20th century.
Born 25 January 1889, in Bremen.
Painter.

Gustav Adolf Schreiber attended the art academy in Dresden.

SCHREIBER, Hans
German, 19th - 20th century.
Born 20 April 1860, in Filehne.
Stained glass painter.

Hans Schreiber lived and worked in Berlin.

SCHREIBER, Hans
German, 20th century.
Born 28 August 1894, in Hanau (Hesse).
Draughtsman.

Hans Schreiber lived and worked in Wuppertal-Eberfeld.

SCHREIBER, Hans Georgi
Swiss, 18th century.
Active c. 1777.
Painter.

SCHREIBER, Hans Sebastian. See **RAMMINGER**

SCHREIBER, Henning
German, 17th century.
Died 13 October 1640, in Clausthal.
Medallist.

SCHREIBER, Hermann
German, 19th - 20th century.
Born 13 May 1864, in Wald, near Solingen (Ruhr).
Painter. Landscapes.
Hermann Schreiber was a pupil of Eugen Bracht.

SCHREIBER, Joachim
German, 17th century.
Painter.

SCHREIBER, Johann Georg
German, 18th century.
Born 1676, in Spremberg; died 31 July 1750, in Leipzig.
Engraver (burin). Urban views.
MUSEUMS AND GALLERIES:
LEIPZIG (Stadtgeschichtliches Mus.): *Views of Leipzig* (several engravings); *Cards* (several engravings).

SCHREIBER, Johann Heinrich, Jesaias and Johann Nikolaus. See the entry **SCHREIBER**, family of artists

SCHREIBER, Johann Leonhard
German, 18th century.
Stucco artist.
In 1735 Johann Schreiber worked in the castle at Blankenburg in the Harz and in 1749 at the church of St James in Nordhausen.

SCHREIBER, Johann von, or Schreibern
German, 18th - 19th century.
Born at the end of the 18th century, in Villach.
Painter.
Johann von Schreiber was a landscape artist and also painted stage-sets.
MUSEUMS AND GALLERIES:
KLAGENFURT (Church of St-Egyde): *Coronation of the Virgin*.

SCHREIBER, Johannes
German, 17th century.
Active in Freising and then in Munich from 1661.
Painter. History painting, portraits.
MUSEUMS AND GALLERIES:
MUNICH (Stadtmus.): *Bishop Albert Sigismund von Freising* (portrait).

SCHREIBER, Johannes
German, 18th - 19th century.
Born 4 July 1755, in Ulm; died 17 December 1827, in Ulm.
Painter, lithographer. Portraits, landscapes.
MUSEUMS AND GALLERIES:
GEISLINGEN (Church): *Portrait of Luther* - ULM (Ulmer Mus.): *Self-portrait; Portrait of the Artist's Wife; Portrait of the Artist's Daughter.*

SCHREIBER, Joseph
German, 17th century.
Born to a family originally from Augsburg.
Active in Bruck (Bavaria) c. 1600.
Painter.

SCHREIBER, Kirstan
German, 15th century.
Died before 9 July 1420, in Danzig (now Gdansk, Poland).
Active in Danzig.
Painter.

SCHREIBER, Lorenz
Swiss, 17th century.
Born to a family originally from Basel.
Cabinet maker, sculptor.
Lorenz Schreiber was a citizen of Schaffhausen in about 1650 and was responsible for the main door of the old guilds' house in Schaffhausen.

SCHREIBER, Matthias
German, 17th century.
Active in Weilheim.
Painter.

SCHREIBER, Michael
German, 20th - 21st century.
Born 1949, in Bremen.
Also active in Italy.
Painter (mixed media), collage artist.
Michael Schreiber trained in Bielefeld and Berlin between 1971 and 1981. He lives and works in Berlin and Italy. He integrates Abstract and Matterist elements on a figurative background. He had solo shows at the Galerie Kurze, Gütersloh (1977, 1979, 1981, 1982, 1984, 1986, 1988), at the Weniger Gallery, Boston and Providence (1987), at Galerie Götz, Stuttgart (1989, 1990), at the Emslandmuseum (1990), at Villa Openheim, Berlin (1992) and at the Galerie Amiot, Paris (1993).

SCHREIBER, Moritz
German, 16th century.
Born to a family originally from Leipzig; died 1556, in Leipzig.
Painter.
Leipzig School.
In collaboration with Heinrich Schmidt, Moritz Schreiber worked for the town of Leipzig from 1539 to 1556. It would seem from the archives that Schreiber played the senior role in this partnership.

SCHREIBER, Otto Andreas
German, 20th century.
Born 30 November 1907, in Deutsch Cekzin (Prussia).
Painter, engraver.
Otto Andreas Schreiber studied at the art academy in Breslau (now Wroclaw, Poland), the industrial school in Düsseldorf and the art academy in Königsberg (now Kaliningrad, Russia). He lived and worked in Berlin.

He was influenced by Munch and Nolde. His works are now owned by the artistic associations of Kaliningrad and Berlin, and by the town of Hanover.

SCHREIBER, Paul
Austrian, 19th century.
Active in Vienna.
Engraver (stone).
MUSEUMS AND GALLERIES:
VIENNA (Kunsthistorisches Mus.): *Portrait of Emperor Franz Josef I as Young Man*.

SCHREIBER, Pius
Austrian, 19th century.
Born 1814, in Vienna.
Engraver.
Pius Schreiber attended the academy from 1830 and exhibited from 1836 to 1837.

SCHREIBER, Richard
German, 20th century.
Born 1904, in Hindenburg (Upper Silesia).
Watercolourist. Figures.

Richard Schreiber trained in Berlin from 1924, and later in Paris under Othon Friesz from 1928 to 1932. He lived and worked in Düsseldorf from 1933. He exhibited in Germany and abroad, notably at the 1962 exhibition *Artists of Düsseldorf* at the art museum in Ostend.

A skilled draughtsman, he portrayed people in watercolour in a stylised manner.

SCHREIBER, Vasili Pavlovich, or Shreiber
Russian, 19th century.
Born 1850.
Painter, decorative artist.
Vasili Pavlovich Schreiber studied at the art academy in St Petersburg. In 1888, he became a teacher of porcelain painting at the school of painting in St Petersburg.

SCHREIBER, Wentzeslaus
German, 17th century.
Painter.
Wentzeslaus Schreiber was a porcelain decorator at the factory in Hanau from 1684 to 1690.

SCHREIBER, Werner, or Schriewer
German, 18th century.
Born after 1711.
Active in Bremen.
Sculptor.

SCHREIBER DE GRAHL, Hannah
German, 19th - 20th century.
Born 23 April 1864, in Wulfsdorf (Schleswig-Holstein).
Painter. Landscapes, flowers.
A pupil of Karl Hagemeister, Hannah Schreiber de Grahl lived and worked in Potsdam.
MUSEUMS AND GALLERIES:
POTSDAM: two works.

SCHREIDER, Egor Egorovitch, or Shreider
Russian, 19th century.
Born 1844.
Painter. Landscapes.
Egor Egorovitch Schreider studied at the art academy in St Petersburg. He continued his studies in Düsseldorf and Paris, where he studied under Corot. He was the director of a school of painting in Kharkov in the Ukraine.

SCHREIER, David. See **SCHREYER**

SCHREIER, Ulrich
Austrian, 15th century.
Born c. 1430; died c. 1490.
Miniaturist.
Salzburg School.
Ulrich Schreier worked from 1469 for Archbishop Bernhard von Rorh in Salzburg. He illustrated the bible written by Erasmus Stratter in 1469 and a Vulgate (Latin bible) in 1472. The art of engraving clearly had a decisive influence on his miniatures.

SCHREINER, Carl
German, 19th century.
Born to a family originally from Dresden.
Painter.
In 1824 Carl Schreiner taught at the porcelain factory in Meissen.

SCHREINER, Carl Moritz
German, 20th century.
Born 17 October 1889, in Barmen.
Sculptor.
A self-taught sculptor, Carl Moritz Schreiner lived and worked in Düsseldorf. The memorial to *Theodor Körner* in Barmen and a lion in the stadium in Düsseldorf are both his work.
MUSEUMS AND GALLERIES:
DÜSSELDORF: *Cat* (marble) - ELBERFELD: *Cat* (bronze).

SCHREINER, Eduard
German, 19th century.
Active in Munich.
Draughtsman.
Eduard Schreiner was the son of Johann Georg.

SCHREINER, Friedrich Wilhelm
German, 19th century.
Born 1836, in Cologne.
Active in Düsseldorf.
Landscape artist.
Friedrich Schreiner was a pupil of J.W. Lindlar.

SCHREINER, Georg
German, 16th - 17th century.
Active in Nördlingen at the end of the 16th and the beginning of the 17th century.
Sculptor.

SCHREINER, Georg
German, 20th century.
Born 1871, in Regensburg.
Sculptor.
Georg Schreiner was a pupil of Wilhelm von Rumann. He lived and worked in Munich and sculpted many altar figures for local churches.

SCHREINER, Johann Baptist
German, 19th - 20th century.
Born 19 December 1866, in Munich.
Sculptor, medallist.
Johann Baptist Schreiner trained under Wilhelm von Rumann. He lived in Cologne from 1894.

He sculpted figures on the tower of the town hall in Cologne, where there is also a memorial erected in memory of the Catholic theologian Adolf Kolping.

SCHREINER, Johann Georg
German, 19th century.
Born 1801, in Mergelstetten; died 1859, in Munich.
Draughtsman, lithographer.
Johann Schreiner drew a portrait of the young poet, Eduard *Mörike* in 1825 and made lithographs of the frescoes of the church of the Holy Trinity in Munich (1837-1841).

SCHREINER, Johann Wilhelm
German, 18th century.
Active in Lauingen.
Painter.

SCHREINER, Joseph
German, 18th century.
Sculptor.

SCHREINZER, Karl August Matveevich
Russian, 19th century.
Born 1819; died 10 May 1887, in St Petersburg.
Miniaturist.

SCHREITER, Benjamin, or Schretter
German, 18th century.
Active in Hengersberg.
Sculptor, stucco artist.
Benjamin Schreiter decorated several Bavarian churches.

SCHREITER, Lorenz
German, 18th century.
Active in Hengersberg.
Stucco artist.

SCHREITMULLER
German, 18th century.
Of Swabian origin.
Painter. Flowers.

Schreitmuller worked at the porcelain factory in the castle of Bruckberg, near Ansbach.

SCHREITMULLER, August
German, 19th - 20th century.
Born 2 October 1871, in Munich.
Sculptor.
The son of artist Johannes Daniel Schreitmuller, August Schreitmuller trained under Eberle and Robert Diez. He lived and worked in Dresden, where he also taught.

He sculpted figures on the town hall in Dresden and the fountain of peace in Mittweida.

MUSEUMS AND GALLERIES:
BAUTZEN - DRESDEN.

SCHREITMULLER, Johannes Daniel
German, 19th century.
Born 23 February 1842, in Bruckberg, near Ansbach; died 30 May 1885, in Genthin.
Sculptor.
The father of August, Johannes Schreitmuller was the pupil of A. Kreling and taught at the art school in Dresden. He worked on the fabric of the academy in Munich.

SCHREITTER, Zacharias
Austrian, 18th - 19th century.
Born 2 August 1737, in Vienna; died 15 October 1821, in Vienna.
Painter. Portraits.
MUSEUMS AND GALLERIES:
MUNICH (Residenzmus.): *Joseph II* (portrait).

SCHREITTER VON SCHWARZENFELD, Adolf, the Younger
Austrian, 20th century.
Born 28 February 1885, at Tuchern Castle, near Cilli.
Painter, engraver.
The son of Adolf Franz Christian Schreitter von Schwarzenfeld, Adolf the Younger lived and worked in Prague.
AUCTION RECORDS:
LONDON, 20 Oct 1978, *Soldier's Sweetheart* (oil on canvas, 28 x 21 ins / 71 x 52.5 cm) GBP 800.

SCHREITTER VON SCHWARZENFELD, Adolf Franz Christian
Austrian, 19th - 20th century.
Born 10 November 1854, in Oberlautensdorf (Bohemia); died c. 1913.
Painter. Portraits, genre scenes.
Adolf Franz Christian Schreitter von Schwarzenfeld began his career as an officer, and later studied under Jakobides and Diez. He worked in Munich, Vienna and Graz.
AUCTION RECORDS:
HANOVER, 29 Sept 1979, *Young Peasant Playing the Trombone* (oil on canvas, 22 x 27 1/4 ins / 55 x 69 cm) DEM 6,500.

SCHREIVOGEL. See **SCHREYVOGEL**

SCHREMMEL, Erhard. See **SCHRÄMMEL**

SCHREMPF, Veit
German, 18th century.
Active in Stuttgart 1744-1773.
Engraver. Armorials, coins.

SCHRENCK, Hermann von
German, 19th century.
Born 20 June 1847, in Tartu; died 7 January 1897, in Bonn.
Engraver. Landscapes.
Hermann von Schrenk was the pupil of Stan. von Kalckreuth.

SCHRENDER, Bernhard
Dutch, 18th century.
Died 13 October 1780, in Hoorn.
Engraver.
Bernhard Schrender was an assistant to Ploos van Amstel.

SCHRENEL. See **SCHREUEL**

SCHRENER, Wilhelm
German, 19th - 20th century.
Born 28 September 1866, in Wesel.
Painter. Genre scenes.
Wilhelm Schrener grew up in Cologne. He studied drawing at the Düsseldorf art academy.

His work featured in exhibitions in Paris, and he received a commendation in 1900 at the Exposition Universelle.

MUSEUMS AND GALLERIES:
COLOGNE: *Cologne Carnival.*

SCHRENK, Jacob
Austrian, 18th - 19th century.
Born 1757; died 22 January 1830, in Vienna.
Engraver (burin).

SCHRETER, Zygmunt, or Schretter, pseudonym of Szreter
Polish, 20th century.
Born 1896, in Lódz; died 1977.
Active from 1933 then in 1960 naturalised in France.
Painter. Portraits, landscapes, seascapes, still-lifes, flowers.
Zygmunt Schreter was on his way to France when the war caught up with him in Berlin where he remained for a while. He was a student of Corinth, whose influence on his work was definitive. After moving on to Paris, he was associated with central European painters of the Paris School (Pougny, Kisling, Soutine, Segal, Kremègne and Kikoïne). The French state acquired a number of his works.

Work by him was exhibited for the first time in Lódz, in 1927, and only once in Berlin, in 1929. It did however feature at a number of the annual salons in Paris, including the Salon d'Automne and the Salon des Tuileries, and several group exhibitions, in Amsterdam (1935), Paris (1936), Brussels (1937) and Honfleur (1939). There have also been solo exhibitions of his work, in Paris, London, Zurich, Helsinki, New York, Jerusalem, Tel-Aviv and various museums in Israel.

Schreter published two albums: *The First Bach-Casals Festival in Prades* and *The Negev Desert.*

BIBLIOGRAPHY:
Schreter, exhibition leaflet, La Palette bleue, Paris, 1967. Nieszawer, Nadine/Boyé, Marie/Lanzmann, Claude (preface), *Peintres juifs de l'école de Paris 1905-1939*, Denoël, Paris, 2001.

AUCTION RECORDS:
PARIS, 8 April 1990, *Still-life* (oil on canvas, 15 x 18 ins / 38 x 46 cm) FRF 10,000. PARIS, 14 April 1991, *The Country Road* (oil on canvas, 21 1/4 x 28 3/4 ins / 54 x 73 cm) FRF 13,000. TEL AVIV, 12 June 1991, *Figure in a Landscape* (oil on canvas, 13 x 22 ins / 33 x 55 cm) USD 1,100. PARIS, 17 June 1991, *Undergrowth* (oil on card, 15 x 22 ins / 38 x 55 cm) FRF 4,500. PARIS, 17 May 1992, *Landscape* (oil on canvas, 19 3/4 x 25 1/2 ins / 50 x 65 cm) FRF 5,000. PARIS, 24 March 1996, *Portrait of Yvette Moch* (oil on canvas, 19 3/4 x 15 3/4 ins / 50 x 40 cm) FRF 4,500.

SCHRETTER
19th - 20th century.
Painter. Military subjects.
Schretter was a military artist, who is mentioned in Art Prices Current.
AUCTION RECORDS:
LONDON, 15 July 1910, *The Ancient Imperial Bavarian Guard; Horsemen,* GBP 30.

SCHRETTER, Benjamin. See **SCHREITER**

SCHRETTER, Josef
Austrian, 19th century.
Born 18 March 1856, in Inzing (Tyrol); died 18 March 1909, in Innsbruck.
Painter.
Josef Schretter studied under F. Plattner at the art school in Innsbruck from 1868 to 1872. From 1874 to 1877 he attended the academy in Vienna with Leop. K. Miller, K. von Blaas and H. Makart. From 1881 to 1886 he went on a study tour to Italy and Tunisia with his master L.K. Muller. His numerous landscapes and Italianate or Tunisian studies go back to this period. In 1891 he settled permanently in Innsbruck. The handling of light in his pastels won him a considerable reputation. Most of his output has remained in his family.
MUSEUMS AND GALLERIES:
INNSBRUCK - SCHWERIN.

SCHRETTHAUSER, Hans Georg
German, 18th century.
Sculptor (wood).

SCHRETTINGER, Willibald Martin
German, 18th - 19th century.
Born 17 June 1772, in Neumarkt; died 12 April 1851, in Munich.
Engraver, lithographer, writer.

SCHREUDER, Bernhard
Dutch, 18th century.
Died 13 October 1780, in Hoorn.
Engraver.
Bernhard Schreuder produced mezzotints.

SCHREUDER VAN DE COOLWIJK, Jan W. H. See **COOLWIJK**

SCHREUEL, Albert Friedrich Carl
German, 18th - 19th century.
Born 24 June 1773, in Maastricht; died 1853, in Dresden.
Painter.
Initially an officer, Albert Schreuel went to Berlin to study painting and in about 1805 transferred to Dresden where he studied miniature painting with Josef Grassi. He made many copies of the works of Correggio and Raphael in miniature. His expertise extended to oil painting.

SCHREUER, Wilhelm von
German, 19th - 20th century.
Born 28 September 1866, in Wesel; died 11 November 1933, in Düsseldorf.
Painter. Figures, scenes with figures, local scenes, urban landscapes.
Wilhelm von Schreuer lived and worked in Düsseldorf. He painted street scenes and war scenes from 1914 in Belgium.

MUSEUMS AND GALLERIES:
BERLIN (Nationalgal.): *Service Corps Train in Flanders* - COLOGNE: *Cologne Carnival* - DÜSSELDORF: *In the Trenches; Uhlans on the Attack* - MÜNSTER: *The Kingdom of Heaven in Cologne* - WUPPERTAL: *Napoleon I in Düsseldorf.*
AUCTION RECORDS:
COLOGNE, 5 May 1966, *At the Café,* DEM 3,600. COLOGNE, 21 April 1967, *Dance Hall,* DEM 5,500. BONN, 19 May 1971, *The Boat* (gouache and watercolour) DEM 4,200. COLOGNE, 16 June 1972, *Peasants Sitting outside an Inn,* DEM 6,000. COLOGNE, 29 March 1974, *Hussar Regiment Entering Düsseldorf,* DEM 22,000. COLOGNE, 27 June 1974, *Romantic Scene* (watercolour) DEM 4,000. COLOGNE, 25 June 1976, *Coffee in the Castle Garden* (oil on paper remounted on board, 26 3/4 x 32 ins / 68 x 81 cm) DEM 16,000. COLOGNE, 25 Nov 1976, *Sunday Walk by the Rhine* (mixed media/mounted paper, 20 x 24 ins / 50.5 x 61 cm) DEM 6,000. COLOGNE, 11 May 1977, *The Dance Hall* (mixed media/mounted paper/canvas, 35 1/2 x 47 1/4 ins / 90 x 120 cm) DEM 5,000. COLOGNE, 21 Oct 1977, *View of Cologne* (1903, oil on paper remounted/canvas, 15 1/2 x 24 ins / 39.5 x 61 cm) DEM 5,000. COLOGNE, 30 March 1979, *The Banquet* (oil on canvas, 30 3/4 x 39 3/4 ins / 78 x 101 cm) DEM 26,000. COLOGNE, 20 Nov 1980, *Open-air Hostelry* (mixed media/mounted paper/card, 23 1/2 x 31 1/2 ins / 60 x 80 cm) DEM 13,000. LONDON, 24 June 1981, *Düsseldorf Synagogue* (oil on canvas, 34 x 34 ins / 86.5 x 86.5 cm) GBP 1,400. COLOGNE, 24 May 1982, *Concert at the Castle* (mixed media/mounted paper/panel, 11 1/2 x 14 1/4 ins / 29 x 36.5 cm) DEM 8,500. COLOGNE, 30 March 1984, *Open-air Café* (mixed media/mounted paper/card, 18 3/4 x 25 1/2 ins / 47.5 x 65 cm) DEM 27,000. LONDON, 28 Nov 1984, *Ladies and Gentlemen of Fashion in an Interior* (1904, oil on paper remounted/canvas, 25 x 21 ins / 63.5 x 53.5 cm) GBP 4,000. COLOGNE, 22 March 1985, *Street Scene, Old Düsseldorf* (mixed media/mounted paper/canvas, 31 1/2 x 47 1/4 ins / 80 x 120 cm) DEM 17,000. COLOGNE, 14 March 1986, *Scene in a Tavern* (mixed media/paper, 26 3/4 x 25 1/2 ins / 68 x 65 cm) DEM 4,500. COLOGNE, 3 July 1987, *People Sitting by the Rhine* (mixed media, 27 1/2 x 35 1/4 ins / 70 x 89.5 cm) DEM 15,000. COLOGNE, 20 Oct 1989, *Fishing Harbour* (mixed media, 37 1/2 x 49 1/4 ins / 95 x 125 cm) DEM 3,700. COLOGNE, 23 March 1990, *Concert in the Castle Park in Benrath* (mixed media, 55 x 70 3/4 ins / 140 x 180 cm) DEM 18,000. COLOGNE, 29 June 1990, *Café Terrace* (1913, mixed media, 17 1/4 x 23 1/4 ins / 44 x 59 cm) DEM 12,000. COLOGNE, 28 June 1991, *Card Players* (mixed media, 32 x 25 1/2 ins / 81 x 65 cm) DEM 7,500. MUNICH, 25 June 1996, *Inspection of the Cavalry* (1901, oil on canvas, 11 1/2 x 11 1/2 ins / 29.5 x 29.5 cm) DEM 3,360. DÜSSELDORF, 4 March 1999, *Playing Trick-Track* (oil on board, 33 x 25 ins / 85 x 64 cm) DEM 5,000. COLOGNE, 26 June 1999, *Lore on Rhein by Oestrich* (mixed media, 20 x 21 ins / 50 x 54 cm) DEM 7,000. COLOGNE, 29 June 2000, *Officer on a Horse* (mixed media, 28 x 19 ins / 70 x 48 cm) DEM 4,800. COLOGNE, 30 Nov 2000, *Oberkasseler Bridge, Dusseldorf* (1899, mixed media, 28 x 37 ins / 72 x 95 cm) DEM 5,500. HAMBURG, 23 June 2001, *Interior with Elegant Party* (mixed media, 29 x 20 ins / 74 x 52 cm) DEM 11,000. COLOGNE, 28 June 2001, *Elegant Party in Park* (1903, mixed media, 26 x 38 ins / 67 x 96 cm) DEM 7,000. AHLDEN, 3 May 2002, *Campfire* (watercolour and pastel on board, 31 x 44 ins / 78 x 112 cm) EUR 3,000. COLOGNE, 15 May 2002, *Figures in Park* (mixed media on board, 14 x 18 ins / 35 x 45 cm) EUR 3,000. COLOGNE, 20 Nov 2003, *Ballroom* (mixed media, 30 x 39 ins / 76 x 98 cm) EUR 5,500. COLOGNE, 13 Dec 2003, *In the Coffee House* (oil on canvas, 15 x 20 ins / 38 x 50 cm) EUR 16,000. MUNICH, 26 March 2004, *Dutch People Round a Table* (oil on canvas, 21 x 28 ins / 54 x 71 cm) EUR 4,400. COLOGNE, 1 April 2004, *Vespers* (mixed media, 20 x 24 ins / 50 x 60 cm) EUR 3,000.

SCHREUNER, Franz
German, 18th century.
Active in Haguenau.
Painter (porcelain).

SCHREVELIUS, Elisabeth
Dutch, 18th century.
Painter.
Elisabeth Schrevelius married the artist Petrus Voogd in Amsterdam in 1713.

SCHREVERE, Damas Fortuné
French, 19th - 20th century.
Born in Zuytpeene.
Painter. Portraits.

Damas Fortuné Schrevere first exhibited at the Salon de Paris in 1874.

SCHREYER, Adolf
German, 19th century.
Born 9 July 1828, in Frankfurt; died 29 or 30 July 1899, in Kronberg.
Painter. Landscapes, animals.
Orientalism.

After studying at the Städelsches Kunstinstitut in Frankfurt, Adolf Schreyer attended the academy in Düsseldorf. He visited Stuttgart and Munich and went to Vienna in 1849. During the Crimean War he was a draughtsman. After travelling to France and North Africa to study, he settled in Paris in 1862 where he lived until 1870.

In 1871 he returned to Frankfurt. He was a member of the academies of Amsterdam and Rotterdam and received medals in Paris in 1864, 1865 and 1867 and in Munich in 1876. His various travels provided him with material for his compositions. He was primarily a genre painter who studied peasant life in different countries, including the former Soviet Union and North Africa.

He had a predilection for painting horses from all angles. In this respect his work is perhaps reminiscent of that of Eugène Fromentin - brilliant in colour and bold in touch. His compositions are always very cleverly conceived and the phenomenal success he enjoyed in his lifetime has not completely waned.

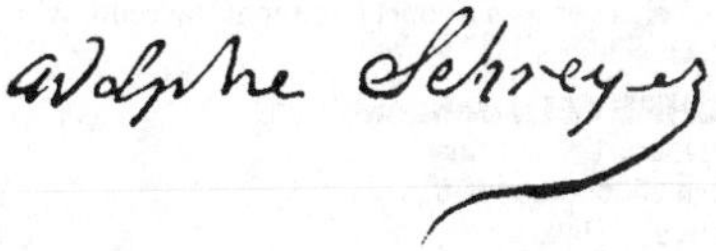

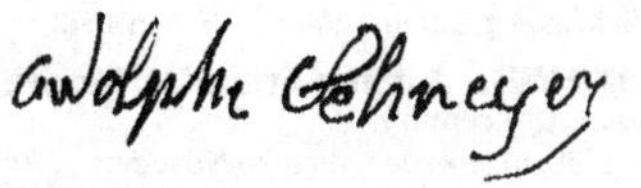

MUSEUMS AND GALLERIES:
BAYONNE: *Arabian Horseman on Sentry Duty* - BOSTON: *Stopping at the Watering Place* - BREMEN: *Sheik* - COLOGNE: *Wallachian Post* - FRANKFURT AM MAIN: *In Wallachia*; *Cart in Wallachia* - HAMBURG: *Wallachian Horses* - MAINZ: *Arabian Horsemen Raiding* - SHEFFIELD: *Nearing Cairo*.

AUCTION RECORDS:
PARIS, 1868, *Arabian Horseman*, FRF 2,100. BRUSSELS, 1873, *Sudden Tug*, FRF 14,600. PARIS, 1874, *Death of An Officer*, FRF 11,000. BRUSSELS, 1874, *Hungarian Team of Horses*, FRF 15,500. BRUSSELS, 1875, *Horses of Irregular Cossacks in Snowy Weather*, FRF 15,000; *Horses Fleeing An Encampment on Fire*, FRF 13,500. BRUSSELS, 1877, *Team of Russian Horses Pursued by Wolves in Snow*, FRF 11,500. NEW YORK, 1879, *Winter in Russia*, FRF 22,500. LONDON, 1881, *Hungarian Team of Horses*, FRF 10,900. NEW YORK, 1885, *Snow Scene*, FRF 22,500. NEW YORK, 1886, *Flight*, FRF 16,200. LONDON, 1888, *Abandoned*, FRF 15,740. NEW YORK, 1889, *Winter in Wallachia*, FRF 13,500. FRANKFURT AM MAIN, 1894, *In the Oasis*, FRF 8,625. LONDON, 1896, *Horses Frightened by Fire*, FRF 13,650. PARIS, 18 Feb 1898, *Caravan*, FRF 14,280. NEW YORK, 1899, *Arab Scout*, FRF 14,500. NEW YORK, 1899, *Hungarian Horses*, FRF 13,250. NEW YORK, 1-2 April 1902, *Arabs Crossing Ford*, FRF 65,000. NEW YORK, 19 June 1906, *Bulgarians*, USD 13,000. NEW YORK, 21-22 Jan 1909, *Watering-place*, USD 8,000. PARIS, 21 April 1910, *Horses under Shelter*, FRF 3,500. LONDON, 21 June 1910, *Fire in Stable*, GBP 651. NEW YORK, 13 Jan 1911, *Chief Arab and Escort*, USD 11,600. PARIS, 7-8 March 1911, *Arab Horsemen*, FRF 8,800. LONDON, 19 May 1922, *Wallachian Carriers*, GBP 273. LONDON, 1 June 1923, *Arab Horsemen*, GBP 110. PARIS, 21-22 June 1923, *Basset Hounds in Kennels*, FRF 200. PARIS, 29-30 June 1927, *Arabian Horseman*, FRF 17,000. NEW YORK, 9 April 1929, *The Outport*, USD 925. NEW YORK, 30 Jan 1930, *Cossacks*, USD 2,500. NEW YORK, 4-5 Feb 1931, *Oasis*, USD 2,200. NEW YORK, 25-26 March 1931, *Wallachian Peasants en Route*, USD 1,750. NEW YORK, 12 Nov 1931, *Covered Waggon*, USD 625. NEW YORK, 26 Oct 1933, *War Advice*, USD 1,850. NEW YORK, 7-8 Dec 1933, *Rearguard*, USD 3,500. PARIS, 14 Dec 1933, *Horse under Shelter in Snow Storm (Wallachia)*, FRF 1,700. NEW YORK, 15 Feb 1934, *Traveller*, USD 1,550. NEW YORK, 29 March 1934, *Arab Charge*, USD 3,600. PARIS, 15 June 1934, *Mounted Officer Carrying the Regimental Colour*, FRF 4,000. NEW YORK, 23 Nov 1934, *Imperial Messenger*, USD 3,000; *Sheik and his Troops*, USD 6,400. PARIS, 28 Dec 1934, *Arabian Horseman as Scout*, FRF 8,020. NEW YORK, 3 Dec 1936, *Snow Storm*, USD 530. NEW YORK, 3 Feb 1938, *Advancing for an Encounter*, USD 1,500. LONDON, 16 Feb 1940, *Mounted Sentries*, GBP 304. NEW YORK, 22 Jan 1942, *Halt for Water*, USD 2,500. NEW YORK, 4-5 June 1942, *Arab Horsemen*, USD 1,000. NEW YORK, 3 Dec 1942, *The Advanced Post*, USD 1,400. NEW YORK, 29 April 1943, *The Outport*, USD 1,900. NEW YORK, 24 May 1944, *Arab Scouts*, USD 1,150. NEW YORK, 19 and 20 Jan 1945, *Arab Cavalry Engagement*, USD 2,000. NEW YORK, 18-19 April 1945, *Arabs Resting*, USD 1,100; *Arab Horsemen Beating Retreat*, USD 2,800. NEW YORK, 2-5 Jan 1946, *Stampede*, USD 2,600; *Return of Foray*, USD 2,900. LONDON, 25 March 1946, *Horsemen*, GBP 170. NEW YORK, 15-16 May 1946, *Arab Horsemen*, USD 2,700. PARIS, July 1946, *Herd of Cattle in Landscape* (attributed) FRF 10,800. LONDON, 8 Nov 1946, *Winter*, GBP 157. PARIS, 8 Dec 1948, *Arab Horseman on Lookout*, FRF 26,000. NEW YORK, 10 Dec 1949, *Arab*, USD 1,000. LONDON, 16 Dec 1949, *Young Berbers*, GBP 273; *Oasis*, GBP 241. PARIS, 6 March 1950, *Algerian Horseman in Countryside*, FRF 12,000. BERLIN, 20 April 1950, *Track in forest* (1867) DEM 1,800. PARIS, 17 May 1950, *Ford*, FRF 4,000. PARIS, 26 May 1950, *Squad in Snow* (1853) FRF 1,000. PARIS, 25 July 1950, *Arabian Horsemen*, FRF 2,100. NEW YORK, 24 Jan 1951, *The Messenger*, USD 675. AMSTERDAM, 13 March 1951, *Arabian Horsemen*, NLG 370. LONDON, 14 March 1951, *Ambush*, GBP 75. PARIS, 16 Nov 1953, *Arabian Horseman*, FRF 18,500. NEW YORK, 23 April 1958, *Russian Post*, USD 1,500. NEW YORK, 21 Oct 1959, *Arab Chief*, USD 1,700. NEW YORK, 4 March 1961, *Train of Beasts of Burden in Wallaby*, USD 1,400. NEW YORK, 29 Nov 1961, *Peasants and Horses in Flight*, USD 3,200. NEW YORK, 15 March 1964, *Mounted Arab Warriors*, USD 4,250. NEW YORK, 24 Nov 1965, *Arab Warriors*, USD 5,250. MUNICH, 22-24 June 1966, *Arab Warrior*, DEM 16,500. NEW YORK, 25 April 1968, *Horses at Watering-place*, USD 7,500. LOS ANGELES, 23 May 1972, *Arab Horses*, USD 9,000. NEW YORK, 10 Oct 1973, *Three Horsemen in Landscape*, USD 8,500. COLOGNE, 14 Nov 1974, *Sleigh Attacked by Wolves*, DEM 36,500. NEW YORK, 15 Oct 1976, *Arab Camp* (gouache, 11 1/2 x 13 1/2 ins / 29 x 34.5 cm) USD 2,200. LONDON, 29 Oct 1976, *Mounted Arabian Horsemen* (oil on canvas, 29 x 54 ins / 73.5 x 137 cm) GBP 13,000. NEW YORK, 28 April 1977, *Arabian Horsemen* (oil on canvas, 31 1/2 x 49 1/4 ins / 80 x 125 cm) USD 25,000. LONDON, 31 March 1978, *The Mounted Abd-el-Kader before Town Gates* (mixed media/mounted paper/canvas, 11 3/4 x 16 1/4 ins / 30 x 41 cm) GBP 1,700. NEW YORK, 12 Oct 1979, *Arab Warrior on Horseback* (oil on canvas, 11 x 14 ins / 28 x 35.5 cm) USD 17,000. LONDON, 25 Nov 1981, *Arab Warrior* (oil on canvas, 28 1/2 x 38 3/4 ins / 72.5 x 98.5 cm) GBP 22,500. NEW YORK, 27 Oct 1983, *Arab Warriors Leading Horses to Watering-place* (oil on canvas, 29 x 38 1/4 ins / 73.6 x 97.1 cm) USD 88,000. LONDON, 20 March 1985, *Arabi-*

an Horsemen at Well (oil on canvas, 26 1/2 x 39 ins / 67 x 99 cm) GBP 70,000. NEW YORK, 29 Oct 1986, *Caravan in Winter* (oil on canvas, 27 1/4 x 32 1/2 ins / 69.5 x 82.5 cm) USD 25,000. NEW YORK, 24 May 1988, *Arabian Horsemen in Landscape* (oil on canvas, 20 1/2 x 33 ins / 52.3 x 83.8 cm) USD 7,750. NEW YORK, 22 Feb 1989, *Arabian Horsemen* (oil on canvas, 34 x 46 3/4 ins / 86.6 x 118.8 cm) USD 148,500. NEW YORK, 23 Feb 1989, *Troïka on Snowy Evening* (oil on canvas, 29 x 39 ins / 73.6 x 99 cm) USD 28,600. NEW YORK, 24 Oct 1989, *Arabian Horsemen Descending Hills* (oil on canvas, 20 x 33 ins / 50.8 x 83.8 cm) USD 66,000. MUNICH, 29 Nov 1989, *Horsemen in Forest in Winter* (oil on canvas, 31 1/2 x 25 1/4 ins / 80 x 64 cm) DEM 33,000. NEW YORK, 1 March 1990, *Arabian Horsemen Advancing* (oil on canvas, 32 x 50 ins / 81.3 x 127 cm) USD 77,000. NEW YORK, 24 Oct 1990, *Arabian Horsemen at Water Hole* (oil on canvas, 20 x 33 ins / 51 x 83.8 cm) USD 38,500. NEW YORK, 23 May 1991, *Arabian Horseman near Water Hole* (oil on canvas, 32 1/4 x 26 ins / 82 x 66 cm) USD 52,800. NEW YORK, 19 Feb 1992, *Arabian Horsemen at Water Hole* (oil on canvas, 34 x 47 ins / 86.6 x 119.4 cm) USD 121,000. NEW YORK, 26 May 1992, *Cartload of Hay* (oil on panel, 13 x 19 3/4 ins / 33 x 50.2 cm) USD 7,700. NEW YORK, 30 Oct 1992, *Wallachian Horsemen in Snow* (oil on canvas, 34 1/4 x 59 1/4 ins / 87 x 150.5 cm) USD 16,500. NEW YORK, 14 Oct 1993, *Bedouins on a Track* (oil on canvas, 31 1/2 x 50 ins / 80 x 127 cm) USD 134,500. NEW YORK, 12 Oct 1994, *Arabian Horsemen Advancing* (oil on canvas, 44 1/4 x 38 1/2 ins / 112.4 x 97.8 cm) USD 172,500. LONDON, 17 Nov 1994, *At the Watering-place* (oil on canvas, 25 x 39 1/4 ins / 63.7 x 100 cm) GBP 36,700. LONDON, 17 Nov 1995, *Attack* (oil on canvas, 23 1/4 x 32 ins / 59 x 81.2 cm) GBP 25,300. NEW YORK, 23-24 May 1996, *Arab Horseman* (1863, oil on canvas, 46 x 35 1/2 ins / 116.8 x 90 cm) USD 46,000. LONDON, 14 June 1996, *Arab Horsemen in Encampment* (oil on canvas, 27 1/2 x 47 1/4 ins / 70 x 120 cm) GBP 32,200. VIENNA, 29-30 Oct 1996, *Hungarian Peasants and Horse-drawn Cart* (oil on canvas, 32 1/4 ins / 82 cm, 2 x 50 3/4 ins/5 x 129 cm) ATS 172,500. NEW YORK, 22 Oct 1997, *Knight of Gelding* (oil on canvas, 18 3/4 x 29 1/4 ins / 47.6 x 74.3 cm) USD 11,500. LONDON, 21 Nov 1997, *Arab Horsemen* (oil on canvas, 32 x 51 ins / 81.3 x 129.5 cm) GBP 19,975. NEW YORK, 12 Feb 1998, *Arabian Horsemen* (oil on canvas, 34 1/4 x 47 1/4 ins / 87 x 120 cm) USD 36,800. NEW YORK, 18 March 1998, *Mounted Arabian Horseman* (oil on canvas, 16 x 12 1/2 ins / 40.6 x 31.8 cm) USD 20,700. PARIS, 26 March 1998, *Meeting between the Two Caïds* (oil on canvas, 32 1/4 x 25 1/2 ins / 82 x 65 cm) FRF 290,000. NEW YORK, 1 Nov 1999, *Advancing Guard* (oil on canvas, 34 x 48 ins / 87 x 121 cm) USD 110,000. NEW YORK, 2 Nov 1999, *Fleeing Wallachian Horses* (oil on canvas, 40 x 67 ins / 102 x 171 cm) USD 75,000. LONDON, 21 June 2000, *Return of Pasha* (oil on canvas, 34 x 46 ins / 86 x 118 cm) GBP 50,000. DETROIT, 21 Oct 2000, *Arab Horseman* (oil on canvas, 28 x 40 ins / 71 x 102 cm) USD 120,000. LONDON, 21 June 2001, *Arab Horseman* (oil on panel, 22 x 33 ins / 55 x 84 cm) GBP 48,000. NEW YORK, 31 Oct 2001, *The Chase* (1863, oil on canvas, 44 x 67 ins / 112 x 171 cm) USD 200,000. LONDON, 20 June 2002, *Arab Warriors on Horseback* (oil on panel, 27 x 39 ins / 69 x 100 cm) GBP 32,000. PARIS, 16 Dec 2002, *The Watchmen* (oil on canvas, 23 x 33 ins / 59 x 83 cm) EUR 45,000. LONDON, 3 June 2003, *Desert Canter* (oil on canvas, 28 x 40 ins / 71 x 102 cm) GBP 18,000. LONDON, 18 June 2003, *Victor* (oil on canvas, 48 x 80 ins / 122 x 202 cm) GBP 9,000. MUNICH, 17 March 2004, *Arabs on Horseback in Landscape* (oil on canvas, 34 x 46 ins / 87 x 118 cm) EUR 44,000. NEW YORK, 22 April 2004, *Scout's Report* (oil on canvas, 28 x 40 ins / 71 x 101 cm) USD 50,000.

SCHREYER, David, or Schreier

German, 17th century.
Died 28 April 1648, in Freiberg (Saxony).
Painter, architect.

David Schreyer worked as a painter in Meissen in 1625.

SCHREYER, Franz

German, 19th century.
Born 7 April 1858, in Leipzig.
Active in Dresden.
Painter. Landscapes.

After attending the academy in Leipzig, Franz Schreyer was taught by F. Preller the younger at the academy in Dresden. Afterwards he settled in Blasewitz near Dresden.

MUSEUMS AND GALLERIES:

LEIPZIG: *Lüneburg Heath.*

AUCTION RECORDS:

MUNICH, 29 May 1980, *Landscape* (1894, oil on canvas, 9 1/2 x 15 3/4 ins / 24 x 40 cm) DEM 2,200. PORTLAND, 4 Aug 1999, *Roman Countryside* (oil on canvas, 9 x 22 ins / 23 x 56 cm) USD 1,800. LONDON, 14 Oct 1999, *Capri, As Seen from Terimini* (1904, oil on canvas, 20 x 29 ins / 52 x 73 cm) GBP 3,000. VIENNA, 23 May 2000, *Landscape with Ruins, Acqua Claudia* (oil on canvas, 30 x 59 ins / 77 x 149 cm) ATS 120,000. HEIDELBERG, 7 Oct 2000, *Gulf of Sorrento* (1887, oil on canvas, 13 x 21 ins / 33 x 53 cm) DEM 9,200.

SCHREYER, Gabriel

German, 17th - 18th century.
Born 1666; died 1730, in Bayreuth.
Painter.

Gabriel Schreyer was a court painter at Bayreuth who painted church ceilings.

SCHREYER, Johann

German, 17th century.
Born 1596; died 1676.
Active in Hall.
Painter.

Johann Schreyer painted a *View of Hall* in 1643.

SCHREYER, Johann Friedrich Moritz

German, 18th century.
Born 1768, in Dresden; died 20 November 1795, in Dresden.
Draughtsman, engraver (burin).

Johann Schreyer was taught by Christian Gottfried Schulze.

MUSEUMS AND GALLERIES:

BERLIN (Kupferstichkabinet): several drawings.

SCHREYER, Johann Michael

German, 18th century.
Sculptor.

Johann Schreyer settled in Allersberg and completed the work begun by Joh. Mich. Berg on the altars and the pulpit of the church at Sulzburg.

SCHREYER, Lothar

German, 20th century.
Born 19 August 1886, in Blasewitz, near Dresden; died 1966, in Hamburg.
Painter, engraver, director, writer. Religious subjects, figures.

Lothar Schreyer studied history of art and law in Heidelberg, Berlin and Leipzig. In 1910 he became a doctor of law. From 1911 to 1918 he was assistant director at the theatre in Hamburg. From 1916 to 1928 he was chief editor of the avant-garde art journal *Der Sturm* (*The Storm*). In 1919 he founded the 'Sturmbühne' (Theatre of the Storm)in Berlin and the Theatre of Combat in Hamburg. From 1921 to 1923 he directed the Bauhaus theatre studio. He was the director of the art school *Der Weg* (*The Way*) in Berlin and Dresden from 1924 to 1927 and editor-in-chief of the Hanseatischer Verlaganstalt, a publishing house in Hamburg, from 1928 to

1931. In 1933 he converted to Catholicism and settled in Hamburg, from then on focusing on painting and engraving.

He produced a number of studies on theatre and art. He produced, notably, 77 wood engravings of the Crucifixion, which were published in Berlin in 1920.

BIBLIOGRAPHY:

Leymarie, Jean/Herzogenrath, Wulf/Grote, Ludwig/Gropius, Walter, *Le Bauhaus*, exhibition catalogue, Württembergischer Kunsteverein, Stuttgart, Musée national d'Art moderne, Paris, 1969. *Geometrische Abstraktion 1910-1990*, exhibition catalogue, Gal. Eremitage, Berlin, 1991.

AUCTION RECORDS:

PARIS, 4 Dec 1972, *Night* (gouache) FRF 4,100. HAMBURG, 9 June 1979, *The Annunciation* (1923, gouache, 12 3/4 x 7 3/4 ins / 32.3 x 20 cm) DEM 3,200. COLOGNE, 17 May 1980, *Composition with Circles* (1923, pen, 12 x 16 1/2 ins / 30.6 x 42.2 cm) DEM 2,600. MUNICH, 29 June 1983, *Paschal Lamb* (1924, gouache and silver, 9 3/4 x 7 1/2 ins / 25 x 19 cm) DEM 4,200. PARIS, 12 May 1993, *Study for a Bauhaus Theatre Set* (1923, watercolour/paper, 13 3/4 x 10 ins / 35 x 24.5 cm) FRF 3,500. LONDON, 20 May 1993, *Mermaid* (1925, oil on canvas, 31 x 20 ins / 78.7 x 50.5 cm) GBP 7,475. COLOGNE, 29 May 1999, *Untitled* (1927, bodycolour over pencil, 20 x 11 ins / 50 x 28 cm) DEM 8,500. ZURICH, 16 Nov 1999, *Blue Tones 3* (1921, gouache, 14 x 10 ins / 36 x 25 cm) CHF 5,500. ROME, 18 April 2002, *Composition with Circles* (1923, 12 x 17 ins / 31 x 42 cm) EUR 2,000. BERN, 20 June 2002, *Female Drive. Male Intellect. Cross of Birth* (colour lithograph heightened with gold, three, 16 x 11 ins / 40 x 29 cm) CHF 9,500.

SCHREYER, Michael

German, 18th century.

Painter, engraver (burin).

Michael Schreyer is mentioned on 5 July 1715 in Leipzig.

SCHREYER, Wilhelm

German, 20th century.

Born 31 January 1890, in Plauen.

Painter. Portraits, landscapes.

Wilhelm Schreyer lived and worked in Munich.

SCHREYÖGG, Georg

German, 20th century.

Born 13 August 1870, in Mittenwald; died July 1934, in Karlsruhe.

Sculptor. Figures. Busts.

Georg Schreyögg trained under Wilhelm von Rumann. From 1909 he taught at the art school in Karlsruhe. He was the sculptor of the *Barbara Fountain* in Koblenz and a *Christ Giving his Blessing* at the Victoria Monastery in Karlsruhe.

MUSEUMS AND GALLERIES:

FREIBURG: *David* (marble) - KARLSRUHE: *Vase Carrier*; bronze bust.

SCHREYVOGEL, Charles

American, 19th - 20th century.

Born 4 January 1861, in New York; died 27 January 1912, in Hoboken (New Jersey), of blood poisoning.

Active in Hoboken (New Jersey).

Painter, watercolourist, sculptor, draughtsman, lithographer, illustrator. Western scenes, portraits, scenes with figures, genre scenes, landscapes.

Charles Schreyvogel carved Meerschaum pipes as a boy in Hoboken, New Jersey. He taught himself to draw and was apprenticed to a gold engraver, a die sinker, and in 1877, a lithographer. In the late 1870s he met H. August Schwabe, president of the Newark Art League, who persuaded him to enroll in art classes there. By 1880, Schreyvogel was teaching drawing and painting from his rooftop studio. In 1887, with the encouragement of Schwabe, Schreyvogel left to study under Karl von Marr and Frank Kirchbach at the Munich Art Academy for the next three years.

When he returned to Hoboken in 1890, he continued as a lithographer and painted portraits, landscapes and ivory miniatures to make a living. After sketching Native Americans, cowboys and horses who worked with *Buffalo Bill's Wild West Show* in New York, he made his first visit West in 1893. For five months, Schreyvogel created field sketches on the Ute Reservation at Ignacio, Colorado. He observed the Apache, Navajo, Utes, and other tribes who came to receive their government allotments, and listened to their stories of the Plains Indian wars. He collected great quantities of Native American and cavalry artifacts which he later used in paintings. During the same trip, he visited Arizona where he sketched cowboys.

Schreyvogel returned to Hoboken in the Autumn of 1893 and began painting Western canvases depicting the events of the Plain Indian wars. The artist carefully researched his subjects through clay modelling and the use of live models. His Western scenes did not sell initially, and he continued as a lithographic artist and portrait painter to earn a living. Over the next ten years he travelled to the West several times, including to the Dakotas, the Blackfeet Reservation in Montana, and the Ute, Sioux and Crow Reservations, and was witness to a council of more than 10,000 Crow, Blackfeet, Sioux and Chippewa Indians held at the Standing Rock Reservation.

In the late 1890s Schreyvogel entered the landscape painting *Close of an Autumn Day* in the 60th Annual Exhibition of the Pennsylvania Academy of Fine Arts in Philadelphia, and in 1897 he entered *Over a Dangerous Pass* in the annual exhibition of the National Academy of Design in New York. Despite not having had previous success, he reluctantly entered *My Bunkie* into the annual exhibition of the National Academy of Design in 1900. He won the Thomas B. Clarke Award for the best American figure composition and gained immediate national recognition. *My Bunkie* went on to win a bronze medal at the Paris Exposition and another medal at the Pan-American Exposition in Buffalo. In 1903, Schreyvogel was made an associate of the National Academy of Design.

Custer's Demand was unveiled in April 1903 at the Knoedler Art Galleries in New York. A fellow Western artist, Frederic Remington, publicly criticized it for its historical inaccuracies, but Schreyvogel was vindicated when numerous supporters defended his work including Custer's widow, soldiers, and President Theodore Roosevelt. In 1904, *Custer's Demand* won the St Louis World Fair Exposition Bronze Medal.

Schreyvogel's output was limited to relatively few major works per year because of the number of his research trips and the large-scale, meticulous nature of his works. Schreyvogel completed fewer than 100 of his Western paintings.

BIBLIOGRAPHY:

Schreyvogel, Charles, *My Bunkie and Others: Pictures of Western Frontier Life*, Moffat, Yard and Company, New York, 1909. Horan, James David, *The Life and art of Charles Schreyvogel, painter-Historian of the Indian-fighting army of the American West*, Crown Publishers, New York, 1969. Carothers, Archie D., '*The Charles Schreyvogel Memorial Studio Collection*' in *Persimmon Hill*, Journal article, Fall 1970. Stewart, Rick, *The American West: Legendary Artists of the Frontier*, Hawthorne Publishing Company, 1986. '*Charles Schreyvogel*' in *Salon d'Automne*, exhibition catalogue, Paris, 1987. Schulze Thulin, Axel/Bisazki, Sabine, *Indianer des Westens Nordamerikas (1870-1900): die Schreyvogel-Samlung im Linden-Museum Stuttgart*, catalogue, Diederichs, Munich, 1992.

MUSEUMS AND GALLERIES:
CORNING (Rockwell Mus. of Western Art): *An Unexpected Enemy* (1900, oil on canvas); *The Last Drop* (1903, Bronze) - NEW YORK (Metropolitan Mus. of Art): *In Hot Pursuit* (after 1900, oil on canvas); *My Bunkie* (1899, oil on canvas) - OKLAHOMA CITY (National Cowboy and Western Heritage Mus.): *On the Skirmish Line* (1900, oil on canvas); *Ready for Battle* (1913); *The Arrival at the Fort* (1902); *The last Drop* (1903); *Going Into Action* (1912, oil on canvas).
AUCTION RECORDS:
NEW YORK, 14 to 17 March 1911, *Soldiers Attacked by Indians,* USD 600. NEW YORK, 26 and 27 Feb 1917, *Surprise Attack,* USD 1,200; *Cavalry,* USD 775. NEW YORK, 29 Jan 1964, *Cavalry Charge,* USD 20,000. NEW YORK, 27 Jan 1965, *Dead Sure,* USD 7,750. LOS ANGELES, 9 June 1976, *Rider Watering his Horse* (1905, bronze, l. 18 ins / 45.7 cm) USD 10,000. NEW YORK, 27 Oct 1977, *The Last Drop* (1903, green-patinated bronze, h. 12¼ ins / 31 cm, l. 18¼ ins/46.3 cm) USD 12,500. NEW YORK, 20 April 1979, c. 1890, oil on canvas remounted on hardboard, 18¾ x 14½ ins / 47.6 x 36.8 cm) USD 5,250. NEW YORK, 17 Oct 1980, *White Eagle* (1899, brown-patinated bronze, h. 19½ ins / 49.5 cm) USD 26,000. NEW YORK, 23 April 1982, *The Last Drop* (1903, brown-patinated bronze, h. 12 ins / 30.5 cm) USD 20,000. LOS ANGELES, 29 June 1982, *Landscape* (oil on canvas remounted on board, 18¼ x 14½ ins / 46.5 x 37 cm) USD 6,250. NEW YORK, 2 June 1983, *Doomed* (1901, oil on canvas, 25 x 34 ins / 63.5 x 86.3 cm) USD 180,000. NEW YORK, 2 June 1983, *White Eagle* (1899, bronze, h. 20½ ins / 52.1 cm) USD 11,500. NEW YORK, 4 Dec 1986, *The Last Drop* (1900, gold and brown patinated bronze, h. 11¾ ins / 29.8 cm) USD 15,000. NEW YORK, 17 March 1988, *Indian Hut on the Plain* (oil on canvas, 9¾ x 8 ins / 25 x 20.6 cm) USD 7,150. NEW YORK, 30 Nov 1989, *The Last Drop* (1903, greenish-brown-patinated bronze, h. 12¼ ins / 31.1 cm) USD 19,800. NEW YORK, 27 May 1993, *The Indian White Eagle* (bronze, h. 19½ ins / 49.5 cm) USD 29,900. NEW YORK, 2 Dec 1993, *The Messenger* (1912, oil on canvas, 34 x 24 ins / 86.4 x 61 cm) USD 255,500. NEW YORK, 30 Nov 1995, *The Last Drop* (1903, bronze, h. 12 ins / 30.4 cm) USD 41,400.

SCHREYVOGEL, Joachim, or Schreivogel
German, 17th century.
Died 1633.
Active in Dresden.
Painter, sculptor (?).
After a three-month trip to Italy, Joachim Schreyvogel was recommended by the Prince-Elector of Saxony to the King of Denmark. He settled in Dresden in 1620.

SCHREYVOGEL, Joachim Franz, or Schreivogel
German, 17th century.
Born 18 November 1624, in Dresden; died 18 February 1688.
Painter.
Joachim Franz Schreyvogel was the son of Joachim.

SCHRIBER, Ulrich
French, 15th century.
Active in Strasbourg.
Illuminator.
Ulrich Schriber illuminated the manuscript of the *History of the World by Rudolph von Ems* (1422) which is now in the municipal library of Augsburg.

SCHRICK, F. van der
Flemish School, 18th century.
Sculptor, designer of ornamental architectural features.
F. van der Schrick worked at the court of Charles of Lorraine in Brussels in 1768.

SCHRIECK, Otto Marseus van.
See **MARSEUS VAN SCHRIECK Otto**

SCHRIEDER, Jacob, or Schrider
Dutch, 18th century.
Active in Amersfoort in 1709 and Utrecht in 1760.
Painter. Portraits.
AUCTION RECORDS:
LINDAU, 5 May 1982, *Five Children before a Balustrade* (1733, oil on canvas, 44 x 51¼ ins / 112 x 130 cm) DEM 15,000.

SCHRIEWER, Werner. See **SCHREIBER**

SCHRIJNDER, Jo
Dutch, 20th century.
Born 1894; died 1968.
Painter. Animals, birds, landscapes.
AUCTION RECORDS:
AMSTERDAM, 10 Feb 1988, *Black Grouse in the Moorland* (oil on canvas, 15¾ x 20 ins / 40 x 51 cm) NLG 1,380. AMSTERDAM, 5 June 1990, *Pheasant on a Hedge* (oil on canvas, 16 x 20 ins / 40.5 x 50.5 cm) NLG 2,300. AMSTERDAM, 14 Sept 1993, *Ducks on a Frozen Lake* (oil on canvas, 16 x 20 ins / 40.5 x 50.5 cm) NLG 4,025. AMSTERDAM, 19-20 Feb 1997, *Hare in a Forest of Silver Birches* (oil on canvas, 27¾ x 23¾ ins / 70.5 x 60.5 cm) NLG 3,459.

SCHRIJVER, Émile de. See **SCHRYVER**

SCHRIKKEL, Louis
Dutch, 20th century.
Born 1902.
Painter (gouache). Scenes with figures, landscapes with figures.
AUCTION RECORDS:
AMSTERDAM, 25 April 1978, *Purchaser* (1936, oil on canvas, 23¼ x 27¼ ins / 59 x 69.5 cm) NLG 2,900. AMSTERDAM, 31 Oct 1979, *Thieves in a Car, Paris* (1927, oil on canvas, 23¼ x 27¼ ins / 59 x 69 cm) NLG 5,400. AMSTERDAM, 10 April 1989, *Farmyard* (1939, oil on canvas, 27¼ x 19¼ ins / 69 x 49 cm) NLG 2,300. AMSTERDAM, 12 Dec 1990, *Car Thieves in Paris* (1927, oil on canvas, 23½ x 27½ ins / 60 x 70 cm) NLG 9,775. AMSTERDAM, 24 Sept 1992, *Happy Farmers* (oil on canvas, 19¾ x 27¾ ins / 50 x 70.5 cm) NLG 5,175. AMSTERDAM, 9 Dec 1992, *Accident* (1926, gouache and colouring pencil/paper/card, 9 x 13¾ ins / 22 x 35 cm) NLG 1,495. AMSTERDAM, 8 Dec 1993, *A Fisherman with Sailing Boats in the Background* (oil on canvas, 23½ x 19¾ ins / 60 x 50 cm) NLG 1,610. AMSTERDAM, 31 May 1995, *The Rose* (1943, oil on panel, 11½ x 6 ins / 29 x 15.5 cm) NLG 1,180.

SCHRIKKER, Cornelis or Kees
Dutch, 20th century.
Born in Amsterdam.
Painter, sculptor. Urban landscapes, landscapes.
Cornelis Schrikker exhibited at the Paris Salon d'Automne and mainly painted landscapes from areas around the French capital.

SCHRIMPER, Fr. Ad.
German, 19th century.
Active in Bremen.
Painter.
Twelve of Fr. Ad. Schrimper's drawings representing landscapes were sold at an auction in 1832.

SCHRIMPF, Georg
German, 20th century.
Born 13 February 1889, in Munich; died 1938, in Berlin.
Painter, engraver.
Neue Sachlichkeit (New Objectivity).
Georg Schrimpf was a militant in the Anarchist movement, and was employed at a bakery in Passau in 1902. In 1916 he married the painter Maria Uhden. He settled in Berlin in 1915, and in 1918 moved to Munich, where he became a

member of the Novembergruppe (November Group) and subsequently the New Secession in Berlin. A visit to Italy in 1922 proved to be a turning point in his career, and the former Futurist Carlo Carra dedicated a monograph to him in 1924.

Schrimpf taught mural decoration in Munich from 1927, and at a Berlin art school from 1933. He was forced to resign by the Nazis shortly before his death.

His painted works fell into two distinct periods. His early works were very linear, the coloured shapes clearly outlined. He had come into contact with modern art as a young painter in Berlin in 1915. Until 1917 his early style was also influenced by the Expressionist movement, all the more so as a result of his acquaintance with Franz Marc. A far-left militant, when he travelled to Italy he made contact with the Social Neo-Realist group of artists formed around the journal *Valori Plastici*.

In his second period, Schrimpf adopted the principles of Social Realism. Abandoning colour, he strove to represent the concrete nature of objects from daily life and from his environment; mostly modest interiors and workers' districts. The sobriety of the paintings of this second period gives them an undeniable monumentality reminiscent of the work, albeit geographically distant, of Mexican artist Diego Rivera.

He was a representative of the Neue Sachlichkeit (New Objectivity); a pictorial movement with clearly expressed political intentions. Within this movement, he brought a very personal, Neo-Romantic note; the vision of an authentic manual worker, with fewer ambitious intentions, and close to concrete, everyday reality. This approach was very different to that of the visionaries of abjection, Otto Dix and Georg Grosz. Works from his second period include: a *Self-portrait*, a *Portrait of Oscar-Maria Graf* from 1918, the 1923 painting *Mother and Child in a Yard*, and *Landscape of the Bavarian Forest* from 1933.

In 1925 his work featured in the first *Neue Sachlichkeit (New Objectivity)* exhibition organised by Gustav Hartlaub at the Mannheim Kunsthalle, and in 1933 at the *New German Romanticism* exhibition in Hanover. In 1915, a first solo exhibition of his works was held by the *Sturm* revue gallery set up by a Berlin group of the same name which promoted the avant-garde, and German Expressionism in particular.

G Schrimpf

BIBLIOGRAPHY:

Carra, Carlo, *Georg Schrimpf*, Valori Plastici, Rome, 1924. Brion, Marcel, *La Peinture allemande*, Éd. Pierre Tisné, Paris, 1959. *Réalismes en Allemagne 1919-1923*, exhibition catalogue, Musée d'Art et d'Industrie, Saint-Étienne, musée d'Art et d'Histoire, Chambery, 1974. Halturin, Aleksandr/Hulten, Pontus/Gunar, Karl (ed.), *Paris-Moscou*, group exhibition catalogue, Éd. du Centre Georges-Pompidou, Paris, 1979. Hofmann, Karl-Ludwig/Praeger, Chrismut, *Wolfgang Storch, Georg Schrimpf und Maria Uhden. Leben und Werk Werkverzeichnis*, catalogue raisonné, Charlottenpresse, Frölich und Kaufmann, Berlin, 1985.

MUSEUMS AND GALLERIES:

BASEL (Kunstmus.): *Young Girl at the Window, Morning* (1925) - MUNICH (Bayerische Staatsgemaldesammlungen): *Landscape of the Bavarian Forest* (1933); *Portrait of Mrs Schrimpf* (1922) - MUNICH (Neue Pinakothek): *At the Balcony* (1927).

AUCTION RECORDS:

MUNICH, 27 Nov 1973, *Young Girl by the Water*, DEM 25,500. COLOGNE, 3 Dec 1976, *Porto Ronco* (oil on canvas, 26 x 23¼ ins / 66 x 59 cm) DEM 3,000. MUNICH, 31 May 1979, *Two Young Girls Sleeping in the Fields* (1932, oil on canvas, 20¾ x 32¼ ins / 53 x 82 cm) DEM 34,000. MUNICH, 30 Nov 1979, *View of the Chiemsee* (1936, gouache, 25½ x 19¼ ins / 65 x 49 cm) DEM 11,500. LONDON, 2 Dec 1980, *Young Woman and Horses* (c. 1922-1924, charcoal, 14 x 16 ins / 35.5 x 40.6 cm) GBP 700. LONDON, 27 March 1984, *Looking Out* (1931, oil on canvas, 31 x 25¼ ins / 79 x 64 cm) GBP 45,000. LONDON, 27 June 1984, *Man and Dog; Woman at the Window* (colouring pencil, brush and ink, two drawings, 8 x 6 ins / 20.3 x 15.3 cm and 8¼ x 6¼ ins/21 x 16 cm) GBP 1,500. COLOGNE, 8 Dec 1984, *Young Girl at the Window* (1927, watercolour, 15¼ x 11¾ ins / 39 x 30 cm) DEM 20,000. MUNICH, 11 June 1985, *Young Girl and Bird* (1919, watercolour, 12¾ x 10 ins / 32.5 x 25.5 cm) DEM 19,000. MUNICH, 3 June 1986, *Bavarian Landscape* (1933, oil on canvas, 35½ x 63 ins / 90 x 160 cm) DEM 95,000. NEW YORK, 13 May 1987, *Staffelsee* (1933, oil on canvas, 23 x 37½ ins / 58.4 x 95.3 cm) USD 48,000. COLOGNE, 30 May 1987, *Nude Standing* (pencil, 20 x 14¼ ins / 51 x 36.3 cm) DEM 2,200. MUNICH, 7 June 1989, *Portrait of a Woman with a Dog* (1924, oil on canvas, 29¾ x 22¾ ins / 75.5 x 58 cm) DEM 154,000. LONDON, 19 March 1991, *Osterseen* (1925, oil on canvas, 15¾ x 23½ ins / 40 x 60 cm) GBP 27,500. MUNICH, 26-27 Nov 1991, *Portrait of Oskar Maria Graf* (1918, oil on canvas, 25½ x 18½ ins / 65 x 47 cm) DEM 178,250. MUNICH, 1-2 Dec 1992, *Young Woman Dressing* (chalk and pencil, 8½ x 6¼ ins / 21.5 x 16 cm) DEM 1,495. NEW YORK, 24 Feb 1995, *Road Round a Village* (1927, watercolour and pencil/paper, 9½ x 13½ ins / 24.4 x 34 cm) USD 2,645. LONDON, 25 June 1996, *Still-life with Rubber* (1924, oil on canvas, 23 x 20 ins / 58.5 x 50.5 cm) GBP 18,975. HAMBURG, 12 June 1999, *Lake Landscape, Langbuergner See* (1930, oil on canvas, 22 x 35 ins / 55 x 90 cm) DEM 42,000. BERLIN, 26 Nov 1999, *Extensive Wooded Landscape* (1937, oil on canvas, 27 x 39 ins / 68 x 100 cm) DEM 65,000. COLOGNE, 7 June 2000, *Grimmelshausen Simplicissimus* (watercolour and pen, 9 x 6 ins / 22 x 14 cm) DEM 4,800. MUNICH, 19 May 2001, *Animals in the Forest* (c. 1918, watercolour and pen on board, 11 x 6 ins / 28 x 16 cm) DEM 27,000. MUNICH, 1 Dec 2001, *Girl with Mirror* (1930, watercolour, 11 x 10 ins / 29 x 25 cm) DEM 21,000. HAMBURG, 23 March 2002, *Diessen Shore on Ammersee* (watercolour, 11 x 19 ins / 29 x 49 cm) EUR 2,500. MUNICH, 27 June 2003, *Pre-alpine Landscape with Lake* (1905, oil on canvas, 35 x 66 ins / 89 x 168 cm) EUR 42,000. BERLIN, 29 Nov 2003, *Bathers* (1924, watercolour over pencil) EUR 2,200. LONDON, 3 Feb 2004, *Landscape with Figures* (1924, oil on canvas, 26 x 34 ins / 66 x 86 cm) GBP 130,000.

SCHRIMPF, Johann Georg

German, 18th century.

Active in Nymphenburg, Ludwigsburg and Kassel.

Painter (porcelain).

SCHRO, Dietrich

16th century.

Active in Mainz between 1545 and 1568.

Sculptor.

Schro's work includes the tombs of Prince Elector Albert of Brandenburg, Sebastian of Heusenstamm and Georg Goler of Regensburg in Mainz Cathedral.

SCHROBILTGEN, Paul

Belgian, 20th century.

Born 1923, in Messancy-lez-Arlon; died 1980, in Ukkel.

Painter, lithographer.

A member of the Luxembourg Academy, Paul Schrobiltgen studied at the Arlon Academy between 1937 and 1944. He illustrated a collection of poems by J. C. Morgen. His work features in collections held by the Belgian state, and was the subject of a retrospective in Belgium in 1991.

His work spanned the Cubist and Expressionist periods, before developing into sensitive abstraction, and later kinetic art.

SCHRÖCK, Michael, or Schreck
German, 17th century.
Born 1670, in Presburg; died 1706, in Berlin.
Painter. Portraits.
Michael Schröck studied in Venice and worked from 1698 in Berlin.

SCHRÖCK, Stephan, or Schröcker
German, 17th - 18th century.
Active in Laufen 1686-1723.
Painter.

SCHRÖCKER, Hans
Austrian, 18th century.
Painter.

SCHRÖCKER, Hartmann
German, 18th - 19th century.
Born 7 March 1745, in Neresheim; died 3 February 1827, in Neresheim.
Cabinet maker.

SCHRÖCKER, Stephan. See **SCHRÖCK**

SCHRÖDER
German, 17th century.
Active in Wittenberg.
Painter.

SCHRÖDER, A.
German, 19th century.
Active in Berlin.
Painter. Portraits, landscapes, animals.
A. Schröder was the pupil of J. Kirchoff and exhibited from 1832 to 1848.
AUCTION RECORDS:
LONDON, 22 Nov 1996, *Horseman* (1894, oil on panel, 10 x 8 ins / 25.4 x 20.3 cm) GBP 1,150.

SCHRØDER, Abel I
Danish, 16th century.
Died 1602, in Nastved.
Active in Nastved (Seeland).
Sculptor (wood).
Abel Schrøder I was probably the father of Abel Schrøder II.

SCHRØDER, Abel II
Danish, 17th century.
Born 1602 or 1603, in Nastved; died 5 March 1676, in Nastved.
Sculptor (wood).
Schrøder was probably the son of Abel Schrøder I. He sculpted numerous altars.

SCHRÖDER, Albert
German, 17th century.
Cabinet maker.

SCHRÖDER, Albert Friedrich
German, 19th - 20th century.
Born 3 November 1854, in Dresden; died 1939, in Dresden.
Active in Munich.
Painter, illustrator. Figures, portraits, genre scenes.
Albert Friedrich Schröder was a pupil of C. Verlat and F. Pauwels.

A.Schröder

MUSEUMS AND GALLERIES:
DUISBURG - MAGDEBURG.
AUCTION RECORDS:
NEW YORK, 26 and 27 Feb 1947, *Card Game*, USD 750. LONDON, 21 Oct 1970, *Audience*, GBP 750. LONDON, 22 Oct 1971, *Dessert Wine; Card Players*, Gns 2,000. LONDON, 12 May 1972, *Good Story*, Gns 1,200. VIENNA, 22 May 1973, *Drink among Friends*, ATS 110,000. LONDON, 14 June 1974, *Horseman* (1888) Gns 1,700. NEW YORK, 14 May 1976, *Duo* (1894, oil on canvas, 18 1/2 x 25 1/4 ins / 47 x 64 cm) USD 5,250. NEW YORK, 4 May 1979, *Pipe Smoker* (1891, oil on panel, 11 x 7 3/4 ins / 28 x 20 cm) USD 5,000. LONDON, 22 May 1981, *After the Lesson* (1890, oil on panel, 12 x 15 ins / 30.5 x 38.2 cm) GBP 1,500. NEW YORK, 29 Feb 1984, *Gentleman with a Mandoline* (oil on panel, 13 1/2 x 17 ins / 34 x 43 cm) USD 4,500. VIENNA, 20 March 1985, *Merry Companions* (oil on panel, 15 3/4 x 19 3/4 ins / 40 x 50 cm) ATS 75,000. NEW YORK, 28 Oct 1986, *Wounded Horseman* (1899, oil on canvas, 28 1/2 x 39 3/4 ins / 72.4 x 101 cm) USD 9,000. LONDON, 14 Feb 1990, *Eating in Merry Company* (oil on panel, 15 1/2 x 19 3/4 ins / 39.5 x 50 cm) GBP 8,580. NEW YORK, 20 Jan 1993, *Young Man with a Pipe* (oil on panel, 9 1/2 x 12 3/4 ins / 24.1 x 32.4 cm) USD 3,450. LONDON, 17 Nov 1993, *Woman Playing the Mandolin* (oil on panel, 16 1/4 x 12 ins / 41 x 30.5 cm) GBP 4,370. MUNICH, 7 Dec 1993, *Playing Backgammon; Navigators Studying a Map* (oils/panel, a pair, each 26 1/4 x 21 1/2 ins / 66.5 x 54.5 cm) DEM 29,900. NEW YORK, 20 July 1994, *Little Girl Dancing* (1887, oil on panel, 12 3/4 x 17 1/4 ins / 32.7 x 43.8 cm) USD 6,325. LONDON, 10 Feb 1995, *Lively Banter in an Interior* (1890, oil on panel, 15 3/4 x 11 1/2 ins / 40 x 29.2 cm) GBP 5,175. LONDON, 15 March 1996, *Recounting a Tale* (oil on panel, 18 x 21 ins / 45.7 x 53.4 cm) GBP 7,130.

SCHRÖDER, Anton Julius
Danish, 20th century.
Born 16 September 1893, in Kolding (Jutland).
Active in Kolding.
Painter. Landscapes.

SCHRØDER, Bernhard
Danish, 19th century.
Born 11 October 1832, in Copenhagen; died 21 March 1888, in Copenhagen.
Painter, decorative artist.
Schrøder was the brother of the architect Johan Schrøder. In 1858, he founded a company with Nielsen and Hansen, which still exists today. He was responsible for some of the decoration of Frederiksborg castle.

SCHRÖDER, Carl Julius Hermann
German, 19th century.
Born 1802, in Brunswick; died 13 May 1867, in Brunswick.
Painter, engraver. Figures, portraits, genre scenes.
Carl Schröder attended the academy in Dresden and worked in Munich. His works became popular through lithography.
MUSEUMS AND GALLERIES:
BRUNSWICK - KALININGRAD: *Dance of Bavarian Peasants*.
AUCTION RECORDS:
PARIS, 23 April 1897, *Dialogue*, FRF 700. LONDON, 24 March 1982, *Reverie* (1836, oil on canvas, 15 1/4 x 11 3/4 ins / 39 x 30 cm) GBP 1,500. MUNICH, 17 Oct 1984, *Stroke of Genius* (oil on canvas, 19 x 15 3/4 ins / 48.5 x 40 cm) DEM 9,500. COPENHAGEN, 16 May 1994, *Southern Landscape with Cascade* (1866, oil on canvas, 21 1/4 x 17 1/4 ins / 54 x 44 cm) DKK 10,500. NEW YORK, 17 Jan 1996, *Old Man Smoking Pipe and Conversing with Bird* (oil on canvas, 10 3/4 x 9 1/4 ins / 27.3 x 23.5 cm) USD 1,955. ANTWERP, 22 March 1999, *Leaving* (1854, oil on canvas, 45 x 63 ins / 115 x 160 cm) BEF 140,000. MUNICH, 29 Sept 1999, *Did I Hear Right?* (oil on canvas, 15 x 12 ins / 37 x 30 cm) DEM 15,000. LONDON, 11 June 2002, *Portrait of a Young Lady* (1853, oil on canvas, 26 x 20 ins / 65 x 51 cm) GBP 1,000.

SCHRÖDER, Caspar or Kaspar
Swedish, 18th century.
Born near Värjö; died November 1710, in Stockholm.
Sculptor.
Schröder worked with Nicolas Schultz in 1672, and with Henrik Scutz. He adopted Bernini's style, which was in vogue in Sweden at the time, in his work for castles.

SCHRÖDER, Christian Johann, or Schroeter
Bohemian School, 17th - 18th century.
Born in Goslar; died at the beginning of the 18th century, in Prague.
Painter, decorative artist.
Christian Johann Schröder studied in Rome from 1682 to 1684, and in Venice. He became a painter at the Bohemian court in 1684 and decorated the Spanish hall of the Hradschin in Prague.

SCHRÖDER, Dora
German, 19th century.
Born 1851, in Itzehoe; died 1873, in Itzehoe.
Painter.
MUSEUMS AND GALLERIES:
KIEL: *Flowers.*

SCHRØDER, Ejler
Danish, 17th century.
Died between 1628 and 1630, in Nastved.
Active in Nastved.
Sculptor (wood).
Schrøder was the son of Abel Schrøder I. He sculpted mostly church chairs.

SCHRÖDER, Franz Adam
German, 19th century.
Born 20 March 1809, in Hamburg; died 24 June 1875, in Hamburg.
Engraver (burin).

SCHRÖDER, Georg. See **SCHRÖTER**

SCHRÖDER, Georg Engelhardt
Swedish, 18th century.
Born 31 May 1684, in Stockholm; died 17 May 1750.
Painter. History painting, genre scenes, landscapes.
Schröder was a pupil of David von Krafft. He travelled to Brunswick and Venice from 1710 to 1715, and to Rome, Munich and London from 1718 to 1725. He devoted himself mostly to portraits, but also composed some mythological scenes. He was a painter to the court. He left Sweden during the wars, and was replaced by Taraval, a Frenchman, who helped to found the royal Swedish academy. An artist of conservative taste, he did not have a great influence on the development of Swedish painting. He returned to Sweden in 1726, after having visited Germany, France, Italy and Britain.
MUSEUMS AND GALLERIES:
GÖTEBORG: *Portrait of Nic. Keder; Apelle Painting Venus* - STOCKHOLM (Kungliga Akademien): *Portraits of the Artist and the Painter Johan Philippe Lemke* - STOCKHOLM (Nationalmus.): *The Four Elements* - VÄXJÖ: *Portrait of A. von Aschberg.*
AUCTION RECORDS:
STOCKHOLM, 11 April 1984, *Portrait of a Lady of Quality* (oil on canvas, 30 1/4 x 25 1/4 ins / 77 x 64 cm) SEK 11,500. STOCKHOLM, 19 April 1989, *Portrait of a Foreign Officer* (oil on canvas, 50 x 40 1/4 ins / 127 x 102 cm) SEK 24,000. STOCKHOLM, 19 May 1992, *Portrait of Cardinal de Fleury* (oil on canvas, 62 1/4 x 50 1/2 ins / 158 x 128 cm) SEK 18,500. STOCKHOLM, 3 Dec 2002, *Portrait of Count Nils Bjelke* (oil on canvas, 31 x 26 ins / 79 x 65 cm) SEK 78,000. STOCKHOLM, 4 Dec 2002, *Portraits of Fredrik I and Ulrika Eleonora the Younger* (oil on canvas, a pair, 87 x 52 ins / 220 x 133 cm) SEK 75,000. STOCKHOLM, 4 June 2003, *Portrait of Admiral Johan von Utfall and his Wife Maria Helena* (oil on canvas, a pair, 31 x 25 ins / 79 x 63 cm) SEK 41,000. STOCKHOLM, 2 Dec 2003, *Portrait of King Fredrik I* (oil on canvas, 76 x 56 ins / 194 x 142 cm) SEK 155,000.

SCHRÖDER, Hans
German, 17th century.
Active in Lüneburg 1604-1618.
Sculptor, painter.
Hans Schröder carried out five stone figures for the Rathaus at Luneburg.
MUSEUMS AND GALLERIES:
LÜNEBURG (Ostpreussisches Landesmus.): *Bust of Anna von Weihe.*

SCHRÖDER, Hans
German, 17th century.
Died 10 October 1628.
Active in Hamburg.
Painter.
Hans Schröder became a master in 1605.

SCHRÖDER, Heinrich
German, 20th century.
Born 12 July 1881, in Krefeld.
Painter, engraver.
Heinrich Schröder studied in Berlin, Weimar and Paris before settling in Munich.
MUSEUMS AND GALLERIES:
DÜSSELDORF.

SCHRÖDER, Hubert
British, 19th - 20th century.
Born 1867.
Painter, engraver.
Hubert Schröder was active as an engraver in Bournemouth and London.

SCHRÖDER, Ivan Nikolaevich or Pavlovich, or Chredér
Russian, 19th century.
Born 1835.
Sculptor.
Ivan Schröder studied under Baron Petr Karlovich Klodt and at the art academy in St Petersburg under Pimenov. He travelled in South America from 1865 to 1869 and settled in St Petersburg in 1869. He produced the memorial monuments to *Admiral Krusenstern* and *Prince Peter Oldenburg* in St Petersburg.

SCHRØDER, J. N.
Danish, 18th century.
Born probably in 1715; died after 1745.
Engraver (burin).
Schrøder engraved views of cities and Danish castles.

SCHRÖDER, Jacob
German, 17th century.
Active in Stade.
Medallist.

SCHRÖDER, Johann Heinrich
German, 18th - 19th century.
Born 28 August 1757, in Meiningen; died 29 January 1812, in Meiningen.
Painter. Portraits.
The pupil of Tischbein in Kassel, Johann Schröder worked in Hanover and Brunswick and went to the Netherlands and England. He painted the portraits of several crowned heads.
MUSEUMS AND GALLERIES:
BERLIN (Mus. Hohenzollern): *The Duke of York and Rederick, Duchess of York; Mme Selle, Wife of the Doctor to Friedrich II* - BERLIN (Nationalgal.): *Karl August, Prince of Hardenberg* - BERLIN (Palace): *Queen Louise* - BLANKENBURG (Mus. Kleines Schloss): *Duke Karl Wilhelm Ferdinand and Duchess*

Maria - BRUNSWICK: *Duke Frederick August von Brunswick* - BRUNSWICK (Herzog Anton Ulrich-Mus.): *Duchess Philippine Charlotte d'Orléans and Duchess Frederique Louise Wilhelmina* - BRUNSWICK (Städtisches Mus.): *King Friedrich Wilhelm II; Duchess Maria von Baden; Portrait of the Artist* - ROHRBECK (Castle): *Karl Friedrich Leopold von Gerlach* - SCHWEIKERSHEIM (Schloss): *Count August Neale; Countesses Pauline and Sophia Neale; Caroline von Bergh* - WEIMAR (Schlossmus.): *Wilhelmina von Orange* - WOLFSBERG: *Charles August, Prince of Hardenberg*.

SCHRÖDER, José-Maria
German, 20th century.
Born c. 1887; died after 1938.
Painter. Portraits, landscapes.

José-Maria Schröder studied in Düsseldorf until 1908. He lived in Naples from 1924 to 1927 and it was there that he met and became friends with the author and philosopher Jean Grenier, who featured in *Voir Naples* (*See Naples and Die*). Schröder painted a portrait of Grenier and his young partner and Schröder himself married an Italian girl, with whom he had a daughter, born in 1926. In 1927 he left his Italian family and settled in Paris. In all probability thanks to Grenier, he was introduced to various luminaries in Paris, including Louis Guilloux and André Chamson. Schöder returned to Düsseldorf in 1927 and settled there, living with his three sisters and exhibiting at the Flechtheim Gallery in 1928.

His views of Naples reveal him to be a competent painter who painted in a conventional manner, albeit with some Expressionist overtones. He himself described his work from this period as a 'tragic symphony'. It was in the Bavarian Alps, however, that he found his true inspiration. Overall, his paintings owe much to the model of Rembrandt.

SCHRÖDER, Josef
Austrian, 19th century.
Active in Innsbruck.
Sculptor.

Josef Schröder sculpted the statue of Pope Pius in 1824.

SCHRÖDER, Karl
German, 18th - 19th century.
Born 18 October 1760, in Brunswick; died 6 April 1844, in Brunswick.
Painter, engraver, draughtsman. Genre scenes.

Karl Schröder studied in Augsburg and Paris.

MUSEUMS AND GALLERIES:
BERLIN (Kupferstichkabinet): engravings.

SCHRÖDER, Karl
Danish, 19th - 20th century.
Born 13 July 1870.
Active in Lilleröd.
Painter, potter, draughtsman.

Karl Schröder was the brother of Rolf Schröder and a pupil of the painters Otto Bache and Frederick Vermehren. He also designed furniture.

AUCTION RECORDS:
MUNICH, 1 and 2 Dec 1992, *Bouquet of Wild Flowers* (oil on canvas, 33 1/2 x 29 1/2 ins / 85 x 75 cm) DEM 4,025.

SCHRÖDER, Karl, or Schröder-Tapiau
German, 19th - 20th century.
Born 25 October 1870, in Tapiau, East Prussia (now Gvardeysk, Russia); died 1945, in Munich.
Active in Dachau.
Painter.

SCHRÖDER, L. (Frau). See **MÜLLER Louise**

SCHRÖDER, Liska
Maiden name: Kurz
German, 19th century.
Born 30 March 1834, in Frankfurt an der Oder.
Active in Charlottenburg.
Landscape painter.

The pupil of Paul Flickel and Carl Ludwig, Liska Schröder was initially in Berlin and from 1897 in Charlottenburg. She exhibited in Berlin from 1884.

SCHRÖDER, Matthias. See **SCHRÖTER**

SCHRÖDER, Povl
Danish, 20th century.
Born 17 July 1894, in Copenhagen; died 1957.
Painter. Figures, interiors with figures, landscapes, still-lifes, flowers. Frescoes.

Povl Schröder painted frescoes for the Ritz Hotel in Copenhagen.

AUCTION RECORDS:
COPENHAGEN, 29 April 1976, *Still-life* (oil on canvas, 26 1/2 x 39 1/4 ins / 67 x 100 cm) DKK 3,500. COPENHAGEN, 8 March 1979, *Interior with Seated Woman* (oil on canvas, 31 1/2 x 23 1/2 ins / 80 x 60 cm) DKK 6,500. COPENHAGEN, 20 Sept 1989, *Reclining Model* (oil on canvas, 31 x 36 1/2 ins / 79 x 93 cm) DKK 16,000. COPENHAGEN, 30 May 1990, *Flowers in a Vase* (oil on canvas, 24 3/4 x 20 1/2 ins / 63 x 52 cm) DKK 6,000. STOCKHOLM, 14 June 1990, *Interior with Reclining Nude* (oil on canvas, 31 1/2 x 36 1/2 ins / 80 x 93 cm) SEK 21,000. COPENHAGEN, 4 Dec 1991, *Still-life with Books on a Table* (oil on canvas, 35 x 46 ins / 89 x 116 cm) DKK 21,000. COPENHAGEN, 2 April 1992, *Still-life with Flowers* (oil on canvas, 37 1/2 x 26 ins / 95 x 66 cm) DKK 12,000. COPENHAGEN, 21 Oct 1992, *Interior* (oil on canvas, 35 1/2 x 28 ins / 90 x 71 cm) DKK 26,000. COPENHAGEN, 21 April 1993, *Still-life with Bottles on a Table* (oil on canvas, 30 3/4 x 36 1/4 ins / 78 x 92 cm) DKK 8,000. COPENHAGEN, 27 April 1995, *Still-life on a Table* (oil on canvas, 25 1/2 x 31 1/2 ins / 65 x 80 cm) DKK 10,000. COPENHAGEN, 17 April 1996, *Still-life* (oil on canvas, 21 1/4 x 25 1/2 ins / 54 x 65 cm) DKK 8,600. COPENHAGEN, 20 Feb 2002, *Interior* (oil on canvas, 31 x 39 ins / 80 x 100 cm) DKK 17,000. COPENHAGEN, 10 April 2002, *Still-life with Vase and Fruit on Table* (oil on canvas, 45 x 37 ins / 115 x 95 cm) DKK 26,000. COPENHAGEN, 1 April 2003, *Girl on Sofa* (oil on canvas, 39 x 34 ins / 100 x 86 cm) DKK 11,000. COPENHAGEN, 29 March 2004, *Portrait of a Seated Woman* (oil on canvas, 40 x 30 ins / 102 x 75 cm) DKK 12,000. COPENHAGEN, 29 March 2004, *Still-life with Chair and View to Garden* (oil on canvas, 39 x 28 ins / 98 x 72 cm) DKK 15,000.

SCHRÖDER, Sierk
Dutch, 20th century.
Born 1903; died 2002.
Painter, watercolourist, pastellist. Figures, nudes, portraits, still-lifes.

Sierk Schröder studied at the fine arts academy in The Hague from 1922 to 1925, then completed his studies under André Lhote in Paris before returning to live and work in The Hague. From 1960 to 1968, Schröder taught at the national academy of fine arts in Amsterdam. A foundation dedicated to him and his work was established in Zuidwijk in 1995.

Schröder's compositions - 'figurations' - are examples of a classicist approach modulated by post-war Impressionist influences.

BIBLIOGRAPHY:
Kreeftenberg, Willemijn, *Sierk Schröder* (text in French, German, English and Italian).

AUCTION RECORDS:
AMSTERDAM, 10 April 1989, *Reclining Nude* (1976, pastel, 18 1/4 x 25 3/4 ins / 46.5 x 65.5 cm) NLG 3,910. AMSTERDAM, 17 Sept 1991, *Young Girl Reading* (1977, watercolour/paper, 19 3/4 x 17 3/4 ins / 50 x 45 cm) NLG 5,175. AMSTERDAM, 9 Dec 1992, *Young Girl Reading* (watercolour/paper, 13 1/4 x 16 1/4 ins / 33.5 x 41 cm) NLG 2,875. AMSTERDAM, 26 May 1993,

Reclining Nude (1935, oil on canvas, 23 1/2 x 31 3/4 ins / 60 x 80.5 cm) NLG 6,325. AMSTERDAM, 9 Dec 1993, *Woman Resting* (watercolour/paper, 17 x 23 1/4 ins / 43 x 59 cm) NLG 1,955. AMSTERDAM, 1 June 1994, *Young Woman* (1981, black chalk heightened with white, 18 1/2 x 23 1/2 ins / 47 x 60 cm) NLG 2,070. AMSTERDAM, 8 Dec 1994, *Two Fish* (1979, watercolour/card, 11 1/2 x 15 ins / 29 x 38 cm) NLG 3,335. AMSTERDAM, 6 Dec 1995, *Full-length Nude Looking out of a Window* (1963, watercolour/paper, 20 1/2 x 17 ins / 52 x 43 cm) NLG 6,325. AMSTERDAM, 5 June 1996, *Reclining Nude* (1975, ink and watercolour/paper, 18 x 23 ins / 45.5 x 57.5 cm) NLG 8,625. AMSTERDAM, 19-20 Feb 1997, *Young Woman* (1976, watercolour/paper, 19 3/4 x 15 3/4 ins / 50 x 40 cm) NLG 4,036. GRAVENHAGE, 28 April 1999, *Sketching Model* (1976, watercolour, 17 x 14 ins / 42 x 36 cm) NLG 5,500. AMSTERDAM, 10 June 1999, *Lady Reclining in Front of Mirror* (1978, watercolour on card, 28 x 35 ins / 70 x 90 cm) NLG 16,000. AMSTERDAM, 30 Nov 2000, *Seated Nude Seen from Behind* (1955, charcoal, 22 x 18 ins / 57 x 45 cm) NLG 5,500. AMSTERDAM, 3 Dec 2001, *Nude Reading* (1972, watercolour, 9 x 14 ins / 23 x 36 cm) NLG 5,000. AMSTERDAM, 28 May 2002, *Seated Nude* (charcoal and watercolour, 19 x 14 ins / 47 x 35 cm) EUR 3,500. AMSTERDAM, 28 May 2002, *Seated Nude* (1986, pastel, 27 x 31 ins / 68 x 79 cm) EUR 6,500. AMSTERDAM, 25 Nov 2003, *Lady in a Blue Kimono* (1986, watercolour, 19 x 14 ins / 49 x 36 cm) EUR 7,500. AMSTERDAM, 2 Dec 2003, *Toilette* (oil on canvas, 28 x 20 ins / 70 x 50 cm) EUR 10,000. AMSTERDAM, 9 June 2004, *Seated Nude* (1974, watercolour and black chalk, 23 x 17 ins / 58 x 44 cm) EUR 4,000. AMSTERDAM, 9 June 2004, *Seated Nude* (1979, watercolour and black chalk, 20 x 16 ins / 51 x 41 cm) EUR 4,200.

SCHRÖDER, Simon. See **SCHRÖTER**

SCHRÖDER, W.

German, 19th century.

Painter. Landscapes, seascapes.

W Schröder exhibited from 1860 to 1870 in Berlin.

SCHRÖDER-SONNENSTERN, Friedrich or Emil, or Schroeder-Sonnonnenstern

Lithuanian, 20th century.

Born 11 September 1892, in Kaukehmen (now Jasnoje) or Tilsit (now Sovetsk); died 1982.

Active in Germany.

Painter, draughtsman, poet.

Symbolism.

The details of Friedrich Schröder-Sonnenstern's biography are not easy to check and are known essentially from the artist himself. He was apparently born into a large family, and his father was a postilion. He was placed in a reform school at an early age, and his various professions - circus stable boy, smuggler, healer - made for a colourful existence. More certain information is available from the periods spent in prison and psychiatric hospitals that punctuated his life.

It was only in 1949, at the age of 57, that he began to draw, in coloured pencils, while living among the ruins in Berlin. Only a decade or so later, Hans Bellmer introduced him to his Surrealist friends, who immediately invited him to exhibit it at the Surrealist exhibition in Paris in 1959. His work was subsequently shown on many occasions, either at exhibitions given over to Surrealist and Fantastical art, or at exhibitions of Art Brut, mainly in Basel, Frankfurt am Main, Paris and Hamburg. In 1969, he exhibited in Vienna, Paris and Venice.

Drawing on images from a huge bestiary, whose figures, pregnant with symbolism, are reminiscent of Victor Brauner's imaginings, Schröder-Sonnenstern drew up an endless catalogue of his obsessions. These revolved around the problems of relations between human beings, particularly those of a sexual nature.

BIBLIOGRAPHY:

'*Schröder-Sonnenstern*' in *Chroniques de l'Art Vivant*, periodical, Maeght, Paris, July 1969.

AUCTION RECORDS:

HAMBURG, 4 June 1976, *Moon Tale* (1954, coloured pencil, 19 1/4 x 27 1/2 ins / 48.7 x 69.7 cm) DEM 10,000. NEW YORK, 17 May 1979, *The Race between Life and Death* (1958, pencil and graphite, 18 1/2 x 27 ins / 47 x 68.5 cm) USD 5,500. ZURICH, 17 May 1980, *Flight from Woman* (1959, mixed media, 14 1/2 x 20 ins / 36.6 x 51 cm) CHF 2,500. ZURICH, 30 Oct 1980, *Dance of the Swan Puppets, or the Swans' Moral Incantation* (1956, coloured pencil, 19 x 27 1/2 ins / 48 x 70 cm) CHF 4,000. ZURICH, 28 Oct 1981, *Hearts in the Snow* (1964, coloured pencil, 19 1/4 x 27 1/4 ins / 49 x 69 cm) CHF 4,600. ZURICH, 14 May 1983, *Fidgeting and Spitting Elks* (1959, wax crayon, 20 x 28 1/4 ins / 51 x 72 cm) CHF 2,800. MILAN, 9 June 1983, *The Scales of Moon-World Moral Justice* (1959, mixed media/card, 35 1/2 x 24 ins / 90 x 61 cm) ITL 3,500,000. LONDON, 25 June 1985, *The Swan-Doll* (1961, coloured pencil and graphite, 28 1/2 x 20 ins / 72.5 x 51 cm) GBP 3,200. LONDON, 28 May 1986, *Der Mondmoralische Tiervogel* (*The Moon-Moral Bird-Animal*) (1959, wax crayon/pencil outlines in colour, 28 3/4 x 20 ins / 73 x 51 cm) GBP 1,600. LOKEREN, 12 Dec 1987, *The Moon-Moral Decorative Bird* (1960, pastel, 28 3/4 x 20 ins / 73 x 51 cm) BEF 75,000. ZURICH, 25 Oct 1989, *Upside-down or Acrobatic Moon Conscious* (mixed media and gilded bronze, h. 20 3/4 ins / 53 cm) CHF 1,800. PARIS, 18 Feb 1990, *The Funny Immoral Moon Airbridge* (1956, colouring pencil, 23 x 34 1/2 ins / 58.5 x 87.5 cm) FRF 70,000. NEW YORK, 21 Feb 1990, *Requesting a Hand for a Lunar and Diplomatic Marriage* (1965, colouring pencil/card, 28 1/2 x 20 ins / 72.7 x 50.8 cm) USD 9,350. STOCKHOLM, 30 May 1991, *Psyche and Nabamor* (1956, coloured chalk/paper, 28 3/4 x 39 3/4 ins / 73 x 101 cm) SEK 16,500. STOCKHOLM, 30 Nov 1993, *Being Following Its Destiny* (coloured chalk/paper, 19 3/4 x 28 1/4 ins / 50 x 72 cm) SEK 16,500. NEW YORK, 24 Feb 1995, *The Swan-Doll* (graphite and colouring pencil/card, 20 x 28 1/2 ins / 50.8 x 72.7 cm) USD 2,645. COPENHAGEN, 7 June 1995, *Lunar Inventory* (1964, soft chalks, 20 x 28 1/4 ins / 51 x 72 cm) DKK 9,500.

SCHRÖDER-TAPIAU, Karl. See **SCHRÖDER Karl**

SCHRÖDL, Anton

Austrian, 19th - 20th century.

Born 24 February 1820, in Schwechat; died 5 July 1906, in Vienna.

Painter. Landscapes, animals.

Anton Schrödl studied at the academy in Vienna and spent time in Germany and Hungary before settling in the Austrian capital.

MUSEUMS AND GALLERIES:

MUNICH (Neue Pinakothek): *Landscape* - VIENNA: *Ram on the Foreshore*; *Cattle in front of a Shepherd's Hut*; *Two Sheep in a Cowshed*.

AUCTION RECORDS:

PARIS, 18 April 1950, *Mountain Landscapes* (two paintings) FRF 1,850. VIENNA, 17 March 1970, *Alpine Landscape*, ATS 20,000. VIENNA, 30 Nov 1971, *Cowshed Interior*, ATS 50,000. BRUSSELS, 5 Oct 1976, *Still-life* (oil on canvas, 27 1/4 x 39 ins / 69 x 99 cm) ATS 18,000. COLOGNE, 11 June 1979, *Rustic Interior* (oil on card, 13 x 17 3/4 ins / 33 x 45 cm) DEM 4,400. VIENNA, 18 May 1983, *Kitchen Interior* (oil on card, 11 x 17 1/4 ins / 28 x 43.5 cm) ATS 35,000. LONDON, 26 Feb 1988, *Sheep in a Fold* (oil on canvas, 15 1/2 x 21 3/4 ins / 39.5 x 55.4 cm) GBP 1,650. MUNICH, 25 June 1996, *Milkmaid* (oil on card, 5 1/2 x 10 ins / 14 x 25.5 cm) DEM 1,080.

SCHRÖDL, Leopold
Austrian, 19th century.
Born 7 July 1841, in Währing near Vienna; died 5 December 1908, in Vienna.
Sculptor.
Leopold Schrödl was the son of Norbert Michael Michael.

SCHRÖDL, Norbert
Austrian, 19th - 20th century.
Born 16 July 1842, in Vienna; died 25 February 1912, in Kronberg.
Painter. Portraits.
Norbert Schrödl was the son of Norbert Michael Schrödl. He studied in St Petersburg under Zichy and in Frankfurt under Becker von Worms, before going on to work in Dresden, Berlin, Paris and Italy.
MUSEUMS AND GALLERIES:
FRANKFURT AM MAIN: *Portrait of Empress Frederika; Portrait of the Painter Anton Burger; Portrait of the Painter Adolf Schreyer.*
AUCTION RECORDS:
HEIDELBERG, 11 April 1981, *Harvest Scene* (pen and wash, 5 3/4 x 9 1/4 ins / 14.5 x 23.5 cm) DEM 1,800.

SCHRÖDL, Norbert Michael
Austrian, 19th century.
Born 16 April 1816, in Schwechat, near Vienna; died 1 December 1890, in Dresden.
Sculptor (ivory).
Norbert Schrödl was the father of Leopold and Norbert.

SCHRODT, Johann Georg
German, 18th century.
Active in Wasserburg.
Painter.

SCHRÖDTER, Adolf, or Chrodter
German, 19th century.
Born 28 June 1805, in Schwedt; died 9 December 1875, in Karlsruhe.
Painter, engraver. Genre scenes.
Biedermeier.
Adolf Schrödter attended the academy in Berlin and was taught by Schadow in Düsseldorf. In 1835 he was made a member of the academy in Berlin and in 1859 he received a gold medal. He engraved genre subjects, vignettes and various illustrations.

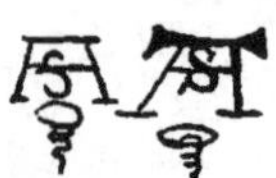

MUSEUMS AND GALLERIES:
AMSTERDAM (Stedelijk Mus.): *Don Quixote in his Study* - BERLIN (Nationalgal.): *Wine Tasting; Triumph of his Majesty the Wine* (two paintings); *Peasant Celebration; Rhenish Landscape; Till Eulenspiegel; Forest Forge; Herbarium Ornatum; Don Quixote Studying the Romances of Chivalry; Scene from Shakespeare's Henry IV* - COLOGNE: *Don Quixote* - DÜSSELDORF: *Peasant Celebration* (two paintings); *Don Quixote and his Dulchinea* - FRANKFURT AM MAIN (Städel): *Downcast Tanners; The Four Principal Drinks: Hock, Champagne, Punch and May Wine* - HAMBURG: *Munchhausen, Recounting his Adventures* - KALININGRAD: *How Till Eulenspiegel Tricked the Wine Waiter for a Jug of Wine* - KARLSRUHE: *The Four Seasons* - MÜNSTER: *Falstaff Inspecting the Recruits; Falstaff with the Justice of the Peace Schaal.*
AUCTION RECORDS:
LONDON, 21 Oct 1983, *As you Like It, Act 3, Scene 4* (1851, oil on canvas, 23 x 26 1/2 ins / 58.4 x 67.2 cm) GBP 1,900. BERLIN, 5 Dec 1986, *Triumph of Bacchus* (watercolour/pencil outlines/card, 12 x 37 1/2 ins / 30.2 x 95 cm) DEM 8,000. COLOGNE, 17 May 2003, *Wood Nymph* (1854, watercolour, 13 x 12 ins / 34 x 30 cm) EUR 8,200.

SCHRÖDTER, Alwine
Maiden name: Heuser
German, 19th century.
Born 13 February 1820, in Gummersbach (Rhineland); died 12 April 1892, in Karlsruhe.
Painter. Flowers.
In 1840 Alwine married the painter Adolf Schrödter.

SCHRÖDTER, Hans
German, 19th - 20th century.
Born 14 July 1872, in Karlsruhe.
Active in Donaueschingen.
Painter, engraver, illustrator.
Hans Schrödter was the uncle of Adolf Schrödter and a pupil of Leopold von Kalckreuth and Hans Thoma.

SCHROEDER, Erich
German, 17th century.
Active in Hamburg 1659-1681.
Painter.

SCHROEDER, Friedrich
German, 18th - 19th century.
Born 1768, in Hessen-Kassel; died 1839, in Paris.
Engraver, reproductions engraver.
The pupil of Klauber in Augsburg, Friedrich Schroeder engraved landscapes after Swanevilt, Vernet, La Hire and Karel du Jardin. He imitated the style of Woollett, notably in his works after Bemmel. He often engraved for other artists, executing the background and minor details for Massard and Toschi.

SCHROEDER, Louis Jean Désiré
French, 19th century.
Born 24 December 1828, in Paris; died 1898.
Sculptor.
His masters were François Rude and Dantan the Elder. He first exhibited at the Salon in 1848 and won a second-class medal in 1852.
MUSEUMS AND GALLERIES:
DIJON: *Oedipus and Antigone* - TOURS: *Falling Leaves.*

SCHROEDER, Max
German, 19th century.
Born 3 March 1858, in Greifswald.
Active in Berlin.
Painter. Seascapes.

SCHROEDER, Minna
German, 19th - 20th century.
Died 22 February 1931, in Leipzig.
Miniaturist.
Minna Schroeder was a pupil of Walter Tiemann. She is noted for portraits of Princess Margaret and Prince and Princess Johann Georg of Saxony.

SCHROEDER, Nathanael
German, 17th century.
Born 1630, in Danzig (now Gdansk, Poland); died 1685, in Danzig.
Draughtsman, engraver.
Nathanael Schroeder was an amateur.

SCHROEDER, Ulrich Anton
German, 19th century.
Born 24 April 1805, in Güstrow; died 1837, in Munich.
Painter. Figures, portraits.
Ulrich Schroeder attended the academy in Dresden.

SCHROEDER, William Howard
British, 19th century.

Died August 1892, in Pretoria.
Draughtsman, caricaturist.
William Howard Schroeder settled in South Africa, where he became extremely successful. A large number of his caricatures were reproduced in the English press.

SCHROEDER-SONNENSTERN, Friedrich or Emil. See **SCHRÖDER-SONNENSTERN**

SCHROEDTER, Anton
German, 19th - 20th century.
Born 9 February 1879, in Koblenz.
Sculptor.
Anton Schroedter was a pupil of Ludwig Habich. He spent time in Rome between 1907 and 1914 before going on to live and work in Darmstadt. He is noted for his decorations for the façade of the commercial college in Cologne.

SCHROEGER, Efraim
Polish, 18th century.
Born 18 February 1727, in Thorn (now Torun); died 16 August 1783, in Warsaw.
Draughtsman, architect.
Efraim Schroeger studied architecture under Captain Deybel. He was a draughtsman and an architect at the court of Stanislas-August. He rebuilt the Carmelite church in Warsaw, and also designed a palace for a primate, as well as the Skiernievice chapel. In the chapel was a statue of Ostrovski, which was sculpted by Monaldi from Schroeger's drawings.

SCHROEKH, Michael. See **SCHRÖCK**

SCHROER, Hans, or Schöer or Schrorer
Belgian, 16th century.
Born to a family originally from Liège; died 1601, in Kassel.
Painter, modeller, sculptor, stucco artist.
Until 1572 Hans Schroer was in the service of Landgrave Wilhelm IV of Hessen-Kessel, for whom he drew the plans of a fountain. In 1572 he went to work for Prince Elector Augustus of Saxony. Between 1573 and 1577 he painted 28 murals for Freudenstein Castle, Freiberg. In 1575 he did paintings for Dresden Castle and finally went to Augsburg, where he painted portraits of the dukes of Württemberg.

SCHRÖER, Rudolf
Austrian, 19th - 20th century.
Born 1 October 1864, in Vienna.
Sculptor.
Rudolf Schröer was a pupil of E. Hofmann.

SCHROETER, C.
German, 19th century.
Active in Berlin c. 1817.
Lithographer.

SCHROETER, Carolina von
Maiden name: Grasselli
Italian, 19th century.
Born 1803, in Rome.
Miniaturist.

SCHROETER, Christian Johann.
See **SCHRÖDER**

SCHROETER, Constantin Johann Friedrich Carl. See **SCHRÖTER**

SCHROETER, Gottlieb Heinrich von
German, 19th century.
Born 25 March 1802, in Rendsburg; died after 1866.
Painter. History painting, religious subjects.
Gottlieb Schroeter studied in Dresden and from 1821 to 1827 lived in Rome, where he evolved under the influence of Overbeck. He was also a writer and his wife Carolina, née Grasselli, was a miniature painter.

AUCTION RECORDS:
LONDON, 14 Feb 1990, *The Return of Judith after the Murder of Holofernes* (1835, oil on canvas, 31 3/4 x 24 3/4 ins / 80.5 x 63 cm) GBP 2,860.

SCHROETER, Johann Friedrich, or Schioter
German, 18th - 19th century.
Born 11 December 1770, in Leipzig; died 2 April 1836, in Leipzig.
Engraver (burin), draughtsman.
The pupil of Bause, Johann Schroeter was appointed Engraver at the University of Leipzig in 1813. He engraved portraits and genre scenes, especially after Rembrandt but his output is mainly anatomical.

SCHROETER, Johann Gottlob
German, 19th century.
Died 1818.
Active in Dresden.
Painter.

SCHROETER, Paul K.
German, 19th - 20th century.
Born 26 October 1866, in Kempen.
Active in Berlin.
Painter, engraver.
Paul K. Schroeter was a pupil of Peter Janssen and E. von Gebhardt.

SCHROETER, Richard
German, 19th - 20th century.
Born 15 February 1873, in Breslau (now Wroclaw, Poland).
Painter. Landscapes, seascapes.
Richard Schroeter studied under W. Friedrich and Friedrich Kallmorgen and went on to live and work in Berlin, where examples of his work can be seen in various municipal collections and, most notably, in the town hall of Berlin-Schöneberg.

SCHROETTER, Richard
German, 20th century.
Born 1893, in Prerau, near Olmütz (now Olomouc, Czech Republic).
Active in France.
Painter.
Richard Schroetter was a pupil of Franz Thiele. He exhibited at the Salon des Tuileries in Paris.
MUSEUMS AND GALLERIES:
PRAGUE (Národní Gal.): three works.

SCHROEVENS, Cesar
Belgian, 20th century.
Born 25 February 1884, in Antwerp.
Sculptor. Figures. Busts.
Cesar Schroevens was a pupil of Frans Joris and Jef Lambeaux. He is noted for 10 busts sculpted for the foyer of the Flemish Lyric Theatre in Antwerp and for a bust of *Verhaeren* housed in the Maison du People in Brussels.
MUSEUMS AND GALLERIES:
ANTWERP: *Bust of Jef Lambeaux* (bronze); *Bust of Verhaeren* (marble) - IXELLES: *Head of a Woman.*
AUCTION RECORDS:
LOKEREN, 21 March 1992, *Embrace* (1943, plaster sculpture, h. 16 1/2 ins / 42 cm, w. 22 ins/55 cm) BEF 33,000.

SCHROFF
German, 18th century.
Active c. 1770.
Sculptor (wood).

SCHROIDER, G.
British, 18th century.
Active in London.
Painter. Portraits.

SCHROM, Sidonius von
Austrian, 20th century.
Born 22 November 1887, in Vienna.
Active in Innsbruck.
Painter, engraver.

SCHRÖNER, A.
German, 19th century.
Active c. 1839.
Miniaturist.
MUSEUMS AND GALLERIES:
HAMBURG (Mus. für Kunst und Gewerbe): *Portrait of Dr Johann Schleiden* (watercolour).

SCHROP, Thomas
German, 17th century.
Born to a family originally from Augsburg.
Active in Bergen in Norway in 1618.
Cabinet maker.

SCHROPP, Anton
German, 18th century.
Cabinet maker.

SCHROPP, Johann Daniel
Austrian, 18th century.
Painter.
Johann Schropp mainly painted landscapes at the porcelain factory in Vienna from 1771-1791.

SCHROPP, Karl
German, 19th century.
Born 1794; died 1876.
Modeller.
Karl Schropp worked at the Neue Residenz in Bamberg.

SCHROPP, Karl
German, 20th century.
Born 22 April 1899, in Heidelberg.
Active in Geneva.
Painter.
Karl Schropp studied under Friedrich Fehr and Albert Haueisen. Several examples of his work were acquired by the city of Heidelberg and the regional collection of Baden-Württemberg.
MUSEUMS AND GALLERIES:
MANNHEIM - NUREMBERG.

SCHROPP, Simon
German, 17th century.
Cabinet maker.
Simon Schropp furnished the cells for the monks in the Ottobeuren monastery, where he stayed from 1684.

SCHRORER, Hans. See **SCHROER**

SCHRORER, Hans Friedrich, or Schrorrer
German, 17th century.
Active in Augsburg 1609-1649.
Painter, engraver.
Confusion persists between this artist and Hans Friedrich Schorer the Elder, painter and engraver in Augsburg, who studied at the end of the 16th century in Venice and who worked between 1600 and 1639 in Nuremberg and Augsburg.

SCHRORER, Hans Friedrich, the Younger, or Schrorrer
German, 17th century.
Born 1610.
Active in Augsburg.
Painter.

SCHROT, Augustin, or Schrott
Austrian, 16th century.
Active in Vienna.
Painter.
Augustin Schrot became a burgher of Kempten in 1567 and settled in Vienna in 1573.

SCHROT, Christian. See **SGROOTEN**

SCHROTBANCK, Hanns
French, 15th - 16th century.
Painter, engraver.
School of Alsace.
There is evidence of Hanns Schrotbanck in Strasbourg in 1483, 1490 and 1502. There is no doubt that he engraved monograms.
MUSEUMS AND GALLERIES:
BERLIN (Deutsches Staatsbibliothek): *Calendar for 1490* (engraving/wood, attributed).

SCHRÖTEL, W.
German, 18th century.
Active in the middle of the 18th century.
Painter.
W. Schröter painted the portrait of Marshal Friedrich Ferdinand August, count of Würzburg.

SCHRÖTER, Bernhard
German, 19th - 20th century.
Born 1 October 1848, in Meissen; died 21 July 1911, in Meissen.
Painter. Figures, portraits, landscapes.
Bernhard Schröter was a pupil of C. Verlat and J. Hubner.

SCHRÖTER, Constantin Johann Friedrich Carl
German, 19th century.
Born 21 March 1795, in Schkeuditz; died 18 October 1835, in Berlin.
Painter. Genre scenes, portraits.
Constantin Schröter attended the drawing academy in Leipzig and was taught by Pochmann in Dresden. In 1819 he returned to Leipzig, establishing himself as a portrait painter. He also painted genre scenes. In 1826 he went to Berlin where his career came to an end.
AUCTION RECORDS:
COLOGNE, 21 Nov 1985, *Huntsman before Dead Stag* (1829, oil on panel, 19 x 15 ins / 48 x 38 cm) DEM 15,000.

SCHRÖTER, Corona Elise Wilhelmine
German, 18th century.
Born 11 January 1751, in Guben; died 23 August 1802, in Ilminau.
Painter.
Goethe requested Corona Schröter's presence in Weimar.
MUSEUMS AND GALLERIES:
WEIMAR (Goethe-Nationalmus.): *Self-portrait* (two versions).

SCHRÖTER, Friedrich
Swiss, 17th century.
Died 31 May 1660, in Altdorf (Suisse).
Active in Freiburg im Brisgau.
Painter.
Friedrich Schröter decorated the churches of Silenen and Attinghausen.

SCHRÖTER, Georg, or Schröder or Schroter or Schrotter
German, 16th century.
Born c. 1535, in Torgau; died 1586, in Torgau.
Sculptor.
Georg Schröter was a pupil of his father Simon Schröter the Elder. He worked solely in sandstone and alabaster.

SCHRÖTER, Johann, or Sckretar
German, 17th century.
Painter.
Johann Schröter painted the 12 Apostles and St Saturnin for the cathedral in Frauenburg (now Frombork).

SCHRÖTER, Johann Heinrich
German, 18th century.
Active in Zerbst c. 1723.
Painter (glazed earthenware).

SCHRÖTER, Ludwig
Swiss, 19th - 20th century.
Born 23 August 1861, in Esslingen; died 18 January 1929, in Zurich.
Draughtsman.

SCHRÖTER, Marianne von
German, 19th century.
Painter.
MUSEUMS AND GALLERIES:
ROSTOCK (Kunsthalle): two portraits.

SCHRÖTER, Matthias, or Schröder
German, 19th century.
Painter. Religious subjects, portraits, landscapes with figures.
Nazarenes group (related to).
Born in southern Bavaria, Matthias Schröter became a Benedictine monk and painted portraits and religious subjects in the Nazarene style.
AUCTION RECORDS:
LOS ANGELES, 17 March 1980, *Recumbent Nude and Lyre Player* (1906, oil on canvas, 28¾ x 36¼ ins / 73.2 x 92 cm) USD 1,300. LONDON, 31 Oct 1996, *Fishing in A River* (1868, oil on canvas, 13¾ x 19¼ ins / 35 x 49 cm) GBP 1,150.

SCHRÖTER, Simon, the Elder, or Schröder or Schroter or Schrotter
German, 16th century.
Died 10 August 1568.
Active in Torgau.
Sculptor.
Simon Schröter the Elder was the father of Georg and Simon Schröter the Younger. He was one of the most famous Saxon sculptors of the Renaissance, and was responsible for the portal of the church of Gotha Castle.

SCHRÖTER, Simon, the Younger, or Schröder or Schroter or Schrotter
German, 16th century.
Born c. 1545, in Torgau; died probably 1573.
Sculptor.
Simon Schröter the Younger was the son of Simon Schröter the Elder.

SCHRÖTER, Theodor
Austrian, 17th century.
Painter.

SCHROTER, Wilhelm, or Schroeter, called Winter-Schroeter
German, 19th century.
Born 24 February 1849, in Dessau; died 1904, in Karlsruhe.
Painter. Landscapes.
Wilhelm Schroter was the pupil of C.F. Lessing and H. Gude.
MUSEUMS AND GALLERIES:
ALTENBURG - CHEMNITZ - DESSAU - DONAUESCHINGEN - PFORZHEIM.
AUCTION RECORDS:
COLOGNE, 26 March 1976, *Forest Interior* (1895, oil on canvas, 35½ x 53¼ ins / 90 x 135 cm) DEM 1,500. COLOGNE, 11 June 1979, *Winter Landscape* (oil on canvas, 32¼ x 47¼ ins / 82 x 120 cm) DEM 3,200. ZURICH, 21 March 2000, *Winter Landscape with Stream* (1899, oil on canvas, 32 x 24 ins / 82 x 62 cm) CHF 3,500. SAN FRANCISCO, 15 Nov 2000, *Extensive Winter Landscape with Figure Walking along Stream* (1889, oil on canvas, 32 x 47 ins / 81 x 119 cm) USD 5,000. AMSTERDAM, 23 April 2001, *Winter Landscape* (1893, oil on canvas, 33 x 50 ins / 85 x 126 cm) NLG 19,000.

SCHROTH, Andreas, or Schrott
Austrian, 19th century.
Born 1791, in Vienna.
Sculptor, painter.
Andreas Schroth attended the academy of Vienna from 1809 and exhibited from 1820 to 1850.

SCHROTH, Jakob
Austrian, 18th - 19th century.
Born 1773, in Pest; died 22 February 1831, in Vienna.
Sculptor.
Jakob Schroth sculpted figures for the castle at Weilburg and the castle founded by the Scots in the vicinity of Vienna.

SCHROTH, Johann, the Elder, or Schrott
Austrian, 19th century.
Born 1789; died 1857, in Vienna.
Architect, sculptor.

SCHROTH, Johann, the Younger, or Schrott
Austrian, 19th century.
Born 1819, in Vienna.
Sculptor.
Johann Schroth was the son of Johann the Elder.

SCHROTH, Johann Friedrich, or Schrott
Austrian, 15th century.
Active in Vienna.
Sculptor.
Johann Friedrich Schroth worked for Count Esterhazy and carved the high altar of the church of Oberndorf, near Raabs.

SCHROTH, Josef
Austrian, 18th century.
Born 2 January 1764, in Pest; died 16 September 1797, in Vienna.
Sculptor.

SCHROTT. See also **SCHROT** and **SCHROTH**

SCHROTT, Andreas. See **SCHROTH**

SCHROTT, Augustin. See **SCHROT**

SCHRÖTT, Erasmus
Hungarian, 18th century.
Born 1755, in Göbel; died 20 February 1804, in Kassa (now Košice, Slovakia).
Painter, engraver.
Erasmus Scrött painted an *Allegory of Hungarian Law* for the town hall in Kassa.

SCHROTT, G.
18th century.
Silhouettist.

SCHROTT, Johann. See **SCHROTH**

SCHROTT, Johann Friedrich. See **SCHROTH**

SCHROTT, Maximilian
German, 19th century.
Born 1783, in Landshut; died 1822, in Munich.
Miniaturist, draughtsman. Landscapes.
Schrott was a pupil of H. Mitterer.
MUSEUMS AND GALLERIES:
MUNICH (Stadtmus.): landscape drawing.

SCHROTT, Othmar, or Schrott-Vorst
German, 20th century.

Born 24 April 1883, in Innsbruck.
Sculptor, engraver.
Othmar Schrott was a pupil of A. Brenck and W. von Rumann.

SCHROTTA, Janos Frigies or Johann Friedrich
Hungarian, 20th century.
Born 13 May 1898, in Kispest.
Sculptor.
Janos Frigies Schrotta lived and worked in Budapest. His works include a memorial monument to the war dead in Tasabanya.

SCHRÖTTER, Alfred von
Austrian, 19th - 20th century.
Born 12 February 1856, in Vienna; died 1935.
Painter, illustrator. Figures, landscapes.
Alfred von Schrötter studied under Canon and Loefftz at the academy in Vienna and went on to teach at the fine arts school in Graz. He is noted for his decorations in the Stephanie Chamber in Graz.
MUSEUMS AND GALLERIES:
GRAZ: *Country Road* - MAGDEBURG - OPAVA - WEIMAR.
AUCTION RECORDS:
VIENNA, 16 Nov 1983, *Portrait of a Hunter* (1886, oil on panel, 11 x 7¼ ins / 28 x 18.5 cm) ATS 110,000. NEW YORK, 17 Oct 1991, *Hunter* (1889, oil on panel, 15 x 12 ins / 38.1 x 30.5 cm) USD 8,250.

SCHRÖTTER, Bernhard von
Austrian, 18th - 19th century.
Born 29 August 1772, in Vienna; died 4 July 1842, in Vienna.
Painter, lithographer. Portraits.
Bernhard von Schrötter exhibited from 1813 to 1840 at Ste-Anne and mainly painted actors in their roles.
MUSEUMS AND GALLERIES:
GRAZ (Gallery of theatre portraits).

SCHRÖTTER, Georg
German, 17th - 18th century.
Born 1650; died 1717.
Active in Grüssau (now Krzeszow, Poland).
Sculptor.

SCHROTTER, Georg. See also **SCHRÖTER**

SCHROTZBERG, Franz
Austrian, 19th century.
Born 2 April 1814, in Vienna, in 1811 according to some sources; died 29 May 1889, in Graz.
Painter. Mythological subjects, portraits.
After attending the academy in Vienna, Schrotzberg studied in Italy, Germany and Belgium and spent time in Paris and London. On his return to Vienna, he became an academy member there.
MUSEUMS AND GALLERIES:
MUNICH: *Theresia, Gräfin von Würzburg; Elisabeth, Empress of Austria, born Princess of Bavaria; Mathilde, Archduchess of Austria* - VIENNA: *Leda; The Artist* - VIENNA (Czernin'sche Gemäldegal.): *Countess Czernin of Chudentz; Count Czernin; Countess Caroline Czernin.*
AUCTION RECORDS:
VIENNA, 14 March 1978, *Portrait of Countess Nako of Hagy* (1850, oil on canvas, 28 x 22½ ins / 71 x 57 cm) ATS 25,000. VIENNA, 11 Sept 1985, *Portrait of Little Girl* (oil on canvas, 62¼ x 43¼ ins / 158 x 110 cm) ATS 50,000. LONDON, 22 Nov 1990, *Leda and the Swan* (oil on canvas/panel, 53 x 40 ins / 134.6 x 101.6 cm) GBP 3,850. VIENNA, 19 Oct 1999, *Portrait of Woman in White Dress* (1849, oil on canvas, oval, 53 x 41 ins / 134 x 105 cm) ATS 140,000. LONDON, 13 Jan 2000, *Flora* (oil on canvas, painted in a circle, 31 x 31 ins / 80 x 80 cm) GBP 1,000. VIENNA, 22 March 2001, *Die Emancipierte (Portrait of a Young Viennese Woman in a Riding Outfit)* (oil on canvas, 44 x 21 ins / 111 x 54 cm) ATS 90,000. VIENNA, 9 April 2002, *Grafin Nabo de Nagy Szt Miklos* (1850, oil on canvas, 28 x 23 ins / 72 x 58 cm) EUR 2,600.

SCHROTZBERG, Peter von
Austrian, 20th century.
Miniaturist.

SCHROWDER, Benjamin
British, 18th - 19th century.
Born c. 1757, in Winchelsea; died 1826, in Dublin.
Sculptor.
Benjamin Schrowder was E. Foley's first teacher.

SCHRUERS, Xavier, or Scruers
Belgian, 19th century.
Sculptor. Busts.
Xavier Schruers was a pupil of G.L. Godecharle. He exhibited a bust at the Brussels Salon in 1813.

SCHRUTEK DE MONTE SYLVA, Franz von
Austrian, 19th century.
Born c. 1800, in Bohemia; died 1861, in Estonia, as the result of an accident.
Painter.

SCHRYBER, Bernhardin
Swiss, 17th century.
Died 14 June 1654, in Schaffhausen.
Active in Schaffhausen.
Painter (glass).

SCHRYBER, Tobias
Swiss, 17th century.
Died 4 November 1610, in Schaffhausen.
Active in Schaffhausen.
Painter (glass).

SCHRYVER, Émile de
Belgian, 20th century.
Born 16 July 1891, in Brussels; died 1957.
Painter. Interiors, urban landscapes.
Émile de Schryver was a self-taught painter who began working in 1948. He exhibited at the Salon d'Automne in Paris and was an Officier of the Légion d'Honneur.
MUSEUMS AND GALLERIES:
PARIS (MAMVP).

SCHRYVER, Louis Marie de
French, 19th - 20th century.
Born 12 October 1862, in Paris; died 6 December 1942, in Paris.
Painter (gouache), watercolourist, pastellist, draughtsman. Religious subjects, portraits, nudes, genre scenes, landscapes, urban landscapes, still-lifes (flowers).
Louis Marie de Schryver was of Belgian descent and his early promise was encouraged by his father, a Parisian journalist who belonged to the republican intellectual movement, centred around the friends of Victor Hugo, that opposed the regime of Napoleon III. He flourished in the fine art world with the help of his father's acquaintances, who included Gustave Courbet, Rosa Bonheur and Gabriel Ferrier, whose pupil he became. He was appointed an honorary member of the Society of Arts of Canada, Montreal, in 1893. With Émile Auguste Carolus-Duran and Augustin Zwiller he created the Exhibition of Painting and Sculpture at the French Automobile Club. In 1919 he was sent to occupied Germany for five years as a painter on a cultural mission to Ludwigshafen-am-Rhein (Rhineland Palatinate). He returned to Paris in 1925 to live, as he wished, in retirement, but without abandoning painting.

He exhibited in group exhibitions, including: from 1872, at the age of thirteen, the Salon de Paris, then the Salon des Artistes Français, of which he became a member in 1896; from 1903 to 1922, the Salon d'Automobile Club de France; from 1940 to 1942, the Salon des Indépendants, Paris. He held a solo show at the Galerie Tedesco Frères, Paris, that then travelled to Belgium, Germany, Austria, Russia and North America. He received a number of awards, including: 1879, a second-class medal at the World Exhibition, Sydney; 1886, an honourable mention, Paris; 1889, an honourable mention at the Exposition Universelle, Paris; 1891, a third-class medal, Paris; 1896, a second-class medal Paris; 1900, a silver medal at the Exposition Universelle, Paris.

While still very young he found a style that was to ensure his future success - Paris street scenes of the turn of the century, with pretty women in the costume of the period walking among stallholders, street sweepers on the Champs-Élysées, flower-sellers on the Île de la Cité. With *An 18th-century Market* (the market of St Germain) he began a short series of colourful `costume' paintings at the request of the Galerie Tedesco. In a quite different style, he depicted the start of the period of automobile racing in works such as *At Speed* (1906) and *The Victor's Arrival* (1907), which were forerunners of the Futurism of Carlo Carra and Giacomo Balla.

At the same time he painted portraits and subjects that were inspired by the literature of the time: *Women of Lesbos, Christian Martyr, Sacred Love, Profane Love,* and some fashionable portraits: *Mlle de Valmont, Mme la Contesse de Boubée, Mme la Marquise de Beauchamp and her Daughter, Dr Poirier.* After World War I he painted less and abandoned some of the subjects that had established his reputation. While in the Rhineland he painted in a variety of techniques some landscapes, orchards in flower, gardens, still-lifes and flowers: *The Alphabet, Children with Spinning Tops, The Flag.* When he returned to Paris he took up again his favourite subjects - views of the city, often with figures; some of these paintings he signed with his name, some with a pseudonym.

Louis de Schryver

Louis de Schryver

Louis de Schryver

BIBLIOGRAPHY:

Hovald, Patrice, '*Le Peintre Louis de Schryver, en entretien avec sa fille, Mme Émile Hert*' in *La Maison d'Alsace* n° 15, periodical, Mulhouse, 1978.

MUSEUMS AND GALLERIES:

CAMBRAI: *Open-air Stallholder* (1895) - COMPIÈGNE (Mus. national de la Voiture et du Tourisme): *Arrival of the Victor at the Premier Prix of the Automobile Club* - PARIS (MAMVP): *Porte de Paris* - PARIS (Mus. de l'Armée): *The Flag* - PONTOISE (Mus. Tavet-Delacour): *Still-life* (1879) - TOURCOING: *My Last Flowers* (1886).

AUCTION RECORDS:

PARIS, 3 June 1898, *Flower Seller* (drawing) FRF 150. NEW YORK, 7 Feb 1907, *Bridge,* USD 200. PARIS, 29-30 Dec 1924, *Fishing,* FRF 160. PARIS, 13 Feb 1950, *Basket of Flowers* (gouache) FRF 3,200. PARIS, 10 Dec 1954, *Flower Seller, Avenue de l'Opéra,* FRF 64,500. COLOGNE, 24 March 1972, *Walk,* DEM 3,000. LOS ANGELES, 13 Nov 1972, *Couple in a Garden,* USD 2,100. LONDON, 14 Oct 1973, *Flower Seller, Avenue de l'Opéra,* GBP 2,100. NEW YORK, 12 Jan 1974, *Flower Seller* (oil on canvas, 20 x 15 ins / 51 x 38 cm) USD 2,300. NEW YORK, 15 Oct 1976, *Fish Seller* (1901, oil on canvas, 27½ x 18 ins / 70 x 46 cm) USD 3,200. NEW YORK, 21 Jan 1978, *Picking Apple Blossoms* (1900, fan-shaped watercolour, 27½ x 11 ins / 70 x 28 cm) USD 850. LONDON, 6 May 1981, *The Flower Market on the Île de la Cité, Paris* (oil on canvas, 36 x 28¼ ins / 91.5 x 72 cm) GBP 3,600. ENGHIEN-LES-BAINS, 22 Nov 1981, *Tea* (28¾ x 36¼ ins / 73 x 92 cm) FRF 18,500. NEW YORK, 23 Feb 1983, *Basket of Plums* (watercolour and gouache, 11½ x 17½ ins / 29.2 x 44.5 cm) USD 1,100. PARIS, 8 June 1984, *Portrait of Madame Fénéon* (1904, oil on canvas, 56 x 52 ins / 142 x 132 cm) FRF 11,000. CLERMONT-FERRAND, 13 June 1984, *Place de l'Opéra* (c. 1932, oil on canvas, 19¾ x 25½ ins / 50 x 65 cm) FRF 36,000. LONDON, 19 June 1985, *Avenue de l'Opéra, Paris* (1895, oil on canvas, 10¼ x 13½ ins / 26 x 34.5 cm) GBP 15,000. LONDON, 3 Dec 1985, *Flower Market, Rue du Havre* (1893, oil on canvas, 35¾ x 28 ins / 91 x 71 cm) GBP 58,000. NEW YORK, 28 Oct 1986, *Flower Seller, Rue de Rivoli* (1893, oil on canvas, 23¼ x 27½ ins / 59 x 69.9 cm) USD 130,000. LONDON, 25 March 1987, *A Parisian Flower Seller* (1897, oil on panel, 8½ x 6 ins / 21.5 x 15 cm) GBP 12,000. LONDON, 24 March 1988, *Flower Seller, Avenue de l'Opéra* (1911, oil on canvas, 22½ x 36¼ ins / 57 x 92 cm) GBP 23,100. MONACO, 2 Dec 1988, *Spring Day on the Champs-Élysées, Paris* (1907, watercolour and gouache, 5¾ x 8¼ ins / 14.5 x 21 cm) FRF 22,200. NEW YORK, 23 Feb 1989, *Pretty Young Woman* (1902, oil on canvas, 24¼ x 20 ins / 61.6 x 50.5 cm) USD 11,000. LONDON, 7 June 1989, *The Grasshopper and the Ant* (oil on canvas, 28¼ x 17¾ ins / 71.5 x 45 cm) GBP 6,380. RHEIMS, 22 Oct 1989, *Montmartre and Le Lapin Agile* (oil on canvas, 38¼ x 51¼ ins / 97 x 130 cm) FRF 40,000. NEW YORK, 22 May 1990, *Flower Seller in a Paris Street* (1897, oil on canvas, 20 x 28 ins / 50.8 x 71.1 cm) USD 209,000. LONDON, 21 June 1991, *Roses in a vase, with two pears on a plate and fruit and flowers on a ledge* (1896, oil on canvas, 35¾ x 32¼ ins / 90.8 x 81.9 cm) GBP 12,100. NEW YORK, 16 Oct 1991, *Flower Seller at the Madeleine* (1891, oil on canvas, 21½ x 25¾ ins / 54.6 x 65.4 cm) USD 114,400. NEW YORK, 27 May 1992, *Summer flowers* (1888, oil on canvas, 40½ x 62 ins / 102.8 x 157.5 cm) USD 165,000. NEW YORK, 30 Oct 1992, *Avenue in the Bois de Boulogne on a Spring Morning* (oil on canvas, 27¾ x 40½ ins / 70.5 x 102.9 cm) USD 132,000. PARIS, 22 March 1993, *Two Friends* (1904, oil on canvas, 33¾ x 27½ ins / 86 x 70 cm) FRF 38,000. NEW YORK, 26 May 1993, *Flower Seller near the Élysée* (1896, oil on canvas, 22 x 18½ ins / 55.9 x 47 cm) USD 140,000. NEW YORK, 12 Oct 1994, *Flower Seller and his Young Daughter, Place du Carrousel, Paris* (oil on canvas, 20½ x 22¾ ins / 52.1 x 58.1 cm) USD 35,650. LONDON, 14 June 1995, *Still-life with Flowers* (1896, oil on canvas, 12½ x 15¾ ins / 32 x 40 cm) GBP 6,900. NEW YORK, 3 Nov 1999, *Flower Seller, Avenue de L'Opera, Paris* (1890, oil on canvas, 28 x 36 ins / 70 x 92 cm) USD 80,000. NEW YORK, 3 Nov 1999, *Purchase of Fresh Flowers, Avenue de L'Opera, Paris* (1895, oil on canvas, 10 x 13 ins / 26 x 34 cm) USD 100,000. NEW YORK, 31 Oct 2000, *Beauty Amid Rose Petals* (1901, oil on canvas, oval, 24 x 31 ins / 60 x 80 cm) USD 20,000. NEW YORK, 22 May 2001, *Parisian Flower Seller* (oil on canvas) USD 30,000. NEW YORK, 2 Nov 2001, *Flower Seller at the Place de L'opera, Paris* (oil on canvas, 20 x 26 ins / 50 x 65 cm) USD 26,000. PARIS, 26 June 2002, *Gallant Scene* (1907, watercolour, 6 x 9 ins / 15 x 22 cm) EUR 4,000. PARIS, 26 June 2002, *Flower Market* (watercolour, 6 x 9 ins / 15 x 22 cm) EUR 4,000. NEW YORK, 24 April 2003, *Flower Seller, Champs Elysees, Rampart Gardens* (1897, oil on canvas/board, 21 x 29 ins / 53 x 74 cm) USD 120,000. SAN FRANCISCO, 19 Nov 2003,

Flower Seller (1898, oil on canvas, 22 x 17 ins / 57 x 43 cm) USD 50,000. MILFORD, 6 May 2004, *On the Boulevard* (1927, oil on canvas, 13 x 18 ins / 33 x 46 cm) USD 11,000. NEW YORK, 27 Oct 2004, *The Flower Girl* (1896, oil on panel, 6 x 4 ins / 15 x 11 cm) USD 12,000.

SCHTEINBERG, Edik Arkadievich.
See **STEINBERG**

SCHUBACK, Elisabeth
German, 19th century.
Active c. 1827.
Lithographer.

SCHUBACK, Emil Gottlieb
German, 19th century.
Born 28 June 1820, in Hamburg; died 14 March 1902, in Düsseldorf.
Painter, lithographer. Portraits, genre scenes.

Schuback was taught by G. Hardoff in Hamburg, Cornelius and Hess in Munich, and Rudolf Jordan in Düsseldorf. He worked in Rome between 1843 and 1846 before moving to Düsseldorf in 1856. His key work is *Christ on the Mount of Olives*.

AUCTION RECORDS:
NEW YORK, 17 May 1984, *Broken Toy* (oil on canvas, 26 1/4 x 22 1/2 ins / 66.5 x 57 cm) USD 6,500. NEW YORK, 28 Oct 1986, *Children Playing in Interior* (1866, oil on canvas, 22 x 20 ins / 56 x 51 cm) USD 9,500. MUNICH, 6 Dec 2000, *Farewell* (oil on canvas, 22 x 18 ins / 56 x 46 cm) DEM 5,000.

SCHUBART
German, 19th century.
Died c. 1815, in Hamburg.
Miniaturist.

Schubart was a pupil of Camerata in Dresden.

SCHUBART, Christian Friedrich, or Schuberth
German, 18th century.
Active in Dresden 1730-1760.
Painter. Flowers, fruit.

SCHUBART, Christian Ludwig
German, 19th century.
Born 1807, in Dresden.
Active in Dresden.
Painter. Portraits.

SCHUBART, Christopher
German, 17th century.
Born in Ingolstadt.
Painter.

Christopher Schubart worked in Munich and painted a portrait of Queen Anne of England.

SCHUBART, David, or Schubert or Schuberth
German, 16th - 17th century.
Died 1607, in Wurzen.
Active in Oschatz 1587-1606.
Painter.

SCHUBART, Karl Ludwig
German, 19th century.
Born 16 July 1820, in Frankenthal; died 17 March 1889, in Speyer.
Painter, lithographer.

After attending the academy in Munich, Karl Schubart worked in Zweibrücken and, from 1874, in Spire.

MUSEUMS AND GALLERIES:
FRANKENTHAL (Mus.): *Self-portrait*.

SCHUBART, Samuel
German, 17th century.
Active in Dresden.
Painter.

SCHUBAUER, Christoph, or Schupauer
German, 16th century.
Active in Munich c. 1569.
Painter.

SCHUBAUER, Friedrich Leopold
German, 19th century.
Born 1795, in Dresden; died 28 April 1852, in Kahnsdorf, near Borna.
Painter. Military subjects, battles, portraits.

Schubauer was the pupil of Gustave Ad. Hennig in Leipzig and an officer. He painted a portrait of King Albert in 1847.

MUSEUMS AND GALLERIES:
DRESDEN (Militärhistorisches Mus.): *Battle of Podobna; The Cuirassiers of the Royal Guard in Friedland in 1807; Battle of Kalisch* - LEIPZIG: *Episode from the Battle of Moskva*.

AUCTION RECORDS:
NEW YORK, 19 May 1993, *Storming of Trinidad Salcedo* (oil on panel, 12 3/4 x 16 ins / 32.5 x 39.7 cm) USD 23,000.

SCHÜBEL, Leo
German, 20th century.
Born 12 May 1888, in Ansbach.
Painter, engraver.

Leo Schübel studied at the fine arts academy in Munich. The town hall of Ansbach has his *Ansbach of Old*.

SCHÜBELER, Heinrich
Danish, 19th - 20th century.
Born 19 June 1865, in Copenhagen; died 4 April 1933, in Copenhagen.
Painter.

Heinrich Schübeler specialised in decorative compositions.

SCHUBERG, Clara
German, 19th - 20th century.
Born 28 October 1862, in Karlsruhe.
Active in Karlsruhe.
Painter. Still-lifes.

Clara Schuberg was a pupil of Margarete Hormuth-Kallmorgen and Friedrich Kallmorgen.

SCHUBERT, August
Austrian, 19th century.
Born 16 January 1844, in Vienna.
Draughtsman, illustrator. Portraits.

August Schubert attended the academy in Vienna between 1858 and 1859 and studied under V. Katzler.

SCHUBERT, Benjamin
German, 19th century.
Active in Dessau.
Sculptor.

Benjamin Schubert erected a fountain, no longer extant, in Dresden market square.

SCHUBERT, Carl
Austrian, 19th century.
Born 6 November 1795, in Vienna; died 20 March 1855, in Vienna.
Painter, draughtsman, engraver, lithographer. Landscapes.

Carl Schubert was the brother of the composer Franz Schubert and father of the painters Ferdinand and Heinrich Carl.

MUSEUMS AND GALLERIES:
VIENNA (Akademie der Bildenden Künste): several drawings - ZURICH (Kunsthaus): two works.

SCHUBERT, David. See **SCHUBART**

SCHUBERT, Ernö or Ernst
Hungarian, 20th century.
Born 17 December 1903, in Bacsfa; died 1960, in Budapest.
Painter, draughtsman, engraver.

Ernö Schubert attended the fine arts school in Budapest in around 1920 and was active with the UME and KUT groups. From 1948 to 1952, he was director of the decorative arts academy in Budapest. Work by him was shown at the exhibition *L'Avant-garde hongroise 1910-1930* (*The Avant-Garde in Hungary, 1910-1930*) at the Galerie Franka Berndt in Paris in 1984. His first solo exhibition, of abstract works, took place at the Tamàs Gallery in Budapest in 1932.

SCHUBERT, Ferdinand
Austrian, 19th century.
Born 15 August 1824, in Vienna; died 15 August 1853, in Vienna.
Painter. History painting, figures, portraits.
Ferdinand Schubert was taught by H. Schwemminger, Karl Mayer and Amerling, and went to Rome. He carried out engravings for Images for Booksellers and Printers.
MUSEUMS AND GALLERIES:
VIENNA (Schubert Mus.): *Portrait of Ferdinand; Portrait of Carl Schubert* - VIENNA (SM): *Walls of Hapsburg* - ZURICH: *Fisherman and Mermaid; Portrait of the Werdmuller Family.*
AUCTION RECORDS:
LINDAU, 2 Oct 1985, *Psyche* (oil on canvas, 51 1/2 x 37 1/2 ins / 131 x 95 cm) DEM 8,500.

SCHUBERT, Franz August
German, 19th century.
Born 10 November 1806, in Dessau; died 1893, in Dessau.
Painter, engraver (etching). History painting.
After attending the academy in Dresden, Franz Schubert visited Italy. On his return he lived and taught for 10 years in Dessau before moving to Berlin in 1850. He engraved biblical subjects, notably 25 plates after Raphael's *Story of Psyche*. He also worked on the fresco of the *Ascension of Christ* in the Protestant church in Munich.
AUCTION RECORDS:
NEW YORK, 24 Jan 1980, *Meeting of Jacob and Rachel* (1835, oil on canvas, 39 x 55 1/4 ins / 99 x 140.5 cm) USD 14,000. STUTTGART, 19 March 1999, *Seated Angel* (oil on canvas, 39 x 26 ins / 100 x 65 cm) DEM 3,500. PARIS, 5 Dec 2001, *Christ Welcoming the Unfortunate* (1842, oil on canvas, 39 x 53 ins / 99 x 135 cm) FRF 34,000.

SCHUBERT, Gustav Wilhelm
German, 19th - 20th century.
Born 21 August 1875, in Freiberg (Saxony).
Active in Freiberg.
Painter.

SCHUBERT, Gyula or Julius
Hungarian, 20th century.
Born 28 April 1888, in Presburg (now Bratislava, Slovakia).
Painter. Figures, landscapes.
Schubert studied in Budapest.
MUSEUMS AND GALLERIES:
BRATISLAVA (Mestské Múz.).

SCHUBERT, Hanns
German, 20th century.
Born 1 July 1887, in Greifswald.
Painter, engraver. Religious subjects, figures.
Hanns Schubert was a pupil of Bentzer at the academy in Dresden and of Köpping at the academy in Berlin. He produced paintings on glass for churches in Zullchow and Sydowsane (near Szczecin) and decorations for the Deaconnes Chapel in Szczecin-Finkelwalde.

SCHUBERT, Heinrich Carl
Austrian, 19th century.
Born 23 July 1827, in Vienna; died 12 February 1897, in Vienna.
Painter, watercolourist. Landscapes, farmyard scenes, flowers.
Heinrich Schubert was the pupil of Th. Ender and Steinfeld, the son of Carl and the brother of Ferdinand.
AUCTION RECORDS:
VIENNA, 9 June 1970, *Austrian Landscape*, ATS 32,000. VIENNA, 19 June 1979, *Meadow Flowers* (watercolour, 24 3/4 x 17 1/4 ins / 63 x 44 cm) ATS 25,000. VIENNA, 14 Sept 1983, *Farmyard* (1863, oil on canvas, 20 3/4 x 26 1/2 ins / 53 x 67 cm) ATS 35,000. MUNICH, 21 June 1994, *Friedau Castle in the Environs of Biel* (1880, watercolour/paper, 17 1/4 x 22 1/4 ins / 43.5 x 56.5 cm) DEM 3,450. VIENNA, 11 June 2002, *Hunting Mountain Goats with Alpine Views* (1868, watercolour and pencil, 19 x 25 ins / 48 x 64 cm) EUR 3,000.

SCHUBERT, Hermann
German, 19th - 20th century.
Born 12 June 1831, in Dessau, near Halle; died 24 January 1917, in Dresden.
Sculptor. Figures. Busts, monuments.
Hermann Schubert was the son of Benjamin Schubert and the father of the architect Otto Schubert. He studied at the fine arts academy in Munich between 1849 and 1852, then spent the period from 1856 to 1872 in Rome. His body of work includes the Jubilee Fountain in Dresden and monuments in Dresden dedicated to the memory of *W. Müller* and *Friedrich Schneider*, together with a *Jacob Fighting with the Angel* in the Dresden church of St Sophia.
MUSEUMS AND GALLERIES:
INNSBRUCK (Tiroler Landesmus. Ferdinandeum): *Bust of Alois Flir.*

SCHUBERT, Hugo
Austrian, 19th - 20th century.
Born 13 October 1874, in Vienna; died 19 October 1913, in Vienna.
Painter, miniaturist, engraver, illustrator.
Hugo Schubert studied under his brother August Schubert, under William Unger, and under Siegmund L'Allemand and Franz Rumpler at the fine arts academy in Vienna.

SCHUBERT, Johann David
German, 18th - 19th century.
Born 1761, in Dresden; died 1822, in Dresden.
Painter, engraver, draughtsman. History painting.
Johann Schubert was the pupil of F. Hutin and K.-C. Klass. He taught painting, history, and painting on porcelain in Meissen in 1781, and was director of the academy in Dresden. He also carried out engravings for the booktrade. The Kupferstichkabinett conserves his preparatory drawings for illustrations for novels of the period.
MUSEUMS AND GALLERIES:
BERLIN (Kupferstichkabinet): engravings - DRESDEN (Stadtmus.): *Announcement of the Peace of Teschen.*
AUCTION RECORDS:
PARIS, 24 June 1929, *The King and the Sower* (drawing) FRF 110. MUNICH, 29 June 1982, *Meeting between Frederick the Great and Emperor Joseph II* (pen drawing and gouache, 22 3/4 x 35 ins / 58 x 88 cm) DEM 5,600. MUNICH, 28 June 1983, *The Meeting of Frederick the Great with Emperor Joseph II* (pen and gouache, drawing, 22 3/4 x 35 ins / 58 x 88 cm) DEM 3,000.

SCHUBERT, Josef, or Schuberth
German, 18th century.
Sculptor.
Josef Schubert worked in Mährisch-Trubau in 1783 and sculpted several church altars.

SCHUBERT, Joseph
Belgian, 19th century.
Born 19 December 1816, in Brussels; died 25 November 1885, in Brussels.
Draughtsman, lithographer.

SCHUBERT, Karl Gottlieb
German, 18th century.
Born to a family originally from Gräbel (Silesia); died 1804, in Fürstenberg.
Sculptor.
Karl Schubert was a modeller at the porcelain factory of Fürstenberg from 1775.

SCHUBERT, Otto
German, 20th century.
Born 29 January 1892, in Dresden.
Active in Dresden.
Painter, engraver.
MUSEUMS AND GALLERIES:
DRESDEN: several paintings.

SCHUBERT VON EHRENBERG, Peter. See **EHRENBERG Peter Schubert von**

SCHUBERT-SOLDERN, Victor von
Hungarian, 19th - 20th century.
Born 15 August 1834, in Prague; died 30 June 1912, in Dresden.
Painter. History painting, genre scenes, portraits.
Victor von Schubert-Soldern was a student at the fine arts academy in Prague. He subsequently worked in Antwerp, and then for Cogniet in Paris, in 1861 and 1862. In 1870, he settled in Dresden, where he exhibited nearly every year.

SCHUBERTH, Christian Friedrich. See **SCHUBART**

SCHUBERTH, Josef. See **SCHUBERT**

SCHUBIN, Fedor Ivanovitch. See **CHUBIN Fiodor Ivanovich**

SCHUBLER, A. G. J.
German, 17th century.
Painter, engraver. Portraits.
Schubler carried out engravings for the booktrade. Noteworthy are his plates for *Images for Booksellers and Printers*, a work published in Altdorf and Nuremberg in 1626. Despite the dates, he could be compared to Andreas Georg.

SCHÜBLER, Andreas Georg
German, 18th century.
Engraver.
The pupil of M. Renz, Schübler worked in Nuremberg from 1725 to 1750. He carried out a line engraving of *Professor Ole Norm*.

SCHUBNEL, Jean
French, 20th century.
Born 1894, in Château-la-Vallière.
Painter.
Jean Schubnel, a self-taught painter, certainly exercised some professional activity, but the sources do not tell us what it was. He lived and worked in the Touraine and exhibited in Paris for the first time in 1952. He painted the keeps and châteaux of his native region in a naively romantic style.
BIBLIOGRAPHY:
Bihalji-Merin, Oto, *Les Peintres naïfs*, Delpire, Paris, 1960.
MUSEUMS AND GALLERIES:
VICQ (Mus. International d'Art Naïf).

SCHUBRING, Richard
German, 19th century.
Born 14 December 1853, in Dessau.
Painter. Portraits, landscapes.
Schubring was a pupil of E. Hildebrand and L. Pohle who worked in Berlin and Munich.
MUSEUMS AND GALLERIES:
ERFURT (Angermus.): *Surf*.

SCHUBRUCK, Pieter. See **SCHOUBROECK**

SCHUCH, Andreas, or Schuchel, Schuech, Schuoch
German, 17th century.
Active in Ulm 1645-1680.
Painter.

SCHUCH, August Fridrikovich, or Chukh
Estonian, 19th century.
Born in Estonia; died 1850, in St Petersburg.
Painter, lithographer.
August Fridrikovich Schuch studied under Carl Adolf Senff.

SCHUCH, Johann Thomas
Austrian, 18th century.
Died 1785.
Active in Brno.
Engraver.
Schuch became a master in Brno in 1748.

SCHUCH, Karl
Austrian, 19th century.
Born 30 September 1846, in Vienna; died 13 September 1903, in Vienna.
Painter. Portraits, genre scenes, landscapes, still-lifes, animals.
Karl Schuch attended the academy in Vienna, and in 1869 went to Munich where he was in contact with Thoma and Trübner and worked with Leibls. He then went to Paris where he came under the influence of Courbet, and in 1872 visited Italy and the Netherlands. His works figured in the exhibition *Chefs-d'œuvre du Belvédère de Vienne* (*Masterpieces from the Belvedere in Vienna*) in the Musée Marmottan in Paris.
MUSEUMS AND GALLERIES:
AACHEN: *Still-life with Roses* - BERLIN (Nationalgal.): *Still-lifes with Lobster and Apples; Peasants' Houses at Ferch; Flowers; Landscape* - BREMEN: *Still-lifes with Fox and Apples; At the Edge of Wessling Lake* - COLOGNE (Wallraf-Richartz Mus.): *Still-life with Mallard* - DRESDEN (Gemäldegal. Neue Meister): *Large Still-life; Basket of Rhododendrons* - DÜSSELDORF: *Birch Forest; Mallard* - HALLE: *Still-life with Apples* - HAMBURG: *Street in Olevano; Sawyard; Mallard* - HANOVER: *Landscape with Ruined Bridge; Monastery in Verdure; Church at Olevano; View of Olevano; Donkey; Portrait of Karl Hagemeister; Schuch's Studio in Venice; Still-life with Pewter Picher; Courtyard of the Abbey of St Gregory in Venice; Ferch Landscape; Still-life; Dead Man's Head; Wooden Scaffolding; Peasant House at Edge of Lake; Mallards; Apples; Water-mill* - KREFELD: two still-lifes - LEIPZIG: *Glade near Bernried by Lake Starnberg* - MAGDEBURG (Kulturhistorisches Mus.): *Enten-Stilleben* (*Still-life with Duck*) - MANNHEIM: *Liederlahner Inn; Gladioli and Oranges* - MUNICH: *Apples in Pewter Dish; Peonies; Chicken; Asparagus; Mountain Landscape* - NUREMBERG: *Azaleas; Stormy Atmosphere at Ferch* - POZNAN: *Peonies* - STUTTGART: *Street in Olevano; Cheese, Apples and Bottle; Peonies* - SZCZECIN: *Landscape near Kähnsdorf; Stream on Banks of Lake; Prags Landscape; Doubs; Leeks and Cheese; Roses and Azaleas* - VIENNA (Österreichische Gal. Belvedere): *Mountain Landscape in Italy; Rocks near Olevano; Skirt of Forest near Purkersdorf; Self-portrait; Sailing Boat on the Havel; Kitchen; Reeds on the Banks of the Havel; Melons, Peaches and Grapes; Cheese, Apples and Bottle; Forest Interior* - WROCLAW (Muz. Narodowe): *High Mountain near Prags in the Tyrol; Still-life* - WUPPERTAL: *Ducks; Lobster and Leeks; Horse and Mule* - WUPPERTAL (Ruhmeshalle): *Water-mill with Ducks near Prags* - ZURICH (Henneberg Gal.): *Duck; Still-life; Landscape; Julienne*.
AUCTION RECORDS:
VIENNA, 4 Dec 1962, *After the Rain*, ATS 40,000. COLOGNE, 15 April 1964, *Still-life with Apples and Plates*, DEM 14,000. VIENNA, 12 Sept 1967, *After the Rain*, ATS 70,000. VIENNA, 30 Nov 1971, *Still-life*, ATS 300,000. COLOGNE, 15 Nov 1972,

Still-life with Pheasants, DEM 80,000. COLOGNE, 6 June 1973, *Still-life with Fox,* DEM 44,000. COLOGNE, 27 June 1974, *Still-life with Game,* DEM 34,000. MUNICH, 25 Nov 1976, *Self-portrait* (oil on canvas, 12½ x 10¼ ins / 32 x 26 cm) DEM 8,500. VIENNA, 15 Sept 1981, *View of Roman Countryside* (1870, oil on canvas, 10½ x 8½ ins / 26.5 x 21.5 cm) ATS 65,000. MUNICH, 5 June 1984, *Still-life with Apples and Cheese* (oil on canvas, 24 x 31 ins / 61 x 79 cm) DEM 300,000. MUNICH, 23 Oct 1985, *Still-life* (oil on canvas, 35½ x 23½ ins / 90 x 60 cm) DEM 40,000. MUNICH, 5 June 1986, *Ruins of Castle at Seaside* (1869, pencil, 5½ x 6¾ ins / 14 x 17 cm) DEM 1,900. LONDON, 4 April 1989, *Self-portrait, Evening* (oil on card, 10¾ x 14 ins / 27.5 x 35.5 cm) GBP 18,700. LONDON, 21 June 1991, *Still-life with Pheasant and other Game Birds on Stone Mantelpiece* (1885, oil on canvas, 23¼ x 31 ins / 59 x 79 cm) GBP 29,700. NEW YORK, 26 May 1993, *Fisherman in Alpine River* (oil on canvas, 41 x 30 ins / 104.1 x 76.2 cm) USD 6,900. HEIDELBERG, 15-16 Oct 1993, *Forest Interior* (oil on panel, 11½ x 9¼ ins / 29.5 x 23.5 cm) DEM 8,000. VIENNA, 29-30 Oct 1996, *Forest* (1878, oil on paper/card, 12½ x 15¾ ins / 32 x 40 cm) ATS 218,500. MUNICH, 27 Feb 1999, *Old Smithy in Wessling* (oil on canvas, 20 x 24 ins / 50 x 62 cm) DEM 32,000. MUNICH, 27 Feb 1999, *Still-life of Wild Duck on a Wooden Plank* (oil on canvas, 20 x 31 ins / 50 x 80 cm) DEM 55,000. DÜSSELDORF, 31 Jan 2000, *Deep in Woods* (oil on canvas/board, 24 x 32 ins / 61 x 82 cm) DEM 180,000. LONDON, 27 Oct 2000, *Still-life of Flowers* (oil on canvas, 22 x 26 ins / 56 x 67 cm) GBP 60,000. VIENNA, 12 Oct 2004, *Flowerpot with White Azaleas and Basket of Pansies* (oil on canvas, 24 x 31 ins / 61 x 78 cm) EUR 150,000.

SCHUCH, Werner Wilhelm Gustav
German, 19th - 20th century.
Born 2 October 1843, in Hildesheim; died 24 April 1918, in Berlin.
Painter. Historical subjects, battles, portraits, equestrian portraits, landscapes, still-lifes.

Werner Wilhelm Gustav Schuch studied painting in Düsseldorf and Munich. He was awarded a gold medal in Berlin in 1886.

MUSEUMS AND GALLERIES:
BERLIN (Deutsches Historisches Mus.): *General Zieten at Hennersdorf; General Seydlitz at Rossbach; Charge of the Brandenburg Hussars at Möckern; Battle of the Nations at Leipzig* - BERLIN (Nationalgal.): *Equestrian Portrait of Wilhelm II* (1890); *Years of Want* (1876) - DRESDEN (Gemäldegal. Neue Meister): *Tomb of Huns* - HAMBURG: *Foreshore Landscape* - HILDESHEIM (Roemer und Pelizaeus Mus.): *Attack on a Village* - KALININGRAD: *Hawkers during the Thirty Years' War* - MÜNSTER: *Winter Quarters* - NUREMBERG: *Cortège of Gustavus Adolphus at Wolgast* - OLDENBURG: *Legacy; Foreshore* - WIESBADEN: *Killjoy* - WROCLAW (Muz. Narodowe): *Seydlitz on Patrol.*

AUCTION RECORDS:
NEW YORK, 11-12 March 1909, *Retreat,* USD 195. FRANKFURT AM MAIN, 11-13 May 1936, *Landscape,* DEM 3,000; *Still-life,* DEM 6,400. NEW YORK, 4 June 1971, *Scene from the Thirty Years' War,* USD 1,100. LUCERNE, 2 June 1981, *Horseman* (1884, oil on canvas, 27½ x 20¾ ins / 70 x 53 cm) CHF 4,600.

SCHUCHAIEFF, Wassili Ivanovitch.
See **SHUKHAEV Vasili Ivanovich**

SCHUCHARDT, Michael, or Schugardt
German, 18th century.
Painter (porcelain).

Schuchardt worked in Klosterweilsdorf in 1716, and in Katzhutte and Wallendorf from 1764 and 1765.

SCHUCHART, Johann Tobias
German, 17th - 18th century.
Died 1711, in Dessau.
Active in Anhalt.
Sculptor, architect.

In 1695 Johann Schuchart participated in the building of the Johanneskirche in Dessau.

SCHUCHBAUER, Anton
German, 18th century.
Born c. 1720.
Sculptor.

Schuchbauer worked mostly for the church in Klausenburg (now Cluj-Napoca, Romania).

SCHUCHBAUR, J. G.
German, 18th century.
Painter.

MUSEUMS AND GALLERIES:
KLOSTERLECHFELD (Church of Maria Hilf): *Adoration of the Magi* (1761).

SCHUCHEL, Andreas. See **SCHUCH**

SCHÜCHLIN, Hans, or Schyechlin, Schuelin, Schielin
German, 15th century.
Born c. 1440, in Ulm (Baden-Württemberg); died 1505, in Ulm.
Painter. Religious subjects, portraits. Decorative schemes.
Swabian School.

It is thought that Hans Schüchlin studied in Nuremberg and was a pupil, at the same time as Michael Wolgemut, of Hans Pleydenwurff. In 1493 he was head of the painters' guild of Ulm.

Schüchlin's carefully painted works are influenced by Flemish art, especially Roger van der Weyden, and reveal great skill in form and an elegant sensibility. By 1469 his reputation was established enough for the Gemming family to commission from him an altarpiece for their funerary chapel in the church of Tiefenbronn, in which there is also a retable by Lucas Moser. Among his other works are an altarpiece painted in collaboration with his son-in-law Bartholomaüs Zeitbloom in the church of Münster, and a painting in the church of St Maurice in Lorch. A *Crucifixion,* painted before 1469 in the church of St George in Dunkelsbuhl, is also attributed to him.

uud· von Hans Schülein
B Zeitblom zu: im gemacht 18

MUSEUMS AND GALLERIES:
BUDAPEST: *Death of the Virgin* (in collaboration with B. Zeitblom); *St Gregory, St John and St Augustine; St Florian, St John the Baptist and St Sebastian* - MAINZ: *Moritz Ensinger* - MUNICH (Bayerisches Nationalmus.): *Double Portrait* - PRAGUE (Národní Gal. V Praze): *Beheading of St Barbara* - STUTTGART: *Zachariah at the Temple.*

AUCTION RECORDS:
LONDON, 11 May 1934, *Portrait of a Woman,* GBP 199.

SCHUCHMANN, J. E.. See **SCHUMANN Johan Ehrenfried**

SCHUCHWOSTOV, Stepan Mikhailovitch.
See **SHUKHVOSTOV Stepan Mikhailovich**

SCHUCKMANN, Ernst Friedrich von
German, 19th century.
Born 22 October 1808, in Schwasdorf (Mecklemburg-Schwerin).
Painter. History painting, portraits, genre scenes.

Schuckmann was the pupil of Herbig in Berlin, and of Schadow and Hildebrandt in Düsseldorf. His career was spent in Hamburg.

SCHUCZTEUFFEL, Georg
German, 16th century.
Active in Hermannstadt (now Sibiu, Romania).
Painter.

SCHUDDER
French, 20th century.
Died July 1915; on active service.
Painter.

SCHUDE, Sebastian, or Schuden
French, 15th century.
Born to a family originally from Magdeburg.
Active in Strasbourg 1476-1478.
Painter.

SCHUDT, Johann Ludwig
German, 19th century.
Born 6 March 1842, in Höchst-am-Main; died 17 August 1904, in Frankfurt am Main.
Painter.

Schudt was the pupil of Ferdinand Keller.

SCHUECH, Andreas. See **SCHUCH**

SCHUECHBAUR, Beno
German, 18th century.
Sculptor.

SCHUECHMACHER, Hans.
See **SCHUHMACHER**

SCHUELER, Anton. See **SCHÜLER**

SCHUELER, Jon
American, 20th century.
Born 1916, in Milwaukee (Wisconsin); died 1992.
Painter.

Jon Schueler graduated in English Literature at the University of Wisconsin. After having been a pilot in the American Air Force during World War II he studied painting under the direction of Clifford Still in San Francisco from 1948 until 1951. He included memories of his impressions as a pilot in his works. He settled in New York, and spent some time in Scotland and Paris between 1957 and 1959.

Schueler took part in many group exhibitions, including: *Nature in Abstraction* and *New Talent in the USA* both at the Whitney Museum in New York in 1958; the Maryland Institute in Baltimore in 1961 and 1962; and the Whitney Museum in 1963, among others. He put on his first solo exhibition in San Francisco in 1950 and held several other solo exhibitions in New York.

BIBLIOGRAPHY:

Nordland, Gerald, *Jon Schueler: To the North*, Merrell, London, 2002.

SCHUELER, P.
Swiss, 18th century.
Born in Fribourg.
Engraver. Armorials.

SCHUELIN, Hans. See **SCHÜCHLIN**

SCHUER, Theodorus Cornelisz. van der, or Schuur, known as Vriendschap
Dutch, 17th - 18th century.
Born 1628, in The Hague; died December 1707, in The Hague.
Painter, draughtsman. Allegorical subjects, mythological subjects.

Theodorus Cornelisz. van der Schuer travelled to Paris at a very early age, where he studied under Sébastian Bourdon. He was appointed head of the Pictura fraternity on 20 November 1673, and dean on 20 November 1688. One of the five founder members of the academy of design in Brussels, he marked the occasion with a corner painting for the ceiling of the great hall. He worked in Rome in 1665. He lost his fortune on the grounds of incitement to war and his possessions were seized.

MUSEUMS AND GALLERIES:
AMSTERDAM: cupola ceiling - LEIDEN: *Justice with a Crown in her Right Hand and a Sword in her Left*; *Minerva*; *View of the Plague Hospice in 1682* - THE HAGUE (Gemeentemus.): *Hercules* (ceiling in the Commissions Chamber); painted overmantel representing Hercules.

AUCTION RECORDS:
AMSTERDAM, 18 May 1988, *Minerva Visiting the Muses on Mount Helicon* (1675, oil on canvas, 79 3/4 x 58 1/2 ins / 202.5 x 148.5 cm) NLG 29,900.

SCHUERECHT
Austrian, 18th century.
Active in Vienna.
Painter.

SCHUEREN, Anthony van der
German, 17th century.
Active in Dordrecht 1689-1693.
Painter.

SCHUERMANS, Jan. See **SCHOORMAN**

SCHUERMANS, Karel
Belgian, 19th - 20th century.
Born 1869, in Antwerp; died 1955, in Antwerp.
Sculptor.

Karel Schuermans studied at the fine arts academy in Antwerp.

MUSEUMS AND GALLERIES:
ANTWERP.

SCHUESSELE, Christian. See **SCHUSSELE**

SCHUFFELIN, Hans, the Younger.
See **SCHÄUFFELIN**

SCHUFFENECKER, Claude-Émile
French, 19th - 20th century.
Born 8 December 1851, in Fresne-St-Mamès; died 31 July 1934, in Paris.
Painter, draughtsman, pastellist, architect. Figures, portraits, landscapes, landscapes with figures, seascapes.
Symbolism.
School of Pont-Aven.

As a young man Claude-Émile Schuffenecker was a pupil of Grellet, Paul Baudry and Carolus-Duran, but he did not immediately follow up his artistic vocation. Working in a stockbroker's to make a living, he met Gaugin, who was in exactly the same situation. They both abandoned security for the artistic adventure and remained friends, though a modest inheritance enabled Schuffenecker to begin a small collection of works of art. In 1883 he gained a licence to teach art in schools and colleges and went to work at the lycée of Vannes. He gave up teaching in 1914. In 1883 he attended the Académie Colarossi, and he met Manet, Pissarro and Mallarmé. In 1886 he introduced Émile Bernard to his friend Gaugin, a meeting that led to `cloisonnism' and the dispute about primacy that arose from it. He joined Gaugin again near Pont-Aven, Brittany, and in 1887 stayed in Étretat and Yport, where he lodged Gaugin and entertained Van Gogh.

About 1892 he joined the *Rose + Croix* (*Rose + Cross*) movement and collaborated with Émile Bernard on the esoteric review *Le Coeur.* In 1893 he joined Madame Blavatsky's theosophical movement.

He exhibited for the first time at the Salon des Artistes Français of 1877, then in 1884 at the Salon des Indépendants, of which he was a co-founder. In 1886 he exhibited at the 8th and last exhibition of the Impressionists and in 1888 with Gaugin at the `synthesist' exhibition organised by Theo van Gogh at Boussaud et Valadon. In 1889 he organised an exhibition of works by Gaugin, Émile Bernard, Anquetin, Louis Roy and himself at the Café Volponi. In 1891 he exhibited at the first exhibition of *Peintres impressionistes et symbolistes* (*Impressionist and Symbolist Painters*) at Le Barc, Bouteville, and in 1900, with Émile Bernard, at the first exhibition of the Esoteric Group. He was represented in 1934 in *Gaugin et ses amis, l'École de Pont-Aven et l'Académie Julian* (*Gaugin and his Friends, the Pont-Aven School and the Académie Julian*).

The only solo show he held took place at the Librairie de l'Art Indépendant d'Edmond Bailly in 1896. A retrospective was organised jointly by the Musée Departmental and the Museum of Pont-Aven in 1996, and this went also to the Museum of St-Germain-en-Laye.

Schuffenecker was well informed about the state of knowledge in his own time. He was a scholarly man and his letters show he had a gift for writing. His company was much sought after. Although he started to paint in an entirely classical style, he joined the Impressionists, or, rather, the Neo-Impressionists. His clear head and bold spirit led him to adopt their essential principles, which he put to work in landscapes and seascapes, almost always of Brittany, and in infrequent portraits. His painting *Hymn to the Sun* is often referred to. From 1890 to 1896 he painted what can rightly be called Symbolist pictures. Regretting the fate of an artist who seemed destined for high renown, André Salmon wrote, `Was it not the drudgery that paralysed him? He earned his living and wasted his time teaching school kids to draw from plaster models; it is said that he spoke to them in the same way you would to college students you wanted to discourage from entering for the Prix de Rome'.

Schuffenecker

BIBLIOGRAPHY:

Le Paul, Charles-Guy, '*Gauguin et Schuffenecker*' in *Bulletin des Amis du Musée de Rennes* n° 2, special edition on Pont-Aven, periodical, Rennes, 1978. Grossvogel, Jill-Elyse, *Claude-Emile Schuffenecker. Margin and Image,* exhibition catalogue, The University Art Gall., Binghamton (NY), 1980. Porro, René, '*Claude-Émile Schuffenecker*' in vol. I, catalogue raisonné, Art Conseil, Fédry, 1992. Grossvogel, Jill-Elyse/Puget, Catherine/Delannoy, Agnès, *Claude-Émile Schuffenecker,* exhibition catalogue, Musée départemental Maurice-Denis, St-Germain-en-Laye, 1996. Grossvogel, Jill-Elyse, '*Claude-Emile Schuffenecker*' in vol. I, catalogue raisonné, Alan Wofsy Fine Arts, San Francisco, 2000.

MUSEUMS AND GALLERIES:

CINCINNATI (AM): *Road beneath Trees* (1895, oil on canvas) - FÉCAMP (Mus. des Arts et de l'Enfance): *Rocks in Yport* (1889, oil on canvas) - PARIS (MAMVP): *Young Girl* - PONT-AVEN: *Portrait of Madame Félicien Champsaur* - QUIMPER (MBA): *Rocky Coast in Brittany* (1886, oil on canvas) - ST-GERMAIN-EN-LAYE (Mus. du Prieuré-Maurice-Denis): *Inspired Woods* (c. 1895-1900).

AUCTION RECORDS:

PARIS, 8 June 1909, *Cliffs, Dieppe,* FRF 125; *Spring Landscape,* FRF 110. PARIS, 6 Nov 1924, *Road on a High Plateau,* FRF 600. PARIS, 3 Dec 1927, *Spring by the Sea,* FRF 220. PARIS, 21 April 1943, *Rock,* FRF 820. PARIS, 9 April 1945, *Landscape* (pastel) FRF 1,650; *Notre Dame in Snow* (1889) FRF 3,550. PARIS, Oct-July 1946, *Summer Landscape at the Day's End,* FRF 4,000; *Avenue with Tall trees,* FRF 2,000. PARIS, 27 Nov 1946, *The Cliff, Yport,* FRF 5,000; *Snow Scene* (1887) FRF 13,500. PARIS, 22 March 1955, *Road in Snow,* FRF 155,000. LONDON, 22 March 1961, *Portrait of Émile Bernard* (pastel) GBP 280. NEW YORK, 26 April 1961, *Notre Dame, Paris, in Snow,* USD 1,000. PARIS, 29 March 1963, *Breton Seascape,* FRF 4,100. VERSAILLES, 13 May 1964, *Fisherman at the Foot of Cliffs,* FRF 8,000. GENEVA, 22 May 1964, *Child Leaving School* (pastel) CHF 4,000. PARIS, 22 March 1965, *Young Woman Reading in a Meadow,* FRF 50,000. LONDON, 24 June 1966, *Port,* Gns 1,400. LONDON, 30 April 1969, *Portrait of the Painter Fernand Guignou,* GBP 4,000. PARIS, 25 June 1969, *Ballerina* (pastel) FRF 9,000. VERSAILLES, 15 March 1970, *Cliffs by the Sea,* FRF 20,000. BREST, 2 May 1974, *Western Wise Man,* FRF 20,000. LONDON, 8 April 1976, *Mother and Child on the Beach, Étretat* (c. 1888, oil on canvas, 36 3/4 x 25 ins / 93.5 x 63.5 cm) GBP 2,100. PARIS, 21 June 1976, *Landscape* (pastel, 12 1/2 x 18 ins / 32 x 46 cm) FRF 2,900. BREST, 15 May 1977, *Breton Sea Coast* (oil on canvas, 19 3/4 x 15 ins / 50 x 38 cm) FRF 7,000. MUNICH, 24 May 1978, *Landscape with a Large Tree* (pastel, 18 1/2 x 23 3/4 ins / 46.7 x 60.5 cm) DEM 5,600. PARIS, 9 May 1979, *Road between Trees* (pastel, 18 x 14 1/4 ins / 46 x 36 cm) FRF 12,000. BREST, 16 Dec 1979, *Red Trees* (1896, lithograph, 16 1/2 x 12 1/4 ins / 42 x 31 cm) FRF 5,800. BREST, 16 Dec 1979, *Wash-house in Bas-Meudon* (oil on canvas, 18 x 22 ins / 46 x 55 cm) FRF 46,600. NEW YORK, 21 Nov 1980, *Portrait of a Woman* (black chalk, 25 x 19 ins / 63.5 x 48.2 cm) USD 1,800. BREST, 3 March 1981, *Landscape* (oil on canvas, 25 1/2 x 32 ins / 65 x 81 cm) FRF 29,000. ENGHIEN-LES-BAINS, 26 June 1983, *Breton House Overlooking the Sea* (1886, oil on canvas, 19 3/4 x 24 ins / 50 x 61 cm) FRF 150,000. LONDON, 7 Dec 1983, *Self-portrait* (charcoal, 10 x 7 1/4 ins / 25.4 x 18.7 cm) GBP 800. LONDON, 27 March 1984, *Portrait of a Man* (pastel/paper, 16 3/4 x 21 1/2 ins / 42.5 x 54.5 cm) GBP 1,100. BREST, 19 May 1985, *Morning Mist* (pastel, 19 3/4 x 15 3/4 ins / 50 x 40 cm) FRF 10,000. PARIS, 26 June 1986, *Young Boy under the Cliffs of Étretat* (1886 ou 1888, oil on canvas, 21 1/4 x 25 1/2 ins / 54 x 65 cm) FRF 250,000. PARIS, 11 Jan 1988, *The Last Peasant in Meudon* (oil on canvas, 22 1/2 x 15 3/4 ins / 57 x 40 cm) FRF 35,000. PARIS, 19 March 1988, *Fisherman in Yport* (pastel, 7 3/4 x 5 ins / 20 x 13 cm) FRF 5,800. PARIS, 2 June 1988, *Figure Standing in front of the Sea and Rocks at Low Tide* (oil on canvas, 24 1/2 x 20 ins / 62 x 50.5 cm) FRF 220,000. NEW YORK, 6 Oct 1988, *By the Sea* (pastel/paper, 9 1/2 x 12 1/4 ins / 24 x 31.2 cm) USD 6,600. LONDON, 21 Oct 1988, *Paris: the Seine at the Île St-Louis* (oil on canvas, 10 3/4 x 16 1/4 ins / 27.5 x 41 cm) GBP 10,450. PARIS, 27 Oct 1988, *Bay in Brittany* (oil on canvas, 18 x 24 ins / 46 x 61 cm) FRF 83,000. LONDON, 21 Feb 1989, *Bouquet of Flowers and a Fan* (1886, oil on canvas, 16 1/4 x 12 3/4 ins / 41 x 32.5 cm) GBP 16,500. PARIS, 10 April 1989, *Women at the Wash-house* (oil on canvas, 18 x 15 ins / 46 x 38 cm) FRF 220,000. NEW YORK, 11 May 1989, *Hayricks* (1886, oil on canvas, 18 x 22 ins / 45.5 x 56 cm) USD 30,800. NEW YORK, 6 Oct 1989, *Étretat: Pointe d'Aval (front); Pointe de Hoche (back)* (pastel/paper, 8 1/4 x 10 3/4 ins / 21 x 27.3 cm) USD 8,800. NEW YORK, 16 Nov 1989, *Flowers and Fruit* (1880, oil on canvas, 25 1/2 x 21 1/4 ins / 64.7 x 54 cm) USD 132,000. PARIS, 23 Nov 1989, *The Cliffs, Étretat* (c. 1896, pastel, 5 3/4 x 9 ins / 14.5 x 23 cm) FRF 38,000. PARIS, 26 Nov 1989, *Village in Snow* (oil on canvas, 18 x 21 1/2 ins / 45.5 x 54.5 cm) FRF 140,000. PARIS, 20 Feb 1990, *Woman Sewing* (oil on canvas, 16 1/4 x 13 ins / 41 x 33 cm) FRF 42,000. NEW YORK, 26 Feb 1990, *Seated Woman* (pastel/paper/card, 24 1/2 x 18 ins / 62.5 x 45.6 cm) USD 13,200. PARIS, 3 April 1990, *Elephant Rock, Étretat* (1892, oil on canvas, 17 x 22 ins / 43 x 55 cm) FRF 28,000. LA VARENNE-ST-HILAIRE, 20 May 1990, *Rocky Coast* (pastel, 13 1/2 x 19 ins / 34 x 48 cm) FRF 29,500. NEW YORK, 14 Feb 1991, *Breton Cliffs* (pastel/paper/card, 15 x 18 1/2 ins / 38.1 x 47 cm) USD 15,400. PARIS, 20 June 1991, *Brittany, Road across a Heath* (oil on canvas, 18 x 22 ins / 46 x 55 cm) FRF 82,000. NEW YORK, 12 May 1993, *Workers in the Fields* (oil on canvas, 32 x 40 ins / 81 x 101.9 cm) USD 18,400. LONDON, 30 Nov 1994, *Children Playing with a Balloon* (oil on canvas, 32 1/4 x 26 ins / 82 x 66 cm) GBP 41,100. PARIS, 12 June 1995, *The Gardener* (1888, oil on canvas, 20 x 22 ins / 50.5 x 56 cm) FRF 67,000. PARIS, 13 Nov 1996, *Washerwomen* (c. 1895, pastel, 9 x 11 3/4 ins / 22 x 30 cm) FRF 18,000. PARIS, 2 Dec 1996, *Woman beneath a Tree* (pastel/paper, 13 x 16 3/4 ins / 33 x 42.6 cm) FRF 2,760. PARIS, 20 Jan 1997, *Woman with a Basket* (pastel, 8 1/2 x 5 ins / 21.5 x 13 cm) FRF 4,500. TEL AVIV, 26 April 1997, *Cliffs, Étretat* (oil on canvas, 24 x 29 ins / 61 x 73.7 cm) USD 17,250. PARIS, 30 Nov 1998, *Child Dreaming in Front of the Sea at Sunset* (1884, oil on canvas, 21 x 26 ins / 54 x 65 cm) FRF 490,000. PARIS, 14 Dec 1999, *The Washerwomen* (oil on canvas, 18 x 15 ins / 45 x 38 cm) FRF 170,000. PARIS, 17 Aug 2000, *The Washerwomen* (oil on canvas, 18 x 15 ins / 45 x 38 cm) FRF 195,000. CALAIS, 30 Sept 2001, *Tree-lined Alley* (pastel/paper, 17 x 14 ins / 44 x 35 cm) FRF 19,000. LONDON, 9 April 2002, *Women Sewing at the Window* (1895, pastel/paper, 25 x 19 ins / 63 x 49 cm) GBP 6,000. PARIS, 18 Dec 2003, *Women in Brittany* (1890, oil on canvas, 21 x 26 ins / 54 x 65 cm) EUR 40,000. PARIS, 26 June 2003, *Banks of the Pond* (oil on canvas, 21 x 26 ins / 54 x 65 cm) EUR 32,000. NEW YORK, 6 May 2004, *Snow-covered Road* (1887, oil on canvas, 18 x 22 ins / 46 x 55 cm) USD 40,000.

SCHUFFENECKER, Jacques
French, 20th century.
Born 21 November 1941.
Painter, draughtsman. Figures, interiors with figures, still-lifes.

Jacques Schuffenecker is the grandson of Claude-Emile Schuffenecker. He studied under Chapelain-Midy and Brayer at the École des Beaux-Arts in Paris and went on to take part in a number of exhibitions in Paris. He was awarded a commendation by the Eugène Carrière Prize jury.

Jacques Schuffenecker's style is that of a Realist with hints of Post-Cubism. One of his favourite themes is that of young artists in discussion in a communal studio, notably in the presence of his own teachers at the École des Arts.

BIBLIOGRAPHY:
Jacques Schuffenecker, exhibition catalogue, Maître Claude Robert, Paris, November 1969.

AUCTION RECORDS:
VERSAILLES, 14 Dec 1980, *Washerwomen by the River* (oil on canvas, 18 x 15 ins / 46 x 38 cm) FRF 18,000.

SCHÜFFNER
German, 18th century.
Engraver.

SCHUFINSKY, Viktor
Austrian, 19th - 20th century.
Born 28 July 1876, in Vienna.
Painter, draughtsman.

Viktor Schufinsky studied under Karl Hrachowina, Ludwig Minnigerode and Felicien Myrbach-Rheinfeld at the fine arts academy in Vienna. He produced several lithographs depicting scenes of World War I.

SCHUFRIED, Dominik, or Schuhfried
Austrian, 19th century.
Born 1810, in Vienna; died c. 1875 according to some sources, after 1888 according to others, in Vienna.
Painter. Genre scenes, landscapes.

He attended the academy in Vienna and exhibited from 1838 to 1857, and from 1869 to 1871. He painted a *Family of Peasants* that was formerly in the Imperial Palace in Vienna.

AUCTION RECORDS:
VIENNA, 16 March 1971, *Summer Landscape*, ATS 32,000. VIENNA, 27 May 1974, *Alpine Landscape*, ATS 30,000. LONDON, 29 Oct 1976, *Wooded Landscape with Staffage* (1871, oil on canvas, 28 1/2 x 38 1/2 ins / 72.5 x 98 cm) GBP 1,400. VIENNA, 14 June 1977, *Wooded Landscape at Twilight with Staffage* (1871, oil on canvas, 29 1/4 x 40 ins / 74.5 x 101.5 cm) ATS 80,000. COLOGNE, 21 March 1980, *Farmyard* (oil on canvas, 16 3/4 x 22 3/4 ins / 42.5 x 58 cm) DEM 8,000. VIENNA, 15 Dec 1981, *Country Scene* (oil on canvas, 16 3/4 x 22 3/4 ins / 42.5 x 58 cm) ATS 70,000. COLOGNE, 23 March 1990, *Storm on the Coast of Normandy* (1875, oil on canvas, 19 3/4 x 32 1/4 ins / 50 x 82 cm) DEM 2,200. NEW YORK, 1 Nov 1995, *Rustic Scene in Bavaria* (1868, oil on canvas, 30 x 40 ins / 76.2 x 101.6 cm) USD 9,200. VIENNA, 22 May 2003, *Landscape with Figures* (1859, oil on panel, 14 x 18 ins / 36 x 46 cm) EUR 4,000. VIENNA, 24 Nov 2003, *Rest in the Wood* (oil on canvas, one of a pair, 25 x 31 ins / 63 x 80 cm) EUR 4,000.

SCHUFRIED, Jakob, or Schuhfried, Schulfried, Schurfried
Austrian, 19th century.
Born 1785, in Vienna; died 12 May 1857, in Vienna.
Painter (porcelain).

The father of Dominik, Jakob Schufried was employed at the porcelain factory in Vienna, initially as a painter of figures, and from 1805 as a landscape painter.

SCHUGARDT, Michael. See **SCHUCHARDT**

SCHUH, Franz Peter
German, 18th century.
Born 1734, in Burgkundstadt; died 9 January 1803, in Bayreuth.
Sculptor.

SCHUH, Gotthard
Swiss, 20th century.
Born 1897; died 1969.
Painter.

MUSEUMS AND GALLERIES:
AARAU (Aargauer Kunsthaus): *Day* (1920); *Girl in a Room* (1924).

SCHUHBAUER, Beno. See **SCHUECHBAUR**

SCHUHFRIED, Dominik and Jakob. See **SCHUFRIED**

SCHUHLER, Johann. See **SCHULER**

SCHÜHLY, Hans
Austrian, 19th century.
Born 1850, in Schönnbrunn, near Vienna; died 23 August 1884, in Vienna

Schühly was taught by A. Zimmermann and of E. von Lichtenfels.

AUCTION RECORDS:
VIENNA, 27 May 1974, *Temptestuous Landscape*, ATS 25,000.

SCHUHMACHER. See also **SCHUMACHER**

SCHUHMACHER, Albert, or Schomaker
German, 18th century.
Died 1746.
Active in Bremen.
Painter.

Schuhmacher painted flowers and decorated ceilings.

SCHUHMACHER, Alfred
Swiss, 20th century.
Born 15 or 17 June 1883, in Zurich.
Painter. Landscapes.

Alfred Schuhmacher was self-taught.

SCHUHMACHER, Daniel
German, 17th - 18th century.
Born 1663; died 1728.
Active in Ansbach.
Cabinet maker.

SCHUHMACHER, Esaias
German, 17th century.
Active in Stettin (now Szczecin, Poland).
Painter.

MUSEUMS AND GALLERIES:
ANKLAM (Church of St Nikolai): *Portrait of Officer Franc. Buddeus* (1695).

SCHUHMACHER, Hans, or Schuechmacher
German, 16th century.
Active in Munich 1556-1580.
Engraver, medallist.
Munich School.

SCHUHMACHER, Hugo
Swiss, 20th century.
Born 1939, in Zurich.
Painter (gouache), draughtsman. Figures, still-lifes, landscapes, animals.

Hugo Schuhmacher studied graphic design in Zurich. He visited Spain in 1962-1964 and spent 1964-1967 in Paris, followed by time in the Canary Islands in 1965-1966. He took up painting and photography while living in Spain and the Canaries.

Schuhmacher started out as an exponent of Art Informel. From around 1966, however, he stopped painting expressive landscapes and turned towards themes associated with industry, starting to develop a Pop Art approach which inevitably implied a radical change of technique, notably in the use of airbrush work. Initially, he worked in a 'neutral' vein, painting automotive accessories such as hubcaps and headlights for no other apparent reason than an unmitigated aesthetic delight in their purity of form and colour or because they 'held up a mirror' to the urban environment in which they featured, such as in his *Auto-Landscapes* painted in 1968 and 1971.

He subsequently refined his approach to incorporate a more pronounced element of social commentary directed against the age of technology. His automotive portraits took on a more aggressive ('macho') aspect, where the automobile is identified with prestige, wealth and power and with the erotic potential it generates. This new approach encouraged him to move away from a slavish 'reflection' of the world at large and, increasingly, towards a sexually symbolic rendering of the automotive theme, creating marketing and advertising-inspired associative juxtapositions between the motor car and female nudes or even producing quasi-Surrealist versions of the automobile in the form of the female anatomy. An example of this is his *Queen* series, where the engine takes on the contours of a woman's breasts.

Overall, Schuhmacher's work emerges as a concerted protest against the commercialisation of society and the exploitation of humanity in general and of womankind in particular as little less than an object of merchandising.

He was invited to participate in the Paris Biennale in 1969. His work is exhibited predominantly in Switzerland (Zurich, St Gall, Bern), but he has also shown work in Düsseldorf.

BIBLIOGRAPHY:
Kneubühler, Theo, *Kunst: 28 Schweizer*, exhibition catalogue, Gal. Raeber, Lucerne, 1972.

MUSEUMS AND GALLERIES:
AARAU (Aargauer Kunsthaus): *Free Everybody Free* (1972); *Landscape (Sihlochstrasse)* (1976).

AUCTION RECORDS:
ZURICH, 14-16 Oct 1992, *Sea Trout* (pencil, 27 1/4 x 39 1/4 ins / 69.3 x 99.5 cm) CHF 2,000.

SCHUHMACHER, Immanuel Friedrich
German, 18th - 19th century.
Born 29 June 1754, in Ansbach; died 16 December 1824, in Bayreuth.
Painter. Religious subjects.

Immanuel Schuhmacher was court painter at Bayreuth.

MUSEUMS AND GALLERIES:
BAYREUTH (Church): *Christ in the Temple*.

SCHUHMACHER, Karl Jakob
Baltic School, 19th century.
Born 1786, in Riga; died February 1824, in Riga.
Painter. Portraits.

SCHUHMACHER, Meta (Mrs). See **OELRICHS Meta**

SCHUHMACHER, Wim, or Schumacher
Dutch, 20th century.
Born 1894, in Amsterdam; died 1986.
Painter, draughtsman. Nudes, portraits, landscapes, still-lifes.

Considerable uncertainty surrounds Wim Schuhmacher's biographical details. Some less than reliable sources claim that he was born in the USA in 1870 - in Boston, to be more precise - and that he was baptised William E. or Willem. It is also suggested that he died in 1930. What can be said with some degree of certainty, however, is that he studied at the fine arts academy in Amsterdam and that he travelled extensively in Europe, spending some time in Paris. The influence of La Fauconnier is apparent in the forceful structure of Schuhmacher's landscapes and still-lifes, which are in a distinct Magic Realist style. He was captivated by the changing light of southern Europe and was acknowledged as a master of grey tones.

Schuhmacher's work featured in *De Blijvende Verlokking: Nederlandse Kunstenaars in Italië, 1806-1940* (*Lasting Attraction: Dutch Artists in Italy, 1806-1940*) at the Kunsthal in Rotterdam in 2003.

BIBLIOGRAPHY:
Van Geest, Jan, *Wim Schuhmacher, de Meester van het grijs*, Jan Brand Boeken, Arnhem, 1991.

MUSEUMS AND GALLERIES:
ROTTERDAM (Mus. Boijmans Van Beuningen): *Port of Palma* (1913).

AUCTION RECORDS:
AMSTERDAM, 25 April 1978, *View of Saignon Village* (oil on canvas, 25 3/4 x 34 1/4 ins / 65.5 x 87 cm) NLG 12,000. AMSTERDAM, 24 April 1979, *Provençal Landscape* (oil on canvas, 25 x 31 ins / 63.5 x 79 cm) NLG 3,800. AMSTERDAM, 14 June 1979, *Self-portrait* (1942, pen, 12 1/2 x 9 1/2 ins / 31.5 x 24 cm) NLG 4,200. AMSTERDAM, 18 March 1985, *View of Corte (Corsica)* (oil on canvas, 55 1/2 x 33 1/2 ins / 141 x 85 cm) NLG 20,000. AMSTERDAM, 10 April 1989, *Piet Tiggers' Children* (oil on canvas, 27 1/4 x 22 1/2 ins / 69 x 57 cm) NLG 5,175. AMSTERDAM, 24 May 1989, *Portrait of a Woman* (1939, oil on canvas, 13 x 22 ins / 33 x 55 cm) NLG 29,900. AMSTERDAM, 22 May 1990, *Portrait of the Artist's Wife* (oil on canvas, 39 3/4 x 30 3/4 ins / 101 x 78 cm) NLG 41,400. AMSTERDAM, 12 Dec 1990, *Reclining Nude* (ink/paper, 9 3/4 x 14 ins / 25 x 35.5 cm) NLG 4,370; *Courtyard of Cervantes' Inn in Toledo* (oil on canvas, 26 x 31 1/2 ins / 66 x 80 cm) NLG 40,250. AMSTERDAM, 5-6 Feb 1991, *Reclining Nude* (black chalk/paper, 14 x 23 1/2 ins / 35.5 x 60 cm) NLG 1,035. AMSTERDAM, 23 May 1991, *Tree* (oil on canvas/card, 13 3/4 x 18 3/4 ins / 35 x 47.5 cm) NLG 13,800. AMSTERDAM, 11 Dec 1991, *Winter Landscape* (1915, oil on canvas, 18 1/2 x 37 ins / 47 x 94 cm) NLG 25,300. AMSTERDAM, 18 Feb 1992, *Portrait of a Baby* (pencil/paper, 14 x 14 1/4 ins / 35.5 x 36.5 cm) NLG 1,035. AMSTERDAM, 21 May 1992, *Orchard in Blossom* (1920, oil on canvas, 42 3/4 x 37 1/2 ins / 108.5 x 95.4 cm) NLG 57,500. AMSTERDAM, 26 May 1993, *Still-life with Dead Birds, Eggs and Green Pears on a Table* (1932, oil on

canvas, 21 1/4 x 25 1/2 ins / 54 x 65 cm) NLG 97,750. AMSTERDAM, 31 May 1994, *View of Notre-Dame in Paris* (oil on canvas, 23 1/2 x 28 1/2 ins / 59.5 x 72.5 cm) NLG 40,250. AMSTERDAM, 6 Dec 1995, *Female Nude* (black ink/paper, 63 x 45 1/4 ins / 160 x 115 cm) NLG 7,475. AMSTERDAM, 4 June 1996, *Fountain in Corte (Corsica)* (1929, oil on canvas, 25 1/2 x 32 ins / 65 x 81 cm) NLG 73,160. AMSTERDAM, 17-18 Dec 1996, *Landscape with Telephone Poles* (oil on canvas, 13 x 17 1/2 ins / 33 x 44.5 cm) NLG 23,010. AMSTERDAM, 2 Dec 1997, *Portrait of Melitta* (c. 1927-1929, oil on canvas, 11 3/4 x 9 ins / 30 x 23 cm) NLG 115,320. AMSTERDAM, 10 June 1999, *View of Teruel, Spain* (c. 1936, Indian ink, 19 x 24 ins / 49 x 60 cm) NLG 110,000. AMSTERDAM, 1 Dec 1999, *Quiet Street, Palma de Mallorca* (oil on canvas, 32 x 26 ins / 81 x 65 cm) NLG 170,000. AMSTERDAM, 8 June 2000, *Self-portrait* (Indian ink, circular, 9 x 9 ins / 23 x 23 cm) NLG 80,000. AMSTERDAM, 30 Nov 2000, *Woman in the Dunes* (oil on canvas, 39 x 32 ins / 100 x 81 cm) NLG 200,000. AMSTERDAM, 12 June 2001, *Self-portrait* (c. 1942, pen and black ink, 13 x 10 ins / 33 x 25 cm) NLG 95,000. AMSTERDAM, 3 Dec 2001, *Bosven, omstreken schoorl* (oil on canvas, 20 x 24 ins / 52 x 61 cm) NLG 42,000. AMSTERDAM, 16 April 2002, *Reclining Woman, Melitta* (oil on canvas, 13 x 22 ins / 33 x 55 cm) EUR 42,000. AMSTERDAM, 28 May 2002, *Herfstbos* (1915, oil on canvas, 19 x 28 ins / 47 x 70 cm) EUR 26,000. AMSTERDAM, 3 June 2003, *Still-life with Fruit and Fish* (1931, oil on canvas, 26 x 32 ins / 65 x 81 cm) EUR 50,000. AMSTERDAM, 25 Nov 2003, *Portrait of a Man from Senegal* (1929, black chalk, 39 x 32 ins / 100 x 81 cm) EUR 10,000. AMSTERDAM, 8 June 2004, *Jan Wiegers and Model, Schets* (oil on canvas, 22 x 16 ins / 55 x 41 cm) EUR 4,400. AMSTERDAM, 1 Dec 2004, *Still-life with Fish and Lemon* (1931, oil on canvas, 32 x 39 ins / 81 x 100 cm) EUR 50,000.

SCHUHMANN. See **SCHUMANN**

SCHUIL, Han
Dutch, 20th - 21st century.
Born 1958, in Voorshoten.
Painter.

Han Schuil lives and works in Amsterdam. His abstraction is based on reality, from which he borrows materials (wood, metal, fabric). Using geometric forms in complementary colours or pastel tones, he establishes a rhythm, working on movement, at the heart of a composition that is very straightforward because it is simple and purified. He has had solo shows in Rotterdam (1985), at the Museum of Contemporary Art in Montreal (1987) and in Bruges (1992).

MUSEUMS AND GALLERIES:
HEERLEN (Stadsgalerij): *Untitled* (1989, oil/aluminium).

SCHUITEN, Robert
French, 20th century.
Born 1912; died 1997.
Architect, painter, draughtsman, watercolourist.

Robert Schuiten is best known as an architect, the inventor of the first 'ecological houses' in the 1940s and 1950s. Painting was, however, his first calling, and he pursued it, seeking effects of light and colour. His architectural plans were accompanied by numerous graphic or painted works.

BIBLIOGRAPHY:
Cluvot, Maurice/Strauven, Francis/Lamy, Dominique, *Robert Schuiten: architecte et peintre*, Archives d'Architecture Moderne, Brussels, 2002.

SCHUKAYEFF, Stepan Grigorievitch. See **CHUKAEV Stepan Grigorievich**

SCHUKOWSKIJ. See **JOUKOVSKI Pavel Vassiliévitch von**

SCHULD, Gerhard. See **SCHULT**

SCHULDES, Wenzel
Austrian, 19th century.
Born 1777, in Tabor; died 1 November 1828, in Prague.
Engraver (aquatint).

Schuldes worked in Vienna.

SCHULDHESS, Jörg Shimon Anton, or Jörg Simon Anton
Swiss, 20th - 21st century.
Born 1941, in Basel.
Active from 1979 to 1983 and naturalised in Israel.
Painter, watercolourist, draughtsman, sculptor, engraver. Figures, scenes with figures, landscapes.

Jörg Schuldhess was of Italian Jewish descent. He had a Christian education, before converting to Judaism in 1968. At the age of 23 he went to India to teach as a missionary for a while, returning there several times. He travelled continually, particularly in Asia (including Hong Kong and Sri Lanka), Africa (including Morocco, Uganda and Tanzania) and South America (including Mexico and Argentina). He then settled in Israel, becoming an Israeli national, but gave up his citizenship in 1983 and returned to Switzerland.

As a militant artist, his aim is to present the needs and hopes of humanity in visual form, in particular producing a whole body of work relating to the political situation in the Middle East. His stylised, brightly coloured compositions, in which lines predominate, depict screaming faces and broken bodies, as well as views of towns, particularly places of worship (mosques). The structures he uses, with emphasis on symmetry, the circular form, and the laws of mathematics, resemble the mandalas, establishing parallels between different religions (the star of David, yin and yang, the cross and the Ten Commandments).

Schuldhess has taken part in numerous group exhibitions: 1968, 1970 Bradford Biennale; 1972 Venice Biennale and Tokyo Biennale; 1979 Cracow Biennale; 1980 Ljubljana Biennale; winning various awards. There have also been a vast number of solo exhibitions, many of them sponsored by various embassies; a prospectus mentions more than 380 such exhibitions between 1960 and 1987.

BIBLIOGRAPHY:
Schuldhess, Jörg Simon Anton, '*For Abel, the Mark of Cain*' in *7 vol*, Ziona Schuldhess-Wettstein, Liestal, 1986.

MUSEUMS AND GALLERIES:
PARIS (BNF): *Father* (1980, etching).

SCHULDT, F. L.
German, 19th century.
Active during the first half of the 19th century.
Painter.

MUSEUMS AND GALLERIES:
DARMSTADT (Schlossmus.): *Portrait of Prince Emil von Hessen; Countryside Scene of 1815.*

SCHÜLDT, Fritiof Johannes
Swedish, 20th century.
Born 9 June 1891, in Stockholm; died 1978.
Painter. Figures, nudes, interiors with figures, landscapes.

Fritiof Johannes Schüldt studied at the fine arts academy in Stockholm from 1910 to 1912.

MUSEUMS AND GALLERIES:
GÖTEBORG - STOCKHOLM.

AUCTION RECORDS:
STOCKHOLM, 24 April 1947, *Reclining Nude*, SEK 2,400. STOCKHOLM, 6 April 1951, *View through a Window* (1948) SEK 5,000; *Young Girl Seated*, SEK 4,300. NEW YORK, 8 Nov 1979, *Self-portrait* (c. 1940, oil on canvas, 32 x 25 3/4 ins / 81 x 65.5 cm) USD 1,600. STOCKHOLM, 14 June 1990, *Interior with a Woman Reading near a Window Facing out to Sea* (oil on canvas, 23 1/4 x 28 1/4 ins / 59 x 72 cm) SEK 8,500. STOCKHOLM, 13 April 1992, *Norwegian Girl Seated in an Interior* (oil on canvas, 31 x 25 1/4 ins / 79 x 64 cm) SEK 12,000. STOCKHOLM, 6 Nov 2002, *Harbour at Ischia* (oil on panel, 22

x 26 ins / 55 x 65 cm) SEK 18,000. STOCKHOLM, 4 Nov 2003, *Still-life with Jugs, Flowers and Brushes* (1946, oil on canvas, 29 x 37 ins / 73 x 93 cm) SEK 15,000. STOCKHOLM, 26 April 2004, *View from the Terrace of the Villa by the Sea, Smedsudden* (1920, oil on canvas, 17 x 13 ins / 44 x 32 cm) SEK 82,000. STOCKHOLM, 3 Nov 2004, *Studio at Rue Daguerre* (oil on canvas, 46 x 35 ins / 116 x 89 cm) SEK 18,000.

SCHULDTNER
German, 18th century.
Active towards the middle of the 18th century.
Painter. Religious subjects.
MUSEUMS AND GALLERIES:
VIECHTACH (Church): *Holy Family Surrounded by Angels.*

SCHULE, Albert Johann Christian
German, 19th century.
Born 8 June 1801, in Leipzig; died 8 December 1875.
Active in Leipzig.
Engraver (burin).
Albert Schule was the son of Christian.
MUSEUMS AND GALLERIES:
LEIPZIG (Stadtgeschichtliches Mus.): portraits; landscapes.

SCHULE, Christian Georg
German, 18th - 19th century.
Born 7 October 1764, in Copenhagen; died 9 August 1816, in Leipzig.
Engraver.
Christian Schule attended the Kunstakademi in Copenhagen and was taught by J.F. Clemens, becoming his apprentice in 1781. Between 1787 and 1816 he lived in Leipzig where he worked for booksellers.

SCHULE, F.
German, 19th century.
Born 1795, in Leipzig.
Active in Russia 1845-1848, and thereafter in Leipzig.
Painter. Portraits.

SCHÜLEIN, Julius Wolfgang
German, 20th century.
Born 28 May 1881, in Munich.
Painter, engraver. Urban landscapes.
Julius Wolfgang Schülein was a pupil of Hugo von Habermann.
MUSEUMS AND GALLERIES:
MUNICH (Städtische Gal. im Lenbachhaus): *At the Montparnasse Railway Station.*

SCHÜLEIN, Suzanne
Maiden name: Carvallo
French, 20th century.
Born 1 July 1883, in Paris.
Active in Germany.
Painter, engraver. Portraits, genre scenes, landscapes.
Suzanne Schülein, the wife of Julius W. Schülein, lived and worked in Munich. She exhibited in Paris at the Salon des Indépendants in 1907, 1909 and 1910, at the Salon d'Automne in 1913, and at the Salon des Tuileries in 1934 and 1935.

SCHULER, Adam
School of Alsace, 17th century.
Born 1645.
Painter.
In 1678 Adam Schuler married Marie Elisabeth, daughter of the painter Rudolf Sturm von Waldkirch.

SCHÜLER, Alfred
German, 19th - 20th century.
Born 21 October 1858, in Elberfeld.
Active in Hamburg.
Painter. Portraits, landscapes.
Alfred Schüler studied at the fine arts academy in Munich.
MUSEUMS AND GALLERIES:
HAMBURG (Rathaus): *Portrait of J. Halben.*

SCHÜLER, Anton, or Schueler
Austrian, 18th century.
Of Tyrolean origin.
Painter.

SCHÜLER, Arthur
German, 19th - 20th century.
Born 1877, in Berlin.
Active in Berlin.
Painter. Landscapes.
Arthur Schüler studied at the fine arts academy in Berlin.

SCHÜLER, Ch.
German, 19th century.
Active in Darmstadt between 1835 and 1836.
Engraver (wood).

SCHULER, Charles Auguste
French, 19th century.
Born 11 March 1804, in Strasbourg; died 23 October 1859, in Strasbourg.
Engraver.
His teachers were his father, Guérin and Gros. He was admitted to the École des Beaux-Arts on 6 April 1822. His first Salon exhibition was in 1824, and he won a third-class medal in 1846.

SCHULER, Charles Louis
French, 19th century.
Born 1785, in Strasbourg; died 1852, in Lichtenthal, near Baden-Baden, Germany.
Engraver, draughtsman.
This artist was a pupil of Guérin in Paris. He started off working in Strasbourg, producing small engravings for almanacs and other local publications of that nature. Later he moved to Karlsruhe (south-west Germany), and worked on more highbrow engravings after the Italian Old Masters.
MUSEUMS AND GALLERIES:
STRASBOURG (Mus. des Arts Appliqués): *Portrait of a Lady.*

SCHÜLER, Chr.
German, 19th century.
Active in Darmstadt c. 1852.
Engraver (steel).

SCHULER, Dominik
Swiss, 19th century.
Born 5 June 1840, in Sattel; died 11 January 1891, in Schwyz.
Sculptor, designer of ornamental architectural features.

SCHULER, Édouard
French, 19th century.
Born 19 August 1806, in Strasbourg; died 1882, in Lichtenthal, near Baden-Baden, Germany.
Engraver, sculptor.
The son of Charles Louis Schuler, Édouard Schuler learned his craft from his father and from Baron Gros. He worked in Strasbourg, engraving religious subjects and genre scenes. He contributed to a collection of engravings of works by the finest modern painters. These were engraved on steel by the most skilful artists of the day, under the direction of MC Frommel (in Karlsruhe, south-west Germany, in 1833).

SCHULER, Gottfried
German, 20th century.
Active in Weimar.
Engraver.
Examples of Gottfried Schuler's work featured in *De Bonnard à Baselitz: Dix Ans d'Enrichissements du Cabinet des Estampes 1978-1988* (From Bonnard to Baselitz: A Decade

of Acquisitions by the Prints Collection 1978-1988), an exhibition held at the Bibliothèque Nationale in Paris in 1992.
MUSEUMS AND GALLERIES:
PARIS (BNF): *Village Outskirts in Winter I* (1981, dry-point).

SCHULER, Hans, or Schuller
French, 19th - 20th century.
Born 25 May 1874, in Morange (Lorraine); died 1951.
Active in the USA.
Sculptor.
Schuler was taught by Charles Raoul Verlet. From 1925 he was director of the Maryland Institute. He lived and worked in Baltimore.

He exhibited in Paris, at the Salon des Artistes Français, and received a third-place medal in 1901.

His most notable works include *Paradise Lost* and the monument of *John Hopkins* in Baltimore and *Ariadne*.
MUSEUMS AND GALLERIES:
ST LOUIS: *Paradise Lost*.
AUCTION RECORDS:
LONDON, 6 Nov 1986, *Nude Lying on a Rock* (patinated bronze, h. 14¼ ins / 36 cm) GBP 1,800.

SCHULER, Heinrich
German, 19th century.
Born 1857, in Mainz; died 1885, in Munich.
Active in Mainz and Munich.
Painter.
MUSEUMS AND GALLERIES:
MAINZ: *Main Square and Fountain in Mainz with Famous Figures*.

SCHULER, Johann
French, 17th century.
Born 1648; died 1704.
Painter.
Johann Schuler was the grandfather of the Strasbourg printer Johann Friedrich Schuler, who was born in 1748.

SCHULER, Johann, or Schuhler
Austrian, 18th century.
Of Tyrolean origin.
Active in Basel and Zurich.
Stucco artist.

SCHULER, Jules Théophile or Théophile
French, 19th century.
Born 18 June 1821, in Strasbourg; died 26 January 1878, in Strasbourg.
Painter, draughtsman, illustrator. Historical subjects, portraits, genre scenes, interiors with figures, landscapes with figures, landscapes.
Schuler was a student of Michel Drolling and Paul Delaroche in Paris, and he also studied in Munich. He lived in Neuchâtel, Switzerland, for a few years, then moved back to his home town of Strasbourg. He first exhibited at the Paris Salon in 1845.

He worked on several magazines and provided numerous illustrations for the works of Victor Hugo, Jules Verne and Erckmann-Chatrian.

MUSEUMS AND GALLERIES:
BERN: *The Mayor of Strasbourg Receiving the Swiss Deputation during the Siege of 1870* - COLMAR: *The Chariot of Death; Woodcutters in the Vosges* - MULHOUSE: *Kuss, Mayor of Strasbourg; Studio Interior; Major Sers* - NEUCHÂTEL: *Snowplough; Floats at Montboron on the Sarine* (grisaille) - STRASBOURG: *Young Alsatians in the 18th Century; Prayer of the Miners in Preuschdorf; Orchard; A Sunday Evening in Preuschdorf; Winter in Alsace; Portrait of Mademoiselle Rose Schuler*.
AUCTION RECORDS:
PARIS, 22 June 1945, *Dr Kuss, Mayor of Strasbourg* (graphite drawing, scaled-down version of the painting, sold with a Kauffmann drawing 'On The Market') FRF 300.

SCHULER, Karl
German, 19th century.
Born 11 January 1847, in Nuremberg; died 13 April 1886, in Berlin-Friedenau.
Sculptor.
Karl Schuler studied in Nuremberg, Berlin, Rome and Dresden. His sculptural works included a bronze statue of Prince Adalbert in Wilhelmshaven, a colossal statue of Friedrich Wilhelm IV in Berlin and a monument of Luther in Nordhausen.

SCHÜLER, Karl Ludwig
Austrian, 19th century.
Born 1790 or 1791, in Fünfkirchen; died 1852, in Vienna.
Miniaturist, lithographer.
Schüler attended the academy in Vienna.

SCHÜLER, Max
German, 19th - 20th century.
Born 26 June 1854, in Gesecke (Württemberg).
Active in Frankfurt am Main.
Painter. Portraits.
MUSEUMS AND GALLERIES:
STRASBOURG: *Portrait of Field Marshal Van Manteuffel* (1883).

SCHULER, Wilhelm
German, 19th - 20th century.
Born 28 May 1875, in Karlsruhe.
Draughtsman.
Wilhelm Schuler studied in Karlsruhe, Stuttgart and Paris.
MUSEUMS AND GALLERIES:
AACHEN (Suermondt-Ludwig Mus.): several drawings.

SCHULFRIED, Jakob. See **SCHUFRIED**

SCHULIN, Carl
German, 19th century.
Active in Berlin.
Engraver (copper/steel).
Schulin exhibited in Berlin between 1838 and 1848.

SCHULKOV, Leonti
Russian, 18th century.
Active during the second half of the 18th century.
Icon painter.
Leonti Schulkov worked for the Russian court from 1674 to 1686.

SCHULLER, Betty
German, 19th century.
Born 11 March 1860, in Schässbourg; died 8 August 1904.
Painter.
Betty Schuller was the daughter of Ludwig F. Schuller.

SCHÜLLER, F.
German, 18th century.
Active c. 1730.
Painter.
Schüller's *Judgement Day* is in Burstadt Rathaus. He may be the same artist as F. Schuller.

SCHULLER, F.
German, 18th century.
Painter.

Three pictures of palatine princes born in Neuburg an der Donau are signed by F. Schuller.

SCHULLER, Franz Bernhard. See **SCHILLER**

SCHULLER, Georg, or Schuler
German, 17th century.
Active in Hermannstadt (now Sibiu, Romania).
Medallist, goldsmith.

SCHULLER, Gottlieb
Austrian, 19th - 20th century.
Born 10 December 1879, in Auffach (Kufstein).
Painter.

Gottlieb Schuller served as artistic director of a glass-painting school in the Tyrol.

SCHULLER, Joseph Carl Paul
French, 19th century.
Born in Husseren (Haut-Rhin).
Painter. Landscapes, animals, flowers.

His masters were Pierre Emmanuel Damoye and Emmanuel Benner. He made his debut at the Paris Salon in 1880 and became a member of the Société des Artistes Français in 1888. He received an honourable mention in 1885 and a bronze medal in 1889 at the Exposition Universelle in Paris.

He painted birds and flowers.

MUSEUMS AND GALLERIES:
CAEN: *Chrysanthemums* - MULHOUSE.

AUCTION RECORDS:
LONDON, 19 March 1986, *Hollyhocks on the Riverbank* (1890, oil on canvas, 55 x 39 3/4 ins / 140 x 101 cm) GBP 5,000. VERSAILLES, 19 Nov 1989, *Garden in Bloom* (oil on panel, 16 x 11 ins / 40.5 x 28 cm) FRF 4,200. LONDON, 24 Nov 1989, *Courtyard in Bloom* (1892, oil on panel, 19 3/4 x 12 3/4 ins / 50 x 32.5 cm) GBP 9,900. PARIS, 25 March 1993, *Wild Flowers* (oil on panel, 16 1/4 x 11 ins / 41 x 28 cm) FRF 3,300.

SCHÜLLER, Karl
Austrian, 19th century.
Born 14 June 1852, in Taus, Bohemia; died 23 October 1901, in Vienna.
Painter.

The pupil of F. Laufberger and A. Eisenmenger, Karl Schüller painted several portraits of *Franz Josef I*.

SCHULLER, Ludwig Friedrich
Austrian, 19th century.
Born 18 January 1826, in Feffernitz, Carinthia; died 18 March 1906, in Schässbourg.
Painter.

The father of Betty, Ludwig Schuller studied in Paris, Vienna and Rome between 1854 and 1855.

MUSEUMS AND GALLERIES:
SIBIU.

SCHULLERUS, Fritz
German, 19th century.
Born 22 July 1866, in Fogarasch; died 22 December 1898, in Gross Schenk.
Painter. Portraits, landscapes.

Schullerus was the pupil of G. Hackl and L. von Löfftz.

MUSEUMS AND GALLERIES:
SIBIU: several works and studies.

SCHULMAN, David
Dutch, 20th century.
Born 31 October 1881, in Hilversum; died 21 October 1966, in Laren.
Painter. Landscapes, landscapes with figures, urban landscapes, winter landscapes, harbour scenes.

David Schulman's style vacillates between Naturalism and Impressionism. He painted a large number of Dutch landscapes. He exhibited on numerous occasions both in the Netherlands and abroad and was awarded a silver medal at the San Francisco International Exhibition of 1915.

AUCTION RECORDS:
AMSTERDAM, 27 April 1976, *Amsterdam in Winter* (oil on canvas, 18 x 28 ins / 45.5 x 71 cm) NLG 5,200. AMSTERDAM, 15 Sept 1977, *River Landscape* (oil on canvas, 23 1/4 x 31 ins / 59 x 79 cm) NLG 2,500. AMSTERDAM, 20 March 1978, *Boats in Port* (oil on panel, 12 1/2 x 19 ins / 32 x 48 cm) NLG 3,000. AMSTERDAM, 31 Oct 1979, *Port of Volendam* (1924, oil on canvas, 19 1/4 x 27 1/4 ins / 49 x 69 cm) NLG 3,000. AMSTERDAM, 19 May 1981, *Amsterdam in Winter* (oil on canvas, 16 3/4 x 24 1/2 ins / 42.5 x 62.5 cm) NLG 4,600. AMSTERDAM, 30 Aug 1988, *Sunset over a Hamlet in Winter* (oil on canvas, 23 1/2 x 39 1/4 ins / 60 x 100 cm) NLG 5,750. AMSTERDAM, 3 Sept 1988, *Rhine View with the Belfry of Cunera Church in the Distance* (oil on canvas, 17 1/4 x 35 ins / 44 x 88 cm) NLG 1,725. AMSTERDAM, 16 Nov 1988, *Village in Winter* (oil on canvas, 16 1/4 x 30 ins / 41 x 76 cm) NLG 4,830. AMSTERDAM, 28 Feb 1989, *View of Monnikendam* (oil on panel, 18 1/4 x 30 ins / 46.5 x 76 cm) NLG 1,725. AMSTERDAM, 19 Sept 1989, *Winter Afternoon at Blaricum* (oil on canvas, 15 1/4 x 22 ins / 39 x 55 cm) NLG 3,680. AMSTERDAM, 25 April 1990, *Winter at Laren* (oil on canvas, 20 3/4 x 33 ins / 53 x 84 cm) NLG 5,750. AMSTERDAM, 6 Nov 1990, *Schreijerstoren Towers in Amsterdam* (oil on canvas, 11 x 16 1/4 ins / 28 x 41.5 cm) NLG 3,450. AMSTERDAM, 5-6 Feb 1991, *Boarding Moored Sailing Boats, with Edam Church in the Background* (oil on canvas, 12 3/4 x 19 ins / 32.5 x 48.5 cm) NLG 1,150. AMSTERDAM, 24 April 1991, *Winter View of Blaricum* (oil on canvas, 22 x 33 ins / 56 x 84 cm) NLG 5,750. AMSTERDAM, 17 Sept 1991, *Overcast Day on the Foreshore* (oil on canvas, 14 1/2 x 20 3/4 ins / 37 x 53 cm) NLG 1,380. AMSTERDAM, 5-6 Nov 1991, *Blaricum in the Snow* (oil on canvas, 13 3/4 x 25 1/4 ins / 35 x 64 cm) NLG 5,980. AMSTERDAM, 18 Feb 1992, *Panoramic View of Amsterdam, with the Central Station and the Church of St Nicholas* (oil on canvas, 19 3/4 x 27 1/2 ins / 50 x 70 cm) NLG 13,800. AMSTERDAM, 14-15 April 1992, *Winter View of Laren* (oil on canvas, 25 1/2 x 46 ins / 65 x 116 cm) NLG 7,130. AMSTERDAM, 9 Nov 1993, *View of Gelder Quay in Amsterdam* (oil on canvas, 18 1/4 x 29 1/4 ins / 46.5 x 74.5 cm) NLG 6,325. MONTREAL, 23-24 Nov 1993, *Sowing Season* (oil on canvas, 13 x 19 ins / 33 x 48.2 cm) CAD 1,000. AMSTERDAM, 11 April 1995, *Midday in Winter* (oil on canvas, 23 1/2 x 38 3/4 ins / 60 x 98.5 cm) NLG 5,664. AMSTERDAM, 4 June 1996, *Port of Amsterdam* (oil on canvas, 17 1/2 x 28 3/4 ins / 44.5 x 73 cm) NLG 4,720. AMSTERDAM, 18 June 1996, *Winter in Laren* (oil on canvas, 22 1/2 x 33 ins / 57 x 84 cm) NLG 8,050. AMSTERDAM, 19-20 Feb 1997, *View of a Town in Winter, with a Peasant Woman in a Snow-covered Square* (oil on panel, 11 x 8 1/4 ins / 27 x 21 cm) NLG 3,228. AMSTERDAM, 28 April 1999, *Laren in Winter* (oil on canvas, 19 x 30 ins / 48 x 76 cm) NLG 9,200. AMSTERDAM, 7 July 1999, *Winter in Laren* (oil on canvas, 15 x 21 ins / 37 x 53 cm) NLG 14,000. THE HAGUE, 9 May 2000, *Amsterdam in Winter with View of the Westertoren* (oil on canvas, 23 x 31 ins / 58 x 78 cm) NLG 10,000. AMSTERDAM, 25 Oct 2000, *Early Morning* (1905, oil on canvas, 15 x 13 ins / 37 x 33 cm) NLG 4,000. AMSTERDAM, 11 Feb 2001, *Midday in Winter at Blaricum* (oil on canvas, 28 x 39 ins / 70 x 100 cm) NLG 12,000. AMSTERDAM, 4 Sept 2001, *Blaricum in Winter* (oil on canvas, 22 x 33 ins / 55 x 85 cm) EUR 7,500. AMSTERDAM, 12 March 2002, *View of Wijk bij Duurstede* (oil on canvas, 24 x 39 ins / 60 x 99 cm) EUR 8,500. AMSTERDAM, 21 Oct 2002, *Farm in the Snow* (oil on canvas, 21 x 33 ins / 54 x 84 cm) EUR 3,200. AMSTERDAM, 10 March 2003, *Betuwe* (oil on canvas, 32 x 37 ins / 82 x 94 cm) EUR 3,200. AMSTERDAM, 2 Sept 2003, *Towards Evening*

in Blaricum (oil on canvas, 24 x 31 ins / 60 x 80 cm) EUR 5,000. AMSTERDAM, 15 March 2004, *View of the Prins Hendrikkade, Amsterdam* (oil on canvas, 20 x 28 ins / 51 x 71 cm) EUR 4,600. AMSTERDAM, 28 June 2004, *View of Laren in Winter* (oil on canvas, 24 x 31 ins / 60 x 80 cm) EUR 6,500.

SCHULMAN, Léon Gaspard. See **GASPARD Leon Schulman**

SCHULMAN, Lion
Dutch, 19th - 20th century.
Born 1851; died 1943.
Painter. Scenes with figures, landscapes, flowers.

AUCTION RECORDS:
AMSTERDAM, 16 Nov 1988, *Forest of Viersprong Oosterbeek, with a Horseman and a Peasant Fishing in a Pond* (1878, oil on canvas, 31 1/2 x 45 1/2 ins / 80 x 115.5 cm) NLG 8,625. AMSTERDAM, 19 Sept 1989, *Peasant Woman and Child Walking on a Road near a Farm* (oil on canvas, 20 1/4 x 16 1/4 ins / 51.5 x 41.5 cm) NLG 1,265. AMSTERDAM, 11 Sept 1990, *Dahlias in an Earthenware Jug* (oil on canvas, 39 3/4 x 26 3/4 ins / 101 x 68 cm) NLG 1,495. AMSTERDAM, 6 Nov 1990, *Winter Landscape near Graveland, with Figures on a Path* (1885, oil on panel, 12 1/2 x 10 ins / 32 x 25.5 cm) NLG 6,325. AMSTERDAM, 23 April 1991, *Figures in a Creek* (oil on panel, 5 1/2 x 4 1/4 ins / 14 x 11 cm) NLG 2,415. AMSTERDAM, 18 Feb 1992, *Wooded Landscape near Oosterbeek with Peasants on a Path* (1886, oil on canvas, 15 1/4 x 20 1/2 ins / 39 x 52 cm) NLG 3,220. AMSTERDAM, 21 April 1994, *On a Path near Oosterbeek* (1896, oil on canvas, 31 3/4 x 43 1/2 ins / 80.5 x 110.5 cm) NLG 3,680. AMSTERDAM, 2 Sept 1997, *Wooded Landscape with a Horse and Vehicle near a Cottage* (oil on panel, 6 x 4 1/2 ins / 15.5 x 11.5 cm) NLG 518.

SCHULMEISTER, Willibald
German, 19th century.
Born 1851, in Deutsch-Lodenitz, near Sternberg; died 1909.
Painter, engraver. Landscapes.

The pupil of William Unger, Schulmeister taught drawing at the school of applied arts in Vienna.

SCHULPLE, Simon. See **SCHILPLI**

SCHULSTRÖM, Isak
Swedish, 18th century.
Born c. 1712; died 15 October 1778, in Svanskog.
Active in Karlstad.
Engraver (wood).

SCHULT, Émile
20th century.
Mixed media. Artists' books.

Schult exhibited a book at the 1992 exhibition *De Bonnard à Baselitz - Dix Ans d'enrichissements du cabinet des estampes* (*From Bonnard to Baselitz: A Decade of Acquisitions by the Prints Collection 1978-1988*) at the Bibliothèque Nationale in Paris.

SCHULT, Friedrich
German, 20th century.
Born 18 February 1889, in Schwerin.
Sculptor.

Friedrich Schult studied at the school of applied arts in Hamburg. He worked primarily in wood.

SCHULT, Gerhard
German, 19th century.
Active in Cologne.
Painter. Genre scenes, portraits.

Schult studied under Th. Hildebrandt in 1838.

SCHULT, Geuert
Danish, 17th century.
Born to a family originally from Odense.
Sculptor (wood).

SCHULT, Ha
German, 20th century.
Born 24 June 1939, in Parchim (Mecklenburg).
Active in the USA from 1959.
Painter, performance artist.

Ha Schult studied until 1961 under Karl Otto Gotz at the fine arts academy in Düsseldorf, but it was not until 1968 or thereabouts that he took up painting seriously, having already worked at a variety of odd jobs, including a spell on the railroads and stints as a farmer and as an art director in an advertising firm. He settled in New York in 1959 and became artist-in-residence at the fine arts academy in Kassel in 1971.

Schult's influences include Yves Klein, Nam June Paik and Jackson Pollock. In the course of his 'happenings', he focuses above all on the notion and process of destruction and pollution, explored in what he himself terms 'bio-kinetic environments'. He reconstitutes desolate urban landscapes in the guise of a 'no-man's land' of automobile wrecks and assorted urban detritus.

Schult has taken part in a large number of group exhibitions, including at the following: Munich (1968, 1972, 1974); the Kunsthalle in Cologne (1970, 1974); Documenta V in Kassel (1972); the Kunsthalle in Nuremberg (1976); the Wilhelm-Lehmbruck-Museum in Duisburg (1979); Nice (1982); and the National Galerie in Berlin (1982). He has also exhibited solo on a number of occasions since 1968, including at the following: Munich (1970); Heidelberg (1971); the Folkwang Museum in Essen (1974); Kiel (1974); Stuttgart (1974); Munich (1974); the Palazzo Spaletti in Naples (1977); the Museum am Ostwall in Dortmund (1978); and the Museum Ludwig in Cologne (1980).

MUSEUMS AND GALLERIES:
DORTMUND (Mus. am Ostwall) - DUISBURG (Wilhelm Lehmbruck Mus.) - KIEL (Kunsthalle) - MANNHEIM (Städtische Kunsthalle) - NUREMBERG (Kunsthalle) - RECKLINGHAUSEN (Kunsthalle).

SCHULT, Jacob
German, 16th century.
Active in Trondheim at the time of Christian II 1513-1523.
Medallist.

SCHULT, Johann
German, 20th century.
Born 28 February 1889, in Kirch-Jesar (Mecklenburg Schwerin).
Painter, illustrator. Portraits.

Johann Schult studied from 1908 to 1911 at the fine arts academy in Munich. He was a civilian prisoner in Russia from 1914 to 1918. He was a contributor to the periodical *Ortie* (*Stinging Nettle*) from 1931.

MUSEUMS AND GALLERIES:
MUNICH (Acad.): *Self-portrait* (1910).

AUCTION RECORDS:
MUNICH, 10 May 1989, *Peasant Girl* (oil on canvas, 33 3/4 x 25 1/2 ins / 86 x 65 cm) DEM 11,000.

SCHULT, Jost or Joost. See **SCHUTZE**

SCHULTE, Antoinette
American, 20th century.
Born 1897; died 1981.
Active in France.
Painter, watercolourist. Portraits, landscapes, still-lifes.
Poetic Reality.

Antoinette Schulte lived in Paris, where her circle of friends included Despiau, Dunoyer de Segonzac, Charles Dufresnes, Roland Oudot, and Legueult, among others. This friendship was celebrated around 1970 in an exhibition in which her own works were included in a collection of works by Parisian artists. She exhibited at the Salon d'Automne in Paris.

Schulte's painting style can be described as 'poetic reality', the discreet and sensitive interpretation of the natural world. Although she mainly painted landscapes and still-lifes she also left sketches, heightened with watercolour, of her artist friends at work.

SCHULTE, August von
German, 19th century.
Born 1800, in Hanover; died in Hanover.
Painter.

Schulte's painting *Dragonfly* is signed *ASV, Düsseldorf.*

MUSEUMS AND GALLERIES:
HANOVER (Niedersächsisches Landesmus.): *Dragonfly.*

SCHULTE, Johan de
Dutch, 16th century.
Active in Breda.
Sculptor.

SCHULTE, Malkin
German, 20th century.
Active in the 1970s.
Mixed media.

A book of illustrations by Malkin Schulte was shown at *De Bonnard à Baselitz - Dix Ans d'enrichissements du cabinet des estampes* (*From Bonnard to Baselitz: A Decade of Acquisitions by the Prints Collection 1978-1988*), an exhibition featuring a decade of acquisitions by the Prints Collection, held at the Bibliothèque Nationale in Paris in 1992.

SCHULTE IM HOFE, Rudolf
German, 19th - 20th century.
Born 9 January 1865, in Uckendorf (Westphalia); died 18 February 1928, in Berlin.
Painter, engraver. Portraits, landscapes.

Rudolf Schulte im Hofe was a pupil of Ludwig Schmid-Reutte, Gabriel von Hackl and Ludwig von Loefftz.

MUSEUMS AND GALLERIES:
BERLIN (Nationalgal.): *Houses at Sonnenburg* - HAMBURG: *Gertrude Troplovitz* - MÜNSTER: *Sonnenburg.*

SCHULTEN, Arnold
German, 19th century.
Born 1809, in Düsseldorf; died 30 July 1874, in Düsseldorf.
Painter, watercolourist. Landscapes with figures, landscapes.

Schulten attended the academy in Düsseldorf and was a pupil of Schirmer. His repertoire consisted of German, Swiss, Bavarian and Italian landscapes.

MUSEUMS AND GALLERIES:
BREMEN: *Swiss Landscape* (watercolour) - HANOVER: *Chapel in Forest.*

AUCTION RECORDS:
NEW YORK, 2 April 1976, *Summer Landscape with Flock* (oil on canvas, 10¼ x 14¼ ins / 26 x 36 cm) USD 750. SAN FRANCISCO, 24 June 1981, *Bavarian Landscape* (1845, oil on canvas, 45 x 59¾ ins / 114 x 152 cm) USD 8,000. COLOGNE, 18 March 1983, *Mountainous Landscape with Mill* (oil on canvas, 28 x 38½ ins / 71 x 98 cm) DEM 4,750. BREMEN, 11 Dec 1999, *Herders Resting under Oak Tree by River* (1868, oil on canvas, 30 x 44 ins / 75 x 112 cm) DEM 3,300. DÜSSELDORF, 31 Jan 2000, *Romantic Rhine Landscape* (oil on canvas, 16 x 23 ins / 40 x 58 cm) DEM 15,000. COLOGNE, 3 July 2003, *Swiss Mountain Lake in Summer* (1861, oil on canvas, 8 x 13 ins / 21 x 32 cm) EUR 1,500.

SCHULTEN, F. Cornel
Dutch, 18th century.
Active c. 1756.
Painter, draughtsman.

SCHULTES, Benno Kassian
Austrian, 18th century.
Born to a family originally from Imst (Tyrol); died 17 May 1777, in Munich.
Sculptor.

SCHULTES, Hans I, or Schultess, Schulthes, Schultheiss
German, 16th century.
Active in Augsburg during the last third of the 16th century.
Engraver (wood).

SCHULTES, Hans II, or Schultess, Schulthes, Schultheiss
German, 16th - 17th century.
Active in Augsburg.
Painter. Monograms.

SCHULTES, Lorenz, or Schulthess, Schultheiss
German, 17th century.
Active in Augsburg c. 1600.
Painter.

SCHULTES, Matthäus
German, 17th century.
Active in Ulm 1652-1679.
Painter, engraver (wood). Monograms.

SCHULTES, Wolff. See **SCHULTHESS**

SCHULTHEISS, Albrecht
German, 19th - 20th century.
Born 7 March 1823, in Nuremberg; died 14 September 1909, in Munich.
Engraver, draughtsman. Portraits.

Albrecht Schultheiss was the father of the painter Karl Schultheiss. He studied under Peter Carl Geissler in Nuremberg, Lazarus G. Sichling in Leipzig, and also in Berlin. He settled in Munich in 1850.

SCHULTHEISS, Hans
German, 17th century.
Died 1658.
Active in Wurzach.
Painter.

Schultheiss worked for the church in Aulendorf.

SCHULTHEISS, Hans. See also **SCHULTES**

SCHULTHEISS, Karl
German, 19th - 20th century.
Born 21 July 1852, in Munich; died 1944.
Painter, designer. Portraits, landscapes.

Karl Schultheiss was the son of Albrecht Schultheiss and the husband of Natalie Schultheiss. He studied under Georg Raab and Wilhelm von Diez and went on to provide decorative compositions for various public buildings in Munich.

MUSEUMS AND GALLERIES:
MUNICH: *Head of a Young Girl* - NUREMBERG: *Grandfather and Grandmother* - WUPPERTAL: *Watermill.*

AUCTION RECORDS:
NEW YORK, 13 Feb 1985, *In a Garden* (1905, oil on canvas mounted on card, 30½ x 40½ ins / 77.5 x 103 cm) USD 3,750.

SCHULTHEISS, Karl Max
German, 20th century.
Born 4 August 1885, in Nuremberg; died in Munich.
Painter, illustrator, engraver. Figures, portraits, landscapes.

Karl Max Schultheiss studied in Nuremberg and in Munich under Herterich, Wilhelm von Diez and Angelo Janck. He illustrated numerous publications, among them the collected works of Théophile Gauthier.

AUCTION RECORDS:
COLOGNE, 23 March 1990, *Wine Harvest on the Moselle* (oil on canvas, 11 x 16 1/4 ins / 27 x 41.5 cm) DEM 1,300. NEW YORK, 17 Feb 1994, *Landscape with an Elegant Old Lady* (oil on canvas, 42 x 32 ins / 106.7 x 81.3 cm) USD 4,600.

SCHULTHEISS, Lorenz. See **SCHULTES**

SCHULTHEISS, Natalie
Maiden name: Hampel
Austrian, 19th - 20th century.
Born 1865, in Vienna; died 1932 or 1952.
Painter. Still-lifes.
Natalie Schultheiss was the wife of the painter Karl Schultheiss and the sister of the painter Charlotte Hampel. She studied at the fine arts school in Munich.
AUCTION RECORDS:
SAN FRANCISCO, 8 Oct 1980, *Still-life with Cherries* (1923, oil on canvas, 16 1/2 x 24 1/4 ins / 42 x 61.5 cm) USD 1,500. NEW YORK, 13 Oct 1993, *Still-life with Grapes and Pomegranates* (1911, oil on canvas, 24 x 32 1/4 ins / 61 x 81.9 cm) USD 4,600. MUNICH, 7 Feb 2001, *Still-life with Fruit* (1904, oil on canvas, 25 x 38 ins / 64 x 96 cm) DEM 3,800. MUNICH, 7 Nov 2001, *Still-life with Pumpkin and Peaches* (oil on canvas, 28 x 43 ins / 72 x 109 cm) DEM 4,500. VIENNA, 16 May 2002, *Still-life with Oranges and Yellow Tulips* (oil on canvas, 28 x 37 ins / 70 x 94 cm) EUR 4,000. VIENNA, 28 Nov 2002, *Bunch of Gladioli* (1895, oil on canvas, 35 x 24 ins / 90 x 60 cm) EUR 7,500. VIENNA, 10 April 2003, *Still-life with Peaches, Melon and Grapes on a Silver Plate* (oil on canvas, 23 x 33 ins / 59 x 85 cm) EUR 3,400. VIENNA, 27 May 2004, *Still-life with Cherries* (oil on canvas, 21 x 15 ins / 54 x 39 cm) EUR 2,600.

SCHULTHEISS, Sixt
German, 16th century.
Died at the end of 1526; or at the beginning of 1527 according to some sources.
Active in Schlettstadt (now Sélestat, France).
Sculptor. Portraits.

SCHULTHES, Hans and Lorenz.
See **SCHULTES**

SCHULTHESS, Caspar Hans
Swiss, 19th century.
Born 1798, in Zurich; died 1841.
Painter, watercolourist. Hunting scenes, landscapes.
The society of arts in Zurich conserves five of Schulthess' watercolours representing landscapes and hunting scenes. He was also a heraldist.

SCHULTHESS, Conrad Hans
Swiss, 19th century.
Born 1785, in Zurich; died 1849.
Painter, engraver.

SCHULTHESS, Dorothea
Swiss, 19th century.
Born 1776, in Zurich; died 1853, in Zurich.
Painter, watercolourist. Portraits, flowers. Miniatures.
Dorothea Schulthess was the sister of Leonhard.
MUSEUMS AND GALLERIES:
ZURICH (Society of Art Collection): seven watercolours.

SCHULTHESS, Emil and Ludwig (brothers)
Swiss, 19th century.
Emil born 1805, in Zurich; Emil died 1855, in Zurich, Ludwig died 1844.
Painters. Urban landscapes, architectural views.
Emil and Ludwig Schulthess were amateurs. The society of arts in Zurich conserves about 100 views of old Zurich by Emil.
MUSEUMS AND GALLERIES:
ZURICH (Society of Art Collection).

SCHULTHESS, Heinrich
Swiss, 19th century.
Born 1783, in Zurich; died 1832, in Zurich.
Landscape artist.

SCHULTHESS, Karl Johann Jakob
Swiss, 19th century.
Born 24 February 1775, in Neuchâtel; died 20 April 1854, in Zurich.
Painter. Genre scenes, portraits.
Karl Schulthess initially taught drawing in his native town, then worked in Dresden and Paris. Later, he settled definitively in Neuchâtel where he taught drawing at the municipal school.
MUSEUMS AND GALLERIES:
BERN (Kunstmus.): *Costume of Lady from Zurich*.

SCHULTHESS, Leonhard
Swiss, 19th century.
Born 1775, in Zurich; died 1841, in Zurich.
Painter. Flowers.
Leonhard Schulthess was the brother of Dorothea.
MUSEUMS AND GALLERIES:
ZURICH (Society of Art Collection): a watercolour.

SCHULTHESS, Ludwig. See **SCHULTHESS Emil** and **Ludwig**

SCHULTHESS, Wilhelm
Swiss, 19th century.
Born 1791, in Zurich; died 1873, in Zurich.
Engraver (wood), painter.
Wilhelm Schulthess studied in Berlin with Gubitz.
MUSEUMS AND GALLERIES:
ZURICH (Society of Art Collection): a gouache.

SCHULTHESS, Wolff
Austrian, 16th century.
Sculptor.

SCHULTHEUS, Wolfgang
17th century.
Engraver, designer of ornamental architectural features.

SCHULTS, Daniel Jerzy. See **SCHULTZ**

SCHULTZ
Danish, 19th century.
Born in Denmark.
Sculptor.
Schultz participated in exhibitions in Paris. He won a silver medal at the Exposition Universelle in 1889.

SCHULTZ. See also **SCHULTZE**

SCHULTZ, Albert
French, 19th - 20th century.
Born 15 April 1871, in Strasbourg.
Sculptor.
Schultz was taught by Wilhelm von Ruemann. He created the *French Cockerel* on the Kehl bridge, *Goose Keeper* in the Strasbourg Orangerie and the monuments to the dead in Rosheim, Guebwiller, Woerth and Geisberg near Wissembourg.
MUSEUMS AND GALLERIES:
HAGUENAU: *Frederick Barbarossa*.

SCHULTZ, Alexander
Norwegian, 20th century.
Born 1901, in Christiania (now Oslo), to Russian parents.
Painter. Landscapes, flowers.
Alexander Schultz was the son of a Russian oceanographer. His childhood was divided between Russia and Norway. He was a pupil of the Norwegian painter Oluf Wold-Torne and, during his years spent in Paris from 1922 to 1928, also stud-

ied under another Norwegian artist, Henrik Sörensen, and under Othon Friesz. (in all probability at the Scandinavian Academy in Paris). He spent extended periods of his life in Italy. In 1954 he was appointed to a teaching post at the fine arts academy in Oslo and became principal of that institution in 1958.

His work betrays the influence of the Danish painter Georg Jacobsen, whose theories on geometric composition Schultz espoused. After 1945, Schultz adhered to those principles of rigorously geometrical composition although, in time, his style grew appreciably lighter.

An extensive exhibition of Schultz's work was mounted in 1950 by the Royal Scottish Academy.

MUSEUMS AND GALLERIES:
OSLO (Nasjonalgal.).

SCHULTZ, Anton
Danish, 18th century.
Active between 1707 and 1723 in Copenhagen, and between 1724 and 1735 in Russia.
Medallist.

SCHULTZ, Asta
Maiden name: Ring
Danish, 20th century.
Born 24 September 1895, in Vejle (Jutland).
Painter, engraver.
Asta Schultz studied at the Kunstakademi in Copenhagen. Her work was influenced by that of Jens Ferdinand Willumsen and Ernst J. Zeuthen.

SCHULTZ, C.
German, 19th century.
Draughtsman. Portraits.
Schultz was active in Marburg around 1840, and Kassel in 1841. He requires comparison with Christian Schulz.

SCHULTZ, Christian Benjamin. See **SCHULZ**

SCHULTZ, Daniel, the Elder
Polish, 17th century.
Died 1646, in Danzig (now Gdansk).
Active in Danzig.
Painter. History painting, portraits.

SCHULTZ, Daniel
Polish, 18th century.
Born c. 1680, in Danzig (now Gdansk).
Painter, draughtsman, engraver.
Daniel Schultz produced engravings of animals, particularly birds.

SCHULTZ, Daniel Jerzy, or Schults or Schulz, called the Younger
Polish, 17th century.
Born c. 1615, in Danzig (now Gdansk); died 1683, in Danzig.
Painter. Portraits, genre scenes, still-lifes.
Daniel Schultz studied in Paris and Breslau (now Wroclaw). He worked mainly in Russia and Poland. He painted still-lifes, genre scenes and portraits. His most famous portrait represents *John Casimir*, in Polish costume, and is now in the art collection of Crispholm castle in Sweden. The town hall in Gdansk owns his portraits of *John Casimir*, *Michael Korybut* and *John III*. Daniel Schultz's work shows Dutch influence. He is considered among the best Polish painters of the 17th century.

MUSEUMS AND GALLERIES:
GDANSK: *Duck Hunt; Tartar Nobleman with his Sons; Portrait of Constantin von Schumann; Farmyard; Fox and Grapes* - STOCKHOLM: *Game Seller.*

AUCTION RECORDS:
PARIS, 1888, *Farmyard,* FRF 2,450. STUTTGART, 20 Sept 2001, *Portrait of an Old Woman* (oil on canvas, 31x25 ins / 78x64 cm) DEM 4,550.

SCHULTZ, Elisabeth
German, 19th century.
Born 12 May 1817, in Frankfurt am Main; died 26 September 1898, in Frankfurt am Main.
Painter. Flowers.
Elisabeth Schultz was taught by V. Prestel, Nik. Hoff and Th. Huth.

SCHULTZ, Erdmann, or Schulze
German, 19th century.
Born c. 1810.
Painter. Still-lifes (flowers/fruit).
Erdmann Schultz was the pupil of Völker in Berlin where he worked.

AUCTION RECORDS:
NEW YORK, 30 Oct 1992, *Still-life with Vase of Roses and Foliage surrounded by Fruit on Marble Mantelshelf* (oil on canvas, 14 x 17 3/4 ins / 35.6 x 45.3 cm) USD 8,800.

SCHULTZ, Georg
Polish, 17th century.
Active in Danzig (now Gdansk).
Painter.

SCHULTZ, George F.
American, 19th - 20th century.
Born 17 April 1869, in Chicago; died 1934.
Painter. Landscapes, seascapes.
George Schultz was a member of the Water Color Club. His works include *Seascape*, at the Union League Club in Chicago, and *Shadows at Dusk*, at the Archie Club.

Geo F Schultz

AUCTION RECORDS:
LONDON, 10 March 1910, *Summer Morning,* GBP 9. NEW YORK, 22 June 1984, *By the Brook* (oil on canvas, 30 x 40 ins / 76.2 x 101.6 cm) USD 3,250. NEW YORK, 31 May 1990, *Testing Waters* (oil on canvas, 24 x 20 ins / 60.9 x 50.8 cm) USD 2,420.

SCHULTZ, Gottfried
German, 19th century.
Born 4 February 1842, in Darfeld (Westphalia).
Painter. Portraits, still-lifes.
Gottfried Schultz was the pupil of J. W. Preyer in Düsseldorf where he worked.

G. Schultz

AUCTION RECORDS:
COLOGNE, 28 June 1991, *Still-life of Asters, Chrysanthemums and other Flowers in China Bowl* (oil on canvas, 38 1/2 x 4 3/4 ins / 98 x 12 cm) DEM 2,600. LONDON, 19 March 1993, *Still-life of Grapes, Peaches, Plums and Hazel Nuts with Glass of Champagne on Marble Mantelshelf* (1876, oil on canvas, 13 3/4 x 17 3/4 ins / 35 x 45 cm) GBP 9,200. ZOFINGEN, 31 May 2002, *Still-life of Red Berries, Peaches and Strawberries* (oil on canvas, 7 x 8 ins / 18 x 21 cm) CHF 16,000. ZOFINGEN, 31 May 2002, *Still-life of Grapes and Peaches* (oil on panel, 7 x 8 ins / 18 x 21 cm) CHF 16,000.

SCHULTZ, Harry
German, 19th - 20th century.
Born 14 March 1874, in Elbing (now Elblag, Poland).
Active in Munich.
Painter. Nudes, portraits, landscapes, seascapes.

Harry Schultz studied at the fine arts academies of Königsberg (now Kaliningrad, Russia) and Munich.
MUSEUMS AND GALLERIES:
KALININGRAD: *Nude Child*.
AUCTION RECORDS:
COLOGNE, 18 March 1989, *Seascape* (oil on canvas, 22 x 25 1/2 ins / 55 x 65 cm) DEM 1,500. AMSTERDAM, 19 Sept 1989, *Nude on a Rock by the Sea* (1917, oil on canvas, 20 x 16 1/4 ins / 51 x 41 cm) NLG 2,760.

SCHULTZ, Harry
Russian, 20th century.
Born 1 January 1900, in Sebastopol.
Active in the USA.
Painter.
Harry Schultz was a student of John Sloan and Kenneth Miller, and was a member of the Independent Artists' Society.

SCHULTZ, Heinrich Joachim
German, 18th century.
Active in Haveberg.
Sculptor.

SCHULTZ, Hermann Theodor
German, 19th century.
Born 1816, in Wittstock; died 22 February 1862, in Berlin.
Painter.
The pupil of K. Wach and K. Blechen, Hermann Schultz contributed to the decoration of the chapel in the castle of Berlin, and to the vestibule of the Altes Museum.

SCHULTZ, J. A.
Dutch, 19th century.
Born in Zealand; died c. 1865, in Utrecht.
Painter, engraver (etching).
J. A. Schultz engraved genre scenes.

SCHULTZ, J. Theodor
German, 19th century.
Born 1817, in Hamburg; died 29 April 1893, in Hamburg.
Painter.

SCHULTZ, Johann Bernhard. See **SCHULZ**

SCHULTZ, Johann Friedrich
German, 18th century.
Born c. 1711, in Züllichau; died 16 January 1761, in Ofen.
Painter.
Johann Schultz worked for the church of St Anne in Ofen.

SCHULTZ, Johann Karl
German, 19th century.
Born 5 May 1801, in Danzig (now Gdansk, Poland); died 12 June 1873, in Danzig.
Painter, engraver, lithographer. Architectural views.
Johann Karl Schultz attended the art academy in Danzig and the academy in Berlin with Hummel. He continued his artistic education in Rome from 1824 to 1828, and after working in Berlin between 1828 and 1832, became director of the art academy in Danzig. He mainly painted church interiors; several of his paintings were bought by Friedrich Wilhelm IV, in particular, nine views of Marienburg.
MUSEUMS AND GALLERIES:
BERLIN (Palace): *Interior of Church* - GDANSK: *Long Bridge; View of Danzig* - KALININGRAD: *Choir of Königsberg Cathedral*.

SCHULTZ, Johann Kaspar or Kaspar, or Schultze
German, 17th century.
Engraver (burin).
Johann Kaspar Schultz lived in Bremen between 1664 and 1680.

SCHULTZ, Johannes Christoffel
Dutch, 18th - 19th century.
Born 1749, in Amsterdam; died 1812, in Amsterdam.
Painter, engraver (etching). Landscapes.
Johannes Christoffel Schultz was a pupil of his father, a tapestry designer. H. Stovisch was his pupil. His engravings include a *Self-portrait*.

SCHULTZ, Julius Vilhelm
Danish, 19th century.
Sculptor.
Several of Schultz's works are in the museum in Copenhagen, including *Adam and Eve, The Young Oehlenschlager* and *Jans Baggesen*.

SCHULTZ, Karl Friedrich. See **SCHULZ**

SCHULTZ, Karl Johann Stephan
Baltic School, 19th century.
Born 4 September 1823, in Riga; died 3 June 1859, in Litau (now Jelgava) Latvia.
Painter. Genre scenes.
Karl Schultz was a student at the art academy in St Petersburg in 1843, and in Dresden from 1845 to 1847. He worked in Litau. The museum in Riga owns two of his works, *Portrait of a Woman* and *Study of a Head*.

SCHULTZ, Leff
Russian, 20th century.
Born 6 November 1897, in Rostov-on-Don; died 25 December 1970, in Paris.
Active from 1927 in France.
Painter, sculptor (bronze), designer. Stage sets.
Leff Schultz initially studied at the fine arts school in Petrograd (now St Petersburg), then, fleeing the Revolution, in Ljubljana, Yugoslavia, where he subsequently worked as a designer at the Novi Sad Theatre. He arrived in France in 1927, and apparently mixed in Surrealist circles while studying at the Académie de la Grande Chaumière and the Académie Julian. He spent the inter-war period in Algeria, then moved to Morocco before finally returning to Paris in 1951.

Schultz's works vacillate in style between those influenced by Post-Cubism and Gromaire, with a pointillist approach, to those that are surreal in vein, characterised by the superimposition on the same level of several layers of transparent images. Perhaps the most curious part of his output is the pictures encrusted with mother of pearl and precious stones, which take their inspiration from popular Russian, Persian and Indian art.
AUCTION RECORDS:
ENGHIEN-LES-BAINS, 29 Oct 1978, *Eagle* (black-patinated bronze, h. 12 1/4 ins / 31 cm) FRF 6,300.

SCHULTZ, Martin Friedrich. See **SCHULZE**

SCHULTZ, Nikolaus
Belgian, 17th century.
Of Brabant origin.
Sculptor.

SCHULTZ, Otto
German, 19th - 20th century.
Born 16 December 1848, in Berlin; died 13 August 1911.
Active in London and Berlin.
Sculptor, medallist.
Otto Schultz was a pupil of Edward Wittig and Wilhelm Kullrich. He was assistant medal-maker at the Royal Mint.

SCHULTZ, Petter or Peter
Danish, 17th century.
Born 1647, in Stockholm; died 1689, in Stockholm.
Sculptor.
Schultz sculpted allegorical figures of women, including *Love* and *Reason*.

SCHULTZ, Theodor
German, 19th century.
Born 1814, in Vienenburg; died 20 July 1849, in Highland (Illinois), USA.
Painter. Portraits.
Theodor Schultz attended the academy in Munich from 1837 to 1839. He worked in Goslar, Dresden, Wroclaw (Breslau), Vienna and Italy, and in 1847 went to America.

SCHULTZ, Urban, called Urban Snikare
Swedish, 16th century.
Of Silesian origin.
Sculptor. Portraits.
Urban Schultz emigrated to Sweden where, with Markus Ulfrum, he carved the fine sculptures in King Erick's bedchamber in Kalmar Castle. In 1566 he was appointed director of works at Uppsala Castle.

SCHULTZ, Walter
Dutch, 17th century.
Active in Haarlem in 1676.
Engraver.

SCHULTZ-DAL, Jacques Georges
French, 20th century.
Born 13 November 1894, in Paris.
Painter, engraver, draughtsman. Urban landscapes.
Schultz-Dal worked in Paris, at the Académie Julian, then came first in the competitive exam of the École des Beaux-Arts in 1920. The same year he made his debut at the Salon des Artistes Français, where he continued to exhibit over the next fifteen years. He was awarded a bronze medal in 1922, silver in 1923, gold in 1928 and the Prix Belin-Dollet. In 1925 the Académie des Beaux-Arts, which had already selected him for the Prix Chenavard, Prix Roux and Prix de la Société Française de Gravure, gave him one of its highest honours, the Grand Prix Leguay-Lebrun for drawing. The Académie also sent him to London on two study assignments, and he returned with numerous paintings portraying modern aspects of the city. After 1935 he exhibited only occasionally.

As well as having a large repertoire of engravings to his name, he published a small number of studies in reviews.

SCHULTZ-WALBAUM, Theodor
German.
Born in Gustedt.
Active in Bremen.
Painter, engraver.
Schultz-Walbaum painted a series of 17 panels of the sea and the Fresian coast, and another series illustrating the adventures of Robinson Crusoe. Both series were hung in Peter's House in Bonn.

SCHULTZ-WETTEL, Fernand, or Schult-Wettel
French, 19th - 20th century.
Born 6 August 1872, in Mulhouse.
Painter, illustrator.
Art Nouveau.
Schultz-Wettel studied at the academy of fine arts in Berlin and was taught by Jules Lefebvre and Bouguereau at the Académie Julian in Paris. He lived in Oberehnheim in Alsace. He exhibited at the Salon de la Société Nationale des Beaux-Arts in Paris, and in Berlin and Munich.

He created posters and illustrated the *Thousand and One Nights* and Casanova's *Memoirs*.

BIBLIOGRAPHY:
Osterwalder, Marcus (ed.), *Dictionnaire des illustrateurs 1800-1914*, Ides et Calendes, Neuchâtel, 1989.

SCHULTZBERG, Anselm, or Anshelm Leonard
Swedish, 19th - 20th century.
Born 28 September 1862; died 1945.
Painter. Landscapes.
Anselm Schultzberg studied under Edward Perseus at the fine arts school in Stockholm, then under Hahn and Fernand Cormon. He lived for a period in Italy and in Paris (where he exhibited at the Salon des Artistes Français). He received an honourable mention at the Exposition Universelle of 1889 and a bronze medal in 1891. He was a member of the fine arts academy of Sweden.

MUSEUMS AND GALLERIES:
COPENHAGEN (Statens Mus. for Kunst): *Winter's Day* - STOCKHOLM: *Winter Morning after a Fall of Snow*; *Walpurgis Night in the Dalarna Mountains of Central Sweden*.

AUCTION RECORDS:
NEW YORK, 22-25 May 1946, *Winter Sunset in a Forest*, USD 450. STOCKHOLM, 22 March 1950, *Isba in the Snow*, SEK 3,500. LONDON, 10 March 1971, *Winter Evening on a Riverbank*, GBP 460. STOCKHOLM, 8 Nov 1972, *Winter Landscape*, SEK 10,500. STOCKHOLM, 24 April 1974, *Winter Landscape*, SEK 19,800. LONDON, 19 May 1976, *Snow-covered Landscape at Dusk* (1902, oil on canvas, 39 1/4 x 51 1/2 ins / 100 x 131 cm) GBP 2,500. MALMÖ, 2 May 1977, *Stockholm in the Snow* (1935, oil on canvas, 23 1/4 x 28 3/4 ins / 59 x 73 cm) SEK 15,000. GÖTEBORG, 7 Nov 1979, *Snowy Landscape* (1909, oil on canvas, 36 1/4 x 28 1/4 ins / 92 x 72 cm) SEK 20,000. STOCKHOLM, 22 April 1981, *Forest in the Snow* (1888, oil on canvas, 35 x 47 ins / 88 x 118.5 cm) CHF 71,000. NEW YORK, 24 May 1984, *Peasant Woman in a Cabbage Field* (1891, oil on canvas, 65 x 92 ins / 165.1 x 233.8 cm) USD 28,000. STOCKHOLM, 28 Oct 1985, *Young Girl in a Wooded Landscape* (1890, oil on canvas, 57 1/2 x 41 3/4 ins / 146 x 106 cm) SEK 345,000. STOCKHOLM, 4 Nov 1986, *Summer Landscape* (1916, oil on canvas, 48 3/4 x 98 1/2 ins / 124 x 250 cm) SEK 180,000. STOCKHOLM, 19 Oct 1987, *Winter Landscape* (oil on canvas, 28 x 39 1/4 ins / 71 x 100 cm) SEK 620,000. STOCKHOLM, 15 Nov 1988, *Winter: Snow-covered Pine Forest near Vika* (oil, 33 3/4 x 43 ins / 86 x 109 cm) SEK 200,000. STOCKHOLM, 19 April 1989, *Winter at the Presbytery near Damshöjden* (oil on canvas, 27 1/2 x 43 1/4 ins / 70 x 110 cm) SEK 170,000. GÖTEBORG, 18 May 1989, *Winter at Knifvadalen-Wika, Dalarna* (1917, oil on canvas, 31 1/2 x 45 1/4 ins / 80 x 115 cm) SEK 195,000. STOCKHOLM, 15 Nov 1989, *Bärholmarna and Lake Vessman* (1924, oil on canvas, 20 3/4 x 28 1/4 ins / 53 x 72 cm) SEK 42,000. LONDON, 29 March 1990, *Winter Morning in a Frozen Forest* (1923, oil on canvas, 32 x 46 ins / 81 x 116 cm) GBP 11,000. STOCKHOLM, 16 May 1990, *Summer at Harven on the Outskirts of Hallends Väderö* (oil on panel, 18 x 23 1/2 ins / 46 x 60 cm) SEK 17,000. NEW YORK, 23 Oct 1990, *Stone Steps in an Orchard* (1889, oil on canvas, 18 1/2 x 14 1/2 ins / 47 x 36.8 cm) USD 17,600. STOCKHOLM, 14 Nov 1990, *Winter Sunset over a Mountain Landscape with a Fir Forest*. STOCKHOLM, 29 May 1991, *Tree-lined Avenue in the Spring Sun* (1886, oil on canvas, 44 x 56 3/4 ins / 112 x 144 cm) SEK 175,000. STOCKHOLM, 13 April 1992, *Sunny Mountain Village in Gavinana in Northern Italy* (1911, oil on canvas, 33 3/4 x 39 1/4 ins / 86 x 100 cm) SEK 18,000. STOCKHOLM, 5 Sept 1992, *Snow-covered Forest in the Dalarna Mountains on a Winter Evening* (oil on canvas, 33 1/2 x 42 1/2 ins / 85 x 108 cm) SEK 67,000. STOCKHOLM, 10-12 May 1993, *Sun over Snow-clad Firs in the Region of Filipstad Bergslag* (oil on canvas, 26 3/4 x 41 1/4 ins / 68 x 105 cm) SEK 36,000. STOCKHOLM, 30 Nov 1993, *Snow-covered Fir Forest in the Sun* (oil on canvas, 31 1/2 x 45 1/4 ins / 80 x 115 cm) SEK 67,000. LONDON, 14 June 1995, *Snow-covered Landscape* (1893, oil on canvas, 11 1/4 x 17 3/4 ins / 28.5 x 45 cm) GBP 2,990. NEW YORK, 17 Jan 1996, *Snow-covered Forest* (1822, oil on canvas, 36 x 28 ins / 91.4 x 71.1 cm) USD 2,760. STOCKHOLM, 18 May 1999, *Evening*

Sunshine in Wood: Winter from Hogakt near Falun (oil on canvas, 35 x 43 ins / 89 x 110 cm) SEK 60,000. STOCKHOLM, 26 May 1999, *January Evening in a Wood* (1918, oil on canvas, 32 x 46 ins / 81 x 116 cm) SEK 64,000. STOCKHOLM, 28 Nov 2000, *Sunny Winter's Day, Tunaslatten, Dalarna* (oil on canvas, 27 x 41 ins / 68 x 105 cm) SEK 105,000. STOCKHOLM, 5 Dec 2000, *Evening in May* (1896, oil on canvas, 29 x 40 ins / 74 x 101 cm) SEK 74,000. STOCKHOLM, 29 May 2001, *Frost, Grez-sur-Loing* (1890, oil on canvas, 28 x 39 ins / 71 x 99 cm) SEK 320,000. STOCKHOLM, 4 Dec 2001, *Trees in Autumn Sunshine* (1889, oil on canvas) SEK 78,000. STOCKHOLM, 28 May 2002, *Winter Landscape with Evening Sunshine* (1902, oil on canvas, 56 x 69 ins / 143 x 176 cm) SEK 48,000. STOCKHOLM, 28 May 2002, *June Evening in the Garden* (oil on canvas, 29 x 40 ins / 74 x 101 cm) SEK 86,000. STOCKHOLM, 2 Dec 2003, *Trees in Autumn Sunshine* (1889, oil on canvas, 16 x 11 ins / 41 x 29 cm) SEK 60,000. STOCKHOLM, 3 Dec 2003, *Midwinter: Landscape from Bjursastrakten* (oil on canvas, 31 x 46 ins / 80 x 116 cm) SEK 58,000. LONDON, 18 Nov 2004, *Midsummer Night in Dalarna, Sweden* (oil on canvas, 48 x 65 ins / 121 x 166 cm) GBP 6,000. STOCKHOLM, 30 Nov 2004, *Winter Landscape near an Old Coal Shed* (oil on canvas, 33 x 43 ins / 85 x 110 cm) SEK 47,000.

SCHULTZE, Andreas

German, 17th century.
Active in Torgau.
Sculptor.

Schultze sculpted a number of pulpits.

SCHULTZE, Bernhard, or Bernard

German, 20th century.
Born 31 May 1915, in Schneidemühl (now Pila), Poland.
Painter, watercolourist, draughtsman, collage artist, sculptor, assemblage artist, environmental artist.
Quadriga Group.

Bernhard Schultze studied from 1933 to 1939 at the fine arts academy in Berlin under Willy Jaeckel and at the fine arts academy in Düsseldorf. From 1939 to 1945 he served in World War II, notably in Russia and North Africa. He spent time in Paris from 1945 to 1947 and again in 1952 and 1953, where he was involved with the Phases group. He moved to Frankfurt am Main where, in 1952, he was one of the co-founders - alongside Karl-Otto Götz, Otto Greis and Heinz Kreutz - of the so-called Quadriga group which advocated abstraction in the broadest sense of that term. He visited New York for the first time in 1964 and subsequently travelled as far afield as Ceylon (now Sri Lanka), Thailand and Burma. 1975 saw him in Mexico and Guatemala. He settled in Cologne in 1968 and became a member of the fine arts academy of Berlin in 1972. He married the artist Ursula Schultze-Bluhm.

Schultze's early work was Expressionist tinged with Surrealist influences. (His earliest work, however, was destroyed in the bombing of Berlin.) In the 1950s, he was influenced - like so many of his fellow artists worldwide - by the Art Informel approach adopted by artists such as Wols, Lanskoy, Riopelle and others. Around this time, his painting began to incorporate heterogeneous elements such as tree branches and straw. From 1956 he started to produce low reliefs, albeit still with a canvas base. In 1959, however, with his *Tabuskris* series, he started to produce progressively stand-alone reliefs in the guise of single or multiple sculptures often organised into 'environments' for which he coined the term 'Migofs'. These strange forms vacillated between the vegetal and the inorganic, often featuring cheap jewellery representing decaying items of fruit and sweetmeats which, in turn, symbolise death in much the same way as the *vanitas* or *memento mori* of yesteryear.

Schultze's work featured in numerous group exhibitions, including at the following: the International Biennale of Colour Lithography at the Cincinnati Art Museum (1954); Documenta in Kassel (1959, 1964, 1977); New York's Guggenheim Museum (1960); the Kunsthalle in Baden-Baden (1963); the fine arts academy of Berlin (1966); New York's Museum of Modern Art (1968); the Kunsthalle in Düsseldorf (1975, 1978); and the Kunsthaus in Zurich (1979). Solo exhibitions include those at the following: Hamburg (1947); the Egon Günther Gallery in Mannheim (regularly from 1948 to 1951); the Zimmergalerie Franck in Frankfurt am Main (1949-1958); the Galerie Daniel Cordier in Paris (1958, 1962); the Städtische Kunstmuseum in Duisburg (1958, 1962); the Kunsthalle in Baden-Baden (1961); the fine arts museum in La Chaux-de-Fonds (1962); das Städtische Museum in Wiesbaden (1962); the Kunstverein in Wuppertal (1962); the Kestner-Gesellschaft in Hanover (1966); the Museum of Modern Art in New York (1966); the Kunstverein in Cologne, Brunswick and Darmstadt (1968); the Palais des Beaux-Arts in Brussels (1969); the Baukunst Galerie in Cologne (1969, 1973, 1977, 1982, 1985, 1988, 1989); the museum of Bochum (1970); the Centre National d'Art Contemporain in Paris (1971); the Boymans van Beuningen Museum in Rotterdam (1974); the Kunsthalle in Baden-Baden (1974); the Städtische Museum in Leverkusen (1979); the Künstlerhaus in Vienna (1979); the Kunsthalle in Düsseldorf (1980); the fine arts academy of Berlin (1981); the Kunstverein in Frankfurt am Main (1981); the Saarland Museum in Saarbrücken (1981); the Graphische Sammlung Albertina in Vienna (1982); and the Henze & Ketterer Gallery in Bern (2000). Schultze was awarded the Darmstadt City Prize in 1967, the Cologne City Prize in 1969, the Cultural Prize of Hessen in 1984 and the Lovis-Corinth Prize in 1986.

BIBLIOGRAPHY:

Bernhard Schultze, exhibition catalogue, Centre national d'Art contemporain, Paris, 1971. '*Bernhard Schultze ou l'Univers labyrinthique*' in *Chroniques de l'Art Vivant*, periodical, Maeght, Paris, February 1971. *Bernhard Schultze - Retrospektive 1953-1989*, exhibition catalogue, Baukunst Gal., Cologne, 1989. Heuer, Egon, *Bernard Schultze. Die Druckgrafik*, Märkisches Museum der Stadt, Witten, 1990. Romain, Lothar/Wedewer, Rolf, *Bernhard Schultze*, Hirmer, Munich, 1991.

MUSEUMS AND GALLERIES:

BOCHUM: *Migof Vanitas* (1964, collage) - COLOGNE (Mus. Ludwig): *Migof: Parthenon II* (1972) - COLOGNE (Wallraf-Richartz Mus.) - DARMSTADT (Hessisches Landesmus.) - DUISBURG (Wilhelm Lehmbruck Mus.): *Relief Painting* (1964) - FRANKFURT AM MAIN (Mus. für Moderne Kunst): *Colossus of...* (1977) - HAMBURG (Kunsthalle): *Heroic Landscape* (1979) - MANNHEIM (Städtische Kunsthalle) - MUNICH (Neue Pinakothek): *Grotesque Promenade* (1964) - PARIS (MNAM-CCI): *Malone Memo* (1961) - ROTTERDAM (Mus. Boijmans Van Beuningen) - WUPPERTAL: *Obit* (1958, collage).

AUCTION RECORDS:

COLOGNE, 5 Dec 1969, *Torsyt*, DEM 6,000. HAMBURG, 10 June 1972, *Floral*, DEM 5,800. ANTWERP, 6 April 1976, *Hanged Migof* (1966, iron wire, 39 1/4 x 39 1/4 ins / 100 x 100 cm) BEF 50,000. MUNICH, 25 May 1976, *Enchanted Landscape* (1958, watercolour and pen, 17 1/4 x 24 1/4 ins / 44 x 61.5 cm) DEM 2,700. LONDON, 1 July 1980, *Untitled* (1961, mixed media/mounted paper/canvas, 65 x 39 1/4 ins / 165 x 100 cm) GBP 2,000. MUNICH, 8 June 1982, *Barrier* (1965, mixed media and collage, 19 x 24 3/4 ins / 48 x 63 cm) DEM 2,850. HAMBURG, 12 June 1982, *Migof* (c. 1961, iron wire, polyester, textile and oil, h. 23 1/2 ins / 60 cm, w. 15 3/4 ins/40 cm) DEM 3,200. HAMBURG, 9 June 1984, *Migof Group* (1960, wood, iron wire, textile, polyester and oil, 17 x 28 1/2 x 18 1/4 ins / 43 x 72.5 x 46.5 cm) DEM 3,200. MUNICH, 27 Nov 1984, *Under a Green Symbol* (1968, mixed media and coloured pencil, 47 1/2 x 35 1/2 ins / 120.5 x 90 cm) DEM 5,000. MUNICH,

11 June 1985, *Abstract Composition* (1961, pen, coloured chalk and mixed media, 22 1/2 x 30 1/4 ins / 57.2 x 76.8 cm) DEM 2,700. DÜSSELDORF, 9 Nov 1985, *Ormit* (1959, object). COLOGNE, 31 May 1986, *Abstract Composition* (pencil, 24 x 17 ins / 61 x 43 cm) DEM 2,800. MILAN, 27 Oct 1986, *Migof Composition* (colour relief/canvas, 22 x 48 ins / 55 x 122 cm) ITL 13,000,000. BERLIN, 23 May 1987, *Abstract Composition* (1957, mixed media/mounted paper/canvas, 19 3/4 x 25 1/2 ins / 50 x 65 cm) DEM 5,000. PARIS, 20 March 1988, *Hand and Foot in Violet* (1964, collage and oil on canvas, 29 1/2 x 48 ins / 75 x 121 cm) FRF 39,000. LONDON, 30 June 1988, *Homage to Ossian* (1955, oil/synthetic resin, 46 1/4 x 40 3/4 ins / 117.5 x 103.5 cm) GBP 27,500. LONDON, 6 April 1989, *Untitled* (1956, oil on canvas, 39 1/4 x 31 1/2 ins / 100 x 80.3 cm) GBP 17,600. PARIS, 1 Oct 1990, *Composition* (1964, pen and Indian ink drawing, 14 1/2 x 23 ins / 37 x 58.5 cm) FRF 6,000. ZURICH, 7-8 Dec 1990, *Abstraction* (mixed media/muslin, 13 1/2 x 7 3/4 ins / 34.5 x 20 cm) CHF 4,600. LONDON, 27 June 1991, *Vitality* (1955, oil on canvas, 45 1/4 x 31 3/4 ins / 115 x 80.5 cm) GBP 33,000. ZURICH, 16 Oct 1991, *Homage to Stifter* (1980, watercolour/card, 28 3/4 x 40 1/4 ins / 73 x 102 cm) CHF 13,000. AMSTERDAM, 21 May 1992, *Untitled* (1957, watercolour and coloured pencil/paper, 19 1/4 x 24 1/2 ins / 49 x 62.5 cm) NLG 7,475. AMSTERDAM, 9 Dec 1992, *Untitled* (1958, watercolour, coloured pencil and pencil/paper, 17 3/4 x 24 1/2 ins / 45 x 62 cm) NLG 7,820. AMSTERDAM, 9 Dec 1993, *Untitled* (1958, mixed media/card, 20 x 28 1/2 ins / 51 x 72.7 cm) NLG 34,500. LONDON, 21 March 1996, *Green and Red Matter* (1956, collage of canvas and oil on canvas, 47 1/4 x 47 1/4 ins / 120 x 120 cm) GBP 11,500. PARIS, 5 Dec 1997, *Tabuskri 6* (oil on canvas, 31 1/2 x 43 1/4 ins / 80 x 110 cm) FRF 60,000. PARIS, 19 Dec 1997, *Untitled* (ink, 18 1/2 x 24 3/4 ins / 47 x 63 cm) FRF 6,500. PARIS, 11 March 1998, *Untitled* (1959, watercolour/paper, 17 x 24 1/2 ins / 43 x 62 cm) FRF 4,500. HAMBURG, 11 June 1999, *Geographical Situation I* (1955, mixed media on board, 50 x 40 ins / 127 x 101 cm) DEM 58,000. COLOGNE, 12 Nov 1999, *Tannhauser* (1989, oil on canvas, 79 x 55 ins / 200 x 140 cm) DEM 56,000. COLOGNE, 10 Nov 2000, *Cruont* (1958, oil on material, 39 x 39 ins / 100 x 100 cm) DEM 36,000. BERLIN, 25 Nov 2000, *Migof, Centaur* (1975, oil on canvas, 65 x 98 ins / 164 x 250 cm) DEM 35,000. COLOGNE, 2 June 2001, *From the Top Down* (1986, oil on canvas, 79 x 55 ins / 200 x 140 cm) DEM 40,000. BERLIN, 1 Dec 2001, *Freethinker* (1988, oil on canvas, 39 x 31 ins / 100 x 80 cm) DEM 18,000. MUNICH, 6 Dec 2002, *On the Shore* (1956, oil on canvas, 47 x 39 ins / 120 x 100 cm) EUR 12,000. COLOGNE, 27 Nov 2003, *Dance of the Grimaces around Atom Fear* (1987, oil on canvas, 79 x 102 ins / 200 x 260 cm) EUR 20,000. MUNICH, 5 Dec 2003, *With Blue* (oil, sand and varnish on canvas, 47 x 39 ins / 120 x 100 cm) EUR 16,000. COLOGNE, 4 June 2004, *Tabuskri* (1960, oil on canvas, 47 x 20 ins / 120 x 50 cm) EUR 7,500. BERLIN, 11 June 2004, *Wailing Wall* (1953, oil on masonite, 53 x 40 ins / 135 x 101 cm) EUR 34,000.

SCHULTZE, Franz

German, 19th - 20th century.
Born 12 June 1842, in Berlin; died 15 April 1907, in Weimar.
Painter. Portraits, genre scenes.

Franz Schultze studied under Eduard Daege in Berlin, Micaise de Keyser in Antwerp and August W. Sohn in Düsseldorf, where he worked from 1869 to 1890, prior to settling in Weimar.

SCHULTZE, Franziska

German, 19th century.
Born 11 April 1805, in Weimar; died 15 April 1864, in Weimar.
Painter. Flowers.

Franziska Schultze was inspired by Huysum, Seghers, Mignon and Heem.

SCHULTZE, Karl

German, 19th - 20th century.
Born 17 August 1856, in Düsseldorf.
Painter. Landscapes.

AUCTION RECORDS:

LONDON, 29 May 1985, *Boat Trip* (1882, oil on canvas, 44 x 60 1/2 ins / 111.5 x 153.5 cm) GBP 4,000.

SCHULTZE, Kaspar. See **SCHULTZ Johann Kaspar**

SCHULTZE, Klaus

German, 20th century.
Born 1927, in Frankfurt am Main.
Sculptor, sculptor of assemblages, potter. Figures.

Following an initial period of experimentation with various types and techniques of inlays, Klaus Schultze started to produce spherical or ovoid 'heads' mounted on cylinders which represent necks, together with busts mounted on a stele to reinforce their monumental character. There are two principal points of reference in Schultze's work: first, that his sculptures interlock like pieces of a three-dimensional jigsaw puzzle and, second, that he uses brilliant enamels to achieve a sumptuously polychromatic finish. His work featured in numerous group exhibitions and solo shows in Germany, Switzerland and, on several occasions, Paris.

SCHULTZE, Marie

German, 18th century.
Born 1721, in Berlin; died 1794, in Berlin.
Painter, art restorer. Portraits.

Marie Schultze was taught by Heinrich Hasselhorst.

SCHULTZE, Robert

German, 19th century.
Born 30 March 1828, in Magdeburg.
Painter. Landscapes with figures, landscapes, waterscapes.

Robert Schultze worked in Munich after attending the academies in Dresden in 1845, and Düsseldorf in 1847.

MUSEUMS AND GALLERIES:

ALTENBURG: *Starnberg Lake*.

AUCTION RECORDS:

BERN, 23-24 Oct 1964, *Alpine Lake*, CHF 7,000. LONDON, 30 Jan 1980, *Farm in Mountainous Landscape* (oil on canvas, 37 x 54 1/4 ins / 94 x 137.5 cm) GBP 1,400. MUNICH, 31 May 1990, *Fishermen on Alpine Lake* (oil on canvas, 37 1/2 x 57 1/2 ins / 95.5 x 146 cm) DEM 22,000. NEW YORK, 19 July 1990, *Tyrolese Landscape with Huts* (oil on card, 14 x 17 1/2 ins / 35.6 x 44.6 cm) USD 1,320. NEW YORK, 20 Jan 1993, *Lake Maggiore* (oil on canvas, 26 x 39 1/2 ins / 66 x 100.3 cm) USD 3,450. BILLINGSHURST, 18 May 1999, *Menton, Southern France* (oil on canvas, 26 x 39 ins / 65 x 98 cm) GBP 5,000. BILLINGSHURST, 18 May 1999, *Lone Rower in a Fjord* (oil on canvas, 26 x 39 ins / 65 x 98 cm) GBP 5,500. COLOGNE, 30 Nov 2000, *Shore Scene, Lake Lugano* (oil on canvas, 28 x 22 ins / 71 x 55 cm) DEM 4,000. VEJLE, 16 Jan 2001, *Coastal Landscape with Cliffs* (oil on canvas, 26 x 35 ins / 65 x 90 cm) DKK 15,000. ZURICH, 30 March 2001, *Hay Harvest* (1863, oil on canvas, 25 x 37 ins / 63 x 94 cm) CHF 6,500. VIENNA, 22 May 2003, *View of Wallensee, Kanton St Gallen* (oil on canvas, 21 x 28 ins / 54 x 70 cm) EUR 2,800. AMSTERDAM, 10 Dec 2003, *Alpine Glory, Alps in Summer at Lauterbrunnen, Switzerland* (oil on panel, 15 x 19 ins / 37 x 49 cm) EUR 1,500. VIENNA, 24 Feb 2004, *Norwegian Coast* (oil on canvas, 28 x 44 ins / 70 x 111 cm) EUR 2,400.

SCHULTZE, Siegfried

German, 17th century.

Active in Hildesheim.
Painter.

SCHULTZE-BANK, Fritz
German, 19th - 20th century.
Born 10 June 1874, in Berlin.
Active in Potsdam.
Painter, illustrator. Portraits.

Fritz Schultze-Bank was a pupil of Paul F. Meyerheim and Max Koner.

SCHULTZE-BERTALLO, Maximilian
German, 19th - 20th century.
Born 1 September 1866, in Berlin.
Active in Strasbourg and Leipzig.
Painter. Portraits.

Maximilian Schultze-Bertallo studied at the fine arts academies in Berlin and Munich and at the Académie Julian in Paris.

SCHULTZE-JASMER, Theodor
German, 20th century.
Born 7 July 1888, in Oschatz.
Painter, engraver.

Theodor Schultze-Jasmer worked at the fine arts academy in Leipzig.

SCHULTZE-THEWIS, Walter, or Schulze-Thewis
German, 19th - 20th century.
Born 3 January 1872, in Berlin.
Sculptor.

Walter Schultze-Thewis won the Prix de Rome in 1903.

SCHULTZENDORFF, Wilhelm Albert Sigismund von
German, 19th century.
Born 1830, in Berlin.
Painter. Genre scenes.

Initially a cavalry officer, Wilhelm von Schultzendorff subsequently became the pupil of Pauwels and Verlat in Weimar. His career was spent in Dresden.

SCHULZ
German, 18th century.
Sculptor.

Schulz was the pupil of Fr. W.E. Döll.

SCHULZ, Adrien
French, 19th - 20th century.
Born 10 February 1851, in Paris; died 15 January 1931.
Painter, potter. Landscapes, waterscapes, animals.

Schulz was taught by Emile Dardoize and Hector Hanoteau. He lived in Montigny-sur-Loing, where Sisley was his neighbour. The influence of Impressionism can be seen through his use of a spectrum of light colours in his numerous paintings of Fontainebleau forest and the banks of the Marne. He also painted landscapes on earthenware. Schulz exhibited at the Salon in Paris from 1876, then at the Salon des Artistes Français, Salon d'Automne, of which he was one of the founding members, and the Salon d'Hiver. In 1931 a posthumous retrospective of his work was organised at the Salon d'Automne in Paris.

AUCTION RECORDS:

NEW YORK, 12-14 March 1906, *View of Montigny*, USD 120. PARIS, 14 Dec 1908, *View of the Banks of the Rhine*, FRF 260. PARIS, 12 March 1919, *Pond in Fontainebleau Forest in Autumn*, FRF 180. PARIS, 18 Jan 1924, *After the Storm, Fontainebleau Forest*, FRF 360. PARIS, 28 Jan 1943, *Undergrowth in Autumn in Fontainebleau*, FRF 3,000. PARIS, 6 Dec 1946, *Herd at the Pond (Barbizon)*, FRF 4,000. CLERMONT-FERRAND, 13 Oct 1948, *Fisherman in a Boat*, FRF 2,800. NEW YORK, 30 May 1980, *Man Collecting Firewood on a Country Road* (1901, oil on canvas, 21 x 25 1/4 ins / 53.3 x 64.2 cm) USD 1,700. NEW YORK, 23 Oct 1990, *River Bank* (oil on canvas, 39 1/4 x 83 1/2 ins / 99.7 x 212.1 cm) USD 14,300. CALAIS, 24 March 1996, *Washerwoman at the River Bank* (oil on canvas, 15 x 22 ins / 38 x 55 cm) FRF 9,200. PARIS, 25 April 1996, *Geese* (oil on panel, 24 x 9 ins / 61 x 23 cm) FRF 4,600.

SCHULZ, Anton Franz Josef
Austrian, 18th century.
Painter.

Anton Schulz decorated porcelain at the factory in Vienna between 1726 and 1742.

SCHULZ, Arthur
German, 19th - 20th century.
Born 15 August 1873, in Berlin.
Sculptor. Portraits. Monuments.

Arthur Schulz was a pupil of Gerhard A. Janensch. He is noted for his fountain for the town hall in Quedlinburg and for monuments to Emperor Frederick near Szczecin and for Duchess Frederika in Copenhagen Castle.

SCHULZ, August Traugott
German, 18th century.
Painter.

August Schulz decorated porcelain at the factory in Meissen around 1750.

SCHULZ, Bruno
Polish, 20th century.
Born 1893, in Galicia; died at the end of 1942, in Drohobycz, Ukraine.
Painter, draughtsman, illustrator, engraver. Figures, nudes, scenes with figures.

After studying in Vienna, Bruno Schulz taught drawing in Drohobycz, Ukraine. He then turned to writing, in which he brought to life a whole universe where the fantastical sprang directly from his observation of life in a small town and patriarchal Jewish mores, an approach that can be likened to that of Kafka. In a letter to his friend Witkiewicz, Schulz wrote: 'The beginnings of my drawings are lost in a mythological mist.' Many of his drawings are in some way intended to constitute a natural foil to the novellas contained in the two collections *The Cinnamon Shops* and *The Pall-bearers' Sanatorium*. Schulz's drawings, which are as striking as his writing, vacillate between the comic and the anguished: nearly all the figures in them, who appear to be caricatures, though are in fact not, constitute a gallery of self-portraits by Schulz. Through them, Schulz, who was physically ugly, depicts his deformed body, set against the power of the beautiful face and magical glance. He illustrated and translated Kafka's *The Trial*.

Work by him was shown in 1983 in the context of an exhibition entitled *Présences polonaises* (*Polish Presences*) at the Centre Georges Pompidou, Paris. There have been solo exhibitions of his work, at the Musée Cantini in Marseille (1988), and at the Musée des Beaux-Arts in Nantes (1989).

BIBLIOGRAPHY:

70 Dessins de Bruno Schulz, exhibition catalogue, Centre de civilisation polonaise de la Sorbonne, Paris, 1975. *Bruno Schulz*, exhibition catalogue, Actes Sud, Arles, Musées de Marseille, Marseilles, 1988.

SCHULZ, Christian
German, 19th century.
Born 1817, in Kassel.
Lithographer.

Christian Schulz studied in Munich in 1839 and was active in Kassel. He is to be compared to C. Schultz.

SCHULZ, Christian Benjamin, or Schultz
German, 19th (?) century.
Active in Heilsberg in East Prussia.
Sculptor.

SCHULZ, Daniel Jerzy. See **SCHULTZ**

SCHULZ, Dominique
French, 20th - 21st century.
Born 1950.
Painter.

Dominique Schulz studied in the 1970s at the Académie Charpentier and the American Center in Paris before going on to enrol at the Art Students' League in New York. He now works in southern France and Paris.

His vividly-coloured decorative work is typically produced over a white monochrome base and features powerful single-colour curves which convey a strong sense of movement.

SCHULZ, Édouard, or Schulze
German, 19th century.
Painter, lithographer. Portraits, genre scenes.

Édouard Schulz attended the academy in Berlin between 1822 and 1826.

AUCTION RECORDS:
HEIDELBERG, 13 Oct 1979, *2 Still-lifes* (1897, oil on canvas mounted/card and oil on panel, each 8¼ x 11 ins / 21 x 28 cm) DEM 1,700.

SCHULZ, Emil
German, 19th - 20th century.
Born 1822, in Wolfenbüttel; died 8 January 1912, in Brunswick.
Painter. Portraits.

Emil Schulz was a pupil of Hans H. J. Brandes and Ferdinand T. Hildebrandt. He worked in Dresden from 1840 to 1844, in Munich from 1844 to 1848, in Düsseldorf in 1849 and thereafter in Brunswick.

SCHULZ, Emma von, or Schoultz
German, 19th century.
Born in Dunamunde, near Riga; died May 1882, in Berlin.
Painter. Genre scenes, portraits.

Emma von Schulz was the pupil of Fr. Kraus.

SCHULZ, Ferdinand R.
Austrian, 19th century.
Born 1804, in Vienna.
Painter. Religious subjects.

Ferdinand Schulz exhibited in Vienna in 1828 and 1841.

SCHULZ, Franz
Austrian, 18th - 19th century.
Painter.

Franz Schulz decorated porcelain at the factory in Vienna from 1785 to 1847.

SCHULZ, Friedrich or Fritz
German, 19th century.
Born c. 1823; died 22 August 1875.
Painter, draughtsman. Military subjects, battles.

Friedrich Schulz was the pupil of H. Vernet in Paris. He worked in Berlin and drew the campaigns of 1864, 1866 and 1870.

AUCTION RECORDS:
COLOGNE, 26 March 1976, *Petition* (1864, oil on canvas, 39¼ x 31½ ins / 100 x 80 cm) DEM 2,800. AHLDEN, 8 May 2004, *Prince Friedrich Carl of Prussia at the Battle of Sedan* (oil on canvas, 29 x 23 ins / 73 x 59 cm) EUR 3,900.

SCHULZ, Friedrich Sigmund
German, 18th century.
Born 1733, in Torgau; died 1776, in Görlitz.
Painter. Portraits.

SCHULZ, Georg. See **SCHOLZ**

SCHULZ, Ida
German, 19th - 20th century.
Born 28 November 1870, in Buckau, near Magdeburg.
Painter, engraver.
Worpswede Artists' Colony.

Ida Schulz worked in Worpswede (1903-1904), then in Paris (1908-1909 and 1912-1913) and, finally, in Basel (from 1913).

SCHULZ, Ilona or Helen
Hungarian, 20th century.
Born 14 June 1887, in Reichenberg (now Liberec, Czech Republic).
Painter.

Ilona Schulz studied in Budapest, but mainly lived in London.

SCHULZ, Joachim Christian
German, 18th century.
Born 1721; died 1786.
Active in Berlin.
Painter. Portraits, flowers.

Joachim Schulz was the pupil of Augustin Dubuisson.

SCHULZ, Johann
German, 18th century.
Active in Göttingen, Lower Saxony.
Painter. Portraits.

Johann Schulz painted the portrait of Professor A.G. Richter in the lecture room of Göttingen University.

SCHULZ, Johann Bernhard, or Schultz
German, 17th century.
Died 1695.
Engraver.

From 1685, Johann Bernhard Schulz engraved medals for the mint in Berlin in honour of the Prince-Elector Friedrich III, Sophie Charlotte, and for Halle University.

SCHULZ, Johann Caspar
German, 18th century.
Active in Leipzig between 1735 and 1750.
Painter, engraver. Portraits.

SCHULZ, Johann Christian
German, 18th century.
Born c. 1700, in Dresden.
Painter. Portraits.

Johann Christian Schulz settled in Leipzig in 1750.

SCHULZ, Johann Gottfried
German, 18th century.
Active in Dresden.
Sculptor.

Johann Gottfried Schulz was the pupil of Kretzschmar.

SCHULZ, Johann Gottlieb
German, 18th century.
Active in Dresden 1750-1760.
Painter. Portraits.

SCHULZ, Johann Heinrich Karl
German, 19th century.
Born 1813, in Stade; died 1836, in Munich.
Painter, engraver. Portraits.

Johann Heinrich Schulz was the pupil of J.J.C. Dahl.

SCHULZ, Johann Ludwig
German, 19th century.
Painter. Portraits, landscapes.

Johann Ludwig Schulz lived in Riga from 1812 to 1830, and thereafter in St Petersburg.

MUSEUMS AND GALLERIES:
RIGA (Mus.): *Suburbs of Riga before the Fire of 1812; Portrait of J.K.D. Muller.*

SCHULZ, Johann Ludwig Ernst
German, 18th - 19th century.
Born 1758, in Brunswick; died 9 May 1826, in Mainz.
Painter.

Johann Ludwig Ernst Schulz worked in Mainz and Brunswick.
MUSEUMS AND GALLERIES:
MAINZ: *Old House on the Brand.*

SCHULZ, Julius
German, 19th century.
Born 1808, in Karlsruhe; died 1896, in Zurich.
Painter. Portraits.
Julius Schulz studied in Munich and worked in Zurich from 1858.

SCHULZ, Julius Carl
German, 19th century.
Active in Berlin.
Painter, engraver.
Julius Carl Schulz sent hunting scenes and military pictures to the academy in Berlin between 1824 and 1846.

SCHULZ, Karl
German, 19th century.
Born 1811, in Wildungen; died 1871, in Arolsen.
Sculptor.
Karl Schulz executed a colossal bust of Christian Rauch in front of the house where he was born in Arolsen.

SCHULZ, Karl Anton
German, 19th century.
Born 1831, in Frankfurt am Main.
Active in Dorpat (now Tartu, Estonia) and Riga.
Painter, engraver, lithographer. Portraits, urban landscapes.

SCHULZ, Karl Friedrich, or Schultz
German, 19th century.
Born 2 November 1796, in Selchow; died 3 March 1866, in Berlin.
Painter. History painting, genre scenes, hunting scenes, still-lifes.
The son of a baker, Karl Friedrich Schulz participated in the campaigns of 1814 and 1815. He was the pupil of Boulanger in Paris and attended the academy in Berlin, becoming a member there in 1831 and a teacher in 1840.
MUSEUMS AND GALLERIES:
KALININGRAD: *Game Merchant; Dead Woodcock and Two other Birds* - MUNICH: *Genre Painting* - WEIMAR: *Mousetrap Merchant Chatting with Peasant Woman.*
AUCTION RECORDS:
VIENNA, 5 Dec 1984, *After the Battle* (1827, oil on panel, 16 1/2 x 20 1/4 ins / 42 x 51.5 cm) ATS 55,000. MUNICH, 25 June 1992, *Fight between the Prussian Uhlans and the French Cuirassiers* (oil on wood, 11 1/4 x 15 1/2 ins / 28.5 x 39.5 cm) DEM 4,520. NEW YORK, 22-23 July 1993, *Mill* (1835, oil on canvas, 12 3/4 x 15 ins / 32.4 x 38.1 cm) USD 920. MUNICH, 7 Dec 1993, *Encounter between the Ulhans and the Dragons; Uhlan near Spirited Horse* (1850, a pair, h/t 30 x 37 1/2 ins / 76 x 95 cm) DEM 32,200. LONDON, 14 July 1999, *Russian Grenadier Regiments on Manoeuvres* (1849, oil on canvas, 30 x 37 ins / 76 x 95 cm) GBP 10,000. LONDON, 14 July 1999, *Life-guards, Atamanskii Cossack Regiment on Manoeuvres* (1847, oil on canvas, 30 x 37 ins / 76 x 95 cm) GBP 13,000. AMSTERDAM, 12 March 2002, *Military Regiment* (1848, oil on canvas, 30 x 37 ins / 76 x 95 cm) EUR 25,000. COLOGNE, 21 Nov 2002, *Meeting on Country Track in Winter* (1845, oil on panel, 24 x 32 ins / 61 x 81 cm) EUR 4,800. NEW YORK, 23 April 2003, *Officers Standing before their Regiments. Ulans Setting-out on Horseback* (1850, oil on canvas, a pair, 30 x 38 ins / 77 x 97 cm) USD 140,000.

SCHULZ, Karl Friedrich Moritz
German, 19th century.
Born 29 March 1832, in Dresden.
Painter.
Karl Friedrich Schulz was the pupil of L. Richter.

SCHULZ, Karl Hermann
German, 19th - 20th century.
Born 9 March 1874, in Löbau.
Active in Dresden.
Painter.
Karl Hermann Schulz studied at the fine arts academy in Dresden.

SCHULZ, Léon
French, 19th - 20th century.
Born 13 February 1872, in Lyons.
Painter, watercolourist, engraver.
Schulz exhibited at the Salon des Artistes Français in Paris from 1924 and was made Chevalier of the Légion d'Honneur.

SCHULZ, Leopold
Austrian, 19th century.
Born 1804, in Vienna; died 6 October 1873, in Heiligenstadt.
Painter. History painting.
Leopold Schulz attended the academy in Vienna and was taught by Cornelius and J. Schnor von Karolsfeld. He worked in Munich, Rome and Vienna and was curator at the academy in Vienna. Noteworthy among his works are the *Portrait of Gregory XVI*, scenes from Homer and Theocritus for the new palace in Munich, and in Vienna, *Ludwig von Bayern Visiting Friedrich der Schöne von Österreich in the Prison of Schloss Trausnitz, Proposing to Share the Crown with him.*
MUSEUMS AND GALLERIES:
VIENNA: *Ludwig von Bayern Visiting Friedrich der Schöne in Prison.*

SCHULZ, Louis
German, 19th century.
Born c. 1843, in Leipzig.
Engraver (burin).
Louis Schulz worked in Rome from 1866 to 1871, then in Leipzig.

SCHULZ, Ludwig
German, 19th century.
Born 1810, in Kassel.
Active in Kassel.
Painter. Portraits, genre scenes.
Ludwig Schulz studied in Munich.

SCHULZ, Martin
German, 17th century.
Painter.
Court painter at Brandenburg, Martin Schulz painted portraits of numerous princely figures.

SCHULZ, Michael
German, 18th - 19th century.
Painter.
Michael Schulz is known for his paintings of flowers on porcelain executed at the porcelain factory of Vienna at the end of the 18th and beginning of the 19th centuries.

SCHULZ, Mieczyslaw
Polish, 20th century.
Born 25 March 1895, in Warsaw.
Painter. Religious subjects. Murals.
Mieczyslaw Schulz was a student in Warsaw. He concentrated on fresco painting and decorated several churches.

SCHULZ, Moritz
German, 19th century.
Born 4 November 1825, in Leobschütz; died 17 December 1904, in Berlin.
Sculptor.

Moritz Schulz was taught by Posen at the art academy and by Drake at the academy in Berlin, and later went to Rome. His *Battle of Sadowa* is in the Siegesallee (Victory Avenue).
MUSEUMS AND GALLERIES:
BERLIN: *Maternal Love*.

SCHULZ, P. F.
German, 18th century.
Active in Nuremberg during the first half of the 18th century.
Painter, engraver.
P. F. Schulz was a pupil of Tyroff.

SCHULZ, Paul
German, 19th - 20th century.
Born 26 October 1868, in Berlin.
Active in Rome 1898-1915.
Sculptor.
Paul Schulz was a pupil of Ernst Herter.

SCHULZ, Paul
German, 19th - 20th century.
Born 13 January 1875, in Tschirnau.
Sculptor. Nudes. Monuments.
Paul Schulz was a pupil of Christian Behrens and, subsequently, of Auguste Rodin at the Académie Julian in Paris. He is noted for a monument to Martin Luther at Reichenbach (Silesia).
MUSEUMS AND GALLERIES:
WROCLAW: *Nude*.

SCHULZ, Toni
German, 19th - 20th century.
Born 1858, in Berlin; died 1918, in Arolsen.
Painter, watercolourist.

SCHULZ, Wilhelm
German, 19th - 20th century.
Born 23 December 1865, in Lüneburg; died 16 March 1952, in Munich.
Draughtsman.
Wilhelm Schulz studied at the fine arts academies of Hamburg, Berlin, Karlsruhe and Munich and was a regular contributor to the satirical review *Simplicissimus* from 1897. He also produced drawings to illustrate his own prose and poems.
AUCTION RECORDS:
LONDON, 20 June 1980, *Return from the Fields* (oil on canvas, 30 3/4 x 24 1/4 ins / 78.1 x 61.5 cm) GBP 2,500. MUNICH, 29 May 2001, *Rabble Rousers* (Indian ink, watercolour, chalk and colour pen, 13 x 9 ins / 34 x 24 cm) DEM 4,200.

SCHULZ LE CRECHT, Wilhelm
German, 18th - 19th century.
Born 1774, in Meiningen; died 1864, in Meiningen.
Sculptor (ivory).
Several of Schulz le Crecht's works are in the museum of Berlin castle and in Dresden and Weimar.

SCHULZ-BRIESEN, Édouard
German, 19th century.
Born 11 May 1831, in Neuss; died 21 February 1891, in Düsseldorf.
Painter. Genre scenes, portraits.
Schulz-Briesen was a pupil of Sohn, Schadow, Vautier, Dykmann and Wappers. In 1848 he worked in the academy in Düsseldorf, and in 1851 settled in Antwerp where he was to remain for several years. After several sojourns in France and Germany he returned to Düsseldorf. He received a bronze medal in London in 1890.
MUSEUMS AND GALLERIES:
DÜSSELDORF: *Imprisonment*; *Daydreaming* - LIÈGE: *Inquiry*.
AUCTION RECORDS:
COLOGNE, 22 Oct 1971, *Café Scene*, DEM 15,000.

SCHULZ-MATAN, Walter
German, 20th century.
Born 23 September 1883, in Apolda.
Painter. Portraits.
Walter Schulz-Matan was a part-time painter.
MUSEUMS AND GALLERIES:
DARMSTADT: *Mrs Maria Schrimpf* - MUNICH: *Self-portrait* - OLDENBURG: *Harlequin*.

SCHULZE, Adolf Otto Wolfgang. See **WOLS**

SCHULZE, Andreas
German, 20th - 21st century.
Born 1955, in Hanover.
Painter. Interiors, landscapes, still-lifes, flowers.
Andreas Schulze lives and works in Hanover. His paintings depict everyday objects, and more specifically the structure of those objects that form the backdrop to a person's life, removing them from their context, resulting in rather strange, decorative works. He has taken part in various group exhibitions including the Nouvelle Biennale de Paris in 1985. There have also been a number of solo exhibitions: 1982 Düsseldorf; 1982, 1987 Munich; 1983 Stuttgart, Museum voor hedendaagse Kunst in Ghent; 1983, 1984, 1988 Cologne; 1984 Hamburg; 1988 the Museo de Arte Contemporaneo in Seville, Fondation Caixa de Pensiones in Valencia, the Museo de Bellas Artes in Bilbao; 1989 Kunstverein in Lucerne and Munich; 1997 Le Parvis, Pau.
BIBLIOGRAPHY:
Nouvelle Biennale de Paris, exhibition catalogue, Electa, Le Moniteur, Paris, 1985. Schipper, Esther, "*Andreas Schulze - Du tableau au-dessus d'un canapé*' in *Art Press*, periodical, Paris, 1989. Arnaudet, Didier, "*Andreas Schulze*' in *Art Press* no. 229, periodical, Paris, November 1997.
AUCTION RECORDS:
NEW YORK, 27 Feb 1992, *Untitled* (acrylic/canvas, diptych, 82 1/2 x 141 1/2 ins / 209.5 x 359.4 cm) USD 5,500. NEW YORK, 6 May 1992, *Untitled* (1982, acrylic/canvas, diptych, in all 78 3/4 x 157 1/2 ins / 200 x 400 cm) USD 6,050. NEW YORK, 25-26 Feb 1994, *Untitled* (1985, acrylic/canvas, 108 x 114 ins / 274.3 x 289.6 cm) USD 4,600. NEW YORK, 1 Nov 1994, *Untitled* (1984, oil on canvas, diptyque 70 3/4 x 141 3/4 ins / 180 x 360 cm) USD 2,300. PARIS, 23 June 1999, *Untitled* (1987, oil on canvas, 87 x 134 ins / 220 x 340 cm) FRF 55,000. LONDON, 8 Dec 1999, *Untitled, Spheres* (acrylic on linen, diptych, 79 x 157 ins / 200 x 400 cm) GBP 10,000. HAMBURG, 8 June 2000, *Untitled* (1986, acrylic on cloth, diptych, 91 x 134 ins / 230 x 340 cm) DEM 21,000. HAMBURG, 7 Dec 2001, *Untitled* (1984, oil on canvas, diptych, a pair, 71 x 142 ins / 180 x 360 cm) DEM 7,500. HAMBURG, 7 Dec 2001, *Small Brothel* (1986, acrylic on canvas, 79 x 79 ins / 200 x 200 cm) DEM 8,000. COLOGNE, 4 June 2004, *Untitled* (1982, acrylic on cotton, 79 x 157 ins / 200 x 400 cm) EUR 8,500. VIENNA, 12 Oct 2004, *Untitled* (1984, oil on canvas, diptych, 79 x 157 ins / 200 x 400 cm) EUR 5,000.

SCHULZE, Arend
German, 17th century.
Active in Celle.
Sculptor (wood).

SCHULZE, Christian Gottfried or Chrétien Théophile
German, 18th - 19th century.
Born 1749, in Dresden; died 1819.
Draughtsman, engraver.
Christian Schulze initially learned engraving with Carl Hunn, then worked with Giuseppe Camerata, and thereafter was in Paris under the supervision of J.-G. Wille, thus benefiting from the guidance of one of the foremost French engravers. On returning to his native town he produced

several portraits. He also engraved a number of paintings in the gallery in Dresden.

SCHULZE, Emil
German, 19th - 20th century.
Born 22 February 1863, in Guckelsberg, near Chemnitz.
Active in Dresden and Zurich.
Painter, designer.

SCHULZE, Erdmann. See **SCHULTZ**

SCHULZE, Ernst August
German, 18th century.
Born 1684.
Painter.
Ernst August Schulze worked in Hildesheim from 1721 to 1738.

SCHULZE, Ernst Friedrich
German, 18th - 19th century.
Born December 1773, in Gotha; died 26 February 1826, in Coburg.
Painter.
Ernst Friedrich Schulze was court painter at Saxe-Coburg and executed the monument of Queen Louise in the park of the castle of Hildburghausen in 1815.

SCHULZE, Fritz
German, 19th - 20th century.
Born 17 July 1838, in Rendsburg; died 23 December 1914, in Munich.
Sculptor.
Fritz Schulze attended courses at the Kunstakademi in Copenhagen in 1856 and visited Rome in 1863.

SCHULZE, Johann Daniel
German, 19th century.
Born 1 October 1786, in Berlin; died 18 January 1836, in Frankfurt am Main.
Painter. Flowers. Frescoes.

SCHULZE, Johann Friedrich
German, 18th - 19th century.
Born 1748, in Berlin; died 1824, in Berlin.
Painter (porcelain).
The pupil of C. Clauze, Johann Friedrich Schulze worked at the porcelain factory in Berlin from 1762 to 1823.

SCHULZE, Johann Wilhelm
German, 18th century.
Born 1733, in Berlin.
Active in Potsdam.
Sculptor.
Johann Wilhelm Schulze was taught by B. Giese. He provided a few groups of children for the Königskolonnaden (Royal Colonnades) of Karl von Gontard in Berlin from 1777 to 1780.

SCHULZE, Karl
German, 19th century.
Active in Berlin 1824-1827.
Painter. Genre scenes, flowers, fruit.
AUCTION RECORDS:
AMSTERDAM, 21 April 1993, *Imposing Floral Arrangement in Vase with Peaches and Grapes on Table* (1827, oil on canvas, 20 1/2 x 16 1/4 ins / 52 x 41 cm) NLG 46,000.

SCHULZE, Ludwig Johann August
German, 19th century.
Painter. Genre scenes.
Ludwig Schulze attended the academies of Berlin and Munich from 1841 to 1842 and worked in Berlin.

SCHULZE, Martin Friedrich, or Schultz
German, 18th century.
Born 1721, in Berlin; died 1794, in Berlin.
Painter, art restorer. Portraits.
Martin Schulze was the pupil of Th. Huber.

SCHULZE, Otto
German, 20th century.
Born 5 September 1893, in Hanover; died 21 March 1919, in Dresden.
Painter, engraver.
Otto Schulze was a pupil of Oskar Zwintscher and Robert Sterl.

SCHULZE-NAUMBURG, Paul
German, 19th - 20th century.
Born 10 June 1869, in Naumburg Almrich.
Active in Saaleck, near Kösen.
Painter. Architectural views, landscapes.
Paul Schulze-Naumburg studied at the fine arts academy in Karlsruhe in 1887 and went on to become a pupil of Ferdinand von Keller from 1891 to 1893. He became a member of the architectural school and director of the fine arts school in Weimar. He was a practising architect and an art critic.
MUSEUMS AND GALLERIES:
LEIPZIG: *Plaul Castle.*

SCHULZE-ROSE, Wilhelm
German, 19th - 20th century.
Born 10 January 1872, in Dahgme.
Painter. Scenes with figures, landscapes.
Wilhelm Schulze-Rose studied at the fine arts academies of Dresden and Königsberg (now Kaliningrad, Russia) before going on to work in Leipzig and, from 1913, in Lomnitz near Görlitz.
MUSEUMS AND GALLERIES:
DESSAU: *Mature Lime Trees* - ZITTAU: *Night before a Fête.*
AUCTION RECORDS:
DÜSSELDORF, 13 Nov 1973, *Bible Reading,* DEM 2,000.

SCHULZE-SÖLDE, Max Wilhelm, or Schulze-Soelde
German, 20th century.
Born 25 January 1887, in Dortmund.
Painter.
Max Wilhelm Schulze-Sölde initially studied law before enrolling at the fine arts academy in Düsseldorf. He moved to Paris in 1914 to study under Othon Friesz. and was interned for four and a half years during World War I. He subsequently lived and worked in Hamm (Westphalia).
MUSEUMS AND GALLERIES:
DÜSSELDORF - HAMM - MÜNSTER - RECKLINGHAUSEN.
AUCTION RECORDS:
COLOGNE, 30 March 1979, *Winter Landscape* (oil on card, 23 1/4 x 35 1/2 ins / 59 x 90 cm) DEM 3,500. COLOGNE, 20 Oct 1989, *Landscape in Westphalia* (1939, tempera/panel, 9 1/2 x 18 ins / 24 x 45.5 cm) DEM 1,100.

SCHULZENHEIM, Ida Eleonora de
Swedish, 19th - 20th century.
Born 8 January 1859, in Skedi; died 1940.
Painter. Animals.
Ida Eleonora de Schulzenheim was a pupil of Jules Lefebvre and Julien Dupré. She exhibited her work at various Paris Salons, receiving an honourable mention at the Exposition Universelle in 1889 and 1892.
MUSEUMS AND GALLERIES:
STOCKHOLM.
AUCTION RECORDS:
LONDON, 17 June 1992, *Young Boy with Two Greyhounds* (1890, oil on canvas, 50 3/4 x 74 1/2 ins / 129 x 189 cm) GBP 3,080.

SCHUM, Kaspar
German, 19th century.
Born 1792, in Lichtenfels or in Birkenhammes, near Karlsbad (now Karlovy Vary, Czech Republic).

Painter (including porcelain). Landscapes.
Schum worked at the porcelain factory in Munich from 1810.

SCHUMACHER
German, 18th century.
Painter. Portraits.
MUSEUMS AND GALLERIES:
EMDEN (Ostfriesisches Landesmus.): *Half-length Portrait of Old Man*.

SCHUMACHER, Bernhard, or Bernard
German, 19th - 20th century.
Born 11 December 1872, in Kassel.
Engraver, watercolourist.
Bernhard Schumacher studied at the Royal Academy in London from 1893 to 1897 and was also a pupil of Frank Short. He lived and worked in Bremen, Hamburg and Neumunster.
AUCTION RECORDS:
LONDON, 28 March 1990, *Portrait of Miss Voight* (1901, oil on canvas, 50 1/2 x 33 3/4 ins / 128 x 86 cm) GBP 11,000.

SCHUMACHER, Emil
German, 20th century.
Born 1912, in Hagen; died 1999.
Painter (mixed media), sculptor of assemblages, engraver.
Quadriga Group.
On leaving secondary school, Emil Schumacher studied from 1932 to 1939 at the college of decorative arts in Dortmund, where he developed a passion for both the German Primitives and the 1910-vintage Expressionists. During World War I, he worked as an industrial designer in an armaments plant. He taught at the fine arts academy in Hamburg from 1958, and then taught at the fine arts school in Karlsruhe from 1966 to 1977. He was a member of the Berlin Academy of Arts from 1968.

Between 1935 and the outbreak of World War II, Schumacher painted figurative compositions influenced by Christian Rohlfs. These attracted little attention. From 1945, however, his work became progressively abstract, influenced no doubt by the work of Wols. By the 1950s he was increasingly influenced by the Art Informel artistic currents emanating from Paris. His work began to exhibit a progressive interest in colour as matter and, from 1952, he started to introduce tactile elements into his compositions, such as sand, rusty nails, scraps of fabric, wire netting and paper clippings. This approach brought him to the attention of the critics and a wider public, who were fascinated by the fact that the contours of a landscape appeared to emerge from his compositions when they were viewed from a distance. His work from this period had none of the vicious sophistication of an Alberto Burri; instead, he sought to impart a raw edge to his work, insisting that it could be appreciated 'even by the blind'.

Schumacher stopped producing these reliefs in 1958 and reverted to oils as his principal medium. That said, expression and varied surface texture remained essential elements in his work. Thus, his *Little by Little* is typical of his sensual style of the 1960s, where colour, structure and incised lines dominate the canvas. These incisions are important on two levels: the first is essentially visual in terms of flourishes and symbols, the second - as his close friend and biographer Werner Schmalenbach pointed out - is in terms of the underlying intent. These compositions draw on the implicit duality that exists between the stability of the work and the impact and intervention of the artistic gesture.

It is never easy to define Schumacher's style. Elements of Art Informel are ever present, particularly in the bold use of blacks and reds which yield a dense and kneaded surface texture. The incisions in the form of gouges, scores and scratches emerge and disappear in an elegant calligraphy hinting at sacred hieroglyphs. The whole is reinforced by jagged slashes of black, sudden splashes of white and occasional and violent use of the palette knife. At times, this permutation of thickly applied paint and intermittent graffiti dissipates into dull greenish-blues which evoke the calm of an undersea world from which Schumacher, the erstwhile Expressionist, permits the vague contours of a human form to emerge from the primal ooze.

Schumacher took part in group exhibitions, notably those of the Zen 49 group in both Germany and the USA. Other notable group exhibitions include those at the following: the Stedelijk Museum in Amsterdam (1954); the Venice Biennale (1958, 1962); the International Exhibition of Contemporary Painting and Sculpture at the Carnegie Institute in Pittsburgh (1958, 1967, 1970); Documenta in Kassel (1959, 1964, 1977); the São Paulo Biennale (1959, 1963); the National Museum in Tokyo (1960, 1966); the International Engraving Exhibition at the Moderna Galerija in Ljubljana (1961, 1965, 1967); the cantonal museum in Lausanne (1963); the Sydney Biennial (1973); the Kunsthaus in Zurich (1980); and the art fair in Cologne (1981).

Among his solo exhibitions, the most notable include those at the following: Wuppertal (1947, 1956, 1957); Münster (1956); Düsseldorf (1957); Hanover, Paris and Hagen (1958); Berlin (1958, 1961); Munich (1958, 1959, 1960); Rome and Stuttgart (1959); New York (1959, 1960); the Westfälischer Kunstverein in Münster (1962); the Kunstverein in Hamburg (1962); the Wilhelm Lehmbruck Museum in Duisburg (1962); the Kunstverein in Freiburg (1962); the Biennale in São Paulo (1963); the Nardodni Gallery in Prague (1967); the Kunstverein in Düsseldorf (1971); the Neue Galerie in Linz (1976); the Kunstverein in Brunswick (1978); the Kunsthalle in Bremen (1984); the Nationalgalerie in Berlin (1988); the Pinacoteca in Locarno (1994); and the Galerie Nationale du Jeu de Paume in Paris (1997).

Schumacher was the recipient of numerous prizes and awards, including the Jungen Wesen Prize (1948), the Osthaus Prize (1958), the Cardazzo Prize at the 31st Venice Biennale (1962), and the Tokyo International Engraving Award (1966). He was put forward in 1958 for the Guggenheim National Section Award.

Schumacher

BIBLIOGRAPHY:
Ier Salon international des Galeries Pilotes, exhibition catalogue, Musée cantonal, Lausanne, 1963. Schmalenbach, Werner, '*Emil Schumacher*' in *Quadrum*, periodical, Brussels, c. 1969. Schmalenbach, Werner, *Emil Schumacher*, DuMont, Cologne, 1981.
MUSEUMS AND GALLERIES:
BELGRADE (Muz. savremene umetnotsi) - BERLIN (Nationalgal.) - BONN (Kunstmus.) - BUFFALO (Albright-Knox AG) - CHICAGO (AI) - DÜSSELDORF (Kunstsammlung Nordrhein-Westfalen): *Large Red Painting* (1965); *Macumba* (1973-1974) - HANOVER: *Kuomi* (1961) - LAUSANNE (Cantonal MFA) - LINZ (Neue Gal. der Stadt) - LJUBLJANA (Moderna Gal.) - LONDON (Tate Collection): works on paper - NEW YORK (Solomon R. Guggenheim Mus.): *Florian* (1960) - PITTSBURGH (Carnegie MA): *9 May 1967* (1967, on brown paper); *B-5/1969* (1969, acrylic on paper on canvas); *Feno* (1960, oil on canvas) - VIENNA (Mus. Moderner Kunst, Ludwig Foundation Bequest).
AUCTION RECORDS:
DÜSSELDORF, 14 Nov 1973, *Tettix*, DEM 14,000. ZURICH, 18 Nov 1976, *Composition* (oil and tar/panel, 75 1/2 x 80 1/4 ins / 192 x 204 cm) CHF 20,000. MUNICH, 23 May 1978, *Compo-*

sition (1958, gouache, oil and plaster/card, 13 x 10 1/4 ins / 33 x 26 cm) DEM 4,800. COLOGNE, 5 Dec 1979, *Composition* (1954, oil on canvas, 15 x 18 ins / 38 x 46 cm) DEM 6,400. HAMBURG, 13 June 1981, *Zessa* (1959, oil on canvas, 48 x 38 ins / 121 x 96.5 cm) DEM 42,000. LONDON, 6 Dec 1983, *Gingo* (1958, oil and sand/canvas, 66 3/4 x 51 3/4 ins / 169.5 x 131.5 cm) GBP 16,000. LONDON, 4 Dec 1984, *Untitled* (1961, collage and gouache/card, 23 1/4 x 15 1/4 ins / 59 x 38.5 cm) GBP 3,100. ZURICH, 8 June 1985, *Composition* (1961, mixed media/canvas, 13 1/4 x 9 1/2 ins / 33.5 x 24 cm) CHF 10,000. COLOGNE, 10 Dec 1986, *Breakthrough* (1955, oil on canvas, 31 1/2 x 23 1/2 ins / 80 x 60 cm) DEM 65,000. LONDON, 30 June 1988, *Kalimbi IV* (1959, mixed media, 39 1/4 x 31 1/2 ins / 100 x 80 cm) GBP 28,600; *Biros* (1960, mixed media/canvas, 31 1/2 x 23 1/2 ins / 80 x 60 cm) GBP 48,400. LONDON, 25 May 1989, *Tarquinia* (1961, sand and oil on canvas, 31 1/2 x 23 1/2 ins / 80 x 60 cm) GBP 37,400. LONDON, 22 Feb 1990, *Untitled* (1972, gouache and oil on irregular paper, 27 1/4 x 22 ins / 69 x 56 cm) GBP 16,500. LONDON, 5 April 1990, *Untitled* (1963, oil and mixed media/canvas, 23 1/2 x 15 3/4 ins / 60 x 40 cm) GBP 38,500. LONDON, 6 Dec 1990, *Little by Little* (1960, oil and coating/canvas, 39 1/4 x 31 1/2 ins / 100 x 80 cm) GBP 66,000; *Untitled* (1958, oil and mixed media/canvas, 67 x 52 ins / 170 x 132 cm) GBP 90,200. ROME, 13 May 1991, *Untitled* (1959, mixed media/paper/card, 20 1/2 x 14 1/2 ins / 52 x 37 cm) ITL 20,700,000. LONDON, 27 June 1991, *Untitled* (1957, oil and mixed media/canvas, 67 x 52 ins / 170 x 132 cm) GBP 88,000. MUNICH, 26-27 Nov 1991, *Composition* (1960, oil on card, 24 1/2 x 19 1/2 ins / 62 x 49.5 cm) DEM 40,250. LONDON, 26 March 1992, *Tecins* (1962, oil on card, 30 1/4 x 71 1/4 ins / 77 x 181 cm) GBP 90,200. LONDON, 20 May 1993, *Untitled* (1962, gouache, oil, pencil and ink/craft paper, 25 x 19 3/4 ins / 63.5 x 50.3 cm) GBP 12,650. LONDON, 2 Dec 1993, *Mabudin* (1965, oil, texture and canvas/panel, 30 1/2 x 70 1/4 ins / 77.5 x 178.5 cm) GBP 69,700. LONDON, 1 Dec 1994, *Cadmo* (1976, oil on canvas, 63 x 51 1/4 ins / 160 x 130 cm) GBP 117,000. LONDON, 26 Oct 1995, *Untitled* (1959, mixed media/embossed paper, 21 x 18 3/4 ins / 53.5 x 47.7 cm) GBP 9,200. MILAN, 2 April 1996, *Desert* (1962, oil on canvas, 26 1/2 x 18 ins / 67.5 x 45.5 cm) ITL 48,300,000. LONDON, 23 May 1996, *Composition in Red and Black* (1965, mixed media/canvas, 19 3/4 x 27 1/2 ins / 50 x 70 cm) GBP 49,900. LONDON, 24 Oct 1996, *Belau* (1967, oil and pigment/wood, 52 3/4 x 39 1/4 ins / 134 x 100 cm) GBP 122,500. LONDON, 6 Dec 1996, *Mila* (1965, oil on canvas, 39 1/2 x 31 3/4 ins / 100.5 x 80.5 cm) GBP 41,100. LONDON, 25 June 1997, *Painting* (1961, oil on canvas, 39 1/2 x 79 ins / 100.3 x 200.7 cm) GBP 161,000. LONDON, 26 June 1997, *Rome VII* (1963, oil on canvas, 17 3/4 x 27 1/4 ins / 45 x 69.2 cm) GBP 27,600. LONDON, 27 June 1997, *Mora* (1965, oil and canvas/canvas, 28 x 19 3/4 ins / 71 x 50 cm) GBP 13,800. LONDON, 23 Oct 1997, *Zills* (1965, oil on canvas, 31 1/2 x 39 1/4 ins / 80 x 100 cm) GBP 51,000. BERLIN, 4 June 1999, *Grisolet* (1957, oil on cardboard, 39 x 31 ins / 99 x 80 cm) DEM 110,000. BERLIN, 26 Nov 1999, *Untitled* (1956, oil on board, 39 x 31 ins / 99 x 79 cm) DEM 150,000. COLOGNE, 10 Nov 2000, *Mandalay* (1958, oil on canvas, 28 x 20 ins / 70 x 50 cm) DEM 200,000. MUNICH, 2 Dec 2000, *Acheron* (mixed media, oil and sand on canvas, 67 x 52 ins / 170 x 131 cm) DEM 250,000. LONDON, 10 Oct 2001, *Rofos II* (1961, oil on canvas, 39 x 31 ins / 100 x 80 cm) GBP 90,000. COLOGNE, 5 Dec 2001, *Dades* (1978, oil, asphalt and sand on canvas, 39 x 63 ins / 100 x 160 cm) DEM 250,000. BERLIN, 7 June 2002, *Tecnis* (1962, oil on panel, 30 x 71 ins / 76 x 180 cm) EUR 180,000. COLOGNE, 4 Dec 2002, *Sur* (1964, oil on canvas, 39 x 31 ins / 100 x 80 cm) EUR 80,000. COLOGNE, 27 Nov 2003, *Soman* (1962, oil and sand on canvas, 39 x 31 ins / 100 x 80 cm) EUR 165,000. COLOGNE, 13 Dec 2003, *GC 11* (1990, mixed media, 21 x 28 ins / 53 x 70 cm) EUR 40,000. COLOGNE, 4 June 2004, *Untitled* (1984, gouache, oil and chalk on packing paper, 21 x 26 ins / 54 x 65 cm) EUR 24,000. BERLIN, 26 Nov 2004, *Gregor* (1967, oil on canvas, 32 x 39 ins / 81 x 100 cm) EUR 100,000.

SCHUMACHER, Franz

Swiss, 17th century.
Born 8 February 1629, in Baar, near Zoug.
Sculptor. Portraits.

Franz Schumacher studied in Rome.

SCHUMACHER, Fritz or Fritz Wilhelm

German, 19th - 20th century.
Born 4 November 1869, in Bremen; died 5 November 1947, in Hamburg.
Architect, draughtsman, town planner.

Franz Schumacher spent part of his childhood in Bolivia and in the USA as his father was a diplomat. He studied mathematics and natural sciences then turned towards architecture which he studied under the direction of Friedrich von Thiersch. He was appointed in 1896 to the administration of the architecture of the city of Leipzig then in 1909 to the administration of the architecture of Hamburg whose urban development up to 1933 has been greatly marked by his imprint. At the same time he was a teacher at the Technical High School in Dresden from 1901 to 1909. He was a member of the Academy of Fine Art of Vienna and of the Academy of Art in Dresden and in his teaching he stressed the importance of drawing in architecture. Among his pupils were Erich Heckel and Ernst Ludwig Kirchner. Since 1949 there has been a 'Fritz-Schumacher Prize' which is awarded to a person remarkable in the domain of architecture and urbanism. He had a great influence on the reform of the arts at the turn of the century and made several contacts with visual artists. He published committed writings, for example, *Kampf um die moderne Kunst* (*Struggle for Modern Art*); studies of utopian architecture and organised several exhibitions of applied arts, chiefly the Third German Art Exhibition of Dresden in 1906. This exhibition marked a turning point in the history of the applied arts in Germany, surpassing the floral and ornamental line of the Jugendstil type with a functional art thought to be more suitable to the material used. He can be placed among the co-founders in 1907 of the Deutscher Werkbund at Munich. An association founded by architects, designers and industrialists who proposed the use of simple and solid shapes to be applied as much in architecture as in consumer goods. His work as architect made him a representative of 'the Expressionism of brick', a reinterpretation of the traditional architecture of the Hanseatic North of Germany. His style evolved from a contained historicism to a language linked to new forms of construction. He was consulted for the creation of the Dresden-Hellerau of the Deutsche Werkstätten für Hausrat.

BIBLIOGRAPHY:

Ockert, Erwin, *Fritz Schumacher: Sein Schaffen als Stadtebauer und Landesplaner*, Ernst Wasmuth, Tübingen, 1950. Frank, Hartmut/Weller, Christian, *Fritz Schumacher: Reformkultur und Moderne*, Hatje, Stuttgart, 1994. Löbert, Dagmar, *Fritz Schumacher, Reformarchitekt zwischen Tradition und Moderne*, Donat, Bremen, 1999.

SCHUMACHER, Gereon

German, 18th century.
Born 1716; died 13 August 1792, in Cologne.
Active in Cologne.
Painter.

Gereon Schumacher belonged to the Society of Jesus. Two of his paintings are in the church of the Assumption in Cologne: *St Ignatius Kneeling before the Virgin* and *St Ignatius Kneeling before the Saviour*.

SCHUMACHER, Hans

German, 17th century.

Active in Wollin.
Sculptor.

SCHUMACHER, Harald Peter William
Danish, 19th century.
Born 23 March 1826, in Copenhagen; died 20 January 1912, in Copenhagen.
Painter. Architectural views, landscapes.

Schumacher was a pupil of Frederik F. Helsted, and also studied at the Kunstakademi in Copenhagen.

MUSEUMS AND GALLERIES:
COPENHAGEN (Bymus.).

AUCTION RECORDS:
VIENNA, 14 March 1984, *The Cross on the Side of the Road* (1877, oil on canvas, 24 x 37 3/4 ins / 61 x 96 cm) ATS 35,000. COPENHAGEN, 1 June 1999, *Coastal Landscape, Ellekilde North of Helsingør* (oil on canvas, 19 x 32 ins / 48 x 82 cm) DKK 12,000. BERLIN, 26 Nov 1999, *Boy under Pergola with View of Vesuvius and Bay of Naples* (oil on canvas, 15 x 24 ins / 38 x 61 cm) DEM 3,200. VEJLE, 19 Jan 2000, *View of Rome with St Peter's in Background* (oil on canvas, 22 x 33 ins / 56 x 84 cm) DKK 14,000. COPENHAGEN, 3 Sept 2001, *Landscape with Large Trees, Hunter Shooting at Flock of Birds* (oil on canvas, 23 x 28 ins / 58 x 70 cm) DKK 16,000. COPENHAGEN, 3 June 2002, *Small Boy with Fishing Rod on Bridge in Landscape, Jylland* (oil on canvas, 23 x 37 ins / 58 x 94 cm) DKK 40,000.

SCHUMACHER, Hugo. See **SCHUHMACHER**

SCHUMACHER, Karl
German, 19th - 20th century.
Born 5 December 1869, in Arolsen; died 1919.
Active in England and Norway.
Painter. Portraits.

Karl Schumacher studied under Fritjof Smith in Weimar.

SCHUMACHER, Karl Georg Christian
German, 19th century.
Born 14 May 1797, in Doberan; died 22 June 1869, in Dresden.
Painter, engraver, lithographer. History painting.

Karl Schumacher attended the academy in Dresden between 1819 and 1821. An interlude in Italy was followed by a period of residence in Dresden from 1826 to 1830. After further travels, he settled in Schwerin, where he was appointed court painter at Mecklenburg Schwerin. A number of his works are to be found in the Staatlisches Museum in Schwerin: *Holy Family, Adoration of the Kings, The Departure of Heinrich the Pilgrim, The Return of Heinrich the Pilgrim* and the *Battle of Gransee*.

SCHUMACHER, Ludwig
German, 18th century.
Painter. Genre scenes.

The gallery of Salzdahlum received three works by Ludwig Schumacher.

SCHÜMACHER, M.
Dutch, 18th century.
Painter.

SCHUMACHER, Matthias
German, 18th century.
Died c. 1760.
Active in Cologne.
Painter. History painting.

MUSEUMS AND GALLERIES:
COLOGNE (Basilika St. Aposteln): *Christ Driving the Moneychangers from the Temple*.

SCHUMACHER, Max
Chilean, 20th century.
Born 11 November 1885, in Lola.
Active in Germany.
Sculptor.

Max Schumacher lived and worked in Berlin.

SCHUMACHER, Philipp
Austrian, 19th - 20th century.
Born 20 May 1866, in Innsbruck.
Painter, illustrator. Religious subjects.

Philipp Schumacher studied from 1888 to 1895 under Josef Matthias von Trenkwald at the fine arts academy in Vienna before working successively in Rome (1895-1900), Berlin (1900-1906) and Munich (from 1906).

SCHUMACHER, Tony, short for Antonie
German, 19th - 20th century.
Born 17 May 1848, in Louisburg; died 10 July 1931, in Louisburg.
Illustrator.

Tony Schumacher specialised in the illustration of children's books and on occasion also wrote texts to accompany her illustrations.

BIBLIOGRAPHY:
Osterwalder, Marcus (ed.), *Dictionnaire des illustrateurs 1800-1914*, Ides et Calendes, Neuchâtel, 1989.

SCHUMACHER, William E. or Willem.
See **SCHUHMACHER Wim**

SCHUMACHER-SALIG, Ernst
German, 20th century.
Born 11 July 1900, in Mönchengladbach.
Active in Düsseldorf.
Painter. Landscapes.

SCHUMANN, Albert
German, 19th century.
Active c. 1833.
Miniaturist.

SCHUMANN, Albert
German, 19th century.
Active in Berlin.
Painter. Still-lifes.

Albert Schumann exhibited at the academy in 1844.

SCHUMANN, Andreas, the Elder
German, 17th - 18th century.
Born c. 1662; died 16 August 1729.
Engraver.

Andreas Schumann the Elder and his son Andreas worked together in Berlin as glass engravers.

SCHUMANN, Andreas, the Younger
German, 18th century.
Born 1710; died after 1738.
Engraver.

Andreas Schumann the Younger worked with his father Andreas as a glass engraver.

SCHUMANN, Anton
Austrian, 18th century.
Active in Prague c. 1790.
Sculptor.

SCHUMANN, August
German, 17th century.
Died September 1677.
Painter.

August Schumann was court painter in Dresden and painted a still-life with musical instruments in 1662.

SCHUMANN, Christian
German, 18th century.
Draughtsman.

Christian Schumann drew views of Augsburg and its surroundings.

SCHUMANN, Christian
American, 20th - 21st century.
Born 1970, on Rhode Island.
Active in New York and Los Angeles.
Painter, collage artist.

Christian Schumann grew up in Texas and studied at the San Francisco Art Institute, graduating in 1992. Though he experimented with other media, as in *A Tender Moment*, a handmade rug with a woman's face, an aeroplane, two zeros and the word 'SUNNY' (1996), Schumann went on to concentrate on painting and collage. He produces gaudily coloured, cartoon-Expressionist images with an undercurrent of social commentary and personal suffering. A Hieronymous Bosch for an age obsessed with advertising, the internet and the media, Schumann recycles the visual detritus from the information-charged environment into ambiguous allegories with, in his words, 'hopeless optimism'. Where Bosch saw evil beings lurking around every corner prepared to exploit human folly, Schumann presents slobbering businessmen, flying houses, impossible gunboats, surly comic characters and an anatomically precise rendition of a chicken's digestive tract. The visual raconteur of this chaotic era, Schumann works hard to capture the self-replicating, ubiquitous, pervasive structure of 21st-century information glut.

Schumann's candy-coloured, hallucinatory canvases are intensely original in their portrayal of the universal condition of message overload. His bizarre sense of humour emerges at every turn: in the images of two Asian girls, their hats emblazoned with the words 'Ham' and 'Eggs', and in the cheesy depiction of a serenading musician, the spitting image of a young Ronald Reagan. He likes penning lists, copying the lyrics of entire songs or writing down passages of original prose on his paintings, producing scarified palimpsests. Works include *Ahoa Oe* (2000), *Bamboo Taboo* (2000), *Blob Lab* (2001), *Fallen* (2001) and *Doubletime Horrostick* (2003).

Schumann featured in several group exhibitions from 1991 in the USA and in Europe, including Venice, Paris, Liverpool and Berlin. Solo exhibitions include those at *Arid Flowers of Gongorism* at the DOG in San Francisco (1991); the Postmasters Gallery in New York (from 1992); the Daniel Weinberg Gallery in San Francisco (1994); the Anti-Matter Gallery in San Francisco (1992); Il Capricorno in Venice (1996); the Jay Joplin/White Cube Gallery in London (1997); the Galerie Carlier-Gebauer in Berlin (from 1999); the Gagosian Gallery in Los Angeles (2001); *Energy Regulations* with Gary Panter at the Sandra Gering Gallery in New York (2002); *Levels, Platforms, Paths and Obstacles* at the Dunn and Brown Contemporary Gallery in Dallas (2003); and the Patrick Painter Gallery in Santa Monica (2004).

BIBLIOGRAPHY:

Saltz, Jerry, '*C. Schumann at Postmasters, New York*' in *Art in America*, journal article, March 1993. Johnson, Ken, '*Big Top Whitney*' in *Art in America*, journal article, June 1995. Bates, Rob, '*The Schumann Show*' in *Smock Magazine*, no. 2, journal article, fall/winter 2000. Leffingwel, Edward, '*Christian Schumann*' in *Art in America*, journal article, February 2000.

AUCTION RECORDS:

NEW YORK, 19 May 1999, *Untitled* (1995, acrylic, paper and pencil on canvas, 78 x 60 ins / 198 x 152 cm) USD 30,000. NEW YORK, 17 Nov 1999, *Untitled: Some Spirits I Let Out One Afternoon* (1998, oil on canvas, 26 x 40 ins / 66 x 101 cm) USD 4,200. NEW YORK, 18 May 2000, *Cream Corn Circus* (1993, acrylic and paper collage on canvas, 60 x 72 ins / 152 x 183 cm) USD 40,000. NEW YORK, 17 Nov 2000, *Untitled: Faces* (1994, oil, acrylic, graphite, ink and paper collage on canvas, 72 x 108 ins / 183 x 274 cm) USD 38,000. NEW YORK, 15 May 2001, *Untitled: Congeal Ed* (1993, acrylic, graphite and paper collage on canvas, 72 x 60 ins / 183 x 152 cm) USD 18,000. NEW YORK, 16 May 2002, *Untitled: Gaping Hole* (1994, oil on canvas, 24 x 18 ins / 61 x 46 cm) USD 3,000. NEW YORK, 16 May 2002, *Dirty World* (1999, acrylic on canvas, 60 x 72 ins / 152 x 183 cm) USD 12,000. NEW YORK, 16 May 2003, *Summer Rust* (2001, acrylic, paper collage, graphite and colour pencil on canvas, 38 x 50 ins / 96 x 126 cm) USD 19,000. NEW YORK, 14 Nov 2003, *Untitled* (1992, acrylic, gouache, graphite and paper collage on canvas, 65 x 117 ins / 164 x 296 cm) USD 35,000. NEW YORK, 13 May 2004, *Useless* (1999, acrylic, mixed media and collage on canvas, 65 x 72 ins / 166 x 183 cm) USD 17,000. NEW YORK, 14 May 2004, *Flatbush* (1999, acrylic, gouache, pen, ink and collage on canvas, 72 x 60 ins / 183 x 152 cm) USD 16,000.

SCHUMANN, Daniel Johann
German, 18th - 19th century.
Born 1752; died after 1809.
Active in Potsdam.
Sculptor.

Daniel Schumann was the pupil of A.L. Kruger and the Räntz brothers in Potsdam with whom he worked for five years. He completed his studies at the Kunstakademi in Copenhagen.

SCHUMANN, Ernst
German, 17th century.
Painter.

MUSEUMS AND GALLERIES:

QUEDLINBURG (Rathaus): *Susanna Justified by Daniel.*

SCHUMANN, Frieda
Swiss, 20th - 21st century.
Born 14 December 1967, in Sorengo.
Active in France.
Sculptor, installation artist.

Frieda Schumann lives and works in Nice and Paris. She produces installations that combine individual and universal themes, particularly concerning the female sex, expressed through techniques such as embroidery and sewing and using items of furniture (coat stand, dishes, armchairs). She creates warm, decorative 'living' spaces, choosing either old-fashioned objects found at flea markets which have the charm of the remembered or the familiar, or objects that she herself has roughly sculpted, such as a wooden typewriter.

Frieda Schumann has taken part in various group exhibitions: 1992, Nice, Paris, Cologne, New York; 1993, Salon de Montrouge; 1994, Nice, Villeurbanne. There have also been a number of solo exhibitions of her works: 1993, gallery of the Villa Arson school in Nice; 1994, Galerie La Tête d'Obsidienne in La Seyne-sur-Mer; 2001, *Y?*, as part of the *Play* event at the Musée d'Art Moderne et Contemporain in Geneva.

BIBLIOGRAPHY:

Macchi, Catherine, *Frieda Schumann*, exhibition leaflet, Villa Arson-Centre national des Arts plastiques, Nice, Gal. La Tête d'obsidienne, La Seyne-sur-Mer, 1993-1994. Lions, Marie Laure, ''*Frieda Schumann*' in *Art Press* no. 199, periodical, Paris, February 1995.

SCHUMANN, Johan Ehrenfried
German, 18th century.
Born 25 February 1732, in Weimar; died 28 October 1787, in Weimar.
Painter. Scenes with figures, portraits, landscapes.
Stage sets, decorative panels.

Johan Ehrenfried Schumann became court painter to Anna Amelia of Saxe-Weimar on 3rd April 1764, and executed landscapes and painted stage sets. In the castle of Stedtfeld he painted panels of Thuringian landscapes and popular scenes.

MUSEUMS AND GALLERIES:
EISENACH (Schloss): *Portrait of Duke Karl August in Hunter's Garb.*

SCHUMANN, Johann Gottfried
German, 18th century.
Active in Wittenberg during the first half of the 18th century.
Draughtsman, engraver.

SCHUMANN, Johann Gottlob
German, 18th - 19th century.
Born 1761, in Dresden; died 11 November 1810.
Painter, engraver (burin).
Johann Gottlob Schumann became a member of the academy in Dresden in 1805. He engraved portraits and landscapes and spent part of his career in London where he collaborated with W. Byrne.

J. Sch

SCHUMANN, Karl Franz Jakob
German, 18th - 19th century.
Born 8 August 1767, in Berlin; died 27 September 1827.
Painter, watercolourist. Historical subjects, still-lifes.
The pupil of J. C. Frisch, Karl Schumann also studied in Italy and in 1801 was appointed Professor of Anatomy at the academy in Berlin. His repertoire consisted of scenes from the history of Brandenburg, many of which are in the royal castle in Berlin.

AUCTION RECORDS:
LONDON, 27 Nov 1987, *Still-life with Vase of Flowers* (1894, watercolour heightened with white, 25 x 18¼ ins / 63.5 x 46.2 cm) GBP 1,800.

SCHUMANN, Nikolaus
German, 16th century.
Sculptor. Portraits.

SCHUMANN, Th., or Schuhmann
German, 19th century.
Active in Karlsruhe between 1824 and 1828.
Lithographer.

SCHUMANN, Urban
German, 16th century.
Sculptor.
Urban Schumann was a monk.

SCHUMANN, Wilhelm
German, 19th century.
Active in Berlin.
Painter. Genre scenes, portraits.
Wilhelm Schumann was the pupil of Brucke and contributed to exhibitions at the academy in Berlin from 1830 to 1844.

SCHUMER, Joannes
Dutch (?), 17th century.
Born c. 1670.
Painter, engraver (etching). History painting, animals.
The following engravings are attributed to Joannes Schumer: *Peasant with Two Hunting Dogs; Peasant with Two Cows; Cow at a Drinking Place; Cow with Sleeping Cowherd*; and *Small Group of Livestock.*

SCHUMM, Georg Joseph
French, 18th century.
Active in Strasbourg.
Painter.
Georg Joseph Schumm received first prize in 1788 as a pupil at the art school in Strasbourg.

SCHUMM, Theresa. See **RUDHART**

SCHUMWAY, Henry Colton, or Shumway
American, 19th century.
Born 4 July 1807, in Middletown; died 6 May 1884, in New York.
Miniaturist, painter. Portraits, landscapes.
Henry Colton Schumway studied in New York and established himself there in 1829 as a painter of miniatures. Although he appears to have successfully mastered this genre, he abandoned it in favour of portrait painting in oils and was highly successful. In 1831 he was made an associate of the National Academy of Design in New York, and was admitted as a member the following year. He also painted a few landscapes.

SCHUNCKO, Anton
Austrian, 18th century.
Born in Tepl (Bohemia).
Painter.
Schuncko worked in Vienna.

SCHÜNEMANN, Gregorius or Jacobus
German, 17th century.
Painter. Portraits.
The portrait *Heinrich Adrian von Veltheim* is by Schünemann.

AUCTION RECORDS:
LONDON, 15 Nov 1989, *Portrait of Robert Macgill, 2nd Viscount of Oxford* (oil on canvas, oval, 29¼ x 24½ ins / 74 x 62 cm) GBP 5,500.

SCHUNKO, Franz
Austrian, 18th century.
Of Bohemian origin; died 27 December 1770.
Painter.
Schunko became a member of the academy in Vienna in 1762.

SCHÜNNEMANN, Johannes, or Hans
Dutch, 17th century.
Active in the Netherlands.
Sculptor.

SCHÜNZEL, Karl
German, 19th - 20th century.
Born 28 July 1875, in Lauscha (Thuringia).
Active in Munich.
Painter.
Karl Schünzel was a pupil of Karl Raupp.

SCHUOCH, Andreas. See **SCHUCH**

SCHUPAUER, Christoph. See **SCHUBAUER**

SCHUPISSER, Peter
Belgian, 20th - 21st century.
Born 1951, in Ixelles (Brussels).
Painter. Murals.
Peter Schupisser trained at the art academy in Watermael-Boitsfort.

SCHUPP, Johann
German, 17th - 18th century.
Born 1631; died 1713.
Active in Villingen.
Sculptor.

SCHUPP, Joseph Anton
German, 17th - 18th century.
Born 1664; died 1729.
Active in Villingen.
Sculptor.

SCHÜPPEL, Fr.
German, 19th century.
Active c. 1800.
Painter.

SCHÜPPEL, Karl
German, 19th - 20th century.
Born 25 November 1876, in Oberlungwitz (Saxony).
Active in Oberlungwitz.
Sculptor.
Karl Schüppel studied at the fine arts academy in Dresden and subsequently at the Académie Julian in Paris.

SCHUPPEN, H. van
Flemish School, 16th - 17th century.
Active in Rome 1594-1620.
Engraver.
H. van Schuppen is referred to by Ris-Paquot.

HV

SCHUPPEN, Jacob van, or Souppen
Dutch, 17th - 18th century.
Born 26 January 1670, in Fontainebleau; died 29 January 1751, in Vienna.
Active in France and Austria.
Painter. History painting, portraits, genre scenes.
Jacob van Schuppen was a pupil of his father Pieter van Schuppen and his uncle Nicolas de Largillière, whose style he imitated. He became an academician in 1704 and married Marie-Françoise Thierry in 1705. Van Schuppen was resident in Paris and Lunéville until 1719. He became naturalised in the French region of Lorraine, and was court painter to Duke Leopold before being taken to Vienna by Archduke Charles (the future Charles VI of Austria) as a painter to the court and privy chamber. With Count Anhalt, he co-founded the Hebung Institute, for which he received a pension of 4000 gulden from 1744.

MUSEUMS AND GALLERIES:
AMSTERDAM: *Prince Eugène of Savoie* - BESANÇON: *Portrait of the Astronomer Boulle* - BRUNSWICK: *Meleager Slaying the Calydonian Boar* (sketch) - DIJON: *Portrait of a Woman* - ÉPINAL: *Charles Alexander, Son of the Duke of Lorraine* - GRAZ: *Portrait of Charles VI and Empress Elisabeth* - LA FÈRE: *Family Portrait* - MONTPELLIER: *Meleager Slaying the Calydonian Boar* - NANCY (Mus. Lorrain): *Self-portrait; Leopold of Lorraine with his Family* - SIBIU: two still-lifes; *Portrait of Henri de Seilen* - TURIN: *Eugène of Savoie on Horseback* - VIENNA: *Portrait of an Elderly Man* - VIENNA (Akademie der Bildenden Künste): *Self-portrait; Portrait of Charles VI* - VIENNA (Kunsthistorisches Mus.): *Self-portrait* - VIENNA (Liechtenstein Mus.): *Self-portrait* - VIENNA (Österreichische Gal. Belvedere, Barockmuseum): *Portrait of the Painter Parrocel.*

AUCTION RECORDS:
PARIS, 1897, *Self-portrait,* FRF 1,450. PARIS, 17 April 1920, *Romantic Pastoral,* FRF 3,800. PARIS, 27 April 1928, *Romantic Pastoral,* FRF 2,800. LONDON, 13 March 1963, *Allegory of Beauty,* GBP 600. VIENNA, 16 Sept 1969, *Portrait of a Gentleman,* ATS 20,000. VIENNA, 22 June 1976, *Emperor Charles VI* (oil on canvas in grisaille, 27 1/2 x 21 1/4 ins / 70 x 54 cm) ATS 40,000. NEW YORK, 17 June 1982, *Self-portrait* (oil on canvas, 52 x 45 ins / 132 x 114.5 cm) USD 6,000. LONDON, 12 Dec 1984, *Self-portrait* (oil on canvas, 51 1/2 x 44 ins / 131 x 112 cm) GBP 5,000. LONDON, 10 July 1992, *Portrait of Victor, Count of Philippi, General-in-Chief of a Regiment of the Dragoons* (1723, oil on canvas, 57 1/4 x 48 1/2 ins / 145.4 x 123.2 cm) GBP 6,050. PARIS, 1 April 1996, *Young Children Playing in front of a Fountain of Neptune* (oil on panel, 23 1/4 x 17 1/4 ins / 59 x 44 cm) FRF 60,000. PARIS, 23 March 2000, *Gentlemen Meeting around a Table in an Interior* (oil on canvas, 29 x 37 ins / 74 x 93 cm) FRF 180,000. TURIN, 18 Oct 2000, *Elegant Company in an Interior* (1703, oil on canvas, 39 x 50 ins / 98 x 128 cm) ITL 72,000,000.

SCHUPPEN, Jacques van
French, 19th century.
Born 8 September 1825, in Paris.
Painter. History painting.
A pupil of Gleyre, he entered the École des Beaux-Arts on 5 April 1843. His first Salon exhibition was in 1850; he won a third-class medal in 1851, and a second-class medal in 1861.

SCHUPPEN, Pieter Louis van
Flemish School, 17th century.
Born 5 September 1627, in Antwerp; died 7 March 1702, in Paris.
Draughtsman, engraver (burin).
Pieter Louis van Schuppen was a pupil in Antwerp in 1639, and a guild master in the same city in 1651. He married Elisabeth de Mesmaker and moved to Paris shortly afterwards, where he became a pupil of Nanteuil and a member of the Académie Royale in 1663. His accomplished technique earned him the nickname *Petit Nanteuil* (Little Nanteuil). He engraved a large number of portraits, including several after his own drawings: *Philippe de Champagne; Claude Lefebvre;* and *Nanteuil.* 140 works by Van Schuppen, including 17 drawings, are catalogued at the Albertina in Vienna.

In 2001 some of his portraits featured in the exhibition *Painted Ladies. Women at the Court of Charles II* at the National Portrait Gallery in London.

P v S f

BIBLIOGRAPHY:
MacLeod, Catharine/Marciari Alexander, Julia/Sharpe, Kevin/Dethloff, Diana/Wynne, Sonya, *Painted Ladies. Women at the Court of Charles II,* exhibition catalogue, National Portrait Gall., London, 2001.

MUSEUMS AND GALLERIES:
LONDON (National Portrait Gal.): *Margaret Cavendish, Duchess of Newcastle* (c. 1655-1658, engraving, after Abraham van Diepenbeeck).

SCHUPPIUS, Gustav
German, 18th century.
Born c. 1722; died 1759.
Sculptor.
Schuppius was a court sculptor in Plön at the time of Friedrich Karl.

SCHUPPLI, Adèle
Maiden name: Gindrez
Swiss, 19th century.
Born 8 July 1831, in Montet; died 22 March 1899, in Bern.
Painter. Flowers.

SCHUPPNER-HAMM, Robert
German, 20th century.
Born 26 January 1896, in Hamm.
Painter. Portraits, landscapes.
Robert Schuppner-Hamm was self-taught. He travelled extensively in France, Italy and Spain before settling down to work in Berlin and Hamburg. An artist identified only as 'Schüppner' exhibited abstract compositions at the Salon des Réalités Nouvelles in Paris in 1952, 1953 and 1955.

MUSEUMS AND GALLERIES:
MULHOUSE (MBA): *Young Girl Seated.*

AUCTION RECORDS:
PARIS, 7 May 1943, *Painter,* FRF 1,000; *Seaside Landscape,* FRF 1,400. PARIS, 5 Oct 2004, *Untitled* (oil on canvas, 26 x 20 ins / 65 x 50 cm) EUR 2,100. PARIS, 5 Oct 2004, *Magnetic Reflection* (oil on canvas, 26 x 21 ins / 65 x 54 cm) EUR 4,100.

SCHURAVLEF, Thyrsus Sergejvitch.
See **JURAVLEV Firs Sergeevich**

SCHÜRCH, Johann Robert
Swiss, 20th century.
Born 1895, in Aarau; died 1941, in Ascona.
Painter, watercolourist, draughtsman. Figures, scenes with figures, landscapes.

Johann Robert Schürch is credited with numerous wash compositions, frequently depicting circus scenes.

MUSEUMS AND GALLERIES:

AARAU (Aargauer Kunsthaus): *Clown* (1921); *Harlequin* (1924); *Salome* (1925); *Portrait of a Woman* (1925); *Couple* (c. 1925).

AUCTION RECORDS:

BERN, 22 Oct 1976, *Bathers* (oil on canvas, 32 x 25 1/2 ins / 81 x 65 cm) CHF 1,800. ZURICH, 20 May 1977, *Alpine Landscape with the Eiger, Mönch and Jungfrau* (1933, oil on canvas, 12 1/2 x 15 1/2 ins / 32 x 39.5 cm) CHF 6,000. ZURICH, 21 May 1977, *Old Woman* (watercolour and pen, 12 3/4 x 9 ins / 32.7 x 22.7 cm) CHF 3,200. BERN, 25 Oct 1979, *Landscape in the Valais* (1930, oil on canvas, 30 x 37 3/4 ins / 76 x 96 cm) CHF 2,200. ZURICH, 16 May 1981, *Absinthe* (pencil, 16 3/4 x 11 1/4 ins / 42.5 x 28.5 cm) CHF 4,000. ZURICH, 30 Oct 1982, *Portrait of Ferdinand Hodler* (1917, oil on panel, 17 x 12 1/2 ins / 43 x 32 cm) CHF 5,000. BERN, 22 Oct 1983, *View of Lugano* (oil on canvas, 15 x 22 ins / 38 x 55 cm) CHF 3,800. BERN, 27 Oct 1984, *Landscape in the Ticino* (oil on canvas, 22 x 18 ins / 55 x 46 cm) CHF 5,500. ZURICH, 10 Nov 1984, *Woman Doing her Hair* (Indian ink wash, 11 x 8 1/4 ins / 27 x 21 cm) CHF 3,400. ZURICH, 1 Dec 1984, *Self-portrait with Pipe* (1930, gouache, 11 x 8 1/4 ins / 27 x 21 cm) CHF 3,500. ZURICH, 8 June 1985, *Two Young Women* (1928, Indian ink wash, 10 1/2 x 8 1/4 ins / 26.5 x 20.7 cm) CHF 3,600. BERN, 26 Oct 1988, *Tree in Blossom* (oil on canvas, 14 1/4 x 18 ins / 36 x 46 cm) CHF 3,100. BERN, 12 May 1990, *View of Salève* (oil on card, 15 x 20 ins / 37.2 x 51 cm) CHF 1,400. ZURICH, 29 April 1992, *Three Women* (ink and wash, 8 1/4 x 11 ins / 21 x 27 cm) CHF 4,200. ZURICH, 4 June 1992, *At the Circus* (1927, ink/paper, 11 x 8 1/4 ins / 27 x 21 cm) CHF 2,938. ZURICH, 9 June 1993, *Circus Performer* (ink/paper, 11 x 8 1/4 ins / 27 x 21 cm) CHF 3,680. ZURICH, 24 June 1993, *Bather* (wash, 10 1/4 x 8 1/4 ins / 26 x 21 cm) CHF 3,200. LUCERNE, 20 Nov 1993, *Ticino Woman with a Child* (oil on reinforced canvas, 12 1/4 x 9 ins / 31 x 23 cm) CHF 2,000. ZURICH, 24 Nov 1993, *Model* (1927, ink/paper, 11 x 8 1/4 ins / 27 x 21 cm) CHF 3,450. ZURICH, 13 Oct 1994, *By the Deathbed* (ink and wash, 7 3/4 x 10 ins / 19.5 x 25.5 cm) CHF 2,000. ZURICH, 8 Dec 1994, *Black Cat* (1930, ink/paper, after Edgar Allan Poe, 8 1/4 x 11 ins / 21 x 27 cm) CHF 4,025. ZURICH, 7 April 1995, *España* (1938, ink wash, 11 1/2 x 8 ins / 29 x 20.5 cm) CHF 1,900. ZURICH, 3 April 1996, *Mother and Child* (oil on canvas, 24 1/2 x 18 ins / 62.5 x 45.8 cm) CHF 3,400. LUCERNE, 23 Nov 1996, *Adam and Eve* (pen with watercolour/paper, 17 3/4 x 13 ins / 45 x 33 cm) CHF 4,000. ZURICH, 23 March 1999, *By the Road* (ink, 11 x 8 ins / 27 x 21 cm) CHF 2,800. ZURICH, 23 March 1999, *Unemployed Man and Family* (1929, pencil, 19 x 14 ins / 48 x 35 cm) CHF 3,000. BERN, 12 May 2000, *Morcote, Lake Lugano* (oil on canvas, 15 x 22 ins / 38 x 55 cm) CHF 2,700. ZURICH, 7 Dec 2000, *Zarathustra* (1920, oil on canvas, 24 x 20 ins / 61 x 50 cm) CHF 15,000. ZURICH, 19 June 2001, *Man with Horse* (Indian ink and watercolour, 13 x 19 ins / 33 x 48 cm) CHF 5,000. BERN, 9 Nov 2001, *Portrait of a Bearded Man with Glasses and Hat* (watercolour and gouache, 20 x 15 ins / 50 x 38 cm) CHF 2,900. LUCERNE, 1 June 2002, *Couple with Child* (Indian ink, brush and watercolour, 8 x 10 ins / 21 x 26 cm) CHF 2,400. ZURICH, 25 Nov 2002, *Standing Female Nude* (oil on panel, 19 x 8 ins / 49 x 20 cm) CHF 2,800. ZURICH, 25 Nov 2003, *Female Nude* (1940, watercolour over Indian ink, 19 x 12 ins / 47 x 31 cm) CHF 2,300. ZURICH, 9 Dec 2003, *Two Women* (oil on board, 21 x 16 ins / 54 x 41 cm) CHF 11,000. ZURICH, 29 Nov 2004, *Lovers* (ink and watercolour, 11 x 8 ins / 27 x 21 cm) CHF 3,000. ZURICH, 29 Nov 2004, *Man Playing an Accordion* (ink and watercolour, 11 x 8 ins / 27 x 21 cm) CHF 3,000.

SCHURCH, Paul
Swiss, 20th century.
Born 14 February 1886, in Wangen, near Otten; died 1939.
Active in Ascona.
Painter, illustrator.

Paul Schurch studied at the fine arts academies of Karlsruhe and Munich, then at the Académie Colarossi in Paris.

AUCTION RECORDS:

BERN, 6 May 1983, *Mountain Landscape of San Bernardino* (1933, oil on canvas, 22 x 23 1/4 ins / 55 x 59 cm) CHF 4,300. LUCERNE, 14 Nov 2001, *Peaceful Corner* (1914, oil on canvas, 26 x 21 ins / 66 x 53 cm) CHF 2,600. BERN, 1 May 2002, *Mountain Landscape in Evening Sun* (oil on canvas, 19 x 24 ins / 48 x 61 cm) CHF 4,600. ZOFINGEN, 4 June 2004, *San Bernardino* (oil on canvas, 16 x 24 ins / 40 x 60 cm) CHF 2,300.

SCHURDA, Antalou Anton von
German, 19th - 20th century.
Born 1854, in Kesmark.
Painter. Landscapes.

SCHURDER, Henri
French, 20th century.
Born in Morocco.
Painter. Animals, still-lifes.
Groupe Art-Cloche.

Schurder lived and worked in Paris from 1976. He was a member of Art Cloche, an informal, anti-establishment group that was founded in 1981 in the name of Dada and Fluxus, and squatted in a building in Rue d'Arcueil in Paris. He participated in the group's exhibitions from 1981 to 1988.

BIBLIOGRAPHY:

Art cloche. Élément pour une rétrospective. Squatt artistique, auction catalogue, Maître Pierre Cornette de Saint-Cyr, Paris, 30 January 1989.

AUCTION RECORDS:

PARIS, 30 Jan 1989, *White Bird* (oil on canvas, 31 1/2 x 53 1/4 ins / 80 x 135 cm) FRF 3,100. PARIS, 21 Sept 1989, *Still-life* (1989, oil on panel, 31 1/2 x 41 3/4 ins / 80 x 106 cm) FRF 4,000. CALAIS, 8 July 1990, *Still-life* (1989, mixed media/panel, 27 1/2 x 30 ins / 70 x 76 cm) FRF 8,000.

SCHÜRER, Johann Christoph
German, 17th century.
Active in Dresden.
Painter.

SCHÜRER, Paul
German, 16th - 17th century.
Died probably in 1609.
Painter.

Paul Schürer was probably the father of Johann Christoph. He painted many portraits.

SCHÜRER, Wolfgang
German, 16th century.
Painter.

SCHURFRIED, Jakob. See **SCHUFRIED Jakob**

SCHURICHT
Austrian, 18th century.
Active in Vienna c. 1710.
Enameller.

SCHURICHT, Christian Friedrich
German, 18th - 19th century.
Born 5 March 1753, in Dresden; died 2 September 1832, in Dresden.
Draughtsman, architect.

Christian Schuricht was the pupil of Krubsacuis and attended the academy in Dresden in 1777.

SCHURIG, Felix
German, 19th - 20th century.
Born 14 February 1852, in Dresden; died at the end of July 1907, in Iowa City, USA.
Active in the USA from 1901.
Painter. Portraits, genre scenes.
Felix Schurig studied under his father Karl Wilhelm Schurig and Ferdinand W. Pauwels. Examples of his work were exhibited by the Royal Scottish Academy in 1880.
AUCTION RECORDS:
LONDON, 23 Feb 1977, *Clandestine Affair* (1876, oil on canvas, 30 1/4 x 24 1/2 ins / 77 x 62 cm) GBP 600.

SCHURIG, Karl Wilhelm
German, 19th century.
Born 17 December 1818, in Leipzig; died 10 March 1874, in Dresden.
Painter, illustrator. History painting.
After studying in Leipzig and Dresden with Bendemann, Schurig continued his artistic education in Italy. He executed a number of drawings after old masters and taught at the academy in Dresden in 1857.
MUSEUMS AND GALLERIES:
DRESDEN (Gemäldegal. Neue Meister): *Scene from the Persecution of the Jews in Spire*.
AUCTION RECORDS:
COPENHAGEN, 9 Nov 1983, *Rustic Scene* (1847, oil on canvas, 17 3/4 x 33 1/2 ins / 45 x 85 cm) DKK 14,000.

SCHURIKOV, Fedor
Russian, 19th century.
Active during the first half of the 19th century.
Painter.
Fedor Schurikov studied at the St Petersburg academy.

SCHURITZ, J. C.
German, 18th century.
Cabinet maker.

SCHURMAN, Anna Maria van
German, 17th century.
Born 5 November 1607, in Cologne; died 4 May 1678, in Wiewerd.
Painter, engraver. Portraits.
The daughter of Netherlandish parents who had emigrated following religious persecution, Anna Maria van Schurman was attracted to the arts and sciences from an early age. She came with her parents to Utrecht in 1615, and in 1620 to Franeker. On the death of her parents she returned to Utrecht, refused to marry the poet Cats, and in 1653 returned to Cologne, later transferring to Middelburg. Through her brother she came into close contact with the Pietist, Johann de Labadie, in 1661, summoning him to Middelburg in 1666 and marrying him in secret. She accompanied him to Altona when he had to emigrate. On his death in 1674 she settled in Wiewarden in southern Friesland. A painter and sculptress, her talents extended to poetry, music and languages and she was also acquainted with mathematics and theology. She was one of the first supporters of the emancipation of women. Her works were signed *A.S.* and sometimes *A.M.S.*
MUSEUMS AND GALLERIES:
FRANEKER: 21 painted or engraved portraits - UTRECHT: *Portrait of Voetius, M. Schotanus and C. Dematius.*

SCHURMAN, Jan. See **SCHOORMAN**

SCHÜRMAN, Johan
German, 17th century.
Active in Bremen.
Engraver. Portraits.
MUSEUMS AND GALLERIES:
BREMEN (Focke-Mus.): *The Flight into Egypt* (miniature).

SCHURMAN, John, or Schoerman
German, 17th century.
Born in Emden.
Sculptor. Statues, monuments.
In 1638 and 1654 John Schurman was active in England where he sculpted the tomb of Sir Simon Baskerville in St Paul's Cathedral in London for Nicholas Stone. He also carried out two statues of herdsmen for Sir John Danvers in Chelsea, London, a *Sphinx*, a *Hercules* and an *Antaeus*. His works probably came from the workshop of Nicholas Stone.

SCHURMANN
French, 20th - 21st century.
Born 1950, in Paris.
Draughtsman, engraver.
Schurmann lives and works in La Roche-Guyon. Examples of his work featured in *De Bonnard à Baselitz - Dix Ans d'enrichissements du cabinet des estampes 1978-1988* (*From Bonnard to Baselitz: A Decade of Acquisitions by the Prints Collection 1978-1988*), an exhibition held in 1993 at the Bibliothèque Nationale in Paris.
MUSEUMS AND GALLERIES:
PARIS (BNF): *Star-Flowers* (1981, dry-point and mezzotint).

SCHURMANN, Friedrich
German, 19th century.
Born 26 December 1840, in Dorstfeld, near Dortmund.
Active in Marburg.
Watercolourist, lithographer.

SCHURMANN, Fritz, or Schuremann
German, 19th - 20th century.
Born 27 February 1863, in Düsseldorf.
Active in Düsseldorf.
Painter. Scenes with figures.
Fritz Schurmann was a pupil of Carl F. Deiker. He specialised in hunting scenes.
AUCTION RECORDS:
AMSTERDAM, 5 June 1990, *Stag near a Stream in Autumn* (1920, oil on card, 19 x 24 1/2 ins / 48 x 62 cm) NLG 1,150.

SCHURMANN, Hans
Swiss, 17th century.
Sculptor.
Hans Schurmann was a member of the Brotherhood of St Luke in Lucerne.

SCHURR, Claude
French, 20th century.
Born 1921, in Paris.
Painter, watercolourist, illustrator. Scenes with figures, portraits, nudes, interiors, landscapes, urban landscapes, seascapes, harbour scenes, still-lifes.
Murals, designs for tapestries, designs for mosaics.
Schurr studied at the École des Beaux-Arts in Paris from 1938 to 1942. He was awarded a scholarship for the Casa Velázquez in 1949. He travelled in Europe. He has taught at the Académie Ranson and the École des Arts et Métiers in Paris. He was awarded the Prix Antral in 1948 and the Grand Prix National des Arts in 1950.

Above all a landscape, seascape and still-life painter, he sometimes painted compositions with figures and portraits. His facet compositions bring him close to the Post-Cubist movement. His range of light, fresh tones denote his preference for the light in Brittany and the coasts of northern France. His numerous wall decorations adorn the Harcourt studios in Paris, the psychiatric hospital in Ville-Evard, the Science Faculty of Nice, the liners Clément Ader, Raymond Poincarré and Foch. He has also realised lithographs and illustrated books, including *La Grand'route* de Blaise Cendrars (1952); *L'Ensorcelée* (*The Bewitched*) by Barbey d'Aurevilly (1955), *Les Philippes* by Jules Renard (1958); *Le Petit Ami* by Paul Léautaud (1960); *Moderato Cantabile* by Marguerite Duras (1964); *Regain* by Jean Giono (1965); *Viper in the Fist* by Hervé Bazin (1965) and *Hélène* by Robert Marteau (1973).

Schurr has taken part in the various Salons in Paris: Salon des Moins de Trente Ans in 1941; the Salon d'Automne, where he has been a member, from 1942; Salon des Indépendants, Salon des Tuileries, Salon de la Société Nationale des Beaux-Arts, Salon Comparaisons, Salon du Dessin et de la Peinture à l'Eau, and, from 1955, the Salon des Peintres Témoins de Leur Temps. He also participated in numerous group exhibitions in the rest of France and abroad: in 1961 at the Palais de la Méditerranée in Nice, the museums of Tours and Nancy, the São Paulo Biennale and the Menton Biennale. He regularly exhibited his work in solo shows in Paris from 1946, and has also exhibited in the USA since 1946, then in Belgium and Switzerland.

CLAUDE SCHURR

BIBLIOGRAPHY:
Harambourg, Lydia, *L'École de Paris 1945-1965. Dictionnaire des peintres*, Ides et Calendes, Neuchâtel, 1993.
MUSEUMS AND GALLERIES:
PARIS (MAMVP) - PARIS (MNAM-CCI).
AUCTION RECORDS:
MARSEILLES, 6 Dec 1980, *15 August Procession in St-Guénolé* (oil on canvas, 28 3/4 x 39 1/4 ins / 73 x 100 cm) FRF 7,500. MEGÈVE, 16 July 1983, *Caquetage à la Herra-Dura* (*Prattling at Herra-Dura*) (oil on canvas, 32 x 39 1/4 ins / 81 x 100 cm) FRF 13,000. PARIS, 20 June 1988, *Port in Brittany* (oil on canvas, 31 1/2 x 39 1/4 ins / 80 x 100 cm) FRF 9,000. PARIS, 29 Nov 1989, *Juan-les-Pins* (oil on canvas, 22 x 29 1/2 ins / 56 x 75 cm) FRF 12,000. PARIS, 25 June 1990, *Seascape* (oil on canvas, 25 1/2 x 36 1/4 ins / 65 x 92 cm) FRF 7,600. PARIS, 18 July 1990, *Pensive Boat* (oil on canvas, 35 1/2 x 28 3/4 ins / 90 x 73 cm) FRF 9,000. FONTAINEBLEAU, 18 Nov 1990, *The Flower Market in Nice's Old Town* (oil on canvas, 23 1/2 x 28 3/4 ins / 60 x 73 cm) FRF 22,500. NEUILLY, 20 May 1992, *Prélassement* (*Lounging*) (oil on canvas, 51 1/4 x 38 1/4 ins / 130 x 97 cm) FRF 23,000. LE TOUQUET, 8 June 1992, *Bay of Porquerolles* (oil on canvas, 28 3/4 x 36 1/2 ins / 73 x 93 cm) FRF 20,000. LE TOUQUET, 30 May 1993, *Le Pardon de saint Guénolé* (*The Pardon of St Guénolé*) (oil on canvas, 32 x 39 1/4 ins / 81 x 100 cm) FRF 17,000. NEUILLY, 19 March 1994, *The Flower Market in Cannes* (oil on canvas, 24 x 19 3/4 ins / 61 x 50 cm) FRF 11,000. LOKEREN, 10 Dec 1994, *Winter Morning in Cannes* (oil on canvas, 36 1/4 x 28 3/4 ins / 92 x 73 cm) BEF 140,000. PARIS, 26 March 1995, *Female Confidences* (oil on canvas, 35 x 46 ins / 89 x 116 cm) FRF 8,000. CALAIS, 15 Dec 1996, *Venice, the Rialto* (oil on canvas, 13 x 18 ins / 33 x 46 cm) FRF 13,800. PARIS, 22 March 1998, *The Cliffs of Yport* (1967, oil on canvas, 45 x 63 3/4 ins / 114 x 162 cm) FRF 4,800. LILLE, 27 Oct 2001, *Red Regattas in Cannes* (oil on canvas, 18 x 22 ins / 46 x 55 cm) FRF 11,000. CALAIS, 9 Dec 2001, *Douarnenez Port* (oil on canvas, 24 x 32 ins / 60 x 81 cm) FRF 14,000. CALAIS, 19 May 2002, *Ambiance rouge au suquet* (oil on canvas, 32 x 39 ins / 81 x 100 cm) EUR 1,800. CALAIS, 16 March 2003, *Sailingboats at Audierne* (oil on canvas, 39 x 32 ins / 100 x 81 cm) EUR 2,000. NEW YORK, 25 Feb 2004, *Port at Nice* (oil on canvas, 39 x 32 ins / 100 x 81 cm) USD 5,500.

SCHURRIUS, Georg Wilhelm, the Elder. See **SCHORIGUS**

SCHÜRSTAB, Hans, or Schurstab
German, 15th century.
Died before 20 December 1494.
Active in Nuremberg.
Painter. Maps.

SCHÜRSTAB, Leonhart, the Younger, or Schurstab
German, 16th century.
Active in Nuremberg 1516-1527.
Painter.
Nuremberg School.

Leonhart Schürstab the Younger was the son of Leonhart Schürstab the Elder.

SCHÜRSTAB, Leonhart or Lienhart, the Elder, or Schurstab
German, 16th century.
Died before 14 September 1519.
Active in Nuremberg.
Painter.

Leonhart Schürstab the Elder was the brother of Hans Schürstab.

SCHURTENBERGER, Ernst
Swiss, 20th century.
Born 1931.
Painter. Figures, portraits.

AUCTION RECORDS:
LUCERNE, 26 Nov 1994, *Standing Female Figure* (1964, oil on canvas, 15 x 11 3/4 ins / 38 x 30 cm) CHF 1,000. LUCERNE, 20 May 1995, *Portrait* (1978, oil on canvas, 15 3/4 x 11 3/4 ins / 40 x 30 cm) CHF 1,500. LUCERNE, 5 June 1999, *Untitled* (1988, oil on canvas, 29 x 34 ins / 73 x 86 cm) CHF 2,800. LUCERNE, 1 June 2002, *Still-life* (1962, oil on canvas, 21 x 26 ins / 54 x 65 cm) CHF 2,500.

SCHURTH, Ernst
German, 19th century.
Born 1 May 1848, in Neustadt (Black Forest); died 11 July 1910, in Karlsruhe.
Painter.

Schurth studied in Nuremberg, Munich, Dresden, Vienna and Karlsruhe with Ferdinand Keller. From 1885 he taught at the art academy in Karlsruhe and contributed to the decoration of the Technische Universität there.

SCHURTZ, Cornelius Nicholas
German, 17th century.
Active in Nuremberg c. 1670-1689.
Engraver (burin), draughtsman.

Schurtz engraved portraits of famous physicians and small emblematic subjects. He signed his works *C.N.S.*

SCHURYGIN, Arsseniz Nikolaievitch. See **CHURYGIN Arsenii Nicolaievich**

SCHÜRZFÜRGEN. See **RATGEB Jerg**

SCHÜRZJÜRGEN. See **RATGEB Jerg**

SCHUSCHARDT, Christian
German, 19th century.
Died 1870, in Weimar.
Painter.

Schuschardt was director of the drawing school in Weimar.

SCHUSEIL, Friedrich Hermann
German, 19th century.
Born 1822.
Engraver (wood).

Schuseil was the pupil of F. W. Gubitz.

SCHUSSEL, Gottlob
German, 20th century.
Born 24 March 1892, in Segringen.
Active in Kempten.
Painter, engraver.

SCHUSSELE, Christian, or Schuessle, Schuessele
French, 19th century.
Born c. 1824, in Alsace; died 21 August 1879, in Merchantville (New Jersey), USA.
Painter. History painting, portraits.

He studied with Yvon in Paris. In 1847 he went to live in the USA.

MUSEUMS AND GALLERIES:

MINNEAPOLIS: *General Jackson before Judge Hall.*

AUCTION RECORDS:

NEW YORK, 14 Dec 1933, *Metty Reading the Scriptures to the Indians,* USD 600. BOLTON, 17 July 1980, *Washington Irving and His Literary Friends* (oil on canvas, 52 x 78 1/4 ins / 132 x 198.5 cm) USD 18,000. PORTLAND, 4 April 1981, *The New Percussionist* (ink wash, 7 1/4 x 11 ins / 18.5 x 27 cm) USD 1,200. NEW YORK, 23 April 1981, *The Father's Return* (1853, oil on canvas, 36 x 29 ins / 91.5 x 73.6 cm) USD 7,000. NEW YORK, 22 June 1984, *King Solomon and the Iron Worker* (1863, oil on canvas, 46 1/4 x 62 1/4 ins / 117.7 x 158.1 cm) USD 6,000. NEW YORK, 22 May 1996, *Little Boys Playing Soldiers* (1853, oil on canvas, 36 x 29 ins / 91.4 x 73.7 cm) USD 10,350.

SCHUSSER, Josef
Czech, 19th - 20th century.
Born 10 March 1864.
Painter.

Josef Schusser studied from 1893 to 1897 at the Prague academy with Voytech Hynais, and then in Munich. He was professor at the fine arts school in Prague from 1903 onwards.

MUSEUMS AND GALLERIES:

PRAGUE (Národní Gal.): *May Evening; Woman with Red Parasol.*

SCHÜSSLER
German, 18th century.
Sculptor.

Schüssler worked on the high altar of the church in Mönchberg.

SCHÜSSLER, Alfred von, or Ludwig Hermann Alfred
German, 19th century.
Born 7 April 1820; died 22 November 1849, in Rome.
Painter. History painting, architectural views.

Schüssler entered the academy in Dresden in September 1835, and between 1840 and 1848 was taught by Ed. Bendemann. From 1843 he worked in Rome, and from 1840 to 1848 exhibited in Dresden.

SCHUSSLER, Heinrich
German, 16th century.
Active in Neustadt or Eibelstadt.
Sculptor (wood).

SCHUSTER
German, 18th century.
Painter.

Schuster was court painter at Weimar around 1734 and painted frescoes in the Schloss Belvedere in Weimar.

SCHUSTER, Adam
German, 18th century.
Painter (glazed earthenware).

Adam Schuster worked at the porcelain factory in Nuremberg around 1719.

SCHUSTER, Anton
German, 19th century.
Born c. 1785, in Mindelheim.
Sculptor.

Anton Schuster was active in Mindelheim and Landsberg.

SCHUSTER, Arnold
German, 19th century.
Born c. 1810, in Mönchsroth, near Dinkelsbühl.
Painter, lithographer.

Arnold Schuster was a pupil at the academy in Munich.

SCHUSTER, Berthe
French, 20th century.
Painter.

Schuster took part in the Salon des Tuileries in Paris.

SCHUSTER, Dominicus
Austrian, 18th century.
Active in Leoben.
Painter.

SCHUSTER, Donna N.
American, 20th century.
Born 1883; died 1953.
Painter.

Donna Schuster studied under Edmond C. Tarbell and William M. Chase. She was a member of the Society of Independent Artists, and received many awards.

AUCTION RECORDS:

LOS ANGELES, 15 Oct 1979, *In the Garden* (oil on canvas, 35 x 35 ins / 89 x 89 cm) USD 3,100. LOS ANGELES-SAN FRANCISCO, 7 Feb 1990, *Village on the Hill* (oil on canvas, 8 1/4 x 11 ins / 21 x 27 cm) USD 8,800. LOS ANGELES-SAN FRANCISCO, 10 Oct 1990, *Fetching Water from the Well* (oil on canvas, 20 x 24 ins / 51 x 61 cm) USD 4,950. PASADENA, 19 Oct 1999, *Still-life of Bouquet of Flowers in Decorated Vase* (oil on canvas, 20 x 26 ins / 51 x 66 cm) USD 2,750. LOS ANGELES, 9 Dec 1999, *Lady with Pekingese* (oil on canvas, 34 x 35 ins / 86 x 88 cm) USD 7,000. SAN FRANCISCO, 14 June 2000, *The Breakfast Table* (oil on canvas, 25 x 30 ins / 63 x 76 cm) USD 16,000. PASADENA, 13 Feb 2001, *Landscape, Yosemite Falls* (oil on canvas on masonite, 24 x 18 ins / 61 x 46 cm) USD 2,500. MILFORD, 25 Oct 2001, *Path to a House* (oil on canvas, 17 x 17 ins / 43 x 43 cm) USD 9,500. PASADENA, 18 Feb 2003, *Canal in Venice* (oil on board, 9 x 7 ins / 23 x 18 cm) USD 5,500. PASADENA, 18 Nov 2003, *Mending Nets, probably Terminal Island, Wilmington, CA* (watercolour, 15 x 21 ins / 38 x 53 cm) USD 5,000. PASADENA, 15 June 2004, *Golden Hills, California* (oil on board, 12 x 16 ins / 30 x 41 cm) USD 12,000.

SCHUSTER, Franz
Austrian, 18th century.
Active in Vienna.
Sculptor.

SCHUSTER, Franz, or Ferenc
Austrian, 19th - 20th century.
Born 24 December 1870, in Weisskirchen, Hungary; died 14 June 1903, in Vienna.
Engraver.

Franz Schuster studied at the fine arts academy in Vienna and is noted for two series of engravings entitled *Mother* and *Saviour.*

SCHUSTER, Georg Kurt Rudolf
German, 19th - 20th century.
Born 1 February 1866, in Bockwa, near Zwickau.
Active in Leipzig.
Painter, engraver.

Georg Kurt Rudolf Schuster was a pupil of Fritjof Smith.

SCHUSTER, Hans
Bohemian School, 18th century.
Sculptor.

SCHUSTER, J. F.
German, 18th century.
Active in Berlin.
Engraver (burin).

J. F. Schuster engraved views of Potsdam.

SCHUSTER, Johann
German, 17th - 18th century.
Born probably in 1666, in Schleiz; died 10 December 1724, in Coburg.
Painter.
Johann Schuster was at the Saxon court.

SCHUSTER, Johann Martin
German, 17th - 18th century.
Born c. 1667, in Nuremberg; died 1738, in Nuremberg.
Painter.
The pupil of his uncle Johann Murrer, Johann Martin Schuster studied in Venice between 1690 and 1693, and in Rome between 1693 and 1703. After a three-year period in Vienna, he settled in Nuremberg where he was appointed director of the painting academy.
MUSEUMS AND GALLERIES:
NUREMBERG (Germanisches Nationalmus.): *Portrait of Maria von Bernern.*

SCHUSTER, Josef
Austrian, 19th century.
Born 17 June 1812, in Graz; died 15 March 1890, in Vienna.
Painter. Portraits, still-lifes (flowers/fruit).
Josef Schuster was the pupil of Mossmer, Wegmayer and Franz Petter at the academy in Vienna.
MUSEUMS AND GALLERIES:
VIENNA: *Flora of the Alps.*
AUCTION RECORDS:
VIENNA, 22 March 1966, *Flowers of the Alps,* ATS 38,000. NEW YORK, 25 April 1968, *Still-life,* USD 1,400. NEW YORK, 24 Feb 1971, *Still-life with Flowers and Fruits,* USD 3,100. VIENNA, 20 March 1973, *Alpine Flowers,* ATS 100,000. LONDON, 20 July 1977, *Alpine Flowers* (1869, oil on panel, 12 x 9½ ins / 30.5 x 24 cm) GBP 900. COLOGNE, 1 June 1978, *Still-life with Flowers* (1849, oil on panel, 13¾ x 12¼ ins / 35 x 31 cm) DEM 12,000. VIENNA, 15 May 1979, *Still-life with Flowers* (1874, oil on canvas, 19¾ x 31 ins / 50 x 79 cm) ATS 35,000. VIENNA, 19 May 1981, *Roses and Birds* (1874, oil on canvas, 19¾ x 31 ins / 50 x 79 cm) ATS 80,000. VIENNA, 22 June 1983, *Calvary with Alpine Flowers* (1873, oil on canvas, 26¾ x 22 ins / 68 x 56 cm) ATS 25,000. VIENNA, 20 March 1985, *Flowers of the Alps* (oil on panel, 13 x 10¼ ins / 33 x 26 cm) ATS 70,000. VIENNA, 23 Feb 1989, *Albino Peacock* (1838, oil on canvas, 22¼ x 17¾ ins / 56.5 x 45 cm) ATS 154,000. LONDON, 28 Nov 1990, *Still-life of Roses and Carnations in Castle Park in Bohemia* (1868, oil on canvas, 26 x 20½ ins / 66 x 52 cm) GBP 6,050. LONDON, 16 March 1994, *Still-life with Pitcher of Wine* (1847, oil on canvas, 9¼ x 12½ ins / 23.5 x 32 cm) GBP 4,370. LONDON, 22 Feb 1995, *Portrait of Lady with Parasol* (oil on canvas, 21¼ x 16¼ ins / 54 x 41 cm) GBP 862. LONDON, 9 Oct 1997, *Still-life with Tea Service; Supper of Herring* (oil on panel, a pair, each, 5 x 4 ins / 13 x 10 cm) GBP 1,495. VIENNA, 5 Oct 1999, *Still-life of Alpine Flowers* (oil on panel, 8 x 6 ins / 20 x 15 cm) ATS 45,000. NEW YORK, 1 Nov 1999, *Cockatoo, Grapes, Figs, Plums, Peach on Marble Ledge* (1851, oil on canvas, 25 x 31 ins / 63 x 79 cm) USD 26,000. VIENNA, 30 Oct 2001, *Still-life with Grapes, Peaches and Tankard* (1844, oil on panel, 20 x 16 ins / 50 x 40 cm) ATS 38,000. VIENNA, 29 Nov 2001, *Alpine Flowers* (oil on panel, 6 x 5 ins / 16 x 13 cm) ATS 35,000. PORTLAND, 31 July 2002, *Mountain Wildflowers* (oil on board, 19 x 15 ins / 48 x 39 cm) USD 2,500. ZURICH, 23 June 2003, *Still-life with Flowers and Ivy* (1848, oil on panel, 17 x 13 ins / 42 x 34 cm) CHF 6,000. ZURICH, 23 June 2003, *Still-life with White Grapes and Tankard* (1848, oil on panel, 17 x 13 ins / 42 x 34 cm) CHF 6,000.

SCHUSTER, Joseph
German, 18th century.
Active in Neustadt.
Painter.

SCHUSTER, Karl Friedrich H.
German, 19th - 20th century.
Born 30 January 1854, in Freiburg im Breisgau; died 2 August 1925.
Painter. Landscapes.
Karl Friedrich H. Schuster was a pupil of Gustav Schönleber.

CARL SCHVSTER

MUSEUMS AND GALLERIES:
FREIBURG IM BREISGAU.

SCHUSTER, Karl Maria
Austrian, 19th - 20th century.
Born 13 September 1871, in Purkersdorf; died 1953.
Active in Vienna.
Painter, illustrator.
Karl Maria Schuster was a pupil of Julius Berger, Leopold K. Müller, Josef M. Trenkwald and Siegmund L'Allemand.
AUCTION RECORDS:
MUNICH, 31 May 1979, *Interior with a Young Woman at her Embroidery* (oil on panel, 17¾ x 15 ins / 45 x 38 cm) DEM 2,000. LONDON, 18 June 1986, *Young Girl Gathering Peonies* (1896, oil on canvas, 61 x 39 ins / 155 x 99 cm) GBP 7,500. NEW YORK, 24 May 1988, *Reading on a Terrace in Capri* (1904, oil on canvas, 35½ x 50½ ins / 90.2 x 128.3 cm) USD 60,500. NEW YORK, 1 March 1990, *New Gloves* (1909, oil on canvas, 39¼ x 30¼ ins / 99.6 x 76.8 cm) USD 8,800. PARIS, 21 March 1990, *Marishka Villa* (1927, oil on canvas, 26 x 33¾ ins / 66 x 86 cm) FRF 40,000. NEW YORK, 22 May 1991, *Breakfast* (1925, oil on canvas, 32 x 25½ ins / 81.3 x 64.8 cm) USD 5,500. VIENNA, 5 Oct 1999, *Arab with Laden Camel* (1900, oil on canvas, 29 x 23 ins / 74 x 58 cm) ATS 28,000. VIENNA, 25 Jan 2000, *Oriental Pictures* (oil on canvas, two, 18 x 13 ins / 46 x 34 cm) ATS 25,000. SAN FRANCISCO, 17 May 2000, *New Melody* (1921, oil on canvas, 30 x 23 ins / 77 x 58 cm) USD 2,750. VIENNA, 6 March 2001, *Lower Austria* (1911, oil on canvas, 15 x 20 ins / 39 x 50 cm) ATS 25,000. LINZ, 27 May 2002, *Flower Garden by Worthersee* (1932, oil on canvas, 24 x 30 ins / 62 x 77 cm) EUR 1,900. VIENNA, 29 April 2003, *On the Verandah in Capri* (1904, oil on canvas, 27 x 21 ins / 69 x 53 cm) EUR 10,000. VIENNA, 29 April 2003, *Rome* (1900, oil on canvas, 16 x 35 ins / 41 x 90 cm) EUR 12,000. SALZBURG, 14 Oct 2004, *Landscape in St Jacob, Defreggental* (1941, oil on canvas, 39 x 31 ins / 100 x 80 cm) EUR 1,500.

SCHUSTER, Ludwig
Austrian, 19th century.
Born 1820, in Vienna.
Still active in 1873.
Painter. Genre scenes, landscapes, flowers.

SCHUSTER, Ludwig Albrecht
German, 19th century.
Born 9 May 1824, in Stolpen; died 14 May 1905, in Dresden.
Painter. Battles.
Ludwig Albrecht Schuster taught at the academy in Dresden.
MUSEUMS AND GALLERIES:
BAUTZEN (Stadtmus.): *Battle near Grossbeeren* - DRESDEN (Gemäldegal. Neue Meister): *At the Battle of Borodino; Saxon Grenadiers at the Battle of Jena.*
AUCTION RECORDS:
COLOGNE, 17 March 1978, *Cavalry Charge* (oil on panel, 7½ x 11 ins / 19 x 27 cm) DEM 2,400.

SCHUSTER, Maximilian
German, 19th century.
Born 10 October 1784; died 10 December 1848, in Oberdettingen.
Sculptor.

The son of Michaël Schuster, Maximilian painted and sculpted cherubins in Swabian churches.

SCHUSTER, Michaël Johann
German, 18th century.
Active in Augsburg.
Sculptor.
Michaël Schuster worked in Oberdettingen.

SCHUSTER, Reinhardt
Romanian, 20th century.
Born 1 September 1936, in Bod.
Active since 1983 in Germany.
Painter.
Reinhardt Schuster was a student at the N. Grigorescu Art Institute in Bucharest in 1964. He then taught at the F. Schiller Cultural Centre in Bucharest, and lived and worked in Düsseldorf from 1983. Schuster's paintings are very structured, built on geometrical forms painted in areas of flat colour which are nevertheless reminiscent of landscapes and architectural views. He puts static and dynamic elements together, plays with the contrasts between colours, and has an interest in movement.

His work has been shown in group exhibitions in Europe and Japan, and there have been solo exhibitions of his work, in Bucharest (regularly from 1967, notably at the F. Schiller Cultural Centre in 1970 and 1981); in Düsseldorf and the Siebenbürgisches Museum in Gundelsheim (1978); in Berlin (1979); at the Romanian Academy in Rome and London (1981); and in Frankfurt am Main (1985).

BIBLIOGRAPHY:
Ionel Jianou, *Romanian Artists and the West,* American Romanian Academy of Arts and Sciences, Los Angeles, 1986.

SCHUSTER, Rudolf Heinrich
German, 19th century.
Born 1 September 1848, in Markneukirchen; died 30 June 1902, in Markneukirchen.
Painter, illustrator. Genre scenes, landscapes, landscapes with figures.
Rudolf Schuster was the pupil of Ludwig Richter at the academy in Dresden. He visited French Switzerland, Harz, Turingen, the Alps of Swabia and Bohemia, and worked in Italy and a number of German towns.

MUSEUMS AND GALLERIES:
CHEMNITZ - DRESDEN - WIESBADEN - WROCLAW: *Winter Landscape on the Elba.*

AUCTION RECORDS:
MUNICH, 19 Sept 1979, *Harvesters' Rest* (1877, oil on canvas, 15 3/4 x 23 1/2 ins / 40 x 60 cm) DEM 18,000. LONDON, 30 Jan 1980, *Grape Harvest Scene* (1881, oil on canvas, 16 1/2 x 26 1/2 ins / 42 x 67 cm) GBP 950. NEW YORK, 30 June 1981, *Promenade in the Hills* (1897, oil on canvas, 15 x 23 1/4 ins / 38 x 59 cm) USD 5,250. AMSTERDAM, 28 Oct 1992, *Summer Landscape with Encampment of Bohemians at foot of Cliff* (1876, oil on canvas, 20 1/4 x 30 3/4 ins / 51.5 x 78 cm) NLG 2,530. NEW YORK, 17 Feb 1994, *Gypsies' Caravan in Rocky Landscape at Twilight* (1876, oil on canvas, 20 1/4 x 30 3/4 ins / 51.5 x 78 cm) USD 2,875.

SCHUSTER, Sigmund
German, 19th century.
Born 1807, in Mönchsroth, near Dinkelsbühl.
Painter. Portraits.
Sigmund Schuster attended the academy in Munich.

SCHUSTER VON BÄRNODE, Robert
Austrian, 19th century.
Born 28 March 1845, in Podgorze (Galicia).
Active in Vienna.
Painter. Genre scenes.
Schuster von Bärnode attended the academy at Vienna with Oengerth.

SCHUSTER WITTEK, Johanna von
Austrian, 20th century.
Born 19 October 1860 or 1863, in Vienna.
Painter, watercolourist. Flowers.
Johanna von Schuster Wittek was a pupil of Emil J. Schindler.

SCHUSTER-SCHÖRGARN, Marie, wife of Sieger
Austrian, 19th - 20th century.
Born 15 April 1869, in Vienna.
Painter. Landscapes.
Marie Schuster-Schörgarn was a pupil of Hugo Darnaut.

MUSEUMS AND GALLERIES:
GRAZ.

SCHUSTER-WEIDENBERG, Johann August
German, 19th - 20th century.
Born 27 September 1858, in Weidenberg.
Painter.
Johann August Schuster-Weidenberg studied between 1882 and 1889 at the fine arts academy in Munich.

SCHUSTER-WOLDAN, Georg
German, 19th - 20th century.
Born 7 December 1864, in Nimptsch, Silesia.
Painter.
Georg Schuster-Woldan was the brother of Raffael Schuster-Woldan. He studied in Stuttgart, Munich (where he subsequently lived and worked) and Frankfurt am Main.

SCHUSTER-WOLDAN, Raffael
German, 19th - 20th century.
Born 7 January 1870, in Striegau.
Painter. History painting, portraits.
Raffael Schuster-Woldan was the brother of Georg Schuster-Woldan. He studied at the fine arts academy in Berlin and went on to live and work in Munich, where he was awarded a medal in 1897. He painted predominantly portraits of society women.

MUSEUMS AND GALLERIES:
GDANSK - GERA - WEIMAR.

SCHUSTLER, Karl
Austrian, 19th century.
Painter. Portraits, genre scenes, landscapes.
Schustler worked in Vienna where he exhibited from 1841 to 1847.

SCHUSTOFF. See **SHUSTOV Afinoghen Loghinovich**

SCHUT, A.
Dutch, 18th century.
Active c. 1713-1733.
Draughtsman, engraver.
A. Schut produced engravings for booksellers.

SCHUT, C. W.
German or Dutch, 17th century.
Active in Dordrecht.
Painter. Seascapes.

MUSEUMS AND GALLERIES:
HAMBURG: *Seascape with Dordrecht in the Background.*

SCHUT, Cornelis I
Flemish School, 17th century.
Born 13 May 1597, in Antwerp; died 29 April 1655, in Antwerp.
Painter, engraver. Religious subjects. Designs for tapestries.
Cornelis Schut I was possibly a pupil of Wenceslas Coeberger and Rubens. He became a guild master in 1618 and a

member of the 'Wallflower' rhetorical society in 1630. He married Catharine Geensins in 1631, and Anastasia Scelliers in 1638. He produced decorative works for the entry of Cardinal Jufant into Ghent in 1635 and an altarpiece for the arquebusiers' guild in 1643. Upon the death of Rubens, he became one of Antwerp's most celebrated painters. Schut collaborated with Daniel Seghers, J. Wildens and V. Nieffs. His pupils were H. Brant in 1634, J. Havick in 1636, J. B. and Adam Kerckhoven in 1641, P. Verbeeck in 1642, Jan Popels, J. Witdoeck and J. Vinck.

In 2000 his work featured in *Dans la Lumière de Rubens: Peintres Baroques des Pays-Bas du Sud (In the Light of Rubens. Baroque Painters of the Southern Netherlands)* at the Musée des Beaux-Arts in Valenciennes, an exhibition highlighting the work of less well-known Flemish Baroque artists, so often eclipsed by Rubens, Van Dyck and Jordaens.

BIBLIOGRAPHY:
Wilmers, Gertrude, *Cornelis Schut (1597 - 1655): a Flemish painter of the High Baroque*, Brepols, Turnhout, 1996. Limousin, Isabelle/Ramade, Patrick/Cordier, Gaëlle, *Dans la lumière de Rubens: peintres baroques des Pays-Bas du Sud*, exhibition catalogue, Musée des beaux-arts, Valenciennes, 2000.

MUSEUMS AND GALLERIES:
AMSTERDAM: *Glorification of the Virgin* - ANTWERP: *Portiuncula; Beheading of St George; Purification of the Virgin* - BRUNSWICK: *Festival of Venus* - BRUSSELS: *Martyrdom of St James*; sketch - COLOGNE: *Resurrection* - COPENHAGEN: sketch - GLASGOW: *Holy Family* - LILLE: *Alexander Cutting the Gordian Knot* - MUNICH: *Vulcan at his Forge* - NANTES: *The Child Jesus Surrounded by a Garland of Flowers* (grisaille, in collaboration with D. Seghers) - ROHRAU (Schlossmus., Graf Harrach'sche Familiensammlung): *Garland* - ST PETERSBURG (Hermitage): *Adoration of the Shepherds* - VIENNA: *Temple of Time; Hero and Leander* - VIENNA (Czernin'sche Gemäldegal.): *Holy Family in a Forest.*

AUCTION RECORDS:
AMSTERDAM, 1705, *Europa Taking Leave of the Virgins,* FRF 220. PARIS, 1777, *Jesus Carrying his Cross,* FRF 1,402. PARIS, 1787, *Holy Family with St John,* FRF 599. PARIS, 1843, *St John Sleeping,* FRF 909. PARIS, 1882, a painting, subject unspecified) FRF 1,000. PARIS, 1890, *Holy Family,* FRF 1,400. PARIS, 19 Sept 1892, *Adoration of the Shepherds,* FRF 800. PARIS, 21 Nov 1900, *Holy Family,* FRF 205; *Holy Family* (in collaboration with Seghers) FRF 4,900. NEW YORK, 1 Feb 1911, *Horsemen,* USD 65. LONDON, 5 May 1911, *Holy Family* (in collaboration with J. van Kessel) GBP 45; *The Child Jesus* (in collaboration with D. Seghers) GBP 10. PARIS, 2-3 June 1919, *Banks of the Rhine with Figures,* FRF 370. PARIS, 16 Feb 1923, *St Joachim and the Angel,* FRF 160. PARIS, 13 Oct 1948, *Christ before Pilate* (attributed) FRF 15,000. PARIS, 19 June 1950, *Beheading of St George* (wash) FRF 2,900. PARIS, 4 June 1951, *Plenty* (attributed) FRF 51,000. AMSTERDAM, 18 Nov 1985, *Entombment of Christ* (brush, brown ink and wash heightened with white and pink/outlines in black chalk, 13 x 10 ins / 32.8 x 25.3 cm) NLG 62,000. LONDON, 19 Dec 1985, *Adoration of the Magi* (oil on canvas, 49 1/2 x 69 ins / 126 x 175 cm) GBP 8,300. NEW YORK, 14 Jan 1988, *Virgin and Child* (oil on canvas, 57 1/2 x 76 3/4 ins / 146 x 195 cm) USD 35,200. NEW YORK, 4 April 1990, *Assumption of Mary Magdalene* (oil/copper, 15 x 11 1/2 ins / 38.1 x 29.2 cm) USD 4,180. LONDON, 3 July 1991, *Rape of Europa* (oil on canvas, 64 x 106 ins / 162.5 x 269 cm) GBP 27,500. LONDON, 8 July 1994, *Virgin and Child with St John the Baptist as a Child, St Elizabeth and Angels* (oil on canvas, 66 1/4 x 91 1/2 ins / 168.5 x 232.5 cm) GBP 17,250. LONDON, 9 Dec 1994, *Virgin and Child with St Anne* (oil on canvas, 62 3/4 x 47 1/2 ins / 159.2 x 120.9 cm) GBP 18,400. LYONS, 7 April 1997, *Apotheosis of the Virgin* (oil on canvas, 65 3/4 x 48 ins / 167 x 122 cm) FRF 90,000. LONDON, 2 July 1997, *St Francis and St Catherine Holding a Picture of the Virgin and Child Surrounded by Putti Holding Garlands of Flowers* (c. 1650, oil/copper, in collaboration with Frans Ijkens, 38 1/2 x 31 1/2 ins / 97.8 x 80 cm) GBP 11,500. LONDON, 12 July 2001, *Allegory of Plenty* (oil on panel, 18 x 25 ins / 46 x 64 cm) GBP 8,500. LONDON, 7 July 2004, *Suzanna and the Elders* (oil on canvas, 47 x 42 ins / 119 x 107 cm) GBP 110,000.

SCHUT, Cornelis II
Flemish School, 17th century.
Active in Rome 1624-1627.
Painter.

Cornelis Schut II is possibly identifiable as a painter of the same name, recorded as a guild master in Antwerp around 1628, who died in Rome on 12 October 1636 aged 28.

SCHUT, Cornelis III, or Escut, Scut
Flemish School, 17th century.
Born c. 1629, in Antwerp; died 1685, in Seville.
Painter.
Seville School.

Cornelis Schut III was a pupil of his uncle Cornelis Schut I. He travelled to Seville, where he was co-founder and president (1670-1674) of the academy of painting. The city museum in Seville has his portrait of the Dominican *Domingo de Bruselas*.

SCHUT, Pieter Hendricksz.
Dutch, 17th century.
Born c. 1619; died after 1660, in Amsterdam.
Draughtsman, engraver.

Pieter Hendricksz. Schut was a pupil of Claes Jansz. Visscher in Amsterdam in 1635. His engravings include the following: *Embarkation of Charles II of England at Scheveningen in 1660; Eight Street Plans of Amsterdam; Churches and Monuments of Amsterdam* (8); *Notable Cities of Europe* (24); *Towns and Monuments of Zealand* (36); *Biblical Stories* (42); and *Verscheyde Aerdige Compartimenten en Tafels Nieuwelyckx Geinventeert*... with G. van der Esckhout.

SCHÜTKY, Waldemar
Russian, 20th century.
Born 12 June 1881, in St Petersburg.
Sculptor, medallist.

Waldemar Schütky was a student of Wilhelm von Ruemman. He lived and worked in Munich.

SCHUTT, Elemer
Hungarian, 20th century.
Born 1881, in Budapest; died 18 July 1907, in Budapest.
Painter. Portraits, landscapes.

SCHÜTT, Gustav
Austrian, 20th century.
Born 9 May 1890, in Vienna.
Painter, lithographer. Landscapes.

Gustav Schütt studied at the fine arts academy in Vienna.

MUSEUMS AND GALLERIES:
MÖDLING - VIENNA (MM).

SCHÜTTE, Ernst Heinrich Conrad
German, 20th century.
Born 5 April 1890, in Hanover.
Painter, architect.

SCHUTTE, Hans, or Schute
Danish, 17th century.
Born to a family originally from Odense.
Active between 1647 and 1680 in Denmark.
Painter.

Schutte produced numerous epitaphs.

SCHÜTTE, Oscar Carl Laurits
Danish, 19th - 20th century.
Born 2 January 1837, in Jutland; died 19 May 1913, in Copenhagen.
Painter. Portraits, genre scenes.

Oscar Carl Laurits Schütte studied under Harald F. Foss, Wenzel Tornöe and P. H. Kristian Zahrtmann. He is noted for his portraits in Rosenholm Castle.

MUSEUMS AND GALLERIES:
HORSENS: portraits.

SCHÜTTE, Thomas, or Shütte
German, 20th - 21st century.
Born 1954, in Oldenburg.
Painter, watercolourist, installation artist, sculptor (steel/bronze/ceramics), draughtsman. Scenes with figures, figures, architectural views, still-lifes. Stage sets.
Düsseldorf Constructive Sculpture.

Thomas Schütte was a pupil of Klaus Rinke, Gerhard Richter and Fritz Schwegler from 1973 to 1981 at the Kunstakademie in Düsseldorf, where he lives and works. Staging is a key element of his creations. His works tell stories, suggesting the world of childhood, through different media: simple architectural models, watercolours, sculptures, monuments and so on. He is particularly interested in contrasts in scale, from the infinitely large to the infinitely small, for example placing a miniature man, a puppet or a wooden silhouette, based on familiar figures - Renaissance statues, figures from Daumier's works, Géricault's lunatics - inside a monumental architectural work. Humour and wordplay are key elements in his drawings, which are based on a daily diary and include written language.

Schütte has taken part in various group exhibitions: 1979, Rheinisches Landesmuseum, Bonn; 1979, Kunstverein, Düsseldorf; 1981, 1985, ARC, Musée d'Art Moderne de la Ville de Paris; 1982, Nouvelle Biennale de Paris; 1982, Kunstmuseum, Düsseldorf; 1985, Museum Haus Lange, Krefeld; 1986, Stedelijk Museum, Amsterdam; 1987, Centro de Arte Reina Sofia, Madrid; 1987, Museum Folkwang, Essen; 1987, 1992, Documenta, Kassel; 1989, Musée d'Art Contemporain, Montreal; 1990, Institute of Contemporary Art and Serpentine Gallery, London; 1990, Musée des Beaux-Arts, Tourcoing; 1991, IVAM, Valencia; 1992, Moderna Galerija, Ljubljana; 1993, Middelheim Park, Antwerp; 1997, *Skulptur. Projekte in Münster 1997* (*Sculpture. Projects in Münster 1997*); 2003, *Esprit des Lieux* (*The Spirit of Places*), L' Œuvre Contemporaine et son Espace de Présentation, Palais des Papes, Avignon and *Bandes à part: le cinéma dans l'art contemporain* (*On the Fringes: Cinema in Contemporary Art*), Musée d'Art Moderne et Contemporain, Strasbourg, two exhibitions forming part of *Trésors publics, 20 ans de création dans les Fonds régionaux d'art contemporain* (*Public Treasury, 20 Years of Creation in the Regional Collection of Contemporary Art*).

There have been solo exhibitions of his works: 1979, Arno Kohnen gallery, Düsseldorf; 1980, 1982, 1986, 1990, Rüdiger Schöttle, Munich; from 1981 onwards regular exhibitions at the Konrad Fischer gallery in Düsseldorf; 1985, Art Gallery of Ontario, Toronto; 1985, Grande Halle de la Villette, Paris; 1985, Nationalgalerie, Berlin; 1986, 1990, Museum Haus Lange, Krefeld; 1987, Landesmuseum, Amsterdam; 1988, Staatliche Kunsthalle, Baden-Baden; 1989, Clamecy museum; 1989, 1990, Museum Haus Esters, Krefeld; 1990, Kunsthalle, Bern; 1990, Galerie Crousel-Robelin and Musée d'Art Moderne de la Ville de Paris; 1990, Stedelijk Van Abbemuseum, Eindhoven; 1991, Kunstverein, Kassel; 1991, Vereeniging voor het Museum, Ghent; 1994, Kunsthalle in Hamburg and Stuttgart; 1994, Carré d'Art, Nîmes; 1998, Whitechapel Art Gallery, London; 1999, Dia Foundation for the Arts, New York; 2002, *Dürer*, Galerie Nelson, Paris; 2003, Musée de Grenoble; 2004, K21 Kunstsammlung Nordrhein-Westfalen, Düsseldorf.

BIBLIOGRAPHY:
Pagé, Suzanne/Zacharopoulos, Denys/Javault, Patrick, *Dispositif-Sculpture - J. Drescher, H. Klingelhöller, R. Mucha, T. Schütte*, exhibition catalogue, ARC Musée d'Art Moderne de la Ville de Paris, Paris, 1985. Richard, Anne, "*Thomas Schütte*' in *Opus international* no. 120, periodical, Paris, July-August 1990. Gintz, Claude, "*Thomas Schütte*' in *Art Press* no. 150, periodical, Paris, September 1990. *Thomas Schütte*, exhibition catalogue, Carré d'Art-Musée d'Art contemporain, Nîmes, 1994. Rudolph, Karen, '*Thomas Schütte*' in *Beaux-Arts Magazine* no. 128, periodical, Paris, November 1994. Avgikos, Jan/Cooke, Lynne/Kluge, Alexander/Sandqvist, Gertrud/Schütte, Thomas/Stewart, Susan, *Thomas Schütte*, exhibition catalogue, Dia Center for the Arts, New York, 2001.

MUSEUMS AND GALLERIES:
DARMSTADT (Hessisches Landesmus.): *Model and Views* (1982) - DUNKIRK (FRAC Nord-Pas de Calais): *Bank* - LYONS (FRAC Rhône-Alpes): *Bath* (1984) - MONTPELLIER (FRAC Languedoc Roussillon): *No Respect* (1995) - NÎMES (Carré d'Art, MAC): *Four Tables (Studio, House, Gallery Fischer, Museum Haus Lange)* (1996).

AUCTION RECORDS:
PARIS, 16 Oct 1988, *Fruit* (1985, watercolour/paper, 51 1/4 x 43 1/4 ins / 130 x 110 cm) FRF 11,000. PARIS, 8 Oct 1989, *Untitled* (Indian ink, 51 1/4 x 43 1/4 ins / 130 x 110 cm) FRF 41,000. LONDON, 25 March 1993, *Untitled (Melon)* (1986, watercolour and varnish/paper, 56 1/4 x 43 ins / 142.9 x 109.2 cm) GBP 1,610. FRANKFURT AM MAIN, 14 June 1994, *Children's Book* (1991, 12 watercolours, each 7 3/4 x 11 ins / 19.5 x 27 cm) DEM 22,000. ZURICH, 30 Nov 1995, *Self-portrait* (1995, photograph, with title, signature and date on the back of the frame with a sculpture in Altuglas, 9 1/4 x 6 ins / 23.5 x 15.2 cm and 19 x 7 1/2 x 6 3/4 ins/48 x 19 x 17 cm) CHF 8,625. NEW YORK, 20 May 1999, *Picture Book of Late Night* (1996, ink and watercolour, twelve, 17 x 12 ins / 44 x 30 cm) USD 48,000. LONDON, 29 June 1999, *Boats* (1986, painted wood, a pair, 63 x 67x157 ins / 160 x 170x400 cm) GBP 32,000. LONDON, 27 June 2000, *Ghosts* (aluminium, three, 18 x 9x6 ins / 46 x 23x15 cm) GBP 36,000. NEW YORK, 17 Nov 2000, *Flowers, Pink, Orange, Blue, Yellow* (1995, watercolour and ink, four, 11 x 8 ins / 28 x 20 cm) USD 12,000. LONDON, 28 June 2001, *Rosa Kacheln, Pink Tiles* (1980, varnish and plastic, h. 118 ins / 300 cm) GBP 29,000. NEW YORK, 15 Nov 2001, *Urn* (1999, ceramic, 30 x 12x10 ins / 76 x 30x25 cm) USD 25,000. LONDON, 23 Oct 2002, *Sketch for Sculpture* (1985, enamel on paper, 51 x 43 ins / 130 x 110 cm) GBP 11,000. COLOGNE, 3 Dec 2002, *Lemon with Blue, Yellow and Black - and Red* (varnish, gouache and colour chalk on board, 56 x 43 ins / 141 x 110 cm) EUR 14,500. LONDON, 26 June 2003, *Study for The Foreigners* (1992, pencil, 43 x 78 ins / 108 x 197 cm) GBP 35,000. NEW YORK, 12 Nov 2003, *Big Heads* (1992, graphite, ink and yellow paper, diptych, 39 x 28 ins / 100 x 70 cm) USD 35,000. NEW YORK, 13 May 2004, *Urns* (1999, painted ceramic vessel, two parts, 31 x 14x14 ins / 80 x 35x35 cm) USD 18,000. NEW YORK, 8 Nov 2004, *Thomas Schütte* (black and white, 31, 27 x 19 ins / 69 x 47 cm) USD 160,000.

SCHUTTENHELM, Heinrich, or Schittenhelm
German, 15th century.
Painter.

Between 1430 and 1440 Heinrich Schuttenhelm painted the Passion cycle in the Carmelite church of Nördlingen.

SCHUTTENHELM, Lukas, or Schittenhelm
German, 16th century.
Active in Nördlingen.
Painter.

SCHUTTER, Jean Louis de
Belgian, 20th century.
Born 14 February 1910, in Antwerp.
Sculptor, painter. Animals. Busts.
Jean Louis de Schutter studied sculpture under Jozué Dupon and painting under Julien Creytens and Eugen van Mieghem. He started painting in 1925 but devoted himself to sculpture from 1931. He is noted among other things for his *Monty* (an elephant), *Thinker* (a monkey), figures of birds, busts of children and busts of his father and his uncle, *Louis de Schutter* and *Hesman de Schutter* respectively. He exhibited in Antwerp, Brussels, Amsterdam and Ghent (at the triennial Salon of 1938) and was awarded first prize at Antwerp's Koninklijke Academie voor Schone Kunsten.

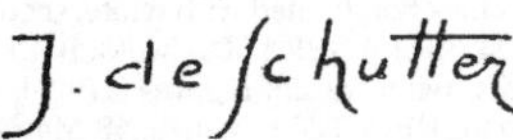

AUCTION RECORDS:
LOKEREN, 20 April 1985, *Maya* (patinated bronze, h. 41 3/4 ins / 106 cm) BEF 360,000.

SCHUTTER, Theodorus Cornelis
Belgian, 18th century.
Active c. 1760.
Draughtsman.
The city museum of Brussels has three city views by Theodorus Cornelis Schutter.

SCHUTTER, W.
German, 19th century.
Active in Groningen c. 1828.
Medallist.

SCHUTTERLIN, Jacob
French, 17th century.
Active in Strasbourg.
Cabinet maker.
Jacob Schutterlin built the structure of the upper floor of the town hall in Wiesbaden.
MUSEUMS AND GALLERIES:
WIESBADEN (Wiesbaden Mus.): several works.

SCHÜTZ
German, 19th century.
Active in Düren c. 1832.
Lithographer.

SCHÜTZ. See also **SCHÜZ**

SCHÜTZ, Adolph Johann
German, 19th century.
Born 24 June 1796, in Dresden.
Active in Dresden.
Painter. Portraits.
Adolph Schütz was a pupil at the academy in Dresden with Toscani and J. D. Schubert.

SCHUTZ, Anton Joseph Friedrich
German, 20th century.
Born 19 April 1894, in Berndorf (Rhineland).
Engraver.
Anton Joseph Friedrich Schutz studied under Hermann Groeber and Peter Halm at the fine arts academy in Munich. He became a member of the American Federation of Arts.
MUSEUMS AND GALLERIES:
LONDON (British Mus.) - PARIS (BNF) - WASHINGTON DC (NGA): *prints* - WASHINGTON DC (Smithsonian American AM): *New York Stock Exchange* (1925, etching); *Spirit of Chicago* (no date, etching).

SCHÜTZ, C.
German, 19th century.
Active during the first half of the 19th century.
Miniaturist.

SCHUTZ, Charles Nicolas
French, 20th century.
Born in Arschivilier.
Engraver.
Schutz was taught by Tony Robert-Fleury and Georges Profit. He was a member of the Salon des Artistes Français from 1905, having exhibited there from 1889. He received an honourable mention in 1889, a third-class medal in 1905 and a silver medal in 1921.

SCHUTZ, Edda
French, 20th century.
Born 5 March 1932, in Mulhouse.
Painter. Still-lifes, flowers, fruit.
Schutz studied at the École des Beaux in Mulhouse. She exhibited at the Salon des Artistes Français in Paris, where she was a member from 1976, the Salon des Indépendants, where she was a member from 1980, as well as in regional group exhibitions, receiving various distinctions. She also showed her paintings in numerous private galleries in Mulhouse, Paris, Balen, Geneva, Rome, New York, Dallas and Tokyo.
Her bouquets of flowers and fruit compositions are painted with a meticulous attention to detail.

SCHÜTZ, G. F.
German, 19th century.
Born to a family originally from Altona.
Active c. 1820 in Heidelberg.
Painter. Portraits.

SCHÜTZ, Georg
German, 17th century.
Born to a family originally from Wessobrunn.
Active in Munich.
Sculptor.

SCHÜTZ, Heinrich
German, 19th - 20th century.
Born 3 March 1875, in Offenbach am Main (Hesse).
Active in Munich.
Painter. Scenes with figures, animals.
MUSEUMS AND GALLERIES:
MUNICH (Ministry of Agriculture): *Peasant at Work.*
AUCTION RECORDS:
BERN, 6 May 1983, *Leaving for the Fields* (1919, oil on card, 19 3/4 x 27 1/2 ins / 50 x 70 cm) CHF 3,200. NEW YORK, 10 Feb 1998, *Driving a Cart* (oil on panel, 22 x 29 ins / 56 x 73.5 cm) USD 1,380.

SCHÜTZ, Hermann
German, 19th century.
Born 1807, in Bückeburg; died 12 April 1869, in Munich.
Engraver of reproductions.
Hermann Schütz was the pupil of C. A. Schwerdgeburth and S. Amsler. He was aquainted with the poet August Graf von Platen and M. von Schwiad.

SCHÜTZ, Joannes, or Jan, Johan Frederick
Dutch, 19th century.
Born 2 December 1817; died 27 February 1888, in Middelburg.
Painter. Landscapes, seascapes.
Joannes Schütz was the father of Willem Joannes Schütz. He was a pupil and then teacher at the school of design in Middelburg.
MUSEUMS AND GALLERIES:
THE HAGUE: *Flessingen Coast.*
AUCTION RECORDS:
LONDON, 4 May 1973, *Boats at Sea*, Gns 1,700. AMSTERDAM, 22 Oct 1974, *Boats in Heavy Seas* (1882) NLG 7,200. LONDON, 24 Nov 1976, *Sailing Ships in Calm Seas* (1874, oil on canvas, 26 1/2 x 40 3/4 ins / 67.5 x 103.5 cm) GBP 1,800. LONDON, 4 May

1977, *Sailing Ships in Calm Seas* (1875, oil on canvas, 27 1/4 x 41 ins / 69 x 104 cm) GBP 2,100. LONDON, 3 June 1983, *Shipwreck* (1846, oil on canvas, 20 1/4 x 28 ins / 51.4 x 71.1 cm) GBP 1,800. BRUSSELS, 30 Oct 1985, *Seascape* (1873, oil on canvas, 26 3/4 x 40 1/4 ins / 68 x 102 cm) BEF 200,000. STOCKHOLM, 16 May 1990, *Seascape with Sailing Boats* (1874, oil on canvas, 24 1/2 x 39 ins / 62 x 99 cm) SEK 16,000. AMSTERDAM, 30 Oct 1991, *Mariners near a Boat on a Beach* (1861, oil on panel, 6 x 10 ins / 15.5 x 24.5 cm) NLG 2,990. AMSTERDAM, 18 Feb 1992, *Fishermen on a Beach* (1887, oil on panel, 6 1/4 x 5 ins / 16 x 12.5 cm) NLG 1,840. AMSTERDAM, 24 Sept 1992, *Boat in Full Sail in Calm Weather* (1867, oil on panel, 10 1/2 x 12 1/2 ins / 26.5 x 31.5 cm) NLG 6,325. AMSTERDAM, 19 Oct 1993, *Sailing Ships in a River Estuary* (oil on panel, 7 1/4 x 10 ins / 18.5 x 24.5 cm) NLG 1,840. AMSTERDAM, 11 April 1995, *Sailing in an Estuary* (oil on panel, 17 1/4 x 23 1/2 ins / 44 x 60 cm) NLG 13,570. LONDON, 30 May 1996, *Calm Weather* (1880, oil on canvas, 27 1/4 x 41 1/4 ins / 69 x 105 cm) GBP 13,800. AMSTERDAM, 18 June 1996, *Fishing Boats Hauling In their Sails in Calm Weather* (oil on canvas, 19 x 28 3/4 ins / 48.5 x 73 cm) NLG 2,530. AMSTERDAM, 5 Nov 1996, *Raft* (1857, oil on canvas, 28 x 35 ins / 71 x 89 cm) NLG 5,900. LONDON, 26 Jan 2000, *Becalmed* (1879, oil on canvas, 27 x 41 ins / 69 x 105 cm) GBP 4,800. BERN, 11 May 2000, *Seascape* (1882, oil on panel, 9 x 16 ins / 24 x 40 cm) CHF 3,600. LONDON, 24 May 2001, *Flat Calm offshore* (1876, oil on canvas, 28 x 41 ins / 70 x 105 cm) GBP 5,500. AMSTERDAM, 22 Oct 2001, *Pilot Ship in Full Sail on the Schelde* (1871, oil on canvas, 27 x 41 ins / 69 x 103 cm) NLG 16,000. AMSTERDAM, 23 April 2002, *Pink and Schooner in a Breeze* (1876, oil on canvas, 21 x 30 ins / 53 x 75 cm) EUR 9,500. COLOGNE, 16 Nov 2002, *Fishing Cutter in Calm Seas* (1877, oil on canvas, 28 x 41 ins / 72 x 104 cm) EUR 9,000. LONDON, 5 June 2003, *Coastal Trader and Fishing Barge in Calm Waters at Dawn* (1878, oil on canvas, 28 x 42 ins / 71 x 107 cm) GBP 7,000. LONDON, 16 Sept 2003, *Dutch Small Craft and Brig Drying Their Sails in a Calm* (1878, oil on canvas, 28 x 41 ins / 70 x 105 cm) GBP 8,500.

SCHÜTZ, Johann
German, 18th century.
Stucco artist.

After completing his apprenticeship in the workshop of Dom. Zimmermann in Landsberg, Johann Schütz worked as a stucco artist in the Catholic church in Urlau.

SCHÜTZ, Johann Georg, or Schüz
German, 18th - 19th century.
Born 1755, in Frankfurt; died 1813.
Painter, engraver. Mythological subjects, genre scenes, landscapes.

Johann Georg Schütz was first taught by his father, Christian Georg Schütz, then attended the academy in Düsseldorf. He later travelled to Rome.

MUSEUMS AND GALLERIES:

FRANKFURT AM MAIN (Historisches Mus.): *Bombardment of Mainz by Night* - GRAZ: *Venis and Adonis* - LVIV: *Sacrifice of Iphigenia* - WEIMAR: *The Castle of Tiefurt near Weimar.*

AUCTION RECORDS:

PARIS, 22 Dec 1948, *River Scenes* (two pendants) FRF 59,100. PARIS, 24 Dec 1948, *Mountain Scenes* (two pendants) FRF 30,600; *Rhenish Landscape,* FRF 11,100. PARIS, 8 April 1949, *View of the Banks of the Rhine,* FRF 9,500. PARIS, 16 June 1950, *Peasants in the Country* (two pendants) FRF 11,000. PARIS, 15 June 1951, *Peasants on River Bank,* FRF 38,000. PARIS, 27 June 1951, *Smugglers,* FRF 19,000. PARIS, 7 Dec 1951, *Morning; Evening* (two pendants) FRF 70,000. VIENNA, 16 March 1976, *Shepherds in River Landscape* (oil on panel, 11 1/2 x 14 1/2 ins / 29.5 x 36.8 cm) ATS 80,000. LYONS, 6 Dec 1983, *Landscape with River Bank* (oil on wood, 16 1/4 x 22 ins / 41 x 55 cm) FRF 63,000. MONACO, 17 June 1989, *Landscapes of the Rhine Valley* (1764, oil on panel, a pair, each 12 3/4 x 16 1/2 ins / 32.5 x 42 cm) FRF 177,600. MONACO, 5-6 Dec 1991, *Rhenish Landscape* (oil on canvas, 8 1/2 x 11 1/2 ins / 21.5 x 29 cm) FRF 27,750. PARIS, 11 Dec 1991, *Bank of the Rhine* (oil on canvas, 15 x 18 1/2 ins / 38 x 47 cm) FRF 38,000. MONACO, 18-19 June 1992, *River Landscape with Castle* (oil on canvas, 9 x 11 3/4 ins / 23 x 30 cm) FRF 19,980. MONACO, 19 June 1994, *Landscape with River Bank* (oil on canvas, 15 3/4 x 21 1/4 ins / 40 x 54 cm) FRF 27,750. PARIS, 22 Oct 1997, *River Landscape with Mill* (canvas, 15 1/4 x 21 ins / 39 x 52.5 cm) FRF 27,000. ERLANGEN, 13 March 1999, *Romantic and Extensive View of Mainz* (1787, oil on panel, 10 x 15 ins / 26 x 39 cm) DEM 22,000. LONDON, 5 July 2000, *Apollo and Mercury. Apollo Slaying Python. Allegory of the Arts. Toilette of Venus* (black chalk heightened with white, set of four works, 12 x 7 ins / 30 x 19 cm) GBP 1,500. MUNICH, 21 March 2001, *Ruin Landscape with Peasant Figures* (1798, gouache, 7 x 9 ins / 17 x 24 cm) DEM 3,200. BERLIN, 18 May 2001, *Cestius Pyramid in Rome at Night* (1788, pen, brush and Indian ink, 14 x 20 ins / 36 x 51 cm) DEM 14,000. VIENNA, 24 March 2004, *Rhine Landscape* (oil on panel, 9 x 13 ins / 24 x 32 cm) EUR 7,000.

SCHÜTZ, Johannes
German, 17th - 18th century.
Active at the end of the 17th and beginning of the 18th centuries.
Painter (glazed earthenware).

Johannes Schütz worked from 1699 to 1723 at the factory in Hanau.

SCHÜTZ, Joseph
Austrian, 19th century.
Active in Vienna.
Draughtsman, engraver.

SCHÜTZ, Julia
Hungarian, 19th century.
Born 7 November 1859, in Budapest.
Active in Budapest.
Landscape artist.

SCHUTZ, Karl, or Schytz
German, 18th century.
Active in 1775.
Painter, engraver.

Karl Schutz is mentioned by Ris-Paquot.

SCHÜTZ, Karl, or Schytz
Austrian, 18th century.
Born 2 November 1745, in Laibach (now Ljubljana, Slovenia); died 14 March 1800, in Vienna.
Draughtsman, engraver, architect.

Karl Schütz engraved landscapes and military scenes as well as illustrating scenes from the *Iliad* and Scarron's *New.*

SCHÜTZ, Karl Balthasar Ernst
German, 19th century.
Born 1808, in Heilbronn (Baden-Württemberg).
Painter. Portraits, genre scenes.

SCHÜTZ, Mathias, or Schiz
German, 17th century.
Born c. 1610, in Fürstenfeldbruck; died 1683.
Sculptor.

Mathias Schütz was a master in Munich in 1640. The Bayerisches Nationalmuseum in Munich conserves several decorative elements that he executed for the papal chambers of the Residenz.

MUSEUMS AND GALLERIES:

MUNICH (Bayerisches Nationalmus.).

SCHÜTZ, Nikolas
German, 17th century.
Active in Kiel c. 1692.
Draughtsman. Portraits.

SCHÜTZ, Nikolaus, or Schyz
German, 18th century.
Born to a family originally from Wessobrunn; died 13 December 1785, in Landsberg.
Stucco artist, architect.

In 1719 Nikolaus Schütz was in charge of the decoration of the celebrations hall in the abbey at Nersheim.

SCHÜTZ, Oskar
German, 19th - 20th century.
Born 12 January 1842, in Leipzig; died 15 March 1916, in Dresden.
Painter.

SCHÜTZ, Sebastian. See the entry **SCHYZ**

SCHÜTZ, Tobias
Austrian, 18th century.
Born in Bohemia; died before 1726.
Active in Olmütz (now Olomouc, Czech Republic).
Sculptor.

Tobias Schütz married in 1723.

SCHÜTZ, Willem Joannes
German, 19th - 20th century.
Born 18 August 1854, in Middelburg; died 1933.
Active in Middelburg.
Painter, watercolourist. Seascapes.

Willem Joannes Schütz was the son and pupil of the painter Johannes Schütz.

MUSEUMS AND GALLERIES:

HAARLEM (Frans Halsmus.) - MIDDELBURG.

AUCTION RECORDS:

LONDON, 9 May 1979, *Landscape near Dordrecht* (oil on canvas, 17 x 31 ins / 43 x 79 cm) GBP 2,000. AMSTERDAM, 14 June 1994, *Sailing Vessels off the Coast* (oil on canvas, 11 3/4 x 20 ins / 30 x 50.5 cm) NLG 2,070.

SCHUTZBACH, Erwin
German, 20th century.
Born 1909, in Balingen.
Sculptor, potter.

Erwin Schutzbach studied in Munich and under Edwin Scharff at the fine arts academy in Cologne. He completed his studies during a series of trips to Italy and France, notably to Paris, where he received advice and encouragement from Constantin Brancusi. He went on to teach at the school of applied arts in Wiesbaden. He worked in wood, bronze and, from around 1960, predominantly in terracotta. His subject matter is akin to that of Brancusi or Lipsi in terms of its elementarity and patination, not to mention its permutation of the everyday and the ritualistic. He exhibited mainly in Freiburg im Breisgau, Cologne and Munich and within the framework of group exhibitions.

BIBLIOGRAPHY:

Ier Salon international des Galeries Pilotes, exhibition catalogue, Musée cantonal, Lausanne, 1953.

SCHÜTZE, Albert
German, 19th - 20th century.
Born 11 July 1827; died 1908, in Berlin.
Painter. Portraits, genre scenes.

SCHÜTZE, August
German, 19th century.
Born 14 April 1805, in Hamburg; died 1847, in Hungary.
Painter. Genre scenes.

August Schütze was the pupil of F. Waldmuller.

AUCTION RECORDS:

NEW YORK, 13 Oct 1993, *Little Girl Feeding Grass to Rabbits; Little Boy Playing with Squirrel* (1837, oil on canvas, a pair, each 9 1/2 x 8 1/4 ins / 24.4 x 21 cm) USD 13,800.

SCHÜTZE, Christoph. See **SCHÜZ**

SCHÜTZE, Georg, or Schutze, called Georgius or Gregorius Aurifaber Pomeranus
German, 16th century.
Born to a family originally from Pomerania.
Active in the second half of the 16th century.
Miniaturist, goldsmith.

Georg Schütze was court painter to Prince Jehan Sigismond of Transylvania and worked in Karlsburg, Bistritz and Fogoras.

SCHÜTZE, Johann Christoph
German, 18th century.
Died 31 May 1765, in Weissenfels.
Painter, architect.

From 1719 to 1745, Johann Schütze was architect to the dukes of Saxe-Weissenfels at Zerbst, and worked from 1720 on the town's castle. He painted portraits of *Aug. Lebrecht von Erlach*, the princess *Johanna Elisabeth von Anhalt*, *A Lady*, *Catherine II of Russia* and the tsar *Peter III*.

SCHUTZE, Jost or Joost, or Scheutze, Schult, Schütz, Schütze, Schytt, Skytt, Skytts
Swedish, 17th century.
Died 1674.
Sculptor. Monuments.

Schutze was associated with the admiralty of Stockholm. He worked at the Rosenhane castle in Stockholm around 1650, as well as on the tomb of *Charles X* at the church of Riddarholm in 1660.

SCHÜTZE, Ludwig
German, 19th century.
Born c. 1807, in Dresden; died 1872, in Wiesa (Saxony).
Engraver, draughtsman.

Ludwig Schütze studied with J. Ph. Veit and A. Reindel and carried out line engravings on steel.

AUCTION RECORDS:

MUNICH, 10 Dec 1992, *Clump of Trees* (pencil/paper, 16 1/2 x 13 1/2 ins / 42 x 34.4 cm) DEM 2,825.

SCHÜTZE, Wilhelm
German, 19th century.
Born 19 July 1840, in Kaufbeuren; died 31 May 1898, in Munich.
Painter, engraver. Genre scenes.

Wilhelm Schütze executed lithographs like his master, Alex. Wagner.

MUSEUMS AND GALLERIES:

CHEMNITZ: *Children with Cats* - MUNICH (Pinakothek): *Portrait of Child*.

AUCTION RECORDS:

NEW YORK, 1899, *Blind-man's Buff*, FRF 1,250. NEW YORK, 11 - 12 March 1909, *The Blind One*, USD 400. PARIS, 7 - 8 March 1911, *Cat Lying in Wait*, FRF 270. LONDON, 15 Feb 1967, *Romantic Secrets*, GBP 320. BERLIN, 30 Sept 1977, *Children Peeling Potatoes* (oil on canvas, 20 1/2 x 24 ins / 52 x 61 cm) DEM 7,000. LONDON, 18 Jan 1980, *Child Peeling Vegetables* (oil on canvas, 19 3/4 x 23 3/4 ins / 50.2 x 60.3 cm) GBP 3,400. NEW YORK, 27 May 1982, *Little Girls Playing Mothers* (1884, oil on canvas, 23 1/4 x 29 1/4 ins / 59 x 74 cm) USD 24,000. LONDON, 21 June 1985, *Girl at the Window* (oil on canvas, 15 3/4 x 12 1/2 ins / 40 x 32 cm) GBP 8,500. LON-

DON, 27 Nov 1987, *Adorable Kittens* (oil on canvas, 29 1/2 x 24 1/2 ins / 75 x 62 cm) GBP 32,000. MUNICH, 12 Dec 1990, *Young Musicians shortly after Concert* (oil on canvas, 15 3/4 x 16 1/2 ins / 40 x 42 cm) DEM 13,200. NEW YORK, 29 Oct 1992, *Little Girls Attending to Cat's Paw* (oil on canvas, 16 x 13 ins / 40.6 x 33.3 cm) USD 25,300. NEW YORK, 18 March 1998, *Halt! Who goes there?* (oil on canvas, 29 x 36 ins / 73.7 x 91.4 cm) USD 68,500. LUCERNE, 13 Oct 1999, *The Cats' Mother* (oil on canvas, 30 x 36 ins / 75 x 92 cm) CHF 120,000. LONDON, 22 June 2000, *Pink Roses in a Vase* (oil on board, oval, 22 x 19 ins / 57 x 47 cm) GBP 3,800. MUNICH, 5 July 2000, *Still-life of Fruit with Wine Glass* (1869, oil on canvas, 25 x 37 ins / 64 x 93 cm) DEM 4,000. LINDAU, 4 Oct 2001, *Country Children at Play with Cat and Mouse* (oil on canvas, 30 x 25 ins / 77 x 63 cm) DEM 105,000. LUCERNE, 14 Nov 2001, *Cat Breakfast* (oil on canvas, 16 x 13 ins / 41 x 32 cm) CHF 35,000. KEMPTEN, 11 July 2002, *Still-life with White and Red Roses* (oil on canvas, 22 x 31 ins / 56 x 79 cm) EUR 2,300. AUGSBURG, 21 March 2003, *Boy and Girl by Farmstead* (oil on canvas, 31 x 25 ins / 79 x 63 cm) EUR 9,500. LUCERNE, 4 June 2003, *Entry Forbidden* (oil on canvas, 29 x 36 ins / 73 x 92 cm) CHF 110,000.

SCHÜTZE, Wilhelm Johann

German, 19th century.

Born 1814, in Berlin; died 1878.

Painter, fresco artist. Portraits, genre scenes.

Wilhelm Johann Schütze was the pupil of Aug. von Kloeber and taught at the academy in Berlin. He collaborated with Carl Eggers on fresoes designed by Schinkel in the vestibule of the Berlin Altes Museum.

SCHÜTZE POMERANUS, Georgius.
See **SCHÜTZE Georg**

SCHÜTZE-SCHUR, Ilse

German, 19th - 20th century.

Born 21 August 1868, in Berlin-Charlottenburg; died 1923.

Painter, engraver.

Ilse Schütze-Schur was the wife of the poet Ernst Schur. She is noted for her illustrations of children's books written by her husband and for her art criticism.

SCHÜTZENBERGER, Louis Frédéric

French, 19th century.

Born 8 September 1825, in Strasbourg; died 17 April 1903, in Strasbourg.

Painter. Religious subjects, allegorical subjects, nudes, portraits, genre scenes.

Louis Schützenberger was admitted to the École des Beaux-Arts in Paris in 1843 where his masters were Charles Gleyre and Paul Delaroche. His work appeared at the Paris Salon from 1850 onward. He won a third-class medal in 1851, a second-class medal in 1861 and a *Dusk* in 1863. He was made a Chevalier of the Légion d'Honneur in 1870.

MUSEUMS AND GALLERIES:

ARRAS: *Rape of Europa* - LUXEMBOURG: *Centaurs Hunting a Wild Boar* - MULHOUSE: *Memory of Italy; Evening; Caesar and Ariovistus Meeting in Alsace; Exodus: Alsatian Family Leaving Their Country* - STRASBOURG: *Old Man Reading; Hunter with a Hunting Horn; Roman Slaves; Portrait of Madame Weber-Schlumberger; Young Girl in the Bath; Father of the Artist; Wife of the Artist; Hunters; Two Nudes* - VALENCIA: *The Foolish Virgins*.

AUCTION RECORDS:

PARIS, 1900, *Draped Woman* (study) FRF 23. PARIS, 21 May 1904, *Mariata*, FRF 145. NEW YORK, 5 March 1981, *Couple in a Garden* (oil on canvas, 51 1/2 x 38 1/2 ins / 131 x 98 cm) USD 4,200. NEW YORK, 23 May 1985, *Picking Flowers* (oil on canvas, 51 1/2 x 38 1/2 ins / 131 x 98 cm) USD 4,000. PARIS, 30 Nov 1987, *Suzanna and the Elders* (oil on card, 11 x 9 ins / 27 x 22 cm) FRF 2,200. LONDON, 20 Sept 2001, *Tinker in a French Street* (1869, oil on canvas, 77 x 60 ins / 195 x 152 cm) GBP 1,500.

SCHÜTZENBERGER, Paul René

French, 19th - 20th century.

Born 29 July 1860, in Mulhouse; died 31 December 1916, in Paris.

Painter. Genre scenes, landscapes.

Schützenberger was taught by J.P. Laurens. He featured at the Salon des Artistes Français, where he exhibited *Girl Reading at the Window* (1891). He received an honourable mention at the 1900 Exposition Universelle and exhibited at the Salon des Indépendants from 1902 and the Nationale des Beaux-Arts from 1910.

MUSEUMS AND GALLERIES:

SOISSONS: *Girl Reading at the Window*.

AUCTION RECORDS:

PARIS, 29 June 1942, *Female Nude* (1914) FRF 450. PARIS, 5 Feb 1951, *Nude Standing*, FRF 450. HONFLEUR, 17 July 1983, *Young Female Nude in Tulle Skirt* (1906, oil on canvas, 32 x 21 1/2 ins / 81.5 x 54.5 cm) FRF 10,500. PARIS, 8 April 1998, *Nu à sa coiffure* (oil on canvas, 48 x 35 3/4 ins / 121 x 91 cm) FRF 40,000.

SCHÜTZERCRANTZ, Adolph Ulric

Swedish, 19th century.

Born 25 March 1802, in Stockholm; died 9 October 1854, in Stockholm.

Draughtsman, lithographer, painter.

Schützercrantz was an officer.

MUSEUMS AND GALLERIES:

STOCKHOLM (Nationalmus.): several drawings.

SCHUUR, Theodorus Cornelisz. van der.
See **SCHUER**

SCHUURMANN

Dutch, 17th century.

Painter. Portraits.

SCHUURSMA, Frans

Dutch, 20th century.

Born April 1938, in Amsterdam.

Painter, musician. Landscapes with figures.

Frans Schuursma studied at the fine arts college in Tillburg and at the fine arts academy in Antwerp. His unusual compositions often feature landscapes peopled with amputees and deformed figures. He exhibited his work in solo shows in Amsterdam, Antwerp, The Hague and Patis (at the Dutch Institute).

SCHUYCK. See **SCHAYCK**

SCHUYFF, Peter

Swiss, 20th - 21st century.

Born 1958.

Painter, watercolourist.

Neo-Conceptual Art, Appropriation Art.

Peter Schuyff's works are abstract, with an emphasis on rhythm, created mainly by the relief of the canvas and alternating strips. He has taken part in group exhibitions including 2001, *L'Esprit de famille* (*Family Spirit*), Villa du Parc, Annemasse. There have also been solo exhibitions of his works: 1990 Galerie Gilbert Brownstone in Paris; 1992 Art&Public in Geneva.

BIBLIOGRAPHY:

Donovan, Keith, *Peter Schuyff - Watercolors*, exhibition catalogue, Gal. Art et Public, Geneva, 1992.

MUSEUMS AND GALLERIES:

GENEVA (Mamco).

AUCTION RECORDS:

PARIS, 15 June 1988, *Untitled* (1988, acrylic/canvas, 73 3/4 x 73 3/4 ins / 187.5 x 187.5 cm) FRF 75,000. NEW YORK, 10 Nov

1988, *Untitled* (1984, acrylic/canvas, 90 x 66 1/4 ins / 228.8 x 168 cm) USD 15,400. NEW YORK, 4 May 1989, *Untitled* (1985, acrylic/fabric, 90 x 66 1/4 ins / 228.6 x 168.3 cm) USD 33,000. NEW YORK, 5 Oct 1989, *Untitled* (1984, acrylic/canvas, 66 x 46 ins / 167.7 x 117 cm) USD 23,100. NEW YORK, 23 Feb 1990, *Untitled* (1986, acrylic/fabric, 75 x 75 ins / 190.5 x 190.5 cm) USD 17,600. NEW YORK, 27 Feb 1990, *Untitled* (1984, acrylic/fabric, 90 x 66 ins / 228.6 x 167.6 cm) USD 23,100. AMSTERDAM, 22 May 1990, *Composition with Lips* (1983, pencil and watercolour/paper, 30 x 22 1/4 ins / 76 x 56.5 cm) NLG 3,220. NEW YORK, 5 Oct 1990, *The World of a Yellow Man* (1984, oil on panel, diptych, 90 x 132 1/4 ins / 228.9 x 335.9 cm) USD 12,100. NEW YORK, 13 Feb 1991, *Untitled* (1987, acrylic/fabric, 12 x 12 1/4 ins / 30.5 x 30.8 cm) USD 1,320. NEW YORK, 7 May 1991, *Untitled* (1984, acrylic/canvas, 66 x 46 1/4 ins / 167.8 x 117.2 cm) USD 4,950. NEW YORK, 3 Oct 1991, *Untitled* (1985, acrylic/fabric, 120 x 120 ins / 304.8 x 304.8 cm) USD 8,800. NEW YORK, 13 Nov 1991, *Dominant Tonality* (1985, acrylic/fabric, 120 1/4 x 120 ins / 305.2 x 304.6 cm) USD 7,700. NEW YORK, 8 Oct 1992, *Untitled* (1991, acrylic/canvas, 96 x 66 ins / 243.9 x 167.7 cm) USD 5,500. NEW YORK, 22 Feb 1993, *Untitled* (1986, oil on canvas, 75 x 75 ins / 190.5 x 190.5 cm) USD 3,080. NEW YORK, 7 May 1993, *Untitled* (1985, acrylic/fabric, 90 1/4 x 60 1/2 ins / 229.3 x 153.6 cm) USD 4,600. NEW YORK, 11 Nov 1993, *Untitled* (1987, oil on canvas, 75 x 75 ins / 190.5 x 190.5 cm) USD 6,325. NEW YORK, 3 May 1995, *Wilma* (1984, acrylic/canvas, 96 x 66 ins / 243.8 x 167.6 cm) USD 6,325. NEW YORK, 10 Oct 1996, *Untitled* (1989, acrylic with traces of charcoal/canvas, 75 x 25 ins / 190.5 x 63.5 cm) USD 2,875. PARIS, 29 April 1997, *Red and Blue Composition* (acrylic/canvas, 72 1/2 x 34 3/4 ins / 184 x 88.5 cm) FRF 16,000. LONDON, 23 Oct 1997, *Untitled* (1990, acrylic/canvas, 20 x 16 ins / 50.8 x 40.6 cm) GBP 1,150. NEW YORK, 28 Dec 1999, *Untitled* (acrylic on canvas, 75 x 46 ins / 191 x 117 cm) USD 4,500. PARIS, 26 Feb 2003, *Untitled* (acrylic on paper on cardboard, 63 x 91 ins / 160 x 230 cm) EUR 3,350. NEW YORK, 14 May 2004, *Untitled* (1986, acrylic on canvas, 95 x 94 ins / 241 x 240 cm) USD 5,000. NEW YORK, 13 Dec 2004, *Untitled* (acrylic on linen, 120 x 120 ins / 305 x 305 cm) USD 11,000.

SCHUYL, F.
Dutch, 17th century.
Painter, engraver (etching).

F. Schuyl is possibly identifiable as the botanist and doctor Professor Florentius Schuyl of Leiden (1619-1669). He is noted for his print *Death and the Newborn Baby*.

SCHUYL VAN DER DOES, Cecile Dorothea (Countess). See **NAHUYS**

SCHUYLENBERGH, André van
Belgian, 20th - 21st century.
Born 1952.
Painter (including gouache). Figures.

AUCTION RECORDS:
LUCERNE, 24 Nov 1990, *Couple* (1986, gouache/paper, 26 1/2 x 19 1/4 ins / 67 x 49 cm) CHF 1,600. LUCERNE, 15 May 1993, *Movement* (1986, acrylic/canvas, 35 1/2 x 27 1/2 ins / 90 x 70 cm) CHF 4,000.

SCHUYLENBURCH, Maria Machteld van, also known as Lennep
Maiden name: van Sypesteyn
Dutch, 18th century.
Born 1724; died 1774.
Miniaturist. Historical figures.

Daniel van Lennep was the second husband of Maria Machteld van Schuylenburch.

MUSEUMS AND GALLERIES:
AMSTERDAM: *William IV of Orange-Nassau* (miniature).

SCHUYLENBURGH, Hendrik van
Dutch, 17th century.
Died 1689, in Middelburg.
Painter. Landscapes, urban landscapes.

Hendrik van Schuylenburgh was a member of the guild of Middelburg in 1642.

MUSEUMS AND GALLERIES:
AMSTERDAM: *Headquarters of the Dutch East India Company at Hugh; Bengal; Plantation in Bengal.*

SCHÜZ. See also **SCHÜTZ**

SCHÜZ, Christian Georg I, the Elder, or Schütz
German, 18th century.
Born 27 September 1718, in Flörsheim; died 1791, buried 6 December in Frankfurt am Main.
Painter. Genre scenes, landscapes with figures.

Christian Georg Schüz studied in Frankfurt with Hugo Schlegel in 1731 and also worked with Apiani. The figures of his landscapes, as well as the animals, were added by W. F. Hirt and later by Pforr. He was the father of Franz, Heinrich and Philippine Maria Schüz or Schütz.

MUSEUMS AND GALLERIES:
ASCHAFFENBURG: four views of Mainz; *The Main at Hochheim; The Rhine at Mainz*; three landscapes with ruines - BERN: *Landscape with Cows Crossing under Bridge; The Staubbach and the Virgin; The Glaciers of Grindelwald* - BUDAPEST: *Landscape* - DARMSTADT: *River; Landscape with Flock; Interior of Church* - DESSAU: three landscapes of the Rhine; *View of Frankfurt and Sachsenhausen; Bridge over the Main at Frankfurt* - FRANKFURT AM MAIN (Städel): two landscapes of the Rhine; *Forest Nook near Oberrad; View of Aschaffenburg; Schloss Schönbusch near Aschaffenburg*; two landscapes with ruins; *Landscape with Animals; Mountain Landscape with Cows; Interior of the Church of Our Lady; The Römerberg; Devils Bridge; Grazing; Highway; Beach; The Liebraufenberg; Guard-house at Frankfurt* - GENEVA (Mus. Ariana): *View of Spot on the Banks of the Rhine* - GRAZ: *Venus and Adonis* - HEIDELBERG: *River Landscape* - KASSEL: *Part of the New Lower Town of Kassel in Second Half of 18th Century; River Landscape with Town in Background; Landscape with Windmill at Water's Edge* - KOBLENZ: *Flight into Egypt* - MAINZ: two landscapes near the Main; *three Italian ruins* - MUNICH: *View of Rhine near Mainz; View of Mainz taken from East; View of Weisenau, near Mainz* - OSLO: two Rhenish landscapes - SPEYER: *View of Oppenheim; The Salt Tower* - STUTTGART: two small landscapes.

AUCTION RECORDS:
PARIS, 15 Dec 1922, *Watermill; Hamlet* (both) FRF 580. PARIS, 28 - 29 Nov 1923, *Fountain; Promenade on the Terrace* (both) FRF 2,500. PARIS, 19 March 1924, *Bargemen Unloading their Goods; Villagers Carrying their Goods for Shipping* (both) FRF 4,200. PARIS, 7 - 8 Nov 1928, *River Bank with Village and Figures*, FRF 2,500. PARIS, 14 Dec 1935, *Palace Court*, FRF 650. PARIS, 23 Dec 1936, *Farm at Bank of River; Cascade* (both) FRF 1,900. PARIS, 26 Jan 1944, *Landscapes* (two pendants) FRF 23,500. PARIS, 3 April 1950, *Cascade*, FRF 5,200. PARIS, 27 April 1950, *Mountain Landscape; River Bank* (1764, two pendants) FRF 70,000. LONDON, 2 March 1951, *Swiss Panorama* (1774) GBP 73. PARIS, 30 April 1951, *Town on the Danube* (1754) FRF 37,000. LONDON, 29 May 1959, *View of Valley*, GBP 609. LUCERNE, 21 - 27 Nov 1961, *Crossing the Moselle*, CHF 7,200. COLOGNE, 21 Oct 1966, *Banks of Rhine*,

DEM 12,000. LONDON, 29 July 1970, *Two Paintings* (two paintings/metal) GBP 1,750. MUNICH, 17 Nov 1971, *Mountainous Landscape,* DEM 17,200. LONDON, 6 Dec 1972, *Romantic Landscapes* (two gouaches) Gns 1,000. HEIDELBERG, 8 Feb 1974, *River Landscape,* DEM 10,500. PARIS, 25 Feb 1976, *Landscape with Figures* (oil on panel, 10 x 12 3/4 ins / 25.5 x 32.5 cm) FRF 23,000. COPENHAGEN, 7 Dec 1976, *Landscape with Bridge* (oil on panel, 9 x 12 ins / 22 x 30.5 cm) DKK 22,000. VIENNA, 15 March 1977, *Self-portrait* (oil on canvas, 36 1/4 x 30 ins / 92 x 76 cm) ATS 60,000. COLOGNE, 1 June 1978, *Banks of the Main* (oil on panel, 13 1/2 x 19 ins / 34 x 48.5 cm) DEM 17,000. LONDON, 7 Feb 1979, *Huntsmen in Fantastic Landscape on Banks of Rhine.* HEIDELBERG, 12 Oct 1979, *Rhenish Landscape* (c. 1783, etching, 10 x 12 1/2 ins / 24.5 x 32 cm) DEM 2,000. VIENNA, 15 Sept 1981, *Village in Winter* (oil on canvas, 9 x 19 3/4 ins / 23 x 50 cm) ATS 160,000. COLOGNE, 22 Nov 1984, *Scene at River Bank* (oil on panel, 13 1/2 x 17 3/4 ins / 34 x 45 cm) DEM 24,000. PARIS, 16 Oct 1985, *Views of the Rhine Valley* (oil on panel, pendants, 15 1/4 x 22 ins / 39 x 55 cm) FRF 220,000. LONDON, 2 July 1986, *Landscape of Banks of the Rhine* (1767, oil/copper, 17 x 22 ins / 43 x 56 cm) GBP 21,000. PARIS, 21 Dec 1987, *Landscape near the Rhine* (oil on canvas, 15 x 18 1/2 ins / 38 x 47 cm) FRF 40,000. NEW YORK, 15 Jan 1988, *Herdsman with Cows near Pool in a Glade* (1785, oil/copper, 16 3/4 x 21 1/2 ins / 42.5 x 54.6 cm) USD 6,600. PARIS, 16 March 1988, *Landscape with Peasants and Flock near Roman Ruins* (oil on canvas, 83 3/4 x 81 ins / 213 x 206 cm) FRF 400,000. MORLAIX, 15 Aug 1988, *Torrent* (oil on canvas, 15 3/4 x 20 1/2 ins / 40 x 52 cm) FRF 57,500. NEW YORK, 21 Oct 1988, *Christ Healing the Sick Man at Bathesda* (oil on panel, 12 1/4 x 18 ins / 31 x 45.5 cm) USD 2,475. NEW YORK, 12 Jan 1989, *Extensive River Landscape* (oil on canvas, 9 1/4 x 13 3/4 ins / 23.5 x 35 cm) USD 9,350. NEW YORK, 7 April 1989, *Extensive River Landscape* (oil on panel, 9 3/4 x 13 3/4 ins / 25 x 35 cm) USD 3,575. PARIS, 11 Dec 1989, *Landscapes of the Rhine Valley* (pair of oak panels, 9 1/4 x 13 1/2 ins / 23.5 x 34 cm) FRF 200,000. LYONS, 21 March 1990, *Chamonix Valley* (oil on canvas, 16 1/2 x 22 3/4 ins / 42 x 58 cm) FRF 59,000. LONDON, 11 April 1990, *Rhenish Landscape* (oil on panel, 7 3/4 x 10 ins / 19.5 x 25.2 cm) GBP 19,800. COLOGNE, 29 June 1990, *Romantic River Landscape with Figures* (oil on canvas, 31 1/2 x 39 1/4 ins / 80 x 100 cm) DEM 7,500. LONDON, 20 July 1990, *Rhenish Landscape with Peasants on Rocky Path Leading up to Chapel* (oil on panel, 10 x 12 3/4 ins / 25.7 x 32.5 cm) GBP 12,100. NEW YORK, 10 Oct 1991, *Extensive Rhenish Landscape with Castle on Promontory and Village in Valley with Peasants* (oil on canvas, 11 1/4 x 15 1/4 ins / 28.6 x 38.7 cm) USD 19,800. PARIS, 15 April 1992, *Winter Landscape* (oil on canvas, 28 x 45 1/4 ins / 71 x 115 cm) FRF 71,000. PARIS, 22 June 1992, *View of Rhine Valley* (oil on canvas, 15 x 22 1/2 ins / 38 x 57 cm) FRF 90,000. MUNICH, 25 June 1992, *Idealized Rhenish Landscapes* (oil/copper, a pair, each 7 x 8 1/2 ins / 18 x 21.5 cm) DEM 45,200. LONDON, 8 July 1992, *Rhenish Landscape* (oil on panel, a pair, each 8 x 11 1/2 ins / 20.5 x 29 cm) GBP 18,700. AMSTERDAM, 10 Nov 1992, *Rhenish Landscape with Boat Berthed at Quay, and Town in Distance in Twilight* (1785, oil on panel, 10 1/2 x 14 1/2 ins / 26.5 x 36.7 cm) NLG 44,850. LONDON, 9 Dec 1992, *Landscape at Nightfall with Figures Resting near House* (1787, oil on canvas, 26 x 43 3/4 ins / 66 x 111 cm) GBP 13,200. PARIS, 15 Dec 1992, *Banks of the Rhine* (oil on canvas, a pair, 12 1/4 x 15 1/2 ins / 31 x 39.5 cm) FRF 80,000. NEW YORK, 14 Jan 1993, *Extensive Rhenish Landscape with Travellers on Path leading to Castle* (1775, oil/copper, 18 3/4 x 23 3/4 ins / 47.8 x 60.6 cm) USD 60,500. LONDON, 21 April 1993, *Fluvial Landscape with Figures on Bank near Houses* (1748, oil on canvas, 16 x 22 1/4 ins / 40.8 x 56.5 cm) GBP 9,200. LONDON, 6 July 1994, *Cavalry Engagement in Rhenish Landscape* (oil on panel, 24 x 38 3/4 ins / 61.2 x 98.4 cm) GBP 23,000. AMSTERDAM, 15 Nov 1995, *Capriccio of Rhenish Landscape with Town at River Bank and Merchants Unloading Barges* (black chalk and wash, 6 x 8 3/4 ins / 15.2 x 22.3 cm) NLG 1,180. PARIS, 26 March 1996, *View of German Village on the Bank of the Rhine* (oil on canvas, 45 1/2 x 56 3/4 ins / 115.5 x 144 cm) FRF 115,000. LONDON, 17 April 1996, *Village Burning at Night* (oil on panel, a pair, each 15 1/4 x 20 ins / 39 x 50.8 cm) GBP 4,830. LONDON, 11 Dec 1996, *Rhenish Landscape; Capriccio* (oil on panel, a pair, 10 x 12 1/2 ins / 25.5 x 32 cm) GBP 21,850. LONDON, 16 April 1997, *Boats and People in Rhenish River Landscape* (oil on panel, 7 3/4 x 10 ins / 19.5 x 25.5 cm) GBP 8,050. STUTTGART, 25 June 1999, *Figures on Riverbank near Wooden Bridge, leading to Fortified-town* (oil on canvas, 44 x 59 ins / 112 x 150 cm) DEM 50,000. ZURICH, 8 Sept 1999, *Landscape with Ruins and Travellers* (1767, oil on copper, 15 x 21 ins / 38 x 53 cm) CHF 80,000. LONDON, 18 April 2000, *Rhenish Landscapes with Travellers on the Banks of a River* (oil on copper, a pair, 6 x 7 ins / 14 x 18 cm) GBP 7,000. STUTTGART, 30 June 2000, *View of a Mountain Stream with Two Anglers* (1765, oil on canvas, 17 x 13 ins / 44 x 33 cm) DEM 33,000. TOESTORF, 3 Nov 2001, *Arcadian Landscape with Figures* (1778, oil on copper, 13 x 18 ins / 34 x 46 cm) DEM 18,000. COLOGNE, 17 Nov 2001, *Wide River Landscape* (oil on panel, 14 x 18 ins / 35 x 45 cm) DEM 17,000. LONDON, 17 April 2002, *Rhenish Landscapes with Figures on Track* (oil on copper, a pair, 14 x 17 ins / 35 x 44 cm) GBP 38,000. MUNICH, 6 Dec 2002, *Idealised Rhine Landscape* (oil on panel, 10 x 13 ins / 26 x 33 cm) EUR 18,000. BREMEN, 28 June 2003, *Rhine Landscape* (oil on canvas, 17 x 20 ins / 42 x 51 cm) EUR 7,500. ZURICH, 8 Dec 2003, *Mountain Landscape with Waterfall, Figures and Animals* (1764, oil on panel, 13 x 17 ins / 33 x 42 cm) CHF 6,000. MUNICH, 26 March 2004, *River Landscape with Hill-top Fortress* (oil on panel, 11 x 15 ins / 27 x 37 cm) EUR 7,100. PARIS, 21 June 2004, *View from Edge of the Rhine* (1764, oil on copper, 15 x 19 ins / 38 x 48 cm) EUR 8,000.

SCHÜZ, Christian Georg II, or Schütz

German, 18th - 19th century.

Born 1755 or 1758, in Flörsheim; died 10 April 1823, in Frankfurt.

Painter, watercolourist, engraver. Landscapes.

Christian Georg Schüz II was the nephew and pupil of Christian Georg Schüz the Elder. Initially he made copies of his uncle's works, then dedicated himself to painting Rhenish landscapes, mainly in watercolours. He was appointed curator of the museum at Frankfurt around 1789, abusing his position by fraudulently selling a work attributed to Holbein. The museum later recovered the stolen painting.

MUSEUMS AND GALLERIES:

DARMSTADT: *Landscape; Ruined Temple* - FRANKFURT AM MAIN (Städel): *View of Frankfurt above Sachsenhausen; The Lorelei at Sunset; The Lorelei in the Morning Mist; The Rock of Baudouin; The Environs of Meissner; Frankfurt seen from Muhlberg; The Rhine near Braubach* - KASSEL: two Rhenish landscapes - MAINZ: a watercolour - MÜNSTER: two market scenes - WIESBADEN: *View of Frankfurt; View of Mainz.*

AUCTION RECORDS:

COLOGNE, 11 Nov 1964, *View of Mainz,* DEM 4,500. LONDON, 5 March 1969, *View of Rhine Valley,* GBP 800. LONDON, 6 Dec 1972, *Landscapes* (two pendants) GBP 6,500. VIENNA, 12 March 1974, *Fluvial Landscape,* ATS 50,000. NEW YORK, 19 Jan 1984, *Mountain Landscape and a River with Figures* (oil on panel, 8 1/2 x 12 ins / 21.5 x 30.5 cm) USD 4,500. MUNICH, 14 May 1986, *Horseman and Travellers in River Landscape* (oil on canvas, 22 1/4 x 35 ins / 56.5 x 88 cm) DEM 16,000. COLOGNE, 15 Oct 1988, *Landscape with Figures and Ruined Church on Lake Shore and Mountains in Background* (oil on canvas, 20 1/2 x 28 1/4 ins / 52 x 72 cm) DEM 5,500. VERSAILLES, 19 March 1989, *River Landscape with Figures* (oil on canvas, 13 3/4 x 17 ins / 35 x 43 cm) FRF 28,000. PARIS, 25 April 1990, *Fishermen on River Bank* (oil on canvas, 9 1/2 x 12 1/2 ins / 24 x 31.5 cm) FRF 18,000. STOCKHOLM, 19 May 1992, *Landscape with Figures and Windmill* (oil on panel, 9 3/4 x 13 1/2 ins / 25 x 34.5 cm) SEK 25,500. LONDON, 11 Dec 1992, *Windmill in Extensive Landscape with Peasants on River Bank* (oil on panel, 9 3/4 x 13 1/2 ins / 24.8 x 34.6 cm) GBP 2,530. LONDON, 26 Oct 1994, *Church in Suburbs of Town* (oil on panel, 8 1/2 x 11 1/4 ins / 21.5 x 28.5 cm) GBP 5,750. LONDON, 11 Oct 1995, *River Landscape with Figures* (oil on panel, 12 x 15 1/2 ins / 30.5 x 39.5 cm) GBP 9,200. PARIS, 17 June 1997, *Panoramic View of Rhine Valley* (canvas, 49 x 64 1/4 ins / 124.5 x 163 cm) FRF 175,000. LONDON, 28 Oct 1999, *River Landscape with Travellers on Bridge* (oil on panel, 9 x 12 ins / 23 x 31 cm) GBP 5,500. ZURICH, 4 Nov 2000, *Fantasy Rhine Landscape with Boats, Tower and Church* (oil on panel, 12 x 16 ins / 31 x 41 cm) CHF 34,000. COLOGNE, 25 Nov 2000, *River Landscape with High Fortress* (oil on canvas, 67 x 80 ins / 169 x 204 cm) DEM 42,000. BREMEN, 28 June 2003, *Feldberg, Taunus at Sunset* (oil on canvas, 13 x 16 ins / 32 x 40 cm) EUR 6,500. MUNICH, 5 Dec 2003, *Idyllic Landscape* (oil on panel, 13 x 17 ins / 33 x 44 cm) EUR 6,200.

SCHÜZ, Christian Georg III, or Schütz
German, 19th century.
Born 16 April 1803, in Frankfurt am Main;
died May 1821.
Painter.

Christian Georg Schüz III was a relation - perhaps the son - and pupil of Christian Georg Schüz II.

SCHÜZ, Christoph, or Schütze
German, 18th century.
Died c. 1726.
Active in Leipzig.
Painter.

SCHÜZ, Franz, or Schütz
German, 18th century.
Born 16 December 1751, in Frankfurt; died 14 May 1781, in Sacconnex.
Painter, engraver. Landscapes with figures, landscapes.

Franz Schüz studied under his father, Christian Georg Schüz the Elder, and painted numerous views of Switzerland. A journey to Milan and its environs was to exert a positive influence. He is routinely represented as a jovial companion who enjoyed music and fine wine.

MUSEUMS AND GALLERIES:
BERN: three imaginary landscapes; *Church by Stream*; *Windmill* - GRAZ: *Landscape of High Mountains with Stream.*

AUCTION RECORDS:
NEW YORK, 7 June 1978, *Swiss Landscape* (oil on panel, 10 1/4 x 15 3/4 ins / 26 x 40 cm) USD 3,600. ZURICH, 2 Nov 1979, *Fishermen by Mountain Torrent* (oil/copper, 23 1/4 x 17 ins / 59 x 43 cm) CHF 15,000. COPENHAGEN, 22 April 1982, *River Landscapes with Figures* (oil on panel, a pair, 14 1/4 x 19 ins / 36 x 48 cm) DKK 130,000. STOCKHOLM, 31 Oct 1984, *River Landscape with Figures* (oil on panel, 18 x 28 1/4 ins / 46 x 72 cm) SEK 110,000. MUNICH, 23 Oct 1985, *Rhenish Landscapes* (oil on canvas, a pair, 14 1/4 x 18 3/4 ins / 36 x 47.5 cm) DEM 85,000. AMSTERDAM, 13 Nov 1995, *Travellers Crossing Bridge near Cascade* (1775, oil on canvas, 35 3/4 x 42 1/4 ins / 90.7 x 107.5 cm) NLG 10,350. VIENNA, 22 March 2001, *Wooded Landscape with River and Herders* (oil on canvas, 11 x 15 ins / 28 x 37 cm) ATS 80,000. COLOGNE, 19 May 2001, *River Landscapes* (oil on canvas, 11 x 14 ins / 27 x 35 cm) DEM 30,000. VIENNA, 27 March 2003, *Houses on River and Figures* (oil on panel, 7 x 11 ins / 19 x 28 cm) EUR 5,000.

SCHÜZ, Friedrich, or Schütz
German, 19th - 20th century.
Born 17 July 1874, in Düsseldorf; died 1954, in Tübingen.
Painter, engraver.

Friedrich Schüz was the brother of Hans Schüz and the son of Theodor Schüz. He was a pupil of Heinrich Lauenstein, Peter J. Janssen and Karl F. E. von Gebhardt.

MUSEUMS AND GALLERIES:
DÜSSELDORF - HAIGENLOCH (Schütz Mus.).

AUCTION RECORDS:
HAMBURG, 14 June 1980, *Landscape* (oil on card, 27 1/2 x 38 1/2 ins / 70 x 98 cm) DEM 4,000. NEWBURY, 10 Oct 2001, *View of Salzburg* (oil on panel, 20 x 26 ins / 51 x 66 cm) GBP 3,800.

SCHÜZ, Hans
German, 20th century.
Born 21 February 1883, in Düsseldorf; died 3 January 1922, in Stuttgart.
Painter, engraver. Religious subjects.

Hans Schüz was the son of Theodor Schüz and the brother of Friedrich Schüz. He studied in Düsseldorf under Peter J. Janssen, in Karlsruhe under Ludwig Schmid-Reutte and Walter Conz, and in Munich under Carl von Marr and Ludwig von Loefftz.

MUSEUMS AND GALLERIES:
DÜSSELDORF: *Flight into Egypt* - WUPPERTAL: *Wedding Feast at Cana.*

SCHÜZ, Heinrich Joseph, or Schütz
German, 18th - 19th century.
Born 17 September 1760, in Frankfurt am Main; died 2 July 1822, in Frankfurt am Main.
Draughtsman, engraver (aquatint).

Heinrich Schüz was the son of Christian Georg Schüz I and the pupil of J. G. Prestel.

SCHÜZ, Johann Georg. See **SCHÜTZ**

SCHÜZ, Josef
German, 18th century.
Active c. 1758.
Painter.

MUSEUMS AND GALLERIES:
HOHENDILCHING (Church): *Joseph and the Christ Child; Anne Teaching the Infant Virgin.*

SCHÜZ, Joseph Antoni
German, 18th century.
Born 1746, in Neresheim.
Painter.

Joseph Schüz studied in Vienna and worked in Munich.

MUSEUMS AND GALLERIES:
GRIESSTÄTT (Kloster Altenhohenau, St. Peter und Paul): *St Anne and the Virgin; St Peter and St Paul; St Anne and the Virgin; St Xavier and St Dominic.*

SCHÜZ, Philippine Maria
German, 18th century.
Born 1767; died 1797.
Painter. Landscapes with figures.

Philippine Maria Schüz was the daughter of Christian Georg Schüz I.

AUCTION RECORDS:
VIENNA, 16 May 1984, *Banks of the Rhine with Figures* (oil on canvas, 9 1/2 x 12 1/2 ins / 24.2 x 31.5 cm) ATS 60,000.

SCHÜZ, Theodor
German, 19th century.
Born 26 March 1830, in Thumlingen; died 17 June 1900, in Düsseldorf.
Painter, illustrator. Portraits, genre scenes, landscapes.

Theodor Schüz was taught by Rustige, Neher and Steinkopf at the art academy in Stuttgart, then by Piloty in Munich. He settled in Düsseldorf in 1860.

MUSEUMS AND GALLERIES:
DÜSSELDORF: *Promenade at Easter* - FRANKFURT AM MAIN (Städel): *Landscape* - STUTTGART: *Midday Prayer during Harvest; Sermon Listeners before Church* - ULM: *Evening Prayer.*

AUCTION RECORDS:
STUTTGART, 6 March 1981, *Couple in Garden* (oil on canvas, 51 1/2 x 38 1/2 ins / 131 x 98 cm) DEM 4,200. PARIS, 12 Dec 1984, *Harvest* (oil on canvas, 10 x 14 1/2 ins / 24.5 x 37 cm) FRF 15,000. LONDON, 8 Oct 1986, *View of Farm* (oil on canvas, 27 1/4 x 37 1/2 ins / 69 x 95 cm) GBP 26,000. AMSTERDAM, 2 May 1990, *Young Friends* (1896, oil on canvas, 18 3/4 x 23 ins / 47.5 x 57.5 cm) NLG 20,700. VERSAILLES, 12 June 1994, *Procession, Spring Song* (1859, oil on canvas, 48 x 63 3/4 ins / 122 x 162 cm) FRF 840,000. COLOGNE, 4 Dec 1999, *Alpine Landscape with Resting Walkers* (1897, oil on board, 13 x 10 ins / 33 x 25 cm) DEM 6,000. COLOGNE, 20 May 2000, *Mountain Landscape with Stream* (1895, oil on canvas, 17 x 31 ins / 44 x 80 cm) DEM 13,000. STUTTGART, 20 Sept 2001, *Grand-father's Visit* (oil on canvas, 30 x 25 ins / 75 x 63 cm) DEM 10,000. LUCERNE, 4 June 2003, *Swabian Alb Landscape* (1891, oil on board, 7 x 10 ins / 19 x 25 cm) CHF 6,000. STUTTGART, 19 Sept 2003, *Children Playing near Haigerloch* (oil on board, 4 x 7 ins / 11 x 17 cm) EUR 2,500.

SCHVANCK, Wilhelmine
Latvian, 19th century.
Born 2 August 1844, in Volmer.
Active in Germany.
Painter. Portraits, still-lifes.
Wilhelmine Schvanck studied under Anton M. L. Kriebel in Dresden and was active in Altenburg.
AUCTION RECORDS:
LONDON, 27 Nov 1985, *Young Girl Chasing a Butterfly* (1877, oil on canvas, oval, 29 1/2 x 26 1/4 ins / 75 x 66.5 cm) GBP 2,200.

SCHVEDE, Fedor Fedorovich
Russian, 19th century.
Born 1819; died 7 September 1863, in St Petersburg.
Landscape artist.
Fedor Fedorovich Schvede was the cousin of Robert Schvede and studied at the art academy in St Petersburg.

SCHVEDE, Robert, or Chvede
Russian, 19th century.
Born 6 December 1806, in Moiseküll; died 28 July 1874, in Gräfenfeld.
Portrait artist.
Robert Scheve studied at the art academy in St Petersburg, and was taught by K.T. von Neff.
MUSEUMS AND GALLERIES:
RIGA (MM): *Portrait of a Lady*.

SCHWAB
German, 18th century.
Sculptor.

SCHWAB
German, 18th century.
Born to a family originally from Lohr-am-Main.
Stucco artist.
Schwab decorated the castle of Birstein.

SCHWAB, André Pierre
French, 20th century.
Born 6 August 1883, in Nancy.
Sculptor, engraver, medallist.
Schwab was taught by Jules Clément Chaplain and Marius Jean A. Mercié. He exhibited in Paris, at the Salon des Artistes Français, where he was a member presented hors-concours (outside of the competition); he won the gold medal in 1926.

SCHWAB, Cölestin (Pater)
German, 18th century.
Art lover.
Cölestin Schwab was in charge of the building works of the church in Bruchsal in 1737 and 1738.

SCHWAB, Eigil Wilhelm
Swedish, 20th century.
Born 28 March 1882, in Stockholm; died 1952.
Painter, draughtsman, engraver. Portraits, landscapes, still-lifes.
Eigil Wilhelm Schwab studied at the fine arts academy from 1903 to 1907. He specialised in portraiture and caricatures.
AUCTION RECORDS:
STOCKHOLM, 6 June 1988, *Still-life with Flowers on a Blue Table* (oil, 21 1/4 x 17 1/4 ins / 54 x 44 cm) SEK 5,500; *Courtyard in the Late Winter Sun* (1908, oil, 17 x 21 1/4 ins / 43 x 54 cm) SEK 3,500. STOCKHOLM, 6 Dec 1989, *Still-life of a Floral Composition with Lilies* (oil on panel, 24 x 17 3/4 ins / 61 x 45 cm) SEK 4,000.

SCHWAB, Ernst
German, 18th century.
Active in Würzburg.
Painter.
Ernst Schwab painted the decoration of the Residenz at Würzburg.

SCHWAB, Hans. See **WERTINGER Hans**

SCHWAB, Hélène Louise
French, 20th century.
Born 22 November 1878, in Beaume-les-Dames (Doubs).
Painter. Figures, landscapes.
Schwab was taught by Fernand Humbert. From 1921 she exhibited in Paris, at the Salon des Artistes Français, where she was a member.

SCHWAB, Johann Caspar or Jean Gaspard
Austrian, 18th century.
Born 1727, in Vienna.
Engraver (burin).
Johann Schwab was the pupil of Wille in Paris where he worked from 1765. He was still alive in 1810.

SCHWAB, Jorg. See **DIEF Jorg**

SCHWAB, Karl Philipp
German, 19th century.
Born to a family originally from Schwetzingen.
Painter. Genre scenes, landscapes, flowers.
Karl Schwab attended the academy in Munich around 1823, then worked in Mosbach.

SCHWAB, P. C.
German, 18th century.
Painter.
P. C. Schwab worked in the glazed earthenware factory in Nuremberg between 1725 and 1730.
MUSEUMS AND GALLERIES:
WÜRZBURG (Mainfränkisches Mus.): two plates.

SCHWABE, Aleksandr Johann Gotlieb, or Shvabe Aleksandr Petrovich
Latvian, 19th century.
Born 14 September 1818, in Riga; died 30 May 1872, in Reval (now Tallinn).
Painter. Historical subjects, battles, figures, animals.
Aleksandr Johann Schwabe studied at the art academy in St Petersburg with Sauerweid, and became a teacher there in 1861.
MUSEUMS AND GALLERIES:
MOSCOW (State Tretyakov Gal.): *Parliamentarians*.
AUCTION RECORDS:
LONDON, 10 Oct 1990, *Two Cossack Sentinels Talking* (oil on canvas, 22 3/4 x 18 1/4 ins / 57.8 x 46.4 cm) GBP 8,800. LONDON, 27 Nov 1992, *Two Cossack Sentinels Talking* (1841, oil on canvas, 22 3/4 x 18 1/4 ins / 57.8 x 46.4 cm) GBP 4,400. LONDON, 20 Nov 2002, *At the Races* (1853, oil on canvas, 29 x 42 ins / 73 x 106 cm) GBP 32,000.

SCHWABE, Carlos, or Charles
German, 19th - 20th century.
Born 21 July 1866, in Altona; died 1926, in Paris.
Active in Switzerland from 1870, naturalised in 1888, also active in France from 1884.
Painter (including gouache), watercolourist, engraver, draughtsman, illustrator, designer. Religious subjects, allegorical subjects, genre scenes, nudes, portraits, landscapes. Designs (wallpapers).
Symbolism.

Carlos Schwabe's family settled in Geneva in 1870 and Carlos studied under J. Mittey and Barthélemy Menn at the fine arts school there. Schwabe moved to Paris in 1884.

He was a highly successful decorative painter, noted perhaps above all for his wide range of stylised floral wallpaper patterns. He was also an accomplished illustrator whose formal approach contains echoes of Dürer and Mantegna. He is particularly noted for his illustrations, among others, of Émile Zola's *Le Rêve* (*The Dream*), Charles Baudelaire's *Les Fleurs du Mal* (*The Flowers of Evil*), and Maurice Maeterlinck's *Pelleas and Melisande*. Towards the end of his life, his powerful Symbolism became distinctly more muted.

He exhibited in Paris at the Salon de la Société Nationale des Beaux-Arts (initially in 1891 with *Evening Bells*), the Salon des Artistes Français and the Rose-Croix (Rosicrucian) exhibition of 1892 at the Galerie Durand-Ruel, for which he designed the poster. Several of Schwabe's works were shown in 1993 at the *L'Âme au Corps* (*Body and Soul*) exhibition mounted at the Galeries Nationales du Grand Palais in Paris. The Musée d'Orsay devoted an exhibition to him in 1994 entitled *Symbolisme et Naturalisme: Carlos Schwabe Illustrateur du 'Rêve' de Zola* (*Symbolism and Naturalism: Carlos Schwabe, Illustrator of Zola's 'Dream'*). Schwabe was awarded a gold medal at the Exposition Universelle in Paris in 1900 and, the following year, was made a Chevalier of the Légion d'Honneur.

Bibliography:

Osterwalder, Marcus (ed.), *Dictionnaire des illustrateurs 1800-1914*, Ides et Calendes, Neuchâtel, 1989. Jumeau-Lafond, Jean-David, *Carlos Schwabe, symboliste et visionnaire*, ACR Édition, Courbevoie, 1994. '*Carlos Schwabe, symboliste et visionnaire*' in *Art et Métiers du Livre*, no. 186, p 52, periodical, Paris, 1994.

Museums and Galleries:

Amsterdam (Van Gogh Mus.): *Virgin of the Lilies* - Geneva (MAH): *Passion* - Geneva (Mus. Ariana): *Passion* - Paris (Louvre): *Death of the Gravedigger* - Rio de Janeiro (Mus. Nacional de Belas Artes): *All Souls' Day* (1893).

Auction Records:

Paris, 4 March 1925, *Scene of Spiritism* (watercolour) FRF 20. Paris, 26 Feb 1931, *Woman with Lute* (watercolour); *Art and Idea* (Indian ink wash, two) FRF 52. Paris, Oct 1945-July 1946, *Dauphiné Landscape*; *Alsace Landscape* (two gouaches) FRF 600. Paris, 9 Dec 1974, *Mother and Child in Paradise* (gouache) FRF 74,500. Monte Carlo, 16 Dec 1978, *Muse* (watercolour, 19 x 12 1/2 ins / 48.5 x 32 cm) FRF 36,000. Paris, 4 April 1979, *Waves* (1908, watercolour drawing, 9 x 6 1/4 ins / 22 x 16 cm) FRF 12,000. Paris, 26 June 1979, *Woman Bathing* (1903, oil on panel, 17 x 7 1/2 ins / 43 x 19 cm) FRF 30,000. London, 26 Nov 1980, *Dusk by the Sea* (1916, pastel, round, diam. 4 3/4 ins / 12 cm) GBP 3,000. New York, 26 May 1983, *Ideal* (1913, oil on canvas, 78 x 45 ins / 198 x 114 cm) USD 15,000. Paris, 19 Oct 1983, *Allegory of Time* (pencil/grey paper, 9 x 6 ins / 22 x 15 cm) FRF 29,000. London, 10 Sept 1984, *Virgin and Child; Symbols of the Passion* (1895, watercolour and pencil heightened with gold, a pair, 13 1/2 x 10 1/4 ins / 34 x 26 cm) GBP 8,500. Paris, 27 Sept 1985, *Illustration for 'Les Fleurs du Mal'* (1893, wash drawing heightened with gouache/two joined sheets, 7 1/2 x 5 ins / 19 x 13 cm) FRF 9,500. Paris, 18 April 1989, *Apple Trees in Blossom at St-Malo de La Lande* (1912, 18 x 24 ins / 46 x 61 cm) FRF 20,000. London, 1 Dec 1989, *Apple Blossom* (1912, oil on canvas, 39 1/4 x 28 3/4 ins / 100 x 73 cm) GBP 6,820. Monaco, 3 Dec 1989, *Fate* (1894, watercolour and gouache, 17 1/2 x 26 1/2 ins / 44.7 x 67.5 cm) FRF 800,000. Monaco, 8 Dec 1990, *Pelleas and Melisande* (1923, watercolour, 8 3/4 x 6 1/4 ins / 22.5 x 16 cm) FRF 66,600. Paris, 11 Dec 1991, *Virginity* (1909, gouache and watercolour, 5 1/2 x 4 ins / 14 x 10 cm) FRF 4,300. London, 11 April 1995, *Childhood* (1889, ink and watercolour, 26 1/2 x 17 1/4 ins / 67 x 44 cm) GBP 3,450. Zurich, 12 June 1995, *Portrait of a Woman* (red chalk/paper, 23 1/2 x 18 ins / 60 x 46 cm) CHF 2,070. Amsterdam, 4 June 1996, *Fruit Tree in Blossom* (1912, oil on canvas, 39 1/4 x 28 3/4 ins / 100 x 73 cm) NLG 6,844. London, 26 March 1997, *Homer in the Elysian Fields* (c. 1910, oil on canvas, 51 1/4 x 63 ins / 130 x 160 cm) GBP 18,400. London, 17 Feb 1999, *Rosicrucian Composition* (1894, watercolour and ink, 13 x 9 ins / 33 x 22 cm) GBP 1,800. Paris, 12 Dec 1999, *Virgin of the Lys* (1912, watercolour, 13 x 9 ins / 33 x 23 cm) FRF 201,000. Paris, 16 March 2001, *Apple Trees in Blossom* (1912, oil on canvas, 39 x 29 ins / 100 x 73 cm) FRF 95,000. Paris, 30 March 2001, *Virgin with Rose* (crayon and pencil on gold ground) FRF 62,000. Paris, 5 June 2002, *Game* (1892, watercolour and ink, 12 x 9 ins / 30 x 22 cm) EUR 9,500. New York, 29 Oct 2002, *Elysian Fields* (1903, pencil, watercolour and gouache, 19 x 12 ins / 47 x 30 cm) USD 35,000. Paris, 6 June 2003, *Metje in Switzerland* (oil on panel, 11 x 14 ins / 28 x 35 cm) EUR 1,500. Paris, 27 Nov 2003, *Judgement of Paris* (1924, oil on canvas, 66 x 116 ins / 168 x 295 cm) EUR 19,500. Neuilly, 11 June 2004, *Faun* (1923, pastel, red chalk, charcoal and colour crayon, 12 x 19 ins / 31 x 48 cm) EUR 5,500.

SCHWABE, Emil
German, 19th - 20th century.
Born 12 June 1856, in Zielenzig.
Painter. Portraits, genre scenes.

Emil Schwabe studied at the fine arts academy in Düsseldorf.

Museums and Galleries:

Düsseldorf: *Political Issues*; *Portrait of an Old Woman*.

SCHWABE, Heinrich
German, 19th - 20th century.
Born 30 October 1847, in Wiesbaden.
Sculptor.

Heinrich Schwabe studied under August von Kreling at the fine arts school in Nuremberg and went on to teach there from 1875 to 1907.

SCHWABE, Heinrich August
German, 19th - 20th century.
Born 2 February 1843, in Oberweissbach (Turingen); died 8 February 1916, in South Orange (New York).
Active in the USA from 1871.
Painter. Designs for stained glass.

Heinrich August Schwabe lived and worked in Newark (New Jersey), having moved to the USA in or around 1871 after studying design in New York, Munich and Paris and starting out as a glass painter in Stuttgart.

SCHWABE, Leonhard
Danish, 18th century.
Active in Copenhagen.
Sculptor.

Schwabe worked on the decoration of Frederiksborg and Rosenborg castles.

SCHWABE, Nikolaus or Nickel
German, 16th century.
Active in Copenhagen.
Medallist, engraver.

Nikolaus Schwabe was initially apprenticed in Nuremberg. He entered the service of Christian IV of Denmark in 1596.

SCHWABE, Randolph
British, 20th century.
Born 9 March 1885, in Manchester; died 19 September 1948, in Helensburgh.
Painter, watercolourist, draughtsman, engraver, illustrator. Mythological subjects, military subjects, figures, landscapes, urban landscapes, architectural views, costume studies.

Randolph Schwabe trained in London at the Royal College of Art in 1899, the Slade School of Fine Art from 1900-1905 and the Académie Julian in Paris in 1906. He became a member of the London Group in 1915 and the Royal Society of Painters in Watercolours in 1939. Schwabe taught at Camberwell and Westminster Schools of Art, and succeeded Henry Tonks as professor and principal of the Slade School in 1930. He exhibited with the New English Art Club from 1909, becoming a member in 1917. Schwabe also exhibited with the Royal Scottish Academy in 1925, 1939 and 1945. He was an Official War Artist from 1914-1918, and produced a number of drawings of the Women's Land Army. He collaborated with F.M. Kelly on two books: *Historic Costume* in 1925 and *A Short History of Costume and Armour* in 1931.

MUSEUMS AND GALLERIES:
LONDON (Tate Collection): *Hampstead High Street* (1928); *The Radcliffe Observatory, Oxford* (1942).

AUCTION RECORDS:
LONDON, 3 May 1990, *Nymphs Picking Apples* (oil on canvas, 48 x 96 ins / 122 x 244 cm) GBP 2,640. LONDON, 2 May 1991, *Nymphs Picking Apples* (oil on canvas, 48 x 96 ins / 122 x 244 cm) GBP 2,200. LEOMINSTER, 15 Aug 2001, *Portrait of a Young Girl Seated Close to River Bridge in Landscape* (oil on canvas, 39 x 28 ins / 99 x 71 cm) GBP 1,500.

SCHWABEDA, Johann Michael
German, 18th century.
Born 1734, in Erfurt; died 1794, in Ansbach.
Painter. Landscapes, flowers, fruit.

After a period spent as a wax modeller, Johann Schwabeda was court painter at Ansbach and also worked at Fulda and Würzburg. His key work is the portrait of *Seckendorf Aberdar* in the castle of Strössendorf near Ansbach.

SCHWABENMAJER, Gustav. See **MAJER Gustav**

SCHWABENTALER, Hans.
See **SCHWANTHALER**

SCHWACH, Heinrich August
Austrian, 19th century.
Born 19 September 1829, in Neutitschein; died 6 May 1902, in Graz.
Painter. History painting, battles, portraits.

The pupil of Waldmuller and Rahl at the academy in Vienna, Schwach went to study in Belgium and worked with Dijkmans in Antwerp. He taught at the art academy in Graz and in Austria enjoyed a considerable reputation as a restorer of old paintings.

SCHWACHHOFER, Johann Joseph, or Johannes Josephus
German, 18th - 19th century.
Born 1772, in Mainz; died after 1828.
Painter. History painting, portraits.

Schwachhofer was the pupil of J. Knyper in Amsterdam where his presence is recorded until 1828.

SCHWACKE, Brigitte
German, 20th - 21st century.
Born 1957, in Marl.
Sculptor, draughtswoman, installation artist.

Brigitte Schwacke studied design in Münster, attended the Akademie der Bildende Künste in Munich from 1983 to 1989, was a pupil in Paolozzi's studio in 1989, and a student at the Royal College of Art in London from 1991 to 1992. In 1992 she was a research assistant at the Slade School of Fine Art in London. She lives and works in Munich.

She produces drawings, geometric figures and delicate interlaced lines on the exhibition walls. She also creates iron wire sculptures and abstract drawings in bitumen on paper. Her work is concerned with the relationship between man and time.

She has taken part in various group exhibitions: in Munich on a regular basis since 1984; 1986, Sarajevo; 1987-1988, Kunsthalle in Mannheim and Kunstverein in Stuttgart; 1988, Skulpturenmuseum Glaskasten in Marl and Kunstverein in Dorsten and Bonn; 1991, Edinburgh; 1992, EXPO 92 in Seville and Royal College of Art in London. There have been regular solo exhibitions of her works at the Hasenclever gallery in Munich since 1989, and others including 1991, Kunstinstitut in Stuttgart; 1992, Städtische Galerie in Villingen-Schwenningen; 1993, Kunstinstitut in Heidenheim; 1994, Brussels; 1995, 2004, Galerie Pierre Brullé in Paris.

BIBLIOGRAPHY:
Brigitte Schwacke - Skulpturen, Installationen, exhibition catalogue, Gal. der Künstler, Munich, 1993.

SCHWADE, Heinrich
German, 19th century.
Born 27 November 1843, in Erfurt; died 26 September 1899, in Munich.
Sculptor.

Schwade attended the academy in Munich with Widmann and sculpted the statues of the 12 apostles for the church of St Michael in Breslau (now Wroclaw, Poland).

SCHWAGER, H.
Austrian, 19th century.
Born 3 April 1822, in Duppau (Bohemia); died 8 September 1880, in Rodaun, near Vienna.
Miniaturist. Portraits.

Schwager attended the academy in Vienna in 1847 and devoted himself to portrait painting under the guidance of Kupelwieser. He travelled in Germany, France, Belgium, England and Russia where he received numerous portrait commissions. One of the last miniaturists of the group led by the Austrian painter, Moritz Michael Daffinger, he excelled in the portrayal of children's heads.

SCHWAIGER. See also **PETEL Clement**

SCHWAIGER, Georg and Philipp (brothers)
German, 16th - 17th century.
Active in Amberg.
Sculptors.

One of the Schwaiger brothers was working between 1596 and 1601, the other around 1615.

SCHWAIGER, Hans
Austrian, 16th century.
Active in Graz.
Painter.

SCHWAIGER, Hans
Czech, 19th - 20th century.
Born 28 June 1854, in Jindrichuv Hradec; died 17 June 1912, in Prague.
Painter, watercolourist, draughtsman, engraver.
Historical subjects, genre scenes.

Hans Schwaiger was a student of Josef M. Trenkwald and Carl Wurzinger at the Akademie der Bildenden Künste in Vienna. His output was prolific, and he produced mainly watercolours in Vienna, Brno and Prague. His most famous works became the property of President Masaryk and Prince Liechtenstein.

Museums and Galleries:
Vienna: *The Water Sprite* (watercolour).

SCHWAIGER, Johann
Austrian, 17th - 18th century.
Born 17 June 1657, in Reichenhall; died 10 May 1734.
Active in Reichenhall.
Sculptor. Religious subjects.
Johann's Schwaiger's repertoire is mainly religious in inspiration.

SCHWAIGER, Josef
German, 17th century.
Born near Munich.
Active in Munich c. 1685.
Painter.

SCHWAIGER, Philipp. See **SCHWAIGER Georg** and **Philipp**, brothers

SCHWALB. See **KIPRENSKY Orest Adamovich**

SCHWALBACH, Carl
German, 20th century.
Born 18 May 1885, in Mainz; died 1983.
Active in Munich.
Painter, engraver. Nudes, scenes with figures.
Carl Schwalbach studied at the fine arts school and academy in Munich. He painted predominantly nude groups against landscape backgrounds.
Museums and Galleries:
Darmstadt - Mainz - Munich - Nuremberg - Oberschleissheim (Neues Schloss Schleissheim, Staatsgal.).
Auction records:
São Paulo, 15 Sept 1982, *Fruits of the Earth* (1922, oil on canvas, 37 x 31 1/2 ins / 94 x 79.8 cm) BRL 480,000. Munich, 6 June 1984, *Women Bathing* (1927, oil on canvas, 41 1/4 x 26 ins / 105 x 66 cm) DEM 4,800.

SCHWALBE, Heinrich Wilhelm Christian
German, 19th century.
Born 28 September 1790, in Brunswick; died 10 February 1831, in Berlin.
Painter. Genre scenes, portraits.
Schwalbe attended the academy in Munich from 1820 to 1822, and studied in Rome from 1824 to 1825. He worked in Berlin, and after 1828, in Brunswick.
Museums and Galleries:
Brunswick (Herzog Anton Ulrich-Mus.): *The Annunciation*.

SCHWALBE, Ole
Danish, 20th century.
Born 1929, in Copenhagen.
Painter. Designs for tapestries.
Ole Schwalbe became a member of the Den Frie group in 1969. He wrote several books on art history. He was commissioned to produce decorative compositions for a variety of public buildings, notably schools. His style is precise, pure and geometric (squares and circles), his colour palette minimal. He participated in group exhibitions, including the 1945 Spring Salon in Copenhagen and *Art Danois* (*Danish Art*), an exhibition held at the Grand Palais in Paris in 1973.
Bibliography:
Galy-Carles, Henry, *Art danois, 1945-1973*, exhibition catalogue, Gal. nationales du Grand Palais, Paris, 1973.
Museums and Galleries:
Aalborg (Nordjyllands Kunstmus.): *Composition* (1953); *Sign* (1956-1960); *For Anna* (1961-1962) - Copenhagen (Kunstindustrimus.): *Red Mirage* (1969).
Auction records:
Copenhagen, 29 April 1976, *Composition* (oil on canvas, 12 1/2 x 28 ins / 32 x 71 cm) DKK 3,200. Copenhagen, 6 March 1980, *Compositions* (1956, oil on canvas, three items, 23 1/2 x 19 1/4 ins / 60 x 49 cm) DKK 18,000. Copenhagen, 2 March 1988, *Composition* (46 x 31 1/2 ins / 116 x 80 cm) DKK 10,600. Copenhagen, 22 Nov 1989, *Composition* (1957, oil on canvas, 24 x 19 3/4 ins / 61 x 50 cm) DKK 8,500. Copenhagen, 14-15 Nov 1990, *Night* (1985, oil on canvas, 35 3/4 x 33 ins / 91 x 84 cm) DKK 8,000. Copenhagen, 4 March 1992, *Study* (oil/synthetic resin, 9 3/4 x 17 3/4 ins / 25 x 45 cm) DKK 4,000. Copenhagen, 20 May 1992, *Composition* (oil on canvas, 41 1/4 x 48 ins / 105 x 121 cm) DKK 7,000. Copenhagen, 3 Nov 1993, *Roman Night* (oil on canvas, 28 3/4 x 23 1/2 ins / 73 x 60 cm) DKK 8,000. Copenhagen, 2 March 1994, *Antonio* (oil on canvas, 28 3/4 x 23 1/2 ins / 73 x 60 cm) DKK 7,000. Copenhagen, 12 March 1996, *Steccato* (oil on canvas, 25 1/4 x 25 1/2 ins / 64 x 65 cm) DKK 5,500. Copenhagen, 22-24 Oct 1997, *Composition* (1988, oil on canvas, 36 1/4 x 32 3/4 ins / 92 x 83 cm) DKK 8,000. Copenhagen, 29 Sept 1999, *Composition* (1956, oil on masonite, 51 x 38 ins / 130 x 97 cm) DKK 15,000. Copenhagen, 9 Feb 2000, *Mabillon* (1960, oil on canvas, 24 x 47 ins / 60 x 120 cm) DKK 90,000. Copenhagen, 30 Aug 2000, *Landmark* (painted wood in several pieces on circular platform, 118 x 79 ins / 300 x 200 cm) DKK 25,000. Copenhagen, 19 June 2001, *Trinity* (1954, oil on masonite, 48 x 28 ins / 122 x 70 cm) DKK 18,000. Copenhagen, 19 June 2001, *Roman Light* (1966, oil on canvas, 29 x 24 ins / 73 x 60 cm) DKK 25,000. Copenhagen, 10 April 2002, *Concrete Composition: White, Red and Black* (1966, oil on canvas, 40 x 26 ins / 101 x 67 cm) DKK 30,000. Copenhagen, 18 June 2002, *Composition* (1961, oil on canvas, 21 x 18 ins / 54 x 46 cm) DKK 40,000. Copenhagen, 17 Sept 2003, *Study for Mabillon* (1959, oil on canvas, 13 x 26 ins / 33 x 65 cm) DKK 15,000. Copenhagen, 5 Oct 2004, *Study* (1958, oil on masonite, 10 x 18 ins / 25 x 45 cm) DKK 20,000. Copenhagen, 5 Oct 2004, *Composition* (1951, oil on masonite, 20 x 15 ins / 51 x 39 cm) DKK 65,000.

SCHWALLER, Franz Michael
Swiss, 18th century.
Died 2 March 1792.
Painter.
Schwaller belonged to the guild of Solothurn in 1744.

SCHWALLINGER, Johann Ludwig
German, 17th century.
Active in Saarbrücken in 1623, and in Zweibrücken in 1635.
Painter. Portraits.

SCHWALM, J.
German, 19th century.
Active in Kassel c. 1825.
Draughtsman.

SCHWAMBERGER
Austrian, 18th century.
Active in Vienna.
Painter.

SCHWAMBERGER, Gregor
German, 17th century.
Active in Augsburg.
Sculptor.

SCHWAN, Balthasar
German, 17th century.
Died 1624.
Engraver (burin).
Schwan was granted citizenship in Frankfurt am Main in 1620.

SCHWAN, Friedrich Karl
German, 19th - 20th century.
Born 25 February 1875, in Zeckritz, near Torgau.
Active in Dresden.
Sculptor.

SCHWAN, H.
German, 19th century.
Painter. Urban landscapes.
H. Schwan contributed to exhibitions at the academy in Berlin from 1856 to 1876.

SCHWAN, Johann Daniel
German, 18th century.
Sculptor.

SCHWAN, Peter
German, 17th century.
Active in Cologne 1626-1638.
Painter.

SCHWAN, Wilhelm
German, 17th century.
Active in Brunswick 1621-1641.
Painter, engraver (burin).

SCHWANCK, Martin Johann, or Schwang
German, 18th century.
Died 1794, in Mainz.
Active in Mainz.
Sculptor.
Schwanck had a hand in the restoration of the Castle at Koblenz in 1787.

SCHWANDA, Joseph
Austrian, 19th century.
Born 1796, in Brunn; died 7 June 1829, in Brunn.
Painter. Portraits.
Schwanda attended the academy in Vienna. The museum in Brunn conserves his portrait of Pastor Fricay.

SCHWANDALLER, Hans.
See **SCHWANTHALER**

SCHWANDER, Joseph
Swiss, 18th - 19th century.
Born 1775, in Emmen; died 16 April 1816, in Zurich.
Painter. Genre scenes.

SCHWANFELDER, Charles Henry
British, 18th - 19th century.
Born 11 January 1774, in Leeds; died 1837.
Painter. Portraits, sporting subjects, landscapes with figures, animals.
Charles Henry Schwanfelder was official animal painter to King George III and the Prince Regent. He exhibited in London from 1809 to 1826, showing compositions with sporting themes, typically at the Royal Academy and the British Institution.

BIBLIOGRAPHY:
Mackerness, Eric David, *'Art and Art Instruction in a Nineteenth-Century City: Sheffield'* in *Art History 1, 3*, September 1978. Budge, A., ' *C.H. Schwanfelder - animal painter to the Prince Regent*' in *Leeds Art Calendar, 85*, 1979.

MUSEUMS AND GALLERIES:
LEEDS (City AG): *Pointer and Two Setters* (oil on canvas); *Landscape with Waterfall* (oil on canvas); *Portrait of City Councillor Benjamin Goodman* (1816, oil on canvas); *Self-portrait* (oil on canvas); *Portrait of William and Charles Chadwick at Burley Lodge* (1824, oil on canvas); *Portrait of George Linley* (oil on canvas); other paintings of dogs and landscapes (watercolours) - NOTTINGHAM (Castle Museum and Art Gallery): *Mountain, River, Bridges and Little Houses.*

AUCTION RECORDS:
LONDON, 3 Dec 1926, *Capercaillie Shoot*, GBP 50. LONDON, 27 March 1929, *Landscape with Hunter*, GBP 60. PARIS, 6 June 1951, *Taking the Fox* (1825) FRF 11,500. LONDON, 15 July 1964, *Landscape*, GBP 580. LONDON, 19 July 1972, *Landscape with the Horse 'St. Mark'*, GBP 420. LONDON, 26 March 1976, *Landscape with Horse and Spaniel* (1832, oil on canvas, 24 1/4 x 29 1/4 ins / 61.5 x 74 cm) GBP 1,300. LONDON, 15 March 1978, *Landscape with Gentleman riding a Thoroughbred* (oil on canvas, 20 x 29 1/4 ins / 51 x 74 cm) GBP 2,600. LONDON, 11 April 1980, *Two Thoroughbreds in a Wooded Landscape* (oil on canvas, 21 3/4 x 29 3/4 ins / 55.2 x 75.6 cm) GBP 750. LONDON, 26 June 1981, *Landscape with Hunters and Hounds* (1812, oil on canvas, 25 x 32 ins / 63.5 x 81.2 cm) GBP 1,400. LONDON, 14 March 1984, *Hunting Scene: Capercaillie Shoot in Yorkshire* (oil on canvas, 39 1/4 x 49 1/4 ins / 100 x 125 cm) GBP 20,000. LONDON, 20 Nov 1985, *Bay Horse and Dog in a Wooded Landscape* (1819, oil on canvas, 25 1/4 x 32 3/4 ins / 64 x 83 cm) GBP 7,500. NEW YORK, 9 June 1988, *Hunting on the Foreshore* (1826, oil on canvas, 28 x 35 ins / 71.1 x 88.9 cm) USD 14,300. LONDON, 18 May 1990, *Portrait of Miss Jane Caroline Eadon; Portrait of Mrs. Mary Ann Hare* (oil on canvas, pair, each 21 x 17 ins / 53.3 x 43.2 cm) GBP 1,980. LONDON, 12 July 1990, *Grouse Shoot* (oil on canvas, 27 x 36 1/4 ins / 68.5 x 92 cm) GBP 6,600. LONDON, 31 Oct 1990, *Hunters and Hounds in a Vast Landscape* (oil on canvas, 17 1/4 x 23 1/2 ins / 44 x 60 cm) GBP 1,650. LONDON, 10 April 1991, *Pack Hound and Two Spaniels in a Park* (oil on canvas, 17 x 23 1/4 ins / 43 x 59 cm) GBP 9,350. LONDON, 12 April 1991, *Dapple-Grey Horse, Bay and Spaniel in a Vast Landscape* (1812, oil on canvas, 26 x 34 1/2 ins / 66 x 87.5 cm) GBP 7,700. PERTH, 26 Aug 1991, *Hunting in the Wilds* (oil on canvas, 33 x 44 ins / 84 x 111.5 cm) GBP 7,700. NEW YORK, 5 June 1992, *Chestnut Trotter* (1826, oil on canvas, 23 x 30 ins / 58.4 x 76.2 cm) USD 4,400. LONDON, 7 April 1993, *Vast Mountain Landscape with Figures Fishing by a Fast-Moving Stream* (oil on canvas, 32 3/4 ins / 83 cm, 3 1/4 x 44 ins/8 x 111.9 cm) GBP 6,900. PERTH, 31 Aug 1993, *Hunting in the Wilds* (oil on canvas, 33 x 44 ins / 84 x 111.5 cm) GBP 9,430. LONDON, 27 May 1999, *John Spence Clearing Last Hurdle* (1817, oil on canvas, 44 x 56 ins / 112 x 143 cm) GBP 65,000. LONDON, 14 July 1999, *Two Greyhounds in Landscape with Prey* (oil on canvas, 57 x 71 ins / 144 x 180 cm) GBP 40,000.

SCHWANG, Martin Johann. See **SCHWANCK**

SCHWANHARD, Georg, the Elder, or Schwanhardt or Schwanhart
German, 17th century.
Born 1601, in Nuremberg; died 3 April 1667.
Engraver (glass).
Georg Schwanhard the Elder was the pupil of Kaspar Lehmann in Prague and settled in Nuremberg in 1622.

SCHWANHARD, Georg, the Younger, or Schwanhardt or Schwanhart
German, 17th century.
Died 4 February 1676, in Nuremberg.
Engraver (glass).
Georg Schwanhard the Younger was the son of Georg the Elder.

SCHWANHARD, Heinrich
German, 17th century.
Died 2 October 1693, in Nuremberg.
Engraver (glass). Figures and landscapes.

SCHWANHARD, Katharina
German, 17th century.
Died 22 April 1701, in Nuremberg.
Engraver (glass).
Katharina Schwanhard was the wife of Georg the Younger.

SCHWANHARD, Marie
German, 17th century.
Died 1 March 1658.
Active in Nuremberg.
Engraver (glass).
Marie Schwanhard was the daughter of Georg the Elder.

SCHWANHARD, Sophie
German, 17th century.

Died 4 July 1657.
Active in Nuremberg.
Engraver (glass).
Sophie Schwanhard was the daughter of Georg the Elder.

SCHWANHARD, Susanna, later Frau Morbach
German, 17th century.
Died 2 April 1669.
Active in Nuremberg.
Engraver (glass).
Susanna Schwanhard was the daughter of Georg the Elder.

SCHWANTHALER, Basilius
Austrian, 17th century.
Born 4 March 1670, in Ried.
Sculptor.
Basilius Schwanthaler was the son of Thomas and brother of Johann Josef or Johann Franz Schwanthaler. He worked for the abbey of Heiligenkreuz near Vienna.

SCHWANTHALER, Bonaventura
Austrian, 18th century.
Born 14 July 1678, in Ried.
Sculptor.
Bonaventura Schwanthaler sculpted *St Leonard* and *St Antony* in the church in Ried.

SCHWANTHALER, Franz Anton
Austrian, 18th - 19th century.
Born 10 May 1767, in Ried; died 1833, in Munich.
Sculptor.
Franz Anton Schwanthaler was the son of Peter the Elder and brother of Johann Peter the Younger and Franz (or Franz Jakob) Schwanthaler. He settled in Munich in 1785.

SCHWANTHALER, Franz I, or Johann Franz
Austrian, 18th century.
Born 16 August 1683, in Ried; died 3 July 1762, in Ried.
Sculptor.
Franz Schwanthaler I was the son of Thomas, the brother of Basilius and Johann Josef, and the father of Franz Mathias and Johann Peter Schwanthaler the Elder. He is associated with sculptural groups of small dimensions executed in the late Baroque style.
MUSEUMS AND GALLERIES:
VIENNA (Österreichische Gal. Belvedere, Barockmuseum).
AUCTION RECORDS:
VIENNA, 15 March 1978, *Christ* (c. 1720, lime wood, h. 30 ins / 76 cm) ATS 110,000. VIENNA, 5 Oct 2001, *St Florian* (gilded and painted wood, h. 44 ins / 113cms) ATS 350,000. VIENNA, 3 Oct 2002, *God, the Father with Angels and Star-burst* (gilded and silvered wood) EUR 16,000. VIENNA, 3 Oct 2002, *Madonna on Cloud with Crescent Moon* (gilded and painted panel, h. 45 ins / 215 cm) EUR 18,000. VIENNA, 25 March 2003, *Resurrected Christ* (gilded wood, h. 30 ins / 75 cm) EUR 6,000. VIENNA, 25 March 2003, *Madonna with Child* (low relief, h. 32 ins / 82 cm) EUR 19,000.

SCHWANTHALER, Franz II, or Franz Jakob
German, 18th - 19th century.
Born 2 August 1760, in Ried; died 4 December 1820, in Munich.
Sculptor.
Franz Schwanthaler II was the son of Johann Peter the Elder, the brother of Johann Peter the Younger and Franz Anton Schwanthaler the Elder, and possibly the father of Ludwig Michael. He worked in Ried and Salzburg, settling in Munich in 1785. An early exponent of Classicism in Munich, he sculpted numerous funerary monuments and statues as well as executing decorative sculptures, largely in Munich.
MUSEUMS AND GALLERIES:
MUNICH (Bayerisches Nationalmus.): *Bust of Queen Caroline*.

SCHWANTHALER, Franz Jakob
Austrian, 18th century.
Born 3 July 1760, in Ried; died 1801, in Ried.
Sculptor.
Franz Jakob Schwanthaler was the son of Franz Mathias.

SCHWANTHALER, Franz Mathias
Austrian, 18th century.
Born 20 June 1714, in Ried; died 16 April 1782, in Ried.
Sculptor.
Franz Mathias Schwanthaler was the son of Franz or Johann Franz, the brother of Johann Peter the Elder and the father of Franz Jakob Schwanthaler. He worked for the churches of Waldzell and Aspach.

SCHWANTHALER, Hans, or Schwanthaller or Schanenthaller or Schwandaller or Schwabenthaler or Schwabentaler
German, 17th century.
Born in Oberland (Baden-Württemberg); died 20 November 1656, in Ried.
Active during the first half of the 17th century.
Sculptor (wood).
The father of Thomas, Hans Schwanthaler originated the extensive dynasty of the Schwanthaler, the Ried sculptors. He founded a sculpture workshop in Ried (upper Austria) in 1632.

SCHWANTHALER, Johann Ferdinand
Austrian, 18th century.
Born 19 October 1722, in Ried.
Sculptor.
Johann Ferdinand Schwanthaler sculpted a tabernacle in Rococo style in the church of Gurten in 1775.

SCHWANTHALER, Johann Georg
Austrian, 18th century.
Born 1740; died 1810.
Sculptor. Religious subjects. Groups, low reliefs, figurines.
Johann Georg Schwanthaler worked in Gmunden from 1773 to 1709 and sculpted crib figurines.
AUCTION RECORDS:
VIENNA, 3 Dec 1971, *St Anne Teaching the Infant Virgin to Read*, ATS 35,000. LONDON, 8 July 1976, *St John the Baptist Preaching in the Wilderness* (1783, wood, high relief, 9 x 12 1/2 ins / 22 x 32 cm) GBP 1,600.

SCHWANTHALER, Johann Josef
Austrian, 18th century.
Born 12 February 1681, in Ried; died 24 June 1743, in Ried.
Sculptor.
Johann Josef Schwanthaler was the son of Thomas and the brother of Basilius and Franz (or Johann Franz) Schwanthaler. He worked in Ried, Eitzing, Auleiten and Gonetreit.

SCHWANTHALER, Johann Peter, the Elder
Austrian, 18th century.
Born 20 June 1720, in Ried; died 20 July 1795, in Ried.
Sculptor.
Johann Peter Schwanthaler the Elder was the son of Johann Franz, the brother of Franz Mathias and the father of Johann Peter the Younger, Franz (or Franz Jakob) and Franz Anton Schwanthaler. He was one of the principal exponents of the Rococo style in Austria and produced the five altars in the church in Hohenzell.
MUSEUMS AND GALLERIES:
VIENNA (Österreichische Gal. Belvedere, Barockmuseum): *Pietà*.
AUCTION RECORDS:
VIENNA, 16 March 1977, *The Virgin and the Angel of the Annunciation* (sculpture in polychr. lime wood, the pair, h. 6 1/4 ins / 16 cm the Virgin Saint, 9 1/4 ins/23.4 cm the angel) ATS

120,000. VIENNA, 6 Oct 2000, *Cross. Mary* (lime wood, two works, h. 22 ins / 57 cm) ATS 140,000. VIENNA, 22 March 2002, *The Risen Christ* (painted wood, h. 27 ins / 68 cm) EUR 9,000.

SCHWANTHALER, Johann Peter, the Younger
Austrian, 18th - 19th century.
Born 2 July 1762, in Ried; died 10 June 1838, in Ried.
Sculptor.

Johann Peter Schwanthaler the Younger was the son of Johann Peter the Elder, the brother of Franz (or Franz Jakob) and Franz Anton Schwanthaler and the father of Xaver. He sculpted funerary monuments, tabernacles and cribs.

MUSEUMS AND GALLERIES:
RIED (Mus.): a crib.

SCHWANTHALER, Ludwig Michael von
German, 19th century.
Born 26 August 1802, in Munich; died 14 November 1848, in Munich.
Sculptor, draughtsman. Groups, statues.

Ludwig Michael von Schwanthaler was the son of the sculptor Franz Anton (or Franz Jakob) Schwanthaler. He taught at the academy in Munich in 1834 and was an exponent of classical sculpture in south Germany.

MUSEUMS AND GALLERIES:
MUNICH (Schwanthaler Mus.).

AUCTION RECORDS:
MUNICH, 28 Nov 1985, *Scene from the History of Ancient Greece* (pen drawing and pencil, series of fifteen, 4 1/4 x 3 1/2 ins / 11 x 9 cm and 7 3/4 x 19 ins/20 x 48 cm and 7 3/4 x 14 1/4 ins/20 x 36 cm) DEM 14,000. HEIDELBERG, 9 Oct 1992, *Amor and Psyche Intertwined; Sleeping Cupid discovered by Psyche* (ink and pencil, a pair, each 7 3/4 x 13 ins / 19.5 x 33 cm) DEM 2,400. ZURICH, 8 Sept 1999, *Erato, Muse of Love-poetry and Lyric, Holding Lyre and Scroll* (white Carrara marble, h. 63 ins / 160 cm) CHF 33,000.

SCHWANTHALER, Rudolf
German, 19th century.
Born 4 April 1842, in Munich; died 27 April 1879, in Munich.
Sculptor.

Rudolf Schwanthaler studied under M. Widnmann and J. von Halbig at the academy in Munich. His repertoire consisted of busts and statues for funerary monuments.

SCHWANTHALER, Thomas
Austrian, 17th century.
Born 5 June 1634, in Ried; died 13 February 1707, in Ried.
Sculptor.

Thomas Schwanthaler was the son of Hans and father of Basilius, Johann Josef and Franz (or Johann Franz). An exponent of Baroque Austrian sculpture, he is associated with altars, funerary monuments and statues for churches in upper Austria.

SCHWANTHALER, Xaver or Franz Xaver or Xavier
German, 19th century.
Born 16 November 1799, in Ried; died 24 September 1854, in Munich.
Sculptor.

Xaver Schwanthaler was the son of Johann Peter the Younger. From 1816 he worked in Munich where he sculpted numerous statues and decorations.

MUSEUMS AND GALLERIES:
SALFORD (Museum and AG): *Schwanhilda*.

SCHWAR, Wilhelm
German, 19th - 20th century.
Born 1860; died 1943.
Active in Munich.
Painter. Genre scenes.

AUCTION RECORDS:
HANOVER, 20 Sept 1980, *Cat and Kitten* (1911, oil on canvas, 16 1/4 x 20 ins / 41 x 51 cm) DEM 11,000. NEW YORK, 1 April 1981, *Collie Dog and Kittens* (oil on canvas, 16 x 20 ins / 40.6 x 50.8 cm) USD 3,750. LONDON, 18 Dec 1997, *Best of Friends* (1906, oil on canvas, 16 x 20 ins / 40.6 x 50.8 cm) GBP 10,580.

SCHWARCMANN, Johann Jakob.
See **SCHWARZMANN**

SCHWARTING, Friedrich
German, 20th century.
Born 1883, in Oldenburg; died August 1918; on the front.
Painter.

Friedrich Schwarting was a pupil of Hermann Schaper.

SCHWARTZ. See also **SCHWARZ**

SCHWARTZ, Adolf, or Schwarz
Austrian, 19th - 20th century.
Born 11 June 1869, in Vienna; died 15 August 1926, in Vienna.
Painter. Landscapes, seascapes.

Adolf Schwartz studied under Adolf Kaufmann at the fine arts academy in Vienna.

MUSEUMS AND GALLERIES:
GRAZ: *Valley View*.

AUCTION RECORDS:
VIENNA, 8 Feb 1990, *Danube Port* (oil on canvas, 27 1/2 x 39 3/4 ins / 70 x 101 cm) ATS 60,000. VIENNA, 4 April 2001, *Field with Figures* (oil on canvas, 19 x 31 ins / 47 x 80 cm) ATS 25,000.

SCHWARTZ, Alfred or Albert Gustav, or Schwarz
German, 19th century.
Born 6 July 1833, in Berlin.
Painter. Portraits, genre scenes.

Alfred Schwartz attended the art academy in Berlin where he exhibited from 1859 to 1878.

AUCTION RECORDS:
NEW YORK, 8-10 Jan 1909, *Nathalie*, USD 575. NEW YORK, 22 May 1991, *Childish Pranks* (1896, oil on canvas, 24 x 31 3/4 ins / 61 x 80.6 cm) USD 8,800.

SCHWARTZ, Andrew Thomas
American, 19th - 20th century.
Born 20 January 1867, in Louisville (Kentucky); died 1942.
Painter. Landscapes, waterscapes. Murals.

Andrew Schwartz studied in Cincinnati and at the Art Students' League in New York. He was a member of the artistic club of Rome, the Salmagundi Club and the American Federation of Arts.

MUSEUMS AND GALLERIES:
CINCINNATI - KANSAS CITY.

AUCTION RECORDS:
NEW YORK, 1 Dec 1988, *Landscape with Houses beside a River* (1911, oil/synthetic resin, 40 x 51 3/4 ins / 101.6 x 131.5 cm) USD 22,000. NEW YORK, 12 March 1992, *River Annisquam* (1911, oil on canvas, 32 1/4 x 36 1/4 ins / 82 x 92 cm) USD 9,900. NEW YORK, 11 March 1993, *Landscape with Houses beside a River* (1911, oil/synthetic resin, 40 x 51 3/4 ins / 101.6 x 131.5 cm) USD 19,550. NEW YORK, 21 Sept 1994, *Sunny Morning in the Blue Ridge Mountains of Virginia* (1912, oil on canvas, 24 x 30 ins / 61 x 76.2 cm) USD 6,037. CONNECTICUT, 24 May 1999, *Mother and Child by River* (oil on canvas, 24 x 30 ins / 61 x 76 cm) USD 1,700. NEW YORK, 26 May 1999, *California Hillside* (oil on canvas, 30 x 40 ins / 76 x 102 cm) USD 8,000. NEW YORK, 28 Nov 2000, *Les Callanques near Cassis, Marseilles, France. Running Stream* (oil on canvas, a pair) USD 1,900. LAMBERTVILLE, 19 May 2001, *Young Woman with Long Dark Hair* (oil on canvas, 20 x 22 ins / 51 x 56 cm) USD 2,400. NEW ORLEANS, 26 May 2001, *View of the Hudson River Valley* (oil on canvas, 32 x 36 ins / 81 x 91 cm) USD 6,000. NEW ORLEANS, 12 Oct 2002, *View of the Hudson River Valley* (oil on canvas, 32 x 36 ins / 81 x 91 cm) USD 6,500. CEDAR FALLS, 23 Nov 2002, *Spring Plowing* (oil on canvas, 24 x 30 ins / 61 x 76 cm) USD 3,700. NEW YORK, 21 May 2003, *Brooklyn Bridge* (oil on canvas, 16 x 12 ins / 41 x 30 cm) USD 1,700. NEW YORK, 21 May 2003, *The Summit. Country Home* (1932, oil on canvas, 16 x 20 ins / 41 x 51 cm) USD 2,250.

SCHWARTZ, C.
American, 19th century.
Active in Baltimore in 1814.
Engraver. Portraits.

C. Schwartz engraved a portrait of the bishop *James Kemp*.

SCHWARTZ, Charles Auguste
French, 19th century.
Born 1841, in Strasbourg; died c. 1900, in Paris.
Painter. Urban landscapes.

MUSEUMS AND GALLERIES:
STRASBOURG: *Strasbourg in August 1860*.

SCHWARTZ, Christoph, or Schwarz
German, 16th century.
Born c. 1545, in Munich; died 15 April 1592, in Munich.
Painter, draughtsman. Mythological subjects, religious subjects, portraits.
Munich School.

Christoph Schwartz was a pupil of Bocksperger in Munich and then of Titian in Venice. When he returned to Munich he was appointed court painter, a post which he held until his death. He decorated several public buildings in Munich, and Jan Sadeler engraved several of his works.

MUSEUMS AND GALLERIES:
BRNO: *Defeat of Senacherib* - BRUNSWICK: *Portrait* - DRESDEN: *Crucifixion* - FLORENCE: *Self-portrait* - HANOVER: *Christ on the Cross* - LANDSHUT (Church of St Martin): *Crucifixion* - MUNICH: *The Artist's Daughter; Crucifixion; Virgin and the Child Jesus on Clouds; St Jerome and St Catherine* - NUREMBERG (Germanisches Nationalmus.): *Virgin with Child, St Catherine and St Jerome* - RENNES: *Jesus on the Cross between the Two Thieves* - VIENNA: *Women Bathing; Death of Adonis; Flagellation; Entombment; Last Judgement* - WROCLAW: *Entombment*.

AUCTION RECORDS:
COLOGNE, 1862, *Portrait of a Young Man*, FRF 127. PARIS, 12 May 1919, *Neptune's Chariot* (drawing) FRF 85. NEW YORK, 5 June 1985, *Adoration of the Shepherds* (oil on canvas, 23 x 62 1/2 ins / 57.5 x 159 cm) USD 30,000. MUNICH, 28 Nov 1985, *Kneeling Angel Holding a Candle* (pen and wash, 11 x 7 ins / 28 x 18 cm) DEM 6,000. LONDON, 8 April 1986, *St Michael Defeating the Rebellious Angels* (black chalk, pen and wash, 11 3/4 x 6 3/4 ins / 29.9 x 17 cm) GBP 4,800. PARIS, 31 Jan 1991, *Last Judgement* (oil on panel, 38 3/4 x 58 ins / 98.5 x 147.5 cm) FRF 37,000.

SCHWARTZ, Ernst
German, 20th century.
Born 3 March 1883, in Breslau (now Wroclaw, Poland); died 19 January 1932, in Berlin.
Active in Munich, Berlin and in Stettin (now Szczecin, Poland).
Painter, engraver.

Ernst Schwartz studied under Siegfried Haertel in Breslau and at the fine arts academy in Stuttgart.

SCHWARTZ, Esther
French, 19th - 20th century.
Born in Nancy.
Engraver.

Schwartz was a wood engraver and featured at the Salon des Artistes Français in Paris, where she had an honourable mention in 1904.

SCHWARTZ, Eva
Polish, 20th century.
Born 1900, in Warsaw; died October 1974.
Active from 1926 in France.
Painter, sculptor.

Eva Schwartz studied sculpture in Frankfurt am Main, then settled in Paris in 1926, where she exhibited at the Salon des Artistes Indépendants, among other places. In 1964, there was a large exhibition of her paintings and sculptures in Warsaw.

SCHWARTZ, Frantz, or Johan Georg Frans.
See **SCHWARZ**

SCHWARTZ, Gustav, or Schwarz
German, 19th century.
Born c. 1800, in Berlin.
Painter. Military subjects, portraits, genre scenes.

From 1850 Gustav Schwartz spent most of his career in Russia, in particular as court painter. He exhibited in Berlin from 1834 to 1842 where a number of his works are conserved in the old castle.

AUCTION RECORDS:
LONDON, 27 Nov 1981, *Tsar Nicholas I Returning to Krasnoe Selo* (1848, oil on canvas, 26 1/2 x 43 1/2 ins / 67 x 110.5 cm) GBP 4,500.

SCHWARTZ, Hans. See also **MALER Hans**

SCHWARTZ, Hans
German, 16th century.
Active in Œttingen in the second half of the 16th century.
Painter.

Hans Schwartz painted biblical scenes and equestrian battles after Albrecht Dürer.

SCHWARTZ, Hans
German, 16th - 17th century.
Active in Habersdorf.
Painter.

Hans Schwartz was a burgher of Dresden in 1583.

SCHWARTZ, Hans
Swedish, 17th century.
Active in Göteborg (?) during the second half of the 17th century.
Sculptor.

Schwartz sculpted altars.

SCHWARTZ, Heinz
Swiss, 20th century.
Born 1920.
Sculptor.

Heinz Schwartz worked in plaster and bronze.

Museums and Galleries:
Aarau (Aargauer Kunsthaus): *Large Torso* (1947-1949); *Renée* (1962); *Standing Female Nude.*
Auction records:
Zurich, 22 Nov 1978, *Standing Nude* (bronze, h. 69 1/4 ins / 176 cm) CHF 15,000. Bern, 6 Nov 2002, *Standing Female Nude with Long Hair* (1974, h. 71 ins / 180 cm) CHF 14,000. Bern, 7 Nov 2003, *Female Nude* (light patinated bronze, h. 28 ins / 72 cm) CHF 4,400.

SCHWARTZ, Istvan, or Stefen, Stefan
Austrian, 19th - 20th century.
Born 20 August 1851, in Neutra; died 31 July 1924, in Raabs.
Sculptor, medallist.
Istvan Schwartz took part in various Expositions Universelles in Paris, notably in 1900, when he was awarded a gold medal.

SCHWARTZ, Johann Christian August
German, 18th - 19th century.
Born 1756, in Hildesheim; died 7 March 1814, in Brunswick.
Painter, pastellist, miniaturist. Portraits.
Johann Christian Schwartz worked in Brunswick, Dresden, Hamburg and Berlin.
Museums and Galleries:
Brunswick (Herzog Anton Ulrich-Mus.): *Queen Louise of Prussia; Portrait of Lady* - Brunswick (Städtisches Mus.): *Herzog Karl-Wilhelm Ferdinand von Brunswick.*
Auction records:
Brussels, 21 May 1951, *Portrait of Lady* (1785, pastel) BEF 3,600. Paris, 28 Jan 1985, *Portrait of Mathematician* (1798, gouache, 11 1/2 x 9 ins / 29 x 23 cm) FRF 21,000.

SCHWARTZ, Johann Heinrich
German, 17th - 18th century.
Active in Berlin.
Painter.
Johann Heinrich Schwartz may be the same as Johan Heinrich Swartze who was active in Lübeck around 1690.

SCHWARTZ, Johannes, called Vredemann and Niger
Dutch, 15th - 16th century.
Born c. 1480, in Groningen.
Engraver.
Johannes Schwartz is referred to by Ris-Paquot.

S$

SCHWARTZ, Josef Anton
Austrian, 18th century.
Born c. 1700, in Budejovice; died 26 September 1759, in Olmütz (now Olomouc, Czech Republic).
Painter.
Josef Anton Schwartz executed two altar paintings in the church in Zwittawka (Moravia).

SCHWARTZ, József
Hungarian, 19th century.
Died 1823, in Budapest.
Painter.
József Schwartz painted altarpieces for churches in Budapest. The municipal museum in Budapest owns works by him.

SCHWARTZ, Léonard. See **LEONARD**

SCHWARTZ, M.
French, 20th century.
Painter.
Schwartz participated in the exhibition *De Bonnard à Baselitz - Dix Ans d'enrichissements du cabinet des estampes 1978-1988* (*From Bonnard to Baselitz: A Decade of Acquisitions by the Prints Collection 1978-1988*) at the Bibliothèque Nationale de Paris in 1992.

SCHWARTZ, Manfred
American, 20th century.
Born 11 November 1908, in Germany; died 1970.
Painter, illustrator.
Manfred Schwartz studied under John Sloan and George Bridgman. He was a member of the Society of Independent American Artists and the Société des Artistes Indépendants in Paris.

SCHWARTZ, Martin. See **SCHWARZ**

SCHWARTZ, Michael
German, 16th century.
Active at the beginning of the 16th century.
Painter. History painting.
Michael Schwartz was an imitator of Dürer. In 1512 he painted scenes from the *Passion* and the *Life of the Virgin* for the church of St Mary in Danzig (now Gdansk).

SCHWARTZ, Mommie, or Schwarz
Dutch, 19th - 20th century.
Born 1876; died 1942.
Painter. Landscapes, still-lifes.
Auction records:
Amsterdam, 20 March 1978, *Adriatic Coastal Landscape* (oil on canvas, 30 1/4 x 39 1/2 ins / 77 x 100.5 cm) NLG 3,400. Amsterdam, 10 April 1989, *Railway Bridge* (oil on canvas, 28 x 27 ins / 71 x 68.5 cm) NLG 4,600. Amsterdam, 21 May 1992, *Still-life* (oil on canvas, 17 3/4 x 22 ins / 45 x 55 cm) NLG 14,950. Amsterdam, 10 Dec 1992, *Thaw* (oil on canvas, 39 1/4 x 31 1/2 ins / 100 x 80 cm) NLG 4,830. Amsterdam, 27-28 May 1993, *Olive Trees in Mallorca* (oil on canvas, 25 1/2 x 22 ins / 65 x 55 cm) NLG 12,075. Amsterdam, 7 Dec 1995, *Work in the Fields* (oil on canvas, 24 1/2 x 20 1/2 ins / 62 x 52 cm) NLG 59,000. Amsterdam, 2-3 June 1997, *Magnolias in a Vase* (oil on canvas, 33 3/4 x 31 ins / 86 x 78.5 cm) NLG 8,024. Amsterdam, 2 Dec 1997, *Still-life with Fruit* (c. 1913-1914, oil on canvas, 17 3/4 x 22 ins / 45 x 55 cm) NLG 46,128. Amsterdam, 7 June 1999, *Still-life with Painted Pallet* (oil on panel, 24 x 21 ins / 60 x 54 cm) NLG 20,000. The Hague, 9 May 2000, *Still-life with Flowers* (oil on canvas, 32 x 25 ins / 81 x 64 cm) NLG 18,000. Amsterdam, 8 June 2000, *View in Bergen* (oil on canvas, 33 x 28 ins / 83 x 72 cm) NLG 22,000. Amsterdam, 3 Dec 2001, *Still-life with Flowers* (oil on cardboard, 37 x 26 ins / 94 x 65 cm) NLG 9,000. Amsterdam, 28 May 2002, *Still-life with Flowers. Landscape* (oil on board, double-sided, 32 x 26 ins / 82 x 66 cm) EUR 42,000. Amsterdam, 3 June 2003, *Alley, possibly in Bergen* (oil on canvas, 19 x 15 ins / 49 x 38 cm) EUR 8,000. Amsterdam, 24 Nov 2003, *Broadway, Hat of Distinction* (gouache and collage, 19 x 13 ins / 48 x 32 cm) EUR 2,400. Amsterdam, 9 June 2004, *Farmyard. Still-life with Fruit on a Table* (oil on plywood, double-sided, 17 x 22 ins / 42 x 56 cm) EUR 6,000.

SCHWARTZ, Nikolaus
German, 17th century.
Active in Gera at the beginning of the 17th century.
Sculptor (wood).

SCHWARTZ, Paul Wolfgang. See **SCHWARZ**

SCHWARTZ, Philippe
French, 20th - 21st century.
Born 1950, in Paris.
Draughtsman, engraver. Mythological subjects.
Examples of work by Philippe Schwartz featured in *De Bonnard à Baselitz - Dix Ans d'enrichissements du cabinet des estampes 1978-1988* (*From Bonnard to Baselitz: A Decade of Acquisitions by the Prints Collection 1978-1988*), an exhibition held in 1993 at the Bibliothèque Nationale in Paris.

MUSEUMS AND GALLERIES:
PARIS (BNF): *Phoenix* (1980, dry-point).

SCHWARTZ, Raphaël. See **RAPHAEL-SCHWARTZ**

SCHWARTZ, Reiner
German, 20th century.
Born 1940.
Painter.

AUCTION RECORDS:
MUNICH, 25 May 1976, *Dirndl* (1972, oil on canvas, 35 1/2 x 27 1/2 ins / 90 x 70 cm) DEM 4,000.

SCHWARTZ, Sol
American, 20th century.
Born 1899; died c. 1960.
Painter. Portraits, landscapes, flowers.

Sol Schwartz studied at the Pratt Institute and the Art Students' League in New York. He was an eclectic artist who in turn practised both Figuration and Abstraction. He painted many portraits of famous people, including Einstein, Picasso and Churchill.

SCHWARTZ, Walter
Danish, 20th century.
Born 17 April 1889, in Skagen.
Active in Copenhagen.
Painter, engraver. Portraits, landscapes, still-lifes.

Walter Schwartz also worked as a journalist.

AUCTION RECORDS:
COPENHAGEN, 21 April 1993, *French Can-can Dancers* (oil on canvas, 31 x 37 ins / 79 x 94 cm) DKK 4,800. LONDON, 8 Feb 2001, *Sunlit Interior* (1918, oil on canvas, 27 x 35 ins / 69 x 88 cm) GBP 3,500.

SCHWARTZ, Wenzel
German, 17th century.
Died 29 March 1686.
Active in Breslau (now Wroclaw).
Painter.

SCHWARTZ, Wilhelm
German, 17th century.
Active in Breslau (now Wroclaw) in the mid-seventeenth century.
Painter, illustrator, calligrapher.

SCHWARTZ, William Samuel
American, 20th century.
Born 1896, in Smorgon; died 1977, in Chicago.
Active in the USA.
Painter. Genre scenes.

Willam Samuel Schwartz was a student at Vilna (now Vilnius) and then at the Art Institute in Chicago, and his work was shown at Carnegie Foundation exhibitions in Pittsburgh. His works are often lively New York street scenes.

MUSEUMS AND GALLERIES:
CHICAGO (AI) - DALLAS (MA): *Still-life* (c. 1929, oil on canvas); *Symphonic Forms in Grey* (oil on canvas) - DETROIT (IA).

AUCTION RECORDS:
NEW YORK, 11 Oct 1979, *Toilers of the Soul* (oil on canvas, 40 x 50 ins / 101.5 x 127 cm) USD 2,800. NEW YORK, 31 May 1985, *Still-life with Abstract Flowers* (watercolour/mounted paper/card, 19 3/4 x 15 3/4 ins / 50.3 x 40 cm) USD 1,000. NEW YORK, 30 Sept 1988, *My Model* (1928, oil on canvas, 30 x 36 1/4 ins / 76.4 x 91.8 cm) USD 7,700; *Fishing for Crabs* (gouache/card, 18 x 22 ins / 45.7 x 56 cm) USD 2,310. NEW YORK, 16 March 1990, *Self-portrait* (1930, oil on canvas, 36 x 30 ins / 91.5 x 76.2 cm) USD 8,250. NEW YORK, 12 March 1992, *The Organ Player from the Barbary Coast* (1929, oil on canvas, 36 1/4 x 40 1/4 ins / 92 x 102 cm) USD 13,200. NEW YORK, 25 Sept 1992, *Solitude* (oil on canvas, 40 x 30 ins / 101.6 x 76.2 cm) USD 7,700. NEW YORK, 17 March 1994, *Road in a Village* (1929, oil on canvas, 28 x 30 ins / 71.1 x 76.2 cm) USD 18,400. NEW YORK, 21 Sept 1994, *Apartments in West Side* (1927, oil on canvas, 28 x 34 ins / 71.1 x 86.4 cm) USD 9,200. NEW YORK, 21 May 1996, *The Last Rays* (oil on canvas, 32 x 28 ins / 81.3 x 71.1 cm) USD 2,300. NEW YORK, 27 Sept 1996, *My Model* (1928, oil on canvas, 30 x 36 ins / 76.2 x 91.5 cm) USD 5,750; *Fruit on a Table* (1930, oil on canvas, 32 x 36 ins / 81.3 x 91.4 cm) USD 2,300.

SCHWARTZ, Wolf
German, 17th century.
Active in Stuttgart c. 1620.
Sculptor.

SCHWARTZ ABRYS, Léon. See **SCHWARZ-ABRYS**

SCHWARTZ-WALDEGG, Fritz
Austrian, 20th century.
Born 1 March 1889, in Vienna.
Painter.

Fritz Schwartz-Waldegg was a pupil of Christian Griepenkerl and Rudolf Bacher.

MUSEUMS AND GALLERIES:
VIENNA.

SCHWARTZBACH, Christian
German, 17th century.
Died 1704.
Active in Danzig (now Gdansk, Poland).
Portrait artist.

SCHWARTZE, Georgine Elisabeth
Dutch, 19th - 20th century.
Born 12 April 1854, in Amsterdam.
Sculptor. Figures.

Georgine Elisabeth Schwartze was the daughter of the painter Johan Georg Schwartze and a pupil of Frans Stracke and Ferdinand Leenhoff. She received an honourable mention at the Exposition Universelle in Paris in 1900.

MUSEUMS AND GALLERIES:
AMSTERDAM (Stedelijk Mus.): *Choirboy*; *Children Sleeping*.

SCHWARTZE, Johan Georg
Dutch, 19th century.
Born 20 October 1814, in Philadelphia; died 28 August 1874, in Amsterdam.
Painter, draughtsman. Portraits.

Johan Georg Schwartze was the father of Georgine Elisabeth and Thérèse Schwartze. He studied first in America and later in Düsseldorf under Leutze, Lessing and Schadow.

MUSEUMS AND GALLERIES:
AMSTERDAM (Rijksmus.): *Self-portrait*; *Portrait of Johann Rive*; *Portrait of the Artist's Daughters* - AMSTERDAM (Stedelijk Mus.): *Woman at Prayer* - THE HAGUE (Gemeentemus.): *Portrait of Thérèse Schwartze* - UTRECHT (Centraal Mus.): *Portrait of Doctor Fles*.

AUCTION RECORDS:
AMSTERDAM, 5 June 1990, *Portrait of Jimmy Barge Aged One, Wearing a White Shirt* (1865, oil on canvas, 20 1/2 x 15 3/4 ins / 52 x 40 cm) NLG 1,610. AMSTERDAM, 3 Sept 2002, *Portrait of Johanna Louise van Eeghen-den Tex* (1850, oil on canvas, 36 x 30 ins / 91 x 75 cm) EUR 4,200. GRAVENHAGE, 6 Nov 2002, *Poet* (1855, oil on canvas, 26 x 33 ins / 66 x 83 cm) EUR 2,400.

SCHWARTZE, Thérèse, wife of Van Duyl
Dutch, 19th - 20th century.
Born 20 December 1852, in Amsterdam; died 23 December 1918, in Amsterdam.
Painter (gouache), pastellist, draughtswoman. Figures, portraits, genre scenes, interiors with figures.

Thérèse Schwartze studied under her father Johan Georg Schwarz, under Gabriel Max and, in Munich, under Carl

Theodor Piloty and Franz Seraph Lenbach. She subsequently moved to Paris, where she pursued her studies under Denis Pierre Bergeret and Jean Jacques Henner. She made her Paris Salon debut in 1879 and went on to receive an honourable mention in 1884, a bronze medal in 1889, and silver medals at the Exposition Universelle in Paris in 1889 and 1900.

Th.Schwartze.1900

Th. Schwartze

MUSEUMS AND GALLERIES:

AMSTERDAM: *Three Young Girls in an Amsterdam Orphanage; Puck; F.D.O. Obreens; J.L. Dusseau; J. Joubert; Self-portrait* - AMSTERDAM (Stedelijk Mus.): *Head of a Little Girl; He Comes; Dead Child; Lutheran Converts* - DÜSSELDORF: *Mirror* - FLORENCE (Uffizi): *Self-portrait* - LEIDEN: *L. M. de Laat de Kanter; Joanis Mathias Schrant* - ROTTERDAM (Mus. Boijmans Van Beuningen): *Five Orphans* - SYDNEY - THE HAGUE (Gemeentemus.): *Daydreamer* - VALENCIENNES: *Henri Harpignies.*

AUCTION RECORDS:

LONDON, 29 May 1910, *He Comes* (1882) GBP 33. PARIS, 14 Feb 1945, *Portrait of a Woman* (1883) FRF 1,250. AMSTERDAM, 25 May 1976, *Harpist* (pastel, 33 1/2 x 26 ins / 85 x 66 cm) NLG 2,500. AMSTERDAM, 31 Oct 1977, *Portrait of Lizzy Ansingh* (1902, oil on canvas, 30 3/4 x 24 1/2 ins / 78 x 62 cm) NLG 9,000. AMSTERDAM, 24 March 1980, *Portrait of Maria Agnes van Riemsdijk* (watercolour and gouache, 28 3/4 x 22 1/2 ins / 73 x 57 cm) NLG 4,000. AMSTERDAM, 6 June 1983, *Interior with Young Women* (1873, oil on canvas, 41 x 53 3/4 ins / 104 x 136.5 cm) NLG 4,000. AMSTERDAM, 5 March 1984, *Young Girl Seated* (1876, oil on canvas, 31 1/2 x 26 1/2 ins / 80.2 x 67 cm) NLG 2,500. COLOGNE, 30 March 1984, *Portrait of a Young French Peasant Woman* (oil on canvas, 23 1/2 x 19 3/4 ins / 60 x 50 cm) DEM 3,500. LONDON, 10 Sept 1984, *Young Woman with a Guitar* (pastel/mounted paper/canvas, 24 x 32 ins / 61 x 81 cm) GBP 850. AMSTERDAM, 3 May 1988, *Portrait of the Painter Bramine Hubrecht* (pastel and oil on paper, 22 1/2 x 17 1/4 ins / 57 x 44 cm) NLG 5,750. AMSTERDAM, 30 Oct 1990, *Little Girl at Prayer* (1874, oil on canvas, 27 x 20 1/2 ins / 68.5 x 52 cm) NLG 1,495. AMSTERDAM, 14-15 April 1992, *Portrait of a Young Girl with a Hat* (black chalk heightened with white, 14 3/4 x 10 3/4 ins / 37.5 x 27.5 cm) NLG 2,990. AMSTERDAM, 28 Oct 1992, *Head and Shoulders of a Child Resting on Cushions* (pastel/paper, 14 1/4 x 19 3/4 ins / 36 x 50 cm) NLG 1,380. AMSTERDAM, 3 Nov 1992, *Portrait of Mrs Ansingh-Weber* (1905, black chalk, 23 1/2 x 18 ins / 60 x 46 cm) NLG 1,323. AMSTERDAM, 20 April 1993, *Portrait of a Seated Lady* (1893, oil on canvas, 68 1/4 x 50 3/4 ins / 173.5 x 129 cm) NLG 5,520. NEW YORK, 17 Feb 1994, *Peasant Woman with a Blue Bonnet* (oil on canvas, 21 3/4 x 17 1/2 ins / 55.4 x 44.5 cm) USD 2,760. AMSTERDAM, 21 April 1994, *Lost* (1903, oil on canvas, 39 3/4 x 24 1/4 ins / 101 x 61.5 cm) NLG 18,400. AMSTERDAM, 18 June 1996, *Portrait of a Little Girl* (pencil, coloured chalk and gouache/paper/canvas, 22 x 17 1/4 ins / 55 x 44 cm) NLG 1,725.

SCHWARTZENBACH.
See **SCHWARZENBACH**

SCHWARTZENBERG, Simon

Romanian, 20th century.
Born 20 September 1895, in Harlan.
Active in France.
Painter. Urban landscapes.

Simon Schwartzenberg was director of a hosiery factory. He was profoundly traumatised by the murder of his two sons by Nazi soldiers, and there may be a link between this and the fact that he started to paint in 1952, as well as developing a passionate interest in music. Schwartzenberg mainly paints the old stonework of Parisian monuments, which places him together with Louis Vivin, in so far as he depicts the stonework in great detail, down to the paving stones of the streets. His style is lighter and more playful than that of Vivin, and it does not attain the gravitas of Vivin's work.

Work by him was exhibited for the first time in 1959, at the Maison de la Pensée in Paris, then at the exhibition *Les Naïfs du Douanier Rousseau à nos jours* (*Naive Painters from Douanier Rousseau to the Present Day*). Other groups exhibitions followed in Paris, at the Salon des Réalités Nouvelles (1963); at *Quatre Peintres Naïfs* (*Four Naive Painters*), curated by Anatole Jakovsky, and *Quinze Peintres Naïfs* (*Fifteen Naive Painters*); at the Galerie Charpentier (1965). Group exhibitions abroad included ones in Japan, *From Douanier Rousseau to Today* (1966); in Yugoslavia, Italy, Brussels and Basel (1969); and at the Kunsthaus in Vienna, at *Die Naïve, Aufbruch ins verlorene Paradies* (*The Naïve Painters, Journey to a Lost Paradise*). There were solo exhibitions in Paris from 1963.

BIBLIOGRAPHY:

Die Naïve, aufbruch ins verlorene paradies, exhibition catalogue, Kunsthaus, Vienna, 2001 (text in German and English).

MUSEUMS AND GALLERIES:

BÖNNIGHEIM (Mus. Charlotte Zander) - PARIS (MNAM-CCI): *Orange: the Roman Theatre.*

SCHWARTZENWALDER, Martin.
See **SCHWARZWALDER**

SCHWARTZKOPF. See also **SCHWARZKOPF**

SCHWARTZKOPF, Richard

German, 20th century.
Born 11 April 1893.
Active in Düsseldorf.
Engraver (wood), calligrapher. Military subjects.

Richard Schwartzkopf was a calligrapher and, above all, a woodcut engraver who worked in the style of German engraving that had been followed since the Middle Ages. He made no attempt to develop the deliberately archaic style espoused by engravers in Die Brücke but was intent instead on producing the stylised images which characterised German philately during the Third Reich. He is particularly noted for *German Passions*, a suite of engravings depicting the aggressive parades and rippling swastika standards which typified Hitler's 'Brown Shirts'.

His work featured in the exhibition of 'authorised' German art which was held concurrently with the exhibition of *Entartete Kunst* (*Degenerate Art*) proscribed by Adolf Hitler in Munich in 1937.

SCHWARTZMANN, Andreas and Johann Jakob. See **SCHWARZMANN**

SCHWARZ. See also **SCHWARTZ** and **SWARTZ**

SCHWARZ, Adolf. See **SCHWARTZ**

SCHWARZ, Alfred

German, 19th - 20th century.
Born 1867; died 1951.
Painter. Portraits, genre scenes.

AUCTION RECORDS:

LUCERNE, 25 May 1982, *Maternal Bliss* (oil on canvas, 24 3/4 x 45 ins / 63 x 114 cm) CHF 3,400. LONDON, 30 March 2001, *Portrait of a Young Girl with a Parasol* (1903, oil on panel, 39 x 29 ins / 100 x 73 cm) GBP 14,000. VEJLE, 10 March 2003, *Young Woman and Cupid* (oil on canvas, 38 x 28 ins / 96 x 70 cm) DKK 31,000. LONDON, 17 June 2003, *Fresh from the Garden* (1915, oil on canvas, 46 x 39 ins / 117 x 100 cm) GBP

4,500. STAUFEN, 25 March 2004, *Portrait of a Debutant* (1896, oil on panel, 13 x 10 ins / 33 x 26 cm) EUR 3,300.

SCHWARZ, Alfred. See also **SCHWARTZ**

SCHWARZ, Alfred or Albert Gustav. See **SCHWARTZ**

SCHWARZ, Armand
Swiss, 20th century.
Born 17 January 1881, in Delsberg.
Painter. Landscapes, animals.

Armand Schwarz studied art in Bern and at the fine arts academy in Düsseldorf.

MUSEUMS AND GALLERIES:
BERN: *Cattle in a Forest*.

SCHWARZ, Bernhard
German, 16th century.
Sculptor.

Bernhard Schwarz was a pupil of Hans Dauher in Augsburg in 1521.

SCHWARZ, Caintat or Cajetan?
German, 17th century.
Active during the first half of the 17th (?) century.
Engraver (burin). Religious subjects.

SCHWARZ, Charles or Carl Benjamin
German, 18th - 19th century.
Born 1757, in Leipzig; died 21 October 1813, in Leipzig.
Painter, draughtsman, watercolourist, engraver (etching).

Charles Schwarz was a pupil of Oeser. He engraved landscapes and allegorical subjects.

MUSEUMS AND GALLERIES:
LEIPZIG (Stadtgeschichtliches Mus.): *View of Market*.

SCHWARZ, Christian
German, 17th century.
Born 1645, in Dresden; died 1684, in Reichstadt, near Dippoldiswalde.
Active in Dresden.
Painter.

Christian Schwarz studied under J.C. Patenti in Hamburg, then in Vienna.

SCHWARZ, Christian Jacob
German, 18th century.
Active in Leipzig at the end of the 18th century.
Painter, engraver.

Christian Jacob Schwarz worked as an engraver of architectural views.

SCHWARZ, Christoph. See **SCHWARTZ**

SCHWARZ, Damaszen
Austrian, 18th century.
Born 1721.
Active in Brno.
Painter.

Damaszen Schwarz was a Dominican friar who executed statues for the high altar of the Dominikanerkirche in Brunn in 1743.

SCHWARZ, Elsa, wife of Beck
Austrian, 20th century.
Born 26 April 1888, in Vienna.
Painter. Landscapes, still-lifes.

SCHWARZ, Emmanuel Jacob
German, 18th century.
Born c. 1724; died 1791, in Augsburg.
Active in Augsburg.
Sculptor.

Emmanuel Schwarz executed funerary monuments and architectural structures.

SCHWARZ, Eugen
German, 19th century.
Born May 1851, in Bürgeln; died 1904, in Berlin.
Painter. Portraits.

Eugen Schwarz studied under Ferdinand Keller in Karlsruhe and Hans Canon in Vienna; from 1896 he was active in Berlin.

SCHWARZ, Frantz, or Johan Georg Frans, or Schwartz
Danish, 19th - 20th century.
Born 18 July 1850, in Copenhagen; died 13 February 1917, in Copenhagen.
Painter, engraver. Portraits.

Frantz Schwarz studied at the Kunstakademi in Copenhagen.

MUSEUMS AND GALLERIES:
COPENHAGEN: *Self-portrait* - HILLERØD (Frederiksbörg Slot): *King Frederik III and the Four Estates; Self-portrait*.

AUCTION RECORDS:
COPENHAGEN, 8 June 1977, *Egg Seller* (1887, pastel, 26 x 22 ins / 66 x 56 cm) DEM 13,000. NEW YORK, 13 June 1980, *Perspective* (1912, pen heightened with white and silver, 9 3/4 x 9 3/4 ins / 25 x 25 cm) USD 1,900. LONDON, 16 March 1989, *Lace Maker* (1886, oil on panel, 11 1/4 x 9 ins / 28.5 x 22 cm) GBP 5,500.

SCHWARZ, Franz Joseph
German, 19th century.
Born 1841, in Dresden.
Sculptor.

Franz Joseph Schwarz executed statues in the cathedral at Halberstadt and in the church of Grottau.

AUCTION RECORDS:
LONDON, 23 Feb 1977, *Farmyard* (oil on panel, 25 1/4 x 30 1/2 ins / 64 x 77.5 cm) GBP 1,250.

SCHWARZ, Georg
Austrian, 17th - 18th century.
Sculptor (wood).

The son of Konrad Schwarz, Georg sculpted the choir stalls in the church in Hüttau.

SCHWARZ, Gustav. See **SCHWARTZ**

SCHWARZ, Heinrich
German, 20th century.
Born 19 December 1903, in Berlin.
Painter, engraver. Portraits, animals.

SCHWARZ, J.
German, 17th century.
Sculptor (wood).

J. Schwarz sculpted a statue of *St Sebastian* at Gmund in 1662.

SCHWARZ, Jakob
German, 18th century.
Died 1750.
Active in Munich.
Painter.

SCHWARZ, Jakob Eberhard
German, 17th century.
Active in Stuttgart in the middle of the 17th century.
Sculptor (wood).

Jakob Eberhard Schwarz sculpted a *Christ on the Cross* in the church in Schönaich in 1650.

SCHWARZ, Jeremias
German, 16th century.
Active in Leonberg at the end of the 16th century.
Sculptor.

Jeremias Schwarz carved the tomb of Ludwig VI in the church of the Holy Spirit, Heidelberg.

SCHWARZ, Johann Christof
German, 17th - 18th century.
Born c. 1660; died 1714.
Active in Bayreuth.
Painter, calligrapher.

SCHWARZ, Johann Georg
German, 18th century.
Active in the middle of the 18th century.
Sculptor (wood).
Johann Georg Schwarz sculpted the choir stalls in the church at Weilheim in 1751.

SCHWARZ, Johann Gottlieb, or Chvarts
German, 18th century.
Born 1736, in Germany; died 31 December 1804, in St Petersburg.
Sculptor (wood), designer of ornamental architectural features.
Johann Gottlieb Schwarz taught at the art academy in St Petersburg from 1770.

SCHWARZ, Johann Israel
Austrian, 17th century.
Active in Vienna 1639-1674.
Painter, engraver. Seals.

SCHWARZ, Johann Jakob
German, 18th century.
Active in Nuremberg 1725-1758.
Draughtsman, engraver.
Johann Jakob Schwarz engraved architectural views and landscapes as well as executing preliminary drawings for line engavings.

SCHWARZ, Johann Jakob
Swiss, 18th century.
Born c. 1765, in Nuremberg.
Active in Switzerland.
Engraver.

SCHWARZ, Johann or Hans
Swiss, 19th century.
Died 1811, in Klein-Hüningen, near Basel.
Watercolourist.
Johann Schwarz painted popular scenes and caricatures and may be identical with Johann Jakob Schwarz, born in Nuremberg around 1765.

SCHWARZ, Johann Samuel
German, 18th century.
Active in Gransee in 1776.
Engraver.

SCHWARZ, Jörg
German, 16th century.
Active in Nuremberg during the second half of the 16th century.
Sculptor (wood).
Jörg Schwarz carved a ceiling and a door in a room of the university of Würzburg in 1585.

SCHWARZ, Joseph
German, 18th century.
Active in Passau 1725-1734.
Painter.
Joseph Schwarz executed the ceiling painting of the church in Untergriesbach in 1725.

SCHWARZ, Joseph
German, 18th century.
Died 1765, in Buchloe.
Painter.
Joseph Schwarz sculpted a calvary for the church in Buchloe.

SCHWARZ, Joseph
Austrian, 18th century.
Born c. 1750, in Nixdorf.
Sculptor (stone/wood), designer of ornamental architectural features.
Joseph Schwarz studied under Wilhelm Müller in Dresden and may have been identical to Johann Gottlieb Schwarz.

SCHWARZ, Karl Friedrich
German, 19th century.
Born 1797, in Leipzig.
Active in Dresden.
Painter, decorative designer. Landscapes, architectural views.

SCHWARZ, Konrad
Austrian, 17th century.
Died 1702.
Sculptor (wood).
Konrad Schwarz was the son of Wolf Schwarz who died in 1652. He sculpted pulpits and choir stalls for churches in the Salzburg area.

SCHWARZ, Lukas or Lux
Swiss, 15th - 16th century.
Died before 1526.
Active in Bern from 1498.
Glass painter.
Bern School.
Lukas Schwarz painted many windows for churches and domestic buildings.

SCHWARZ, Martin
German, 15th - 16th century.
Active in Rothenburg 1480-1522.
Painter. History painting.
Martin Schwarz's works have been attributed to Martin Schongauer. Among his principal paintings, now lost, were a *Christ on the Cross* for the church of Schwebach, near Nuremberg, and an altarpiece for the Dominican chuch of Rothenburg.
MUSEUMS AND GALLERIES:
BAMBERG (Municipal Mus.): *Virgin with St Margaret, St Catherine and Other Saints*; *Departure of the Apostles* - NUREMBERG (Germanisches Nationalmus.): *Annunciation*; *Nativity*; *Adoration of the Magi*; *Death of the Virgin* - WÜRZBURG: *St Margaret and St Apollina*.

SCHWARZ, Martin
German, 17th century.
Died 1644, in Leipzig.
Painter.
Martin Schwarz was a sexton in the Thomaskirche in Leipzig.
MUSEUMS AND GALLERIES:
LEIPZIG (Stadtgeschichtliches Mus.): *Christ in the Garden of Gethsemane*.

SCHWARZ, Martin
Swiss, 20th - 21st century.
Born 1946, in Winterthur.
Painter, photomontage artist. Scenes with figures, figures.
Citationism.
In 1984, at the time when Martin Schwarz was a painter of scenes with figures, landscapes and flowers, he had a solo exhibition at the Kunstmuseum in Winterthur. However, by then he was already working on photomontages. He then went on to practise 'modification'. From Gironella to Herman Braun-Vega, from Picasso to Velázquez and Manet, his strategy of modification has earned him approval. Going beyond the traditional techniques of the episcope or collage, modern computer-aided methods allow original documents to be spectacularly tranformed into perfectly executed paint-

ings in a short space of time, creating a sense of rapture and fantasy. Schwarz makes the most of these techniques, using them for various purposes: the rumpled bed that appears still warm, which Goya's Maja has just got out of, is poetically treated, but his purpose is simply mischievous in the case of David's Napoleon, whose hand he has moved so that it is touching the front of his trousers.

SCHWARZ, Mommie. See **SCHWARTZ Mommie**

SCHWARZ, Otto Gottlieb
German, 19th century.
Born in Werro.
Active in Riga during the first half of the 19th century.
Lithographer.

SCHWARZ, Paul Wolfgang, or Schwartz
German, 18th - 19th century.
Born 1766, in Nuremberg; died c. 1815, in Nuremberg.
Engraver (aquatint/stippling). History subjects and landscapes.

Paul Wolfgang Schwarz was the pupil of Ch. De Mechel. In 1789 he was appointed court engraver to the duke of Saxe-Coburg-Saalfeld.

SCHWARZ, Philipp
German, 19th - 20th century.
Born 12 February 1874, in Darmstadt; died December 1924, in Darmstadt.
Sculptor.

SCHWARZ, Pierre
Belgian, 20th - 21st century.
Born 1950.
Painter, engraver.

Pierre Schwarz trained at the art academies in Brussels and Watermael-Boitsfort, then with Kokoschka in Salzburg.

SCHWARZ, Rudolf
Austrian, 19th - 20th century.
Born 1856, in Vienna; died 14 April 1912, in Indianapolis.
Active in the USA.
Sculptor.

SCHWARZ, Rudolf
German, 19th - 20th century.
Born 21 October 1878, in Kaiserslautern.
Active in Munich.
Sculptor.

Rudolf Schwarz studied under Wilhelm von Ruemann and at the fine arts academy in Munich.

MUSEUMS AND GALLERIES:
MULHOUSE (MBA): *Reichsautobahn No. 43.*

SCHWARZ, Sigrid Katharina
Swiss, 20th century.
Born 1914, in Basel; died 1992, in Basel.
Painter. Still-lifes, flowers.

AUCTION RECORDS:
ZURICH, 4 June 1992, *Still-life with a Lady's Slipper Orchid* (oil on card, 17 3/4 x 14 3/4 ins / 45 x 37.5 cm) CHF 791.

SCHWARZ, Stephan
German, 15th - 16th century.
Active in Augsburg 1493-1535.
Sculptor.

SCHWARZ, Viatcheslav Grigorievitch, or Chvarts
German, 19th century.
Born 22 September 1838, in Kursk; died 29 March 1869, in Russia.
Painter, engraver (etching). Battles.

Viatcheslav Schwarz attended the academy in Berlin and became painter to Nicholas II, Tsar of Russia.

MUSEUMS AND GALLERIES:
MOSCOW (State Tretyakov Gal.): *Ivan the Terrible and his Dead Son; The Russian Ambassador at the Court of the Roman Emperor; The Patriarch Nikon in New Jerusalem; 16th-century Coach; Spring Procession of the Tsarina on Pilgrimage at the time of Aleksei Mikhailovitch; Battle* (pen, four illustrations for A. K. Tolstoï's novel: Prince Serebriany, and seven illustrations for Lermontov's poem: The Song of Kalachnikov) - ST PETERSBURG (Hermitage): *Chess Game.*

SCHWARZ, Wenzel, or Franz Wenzel, called Wenzel-Schwartz
German, 19th - 20th century.
Born 24 October 1842, in Spittelgrund; died 31 May 1919, in Dresden.
Painter. History painting, portraits.

Wenzel Schwarz studied at the fine arts academies of Dresden and Antwerp and travelled extensively in Germany, Italy and Algeria before settling back in Dresden, where he was awarded a silver medal in 1863. Various examples of works by Schwarz are to be found in churches in Dresden and Bauzen.

SCHWARZ, Wilhelm, or Willi Franz
German, 20th century.
Born 10 September 1889, in Gruorn, near Urach.
Painter. Landscapes.

Wilhelm Schwarz studied at the fine arts academy in Stuttgart and under Gustav Bechler.

SCHWARZ, Wolf
Austrian, 17th century.
Died 1652.
Sculptor (wood).

Wolf Schwarz was the father of Konrad; he sculpted pulpits and altars for churches in Werfen.

SCHWARZ-ABRYS, Léon, or Schwartz-Abrys
French, 20th century.
Born 1905; died 1990.
Painter. Scenes with figures, figures, portraits, landscapes, seascapes, animals.

Schwarz-Abrys featured at the Salon des Indépendants in Paris in 1939. The working-class area of Ménilmontant, from where he hailed, was one of his favourite subjects; he often gave a tragic vision as he painted its characteristic small houses in a dramatic light. He also painted portraits of patients of St Anne psychiatric hospital in Paris, and galloping horses.

BIBLIOGRAPHY:
Schwarz-Abrys, Thibaud, Paris, 1988.

AUCTION RECORDS:
PARIS, 26 May 1971, *Rue des Grands-Champs,* FRF 1,400. PARIS, 21 March 1974, *Old Houses,* FRF 3,000. VERSAILLES, 28 March 1976, *Ménilmontant Train Station* (oil on canvas, 21 1/4 x 25 1/2 ins / 54 x 65 cm) FRF 4,000. PARIS, 30 May 1988, *Village* (oil/hardboard, 21 1/4 x 25 1/2 ins / 54 x 65 cm) FRF 1,700. PARIS, 12 July 1988, *Boats in the Gulf* (oil on panel, 19 3/4 x 24 ins / 50 x 61 cm) FRF 3,500. PARIS, 16 Jan 1989, *Street in Ménilmontant* (oil/hardboard, 19 3/4 x 24 ins / 50 x 61 cm) FRF 3,400. PARIS, 16 Nov 1990, *Train Station* (oil/hardboard, 20 3/4 x 24 3/4 ins / 53 x 63 cm) FRF 4,500. PARIS, 10 June 1991, *Train Station* (oil/hardboard, 21 1/4 x 25 1/2 ins / 54 x 65 cm) FRF 4,000.

SCHWARZBAUER, Joseph Anton
Austrian, 18th century.
Born 1766; died 6 August 1800.
Active in Vienna.
Portrait artist.

SCHWARZBAUR, Christoph
German, 18th century.
Painter.
Christoph Schwarzbaur painted a *Christ Crucified* in the church of Ochsenhausen.

SCHWARZBECK, Fritz
German, 20th century.
Born 23 December 1902, in Wicklesgreuth.
Sculptor. Busts.
Fritz Schwarzbeck studied at the fine arts academies of Düsseldorf and Kassel.

SCHWARZBÖCK, Georg
Austrian, 19th - 20th century.
Born 5 April 1877, in Vienna.
Sculptor, engraver. Medals.

SCHWARZBURGER, Carl
German, 19th - 20th century.
Born 7 July 1850, in Leipzig.
Active in Brooklyn (New York) from 1874.
Engraver (burin).

SCHWARZE. See also **SCHWARTZE**

SCHWARZE, Paul
German, 19th century.
Born March 1784, in Leipzig; died 8 March 1824, in Leipzig.
Engraver (burin).
Schwarze attended the academy in Dresden and engraved landscapes, genre scenes and historical subjects.

SCHWARZENBACH, Jacob, or Schwartzenbach
Dutch, 18th century.
Born 19 January 1763, in Middelburg; died 7 May 1805, in Véré.
Painter, engraver (etching). Portraits.
Jacob Schwarzenbach engraved portraits.
Museums and Galleries:
Amsterdam (Rijksmus.): two seascapes.

SCHWARZENBACH, Peter
German, 15th century.
Active in Ulm in 1473.
Sculptor.
Peter Schwarzenbach was also a metal embosser.

SCHWARZENBERG, Ernst von (Prince)
Austrian, 18th - 19th century.
Born 25 May 1773; died 14 March 1821.
Draughtsman.

SCHWARZENBERG, Johanna Elisabeth. See **SCHMERFELD Johanna Elisabeth von**

SCHWARZENBERG, Melchior
German, 16th century.
Active in Rostock and Wittenberg 1516-1550.
Draughtsman, engraver (wood).
Melchior Schwarzenberg made engravings for a bible in Wittenberg in 1534.

SCHWARZENBERG, Pauline Charlotte Iris
Maiden name: Princess d'Arenberg
Austrian, 18th - 19th century.
Born 2 September 1774; died 1 July 1810, in Paris.
Draughtsman, engraver.
Pauline Schwarzenberg drew and engraved views of the castles of the Schwarzenberg family in Bohemia.

SCHWARZENBERGER, Adolph
German, 18th century.
Born c. 1714; died March 1738.
Active in Frankfurt.
Sculptor.

SCHWARZENBERGER, Franz
German, 18th century.
Born c. 1699; died November 1735.
Active in Frankfurt.
Sculptor.
Franz Schwarzenberger was the son of Johann Bernhard.

SCHWARZENBERGER, Hans, or Schwarzperger
German, 16th century.
Active in Augsburg, Nuremberg and Regensburg 1528-1538.
Engraver (wood).

SCHWARZENBERGER, Johann
German, 18th century.
Active in Ambling and Prien in 1739.
Stucco artist.

SCHWARZENBERGER, Johann Bernhard, or Schwarzenburger
German, 17th - 18th century.
Born 4 June 1672, in Frankfurt; died July 1741, in Frankfurt.
Sculptor, cameo engraver.
Johann Bernhard Schwarzenberger was the father of Adolf, Franz and Valentin Schwarzenberger. He collaborated with his sons and sculpted statues.

SCHWARZENBERGER, Johann Peter
German, 17th century.
Active c. 1697.
Portrait artist.
Johann Peter Schwarzenberger was the brother of Johann Bernhard.

SCHWARZENBERGER, Rupert
Austrian, 19th century.
Died 25 March 1900, in Innsbruck.
Painter, glassmaker, architect, illustrator. Interiors.

SCHWARZENBERGER, Valentin
German, 18th century.
Born 1692, in Frankfurt am Main (?); died 5 February 1754, in Leipzig.
Sculptor.
Valentin Schwarzenberger was the pupil of Permoser in Dresden; he sculpted the pulpit in the church of St Paul in Dresden.

SCHWARZENBERGER, Valentin
German, 18th century.
Born c. 1704; died April 1732.
Active in Frankfurt.
Sculptor.
Valentin Schwarzenberger was the son of Johann Bernard.

SCHWARZENBURGER, Johann Bernhard. See **SCHWARZENBERGER**

SCHWARZENFELD, Schreitter von. See **SCHREITTER VON SCHWARZENFELD**

SCHWARZENHORN, Johann Rudolf Schmid von. See **SCHMID Johann Rudolf**

SCHWARZER, Karl Josef
German, 19th century.
Born c. 1825, in Heinrichswalde; died 10 May 1896, in Rome.
Painter, copyist.

SCHWARZER, Ludwig
Austrian, 20th century.
Born 1912, in Vienna.
Painter.

Ludwig Schwarzer studied from 1932 to 1936 at the fine arts academy in Vienna and went on to participate in group exhibitions, notably the Menton Biennale.

AUCTION RECORDS:

VIENNA, 18 March 1977, *Homing Pigeon* (1976, oil on mounted canvas/panel, 12 1/4 x 16 1/4 ins / 31 x 41 cm) ATS 40,000. VIENNA, 16 March 1979, *Target* (1978, oil on panel, 15 3/4 x 11 3/4 ins / 40 x 30 cm) ATS 38,000. VIENNA, 17 March 1987, *Visit* (1973, tempera, 15 1/4 x 11 3/4 ins / 39 x 30 cm) ATS 22,000. VIENNA, 15 June 1999, *Road to Exenschlager* (oil on canvas, 31 x 47 ins / 80 x 120 cm) ATS 67,000. VIENNA, 18 April 2001, *Circe* (1967, oil on board, 11 x 8 ins / 27 x 20 cm) ATS 80,000. LINZ, 27 Nov 2003, *Private Theatre Box* (oil on panel, 14 x 20 ins / 36 x 50 cm) EUR 3,000.

SCHWARZHUBER, Aventin
German, 18th - 19th century.
Active in Munich.
Painter.

Aventin Schwarzhuber was the pupil of Johann Kaspar Sing; he worked for churches in Amberg, Ingolstadt and Stadtamhof.

SCHWARZINGER, Franz
Italian, 20th century.
Painter.

Franz Schwarzinger held a solo exhibition of his work in 1988 at the Galleria Fabi Basaglia in Bologna.

SCHWARZKOGLER, Rudolf
Austrian, 20th century.
Born 1940; died 1969.
Performance artist.
Aktionismus group.

Rudolf Schwarzkogler's 'actions' and 'happenings' were provocative and repulsive in the extreme, a constant challenge to man in his social state and a reflection of the sense of morbid depression that appears to have typified mid-1960s Vienna. He took it upon himself to express his outrage and derision. In an act of supreme negation (rather than one of despair), he effectively committed suicide as a result of one of his 'actions', which saw him perform a series of crude amputations on his own person.

Schwarzkogler's 'actions' and 'happenings' have been the subject of numerous group exhibitions since his death in 1969, notably at Documenta V in Kassel in 1972 and later at the following: *La Peinture comme Crime ou la Part Maudite de la Modernité* (*Painting as Crime or the Curse of Modernity*) at the Louvre in Paris (2001); *Selbst und Andere: Das Bildnis in der Kunst nach 1960* (*Self and Others: Portraiture since 1960*) at the Rupertinum in Salzburg (2003); and *Phantom der Lust. Visionen des Masochismus in der Kunst* (*Phantom of Desire. Visions of Masochism in Art*), an exhibition devoted to Sacher-Masoch and held at the Neue Galerie am Landesmuseum in Graz (2003).

Schwarzkogler retrospectives include those at the following: Vienna (1970); Innsbruck (1976); the Museum Moderner Kunst Stiftung Ludwig in Vienna (1992); and *Rudolf Schwarzkogler: Photographies d'Actions, Vienne, 1965-1966* (*Rudolf Schwarzkogler: Photographs of Actions, Vienna, 1965-1966*) at the Musée National d'Art Moderne in Paris (1993).

BIBLIOGRAPHY:

Michel, Régis, *La peinture comme crime ou la part maudite de la modernité*, group exhibition catalogue, Musée du Louvre, Réunion des Musées Nationaux, Paris, 2001. Weibel, Peter (ed.), *'Phantom der Lust. Visionen des Masochismus in der Kunst'* in *2 vol*, exhibition catalogue, Neue Galerie am Landesmuseum, Graz, Belleville Verlag, Munich, 2003.

SCHWARZKOPF, Karl Heinrich
German, 18th - 19th century.
Born c. 1763; died 1 December 1846.
Modeller.

Schwarzkopf worked in the porcelain factories of Berlin, Brunswick and Furstenberg.

SCHWÄRZLER, Alois Konrad
Austrian, 19th - 20th century.
Born 17 November 1874, in Kufstein.
Active in Kramsach (North Tyrol).
Engraver. Landscapes.

Alois Konrad Schwärzler is noted for engravings of landscapes in the Engadine region of Switzerland and the South Tyrol.

SCHWARZMANN, Andreas, or Schwartzmann
German, 18th century.
Born to a family originally from Waldsassen; died 30 August 1739, in Fulda.
Stucco artist.

Andreas Schwarzmann worked for the cathedral and castle of Fulda.

SCHWARZMANN, Johann Jakob, or Schwartzmann or Schwarcmann
Austrian, 18th century.
Born 23 May 1729, in Schnifis, near Ferldkirch; died 12 July 1784, in the same area.
Stucco artist, sculptor.

Johann Schwarzmann executed numerous works in the churches of Austria and southern Germany and was employed at the Hohenzollern Court.

SCHWARZMANN, Joseph
Swiss, 18th century.
Born c. 1724, in Coire; died 16 September 1793, in Rome.
Engraver (burin/wood).

The father of Joseph Anton Schwarzmann.

SCHWARZMANN, Joseph Anton
Italian, 18th century.
Born 22 March 1754, in Rome.
Engraver (wood).

Joseph Anton Schwarzmann was the son of Joseph Schwarzmann and husband of the engraver Laura Piranesi, the daughter of G. B. Piranesi.

SCHWARZMANN, Joseph Anton
Austrian, 19th century.
Born 1 February 1806, in Prutz; died 18 July 1890, in Munich.
Painter, decorative designer.

Joseph Anton Schwarzmann studied under Schönherr and H. Hess in Munich. He painted decorations in a number of castles in Munich and in the Pinakothek, as well as in the castle at Athens.

SCHWARZMAYR, Joseph
German, 18th century.
Active in Reisbach 1765-1769.
Sculptor (wood).

Joseph Schwarzmayr sculpted the high altar in the Mariakirche.

SCHWARZPECKH, Hans
Austrian, 17th century.
Sculptor (wood).

Schwarzpeckh executed several statues in the church of Prazoll near Bozen (now Bolzano, Italy) around 1650.

SCHWARZPERGER, Hans.
See **SCHWARZENBERGER**

SCHWARZSCHILD, Alfred
German, 19th - 20th century.
Born 14 November 1874, in Frankfurt am Main.
Painter. Genre scenes.

Alfred Schwarzschild exhibited at the Salon des Artistes Français, where he received an honourable mention in 1903, and at the Salon de la Société Nationale des Beaux-Arts.

AUCTION RECORDS:
LINDAU, 7 May 1980, *Woman and Children in Fields* (oil on canvas, 39 1/4 x 59 ins / 100 x 150 cm) DEM 4,200. LUCERNE, 6 Nov 1986, *Two Nudes Carrying a Bowl of Fruit* (1909, oil on canvas, 68 x 40 1/2 ins / 173 x 103 cm) CHF 8,500. LONDON, 5 May 1989, *Farewell* (1911, oil on canvas, 51 x 34 1/2 ins / 129.5 x 87.5 cm) GBP 5,500. MUNICH, 29 Nov 1989, *South Wind* (1903, oil on canvas, 36 3/4 x 83 3/4 ins / 93.5 x 213 cm) DEM 16,500. LONDON, 18 March 1994, *Centre of Attention* (1902, oil on canvas, 29 1/4 x 59 3/4 ins / 74 x 152 cm) GBP 9,200. NEW YORK, 1 Nov 1995, *Summer's End* (1903, oil on canvas, 84 x 37 1/2 ins / 213.4 x 95.3 cm) USD 19,550. MUNICH, 3 Dec 1996, *Children with Garlands of Flowers* (1902, oil on canvas, 37 3/4 x 50 ins / 96 x 127 cm) DEM 4,800. NEW YORK, 18 March 1998, *Sweetest Nectar* (1928, oil on canvas, 27 3/4 x 47 1/2 ins / 70.5 x 120.7 cm) USD 5,750. VIENNA, 27 May 2004, *Children Playing* (1902, oil on canvas, 29 x 60 ins / 73 x 153 cm) EUR 5,000.

SCHWARZT, Frank H.
American, 20th century.
Born 21 June 1894, in New York; died 1951.
Painter, draughtsman.

Frank Schwarzt studied under Harry Mills Walcott. He was a member of the Salmagundi Club in New York.

SCHWARZWALDER, Martin, or Schwartzenwalder
Austrian, 17th century.
Active in Vienna during the second half of the 17th century.
Sculptor (wood), painter. Figures.

Martin Schwarzwalder sculpted the altar dedicated to St Joseph in the abbey of Heiligenkreuz in 1689.

SCHWARZWALDER, Max
German, 18th century.
Sculptor (wood).

Max Schwarzwalder sculpted altars, choir stalls and confessional boxes in the church of St Stephen in Mindelheim.

SCHWATHE, Hans
Swiss, 19th - 20th century.
Born 28 May 1870, in Strachwitztal.
Sculptor, medallist. Religious subjects. Busts.

Hans Schwathe sculpted tombs, busts and altars for churches in Vienna and other Austrian towns and cities.

SCHWATZER, Erhard, or Swatzer
German, 15th - 16th century.
Painter. Religious subjects.

Erhard Schwatzer worked for the bishops of Bamberg.

SCHWATZER, Erhard I
German, 16th century.
Active in Nuremberg in 1529.
Painter.

SCHWATZER, Erhard II, or Schwetzer or Schweitzer or Svetzer
German, 16th century.
Born 1505.
Active in Nuremberg.
Painter. Portraits.

Erhard Schwatzer II may have been the son of Erhard Schwatzer I.

SCHWAYER. See **SCHWAIGER**

SCHWAZ, Hans. See **MALER**

SCHWEBACH, Johann Jakob. See **SWEBACH**

SCHWEBEL, Ivan
Israeli and American, 20th century.
Born 1932, in West Virginia in the USA.
Active in Israel since 1963.
Painter (mixed media), illustrator. Figures, scenes with figures.

Ivan Schwebel studied history of art at New York University and also attended courses at the Institute of Fine Art. He paints religious and historical subjects, such as King David, taken out of their traditional context and reinterpreted in a modern environment. He has taught at the Bezalel Academy of Art and Design in Jerusalem and has illustrated the works *Retrievements, a Jerusalem Anthology* (1968) and *Arena of Jerusalem* (1987). He has also painted a mural in a garden in Tel Aviv.

Schwebel's work was shown at the exhibition *Young and Old Masters of Israeli and International Art* at the Safrai Fine Art Gallery in Jerusalem. In 1971 he had a solo exhibition, *Ha-oman be-sadnato*, at the Israel Museum in Jerusalem.

BIBLIOGRAPHY:
Friedman, Ina, '*Arts: Painting the Hate*' in *The Jérusalem Report. com*, Jerusalem. *Ha-oman be-sadnato*, exhibition catalogue, Israel Museum, Jerusalem, 1971.

AUCTION RECORDS:
TEL AVIV, 2 Jan 1989, *Figures* (oil on canvas, 35 1/4 x 39 1/4 ins / 89.5 x 100 cm) USD 2,200. TEL AVIV, 3 Jan 1990, *Last Showing at the Zion Cinema* (1979, oil and pencil/canvas, 35 1/2 x 41 1/4 ins / 90 x 105 cm) USD 6,380. TEL AVIV, 19 June 1990, *Painting-sculpture in the Environment* (1974, mixed media/paper, 39 x 27 ins / 99 x 68.5 cm) USD 2,090. TEL AVIV, 1 Jan 1991, *Man and Woman* (1988, oil on paper/canvas, 23 x 27 1/4 ins / 57.5 x 69 cm) USD 1,210. TEL AVIV, 5 Jan 1999, *Figures at Doorway, View of Jerusalem Hills* (c. 1973, oil on canvas, 29 x 20 ins / 73 x 73 cm) GBP 1, 463. TEL AVIV, 5 Jan 1999, *Self-portrait and Figures in a Landscape* (oil on board, 26 x 38 ins / 67 x 97 cm) GBP 976.

SCHWEBEL, João André
Portuguese, 18th century.
Active from 1750 to 1757.
Draughtsman, architect.

João André Schwebel drew geographical maps.

SCHWEBLIN. See **MORANDT Conrad**

SCHWECHTEN, Friedrich Wilhelm
German, 19th century.
Born 2 December 1796, in Berlin; died 28 April 1879, in Meissen.
Glass painter, draughtsman, engraver (etching), architect.

Schwechten engraved views of Athens, the cathedral at Meissen and historical subjects.

SCHWED, Lorenz
Austrian, 18th century.
Born 1746; died 19 August 1805, in Vienna.
Active in Vienna.
Sculptor.

SCHWEDAR, Julius
Austrian, 19th - 20th century.
Born 8 December 1854, in Pavia; died 23 February 1929, in Klagenfurt.
Painter. Landscapes.

Julius Schwedar studied in Graz under Alfred Zoff.

SCHWEDE, R.
German, 16th century.
Active in Bamberg (Bavaria), at the beginning of the 16th century.
Painter.
In collaboration with Georg Glaser, R. Schwede painted murals in the cloister of the Carmelite monastery of Frankfurt.

SCHWEDER, G. F. Theodor
German, 19th century.
Born 23 February 1812, in Magdeburg.
Sculptor.
Theodor Schweder studied under Josef Klieber in Vienna, under Rauch in Berlin and under Schwanthaler in Munich, later settling in Valparaíso.

SCHWEDER, Hermann
German, 19th century.
Painter. History painting, genre scenes.
Hermann Schweder was the pupil of J. Schrader and exhibited in Berlin from 1860 to 1866.

SCHWEDESKY, Ralf
German, 20th - 21st century.
Born 1952, in Belzig.
Painter, engraver (etching).
Ralf Schwedesky took part in the exhibition *De Bonnard à Baselitz - Dix Ans d'enrichissements du cabinet des estampes* (*From Bonnard to Baselitz: A Decade of Acquisitions by the Prints Collection 1978-1988*) in 1992 at the Bibliothèque Nationale in Paris.
MUSEUMS AND GALLERIES:
PARIS (BNF): *Stone Age II: Resurrection* (1984, etching).

SCHWEDLER, Robert
German, 19th century.
Born in Küstrin (now Kostrzyn, Poland).
Active in Berlin and Lüneburg 1846-1868.
Painter. Genre scenes.

SCHWEER, Charles
French, 20th century.
Born 1 August 1877, in Mulhouse.
Engraver.
Schweer exhibited from 1906, at the Salon des Artistes Français in Paris.

SCHWEGERLE, Hans
German, 20th century.
Born 2 May 1882, in Lübeck.
Sculptor, illustrator. Busts.
Hans Schwegerle studied under Wilhelm von Ruemann and at the fine arts academy in Munich.
MUSEUMS AND GALLERIES:
MUNICH (NG): *Bust of Martin Luther* - MUNICH (Städtische Gal. im Lenbachhaus): *Melusina* - NUREMBERG (Municipal Gal.): *Bust of Thomas Mann*.

SCHWEGERLE, Jakob
German, 19th century.
Born c. 1811; died 1864, in Augsburg.
Lithographer.

SCHWEGLER, Fritz
German, 20th century.
Born 1935, in Breech.
Active in Düsseldorf.
Painter, sculptor, engraver.
Examples of Fritz Schwegler's work featured in *De Bonnard à Baselitz: Dix Ans d'Enrichissements du Cabinet des Estampes 1978-1988* (*From Bonnard to Baselitz: A Decade of Acquisitions by the Prints Collection 1978-1988*) at the Bibliothèque Nationale in Paris in 1992.

SCHWEGLER, Jakob
German, 16th century.
Active in Ostrach (Baden-Württemberg), at the end of the 16th century.
Sculptor (wood), cabinet maker.
With Melchior Binder, Jakob Schwegler carved the stalls of the church of Salem between 1589 and 1593.

SCHWEGLER, Jakob
Swiss, 19th century.
Born 2 May 1793, in Hergiswil; died 7 January 1866, in Lucerne.
Painter, miniaturist, lithographer, sculptor. Genre scenes.
Jakob Schwegler studied painting with Willisan and sculpture with Schlatt, settling in Lucerne where he taught drawing. He was followed by his two sons, the lithographer Joseph Schwegler, and the painter Xaver Schwegler.
MUSEUMS AND GALLERIES:
SOLOTHURN (Kunstmus.): *Tinsmith*.
AUCTION RECORDS:
LUCERNE, 7 Nov 1985, *Under the Egg* (1859, oil on canvas, 18 x 23 3/4 ins / 45.5 x 60.5 cm) CHF 17,000.

SCHWEGLER, Joseph
Swiss, 19th century.
Born 31 May 1831, in Lucerne.
Lithographer.
Joseph Schwegler was the son of Jakob; he settled in New York in 1873.

SCHWEGLER, Philipp Jakob
German, 18th century.
Born 1702, in Söflingen; died 1738, in Söflingen.
Painter.

SCHWEGLER, Xaver
Swiss, 19th century.
Born 3 December 1832, in Lucerne; died 16 January 1902, in Lucerne.
Painter, miniaturist, draughtsman. Hunting scenes, figures, portraits, landscapes, waterscapes, interiors, still-lifes.
Xaver Schwegler was first taught by his father Jakob, then went to Munich where he made numerous copies after the old masters. After a Parisian interlude he returned to Switzerland, settling in Lucerne, and taught in the drawing school of the Canton there.
MUSEUMS AND GALLERIES:
BASEL: *Huntsman with Animal Pelts on Sleigh; Still-life, Game* - BERN: *16th- and 17th-century Cups* - LAUSANNE: *Snow Scene: Sliding*.
AUCTION RECORDS:
LUCERNE, 17 June 1950, *Vierwaldstättersee*, CHF 1,600. BERN, 22 Oct 1976, *View of the Vierwaldstättersee* (1850, oil on paper remounted on board, 13 x 17 1/4 ins / 33 x 44 cm) CHF 2,000. BERN, 28 April 1978, *Tinsmith* (oil on paper remounted/canvas, 12 1/2 x 15 1/4 ins / 32 x 38.5 cm) CHF 2,800. SAN FRANCISCO, 21 June 1984, *Still-life with Hare and Pheasant* (oil on canvas, 11 3/4 x 9 1/4 ins / 30 x 23.5 cm) USD 1,500. LUCERNE, 3 Oct 1986, *Views of Lucerne, Zinen, Hasli, etc.* (watercolour, series of fourteen) CHF 32,000. LUCERNE, 13 Oct 1999, *Outer Weggistor in Lucerne* (oil on canvas, 13 x 23 ins / 34 x 58 cm) CHF 16,000. LUCERNE, 8 Nov 2000, *Still-life with Game* (oil on canvas, 27 x 21 ins / 68 x 54 cm) CHF 7,200. LUCERNE, 2 May 2001, *Hunting Still-life* (oil on canvas, 12 x 15 ins / 30 x 37 cm) CHF 5,200. LUCERNE, 19 Nov 2003, *Ennetburgen* (1851, oil on paper/canvas, 13 x 20 ins / 34 x 50 cm) CHF 2,400. LUCERNE, 19 Nov 2003, *Interior with Dead Birds on Chair* (oil on canvas, 13 x 10 ins / 32 x 26 cm) CHF 2,400.

SCHWEGMAN, Hendrik
Dutch, 18th - 19th century.
Born 1761, near Haarlem; died 1816, near Haarlem.
Painter, engraver (etching). Still-lifes, flowers.

Hendrik Schwegman was a pupil of P. van Loo. He joined the guild of Haarlem in 1791. He was a prolific engraver, noted for his coloured plates for the *Icones Planlarum Rariorum*. He also engraved landscapes in the manner of Antony Waterloo. He died an alcoholic.

MUSEUMS AND GALLERIES:

BRUSSELS: drawings - HAARLEM: drawings.

SCHWEICH, Carl or Karl

German, 19th century.

Born 6 December 1823, in Darmstadt; died 23 April 1898, in Düsseldorf.

Painter. Portraits, landscapes.

Schweich studied under Aug. Lucas in Darmstadt, under Rottman in Munich and under Dyckmans and Wappers in Antwerp. He liked to depict clouds and the effects of storms and squalls.

MUSEUMS AND GALLERIES:

DARMSTADT (Hessisches Landesmus.): a work.

SCHWEICKARDT, Hendrik Willem or Heinrich Wilhelm, or Schweickhardt, Scheickhardt

German, 18th century.

Born 1746, in Brandenburg; died 8 July 1797, in London.

Painter, watercolourist, engraver, draughtsman.

Portraits, landscapes, landscapes with figures. Designs for tapestries.

Schweickardt was the pupil of Girolamo Lapis and produced etchings. He went to The Hague in 1775 and to London in 1786. His son, Lodevyk Schweickardt, was an engraver.

MUSEUMS AND GALLERIES:

BLACKBURN: *Live-stock* - HAMBURG: *Italian Landscape* - LONDON (NG): *Cattle* (1794, oil/wood) - MONTREAL (Learmont): *Landscape* - PARIS (Louvre): *Skaters on Canal* - ROHRAU (Schlossmus., Graf Harrach'sche Familiensammlung): *Landscape* - THE HAGUE (Gemeentemus.): *Fruit-seller.*

AUCTION RECORDS:

PARIS, 18-23 March 1901, *View of Canal in Holland,* FRF 640. LONDON, 11 March 1911, *Frozen River* (1793) GBP 39. PARIS, 20 May 1925, *Skaters on Canal in Holland,* FRF 820. LONDON, 19 July 1929, *Scene of Frozen River,* GBP 65. LONDON, 20 Dec 1946, *Scene of Frozen River,* GBP 94. LONDON, 9 June 1967, *Skaters on Frozen River,* Gns 1,100. LONDON, 29 Nov 1968, *Winter Landscape with Skaters,* Gns 2,600. AMSTERDAM, 10 Nov 1970, *Winter Landscape with Skaters,* NLG 40,000. AMSTERDAM, 14 Nov 1972, *Winter Landscape with Figures,* NLG 16,000. LONDON, 30 Nov 1973, *Peasants and Flocks at River Bank,* Gns 3,800. LONDON, 18 July 1974, *Italian Landscape* (1780) Gns 2,800. PARIS, 12 March 1976, *Skaters; River Banks* (oil on panel, a pair, 7 1/2 x 10 1/4 ins / 19 x 26 cm) FRF 16,500. LONDON, 25 March 1977, *Winter Landscape with Skaters* (oil on panel, 11 x 15 ins / 28 x 38 cm) GBP 6,000. LONDON, 19 April 1978, *Peasants and Flocks in Landscape* (oil on panel, 17 x 25 1/4 ins / 43 x 64 cm) GBP 1,000. LONDON, 9 May 1979, *Winter Landscape with Frozen River* (oil on canvas, 17 1/4 x 23 1/4 ins / 44 x 59 cm) GBP 3,600. VERSAILLES, 18 May 1980, *Peasants Returning from Fields* (pen and watercolour, 10 1/2 x 9 ins / 26.5 x 22 cm) FRF 4,400. AMSTERDAM, 16 Nov 1981, *Winter Landscape with Skaters* (pen and wash/blue paper, 11 x 7 1/4 ins / 28 x 18.1 cm) NLG 2,300. LILLE, 12 Dec 1982, *Skating Scene* (oil on wood, 7 x 11 ins / 18 x 28 cm) FRF 18,000. VIENNA, 16 Nov 1983, *Winter Landscape with Skaters* (oil on panel, 8 x 11 ins / 20.3 x 28 cm) ATS 200,000. LONDON, 25 Oct 1985, *Skaters in River Landscape* (1791, oil on panel, 20 x 28 ins / 50.8 x 71.1 cm) GBP 15,000. MONTE CARLO, 22 Feb 1986, *River Landscape in Summer, Holland; Fishing Scene; Family of Shepherds by Cascade; Shepherds Leading their Flock to Drinking-trough; Moonlit River Landscape; Skating Scene* (1776, oil on canvas, six canvases, 104 3/4 x 102 3/4 ins / 266 x 261 cm, 104 1/4 x 104 1/4 ins/265 x 265 cm, 104 x 36 ins/264 x 90.5 cm, 65 x 37 ins/165 x 94 cm, 104 1/4 x 41 1/4 ins/265 x 104.5 cm and 104 1/4 x 4 1/4 ins/265 x 11 cm) FRF 1,000,000. LONDON, 19 May 1989, *Winter Landscape with Skaters in Estuary* (oil on canvas, 15 x 18 3/4 ins / 37.2 x 47.6 cm) GBP 6,600. AMSTERDAM, 9 Nov 1993, *Hay-making in Dutch Landscape* (1779, oil on panel, 15 3/4 x 21 ins / 40 x 52.5 cm) NLG 7,130. LONDON, 22 April 1994, *Putti with Flowers* (oil on panel, 9 1/2 x 6 3/4 ins / 24.3 x 17.2 cm) GBP 1,840. AMSTERDAM, 17 Nov 1994, *Winter Landscape with Men Pulling Sleigh on Snowy Bank with Skaters in the Distance* (oil on canvas, 28 1/4 x 38 1/2 ins / 71.5 x 98 cm) NLG 50,000. AMSTERDAM, 13 Nov 1995, *Country Wedding* (1782, oil on canvas, 29 1/2 x 40 ins / 74.8 x 101.8 cm) NLG 69,000. AMSTERDAM, 6 May 1996, *Putti Playing in Park* (oil on canvas in pink grisaille, a pair, each 31 3/4 x 41 1/2 ins / 80.5 x 105.5 cm) NLG 37,760. NEW YORK, 16 Oct 1997, *Winter Landscape with Skaters and other Figures on Frozen Pond* (1793, oil on panel, 13 x 17 1/2 ins / 33 x 44.4 cm) USD 107,000. LONDON, 3-4 Dec 1997, *Pastoral Scene with Peasants and Cows near River* (oil on panel, 17 x 24 ins / 43.2 x 60.8 cm) GBP 10,350. LONDON, 14 June 2001, *Groom with Two Saddled Chestnut Hunters* (oil on panel, 12 x 16 ins / 30 x 40 cm) GBP 2,400. PARIS, 12 Oct 2001, *Bringing in the Hay* (oil on panel, 17 x 22 ins / 42 x 57 cm) FRF 19,000. AMSTERDAM, 14 May 2002, *Wedding Dance in a Village* (1782, oil on canvas, 30 x 40 ins / 75 x 102 cm) EUR 30,000. LONDON, 9 July 2002, *Frozen Canal with a Washerwoman, Horse-drawn Cart, Skaters and a Bridge beyond* (oil on panel, 18 x 24 ins / 46 x 61 cm) GBP 38,000. AMSTERDAM, 4 Nov 2003, *Canal Landscape with Peasant Family by their Cottage, and Piles of Peat* (1785, oil on canvas, 18 x 26 ins / 45 x 65 cm) EUR 16,000. LONDON, 10 Dec 2003, *Three Putti Holding Garlands of Flowers beside Classical Column* (oil on canvas, shaped top, 31 x 43 ins / 78 x 108 cm) GBP 2,800. NOTTINGHAM, 5 Feb 2004, *Dutch Winter Scene with Skaters* (1783, oil on panel, 11 x 15 ins / 28 x 37 cm) GBP 41,000. LONDON, 9 July 2004, *Winter Landscape with Peasants Skating* (oil on canvas, 28 x 39 ins / 72 x 99 cm) GBP 9,500.

SCHWEICKARDT, Katharina

British, 18th century.

Painter. Flowers.

Katharina Schweickardt was the daughter of Hendrik Willem Schweickardt.

SCHWEICKARDT, Louis or Lodevyk

British, 18th century.

Engraver (burin).

Son of Hendrik Willem Schweickardt, Louis Schweickardt engraved illustrations of military uniforms.

SCHWEICKART, Johann Adam, or Schweikart

German, 18th century.

Born 19 October 1722, in Nuremberg; died 15 October 1787, in Nuremberg.

Engraver (burin), draughtsman.

Johann Schweickart studied with Preissler, then completed his training in Italy, spending 18 years in Florence where he produced several plates of jewels in the collection published by Stosch. On his return, he engraved a number of reproductions of paintings by the masters. He was also known for his copies of drawings.

MUSEUMS AND GALLERIES:

BERLIN (Kupferstichkabinet): *Self-portrait.*

AUCTION RECORDS:

LONDON, 12 May 1972, *Landscape with Frozen River,* Gns 1,600.

SCHWEICKART, Lothar Ignaz

German, 18th century.

Born 1702; died 1779.

Active in Bruchsal.

Painter.

Lothar Schweickart painted for the town of Bruchsal and for bishops.

SCHWEICKER, Johann
German, 19th century.
Born c. 1799, in Lindau.
Engraver (burin), lithographer.
Schweicker studied under A. Reindel and attended the academy in Nuremberg.

SCHWEICKER, Thomas, or Schweiker
German, 16th century.
Born 1541, in Schwäbisch Hall; died 1602 or 1608.
Painter.
Heilbronn Museum owns a *Self-portrait* by Schweicker.

SCHWEICKLE, Konrad Heinrich
German, 19th century.
Born 28 March 1779, in Stuttgart; died 2 June 1833.
Sculptor.
Schweickle was a pupil of Scheffauer and also studied in Paris and Rome.

SCHWEIGART, Johann Joseph
German, 19th century.
Born 1789, in Dresden.
Painter.
Schweigart was the pupil of Josef Grassi and painted landscapes, portraits and military scenes.

SCHWEIGEL. See also **SCHEUBEL**

SCHWEIGEL, Andreas
German, 18th - 19th century.
Born 30 November 1735, in Brünn (now Brno, Czech Republic); died 23 March 1812, in Brünn.
Sculptor.
Andreas Schweigel was the son of Anton and brother of Johann and Thomas Stefan Schweigel.
MUSEUMS AND GALLERIES:
OPAVA (Provincial Mus.): *St Helen and Constantine* (two statues).

SCHWEIGEL, Anton I
Austrian, 18th century.
Born 1700, in Gaiming; died 24 April 1761, in Brno.
Active from 1725.
Sculptor.
Anton Schweigel I was the father of Andreas.

SCHWEIGEL, Anton II
Austrian, 19th century.
Born 1786; died 28 November 1846.
Active in Brno.
Sculptor.
Anton Schweigel II was the son of Thomas Stefan.

SCHWEIGEL, Johann
Austrian, 18th century.
Born 28 September 1740.
Active in Brno.
Sculptor.
Johann Schweigel was the brother of Andreas.

SCHWEIGEL, Johann Joseph.
See **SCHEUBEL**

SCHWEIGEL, Josef
Austrian, 19th century.
Born 9 January 1775.
Active in Brno.
Sculptor.
Josef Schweigel was the son and collaborator of Thomas Stefan.

SCHWEIGEL, Thomas Stefan
Austrian, 18th - 19th century.
Born 21 December 1743; died 12 September 1814.
Active in Brno.
Sculptor.
Thomas Schweigel was the brother and collaborator of Andreas.

SCHWEIGER. See also **SCHWAIGER**

SCHWEIGER, Johan Friedrich
Norwegian, 18th century.
Born in Helmstedt; died 1788, in Trondheim.
Painter.
Schweiger settled in Norway in 1740. He painted portraits and landscapes.

SCHWEIGERT, Mathias
German, 18th century.
Born 1691, in Weissenhorn; died 2 August 1725, in Weissenhorn.
Painter.
Schweigert was court painter in Munich.

SCHWEIGGER. See also **SCHWAIGER**

SCHWEIGGER, Emanuel I
German, 17th century.
Born 9 October 1583, in Grötzingen; died 27 August 1627, in Rome.
Painter.

SCHWEIGGER, Emanuel II
German, 17th century.
Died 21 October 1634.
Active in Nuremberg.
Sculptor.
Emanuel Schweigger II was the father of Georg.
MUSEUMS AND GALLERIES:
BERLIN (Kupferstichkabinet): a drawing.

SCHWEIGGER, Georg or Georges
German, 17th century.
Born 6 April 1613, in Nuremberg; died 13 June 1680, in Nuremberg.
Sculptor, founder. Statues.
Georg Schweigger was the son and pupil of Emanuel II Schweigger von Nuremberg and made statues of important figures of the time.

MUSEUMS AND GALLERIES:
BRUNSWICK: *Equestrian Statuette of Gustav Adolph* - HAMBURG: *Tomb of Gustave Adolph* (model) - VIENNA: *Medal with Effigy of Ferdinand III; Bust of Ferdinand III* - WÜRZBURG: *Christ Shown to the People.*

SCHWEIGGER, Hans
German, 15th century.
Active in Ulm during the first half of the 15th century.
Sculptor, painter.

SCHWEIGHOEUSER, Louis or François Louis
French, 18th century.
Born 1760, in Strasbourg.
Sculptor.
Louis Schweighoeuser studied under Luc Breton. In 1782 he won first prize in the competition at the school of painting and sculpture in Besançon with his *Death of Epaminondas.*
MUSEUMS AND GALLERIES:
BESANÇON: *Death of Epaminondas.*

SCHWEIGHOFER, August
Austrian, 19th - 20th century.

Born 5 June 1879, in Imst; died 23 May 1935, in Imst.
Painter.

SCHWEIGHOFER, Franz
Austrian, 19th century.
Born 25 March 1797, in Brixen (now Bressanone, Italy); died 4 December 1861, in Bozen, South Tyrol (now Bolzano, Italy).
Lithographer. Panoramas, landscapes, mountainscapes, architectural views.
Schweighofer worked in Vienna and Innsbruck and engraved castles, mountains and panoramas.

SCHWEIGL. See **SCHWEIGEL**

SCHWEIGLÄNDER, Alois, or Schweiglender
German, 18th - 19th century.
Born 19 July 1740, in Ottingen; died 1812?, in Nuremberg.
Painter.
Schweigländer executed altar paintings in the abbey of Reichenbach.
MUSEUMS AND GALLERIES:
AUGSBURG (Maximilianmus.): cible - ULM (Ulmer Mus.): *Coronation of the Virgin*.

SCHWEIKART, Karol or Karl Gottlieb
Polish, 18th - 19th century.
Born 28 February 1772, in Ludwigsburg; died 16 April 1855, in Tarnopol (Galicia).
Miniaturist. Figures, portraits, landscapes, animals.
Karl Schweikart studied in Karlsruhe, Stuttgart, and later in Vienna.
MUSEUMS AND GALLERIES:
CRACOW (Muz. Narodowe): *Portrait of the Doctor Joseph Sei* - LVIV (Lubomirski Mus.): *The Actor Ant. Bensa; P. Romanowicz and Family; D. Schaffel; Louise von Koller* - LVIV (Municipal Mus.): *Self-portrait; The Artist's Wife; The Singer Skibinska; Self-portrait; The Artist's Wife; Two Landscapes; Dead Bustards* - SALZBURG (Mozart Mus.): *Portrait of Mozart* - WARSAW (Muz. Narodowe): *Portrait of L. Rulikowski.*

SCHWEIKHARDT. See **SCHWEICKARDT**

SCHWEINBERGER, Anton
German, 16th - 17th century.
Goldsmith.
Prague School..
Anton Schweinberger was the court jeweller of Emperor Rudolf II (1552-1612, Emperor from 1576). He worked in Prague and added to the imperial collection of *mirabilia*, unusual natural objects sometimes refashioned into *objets d'art*. He created his most famous work, a large gold-encrusted water jug, from a double coconut brought back from the Seychelles by the Dutch admiral Hermanzen. The jug is now kept in the Kunsthistorisches Museum in Vienna.

SCHWEINFURTH, Ernst
German, 19th century.
Born 2 March 1818, in Karlsruhe; died 24 October 1877, in Rome.
Painter, engraver (etching). Landscapes.
Schweinfurth studied under C. L. Frommel and at the academy in Munich.
MUSEUMS AND GALLERIES:
DONAUESCHINGEN: *Schloss Hohenbaden* - KARLSRUHE (Staatliche Kunsthalle): *The Bay of Cattaro* - MUNICH (Schack-Gal.): *Landscape near Cervetri; The Lateran Cloister* - RIGA (MM): *Roman Countryside.*

SCHWEINFURTH, Eva Margarethe, wife of Bochert
German, 19th - 20th century.
Born 8 May 1878, in Riga.
Painter.
Eva Margarethe Schweinfurth completed her studies in Riga, Paris and Munich.

SCHWEINHEIM, Conrad, or Sweinheim
German, 15th century.
Active in 1478.
Engraver. Cards.
Schweinheim collaborated with A. Bucking.

SCHWEINHUBER, Franz Xaver
German, 18th - 19th century.
Painter. Religious subjects.
Franz Schweinhuber worked in Rothenburg-ob-der-Tauber in 1794 and executed paintings for churches in Eichstätt and Hohendorf.

SCHWEINHUBER, Johann Anton
German, 18th century.
Born c. 1729; died 8 May 1773.
Active in Rothenburg-ob-der-Tauber.
Painter.

SCHWEINHUBER, Xaver
German, 19th century.
Born 1 July 1813.
Painter.
Xaver Schweinhuber was the brother of Franz and also worked in Rothenburg-ob-der-Tauber.

SCHWEINITZ, Rudolf or Karl Rudolf
German, 19th century.
Born 15 January 1839, in Charlottenburg; died 7 January 1896, in Berlin.
Sculptor. Figures. Statues.
Schweinitz studied under Schievelbein at the academy in Berlin and was in Paris, Italy and Copenhagen.
MUSEUMS AND GALLERIES:
BERLIN: *Endangered love.*
AUCTION RECORDS:
PARIS, 22 April 1994, *Oriental Dancer* (1885, white marble, h. 49 1/4 ins / 125 cm) FRF 35,100.

SCHWEINZER, Mathias
German, 18th - 19th century.
Born 20 September 1768, in Vienna; died 11 November 1837, in Vienna.
Painter.

SCHWEIPEL, Johann Joseph.
See **SCHEUBEL**

SCHWEISSINGER, Georg Karl
German, 19th century.
Born 14 November 1822, in Königsberg (now Kaliningrad, Russia).
Painter, lithographer.
Georg Schweissinger was the brother of Theodor; he attended the academy in Leipzig.
MUSEUMS AND GALLERIES:
LEIPZIG (Stadtgeschichtliches Mus.): drawings.

SCHWEISSINGER, Theodor or Johann Friedrich Theodor
German, 19th century.
Born 7 April 1819, in Königsberg (now Kaliningrad, Russia).
Painter, lithographer.
Theodor Schweissinger was the brother of Georg Karl; he attended the academy in Leipzig and worked in the same city.

SCHWEITZER. See also **SCHWEIZER**

SCHWEITZER, Adolf Gustav
German, 19th - 20th century.
Born 19 April 1847; died February 1914, in Düsseldorf.
Painter. Landscapes.

Adolf Gustav Schweitzer studied at the fine arts academy in Düsseldorf and returned to live and work there after travelling extensively through France, Belgium and Norway.
Museums and Galleries:
Düsseldorf: *Winter's Day.*
Auction records:
Berlin, 7 July 1971, *Boats in a Fjord,* DEM 2,500. New York, 22 Jan 1982, *Frozen Pond by Moonlight* (1875, oil on canvas, 30 x 49¼ ins / 76 x 125 cm) USD 3,400. New York, 25 May 1984, *Winter Landscape at Dusk* (oil on canvas, 21 x 33¼ ins / 52.4 x 84.5 cm) USD 1,900. Amsterdam, 20 April 1993, *Rocky Torrent in a Forest* (oil on canvas, 48 x 37 ins / 122 x 94 cm) NLG 4,600.

SCHWEITZER, Alfred
German, 20th century.
Born 2 December 1882, in Munich.
Painter, engraver. Landscapes.
Alfred Schweitzer was the son of the painter Cajetan Schweitzer and a pupil of Wilhelm von Diez, Ludwig Herterich, Ludwig von Loefftz and Christian Jank.
Auction records:
Munich, 24 March 1993, *Landscape* (23½ x 31½ ins / 60 x 80 cm) DEM 700.

SCHWEITZER, Cajetan
German, 19th - 20th century.
Born 4 June 1844, in Munich; died 18 October 1913.
Painter. History painting.
Cajetan Schweitzer was the father of the painters Alfred and Reinhold Schweitzer. He was a pupil of Friedrich J. Voltz, Wilhelm von Kaulbach and Moritz von Schwind.

SCHWEITZER, Christoph, or Schweytzer or Schweizer or Schwitzer
Swiss, 16th century.
Active in Zurich.
Engraver (wood).
Christoph Schweitzer engraved book illustrations.

SCHWEITZER, Émile
French, 19th century.
Born 24 July 1837, in Strasbourg; died 28 November 1903, in Strasbourg.
Draughtsman, watercolourist.
He was a student of Théophile Schuler and Petit-Gérard in Paris. He drew anatomical studies, landscape views and historical scenes.
Museums and Galleries:
Strasbourg (Prints Collection): several works.

SCHWEITZER, Erhart. See **SCHWATZER**

SCHWEITZER, Erwin
German, 20th century.
Born 30 April 1887, in Stuttgart.
Painter, engraver.
Erwin Schweitzer was a pupil of Christian Adam Landenberger and Angelo Janck.

SCHWEITZER, Franz Xaver
German, 18th century.
Died May 1773, in Cologne.
Painter.
Franz Schweitzer painted *The Massacre of the Innocents* in the church of the Minoritenkirche in Cologne.

SCHWEITZER, Gaston Auguste
French, 19th - 20th century.
Born 1 September 1879, in Montreuil-sous-Bois.
Sculptor.
Schweitzer was taught by Jean A.J. Falguière, Paul C. Auban and Victor Peter at the École des Beaux-Arts de Paris. He exhibited at the Salon des Artistes Français in Paris from 1903.

SCHWEITZER, Georg
Austrian, 18th century.
Sculptor.
Georg Schweitzer sculpted the tabernacle and pulpit (?) of the church in Rust in 1774.

SCHWEITZER, Hans Heinrich, or Schwyzer
Swiss, 17th century.
Born 1618, in Zurich; died 1673.
Painter, engraver (burin).
Hans Schweitzer painted family trees, armorial bearings and portraits.

SCHWEITZER, Henrik
Hungarian, 18th century.
Died 12 January 1781, in Kassa (now Košice, Slovakia).
Painter.
Henrik Schweitzer painted an altarpiece for the chapel at Sztropko castle.

SCHWEITZER, Johann I
German, 17th century.
Born 23 June 1588, in Frankfurt am Main; died 1642.
Painter.

SCHWEITZER, Johann II
German, 17th century.
Born 21 November 1613, in Frankfurt am Main; died 1639.
Painter.

SCHWEITZER, Mathias
German, 16th century.
Born in Frankfurt am Main; died 1604, in Frankfurt am Main.
Painter.
Frankfurt School.

SCHWEITZER, Reinhold
German, 19th - 20th century.
Born 30 September 1876, in Munich.
Painter, engraver.
Reinhold Schweitzer was the son and pupil of Cajetan Schweitzer. He completed his studies at the fine arts academy in Düsseldorf.

SCHWEITZER, Simon
German, 16th - 17th century.
Active in Baligen from 1593 to 1613.
Sculptor.
Simon Schweitzer carved tombs and altars for the churches of Balingen and Haigerloch. Stuttgart Museum has a *Statue of a Woman* in wood by him.

SCHWEIZER. See also **SCHWEITZER**

SCHWEIZER, Albert
Swiss, 20th century.
Born 19 March 1885, in Baerenwill; died 1948.
Painter. Landscapes.
Museums and Galleries:
Aarau (Aargauer Kunsthaus): *Hilly Landscape.*
Auction records:
Zofingen, 12 June 1993, *Village Street in Egerkingen* (oil on panel, 13 x 16¼ ins / 33 x 41 cm) CHF 1,700.

SCHWEIZER, Alois
Austrian, 19th century.
Born 1816, in Linz.
Painter. Genre scenes, landscapes.
Alois Schweizer attended the academy in Munich.

SCHWEIZER, Andréas
Swiss, 20th - 21st century.
Born 1961.
Painter.
Andréas Schweizer lives and works in Nyon. He revitalises abandoned sites through photography or painting. In 1992 he took part in the Salon Découverte in Paris organised by the Galerie Rivolta in Lausanne.

SCHWEIZER, Christoph. See **SCHWEITZER**

SCHWEIZER, Ernst
Swiss, 19th - 20th century.
Born 16 March 1874, in Zurich; died 21 August 1929, in Zurich.
Painter. Portraits, landscapes, still-lifes.
Ernst Schweizer was the brother of Otto and Paul Schweizer. He studied in Zurich, Munich and Rome and was influenced by the work of Arnold Böcklin.

SCHWEIZER, Helmut
German, 20th - 21st century.
Born 1946, in Stuttgart.
Painter, video artist. Multimedia.
Helmut Schweizer is active not only as a painter but also as a photographer and video artist. He exhibited an artists' book at the exhibition *De Bonnard à Baselitz - Dix Ans d'enrichissements du cabinet des estampes 1978-1988* (*From Bonnard to Baselitz: A Decade of Acquisitions by the Prints Collection 1978-1988*) in 1992 at the Bibliothèque Nationale in Paris.

SCHWEIZER, J. Otto, or Otto
Swiss, 19th - 20th century.
Born 27 March 1863, in Zurich.
Active in Philadelphia, USA, from 1895.
Sculptor. Portraits. Monuments.
J. Otto Schweizer was the brother of Ernst and Paul Schweizer. He studied at the fine arts school in Zurich and under Johannes Schilling at the royal academy of fine arts in Dresden before going on to complete his artistic education in Florence, Paris and Rome. He was a member of the American Federation of Art. He sculpted a number of commemorative monuments and numerous portraits of leading figures in American society of the day.

SCHWEIZER, Jakob or Hans Jakob
Swiss, 19th century.
Born 29 June 1800, in Zurich; died 15 March 1869, in Zurich.
Painter. Portraits, genre scenes, landscapes.
Jakob Schweizer studied in Vienna and Munich.
MUSEUMS AND GALLERIES:
ZURICH (Kunsthaus): *Portrait of a Man*; five watercolours.

SCHWEIZER, Johann
German, 17th century.
Born 18 April 1625, in Zurich; died 16 October 1670, in Darmstadt.
Draughtsman, engraver (burin). Portraits and architectural views.

SCHWEIZER, Johann
German, 17th century.
Born in Heidelberg; died 1679.
Engraver.
Johann Schweizer is mentioned around 1660 working for the book trade. He primarily engraved plates after his drawings and the frontispiece for *Parnassus Heibelbergensis*.

SCHWEIZER, Johann Jacob
German, 18th century.
Born 24 March 1700.
Active in Deggingen.
Sculptor, stucco artist.
Johann Jacob Schweizer was the son and collaborator of Ulrich Schweizer and executed, with his father, the pulpit in the church of Our Lady in Reutlingen.

SCHWEIZER, Julius
German, 19th century.
Born 1814, in Rauenstein.
Painter.
Julius Schweizer attended the academies in Berlin and Munich and was in Italy in 1845.

SCHWEIZER, Paul
Swiss, 19th - 20th century.
Born 7 April 1877, in Zurich.
Active in Florence and Zurich.
Painter.
Paul Schweizer was the brother of Ernst and Otto Schweizer. He studied under Ernst Schurth at the fine arts academy in Karlsruhe and under Ludwig Herterich and Carl von Marr at the fine arts academy in Munich.

SCHWEIZER, Ulrich
German, 17th - 18th century.
Born 2 April 1674.
Active in Deggingen.
Sculptor, stucco artist.
Ulrich Schweizer was the father of Johann Jacob; he sculpted the altars in the church of Balgheim in 1738.

SCHWEIZER, Wilfried
Swiss, 20th century.
Born 11 October 1884, in Zurich.
Draughtsman.
Wilfried Schweizer was an amateur graphic artist best known for his caricatures.

SCHWEIZER, Wilhelm
Swiss, 19th century.
Born 1809, in Zurich; died 1837.
Engraver (burin). Landscapes.
Wilhelm Schweizer attended the academy in Munich.

SCHWELLBACH
German, 19th century.
Active in Karlsruhe in 1811.
Lithographer.

SCHWEMER, Paul
German, 20th century.
Born 26 December 1889, in Neubukow; died 1938.
Active in Hamburg.
Painter, engraver. Portraits.
Paul Schwemer was a pupil of Arthur Illies.
MUSEUMS AND GALLERIES:
HAMBURG (Kunsthalle): *Portrait of the Poet Karl Lorenz*.

SCHWEMKORDT, Michael
German, 16th century.
Active in Pirna at the end of the 16th century.
Sculptor.
Schwemkordt carved fonts for the church of St Michael, Bautzen.

SCHWEMMINGER, Anton
Austrian, 18th century.
Born 1764; died 5 May 1808, in Vienna.
Painter (porcelain).
Anton Schwemminger worked at the porcelain factory in Vienna from 1793 to 1806.

SCHWEMMINGER, Heinrich
Austrian, 19th century.
Born 7 January 1803, in Vienna; died 3 March 1884, in Vienna.
Painter. History painting.

Heinrich Schwemminger was the son of Anton. He studied at the academy in Vienna, becoming a member there in 1848 and later a teacher.
MUSEUMS AND GALLERIES:
VIENNA: *The Dying Singer Ibykus Summons the Cranes to Avenge Him.*

SCHWEMMINGER, Josef
Austrian, 19th century.
Born 21 June 1804, in Vienna; died 12 January 1895, in Vienna.
Painter. Rustic scenes, landscapes, mountainscapes, waterscapes.
Josef Schwemminger attended the academy in Vienna.
MUSEUMS AND GALLERIES:
VIENNA (Historisches Mus.): *The Ortlerspitze in the Tyrol.*
AUCTION RECORDS:
VIENNA, 11 March 1980, *Flock at Water's Edge* (1850, oil on canvas, 33 3/4 x 49 3/4 ins / 86 x 126.5 cm) ATS 40,000. VIENNA, 13 Oct 1981, *Farmyard Scene* (oil on canvas, 28 1/4 x 39 ins / 72 x 99 cm) ATS 35,000. LONDON, 30 May 1984, *Alpine Valley* (1838, oil on panel, 23 x 28 3/4 ins / 58.5 x 73 cm) GBP 6,000. VIENNA, 20 Feb 2001, *Krimhilds' Dream* (oil on canvas, 22 x 28 ins / 55 x 70 cm) ATS 50,000. VIENNA, 6 March 2001, *Castle* (watercolour, 9 x 9 ins / 22 x 23 cm) ATS 40,000.

SCHWEMMINGER, Joseph
Austrian, 18th century.
Born 1740; died 25 October 1770, in Vienna.
Painter. Flowers.

SCHWEMMINGER, Karl
Austrian, 18th century.
Born 1738; died 6 May 1806, in Vienna.
Painter (porcelain).
Karl Schwemminger worked at the porcelain factory in Vienna from 1762.

SCHWENCK. See **SCHWENK** and **SCHWENKE**

SCHWENCKE, Theodor, or Schwenke
German, 19th century.
Active in the first half of the 19th century.
Painter. Landscapes, architectural views.
Schwencke studied under Wach in Berlin.
AUCTION RECORDS:
LONDON, 27 Nov 1992, *The Thermal Baths of Lucca, Italy* (oil on canvas, 29 1/2 x 65 ins / 75 x 165 cm) GBP 29,700.

SCHWENDER, Hans Isaak, or Schwenter
German, 17th century.
Active in Regensburg at the beginning of the 17th century.
Painter.

SCHWENDER, Isaak, or Schwenter
German, 16th century.
Born 1543, in Kelheim; died 1609, in Regensburg.
Painter. Religious subjects.
Isaak Schwender painted an altarpiece for the church of St Oswald, Regensburg, in 1604.

SCHWENDER, Jakob, or Schwenter
German, 16th century.
Active in Regensburg in 1592.
Painter.
Jacob Schwender worked for the Town Hall of Regensburg.

SCHWENDER, Paul or Johann Paul, or Schwenter
German, 17th century.
Active in Regensburg in 1619.
Painter. Religious subjects.

SCHWENDIMANN, Joseph Irenäus
Swiss, 18th century.
Born in Ebikon, near Lucerne; died 1754 or 1756.
Engraver (burin), cabinet maker.
Joseph Irenäus Schwendimann was the father and master of Joseph.

SCHWENDIMANN, Joseph or Caspar Joseph
Swiss, 18th century.
Born 6 December 1721, in Ebikon, near Lucerne; died 1 December 1786, in Rome.
Medallist, engraver (burin).
Joseph Schwendimann was the son of Joseph Irenäus. He settled in Rome in 1772 where he engraved and embossed medals of effigies of the popes and other contemporary figures.

SCHWENDT, Anton
Austrian, 19th century.
Active in Vienna 1828-1864.
Painter. Figures.
Schwendt was a painter at the porcelain factory in Vienna.

SCHWENDY, Albert
German, 19th century.
Born 20 October 1820, in Berlin; died 17 August 1902, in Dessau (Saxony-Anhalt).
Painter, draughtsman. Landscapes, landscapes with figures, urban landscapes, architectural views.
Schwendy was initially a pupil of Eduard Biermann at the art academy in Berlin, then studied at the art academy in Munich and at Eugène Lepoittevin's workshop in Paris. He lived in Berlin between 1848 and 1871, subsequently settling in Dessau where he taught drawing. He specialised in views of cathedral interiors and exteriors as well as market places.
MUSEUMS AND GALLERIES:
DESSAU (Mus. für Stadtgeschichte): *Old Market Place in Dessau.*
AUCTION RECORDS:
LONDON, 15 March 1974, *Market Place in Rouen,* Gns 1,150. COLOGNE, 25 June 1976, *Street in Nuremberg* (1886, oil on canvas, 35 3/4 x 26 1/2 ins / 91 x 67 cm) DEM 9,500. MUNICH, 27 Nov 1980, *Market Place in Nuremberg* (1889, oil on card, 14 x 11 1/2 ins / 35.5 x 29 cm) DEM 18,000. COLOGNE, 25 March 1999, *Market in Halberstadt* (1899, oil on canvas, 21 x 25 ins / 53 x 63 cm) DEM 10,500. LONDON, 5 Sept 2000, *Figures by River, a Townscape beyond. Rowing before a Continental Town* (1883, oil on board, a pair, 8 x 11 ins / 20 x 28 cm) GBP 1,700. MUNICH, 21 March 2001, *Old Harbour City, possibly in Brittany* (1852, oil on canvas, 20 x 26 ins / 52 x 65 cm) DEM 8,000. AHLDEN, 3 May 2002, *Old Town of Goslar* (1870, oil on panel, 6 x 9 ins / 15 x 22 cm) EUR 3,800. BERLIN, 29 Nov 2003, *City* (1847, oil on canvas, 19 x 15 ins / 47 x 39 cm) EUR 4,500.

SCHWENINGER, Karl, the Elder
Austrian, 19th century.
Born 30 October 1818, in Vienna; died 13 October 1887, in Vienna.
Painter. Landscapes, landscapes with figures, mountainscapes, animals.
It is not known under whom Karl Schweninger the Elder studied. After a number of journeys he settled in his native city.

Museums and Galleries:
Vienna: *Farmer; Italian Landcape.*
Auction records:
Vienna, 16 March 1950, *Flock being Ferried across Lake,* ATS 3,500. Vienna, 9 June 1970, *Landscape at Nightfall,* ATS 20,000. Vienna, 16 March 1971, *Alpine Village,* ATS 35,000. Vienna, 20 March 1973, *Landscape with Lake; Traunkirchen,* ATS 80,000. Stuttgart, 10 June 1977, *Landscape of High Mountains* (oil on canvas, 24½ x 31 ins / 62 x 79 cm) DEM 4,500. London, 28 Nov 1980, *Peasants and Flock on Country Track* (oil on card, 16½ x 24½ ins / 42 x 62 cm) GBP 3,500. London, 24 June 1981, *Flock Drinking in Alpine Lake* (oil on canvas, 25 x 33¼ ins / 63.5 x 84.5 cm) GBP 2,500. London, 30 May 1984, *Artist and Model* (oil on canvas, 23 x 19 ins / 57.5 x 48 cm) GBP 2,600. Vienna, 20 May 1999, *Refuge in Mountain Landscape, Cimone della Pala beyond* (oil on canvas, 20 x 26 ins / 50 x 65 cm) ATS 60,000. New York, 2 Nov 1999, *In the Atelier* (oil on canvas, 20 x 26 ins / 51 x 65 cm) USD 40,000. Lindau, 4 Oct 2000, *River Landscape* (oil on canvas, 27 x 41 ins / 69 x 105 cm) DEM 3,800. Munich, 6 Dec 2000, *Romantic Moonlit Landscape with Shepherd and Flock* (oil on canvas, 15 x 19 ins / 38 x 47 cm) DEM 3,500. Vienna, 28 May 2001, *Konigsee* (oil on canvas, 10 x 50 ins / 25 x 127 cm) ATS 70,000. Vienna, 29 Nov 2001, *Storm-clouds over Mountain Farmstead* (1847, oil on canvas, 25 x 31 ins / 63 x 79 cm) ATS 60,000. London, 1 Oct 2003, *Moment to Herself* (oil on canvas, 32 x 23 ins / 82 x 58 cm) GBP 2,000. Budapest, 9 Dec 2003, *Landscape* (oil on canvas, 26 x 33 ins / 66 x 85 cm) HUF 500,000.

SCHWENINGER, Karl or Carl, the Younger

Austrian, 19th century.
Born 17 May 1854, in Vienna; died 1903, in Vienna.
Painter. Figures, portraits, genre scenes.

The son of Karl Schweninger the Elder, Karl the Younger painted genre scenes with figures in rococo costume.

Schweninger

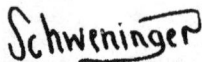

Auction records:
New York, 12 March 1969, *Poem,* USD 1,100. London, 4 June 1970, *Conspirator,* Gns 750. London, 13 June 1974, *Merry company in Park,* Gns 4,000. New York, 2 April 1976, *The Painter's Studio* (oil on canvas, 22 x 31½ ins / 55 x 80 cm) USD 4,750. Vienna, 13 April 1976, *Bacchus and Ariadne* (1875, oil on canvas, 70¾ x 48 ins / 180 x 122 cm) ATS 32,000. New York, 12 May 1978, *Duet* (oil on canvas, 39 x 30 ins / 99 x 76 cm) USD 4,250. Vienna, 10 June 1980, *Honeymoon* (oil on canvas, 22½ x 17½ ins / 57 x 44.5 cm) ATS 15,000. Vienna, 19 May 1981, *Painter and his Model* (oil on canvas, 27½ x 17½ ins / 70 x 44.5 cm) ATS 70,000. New York, 23 Feb 1989, *Recital* (oil on panel, 15½ x 12¼ ins / 39.4 x 31.1 cm) USD 8,250. New York, 23 May 1989, *Sylvia* (oil on canvas, 19 x 23¾ ins / 48.2 x 60.3 cm) USD 30,250. London, 6 Oct 1989, *Tête-à-tête* (oil on panel, 13¼ x 10½ ins / 33.5 x 26.5 cm) GBP 3,080. New York, 1 March 1990, *Reception in Park* (oil on canvas, 29½ x 39¾ ins / 75 x 101 cm) USD 26,400. New York, 23 May 1990, *Secret* (oil on canvas, 25 x 20 ins / 63.5 x 50.8 cm) USD 7,700. New York, 23 May 1991, *Chess Game* (oil on canvas, 29¼ x 40 ins / 74.3 x 101.3 cm) USD 8,250. London, 29 Nov 1991, *Moment of Idle Chatter* (1887, oil on canvas, 27 x 37¼ ins / 68.5 x 94.6 cm) GBP 12,100. London, 19 June 1992, *Sylvia* (oil on canvas, 19 x 23¾ ins / 48.2 x 60.4 cm) GBP 13,200. New York, 29 Oct 1992, *Happy Hours* (oil on panel, a pair, each 21 x 32 ins / 53.3 x 81.3 cm) USD 13,750. London, 11 April 1995, *Flirt in Park* (oil on canvas, 36½ x 28 ins / 93 x 71 cm) GBP 3,450. London, 21 Nov 1996, *Afternoon on Terrace* (oil on canvas, 29¼ x 40 ins / 74.5 x 100.7 cm) GBP 35,600. London, 26 March 1997, *Lady with Butterflies* (1887, oil on canvas, 35½ x 17¾ ins / 90 x 45 cm) GBP 6,210. London, 21 Nov 1997, *Portrait after the Original* (oil on canvas, 20 x 26¾ ins / 51 x 68 cm) GBP 9,200. Vienna, 5 Oct 1999, *Deer with Cows, Drinking* (oil on canvas, 46 x 36 ins / 118 x 91 cm) ATS 45,000. London, 14 Oct 1999, *Alpine Lake Landscape with Figures by the Shore* (oil on canvas, 37 x 50 ins / 95 x 127 cm) GBP 2,300. Milan, 13 June 2000, *Female Nudes* (oil on canvas, 33 x 48 ins / 85 x 122 cm) ITL 32,000,000. New York, 30 Oct 2001, *Garden Party* (oil on canvas, 29 x 39 ins / 74 x 100 cm) USD 22,000. Budapest, 11 Sept 2002, *In the Castle* (oil on canvas, 25 x 20 ins / 63 x 50 cm) HUF 800,000. New York, 5 Feb 2003, *Courtship* (oil on canvas, 37 x 28 ins / 94 x 72 cm) USD 3,500. Philadelphia, 7 Dec 2003, *Flowers from an Admirer* (oil on panel, 17 x 12 ins / 43 x 30 cm) USD 2,100. Berlin, 27 March 2004, *Young Couple with Baby on Terrace* (oil on canvas, 31 x 24 ins / 80 x 60 cm) EUR 3,000. Lindau, 23 Sept 2004, *Landscape in Late Summer Light* (oil on canvas, 19 x 25 ins / 47 x 63 cm) EUR 2,000.

SCHWENINGER, Rosa

Austrian, 19th century.
Born 11 February 1849, in Vienna.
Painter, pastellist. Portraits, genre scenes.

Rosa Schweninger was the daughter of Karl the Elder.
Auction records:
Zurich, 3 June 1983, *Antiquary* (oil on panel, 17½ x 21½ ins / 44.5 x 54.5 cm) CHF 7,500. New York, 23 Feb 1989, *Little Girl with Brood of Rabbits* (oil on card, 16½ x 20½ ins / 42 x 52 cm) USD 17,600. London, 16 Nov 1994, *Bouquet Arrangement* (pastel, 37 x 26¾ ins / 94 x 68 cm) GBP 2,070. Vienna, 30 Nov 2000, *Two Men Looking at a Gun* (oil on panel, 10 x 13 ins / 25 x 33 cm) ATS 40,000. Vienna, 29 Nov 2001, *Proud Mother of Puppies* (oil on canvas, 22 x 27 ins / 55 x 69 cm) ATS 150,000.

SCHWENK, Carl Eugen

German, 20th century.
Born 19 December 1894, in Stuttgart.
Active in Leipzig.
Painter, engraver.

Carl Eugen Schwenk was the husband of Johanna Schwenk and a pupil of Heinrich Altherr.

SCHWENK, Georg

German, 19th - 20th century.
Born 3 June 1863, in Dresden; died 26 May 1936.
Painter. History painting, portraits, genre scenes.

Georg Schwenk followed courses at the fine arts academy in Dresden and was awarded a silver medal in 1886.
Museums and Galleries:
Leipzig (Stadtgeschichtliches Mus.): *Portrait of Doctor Radius and his Wife.*

SCHWENK, Johanna

Maiden name: Baldeweg
German, 20th century.
Born 19 September 1890, in Leipzig.
Painter, engraver, designer.

Johanna Schwenk was the wife of the painter Carl Eugen Schwenk.

SCHWENK, Johannes I

German, 17th - 18th century.
Active in Ulm 1691-1703.
Draughtsman.

SCHWENK, Johannes II

German, 18th century.
Born 1699; died after 1735.
Active in Ulm.
Draughtsman.

SCHWENK, Marthe. See **BAUMEL-SCHWENCK**

SCHWENK, Wilhelm or Friedrich Wilhelm
German, 19th century.
Born 31 January 1830, in Dresden; died 24 February 1871, in Dresden.
Sculptor.
Wilhelm Schwenk studied under E. Titeschel at the academy in Dresden and specialised in busts and religious statues.

SCHWENKE, Daniel
German, 17th century.
Born beginning February 1596, in Pirna; died end October 1623, in Pirna.
Sculptor.
Daniel Schwenke was the son of Michael and worked with his brother Hans.

SCHWENKE, David, or Schwencke
German, 17th century.
Born end September 1575, in Pirna; died beginning November 1620, in Pirna.
Sculptor.
David Schwenke was the brother and successor of Michael Schwenke. He sculpted numerous funerary monuments and altars as well as incising epitaphs.

SCHWENKE, Gottlieb, or Schwencke
German, 19th century.
Born to a family originally from Saxony; died 1821, in Munich.
Portrait artist.
Gottlieb Schwenke worked in Mitau (now Jelgava, Latvia) and St Petersburg.
MUSEUMS AND GALLERIES:
JELGAVA: *Portrait of Heinrich von Offenberg.*

SCHWENKE, Hans, or Schwencke
German, 17th century.
Born c. 15 December 1589, in Pirna; died beginning August 1634, in Pirna.
Sculptor.
Hans Schwenke was the pupil of Michael Schwenke. He sculpted altars and funerary monuments as well as incising epitaphs.

SCHWENKE, Michael, or Schwenck or Schwencke
German, 16th - 17th century.
Born end May 1563, in Pirna; died 10 July 1610, in Pirna.
Sculptor.
Michael Schwenke worked in the shop of Christopher Walter II in Dresden and was one of the finest Saxon sculptors of his time. He carved fonts, altars, tombs and low reliefs.

SCHWENN, Carl Joseph
Danish, 20th century.
Born 7 January 1888, in Aarhus.
Painter. Portraits, landscapes.
Carl Joseph Schwenn studied in Copenhagen and Paris.

SCHWENSEN, Hans Henrik Wolder
Danish, 19th century.
Born 29 January 1837, in Frørup; died 20 November 1876, in Roskilde.
Landscape artist.
Schwensen was a pupil at the Kunstakademi in Copenhagen. He worked in Munich and in Switzerland.

SCHWENTER. See also **SCHWENDER**

SCHWENTER, Arfwid Sigmund
German, 17th - 18th century.
Born 1649; died 1720, in Bayreuth.
Sculptor.
Schwenter was probably the pupil of Brenk-Schlehendorn. He settled in Wunsiedl.

SCHWENTERLEY, Heinrich or Christian Heinrich
German, 18th - 19th century.
Born 14 February 1749, in Göttingen (Lower Saxony); died February 1815, in Göttingen (Lower Saxony).
Engraver (burin), painter, miniaturist.
Schwenterley engraved portraits of professors at the University of Göttingen.
MUSEUMS AND GALLERIES:
GÖTTINGEN (Städtische Mus.): *Portrait of the Artist; Portrait of the Bookseller Aderholz.*

SCHWENZENGAST, Gregor
Austrian, 17th - 18th century.
Sculptor, stucco artist.
Schwenzengast sculpted funerary monuments and decorations for churches and citizens' houses in the Tyrol.

SCHWENZER, Karl
German, 19th century.
Born 26 February 1843, in Löwenstein; died 29 November 1904, in Stuttgart.
Sculptor, medallist.
Schwenzer was the pupil of August von Kreling in Nuremberg, Paulin Tasset in Paris and Wyon in London, and became court medallist in Stuttgart.

SCHWEPPE, Johann Gottlieb
German, 18th century.
Born 1763; died 1809.
Active in Stuttgart.
Miniaturist.
MUSEUMS AND GALLERIES:
STUTTGART (Schloss Mus.): *Portrait of Friedrich von Wurtemberg.*

SCHWER, Georg
German, 19th century.
Born 26 March 1827, in Nuremberg; died 7 July 1877, in Düsseldorf.
Painter. Genre scenes, landscapes.
Georg Schwer was the pupil of C.F. Sohn and Jordan.

SCHWER, Joseph
Austrian, 19th century.
Active in Vienna during the first half of the 19th century.
Painter. Still-lifes.
Joseph Schwer exhibited in Vienna from 1820 to 1830.

SCHWERAK, Joszef, called Banati-Schwerak
Hungarian, 20th century.
Born 6 October 1897, in Temesvár (now Timisoara, Romania).
Painter. Figures, landscapes.
Schwerak studied in Budapest.
MUSEUMS AND GALLERIES:
BUDAPEST (Fővárosi Képtár): *After the Bath.*

SCHWERDFEGER. See **SCHWERDTFEGER**

SCHWERDGEBURTH, Charlotte Amalia
German, 19th century.
Born 22 May 1795, in Dresden; died 13 October 1831, in Dresden.
Painter. Portraits and historical scenes.
Charlotte Schwerdgeburth was taught by her father and attended the academy in Dresden.

SCHWERDGEBURTH, Johann Burkhard
German, 18th century.
Born 1759, in Dresden.

Active in Dessau, Weimar, Gera and Dresden.
Painter (?), draughtsman. Landscapes.

SCHWERDGEBURTH, Karl or Carl August
German, 19th century.
Born 5 August 1785, in Dresden; died 25 October 1878, in Weimar.
Painter, draughtsman, engraver.

Karl Schwerdgeburth attended the academy in Dresden and engraved religious subjects and portraits. His key work is *Luther at the Diet of Worms.*

SCHWERDGEBURTH, Otto
German, 19th century.
Born 5 March 1835, in Weimar; died 22 December 1866, in Weimar.
Painter. History painting, genre scenes.

Otto Schwerdgeburth was taught by his father Karl and by Preller. He worked in Antwerp for the Hôtel de Ville and for the church of St Nicholas. He settled permanently in Weimar in 1860.

MUSEUMS AND GALLERIES:
BREMEN: *Last Look of the Protestants of Salzburg towards their Hearths* - COLOGNE: *Promenade of Faust* - WEIMAR: *Promenade of Faust on Easter Morning; On the Ramparts of Mantua*.

SCHWERDTFEGER, Kurt
German, 20th century.
Born 20 June 1897, in Deutsch-Puddiger (Pomerania); died 1966, in Himmelsthür-Hildesheim.
Sculptor, potter. Animals. Busts.
Groups: Novembergruppe, Deutscher Werkbund.

Kurt Schwerdtfeger studied philosophy and art history in Königsberg (now Kaliningrad, Russia) and Jena in 1919-1920 before going on to study sculpture at the Bauhaus School from 1920 to 1924. Between 1925 and 1937, Schwerdtfeger taught sculpture at the Werkkunstschule (college of applied arts) in Szczecin. He became a member of the Novembergruppe and the Deutscher Werkbund. 1946 saw him teaching again, this time in Alfeld am Leine.

In 1922, during his time spent at the Bauhaus, Schwerdtfeger worked on coloured light effects that may be regarded as precursors of the lumino-kinetic experimentation that took place in the 1960s.

BIBLIOGRAPHY:
Schreyer, Lothar, *Kurt Schwerdtfeger*, Delpesche Verlagsbuchhandlung, Munich, 1962. Leymarie, Jean/Herzogenrath, Wulf/Grote, Ludwig/Gropius, Walter, *Le Bauhaus*, exhibition catalogue, Württembergischer Kunsteverein, Stuttgart, Musée national d'Art moderne, Paris, 1969. Popper, Frank, *L'Art cinétique*, Gauthier-Villars, Paris, 1970.

MUSEUMS AND GALLERIES:
SZCZECIN (Mus. Stadt): *Bust of Adolf Hitler; Bust of Georg Buschan*; several animal sculptures.

SCHWERDTFEGER, Mathaes, called Newer Schmidt
German, 16th century.
Active in Dresden.
Engraver (steel).

The Stadtmuseum in Dresden has a saw engraved by Schwerdtfeger and dated 1564.

SCHWERDTFEGER, Max
German, 20th century.
Born 16 May 1881, in Wensin.
Active in Frankfurt am Main.
Painter. Genre scenes, still-lifes.

Max Schwerdtfeger studied under Filadelfo Simi in Florence and at the Académie Julian in Paris.

MUSEUMS AND GALLERIES:
FRANKFURT AM MAIN (Städel): *Shepherd's Dream* - WORMS (Mus. der Stadt): *Still-life.*

SCHWERDTNER, Johann
Austrian, 19th - 20th century.
Born 14 July 1834, in Vienna; died 15 March 1920, in Vienna.
Sculptor, medallist.

Johann Schwerdtner was a pupil of Wenzel Seidan.

SCHWERDTNER, Karl Maria
Austrian, 19th - 20th century.
Born 27 May 1874, in Vienna.
Sculptor, medallist. Portraits.

Karl Maria Schwerdtner studied under his father Johann Schwerdtner and under Edmund Hellmer.

SCHWERER, Jósef
Hungarian, 18th century.
Sculptor (wood).

Jósef Schwerer sculpted the stalls of the cathedral in Pécs in 1762.

SCHWERI, Albin
Swiss, 20th century.
Born 1 March 1885, in Ramsen.
Painter. Designs for stained glass, murals.

Albin Schweri studied fine arts at the academies of Zurich and Munich and went on to produce numerous stained glass windows for churches in Switzerland.

SCHWERIN, Amélie Ulrika Sofia von
Maiden name: Chrysander
Swedish, 19th century.
Born 2 April 1819, in Skåne; died 26 January 1897, in Düsseldorf.
Painter. Landscapes.

Schwerin studied in Düsseldorf and in Munich, where she was a pupil of Friedrich Voltz.

AUCTION RECORDS:
GÖTEBORG, 3 Nov 1982, *Summer Landscape* (1869, oil on canvas, 35 1/2 x 51 1/4 ins / 90 x 130 cm) SEK 23,500. GÖTEBORG, 13 April 1983, *Landscape in the Alps* (1868, oil on canvas, 32 3/4 x 42 1/2 ins / 83 x 108 cm) SEK 27,000. STOCKHOLM, 14 Nov 1990, *Starnberger Lake* (1875, oil on canvas, 32 1/4 x 48 3/4 ins / 82 x 124 cm) SEK 15,000. STOCKHOLM, 19 May 1992, *Wooded Prairie with Cattle by a Stream and Mountains in the Background* (oil on canvas, 35 1/2 x 53 1/4 ins / 90 x 135 cm) SEK 33,000. STUTTGART, 17 March 2000, *Cows by River Surrounded by Huge Oak Trees* (1864, oil on canvas, 38 x 51 ins / 97 x 130 cm) DEM 6,500. STOCKHOLM, 16 June 2003, *Arasof, Farlovs Parish, Skåne* (1857, oil on canvas, 18 x 23 ins / 46 x 59 cm) SEK 14,500. STOCKHOLM, 26 May 2004, *Cattle Watering* (oil on canvas, 51 x 75 ins / 129 x 191 cm) SEK 40,000.

SCHWERTER, Rudolf
Swiss, 17th century.
Active in Baden (Aargau).
Painter.

Schwerter painted the façade of the school in Bruges in 1640.

SCHWERTFEGER. See **SCHWERDTFEGER**

SCHWERTFURER, Rudolph
German, 19th century.
Born 18 June 1831, in Linz (River Rhine).
Active in Stuttgart.
Engraver (wood).

Schwertfurer was the pupil of H. Bürkner.

SCHWERTLE, Franz Karl
German, 18th century.
Born 1716, in Dillingen; died 24 July 1768, in Dillingen.
Sculptor.

Probably taught by Stephan Luidl, Schwertle executed numerous sculptures for the churches of Dilligen and the surrounding area.

SCHWERTNER, Franz
Austrian, 19th - 20th century.
Born 17 March 1858, in Schönfeld (Bohemia).
Engraver.
Franz Schwertner was a pupil of Franz Wielsch and specialised in etching. He also worked as an architect.

SCHWERTSCHKOFF, Wlad
Painter. History painting, genre scenes.
Schwertschkoff painted several copies after Italian and Dutch masters.
MUSEUMS AND GALLERIES:
HELSINKI.

SCHWERZEK, Karl
Austrian, 19th - 20th century.
Born 16 October 1848, in Friedk; died February 1919, in Vienna.
Sculptor. Allegorical subjects. Statues, monuments.
Karl Schwerzek sculpted monuments and statues for public buildings in Vienna.
MUSEUMS AND GALLERIES:
OPAVA: *Painting; Architecture; Sculpture.*

SCHWERZL, Sigismund, or Schwerzel
German, 17th century.
Active in Leipzig during the first half of the 17th century.
Glass painter.

SCHWERZMANN, Joseph Roman
Swiss, 19th - 20th century.
Born 23 May 1855, in Zug.
Sculptor. Religious subjects.
Joseph Roman Schwerzmann carved compositions in wood for churches in Langau, Varese and Zug.

SCHWERZMANN, Wilhelm
Swiss, 19th - 20th century.
Born 21 June 1877, in Zug.
Sculptor. Statues.
Wilhelm Schwerzmann was a pupil of Adolf Meyer. He sculpted figures for fountains and public buildings.

SCHWESIG, Karl
Swiss, 20th century.
Born 1898, in Baraubauerschaft.
Active in Düsseldorf.
Painter, engraver (etching).
Das Junge Rheinland (Young Rhineland group).
Karl Schwesig was a member of Das Junge Rheinland in Düsseldorf.

SCHWESSINGER, Georg
German, 19th - 20th century.
Born c. 1874; died March 1914, in Munich.
Sculptor. Religious subjects.
Georg Schwessinger was a pupil of Jakob Bradl and Wilhelm von Ruemann. He is noted for sculptures in the Protestant church in Forchheim.

SCHWESTER, Anton
Austrian, 19th - 20th century.
Engraver (burin).
Anton Schwester studied at the fine arts academy in Vienna.

SCHWESTERMÜLLER, David
German, 17th century.
Born October 1596, in Ulm; died 12 August 1678, in Augsburg.
Painter, draughtsman, modeller (wax).
Schwestermüller studied in Rome and was also a goldsmith.
MUSEUMS AND GALLERIES:
STOCKHOLM (Nationalmus.): *Statuette of Gustavus Adolphus* (drawing).

SCHWETTE, Alexandre Samuel, or Chévtté
Russian, 20th century.
Born 1880, in Riga.
Painter.
Alexandre Samuel Schwette studied in Riga and then in New York. Work by him was exhibited in Paris, at the Salon d'Automne, the Salon des Indépendants, and the Société Coloniales des Artistes Français.

SCHWETZ, Karl
Austrian, 20th century.
Born 4 August 1888, in Kanitz.
Painter, engraver, illustrator, sculptor, potter.
Karl Schwetz was the husband of Ida Schwetz-Lehmann. He studied at the fine arts school in Vienna and went on to produce book illustrations and various designs for the Viennese porcelain factory.

SCHWETZ-LEHMANN, Ida
Austrian, 20th century.
Born 26 April 1883, in Vienna.
Sculptor, potter.
Ida Schwetz-Lehmann studied at the fine arts school in Vienna. She was the wife of Karl Schwetz. She worked at the Wiener Werkstätte (Viennese Workshops) founded in 1903 by Josef Hoffmann, Koloman Moser and the industrialist Fritz Wärndorfer, who was a strong advocate of the arts and crafts movement and its practical applications.

SCHWETZER, Erhard. See **SCHWATZER**

SCHWEYER. See also **SCHWAIGER**

SCHWEYER, Jeremias Paul
German, 18th - 19th century.
Born 3 November 1754, in Nuremberg; died 16 December 1813, in Frankfurt am Main.
Painter, engraver (burin).
Schweyer painted popular motifs and society scenes as well as engraving portraits.
MUSEUMS AND GALLERIES:
SPEYER (Historisches Mus. der Pfalz): two genre scenes.

SCHWEYGER. See **SCHWEIGER**

SCHWICHTENBERG, Bernhard
Swiss, 20th century.
Painter (mixed media).
Bernhard Schwichtenberg teaches at the fine arts school in Kiel. As a designer, his principal preoccupations are light and kinetics. He produces 'material paintings', examples of which include his *Platitudes*, where soft-drink cans are crushed before being harmoniously positioned on a rice-paper base. Examples of Schwichtenberg's work were shown at the Goethe Institute in Paris in 1991.

SCHWICHTENBERG, Martel
German, 20th century.
Born 1896, in Hanover; died 1945, in Salzburg.
Painter. Figures, still-lifes.
AUCTION RECORDS:
MUNICH, 28 May 1976, *Still-life with Doll* (oil on canvas, 30 x 23 1/2 ins / 76 x 60 cm) DEM 1,650. MUNICH, 30 May 1980, *Still-life with Japanese Doll* (oil on canvas, 30 x 23 1/2 ins / 76 x 60 cm) DEM 2,000. MUNICH, 3 June 1980, *House* (1922, watercolour/pencil outlines, 17 3/4 x 23 ins / 45 x 58.6 cm) DEM 2,000. NEW YORK, 19 May 1981, *Little Girl in a Red Dress* (pencil and oil on card, 27 3/4 x 19 1/2 ins / 70.8 x 49.8 cm) USD 1,800. HAMBURG, 12 June 1982, *From Pomerania* (1923, lithographs, set of six) DEM 2,400. MUNICH, 25 Nov 1983, *Santa Margarita* (c. 1925, oil on canvas, 29 1/2 x 23 1/2 ins / 75 x 60

cm) DEM 4,200. MUNICH, 11 June 1985, *Still-life with Fruit* (oil on canvas, 23¾ x 29½ ins / 60.5 x 75 cm) DEM 7,000. MUNICH, 26-27 Nov 1991, *Still-life with Japanese Doll* (oil on canvas, 30 x 23½ ins / 76 x 60 cm) DEM 4,370. LONDON, 18 Oct 2000, *Girl in a Red Striped Shirt* (c. 1920, oil on cardboard, 28 x 20 ins / 71 x 50 cm) GBP 18,000. MUNICH, 4 June 2002, *Reclining Female Nude: Tilla Durieux* (oil on canvas, 31 x 37 ins / 79 x 94 cm) EUR 1,800. MUNICH, 4 June 2002, *Ponte Decimo* (oil on canvas, 31 x 37 ins / 79 x 93 cm) EUR 2,500. BERLIN, 24 April 2004, *Untitled* (oil on board, double-sided, 28 x 20 ins / 70 x 50 cm) EUR 10,000. MUNICH, 13 May 2004, *Cacti* (oil on canvas, 23 x 19 ins / 59 x 49 cm) EUR 4,000.

SCHWIERING, Heinrich

German, 19th - 20th century.

Born 23 August 1860, in Buckerburg.

Painter. Genre scenes.

Heinrich Schwiering studied under Peter J.T. Janssen and August W. Sohn at the fine arts academy in Düsseldorf.

SCHWIERKIEWICZ, Robert

Hungarian, 20th century.

Screen printer.

A silk-screen painting by Robert Schwierkiewicz was featured at the exhibition in 1992 at the Bibliothèque Nationale in Paris, *De Bonnard à Baselitz: Dix Ans d'enrichissements du cabinet des estampes* (*From Bonnard to Baselitz: A Decade of Acquisitions by the Prints Collection 1978-1988*).

SCHWIEZER, Peter. See **SCHWITZER**

SCHWILL, William Valentine. See **SCHEVILL**

SCHWIMBECK, Fritz

German, 20th century.

Born 30 January 1889, in Munich.

Painter, engraver, illustrator.

Fritz Schwimbeck illustrated books.

SCHWIMMER, Max

German, 20th century.

Born 9 December 1895, in Leipzig; died 1960.

Painter, engraver. Portraits, urban landscapes.

Max Schwimmer was self-taught. He was strongly influenced by the work of Henri Matisse.

MUSEUMS AND GALLERIES:

LEIPZIG: *Automobile Garage; Portrait of Makke.*

SCHWIND, Édouard

French, 19th century.

Painter. History painting, portraits, genre scenes.

His work was exhibited at the Salon between 1839 and 1846.

MUSEUMS AND GALLERIES:

POITIERS: *Portrait of Drouet, Count of Erlon and Marshal of France* - RHEIMS: *Portrait of Drouet, Count of Erlon and Marshal of France.*

SCHWIND, Ernestine. See **QUANTIN**

SCHWIND, Moritz Ludwig von

Austrian, 19th century.

Born 21 January 1804, in Vienna; died 8 February 1871, in Munich.

Painter, fresco artist, engraver, draughtsman. Religious subjects, genre scenes. Designs for stained glass. Biedermeier.

Nazarenes group (related to).

Moritz von Schwind attended the Akademie der Bildende Künste in Vienna from 1821 to 1823 where he was taught by Ferdinand Schnorr von Carolsfeld, and also studied under Cornelius in Munich. In 1828 he was commissioned to paint 20 frescoes inspired by the poet Tieck for King Ludwig's new palace, and from 1853 to 1855 painted a series of compositions from the life of St Elisabeth of Hungary. In 1859 he provided the cartoons for the 26 windows in Glasgow Cathedral, Scotland. His output also included an altar painting for the Frauenkirche in Munich, decoration for the Opera in Vienna in 1869, and paintings for the Neue Pinakothek. He also engraved genre scenes and vignettes. A member of the Dresden Akademie from 1846, and those of Vienna and Berlin from 1866, he later became correspondent for the Académie des Beaux-Arts in Paris.

Von Schwind is arguably the key figure among Romantic German artists who emulated the distant past of Germany with its mystique, chivalry and intrinsic picturesqueness - desires that can be conflated in the untranslatable German term Sehnsucht ('yearning'), which was to take on its full meaning in the Romantic period. This was anticipated in Goethe's first novella, *The Sorrows of the Young Werther*, as well as the work of Tieck, Joseph von Eichendorf, Eduard Möricke, Clemens Maria Brentano, Arnim, Novalis and Kleist. In an attempt to evoke such themes, the art of Von Schwind is narrative in spirit, sometimes bringing to mind details of illuminators of the past, which were inspirational in his decorative cycles, such as the historical or legendary frescoes that he painted in 1854 for the seat of German history - the castle at Wartburg.

Apart from the great historical compositions, the work of Von Schwind is also characterised by his apparent preference for the more familiar subjects of popular legends and fairytales, such as the *Beautiful Melusina*, the *Legend of the Seven Crows*, the *Legend of the Seven Ravens*, and the *Songs of the Marvellous Horn-player*, as well as scenes of bourgeois daily life, or the lords of Germany in the Middle Ages. His partiality for the Romantic writers manifests itself in, for example, the *Honeymoon*. For Von Schwind the simple, the real and the quotidian coalesce gracefully with the epic, the fabulous and the historical.

Handzeichnung von Moritz von Schwind
(Aus dem Familiennachlass).

Stamp of sale

BIBLIOGRAPHY:

Koskchatzky, Sottrifer, *Die Kunst von Steim*, Albertina, Vienna, 1985. Giesen, Sebastian/Gross, Friedrich, *Moritz von Schwind. Meister der Spätromantik*, Cantz Publishers, Ostfildern, 1996.

MUSEUMS AND GALLERIES:

BERLIN: *The Rose or the Journey of the Artist; Leaving at Dawn; Adventure of the Painter Binder; Duchess of Orléans and Schwind; Sabine von Steinbach; Portrait of Young Man;* sketch - DARMSTADT: *Amazon and Page; Early Morning; Midday* - EISENACH: *Portraits of the Great Duke Karl Alexander, the Grand Duchess Sophia and the Commander von Armwold* - ESSEN: *Wealth* - FRANKFURT AM MAIN: *Singing Masters at the Warthburg; Lady of the Elves in the Alders; Terpsichore; Dante and Beatrice* - HALLE: *The Dream of Adam* - HAMBURG: *The Elders of Schnorr von Karolsfeld; Water Sprites Watering Stag; The Cantatrice Caroline Hetzenecker; Fidelio; The Magic Flute* - KARLSRUHE: *Portraits of Wilhelm Sachs, Jules Sachs and Frau Sachs* - LEIPZIG: *The Horseman Kuno von Falkenstein Riding* - MUNICH: *Symphony* (1852); *Dance of the Elves* (1844); *Cinderella; Valley near Wartburg; In the Artist's House* - NUREMBERG (Modern Gal.): *Two Portraits of Girls* - STUTTGART: *Father Rhine and Affluents; The Three Hermits* - VIENNA: *Emperor Max; Diana with her Nymphs Hunting; Cutters of Bread; The Beautiful Melusina* (series of 11 watercolours); nine cartoons for paintings for the foyer of the Opera House of Vienna - WEIMAR: *St Elisabeth's Glove*; Scenes from the story of the Countess of Thuringia; six sketches of frescoes; *The Six Crows and the Faithful Sister*; 15 watercolours - ZURICH: *Portrait of a Woman.*

AUCTION RECORDS:

MUNICH, 14-16 Oct 1964, *Poet at Warthburg Court,* DEM 27,000. COLOGNE, 22 Nov 1973, *Portrait of Cavalier,* DEM 12,500. LONDON, 17 July 1979, *The Wondrous Saint* (watercolour, pencil and pen, 13 1/4 x 5 1/4 ins / 33.7 x 13.4 cm) GBP 3,000. MUNICH, 29 Nov 1979, *The Artist with his Family in Landscape* (1864, oil on canvas, 59 1/2 x 32 3/4 ins / 151 x 83 cm) DEM 48,000. LONDON, 19 March 1981, *Night* (pen, 10 1/4 x 8 1/4 ins / 26.2 x 21.2 cm) GBP 700. LONDON, 16 March 1983, *Study of Karoline Hetzenbecker as Iphigenia* (pencil heightened with white and gold gouache, 16 1/4 x 9 ins / 41 x 23 cm) GBP 800. LONDON, 27 Nov 1984, *Kaiser Otto I Celebrating Whitsun Holiday in Quedlingburg* (1850, oil on canvas, 39 1/4 x 30 1/4 ins / 100 x 77 cm) GBP 35,000. MUNICH, 28 Nov 1985, *Reunion* (watercolour, 13 x 9 1/4 ins / 33 x 23.5 cm) DEM 3,600. NEW YORK, 26 Oct 1990, *Portrait of Lanzendorf* (1842, pencil/paper, 7 x 5 ins / 17.8 x 12.7 cm) USD 4,400. MUNICH, 1 - 2 Dec 1992, *Sketch of Nymph Walking* (pencil, 9 x 5 1/2 ins / 23 x 14 cm) DEM 1,150. MUNICH, 10 Dec 1992, *Monk Chaperoning Young Couple into Garden of Church* (pencil and black ink/paper, 5 1/2 x 8 ins / 14 x 20.5 cm) DEM 9,266. HEIDELBERG, 8 April 1995, *Face of Young Woman seen in profile from right* (black chalk and pencil, 11 1/4 x 8 ins / 28.5 x 20.5 cm) DEM 2,200. LONDON, 11 Oct 1995, *Sketch for the Illustration for the Counts of the Seven Ravens* (pencil and black and white chalk/bistre-coloured paper, 77 1/2 x 35 ins / 197 x 89 cm) GBP 5,980. NEW YORK, 27 Jan 1999, *Sabina of Steinbach Sculpting Synagogue* (pen and brown ink over graphite, heightened with white, 11 x 11 ins / 29 x 28 cm) USD 30,000. MUNICH, 30 Nov 1999, *Christ is Brought to the Temple* (pencil heightened with white, 19 x 9 ins / 47 x 23 cm) DEM 8,500. LONDON, 22 June 2000, *Song Contest on the Wartburg* (oil on canvas, 17 x 17 ins / 43 x 42 cm) GBP 20,000. FRANKFURT, 2 Sept 2000, *Spring. Summer. Autumn. Winter* (four works on paper, 27 x 26 ins / 68 x 65 cm) DEM 12,000. COLOGNE, 19 May 2001, *Two Cupids Playing by Stream* (oil on panel, 20 x 15 ins / 50 x 38 cm) DEM 50,000. COLOGNE, 24 Nov 2001, *Glove of St Elizabeth* (oil on canvas, 29 x 58 ins / 74 x 147 cm) DEM 10,000. VIENNA, 11 June 2002, *Queen of the Night* (watercolour, 16 x 12 ins / 41 x 31 cm) EUR 6,000. VIENNA, 11 June 2002, *Monostatos Approaching Pamina to Kiss her* (watercolour and Indian ink, semi circular, 11 x 21 ins / 28 x 53 cm) EUR 10,000. MUNICH, 19 March 2003, *Seven Silhouette Cut-outs* (board, 11 x 14 ins / 27 x 36 cm) EUR 1,700. HEIDELBERG, 11 April 2003, *Rider* (watercolour and pen over pencil, 7 x 29 ins / 17 x 73 cm) EUR 4,200. NEW YORK, 22 Jan 2004, *Four Nymphs Tying Pan to a Tree* (1851, black chalk, pen, brown and grey ink and watercolour, 8 x 14 ins / 21 x 36 cm) USD 13,000. SAARBRÜCKEN, 9 July 2004, *Portrait of the Music Conductor, Franz Lachner* (1849, oil on canvas, 23 x 20 ins / 58 x 52 cm) EUR 9,000.

SCHWIND, Wilhelm

German, 19th - 20th century.
Born 14 September 1853, in Goldstein; died 1 May 1906.
Sculptor. Allegorical subjects. Busts.

Wilhelm Schwind studied at the Städelsches Kunstinstitut in Frankfurt am Main and at the fine arts academy in Berlin.

SCHWINDRAZHEIM, Hugo

German, 19th - 20th century.
Born 21 June 1869, in Hamburg.
Draughtsman.

Hugo Schwindrazheim was a caricaturist.

SCHWINDRAZHEIM, Oskar

German, 19th - 20th century.
Born 16 April 1865, in Hamburg.
Painter, art critic.

SCHWINDT, Karl

German, 19th century.
Born 28 September 1797, in Breslau (now Wroclaw, Poland); died 10 July 1867, in Gomba, near Pest, Hungary.
Painter, lithographer.

A painter of portraits and street scenes, Schwindt also carried out numerous illustrations, predominantly in Budapest.

SCHWINGE, Friedrich Wilhelm

German, 19th - 20th century.
Born 30 March 1852, in Hamburg; died 22 October 1913.
Painter. Landscapes, seascapes.

Friedrich Wilhelm Schwinge studied under Peter J. Janssen and Eugène G. Drücker at the fine arts academy in Düsseldorf.

MUSEUMS AND GALLERIES:

BRUNSWICK (Städtisches Mus.).

AUCTION RECORDS:

COLOGNE, 18 March 1983, *Wash Day* (watercolour, 23 1/4 x 31 1/4 ins / 59 x 79.5 cm) DEM 4,000.

SCHWINGEN, Peter

German, 19th century.
Born 14 October 1813, in Muffendorf near Bad Godesberg (north Rhine-Westphalia); died 6 May 1863, in Düsseldorf.
Painter, lithographer, draughtsman.

Schwingen was the pupil of Th. Hildebrandt and K. F. Sohn at the academy in Düsseldorf. He also executed preparatory drawings for wood engravings.

MUSEUMS AND GALLERIES:

DÜSSELDORF (Kunstmus.): *Woman at Window; St Martin Visiting the Children in Düsseldorf; Schmitz the Tailor* - GODESBERG (Municipal Mus.): *Portrait of the Artist.*

AUCTION RECORDS:

COLOGNE, 18 Oct 1974, *Seizure,* DEM 12,000. COLOGNE, 16 June 1978, *Old Couple in Interior* (1837, oil on canvas, 15 1/2 x 13 1/2 ins / 39.5 x 34.5 cm) DEM 22,000. MUNICH, 29 Sept 1999, *Woman's Portrait* (1859, oil on canvas, one of a pair, 33 x 26 ins / 84 x 67 cm) DEM 3,300.

SCHWINTER, Johann

German, 17th century.
Painter.

Schwinter painted a *Holy Family* in the cathedral at Constance in 1670.

SCHWITER, Ludwig August de, or Louis Auguste (Baron)

German, 19th century.
Born 1 February 1805, in Nienburg (Hanover); died 20 August 1889, in Salzburg.
Also active in France.
Painter. Portraits, landscapes.

Schwiter studied in Paris where he lived and worked for nearly 40 years. A successful painter, he was in close contact with Eugène Delacroix who left him a painting by Watteau, another by Chardin and an incomplete canvas by Th. Fielding. He exhibited in the Salon de Paris from 1831 to 1859, winning a third-class medal in 1845.

MUSEUMS AND GALLERIES:

NANCY: *Emma von Schreokinger* - VERSAILLES: *Jacques-Maurice Hatry, Major; Jacques-Maurice Hatry, General-in-chief of the Dutch Army.*

AUCTION RECORDS:
PARIS, 5 May 1928, *Portrait of a Man*, FRF 2,000. PARIS, 3 Nov 1983, *Portrait of the Duchess of Montmorency-Luxembourg in the park of the Château de St-Cloud* (1855, oil on canvas, 98 1/2 x 65 1/4 ins / 250 x 166 cm) FRF 90,000.

SCHWITTERS, Kurt
German, 20th century.
Born 20 June 1887, in Hanover; died 8 January 1948, in Ambleside (Cumbria), England.
Painter, collage artist, assemblage artist, draughtsman, sculptor, engraver. Portraits, landscapes, still-lifes.
Dadaism.
Hanover Dadaist Group.

Nothing in Kurt Schwitters' early work gave any indication of his subsequent career as an innovator. He completed his secondary school studies in Hanover and enrolled at the fine arts academy in Dresden, where he duly attended classes given by K. Banzer, G. Kuehl and E. Hegenbarth. It would appear that he visited Munich in 1913 and, if that was indeed the case, he may have been influenced by the Expressionists of the Die Brücke group. He served in World War I but, by all accounts, his behaviour was so strange and erratic that he was assigned permanently to a menial desk job. In 1915, while still on active service, he settled in Hanover.

By 1917, Schwitters was painting and writing poetry. His first collection of poems, *Anna Blume*, appeared in 1917. In 1920 he made the acquaintance of leading Dadaists Raoul Hausmann from the Berlin Dadaist chapter and Hans Arp from its counterpart in Zurich. Schwitters was denied access to the Berlin Dadaist circle, ostensibly on the grounds that he had contributed not only to the review *Der Zeitweg* but also to another review, *Der Sturm*, which had come out strongly against the German Dadaists and their anti-art credo. Nevertheless, he, together with Hausmann and Hannah Köch, participated in Fmsbw, a Dadaist conference in Prague that served as a point of departure for his subsequent poem *Ursonate*, which he described as a 'composition in oral sounds'. 1922 saw Schwitters on a Dadaist 'promotional tour' again, this time in the Netherlands, in the course of which he met up with Theo and Nelly van Doesburg who introduced him to the tenets of the De Stijl group, the forerunners of Piet Mondrian's Neo-Plasticism.

The first issue of Schwitters' publication *Merz* (1923) was devoted to the activities of the Dutch Dadaists. The term 'Merz', incidentally, was a nonsense word that Schwitters had taken from one of his own collages, where the German word 'Kommerz' had been partially obscured. A year previously, Schwitters had finally been welcomed into the bosom of the Dadaist movement to the extent that he had been admitted to the Dada Congress in Weimar. At the time, he was also a contributor to Theo van Doesburg's periodical *Mécano*.

He spent a short time in Paris in 1927, where he met with leading abstract artists of the day, among them Michel Seuphor. His commitment to membership of the Cercle et Carré (Circle and Square) and Abstraction-Création groups in 1930 and 1932 respectively would seem to suggest that his commitment was to positive Abstraction rather than to the negative/nihilistic variant espoused by the Dadaists as a whole.

Schwitters had long harboured the notion of building a 'cathedral' of everyday objects and had worked assiduously on his gigantic so-called *Merzbau* (*Merz Building*), a wood and plaster structure embellished with found objects, which he frequently referred to as his 'Cathedral of Erotic Misery'. This structure, which gradually took over his apartment in Hanover, was destroyed during World War II. Schwitters had in any event found himself obliged to abandon the project when, with the imminent ascent to power of the Nazis, he elected to leave Germany in 1933 or, as some sources suggest, 1937. He moved to Norway, settling in Lysaker near Oslo, where he promptly set about building a second *Merzbau*, which was destroyed by fire in 1951. When Germany invaded Norway, Schwitters was forced into exile yet again. This time he escaped to England, where he was initially interned for a time as a German national but was eventually able to settle down on a farm in Ambleside in the Lake District, thanks in no small part to a stipend from New York's Museum of Modern Art. He began work on a third *Merzbau* but died before completing it. It is now preserved in the University of Newcastle.

The approach Schwitters applied to his wittily selective *Merz* collages of urban detritus (train tickets, postage stamps, spools of wire, jar lids, algae, fragments of leaflets, corrugated paper, envelopes, and so on, including the occasional allusion to his closest friends - Theo van Doesburg's tie, a pencil used by Mies van der Rohe, or a lock of Hans Richter's hair) was gradually extended to apply to the whole of his artistic output, although it should be noted that he continued to paint in a more conventional manner, producing a large number of oils (landscapes and portraits) which vacillated between Romanticism, Naturalism and Expressionism. Equally, Schwitters worked successfully as a commercial designer and typographer. In effect, his *Merz* experience was instrumental in developing his ability to work, notably from 1922, in a sort of Neo-Constructivist style.

The two- and three-dimensional works by Schwitters - not to mention his literary output - proved a significant influence on generations which followed and that influence is now widely recognised. In that context, reference can be made to artists such as Arman, Spoerri, Hains and others, including Robert Rauschenberg and his 'combine paintings'. Moreover, Schwitters pointed forward to the 'happenings' of Allan Kaprow and the work of Kienholz.

Whether working as a Cubist-Dadaist or an Abstract-Dadaist, however, Schwitters' prime preoccupation was with light. In *Kurt Schwitters. Das Literarische Werk* (*Kurt Schwitters: The Literary Works*), Friedhelm Lach cites a key passage where Schwitters declares himself to be first and foremost an Impressionist. He explains: 'Whether or not I work from nature or in the abstract, light is essential to me. It is the hyphen that brings my work together. Abstraction is the art of offering opposition to nature... As to how many phases I have gone through, all I can say is that I am not ashamed of my ability to paint a decent portrait and that I will continue to do so. There is nothing avant-garde about that.'

Schwitters took part in a very large number of group exhibitions, starting with the September Salon organised by the Kunstverein (Artists' Association) in Hanover in 1911. From 1913, he exhibited on a regular basis at the Grosse Kunstausstellung (Great Exhibition) organised by the same group. He also showed his work at an early exhibition mounted by the Kestner-Gesellschaft in Hanover in 1917. Other exhibitions include those at the following: *Deutscher Expressionismus* (*German Expressionism*) at the Mathildenhöhe in Darmstadt (1920); the Société Anonyme in New York, an organisation driven in large part by Marcel Duchamp (1920, 1921); *Abstract and Surrealist Painting and Sculpture* at the Kunsthaus in Zurich (1929); the Städtische Kunsthalle in Mannheim (1927); the Kunsthaus in Zurich (1929); the Salon 1940 at the Parc des Expositions in Paris (1932); *Cubism and Abstract Art* and *Fantastic Art, Dada, Surrealism* at the Museum of Modern Art in New York (1936); and the Galerie Charpentier in Paris (1939). After his death, his works continued to be shown in group exhibitions at the following: the Museum of Modern Art in New York (1948, 1957, 1961, 1968); the Kunsthalle in Bern (1956); the Kunsthalle in Düsseldorf (1958); the Venice Biennale (1960); the Kunstverein in Hanover (1962); the Kunsthaus in Zurich (1966, 1983); the Städtische Galerie in Frankfurt am Main (1977, 1986); the Neue Nationalgalerie in Berlin (1977); the Westfälisches

Landesmuseum in Münster (1980); the Royal Academy of Arts in London (1985); the Sprengel Museum in Hanover (1987, 1991); the Centro de Arte Reina Sofia in Madrid (1989); the Musée National d'Art Moderne and the Centre Georges-Pompidou in Paris (1990); the Institute of Contemporary Art in Boston (1992); the Kunstsammlung Nordrhein-Westfalen in Düsseldorf (1992); the Biennale d'Art Contemporain in Lyons (1993); the Centre de la Vieille Charité in Marseilles (1993); the Kunsthalle der Hypo-Kulturstiftung in Munich (1993); the Carré d'Art in Nîmes (1993); and the Palazzo delle Esposizioni in Rome (1994).

Schwitters' work was also the subject of numerous solo exhibitions. During his lifetime, these included one-man shows in 1920 at the Galerie Der Sturm in Berlin, in 1926-1927 at the Kunstverein für Böhmen (Bohemian Art Federation) in Prague, and in 1944 at the Modern Art Gallery in London. Posthumous solo exhibitions include those held at the following: the Modern Art Gallery in Basel (1948); the Pinacotheca Gallery in New York (1948); the London Gallery in London (1950); the Sidney Janis Gallery in New York (1952, 1956, 1959); the Galerie Berggruen in Paris (1954); the Stedelijk Museum in Amsterdam (1956); the Palais des Beaux-Arts in Brussels (1956); the Kestner-Gesellschaft in Hanover (1956); the Philips Gallery in Washington (1957); Lord's Gallery in London (1958); the Galerie Schmela in Düsseldorf (1959); the Arts Council of Great Britain in London (1959); the Galleria Schwarz in Milan (1961, 1963); the Museu d'Arte Moderna in São Paulo (1961); a travelling exhibition organised by the Art Museum of Pasadena and the Konstnärshuset in Stockholm (1962); the Malborough Gallery in London (1963, 1972, 1981, 1985); the Wallraf-Richartz Museum in Cologne (1963); the Chalette Gallery in New York (1963); the Tonelli-Arte Moderna in Milan (1964); the Boymans van Beuningen Museum in Rotterdam (1964); a travelling exhibition organised by the Museum of Fine Arts in Dallas (1965); a travelling exhibition organised by the Städtische Kunsthalle in Düsseldorf (1971); the Museum of Modern Art in New York (1972, 1985); the FIAC (Foire Internationale d'Art Contemporain) in Paris, presented by the Galerie Gmurzynska in Cologne (1980); the Fundacio Juan March in Madrid (1982, 1999); a travelling exhibition organised by the Seibu Museum of Art in Tokyo (1983); the Museum Ludwig in Cologne (1985); the Tate Gallery in London (1985); the Sprengel Museum in Hanover (1986, 1990); the Stadtbibliothek in Hanover (1987); the National Gallery of Art Library in Washington (1993); the Galerie Lelong in Zurich (1994); a travelling exhibition organised by the Centre Georges-Pompidou and the Musée National d'Art Moderne in Paris and presented at the museum in Grenoble (1994); the Contemporary Art Pavilion in Milan (2001); the Abbot Hall Art Gallery in Kendal in Britain, with Hilde Goldschmidt (2003); and *Kurt Schwitters: MERZ, A Total Vision of the World* at the Tinguely Museum in Basel (2004).

Kurt Schwitters

K.S.
41

Bibliography:

Arp, Hans/Lissitzky, El, *Die Kunstismen [Les Ismes de l'art]*, E. Rentsch, Leipzig, Erlenbach, Zurich, 1925. Moholy-Nagy, Laszlo, *Vision in Motion*, P. Theobald, Chicago, 1947. *Kurt Schwitters*, exhibition catalogue, Gal. Berggruen, Paris, 1954. Themerson, Stefan, *Kurt Schwitters in England*, Gaberbocchus, London, 1958. *Kurt Schwitters: A Retrospective Exhibition, November 10-December 12, 1965*, Dallas Museum of Fine Arts, Dallas, 1965. Schmalenbach, Werner, *Kurt Schwitters*, Prestel, Munich, 1967 (Abrams, New York, DuMont Schauberg, Köln, 1984). Lach, Friedhelm, *Der Merz Künstler Kurt Schwitters*, DuMont Schauberg, Cologne, 1971. *Kurt Schwitters: Works in the Museum Collections*, Museum of Modern Art, New York, 1972. Last, Rex W., *German Dadaist Literature: Kurt Schwitters, Hugo Ball, Hans Arp*, Twayne Publishers, New York, 1973. Lach, Friedhelm, *'Kurt Schwitters. Das literarische Werk'* in *5 vol*, M. DuMont Schauberg, Cologne, 1973-1981. Elderfield, John, *Kurt Schwitters*, Thames & Hudson, London, 1985. Morton, Colin, *The Merzbook: Kurt Schwitters Poems*, Quarry Press, Kingston (Ontario), 1987. *Typographie kann unter Umstanden Kunst sein, Kurt Schwitters*, exhibition catalogue, Museum Wiesbaden, Wiesbaden, 1990. Bailly, Jean-Christophe, *Kurt Schwitters*, Hazan, Paris, 1993. Dietrich, Dorothea, *The Collages of Kurt Schwitters. Tradition and innovation*, Cambridge University Press, New York, 1993. Lemoine, Serge/Barré, François, *Kurt Schwitters*, exhibition catalogue, Réunion des musées nationaux, Centre Georges-Pompidou, Paris, 1994. Lemoine, Serge/Nobis, Beatrix/Haldenwanger, Maria, *Kurt Schwitters*, exhibition catalogue, Instituto Valenciano de Arte Moderno (IVAM) Centro Julio González, Valencia, 1995. Webster, Gwendolen, *Kurt Merz Schwitters*, University of Wales Press, Cardiff, 1997. Orchard, Karin/Schulz, Isabel, *Kurt Schwitters. Werke und Dokumente, Verzeichnis der Bestände im Sprengel Museum Hannover (Catalogue of the works and documents in the Sprengel Museum Hannover)*, exhibition catalogue, Sprengel Museum, Hanover, 1998 (text in German and English). Schulz, Isabel/Orchard, Karin, *Kurt Schwitters 1905-1922*, catalogue raisonné, Hatje Cantz, Ostfildern-Ruit, 2000. Meyer-Büser, Suzanne/Orchard, Karin, *In the beginning was Merz, from Kurt Schwitter to the present day*, exhibition catalogue, Sprengel Museum, Hannover, Hatje Cantz, Ostfildern-Ruit, 2000 (text in English). *'Der Nachlass von Kurt und Ernst Schwitters'* in *Patrimonia*, no. 222, catalogue, Sprengel Museum, Hanover, 2002. *Kurt Schwitters. MERZ, a total vision of the world*, exhibition catalogue, Benteli, Bern, 2004 (text in English and German).

Museums and Galleries:

Amsterdam (Stedelijk Mus.): *Merz 30, 39 (Mauxio)* (1930) - Basel (Kunstmus.): *Merz 20b. The Springtime Picture* (1920) - Basel (Kunstmus., Prints Collection): *Mz 344. Dordrecht* (1922); *Photogram I* (c. 1923-1929); *Homage to Jean Arp* (1924) - Berlin (Nationalgal.): *Little Column* (c. 1922); *Large Schnurchell* (1923) - Berlin (Staatliche Mus.): *Gone with the Wind C 77* (1946) - Bern (Kunstmus.): *Disjointed Forces* (1920) - Buffalo (Albright-Knox AG): *Difficult* (c. 1942-1943) - Cologne (Mus. Ludwig): *Merz Picture 9b. The Big Picture-I* (1919) - Cottbus (Brandenburgische Kunstsammlungen): *Relief with Yellow Rectangle-2* (1928) - Düsseldorf (Kunstsammlung Nordrhein-Westfalen): *Mz 150. Oskar* (1920); *Merz 169: Forms in Space* (1920); *Merz 271: Room* (1921); *Wood on Black* (c. 1943-1946) - Göteborg (Konstmus.): *Self-portrait* (1947) - Grenoble: *De Stijl* (1947); *Heights of Langdale* (1945) - Hamburg (Kunsthalle): *Mz 600. Leiden* (1923) - Hanover (Kestner-Mus.): *Inlaid Box Anna* (1920-1921); *With String* (1923-1926) - Hanover (Sprengel Mus.): *Houses in the Snow* (1918); *The Bookseller Julius Beeck* (1919); *Merz Picture 31* (1920); *Mz 158. Kots Painting* (1920); *Mz 410. Something Like That* (1922); *Vertical* (1923); *Mz 1926, 5. With Velvet Lilac* (1924); *Painting 1926, 3. Cicero* (1926); *Drawing-i Horse* (1928); *Dedicated to 8s* (1929); *Postage Due* (1931-1932); reconstruction made in 1983*Der Merzbau* (c. 1923-1936); *Portrait from Another Era* (1937-1938); *Recommended* (1939); *Coloured Half-moon* (1940); *Cathedral* (1941-1942); *Little Dog* (1943-1944); *Pebble Sculpture* (1946-1947); *Two Forms in Rhythm* (1947) - London (Tate Collection): *Picture of Spatial Growths - Picture with Two Small Dogs* (1920-

1939, mixed media collage/board); *The Autumn Crocus* (1926-1928, reconstructed 1958, painted concrete, sculpture); *Chicken and Egg* (1946, mixed media, sculpture); *Painted Stone* (1945-1947, painted stone); *(Togetherness)* (c. 1945-1947, mixed media, sculpture); *Lofty* (c. 1945-1947, painted plaster, sculpture) - LOS ANGELES (County MA): *Construction for High-born Ladies* (1919) - MADRID (Mus. Thyssen-Bornemisza): *Merz Picture I A (The Alienist)* (1919); *Merz 1925. 1 Relief in a Blue Square* (1925) - MÜNSTER (Westfälisches Landesmus.): *Merz Picture with Green Ring* (1926-1937) - NAGOYA (City AM): *Merz 52. Beauty Care* (1920) - NEUSS (Stiftung Insel Hombroich) - NEW HAVEN (AG, Yale University): *Merz 1003. Peacock Wheel* (1924); *Relief with Red Segment* (1927) - NEW HAVEN (Société Anonyme Collection): *Merz 19* (1920) - NEW YORK (MoMA): *Drawing A2 Hansi* (1918); *Picture with a Clear Centre* (1919); *.fec* (1920); *Mz 252. Coloured Squares* (1921); *Merz Picture 32 A. Cherry Picture* (1921) - NEW YORK (Solomon R. Guggenheim Mus.): *Merz Picture 5 B* (1919); *Mz 163 with Perspiring Woman* (1920) - PARIS (MAMVP): *Mirror Collage* (1920-1921); *Two Black Angles* (1944) - PARIS (MNAM-CCI): *Gold* (1924); *Collage* (1924); *Merz 1926, 2 (Even Up There)* (1926); *Memory of Norway* (1930); *Dotting the I* (1939) - PHILADELPHIA (MA): *Merz Construction* (1921) - ST PETERSBURG, FL: *Red Feather (for Lisker)* (1921) - ST-ÉTIENNE (Mus. d'Art et d'Industrie): *Untitled* (1939) - STOCKHOLM (Moderna Mus.): *Horizontal* (1947) - STRASBOURG (Mus. d'Art Moderne et Contemporain): *Bag for the Shipwrecked* (1921); *Mz Herbin* (1923-1924) - STUTTGART (Staatsgal.): *Picture-And* (1919) - TOKYO (Sezon MMA): *Red Rubber Ball Picture* (1942) - UKUYAMA (MA): *Abstraction 19 (Unveiling)* (1918); *Z 77 Industrial Site* (1918); *Z 1927 Street at Night* (1918) - VALENCIA (IVAM Centre Julio González): *Plastic Merz Drawing* (1931); *Unititled* (c. 1943-1945) - ZURICH (Kunsthaus): *Hans Arp's Watch* (1928).

AUCTION RECORDS:

MILAN, 21 Nov 1961, *In the Kitchen*, ITL 5,800,000. MILAN, 1 Dec 1964, *Commerce and Banking*, ITL 1,200,000. NEW YORK, 14 Oct 1965, *Aerial Painting*, USD 8,000. GENEVA, 27 June 1969, *Composition* (watercolour and collage) CHF 9,000. BERN, 12 June 1971, *Metallurgist with Benesch*, CHF 17,000. COPENHAGEN, 14 March 1972, *Cubist Chest in Rosewood*, DKK 32,000. LONDON, 29 Nov 1972, *Mz 281: Fifty-eight*, GBP 5,200. NEW YORK, 4 May 1973, *Little Dog* (wood and plaster) USD 7,000. LONDON, 3 April 1974, *Composition* (1947) GBP 3,600. HAMBURG, 4 June 1976, *War and Peace* (1947, collage and oil, 7 1/4 x 5 1/4 ins / 18.3 x 13.2 cm) DEM 21,000. BERN, 9 June 1977, *Merz Folder 3* (1923, lithograph, 21 3/4 x 17 1/2 ins / 55.5 x 44.5 cm) CHF 9,200. BERN, 9 June 1977, *Blacksmith* (1921, collage of paper and fabric/card, 7 x 5 1/2 ins / 18 x 14.2 cm) CHF 54,000. COLOGNE, 19 May 1979, *Head Profile* (1921, lithograph, 9 1/2 x 7 3/4 ins / 24 x 20 cm; 15 1/4 x 10 3/4 ins/39 x 27.5 cm) DEM 2,200. MUNICH, 29 May 1979, *Factories* (1918, charcoal, 6 1/2 x 4 1/4 ins / 16.3 x 11 cm) DEM 7,000. BERN, 22 June 1979, *Merz Picture I C* (1920, collage, 6 1/4 x 5 1/2 ins / 15.6 x 13.7 cm) CHF 114,000. LONDON, 3 Dec 1980, *1947* (gouache and collage, 12 x 8 1/2 ins / 30.5 x 21.5 cm) GBP 6,000. NEW YORK, 19 May 1981, *Chocolate* (1947, oil and collage, 17 1/4 x 15 1/4 ins / 44 x 39 cm) USD 30,000. NEW YORK, 20 May 1982, *Invisible Ink* (1947, collage and gouache, 11 1/2 x 9 ins / 29 x 22.7 cm) USD 14,000. MUNICH, 29 Nov 1983, *Untitled* (1922, oil and collage/card, 15 1/2 x 12 1/2 ins / 39.5 x 31.5 cm) DEM 155,000. LONDON, 27 June 1984, *Anna Blume* (1922, mixed media, 8 x 6 1/4 ins / 19.4 x 15.9 cm) GBP 5,000. NEW YORK, 16 May 1985, *Design: Kurt Schwitters* (1931, pen, graphite and collage/paper, 12 1/2 x 9 3/4 ins / 32 x 25 cm) USD 11,500. LONDON, 23 June 1986, *Red Circle* (1942, oil and collage/wood, 43 x 36 ins / 109 x 91.5 cm) GBP 56,000. LONDON, 19 Oct 1988, *Ambleside* (1942, oil on panel, 11 x 12 3/4 ins / 27 x 32.3 cm) GBP 2,200. LONDON, 21 Oct 1988, *Portrait of Beatrice Bradley* (1945, oil on card, 25 3/4 x 20 3/4 ins / 65.3 x 52.7 cm) GBP 3,520. NEW YORK, 12 Nov 1988, *Untitled* (1922, mixed media collage/card, 6 x 5 ins / 14.3 x 11.8 cm) USD 38,500. PARIS, 20 Nov 1988, *Flying* (1920, Merz-collage) FRF 440,000; *Mirror Collage* (collage/mirror, h. 11 1/4 ins / 28.5 cm) FRF 2,100,000. AMSTERDAM, 8 Dec 1988, *Composition* (1928, collage, 4 3/4 x 3 3/4 ins / 12 x 9.6 cm) NLG 59,800. LONDON, 5 April 1989, *England's Lake District* (1942, oil on card, 21 x 17 ins / 52.5 x 43 cm) GBP 22,000. NEW YORK, 10 May 1989, *Asbestos Mat* (1944, oil on wood and asbestos, 19 1/2 x 15 1/2 ins / 49.8 x 39.4 cm) USD 115,500. PARIS, 17 June 1989, *Mainly Blue* (1908, collage, oil and pencil, 7 3/4 x 6 1/2 ins / 20 x 16.3 cm) FRF 250,000. LONDON, 28 June 1989, *Mountain Range in Oye* (1930, oil, wood and metal/reinforced canvas, 20 3/4 x 18 ins / 53 x 45.5 cm) GBP 148,500. PARIS, 7 Oct 1989, *Out of the Dark* (1943, collage/card, 9 x 7 1/2 ins / 23 x 19 cm) FRF 280,000. NEW YORK, 13 Nov 1989, *Apollo in February* (collage/card, 7 1/4 x 6 ins / 18.4 x 14.3 cm) USD 66,000. LONDON, 29 Nov 1989, *Collage* (1947, collage/paper, 9 x 7 ins / 22.8 x 17.7 cm) GBP 77,000. LONDON, 4 April 1990, *Constructivist Composition* (oil on canvas, 24 3/4 x 19 3/4 ins / 63 x 50 cm) GBP 82,500. NEW YORK, 16 May 1990, *Composition: Ashoff, Ellen* (1922, paper collage with ink and gold paint/card/black paper, 11 1/4 x 8 3/4 ins / 28.5 x 22.3 cm) USD 148,500. NEW YORK, 14 Nov 1990, *Mountain Peaks* (1918, black chalk/paper, 8 x 1 1/2 ins / 19.4 x 4 cm) USD 14,300. PARIS, 25 Nov 1990, *Composition* (1923, collage, 9 x 6 ins / 22 x 15 cm) FRF 550,000. AMSTERDAM, 23 May 1991, *Langdale Pikes* (1945, oil on card, 15 x 19 3/4 ins / 38 x 50 cm) NLG 19,550. NEW YORK, 6 Nov 1991, *Merz Picture 9A* (assemblage with collage and oil on card, with a counter from a game of draughts, 6 1/4 x 8 ins / 16 x 19.4 cm) USD 242,000. LONDON, 4 Dec 1991, *Mz 30, 3* (1930, collage, 6 x 5 ins / 15.4 x 12.4 cm) GBP 38,500. LONDON, 25 March 1992, *Collage* (1947, 10 1/2 x 8 3/4 ins / 26.4 x 22.4 cm) GBP 15,400. NEW YORK, 9 May 1992, *Refuge near the Djupvasshytta Hotel* (1938, oil on panel, 9 1/4 x 7 ins / 23.2 x 17.5 cm) USD 1,870. NEW YORK, 14 May 1992, *C. 68 Wanteeside* (1945, oil and assemblage/wood/plywood, 5 3/4 x 7 1/4 ins / 14.9 x 18.4 cm) USD 77,000. BERLIN, 27 Nov 1992, *Mz 103* (collage and pencil, 4 3/4 x 3 3/4 ins / 12.3 x 9.5 cm) DEM 101,700. LONDON, 22 June 1993, *Disparate Construction with Candle* (assemblage of painted wood, wax and fabric, 11 x 11 ins / 27 x 27 cm) GBP 243,500. NEW YORK, 4 Nov 1993, *Players* (1934, collage/paper, 6 1/4 x 5 ins / 15.9 x 13 cm) USD 48,300. NEW YORK, 11 May 1994, *Sole of a Shoe* (1945, oil and assemblage relief/plywood, 21 1/4 x 17 3/4 ins / 54 x 45.1 cm) USD 244,500. PARIS, 30 March 1995, *Collage* (glued paper, 13 1/2 x 9 1/2 ins / 34 x 24.4 cm) FRF 190,000. LONDON, 11 Oct 1995, *Red Square* (1926, collage of leaf, pen and paper/paper, 9 x 7 1/4 ins / 23 x 18.4 cm) GBP 20,700. NEW YORK, 1 May 1996, *Untitled* (1926, collage/card, 6 1/2 x 5 ins / 16.5 x 13 cm) USD 46,000. LONDON, 25 June 1996, *Untitled* (1939, collage, 6 1/2 x 4 3/4 ins / 16.3 x 12.2 cm) GBP 17,250. LONDON, 23 Oct 1996, *Square B* (1922-1925, collage, 6 x 5 ins / 15 x 13 cm) GBP 9,200. LONDON, 3 Dec 1996, *Ord U* (1945, collage, 13 x 10 ins / 33 x 25.4 cm) GBP 16,100. AMSTERDAM, 10 Dec 1996, *Linda* (1926, collage/paper) NLG 86,490. MILAN, 10 Dec 1996, *Mz Heart 253* (1921, collage, 7 x 5 3/4 ins / 18 x 14.5 cm) ITL 53,590,000. LONDON, 25 June 1997, *Merz XI 3 Art* (1947, collage/card/panel, 5 x 3 3/4 ins / 12.5 x 9.8 cm) GBP 12,650. LONDON, 22 Oct 1997, *Mz 307* (1921, collage, 7 x 5 3/4 ins / 17.5 x 14.5 cm) GBP 41,100. LONDON, 7 Oct 1999, *Yellow Mark: Merz 247* (1921, paper, textile and collage, 6 x 4 ins / 14 x 11 cm) GBP 52,000. NEW YORK, 9 Nov 1999, *Mz 325, Blitznadeln* (1921, fabric, paper, collage and black gouache on board, 7 x 5 ins / 17 x 13 cm) USD 150,000. NEW YORK, 9 May 2000, *Fernspr Mz 26,53* (1926, collage on board on paper, 9 x 7 ins / 22 x 17 cm) USD 120,000. LONDON, 28 June 2000, *Green Rectangle* (1921, oil, glass, fabric, cotton wool and glass on paper, 6 x 5 ins / 15 x 13 cm) GBP 50,000. NEW YORK, 23 Feb 2001, *Delco* (1942, collage, 7 x 6 ins / 17 x

14 cm) USD 45,000. NEW YORK, 5 Nov 2001, *Merzbild 49 A, Galerie van Gervens* (1922, assemblage on board, 17 x 13 ins / 44 x 32 cm) USD 170,000. NEW YORK, 21 Feb 2002, *MZ201 1 Ulice* (1926, collage on board, 10 x 8 ins / 26 x 21 cm) USD 47,500. ZURICH, 4 Dec 2002, *Aufunterbrief* (1920, collage and oil on paper on board, 9 x 7 ins / 23 x 17 cm) CHF 92,000. LONDON, 3 Feb 2003, *Mz er* (1922, collage, 12 x 9 ins / 31 x 23 cm) GBP 90,000. BERN, 20 June 2003, *Gaahden - Merz 347* (1922, collage on paper with text, 7 x 5 ins / 19 x 13 cm) CHF 95,000. BERN, 18 June 2004, *Collage* (1921, collage, paper, material and oil, 6 x 5 ins / 16 x 13 cm) CHF 190,000. COLOGNE, 4 Dec 2004, *Relief with Yellow Rectangle 2* (1928, oil, plaster, panel and metal on wood, 26 x 18x7 ins / 65 x 46x18 cm) EUR 1,200,000.

SCHWITZER, Hans
Swiss, 16th century.
Active in Bern from 1506 to 1513.
Painter.

SCHWITZER, Peter, or Schwiezer, Schwizer, Suizer, Svitzer
French, 18th century.
Born in Strasbourg.
Active in the middle of the 18th century.
Sculptor, designer of ornamental architectural features.
Peter Schwitzer worked for the castles of Potsdam.

SCHWOB
French, 19th - 20th century.
Painter.
Schwob exhibited in Paris at the Salon de la Rose-Croix, a meeting point for those painters interested in the Italian Primitives and Mannerists, in particular Botticelli.

SCHWOB, Lucien
Swiss, 20th century.
Born 1895, in La Chaux-de-Fonds; died 1985.
Painter.
Lucien Schwob studied in Paris under Bernard Naudin.

SCHWOERER, Friedrich. See **SCHWÖRER**

SCHWOISER, Eduard
German, 19th century.
Born 18 March 1826, in Brusau; died 3 September 1902, in Munich.
Painter. History painting, genre scenes.
Schwoiser was a pupil of Foltz who travelled to England, France, Italy, the Netherlands and Spain to study. Decorated with many orders, he settled and taught in Munich. Some of his cartoons and frescoes are conserved in the museum there.
MUSEUMS AND GALLERIES:
MUNICH: *Eight Scenes from the History of Bavaria; Henry IV at Canossa.*

SCHWOLL, Joachim van, or Zwoll
Dutch, 16th century.
Died 1575 or 1586, in Hamburg.
Painter.
Schwoll lived in Hamburg from 1566 to 1575.

SCHWÖRER, Friedrich, or Schwoerer
German, 19th century.
Born 9 January 1833, in Weil (Baden); died 25 March 1891, in Munich.
Painter, illustrator. History painting.
Schwörer was taught by Foltz at the academy in Munich, and by Cogniet in Paris.
MUSEUMS AND GALLERIES:
MUNICH: frescoes.

SCHWORMSTÄDT, Felix
German, 19th - 20th century.
Born 16 September 1870, in Hamburg; died 1938.
Draughtsman, illustrator, painter (gouache).
Felix Schwormstädt studied at the fine arts academy in Karlsruhe and then under Carl von Marr at the fine arts academy in Munich.

SCHWYZER. See also **SCHWEIZER** and **SCHWITZER**

SCHWYZER, Hans Heinrich.
See **SCHWEITZER**

SCHWYZER, Julius
Swiss, 20th century.
Born 1876, in Pfaffnau; died February 1929, in Zurich.
Sculptor. Figures. Statues.
Julius Schwyzer was a pupil of Louis Wethli; he sculpted cement statues and fountains.
MUSEUMS AND GALLERIES:
AARAU (Aargauer Kunsthaus): *Female Head* - ZURICH (Kunsthaus): *Head of a Young Girl.*

SCHYECHLIN, Hans. See **SCHÜCHLIN**

SCHYL, Jules
Swedish, 20th century.
Born 1893; died 1977.
Painter. Figures, scenes with figures, landscapes, still-lifes.
AUCTION RECORDS:
STOCKHOLM, 6 June 1988, *Violinists* (oil, 19 1/4 x 17 3/4 ins / 49 x 45 cm) SEK 15,500. STOCKHOLM, 22 May 1989, *Composition: Mountains, Buildings and Lake* (oil on canvas, 19 1/4 x 27 1/4 ins / 49 x 69 cm) SEK 32,000. STOCKHOLM, 6 Dec 1989, *Artist's Model wearing a Black Hat* (oil on canvas, 22 x 18 1/2 ins / 55 x 47 cm) SEK 30,000. STOCKHOLM, 5-6 Dec 1990, *Marmmorkirken, Copenhagen* (oil on canvas, 19 x 16 1/2 ins / 48 x 42 cm) SEK 10,500. STOCKHOLM, 21 May 1992, *Still-life with Bouquet of Flowers* (oil on canvas, 29 1/2 x 24 ins / 75 x 61 cm) SEK 8,000. STOCKHOLM, 30 Nov 1993, *Gondolas on the Lido* (oil on canvas, 23 1/2 x 31 ins / 60 x 79 cm) SEK 11,000. STOCKHOLM, 27 April 1999, *Shy Nude Model* (1935, oil on canvas, 44 x 22 ins / 111 x 56 cm) SEK 26,000. STOCKHOLM, 27 April 1999, *Lady in a Hat* (1927, oil on canvas, 39 x 18 ins / 100 x 46 cm) SEK 30,000. MALMÖ, 8 April 2000, *Cubist Composition with Musical Instruments* (1961, oil on canvas, 29 x 32 ins / 73 x 82 cm) SEK 32,000. STOCKHOLM, 7 Nov 2000, *Nude Female Model* (1925, oil on canvas, 39 x 27 ins / 99 x 69 cm) SEK 39,000. STOCKHOLM, 2 May 2001, *Still-life with Apples and Top Hat* (oil on canvas, 19 x 22 ins / 49 x 55 cm) SEK 21,000. STOCKHOLM, 21 May 2001, *Self-portrait* (1921, oil on panel, 17 x 13 ins / 44 x 32 cm) SEK 23,000. STOCKHOLM, 23 April 2002, *Southern Harbour* (oil on canvas, 22 x 31 ins / 57 x 80 cm) SEK 27,000. MALMÖ, 27 Nov 2002, *Reclining Model* (oil on canvas, 25 x 31 ins / 64 x 79 cm) SEK 28,000. STOCKHOLM, 28 April 2003, *Southern Landscape* (oil on canvas, 22 x 34 ins / 56 x 86 cm) SEK 32,000. STOCKHOLM, 4 Nov 2003, *Cubist Model* (oil on canvas, 21 x 26 ins / 54 x 65 cm) SEK 19,500. STOCKHOLM, 27 April 2004, *San Salute* (1954, oil on canvas, 32 x 23 ins / 81 x 58 cm) SEK 32,000. STOCKHOLM, 2 Nov 2004, *By the River* (1921, oil on canvas, 24 x 20 ins / 61 x 51 cm) SEK 20,000.

SCHYNDEL, Anna van. See **SCHENDEL**

SCHYNDEL, Bernardus van. See **SCHENDEL**

SCHYNDEL, C. L. van, or Schendel
Dutch, 17th century.
Active in 1650.
Painter. Figure compositions, scenes with figures.
AUCTION RECORDS:
COLOGNE, 1862, *Group of People Making Music,* FRF 195. COLOGNE, 26 Nov 1970, *Tavern Scene,* DEM 6,500.

SCHYNDEL, J. van. See **SCHENDEL** or **SCHEYNDEL**

SCHYNVOOT, Jacobus, or Schynvoet
Dutch, 18th century.
Active in Amsterdam and London.
Draughtsman, engraver (burin).

Jacobus Schynvoot was the brother or son of Simon Schynvoot. He is thought to have travelled to London in 1700. He engraved landscapes and views of country seats after his own drawings, in a style reminiscent of John Kip. He was still active in 1733.

SCHYNVOOT, Simon
Dutch, 17th - 18th century.
Born 1653, in The Hague; died 24 August 1727, in Amsterdam (?).
Engraver, draughtsman.

Simon Schynvoot was the husband of Cornelia de Ryck. He was known as a collector, garden designer and poet.

SCHYRGENS, Antoine
Belgian, 20th century.
Born 1890, in Liège; died 1981.
Painter, watercolourist, draughtsman, engraver. Seascapes.

Antoine Schyrgens taught watercolours at the fine arts academy in Ostend.

MUSEUMS AND GALLERIES:
OSTEND.

SCHYSELER, Gregorius, or Schysseler
Dutch, 17th century.
Sculptor (wood).

Gregorius Schyseler carved an organ loft for the parish church at 's-Hertogenbosch and a crucifix for the church at Venloo. Stylistic similarities suggest a common identity with the artist Grégoire Schiffelers.

SCHYTT, Jost or Joost. See **SCHUTZE**

SCHYTZ, Charles. See **SCHUTZ**

SCHYTZ, Karl. See **SCHUTZ**

SCHYVINCK, Firmin
Belgian, 20th century.
Born 1933, in Adegem.
Painter.

Firmin Schyvinck studied at St Luke's fine arts academy in Ghent.

SCHYZ. See also **SCHUTZ**

SCHYZ, Sebastian
German, 17th century.
Draughtsman.

Schyz may have been identical to the painter Schütz, pupil of Jobst Harrich in Nuremberg from 1608 to 1613.

MUSEUMS AND GALLERIES:
BERLIN (Kupferstichkabinet): a drawing.

SCIACCO, Tommaso, or Sciacca
Italian, 18th century.
Born 1734, in Mazzara; died in Lendinara.
Painter. History painting.

Tommaso Sciacco executed works for churches with Cavalucci and Agostino Masucci in Rome and also in Rovigo.

MUSEUMS AND GALLERIES:
ÁSCOLI PICENO (Pinacoteca Civica): *St Teresa* - ROVIGO (Pinacoteca): *St Thaddeus*.

SCIALLERO, Luigi
Italian, 19th - 20th century.
Born 4 March 1829, in Genoa; died 29 January 1920, in Genoa.
Painter. Scenes with figures.

Luigi Sciallero was a student at the academy of fine arts in Genoa.

MUSEUMS AND GALLERIES:
GENOA (Gal. d'Arte Moderna): *Death of Columbus*.

SCIALOJA, Toti, or Scialoia
Italian, 20th century.
Born 1914, in Rome; died 1 March 1998, in Rome.
Active in France and in the USA.
Painter, scenographer, art critic. Figures, landscapes, still-lifes. Stage costumes and sets.

Toti Scialoja taught at the academy of fine arts in Rome, of which he later became the director.

He was originally influenced by the Expressionist style of the painters working in Rome in the 1930s but his work began to develop in new directions, particularly after 1958, when he produced a succession of imprints on canvas where the density of colour gradually fades as the imprint is repeated over time. He abandoned paintbrushes altogether in favour of cloths dipped in paint after meeting Willem de Kooning and Franz Kline in New York. Scialoja was also a writer and art critic.

He took part in many collective exhibitions including: Rome Quadriennale (1939, 1943, 1948, 1955 and 1959); São Paulo Biennale (1951); Venice Biennale (regularly between 1952 and 1958); International Exhibition of the Carnegie Foundation, Pittsburgh (1955 receiving a mention and 1958); Documenta, Kassel (1959).He held several solo exhibitions from 1941 including: New York (1956) Galleria Nazionale d'Art Moderna e Contemporanea, Rome (1991). A number of posthumous retrospectives have been organised including one at Palazzo dei Diamanti, Ferrara (2002).

BIBLIOGRAPHY:
Di Meo, Philippe, '*Toti Scialoja*' in *Art Press* n° 161, periodical, Paris, September 1991. Curcio, Renato, *À visage découvert: entretien avec Mario Scialoja*, Lieu commun, Paris, 1993. *Toti Scialoja: Opere 1955-1963*, exhibition catalogue, Galleria dello Scudo, Verona, Skira, Milan, 1999.

MUSEUMS AND GALLERIES:
AMSTERDAM (Stedelijk Mus.) - PITTSBURGH (Carnegie MA): *Mattino D'Inverno* (*Winter Morning*) (lithograph) - ROME (Gal. Nazionale d'Arte Moderna).

AUCTION RECORDS:
MILAN, 12 June 1984, *Intermittences* (1966, mixed media/canvas, 25 1/4 x 53 1/2 ins / 64 x 136 cm) ITL 3,000,000. ROME, 23 April 1985, *In the Dark* (1957, oil and sand/canvas, 62 1/2 x 75 1/4 ins / 159 x 191 cm) ITL 4,800,000. MILAN, 8 June 1988, *Cross* (1958, mixed media, 30 1/4 x 16 ins / 77 x 40.5 cm) ITL 6,200,000. ROME, 15 Nov 1988, *Landscape with Houses* (1946, oil on canvas, 23 1/2 x 31 1/2 ins / 60 x 80 cm) ITL 6,200,000. MILAN, 14 Dec 1988, *Composition* (1962, mixed media on board, 19 x 28 ins / 48.5 x 71 cm) ITL 5,000,000. ROME, 17 April 1989, *Harlequin* (1952, oil on canvas, 55 x 23 1/2 ins / 140 x 60 cm) ITL 6,000,000. ROME, 28 Nov 1989, *Factory near the Tiber* (1946, oil on canvas, 23 1/2 x 27 1/2 ins / 60 x 70 cm) ITL 11,500,000. NEW YORK, 21 Feb 1990, *Untitled* (1954, acrylic/canvas, 25 1/2 x 39 1/2 ins / 64.8 x 100.3 cm) USD 4,125. ROME, 30 Oct 1990, *Sleeping Man* (1953, oil on canvas, 39 1/4 x 31 1/2 ins / 100 x 80 cm) ITL 5,500,000. MILAN, 13 Dec 1990, *Schemes* (1987, oil on canvas, 55 1/4 x 55 1/4 ins / 140.5 x 140.5 cm) ITL 11,000,000. ROME, 9 April 1991, *Four Imprints* (1959, mixed media/hemp, 44 1/2 x 95 ins / 113 x 241 cm) ITL 7,000,000. MILAN, 14 Nov 1991, *Composition* (cement on board, 28 x 39 3/4 ins / 71 x 101 cm) ITL 6,000,000. ROME, 9 Dec 1991, *Still-life* (1954, oil on canvas, 39 1/4 x 25 1/2 ins / 100 x 65 cm) ITL 9,200,000. ROME, 25 May 1992, *Still-life* (1954, oil on canvas, 23 1/2 x 32 ins / 60 x 81 cm) ITL 7,475,000. MILAN, 9 Nov 1992, *Composition* (1982, mixed media and collage/mounted paper, 17 x 38 1/2 ins / 43 x 98 cm) ITL 2,600,000. ROME, 19 Nov 1992, *Still-life with Flowers and*

Fruit (1942, oil on canvas, 15 3/4 x 19 3/4 ins / 40 x 50 cm) ITL 6,500,000. ROME, 14 Dec 1992, *A Mild Winter* (1955, oil on canvas, 31 x 33 3/4 ins / 79 x 86 cm) ITL 6,900,000. NEW YORK, 22 Feb 1993, *Surprise* (1958, oil on canvas, 21 1/2 x 29 1/2 ins / 54.5 x 75 cm) USD 2,090. MILAN, 22 Nov 1993, *Children's Book* (1955, oil on canvas, 39 1/4 x 31 1/2 ins / 100 x 80 cm) ITL 9,192,000. ROME, 28 March 1995, *View of Turin* (1943, oil on canvas, 15 3/4 x 19 3/4 ins / 40 x 50 cm) ITL 7,820,000. MILAN, 2 April 1996, *Still-life* (1942, oil on canvas, 15 3/4 x 23 1/2 ins / 40 x 60 cm) ITL 9,775,000. MILAN, 11 April 2000, *Teutoco* (1988, oil on canvas, 55 x 80 ins / 139 x 204 cm) ITL 10,000,000. PRATO, 24 Nov 2000, *Untitled* (pigment and glue on canvas, 39 x 28 ins / 100 x 71 cm) ITL 7,500,000. FLORENCE, 19 Nov 2001, *Three Black* (1959, sand and mixed media on canvas, 17 x 46 ins / 43 x 116 cm) ITL 9,500,000. FLORENCE, 19 Nov 2001, *Witch 3* (1963, sand, mixed media and collage on canvas, 35 x 93 ins / 90 x 235 cm) ITL 18,000,000. FLORENCE, 16 May 2002, *Repetition* (1959, mixed media on canvas, 45 x 96 ins / 114 x 244 cm) EUR 14,000. PRATO, 25 May 2002, *Metro Barbes* (1948, oil on canvas, 26 x 20 ins / 65 x 50 cm) EUR 6,200. VERCELLI, 1 May 2003, *Composition* (1989, glue on canvas, 39 x 28 ins / 100 x 72 cm) EUR 6,500. MILAN, 24 Nov 2003, *Red One* (1972, acrylic, 69 x 92 ins / 175 x 234 cm) EUR 8,500. MILAN, 19 May 2004, *Composition* (1990, mixed media and glue on card, 20 x 14 ins / 50 x 35 cm) EUR 2,000. MILAN, 14 June 2004, *Still-life* (1949, oil on canvas, 20 x 29 ins / 50 x 73 cm) EUR 15,500.

SCIAMERONE, Pippo. See **FURINI Filippo**

SCIAMINOSSI, Raffaello.
See **SCHIAMINOSSI**

SCIAMPAGNA, Giovanni. See **CHAMPAGNE Jean**

SCIANZI, Giacomo, or erroneously known as Schanzi or Schanz
German, 17th - 18th century.
Active in Breslau (now Wroclaw, Poland) 1680-1700.
Painter, architect. Landscapes.

Scianzi painted the dome frescoes of the cathedral in Breslau.

AUCTION RECORDS:
PARIS, 4 Nov 1943, *Bay of Naples,* FRF 580.

SCIARA, Ketty di, pseudonym of Balletti Notarbartolo di Sciara, Ketty
Italian, 20th century.
Born in Palermo.
Painter, sculptor. Figures, nudes, interiors, landscapes, still-lifes.

Ketty di Sciara lived and worked in Palermo and Rome. She knew De Chirico, who advised her in her work. She has held many solo exhibitions in Italy and also abroad, in Paris, Toronto, São Paulo, New York and Tunis.

AUCTION RECORDS:
PARIS, 12 Oct 1992, *Landscape at Sunset* (oil on canvas, 35 1/2 x 47 1/4 ins / 90 x 120 cm) FRF 2,900.

SCIARANO. See **SCHERANO**

SCIARRA, Giuseppe
Italian, 17th century.
Active in Tricarico in 1648.
Painter.

Sciarra painted the *Legend of St Anthony of Padua* in the cloisters of the monastery of St Anthony in Tricarico.

SCIAVARRELLO, Nunzio
Italian, 20th century.
Born 1918, in Bronte (Sicily).
Painter, engraver, draughtsman. Nudes, still-lifes. Stage sets.

Nunzio Sciavarrello's work featured in the exhibition *Il Sentimento delle Cose* (*The Feeling of Things*) held at the Biblioteca Civica in Verolanuova in Lombardy in 1993.

His engravings of nudes are full of a feeling of movement, the sharp lines cut deep into the engraved plate.

BIBLIOGRAPHY:
Il Sentimento delle cose - Un percorso della grafica italiana contemporanea, exhibition catalogue, Biblioteca civica, Ed. Gall. civica d'arte moderna e contemporanea, Verolanuova, 1993.

SCIBELLI, Vinzenzo
Italian, 18th century.
Active in Naples.
Painter.

Scibelli was the pupil of F. Solimena.

SCIBEZZI
Italian, 20th century.
Painter. Landscapes.

Scibezzi was awarded third prize in the Burano painting competition in 1946.

SCIENZIA, Vettore
Italian, 16th century.
Born in Feltre (Belluno); died 1547 or 1548, in Venice.
Sculptor (wood).

Working in collaboration with Vincenzo da Trento, Vettore Scienzia carved the ceiling of the civic hospital in Venice in 1519.

SCIEPMANS, Gauthier. See **SCHIPMANS**

SCIFFELIN, Hans. See **SCHÄUFFELIN**

SCIFONI, Anatolio
Italian, 19th century.
Born 2 May 1841, in Florence; died 1884, in Rome.
Painter. Portraits, genre scenes, scenes with figures, interiors with figures, landscapes.

Anatolio Scifoni was a student at the Surikov Institute of Fine Art in Moscow and became a member of the Russian Union of Artists. He exhibited in Rome and, abroad, at the salons of Paris, Vienna, London, Monaco and Philadelphia.

AUCTION RECORDS:
NEW YORK, 12 Jan 1974, *The Artist's Studio,* USD 6,000. ROME, 24 May 1988, *Juno's Sacred Peacocks Feeding* (oil on canvas, 30 3/4 x 22 1/2 ins / 78 x 57 cm) ITL 6,000,000. LYONS, 4 March 2001, *Young Beggar Girl* (oil on canvas) FRF 20,000.

SCIFONI, Enrico
Italian, 19th - 20th century.
Painter, draughtsman. Religious subjects, portraits, still-lifes.

Enrico Scifoni studied drawing with Tommaso Minardi and painting with Francesco Podesti, Luigi Fontana and Capaldi. He also attended the art school in Rome. The King of Italy made him a knight of the Order of St Maurice. Later, having painted portraits of Princes of Naples, he was awarded the Order of the Cross, and Prince Nico of Montenegro awarded him the Order of St Daniel. He entered the Alinari art competiton of 1900 with his painting *Madonna and Child*.

AUCTION RECORDS:
MILAN, 14 May 1988, *Still-life with Figs* (1929, ink and pencil, 8 1/2 x 11 ins / 21.5 x 28 cm) ITL 9,000,000. PARIS, 2 Dec 1992, *Portrait of a Man with Decorations* (oil on canvas, 50 1/2 x 34 1/4 ins / 128 x 87 cm) FRF 3,600.

SCIFRONDI, Antonio. See **CIFRONDI Antonio**

SCILLA, Agostino, or Silla
Italian, 17th century.
Born 10 August 1629, in Messina; died 31 May 1700, in Rome.

Painter. Portraits, genre scenes, landscapes, still-lifes. Scilla was the pupil of Antonio Ricci, known as Il Barbalunga. Thanks to the influence of his master, he was awarded a grant by the Senate in Messina to continue his studies in Rome, where he studied under Andrea Sacchi for four years. On returning to his native city he opened a very popular academy, but political upheavals there obliged him to leave for Rome, where he ended his career.

He painted interesting landscapes with animals and excelled in the depiction of heads of old men, the realism of which is much admired. He was also a poet, numismatist and scholar.

He was represented in a collective thematic exhibition devoted to still-life in Italy entitled *Stille Welt. Italienische Stilleben aus drei Jahrhunderten* (Still World. Three Centuries of Italian Still-life) mounted at the Kunsthalle der Hypo-Kulturstiftung in Munich in 2003.

BIBLIOGRAPHY:
Hyerace, Luigi, *Agostino Scilla: per un catalogo delle opere*, Societa messinese di storia patria, Messina, 2001. Gregori, Mina/Prinz, Johann Georg, *Stille Welt. Italienische Stilleben aus drei Jahrhunderten*, exhibition catalogue, Kunsthalle der Hypo-Kulturstiftung, Munich, 2003.

MUSEUMS AND GALLERIES:
BOSTON (MFA): *Portrait of the Painter Andrea Sacchi* - ROME (Gal. dell'Accademia Nazionale di S Luca): *St Jerome.*

AUCTION RECORDS:
LONDON, 1 Nov 1991, *Still-life with a Hare and a Pair of Dead Plovers, Red Mullet, Oysters and Lemons on a Stone Entablature* (oil on canvas, 27 1/4 x 37 3/4 ins / 69.5 x 96 cm) GBP 5,280.

SCILLA, Giacinto
Italian, 17th - 18th century.
Born in Messina; died 1711, in Rome.
Painter. Animals.
Giacinto Scilla was the younger brother and assistant of Agostino Scilla.

SCILLA, Giacomo. See **LONGHI Silla** or **Scilla Giacomo**

SCILLA, Saverio
Italian, 17th - 18th century.
Born 14 April 1673, in Messina; died 1748.
Painter.
Saverio Scilla, a numismatist and scholar, was the son of Agostino Scilla.

SCILLE MONNERET, Mireille.
See **MONNERET SCILLE**

SCILLEMAN, Ariaen
Dutch, 15th - 16th century.
Active in Antwerp from 1494 to 1517.
Painter.
Scilleman was a pupil of Quentin Matsys and is perhaps the same artist as the Master of the Morrison Triptych.

SCILTIAN, Gregorio
Russian-Armenian, 20th century.
Born 20 August 1900, in Rostov-on-Don; died 1 April 1985, in Rome.
Active from 1923 in Italy.
Painter, illustrator, watercolourist, designer.
Allegorical subjects, mythological subjects, figures, nudes, portraits, interiors, still-lifes. Stage sets.
Gregorio Sciltian left Russia in 1919 and went to Vienna, where he studied at the Akademie der Bildenden Künste. In 1923, he left for Italy and settled in Rome. Initially influenced by Cubism, Sciltian then abandoned this style for what George Waldemar has called 'the recall to order' and which was in fact a return to a scrupulous form of representation. Although he makes much of the potential of trompe-l'œil, his output cannot be considered realist. The world he represents is sometimes one of allegorical make-up, such as in his works *The School of Modernity* (1955) and *The Eternal Illusion* (1967), and occasionally he refers to historical genres: Classical still-lifes, conceits, and Caravaggesque scenes, such as *Trasteverino: Bacchus in the Inn* (1935). The ambiguity that marks Sciltian's output no doubt derives from these works, and leads some to deem him a Surrealist. Sciltian's very theatrical settings are more comprehensible when one realises that he was also a set painter: he worked for La Scala in Milan, and the Florence festival. As a decorative painter he also designed pictures for an Italian cruise ship.

Between 1926 and 1933, work by him was shown on several occasions in Paris (at the Salon d'Automne, the Salon des Indépendants and the Salon des Tuileries), from 1952 on several occasions in Rome (at the Quadriennale) and Venice (at the Biennale). Following his first solo exhibition, in Rome in 1925, there were frequent exhibitions of his work, in Milan (1933, 1936, 1938, 1949, 1953), Paris (1929, 1920, 1932, 1949, 1953, 1958, 1966), Venice (1955, 1958, 1973), New York (1966), and Ferrara (1986, at the Palazzo dei Diamanti).

G. Sciltian

BIBLIOGRAPHY:
Civello, Renato, *Sciltian - Opera Omnia*, Verico Hoepli, Milan, 1986.

MUSEUMS AND GALLERIES:
PARIS (former Mus. du Luxembourg): *The Florist.*

AUCTION RECORDS:
MILAN, 25 Nov 1980, *Vase of Flowers* (oil on canvas, 35 1/2 x 23 1/2 ins / 90 x 60 cm) ITL 7,200,000. MILAN, 16 June 1981, *Still-life* (mixed media/brown paper, 8 1/2 x 10 3/4 ins / 21.5 x 27.5 cm) ITL 4,200,000. MILAN, 25 Nov 1982, *Seated Model* (pen drawing heightened with white, 19 1/2 x 12 3/4 ins / 49.5 x 32.5 cm) ITL 1,600,000. MILAN, 4 April 1984, *Fugue* (watercolour and tempera/mounted card, 13 3/4 x 20 1/4 ins / 35 x 51.5 cm) ITL 2,800,000. ROME, 3 Dec 1985, *Still-life with Pistols and Playing Cards* (1952, oil on canvas, 24 3/4 x 19 ins / 63 x 48 cm) ITL 10,500,000. ROME, 20 May 1986, *Still-life with Vase of Flowers* (1922, oil on canvas, 29 1/2 x 35 3/4 ins / 75 x 91 cm) ITL 7,500,000. ROME, 17 April 1989, *Still-life with a Plate of Patisserie* (oil on canvas, 6 3/4 x 9 ins / 17 x 22 cm) ITL 16,000,000. ROME, 8 June 1989, *Still-life with Crayfish* (oil on panel, 15 x 22 ins / 38 x 55 cm) ITL 28,000,000. MILAN, 7 Nov 1989, *Nude from Behind with a Mirror* (oil on canvas, 35 1/2 x 25 1/2 ins / 90 x 65 cm) ITL 34,500,000. ROME, 6 Dec 1989, *Still-life* (1932, oil/plywood, 19 3/4 x 15 3/4 ins / 50 x 40 cm) ITL 20,700,000. MILAN, 12 June 1990, *The Magical Library* (oil on canvas, 41 1/2 x 45 1/4 ins / 105.5 x 115 cm) ITL 70,000,000. MILAN, 13 Dec 1990, *Still-life* (1937, oil on panel, 14 1/4 x 22 ins / 36.5 x 55 cm) ITL 31,000,000. ROME, 13 May 1991, *Still-life with Candle and Book* (oil on canvas, 9 3/4 x 14 1/4 ins / 25 x 36 cm) ITL 9,200,000. MILAN, 19 Dec 1991, *Portrait of a Woman* (oil on panel, 21 1/4 x 17 3/4 ins / 54 x 45 cm) ITL 17,000,000. MILAN, 9 Nov 1992, *The Artist's Studio* (oil on canvas, 25 1/2 x 29 1/2 ins / 65 x 75 cm) ITL 44,000,000. ROME, 19 Nov 1992, *The Departure* (1944, oil on panel, 41 x 29 1/4 ins / 104 x 74 cm) ITL 46,000,000. MILAN, 15 Dec 1992, *The Magical Library* (oil on canvas, 41 1/2 x 45 1/4 ins / 105.5 x 115 cm) ITL 95,000,000. MILAN, 16 Nov 1993, *Head of a Young Girl* (oil on canvas, 15 3/4 x 13 3/4 ins / 40 x 35 cm) ITL 26,450,000. MILAN, 24 May 1994, *Still-life* (1938, oil on canvas, 20 x 27 1/2 ins / 50.5 x 70 cm) ITL 24,150,000. MILAN, 22 June 1995, *Portrait of Lisetta Ponti* (oil on canvas, 15 x 11 1/2 ins / 38 x 29 cm) ITL 11,500,000. MILAN, 28 May 1996, *Cosmos and Microcosmos* (oil on canvas, 41 1/4 x 37 1/2 ins / 105 x 95 cm) ITL 80,400,000. MILAN, 25 Nov 1996, *The Bibliophile* (oil on canvas, 19 1/4 x 16 1/4 ins / 49 x 41.5 cm) ITL 13,800,000. ROME, 27 April 1999, *Magician* (oil on canvas,

24 x 16 ins / 60 x 40 cm) ITL 25,000,000. VENICE, 13 Nov 1999, *Lady by Red Curtain* (oil on panel, 21 x 17 ins / 54 x 44 cm) ITL 25,200,000. MILAN, 30 May 2000, *Rustic Kitchen* (oil on canvas, 33 x 37 ins / 85 x 95 cm) ITL 35,000,000. MILAN, 12 Dec 2000, *Still-life with Curtain and Mandolino* (oil on canvas, 33 x 28 ins / 85 x 70 cm) ITL 33,000,000. MILAN, 20 Nov 2001, *Portrait of Woman* (oil on canvas, 20 x 14 ins / 50 x 35 cm) ITL 6,000,000. FLORENCE, 16 May 2002, *Man from Trastevere* (1970, oil on canvas, 34 x 26 ins / 86 x 65 cm) EUR 24,000. MILAN, 21 May 2002, *Still-life with Pomegranates* (oil on canvas, 35 x 35 ins / 90 x 90 cm) EUR 14,000. MILAN, 27 May 2003, *Journey on Mysterious Island* (oil on board, 43 x 65 ins / 110 x 165 cm) EUR 25,000. MILAN, 28 Oct 2003, *Composition with Shell, Monocular in Seascape* (oil on board, 28 x 22 ins / 70 x 55 cm) EUR 10,000. NEW YORK, 6 May 2004, *Corsican Landscape* (oil on canvas, 24 x 20 ins / 61 x 50 cm) USD 14,000. MILAN, 24 May 2004, *Self-portrait* (oil on canvas, 18 x 14 ins / 45 x 35 cm) EUR 14,000.

SCIORINI, Lorenzo, also known as Lorenzo della Sciorina, called Vaiani
Italian, 16th century.
Born between 1540 and 1550, in Florence; died 1 June 1598, in Florence.
Painter.

A pupil of Allori, Lorenzo Sciorini worked on the decoration of Michelangelo's catafalque.

MUSEUMS AND GALLERIES:
FLORENCE (Mus. Mediceo): *Portrait of Eleonora of Toledo; Portrait of Don Garcia.*

SCIORTINI, Gaetano. See **SORTINO**

SCIORTINO, Antonio or Anthony
British, 20th century.
Born 12 February 1881, in Malta.
Sculptor. Busts, statues.

Antonio Sciortino trained at the Institute of Fine Art in Rome. He specialised in tombs and funerary effigies, and exhibited a work with the Royal Academy in 1925.

MUSEUMS AND GALLERIES:
JOHANNESBURG (Art Gallery): *Bust of Adrian Dingle.*

AUCTION RECORDS:
LOS ANGELES, 22 Oct 1980, *Rythmi Vitæ* (1927, bronze, h. 21 ins / 53.5 cm) USD 1,100.

SCIORTINO, Stéphane
French, 20th century.
Born 28 March 1925, in Paris.
Painter. Landscapes.

Sciortino was a student at the École des Beaux-Arts de Paris. As of 1954 he participated in regional group exhibitions, where he was honoured with numerous distinctions. He also regularly exhibited in Paris, including at the Salon d'Automne, of which he was a member from 1972, Salon des Indépendants from 1970, Salon des Artistes Français and Salon des Terres Latines from 1971, Salon des Peintres Témoins de Leur Temps in 1972, Salon de la Société Nationale des Beaux-Arts from 1975 and the Salon de la Marine from 1992.

MUSEUMS AND GALLERIES:
ALÈS - PARIS (MAMVP).

AUCTION RECORDS:
RHEIMS, 23 Oct 1988, *Paimpol* (oil on canvas, 18 x 24 ins / 46 x 61 cm) FRF 4,500. RHEIMS, 5 March 1989, *Audierne, the Fishing Port* (oil on canvas, 24 x 15 ins / 61 x 38 cm) FRF 4,500. VERSAILLES, 10 Dec 1989, *New York Transparencies* (1989, oil on canvas, 32 x 39 1/4 ins / 81 x 100 cm) FRF 21,000.

SCIOVINO, Niccolò
Italian, 16th century.
Active in Ferrara.
Marquetry worker.

Niccolò Sciovino made the choir stalls in the church of S Benedetto in Ferrara.

SCIPIO
Dutch (?), 15th century.
Painter (?). Religious subjects.

Scipio is the supposed surname or forename of a master active in Paris about 1490.

MUSEUMS AND GALLERIES:
PARIS (Louvre): *Descent from the Cross.*

SCIPION
16th century.
Died 22nd December 1578, in Mechelen.
Painter.

SCIPION, Jehan
French, 16th century.
Active in Paris c. 1558.
Painter. Portraits.

Jehan Scipion painted a portrait that was bought by Caterina de' Medici for the château of Monceaux. He may be the same artist as the painter Scipion who died in Mechelen.

SCIPIONE, pseudonym of Gino Bonichi
Italian, 20th century.
Born 1904, in Macerata (Marche); died 1933, in Arco.
Painter, draughtsman, illustrator. Allegorical subjects, mythological subjects, figures, portraits, urban landscapes, animals.
School of Rome group, Scuola di via Cavour group.

Famous in his lifetime as a larger-than-life personality, the extremely handsome Scipione (Scipio) took his nickname from his resemblance to a Roman warrior. He was a mystical yet practical bohemian who suffered from tuberculosis. His influence, a reaction against the often gratuitous formalism of the Novecento group, was beginning to make itself felt at the time of his premature death and is still important today. He sought to show the value not so much of the neo-Romanticism that he advocated, as of the fully-mastered art of painting itself. His combination of a romantic sensibility and a more modern expressionist language resulted in a number of powerful works such as his *Roman Courtesan* and *Piazza Navona,* both of 1930. He worked as an illustrator for the journal *La Fiera Letteraria* (*The Literary Fair*) and composed a number of poems.

Scipione participated in a number of collective exhibitions including the Venice Biennale (1930) and the Rome Quadriennale (1931). In his lifetime he held solo exhibitions from 1928 at the Galleria d'Arte Moderna in Rome. Posthumous retrospectives of his work were mounted at the art gallery in Macerata after his death, one in 1948 at and another to mark the fiftieth anniversary of his birth in 1954.

MUSEUMS AND GALLERIES:
MONTEVIDEO (MMA) - ROME (Gal. Nazionale d'Arte Moderna) - TEL AVIV (MMA) - TURIN (Gal. Civica d'Arte Moderna e Contemporanea).

AUCTION RECORDS:
MILAN, April 1950, *Horse,* ITL 500,000. MILAN, 29 March 1977, *Argument* (1929, pen and red ink, 11 1/2 x 12 1/4 ins / 29 x 31 cm) ITL 1,700,000. MILAN, 7 June 1977, *Poetess* (hardboard, 17 3/4 x 14 1/4 ins / 45 x 36 cm) ITL 18,000,000. LONDON, 28 June 1977, *Portrait of a Seated Woman* (1909, pencil and coloured chalks, 18 x 12 1/2 ins / 45.5 x 31.5 cm) GBP 4,500. MILAN, 25 Nov 1980, *St John Lateran* (1932, oil on canvas,

17¾ x 20 ins / 45 x 51 cm) ITL 46,000,000. MILAN, 17 Nov 1981, *Collepardo* (pen, 6¼ x 8½ ins / 16 x 21.7 cm) ITL 2,000,000. MILAN, 15 Nov 1983, *Ill Assorted Couple* (pen and bistre ink, 12¾ x 8½ ins / 32.5 x 21.3 cm) ITL 12,500,000. ROME, 5 Dec 1983, *Temptation of Eve* (1930, oil on panel, 15¼ x 19¼ ins / 39 x 49 cm) ITL 75,000,000. ROME, 3 Dec 1985, *Female Nude in an Interior* (1925, sepia ink and watercolour, 10¾ x 12 ins / 27.5 x 30.5 cm) ITL 14,500,000. MILAN, 15 May 1986, *Still-life with Figs* (1929, pen and pencil, 8½ x 11 ins / 21.5 x 28 cm) ITL 13,000,000. MILAN, 19 May 1987, *The Present* (1929, pen, 8½ x 8¼ ins / 21.5 x 21 cm) ITL 15,000,000. ROME, 28 Nov 1989, *Diana and Actaeon* (1927, oil on panel, 9 x 12¾ ins / 23 x 32.5 cm) ITL 72,000,000. MILAN, 17 May 1999, *Ox and Calf* (charcoal, 12 x 16 ins / 31 x 41 cm) ITL 11,000,000. MILAN, 17 Nov 1999, *Circe the Sorceress* (1929, ink, 10 x 9 ins / 25 x 23 cm) ITL 11,000,000. ROME, 18 April 2000, *Washerwomen* (sepia ink and watercolour, 6 x 7 ins / 16 x 19 cm) ITL 10,000,000. MILAN, 28 Nov 2000, *The Hunters' Inn* (Indian ink, 9 x 13 ins / 22 x 32 cm) ITL 7,500,000. PRATO, 29 May 2004, *Nudes in Ponte Sant'Angelo* (ink and watercolour on paper laid on cardboard, 7 x 9 ins / 18 x 22 cm) EUR 7,000. MILAN, 8 June 2004, *Apocalypse* (pencil, 18 x 24 ins / 45 x 60 cm) EUR 3,500.

SCIPIONE, Gaetano. See **POLZONE Scipio**

SCIPIONE DA AVERARA
Italian, 16th century.
Active in Bergamo during the first half of the 16th century.
Painter.

SCIPIONE DA CARONA. See **CASELLA Scipione da Carona**

SCIPIONE DI GUIDO
Italian, 16th - 17th century.
Active in Naples.
Sculptor (wood).
Scipione di Guido carved the choir stalls in Catania Cathedral.

SCIPIONI, Antonio
Italian, 15th century.
Died before 1488.
Active in Averara.
Painter.
Antonio Scipioni was the father of Battista, Giacomo and Jacopino Scipioni.

SCIPIONI, Battista or Giovanni Battista
Italian, 15th century.
Active in Bergamo from 1486 to 1488.
Painter.
The son of Antonio Scipioni, Battista Scipioni worked with his brothers Giacomo and Jacopino.

SCIPIONI, Giacomo
Italian, 16th century.
Died after 1529.
Active in Averara.
Painter.
Giacomo Scipioni was the son of Antonio Scipioni.

SCIPIONI, Jacopino
Italian, 16th century.
Died between 13 March 1532 and 4 August 1543.
Active in Averara and in Bergamo.
Painter.
The son of Antonio Scipioni, Jacopino Scipioni painted many frescoes in the churches of Bergamo.

SCIPTIUS, Georg Christian. See **SEIPTIUS**

SCISLO, Jan
Polish, 18th century.
Born c. 1729; died 6 July 1804.
Painter.
Jan Scislo is thought to have studied under M. Bacciarelli. He produced paintings of several castles. The National Museum in Warsaw owns two landscapes by him.

SCITA, Pietro. See **SITA**

SCITIVAUX DE GREISCHE, Anatole de, or de Greysche
French, 19th century.
Born 1812, in Nancy.
Painter, watercolourist. Hunting scenes, horses.
He made his Salon debut in 1857 and was active until 1876.

SCITIVAUX DE GREISCHE, Roger de, or de Greysche
French, 19th century.
Born 20 October 1830, in Nancy; died 6 February 1870, in Paris.
Painter. Genre scenes, portraits.
A pupil of Couture, this artist debuted at the Salon in 1857. The Musée de Nancy, eastern France, has a *Study of the Head of a Young Girl* by him.

SCIULLO, Bernard di
French, 20th century.
Born 1930.
Painter.
Sciullo participated in the Salon des Réalités Nouvelles in Paris, most notably in 1986, 1988 and 1989, as well as in Groupe 190. His style and the pictorial feel of his work approach Expressionism, and an anthropomorphic aspect can be read in the gestural lines, at least in the faces.

SCIUTI, Giuseppe, or Patti Sciuto
Italian, 19th - 20th century.
Born 5 March 1834, in Zafferana Etnea (Sicily); died 14 March 1911, in Rome.
Painter (mixed media). Mythological subjects, figures, genre scenes, landscapes.
Originally intending to become a doctor, Giuseppe Sciuti abandoned his studies to become an artist. He was a pupil of Gandalfo.

He participated in a number of major exhibitions, often abroad and including Vienna and London. The Royal Scottish Academy in Edinburgh showed his work in 1872. He painted sets for the theatre in Palermo for a production of *The Triumph of King Ruggero the Norman*.

MUSEUMS AND GALLERIES:
CATANIA (Mus. Civico di Castello Ursino): *The Widow*; *Betrayed* - MILAN (Gal. d'Arte Moderna): *Pindar Singing the Praises of a Victor at the Olympic Games* - MILAN (Pinacoteca di Brera): *Greek Wedding* - PALERMO (Gal. d'Arte Moderna): *Funeral of Timoleon* - ROME (Gal. Nazionale d'Arte Moderna): *Restauratio Aerarii*; *In the Temple of Venus* - ZAFFERANO (Etna): *Etna Erupting*.

AUCTION RECORDS:
ROME, 14 Dec 1988, *Woman in Traditional Costume* (oil on canvas, 17½ x 13 ins / 44.5 x 33 cm) ITL 900,000. STOCKHOLM, 15 Nov 1989, *Interior with Women and Two Children* (oil, 25½ x 20 ins / 65 x 51 cm) SEK 47,000. ROME, 28 May 1991, *Girl Playing a Cithara* (mixed media/grey paper, 11¼ x 8¼ ins / 28.5 x 21 cm) ITL 2,400,000. ROME, 14 Nov 1991, *Temple of Venus* (oil on canvas, 21¼ x 29¼ ins / 54 x 74 cm) ITL 40,250,000. ROME, 27 April 1993, *Roman Lady* (oil on canvas, 15¾ x 14¼ ins / 40 x 36 cm) ITL 2,927,700. ROME, 13 May 2000, *Post Prandium* (oil on canvas, 18 x 24 ins / 46 x 61 cm) ITL 15,000,000. VENICE, 8 July 2000, *Mythological Figures* (oil on canvas, 24 x 18 ins / 62 x 45 cm) ITL 12,000,000. MILAN, 5 June 2001, *Roman Scene: Concert* (oil on canvas, 21 x 26 ins / 53 x 66 cm) ITL 29,000,000. LONDON, 19 Nov 2003, *Tribute to Caesar* (oil on canvas, 29 x 53 ins / 74 x 135 cm) GBP 12,000.

ROME, 23 June 2004, *Bust of Ancient Roman* (oil on canvas, 37 x 23 ins / 93 x 59 cm) EUR 3,800.

SCKELL, Carl August, or Skell
German, 19th century.
Born 14 November 1793, in Karlberg, near Zweibrücken; died 10 July 1840, in Munich.
Lithographer.

Sckell engraved architectural views and views of gardens. He was also a horticulturist.

SCKELL, Fritz, or Skell
German, 20th century.
Born 1 August 1885, in Munich.
Painter, draughtsman, illustrator. Figures, landscapes, animals.

Fritz Sckell produced illustrations for medical, biological and zoological publications; he travelled extensively in the Far East.

AUCTION RECORDS:
ZURICH, 7 June 1980, *Lake Landscape* (1929, oil on canvas, 31 x 37 1/2 ins / 78.5 x 95.5 cm) CHF 4,600. MUNICH, 28 March 2001, *Batakmutter* (oil on canvas, 49 x 29 ins / 125 x 73 cm) DEM 4,000. MUNICH, 4 July 2001, *Holy Night* (oil on board, 31 x 39 ins / 80 x 100 cm) DEM 4,000. LUCERNE, 16 June 2004, *Malayasian Bathing Scene* (oil on canvas, 31 x 56 ins / 78 x 142 cm) CHF 2,600.

SCKELL, Louis
German, 19th - 20th century.
Born 1869, in Munich; died 1950, in Bad Tölz.
Painter. Landscapes.

Louis Sckell was the son of Ludwig Sckell; he painted landscapes, chiefly of forests.

AUCTION RECORDS:
COLOGNE, 20 Oct 1989, *Hunting Party* (oil on panel, 8 1/2 x 11 1/4 ins / 21.5 x 28.5 cm) DEM 3,500. VIENNA, 14 March 2000, *Moonlit Pond* (oil on canvas, 31 x 26 ins / 78 x 65 cm) ATS 28,000. MUNICH, 2 July 2003, *Mountain Farmstead by a Stream* (oil on canvas, 22 x 27 ins / 55 x 68 cm) EUR 1,500.

SCKELL, Ludwig, or Skell
German, 19th century.
Born 1842, in Obergünzburg; died 31 March 1905, in Munich.
Painter. Portraits, genre scenes, landscapes.

AUCTION RECORDS:
NEW YORK, 18 Sept 1981, *Alpine Landscape* (oil on panel, 8 1/4 x 11 ins / 21 x 27 cm) CAD 2,900. VIENNA, 16 Nov 1983, *Stags in Mountain Landscape* (oil on canvas, 19 3/4 x 27 1/2 ins / 50 x 70 cm) ATS 50,000. MUNICH, 14 March 1985, *Isartal* (oil on canvas, 16 1/4 x 26 ins / 41 x 66 cm) DEM 14,000.

SCKELL, Ludwig, or Ludwig von, or Skell
German, 19th - 20th century.
Born 14 October 1833, in Schloss Berg (Starnberger See); died 23 February 1912, in Pasing, near Munich.
Painter. Mountainscapes, waterscapes, landscapes.

Son of a royal gardener and father of Louis Sckell, Ludwig Sckell studied at the fine arts academy in Munich under Richard Zimmermann. He is a representative of German landscape Romanticism influenced after 1860 by Eduard Schleich the Elder, notably by the latter's use of harmonious warm browns.

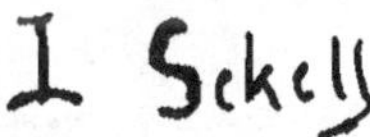

MUSEUMS AND GALLERIES:
MAINZ: *Landscape.*

AUCTION RECORDS:
MUNICH, 11 Dec 1968, *Mountain Landscape*, DEM 3,600. COLOGNE, 23 March 1973, *Waterfall*, DEM 4,500. LONDON, 12 June 1974, *Landscape with Flock*, GBP 1,400. NEW YORK, 2 April 1976, *Mountain Village* (oil on canvas, 25 1/2 x 34 ins / 65 x 85.5 cm) USD 3,900. STUTTGART, 23 Feb 1978, *Farmhouse near a River* (oil on canvas, 25 1/2 x 33 1/2 ins / 65 x 85 cm) DEM 17,800. MUNICH, 6 Nov 1981, *Storm-Tossed Landscape* (oil on panel, 10 x 12 1/2 ins / 24.5 x 32 cm) DEM 6,800. LUCERNE, 19 May 1983, *Couple of Peasants on a Country Road* (oil on canvas, 16 1/2 x 23 1/2 ins / 42.2 x 60 cm) CHF 17,000. COPENHAGEN, 7 Nov 1984, *Mountainous Landscape* (oil on canvas, 21 1/4 x 29 1/4 ins / 54 x 74 cm) DKK 40,000. LONDON, 27 Nov 1985, *River Landscape* (oil on canvas, 20 1/2 x 30 3/4 ins / 52 x 78 cm) GBP 4,000. MUNICH, 10 Dec 1992, *Landscape with Peasant Monks* (oil on panel, 5 x 10 1/4 ins / 13 x 26 cm) DEM 11,300. MUNICH, 27 June 1995, *Wooded River Landscape near Regen* (oil on canvas, 17 1/4 x 35 1/2 ins / 44 x 90 cm) DEM 11,500. VIENNA, 29-30 Oct 1996, *Little Girl Feeding Ducks* (1880, oil on canvas, 21 x 35 ins / 52.5 x 88 cm) ATS 149,500. MUNICH, 2 Dec 1997, *Mating Season in the Marshlands* (oil on wood, 6 1/4 x 9 1/2 ins / 16 x 24 cm) DEM 4,800.

SCKRETAR, Johann. See **SCHRÖTER**

SCKTTI, Ivan, or Scotti
Russian, 19th century.
Died 1832, in St Petersburg.
Painter, decorative designer.

SCLATER, Robert
British, 19th century.
Active in Edinburgh from 1826 to 1838.
Medallist.

SCLIAR, Carlos
Brazilian, 20th century.
Born 1920.
Painter, draughtsman. Military subjects, figures, landscapes, Still-lifes.

Carlos Scliar fought in Italy in World War II.

Under the influence of Candido Portinari and Lasar Segall, his earliest painting was social, dominated by the human figure, also expressionist affected by Cubism. He brought lyrical drawings in Indian ink back from the Italian front then developed his work with still-lifes.

AUCTION RECORDS:
SÃO PAULO, 11 Aug 1981, *Boats* (1975, oil/hardboard, 14 1/2 x 22 ins / 37 x 56 cm) BRL 200,000. RIO DE JANEIRO, 7 Dec 1983, *Fruit* (1964, vinyl and collage, 25 1/2 x 39 1/4 ins / 65 x 100 cm) BRL 2,050,000.

SCLIEF, Pierre. See **SCHLEIFF**

SCLOBAS, Charles Joseph
Flemish School, 18th century.
Born 5 February 1753.
Active in Mons.
Sculptor.

Charles Joseph Sclobas was the brother of Jean-Baptiste Sclobas.

SCLOBAS, Jean-Baptiste
Flemish School, 18th century.
Born 7 April 1744.
Active in Mons.
Sculptor.

Jean-Baptiste Sclobas was the brother of Charles Joseph Sclobas.

SCLOPIS, Ignazio
Italian, 18th century.
Born in Turin; died 4 October 1793.

Draughtsman, engraver (burin). Urban landscapes, panoramas.
Sclopis engraved panoramic views of Italian towns.
Auction records:
Bern, 21 June 1985, *Prospetto generale della Città di Napoli* (1764, etching/three continuous sheets, 17 1/4 x 82 ins / 44 x 208.5 cm) CHF 5,200.

SCOBL, Michael. See **SKOBL Mikhail**

SCOCCHERA, Alfredo
Italian, 20th century.
Born 1887, in Baselice (Abruzzi); died 1955, in Milan.
Painter. Religious subjects, genre scenes, landscapes.
A pupil of Francesco Paolo Michetti, Alfredo Scocchera executed the decorative paintings in Milan cemetery and in the churches in Assisi and Loreto.
Auction records:
Milan, 29 Oct 1992, *View of a Lake in Lombardy* (oil on canvas mounted to board, 9 3/4 x 13 1/2 ins / 25 x 34.5 cm) ITL 2,800,000. Milan, 9 Nov 1993, *Palazzo Sforzesco in Milan* (oil on panel, 15 3/4 x 11 3/4 ins / 40 x 30 cm) ITL 1,150,000. Milan, 18 Dec 1996, *Horses on the Tow-Path, Milan* (1926, oil on panel, 10 3/4 x 8 ins / 27.5 x 20.5 cm) ITL 1,747,000.

SCOCCIANTI, Andrea di Angelo, called Il Raffaello delle Fogliarelle or Il Pulcinella
Italian, 17th - 18th century.
Born 1640, in Massaccio; died 1730.
Sculptor, stucco artist.
Andrea Scoccianti worked in Rome, Modena and Massaccio.

SCOCCIANTI, Angelo
Italian, 17th - 18th century.
Born 1672; died 1762.
Sculptor, stucco artist.
Angelo Scoccianti, the son of Andrea Scoccianti, worked in Rome.

SCOCCIANTI, Cosmo or Cosma or Cosimo
Italian, 17th - 18th century.
Born 1642, in Massaccio; died 1720.
Sculptor, stucco artist.
Cosmo Scoccianti was the brother of Andrea di Angelo Scoccianti.

SCODA, Guillermo. See **SCADA**

SCOENENBERGHE, Hendryck van, or Schoenenberghe
Flemish School, 15th century.
Died between 1492 and 1494.
Active in Louvain.
Glass painter.
Son of Jan van Scoenenberghe, Hendryk van Scoenenberghe was a master in 1450, and worked for the Town Hall of Louvain in 1487, the church of St Sulpice, Diest, in 1492, and the Parc Abbey in Louvain.

SCOENENBERGHE, Jan van, or Schoenenberghe
Flemish School, 15th century.
Died before 4 April 1458.
Glass painter.
Jan van Scoenenberghe was the father of Hendryck and Tilman Scoenenberghe, worked in Louvain from 1426, and painted windows for the church of Averbode in 1434, for the 'Blauscœsen Put' in 1441, the church of Werchter in 1446, and the church of St Quentin in 1453.

SCOENENBERGHE, Tilman van, or Schoenenberghe
Flemish School, 15th century.
Died 1484.
Active in Louvain.
Glass painter.
Tilman van Scoenenberghe was a son of Jan van Scoenenberghe.

SCOENERE. See **STOEVERE**

SCOEUWESHUESEN, Hinrich
German, 16th century.
Born to a family originally from Bremen.
Active c. 1580.
Sculptor.
Scoeuweshuesen carved a *Last Judgement* in the central porch of the church of Our Lady, Lünenburg.

SCOFIELD, William Bacon, or Schofield
American, 19th - 20th century.
Born 8 February 1864, in Hartford; died 22 January 1930, in Worcester.
Painter, sculptor.
William Scofield studied under Gutzon Borglum. He was also a writer.

SCOGNAMIGLIO, Antonio Giovanni
Italian, 18th - 19th century.
Painter. Scenes with figures, genre scenes.
Scognamiglio was one of the painters engaged by the prince-archbishop of Naples to copy the great masters.
Museums and Galleries:
Naples (Mus. di Capodimonte): *Bohemian Woman*.
Auction records:
London, 2 April 1980, *Bedouin Encampment* (oil on canvas, 25 1/2 x 53 1/4 ins / 65 x 135 cm) GBP 600. London, 25 Nov 1983, *Arab Encampment* (oil on canvas, 26 x 53 ins / 66 x 134.7 cm) GBP 11,000. London, 4 Oct 1989, *Nomad Encampment in the Desert* (1883, oil on canvas, 17 x 35 ins / 43 x 89 cm) GBP 2,200. Rome, 28 May 1991, *Jousting* (oil on panel, 9 1/2 x 13 1/2 ins / 24 x 34 cm) ITL 1,200,000. New York, 16 July 1992, *Gypsy Musicians in a Barn* (oil on canvas, 29 1/2 x 19 1/4 ins / 74.9 x 48.9 cm) USD 3,300. London, 11 April 1995, *Sudden Tiredness* (oil on canvas, 36 1/4 x 22 ins / 92 x 56 cm) GBP 2,300. London, 12 June 1996, *Fortune Teller* (oil on canvas, 41 1/4 x 61 ins / 104.5 x 155 cm) GBP 8,625. Ickworth, 12 June 1996, *Bohemian Woman* (oil on canvas, after Correggio, 19 x 16 ins / 48.5 x 40.5 cm) GBP 8,050. London, 8 Oct 2002, *Reading Lesson* (oil on canvas, 41 x 29 ins / 104 x 74 cm) GBP 1,600. London, 18 Sept 2003, *Fishing in the Shadow of Vesuvius* (oil on canvas, 28 x 40 ins / 72 x 102 cm) GBP 2,200.

SCOHY, Jean
French, 19th century.
Born 1824, in Lyons; died 1896 or 1897, in Lyons.
Painter. Religious subjects, figures, portraits, genre scenes. Murals.
He was the pupil of Claude Bonnefond and Augustin Thierriat at the École des Beaux-Arts in Lyons. He exhibited at the Lyons Salon from 1848 to 1891.

He produced decorative panels for the Palais de la Bourse and the ceiling of the Bellecour theatre in Lyons. He also painted a commemorative plaque for the church of Notre-Dame St-Louis-de-la-Guillotière, in remembrance of the floods that hit La Guillotière on 31 May 1856.
Museums and Galleries:
Lyons (MBA): *Blonde Woman*.

SCOIDON, Richard
German, 18th century.
Active c. 1700 (?).
Painter.
Scoidon painted a *Still-life with Flowers and Rabbit*

SCOLAIO DI GIOVANNI
Italian, 15th century.

Active in Florence during the first half of the 15th century.
Painter.
Scolaio di Giovanni painted frescoes in the house of Francesco Datini in Prato.

SCOLARI, Giuseppe
Italian, 16th century.
Born in Vicenza.
Active in the second half of the 16th century.
Painter, fresco artist, engraver. Religious subjects, mythological subjects.
A pupil of J.B. Maganza, Giuseppe Scolari executed oil paintings and frescoes for churches in Venice, Verona and Vicenza. He also made engravings and woodcuts.
AUCTION RECORDS:
LONDON, 27 April 1977, *St Jerome* (woodcut, 21 x 15 ins / 53.1 x 37.2 cm) GBP 850. MUNICH, 29 May 1978, *Entombment* (woodcut) DEM 6,800. LONDON, 6 Dec 1983, *St George* (woodcut, 20 x 14 ins / 50.8 x 35.7 cm) GBP 1,600. LONDON, 26 June 1985, *St Jerome* (woodcut, 21 3/4 x 15 ins / 55.2 x 37.2 cm) GBP 1,900. PARIS, 26 March 1996, *Rape of Persephone* (woodcut) FRF 13,500.

SCOLARI, Stefano
Italian, 16th - 17th century.
Active in Venice.
Engraver. Maps.

SCOLARI, Stefano Mozzi
Italian, 17th century.
Active in Venice from 1650 to 1687.
Engraver. Cards.

SCOLES, John
American, 18th - 19th century.
Active in New York 1793-1844.
Engraver. Portraits, genre scenes.

SCOLES, Joseph John
British, 19th century.
Born 27 June 1798, in London; died 29 December 1863, in London.
Architect, draughtsman.
Joseph John Scoles was a celebrated architect who produced remarkable drawings of Greece and Syria during a study trip to the region. He also penned several works on Egypt and the Holy Land.

SCOLOPIS, Ignazio. See **SCLOPIS**

SCOMPARINI, Eugenio
Italian, 19th - 20th century.
Born 1845, in Trieste; died 18 March 1913.
Painter. Figures, portraits, genre scenes.
MUSEUMS AND GALLERIES:
TRIESTE (Civico Mus. Revoltella): *Marguerite Gauthier; Lady with Dog; Odalisque; Allegory Commemorating the Founder of the Museum.*
AUCTION RECORDS:
LONDON, 3 Oct 1979, *Ophelia Gathering Flowers* (1872, oil on canvas, 89 1/4 x 59 ins / 227 x 150 cm) GBP 1,100. MILAN, 13 June 2000, *Romantic Scene from Antiquity* (oil on canvas, oval, 27 x 35 ins / 68 x 89 cm) ITL 6,800,000. TRIESTE, 4 Dec 2001, *Beauty* (oil on canvas, 21 x 40 ins / 54 x 102 cm) ITL 24,000,000. VENICE, 12 April 2002, *Portrait of Woman with Bunch of Roses* (1876, oil on canvas, 37 x 28 ins / 95 x 70 cm) EUR 2,200. VENICE, 12 April 2002, *Man with Beard* (oil on canvas, 26 x 20 ins / 66 x 52 cm) EUR 2,800. TRIESTE, 20 Feb 2004, *Venice* (1868, oil on canvas, 20 x 24 ins / 50 x 62 cm) EUR 5,000.

SCONZANI, Ippolito
Italian, 18th century.
Of Bolognese origin.
Painter, decorative artist, fresco artist.
Ippolito Sconzani worked for the abbeys of Melk and St Florian in Austria.

SCONZANI, Leonardo, or Sconzain
Italian, 18th century.
Born 1695, in Bologna; died 1735, in Bologna.
Painter, miniaturist, designer of ornamental architectural features.
Leonardo was the nephew of Ippolito Sconzani and the pupil of Raimondo Manzini.

SCOPAS
4th century BC.
Born in Paros.
Active during the first half of the 4th century BC.
Sculptor, architect.
Ancient Greek.
Scopas worked with Bryaxis, Leochares and Timotheus on the sculptural decoration of the Mausoleum at Halicarnassus (c. 350 BC), his contribution being the *Battle of Greeks and Amazons*. Each group of this frieze is a miracle of balance and clarity, sufficient in itself, yet following through to the next group with great skill in a movement that is both ordered and impetuous. Remarkably, Scopas succeeds in giving new life to all the traditional schemas of a theme that had been repeated so many times before. Despite his innovations, Scopas' art seems restrained compared to that of Bryaxis and Leochares who, wishing to go further, carved figures full of violence and pathos.

The other works of Scopas are said to have included statues of *Aphrodite Pandemus; Hecate; Bacchante with a Slain Goat;* and *Apollo Cytharoedus* (Apollo with Lyre). His statues of figures in repose - one of the most difficult poses to do successfully - have a natural ease, and can express emotions such as the languor of love or unsatisfied waiting, as in the figure of *Pothos* (Longing).

Scopas may also have collaborated in work on the Artemisium at Ephesus and made structures for the temple at Tegea where he made the pediments. The decorative wealth of this temple reveals an imagination very different from anything in the 5th century BC. Scopas seeks constantly for sharply contrasted effects, and is quite prepared to add a degree of pathos to figures such as that of *Meleager*, taken from the sculpture on the pediment at Tegea. By carving the eye so that the eyeballs lie deep beneath the lids and depressed within the eye socket, he manages to convey the anguish of his figures without having to accompany the expression with the more usual frowning brow, giving the features instead a regularity that is still close to the classical ideal. A copy of his *Maenad* in Dresden shows his skill with a figure in movement, where the emphasis does not exclude gracefulness.

Although Scopas turns his back on the classical spirit of the preceding century, moving towards a kind of violence and extreme religious tension, his work is sufficiently restrained and graceful to retain an energetic and natural character that has nothing to do with the excesses of the future. He seems rather to define a new classical art, more daring than that which went before, with a more realistic handling of space.
BIBLIOGRAPHY:
Norman, N.J., *'The Temple of Alea Athena at Tegea'* in *American Journal of Archaeology, lxxxvii (1984) pp.169-194.* Palagia, Olga, *'The Hope Heracles Reconsidered'* in *Oxford Journal of Archaeology iii (1984) pp.169-194.* Arias, P.E., *Skopas*, L'Erma, Rome, 1952. Charbonneaux, Jean, *La Sculpture grecque classique*, Gonthier, Paris, 1964. Stewart, A.F., *Skopas of Paros*, Noyes Press, Park Ridge, 1977. Stewart, A.F., *Greek Sculpture: An Exploration*, Yale University Press, New Haven and London, 1990.

SCOPETA, Domingos Antonio. See **SCHIOPETTA**

SCOPETTA, Pietro. See **SCAPPETTA**

SCOPFT, Bernardo, or Scopfet or Scopet
Italian, 18th century.
Active in Genoa in the middle of the 18th century.
Sculptor (wood).
Scopft was the successor and possibly the pupil of A.M. Maragliano; he sculpted numerous figurines for nativity scenes in Genoese churches.

SCOPOLI, Andreas
Austrian, 18th century.
Born 1725, in Cavalese (?); died 12 October 1785, in Vienna.
Painter.

SCOPOLI, Anton
Austrian, 18th century.
Born in Cavalese; died 1766, in Vienna.
Painter.
Anton Scopoli studied in Vienna and was a pupil of Franz Unterberger.

SCOPPA, Giuseppe Gustavo
Italian, 19th century.
Born 7 March 1856, in Naples.
Painter. Landscapes with figures, landscapes, seascapes.
The son and pupil of Raimondo Scoppa, Giuseppe Scoppa later became a student at the Accademia di Belle Arti in Naples.
AUCTION RECORDS:
LONDON, 4 March 1981, *View of Sorrento* (gouache, 11 x 15½ ins / 28 x 39.5 cm) GBP 800. MILAN, 27 March 1984, *Amalfi Coast* (tempera, 16½ x 24¾ ins / 42 x 63 cm) ITL 2,600,000. LONDON, 22 March 1985, *View of Naples from the Carmine* (gouache, 16½ x 25 ins / 42 x 63.5 cm) GBP 2,000. LONDON, 25 March 1988, *View of the Jetty in Naples* (gouache, 19¾ x 28¼ ins / 50 x 72 cm) GBP 3,080; *Posillipo Castel dell'Ovo* (oil on canvas mounted on board, a pair, 6¼ x 9 ins / 16 x 22 cm) ITL 2,300,000. ROME, 12 Dec 1989, *Countryside* (oil on canvas, 13½ x 20¾ ins / 34.5 x 53 cm) ITL 2,000,000. ROME, 31 May 1990, *Fishing Boat in the Bay of Naples* (oil on canvas, 6 x 14¾ ins / 15.5 x 37.5 cm) ITL 750,000. ROME, 4 Dec 1990, *Fishermen at Sea near Castel dell'Ovo* (oil on panel, 9 x 12¼ ins / 22 x 31 cm) ITL 950,000. BRUSSELS, 23 June 1999, *Views of the Bay of Naples* (gouache, a pair, 15 x 21 ins / 39 x 53 cm) BEF 320,000. PARIS, 26 Nov 1999, *View of Naples* (gouache, 20 x 36 ins / 51 x 91 cm) FRF 58,000. BRUSSELS, 15 Feb 2000, *View of the Temples of Paestum* (gouache, 19 x 27 ins / 48 x 68 cm) BEF 90,000. LONDON, 29 Nov 2000, *Piazza del Colosseo* (gouache, 21 x 31 ins / 53 x 79 cm) GBP 1,400. LONDON, 8 Oct 2003, *Carriages and Figures on the Via della Riviera di Chiaia, Naples* (gouache, 18 x 34 ins / 46 x 86 cm) GBP 3,400. LINDAU, 23 Sept 2004, *View of a Southern Coastal Harbour and Village* (gouache, 19 x 33 ins / 47 x 85 cm) EUR 5,200.

SCOPPA, Raimondo
Italian, 19th century.
Born 22 March 1820, in Naples; died 1890.
Painter. Genre scenes, landscapes with figures.
A pupil of Smargiassi and Pottola, Raimondo Scoppa exhibited work in Naples, Florence, Turin and Milan.
AUCTION RECORDS:
NEW YORK, 30 May 1980, *Port Scene* (oil on board, 8½ x 13½ ins / 21.6 x 34.3 cm) USD 850. ROME, 6 Dec 1994, *Fishermen in the Bay* (1866, oil on canvas, 19¾ x 26½ ins / 50 x 67 cm) ITL 6,482,000. VENICE, 16 June 2000, *View of Sorrento* (oil on canvas, 20 x 30 ins / 50 x 76 cm) ITL 9,000,000. MILAN, 5 June 2001, *Along the Coast* (oil on canvas, 20 x 30 ins / 50 x 76 cm) ITL 13,000,000.

SCOPPA, Ridolfo
Italian, 18th century.
Active in Naples.
Painter. Flowers, fruit.
Scoppa was the pupil of Onofrio Loth.

SCOPULA, Giovanni Maria
Italian, 13th century.
Born in Irunto.
Painter.
There is a triptych by this painter in the Campana Collection of the Louvre that depicts *The Annunciation, The Visitation* and *The Nativity*, and carries the inscription *Joanes Maria Scopula de Irunto pinxit in Otranto* (*Giovanni Maria Scopula painted this picture in Otranto*).

SCORDIA, Antonio
Italian, 20th century.
Born 1918, in Santa Fe, Argentina, to Italian parents; died 1998.
Painter, engraver, sculptor, ceramicist. Nudes, landscapes, still-lifes.
Antonio Scordia lived and worked in Rome. He worked in a post-Cubist style with a colour palette characteristic of the Expressonists.
He participated in several collective exhibitions including: Venice Biennale (1952, 1954 and 1956 obtaining a prize for rdrawing); São Paulo Biennale (1957); Tokyo Biennale (1961). He won the Faenza prize for ceramics in 1952.

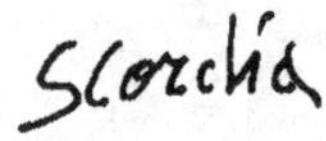

MUSEUMS AND GALLERIES:
BUENOS AIRES - CÓRDOBA - RICHMOND - ROME (Gal. Nazionale d'Arte Moderna) - SYDNEY - VENICE.
AUCTION RECORDS:
ROME, 2 Dec 1980, *Still-life with Teapot* (1953, oil on canvas, 39¼ x 30¾ ins / 100 x 78 cm) ITL 1,600,000. ROME, 17 April 1989, *Female Nude* (19582, oil on board, 17½ x 27½ ins / 44.5 x 70 cm) ITL 2,200,000. ROME, 10 April 1990, *Summer* (1975, oil on canvas, 51¼ x 41¼ ins / 130 x 105 cm) ITL 7,500,000. ROME, 25 March 1993, *Beached Boat* (1949, oil on canvas, 19¾ x 23½ ins / 50 x 60 cm) ITL 2,400,000. ROME, 3 June 1993, *Windows in Rome* (1952, oil on canvas, 31½ x 39¼ ins / 80 x 100 cm) ITL 3,200,000. LONDON, 26 Oct 1994, *Night Landscape* (1957, oil on canvas, 35½ x 29½ ins / 90 x 75 cm) GBP 2,185. ROME, 28 March 1995, *Still-life* (1954, oil on canvas, 25½ x 21¼ ins / 65 x 54 cm) ITL 3,220,000. NEW YORK, 10 Oct 1996, *Valentina in an Armchair* (1955, charcoal/paper, 26 x 19 ins / 66 x 48.3 cm) USD 1,035. MILAN, 10 Dec 1996, *Roofs in Rome* (oil on canvas, 10¼ x 12½ ins / 26 x 32 cm) ITL 2,213,000.

SCORE, Étienne Rodolphe, or Scores, Scorr, Scort, Secorps
French, 17th century.
Born c. 1645, in Angers; died 28 September 1668, in Angers.
Painter.
Étienne Rodolphe Score was the second son of Jacob Rodolphe Score.

SCORE, Jacob Rodolphe, or Scores, Scorr, Scort, Secorps
French, 17th century.
Born 1621, of Flemish origin; died March 1671, in Angers.
Painter.

Jacob Rodolphe Score was in charge a large part of the decoration work for the entry of the count of Harcourt into the town of Angers.

SCORE, William
British, 18th century.
Born in Devon.
Active at the end of the 18th century.
Painter, engraver. Portraits.

William Score was a pupil of Reynolds and responsible for painting drapes and soft furnishings in the latter's portraits. He exhibited at the Royal Academy from 1781 to 1794, typically with mezzotint engravings.

AUCTION RECORDS:
LONDON, 7 Feb 1910, *Portrait of J. Quick and John Sinclair* (on panel) GBP 2.

SCOREL, Jan van, or Scoreel, Schorel, Schoreel, Schoorel, Schooreel, Schoorl, Scorelius, Scorellius, also known as Master of the Death of Mary
Dutch, 16th century.
Born 1 August 1495, in Scorel, near Alkmaar; died 6 December 1562, in Utrecht.
Painter, engineer, architect. History painting, portraits, group portraits.
Utrecht School.

Jan van Scorel worked until he was 14 in the workshop of Cornelis Buys the Elder in Alkmaar, and from 1510 to 1512 with Cornelis Willemsz. in Haarlem. He then went to Amsterdam and joined Jacob Cornelisz. van Ootsanen, whose 12-year-old daughter fell in love with him. He worked with various masters in several cities, including Antwerp, and about 1517 he was in Utrecht with Jan Mabuse (Gossart). There are also references to him in Cologne, Spire, Strasbourg, Basel, and with Albrecht Dürer in Nuremberg. However, there is no evidence at all that he ever joined a guild or became a master. In 1517 he worked in Stiers, Corinthia, for a baron who also wanted him to marry his daughter. He went to Venice, where he made contact with painters from Antwerp, and went on to Jerusalem. In 1520 he was in Rhodes and on the return journey visited Italy. He arrived in Rome during the pontificate of Adrian VI and a few months after this pope's death he returned to the Netherlands via France (1524). He turned down an invitation from Francis I to work at the French court. He moved to Utrecht and then, in 1525, to Haarlem where M. van Heemskerk worked with him. By 1528, when he became a canon of the church of St Mary, Utrecht, he had a considerable reputation. He worked from 1536 to 1538 at Breda Castle, and in 1540 and 1549 for the visits of Charles V and Philip II to Utrecht. He also worked for the King of Sweden and in 1550, in collaboration with Lancelot Blondeel, he restored the Van Eyck triptych in Ghent. From 1530 he lived with Agatha van Schoonhoven, who bore him six children. He was also an engineer, a musician and a poet.

Previously the painting *The Death of Mary* and the Rheinhold altar were attributed to Jan van Scorel. Some historians identified the Master of the Death of Mary with Jan Joost van Calcar, others with the Cologne painter Johain Voss, or with Johann van Duren. Today it is considered that the Master of the Death of Mary is the Flemish painter Joss van Cleve, also called Joos van der Beke. Dr von Würbach, who studied the matter at length, believed that the small *Death of Mary* was painted in Antwerp by Jan Scorel in 1515 in the workshop of Jan (brother of Jacob) Cornelisz. of Amsterdam, and, indeed, the monogram is characteristic of Antwerp painters. The Rheinhold altar bears exactly the same monogram with the first letter missing. It could have been painted in the same workshop in 1516, with the extensive collaboration of Jan Scorel. The Utrecht exhibition of 1955 has enabled a better account of his works to be established. In his early years, about 1520-1521, the Dutch taste for costume detail, décor, faces and hands is notable, as seen in the triptych of Orbervellach, painted originally for the Falkenstein Castle in 1520, a painting clearly still influenced by Jacob Cornelisz. of Amsterdam. The wings of this triptych recall Dürer's style and may come from a different retable. Van Scorel soon began to show a predilection for landscapes bathed in a misty light, suggestive of Venetian painting; this is especially evident in the *Tobias and the Angel* of 1521. But soon Rome, antique art, and, above all, Raphael had their effects on him; his landscapes become exotic and are packed with references to what he had seen and sketched on his journey to Jerusalem. A good example is *Christ's Entry into Jerusalem* (Utrecht, 1525-1527), the central panel of the Van Lachorst triptych, in which a busy foreground contrasts with a distant, peaceful and hazy background. The Amsterdam *Bathsheba* has an exotic background of Italian palaces that Van Scorel has rendered with fluid, light and transparent strokes. The same touch is found in the face of *Mary Magdalene* (1529), a painting not dissimilar to Dürer's art, which has a landscape background that moves from brown to a bluish-green as it recedes into the distance, and that is reminiscent of the contemporary works of Jean Coussin. The painting that shows most clearly his attempt to rival the work of Raphael is the Vienna *Presentation in the Temple*. It is in portraiture that he reveals his full sensitivity. The most significant example is the portrait of his companion *Agatha van Schoonhoven* (1529), a moving and penetrating painting that is generous in its forms and refined in its use of colour. The *Portrait of a Man in a Red Beret* (1531) is also transparent in colour, but the attribution is sometimes disputed. In 1965 the *St Stephen* polyptych (Douai) was discovered, a painting that is a kind of synthesis of his skills, showing his taste for the antique in its drapery and nudes, for Rome and its architecture, and for composite landscapes. Jan van Scorel was a cosmopolitan man who travelled widely, who never chose to be a member of a guild or confraternity, and who produced a universal art worthy of his humanism.

In 2001 his work was represented in the exhibition *Tekenen van warmte: 17de-eeuwse Nederslandse tekenaars in Italië* (*Drawn to Warmth. 17th-century Dutch Draughtsmen in Italy*) at the Rijksmuseum, Amsterdam.

BIBLIOGRAPHY:
Hoogewerff, G.-J., *Jan Van Scorel, peintre de la renaissance hollandaise*, M. Nijhoff, The Hague, 1923. Jonge, Caroline Henriette de, *Jan Van Scorel*, H.J.W. Becht, Amsterdam, 1940. Hoogewerff, Godefridus Joannes, *Jan Van Scorel, peintre de la renaissance hollandaise*, M. Nijhoff, The Hague, 1941. Leymarie, Jean, *La Peinture hollandaise*, Skira, Geneva, 1956.

MUSEUMS AND GALLERIES:
AMSTERDAM: *Mary Magdalene; Solomon and the Queen of Sheba; Bathsheeba* (nine panels representing the Last Judgement and scenes from the Old Testament, vault paintings) - BASEL: *David Joris* - BERGAMO (Accademia Carrara): *Virgin and Child* - BERLIN: *C. A. Van der Dussen; Virgin and Child; Baptism of Christ* - BLOOMFIELD HILLS (Cranbrook AM): *Portrait of a Pilgrim* - BONN: *Crucifixion* - COLOGNE: *Portrait of a Man* - DORDRECHT: *Holy Family and Donors* - DOUAI: *St*

Stephen Polyptych - DRESDEN: *David Beheading Goliath* - FRANKFURT AM MAIN: *Portrait of a Man* - HAARLEM: *Confraternity of the Knights of the Holy Land in Haarlem; Adam and Eve; Baptism of Christ; St Cecilia Playing the Organ* - KASSEL: *Transfiguration of Christ on Mount Tabor; Family Portrait; Virgin and Child* - LA FÈRE: *Mary Magdalene Praying* - OBERVELLACH (Pfarrkirche): *Frangipani Triptych* - OLDENBURG: *Venetian Aristocrat* - ROME (Palazzo Doria Pamphili): *Agatha van Schoonhoven* - ROTTERDAM: *Portrait of a Young Man; Virgin and Child; St Sebastian* - TURIN: *Portrait of a Scholar* - UTRECHT: *Triptych of the Vischer van der Gheer Family; Twelve Members of the Confraternity of Jerusalem in Utrecht; Twelve Members of the same confraternity; Nine Members; Five Members* - VIENNA (Kunsthistorisches Mus.): *The Presentation in the Temple* - VIENNA (Liechtenstein Mus.): *Portraits of a Man and a Woman.*

AUCTION RECORDS:

COLOGNE, 1862, *Christ on the Cross between the Virgin; St John and St Mary Magdalene,* FRF 360. PARIS, 1881, *Descent from the Cross,* FRF 1,600. PARIS, 1899, *Ernest Jean; Duke of Courlande,* FRF 620. BRUSSELS, 1900, *Pietà,* FRF 4,600. PARIS, 3 May 1910, *Portrait of a Young Woman,* FRF 1,185. LONDON, 11-12 May 1911, *Burghermaster and His Wife,* GBP 110. LONDON, 25-26 May 1911, *Virgin and the Child Jesus,* GBP 21. LONDON, 1 June 1911, *Flight into Egypt,* GBP 15. PARIS, 9-11 Dec 1912, *Virgin and Child,* FRF 3,100. LONDON, 23-24 May 1922, *Crucifixion* (drawing) GBP 21. LONDON, 10 July 1925, *Old Woman,* GBP 56. LONDON, 4 Dec 1925, *St John the Baptist Preaching in the Desert,* GBP 60. LONDON, 17-18 May 1928, *Portrait of a Gentleman,* GBP 1,050. NEW YORK, 27-28 March 1930, *Isaac and Jacob,* USD 300. LONDON, 11 July 1930, *Hermanmus van Mettechoven,* GBP 220. PARIS, 27 May 1932, *Virgin and Child* (attributed) FRF 27,000. BRUSSELS, 20 June 1938, *Adoration of the Shepherds,* BEF 3,900. LONDON, 16 July 1943, *Edmund, Lord Sheffield,* GBP 1,575. PARIS, 5 March 1945, *Adoration of the Child* (school of Jan van Scorel) FRF 20,000. LONDON, 1 May 1946, *Young Woman,* GBP 320. PARIS, 25 April 1951, *Portraits of Jacob and Jan Bruinsen van der Dussen.* PARIS, 15 June 1951, *St Mary Magdalene Seated in a Landscape* (variation of the painting in the Rijksmuseum, attributed) FRF 42,000. PARIS, 27 June 1951, *Baptism of Christ* (attributed) FRF 50,000. PARIS, 7 June 1955, *Portrait of a Young Woman,* FRF 1,020,000. LONDON, 20 March 1959, *Madonna and Child in a Landscape,* GBP 2,100. LONDON, 27 June 1962, *Portrait of a Young Man,* GBP 1,100. PARIS, 26 March 1963, *Nativity* (triptych) FRF 126,000. LONDON, 6 July 1966, *Portraits of a Young Man and a Young Woman* (two pendants) GBP 5,000. BERN, 17 Nov 1967, *Virgin and Child,* CHF 27,000. AMSTERDAM, 9 June 1977, *Holy Family* (oil on panel, 31 1/2 x 24 ins / 80 x 61 cm) NLG 46,000. LONDON, 16 April 1980, *Adoration of the Magi* (oil on panel, 38 1/2 x 28 1/2 ins / 98 x 72.5 cm) GBP 14,000. LONDON, 5 July 2000, *The Death of St Hilary* (pen/ink wash, 9 x 8 ins / 24 x 20 cm) GBP 45,000.

SCORES. See **SCORE**

SCORIEL, Jean-Baptiste

Belgian, 20th century.

Born 1883, in Lambusart; died 1956.

Painter. Landscapes, seascapes.

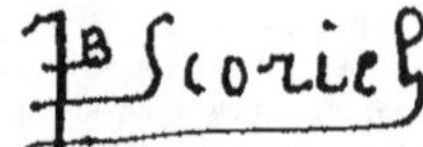

AUCTION RECORDS:

BRUSSELS, 12 June 1990, *Landscape* (oil on canvas, 25 1/2 x 27 1/2 ins / 65 x 70 cm) BEF 85,000. BRUSSELS, 7 Oct 1991, *Village in the Snow* (1942, oil on canvas, 33 1/2 x 37 1/2 ins / 85 x 95 cm) BEF 110,000. LOKEREN, 23 May 1992, *Orchard in Spring* (oil on canvas, 19 3/4 x 31 1/2 ins / 50 x 80 cm) BEF 150,000. LOKEREN, 11 Oct 1997, *Fishing Port (Dieppe)* (1920, oil on canvas, 39 1/4 x 47 1/4 ins / 100 x 120 cm) BEF 110,000. BRUSSELS, 10 June 2002, *Fog Clears by the Sambre* (1928, oil on canvas, 48 x 39 ins / 123 x 98 cm) EUR 1,600. BRUSSELS, 8 Nov 2004, *Snowy Landscape* (oil on canvas, 39 x 47 ins / 100 x 120 cm) EUR 3,000.

SCORODUMOV, Gavril Ivanovich, or Scrudomov

Russian, 18th century.

Born 12 March 1755, in St Petersburg; died 12 July 1792, in St Petersburg.

Draughtsman, engraver (burin), miniaturist.

Gavril Ivanovich Scorodumov was the son of Ivan Scorodumov and studied at the art academy in St Petersburg. As a very young man, he lived in England and studied under Bartolozzi, whose style he imitated. He is considered to have been the first Russian engraver to acquire a reputation as a serious artist. He lived in London from 1775 to 1782, and engraved several works by well-known artists of that time. After returning to St Petersburg, he worked for the court as a miniaturist, and painted portraits of members of the Imperial family on a large number of snuffboxes and rings. He produced a *Portrait of the Empress Catherine the Great* in the style of F. Rokotov.

SCORODUMOV, Ivan Ivanovich

Russian, 18th century.

Born 1729; died after 1790.

Painter, decorative designer.

Ivan Ivanovich Scorodumov was the father of Gavril Ivanovitch Scorodumov. He worked for palaces in St Petersburg, Peterhof and Tsarskoe-Selo.

SCORR. See **SCORE**

SCORRANO, Luigi

Italian, 19th - 20th century.

Born 13 June 1842, in Lecce (Apulia); died 15 June 1924, in Urbino.

Painter. Genre scenes.

A student at the academy of fine arts in Naples, Luigi Scorrano exhibited mainly in that city.

SCORSINI, Pietro. See **SCORZINI**

SCORT. See **SCORE**

SCORTELL, Bernardo

Spanish, 15th century.

Active in Valencia at the end of the 15th century.

Painter.

Bernardo Scortell painted some works in Valencia Cathedral.

SCORTESCO, Paul

Romanian, 20th century.

Born 10 May 1895, in Iasi, Moldavia (now Romania).

Active and from 1924 naturalised in France.

Painter. Figures, nudes, scenes with figures, landscapes, still-lifes, flowers.

Paul Scortesco was a pupil of Jean-Paul Laurens and Fernand Cormon at the École Nationale des Beaux-Arts in Paris. Notable among his figurative and landscape paintings are *The Fratellini* and *The Old Port at St Tropez,* as well as views of Venice, Palestine, Spain, Hungary and the Camargue, where he specialised in painting gipsies.

Work by him was shown at group exhibitions in Paris - at the Salon des Tuileries from 1926, then at the Salon des Indépendants, and the Société Nationale des Beaux-Arts, of which he was a member - and abroad, in Rome, Athens, Cairo, Lison, Rio de Janeiro, Buenos Aires and elsewhere.

MUSEUMS AND GALLERIES:

ATHENS - CAIRO - LISBON - PARIS.

Auction records:
Paris, 30 April 1945, *The Old Port at St Tropez,* FRF 1,300. Paris, 12 Dec 1946, *Flowers in an Interior,* FRF 4,600. Paris, 19 Nov 1948, *Gitane - Landscape - Nude Lying Down* (three oils on canvas) FRF 5,900. Paris, 28 Feb 1949, *The Circus at the Fairground,* FRF 7,100. Paris, 28 June 1950, *Landscapes* (two pendants) FRF 2,150.

SCORTICONE, Domenico
Italian, 17th century.
Died c. 1650, in Genoa.
Sculptor, architect.
Scorticone was the pupil of Taddeo Carlone; he executed works for the churches of Genoa.

SCORZA, Juan Bautista. See **CASTELLO Giovanni Battista called il Genovese**

SCORZA, Sinibaldo
Italian, 17th century.
Born 16 July 1589, in Voltaggio (Genoa); died 1631, in Genoa.
Painter, engraver, draughtsman. Religious subjects, mythological subjects, landscapes.
Sinibaldo Scorza had lessons with G.B. Corrosio and G.B. Paggi. He began executing pen drawings with such talent that it was possible to mistake his copies of Albrecht Dürer for originals. He then studied the art of the miniature, worked for Cavalerio Marini and was employed at the court in Turin, where he executed ten miniatures of the *Creation of the World* in such a manner as to invite comparison with those of Julio Clovi. Scorza settled in Rome, where a large number of easel paintings in oils brought him fame and fortune. He also produced etchings. His paintings have become fairly rare.His work was featured in the collective exhibition on the theme of still-life in Italy, *Stille Welt. Italienische Stilleben aus drei Jahrhunderten* (*Still World: Three Centuries of Italian Still-life Painting*), at the Kunsthalle der Hypo-Kulturstiftung in Munich in 2003.
Bibliography:
Biole, Mario, *Sinibaldo Scorza: pittore, miniaturista, incisore,* Liguria, 1981. Gregori, Mina/Prinz, Johann Georg, *Stille Welt. Italienische Stilleben aus drei Jahrhunderten,* exhibition catalogue, Kunsthalle der Hypo-Kulturstiftung, Munich, 2003.
Museums and Galleries:
Florence: *The Artist* - Genoa (Palazzo Rosso): *Landscape with Animals; Sacrifice of Noah after the Flood; Parting of Abraham and Agar; Pigeons* - Rome (GA Antica di Palazzo Corsini): *View of the Square in Pasquino.*
Auction records:
Paris, 25 Feb 1924, *Bacchanalian Feast* (sepia wash) FRF 500. Paris, 16 May 1925, *Orpheus Charming the Animals* (pen) FRF 220. Paris, 4 June 1973, *Orpheus Charming the Animals,* FRF 15,500. Monaco, 15 June 1990, *Orpheus Charming the Animals* (ink, 16 x 22 1/4 ins / 40.6 x 56.8 cm) FRF 122,100. New York, 9 Jan 1996, *Horse's Head; Woman with her Sleeping Child and a Calf Standing Nearby* (ink and black chalk, two drawings, 6 x 5 ins / 15.5 x 13 cm and 4 1/4 x 6 1/4 ins/10.8 x 16 cm) USD 2,415. Venice, 19 Feb 2000, *Noah's Ark* (oil on canvas, 22 x 27 ins / 55 x 68 cm) ITL 8,000,000. London, 11 July 2001, *Studies of the Skeleton and Skull of a Horse* (pen and brown ink, 8 x 11 ins / 20 x 29 cm) GBP 8,000. Milan, 17 Dec 2001, *Seascape with Boats* (oil on canvas, 24 x 30 ins / 62 x 75 cm) ITL 39,000,000. Paris, 27 March 2003, *Studies of Dogs* (pen and ink, 5 x 9 ins / 13 x 24 cm) EUR 4,500. Paris, 25 June 2003, *Animals Entering the Ark* (oil on canvas, 69 x 91 ins / 175 x 230 cm) EUR 18,000.

SCORZELLI, Eugenio
Argentinian, 20th century.
Born 1890, in Buenos Aires; died 1958, in Naples.
Active in Italy.
Painter. Scenes with figures, landscapes.

Eug-Scorzelli

Auction records:
Rome, 25 May 1988, *In the Café* (oil on card, 10 3/4 x 15 1/4 ins / 27.5 x 38.5 cm) ITL 1,300,000. Milan, 6 Dec 1989, *View of St Mark's from the Lagoon* (oil on panel, 7 3/4 x 11 3/4 ins / 20 x 30 cm) ITL 2,200,000. London, 14 Feb 1990, *The Turkey Market in Naples* (oil on canvas/card, 11 x 15 ins / 28 x 38 cm) GBP 3,080. Milan, 21 Nov 1990, *The Seaside at Dusk* (oil on canvas, 19 3/4 x 32 ins / 50 x 81.5 cm) ITL 3,000,000. Rome, 16 April 1991, *At the Races* (oil on canvas, 19 3/4 x 27 1/2 ins / 50 x 70 cm) ITL 11,500,000. Milan, 7 Nov 1991, *Flock by Fittleworth Village* (oil on canvas, 19 3/4 x 15 3/4 ins / 50 x 40 cm) ITL 2,000,000. Rome, 24 March 1992, *Paris; On the Seine* (oil on canvas/card, each 7 3/4 x 11 3/4 ins / 20 x 30 cm) ITL 11,500,000. Milan, 16 June 1992, *The Porte St-Denis in Paris* (oil on canvas, 17 1/4 x 24 ins / 44 x 61 cm) ITL 8,500,000. Rome, 19 Nov 1992, *River Landscape, perhaps near Paris* (oil on card, 10 x 13 1/2 ins / 24.5 x 34.5 cm) ITL 1,035,000. Milan, 17 Dec 1992, *City Landscape* (oil on canvas, 7 3/4 x 11 3/4 ins / 20 x 30 cm) ITL 4,400,000. Milan, 8 June 1993, *The Campania at Santa Maria Capua Vetere* (1950, oil on canvas/card, 10 x 13 1/2 ins / 24.5 x 34.5 cm) ITL 5,000,000. Milan, 20 Dec 1994, *Narrowboats on the Seine in Paris* (oil on panel, 12 1/4 x 16 1/2 ins / 31 x 42 cm) ITL 5,750,000.

SCORZINI, Alessandro
Italian, 19th - 20th century.
Born 22 April 1858, in Calcara di Crespellano (Emilia Romagna).
Painter.
A pupil of Antonio Piccinelli, Alessandro Scorzini lived and worked in Bologna.

SCORZINI, Luigi
Italian, 19th century.
Born 5 September 1799, in Milan; died 28 November 1839, in Milan.
Sculptor, goldsmith.
A student at the Accademia di Belle Arti di Brera in Milan, Luigi Scorzini carved ten statues for the Duomo in Milan.
Museums and Galleries:
Milan (Gal. d'Arte Moderna): *Aeneas, Anchises and Ascanius.*

SCORZINI, Pietro
Italian, 18th century.
Active c. 1720.
Painter, decorative artist. Church decoration.
Scorzini executed works for churches in Lucca.

SCOT, Robert
American, 18th century.
Active in Philadelphia from 1783.
Engraver. Portraits. Coins.

SCOTIN, François Gérard
French, 18th century.
Born 17 January 1703.
Engraver.
François Gérard Scotin was the son of Jean-Baptiste Scotin I and the brother of Louis François Scotin.

SCOTIN, Gérard, the Elder
French, 17th - 18th century.
Born 1643, in Antwerp (?); died 16 November 1715, in Paris.
Engraver. Religious subjects.

Gérard Scotin the Elder was the son of the sculptor Pierre Scotin and was apprenticed to François de Poilly the Elder, whose style he imitated. In 1665 he was working for the Gobelins manufactory. He was married to Geneviève Bailleu, with whom he had four children: Gérard Jean-Baptiste, Jean-Baptiste, Marie Nicolas and Marie Catherine.

He engraved religious subjects.

SCOTIN, Gérard Jean-Baptiste I
French, 17th - 18th century.
Born 24 December 1671, in Paris; died 1 February 1716, in Paris.
Engraver.

Gérard Jean-Baptiste Scotin I was the son of Gérard Scotin the Elder and the brother of Jean-Baptiste Scotin I and Marie Nicolas Scotin.

He engraved portraits, paintings and ornaments after Rigaud, Boucher, Watteau, Lancret, and Pater, among others. Several works by him are dated 1710. He married Geneviève Michez on 9 October 1695.

SCOTIN, Gérard Jean-Baptiste II
French, 18th century.
Born 13 September 1698, in Paris.
Engraver.

Gérard Jean-Baptiste Scotin II is cited as the son and pupil of Gérard Jean-Baptiste Scotin I. He is believed to have gone to England. It is possible that he and Louis Gérard Scotin (who is also reported to have visited England) may have been the same person.

SCOTIN, Jean-Baptiste I
French, 17th - 18th century.
Born 9 July 1678.
Engraver.

Jean-Baptiste Scotin I was the son of Gérard Scotin the Elder and the father of François Gérard and Louis François Scotin.

He engraved portraits, views of Paris and Rheims Cathedral, along with some vignettes.

SCOTIN, Jean-Baptiste II
French, 18th century.
Born 1729.
Active in St Petersburg.
Engraver.

SCOTIN, Louis François
French, 18th century.
Born 4 March 1769.
Engraver.

Louis François Scotin was the son of Jean-Baptiste Scotin I and the brother of François Gérard Scotin.

SCOTIN, Louis Gérard
French, 18th century.
Born 1690, in Paris; died after 1755.
Engraver.

Louis Gérard Scotin studied under his uncle Gérard Scotin or under Gérard Jean-Baptiste Scotin I. He may have been the same person as Gérard Jean-Baptiste Scotin II.

He engraved religious subjects and genre scenes. From 1733 he worked in London on a reproduction of Bernard Picard's religious ceremonies. In 1745 he executed two of the six plates of the *Fashionable Wedding* and several plates after Frank Hayman.

SCOTIN, Marie Nicolas
French, 18th century.
Died after 1716.
Active in Paris.
Illuminator.

Marie Nicolas Scotin was the son of Gérard Scotin the Elder and the brother of Jean-Baptiste Scotin I and Gérard Jean-Baptiste Scotin I. He married Catherine Jacquin on 30 August 1700. On 2 February 1716 he witnessed the death certificate of his brother Gérard Jean-Baptiste I.

SCOTIN, Pierre
French, 17th century.
Born c. 1618; died 12 February 1681, in Paris.
Sculptor.

Pierre Scotin was the father of Gérard Scotin the Elder, the first in a respectable line of Scotin engravers.

SCOTINKOV, Egor or Georg.
See **SKOTNIKOV Egor Ossipovich**

SCOTIS, Gottardo de and Melchiorre de.
See **SCOTTI**

SCOTNEY, Francis
British, 19th century.
Active in London during the first half of the 19th century.
Painter, miniaturist. Portraits, landscapes, architectural views.

Francis Scotney exhibited in London from 1811 to 1833.

SCOTO, or Schoto
Italian, 16th century.
Active in Pistoia.
Painter.

Scoto painted a *Virgin and Child* in fresco.

SCOTO, Gottardo. See **SCOTTI**

SCOTT
British, 18th century.
Active in London in 1770.
Painter. Flowers.

SCOTT
British, 18th century.
Active in London in 1786.
Painter.

SCOTT, Adam Sherriff, or Sherriff-Scott, Adam
British, 20th century.
Born 1887, in Scotland; died 1980.
From c. 1910 active in Canada.
Painter. Local scenes, landscapes, local figures. Murals.

Adam Scott taught at the Royal Academy of Fine Art in Montreal. His genre paintings feature scenes from the everyday lives of Canadian families, Eskimo peoples (especially the Inuit) and white settlers.

BIBLIOGRAPHY:

Reid, Dennis, *A Concise History of Canadian Painting*, Oxford University Press, Toronto, 1988.

AUCTION RECORDS:

TORONTO, 15 May 1978, *Ice-fishing* (oil on canvas, 30 x 24 ins / 76.2 x 61 cm) CAD 1,500. TORONTO, 14 May 1979, *Eskimo with Sledge* (oil on canvas, 24 x 29½ ins / 61 x 75 cm) CAD 1,050. TORONTO, 28 May 1985, *The Fallen Giant, Ile de Orleans (sic)* (oil on canvas, 15¾ x 19¾ ins / 40 x 50 cm) CAD 3,400. TORONTO, 18 Nov 1986, *Village Winter Scene* (oil on canvas, 23¼ x 28¾ ins / 58.8 x 73.1 cm) CAD 6,250. MONTREAL, 25 April 1988, *River and Landscape* (oil on canvas, 20 x 24 ins / 51 x 61 cm) CAD 2,700; *Portrait of an Eskimo* (oil on canvas, 24 x 18 ins / 61 x 46 cm) CAD 2,800. MONTREAL, 17 Oct 1988, *Mother* (oil on canvas, 32 x 24 ins / 81 x 61 cm) CAD 2,200; *Returning to the Igloo* (oil on canvas, 24 x 30 ins / 61 x 76 cm) CAD 5,200. MONTREAL, 30 Oct 1989, *Portrait of an Indian* (oil on canvas, 20 x 16¼ ins / 51 x 41 cm) CAD 3,300. MONTREAL, 30 April 1990, *Inuit Family Resting* (oil on canvas, 24 x 30 ins / 61 x 76 cm) CAD 4,400. MONTREAL, 5 Nov 1990, *Moving Camp* (oil on canvas, 24 x 35¾ ins / 61 x 91 cm) CAD 3,740. MONTREAL, 4 June 1991, *Fishing in the Shelter of a Bridge* (oil on canvas, 16 x 20 ins / 40.5 x 50.8 cm) CAD 1,200.

MONTREAL, 23-24 Nov 1993, *Summer's Day at the Beach* (oil on panel, 12 1/2 x 14 1/2 ins / 31.6 x 36.6 cm) CAD 2,400. MONTREAL, 21 June 1994, *Maple Syrup* (oil on panel, 30 1/2 x 38 ins / 77.5 x 96.5 cm) CAD 13,000.

SCOTT, Anne (Lady)
British, 19th century.
Painter, miniaturist. Flowers.

Anne Scott exhibited examples of her work at the Royal Academy from 1802 to 1807.

AUCTION RECORDS:
LONDON, 19 May 1926, *Bouquet of Flowers*, GBP 70.

SCOTT, B. F.
British, 18th century.
Active in London.
Miniaturist, engraver (mezzotint).

An artist identified as B.F. Scott exhibited miniatures at London's Royal Academy and the Society of Artists from 1790 to 1792. He is probably the same mezzotint engraver cited by John Choloner Smith as having engraved a portrait from an original by John Raphael Smith. A painter of mountain views called B.F. Scott also exhibited at the Royal Academy and the Suffolk Street Gallery in London from 1833 to 1849; it is possible that he was related to the present artist although highly improbable that they are one and the same.

SCOTT, Charles James
British, 19th century.
Painter. Landscapes.

Charles James Scott exhibited in Brighton and London from 1819 to 1830.

SCOTT, Charlotte H.
American, 20th century.
Born in Worcester.
Painter.

Charlotte Scott studied at the art school at the museum in Worcester, then under André Lhote and Fernand Léger in Paris. She exhibited her work in Paris, at the Pennsylvania Academy of Fine Arts and in Worcester.

SCOTT, David
British, 19th century.
Born 10 October 1806, in Edinburgh; died 5 March 1849, in Edinburgh.
Painter, engraver. History painting.

David Scott was the son of the engraver Robert Scott. He started out producing prints from original drawings by Stolbard to illustrate Thomson's *Scottish Melodies*. From 1828 he devoted himself exclusively to painting. He was admitted to associate membership of the Scottish Academy in 1830 and to full membership in 1832 (on his return from an extended visit to Italy). In 1842 Scott competed unsuccessfully in the competition to decorate the Houses of Parliament, much to his chagrin; he was given to vast and highly demanding allegorical canvases and it may be that his ambition exceeded his ability. As an engraver, however, his smaller-scale compositions proved excellent, particularly in the vase of his 25 etchings done in 1837 to illustrate Samuel Taylor Coleridge's *Rime of the Ancient Mariner*. Here, his bold linear approach attests to his familiarity with the work of William Blake.

BIBLIOGRAPHY:
Irwin, David, *Scottish Painters at Home and Abroad, 1700-1900*, Faber and Faber, London, 1975. Irwin, David, *'David Scott: Illustratons of Mysticism and the Supernatural'* in *Studies in Romanticism, 15, 3*, 1976. Hardie, W.R., *Scottish Painting 1837-1939*, Studio Vista, 1976. *Early Victorian Draughtsman and the Rise of the Scottish Academy*, exhibition catalogue, 1981. Errington, Lindsay, *Sunshine and Shadow: The David Scott Collection of Victorian Paintings*, exhibition catalogue, Edinburgh, 1991.

MUSEUMS AND GALLERIES:
EDINBURGH (Nat. Gal. of Scotland): *Alchemist Paracelsus lecturing on the Elixir of Life* (oil on canvas); *Vintner* (oil on canvas); *Puck Fleeing the Dawn* (1837, oil on canvas, inspired by Shakespeare's 'A Midsummer Night's Dream'); *Ariel and Caliban* (1837, oil on canvas); *Traitor's Gate* (oil/panel); *Dr Samuel Brown* (oil on canvas) - EDINBURGH (Nat. Gal. of Scotland, Print Room): *The Murder of Rizzio* (watercolour) - EDINBURGH (Royal Scottish Academy): *Cain Degraded* (1831, oil on canvas) - PAISLEY (Museum and Art Gallery): *William Wallace, Scottish Patriot* - SUNDERLAND: *Achilles Invoking Patrocles over Hector's Dead Body*.

AUCTION RECORDS:
EDINBURGH, 2 July 1981, *Nimrod* (oil on canvas, 70 x 55 1/2 ins / 178 x 141 cm) GBP 1,200. EDINBURGH, 25 Aug 2000, *Robert Burns* (oil on canvas, 16 x 11 ins / 41 x 29 cm) GBP 3,700. LONDON, 7 March 2002, *Morar Triptych* (1881, oil on canvas, triptych, 30 x 60 ins / 76 x 152 cm) GBP 2,200. LONDON, 7 March 2002, *Loch Morar* (1881, oil on board, set of four, 46 x 16 ins / 117 x 41 cm) GBP 4,200. LONDON, 20 Feb 2003, *Study for 'Deposition'* (oil on card on board, 19 x 16 ins / 49 x 41 cm) GBP 3,800. TUNBRIDGE WELLS, 19 Nov 2003, *Family of Cheetahs* (acrylic on board, 40 x 40 ins / 101 x 101 cm) GBP 2,500.

SCOTT, Edmund
British, 18th - 19th century.
Born c. 1746, in London; died c. 1810, in London.
Engraver (burin), draughtsman.

Edmund Scott was a pupil of Baryolozzi. He engraved historical subjects and genre scenes.

AUCTION RECORDS:
LONDON, 13 Nov 1997, *Como and the Spirits; Sabrina Freeing the Lady from the Magic Chair; and others* (1793, dry-point) GBP 5,290.

SCOTT, Edwin or Frank Edwin
American, 20th century.
Born 1862, in Buffalo (New York State); died 24 December 1929, in Paris.
Active in France.
Painter. Urban landscapes.

Edwin Scott lived in Paris for much of his life. He painted urban landscapes, particularly of the St-Germain-des-Prés quarter in Paris, and views of Venice. He also painted views of Paris.

Scott took part in the Salon de la Société Nationale des Beaux-Arts. A work entitled *Place des Pyramides* was presented by the Royal Scottish Academy in 1914. His work was included in the exhibition *L'Impressionisme américain 1880-1915* (*American Impressionism 1880-1915*) at the Fondation de l'Hermitage in Lausanne.

BIBLIOGRAPHY:
Paintings by Edwin Scott from the Alice Pyke Barney Memorial Collection, exhibition catalogue, Smithsonian Institute, Washington DC, 1970. Cikovski, Nicolai/Hauptman, William, *L'Impressionnisme américain 1880-1915*, exhibition catalogue, Fondation de l'Hermitage, Lausanne, 2002.

AUCTION RECORDS:
PARIS, 5 Nov 1926, *Place de la Concorde* FRF 125. PARIS, 24 Jan 1945, *La Porte St-Denis* FRF 1,150. NEW YORK, 26 May 1988, *Church of Santa Maria della Salute, Venice* (oil on canvas, 21 1/2 x 18 1/4 ins / 54.8 x 46.3 cm) USD 3,520. PARIS, 23 June 1988, *Cabs on the Boulevard des Batignolles* (oil on panel, 16 1/4 x 12 1/2 ins / 41 x 32 cm) FRF 15,000. NEW YORK, 25 Sept 1992, *Grey Day in Paris* (oil on panel, 14 x 10 1/2 ins / 35.6 x 26.7 cm) USD 935. MILAN, 8 June 2004, *Street in Paris* (oil on canvas, 32 x 25 ins / 81 x 64 cm) EUR 2,000.

SCOTT, Emily Mary Spafard
American, 19th - 20th century.
Born 27 August 1832, in Springwater; died 9 April 1915, in New York.

Painter. Flowers, fruit.
Emily Scott studied in New York and Paris.
MUSEUMS AND GALLERIES:
BROOKLYN, NY - NEW YORK (Metropolitan Mus. of Art).

SCOTT, Evans de. See **EVANS DE SCOTT**

SCOTT, G.
British, 19th century.
Engraver. Portraits.
Active c. 1800.

SCOTT, George Gilbert (Sir)
British, 19th century.
Born 1811, in Gawcott, Buckinghamshire; died 27 March 1878, in London.
Draughtsman. Landscapes.
George Gilbert Scott was an eminent Victorian architect who played a key role in the preservation and restoration of ancient monuments. He drew assiduously in the course of frequent travels in Europe - notably in Germany - producing topographic studies which, in the eyes of some critics, rival the charming sketches of Samuel Pront. Scott is also reputed to have painted at least one portrait in oils. He was knighted in 1878.
BIBLIOGRAPHY:
Scott, George Gilbert, *Personal and Professional Recollections*, P. Watkins, Stamford, 1995. Miele, Chris, *'Icon of Victorial Modernity'* in *Country Life*, vol. 193, 2, 1999.

SCOTT, Georges Bertin, called Scott de Plagnolles
French, 19th - 20th century.
Born 10 June 1873, in Paris; died 1942.
Painter (gouache), watercolourist, draughtsman, illustrator. History painting, military subjects, figures, nudes, portraits, flowers, landscapes.
Scott was taught by Edouard Detaille. During World War I he was a war painter. He exhibited in Paris, at the Salon des Artistes Français, where he was a member from 1897. He was made a Chevalier of the Légion d'Honneur in 1912 and an Officier in 1928. He was a regular contributor to the review *L'Illustration*, which covered topical issues in text and image.
Although primarily a painter, watercolourist and draughtsman of military subjects, either of scenes witnessed during the war or historical reconstructions, he also painted a variety of subjects, generally in watercolours, such as figures in the corrida, flowers, nudes, landscapes of Spain and Holland, views of beaches and ports in the north of France and Brittany.

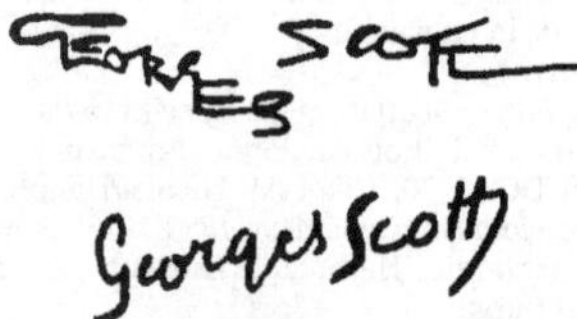

MUSEUMS AND GALLERIES:
BRISTOL (City Mus. & AG): *H.M. King George V* (oil on canvas) - PARIS (Mus. de l'Armée) - ROME (Gal. Nazionale d'Arte Moderna): *Portrait of Mussolini*.
AUCTION RECORDS:
PARIS, 4-5 March 1920, *German Prisoners in a Church*, FRF 3,200. PARIS, 20 April 1928, *Lancer* (watercolour) FRF 300. PARIS, 16 Feb 1931, *Poilu* (*First World War Soldier*, FRF 150. PARIS, 23 March 1945, *Cavalryman*, FRF 6,800. PARIS, Oct 1945 - July 1946, *Officers of Cavalrymen Saluting the Flag* (1919) FRF 24,000; *Burial of Her Majesty the Queen Victoria* (1901, watercolour and gouache) FRF 50,000; *Egyptian Campaign: Bonaparte's Army Camping in front of the Sphinx* (1932, watercolour) FRF 69,000; *Dawn Roll Call* (1917, graphite and pen) FRF 4,000; *Étretat Beach* (1928, watercolour) FRF 9,500. PARIS, 24 Nov 1948, *Foot Soldiers* (1914) FRF 3,500. PARIS, 7 Feb 1951, *Napoleon I the Equestrian* (1927, watercolour and sepia wash) FRF 20,000. PARIS, 24 March 1976, *Don Quixote* (1928, oil on panel, 31 x 39 1/4 ins / 79 x 100 cm) FRF 2,000. EDINBURGH, 14 Nov 1978, *Surrender of General Kronje to General Roberts* (oil on canvas, 44 x 69 1/4 ins / 112 x 176 cm) GBP 800. LONDON, 14 Feb 1979, *Algeria, the Presidential Convoy Escorted by Arab Horsemen* (1903, pencil and wash heightened with white, 15 1/2 x 52 3/4 ins / 39.5 x 134 cm) GBP 1,500. PARIS, 23 Feb 1979, *Bather Near the Temple of Love* (1922, oil on canvas, 67 3/4 x 45 ins / 172 x 114 cm) FRF 6,200. ENGHIEN-LES-BAINS, 26 June 1983, *Fantasia* (1930, watercolour heightened with gouache, 26 1/2 x 39 ins / 67 x 99 cm) FRF 61,000. VERSAILLES, 13 May 1984, *Conquest of Holland (1794-1795) by the Armies of the North Commanded by General Pichegru* (1909, oil on canvas, 45 1/4 x 79 1/4 ins / 115 x 201 cm) FRF 32,000. LONDON, 28 Nov 1985, *Parade in Honour of the President Emile Loubet* (1903, watercolour and gouache, 14 1/4 x 18 1/2 ins / 36.5 x 47 cm) GBP 3,600. PARIS, 4 Dec 1986, *Arab Dignitary on Horseback Before His People* (1905, oil on canvas, 76 x 63 3/4 ins / 193 x 162 cm) FRF 80,000. BREST, 13 Dec 1987, *Young Bretons Packing Sardines at St-Guénolé, Penmarch* (watercolour and gouache, 13 3/4 x 9 3/4 ins / 35 x 25 cm) FRF 13,500. PARIS, 8 Dec 1989, *Fantasia* (watercolour, gouache and charcoal, 26 3/4 x 39 ins / 68 x 99 cm) FRF 19,000. PARIS, 13 Dec 1989, *Triumph of Picador* (1900, watercolour and gouache, 19 1/2 x 14 3/4 ins / 49.5 x 37.5 cm) FRF 16,000. RHEIMS, 18 March 1990, *Wounded Soldiers Waiting to be Relieved* (1910, oil on canvas, 29 1/4 x 22 ins / 74 x 56 cm) FRF 6,000. PARIS, 6 April 1990, *Charge of the Cavalry* (watercolour, 16 1/2 x 13 1/2 ins / 42 x 34 cm) FRF 24,000. PARIS, 23 April 1993, *Nude with Roses* (1822, oil on canvas, 67 x 45 ins / 170 x 114 cm) FRF 25,000. PARIS, 8 Nov 1993, *Le Cavalier au Cheval Blanc* (1934, watercolour, 11 1/2 x 9 ins / 29 x 23 cm) FRF 4,500. PARIS, 14 Nov 1995, *Hunters' Boat at Dawn* (1921, watercolour, 28 1/4 x 38 3/4 ins / 71.5 x 98.5 cm) FRF 7,100. PARIS, 10 April 1996, *Beach Scene* (1920, watercolour and gouache, 17 1/4 x 24 1/2 ins / 44 x 62.5 cm) FRF 10,000. PARIS, 26 March 1998, *The Palace Guard* (oil on panel, 17 3/4 x 22 ins / 45 x 55 cm) FRF 31,000. PARIS, 23 June 2000, *Quarzazat* (1935, oil on board, 17 x 20 ins / 43 x 52 cm) FRF 22,000. PARIS, 30 Jan 2002, *Tunis, Flower Seller* (oil on canvas, 18 x 13 ins / 45 x 33 cm) EUR 2,745.

SCOTT, Gerald
Canadian, 20th century.
Born 1926.
Painter.
Gerald Scott took part in a collective exhibition representing new trends: *Four Young Canadians*, with Michael Snow, William Ronald and Robert Varvarande, in Toronto in 1956. At that time he painted figurative works.

SCOTT, Henri Louis
French, 19th century.
Born c. 1846, in Le Havre; died May 1884, in Paris.
Painter, draughtsman. Landscapes.
A pupil of Herbes, this artist first exhibited at the Salon in 1872.
AUCTION RECORDS:
PARIS, 7 Feb 1891, *Terreplein on the Pont-Neuf*, FRF 110. PARIS, 11 March 1925, *Old Houses in Nantes* (pen and wash) FRF 90. LONDON, 7 Nov 1973, *Three-masters*, GBP 600. BENNINGTON (NEW HAMPSHIRE), 25 Aug 1979, *Off the Eddystone* (oil on canvas, 23 1/4 x 35 1/4 ins / 59 x 89.5 cm) USD 3,500.

SCOTT, Henry
British, 20th century.
Painter. Seascapes.
Henry Scott was active from 1950-1966.

Auction records:
London, 12 Nov 1976, *The Titania at Sea* (oil on canvas, 24 x 36 ins / 61 x 91.5 cm) GBP 850. London, 18 May 1977, *Naval Battle* (1966, oil on canvas, 27 1/4 x 41 1/4 ins / 69 x 104.5 cm) GBP 1,500. London, 4 Nov 1983, *The Clipper Jessie Readman* (oil on canvas, 40 x 48 ins / 101.6 x 122 cm) GBP 2,600. London, 31 May 1989, *The Thomas Stevens at Sea* (oil on canvas, 20 x 30 ins / 51 x 76 cm) GBP 990. London, 5 Oct 1989, *The Frigate Light Brigade in Full Sail* (1966, oil on canvas, 24 x 36 ins / 61 x 91.5 cm) GBP 3,520. London, 18 Oct 1990, *The Galatea in Full Sail; The Crusader by Moonlight* (oil on canvas, a pair, 14 x 20 ins / 35.5 x 51 cm) GBP 1,870. London, 22 May 1991, *The Star of Persia* (oil on canvas, 20 x 30 ins / 51 x 76 cm) GBP 1,760. London, 16 July 1993, *The Tea-ship Caliph, Thirty Days Out* (oil on canvas, 13 3/4 x 20 ins / 35 x 50.5 cm) GBP 2,415. London, 11 May 1994, *Full Steam Ahead!* (oil on canvas, 23 x 34 ins / 58.5 x 86.5 cm) GBP 1,092. London, 30 May 1996, *The Clipper Battle Abbey Guiding the Star of Bengal* (1966, oil on canvas, 23 1/2 x 36 ins / 60 x 90.5 cm) GBP 2,300. London, 13 May 1999, *Tea Clippers Ariel and Taeping off the Lizard* (oil on canvas, 28 x 42 ins / 71 x 107 cm) GBP 4,500. London, 13 May 1999, *China Clipper, Highflyer* (oil on canvas, 24 x 36 ins / 61 x 91 cm) GBP 5,800. New York, 8 March 2000, *Clipper, Glory of the Seas, Outward Bound* (oil on canvas, 28 x 42 ins / 71 x 107 cm) USD 10,000. New York, 8 March 2000, *Frigate USS Constitution and British Frigate Java in Battle* (oil on canvas, 20 x 30 ins / 51 x 76 cm) USD 12,000. New York, 31 July 2001, *Ariel and Taeping Racing up Channel* (oil on canvas, 28 x 42 ins / 71 x 106 cm) USD 8,500. New York, 31 July 2001, *Outward bound. Homeward Bound* (oil on canvas, a pair, 24 x 36 ins / 61 x 91 cm) USD 9,000. New York, 30 July 2002, *Bolton Abbey Stormy Night - The Starboard Light* (oil on canvas, 20 x 30 ins / 51 x 76 cm) USD 7,000. London, 31 Oct 2002, *Flying Cloud Rounding Cape Horn* (oil on canvas, 20 x 30 ins / 51 x 77 cm) GBP 2,600. London, 18 June 2003, *Night Watch - Iron clipper Ivanhoe Leading Spindrift* (oil on canvas, 24 x 39 ins / 61 x 100 cm) GBP 4,500. New York, 29 July 2003, *Tranquil Morning Foochow* (oil on canvas, 14 x 20 ins / 36 x 51 cm) USD 4,500. New York, 10 Feb 2004, *Homeward Run, Tea Clipper, Crest of the Wave Running up the Channel* (oil on canvas, 28 x 42 ins / 71 x 107 cm) USD 16,000. New York, 29 July 2004, *American Clipper Glory of the Seas* (1967, oil on canvas, 26 x 39 ins / 66 x 100 cm) USD 15,000.

SCOTT, James
British, 19th century.
Painter. Portraits.

James Scott exhibited in London from 1821 to 1844, showing principally portrait miniatures.

SCOTT, James
British, 19th century.
Born 1809.
Painter, engraver. Portraits.

James Scott exhibited in London from 1858 to 1889.

SCOTT, James
American, 20th century.
Born 3 September 1883, in Racine (Wisconsin).
Painter.

James Scott studied at the Art Students' League in New York, at the Académie Julian, the Académie Colarossi and the Académie de la Grande Chaumière in Paris. He was a member of the Salmagundi Club.

SCOTT, James Fraser
New Zealander, 19th - 20th century.
Born 1878, in Dunedin; died 26 April 1932, in London.
Painter. Landscapes.

James Fraser Scott went to Europe in 1898 and studied in Paris at the Académie Julian and also in Munich, Antwerp and in Italy. He returned to New Zealand in about 1907 but moved Sydney, Australia, two years later. After World War I he went to London where he painted war pictures for the Australian War Museum.

Auction records:
Sydney, 3 July 1989, *Riverbank* (oil on canvas, 22 x 17 ins / 56 x 43 cm) AUD 6,500. Sydney, 20 April 1999, *Australian Pavilion Looking Towards Indian Pavilion, British Empire Exhibition, Wembley 1924/5* (oil on canvas, 16 x 24 ins / 41 x 61 cm) AUD 4,500. Victoria, 4 April 2000, *Spring Rite* (oil on canvas, 24 x 19 ins / 60 x 49 cm) AUD 3,900.

SCOTT, Jeannette
Canadian, 19th - 20th century.
Born 26 September 1864, in Rincardine (Ontario).
Painter.

Jeannette Scott studied at the Philadelphia Academy of Fine Arts and also in Paris. She was a member of the American Federation of Arts.

SCOTT, John
British, 18th - 19th century.
Born 12 March 1774, in Newcastle; died 1828, in Chelsea.
Painter, engraver. Animals.

John Scott was a pupil of Pollard. He contributed to a large number of publications. His accomplished cold-chisel engravings of horses and dogs proved highly popular.

Museums and Galleries:
London (British Mus.): some 400 sketches.

SCOTT, John
British, 19th century.
Painter. History painting, genre scenes, seascapes.

John Scott exhibited in London from 1862 to 1904.

Auction records:
London, 15 Oct 1976, *Sailship 'Ironside' off the Dover Coast* (1861, oil on canvas, 26 1/2 x 47 ins / 67.3 x 119.3 cm) GBP 1,800. London, 6 Dec 1977, *The 'Ocean Bride' off the Coast* (1865, oil on canvas, 29 1/2 x 48 ins / 75 x 121 cm) GBP 1,100. London, 6 June 1984, *Clipper Ship 'Marlborough' of Tynemouth* (1862, oil on canvas, 31 1/2 x 48 ins / 80 x 121 cm) GBP 7,800. London, 5 June 1985, *Vessels of the Royal Yacht Squadron* (oil on canvas, 22 3/4 x 35 ins / 58 x 89 cm) GBP 2,800. London, 15 June 1988, *Daydreaming* (oil on canvas, 33 3/4 x 19 1/4 ins / 86 x 49 cm) GBP 1,650. London, 31 May 1989, *Snow Sisters* (1864, oil on canvas, 27 1/4 x 36 ins / 69 x 91.5 cm) GBP 12,650. London, 3 Nov 1989, *The 'Flying Cloud' off Whitby* (1871, oil on canvas, 27 1/4 x 42 1/4 ins / 69 x 107 cm) GBP 17,600. London, 30 May 1990, *The Three-Masted Steamship 'Arratoon Apcar'* (1873, oil on canvas, 27 x 42 1/4 ins / 68.5 x 107 cm) GBP 6,050. London, 11 May 1994, *The Paddle-Steamer 'Akcan' off Tynemouth* (1869, oil on canvas, 24 1/4 x 36 ins / 61.5 x 91.5 cm) GBP 5,520.

SCOTT, John
British, 19th - 20th century.
Born 1850, in Carlisle; died 1919, in Barnet.
Painter, watercolourist. Scenes with figures.

John Scott was a member of the Royal Society of British Artists, and of the Royal Institute of Painters in Watercolour.

Auction records:
London, 14 June 1977, *Spilt Milk* (oil on canvas, 38 1/4 x 63 ins / 97 x 160 cm) GBP 750. London, 25 May 1979, *Reverie* (oil on canvas, 16 1/4 x 29 3/4 ins / 41.2 x 75.6 cm) GBP 900. London, 18 Feb 1983, *Freyja's First Task* (oil on canvas, 60 x 36 1/4 ins / 152.5 x 92 cm) GBP 2,400. London, 25 March 1994, *After a Tennis Match* (pencil and watercolour, 11 3/4 x 20 ins / 30.1 x 50.8 cm) GBP 7,475. London, 7 June 1995, *The New Pretender* (1913, oil on canvas, 14 1/4 x 22 1/2 ins / 36.5 x 57 cm) GBP 1,150.

SCOTT, John Douglas
British, 19th century.
Painter. Landscapes, waterscapes.
John Douglas Scott worked in Edinburgh and exhibited frequently in London from 1871 to 1881, typically at the Royal Academy and the Suffolk Street Gallery.
MUSEUMS AND GALLERIES:
SUNDERLAND: *Plockton, Ross-Shire; Highland Loch; Ross-Shire.*
AUCTION RECORDS:
LONDON, 10 Dec 1910, *Westminister from the Terrace of the Adelphi,* GBP 94; *Westminster, Seen from the River Thames,* GBP 52; *Westminster, seen from the River Thames,* GBP 54. LONDON, 11 Feb 1911, *Old Westminster Bridge,* GBP 52. LONDON, 29 April 1911, *Calm Evening* (1876) GBP 10.

SCOTT, John Henderson
British, 19th century.
Born 10 February 1829, in Brighton; died 6 December 1886, in Brighton.
Painter, watercolourist. Landscapes, seascapes.
John Henderson Scott was the son of William Henry Scott. He exhibited in London and Brighton, typically with views of Sussex and Normandy.
AUCTION RECORDS:
NEW YORK, 30 April 1969, *Seascape,* USD 1,300.

SCOTT, John White Allen
British, 19th century.
Born 1815, in Dorchester; died 4 March 1907, in Cambridge.
Painter. Landscapes, rustic scenes, still-lifes (flowers/fruit).
AUCTION RECORDS:
NEW YORK, 29 April 1976, *Mount Chocorua* (oil on canvas, 30 x 50 ins / 76.2 x 127 cm) USD 3,250. NEW YORK, 12 Oct 1978, *New England Landscape in Autumn* (1866, oil on canvas, 30 x 50 ins / 76.2 x 127 cm) USD 4,000. NEW YORK, 23 Sept 1981, *Harvest Scene* (oil on canvas, 20 x 30 ins / 50.8 x 76.2 cm) USD 4,250. NEW YORK, 18 Dec 1991, *Still-life with Fruit on a Table* (oil on canvas, 14 x 20 ins / 35.6 x 50.8 cm) USD 1,045. NEW YORK, 25 March 1997, *Landscape with Haystacks* (oil on canvas, 12¼ x 18 ins / 30.8 x 46 cm) USD 2,070.

SCOTT, Julian
American, 19th century.
Born 14 February 1846, in Johnson; died 4 July 1901, in Plainfield.
Painter. Military subjects, battles, genre scenes, landscapes.
Julian Scott was an associate of the National Academy of Design in New York.
AUCTION RECORDS:
LONDON, 5 March 1910, *Prussian Soldiers in the Time of Frederick the Great,* GBP 7. LONDON, 3 Dec 1910, *Launch of a Warship,* GBP 16. NEW YORK, 7 March 1911, *Captain Molly Pitcher,* USD 85. LONDON, 12 April 1911, *London Town Hall,* GBP 16. NEW YORK, 30 April 1980, *Young Drummers Playing Cards* (1886, oil on canvas, 25 x 30 ins / 63.5 x 76.2 cm) USD 7,000. PORTLAND, 11 July 1981, *Captain John Jupa, California* (1891, oil on board, 12 x 9¾ ins / 30.2 x 25 cm) GBP 4,250. NEW YORK, 2 June 1983, *Vermont Division at the Battle of Chancellorsville* (1871-1872, oil on canvas, 48¼ x 72 ins / 122.6 x 182.9 cm) USD 30,000. NEW YORK, 14 March 1986, *Yankee Decoys* (1872, oil on canvas, 16 x 20 ins / 40.5 x 51 cm) USD 6,500. NEW YORK, 31 May 1990, *Major General William F. Smith and his Staff* (1882, oil on canvas, 12 x 20 ins / 30.5 x 50.8 cm) USD 4,400. NEW YORK, 2 Dec 1992, *Major General William F. Smith and his Staff* (1882, oil on canvas, 12 x 20 ins / 30.5 x 50.9 cm) USD 3,520. NEW YORK, 9 March 1996, *Returning Home* (1887, oil on canvas, 179¼ x 24 ins / 455.1 x 61 cm) USD 11,500.

SCOTT, Katharine H.
American, 20th century.
Born in Burlington (Ohio).
Painter, miniaturist.
Katharine Scott studied under John H. Vanderpoel and William M. Chase. She was a member of the American Federation of Arts.

SCOTT, Louise
Canadian, 20th century.
Painter. Scenes with figures, figures.
Louise Scott studied at the École des Beaux-Arts in Montreal, and in 1958 she under Oskar Kokoshka in Salzburg. She seemed to have formulated the characteristics of her work by the beginning of the 1960s, defining her world with simplified scenery and plumpish figures, painted at an angle.
MUSEUMS AND GALLERIES:
KITCHENER (Kitchener-Waterloo AG) - OSHAWA (Robert McLaughlin Gal.) - OTTAWA (Nat. Gal. of Canada).

SCOTT, Margaret (Mrs). See **GATTY**

SCOTT, Maria, later Mrs Brooksbank
British, 19th century.
Painter, watercolourist. Flowers, fruit.
Maria Scott was the daughter of William Henry Scott. She was a member of the Society of Painters in Watercolours, and exhibited in Brighton from 1830 to 1839 under her married name of Brookbank.

SCOTT, Marian D.
Canadian, 20th century.
Born June 1906, in Montreal; died 1993.
Painter.
Marian Scott studied at the Art Association and the École des Beaux-Arts in Montreal, then at Slade School in London, where her teacher was Henry Tonks. She taught painting at the Saint Georges school and the museum of fine arts in Montreal, and was a member of the Canadian Group and the Contemporary Arts Society. All her work is inspired by a Surrealist vision of things and how they are made and tends towards abstraction. She painted a mural at the McGill University in Montreal in 1943.

Scott took part in important exhibitions of contemporary Canadian art in Canada, the USA and Great Britain. She also showed her works in several private exhibitions.
BIBLIOGRAPHY:
Reid, Dennis, *A Concise History of Canadian Painting,* Oxford University Press, Toronto, 1988.
MUSEUMS AND GALLERIES:
HAMILTON, NJ (AG) - JERUSALEM (Israel Mus.): *Group 7* - LONDON: *Fossil Forms; Cell and Fossil* - MONTREAL: *Steep Path; Group 5* - OSHAWA (Robert McLaughlin Gal.) - OTTAWA (Nat. Gal. of Canada) - QUEBEC: *Fire Escape* - TORONTO (AG of Ontario): *Atom, Bone and Embryo; Cell and Crystals* - WINNIPEG (AG).

SCOTT, Patrick
Irish, 20th century.
Born 1921, in County Cork.
Painter. Scenes with figures.
Patrick Scott studied architecture in Ireland but was a self-taught painter. His compositions, often rural scenes with peasants, are characterised by their robust simplicity. Scott became professor of drawing in Dublin. His work has featured in a number of group exhibitions, including the 1960 Venice Biennale. He held a one-man show in Dublin in 1944, and subsequently exhibited in Ireland, London, Germany and the US. A retrospective was held in 2002 at the Hugh Lane Gallery in Dublin.
MUSEUMS AND GALLERIES:
NEW YORK (MoMA): *Woman Carrying Grass.*

SCOTT, Peter (Sir)
British, 20th century.
Born 14 September 1909; died 1989.
Painter, illustrator. Landscapes, animals.

Peter Scott was the son of the polar explorer Captain R.F. Scott and of the artist Kathleen Kennet, who sculpted the statue of Peter Pan in Kensington Gardens. He was educated at Oundle School in Northamptonshire, where the headmaster K. Fisher, brother of James Fisher the ornithologist, encouraged his interest in the natural world and in birds. He continued his education at Cambridge and trained at the Royal Academy and in Munich. Sir Peter Scott's main interest was in the environment and conservation, and he used his artistic talent to fund his projects, which included the Wildfowl Trust in Slimbridge in Gloucestershire. He painted mainly, but not exclusively, birds (the panda on the Worldwide Fund for Nature's logo was inspired by one of his paintings), with a preference for geese in full flight against a sunset or a dawn scene. This became known as 'Scott's standard formula'.

He was very active as an illustrator, painting work noted for both its attractiveness and its accuracy; contributions include: *The Handbook of Birds of Europe, the Middle East and North Africa* and *The Birds of Western Paleartic*. Scott also published and illustrated his own books (*Morning Flight* and *Wild Chorus*) and contributed plates to Paul Gallico's *Snow Goose* (1946) and to the *Avicultural Magazine* (1956, 1947 and 1950).

Sir Peter Scott features in the De Witt library of reproductions and illustrations at the Courtauld Institute in London and his correspondence with the painter Keith Shackleton (which dates from c.1937-1987) is in Cambridge University Library, Manuscript and Archive Department. He held a solo exhibition at Ackerman's Gallery, London in 1933 and featured in a retrospective in Cheltenham in 1989.

Peter Scott

Peter Scott 1938

BIBLIOGRAPHY:
The Art of Peter Scott: Images from a Lifetime, London, 1992 (selection and captions by Ph. Scott). Huxley, Elspeth, *Sir Peter Scott, Painter and Naturalist*, London, 1993.

MUSEUMS AND GALLERIES:
HALLAND NEAR LEWES (Bentley Wildfowl Park): *Pink Footed Geese in Flight over Black and White Furrowed Field* - OXFORD (Edward Grey Institute of Field Ornithology): *King Eider: Male, Head. Perry River* - WALLSWORTH HALL, GLOS. (Nature in Art Museum): *Pintail in Pursuit at Sunrise* (signed and dated 1987, oil on canvas) - WAUSAU, WISCONSIN (Leigh Yawkey Woodson Art Museum): *Honkers Against a Cumulus Sky* (1980, oil on wood); *Egyptian Geese in a Morning Mist* (1982, oil on canvas); *Bahama Pintails in the Reeds* (1954, oil on canvas) - WOBURN ABBEY: *Ducks* (oil on canvas).

AUCTION RECORDS:
LONDON, 12 Nov 1976, *Swans in a Winter Sky* (1934, oil on canvas, 35 x 62 1/2 ins / 88 x 159 cm) GBP 400. NEW YORK, 20 June 1978, *Birds in Flight* (1966, hardboard, 48 x 72 ins / 122 x 183 cm) USD 1,500. NEW YORK, 28 May 1980, *Hawking* (1938, oil on canvas, 61 x 119 1/2 ins / 155 x 303.5 cm) USD 1,200. LONDON, 12 June 1981, *Ducks and Other Birds* (1940, oil on canvas, 20 x 30 ins / 50.8 x 76.2 cm) GBP 2,200. LONDON, 4 March 1983, *Pink Footed Geese Coming out From the Fields* (1945, oil on canvas, 36 x 60 ins / 91.5 x 152.5 cm) GBP 5,800. NEW YORK, 7 June 1985, *Caspan Marsch Pintails and Greylags Coming in* (1944, oil on canvas, 20 x 30 ins / 50.8 x 76.2 cm) USD 5,500. LONDON, 9 June 1988, *Wild Ducks Landing on a Pond* (1955, oil on card, 23 x 38 1/2 ins / 57.5 x 97.5 cm) GBP 4,620. EDINBURGH, 30 Aug 1988, *Wilds Ducks Taking Flight* (1940, oil on canvas, 20 x 30 ins / 51 x 76 cm) GBP 4,400. GLASGOW, 7 Feb 1989, *Ducks in Formation Ready for Migration* (1947, oil on canvas, 20 x 24 ins / 51 x 61 cm) GBP 5,500. PERTH, 28 Aug 1989, *Mallards in Flight and a Rainbow* (1952, oil on canvas, 25 x 36 ins / 63.5 x 91.5 cm) GBP 7,150. SOUTH QUEENSFERRY, 1 May 1990, *Black Ducks in Flight above a Frozen Pond* (1952, oil on canvas, 25 1/4 x 36 1/4 ins / 64 x 92 cm) GBP 7,700. PERTH, 27 Aug 1990, *Wild Ducks in Flight in Gloucestershire* (1947, oil on canvas, 42 1/4 x 97 1/4 ins / 107 x 247 cm) GBP 13,200. GLASGOW, 5 Feb 1991, *Seven Wild Ducks in Flight* (1956, oil on canvas, 24 x 20 ins / 61 x 51 cm) GBP 1,320. SOUTH QUEENSFERRY, 23 April 1991, *Ducks and Teals in Flight* (1953, oil on card, 23 1/2 x 40 1/4 ins / 60 x 102 cm) GBP 2,200. PERTH, 26 Aug 1991, *Duck Snare on a River* (1947, oil on canvas, 25 x 30 ins / 63.5 x 76 cm) GBP 5,720. GLASGOW, 4 Dec 1991, *Ducks in Flight* (1952, oil on canvas, 25 x 36 ins / 63.5 x 91.5 cm) GBP 4,180. NEW YORK, 5 June 1992, *A Pearly Dawn* (1939, oil on canvas, 15 x 18 ins / 38.1 x 45.7 cm) USD 4,950. PERTH, 1 Sept 1992, *Ducks in Flight above Chew Valley Lake at the End of the Afternoon* (1975, oil on canvas, 28 x 36 ins / 71 x 91.5 cm) GBP 8,250. LONDON, 16 March 1993, *Red Footed Geese* (1954, oil on canvas, 19 1/4 x 23 1/4 ins / 48.9 x 59 cm) GBP 6,325. ST ASAPH, 2 June 1994, *Migrating Duck by the Mountains in Persia* (1938, oil on canvas, 20 x 30 ins / 51 x 76 cm) GBP 4,830. LONDON, 22 Nov 1995, *Red Footed Geese in Flight* (1958, oil on canvas, 33 1/2 x 55 ins / 85 x 139.5 cm) GBP 2,760. LONDON, 14 May 1996, *Siesta: Ducks asleep in the Reeds by the Riverbank* (1951, oil on canvas, 17 1/2 x 15 ins / 44.5 x 37.2 cm) GBP 4,830. BILLINGSHURST, 23 Feb 1999, *Mallards that Leave Island Pool in Morning* (1937, oil on canvas, 15 x 17 ins / 37 x 44 cm) GBP 6,500. DERBY, 8 Dec 1999, *Evening Flight, Snow Geese above a Headland with Lighthouse* (1946, oil on canvas, 20 x 30 ins / 51 x 76 cm) GBP 4,100. CANTERBURY, 11 April 2000, *Greylags Alighting* (1941, oil on canvas, 20 x 30 ins / 51 x 76 cm) GBP 4,200. LONDON, 17 May 2000, *Evening Flight* (1961, oil on canvas, 28 x 35 ins / 71 x 90 cm) GBP 2,400. LONDON, 16 Oct 2001, *A Skein of Geese over Wetlands* (1947-1990, oil on canvas, 26 x 67 ins / 65 x 170 cm) GBP 4,100. CARLISLE, 25 Oct 2001, *Bewick Swans Flying from the House Pond at Eastpark, Caerlaverock* (1979, oil on canvas, 17 x 14 ins / 43 x 36 cm) GBP 3,600. LONDON, 6 Nov 2002, *If the Nights are Moonless, only the Last Little Bunches of Pink Feet Pass across Dawn* (1936, oil on canvas, 15 x 18 ins / 38 x 46 cm) GBP 2,800. AYLSHAM, 13 Dec 2002, *Mallards Rising from Pool* (1935, oil on canvas, 19 x 29 ins / 48 x 74 cm) GBP 4,500. LONDON, 12 June 2003, *Snow Geese before the Squall* (1949, oil on canvas, 30 x 50 ins / 76 x 127 cm) GBP 9,500. LONDON, 26 Nov 2003, *Pink Feet in the Severn Estuary* (1961, oil on canvas, 28 x 36 ins / 71 x 91 cm) GBP 6,500. LONDON, 10 June 2004, *Snow Geese* (1939, oil on canvas, 30 x 44 ins / 76 x 112 cm) GBP 9,000. LONDON, 3 Nov 2004, *Geese in Flight* (1945, oil on canvas, 20 x 30 ins / 51 x 76 cm) GBP 8,500.

SCOTT, Robert Bagge
British, 19th century.
Born 1849; died 1925.
Active in Norwich.
Painter. Landscapes.

Robert Bagge Scott exhibited in London from 1886 to 1896, chiefly at the Royal Academy.

MUSEUMS AND GALLERIES:
NORWICH (Castle Mus. and AG): *By the Riverside*.

SCOTT, Robert Lauder
British, 18th - 19th century.
Born 13 November 1771, in Lanark; died January 1841, in Edinburgh.

Engraver. Landscapes, architectural views.
Robert Scott is widely regarded as the best of the 19th century Scottish engravers. He studied under Alexander Robertson in 1787 while concurrently attending the Trustees' Academy in Edinburgh. He made his mark early on with an exceptional series of 12 views of the Scottish capital. He was a frequent and prolific contributor to *Scott's Magazine*. Not least, Robert Scott passed on his knowledge to a number of pupils who would subsequently emerge as master engravers in their own right - among them John Burnett, James Stewart, John Horsburgh, Thomas Brown and William Douglas.

BIBLIOGRAPHY:
Errington, Lindsay, *Master Class: Robert Scott Lauder and his Pupils*, exhibition catalogue, Aberdeen Art Gallery and Museums, 1985.

SCOTT, Samuel
British, 18th century.
Born 1703, in London; died 12 October 1772, in Bath.
Painter, watercolourist. Seascapes, landscapes, architectural views.
Samuel Scott moved to London some time after 1725 and became a close friend of William Hogarth. Scott's own sea and cityscapes were widely acclaimed. He exhibited in London from 1761, principally at the Society of Artists, the Free Society, the Royal Academy and the Spring Gardens Rooms. Samuel Scott retired to Bath towards the end of his career, by which time he had been acknowledged as one of England's leading watercolourists.

BIBLIOGRAPHY:
Cordingly, David, *Marine Painting in England, 1700-1900*, Studio Vista, London, 1974. Kingzett, Richard, '*A Catalogue of the Works of Samuel Scott*' in *Walpole Society, 48*, 1980-1982.

MUSEUMS AND GALLERIES:
LONDON (NG): *A View of London Bridge before the Late Alterations* (before 1758, oil on canvas); *An Arch of Old Westminster Bridge* (c. 1750, oil on canvas, two paintings); *A View of Westminster Bridge and Parts Adjacent* (before 1758, oil on canvas); *A Sunset, with a View of Nine Elms* (c. 1750-1760, oil on canvas) - LONDON (Victoria and Albert Mus.): *Thames, Blackfriars and St Paul's*; *Thames, Port of Westminster* - MANCHESTER: *Thames at Twickenham* (watercolour).

AUCTION RECORDS:
LONDON, 1877, *View of London*, FRF 2,550. LONDON, 19 March 1890, *Scenes in a Park* (two pendants) FRF 2,625. NEW YORK, 23 and 24 Feb 1906, *Old Tower, Sawy*, USD 350. LONDON, 12 March 1910, *View of Westminster Bridge*; *Old London Bridge*, GBP 168. LONDON, 23 March 1910, *Greenwich Hospital*, GBP 8. LONDON, 25 Nov 1921, *Horse Guards' Parade*, GBP 173. LONDON, 4 and 5 May 1922, *St Paul's Cathedral*, GBP 147; *Blackfriars Bridge*, GBP 94. LONDON, 26 Jan 1923, *Westminster from the Thames*, GBP 399. LONDON, 2 March 1923, *Lambeth Place and Somerset House* (both) GBP 199. LONDON, 27 June 1924, *Naval Battle against the Spaniards*, GBP 168. LONDON, 4 July 1924, *View of Westminster*, GBP 378. LONDON, 4 March 1927, *Capture of the 'Acapulco'*, GBP 483. LONDON, 27 May 1927, *Old Northumberland House*, GBP 357. LONDON, 8 July 1927, *View of Whitehall*, GBP 1,365. LONDON, 9 June 1944, *Port of London: Construction of Westminster Bridge*, GBP 3,990. LONDON, 15 Nov 1944, *Warships*, GBP 250. LONDON, 20 April 1945, *Westminster and Bridge*, GBP 241. LONDON, 23 Jan 1946, *Westminster Bridge*, GBP 320. LONDON, 25 Jan 1946, *Bridge and Abbey of Westminster*, GBP 1,732. LONDON, 5 April 1946, *Thames View* (two pendants) GBP 315. LONDON, 12 June 1950, *View of the Thames and Westminster Abbey* (1745) GBP 2,047. LONDON, 23 June 1950, *Horse Guards' Parade*, GBP 210. LONDON, 18 Oct 1950, *Horse Guards' Parade*, GBP 500. LONDON, 27 June 1958, *London from Westminster Bridge*, GBP 2,100. LONDON, 24 June 1960, *Old Westminster Bridge*, GBP 2,835. LONDON, 30 June 1961, *Old Westminster Bridge*, GBP 945. LONDON, 27 Oct 1961, *The Building of Westminster Bridge*, Gns 7,000. LONDON, 28 June 1963, *St James's Park*, Gns 11,000. LONDON, 8 Dec 1965, *Banks of the Thames and the Tower of London*, GBP 33,000. LONDON, 12 May 1967, *William III arriving in Torbay*, Gns 6,500. LONDON, 20 Nov 1968, *Horse Guards' Parade*, GBP 28,000. LONDON, 24 June 1970, *Building Westminster Bridge*, GBP 40,000. LONDON, 23 June 1972, *Thames at Westminster*, Gns 18,000. NEW YORK, 1 June 1974, *Yachts and Fishing Boats*, USD 44,000. LONDON, 14 July 1976, *Thames at Westminster* (oil on canvas, 21 x 43 ins / 53.5 x 109 cm) GBP 15,000. LONDON, 24 March 1977, *View of the Thames, London* (watercolour, 11 1/2 x 24 1/2 ins / 29 x 62 cm) GBp 3,600. LONDON, 27 June 1980, *Ludford Bridge* (1767, oil on canvas, 13 3/4 x 17 1/4 ins / 35 x 43.8 cm) GBP 2,400. LONDON, 27 March 1981, *Naval Battle* (oil on canvas, 30 x 48 1/2 ins / 76.2 x 123.2 cm) GBP 7,500. LONDON, 21 Nov 1984, *Francis, Duke of Lorraine, leaving England* (1731-1732, oil on canvas, 49 x 73 ins / 124.5 x 185.5 cm) GBP 30,000. LONDON, 20 Nov 1985, *Men-of-War and other craft Becalmed off the Coast* (1731, oil on canvas, 28 x 50 1/2 ins / 71 x 128.5 cm) GBP 11,500. LONDON, 12 March 1986, *Warshops and other Vessels in Open Sea* (oil on canvas, 10 3/4 x 13 1/2 ins / 27.5 x 34 cm) GBP 4,500. LONDON, 12 July 1989, *Capture of two French Warships by 'Bridgewater' and 'Sheerness' in 1745* (oil on canvas, 47 1/4 x 83 ins / 120 x 211 cm) GBP 47,300. LONDON, 15 Nov 1989, *Thames at Twickenham* (oil on canvas, 18 x 36 ins / 46 x 91.5 cm) GBP 69,300. LONDON, 10 Nov 1993, *Warship and other Craft on a Calm Sea* (1760, oil on canvas, 10 3/4 x 13 1/2 ins / 27.5 x 34 cm) GBP 6,325. LONDON, 9 Nov 1994, *Old Westminster Bridge* (oil on canvas, 37 1/4 x 59 1/2 ins / 94.5 x 151 cm) GBP 111,500. LONDON, 5 July 1996, *Naval Engagement off Lizard Point: The 'Lion' and the 'Elizabeth' and, in the distance, the Frigate 'Du Theilly' with the Young Pretender on Board, July 20, 1745* (oil on canvas, 40 1/2 x 60 ins / 102.7 x 152.3 cm) GBP 51,000. LONDON, 13 Nov 1996, *His Majesty's Ship 'William' and other Craft on a Calm Sea* (oil on canvas, 48 x 73 1/2 ins / 122 x 186.5 cm) GBP 47,700. LONDON, 6 July 1999, *Morning Gun - English Men o'War and Coastal Craft off Portsmouth Harbour* (oil on canvas, 28 x 60 ins / 71 x 152 cm) GBP 9,800. PARIS, 17 Aug 1999, *Portsmouth Harbour* (oil on canvas, 28 x 60 ins / 71 x 152 cm) FRF 184,000. CREWKERNE, 15 Feb 2001, *Covent Garden: the Hustings* (oil on canvas, painted with another artist, 40 x 61 ins / 101 x 154 cm) GBP 38,000. LONDON, 10 July 2001, *Thames at Westminster Bridge Looking East* (oil on canvas, 36 x 56 ins / 92 x 141 cm) GBP 34,000. NEW YORK, 24 Jan 2002, *View of the Thames at Westminster* (oil on canvas, 22 x 44 ins / 56 x 112 cm) USD 160,000. LONDON, 31 Oct 2002, *Historic Encounter between HMS Lion and Two French Vessels* (oil on canvas, 41 x 60 ins / 103 x 152 cm) GBP 80,000.

SCOTT, Septimus E.
British, 20th century.
Born 1879; died 1962.
Painter. Figures, portraits, landscapes, seascapes.
Septimus E. Scott was a member of the Royal Academy, where he exhibited from 1905 to 1952.

Sep E Scott

AUCTION RECORDS:
LONDON, 6 June 1984, *Tales of the Sea* (oil on canvas, 35 3/4 x 24 3/4 ins / 91 x 63 cm) GBP 2,000. LONDON, 23 Sept 1988, *Una and the Lion* (1903, oil on canvas, 16 1/2 x 24 1/2 ins / 42 x 62 cm) GBP 2,860. LONDON, 6 March 1992, *Henley Regatta* (watercolour and gouache, 15 x 12 ins / 38 x 30.5 cm) GBP 6,050. BRISTOL, 2 Oct 2001, *Tennis Player* (oil on canvas, 39 x 54 ins

/ 100 x 136 cm) GBP 1,900. BRISTOL, 2 Oct 2001, *Footballer* (oil on canvas, 39 x 54 ins / 100 x 136 cm) GBP 2,000. LONDON, 4 Dec 2002, *On the Beach* (oil on canvasboard, 12 x 15 ins / 30 x 39 cm) GBP 4,500. LONDON, 4 Dec 2002, *Sunday Morning* (oil on canvasboard, 12 x 15 ins / 30 x 39 cm) GBP 5,500. CHESTER, 27 Feb 2003, *Company of Soldiers Marching Past a Ploughman and his Boy* (watercolour, 19 x 27 ins / 48 x 68 cm) GBP 1,950.

SCOTT, Thomas D. or Tom
British, 19th - 20th century.
Born 1854, in Selkirk; died 31 July 1927, in Selkirk.
Painter, watercolourist, miniaturist. Portraits, genre scenes, landscapes.

Thomas D. Scott was a member of the Royal Scottish Academy and the Royal Scottish Watercolours Society. He exhibited in London from 1887.

MUSEUMS AND GALLERIES:
EDINBURGH (Royal Scottish Academy): *Chill November's Surly Blast* (1902, watercolour).

AUCTION RECORDS:
LONDON, 26 June 1929, *A Fresh Entry*, GBP 180. LONDON, 29 Nov 1930, *The Legend of Ladywood* (watercolour) GBP 63; *Oakwood Tower* (watercolour) GBP 115. AUCHTERARDER, 30 Aug 1983, *Troops on the March* (watercolour, 30 x 50 ins / 76 x 127 cm) GBP 1,000. WEST LOTHIAN, 30 April 1985, *Goldielands, the Watch Tower of Branklholme* (1908, watercolour, 39 3/4 x 53 1/4 ins / 101 x 135 cm) GBP 3,500. EDINBURGH, 30 April 1986, *St Mary's Loch, Selkirkshire* (1904, watercolour, 24 x 36 ins / 61 x 91.4 cm) GBP 1,800. AUCHTERARDER, 1 Sept 1987, *St Mary's Loch* (1912, watercolour, 19 1/4 x 32 3/4 ins / 49 x 83 cm) GBP 1,500. PERTH, 28 Aug 1989, *Traquair House in Peebleshire* (1923, watercolour, 17 3/4 x 23 1/2 ins / 45 x 59.5 cm) GBP 3,520. PERTH, 27 Aug 1990, *Street in Tunis at Midday* (1889, watercolour, 12 x 18 ins / 30.5 x 45.5 cm) GBP 2,200. GLASGOW, 5 Feb 1991, *Whitmur Loch* (1884, watercolour and gouache, 15 x 22 ins / 38 x 55 cm) GBP 1,650. SOUTH QUEENSFERRY, 23 April 1991, *Kirkwall* (1900, watercolour, 11 x 9 ins / 28 x 22 cm) GBP 2,090. EDINBURGH, 2 May 1991, *Portrait of an Artist, thought to be William Duthie, at his easel in a sunny landscape* (1886, watercolour heightened with white, 7 1/4 x 11 1/4 ins / 18.4 x 28.6 cm) GBP 2,035. PERTH, 1 Sept 1992, *The Way Home* (watercolour, 17 3/4 x 23 1/4 ins / 45 x 59 cm) GBP 990. GLASGOW, 1 Feb 1994, *The Bridge on the Quair at Traquair House* (1903, watercolour, 10 x 14 ins / 25.5 x 35.5 cm) GBP 862. PERTH, 26 Aug 1996, *St Mary's Loch* (1917, watercolour, 10 x 13 1/2 ins / 24.5 x 34.5 cm) GBP 1,380. EDINBURGH, 15 May 1997, *Sunlit Landscape with a Shepherd and his Dog on a Path* (1919, watercolour, 13 3/4 x 12 ins / 35 x 30.5 cm) GBP 2,300.

SCOTT, Tim
British, 20th century.
Born 18 April 1937, in Richmond (Surrey).
Sculptor.
New Generation Sculpture.

Tim Scott spent his childhood in Lausanne (Switzerland), and trained with the Architectural Association in London before studying at St Martin's School of Art under the sculptor Anthony Caro. He was subsequently active in the studio of Le Corbusier-Wegenscky in Paris, where he lived from 1959 to 1961. He was head of the department of sculpture at St Martin's in London, where he settled. Scott's early works are characterised by simple, solid forms inspired by the work of Brancusi. Later pieces are more fragile, based on a range of polychromed materials such as sheets of synthetic resin, fibreglass, metal and glass tubes, highlighting the particular characteristics of the individual elements through a play of contrasts. Since 1975 he has worked exclusively in stainless steel.

Scott's work has featured in a number of group exhibitions: 1958, 1959, RBA Gallery, London; 1961, Institute of Contemporary Arts, London; 1965, 1981, Whitechapel Art Gallery, London; 1966, Jewish Museum, New York; 1967, Kunsthalle, Bern; 1968, Akademie der Künste, Berlin; 1970, National Museum of Modern Art, Tokyo; 1976, Palazzo Reale, Milan. His work has also been the subject of a number of solo exhibitions, including: 1967, Whitechapel Art Gallery, London; 1969, Museum of Modern Art, Oxford; 1971, Tate Gallery, London; 1972, Museum of Fine Arts, Boston; 1973, Corcoran Gallery of Art, Washington; 1976, Art Gallery of Windsor, Ontario; 1979, Kunsthalle, Bielefeld; 1981, Kunsthalle, Hamburg.

BIBLIOGRAPHY:
Tim Scott, exhibition catalogue, Kunsthalle, Bielefeld, 1979. Blume, Dieter/Bojescul, Wilhelm, *Tim Scott: Skulpturen*, exhibition catalogue, Kunstverein, Braunschweig, 1988 (text in German and English). *Tim Scott, Skulturen, Zeichnungen*, exhibition catalogue, Gal. Winkelmann, Düsseldorf, 1997.

MUSEUMS AND GALLERIES:
BOSTON (MFA) - LISBON (Centro de Arte Moderna José de Azeredo Perdigão, Fundação Calouste Gulbenkian) - LONDON (Tate Collection): *Dulcimer* (1961, mixed media) - MELBOURNE (Nat. Gal. of Victoria) - NEW YORK (MoMA) - WASHINGTON DC (Hirshhorn Mus. and Sculpture Garden): *Utica IV* (1977, welded mild steel).

AUCTION RECORDS:
LONDON, 18 Oct 1990, *Rupavali* (1977, welded steel, 27 x 48 1/2 x 37 1/2 ins / 68.6 x 123.2 x 95.3 cm) GBP 5,060. LONDON, 17 Oct 1991, *Nrtta VI* (1980, welded steel, 24 1/2 x 17 1/4 x 18 1/2 ins / 62 x 44 x 47 cm) GBP 1,650. LONDON, 8 Nov 1991, *Counterpoint VI 1972-73* (oersoex and metal, 48 x 61 x 31 1/2 ins / 122 x 155 x 80 cm) GBP 3,080. LONDON, 26 March 1992, *Shruti XI* (1978, welded steel, 19 1/2 x 17 3/4 ins / 49.5 x 45 cm) GBP 1,100. LONDON, 26 March 1993, *Nrtta V 1980* (steel, h. 27 ins / 68.5 cm) GBP 1,150.

SCOTT, Walter
British, 19th - 20th century.
Born 1851, in Coventry; died 1925, in Coventry.
Painter, watercolourist. Landscapes.

Walter Scott trained and later taught at the Coventry School of Art, then became the headmaster at Norwich Art School. He painted in Gloucestershire, Wales, Lake District, Warwickshire, and Norfolk. In his early days he also designed watch cases.

MUSEUMS AND GALLERIES:
COVENTRY (Coventry Art Gallery).

SCOTT, William
British, 19th - 20th century.
Born 1848; died 20 April 1918.
Active in London.
Engraver (etching), architect.

SCOTT, William
British, 19th - 20th century.
Born 1868, in Northumberland.
Painter.

William Scott was a coal miner whose paintings, such as *Bedlington Terrier*, earned him a reputation as one of Britain's leading naive artists.

SCOTT, William Bell
British, 19th century.
Born 12 September 1811, in Edinburgh; died 22 November 1890, in Penkill Castle.
Painter, watercolourist, engraver, draughtsman.
History painting, figures, genre scenes, still-lifes.
Symbolism.
Pre-Raphaelite.

William Bell Scott was the son of the engraver Robert Scott and a great-nephew of the sculptor Gowan. He studied engraving under his father and appears to have worked alongside him until 1837, when he left for London. Henceforth, after a few forays into engraving, he devoted himself exclusively to painting.

William Bell Scott made his exhibition debut as a painter at the Scottish Academy in 1833. He enjoyed considerable success with *The Old English Ballad Singer, Jester* (1840) and *King Alfred disguised as a Harpist*. In 1842, however, he experienced a setback when both the Royal Academy and the British Institution declined to exhibit his work. He was offered a teaching post in Newcastle, almost by way of compensation, and from 1843 to 1858 was preoccupied by his duties there. He re-entered the fray again in June 1861, when a one-man show was organised. The following year Scott visited Italy; he was destined to return there in 1873. Following his solo exhibition in 1861, however, he again began exhibiting at the Royal Academy, the British Institution and the Suffolk Street Gallery. He continued to do so until 1869.

After the death of his brother David in 1849, William Bell Scott aligned himself with the Pre-Raphaelites, although his sympathy with their credo and his personal affection for Rossetti and William Holman Hunt does not appear to have impacted to any considerable degree on his own artistic output. Scott was also a poet and an author of some distinction. He repeatedly expressed admiration for the painters of the Italian Renaissance, but his own work was influenced much more by German art, especially the engravings of Dürer. His own murals also betray the influence of German Romantics such as Caspar David Friedrich. Scott penned three books on this subject - a life of Dürer in 1869, a monograph on contemporary German painting in 1873 and an introductory chapter to a work entitled *Minor Masters*, published in 1879. He amassed a major engravings collection where, predictably, German engravers were particularly well represented.

BIBLIOGRAPHY:

Hall, Michael, '*Penkill Castle, Ayrshire, Home of Dr Elton A. Eckstrand*' in *Country Life*, vol. 185, 1991. Dare, Robert, '*History, Progress and Industry: William Bell Scott's Iron and Coal*' in *Word and Image*, vol. 12, 3, London, 1996.

MUSEUMS AND GALLERIES:

EDINBURGH (Nat. Gal. of Scotland): *The Nativity* (1872, oil on canvas); *Albrecht Dürer in Nurnberg* (oil on canvas); *Una and the Lion* (oil on canvas, exhibited in 1860) - LONDON (Tate Collection): *The Eve of the Deluge* (1865, oil on canvas) - LONDON (Victoria and Albert Mus.): eleven watercolours - SUNDERLAND: *Funeral of the Sea King*.

AUCTION RECORDS:

LONDON, 9 March 1976, *Dusk by the Sea* (1861, oil on canvas, 13 x 19 ins / 33 x 48 cm) GBP 750. LONDON, 6 Dec 1977, *Twilight* (1862, oil on canvas, 13 x 19 ins / 33 x 48.5 cm) GBP 2,000. LONDON, 14 Feb 1978, *Harvest Scene near the Sea* (oil on canvas, 13½ x 19¾ ins / 34 x 50 cm) GBP 1,700. LONDON, 18 April 1978, *Rending of the Veil* (1867-1868, watercolour, 28½ x 23½ ins / 72.5 x 60 cm) GBP 1,700. GLASGOW, 10 April 1980, *Eve of the Deluge* (1865, oil on canvas, 28¾ x 55 ins / 73 x 140 cm) GBP 12,000. GLASGOW, 1 Oct 1981, *Chaucer reading one of his Poems* (oil on canvas, rounded at the top, 25¼ x 35 ins / 64 x 89 cm) GBP 4,000. LONDON, 15 June 1982, *'Thou hast left me ever, Jamie, Thou hast left me ever' (Robert Burns)* (watercolour heightened with gouache, 16½ x 26 ins / 42 x 66 cm) GBP 2,400. LONDON, 21 June 1983, *Fair Rosamund Alone in her Bower* (1856, oil on canvas, 26½ x 20 ins / 67.5 x 51 cm) GBP 8,000. LONDON, 24 May 1984, *Market Square, Hexham* (1853, watercolour heightened with white, 19 x 22¾ ins / 48 x 58 cm) GBP 2,200. LONDON, 26 Nov 1986, *Seaside at Sunset* (oil on canvas, 14 x 20 ins / 35.5 x 51 cm) GBP 7,500. NEW YORK, 28 Feb 1990, *Twilight in Berwickshire* (1862, oil on canvas, 13 x 19 ins / 33 x 48.3 cm) USD 44,000. LONDON, 25 March 1994, *Proserpine Picking Flowers* (pencil and watercolour heightened with gouache, 27½ x 17¼ ins / 69.9 x 43.8 cm) GBP 2,300. LONDON, 3 June 1994, *King of the Sea's Oath: 'You can see, fair lady, that this sword can secure the ransom of a king'* (1860, pencil and watercolour, 10½ x 13¼ ins / 26.5 x 33.5 cm) GBP 3,450. LONDON, 29 March 1995, *Harvest Time at the Poet's House* (oil on canvas, 18 x 24 ins / 46 x 61 cm) GBP 2,760. LONDON, 6 Nov 1995, *Chaucer reading from his Poem 'The Flower and the Leaf' to his Patron John of Gaunt and their wives Catherine and Philippa* (oil on canvas, rounded at the top, 26 x 35½ ins / 66 x 90 cm) GBP 4,600. LONDON, 23 Oct 1996, *Still-life* (1973, oil on canvas, 48 x 78 ins / 122 x 198 cm) GBP 51,000. BILLINGSHURST, 26 Jan 1999, *The Basin of St Mark's from the Campanile* (watercolour heightened with gouache, 9 x 14 ins / 24 x 35 cm) GBP 4,000. LONDON, 8 Feb 2000, *Messengers of Summer* (1841, watercolour heightened with scratching out, 4 x 6 ins / 11 x 16 cm) GBP 4,400. LONDON, 28 Nov 2000, *Fatal Sisters Select the Doomed at the Battle* (pencil, four joined sheets, 31 x 60 ins / 79 x 152 cm) GBP 1,500. LONDON, 20 Feb 2003, *Messenger of the New Faith* (1867, oil on canvas, 29 x 45 ins / 73 x 115 cm) GBP 6,500. SYDNEY, 15 May 2004, *Study of a Young Woman's Head* (pencil, 14 x 10 ins / 35 x 25 cm) AUD 7,000. LONDON, 9 June 2004, *Eve of the Deluge* (1865, oil on canvas, 29 x 45 ins / 74 x 115 cm) GBP 30,000.

SCOTT, William Edward

American, 20th century.

Born 1884, in Indianapolis (Indiana); died 1964, in Chicago.

Painter, illustrator. Figures, portraits, genre scenes, fishing scenes, landscapes. Murals.

William Edward Scott studied at the Chicago Art Institute, then at the Académie Julian and the Académie Colarossi in Paris between 1909 and 1914. He also studied under Henry O. Tanner in France. He travelled to Haiti in 1931.

He painted many genre scenes in France and Haiti, and several portraits of Booker T. Washington. He produced illustrations for the Afro-American magazine *The Crisis*. His murals decorate many public buildings in America (in Virginia, Illinois, for example at the Wabash YMCA in Chicago, Indiana and New York). He began painting them in 1932, later producing them as part of the Works Progress Administration, which offered work to the unemployed. His sensitive, humanistic realism was influenced by the Impressionists.

Scott exhibited his work in the Paris Salon in 1912; at the Royal Academy in London in 1913; the Harmon Foundation in New York in 1928, 1931 and 1933; the Salon d'Automne in Paris in 1931; and the South Side Community Center in Chicago in 1940. His work has appeared posthumously in themed collective exhibitions, including: *Two Centuries of Black American Art* at the Los Angeles County Museum, Los Angeles, in 1976; *A Shared Heritage: Art by Four African Americans* at the Indianapolis Museum of Art, Indianapolis (Indiana), in 1996; and *To Conserve a Legacy. American Art from Historically Black Colleges and Universities*, Addison Gallery of Art, Phillips Academy, Andover (Massachusetts), in 1999. He also showed his work in private exhibitions, as in Port-au-Prince in 1931.

BIBLIOGRAPHY:

Lewis, Samella, *African American Art and Artists*, University of California Press, Berkeley, 1993. Taylor, William E., et al., *A Shared Heritage: Art by Four African-Americans*, group exhibition catalogue, Indianapolis Museum of Art, Indiana University Press, Indianapolis, 1996. Powell, Richard J./Reynolds, Jock, *To conserve A Legacy. American Art from Historically Black Colleges and Universities*, group exhibition catalogue, Addison Gall. of Art, Phillips Academy, Andover (MA), 1999.

MUSEUMS AND GALLERIES:
CHICAGO (DuSable Mus. of African American History) - INDIANAPOLIS (MA): *Rainy Night- Etaples* (1912, oil on canvas).

SCOTT, William George
British, 20th century.
Born 15 February 1913, in Greenock, Scotland; died 28 December 1989, in Coleford.
Painter. Scenes with figures, figures, nudes, landscapes, still-lifes. Murals.

The son of an Irish father and a Scottish mother, William Scott spent his childhood in Enniskillen in Northern Ireland, and studied classics at Belfast College before enrolling at Belfast College of Art in 1933. He subsequently trained at the Royal Academy in London, winning prizes for both painting and sculpture. From 1937 to 1939 he worked in Italy and France, and settled at Pont-Aven in Brittany in 1938 with his wife, the painter and sculptor Mary Lucas. At Pont-Aven, he met Emile Bernard. Scot was also active in Cagnes-sur-Mer, in southern France. He served for four years during World War II, and was subsequently appointed Senior Painting Master at the Bath Academy of Art, in Corsham, a post he held until 1956.

Scott's mature works are mainly still-lifes, but he has produced compositions approximating to figure paintings, often using his wife as a model (although their subject-matter is rendered progressively unidentifiable in the finished work). In this respect his art is comparable to that of Estève, whose own process of abstraction parallels Scott's. However, Estève's bright, Bonnard-inspired palette is in marked contrast to Scott's sobre, muted colours and thickly applied layers of workmanlike brushwork, which are perhaps more reminiscent of the careful, measured art of Poliakoff. The surface of his works is divided into a number of forms, freely positioned one inside the other in solidly balanced compositions. In the early 1950s some of his work veered towards abstraction.

During his trip to the US in 1953, Scott's encounters with the modern American school - Jackson Pollock, Franz Kline, De Kooning and others - led gradually to his eschewing abstraction and returning to a more representational style. He nevertheless remained faithful to the unalterable structure of the still-life, with forms based on plates or cooking-vessels, often reduced to a simple outline, as in *Berlin Blues 6* (1966), with irregular shapes flatly painted in separate tiers, or in *Grey Still-life* (1969). These forms are richly painted with successive layers of creamy whites, and blue tones obtained by the application of layers of white paint on a vividly coloured base.

Scott exhibited at the Salon d'Automne in Paris, of which he became a member from 1938. His work also featured in major exhibitions of British contemporary art in Britain and abroad: 1947, 1953 Institute of Contemporary Art, London; regularly since 1950 at the Solomon R. Guggenheim Museum, New York; 1953, Brooklyn Museum, New York; 1955, 1958, 1964 Documenta, Kassel; 1955, 1958, 1961 Carnegie Institute, Pittsburgh; 1955 Museum of Modern Art de New York; 1956, 1986 Tate Gallery, London; 1959 Museum of Art, Baltimore; 1960, Pushkin Museum, Moscow; 1962 National Gallery of Canada, Ottawa, San Francisco Museum of Art, Museum of the Twentieth Century, Vienna; 1964, Calouste Gulbenkian Foundation, Lisbon; 1967, National Museum of Modern Art, Tokyo; 1970, National Gallery of Art, Washington; 1977, Royal Academy, London, city museum, Madrid; 1984, Victoria and Albert Museum, London; 1987, Musée d'Art Moderne de Saint-Étienne. Scott's work has also been the subject of a number of solo exhibitions, including: 1942, 1948, 1951, 1953, 1954, 1956, 1959, 1961, 1963, London; 1953, 1961 São Paulo Biennale; from 1956 on, New York; 1958 Venice Biennale and the Musée d'Art Moderne de la Ville de Paris, the Wallraf-Richartz Museum, Cologne, Palais des Beaux-Arts, Brussels, the Zurich Kunsthaus, Museum Boymans Van Beuningen in Rotterdam; 1960, Kestner-Gesellschaft, Hanover and the Kunstverein, Freiburg, Museum am Ostwall, Dortmund and the Städtische Galerie, Munich; 1963 Kunsthalle, Bern and the Ulster Museum, Belfast; 1972 Tate Gallery, London; 1975 Albright-Knox Art Gallery, Buffalo; 1981, Imperial War Museum, London; 1986, Ulster Museum, Belfast; 1991, Kerlin Gallery, Dublin; 1992, Andre Emmerich Gallery, New York.

BIBLIOGRAPHY:
Alley, Ronald, *William Scott,* Methuen, London, 1962. *William Scott - Paintings, Drawings, Gouaches,* exhibition catalogue, Tate Gall., London, 1972. Alley, Ronald/Flanagan, Terence, *William Scott,* Council of Northern Ireland, Belfast, 1986. Lynton, Norbert, '*William Scott*' in *coll. Modern British Masters,* vol. I, Bernard Jacobsen, London, 1990. *William Scott - Paintings on Paper and Canvas,* exhibition catalogue, André Emmerich Gall., New York, 1992.

MUSEUMS AND GALLERIES:
ABERDEEN (AG): *Composition with Blue and Black* (*Composition with Blue and Black*); *Seated Nude*; *The Border Widow* - ADELAIDE (AG of South Australia) - BALTIMORE (MA) - BELFAST (Ulster Mus.): *Still-life* (1949, oil on canvas); *Brown Still-life* (1958, oil on canvas); *White with Red Lines* (1962, oil on canvas); *Egypt Series No. 3* (1972, oil on canvas) - BIRMINGHAM (Mus. and AG): *Still-life: Flowers and a Jug* (1946, oil on canvas); *Brown and Black* (oil on canvas) - BRISTOL (City Mus. and AG): *Still-life with Fish, Mushrooms, Knife* (oil on canvas); other paintings - BUFFALO (Albright-Knox AG) - CAMBRIDGE (Fitzwilliam Mus.) - CAMBRIDGE (Kettle's Yard, University of Cambridge): *Still-life with White Mug* (1957, oil on canvas); *Bowl* (1962, oil on canvas) - EDINBURGH (Scottish Nat. Gal. of Modern Art) - GENOA (Gal. d'Arte Moderna) - HAMBURG (Kunsthalle) - HOUSTON (MFA) - LISBON (Museu Calouste Gulbenkian) - LONDON (Imperial War Mus.) - LONDON (Tate Collection): *Seated Nude* (1939, oil on canvas); *White, Sand and Ochre* (1960-1961, oil on canvas); *Berlin Blues 4* (1965, oil on canvas); *Permutations Ochre* (1978, oil on canvas) - LONDON (Victoria and Albert Mus.) - MELBOURNE (Nat. Gal. of Victoria) - NEW YORK (MoMA) - NEW YORK (Solomon R. Guggenheim Mus.): *Composition in Yellow and Black* (1953) - OTTAWA (Nat. Gal. of Canada) - PARIS (MNAM-CCI) - PITTSBURGH (Carnegie MA): *Seated Figure* (1954, oil on canvas) - ROME (Gal. Nazionale d'Arte Moderna) - SANTA BARBARA (MA): *Composition, Ceruleum* (1960, watercolour and gouache); *Still-life* (1988, coloured lithograph) - SÃO PAULO (Museum of Modern Art) - SOUTHAMPTON (City AG): *Gouache* (1963) - SYDNEY (AG of New South Wales) - TOLEDO (MA) - TORONTO (AG of Ontario) - TURIN (Galleria Civica D'arte Moderna e Contemporanea) - VIENNA (Mus. Moderner Kunst Stiftung Ludwig) - WASHINGTON DC (Hirshhorn Mus. and Sculpture Garden): *Black And White Forms* (1953, oil on canvas).

AUCTION RECORDS:
LONDON, 4 Dec 1963, *Still-life,* GBP 340. LONDON, 17 March 1965, *Still-life with Eggs on a Dish,* GBP 420. NEW YORK, 25 Sept 1968, *Up and Across,* USD 3,000. LONDON, 27 Oct 1972, *Young Girl on the Beach,* Gns 6,000. LONDON, 3 April 1974, *Orange and White* (1960) GBP 3,600. LONDON, 16 March 1977, *Berlin Blues* (1965, oil on canvas, 20 x 20 ins / 51 x 51 cm) GBP 580. LONDON, 14 March 1979, *Blue Still-life* (1957, oil on canvas, 29 3/4 x 35 1/2 ins / 75.5 x 90 cm) GBP 1,200. LONDON, 23 May 1984, *Still-life with Bottles* (1955, black chalk, 19 x 25 1/2 ins / 48 x 65 cm) GBP 2,200. LONDON, 6 Dec 1984, *Yellow Still-life* (1958, oil on canvas, 40 1/4 x 50 ins / 102 x 127 cm) GBP 7,000. LONDON, 24 April 1985, *View of a Village* (1941, watercolour/pencil outlines, 16 x 19 ins / 40.5 x 48 cm) GBP 900. LONDON, 21 May 1986, *Seated Nude* (1946, oil on canvas, 31 x 18 1/2 ins / 79 x 47 cm) GBP 9,000. LONDON, 9 June 1988, *Still-life with Dark Blue and White* (oil on canvas, 11 3/4 x 13 3/4

ins / 30 x 35 cm) GBP 1,155. BELFAST, 28 Oct 1988, *Mandarin Orange III* (1969, watercolour and gouache, 26 3/4 x 40 ins / 68.2 x 101.3 cm) GBP 3,960. LONDON, 9 June 1989, *Seated Young Girl* (oil on canvas, 20 x 15 ins / 50.8 x 38.2 cm) GBP 12,650. LONDON, 10 Nov 1989, *On Pale Grey* (1963, oil on canvas, 34 x 44 ins / 86.5 x 111.8 cm) GBP 19,800. LONDON, 9 March 1990, *Harbour* (oil on card, 10 1/2 x 14 ins / 26.7 x 35.6 cm) GBP 12,650. NEW YORK, 5 Oct 1990, *Composition* (oil on canvas, 20 x 24 ins / 50.8 x 61 cm) USD 22,000. LONDON, 9 Nov 1990, *Black, Navy-blue and Brown* (1960, oil on paper, 19 1/2 x 24 1/4 ins / 49.5 x 61.5 cm) GBP 8,800. LONDON, 8 March 1991, *Abstract Composition* (pastel, 14 1/2 x 13 1/2 ins / 37 x 34.5 cm) GBP 3,520. LONDON, 7 June 1991, *Three Forms* (1971, oil on canvas, 48 x 48 ins / 121.9 x 121.9 cm) GBP 25,300. LONDON, 8 Nov 1991, *Poem for a Jug, Blue on White* (1978, oil on canvas, 20 x 20 ins / 50.8 x 50.8 cm) GBP 8,580. LONDON, 26 March 1993, *Brown, Black and White* (1973, oil on canvas, 25 x 25 ins / 63.5 x 63.5 cm) GBP 8,050. NEW YORK, 5 May 1993, *Blue in Brown* (oil/synthetic resin, 22 1/4 x 26 3/4 ins / 56.4 x 68 cm, 1 1/4 ins/3 cm) USD 13,800. LONDON, 25 Nov 1993, *Young Woman in Front of a Table* (1938, oil on canvas, 24 x 30 ins / 61 x 76 cm) GBP 45,500. LONDON, 26 Oct 1994, *Aegean Light* (1973, oil on canvas, 66 1/4 x 68 ins / 168 x 173 cm) GBP 40,000. LONDON, 30 May 1997, *Still-life with Fish IV* (1956, pencil and charcoal, 22 x 30 ins / 55.9 x 76.2 cm) GBP 5,520; *Gaelic Landscape* (1961-1962, oil on canvas, 63 x 68 1/2 ins / 160 x 174 cm) GBP 58,700. LONDON, 22 Oct 1997, *Still-life with Sandy Background* (1971, oil on canvas, 48 x 72 ins / 122 x 183 cm) GBP 29,325. LONDON, 11 Dec 1997, *Seated Nude* (1956, charcoal/paper, 25 x 19 ins / 63.5 x 48.2 cm) GBP 2,530. LONDON, 5 March 1999, *Fish and Eggs* (1950, oil on canvas, 13 x 16 ins / 33 x 41 cm) GBP 58,000. LONDON, 4 June 1999, *Table with Still-life No. 1* (1958, oil on canvas, 40 x 50 ins / 101 x 127 cm) GBP 24,000. LONDON, 21 June 2000, *Mother and Child* (1942, oil on canvas, 20 x 24 ins / 51 x 61 cm) GBP 55,000. LONDON, 24 Nov 2000, *Opposite and Equal* (1961, oil on canvas, 68 x 67 ins / 173 x 169 cm) GBP 42,000. LONDON, 13 June 2001, *Dark Blue, Light Blue and White* (1964, oil on canvas, 74 x 48 ins / 187 x 123 cm) GBP 80,000. LONDON, 13 June 2001, *Still-life* (1957, oil on canvas, 54 x 71 ins / 138 x 181 cm) GBP 140,000. LONDON, 17 May 2002, *Still-life with Frying Pan* (c. 1947-1948, oil on canvas, 26 x 32 ins / 67 x 81 cm) GBP 135,000. LONDON, 7 June 2002, *Figure Divided* (1965, oil on canvas, 66 x 78 ins / 167 x 198 cm) GBP 65,000. LONDON, 6 June 2003, *White, Brown and Black* (1959, oil on canvas, 16 x 20 ins / 40 x 50 cm) GBP 75,000. LONDON, 21 Nov 2003, *Bowl and Frying Basket* (1950, oil on canvas, 20 x 24 ins / 51 x 61 cm) GBP 165,000. LONDON, 4 June 2004, *Orchre Still-life II* (oil on canvas, 48 x 48 ins / 122 x 122 cm) GBP 82,000. LONDON, 4 June 2004, *Harbour, Port Manech* (1939, oil on canvas, 20 x 24 ins / 51 x 61 cm) GBP 100,000.

SCOTT, William Henry Stothard
British, 19th century.
Born 7 March 1783, in Brighton; died 27 December 1850.
Painter, watercolourist, lithographer. Interiors, waterscapes, urban views, architectural views.

William Henry Stothard Scott was an Associate Member of the Society of Painters in Watercolours. He worked in Brighton and painted numerous views of Sussex and Surrey.

MUSEUMS AND GALLERIES:

MANCHESTER: *Severn Valley* (watercolour).

AUCTION RECORDS:

LONDON, 4 and 5 May 1922, *Rhine View* (drawing) GBP 23; *Sussex Views* (two drawings) GBP 75; *River Thames at Richmond; View of Pau* (two drawings) GBP 92. LONDON, 9 Feb 1923, *Shoreham; Snowdon* (drawing, both) GBP 48. LONDON, 18 March 1980, *Pulborough* (watercolour, 21 3/4 x 31 ins / 55.5 x 79 cm) GBP 650. LONDON, 10 July 1984, *Cottage at Old Shoreham* (watercolour pencil and touches of white, 21 x 28 1/4 ins / 53.5 x 72 cm) GBP 700.

SCOTT, William Wallace
American, 19th century.
Born 1819; died 6 October 1905, in New York.
Watercolourist.

William Wallace Scott worked in London until 1859, then moved to New York.

SCOTT-SMITH, Jessie (Miss)
British, 19th century.
Miniaturist.

Jessie Scott-Smith worked in Balham and exhibited at London's Royal Academy and the New Water-Colour Society as of 1883; she is not to be confused with the American painter Jessie Wilcox Smith.

SCOTTI
Italian, 19th century.
Active in Italy.
Painter.

Scotti's work appeared in exhibitions in Paris. He received an honourable mention at the Exposition Universelle of 1900 in Paris.

SCOTTI. See also **SCOTTO**

SCOTTI, Anton Marcell
Austrian, 18th century.
Born 1765, in Kosel; died 10 June 1795, in Vienna.
Draughtsman, engraver.

Scotti was a pupil of Weirotter.

SCOTTI, Antonio
Russian, 19th century.
Died 1827, in Odessa.
Active in Venice.
Painter. Stage sets.

Antonio Scotti worked in Warsaw from 1803.

SCOTTI, Bartolomeo
Italian, 18th century.
Born 1727, in Laino.
Painter.

Bartolomeo Scotti, the brother of Giosuè Scotti, was court painter to the dukes of Württemberg.

SCOTTI, Carlo
Italian, 17th century.
Engraver (burin).

Carlo Scotti worked in Venice, Bologna and Modena. He engraved vignettes and portraits.

SCOTTI, Domenico
Italian, 18th century.
Active in Naples.
Painter.

SCOTTI, Domenico or Dementij
Italian, 19th century.
Born 1780.
Painter, draughtsman.

Domenico Scotti drew battle scenes and made drawings for engravings.

SCOTTI, Ernesto M.
Argentinian, 20th century.
Born 1900, in Buenos Aires.
Painter. Nudes, portraits.

SCOTTI, Felice, or Scotto
Italian, 15th century.
Active at the end of the 15th century.
Painter, glass painter. Religious subjects. Frescoes.

Some of Felice Scotti's works are in private collections in Como, while in the church of S Croce is his fresco cycle depicting the *Life of St Bernard*.

SCOTTI, Francesco Emmanuele. See **SCOTTO**

SCOTTI, Giorgio
Italian, 15th century.
Active in Como in 1464.
Painter.

SCOTTI, Giosuè
Italian, 18th century.
Born 1729, in Laino; died 1785, in St Petersburg.
Painter.
The son of Pietro Scotti, Giosuè Scotti also worked in Stuttgart and in Russia.

SCOTTI, Giovanni Pietro. See **ZAIST Giovanni Battista**

SCOTTI, Girolamo. See **SCOTTO**

SCOTTI, Gottardo, or de Scotis, Schotis, Scoto
Italian, 15th century.
Born in Piacenza; died 1485, in Milan.
Painter, sculptor. History painting.
Lombard School.
Gottardo Scotti carried out decorative work in Milan in 1457 and 1458. He belonged to the guild of painters and was frequently employed at the Castello and the cathedral.
Museums and Galleries:
Milan (Mus. Poldi Pezzoli): triptych, signed.

SCOTTI, Luigi
Italian, 18th - 19th century.
Active in Florence.
Draughtsman.

SCOTTI, Melchiorre, or de Scotis, Schotis
Italian, 15th century.
Born in Piacenza.
Active in Milan from 1430 to 1451.
Painter.
Lombard School (Milan).
Melchiorre Scotti was employed to carry out work in Milan Cathedral.

SCOTTI, Nicola
Italian, 20th century.
Born 25 September 1938, in Casamicciola Terme (island of Ischia, Naples).
Active in Belgium from 1965.
Painter, sculptor.
From 1962 to 1965, Nicola Scotti attended courses at the Accademia Artisti Associati (3A) in Milan and then, briefly, evening classes at the academy in Ixelles, Belgium. His painting is derived from Expressionism while his sculpture is anthropomorphic.

He participated in collective exhibitions, frequently at the Salon du Bon Vouloir at the Musée des Beaux-Arts in Mons. His work was presented in a solo exhibition in 1969 at the Roggemans Gallery in Brussels and at the Cour Royale in Brussels in 2001.
Museums and Galleries:
Brussels (Archives et Mus. de la Vie flamande) - Mouscron (Mus. de Folklore Léon Maes) - Tournai (MBA).

SCOTTI, Pietro
Italian, 18th century.
Active in Laino during the first half of the 18th century.
Painter.
Pietro Scotti executed works for the Ludwigsburg palace in Württemberg.

SCOTTIE, Wilson. See **WILSON Scottie**

SCOTTINI, Francesco
Italian, 18th century.
Active in Florence from 1732 to 1737.
Sculptor, stucco artist.

SCOTTISH CHURCH IN VIENNA, Master of the. See **MASTERS**

SCOTTO. See also **SCOTTI**

SCOTTO, Felice. See **SCOTTI**

SCOTTO, Francesco Emmanuele, or Scotti
Italian, 18th - 19th century.
Born 1756, in Genoa; died 23 May 1826, in Genoa.
Painter, engraver (burin).
Scotto was the pupil of C.G. Ratti and studied at the academy in Genoa. He painted and engraved portraits and religious subjects.

SCOTTO, Girolamo, or Scotti
Italian, 19th century.
Born c. 1787.
Engraver.
A pupil of R. Morghen and Longhi, Girolamo Scotto made engravings of religious subjects, historical scenes and portraits.

SCOTTO, Stefano
Italian, 15th century.
Active in Milan at the end of the 15th century.
Painter.
Stefano Scotto was reputed to be an expert painter of grotesques. He was the master of Gaudenzio Ferrari and, it is thought, of Bernardino Luini.

SCOTTUS, Karol
German, 17th century.
Active in Danzig (now Gdansk, Poland) 1692.
Engraver.

SCOUFLAIRE, Fernand
Belgian, 20th century.
Born 1885, in Brussels.
Painter. Genre scenes, figures, landscapes. Stage sets.

SCOUGALL, David, or Scougal
British, 17th century.
Painter. Portraits.
David Scougall was active in Scotland during the latter half of the 17th century. He was first and foremost a portrait painter.
Auction records:
London, 18 Oct 1989, *Portrait of Mrs Thomas Craig of Riccarton in Midlothian, wearing a yellow gown and a blue cape* (oil on canvas, 26 1/2 x 23 ins / 67.5 x 58.5 cm) GBP 2,200. Haddington, 21-22 May 1990, *Portrait of George, 2nd Earl of Dalhousie, wearing armour and a white scarf* (oil on canvas, 26 1/2 x 29 3/4 ins / 67 x 75.5 cm) GBP 5,940.

SCOUGALL, George
British, 17th - 18th century.
Painter. Portraits.
George Scougall was the son of John Scougall. He painted in the manner of Peter Lely.

SCOUGALL, John
British, 17th - 18th century.
Born c. 1645, perhaps in Leith (Edinburgh); died c. 1730, in Prestonpans (East Lothian).
Painter. Portraits.
Little is known about John Scougall other than that he is traditionally alleged to have been the favourite painter of James VI - a claim that may or may not be justified.

Museums and Galleries:
Edinburgh: *Portrait of the Artist* - Glasgow: *King William III; Queen Mary; Queen Anne.*
Auction records:
London, 18 May 1990, *Portrait of David Carnegie in Armour and wearing a White Cravat* (oil on canvas, oval, 29 x 24 ins / 73.5 x 61 cm) GBP 1,980. London, 10 April 1992, *Portrait of Lady Susanna Hamilton in a Yellow Satin Gown with a White Border; Portrait of Margaret, Countess of Rothes, wearing a grey satin gown and a blue stole* (oil on canvas, pair, oval, 13 1/4 x 11 1/4 ins / 33.6 x 28.6 cm and 13 3/4 x 11 1/4 ins/35 x 28.6 cm) GBP 3,850. London, 9 Sept 1999, *Portrait of Gentleman in Armour with White Jabot* (oil on canvas, oval, 29 x 23 ins / 74 x 58 cm) GBP 1,600.

SCOULAR, William
British, 19th century.
Born 1796; died after 1846.
Sculptor.
William Scoular was possibly related to James Scouler. He studied at the Royal Academy in London and went on to sculpt portraits, chiefly of leading figures in Scottish public life.

SCOULER, James, or Scoular
British, 18th century.
Born 1741; died 1787.
Active in London.
Miniaturist.
James Scouler was a Society of Arts prize-winner at the age of 14. He exhibited on a regular basis between 1769 and 1787 at the Royal Academy and also produced pencil portraits.
Museums and Galleries:
Glasgow: *Flora* (miniature/ivory).

SCOUPREMAN, Pierre
Belgian, 19th - 20th century.
Born 18 November 1873, in Brussels; died 1960.
Painter. Interiors, landscapes, still-lifes.
Pierre Scoupreman was self-taught; he exhibited at the Cercle Artistique (Arts Circle) in Brussels and at the Belgian Triennale.

P. Scoupreman

Auction records:
Brussels, 27 March 1990, *Still-life* (1922, oil on canvas, 22 1/2 x 22 1/2 ins / 57 x 57 cm) BEF 35,000. Brussels, 12 June 1990, *Garden Entrance* (1921, oil on panel, 15 1/2 x 13 1/2 ins / 39.5 x 34.5 cm) BEF 35,000.

SCOVOLO, Mario di
Italian, 19th century.
Born 27 September 1840, in Provezze (Lombardy); died 1884, in Modena.
Active in Bologna.
Painter.
Mario di Scovolo was a pupil of Faustino Joli.
Museums and Galleries:
Brescia (Pinacoteca Tosio-Martinengo): *Cimabue Observing the Young Giotto; Captivity of Arnaldo da Brescia* - Trieste (Civico Mus. Revoltella): *After the Battle.*

SCOZIA, Vincenzo
Italian, 18th century.
Active in Venice during the second half of the 18th century.
Painter.
Vincenzo Scozia was the pupil of Fr. Fontebasso.

SCPROTTER, Adolphe
19th century.
Active c. 1833.
Painter.
Scprotter is mentioned in Ris-Paquot.

SCRAVEN, Pieter
Flemish School, 16th century.
Painter.
Mechelen School, Amsterdam School.
In 1582 Scraven was a member of the Guild of Dordrecht and in 1591 a burgher of Amsterdam.

SCREMIN, Giambattista
Italian, 19th century.
Born 1821, in Padua; died 1908.
Painter.
A pupil of Vincenzo Gazzotto, Giambattista Scremin worked as a painter of stage sets in Pisa, Florence, Rome, Naples, Palermo and Paris.

SCRETA. See also **SKRETA**

SCRETA, Karel or Karl (Count Sotnowsky von Zoworzie), or Skreta, Creeten
Moldovan Czech, 17th century.
Born 1610, in Prague; died 1674, in Prague.
Painter, engraver, draughtsman, illustrator. History painting, religious subjects, mythological subjects, portraits.
Bohemian School.
Karel Screta came from a Moldovan family. He began studying painting in Prague with artists linked to the court of Rudolph II, and then went to Stuttgart for religious reasons. He appears to have then continued his artistic training in Italy, and lived for several years in Venice, Bologna and Florence. In 1634, he met Nicholas Poussin in Rome. He was appointed as a teacher at the academy of fine arts in Bologna. On returning to Prague around 1638, having converted to Catholicism, he was nominated a member of the art academy, and became its director in 1652.

Several of his drawings were engraved by Matthäus Merian and Wenzel Hollar. He produced several engravings that were made into prints. Many of his paintings are of religious scenes, in particular the lives of saints. He worked for various churches in Prague. He produced a cycle of 30 paintings, which have since been lost, portraying the life of St Wenceslas. He painted portraits of dignitaries, including *The Empress Eleonore, Poussin,* and *Joachim von Sandrart.* He painted figures in monumental, sober compositions, and was able to give the figures personality without losing the overall melancholic, or Romanesque atmosphere of the work. His work featured in an exhibition entitled *Lumière et ténèbres, art et civilisation du Baroque en Bohême* (*Light and Shadow, Baroque Art and Civilisation in Bohemia*) at the Palais des Beaux-Arts in Lille (2002).
Bibliography:
Pazaurek, Gustav E., *Carl Screta (1610-1674), ein Beitrag zur Kunstgechichte des XVII. Jahrhundertes*, B. Knauer, Prague, 1889. Blazicek, Oldrich J., *Karel Skréta: die Familie des Edelsteinschneiders*, Artia, Prague, 1964. Neumann, Jaromír, *Skrétové. Karel Skréta a jeho syn*, Akropolis, Prague, 2000. Vlnas, Vit (ed.), *Lumière et ténèbres, art et civilisation du Baroque en Bohême*, exhibition catalogue, Palais des Beaux-Arts, Lille, Réunion des musées nationaux, Paris, 2002.
Museums and Galleries:
Darmstadt (Hessisches Landesmus.): *Portrait of a Man* - Dresden (Gemäldegal.): *Moses with the Tablets of the Law; St Paul; St Gregory; St Ambrose; St Jerome; St Mark; St Matthew; St Luke; St John the Baptist; Portrait of Bernard de Wit-*

te and the Count von Terzky - OBERSCHLEISSHEIM (PG): *Christ and the Samaritan* - PRAGUE (Church of Our Lady of Týn): *St Luke Painting the Virgin* - PRAGUE (Church of St Martin): *St Giles* - PRAGUE (Church of St Nicholas) - PRAGUE (Church of St Stephen) - PRAGUE (Rudolfinum Gal.): *St Luke Painting the Virgin; St Martin Divides his Cloak; Christ before Pilate; Flagellation; St Wenceslas* (two); *Birth of a Saint* - VIENNA (Czernin'sche Gemäldegal.): *Madonna and Child; St Augustine* - VIENNA (Liechtenstein Mus.): *St Wenceslas Tearing Down the Idols.*

AUCTION RECORDS:

NEW YORK, 16 Jan 1986, *Studies for the Adoration of the Shepherds* (red chalk on first side, and red chalk and pen on the back, 12 1/2 x 15 1/4 ins / 32 x 39 cm) USD 3,500. NEW YORK, 11 Jan 1994, *Apollo and the Muses* (black chalk, ink and wash, design of a title page for a music book, 5 1/2 x 7 3/4 ins / 14.2 x 19.6 cm) USD 6,325.

SCRIBE, Ferdinand or Fernand
Belgian, 19th - 20th century.
Born 1851; died 1913, in Ghent.
Painter. Landscapes.
Orientalism.

MUSEUMS AND GALLERIES:

GHENT.

SCRIBE, Ovide Léon or Léon Ovide
French, 19th century.
Born 14 September 1841, in Albert (Somme).
Painter, potter. Portraits, genre scenes, landscapes.

His masters were Boischevalier, Ingres and Henner. He made his Salon debut in 1868.

SCRILLI, Bernardo Sansone. See **SGRILLI**

SCRIVE, Philippe
Canadian, 20th century.
Born 17 August 1927, in Ville-Marie (Quebec).
Active since 1974 and naturalised in France.
Sculptor.

Philippe Scrive studied at the École des Beaux-Arts in Quebec from 1944 until 1946, then at the École des Beaux-Arts in Paris from 1946 until 1952. He met Brancusi in 1948, the architects Neutra and Frank Lloyd Wright in the USA in 1952, and Le Corbusier in 1954.

During the early part of Scrive's career, after 1946, he worked mainly with stone and wood, intuitively carving structures with solidly balanced shapes in the manner of the most primitive art forms. In the second stage of his development he began to use concrete and metal, particularly after he had collaborated with architects such as J. Willerval, J. Faugeron, R. Génermont, Legrand-Rabinel, M. Marty and G. Maillols. Using metal opened up more aerial possibilities and he soon began to use it in sculptures not specifically designed for architectural purposes.

Although some of Scrive's most recent works are once more reminiscent of ancient sculptures carved from solid masses, often made up from clearly visible elements rigorously fitted together, others are composed of flowing petal-like forms resting one against another. The shining finish of the metal, often polished aluminium, accentuates its elegance. He has also created many monumental works, including sandstone cladding for the façade of Montparnasse station in Paris in 1964; two sculptures in wood for the church in Nevers in 1965; a sculpture in wood for the ENA in Villeneuve-d'Ascq in 1973; and a fountain sculpture for the Place Jean Jaurès for the town hall in Montreal in 1975.

Scrive has taken part in collective exhibitions, including the Quebec Symposium in 1969, and also regularly in the Paris Salons, particularly the Salon de la Jeune Sculpture since 1958. He has also shown his works in private exhibitions, in Paris in 1958, 1968 and 1972; Montreal in 1960; Caracas and Neuchâtel in 1974; and at the Services Culturels du Québec in Paris in 1987. He has won many prizes, including the Prix des Vikings in Paris in 1953 and the Prix de la Jeune Sculpture in Paris in 1972.

SCRIVEN, Edward
British, 19th century.
Born 1775, in Alcester; died 23 August 1841, in London.
Engraver (burin).

Edward Scriven was a portrait engraver, the pupil of Robert Thew.

SCRIVER, Robert M.
American, 20th century.
Born 1914; died 1999.
Sculptor. Local scenes, animals.

Robert Scriver worked in bronze.

BIBLIOGRAPHY:

Paladin, Vivian A., *Scriver*, Montana Historical Society, Helena (MT), 1972. Scriver, Bob/Cochran, Bill/Krakel, Dean/Hedgepeth, Don, *An honest try*, Lowell Press, Kansas City, 1975. '*Robert M. Scriver*' in *Salon d'Automne*, exhibition catalogue, Paris, 1987. *The Blackfeet: artists of the Northern Plains: the Scriver collection of Blackfeet Indnia artifacts and related objects, 1884-1990*, Lowell Press, Kansas City, 1990.

MUSEUMS AND GALLERIES:

OKLAHOMA CITY (National Cowboy and Western Heritage Mus.): *Laudable Effort* (1970); *Winnings* (1971).

AUCTION RECORDS:

LOS ANGELES, 9 June 1988, *King of Winter* (bronze, h. 1 1/2 ins / 3.575 cm) USD 3,575. NEW YORK, 17 Dec 1990, *Prize of a Scalp* (1963, brown-patinated bronze, h. 13 1/2 ins / 34.4 cm) USD 1,210. HAYDEN, 31 July 1999, *Elk. Moose. Mule Deer. Whitetail Deer* (bronze, four, h. 11 ins / 28 cm) USD 4,750. SANTA FE, 3 June 2000, *The Buffalo Runner* (bronze, h. 11 ins / 28 cm) USD 4,000. HAYDEN, 29 July 2000, *Herd Bull* (bronze, h. 20 ins / 51 cm) USD 7,000. SAN FRANCISCO, 9 June 2002, *Moving On* (brown patinated bronze, h. 13 ins / 33 cm) USD 3,750. SANTA FE, 9 Nov 2002, *Too Late for the Hawken* (bronze, 22 x 29x28 ins / 56 x 74x71 cm) USD 5,000. MONTANA, 1 March 2003, *Lewis, Clark and Sacajawea* (bronze, 25 x 15x18 ins / 64 x 38x46 cm) USD 23,000. HAYDEN, 26 July 2003, *Return of the Blackfeet Riders* (bronze, h. 16 ins / 41 cm) USD 14,000. HAYDEN, 24 July 2004, *Old Timers. Cowboy on a Horse* (bronze, a pair, 13 x 12x6 ins / 33 x 30x15 cm) USD 7,000. HAYDEN, 24 July 2004, *Reride. Buffalo Hunter* (bronze, a pair, 20 x 20x7 ins / 51 x 51x18 cm) USD 13,000.

SCRIVERE, Jean
Flemish School, 14th century.
Active in Ghent from 1344 to 1347.
Painter.

SCRIVERE, Liévin
Flemish School, 14th century.
Active in Ghent from 1344 to 1347.
Painter.

SCRIVERE, Macaire de
Flemish School, 14th century.
Active in Ghent from 1344 to 1347.
Painter.

SCROETS, Willem. See **SCROTS Willem** or **Guillaume**

SCROOT, Christian. See **SGROOTEN**

SCROPE, William
British, 18th - 19th century.
Born 1772, in Castle Combe, (Wiltshire); died 20 July 1852, in London.
Painter, draughtsman, writer. Landscapes, landscapes with figures.

William Scrope published a number of works he had himself illustrated, including *The Landscape, Scenery of Scotland, Days and Nights of Salmon Fishing* and *Days of Deerstalking*. He exhibited occasionally at the Royal Academy and the British Institution.

AUCTION RECORDS:

LONDON, 23 Nov 1979, *Flock in a Wooded Landscape* (oil on canvas, 35¾ x 47¾ ins / 90.7 x 121.3 cm) GBP 850.

SCROSATI, Luigi
Italian, 19th century.
Born 21 June 1815, in Milan; died 3 December 1869, in Milan.
Painter, watercolourist. Church interiors, animals, farmyard scenes, still-lifes, flowers. Decorative schemes.

MUSEUMS AND GALLERIES:

MILAN (Pinacoteca di Brera): paintings - TURIN: paintings.

AUCTION RECORDS:

MILAN, 16 March 1972, *Hen House*, ITL 1,100,000. MILAN, 12 June 1973, *Vase of Flowers*, ITL 1,400,000. MILAN, 13 Oct 1987, *Flowers* (1862, watercolour, 20½ x 14 ins / 52 x 35.5 cm) ITL 5,000,000. MILAN, 6 Dec 1989, *Still-life* (oil on board, 6 x 9½ ins / 15 x 24 cm) ITL 1,100,000. MILAN, 29 March 1995, *Flowers* (oil on canvas, 15¾ x 11¾ ins / 40 x 30 cm) ITL 12,650,000. MILAN, 14 June 1995, *Interior of a Church* (1856, watercolour/paper, 19 x 14¼ ins / 48 x 36 cm) ITL 2,760,000. MILAN, 23 Oct 1996, *Red Lillies* (oil on canvas, 29¼ x 23¼ ins / 74 x 59 cm) ITL 6,990,000.

SCROSATO, Cristoforo
Italian, 15th century.
Active in Brescia in 1432.
Painter, illuminator.
Lombard School.

Cristoforo Scrosato worked in Milan Cathedral.

SCROTS, Willem or Guillaume, or Scroets
Dutch, 16th century.
Active c. 1537.
Painter. Portraits.

Scrots was Court Painter to Maria of Hungary in 1537. He painted portraits of the Empress Elizabeth, his patron's mother, and Charles V, but these works are now lost.

SCROUDOMOFF, Gabriel.
See **SCORODUMOV Gavril Ivanovich**

SCRUERS, Xavier. See **SCHRUERS**

SCRUGGS, Margaret Ann
American, 20th century.
Born 18 February 1892, in Dallas; died 1988.
Engraver, illustrator.

Margaret Scruggs was a member of the American Federation of Arts and the American League of Artist Teachers.

SCRYMGEOUR, J.
British, 17th century.
Active in London during the first half of the 17th century.
Painter. History painting, portraits.

J. Scrymgeour exhibited in London from 1832 to 1836.

SCUDANIGLIO, Annibale
Italian, 16th - 17th century.
Active in Trapani from 1581 to 1615.
Sculptor.

MUSEUMS AND GALLERIES:

TRAPANI: lectern (bronze).

SCUDDER, Alice Raymond
American, 20th century.
Born in New Orleans.
Painter, engraver.

Alice Scudder studied at the art school in Newcomb under Chase and Francis Luis Mora. She was a member of the American Federation of Arts.

SCUDDER, Janet or Netta Deweze Frazee
American, 20th century.
Born 27 October 1875, in Terre Haute (Indiana); died 1940.
Sculptor, medallist. Scenes with figures, allegorical subjects, mythological subjects, figures, animals.

Janet Scudder studied under Lorado Taft in Chicago and Frederick W. Macmonnies in Paris. She was a member of the American Federation of Arts, and received many awards, including an honourable mention at the Salon des Artistes Français in Paris in 1911. She was decorated with the Légion d'Honneur in 1925.

She carved sculptures for fountains and medallions.

MUSEUMS AND GALLERIES:

CHICAGO (AI): *Lovers' Tiff* - NEW YORK (Metropolitan Mus. of Art): *Fountain with Frogs* - PARIS (MAM): *Child and Fish*.

AUCTION RECORDS:

NEW YORK, 29 Sept 1977, *Young Girl with a Bow* (patinated bronze, h. 26¾ ins / 68 cm) USD 1,200. NEW YORK, 21 Oct 1983, *Frog Fountain* (dark-green-patinated bronze, h. 12¼ ins / 31.1 cm) USD 4,500. NEW YORK, 6 Dec 1985, *Young Pan* (brown-patinated bronze, h. 14 ins / 35.5 cm) USD 5,000. NEW YORK, 30 May 1986, *Shell Fountain* (c. 1918, brown-patinated bronze, h. 16 ins / 40.6 cm) USD 5,500. NEW YORK, 29 May 1987, *Little Lady of the Sea* (bronze, h. 32¼ ins / 82.2 cm) USD 60,000. NEW YORK, 28 Sept 1989, *Child with Frogs* (bronze fountain, h. 12½ ins / 31.8 cm) USD 8,250. NEW YORK, 26 Sept 1990, *Child with Frogs* (brown-patinated bronze fountain, h. 12¼ ins / 31.1 cm) USD 14,300. NEW YORK, 27 Sept 1990, *Victory* (allegory in bronze balanced on a marble ball, h. 31½ ins / 80 cm) USD 3,850. NEW YORK, 26 Sept 1991, *Child with Frogs* (lead fountain, h. 12½ ins / 31.8 cm) USD 5,060. NEW YORK, 6 Dec 1991, *Child with Frogs* (bronze, h. 12½ ins / 31.8 cm) USD 13,200. NEW YORK, 21 Sept 1994, *Young Pan* (bronze, h. 14½ ins / 36.8 cm) USD 9,775. NEW YORK, 25 May 1995, *Child with Frogs (Fountain)* (bronze, h. 38 ins / 96.5 cm) USD 46,000. NEW YORK, 23 April 1997, *Tortoise* (greenish-brown-patinated bronze, group, fountain, h. 17 ins / 43.2 cm) USD 14,950. NEW YORK, 15 June 2000, *Girl with Frog Fountain* (1916, brown patinated bronze, h. 40 ins / 102 cm) USD 7,000. NEW YORK, 6 June 2001, *Figural Fountain* (weathered patinated bronze, h. 41 ins / 103 cm) USD 21,000. NEW YORK, 3 Oct 2001, *Boy with Snail* (greenish black patinated bronze, h. 31 ins / 79 cm) USD 19,000. NEW YORK, 5 Dec 2002, *Young Diana* (1910, brown patinated bronze, h. 27 ins / 69 cm) USD 38,000. NEW YORK, 5 Dec 2002, *Flying Cupid* (c. 1912, verdigris patinated bronze, h. 52 ins / 133 cm) USD 55,000.

SCULLY, Harold, or Harry
Irish, 19th - 20th century.
Born 1860, in Cork; died 1935.
Painter, watercolourist. Landscapes, interiors, figures.

Harry Scully trained at the School of Art in Cork, at Heatherley's Academy in London and then in Paris. He may have met William Gerard Barry in Cork about 1885 and perhaps Barry himself encouraged him to join the artist colony at Étaples in Normandy.

Scully was equally skilled as a watercolour artist as with oils. In 1893, he established a studio at Emmet Place in Cork where he offered instruction in the art of painting. He travelled to Normandy, Brittany, Italy, Holland and England. His subject matter was wide-ranging and recurring themes include atmospheric moonlight and evening scenes; marshlands and rivers; cottage and church interiors; farmyards and rural scenery. He visited the artist colony at Newlyn between 1880 and 1900 and eventually settled in Kent until his death.

Scully's works include: *Washing Place at Quimperlé, Washing Place, Brittany, Evening at Newlyn, Interior of St Fiacre, Brittany* (1906), *Two Breton Children in a Church* (1911), *Young Girl in a Church* (1896), *Mother and Child* (1907), *Washing Day in Cornwall.*

Scully exhibited with the New Water-Colour Society from 1897 to 1893, and with the main London galleries from 1887. A member of the Royal Hibernian Academy from 1906, he exhibited there until 1932. Scully's work has traditionally been compared to that of Walter Osborne.

SCULLY, Sean

Irish, 20th century.

Born 30 June 1945, in Dublin.

Active in the USA from 1975, naturalised in 1983.

Painter, watercolourist, pastellist, photographer.

Sean Scully's family moved to London from Ireland in 1949. He was an apprenticed typographer and studied at evening classes at the Central School of Art in London from 1962 to 1965. From 1965 to 1968 he studied at the Croydon College of Art and from 1968 to 1972 at the university of Newcastle where he became an assistant teacher. In 1969 he spent time in Morocco. From 1973 to 1975 he taught at the Chelsea School of Art and at Goldsmith's College in London. From 1977 to 1983 he taught at Princeton University. In 1987 he travelled in Mexico. Since 1975 he has lived and worked in New York, spending regular periods in London and Barcelona, where he has studios.

From the start of his career, Scully was deeply influenced by the American Abstract Expressionists, Rothko in particular, but also by Mondrian. He rejected Figuration and turned instead to the basic principles of Neo-Plasticism as seen in the work of Rothko and Mondrian, using rectangles and vertical and horizontal lines and a limited palette. Paul Klee and his chequered compositions of the 1930s were another influence. During the 1970s Scully adopted the optical approach favoured by Bridget Riley, creating the illusion of structures in relief and producing a sensation of movement through superposition within a work in flat tints. Through the combination of coloured bands and lines - sometimes humorously suggestive of Scottish tartans - Scully draws attention to the relative spatial nature of the perception of colours; yellows and oranges appear closer to us than greens, blues and violets.

By 1975 he had turned away from the use of a grid effect in favour of work structured through the repetition of horizontal and vertical bands. Scully described himself as purging his work of all that he could, including colour, although he considered himself a colourist. The only thing that he could not bear to abandon was the fundamental element of structure; the band, line, stripe or whatever this element was. The visual structure became all important. His work now bore similarities with Minimal Art and he exploited the notion of seriality within the work itself through the repetition of bands (primary geometric forms), anonymity of execution (using tape to create the bands) and the use of neutral colours, if any, such as black and white.

In 1982 Scully again changed direction, assembling pieces of painted wood in a variety of formats to create a canvas but leaving the initial fragmentation of the piece visible. These pieces display relief effects and superposition and break out of the conventional rectangle of the frame. He also used a greater range of colours, with each unit possessing its own colour rhythm - a tension born of the union of blocks of different coloured bands, size and orientation (vertical or horizontal) on the same plane. The rhythm is broken, the picture is born in the picture and affirms its independence while being disturbed by the proximity of similar motifs and evoking other 'spaces'. Near and far become confused and trouble the eye.

In the 1990s Scully worked with chequered structures and began to tackle volume in his *Floating Paintings*, metallic structures attached to and projecting from the wall (with 3 sides showing), usually arranged as triptychs and painted in oils in continuous bands in such a way that the identical surfaces continue without interruption.

Whatever the structure chosen - and this fundamentally hardly varies - Scully pays particular attention to the treatment of colour. He superposes layer upon layer of different colours, visible through the effect of transparency (a dull blue reveals the orange of the layer below and this in turn reveals the red below that), and thus obtains unique tones of great depth. Each band is treated individually and is subject to many variations, with deliberate brushmarks and colour spilling over so that no band is identical to another of the same colour and each possesses its own autonomy, power, personality and character, independent of other elements. Through this process Scully affirms his rejection of a mechanical form of painting that ignores the craftsman, in favour of one that reveals the act of the painting coming into being. This superposition of richly spread colours gives the work 'volume' (in that the surface loses its flatness) as well as an intensity and vibration. This is not just about matter; the colours evoke the sensibility of a moment, the perception of a light, the evocation of a place, a work of literature (Nabokov, Beckett, Conrad), or a person, as the titles reveal. The series Scully began showing in 1979, the *Catherine Paintings*, consists of a series of particular, typical canvases dedicated to his wife, the painter Catherine Lee, and chosen with her each year from among his current work. These are works of great sensuality and warmth and, free from the perfectionism of some Abstract art, they express an emotion born of difference at the heart of repetition, which Scully sees as 'sexual'. Scully has said that he believes his paintings are highly sexual in the way they are painted, that these are surfaces that can be touched and that this makes them sexy and exciting.

Scully has taken part in many group exhibitions, including at the following: *Peinture Anglaise Aujourd'hui* (*English Painting Today*) at the Musée d'Art Moderne de la Ville de Paris (1973); the Brooklyn Museum of Art (1986); the Corcoran Gallery of Art in Washington (1986); the Pratt Institute in New York (1988); the museum of Albuquerque (1989); the National Gallery of Art in Washington (1989); and the Victoria and Albert Museum in London (1991).

Scully has also shown his work in numerous solo exhibitions, including at the following: the Rowan Gallery in London (regularly during the period 1973-1987); the Tortue Gallery in Santa Monica in California (1975); the Museum für (Sub)Kultur in Berlin (1981); the David McKee Gallery in New York (regularly from 1983); the Carnegie Institute in Pittsburgh (1985); the Museum of Fine Art in Boston (1985); the Art Institute in Chicago (1987); the Whitechapel Art Gallery in London (1989); the Städische Galerie im Lenbachhaus in Munich (1989); the Palacio de Velázquez del Retiro in Madrid (1989); the Modern Art Museum in Fort Worth (1993); the Palais des Beaux-Arts in Brussels (1995); a touring exhibition organised by the Hirshhorn Museum and Sculpture Garden in Washington (1995); the Kunsthalle in Beifeld (1995); the Villa delle Rose Modern Art Gallery in Bologna (1996); the Galerie Nationale du Jeu de Paume in Paris (1996); the City Art Gallery in Manchester (1997); the Galerie Lelong in Paris (1997, 1999); a retrospective at the Musée Jenisch in Vevey in Switzerland (2001); *Pinturas, Pasteles, Acuarelas y Fotografías* (*Paintings, Pastels, Watercolours and Photographs*) at IVAM at the Centro Julio González in Valencia (2002); and the Hôtel des Arts in Toulon (2003).

Scully has received numerous prizes: the Peter Stuyvesant Foundation Prize (1970); the prize awarded at the *Northern Young Contemporaries* exhibition at the Whitworth Art Gallery in Manchester (1971); the John Knox bursary which enabled him to spend time at Harvard University (1972); the Harkness bursary (1975); a Guggenheim Foundation bursary (1983); and the National Endowment for the Arts bursary awarded by the American government (1984).

BIBLIOGRAPHY:

Scully, exhibition catalogue, Art Institute of Chicago, Chicago, 1987. *Scully*, exhibition catalogue, Whitechapel Art Gall., London, 1989. Poirier, Maurice, *Sean Scully*, Hudson Hills Press, New York, 1990. *Scully: the Catherine Paintings*, exhibition catalogue, Modern Art Museum, Fort Worth, 1993. *Scully - Twenty Years, 1976-1995*, exhibition catalogue, High Museum of Art, Atlanta, Thames & Hudson, London, 1995. Durand, Régis, '*Sean Scully: une abstraction ancrée dans le monde*' in *Art Press*, no. 155, periodical, Paris, February 1995. Eccher, Danilo, *Scully*, exhibition catalogue, Villa delle Rose, Bologna, Charta, Milan, 1996. *Scully*, exhibition catalogue, Gal. nationale du Jeu de Paume, Paris, 1996. Frémon, Jean, '*Scully*' in *coll. Repères. Cahiers d'Art Contemporain*, no. 91, Gal. Lelong, Paris, 1997. Yau, John, '*Scully*' in *coll. Repères. Cahiers d'Art Contemporain*, no. 101, Gal. Lelong, Paris, 1999. Carrier, David, *Sean Scully*, Thames-&-Hudson, Paris, 2004.

MUSEUMS AND GALLERIES:

BELFAST (Ulster Mus.): *Fourth Layer* (1973, acrylic/canvas) - BERLIN (Mus. für Sub Kultur) - BIELEFELD (Kunsthalle) - BOSTON (MFA) - BUFFALO (Albright-Knox AG) - CAMBRIDGE (Fitzwilliam Mus.): *Painting 20/7/74, No. 3/3* (1974, acrylic/canvas) - CANBERRA (Nat. Gal. of Australia): *Omaha Snow Door* (2000, type C colour photograph); *Art Horizon* (photographs of Scully's own paintings) - CHICAGO (AI) - CLEVELAND (MA) - DENVER (AM) - ESSEN (Folkwang Mus.) - FORT WORTH (MMA): *Wall of Light Desert Night* (1999, oil/linen); *Pale Fire* (1988, oil on canvas) - HUMLEBÆK (Louisiana Mus. for Moderne Kunst) - LONDON (Tate Collection): *Fort 2* (1980, oil on canvas); *Paul* (1984, oil on canvas) - LONDON (Victoria and Albert Mus.) - MADRID (Mus. Nacional Centro de Arte Reina Sofía) - MANCHESTER (City AG) - MELBOURNE (Nat. Gal. of Victoria) - MEXICO CITY (Centro Cultural Arte Contemporáneo) - MINNEAPOLIS (Walker Art Center) - MUNICH (Städtische Gal. im Lenbachhaus): *Stone Light* (1992) - NAGOYA (City AM) - NEW YORK (Brooklyn Mus.) - NEW YORK (MoMA) - PITTSBURGH (Carnegie MA): *Sign* (1987, oil on canvas) - SYDNEY (MCA): *Orange Print* (1971-1972) - WASHINGTON DC (Hirshhorn Mus. and Sculpture Garden): *Why And What (Yellow)* (1988, oil on canvas with steel panel).

AUCTION RECORDS:

NEW YORK, 9 May 1984, *Fort No. 2* (1980, oil on canvas, mounted on two joined panels, 84 x 84 ins / 213.5 x 213.5 cm) USD 8,000. LONDON, 6 Dec 1985, *Untitled No. 5* (1979, oil/acrylic/canvas, 48 x 48 ins / 122 x 122 cm) GBP 3,500. LONDON, 26 June 1986, *Untitled No. 4* (1979, oil on canvas, 48 x 48 ins / 122 x 122 cm) GBP 3,000. LONDON, 23 Feb 1989, *Square No. 6* (1974, acrylic/paper, 26 x 26 ins / 66 x 66 cm) GBP 1,320. LONDON, 6 April 1989, *Studies in Four Diagonals* (acrylic and collage/paper, 27 x 20 ins / 68.5 x 51 cm) GBP 1,760. NEW YORK, 4 May 1989, *Small Brown Painting 2* (1978, acrylic/canvas, 15 x 15 ins / 38.4 x 38.4 cm) USD 22,000. LONDON, 22 Feb 1990, *Black x 5* (1975, oil and braid/paper, 19 x 30 1/4 ins / 48 x 77 cm) GBP 11,000. NEW YORK, 8 May 1990, *Untitled* (1985, oil/three panels, 72 x 112 ins / 183 x 284.5 cm) USD 341,000. NEW YORK, 9 May 1990, *Two* (1986, oil, primer and glue/fabric, 48 x 56 ins / 122 x 142.3 cm) USD 115,500. NEW YORK, 2 May 1991, *Star* (1982, oil on card, 26 1/2 x 15 1/4 ins / 67.3 x 39 cm) USD 55,000. NEW YORK, 3 Oct 1991, *Zembra* (1985, oil on canvas, 30 x 30 ins / 76 x 76 cm) USD 41,800. NEW YORK, 12 Nov 1991, *Manus II* (1983, oil on canvas, 60 x 51 3/4 ins / 152.4 x 131.5 cm) USD 176,000. NEW YORK, 7 May 1992, *For Charles Choset* (1988, oil on canvas, 75 x 90 1/2 ins / 190.5 x 229.9 cm) USD 93,500. PARIS, 15 June 1992, *Untitled* (1971, gouache, 17 1/4 x 24 1/2 ins / 44 x 62 cm) FRF 14,000. NEW YORK, 17 Nov 1992, *Now* (1987, oil on canvas, 96 x 108 ins / 243.8 x 274.3 cm) USD 99,000. NEW YORK, 18 Nov 1992, *The Dark Side* (1986, three joined panels, 111 1/2 x 93 x 7 1/4 ins / 283.5 x 236.4 x 18.6 cm) USD 93,500. NEW YORK, 4 May 1993, *Abacus* (1988, oil/fabric, assemblage of two paintings, 65 1/4 x 79 ins / 165.7 x 200.7 cm) USD 107,000. NEW YORK, 3 May 1994, *Some Questions* (1984, oil on canvas, 102 1/2 x 128 ins / 260.3 x 325 cm) USD 79,500. PARIS, 4 May 1994, *Untitled* (1984, mixed media/paper, 22 x 30 ins / 56 x 76 cm) FRF 39,000. NEW YORK, 15 Nov 1995, *Black Stripes* (1984, oil on canvas, 84 x 84 ins / 213.4 x 213.4 cm) USD 57,500. LONDON, 30 Nov 1995, *Two in One* (1985, oil on canvas, 90 x 108 ins / 228.6 x 274.3 cm) GBP 51,000. NEW YORK, 5 May 1996, *Panel I* (1986, coloured woodcut, 40 x 29 1/2 ins / 101.5 x 75 cm) USD 4,312. LONDON, 23 Oct 1996, *Untitled I* (1979, oil/acrylic/canvas, 42 x 42 ins / 106.7 x 106.7 cm) GBP 24,150. NEW YORK, 19 Nov 1996, *Untitled* (1975, watercolour and adhesive tape/paper, 22 3/4 x 31 ins / 57.8 x 78.8 cm) USD 4,600. NEW YORK, 19 Nov 1996, *Darkness and Heat* (1988, oil on canvas, 80 x 108 ins / 203.2 x 274.3 cm) USD 101,500. NEW YORK, 20 Nov 1996, *Untitled* (1989, pastel/paper, 30 x 38 1/4 ins / 76.2 x 97.2 cm) USD 27,600. NEW YORK, 21 Nov 1996, *Mirror* (1990, oil on canvas, four joined canvases, 96 1/4 x 72 x 6 ins / 244.5 x 182.8 x 14.3 cm) USD 123,500. LONDON, 6 Dec 1996, *Diagonal Series No. 6* (1973, acrylic, adhesive tape and pencil/paper, 22 1/4 x 29 3/4 ins / 56.8 x 75.8 cm) GBP 1,495. NEW YORK, 7 May 1997, *Black Ridge* (1984, 84 x 84 ins / 213.4 x 213.4 cm) USD 70,700. LONDON, 26 June 1997, *Traveller* (1983, oil on canvas, in three parts, 69 x 93 1/4 x 5 3/4 ins / 175 x 237 x 14.5 cm) GBP 56,500. BERLIN, 5 June 1999, *Untitled* (1991, watercolour and pencil, 10 x 14 ins / 25 x 35 cm) DEM 10,000. NEW YORK, 17 May 2000, *Close* (1986, oil on canvas, three, attached, 96 x 69 ins / 244 x 175 cm) USD 70,000. NEW YORK, 19 May 2000, *Fort Five* (oil on canvas, 41 x 41 ins / 104 x 104 cm) USD 32,000. NEW YORK, 16 May 2001, *Music* (1986, oil on canvas, two parts, 108 x 96 ins / 274 x 244 cm) USD 105,000. LONDON, 28 June 2001, *Untitled* (1987, charcoal and pastel, 22 x 30 ins / 57 x 75 cm) GBP 12,000. LONDON, 8 Feb 2002, *Untitled* (1990, pastel and charcoal, 48 x 60 ins / 122 x 153 cm) GBP 42,000. NEW YORK, 13 Nov 2002, *Arrest* (1987, oil on canvas, two parts, 84 x 108 ins / 213 x 274 cm) USD 100,000. LONDON, 22 Oct 2003, *Enter 6* (lithograph, six, 18 x 13 ins / 45 x 34 cm) GBP 7,000. NEW YORK, 12 Nov 2003, *Stranger* (1987, oil on canvas, three, attached, 96 x 124 ins / 244 x 315 cm) USD 130,000. NEW YORK, 12 Feb 2004, *Untitled* (1983, pastel, 22 x 30 ins / 57 x 76 cm) USD 27,000. LONDON, 23 June 2004, *Dead Sea* (1989, oil on canvas, 96 x 72 ins / 244 x 183 cm) GBP 125,000.

SCULTORI, Adam or Adamo, called Mantovano
Italian, 16th century.
Born c. 1530, in Mantua; died 1585.
Engraver (burin).

Adam Scultori was the son of Giovanni Battista Scultori.

SCULTORI, Diana, called Mantovana
Italian, 16th century.
Born c. 1530, in Mantua; died 1585.
Engraver (burin).

Diana Scultori was the sister of Adam Scultori.

AUCTION RECORDS:

LONDON, 5 Dec 1985, *Christ and the Woman Taken in Adultery* (1575, engraving/copper, 16 3/4 x 23 ins / 42.4 x 58.5 cm) GBP 1,600.

SCULTORI, Giovanni Battista, or Scultore or Sculptor, called Mantovano
Italian, 16th century.
Born 1503, in Mantua; died 29 December 1575, in Mantua.
Sculptor, engraver (burin).

A pupil of Giulio Romano, Giovanni Battista Scultori worked in Mantua. He was the father of Adam Scultori.

AUCTION RECORDS:

LONDON, 18 June 1982, *Resurrection* (1537, engraving/copper) GBP 480. NEW YORK, 3 May 1983, *Naval Battle between the Greeks and the Romans* (1538, engraving/copper, 16 1/4 x 23 ins / 41 x 58.4 cm) USD 2,500. LONDON, 7 March 1985, *David and Goliath; Mars and Venus* (engraving/copper, a pair) GBP 1,150.

SCUPOLA, Giovanni Maria, or Scupula
Italian, 16th century.
Born in Otranto.
Active c. 1500.
Painter.

MUSEUMS AND GALLERIES:

BOLOGNA (Pinacoteca Nazionale): *Deposition; Entombment* (two triptychs) - COLMAR: *Crucifixion and Ecce Homo* - NAPLES (Mus. di Capodimonte): retable composed of 16 panels - PARIS (Louvre): triptych.

SCURI, Enrico
Italian, 19th century.
Born 26 April 1805, in Bergamo; died 4 May 1884, in Bergamo.
Painter. Religious subjects, portraits.

The father of Selene Scuri, Enrico Scuri was a pupil of Diotti. He specialised in painting scenes from religious history for Italian churches.

AUCTION RECORDS:

MILAN, 17 June 1982, *Diana and Endymion* (oil on canvas, 33 1/4 x 24 3/4 ins / 84.5 x 63 cm) ITL 5,000,000. MILAN, 18 Oct 1995, *Portrait of Simone Mayr* (oil on paper/canvas, 13 1/2 x 10 1/2 ins / 34.5 x 26.5 cm) ITL 4,370,000.

SCURI, Selene, married name Galizzi
Italian, 19th century.
Born 3 June 1845, in Bergamo.
Painter. History painting, genre scenes.

The daughter and pupil of Enrico Scuri, Selene Scuri exhibited some of her paintings in Parma in 1870.

SCURTI, Franck
French, 20th - 21st century.
Born 1965, in Lyons.
Sculptor, mixed media, installation artist, video artist.
Conceptual Art, Art Narratif.

Franck Scurti lives and works in Paris. He selects his themes from everyday life but embellishes his subject matter by the discreet use of humour, irony and allusions to art history. The items of furniture in his *Chairs*, for example, appear to be typical of the 1960s but are actually a blown-up rendering of a sardine can lid. His images and objects are drawn from the media and from the streets: an example is his *Café Erika* of 2000, which is based on a drawing of the wreck of the petrol tanker Erika, while his *Sandwich* of 1988 is in reality the glass door to a baker's shop adorned with credit card and luncheon voucher stickers. Scurti's *Smoke* 'installation' of 1995 was inspired by 'soft' drugs, where the viewer is invited to participate in a disorienting 'floating' experience. Similarly, his 2001-2002 video *Linea* features the transposition of a pessimistic 1970s cartoon character of that name into the volatile world of contemporary international banking and financial services.

He has shown examples of his work at group exhibitions, among them: in 1997, at *Coincidences, Coincidences,* hosted at the Cartier Foundation in Paris; in 1997, at *Transit - 60 artistes nés après 60 - Œuvres du Fonds National d'Art Contemporain* (*Transit - 60 Artists Born After 60 - Works from the National Collection of Contemporary Art*), held at the École des Beaux-Arts in Paris; and, in 2003, at *L'Etat des Choses* (*The State of Things*), an exhibition focusing on everyday objects in contemporary art, presented within the framework of *Public Treasury, 20 Years of Creation in the Regional Collection of Contemporary Art (FRAC)* at the Musée des Beaux-Arts in Nantes.

Scurti has also exhibited solo, notably: in 1993, at the Galeries Contemporains of the Centre Pompidou in Paris; in 1996, at the Jules Verne Art Centre in Brétigny-sur-Orge; in 1997, at the Centre for Contemporary Creativity (CCC) in Tours; in 1997, at the Galerie Anne de Villepoix in Paris; in 2002, at *Flags Vision,* in Caen; in 2002, at *Franck Scurti: Before and After,* held at the Palais de Tokyo in Paris; and, also in 2002, at the Centre Nationale de la Photographie in Paris.

BIBLIOGRAPHY:

Franck Scurti, exhibition catalogue, Centre d'art de l'Espace Jules-Verne, Brétigny-sur-Orge, 1996. Zahm, Olivier (preface), et al., *Trésors publics, 20 ans de création dans les Fonds régionaux d'art contemporain,* Flammarion, Paris, 2003 (text in French and English). Piron, François, "*Franck Scurti. Valeurs & Usages*' in *Art Press* n° 286 p. 32, periodical, Paris, January 2003.

MUSEUMS AND GALLERIES:

BORDEAUX (FRAC Aquitaine): *Mobilis in Mobili* (1996) - MARSEILLES (FRAC Provence-Alpes-Côte d'Azur): *Calendar* (1992) - PARIS (FNAC): *Smoke* (1995, resin, plaster, steel, foam).

SCUT, Cornelis. See **SCHUT**

SCUTARINI, Pietro
Italian, 17th century.
Active in Venice in 1646.
Mosaicist.

Scutarini worked for St Mark's church in Venice.

SCUTARIO, Filippo di maestro Giovanni
Italian, 13th century.
Active in Venice c. 1230.
Painter.

SCUTELLARI
Italian, 18th century.
Active in Bologna.
Sculptor.

SCUTELLARI, Andrea, or Scutalario or Scutelari, called Andrea da Viadana
Italian, 16th century.
Born 1560, in Viadana.
Painter.

The nephew of Francesco Scutellari and pupil of Bernardo Campi, Andrea Scutellari executed paintings for the churches of Cremona.

SCUTELLARI, Francesco
Italian, 16th century.
Active in Viadana during the first half of the 16th century.
Painter.

Francesco Scutellari executed paintings in the churches of Viadana.

SCUTENAIRE, Léon
Belgian, 20th century.
Died July 1965, in Brussels.
Painter.

SCUTIFIER, Marcus
Flemish School, 16th century.
Illuminator.

Scutifier painted the initials and illuminations of the magnificent missal that bears the arms of Croy and is now in the Library of Cambrai.

MUSEUMS AND GALLERIES:

CAMBRAI (Bibliothèque municipale): missal illumination.

SCWARTZ, Michel

French, 20th century.

Born in Seloncourt (Doubs).

Painter. Landscapes.

Scwartz took part in group exhibitions, most notably the Salon de Peinture Franc-Comtoise in Lons-le-Saunier in the Jura in 1973.

SCYLAX

1st (?) century.

Cameo engraver, painter (?). Mythological subjects.

Ancient Greek.

Scylax is represented by three cameos showing characters from Greek mythology.

SCYLLIS

6th century BC.

Active in Crete at the beginning of the 6th century BC.

Sculptor.

Ancient Greek.

Scyllis collaborated with his brother Dipoenus. He worked chiefly in wood, making statues clad with ivory and gold.

SCYMNUS

5th century BC.

Active in the middle of the 5th century BC.

Sculptor.

Ancient Greek.

Scymnus was a pupil of Critius.

SCYTHES

6th century BC.

Active c. 510 BC.

Vase painter.

Ancient Greek.

Three vases have been attributed to Scythes, one of which (a fragment) is in the Louvre in Paris.

SCZ. See **SZCZ for the names starting by these letters**

SDRUSCIA, Achille

Italian, 20th century.

Died 1994.

Painter. Landscapes.

AUCTION RECORDS:

ROME, 15 Nov 1988, *Periphery and Gasometer* (1952, oil on panel, 11¾ x 15¾ ins / 30 x 40 cm) ITL 1,400,000; *Resting Puppets* (1942, oil/synthetic resin, 24½ x 38¼ ins / 62 x 97 cm) ITL 2,400,000. ROME, 17 April 1989, *Corso Vittorio Emmanuele* (oil on canvas, 19¾ x 27½ ins / 50 x 70 cm) ITL 2,200,000. ROME, 28 Nov 1989, *Piazza Navona; Campo dei Fiori* (oil on canvas, a pair, each 19¾ x 23½ ins / 50 x 60 cm) ITL 2,200,000. ROME, 10 April 1990, *View of Rome* (oil on canvas, 15¾ x 19¾ ins / 40 x 50 cm) ITL 1,100,000. ROME, 30 Oct 1990, *Bar Interior* (oil on canvas, 22 x 28 ins / 55 x 71 cm) ITL 1,400,000. ROME, 19 April 1994, *View of the Campo dei Fiori* (oil on canvas, 27½ x 39¼ ins / 70 x 100 cm) ITL 2,760,000. ROME, 13 June 1995, *Puppets* (1949, oil/synthetic resin, 24 x 37½ ins / 61 x 95 cm) ITL 1,380,000.

SEABORNE, William

American, 19th - 20th century.

Born 1849; died 11 March 1917, in New York.

Sculptor.

SEABROOKE, Elliott

British, 20th century.

Born 31 May 1886, in Upton Park; died 6 March 1950, in Nice, France.

Painter, draughtsman. Landscapes, still-lifes.

Elliott Seabrooke trained at the Slade School of Fine Art, London, from 1906 to 1911. He was active in Epping Forest and the Lake District, and subsequently travelled to Holland, France and Italy. He served in the British Red Cross from 1914 to 1918, and was an Official War Artist on the Italian Front. Seabrooke exhibited with the New English Art Club from 1909 to 1920, and the London Group from 1919 (he became a member in 1920, and was president from 1943 to 1948 and vice-president from 1949 to 1950). He held his first one-man show in 1912 at the Carfax Gallery, London. Seabrooke's work was influenced by Cézanne. His mature paintings reflect the Pointillist technique of Seurat.

MUSEUMS AND GALLERIES:

LONDON (Tate Collection): *Old Shipping in Heybridge Basin* (1947); *Evening at Zandvoort* (1949).

AUCTION RECORDS:

LONDON, 29 July 1988, *Dutch Landscape* (1939, oil on canvas, 23½ x 17½ ins / 60 x 44.5 cm) GBP 440. AMSTERDAM, 12 Dec 1990, *A Mediterranean Village* (1929, oil on canvas, 16¼ x 21¾ ins / 41 x 55.5 cm) NLG 3,680. LONDON, 18 Dec 1991, *Coastal Landscape in France* (pencil and watercolour, 12 x 19 ins / 30.5 x 48 cm) GBP 440. LONDON, 24 Nov 2004, *Sunlit Garden. Harbour Scene* (oil on board, a pair, 10 x 13 ins / 26 x 32 cm) GBP 1,000.

SEABY, Alan William or Allen

British, 19th - 20th century.

Born 1867, in London; died 1953, in Reading.

Painter (gouache), watercolourist, engraver. Animals.

Alan Seaby was active in Reading, as a painter and wood-engraver. His work featured at exhibitions of the Royal Scottish Academy in 1925 and 1945.

AWSEABY

AUCTION RECORDS:

LONDON, 16 March 1993, *A White-tailed Eagle and its Prey* (watercolour and gouache/material, 20½ x 29 ins / 52.3 x 73.7 cm) GBP 4,025. PERTH, 31 Aug 1993, *Grouse* (watercolour and gouache/material, 18¾ x 25½ ins / 47.5 x 65 cm) GBP 1,092. LONDON, 15 March 1994, *Long-crested Tits* (watercolour and gouache, 9¾ x 7¼ ins / 24.7 x 18.4 cm) GBP 2,300. LEYBURN, 22 July 2004, *Woodcock Nesting Amongst Bracken. Bird Amongst Reeds* (pencil and watercolour heightened with white, a pair, 11 x 15 ins / 28 x 39 cm) GBP 1,100.

SEAFORTH, Charles Henry

British, 19th century.

Born 1801; died after 1853.

Painter. Seascapes.

Charles Henry Seaforth worked most of his life in London but moved to Naples in 1952, shortly before his death.

AUCTION RECORDS:

PARIS, 9 Dec 1949, *Vessels in Sight of the Coast*, FRF 15,000; *Harbour View; Bay of Naples* (two pendants) FRF 4,100. LONDON, 26 March 1976, *Battle of Trafalgar* (1849, oil on canvas, 70 x 105 ins / 177.7 x 266.6 cm) GBP 6,000. TORQUAY, 13 June 1978, *Embarking Cavalry on a Troopship* (oil on canvas, 48 x 82 ins / 122 x 208.5 cm) GBP 6,000. LONDON, 3 Oct 1984, *The 'Victory' off the Mediterranean Coast* (oil on canvas, 19½ x 29½ ins / 49.5 x 75 cm) GBP 2,400. LONDON, 20 April 1990, *Dutch Three-Master and other Craft cCaught in an Offshore Storm* (oil on canvas, 47¾ x 72 ins / 121.5 x 183 cm) GBP 11,000. LONDON, 22 Nov 1991, *Merchantman off the Indian Coast at Dawn* (1867, oil on canvas, 19¾ x 29½ ins / 50.2 x 74.8 cm) GBP 3,520. LONDON, 8 April 1992, *Admiral's Rowboat Returning Ashore* (oil on canvas, 29½ x 41¼ ins / 75 x 105 cm) GBP 9,350. LONDON, 3 May 1995, *Two-Master enter-*

ing Harbour (1861, oil on canvas, 16 x 30 ins / 40.5 x 76.5 cm) GBP 20,700.

SEAGE, Lucas
South African, 20th - 21st century.
Born 1956, in Newclare (Johannesburg).
Painter (mixed media).

Lucas Seage won the National Art Competition 1981 for Black Artists and Art Students run by the Haenggi Foundation. He received a bursary to study in Düsseldorf for two years. In 1994 Seage took part in *Un Art Contemporain d'Afrique du Sud* (*Contemporary Art of South Africa*) at the Galerie de l'Esplanade in La Défense in Paris.

SEAGER, Sarah
American, 20th century.
Installation artist, lithographer. Artists' books.

Sarah Seager took part in the exhibition *Pure Beauty* at the American Center in Paris in 1994.

She arranged letters left by the former owner of her house as a work of art, which she presents in exhibitions accompanied by requests she has made to the Archives of American Art for this correspondence to be recognised.

BIBLIOGRAPHY:
Cuvelier, Pascaline, '*Texte*' in *Beaux-Arts Magazine* n° 126, periodical, Paris, September 1994.

SEAGHAN MAC CATHMHAOIL.
See **CAMPBELL John Patrick**

SEAGO, Edward Brian
British, 20th century.
Born 31 March 1910; died 1974.
Painter, watercolourist. Seascapes, landscapes, flowers.

Edward Seago was a member of the Royal Society of British Artists from 1946, and the Royal Society of Painters in Watercolours from 1959. He painted numerous English landscapes, notably in Norfolk, where he settled, but also produced a large body of work abroad. His work also includes a number of flower paintings. Much of his work was Post-Impressionist in atmosphere. His rapid brushwork captures reflections of light, occasionally enveloping his subjects in a diffuse, Turner-esque haze. He exhibited in London, Glasgow, New York, Toronto, Montreal, Los Angeles, Oslo and Brussels. He held his first solo exhibition in London in 1944; two years later, he exhibited paintings depicting the war in Italy when he was Official Artist to the Italian Campaign. A later exhibition, at St James's Palace in 1957, featured a series of paintings executed during a world tour accompanying the Duke of Edinburgh.

Edward Seago

BIBLIOGRAPHY:
Hawcroft, Francis W., *Edward Seago*, Collins, London, 1965.
Reid, J.W., *Edward Seago the Landscape Art*, Collins, London, 1991.

AUCTION RECORDS:
LONDON, 20 May 1970, *View of Venice*, GBP 1,500. LONDON, 17 Feb 1971, *The Ornamental Pond in the Jardin des Tuileries*, GBP 1,300. LONDON, 11 May 1973, *June in Norfolk*, Gns 1,400. SCOTLAND, 30 Aug 1974, *Seashore Scene*, GBP 2,800. LONDON, 5 March 1976, *Yachts in Ramsgate Harbour* (oil on card, 14 x 20 ins / 35.5 x 51 cm) GBP 2,600. LONDON, 12 Nov 1976, *The Pont Alexandre III, Paris* (watercolour, 11 x 15 ins / 27 x 38 cm) GBP 650. LONDON, 4 March 1977, *Flooded Marsh* (watercolour, 14 x 21 1/2 ins / 35.5 x 54.5 cm) GBP 1,100. LONDON, 16 Nov 1977, *The Lieutenance at Honfleur* (oil on card, 19 1/2 x 29 1/2 ins / 49.5 x 75 cm) GBP 4,500. LONDON, 19 Oct 1979, *Village in the High Atlas, Morocco* (watercolour, 13 1/4 x 20 1/4 ins / 33.5 x 51.5 cm) GBP 2,200. LONDON, 19 Oct 1979, *Yachts on the River Ant* (oil on card, 16 x 24 ins / 40.5 x 61 cm) GBP 11,000. LONDON, 6 Nov 1981, *Village on the Banks of a River in Norfolk* (oil on card, 11 1/2 x 16 ins / 29.5 x 40.5 cm) GBP 3,500. LONDON, 3 Nov 1982, *An Old Fortress on the Italian Coast* (watercolour and pencil, 9 3/4 x 14 3/4 ins / 25 x 37.5 cm) GBP 1,200. LONDON, 10 June 1983, *Pin Mill* (oil on card, 26 x 36 ins / 66 x 91.5 cm) GBP 15,000. LONDON, 4 Nov 1983, *The Hôtel de Ville, Honfleur* (watercolour, 14 1/2 x 20 1/2 ins / 37 x 52 cm) GBP 1,600. LONDON, 15 March 1985, *Fishing-boats at Chioggia* (watercolour/pencil outline, 11 x 14 1/2 ins / 27 x 37 cm) GBP 2,800. LONDON, 12 June 1986, *The Butt and Oyster* (oil on card, 21 1/2 x 35 1/2 ins / 54.5 x 90 cm) GBP 15,500. LONDON, 9 June 1988, *Model Boats on the Ornamental Pond in the Jardin des Tuileries, Paris* (oil on card, 17 1/2 x 23 1/2 ins / 44.6 x 60 cm) GBP 8,800; *Piccadilly, London, June 1953* (oil on canvas, 17 3/4 x 23 1/2 ins / 45 x 60 cm) GBP 17,600. LONDON, 29 July 1988, *View of Whitby* (watercolour, 19 1/2 x 13 1/2 ins / 49.5 x 34.5 cm) GBP 1,265. LONDON, 2 March 1989, *In the Mud at Pin Mill* (oil on card, 11 x 15 3/4 ins / 27.8 x 40.3 cm) GBP 11,000. LONDON, 8 June 1989, *Fishing-boats in the Harbour at Ponza* (oil on panel, 20 x 30 ins / 50.8 x 76.1 cm) GBP 25,300. LONDON, 8 March 1990, *Yachts in the Harbour at Dieppe* (oil on card, 19 1/2 x 29 1/2 ins / 49.4 x 75 cm) GBP 39,600. LONDON, 7 June 1990, *Sunny Afternoon in Honfleur* (oil on card, 10 1/2 x 14 ins / 26.8 x 35.6 cm) GBP 19,250. LONDON, 8 Nov 1990, *Porto Cervo in Sardinia* (1969, oil on card, 13 1/2 x 19 1/4 ins / 34.5 x 49 cm) GBP 13,750. LONDON, 25 Jan 1991, *Summer Breeze* (oil on canvas, 17 1/2 x 23 1/2 ins / 44.5 x 59.5 cm) GBP 9,350. LONDON, 7 March 1991, *Barges on the Thames at Low Tide, at Pin Mill* (oil on card, 16 x 24 ins / 40.5 x 61 cm) GBP 19,800. LONDON, 6 June 1991, *Sampans in Tai Po* (oil on card, 19 1/2 x 29 1/2 ins / 49.5 x 75 cm) GBP 19,800. NEW YORK, 17 Oct 1991, *A Norfolk Barn* (oil on card, 20 x 30 ins / 50.8 x 76.2 cm) USD 13,200. LONDON, 18 Dec 1991, *Drumlanrig in Scotland* (ink and watercolour, 11 x 15 ins / 28 x 38 cm) GBP 1,760. LONDON, 6 March 1992, *Flowers in a Glass Vase* (oil on card, 23 1/2 x 17 1/2 ins / 59.5 x 44.5 cm) GBP 6,050; *Hazels along the Champs-Elysées* (oil on canvas, 26 x 36 ins / 66 x 91.5 cm) GBP 22,000. LONDON, 12 March 1992, *Sunny Spell at Brightlingsea* (oil on card, 20 x 29 1/2 ins / 51 x 75 cm) GBP 16,675. LONDON, 6 Nov 1992, *Marshland Mill* (oil on canvas, 20 x 24 ins / 50.7 x 61 cm) GBP 11,000. NEW YORK, 3 June 1994, *Diana Pelly Showing Belinda, Accompanied by her Dog Taffy* (1930, oil on canvas, 25 x 30 ins / 63.5 x 76.2 cm) USD 34,500. NEW YORK, 18-19 July 1996, *Herring Fishers Leaving Yarmouth Harbour* (oil on card, 12 1/4 x 16 ins / 30.8 x 40.6 cm) USD 4,025. LONDON, 5 Nov 1999, *Champs-Élysées, Paris* (c. 1952, oil on canvas, 26 x 36 ins / 66 x 91 cm) GBP 68,000. MELBOURNE, 23 Nov 1999, *Champs Élysées, Paris* (oil on board, 19 x 29 ins / 48 x 74 cm) AUD 65,000. PARIS, 26 March 2000, *Venice, View of the Grand Canal busy with a Number of Gondolas* (oil on panel, 26 x 35 ins / 65 x 90 cm) FRF 560,000. LONDON, 24 Nov 2000, *Shipping in Hong Kong Harbour* (1962, oil on board, 22 x 32 ins / 55 x 81 cm) GBP 46,000. LONDON, 8 June 2001, *Chestnut Trees, Champs Elysees* (c. 1952, oil on canvas, 14 x 36 ins / 35 x 91 cm) GBP 68,000. LONDON, 23 Nov 2001, *White Mill, Thurne, Norfolk* (oil on board, 20 x 26 ins / 51 x 66 cm) GBP 35,000. MELBOURNE, 30 April 2002, *English Countryside - Suffolk Farm* (oil on board, 26 x 36 ins / 65 x 92 cm) AUD 72,500. LONDON, 3 July 2002, *Summer on the Norfolk Broads* (oil on canvas, 26 x 36 ins / 66 x 91 cm) GBP 46,000. LONDON, 21 Nov 2003, *Blythburgh, Suffolk* (oil on canvas, 28 x 40 ins / 71 x 102 cm) GBP 42,000. LONDON, 21 Nov 2003, *Morning Sunlight, Honfleur* (oil on canvas, 28 x 40 ins / 71 x 102 cm) GBP 48,000. LONDON, 21 May 2004, *Derby Day* (1936, oil on panel, 22 x 30 ins / 56 x 76 cm) GBP 280,000. LONDON, 4 June 2004, *Circus Encampment* (1931, oil on panel, 25 x 30 ins / 63 x 76 cm) GBP 45,000.

SEAH, Kim Joo
Singaporean, 20th century.

Born 1939.
Painter. Scenes with figures, figures.
Kim Joo Seah is best known for his illustrations of contemporary life executed in batik. A wall-painting by Seah decorated the Singapore Pavilion at the 1970 Expo International. His batik paintings won numerous prizes in Malaysia in the 1970s.
AUCTION RECORDS:
SINGAPORE, 5 Oct 1996, *Indonesian Beauties* (batik on cotton, a pair, each 33 1/2 x 12 1/2 ins / 85 x 32 cm) SGD 3,680.

SÉAILLES, Andrée
French, 20th century.
Born 1891, in Paris; died 19 September 1983.
Painter. Figures, landscapes, flowers. Murals.
Séailles, daughter of the writer Gabriel Séailles and painter Octavie 'Charles Paul' Séailles, was taught by Paul Baudoin. She featured at the Salon de la Société Nationale des Beaux-Arts and Salon des Indépendants in Paris.

The rapid strokes of her small-format paintings of oil on paper ally her to the pointillist school and are reminiscent of the landscapes of Barbizon.

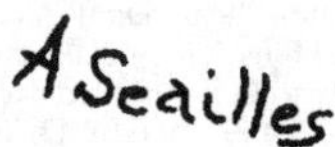

SÉAILLES, Octavie, also known as Charles-Paul
French, 19th - 20th century.
Born 1855, in Douai; died 1944, in Barbizon.
Painter. Figures, nudes, portraits, landscapes.
Séailles was the wife of the philosopher Gabriel Séailles. She signed Charles-Paul Séailles in homage to her father. She was taught by Paul Parrot and was also a student and friend of Eugène Carrière, who, along with Jean-Jacques Henner, advised her in her work.

She exhibited at the Salon d'Automne in Paris, becoming a member in 1905, and the Salon des Indépendants. Several of her pieces were exhibited at the Galerie Weil in Paris in 1974. Her landscapes could be seen to bring her close to the Barbizon School.

SEALE, Barney
British, 20th century.
Born 16 March 1896, in London; died 22 July 1957.
Sculptor, painter. Military subjects, figures.
Barney Seale studied under Frith and Henry Massey. He lived and worked in London. Seale's works were shown at the Royal Scottish Academy in 1936, 1937 and 1938, and by the Royal Academy from 1937 to 1941. He is noted for a self-portrait, a *Judas*, and a bronze bust of *Augustus E. John RA*.
AUCTION RECORDS:
LONDON, 12 Nov 1986, *Christopher Richard Wynne Nevinson* (1930, bronze, h. 22 ins / 56 cm) GBP 650.

SEALEY, Alfred
American, 19th century.
Born in the USA; died c. 1862, in Canada.
Active in Philadelphia.
Engraver (burin).
Alfred Sealey mostly engraved banknotes.

SEALEY, Doug, or Sealy
Australian, 20th century.
Painter. Landscapes.
AUCTION RECORDS:
ROSEBERY, 7 Sept 1976, *Sofala Valley* (1974, oil on card, 23 1/2 x 29 1/2 ins / 59.5 x 75 cm) AUD 450. SYDNEY, 3 July 1989, *Sofala Valley* (oil on card, 23 1/2 x 30 ins / 60 x 76 cm) AUD 850.

SEALY, Allen Culpepper
British, 19th - 20th century.
Born 1850; died 1927.
Painter. Horse racing scenes.
Allen Sealy is noted for his numerous paintings of racing scenes.
AUCTION RECORDS:
LONDON, 11 June 1986, *Jest with Jockey Up; Hulcot with Jockey Up* (1899, oil on canvas, a pair, 20 x 24 ins / 51 x 61 cm) GBP 12,000. NEW YORK, 5 June 1992, *The Rendez-vous* (1892, oil on canvas, 20 1/2 x 26 1/2 ins / 52.1 x 67.3 cm) USD 16,500. NEW YORK, 4 June 1993, *Pureblood with Jockey Up* (1905, oil on canvas, 21 x 25 1/2 ins / 53.3 x 64.8 cm) USD 8,338. LONDON, 3 June 1994, *Norman III, Winner of the 1908 Guineas Prize at Newmarket* (1908, oil on canvas, 20 x 25 ins / 50.8 x 63.5 cm) GBP 2,530. LONDON, 12 Nov 1997, *Mr Leopold de Rothschild's Bay Foal Hulcot with Jockey Up, at Newmarket; Mr Leopold de Rothschild's Bay Filly Jest with Jockey Up, at Newmarket* (1899, oil on canvas, a pair, each 20 x 24 ins / 51 x 61 cm) GBP 11,500.

SEALY, Colin
British, 20th century.
Born 1900; died 1976.
Painter. Landscapes, still-lifes.
Colin Sealy's work was shown at the Royal Academy from 1923 to 1940.
AUCTION RECORDS:
LONDON, 21 Sept 1989, *Houses at St Ives in the Early Morning* (oil on card, 18 x 14 ins / 45.5 x 35.6 cm) GBP 1,100. LONDON, 28 June 2000, *Cornish Town* (oil on board, 20 x 26 ins / 51 x 66 cm) GBP 1,900.

SEALY, Doug. See **SEALEY**

SEALY, J.
British, 19th century.
Active in London from 1809 to 1811.
Sculptor.

SEAMAN, Abraham, Noah and W.
British, 18th century.
Painters. Portraits. Miniatures.
Both artists are in all probability from the same family.

SEARCY, Elisabeth
American, 20th century.
Born in Memphis (Tennessee).
Painter, engraver. Landscapes.
Elisabeth Searcy was a member of the Pen and Brush Club and the American Federation of Arts.

SEARLE, A. H.
British, 19th century.
Painter. Landscapes.
A.H. Searle was an exhibitor at London's Suffolk Street Gallery in 1888.

SEARLE, Alice T.
American, 19th - 20th century.
Born 8 February 1869, in Troy.
Active in Brooklyn.
Miniaturist.
Alice Searle began her studies in New York, then went to Paris where she studied at the Académie Colarossi and with Mme Debillemont-Chardon. She was awarded a bronze medal in St Louis in 1904.

SEARLE, Ronald
British, 20th century.
Born 3 March 1920, in Cambridge.
Active since 1961 in France.
Painter, draughtsman, humorist. Scenes with figures.
Ronald Searle was born into a working-class family and took a job with a packaging firm to earn money for art classes. At the age of fifteen he began his career as an illustrator, producing cartoons for the *Cambridge Daily News*; this work

helped to finance his fine art studies. He went on to draw for *Punch,* and contributed reports on Alaska and the USA to *Life* magazine. In 1939 he gained a Minister of Education Drawing Diploma and enlisted in the Territorial Army as an architectural draughtsman. During World War II he produced the prototype St Trinian's panel for *Lilliput* (in October 1941), but after the British surrender to the Japanese at Singapore he entered the Changi prison camp, and was forced to work on the construction of the Ban Pong-Burma railway. He recorded the atrocities witnessed there. In October 1945 he returned to Cambridge, and married in 1946.

Since his first illustrated books were not financially successful, Searle concentrated on cartoons, including publication of *Hurrah for St Trinians* in 1948. Two years later he was engaged as illustrator for *Punch's* theatre column, and rose to become one of England's foremost illustrators, founding his own publishing company, Perpetua Books, which collected his cartoons in book form. In 1960 he became the first non-American illustrator to receive the National Cartoonist Society's Reuben Award.

In 1961, tired of popular acclaim however, he left for Paris, where he produced a series of paintings of violent and disturbing subject-matter. In 1967 he married his second wife, Monica, with whom he moved to a small village in Haute-Provence, where he produced lithographs and albums of drawings, including *It Must be True; Pardon Monsieur; Those Magnificent Men in their Flying Machines; Searle's Cats; The Square Egg and The Vicious Circle; Les Filles de Hambourg (Secret Sketchbook: The Backstreets of Hamburg); Hello, Where Did All the People Go?; Entre Vielles Connaissances; Homage to Toulouse-Lautrec.* He has since designed commemorative medals for the French mint, designed the animated opening sequences for the film, *Those Magnificent Men in Their Flying Machines,* done almost 40 covers for the *New Yorker,* and also drawn for the *New York Times* and the *International Herald Tribune* and *Le Monde.*

Searle's experience in prisoner-of-war camps forged his distinctive brand of black humour and highly personal style. His later drawings are less 'dark' in character but remain bitingly satirical, deliberately absurd and irreverent. His skillful use of rapid, freely-drawn lines, arabesques and tangled, expressive scribbles highlights select details and contours with remarkable economy.

Ronald Searle's work was shown at the Royal Scottish Academy in 1941 and 1954. Searle was also the subject of a solo exhibition at the Bibliothèque Nationale de France, Paris, in 1973.

BIBLIOGRAPHY:

Ronald Searle, exhibition catalogue, Bibliothèque nationale de France, département des estampes, Paris, 1973. Davies, Russell, *Ronald Searle: A Biography,* Sinclair-Stevenson, London, 1990. *Ronald Searle dans 'Le Monde'*, Le Cherche Midi Éditeur, Paris, 1998.

MUSEUMS AND GALLERIES:

BREMEN (Kunsthalle) - HANOVER (Wilhelm-Busch Museum) - LONDON (British Mus.) - LONDON (Victoria and Albert Mus.) - MUNICH (Stadtmus.) - NOTTINGHAM (Castle Musem and Art Gallery).

AUCTION RECORDS:

LONDON, 7 June 1985, *The Crazy Horse, Paris* (1960, pen and wash, 14 1/2 x 15 1/2 ins / 37 x 39.5 cm) GBP 1,400. LONDON, 17 Dec 1999, *The Glorious 12th* (1992, pencil, pen, ink and watercolour, 19 x 19 ins / 47 x 49 cm) GBP 3,000. LONDON, 17 Dec 1999, *St Andrews* (1995, pen, black ink and watercolour, 17 x 24 ins / 42 x 60 cm) GBP 5,000. LONDON, 8 Dec 2000, *Man's Best Friend* (1954, pen, ink and wash, 22 x 15 ins / 55 x 37 cm) GBP 5,000. LONDON, 8 Dec 2000, *First Glass* (1955, pencil, pen and ink, 12 x 13 ins / 30 x 33 cm) GBP 6,000. LONDON, 14 June 2001, *It's THEM from THERE* (1956, pen and black ink heightened with white, 10 x 11 ins / 25 x 29 cm) GBP 3,600. NEW YORK, 10 Nov 2001, *Waiter Bringing Tray of Elaborate Meal into Dining Room, Bird Atop* (pen, ink and watercolour, 17 x 13 ins / 43 x 33 cm) USD 4,750. LONDON, 4 Dec 2002, *St Trinians* (1950, pencil, pen, black ink, watercolour and crayon, 14 x 14 ins / 35 x 35 cm) GBP 3,800. LONDON, 4 Dec 2002, *Nigel Molesworth and the Karackter Kup* (1958, pencil, pen and black ink, 4 x 10 ins / 11 x 25 cm) GBP 4,500. LONDON, 3 July 2003, *Wicked World of Bookselling: Nice Set, but One Volume Missing* (pencil, pen, black ink and watercolour, 13 x 10 ins / 32 x 25 cm) GBP 3,800. LONDON, 3 Dec 2003, *Dented at Head* (pencil, black ink and watercolour, 12 x 9 ins / 31 x 23 cm) GBP 4,200. LONDON, 1 July 2004, *Winston Churchill Speaking at the Guildhall, Cambridge* (1939, pencil, 8 x 6 ins / 21 x 16 cm) GBP 2,300. LONDON, 1 July 2004, *Molesworth: Great Escape Routes* (1953, pencil and black ink, 13 x 10 ins / 34 x 25 cm) GBP 2,600.

SEARS, Charles Payne

British.

Painter. Landscapes.

Sears was mentioned by Miss Florence Levy.

AUCTION RECORDS:

NEW YORK, 9 and 10 March 1911, *In the Woods,* USD 50.

SEARS, M. U.

British, 19th century.

Born c. 1800, in London.

Engraver (wood).

M.U. Sears worked initially in London, then in Leipzig and Paris.

SEARS, Philip Shelton

American, 19th - 20th century.

Born 12 November 1867, in Boston (Massachusetts); died 1953.

Sculptor. Busts, monuments.

Phlip Sears studied under Daniel C. French and at the school of fine arts in Boston. He was a member of the American Federation of Arts. He created busts of American personalities and commemorative monuments.

SEARS, Sarah Choate

Maiden name: Choate

American, 19th - 20th century.

Born 5 May 1858, in Cambridge; died 1935.

Painter, pastellist, watercolourist. Genre scenes, flowers.

Sarah Sears studied under Ross Turner, Joseph de Camp, Demirs M. Bunker, Edmund, C. Tarbell and George de Forest Briesh. She was a member of the New York Water Colors Club and the Boston Water Colors Club, and lived and worked in Boston.

Sears was awarded a medal in Chicago in 1893, an honourable mention in Paris in 1900 at the Exposition Universelle (Universal Exhibition), a medal for watercolours in Buffalo in 1901, a silver medal in Charleston in 1902 and a silver medal in St Louis in 1904.

SEARS, Taber

American, 19th century.

Died 1870, in Boston.

Active in New York.

Painter. Decorative schemes.

Taber Sears studied in Boston, Paris, Florence and Rome.

SEATON, Christopher

British, 18th century.

Died 6 October 1768.

Active in London.

Cameo engraver.

Christopher Seaton was a pupil of Christopher Reisen. He also sculpted portraits.

SEATON, John Thomas. See **SETON John Thomas**

SEAVER, Elizabeth A.
American, 20th century.
Active from 1930 until 1940.
Sculptor.

AUCTION RECORDS:
NEW YORK, 26 Sept 1991, *Adagio* (bronze figure, h. 28 3/4 ins / 73 cm) USD 4,290.

SEAWELL, Henry Washington
American, 20th century.
Born in San Francisco.
Painter, illustrator.

Henry Seawell studied under Laurens and Constant in Paris. He was a member of the American Artistic Association in Paris.

SEBAG, Alain
American, 20th - 21st century.
Born 1948.
Painter.

Alain Sebag uses large blurry coloured areas to achieve a kind of Abstract Landscapism reminiscent of the Nuagistes.

SEBALD, Johann Georg
German, 18th century.
Active in Würzburg in the middle of the 18th century.
Draughtsman, calligrapher.

SEBALD, Martin
German, 19th century.
Born 18 December 1807, in Augsburg; died 17 December 1889, in Augsburg.
Medallist.

Martin Sebald attended the art school in Augsburg and the academy in Munich.

SEBALDT, Otto Friedrich Wilhelm
French, 19th - 20th century.
Born 24 January 1873, in Nancy.
Active in Germany.
Painter, illustrator, art writer.

Sebaldt was taught by R. Poetzelberger, L. von Kalckreuth and O. Gussow. He lived and worked in Dresden.

MUSEUMS AND GALLERIES:
DRESDEN (Stadtmus.).

SEBALT
German, 16th century.
Painter.

Sebalt worked in Pegau in 1515.

SEBASTIAN
Austrian, 15th century.
Active in Linz.
Painter.

Sebastian painted a fresco of *St Christopher* in the church of Obermauern in 1468.

SEBASTIAN
Spanish, 16th century.
Sculptor.

Sebastian collaborated with Felipe Vigarni on the making of the high altar for the Capilla Real in Granada in 1521.

SEBASTIAN
French, 19th century.
Draughtsman. Portraits.

MUSEUMS AND GALLERIES:
BÉZIERS: *Portrait of Gounod* (drawing).

SEBASTIAN, Franz Anton. See **SEBASTINI**

SEBASTIAN, Georg
German, 18th century.
Active at the beginning of the 18th century.
Painter.

Sebastian executed the altar painting in the church in Marktheidenfeld.

SEBASTIAN, José
Spanish, 18th century.
Active in Villarreal at the beginning of the 18th century.
Sculptor.

José Sebastian carved the high altar of the church of Sta Agueda la Yusana in Jérica (Castellón) in 1704.

SEBASTIAN DE ALEXOS
Spanish, 16th century.
Died before 27 February 1519.
Active in Seville.
Painter. Religious subjects.

Sebastian de Alexos is known through an inventory of his property.

SEBASTIAN DE BURGOS
Spanish, 16th century.
Born 1539.
Active in Valladolid.
Sculptor.

SEBASTIANI, Antonio
Italian, 18th - 19th century.
Born 1743; died 1818.
Painter.

Antonio Sebastiani was active in Parma.

SEBASTIANI, Lazzaro di Jacopo. See **BASTIANI**

SEBASTIANI, Sebastiano
Italian, 17th century.
Born in Camerino; died before 8 August 1626.
Sculptor, caster.

Sebastiano Sebastiani, the pupil of Girolamo Lombardi, executed works for the cathedrals in Loreto and Ripatransone.

SEBASTIANI, Thomas
French, 19th century.
Painter. History painting.

He exhibited at the Salon between 1841 and 1846.

SEBASTIANI MANCINI, Giuseppe, called Giuseppino, or Giuseppino of Macerata
17th century.

SEBASTIANO
Italian, 15th century.
Active in 1447.
Illuminator.

Sebastiano was a Franciscan monk.

SEBASTIANO, or Bastiano di Niccolò di Bastiano da Montecarlo
Italian, 16th century.
Died 10 February 1563.
Active in Pescia.
Painter.

A pupil of Raffaellino del Garbo, Sebastiano worked in Florence. He was probably the son of Bastiano di Niccolò da Montecarlo.

SEBASTIANO, Aquilano
Italian, 16th century.
Sculptor.

Aquilano Sebastiano carved a *Madonna Adoring the Holy Child* for the church at Arquata del Tronto.

SEBASTIANO, Niccolo
Italian, 18th century.
Painter (porcelain).

Niccolo Sebastiano worked at the Ginori porcelain factory at Doccia, signing himself NS.

SEBASTIANO, Schiavone (fra).
See **SCHIAVONE Sebastiano**

SEBASTIANO BRESCIANO.
See **ARAGONESE DI GHEDI Sebastiano**

SEBASTIANO DA COMO
Italian, 16th century.
Active during the first half of the 16th century.
Sculptor.
Sebastiano da Como was responsible for a number of statues of 1532 in the chapel of the Holy Sacrament in the church at Campli.

SEBASTIANO DA IMOLA
Italian, 16th century.
Active during the first half of the 16th century.
Painter.
Sebastiano da Imola assisted Innocenzo Frantucci in painting the frescoes in the church of S Michele in Bosco in Bologna.

SEBASTIANO DA LUGANO, also known as
Sebastiano Mariani di Giacomo
Italian, 16th century.
Died before December 1518.
Active in Lugano (Ticino), Switzerland.
Sculptor, architect.
Sebastiano da Lugano was involved in the building of the basilica of S Giustina in Padua and S Giovanni Crisostomo in Venice. He carved several marble statues in the chapel of S Antonio in Padua. As an architect, he took an active role in fortifying the town against Louis XII of France. He also worked for St Mark's in Venice.

SEBASTIANO DA PLURIO
Italian, 16th century.
Painter.
Sebastiano da Plurio executed paintings in the church of S Giacomo di Livo in Como.

SEBASTIANO DA REGGIO. See **RE Sebastiano di**

SEBASTIANO DA ROVIGNO (fra).
See **SCHIAVONE Sebastiano**

SEBASTIANO DEL GARZATORI.
See **GARZATORI**

SEBASTIANO DEL PIOMBO (Fra), real name:
Sebastiano de Luciani or Lucianis
Italian, 16th century.
Born 1485, probably in Venice; died 21 June 1547, in Rome.
Painter. History painting, portraits.
At the age of 46, Sebastiano del Piombo asked the Pope to appoint him to the position he was to hold until his death at the age of 62, maker of the lead seals for papal bulls, which required the holder to take holy orders and the monk's habit. In this way, he acquired the name by which he is generally known, Sebastiano del Piombo ('of the lead').At the age of 15, before studying painting, Sebastiano was already a well-known singer and lutenist, much sought after in Venetian society. He began his apprenticeship in the studio of Giovanni Bellini and later asked for lessons from his elder by eight years, Giorgione. He assimilated Giorgione's style so effectively that his *St John Chrysostom* in Venice was attributed for many years to the older man.

By about 1512, portraits and paintings by Sebastiano had begun to establish his reputation in Rome and the banker Chigi asked him to carry out some work in his palazzo in Rome, later known as the Villa Farnesina. Baldassare Peruzzi had already decorated part of the palazzo, and Sebastiano added subjects from fables, painting them in a Venetian style that contrasted with the other works in the Roman style. He was not overawed by Raphael's *Galatea*; on the contrary, he painted a pendant to it, *Polyphemus*, now lost. Sebastiano was particularly influenced by Raphael at this time, as can be seen from his portraits *La Fornarina* (Florence), the *Violinist, Cardinal Carondelet, Tebaldeo the Poet* and *Dorothea* (Berlin).However, Sebastiano then became a supporter of Michelangelo, who in turn promoted the Venetian's work and may perhaps even have provided him with designs. It was at about this period that he painted a *Pietà* for the chapel of S Francesco in Viterbo for which Michelangelo supplied the drawing. Sebastiano added colours, with beautiful and harmonious tones, using the sombre and desolate landscape in the background to emphasise the dark-skinned body of Christ. Another of his works based on drawings by Michelangelo is a *Flagellation* in oils on the wall of the church of S Pietro in Montorio in Rome. The use of oil paint instead of the normal fresco technique proved to be a mistake for, unlike fresco, the paint has darkened with time and today the *Flagellation* has lost much of its energy. In the same chapel, he painted - in fresco - *St Peter, St Francis, Two Prophets* and *The Transfiguration*. In *The Transfiguration* we see the manner of Michelangelo in the massive figures.

Sebastiano devoted six years to these works, the success of which resulted in a commission from Pope Julius II, at the instigation of Michelangelo, for a *Raising of Lazarus*. Raphael had just completed his *Transfiguration* (his last work, after the artist's death placed on the high altar of S Pietro in Montorio). Supported by Michelangelo, Sebastiano was not afraid to enter into competition with Raphael and it was on a panel 4 metres by 2 metres 78 centimetres, the same dimensions as Raphael's work, that Sebastiano began to paint his *Raising of Lazarus*. Michelangelo offered assistance and advice at every stage. Raphael was not deceived and was able to reveal the collaborative nature of the work. *Raising of Lazarus* was painted in Rome between 1517 and 1519 and then sent by Pope Clement VII to Narbonne Cathedral in France. It later belonged to the Duke of Orléans, who took it to England where it was acquired by the National Gallery in London in 1824.Sebastiano is credited with having invented a way of painting on walls in oils, a procedure involving spreading a special coating on the rough walls giving a suitable surface for oil paint. It is possible that this gave rise to his quarrel with Michelangelo. Vasari relates the event:'Having persuaded the pope to have the *Last Judgement* painted in oils, Sebastiano prepared a coating for this, despite the objections of Michelangelo who would only work in fresco, saying that the art of oil painting was only for women, good only for lazy and cowardly people like Sebastiano himself. Soon after, Michelangelo had the surface of the wall prepared as he wished it but did not forget the insult that he felt he had received.'Sebastiano applied his invention to stone tablets so that they could be used like canvases, but the procedure quickly fell out of favour because of the difficulty of transporting heavy pieces of stone. The method had already been used in the early 14th century for a number of paintings that were later passed off as antique.

An important work by Sebastiano, though not of the quality of the *Raising of Lazarus*, now in the Louvre in Paris, is the *Visitation of the Virgin*. It is signed and dated ' *Sebastianus Venetus faciebat, Romae, M. D. XXI* '. Once part of the collection of François I, this work for a long time decorated the royal palaces of Fontainebleau, Versailles and the Louvre. According to tradition, the face of the Virgin was a portrait of Michelangelo. François I, who already owned the *Visitation*, commissioned Sebastiano to paint a *St Michael Defeating the Dragon* so that he could hang it alongside the same subject painted by Raphael, which he already owned. Sebastiano never finished this painting.

Sebastiano del Piombo's portraits present his subjects with simplicity and livliness. As in his other works, his technique in the application of paint is admirable, the colours rich and sombre, the draughtsmanship broad and majestic. The best include the portraits of *Marcantonio Colonna, Ferdinand, Marquis of Pescara* and *Vittoria Colonna.* He also painted Pope *Hadrian VI.* The portrait of an unknown woman in the Uffizi in Florence recalls the style of Titian.

It is clear that Michelangelo had a major influence on Sebastiano's work, the effect of which was to make it heavier and more massive. Vasari suggests that Sebastiano also had a significant influence on Michelangelo's use of paint and colour, saying that Sebastiano gave much advice to Michelangelo while Michelangelo 'was to make the fortune and fame of Sebastiano'. Later he writes:

'The right choice of tone, the precise meeting in contrast and in the union of intermediate tints, without which it is not possible to endow such a large mass with the necessary clarity, simplicity and volume and the complicated detail with the necessary precision, emphasis and expression - none of these things can be achieved by any but the most talented artist. To be successful, he must have in addition an instinct for colour and experience in using it, an understanding of its essence, its behaviour, its range, its advantages and its limits.' Since the painting in the Sistine Chapel indubitably provides an example of the choice and distribution of colours as we have described, since everywhere we can admire the decisive use of pure tonality quite apart from the state of the form that the colours are required to fill, we can conclude that Michelangelo had absorbed, in so far as he required it for his ends, all that which he could learn from Venetian art. Although Sebastiano did not touch Michelangelo's work, he can rightly claim a part in it. This was no small honour and not one to be sneered at, particularly for a good-natured companion like Sebastiano, a man who seems never to have suffered from strong feelings of envy or ambition.

In accordance with his last wishes, Sebastiano del Piombo was buried without ceremony, without mourners or candles, in the church of S Maria del Popolo. The money that would have been spent on the ceremony was distributed to the poor.

Del Piombo had many pupils, including the Sicilian Tommaso Laureti, and numerous direct or indirect imitators such as Giuseppe Valeriani and Francisco da Ribalta.

BIBLIOGRAPHY:

Gould, C., *Sebastiano del Piombo's 'The Raising of Lazarus,* National Gallery Publications, London, 1967. Pignatti, Terisio, *The golden century of Venetian painting,* exhibition catalogue, County Museum of Art, Los Angeles, 1979. Hirst, Michael, *Sebastiano Del Piombo,* Oxford University Press, Oxford, 1981. Gentili, Augusto/Bertini, Chiara, *Sebastiano del Piombo: pala di San Giovanni Crisostomo,* Arsenale editrice, Venice, 1985. Juncic, J., *'Joachimist Prophecies in Sebastiano del Piombo's Borgherini Chapel and Raphael's Transfiguration'* in *Journal of the Warburg & Courtauld Institutes,* vol 51, 1988. Howard, E., *'New Evidence on the Italian Provenance of a Portrait by Sebastiano del Piombo'* in *Burlington Magazine,* vol 130, 1988. Joannides, Paul, *Raphäel et son temps,* exhibition catalogue, Palais des Beaux Arts, Lille, 2002.

MUSEUMS AND GALLERIES:

AIX-EN-PROVENCE (Mus. Granet): *Head of an Old Man* (attributed) - AUSTIN (Jack S. Blanton MA, University of Texas): *Portrait of a Man* (c. 1516) - BERLIN: *Young Roman Woman, known as Dorothea; Judith; Knight of the Order of St James* - BUDAPEST: *Portrait of a Young Man* - BUDAPEST (Ráth Gyorgy Múz.): *Portrait of a Girl* - CAMBRIDGE (Fitzwilliam Mus.): *Adoration of the Shepherds* (1511-1512, oil on canvas) - CHÂTEAU-GONTIER: *Martyrdom of St Agnes* - DETROIT: *Portrait of a Young Man with Two Ladies* - DUBLIN: *Portrait of Cardinal del Monte* - FLORENCE (Palazzo Pitti): *Concert; Martyrdom of St Agatha; Portrait of Baccio Valori* - FLORENCE (Uffizi): *Lamentation over the Dead Adonis; La Fornarina; Portrait of a Man* - FORT WORTH (Kimbell AM): *Head of a Woman* (early 1530s, oil/panel) - HANOVER (Kestner-Mus.): *Portrait of a Girl* - LILLE (MBA, Wicar Collection): *Polyphemus* (1511, pen and ink) - LONDON (NG): *The Daughter of Herodias* (1510, oil/wood); *The Raising of Lazarus* (1517-1519, oil on wood transferred to canvas); *The Madonna and Child with Sts Joseph and John the Baptist and a Donor* (c. 1530, oil/wood); *The Entombment* (after 1512, oil/wood, formerly attributed, work of Andrea Busati) - LOS ANGELES (Getty Mus.): *Pope Clement VII* (c. 1531, oil/slate) - MADRID: *Christ Descending into Purgatory; Christ Carrying the Cross* - NAPLES: *Madonna of the Veil; Portrait of Clement VII without a Beard; Portrait of Clement VII with a Beard* - NARBONNE: *Portrait of a Scholar; Study of a Head* (attributed) - NEW YORK (Metropolitan Mus. of Art): *Portrait of a Man, said to be Christopher Columbus* (1519) - PARIS (Louvre): *Double Portrait; Visitation; Portrait of Caterina Colonna* (attributed) - PARMA: *Portrait of Clement VII and Pietro Carnesecchi* - ROME (Church of S Pietro in Montorio): *Transfiguration; Flagellation* - ROME (Farnesina): *Frescoes* - ROME (Gal. Nazionale d'Arte Antica di Palazzo Barberini): *Portrait of a Woman* - ST PETERSBURG: *Entombment; Portrait of Cardinal Polo; Christ Carrying the Cross* - VENICE: *Two Saints* - VIENNA: *Portrait of a Cardinal* - VITERBO: *Pietà; Flagellation.*

AUCTION RECORDS:

LONDON, 2 March 1923, *Circumcision,* GBP 199. LONDON, 13 July 1923, *Ferry Carondelet and his Secretary,* GBP 3,255. PARIS, 11 April 1924, *Head of a Man* (black chalk) FRF 330. LONDON, 20 May 1927, *Portrait of a Woman,* GBP 714. LONDON, 27 July 1928, *Man Dressed in Black,* GBP 682. PARIS, 22 and 23 Feb 1929, *Study of a Leg* (pen) FRF 200. NEW YORK, 27 March 1930, *Woman Taken in Adultery,* USD 475. NEW YORK, 22 Jan 1931, *A Cardinal and his Secretaries,* USD 10,500; *Holy Family,* USD 11,500. LONDON, 18 April 1932, *Annibale Ciro,* GBP 460. LONDON, 1 June 1945, *Chevalier Bayier,* GBP 546. LONDON, 25 Oct 1946, *St Lucy,* GBP 315. LONDON, 5 April 1977, *Prophet and Angel* (black chalk, wash heightened with white/blue paper, 12 1/2 x 10 ins / 31.8 x 25.1 cm) GBP 104,000. LONDON, 2 July 1984, *Prophet* (black chalk heightened with white, 7 3/4 x 6 ins / 20 x 15.5 cm) GBP 21,000. ROME, 5 Dec 1985, *Portrait of Clement VII de' Medici* (c. 1530-1532, oil on panel, 23 1/2 x 17 1/4 ins / 60 x 44 cm) ITL 25,000,000. LONDON, 11 Dec 1987, *Portrait of Pope Clement VII* (oil/slate, 41 1/2 x 34 1/2 ins / 105.5 x 87.5 cm) GBP 380,000. LONDON, 2 July 1990, *Christ as a Beggar* (black chalk heightened with white, 7 3/4 x 6 ins / 20 x 15.5 cm) GBP 66,000.

SEBASTIANO DI COLA DA CASENTINO

Italian, 15th century.
Died 1506.
Active in L'Aquila.
Painter, sculptor (wood).

Probably identical with Sebastiano Aquilano, Sebastiano di Cola da Casentino worked at Aquila Cathedral and in other churches in the area.

SEBASTIANO DI RIDOLFO DELLA PIETRA

Italian, 15th century.
Born in Perugia; died between 1507 and 1509.
Painter.

Sebastiano di Ridolfo della Pietra painted an altarpiece for the church of S Onofrio in Monterosso near Sassoferrato depicting *The Virgin with Sts Onofrio, Sebastian, Roch and Dominic.* He also painted an altarpiece for the church of Ponte San Giovanni near Perugia.

SEBASTIANO LUCIANI. See SEBASTIANO DEL PIOMBO

SEBASTIANO VERONESE
Italian, 16th century.
Active in the middle of the 16th century.
Painter.
Sebastiano Veronese was one of the painters involved in the painting of the portico in the Palazzo Vecchio in Florence.

SEBASTIANONE
Italian, 17th century.
Painter. Portraits, genre scenes.
Sebastianone, the pupil of Alessandro Magnasco, worked in Milan.
MUSEUMS AND GALLERIES:
MILAN (Pinacoteca di Brera): *Self-portraits.*
AUCTION RECORDS:
MILAN, 12 Dec 1988, *Quarrel during a Meal* (oil on canvas, 29 1/2 x 35 1/2 ins / 75 x 90 cm) ITL 11,000,000.

SEBASTIEN, pseudonym of Gab-Simo
French, 20th century.
Born 28 March 1909, in Paris; died 2 July 1990, in Paris.
Painter, sculptor, poet. Figures, landscapes.
Symbolism.
Sébastien trained at the École Boulle in Paris from 1924 to 1928. He was initially interested in decoration and architecture, then photography, and taught himself to paint and sculpt. He travelled in Morocco, Yugoslavia (now Serbia and Montenegro) and Venice, as well as on French soil, in Brittany. In 1940, after being demobilised, he took refuge in Vallauris (near Nice), where he met Marguerite and Aimé Maeght. The Centre d'Art Sébastien opened in St-Cyr-sur-Mer in 1993.

An award winner for thought on French art at the American Blumenthal Foundation in 1936 for his painted and sculpted work as a whole, he went on to receive several medals from the various Parisian Salons. He painted his first pieces - portraits and still-lifes - in Pornic (on the coast near Nantes), Paris and Le Pouldu in Brittany, and his first sculptures in Ourika, Morocco in 1930. From the 1940s his coloured paintings tend towards a Symbolism of naive inspiration, in particular in his landscapes, or more markedly allegorical with the sculptures *Les Retrouvés* and *Love*.

He featured in group exhibitions including the Salon d'Automne in Paris, where he became a member, from 1929 to 1989; Salon de Vincennes in 1933; Salon des Artistes Décorateurs, Paris, from 1934 to 1960; the Exposition Universelle in Paris in 1937; the World Fair in New York and San Francisco in 1939; the Milan Triennale in 1939; the Salon de l'Imagerie and Salon des Tuileries in 1945; Salon de la Marine in Paris in 1950; Salon d'Art Sacré in Paris in 1952; the Exposition Universelle in Brussels in 1958 and the Salon des Indépendants in Paris from 1970 to 1987.

He exhibited his work in solo shows including at the Musée de Castres in 1951, a retrospective at the Palais des Arts et de la Culture in Brest in 1977, *Homage to Sébastien* at the Mairie of the 13th arrondissement in Paris in 1991.
BIBLIOGRAPHY:
Catalogue de l'œuvre de Sébastien, Maeght, Paris, 1991.
MUSEUMS AND GALLERIES:
ORLÉANS - PARIS (Mus. de la Marine) - PARIS (Mus. des Arts décoratifs) - PONT-AVEN - RABAT - ST-CYR-SUR-MER (Centre d'Art Sébastien).

SEBASTIEN, Henri
French, 17th century.
Born in Auxonne.
Painter. History painting, religious subjects.
MUSEUMS AND GALLERIES:
ORCHAMPS-VENNES (Church of Sts Pierre et Paul): *Holy Family.*

SEBASTIEN-LAURENT, Maurice.
See **LAURENT Maurice Sébastien**

SEBASTINI, Franz Anton, or Sebastian or Sebastiani, Schebesta
Austrian, 18th century.
Born c. 1725; died before 24 March 1789.
Painter, fresco artist. Religious subjects.
Sebastini spent most of his career in Kojetein. He executed frescoes and altar paintings for numerous churches in Moravia and Silesia.

SEBAULT, T.
French, 18th century.
Active in St-Barthélemy (now in the Maine-et-Loire).
Sculptor.
T. Sebault sculpted a sundial for the church in St-Barthélemy.

SEBBA, Siegfried Shalom
Israeli, 20th century.
Born 1897; died 1975.
Painter. Scenes with figures, figures.
Siegfried Shalom Sebba lived and worked in Tel Aviv.
BIBLIOGRAPHY:
Gabler, K., *Das Erste Buch über Siegfried Shalom Sebba, den Wahrscheinlich Bedeutensten Künstler Israels*, 1981.
AUCTION RECORDS:
TEL AVIV, 20 June 1990, *Young Woman Standing* (oil on canvas, 39 1/2 x 16 ins / 100.5 x 40.5 cm) USD 7,260. TEL AVIV, 1 Jan 1991, *Trucks* (1931, oil on canvas, 27 3/4 x 24 ins / 70.5 x 61 cm) USD 5,720.

SEBBERS, Julius Ludwig
German, 19th century.
Born 1804, in Brunswick; died after 1837, in Berlin (?).
Painter (porcelain).
Sebbers worked in the porcelain factories of Munich and Brunswick.
MUSEUMS AND GALLERIES:
WEIMAR (Goethe-Nationalmus.): a cup in effigy to 'Goethe'.

SEBELON, Claude Marius
French, 19th century.
Born 1819, in Meximieux (Ain); died 1865, in Lyons.
Painter. Portraits.
MUSEUMS AND GALLERIES:
LYONS: *Portrait of Bonnefond; Portrait of Vibert.*

SEBEN, Henri van
Belgian, 19th - 20th century.
Born 15 November 1825, in Brussels; died 23 November 1913, in Ixelles (Brussels).
Painter, watercolourist. Portraits, genre scenes, landscapes.
Henri van Seben studied in The Hague under B.J. van Hove and lived and worked in Brussels from 1952.

MUSEUMS AND GALLERIES:
BRUSSELS: *Outskirts of The Hague.*
AUCTION RECORDS:
LONDON, 4 April 1910, *Genre Composition* (1857) GBP 5. LONDON, 8 Nov 1972, *Skaters*, GBP 420. LONDON, 1 Nov 1973, *Harvesting Apples*, Gns 2,000. AMSTERDAM, 22 Oct 1974, *Harvesting Apples* (1859) NLG 16,000. NEW YORK, 2 April 1976, *Soap Bubbles* (1859, oil on canvas, 23 1/2 x 19 3/4 ins / 60 x 50 cm) USD 1,100. COLOGNE, 11 May 1977, *Soap Bubbles* (1859, oil on canvas, 23 3/4 x 20 ins / 60.5 x 50.5 cm) DEM 3,000. LONDON, 19 March 1980, *Two Young Skaters* (oil on canvas, 23 1/2 x 19 3/4 ins / 60 x 50 cm) GBP 1,200. BRUSSELS, 25 Nov 1981, *Near the Well* (1855, oil on panel, 12 1/2 x 15 3/4

ins / 32 x 40 cm) BEF 95,000. NEW YORK, 29 Feb 1984, *Vow* (oil on panel, 13 x 9 3/4 ins / 33 x 25 cm) USD 4,500. LONDON, 9 Oct 1985, *Children Collecting Firewood* (oil on canvas, 20 3/4 x 26 ins / 53 x 66 cm) GBP 1,800. BERN, 30 April 1988, *Children Gathering Wild Flowers* (oil on canvas, 24 1/2 x 36 1/4 ins / 62 x 92 cm) CHF 4,000. VERSAILLES, 5 March 1989, *Encampment on the Plain in the Snow* (1876, oil on canvas, 20 x 26 1/2 ins / 50.5 x 67 cm) FRF 13,500. NEW YORK, 17 Jan 1990, *Skating on the Frozen Canals* (oil on canvas, 19 1/4 x 28 ins / 48.7 x 71.2 cm) USD 3,300. AMSTERDAM, 25 April 1990, *Apple Thieves* (1859, oil on canvas, 27 1/2 x 35 1/2 ins / 70 x 90 cm) NLG 27,600. AMSTERDAM, 23 April 1991, *Picking Flowers* (1874, oil on panel, 5 x 4 1/4 ins / 12.5 x 11 cm) NLG 4,830. NEW YORK, 26 May 1992, *Children Playing with a Hoop* (1858, oil on canvas, 28 1/2 x 24 1/2 ins / 72.3 x 62.2 cm) USD 3,080. AMSTERDAM, 24 Sept 1992, *Village Path in Winter* (oil on canvas/panel, 15 3/4 x 12 ins / 40 x 30.5 cm) NLG 1,150. NEW YORK, 16 Feb 1993, *Cold Winter Afternoon* (oil on panel, 19 1/2 x 14 1/2 ins / 49.7 x 36.8 cm) USD 1,650. LONDON, 19 March 1993, *Late for School* (1857, oil on canvas, 15 3/4 x 27 1/2 ins / 40 x 70 cm) GBP 6,325. AMSTERDAM, 9 Nov 1994, *Figures on a Frozen River* (watercolour, 12 1/2 x 17 1/4 ins / 31.5 x 44 cm) NLG 2,760. PARIS, 27 May 1997, *Romantic Winter Outing* (1876, oil on canvas, 30 x 44 ins / 76.5 x 112 cm) FRF 60,000. GLASGOW, 25 Feb 1999, *Skating Party* (1865, oil on canvas, 24 x 20 ins / 60 x 50 cm) GBP 4,400. AMSTERDAM, 16 March 1999, *Orphans at the Hooglandse Kerkgracht in Leiden* (oil on canvas, 29 x 26 ins / 74 x 65 cm) NLG 14,000. NORTH BETHESDA, 10 March 2000, *Faggot Gatherer in Winter* (oil on panel, 9 x 6 ins / 23 x 15 cm) USD 2,900. BRUSSELS, 19 June 2000, *Harvesters Before the Storm* (oil on canvas, 26 x 36 ins / 65 x 92 cm) BEF 270,000. BRUSSELS, 20 March 2001, *Fishing Village in the Dunes* (oil on canvas, 48 x 35 ins / 123 x 90 cm) BEF 150,000. BRUSSELS, 8 May 2001, *Young Anglers by a Pool* (1859, oil on canvas, 24 x 20 ins / 60 x 50 cm) BEF 260,000. LOKEREN, 11 May 2002, *Two Children in the Snow* (oil on panel, 17 x 13 ins / 44 x 34 cm) EUR 3,300. BRUSSELS, 18 Nov 2003, *Little Thieves at the Greengrocer's* (1852, oil on canvas, 24 x 36 ins / 61 x 91 cm) EUR 2,700. BRUSSELS, 9 Dec 2003, *Farmyard with Figures* (1855, oil on mahogany panel, 13 x 16 ins / 32 x 40 cm) EUR 2,000. AMSTERDAM, 3 Feb 2004, *Figures and Animals in a Small Street, Arnemuiden* (oil on canvas, 48 x 35 ins / 123 x 90 cm) EUR 2,600. BRUSSELS, 13 Sept 2004, *Children Playing at Home Time* (oil on panel, 20 x 26 ins / 51 x 65 cm) EUR 3,400.

SEBERGER, Adam
Austrian, 18th century.
Active in Linz in 1732.
Painter.

Seberger painted three Still-lifes of flowers for the abbey of St Florian.

SEBERT, or Ceber or Seber
French, 17th century.
Painter.

Sebert studied at the Académie Royale in Paris.

MUSEUMS AND GALLERIES:

DIJON (Palais Épiscopal): *Abraham and Melchisedech.*

SEBERT, Hans Matthes, or Seber, Seberth, Sewert, or erroneously known as Seconet
German, 17th century.
Died 23 April 1665, in Bamberg.
Active in Bamberg (Bavaria).
Sculptor.

Sebert worked for the cathedral of Bamberg where he executed altars and tombs.

SEBES, Laurent
French, 20th - 21st century.
Born 12 June 1959, in Paris.
Painter, sculptor.

Laurent Sebes studied at the École Boulle in Paris and was an Ile-de-France scholarship laureate in 1986. He produces sculptures in crumpled metal sheet, part-painted to enhance effects of light and shade.

He has shown work at group exhibitions: in 1986 and 1988, at the Salon de Montrouge; in 1987, at the International Contemporary Arts Fair in Paris; and, in 1989, at the Frankfurt International Fair. Solo exhibitions by Sebes have included those held in 1985, 1986, 1987 and 1989 at the Galerie Charles Sablon in Paris.

SEBES, Pieter Willem
Dutch, 19th century.
Born 1830 or 1839, in Harlingen; died 1906.
Active in Louvain, Brussels and Leeuwarden.
Painter. Genre scenes, interiors with figures.

Pieter Willem Sebes was a pupil of Jurgen and De Jong.

AUCTION RECORDS:

AMSTERDAM, 30 Oct 1979, *Interior Scene* (1876, oil on panel, 22 x 17 1/4 ins / 55 x 44 cm) NLG 10,000. LONDON, 2 Oct 1992, *Interior with a Mother and Child* (1879, oil on canvas, 27 3/4 x 40 ins / 70.5 x 100.7 cm) GBP 4,400. LONDON, 2 Oct 1992, *Interior with a Mother and Child* (1879, oil on canvas, 27 3/4 x 40 ins / 70.5 x 100.7 cm) GBP 4,400. AMSTERDAM, 5 Nov 1996, *Interior with Laughing Child* (oil on panel, 13 x 18 ins / 33 x 45.5 cm) NLG 6,136. AMSTERDAM, 27 Oct 1997, *Good Friends* (1891, oil on canvas, 21 x 26 1/2 ins / 52.5 x 67 cm) NLG 7,080. SAN FRANCISCO, 26 May 1999, *Debts* (oil on canvas, 32 x 26 ins / 82 x 65 cm) USD 6,500. LONDON, 14 Dec 1999, *Tea in the Conservatory* (oil on canvas, 28 x 39 ins / 71 x 99 cm) GBP 3,000. ZURICH, 2 May 2001, *Young Woman Reading* (oil on panel, 21 x 16 ins / 53 x 40 cm) CHF 3,000. LONDON, 18 June 2003, *Important Letter* (1858, oil on panel, 18 x 15 ins / 46 x 39 cm) GBP 5,800. AMSTERDAM, 3 Feb 2004, *Pretty Dress* (1874, oil on canvas, 32 x 26 ins / 82 x 65 cm) EUR 1,800. SAN FRANCISCO, 18 May 2004, *Debts* (oil on canvas, 33 x 26 ins / 83 x 66 cm) USD 4,750.

SEBESTYEN, Zoltan
Romanian, 20th - 21st century.
Born 1954, in Budapest.
Painter.

Zoltan Sebestyen studied at the school of fine arts in Budapest. His paintings are abstract and gestural and represent the trend known as the 'New Awareness'. He is known for his *Parapet* series. He has exhibited in Hungary, Nuremberg and Moscow.

SEBILLAU, Paul, or Sébilleau
French, 19th century.
Born in Bordeaux; died 30 January 1907, in Bordeaux.
Painter. Landscapes.

This artist was a pupil of Louis-Augustin Auguin. He debuted at the Salon in 1877; he was awarded an honourable mention in 1884, a bronze medal in 1889 (at the Exposition Universelle), and a second-class medal in 1899.

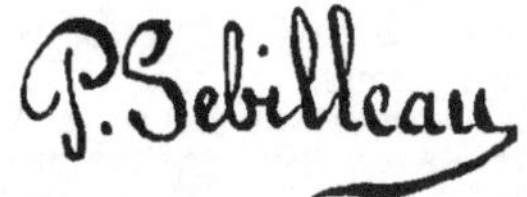

MUSEUMS AND GALLERIES:

BORDEAUX: *Morning, Golfe Juan* - PÉRIGUEUX: *Woodland Clearing in Breda* - ROCHEFORT: *Mortefontaine.*

AUCTION RECORDS:

PARIS, 1900, *Dunes at Soulac, Gironde,* FRF 35. PARIS, 13 Dec 1937, *September Night in St-Georges de Divonne, Charente,* FRF 22. PARIS, July 1946, *Chartres in 1889,* FRF 2,000; *Landscape with Misty Sky,* FRF 2,000. PARIS, 21 Feb 1949, *Marsh-*

es, FRF 3,600; *On the Clifftop,* FRF 2,000. PARIS, 19 March 1951, *Landscape,* FRF 2,000.

SÉBILLE, Albert

French, 19th - 20th century.
Born 1874, in Marseilles; died 1953.
Painter (gouache), watercolourist. Urban landscapes, waterscapes, seascapes.

Sébille was taught by his father, Octave Sébille, then by Jean Léon Gérôme at the École des Beaux-Arts in Paris. He was an official painter for the navy.

He featured at the Salon des Artistes Français in Paris and received an honourable mention at the 1900 Exposition Universelle.

AUCTION RECORDS:
PARIS, 10 July 1983, *Paris* (watercolour, 41 x 28 3/4 ins / 104 x 73 cm) FRF 21,000. ORLÉANS, 16 May 1987, *The 'Champlain' Leaving Le Havre* (1931, watercolour, 19 x 24 ins / 48 x 61 cm) FRF 31,000. PARIS, 9 Dec 1988, watercolour, 41 x 28 3/4 ins / 104 x 73 cm) FRF 62,000. PARIS, 6 Dec 1990, *Frigate in Difficulty Being Visited by a Flagship* (gouache, 10 1/4 x 13 1/2 ins / 26 x 34.5 cm) FRF 5,500. MONACO, 22 June 1991, *French Squadron off the Coast of Spain* (1908, black chalk and watercolour, 25 3/4 x 39 1/4 ins / 65.4 x 99.5 cm) FRF 26,640. PARIS, 26 Oct 1992, *The Liner 'France' Leaving the Quai Southampton in Le Havre* (gouache, 26 x 39 1/4 ins / 66 x 100 cm) FRF 102,000. LE HAVRE, 10 July 1995, *Victim of a Seagoing Navigation Freighter* (1940, watercolour, 25 1/2 x 38 1/2 ins / 65 x 98 cm) FRF 18,200. PARIS, 17 Oct 1997, *Battleship* (watercolour, 19 1/4 x 12 3/4 ins / 49 x 32.5 cm) FRF 24,000. PARIS, 21 March 2003, *Ile de France, Liner* (oil on canvas, 24 x 19 ins / 60 x 48 cm) EUR 2,500. LE HAVRE, 26 Oct 2003, *Royal Squadron* (oil on canvas, 53 x 98 ins / 135 x 250 cm) EUR 3,500.

SEBILLE, Fernand Pierre Émile

French, 19th century.
Born 19th century, in Avallon (Yonne).
Engraver.

He was taught by M Fanchon. His work was shown at the Salon of the Société des Artistes Français and he was awarded an honourable mention in 1906.

SÉBILLE, Gysbert. See SIBILLA Gijsbert Jansz.

SEBILLE, Octave

French, 20th century.
Born 9 November 1896, in Paris.
Painter.

Sébille was a turner and tool-maker then a taxi driver. He lived and worked in Montreuil, an eastern suburb of Paris. From 1935 he painted views of the countryside he had visited and views of Montreuil. His technique, although naive, shows that he had observed paintings by the masters and read specialist works.

SEBILLEAU, Paul. See SEBILLAU

SÉBILLOT, Paul

French, 19th - 20th century.
Born 6 February 1843, in Matignon (Côtes-d'Armor, now Côtes-du-Nord); died 1918, in Paris.
Painter, engraver. Waterscapes, seascapes.

Sébillot was taught by François Feyen-Perrin. He exhibited at the Salon de Paris from 1870, then at the Salon des Artistes Français. He was made Chevalier of the Légion d'Honneur. He had some poems published and founded reviews on the legends and traditions of his native region. His landscapes and etchings also depict Brittany exclusively.

MUSEUMS AND GALLERIES:
ST-BRIEUC: *Mouth of the Trieux.*

AUCTION RECORDS:
PARIS, 23 May 1941, *Rocks at the Seaside,* FRF 280.

SÉBIRE, Gaston

French, 20th century.
Born 18 August 1920, in St-Samson (Calvados); died 2001.
Painter, engraver, pastellist. Figures, landscapes, urban landscapes, seascapes, still-lifes, flowers. Stage costumes and sets.

After studying in Rouen, Sébire joined the Post Office, where he chose to work at night in order to learn to paint during the day. He settled in Paris in 1951. He was made an official painter of the French navy in 1973. He created the costumes and sets for *Ange gris* (*Grey Angel*) (music by Debussy) for the ballets of the Marquis de Cuevas in 1953. He then settled in Normandy.

In the works from his first period, the range of refined greys employed places him in the Neo-Realist movement that followed the death of Françis Grüber. He is renowned for his seascapes and seasides of Post-Impressionist style, and also painted verdant landscapes gaily filled with light and flowers, which nonetheless have a note of melancholy.

He took part in group exhibitions including, in Paris, the Salon des Indépendants, Salon d'Automne from 1956, Salon des Tuileries, Salon Comparaisons from 1962, and the Salon des Artistes Français from 1964. He featured in other group shows in London with Lorjou and Clavé, in Munich, Washington, Japan, various exhibitions of the Paris School at the Galerie Charpentie in Paris from 1953 to 1958, and 1961, and at the Biennale des Jeunes at the Pavillon de Marsan in 1957.

His solo exhibitions include 1944, first exhibition, Galerie Gosselin, Rouen; 1952, Galerie Visconti, Paris; 1956, Galerie Charpentier, Paris, 1961, Galerie Combes, Clermont-Ferrand; 1962, 1965 and 1968, Galerie Drouant, Paris; 1964, Musée de Rouen; 1965, and regularly thereafter, Wally Findlay Galleries, New York, Paris, Chicago; 1971, Wally Findlay Galleries, Paris; 1976, Centre Culturel Le Mesnis-Esnard; 1986, retrospective, Musée des Beaux-Arts, Rouen; 1991 with Cacheux, Association Roger Worms, Ville de Montfermeil; 1992, Wally Findlay Galleries, Paris. He received the Prix de la Casa Velázquez, the Critics' Prize in 1953, the Greenshields Prize in 1957, the gold medal at the Salon des Artistes Français in 1968.

BIBLIOGRAPHY:
Osenat, Pierre, '*Sebire*' in *coll. Éloges,* Les Heures Claires, Paris. Osenat, Pierre, *Gaston Sébire,* exhibition leaflet, Palais des arts et de la culture, Brest, 1973. *Sebire: Mers et Jardins,* exhibition leaflet, Wally Findlay Gall., Paris, 1983. Harambourg, Lydia, *L'École de Paris 1945-1965. Dictionnaire des peintres,* Ides et Calendes, Neuchâtel, 1993.

MUSEUMS AND GALLERIES:
NORWICH (Castle Mus. and AG): *Environs de Madrid* - PARIS (MAMVP) - ROUEN (MBA).

AUCTION RECORDS:
ROUEN, 12 Feb 1972, *Seascape at Le Havre,* FRF 4,500. VERSAILLES, 9 May 1973, *Walkers on the Beach at Cabourg,* FRF 5,900. VERSAILLES, 28 April 1974, *Trouville, the Beach,* FRF 6,000. ROUEN, 5 Dec 1976, *Trouville Beach* (oil on canvas, 21 1/4 x 31 1/2 ins / 54 x 80 cm) FRF 6,000. ROUEN, 5 Nov 1978, *Seascape* (oil on canvas) FRF 8,500. VERSAILLES, 5 Oct 1980, *Sailing Boats in Ouistreham* (oil on canvas, 32 x 39 1/4 ins / 81 x 100 cm) FRF 8,400. ROUEN, 12 Nov 1983, *On the Beach* (oil on canvas, 39 1/4 x 25 1/2 ins / 100 x 65 cm) FRF 13,000. ROUEN, 15 Dec 1985, *Bouquet of Flowers* (oil on canvas) FRF 15,000. LA VARENNE-ST-HILAIRE, 29 May 1988, *Country Road* (oil on canvas, 23 1/2 x 32 ins / 60 x 81 cm) FRF 6,800. PARIS, 30 May 1988, *Still-life with Fruit* (oil on canvas, 15 x 18 ins / 38 x 46 cm) FRF 6,200. PARIS, 6 June 1988, *Beach* (oil on canvas,

20½ x 28¾ ins / 52 x 73 cm) FRF 13,500. PARIS, 4-6 July 1988, *Village Road* (oil on canvas, 32 x 39¼ ins / 81 x 100 cm) FRF 7,500. VERSAILLES, 25 Sept 1988, *Vase of Roses* (oil on canvas, 24 x 18 ins / 61 x 46 cm) FRF 6,500. FONTAINEBLEAU, 18 Dec 1988, *Huts in Arcachon* (1962, oil on canvas, 28¾ x 39¼ ins / 73 x 100 cm) FRF 20,000. PARIS, 26 May 1989, *Les Meules* (oil on canvas, 28¾ x 36¼ ins / 73 x 92 cm) FRF 8,000. LONDON, 25 Oct 1989, *Landscape and Hills* (1955, oil on canvas, 34¾ x 46 ins / 88.5 x 116 cm) GBP 13,200. VERSAILLES, 28 Jan 1990, *Vase of Flowers* (oil on canvas, 32 x 23¾ ins / 81 x 60.5 cm) FRF 19,500. PARIS, 26 April 1990, *Little House on the Prairie* (oil on canvas, 25½ x 32¼ ins / 65 x 82 cm) FRF 22,000. PARIS, 7 Nov 1990, *Cabins in Le Havre* (oil on canvas, 31½ x 39¼ ins / 80 x 100 cm) FRF 23,000. FONTAINEBLEAU, 18 Nov 1990, *Still-life in a Garden* (oil on canvas, 28¾ x 36¼ ins / 73 x 92 cm) FRF 27,500. DOUAI, 24 March 1991, *Landscape* (oil on canvas, 31½ x 39¼ ins / 80 x 100 cm) FRF 12,200. NEW YORK, 27 Feb 1992, *Vase of Flowers* (oil on canvas, 21½ x 15 ins / 54.6 x 38 cm) USD 2,860. LE TOUQUET, 8 June 1992, *Landscape near Collioures* (oil on canvas, 51¼ x 38¼ ins / 130 x 97 cm) FRF 20,000. NEW YORK, 10 Nov 1992, *Rue du Mont-Cenis with the Sacré-Coeur* (oil on canvas, 64 x 51½ ins / 162.5 x 130.5 cm) USD 1,100. NEW YORK, 22 Feb 1993, *Blue Tent* (oil on canvas, 28¾ x 36¼ ins / 73 x 92 cm) USD 3,850. PARIS, 6 April 1993, *Mountainous Landscape* (oil on canvas, 38¼ x 51¼ ins / 97 x 130 cm) FRF 9,500. NEW YORK, 29 Sept 1993, *Roses et Fleurs Blanches* (oil on canvas, 25½ x 20 ins / 64.8 x 50.8 cm) USD 2,070. PARIS, 25 May 1994, *Table in the Garden* (oil on canvas, 40¼ x 32¼ ins / 102 x 82 cm) FRF 19,000. NEW YORK, 10 Oct 1996, *Window Overlooking the Beach* (oil on canvas, 57½ x 45 ins / 146.1 x 114.3 cm) USD 4,025. PARIS, 12 Dec 1996, *Seaside Village* (oil on canvas, 32 x 39¼ ins / 81 x 100 cm) FRF 11,000. PARIS, 25 May 1997, *Hut on the Beach* (oil on canvas, 19¾ x 25½ ins / 50 x 65 cm) FRF 6,000. CONNECTICUT, 22 Feb 1999, *Still-life* (oil on canvas, 57 x 39 ins / 145 x 99 cm) USD 3,750. CONNECTICUT, 22 Feb 1999, *Bouquet of Flowers* (oil on canvas, 51 x 37 ins / 130 x 94 cm) USD 3,750. PARIS, 15 Aug 2000, *Still-life with Bottles and Fruit* (c. 1955, oil on canvas, 29 x 36 ins / 73 x 91 cm) FRF 17,000. NEUILLY, 16 Nov 2000, *Normandy Beach* (oil on canvas, 29 x 36 ins / 73 x 92 cm) FRF 11,800. FLORIDA, 20 March 2001, *Meadow with Magnolia* (oil on canvas, 51 x 64 ins / 130 x 163 cm) USD 3,750. FLORIDA, 17 April 2001, *Garden and Parasol* (oil on canvas, 64 x 51 ins / 163 x 130 cm) USD 4,000. ST. LOUIS, 8 June 2002, *Parisian Street Scene* (oil on canvas, 34 x 42 ins / 86 x 107 cm) USD 2,600. CALAIS, 7 July 2002, *Normandy Landscape* (oil on canvas, 29 x 39 ins / 73 x 100 cm) EUR 3,100. PARIS, 26 Sept 2003, *Landscape near Collioure* (oil on canvas, 38 x 51 ins / 96 x 130 cm) EUR 4,100. PARIS, 13 Dec 2003, *Grey Sky over Beach* (oil on canvas, 18 x 26 ins / 46 x 65 cm) EUR 2,700. LONDON, 24 March 2004, *Menton, Morning* (oil on canvas, 29 x 36 ins / 73 x 92 cm) GBP 3,200. DEAUVILLE, 21 Aug 2004, *Landscape* (oil on canvas, 76 x 51 ins / 194 x 130 cm) EUR 2,500.

SEBOTH, Josef

Austrian, 19th century.
Born 12 February 1814, in Vienna; died 28 April 1883, in Graz.
Painter. Flowers.

Josef Seboth worked at the porcelain factory in Vienna.

MUSEUMS AND GALLERIES:

GRAZ (Landesmus. Joanneum): still-lifes.

SEBOTH, Joseph

Austrian, 18th century.
Born 16 March 1764, in Vienna; died 16 January 1806, in Vienna.
Painter.

SEBREE, Charles

American, 20th century.
Born 1912, in Madisonville (Kentucky); died 1985.
Painter (including gouache), watercolourist, illustrator. Religious subjects, figures, portraits, still-lifes. Stage costumes and sets.

Charles Sebree studied at the Art Institute of Chicago. From 1936 to 1939, he worked in Illinois for the Federal Art Project (the federal government programme set up to help artists during the Depression). He lived on the South Side of Chicago before retiring to Washington DC.

Sebree painted figures with stylised features and massive forms, outlined in black, representing figures from the Bible or the African-American community. He also illustrated a children's book, Countee Cullen and Christopher Cat's *The Lost Zoo (a rhyme for the young, but not too young)* (London, New York: Harper & Brothers, 1940).

Sebree took part in various group exhibitions, such as: at the Federal Art Project Gallery, Chicago (1937); the American Negro Exposition, Chicago (1940); at the Institute of Modern Art, Boston (1943); and at the South Side Community Art Center, Chicago (1945). After his death, his work was included in such thematic group exhibitions as *Narratives of African Art and Identity. The David C. Driskell Collection*, High Museum of Art, Atlanta (1998); and *To Conserve A Legacy: American art from historically Black Colleges and Universities*, Addison Gallery of Art, Phillips Academy, Andover, Massachusetts (1999). He also had a number of solo exhibitions, including at the Roko Gallery, New York (1949); and a posthumous retrospective of his work was held in 1984 at the Evan-Tibbs Collection, Washington DC.

BIBLIOGRAPHY:

National Negro Art Exhibition, group exhibition catalogue, South Side Community Art Center, Chicago, 1945. Dover, Cedric, *American Negro Art*, New York Graphic Society, Greenwich, 1960. Dickason Cederholm, Theresa, *Afro-American Artists. A Bio-Bibliographical Directory*, Trustees of the Boston Public Library, Boston, 1973. Powell, Richard J./Reynolds, Jock, *To Conserve A Legacy: American Art from historically Black Colleges and Universities*, group exhibition catalogue, Addison Gall. of Art, Phillips Academy, Andover, 1999.

MUSEUMS AND GALLERIES:

CHICAGO (AI): *Ritual Woman* - WASHINGTON DC (GA, Howard University): *War Worker* (1949, painting on card).

AUCTION RECORDS:

PITTSFIELD, 8 Sept 2001, *Dream of Pearls* (1948, tempera on masonite, 20 x 24 ins / 51 x 61 cm) USD 12,000. CINCINNATI, 7 June 2003, *Woman in a White Turban* (c. 1960, oil on foam-board, 6 x 4 ins / 15 x 10 cm) USD 2,000. CHICAGO, 11 Sept 2004, *Head of a Man* (tempera on canvas, 24 x 30 ins / 61 x 76 cm) USD 10,200.

SEBREGONDI, Nicolo, or Sebregundio or Subregundi

Italian.
Born in the Valtellina Valley.
Painter, architect.

Sebregondi worked in Mantua from 1613 to 1651.

SEBREGTS, Lode

Belgian, 20th century.
Born 1906, in Antwerp; died 2002.
Painter, draughtsman. Figures, portraits, urban landscapes, flowers.

Lode Sebregts studied at the Koninklijke Academie voor Schone Kunsten and the Hoger Instituut voor Schone Kunsten in Antwerp and taught in Antwerp; he is noted for his paintings of the old district.

MUSEUMS AND GALLERIES:

ANTWERP.

SÉBRON, Hippolyte Victor Valentin

French, 19th century.

Born 21 August 1801, in Caudebec-en-Caux (Seine-Maritime); died 1 September 1879, in Paris.
Painter, watercolourist, draughtsman. Religious subjects, portraits, interiors, architectural views, landscapes, waterscapes. Panoramas.

Hippolyte Sébron was a student at the École des Beaux-Arts in Paris, where he was taught first by Louis Daguerre and then by Léon Cogniet. He lived in the USA from 1849 to 1855. Between 1831 and 1878 he regularly exhibited at the Paris Salon.

He was initially employed as a painter of dioramas. Later in his career he produced a great many canvases, particularly church interiors, ruins and other architectural subjects.

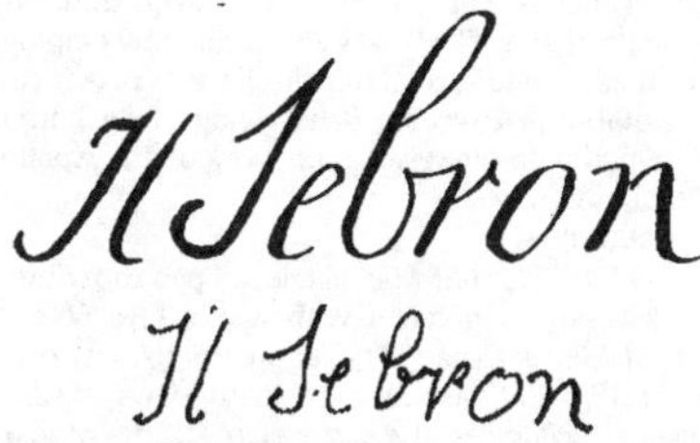

MUSEUMS AND GALLERIES:
ARRAS: *Interior of St Maurice Cathedral* - BRUSSELS (MBA): *Interior of the Church of St James in Antwerp* - LE HAVRE: *View of Grenada* - POITIERS: *Pius IX Officiating at St Peter's in Rome* - ROUEN (MBA): *Interior of St Mark's in Venice; Street in New York; Niagara Falls; Interior of St Catherine's in Brussels* - ST-ÉTIENNE (Mus. d'Art et d'Industrie): *Christ in the Garden of Gethsemane* - TROYES: *Ruins of Baalbek (Ancient Heliopolis)* - VERSAILLES (Château): *Baptism of Albert of Orleans on 2 May 1841 in Paris, at Notre Dame Cathedral.*

AUCTION RECORDS:
PARIS, 1850, *Interior of Windsor Chapel* (with Queen Victoria, Prince Albert and the Duke of Wellington) FRF 2,540. PARIS, 1890, *Landscape with Figures,* FRF 965. PARIS, 20 Feb 1931, *Château de Vendoire (Dordogne),* FRF 350. PARIS, 23 June 1943, *Quays of the Seine at the Louvre* (1837) FRF 33,500. NEW YORK, 10 May 1974, *Niagara Falls in Winter,* USD 2,000. VERSAILLES, 4 Nov 1979, *Tangiers* (1830, oil on canvas, 15 x 22 ins / 38 x 55 cm) FRF 4,000. AMSTERDAM, 6 June 1983, *Interior of St Jacob's Church in Antwerp* (1857, oil on canvas, 32 1/2 x 25 1/2 ins / 82.5 x 64.5 cm) NLG 16,000. LONDON, 21 June 1984, *The Chinese Pavilion at the Gateway to Topkapi, Constantinople* (1866, watercolour, 11 x 16 1/2 ins / 28 x 42 cm) GBP 3,000. NEUILLY, 7 April 1991, *Ste-Geneviève-du-Mont* (1936, oil on canvas, 35 x 25 1/2 ins / 89 x 65 cm) FRF 25,500. PARIS, 13 April 1992, *Fountain of Selim III in Constantinople* (1864, watercolour, 12 1/2 x 19 ins / 32 x 48 cm) FRF 21,000. PARIS, 23 Oct 1992, *Three Views of the Alcazar in Segovia* (lead pencil, 11 1/2 x 15 1/4 ins / 29 x 38.5 cm) FRF 8,200. NEW YORK, 22-23 July 1993, *Interior of a Church* (1838, oil on canvas, 35 1/2 x 24 1/2 ins / 90.2 x 62.2 cm) USD 3,738. NEW YORK, 30 Oct 1996, *Winter Storm, Niagara Falls* (1856, oil on canvas, 25 3/4 x 39 ins / 65.4 x 99.1 cm) USD 4,600. NEW YORK, 18 March 1998, *Baptism of Albert of Orleans, on 2 May 1841 in Paris* (oil on canvas, 16 x 12 3/4 ins / 40.6 x 32.4 cm) USD 8,625. PARIS, 27 March 2003, *Golden Horn* (1864, watercolour, 8 x 17 ins / 21 x 44 cm) EUR 2,700. NEW ORLEANS, 6 Dec 2003, *Study for Giant Steamboats* (oil on canvas, 16 x 19 ins / 41 x 48 cm) USD 17,500.

SECANE, Luis
Argentinian, 20th century.
Born c. 1915, in Buenos Aires.
Painter, engraver, lithographer, illustrator. Wall decorations.

In spite of some coincidences, Luis Secane is probably not identical with Luis Seoane.

Luis Secane completed his studies in Spain and returned to Argentina in 1938. He lived and worked in Buenos Aires. He was a well-known graphic artist and produced several mural decorative works, including those in the gallery at Santa Fé and in the Teatro Municpal General San Martin in Buenos Aires.

His work featured in numerous collective exhibitions, including: the National Gallery in Washington (1956); the Venice Biennale (1956); selection for the Palanza Prize (1956-1957); the *Panamerican Biennale* in Mexico (1958); the Argentinian pavilion in the *Exposition Internationale* in Brussels (1958); the *Biennale of Lithography* in Cincinnati (1958); *Exhibition of Argentinian Painting* in La Paz and Lima (1958); Biennale at São Paulo (1959); *Exhibition of South-American Painting* in Dallas Museum (1959); *International Exhibition of Modern Art* in Buenos Aires (1960); *150 Years of Argentinian Painting* (1961). He had several solo exhibitions after he returned from Spain.

MUSEUMS AND GALLERIES:
BUENOS AIRES (Mus. Nacional de Bellas Artes) - CÓRDOBA (MBA Genaro Pérez) - MONTEVIDEO (MM) - NEW YORK (MoMA).

SECANO, Gerónimo or Jerónimo
Spanish, 17th - 18th century.
Born 1638, in Saragossa; died 1710, in Saragossa.
Painter, sculptor.

Gerónimo Secano learned to paint in Saragossa before going to study the old masters in the royal collection in Madrid. He returned to Saragossa where he painted frescoes for the church of S Pablo and had many pupils.

SECARD, Louis
French, 18th century.
Painter.

Louis Secard was admitted into the Académie de St-Luc on 17 October 1753 in return for four hundred francs and one history painting. Bellier de la Chavignerie mentions him in his general dictionary of French artists.

SECCADENARI, Ercole
Italian, 16th century.
Died 1540, in Bologna.
Sculptor, architect.

Ercole Seccadenari carved portals and statues for a number of churches in Bologna.

SECCANTE, Giacomo, or Secante, called Trombon
Italian, 16th century.
Died 22 December 1585.
Painter.

Giacomo Seccante painted many altarpieces for Udine Cathedral and churches in Moruzzo, Ronchis, Nogaro, Asio and Folignano.

SECCANTE, Giacomo
Italian, 17th century.
Born 25 September 1617.
Active in Udine.
Painter.

Giacomo Seccante was the son of Pomponio Seccante.

SECCANTE, Pomponio
Italian, 16th century.
Born c. 1570.
Active in Udine (Veneto).
Painter.

The son of Sebastiano Seccante the Younger, Pomponio Seccante painted the altarpiece in the church at Trivignano.

SECCANTE, Sebastiano, the Elder
Italian, 16th century.
Died 1581, in Udine (Veneto).
Painter. Religious subjects.
The brother of Giacomo Seccante, Sebastiano Seccante painted altarpieces for the cathedrals of Cividale and Udine.

SECCANTE, Sebastiano, the Younger
Italian, 16th century.
Born in Udine (Veneto).
Active at the beginning of the 16th century.
Painter. History painting, portraits.
Pupil and son-in-law of Pomponio Amalteo, Sebastiano Seccante painted a *Christ Carrying the Cross* for the church of S Giorgio in Udine.

SECCANTE, Seccante
Italian, 16th - 17th century.
Born 23 September 1571, in Udine (Veneto).
Painter.
Seccante Seccante painted altarpieces for the churches in Gemona and for Grado Cathedral.

SECCHI, Giovanni Andrea
Italian, 16th century.
Active in Cremona during the first half of the 16th century.
Painter.

SECCHI, Giovanni Battista, called Il Carravaggio or Il Caravaggino
Italian, 17th century.
Active c. 1619.
Painter.
Secchi was baptised in Caravaggio. Lanzi attributes to him an *Ephiphany* in the church of S Pietro at Gessi.

SECCHI, Luigi
Italian, 19th - 20th century.
Born 1853, in Cremona; died 24 April 1921, in Miazzina (Veneto).
Sculptor, medallist.
Luigi Secchi exhibited in Milan and Turin.
MUSEUMS AND GALLERIES:
GENOA: *Rest* (bronze) - ROME (Gal. Nazionale d'Arte Moderna): *Ocarina*; *Resting*.
AUCTION RECORDS:
MILAN, 6 Nov 1980, *Nude* (bronze, h. 15 3/4 ins / 40 cm) ITL 900,000.

SECCHIARI, Giulio
Italian, 17th century.
Born in Modena; died 1631, in Sassuolo (Emilia-Romagna).
Painter.
Secchiari was the pupil of the Carracci brothers in Bologna. He worked in Rome and Mantua and for churches in Modena. Most of his works have been destroyed.

SECCI, Antonio
Italian, 20th century.
Born 1944, in Dorgali (Nuoro).
Painter.
Antonio Secci settled in Milan early in his life. He travelled in France, Belgium, Switzerland and the USA.

From 1966 to 1972 he worked in collaboration with Roberto Crippa. His painting can be described as having the 'strength of coordination' and of 'abstract spaces' in the sense of the theories of Bertrand Russell, and springs solely from the creative mind of the artist. In it antagonistic shapes balance and counterbalance in harmonious rhythm.

His work was shown in several collective exhibitions, including the Menton Biennale and in many solo shows.

SÉCHAN, Charles or Polycarpe Charles
French, 19th century.
Born 29 June 1803, in Paris; died 14 September 1874, in Paris.
Painter, draughtsman, decorative designer.
Landscapes, urban landscapes, architectural views. Murals.
Charles Séchan's masters were Jules Lefebvre and Charles Cicéri. He was appointed set designer to the Garnier Opera in Paris and was also made a Chevalier of the Légion d'Honneur.

He was one of the first set designers of his time and, independently of his work at the Opera, he made sets for the Comédie Française and the Porte St-Martin and Ambigu theatres in Paris as well. He was also frequently employed to decorate theatre auditoriums in the French provinces and abroad: notably in Dresden, Brussels and Constantinople. He also helped with the restoration work on the Apollo Gallery at the Louvre.
AUCTION RECORDS:
PARIS, 1883, *The Mont St-Michel* (eleven pen drawings with Indian ink wash, heightened with white) FRF 500. PARIS, 1890, *The St-Martin Canal*; *Tumbledown Houses* (two studies together) FRF 510. PARIS, 29 June 1949, *Views of Churches and Various Structures in Caen* (set of 12 drawings) FRF 10,000.

SÉCHAS, Alain
French, 20th - 21st century.
Born 1955, in Colombes.
Painter, sculptor, draughtsman, installation artist, video artist. Figures, scenes with figures, animals. Animated films.
Alain Séchas lives and works in Paris. He works across a broad range of disciplines - painting, sculpture, drawings, installations, video, and cartoons - to create a comic strip-cum-television world peopled with colourful and appealing characters, such as absent-minded professors and children, animals such as cats and spiders, and other elements that evoke a childlike world. He employs everyday objects and materials such as polyester, plastic to develop a world of banal anecdote (a painting lesson, perhaps, as in *Papas* of 1995), but also to hint at underlying angst or sexual aggression, as seen in *Rape* (1988), or *Exhibitionist* (1991) and broad social themes such as the use and abuse of violence and power.

He has shown examples of his work at a number of group exhibitions: in 1985, at the Lothringer Strasse Gallery in Munich; in 1990, at the Venice Biennale (Open Section); in 1991, at the Contemporary Art Biennale in Lyons; in 1992, at the Hôtel des Arts in Paris; in 1996, at the Centre d'Art Contemporain in Grenoble; in 2000, at *Présumés innocents: l'art contemporain et l'enfance* (*Presumed Innocent: Contemporary Art and Childhood*), at the Capc Musée d'Art Contemporain in Bordeaux; and, in 2003, at *L'Etat des Choses* (*The State of Things*), a reflection on everyday objects in contemporary art presented within the framework of *Public Treasury, 20 Years of Creation in the Regional Collection of Contemporary Art (FRAC)*, held at the Musée des Beaux-Arts in Nantes.

Solo exhibitions by Alain Séchas have included those in 1985, 1988 and 1995 at the Galerie Ghislaine Hussenot in Paris; in 1987 at APAC in Vevers; in 1990, at the La Criée Halle d'Art Contemporain in Rennes; in 1995, at the Creux de l'Enfer Centre d'Art Contemporain in Thiers; in 1996, at the São Paulo Biennale and the Musée d'Art Contemporain in Lyons; in 1997, at the École des Beaux-Arts in Nîmes and at the Fondation Cartier pour l'Art Contemporain in Paris; and, in 2001, at the Musée d'Art Moderne et Contemporain in Strasbourg.

BIBLIOGRAPHY:
Javault, Patrick, *Alain Séchas*, Association pour l'art contemporain, Nevers, 1988. *Alain Séchas*, exhibition catalogue, Hôtel des Arts, Paris, 1992. Francblin, Catherine, "*Interview: Alain Séchas. Si c'est beau, c'est beau pour tout le monde*' in *Art Press* n° 212, periodical, Paris, April 1996. Bernadac, Marie-Laure/Moisdon-Tremblay, et al., *Présumés innocents: l'art contemporain et l'enfance*, exhibition catalogue, Capc Musée d'Art contemporain, Bordeaux, 2000. '*D'entre ses chats. Entretien avec Alain Séchas*' in *L'Œil* n° 541, periodical, Paris, November 2002. Zahm, Olivier (preface), et al., *Trésors publics, 20 ans de création dans les Fonds régionaux d'art contemporain*, Flammarion, Paris, 2003 (text in French and English).
MUSEUMS AND GALLERIES:
ANGOULÊME (FRAC Poitou-Charentes): *PacMan* (1984) - CLERMONT-FERRAND (FRAC Auvergne): *Octopus* (1990, polyester, plexiglas, stainless steel) - LIMOGES (FRAC Limousin): *Chromes* (1988) - PARIS (FNAC): *Professor Suicide* (1995, installation) - PARIS (MNAM-CCI): *Bicycle* (1985); *Mannequin* (1985) - VILLEURBANNE (FRAC Rhône-Alpes).

SECHEHAYE, Félix
Swiss, 19th century.
Born 20 April 1839, in Geneva.
Painter.
Félix Sechehaye was taught by Calame and exhibited in Geneva until 1880.

SECHEHAYE, Jacques René
Swiss, 18th century.
Born 7 November 1758, in Geneva; died 3 March 1786, in Geneva.
Enameller.
Jacques Sechehaye was the pupil of P.F. Marcinhes.

SECHER, Valdemar
Danish, 20th century.
Born 24 June 1885, in Skaarup, near Rönde; died 1976.
Active in Copenhagen.
Painter. Portraits, landscapes.
Valdemar Secher was a pupil of N.V. Dorph.
MUSEUMS AND GALLERIES:
COPENHAGEN - HULL.

SECK, Amadou
Senegalese, 20th - 21st century.
Born 1950, in Dakar.
Painter.
Amadou Seck uses a combination of clay and sand to emulate the forms and themes of ancient African statuary.

SECK-CARTON, Heinrich Josef Anton Maria
German, 20th century.
Born 6 October 1888, in Flörsheim; died 1943, in Mainz.
Painter, fresco artist. Religious subjects.
Heinrich Seck-Carton painted frescoes for churches in and around Mainz, where he lived and worked.
MUSEUMS AND GALLERIES:
MAINZ (MG).

SECKEL, Chr.
Austrian, 18th century.
Painter.
Chr. Seckel was the father or brother of Norbert Seckel and painted four architectural views of Seehof Castle near Bamberg.

SECKEL, Josef
Dutch, 20th century.
Born 23 December 1881, in Rotterdam; died 1945.
Active in The Hague.
Painter. Figures, still-lifes.
MUSEUMS AND GALLERIES:
ROTTERDAM (Mus. Boijmans Van Beuningen) - THE HAGUE (Gemeentemus.).
AUCTION RECORDS:
AMSTERDAM, 14 Sept 1993, *Zinnias* (oil on canvas, 15 3/4 x 10 1/4 ins / 40 x 26 cm) NLG 1,495.

SECKEL, Norbert
Austrian, 18th century.
Born 1725, in Prague; died c. 1800.
Painter. Landscapes, architectural views, flowers.
Norbert Seckel executed frescoes for the Spanish Hall in Prague Castle.

SECKELMAN, Hans
German, 19th - 20th century.
Painter.
Hans Seckelman is noted for a *Portrait of Karl Marx*.

SECKENDORF, Götz von
German, 20th century.
Born 3 October 1889, in Brunswick; died 24 August 1914, near Cambrai, on the front.
Painter. Landscapes.
Götz von Seckendorf studied in Paris under Ranson.
MUSEUMS AND GALLERIES:
BRUNSWICK: *Young Woman Bathing; Landscape near Friedersdorf* - HAMBURG (Kunsthalle): *Landscape near Tangiers*.
AUCTION RECORDS:
VIENNA, 29-30 Oct 1996, *View of Pegli* (oil on panel, 19 1/4 x 25 1/4 ins / 49 x 64 cm) ATS 86,250.

SECLIERS, Ingelbert Lievin van.
See **SICLERS**

SECO, Simão, or Sequo
Portuguese, 16th century.
Painter, illuminator.
Active in Lisbon in the early and mid-16th century, Simão Seco was an Augustinian monk. He executed a *Missal* for Braga Cathedral in 1529. He worked for King John III between 1551 and 1554.

SECOLA, A.
Painter. Genre scenes.
Secola was mentioned by Miss Florence Lévy.
AUCTION RECORDS:
NEW YORK, 27 Jan 1906, *Music*, USD 100. AMSTERDAM, 28 Feb 1989, *Villager Chatting by the Well* (oil on canvas, 26 3/4 x 18 3/4 ins / 68 x 47.5 cm) NLG 1,092. NEW YORK, 21 May 1991, *Village Fête* (oil on canvas, 20 x 32 ins / 50.8 x 81.3 cm) USD 4,620. NEW YORK, 20 July 1994, *Dancing at the Inn* (oil on canvas, 19 3/4 x 32 1/4 ins / 50.2 x 81.9 cm) USD 1,840. NEW YORK, 15 June 1999, *Tired Professor* (oil on canvas, 20 x 32 ins / 51 x 81 cm) USD 5, 000. CHICAGO, 6 May 2000, *Typical Afternoon* (oil on canvas, 19 x 32 ins / 48 x 81 cm) USD 2, 400. SHREWSBURY, 11 April 2001, *Elegant Lady Wearing a Striped Satin Dress Holding Flowers* (oil on panel, 39 x 13 ins / 100 x 33 cm) GBP 2, 000.

SECOND, Louis. See **FÉRÉOL**

SECONDINO, Pompeo, or Secondiano
Italian, 17th century.
Born to a family originally from Vercelli.
Painter.
Secondino was active from 1603 onwards. He worked for the ducal court in Turin.

SECONET, Hans Matthes. See **SEBERT**

SECORPS. See **SCORE**

SECQUEVILLE, Maxime
French, 20th century.
Born 1935; died 1996.
Painter. Landscapes, urban landscapes, waterscapes.

École des Bords de Marne.

Auction records:

La Varenne-St-Hilaire, 6 March 1988, *Walkers on the Banks of the Marne in Champigny* (oil on canvas, 23 1/2 x 28 3/4 ins / 60 x 73 cm) FRF 7,500. La Varenne-St-Hilaire, 29 May 1988, *The Marne in La Varenne St-Hilaire* (oil on canvas, 23 1/2 x 28 3/4 ins / 60 x 73 cm) FRF 6,000. La Varenne-St-Hilaire, 21 May 1989, *Little Branch of Polangis* (oil on canvas, 25 1/2 x 31 1/2 ins / 65 x 80 cm) FRF 6,800. Versailles, 24 Sept 1989, *Moret-sur-Loing* (oil on canvas, 19 3/4 x 24 ins / 50 x 61 cm) FRF 7,000. Versailles, 10 Dec 1989, *Landscape in the Perche* (oil on canvas, 19 3/4 x 24 ins / 50 x 61 cm) FRF 4,500. Versailles, 22 April 1990, *Camaret, the Mauritanian of Armorica* (oil on canvas, 21 1/4 x 25 1/2 ins / 54 x 65 cm) FRF 4,200. La Varenne-St-Hilaire, 20 May 1990, *Autumn Light* (oil on canvas, 23 1/2 x 28 3/4 ins / 60 x 73 cm) FRF 7,000.

SEDAZZI, Giuseppe

Italian, 18th century.
Born 1757, in Bologna.
Painter.

Sedazzi was the pupil of G.G. Barozzi and G. Varotti.

SEDDING, John Dando

British, 19th century.
Born 13 April 1838, in Eton; died 7 April 1891, in Winsford.
Architect, designer, draughtsman, art writer. Designs for embroidery and wallpapers.

John Dando Sedding was a practising architect who was also an accomplished designer of embroidery patterns, wallpapers and the like. His intimate knowledge of plant life resulted in leaf and flower designs of an unusual sensitivity.

SEDDON, John Pollard

British, 19th century.
Born 19 September 1827, in London; died 1 February 1906.
Designer, lithographer, architect, art writer.

John Pollard Seddon was the brother of Thomas Seddon. He engraved landscapes and architectural subjects.

SEDDON, Thomas

British, 19th century.
Born 28 August 1821, in London; died 23 November 1856, in Cairo.
Painter. Landscapes, landscapes with figures, local scenes.
Orientalism.

Thomas Seddon was the son of a major London-based furniture manufacturer. He studied in Paris from 1841 and went to work as a draughtsman in his father's factory. Seddon was one of the founders of the North London School of Drawing and Modelling, where he also taught. He started painting in 1851 and exhibited his first canvas, *Penelope*, in 1852. He turned increasingly towards landscape work. Seddon visited the East in 1853 and again in 1854, in the company of Holman Hunt. He died in the course of a third visit in 1856.

Seddon

Bibliography:

Landow, P., '*Thomas Seddon's Moriah and His Jerusalem and the Valley of Jehosophat*' in *Journal of Pre-Raphaelite and Aesthetic Studies*, 1987. Gilbert, Christopher, '*Seddon, Sons and Shackleton*' in *Furniture History*, vol. 33, 1997.

Museums and Galleries:

London (Tate Collection): *Jerusalem and the Valley of Jehoshaphat from the Hill of Evil Counsel* (1854-1855, oil on canvas).

Auction records:

London, 28 Nov 1972, *Penelope*, GBP 3,600. London, 18 Oct 1974, *Dromedary and Arabs in the Desert*, Gns 450. New York, 22 May 1985, *Arab Sheikh (Sir Richard Burton in Arab Dress)* (1854, oil on canvas, 18 1/4 x 14 1/4 ins / 46.4 x 36.2 cm) USD 37,500. London, 19 Feb 2003, *Arabs at Prayer in the Desert* (oil on canvas, 25 x 44 ins / 63 x 112 cm) GBP 55,000.

SEDEJ, Maksim

Slovene, 20th century.
Born 1909, in Dobracevo.
Painter.

Maksim Sedej was influenced by the modern French school. His *Circus* was shown at the exhibition in Paris organized by UNESCO in 1946.

SEDELMAYER. See also **SEDELMAYR**

SEDELMAYER, Ferdinand von

Austrian, 19th century.
Active in Vienna c. 1820.
Portrait artist.

SEDELMAYER, Jakob

German, 17th century.
Born in Friedberg (Bavaria).
Active in Augsburg in 1695.
Painter. Religious subjects, contemporary events and landscape.

SEDELMAYER, Joseph Anton

German, 19th century.
Born 1797, in Munich; died 1863.
Painter, engraver (etching), lithographer. Landscapes.

The pupil of Kobel and G. von Dillis in Munich, Joseph Sedelmayer executed engravings after pictures in galleries in Schleissheim and Munich.

Auction records:

Munich, 14 March 1985, *Mountainous Landscape with Wooden Bridge* (1830, oil on canvas, 22 1/4 x 29 1/4 ins / 56.5 x 74.5 cm) DEM 5,000. Munich, 27 Sept 2000, *Wesslinger See* (1825, oil on panel, 15 x 18 ins / 39 x 46 cm) DEM 9,500. Munich, 26 June 2002, *Starnberger See - Ammerland* (oil on canvas, one of a pair, 16 x 19 ins / 40 x 47 cm) EUR 2,500. Munich, 26 June 2002, *Schloss Ammerland on Starnberger See* (oil on canvas, one of a pair, 16 x 19 ins / 40 x 47 cm) EUR 3,000.

SEDELMAYER, Martin

Austrian, 18th century.
Born 1766; died 31 May 1799, in Vienna.
Draughtsman. Plants.

SEDELMAYR. See also **SEDELMAYER**

SEDELMAYR, Eleonora Katharina. See **REMSHARD**

SEDELMAYR, H.

Austrian, 18th century.
Engraver (etching).

H. Sedelmayr engraved a leaf bearing the effigy of Emperor *Charles VI*, which is conserved in the national library in Vienna.

SEDELMAYR, Jeremias Jakob, or Sedelmayer

German, 18th century.
Born 1706, in Augsburg; died 1761, in Augsburg.
Miniaturist, draughtsman, engraver. Religious subjects, portraits and genre scenes.

In addition to his other subjects, Jeremias Sedelmayr is known for his views of the imperial library in Vienna, which were engraved after his own drawings and published in 1737.

AUCTION RECORDS:

MUNICH, 29 Oct 1985, *The Stoning of St Stephen* (1739, pen and wash/traces of red chalk and pencil, 14 1/4 x 8 3/4 ins / 36 x 22.5 cm) DEM 2,500.

SEDELMAYR, Joseph

Austrian, 19th century.
Born 1805, in Gars am Kamp.
Active in Munich, Germany.
Lithographer.

Joseph Sedelmayr studied under H. Mitterer in Munich.

SEDELMAYR, Sabina

German, 18th century.
Born c. 1700, in Augsburg; died 1775, in Augsburg.
Miniaturist, watercolourist.

Sabina Sedelmayr was the sister of Jeremias Jakob Sedelmayr and Eleonara Katharina Remshard.

SEDERBOOM. See **QUELLIN Jan Erasmus**

SEDGLEY, Peter

British, 20th century.
Born 1930.
Painter.
Op Art, Lumino-Kinetic Art.
Space Limited Group.

Peter Sedgley studied architecture from 1944-1947 and worked as an architect from 1947 to 1959. In 1960-1962 he created a co-operative of design and construction technicians with the British abstract painter Bridget Riley. He began painting relatively late in his career, in 1963. Sedgley's paintings explore optical effects and effects of light and movement, forming a close parallel to the work of Bridget Riley.

His work has featured in a number of group exhibitions in the same vein, including: 1965, *The Responsive Eye*, MoMA, New York; 1965, Salon des Réalités Nouvelles, Paris; 1966, *Kinetic Art*, Coventry; 1966, *Aspects of New British Art*, a touring exhibition in Australia; 1967, *Light in Movement*, Dublin and Bristol; 1968, *British Print-making*, MoMA, New York. Sedgely's work has also been the subject of a number of solo exhibitions, including: 1965, 1966, London; 1965, 1966, New York; 1966, Chicago; 1968, Hamburg.

BIBLIOGRAPHY:

Cyril Barrett, *Peter Sedgley, painting, objects, installations 1963-1980*, exhibition catalogue, Kelpras-Studios, London, 1980. *Peter Sedgley: acts of light. Paintings, kinetic pieces, works on paper and prints*, exhibition catalogue, Desmond Fine Art, London, 2000.

MUSEUMS AND GALLERIES:

BRISTOL (City Museum and Art Gallery): *Blue Pulse* (1972).

AUCTION RECORDS:

NEW YORK, 13 Feb 1991, *Suspense* (1966, acrylic on preformed canvas, 60 x 52 ins / 152.4 x 132.1 cm) USD 2,200. LEEDS, 21 Nov 2000, *Blue Point 1978* (oil on canvas, 40 x 39 ins / 102 x 100 cm) GBP 1,850. LONDON, 6 Dec 2000, *Blue and Green Modulation 1964* (1964, emulsion on board, 39 x 39 ins / 100 x 100 cm) GBP 2,500. LONDON, 4 July 2001, *Event* (1966, oil on canvas) GBP 2,000. LONDON, 3 June 2003, *Colour Study* (1966, emulsion on board, 30 x 30 ins / 76 x 76 cm) GBP 1,800. LONDON, 19 May 2004, *Study in Blue and Yellow* (1973, acrylic on card, 20 x 20 ins / 50 x 50 cm) GBP 1,100. LONDON, 14 Sept 2004, *Blue Nimbus. Red Planet* (1967, mixed media on paper, two, 10 x 10 ins / 25 x 25 cm) GBP 1,200.

SEDGWICK, John (Mrs). See **OLIVER Emma Sophie**

SEDGWICK, William

British, 18th century.
Born 1748, in London; died c. 1800.
Engraver (stippling), painter. Landscapes.

William Sedgwick was influenced by Bartolozzi.

SEDILLE, Jules or Charles Jules

French, 19th century.
Born 26 March 1807, in Paris; died 30 July 1871, in Paris.
Painter, architect. Battles.

He was the father of Paul Sedille and the pupil of Vaudoyer and Le Bas.

SEDILLE, Paul

French, 19th century.
Born 1836, in Paris; died 6 January 1900, in Paris.
Painter, architect, decorative designer, art writer.
Landscapes with figures, landscapes, urban landscapes.

He was the son of Jules Sedille and the pupil of Lanoue, Guénepin and Renié.

AUCTION RECORDS:

PARIS, 1872, *Autumn in the Woods*, FRF 160. PARIS, 1880, *Landscape*, FRF 107. PARIS, 6 July 1949, *Landscapes, Views of a Town, Military Review* (set of paintings) FRF 2,000. PARIS, 15 Feb 1950, *Dusk*, FRF 1,700; *Landscape*, FRF 1,200. VIENNA, 10 June 1980, *Path through a Forest* (oil on panel, 16 x 12 1/2 ins / 40.5 x 31.5 cm) ATS 18,000.

SEDILLOT, Anna

French, 19th - 20th century.
Born in Paris.
Pastellist.

Sédillot was a member of the Artistes Français from 1899 and featured at the Salon, where she received an honourable mention in 1900.

SEDIVA, Emanuela

Czech, 20th century.
Born 1880, in Hostivice.
Painter.

SEDIVY, Franz Joseph

Danish, 20th century.
Born 26 November 1888, in Copenhagen.
Painter, designer.

Franz Joseph Sedivy was the son of Franz Maria Sedivy.

SEDIVY, Franz Joseph Xaver

Czech, 19th - 20th century.
Born 23 October 1838, in Goltsch-Jenikau (now Golcuv-Jenikov); died 22 September 1919, in Copenhagen.
Engraver (wood).

Franz Joseph Xaver Sedivy was the father of Franz Maria Sedivy; he settled in Copenhagen in 1870.

SEDIVY, Franz Maria

Danish, 19th - 20th century.
Born 2 December 1864, in Prague; died 1945.
Illustrator, lithographer.

Son of Franz Joseph Xaver Sedivy and father of Franz Joseph Sedivy, he studied at the Kongelige Danske Kunstakademi in Copenhagen.

MUSEUMS AND GALLERIES:

COPENHAGEN - HILLERØD (Frederiksborg Slot).

SEDIVY, Karel

Danish, 19th - 20th century.
Born 29 August 1860, in Prague; died 7 November 1906, in Copenhagen.
Painter, engraver, draughtsman, illustrator.
Landscapes.

Brother of Franz Maria Sedivy, Karel Sedivy worked as a woodcut engraver and illustrator.

MUSEUMS AND GALLERIES:

COPENHAGEN.

SEDLACEK, Franz, or Sedlazer
German, 20th century.
Born 21 January 1891, in Breslau (now Wroclaw, Poland); died 1944.
Active in Vienna.
Painter, engraver.

Franz Sedlacek was a a member of the Secession Group.

MUSEUMS AND GALLERIES:
LINZ: *Librarian.*

AUCTION RECORDS:
COLOGNE, 19 Nov 1981, *Tête-à-Tête* (oil on panel, 17 3/4 x 13 1/4 ins / 45 x 33.5 cm) DEM 4,600. VIENNA, 21 June 1983, *Flying Fish* (1916, Indian ink, 6 1/2 x 10 1/4 ins / 16.5 x 26 cm) ATS 18,000. VIENNA, 31 March 1984, *Salzburg or Landscape with Hunter* (1926, oil on card, 25 1/2 x 21 1/4 ins / 65 x 54 cm) ATS 120,000. VIENNA, 10 Sept 1985, *Storm* (1932, charcoal and stump, 17 1/4 x 14 1/2 ins / 43.5 x 37 cm) ATS 22,000. NEW YORK, 24 Feb 1995, *Female Visitor* (1925, oil on panel, 21 x 25 1/2 ins / 53.3 x 64.8 cm) USD 31,050. LONDON, 15 March 1996, *Sweetmeat Vendor, Scutari, Turkey* (oil on canvas, 32 1/4 x 51 ins / 82 x 129.5 cm) GBP 6,325. NEW YORK, 10 Oct 1996, *Shape above the Trees* (1928, oil on panel, 17 3/4 x 20 ins / 45.1 x 49.9 cm) USD 37,375. AHLDEN, 17 Sept 1999, *Inn Interior with Noble Couple Entering* (oil on canvas, 22 x 27 ins / 55 x 68 cm) DEM 4,800. VIENNA, 14 May 2002, *Mountain Landscape* (1933, charcoal heightened with white, 10 x 13 ins / 26 x 34 cm) EUR 4,500. VIENNA, 25 Nov 2002, *Author* (1937, lithograph, 20 x 14 ins / 50 x 35 cm) EUR 26,000. VIENNA, 29 April 2003, *Skeletons* (gouache, 9 x 17 ins / 23 x 43 cm) EUR 5,000. LINZ, 14 May 2003, *In Flight* (1915, pen, 6 x 7 ins / 16 x 18 cm) EUR 3,600. VIENNA, 21 April 2004, *Hallstatter Glacier* (1938, pencil, 11 x 9 ins / 29 x 23 cm) EUR 3,600. VIENNA, 12 Oct 2004, *Industrial Landscape* (1934, oil on plywood, 19 x 30 ins / 48 x 75 cm) EUR 130,000.

SEDLACEK, Peter
German, 20th century.
Born 1939, in Hamburg.
Also active in France and in Spain.
Painter.

Peter Sedlacek divides his time between Hamburg, Ibiza and Vence and has exhibited in Vence. His style is close to Surrealism and his compositions feature a diffuse and visionary 'cellular' landscape set in indeterminate space.

SEDLACEK, Stephan
Austrian or Czechoslovakian, 19th - 20th century.
Painter. Genre scenes, interiors with figures.

AUCTION RECORDS:
ENGHIEN-LES-BAINS, 4 March 1984, *Slave Merchant* (oil on canvas mounted/panel, 31 x 23 1/4 ins / 79 x 59 cm) FRF 18,000. LONDON, 21 June 1989, *Harem Scene* (oil on canvas, 31 x 48 3/4 ins / 78.5 x 124 cm) GBP 4,400. LONDON, 14 Feb 1990, *In the Harem* (oil on canvas, 31 x 48 3/4 ins / 78.5 x 124 cm) GBP 8,250. AMSTERDAM, 25 April 1990, *Interesting Tale* (oil on canvas, 20 3/4 x 26 1/2 ins / 53 x 67 cm) NLG 8,050. AMSTERDAM, 23 April 1991, *Musical Reunion* (oil on canvas, 20 1/2 x 26 ins / 52 x 66 cm) NLG 4,830. AMSTERDAM, 24 April 1991, *Recital in a Rococo Interior* (oil on canvas, 22 x 26 3/4 ins / 55 x 68 cm) NLG 3,450. LONDON, 17 June 1992, *Billiards* (oil on canvas, 28 1/4 x 45 ins / 72 x 114 cm) GBP 2,750. AMSTERDAM, 20 April 1993, *Cardinals in Conversation* (oil on canvas, 21 1/4 x 26 3/4 ins / 54 x 68 cm) NLG 1,725.

SEDLACEK, Vojtech or Adalbert
Czech, 20th century.
Born 9 September 1892.
Painter (including gouache), watercolourist, engraver.

Sedlacek was a student of J. Preissier and M. Svabinsky. He continued his studies in Berlin, Dresden, Munich and Vienna. Work by him was shown at exhibitions in Milan, the USA, Japan, Cracow, Warsaw, London, and at the international exhibition in Paris in 1937, where he received a *diplôme d'honneur*. There were several solo exhibitions in Prague, from 1925, and he was the recipient of further important awards in 1954, 1959 and 1964.

Like V. Rabas, he produced touching local landscapes.

BIBLIOGRAPHY:
Fifty years of Czechoslovak Painting from the Collections of the Galleries, 1918-1958, exhibition catalogue, Slovenska Narodna Gal., Bratislava, 1968 (in commemoration of the 50th anniversary of the Republic of Czechoslovakia).

MUSEUMS AND GALLERIES:
PRAGUE (Národní Gal.): watercolours and gouaches.

SEDLACZEK, Joseph, or Sedlatschek
Austrian, 19th century.
Born 1789; died 11 June 1845, in Vienna.
Engraver (burin).

Sedlaczek produced an engraving of a view of Hartberg in Styria, Austria.

SEDLCANSKY, Johann Jakob
Bohemian School, 17th century.
Active in Prague.
Illuminator, calligrapher.

Johann Sedlcansky illuminated a Psalter from 1620 to 1623.

SEDLEZKY, Balthazar Sigismond.
See **SETLEZKY**

SEDLMAIER, Thekla Crescentia
Maiden name: Karth
German, 19th century.
Active in Munich c. 1830.
Painter. Portraits, genre scenes.

Sedlmaier studied under J. Muxel.

SEDLMAYER. See also **SEDELMAYER** and **SEDELMAYR**

SEDLMAYR
German, 18th century.
Died 1798.
Active in Munich.
Landscape artist.

SEDMIGRADSKY, E.
Painter. History painting.

MUSEUMS AND GALLERIES:
HELSINKI: *Alexander the Great at Darius' Tent.*

SEDOV, Grigory Semenovich, or Sedov, Siedov
Russian, 19th century.
Born 1836; died 1884 or 1886.
Painter, engraver. Figures, genre scenes.

Grigory Semenovich Sedov studied at the art academy in St Petersburg. He also worked as a lithographer. Hwe sometimes signed his work *Sedoff* in Latin script.

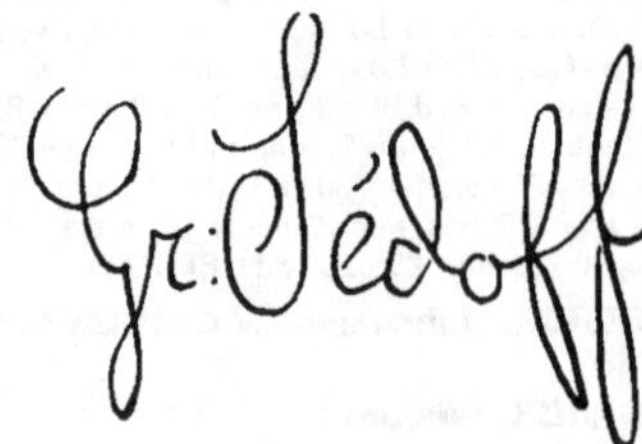

MUSEUMS AND GALLERIES:
MOSCOW (State Tretyakov Gal.): *A Bourgeois woman from Kursk* - ST PETERSBURG (Gosudarstvennyj Russkij Muz.): *Ivan the Terrible Admiring his Wife Vassilissa Milentieva.*
AUCTION RECORDS:
LONDON, 14 Dec 1995, *Ivan the Terrible Taking Advice from Oprichnik Malyuta Skuratov, his Favourite* (oil on canvas, 56 x 42 ins / 142.5 x 106.5 cm) GBP 17,250.

SEDRAC, Serge

Russian, 20th century.
Born 1878, in Tbilisi, Georgia; died 1974, in Paris.
Active from 1926 in France.
Painter. Genre scenes, landscapes, landscapes with figures, mountainscapes.

Serge Sedrac studied at the fine arts school in Moscow. He continued his studies in Paris, where he finally settled in 1926. He painted mainly mountain landscapes, often of the Alps.
AUCTION RECORDS:
PARIS, 25 June 1947, *Megève,* FRF 2,000. PARIS, 27 Jan 1950, *Sun on the Snow,* FRF 7,800. PARIS, 12 Feb 1989, *Leaving Chez Maxim* (oil on canvas, 11 x 13 3/4 ins / 27 x 35 cm) FRF 7,000. PARIS, 4 April 1989, *The Balloon Seller* (oil on canvas, 11 x 13 3/4 ins / 27 x 35 cm) FRF 5,000. SCEAUX, 11 March 1990, *Beach Scene* (oil on canvas, 6 1/4 x 11 ins / 16 x 28 cm) FRF 5,800. PARIS, 12 Dec 1990, *Sun Setting on the Snow at St Maurice* (oil on card/canvas, 18 x 21 ins / 46 x 53.5 cm) FRF 9,000.

SEE, Mathilde

French, 20th century.
Born in Paris.
Painter, designer. Flowers.

Mathilde See worked in Paris. She exhibited at the Société Nationale des Beaux-Arts.

MUSEUMS AND GALLERIES:
PARIS.
AUCTION RECORDS:
PARIS, 16 June 1925, *Still-life: Peaches, Grapes, Figures and Cups* (watercolour) FRF 130. PARIS, 14 and 15 Dec 1927, *Platter of Peaches* (watercolour) FRF 180. PARIS, 29 Nov 1937, *Bouquet of White Roses* (watercolour) FRF 45. PARIS, 24 April 1943, *Peaches,* FRF 800. PARIS, 23 March 1944, *Flowers and Basket of Fruit* (two watercolours) FRF 2,200. PARIS, 24 May 1944, *Tea Roses* (watercolour) FRF 850. PARIS, 31 Jan 1945, *Roses in a Vase* (watercolour) FRF 950; *Still-life: Porcelain and Tea Roses* (watercolour) FRF 1,200. PARIS, July 1946, *Pink Roses in a Vase* (watercolour) FRF 4,000. PARIS, 28 Feb 1951, *Flowers* (watercolour) FRF 1,800.

SEE, Raymonde

French, 20th century.
Born in Paris.
Painter, draughtsman.

See was a student of Conrad Kickert and Morisset. She exhibited at the Salon des Tuileries in Paris.

SEEBACH, Adam

Swedish, 17th century.
Of German origin.
Active in Nyköping from 1629 to 1655.
Painter.

Seebach worked for the Swedish court.

SEEBACH, C. H.

Danish, 18th century.
Active c. 1750.
Draughtsman.

Seebach is known for his portrait of *Frederik V of Denmark.*

SEEBACH, Hans Georg

Swiss, 16th century.
Born to a family originally from Zurich.
Glass painter.

Hans Georg was the son of Ulrich Seebach and was active from 1542 to 1570. He worked for the city of Zurich and moved to Strasbourg in 1567.

SEEBACH, Lothar von

French, 19th - 20th century.
Born 26 March 1853, in Fessenbach; died 23 September 1930, in Strasbourg.
Painter, engraver, draughtsman. Figures, portraits, genre scenes, scenes with figures, interiors, landscapes, architectural views.

Seebach was a student of Ferdinand Keller. He settled in Strasbourg in 1875. He regularly travelled in Italy.
MUSEUMS AND GALLERIES:
BERLIN (Nationalgal.): *Detail of Strasbourg Port; Bridge at Sarrebourg; Old Linen Maid* - KARLSRUHE: *At the Potter's* - STRASBOURG: *St-Pierre de Rome Church; Portrait of the Antique Dealer Brion; Charity at St Marc.*
AUCTION RECORDS:
LINDAU, 5 May 1982, *Bouquet of Autumn Flowers* (oil on canvas, 30 x 38 1/4 ins / 76 x 97 cm) DEM 4,300. STRASBOURG, 11 March 1989, *Young Blonde Girl in Mauve Suit* (oil on canvas, 39 1/4 x 32 ins / 100 x 81 cm) FRF 16,000. BERN, 12 May 1990, *Portrait of a Woman in a Hat* (oil on canvas, 31 1/2 x 25 1/4 ins / 80 x 64 cm) CHF 2,600.

SEEBACH, Peter

Swiss, 16th century.
Born c. 1540, in Zurich; died 2 August 1605, in Zurich.
Glass painter.
Zurich School.

Peter Seebach painted many large and small windows containing coats-of-arms for domestic buildings in Zurich.

SEEBACH, Ulrich

Swiss, 16th century.
Died 1552, in Zurich.
Active in Kybourg.
Glass painter.

Father of Hans Georg Seebach, Ulrich Seebach painted windows depicting coats-of-arms.

SEEBACHER, Ferdinand

German, 19th century.
Born 10 March 1831, in Munich; died 29 September 1904, in Munich.
Painter, decorative designer.

Seebacher produced decorative artwork for churches.

SEEBER, Johann Stefan

German, 18th century.
Born c. 1708; died 1792.
Active in Dresden.
Engraver.

Johann Stefan Seeber was court engraver at Dresden and produced flowers and various ornamental motifs.

SEEBER, Karl Andreas

German, 19th century.
Born 30 November 1855, in Sbitschin.
Active in Berlin.
Painter. Portraits, genre scenes.

Karl Andreas Seeber studied under Anton von Werner.

AUCTION RECORDS:
AMSTERDAM, 2 May 1990, *Daily Life in a District of Rome* (1885, oil on canvas, 31 1/2 x 24 1/2 ins / 80 x 62 cm) NLG 6,670.

SEEBERGER, Gustav
German, 19th century.
Born 1812, in Redwitz (Franconia or Franken); died 22 April 1888, in Munich.
Painter, lithographer. Architectural views.
Seeberger attended the art academy in Nuremberg, Germany. In 1840, he settled in Munich, where he became a teacher at the academy in 1854. He produced engravings of Bavarian landscapes.

SEEBLUMER, Franz Karl
Austrian, 17th century.
Active in Pilsen (now Plzen, Czech Republic) during the second half of the 17th century.
Painter.
Seeblumer painted frescoes and altarpieces for the churches of Unter-Rutschow, Tepl and Plass.

SEEBOECK, Ferdinand
Austrian, 19th - 20th century.
Born 28 March 1864; died 1953.
Sculptor.
Ferdinand Seeboeck was a pupil of Hellmer and Ad. Hildebrand.
MUSEUMS AND GALLERIES:
MUNICH (Schack-Gal.): *Portrait of Count Schach* - STRASBOURG: *Bust of Puttkamer.*

SEEBOLD, Rudolf
German, 20th century.
Died June 1918.
Painter. Figures.

SEECK, Hans
German, 16th century.
Died 1583.
Active in Brunswick.
Sculptor.
Seeck carved tombs, low reliefs and pulpits.

SEECK, Marie
German, 19th - 20th century.
Born 11 September 1861, in Königsberg (now Kaliningrad, Russia); died 1935.
Painter, engraver. Landscapes, architectural views.

SEECK, Otto
German, 19th - 20th century.
Born 7 March 1868, in Berlin; died 1937.
Painter, lithographer.
Otto Seeck studied under Knille at the fine arts academy in Berlin; he produced decorative compositions.

SEED, T.S.
British, 18th - 19th century.
Active in Southampton from 1795 to 1820.
Engraver. Portraits. Armorials.

SEEFISCH, Hermann Ludwig
German, 19th century.
Born 1816, in Potsdam; died 1879.
Painter. Portraits, genre scenes, landscapes.
Seefisch worked in Wilhelm Wachs' studio in Berlin, where he also attended the art academy, in 1832. He perfected his skills in Paris before settling permanently in Berlin.
AUCTION RECORDS:
NEW YORK, 3 May 1979, *Chalet by a Mountain Lake* (1850, oil on canvas, 26 1/2 x 37 ins / 67 x 94 cm) USD 3,500. BERN, 17 May 1999, *Isola Bella* (1849, oil on canvas, 31 x 41 ins / 80 x 105 cm) CHF 20,000. AMSTERDAM, 7 July 1999, *Vierwaldstattersee* (1845, oil on canvas, 30 x 41 ins / 75 x 105 cm) NLG 6,500. VIENNA, 23 May 2000, *Mountain Landscape with House and Sailing Boat* (1845, oil on canvas, 29 x 41 ins / 73 x 105 cm) ATS 80,000. BERN, 14 Nov 2002, *Isola Bella* (1849, oil on canvas, 31 x 41 ins / 80 x 105 cm) CHF 14,000. STAUFEN, 6 Dec 2002, *Isola Bella and Lago Maggiore* (oil on canvas, 27 x 38 ins / 69 x 96 cm) EUR 5,900. MUNICH, 17 May 2003, *Mountain Village in Aosta Valley with View of Mont Blanc* (1841, oil on canvas, 24 x 29 ins / 60 x 73 cm) EUR 5,100. AHLDEN, 19 Sept 2003, *Vierwaldstadtersee* (1845, oil on canvas, 22 x 27 ins / 55 x 68 cm) EUR 4,000.

SEEFRIED, Anton or Peter Anton, or Seyfrid
German, 18th - 19th century.
Born c. 1742, in Otting, near Monheim; died 27 March 1812, in Munich.
Modeller (porcelain).
Anton Seefried studied under Franz Anton Bustelli (1727 - 1763) and was the father of Georg Seefried. He worked for the German porcelain manufactories in Nymphenburg and Kelsterbach.

SEEFRIED, Friedrich, or Seyfried
German, 16th century.
Born 1549, in Nordlingen; died 1609.
Painter, draughtsman. Portraits. Armorials.
Friedrich Seefried may be identical with Michael Seefried. He worked for Wilhelm V of Bavaria.

SEEFRIED, Georg
German, 19th century.
Born c. 1786; died 20 July 1817, in Munich.
Painter (porcelain). Landscapes.
Georg Seefried was the son of Peter Anton. He worked for the Nymphenburg porcelain manufactory in Germany.

SEEFRIED, Johann Kaspar
German, 17th - 18th century.
Active in Nördlingen from 1681 to 1724.
Sculptor.
Johann Kaspar Seefried produced mainly funerary monuments, as well as sculptures for Schrattenhofen castle, Germany.

SEEFRIED, Michael
German, 16th century.
Active in Nordlingen from 1575 to 1576.
Painter.
Michael Seefried may be identical with Friedrich Seefried.

SEEGEN, Bartholomäus
Austrian, 18th century.
Born 1684, in Vienna; died 2 December 1761, in Vienna.
Sculptor.
Bartholomäus Seegen was probably the father of Franz Xaver.

SEEGEN, Franz Xaver, or Segen
Austrian, 18th century.
Born 5 October 1724, in Vienna; died 1780, in Vienna.
Sculptor.
Franz Xaver was probably the son of Bartholomäus Seegen. He attended the art academy in Vienna and produced religious statues, low reliefs and crucifixes.

SEEGEN, Johann Bartholomäus
Austrian, 18th century.
Born 1726, in Vienna; died 17 March 1804, in Vienna.
Sculptor.
Johann Bartholomäus was the brother of Franz Xaver Seegen.

SEEGER, Hermann
German, 19th century.
Born 15 October 1857, in Halberstadt (Saxony-Anhalt); died 1920.
Active in Berlin.

Painter, engraver. Figures, genre scenes, landscapes with figures.

Hermann Seeger studied under Thumann and Gussow at the art academy in Berlin.

Museums and Galleries:

Görlitz (Städtische Kunstsammlungen): *Taking a Rest during the Flight.*

Auction records:

Munich, 1 Dec 1976, *Young Girl on the Beach* (oil on canvas, 20 1/2 x 28 3/4 ins / 52 x 73 cm) DEM 830. London, 5 Oct 1979, *Love Letter* (oil on canvas, 33 x 46 3/4 ins / 84 x 118.7 cm) GBP 900. London, 26 Nov 1986, *Young Girl Sitting on the Beach* (oil on canvas, 20 x 28 1/4 ins / 51 x 72 cm) GBP 3,800. Paris, 30 May 1988, *Man with Pipe* (oil on canvas, 25 1/2 x 39 1/4 ins / 65 x 100 cm) FRF 3,500. New York, 17 Jan 1990, *Relaxing on the Beach* (oil on canvas, 33 1/2 x 43 ins / 85.2 x 109.2 cm) USD 29,700. New York, 23 May 1990, *Confidences* (1901, oil on panel, 256 1/4 x 26 1/2 ins / 650.8 x 67.3 cm) USD 8,250. Amsterdam, 5 June 1990, *Young Woman Sewing in an Interior* (1914, oil on canvas, 16 3/4 x 13 1/2 ins / 42.5 x 34 cm) NLG 7,475. Stockholm, 14 Nov 1990, *Young Children Lost in the Forest* (oil on canvas, 35 1/2 x 28 ins / 90 x 71 cm) SEK 21,000. Munich, 12 Dec 1990, *Young Girls in the Dunes* (oil on canvas, 26 x 40 1/4 ins / 66 x 102 cm) DEM 17,600. London, 19 June 1992, *Summer Pleasures* (1899, oil on canvas, 35 1/2 x 27 1/2 ins / 90 x 70 cm) GBP 18,700. Amsterdam, 21 April 1993, *Lilacs* (oil on canvas, 32 x 24 3/4 ins / 81 x 63 cm) NLG 5,175. London, 18 June 1993, *On the Beach* (oil on canvas, 33 1/2 x 42 1/2 ins / 85 x 108 cm) GBP 5,175. New York, 16 Feb 1994, *On the Beach* (oil on canvas, 31 x 46 1/2 ins / 78.7 x 118.1 cm) USD 26,450. London, 17 March 1995, *Picking Daisies* (1905, oil on canvas, 35 1/2 x 29 1/4 ins / 90.2 x 74.3 cm) GBP 40,000. Munich, 25 June 1996, *Two Young Girls in the Dunes* (oil on canvas, 33 1/2 x 47 1/2 ins / 85 x 120.5 cm) DEM 15,600. Munich, 23 June 1997, *Young Girls Dancing on the Beach* (oil on canvas, 31 3/4 x 47 1/2 ins / 80.5 x 120.5 cm) DEM 17,227. Bremen, 11 Dec 1999, *Women Talking* (oil on canvas, 34 x 47 ins / 86 x 120 cm) DEM 9,000. Vlaamse Kaai, 4 April 2000, *Young Boy and Girl Holding Hands in the Woods* (oil on canvas, 43 x 28 ins / 110 x 70 cm) BEF 260,000. London, 12 Oct 2000, *Two Girls among Sand Dunes* (oil on canvas, 34 x 48 ins / 86 x 121 cm) GBP 7,000. Staufen, 21 Sept 2001, *Fishermen with Boat* (oil on canvas, 13 x 18 ins / 34 x 45 cm) DEM 4,500. Berlin, 7 Dec 2002, *Two Teenage Girls Playing a Lute on the Dunes* (oil on canvas, 31 x 47 ins / 80 x 120 cm) EUR 10,500. Amsterdam, 29 April 2003, *Looking out to Sea* (oil on board, 19 x 27 ins / 49 x 69 cm) EUR 10,000. Cologne, 20 Nov 2003, *Tete-a-tete* (oil on panel, 7 x 9 ins / 18 x 23 cm) EUR 2,600. Munich, 26 March 2004, *Girls Picking Flowers* (oil on canvas, 10 x 13 ins / 26 x 32 cm) EUR 3,000. Cologne, 22 May 2004, *Young Goethe and Friederike Brion in Pfarr Garden, Sesenheim* (1898, oil on canvas, 32 x 23 ins / 81 x 59 cm) EUR 4,600.

SEEGER, Johann

German, 18th century.

Active in the middle of the 18th century.

Potter.

Johann Seeger worked for the Niederweiler manufactory in Germany in 1759.

SEEGER, Karl Ludwig

German, 19th century.

Born 15 July 1808, in Alzey; died 20 August 1866, in Darmstadt.

Active in Mainz, Munich and Darmstadt.

Painter. Landscapes with figures, landscapes.

Museums and Galleries:

Darmstadt: *By the Lake; Peasants Returning* - Mainz: *Swabian Landscape* - Munich: *Landscape of the Rhineland.*

Auction records:

Lucerne, 19 May 1983, *Ammersee Landscape* (1831, oil on canvas, 24 x 32 ins / 61 x 81.5 cm) CHF 49,000. Heidelberg, 9 Oct 1992, *Mossy Rock* (oil on paper, 6 1/2 x 9 1/2 ins / 16.5 x 24.4 cm) DEM 3,000.

SEEGER, Paul, or Seger

German, 18th century.

Active 1723-1743.

Painter. Religious subjects.

Paul Seeger was the abbot of Gengenbach monastery in Germany.

Museums and Galleries:

Gengenbach (Monastery church): *Birth of the Virgin* (1723).

SEEGER, Samuel

German, 18th century.

Born c. 1727, in Rathenow (Brandenburg); died 5 June 1763, in Bayreuth (Bavaria).

Sculptor.

SEEGERS. See **SEGHERS**

SEEGERT, Alwin

German, 20th century.

Born 27 October 1862, in Berlin.

Painter. Portraits, architectural views.

Alwin Seegert was a pupil of C.G. Hellqvist.

SEEGMÜLLER, Franz Christian, or Segmüller or Segmiller

Austrian, 17th century.

Died 28 April 1696, in Graz.

Active in Graz, Austria, from 1669.

Painter.

SEEGMÜLLER, Franz Josef

Austrian, 18th century.

Active in Graz, Austria, from 1727 to 1733.

Painter.

Franz Josef was the son of Franz Christian Seegmüller.

SEEHAS, Christian Ludwig

German, 18th century.

Born 1753, in Schwerin (Mecklenburg-West Pomerania); died 26 July 1802, in Schwerin.

Painter, engraver (burin). Architectural views and portraits.

Seehas attended the art academy in Dresden.

Museums and Galleries:

Schwerin: *Portraits of Joseph Haydn; Portrait of Hofmeister; View of the Coliseum; Egeria's Grotto, Rome.*

SEEHAUS, Paul Adolf

German, 20th century.

Born 7 September 1891, in Bonn; died 13 March 1919, in Hamburg.

Painter, engraver, draughtsman. Figures.

Museums and Galleries:

Berlin (National Mus.): *Magdeburg Cathedral* - Düsseldorf (Kunstmus.): *Mountain Town* - Wuppertal (Von der Heydt Mus.): *Harbour; Banks of the Rhine near Bonn.*

Auction records:

Cologne, 5 Dec 1981, *Couple* (pen, 7 1/4 x 9 1/4 ins / 18.1 x 23.8 cm) DEM 1,500. Cologne, 11 Nov 2000, *Red Towers* (oil on canvas, 31 x 35 ins / 78 x 90 cm) DEM 80,000. Königstein, 4 June 2003, *View over Thine with Figures and Ships* (Indian ink and brush, 14 x 12 ins / 35 x 30 cm) EUR 1,400.

SEEHUSEN, Johann Christoffer

Danish, 18th - 19th century.

Born 20 May 1762, in Steinberg; died 25 September 1824, in Birkerød.
Engraver (burin), draughtsman.
Seehusen was the father of Peter Johann Seehusen.

SEEHUSEN, Peter Johann
Danish, 19th century.
Born 1 April 1791, in Birkerød; died 1 November 1863, in Copenhagen.
Engraver.
Seehusen was the son of Johan Christoffer Seehusen.

SEEHUSEN, R. J. P.
Danish, 19th century.
Active in Tranekjær c. 1800.
Engraver (burin), draughtsman.

SEEKATZ, E. Karl
German, 19th century.
Born 1785; died 12 October 1839, in Darmstadt.
Painter, lithographer.
Karl Seekatz produced work for the court of Darmstadt and engravings of uniforms.

SEEKATZ, Friedrich Heinrich
German, 18th century.
Active in Worms 1742-1752.
Painter.
Friedrich Heinrich was the son of Georg Christian Seekatz I and produced sculptures for the church of Löhnberg (Germany).

SEEKATZ, Georg Christian I
German, 18th century.
Born December 1683, in Westerburg; died 1750, in Weilburg.
Painter.
Georg Christian I was the father of Friedrich Heinrich Seekatz. He produced paintings for the church and castle at Weilburg in Germany.

SEEKATZ, Georg Christian II
German, 18th century.
Born 1722, in Grünstadt (Rhineland Palatinate); died 1788, in Darmstadt.
Active in Darmstadt.
Painter, gilder.
Georg Christian II was the son of Johann Martin and the brother of Johann Ludwig Seekatz.

SEEKATZ, Johann Ludwig
German, 18th century.
Born 1711, in Grünstadt (Rhineland Palatinate).
Painter.
Johann Ludwig was the son of Johann Martin and the brother of Georg Christian Seekatz. He produced paintings for the German court of Worms.

SEEKATZ, Johann Martin
German, 17th - 18th century.
Born 1669, in Westerburg; died 1729, in Worms.
Painter.
Johann Martin Seekatz was the father of Johann Ludwig and Georg Christian Seekatz II, and at 50 years his senior, the elder brother of Johann (otherwise known as Joseph Konrad or Conrad Seekatz). He produced paintings for the church of the Trinity at Worms from 1725.

SEEKATZ, Johann, or Joseph Konrad, or Conrad
German, 18th century.
Born 4 September 1719, in Grünstadt (Rhineland Palatinate); died 25 August 1768, in Darmstadt.
Painter. Religious subjects, military subjects, genre scenes, landscapes with figures.

Joseph Konrad Seekatz was the younger brother and pupil of Johann Martin Seekatz, who was 50 years his senior. He was court painter at Hesse in Germany in 1753, and also worked for the count of Thoranc at his town house in Grasse (Provence, France) on the recommendation of a French officer leading the occupation troops. Before discovering France, Seekatz painted in the style of the Flemish painter Adriaen Brouwer (1605/06 - 1638), who was famous for his tavern scenes. He later discovered the paintings of Jean Honoré Fragonard, the French painter and engraver (1732 - 1806) famous for his galant and genre scenes and portraits, and was deeply affected by the light peculiar to the South of France. On his return to Germany, Seekatz had become transformed into a painter whose work was bathed in sunlight.

MUSEUMS AND GALLERIES:
AACHEN: *Boilermaker* - AUGSBURG: *Liberation of St Peter; Jesus before Pilate* - BASEL: *Ratcatcher* - BERLIN (Bodemus.): *Return from Egypt* - CONSTANCE: *The Wassenberg Household* - DARMSTADT: *Self-portrait; Landgrave Ludwig VIII; Portrait of Johann Kupetzky; Four Scenes from the Life of Christ; Flight into Egypt; St Peter's Mission; Twelfth Night; Dead Hare; Beggars by the Fountain; Musician; Queen of Sheba before Solomon; Procession of Bacchus; Diana and Actaeon* - FRANKFURT AM MAIN: *Dog and Child; Taking a Rest during the Battle; Young Girl with a Light; Dulcimer Player* - MAGDEBURG (Kulturhistorisches Mus.): *Angelnde Knaben (Boys Fishing)* - MAINZ: *Joseph and Potiphar's Wife; Jews Wanting to Stone the Saviour; Christ and the Woman Taken in Adultery; Christ and Caiaphas; The Jews Leaving Egypt; Emissaries with Grapes in the Promised Land* - MANNHEIM: *Self-portrait* - NUREMBERG (Germanisches Nationalmus.): *Landscape with Family of Beggars* - OSLO (Nasjonalgal.): *Landscape with Peasants* - SPEYER: *War and Peace; Taking a Rest on the Way; Bohemians Taking a Rest; Rebecca by the Fountain* - WEIMAR (Goethe-Nationalmus.): *Councillor Goethe's Family* - WEIMAR (Schlossmus.): *Young Woman and Fortune-Teller; Denial of St Peter* - WÜRZBURG: *Landscape by Moonlight* - ZURICH: *Self-portrait.*

AUCTION RECORDS:
PARIS, 28 Nov 1923, *Village Celebration,* FRF 1,200; *Grape Harvest and the Little Gardeners* (two) FRF 1,000. MUNICH, 4-6 Oct 1961, *The Market,* DEM 4,800. LONDON, 4 March 1966, *Twelfth Night,* Gns 750. VIENNA, 18 Sept 1973, *Christ's Arrest,* ATS 38,000. NEW YORK, 12 Jan 1979, *Strolling Minstrel* (oil on canvas, 15 1/4 x 12 1/2 ins / 39 x 32 cm) USD 5,500. LONDON, 17 July 1981, *Jacob and Rachel at the Well* (oil on panel, 8 1/4 x 11 1/4 ins / 21 x 28.6 cm) GBP 1,800. PARIS, 6 June 1984, *Landscape with Figures* (oil on canvas, 25 1/2 x 18 3/4 ins / 65 x 47.5 cm) FRF 28,000. LONDON, 3 July 1985, *Children Playing Music; Children Playing with a Marmot* (oil on canvas remounted/panel, a pair, 10 x 7 ins / 25.5 x 18 cm) GBP 15,000. PARIS, 16 March 1988, *Portrait of Goethe as a Child* (oil on canvas, 22 1/2 x 19 ins / 57 x 48 cm) FRF 350,000. PARIS, 16 March 1988, *Portrait of Goethe as a Child; Allegory of the Air* (oil on canvas, 22 1/2 x 19 ins / 57 x 48 cm) FRF 350,000. PARIS, 15 March 1989, *Serenade; Tea in the Park* (oil on canvas, a pair, 13 x 9 1/2 ins / 33 x 24 cm) FRF 550,000. LONDON, 21 July 1989, *Young Boys Playing Dice; Young Boys Playing Cards* (oil on canvas, a pair, each 10 x 9 ins / 25.7 x 22 cm) GBP 6,050. COLOGNE, 20 Oct 1989, *Young Fishermen by the Stream* (oil on canvas, 9 x 9 1/4 ins / 23 x 23.5 cm) DEM 13,000. LONDON, 11 April 1990, *Judgement of Paris* (oil on canvas, 14 1/4 x 19 1/4 ins / 36.5 x 49 cm) GBP 66,000. LONDON, 1 April 1992, *Young Peasant and his Dog Holding a Lighted Brand; Young Peasant Boy Carrying a Hurdy-Gurdy and Smoking a Pipe* (oil on canvas, a pair, each 19 3/4 x 15 1/4 ins / 50 x 38.5 cm) GBP 14,850. LONDON, 10 July 1992, *Christ and the Samaritan Woman near the Well* (oil on panel, 8 3/4 x 11 1/2 ins / 22.5 x 29.5 cm) GBP 4,180. NEW YORK, 14 Jan 1994, *Soldiers and*

Villagers in an Encampment (oil on canvas, 11 x 15 3/4 ins / 27.9 x 40 cm) USD 60,250. DIJON, 15 May 1994, *Landgrave Ludwig VIII's Hunt* (oil on canvas, 17 3/4 x 25 1/2 ins / 45 x 65 cm) FRF 560,000. PARIS, 16 Dec 1994, *Bohemian Camp in the Moonlight* (oil on canvas, 11 1/2 x 13 1/2 ins / 29 x 34.5 cm) FRF 27,000. VIENNA, 29-30 Oct 1996, *Children by the Fountain* (oil on canvas, 14 1/2 x 12 1/2 ins / 37 x 32 cm) ATS 575,000. AMSTERDAM, 10 Nov 1997, *Orpheus Charming the Animals; Mercury Playing the Flute whilst Argus Falls Asleep* (oil on panel, a pair, 9 1/2 x 12 ins / 23.9 x 30.3 cm and 9 1/2 x 12 ins/24.1 x 30.2 cm) NLG 55,353. VIENNA, 24 March 1999, *Christ and the Samaritan Woman at a Fountain* (oil on panel, 9 x 11 ins / 22 x 29 cm) ATS 90,000. LONDON, 7 July 1999, *Game Seller. Greengrocer* (oil on panel, a pair, 9 x 9 ins / 22 x 24 cm) GBP 4,800. LONDON, 5 July 2000, *Soldiers Returning from Battle* (oil on canvas, 15 x 20 ins / 39 x 52 cm) GBP 13,000. MUNICH, 8 Nov 2000, *Finding of Moses* (oil on canvas, 12 x 9 ins / 30 x 22 cm) DEM 48,000. NEW YORK, 25 Jan 2001, *Print Seller* (oil on canvas/panel, 9 x 7 ins / 23 x 18 cm) USD 22,000. LONDON, 10 Dec 2001, *Landscape with Horse and Cart and Other Travellers near Ruins* (oil on canvas, 26 x 36 ins / 66 x 91 cm) GBP 5,500. LONDON, 12 July 2002, *Young Peasant Family Disporting with a Billy Goat in a Farmyard* (oil on canvas, 16 x 13 ins / 41 x 32 cm) GBP 7,500. MUNICH, 4 Dec 2002, *Covenant of Peace of Jacob and Esau* (oil on canvas, 16 x 20 ins / 40 x 51 cm) EUR 10,000. LONDON, 20 Feb 2003, *Lady with Parrot at a Casement* (oil on panel, 10 x 9 ins / 26 x 22 cm) GBP 3,000. MUNICH, 19 Sept 2003, *Organ Grinder Resting in the Evening with Children by the Fire* (oil on canvas, 20 x 15 ins / 50 x 37 cm) EUR 14,000.

SEEKATZ, Philipp Christian
German, 18th century.
Born 1750, in Worms.
Painter, draughtsman.

Philipp Christian was the son of Friedrich Heinrich Seekatz.

MUSEUMS AND GALLERIES:
DARMSTADT (Schlossmus.): two genre scenes.

SEEL, Adolf
German, 19th century.
Born 1 March 1829, in Wiesbaden; died 14 February 1907, in Dillenburg.
Painter, watercolourist. Portraits, genre scenes, church interiors, architectural views.
Orientalism.

Seel attended the art academy in Düsseldorf. He visited France, Italy, Spain, Portugal and part of Africa - bringing back some orientalist pictures from Spain and Cairo - and in 1873 and 1874, travelled to the East. He exhibited at the international watercolour exhibition in Dresden in 1892.

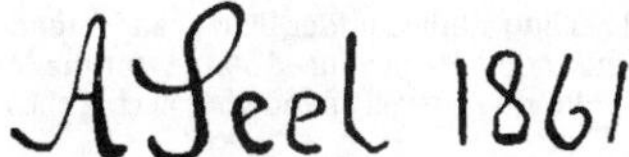

MUSEUMS AND GALLERIES:
DÜSSELDORF: *Interior of St Mark's in Venice; Interior of a Harem; Portrait of the Painter Th. Mintrop* - HANOVER: *Village Sexton* - OSLO: *Path Crossing in front of a Conventual Church.*

AUCTION RECORDS:
BERLIN, 19 Sept 1968, *The Harem*, DEM 3,400. NEW YORK, 23 May 1985, *A Nubian Guard* (oil on canvas remounted on hardboard, 37 x 23 ins / 94 x 58.5 cm) USD 8,000. NEW YORK, 28 Oct 1986, *An Interior Courtyard at the Alhambra* (1870, oil on paper remounted/panel, 26 3/4 x 16 3/4 ins / 68 x 42.5 cm) USD 5,000. NEW YORK, 23 Feb 1989, *Slave Sale in Cairo* (oil on canvas, 38 3/4 x 50 1/4 ins / 98.4 x 127.6 cm) USD 46,200. LONDON, 24 Nov 1989, *Woman Orange-Seller* (oil on canvas, 38 1/4 x 27 ins / 97 x 68.5 cm) GBP 17,600. LONDON, 14 Feb 1990, *Peasants in a River Landscape* (oil on canvas, 27 3/4 x 37 1/2 ins / 70.5 x 95 cm) GBP 3,520. LONDON, 21 June 1991, *Woman Orange-Seller* (oil on card, 26 1/4 x 19 ins / 66.4 x 48.3 cm) GBP 8,800. NEW YORK, 20 July 1995, *The Sentry* (1873, watercolour/traces of pencil, 13 3/4 x 9 ins / 34.9 x 22.9 cm) USD 4,600. NEW YORK, 23-24 May 1996, *Night Watchmen* (1873, oil on canvas, 42 1/2 x 31 1/2 ins / 108 x 80 cm) USD 85,000. LONDON, 21 Nov 1997, *In the Courtyard* (oil on canvas, 45 x 60 1/2 ins / 114.2 x 153.8 cm) GBP 12,650. COLOGNE, 26 June 1999, *Street Scene with Oriental Tea House* (1885, oil on canvas, 34 x 24 ins / 87 x 60 cm) DEM 14,000. AMSTERDAM, 24 Oct 2000, *Confession* (1867, oil on canvas, 37 x 30 ins / 94 x 77 cm) NLG 10,000. DRIFFIELD, 20 Aug 2004, *Arabian Bath Scene with Solitary Female Figure* (1973, watercolour, 23 x 18 ins / 58 x 46 cm) GBP 2,000.

SEEL, C.
Painter. Military subjects.

MUSEUMS AND GALLERIES:
LIÈGE (Mus.): *Retreating Infantry.*

SEEL, Louis
German, 20th century.
Born 25 April 1881, in Wiesbaden (Hesse); died 13 November 1958.
Active in France.
Painter, watercolourist. Figures, landscapes.

Louis Seel studied at the fine arts academy in Karlsruhe from 1899 to 1901, then at the Städel Institute in Frankfurt am Main (1901-1902). He moved to Holland and subsequently spent 14 years in France - from 1905 to 1914, when he worked in the same atelier as Matisse, Bonnard, Derain and Marie Laurencin, and again from 1919 to 1925, when he lived in Provence. He also visited Spain and spent the war years there (1914-1919).

Seel painted numerous landscapes of the region around Avignon and Arles, one of his favourite themes being peach trees in blossom.

MUSEUMS AND GALLERIES:
STUTTGART (Staatsgal.).

SEEL, Mahy van
Dutch, 17th century.
Active during the first half of the 17th century.
Sculptor (wood).

Mahy van Seel carved a figure of *Justice* for the town hall of Middelburg.

SEEL, Paul
Austrian, 17th century.
Active in Salzburg, Austria, 1642-1695.
Medallist, engraver (burin).

Paul Seel worked for the archbishop princes of Salzburg. He engraved medals to commemorate various pilgrimages.

SEEL, Peter
Austrian, 17th century.
Born 1592; died 1669.
Active in Salzburg, Austria.
Medallist. Religious subjects.

SEEL, Richard or Johann Richard
German, 19th century.
Born 2 February 1819, in Elberfeld; died 12 February 1875, in Elberfeld.
Painter. Portraits.

Richard Seel studied under K. F. Sohn at the art academy in Düsseldorf.

MUSEUMS AND GALLERIES:
DÜSSELDORF (Stadtmus.): *Portrait of Mrs Köster.*

SEELAND, Edmund
German, 18th century.
Born in Weisenau, near Mainz.

Active during the second half of the 18th century.
Painter.
Edmund Seeland produced altar paintings and portraits for the court of Mainz in Germany.
MUSEUMS AND GALLERIES:
ASCHAFFENBURG: *Portrait of the Elector of Mainz.*

SEELÄNDER, Nikolaus
German, 18th century.
Born c. 1690, in Erfurt; died 1744, in Hanover.
Engraver (burin), medallist.
Seeländer was court painter in Hanover, Germany. He produced engravings of portraits and family trees, and as a numismatist (coins and medals), engraved medals bearing the image of contemporary princes.

SEELDRAYERS, Émile
Belgian, 19th - 20th century.
Born 24 January 1847, in Ghent; died 21 May 1933, in Brussels.
Painter, illustrator. Portraits, genre scenes, landscapes.
Émile Seeldrayers studied in Ghent, Munich and Düsseldorf and contributed illustrations to works by Camille Lemonnier.

SEELE, Alexander Cäsar
German, 19th - 20th century.
Born 14 April 1849, in Dresden; died 13 October 1922, in Munich.
Painter. Landscapes.
Alexander Seele was a pupil of Ludwig Gebhardt; he sometimes painted on glass.
AUCTION RECORDS:
COPENHAGEN, 16 Nov 1994, *Young Woman Standing under a Tree* (painting on glass, 4 1/4 x 3 1/2 ins / 11 x 9 cm) DKK 3,400.

SEELE, Johann Baptist
German, 18th - 19th century.
Born 27 June 1774, in Messkirch; died 27 August 1814, in Stuttgart (Baden-Württemberg).
Painter, engraver. Military subjects, battles, portraits.
Johann Baptist Seele studied under Philipp Friedrich Hetsch at the art academy in Stuttgart. He was court painter in Wurtemberg, and in 1804, was appointed director of the royal gallery in Stuttgart. He produced portraits of members of Duke Friedrich's court and paintings of battle scenes, including, in 1806 and 1809, the exploits of the Wurtemberg cavalry regiment (German unit in French pay), which reveal his skill in chiaroscuro.
MUSEUMS AND GALLERIES:
CONSTANCE: *Portrait of Dean Strasser* - DONAUESCHINGEN: *Several Self-portraits; Military Scenes and Equestrian Battles; Portraits of Members of the Princely Family; The Artist's Parents* - KARLSRUHE (Staatliche Kunsthalle): *Crossing a River during the Night* - MUNICH (Neue Pinakothek): *Portrait of Inspector Johann Christian von Mannlich* - MUNICH (Städtische Gal. im Lenbachhaus): *Portrait of the Director J. J. Dorner* - STUTTGART (Staatsgal.): *Archduke Charles; French Vanguard; Four Skirmishes on Horseback; Portrait of a Lady; Battle on Devil Bridge; The Wild Hunter; Hymn to Fidelity; Dr Klein's Family* - VERSAILLES: *Count L. W. Otto* - VIENNA (Heeresgeschichtliches Mus.): *Archduke Charles of Austria.*
AUCTION RECORDS:
PARIS, 1823, *The Great Stag Hunt at Stuttgart* (pen and sepia drawing) FRF 14. PARIS, 1859, *Cabaret Scene* (drawing in red pencil) FRF 19. LYONS, 13 May 1980, *Horseman* (1807, oil on panel) FRF 14,000. LONDON, 24 Nov 1989, *Portrait of Archduke Karl Wearing Military Uniform with Sword at his Side* (1800, oil on canvas, 82 x 53 3/4 ins / 208.5 x 136.5 cm) GBP 9,900. HEIDELBERG, 8 April 1995, *Austrians Returning from Plunderage* (oil on panel, 12 1/2 x 8 3/4 ins / 31.5 x 22.5 cm) DEM 6,300. LINDAU, 4 May 1999, *Many Figures beside a Large Tented Camp* (1789, oil on canvas, 24 x 32 ins / 61 x 82 cm) DEM 5,500. LINDAU, 4 May 1999, *Hunting Party Resting by a Pond in a Hilly Landscape* (oil on canvas, 24 x 32 ins / 62 x 82 cm) DEM 5,500. MUNICH, 27 June 2001, *French Soldiers* (watercolour heightened with white, 7 x 11 ins / 18 x 27 cm) DEM 3,300.

SEELE, Johann Mich
German, 18th century.
Active in Nuremberg 1740-1762.
Painter, engraver. Religious subjects and portraits.

SEELE VON
German, 19th century.
Active c. 1840.
Silhouettist.

SEELIG, Franz
German, 18th century.
Active in Breslau (now Wroclaw), Poland, in 1701.
Painter.

SEELIG, Johann
German, 17th century.
Active in Landshut (Bavaria) in 1680.
Painter.

SEELIG, Julius Moritz
German, 19th century.
Born 25 December 1809, in Annaberg (Saxony); died 12 September 1887, in Cotta, near Dresden.
Sculptor.

SEELIGER, Franz Gabriel
German, 17th - 18th century.
Active in Breslau (now Wroclaw), Poland, 1699-1713.
Painter.

SEELIGER, Friedrich
German, 18th century.
Active in Berlin at the end of the 18th century.
Painter, miniaturist.

SEELIGER, Karl Wilhelm
German, 18th - 19th century.
Born 1766, in Berlin; died 28 August 1821, in St Petersburg, Russia.
Active in Riga (Latvia) and St Petersburg.
Painter, miniaturist, engraver (burin).
MUSEUMS AND GALLERIES:
RIGA (Municipal Library): *Portrait of a Man.*

SEELING, Bernhard Otto
Czech, 19th century.
Born 1850, in Prague; died 20 April 1895, in Prague.
Sculptor.
Bernhard Seeling studied under Platzer and attended the art academy in Prague. He produced statues for the Museum of Bohemia in Prague as well as for several churches in Bohemia.

SEELINGER, Alfred
German, 19th century.
Born in Bavaria; died 1873, in Rio de Janeiro, Brazil.
Painter. History painting.
Seelinger painted *Spartacus, Gladiator.*

SEELMANN, Franz von
German, 19th century.
Active in Offenbach (Hesse) Germany, at the beginning of the 19th century.
Engraver (burin). Architectural views.

SEELMANN, Heinrich
German, 18th century.
Born in Staffelstein.
Active 1764-1792.

Stucco artist.

Heinrich Seelmann studied under J. M. Feichtmayr. He produced ceilings and decorative works coated with stucco for northern Bavarian castles.

SEELMANN, Otto or August Otto

German, 19th century.

Born 13 July 1827, in Dessau (Saxony-Anhalt); died 15 February 1909, in Dessau.

Painter. Portraits, landscapes, animals.

Otto Seelmann attended the art academy in Berlin and produced work for the court of Dessau.

MUSEUMS AND GALLERIES:

DESSAU (Anhaltische Gemäldegal.): *Before the Ride on Horseback* - DESSAU (Mus. für Stadtgeschichte): *Horses Grazing.*

SEELMAYER, Franz. See **SELLMAYER**

SEELOS, Franz I

Austrian, 19th - 20th century.

Born 27 December 1873, in Zirl.

Painter, designer. Landscapes.

Franz Seelos I was the father of Franz Seelos II; he painted decorations and landscapes for crèches (cribs).

SEELOS, Franz II

Austrian, 20th century.

Born 5 February 1905, in Zirl.

Painter, designer.

Franz Seelos II was the son of Franz Seelos I; he painted decorative compositions for churches and bourgeois houses in the Austrian Tyrol.

SEELOS, Gottfried

Austrian, 19th century.

Born 9 January 1829, in Bozen, South Tyrol (now Bolzano, Italy); died 13 March 1900, in Vienna.

Painter, engraver. Landscapes, seascapes, architectural views.

Gottfried Seelos studied under Joseph Selleni and Jan Nowopacky. He became an honorary member of the Société Royale Belge des Aquarellistes (Belgian Royal Society of Watercolourists).

MUSEUMS AND GALLERIES:

INNSBRUCK (Tiroler Landesmus. Ferdinandeum): *Landscape near Meran* - VIENNA (Kunsthistorisches Mus.): *Chestnut Gatherers in the South Tyrol;* five watercolours depicting architectural subjects; 35 watercolour representations of the lighthouses and port entrances along the Istrian and Dalmation coast.

AUCTION RECORDS:

VIENNA, 5 Oct 1976, *Mountainous Landscape at Dawn* (1867, oil on canvas, 17 3/4 x 24 3/4 ins / 45 x 63 cm) ATS 10,000. VIENNA, 17 Feb 1981, *Farmyard* (1872, oil on panel, 15 1/4 x 20 1/2 ins / 38.5 x 52 cm) ATS 80,000. VIENNA, 22 May 1982, *Alpine Landscape* (watercolour, 14 1/4 x 10 ins / 36 x 25.6 cm) ATS 25,000. VIENNA, 12 Sept 1984, *View of a Castle in a Wooded Landscape* (1863, watercolour, 11 1/2 x 17 1/4 ins / 29.5 x 44 cm) ATS 18,000. MUNICH, 27 June 1995, *Italian Landscape* (1862, oil on panel, 13 3/4 x 19 1/4 ins / 35 x 49 cm) DEM 16,100. MUNICH, 29 Sept 1999, *Southern Tyrol Landscape* (1854, pencil and wash heightened with white, 8 x 11 ins / 21 x 27 cm) DEM 4,400. VIENNA, 29 Nov 2001, *Farmstead with Figures* (1873, oil on panel, 15 x 20 ins / 39 x 52 cm) ATS 40,000. VIENNA, 29 Nov 2001, *Southern Tyrolean Scene* (1873, oil on panel, 15 x 20 ins / 38 x 52 cm) ATS 100,000. VIENNA, 29 Oct 2002, *Sicilian Day* (oil on canvas, 12 x 10 ins / 30 x 25 cm) EUR 3,200. VIENNA, 28 Nov 2002, *Mountain Landscape* (1877, oil on canvas, 23 x 37 ins / 59 x 94 cm) EUR 13,000. VIENNA, 23 Sept 2003, *Three Pinnacles* (watercolour, 21 x 17 ins / 53 x 42 cm) EUR 2,800. VIENNA, 26 March 2004, *Zenoburg near Meran* (1850, pencil and watercolour, 13 x 17 ins / 32 x 42 cm) EUR 2,000.

SEELOS, Gustav

Austrian, 19th - 20th century.

Born 12 September 1831, in Bozen (now Bolzano, Italy); died 14 January 1911, in Innsbruck.

Painter, engineer.

Gustav Seelos was the brother of Gottfried and Ignaz Seelos; he painted watercolour landscapes of the Austrian Tyrol.

SEELOS, Ignaz

Austrian, 19th century.

Born 14 October 1827, in Bozen, South Tyrol (now Bolzano, Italy); died 7 July 1902, in Vienna.

Painter, draughtsman, lithographer. Flowers.

Ignaz was the brother of Gottfried and Gustav Seelos. He studied under Selleni.

MUSEUMS AND GALLERIES:

VIENNA (Kunsthistorisches Mus.): *Homage to the Alps* (watercolour).

AUCTION RECORDS:

VIENNA, 11 Dec 1985, *Alpine Flowers* (oil on panel, 13 x 17 3/4 ins / 33 x 45 cm) ATS 60,000. MUNICH, 6 Dec 2002, *Still-life with Flowers* (oil on panel, 15 x 22 ins / 37 x 55 cm) EUR 2,800.

SEELOS, Josef

Austrian, 19th century.

Born in Imst; died 1836.

Sculptor.

MUSEUMS AND GALLERIES:

INNSBRUCK (Tiroler Landesmus. Ferdinandeum): *Alexander Taming Bucephalas.*

SEEMANN, Abel

German, 17th century.

Active in Königsberg, East Prussia (now Kaliningrad, Russia) during the second half of the 17th century.

Painter. Battles.

SEEMANN, Dora

German, 19th - 20th century.

Born 20 February 1858, in Insterburg; died 20 February 1923, in Breslau (now Wroclaw, Poland).

Active in Breslau.

Painter. Landscapes.

Dora Seemann was a pupil of C. Schirm.

MUSEUMS AND GALLERIES:

GÖRLITZ - WROCLAW.

SEEMANN, Enoch, the Elder, or Seeman or Zeeman

German, 17th century.

Born c. 1661, in Elbing (now Elblag, Poland).

Painter. Portraits, landscapes.

Enoch Seeman the Elder settled in Danzig (now Gdansk, Poland) in 1683, and then in London around 1704. He was probably the father of Isaac Seemann the Elder, who was therefore likely to have been born after 1683, in Danzig.

SEEMANN, Enoch, the Younger, or Seeman or Zeeman

Polish, 18th century.

Born c. 1694, in Danzig (now Gdansk); died 1744, in London.

Painter. Portraits.

Enoch Seeman was the younger brother and the student of Isaac Seemann. He also studied in London, where he painted portraits and heads of old men in the style of Denner. Several of his works were engraved by Barsset, Berningeroth, Biedendorf and Simon.

MUSEUMS AND GALLERIES:
DRESDEN: *Self-portrait* (1716) - HANOVER: *Portrait Believed to be of General Bisset* - LONDON (National Portrait Gal.): *Abraham Tucker* (1739, oil on canvas, feigned oval); several other portraits.
AUCTION RECORDS:
LONDON, 15 June 1928, *William Vaugham*, GBP 73. LONDON, 11 July 1930, *The Viscount Lewisham, Lord North and Lord Brownlow North as Children, in a Landscape*, GBP 115. LONDON, 11 June 1969, *Portraits of George and John Campbell*, GBP 600. LONDON, 4 April 1973, *Portrait of a Young Girl*, GBP 500. HARROGATE, 16 Oct 1973, *Portrait of a Gentleman*, GNS 700. LONDON, 18 March 1977, *Portrait of the Giant Cajanus* (oil on canvas, 123 x 71 ins / 312.3 x 180.2 cm) GBP 1,200. LONDON, 11 July 1984, *Portrait of an Arab Ambassador* (oil on canvas, 93 1/2 x 57 1/2 ins / 237.5 x 146 cm) GBP 26,000. LONDON, 22 Nov 1985, *Portrait of Mary, the Daughter of Sir Thomas Slingsby* (oil on canvas, 61 x 50 ins / 155 x 127 cm) GBP 2,600. LONDON, 21 Nov 1986, *Portrait of Edward Wood* (oil on canvas, 90 1/2 x 54 1/2 ins / 230 x 138.5 cm) GBP 7,500. LONDON, 18 Nov 1988, *Group of Six Children with their Mother and Two Dogs* (oil on canvas, 70 1/4 x 93 3/4 ins / 178.4 x 238 cm) GBP 4,950; *Bust-length Portrait of a Lady Dressed in Red* (oil on canvas, oval, 29 3/4 x 25 1/4 ins / 75.6 x 64 cm) GBP 1,100. LONDON, 10 July 1991, *Portrait of Anne Dashwood, Seated, Dressed in a Dark Blue Dress over a White Blouse* (oil on canvas, 49 1/4 x 39 1/4 ins / 125 x 99.5 cm) GBP 5,280. LONDON, 15 Nov 1991, *Portrait of Mary Rand, Seated in Three-quarter Profile and Wearing a White Satin Dress Decorated with Lace and Blue Ribbons and Holding a Pearl Necklace* (1742, oil on canvas, 50 x 40 ins / 127 x 101.9 cm) GBP 6,050. LONDON, 8 April 1992, *Portrait of a Gentleman Wearing a Red Coat over a Gold-embroidered Waistcoat* (oil on canvas, oval, 29 1/2 x 24 1/4 ins / 75 x 61.5 cm) GBP 1,870. LONDON, 7 Oct 1992, *Portrait of a Young Woman, Believed to be Jane Middleton* (oil on canvas, 29 1/2 x 24 1/2 ins / 75 x 62 cm) GBP 1,155. LONDON, 7 April 1993, *Group of Six Children with their Mother and Two Dogs in a Landscape* (oil on canvas, 70 1/4 x 93 3/4 ins / 178.4 x 238 cm) GBP 6,325. NEW YORK, 8 Oct 1993, *Portrait of a Lady Dressed as a Cavalier* (oil on canvas, 49 x 39 ins / 124.5 x 99.1 cm) USD 6,900. LONDON, 30 May 1997, *Portrait of Thomas Best of Chilston* (oil on canvas, 48 3/4 x 39 1/4 ins / 124 x 100 cm) GBP 6,670. LONDON, 9 July 1997, *Portrait of a Young Boy and his Two Sisters* (oil on canvas, 59 1/4 x 69 3/4 ins / 150.5 x 177 cm) GBP 16,100. LONDON, 12 Nov 1997, *Portrait of Catherine Baldwyn and Ann Woodruffe* (oil on canvas, 45 1/4 x 57 3/4 ins / 115 x 147 cm) GBP 14,950. VENICE, 27 June 1999, *Portrait of a Young Lady Standing by a Spinnet* (1733, oil on canvas, 50x40 ins / 127x101 cm) ITL 11,500,000. LONDON, 15 June 2000, *Portrait of Margaret North* (oil on canvas, 49x37 ins / 124x93 cm) GBP 5,200. LONDON, 1 Dec 2000, *Portrait of Lady Caroline D' Arcy, Countess of Ancram, in a Grey Satin Dress, Landscape beyond* (oil on canvas, 96x60 ins / 245x153 cm) GBP 10,000. LEWES, 25 Oct 2002, *Portrait of a Young Man* (oil on canvas, 18x17 ins / 46x43 cm) GBP 4,400. LONDON, 26 Nov 2002, *Portrait of a Gentleman Loading His Gun with a Spaniel by His Side* (oil on canvas, 93x59 ins / 237x149 cm) GBP 18,000. LONDON, 25 Nov 2003, *Portrait of Mary Rand, Seated in an Oyster Satin Dress with Blue Ribbons in an Interior* (oil on canvas, 50x40 ins / 127x102 cm) GBP 7,000. LONDON, 27 Nov 2003, *Portrait of Thomas Plumer Byde and His Brother John Byde* (oil on canvas, 50x40 ins / 126x101 cm) GBP 7,500. LONDON, 25 Nov 2004, *Portrait of Miss Bacon* (oil on canvas, 31x32 ins / 78x82 cm) GBP 22,000.

SEEMANN, Heinrich or Heini
Swiss, 16th century.
Active in Thun, from 1577 to 1595.
Glass painter.

SEEMANN, Isaac, the Elder
Polish, 18th century.
Born in Danzig (now Gdansk); died c. 1730, in London.
Painter. Portraits.

Isaac Seeman the Elder was born in Danzig in 1683, and was probably the son of Enoch Seeman the Elder. From 1700 he was in London, where he painted several portraits. His portrait of *W. Thomson* was engraved by Fabre, and his portrait of *Attilio Ariosto* was engraved by Simon.

SEEMANN, Isaac, the Younger
Polish, 18th century.
Died 4 April 1751, in London.
Painter. Portraits.

Isaac Seemann was the eldest son and the student of Isaac Seemann the Elder. He studied in London and painted mostly portraits.

SEEMANN, Johann Leonhard
German, 18th century.
Active in Danzig c. 1720.
Painter.

SEEMANN, Paul
British, 18th century.
Painter.

Son of Isaac Seemann the Younger, Paul Seemann; lived and worked in London.

SEEMANN, R. Max
German, 19th century.
Born 9 April 1838, in Kraupischkehmen, East Prussia; died 18 October 1907, in Berlin.
Painter, engraver (etching).

Max Seemann studied in Königsberg, East Prussia (now Kaliningrad, Russia), and Dresden, Germany. He settled in Berlin in 1868.

SEEMANN, Richard
German, 19th - 20th century.
Born 15 February 1857, in Stuttgart.
Painter. Figures, still-lifes.

Richard Seemann was a pupil of Herterich, Igler and Haug.

SEEMANNS, G.
Dutch, 17th century.
Painter.

G. Seemanns is noted for hunting scenes and paintings of birds.

SEEMING, Robert
French, 19th century.
Born in Paris.
Painter. Seascapes.

His masters were Lalanne and Chouppe. He debuted at the Salon in 1872.
MUSEUMS AND GALLERIES:
ORLÉANS: *Rocks in Brittany* (watercolour).

SEENER, Bruno Paul
German, 19th century.
Died 9 January 1893, in Nuremberg.
Active in Chemnitz (Saxony).
Engraver.

Seener engraved illustrations for Goethe's *Walpurgis Night* in 1921.

SEER, Jakob, or Sehr
Austrian, 18th century.
Active in Eggenburg, Austria, during the first half of the 18th century.
Sculptor.

Seer produced statues for churches and fountains.

SEERY, John
American, 20th century.

Born 1941, in Cincinnati (Ohio).
Painter.

John Seery's painting comes straight out of Tachism. He paints forms floating in space apparently free of all constraints. Far from frenzied action painting, these works evoke a light-hearted calm. He uses bright, acidic colours and sweeping generous strokes. Seery held solo exhibitions in New York in 1970, 1972 and 1974; in Chicago in 1970 and 1972; in Cleveland, in 1971; in Sydney in 1974; in Zurich in 1975.

Museums and Galleries:

Baltimore (MA) - Boston (ICA) - Canberra (National MA) - Chicago (AI) - Cincinnati (Contemporary Arts Center) - Houston (Contemporary Arts Mus.) - Sydney (MCA) - Washington DC (Hirshhorn Mus. and Sculpture Garden): *Ground Sea* (1970, acrylic/canvas).

Auction records:

New York, 25 Oct 1974, *Soft Entry,* USD 1,800. New York, 18 May 1979, *Side Look II* (1970, acrylic/canvas, 57 x 43 ins / 145 x 109 cm) USD 3,100. New York, 13 May 1981, *Ty's Day* (1970, acrylic/canvas, 55 x 49 ins / 139.5 x 124.5 cm) USD 1,900. New York, 2 Nov 1984, *Wah Binger Dah* (1971, acrylic/canvas, 110 x 88 ins / 279.5 x 223.5 cm) USD 3,000. New York, 12 Nov 1991, *Yankee Clipper* (1976, acrylic/canvas, 30 x 29 ins / 76.2 x 73.6 cm) USD 2,200. New York, 27 Feb 1992, *Cliffs* (1980, acrylic/canvas, 40 x 78 ins / 101.6 x 198.4 cm) USD 1,100. Hayden, 28 July 2001, *Before the Storm* (oil on canvas, 36 x 24 ins / 91 x 61 cm) USD 16,000.

SEEST, Christian

Danish, 18th century.
Active from 1741 to 1768.
Sculptor.

Seest worked in Paris and London, and in Copenhagen, where he was a painter at the court.

SEEVAGEN, Lucien

French, 20th century.
Born 29 January 1887, in Chaumont; died 25 June 1959, on the island of Bréhat.
Painter (gouache), engraver. Landscapes, urban landscapes, waterscapes, seascapes, architectural views.

Seevagen studied at the École des Arts Décoratifs in Paris and was also taught by Eugène Charvot. He worked most of the time on the island of Bréhat. A skilled landscapist, he painted Brittany, Normandy, in particular Honfleur, the sea, fishing boats, and the peaceful villages inland, depicting the most diverse aspects according to the season or the weather.

Seevagen exhibited in various Parisian salons, regularly at the Salon des Indépendants, Salon d'Automne and Salon des Tuileries.

Auction records:

Paris, 23 Dec 1927, *Boulevard Edgar-Quinet,* FRF 400. Paris, 27 March 1931, *Springtime in Morvan* (gouache) FRF 360. Paris, 7 April 1943, *Village in Brittany,* FRF 6,000; *House in Ruins,* FRF 9,600. Paris, 24 March 1947, *The Seine at the Quai de l'Hôtel de Ville,* FRF 6,000. Paris, 4 May 1951, *View of Brittany,* FRF 3,000. Versailles, 22 April 1990, *Port in Brittany* (oil on canvas, 15 x 18 ins / 38 x 46 cm) FRF 9,200. Versailles, 21 Oct 1990, *Cottages Near the Coast* (oil on canvas, $14\frac{1}{4}$ x $36\frac{1}{4}$ ins / 36.5 x 92 cm) FRF 7,500. Paris, 10 June 1992, *Boats at Anchor* (oil on canvas, 17 x $28\frac{1}{4}$ ins / 43 x 72 cm) FRF 4,200. Paris, 20 March 1996, *Fishing Boats in Paimpol* (oil on panel, 15 x 18 ins / 38 x 46 cm) FRF 5,500; *Le Moulin à Mer* (oil on canvas, $21\frac{1}{4}$ x $25\frac{1}{2}$ ins / 54 x 64.5 cm) FRF 11,500; *Bréhat, Boats on the Shore* (oil on canvas, $25\frac{1}{2}$ x 36 ins / 65 x 91.5 cm) FRF 9,000. Calais, 7 July 1996, *Paris, the Seine on a Snowy Day* (oil on canvas, $19\frac{3}{4}$ x 24 ins / 50 x 61 cm) FRF 6,000. Paris, 26 Jan 1998, *View of Etna* (1931, oil on canvas, 11 x 9 ins / 27 x 22 cm) FRF 3,500. Paris, 21 April 1999, *Low Tide, Brehat* (oil on canvas, 20 x 39 ins / 50 x 100 cm) FRF 11,000. Paris, 18 June 2001, *Patio in Moorish Villa, Medeah* (oil on panel, 11 x 15 ins / 29 x 37 cm) FRF 15,000. Rennes, 1 Dec 2002, *Ile de Brehat* (oil on canvas, 20 x 26 ins / 50 x 65 cm) EUR 2,050. Brest, 16 May 2004, *Discussion by the Cottages at Brehat* (oil on canvas, 15 x 36 ins / 37 x 92 cm) EUR 1,500.

SEEWAGEN, Heini or Heinrich, or Sewagen

Swiss, 16th century.
Born possibly in Schaffhausen; died after 1544.
Sculptor (wood), cabinet maker.

Between 1522 and 1525 Seewagen carved the stalls of Bern Cathedral in collaboration with Jakob Russ.

SEEWALD, Richard

German, 20th century.
Born 4 May 1889, in Arnswalde; died 1976, in Ronco.
Active in Cologne.
Painter, engraver, illustrator, writer.

Richard Seewald was an illustrator of classical texts, among them Virgil's *Eclogues,* and also illustrated travel books.

Bibliography:

Jentsch, Ralph, *Richard Seewald. Das graphische Werk,* Verlag Kunstgalerie, Esslingen, 1973. Kinkel, Hans/Jentsch, Ralph, *Richard Seewald. Radierungen, Holzschnitte, Lithographien,* Verlag Hatje Cantz, Stuttgart, 1991.

Museums and Galleries:

Ann Arbor (University of Michigan Mus. of Art): *In the Meadows* (coloured lithograph) - Cologne (Wallraf-Richartz Mus.): *Girgenti; Landscape with Dog* - Szczecin: *Tuscan Landscape.*

Auction records:

Cologne, 3 June 1969, *Church,* DEM 4,200. Munich, 26 Nov 1977, *Milkmaid, Positano* (1924, watercolour, $22\frac{1}{2}$ x $19\frac{1}{4}$ ins / 57 x 49 cm) DEM 5,100. Zurich, 26 May 1978, *Maona Quies* (oil on panel, verso: a landscape study, $19\frac{3}{4}$ x $24\frac{3}{4}$ ins / 50 x 63 cm) CHF 3,600. Cologne, 19 May 1979, *Waterfalls* (1940, oil on panel, $29\frac{1}{2}$ x 32 ins / 75 x 81 cm) DEM 6,000. Munich, 30 May 1980, *Young Man with a Straw Hat* (1924, watercolour, $23\frac{3}{4}$ x 18 ins / 60.5 x 46 cm) DEM 3,400. Munich, 8 June 1982, *Landscape* (1921, oil on canvas, $30\frac{3}{4}$ x $22\frac{3}{4}$ ins / 78 x 58 cm) DEM 6,500. Munich, 25 Nov 1983, *Ascona* (1915, pen and watercolour with pencil outlines, 11 x $13\frac{1}{2}$ ins / 27 x 34 cm) DEM 2,400. Munich, 29 May 1984, *Shepherd* (1918, watercolour and pen with pencil outlines, $8\frac{1}{4}$ x $8\frac{1}{4}$ ins / 21 x 21 cm) DEM 3,400. Zurich, 7 June 1986, *Aegina* (oil on canvas, 20 x $31\frac{1}{2}$ ins / 51 x 80 cm) CHF 13,000. Munich, 8 June 1988, *Sunflowers* (oil on canvas, $27\frac{3}{4}$ x $23\frac{1}{2}$ ins / 70.5 x 60 cm) DEM 13,200. Munich, 7 June 1989, *Portrait of Theodor Haecker* (1913, oil on card, $27\frac{1}{4}$ x $19\frac{3}{4}$ ins / 69 x 50 cm) DEM 6,600; *Ronco Church* (1913, oil on canvas, 31 x $23\frac{1}{4}$ ins / 79 x 59 cm) DEM 19,800. Heidelberg, 15-16 Oct 1993, *Villa of Quintillius Varus, Tivoli* (ink, 10 x $12\frac{3}{4}$ ins / 25.5 x 32.6 cm) DEM 1,050. Heidelberg, 15 Oct 1999, *National Feast Day in Cassis, Southern France* (1914, watercolour and pencil, 11 x 14 ins / 28 x 35 cm) DEM 4,800. London, 9 Oct 2002, *Eberhard Reinacher* (1928, pencil, 25 x 19 ins / 64 x 48 cm) EUR 2,000.

SEFER, Lienhart. See **SEYFER**

SEFERIAN, Chouchanik

20th century.
Painter.

Seferian's painting tends towards the abstract; it is highly structured and colourful, and characterised by sensual cut-outs. He has had a number of solo exhibitions, including one at the Galerie Dutko in Paris in 1988.

SEFEROV, Vicko, or Sefer
Bosnian, 20th century.
Born 21 February 1895, in Mostar (now in Bosnia and Herzegovina).
Painter.

Vicko Seferov was a student of Zempliny and Rety in Budapest.

SEFFAJ, Saad
Moroccan, 20th century.
Born 1937, in Tétouan.
Painter.

Saad Seffaj was a professor at the school of fine arts in Tétouan. Along with Meki Meghara, he was an active member of the group of Tétouan artists who considered themselves to stand in a Hispanicist tradition and who preserve some of its aspects, such as the liking for abundant and sandy materials and the creation of collages from heterogeneous materials. He draws inspiration from the ornamental motifs of archaeological earthenware from the Rif mountains, which he integrates as structured elements in the informal context of his rudimentary and deliberately cracked pedestals.

BIBLIOGRAPHY:
M' Rabet, Khalil, *Peinture et identité - L'Expérience marocaine*, L'harmattan, Rabat, apr. 1986.

SEFFER-GUERRA, Alessandro
Italian, 19th century.
Born 1832, in Belluno (Veneto); died 1905, in Belluno.
Painter.

SEFFNER, Karl Ludwig
German, 19th - 20th century.
Born 19 June 1861, in Leipzig; died 2 October 1932, in Leipzig.
Sculptor.

Karl Seffner studied at the academy in Leipzig and under Emil Hundrieser and Schuler in Berlin; he settled in Leipzig in 1891 after completing his studies in Italy.

MUSEUMS AND GALLERIES:
BAUTZEN (Stadtmus.): *Bust of King Albert* - BREMEN: *Bust of Carl Schutte; Schiller Medallion* - DRESDEN (Albertinum): *Busts of Kings Albert and Georg of Saxony; Bust of Max Klinger* - LEIPZIG: *Fly-Catcher; Albert of Saxony; Karl Ludwig; Queen Caroline of Saxony* - MAGDEBURG (Kulturhistorisches Mus.): *Eve* - WEIMAR (Schlossmus.): *Goethe at the Age of Fifty-Eight Years* (bronze, bust).

AUCTION RECORDS:
COLOGNE, 22 June 1979, *Fly-Catcher* (bronze, h. 13½ ins / 34 cm) DEM 3,500. COLOGNE, 18 Nov 2004, *Dancing Faun* (bronze, h. 33 ins / 83 cm) EUR 2,200.

SEFIK BURSALI. See **BURSALI Sefik**

SEGA, Giovanni Del
Italian, 16th century.
Died between 19 February and 29 August 1527, possibly in Carpi.
Active in Forlì.
Painter.

Giovanni Del Sega painted frescoes in the churches of S Croce and S Niccolò in Carpi.

SEGAL, Arthur
Romanian, 20th century.
Born 13 June 1875, in Iasi, Moldavia (now Romania); died 23 June 1944, in London.
Active in England after 1936.
Painter, sculptor, engraver.
Dadaism, Op Art.

Arthur Segal initially studied at the Akademie der Künste in Berlin, and then at the Akademie der Bildenden Künste in Munich, from 1896. He travelled in Italy and France from 1902 to 1903 and settled in Berlin in 1904. He became friends with the painter Adolf Hölzel. During World War I he took refuge in Ascona among the Monte Verità commune, where he met Arp, and then in Zurich, where he met up with Jawlensky and the prime movers of the Dada movement. As a result, he collaborated on the *Dada Review* in 1916, providing a woodcut; on *Dada 3* in 1918; and on the Dada review *Der Zeltweg*, in which he expounded his theory of equivalences for a non-hierarchical understanding of vision. At the end of 1919, he returned to Berlin, where he met up again with Raoul Hausmann, and became a member of the Novembergruppe. In 1927, he collaborated on the constructivist review *i 10* founded by Arthur Lehning in Amsterdam. Fleeing the rise of Nazism, he arrived in Las Palmas, Majorca, in 1933; in 1936 he settled in London. In 1929, he published a theoretical work entitled *The Impersonal Laws of Painting*.

Segal was the creator of what he called the 'simultaneous picture', a picture divided into a dozen or so squares, in each of which a different subject was painted. This procedure is similar to comics strips, and can be considered the precursor of the techniques from which Pop Art would spring in the 1960s. There were several innovations in his work after 1919. One such was spectralism, whereby he painted objects in red, green and yellow stripes, a procedure that is a sort of prismatic decomposition of light and which may be compared with Larionov's rayonism. Segal also produced sculptures that played with the same effects. With his 'eye-catchers', he only painted part of an object, the rest of the image remaining fuzzy; this is presumably to correlate with the physiological fact that one can only focus with precision on one point in the field of vision. Around 1927, he applied the term 'new naturalism' to his works, which at that time were close in structure to divisionist works.

In Berlin he exhibited with the Berlin Secession, and was then a member of a grouping of expressionist painters akin to those of the Die Brücke group, known as the Neue Secession, with whom he also exhibited. In 1916, work by him was shown at the Cabaret Voltaire exhibition in Zurich, the birthplace of Dada, and in 1917 at the Dada Gallery. Work by him was also shown at exhibitions of the Novembergruppe, and at the exhibition *Wege und Richtungen Abstrakter Malerei in Europa* (*Paths and Directions in Abstract Painting in Europe*) in 1927 at the Städtische Kunsthalle in Mannheim. There were also solo exhibitions, the first at the Altmann Gallery in Berlin (1920), then in Rotterdam and The Hague (1926). After his death, there were retrospectives at Royal Society of British Artists (1945), and the Kunstverein, Cologne (1987).

A.Segal

BIBLIOGRAPHY:
Dorival, Bernard/Hoog, Michel, *Dada*, exhibition catalogue, Musée national d'Art moderne, Paris, 1966. Liska, Pavel, *Arthur Segal 1875-1944*, Argon Verlag, Berlin, 1987. Dachy, Marc, '*Dada et les Dadaïsmes*' in *coll. Folio essais*, Gallimard, Paris, 1994.

MUSEUMS AND GALLERIES:
BERLIN (Berlinische Gal.): *Helgoland* (1923) - BERLIN (Nationalgal.) - COLOGNE (Mus. Ludwig) - GENEVA (Petit Palais) - MANNHEIM - THE HAGUE (Gemeentemus.) - ZURICH (Kunsthaus).

AUCTION RECORDS:
LONDON, 4 Dec 1968, *The Tutor*, GBP 450. LONDON, 30 April 1969, *Landscape and Still-life*, GBP 650. LONDON, 16 April

1970, *Zeppelin above Chicago,* GBP 1,800. LONDON, 30 Nov 1972, *House I,* GBP 1,000. LONDON, 7 Dec 1973, *Prismatic Construction,* Gns 1,700. LONDON, 4 July 1974, *Prismatic Construction* (1923) GBP 2,000. ZURICH, 18 Nov 1976, *Where are you, Adam?* (oil on canvas, 27¼ x 35½ ins / 69.5 x 90 cm) CHF 8,800. ZURICH, 23 Nov 1977, *Potsdamer Platz* (1912, oil on card, 32 x 24½ ins / 81 x 62 cm) CHF 10,000. BERN, 22 June 1979, *Still-life* (1918, oil on canvas, 20 x 24¾ ins / 51 x 63 cm with the frame) CHF 27,000. ZURICH, 13 May 1982, *Farm Work* (mixed media, 16¾ x 22 ins / 42.6 x 56.1 cm) CHF 4,000. LONDON, 6 Dec 1983, *Housework* (1921, oil on panel, 24¼ x 32 ins / 61.5 x 81 cm) GBP 4,800. LONDON, 4 Dec 1985, *Still-life with Bottle* (1924, oil on canvas, 27¼ x 31½ ins / 69 x 80 cm) GBP 18,000. LONDON, 24 Feb 1988, *Still-life* (1908, oil on canvas, 14¾ x 18 ins / 37.5 x 45.5 cm) GBP 8,800. LONDON, 21 Oct 1988, *Still-life with Apples in Perspective* (oil on card, 23½ x 31¼ ins / 60 x 79.5 cm) GBP 3,520. LONDON, 4 April 1989, *Street Scene* (1923, oil on card, 19¾ x 23½ ins / 50 x 60 cm) GBP 49,500. LONDON, 20 Oct 1989, *Tulips* (1908, oil on canvas, 13 x 14 ins / 33 x 35.5 cm) GBP 7,150. LONDON, 29 Nov 1989, *Winter Landscape* (1918, oil on card in a painted frame, in all 21¼ x 27½ ins / 54 x 69.8 cm) GBP 20,900. LONDON, 3 April 1990, *Sailing Ship in a Port* (1912, oil on canvas, 24½ x 32¼ ins / 62.5 x 82 cm) GBP 30,800. PARIS, 30 May 1990, *Sailing Ships in a Port* (oil on canvas, 24½ x 32¼ ins / 62.5 x 82 cm) FRF 250,000. TEL AVIV, 31 May 1990, *The Street at Night* (oil on card, including frame 37¾ x 30 ins / 96 x 76 cm) USD 74,800. TEL AVIV, 26 Sept 1991, *Vase of Thistles* (oil on panel, 28¾ x 22½ ins / 73 x 57 cm) USD 5,500. LONDON, 4 Dec 1991, *Woman Sleeping* (1925, oil on card, 31¼ x 38¾ ins / 79.2 x 98.5 cm) GBP 35,200. TEL AVIV, 6 Jan 1992, *At the Circus* (watercolour, 11¾ x 9 ins / 30 x 22 cm) USD 3,850. LONDON, 23 June 1993, *Woman in the Mirror of Time* (oil on canvas, 30 x 37½ ins / 76 x 95.5 cm) GBP 29,900. TEL AVIV, 4 Oct 1993, *Village* (1928, oil on card, 25 x 32¼ ins / 63.7 x 81.8 cm) USD 34,500. LONDON, 11 Oct 1995, *Self-portrait* (1909, oil on card, 20 x 14¼ ins / 50.5 x 36 cm) GBP 13,800. PARIS, 10 Dec 1996, *Composition: Helgoland* (c. 1925, oil on canvas, 29¼ x 36¼ ins / 74 x 92 cm) FRF 170,000. TEL AVIV, 24 April 1997, *Interior* (1942, oil on card, 32 x 24¼ ins / 81.2 x 61.3 cm) USD 15,000. LONDON, 9 Oct 1997, *People Walking in the Park* (1913, oil on paper, 32 x 24½ ins / 81.3 x 62.2 cm) GBP 9,200. LONDON, 30 April 1999, *The Milkmaid* (1919, oil on canvas, 17 x 22 ins / 44 x 57 cm) GBP 13,000. BERLIN, 5 June 1999, *Landscape in Sunset* (c. 1918, gouache, 14 x 19 ins / 35 x 47 cm) DEM 49,000. NEW YORK, 12 May 2000, *Still-life with Candle Holder and Box* (oil on panel, 32 x 39 ins / 81 x 100 cm) USD 90,000. LONDON, 17 Oct 2000, *Still-life with Flowers* (1911, oil on board, 41 x 28 ins / 105 x 71 cm) GBP 20,000. STOCKHOLM, 26 April 2001, *Unüberwindlicher Abgrund* (1918, oil on canvas, 20 x 25 ins / 51 x 63 cm) SEK 310,000. STOCKHOLM, 26 April 2001, *Separation* (1918, oil on canvas, 19 x 24 ins / 49 x 61 cm) SEK 330,000. TEL AVIV, 6 April 2002, *The Bridge in Rugenwaldermunde* (1925, oil on canvas, 27 x 35 ins / 69 x 90 cm) USD 45,000. ZURICH, 4 June 2002, *Houses* (1918, oil on canvas, 17 x 22 ins / 44 x 55 cm) CHF 58,000. BERLIN, 31 May 2003, *Street Scene* (1916, oil on canvas, 28 x 35 ins / 70 x 90 cm) EUR 28,000. BERLIN, 29 Nov 2003, *Still-life with Bottles* (1942, oil on panel, 16 x 20 ins / 40 x 50 cm) EUR 15,000. NEW YORK, 18 March 2004, *Narcissen* (1908, oil on canvas, 19 x 11 ins / 49 x 29 cm) USD 6,500. LONDON, 20 Oct 2004, *Self-portrait in the Studio* (c. 1940, oil on board, 13 x 11 ins / 34 x 28 cm) GBP 2,200.

SEGAL, George

American, 20th century.

Born 26 November 1924, in New York; died 10 June 2000.

Sculptor, painter, pastellist. Figures, nudes.

George Segal studied at the Pratt Institute of Design in Brooklyn in 1947. He completed his education at the University of New York in 1948-1949 under the direction of Tony Smith and William Baziotes. In 1949 he bought a chicken farm so that he could set up a poultry factory not far from the one owned by his father. He met Allan Kaprow in 1953, who was a lecturer at Rutgers University at the time and the founder of the Hansa Gallery, where he met other artists and began to paint seriously. In 1956 he became the artistic advisor to the Art Club at Rutgers University. After experiencing financial difficulties he sold his chickens in 1958 and converted his factory buildings into an art studio. He was awarded a degree from Rutgers University in 1963, and the same year travelled to Europe where he met Alberto Giacometti. He taught art in various schools.

In the early part of Segal's career he was a painter, of nudes in particular, then of abstract works influenced by Matisse and Bonnard. It was his rather unusual career as a poultry farmer which inspired the famous 'Chicken Happening' in Philadelphia in 1962 by Allan Kaprow, an artist without whom Pop Art might never have come about. He probably had an influence on Segal, who, having been a fairly conventional artist, suddenly abandoned painting. Having taken up sculpture he appeared as one of the first creators of Pop Art in 1962, alongside fellow sculptors Kienholz and Oldenburg, and painters Lichtenstein, Rosenquist and Warhol. He also gained appreciation for the pastels he created in the 1960s.

Although he had already begun to create sculptures using materials such as plaster, canvas and wire, he discovered a technique of moulding from living models, courtesy of the pharmacist husband of one of his students, by applying bandages impregnated with plaster as used in medical practice. He did not devote himself completely to sculpture until 1964, when articles praising his work appeared in the art reviews *Artforum*, *Artnews* and *Art International*. After that he created life-size models of figures, usually nudes, in the most ordinary poses, which he placed in everyday situations of his choosing, such as a couple entwined on an unmade bed, a petrol station attendant next to his pump, a man going to the cinema in the entrance of a real cinema with its neon sign, the figure of a man climbing a real staircase, a pinball player with the machine switched on, a cinema cashier at a glass-fronted cash desk, a man drinking, sitting at a real table on a real chair, and others. In fact, in the environments he created everything was real except for the human beings, which were fixed and immobile figures moulded in slightly disturbing pallid white plaster.

After 1976 Segal cast his sculptures in bronze with a white or dark patina. They give an even more arresting impression of the attitudes, faces and physical presence of the figures and their seemingly impossible social relationships. Many are pieces that have been commissioned by public institutions or private groups. It would be wrong to try to compare him with Kienholz, for with the latter the intention is always violent political or social denunciation, whilst Segal's work is simply a cold statement, usually of solitude and the poverty of the human being.

Segal took part in collective exhibitions, including the Boston Art Festival in 1956; *The New York School: Second Generation* organised by Meyer Schapiro at the Jewish Museum, New York, in 1957; *18 Happenings in 6 Parts* at the Reuben Gallery and the Hansa Gallery, New York, in 1959; his first appearance at the *Annual Exhibition of Contemporary American Painting* at the Whitney Museum of American Art, New York, in 1959; and the São Paulo Biennale in 1963 and 1967. He appeared in many major exhibitions dedicated to Pop Art or American contemporary art in general throughout the world.

Segal also exhibited in solo exhibitions, for example at the Hansa Gallery, New York, where he was a member of the cooperative, from 1956 until 1959; the Richard Bellamy Gallery,

New York, in 1960; Douglass College, Rutgers University, New Brunswick, in 1963; Galerie Ileana Sonnabend, Paris, also in 1963; Sidney James Gallery, New York, in 1965; *George Segal: 12 Human Situations*, at the Museum of Contemporary Art, Chicago, in 1968; Paris in 1969; a travelling exhibition in Europe organised by the Kunsthaus in Munich, visiting Munich, Cologne, Rotterdam and Paris, in 1971-1972; an exhibition of pastels at California State University, Long Beach, in 1977; Walker Art Center, Minneapolis, in 1978; and the Galerie Beaubourg, Paris, in 1990.

Segal won the Neysa McMein Purchase Award from the Whitney Museum of American Art in 1965 and the Frank G. Logan first prize in 1966.

BIBLIOGRAPHY:

Friedman, Martin (preface), *George Segal*, exhibition catalogue, Gal. Speyer, Paris, 1971. *George Segal*, exhibition catalogue, Centre national d'Art contemporain, Paris, 1972. Tuchman, Phyllis, *'Segal'* in *coll. Modern Masters*, Abbeville Press, New York, 1983. *George Segal: the Drawings*, exhibition catalogue, Butler Institute of American Art, Youngstown, 1985. Price, Marla, *George Segal: Still Lifes and Related Works*, exhibition catalogue, Modern Art Museum, Fort Worth, 1990. Livingstone, Marco, *George Segal, Retrospective: Sculptures, Paintings, Drawings*, exhibition catalogue, Montreal Museum of Fine Arts, Montreal, 1997. *George Segal: Bronze*, exhibition catalogue, Mitchell-Innes and Nash, New York, 2003.

MUSEUMS AND GALLERIES:

AACHEN (Ludwig Forum für Internationale Kunst) - AMSTERDAM (Stedelijk Mus.) - BUFFALO (Albright-Knox AG) - CHICAGO (AI) - CHICAGO (MCA): *Man in Bar* (1969, mixed media) - CLEVELAND (MA) - COLOGNE (Stadtmus.) - COLOGNE (Wallraf-Richartz Mus.) - DARMSTADT (Hessisches Landesmus.) - DES MOINES (Art Center) - DETROIT (IA) - HARTFORD (Wadsworth Atheneum): *Trapeze* (plaster/wood/metal/rope) - KREFELD (Kaiser Wilhelm Mus.) - MEXICO CITY (MAC International Rufino Tamayo) - MINNEAPOLIS (Walker Art Center) - MÖNCHENGLADBACH (Mus. Abteiberg) - MUNICH (Staatsgal. Moderne Kunst) - NEW YORK (Metropolitan Mus. of Art) - NEW YORK (MoMA) - NEW YORK (Solomon R. Guggenheim Mus.) - NEW YORK (Whitney Mus. of American Art) - OSAKA (National MA) - OTTAWA (NG. of Canada) - PARIS (MNAM-CCI) - PHILADELPHIA (MA) - PITTSBURGH (Carnegie MA): *The Tightrope Walker* (1969, plaster and rope) - ROTTERDAM (Mus. Boijmans Van Beuningen) - SAN FRANCISCO (MoMA): *Hot Dog Stand* (1978, mixed media) - STOCKHOLM (Moderna Mus.) - SYRACUSE (Everson MA): *Untitled* (1973, silk screen print/paper) - TOKYO (Seibu MA) - WASHINGTON DC (Hirshhorn Mus. and Sculpture Garden) - WILMINGTON, DE (Delaware AM): *Swan Motel* (oil on canvas) - ZURICH (Kunsthaus).

AUCTION RECORDS:

PARIS, 12 March 1972, *Girl on a Chair* (plaster and wood) FRF 1,500. NEW YORK, 18 Oct 1973, *Farmer* (plaster, glass, wood and imitation brick) USD 10,000. MILAN, 6 Nov 1973, *Girl on a Red Chair* (pastel) ITL 1,200,000. NEW YORK, 4 May 1974, *Head* (plaster) USD 1,600. NEW YORK, 21 Oct 1976, *Woman Looking through a Window* (1969, plaster, wood and Celotex, 60 x 24 x 12 ins / 152.5 x 61 x 30.5 cm) USD 16,500. PARIS, 22 March 1977, *Girl on a Chair* (1970, plaster and wood, 35 3/4 x 24 x 15 ins / 91 x 61 x 38 cm) FRF 5,000. NEW YORK, 19 Oct 1979, *Seated Nude* (1957, pastel, 18 x 12 ins / 45.7 x 30.5 cm) USD 1,500. LONDON, 5 Dec 1979, *His Hand on her Back* (1973, plaster, h. 41 1/4 ins / 105 cm, w. 28 1/2 ins/72.5 cm) GBP 2,000. NEW YORK, 31 Oct 1984, *Girl in an Armchair* (1982, plaster, wood and willow, 45 x 37 x 52 ins / 114.3 x 94 x 132 cm) USD 80,000. NEW YORK, 6 Nov 1985, *Blue Girl in Black Doorway* (1979, construction). LONDON, 5 Dec 1985, *Female Nude* (1970, pastel, 19 x 15 ins / 48.3 x 38 cm) GBP 3,000. NEW YORK, 11 Nov 1986, *Portrait of Robert and Ethel Scull* (1965, plaster, wood, canvas and fabric, 84 1/4 x 72 x 72 ins / 213.8 x 182.8 x 182.8 cm) USD 140,000. NEW YORK, 11 Nov 1986, *Woman in Dress No2* (1981, pastel/paper, 18 x 12 ins / 45.7 x 30.5 cm) USD 7,000. NEW YORK, 7 Oct 1987, *Woman Straddling Red Chair* (1985, painted plaster and wood, 39 x 26 x 21 1/2 ins / 99 x 66 x 54.6 cm) USD 67,500. PARIS, 4 Dec 1987, *Seated Woman* (pastel/red paper, 17 1/4 x 11 3/4 ins / 44 x 30 cm) FRF 12,000. PARIS, 4 Dec 1987, *Seated Woman* (1965, pastel/red paper, 17 1/4 x 11 3/4 ins / 44 x 30 cm) FRF 12,000. NEW YORK, 3 May 1988, *Machine of the Year* (mixed media sculpture, 96 x 144 x 96 ins / 243.8 x 365.8 x 243.8 cm) USD 187,000. LONDON, 20 Oct 1988, *Seated Woman* (1965, pastel/paper, 17 1/4 x 11 3/4 ins / 44 x 30 cm) GBP 1,980. NEW YORK, 9 Nov 1988, *Girl on a Blanket, with a Finger on her Chin*. NEW YORK, 14 Feb 1989, *Untitled* (1962, chalks/paper, 12 x 18 ins / 30.5 x 45.7 cm) USD 3,850. NEW YORK, 2 May 1989, *Three Swimmers with a Birch* (1980, plaster and wood, 50 x 54 x 13 ins / 127 x 137.2 x 33 cm) USD 187,000. LONDON, 25 May 1989, *Woman Sitting on a Chair* (1970, wood and plaster, 35 3/4 x 24 x 13 3/4 ins / 91 x 61 x 35 cm) GBP 3,520. NEW YORK, 7 Nov 1989, *Metro* (plaster, metal, pane of glass, rattin, electric lightbulbs and map, 88 1/2 x 113 x 51 ins / 224.8 x 287 x 129.5 cm) USD 528,000. MILAN, 8 Nov 1989, *Untitled* (1970, soft pastel and charcoal/paper, 24 3/4 x 18 3/4 ins / 63 x 47.5 cm) ITL 46,000,000. PARIS, 17 Dec 1989, *Self-portrait of Head and Body* (1968, sculpture in plaster and wood, h. 66 1/4 ins / 168 cm) FRF 3,000,000. LONDON, 22 Feb 1990, *Woman on a Chair* (1970, wood, plaster and paint, 35 3/4 x 24 x 14 1/2 ins / 91 x 61 x 37 cm) GBP 10,450. PARIS, 5 April 1990, *Figure* (1986, bronze painted white, h. 23 3/4 ins / 60.5 cm) FRF 250,000. PARIS, 11 June 1990, *Nude with Violin* (pastel/paper, 12 x 18 ins / 30.5 x 45.7 cm) FRF 45,000. MILAN, 23 Oct 1990, *Restaurant Window II* (1971, gesso, 50 3/4 x 54 1/4 x 40 1/2 ins / 129 x 138 x 103 cm) ITL 380,000,000. LUGANO, 28 March 1992, *Fragment of Girl Resting* (1970, plaster, h. 14 1/2 ins / 37 cm) CHF 10,000. NEW YORK, 6 May 1992, *Low Relief II (Hands Clasped behind his Back)* (1971, plaster moulded in a frame, 30 3/4 x 22 ins / 78.4 x 55.6 cm) USD 61,600. NEW YORK, 7 May 1992, *Jacket* (1988, painted plaster and wood, 75 x 22 x 7 ins / 190.5 x 55.9 x 17.8 cm) USD 27,500. LOKEREN, 23 May 1992, *Composition with Shoe* (1975, pastel, 24 1/2 x 18 1/2 ins / 62.5 x 47 cm) BEF 190,000. NEW YORK, 17 Nov 1992, *Girl Washing with one Foot on a Chair* (1967, plaster and wooden chair, in all 48 x 46 x 24 ins / 121.9 x 116.8 x 61 cm) USD 187,000. LOKEREN, 20 March 1993, *Young Girl Thinking* (1975, polyester, h. 19 ins / 48.5 cm, w. 10 1/2 ins/26.5 cm) BEF 130,000. NEW YORK, 4 May 1993, *Woman Drying herself with one Foot on a Stepladder* (plaster and metal, 54 x 19 x 45 ins / 137.2 x 48.3 x 114.3 cm) USD 90,500. NEW YORK, 4 May 1993, *Young Woman on a Green Kitchen Chair* (1964, plaster and painted wood, 41 x 30 x 38 ins / 104.4 x 76.2 x 96.5 cm) USD 200,500. NEW YORK, 3 May 1994, *Young Woman Looking through the Window* (1979, wall relief in oil/plaster with a wooden support, 50 x 22 1/2 x 29 ins / 127 x 57 x 73.7 cm) USD 68,500. LONDON, 27 Oct 1994, *Untitled* (1964, pastel/card, 17 3/4 x 12 ins / 45 x 30.5 cm) GBP 2,875. LONDON, 26 Oct 1995, *Girl and Pendulum* (1972, plaster and electric 'Bulova' pendulum and wood, 35 x 24 1/4 x 23 1/4 ins / 89 x 61.5 x 59 cm) GBP 41,100. NEW YORK, 14 Nov 1995, *Metro* (1968, plaster, metal, glass, bulbs and electric wires, map and muslin, 88 1/2 x 113 x 51 ins / 224.8 x 287 x 129.5 cm) USD 310,500. LONDON, 30 Nov 1995, *Artist's Studio* (plaster, wood, metal, paint and mixed media, 96 x 72 x 108 ins / 244 x 183 x 274.4 cm) GBP 111,500. PARIS, 11 Dec 1997, *Sleeping Woman* (1970, multiple of 125 editions, h. 19 3/4 ins / 50 cm, w. 15 ins/38 cm, depth 9 ins/22 cm) FRF 6,000. LONDON, 11 Dec 1997, *Girl on a Chair* (1970, painted wood and plaster, 36 x 24 x 12 ins / 91.5 x 61 x 30.5 cm) GBP 2,530. LOS ANGELES, 9 June 1999, *Man on Bench* (1985, painted plaster, steel and wood, 51 x 60x36 ins / 129 x 152x92 cm) USD 45,000. NEW YORK, 9 Nov 1999, *Girl on Green Chair* (plaster and painted wood, 45 x 30x38 ins / 114 x 76x96 cm) USD 190,000. NEW YORK, 17 May 2000, *Movie Poster* (1967, plaster figure on panel, 72 x 26x15 ins / 183 x

65x37 cm) USD 320,000. NEW YORK, 16 Nov 2000, *Woman in Red Wicker Chair* (1964, white plaster over armature wicker chair, 43 x 42x25 ins / 109 x 107x63 cm) USD 220,000. NEW YORK, 16 May 2001, *Helen Against Wall with Door* (1987, painted plaster on wood, 38 x 55 ins / 96 x 140 cm) USD 230,000. NEW YORK, 14 Nov 2001, *Chance Meeting* (c. 1989, brown patinated bronze, aluminium post and painted metal sign, 122 x 46x76 ins / 310 x 117x193 cm) USD 600,000. NEW YORK, 14 May 2002, *Laundromat* (1966-1967, plaster, plastic and metal, 85 x 97x43 ins / 217 x 247x110 cm) USD 300,000. MILAN, 5 June 2002, *Man on a Bench* (white patinated bronze, 52 x 47x39 ins / 132 x 120x100 cm) EUR 160,000. NEW YORK, 12 Nov 2003, *Girl with Arm on a Chair* (1971, plaster and wood low relief, wall relief, 34 x 25x7 ins / 86 x 64x18 cm) USD 45,000. NEW YORK, 12 Nov 2003, *Portrait - Vera List* (1965, plaster and metal, 52 x 27x40 ins / 132 x 69x102 cm) USD 95,000. NEW YORK, 12 May 2004, *The Artist in his Loft* (1969, plaster, wood, glass, porcelain and metal, 90 x 69x60 ins / 229 x 175x152 cm) USD 350,000. PARIS, 18 July 2004, *Man Looking Through the Window* (1985, patinated bronze, 96 x 37x28 ins / 244 x 94x71 cm) EUR 150,000.

SEGAL, Jacques

French, 20th century.

Born 21 September 1933, in Paris.

Painter (gouache), draughtsman. Scenes with figures, figures, nudes, still-lifes, landscapes, seascapes, animals.

Segal studied in Paris with Mac Avoy and at the École des Arts Appliqués and the Académie de la Grande Chaumière. He paints traditional subjects but with a particular sense of colour and light which at times veers towards unreality. He exhibited at the Salon d'Automne in Paris. He gave solo shows in 1984 at Mandragore Internationale in Paris, the Galerie Hautefeuille from 1988 to 1990 in Paris, the Musée de Provins et du Provinois in 1999 and at the Espace Paul Valéry in Plessis-Trévise in 2001.

BIBLIOGRAPHY:

Jacques Segal. Peintures et dessins, exhibition catalogue, Musée de Provins et du Provinois, Provins, 1999.

SEGAL, Simon

Ukrainian, 20th century.

Born 3 October 1898, in Bielostok Kiev; died 1969, in Arcachon, France.

Active from 1925 then naturalised in 1949 in France.

Painter, illustrator. Figures, landscapes, landscapes with figures. Designs for tapestries.

Simon Segal initially intended to become a fully qualified engineer in Russia. He spent time in Warsaw in 1918, arrived in Berlin in 1920, and then in Paris in 1925, where he had various jobs. He painted in Toulon from 1926 to 1933, then came to Paris, where he painted in various picturesque corners of the inner areas. During World War II, he remained in the Creuse département, then moved his studio to the Channel, at Jobourg.

In 1935, in an almost visionary act, he presented a collection of gouches on World War I at the Galerie Billiet-Vorms, in Paris. They were all bought the day they were put up by an American collector, Frank Altschul. In 1936 and 1939, he painted workers and tramps. Although Segal was born in Russia and spent the whole of his youth there, his work ultimately acquired a singularly French flavour, and Segal became one of the most faithful painters of the countryside and people of France. However, he also produced work in a more serious vein: in 1949, he made cartoons for tapestries for the Gobelins factory; in 1956 he produced forty-two watercolours of the Bible; and in 1968 he illustrated the *Apocalypse*.

Work by him was shown often at the salons in Paris, at the Salon des Indépendants, the Salon d'Automne, the Salon des Tuileries, the Salon des Peintres Témoins de leur Temps, the Salon des Grands et Jeunes d'Aujourd'hui, and the Salon de Mai (early on in his career). There were also solo exhibitions, including at the Galerie Billiet-Vorms, Paris (1935); at the Galerire Drouant, Paris (1950, 1968); in Toulon (1951); at the Galerie Bassano, Paris (1953, 1954, 1955, 1957, 1962); a retrospective at the Albi Museum (1951); at the Musée Bourdelle, Paris (1958-59); and the Museu de Arte Moderna in São Paulo (1958-59). After his death, there were retrospectives at the Palais des Arts et de la Culture in Brest (1970); in Valréas (1972); at the Musée du Luxembourg; and at the Espace Expo 2000 in Arcachon (1997).

BIBLIOGRAPHY:

Bouret, Jean, *Simon Segal*, Presses littéraires de France, Paris, 1950. *Simon Segal*, exhibition catalogue, Musée du Luxembourg, Paris, 1989. Harambourg, Lydia, *L'École de Paris 1945-1965. Dictionnaire des peintres*, Ides et Calendes, Neuchâtel, 1993. *Simon Segal*, exhibition catalogue, Ville d'Arcachon, 1997. Nieszawer, Nadine/Boyé, Marie/Lanzmann, Claude (preface), *Peintres juifs de l'école de Paris 1905-1939*, Denoël, Paris, 2001.

MUSEUMS AND GALLERIES:

AUPS (Musée Simon-Segal) - PARIS (FNAC).

AUCTION RECORDS:

PARIS, 20 Dec 1954, *Thérèse with Doll*, FRF 56,000. VERSAILLES, 17 April 1988, *Self-portrait* (oil on card, 18 x 14¾ ins / 45.5 x 37.5 cm) FRF 4,400. PARIS, 17 June 1991, *Breton Landscape* (watercolour and gouache, 12¼ x 16 ins / 31 x 40.5 cm) FRF 4,000.

SEGALA, Antonio

Italian, 18th century.

Of Veronese origin.

Sculptor, architect.

Antonio Segala was active about 1740. He sculpted the tabernacle in the church of SS Quirico e Giulietta in Verona.

SEGALA, Francesco, or Segalino

Italian, 16th century.

Died possibly c. 1593.

Active in Padua.

Sculptor, founder.

Francesco Segala worked in Padua, at St Mark's Basilica in Venice and for the Habsburgs.

MUSEUMS AND GALLERIES:

UDINE: *Bust of Tiberio Deciano* - VIENNA (Kunsthistorisches Mus.): *Portrait of Archduke Ferdinand of Tyrol*; *Portrait of a Gentleman*.

AUCTION RECORDS:

LONDON, 12 May 1970, *Hercules*; *Omphale* (two bronzes) Gns 2,000.

SEGALA, G.

Italian, 18th century.

Active during the first half of the 18th century.

Sculptor, architect.

Segala sculpted the Dionisi altar in the cathedral in Verona.

SEGALA, Giorgio

Italian, 18th century.

Born in Venice.

Sculptor.

Giorgio Segala, the pupil of Pietro Pisani in Florence, was active in the late 18th century.

SEGALA, Giovanni, or Segalla

Italian, 17th - 18th century.

Born 1663, in Murano; died 1720, in Venice.

Painter. Religious subjects.

Giovanni Segala was the pupil of Antonio Zanchi and Pietro Vecchia.

MUSEUMS AND GALLERIES:

VENICE (Gal. dell'Accademia): *Carita*.

Auction records:
Milan, 12 June 1989, *Flight into Egypt* (oil on canvas, 104¼ x 88¼ ins / 265 x 224 cm) ITL 32,000,000. London, 17 April 1991, *Jacob Depriving Esau of his Birthright* (oil on canvas, 37½ x 51¼ ins / 95.5 x 130 cm) GBP 5,500.

SEGALA, Luigi
Italian, 20th century.
Born 8 March 1880, in Grosseto (Tuscany); died 1956.
Painter. Landscapes.
Luigi Segala was a pupil of Maineri.

SEGALAT, Jean
French, 20th century.
Painter.
Segalat studied at the École des Beaux-Arts in Paris for two years. He lived and worked in Bordeaux.

He was influenced by Toulouse-Lautrec and the early work of Picasso.

Museums and Galleries:
Bordeaux.

SÉGALEN
French, 20th century.
Born 1939, in Brest.
Painter. Landscapes with figures, seascapes, landscapes.
Ségalen studied at the École des Beaux-Arts in Brest until 1956, then at the École des Beaux-Arts de Rennes. He lived and worked in Melon (Côtes des Légendes) in Brittany. Ségalen painted coastal scenes of life in Brittany, depicting typical views with a stylised look which at times tends toward the dreamlike or even the fantastic.

He took part in group exhibitions including at the École des Beaux-Arts, Brest in 1956; Salon des Artistes Bretons in 1959; Salon d'Automne in Paris in 1973; Salon Grands et Jeunes d'Aujourd'hui in 1974; Brest International Biennale in 1978; Salon des Indépendants in Paris in 1982, 1983 and 1986; and in 1982, the Salon de la Marine. His first solo show was in Brest in 1957, after which he went on to show his work at the Musée de Morlaix in 1976 and the Hôtel de Ville of Pont-Aven in 1984.

SEGALINO, Francesco. See **SEGALA**

SEGALL, Lasar
Lithuanian, 20th century.
Born 7 July 1890, in Vilnius; died 2 August 1957, in São Paulo.
Active then in 1923 naturalised in Brazil.
Painter, sculptor, engraver, lithographer.
From 1906 to 1909, Lasar Segall was a student of Lovis Corinth at the Akademie der Künste in Berlin. With the intention of divesting himself of the academic approach he had acquired, he continued his studies at the academy in Dresden in 1910, as a *Meisterschuler* (master-pupil), with a studio of his own. He travelled, notably to the Netherlands and, in 1913, to Brazil and São Paulo, where he mounted an exhibition of his works, remarkable for having been the first exhibition of modern art in Brazil. He returned to Germany in 1913, and on the outbreak of World War I was made a civil prisoner, being a Russian citizen, and exiled to Meissen. He was given permission to move to Dresden, where he was a member of the Dresden Secession group in 1919, together with Conrad Felizmüller, Otto Dix and Otto Lange. In 1923, Segall settled permanently in Brazil, taking Brazilian nationality. For a while, he was considered the most prominent figure of the Brazilian school of painting; in 1932, he founded the Modern Art Society.

Active in German artistic life at the start of the 20th century, Segall was influenced by expressionism - all the more because the style suited his temperament. This influence is confirmed by his output: the figures in his compositions are stylised, and have out-sized heads with large, almond-shaped eyes, and the colours are cold. Although the angularity apparent in the paintings of 1912 to 1923 expresses the morbid psychology of the distraught and half-starved figures in them, and can be said to have been influenced by expressionism, these paintings are nevertheless characterised by attention to detail in the construction of form, and can therefore be compared with the work of the fauves in Paris. His output in Brazil - landscapes, etchings of women - was calmer in spirit, though still as compositionally rigorous. Though Segall was far removed from Europe, most of his output was always given over to his Russian Jew's childhood reminiscences: emigrants, vulnerable and wandering women, and broken families, as in *Sick Family, Destitute Family, Street,* and *Pregnant Women.* The social problems raised by these images and are familiar also from the work of Di Cavalcanti and Tarsila; in Brazil these problems would be at the root of the 1930 revolution. Segall was an active member of the Modern Art Society, and together with other artists, he produced murals for the Society's headquarters that were both popular and fairy-tale like in atmosphere. In around 1930, Segall began to produce small sculptures in bronze or marble, representing figures (such as *Motherhood*) and groups. He was later to show himself particularly sensitive to the plight of the people of Israel, and the works from this period are among his best known: *Pogrom, Concentration Camp, Exodus,* and *The Ship of Emigrants.* Occasionally, the tormented spirit of this sincere and emotional man would find respite in calm subjects, such as the various works entitled *Forest* of 1950 to 1955, or the rather beautiful renditions of *Motherhood* that punctuate his output. Segall published series of etchings and lithographs, including *Memories of Vilnius* (1919); *Bubu,* after Carles-Louis Philippe's novel *Bubu of Montparnasse* (1921); *The Gentlewoman,* after the novel *Krotkaya* by Dostoyevsky (1921); *Mango* (1944); *Cançao da partida* after Jacintha Passos (1945); and *Poemas Negros* (*Black Poems*) by Jorge de Lima (1946).

Work by Segall was shown at group exhibitions, including the Freie Sezession in Berlin (1909, where he was awarded the Liebermann Prize); the 1st São Paulo biennale (1951, where a whole room was given over to his work); and the 2nd and 3rd São Paulo biennales (1953 and 1955, for the latter of which he was not part of the competition). Exhibitions featuring Segall's work after his death were the fourth São Paulo biennale (1957, which acted as retrospective in his memory); the Venice biennale (1958); and the exhibition *Modernidade: Art Brésilien du XXe Siècle* (*Modernity: Brazilian Art in the 20th Century*) at the Musée d'Art Moderne de la Ville de Paris (1987). There were also solo exhibitions, the first taking place in the Gurlitt Gallery in Dresden in 1910, including ones at São Paulo and Campinas (1913); the Folkwang Museum in Hagen (1920); at the Schames Gallery in Frankfurt am Main (1921); at the Print Collection in Leipzig (1923); in São Paulo (1924); at the Neumann-Nierendorf Gallery in Berlin (1926); at *People and Personnages of Brazil* in São Paulo (1926-27); Rio de Janeiro (1928); the Galerie Vignon in Paris (1931); the Pro Arte Gallery in Rio de Janeiro (1933); the Bragaglia Gallery in Rome (1933); New York (1938); a retrospective at the Museu Nacional in Rio de Janeiro (1943); at the American Artists' Association in New York (1943); a retrospective at the Museu de Arte Moderna in São Paulo (1951); retrospectives at the Palacio de la Virreina in Barcelona and the Museo Nacional Centro de Arte Reina Sofía in Madrid (1958); and a travelling exhibition organized by the Musée d'Art et d'Histoire du Judaïsm in Paris (1988-2000).

BIBLIOGRAPHY:
Dauebler, Theodor, *Lasar Segall*, Fritz Gurlitt, Berlin, 1922. Fierens, Paul, *Lasar Segall*, Chroniques du jour, Paris, 1938. Horta Beccari, Vera d', *Lasar Segall e o modernismo paulista*, dissertation, Brasiliense, São Paulo, 1984. *A gravura de Lasar Segall*, exhibition catalogue, Museum Lasar Segall, São Paulo, 1988. *Lasar Segall e o Rio de Janeiro*, exhibition catalogue, Museu de Arte Moderna, Rio de Janeiro, 1991 (text in Portuguese and English). Valladão de Mattos, Cláudia, *Lasar Segall*, dissertation, Edusp, São Paulo, 1997. d'Alessandro, Stéphanie, *Lasar Segall: nouveaux mondes*, Adam Biro, Paris, 2000.

MUSEUMS AND GALLERIES:
BERLIN (Jüdisches Mus.): *Silver Birch at Thera, Brazil* (1922, gouache) - ESSEN (Folkwang Mus.): *Widow* (1919, oil on canvas) - NEW YORK (Jewish Mus.): *Exodus* (1947, oil on canvas) - SÃO PAULO (Mus. Lasar Segall) - SÃO PAULO (Pinacoteca do Estado): *Banana Plantation* (1927, oil on canvas).

AUCTION RECORDS:
NEW YORK, 15 Jan 1969, *Landscape*, USD 1,050. COLOGNE, 4 Dec 1985, *Abstract Composition* (tempera, 16¼ x 21¼ ins / 41 x 54 cm) DEM 6,500. NEW YORK, 21 Nov 1988, *Mother and Son* (1945, ink/paper, 19 x 13 ins / 48.4 x 33 cm) USD 2,860. NEW YORK, 21 Nov 1995, *Still-life* (1924, oil on card, 27¼ x 20¾ ins / 69.5 x 52.7 cm) USD 96,000. PARIS, 19 June 1996, *Figures* (c. 1918, oil on canvas, 25½ x 33 ins / 65 x 84 cm) FRF 580,000. NEW YORK, 28 May 1997, *Two Figures* (c. 1935, pastel and wax/paper, 20 x 15¾ ins / 50.8 x 40 cm) USD 55,200.

SEGALMAN, Richard

American, 20th century.
Born 1934.
Sculptor, pastellist.

Richard Segalman attended the Parsons School of Design in New York between 1951 and 1955, then worked at the Art Students' League around 1960.

MUSEUMS AND GALLERIES:
BOSTON (MFA) - WASHINGTON DC (Hirshhorn Mus. and Sculpture Garden) - YOUNGSTOWN (Butler Institute of American Art).

AUCTION RECORDS:
NEW YORK, 28 Nov 1995, *Lucy* (pastel/paper, 30 x 22 ins / 76 x 55.8 cm) USD 1,725. NEW YORK, 29 Oct 2002, *Sunday. Raymond. Mario* (pencil and watercolour, three, 11 x 15 ins / 29 x 38 cm) USD 2,000. NEW YORK, 29 Oct 2002, *Two Portraits of David. Man Rowing* (pencil and watercolour, 20 x 15 ins / 52 x 38 cm) USD 2,250.

SEGANTINI, Giovanni

Italian, 19th century.
Born 15 January 1858, in Arco del Garda (Trentino); died 28 September 1899, near Pontresina (Ober Engadin, Switzerland).
Also active in Switzerland.
Painter (including gouache), watercolourist, pastellist. Religious subjects, allegorical subjects, figures, rustic scenes, genre scenes, local scenes, interiors with figures, mountainscapes, waterscapes, still-lifes, animals, flowers.
Symbolism.
Macchiaioli group.

When he was four years old, Giovanni Segantini's mother died and his father took him to Milan and left him to be looked after by an impoverished female relative. He then disappeared without trace and Giovanni heard nothing more from him. Since his relative was out most of the time trying to earn a living, the small boy lived for two years almost entirely on his own. When she was there, he is more likely to have been ill-treated than spoiled by her. One day he ran away into the mountains. Taken in by some kindly peasants, he looked after their animals (work that the young Giotto may also have done).

As he grew up in these humble surroundings, his gifts as an artist began to emerge and he acquired some patrons who paid for him to go to Milan to study painting. Despite their generosity, life for Segantini was very difficult. He had just enough money to pay for his studies and attic lodgings. He was 19 when he produced his first oil painting, *The Choir of the Church of S Antonio*. He stayed on in Milan for a few more years, his efforts soon finding a reward in his increasing success; he was greatly assisted by Vittore Grubicy, a generous patron of Milanese artists who was always ready with financial help and good advice.

Without leaving Milan, Segantini studied the works of contemporary painters. As soon as he felt confident of his mastery of technique, he went to live in Brianza, an area in the mountains that reminded him of his childhood. There, between 1881 and 1886, living close to the shepherds who were the subjects of his paintings, he produced works of deeply-felt sincerity. In 1886, as if Brianza were not remote enough, he moved yet higher into the mountains, to the village of Savognin, painting there until 1894 when he died very suddenly while he was at work. He had had a hut built for him near the mountain top at an altitude of 8,900 feet (2,700 metres), close to the Schafberg refuge. It was here that, surrounded by snow, he was working on a major triptych intended for the Paris Salon. Suddenly taken ill, he died of the effects of trying to quench his thirst with snow. He was barely 40.

His early works were painted in dark colours but as he adopted the neo-Impressionists' experiments with the division of colours, a technique to which he had been introduced by Vittore Grubicy in about 1886, his palette lightened. His technique became more personal, combining neo-Impressionist divisionism with the more flexible technique of the Macchiaioli. A complex painter, he produced not only alpine landscapes but also subjects inspired by the lives of the peasants who worked in the mountains. In these paintings, following, in his own personal manner, the ideas of Bastien Lepage and, particularly, Jean-François Millet, he represented religious and symbolic subjects with images that recall the naivety of medieval art.

In 1883, he was awarded a gold medal in Amsterdam for his painting *Ave Maria a trasbordo* (*Ave Maria on the Boat*). His works met with great success not only in Italy but also abroad, in Dresden and Berlin for example. Several retrospective exhibitions have been held since his death including: *Giovanni Segantini*, Museum des 20. Jahrhunderts, Vienna (1981); *75 Jahre Museum Segantini, St Moritz, 1908-1983. 125 Jahre Giovanni Segantini, 1858-1899*, St Moritz (1983); *Giovanni Segantini 1858-1899*, Kunsthaus, Zurich (1990); *Giovanni Segantini: opere giovanili nelle collezioni del Trentino* (*Giovanni Segantini: Early Works from the Collections in the Trentino Region*), Cassa Rurale di Arco-Garda (1999); *Giovanni Segantini: luce e simbolo* (*Giovanni Segantini: Light and Symbol*), Peggy Guggenheim Collection, Venice (2000).

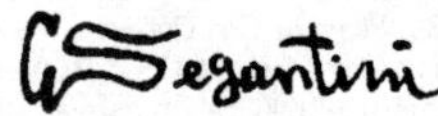

Bibliography:
Quinsac, Annie-Paule, *'Segantini: catalogo general'* in *2 vol.*, Electa, Milan, 1982. *75 Jahre Museum Segantini, St. Moritz, 1908-1983. 125 Jahre Giovanni Segantini, 1858-1899*, exhibition catalogue, Museum Segantini, St Moritz, 1983 (text in German and Italian). Frehner, Matthias/Klemm, Christian, et al., *Giovanni Segantini 1858-1899*, Hatje Cantz, Ostfildern, 1999. Quinsac, Annie-Paule, *Giovanni Segantini: luce e simbolo*, exhibition catalogue, Peggy Guggenheim Collection, Venice, 2000 (text in Italian and English). Quinsac, Annie-Paule, *'Segantini's centennial celebrations. An afterthought'* in *Apollo* n° 468 p. 47, London, February 2001.

Museums and Galleries:
Amsterdam: a pastel - Basel: *Drinking Tough* - Berlin: *Nightfall; Coming Home* - Bern: *Returning from the Forest* - Brussels: *Sheepfold* - Hamburg: *Meadowsi in the Engadin Valley* - Leipzig: *Vittore Grubicy du Dragon* - Liverpool: *Punishment of Lust* - Milan (Gal. d'Arte Moderna): *Two Mothers* - Munich (Neue Pinakothek): *Labourer in the Engadin Valley* - Rome (Gal. Nazionale): *At the Helm* - St Moritz (Segantini Mus.): *Haymaking* (1899); *Nature, Life and Death*; Other Works - The Hague (Mus. Mesdag): *Two Mothers; Homecoming of the Flocks* - Vienna (Österreichische Gal. Belvedere): *Bad Mothers; Pasture with White Cow* - Zurich (Kunsthaus): *Girl by a Fence; Musical Allegory.*

Auction records:
London, 29 April 1927, *Idyll*, GBP 3,570. London, 16 Dec 1929, *Flocks*, GBP 110. Paris, 20 Jan 1947, *Hut in the Mountains* (attributed) FRF 50,000. Paris, 20 Dec 1948, *Landscape*, FRF 80,000. Geneva, 27 Nov 1965, *Still-life*, CHF 30,000. London, 30 June 1967, *Sick Child* (watercolour/grey paper) Gns 420. Lucerne, 30 Nov 1968, *Peasant Woman in a Winter Landscape*, CHF 50,000. Geneva, 24 April 1970, *The Artist's Wife when Ill* (watercolour) CHF 10,000; *Village in the Snow*, CHF 40,000. Zurich, 11 June 1971, *Peasant woman Carrying a Load in a Mountain Landscape*, CHF 74,000. Lucerne, 18 June 1971, *Sick Girl* (gouache) CHF 15,000. Milan, 29 March 1973, *Hunting Trophies: Pheasant and Woodcock* (two pendants) ITL 3,400,000. Zurich, 8 Nov 1974, *Embracing the Cross* (pastel) CHF 62,000. Rome, 12 Nov 1974, *View of the Holy City*, ITL 7,500,000. Bern, 10 June 1976, *Ave Maria in Trasbordo* (*Ave Maria on the Boat*) (1882, pen, 12 x 9 ins / 30.3 x 22.8 cm) CHF 20,000. Zurich, 12 Nov 1976, *Shepherdess and Flock in the Moonlight* (1882, oil on canvas, 32½ x 21 ins / 82.5 x 53.5 cm) CHF 48,000. Zurich, 12 May 1977, *Horse at a Drinking Trough* (oil on canvas, 26½ x 46¼ ins / 67.5 x 117.5 cm) CHF 22,000. Zurich, 19 May 1979, *Labourer* (c. 1892, charcoal, 19¾ x 14¾ ins / 50.3 x 37.5 cm) CHF 30,000. Bern, 22 June 1979, *Ave Maria in Trasbordo* (1888-1890, pastel, 16¼ x 24 ins / 41.5 x 61 cm) CHF 74,000. Bern, 22 Nov 1979, *Still-life* (oil on canvas, 23½ x 31½ ins / 60 x 80 cm) CHF 30,000. London, 23 June 1981, *Ave Maria in Trasbordo* (c. 1888-1890, charcoal and pastel/paper, 16¼ x 21¼ ins / 41.5 x 54 cm) GBP 30,000. Munich, 30 June 1982, *Fruit of Love* (oil on canvas, 34¼ x 20½ ins / 87 x 52 cm) DEM 110,000. Zurich, 2 June 1983, *Still-life with Sausages and Cheese* (1880, oil on canvas, 45¼ x 20¾ ins / 115 x 53 cm) CHF 70,000. London, 21 June 1984, *On the Balcony* (c. 1892, lead pencil and grey wash, 10½ x 7 ins / 26.5 x 17.5 cm) GBP 4,200. London, 28 Nov 1985, *Ave Maria in Trasbordo* (1883, pen and black ink, 12 x 9 ins / 30.5 x 22.8 cm) GBP 30,000. Zurich, 29 Nov 1985, *Peasant Girl Carrying Wood* (oil on canvas, 24 x 16¼ ins / 61 x 41 cm) CHF 220,000. Milan, 18 Dec 1986, *Bell-Ringer* (1879-1880, oil on canvas, 46 x 24 ins / 117 x 61 cm) ITL 120,000,000. Milan, 23 March 1988, *Priest Going up the Steps* (oil on canvas, 13 x 11¼ ins / 33 x 28.5 cm) ITL 65,000,000. Rome, 6 Dec 1989, *Hare* (oil on canvas, 26½ x 19¾ ins / 67 x 50 cm) ITL 218,500,000. Milan, 18 Oct 1990, *Floral Decoration* (oil on canvas, 19¾ x 39¼ ins / 50 x 100 cm) ITL 66,000,000. Zurich, 7-8 Dec 1990, *Portrait of the Artist's Sister-in-Law: Irene* (1881, oil on panel, 13 x 9¼ ins / 33 x 23.6 cm) CHF 34,000. Milan, 12 March 1991, *Scene in an Interior* (oil on canvas, 30 x 23½ ins / 75.3 x 60 cm) ITL 49,000,000. New York, 22 May 1991, *Cowherd* (pencil pencil and charcoal on paper mounted to board, 9¼ x 7 ins / 23.5 x 17.8 cm) USD 19,800. Milan, 6 June 1991, *Landscape around Brianza* (oil on board, 7 x 4¾ ins / 18 x 12 cm) ITL 12,000,000. Milan, 17 Dec 1992, *Cobbler* (oil on canvas, 37¾ x 28¾ ins / 96 x 73 cm) ITL 200,000,000. Milan, 16 March 1993, *Two Cows in a Shed* (oil on canvas, 19¾ x 29¾ ins / 50 x 75.5 cm) ITL 40,000,000. Zurich, 24 Nov 1993, *Woman with Umbrella* (oil on canvas, 11¼ x 6½ ins / 28.5 x 16.5 cm) CHF 131,350. Zurich, 8 Dec 1994, *Still-life with Roses* (oil on canvas, 11¼ x 21½ ins / 28.5 x 54.5 cm) CHF 63,250. Zurich, 12 June 1995, *Study of the Seine* (charcoal and pencil/paper, 31½ x 53½ ins / 80 x 136 cm) CHF 317,800. Milan, 19 Dec 1995, *Roses* (oil on canvas, 17¾ x 9¾ ins / 45 x 25 cm) ITL 14,375,000. Zurich, 10 Dec 1996, *Edelweiss* (charcoal/paper, 26½ x 15 ins / 67.5 x 38 cm) CHF 176,550. Zurich, 4 June 1997, *Agony of Comala* (1895, pencil and chalk/paper, 8¼ x 11½ ins / 21 x 29.5 cm) CHF 137,000. Milan, 20 Oct 1999, *The Herdsman* (1882-1883, oil on canvas, 17 x 24 ins / 44 x 62 cm) ITL 112,261,000. New York, 9 Nov 1999, *Springtime in the Alps* (1897, oil on canvas, 46 x 89 ins / 116 x 227 cm) USD 8,700,000. London, 27 Oct 2000, *Alpine Landscape* (1898-1999, oil on canvas, 20 x 35 ins / 51 x 90 cm) GBP 70,000. Zurich, 12 Dec 2000, *Love on the Mountain* (c. 1881-1882, oil on canvas, 30 x 21 ins / 77 x 53 cm) CHF 540,000. Munich, 17 May 2001, *Ave Maria a Trasbordo* (Indian ink, 12 x 9 ins / 30 x 23 cm) DEM 400,000. Zurich, 19 June 2001, *Fruit of Love* (1892, ochre and gold dust, 19 x 11 ins / 48 x 29 cm) CHF 115,000. New York, 23 Jan 2002, *Return to the Sheepfold* (black and white chalk, 8 x 10 ins / 20 x 25 cm) USD 86,000. Zurich, 25 March 2002, *Portrait of Leopoldina Grubicy* (c. 1880, oil on canvas, 17 x 14 ins / 42 x 35 cm) CHF 180,000. Zurich, 26 May 2003, *La Radice* (*The Root*) (oil on canvas, 22 x 31 ins / 55 x 80 cm) CHF 160,000. Zurich, 29 Sept 2003, *Landscape at Dusk* (oil on canvas, 31 x 39 ins / 80 x 100 cm) CHF 60,000. Milan, 8 June 2004, *Midday in the Alps* (1892, pastel, 15 x 9 ins / 37 x 22 cm) EUR 30,000.

SEGANTINI, Gottardo

Italian, 20th century.

Born 25 May 1882, in Puisano (Lombardy); died 1974, in Maloja (Abruzzi).

Painter, engraver. Landscapes, seascapes.

The son of Giovanni Segantini, Gottardo Segantini studied at the Accademia di Belle Arti di Brera in Milan and with Hermann Gattiker. He made etchings after his father's paintings and also painted alpine scenes and seascapes. He also wrote about art.

Auction records:
London, 13 March 1964, *Shepherdess with Flocks in an Alpine Landscape*, Gns 320. Zurich, 25 May 1979, *Summer Landscape, Sils* (1955, hardboard, 32¼ x 43¼ ins / 82 x 110 cm) CHF 9,000. Zurich, 11 Nov 1981, *Dawn, Silersee* (1936, oil on canvas, 35½ x 47¼ ins / 90 x 120 cm) CHF 14,000. Zurich, 3 June 1983, *Winter Landscape* (1952, oil/Pavatex, 19½ x 25½ ins / 49.5 x 64.5 cm) CHF 16,000. Zurich, 8 June 1985, *In the Engadin Valley* (1944, oil/hardboard, 36¼ x 28 ins / 92 x 71 cm) CHF 9,000. London, 24 June 1986, *Basilica of Constantine, Rome* (1912, oil on canvas, 31½ x 31½ ins / 80 x 80 cm) GBP 8,000. Rome, 7 April 1988, *Eternal Beauty* (1912, oil on canvas, 39¼ x 61 ins / 100 x 155 cm) ITL 14,000,000. London, 30 March 1990, *Bittaberg Lake* (1923, oil on canvas,

46 1/2 x 71 1/4 ins / 118 x 181 cm) GBP 24,200. LONDON, 21 June 1991, *Grap da Corn with Piz Corvatsch and a Lake in the Foreground* (1954, oiol on board, 33 x 48 ins / 84 x 122 cm) GBP 15,400. ZURICH, 24 Nov 1993, *Summer Landscape near Maloja* (1957, oil/synthetic resin, 33 1/2 x 44 ins / 85 x 111.5 cm) CHF 46,000. ZURICH, 2 June 1994, *Peace of the Mountains* (1939, oil on canvas, 39 1/4 x 31 1/2 ins / 100 x 80 cm) CHF 34,500. ZURICH, 12 June 1995, *Mountain Lake and Pic de la Margna* (1927, oil on canvas, 32 x 39 1/4 ins / 81 x 100 cm) CHF 51,750. ZURICH, 30 Nov 1995, *Piz Forno near Maloja* (1953, oil/synthetic resin, 22 x 29 1/4 ins / 55 x 74 cm) CHF 59,800. ZURICH, 5 June 1996, *Impression* (1938, oil on canvas, 28 3/4 x 23 ins / 73 x 58.5 cm) CHF 69,000. ZURICH, 10 Dec 1996, *Cavaloccio Lake in the Morning* (1926, oil on canvas, 32 x 45 1/4 ins / 81 x 115 cm) CHF 125,700. ZURICH, 4 June 1997, *Winter Landscape* (1924, oil on canvas, 31 x 26 1/4 ins / 78.5 x 66.5 cm) CHF 97,45. ZURICH, 18 March 1999, *Autumn in Lake Cavloccio in Upper Engadine* (1927, oil on canvas, 35 x 47 ins / 90 x 119 cm) CHF 110,000. ZURICH, 23 March 1999, *Silsersee with Piz Corvatsch* (1942, oil on board, 29 x 43 ins / 73 x 110 cm) CHF 185,000. ZURICH, 21 March 2000, *Piz Margna at Sunset* (1925, oil on canvas, 39 x 30 ins / 100 x 75 cm) CHF 90,000. ZURICH, 7 June 2000, *Landscape in Engadine with Cow* (1945, oil on board, 33 x 25 ins / 83 x 63 cm) CHF 40,000. ST GALL, 21 Nov 2001, *Summer Landscape near Maloja* (1957, oil on board, 33 x 44 ins / 85 x 111 cm) CHF 48,000. ZURICH, 3 Dec 2001, *St Lorenz Church, Sils Baselgia, Engadine* (1942, oil on panel, 18 x 22 ins / 46 x 55 cm) CHF 62,000. ZURICH, 3 June 2002, *Spring in the High Mountains* (1944, oil on plate, 37 x 48 ins / 95 x 122 cm) CHF 155,000. ZURICH, 25 Nov 2002, *Shepherd with Flock in the Mountains* (1960, oil on board, 26 x 33 ins / 66 x 84 cm) CHF 85,000. ZURICH, 26 May 2003, *Rome* (oil on canvas, two, 26 x 31 ins / 65 x 80 cm) CHF 40,000. ROME, 11 June 2003, *Landscape of Engadine* (oil on canvas, 41 x 47 ins / 105 x 120 cm) EUR 44,000. ZOFINGEN, 4 June 2004, *White Church, Maloya* (1914, oil on canvas, 35 x 24 ins / 89 x 61 cm) CHF 35,000. ZURICH, 23 June 2004, *Church of St Moritz* (1945, oil on panel, 32 x 36 ins / 81 x 91 cm) CHF 70,000.

SEGANTINI, Mario
Italian, 20th century.
Born 31 March 1885, in Milan; died February 1916, in Maloja.
Sculptor, painter, engraver.

The son of Giovanni Segantini, Mario Segantini was a pupil at the Accademia di Belle Arti di Brera in Milan and of E. Quadrelli and G. Gurschner. He made engravings of his father's works.

AUCTION RECORDS:
ZURICH, 30 Nov 1981, *Bather* (oil on canvas, 23 1/2 x 59 ins / 60 x 150 cm) CHF 14,500. ZURICH, 13 Nov 1982, *Grazing Sheep* (oil on canvas, 17 x 25 1/4 ins / 43 x 64 cm) CHF 4,400. ROME, 17 April 1989, *Segantini Chalet at Passo Rolle* (1925, oil on board, 19 3/4 x 26 ins / 50 x 66 cm) ITL 6,000,000. BERN, 14 Nov 2002, *Portrait of Young Blonde Man* (1903, oil and gold on bronze, 26 x 21 ins / 65 x 54 cm) CHF 3,500.

SÉGAR. See also **SÉGART**

SEGAR, Francis, or Seigar
British, 16th century.
Active in 1598.
Painter.

Francis Segar was the brother of William Segar.

SEGAR, William, or Seigar
British, 16th century.
Painter, engraver. Portraits.

The brother of Francis Segar, William Segar was working in 1598. He engraved books of heraldry.

AUCTION RECORDS:
LONDON, 19 Nov 1986, *Portrait of Elizabeth Stafford, Lady Drury* (oil on panel, oval, 27 x 21 ins / 68.5 x 52.5 cm) GBP 21,000.

SEGARD, Aljoscha
Bulgarian, 20th century.
Born 1942, in Sofia.
Active in Switzerland and in France.
Painter.

Aljoscha Segard paints small abstract or figurative symbols which he then mixes up before arranging in a very particular order. His art also draws on the effects of the materials he uses. He has had several solo exhibitions, including: 1977, Claudia Meyer Gallery, Zurich; 1979 Schindler Gallery, Bern; 1982 Galerie Karl Flinker, Paris.

SÉGARD, Jean
French, 14th century.
Active in Lille from 1341 to 1348.
Illuminator.

SÉGARD, Jean. See also **SÉGART**

SEGARD, Louis
French, 18th century.
Painter. Landscapes.

Louis Segard was admitted into the Académie de St-Luc in Paris on 17 October 1753.

AUCTION RECORDS:
PARIS, 31 March 1995, *Pond below the Ramparts* (oil on canvas, 20 3/4 x 31 1/2 ins / 53 x 80 cm) FRF 18,000.

SEGARO, Giambattista
Italian, 17th century.
Active in Genoa at the beginning of the 17th century.
Miniaturist.

SEGARO, Giuseppe
Italian, 17th century.
Active in Genoa c. 1605.
Miniaturist.

SEGARRA, Jayme or Jaime
Spanish, 16th century.
Painter.

In 1530, Jayme Segarra painted an altarpiece for the church of Our Lady of Belen in Reus, Calalonia.

SÉGART, Jean, or Ségar or Ségard
French, 16th century.
Born in Arras.
Painter, gilder.

Jean Ségart was the father of Luc Ségart. In 1570 he settled in Tournai, where he worked from 1570 to 1598.

SÉGART, Luc
Flemish School, 16th - 17th century.
Active in Tournai from 1576 to 1637.
Painter.

Luc Ségart was the son and pupil of Jean Ségart and he painted religious subjects and decorations.

SÉGART, Pierre
Flemish School, 17th century.
Active in Tournai, Belgium, in 1635.
Painter. Waterscapes.

Pierre Ségart was the grandson of Jean Ségart.

AUCTION RECORDS:
PARIS, 23 Feb 1978, *Landscape with Lake* (oil on panel, 22 1/2 x 33 1/4 ins / 57 x 84.5 cm) FRF 12,000.

SEGATO, Girolamo
Italian, 19th century.
Born 13 June 1792, in Vedana (Veneto); died 3 February 1836, in Florence.
Engraver (burin).

SEGAUD
French, 18th century.
Active in Paris.
Painter.
Segaud featured at the 1793 Salon with several portraits and one drawing.

SÉGAUD, Armand Jean-Baptiste
French, 20th century.
Born 1 August 1875, in Moulins (Allier).
Painter, draughtsman, illustrator. Mythological subjects, landscapes. Murals.
Ségaud was a student of Pierre Victor Galland and Georges Callot. He regularly exhibited at the Salon des Artistes Français in Paris, and was a member of the jury.

He made decorative paintings for the Monte Carlo casino (*Apollo and the Muses*), and in Paris. He also worked as a bookbinder.

AUCTION RECORDS:
PARIS, 22 June 1992, *Port of Nafta in Tunisia* (1899, oil on canvas, 24 x 17 1/4 ins / 61 x 43.5 cm) FRF 7,000.

SEGAWA, Kazu
Japanese, 20th - 21st century.
Born 1949, in Kobe.
Since 1978 active in France.
Painter. Landscapes, urban landscapes.
Kazu Segawa paints the landscapes of the south or the banks of the Marne. He has shown his works in personal exhibitions including 1986, 1989 and 1991 at the Tokyu Gallery in Yokohama, in 1989 at the Chalgrin Gallery in Paris, in 1990 at the Alias Gallery in Paris, in 1992 at the Emon Gallery in Tokyo and in 1993 at the Triangle Gallery in Paris.

SÉGÉ, Alexandre
French, 19th century.
Born 1818, in Paris; died 27 October 1885, in Coubron (Seine-St-Denis).
Painter, engraver. Waterscapes, landscapes.
Alexandre Ségé was a pupil of Léon Cogniet and Camille Flers at the École des Beaux-Arts in Paris.

His work was first shown at the Paris Salon in 1844 and he exhibited his etchings there for the first time in 1855. He won a second-class medal in 1873 and a third-class medal at the Exposition Universelle of 1878. He was made a Chevalier of the Légion d'Honneur in 1874.

He chose as his subjects landscape views of Beauce, northwest France, and the banks of the River Oise. He began making etchings of a number of his own landscapes in 1848.

MUSEUMS AND GALLERIES:
AMIENS (Mus. de Picardie): *After the Rains* - CHARTRES: *Rocks at Piégud; In Chartres Country* - PÉRIGUEUX: *Panorama of Paris* - RENNES: *Pines at Plédélioc.*

AUCTION RECORDS:
PARIS, 1879, *The Chartres Plain,* FRF 1,620; *Field of Carnations,* FRF 490; *Country Valley,* FRF 720; *Wild Grasses,* FRF 550. PARIS, 2 April 1897, *By the Sea,* FRF 325. PARIS, 4-5 Dec 1918, *Landscape,* FRF 110. PARIS, 28 March 1927, *Return to the Village,* FRF 330. PARIS, 14 April 1937, *Village by the Water's Edge,* FRF 300. PARIS, 24 May 1944, *Valley,* FRF 1,250. PARIS, 28 March 1945, *Landscape,* FRF 1,600. PARIS, 31 Jan 1949, *Excursion High up in the Mountains,* FRF 8,500. PARIS, 11 Dec 1950, *Hunters,* FRF 500. NEW YORK, 2 May 1979, *Flock in a Riverscape* (oil on canvas, 19 3/4 x 30 1/2 ins / 50.2 x 77.5 cm) USD 1,800.

SEGEBARTH, Ludwig
German, 20th century.
Born 24 September 1879, in Stettin (now Szczecin, Poland).
Painter, draughtsman, writer.
Ludwig Segebarth was a pupil of Schlabitz and Müller-Schönfeld.

SEGELCKE, Severin
Norwegian, 19th - 20th century.
Born 12 July 1867, in Christiania (now Oslo); died 1940.
Painter, engraver. Portraits, landscapes.
Severin Segelcke studied in Paris under Roll.

SEGELLON
French, 18th - 19th century.
Painter.
Segellon figures in annual auction records.

AUCTION RECORDS:
PARIS, 13 June 1947, *Inside a Sheepfold* (1797) FRF 12,800.

SEGEN. See **SEEGEN**

SEGEN VON SECHTEN, Ludwig.
See **SIEGEN VON SECHTEN**

SEGENSCHMID, Conrad
German, 15th century.
Active in Heimenkirch near Lindau in the middle of the 15th century.
Illuminator, calligrapher.
The Prints Department of Berlin has a *War of Troy* illuminated by Segenschmid.

SEGER, Anna, or Seghers or Segher
Flemish School, 16th century.
Died before 1566.
Active in Antwerp c. 1550.
Miniaturist.
In his interesting *Dictionary of the Miniaturists* Bradley says that Anna Seger was probably the daughter of Daniel Seghers. This is mistaken, because the famous Antwerp Jesuit was not born until 1590. It could be that she was Pieter Seghers's sister, though there is no documentary evidence to support such a hypothesis. It has even been thought she was the daughter of an Antwerp doctor. Anna Seger had a considerable reputation in her own time. The Liechtenstein Gallery of Vienna has several pen drawings that bear her signature.

SEGER, Ernst
German, 19th - 20th century.
Born 18 September 1868, in Neurode, Silesia; died 1939.
Sculptor, medallist. Statues, busts, monuments.
Ernst Seger was a pupil of Christian Behrens; he sculpted war memorials.

MUSEUMS AND GALLERIES:
COLOGNE (Wallraf-Richartz Mus.): *Wrestler* - KARLSRUHE (Staatliche Kunsthalle): *Mignon and Felix* - WROCLAW (Muz. Narodowe): *Bust of a Young Woman; Young Roman; Female Centaur and Satyrs; Nude.*

AUCTION RECORDS:
COLOGNE, 24 June 1983, *Bathers* (1906, bronze, h. 29 1/2 ins / 75 cm) DEM 3,600. MONTREAL, 7 Dec 1995, *Salome* (bronze, h. 11 ins / 28 cm) CAD 1,600. WARSAW, 30 May 1999, *Young Girl* (c. 1910, patinated bronze, h. 30 ins / 75 cm) PLN 16,000. BERLIN, 18 Sept 1999, *Female Nude* (c. 1900, alabaster, h. 11 ins / 29 cm) DEM 3,600. MUNICH, 18 Nov 2000, *Phryne* (ivory and bronze, h. 11 ins / 27cm) DEM 15,000. STOCKHOLM, 5 Dec 2000, *Woman Dancing* (marble, h. 69 ins / 175 cm) SEK 90,000. AHLDEN, 5 May 2001, *Phryne* (marble and patinated bronze, h. 8 ins / 21 cm) DEM 14,000. FLORIDA, 14 Jan 2002, *Dancer* (ivory and marble, h. 10 ins / 25 cm) USD 2,000. COLOGNE, 9 March 2002, *Fauns Fighting* (1921, patinated bronze, 22 x 12x6 ins / 55 x 31x14 cm) EUR 3,500. HAMBURG, 4 Dec 2003, *Dancer* (brown patinated bronze, h. 18 ins / 45 cm) EUR 1,600. HAMBURG, 4 Dec 2003, *Young Woman* (alabaster and ivory, h. 8 ins / 21 cm) EUR 2,200. LONDON, 9 Nov

2004, *Standing Nude* (white marble, h. 23 ins / 59 cm) GBP 1,900. HARROGATE, 25 Nov 2004, *Semi-nude Female* (bronze and alabaster, h. 24 ins / 61 cm) GBP 2,800.

SEGER, Hermann August
German, 19th century.
Born 26 December 1839, in Poznan, Poland; died 30 November 1893, in Berlin.
Ceramicist.

Hermann August Seger was director of the Research Department of the Royal Porcelain Factory (KPM) in Berlin from 1878 and saw its evolution. He invented a procedure known under the name of 'Seger porcelain' which allows the use of a vast palette of fluid colours in decoration inclined towards abstract art.

BIBLIOGRAPHY:
Hecht, H./Cramer, E./Bleininger, Albert (ed.), *The collected writings of Hermann August Seger*, American Ceramic Society, Easton (Pa), 1902.

MUSEUMS AND GALLERIES:
CLEVELAND (MA): *Vase* (1900).

SEGER, Josef
Austrian, 20th century.
Born 12 June 1908, in Alt-Karlsthal.
Active in Vienna.
Engraver.

Josef Seger was a pupil of Alfred Cossmann.

SEGER, Martin
German, 16th century.
Died after 1580.
Active in Würzburg.
Painter.

Martin Seger worked for the cathedral and Town Hall of Würzburg.

SEGER, Paul. See **SEEGER**

SEGERMAN, Jan
Dutch, 17th century.
Active in Utrecht 1611-1619.
Painter.

SEGERS. See also **SEGHERS**

SEGERS, Adrien, or Seghers
Belgian, 20th century.
Born 1876; died 1951, in Rouen.
Active from 1914 in France.
Painter. Landscapes, waterscapes.

Adrien Segers moved to the region around Rouen in 1914 and painted views of the Seine.

AUCTION RECORDS:
ROUEN, 22 March 1981, *St-Romain Festival, Rouen* (1923, oil on canvas, 23 1/2 x 28 3/4 ins / 60 x 73 cm) FRF 10,000. ROUEN, 15 Dec 1985, *St-Maclou Gate, Rouen* (1937, oil on canvas, 21 1/4 x 18 ins / 54 x 46 cm) FRF 15,000. PARIS, 25 March 1991, *Ru Ruissel, Rouen* (oil on canvas, 28 3/4 x 23 1/2 ins / 73 x 60 cm) FRF 16,000. PARIS, 19 Nov 1995, *Barges on the Seine* (oil on panel, 9 x 16 1/4 ins / 22 x 41 cm) FRF 13,500. PARIS, 21 Nov 1995, *Fishing in the Seine near Giverny* (1941, oil on canvas, 25 1/2 x 21 1/4 ins / 65 x 54 cm) FRF 5,000. PARIS, 25 May 1997, *Rouen: Street Scene in the Snow* (1934, oil on canvas, 8 1/2 x 13 3/4 ins / 21.5 x 35 cm) FRF 7,500. VERSAILLES, 3 Dec 2000, *Seine near Rouen* (1920, oil on canvas, 20 x 25 ins / 50 x 64 cm) FRF 32,500. STOCKHOLM, 3 Dec 2002, *Seine at Port St Queen* (oil on canvas, 18 x 26 ins / 46 x 65 cm) SEK 18,000.

SEGERS, Maria
Belgian, 20th century.
Born 1922, in Antwerp; died 1979.
Painter, engraver.

Maria Segers studied at the Koninklijke Academie voor Schone Kunsten and the Nationaal Hoger Instituut voor Schone Kunsten in Antwerp.

MUSEUMS AND GALLERIES:
ANTWERP (Prentenkabinet) - BRUSSELS (Bibliothèque royale Albert Ier, Prints Collection) - HILVERSUM (Prints Collection).

SEGERSTRALE, Lennart
Finnish, 20th century.
Born 17 June 1892; died 1975.
Painter, engraver.

SEGERSTRÖM, Abraham
Swedish, 18th century.
Painter.

Segerstrom was assistant to Carl Hofverberg in Angermanland in 1758.

SEGERWALL, Sven
Swedish, 18th century.
Active from 1714 to 1719.
Sculptor (wood).

Segerwall sculpted an altarpiece and a *Christ on the Cross* for the church of Hjortsberga.

SEGESDY, György
Hungarian, 20th century.
Born 1939.
Sculptor.

Gyorgy Segesdy was a student of Ivan Szabo, Andras Beck and Zsigmond Kisfaludi Strobl at the fine arts academy in Budapest, from 1949 to 1954. He lives and works in Budapest. Work by him has been shown frequently at various exhibitions in Hungary and abroad. In 1963, he represented young Hungarian artists at the Paris biennale, exhibited at the Venice biennale in 1964, and 1969 at the constructivist biennale in Nuremberg. He was awarded the Munkácsy Prize.

Segesdy's output consists mainly of large-scale statues, which may be seen in several towns in Hungary. At the Nuremberg constructivist biennale, he exhibited several sculptures. Although Hungarian critics considered him to be a contemporary constructivist artist, western European critics have seen in his work a tendency towards ornamental Baroque, which is emphasized by the richness of carefully polished materials, such as steel, chrome, copper, and plexichrome, often all present in the same work.

BIBLIOGRAPHY:
Hongrie 68, Pannonia, Budapest, 1968. Csorba, Géza, *Art hongrois contemporain*, exhibition catalogue, Musée Galliera, Paris, 1970.

SEGESSER, Marguerite von (Countess Crivelli)
Swiss, 19th - 20th century.
Born 7 April 1843, in Lucerne; died 26 July 1910, in Bern.
Painter, embroiderer.

Marguerite von Segesser was a pupil of Alb. Von Keller, Brunet-Debaines, Otterstädt and Dagnan-Bouveret.

SEGEWITZ, Eugen von
German, 20th century.
Born 1878, in Karlsruhe.
Painter. Landscapes, waterscapes, still-lifes.

Eugen von Segewitz studied under Friedrich Fehr.

MUSEUMS AND GALLERIES:
KARLSRUHE (Staatliche Kunsthalle): *Winter; Still Life* - PFORZHEIM (Gal.): *Landscape on Lake Constance*.

SEGGERSDORF, Leonhard
German, 18th century.

Active during the first half of the 18th century.
Sculptor.
Seggersdorf produced altars for the church of Schleiden in Germany in 1715.

SEGHER, Anna. See **SEGER**

SEGHERS, Alice
Belgian, 20th century.
Born 1887, in Ixelles (Brussels); died 1946.
Painter. Figures, portraits.
Daughter of the painter Franz Seghers, Alice Seghers studied in Brussels under Blanc-Garin and completed her studies in Florence.

SEGHERS, Cornelius Johannes Adrianus
Belgian, 19th century.
Born 28 May 1814, in Antwerp; died 1875.
Painter, lithographer, engraver (etching). History painting.
Cornelius Johannes Adrianus Seghers engraved genre scenes and frontispieces. The Plantin-Moretus Museum in Antwerp has a plate by him showing the *Invention of the Printing Press*.

Stamp of sale

AUCTION RECORDS:
VERSAILLES, 30 Oct 1983, *Scene of Love from the Romantic Era* (1844, oil on canvas, 27½ x 22 ins / 70 x 56 cm) FRF 23,600. BRUSSELS, 16 May 2000, *Portrait of a Man and a Woman* (oil on canvas laid down, 39 x 34 ins / 100 x 86 cm) BEF 120,000.

SEGHERS, Daniel, or Zeghers, known as The Jesuit of Antwerp
Flemish School, 17th century.
Born 5 December 1590, in Antwerp; died 2 November 1661, in Antwerp.
Painter. Religious subjects, portraits, flowers, insects.
Following the death of his father Pieter Seghers, Daniel Seghers was raised in Holland as a Calvinist by his mother. He discovered painting and is cited as a pupil of Jan Brueghel the Elder (nicknamed 'Velvet' Brueghel) in Antwerp. He reconverted to Catholicism and became a guild master in 1611 before entering the Jesuit Order as a novice in Mechelen in 1614. He spent time in Brussels and a year in Rome. He worked for a number of royal patrons. His pupils were P. van Thielen, O. Elliger, N. Verendael, F. Ykeus, J. van Son, H. Galle, J.G. Gillemans, C. Luckx and J. Davidsz. de Heem. He painted the floral motifs in works by his friend Rubens, and in those of Erasmus Quellinus, Van Thulden, Cornelis Schut and Abraham van Diepenbeeck. He travelled to Ghent for health reasons in the winter of 1660 and died upon his return to Antwerp.

For Seghers, still-lifes, genre scenes (often with religious themes, such as the *Vision of St Francis* or the *Holy Family*) or, more frequently, images of saints in tondo form (*St Ignatius* or even the *Christ of Sorrows*) were pretexts for the depiction of decorative flower garlands, executed in the minutely detailed, enamelled style of the Flemish 17th century. Seghers' flower garlands are purely decorative, generally framing a central image by another artist, but are saved from anonymity by his evident depth of botanical knowledge and imaginative compositional sense. The resulting works were clearly conceived as a unified whole, with the central images often painted in grisaille or dark tones, in deliberate contrast to Seghers' varied, delicate palette of whites and carmines complementing the more sobre greens of the foliage. Lilies, roses and columbines are frequently intertwined with brambles, berries and thistles. Two of the finest examples are to be seen at the Mauritshuis in The Hague (*Garland of Flowers with the Virgin and Child* (1645), with a central motif by Bosschaert) and at the Capodimonte Museum in Naples (*Garland of Flowers* surrounding an image of the Virgin). More conventional flower pieces also feature in Seghers' work, albeit rarely; the 1643 painting of a vase of flowers in the Dresden Gemäldegalerie is a good example. At its most sophisticated, Seghers' work touches on the Baroque, for example in the 1643 *Garland Surrounding a Bust of St Ignatius Loyola* in the city museum of Antwerp. The genre enjoyed considerable success throughout Europe, spawning numerous imitators, from whom Seghers' work is distinguished by its minute observation and refined sense of colour.

Seghers' work featured in *Dans la Lumière de Rubens: Peintres Baroques des Pays-Bas du Sud* (*In the Light of Rubens. Baroque Painters of the Southern Netherlands*) at the Musée des Beaux-Arts in Valenciennes in 2000, an exhibition highlighting the work of the talented Flemish painters so often eclipsed by their illustrious contemporaries Rubens, Van Dyck and Jordaens.

BIBLIOGRAPHY:
Burke-Gaffney, M.W., *Daniel Seghers, 1590-1661: A Tercentenary Commemoration*, Vantage Press, New York, 1961. Hairs, Marie-Louise, *Les Peintres de fleurs flamands au XVIIe siècle*, Lefebvre et Gillet, Brussels, 1985. Limousin, Isabelle/Ramade, Patrick/Cordier, Gaëlle, *Dans la lumière de Rubens: peintres baroques des Pays-Bas du Sud*, exhibition catalogue, Musée des beaux-arts, Valenciennes, 2000.

MUSEUMS AND GALLERIES:
ANTWERP: *Garland of Flowers* (surrounding a 'St Ignatius Loyola' by C. Schut); *Flowers* (surrounding a 'Portrait of a Man' by Gouz Coques); *St Theresa; Virgin* - ARRAS: *Garland of Flowers* - BERLIN: two still-lifes - BIRMINGHAM: *Flowers* - BRUSSELS: *Garland of Flowers; Flowers* (surrounding a 'Jesus' by Quellinus) - BUDAPEST: *Garland of Flowers* - DRESDEN: six flower paintings - FLORENCE: *Garland of Flowers with a Bust of a Man in Chiaroscuro* - GENEVA (Mus. Ariana): *Hermit Surrounded by Orange Blossom and Roses* - NAPLES (Mus. di Capodimonte): *Garland of Flowers* (surrounding a 'Virgin') - OBERSCHLEISSHEIM (Neues Schloss Schleissheim, Staatsgal.): *Roses* - ORLÉANS: *Garland of Flowers Surrounding the Holy Family in a Medallion* - STOCKHOLM: two paintings of flowers - THE HAGUE: *Garlands of Flowers Surrounding Portraits of William of Orange* - THE HAGUE (Mauritshuis): *Garland of Flowers* (1645, surrounding a 'Virgin and Child' by Bosschaert) - VIENNA: *Flowers*.

AUCTION RECORDS:
AMSTERDAM, 1710, *Garland of Flowers*, FRF 420. PARIS, 1777, *Garland of Flowers Surrounding a Medallion*, FRF 200. PARIS, 1840, *Flowers*, FRF 360. PARIS, 11 Aug 1857, *Crown of Thorns* (in collaboration with Gerard Seghers) FRF 2,000. BRUSSELS, 1865, *Garland of Flowers Surrounding a Niche Containing a Fountain*, FRF 350. PARIS, 6-9 March 1872, *Flowers Decorating a Medallion*, FRF 960; *Flowers Decorating a Medallion*, FRF 900. PARIS, 1881, *Virgin Surrounded by Flowers*, FRF 1,000. PARIS, 1881, *Altar Decorated with Flowers*, FRF 2,300. PARIS, 1886, *Virgin and Child Jesus*, FRF

1,200. LONDON, 1889, *Flowers,* FRF 920. PARIS, 1889, *Virgin Surrounded by Flowers,* FRF 750. PARIS, 1891, *Garland of Flowers,* FRF 470. PARIS, 1895, *Flowers in a Vase,* FRF 400. LE HAVRE, 1898, *Portrait of Pieter Paul Rubens Surrounded by a Garland of Flowers* (in collaboration with Schut) FRF 3,200. PARIS, 1900, *St Dominic in a Niche Surrounded by Flowers,* FRF 400. PARIS, 15 June 1904, *Garland of Flowers,* FRF 600. PARIS, 28 June 1905, *Bouquet of Flowers,* FRF 300. PARIS, 23 March 1908, *Flowers Decorating a Stone,* FRF 1,020. PARIS, 1 June 1908, *Flowers,* FRF 700. PARIS, 24 April 1910, *Flowers Surrounding a Cartouche,* FRF 520. LONDON, 11 and 12 May 1911, *Flowers Surrounding the Rape of Europa,* GBP 17. LONDON, 7 July 1911, *Flowers, Butterflies and Insects,* GBP 16. PARIS, 28 Feb 1919, *Holy Family Surrounded by a Garland of Flowers* (in collaboration with Cornelis Schut) FRF 950. PARIS, 19-22 May 1919, *Still-life,* FRF 250. LONDON, 24 March 1922, *River Scene,* GBP 31. PARIS, 5 Dec 1923, *Medallion Surrounded by Flowers,* FRF 970. LONDON, 26 May 1924, *Vision of St Francis,* GBP 52. PARIS, 12 May 1926, *Virgin and Child Jesus in a Frame of Flowers,* FRF 3,800. PARIS, 21 June 1926, *Bowl Decorated with Flowers,* FRF 4,350. PARIS, 25 Jan 1928, *Flowers,* FRF 4,900. PARIS, 8 Nov 1928, *Garland of Flowers Framing a Cartouche,* FRF 5,000. PARIS, 10 Nov 1928, *Virgin and Child Surrounded by a Garland of Flowers, Butterflies and Insects,* FRF 5,200. BRUSSELS, 4 April 1938, *Garland of Flowers,* BEF 4,100. PARIS, 30 June and 1 July 1941, *Garland of Flowers before a Medallion,* FRF 1,500. PARIS, 5 Nov 1941, *Gardener,* FRF 10,000. PARIS, 3 Dec 1941, *Garlands of Flowers Framing Two Medallions, One with Christ, the Other with the Virgin* (collection) FRF 21,000. PARIS, 29 April 1942, *Bouquet of Flowers Surrounding a Medallion,* FRF 95,100. PARIS, 25 Nov 1942, *Susanna and the Elders* (watercolour) FRF 2,000. PARIS, 28 Feb 1945, *Holy Family in a Garland of Flowers and Fruit* (school of Daniel Seghers) FRF 71,000. LONDON, 13 July 1945, *Virgin and St Anne* (in collaboration with Cornelis Schut) GBP 105. PARIS, 20 Dec 1946, *Holy Family in a Garland of Roses* (school of Daniel Seghers and Cornelis Schut) FRF 62,000. PARIS, 26 and 27 June 1947, *Virgin and Child in a Frame of Flowers* (attributed) FRF 24,000. PARIS, 27 Oct 1948, *Medallions Surrounded by Garlands of Flowers; Virgin and Christ* (two pendants, attributed) FRF 17500. PARIS, 8 July 1949, *Flowers in a Crystal Vase* (attributed) FRF 272,000. PARIS, 27 March 1950, *Virgin Presenting the Infant Jesus: Garland of Flowers and Fruit* (school of Daniel Seghers) FRF 32,000. NICE, 13-15 April 1950, *Annunciation: Frame of Flowers* (attributed) FRF 31,000. BRUNSWICK, 21 April 1950, *Virgin and Child in a Frame of Fruit,* DEM 1,000. PARIS, 12 May 1950, *Cupids Presenting Flowers and Fruit* (1645) FRF 35,000. LONDON, 5 June 1950, *Garland of Flowers,* GBP 367. PARIS, 13 Nov 1950, *Children among Flowers and Fruit* (1645) FRF 17,500. PARIS, 25 June 1951, *Cupids, Flowers and Fruit* (1645) FRF 38,000. PARIS, 28 March 1955, *Garland of Flowers,* FRF 410,000. PARIS, 20 June 1957, *Flowers,* FRF 950,000. LONDON, 8 July 1959, *Bouquet of Spring Flowers,* GBP 720. LONDON, 7 Dec 1960, *Summer Flowers* (on metal) GBP 1,400. COLOGNE, 2 and 6 Nov 1961, *Still-life with Flowers,* DEM 14,000. LONDON, 26 June 1964, *Pietà with a Garland of Flowers* (in collaboration with Quellinus Erasmus) Gns 1,600. COLOGNE, 11 Nov 1964, *Virgin and Child in a Flowery Frame,* DEM 60,000. LONDON, 19 March 1965, *Bouquet of Flowers in a Vase,* Gns 6,000. COPENHAGEN, 22 March 1966, *Still-life with Flowers,* DKK 58,000. PARIS, 19 June 1967, *Vase of Flowers,* FRF 60,000. NEW YORK, 12 Feb 1970, *Decorated Cartouche,* USD 11,000. LONDON, 7 July 1976, *Vase of Flowers* (oil on canvas, 22 x 15 1/4 ins / 56 x 38.5 cm) GBP 12,000. LONDON, 30 Nov 1979, *Roses and Tulips in a Vase* (oil/copper, 16 x 12 1/2 ins / 40.7 x 31.8 cm) GBP 75,000. NEW YORK, 11 June 1981, *Virgin and Child in a Niche Surrounded by Bouquets of Flowers* (1646, oil on canvas, 48 1/4 x 36 1/2 ins / 122.5 x 92.8 cm) USD 34,000. MONTE CARLO, 8 Dec 1984, *Garland of Flowers with a Central Medallion of the Virgin* (oil on panel, 30 1/4 x 21 ins / 77 x 53.5 cm) FRF 40,000. NEW YORK, 15 Jan 1985, *Flowers in a Vase* (oil/copper, 10 1/2 x 7 1/2 ins / 26.5 x 19 cm) USD 22,000. PARIS, 8 June 1988, *Garland of Flowers Surrounding a Cartouche with Joseph and the Infant Jesus* (oil on canvas, 61 x 37 3/4 ins / 155 x 96 cm) FRF 80,000. STOCKHOLM, 15 Nov 1988, *Mary and the Infant Jesus in a Garland of Flowers* (oil, 46 1/2 x 35 ins / 118 x 89 cm) SEK 32,000. LONDON, 21 April 1989, *Iris, Roses, a Tulip and Orange Blossom in a Crystal Vase on an Entablature* (oil on panel, 29 1/4 x 19 3/4 ins / 74.5 x 50.2 cm) GBP 63,800. MONACO, 2 Dec 1989, *Garland of Flowers Surrounding the Virgin and Child* (oil on panel, 25 1/2 x 19 ins / 64.5 x 48.5 cm) FRF 355,200. LONDON, 31 Oct 1990, *Portrait of Prince Frederick Hendrik of Orange Surrounded by a Garland of Flowers* (oil on canvas, 36 x 28 3/4 ins / 91.5 x 73 cm) GBP 5,720. PARIS, 26 June 1992, *Roses, Tulips and Orange Blossom in a Crystal Vase on an Entablature* (oil/copper, 10 1/4 x 7 ins / 26.2 x 18 cm) FRF 1,350,000. NEW YORK, 7 Oct 1994, *Still-life with Bouquets of Various Flowers, Tulips, Roses, Peonies* (oil on canvas, a pair, each 12 1/2 x 8 1/4 ins / 32 x 21 cm) USD 28,750. LONDON, 13 Dec 1996, *Garland of Flowers and White Butterflies* (oil on canvas, 51 3/4 x 38 1/2 ins / 131.5 x 98 cm) GBP 20,700. ZURICH, 22 Sept 2000, *Still-life with Flowers* (oil on copper, 11 x 7 ins / 27 x 19 cm) CHF 165,000. LONDON, 14 Dec 2000, *Still-life with Rose, Tulips and Orange Blossom in a Glass Vase with a Red Admiral* (oil on copper, 12 x 7 ins / 31 x 19 cm) GBP 240,000. NEW YORK, 25 Jan 2001, *Wreaths of Roses, Tulips, Daffodils and other Flowers, Suspended from Blue Ribbons* (oil on copper, a pair, 28 x 22 ins / 70 x 56 cm) USD 250,000. COLOGNE, 5 April 2001, *Adoration of the Shepherds* (oil on panel, 26 x 19 ins / 65 x 48 cm) DEM 8,500.

SEGHERS, François, or Franz
Belgian, 19th - 20th century.
Born 29 March 1849, in Brussels; died 1939, in Ixelles (Brussels).
Painter. Flowers.

François Seghers studied at the fine arts academy in Ixelles and under Pierre-Paul Laurent in Paris.

MUSEUMS AND GALLERIES:
IXELLES: *Flowers.*

SEGHERS, Gerard, or Segers, or Zegers
Flemish School, 16th - 17th century.
Baptised 17 March 1591 in Antwerp; died 18 March 1651, in Antwerp.
Also active in Italy.
Painter. History painting, religious subjects, allegorical subjects, mythological subjects.
Antwerp School.

Younger brother of Daniel Seghers, Gerard Seghers was a pupil in 1603, probably of Hent van Balen and Abr. Janssens, and became a master in 1608. He went to Italy and then worked for several years in Madrid for Philip II. He returned to Antwerp and painted part of the Debating Hall. In 1621 he married Catharine Wouters and in 1637 he became Court Painter to Ferdinand. He was doyen of the Guild in 1546 and after the death of Rubens became one of the richest and most famous painters of his time. Among his pupils were Th. Willeborts Bosschaert, Peter Franchois and perhaps Jan Miel. D'Argenville and Deschamps claim that Seghers visited England, but Walpole does not mention this and the English biographers seem to doubt whether it is true.

Bibliography:
Delvingt, Anne, *Quatorze tableaux de Gérard Seghers retrouvés*, Sils Maria, Mons, 2000.

Museums and Galleries:
Brunswick: *Silenus and his Companions; Rape of Europa* - Dijon: *Descent from the Cross* - Florence: *Allegory of the Conception* - Ghent: *The Angel Waking Joseph to Tell Him to Flee* - Oberschleissheim (Neues Schloss Schleissheim, Staatsgal.): *Death of St Dympna* - Rheims (MBA): *Christ after the Flagellation* - Toulouse: *Adoration of the Magi* - Vienna: *Virgin and the Child Jesus*.

Auction records:
Paris, 1756, *St Sebastian,* FRF 24. Paris, 11 Jan 1816, *Flower Garlands Surrounding a low relief,* FRF 100. Paris, 1861, *The Virgin Sleeping,* FRF 610. Paris, 1890, *Holy Family,* FRF 1,400. Paris, 1894, *Infant Bacchus; Blind Man's Buff* (collection) FRF 480. Brussels, 1899, *Adoration of the Magi,* FRF 475; *Still-life,* FRF 6,700. London, 1 April 1960, *Denial of St Peter,* GBP 1,260. London, 29 June 1962, *Music Making,* Gns 300. Versailles, 8 June 1967, *Plighting of Troths or The Five Senses,* FRF 4,300. Stockholm, 16 May 1990, *Sacrifice of Abraham* (oil on canvas, 40 1/4 x 32 3/4 ins / 102 x 83 cm) SEK 30,000. Troyes, 28 Nov 1993, *Denial of St Peter* (oil on canvas, 43 3/4 x 60 1/4 ins / 111 x 153 cm) FRF 160,000. New York, 31 Jan 1997, *Ecstasy of St Francis* (oil on canvas, 72 x 54 1/4 ins / 183 x 137.5 cm) USD 85,000. Bremen, 14 Dec 2001, *Rinaldo and Armida* (oil on canvas, 58 x 78 ins / 147 x 198 cm) DEM 45,000. Antwerp, 18 Nov 2002, *Christ and Nicodemus* (oil on canvas, 45 x 62 ins / 114 x 158 cm) EUR 110,000. Stuttgart, 11 Dec 2003, *Ascension of Christ* (oil on copper, 12 x 9 ins / 31 x 23 cm) EUR 7,000.

SEGHERS, Hendrick

Flemish School, 18th - 19th century.
Born 1780, in Antwerp.
Painter. Portraits, genre scenes.

Hendrick Seghers was a pupil at the academy of Antwerp. The Montreal Museum of Fine Art has a canvas attributable to him, based on information contained within the catalogue.

Museums and Galleries:
Montreal: one canvas.

SEGHERS, Hercules, Herkules or Harcules Pietersz., or Segers, Seegers, Zegers

Dutch, 17th century.
Born c. 1590, in Haarlem, c. 1625 according to Bryan's Dictionary (erroneously); died c. 1638, in Amsterdam, in 1679 according to some sources.
Painter, engraver, draughtsman, art dealer. Religious subjects, scenes with figures, landscapes with figures, landscapes, waterscapes.

Hercules Seghers was probably a pupil of Gilles Coninxloo for a period of months before the latter's death in 1607, when Seghers acquired a number of drawings and prints at the sale of the contents of Coninxloo's studio. He was a member of the guild of Haarlem in 1612 and made an arranged marriage to Anneken van den Brugghen (then aged 40) in 1614. He established himself on the Lindengracht in 1619 and was resident in Amsterdam in 1629, Utrecht in 1631 and The Hague in 1633. Acording to some historians, he travelled to Italy, Dalmatia and Montenegro.

A period of time spent in the Meuse region is reflected in Seghers' work, although it is not possible to identify specific landscapes with any certainty in his paintings or engravings. His paintings are still relatively little-known; only 15 works are attributed to him and their chronology is difficult to establish. His *Landscape in the Meuse* is dated to between 1625 and 1627, featuring a group of Dutch-style houses transposed to the banks of the river Meuse. Here, the supernatural 'inner' radiance of certain passages gives the picture an eerie quality, but there is as yet no hint of the anguish and solitude expressed in such landscapes as his *Rhenen and the Canera Tower* (in Berlin), with its successive, infinite horizons and fantastical skies painted in greens, ochres and yellows. It could be claimed that Seghers opened the way to dramatic landscape, thus presaging the work of Rembrandt. It is notable that Rembrandt showed a liking for Seghers' work, for he owned between 8 and 11 of Seghers' pictures. One painting by Seghers, the *Mountain Landscape* in Florence, has even been attributed to Rembrandt; evidence of the clear spiritual and stylistic links between the two artists. Rembrandt is also said to have based a *Flight into Egypt* on a copper plate of *Tobias and the Angel* engraved by Seghers after Elsheimer. Seghers also painted two still-lifes, including a *Still-life with Book* which shows an aesthetic sensibility close to that of Van Gogh.

Seghers' visionary, fantastical engravings enjoyed renewed acclaim in the 20th century. He is credited with the invention of a new technique, lift-ground etching or sugar-bite aquatint. He experimented at length with the subtleties of different inks and papers, re-touched his prints by hand to create a two-tone effect, and created dissonant colour contrasts based on a palette of pale, somewhat deathly shades of green. He has been characterised as the creator of an 'unreal, dramatic universe' of 'chaotic landscapes featuring arid, rocky outcrops dominating broad valleys, forests, ruins and seascapes' (Jean Adhémar, Michèle Hebert, Jacques Lethève: *Les Estampes*).

Seghers' work is reminiscent of the great German Renaissance engravers (especially Altdorfer) and Romantic painters (Caspar-David Friedrich and Runge, among others). His artistic vocabulary of rocks and vegetation, unique in the history of etching, heralds that of the 19th-century French print-maker Rodolphe Bresdin. Both were fascinated by a sense of the 'inextricable', producing complex intertwined forms and a distinct atmosphere of brooding unease. The rocky strata depicted in Seghers' etchings are evocative of the Rhineland landscapes of Max Ernst.

Bibliography:
Collins, Leo C., *Hercules Seghers*, University of Chicago Press, Chicago, 1953. Leymarie, Jean, *La Peinture hollandaise*, Skira, Geneva, 1956. Van Leusden, Willem, *The Etchings of Hercules Seghers and the Problem of his Graphic Technique*, A. W. Bruna, Utrecht, 1961. *Les Plus Belles Gravures du monde occidental, 1410-1914*, exhibition catalogue, Bibliothèque nationale de France, Paris, 1966. Bouchet, A. du, *'Notes devant Seghers' et Y. Bonnefoy: 'Hercules Seghers'* in *L'Éphémère,* no. 2, periodical, Fondation Maeght, St-Paul-de-Vence, Paris, April 1967. Staël, N. de, ''*La Coupe de la phrase bonne lame' et A. du Bouchet: 'Fragment de montagne''* in *L'Éphémère,* no. 4, periodical, Fondation Maeght, St-Paul-de-Vence, Paris, September 1967. Haverkamp Begemann, Egbert, *Hercules Seghers,* J. M. Meulenhoff, Amsterdam, 1968. Adhémar, J./Hébert, M./Lethève, J., *Les Estampes,* Gründ, Paris, 1973. Haverkamp Begemann, Egbert, *Hercules Segers: the Complete Etchings,* Scheltema en

Holkema, Amsterdam, 1973. Seghers, H./Rowlands, John, *Hercules Seghers*, G. Braziller, New York, 1979.
MUSEUMS AND GALLERIES:
AMSTERDAM (Rijksmus.): *Landscape by a River* - AMSTERDAM (Rijksprentenkabinet): engravings - BERLIN (Bodemus.): *View over Rhenen* - FLORENCE (Uffizi): *Mountain Landscape* - PARIS (BNF, Prints Collection): engravings - ROTTERDAM: *Landscape*.
AUCTION RECORDS:
PARIS, 5 Dec 1892, *Meeting of Officers on Horseback*, FRF 650. PARIS, 26 March 1900, *Holy Family*, FRF 170. LONDON, 27 June 1930, *River Scene*, GBP 2,520. GENEVA, 25 May 1935, *Hilly Landscape*, CHF 8,100. GENEVA, 7 Dec 1935, *Hilly Landscape*, CHF 17,375. GENEVA, 24 June 1949, *Portrait of an Alderman* (attributed) CHF 5,800. LUCERNE, Nov 1950, *Panoramic View of a Town Traversed by a Canal*, CHF 3,200. LONDON, 9 May 1951, *Marshy Landscape*, GBP 7,500. NEW YORK, 18 April 1956, *Landscape with Windmills* (on copper) USD 2,200. LONDON, 6 July 1966, *Landscape with Cottages*, GBP 2,400. AMSTERDAM, 5 Nov 1968, *Red Cabbage*, NLG 32,000.

SEGHERS, Jan Baptist, or Segers, Zeghers
Flemish School, 17th century.
Baptised 31 December 1624 in Antwerp.
Painter.
Jan Baptist Seghers was the son of Gerard Seghers. He was guild master in Antwerp in 1646 and spent three years in Vienna, working for Ottavio Piccolomini-Pieri, Duke of Amalfi.

SEGHERS, Ludwig
Flemish School, 19th century.
Active in Antwerp c. 1846.
Painter. Genre scenes.
AUCTION RECORDS:
LONDON, 19 March 1980, *Music Lesson* (oil on panel, 17 1/2 x 14 1/2 ins / 44.5 x 37 cm) GBP 1,500.

SEGHERS, Maurice
Belgian, 20th century.
Born 1883; died 1959.
Painter, engraver. Landscapes, seascapes.
Maurice Seghers studied at the fine arts academy in Antwerp and painted seascapes of Ostend and Nieuport.

AUCTION RECORDS:
LOKEREN, 15 May 1993, *The Scheldt* (oil on panel, 39 1/4 x 44 1/2 ins / 100 x 113 cm) BEF 60,000. LOKEREN, 11 March 1995, *Cloister Gallery Interior* (1905, oil on panel, 10 3/4 x 14 1/4 ins / 27.5 x 36 cm) BEF 38,000.

SEGHIZZI, Andrea or Giovanni Andrea, or Sighizzi or Sigizzi
Italian, 17th century.
Born 1630, in Bologna; died 1684.
Painter, decorative artist.
Andrea or Giovanni Andrea Seghizzi was the father of Antonio, Francesco and Innocenzo Seghizzi. He was the pupil of Francesco Albano and worked in Ravenna, Modena, Parma and Bologna.

SEGHIZZI, Antonio
Italian, 17th century.
Active in Bologna.
Painter. Frescoes.
Antonio Seghizzi was the son of Andrea Seghizzi.

SEGHIZZI, Francesco
Italian, 17th century.
Active in Bologna.
Painter. Architectural views.
Francesco was the son of Andrea Seghizzi.

SEGHIZZI, Innocenzo
Italian, 17th century.
Active in Bologna.
Painter. Architectural views.
Innocenzo was the son of Andrea Seghizzi.

SEGHIZZI, Stefano
Italian, 16th century.
Active in Modena and in Ferrara in 1547.
Sculptor (wood).

SEGIETH, Paul
German, 20th century.
Born 2 January 1884, in Königshütte; died 1969.
Active in Munich.
Painter.
Paul Segieth studied in Breslau (now Wroclaw, Poland).
AUCTION RECORDS:
MUNICH, 26 May 1992, *Cavalry School* (1913, gouache, 19 1/2 x 18 1/2 ins / 49.5 x 47 cm) DEM 1,725. MUNICH, 11 Nov 2004, *Chinese Tower* (oil on canvas, 19 x 22 ins / 47 x 56 cm) EUR 2,000.

SEGISSER, Paul
German, 19th - 20th century.
Born 24 December 1866, in Karlsruhe; died 1934.
Active in Weizern.
Painter.
Paul Segisser studied at the academy in Karlsruhe and under Ferdinand Keller and W. Trübner.
MUSEUMS AND GALLERIES:
KARLSRUHE (Staatliche Kunsthalle): *Atelier*.

SEGIZZI, Gaspero di Cristoforo, or de Segittii
Italian, 16th century.
Died 8 March 1576, in Venice.
Illuminator.

SEGLA, André
French, 18th century.
Born 1748, in Marseilles; died November 1783, in Rome.
Sculptor.
André Segla studied under Vassé and came second in the Prix de Rome competition in 1772 and first in 1773.

SEGMILLER. See **SEEGMÜLLER**

SEGNA, Nicoletto, also known as Nicoletto da Modena, called del Cogo
Italian, 15th century.
Died 1496, in Ferrara.
Painter.
Nicoletto Segna worked for the court at Ferrara and also painted theatre scenery.

SEGNA DI BUONAVENTURA, Niccolò, or Segna di Tura or Segnor
Italian, 13th - 14th century.
Died before 4 November 1331.
Painter. Religious subjects.
Sienese School.
A pupil of Duccio di Buoninsegna, Niccolò Segna di Bonaventura worked in Siena between 1298 and 1326. Among his works are a *Christ on the Cross* in the abbey of S Fiore and a *Maestà* in the church at Castiglione Fiorentino near Arezzo. A polyptych in the museum in Siena is attributed to Segno di Buonaventura with the exception of the central part which is thought to be by Duccio, an example of the close collaboration between master and pupil. Following the fashion of the time, Segna's figures are, however, sometimes

more elongated than those of his master, as Segna was much attracted to the fashion of the time in Siena.

Bibliography:

Stubblebine, James, '*Segna di Bonaventura and the Image of the Man of Sorrows*' in *Gesta*, vol 8, 1969. Stubblebine, James, '*The Role of Segna di Bonaventura in the Shop of Duccio*' in *Pantheon*, vol 30, 1972. Stubblebine, James H., *Duccio di Buoninsegna and his school*, Princeton University Press, Princeton, 1979.

Museums and Galleries:

Budapest: *St Mary Magdalene* - Moscow (Pushkin MFA): *Christ on the Cross* - Munich (Pinakothek): *St Mary Magdalene* - New York (Metropolitan Mus. of Art): *Madonna and Child, St Benedict, St Silvester Gozzolini* (part of a polyptych) - Siena (Pinacoteca Nazionale): *Madonna with Sts John the Evangelist, Paul and Bernard.*

Auction records:

Paris, 15 June 1951, *St John the Baptist; St Dominic* (two pendants) FRF 61,000. London, 24 March 1965, *Crucifixion*, GBP 4,000. London, 26 Nov 1971, *Virgin and Child*, Gns 4,200. New York, 11 June 1981, *Virgin and Child* (oil on panel with gold background, rounded at the top, 34 1/4 x 23 1/4 ins / 87 x 59 cm) USD 115,000. New York, 11 Jan 1991, *Virgin and Child with St Bartholomew and St Ansanus with a Small Donor Figure Bottom Right* (tempera/panel with gold background, 65 1/2 x 32 ins / 166.4 x 81.5 cm) USD 528,000. London, 5 July 1991, *Virgin and Child* (tempera/panel with gold background, rounded at the top, 34 x 23 1/4 ins / 86.3 x 59 cm) GBP 143,000. London, 10 Dec 1993, *Virgin and Child Enthroned with St Bartholomew and St Ansanus and a Kneeling Female Donor* (tempera/panel with gold background, 70 x 35 1/4 ins / 177.5 x 89.5 cm) GBP 161,000. New York, 19 May 1995, *Head of a St* (tempera/panel with gold background, 12 1/4 x 9 1/4 ins / 31.1 x 23.8 cm) USD 118,000. New York, 12 Jan 1996, *St Margaret of Antioch and St Christopher; St John the Baptist and St Peter* (tempera/panel with gold background, a pair, each 8 1/4 x 7 ins / 21 x 18 cm) USD 43,700. New York, 31 Jan 1997, *Virgin and Child* (tempera/panel with gold background, 26 1/4 x 18 ins / 66.7 x 45.7 cm) USD 79,500. London, 7 July 2000, *Female Martyr* (oil on panel with gold ground, arched top, 27 x 16 ins / 69 x 41 cm) GBP 38,000.

SEGNANI, Francesco

Italian, 19th century.
Born 1804, in Sarzano (Emilia Romagna); died 18 March 1855, in Reggio Emilia.
Painter, engraver (burin).

A pupil of Prospero Minghetti, Francesco Segnani painted a *St Alphonus of Liguori* for the church of S Prospero in Reggio.

SEGNANI, Napoleone

Italian, 19th century.
Active in 1837.
Medallist, goldsmith.

The brother of Francesco Segnani, Napoleone Segnani made a medal with the portrait of *Karoline Unger*.

SEGOFFIN, Victor Joseph Jean Ambroise

French, 19th - 20th century.
Born 5 March 1867, in Toulouse; died 17 October 1925, in Paris.
Sculptor. Busts, statues, monuments.

Segoffin studied at the École des Beaux-Arts in Paris and was taught by the sculptor Cavelier and the very classic sculptor Louis-Ernest Barrias. He received the Prix de Rome in 1897 and was also made Officier of the Légion d'Honneur.

He exhibited at the Salon des Artistes Français in Paris, where he became a member. Having been declared horsconcours (ineligible to take part in its competitions), he was a jury and committee member. He featured in a theme-based group exhibition *Vénus et Caïn. Figures de la Préhistoire 1830-1930* (*Venus and Cain. Prehistoric Figures 1830-1930*), an exhibition showing the emergence of prehistory as a scientific discipline and source of artistic inspiration at the Musée d'Aquitaine in Bordeaux.

He sculpted numerous statues, busts and tombstones. *Time and Genius* decorates the Cour Napoléon of the Louvre.

Bibliography:

Lafont-Couturier, Hélène/Dagen, Philippe/Loizeau, Sigolène, *Vénus et Caïn. Figures de la préhistoire 1830-1930*, exhibition catalogue, Musée d'Aquitaine, Bordeaux, 2003.

Museums and Galleries:

Bayonne (Mus. Bonnat): *The Painter Léon Bonnat* - Lyons: *Man and Human Misery* - Nemours: *Earth, Life, Peace* - Paris (Mus. d'Orsay): *Busts of the Painters H Harpignies, Léon Bonnat, Félix Ziem* - Toulouse: *David Triumphs Over Goliath.*

Auction records:

Paris, 30 Jan 1933, *Bust of Maréchal Foch* (green-patinated bronze) FRF 300; *Bust of Ziem* (patinated bronze) FRF 700; *War Dance* (patinated bronze statue) FRF 1,300. Paris, 13 Dec 1972, *Young Woman Playing the Cymbals* (white marble) FRF 10,500. Paris, 28 March 1974, *Judith and Holofernes* (bronze) FRF 6,300. Paris, 16 June 1978, *War Dance or Holy Dance* (1905, brown-patinated bronze, h. 23 ins / 58.5 cm) FRF 7,500. Bourg-en-Bresse, 27 April 1980, *Nude Girl Begging For Mercy* (1900, green-patinated bronze, h. 70 3/4 ins / 180 cm) FRF 75,000. Enghien-les-Bains, 11 Dec 1983, *Dancers with Cymbals* (1905, brown- and gold-patinated bronze, h. 46 ins / 117 cm) FRF 40,000. Semur-en-Auxois, 17 Feb 1985, *Dancer with Tambourine* (patinated bronze, h. 46 ins / 117 cm) FRF 29,000.

SEGOGELA, Johannes Mashego

South African, 20th century.
Born 1936, in Sekukuniland (Transvaal).
Sculptor, installation artist.

Johannes Segogela's work featured in the 1994 exhibition *Un Art contemporain d'Afrique du Sud* (*Contemporary Art of South Africa*) at the Galerie de l'Esplanade at La Défense, Paris.

SEGOH, Pierre

Togolese, 20th - 21st century.
Born 1980, in Togo.
Painter.

Pierre Segoh is a self-taught artist who produces colourful compositions on unstretched canvas. He has shown in a number of public exhibitions: 2000, Togo Week at the Assemblée Française Nationale in Paris; 2000 and 2001, Salon Grands et Jeunes d'Aujourd'hui, Paris and Luxembourg; 2001, *L'École de Lomé. Artistes togolais d'aujourdhui* (*School of Lomé. Togo Artists of Today*), Espace St-Jean, Melun.

Bibliography:

Persin, Patrick-Gilles, *L'École de Lomé. Artistes togolais d'aujourd'hui*, exhibition catalogue, Association Grands et Jeunes d'Aujourd'hui, Paris, 2001.

SEGOND, Philippe

French, 20th - 21st century.
Born 1961, in Marseilles.
Painter.

Philippe Segond studied visual arts in Aix-en-Provence and worked between 1982 and 1985 in the studio of the sculptor Alfieri Gardone. He now lives and works in Paris. Paintings from his *Oranges* series are originally 'landscapes' which he has subsequently 'decomposed' to reveal their contradictory features. He went on to produce paintings in a range of silver tones, often in diptych format, where the smaller of the two paintings shows a subject's head and the larger painting shows the entire body. Another series - entitled *Post-Nuclear Sfumato* - comprises 40 works exhibited at the Renos Xippas Gallery in 1997. Here, Segond drips paint over powdered material to create notional landscapes.

He has been involved in various group exhibitions, among them: in 1990, at the Salon de Montrouge; in 1991, at *Entre Ciel et Terre* (*Between Earth and Sky*), held at the Hôtel Ephémère in Paris; in 1993, at *Versions of Landscape*, held at the Centre d'Art in Ivry-sur-Seine; and, in 2004, at *Peintures* (*Philippe Segond: Paintings*), also at the Centre d'Art in Ivry-sur-Seine. Solo exhibitions by Segond have included those in 1993, at the La Grange Gallery in St-Julie (Vendée); in 1994, at the Chapelle de l'Hôpital Charles Foix in Ivry-sur-Seine; in 1995, at the Galerie Manu Timoneda in Aix-en-Provence; in 1995, at the Galerie Municipale Édouard Manet in Gennevilliers; and in 1997, 2001 and 2002, at the Galerie Renos Xippas in Paris.

BIBLIOGRAPHY:

Katz, Stéphanie, *Un Œil sous une peau d'argent*, exhibition catalogue, Gal. municipale Édouard-Manet, Gennevilliers, 1995. Suchère, Éric, "*Philippe Segond*' in *Art Press* n° 224, periodical, Paris, May 1997. Hindry, Ann, *Philippe Segond*, exhibition catalogue, Gal. Renos Xippas, Paris, 1999 (text in French and English).

AUCTION RECORDS:

PARIS, 14 April 1991, *Untitled* (mixed media/canvas, 63 3/4 x 51 1/4 ins / 162 x 130 cm) FRF 10,000. PARIS, 21 March 1992, *Landscape with Trees* (1991, mixed media/canvas, 51 1/4 x 63 3/4 ins / 130 x 162 cm) FRF 10,000.

SEGONI, Alcide, pseudonym: Alceste
Italian, 19th century.
Born 25 April 1847, in Florence; died 1894, in Florence.
Painter. Military subjects, figures.

Alcide Segoni studied at the Accademia di Belle Arti in Florence and with the painter Ciceri. He made his debut in about 1870, exhibiting in Florence, Turin, Milan and Venice.

MUSEUMS AND GALLERIES:

PRATO (Mus. Civico): *Discovery of the Body of Catalina after the Battle*.

AUCTION RECORDS:

LONDON, 20 June 1924, *Council of War before Austerlitz*, GBP 68. LONDON, 5 July 1946, *Council of War before Austerlitz*, GBP 99. LONDON, 22 April 1959, *The Queen's Favourite*, GBP 200. LONDON, 9 June 1967, *Napoleon after the Battle of Marengo*, Gns 600. LONDON, 11 Oct 1985, *After the Duel* (oil on canvas, 19 x 28 ins / 48 x 71 cm) GBP 2,000. LONDON, 28 Oct 1992, *The Connoisseur* (oil on canvas, 36 1/4 x 24 1/2 ins / 92 x 62 cm) GBP 3,300. NEW YORK, 2 May 2000, *Suspected* (oil on canvas, 30 x 48 ins / 75 x 123 cm) USD 20,000. NANTWICH, 25 April 2001, *Prussian Soldiers Discussing Business in an Inn* (oil on canvas, 15 x 19 ins / 37 x 49 cm) GBP 3,500. LONDON, 19 June 2001, *Cheat. Found Out* (oil on canvas, a pair, 11 x 14 ins / 29 x 36 cm) GBP 7,500.

SEGONI, Cosimo
Italian, 17th century.
Born in Montevarchi; died after 1660, in Florence.
Painter.

Cosimo Segoni was the pupil of G.B. Vanni.

SEGONI, Giovanni Andrea
Italian, 17th century.
Died 23 September 1695.
Active in Siena.
Potter.

SEGONZAC, André Dunoyer de.
See **DUNOYER DE SEGONZAC André Albert Marie**

SEGORBE, Juan de
Spanish, 15th century.
Active in the middle of the 15th century.
Sculptor.

Juan de Segorbe collaborated in the making of the high altar at Saragossa Cathedral.

SEGOVIA, Andrés
Spanish, 20th century.
Born 25 September 1929, in Buenos Aires, to Spanish parents; died July 1996.
Active in France.
Painter, lithographer. Still-lifes, flowers.

Andrés Segovia had an eventful childhood, moving as a Spanish refugee to South America via Spain, Switzerland, Italy and Germany before finally arriving in France. By 1947, he had decided to devote himself entirely to painting, albeit after working for a brief period as a poster artist under the direction of Paul Colin. Antoni Clavé, with whom he became friends, had a decisive influence on him, although he continued to be essentially self-taught. Segovia's gradual evolution towards Symbolism was underpinned by a sound technique and meticulous execution. Whatever the subject matter - apples, watermelons, a mannequin's wooden head, a machine, an insect, a landscape - Segovia imparts it a subtle change of perception. His light and elegant colour palette adds to the attractiveness of his work that has been described by one art historian as 'scrupulously realistic painting that is somehow distanced from reality'.Segovia's work featured at numerous collective exhibitions in Paris, including: *Peintres Témoins de leur Temps* (*Painters as Witnesses of their Time*) exhibition, Salon de Mai (in the early years), Salon d'Automne and Salon de la Jeune Peinture. On the recommendation of André de Segonzac, his work also featured at an exhibition held at the Galerie du Chêne in Lausanne in 2001.

From 1949, he began to exhibit solo, first in Geneva, then in Paris (from 1951) and, on a regular basis, in New York (1954, 1965, 1967, 1974), Washington (1963), Germany (1967, 1969), Madrid (1969), and in Paris at the 1992 Salon des Arts Graphiques sponsored by Turner Art Editions.

SEGOVIA

AUCTION RECORDS:

NEW YORK, 16 Feb 1961, *Chair and Flowers*, USD 1,000. PARIS, 17 Feb 1988, *Composition* (oil/hardboard, 57 1/2 x 44 1/2 ins / 146 x 113 cm) FRF 21,000. PARIS, 17 March 1988, *Composition* (oil/hardboard, 63 x 50 1/2 ins / 160 x 128 cm) FRF 4,000. PARIS, 8 Nov 1989, *Bouquet of Flowers* (oil on panel, 39 3/4 x 28 3/4 ins / 101 x 73 cm) FRF 19,000. AMSTERDAM, 13 Dec 1989, *Still-life with a Basket on a Cloth-Covered Table* (1955, brown ink and watercolour/paper, 38 1/2 x 28 ins / 98 x 71 cm) NLG 1,380.

SEGOVIA, Antoine
French, 20th century.
Sculptor of assemblages, painter (mixed media).

Segovia was a painter and sculptor, combining the two in his works and using raw materials, scraps, wood, and nets with gestural paintings of abundant colours, streaks of paint and a network of marks which show the work of time.

SEGOVIA, Juan de
Spanish, 17th century.
Active in Madrid in the middle of the 17th century.
Painter. Seascapes.

SEGOVIA, Pedro de. See **PEDRO DE SEGOVIA**

SEGOVIE, Master of. See **A. B., Master with the initials**

SEGRÉ, Sergio
Italian, 20th century.

Born 1932, in Italy.
Active in Israel.
Painter, engraver. Portraits.

Sergio Segré emigrated to Israel in 1950. He studied in Tel-Aviv under Moshe Mokakdy, winning the Kolb Prize in 1961.

His early work was influenced by the expressive qualities of Francis Bacon. Later he developed a series of works consisting of large areas of primary colours. He also produced silk-screen prints.

AUCTION RECORDS:

TEL AVIV, 4 April 1994, *Portrait of a Woman* (1968, oil on canvas, 36 1/4 x 28 3/4 ins / 92 x 73 cm) USD 2,070. NEW YORK, 14 June 1995, *Untitled* (1968, oil on canvas, 32 x 21 1/2 ins / 81.3 x 54.3 cm) USD 920.

SEGRELLES ALBERT, José

Spanish, 20th century.
Born 1885, in Albaida (Valencia); died 3 March 1969.
Painter, watercolourist, engraver, draughtsman, illustrator. Religious subjects, allegorical subjects, portraits, scenes with figures.

José Segrelles Albert studied under José Garnelo y Alda and Antonio Muñoz Degrain at the college of fine arts in Valencia and received additional instruction from A. Cava; he lived initially in Barcelona and then in Madrid. He travelled to New York in 1931 but returned to Spain, settling in Valencia in 1935. He was elected to membership of the fine arts academy of Valencia in the early 1940s.

A talented and imaginative illustrator, he quickly made a name for himself on the international scene. He illustrated a large number of novels, novellas, short stories and other literary and historical works for children, together with adventure stories. Examples include *Famous Pages from History; Great Deeds by Great Men; Tales of the Alhambra;* and *1001 Nights*. Between 1914 and 1921, he provided in excess of one hundred aquatints for Salvat's periodical *Hojas Selectas*. He also contributed to the *Illustrated London News*, which commissioned several series of illustrations on various themes, including *Beethoven, Dante's Inferno, Don Quixote in Pictures, Wagner's Ring Cycle* and *Perrault's Fairy Tales*. His drawings also appeared in several American publications. He executed two series illustrating the lives of St Joseph and St Francis of Assisi, together with another series illustrating the Seven Deadly Sins (which he set against a mysterious marine background) and yet another series on facts and legends drawn from Christian writings and Roman and Greek mythology including Verdaguer y Santalo's *Atlàntida* (*Atlantis*). Between the end of the Spanish Civil War and 1960, José Segrelles painted primarily in oils, a technique he had neglected to a great degree to concentrate on his illustration work. He painted portraits of several leading lights in the new political regime (including one of General Franco) and produced various religious compositions for the churches of San Roque and San Sebastián in Alcoy and the parish church in Albaida. Among his late work, mention should be made of *Pentecost; Martyrdom of San Bernardo; Martyrdom of Zaydiyah and Zorayda* and *Ninth Symphony*.

Segrelles deserves to be remembered for his unfettered flights of fancy grounded in an ability to combine the anecdotal with the baroque.

He featured at various group exhibitions including: National Fine Arts Exhibition, Barcelona (from 1915 to 1928 and receiving a gold medal); Fine Arts Circle, Barcelona (1918 and 1932); Madrid Athenaeum (1923); Fine Arts Circle, Valencia (from 1960 receiving an honorary medal). His work was also shown in solo exhibitions in Madrid, Valencia and Barcelona between 1911 and 1967.

BIBLIOGRAPHY:

Montagud Piera, Bernardo, *J. Segrelles. Biografia pictorica (1885-1969)*, monograph, biography, Alzira, Commissió Fal-la Plaça Major, 1985. Arnáiz, José Manuel/López Jiménez, Javier/Merchán Díaz, Manuel (ed.), '*Cien años de pintura en Espana y Portugal (1830-1930)*' in vol. X, Antiqvaria, Madrid, 1993. *José Segrelles*, Gal. Segrelles, Valencia, 1994.

MUSEUMS AND GALLERIES:

ALBAIDA (Casa-Mus. José Segrelles): *Artist's Family* (1902).

SEGRERA. See SAGRERA

SEGUELA, Harry Jean Guy

French, 20th century.
Born 19 February 1921, in Paris; died 23 February 2001.
Painter. Stage costumes and sets.

Seguela trained under Camille Descossey at the École des Beaux-Arts in Montpellier between 1939 and 1940, and was taught by Mac Avoy at the Académie de la Grande Chaumière in Paris from 1942 to 1953. He designed the costumes and sets for *Phaedra* for the Théâtre de Poche in Paris in 1951. He was made Chevalier of the Légion d'Honneur.

He exhibited regularly in Paris, at the Salon de la Société Nationale des Beaux-Arts, Salon des Peintres Témoins de Leur Temps, where he became a member, as well as at the Salon Comparaisons, Salon de la Marine, Salon des Terres Latines, and the Salon des Grands et Jeunes d'Aujourd'hui. He featured in the 1984 exhibition *Vingt-cinq ans d'acquisitions (1959-1984)* (*25 Years of Acquisitions, 1959-1984*) at the Musée d'Art et d'Histoire in Narbonne.

He gave solo shows at the Galerie Chardin in Paris in 1954, Galerie Bernheim-Jeune in Paris in 1956, Galerie Katia Granoff in 1964 and 1982; Galerie Isy Brachot in Brussels in 1967, and a retrospective in 1977 at the Musée de Courbevoie.

MUSEUMS AND GALLERIES:

AVIGNON (Mus. Calvet) - CASTRES (Mus. Goya) - LA TRONCHE (Mus. Hébert) - LYONS (MBA) - MONTPELLIER (Mus. Fabre) - MULHOUSE (MBA) - NARBONNE (MAH): *Three Boats* - NÎMES (MBA).

SEGUÍ, Antonio

Argentinian, 20th century.
Born 1934, in Córdoba.
From 1963 active in France.
Painter, collage artist, sculptor, engraver, draughtsman, pastellist, illustrator.
Nouvelle Figuration, Figuration Narrative.

Antonio Seguí was born in Córdoba, and from 1950 to 1953 he studied painting and sculpture first in Argentina and then in Europe, in France and Spain. From 1957 to 1961 he lived in Mexico. In 1962 he returned to Argentina. As it was 'much harder to be a provincial from Córdoba in Buenos Aires than an Argentinian in Paris', in 1963 he settled permanently in France, in Arcueil near Paris. He taught for five years at the École des Beaux-Arts in Paris.

Antonio Seguí occupies a major place in graphic art, especially as a print-maker using various techniques: line engraving, wood engraving, etching and aquatint.

In his early period he stood rather apart from the general pop art movement of the 1960s. Not much interested in the modern urban landscape of pop art, he perhaps retained no more of it than its pleasure in drawing, its freedom from formal constraints after decades obsessed with abstraction. In common with the Englishman David Hockney, the German Voss, the Haitian Telemaque, the American Saül, the Swiss Samuel Buri, the Canadian Alleyn, Arroyo the Spaniard, and Frenchmen like Rancillac and Cheval-Bertrand, he celebrated the rediscovery of painting and its narrative function. He was more of a painter than these, both in his vision and technique echoing the monsters and nightmares of Goya, even to the extent of imitating their brownish patina. He also painted large canvases in tones of ochre, black and red, with a consummate perception of ridicule: 'Seguí the President'.

In his second period he cut figures from slabs of wood, and liked to paint these in fluorescent colours and line them up in several planes in front of a background canvas, setting a number of paintings side by side as in a strip cartoon, sometimes creating in-depth scenes with mobile elements, reminiscent of Bertholo's animated painted toys. *Make the Story Yourself* is constructed in this way; it consists of movable plates which the viewer moves and so takes part in the story. Seguí then abandoned his fiercely satirical strain and turned his attention to aspects of the comical, often ridiculous, lives of self-important little people. His figure of 'Gustavo' in his hat, his raincoat, stiff, upright, became the emblem of a society in which the individual, or individualism, is king, each going his own way, thinking others do not exist, thinking himself unique and never seeing how he blends into the mass. Seguí then reverted to a more traditional style, working on boating scenes in the manner of Degas, Manet and Matisse. He also produced a series in pastels, *Persons*, in daylight harmonies and an almost surrealist spirit. He did not abandon his typical figures, but changed their situation; in 1992 skulls began to appear in his pictures, turning them into *vanitates* or even into almost abstract still-lifes.

He won a number of prizes in exhibitions of graphic art, including the 1967 Tokyo Biennale, the Havana International Salon also in 1967, the *Latin-American Salon* in Caracas again in the same year, first prize at the 1968 Cracow Biennale, the 1968 International Salon at San Juan, Puerto Rico, the 1968 Darmstadt International Salon, and others.

He also showed work in very many group exhibitions worldwide, including: Salon de Mai, Paris; 1953, Biennale for Artists under Thirty-Five, Paris; 1961, *International Exhibition of Modern Art*, Buenos Aires; 1963, Biennale des Jeunes Artistes in Paris; 1967, *Exhibition for the Marzotto Prize*; the 32nd Venice Biennale; 1970, Galeries Pilotes in Lausanne; 1970, Musée d'Art Moderne, Paris; 1972, 1973, *L'Estampe contemporaine* (*Contemporary Print-Making*), in the Bibliothèque Nationale, Paris; 1977, Documenta, Basel; 2001, FIAC (International Fair of Contemporary Art) with the Galerie Claude Bernard in Paris. His first solo exhibition was at the Paideia Gallery in Argentina in 1957. This was followed by exhibitions at the following institutions: the City Art Museum, Guatemala (1958); Institute of Contemporary Art, Quito (1961); Museo Emilio Caraffa, Córdoba (1962); Gallery Galatea, Buenos Aires (1963, 1968); Galerie Jeanne Bucher, Paris (1964, 1968); Galerie Claude Bernard, Paris (1964, 1968); Gallery Paul Bruck, Luxemburg (1965); Kunsthalle, Darmstadt (1969); the Cracow Museum, Cracow (1970); Musée d'Art Moderne de la Ville de Paris (1971); Museo Nacional de Bellas Artes, Buenos Aires (1972); the Lefebre Gallery, New York (1975, 1977); Galerie du Dragon, Paris (1978); Museo de Arte Moderno, Caracas (1978); Galerie Nina Dausset, Paris (1979); Nishimura Gallery, Tokyo (1980); Museo nacional de Bellas Artes, Buenos Aires (1991); Centre d'Art Contemporain, Mont-de-Marsan (1992); Centre d'Art Contemporain, Istres (1996); Espace Ecureuil, Marseilles (1996); Musée des Beaux-Arts, Mulhouse (2003).

BIBLIOGRAPHY:

Cantini 69. Naissance d'une collection, exhibition catalogue, Musée Cantini, Marseilles, 1969. Krimmel, B., *Antonio Seguí*, exhibition catalogue, Darmstadt, Kunsthalle, 1969. Krimmel, B., *Antonio Seguí*, exhibition catalogue, Kunsthalle, Darmstadt, 1969. *Vision 24 Pittori et Scultori America Latina*, Istituto Italo-Latino Americano, Rome, 1970. *Seguí*, exhibition catalogue, Museo de Arte Moderno, Caracas Museum, 1978. *Seguí*, exhibition catalogue, Museum of Fine Arts, Caracas, 1978. *Seguí*, exhibition catalogue, New York, Lefebre Gallery, 1979. *Seguí*, exhibition catalogue, Lefebre Gallery, New York, 1979. *Seguí*, exhibition catalogue, Aix-en-Provence Cathedral, Cloître St Louis, 1985 (including interview with H. Le Chénier). *Seguí*, exhibition catalogue, Aix-en-Provence Cathedral, Cloitre St Louis, 1985 (including interview with H. Le Chénier). Glusberg, J., '*Antonio Seguí*' in *Lat. Amer. A., IV/1*, periodical, 1992. Glusberg, J., '*Antonio Seguí*' in *Lat. Amer. A*, vol. iv/1, 1992. '*Antonio Segui. L'Art contemporain en Amérique latine*' in *Opus international*, periodical, Paris, winter 1995. A. M. Escallón, A.M. and others, *Antonio Segui: Hombre de ciudades*, exhibition catalogue, Washington, DC, Art Museum of the Americas; Mexico City, Mus. Rufino Tamayo, 1996-7. Escallón, A. M. and others, *Antonio Seguí: Hombre de ciudades*, exhibition catalogue, A. Mus. Americas, Washington DC, 1996-7. López Anaya, J., *Historia del arte argentino*, Buenos Aires, 1997. López Anaya, J., *Historia del Arte Argentino*, Buenos Aires, 1997.

MUSEUMS AND GALLERIES:

AUSTIN (Jack S. Blanton MA, University of Texas): *El Académico* (*The Academic*) (1963, oil and industrial lacquer/canvas); *Napoleon* (1963, oil on canvas); *Retrato de Kato* (*Portrait of Kato*) (1965, oil on canvas) - BASEL (Kunsthalle) - BILBAO (MBA) - BRATISLAVA (AG) - BUENOS AIRES (ICA) - BUENOS AIRES (MAM) - BUENOS AIRES (Mus. Nacional de Bellas Artes) - BUENOS AIRES (Nat. Institute of Arts) - CARACAS (MBA) - CÒRDOBA (Museo Municipal de Bellas Artes Dr. Genaro Pérez) - CÓRDOBA (Museo Provincial de Bellas Artes Emilio A. Caraffa) - CRÉTEIL (FDAC Val-de-Marne): *Glories of Sport* (1986) - DARMSTADT (Kunsthalle) - GRENOBLE (Mus. de Grenoble) - HAVANA (Casa de Las Americas) - LA PLATA (MBA Bonaerense) - LEVERKUSEN (Schloss Morsbroich, Städtisches Mus.) - LJUBLJANA (Moderna Gal.) - LÓDZ (Muz. Sztuki) - MALDONADO (Mus. de Arte Americano) - MARSEILLES (Mus. Cantini): *Make the Story Yourself* (1965-1968) - NEW YORK (MoMA) - NEW YORK (Solomon R. Guggenheim Mus.) - PARIS (BNF) - PARIS (MAMVP) - PARIS (MNAM-CCI) - PORTO ALEGRE (Mus. de Arte do Rio Grande do Sul) - PRAGUE (Národní Gal.) - QUITO (Mus. de la Casa de la Cultura Ecuatoriana) - RECKLINGHAUSEN (Kunsthalle) - ROTTERDAM (Mus. Boijmans Van Beuningen) - SAN JUAN (Mus. of Engraving) - SANTIAGO (Mus. Nacional de Bellas Artes) - TOKYO (National Mus. of Western Art) - TOURCOING (MBA) - TUCUMAN (Prov. Mus. of Fine Arts) - UTRECHT (Centraal Mus.) - VELA LUKA (MCA) - WASHINGTON DC (Hirshhorn Mus. and Sculpture Garden): *Dona Veronica* (1964, oil/wood) - WASHINGTON DC (Library of Congress).

AUCTION RECORDS:

PARIS, 12 March 1972, *Camping Parade*, FRF 11,000. PARIS, 25 March 1974, *The Great Council* (1964) FRF 12,000. PARIS, 9 June 1976, *Composition* (1964, oil on canvas, 39 3/4 x 31 1/2 ins / 101 x 80 cm) FRF 4,000. NEW YORK, 17 Oct 1979, *Man with a Tie* (1966, mixed media/paper, 29 1/4 x 21 1/2 ins / 74.6 x 54.6 cm) USD 1,800. NEW YORK, 6 Nov 1980, *Twin Composition* (1972, mixed media/canvas, 39 1/2 x 52 3/4 ins / 100.5 x 134.3 cm) USD 2,300. NEW YORK, 5 May 1981, *Landscape and Houses* (1975, charcoal/canvas, 25 1/2 x 32 ins / 65 x 81 cm) USD 2,600. NEW YORK, 7 May 1981, *Landscape* (pastel and charcoal, 78 x 78 ins / 198 x 198 cm) USD 6,750. NEW YORK, 10 June 1982, *Mar del Plata* (1981, oil on canvas, 76 3/4 x 55 ins / 195 x 140 cm) USD 12,000. NEW YORK, 13 May 1983, *Parallel Tales* (1981, oil on canvas, 51 1/2 x 76 1/2 ins / 130.8 x 194.4cm) USD 4,000. NEW YORK, 28 Nov 1984, *Landscape with Figures* (1974, coloured chalks, 58 3/4 x 58 3/4 ins / 149.2 x 149.2 cm) USD 1,500. NEW YORK, 30 May 1985, *Three Figures and a Dog* (1975, coloured chalks/canvas, 13 x 21 1/2 ins / 33 x 54.6 cm) USD 800. PARIS, 4 Dec 1986, *Figure* (1956, brown-patinated bronze, h. 10 1/4 ins / 26 cm) FRF 9,500. PARIS, 4 Dec 1986, *Hace Poco Era Hombre* (1964, oil on canvas, 58 1/4 x 59 ins / 148 x 150 cm) FRF 45,000. PARIS, 3 Dec 1987, *Composition* (oil on canvas, 28 3/4 x 23 1/2 ins / 73 x 60 cm) FRF 26,000. PARIS, 26 Oct 1988, *Portrait of a Man* (1975, pastel and charcoal, 15 3/4 x 11 3/4 ins / 40 x 30 cm) FRF 4,000. PARIS, 20 Nov 1988, *Mirada Incandescente* (1980, oil on canvas, 63 x 59 ins / 160 x 150 cm) FRF 71,000. NEW YORK, 21 Nov 1988, *Coun-*

tryman from the Mountains (1982, mixed media/paper, 39 1/4 x 39 1/4 ins / 100 x 100cm) USD 19,800. PARIS, 16 Dec 1988, *Untitled* (23 x 25 1/2 ins / 58.5 x 64.5 cm) FRF 21,000. PARIS, 12 April 1989, *Elephant* (1972, charcoal/canvas, 46 x 35 1/2 ins / 117 x 90 cm) FRF 33,000. PARIS, 13 April 1989, *Interiors with figures* (1972, mixed media/canvas, 25 1/2 x 32 ins / 65 x 81 cm) FRF 52,000. PARIS, 20 May 1989, *Around the Revolution* (1989, oil on canvas, 39 1/4 x 32 ins / 100 x 81 cm) FRF 60,000. AMSTERDAM, 24 May 1989, *Pedrito* (1962, oil on panel, 17 3/4 x 20 3/4 ins / 45 x 53 cm) NLG 4,600. PARIS, 13 Oct 1989, *Interior and Dog* (1974, oil on canvas, 44 1/2 x 57 ins / 113 x 145 cm) FRF 50,000. NEW YORK, 21 Nov 1989, *Distant View 6* (1976, oil on canvas, 59 x 59 ins / 150 x 150 cm) USD 13,200. LONDON, 22 Feb 1990, *The General* (1963, gouache, pastel and pencil/card, 25 1/2 x 19 1/2 ins / 64.5 x 49.5 cm) GBP 3,520. NEW YORK, 1 May 1990, *Paisage Serrano* (1968, oil on canvas, 38 1/4 x 51 ins / 97 x 129.5 cm) USD 15,400. AMSTERDAM, 22 May 1990, *Marionito* (1963, gouache and colouring pencil/paper, 25 1/4 x 19 ins / 64 x 48 cm) NLG 6,900. PARIS, 30 May 1990, *Figure by a Chair* (mixed media, 30 3/4 x 22 1/2 ins / 78 x 57 cm) FRF 100,000. PARIS, 21 June 1990, *Figure in a Green Tie* (1966, pastel/canvas, 30 1/4 x 22 1/2 ins / 77 x 57 cm) FRF 110,000. PARIS, 28 Oct 1990, *The Men in the Town* (1988, oil on canvas, 28 1/2 x 36 1/4 ins / 72.5 x 92 cm) FRF 125,000. NEW YORK, 19-20 Nov 1990, *Mar del Plata* (1981, acrylic/canvas, 50 3/4 x 76 1/2 ins / 129 x 194 cm) USD 26,400. PARIS, 5 Dec 1990, *Men in the Town* (1990, oil on canvas, 23 1/2 x 28 3/4 ins / 60 x 73 cm) FRF 160,000. AMSTERDAM, 13 Dec 1990, *Bella Vista* (1942, oil on panel, 39 x 39 ins / 99 x 99 cm) NLG 20,700. PARIS, 15 April 1991, *Blood after the Accident* (1990, mixed media/canvas, 32 x 39 1/4 ins / 81 x 100 cm) FRF 53,000. NEW YORK, 15(16 May 1991, *Untitled* (1966, oil on canvas, 25 1/2 x 32 ins / 65 x 81 cm) USD 24,200. NEW YORK, 20 Nov 1991, *Blind People in a Garden* (1980, oil on canvas, 25 1/2 x 36 1/4 ins / 65 x 92 cm) USD 14,300. NEUILLY, 1 Dec 1991, *Untitled* (mixed media/canvas, 45 x 57 ins / 114 x 145 cm) FRF 95,000. NEW YORK, 18-19 May 1992, *Evil Thoughts* (1984, oil on canvas, 51 x 63 1/2 ins / 129.5 x 161.3 cm) USD 24,200. PARIS, 18 Oct 1992, *Untitled (Figure in a Hat)* (1966, watercolour and pastel/paper/canvas, 30 1/4 x 22 1/2 ins / 77 x 57 cm) FRF 20,000. PARIS, 23 March 1993, *An El Cabezow* (1985, oil on canvas, 78 3/4 x 78 3/4 ins / 200 x 200 cm) FRF 95,000. NEW YORK, 18 May 1993, *Elephant* (1979, charcoal and pastel/fabric, 36 1/4 x 28 3/4 ins / 92 x 73 cm) USD 6,900. PARIS, 25 March 1994, *Black on a Grey Background* (gouache and pastel, 19 x 25 1/4 ins / 48.5 x 64 cm) FRF 10,100. NEW YORK, 18 May 1994, *Untitled*. PARIS, 2 June 1994, *Idas y Vueltas* (1983, oil on canvas, 39 1/4 x 32 ins / 100 x 81 cm) FRF 56,000. PARIS, 12 Oct 1994, *Large Town* (1978, oil on paper/canvas, 51 1/4 x 76 3/4 ins / 130 x 195 cm) FRF 90,000. NEW YORK, 15 Nov 1994, *Dog Walk* (1977, pastel/paper, 23 x 32 ins / 58.2 x 81.4cm) USD 23,000. NEW YORK, 16 May 1996, *Untitled* (1989, acrylic and wrapping paper collage/canvas, 45 x 57 1/4 ins / 114.4 x 145.7 cm) USD 27,600. PARIS, 10 June 1996, *Untitled* (1987, gouache and collage/canvas, oval, 20 1/2 x 9 ins / 52 x 22 cm) FRF 15,000. PARIS, 5 Oct 1996, *Country Scene* (acrylic/paper/canvas, 23 1/2 x 47 1/4 ins / 60 x 120 cm) FRF 29,000. NEW YORK, 25-26 Nov 1996, *Untitled* (1976, soft, dry pastel/paper, 22 1/2 x 31 ins / 57.1 x 77.8 cm) USD 6,325. NEW YORK, 28 May 1997, *Paris Roofs* (1983, oil on canvas, 19 1/2 x 59 ins / 49.5 x 149 cm) USD 18,400. NEW YORK, 29-30 May 1997, *City Activity* (1984, oil and acrylic/canvas, 39 1/4 x 31 3/4 ins / 100 x 80.6 cm) USD 20,700. LONDON, 26 June 1997, *Untitled* (1975, pastel and acrylic/paper/canvas, 30 3/4 x 22 1/2 ins / 78.1 x 57.2cm) GBP 4,025. NEW YORK, 24-25 Nov 1997, *Untitled* (1972, oil on canvas, 67 3/4 x 67 3/4 ins / 172 x 172 cm) USD 43,700. PARIS, 3 April 1998, *Distancia de laMirada* (1976, oil on canvas, 59 x 59 ins / 150 x 150 cm) FRF 70,000. MIAMI, 10 Jan 1999, *Busy Town* (1990, oil on canvas, 51 x 64 ins / 130 x 163 cm) USD 29,000. NEW YORK, 2 June 1999, *Hurry* (1992, acrylic on newsprint/canvas, 20 x 59 ins / 50 x 150 cm) USD 15,000. NEW YORK, 1 June 2000, *Boat* (1983, oil on canvas, 20 x 59 ins / 50 x 149 cm) USD 17,000. NEW YORK, 20 Nov 2000, *After Rembrandt* (1977, oil pastel, 75 x 75 ins / 190 x 190 cm) USD 40,000. LILLE, 7 April 2001, *Memories of Isolation* (mixed media, 79 x 79 ins / 200 x 200 cm) FRF 295,000. LONDON, 23 Oct 2001, *Untitled* (1984, oil on canvas, 79 x 79 ins / 200 x 200 cm) GBP 20,000. LILLE, 23 March 2002, *Celebrity* (acrylic on paper/canvas, 47 x 47 ins / 120 x 120 cm) EUR 17,700. PARIS, 26 Oct 2002, *Landscape with Crowd* (acrylic, 79 x 79 ins / 200 x 200 cm) EUR 27,350. PARIS, 29 April 2003, *Bella Vista* (acrylic on panel, 39 x 39 ins / 100 x 100 cm) EUR 9,000. PARIS, 11 Oct 2003, *Distance of the Glance no 1* (1974, oil on canvas, 59 x 59 ins / 150 x 150 cm) EUR 13,000. BUENOS AIRES, 30 March 2004, *Positive-negative* (mixed media on canvas, 29 x 36 ins / 73 x 92 cm) USD 35,000. BUENOS AIRES, 7 Sept 2004, *Composition* (1961, mixed media on canvas, 24 x 28 ins / 60 x 70 cm) USD 22,000.

SEGUI, José

Spanish, 19th century.
Born in Pollensa; died 1821, in Palma (Majorca), Balearics.
Engraver (burin). Scenes with figures.

AUCTION RECORDS:

LONDON, 19 March 1980, *Inn Scene* (oil on panel, 11 1/4 x 15 ins / 28.5 x 38 cm) GBP 2,000.

SEGUI ARECHARALA, Mamerto

Spanish, 19th century.
Born 2 November 1862, in Bilbao; died 1908.
Painter. Genre scenes.

Mamerto Segui Arecharala studied at the school of fine arts in Madrid. In 1881 he visited Rome. He took part in a number of joint exhibitions, including the Vizcaya exhibition of 1882 where he was awarded a silver medal, the Bilbao exhibition of 1883, and the exhibitions of the national fine arts society of Madrid in 1887, 1890 and 1891, receiving a bronze medal in 1887.

He was a painter of genre pieces, finding inspiration in both Italy and his native country of Spain. His typically Spanish subjects, such as *Wedding in Vizcaya*, *A Corner of Vizcaya* and *At the Feria*, reveal the influence of the Romantic painter Pedro de Villegas Marmolejo, particularly in his treatment of bulls, while his landscape backgrounds appear to have been sketched in Italy.

BIBLIOGRAPHY:

Arnáiz, José Manuel/López Jiménez, Javier/Merchán Díaz, Manuel (ed.), '*Cien años de pintura en Espana y Portugal (1830-1930)*' in vol. X, Antiqvaria, Madrid, 1993.

SEGUIER, John

British, 19th century.
Born 1785, in London; died 1856, in London.
Painter. Landscapes, architectural views.

John Seguier was the younger brother of William Seguier. He studied under George Morland and went on to exhibit landscapes at the Royal Academy from 1811 to 1822. In 1843 he succeeded his brother William as curator of the British Institution.

MUSEUMS AND GALLERIES:

CAMBRIDGE (Fitzwilliam Mus.): *Winter Landscape*.

AUCTION RECORDS:

LONDON, 18 June 1976, *Alpha Cottages near Paddington* (oil on panel, 20 x 24 1/2 ins / 51 x 62.2 cm) GBP 650. LONDON, 26 June 1981, *Alpha Cottages near Paddington* (1811?, oil on panel, 20 x 25 ins / 50.8 x 63.5 cm) GBP 1,800. LONDON, 12 April 1991, *View of the Alpha Cottages near Paddington* (oil on canvas, 20 x 25 1/2 ins / 50.8 x 64.8 cm) GBP 4,950.

SEGUIER, William

British, 18th - 19th century.

Born 1771, in London; died 5 November 1843, in Brighton.
Painter, draughtsman. Portraits, landscapes, architectural views.

William Seguier was the brother of John and son of David Seguier, a celebrated art dealer in London at the close of the 18th century. William Seguier was a pupil of George Morland who went on to achieve success as a landscape painter, notably with views of London and the surrounding region. He was also a fine restorer. When the National Gallery was inaugurated in 1824, Seguier was appointed curator ('Keeper'). He also worked as curator of the British Institution.

Bibliography:
Laing, Alastair, '*William Seguier and advice to picture collectors*' in *Studies in the History of Painting Restoration: proceedings of a symposium held in London, 23 February 1996*, Archetype in association with The National Trust, London, 1998.

SEGUIM, Édouard

French, 19th century.
Born in Paris.
Painter. Flowers, fruit.

A pupil of L Mouchet, his first Salon exhibition was in 1877.

SEGUIN

French, 19th century.
Active in Paris.
Enameller.

He exhibited at the Salon of 1806.

SEGUIN, Adrien

French, 20th century.
Born 1926, in Pau.
Painter (gouache), draughtsman. Figures, portraits, still-lifes, landscapes.

Seguin spent his youth in Africa. From 1946 to 1950 he studied at the École des Beaux-Arts de Montpellier, from 1952 to 1955 at the École des Beaux-Arts de Paris, and from 1955 to 1958 at the Académie André Lhote. He won the Prix du Dôme in 1957 (Président Fujita).

The starting point of Seguin's work in the 1950s was a tempered Cubism, which then progressed towards an Expressionism of colour. Séguin employed a chromatic range worked in paste form or with brushes to create 'shape-colours' in a broken up space that remains nonetheless recognisable. Séguin used a variety of materials - oil, acrylic, car paint - on different supports from sheets of wood to polystyrene, and original processes such as panels composed of 'studding'. He painted landscapes of Reunion Island, Martinique, the Camargue and Holland. His drawings of the 1950s and 1960s, principally figures in black and white, in ink or pencil, illustrate an elaborate construction and rigour in form.

Seguin participated in group exhibitions including, in Paris, the Salon des Indépedants, where he was a member, Salon des Terres Latines, Salon d'Automne, Salon de l'Art Libre, Salon des Artistes Françias, Salon de la Jeune Peinture, and the Menton Biennale in 1968. He also had numerous group exhibitions abroad.

The first of his solo shows was in 1952 at the Galerie Gout in Montpellier; he then exhibited at the Galerie des Beaux-Arts in Paris in 1954, the Galerie Vidal in Paris in 1957, the Galerie Bernheim-Jeune, also in Paris, in 1967, the Musée de Toulon in 1972, the Musée de Frontignan in 1980, the Musée de Pézenas in 1986, the Musée Paul Valéry in Sète in 1991, and the Musée des Beaux-Arts-Espace Paul Riquet in Béziers in 2003.

Museums and Galleries:
Frontignan - Les Baux-de-Provence - Montpellier - Oberhausen - Pezensk - Sète - Toulon.

SÉGUIN, Armand or Fortuné Armand

French, 19th century.
Born 1869, in Brittany; died 28 or 29 December 1903, in Châteauneuf-du-Faou (Finistère).
Painter, engraver (wood/etching), illustrator.
Pont-Aven School.

Séguin initially took lessons at the Académie Julian in Paris where he met the artist Paul Gauguin. He then worked with Henry De Groux, whom he had met in Brussels. Gauguin, who also became Séguin's close friend, encouraged him and wrote the preface to his exhibition at the Le Barc de Boutteville gallery in 1895. Gauguin also painted the window and the landscape behind it in Séguin's *Portrait of Marie Jade as a Child*, of 1893, which is now in the Musée National d'Art Moderne in Paris. Séguin was one of the founders of the Nabis group and took part in its early events. He planned to launch a polemical illustrated journal, called *Chut*, as a rival to *Psst*, which was edited by Forain and Caran d'Ache. Contributors to his journal were to include Anatole France, Mirbeau, De Groux, Lautrec, Gauguin and Depaquit. Séguin illustrated Aloysius Bertrand's *Gaspard of the Night* and *Manfred* by Lord Byron. He also wrote for Mithouard's *L'Occident* (The West). Sadly, Séguin's alcoholism caused an end to his career at a young age. During the final years of his life he stayed with Sérusier in Brittany at his home. Séguin was an accomplished artist but he completed only a limited number of works in his short lifetime. Around 80 etchings, drypoints and aquatints survive, and nine lithographs are among his best work.

Museums and Galleries:
Paris (MNAM-CCI): *Portrait of Mademoiselle Charles Morice; Portrait of Marie Jade as a Child* (1893).

Auction records:
Paris, 3 March 1927, *Women in a Terrace Setting* (watercolour) FRF 205. Paris, 1 March 1928, *Houses at the Foot of a Hill*, FRF 300. Paris, 16 May 1929, *Young Breton Woman* (watercolour) FRF 250. Paris, 16 Nov 1976, *Breton Woman* (1893, pastel, 16¼ x 10¼ ins / 41 x 26 cm) FRF 25,100. Brest, 18 Dec 1977, *Breton Woman* (1893, pastel, 16¼ x 10¼ ins / 41 x 26 cm) FRF 40,000. London, 8 Dec 1982, *Apple Trees* (c. 1893, etching and aquatint, 7¼ x 11¾ ins / 18.2 x 30 cm) GBP 2,300. Paris, 19 June 1984, *Boats* (watercolour, fan-shaped, diam. 19¼ ins / 49 cm) FRF 52,000. Paris, 19 June 1984, *House in Brittany* (sketch/canvas, 36¼ x 28¼ ins / 92 x 72 cm) FRF 70,000. Paris, 20 June 1984, *The Bar* (1893, etching and brown aquatint) FRF 55,000. Paris, 21 March 1985, *Fishing* (1893, etching) FRF 5,100. New York, 12 May 1988, *Still-life with Apples* (oil on canvas, 18¼ x 21¾ ins / 46.4 x 55.5 cm) USD 143,000. Paris, 18 April 1991, *Animated Village Street* (oil on canvas, 22 x 18 ins / 55 x 46 cm) FRF 70,000. Paris, 24 Feb 1993, *Evening or The Gleaner* (1894, etching, aquatint and roulette) FRF 14,500. Paris, 11 June 1993, *The Bar* (etching, aquatint, varnish mou (soft varnish) and roulette, 15¼ x 8¾ ins / 39 x 22.3 cm) FRF 45,000. Paris, 23 June 1993, *The Cafe* (etching and roulette) FRF 11,000. Paris, 3 June 1994, *Evening or The Gleaner* (1894, etching, 9 x 9 ins / 23 x 22.8 cm) FRF 7,500. Paris, 17 June 1994, *The Bar* (1893, etching, aquatint and roulette, 15½ x 8¾ ins / 39.3 x 22.2 cm) FRF 13,000. Tours, 19 Nov 1995, *Keeper of the Geese* (oil on canvas, 47¼ x 23½ ins / 120 x 60 cm) FRF 270,000. New York, 2 May 1996, *Keeper of the Geese at Pont-Aven* (1891, oil on canvas, 47 x 23½ ins / 119.4 x 59.7 cm) FRF 96,000. Paris, 13 June 1996, *Evening, or The Gleaner* (1894, etching, 9¼ x 9 ins / 23.2 x 23 cm) FRF 16,500. Paris, 11 April 1997, *Breton Woman by the Sea* (1894, watercolour, 12½ x 9¾ ins / 32 x 24.8 cm) FRF 110,000. London, 20 June 2000, *Pine Trees* (etching, 7 x 12 ins / 18 x 30 cm) GBP 5,200. Bern, 22 June 2000, *Éventail: Breton Couple in a Landscape by the Sea* (zincograph, 7 x 14 ins / 19 x 35 cm) CHF 32,000. Copenhagen, 3 Sept 2001, *Still-life of Fruit on Table* (1904, oil

on panel, 11 x 18 ins / 29 x 45 cm) DKK 25,000. PARIS, 13 Dec 2001, *Landscape with Cows* (1893, etching, 7 x 12 ins / 18 x 30 cm) FRF 40,000. PARIS, 12 March 2002, *On the Railway* (drypoint etching) EUR 3,000. PARIS, 27 March 2002, *Small Valleys in Brittany near Pont-Aven* (wax crayon drawing, 9 x 13 ins / 24 x 34 cm) EUR 12,000. LONDON, 26 June 2003, *Head of a Young Breton Girl* (1896, pastel and charcoal, 21 x 17 ins / 53 x 43 cm) GBP 25,000. PARIS, 29 April 2004, *Woman with Figs* (1899, etching) EUR 6,200.

SEGUIN, C. (Mlle)
French, 19th century.
Active in Rambouillet (Yvelines).
Miniaturist.
She exhibited at the Salon of 1834.

SEGUIN, Camille
French, 20th century.
Born 25 May 1867, in Mulhouse; died 26 March 1952, in Brunstatt (Upper Rhine).
Painter, draughtsman, watercolourist, pastellist. Landscapes, flowers.
Seguin's home town of Mulhouse was famous for its 'indiennes', painted canvases or printed calicoes and he was initially drawn to the craft of textile designer in the Atelier Schaub. Between 1903 and 1913 he worked in Düsseldorf, also taking art classes at the Académie des Beaux-Arts. On his return he immediately turned to painting and poetry. Each of his three hundred poems, written in German, was illustrated by a pastel or charcoal drawing and this work was published in 1944. His first solo exhibition was held in Mulhouse in 1927; a retrospective of his work was shown in 1979 at the home of his daughter, Madame Hueber-Seguin, and another at the Galerie Keiflin in Mulhouse in 1981.

Despite having spent ten years in Germany he was not influenced by Expressionism, remaining faithful to the classic Impressionist roots instilled by his tutor, Corot. He painted landscapes from life, such as the River Ill near Didenheim, the mountains of Moenchsberg and flowery meadows, but also bouquets of flowers, especially peonies, roses and irises.

MUSEUMS AND GALLERIES:
MULHOUSE (MBA): *Bouquet of Roses* (1926).

SEGUIN, F.
French, 18th century.
Miniaturist.

SEGUIN, Geneviève
French, 20th century.
Died 1946.
Painter.

SEGUIN, Gérard or Jean Alfred Gérard, called Gérard Seguin
French, 19th century.
Born 1805, in Paris; died 1875, in Paris.
Painter, illustrator. Religious subjects, historical subjects, portraits.
He was a pupil of M Langlois. His work was shown at the Salon from 1831 to 1868.

MUSEUMS AND GALLERIES:
MULHOUSE: *St Clotilda Giving Alms; Héloïse Receiving the Remains of Abélard* - TROYES: *A Painter's Studio.*

AUCTION RECORDS:
PARIS, 1868, *The Magdalen Repenting,* FRF 300; *June Dew,* FRF 210.

SEGUIN, Henri
Irish, 19th century.
Born 1780, in Dublin.
Engraver (burin).
Henri Seguin was educated at art college in Dublin. He went on to produce *pointillé* engravings for magazines and periodicals.

SEGUIN, Jocelyne
French, 20th century.
Born in the first half of the 20th century.
Painter, engraver. Genre scenes, landscapes.
Seguin was also a teacher and journalist. Her first solo show was in London in 1963. She also exhibited in France, the USA, Italy and Canada. Her paintings convey the light of Mediterranean landscapes.

She paints scenes from life and family scenes, with children as the focal point. The scenes are sometimes in gardens with very gentle blue-green and pearly pink tones.

SEGUIN, José
Spanish, 20th century.
Painter. Landscapes.

SÉGUIN, Marc
Canadian, 20th - 21st century.
Born 20 March 1970, in Ottawa.
Painter, draughtsman, engraver.
Marc Séguin obtained a Baccalaureat in visual arts at Concordia University in 1995. He lives and works in Montreal, and won the Prix Pierre-Ayot de la Ville de Montréal in 1998.

Séguin produces large paintings on the theme of the rose window as a means of sculptural and symbolic reflection on the phenomenon of light. His figures on represented on a white background in a variety of grey tones, like photographic negatives, or in reverse as lighter shades emerging from the emptiness of a black background. His works are diverse in style, ranging from academic to naive, abstract to figurative, and often seem to be puzzles waiting to be solved by the spectator.

Séguin takes part in collective exhibitions, including *De fougue et de passion* (*Spirit and Passion*), at the Musée d'Art Contemporain in Montreal in 1987; *Canada 3 Perspectives* at the Fondazione Bevilacqua La Masa in Venice in 2001; and *Imitations of Life* at the Fondation MontmArt, Paris, in 2003. He has also shown his work in private exhibitions at the Musée d'Art Contemporain in Montreal in 2000; the Centre Culturel Canadien, Paris, (his first exhibition in France) in 2001; and the Jean-Claude Bergeron Gallery, Ottawa, in 2002.

BIBLIOGRAPHY:
Lussier, Réal, *De fougue et de passion,* exhibition catalogue, musée d'Art contemporain, Montreal, 1997. Lussier, Réal, *Marc Séguin: les rosaces,* exhibition catalogue, Musée d'Art contemporain, Montreal, 2000.

MUSEUMS AND GALLERIES:
MONTREAL (MAC) - MONTREAL (MBA) - QUEBEC (Mus. du Quebec).

SEGUIN, Olivier
French, 20th century.
Sculptor.
Seguin lived in Mexico for several years. He lives and works in Touraine.

In 1995 he had a solo show in the Château de Tours. He has created many monumental works in concrete, which were installed in squares and avenues in Mexico City and Guadalajara. Since his return to France he has worked in terracotta, stone, wood and bronze and made sculptures that show the influence of Mayan art.

SEGUIN, Pierre
French, 20th century.
Born 21 January 1872, in Gauriac (Gironde).
Sculptor, designer.
Seguin was a student at the École Supérieure des Arts Décoratifs and later taught at the same school. He exhibited in

Paris, at the Salon de la Société Nationale des Beaux-Arts and the Salon des Artistes Décorateurs. He was an Officier of the Légion d'Honneur.

He created the statue that decorates the façade of the Sacré-Coeur.

SEGUIN, Thomas
Swiss, 18th century.
Born 18 February 1741, in Geneva.
Miniaturist, enameller, engraver (burin).
Seguin exhibited in Paris from 1775 to 1806.

SEGUIN-BERTAULT, Paul
French, 19th - 20th century.
Born 13 March 1869, in Château-Renault (Indre-et-Loire); died 1964.
Painter, engraver. Portraits, landscapes, urban landscapes, still-lifes, flowers. Designs for tapestries.
Seguin-Bertault was taught by Alexandre Cabanel and Gustave Moreau. He spent four years, from 1894 to 1898, in the USA. He exhibited at the Salon des Indépendants from 1909. His output includes designs for tapestries and numerous etchings, and he created an album of ten stamps entitled *La Danse à l'Opéra* (*Dance at the Opera*).

MUSEUMS AND GALLERIES:
PARIS (Manufacture des Gobelins).

AUCTION RECORDS:
PARIS, 24 Feb 1926, *Landscape*, FRF 1,480; *Still-life*, FRF 1,150. PARIS, 4 July 1928, *Tulips*, FRF 3,000. PARIS, 30 March 1968, *Ornamental Lake in the Jardin du Luxembourg*, FRF 10,500. PARIS, 17 Nov 1980, *Foyer of the Opéra* (oil on canvas, 46 x 32 ins / 116 x 81 cm) FRF 56,000. PARIS, 27 Oct 1988, *Place de la Concorde* (oil on canvas, 12 1/2 x 17 3/4 ins / 32 x 45 cm) FRF 14,000. PARIS, 6 Feb 1991, *Place de la Concorde* (oil on canvas, 12 1/2 x 17 3/4 ins / 32 x 45 cm) FRF 9,500. NEW YORK, 27 Feb 1992, *Jardin du Luxembourg* (oil on canvas, 24 x 32 ins / 61 x 81.3 cm) USD 1,760. PARIS, 16 June 1995, *Homage to the Masks, Luxembourg* (1905, oil on canvas, 32 1/4 x 46 ins / 82 x 116 cm) FRF 19,000. PARIS, 30 Oct 2002, *Summer* (oil on canvas, 32 x 22 ins / 81 x 56 cm) EUR 7,000.

SEGUINEAU, Robert
French, 20th century.
Born 1937.
Sculptor. Allegorical subjects.

AUCTION RECORDS:
PARIS, 22 May 1989, *Untitled* (brown-patinated bronze with red and green tones, h. 24 ins / 61 cm) FRF 15,000. PARIS, 30 May 1994, *She is Liberty, the Memory* (reddish-patinated bronze, 27 x 16 1/2 ins / 68.5 x 42 cm) FRF 52,000. PARIS, 30 Sept 1994, *Europe and Liberty no. III* (1990, bronze, h. 19 3/4 ins / 50 cm, width 9 3/4 ins/25 cm) FRF 20,000.

SEGUIRI, José
French, 20th century.
Painter, sculptor.
Seguiri lives and worked in Spain. In 1995 his work was presented at the FIAC (Foire Internationale d'Art Contemporain) in Paris by the Galerie Alain Blondel. In 2001 he showed his work at a solo show, *Chronicles of Mount Olympus*, at the Galerie Alain Blondel in Paris.

He opts for a Neo-Classical aesthetic full of the myths of Antiquity. The subject of his work is the energy of bodies drawn to each other and tormented by desire. The rounded contours of his bronze sculptures of laughing figures and round silhouettes is complemented by gestures tinged with the supernatural grace of the ancient deities.

BIBLIOGRAPHY:
Revilla Uceda, Miguel Angel, '*Jose Seguiri. Pinturas, dibujos y esculturas*' in *coll. Artistas plasticos*, exhibition catalogue, Centro cultural de la Caja general de ahorros, Granada, 1990.

SEGUR, Gustave de, or Louis Gustave Adrien
French, 19th century.
Born 15 April 1820, in Paris; died 9 June 1881, in Paris.
Painter (including gouache), writer. Portraits, landscapes.
He was a pupil of Paul Delaroche. He exhibited at the Salon between 1841 and 1843, and won a third-class medal in 1841.

AUCTION RECORDS:
PARIS, 20 May 1926, *Landscape with Figures* (gouache) FRF 1,950.

SEGURA, Andrés de
Spanish, 16th century.
Active in Seville at the beginning of the 16th century.
Painter.
Andrés de Segura was commissioned to paint some works for an altar in the church of Sta Inés in Seville.

SEGURA, Andrés de
Spanish, 16th century.
Active in Toledo at the beginning of the 16th century.
Painter.
Probably the same as the artist of the same name active in Seville, Andrés de Segura was one of a number of artists who painted works for the altars of Toledo Cathedral.

SEGURA, Antonio de
Spanish, 16th century.
Born in San Millán de la Cogolla (La Rioja); died 1605, in Madrid.
Painter, architect.
Antonio de Segura painted an altarpiece in 1580 for the monastery of St Justus on a commission from Philip II. He also produced a copy of Titian's *Apotheosis of Charles V*.

SEGURA, Esterio
Cuban, 20th - 21st century.
Born 1970, in Santiago de Cuba.
Painter, sculptor, draughtsman, installation artist.
Esterio Segura creates installations based on communication tools and has shown his works in solo exhibitions in France including: Galerie Farideh Cadot, Paris (2001) and Espace EDF Bazacle, Toulouse (2003).

SEGURA, Jean-François
French, 20th - 21st century.
Born 7 February 1955, in Saïda, Algeria.
Painter.
Symbolism.
Jean-François Segura attended courses at the École des Beaux-Arts in Mulhouse in 1978-1979. His painting addresses Symbolist-inspired fantasies, notably featuring dream sequences and madmen.

He has gone on to show his work at group exhibitions, including the 1979 Salon de Strasbourg and the 1980 Salon des Indépendants in Paris. He has also exhibited solo, notably at the Galerie Kaufmann in Mulhouse in 1979 and at the Galerie Corinne Timsit in Paris in 1986.

SEGURA, Juan de
Spanish, 16th century.
Active in Jaca during the first half of the 16th century.
Sculptor.
A pupil of Damián Forment, Juan de Segura carved some statues for Saragossa Cathedral and churches in Huesca. He was also an architect.

SEGURA, Juan José
Mexican, 20th century.
Born 7 September 1901, in Guadalajara (Jalisco).
Active in France and in Brazil.
Painter, engraver. Figures, portraits.

Juan José Segura began to paint in his teens. He studied at the New York School of Fine Art and at the Academia de Bellas Artes de San Fernando in Madrid, then pursued his career in France. He first exhibited in New York in 1926, then in Paris in 1927 at the Salon des Indépendants. He also had frequent shows in the USA, Brazil and Spain. He was a vibrant colourist. His works include: *Madonna of Anxiety*; *My Mother, the Fandango (Portrait of Argentina)*; and effigies of bull-fighters: *Cagancho, Artis, Fuentes, Chicuelo, Lalanda* and *Valencia*.

SEGURA IGLESIAS, Agustín
Spanish, 20th century.
Born 20 February 1900, in Tarifa, near Cádiz; died 4 July 1988, in Madrid.
Painter. Portraits, genre scenes, landscapes, still-lifes.

Agustín Segura Iglesias studied at the college of fine arts in Seville and was awarded a scholarship which enabled him to spend a study year in France and Switzerland; he settled in Madrid in 1919 and exhibited at the National Fine Arts Exhibition in Madrid (obtaining a gold medal in 1945). His body of work comprises portraits of leading personalities of his day, including *José Laguillo, Luis Palomo and Manuel Soto* and *Don Agustín Figueroa, Marquis of Santo Floro*.

BIBLIOGRAPHY:
Arnáiz, José Manuel/López Jiménez, Javier/Merchán Díaz, Manuel (ed.), *'Cien años de pintura en Espana y Portugal (1830-1930)'* in vol. X, Antiqvaria, Madrid, 1993.

AUCTION RECORDS:
LONDON, 23 Nov 1988, *Kitchen Interior with Young Woman Slicing a Ham* (oil on canvas, 43 1/4 x 35 1/2 ins / 110 x 90 cm) GBP 3,300. MADRID, 9 Feb 1999, *Arab Woman with Apples* (oil on canvas, 26 x 21 ins / 65 x 54 cm) ESP 450,000. PARIS, 12 Dec 1999, *The Duchess of Nemours and her dog Teenie* (1958, oil on canvas, 68 x 49 ins / 173 x 124 cm) FRF 26,000. MADRID, 16 Dec 2002, *Girl with Oranges* (oil on canvas, 29 x 24 ins / 73 x 61 cm) EUR 2,000. MADRID, 16 Dec 2002, *Girl with Jug and Flowers* (oil on canvas, 32 x 26 ins / 81 x 65 cm) EUR 2,500. AMSTERDAM, 22 Sept 2003, *Portrait of HRH Princess Marie Christine of Belgium, age 14* (1965, oil on canvas, 28 x 22 ins / 70 x 55 cm) EUR 1,600.

SEGURA Y MONFORTE, Francisco Rafael
Spanish, 19th - 20th century.
Born 3 December 1875, in Barcelona.
Painter, sculptor. Figures, genre scenes, landscapes, animals.

Francisco Rafael Segura y Monforte studied at the fine arts colleges of Madrid, Valencia and Barcelona and under Marcelino de Unceta and Joaquin Sorolla; he taught drawing and painting in Barcelona. Segura painted a range of subjects in very lively colours, but he was particularly attracted to painting animals and, above all, horses. Examples of his work include: *King Alfonso's Horse, Showjumping Competition, Trooping of the Colours* and *Horse Transport at Limpias*. He also authored a *Basic Companion to Drawing and Colouring*.

He featured at various collective exhibitions, including the Barcelona Fine Art Exhibition (1898, 1918, 1919), the National Fine Arts Exhibition in Madrid (from 1901, with a bronze medal award in that year and honourable mentions in 1906 and 1908), the Madrid Autumn Salon (from 1920 to 1930) and the 1933 Salon Parès in Madrid.

BIBLIOGRAPHY:
Arnáiz, José Manuel/López Jiménez, Javier/Merchán Díaz, Manuel (ed.), *'Cien años de pintura en Espana y Portugal (1830-1930)'* in vol. X, Antiqvaria, Madrid, 1993.

MUSEUMS AND GALLERIES:
MADRID (Mus. del Ejercito) - TOLEDO (Mus. de la Academia de Infanteria de Toledo).

SEGURA Y ZABARTE, Elias de
Spanish, 19th century.
Born 16 February 1847, in Madrid.
Painter.

Elias de Segura y Zabarte was a pupil of A. Ferrant.

SEGUVIRA, Domenico de
Portuguese, 18th - 19th century.
Born in Portugal.
Painter.

Domenico de Seguvira gained the protection of a Portuguese minister who sent him to study in Rome. He returned to Portugal in 1810.

SEGUY DE LA GARDE
French, 19th century.
Active at the beginning of the 19th century.
Painter. Landscapes.

He was an officer of the former Royal Guard and also a painter.

SEHER, Joseph
Austrian, 19th century.
Born 1781; died 12 May 1836, in Vienna.
Draughtsman, lithographer, engraver. Portraits, scenes with figures.

Seher produced the engraving *The Fire at Wiener-Neustadt*, dated 1835.

SEHEULT, Michel, or Scheult or Suet
French, 17th century.
Born 1655, in Nantes; died 30 March 1708, in Nantes.
Painter.

SEHEULT, Robert, or Scheult or Suet
French, 18th century.
Active in Nantes 1709-1754.
Painter.

Robert Seheult was the son of Michel Seheult.

SEHGAL, Amar Nath
Indian, 20th century.
Born 5 February 1922, in Western India.
Sculptor.

After advanced study in science, and while still technical director of a major organization, Amar Nath Sehgal attended courses at the fine arts school in Lahore. He was in the USA, where he attended several arts schools and gained a Master's degree, between 1949 and 1952.

Sehgal rapidly gained recognition in India and was given the opportunity to produce some important monuments, notably a memorial monument to Gandhi. His sculpture is directly inspired by his research into Western post-Cubist and abstract styles. Various influences can be detected in his work, but although his art demonstrates remarkable originality, a certain expressionist/decorative tendency detracts from the overall effect (as with Gargallo, when he came under the influence of art deco in the early 1920s). However, some of Sehgal's works, which are more sincere and more modest in approach, are effective, such as the his *Dance of Death*, a group of small almost identical figurines differently oriented in the light.

He had solo exhibitions especially when he was in the USA; a major retrospective was held at the Musée d'Art Moderne, Paris (1965).

SEHILI, Mahmoud
Tunisian, 20th century.
Born 27 July 1931, in Tunis.
Painter.

Mahmoud Sehili was a student at the school of fine arts in Tunis from 1949 to 1952. In 1960, he won the painting diploma at the École des Beaux-Arts in Paris, and he also studied at the Cité des Arts in Paris. He practises an Abstract form of painting in rich and refined coloured harmonies, playing on effects of transparency. His sensual qualities connect him with the Abstraction of the Paris School in the years after World War II.

Sehili took part in collective exhibitions, including the Biennale des Jeunes in Paris (1961, 1963, 1965), and in a large number of groups in Tunisia, the USA, Stockholm, Milan, Paris, London, Bonn and elsewhere. He has held solo exhibitions in Tunis (1972), on the theme of Algeria; in Tunis (1978), on the Sudan; in Sidi Bou Said (1982), on Sidi Bou Said and Medina; and in Tunis (1984), on Morocco.

BIBLIOGRAPHY:
Art contemporain tunisien, exhibition catalogue, Théâtre du Rond-Point, Paris, 1986.

SEHLKE, Johann Heinrich
German, 18th century.
Born in Deutsch-Eylau, Poland.
Active in the middle of the 18th century.
Sculptor.

Sehlke produced sculptures to decorate the tomb of count Finck von Finskenstein in the church of Gilgenburg, Poland. His work can be compared to that of Johann Heinrich Selcke.

SEHLSTEDT, Elias
Swedish, 19th century.
Born 1808, in Härnösand; died 1874, in Sandhamn (near Stockholm).
Painter, poet.

Sehlstedt painted landscapes and seascapes. One of his landscapes is in the museum in Linköping.

SEHR, Jakob. See **SEER**

SEI, Paolo di Matteo
Italian, 15th century.
Active in Siena.
Painter. History painting.

MUSEUMS AND GALLERIES:
BERGAMO (Accademia Carrara): *Mystic Marriage of St Catherine*.

SEIB, Wilhelm
Austrian, 19th - 20th century.
Born 18 May 1854, in Stockerau; died 7 March 1923, in Spannberg.
Sculptor. Statues.

Wilhelm Seib studied in Vienna and Rome and sculpted numerous statues.

MUSEUMS AND GALLERIES:
VIENNA (Kunsthistorisches Mus.): *Emperor Maximilian Carries the Day* - VIENNA (MM): *Rudolf of Habsburg* (equestrian statue).

SEIBELS, Karl
German, 19th century.
Born 1844, in Cologne; died July 1877, in Naples, Italy.
Painter, engraver. Landscapes with figures, landscapes, Italian and Dutch subjects.

Seibels worked with Achenbach and attended the art academy in Düsseldorf.

MUSEUMS AND GALLERIES:
BERLIN (Nationalgal.): *Flock of Sheep* - BREMEN (Kunsthalle): *Pasture* - COLOGNE: *Livestock Grazing*; *Cows Grazing* - DÜSSELDORF (Kunstmus.): *Cows Grazing*; *Village* - ESSEN (Folkwang Mus.): *Farm* - HAMBURG: *Spring in the Village* - SCHWERIN: *Landscape at the Lower Reaches of the Rhine* - WUPPERTAL: *Cows Grazing*.

AUCTION RECORDS:
NEW YORK, 29 Oct 1992, *Cows Quenching their Thirst* (oil on canvas, 11 3/4 x 16 3/4 ins / 29.8 x 42.6 cm) USD 2,640. NEW YORK, 17 Jan 1996, *Cows in a Meadow* (oil on canvas, 24 3/4 x 37 1/2 ins / 62.9 x 95.3 cm) USD 6,325. VIENNA, 28 Nov 2002, *Cows in the Meadow* (oil on canvas, 25 x 37 ins / 63 x 93 cm) EUR 5,000. AHLDEN, 19 Sept 2003, *Cows Grazing by a Pond* (oil on canvas, 24 x 37 ins / 62 x 94 cm) EUR 5,700.

SEIBERT
German, 19th - 20th century.
Born 14 April 1823, in Gross-Umstadt; died 19 January 1914, in Gross-Umstadt.
Active in Brussels, Paris and Italy.
Painter. Portraits.

MUSEUMS AND GALLERIES:
TOULON: *Portrait of Admiral Roze* (1879, signed).

SEIBERTZ, Engelbert
German, 19th century.
Born 21 April 1813, in Brilon (Westphalia); died 2 October 1905, in Arnsberg (north Rhine, Westphalia).
Painter, illustrator, draughtsman. History painting, portraits.

Seibertz attended the art academy in Düsseldorf, and after several trips abroad, settled in Munich, Germany. He produced cartoons for the stained glass windows in Glasgow cathedral.

MUSEUMS AND GALLERIES:
TRIER: *Portrait of the Painter Franz Anton Wyttenbach*.

SEIBEZZI, Fioravante
Italian, 20th century.
Born 1906, in Venice; died 1975.
Painter. Landscapes.

Fioravante Seibezzi specialised in paintings of the Venetian canals.

MUSEUMS AND GALLERIES:
FLORENCE (Gal. d'Arte Moderna): *View of the Grand Canal in Venice*.

AUCTION RECORDS:
VENICE, 30 Oct 1983, *Nude* (1926-1930, oil on board, 15 3/4 x 22 1/2 ins / 40 x 57 cm) ITL 2,000,000. MILAN, 14 Dec 1988, *Landscape* (oil on canvas, 15 3/4 x 20 ins / 40 x 51 cm) ITL 3,000,000. MILAN, 26 March 1991, *Grand Canal* (oil on canvas, 15 3/4 x 23 1/2 ins / 40 x 60 cm) ITL 4,500,000. VENICE, 25 April 1999, *Landscape* (oil on panel, 20 x 32 ins / 51 x 81 cm) ITL 3,700,000. VENICE, 13 Nov 1999, *Auronzo* (oil on canvas, 28 x 41 ins / 70 x 105 cm) ITL 5,500,000. VENICE, 14 April 2000, *Still-life with Watermelons* (oil on panel, 13 x 20 ins / 33 x 50 cm) ITL 3,400,000. MILAN, 7 Nov 2000, *San Marco, Venice* (oil on board, 12 x 16 ins / 30 x 40 cm) ITL 3,500,000. VENICE, 7 July 2001, *Female Nude* (1924, oil on board, 19 x 15 ins / 48 x 38 cm) ITL 4,500,000. VENICE, 16 Dec 2001, *Grand Canal* (1937, oil on canvas, 24 x 20 ins / 60 x 50 cm) ITL 5,000,000. ROME, 10 June 2004, *Spring Landscape* (oil on panel, 24 x 20 ins / 61 x 50 cm) EUR 1,500.

SEIBOLD, Alois Leopold
Austrian, 20th century.
Born 21 January 1879, in Vienna; died 1951.
Painter, engraver (etching).

Alois Seibold was a pupil of V. Jaspar; he was an etcher and occasional art critic.

MUSEUMS AND GALLERIES:
BUCHAREST (Muz. National de Arta al României): *March Evening in the Hanna*.

SEIBOLD, Christian. See **SEYBOLD**

SEIBOLD, Max
German, 20th century.
Born 5 July 1879, in Stuttgart.
Sculptor. Religious subjects, figures. Monuments.

Max Seibold was a pupil of Waderès, and also sculpted war memorials.

SEIBRANDT, Ludwig
German, 16th - 17th century.

Active in Kaufbeure from 1597 to 1609.
Glass painter.

SEIBT, Joseph
German, 18th century.
Active in Schweidnitz (now Swidnica, Poland).
Portrait artist.

SEIDA-LANDENSBERG, Franz Eugen von
German, 18th - 19th century.
Born 23 February 1772, in Rheinberg; died 28 September 1826, in Augsburg (Bavaria).
Engraver. Historical scenes.

SEIDAN, Thomas
Czech, 19th century.
Born 1830, in Prague; died 1890, in Vienna, Austria.
Sculptor.

Thomas Seidan studied under J. von Myslbek.

SEIDAN, Wenzel
Czech, 19th century.
Born May 1817, in Prague; died 29 March 1870, in Vienna, Austria.
Medallist.

Wenzel was Thomas Seidan's brother.

SEIDEL. See also **SEIDL** or **SEYDEL**

SEIDEL, August
German, 19th century.
Born 5 October 1820, in Munich; died 2 September 1904, in Munich.
Active in Munich, Salzburg and other cities.
Painter. Landscapes, landscapes with figures.

August Seidel was influenced by John Constable (1776 - 1837) and the landscape painters of the Barbizon School (a colony of French painters, including Millet and Daubigny, who produced naturalistic pictures of landscapes and peasant life).

MUSEUMS AND GALLERIES:

MUNICH (Neue Pinakothek): *Stormy Landscape with Hunters; Stormy Landscape; Viaduct near Diessen; Landscape near Grosshesselohe; The Old Drinking Trough in Munich* - MUNICH (Städtische Gal. im Lenbachhaus): *Stormy Landscape; Landscape of the Pre-Alps* - PRAGUE (Národní Gal.): *Mountain Pasture by Moonlight* - ROSTOCK (Kunsthalle): *The Zugspitze* - SZCZECIN: *Mountain Pasture* - WROCLAW: *Greek Landscape* - ZURICH (Kunsthaus): *By the Lake at Starnberg.*

AUCTION RECORDS:

PARIS, 13 July 1945, *Profile of a Woman* (pencil, miniature) FRF 650. COLOGNE, 7 June 1972, *Harvest*, DEM 3,600. MUNICH, 30 May 1979, *Alpine Landscape* (1877, oil on card, 7½ x 15½ ins / 19 x 39.5 cm) DEM 8,200. MUNICH, 3 June 1981, *Banks of the Isar at Dusk* (c. 1870, oil on canvas, 13½ x 22 ins / 34.5 x 56 cm) DEM 16,000. BERLIN, 24 May 1984, *Livestock by a Mountain Lake* (1866, oil on canvas, 19 x 29¼ ins / 48 x 74 cm) DEM 33,000. MUNICH, 14 March 1985, *Shepherds and Flock by a Pond* (oil on canvas, 21½ x 29¾ ins / 54.4 x 75.5 cm) DEM 12,000. STOCKHOLM, 14 Nov 1990, *Shepherd and his Sheep by a River in Summer* (oil on canvas, 21¼ x 29½ ins / 54 x 75 cm) SEK 50,000. MUNICH, 10 Dec 1992, *Landscape with a Shepherd and his Flock in a Storm* (oil on canvas, 22 x 29¼ ins / 55 x 74.5 cm) DEM 15,820. LONDON, 17 June 1994, *Ploughing* (1884, oil on card, 9¾ x 17¼ ins / 24.8 x 43.8 cm) GBP 2,760. HEIDELBERG, 8 April 1995, *Winter Landscape* (oil on card, 9¼ x 12 ins / 23.4 x 30.7 cm) DEM 3,700. MUNICH, 27 June 1995, *Lake Como* (oil on canvas, 21 x 26½ ins / 53.5 x 67.5 cm) DEM 5,290. VIENNA, 29-30 Oct 1996, *Travellers in a Stormy Landscape* (1888, oil on canvas, 19 x 31 ins / 48 x 78.5 cm) ATS 230,000. LONDON, 9 Oct 1997, *After the Storm* (1874, oil on panel, 13 x 25½ ins / 33 x 65 cm) GBP 7,475. MUNICH, 2 Dec 1997, *Landscape, Starnberger See* (oil on canvas, 19¼ x 32 ins / 49 x 81 cm) DEM 12,000. MUNICH, 27 Feb 1999, *Mountain Brook during Approaching Thunderstorm* (1891, oil on canvas, 20 x 31 ins / 52 x 80 cm) DEM 12,000. MUNICH, 27 Feb 1999, *View of Mountain Kampenwand in Chiemgau* (oil on canvas, 49 x 60 ins / 125 x 153 cm) DEM 17,000. MUNICH, 12 April 2000, *Evening Landscape* (oil on canvas/board, 8 x 11 ins / 20 x 27 cm) DEM 3,400. MUNICH, 12 April 2000, *Mountain Landscape* (oil sketch on board, 8 x 11 ins / 20 x 27 cm) DEM 3,400. HAMBURG, 24 May 2000, *Midday on the Chiemsee* (1873, oil on canvas, 18 x 32 ins / 45 x 81 cm) DEM 18,000. MUNICH, 6 Dec 2000, *Religous Procession to Upper Bavarian Lake* (oil on canvas, 22 x 30 ins / 56 x 75 cm) DEM 9,000. MUNICH, 27 June 2001, *Chiemsee at Midday* (oil on canvas/board, 19 x 32 ins / 47 x 82 cm) DEM 15,000. MUNICH, 26 Sept 2001, *Mountain Valley with Herder and Cattle* (1883, oil on canvas, 29 x 35 ins / 73 x 88 cm) DEM 6,500. MUNICH, 20 March 2002, *Mountain Pasture* (oil on canvas, 20 x 24 ins / 50 x 60 cm) EUR 3,500. LONDON, 21 March 2002, *Low Tide. Return Home* (oil on canvas, a pair, 22 x 30 ins / 55 x 75 cm) GBP 1,800. AHLDEN, 9 May 2003, *Market* (1868, pencil and watercolour, 10 x 14 ins / 26 x 35 cm) EUR 1,800. MUNICH, 4 Dec 2003, *Harvest by Pre-alpine Lake* (oil on canvas, 21 x 30 ins / 54 x 75 cm) EUR 2,000. MUNICH, 5 Dec 2003, *Mountain Lake with Yachts* (oil on canvas, 22 x 30 ins / 55 x 75 cm) EUR 4,400. MUNICH, 17 March 2004, *Southern Mountain Landscape* (oil on board, 5 x 12 ins / 13 x 31 cm) EUR 3,900. MUNICH, 30 June 2004, *Herder with Cows Returning Home* (oil on panel, 13 x 15 ins / 33 x 39 cm) EUR 4,000.

SEIDEL, Emory P.
American, 20th century.
Born 1881.
Sculptor.

AUCTION RECORDS:

NEW YORK, 31 May 1985, *Two Nymphs Holding Doves* (dark-brown-patinated bronze, h. 9¾ ins / 25 cm and l. 20 ins/50.8 cm) USD 2,000. NEW YORK, 18 Dec 1991, *Bird Bath* (brown-patinated bronze, l. 20¾ ins / 52.7 cm) USD 1,100. NEW YORK, 9 Sept 1993, *Dancer* (1926, bronze, w. 12¾ ins / 32.4 cm) USD 4,600. NEW YORK, 31 March 1994, *Boy and Girl Reading* (bronze, a pair of book ends, h. 9 ins / 22.9 cm) USD 1,955. NEW YORK, 9 March 2004, *Untitled, Two Figures with Birds* (c. 1926, bronze, h. 20 ins / 51 cm) USD 18,000. NEW YORK, 10 Sept 2004, *Atlisa* (c. 1927, bronze candelabra, a pair, h. 19 ins / 48 cm) USD 7,000.

SEIDEL, Franz
German, 19th century.
Born 1818, in Munich; died 14 June 1903, in Munich.
Landscape artist.

Franz Seidel was the brother of August. He was influenced by K. Rottmann.

MUSEUMS AND GALLERIES:

MUNICH (Städtische Gal. im Lenbachhaus): *Stormy Landscape.*

SEIDEL, Gustav
German, 19th century.
Born 28 April 1819, in Berlin; died 19 July 1901, in Rüdersdorf, near Berlin.
Engraver, painter, miniaturist.

Gustav Seidel attended the art academies of Berlin, Buchhorn and Mandel.

SEIDEL, H. von
German, 19th century.
Active c. 1820.
Draughtsman, miniaturist, lithographer. Military portraits.

Von Seidel drew portraits of Russian generals.

SEIDEL, Julie
German, 19th century.
Born 13 May 1791, in Weimar.
Painter.

Julie Seidel studied under Karl Lieber. She exhibited in Weimar from 1818 to 1823.

SEIDEL, Oskar
German, 19th century.
Born 1845, in Löwenberg, Switzerland; died 31 March 1900, in Dresden-Blasewitz.
Painter, illustrator. Figures, landscapes.
Oskar Seidel studied under Julius Schrader.
AUCTION RECORDS:
NEW YORK, 14 Jan 1977, *Riverbanks* (oil on canvas, 18½ x 26½ ins / 47 x 67 cm) USD 1,300. HANOVER, 7 May 1983, *Woman Goatherd and Children in a Landscape* (oil on canvas, 23 x 38¼ ins / 57.5 x 97 cm) DEM 3,800.

SEIDEL, Urban
German, 17th century.
Born in Naumburg-am-Queis (Schlesien).
Active during the second half of the 17th century.
Sculptor.
Urban Seidel produced a sculpture of a crown, which was placed on the tower of Breslau cathedral (now Wroclaw, Poland).

SEIDEL, Wilhelm or Christoph Wilhelm, or Seydel
German, 18th century.
Died December 1761, in Breslau (now Wroclaw, Poland).
Active in Breslau.
Portrait artist.
Wilhelm Seidel attended the art academy in Vienna.
MUSEUMS AND GALLERIES:
WROCLAW (Muz. Narodowe): *Portrait of Johann Heinrich Naumann.*

SEIDELIN, Ingeborg
Danish, 20th century.
Born 30 October 1872, in Copenhagen; died 2 February 1914, in Copenhagen.
Painter. Figures, portraits.
Ingeborg Seidelin was a pupil of Luplau Janssen.
MUSEUMS AND GALLERIES:
AARHUS: *Portrait of K. Hansen-Reistrup, Painter.*

SEIDELMANN. See **SEYDELMANN**

SEIDENBEUTEL, Efroim
Polish, 20th century.
Born 17 June 1903, in Warsaw.
Painter.
Efroim Seidenbeutel was the twin brother of Menasze Seidenbeutel. He studied in Warsaw and Paris, and worked together with his twin. All their paintings are signed with both their names.
MUSEUMS AND GALLERIES:
EDINBURGH - KATOWICE - LÓDZ - MOSCOW.

SEIDENBEUTEL, Josef
Polish, 20th century.
Born 24 October 1894, in Warsaw; died 15 June 1923, in Otwock.
Painter.
Josef Seidenbeutel was a student of St Lentz at the fine arts academy in Warsaw.

SEIDENBEUTEL, Menasze
Polish, 20th century.
Born 17 June 1903, in Warsaw.
Painter. Portraits, landscapes, still-lifes.
Menasze Seidenbeutel was the twin brother and collaborator of Efroim Seidenbeutel.

SEIDENBUSCH, Johann Georg
German, 17th - 18th century.
Born 5 April 1641, in Munich; died 10 December 1729, in Aufhausen.
Painter, poet. Religious subjects.
Seidenbusch was a priest and studied under Sandrart.

SEIDL. See also **SEIDEL** and **SEYDEL**

SEIDL, Alois
German, 20th century.
Born 4 November 1897, in Munich; died 1970.
Painter. Landscapes.
Alois Seidl was self-taught.
MUSEUMS AND GALLERIES:
MUNICH (Städtische Gal. im Lenbachhaus).

SEIDL, Andreas von
German, 18th - 19th century.
Born 1760, in Munich; died 1834, in Munich.
Painter, engraver, lithographer, draughtsman.
Religious subjects, academic studies.
Von Seidl was sent to Rome by the Elector of Bavaria where he won the award of the Accademia di S Luca. He became a member of the art academies of Bologna and Parma in Italy, and in Munich was appointed court painter and a teacher at the academy.
AUCTION RECORDS:
MUNICH, 26 May 1992, *The Good Samaritan* (1791, pen and wash, 7 x 9 ins / 18 x 22 cm) DEM 1,035.

SEIDL, J. M.
German, 18th century.
Active in Deggendorf in the middle of the 18th century.
Painter.
J. M. Seidl produced paintings for the church of Deggendorf in 1748.

SEIDL, Johann
Austrian, 19th century.
Born 1776, in Graz; died 1838, in Budapest, Hungary.
Engraver (burin).

SEIDL, Josef
Austrian, 18th century.
Born 1727; died 24 April 1764, in Vienna.
Painter, miniaturist.
Josef Seidl produced paintings for the church of Gratzen, Austria.

SEIDL, Karl. See **SCHEIDL**

SEIDL, Karl
German, 18th century.
Born 1714; died 1782.
Active in Munich.
Draughtsman, engraver (etching), architect.
Landscapes.

SEIDL, Matthias
German, 17th - 18th century.
Sculptor (wood).
Matthias Seidl carved a pulpit for the church of Hausen (Lower Bavaria), Germany, in 1689, and stalls for the church of Greding (Bavaria), Germany, in 1702.

SEIDL, Michael. See **STEIDL Melchior Michael** or **Martin Melchior**

SEIDLER, Hermann
German, 19th - 20th century.
Born 18 April 1864, in Engen (Baden); died 21 March 1935, in Donauwörth.
Painter, potter.
Hermann Seidler was the brother of Julius Seidler.

SEIDLER, Johann Peter, or Seydler
German, 18th century.
Active in Würzburg (Bavaria) 1700-1715.

Stucco artist.

Johann Seidler carried out work in the summer pavilion of the St Julius Hospital in Würzburg.

SEIDLER, Julius

German, 19th - 20th century.

Born 24 February 1867, in Constance (Baden-Württemberg).

Sculptor.

Brother of Hermann Seidler, Julius Seidler studied under Rümann in Munich and under A. Pruschka, sculpting numerous statues, low reliefs and tombs, chiefly in and around Munich.

SEIDLER, Louise Caroline Sophie or Caroline Louise

German, 19th century.

Born 15 May 1786, in Jena; died 7 October 1866, in Weimar.

Painter, writer. Historical subjects, portraits, mythological subjects, romantic scenes.

Louise Seidler studied under Roue and Goethe (who was an excellent draughtsman), and from 1818 to 1823 was in Italy, where she copied Raphael and Perugino. On her return to Weimar, she became teacher to the princesses Maria and Augusta, and in 1824, was appointed curator of Weimar Gallery. Among her numerous portraits was one of *Goethe*.

MUSEUMS AND GALLERIES:

ALTENBURG: *Portrait of Baron Bernhard von Lindenau* - DRESDEN (Prints Collection): *Portraits of Angelika Facius* - WEIMAR (Goethe-Nationalmus.): *Portrait of Goethe; Alma von Goethe; Minna Herzlieb; B.G. Niebuhr; Figures on the Pediment of the Temple of Phigalia; Raffael Mengs* - WEIMAR (Schlossmus.): *Portraits of Minna Herzlieb and Friedrich Johann Fromann, B.G. Niebuhr and his Wife; Odysseus Arriving on the Island of the Sirens.*

SEIDLER, Lukas

German, 17th century.

Died 1630.

Active in Biberach (Baden-Württemberg).

Painter. Urban landscapes. Coats of arms.

The *Chronicle of Biberach*, which is in Biberach's municipal museum, contains paintings of town views and coats of arms by Lukas Seidler.

MUSEUMS AND GALLERIES:

BIBERACH (Municipal Mus.): *Chronicle of Biberach*.

SEIDLITZ, Johann Georg

Austrian, 18th century.

Born in Koblenz, Germany.

Active during the first half of the 18th century, in Vienna.

Cameo engraver, medallist.

Seidlitz worked for the House of Austria.

SEIDLITZ, Nelly von

Maiden name: von Eichler

German, 20th century.

Born 25 March 1870, in St Petersburg.

Active in Ebenhausen (Bavaria).

Painter, sculptor, engraver. Figures, portraits.

Nelly von Seidlitz was a self-taught artist influenced by the work of Slevogt.

SEIDLMAIR, Georg

Austrian, 17th century.

Sculptor. Religious subjects.

Active in 1628, Seidlmair produced altars for the churches of the southern Tyrol.

SEIF, Guity

20th century.

Painter.

Guity Seif held a solo exhibition at the Blenheim-Jeune Gallery in Paris in 1987.

SEIF, Linus, or Seiff

German, 18th century.

Active in Kempten (Bavaria) during the second half of the 18th century.

Painter. Religious subjects. Decorative schemes.

MUSEUMS AND GALLERIES:

KEMPTEN (Municipal Mus.): *Crucifixion*.

SEIFER, Lienhart. See **SEYFER**

SEIFERT, Alfred

Bohemian School, 19th century.

Born 6 September 1850, in Horovice; died 4 February 1901, in Munich.

Painter. Nudes, portraits, genre scenes.

Alfred Seifert studied under Kirnig in Prague, and was taught by Strähuber, Echter and Raab at the academy in Munich. His works include *Oberon, Titania*, and *Autumn Time*.

Alfred Seifert

MUSEUMS AND GALLERIES:

PRAGUE: *Philippine Welser*.

AUCTION RECORDS:

NEW YORK, 1-2 March 1906, *Head of a Young Girl*, USD 100. NEW YORK, 12-14 March 1906, *A Model Head*, USD 100. NEW YORK, 8 Feb 1935, *Harvest Festival*, USD 210. NEW YORK, 2 April 1976, *Water Carrier; Young Girl with a Basket* (oil on panel, a pair, 17 3/4 x 9 3/4 ins / 45 x 25 cm) USD 1,500. LONDON, 10 Feb 1978, *Portrait of a Young Girl* (oil on panel, 19 x 15 1/4 ins / 48.3 x 38.5 cm) GBP 2,200. LONDON, 9 May 1979, *Summer Flowers* (oil on panel, 19 3/4 x 9 3/4 ins / 50 x 25 cm) GBP 800. NEW YORK, 25 Feb 1983, *Harvest Festival* (oil on canvas, 39 1/2 x 63 1/2 ins / 100.3 x 161.2 cm) USD 30,000. NEW YORK, 30 Oct 1985, *Classic Head* (oil on panel, 13 x 9 1/4 ins / 32.1 x 23.7 cm) USD 1,900. MONACO, 2 Dec 1989, *Sleeping Beauty* (1874, oil on canvas, 34 1/4 x 52 3/4 ins / 87 x 134 cm) FRF 166,500. LONDON, 14 Feb 1990, *Standing Nude* (oil on canvas, 33 1/2 x 24 1/4 ins / 85 x 61.5 cm) GBP 4,950. NEW YORK, 22 May 1990, *Young Beauty on the Steps of a Portal* (oil on canvas, 45 1/4 x 28 ins / 115 x 71.1 cm) USD 18,700. PARIS, 24 May 1991, *Dreaming* (oil on panel, 16 1/2 x 12 1/2 ins / 42 x 32 cm) FRF 25,000. NEW YORK, 15 Oct 1991, *Young Beauty* (oil on panel, 5 1/4 x 4 1/4 ins / 13.5 x 10.5 cm) USD 1,980. AMSTERDAM, 30 Oct 1991, *Dreaming* (oil on canvas, 46 x 39 3/4 ins / 116 x 101 cm) NLG 17,250. LONDON, 15 June 1994, *Promenade* (oil on panel, 20 3/4 x 12 ins / 53 x 30.5 cm) GBP 4,830. LONDON, 9 Oct 1997, *Portrait of a Young Girl Wearing Regional Costume* (oil on panel, 10 1/2 x 8 ins / 26.6 x 20.3 cm) GBP 1,092. LONDON, 23 March 1999, *Portrait of a Young Woman* (oil on panel, 16x12 ins / 41x31 cm) GBP 2,000. SAN FRANCISCO, 26 May 1999, *Simplicity* (oil on panel, 7x6 ins / 18x14 cm) USD 3,250. NEW YORK, 2 May 2000, *The Maiden's Suitor* (oil on canvas, 24x17 ins / 62x42 cm) USD 12,000. BILLINGSHURST, 23 Oct 2000, *Study of a Young Woman* (oil on panel, 16x13 ins / 41x32 cm) GBP 2,600. MUNICH, 13 Dec 2001, *Fortune with Horn of Plenty* (oil on cardboard, 30x18 ins / 76x45 cm) DEM 2,500. ZURICH, 9 Dec 2002, *Portrait of a Young Woman* (oil on panel, 9x7 ins / 24x18 cm) CHF 1,500. LONDON, 17 June 2003, *Innocence* (oil on panel, 22x13 ins / 55x32 cm) GBP 6,000. VIENNA, 24 Nov 2003, *May Time* (oil on canvas, 49x35 ins / 125x88 cm) EUR 13,000. LONDON, 21 Jan 2004, *Portrait of a Girl* (oil on panel, 13x9 ins / 33x23 cm) GBP 3,800.

SEIFERT, Alwin

German, 20th century.

Born 15 June 1873, in Leipzig.

Active in Dresden.

Painter, designer, engraver. Landscapes.
Alwin Seifert studied at the fine arts academies of Leipzig and Düsseldorf.

SEIFERT, Annie
German, 19th - 20th century.
Born 28 June 1863, in Dresden; died 26 January 1913, in Dresden.
Painter. Landscapes, flowers.
Sister of Dora Seifert, Annie Seifert studied under W. Claudius in Dresden and, in Munich, under Hugo von Habermann and Theodor Hummel.

SEIFERT, Carl
German, 20th century.
Born 20 June 1896, in Leipzig; died c. 1958.
Painter, engraver. Landscapes.
Carl Seifert was a pupil of Molitor.
MUSEUMS AND GALLERIES:
LEIPZIG (Mus. der Bildenden Künste): *Mähring Valley.*

SEIFERT, David
Polish, 20th century.
Born 31 December 1896, in Wolanka, or Boryslaw; died 18 January 1980, in Meudon, France.
From 1924 active in France.
Painter, engraver. Figures, landscapes, still-lifes.
David Seifert was a student at the Cracow academy and the graphic arts school in Weimar, where he met Paul Klee. He settled in Paris in 1924, and in Montparnasse got to know Kisling, Chagall, Kikoïne, and Zadkine; he was also Friesz's neighbour. From 1925, his work featured regularly at group exhibitions, at the Salon d'Automne, the Salon des Tuileries, and the Salon des Indépendants.

He produced views of Normandy and the islands of Bréhat in Provence. Around 1925, he painted one of the pillars of the *La Coupole* brasserie in Montparnasse. The French state acquired one of his works in 1939.
BIBLIOGRAPHY:
Nieszawer, Nadine/Boyé, Marie/Lanzmann, Claude (preface), *Peintres juifs de l'école de Paris 1905-1939*, Denoël, Paris, 2001.
MUSEUMS AND GALLERIES:
CHICAGO: *Portrait of the Artist by Himself.*
AUCTION RECORDS:
PARIS, 20 March 1988, *The Village* (oil on canvas, 23 1/2 x 32 ins / 60 x 81 cm) FRF 6,500. PARIS, 30 May 2001, *The Parisienne* (oil on canvas laid on panel, 23 x 14 ins / 59 x 36 cm) FRF 15,000. PARIS, 30 May 2001, *Still-life with Basket* (oil on canvas, 24 x 18 ins / 60 x 46 cm) FRF 15,000.

SEIFERT, Dora
German, 19th - 20th century.
Born 1 February 1861, in Dresden.
Painter, engraver.
Sister of Annie Seifert, Dora Seifert studied in Dresden and Munich.

SEIFERT, Emanuela
German, 19th - 20th century.
Born 1852, in Prague; died 1910, in Munich.
Painter, pastellist. Portraits, genre scenes, still-lifes.

SEIFERT, Franz
Austrian, 19th - 20th century.
Born 2 April 1866, in Vienna; died 1951.
Sculptor. Statues, busts, monuments.
Franz Seifert was a pupil of Kundmann and Hellmer; he sculpted statues, busts and monuments in public gardens.
MUSEUMS AND GALLERIES:
ST LOUIS: *Siegfried.*

SEIFERT, Friedrich or Carl Friedrich
German, 19th - 20th century.
Born 1 January 1838, in Neustadt, near Erfurt; died 27 September 1920, in Langburkersdorf.
Engraver.
Friedrich Seifert studied in Dresden under Hübner and Brückner and in Düsseldorf under Josef Keller.

SEIFERT, Grete
Maiden name: Tschaplowitz
German, 20th century.
Born 17 January 1889, in Proskau (now Proszków, Poland).
Sculptor. Busts.
Grete Seifert was the wife of Carl Seifert and pupil of A. Lehnert; she sculpted portrait busts.

SEIFERT, Hermann Rudolf
Swiss, 20th century.
Born 1885.
Active in Zurich.
Painter, engraver. Posters.

SEIFERT, Max
German, 20th century.
Born 1914, in Düsseldorf.
Painter.
A police officer and self-taught painter, Max Seifert painted highly detailed landscapes which exude charm. Unlike the majority of naive painters, he was remarkably adept at handling perspective and the relative proportions of the various figures, animals, houses and trees that feature in his work, which is reminiscent of an illuminated manuscript.
BIBLIOGRAPHY:
Gans, Louis, *Meesters der Europese naïven*, exhibition catalogue, Centraal Museum, Utrecht, 1970.

SEIFERT, Victor Heinrich
German, 20th century.
Born 19 May 1870, in Vienna; died 1953, in Berlin.
Sculptor. Military subjects. Statues, monuments.
A pupil of Ernst Herter, Ludwig Manzel and Peter Breuer, Victor Seifert sculpted war memorials and statues, principally of a military nature.
MUSEUMS AND GALLERIES:
LEIPZIG: *Young Woman Drinking* (bronze, statuette).
AUCTION RECORDS:
LONDON, 23 Feb 1981, *Surfeit of Books* (bronze, h. 22 ins / 56 cm) USD 1,300. AMSTERDAM, 16 June 1983, *David* (bronze, h. 29 1/2 ins / 75 cm) NLG 3,930. LONDON, 17 April 1984, *Nymph Fishing* (polished bronze, h. 25 3/4 ins / 65.5 cm) GBP 950. COLOGNE, 15 June 1989, *Diana* (bronze on a marble plinth, h. 20 ins / 51 cm) DEM 2,000. NEW YORK, 19 Jan 1995, *Warrior of Old* (bronze, h. 21 ins / 53.3 cm) USD 1,610. LONDON, 13 May 1999, *Young Woman in a Long Dress* (ivory, h. 11 ins / 29 cm) GBP 2,600. WARSAW, 5 Dec 1999, *Girl Fishing* (patinated bronze, h. 32 ins / 82 cm) PLN 43,000. RADOLFZELL, 1 April 2000, *Standing Female Nude Holding an Arrow* (bronze, h. 43 ins / 108 cm) DEM 5,500. AMSTERDAM, 23 May 2000, *Greek Warrior Leaning on His Sword* (green patinated bronze, h. 28 ins / 71 cm) NLG 4,500. LEIPZIG, 6 April 2001, *Female Nude* (bronze, h. 21 ins / 54 cm) DEM 5,500. LINDAU, 8 May 2002, *Thirsty: Standing Female Nude with Water in a Dish* (patinated bronze, h. 28 ins / 70 cm) EUR 5,500. WARSAW, 30 March 2003, *On the Way to School* (c. 1920, patinated bronze, h. 26 ins / 65 cm) PLN 13,000. WARSAW, 30 March 2003, *Female Nude* (c. 1910, patinated bronze, h. 28 ins / 70 cm) PLN 17,000. COPENHAGEN, 2 June 2004, *Standing Youth* (patinated bronze, h. 26 ins / 66 cm) DKK 18,000. AMSTERDAM, 7 June 2004, *Story Time* (brown patinated bronze, h. 21 ins / 53 cm) EUR 3,200. MUNICH, 16 June 2004, *Female Nude with Raised Arms* (bronze, h. 24 ins / 62 cm) EUR 4,000.

SEIFERT-WARTENBERG, Richard
German, 20th century.
Born 23 January 1874, in Brunswick.
Painter. Portraits, landscapes, still-lifes.
Richard Seifert-Wartenberg was also a writer.

SEIFFER. See **SEYFER**

SEIFFERT. See also **SEYFFERT** and **SEYFFERTH**

SEIFFERT, Andreas
German, 17th century.
Glass painter.
The provincial museum of Breslau (now the Muzeum Narodowe, Wroclaw) houses two stained glass windows by Andreas Seiffert, which he produced with Christoph Lengfeldt.
Museums and Galleries:
Wroclaw (Muz. Narodowe): two stained-glass windows.

SEIFFERT, Jeremias, or Seyferth
German, 17th century.
Active in Dresden in 1668.
Painter, architect.
Jeremias Seiffert was the father of Johann Gottfried, and was court painter in Dresden. He designed the plan for the altar in the church of St Paul in Zittau (Saxony), Germany.

SEIFFERT, Johann Gottfried, or Seyferth
German, 18th century.
Active in Querfurt in 1701.
Painter.
Johann Gottfried Seiffert was the son of Jeremias.

SEIFFERT, Johann Gottlieb or Gotthelf. See **SEYFERT**

SEIFFERT, Johann Karl
Polish, 19th century.
Born 1776, in Posen (now Poznan).
Painter. History painting, portraits, landscapes.
Johann Seiffert studied in France, Italy and England.

SEIFFERT, Karl Friedrich
Polish, 19th century.
Born 6 September 1809, in Grünberg; died 25 April 1891, in Berlin, Germany.
Painter. Landscapes.
Karl Seiffert travelled a great deal.
Museums and Galleries:
Berlin (Nationalgal.): *The Grotto of Capri* - Görlitz (Städtische Kunstsammlungen): *Amphitheatre at Taormino.*
Auction records:
Berlin, 23 April 1980, *Mountainous Landscape by the Bridge* (1841, oil on canvas, 14¼ x 21½ ins / 36.5 x 54.5 cm) DEM 4,400. Cologne, 19 May 2001, *On the Ligurian Coast near Porto Venere* (1847, oil on board, 11 x 18 ins / 27 x 45 cm) DEM 14,000. Stuttgart, 6 Dec 2001, *Sicilian Landscape near Cefalu* (oil on canvas, 28 x 46 ins / 70 x 117 cm) DEM 9,000. Vienna, 10 April 2003, *Resting near Mayringen in Late Summer* (1843, oil on canvas, 22 x 27 ins / 56 x 68 cm) EUR 8,000. Vienna, 22 May 2003, *View of Schachental* (oil on canvas, 44 x 75 ins / 111 x 191 cm) EUR 8,500.

SEIFFRID
German, 16th century.
Born in Marburg-an-der-Lahn (?).
Active from 1555 to 1556.
Glass painter.
Seiffrid painted five windows for the Teutonic Knights in Stadelbach.

SEIGAI, real name: Kan Sakumura, nicknames: Zentotsu, Zenjiro, pseudonyms: Utei, Seigai, Usai, Sojunken, Zenno
Japanese, 19th century.
Born 1786; died 1851.
Painter.
Nanga School.
Seigai was a pupil of Katgiri Toin. He was in the service of Honda Nasasukasa Dayu, Lord of the Okazaki Castle in Mikawa (the current prefecture of Aichi). He actually lived and worked mainly in Edo (now Tokyo). He was a great friend of Kazan Watanabe (1793-1841) and began by painting figures but, just like Kazan, soon fell under the influence of Buncho (1763-1840). His best works are his landscapes painted when he was in his 50s, notably a *Landscape*, a vertical scroll in ink and light colours on paper, preserved in the National Museum in Tokyo. The painting is not signed but bears the seal of the painter. Although it belongs to the Nanga School it differs considerably from the early works of this School because of a new Chinese influence on Japanese literati painting and a deeper knowledge of Chinese originals. In fact this landscape could be Chinese and it is difficult to make out the slightest detail which is Japanese. The composition is solid, the brushwork varied and sure and the original texture and the flowing contours confer on the forms a sense of immobility which is interesting. But with technical progress comes a loss of the freshness which is characteristic of the Japanese sensitivity.
Bibliography:
Cahill, James, *Scholar Painters of Japan: the Nanga School*, Asia Society, New York, 1972.
Museums and Galleries:
Tokyo (National Mus.): *Landscape* (ink and colour/paper, roll opening vertically).

SEIGAN, real name: Moi Yanagawa, nicknames: Koto and Musho, nickname: Shinjuro, pseudonyms: Seigan, Tenkoku, Hyakuho, Roryuan and Osekishoin
Japanese, 19th century.
Born 1789, in Mino near Gifu; died 1858.
Painter.
Seigan was a painter and poet of the Nanga School (literati art). He travelled widely in Japan and divided his life between the towns of Edo (now Tokyo) and Kyoto.

SEIGAR, Francis and William. See **SEGAR**

SEIGLE, Henri Julien
French, 20th century.
Born 1911, in Saintes.
Painter. Figures, nudes, still-lifes. Wall decorations.
Seigle spent his childhood in Montauban, then had the opportunity to be advised by Vuillard, who sent him to Paris. There he studied at the École des Arts Décoratifs in 1930. In 1939 he married the painter No Pin, with whom he painted several shared pieces, which were signed *Seigle*. He was represented at exhibitions, including that of the Surrealist group. He created decorative pieces for the French coal board and post office.

SEIGLE

Museums and Galleries:
Paris (MNAM-CCI).
Auction records:
Paris, 14 Dec 1988, *Still-life with Draughtboard* (oil on canvas, 15 x 18 ins / 38 x 46 cm) FRF 17,000. Paris, 8 Nov 1989, *Sail and Net* (oil on canvas, 28¼ x 46 ins / 72 x 116 cm) FRF 195,000. Paris, 4 Dec 1992, *Pitcher on White Background* (1983, oil on canvas, 21¼ x 32 ins / 54 x 81 cm) FRF 5,200. Paris, 4 Nov 1994, *Nude with Tiles* (oil on canvas, 57 x 35 ins / 145 x 88 cm) FRF 8,500. Paris, 28 April 1995, *Model Seated on Red Background* (1957, oil on canvas, 51¼ x 35 ins / 130 x 88 cm) FRF 12,500.

SEIGNAC, Guillaume
French, 19th - 20th century.
Born 1870, in Rennes; died 1924.
Painter. Allegorical subjects, figures, genre scenes. Symbolism.

Seignac was a student of Bouguereau, Tony Robert-Fleury and Gabriel Ferrier. He was a member of the Artistes Français from 1901 and was represented at its Salon, receiving an honourable mention in 1900 and a third class medal in 1903. He enjoyed bringing back to life the canons of classical antiquity in compositions with Symbolist tendencies.

AUCTION RECORDS:
NEW YORK, 3 Feb 1906, *Youth and Love*, USD 1,450. NEW YORK, 22-23 Feb 1907, *Young Girl from Pompeii in a Garden*, USD 925. LONDON, 18 Feb 1911, *The Queen and the Harvest*, GBP 21. NEW YORK, 7 March 1911, *Baby's Bath*, USD 125. PARIS, 11 Feb 1919, *Reverie*, FRF 500. PARIS, 18 Feb 1920, *Pierrot Victorious*, FRF 405. PARIS, 15 April 1924, *Love Disarmed*, FRF 335. PARIS, 20 Feb 1942, *The Wave*, FRF 1,100. PARIS, 25-26 Jan 1943, *Rattle*, FRF 4,200. LILLE, 24-25 May 1943, *Young Nymph*, FRF 3,100. NEW YORK, 7-9 June 1943, *Bather*, USD 430. NEW YORK, 11 Dec 1943, *Psyche*, USD 700. PARIS, 12 Feb 1945, *Water Sprite*, FRF 800. PARIS, July 1946, *Diligence*, FRF 2,300. PARIS, 28 March 1949, *Wave*, FRF 13,500; *Portrait of a Woman*, FRF 5,800. PARIS, 3 July 1950, *Children in the Kitchen*, FRF 34,000. PARIS, 25 June 1951, *Water Sprite*, FRF 37,000. PARIS, 21 Dec 1953, *L'Amour taquin* (*Teasing Love*, FRF 27,000. NEW YORK, 10 May 1961, *Young Girl at the Well*, USD 400. LONDON, 16 Feb 1979, *Portrait of a Beautiful Lady* (oil on canvas, 17 3/4 x 14 1/4 ins / 45 x 36 cm) GBP 1,900. ORLÉANS, 23 May 1981, *Woman Semi-nude* (oil on canvas, 32 x 39 1/4 ins / 81 x 100 cm) FRF 90,000. NEW YORK, 1 March 1984, *Temptress* (oil on canvas, 32 x 39 1/2 ins / 81.3 x 100.3 cm) USD 37,000. LONDON, 9 Oct 1985, *Indolence* (oil on canvas, 28 1/4 x 35 3/4 ins / 72 x 91 cm) GBP 22,000. LONDON, 8 Oct 1986, *Wave* (oil on canvas, 9 x 12 1/2 ins / 23 x 32 cm) GBP 3,400. NEW YORK, 21 May 1987, *Indolence* (oil on canvas, 28 1/4 x 35 3/4 ins / 71.5 x 90.8 cm) USD 40,000. PARIS, 6 June 1988, *Woman Playing the Flute* (oil on panel, 9 x 6 1/4 ins / 22 x 16 cm) FRF 4,200; *Woman Picking Flowers* (oil on panel, 8 3/4 x 6 1/4 ins / 22.1 x 16.1 cm) FRF 4,000. NEW YORK, 24 Oct 1989, *Innocence* (oil on canvas, 39 1/2 x 32 ins / 100.3 x 81.3 cm) USD 99,000. PARIS, 9 Dec 1989, *Pierrot and Columbine* (watercolour and gouache/silk, 14 1/4 x 10 3/4 ins / 36 x 27.5 cm) FRF 30,000. NEW YORK, 17 Jan 1990, *Children's Meal* (oil on card, 15 1/4 x 19 ins / 38.8 x 48.1 cm) USD 6,600. PARIS, 6 April 1990, *The Wave* (oil on canvas, 25 1/2 x 19 3/4 ins / 65 x 50 cm) FRF 42,000. LONDON, 5 Oct 1990, *Casket* (oil on canvas, 24 1/2 x 31 1/2 ins / 62.5 x 80 cm) GBP 13,750. NEW YORK, 28 Feb 1991, *Young Woman from Pompeii in a Garden* (oil on canvas, 61 x 34 1/4 ins / 154.7 x 87 cm) USD 52,800. NEW YORK, 28 May 1992, *Psyche* (oil on canvas, 69 1/4 x 38 ins / 175.9 x 96.5 cm) USD 110,000. LONDON, 17 June 1992, *Wave* (oil on canvas, 19 3/4 x 25 1/2 ins / 50 x 65 cm) GBP 6,600. NEW YORK, 29 Oct 1992, *Confidence* (oil on canvas, 69 x 38 ins / 175.3 x 96.5 cm) USD 49,500. PARIS, 18 Nov 1992, *Odalisque* (oil on canvas, 37 1/2 x 68 1/2 ins / 95 x 174 cm) FRF 150,000. NEW YORK, 17 Feb 1993, *Abandonment* (oil on canvas, 37 3/4 x 68 3/4 ins / 95.9 x 174.9 cm) USD 40,250. NEW YORK, 12 Oct 1994, *Psyche's Hesitation* (oil on canvas, 25 1/2 x 21 1/2 ins / 64.8 x 54.9 cm) USD 23,000. LONDON, 16 Nov 1994, *School Clothes* (oil on panel, 12 1/4 x 9 1/2 ins / 31 x 24 cm) GBP 6,325. NEW YORK, 19 Jan 1995, *Little Girl with a Dog* (oil on canvas, 10 3/4 x 8 3/4 ins / 27.3 x 22.2 cm) USD 4,312. PARIS, 16 June 1995, *Abandonment* (oil on canvas, 19 3/4 x 25 1/2 ins / 50 x 65 cm) FRF 40,000. NEW YORK, 23-24 May 1996, *Daydreams* (oil on canvas, 46 1/2 x 31 1/2 ins / 118.1 x 80 cm) USD 57,500. NEW YORK, 23 May 1997, *Mother and Child* (oil on canvas, 39 1/2 x 28 3/4 ins / 100.3 x 73 cm) USD 40,250. NEW YORK, 9 Feb 1999, *Female Faun* (oil on canvas, 22 x 18 ins / 56 x 46 cm) USD 22,000. NEW YORK, 2 Nov 1999, *Polyhymnia* (oil on canvas, 54 x 31 ins / 138 x 80 cm) USD 95,000. NEW YORK, 3 May 2000, *Nymph with a Mirror* (oil on canvas, 29 x 37 ins / 74 x 93 cm) USD 80,000. PORTLAND, 2 Aug 2000, *Meditation* (oil on canvas, 39 x 27 ins / 99 x 69 cm) USD 62,000. NEW YORK, 24 April 2002, *Nymph* (oil on canvas, 57 x 32 ins / 145 x 82 cm) USD 85,000. MICHIGAN, 18 Sept 2002, *Harlequin* (oil on canvas, 24 x 18 ins / 61 x 46 cm) USD 20,000. PORTLAND, 8 Aug 2003, *Nymph* (oil on canvas, 57 x 33 ins / 145 x 83 cm) USD 70,000. NEW YORK, 28 Oct 2003, *Venus and Cupid* (oil on canvas, 56 x 35 ins / 142 x 89 cm) USD 110,000. LONDON, 15 June 2004, *Odalisque with Doves* (oil on canvas, 18 x 22 ins / 46 x 55 cm) GBP 26,000. NEUILLY, 6 Oct 2004, *Young Woman with Greek Vase* (oil on canvas, 39 x 29 ins / 100 x 73 cm) EUR 33,000.

SEIGNAC, Paul
French, 19th century.
Born 12 February 1826, in Bordeaux; died 1904, in Paris.
Painter. Portraits, genre scenes.

Picot was his master. He made his Salon debut in 1849, and received an honourable mention in 1889.

MUSEUMS AND GALLERIES:
AJACCIO: *The Nun* - RHEIMS: *Young Woman Winding a Clock*.

AUCTION RECORDS:
PARIS, 1872, *The Love of Study*, FRF 410; *The Reprimand*, FRF 1,620. THE HAGUE, 1889, *The Crib*, FRF 460. NEW YORK, 15-16 March 1906, *Book of Little Stories*, USD 125. LONDON, 6 Dec 1909, *Bird's Nest*, GBP 14. LONDON, 13 June 1910, *Young Teacher*, GBP 12. LONDON, 26 Nov 1910, *The Mirror*, GBP 8. LONDON, 25-26 Jan 1911, *Childhood*, GBP 70. LONDON, 4 April 1924, *House of Cards*, GBP 31. PARIS, 4 March 1925, *The Injured Pigeon*, FRF 450; *The Milk Tooth*, FRF 320. PARIS, 9 June 1927, *Young Woman in a Second Empire Interior*, FRF 1,650. LONDON, 20 Feb 1970, *Visiting Grandmother*; *The Gaming Club* (two panels) GBP 1,000. LONDON, 2 Nov 1973, *First Lesson*, Gns 1,900. NEW YORK, 14 Jan 1977, *Children Putting Apples in the Oven* (oil on panel, 10 x 7 1/4 ins / 25.5 x 18.5 cm) USD 2,200. LONDON, 20 April 1979, *Spinner by a Crib* (oil on panel, 11 3/4 x 9 1/2 ins / 29.8 x 24.1 cm) GBP 1,700. NEW YORK, 28 Oct 1981, *Fortune Teller* (oil on panel, 12 1/4 x 9 1/4 ins / 31.2 x 23.2 cm) USD 3,000. LONDON, 3 June 1983, *Servant* (oil on panel, 10 x 7 1/2 ins / 25.4 x 19 cm) GBP 1,500. NEW YORK, 24 May 1985, *Cider-making* (oil on canvas, 25 1/2 x 35 1/2 ins / 64.8 x 90.2 cm) USD 25,000. MONTE CARLO, 22 June 1985, *Currant Branch* (gouache, 6 x 7 3/4 ins / 15.5 x 20 cm) FRF 8,000. MONTE CARLO, 22 June 1986, *Lunch with Friends* (oil on panel, 12 3/4 x 9 1/2 ins / 32.5 x 24 cm) FRF 55,000. NEW YORK, 25 Oct 1989, *Two Children Watching Their Mother Feeding Chicks* (oil on canvas, 14 x 11 ins / 35.5 x 28 cm) USD 13,200. BERN, 12 May 1990, *Two Thirsty Children* (oil on panel, sketch, 12 1/2 x 10 ins / 31.5 x 24.5 cm) CHF 3,800. NEW YORK, 24 Oct 1990, *The Reading Lesson* (oil on panel, 19 x 26 1/4 ins / 48.5 x 66.7 cm) USD

30,800. NEW YORK, 29 Oct 1992, *Grass for the Rabbit* (oil on panel, 14 1/4 x 10 1/2 ins / 36.2 x 26.7 cm) USD 11,550. LONDON, 10 Feb 1995, *A Gift for Grandmother* (oil on canvas, 21 3/4 x 18 ins / 55.5 x 46 cm) GBP 9,775. NEW YORK, 23-24 May 1996, *Young Saleswoman* (oil on panel, 13 3/4 x 10 ins / 34.9 x 25.4 cm) USD 32,200. LONDON, 13 March 1997, *The New Dress* (oil on panel, 14 x 10 1/2 ins / 35.6 x 26.7 cm) GBP 10,120. PORTLAND, 4 Aug 1999, *After Cherry Picking* (oil on canvas, 18 x 22 ins / 46 x 56 cm) USD 19,000. NEW YORK, 2 Nov 1999, *At the Well* (oil on panel, 22 x 17 ins / 55 x 44 cm) USD 13,000. NEWCASTLE, 13 June 2000, *Morning Toilet* (oil on canvas, 13 x 9 ins / 32 x 24 cm) GBP 2,000. SAN FRANCISCO, 15 Nov 2000, *The Young Narcissus* (oil on panel, 14 x 11 ins / 35 x 28 cm) USD 17,000. PORTSMOUTH, 3 Nov 2001, *Morning Porridge* (oil on panel, 15 x 18 ins / 38 x 46 cm) USD 18,000. LONDON, 11 June 2002, *Playmates* (oil on canvas, 14 x 11 ins / 35 x 27 cm) GBP 6,200. LONDON, 21 Nov 2002, *Plate of Cherries* (oil on panel, 16 x 13 ins / 41 x 32 cm) GBP 6,500. LONDON, 20 March 2003, *Learning to Count* (oil on panel, 14 x 11 ins / 35 x 27 cm) GBP 7,500. MILAN, 9 Dec 2003, *Girls* (oil on board, 14 x 11 ins / 36 x 27 cm) EUR 9,000. LONDON, 16 June 2004, *Mother's Little Helper* (oil on canvas, 14 x 11 ins / 36 x 27 cm) GBP 6,000. THOMASTON, 28 Aug 2004, *Cottage Interior with Four Children Reading* (oil on canvas) USD 20,000.

SEIGNE, LA. See **LA SEIGNE Georges**

SEIGNEMARTIN, Jean

French, 19th century.

Born 16 April 1848, in Dijon; died 29 November 1875, in Lyons.

Painter. Local scenes, figures, portraits, landscapes, flowers.

Orientalism.

Lyons School.

Jean Seignemartin was a student at the École des Beaux-Arts in Lyons.

He spent the last two years his life in Algeria which inspired him to paint in a lyrical style, much like Delacroix, whom he greatly admired, but whose work he knew mostly through Guichard. He sometimes worked in collaboration with Vernay. His paintings of bouquets of flowers allowed him to bring enamelled colours to the fore.

MUSEUMS AND GALLERIES:

AMSTERDAM (Stedelijk Mus.): *Smoker* - LYONS: *Portrait of the Artist; Portrait of A Stengelin; Theatre; Flowers;* several landscapes - PARIS (former Mus. du Luxembourg): *Flowers*.

AUCTION RECORDS:

PARIS, 29 March 1943, *Impression of Algiers* (1875) FRF 3,800. PARIS, 29 Nov 1944, *View of Algeria*, FRF 4,600. PARIS, 19 May 1947, *Landscape at Bou Saada* (1879) FRF 5,700. PARIS, 8 May 1950, *Market in Algiers* (1875) FRF 3,100. PARIS, 4 Dec 1950, *Arab Women in South Algeria* (1875) FRF 5,600. LYONS, 8 June 1982, *Vase of Flowers with Allegory of Femininity* (oil on canvas, 36 1/4 x 25 1/2 ins / 92 x 64.5 cm) FRF 11,500. PARIS, 20 Jan 1988, *Death of Lara* (oil on canvas, 38 1/2 x 59 ins / 98 x 150 cm) FRF 50,000. PARIS, 2 June 1997, *Bathers in a Clearing* (oil on canvas, 15 1/4 x 12 1/4 ins / 39 x 31 cm) FRF 9,000. PARIS, 20 Nov 2000, *Worthy and his Favourites* (oil on canvas, 13 x 16 ins / 32 x 41 cm) FRF 14,000. LYONS, 26 Nov 2000, *Dance in the Park* (oil on panel, 13 x 20 ins / 32 x 51 cm) FRF 15,000.

SEIGNEUR

French, 18th century.

Silhouettist.

SEIGNEURET, Antoine Louis

French, 19th century.

Sculptor.

He studied with Petitot and at the École des Beaux-Arts in Orleans, central France. He first exhibited at the Salon in 1870.

SEIGNEURGENS, Ernest Louis Augustin

French, 19th century.

Born in Amiens; died 1904 or 1905.

Painter, illustrator. Figures, genre scenes.

His master was Eugène Isabey. He exhibited at the Salon from 1844 to 1875 and won a third-class medal in 1846.

MUSEUMS AND GALLERIES:

CHÂLONS-EN-CHAMPAGNE: *Duel after the Game* - RHEIMS: *The Grandfather (Man with Dog)*.

AUCTION RECORDS:

PARIS, 8 June 1977, *Romantic Conversation* (oil on canvas, 18 x 15 ins / 46 x 38 cm) FRF 4,000. AMSTERDAM, 22 April 1980, *The Composer* (oil on panel, 6 3/4 x 6 ins / 17 x 15.5 cm) NLG 4,600. PARIS, 24 May 1991, *Harvest* (oil on canvas, 29 1/4 x 36 1/2 ins / 74 x 93 cm) FRF 24,000. AMSTERDAM, 22 Oct 2001, *Difficult Passage* (oil on panel, 10 x 8 ins / 26 x 21 cm) NLG 5,000.

SEIGNEURIE, Nicolas. See the entry **REMBEUR Jean de**

SEIGNEUX, Aloys de

Swiss, 19th - 20th century.

Born 1868, in Geneva; died 1917, in Geneva.

Painter. Landscapes.

Aloys de Seigneux was a pupil of Barthélemy Menn and Nath. Lemaire.

SEIGNIER, O. de

French, 19th century.

Painter. Scenes with figures, animals.

His name is mentioned in public auction catalogues. He seems to have been a painter of burlesque scenes with animal subjects.

AUCTION RECORDS:

PARIS, 2 Dec 1949, *Chicks*, FRF 8,000. PARIS, 3 Nov 1950, *Musician Animals* (two pendants) FRF 7,800.

SEIGNOL

French, 19th - 20th century.

Painter. Landscapes.

AUCTION RECORDS:

CLERMONT-FERRAND, 20 Dec 1950, *Village in the Snow*, FRF 5,000. AVON, 4 April 1976, *Village in Winter* (oil on canvas) FRF 3,500. PARIS, 18 Nov 1994, *Snow on the Banks of the Seine* (1890, oil on canvas, 34 1/4 x 35 3/4 ins / 87 x 91 cm) FRF 22,000. PARIS, 28 May 2003, *Piqueux et griffons vendeens* (oil on canvas, 57 x 39 ins / 145 x 98 cm) EUR 1,800.

SEIGNORET

French, 19th century.

Active in Paris.

Painter. History painting.

A pupil of Regnault, he exhibited at the Salons of 1800 and 1804.

SEIGNORET, Abel

French, 19th century.

Born in Nérac.

Landscape painter.

He debuted at the Salon in 1878.

SEIGYO

Japanese.

Active during the Muromachi period (1338-1593).

Painter.

The details of Seigyo's life are unknown to us, but he belonged to the ink painting school (*suiboku*) of the Muromachi period.

SEIHO, or Tsunekichi
Japanese, 19th - 20th century.
Born 1861, in Kyoto.
Painter.
Seiho was a pupil of Tsuchida Eirin and Bairei (1844-1895). He made a journey to Paris. He is well known for his paintings of cats.
MUSEUMS AND GALLERIES:
BERLIN: *Fish* - PARIS (Louvre): *Rainy Day in Suchou.*

SEIJO RUBIO, José
Spanish, 20th century.
Born 15 October 1881, in Madrid; died 9 September 1970, in La Coruña.
Painter. Religious subjects, genre scenes, landscapes with figures, urban landscapes, waterscapes.
José Seijo Rubio studied at the college of fine arts in Madrid and went on to become curator of the Fine Arts Museum in La Coruña. He painted dramatically-lit landscapes with tiny figures. Examples of his work include *Pilgrims at San Andrés de Teixido, Offering, Calm Sea, Triumphal Arch with Strom clouds, Timber Market* and *Low Tide*.

He featured at various collective exhibitions including: Hispano-French Exhibition, Saragossa (1908 receiving a silver medal), National Society of Fine Arts, Madrid (1926 receiving a bronze medal), Galicia and Buenos Aires.
BIBLIOGRAPHY:
Arnáiz, José Manuel/López Jiménez, Javier/Merchán Díaz, Manuel (ed.), '*Cien años de pintura en Espana y Portugal (1830-1930)*' in vol. X, Antiqvaria, Madrid, 1993.
MUSEUMS AND GALLERIES:
CASTRELOS, GALICIA: *Blinding of St Margaret* - MADRID (Mus. de Arte Moderno): *By the Sea.*

SEIKI, real name: Kizo Yokohama later Seiki, nickname: Seibun, nickname: Shosuke, Shume, pseudonyms: Gogaku, Kibun, Kajo
Japanese, 19th century.
Born 1793, in Kyoto; died 1865.
Painter.
Seiki was a disciple of Keibun (1779-1843), the brother of Goshun. He was part of the Shijo School of Kyoto and from 1855 worked on the decoration of the newly rebuilt Kyoto Castle. He is known as a painter of flowers and birds.

SEIKO, nickname: Tani
Japanese, 19th century.
Active in the Osaka region c. 1810-1820.
Draughtsman, engraver.
Seiko is also known as a maker of illustrated books and *surimono* limited edition prints, published in Osaka, which were used as greetings or announcement cards.

SEIKO, real name: Setsuko Okuhara, pseudonym: Seiko
Japanese, 19th - 20th century.
Born 1837; died 1913.
Painter.
Seiko was a painter of landscapes, flowers and birds, following both the traditional Japanese style and the literati painting of the Nanga School at the same time. He was a disciple of Hirata Shisei. He lived in Tokyo in Kumagaya and in the prefecture of Saitama.

SEIL, A.
Dutch, 17th century.
Active in Amsterdam in 1656.
Engraver.

SEILER
German, 19th century.
Active c. 1810.
Lithographer.

SEILER, Adolf
Polish, 19th century.
Born 25 October 1824, in Gross-Rinnersdorf, near Lüben; died 22 April 1873, in Breslau (now Wroclaw).
Painter (glass).

SEILER, Carl Wilhelm Anton
German, 19th - 20th century.
Born 3 August 1846, in Wiesbaden; died 26 February 1921, in Munich.
Painter. History painting, genre scenes, figures.
Carl Seiler studied at the academy in Berlin and then under Raupp in Munich. He served as a reserve officer in the Franco-Prussian War of 1870 and, after the war, settled in Munich. He became a member of the Berlin Academy in 1895.

Seiler exhibited his work in various venues, including Paris, where he secured an honourable mention in 1903.

C. Seiler

MUSEUMS AND GALLERIES:
BAUTZEN: *Before Dinner* - DRESDEN: *Frederick the Great in Paschwitz Forest* - LEIPZIG: *Discussion* - MELBOURNE: *Standard Bearer* - MUNICH (Neue Pinakothek): *Group of Scholars; Church Interior; Serving Officer* - MUNICH (Städtische Gal. im Lenbachhaus): *Ettal* - WIESBADEN: *At Court.*
AUCTION RECORDS:
LONDON, 5 March 1910, *Reading the News*, GBP 81. NEW YORK, 27 Jan 1911, *Dispatches*, USD 100. LONDON, 9 June 1911, *Rivals* (1883) GBP 117. LONDON, 3 May 1926, *Argument*, GBP 136. LONDON, 4 June 1926, *Card Players*, GBP 173. LONDON, 2 Dec 1927, *Rival Claimants*, GBP 141. COPENHAGEN, 7 Nov 1969, *Interior with Revellers*, DKK 13,000. COLOGNE, 27 Nov 1970, *After Dinner*, DEM 9,000. LONDON, 10 Nov 1971, *Word of Advice*, GBP 1,100. COLOGNE, 25 June 1976, *Tavern Scene* (oil on canvas, 22 x 27 1/4 ins / 55 x 69 cm) DEM 4,000. COLOGNE, 18 March 1977, *Cabaret* (oil on canvas, 16 1/2 x 20 ins / 42 x 51 cm) DEM 4,500. NEW YORK, 12 Oct 1979, *Art Lover* (1893, oil on panel, 10 x 7 3/4 ins / 25.5 x 20 cm) USD 6,250. NEW YORK, 27 Oct 1982, *Old Friends* (oil on panel, 7 1/4 x 9 1/2 ins / 18.5 x 24 cm) USD 8,000. LONDON, 21 Oct 1983, *Interior with Two Men* (1879, oil on panel, 15 x 12 ins / 38.1 x 30.5 cm) GBP 2,200. ZURICH, 6 June 1984, *Art Lover* (oil on panel, 13 x 9 3/4 ins / 33 x 25 cm) CHF 14,000. LONDON, 27 Nov 1985, *Engraver* (1890, oil on panel, 11 x 9 ins / 28 x 23 cm) GBP 4,500. NEW YORK, 25 Feb 1988, *Box of Drawings* (1884, oil on panel, 7 1/4 x 5 1/2 ins / 18.4 x 14 cm) USD 5,500. COLOGNE, 20 Oct 1989, *Military Manoeuvres* (oil on panel, 11 3/4 x 16 ins / 30 x 40.5 cm) DEM 4,000. PARIS, 16 May 1990, *By the Sea* (oil on canvas, 12 1/2 x 9 3/4 ins / 32 x 25 cm) FRF 15,000. LONDON, 28 Nov 1990, *Through the Window* (1886, oil on panel, 7 x 5 1/2 ins / 18 x 14 cm) GBP 3,300. NEW YORK, 21 May 1991, *Rider* (1878, oil on panel, 15 1/4 x 10 ins / 38.7 x 25.4 cm) USD 4,840. LONDON, 4 Oct 1991, *Dandy* (1884, oil on panel, 9 x 3 1/4 x 6 ins / 22 x 8 x 15.2 cm) GBP 1,540. HEIDELBERG, 9 Oct 1992, *Napoleon at the Head of a Cavalry Column during the Russian Campaign* (oil on card, 5 x 9 ins / 12.5 x 23 cm) DEM 1,680. MUNICH, 1-2 Dec 1992, *Farmhouse near Dachau* (oil on card, 10 3/4 x 16 ins / 27.5 x 40.5 cm) DEM 3,220. NEW YORK, 26 May 1993, *Gentleman Reading* (1889, oil on panel, 6 ins / 15 cm, 3/4 x 4 1/4 ins/2 x 10.8 cm) USD 3,680. LONDON, 27 Oct 1993, *Scouting Ahead* (1884, oil on panel, 8 3/4 x 12 ins / 22.5 x 30.5 cm) GBP 2,185. MUNICH, 21 June 1994, *Break during Manoeuvres* (oil on panel, 11 3/4 x 16 ins / 30 x 40.5 cm) DEM 5,750. PARIS, 26 March 1995, *Pipe Smoker Reading* (1880, oil on panel, 6 1/4 x 4 1/2 ins / 16 x 11.2 cm) FRF 8,200. MUNICH, 3 Dec 1996, *Hirschgarten, Munich* (oil on canvas, 20 x 35 1/2 ins / 51 x 90 cm) DEM 48,000.

SEILER, Hans
Swiss, 20th century.
Born 1907, in Neuchâtel; died 4 August 1986.
Active from 1931 in France.
Painter. Figures, portraits, interiors with figures, landscapes, flowers.
Der Schritt Weiter group.

Hans Seiler studied in Bern before enrolling in 1924 at the Beaux-Arts in Lyons to study sculpture. He entered the Académie Ranson in Paris in 1927, where he studied under Bissière. He forged a friendship with Marcel Gromaire in 1928. 1929 saw him back in Bern and the following year found him in France once more, this time in the company of Max von Mühlenen. He settled in Chennevières-on-Marne in 1931 and, a year later, co-founded together with Tonio Ciolina, Albert Lindegger and Max von Mühlenen the group of Abstract artists *Der Schritt Weiter* ('One Step Beyond'). Seiler travelled widely in Holland and England and visited Brittany and Central France on a number of occasions. He was awarded the Bührle Prize in 1952.

Hans Seiler experimented with pure abstraction and Surrealism but in the 1930s turned to the transposition of 'landscapes' by producing post-Cubist ochre-coloured juxtapositions of lines, tiny rectangles, ovals and squares in jigsaw-puzzle format.

Seiler showed his work at numerous group exhibitions, notably in Paris at the Salon de l'Art Français Indépendant of 1929, the Salon d'Automne (1936, 1937, 1944), the Salon des Indépendants (1936, 1937), the Salon de Mai (from 1949) and the 1965 Salon des Réalités Nouvelles. His work also featured in various thematic exhibitions, including the *École de Paris* (Paris School) exhibition at the Galerie Numaga in La Chaux-de-Fonds in 1959 and other *École de Paris* exhibitions at the Galerie Charpentier in Paris in 1957, 1958, 1959 and 1963. Posthumous exhibitions of his work included *Histoires d'Eaux* (*Water Tales*), a group exhibition held in 2002 at the Troisième Oeil Gallery in Paris.

Seeler exhibited solo on several occasions, in 1948 at the Galerie Jeanne Bucher in Paris; in 1951 and 1953 at the Galerie Roque (Paris); in 1952 in London; in 1963, in Oslo; in Paris again, at the Galerie Bongers in 1965 and in 1978, 1980, 1981 and 1988 at the Galerie Bellint; and in 1986, at the Musée Bonnat in Bayonne. Posthumous retrospectives included *Bonjour Monsieur Seiler!*, an exhibition held at the Carrousel du Louvre within the framework of the Art Paris festival of 2002.

BIBLIOGRAPHY:
Courthion, Pierre, *Art indépendant*, Albin Michel, Paris, 1958. Le Sidaner, Jean-Marie, *Hans Seiler: 'au risque de la tradition'*, La Différence, Paris, 1986. Harambourg, Lydia, *L'École de Paris 1945-1965. Dictionnaire des peintres*, Ides et Calendes, Neuchâtel, 1993. Borgeaud, Georges/Valere, Bertrand, *'Hans Seiler: peintre 1907-1986'* in coll. *La Mémoire de l'œil*, J. Genoud, Le-Mont-sur-Lausanne, 1996.

MUSEUMS AND GALLERIES:
BAYONNE (Mus. Bonnat) - BERN (Kunstmus.): *Self-portrait* (1936) - PARIS (MNAM-CCI).

AUCTION RECORDS:
PARIS, 21 Feb 1955, *Interior*, FRF 43,500. PARIS, 30 Nov 1987, *Children* (gouache, 6 1/4 x 22 ins / 16 x 56 cm) FRF 3,400. PARIS, 14 June 1988, *Brittany Landscape* (oil on canvas, 35 1/2 x 69 3/4 ins / 90 x 177 cm) FRF 11,500. NEUILLY, 22 Nov 1988, *Church* (oil on canvas, 31 1/2 x 31 1/2 ins / 80 x 80 cm) FRF 8,500. NEUILLY-SUR-SEINE, 16 March 1989, *Rustic Interior* (oil on canvas, 27 1/4 x 59 ins / 69 x 150 cm) FRF 27,000. NEUILLY, 6 June 1989, *Les Plomarche* (1975, oil on canvas, 46 x 35 ins / 116 x 89 cm) FRF 44,000. PARIS, 4 Dec 1992, *Dutch Canal* (1957, gouache, 5 1/2 x 9 3/4 ins / 14 x 25 cm) FRF 3,500. BOULOGNE, 8 May 1994, *Mauve Flowers* (1976, gouache/paper, 19 3/4 x 12 ins / 50 x 30.5 cm) FRF 4,500. PARIS, 28 Nov 1999, *Rustic Interior* (oil on canvas, 21 x 32 ins / 54 x 81 cm) FRF 11,000. VERSAILLES, 12 Dec 1999, *Breton Port* (1957, oil on canvas, 13 x 21 ins / 32 x 54 cm) FRF 16,500. PARIS, 22 June 2001, *Le Tournant* (1977, oil on canvas, 23 x 28 ins / 59 x 72 cm) FRF 11,000. BERN, 7 Nov 2001, *Abstract Composition with City* (1956, oil on canvas, 15 x 24 ins / 37 x 60 cm) CHF 2,400. VERSAILLES, 29 June 2003, *Untitled* (oil on canvas, 11 x 16 ins / 27 x 41 cm) EUR 1,500. VERSAILLES, 12 Dec 2004, *Beach at Cabourg* (1973, oil on canvas, 18 x 26 ins / 46 x 65 cm) EUR 1,900.

SEILER, Johannes
German, 20th century.
Born 5 August 1871, in Nuremberg.
Sculptor, painter. Landscapes. Busts, monuments.

Johannes Seiler was a pupil of Syrius Eberle and Buttersack; he sculpted war memorials and busts of academics at the universities of Munich and Erlangen.

MUSEUMS AND GALLERIES:
NUREMBERG (Germanisches Nationalmus.): *Bust of Bürgel* - NUREMBERG (Municipal Gal.): *Renunciation* (bronze, statuette).

SEILER, Joseph Albert
Austrian, 19th century.
Painter. Portraits, genre scenes, landscapes, still-lifes.

Joseph Seiler exhibited in Vienna, Austria, from 1837 to 1848.

AUCTION RECORDS:
LOS ANGELES, 28 Feb 1972, *The Fiancée*, USD 1,100. NEW YORK, 15 Oct 1991, *Christmas Morning in St Nepomuk* (oil on canvas, 33 x 25 1/2 ins / 84 x 65 cm) USD 9,900.

SEILER, Pascal
Swiss, 20th - 21st century.
Born 1965, in Steg.
Painter.

Pascal Seiler lives and works in Valais. He paints landscapes in which perspectives are disturbed by marks or criss-crossing. His works have been shown at Galerie La Ferronnerie in Paris.

SEILER, Paul
German, 20th century.
Born 11 June 1873, in La Forêt-Noire; died 9 June 1934, in Frankfurt am Main.
Active in Frankfurt am Main.
Sculptor, designer. Statues, monuments.

Paul Seiler sculpted statues and war memorials in Frankfurt.

SEILHADE, Prosper Jean Émile
French, 19th century.
Died 19 October 1870, in Châteaudun (Eure-et-Loir).
Sculptor. Figures.

In his *Dictionnaire des Sculpteurs de l'École française* (*Dictionary of Sculptors of the French School*), Lami writes 'The name of this artist appears on the monument erected to Henri Regnault in the Cour du Mûrier, at the École des Beaux-Arts'. There is a plaster statue by this sculptor of *Samson Breaking His Bonds*: it was sent to the Musée de Castellane (Alpes de Haute-Provence) by ministerial decree on 21 December 1885.

MUSEUMS AND GALLERIES:
CASTELLANE: *Samson Breaking His Bonds*.

SEILHEAN, Renée
French, 20th century.
Born 18 March 1897, in Bordeaux.
Painter.

Seilhean studied at the Écoles des Beaux-Art in Bordeaux and Roganeau.

She exhibited in Paris from 1923, at the Salon des Artistes Français where she later became a member. She was awarded a silver medal in 1926.

SEILLER, Dietegen
Swiss, 18th century.
Born 15 October 1693, in Schaffhausen; died 1 April 1774.
Engraver, portrait artist.
Dietegen Seiller was the son of Johann Georg.

SEILLER, Johann Georg, or Sailer or Seiler or Seyler
Swiss, 17th - 18th century.
Born 27 August 1663, in Schaffhausen; died 12 January 1740, in Schaffhausen.
Painter, engraver (etching/mezzotint). Portraits, genre scenes.
Johann Seiller studied under Ph. Kilian. He signed his work, *J.G. Seiller Fecit*, or, *J. Georg Seiller Fecit et Ex*, and sometimes, *Jol. Georg Seiller Scafussianus Fecit*.

SEILLIERES, Frédéric
French, 19th century.
Born in Rheims.
Painter, watercolourist. History painting.
A pupil of M Carliez, this artist exhibited at the Salon for the first time in 1875.

SEILMAKER, Jacob. See **SEYLMAKER**

SEIMEI. See **TANYU**

SEIMEN, Johann Conrad. See **SEUMEN**

SEIMERSHEIM-DESGRANGES, Jeanne. See **SELMERSHEIM-DESGRANGES**

SEIMIYA, Naobumi
Japanese, 20th century.
Born 1917, in Tokyo.
Engraver.
Seimiya Naobumi left the department of oil painting at the university of fine arts in Tokyo in 1941 and did not take up engraving again until after the war. In 1954 he began to exhibit with the group Shunyo-kai of which he became a member three years later. He showed his works in several private exhibitions.

SEINIENS, Balthazar van. See **LEMENS**

SEINSHEIM, August Karl von (Count)
German, 19th century.
Born 11 February 1789, in Munich; died 18 December 1869, in Munich.
Painter, lithographer, engraver (etching). Historical subjects.
Von Seinsheim attended the art academy in Munich and studied under Simon Klotz from 1813 to 1816. He started to produce engravings from 1809, and in 1816 went to Italy. On his return to Munich, he painted a *Virgin and Infant Jesus* for the church of Grunbach (Germany), and the *Accusation of St Peter* for the church of Wohburg (Poland). He also produced 10 etchings of religious and genre subjects.

SEIP, Daniel
German, 20th century.
Born 10 May 1893, in Frankfurt am Main.
Painter, engraver (etching). Portraits.
MUSEUMS AND GALLERIES:
FRANKFURT AM MAIN (Town Hall): several portraits.

SEIP, Gertrude
German, 20th century.
Born 19 October 1887, in Darmstadt.
Painter, engraver.
Gertrude Seip studied under W. Bader, A. Beyer-Becker, Albert Hartmann and Richard Hölscher.

SEIPEL, Johann Christian
German, 19th century.
Born 13 August 1821, in Bremen; died 24 May 1851, in Munich.
Painter. Seascapes.
Johann Christian Seipel studied under Wilhelm Krause.

SEIPEL, Ludwig
German, 19th century.
Painter. Stage sets (?).

SEIPP
Austrian, 18th - 19th century.
Active in Vienna, Austria.
Engraver (wood).
Seipp studied under Blasius Höfel.

SEIPP, Alice
American, 20th century.
Born in New York.
Painter, illustrator.
Alice Seipp studied at the Art Students' League in New York and under Douglas and Jane Peterson. She was a member of the Pen and Brush Club and the American Federation of Arts.

SEIPP, Anton
Austrian, 19th century.
Active in Vienna, Austria, c. 1840.
Engraver.
Anton Seipp signed his work *A. Seipp j*

SEIPP, C.
German, 18th century.
Active in Dresden c. 1790.
Engraver (burin).

SEIPTIUS, Georg Christian, or Seipsius or Sciptius
Danish, 18th century.
Born 1744, in Dresden; died 26 June 1795, in Copenhagen.
Painter (porcelain), miniaturist. Historical figures.
Seiptius was a painter at the royal porcelain factory in Copenhagen. He exhibited in London from 1768 to 1780.
MUSEUMS AND GALLERIES:
HILLERØD (Frederiksborg Slot): *Portrait of Queen Juliane Marie of Denmark* (miniature); *Portrait of King Christian VII*.

SEIQUER, Antonio
Spanish, 19th century.
Active in Spain.
Painter.
Antonio Seiquer exhibited in Paris and received a commendation at the Exposition Universelle of 1889.

SEIQUER LÓPEZ, Alejandro
Spanish, 19th - 20th century.
Born 1850, in Murcia; died 19 August 1921.
Painter, draughtsman. Figures, genre scenes, landscapes, animals.
Alejandro Seiquer López was employed until 1875 as a draughtsman at the Ministry of Public Works before applying for a scholarship to study in Paris on the advice of Carlos de Haes.

He painted animals, especially domestic animals, with the influence of Rosa Bonheur immediately evident. His figures are set against a neutral background or sometimes on the bare canvas. Examples include *Donkey, Chicks, Cats Playing, Chicks and a Mousetrap* and *Ducks in Flight*. He also painted genre compositions. His brushwork is subtle yet ample and well-defined; his colours perfectly balanced and reminiscent of the powerful colour sense of the Impressionists. His work featured at various collective exhibitions, including the 1878 Exposition Universelle in Paris and the National Fine Arts Exhibition in Madrid (from 1878 to 1895), where he was awarded a several bronze medals. He was elected president of the painting section of the Madrid Fine Arts Circle in 1902.

BIBLIOGRAPHY:

Arnáiz, José Manuel/López Jiménez, Javier/Merchán Díaz, Manuel (ed.), '*Cien años de pintura en Espana y Portugal (1830-1930)*' in vol. X, Antiqvaria, Madrid, 1993.

SEIRLING, Johannes
German, 18th century.
Active at the beginning of the 18th century.
Portrait artist.

SEIRYU
Japanese, 19th century.
Active in the Osaka region c. 1815.
Print artist.

SEISAI
Japanese, 19th century.
Active in the Osaka region in 1829 or in 1851.
Print artist.

Seisai is known for his portrait of the actor Ichikawa Kakuen, cited by Kuroda.

SEISAI. See also **ICHIGA**

SEISCHI, Ippitsusai. See **BUNCHO**

SEISEI. See **KIICHI Suzuki**

SEISEI-IN. See **KANO Yoshin**

SEISEIDO. See **KORIN**

SEISEIO. See **SHOKADO**

SEISENEGGER, Jakob, or Seisenecker, Seysenegger, Zeyssenecker
Austrian, 16th century.
Born 1505, in Linz; died 1567, in Linz.
Painter. Portraits.

In 1531 Jakob Seisenegger was appointed Court Painter to Ferdinand of Austria, who was later to become emperor, and he painted a portrait of Charles V. He painted in an eclectic style that answered to the pan-European ethos of the court he worked for.

MUSEUMS AND GALLERIES:

BRNO (Moravské zemské Muz.): *Allegory of Justice* - BRUSSELS: *Maximilian of Austria as a Child; His Sister as a Child* - BUDAPEST: *Wilhelm Steynhardt* - THE HAGUE (Mauritshuis): *Elisabeth, Max and Anna, the Children of King Ferdinand* - VIENNA: *Queen Anna; Archduke Ferdinand of the Tyrol; Archduchess Eleanora* - VIENNA (Kunsthistorisches Mus.): *Kaiser Karl V. (Emperor Charles V with Hound)* - WEIMAR: *Count Christopher Magnus.*

AUCTION RECORDS:

LONDON, 13 July 1928, *Child in a White Dress,* GBP 110. LONDON, 23 June 1937, *Maria of Austria,* GBP 66. LUCERNE, 27 Nov 1964, *Portrait of a Lady of Class,* CHF 4,600. MUNICH, 29 and 30 Oct 1965, *Portrait of Queen Anna,* DEM 63,000. VIENNA, 22 Sept 1970, *Portrait of a Young Woman,* ATS 110,000. NEW YORK, 9 June 1983, *Portrait of Two Children* (oil on panel, 17 1/2 x 15 ins / 44.5 x 38 cm) USD 33,000.

SEISLER, Andre
German, 17th century.
Died 1615, in Munich.
Painter.

Seisler studied under Hans von Achen.

SEISON. See **MAEDA Seison**

SEISSEL, Josip, pseudonym: Jo Klek
Croat, 20th century.
Born 1904, in Krapina; died 1987, in Zagreb.
Painter, watercolourist, pastellist, draughtsman, poster artist, scenographer, architect.

Josip Seissel collaborated on the review *Zenit* between 1922 and 1925, producing posters and set designs. He was also a painter; his style was abstract initially, then Surrealist in the 1930s. Two of his most important interests are architecture and town planning. From 1929 to 1939, he was employed as an architect by the city of Zagreb, and in 1937 made the Yugoslavian pavilion for the Exposition Unverselle in Paris. After World War II, he became a professor of town planning.

BIBLIOGRAPHY:

Buzancic, V., *Josip Seissel,* Gal. Umjetnina, Bol. Susovski, Marijan, *Josip Seissel. Slike, crtezi, akvareli, tempere, crtaci blokovi od 1920. do 1987,* exhibition catalogue, Muzej suvremene umetnosti, Zagreb, 1997.

SEISSER, Martin B.
American, 19th century.
Born 1845, in Pittsburgh.
Painter. History painting, portraits.

Martin B. Seisser studied in Munich, where his masters were C. Otto, Piloty and Schwind.

SEITÉ, Jean-Luc
French, 20th century.
Painter. Figures, portraits, landscapes, still-lifes.

Seité's compositions of figures are often close to caricatures. He paints figures and typical scenes of North Africa.

SEITEI, real name: Watanabe Yoshimata, nickname: Ryosuke, pseudonym: Seitei
Japanese, 19th - 20th century.
Born 1851; died 1918.
Active in Tokyo.
Painter.

Seitei painted flowers and birds in the traditional Japanese style. He was a disciple of Kikuchi Yosai.

SEITEL, Wilhelm or Christoph Wilhelm. See **SEIDEL**

SEITER. See also **SEUTTER**

SEITER, Agostino
Italian, 18th century.
Born 27 August 1683, in Rome; died c. 1742, in Rome.
Painter.

Agostino Seiter was the son of Daniel Seiter.

SEITER, Daniel or Joseph Daniel, or Saiter, Seitter, Seuter, Sayter, Seyter, Soiter or Syder, known as il Cavaliere Daniele or Daniele Fiammingo
Austrian, 17th century.
Born 1649 or 1647, in Vienna; died 2 November 1705, in Turin, Italy.
Also active in Italy.
Painter. Religious subjects, mythological subjects, landscapes with figures.

Seiter studied under L. C. Loth, and then under Carlo Maratti (1625 - 1713) in Rome. He was also influenced by the Venetians. Seiter produced work for the court of Turin, and painted numerous altarpieces for Roman and Turin churches.

MUSEUMS AND GALLERIES:

AVIGNON: *Peasants' Meal* - BAMBERG (Municipal Mus.): *Martyrdom of St Erasmus* - BRUNSWICK (Herzog Anton Ulrich-Mus.): *St Jerome* - DRESDEN: *St Jerome* - DÜSSELDORF (Kunstmus.): *Cimon and Pero; Venus Lamenting the Death of Adonis* - MARSEILLES: four paintings representing saints belonging to the Carthusian order; *Head of a Woman; Head of a Man* - MUNICH (Residenzmus.): *Joseph and the Wife of Potiphar* - OBERSCHLEISSHEIM (Neues Schloss Schleissheim,

Staatsgal.): *The Good Samaritan; Noli Me Tangere; Doubting Thomas* - POMMERSFELDEN: *Caritas Romana; Aurora and Cephalus; Venus and Adonis; Triumph of Hercules; Venus, Ceres and Bacchus; St Paul, St Peter and St James; Apostle; Study of a Head* - ROHRAU (Schlossmus., Graf Harrach'sche Familiensammlung): *St John the Baptist* - ROME (Gal. dell'Accademia Nazionale di S Luca): *Caritas Romana; Lot and his Daughters* - TURIN (Pinacoteca): *Christ Dead.*

AUCTION RECORDS:

LONDON, 4 April 1984, *Sine Cerere et Baccho friget Venus (Without Ceres and Bacchus, Venus would Freeze)* (oil on canvas, 46 1/4 x 66 1/2 ins / 117.5 x 169 cm) GBP 6,800. PARIS, 5 Dec 1984, *Diana and Endymion* (pen and wash/sketch in black chalk highlighted with white gouache/grey beige paper, 13 3/4 x 9 3/4 ins / 35 x 24.8 cm) FRF 14,000. MILAN, 16 April 1985, *Death of Pompey* (oil on canvas, 52 x 85 ins / 132 x 216 cm) ITL 20,000,000. PARIS, 17 Dec 1993, *St Bruno* (oil on canvas/panel, 10 3/4 x 7 1/2 ins / 27.5 x 19 cm) FRF 10,000. ROME, 24 Nov 1994, *Nymph in a Wooded Landscape* (oil on canvas, 19 x 25 ins / 48.5 x 63.7 cm) ITL 23,570,000. NEW YORK, 5 Oct 1995, *Martyrdom of St Lawrence* (oil on canvas, 68 1/4 x 53 1/2 ins / 173.3 x 135.8 cm) USD 7,475. ROME, 21 Nov 1995, *Diana and Endymion* (oil on canvas, 38 x 52 1/2 ins / 96.5 x 133.3 cm) ITL 28,284,000.

SEITER, Pietro
Italian, 18th century.
Born 28 June 1687, in Rome.
Engraver (burin), architect.

Pietro Seiter was the son of Daniel Seiter.

SEITGOV, Petr Sikstovich, or Peter, or Pjotr Sikstovich, or Seitgof or Sythov
Russian, 19th century.
Born 1852.
Painter, watercolourist. Landscapes.

Petr Sikstovich Seitgov studied at the art academy in St Petersburg from 1875 to 1878.

MUSEUMS AND GALLERIES:

ST PETERSBURG (Gosudarstvennyj Russkij Muz.): *Pond at Pavlovsk.*

SEITL, Franz, or Seydel or Seydl
Bohemian, 18th century.
Born in Bohemia.
Active in Mährisch-Trübau, Austria, 1730-1760.
Sculptor.

SEITLER, Ludwig
Austrian, 19th century.
Born c. 1812, in Vienna.
Painter, lithographer.

Seitler attended the academies of Vienna and Munich.

SEITLINGER, Bartholomäus or Bartlmä
Austrian, 17th century.
Born 20 August 1632, in Gurk; died 17 April 1683.
Painter.

Bartholomäus was the son of Johann Seitlinger. He painted altarpieces for Gurk Cathedral and the church of Hochfeistritz (Austria).

SEITLINGER, Jacob
Austrian, 17th century.
Active in Tamsweg, Austria, from 1661 to 1680.
Sculptor (wood).

Jacob Seitlinger carved altars for the churches of Tamsweg and the surrounding area.

SEITLINGER, Johann
Austrian, 17th century.
Born 1596; died 10 December 1666.
Active in Gurk, Austria.
Painter.

Johann Seitlinger produced paintings for the altars, pulpit and organs in Gurk Cathedral, Austria.

SEITLINGER, Ulrich I
Austrian, 17th century.
Active in Tamsweg, Austria, from 1617 to 1624.
Sculptor (wood).

Ulrich Seitlinger I carved a rood screen for the church of Tamsweg.

SEITLINGER, Ulrich II
Austrian, 17th century.
Active in Tamsweg, Austria, in 1661.
Sculptor (wood).

Ulrich Seitlinger II carved the high altar for the church of St Leonard near Tamsweg.

SEITOKU, real name: Tokuemon Izutsuya, nickname: Hakuryu, pseudonym: Gion Seitoku
Japanese, 19th century.
Born 1781, in Kyoto; died 1829.
Print artist.

Seitoku is known for his ukiyo-e paintings and his prints of female figures.

SEITON, Filippo, or Seyton
French, 16th century.
Potter.

Seiton was perhaps active in Faenza, but he worked in Lyons from 1581 to 1596.

SEITS, Alexander Maximilian, or Seitz
German, 19th century.
Born 1811, in Munich; died 15 April 1888, in Rome, Italy.
Painter. Religious subjects, mythological subjects, genre scenes.

Seits was the extremely precocious son of Johann Baptist Seitz. He studied under Peter Cornelius and Heinrich Hess, and also worked with Joseph von Führich. Seits exhibited at the Munich museum from the age of 18.

MUSEUMS AND GALLERIES:

FRANKFURT AM MAIN: *Religious Scene* (oil) - HANOVER (Kestner-Mus.): *Children Playing* - MUNICH (Stadtmus.): *Mythological Scene.*

AUCTION RECORDS:

HAMBURG, 4 Dec 1987, *Mary's Education* (1852, tempera/panel, gold background, 16 1/4 x 16 1/4 ins / 41 x 41 cm) DEM 4,000. VIENNA, 29-30 Oct 1996, *Joseph Sold by his Brothers* (1829, oil on canvas, 49 1/4 x 69 3/4 ins / 125 x 177 cm) ATS 1,125,000.

SEITZ. See also **SEIZ**

SEITZ, Anton
German, 19th century.
Born 23 January 1829, in Roth-am-Sand; died 27 November 1900, in Munich.
Painter. Figures, genre scenes, interiors with figures, still-lifes.

Anton Seitz studied under F. Wagner and Reindel, then under Fluggen at the art academy in Munich. He worked in the style of the French painter Ernest Meissonier (1815 - 1891).

Ant Seilz

MUSEUMS AND GALLERIES:

COLOGNE: *Juggler* - LEIPZIG: *The Good Friend* - MAINZ: *Kitchen Scene* - MUNICH: *People Travelling* - NUREMBERG (Germanisches Nationalmus.): *Peasant Woman Writing a Letter* - NUREMBERG (Municipal Mus.): *Player in a Cabaret; The Painter Johann Adam Klein.*

AUCTION RECORDS:
VIENNA, 1881, *The Poultry Merchant*, FRF 4,410. VIENNA, 14 May 1881, *The Widow*, FRF 2,845. PARIS, 1883, *Cabaret*, FRF 3,500. BERLIN, 17 May 1895, *In a Mountain Hut*, FRF 1,312. NEW YORK, 1899, *King of the Carabineers*, FRF 3,900; *Card-Player*, FRF 1,325. NEW YORK, 1899, *Monk Musicians*, FRF 1,300. NEW YORK, 1899, *Strolling Minstrels*, FRF 2,500. LONDON, 22 July 1927, *The Landlord*, GBP 117. LONDON, 11 July 1929, *Flowers in a Sculpted Vase and Birds' Nest*, GBP 89. PARIS, 18 June 1930, *The Little Italian Merchant Girl*, FRF 2,800. NEW YORK, 18 and 19 April 1945, *Without a Homeland*, USD 450. PARIS, 23 May 1945, *Game Lost*, FRF 10,200. AMSTERDAM, 29 and 30 Sept 1965, *Zither Player*, DEM 5,800. VIENNA, 16 March 1971, *Bavarian Peasant Smoking a Pipe*, ATS 22,000. LONDON, 10 Nov 1972, *Cabaret Scene*, Gns 550. COLOGNE, 22 Nov 1973, *Motherhood*, DEM 13,500. MUNICH, 13 March 1974, *The Cheat*, DEM 22,000. ZURICH, 20 May 1977, *Political Discussion* (1864, oil on canvas, 15 x 17 1/4 ins / 38 x 43.5 cm) CHF 23,000. NEW YORK, 26 Jan 1979, *Portrait Artist* (oil on panel, 12 1/2 x 17 1/2 ins / 32 x 44.5 cm) USD 19,000. ZURICH, 6 June 1984, *At the Photographer's* (oil on canvas, 11 x 16 1/2 ins / 28 x 42 cm) CHF 34,000. NEW YORK, 21 May 1986, *Hunting Tale* (1867, oil on panel, 15 x 13 ins / 38.1 x 33 cm) USD 12,000. NEW YORK, 16 Feb 1993, *Artist's Studio* (1872, oil on panel, 8 x 4 ins / 20.4 x 9.9 cm) USD 1,760. MUNICH, 22 June 1993, *At the Court* (oil on wood, 12 1/2 x 15 1/4 ins / 32 x 39 cm) DEM 28,750. MUNICH, 6 Dec 1994, *Family Reunion in a Peasant Interior* (1882, oil on panel, 11 1/2 x 17 3/4 ins / 29 x 45 cm) DEM 46,000. MUNICH, 27 Feb 1999, *Young Farmer's Girl on the Window of a Half-timbered House* (oil on panel, 8 x 7 ins / 20 x 17 cm) DEM 15,000. MUNICH, 29 Sept 1999, *Children Warming Hands on Open Fire* (oil on panel, 14 x 11 ins / 35 x 27 cm) DEM 18,000. BERLIN, 25 March 2000, *Girl at Window* (oil on panel, 7 x 5 ins / 17 x 12 cm) DEM 8,800. SAN FRANCISCO, 17 May 2000, *Peasant Woman Seated in Kitchen Interior* (1894, oil on panel, 13 x 18 ins / 34 x 46 cm) USD 1,800. MUNICH, 5 July 2000, *Peasant Woman Sitting in Kitchen* (1894, oil on panel, 13 x 18 ins / 34 x 45 cm) DEM 9,000. MUNICH, 5 Dec 2001, *Young Woman at Window* (oil on panel, 7 x 5 ins / 17 x 12 cm) DEM 8,000. LUCERNE, 4 June 2003, *Tasting the Milk* (oil on canvas, 30 x 23 ins / 76 x 58 cm) CHF 4,000. MUNICH, 17 March 2004, *Four Children round a Fire in Ruins* (oil on panel, 15 x 11 ins / 38 x 28 cm) EUR 14,000. ZURICH, 26 March 2004, *Girl Reading* (oil on panel, 13 x 9 ins / 34 x 24 cm) CHF 6,000.

SEITZ, Arwed
German, 20th century.
Born 23 February 1874, in Königsberg (now Kaliningrad, Russia).
Painter. Portraits.

Arwed Seitz painted portraits of Königsberg city magistrates and other luminaries.

SEITZ, August
German, 19th century.
Born 1829, in Munich; died 1879, in Munich.
Engraver (burin).

August was the son of Johann Baptist Seitz.

SEITZ, Constantin
German, 17th - 18th century.
Active in Schneeberg, S Tyrol, Italy.
Painter.

Constantin was the father of Karl Heinrich Seitz. He produced work for the churches of Schneeberg.

SEITZ, Franz von
German, 19th century.
Born 31 December 1817, in Munich; died 13 April 1883, in Munich.
Painter, lithographer.

Von Seitz was the son of Johann Baptist and the father of Rudolf Seitz. He studied under Schlotthauer at the art academy in Munich and produced paintings for Munich theatres.

SEITZ, G. C.
German, 17th century.
Engraver (burin). Biblical scenes, portraits.

SEITZ, Georg or Johann Georg
German, 19th century.
Born 14 March 1810, in Nuremberg; died 16 April 1870, in Vienna, Austria.
Painter. Still-lifes (including flowers/fruit).

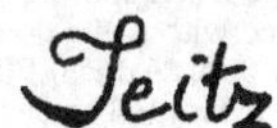

AUCTION RECORDS:
PARIS, 15 Dec 1950, *Flowers and Fruits* (1848) FRF 52,600. VIENNA, 12 Sept 1967, *Still-life with Flowers*, ATS 28,000. LUCERNE, 27 Nov 1971, *Still-life*, CHF 7,000. LONDON, 8 Nov 1972, *Still-life with Flowers and Fruits*, GBP 800. VIENNA, 3 Dec 1974, *Still-life with Fruits*, ATS 50,000. LONDON, 29 Oct 1976, *Still-life with Flowers* (oil on panel, 24 1/2 x 19 ins / 62.5 x 48.2 cm) GBP 1,850. VIENNA, 10 May 1977, *Still-life with Fruits* (oil on panel, 20 x 27 1/4 ins / 50.5 x 69 cm) ATS 22,000. VIENNA, 14 Oct 1980, *Still-life with Fruits* (oil on canvas, 22 x 26 3/4 ins / 55 x 68 cm) ATS 16,000. VIENNA, 15 Sept 1982, *Still-life with Flowers* (1847, oil on panel, 24 1/2 x 19 ins / 62 x 48 cm) ATS 130,000. LONDON, 25 Nov 1983, *Still-life with Flowers and Fruits* (oil on canvas, 18 x 14 1/2 ins / 45.7 x 37 cm) GBP 6,500. VIENNA, 16 Jan 1985, *Still-life with Fruits* (oil on canvas, 16 1/2 x 20 1/2 ins / 42 x 52 cm) ATS 38,000. VIENNA, 10 Sept 1986, *Still-life with Flowers and Fruits* (oil on canvas, 30 1/4 x 24 1/2 ins / 77 x 62 cm) ATS 160,000. NEW YORK, 25 May 1988, *Still-life with Basket of Grapes and Various Fruits Placed on a Console-Table* (oil on canvas, 29 x 39 1/2 ins / 73.6 x 100.4 cm) USD 11,000. LONDON, 17 June 1992, *Still-life with Flowers and Nest on a Marble Entablature* (oil on canvas, 30 1/4 x 24 1/2 ins / 77 x 62 cm) GBP 9,900. VIENNA, 20 May 1999, *Still-life with Fruit on a Table* (oil on canvas, 16 x 20 ins / 41 x 52 cm) ATS 40,000. LONDON, 1 Dec 1999, *Still-life with Flowers, Peaches and Butterflies* (oil on canvas, 23 x 19 ins / 59 x 47 cm) GBP 9,000. VIENNA, 23 May 2000, *Still-life with Fruit* (oil on canvas, 21 x 26 ins / 54 x 67 cm) ATS 35,000. VIENNA, 29 Nov 2001, *Still-life with Fruit on a Marble Slab* (oil on canvas, 22 x 27 ins / 55 x 68 cm) ATS 50,000. VIENNA, 29 Nov 2001, *Still-life with Fruit and Flowers* (1848, oil on canvas, 27 x 22 ins / 68 x 55 cm) ATS 70,000. LONDON, 21 March 2002, *Summer Flowers and Fruit on a Marble Ledge* (oil on canvas, oval, 20 x 25 ins / 51 x 63 cm) GBP 1,800.

SEITZ, Gustav
German, 20th century.
Born 1906, in Neckarau, near Mannheim; died 1969, in Hamburg.
Sculptor. Nudes, portraits.

Gustav Seitz studied in Karlsruhe before becoming a pupil of Wilhelm Gerstel in Berlin, where he studied from 1928 to 1932. He also received advice from Hugo Lederer at the Prussian academy of fine arts. After military service in World War II he taught from 1947 at the fine arts in Berlin-Charlottenburg. He was a member of the fine arts academy of East Berlin from 1950 and, in 1958, was appointed to a teaching post at the fine arts in Hamburg.

Seitz' early work was in many respects close to that of Renoir or Maillol. After the war, however, his style became more robust, even crude. Some of his work - such as *Rosa in Bed* or *Difficult* - equates to little more than rudimentary craftsmanship.

BIBLIOGRAPHY:
Hentzen, Alfred/Grohn, Ursel, *Gustav Seitz. Das plastiche Werk*, Dr. Ernst Hauswedell, Hamburg, 1980. Frenzel, Ursula (preface), *Briefzeichnungen. Gustav Seitz*, Hower, Hamburg, 1999.
AUCTION RECORDS:
HAMBURG, 5 June 1967, *François Villon* (bronze) DEM 3,800. COLOGNE, 6 May 1978, *Bert Brecht, Poet* (bronze, h. 19 3/4 ins / 50 cm) DEM 8,500. HAMBURG, 9 June 1979, *Mykonos* (1965-1969, bronze relief, series of four, 12 x 9 1/4 ins / 30.3 x 23.5 cm and 14 1/4 x 11 1/4 ins/36.3 x 28.5 cm) DEM 10,000. COLOGNE, 1 Dec 1982, *Bertold Brecht* (1959, greenish-brown patinated bronze, h. 9 ins / 22 cm) DEM 10,000. HAMBURG, 9 June 1984, *In Praise of Audacity* (1960, bronze, h. 24 ins / 61 cm) DEM 8,200. COLOGNE, 5 June 1985, *Head* (1949, terracotta, h. 9 ins / 22 cm) DEM 5,000. COLOGNE, 10 Dec 1986, *Crouching Nude* (1947, bronze, h. 6 3/4 ins / 17 cm) DEM 5,600. HEIDELBERG, 15 Oct 1994, *Draped Female Bust* (bronze, h. 7 3/4 ins / 20 cm) DEM 4,400. BERLIN, 5 June 1999, *Bust of Anette* (1948/1958, black patinated bronze, 17 x 14x9 ins / 44 x 35x24 cm) DEM 11,000. BIELEFELD, 23 Sept 1999, *Standing Figure* (dark brown patinated bronze, h. 19 ins / 48 cm) DEM 14,000. COLOGNE, 11 Nov 2000, *Bert Brecht* (ink drawing, 16 x 12 ins / 40 x 30 cm) DEM 3,500. COLOGNE, 11 Nov 2000, *Kathe Kollwitz* (plaster, h. 39 ins / 98 cm) DEM 34,000. HEIDELBERG, 12 Oct 2001, *Woman* (1955, bronze, 4 x 9x4 ins / 9 x 22x10 cm) DEM 10,500. BERLIN, 1 Dec 2001, *Actor* (1961, dark brown patinated bronze, 24 x 7x4 ins / 62 x 18x11 cm) DEM 20,000. HAMBURG, 14 June 2002, *Danae* (bronze, 4 x 9x4 ins / 9 x 22x11 cm) EUR 3,600. HAMBURG, 14 June 2002, *Friends* (bronze relief, 11 x 9x2 ins / 29 x 22x4 cm) EUR 3,800. BERLIN, 26 April 2003, *Seated Nude* (bronze, h. 6 ins / 16 cm) EUR 5,000. BERLIN, 29 Nov 2003, *Kneeling Negro Woman* (brown patinated bronze, h. 21 ins / 54 cm) EUR 16,500. BERLIN, 12 June 2004, *Sappho's Head* (black patinated bronze, h. 13 ins / 32 cm) EUR 17,000. COLOGNE, 4 Dec 2004, *The Last Lovers* (bronze, 14 x 9 ins / 35 x 23 cm) EUR 4,400.

SEITZ, Gustav W.
German, 19th century.
Born 1826, in Hamburg.
Engraver (wood), lithographer.
Gustav Seitz studied in Munich and produced reproductions of paintings using colour lithography.

SEITZ, Johann
Czech, 18th century.
Born in Prague; died after 1809.
Painter, goldsmith. Animals, still-lifes.
MUSEUMS AND GALLERIES:
MANNHEIM (Schloss): *Still-life with Lobster on a Dish.*

SEITZ, Johann Baptist
German, 19th century.
Born 1786, in Munich; died 15 March 1850, in Munich.
Engraver.
Johann Baptist Seitz studied under Roman Boos. He engraved an atlas of Bavaria, Germany.

SEITZ, Johann Daniel
German, 18th century.
Born in Saxony.
Active in the middle of the 18th century.
Painter, sculptor.
Johann Daniel Seitz produced a ceiling and pulpit for the church of Mutterstadt (Germany) around 1756.

SEITZ, Johann or Hans
German, 17th century.
Active in Passau from 1632 to 1681.
Sculptor.
Johann Seitz produced altars and tombs for the churches of Passau and Seitenstetten (Austria).
AUCTION RECORDS:
VIENNA, 24 March 1972, *St Paul* (lime wood) ATS 35,000.

SEITZ, Johann Paul
German, 18th century.
Active in Kaufbeuren (Bavaria) Germany, in the middle of the 18th century.
Sculptor (wood). Religious subjects.
MUSEUMS AND GALLERIES:
BERLIN (Deutsches Historisches Mus.): *St Mary Magdalene* (statue in gold wood).

SEITZ, Joseph
Austrian, 18th - 19th century.
Born 1771, in Nuremberg, Germany; died 9 February 1846, in Vienna.
Painter.

SEITZ, Joseph or Max Joseph
German, 19th century.
Born 1820, in Munich; died 1890, in Munich.
Engraver, metal worker.
Joseph Seitz was the son of Johann Baptist and the father of Otto Seitz.

SEITZ, Julius
German, 19th - 20th century.
Born 27 October 1847, in Külsheim; died 24 May 1912, in Freiberg.
Sculptor.
Julius Seitz sculpted tombs and fountains in Freiberg.

SEITZ, Karl
German, 17th century.
Died 23 April 1652, in Munich.
Painter.
Karl Seitz studied under Hans Pachmair.

SEITZ, Karl
German, 19th century.
Born 29 March 1824, in Munich.
Painter, engraver (burin). Landscapes with figures, landscapes.
Karl Seitz was the son of Johann Baptist Seitz.
AUCTION RECORDS:
VIENNA, 5 Dec 1984, *Boat Trip on the Lake* (oil on canvas, 11 1/2 x 19 1/4 ins / 29.5 x 49 cm) ATS 28,000.

SEITZ, Karl
German, 19th century.
Born March 1851, in Stuttgart.
Painter.
Karl Seitz studied under Alfred Schmidt.

SEITZ, Karl Heinrich
German, 18th century.
Born in Eibenstock.
Active in Eisenberg, c. 1747.
Painter.
Karl Heinrich was the son of Constantin Seitz.

SEITZ, Kaspar
German, 17th century.
Active in Wittenberg (Saxony-Anhalt) in 1637.
Draughtsman.

SEITZ, Ludwig
Italian, 19th century.
Born 11 June 1844, in Rome; died 11 September 1908, in Albano Laziale.
Draughtsman, art writer.
A pupil of his father Alexander Maximilian, Ludwig Seitz came under the influence of P. Cornelius and Overbeck. He

is known particularly for his frescoes in the churches of Loreto, Rome and in Djakovo Cathedral in Slovenia.
MUSEUMS AND GALLERIES:
ZAGREB (Gal.): *Madonna with Angels.*

SEITZ, Martin
German, 17th century.
Died 27 April 1703, in Breslau.
Active in Breslau (now Wroclaw, Poland).
Sculptor.
Martin Seitz produced an altar for the church of St Matthew, Breslau, and statues for the church of the Carmelites of Striegau (Silesia, today south-west Poland).

SEITZ, Maximilian. See **SEITS Alexander Maximilian**

SEITZ, Otto
German, 19th - 20th century.
Born 3 September 1846, in Munich; died 13 March 1912, in Munich.
Painter. Genre scenes.
Otto Seitz was the son of Joseph Seitz and a pupil of Karl von Piloty.

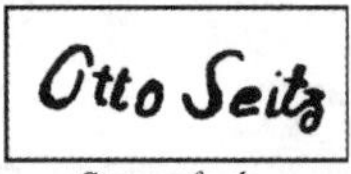
Stamp of sale

MUSEUMS AND GALLERIES:
MUNICH (Municipal Mus.): *Beech Forest* - MUNICH (Neue Pinakothek): *Cheat; Head* (study); *A Genoan; Voyage of Neptune* - WUPPERTAL (Von der Heydt Mus.): *Negro Head.*

SEITZ, Rudolf von
German, 19th - 20th century.
Born 15 June 1842, in Munich; died 18 June 1910, in Munich.
Painter, illustrator, designer.
Son of Franz von Seitz, Rudolf von Seitz studied at the academy in Munich and from 1883 was curator of the national museum of Bavaria.

SEITZ-ZELLER, Justine
Maiden name: Zeller
Swiss, 19th century.
Born 21 June 1856, in Thoune (Bern).
Active in Bern.
Painter. Landscapes, flowers.
Seitz-Zeller studied under Theodor Herr and Jeanne Bauck.

SEIWERT, Franz Wilhelm
German, 20th century.
Born 9 March 1894, in Cologne; died 3 July 1933, in Cologne.
Sculptor, painter, draughtsman, engraver.
Dadaism.
Cologne Dadaist, Stupid Group, Gruppe Progressiver Künstler (Progressive Art Group).
Franz Seiwert studied at the college of applied arts in Cologne and initially practised as an architect. He took up painting partly out of admiration for Van Gogh, Gauguin and Picasso and contributed to various avant-garde reviews, among them *Die Aktion* in Berlin, the *Workers' Dreadnought* in London, *Liberator* (Chicago), *Sept Arts* (Brussels) and the *Bulletin D* edited by Max Ernst and J.T. Baargeld and published in Cologne in November 1919 to coincide with a Dada exhibition mounted by the Cologne art circle. Seiwert refused at the last minute to take part in that exhibition on the grounds that Dadaism was a 'bourgeois undertaking'. The same year, Seiwert found himself working alongside Ernst, Baargeld, Heinrich Hoerle, and Otto Freudlich on the editorial staff of *Der Ventilator,* a pro-Communist journal that was quickly prohibited by the British army of occupation in the Rhineland.

In 1919, he and Hoerle also launched Stupid, a Dadaist splinter group which published a journal of that name. In 1922, when the Dadaists were in the process of linking up with the Constructivists, Seiwert took part in the congress of 'progressives' held in Düsseldorf and attended by Hans Richter, Raoul Hausmann, Hanna Höch, Otto Freudlich, El Lissitzki, Stanislas Kubicki and Ruggero Vasari. He befriended France Herbin and Constantin Brancusi in 1928 and, in 1929, he and Heinrich Hoerle launched yet another artistic group, the *Gruppe Progressiver Künstler* ('Association of Progressive Artists').

Franz Seiwert was both a committed Marxist and a passionate believer in man's supremacy over the machine. His early work evidences Parisian Cubism as represented by Sonia Delaunay. Over time, he evolved towards a more structured Abstractionism.
BIBLIOGRAPHY:
Dorival, Bernard/Hoog, Michel, *Dada,* exhibition catalogue, Musée national d'Art moderne, Paris, 1966. Bohnen, U., *Franz W. Seiwert, 1894-1933,* Glasbilder n° 8, Cologne, 1978.
MUSEUMS AND GALLERIES:
BONN (Kunstmus.) - HAMBURG (Kunsthalle): *Gala Evening* (1925).
AUCTION RECORDS:
COLOGNE, 28 March 1979, *Woman Standing and Holding her Head* (before 1922, enamelled clay, h. 11 ins / 27 cm) DEM 2,500. COLOGNE, 10 Dec 1986, *Head* (c. 1919, Indian ink and watercolour drawing, 10 1/4 x 8 3/4 ins / 26.3 x 22.2 cm) DEM 2,600. AMSTERDAM, 13 Dec 1990, *Untitled* (1922, watercolour and pencil/paper, 11 1/2 x 9 ins / 29 x 22 cm) NLG 19,550. LOKEREN, 9 Oct 1993, *International Worker Aid* (1926, gouache, 22 x 15 ins / 56 x 38 cm) BEF 150,000. LONDON, 13 Oct 1994, *Man and Woman Intertwined* (glass mosaic/card, 10 1/4 x 9 1/4 ins / 26 x 23.8 cm) GBP 12,650. BREMEN, 23 Oct 1999, *Mountain Landscape with Trees* (watercolour, 8 x 10 ins / 20 x 25 cm) DEM 3,300. COLOGNE, 1 June 2001, *Model for the Artist's Parents' Gravestone* (1931, patinated bronze, h. 9 ins / 22 cm) DEM 32,000. COLOGNE, 4 June 2002, *Black Sun on Silver Sky with Tree and House* (tempera on canvas, 13 x 9 ins / 33 x 24 cm) EUR 8,000. COLOGNE, 4 June 2002, *Peasant Battle* (1931, colour chalk and Indian ink, 11 x 14 ins / 27 x 35 cm) EUR 17,000. BERLIN, 12 June 2004, *Created Beings* (1917-1919, woodcut, album of seven, 12 x 10 ins / 30 x 25 cm) EUR 15,000. BERLIN, 26 Nov 2004, *Workers next to a Compressor* (1923, oil on canvas on wood, 18 x 15 ins / 46 x 37 cm) EUR 80,000.

SEIWL, Josef, or Scheiwl
Austrian, 19th - 20th century.
Born 7 April 1833, in Königgrätz (now Hradec Králové, Czech Republic); died 11 June 1912, in Prague.
Painter, illustrator.
Josef Seiwl studied under Eduard von Engerth at the academy in Prague, painted altarpieces for churches in Brandeis, Elbteinitz, Reichenbach, Schwihau and Zales and made decorative stained glass compositions for Königgrätz and Prague Cathedrals.

SEIZ
German, 17th century.
Active in Passau.
Painter.
Seiz painted a *St Nicholas* for the church of Hofkirchen, Germany, in 1686.

SEIZ
German, 18th century.
Active in 1799.
Silhouettist.
Seiz produced silhouettes of members of the princely family of the Palatinate (Germany).

SEIZ. See also **SEITZ**

SEIZ, Thomas
German, 18th century.
Active during the first half of the 18th century.
Stucco artist.
Thomas Seiz worked for the abbey of St Mang in Füssen, Germany, in 1719.

SEIZ, V.
German, 17th - 18th century.
Active in Passau.
Medallist.

SEJDINI, Bukurosh
Albanian, 20th century.
Born 1916.
Painter.
Sejdini's *Dawn: November 17,* which depicts the liberation of Tirana, is in the art gallery in Tirana.

SEJDLITZ, Jan
Polish, 19th century.
Born 1832; died before 1874.
Painter. Landscapes.
Jan Sejdlitz was a student at the art academy in Warsaw.
MUSEUMS AND GALLERIES:
POZNAN (Mielzynski Mus.): *View of the Krakowskie Przedmiescie Suburb in Warsaw* - WARSAW (Muz. Narodowe): *Four Views of Warsaw.*

SEJDLITZ, Jozef Narcyz Kajetan.
See **SEYDLITZ**

SEJKA, Leonid
Yugoslav, 20th century.
Born 14 April 1932, in Belgrade (now in Serbia); died 15 December 1970, in Belgrade.
Painter. Scenes with figures, still-lifes.
Leonid Sejka graduated in architecture, and began to paint in 1950. Sejka's art falls within the wider context of Surrealist figurative art, reacting against the official versions of modernism, and taking the old masters and their systems as a point of reference. Sejka set out his theories of art in his *Treatise on Painting* published in 1964; this work was awarded the Nolit Prize and frequently republished. Sejka's compositions - views onto the outside world through open windows, still-lifes consisting of objects spread out in space or arranged as if on some sort of votive altar - explore the themes of trompe-l'œil in an esoteric context.

He exhibited for the first time in 1953, in Belgrade, alongside Dado Djuric, Uros Toskovic and Sinisa Vukovic. In 1958, he was a founder member of the *Mediala* artists' society. Work by him was shown at *Mediala* and October group exhibitions. There were twelve solo exhibitions of his work during his lifetime, in Belgrade, Munich, Zurich, Basel and Bern. Posthumous exhibitions include ones at the Contemporary Art Museum, Belgrade (1972); the Modern Art Gallery in Valjevo (1987); and the Cultural Centre in Belgrade (1993).
BIBLIOGRAPHY:
Protic, Miodrag B., , Muzej savremene umetnosti (musée d'Art moderne), Belgrade, 1972. Markovic, Srdan, *Leonid Sejka i Mediala,* Prosveta, Nis (Serbia), 1993.
MUSEUMS AND GALLERIES:
BELGRADE (Muz. savremene umetnotsi).

SEJNOST, Josef
Czech, 20th century.
Born 30 May 1878, in Tesenov.
Medallist.
Josef Sejnost lived and worked in Prague. He studied in Bechyne, and in Prague under S. Sucharda.

SEJOURNE, Bernard
Haitian, 20th century.
Born 1945; died 1994.
Painter.
AUCTION RECORDS:
NEW YORK, 21 Nov 1995, *Nights at Comier* (1990, acrylic/synthetic resin, 34 x 39 ins / 86.3 x 99 cm) USD 8,625. PARIS, 12 March 2000, *Mask with Flowers* (oil on panel, 18 x 18 ins / 46 x 46 cm) FRF 33,000.

SEKAL, Zbynek
Czech, 20th century.
Born 12 July 1923, in Prague.
Sculptor, painter, ceramicist, writer.
Zbynek Sekal was arrested in 1941 and deported to Mauthausen. After World War II, in 1945, he became a drawing and painting student of E. Filla and F. Tichy at the institute for decorative arts in Prague. He only began to sculpt in 1948, following a period in Paris in 1947, during which he visited the important international Surrealist exhibition. From 1957, he was a member of the Salon de Mai. Sekal was one of the most important sculptors of his generation in Czechoslovakia. At an early stage, Sekal's sculptures were comparatively figurative, and based on associations between human and plant forms. From 1958, his sculptures lose any relation to reality and become entirely self-sufficient, their form and openwork designs crudely executed, as if with an axe. At the same time, he began to make assemblages for low reliefs, made from old planks, bits of ironwork and all kinds of rubbish, inspired by collage technique, like the *Merz* works developed by Schwitters.

His work was shown at group exhibitions, including *Exhibition D* (1964); the Gmunden ceramics symposium (1964, 1965); at *Transformation in Czech Art* in Liège and Rotterdam (1965); at *Profile 5: Contemporary Czechoslovak Art* at the municipal gallery in Bochum (1965); at *Contemporary Czechoslovak Art* at the fine arts academy in West Berlin (1966); at *Czechoslovak Sculpture from 1900 to Today* at the Folkwang Museum in Essen (1966); at the *International Sculpture Symposium* in Vienna (1966); and at *Contemporary Czechoslovak Art* in Stockholm. There have also been many solo exhibitions, including ones in Prague (1961, 1965), Brno (1965), and Vienna (1965, with Chlupac).

SEKALSKI, Jozef
Polish, 20th century.
Born 1904, in Turek; died 1972.
Active in Scotland from 1940.
Painter.
Jozef Sekalski studied at the University of Vilnius. In 1940, he went to Scotland with what remained of the Polish army. He married there, and lived in St Andrews.
AUCTION RECORDS:
SOUTH QUEENSFERRY, 23 April 1991, *Still-life with Dumb Waiter and Cafetière* (oil on card, 25 1/2 x 34 ins / 65 x 86.5 cm) GBP 770.

SEKATZ, or Seckatz
German, 18th century.
Active probably in Darmstadt.
Painter.
Sekatz exhibited at the Coliseum in 1776.

SEKIEN, real name: Toyofusa Sano, pseudonyms:
Toriyama Sekien, Reiryo, Gesso, Reiryodo, Sengetsudo, sentando

Japanese, 18th century.
Born 1712, in Edo, now Tokyo; died 1788.
Painter, print artist, illustrator.

Sekien was a pupil of Kano Gyokuen and subsequently went moved towards *ukiyo-e* painting and produced illustrations, mainly of pretty women for romances. He also made votive tablets for temples, with those of the Senso-ji temple in Tokyo considered among his best.

SEKIGUCHI, Shungo
Japanese, 20th century.
Born 1 January 1911, in Kobe.
Painter, watercolourist. Landscapes, seascapes.

Sekiguchi lived and worked in Tokyo and in Paris. He studied at the Paris École des Beaux-Arts with Louis Roger from 1935 to 1940. His landscapes depict the French countryside and Breton ports. He exhibited his work in Paris at the Salon des Indépendents, the Salon d'Automne and the Salon des Tuileries.

SEKIHO, real name: Toru Okano, nickname: Genshin, pseudonyms: Sekiho and Unshin
Japanese, 18th century.
Born in Ise.
Painter.

Sekiho was a landscape painter and undoubtedly one of the pioneers of the Nanga School (literati painters) in Japan. He lived in Kyoto around 1768. It is known that he was the author of several works on painting, but they have all been lost.

SEKIMACHI, Kay
American, 20th century.
Born 1926, in San Francisco.
Sculptor.

Kay Sekimachi studied at the California College of Arts and Crafts in Oakland. She gave up graphic arts to become a weaver in 1954 under the direction of Trude Guermonprez. After 1960 she began weaving with nylon filaments, then created her works with elements obtained from three-dimensional transparent shapes.

SEKINE, Nabuo or Nobujo
Japanese, 20th century.
Born 1942.
Painter (mixed media), assemblage artist.

Sekine exhibited his works at the St-Étienne Museum of Modern Art in 1996.

AUCTION RECORDS:
COPENHAGEN, 27 Nov 1986, *Phases of Nothingness* (granite and stainless steel, h. 23 1/2 ins / 60 cm) DKK 15,000. LUCERNE, 20 Nov 1993, *Phases of Nothingness Nos 8-9* (1971, objects/canvas) CHF 1,000.

SEKINE, Shoji
Japanese, 20th century.
Born 1899, in Tokyo; died 1919, in Tokyo.
Painter.

After spending a short time studying at the Taiheyo-gakai Kenkyujo College of Fine Arts, Sekine Shoji turned to Western painting, which he learnt himself.

He took part in the Salons of the Nika-kai group where he established a reputation for the symbolism in his works.

SEKINE, Yoshio
Japanese, 20th century.
Born 1922, in Wakayama Prefecture; died 1985.
Painter.
Gutai group.

After approaching an abstract geometrism, Sekino Yoshio's style followed a hyperrealist tendency. He took part in many collective exhibitions, including: from 1948 at exhibitions of the Han group; from 1949 to 1954 at the *All West Japanese Art Exhibition*; from 1951 to 1955 at Salons of the Nika-kai group; in 1954, exhibitions of avant-garde art in Kobe and Osaka; in 1954 at the Modern Art trade fair organised by the newspaper *Asahai* in Osaka; from 1965 at *International Art of the New Era*, a travelling exhibition in several large Japanese cities with the group Gutai, a group which he subsequently left; in 1966 at the first JAFA (Japan Art Festival Association) in New York, Pittsburgh, Chicago and San Francisco, and in 1968-1969 at the Exhibition of Contemporary Japanese Art in London. He won the Mainichi prize in 1948.

BIBLIOGRAPHY:
Yamamoto, Atsuo, et al., *Gutai: moments de destruction, moments de beauté*, Blusson, Paris, 2002 (text in French and English).

AUCTION RECORDS:
NEW YORK, 13 Feb 1991, *No. 221* (1970, oil and acrylic on canvas, 46 x 36 ins / 116.9 x 90.5 cm) USD 4,950. NEW YORK, 8 Nov 1993, *Untitled* (1965, oil on canvas, 51 1/4 x 76 1/4 ins / 130 x 193.5 cm) USD 3,450. NEW YORK, 24 Feb 1995, *Untitled* (oil on canvas, 64 x 51 1/2 ins / 162.6 x 130.8 cm) USD 3,162. NEW YORK, 10 Oct 1996, *Abacus 341* (1974, oil on canvas, 64 x 51 ins / 162.6 x 129.5 cm) USD 1,725.

SEKINO, Jun'ichiro
Japanese, 20th century.
Born 1914, in Aomori Prefecture; died 1988.
Engraver.
First Thursday Society.

Sekino Jun'ichiro studied engraving and painting with Onchi Kohiro and Munakata Shiko. When he was 21 years old, one of his works, a copper engraving, was accepted at the Slon Teiten (Salon of the Imperial Academy of Fine Arts), following which he took part in the activities of the Japanese Association of Engraving in which he won several prizes, as well as the national academy of painting (Koguka-kai). As a promoter of the movement *Sosaku Hanga* he also took part in the activities of the First Thursday Society directed by Onchi Koshiro. In 1957 he gained several awards at the Afro-Asiatic Exhibition in Cairo and in 1960 at the International Exhibition of East-West Engraving. In 1958 he toured the USA and then went to Europe on a study trip. In 1963 he taught at Oregon State University and in 1965 at Kobe University in Japan.

Sekino's work was represented at the Tokyo International Biennale from its inaugural year, and he frequently took part in the Ljubljana Engraving Biennale, at which he was awarded a prize in 1961. After his death a retrospective, *Woodblock Prints by Sekino Junichiro: the Fifty-Three Stations of the Tokaido* (a contemporary interpretation of the works of Hiroshige), was held at the Museum of Art at the University of Oregon, 1978. He was also represented in thematic exhibitions on Japanese engraving, including in 2002 *Japanese Engraving during the Allied Occupation 1945-1988* at the British Museum in London.

BIBLIOGRAPHY:
Thieme, Ulrich/Becker, Felix, *Allgemeines Lexikon der bildenden Künstler von der Antike bis zur Gegenwart*, Saemann, Leipzig, 1951. Roberts, Laurance P., *A Dictionary of Japanese Artists*, John Weatherhill Inc., New York, 1976. McClain, Robert, *Woodblock prints by Sekino Junichiro: the fifty-three stations of the Tôkaidô*, exhibition catalogue, Museum of Art, University of Oregon, Oregon, ca. 1978. Sekino, Junichiro, *Hanga o_kizuita hitobito: jidenteki Nihon Kindai Hangashi*, Bijutsu Shuppansha, Tokyo, 1979. Merritt, Helen/Yamada, Nanako, *Modern Japanese Woodblock Prints 1900-1975*, exhibition catalogue, University of Hawaï Press, Honolulu, 1992. Smith, Lawrence, *Japanese Prints during the Allied Occupation, 1945-1952: Onchi Kôshirô, Ernst Hacker and the First Thursday Society*, exhibition catalogue, The British Museum Press, London, 2002.

MUSEUMS AND GALLERIES:
CHICAGO (AI) - NEW YORK (MoMA) - SAN FRANCISCO (Asian Art Mus.).

SEKIYA, Yoshimichi
Japanese, 20th century.
Born 1920.
Calligrapher.

Sekiya Yoshimichi studied at the Gifu teacher training college. From 1949 to 1951 he exhibited his work with the institute of artistic calligraphy (Shodo-Geijitsu) and with the Japanese academy of fine arts. He became a member of the Bokujin-kai school in 1952.

In 1953 he took part in the exhibition of *Fine Arts of Today* in Kobe, the *Modern Art Fair* in Osaka and the exhibition of Japanese calligraphy at the Museum of Modern Art in New York, and in 1954 the exhibition of Bokujin-kai in Tokyo, Kyoto and Kobe.

SEKKEI, real name: Sosetsu Yamaguchi, pseudonyms: Sekkei, Baian, Hakuin
Japanese, 17th - 18th century.
Born 1644; died 1732.
Painter.

Sekkei worked in the style of Sesshu (1420-1506) and the Chinese painter Muqi (active in the mid-13th century). He spent the whole of his career in Kyoto.

SEKKEI. See also **SO Shiseki**

SEKKO, real name: Ban Aizawa, nickname: Bun'ei, pseudonyms: Kangaro, Sekko
Japanese, 19th century.
Active around Osaka in the first half of the 19th century.
Print artist.

SEKOTO, Gerard
South African, 20th century.
Born 9 December 1913, near Middelburg (Transvaal); died 1993, in Paris.
Painter.

Gerard Sekoto is a self-taught painter, born at the Botshabelo Mission near Middelburg. His work was shown at annual Salon of South African Art in 1940, where his painting *Yellow Houses* was bought by the Johannesburg Art Gallery. Another work, *Donkeys*, was bought by the South African Railways in 1947. In 1947 Sekoto left South Africa to live in Paris, supporting himself initially by playing jazz. His paintings gradually achieved wider recognition, and the city authorities bought one of his works, *The Little Boy and the Goats*. He remained in Paris for the rest of his life, visiting Senegal for a year in 1966.

Sekoto is recognised as a pioneer of black urban art and social realism. Strong, vivid colours and unusual perspectives convey the vitality, spontaneity and hardship of South African street life in the Johannesburg township of Sophiatown and Cape Town's District Six (where Sekoto lived for a time).

His highly sought-after work featured in a touring exhibition of South African art at the Tate Gallery, London and the Musée Galliera in Paris, as well as Amsterdam, Brussels, Canada and Washington. In 1989 the Johannesburg Art Gallery held a retrospective exhibition of Sekoto's work, and he received an honorary doctorate from the University of Witwatersrand.

SEKULA, Sonja
Swiss, 20th century.
Born 1918, in Lucerne; died 1963, in Zurich.
Naturalised and active from 1934 to 1956 in the USA.
Painter (including gouache), collage artist. Figures, landscapes.

Sonja Sekula studied under Kurt Roesch and Morris Kantor at the Art Students' League in New York. She returned to Zurich in 1956. Her traced landscapes and figures betray the influence of Arshile Gorky and her Surrealist approach is at times close to that of Joan Miro or Roberto Matta.

Sekula participated in group exhibitions, including Surrealist shows in Paris and São Paulo in 1948 and the Brooklyn Biennale of 1949, followed by showings at the Jeanne Bucher Gallery (1951), the Suzanne Bollag Gallery in Zurich (*Collages*, 1958), *Surrealism and Related Movements* (Art Collection, Thun, Switzerland, 1961) and posthumously, *Angelika, Anna and Their Other Sisters*, an exhibition mounted by the Zurich Art Gallery in 1987. She had many solo exhibitions, notably at Peggy Guggenheim's *Art of This Century* in New York (1945), at the Betty Parsons Gallery (1948, 1949, 1951, 1952, 1954, 1957) and at the Suzanne Bollag Gallery (1959, 1961, 1987).

Bibliography:
Schwarz, Dieter/Perret, Roger/Cage, John/Feldman, Morton/Hare, David, *Sonja Sekula, 1918-1963*, exhibition catalogue, Kunstmuseum, Winterthur (CHE), 1996 (text in German and English).

Museums and Galleries:
Aarau (Aargauer Kunsthaus): *Dark and Light Steps* (1961).

Auction records:
Zurich, 22 June 1990, *Composition: Spring* (1961, collage, 19 x 13 1/2 ins / 48 x 34.5 cm) CHF 6,500; *Composition* (1958, collage and pencil, 9 3/4 x 12 1/4 ins / 25 x 31 cm) CHF 2,200. Lucerne, 24 Nov 1990, *Private Totem* (1947, oil on canvas, 16 1/4 x 26 ins / 41 x 66 cm) CHF 4,400. Zurich, 29 April 1992, *Self* (1958, gouache, 20 x 14 ins / 51 x 35.5 cm) CHF 1,500. Lucerne, 15 May 1993, *Untitled* (1961, gouache and collage/black paper, 11 x 15 3/4 ins / 27 x 40 cm) CHF 2,800. Zurich, 13 Oct 1994, *Study in August* (1959, gouache and collage, 9 1/4 x 8 1/2 ins / 23.3 x 21.5 cm) CHF 1,500. Lucerne, 26 Nov 1994, *No. 37* (1956, oil on canvas, 19 3/4 x 13 1/2 ins / 50 x 34 cm) CHF 3,400. Lucerne, 23 Nov 1996, *Zig-Zag* (1962, oil on paper, 9 3/4 x 13 1/4 ins / 25 x 33.5 cm) CHF 2,500. Lucerne, 7 June 1997, *Formation of Thought* (1958, gouache/paper, 27 1/2 x 19 3/4 ins / 70 x 50 cm) CHF 3,800. Zurich, 18 Nov 1997, *Untitled* (1959, collage with sand and gouache, 22 x 11 ins / 55 x 27 cm) CHF 3,000. Zurich, 17 June 1998, *Projection No.10* (1948, oil on canvas, 16 x 12 ins / 40 x 30 cm) CHF 13,000. Lucerne, 27 May 2000, *Announcement* (1969, tempera and crayon, 39 x 18 ins / 98 x 45 cm) CHF 4,200. Lucerne, 24 Nov 2001, *Look - Message* (1956, watercolour and ink, 12 x 8 ins / 31 x 21 cm) CHF 2,500. Zurich, 25 Nov 2002, *New York, Statue of Liberty* (1948, oil on canvas, 38 x 26 ins / 96 x 66 cm) CHF 12,000.

SEKULKIC, Alexander
Serb, 20th century.
Born 2 February 1877, in Veliki Beckerek (Zrenjanin).
Painter.

Alexander Sekulkic studied in Budapest and Munich.

SEL, Jean-Baptiste
American, 19th century.
Active in New Orleans 1820-1830.
Painter. Portraits.

Museums and Galleries:
New Orléans (Louisiana State Mus.): painting.

SÉLASSIÉ, Mickaël, or Mikaël. See **BÉTHÉ-SÉLASSIÉ Micaël**

SÉLAVY, Rrose. See **DUCHAMP Marcel**

SELB, August
German, 19th century.
Born 9 February 1812, in Munich; died 1 November 1859, in Munich.
Draughtsman, lithographer.

August studied under his father Josef Selb and at the academy in Munich.

SELB, Josef or Joseph
German, 19th century.
Born 1784, in Stockach; died 12 April 1832, in Munich.
Painter, lithographer.

Josef Selb was the brother and pupil of Karl. He studied in Düsseldorf and settled in Munich. In 1816, he founded a lithographic institute, and from 1820, worked with Maunlich on reproductions at the Munich gallery. He produced a large number of lithographs in the style of Vernet.

SELB, Karl
German, 18th - 19th century.
Born 1774, in Stockach; died 1819, in Stockach.
Painter.
Karl Selb was the brother of Josef and attended the academies of Düsseldorf and Munich. He painted altarpieces for several churches in the River Lech valley (Austria/Germany).

SELBY, Prideaux John
British, 18th - 19th century.
Born 23 July 1788, in Alnwick (Northumberland); died 27 March 1867, in Twizell (Northumberland).
Painter draughtsman, engraver, illustrator, watercolourist. Birds.
Prideaux John Selby was educated at Durham Grammar School and at University College, Oxford. A wealthy man, he lived as a country gentleman on his estate in Northumberland enjoying country pursuits like watching and shooting birds, collecting insects and fishing. He was also interested in forestry. He became a famed ornithologist and a number of species were named and described by him; he was the founder of the Naturalist Library.

Selby began drawing birds as a child and went on to produce drawings, paintings and etchings that were both informative and decorative. He published *Illustrations in Ornithology* with Sir William Jardine (1825-1841) containing over 200 plates of birds Selby had engraved from his drawings, and illustrated his own *History of British Forest Trees* (1841-1842). He encouraged J.J. Audubon when he came to the UK, and Edward Lear as a young ornithologist.

Selby featured in a collective exhibition of drawing and painting of birds held at the John Rylands University Library, Manchester (2004).

BIBLIOGRAPHY:
Jackson, C.E., *Prideaux John Selby: A Gentleman Naturalist*, Stocksfield, 1992.
MUSEUMS AND GALLERIES:
EDINBURGH (Nat. Gal. of Scotland).
AUCTION RECORDS:
NEW YORK, 25 May 2000, *Common Wild Swan* (watercolour and graphite, 26 x 20 ins / 65 x 52 cm) USD 4,200. LONDON, 30 Nov 2000, *An Assembly of Birds on the Branch of an Oak Tree* (oil on canvas, 30 x 24 ins / 75 x 62 cm) GBP 4,800. LONDON, 8 May 2002, *Birds of the Titmouse Family* (watercolour heightened with gouache and gum arabic, 16 x 9 ins / 40 x 23 cm) GBP 4,200. NEW ORLEANS, 8 June 2002, *Ornithological Studies* (engraving, 25 x 20 ins / 64 x 51 cm) USD 5,200.

SELCK. See **ZYL**

SELCKE, Johann Heinrich
Polish, 18th century.
Born in Danzig (now Gdansk).
Sculptor.
Selcke's work can be compared to that of Johann Heinrich Sehlke. He produced an altar for the church of Deutsch-Eylau, Poland, in 1740.

SELD, Berta von (Baroness)
German, 20th century.
Born 24 December 1860, in Berlin.
Active in Wiesbaden.
Painter. Portraits.
Berta von Seld was a pupil of O. Gussov and K. Kempin.

SELDEN, Henry Bill
American, 20th century.
Born 24 January 1886, in Erie (Pennsylvania); died February 1934, in New London.
Painter, engraver.
Henry Selden studied at the Art Students' League in New York and under Charles Woodbury, Birge Harrison and Duveneck in Cincinnati. He was a member of the Salmagundi Club.

SELDENSLACH, Jacob
Flemish School, 17th - 18th century.
Born 1652, in Breda; died 1735; buried 16 November in Antwerp.
Active in Antwerp.
Painter. Flowers.
Jacob Seldenslach was a pupil of K.P. Verbruggen in 1680. He married Joanna Catherina Pauwels in 1682.

SELDER, Bjorne
Swedish, 20th century.
Sculptor.
Bjorne Selder's work featured at *Street Art*, an exhibition held in Borlänge in 1976 to profile contemporary Swedish sculptors. His sculpture is frequently monumental.

SELDON, John, or Selden
British, 18th century.
Died 12 January 1715, in Petworth.
Sculptor. Portraits.

SELEN, Johannes van
Dutch, 16th century.
Active during the second half of the 16th century.
Engraver.
Selen engraved a series of grotesques in 1590.

SELENICA, David
Albanian, 18th century.
Painter.
David Selenica was an important artistic figure of his time. He decorated the interior of the church of St Nicholas in Voskopojë in southern Albania, then the country's main cultural centre. The interior featured monumental paintings, both *a fresco* and *a secco*, with more than 2000 figures. The figures are well-proportioned, carefully executed and, in a departure from the solemnity of the past, lively and expressive.

SELENSKY, Mikhaïl Mikhaïlovich.
See **ZELENSKY**

SELENZOFF, Kapiton Alekseevich.
See **ZELENTSOV**

SELERONI, Giovanni
Italian, 19th century.
Sculptor.
A pupil of L. Manfredini in Milan, Seleroni was active in Cremona and Milan from 1840. He carried out work for Milan Cathedral and the cemetery in Brescia.
MUSEUMS AND GALLERIES:
CREMONA (Mus. Civico): *Resignation*.

SELEUCUS I
2nd century BC.
Cameo engraver.
Ancient Greek.
Seleucus is known for a cameo representing *Philoctetes Arming*.

SELEUCUS II
1st century.
Painter.
Ancient Roman.

Seleucus painted a number of frescoes depicting lovers and nymphs now in the Museo Nazionale Romano in Rome.

SELEUCUS III
2nd - 3rd century.
Of unknown origin.
Mosaicist.
Ancient Roman.

Seleucus made a mosaic of *Apollo and the Muses*, found in Merida.

SELEY, Jason
Haitian, 20th century.
Born 1919.
Sculptor.

Jason Seley studied with O. Zadkine at the Art Students' League in New York, and then taught sculpture at the Art Centre in Port-au-Prince in Haiti.

He was first influenced by the massive hollowed-out sculptures of Henry Moore. Later he realised that the bumpers of cars provided abstract forms on which he could base his compositions. After various attempts, he finished in 1962 by simply soldering the bumpers, shaping them into severe and complex creations, without turning his back on the tradition of harmony and balance. In 1969-1971 he returned to representational work with *Colleoni II*, a replica of Verrochio's famous equestrian statue, in which he demonstrated the virtuosity he could achieve using nothing but car-bumpers.

AUCTION RECORDS:
NEW YORK, 19 May 1992, *Head of Hector Hyppolite* (moulded aluminium, h. 7 1/4 ins / 18.5 cm) USD 880.

SELEZNEV, Ivan Fedorovich, or Selesnev, Selesnov
Russian, 19th century.
Born 3 January 1856.
Painter. History painting, architectural views.

Ivan Fedorovich Seleznev studied at the art academy in St Petersburg.

MUSEUMS AND GALLERIES:
ST PETERSBURG (Gosudarstvennyj Russkij Muz.): *In Pompei*.

SELF, Colin
British, 20th century.
Born 17 July 1941, in Rackheath, near Norwich.
Painter, sculptor, draughtsman, printmaker.

Colin Self studied at Wymondham College, at Norwich School of Art, where he met Michael Andrews, and at the Slade School of Fine Art in London (1961-1963), where he met and was encouraged by David Hockney and Peter Blake. He travelled in the USA and Canada in the early 1960s. He later taught at the Sheffield College of Art and Norwich School of Art.

Self was influential on the Pop Art movement of the 1960s. He was particularly interested in the issues of self-destructive forces in human behaviour, nuclear weapons and Cold War politics, as seen in his *Guard Dog on a Missile Base No. 1* (1965, pencil drawing), and *Bomber No. 1* (1963, print). His work has also emphasised the evils of consumerism, as when he made a sculpture of a charred hot dog, *Hot Dog Sculpture* (1965), which looked like the remnant of a nuclear holocaust. He redefined the process of etching by inking separate metal plates placed side by side, and by producing unique variants rather than uniform editions of prints. In the mid-1960s, he did a series of collages of female models in Art Deco cinemas, such as his *Cinema 3* (1965). About this time he went to live in Norwich, working in relative isolation. In the 1970s, Self produced what he called 'works of fusion', demonstrating his interest in Norfolk landscape, his children, still-lifes, the art of the past, politics and unemployment. He invented a new process of sculpting by casting liquid concrete into damp sand shaped by his bare hands, as in *Man Scanning the Distance* (1984).

Self has had solo exhibitions at Piccadilly Gallery (1964-1965); Alecto Gallery (1968); Fermoy Centre, King's Lynn (1979); Institute of Contemporary Art, London (1986) and the Tate Gallery, London (1995-1996). Other exhibitions include Galleria Milano, Milan (1965); Camden Arts Centre, London (1967); Tokyo International Print Biennale (1969); Museum of Modern Art, New York (1972-1973); a show touring China and Hong Kong (1982); *Comic Iconoclasm*, Institute of Contemporary Art (1987) and *Continuing the Tradition*, Chappel Galleries, Chappel (1993). The Tate Gallery has extensive holdings of his work in its collection.

BIBLIOGRAPHY:
Colin Self's Colin Selfs, exhibition catalogue, Institute of Contemporary Arts, London, 1986. Collins, I., *Colin Self: From Five Decades*, Norwich, 1999.

MUSEUMS AND GALLERIES:
LONDON: *Out of Focus Object and Flowers 2 (The 1940s)* (1968, lithograph); *Out of Focus Object and Flowers 3 (The 1940s)* (1968, lithograph) - LONDON (Arts Council of Great Britain) - LONDON (Tate Collection): *Bomber No. 1* (1963, print and mixed media on paper); *Margaret in a Chair* (1963, intaglio print); *Leopardskin Nuclear Bomber No. 2* (mixed media sculpture); *Hot Dog Sculpture* (1965, cast polyester resin sculpture); *Picasso's Guernica and the Nazis* (1968, lithograph); *Power and Beauty* (series of screenprints); *Shoe Trees* (1970-1971, etching); *A Letter to Christopher Logue* (1980, lithograph and mixed media); *Shepherd with Lantern* (1983, pastel and mixed media drawing); *The Ploughman* (2001, etching) - MANCHESTER (Whitworth Art Gallery): *Nude* (1971, aquatint); *Lockheed SR-71 Taking Off* (1967, mixed media drawing); *Car Drawing* (1964, pencil and coloured pencil drawing); *Mister* (1968, offset lithograph) - NEW YORK (MoMA) - NORWICH (Castle Mus. and Art Gal.): *Prelude to 1,000 Temporary Objects of our Times* (1971, series of 10 Pop Art etchings).

AUCTION RECORDS:
LONDON, 3 July 1980, *Girl Lying on a Sofa* (1964, colouring pencil and graphite, 12 3/4 x 21 ins / 32.5 x 52.5 cm) GBP 550.
LONDON, 3 July 1987, *Untitled* (1965, collage, pencil, graphite and ink/paper, 21 1/4 x 15 1/4 ins / 54.2 x 38.7 cm) GBP 850.
LONDON, 26 Oct 1994, *Swimming Pool* (1966, pencil, ink and colouring pencil, 9 1/2 x 11 1/2 ins / 24.2 x 29.2 cm) GBP 1,265.
ZURICH, 4 Dec 2002, *Woman Rockets Lolly* (1964, colour pen and pencil, 7 x 17 ins / 17 x 43 cm) CHF 2,600.

SELF-PORTRAITS, Master of. See **MASTERS**

SELIACHUK, Nicolai
Russian, 20th - 21st century.
Born 1947, in Brest, Belarus.
Painter. Scenes with figures.

Nicolai Seliachuk lives in Minsk. His work uses a very precise, figurative technique. Within his ironic compositions, elements from everyday reality co-exist with fabulous inventions.

AUCTION RECORDS:
PARIS, 14 May 1990, *The unexpected Snow* (1989, oil on canvas, 39 1/4 x 31 1/2 ins / 100 x 80 cm) FRF 10,000.

SELIG, Friedrich Wilhelm
German, 19th century.
Died 1810.
Active in Kassel (Hesse).
Draughtsman, engineer.

SELIGER. See also **SEELIGER**

SELIGER, Gall
Austrian, 16th century.
Active in the middle of the 16th century.
Sculptor (stone/wood).

Seliger worked in Graz and carved the pulpit of the church of Villach in 1555.

SELIGER, Hans Karl
German, 20th century.
Born 9 October 1870, in Lottin.
Active in Berlin.
Painter, engraver.

Hans Seliger painted decorative frescoes for churches in Magdeburg, Rügenwalde and Greifenhaegen.

SELIGER, Max
German, 19th - 20th century.
Born 12 May 1865, in Bublitz; died 10 May 1920, in Leipzig.
Painter, designer.

Max Seliger studied under Max Koch and E. Doepler Jr. and produced mosaics, frescoes, stained glass and watercolours in Berlin, Dresden and Leipzig.

SELIGMANN
German, 18th century.
Active in Nuremberg 1765-1779.
Potter.

Seligmann worked for the earthenware manufactory in Nuremberg.

SELIGMANN, Adalbert Franz
Austrian, 19th - 20th century.
Born 2 April 1862, in Vienna; died 1945.
Painter, illustrator.

Adalbert Seligmann was a pupil of Griepenkerl, Wurzinger and Alexander Wagner; he painted compositions for the imperial palace in Vienna and also wrote on art history.

MUSEUMS AND GALLERIES:
VIENNA (Albertina Mus.) - VIENNA (Schubert Mus.).

AUCTION RECORDS:
LONDON, 27 Nov 1985, *Art Critics in the Artist's Studio* (1887, oil on panel, 29 1/4 x 20 ins / 74.5 x 51 cm) GBP 13,000. NEW YORK, 29 Nov 1999, *In the Artist's Studio* (1887, oil on panel, 29 x 20 ins / 74 x 50 cm) USD 10,000. BRUSSELS, 10 Sept 2002, *Still-life with Grapes* (oil on canvas, 39 x 30 ins / 100 x 76 cm) EUR 4,200.

SELIGMANN, Georg Sofus
Danish, 19th - 20th century.
Born 22 April 1866, in Copenhagen; died 20 August 1924, in Montebello, near Helsingør.
Painter.

Georg Seligmann was a pupil of Frans Schwartz, Peter Severin Kröyer and Lauritz Tuxen.

MUSEUMS AND GALLERIES:
COPENHAGEN (Statens Mus. for Kunst): *Weeds* (1888) - HILLERØD (Frederiksborg Slot).

SELIGMANN, Gustaf
Danish, 19th century.
Born in Denmark.
Painter.

Seligmann participated in exhibitions in Paris. He received an honourable mention at the Exposition Universelle in 1889.

SELIGMANN, Johann Michael
German, 18th century.
Born 10 December 1720, in Nuremberg; died 25 December 1762, in Nuremberg.
Engraver. Anatomical and botanical subjects.

Johann Seligmann studied under Preissler and went to Rome and St Petersburg.

SELIGMANN, Kurt
Swiss, 20th century.
Born 20 July 1900, in Basel; died 2 January 1962, in Sugar Loaf (New York), committed suicide.
Active in France then in the USA.
Painter, engraver, writer, illustrator.
Abstraction-Création group, Paris Surrealist group.

Kurt Seligmann studied under Buchner and Ammann at the fine arts academy in Geneva. He returned to Basel, remaining there until 1927 prior to spending three years (1927-1930) studying under André Lhote in Paris and at the fine arts academy in Florence. He travelled to Greece in the company of Le Corbusier.

In 1932, Seligmann aligned himself with the Abstraction-Création group. In 1935, by which time he was in Paris, he encountered the Surrealists, whose ideas strongly influenced his own work. When war broke out in 1939, he moved to the USA together with other artists and writers who formed a circle around André Breton. He became progressively preoccupied with the occult and, in 1948, wrote *The Mirror of Magic*. Between 1950 and 1960, he was attached to the History of Art department of Brooklyn College.

In 1934, Seligmann put together a collection of 15 etchings entitled *Cardiac Protuberances*, prompting critic Anatole Jakovski to write in the preface to their public exhibition in terms of 'Seligmann forms'and a 'Seligmann country'. His meticulously composed constructions emerge as abstract symbols of an 'inner mathematic' and his use of shield-like devices imparts a sort of heraldic symbolism to his work, vacillating between the figurative and the abstract. This is exemplified in his *Unequal Brothers* (1936).

Seligmann illustrated many publications, among them *Heraldic Wanderings* of 1934 and *The Oedipus Myth* (1944). A highlight of his career came at the International Surrealist Exhibition in Paris in 1938, when he showed his notorious *Ultrameuble*, best described as an outlandish item of furniture in the form of a stool supported by two pairs of female legs.

Seligmann's overriding ambition was to draw on his fantasies in order to 'paint as Poussin but from dreams' (paraphrasing Cézanne's celebrated intent to 'paint as Poussin but from nature'). His final exhibition - in New York in 1960 - was inspired by classical mythology and featured transpositions of Polyphemus, Leda, the Sphinx and the Minotaur (as in *Involution*, painted in 1959 or *The King*, dating from 1960).

Seligmann's early compositions were exhibited in Basel, Bern, Brussels, Poland and Tokyo. From 1931, he showed at the Salon des Surindépendants in Paris and also at the major International Surrealist Exhibition held in Paris in 1938. He continued to contribute to the activities of the Surrealists from his self-imposed exile in New York City. His work subsequently appeared at group and thematic exhibitions, including *Hermann Obrist, Louis Soutter, Jean Bloé Nestlé, Kurt Seligmann* at the art museum in Bern in 1967 and *La Révolution Surréaliste* (*The Surrealist Revolution*), held in 2002 at the Pompidou Centre in Paris. The Nierendorf Gallery in New York exhibited his work on a regular basis between 1940 and 1950. Following his death in 1962, solo retrospectives included those at the Helen Serger-La Boetie Gallery in New York (1973), the Jacques Benador Gallery in Geneva (1974), the David Ellis Johns Gallery in London (1975), the Albright-Knox Art Gallery in Buffalo (*Kurt Seligman: Drawings and Prints*, 1982), the museum of art and history in Geneva (*Kurt Seligmann: Engravings*, 1982), the municipal art gallery in Zug (1987) and the Galerie Berggruen in Paris (*Kurt Seligmann: Engravings*, 1998).

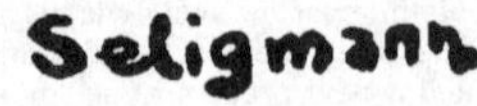

Seligmann

BIBLIOGRAPHY:
Fabre, Gladys C., *Abstraction-Création 1931-1936*, exhibition catalogue, Westfälisches Landesmuseum für Kunst und Kulturgeschichte, Münster, Musée d'Art moderne de la ville de Paris, Paris, 1978. Mason, Rainer Michael/Baum, Timothy/Givaudan, Claude, *Kurt Seligmann. Œuvre gravé*, Musée d'Art et d'Histoire, Cabinet des estampes, Genève, Éd. du Tricorne, Geneva, 1982. Hauser, Stephan E., *Kurt Seligmann. Leben und Werk*, exhibition catalogue, Schwabe, Basel, Kunsthaus, Zug, 1997. Spies, Werner (ed.), *La Révolution surréaliste*, exhibition catalogue, Éd. du Centre Georges-Pompidou, Paris, 2002.
MUSEUMS AND GALLERIES:
AARAU (Aargauer Kunsthaus): *The Superfluous Hand* (1940) - CHICAGO - GENEVA (MAH, Prints Collection): *Wrapped Landscape* (1945) - NEW YORK (Smith College Mus.): *Carnivora* (1944).
AUCTION RECORDS:
NEW YORK, 27 April 1972, *Narcissus*, USD 3,000. LONDON, 5 Dec 1973, *Alchemist*, GBP 8,000. LONDON, 3 Dec 1974, *Torn from the Mirror* (1943) Gns 3,600. ZURICH, 20 May 1977, *Submarine* (c. 1932, oil on panel, 32 x 25½ ins / 81 x 65 cm) CHF 40,000. NEW YORK, 6 Nov 1979, *Effervescence* (oil on canvas, 48 x 60 ins / 122 x 152.5 cm) USD 10,000. NEW YORK, 7 Nov 1979, *Study for Perseus* (pen, 19¼ x 25¾ ins / 49 x 65.5 cm) USD 1,500. BERN, 21 June 1980, *Phantom* (1951, watercolour/pencil outlines, 19¾ x 12½ ins / 50 x 32 cm) CHF 2,600. ZURICH, 30 Nov 1981, *Horseman* (Indian ink, 15¾ x 13 ins / 40 x 33 cm) CHF 2,800. PARIS, 27 Oct 1982, *Outcast* (oil on canvas, 36 x 30 ins / 91.5 x 76.5 cm) FRF 78,000. ZURICH, 9 Nov 1983, *General Staff* (1942, coloured chalks and charcoal, 17¼ x 23 ins / 44 x 58.5 cm) CHF 3,600. LONDON, 8 Feb 1984, *Alaska* (1944, oil on card, 30 x 26 ins / 76 x 66 cm) GBP 2,100. NEW YORK, 21 Feb 1985, *Narcissus* (1944, oil on canvas, 32 x 23¼ ins / 81.3 x 59 cm) USD 3,750. MUNICH, 25 Nov 1986, *The Pythagoreans* (1949, oil on canvas, 22¼ x 48 ins / 56.5 x 122 cm) DEM 19,000. NEW YORK, 29 April 1988, *Indian Myth* (oil on canvas, 27 x 29 ins / 68.5 x 73.5 cm) USD 20,900. LONDON, 29 Nov 1989, *Nocturnal Feast* (1957, oil on canvas, 28¼ x 37¼ ins / 71.5 x 94.5 cm) GBP 18,700. PARIS, 29 March 1990, *Prometheus* (1946, oil on canvas, 35¼ x 48½ ins / 89.5 x 123 cm) FRF 380,000. PARIS, 26 Nov 1990, *Spirit of Conviction* (1943, oil/hardboard, 46 x 57¾ ins / 116 x 147 cm) FRF 180,000. NEW YORK, 11 Nov 1992, *Exorcist* (oil on canvas, 47½ x 58½ ins / 120.7 x 148.6 cm) USD 55,000. NEW YORK, 12 May 1993, *Sleepwalking* (1942, oil/synthetic resin, 44 x 33 ins / 111.8 x 83.8 cm) USD 31,050. NEW YORK, 3 Nov 1993, *Two Heads* (1925, painted wood, construction, h. 20¾ ins / 52.7 cm) USD 36,800; *Initiation* (1946, oil on canvas, 28 x 36 ins / 71 x 91.4 cm) USD 96,000; *Acteon* (1944, oil on canvas, 35 x 30 ins / 88.9 x 76.2 cm) USD 59,700. NEW YORK, 11 May 1994, *Clown* (1931, oil on panel, 36 x 28½ ins / 91.7 x 72.4 cm) USD 32,200. ZURICH, 2 June 1994, *Composition (Aquarium)* (1930, oil on panel, 25½ x 21¼ ins / 65 x 54 cm) CHF 43,700. BERN, 20-21 June 1996, *Heraldic Wanderings* (1934, etching, set of 13 plates, each 20 x 15¼ ins / 51 x 38.5 cm) CHF 2,500. ZURICH, 14 April 1997, *Fauna* (1930, oil on wood, 25½ x 21¼ ins / 64.5 x 53.8 cm) CHF 28,750. NEW YORK, 4 March 1999, *Actaeon* (pen and ink, 22 x 12 ins / 55 x 31 cm) USD 2,600. VERSAILLES, 27 June 1999, *Three Figures* (ink, 28 x 34 ins / 70 x 86 cm) FRF 13,000. NEW YORK, 8 May 2000, *Herold* (oil on panel, 51 x 38 ins / 130 x 96 cm) USD 8,500. PARIS, 9 June 2000, *Idle Alchimist* (1950, oil on canvas, 30 x 20 ins / 77 x 51 cm) FRF 125,000. NEW YORK, 20 Feb 2001, *Indian Myth* (1946, oil on canvas, 27 x 29 ins / 68 x 73 cm) USD 23,000. NEW YORK, 6 Nov 2001, *Head Forms* (c. 1935, oil on panel, 24 x 20 ins / 62 x 51 cm) USD 5,500. PARIS, 27 May 2002, *Untitled* (c. 1941, Indian ink, 22 x 20 ins / 55 x 52 cm) EUR 2,100. PARIS, 24 March 2004, *Lyrical Figure* (ink, 19 x 15 ins / 48 x 38 cm) EUR 1,700. PARIS, 30 June 2004, *Unconcerned, Ulysses Listens to the Siren's Song* (1943, lead pencil and watercolour, 25 x 39 ins / 64 x 98 cm) EUR 11,000.

SÉLIM, Ahmed Fouad
Egyptian, 20th century.
Born 1936, in Cairo.
Painter.

Ahmed Fouad Sélim trained as a lawyer and has also worked as an artistic adviser. The symbolism of his Abstraction, in which he draws truncated geometrical forms, is strongly emphasised by the titles of his works: *Objective*, *Nothingness*. He takes part in collective exhibitions, such as *Visages de l'Art Contemporain Égyptien* (*Aspects of Contemporary Egyptian Art*) at the Musée Galliera in Paris in 1971. He has shown his works in private exhibitions in Cairo, Alexandria and London.
BIBLIOGRAPHY:
Badr El-Din Abou Ghazy, *Visages de l'Art contemporain égyptien*, exhibition catalogue, Musée Galliera, Paris, 1971.
MUSEUMS AND GALLERIES:
ALEXANDRIA (MFA) - CAIRO (Egyptian MMA).

SELIM, Honorine. See **PAUTHONNIER-SELIM**

SELIM TURAN. See **TURAN Selim**

SELIMONOVA, Anna
Russian, 20th - 21st century.
Born 1967.
Painter. Portraits.

Selimonova attended Ugarov's workshop.
AUCTION RECORDS:
PARIS, 10 June 1991, *Portrait of Ala* (oil on canvas, 31½ x 23½ ins / 80 x 60 cm) FRF 7,000.

SELINCART, Henriette
French, 18th century.
Born in Nancy.
Active mostly in Paris.
Painter. History painting.

SELING, Heinrich
German, 19th - 20th century.
Born 1842, in Gesmold, near Osnabrück; died 3 September 1912, in Osnabrück.
Sculptor.

Heinrich Seling studied at the academy in Munich then under Achtermann in Rome. He sculpted the high altar, rood-screen and funerary chapel in Osnabrück Cathedral.

SELINGER, David. See **SELLINGER**

SELINGER, Jean Paul
American, 19th century.
Born 1850, in Boston; died 1909.
Painter.

Jean Paul Selinger was a student at the Lowell Institute in Boston, and was also taught by Leibl in Munich.
MUSEUMS AND GALLERIES:
BOSTON (MFA): *Water Seller*.

SELINGER, Johann Baptist, or Seelinger
German, 18th century.
Born c. 1715; died 14 December 1779, in Inzlingen (Baden-Württemberg).
Active in Merdingen (Baden-Württemberg).
Sculptor.

Selinger studied in Paris, Amsterdam and Antwerp.

SELINGER, Johann Rupert and Michael. See **SELLINGER**

SELINGER, Schelomo
Polish, 20th century.
Born 31 May 1928, in Szczakowa.
Sculptor. Figures (stone/wood), animals.
Schelomo Selinger, an adolescent at the time, knew the horrors of deportation during World War II. After the war in 1945 he in Palestine on a kibbutz. He began sculpture in 1954 and the following year he won the Americo-Isreali 'Norman' prize for sculpture. Since 1956 he has lived and worked in France, in Paris, where he was a pupil of the studio Marcel Gimond aux Beaux-Arts de Paris. He became a Chevalier de la Légion d'Honneur in 1994. In general he expresses sadness - that of his own people and of all the persecuted - in sculptures of hard stone whose representations are inspired at the same time by medieval gargoyles and African totems, but also the victory of life through new birth. He also interprets biblical and metaphysical themes (destiny, light, matter) he has created numerous monumental works, including the *Memorial of the Deportation Camp* at Drancy erected in 1976 at the entrance to the city of La Muette; the *Requiem for German Jews* (1980) at Bosen (Germany) and the *Monument to the Resistance of the Courneuve* (1987). Other monumental sculptures celebrate life, notably *The Dance* (1982) composed of 55 sculptures situated in Basse Square in La Défense (Paris).

L'Espace Rachi Centre of Art and Culture in the rue Broca, Paris, put on a solo exhibition of his works in 2004: *Vivre pour raconter*.

BIBLIOGRAPHY:
Rochefort, Chr./Colan, Barnett D., *Selinger*, Éd. SMI, Paris, 1971. Bonicel, Marie-Françoise, *L'Univers du Sculpteur Shelomo Selinger*, Éd. Ferre, Paris, 1998.

MUSEUMS AND GALLERIES:
PARIS (MAMVP): *Maternité*.

AUCTION RECORDS:
PARIS, 30 Jan 1989, *Nude with Long Hair* (green-patinated bronze, 3 3/4 x 4 x 2 ins / 9.5 x 10 x 5 cm) FRF 3,800. PARIS, 17 June 1991, *Resistance* (1983, bronze, h. 11 1/2 ins / 29 cm) FRF 25,000.

SELIUS
4th century.
Active probably during the 4th century.
Mosaicist.
Ancient Roman.
Selius made a mosaic showing *Diana Bathing with Two Nymphs*, found in Timgad (Algeria).

SELIVANOV, Ivan
Ukrainian, 20th century.
Born 1924, in Kiev.
Painter, engraver.
Ivan Selivanov specialised in depicting the small details and momentous events in the history of communism in Soviet Russia. He is probably the painter J. Selivanov, who exhibited a work entitled *The Insurgents in the Kiev Arsenal*.

BIBLIOGRAPHY:
L'Art russe des Scythes à nos jours, exhibition catalogue, Gal. nationales du Grand Palais, Paris, 1967.

SELIVANOV, Ivan Aleksandrovich
Russian, 19th century.
Born 18 September 1776.
Engraver (burin/mezzotint).
Ivan Aleksandrovich Selivanov studied at the art academy in St Petersburg. He engraved portraits of the Imperial family.

SELKE, F.
German, 18th century.
Active in Cologne in 1792.
Draughtsman.

SELL, Christian, the Elder
German, 19th century.
Born 14 August 1831, in Altona; died 21 April 1883, in Düsseldorf.
Painter, illustrator. Military subjects, battles.
Sell studied under Th. Hilderbrand and Schadow at the academy in Düsseldorf and took a study trip to Germany and Belgium.

Chr. Sell.

MUSEUMS AND GALLERIES:
WROCLAW: *Episode during the Battle of Nachod, 27 June 1866*.

AUCTION RECORDS:
LONDON, 4 Dec 1909, *Scenes from the 1870 Franco-German War* (1879-1880, two pairs) GBP 26. COLOGNE, 6 June 1973, *Scene from the Thirty Years' War*, DEM 9,500. COLOGNE, 26 March 1976, *Rearguard* (1863, oil on canvas, 22 x 32 ins / 55 x 81 cm) DEM 2,700. COLOGNE, 16 June 1977, *War Scene* (1877, oil on panel, 7 x 9 1/2 ins / 18 x 24 cm) DEM 3,000. LONDON, 20 April 1979, *Prussian Soldiers on a Country Road* (oil on panel, 9 1/4 x 12 1/2 ins / 23.5 x 32 cm) GBP 2,400. COLOGNE, 20 March 1981, *Hussars on Patrol* (oil on card, 9 1/4 x 12 1/2 ins / 23.5 x 31.5 cm) DEM 3,800. DÜSSELDORF, 15 June 1983, *Town Siege* (1859, oil on canvas, 16 1/2 x 20 3/4 ins / 42 x 53 cm) DEM 7,000. LONDON, 27 Nov 1985, *Scene from the 1870 Franco-German War* (1883, oil on canvas, 19 x 31 ins / 48 x 78.5 cm) GBP 6,000. MUNICH, 12 June 1991, *Scenes from the 1870-1871 Franco-Prussian War* (1879, oil on wood, four panels, each 4 1/2 x 6 1/2 ins / 11.5 x 16.5 cm) DEM 18,700. NEW YORK, 26 May 1992, *Vanguard Post* (1860, oil on canvas, 20 1/2 x 29 1/4 ins / 52 x 74.2 cm) USD 3,850. AMSTERDAM, 7 Nov 1995, *Soldiers Keeping Watch on the Surrounding Areas* (oil on canvas, 13 1/2 x 21 ins / 34.5 x 53.5 cm) NLG 4,130. NEW YORK, 18-19 July 1996, *Retreat into the Snow; Mountain Observation Post* (1877, oil on canvas, a pair, each 12 1/2 x 16 1/2 ins / 31.8 x 42.2 cm) USD 5,175. JOHANNESBURG, 17 May 1999, *Cavalry Patrol* (1862, oil on canvas, 11 x 13 ins / 28 x 33 cm) ZAR 17,000. HAMBURG, 16 Oct 1999, *Winter Scenes from the Franco-Prussian War* (oil on panel, a pair, 6 x 11 ins / 14 x 27 cm) DEM 6,500. BERN, 10 May 2000, *Wounded Officer* (1870, oil on board, 9 x 13 ins / 24 x 33 cm) CHF 5,800. LONDON, 22 Sept 2000, *Returning from the Thirty Years War* (1852, oil on canvas, 31 x 50 ins / 80 x 128 cm) GBP 6,550. TORONTO, 26 Nov 2001, *Calvary Combat* (1875, oil on panel, 6 x 7 ins / 14 x 18 cm) CAD 3,600. TORONTO, 26 Nov 2001, *Rest at the Front* (oil on panel, 6 x 7 ins / 15 x 18 cm) CAD 3,600. AHLDEN, 29 Nov 2002, *Battle, 1870* (oil on canvas, 12 x 16 ins / 31 x 41 cm) EUR 1,900. LINDAU, 5 Dec 2003, *Prussian Soldier on Horseback* (oil on canvas, 9 x 10 ins / 24 x 26 cm) EUR 1,800. STUTTGART, 25 March 2004, *Signal to Attack* (1875, oil on panel, 5 x 6 ins / 12 x 16 cm) EUR 2,000. AMSTERDAM, 7 Sept 2004, *Prussian Soldiers Resting in a Winter Landscape* (1880, oil on panel, 8 x 11 ins / 20 x 27 cm) EUR 6,500.

SELL, Christian
German, 19th - 20th century.
Born 1854, in Düsseldorf; died 1925, in Gotha.
Painter. Military subjects.

AUCTION RECORDS:
COLOGNE, 12 June 1980, *Scene from the War of 1870* (oil on panel, 6 1/4 x 8 1/4 ins / 16 x 21 cm) DEM 2,400. NEW YORK, 1 March 1984, *Opening Shot* (oil on panel, 5 1/2 x 7 ins / 14 x 17.8 cm) USD 1,200. COLOGNE, 18 March 1989, *Scene from the War of 1870* (oil on card, 8 1/4 x 11 ins / 21 x 27 cm) DEM 1,100.

SELL, Elico
Painter. Genre scenes.

Auction records:
New York, 22 March 1907, *Alchemist,* USD 200.

SELLA, Gabriele De
Italian, 15th century.
Born to a family originally from Finale Ligure.
Active at the end of the 15th century.
Painter.
Probably the same person as Gabriele Da Cella, this artist painted frescoes in the church at Montegrazie in 1498.

SELLAER, Peter van
Flemish School, 16th century.
Active in Antwerp during the second half of the 16th century.
Sculptor.
Peter van Sellaer was possibly the son of Vincent Sellaer.

SELLAER, Vincent, or Zeelare or Zellaer, called Geldersmann
Flemish School, 16th century.
Born in Mechelen.
Active between 1538 and 1544 in Mechelen.
Painter. Religious subjects, allegorical subjects, mythological subjects.
Vincent Sellaer travelled in Italy and was in Brescia in 1525. He then returned to Mechelen, where he is referred to in 1544. His only signed and dated work is the *Let the Little Children Come Unto Me* of 1538, now in Schleissheim Castle, near Munich. This painting shows the influence of Leonardo da Vinci and Sellaer's acquaintance with the Italian mannerists.
Museums and Galleries:
Bern: *Leda and the Swan; Judith Holding the Head of Holofernes* - Bonn: *Lucretia* - Brunswick: *Venus Reclining; Jupiter and Antiope* - Copenhagen (Statens Mus. for Kunst): *The Holy Family with the Infant St John, St Elizabeth and St Anna* - Düsseldorf (Kunstmus.): *War and Peace* - Épinal: *Susanna and the Elders* - Graz: *Madrid; Charity* - Oberschleissheim (Neues Schloss Schleissheim, Staatsgal.): *Let the Little Children Come Unto Me* (1538) - Prague (Rudolfinum Gal.): *Holy Family* - Rouen: *Holy Family* - Stockholm: *Holy Family* - Valenciennes: *Leda and the Swan.*
Auction records:
New York, 20-21 Feb 1946, *Leda and the Swan,* USD 400. London, 26 Nov 1965, *Holy Family with St John the Baptist as a Child,* Gns 600. London, 27 June 1969, *The Virgin and Child with the infant St John the Baptist,* Gns 1,000. London, 17 July 1970, *Virgin and Child,* Gns 1,000. London, 30 Oct 1981, *Holy Family* (oil on panel, 31 1/4 x 41 1/4 ins / 79.3 x 104.6 cm) GBP 4,500. Milan, 26 Nov 1985, *Allegory of the Immaculate Conception* (oil on panel, 44 x 61 ins / 112 x 154 cm) ITL 32,000,000. London, 7 July 1989, *Leda with the Swan and Her Children* (oil on panel, 43 1/2 x 35 ins / 110.5 x 89 cm) GBP 55,000. London, 3 July 1991, *Judith with the Head of Holofernes* (oil on panel, 44 x 35 ins / 112 x 89 cm) GBP 10,780. New York, 17 Jan 1992, *Madonna and Child with St Elizabeth and Other Saints* (oil on panel, 37 1/4 x 42 3/4 ins / 94.6 x 108.6 cm) USD 31,900. London, 17 April 1996, *Venus surrounded by Cherubs* (oil on panel, 37 1/2 x 46 1/2 ins / 95.5 x 118 cm) GBP 12,650.

SELLAIO. See also **FRANCESCO DI NERI DI UBALDO**

SELLAIO, Jacopo Del, or Sellajo
Italian, 15th century.
Born 1441 or 1442, in Florence; died 12 November 1493, in Florence.
Painter. History painting, religious subjects.
Jacopo Del Sellaio was the son of Arcangelo di Jacopo. His works show the influence of the great Florentine masters, particularly Botticelli and Ghirlandaio.
Bibliography:
Horne, H. P., *'Jacopo del Sellaio'* in *Burlington Magazine,* vol 8, 1908. Baskins, C.L., *'Jacopo del Sellaio's Pietà in San Frediano'* in *Burlington Magazine,* vol 81, 1989.
Museums and Galleries:
Bergamo: *Flagellation* - Berlin: *Pietà; Caesar Just Before his Assassination; Murder of Caesar* - Budapest: *Esther and Assuerus* - Prato: *The Visitation.*
Auction records:
Paris, 19-20 April 1921, *Virgin, St Joseph and St John Adoring the Holy Child,* FRF 17,000. London, 14 Dec 1923, *Virgin Adoring the Holy Child,* GBP 68. Paris, 12 and 13 June 1933, *Nativity,* FRF 5,000. New York, 18 and 19 April 1934, *Virgin and Child,* USD 575; *Nativity,* USD 1,150. London, 2 Nov 1934, *Virgin Adoring the Saviour,* GBP 210. London, 19 Dec 1941, *Virgin and Child with St John,* GBP 168. New York, 15 Jan 1944, *Virgin and Child with St John* (school of Jacopo del Sellaio) USD 900. London, 20 Jan 1944, *Virgin and Child with St John,* GBP 157. New York, 31 Jan 1946, *Virgin and Child,* USD 550. London, 18 Nov 1949, *St Mary Magdalene and Two Other Saints,* GBP 304. London, 7 Dec 1960, *Madonna and Child,* GBP 1,200. Versailles, 3 Dec 1961, *Christ Mourned by St John the Evangelist and the Three Maries,* FRF 32,000. Milan, 16 May 1962, *Adoration of the Shepherds with Scenes from the Lives of the Saints in the Background* (tempera/wood) ITL 4,400,000. Milan, 19 Nov 1963, *Virgin and Child,* ITL 4,400,000. London, 19 April 1967, *Esther Before Assureus,* GBP 22,000. New York, 22 Jan 1976, *Virgin Adorning the Holy Child* (oil on panel with a rounded pediment, 39 x 23 1/2 ins / 99 x 60 cm) USD 35,000. London, 12 April 1978, *Virgin Adoring the Holy Child* (oil on panel, rounded at the top, 39 x 24 ins / 99 x 61 cm) GBP 14,000. London, 23 April 1982, *Virgin and Child with the Infant St John the Baptist and an Angel* (oil on panel, round, diam. 33 1/2 ins / 85 cm) GBP 20,000. Monte Carlo, 14 Feb 1983, *Virgin and Child in a Landscape* (oil on panel, 35 x 22 ins / 88 x 56 cm) FRF 410,000. Milan, 8 May 1984, *Virgin and Child* (tempera/panel with gold background, rounded at the top, 48 x 33 1/2 ins / 122 x 85 cm) ITL 50,000,000. London, 13 Dec 1985, *Virgin and Child with the Infant St John the Baptist and an Angel* (oil on panel, 35 3/4 x 24 ins / 91 x 61 cm) GBP 75,000. New York, 21 May 1992, *Holy Family with the Infant St John the Baptist in a Landscape* (oil on panel, tondo, diam. 26 3/4 ins / 68 cm) USD 82,500. Rome, 26 Nov 1992, *Virgin and Child with Angels* (tempera/panel, 17 3/4 x 14 1/2 ins / 45 x 37 cm) ITL 55,000,000. London, 4 July 1997, *Madonna and Child with the Infant St John the Baptist* (tempera/panel, 34 1/4 x 22 1/4 ins / 87 x 56.5 cm) GBP 73,000. Castlecomer, 14 Oct 1999, *Blood of the Redeemer and Adoring Angels* (oil on panel, three in one frame, 10 x 15 ins / 25 x 39 cm) IEP 7,000. Rome, 5 June 2000, *St Jerome* (tempera on panel, 27 x 37 ins / 68 x 93 cm) ITL 310,000,000. Paris, 3 Dec 2001, *John the Baptist* (oil on canvas, 35 x 28 ins / 90 x 71 cm) FRF 135,000. London, 10 Dec 2003, *Madonna and Child, the Young St John the Baptist and an Angel in a Landscape* (tempera on panel) GBP 160,000.

SELLAOUI, Mahfoud
Algerian, 20th century.
Born 28 November 1943, in Algiers.
Active in Switzerland and in Spain since 1966.
Sculptor (wood).
Mahfoud Sellaoui studied at the school of fine arts in Algiers. Having settled in Switzerland in 1966, he participated in theatre and dance projects before going to live in Spain. He won the gold medal at the Cannes Azur 2001 exhibition.

SELLAR, Charles A.
British, 19th century.
Born 1856, in Edinburgh; died 1926, in Perth.
Painter, watercolourist. Portraits, landscapes, coastal views, still-lifes.

After training in law in Edinburgh, Charles Sellar took up art. He lived and worked in Perth from 1888.

He painted views of Perthshire and scenes of the east coast of Scotland such as *East Coast Harbour Scene, probably Crail*, with two young boys on a wall and fishermen; *An East Coast Harbour, Summer* and *Feeding the Hens, Fife*, with a good sense of light.

Sellar featured in exhibitions of the Royal Scottish Society of Painters in Watercolours, the Royal Academy, the Royal Glasgow Institute of Fine Arts and the Royal Hibernian Academy.

BIBLIOGRAPHY:
MacEwan, Peter J., *Dictionary of Scottish Art and Architecture*, 1995.

MUSEUMS AND GALLERIES:
DUNDEE (City Art Academy).

AUCTION RECORDS:
SAN FRANCISCO, 16 Feb 2003, *Young Navigators* (oil on canvas, 20 x 30 ins / 51 x 76 cm) USD 7,000. LONDON, 19 April 2004, *Kitchen Garden* (oil on canvas, 24 x 18 ins / 61 x 46 cm) GBP 4,000.

SELLBACH, E.
German, 19th century.
Born 1822, in Krefeld (North Rhine-Westphalia).
Painter. History painting.
Sellbach attended the academy in Düsseldorf, Germany.

SELLE, Samuel
German, 18th century.
Born c. 1719, in Danzig (now Gdansk, Poland); died after 22 December 1769.
Painter, miniaturist. Coats of arms.

SELLEMOND, Peter
Austrian, 20th century.
Born 14 January 1884, in Felthurns; died 1942.
Sculptor. Figures. Monuments.
Peter Sellemond studied in Klausen under Meraner and in Hall under Bachlechner; he sculpted crucifixions, altars and cribs.

SELLENY, Joseph
Austrian, 19th century.
Born 2 February 1824, in Meidling; died 22 May 1875, in Inzersdorf, of insanity.
Painter, lithographer. Landscapes.
Selleny studied under Ender and Steinfield at the academy in Vienna. He visited the Tyrol and Italy, and from 1857 to 1859, embarked on a long voyage in the company of the crown-prince to Austria, North Africa, the Canary Islands, the Cape Verde Islands and Brazil.

MUSEUMS AND GALLERIES:
GRAZ: *Pine Forest* - VIENNA: *Deserted Farm*; *Stream in the Tyrolean Mountains*; 89 watercolours and drawings, costume studies, and studies of the frigate Novara's tour around the world from 1857 to 1859.

AUCTION RECORDS:
VIENNA, 22 May 1982, *Wooded Landscape* (1870, watercolour, 18 x 23 3/4 ins / 45.9 x 60.5 cm) ATS 60,000. LONDON, 20 June 1985, *View of Gibraltar* (1860, oil on canvas, 23 x 37 1/2 ins / 58.5 x 95.5 cm) GBP 1,400. VIENNA, 9 Feb 1999, *Portrait of a Native Polynesian* (oil on canvas/panel, 9 x 6 ins / 22 x 15 cm) ATS 35,000. VIENNA, 9 May 2000, *Southern Italian Coast* (1854, watercolour and pencil, 8 x 12 ins / 20 x 31 cm) ATS 25,000. VIENNA, 24 Nov 2003, *Woodland Path to Bad Schalders near Brixen, Southern Tyrol* (1871, oil on panel, 21 x 16 ins / 53 x 40 cm) EUR 4,500.

SELLES, Pierre Nicolas
French, 18th - 19th century.
Born 23 May 1751, in Bernay; died 22 June 1831, in Bernay.
Painter. Portraits.

MUSEUMS AND GALLERIES:
BAYEUX: *Portrait of Mademoiselle Delauney known as Mademoiselle Calvados*.

AUCTION RECORDS:
NEW YORK, 11 March 1977, *Young Woman with her Three Children* (oil on canvas, 40 x 48 1/2 ins / 101.5 x 123 cm) USD 1,700.

SELLETH, James. See **SILLETT**

SELLIER, Charles François or Charles Auguste
French, 19th century.
Born 25 December 1830, in Nancy; died 26 November 1882, in Nancy.
Painter. Religious subjects, allegorical subjects, figures, portraits, genre scenes, interiors with figures, landscapes. Murals, church decoration.
His teachers were Louis Le Borgne and Léon Cogniet. He won the Prix de Rome in 1857. He exhibited at the Paris Salon between 1857 and 1882, then became a curator at the Musée de Nancy (eastern France), and director of the Nancy École de Dessin.

MUSEUMS AND GALLERIES:
NANCY (Church of St-Bernard): decoration of the chapelle de St-Denis - NANCY (MBA): *The Magdalen Repenting*; *Leander Dead*; *The Levite of Ephraim*; *Vitellius Visiting the Bedriacum Battlefield*; *The Trickster*; *Kitchen Interior*; *Drawing Room of the Villa Medici in 1862*; *Monk Collecting Alms*; *Madame Victor Massé*; *Italian Woman with a Shell*; *Flight into Egypt*; *Esmeralda in Prison*; study - PARIS (Mus. d'Orsay): *Portrait of E Duget* - TOUL: *Head of a Woman* - TROYES: *Cicada*; *Portrait of the Queen of Italy* (porcelain).

AUCTION RECORDS:
PARIS, 1884, *Residents of the Villa Medici*, FRF 930; *Forge in Andelys*, FRF 7,200; *Interior: at the Alchemist's*, FRF 4,000; *Venus Listening to Cupid*, FRF 1,650; *Slaughter near the Tiber*, FRF 1,450; *Leda*, FRF 1,650. PARIS, 23 Feb 1901, *Italian Woman with Shells*, FRF 250; *Faun and Bacchant*, FRF 205. VERSAILLES, 5 March 1989, *Odalisque with a Hookah* (oil on canvas, 8 1/4 x 15 1/4 ins / 21 x 39 cm) FRF 26,000. PARIS, 2 Dec 1994, *Languid Woman* (oil on canvas, 8 1/4 x 15 1/4 ins / 21 x 39 cm) FRF 42,000. PARIS, 24 April 2002, *Death of Leander* (1861, oil on canvas, 57 x 96 ins / 145 x 245 cm) EUR 4,200.

SELLIER, Dominique
French, 20th - 21st century.
Born 1952, in Le Grand-Lucé (Sarthe).
Painter, engraver, watercolourist.
Dominique Sellier started to paint in 1972 and has since gone on to exhibit her work in Paris. Her painting has the spontaneity of a naive artist in its rendering of a mythical world that seems oddly evocative of the Italian Renaissance. Her work is distinguished by its powerful anecdotal character and a distinct lyrical quality.

SELLIER, François Noël
French, 18th - 19th century.
Born 1737, in Paris.
Engraver (burin).
François Noël Sellier exhibited at the Coliseum in 1776 and at the Salon between 1793 and 1824.

SELLIER, Louis
French, 18th century.
Born 1757, in Paris.
Engraver (burin).
Louis Sellier was the son of François Noël Sellier. He mostly engraved architectural views and ornaments.

SELLIER, Valentin Marie Alexandre
French.
Painter. History painting.
MUSEUMS AND GALLERIES:
TOULON: *Vulcan Chaining up Prometheus on the Top of the Caucasus.*

SELLINGER, David, or Selinger
Austrian, 18th century.
Born 5 January 1766.
Active in Salzburg, Austria.
Painter.
David Sellinger was the son and pupil of Johann Rupert Sellinger.
MUSEUMS AND GALLERIES:
SALZBURG (Carolino Augusteum Mus.): *Portrait of Joh. P. Hofer.*

SELLINGER, Johann Rupert, or Selinger
Austrian, 18th century.
Active in Salzburg, Austria, in 1775.
Painter.
Johann Rupert Sellinger was the father of Michael and David. He restored the altar at the church of Fischach (Bavaria) Austria.

SELLINGER, Michael, or Selinger
Austrian, 18th century.
Born c. 1742.
Active in Salzburg, Austria.
Painter.
Michael was the son of Johann Rupert Sellinger.

SELLITTO, Carlo, or Sellitti or Sollitto
Italian, 17th century.
Born 1581, in Naples; died 1614, in Naples.
Painter.
Earlier documentation relating to Selitto records his name as Sellitti. He was active in Naples.

Sellitto painted altarpieces and portraits which, though inspired by Caravaggio, were in part characterised by Mannerist draughtsmanship. He died young and left only a small number of works. In 2003, he was included in the exhibition on the theme of Neapolitan painting in the 17th and 18th centuries entitled *Les Mystères de Naples. Sublime et triviale: la peinture napolitaine* (*The Mysteries of Naples. The Sublime and the Trivial: Neapolitan Painting*) at the Fesch museum in Ajaccio.
BIBLIOGRAPHY:
Spinosa, Nicolà, et al., *Les Mystères de Naples. Sublime et triviale: la peinture napolitaine*, group exhibition catalogue, Musée Fesch, Ajaccio, 2003.
MUSEUMS AND GALLERIES:
NAPLES (Mus. di Capodimonte): *St Cecilia* (oil on canvas).

SELLITTO, Sebastiano
Italian, 16th century.
Born in Naples.
Painter, gilder.
In 1577, Sebastiano Sellitto painted an altarpiece for the church at Stigliano.

SELLMAYER, Franz
German, 19th century.
Born 1807, in Munich.
Painter (porcelain/enamel).
Sellmayer worked for the porcelain manufactory of Nymphenburg, Germany.

SELLMAYR, Ludwig
German, 19th century.
Born 1834, in Munich; died 6 December 1901, in Munich.
Painter. Landscapes with figures, landscapes, still-lifes.
MUSEUMS AND GALLERIES:
ALTENBURG: *Cows by the Stream.*
AUCTION RECORDS:
LONDON, 6 May 1977, *Livestock in a Wooded Landscape* (oil on panel, 5 1/2 x 11 ins / 14 x 28 cm) GBP 780. LONDON, 26 Nov 1980, *Livestock at a Drinking Trough* (1881, oil on panel, 12 3/4 x 17 1/4 ins / 32.5 x 44 cm) GBP 1,800. LONDON, 19 June 1981, *Livestock at a Drinking Trough* (1881, oil on canvas, 23 1/2 x 39 1/2 ins / 60 x 100.4 cm) GBP 3,000. BREMEN, 22 Oct 1983, *Sheep in the Sheep-Fold* (1876, oil on card, 8 1/4 x 10 3/4 ins / 21.2 x 27.2 cm) DEM 3,600. BERN, 12 May 1990, *Return of the Herd* (oil on panel, 6 3/4 x 11 ins / 17 x 27 cm) CHF 6,000. COLOGNE, 25 March 1999, *Alpine Landscape with Herdsmen, Cows, Goats and Sheep* (oil on canvas, 19 x 26 ins / 49 x 65 cm) DEM 4,500. LINDAU, 4 May 1999, *View of the Monastery and Town of Neresheim* (1892, oil on canvas, 16 x 20 ins / 40 x 52 cm) DEM 5,000. MUNICH, 27 Sept 2000, *Herder with Cows, Goats and Sheep Watering* (oil on canvas, 20 x 35 ins / 50 x 90 cm) DEM 4,000. MUNICH, 22 March 2001, *Wooded Landscape with Deer* (1888, oil on canvas, 22 x 30 ins / 55 x 75 cm) DEM 3,300.

SELLMER, Karl
German, 19th century.
Born 1855, in Landsberg.
Active in Kassel (Hesse).
Painter. Genre scenes, landscapes, animals.

SELLS, Alfred Arthur
British, 19th - 20th century.
Born 1824, in Salisbury; died 1908, in Sevenoaks.
Watercolourist.

SELLSTEDT, Lars Gustaf
American, 19th - 20th century.
Born 30 April 1819, in Sundsvall; died 4 June 1911, in Buffalo.
Painter. Portraits, landscapes, seascapes.
Lars Sellstedt settled in Buffalo in 1842.
MUSEUMS AND GALLERIES:
BUFFALO: *Portrait of the Artist Painted by Himself.*

SELLU, Victor
Romanian, 20th century.
Born 14 November 1943, in Bucharest.
Active in Australia from 1979.
Painter.
Sellu studied in Bucharest at the school of architecture from 1972 to 1974 and at the N. Grigorescu Institute of Fine Arts from 1974 to 1977. He graduated from the City Art Institute in Sydney in 1983. His abstract painting reflects his desire to transpose his varied feelings. With an ethereal sense of line and light scratches, he portrays movements that complement a set of warm colours.

Sellu took part in collective exhibitions in Romania, Athens, England and Australia. He exhibited his works in solo exhibitions including: 1979, at the Friedrich Schiller gallery, Bucharest; 1980, Zeichnungs Gallery, Frankfurt am Main; 1981, Holdsworth Gallery, Sydney; 1983 and 1984, Garry Anderson Gallery, Sydney; 1985 and 1986, Galerie Olivier Nouvellet, Paris.
BIBLIOGRAPHY:
Jianou, Ionel, *Romanian Artists and the West*, American Romanian Academy of Arts and Sciences, Los Angeles, 1986.

SELMA, Fernando
Spanish, 18th - 19th century.
Born 1752, in Valencia; died 8 January 1810, in Madrid.
Engraver.

Fernando Selma was one of Spain's best engravers. He studied under Carmona but was also influenced by the style of Edelinck. His works include a portrait of *Charles V* after Titian and a portrait of *Magellan*. He provided engravings to illustrate *La Conquista de Mejico* (*The Conquest of Mexico*), published in Madrid in 1783, and the *Maritime Atlas of Spain*. He made skilful engravings after Raphael of *Lo Spasimo* (*Christ Falls on the Way to Calvary*), *The Madonna del Pesce* and *Virgin and Child*.

BIBLIOGRAPHY:
De Alcahali, B., *Diccionario biográfico de artistas valencianos*, Imprint de F. Domenech, Valencia, 1897. Esteve Botey, F., *Historia del grabado*, Editorial Labor, Barcelona, 1935. Villena, E., ed, *Fernando Selma el grabador al servicio de la cultura ilustrada*, exhibition catalogue for Calcografia Nacional, Madrid, Fundacion la Caixa, Barcelona, 1993.

SELMERSHEIM-DESGRANGES, Jeanne
French, 20th century.
Born 1877; died 1958.
Painter, watercolourist, draughtswoman. Landscapes, still-lifes, flowers.

Selmersheim-Desgranges was initially a jewellery designer. At the beginning of the twentieth century she became the second wife of Paul Signac. They had a daughter, Geneviève Laure Anaïs, known as Ginette. She exhibited for the first time in 1909 at the Salon des Indépendants in Paris, and continued to feature there regularly. In the 1930s she took part in exhibitions dedicated to Neo-Impressionists.

AUCTION RECORDS:
LOS ANGELES, 20 Nov 1972, *St-Raphaël*, USD 4,000. LONDON, 8 Dec 1977, *Still-life with Flowers* (oil on canvas remounted/panel, 10 1/4 x 13 1/2 ins / 26 x 34 cm) GBP 1,350. LONDON, 4 April 1979, *Vase of Flowers and Fruit* (watercolour and pencil, 15 x 9 3/4 ins / 38 x 25 cm) GBP 500. NEW YORK, 11 May 1979, *Tulips* (1910, oil on canvas, 25 1/2 x 41 1/4 ins / 65 x 105 cm) USD 1,400. NEW YORK, 18 Oct 1985, *Still-life* (oil on canvas, 29 x 36 1/2 ins / 73.6 x 92.7 cm) USD 4,000. LONDON, 19 Oct 1988, *Vase of Flowers* (1927, oil on canvas, 13 1/4 x 16 1/4 ins / 33.5 x 41 cm) GBP 2,420. LONDON, 22 Feb 1989, *Still-life with Chinese Soup Tureen* (oil on canvas, 37 1/2 x 29 1/2 ins / 95 x 75 cm) GBP 20,900. NEW YORK, 5 Oct 1989, *In the Garden* (1909, oil on canvas, 23 1/2 x 28 1/2 ins / 60 x 72.4 cm) USD 38,500. PARIS, 25 June 1990, *Peonies* (oil on panel, 7 1/4 x 9 1/4 ins / 18.5 x 23.5 cm) FRF 4 000. NEW YORK, 8 Oct 1992, *Vase of Flowers* (oil on canvas, 22 1/2 x 17 3/4 ins / 57.2 x 45.3 cm) USD 5,500. LONDON, 13 Oct 1993, *Cathedral as Seen from the Riverbank* (watercolour and pencil, 10 3/4 x 17 1/4 ins / 27.5 x 44 cm) GBP 1,150. PARIS, 14 April 2000, *Clown with Crocodile* (oil on canvas, 21 x 26 ins / 54 x 65 cm) FRF 25,000. PARIS, 14 March 2001, *Bouquet in Red Jug* (oil on canvas on board, 14 x 22 ins / 35 x 57 cm) FRF 25,000. NEW YORK, 8 Nov 2001, *In the Garden* (1909, oil on canvas, 24 x 28 ins / 60 x 72 cm) USD 32,500. NEW YORK, 29 Sept 2004, *Bouquet of Flowers* (oil on canvas on board, 15 x 22 ins / 38 x 55 cm) USD 6,000.

SELMI, Hédi
Tunisian, 20th century.
Sculptor.

Hédi Selmi is considered to be the pioneer of modern sculpture in Tunisia. His sculptures decorate the spaces of many Tunisian public buildings. He was the only artist in the whole of Africa to be selected for the Arts Olympics that took place in Seoul just before the Games of 1988.

SELMOSER, Josef
Austrian, 18th - 19th century.
Active in Vienna, Austria, from 1785 to 1812.
Painter. Interiors with figures.

Selmoser worked for the porcelain manufactory in Vienna.

MUSEUMS AND GALLERIES:
SIBIU (Muz. National Brukenthal): *Interior with Peasants*.

SELMY, Eugène Benjamin
French, 20th century.
Born 7 May 1874, in Clermont-l'Hérault.
Painter. Genre scenes, church interiors.

Selmy was a student of Bonnat, Léon Glaize and A. Maignan. From 1900 he was a member of the Salon des Artistes Français in Paris and exhibited there regularly. He received an honourable mention in 1900, a third-class medal and the Prix Marie Bashkirtseff in 1902, a travel bursary in 1904 and a second-class medal in 1906. He was made Chevalier of the Légion d'Honneur in 1919.

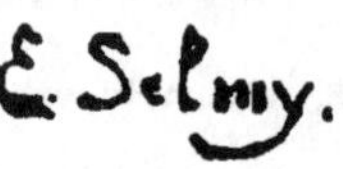

MUSEUMS AND GALLERIES:
BUCHAREST (Muz. National de Arta al României): *Church Interior*.

AUCTION RECORDS:
PARIS, 15 May 1944, *Church Interior* (1905) FRF 200. PARIS, 4 Oct 1950, *Church Interiors* (two canvases) FRF 5,000; *Farmyard*, FRF 1,450. PARIS, 5 Dec 2003, *Marrakech* (oil on canvas, 22 x 18 ins / 55 x 46 cm) EUR 2,500. PARIS, 5 Dec 2003, *Two Women on a Roof* (oil on canvas, 29 x 37 ins / 73 x 93 cm) EUR 3,000.

SELMY, Joseph
French, 18th century.
Active in the middle of the 18th century.
Sculptor, gilder.

Joseph Selmy worked for Toulon Cathedral.

SELOISSE
French, 18th century.
Active in Chantilly in 1707.
Sculptor (wood).

SELORT, Andrés
Spanish, 15th century.
Sculptor (wood).

Andrés Selort worked at Palma Cathedral in Majorca in 1445.

SELORT, Juan
Spanish, 15th century.
Active at the end of the 15th century.
Sculptor (wood), cabinet maker.

Juan Selort worked at Palma Cathedral in Majorca in 1497.

SELOS. See **SEELOS**

SELOUS, Henry Courtney. See **SLOUS**

SELPELIUS, Johannes
German, 17th century.
Died 21 June 1663.
Active in Greding (Germany) and Regensburg, Germany, and Switzerland.
Painter.

Selpelius painted altarpieces for the churches of Amberg (Bavaria), Dissentis (Switzerland), Regensburg (Bavaria) and Straubing (Bavaria).

Museums and Galleries:
Oberschleissheim (Neues Schloss Schleissheim, Staatsgal.): *Caesar and Cleopatra.*

SELSKY, Roman
Ukrainian, 20th century.
Born 21 May 1903, in Sokal, near Lviv.
Painter. Landscapes, still-lifes, flowers.

Between 1918 and 1922, Roman Selsky studied at the fine arts academy in Lviv, where he was a student of Novakivsky. Then from 1922 to 1923, at the fine arts academy in Cracow, where he worked under Julian Mehoffer and in the studio of the Polish painter Joseph Pankiewicz. He then lived in Paris until 1926, metting Bonnard, Matisse, Léger and Picasso. In 1930, he became director of *Artes*, an association of Ukrainian artists that mounted exhibitions in the Ukraine.

The influence of Fauvism is particularly notable in Selsky's painting in the choice of colours (mauves, blue turquoises, oranges) and their treatment, and in the decorative nature of some of his compositions.

Auction records:
Paris, 25 Jan 1993, *A Blue Night* (oil on canvas, 23 1/2 x 36 1/4 ins / 59.5 x 92.2 cm) FRF 10,500. Paris, 23 April 1993, *A Yellow Door* (oil on canvas) FRF 4,800. Paris, 13 Dec 1993, *Women Bathers in the Process of Taking Down a Tent* (oil on remounted paper, 25 1/2 x 34 ins / 64.5 x 86.5 cm) FRF 16,500. Paris, 31 Jan 1994, *The Worries of Autumn* (oil on canvas, 21 1/4 x 25 1/2 ins / 54 x 65 cm) FRF 5,500.

SELTENHORN, Josef Anton
German, 18th century.
Born 10 January 1713, in Pfaffenhausen; died 12 September 1792, in Kraiburg.
Painter.

Seltenhorn painted frescoes on the church ceilings of Pürten (Germany) and Gars (Austria).

Museums and Galleries:
Nuremberg (Germanisches Nationalmus.): drawings.

SELTENHORN, Martin Anton
German, 18th century.
Born 11 November 1741; died 4 May 1809.
Active in Burghausen and Kraiburg (Germany).
Painter.

Martin Anton was the son of Josef Anton Seltenhorn.

SELTER, Johann
German, 18th century.
Active in Mannheim 1700-1716.
Medallist, engraver. Coins.

SELTSAM, Martin
German, 18th century.
Born 1750, in Nuremberg; died 12 October 1808, in Leipzig.
Engraver. Coats of arms, ornaments.

SELTZ, Jules
French, 19th century.
Born 1851, in Héricourt (Haute-Saône); died April 1896, in Neuveville-les-Raon (Vosges).
Painter.

He was a member of the Société des Artistes Français and participated in the exhibitions held by this group.

SELTZAM, Melchior
Austrian, 19th century.
Born 1778, in Vienna; died 30 December 1821, in Vienna.
Painter, engraver. Architectural views.

SELTZER, Olaf Carl
American, 20th century.
Born 1877; died 1957.
Painter (including gouache), watercolourist. Figures, scenes with figures, local scenes, landscapes with figures, landscapes, animals.

Olaf Seltzer specialised in painting the wide open spaces of the American West and the life of cowboys. In this respect his painting is similar to that of Charles Marion Russel.

Bibliography:
Life and Times of Olaf P. Seltzer, 1877-1957: Meticulous Montana Frontier Artist, Montana Historical Society, Helena, 1960. Ladner, Mildred D./Myers, Fred A., *O. C. Seltzer, painter of the Old West*, University of Oklahoma Press, Norman (OK), 1979. '*Olaf Seltzer*' in *Salon d'Automne*, exhibition catalogue, Paris, 1987. Brayshaw, Thomas C./Yascavage, Pam., *Montana in miniature: exhibition of historical works in miniature by O. C. Seltzer*, exhibition catalogue, The Museum, Gret Falls (MT), 1991.

Auction records:
New York, 25 Oct 1973, *Buffalo Herd and Wolves*, USD 17,000. Los Angeles, 4 March 1974, *Roundup in Judith Basin*, USD 15,500. New York, 27 Oct 1977, *Pictograph Painter* (1912, watercolour and ink/card, 20 3/4 x 14 1/4 ins / 52.7 x 36.2 cm) USD 22,000. New York, 27 Oct 1978, *Crow War Party* (oil on canvas, 20 x 30 ins / 51 x 76.2 cm) USD 27,000. New York, 25 Oct 1979, *Indian on Horseback* (1914, watercolour, 13 1/4 x 8 1/2 ins / 33.6 x 21.6 cm) USD 11,000. New York, 25 Oct 1979, *Roping a Steer* (1908, oil on canvas, 20 x 30 ins / 50.8 x 76.2 cm) USD 55,000. New York, 23 April 1981, *Stampeding Herd* (1914, oil on canvas, 15 3/4 x 23 3/4 ins / 40 x 60.3 cm) USD 33,000. New York, 23 April 1982, *Raiding Party* (1907) USD 29,000. New York, 2 June 1983, *The Scouts* (1911, gouache and watercolour, 14 x 22 1/2 ins / 35.5 x 57.1 cm) USD 24,000. New York, 5 Dec 1985, *Indian on Horseback* (watercolour and gouache/paper, 9 3/4 x 13 3/4 ins / 24.7 x 34.9 cm) USD 8,000. New York, 5 Dec 1986, *Indian on Horseback* (watercolour and pencil/card, 12 1/2 x 17 1/2 ins / 31.5 x 44.5 cm) USD 9,000. New York, 1 Dec 1988, *Trail* (gouache/paper, 10 x 14 3/4 ins / 25.4 x 37.5 cm) USD 10,450. New York, 28 Sept 1989, *Lone Wolf* (oil on canvas, 24 x 36 ins / 61 x 91.5 cm) USD 8,800. New York, 1 Dec 1989, *Arriving at Camp* (oil on canvas, 24 x 36 ins / 60.9 x 91.4 cm) USD 88,000. New York, 24 May 1990, *'Crow' Warriors* (1909, gouache and watercolour/card, 17 1/4 x 23 ins / 43.8 x 58.4 cm) USD 27,500. New York, 17 Dec 1990, *Indian Brave* (watercolour/paper, 7 1/2 x 6 3/4 ins / 19.1 x 17.1 cm) USD 8,525. New York, 22 May 1991, *Indian Scout* (oil on card, 13 x 18 1/4 ins / 33 x 46.5 cm) USD 35,200. New York, 23 May 1991, *White Man's Buffalo Carcass* (oil on canvas, 20 x 30 ins / 50.8 x 76.2 cm) USD 41,250. New York, 25 Sept 1991, *The King's Mirror* (1904, oil on canvas, 36 x 48 ins / 91.4 x 121.9 cm) USD 14,300. New York, 26 May 1993, *Indian Warrior* (gouache and pencil/paper, 12 1/4 x 9 1/4 ins / 31 x 23.5 cm) USD 11,500. New York, 1 Dec 1994, *Overlooking the Missouri River* (watercolour/paper, 11 x 16 ins / 27.9 x 40.6 cm) USD 36,800. New York, 13 March 1996, *Indians on the Warpath* (watercolour, gouache and pencil/paper/card, 12 1/2 x 8 1/2 ins / 31.8 x 21.6 cm) USD 14,950. New York, 27 Sept 1996, *Medicine Man* (oil on panel, 12 x 9 ins / 30.5 x 22 cm) USD 16,100. New York, 4 Dec 1997, *Horse Thieves* (oil on canvas, 20 x 30 ins / 50.8 x 76.2 cm) USD 85,000. Cheyenne, 15 March 2002, *Untitled* (watercolour, 7 x 5 ins / 18 x 13 cm) USD 6,000. Cheyenne, 15 March 2002, *Roundup* (1910, oil on canvas, 20 x 30 ins / 51 x 76 cm) USD 46,000. Montana, 1 March 2003, *Untitled* (watercolour, 10 x 4 ins / 25 x 10 cm) USD 8,000. Montana, 1 March 2003, *Indian Scouting Party* (watercolour, 14 x 20 ins / 36 x 51 cm) USD 35,000.

SELTZER, Otto
German, 19th century.
Born 1854, in Gera.
Active in Munich.
Engraver (etching). Landscapes.

SELVA, Attilio
Italian, 20th century.
Born 3 February 1888, in Trieste.
Sculptor. Statues, busts, monuments.

A pupil of Bistolfi, Attlio Selva carved funerary monuments, statues and busts. He lived and worked in Rome.

MUSEUMS AND GALLERIES:
FLORENCE (Gal. d'Arte Moderna): *Portrait of a Girl; Nannina; Camilla* - ROME (Gal. Nazionale): *King Fuad I of Egypt; Claudio* - TURIN (Mus. Civico): *Suzanne.*

SELVA, Francesco
Italian, 17th century.
Sculptor.

Francesco Selva executed works in stucco in the chapel of the Virgin in Foligno cathedral about 1615.

SELVA, G.
Italian, 19th century.
Miniaturist.

MUSEUMS AND GALLERIES:
MILAN (Mus. Teatrale alla Scala): *Portrait of Claudia Cucchi.*

SELVA, Isabel de
French, 20th century.
Painter. Figures, still-lifes.

Selva studied at the École des Beaux-Arts in Paris. She exhibited in Paris, principally at the Salon des Artistes Français, which awarded her the Grand Prix in 1987 and where she was treasurer. She also received the Prix de l'Académie des Beaux-Arts. In addition, she featured at the Salon d'Automne, Salon Comparaisons and Salon du Dessin et de la Peinture à l'Eau in Paris. Her solo exhibitions include a show at the Fondation Taylor in Paris.

Her work bears certain similarities to a meticulous Hyperrealism and shows a true technical mastery, her nudes and still-lifes edging towards a smooth symbolism.

AUCTION RECORDS:
PARIS, 19 April 1996, *Folding Bed* (oil on canvas, 76 3/4 x 51 1/4 ins / 195 x 130 cm) FRF 40,000.

SELVA, Joseph
French, 20th century.
Born 21 August 1909, in Madrid, to French parents.
Painter.

Selva spent his childhood in Paris and started drawing very young. He was imprisoned in 1940. At the end of the war he travelled to South America, and in 1946 returned to Paris, where he met Humblot and the painters of Forces Nouvelles.

He exhibited in South America, in Buenos Aires, as well as in Paris, Luxembourg and Aix-en-Provence.

He was a great poetry lover, and what became his 'paintings of introspection' were paintings of his poetic vision. He only started painting around 1935, when he began his series of *Bas-Fonds* (*The Depths*) while working as set designer in Paris. After the war he returned from Germany with a collection of drawings that were later published under the title *Captivity*.

SELVA, Pino della
Italian, 20th century.
Born 3 January 1904, in Catania.
Active in France from 1931.
Painter (gouache), pastellist, draughtsman, engraver.
Scenes with figures, figures, portraits, landscapes.

A self-taught artist, Pino della Selva worked in Paris from 1931 and was artistic advisor for the Intermondial Ex-Libris Club. He was also a writer and art critic.

In the 1950s, his works tended towards abstraction. As well as portraits of poets, musicians and writers, he produced a number of partly surrealist, partly symbolist paintings.

He regularly took part in collective exhibitions in Paris including: Salon d'Automne (1932 and 1933), Salon des Indépendants (1932 to 1965) and Salon des Réalités Nouvelles (1952 to 1955). In 1969, he had an exhibition of some of his engravings at the Bibliothèque Nationale in Paris. Pino della Selva held regular solo exhibitions in France and abroad.

BIBLIOGRAPHY:
Sciacca Urbano, Sara/Gallo, Francesco/Grassi, Nicolas, *Pino della Selva*, exhibition catalogue, Centro di cultura e arte Aquarius, Catania. Schaube Kock, E./Hortel, François, '*Pino della Selva*' in *coll. Rythmes et couleurs*, Reboulin, Paris, 1961.

AUCTION RECORDS:
ROME, 14 Dec 1988, *On the Beach* (oil on canvas, 13 x 29 ins / 33 x 73.5 cm) ITL 3,400,000. NEUILLY, 5 Dec 1989, *Île de la Cité, Paris* (oil on canvas, 18 1/2 x 22 ins / 47 x 56 cm) FRF 3,500. PARIS, 14 March 1990, *Garden* (1948, oil on canvas, 11 x 9 ins / 27 x 22 cm) FRF 6,200. ROME, 31 May 1994, *Lagoon* (oil on canvas, 12 1/2 x 16 1/2 ins / 32 x 42 cm) ITL 1,532,000. MILAN, 18 Oct 1995, *Country Church* (oil on panel, 11 3/4 x 17 3/4 ins / 30 x 45 cm) ITL 1,035,000.

SELVATICO, Lino
Italian, 20th century.
Born 29 July 1872, in Padua; died 27 July 1924, in Biancade di Roncade (Veneto).
Painter, engraver. Figures, portraits.

The brother of Luigi Selvatico and pupil of Cesare Laurenti, Lino Selvatico made etchings.

MUSEUMS AND GALLERIES:
PALERMO - TRIESTE - UDINE - VENICE.

AUCTION RECORDS:
MILAN, 4 June 1968, *Capriccio*, ITL 600,000. MILAN, 19 June 1979, *Mother and Child* (1920, oil on canvas, 24 1/2 x 19 1/4 ins / 62 x 49 cm) ITL 1,500,000. MILAN, 17 June 1981, *Awakening* (1923, oil on panel, 24 1/2 x 16 1/4 ins / 62 x 41 cm) ITL 8,000,000. MILAN, 26 March 1996, *Beatrice* (oil on canvas, 51 1/4 x 38 1/4 ins / 130 x 97 cm) ITL 28,750,000. LONDON, 1 Dec 1999, *Beatrice* (oil on canvas, 51 x 38 ins / 130 x 97 cm) GBP 15,000. MILAN, 4 Dec 2000, *Female Figure* (oil on board, 7 x 8 ins / 17 x 20 cm) ITL 9,500,000. MILAN, 22 May 2001, *Portrait of Woman in Red Cloak* (oil on canvas, 59 x 39 ins / 150 x 100 cm) ITL 18,000,000. MILAN, 22 May 2001, *The String* (1912, oil on canvas, 31 x 20 ins / 80 x 50 cm) ITL 27,000,000. ROME, 11 Dec 2003, *Lady* (1924, oil on board, 19 x 14 ins / 48 x 36 cm) EUR 2,600.

SELVATICO, Luigi
Italian, 20th century.
Born 5 September 1873, in Venice; died 1938.
Painter, lithographer. Interiors, landscapes.

Luigi Selvatico was the brother of Lino Selvatico and a pupil of Cesare Laurenti.

MUSEUMS AND GALLERIES:
MOSCOW - ROME - VENICE.

SELVATICO, Paolo
Italian, 16th century.
Born c. 1547, in Florence; died 1606, in Parma.
Medallist.

Paolo Selvatico worked for Alfonso d'Este in Modena, for Cesare d'Este in Ferrara and for Ranuccio I Farnese in Parma.

SELVI, Antonio
Italian, 18th century.
Died 1755.
Medallist.

Antonio Selvi was the pupil of Massimiliano Soldani, whose style he adopted. He worked in Florence and in England.

SELVINO, Giovanni Battista or Johann
German, 18th century.

Born c. 1744, in Berlin; died 4 January 1789, in Berlin.
Active from 1760, in Berlin.
Sculptor.

Selvino worked for the court of Berlin and alongside the Räntzen brothers to produce the statue of General von Winterfeld.

SELVINO, Johann Anton
German, 18th - 19th century.
Active in Berlin.
Sculptor.

Johann Anton was the son of Giovanni Battista Selvino. He produced statues in marble and wax, and cast statues into bronze.

SELZ, Dorothée
French, 20th - 21st century.
Born 1946, in Paris.
Painter, sculptor.

Dorothée Selz was involved in a 2002 exhibition entitled *Fridge*, which explored the process of refrigeration at the aptly-named Galerie Fraîch'Attitude in Paris.

Initially, she worked closely alongside Miralda, with whom she organised 'celebrations' in the guise of festivals typically heralding the changing seasons, such as *Fête en Blanc de Verderonne*, celebrating Spring, or *Festival in Black*, purporting to herald the beginnings of Winter and 'nature in mourning'. A feature of these festivals was the accompanying colour-coded meal, at which Selz would use spectacular, and non-toxic, colours to capture the atmosphere of the moment. This thematic approach was continued in her preparation of cake sculptures, which were both entertaining and oddly disquieting. She went on to produce a series of paintings of well-known Parisian monuments which were subsequently coated in meringue, the underlying notion being to capture the Rococo aspects of Parisian architecture. In 1990, Selz used sugar scrolls to illustrate Gouffé's seminal publication *Pastry-Chef Vademecum*.

BIBLIOGRAPHY:
Dreyfus, Laurence, *Fridge*, group exhibition catalogue, Gal. Fraîche'Attitude, Paris, 2002.

SELZAM, Eduard
German, 19th century.
Born 2 October 1859, in Worms.
Active in Utting.
Painter, engraver.

Eduard Selzam studied under L. Löfftz.

MUSEUMS AND GALLERIES:
DARMSTADT (Hessisches Landesmus.): *The Letter.*

SELZAM, J.
Austrian, 18th century.
Active c. 1750.
Engraver (burin).

SELZER, Christian
German, 18th century.
Active in 1785.
Painter.

MUSEUMS AND GALLERIES:
NEW YORK (Metropolitan Mus. of Art): (sideboard with paintings).

SELZER, Karl
German, 19th - 20th century.
Born 8 June 1872, in Passau (Bavaria).
Painter. Still-lifes. Decorative schemes.

Karl Selzer studied at the academy in Munich and under Rudolf von Seitz and built a considerable reputation in his day as a decorative artist.

SELZLIN, Johann. See **STÖLZLIN**

SEM, pseudonym of Goursat

French, 19th - 20th century.
Born 23 November 1863, in Périgueux; died 1934, in Paris.
Painter (gouache), watercolourist, draughtsman, caricaturist, illustrator, designer. Scenes with figures, portraits, genre scenes, animals.

Sem was a committee member of the Salon des Humoristes de Paris and featured there regularly. Two retrospectives have been dedicated to him, at the Musée Carnavalet in Paris, 1979-1980 and the Musée de Périgueux in 1980. He was made Chevalier of the Légion d'Honneur.

He made decorative panels, including for the Théâtre des Champs-Élysées in Paris. He produced around twenty albums as an illustrator: *Album Sem* (1893), *Nightwatch* (1925), *Le Vrai et le faux chic* (*Real and False Chic*) (1914), *Sem at the Seaside*, made of lithographic panels and showcasing a gallery of the celebrities of the day (published between 1898 and 1930). He also created two large series of horses and riders: *Return from the Races* and *Acacias*. His two albums *War Sketches* (1916 and 1917) stand separate from his other work in terms of both form and intention. He also illustrated *Messieurs les Ronds-de-cuir* (*Messrs Penpushers*) by G. Courteline, and his own works such as *Un Pékin sur le Front* (*A Peking on the Forehead*). He worked for various newspapers and magazines, including *Le Gaulois, Le Figaro, Le Rire* and *Le Cri de Paris.*

Sem had a remarkable ability to capture the characteristic feature of a face rather than providing its likeness. His albums of Parisian life authentically reflect the physiognomy of the famous era of the 1900s.

BIBLIOGRAPHY:
Bonnelle, Madeleine/Meneret, Marie José, *Sem*, Éd. Pierre Fanlac, Périgueux, 1979.

AUCTION RECORDS:
PARIS, 1 April 1920, *Horse* (drawing) FRF 500. PARIS, 21 Jan 1924, *Sem Decorated by His Victims* (Indian ink heightened with watercolour) FRF 320. PARIS, 18 Nov 1936, *Portrait of Georges Clemenceau* (watercolour and gouache) FRF 205. PARIS, 24 June 1942, *Soldier on Leave* (watercolour) FRF 320. PARIS, 5 April 1950, *The Deauville Train* (drawing with watercolour) FRF 1,000. PARIS, 28 March 1974, *Hoax Marriage of Mistinguett and Félix Mayol in Deauville in 1913* (watercolour, 12 1/2 x 19 1/4 ins / 32 x 49 cm) FRF 1,200. PARIS, 16 May 1979, *Theatre Troupe on a Bus* (original gouache from the 'Panthéon-Champs Élysées' panel) FRF 7,200. PARIS, 16 May 1979, *In the Bus* (watercolour and gouache, 17 3/4 x 24 ins / 45 x 61 cm) FRF 7,200. PARIS, 25 March 1987, *Portrait of Sacha Guitry* (graphite, 10 x 8 1/4 ins / 25.5 x 21 cm) FRF 15,500. PARIS, 7-12 Dec 1988, *Chez Tourtel* (watercolour, 9 1/2 x 19 ins / 24 x 48.5 cm) FRF 17,500. PARIS, 27 May 1993, *Study of a Dog with a Pink Bow* (oil on card, 12 1/2 x 9 1/4 ins / 31.5 x 23.5 cm) FRF 12,500. PARIS, 12 Dec 2001, *Abbey* (1923, ink, wash, gouache, pencil, 17 x 13 ins / 44 x 33 cm) FRF 13,000. PARIS, 17 Nov 2003, *Cocktail* (watercolour, gouache, 13 x 17 ins / 32 x 42 cm) EUR 2,300.

SEMAN, Pedro
Brazilian, 20th century.
Born 1930.
Engraver.

Pedro Seman was a founder member of NUGRASP (Nucleo de Gravadores de São Paulo). He showed work in the first and second *International Exhibitions of Engraving* in São Paulo and has pieces in several museums.

SEMBACH, A.
German, 19th century.
Painter. Landscapes.
Sembach exhibited in the years following the 1870 war.

SEMBAT, Georgette. See **AGUTTE Georgette**

SEMBERA, Josef, or Schembera
Bohemian, 19th century.
Born 23 April 1794, in Hohenmauth, Bohemia; died 8 August 1866, in Litomisyl (German name: Leitomischl).
Engraver (burin), illustrator. Landscapes.
Sembera attended the academy in Prague and studied under K. Postl.

SEMBOLI, Giovacchino di Giovanni (Maestro). See **GIOACCHINO Di GIOVANNI**

SEMEGHINI, Defendi
Italian, 19th century.
Born 1852, in Nuvolato (Reggio Emilia); died 1891, in Paris.
Illustrator.

SEMEGHINI, Pio
Italian, 20th century.
Born 1878, in Quistello (Ferrara); died 1964, in Verona.
Painter (including mixed media), draughtsman, sculptor, engraver. Portraits, still-lifes, landscapes.
A self-taught artist, Pio Semeghini started as a sculptor. He lived in Modena, Florence, Venice, which he painted many times, Rome, Switzerland and Paris. He also worked in Brittany.

Semeghini exhibited many times at the Venice Biennale (1926, 1928, 1930, 1932, 1934, 1936, 1948, 1950, 1952, 1954) and the Rome Quadriennale (1931, 1939, 1955). In 2003, some of his works were shown at the collective exhibition held at the museum in Lodève, *De Chirico et la peinture italienne de l'entre-deux guerres* (*De Chirico and Italian Painting of the Interwar Period*). He had many solo exhibitions in France and Italy from 1903. He produced more drawings than paintings.

BIBLIOGRAPHY:
Bonito Oliva, Achille/Iovane, Giovanni/Lista, Giovanni, et al., *De Chirico et la peinture italienne de l'entre-deux guerres*, exhibition catalogue, Musée de Lodève, 2003.

AUCTION RECORDS:
MILAN, 25 Nov 1965, *St Mark's Column*, ITL 1,300,000. MILAN, 4 Dec 1969, *Seated Girl*, ITL 2,000,000. MILAN, 26 May 1970, *Venice*, ITL 2,000,000. MILAN, 12 Dec 1972, *Flowers*, ITL 1,500,000. MILAN, 4 June 1974, *Still-life*, ITL 1,500,000. ROME, 27 Jan 1976, *Portrait of a Child* (1954, oil on canvas, 7½ x 9½ ins / 19 x 24 cm) ITL 1,200,000. MILAN, 7 June 1977, *Composition* (1957, oil on panel, 15¾ x 19¾ ins / 40 x 50 cm) ITL 1,700,000. ROME, 13 Nov 1979, *Torcello* (1942, hardboard, 23½ x 28¼ ins / 60 x 72 cm) ITL 6,300,000. ROME, 20 April 1982, *Seated Girl with a Basket of Fruit* (oil on panel, 18½ x 13¾ ins / 47 x 35 cm) ITL 13,500,000. ROME, 5 Dec 1983, *Girl with Red Ribbon (recto); Girl in a White Smock (verso)* (1948, oil on panel, 14½ x 11 ins / 37 x 28 cm) ITL 12,000,000. ROME, 23 April 1985, *Melancholia* (1915, watercolour, 19¾ x 14½ ins / 50 x 37 cm) ITL 14,500,000. MILAN, 19 June 1986, *Seated Woman* (pencil, 6½ x 5 ins / 16.5 x 12.5 cm) ITL 1,400,000. ROME, 28 April 1987, *Maternity* (c. 1948, red chalk, 8½ x 6 ins / 21.5 x 15.5 cm) ITL 1,500,000. MILAN, 8 June 1988, *Flowers and Fruit* (oil on board, 18 x 14½ ins / 45.5 x 37 cm) ITL 5,500,000. MILAN, 14 Dec 1988, *Portrait of a Woman* (1947, oil on panel, 13½ x 8¾ ins / 34 x 22.5 cm) ITL 4,000,000; *View of Torri del Benaco on Lake Garda* (oil/plywood, 14 x 18 ins / 35.5 x 46 cm) ITL 22,000,000. ROME, 21 March 1989, *Girls from Burano (recto-verso)* (oil/plywood, 15¾ x 11¾ ins / 40 x 30 cm) ITL 16,000,000. MILAN, 19 Dec 1989, *Landscape* (1936, oil on panel, 21¼ x 16½ ins / 54 x 42 cm) ITL 23,000,000. MILAN, 27 March 1990, *Little Girl* (1941, oil on panel, 11¼ x 7¼ ins / 28.5 x 18.5 cm) ITL 5,000,000. MILAN, 12 June 1990, *Portrait* (1946, oil on panel, 18½ x 12½ ins / 47 x 32 cm) ITL 14,500,000. MILAN, 24 Oct 1990, *Portrait of a Young Girl with a Jug* (oil on panel, 19 x 12 ins / 48.5 x 30.5 cm) ITL 20,000,000. MILAN, 14 Nov 1991, *Red Roofs* (oil/synthetic resin, 11 x 14¼ ins / 28 x 36 cm) ITL 9,000,000. MILAN, 19 Dec 1991, *Girl with Apple* (oil/panel, 14½ x 11 ins / 37 x 28 cm) ITL 9,500,000. LONDON, 15 Oct 1992, *Portrait of a Woman* (1941, oil on panel, 23½ x 20 ins / 60 x 50.5 cm) GBP 6,050. MILAN, 15 Dec 1992, *Female Portrait* (oil/plywood, 14¼ x 11½ ins / 36 x 29 cm) ITL 9,000,000. ROME, 3 June 1993, *Torri del Benaco* (1946, oil on panel, 14¾ x 17¼ ins / 37.5 x 43.5 cm) ITL 19,000,000. MILAN, 12 Oct 1993, *Burano* (1941, oil/plywood, 20½ x 26½ ins / 52 x 67 cm) ITL 26,450,000. ROME, 8 Nov 1994, *Dressmaking School* (1942, mixed media/paper, 17¼ x 13¼ ins / 44 x 33.5 cm) ITL 6,670,000. MILAN, 22 June 1995, *Still-life with Basket of Fruit* (1948, oil on panel, 9½ x 11¾ ins / 24 x 30 cm) ITL 9,200,000. MILAN, 23 May 1996, *Square in Carpi* (1934, pencil/paper, 6 x 6½ ins / 15 x 16.5 cm) ITL 1,150,000. MILAN, 17 May 1999, *Culagna di Maggio* (1912, oil on panel, 12 x 16 ins / 31 x 40 cm) ITL 15,000,000. MILAN, 9 Nov 1999, *Portrait of Girl* (oil on panel, 11 x 8 ins / 29 x 20 cm) ITL 11,000,000. TURIN, 17 April 2000, *Last Light over the Lagoon* (oil on board, 18 x 23 ins / 46 x 58 cm) ITL 11,000,000. VERCELLI, 17 June 2000, *Head of Young Man* (oil on board, 11 x 8 ins / 28 x 21 cm) ITL 8,000,000. PRATO, 26 May 2001, *Girl with Apple* (1959, oil on board, 24 x 20 ins / 62 x 50 cm) ITL 20,000,000. MILAN, 31 May 2001, *Landscape by Lecco* (1937, oil on board, 16 x 23 ins / 40 x 59 cm) ITL 26,000,000. PRATO, 30 Nov 2002, *White Hat* (1947, oil on board, 20 x 15 ins / 50 x 38 cm) EUR 7,200. ROME, 18 Dec 2002, *Still-life with Pumpkins* (1921, oil on board, 15 x 22 ins / 39 x 55 cm) EUR 14,000. MILAN, 27 May 2003, *Still-life with Mask* (1935, oil on board, 15 x 19 ins / 39 x 47 cm) EUR 9,500. PRATO, 29 Nov 2003, *Houses in Burano* (1940, oil on board, 10 x 13 ins / 25 x 34 cm) EUR 5,000. PRATO, 29 May 2004, *Figures* (1930, oil on board, 12 x 13 ins / 30 x 33 cm) EUR 5,000. PRATO, 29 May 2004, *Portrait* (c. 1950, oil on board, 12 x 19 ins / 31 x 47 cm) EUR 6,500.

SEMELER, Arntz
German, 16th century.
Active in Freiburg.
Sculptor.
Semeler worked for the town of Freiburg and the nearby castle of Neuenberg.

SEMELHAK. See **ZEMELGAK Yakof Ivanovich**

SEMENOFF, Boris
Belgian, 20th century.
Born 1938, in Ixelles (Brussels), of Slavic origin.
Painter.
Boris Semenoff studied at academy of St Luke in Brussels and spent 1959 at the Belgian academy in Rome. He has received various awards and prizes, including the Hélène Jacquet Prize in 1960, the Rik Wouters Prize in 1961, and the Young Belgian Artists Prize in 1963.

Semenoff started as a figurative painter but gradually progressed towards Abstraction. As a rule, his canvases comprise two or three vertical blocks of muted colour (or, on occasion, scarlet) which penetrate a delicate and seemingly infinite black or white ground. The impact is one of formal harmony and grace, a subtle evocation of the female form seen from the front or back, at times nude, at times in the act of love.

Semenoff's work has been shown at a series of solo exhibitions, including at the Galerie Le Zodiaque in Brussels (1965), the Carrefour Gallery in Brussels (1970, 1975), the Theeboom Gallery in Amsterdam (1979, 1981, 1983), the Epsilon Gallery in Brussels (1987, 1988, 1989), the Monochrome Gallery in Brussels (1992) and the Galerie Carole Brimaud in Paris (1993).

Bibliography:

Goyens de Heusch, Serge, *Boris Semenoff,* Éd. Palantines, Quimper, 2001.

Museums and Galleries:

Ixelles.

Auction records:

Brussels, 13 Dec 1990, *Female Nude (Back View)* (ink/paper, 14 1/4 x 11 ins / 36.5 x 27.7 cm) BEF 27,360; *Head on a Pedestal* (1960, watercolour and pencil/paper, 10 1/2 x 14 1/4 ins / 26.6 x 36 cm) BEF 36,480; *Composition* (1961, oil on canvas, 57 x 38 ins / 145 x 96.5 cm) BEF 205,200. Brussels, 7 June 2004, *Composition 3* (1963, oil on canvas, 57 x 45 ins / 146 x 114 cm) EUR 1,500. Brussels, 6 Dec 2004, *Composition* (1972, oil on canvas, 57 x 38 ins / 146 x 97 cm) EUR 1,600.

SEMENOV, Aleksandr

Russian, 20th century.
Born 1890; died 1970.
Painter. Figures, scenes with figures, landscapes with figures.

Aleksandr Semenov studied with Oleg Braz at the St Petersburg academy. He became a member of the Union of Soviet Artists and was named People's Artist. After 1925 he exhibited both at home and abroad. Semenov painted scenes from the circus - rehearsals, performances, scenes onstage and offstage - in a realistic, academic style.

Bibliography:

L'École de Léningrad, auction catalogue, Drouot, Paris, 19 November 1990.

Museums and Galleries:

Brest (MBA) - Kiev (Museum of Russian Art) - Moscow (Ministry of Culture) - Moscow (State Tretyakov Gal.) - Smolensk (MFA) - St Petersburg (Academy) - St Petersburg (Gosudarstvennyj Russkij Muz.).

Auction records:

Paris, 11 June 1990, *Rehearsal on the Ring* (1935, oil on canvas, 14 1/4 x 20 3/4 ins / 36 x 53 cm) FRF 18,000; *Leningrad Circus Entrance Hall* (1933, oil on canvas, 19 1/4 x 25 1/2 ins / 49 x 65 cm) FRF 20,000. Paris, 19 Nov 1990, *Zollo the Clown, before the show* (1934, oil on canvas, 32 x 46 3/4 ins / 81 x 119 cm) FRF 29,000. Paris, 4 March 1991, *Rehearsal on the Ring* (1935, oil on canvas, 14 1/4 x 20 3/4 ins / 36 x 53 cm) FRF 9,100. Paris, 25 March 1991, *Circus Number on a Camel* (1934, oil on canvas, 43 x 46 3/4 ins / 109 x 119 cm) FRF 20,000. Paris, 6 Dec 1991, *Trapeze Artists* (1936, oil on canvas, 22 1/2 x 31 ins / 57 x 79 cm) FRF 25,000.

SEMENOV, Andrei

Russian, 20th - 21st century.
Born 1956.
Painter. Figure compositions, nudes.

Semenov studied at the academy of fine art at the Repin Institute in Leningrad (now St Petersburg). He illustrates scenes of everyday Russian life with ferocity in an Expressionist style similar to the painting of Emile Nolde. He has taken part in collective exhibitions displaying Soviet and contemporary Russian art: 1980 and 1989, Leningrad; 1981, Helsinki; 1982, Tallinn; 1985, Berlin and Turku; 1987, Tokyo; 1988, Berlin; and 1990, Brussels. He held a solo exhibition in Turku in 1985.

Museums and Galleries:

Riga (Valsts Makslas Muzejs/National Gallery of Art) - Rome (Gal. of Contemporary Soviet Art) - St Petersburg (Academy) - St Petersburg (Gosudarstvennyj Russkij Muz.) - Tallinn (Kadrioru Loss - Välikunsti Mus./Palais Kadriorg, Art Gallery).

Auction records:

Paris, 14 May 1990, 1989, oil on canvas, 18 3/4 x 17 1/4 ins / 47.5 x 44 cm) FRF 5,000. Paris, 11 June 1990, *Morning Walk* (oil on canvas, 22 x 23 1/2 ins / 55 x 60 cm) FRF 8,000.

SEMENOV, Viktor

Russian, 20th century.
Born 1933.
Painter (including gouache), watercolourist.
Symbolism.

Viktor Semenov was a student at the fine arts academy (Repin Institute) in Leningrad (now St Petersburg). He was a member of the Leningrad Painters' Association.

He painted abstract compositions in subdued tones that seem to be inspired by the Surrealist approach. He also painted figurative works that are explicitly inspired by symbolism, as his *Two Philosophers* of 1987.

Museums and Galleries:

Moscow (Ministry of Culture) - St Petersburg (Gosudarstvennyj Muz. Istorii) - St Petersburg (Gosudarstvennyj Russkij Muz.).

SEMENOV-MENES, Semion

Russian, 20th century.
Born 1895.
Painter, poster artist. Stage sets.

Semion Semenov-Menes studied between 1915 and 1918 at the art school in Kharkov. Work by him was shown at international group exhibitions, in Paris (1925), New York (1926), Monza (1927); and Cologne (1928). He produced propaganda paintings for trains and boats, as well as cinema posters.

SEMENOVA, Anna

Russian, 20th century.
Born 1888; died 1977.
Active in France.
Painter, sculptor. Figures, flowers.

Anna Semenova was a student of Antoine Bourdelle between 1910 and 1914, and of Ilya Ginsburg in St Petersburg. In 1937, the city of Nantes commissioned a recumbent figure and a bust of Aristide Briand.

Auction records:

Amsterdam, 5 June 1990, *Portrait of a Woman Dressed in Black and Sitting near a Vase of Arums* (oil on canvas, 46 x 39 1/4 ins / 116 x 100 cm) NLG 2,530.

SEMENOWSKY, Eisman, or Semianovski

Russian, 19th - 20th century.
Died 1911.
Painter. Portraits, genre scenes, local scenes.

Eisman Semenowsky is mentioned in Current Art Prices and various other listings of public sales.

Auction records:

Paris, 14 April 1891, *Blondine,* FRF 1,016. London, 6 Dec 1909, *The Garland of Roses,* GBP 16; *Head of a Young Girl,* GBP 6. London, 2 April 1910, *A Catch,* GBP 7. London, 22 April 1911, *The Garland of Roses,* GBP 27. London, 2 May 1924, *Festoon of Flowers,* GBP 42. New York, 15 Jan 1944, *Morning Glory,* USD 280. Antwerp, 1973, *The Bride,* BEF 40,000. London, 27 July 1973, *Portrait of a Woman,* Gns 950. London, 21 July 1976, *Hat with Flowers, Hat with Feathers* (one dated 1884, two oils on panel, 12 1/2 x 9 3/4 ins / 32 x 25 cm) GBP 1,500. London, 23 Feb 1977, *Young Woman Arranging Flowers; Oriental Beauty* (two panels, 33 3/4 x 11 ins / 86 x 27 cm) GBP 1,500. London, 4 May 1977, *Hat with Marguerites* (1887, oil on panel, 14 1/4 x 11 ins / 36 x 27 cm) GBP

600. LONDON, 5 Oct 1979, *Ball on the Deck of the Ship* (oil on panel, 12 3/4 x 7 3/4 ins / 32.5 x 20 cm) GBP 1,300. RHEIMS, 28 Oct 1981, *Young Boy with Hoop* (1889, oil on panel, 19 3/4 x 12 1/2 ins / 50 x 32 cm) FRF 9,000. NEW YORK, 29 Feb 1984, *Harem Beauty* (oil on panel, 21 1/2 x 14 1/2 ins / 54.5 x 37 cm) USD 5,500. LONDON, 21 March 1986, *The Last Touch* (oil on panel, 18 x 7 ins / 45.6 x 17.7 cm) GBP 4,200. NEW YORK, 25 Feb 1988, *Portrait of a Young Woman* (oil on panel, 14 1/4 x 10 1/2 ins / 36.2 x 26.7 cm) USD 2,860. NEW YORK, 23 Feb 1989, *The Hat* (oil on canvas, 12 3/4 x 10 ins / 32.4 x 25.3 cm) USD 24,200. LONDON, 5 May 1989, *Young Gypsy* (1883, oil on panel, 12 1/2 x 10 ins / 32 x 25.5 cm) GBP 2,200. LONDON, 21 June 1989, *Young Girl Delivering a Basket of Flowers* (oil on panel, 22 x 14 3/4 ins / 55 x 37.5 cm) GBP 3,300. LONDON, 4 Oct 1989, *Oriental Beauty* (1889, oil on panel, 12 3/4 x 9 1/2 ins / 32.5 x 24 cm) GBP 3,520. AMSTERDAM, 5-6 Nov 1991, *Young Girl in Oriental Costume* (1890, oil on panel, 10 3/4 x 8 1/2 ins / 27.5 x 21.5 cm) NLG 2,875. NEW YORK, 28 May 1992, *Woman Skating* (1889, oil on panel, 27 3/4 x 17 1/4 ins / 70.5 x 43.8 cm) USD 3,300. AMSTERDAM, 2-3 Nov 1992, *Young Girl among Flowers, with a Butterfly on her Hand* (1893, oil on panel, 19 1/2 x 10 3/4 ins / 49.5 x 27.5 cm) NLG 4,370. NEW YORK, 17 Feb 1993, *Terrace of the Harem* (oil on panel, 14 3/4 x 21 3/4 ins / 37.5 x 55.2 cm) USD 8,913. LONDON, 17 March 1993, *Portraits of Women Wearing Hats* (oil on panel, a pair, each 13 3/4 x 9 3/4 ins / 35 x 25 cm) GBP 5,520. NEW YORK, 27 May 1993, *Oriental Beauties* (oil on panel, a pair, 13 x 9 1/2 ins / 33 x 24 cm) USD 11,500. NEW YORK, 16 Feb 1995, *Roman Beauty* (oil on panel, 34 1/2 x 12 3/4 ins / 87.6 x 32.4 cm) USD 14,950. PARIS, 10 April 1996, *Young Girl with Roses* (1883, oil on panel, 12 1/2 x 10 1/4 ins / 32 x 26 cm) FRF 10,000. NEW YORK, 23 May 1996, *Love Song; Azaleas* (oil on panel, a pair, each 21 3/4 x 14 3/4 ins / 55.2 x 37.5 cm) USD 5,520. NEW YORK, 18-19 July 1996, *The Young Lovers* (oil on panel, 11 1/2 x 15 ins / 29.2 x 38.1 cm) USD 2,875.

SEMENS, Balthazar van. See **LEMENS**

SEMENTI, Giovanni Giacomo, or Sementa or Semenza

Italian, 17th century.

Born 18 July 1580, in Bologna; died 8 September 1636, in Rome.

Painter. History painting.

Sementi, the pupil of Denys Calvaert and Guido Reni, was inspired by the latter and imitated his work with great skill. This is possibly a contributory factor in his success. He executed numerous works in the churches of Bologna, in particular a *Marriage of St Catherine* (in S Francesco), the *Martyrdom of St Cecilia* (in S Elena), a *Crucifixion* (in S Gregorio) and a *St Sebastian* (in S Michele). Sementi also visited Rome, and painted frescoes at the church of S Carlo in Catinari and at S Maria in Aracoeli.

MUSEUMS AND GALLERIES:

BOLOGNA (Pinacoteca Nazionale): *Two Allegorical Figures; Christ Bearing the Cross; Martyrdom of St Eugenia* - MILAN (Pinacoteca di Brera): *Martyrdom of St Victoria* - ROME (Palazzo Doria Pamphili): *Mary Magdalene in Supplication before the Crucifix* - VIENNA: *Marriage of St Catherine*.

SEMENTSOV, Aleksandr or Alexander

Russian, 20th century.

Born 1941, in Suchumi.

Painter. Urban landscapes.

Sementsov trained at the academy of fine art in Tbilisi. He is a member of the Association of Artists of the Former USSR. His painting in a Post-Impressionist style enjoys transposing views of the districts, bridges and monuments of Russian towns, generally treated in cold tones.

SEMENTZEFF, Michel

French, 20th century.

Born 16 February 1933, in Boulogne-Billancourt.

Painter, draughtsman. Figures, landscapes, still-lifes.

Sementzeff featured at group exhibitions in Paris and the rest of France, and in Parisian groups such as the Salon d'Automne, Salon des Artistes Français, Salon Comparaisons, Salon de la Société Nationale des Beaux-Arts, Salon du Dessin and the Salon de la Peinture à l'Eau. He also showed his work in solo exhibitions, including at the Galerie Vendôme in Paris.

His skill as a draughtsman can be seen in his compositions of landscapes or figures, clowns and mime artists, painted or worked with a knife. These pictures introduce us to a world in which the silence becomes a melancholic melody.

AUCTION RECORDS:

VERSAILLES, 8 July 1990, *Snow-covered Vines* (oil on canvas, 28 3/4 x 23 1/2 ins / 73 x 60 cm) FRF 12,000. CALAIS, 7 July 1996, *Carts* (oil on canvas) FRF 5,500.

SEMER, Errico, or Somer

Flemish School, 17th century.

Of Flemish origin.

Active in Naples 1638-1641.

Painter.

Errico Semer painted a *Baptism of Christ* for the church of Santa Maria in Naples.

SEMERARO, Antonio

Italian, 20th - 21st century.

Born 1947, in Taranto (Apulia).

Active since 1974 in France.

Painter, sculptor.

Antonio Semeraro spent less than a year studying at the Turin art college, and apart from this was self-taught. He travelled to Paris to study as well as Amsterdam and New York, and was one of the Ja-na-pa group, whose other members were Christian Bonnefoi, Pierre Dunoyer, Côme Mosta-Heirt and Jean-Luc Vilmouth.

Beginning as he did soon after the early 1970s when American minimalist art was flooding across Europe, Semeraro valued his pictures as objects. By careful analysis he was able to use the frame, thickness and size of each picture to enhance his product. His composition is rigorous, and the extended lines from geometric shapes relate to their point of origin, essential references within restricted space, ground to wall, with the addition of double or triple chromatic effects or sculptural forms. As well as canvas he used metal plates and, from 1978, sheets of wired glass. As these changes proceeded, his questioning work was also being transformed into a matter of shade and light, opaque and transparent areas, where the oblique lines rotating between these elements produced a baroque liveliness. His work refers more and more clearly over the years to the thought and history of Italian painting and its development, to Michelangelo, Rosso and Pontormo, and at the same time to such moderns as Newman and Giacometti. It is a process whereby he seeks to reconcile old and new, or at least to establish links between them.

His work featured at collective exhibitions including: 1976-1978 at the Galerie Mollet-Viéville, Paris; 1977, Ricke gallery in Cologne; 1978, *JA-NA-PA I* at 13 Rue du Vieux Colombier, Paris; 1978, *JA-NA-PA II*, 13 Rue du Vieux Colombier, Paris; 1981, *JA-NA-PA IV*, Galerie Jean Fournier, Paris; 1981, *Baroques*, at the Musée d'Art Moderne de la Ville de Paris; 1984, *Extra Muros* at the botanical gardens in Lille; 1985, *The Abstract Voice* at the Hôtel de Ville, Paris; 1989, the São Paulo Biennale.

His solo shows included: 1976, Galerie Jean-Chauvelin, Paris; 1977, Ricke gallery in Cologne; 1977, Galerie Mollet-Viéville, Paris; 1979, Ursula Schurr gallery in Stuttgart; 1986, Centre d'Art Contemporain in Châteauroux; 1987, Musée des Beaux-Arts, Tourcoing (Lille).

Bibliography:
Stalter, Marcel-André (preface), *Antonio Semeraro 1976-1987*, exhibition catalogue, Musée des Beaux-Arts, Tourcoing, 1987.

SEMERIA, Juan Bautista, or Semetria
Spanish, 16th - 17th century.
Active in Spain from 1586 to 1620.
Sculptor.
Juan Bautista Semeria worked at Toledo Cathedral and at the abbey of Our Lady of Guadalupe.

SEMERNEV, Viktor
Ukrainian, 20th century.
Born 1942, in Odessa.
Painter.
Semernev studied at the school of fine art in Odessa and with Mukin in St Petersburg.
Museums and Galleries:
Kiev (MM) - Moscow - Pvov (MFA).
Auction records:
Paris, 23 Nov 1992, *Sailing Boats* (oil on canvas, 15½ x 20 ins / 39.6 x 50.6 cm) FRF 4,800.

SEMERVILLE
French, 19th century.
Active in Paris in 1830.
Lithographer.

SEMERY, Christophe
French, 17th century.
Died September 1636, in Rheims.
Active in Rheims from 1619.
Painter.

SEMETRIA, Juan Bautista. See **SEMERIA**

SEMETTRE, Jean. See the entry **SMYTERE Jan de**

SEMIAN, Ervin
Czech, 20th century.
Born 24 January 1921, in Devic, Kosovo; died 21 December 1965, in Bratislava.
Painter, illustrator.
Ervin Semian studied from 1939 to 1943 in Bratislava, where he had his first exhibition, in 1943. There were regular exhibitions subsequently, and he also featured at an exhibition in Paris in 1946. His works are charming, illustrative compositions, their style somewhere between that of naive art and an intimism reminiscent of Vuillard.
Bibliography:
Fifty years of Czechoslovak Painting from the Collections of the Galleries, 1918-1958, exhibition catalogue, Slovenska Narodna Gal., Bratislava, 1968 (in commemoration of the 50th anniversary of the Republic of Czechoslovakia).

SEMIGINOWSKI, Jersy or Georges, or Szymonowitz or Eleuter or Elauter
Austrian, 17th - 18th century.
Born c. 1660, in Lemberg (now Lviv, Ukraine); died 1711.
Painter, engraver. Religious subjects, portraits. Murals.
Jersy Semiginowski was sent to Rome to study painting by Jan Sobieski III. He was awarded first prize at the Accademia di S Luca in 1680. From 1687, he worked in Wilanów, where he replaced Claude Callot as director of artistic projects, following the latter's death. He produced a large number of portraits, painted the ceilings of the palace of Wilanów, and also produced paintings for churches. Despite his studies in Rome, his work retained a certain rigidity, linking him to the 'sarmate' tradition. He was ennobled by King John II on 31 July 1688.

SEMIL, Adam
Austrian, 18th century.
Active in Styria, Austria, in the middle of the 18th century.
Painter.
Semil painted two altarpieces in the church of Unterrohr near Hartberg, Austria.

SEMILETOV, Slava
Russian, 20th century.
Born 14 October 1937.
Painter.
There is something symbolist in Slava Semiletov's abstraction. In his *Cosmic Woman*, one can only see her hair, covering the whole of the canvas in elegant arabesques.

SEMILLARD, Valentin
French, 17th century.
Born in Troyes.
Active in Troyes and Orléans 1620-1651.
Painter.

SEMIN, Alessandro. See **SEMINO**

SEMINARIO, Enrique José
Spanish, 19th century.
Born in Guayaquil.
Painter. Landscapes.
Enrique José Seminario was a pupil of Albert Wallet. He exhibited in Paris and was awarded a bronze medal at the Exposition Universelle of 1900.

SEMINI. See also **SEMINO**

SEMINI, Francisco
Spanish, 18th century.
Painter.
Francisco Semini worked at the Buen Retiro porcelain works in Madrid in 1759.

SEMINI, Michele
Italian, 18th century.
Active in Rome c. 1700.
Painter.
Semini was the pupil of Carlo Maratti.

SEMINO, Alessandro, or Semini or Semin
Italian, 16th century.
Died before 28 September 1607.
Active in Genoa.
Painter. History painting.
The son of Andrea Semino, Alessandro Semino worked in collaboration with his brother Giulio Cesare Semino, producing works including a *Martyrdom of St Catherine* for Genoa Cathedral and *St Mary Magdalene at the Feet of Christ* for the sacristy of the church of Santa Maria del Carmine. It is said that, having little success and realising his lack of talent, he abandoned painting.

SEMINO, Andrea, or Semini, called Semino Il Vecchio
Italian, 16th century.
Born 1525 (?), in Genoa; died 1595 (?), in Genoa.
Painter. History painting, religious subjects, portraits.
Son and pupil of Antonio Semino, Andrea Semino studied in Rome. He soon acquired a considerable reputation. He obtained the commission for his first known work, a *Baptism of Christ* of 1552, in the face of competition from painters such as Luca Cambiaso, the Lazzari brothers and Pantaleone Calvi. He produced a large number of works, alone or in collaboration with his brother Ottavio, for the churches and palazzi in Genoa, Milan and Savona. He also painted portraits.
Museums and Galleries:
Turin (Pinacoteca): *Adoration of the Shepherds*.

SEMINO, Antonio, or Semini, Senimo
Italian, 16th century.
Born c. 1485, in Genoa; died after after 1547, probably in 1554 or 1555.
Painter. History painting.

The son of a foreign soldier who settled in Genoa, Antonio was first a pupil of Ludovico Brea, the famous painter from Nice who was then working in Genoa and was to become his assistant. Several works, including a *Martyrdom of St Andrew* in the cathedral dedicated to that saint, bear the signatures of the two artists. The first known work by Antonio Semino is an *Archangel Michael* of 1526 in the church of S Maria della Consolazione. In 1535, he is recorded as being in Savona painting a *Nativity* and a *God the Father* in the Riario family chapel in the church of S Domenico. He painted altarpieces for other churches, including in one in Chiavari. He is last heard of in 1547, but tradition has it that he died in the mid 1550s. His paintings are particularly interesting for their fine landscapes.

SEMINO, Francesco
Italian, 19th century.
Born 1832, in Genoa; died 25 September 1883, in Genoa.
Painter, fresco artist. Religious subjects, allegorical subjects.

A student at the academy of fine art in Genoa, Francesco Semino painted works for a number of churches in that city.

AUCTION RECORDS:
MILAN, 12 Dec 1991, *Allegory of Italy* (oil on canvas, 23 x 20 1/4 ins / 57.5 x 51.5 cm) ITL 5,000,000.

SEMINO, Giovanni Battista
Italian, 16th century.
Active at the end of the 16th century.
Painter.

The son of Ottavio Semino, Giovanni Battista Semino studied at the academy in Florence.

SEMINO, Giulio Cesare
Italian, 17th century.
Active at the beginning of the 17th century.
Painter.

Giulio Semino was commissioned by Philip II to paint works for the Escorial in Madrid. He executed a *Crucifixion* for the church of San Bartolomeo de Sonsoles in Toledo, and is probably the artist known as Cesare Semino, the son of Andrea Semino, who collaborated with his brother Alessandro on the cathedral in Genoa and the sacristy of the church of S Maria del Carmine. According to some of his biographers, Cesare is said to have died about 1615, but this is perhaps more likely to have been the date on which he left Genoa for Spain.

MUSEUMS AND GALLERIES:
GENOA: *Glory of St Stephen; Study for a Head; Glory of a Saint; Ciociaro.*

SEMINO, Ottavio
Italian, 16th century.
Born c. 1520, in Genoa; died 1604, in Milan.
Painter, draughtsman. History painting, religious subjects.
Milanese School.

After studying with his father Antonio, Ottavio Semino went to Rome to continue his training. He collaborated with his brother Andrea but his violent temper put a quick end to this arrangement, Andrea refusing either to live or work with him. Ottavio was to repent of his violent temperament when, after killing one of his apprentices, he was banished from Genoa and not allowed to return until he had paid a large sum in compensation to the boy's parents. Ottavio Semino was a close friend of Luca Cambiaso and the two artists founded a school of painting and drawing. They may both have been very talented artists, but they lacked modesty and attracted harsh criticism from Perino del Vaga. Since the majority of Ottavo Semino's works are in Milan, it seems likely that he only worked in Genoa when young. One the pieces of work executed in Genoa is the decoration of Palazzo Doria, work that Giulio Cesare Procaccino declared worthy of Raphael.

Ottavio Semino had a talented pupil, Camillo Landriani.

MUSEUMS AND GALLERIES:
MILAN (Church of S Angelo): *Life of the Virgin; Life of St Jerome; Christ; Four Doctors of the Church; Four Evangelists* - MILAN (Church of S Marco): *St John the Baptist; Prophets; God the Father; Adoration of the Magi; Marriage and Assumption of the Virgin* - MILAN (Church of S Maria dei Servi): *Annunciation* - MILAN (Church of S Maria delle Grazie, oratory): *St Augustine Banishing the Heretics; Virgin; St John and Angels* - PAVIA (Mus. della Certosa): *Last Supper* - SAVONA: *Archangel Michael* - SAVONA (Church of S Agostino): *Madonna of Mercy.*

AUCTION RECORDS:
NEW YORK, 11 Jan 1989, *Cambyses Learning of the Insurrection of Gaumata* (ink and chalk/blue paper, 9 1/2 x 14 ins / 24.1 x 35.8 cm) USD 5,280.

SEMIONOV, Aleksandr Semenovitch
Russian, 19th century.
Born 1819; died 15 December 1867.
Watercolourist. Portraits.

Aleksandr Semenovitch Semionov studied at the art academy in St Petersburg.

MUSEUMS AND GALLERIES:
ST PETERSBURG (Academy): *Portrait of the Rector Reissig.*

SEMIONOV, Aleksandre
Russian, 20th century.
Born 1922, in Torjok; died 1984.
Painter. Landscapes with figures.

Aleksandre Semionov was a member of the Leningrad Painters' Association.

MUSEUMS AND GALLERIES:
MOSCOW (Ministry of Culture) - ST PETERSBURG (Gosudarstvennyj Muz. Istorii).

AUCTION RECORDS:
PARIS, 26 April 1991, *Leningrad Street in the Rain* (oil on canvas, 23 1/2 x 31 1/4 ins / 60 x 79.5 cm) FRF 6,200. PARIS, 29 May 1991, *Quay on the Neva* (oil on canvas, 32 x 39 1/2 ins / 81 x 100.5 cm) FRF 4,500. PARIS, 24 Sept 1991, *The Anichkov Bridge in St Petersburg* (oil on canvas, 31 x 25 1/4 ins / 79 x 64 cm) FRF 4,000. PARIS, 5 April 1992, *Petrogradskaya Starana, St Petersburg* (1961, oil on canvas, 29 1/4 x 39 ins / 74 x 99 cm) FRF 4,600.

SEMIONOVA, Olga
Russian, 20th - 21st century.
Born 1953.
Painter. Figure compositions.

Semionova is a member of the association of painters. She has exhibited regularly in the former USSR.

AUCTION RECORDS:
PARIS, 8 Dec 1990, *Japanese Melody* (oil on canvas, 19 3/4 x 23 1/2 ins / 50 x 60 cm) FRF 5,500.

SEMITECOLO, Donato
Italian, 14th century.
Active in Venice.
Painter.

Donato Semitecolo was the father of Niccolò Semitecolo.

SEMITECOLO, Niccolò or Nicoletto
Italian, 14th century.
Died after 1400.

Active in Venice during the second half of the 14th century.
Painter. History painting.
Paduan School.

The first dated work by Niccolò Semitecolo is a *Coronation of the Virgin* bearing the inscription *Niccolò Semitecolo MCCCLI* in Venice. In the same collection are 14 small panels by the same artist. A document records his presence in Venice in 1353 where he was working with his father Donato. In 1367, he painted one of the scenes from the *Life of St Sebastian* in the Biblioteca Capitolare in Padua. He was skilful in the rendering of architecture and perspective.

MUSEUMS AND GALLERIES:
PADUA (Biblioteca Capitolare): *Life of St Sebastian* - PADUA (Diocesan Mus. of S Gregorio Barbarigo): *Trinity; Trinity; Virgin* - VENICE (Gal. Reale): *Coronation of the Virgin.*

SEMLER, Adam
German, 17th century.
Born in Leipzig.
Active in the middle of the 17th century.
Painter.

Adam Semler worked for the court and nobility in Sweden.

SEMLER, Heinrich
German, 19th century.
Born 1822, in Coburg (Bavaria).
Painter. Portraits, genre scenes.

Heinrich Semler studied in Munich.

SEMLER, Peter. See **SEMMLER**

SEMMELRAHN, Johannes Ludwig
German, 19th century.
Born c. 1790, in Hamburg.
Engraver. Cards.

Semmelrahn studied under J. Th. Hagemann.

SEMMES, Beverly
American, 20th - 21st century.
Born 1952, in Washington DC.
Sculptor, installation artist.

Beverly Semmes obtained a degree from Yale University in 1987. She lives and works in New York. Her works can be described as 'sartorial' sculptures, in which the length and height seem to be out of proportion. *To be Titled* (1993) is a black velvet dress with seemingly never-ending sleeves that finish in a single heap of fabric; *House Dress* (1991), a dress with very wide shoulders that effectively resembles a rectangular house; *Red Dress* (1992), an evening dress that is so long that it trails on the ground, becoming a blood red river. A feminist angle to some of her works has been proposed, denouncing the inequality of the status of women compared to men, the 'domestic' role of the woman confined to the house or even conjugal violence against women. The architectural concerns that these sculptures raise and the body seen as a landscape are also issues for discussion.

Semmes takes part in collective exhibitions, such as *L'Art au corps. Le corps exposé de Man Ray à nos jours* (*Body Art: The Exposed Body from Man Ray to the Present*), at the Musée d'Art Contemporain, Marseilles, in 1996; and *Almost Warm and Fuzzy: Childhood and Contemporary Art*, an exhibition on the evocation of childhood in contemporary art, P.S.I. Contemporary Art Center, New York, in 2001. She has also shown her work in solo exhibitions, including at the P.S.I. Museum, New York, in 1990; the Institute of Contemporary Art, Philadelphia, in 1993; and the Galerie Gislaine Hussenot, Paris, in 1994.

BIBLIOGRAPHY:
Heartney, Eleanor, '*Beverly Semmes. L'Habit et son alibi*' in *Art Press*, periodical, Paris, February 1994. *Beverly Semmes*, exhibition catalogue, Museum of Contemporary Art, Chicago, 1995. *Beverly Semmes: Directions*, exhibition catalogue, Hirshhorn Museum and Sculpture Garden, Washington DC, 1996.

MUSEUMS AND GALLERIES:
DÔLE (FRAC Franche-Comté): *Landscape* (1993).

SEMMLER, August
German, 19th century.
Born 10 June 1825, in Leipzig; died 16 June 1893, in Dresden.
Engraver.

August Semmler attended the academy in Leipzig and studied under Gustav Adolf Henning. He settled in Dresden.

SEMMLER, Peter, or Semler
German, 16th century.
Active at the end of the 16th century.
Sculptor.

In 1591 Semmler collaborated in the carving of the Way of the Cross in Buchenhüll, near Eichstädt.

SEMON I
6th century BC.
Active at the end of the 6th century BC.
Cameo engraver.
Ancient Greek.

Semon is known for a cameo of black jasper representing a woman bathing, now in Berlin.

SEMON II
Painter.
Ancient Greek.

Semon is described in a papyrus manuscript as the inventor of painting.

SEMONST, Vuillequin, Willequin, Willem or Gauthier. See **SMOUT**

SEMONT, Jean
Flemish School, 15th century.
Active in Tournai in 1413.
Illuminator.

Semont illuminated a copy of St John's Gospel.

SEMOV, Simon
Yugoslavian/Macedonian, 20th century.
Born 1941, in Kavadarci (Macedonia).
Painter.

Semov studied at the academy of fine art in Belgrade until 1964, then took study trips to the former USSR and France. His artistic world, like that of Cemerski, seems torn between the cult of pantheistic tradition associated with mythology and children's legends and dramatic angst. He attempts to express an almost sensual energy of existence, an overlap between animate and inanimate, in paintings with striking colours and with a high impasto that contrasts with smooth, monochrome surfaces.

Semov has taken part in collective exhibitions of contemporary Macedonian art and was invited to the Belgrade Triennale in 1967. He has exhibited his works in many special exhibitions in Belgrade and Skopje from 1965.

SEMPELIUS, D. G., or Stempsius
German, 16th century.
Active c. 1580.
Engraver.

Sempelius copied very successfully several plates by Albrech Dürer. Especially notable is *The Descent into Hell* from *The Life of Christ*, which carries both Dürer's date (1512) and the date of his own printing (1580).

SEMPELS, Georges, called Geo
Belgian, 20th century.
Born 22 October 1926, in Lubbeck or Lubbeek (Brabant); died 25 August 1990, in Vilvoorde.
Painter.

Groups: Zodiaque, Flemish Brabant.
Georges ('Geo') Sempels studied art in Paris from 1945 to 1947 and subsequently in Tienen, Brussels and Aalst (Alost). Until 1967, he was a member of the Zodiaque Group in Brussels and, in 1975, he aligned himself with the Flemish Brabant Group. He was a contributor to *Tijd en Mens* (*Time and Man*) and, latterly, to *Lens*.

Sempels was an abstract artist who worked with warm, thickly applied colours, frequently layered around a central figure. His work communicates a feeling for nature generally and, specifically, for the bond between mankind and the seasons of the year (exemplified in François Jacqmin's poems *Seasons*, which Sempers acknowledged as one of his inspirations). Sempels was involved in various group exhibitions, including those mounted by La Jeune Peinture in Brussels each year between 1960 and 1964. His work also featured at the *Aspects of Recent Flemish Art* exhibition held in Hasselt, Antwerp and Ghent in 1967, at *Contemporary Art* in Mechelen in 1968, at *Contemporary Belgian Art*, an exhibition held in Rio de Janeiro in 1972, at the 1982 exhibition of *Artists from Flemish Brabant*, and at ARCO Arte Contemporáneo in Madrid in 1986.

Sempels' first major one-man show was held at Molenbeek-St-Jean in 1954. This was followed by solo exhibitions at the Galerie Le Zodiaque in Brussels (1960-1964); at the Lambermont Gallery in Brussels (1973); and at the Liège Museum of Modern Art (1986). Since his death, exhibitions of his work have been held in Vilvoorde (1992), Delft-Bornem (1996) and Nieuwenrode (1998). Sempels won the City of Ostend Prize in both 1960 and 1961 and the Knokke Prize in 1963.

Bibliography:
Van Wiemeersch, Albert, *Contemporary Painters and Sculptors in Belgium*, A. Van Wiemeersch, Ghent, 1973. Jong, Casper de, *Schilderslexicon*, Het Spectrum, Utrecht, 1976. Vandenbossche, Hervé, *Geo Sempels*, Artiestenfonds, Antwerp, 1981. Boenders, Frans, *Over Geo Sempels*, Arte-Print, Brussels, 1984. Berckx, Paul, *Geo Sempels*, Lannoo, Tielt, 1988.

SEMPER, Emanuel

German, 19th - 20th century.
Born 6 December 1848, in Dresden; died 16 November 1911, in Dessau.
Sculptor.

Emanuel Semper was a pupil of E.R. Dorer; he sculpted statues and fountains for public squares in several German towns and cities.

SEMPER, Friedrich

German, 17th century.
Born in Zittau (Saxony).
Active in the middle of the 17th century.
Painter.

SEMPER, Gottfried

German, 18th century.
Painter.

Gottfried Semper produced paintings for the high altar of the church of St Blaise in Quedlinburg, Germany.

SEMPERE, Eusebio

Spanish, 20th century.
Born 1924, in Onil (Alicante); died 1985, in Onil.
Active in France between 1948 and 1959.
Painter, collage artist, sculptor, screen printer.
Lumino-Kinetic Art.

Eusebio Sempere studied at the Academia de San Carlos in Valencia and published a manifesto in 1948 on the need to integrate natural light into painting. He lived in Paris between 1940 and 1958 meeting Jean (Hans) Arp and Viktor Vasarely.

Although he receives only the briefest of mentions in Frank Popper's *Kinetic Art*, he is Spain's most important artist in the Op Art and Lumino-Kinetic genres. Until around 1953, his interiors were reminiscent of the Cubists and, above all, of Henri Matisse. At the end of the 1940s, he painted and exhibited abstract compositions with a certain geometric bias but nonetheless closer in spirit to the lyrical and chromatic fantasy of Paul Klee than to optic or even Constructivist art; an example of this was the composition he exhibited at the 1950 Salon des Réalités Nouvelles in Paris. Later, however, he moved firmly in the direction of Op and Kinetic Art. His gouaches, dating from 1953, are studies of geometrical forms in space, starting with the square, then exploring the circle and the triangle. Little by little, Sempere's colours became more intense and his forms progressively complex until, from the late 1960s, the entire canvas was given over to precisely-executed abstract forms.

He experimented with computer-assisted compositions and was also a sculptor; he is remembered in that capacity for his vibrantly colourful chrome-steel composition entitled *Luminous Reliefs*. He featured at collective exhibitions including: Salon de Réalités Nouvelles, Paris (1950, 1956, 1957); São Paulo Biennale (1959, 1961); Brussels and the Venice Biennale in 1960; Tate Gallery, London (1962); Museum of Contemporary Art, Madrid (1965); Museum of Modern Art, New York (1965, 1967); Carnegie Institute, Washington (1966); Louisiana Museum, Humlebae (1968); Nuremberg Biennale (1969); Third Salon International des Galeries Pilotes, Cantonal Museum, Lausanne (1970); Museum of Modern Art, Mexico City (1978) and Galerie René, Paris (1983). He also exhibited solo, notably at the Theo Gallery in Madrid (1980).

Bibliography:
IIIe Salon international des Galeries Pilotes, exhibition catalogue, Musée cantonal, Lausanne, 1970. Corredor-Matheos, José, '*Sempere*' in *Chroniques de l'Art Vivant*, periodical, Maeght, Paris, August 1970. Mélia, Jose, *Sempere*, Éd. Cercle d'Art, Paris, 1977. *Catálogo nacional de arte contemporáneo 1990-1991*, Ibérico 2Mil, Barcelona, 1990-1991.

Museums and Galleries:
Atlanta (MMA) - Barcelona (MAM del Mus. Nacional d'Art de Catalunya) - Bilbao (MBA) - Bolivar (MAM Jesús Soto) - Cambridge, MA (Fogg AM, Harvard University) - Caracas (MBA) - Cuenca (Mus. De Arte Abstracto Español, Fundación Juan March) - London (British Mus.) - Madrid (Biblioteca Nacional) - Madrid (Mus. de Escultura al aire libre) - Madrid (Mus. Nacional Centro de Arte Reina Sofía) - New York (Brooklyn Mus.) - New York (MoMA) - San Francisco (Achenbach Foundation for Graphic Arts) - Santiago (Universitad de Chile, MAC) - Seattle (AM) - Seville (Centro Andaluz de Arte Contemporáneo) - Sofia (Nacionalna chudozestvena galerija) - Valencia (MBA).

Auction records:
Madrid, 28 April 1992, *From Square to Circle* (1968, pencil and gouache/panel, 19 1/4 x 12 3/4 ins / 49 x 32.5 cm) ESP 1,900,000. Madrid, 22 April 1999, *Movement of the S* (1975, oil on panel, 20 x 20 ins / 52 x 50 cm) ESP 1,800,000. Madrid, 20 Dec 1999, *Composition* (oil on canvas laid on panel, 35 x 35 ins / 90 x 90 cm) ESP 850,000. Madrid, 24 April 2000, *Geometric Composition* (1956, oil on board, 26 x 20 ins / 65 x 50 cm) ESP 1,000,000. Madrid, 5 June 2001, *Landscape* (acrylic on paper, 26 x 20 ins / 65 x 50 cm) ESP 1,200,000. Madrid, 17 Dec 2001, *Untitled* (c. 1962, gouache on card, 26 x 20 ins / 65 x 50 cm) EUR 4,210. Madrid, 15 Jan 2002, *Untitled* (gouache) EUR 2,000. Madrid, 16 Dec 2003, *Composition* (1976, gouache, 25 x 19 ins / 64 x 49 cm) EUR 6,000. Madrid, 6 Oct 2004, *Composition* (1984, pencil, gouache and oil on paper, 20 x 20 ins / 52 x 50 cm) EUR 6,500.

SEMPI, P. A. See **SEMPY**

SEMPLICE DA VERONA. See **SEMPLICIO**

SEMPLICIO, also known as Semplice da Verona, called Il Cappuccino Veronese
Italian, 17th century.
Born 1589; died 1654.
Painter. History painting.

Semplicio trained in Verona and became a court painter in Parma. He painted numerous altarpieces and frescoes for churches in northern Italy.

MUSEUMS AND GALLERIES:
FLORENCE (NG): *Dead Christ* - VERONA: *Communion of St Francis*.

SEMPREVIVO, Ranuccio
Italian, 16th - 17th century.
Born to a family originally from Viterbo (Latium).
Painter, mosaicist.

Ranuccio Semprevivo worked in Rome between 1593 and 1619, working especially in St Peter's Basilica and in the Vatican.

SEMPY, P. A., or Sempi
Flemish School, 18th century.
Active at the beginning of the 18th century.
Glass painter.

P. A. Sempy was a pupil and assistant of Michu in Paris.

SEMSER, Charles
American, 20th century.
Born 1922, in Philadelphia.
Sculptor, ceramicist.

Charles Semser went to live in France at the end of the 1940s. He has created coloured sculptures of Baroque figures reminiscent of Niki de St-Phalle's *Nanas* or the creations that appear in processions of Carnival floats, and several monumental works, including a memorial commemorating the bicentenary of the French Revolution in Savigny-le-Temple in 1989, and since the 1940s has produced small-scale works in ceramics and stone, for example: *Holiday* of 1992.

Semser took part in group exhibitions in Paris in the 1970s, including the Salon de Mai, and some years later in 1993 he appeared in the 1st Triennale des Amériques in Maubeuge near Paris. He also shows his works in private exhibitions, for example at the Galerie de l'Odéon, Paris, in 1990, and the Galerie de la Papeterie in Brussels in 1992.

AUCTION RECORDS:
LOKEREN, 11 March 1995, *Two Lovers* (1967, sculpture in painted cement, h. 16 1/2 ins / 42 cm, w. 16 1/2 ins/42 cm) BEF 30,000. LOKEREN, 9 Dec 1995, *Two Lovers* (1967, sculpture in painted cement, h. 16 1/2 ins / 42 cm) BEF 28,000.

SEN. See **SHUNKIN**

SEN, Amulya G.
Hindu School, 20th century.
Born in India.
Painter.

Sen was a painter in the classical Hindu tradition. In 1946, work by him was shown at the international exhibition organized by UNESCO at the Musée d'Art Moderne, Paris.

SEN, Paritosh
Indian, 20th century.
Born 1918, in Dhaka.
Painter, art writer.

Paritosh Sen studied initially at the college of arts and crafts in Madras (now Chennai), and then in Paris, from 1949 to 1954, at André Lhote's studio at the Académie de la Grande Chaumière, as well as at the École des Beaux-Arts. At the same time, he took history of art courses at the École du Louvre. He also spent 1962-1963 in France, at the invitation of the French government. He was a member of the innovative Calcutta Group. He taught at several junctures in his life, notably at the Institute of Printing Technology in Jadavpur, from 1964. He lived and worked in Calcutta (now Kolkata). Sen produced gouache paintings of figures or individuals imbued with a certain feverishness mixed with tension.

Sen's work was shown at collective exhibitions, including: New Delhi national exhibition (1957, 1958, 1961, 1966, 1968, 1973); Commonwealth Arts Festival (1965); São Paulo Biennale (1965). He received the John D. Rockefeller award in 1970.

MUSEUMS AND GALLERIES:
NEW DELHI (NGMA) - SYDNEY (AM).

SENABRE, Ramón
Spanish, 20th century.
Born in Barcelona.
Painter (gouache), watercolourist. Genre scenes, local scenes.
Orientalism.

Ramón Senabre was the younger brother of Louis Jou Senabre. He left Barcelona at the age of 18 and moved to Paris where he worked at various jobs and was able to paint only in his limited free time. He attended evening art school for no more than a month and was otherwise self-taught. In 1925 he was commissioned to provide sets for the Loïe Fuller Ballet Company; he executed textile designs, luminous colour plaques and various accessories.

Only in 1928 was he able to devote himself to painting full-time. His first exhibition, held in a small (and short-lived) gallery in Montparnasse, went unnoticed but, from 1929 to 1932, he featured regularly at collective exhibitions organised by various Paris galleries. He moved to Marseilles and Corsica for a time, but returned to his native Catalonia in around 1935 and continued to paint views of fishermen, seascapes and still-lifes with fish, seafood, fruit and flowers. On 15 February 1936 an exhibition of his work mounted at the Museo de Arte Moderno in Madrid received very positive media coverage. Several of his paintings were acquired by private collectors in Catalonia and from elsewhere in Spain. He returned to Paris around 1950 and exhibited his paintings and watercolours there. His work is now in the hands of private collectors in France, Germany, the Netherlands, the United Kingdom and the USA.

AUCTION RECORDS:
PARIS, 9 Dec 1996, *Musician* (1923, watercolour and gouache, 18 x 17 3/4 ins / 46 x 45 cm) FRF 7,000.

SENACA, Antonio
Spanish, 16th century.
Active at the beginning of the 16th century.
Sculptor (wood).

Antonio Senaca carved the choir stalls in the abbey church of St Eutizio at Valcastoriana near Norica in 1519.

SENADIN
Yugoslavian/Serbian, 20th - 21st century.
Born 1948, in Modrica (Serbia).
Painter (including gouache), engraver, illustrator.

Senadin studied at the school of fine art in Belgrade from 1972 to 1977. His engravings are portrayals of imaginary landscapes, the composition of which is characterised by a prominent feature, contrasting effects of shapes, cold colours and snatches of views. He has produced three bibliophile works and illustrated over 20 books.

Senadin has taken part in collective exhibitions, including: Belgrade Engravers' Group (1977, 1978, 1983); Graficki Kolektiv, Belgrade; Plume d'Or, Pavillon Zuzoric (1977, 1978); *Artistes Yougoslaves*, Centre Français des Arts Graphiques, Paris (1980); Biennale Internationale de la Gravure (International Engraving Biennale), Musée Rimbaud, Charleville-Mézières (1982); May Salon, Belgrade (1983); and IIe Foire Internationale d'Arts Plastiques et du Livre d'Art (2nd International Fine Arts and Art Book Fair), Élancourt. Solo exhibitions including: Graficki Kolektiv gallery, Belgrade (1979, 1984); gallery of fine art, Modrica (1981); cultural centre gallery, Novi Sad (1982); and Galerie Camille Renault, Paris (1984).

SENAILLE. See **SENELLE**

SENAPE, Antonio
Italian, 19th century.
Born 1788; died 1842.
Draughtsman (ink). Landscapes, urban landscapes, urban views, panoramas, architectural views, ruins.

Antonio Senape specialised in drawings of townscapes and panoramas.

AUCTION RECORDS:
LONDON, 19 June 1980, *Temples at Paestum* (pen, 6 1/2 x 17 1/2 ins / 16.5 x 44.5 cm) GBP 600. LONDON, 23 June 1981, *Views of Naples, the Kingdom of the Two Sicilies and Other Italian Landscapes* (pen, sketchbook of 97 drawings, each 10 3/4 x 15 1/4 ins / 27.5 x 38.5 cm) GBP 3,200. LONDON, 22 March 1985, *Views of Italy* (pen ink and pencil, sketchbook of 82 drawings, 9 1/4 x 13 1/2 ins / 23.5 x 34.2 cm) GBP 4,000. LONDON, 19 June 1991, *Panorama of Naples* (1836, ink, four sheets, total 9 1/2 x 57 1/2 ins / 24 x 146 cm) GBP 1,540. LONDON, 16-17 April 1997, *View of Sorrento* (pen and brown and blue inks, 6 x 20 ins / 15.1 x 49.9 cm) GBP 575. NEW YORK, 27 Jan 1999, *Panoramic View of Bay of Naples with Vesuvius Beyond* (pen and brown ink over black chalk, 9 x 85 ins / 23 x 215 cm) USD 14,500. ROME, 7 Dec 1999, *Panoramic View of Naples Seen from San Martino* (pencil, black and colour inks, 10 x 58 ins / 25 x 147 cm) ITL 6,500,000. LONDON, 4 July 2000, *Panoramic View of the Bay of Naples from the Sea* (pencil, pen, blue and brown ink, 9 x 85 ins / 23 x 216 cm) GBP 4,400. LONDON, 4 July 2000, *Panoramic View of the Bay of Naples from Castel Sant'Elmo* (pencil, pen, blue and brown ink, 9 x 56 ins / 23 x 143 cm) GBP 4,500. ROME, 12 Dec 2001, *Posillipo. Naples: Santa Lucia* (pencil, pen and ink, two, 6 x 10 ins / 16 x 25 cm) ITL 4,500,000. MILAN, 14 May 2003, *View of Naples* (Indian ink, 11 x 59 ins / 28 x 149 cm) EUR 3,000. PARIS, 15 Oct 2003, *Views of Naples* (pen and ink, a pair) EUR 2,200.

SÉNARD, Charles
French, 20th century.
Born 1876; died 1934.
Painter, illustrator. Still-lifes, flowers.

Sénard mainly painted bouquets of flowers.

SENARD, Henri
French, 19th century.
Died 30 May 1881, in Lyons.
Active in Roanne.
Painter. Self-portraits, landscapes.
Lyons School.

MUSEUMS AND GALLERIES:
ROANNE: *Self-portrait* (oil on canvas); two landscapes; 7 other canvases.

SENART, pseudonym of Petit, Jean-Marie
French, 20th century.
Born 16 September 1929, in Gardanne.
Sculptor, potter.

Senart studied literature and took lessons at the École des Beaux-Arts in Aix-en-Provence. In 1958 he settled in Paris. He completed a traineeship with Artigas in Galifa in Spain. From 1970 to 1973 he was an assistant in the visual arts department of the University of Marseilles-Luminy. He lived and worked in Soisy-sur-Seine.

Between 1958 and 1969 he made pottery and wood-fired stoneware using direct flames, making the most of the randomness of the fire. From 1970 to 1973 he researched the use of large-sized ceramics. From 1973 he dedicated himself exclusively to sculpture. As with his work in ceramics, in his large sculptures he used Perspex, stainless steel and in particular raw or wrought iron. He created abstract forms, typically with spheres and round shapes. The organisation of the material and his slender structures always show an awareness of the need to maintain a close relationship with space, time and life. He took part in group exhibitions including, in 1966, the International Competition for Contemporary Ceramic Art in Faenza, Italy, where he was awarded a prize; the Montreal Exposition Universelle in 1967, where he represented France; regular presentations at the Salon des Réalités Nouvelles, Salon de la Jeune Sculpture, and Salon des Grands et Jeunes d'Aujourd'hui. He gave solo shows in Paris in 1964, at the American Centre in Paris in 1967 and the Galerie Jaquester in Paris.

SENART, Louis Henri
French, 19th century.
Born in Paris.
Sculptor.

He exhibited at the Salon between 1848 and 1859.

SENAT, Prosper Louis
American, 19th - 20th century.
Born 1852, in Philadelphia; died 1925, in Philadelphia.
Painter. Landscapes.

Prosper Senat studied in Philadelphia, New York, London and Paris.

MUSEUMS AND GALLERIES:
BOSTON: *Street Scene*; *Taormine*.

AUCTION RECORDS:
WASHINGTON DC, 30 Sept 1984, *Fishing Boat at Dusk* (1878, oil on canvas, 21 x 17 ins / 53.5 x 43 cm) USD 1,800. PORTLAND, 28 Sept 1985, *Minori* (watercolour, 25 x 38 ins / 63.5 x 96.5 cm) USD 1,200.

SENATUS, Jean-Louis
Haitian, 20th - 21st century.
Born 1949.
Painter. Scenes with figures.

AUCTION RECORDS:
PARIS, 13 June 1994, *Silhouette on the Island* (1990, oil on canvas, 15 3/4 x 11 3/4 ins / 40 x 30 cm) FRF 6,500. PARIS, 12 June 1995, *The Inhabited Tree* (oil on canvas, 11 3/4 x 15 3/4 ins / 30 x 40 cm) FRF 6,500. PARIS, 1 April 1996, *The Dream* (oil on canvas, 11 3/4 x 15 3/4 ins / 30 x 40 cm) FRF 7,200. PARIS, 25 May 1997, *In the Clouds* (oil on canvas, 7 3/4 x 9 3/4 ins / 20 x 25 cm) FRF 7,000.

SENAU, Pieter
Flemish School, 17th - 18th century.
Possibly of Flemish origin.
Active 1686-1713.
Painter.

Pieter Senau executed the decorative paintings in the theatre at Modena, and two pictures for the town hall in Mons.

SENAULT, François
French, 16th century.
Active in Rouen in 1507.
Sculptor.
Gaillon School.

In 1507 Senault sculpted the escutcheon of Cardinal d' Amboise above the entrance to the Château de Gaillon.

SENAULT, Louis
French, 17th century.
Active in Paris 1669-1680.
Engraver (burin).

SENAVE, Jacques Albert
Belgian, 18th - 19th century.
Born 12 September 1758, in Loo; died 22 February 1829, in Paris.

Painter. Historical subjects, figures, portraits, genre scenes, scenes with figures, market scenes, interiors with figures, landscapes, urban views, animals.

Jacques Albert Senave initially studied under a canon at the abbey of Loo, and later attended the academies in Dunkirk and St-Omer before moving to Paris, where he worked under Julien and Suvée. He was appointed honorary director by the academy of Ypres after presenting a picture of Rembrandt's studio featuring portraits of leading Leiden personalities of the day. He painted traditional Flemish celebrations in the manner of Teniers.

Senave.

Museums and Galleries:

BASEL: *Little Girl Bringing Food to a Cow in a Cowshed; Little Boy Leading a Horse out of a Stable* - GOTHA: *Two Views of Paris* - LOO (parish church): *The Seven Acts of Mercy* - NANTES: *Market in a Public Square; Fruit Market; Interior of a Cottage* - YPRES: *Rembrandt's Studio.*

Auction records:

PARIS, 1817, *Wheelwright's Workshop,* FRF 181; *Green Windmill on the Mont-Rouge Plain,* FRF 244. PARIS, 1833, *Village Schoolmaster Teaching a Group of Forty Children to Read,* FRF 367. PARIS, 1854, *Market by a Village Church,* FRF 410. PARIS, 1861, *Market Scene,* FRF 700. PARIS, 1872, *Dutch Housewife,* FRF 1,010. PARIS, 1885, *Market in Rome,* FRF 1,200; *Blacksmith,* FRF 1,005. PARIS, 23 March 1897, *View of Paris Taken from the Corner of the Old Pont au Change,* FRF 1,600. PARIS, 19 March 1898, *Portrait Thought to be of the Artist with his Son,* FRF 260. PARIS, 13 May 1898, *Farmhouse Interior,* FRF 340. PARIS, 1899, *Woman Selling Curios* (drawing) FRF 400. PARIS, 14 June 1900, *Antique Dealer,* FRF 320. PARIS, 15-16 Jan 1907, *Young Woman Playing a Mandolin,* FRF 225. PARIS, 21 Feb 1919, *Interior of a Flemish Village,* FRF 125. PARIS, 3 June 1921, *Interior of an Inn,* FRF 550. PARIS, 15 Dec 1922, *Happy Mother,* FRF 650. PARIS, 22 Nov 1923, *Les Halles in Paris,* FRF 10,200. PARIS, 12 March 1927, *Happy Mother,* FRF 2,100. PARIS, 9 Feb 1928, *Market,* FRF 20,000. PARIS, 21 Dec 1931, *Market among Ruins,* FRF 3,100. PARIS, 14 Dec 1933, *View of the Louvre and the Pont-Royal,* FRF 3,000. PARIS, 22 Nov 1935, *Sleeping Dairymaid; Horse in a Stable* (two) FRF 2,050. PARIS, 14 Dec 1935, *Shepherds Resting,* FRF 1,250. PARIS, 10 Feb 1943, *Family Meal; Peasant Interior* (collection) FRF 23,000. PARIS, 31 March 1943, *Maternal Happiness* (pen and watercolour) FRF 3,100. PARIS, 7 Oct 1943, *Interior Scene* (attributed) FRF 10,200. PARIS, Oct 1945-July 1946, *Group of Musicians* (1802) FRF 85,500; *A Mother's Care* (1788) FRF 31,500. PARIS, 29 Dec 1948, *Parade of a Travelling Fair* (attributed) FRF 63,000. PARIS, 15 Dec 1949, *Charlatan* (attributed) FRF 43,500. PARIS, 14 June 1951, *Scenes of Family Life* (two pendants) FRF 8,500. PARIS, 29 June 1951, *Mother and Child in a Rustic Kitchen* (attributed) FRF 7,800. PARIS, 2 July 1951, *Village Fair* (school of Jacques Albert Senave) FRF 13,500. PARIS, 2 June 1954, *Market in a Public Square,* FRF 100,000. PARIS, 17 Oct 1968, *Wheelbarow Day,* FRF 17,000. LONDON, 12 March 1969, *Market Scene,* GBP 380. VERSAILLES, 18 July 1973, *Travelling Showmen with a Bear; Travelling Showmen with Trained Monkeys* (two pendants) FRF 6,200. PARIS, 29 Nov 1976, *Cats* (1784, oil on panel, 8½ x 11¼ ins / 21.5 x 28.5 cm) FRF 12,500. LONDON, 23 Feb 1977, *Country Scene* (1791) GBP 3,000. STOCKHOLM, 31 Oct 1979, *At the Butcher's* (1791, oil on panel, 14¼ x 20 ins / 36 x 51 cm) SEK 10,700. ZURICH, 10 Nov 1982, *Artist and Model* (1825, oil on canvas, 22 x 31¼ ins / 55 x 79.5 cm) CHF 10,000. ZURICH, 6 June 1984, *Artist and Model* (1825, oil on canvas, 22 x 31¼ ins / 55 x 79.5 cm) CHF 9,000. PARIS, 1 July 1988, *Kitchen Interior* (oil on panel, 5 x 7¼ ins / 12.5 x 18.5 cm) FRF 36,000. SCEAUX, 10 June 1990, *Loving Couple in a Storeroom* (oil on panel, 13½ x 11 ins / 34 x 27 cm) FRF 13,000. MONTE CARLO, 4 Dec 1993, *Marketplace with a Statue of the Borghese Gladiator* (oil on panel, 17¾ x 22 ins / 45.3 x 56 cm) FRF 62,000. PARIS, 5 March 1994, *Children's Games* (oil on canvas, 8¼ x 10¾ ins / 21 x 27.5 cm) FRF 12,000. PARIS, 31 March 1994, *Market Scene* (oil on panel, 10 x 12½ ins / 24.5 x 32 cm) FRF 29,000. PARIS, 3 April 1995, *Country Fair near a Classical Palace; Young Peasants near a Classical Palace* (oil on panel, a pair, each 10 x 12¾ ins / 24.5 x 32.5 cm) FRF 78,000. LONDON, 15 Nov 1995, *Kitchen Interior* (oil on panel, 28¾ x 24½ ins / 73 x 62 cm) GBP 3,680. PARIS, 28 Oct 1996, *Farmer and her Family in her Kitchen; Time for Supper* (oil on panel, a pair, each 5¾ x 7½ ins / 14.6 x 18.9 cm) FRF 12,000. NEW YORK, 14 Oct 1999, *Young Boy Seated in a Window Niche* (oil on panel, 8 x 6 ins / 21 x 16 cm) USD 8,500. BERN, 1 Nov 2000, *Young Girl with Child in a Courtyard* (1788, oil on panel, 7 x 9 ins / 18 x 24 cm) CHF 10,500. NEUILLY, 17 Dec 2001, *Kitchen Interior* (1788, oil on panel, 7 x 9 ins / 18 x 24 cm) FRF 32,000. PARIS, 8 Dec 2003, *Solving the Puzzle* (oil on panel, 6 x 7 ins / 15 x 18 cm) EUR 1,500.

SENCKEISEN, Johann Gottfried

French, 18th century.
Born c. 1752.
Active in Strasbourg.
Painter, draughtsman.

Museums and Galleries:

STRASBOURG (Mus. des Arts Décoratifs): *Dido and Aeneas* (drawing).

SENCLAT, Jean. See SEUCIAT

SENDAK, Maurice

American, 20th century.
Born 10 June 1928, in Brooklyn (New York City).
Watercolourist, draughtsman, illustrator, decorative designer. Stage costumes and sets.

Maurice Sendak comes from a family of Polish Jews who emigrated to the USA before World War I. While working as a window dresser he attended an evening course at the Art Students' League so that he could become an independent illustrator. He lives and works in Ridgefield (Connecticut).

He became one of the most well known illustrators in the USA in 1964, with the publication of *Where the Wild Things Are,* which he both wrote and illustrated. He was awarded the Caldecott Prize for this work.

Two other cult picture books, *In the Night Kitchen,* in 1970, and *Outside Over There,* in 1981, earned him international recognition. He has written and illustrated about 20 books and has illustrated around 60 other works by various authors. His illustrations are derived from cultural sources, such as Mozart, the Brothers Grimm, Mickey, works by Dürer and Altdorfer. Although Sendak is very well known in the world of children's books he has also created stage sets and costumes for works including Mozart's *Magic Flute* for Houston Grand Opera, *The Love of Three Oranges* by Prokofiev, and *The Cunning Little Vixen* by Janacek for New York City Opera, and for an adaptation of his own book *Where the Wild Things Are.*

Sendak was the first American to receive the Hans Christian Andersen medal for his collective works in 1970. In 1997 he was awarded the National Medal of Arts and in 2005 he exhibited at *Where the Wild Things Are: the Art of Maurice Sendak,* Jewish Museum, New York.

Bibliography:

Lanes, Selma G., *The Art of Maurice Sendak,* Abrams, New York, 1980. Rosenblum, Robert, *The romantic child: from Runge to Sendak,* Thames & Hudson, New York, 1989. Kushner, Tony, *The Art of Maurice Sendak: 1980 to the Present,* Harry N. Abrams, New York, 2003.

Museums and Galleries:
Philadelphia (Rosenbach Mus. and Library).

SENDALL, J.
American, 19th century.
Painter.
Public auction records state that J. Sendall was active in 1826.
Auction records:
New York, 17 Nov 1942, *Newmarket and the Thetford Coach*, USD 300.

SENDIM, Mauricio José do Carmo
Portuguese, 19th century.
Born 1786, in Belem; died 20 October 1870, in Lisbon.
Painter, lithographer.
Mauricio Sendim worked in Belem and painted portraits of the royal family.

SENDIN, Armando
Brazilian, 20th century.
Born in Rio de Janeiro.
Active in Spain and France.
Painter. Figures, seascapes.
Armando Sendin spent his childhood in Spain and studied drawing at the Escuela de Bellas Artes in Cordova. In 1949 he took a degree in philosophy in São Paulo, then specialised in aesthetics at Santiago in Chile. From 1950 to 1952 he continued his study of aesthetics at the Sorbonne in Paris while sitting in on courses at the École des Beaux-Arts. In 1954 he opened an art school in São Paulo. He travelled extensively during the 1970s, and received several prizes for his work.

In a controlled technique, inspired by realism, Sendin painted scenes of city life, the seaside, children playing, always in situations in which people are relaxed and peaceful,a manifestly cheerful art.

He showed work in collective exhibitions including: *Peintres, Sculpteurs, Graveurs* (*Painters, Sculptors and Engravers*) at the École des Beaux-Arts in Paris (1951); at the Salon of modern art in São Paulo (1951-1960); at the principal art Salons in Brazil, in São Paulo, Rio, Brasilia, Belo-Horizonte and others (1966-1973); at the Biennale in São Paulo (1967, 1969, 1973, 1979); at the 7th International Grand Prix in Monaco (1971); at the Salon Figuration Critique in Paris (1983 and 1985).

He had solo exhibitions from 1960, mainly in Brazil, Spain and France, including the Museum of Contemporary Art, Seville (1978) and the Galerie Liliane François in Paris (1981, 1983, 1985, 1992).
Museums and Galleries:
São Paulo (MAM) - São Paulo (Pinacoteca do Estado) - Seville (Centro Andaluz de Arte Contemporáneo) - Washington DC (Art Mus. of the Americas).

SENE
French, 19th century.
Painter. History painting.
He showed his work at the Colisée in 1776 and at the Salon in 1804.

SENE, Étienne
Swiss, 19th century.
Born 3 October 1784, in Geneva; died 21 May 1851, in Geneva.
Sculptor.
Sene produced a relief of the Alps for the English Garden in Geneva.

SÉNÉ, Henry or Henri Charles E.
French, 20th century.
Born 10 June 1889, in Pont-Rémy (Somme); died 10 April 1961, in Paris.
Painter, engraver. Religious subjects, portraits, genre scenes, animals, landscapes with figures, landscapes. Murals.
Orientalism.
Séné studied at the École des Arts et Métiers in Châlons-sur-Marne then, from 1906, he studied under Fernand Cormon at the École des Beaux-Arts in Paris. He travelled several times to Morocco, the Congo, Brazil, Peru and Bolivia, where he was sent to lead a painting workshop at the École des Beaux-Arts de La Paz. His travels abroad provided the inspiration for his exotic landscapes and genre scenes such as *Caravan, Dromedaries, Herd of Llamas, Head of Bolivian Indian*, and so on. He painted frescoes as well as portraits, and, like Géricault, enjoyed painting horses in motion.

Séné exhibited at the Salon des Artistes Français in Paris, where he received an honourable mention in 1913, a silver medal in 1922, the Prix Rosa Bonheur in 1924, a gold medal in 1932 and a medal of honour in 1958.
Museums and Galleries:
Amiens (Mus. de Picardie): *Ecce Homo; Christ Insulted; Death of Roland in Roncevaux; Water Point; Caravan* - Dijon (MBA): *Indians and Llamas* - Honfleur: *The Sailors' Church; Honfleur Basin* - Montevideo: *Head of Bolivian Indian; Herd of Llamas, Lake Titicaca* - Paris (Mus. des Arts d'Afrique et d'Océanie): *Fantasia*.
Auction records:
Paris, 21 Nov 1989, *Two Arab Horsemen* (1934, oil on canvas, 46 x 41 ins / 116 x 104 cm) FRF 23,000. Paris, 6 April 1990, *Kaids* (1934, oil on canvas, 45 1/4 x 41 1/4 ins / 115 x 105 cm) FRF 75,000. Paris, 11 Dec 1995, *Fantasia* (oil on canvas, 23 3/4 x 32 ins / 60.5 x 81 cm) FRF 35,000. London, 13 Oct 1999, *Chleuhs Horsemen in South Morocco* (oil on canvas, 20 x 28 ins / 51 x 70 cm) GBP 2,200. New York, 12 July 2001, *Ox returning to the Fields* (1924, oil on canvas, 60 x 80 ins / 152 x 203 cm) USD 3,250. Paris, 14 June 2004, *La fantasia aux environs de Marrakech* (1941, oil on canvas, 26 x 32 ins / 65 x 81 cm) EUR 9,000. Paris, 25 June 2004, *Cavaliers se preparant pour la fantasia* (oil on canvas, 16 x 28 ins / 40 x 70 cm) EUR 2,600.

SENE, Jean François
Swiss, 19th century.
Born 1 September 1779, in Geneva; died 1 January 1842, in Lancy, near Geneva.
Painter (enamel).

SENÉ, Louis
Swiss, 18th - 19th century.
Born 22 September 1747, in Geneva.
Painter.
Sené exhibited in Paris in 1804.

SENECA, Roland
French, 20th century.
Born 1942, in Chalon-sur-Saône.
Engraver (wood), draughtsman, illustrator.
Roland Seneca is a self-taught engraver whose work was sufficiently impressive to earn him a scholarship to the Casa Velázquez in Madrid. He has lived and worked in Douarnenez since 1968. He favours black and white and makes use of both in his organically-oriented motifs.

He has held a number of solo shows, among them in 1985, at the Musée de Morlaix; in 1989, at the Librairie des Matinaux in Paris; and, in 2000, at the Musée de Vannes.
Bibliography:
Estampes contemporaines. 18 ans d'édition 1982/2001, group exhibition catalogue, Villa Tamaris, Seyne-sur-Mer, 2001. *'Espèces de morceaux'*, Association Cardinaux, Artothèque, Châtellerault, 2001.

Museums and Galleries:
Châteaugiron (FRAC Bretagne) - Dijon (Bibliothèque Mun.) - Morlaix (Mus. des Jacobins) - Paris (BNF) - Quimper (Bibliothèque Municipale) - Quimper (MBA).

SENECHAL, Adrien
French, 20th century.
Born 5 July 1895, in Rheims; died 1974.
Painter, pastellist.

Senechal exhibited in Paris, at the Salon des Artistes Français, where he was a member.

Auction records:
Paris, 5 May 1947, *Seascape,* FRF 2,100. Brest, 15 May 1983, *Interior of a Farm in Brittany* (oil on canvas, 22 3/4 x 18 1/2 ins / 58 x 47 cm) FRF 10,000. Paris, 17 March 1991, *Panoramic View of the town of Rheims* (oil on card, 10 3/4 x 14 1/4 ins / 27.5 x 36 cm) FRF 5,000.

SENECHAL, Marcel
French, 20th century.
Born 24 April 1903, in Malaunay (Seine-Maritime).
Painter. Landscapes, urban landscapes.

Senechal began painting in 1967, after he retired. He regularly participated in group exhibitions in Paris: at the Salon Comparaisons from 1968; from 1969, the Salon des Artistes Français, where he was a member from 1971 and which gave him an honourable mention in 1974; from 1969 the Salon de la Nationale des Beaux-Arts, where he was also a member from 1977; from 1971 the Salon d'Automne, where he was a member from 1975; events devoted to Naive Art, including the 1970 and 1973 Biennales de l'Art Naïf of Zagreb, the 1972 Triennale d'Art Naïf of Bratislava and with the Henri Rousseau Group.

Museums and Galleries:
Vicq (Mus. International d'Art Naïf).

SENECHAL, Nicolas
French, 18th century.
Born 1742, in Paris; died after 1776, in Paris.
Sculptor.

Nicolas Senechal studied under Étienne-Maurice M. Falconet and Jean-Baptiste Lemoyne.

Museums and Galleries:
Besançon (Bibliothèque d'études et de conservation): three relief portraits.

SENEFELDER, Aloys or Alois or Johann Nepomuk Franz Alois
Czech, 18th - 19th century.
Born 6 November 1771, in Prague; died 26 February 1834, in Munich, Germany.
Lithographer, dramatist.

Senefelder was the son of an actor who wanted him to be a lawyer and sent him to the University of Ingolstadt (Bavaria), Germany. Senefelder, however, wanted to be a dramatist and produced a number of unsuccessful plays. When the death of his father deprived him of the means of having his works printed, he looked for a way to reproduce them by a process other than typography, and began a series of experiments with copper-plates, a burin and etching. In order to save himself the expense of copper, he decided to use Kelheim limestone, which he discovered was suitable for the purpose. By chance, in the absence of paper, he scribbled down a laundry list with a grease pencil on the corner of a piece of Bavarian limestone prepared for etching (acid mixture in which a plate is immersed to be bitten or etched), which led him to attempt an engraving in relief, using the areas washed with ink as resistance to the action of the acid instead of the intaglio process used for etching. His first attempt was successful enough for him to take the experiment further, and after a time, due to the special grease pencil, his technique was put into practice. Senefelder sought a commercial footing for his endeavour and became highly successful. In 1818, he published a dissertation, which was translated into French and English.

The success of lithography, particularly in France at that time, is well documented. Senefelder continued his efforts in Germany and strove incessantly to refine his invention. He was assisted by his brothers Clemens, Georg, Theobald and Karl, and by his son Heinrich, who were also lithographers. They shared this new mode of expression with contemporary Belgian artists: Van Brée (1786 - 1871), Verboeckhoven (1798 - 1881), then Wappers (1807 - 1874), Navez (1787 - 1869) and Gallait (1810 - 1887).

Bibliography:
'*Aloys Senefelder, le génie de la lithographie*' in *Art et métiers du Livre* no. 196, periodical, Paris, 1996.

SENEGAT, A.
French, 18th century.
Of French origin.
Active during the first half of the 18th century.
Painter.

Museums and Galleries:
Zurich (Kunsthaus): *Scenes in Joseph's Life* (1715-1716, 11 drawings).

SENEIL. See **SENELLE**

SENELAC, Jehan
French, 15th century.
Active at the end of the 15th century.
Painter. Banners.

Senelac painted *St Barbara and a Boar* on a standard of Louis d'Orléans.

SENELLE
French, 18th century.
Active during the first half of the 18th century.
Sculptor.

Senelle worked on Neptune's Fountain in the park of Versailles.

SENELLE, Jehan, or Senaille or Seneil
French, 17th century.
Born 1603, in Meaux; died before 1671, in Paris (?).
Painter.

Jehan Senelle was probably apprenticed to Valentin de Boulogne. He painted religious subjects for the churches of Meaux and St-Remy-La-Vanne.

Museums and Galleries:
Orléans: paintings.

SENELLE, Pierre
French, 17th century.
Active in Paris 1671-1691.
Sculptor.

Pierre Senelle, the son of Jehan Senelle, was sculptor to the king.

SENELLY
Austrian, 19th century.
Born in Austria.
Painter.

The first part of Senelly's life is believed to have been extremely unhappy and spent in abject poverty. In 1873, when he had just begun to enjoy some success, he went mad.

SENEMONT, François, or Senémon
French, 18th century.
Born 9 February 1720, in Nancy; died 28 March 1782, in Nancy.
Painter, engraver (burin). History painting, genre scenes, portraits.

François Senemont studied at the academy of Nancy. In 1736 he was working on the decoration of the Temple of Hymen in Versailles and, in 1742, on the catafalque of the queen of Poland. He produced many paintings for the churches of Lorraine and executed portraits, including *Fleury, the Actor* and *Gilbert, the Poet*. He was painter in ordinary to the king and painter to the city of Nancy.

AUCTION RECORDS:

NEW YORK, 4 June 1980, *Anna Doublat with J. B. Gillier; Nauss Gillier and Joanna Carola Piclet* (1769, oil on canvas, a pair, 22 1/2 x 17 ins / 57 x 43 cm) USD 3,700.

SENEN, Lorenzo and Vila. See **VILA Lorenzo** and **Senen**

SENEQUIER, Bernard Jacques Christophe

French, 19th century.

Born 1784, in Toulon; died 4 July 1868, in Toulon.

Sculptor, painter.

He was a foreman sculptor in the port of Toulon (Var), France, and also taught at the school of navigation there. He made wooden sculptures for the churches in and around Toulon.

MUSEUMS AND GALLERIES:

TOULON: *Interior of the Église des Cordeliers, in Hyères, before Restoration.*

SENEQUIER, Jules

French, 19th century.

Born in Toulon; died 30 July 1846, in Paris.

Painter (?).

He was the son of Bernard Jacques Christophe Senequier.

SENES, Joseph Anton, or Sennes or Senis

Austrian, 18th century.

Born in Baden, near Vienna; died 7 December 1764, in Munich, Germany.

Sculptor.

Joseph Senes settled in Munich in 1720, where he was court sculptor.

SENES, Romanus

2nd century.

Painter.

Romanus Senes is mentioned in Ris-Paquot.

SENES, Veit, or Sennes

Austrian, 18th century.

Active c. 1700.

Sculptor.

Veit Senes produced the pulpit for the church of Tattendorf, Austria, and an altar for the church of St Stephen, Baden, near Vienna.

SENET PÉREZ, Rafael

Spanish, 19th - 20th century.

Born 7 October 1856, in Seville; died 1926.

Painter, watercolourist. Genre scenes, landscapes with figures, waterscapes.

Rafael Senet Pérez studied under Joaquin Dominguez Becquer and Eduardo Cano de la Preda at the college of fine arts in Seville, then under J. Villegas y Cordero; he completed his formal education in Madrid (where he studied old masters in the Prado) and, from 1881, in Rome. He then travelled extensively in Italy, visiting Florence, Venice and Naples before returning to Seville at the beginning of the 1890s and aligning himself with a group of landscape painters which had formed around Sánchez Perrier. The Tooth's Gallery in London had exclusive sales rights for his work.

He is best known for his genre compositions, examples of which include *Neapolitan Fishermen, Woman Fishing, Watering the Flower Pots, Procession Day, Children with Turkeys, Souvenir of Seville* and *Best Friend*. He also painted light and brightly-coloured views of Venice and the surrounding region. He was involved in various collective exhibitions including: Seville (1869), Cádiz (1879), Madrid (Exposición Nacional de Bellas Artes 1884, at which he was awarded a silver medal), Barcelona (Watercolorists' Society, 1885 and 1907 Exposición Internacional de Bellas Artes) and Munich, where he was awarded a silver medal.

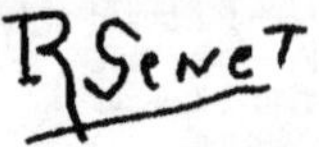

BIBLIOGRAPHY:

Arnáiz, José Manuel/López Jiménez, Javier/Merchán Díaz, Manuel (ed.), '*Cien años de pintura en Espana y Portugal (1830-1930)*' in vol. X, Antiqvaria, Madrid, 1993.

MUSEUMS AND GALLERIES:

MADRID: *Returning with the Catch.*

AUCTION RECORDS:

LONDON, 7 Oct 1966, *Market on the Lagoon, Venice*, Gns 380. LONDON, 15 April 1968, *Grand Canal, Venice*, GBP 920. LONDON, 7 May 1971, *Venice Lagoon*, Gns 320. LONDON, 29 Oct 1976, *Canal in Venice* (oil on canvas, 20 x 12 ins / 51 x 30.5 cm) GBP 3,600. LONDON, 4 Nov 1977, *View of Venice* (oil on canvas, 25 x 59 ins / 63.5 x 150 cm) GBP 2,200. LONDON, 15 June 1979, *View of Venice* (oil on canvas, 20 x 24 ins / 51 x 61 cm) GBP 2,600. NEW YORK, 13 Feb 1981, *Shores of the Mediterranean* (1893, oil on canvas, 18 x 29 1/2 ins / 45.7 x 75 cm) USD 9,500. LONDON, 25 Nov 1983, *Grand Canal, Venice* (oil on canvas, 18 x 31 1/2 ins / 46 x 80 cm) GBP 5,500. NEW YORK, 29 Oct 1986, *View of Venice* (oil on canvas, 18 x 29 3/4 ins / 45.7 x 75.5 cm) USD 13,000. LONDON, 22 June 1988, *Grand Canal, Venice* (1891, oil on canvas, 17 3/4 x 29 1/2 ins / 45 x 75 cm) GBP 26,400. ROME, 14 Dec 1988, *View from Punta della Dogana, Venice* (oil on canvas, 18 x 31 ins / 46 x 79 cm) ITL 31,000,000. LONDON, 21 June 1989, *Walking by the Grand Canal, Venice* (oil on canvas, 13 3/4 x 22 ins / 35 x 55 cm) GBP 14,300. MILAN, 19 Oct 1989, *Gathering Shrimp* (oil on canvas, 13 1/2 x 23 1/2 ins / 34.5 x 60 cm) ITL 15,500,000. NEW YORK, 25 Oct 1989, *The Day's Catch* (oil on panel, 7 1/2 x 13 1/4 ins / 19 x 33.6 cm) USD 12,100. LONDON, 15 Feb 1990, *Jesuits in Venice* (oil on canvas, 14 x 22 ins / 35.6 x 56 cm) GBP 17,600. MILAN, 30 May 1990, *Procession* (oil on canvas, 37 1/2 x 70 ins / 95 x 178 cm) ITL 40,000,000. NEW YORK, 23 Oct 1990, *Bay of Naples* (1891, oil on canvas, 15 x 9 1/4 ins / 38.4 x 23.8 cm) USD 11,000. ROME, 11 Dec 1990, *Canal in Venice* (watercolour, 27 1/4 x 15 ins / 69 x 38 cm) ITL 2,530,000. MILAN, 12 March 1991, *Pastoral Scene in the Campagna Romana* (oil on canvas, 14 3/4 x 22 3/4 ins / 37.5 x 58 cm) ITL 4,000,000. LONDON, 21 June 1991, *The Church of the Jesuits and boats on the Lagoon, Venice* (oil on canvas, 14 x 22 1/2 ins / 35.5 x 57 cm) GBP 11,550. STOCKHOLM, 19 May 1992, *Gypsy Festival with Flamenco Dancers in a Tavern* (oil on canvas, 17 3/4 x 29 1/2 ins / 45 x 75 cm) SEK 77,000. NEW YORK, 30 Oct 1992, *Grand Canal and Rialto Bridge, Venice* (oil on panel, 14 3/4 x 22 1/4 ins / 37.5 x 56.5 cm) USD 23,100. LONDON, 16 June 1993, *Sunny Canal, Venice*. NEW YORK, 16 Feb 1994, *Flamenco Dancer* (1892, oil on canvas, 17 3/4 x 29 3/4 ins / 45.1 x 75.6 cm) USD 43,125. LONDON, 12 June 1996, *View of Venice* (oil on canvas, 18 1/2 x 31 1/2 ins / 47 x 80 cm) GBP 7,130. LONDON, 21 Nov 1996, *Via Sacra and the Arch of Constantine* (1889, oil on panel, 13 1/2 x 20 ins / 34.2 x 51 cm) GBP 6,670. GLASGOW, 20 Feb 1997, *S. Maria della Salute at the Entrance to the Grand Canal, seen from the Walkway leading to St. Mark's Square, Venice* (oil on canvas, 14 1/2 x 22 1/2 ins / 36.8 x 57.2 cm) GBP 7,150. LONDON, 26 March 1997, *Venice Canal Scene in the Sun* (1894, oil on canvas, 22 1/4 x 14 1/4 ins / 56.5 x 36 cm) GBP 11,500.

SENEVAS, de (Baron)

French, 19th century.

Painter. Landscapes.

He exhibited at the Salon between 1834 and 1842.

SENEVAS DE CROIX-MESNIL, Julie de
(Baronne)
French, 19th century.
Painter. Genre scenes.
She exhibited at the Salon between 1834 and 1844.

SENEWALDT, Friedrich Wilhelm
German, 18th - 19th century.
Active in Berlin 1775-1800.
Painter. Portraits, landscapes.
MUSEUMS AND GALLERIES:
BERLIN (Kupferstichkabinet): *Portrait of William of Mechlin* (drawing) - BREMEN (Focke-Mus.): *Miniature Portrait of Mayor Jacob Breuls* - WROCLAW (Mus. of Decorative Arts): *Miniature Portrait of a Countess Stolberg.*

SENEX, John
British, 18th century.
Died 30 December 1740, in London.
Engraver, cartographer.
John Senex was active at least until 1740. He worked as a cold-chisel engraver and cartographer.

SENEZ, Alain
French, 20th - 21st century.
Born 1948, in Paris.
Active in Belgium.
Painter.
Alain Senez studied painting at the École des Beaux-Arts in Paris.

SENEZCOURT, Jules de
French, 19th century.
Born 1818, in St-Omer; died 1866, in Brussels.
Painter. Portraits, genre scenes.
The Musée de Bruxelles has two works by this artist: *The Lute Player* (a self-portrait) and *Head of an Old Man* (a study).
AUCTION RECORDS:
NEW YORK, 2 Dec 1986, *Before the Ball* (oil on panel, 35 x 26 1/4 ins / 89 x 66.5 cm) USD 6,000. PARIS, 1 Dec 1999, *The Swing* (oil on wood, 13 x 17 ins / 33 x 42 cm) FRF 15,200.

SENF, Friedrich Traugott, or Senff
German, 18th - 19th century.
Born 1761, in Dresden; died after 1812.
Painter, miniaturist.
Senf studied under Hutin and Klengel.

SENF, Leon J.
Dutch, 19th - 20th century.
Born 11 March 1860, in Delft; died 1940.
Active in Voorburg, near The Hague.
Painter, engraver, draughtsman. Landscapes with figures.
Leon J. Senf was a pupil of A. Le Comte. He painted on porcelain.
AUCTION RECORDS:
AMSTERDAM, 17 Sept 1991, *Shepherd Leading his Flock* (black chalk and watercolour/paper, 24 1/2 x 36 1/2 ins / 62 x 93 cm) NLG 1,265.

SENFF, Adolf or Karl Adolf
German, 19th century.
Born 17 March 1785, in Halle (Saxony-Anhalt); died 21 March 1863, in Ostrau.
Painter, pastellist. History painting, portraits, genre scenes, landscapes with figures, still-lifes (flowers).
Adolf Senff initially studied theology, then from 1810, devoted himself to painting, studying pastels under Kugelgen in Dresden. Subsequently, he went on a study trip to Italy and stayed in Rome, where he produced several works in the style of Raphael for the castle of Sans-Souci. He was most successful with his paintings of flowers and fruits.
MUSEUMS AND GALLERIES:
COPENHAGEN (Thorvaldsens Mus.): *Flowers* - DRESDEN (Prints Collection): *Self-portrait* - HALLE: *Pumpkins; Child amidst the Flowers; Roman Countryside* - HANOVER (Kestner-Mus.): *Portrait of Thorvaldsen* - LEIPZIG (Stadtgeschichtliches Mus.): *Portrait of Colonel Prensel.*
AUCTION RECORDS:
MUNICH, 10 Dec 1992, *Mother and her Children in a Landscape* (1822, oil on canvas, 52 x 37 1/2 ins / 132 x 95.5 cm) DEM 16,950. COLOGNE, 25 March 1999, *Temple of the Sibyls near Tivoli* (oil on board, 28 x 20 ins / 70 x 51 cm) DEM 26,000. ROME, 4 Dec 2000, *Flowers in a Basket on a Stone Ledge* (oil on canvas, 40 x 30 ins / 101 x 76 cm) ITL 30,000,000. AHLDEN, 20 Sept 2002, *Child's Portrait* (oil on canvas, oval, 25 x 20 ins / 63 x 51 cm) EUR 1,700. LONDON, 16 July 2003, *Flower Studies* (1837, oil on paper/cardboard, 11 x 16 ins / 27 x 40 cm) GBP 8,800. LONDON, 16 July 2003, *Flower Studies* (1837, oil on paper/cardboard, 11 x 16 ins / 27 x 40 cm) GBP 9,500. BERLIN, 13 May 2004, *Plant* (1825, oil on paper, 9 x 7 ins / 22 x 17 cm) EUR 3,200. BERN, 17 June 2004, *Climbing Plant with Yellow Flowers* (gouache, 11 x 7 ins / 29 x 19 cm) CHF 2,300.

SENFF, Karl Julius
Estonian, 19th century.
Born 11 December 1804, in Tartu; died 19 April 1832, in Milan, Italy.
Painter, engraver (burin), lithographer, architect, art writer.
Karl Julius Senff was the son and pupil of Karl August. He studied in Prague and Vienna and published 10 pages about the cathedral of St Guy in Prague.

SENFF, Karl or Karl August
German, 18th - 19th century.
Born 12 March 1770, in Kreypau; died 2 January 1838, in Tartu (Estonia).
Active in Tartu.
Painter, pastellist, watercolourist, lithographer, engraver (burin). Portraits, genre scenes, landscape.
Carl Senff was the brother of Adolf.

SENFF, Karoline. See **SCHILLING Karoline**

SENFFT, Christoph, or Sennfft
German, 17th century.
Active in Laufingen 1602-1615.
Engraver (burin).

SENFFTEL, Johann Jakob
German, 17th - 18th century.
Born c. 1661; died 1729, in Augsburg (Bavaria).
Engraver. Landscapes.
Sensfftel engraved a view of Heidelberg, Germany, in silverpoint in 1689.

SENFT, Melchior
German, 16th century.
Active in Geyersbourg from 1512 to 1515.
Sculptor (wood).
Senft carved the altar of the church of Unter-Münkheim.

SENG, Jakob Christian or Christoph
German, 18th century.
Born 31 March 1727, in Nuremberg; died 11 July 1796, in Nuremberg.
Painter, engraver (etching). Landscapes, battles, hunting scenes, portraits.
Jakob Seng studied under W. I. Prasch.

SENG, Regina Katharina
German, 18th century.
Born 1 November 1756, in Nuremberg; died 30 August 1786, in Nuremberg.
Painter.

Regina Seng was the daughter of Jakob Christian Seng and the wife of Christian Friedrich August von Pilgram.

SENGAI, monastic name: Gibon, nicknames: Sengai or Gai, pseudonyms: Hyakudo, Kyohaku, Muhosai, Amaka Osho, Ayo, Taiho, Temmin
Japanese, 18th - 19th century.
Born 1750, in Mino near Gifu; died 1837.
Monk, painter.

Sengai was the third son of a farmer from the province of Mino in central Japan. He was tonsured and donned the monk's robe at the age of 11. At 19 his Zen Buddhist master authorised him to accomplish his *angya*, the pilgrimage which would lead him from one spiritual master to another until he encountered one with whom he would decide to spend several years to gain a deeper knowledge of Zen. Sengai chose Gessen Zenji, one of the great masters of the period, who lived in Nagata, near the city known today as Yokohama. Senga remained with Gessen for 13 years and when Gessen died he undertook his second *angya*. Tradition has it that he travelled across the north and the centre of the country visiting the different monasteries and even spending some time in the province where he was born. Then he received an invitation to go to Hakata, on the island of Kyushu, where a brother monk, also a disciple of Gessen Zenji, was in charge of a monastery. Sengai accepted and moved into the Shofuku-ji temple of which the patron was the local feudal lord, Kuroda.

In 1811 Sengai resigned his position as abbot of Shokuku-ji and lived an independent life for the next 20 years, during which time he had most contact with ordinary people, and developed his remarkable artistic talents, expressing in his works, which were full of spirit and humour, a deep understanding of Zen. The Shofuku-ji temple is famous for being the first Zen temple built in Japan, by Eisai (1141-1215) on his return from China in 1191. Sengai was the 123rd abbot and he was justifiably elated by this privilege. He was small in stature and nicknamed himself *shikoku-saru*, the monkey of Shikoku, a province known for its small monkeys. He was famous for his detachment, his modest clothes and his charitable sentiments. In 1803, for example, he refused the purple robe, an honour of distinction conferred upon him by imperial order. He renounced it on principle, his ambition being to complete his life as a simple monk dressed in black rags.

A representative collection of the works of Sengai was circulated around European museums from 1960 to 1964, following which the name of this artist became familiar to Westerners. In order to understand it, it is necessary to know that it belongs to Zen Buddhism, which in summary consists of awakening the immediate intuitive sense which lies dormant in the depths of the being of each individual, with a conscious effort to awaken and intensify it. This awakening is called the *satori*, which proposes to grasp the ultimate reality, that is to say a void which is plenitude and a plenitude which is void, not in the intellectual, conceptual or abstract sense, but in the very moment of immediate existence with both feet firmly planted on the ground. In order to attain *satori*, Sengai executed drawings which were both sacred and profane but bursting with deep sincerity, expressing at the same time a certain humour. It was in this way that he aimed to be at the very centre of life in action without allowing his interior freedom to be compromised in any way, and that he affirmed his spiritual liberty. He represented the Universe by the combination circle-triangle-square, the circle representing the infinite at the core of all beings, whilst the triangle was the foundation of all tangible forms and gave birth to the square, which was a double triangle. It was this process of doubling repeated indefinitely which gave the multitude of objects the 'ten thousand elements', to quote the Chinese philosophers, that is to say the Universe. Sengai was a calligrapher and a poet and usually accompanied his works with a haiku for which the painted image was the illustration, or alternatively a haiku which was the Zen commentary of the pictorial representation. Sengai held Basho (1644-1694), the creator of the haiku, in the highest esteem and also often referred to his painting, as in *Basho and the Frog*, which was accompanied by the following haiku: 'An ancient pond, and something jumped into it, Flop'.

BIBLIOGRAPHY:

Teitaro Suzuki, Daisetz, *Sengai, the Zen Master*, Faber and Faber, London, 1971 (notes by Eva van Hoboken, Sazo Idemitsu, Basil Gray, Herbert Read). Suzuki, D. T., *Sengai, the Zen Master*, London, 1971. Addiss, S., *The Art of Zen: Paintings and Calligraphy by Japanese Monks, 1600-1925*, New York, 1989. Suzuki, D.T., *Sengai: The Zen of Ink and Paper*, Shambhala, Boston, 1999. Furata, Shokin, *Sengai: Master Zen Painter*, Kodansha, New York, 2000.

MUSEUMS AND GALLERIES:

TOKYO (Idemitsu MA): many of his works.

AUCTION RECORDS:

NEW YORK, 17 Oct 1989, *Hotei* (kakemono, ink on paper, 19 1/2 x 24 1/2 ins / 49.4 x 62.4 cm) USD 17,600. NEW YORK, 16 Oct 1990, *Kannon Dressed in White* (kakemono, ink/silk, with calligraphy, 32 1/2 x 16 1/2 ins / 82.3 x 41.6 cm) USD 18,700.

SENGE-PLATTEN, Eugen
German, 20th century.
Born 3 September 1890, in Siedlinghausen.
Sculptor.

Eugen Senge-Platten studied at the fine arts academy in Berlin and sculpted war memorials in Winterberg and Schmollenberg.

SENGELAUB, Hans
German, 17th century.
Active in Coburg (Bavaria) Germany, in 1615.
Painter. Landscapes.

Hans Sengelaub was the son of Peter. He painted a panoramic view of the town of Römhild, Germany.

SENGELAUB, Peter
German, 17th century.
Born 5 May 1622, in Coburg (Bavaria).
Painter, architect.

Peter Sengelaub painted portraits, maps and house façades.

SENGENRIEDER, Michael
German, 15th - 16th century.
Active in Munich from 1470 to 1501.
Glass painter.

SENGER, Hans
German, 16th century.
Active probably in Venice c. 1570.
Painter, draughtsman. Sporting subjects.

Senger made drawings for woodcuts.

MUSEUMS AND GALLERIES:

LONDON (British Mus.): *Fencing Scenes* (six engravings/wood) - OXFORD (Ashmolean Mus.): *Fencing Scenes* (eight engravings/wood).

SENGER, Ludwig von
German, 20th century.
Born 6 November 1873, in Waldsassen.
Active in Munich.
Painter.

Ludwig von Senger was a pupil of M. von Diez and L. Herterich.

SENGESPEIK, M. Baltzer
German, 17th century.
Active during the second half of the 17th century.
Sculptor. Religious furnishings.

Sengespeik produced the altar for the church of Wentdorf near Wittenberge (Mecklenburg, west Pomerania), Germany, in 1682.

SENGHER, Philipp, or Sänger
German, 17th century.
Active in Copenhagen, Denmark, and in Florence, Italy, 1681-1694.
Sculptor (ivory), turner.
MUSEUMS AND GALLERIES:
FLORENCE (Mus. Nazionale): several works.

SENGLAUB, Adolf
German, 20th century.
Born 11 March 1873, in Stuttgart.
Painter. History painting.

SENGTHALLER, Hans
German, 20th century.
Born 14 October 1892, in Schellenberg.
Active in Munich.
Painter, engraver.
MUSEUMS AND GALLERIES:
BYTOM: *Alpine Landscape*.

SENGUPTA, Dwijen
Indian, 20th century.
Born in India.
Draughtsman.
Dwijen Sengupta worked mainly in the area of graphic design.

SENIOR, Mark
British, 19th - 20th century.
Born 1862, in Hanging; died 1927.
Painter. Genre scenes.
Mark Senior trained under J.F. Bird, and in London where he attended classes at the Slade School of Fine Art. He was initially influenced by Clausen, whom he counted among his friends, and later by Steer. He exhibited at the Athenaeum Buildings in Leeds in 1886 and the Royal Academy from 1892 to 1924. He is noted for his portraits and scenes painted on the Yorkshire and Dutch coasts.
MUSEUMS AND GALLERIES:
LEEDS (City AG): *Toil* (oil on canvas); *Apple Blossoms* (oil on canvas); *Wild Roses* (1906, oil on canvas); *Spring* (1906, oil on canvas); *Commercial Street, Leeds* (c. 1910, oil on canvas).
AUCTION RECORDS:
LONDON, 17 Oct 1980, *Landscape, Hinderwell* (oil on canvas, 21 x 25 3/4 ins / 53.5 x 65.5 cm) GBP 480. LONDON, 21 May 1986, *Sunlit Houses in Runswick* (oil on canvas, 24 x 20 ins / 61 x 51 cm) GBP 9,500. LONDON, 9 June 1988, *The Coast at Runswick* (oil on panel, 6 1/4 x 9 ins / 15.8 x 22 cm) GBP 902. LEEDS, 30 June 1999, *Picking Apples at Runswick* (oil on canvas, 24 x 20 ins / 61 x 51 cm) GBP 4,500. LEEDS, 30 June 1999, *Runswick Bay* (oil on canvas, 20 x 24 ins / 51 x 61 cm) GBP 13,000. LEEDS, 14 March 2000, *Windy Day* (oil on canvas, 34 x 39 ins / 86 x 100 cm) GBP 9,400. LEEDS, 14 Nov 2000, *Mists Clearing* (1911, oil on canvas, 25 x 30 ins / 63 x 76 cm) GBP 12,500. LEEDS, 13 March 2001, *Morning, Runswick Bay* (oil on canvas, 20 x 24 ins / 51 x 61 cm) GBP 6,500. LEEDS, 20 Nov 2001, *Beach at Brunswick Bay* (1905, oil on panel, 6 x 11 ins / 14 x 28 cm) GBP 9,000. LEEDS, 18 June 2002, *Spring* (oil on canvas, 24 x 20 ins / 61 x 51 cm) GBP 12,500. LEEDS, 19 Nov 2002, *Nymphs Dancing* (1912, oil on canvas, 48 x 54 ins / 122 x 137 cm) GBP 41,000. LEEDS, 25 March 2003, *Rural Landscape with the Sea Beyond. Study of the Rear of a House* (oil on panel, two, 8 x 10 ins / 21 x 26 cm) GBP 6,800. LEWES, 9 Sept 2003, *Figures in a Village Square* (1904, oil on canvas, 20 x 24 ins / 51 x 61 cm) GBP 13,500. LEEDS, 15 June 2004, *Horse Plough at Work* (oil on board, 8 x 10 ins / 20 x 25 cm) GBP 4,200. LEYBURN, 22 July 2004, *Coastal Scene with Fishing Boat Off a Beach* (oil on panel, 9 x 13 ins / 23 x 33 cm) GBP 3,800.

SENIS, Guido da. See **GUIDO DA SIENA**

SENIS, Joseph Anton. See **SENES**

SENIS, Pablo da. See **PABLO DA SENIS**

SENISE, Daniel
Brazilian, 20th - 21st century.
Born 1955.
Painter (mixed media).
Daniel Senise is part of the group of Brazilian artists known by the critics as Generation 80 who were important on the art scene during that decade; members include José Leonilson Bezerra Dias, Nuno Ramos, Jorge Duarte and Fernando Barata. Senise lives and works in Rio de Janeiro. He has taken part in collective exhibitions, including: São Paulo Biennale (1989); *Art from Brazil in New York* travelling exhibition shown in various museums and galleries (1995).
AUCTION RECORDS:
NEW YORK, 17 Nov 1994, *Untitled* (1988, oil on canvas and collage, 35 1/2 x 27 1/2 ins / 90 x 70 cm) USD 9,200. NEW YORK, 25-26 Nov 1996, *Untitled* (1989, oil and plaster/canvas, 83 3/4 x 52 1/4 ins / 212.7 x 132.7 cm) USD 18,400. NEW YORK, 2 June 1999, *Tower of Song, from the series Tower of Song* (1993, acrylic and iron on canvas, 89 x 55 ins / 225 x 140 cm) USD 16,000. NEW YORK, 22 Nov 1999, *Beddangelina* (1990, acrylic and iron on canvas, 58 x 70 ins / 147 x 177 cm) USD 13,000. NEW YORK, 1 June 2000, *Parada* (*Stop*) (pigment and sand on two layers of muslin, 55 x 67 ins / 140 x 170 cm) USD 14,000. NEW YORK, 21 Nov 2000, *Lazaro* (*Lazarus*) (1990, oil on canvas, 46 x 81 ins / 118 x 205 cm) USD 12,000. NEW YORK, 31 May 2001, *Globo* (1992, acrylic on canvas, 64 x 49 ins / 163 x 124 cm) USD 8,000. NEW YORK, 31 May 2001, *Sin titulo* (*Untitled*) (1999, acrylic on canvas, 72 x 94 ins / 184 x 240 cm) USD 12,000. RIO DE JANEIRO, 1 April 2003, *Untitled* (oil on canvas, 94 x 79 ins / 240 x 200 cm) BRL 52,500. RIO DE JANEIRO, 17 June 2003, *Untitled* (1997, oil on canvas, 79 x 94 ins / 200 x 240 cm) BRL 66,150. NEW YORK, 26 May 2004, *Tower of Song* (1993, oil on canvas, 87 x 57 ins / 220 x 146 cm) USD 12,000. RIO DE JANEIRO, 14 Sept 2004, *Untitled* (1985, oil on canvas, 91 x 75 ins / 230 x 190 cm) BRL 68,000.

SENIVAL
French, 15th century.
Miniaturist.
The Musée du Petit Palais, Paris, has a miniature by Senival in the manuscript *The History of Good King Alexander*.

SENKA, artist names: Senka, Sosetsu, Ryoo
Japanese, 16th century.
Active in the Kyoto area at the beginning of the 16th century.
Painter.
Senka was a *suiboku* (ink painting) artist in Kyoto during the Muromachi era.

SENKADO. See **NISHIMURA Shiganaga**

SENKEVICH, Serafina
Russian, 20th century.
Born 1941, in Moldavia.
Painter.
Senkevich studied at the school of fine art in Chishinau.

SENLIS, Jehan de. See **JEHAN DE SENLIS**

SENLIS, Michelle
French, 20th century.
Painter.
Despite her advanced training in drawing, for more than twenty years Senlis wrote fifty or so songs for renowned artists such as Edith Piaf (*C'est à Hambourg*), Jean Ferrat (*No-*

mades) and Daniel Guichard (*Mon Vieux*). She took up painting in 1968 but did not exhibit.

She painted solid, abstract shapes and marks, on superimposed levels, in a range of reduced tones - browns, greens, blues - and with a rigorous composition, emanating a definite spirituality.

In 1978 Pierre Courthion encouraged her to show her work and she gave some solo shows thereafter: 1982, first exhibition, Gertrude van Dyck Gallery in Brussels; in 1988, and regularly from then on, *Les Sortilèges du papier* (*The Curses of Paper*), 2001, Galerie ABC, Brussels; 1998, Galerie Michel Ray, Paris.

SENLIS, Séraphine de, pseudonym of Louis, Séraphine
French, 19th - 20th century.
Born 2 September 1864, in Assy (Oise); died 11 December 1942, in Clermont (Oise).
Painter. Still-lifes (flowers/fruit).

Séraphine's father was a village watchmaker and died young in around 1871; her mother worked as a housekeeper. When Séraphine was young, she looked after sheep. She attended school only irregularly and enjoyed looking after the animals. From the age of thirteen, probably until she was fifteen, she worked as a maid in Paris, then in Compiègne in Picardy for three years. She recounted that in 1882, at the age of eighteen, she joined the convent of St Joseph de Cluny, and spent twenty years there, apparently carrying out menial tasks, rather than as a nun. She left the convent in 1902 and, according to her biographers, went on to become a cleaner as she was too poor to marry. She worked in several houses in the Compiègne region - in St-Just-en-Chaussée and Senlis from 1904. In the countryside at the turn of the century, only those who could provide a dowry of a plot of land were able to marry. It is not clear whether it has simply been deduced in light of this custom and the modesty of Séraphine Louis' means that she never married, or whether she confided this in somebody. There was almost certainly an element of regret and frustration, which slipped into her work in symbolic forms, and the drive behind her creative activity could be attributed to the need to express the dark desires which tormented her and ultimately drove her to madness.

She was discovered by Wilhelm Uhde, a German living in Paris. While staying in Senlis in 1912 he had employed her as a cleaning lady, unaware that she painted. At the house of friends he saw one of her *Bouquets* and learned that she had painted it. The young German was an admirer of the Romantics and thought that he had discovered in her the 'Gothic' miracle. It was fortuitous that Uhde, one of the few admirers of Naive art at the time, happened to cross her path. The still-lifes that she painted in 1912 were confiscated during World War I as the property of an 'enemy subject' and were never found. It was not until 1927 that Uhde saw Séraphine Louis again, at an exhibition of regional painters at Senlis town hall. From then on he bought all of her works, which he kept at his house in Chantilly (Picardy). Uhde's writings are a rich source of first-hand information and exceptionally pertinent views of the artist.

With her technical prowess she is at least in the league of Georges Rouault in the art of a dark ring, the stained glass windows, each facet enamelled with superposed glazes. In his book on *Cinq Maîtres primitifs* (*Five Primitive Masters*) (p130), Wilhelm Uhde hints that he later procured for her the quality materials that she coveted, specifying nevertheless that, 'she doesn't use a single one of the many colours I send her. She gets her own herself and mixes them with gloss. The mystery of this composition remains a secret that she shares with no-one. [...] Often, over the course of the years, painters, for whom no technique remained a secret, begged me to reveal the composition of the splendid paste that Séraphine used in countless paintings.' It is her technique, which is similar to that developed by Gustave Moreau that is astonishing.

Her works featured in numerous exhibitions during her lifetime, including 1929 *Les Peintres du Cœur sacré* (*Painters of the Sacred Heart*) in Paris; 1932 *Les Primitifs modernes* (*The Modern Primitives*); 1937-1938 *Les Maîtres populaires de la réalité* (*Popular Masters of Reality*) in Paris then at the Musée de Grenoble, Zurich Kunsthaus and the Museum of Modern Art, New York; 1938 *Primitives of the 20th Century* in Paris; 1942 *Primitifs du XXe siècle* (*Primitives of the 20th Century*) at the Galerie Drouin in Paris; and after her death in the major exhibitions dedicated to so-called Naive art and in the great exhibitions of French art: 1949 *Peintres primitifs modernes* (*Modern Primitive Painters*) at the Bern Kunsthalle; 1951 *Fifty Years of French Art* at the Royal Academy, London, *Natures Mortes françaises du XVIIe siècle à nos jours* (*French Still-lifes From the 17th Century to the Present Day*) at the Galerie Charpentier in Paris, First Biennale of São Paulo; 1952 *Cinquante Ans de peinture française* (*Fifty Years of French Painting*) at the Musée des Arts Décoratifs de Paris; 1955 *Art of the 20th Century* at the Documenta in Kassel; 1958 *Les Peintres naïfs du Douanier Rousseau à nos jours* (*Naive Painters from Douanier Rousseau to the Present Day*) at the Casino in Knokke-le-Zoute; then *Le Monde des naïfs* (*The World of the Naive Artists*) at the Boymans Museum in Rotterdam; Musée National d'Art Moderne de Paris, an exhibition in which an entire room was dedicated to her; 2001 *Die Naïve, aufbruch ins verlorene paradies* (*The Naïve Painters, Journey to a Lost Paradise*) Vienna Kunsthaus. Exhibitions have been dedicated exclusively to her work, most notably in Paris in 1945 at the Galerie de France, a retrospective in 1951 in connection with the Salon des Femmes Peintres et Sculpteurs, and at the Galerie Pierre Birtschansky in 1962.

BIBLIOGRAPHY:

Uhde, Wilhelm, *Les Peintres du Cœur sacré*, exhibition catalogue, Gal. Quatre Chemins, Paris, 1927. Uhde, Wilhelm, *Séraphine Louis*, Formes, Paris, 1931. Gauthier, Maximilien, *Les Maîtres populaires de la réalité*, exhibition catalogue, Musée d'Art moderne de la Ville de Paris, Paris, 1937. Jakovsky, Anatole, *La Peinture naïve*, Jacques Damase, Paris, 1947. Uhde, Wilhelm, *Cinq Maîtres primitifs*, Philippe Daudy, Paris, 1949. Mathey, François, *Six femmes peintres*, Éd. du Chêne, Paris, 1951. Busse, Jacques, "*Séraphine de Senlis*' in *L'Information artistique*, periodical, Paris, November 1953. Gallot, H.-M., "*Séraphine, bouquetière sans rivale des fleurs maudites de l'instinct*' in *L'Information artistique*, periodical, Paris, May 1957. Bihalji-Merin, Oto, *Das Naïve Bild der Welt*, DuMont Schauberg, Cologne, 1959. Bihalji-Merin, Oto, *Les Peintres naïfs*, Delpire, Paris, 1960. Frank, Nino, "*Séraphine l'obscure*' in *Séraphine de Senlis*, exhibition catalogue, Gal. Pierre Birtschansky, Paris, 1962. Busse, Jacques, "*Séraphine de Senlis*' in *Pour l'Art*, periodical, Lausanne, January-February 1963. Foucher, J.-P., *Séraphine de Senlis*, Éd. du Temps, Paris, 1968. Gallot, H.-M., "*Séraphine: 1864-1942*' in *Séraphine*, exhibition catalogue, Gal. d'Art de la Tradition Populaire, Paris, March 1968. Vircondelet, Alain, *Séraphine de Senlis*, Albin Michel, Paris, 1986.

MUSEUMS AND GALLERIES:

GRENOBLE (Mus. de Grenoble): *Fruit* (c. 1928) - HAMBURG (Kunsthalle): *Blue Séraphine or Great Leaves* - KHARKOV (Municipal Mus.) - KIEV (Chanjenko Mus.) - NEW YORK (MOMA) - ODESSA (Fonds de Cult.) - PARIS (MNAM-CCI): *Pomegranates on Green Background* (c. 1927); *Tree of Paradise* (c. 1929); *Red Tree* (c. 1930).

AUCTION RECORDS:

PARIS, Oct 1945 - July 1946, *Flowers*, FRF 36,000. PARIS, 19 May 1954, *Daisies on Green Background*, FRF 175,000. PARis, 20 March 1964, *Foliage*, FRF 6,000. Paris, 25 March 1968, *Bouquet of Flowers*, FRF 25,000. Paris, 12 June 1969, *Flowers*, FRF 28,000. London, 11 April 1972, *Fruit*, Gns 2,700. Zurich, 1 June 1973, *Cherries on Yellow Background*, CHF 20,000. Paris, 29 Oct 1974, *Wild Flowers*, FRF 36,000. Zurich, 28 May 1976, *Cherries on Yellow Background* (oil on panel, 9 3/4 x 7 1/2 ins / 25 x 19 cm) CHF 4,200. Versailles, 9 March 1980, *Cherry Tree Branch* (oil on panel, 7 3/4 x 9 3/4 ins / 19.5 x 25 cm) FRF 6,500. Paris, 24 March 1981, *Flowers* (oil on panel, 11 x 13 3/4 ins / 27 x 35 cm) FRF 18,000. Zurich, 21 June 1985, *Daisies* (oil on panel, 11 1/2 x 14 ins / 29.5 x 35.5 cm) CHF 5,000. Paris, 27 June 1986, *Spray of Flowers* (oil on panel, 19 1/4 x 23 1/2 ins / 49 x 60 cm) FRF 35,000. Paris, 22 June 1989, *Bouquet* (oil on canvas, 36 1/4 x 28 3/4 ins / 92 x 73 cm) FRF 380,000. Paris, 27 March 1990, *Leaves, Flowers and Fruit, Bouquet* (c. 1929, oil on canvas, 36 1/4 x 23 1/2 ins / 92 x 60 cm) FRF 235,000. Paris, 15 June 1991, *Bouquet of Flowers on Red Background* (oil on canvas, 39 1/4 x 25 1/2 ins / 100 x 65 cm) FRF 250,000. London, 16 Oct 1991, *Flowers on Blue Background* (oil on panel, 8 1/4 x 10 1/4 ins / 21 x 26.1 cm) GBP 4,180. Paris, 3 June 1992, *Flowers and Fruit* (oil on canvas, 51 1/4 x 63 1/2 ins / 130 x 161 cm) FRF 15,000. Paris, 3 July 1992, *Cherries* (oil on canvas, 14 1/4 x 19 1/4 ins / 36 x 49 cm) FRF 18,000. Paris, 26 Nov 1993, *Bouquet of Mimosas* (oil on canvas, 57 x 38 1/4 ins / 145 x 97 cm) FRF 385,000. Paris, 2 June 1995, *Bouquet of Flowers* (oil on canvas, 47 1/4 x 35 1/4 ins / 120 x 89.5 cm) FRF 160,000. Paris, 23 Oct 2000, *Daisies* (oil on panel, 24 x 19 ins / 60 x 49 cm) FRF 40,000. Cannes, 15 Aug 2001, *Basket of Flowers* (oil on canvas, 19 x 24 ins / 47 x 61 cm) FRF 91,000. Paris, 24 April 2002, *Flowers and Fruit* (oil on panel, 11 x 17 ins / 28 x 43 cm) EUR 3,000. Paris, 24 April 2002, *Bunch of Flowers* (oil on canvas, 35 x 28 ins / 90 x 71 cm) EUR 7,000. Paris, 3 Dec 2003, *Cherries* (oil on canvas, 14 x 19 ins / 36 x 49 cm) EUR 3,000. Paris, 3 Dec 2003, *Vase of Lilies* (oil on canvas, 26 x 32 ins / 65 x 81 cm) EUR 3,600. Paris, 26 April 2004, *Branch with Flowers* (oil on panel, 7 x 10 ins / 19 x 25 cm) EUR 2,400.

SENMAN
Japanese, 19th century.
Active in the Osaka area c. 1820.
Print artist.

SENMNO, Antonio. See **SEMINO**

SENN, Christoph or Johann Christoph
German, 18th - 19th century.
Engraver (burin).

Christoph Senn worked first in Christian von Mechel's studio in Basel, Switzerland, then in Dessau and Leipzig in Germany.

SENN, Jakob
Swiss, 19th century.
Born 1790, in Liestal; died 1881, in Basel.
Painter, lithographer.

Jakob Senn studied under his brother Johannes, then under Hieronymus Hess. He painted the façade of the town hall in Basel.

Auction records:
Bern, 24 June 1983, *The Eisengasse in Babel* (c. 1840, coloured lithograph, 17 x 23 1/2 ins / 43 x 60 cm) CHF 3,200.

SENN, Joachim
Swiss, 19th century.
Born 17 July 1810, in Dullikon; died 13 October 1847, in Witznau.
Painter, lithographer.

Joachim Senn studied under M. Disteli.

Museums and Galleries:
Solothurn (Kunstmus.): *Portrait of Disteli*; four other portraits.

SENN, Johannes
Swiss, 19th century.
Born 17 September 1780, in Liestal; died 17 September 1861, in Liestal.
Active in Copenhagen.
Painter, engraver (etching), illustrator, writer. Portraits, genre scenes.

Johannes Senn was the brother of Jakob Senn and studied under Maxim.

SENN, Niklaus
Swiss, 19th century.
Born 16 May 1797, in Buochs; died 1 December 1867, in Bern.
Draughtsman.

SENN, Traugott
Swiss, 20th century.
Born 9 September 1877, in Maisprach; died 1955.
Active in Ins (Bern).
Painter, lithographer.

Traugott Senn studied under L.-O. Merson in Paris.

Museums and Galleries:
Aarau (Aargauer Kunsthaus): *Summer Day* (1935); *Lake Biel* (1938) - Bern - Glaris - La Chaux-de-Fonds - Mannheim - Zurich.

Auction records:
Bern, 25 Oct 1979, *Alpine Landscape* (1911, watercolour and tempera, 13 x 17 1/4 ins / 33 x 44 cm) CHF 1,600.

SENNEP
French, 20th century.
Born 3 June 1894, in Paris; died 9 July 1982, in St-Germain-en-Laye.
Draughtsman, caricaturist.

Going by the name 'Sennep', this man of wit used a pencil as polemists used a quill. He grasped the absurdity of situations more than of people. His verve ran its course in the theatre as well as in the world of politics. He paid homage to H.P. Gassier.

T. SENNEP

SENNES, Franz
Austrian, 18th - 19th century.
Born 1743; died 1814.
Painter (porcelain). Fruits and flowers.

Sennes worked for the porcelain manufactory in Vienna, Austria.

SENNES, Joseph Anton and Veit. See **SENES**

SENNFFT, Christoph. See **SENFFT**

SENNIUS, Titus Sennius Felix
3rd century.
Active in Puteoli.
Mosaicist.
Ancient Roman.

Sennius made a large mosaic of *Apollo and Daphne* from Lillebonne (France), now in Rouen.

Museums and Galleries:
Rouen: *Apollo and Daphne* (mosaic).

SENNO, Pietro
Italian, 19th century.
Born 1831, in Portoferraio (Island of Elba); died September 1904, in Pisa.
Painter. History painting, landscapes with figures, landscapes.

Pietro Senno was pupil of A. Ciseri.

Museums and Galleries:
Prato (Mus. Civico): *Prince Amadeus of Savoy Wounded at Custoza in 1866*; *Landscape at Sunset with Figures*.

AUCTION RECORDS:
NEW YORK, 2 April 1976, *Riders in a Mountainous Landscape* (oil on canvas, 21 1/4 x 32 1/4 ins / 54 x 82 cm) USD 600. MILAN, 6 Nov 1980, *Castello di Caorese* (oil on board, 8 1/4 x 13 1/2 ins / 21 x 34.5 cm) ITL 900,000. ROME, 16 April 1991, *Landscape with an Ox-Cart and Peasants* (oil on canvas, 22 x 29 1/4 ins / 56 x 74 cm) ITL 20,700,000. MILAN, 29 Oct 1992, *At the Edge of a Wood* (1887, oil on canvas, 18 3/4 x 25 1/4 ins / 47.5 x 64 cm) ITL 11,500,000. CONSTANCE, 26 June 1999, *Summer Thunderstorm, Farmer with Red Umbrella at Farmhouse* (oil on canvas, 43 x 32 ins / 108 x 81 cm) DEM 6,600. VERCELLI, 25 May 2002, *Stroll in the Wood* (oil on canvas laid on board, 11 x 15 ins / 29 x 38 cm) EUR 2,500. FLORENCE, 10 June 2003, *Cows at Pasture* (oil on canvas laid on card, 19 x 28 ins / 47 x 70 cm) EUR 3,500. FLORENCE, 10 June 2003, *Re di Noce Beach, Island of Elba* (oil on canvas, 51 x 67 ins / 130 x 170 cm) EUR 60,000.

SENOA, Branko
Croat, 20th century.
Born 7 August 1879, in Zagreb.
Painter, engraver.
Branko Senoa was a student of O. Ivekovic. He was a painter at the National Theatre in Zagreb.

SENONI, Domenico. See **ZENONI**

SENOT, Auguste
French, 17th century.
Painter. History painting.
Auguste Senot painted a *Carrying of the Cross* in St-Ferjeux.

SENS, Georges
Painter. History painting.
MUSEUMS AND GALLERIES:
STRASBOURG: *Tarquinius and Lucretius*.

SENSAI
Japanese, 19th century.
Probably from Ise.
Active in the Osaka area c. 1820.
Print artist.

SENSAI. See also **MARUYAMA Okyo**

SENSASI, Gino Carlo
Italian, 20th century.
Born 26 February 1888, in San Casciano dei Bagni (Tuscany).
Painter, engraver.
A self-taught artist, Gino Carlo Sensasi painted and made woodcuts. He lived and worked in Florence.
MUSEUMS AND GALLERIES:
ROME (Gal. Nazionale d'Arte Moderna).

SENSENEY, George
American, 20th century.
Born 11 October 1874, in Wheeling (Virginia); died 1943.
Active in Holyoke.
Engraver.
George Senseney studied in Washington under H. Helmick. He continued his studies with J.P. Laurens and B. Constant in Paris. He was a member of the Salmagundi Club.

SENSI, Battista di Cristofanello
Italian, 16th century.
Died 1554.
Active in Cortona (Tuscany).
Sculptor, architect.
Battista Sensi carved façades, portals and fireplaces for churches and private homes in Cortona.

SENSI Y BALDACHI, Gaspar
Spanish, 19th century.
Born 1794, in Perugia (Umbria), Italy; died 20 January 1880, in Madrid.
Painter, lithographer.
Gaspar Sensi y Baldachi studied under T. Minardi. He engraved lithographs after paintings in the collections of the king of Spain.

SENSIBILE, Antonio
Italian, 16th century.
Active in Naples during the second half of the 16th century.
Painter.
Antonio Sensibile was a pupil of S. Buono.

SENST, Peter
German, 17th century.
Active at the beginning of the 17th century.
Painter, gilder.
Senst painted the new organs for the cathedral of Magdeburg (Saxony-Anhalt), Germany, in 1604.

SENTENACH Y CABANAS, Narciso
Spanish, 19th - 20th century.
Born 5 February 1853, in Soria (Castilla y León), 6 December 1856 according to some sources; died 26 August 1925, in Madrid.
Painter, sculptor. Portraits, genre scenes, landscapes, flowers.
Narciso Sentenach y Cabanas studied at the academy of fine arts in Seville and secured a scholarship to continue his studies in Rome; he was a member of the academy of fine arts in Madrid.

Examples of his work include *Delilah, Don Miguel de Manara Sheltering an Outcast, Portrait of the Poet Salvador Rueda, Flowers, Winter's End* and *From Bad to Worse*. He was also a major art historian and published books and essays on painting, numismatics and precious metal working techniques in Spain. He featured at various collective exhibitions including the Seville exhibition (1879) and the National Fine Arts Society exhibitions, Madrid (from 1881 to 1910), where he received honourable mentions in 1904, 1906 and 1908.
BIBLIOGRAPHY:
Arnáiz, José Manuel/López Jiménez, Javier/Merchán Díaz, Manuel (ed.), '*Cien años de pintura en Espana y Portugal (1830-1930)*' in vol. X, Antiqvaria, Madrid, 1993.
MUSEUMS AND GALLERIES:
SEVILLE (Biblioteca de la Universidad): *Portrait of Juan de Salinas*.

SENTIER, Bastien or Sébastien
French, 16th century.
Active in Lyons from 1548 to 1554.
Sculptor, painter.

SENTIER, Pierre
French, 16th century.
Active in Lyons from 1544 to 1552.
Sculptor, painter.

SENTIES, Pierre Athasie Théodore
French, 19th century.
Born 23 February 1801, in Paris.
Painter. Religious subjects, portraits.
A Student of both Gros and Régault, Senties was admitted to the École des Beaux-Arts on 28 August 1818. He exhibited at the Salon between 1831 and 1869.
MUSEUMS AND GALLERIES:
VALENCE (Cathedral): *Resurrection*.
AUCTION RECORDS:
BREST, 12 Dec 1995, *Portrait of Simon Bolivar* (1830, oil on canvas, 84 1/4 x 58 1/4 ins / 214 x 148 cm) FRF 350,000.

SENTIS DE VILLEMUR, Joseph Gabriel
French, 19th century.

Born 31 August 1855, in Varennes (Tarn-et-Garonne).
Sculptor.
Works by Joseph Gabriel Sentis de Villemur exhibited at the Salon des Artistes Français from 1890 onwards, received an honourable mention in 1894 and a third class medal in 1897.

SENTOUT, Pierre
French, 18th century.
Active in 1791.
Painter. Portraits.
MUSEUMS AND GALLERIES:
ANGERS: *Self-portrait.*

SENUS, Willem van
Dutch, 18th - 19th century.
Born c. 1770; died 1851, in Amsterdam.
Engraver (burin).
Willem van Senus was a member of the painters' college in Utrecht in 1804. He engraved religious subjects after Van Dyck, and portraits.

SENYARD, George
American, 19th - 20th century.
Died 1924, in Olmstead Falls (Ohio).
Painter.

SENYEI, Karoly
Hungarian, 19th - 20th century.
Born 15 January 1854, in Budapest; died 7 February 1919, in Budapest.
Sculptor.
Karoly Senyei was a student of Knabl and Eberle.
MUSEUMS AND GALLERIES:
BUDAPEST (Szépmuvészeti Múz.): *Coquetry.*

SENZAN, real name: Nagamura Kan, given name: Saimo, artist names: Juzan, Senzan
Japanese, 19th century.
Born 1820; died 1862.
Active in the Kanaya area.
Painter.
A disciple of Watanabe Kazan (1793-1841), Senzan was a Nanga School (literati) painter. Although as a young man he was regarded as a genius, it would seem that in the rest of his career he failed to live up to expectations.

SENZI, Alessandro
Italian, 19th century.
Active in Florence.
Painter. Landscapes.
Alessandro Senzi exhibited mainly in Florence.

SEOANE, Luis
Argentinian, 20th century.
Born 1 June 1910, in Buenos Aires; died 4 April 1979, In La Coruña, Spain.
Active in Spain from c. 1935.
Painter.
In spite of some coincidences, Luis Seoane is probably not identical with Luis Secane.

Seoane settled at La Coruña in Spain and together with Isaac Diaz Pardo he there established the Galician 'Laboratory of Forms'. His painting, influenced by Picasso and Gris, by Miró and perhaps also by Bores, is characterised by its rigorous construction, post-Cubism and strong use of colour. It is representational, restrained, always under geometric and ascetic control. The overall vision, however, is one of hopefulness, most apparent in the *Furtive Portraits* which display a much readier spontaneity.

In 1929 Seoane had his first exhibition at the friends of the art gallery in Santiago de Compostela. After twenty years in Galicia he returned to Buenos Aires where he worked as a journalist for the *Critica* newspaper. In 1940 he was made artistic director of the Emecé editorial and in 1945 the American Institute of Graphic Arts and the Pierpont Morgan Library of New York commissioned him to illustrate numerous editions. Towards the end of the 1940s Seoane travelled to Europe where he met and interviewed Picasso in Paris and Henry Moore in London.

Seoane was granted the medal of the Argentinian Senate of the Nation in 1958 as a result of his success in the Exposition Internationale in Brussels and in 1962 he received the Palanza Prize from the Academia Nacional de Bellas Artes in Buenos Aires. In 1966 he participated in the 5th International Biennale of Engraving in Tokyo and in 1970 in the itinerant *Exhibition of Argentinean Engraving.* He was also part of the 3rd Biennale of Engraving in Cracow (Poland) in 1975 and *Art in Argentina* exhibition at the Wildenstein Gallery in London.
AUCTION RECORDS:
MADRID, 19 Dec 1974, *Figure in Red,* ESP 75,000. NEW YORK, 18 May 1993, *Turning Away from the Sea* (1976, oil on canvas, 29 x 36 1/2 ins / 73.6 x 92.5cm) USD 10,350. MADRID, 18 Feb 1999, *Woman on Horseback* (1945, oil on board, 15 x 19 ins / 39 x 49 cm) ESP 1,100,000. MADRID, 27 April 1999, *Emigrants* (oil on canvas, 23 x 28 ins / 59 x 72 cm) ESP 2,800,000. MADRID, 18 Feb 2000, *Jug and Red Peppers* (oil on canvas, 17 x 28 ins / 44 x 71 cm) ESP 2,000,000. MADRID, 3 Oct 2000, *Abstract Composition* (1967, oil on canvas, 18 x 15 ins / 46 x 38 cm) ESP 1,000,000. MADRID, 8 May 2001, *Figure* (ink wash, 25 x 19 ins / 64 x 49 cm) ESP 460,000. LONDON, 24 June 2002, *Boat and Seagull* (oil on canvas, 20 x 24 ins / 50 x 60 cm) GBP 1,000. BUENOS AIRES, 30 March 2004, *Two Faces* (oil on canvas, 12 x 24 ins / 30 x 60 cm) USD 12,700. BUENOS AIRES, 2 Nov 2004, *Fruit Seller* (1958, pastel, 25 x 18 ins / 64 x 46 cm) USD 11,500.

SEOANNE, Juan de
Spanish, 17th century.
Died 3 May 1680, in Santiago de Compostela.
Sculptor.
Juan de Seoanne carved a statue of *King Ferdinand* for the cathedral of Santiago de Compostela.

SÉON, Alexandre
French, 19th - 20th century.
Born 1855, in Chazelles-sur-Lyons (Loire); died 7 May 1917, in Paris.
Painter, draughtsman, illustrator. Mythological subjects, genre scenes, portraits.
Séon was a pupil of Lehmann, at the Écoles des Beaux-Arts in Lyons, and then of Puvis de Chavannes. He was one of the illustrators of E. Harcourt's *L'Effort* (*The Effort*). His debut was at the 1879 Salon in Paris; he won a silver medal at the 1889 Exposition Universelle, and also featured at the Salon de la Société Nationale des Beaux-Arts. The crispness of his drawing and stylisation is tempered by softer colour schemes.
AUCTION RECORDS:
PARIS, 28 May 1980, *Sphinx* (Indian ink, 10 3/4 x 7 1/4 ins / 27.5 x 18.5 cm) FRF 12,500. NEW YORK, 12 June 1980, *Mythical Island* (oil on canvas, 20 3/4 x 25 1/2 ins / 53 x 65 cm) USD 2,000. PARIS, 13 Dec 1985, *Virgins* (oil on canvas, 10 1/4 x 25 1/4 ins / 26 x 64 cm) FRF 60,000. PARIS, 12 Dec 1988, *Rural Scene* (oil on canvas, 32 1/4 x 54 3/4 ins / 82 x 139 cm) FRF 82,000. PARIS, 20 March 1989, *Narcissus* (1898, pencil/paper, 18 x 12 3/4 ins / 46 x 32.5 cm) FRF 45,500. PARIS, 25 June 1993, *Bust of Woman from Behind* (drawing heightened with white, 18 x 10 3/4 ins / 46 x 27.5 cm) FRF 7,000.

SEOU-SIUE CHAN-JEN. See **SOUXUE SHANREN**

SEPELIUS, Johannes. See **SELPELIUS**

SEPHESHY, Zoltan L., or Szepessy
Hungarian, 20th century.

Born 24 February 1898, in Kassa (now Košice, Slovakia); died 1974.
From c. 1930 also active in the USA.
Painter (gouache), engraver. Landscapes, seascapes.
Zoltan L. Sepheshy studied at the academies in Budapest, Vienna, Prague and Paris. He then lived and worked in Detroit, USA. He was a member of the royal academy in Budapest, and was the recipient of several awards from the same academy, as well as the Carnegie Prize. He also produced woodcut engravings.
Museums and Galleries:
Detroit: *Summer on the Shores of Lake Michigan.*
Auction records:
New York, 9 Sept 1993, *Yesterday's Visitors* (gouache and oil/synthetic resin, 33 x 45 ins / 83.8 x 114.3 cm) USD 1,035.

SEPHTON, Daniel
British, 18th century.
Active in Manchester from 1740 to 1780.
Sculptor.
Daniel Sephton sculpted the *Wright* tomb in Stockport and that of *Price* in Overton-on-Dee.

SEPHTON, George Harcourt
British, 19th century.
Painter. Portraits, genre scenes.
George Harcourt Sephton exhibited in London from 1885 to 1902, typically at the Royal Academy and the Suffolk Street Gallery.
Museums and Galleries:
Sydney: *Black Ox Labouring on the Brighton Downs; Portrait of W. Holman Hunt.*
Auction records:
London, 1 Nov 1990, *Hop-Gathering in Kent* (1891, oil on canvas, 54 x 112 ins / 137 x 284.5 cm) GBP 6,600. New York, 21 May 1991, *Tango* (1911, oil on canvas, 36 x 24 1/2 ins / 91.5 x 62.2 cm) USD 1,540. York, 12 Nov 1991, *Portrait of Charles, Lord Howard of Effingham and Earl of Nottingham* (oil on canvas, 19 1/2 x 15 1/2 ins / 49.5 x 39.5 cm) GBP 2,200.

SEPO, Severo, pseudonym of Pozzati, Severo
Italian, 20th century.
Born 16 March 1895, in Comacchio (Emilia Romagna); died 1983.
Painter, sculptor, poster artist.
A student at the Accademia di Belle Arti in Bologna, Severo Sepo exhibited work in Rome, Bologna and Florence. He received a medal for his posters at the Exposition des Arts Décoratifs in Paris in 1925.

SEPP, Christiaen
Dutch, 18th century.
Died 1775, in Amsterdam.
Engraver. Cartographer.
Christiaen Sepp was the father of Jan Christiaen Sepp.

SEPP, Jan Christiaen
Dutch, 18th - 19th century.
Born 1739, in Amsterdam; died 1811, in Amsterdam.
Painter, engraver (burin). Natural history (insects).
Jan Christiaen Sepp was a member of the Felis Meritis society. He collaborated with his son on engravings for a six-volume *Natural History of the Insects of Holland.*
Auction records:
Amsterdam, 18 Nov 1980, *Duck and its Eggs* (watercolour/traces of black chalk, 16 1/4 x 12 ins / 41 x 30.7 cm) NLG 4,400. Amsterdam, 25 April 1983, *Oriolus Goudmerel* (watercolour/outlines in black chalk, 16 1/4 x 12 1/2 ins / 41 x 31.7 cm) NLG 7,000. Amsterdam, 6 Nov 2001, *Drawings of Falcons* (watercolour, 14 x 13 ins / 36 x 32 cm) NLG 5,000. Amsterdam, 19 May 2004, *Stork* (watercolour and coloured chalk, 16 x 11 ins / 41 x 29 cm) EUR 2,500.

SEPP, Paul
Estonian, 20th century.
Born 15 April 1874, near Dorpat (now Tartu).
Painter. Genre scenes, landscapes.
Paul Sepp was a student of Ilya Repin at the St Petersburg Academy.

SEPPEZZINO, Francesco
Italian, 16th century.
Born 1530; died 1579.
Painter. History painting.
Francesco Seppezzino was a pupil of Luca Cambiaso and Giambattista Castilli.

SEPPI, Cesarina
Italian, 20th century.
Born 1919, in Trento.
Active during the second half of the 20th s.
Painter.
A student at the school of fine art in Venice, Cesarina Seppi completed her studies in 1942.

Her early works are a combination of evocation and abstraction, as in her landscape in beautiful blues and greens, *Morning on the Virgolo,* the sumptuously draped female form of *Nocturne* or her *Cologne Cathedral* of 1958. She moved into a second phase of abstract works using very thick materials and then, in 1968, a third period when she began to produce entirely abstract constructions in which contrasting curves and straight lines enclose surfaces that are often sky blue or sea green with occasional splashes of golden light, evoking memories of sea and sky.

She has exhibited work in various places including Trento (1943, 1946, 1953, 1956, 1959 and 1965) and Milan (1956, 1959, 1966 and 1970).

SEPTGRANGES, Corneille de, or Sept Granges
French, 16th century.
Active in Lyons from 1523 to 1566.
Painter, sculptor, engraver (wood).

SEPTH, Peter. See **SPEETH**

SEPTILICI, Mircea
Romanian, 20th century.
Born 12 August 1912, in Bucharest.
Active since 1984 in Canada.
Painter, draughtsman, watercolourist, pastellist.
Mircea Septilici graduated from the academy of dramatic art in Bucharest in 1937. He is self-taught as a painter. He collaborated on many literary and artistic reviews in Romania, and then lived and worked in Montreal. Both comedian and set painter, Septilici was also active as a painter. As an artist, he works in a traditional vein, nearly always depicting places or precise moments that have brought him pleasure, and which he wished to share.

Work by him was shown at group exhibitions in Romania and Canada; there were also solo exhibitions, including *Theatre in Drawings and Caricatures,* in the foyer of the Comedy Theatre, Bucharest (1941); *Bucharest in Miniature* at the Caminul Artei Gallery in Bucharest (1947); *Impressions of Budapest* in the foyer of the Municipal Theatre in Bucharest

(1960); *Travel Notes* in the foyer of the Comedy Theatre in Bucharest (1967); *Venice in Miniature* in Bucharest (1969); *Impressions of Israel* in the foyer of the Comedy Theatre in Bucharest (1975); *Shapes and Colours* in the foyer of the Comedy Theatre in Bucharest (1983); and *Flowers from Me to Montreal* at the Int'art Contemporary Art Gallery in Montreal (1985).

BIBLIOGRAPHY:

Jianou, Ionel, et al., *Romanian Artists and the West*, American Romanian Academy of Arts and Sciences, Los Angeles, 1986.

SEPULCHRE, Philippe

Belgian, 20th century.
Born 1939, in Liège.
Painter.

Philippe Sepulchre studied architecture at the Académie St-Luc in Tournai and Brussels and painted compositions using densely applied colour.

SEPULVEDA, Mateo Núñez de. See **NÚÑEZ DE SEPÚLVEDA**

SEQUEIRA, Domingos Antonio de

Portuguese, 19th century.
Born 10 March 1768, in Ajuda near Lisbon; died 7 March 1837, in Rome.
Active also in Italy.
Painter, engraver, draughtsman, lithographer.
Religious subjects, portraits.

Domingos Antonio de Sequeira was a pupil of the decorative artist Francisco de Setubal. He was sent to complete his studies in Rome in 1788 at the Accademia di San Luca, where he was taught by Antonio Cavallucci. He achieved considerable fame in Italy and this followed him when he returned to Portugal in 1795. In 1798 he entered the Carthusian monastery of Laveiras as a novice and remained there for three years. After leaving, he was appointed court painter in 1802. In 1805 he became director of the Oporto fine arts academy. He supported the 1820 revolution and, when this failed, was forced to leave Portugal. He went to Paris in 1823 and returned to Rome in 1826 to devote himself to religion. His final years were spent in Rome where he was appointed dean of the Accademia di San Luca. According to tradition, Sequeira was a most unusual character.

For the Carthusian monastery of Laveiras he painted large compositions based on the life of St Bruno including *St Bruno at Prayer*. In 1821 he drew a series of portraits of members of parliament intended for a large format painting (now lost). His historical and religious subjects include *The Final Moments of Camoëns, Torture of Ugolino, Crucifixion, Flight into Egypt* and *Adoration of the Magi*. Sequeira's particular concern with the effects of light associate him with a very 18th-century sensibility.

He exhibited at the Paris Salon of 1824 and was awarded a gold medal. A number of his works featured in the retrospective organised by the Gulbenkian Foundation in Paris in 1983.

BIBLIOGRAPHY:

Correia, V., *Sequeira em Roma: Duas Épocas 1788-1795, 1826-1837*, Imprensa da Universidade, Coimbra, 1923. De Macedo, D., *Domingos Antonio de Sequeira*, Realizacoes Artis, Lisbon, 1956. Kubler G./Soria, M., *Art and Architecture in Spain & Portugal and their American Dominians 1500 to 1800*, Penguin Books, Harmondsworth and Baltimore, 1959. Arnáiz, José Manuel/López Jiménez, Javier/Merchán Díaz, Manuel (ed.), *'Cien años de pintura en Espana y Portugal (1830-1930)'* in vol. X, Antiqvaria, Madrid, 1993.

MUSEUMS AND GALLERIES:

LISBON (Nat. Mus. of Ancient Art): *Descent from the Cross; St Bruno at Prayer; Allegory of the Foundation of the Casa Pia in Belem; Communion of St Onouphrius; The Holy Hermits Anthony and Paul; First Viscount of Santarem; Apotheosis of Wellington; The Portuguese Constitution is Granted in 1822; Egen Mony before Alfonso VII of Castile; Baron de Quintela* - OPORTO (Mus. Nacional de Soares dos Reis): *St Bruno; Allegory with Junot, Bonaparte's Emissary, Rescuing the City of Lisbon; Tribute to Caesar* (rough sketch) - PARIS (Louvre): *Allegory of the Foundation of the Casa Pia in Belem* (sketch) - PARMA (Pinacoteca Giuseppe Stuard): *St John as a Child with a Lamb* - ROME (Gal. dell'Accademia Nazionale di S Luca).

SEQUEIRA, Rico

Portuguese, 20th - 21st century.
Born 1954, in Cebolais de Baixo.
Active in Luxembourg.
Painter.

Rico Sequera studied decoration at a professional school in Luxembourg and trained in Connecticut in the USA. His paintings reflect figuration with an abstract, almost primitive style. The treatment of his work, far from being carefully finished, consists of outlines, tracings and coloured stains rapidly brushed and reflecting action. He invents a world made up of dancing calligraphic forms in ink, moments of struggle, coloured breaks. From beneath this Lyrical Abstraction printing characters, words and motifs show through. He also works on poster cuttings, retaining their irregular shapes.

He has participated in group exhibitions since 1974, regularly in Lisbon and abroad in exhibitions devoted to Portuguese artists. He has shown his work in solo exhibitions: 1983, Castelo Branco, Portugal; 1984 and 1985, S Mamedi gallery, Lisbon; 1986 and 1989, Am Wall gallery, Walshut (Germany); 1988, S Bento gallery, Lisbon; 1991, Brussels.

BIBLIOGRAPHY:

Rico Sequeira, exhibition catalogue, Gal. Michel Vokaer, Brussels, 1991.

SEQUENS, Franz

Czech, 19th century.
Born 28 December 1836, in Pilsen (now Plzen), west Bohemia; died 16 June 1896, in Prague.
Painter.

Sequens attended the academy in Prague, then studied under Kaulbach in Munich. He painted frescoes for the cathedral of St Guy in Prague and produced stained glass windows for the votive church of Vienna.

SEQUERA, Luis de

Spanish, 17th century.
Active in Seville at the beginning of the 17th century.
Sculptor (wood).

Luis de Sequera was commissioned to execute a retable for the church of S Pablo in Seville.

SEQUEVAL, Pascal

French, 18th century.
Active in the middle of the 18th century.
Miniaturist. Religious subjects.

MUSEUMS AND GALLERIES:

BESANÇON (Bibliothèque d'études et de conservation): *Antiphonary* (miniature).

SEQUIN, Otto

Swiss, 20th century.
Born 24 January 1892, in Zurich; died 1959.
Painter, engraver. Still-lifes (flowers).

Otto Sequin was a pupil of Edward Stiefel.

MUSEUMS AND GALLERIES:

WINTERTHUR: *Summer Day*.

AUCTION RECORDS:

ZURICH, 11 May 1978, *Bouquet of Flowers* (1929, oil on canvas, 28 x 22½ ins / 71 x 57 cm) CHF 2,400. ZURICH, 8 Nov 1980, *Bouquet of Flowers* (1929, oil on canvas, 28 x 22½ ins / 71 x 57 cm) CHF 2,000. ZOFINGEN, 28 May 1999, *Still-life with Flowers, Picture, Cloths and Book* (oil on canvas, 18 x 26 ins / 46 x 65 cm) CHF 2,500.

SEQUO, Simon. See **SECO Simão**

SERA, Domenico da
Italian, 16th century.
Active c. 1540.
Engraver, designer of ornamental architectural features.

SERA, Paolo del
Italian, 17th century.
Died 1672, in Florence.
Painter, collector.
Sera was the pupil of Domenico Passignano and T. Tinelli.

SERABAGLIO, Daniele di, or Seravalle, Busti
Italian, 16th century.
Engraver.
Daniele di Serabaglio engraved swords in Milan in the second half of the 16th century.

SERABIA, José de
Spanish, 17th century.
Painter.
José de Serabia was one of the rare disciples of Zurbarán. However, his own works have more in common with the early style of Zurbarán that predates the pre-Cézanne, spiritualised representations of his maturity. The Cordova museum has an interesting collection of strongly Realist rural scenes by Serabia.

SERADOUR, Guy
French, 20th century.
Born 8 October 1922, in Étaples-Le-Touquet (Pas-de-Calais).
Painter, pastellist.
Seradour was a keen painter from a young age. In 1939 he enrolled at the École des Beaux-Arts de Paris, where he stayed for only three months, before choosing to work alone. He liked to convey the movement of his models, using a resolutely drawn technique.

Seradour exhibited at numerous Salons in France and abroad: Belgium, England, the USA, Sweden, Japan and Iran. He was made Chevalier of the Légion d'Honneur. His first solo exhibition was in Algiers in 1940.

Seradour

Guy Seradour

BIBLIOGRAPHY:
Guy Seradour - 20 ans de peinture, Librairie Séguier, Paris, 1990.
MUSEUMS AND GALLERIES:
MARSEILLES (Mus. Cantini) - PARIS (MAM).
AUCTION RECORDS:
LOS ANGELES, 10 March 1976, *Young Girl with a Dog* (oil on canvas, 29 1/4 x 23 1/2 ins / 74 x 59.5 cm) USD 800. DOUAI, 23 Oct 1988, *St-Tropez* (oil on canvas, 25 1/2 x 21 1/4 ins / 65 x 54 cm) FRF 11,800. PARIS, 19 March 1989, *Julien* (oil on canvas, 13 x 7 1/2 ins / 33 x 19 cm) FRF 12,500. VERSAILLES, 20 June 1989, *Young Woman Reading in an Interior* (oil on canvas, 23 1/2 x 28 3/4 ins / 60 x 73 cm) FRF 40,000. DOUAI, 3 Dec 1989, *Boy* (pastel, 19 3/4 x 9 ins / 50 x 23 cm) FRF 13,000. VERSAILLES, 23 Sept 1990, *Still-life with Vase of Flowers and Fruit* (oil on canvas, 28 3/4 x 23 1/2 ins / 73 x 60 cm) FRF 34,500. PARIS, 30 Oct 1991, *Princess* (oil on canvas, 13 3/4 x 11 ins / 35 x 27 cm) FRF 17,000. LE TOUQUET, 14 Nov 1993, *White Egrets* (oil on canvas, 13 x 9 1/2 ins / 33 x 24 cm) FRF 29,500. PROVINS, 30 Jan 1994, *Red Suit* (oil on canvas, 13 x 9 1/2 ins / 33 x 24 cm) FRF 33,000. PARIS, 28 Feb 1994, *Portrait of Anna Maria Countess Guy de Mareschal* (pastel/paper, 16 1/4 x 13 ins / 41 x 33 cm) FRF 5,000. CALAIS, 11 Dec 1994, *Poupy and His Mistress* (oil on canvas, 25 1/2 x 19 3/4 ins / 65 x 50 cm) FRF 35,000. BOULOGNE-SUR-SEINE, 12 March 1995, *Little Girl on the Beach* (oil on canvas, 15 x 18 ins / 38 x 46 cm) FRF 11,500. CALAIS, 15 Dec 1996, *Young Girl with Small Poodle* (oil on canvas, 26 x 20 ins / 66 x 51 cm) FRF 25,000. CALAIS, 23 March 1997, *Young Girl on the Beach* (oil on canvas, 28 3/4 x 21 1/4 ins / 73 x 54 cm) FRF 27,000.

SERAFEDINO, Ebip
Macedonian, 20th - 21st century.
Born 20 November 1952, in Skopje.
Active in France since 1975.
Painter. Scenes with figures, figures.
Ebip Serafedino was self-taught. From 1970 to 1974, he worked mainly in Italy, and in Berlin and Amsterdam; and in 1975 he settled in Paris. Sérafédino's style reflects the many faces of expressionism, and his works go to the limit of abstraction.

Work by him has been shown at group exhibitions since 1980, and there have also been solo exhibitions, at the Galerie Étienne de Causans, Paris, and Saarbrücken (1995), and in Istanbul and Saarbrücken (1996).

SERAFIM, Dumitru, or Séraphin
Romanian, 19th century.
Born 1863, in Bucharest.
Painter. Figures.
Dumitru Serafim studied under Henner, Gérome and Tony Robert-Fleury. His work featured in exhibitions in Paris, where he was awarded a commendation in 1893, and a bronze medal at the 1900 Exposition Universelle. He also painted on porcelain.
MUSEUMS AND GALLERIES:
BUCHAREST (Muz. National de Arta al României): *Head of a Florentine*.
AUCTION RECORDS:
PARIS, 24 Nov 1989, *Elegant Woman in a Sheath Dress* (1914, enamelled porcelain, h. 16 1/4 ins / 41 cm) FRF 4,400.

SERAFIN, Pedro, called El Griego
Spanish, 16th century.
Active in Barcelona.
Painter.
Pedro Serafin painted a *Last Judgement* for the monastery of Montserrat between 1554 and 1578.

SERAFINI, Giulio
Italian, 19th century.
Born 1825, in Venice.
Painter. Religious subjects, genre scenes.
A student at the academies of Venice and Munich, Giulio Serafini painted altarpieces for a number of churches in the Alto Adige.

SERAFINI, Marcantonio
Italian, 16th century.
Born c. 1521, in Verona; died after 1576.
Painter.
The brother of Serafino, Marcantonio Serafini painted frescoes on the façades of houses in Verona.

SERAFINI, Paolo
Italian, 14th - 15th century.
Active in Modena.
Painter. History painting.
The son of Serafino Serafini, Paolo Serafini painted a *Madonna and Child* for Barletta Cathedral, an image that is still

greatly venerated. It bears the inscription *Paulus filius Magistri Seraphini de Seraphinii pictoris de Mutina pinxit*.

SERAFINI, Pro'Valeria, or Pro'Serafini
Italian, 20th century.
Born 21 June 1902, in Rome.
Painter. Portraits, landscapes, still-lifes.

A student at the Accademia di Belle Arti in Rome, Pro'Valeria Serafini was taught by Sigismondo Lipinsky. She painted portraits, still-lifes almost in trompe l'oeil, and landscapes. These are traditional in style and technically skilled.

Her work has appeared in collective exhibitions in Rome and Montecatini Terme. She held solo exhibitions in Rome in 1947 and 1959.

MUSEUMS AND GALLERIES:
LUGANO - MONTECATINI TERME - SALZBURG - VATICAN (Pinacoteca Vaticana).

SERAFINI, Serafino
Italian, 14th century.
Born before 1324, in Modena; died after 10 January 1393.
Painter.

The father of Paolo Serafini, Serafino Serafini is known particularly for the work that he painted for Modena Cathedral. The painting bears his name and the date 1385. Its main subject is the *Coronation of the Virgin*. Lanzi said of this work: 'The composition bears the characteristics of Giotto and his school and conforms closely to the style of the Florentine painter apart from the fact that the figures are more robust, and one could say better fed, than Giotto's.'

SERAFINI, Serafino di Francesco
Italian, 16th century.
Born c. 1533; died between 1595 and 1605.
Active in Verona.
Painter.

The brother of Marcantonio, Serafino Serafini painted some frescoes in the Palazzo dei Rettori in Venice.

SERAFINI, Serafino di Giovanni Francesco
Italian, 15th - 16th century.
Born c. 1457; died soon after 1530.
Active in Verona.
Fresco artist.

Serafino Serafini painted some frescoes in the church of S Maria in Organo in Verona.

SERAFINO DA BERGAMO
Italian, 16th century.
Active in Venice during the first half of the 16th century.
Miniaturist.

Serafino da Bergamo painted some miniatures for St Mark's Basilica in Venice.

SERAFINO DA BRESCIA
Italian, 16th century.
Active in Brescia c. 1530.
Engraver (burin).

Serafino da Brescia worked for King François I of France.

SERAGLIA, Alessandro
Italian, 17th century.
Died 1631.
Active in Modena.
Sculptor.

Seraglia executed sculptures in terracotta and wood.

SERALGI, Ovis. See **SALIGER Ivo**

SERAMBUS
5th century BC.
Active in Aegina probably c. 480 BC.
Sculptor.
Ancient Greek.

Serambus made a statue of one of the victors at Olympia.

SERANCX. See **SERANS**

SERANGELI, Gioacchin Giuseppe
Italian, 18th - 19th century.
Born 1768, in Rome; died 12 January 1852, in Turin.
Also active in France.
Painter, fresco artist. History painting, mythological subjects, portraits, genre scenes. Murals.

Serangeli was a pupil at the school of fine arts in Milan, where he was himself appointed professor at the end of his life, and then studied under Jacques-Louis David in Paris. He exhibited at the Paris Salons between 1796 and 1817, and painted a fresco of the *Legend of Psyche* in the Sommariva villa on Lake Como.

MUSEUMS AND GALLERIES:
CHAMBÉRY: *Caritas Romana* - VERSAILLES: *Napoleon and Alexander I Bidding Farewell at Tilsit; Napoleon Receiving a Deputation from the Army at the Louvre after his Coronation.*

AUCTION RECORDS:
NICE, 18 Feb 1981, *Portrait of Olympe and Colette de Montcabrier in a Park* (1812, oil on canvas, 78$^{3/4}$ x 63 ins / 200 x 160 cm) FRF 76,000. LONDON, 19 June 1985, *Venus, Cupid and the Three Graces* (oil on canvas, 38$^{1/2}$ x 28$^{1/4}$ ins / 98 x 72 cm) GBP 10,000.

SERANS, Heynderic, or Serancx, Zerans
Flemish School, 15th century.
Active in Bruges in 1472.
Painter.

SERANS, Kerstiaen, or Serancx or Zerans
Flemish School, 16th century.
Died 1539, in Bruges.
Painter.

Serans was a pupil of Gheleyn de Wyntere in Antwerp.

SERANVOER, T.
Painter. Still-lifes.

Seranvoer is mentioned in Art Prices Current.

AUCTION RECORDS:
LONDON, 23 March 1910, *Flowers in a Vase*, GBP 5.

SERAPHIM, Juliana
Lebanese, 20th century.
Born 13th April 1934, in Jaffa, Israel.
Painter, draughtsman, engraver.

Juliana Seraphim trained with the painter Jean Khalifié and also won a one-year scholarship to study in Florence (1958-1959), followed by another to study in Paris. She creates a fantastic, fairy-tale world of luxurious landscapes inhabited by half-human, half-plant beings and extraordinary animals. She has produced a portfolio of 27 engravings representing nine Nobel prize-winners, commissioned by a New York editor, and has had works reproduced in the review *Planète*.

She has exhibited in several public exhibitions, including: 1961, 1963, 1968, 1974 and 1982, Sursock Museum, Beirut; 1960s, Biennials, Paris, Alexandria and São Paulo; 1969, Smithsonian Institute, Washington DC; 1978, Musée de Neuilly.

Solo exhibitions include: 1959, International Gallery, Florence; 1960, Amadis Gallery, Madrid; 1960, Vesrière and Forêt galleries, Paris. She was awarded the Viareggio Prize in Italy.

MUSEUMS AND GALLERIES:
NEUILLY (Mus.) - VIAREGGIO (Museo Civico).

SERAPHIN, Dumitru. See **SERAFIM Dumitru**

SERAPHIN, Jules
French, 19th century.
Born in Paris.
Painter, watercolourist. Landscapes.

Seraphin was a pupil of Bauderon and Vermeron. He made his Salon debut in 1879.

SÉRAPHINE, Louis. See **SENLIS Séraphine de**

SERAPION
1st century BC.
Of unknown origin.
Painter.
Ancient Greek.
Serapion is known to have worked in Rome, probably painting landscapes and architectural scenes.

SERATELLI, Alessandro. See **SARATELLI**

SERATRICE, Vincenzo
Italian, 19th century.
Born in Rome.
Painter. Genre scenes.
Vincenzo Seratrice exhibited in Milan and Rome.

SERAUCOURT, Claude
French, 17th - 18th century.
Born 24 November 1677, in L'Arbresle (Rhône); died 15 February 1756, in Lyons.
Engraver (burin).
Claude Seraucourt engraved a plan of the city of Lyons.

SERAVALLE, Daniele di. See **SERABAGLIO**

SERAVITS, Mathias or Matyis. See **SCHERVITZ**

SERBALDI DELLA PESCIA, Pietro or Pier Maria, also known as Mariano da Pescia, or Pier Maria Fiorentino Pescia, called Tagliacarne
Italian, 15th century.
Born 1454 or 1455.
Active in Florence and in Rome.
Sculptor, engraver. Cameos, coins.
Pietro Serbaldi worked in the workshop of Jacopo Tagliacarne. He may be the same person as a painter by the name of Gratiadei.
MUSEUMS AND GALLERIES:
FLORENCE (Gal.): *Venus and Cupid* (porphyry, statuette).

SERBEYRA, Felipe
Portuguese, 17th century.
Active in 1610.
Painter.
Felipe Serbeyra was commissioned to paint the Stations of the Cross in El Porrino.

SERBINOV, Ivan
Russian, 20th - 21st century.
Born 1946.
Painter. Figures, scenes with figures, nudes.
Serbinov studied at the school of fine art in Kichinev and at the academy of fine art in Leningrad (now St Petersburg). He paints his subjects crudely with wide brush-strokes. He is a member of the association of painters of the former USSR and has exhibited from 1974 onwards.

SERCEAU, Jean
French, 17th century.
Sculptor (wood).
Jean Serceau sculpted the stalls in the church of Varize, near Châteaudun, in 1650.

SERCHIOLI, Giorgio
Italian, 17th century.
Active in Carrara in the middle of the 17th century.
Sculptor.
Serchioli sculpted the high altar in the church of St John the Evangelist in Parma in 1660.

SERDA, Émile or Jacques Émile
French, 19th century.
Born in Montpellier; died 1863, in Béziers.
Painter. Landscapes, urban landscapes.
MUSEUMS AND GALLERIES:
BÉZIERS: *Path near La Salvetat; Plaster Kiln; View of Béziers; Landscape.*

SERDYUKOV, Grigori
Russian, 18th century.
Active during the second half of the 18th century.
Painter. Portraits.

SERDYUKOV, Stepan Filippovich
Russian, 18th century.
Born 1748.
Painter. History painting.
Stepan Filippovich Serdyukov studied at the art academy in St Petersburg.

SEREBOURS
German, 19th century.
Active in 1805.
Miniaturist.
Serebours painted *Portrait of a Man.*

SEREBRIAKOV, Alexander, or Serebriakoff Alexandre
Russian, 20th century.
Born 1907; died 10 January 1995.
Active in France.
Watercolourist, painter (gouache/mixed media), draughtsman, designer. Landscapes. Stage sets.
Alexander Serebriakov painted views of Paris and was also a stage set painter. In 2003, work by him was shown at the exhibition *Un été russe à Montmartre. Artistes de Saint-Pétersbourg à Paris au début du XXe siècle* (*A Russian Summer in Montmartre. St Petersburg Artists in Paris at the Beginning of the 20th Century*) at the Musée de Montmartre in Paris.
BIBLIOGRAPHY:
Gérard, Raphaël/Essaïan, Sergeï, et al., *Un été russe à Montmartre. Artistes de Saint-Pétersbourg à Paris au début du XXe siècle*, exhibition catalogue, Musée de Montmartre, Éditions Fragments, Paris, 2003.
AUCTION RECORDS:
NEW YORK, 22 May 1986, *Interior of a Library* (1943, watercolour and gouache, 16 1/2 x 21 3/4 ins / 42 x 55.4 cm) USD 17,000. MONACO, 11 Oct 1991, *Set Design for 'La Sylphide'* (1947, watercolour and ink, 17 x 24 1/2 ins / 43 x 62 cm) FRF 16,650; *The Studio of M. Christian Bérard, in the Rue Casimir Delavigne, Paris* (1948, ink, watercolour and gouache, 15 1/4 x 23 ins / 39 x 57.5 cm) FRF 344,100. LONDON, 17 Nov 1994, *Madeleine Castaing's Stand at the Salon des Antiquaires* (1948, pencil and watercolour, 12 1/4 x 17 ins / 31.4 x 42.9 cm) GBP 14,950. LONDON, 25 Oct 1995, *View of the Louvre* (1931, gouache and watercolour/paper, 24 1/2 x 18 1/2 ins / 62 x 47 cm) GBP 4,025. PARIS, 28 March 1996, *Views towards Passy, the Île des Cygnes, the Pont Mirabeau, the Viaduc d'Auteuil, the Citroën Factories, and the Current Radio-France Site* (1931, watercolour, 28 x 17 3/4 ins / 71 x 45 cm) FRF 18,000. PARIS, 4 June 1999, *The Maze and Temple in the Parc de Groussay* (watercolour, ink and pencil, ten) FRF 120,000. PARIS, 4 June 1999, *The Obelisk and Elephant on the Island of the Parc de Groussay* (watercolour, ink and pencil, seven) FRF 130,000. PARIS, 13 Dec 2002, *Interior in Paris* (1946, watercolour, 24 x 18 ins / 61 x 46 cm) EUR 5,000. LONDON, 21 May 2003, *Grand Drawing Room, Interior* (watercolour, 24 x 19 ins / 62 x 47 cm) GBP 8,500. PARIS, 25 June 2003, *Plan for the Château de Groussay, Side Wall* (1967, brown ink, watercolour, gouache and graphite, 12 x 17 ins / 30 x 43 cm) EUR 4,600. LONDON, 26 May 2004, *Dining Room at Bestegui* (1950,

watercolour over pencil heightened with gouache, 15 x 19 ins / 38 x 49 cm) GBP 5,000. LONDON, 26 May 2004, *Interior Scene, Bestegui* (1950, watercolour and gouache over pencil, 15 x 22 ins / 38 x 57 cm) GBP 8,000.

SEREBRIAKOV, Serebriakoff Alexandre.
See **SEREBRIAKOV Alexander**

SEREBRIAKOVA, Maria
Russian, 20th - 21st century.
Born 1965, in Moscow.
Sculptor, installation artist.
Conceptual Art.

Serebriakova studied between 1977 and 1983 at the Surikov academy of fine art in Moscow, where she lives and workes. She prepared for the entrance examination to the school of fine art, but gave this up, considering the teaching to be too conventional. She travelled the world from 1987, notably living in New York, Turin, Berlin and Paris.

Rejecting official art and Realism, Serebriakova practised a Conceptual Art, frequently including her own photographs. Profoundly influenced by Wittgenstein, she initially worked on language and its structure in Paris, in sculptures and installations constructed from salvaged materials (paper, glass, plexiglas). She assembled these in a Minimalist manner, working on the notion of becoming and the passage of time. She saw art as a sort of ritual that describes the void and shapes it, revealing what words cannot say.

Serebriakova has taken part in many collective exhibitions, notably exhibitions devoted to the young Russian generation: 1987, *Retrospective of Muscovite Artists 1957-1987*, Moscow; 1988, 1989 and 1990, Central Youth Exhibition Centre, Moscow; 1989, Belgrade, Lisbon, Vienna; 1990, Berlin, Ostend, Stedelijk Museum in Amsterdam, New York, Boston, Turin; 1991, PS1 in New York, Cracow; 1992, Documenta in Kassel; 1993, Museum Van Hedendaagse Kunst in Ghent, Kunsthalle in Lophem; and 1994, Bern. Solo exhibitions include: 1991, Skola gallery, Moscow; 1992, Galleria Persano in Turin and Kunstlerhaus Bethanien in Berlin; 1992, 1993, Zeno'X Gallery, Antwerp; and 1995, Centre d'Art Le Creux de l'Enfer (Depths of Hell Art Centre), in Thiers.

BIBLIOGRAPHY:
6 Moskauer Konzeptualisten, exhibition catalogue, Galerie Rigassi, Bern, 1994. Cassagnau, Pascale, *'Maria Serebriakova'* in *Art Press*, n° 199, periodical, Paris, February 1995.

SEREBRIAKOVA, Zinaida Evgenieva, or
Serebyakova Sinaïda Iévgénievna
Russian, 20th century.
Born 1884, in Neskoutchnoe (Kharkov); died 1967, in Paris.
Painter (gouache). Figures, nudes, portraits.

Zinaida Evgenieva Serebriakova was the daughter of the sculptor Eugène Lancerray. She studied at M. Tenicheva's school with Ilya Repin, then in the studio of Osip Braz from 1903 to 1905. From 1902 to 1903, she was in Italy, and she spent time in Paris in 1905 and 1924, in the Crimea in 1911, and in Morocco in 1928 and 1932. She was a member of the Mir Iskusstva (World of Art) group.

In 2003, work by her was shown at the exhibition *Un été russe à Montmartre. Artistes de Saint-Pétersbourg à Paris au début du XXe siècle* (*A Russian Summer in Montmartre. St Petersburg Artists in Paris at the Beginning of the 20th Century*), at the Musée de Montmartre in Paris.

BIBLIOGRAPHY:
Gérard, Raphaël/Essaïan, Sergeï, et al., *Un été russe à Montmartre. Artistes de Saint-Pétersbourg à Paris au début du XXe siècle*, exhibition catalogue, Musée de Montmartre, Éditions Fragments, Paris, 2003.

MUSEUMS AND GALLERIES:
MOSCOW (State Tretyakov Gal.): *At Toilet*; *Laudering the Linen* (1910) - ST PETERSBURG (Gosudarstvennyj Russkij Muz.): *Women Bathing*.

AUCTION RECORDS:
LONDON, 4 March 1982, *Portrait of Yvette Chauviré* (pastel, 23 1/2 x 19 ins / 59.8 x 48.3 cm) GBP 1,150. LONDON, 15 Feb 1984, *Young Moroccan Women Sitting Down* (1928, pastel, 18 x 24 ins / 46 x 61 cm) GBP 750. LONDON, 20 Feb 1985, *Young Moroccan Women* (1932, pastel, 24 x 18 ins / 61 x 45.5 cm) GBP 750. LONDON, 14 Dec 1995, *View of a Village in France* (1926, gouache, 18 x 24 1/2 ins / 46 x 62 cm) GBP 7,130. LONDON, 17 July 1996, *Portrait of Ekaterina N. Geidenreikh* (1929, charcoal and pastel, 24 x 18 1/4 ins / 61 x 46.5 cm) GBP 7,475. LONDON, 19 Dec 1996, *Portrait of Alexandre Benois di Stetto* (1916, gouache, pencil, 25 1/4 x 13 3/4 ins / 64 x 35 cm) GBP 2,300. LONDON, 18 Nov 1999, *Reclining Nude with Cerise Wrap* (1934, pastel, 18 x 24 ins / 46 x 61 cm) GBP 19,000. LONDON, 18 Nov 1999, *Portrait of Mademoiselle Neviadomskaya* (1935, oil on canvas, 24 x 29 ins / 60 x 74 cm) GBP 52,000. LONDON, 10 May 2000, *Sleeping Nude with Stripy Drape* (1934, oil on canvas, 30 x 23 ins / 76 x 59 cm) GBP 50,000. LONDON, 10 May 2000, *Reclining Nude* (1928, oil on canvas, 36 x 25 ins / 92 x 64 cm) GBP 50,000. LONDON, 20 Nov 2001, *Reclining Nude on a Blue Ground* (1927, oil on canvas, 26 x 32 ins / 65 x 81 cm) GBP 195,000. LONDON, 20 Nov 2001, *Russian Bathhouse* (1926, oil on canvas, 54 x 32 ins / 137 x 81 cm) GBP 400,000. LONDON, 20 Nov 2002, *Still-life of Grapes in Basket* (1928, oil on canvas, 21 x 26 ins / 54 x 65 cm) GBP 130,000. LONDON, 20 Nov 2002, *Reclining Nude* (1935, pastel, 20 x 26 ins / 51 x 65 cm) GBP 175,000. NEW YORK, 11 April 2003, *Young Ballerinas* (c. 1921-1924, cyrillic and pastel, unfinished sketch, 25 x 19 ins / 63 x 47 cm) USD 95,000. LONDON, 19 Nov 2003, *Basket of Grapes and Peaches* (1931, oil on canvas, 24 x 29 ins / 60 x 73 cm) GBP 70,000. NEW YORK, 23 April 2004, *Study of Three Peasant Women* (1915, graphite, watercolour and gouache, 17 x 15 ins / 44 x 37 cm) USD 15,000.

SEREBRYAKOV, Gavril Ivanovich
Russian, 18th - 19th century.
Born c. 1745; died 1818.
Painter, miniaturist. Battles, portraits.

Gavril Ivanovich Serebryakov studied and taught at the art academy in St Petersburg.

SEREBRYAKOV, Vasili Aleksandrovich or Alekseevich
Russian, 19th century.
Born 20 December 1810; died 1886.
Painter. History painting, portraits.

Vasili Aleksandrovich Serebryakov studied at the art academy in St Petersburg.

MUSEUMS AND GALLERIES:
MOSCOW (State Tretyakov Gal.): *Fruit*; another painting.

SEREC
French, 19th century.
Active in 1828.
Miniaturist.

A self-portrait of this artist was shown at an exhibition of miniatures in Vannes Museum in 1912.

SERÉE, Janou
French, 20th - 21st century.
Born 27 July 1949, in Brittany.
Painter, sculptor.

Janou Serée attaches her various materials (cardboard, paper or wood) onto wooden supports, creating the effect of material that has weathered over time. She created the Perrier Trophy (European Rowing Cup, La Napoule) in 1987.

She has participated in numerous group exhibitions, including: Menton Biennale, 1980; Triennale of European

Sculpture, Grand Palais, Paris, 1981; UMAM, Galerie des Ponchettes, Musée de Nice, 1982 and 1984; and Concours International de Sculpture, Fondation Paul Ricard, 1987. Her solo exhibitions include: Centre Culturel de Vence, 1988; Centre des Arts et de la Culture, Concarneau, 1992; Institut Français, Rostock (Germany), 1999; and *Murales*, Fondation Taylor, Paris, 2002.

She was awarded the Prize for Excellence of the International Exchange of Franco-Korean-Japanese Art in Tokyo in 1998.

SEREGNI, Luigi
Italian, 19th century.
Born 1819, in Milan.
Active in Venice.
Medallist, engraver. Coins.

SEREGNI, Vincenzo, or Seregno, also known as Vincenzo dell'Orto, called il Seregni
Italian, 16th century.
Born c. 1504 or 1509; died 12 January 1594, in Milan.
Sculptor, architect.

Vincenzo Seregni worked at Milan Cathedral.

SEREGNO, Cristoforo da. See **CRISTOFORO DA SEREGNO**

SEREGNO, Giovanni Angelo
Italian, 15th - 16th century.
Painter.
Lombard School.

Probably the brother of Giovanni Antonio Seregno, Giovanni Angelo Seregno worked in collaboration with him on various projects for Milan Cathedral. He was still in Milan in 1524. He is known to have made a painting of the Virgin in 1486.

SEREGNO, Giovanni Antonio
Italian, 15th - 16th century.
Died after 1524.
Painter.
Lombard School.

Giovanni Antonio Seregno was a relative, perhaps brother, of Giovanni Angelo Seregno and almost always his collaborator. From 1488 they are recorded as working for Milan Cathedral. Giovanni Antonio is also recorded as working with Boltraffio in 1503.

SERENA
German, 18th century.
Active in 1797.
Miniaturist.

Serena's work *Portrait of a Man* was exhibited in Hanover, Germany, in 1918.

SERENA, Basilio
Italian, 18th century.
Born to a family originally from Campione.
Active in 1781.
Stucco artist.

Serena executed ornamental works in stucco in the Palazzo Angeli in Rovigo.

SERENA, Carlo
Austrian, 17th century.
Active during the second half of the 17th century.
Sculptor.

Carlo Serena produced works for the castles of Bohemia and Silesia.

SERENA, Francesco Leone
Austrian, 18th century.
Active during the first half of the 18th century.
Stucco artist.

Francesco Serena worked for the monastery of Ottobeuren (Bavaria, Germany) and the Landhaus in Innsbruck, Austria.

SERENA, Johann Baptist
German, 17th century.
Active in Silesia, 1661-1677.
Stucco artist.

SERENA, Luigi
Italian, 19th - 20th century.
Born 1 August 1855, in Montebelluna; died 12 March 1911, in Treviso.
Painter, watercolourist. Genre scenes.

A pupil of Pompeo Molmenti, Luigi Serena exhibited in Venice, Milan, Turin, Florence and Paris, where he was awarded a bronze medal at the Exposition Universelle of 1889.

MUSEUMS AND GALLERIES:
TREVISO (Mus. Civico L. Bailo).

AUCTION RECORDS:
LONDON, 4 Nov 1977, *Sunday Morning in Venice* (oil on canvas, 47 1/2 x 31 1/2 ins / 120.5 x 80 cm) GBP 1,600. LONDON, 14 Feb 1979, *Couple Resting in a Rustic Interior* (oil on canvas, 39 3/4 x 31 ins / 101 x 78.5 cm) GBP 3,300. ROME, 1 Dec 1982, *Egg-Seller* (oil on canvas, 25 1/2 x 22 ins / 65 x 55 cm) ITL 2,200,000. ROME, 27 April 1993, *Young Washerwoman* (1886, watercolour on artboard, 17 1/4 x 11 1/2 ins / 44 x 29.5 cm) ITL 2,139,500. MILAN, 21 Dec 1999, *Figure in Interior* (oil on panel, 10 x 5 ins / 25 x 13 cm) ITL 7,500,000. PARIS, 17 Dec 2001, *Park Scene* (oil on panel, 10 x 13 ins / 25 x 34 cm) FRF 23,000. VENICE, 11 May 2002, *Portrait of Woman* (1903, oil on canvas, 44 x 28 ins / 113 x 72 cm) EUR 2,100. MILAN, 10 Dec 2003, *Reading on the Terrace* (oil on canvas, 15 x 18 ins / 39 x 45 cm) EUR 12,000. MILAN, 25 May 2004, *Peasant Woman* (oil on canvas, 29 x 20 ins / 74 x 50 cm) EUR 7,100.

SERENA, Vittorio
Italian, 17th century.
Active in 1634.
Engraver (burin).

SERENARI, Gasparo, or Serenario
Italian, 18th century.
Born 1694, in Palermo; died 1759.
Painter, fresco artist. History painting.

Serenari was the pupil of Sebastiano Conca in Rome; he painted the cupola of the Jesuit church and an altarpiece for the Carita monastery in Palermo.

SERENDAT DE BELZIM, Louis
French, 19th - 20th century.
Born 26 June 1854, in Port-Louis (Mauritius Island); died 1933, in Paris.
Painter. Religious subjects, genre scenes, portraits.

Serendat de Belzim was a pupil of Carolus Duran and Alexandre Cabanel. He was an officer of state education. He was President and founder of the Salon d'Hiver in Paris, and exhibited at the Salon des Indépendants, of which he was a founding member. He painted a triptych for Carquefou church.

SERENIO, Alexander, or Serenj
Swiss, 17th century.
Born in Lugano (Ticino); died 1688, in Graz, Austria.
Sculptor, stucco artist.

Alexander Serenio produced decorative work coated in stucco for the sacristies of Mariazell church in Austria.

SERENIO, Josef
Austrian, 18th century.
Died 30 August 1710, in Graz.
Stucco artist.

Josef Serenio was Antonio Quadrio's assistant. He produced work for Styrian castles in Austria.

SERENNE, Célestin André Marie
French, 19th century.
Born 26 May 1846, in Nantes.
Painter. Portraits.
Serenne never received any formal training; he made his debut at the 1876 Salon.

SERENO, Costantino
Italian, 19th century.
Born 1829, in Casal Monferrato (Piedmont); died January 1893, in Turin.
Painter. Genre scenes.
Costantino Sereno exhibited in Turin, Milan and Rome. He painted frescoes in a number of churches in Casale Monferrato and Turin.
MUSEUMS AND GALLERIES:
TURIN (Mus. Civico): several works.

SERES, Johann
Hungarian, 16th century.
Sculptor.
Johann Seres sculpted the portal at the house of the Mikes family in Cluj in Romania.

SÉRÉVILLE, Michel de
French, 20th century.
Born 1922, in Saumur.
Draughtsman, painter (gouache), pastellist, illustrator.
Scenes with figures, figures, nudes, portraits, landscapes, seascapes.
Séréville studied at the École des Beaux-Arts in Paris. He also studied dance, and went on to dance at the Comédie Française in Paris. He also produced numerous circus scenes, in particular with clowns, as well as illustrations for covers of novels.

He showed his work in solo exhibitions, in Paris most notably in 1975 at the Institut National de l'Audiovisuel, and abroad: Kiev, Moscow, Denver, St Petersburg, Cologne and Hilversum.
AUCTION RECORDS:
PARIS, 21 Nov 1988, *Winter* (28¾ x 19¾ ins / 73 x 50 cm) FRF 12,000.

SEREVILLE, Philippe de
French, 19th century.
Born 17 March 1820, in Moulins (Allier).
Painter. Birds.
Philippe Sereville exhibited at the Salon in 1849 and 1850.

SEREX, Philippe
Swiss, 19th - 20th century.
Born 6 October 1871, in Geneva.
Draughtsman.
Philippe Serex was a poster artist and a pupil of Edouard Ravel.

SERFOLIO, Giacomo
Italian, 15th - 16th century.
Born in Fontanabuona.
Active from 1496 to 1502.
Painter.
Giacomo Serfoglio painted an altarpiece in the Santuario del Monte in Genoa in 1498.

SERGARDI, Domenico
Italian, 18th century.
Active during the second half of the 18th century.
Painter.
Sergardi executed frescoes in the cathedral in Spoleto from 1766 to 1768.

SERGE, pseudonym of Féaudierre, Maurice
French, 20th century.
Born 14 December 1909, in Paris.
Painter, draughtsman. Genre scenes.
Serge travelled widely in Europe, visiting England, Holland, Belgium, Italy, Spain, Germany, Poland, Russia and Scandinavia. He was a member of the Salon de l'Araignée and won a Grand Prix at the International Exhibition in Paris in 1937.

Serge was for a long time the most prominent critic and historian attracted by the circus. He also created numerous scenes of Paris life. He always illustrated his countless articles for newspapers and reviews and especially the works that he dedicated almost exclusively to the world of the circus: *Long Live the Circus, The World of the Circus, Panorama of the Circus, History of the Circus, The Road of the Circuses, Magic of Bohemians* and also *Secret London, The Island of Wonder, The Vagabond of Paris, Southern Girls in White Kepis* and *Gypsies and Toreros.*

SERGEANT, Edgar
American, 20th century.
Born 25 November 1877, in New York.
Painter.
Edgar Sergeant studied under Frank Vincent Du Mond and Gifford Beal. He was a member of the American Federation of Arts and the Salmagundi Club.

SERGEEV, Andrei Alekseevich
Russian, 18th - 19th century.
Born 15 June 1771; died 24 November 1837.
Painter. Urban landscapes.
Orientalism.
Andrei Alekseevich Sergeev studied at the art academy in St Petersburg. He painted views of Constantinople.

SERGEIL, Jean
French, 18th century.
Sculptor.
Jean Sergeil exhibited at the 1779 Salon.

SERGEL, Johan Tobias, or Sergell
Swedish, 18th - 19th century.
Born 28 August 1740, in Stockholm; died 26 February 1814, in Stockholm.
Sculptor, engraver, draughtsman. Busts.
Although he was of German origin, Sergel was born in Stockholm. His father was a native of Jena, and arrived in Sweden to work as a saddler and embroiderer for the Swedish army. He settled in Stockholm a year before the birth of Johan Tobias. The young Sergel studied at the German school, and for a short while was apprentice to his father. He then studied drawing with Jean Eric Rehn, and sculptural modelling with Adrien Masreliez. In 1757, he entered the studio of Pierre-Hubert Larchevêque, and soon became his assistant. The following year, he accompanied his master to Paris, where he stayed for seven months, studying at the Académie Royale de Peinture et Sculpture. Larchevêque instilled in him an appreciation for the classical ideal, and upon his return to Stockholm, Sergel would remain in contact with this flourishing French style. Several of his medallions from this period, which are reliefs in the antique style, are still intact. It is also known that he received an 'independent employment connected to the building of the royal castle', and that in 1763, he was accepted as a master in the Kungliga Akademi för de Fria Konsterna in Stockholm.

Several years later, Sergel made his celebrated trip to Rome, which was to have an extraordinary impact on his art and his life. He left for Rome in 1767, and stayed there for 11 years. It was in Rome that he first became successful. During this time, he adhered to the same plan of study that he had set for himself upon his arrival: 'Antiquity during the day, and the study of nature in the evening'. In Rome, he mixed with cosmopolitan society. He socialised with the French artists at the Palazzo Mancini, including Houdon, Boizot, Menageot, Stouf, Clodion, and especially Vincent, with whom he seems to have been particularly close. He also met Füssli, who had arrived in Rome in 1770. Passionately interested in the antique style, he travelled to Naples in 1767, and visited Pompeii and the Herculaneum.

His *Faun* (1770-1774), was the first manifestation of Neo-Classicism in European sculpture, and earned him international renown. In 1778, Gustav III, then King of Sweden, summoned Sergel from Rome. On his way, Sergel stayed in Paris for eight months, receiving acceptance into the Académie Royale de Peinture et Sculpture with his *The Dying Spartan Orthryades*. He stopped in England before arriving in Stockholm in July 1779. The king named him First Sculptor, replacing Larchevêque who had died the preceding year. This began Sergel's official prime, though he did not immediately receive any important commissions. He created several models in marble in the Roman style, participated in the decoration of the opera of Stockholm, and executed a *Bust of Gustav III*, as well as numerous other busts. From 1783 until 1784 he returned to Italy, where he served as a guide for his king. It was well after his return that he began the great work from his Swedish period, the *Statue of Gustav III*. Sketched in 1790, and modelled in 1792, it wasn't cast until 1806. It was inaugurated in 1808, 16 years after the death of the king.

The greatest Swedish sculptor of the end of the 18th century, Johan Tobias Sergel was also one of the precursors of Neo-Classicism. He was in advance of Canova in this respect. Sergel was influenced by apparently contradictory ideas: the classical ideal stemming from the ancient pursuit of perfection, contrasting with the Baroque flourish and dynamic energy of Bernini. This juxtaposition is evident throughout his entire work. The tremendous liberty, the vigour and energy of movement are evident in his preparatory drawings and sketches. Yet equally perceptible are the sudden elements of disciplined, controlled stillness that exemplify the splendid, but often cold, eloquence of Neo-Classic expression. The genesis of *Faun* is revealing in this sense. The sketched drawings, which seem to date from between 1768 and 1769, are free and full of movement, almost rococon in their character. The first terracotta model of 1770, still full of almost palpitating vivacity, is then metamorphosed into the admirably cadenced final marble of 1774. The evolution in Sergel's process is summarised in the expression of Jean-Marie Lannegrand d'Augimont: 'the purity of the perfect, somewhat cold form has absorbed its life'.

Sergel's Roman period engendered candid, if not passionate, preparatory drawings, and his sculptures of couples from the same period are charged with eroticism. This emerged as one of his favourite themes of the period, and is manifested in his *Mercury and Psyche; Jupiter and Juno; Amor and Psyche; Venus and Anchises*; and *Mars and Venus* (1771-1772).

Sergel returned to Sweden having been heaped with honours. Yet he was suffering from an illness, and his drawings of the time reflect his anxieties in the manner of an intimate journal. He is featured in these drawings being assailed by death, and tormented by chimeras, with the immediacy of an already romantic pen. Sergel as a sculptor was clearly in keeping with the taste of his era. He enjoyed great fame during his life, his influence making itself felt well beyond the borders of Sweden. Sergel as a draughtsman, however, revealed a more timeless sensibility. His drawing was earthy, sensual, gleefully anti-clerical, irreverently atheist, sometimes libertine, sometimes painfully melancholy. His unfettered expression had remarkable vitality that was full of humour, even ferocity, and sometimes approached caricature. Sergel the draughtsman was clearly an artist acutely in tune with a society in the very midst of great change.

Bibliography:

Josephson, R., *Sergels fantasi [Sergel's Imagination]*, monograph, Natur och Kultur, Stockholm, 1956. Bjurström, Per, *Sergel. Dessins*, P.-J. Oswald, Paris, 1975. Lannegrand d'Augimont, Jean-Marie, '*Sergel: fougue et mélancolie*' in *Connaissance des Arts* n° 285, periodical, Paris, November 1975. Bjurstrom, Per, *Sergel tecknar [Sergel's Sketches]*, exhibition catalogue, Liber Forlag, Stockholm, 1976. *Johan Tobias Sergel, 1740-1814*, exhibition catalogue, Thorvaldsens Museum, Copenhagen, 1976. O'Brien, E.S., *Johan Tobias Sergel (1740-1814) and Neo-Classicism: the Sculpture of Sergel's Years Abroad, 1767-1779*, dissertation, microfilm, University Microfilms International, Ann Arbor, 1983. *Sergel*, exhibition catalogue, Nationalmuseum, Stockholm, 1990. Olausson, Magnus/Scherf, Guilhem, '*Le Centaure enlaçant une bacchante de Sergel au Louvre*' in *Revue du Louvre* n° 1 p. 56, periodical, Paris, February 2002.

Museums and Galleries:

Copenhagen (Statens Mus. for Kunst): *Faun* - Helsinki: *Reclining Faun* - Kassel: *Frederik II of Hesse-Cassel* - Paris (Louvre): *Drunken Faun; Centaur Enlacing a Nymph* (terracotta) - Stockholm: *Reclining Faun; Apollon; Venus Callipyg; Gustav Adolf II; Gustav III; Sophie-Magdalena, Wife of Gustav III; Gustav Adolf IV as a Child; Charles XIII, then Duke of Sudermannia; Hedwig-Elisabeth-Charlotta, Wife of Charles XIII; Frederik-Adolf, Duke of Ostrogothia; Sophie Albertine; Gustav Adolf IV; Ulrik Scheffer; Gustav-Adolf Reuterholm* (marbles); *The Artist's Father; The Painter Johann Pasch; Diomedes; Tobias; Woman Getting Out of the Bath; Two Lions; Ceres Seeking Proserpina; Cariatyd* (15 terracottas, 14 plaster casts, 61 medallions and 20 sketches) - Stockholm (Nationalmus.): *Achilles and the Chiron centaur* (c. 1770-1772, terracotta); , c. 1775-1778, terracotta); *Centaur Enlacing a Nymph* (c. 1775-1778, graphite, pen and brown ink); *Centaur Enlacing a Nymph* (c. 1775-1778, graphite, pen and brown ink, brown and grey wash); *The Rape of Dejanira by the Centaur Nessus* (c. 1775-1778, red chalk); *The Spartan Othryades Dying* (1779, terracotta); *Achilles on the Strand* (after 1775, terracotta); *Jupiter and Juno* (1772-1773, terracotta); *Mercury and Psyche* (c. 1772, terracotta); *Cupid and Psyche* (c. 1774, terracotta).

Auction records:

London, 19 June 1970, *Bust of King Gustav III of Sweden* (white marble) GBP 2,100. London, 2 July 1985, *Death of an Old Man* (black chalk, pen and wash, 9 3/4 x 13 3/4 ins / 24.8 x 34.8 cm) GBP 750. Stockholm, 28 Oct 1985, *Joakim Beck-Friis* (1793, white marble, h. 30 3/4 ins / 78 cm) SEK 540,000. London, 6 July 1987, *A Sculptor at his Work* (pen and wash heightened with white/grey paper, 16 1/2 x 10 1/2 ins / 42 x 26.8 cm) GBP 4,800. Stockholm, 19 April 1989, *Portrait of Eleonora Lovisa Antoinette Ridderstolpe* (1779, plaster, diam. 26 1/2 ins / 67 cm) SEK 9,000. Stockholm, 29 May 1991, *Bust Portrait of Gustav III* (plaster, h. 25 1/2 ins / 65 cm) SEK 45,000. Stockholm, 26 May 1999, *Fredrik Henrik af Chapman* (painted plaster, circular, 26 x 26x? ins / 67 x 67x? cm) SEK 26,000. Stockholm, 26 May 1999, *Sergel and Annarella* (Indian ink wash, 7 x 11 ins / 18 x 29 cm) SEK 130,000. Stockholm, 16 May 2000, *Mamsell M. with Clerical Collar and Claes with Sabel* (Indian ink/sepia/watercolour, 8 x 13 ins / 20 x 32 cm) SEK 370,000. New York, 24 Jan 2001, *Carciatures of Mechanical Human Bodies and Heads. Man on an Elephant* (pen/brown ink, double-sided, 8 x 13 ins / 20 x 33 cm) USD 8,000. New York, 24 Jan 2001, *Winged Figure Holding a Javelin and Ring, Racing against a Nude Figure* (pen/brown ink, 8 x 13 ins / 21 x 33 cm) USD 13,000. Stockholm, 4 Dec 2002, *Gustav III - Portrait Bust* (painted plaster, h. 21 ins / 54 cm) SEK 55,000. Paris, 9 Dec 2002, *Centaur Embracing a Maenad* (c. 1770, terracotta, 12 x 14x6 ins / 30 x 35x16 cm) EUR

425,000. STOCKHOLM, 2 Dec 2003, *Study of a Fountain* (Indian ink wash, 19 x 16 ins / 48 x 40 cm) SEK 25,000. STOCKHOLM, 2 Dec 2003, *Queen Lovisa Ulrika - Face Mask* (terracotta, h. 7 ins / 19 cm) SEK 84,000.

SERGENT
French, 18th - 19th century.
Active in Salins.
Painter. Still-lifes.

MUSEUMS AND GALLERIES:
LONS-LE-SAUNIER: *Fruit and Birds.*

SERGENT, Antoine Louis François, or Sergeant, also known as Sergent-Marceau
French, 18th - 19th century.
Born 9 October 1751, in Chartres; died 15 July 1847, in Nice.
Painter (gouache), watercolourist, engraver, draughtsman. History painting, portraits.

Antoine Sergent studied under Saint-Aubin but was especially influenced by Alix and produced reasonably well-regarded portrait engravings. He also produced lithographs. During the revolution he showed his republican convictions by becoming the Jacobins' club secretary. In 1794 he married General Marceau's sister after her divorce from Champion de Cernel. During the Terror he took refuge in Switzerland where he lived for two years. Back in Paris he resumed his position among militant artists, driven into a second exile by Bonaparte's 18 Brumaire coup which put an end to the revolution. He settled in Venice and published his *Costumes of Ancient and Modern Peoples.* At the end of his life he became blind.

He exhibited at the Salon from 1793 to 1801 and at the Salon de la Correspondance in 1799.

MUSEUMS AND GALLERIES:
CHARTRES: *The Artist's Wife* - PARIS (Mus. Carnavalet): *Portrait of General Marceau; Portrait of the Artist's Wife.*

AUCTION RECORDS:
PARIS, 1876, *Magnetism* (watercolour) FRF 185. PARIS, 20 May 1899, *Full-length Portrait of General Marceau,* FRF 153. PARIS, 26 Feb 1900, *Storming of the Bastille* (drawing) FRF 355. PARIS, 20 March 1901, *Ill-defended Rose* (watercolour) FRF 110. PARIS, 8-9 Dec 1933, *Tree of Liberty* (1793, graphite) FRF 135. PARIS, 7 Dec 1934, *Charge of the Prince of Lambesc* (watercolour) FRF 3,800. PARIS, 14 May 1936, *Sts-Innocents Market* (pen and watercolour wash) FRF 4,000. PARIS, 5 Nov 1936, *Dauphin and Madame Elisabeth* (drawing) FRF 1,950. PARIS, 27 June 1941, *Prisoners* (Indian ink wash, attributed) FRF 700. PARIS, 11-13 Nov 1942, *Dance around the Tree of Liberty* (watercolour, no forename given, attributed) FRF 21,000. PARIS, 10 Dec 1943, *Sheet of Studies* (wash, no forename given, attributed) FRF 300. PARIS, 31 March 1944, *Revolutionary Dance* (watercolour, attributed) FRF 14,800. PARIS, 10 July 1944, *Studies of Horsemen* (two drawings) FRF 9,100. PARIS, 4 June 1947, *Portrait Presumed to be of Marie-Thérèse Charlotte of France* (gouache, attributed) FRF 2,700. PARIS, 28 March 1963, *Sergent-Marceau Teaching Drawing to his Fiancée* (watercolour) FRF 5,400. PARIS, 22 March 1995, *Flower Seller* (gouache and watercolour, 8½ x 6½ ins / 21.5 x 16.5 cm) FRF 11,500.

SERGENT, Charles
French, 19th century.
Born in Beaumont-sur-Sarthe.
Painter. Portraits, landscapes.

Charles Sergent exhibited at the Salon in 1859 and in 1865.

SERGENT, Francis John. See **SARJENT**

SERGENT, Henri Jean L.
French, 20th century.
Painter.

Sergent exhibited regularly at the Salon des Artistes Français in Paris, receiving an honourable mention in 1932 and a silver medal in 1934.

SERGENT, Lucien Pierre
French, 19th century.
Born 8 June 1849, in Massy (Essonne); died May 1904, in Paris.
Painter, watercolourist. Historical subjects, battles, genre scenes.

Lucien Sergent received formal tuition from Vauchelet, Isidore Pils and Jean-Paul Laurens. He exhibited at the Paris Salon then at the Salon des Artistes Français from 1873 onwards. He was awarded a medal of honour in 1889 and a bronze medal in 1900 at the Exposition Universelle.

Most of his paintings depict battle scenes.

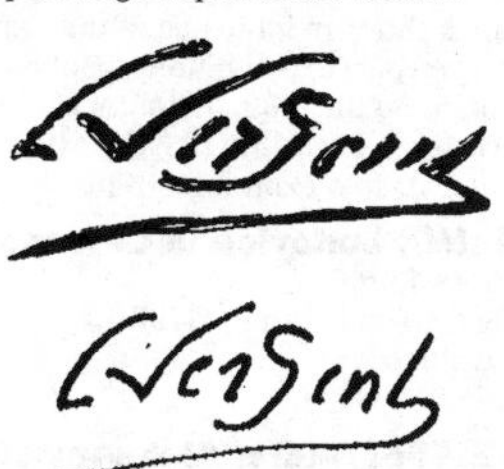

MUSEUMS AND GALLERIES:
ROCHEFORT: *Under Fire* (1870) - SENS: *Scene from the Siege of Thuyen Quan.*

AUCTION RECORDS:
PARIS, 1899, *Defending a House in Bazeilles,* FRF 160; *Sailors in a Trench. Siege of Paris,* FRF 150; *The Chestnut Seller outside the Palais Royal* (watercolour) FRF 810. PARIS, 18 June 1945, *Battle Scene,* FRF 350. LONDON, 4 May 1977, *Retreat of the Prussians* (1898, oil on canvas, 39¼ x 55 ins / 100 x 140 cm) GBP 300. PARIS, 26 Nov 1985, *Fisherman's Family on the Strand* (oil on canvas, 57¾ x 45 ins / 147 x 114 cm) FRF 15,000.

SERGENT-MARCEAU, Antoine Louis François. See **SERGENT**

SERGENT-MARCEAU, Marie Jeanne Louise Françoise Suzanne. See **CHAMPION DE CERNEL**

SERGEYEV, Nicolai
Russian, 20th century.
Born 1908, in Kryukovo; died 1989.
Painter. Landscapes.

Nicolai Sergeyev was a student in the graphic arts department of the polygraphic institute in Moscow in the 1930s. In 1942, he graduated from the Surikov Art Institute in Moscow. He was a member of the USSR Artists' Union.

AUCTION RECORDS:
LONDON, 2 May 1996, *Field of Sunflowers* (1961, oil on canvas, 39 x 67 ins / 99 x 170 cm) GBP 1,725. HELSINKI, 8 May 2004, *The Sparkle* (oil on canvas, 32 x 56 ins / 82 x 142 cm) EUR 80,000.

SERGEYS, François. See **SERGYS**

SERGHINI
Moroccan, 20th century.
Born 1923, in Larache.
Painter.

Serghini lives and works in Tétouan. His work uses the symbol of the door, whether as opening on to the exterior and to escape, or as providing access to the intimacy of the interior or the secret. He draws these doors from the deserted lanes of Tétouan.

BIBLIOGRAPHY:
M' Rabet, Khalil, *Peinture et identité - L'Expérience marocaine*, L'harmattan, Rabat, apr. 1986.

SERGIANT, Thomas Jacobsz.
Dutch, 17th century.
Born c. 1585.
Active in Amsterdam.
Painter.

SERGIOU, Loizos
Cypriot, 20th - 21st century.
Born 1951, in Agia Napia (Famagusta).
Painter.
Sergiou trained at the Accademia di Belle Arti in Florence. He has taught art in secondary schools. His early works dealt with the war during the Turkish invasion of Cyprus. His compositions show an influence of the Expressionist Picasso. He has taken part in exhibitions displaying contemporary Cypriot painting. In 1982, he took part in the Biennale des Jeunes Artistes in Paris. In 1984, the Maison de la Grèce in Paris mounted an solo exhibition of his works.

SERGNANO, Lodovico di Giovanni
Italian, 18th century.
Born 1758; died 28 February 1797.
Active in Belluno.
Painter.

SERGUEIEFF, Andrei Alekseevich. See **SERGEEV**

SERGUEIEFF, Nicolas Alexandrovitch, or Serghéèv
Ukrainian, 19th - 20th century.
Born 1855, in Kharkov.
Active in France.
Painter. Landscapes.
Nicolas Alexandrovitch Sergueieff exhibited in Paris, and received an honourable mention at the Exposition Universelle in 1889.
MUSEUMS AND GALLERIES:
MOSCOW (State Tretyakov Gal.): *By Moonlight.*

SERGUEIEVA, Nina
Ukrainian, 20th century.
Born 1921, in Donetsk.
Painter. Portraits, landscapes, still-lifes.
Socialist Realism.
Nina Sergueieva was a student at the fine arts institute in Kharkov from 1940 to 1945, and then at the Surikov Institute in Moscow, where she worked under Pavel Pavlinov and Ygor Grabar until 1950, the year in which she became a member of the USSR Painters' Union. She painted several group portraits, particularly of women with children.

Work by her was shown at many group exhibitions in the USSR, and at solo exhibitions in Donetsk (1968-1969); Moscow (1972, 1974, 1977, 1980 and 1981); and Czechoslovakia (1978-1979).

BIBLIOGRAPHY:
Tableaux soviétiques, auction catalogue, Salle Drouot, Paris, 3 October 1990.

AUCTION RECORDS:
PARIS, 3 Oct 1990, *Children* (1951, oil on canvas, 29 1/2 x 19 1/4 ins / 75 x 49 cm) FRF 13,000.

SERGYS, François, or Sergeys
Belgian, 19th century.
Born 26 September 1815, in Louvain; died 5 April 1854.
Sculptor.
François Sergys was a pupil of Jean Franck at the academy of Louvain. He exhibited in Ghent in 1838, 1841 and 1845.

SERI, Robert de. See **ROBERT Paul Ponce Antoine**

SERIAKOV, Lavrenti Avksenteevich
Russian, 19th century.
Born 28 January 1824, in Kostrova; died 2 January 1881.
Engraver (wood).
Seriakov studied at the art academy in St Petersburg. He engraved reproductions of paintings in the Hermitage Museum in St Petersburg.

SERICEUS. See **SOYE Philipp de**

SERIN, Harmen, or Hermann, Hendrik Jan
Flemish School, 17th - 18th century.
Born 1678; died c. 1765, in The Hague.
Painter. Religious subjects, portraits.
Harmen Serin was the son of Jan Serin. He is thought to have been a pupil of Jan Erasmus. He was a guild master in The Hague in 1718 and was also active in Ghent.

MUSEUMS AND GALLERIES:
AMSTERDAM: *Dr Louis Trip de Maez* - HOORN: *Meynard Merens.*
AUCTION RECORDS:
AMSTERDAM, 28 Nov 1989, *Bust Portrait of a Gentleman Wearing a Wig on a Balcony, with a Landscape in the Background; Bust Portrait of a Lady Dressed in Blue Holding a Rose on a Balcony, with a Landscape in the Background* (1725, a pair, oval, 33 1/4 x 26 ins / 84.5 x 66 cm) NLG 20,700. TOESTORF, 6 May 2000, *Portrait of a French Duchess* (1728, oil on canvas, oval, 34 x 27 ins / 86 x 68 cm) DEM 7,500. TOESTORF, 11 Nov 2000, *Portrait of a French Duchess* (1728, oil on canvas, oval, 34 x 27 ins / 86 x 68 cm) DEM 8,500. LONDON, 23 April 2004, *Portraits of Gentlemen, One in a Blue Coat and One in a Red Coat* (oil on canvas, a pair, 26 x 20 ins / 66 x 51 cm) GBP 3,500.

SERIN, Jan, or N.
Flemish School, 17th century.
Active in the Netherlands.
Painter. History painting.
Jan Serin was a pupil of Erasmus Quellinus. He is noted for his *St Martin Sharing his Cloak with a Beggar* in the church of St Martin in Tournai.

SERIN, Jan, the Younger
Flemish School, 18th century.
Active c. 1740-1748.
Painter. Portraits.
Jan Serin the Younger was the son of Harmen Serin.

SERIN, Valentino
Italian, 18th century.
Active in Murano.
Painter.

SERINA, Giuseppe
Italian, 16th century.
Active in Alcamo in Sicily in 1579.
Painter.

SERINO, Vincenzo
Italian, 20th century.
Born 17 September 1876, in Naples.
Painter.
Vincenzo Serino studied with Domenico Morelli, Filippo Palizzi and Paolo Vetri.

SERIO, Francesco Antonio
Italian, 18th century.
Active in Naples in the middle of the 18th century.
Painter.
Serio painted the *Madonna of the Rosary* and *The Four Evangelists* for the church of S Maria di Constantinopoli.

SERIO, Giovanni
Italian, 19th - 20th century.
Born 15 April 1872, in Nardó (Apulia).
Painter.
Giovanni Serio was a pupil of Domenico Morelli and Filippo Palizzi. He worked in Nardó.

SERIS, P.B.
French, 20th century.
Born 1915.
Painter.
AUCTION RECORDS:
VERSAILLES, 10 Dec 1989, *The Surrealist City* (oil on canvas, 35 x 46 ins / 89 x 116 cm) FRF 4,800. VERSAILLES, 22 April 1990, *Life is a Tale Told By an Idiot, Full of Sound and Fury, Signifying Nothing (Shakespeare)* (1983, oil on canvas, 36 1/2 x 45 1/4 ins / 93 x 115 cm) FRF 7,000.

SERIZAWA, Keisuke
Japanese, 20th century.
Born 1894 or 1895, in Shizuoka; died 1984.
Painter, designer, illustrator.
Serizawa Keisuke lived and worked at Shizuoka, where he established a studio shortly after World War II. Serizawa is regarded as the master of *kataezome* (stencil dyeing) and Japanese popular art. He used this technique on cloth, paper, screens, book-covers and calendars. In 1956, he was designated a Living National Treasure by the emperor of Japan. After his death, Tohoku Fukushi University in Sendai founded the Serizawa Keisuke Art and Craft Museum in Shizuoka.

His work has been exhibited in a number of museums in the West, such as the Grand-Palais, Paris(1976); the Mingei International Museum, San Diego(1979); the Royal Museum, Edinburgh, in *Japan Festival: Serizawa Keisuke* (2001); and the Cleveland Museum of Natural History, Cleveland and the Riverside Museum, Riverside, California, in *The Art of Keisuke Serizawa: A National Treasure of Japan* (2001).
BIBLIOGRAPHY:
Serizawa, Keisuke, *Serizawa Keisuke: kataezome*, Kodansha. *Keisuke Serizawa*, exhibition catalogue, Réunion des Musées Nationaux, Paris, 1976. Serizawa, Keisuke, *Ayunu: Serizawa Keisuke saosaku to shaushan*, Sikaosha, Shaowa, 1982. Serizawa, Chosuke/Hamada, Shukuko, *The Art of Keisuke Serizawa: A National Treasure of Japan*, exhibition catalogue, Riverside Museum Press, Riverside (CA), 1997.
MUSEUMS AND GALLERIES:
SHIZUOKA (Serizawa Keisuke Mus.): major collection of works.

SERJENT, G. R.. See **SARJENT**

SERLET, Ferdinand
French, 20th century.
Painter.
Ferdinand Serlet received a silver medal at the Salon des Artistes Français in 1937.

SERLIO, Barthelemy. See the entry **SERLIO Sebastiano** or **Sebastien**

SERLIO, Sebastiano or Sebastien
Italian, 16th century.
Born 6 September 1475, in Bologna; died at the end of 1554, in Fontainebleau.
Also active in France.
Painter, architect.
Fontainebleau School.
Sebastiano Serlio worked mainly as an architect, but his writings on architecture became an essential source for the painters of the 16th and especially the 17th centuries. He was the son of Bartolomeo Serlio, a painter of ornaments. Fascinated by geometry, optics and perspective, he was known as a famous theoretician and author of a series of *Books on Architecture*, the first, second and fifth of which were published in Paris between 1545 and 1547, the third and fourth in Venice between 1537 and 1540. A sixth volume was discovered in Munich, the seventh was published, after his death, in Frankfurt am Main in 1575. The eighth volume was never published. A further work, entitled the *Supplementary Book*, had been published in Lyons in 1551. A pupil of Baldassare Peruzzi in Rome, Serlio was inspired by his master's work.

In the early years of his career, he worked at decorative paintings in Pesaro and produced some work for theatrical events in Venice. He seems not to have been involved with any important architectural construction before his arrival in France in 1540-1541 when he was appointed painter and architect at Fontainebleau. Curiously, there is no example of his work at Fontainebleau itself. Nevertheless, he undeniably influenced 16th-century French architecture, particularly by introducing in his books that were accurately translated into French the ideas of Vitruvius. Cardinal d'Este gave him the opportunity to demonstrate his skills with the commission for the *Hôtel de Ferrare* in Fontainebleau, the design of which, known from originals in Munich, anticipates the work of Palladio.

The only entirely surviving work by Serlio is the chateau of Ancy-le-Franc begun c. 1546 which apparently was constructed by Antoine de Clermont from Serlio's designs, rather than Primaticcio's. The question of this attribution, long debated, seems to have been settled in favour of Serlio, but Primaticcio was certainly involved as a painter. The chateau is designed around a square courtyard with Doric pilasters on the exterior and Corinthian on the interior. The original designs for the project, also in Munich, show some difference with the actual building, suggesting that either Primaticcio or Serlio, or both, may have made some changes in the light of local needs and conditions. An example is the use of gabled roofs in the French style instead of the originally intended roof terraces. Not far from Ancy-le-Franc, Serlio was involved with the building of the chateau of Maulnes, now being restored. No known study of this building has been made. Pentagonal in plan, it is surrounded by five towers of different shapes. An alternation of oval and square or rectangular windows continues the unsettling effect of the building's appearance. The façade on the lower side, on the very edge of a cliff, is the most important aspect, dropping down to a nympheum. A central spiral staircase gives access to the interior spaces. Within the staircase is a well shaft reaching the nympheum. The interior layout of the chateau, the base of which is hidden, has rooms distributed in an arbitrary manner at different levels giving no sense of discrete floors. This strange building is a metaphysical folly, a spatial enigma with a symbolist treatment of volume.
BIBLIOGRAPHY:
Dinsmoor, W. B., '*The Literary Remains of Sebastiano Serlio*' in *Art Bulletin*, vol 24, 1942. Gould, C., '*Sebastiano Serlio and Venetian Painting*' in *Journal of the Warburg and Courtauld Institutes*, vol 25, 1962. Rosenfeld, M. N., '*Sebastiano Serlio's Late Style in the Avery Library Version of the Sixth Book on Domestic Architecture*' in *Journal of the Society of Architectural Historians*, vol 28, 1969. Howard, D., '*Sebastiano Serlio's Venetian Copyrights*' in *Burlington Magazine* vol 115, 1973. Hart, V./Day, A., '*A Computer Model of the Theatre of Sebastiano Serlio, 1545*' in *Computers and the History of Art*, vol 5, 1995. Frommel, Sabine, *Sebastiano Serlio architecte (1480-1554)*, Gallimard, Paris, 2002.

SERMADIRAS, Fabien
French, 20th - 21st century.
Born 1956.
Painter, draughtsman.
Fabien Sermadiras lives and works at Vigeois in the Corrèze. Examples of his work featured in *De Bonnard à Baselitz*

- *Dix Ans d'enrichissements du cabinet des estampes 1978-1988* (*From Bonnard to Baselitz: A Decade of Acquisitions by the Prints Collection 1978-1988*), an exhibition held in 1993 at the Bibliothèque Nationale in Paris.

MUSEUMS AND GALLERIES:

PARIS (BNF, Prints Collection): *Uzerche/Berne Junction* (1986, lithograph).

SERMAISE-PERILLARD, Louise
French, 20th century.
Born 26 November 1880, in Paris.
Painter. Still-lifes (flowers/fruit).

Louise Sermaise-Perillard exhibited in Paris at the Salon des Indépendants from 1912, at the Salon de la Société Nationale des Beaux-Arts, Salon d'Automne and Salon des Tuileries in Paris, and in Brussels and Barcelona.

SERMAYER, Yo, known as Savy
Maiden name: Yvonne Serré
French, 20th century.
Born 6 February 1911, in Paris; died 22 September 2003, in Paris.
Painter. Still-lifes.

Yo Sermayer belatedly discovered, in the 1960s, that she was the daughter of Marcel Duchamp. Her mother, Jeanne Chastagnier, had been an artists' model. Sermayer studied at the Académie de la Grande-Chaumière in the 1930s and was a student of André Lhote. She married Jacques Savy in a second marriage and chose to use the name of Savy as her professional name. She mainly painted subjects relating to furniture, such as stools, chairs, armchairs and settees.

In 1967, Marcel Duchamp organised an exhibition for her in New York. On this occasion, he played on the fact that Savy and his own name Sélavy were near homonyms. This was followed by exhibitions of her work at the Kunsthalle in Bern in 1983 (organised by Jean-Hubert Martin), and at the Musée d'Art Moderne et Contemporain in Geneva in 2000. From then on, her studio in Paris, hitherto little known, was much frequented by the followers of 'non-art'.

SERMEI, Cesare (Cavaliere), called Cesare d'Assisi
Italian, 16th century.
Born 1516, in Orvieto; died 3 June 1568, in Assisi.
Painter. Genre scenes.

Cesare Sermei lived mainly in Assisi, producing paintings in oil and fresco. He specialised in works depicting ceremonies and market scenes with many small figures.

SERMEI, Ferdinando
Italian, 16th century.
Active in Orvieto (Umbria) at the end of the 16th century.
Painter, mosaicist.

Ferdinando Sermei executed a mosaic for the façade of Orvieto Cathedral. He also did some work at the church of S Maria Maggiore in Rome.

SERMEI, Giovanni Battista
Italian, 16th - 17th century.
Born 1572, in Fiesole near Florence.
Sculptor.

A pupil of Giambologna, Giovanni Battista Sermei worked in Florence for the Medici family.

SERMEZY DE (Mme). See **DAUDIGNAC Clémence Sophie**

SERMIGLI, Bernardino, or Sermigni
Italian, 17th century.
Born in Umbertide.
Active during the first half of the 17th century.
Painter, architect.

Sermigli decorated the cupola in the church of S Maria della Reggia in Umbertide.

SERMINI, Felix
German, 18th century.
Active during the first half of the 18th century.
Stucco artist.

Sermini produced work for the monastery of Ottobeuren (Bavaria, Germany) in 1723.

SERMINI, Pedro. See **SEXMINI Bartolomé**

SERMON, Paul
British, 20th - 21st century.
Born 1966.
Installation artist, video artist.

Paul Sermon took part in the Lyons Biennale in 1995.

MUSEUMS AND GALLERIES:

LYONS (MAC): *Telematic Vision.*

SERMONDI, Luigi
Italian, 15th century.
Active in Bormio (Lombardy) during the second half of the 15th century.
Painter.

Luigi Sermondi painted an *Adoration of the Kings* for the church of S Spirito in Bormio in 1475.

SERMONET, Virginie. See **LAMBELIN**

SERMONETA, Il. See **SICIOLANTE Girolamo**

SERNA, Bernabé de la and Ismaël Gonzalez de la. See **LA SERNA**

SERNÉ, Adrian
Dutch, 18th - 19th century.
Born 5 July 1773, in Haarlem; died 1847, in Zwolle.
Painter, engraver. Genre scenes, landscapes.

Adrian Serné was the director of the academy at Zwolle, and specialised in producing etchings.

AUCTION RECORDS:

AMSTERDAM, 30 May 1978, *Wooded Landscape with a Church* (oil on panel, 13 1/4 x 17 1/4 ins / 33.5 x 44 cm) NLG 3,800.

SERNEELS, Antoine
Belgian, 20th century.
Born 1909, in Brussels.
Painter. Figures, portraits, landscapes, flowers.

Antoine Serneels studied at the Académie St-Luc in Brussels.

AUCTION RECORDS:

AMSTERDAM, 20 Oct 1976, *Landscape with Shepherd and Shepherdess* (1847, oil on canvas, 20 1/2 x 25 1/4 ins / 52 x 64 cm) NLG 2,800. AMSTERDAM, 10 Feb 1988, *Traveller and Peasant Woman near a Path in the Dunes* (1835, oil on panel, 18 x 14 1/2 ins / 46 x 37 cm) NLG 9,200. BRUSSELS, 12 June 1990, *Amazon* (oil on canvas, 22 3/4 x 18 ins / 58 x 46 cm) BEF 80,000. AMSTERDAM, 19 Oct 1993, *Extensive Landscape with Cattle in a Tree-Lined Meadow, with Peasants Conversing near a Fence* (1836, oil on panel, 15 3/4 x 23 ins / 40 x 58.5 cm) NLG 12,650. LOKEREN, 12 March 1994, *Street Scene, Mexico* (1949, oil on canvas, 28 x 33 3/4 ins / 71 x 86 cm) BEF 36,000.

SERNEELS, Clément
Belgian, 20th century.
Born 1912, in Brussels; died 1991.
Painter. Figures, nudes, landscapes, still-lifes, flowers.

Clément Serneels travelled extensively in Europe, Africa, Asia and Central America.

AUCTION RECORDS:

JOHANNESBURG, 17 March 1976, *Still-life* (1969, oil on canvas remounted on board, 36 x 28 ins / 91.5 x 71 cm) ZAR 650. BRUSSELS, 19 Dec 1989, *Mother and Child* (1935, oil on canvas, 39 1/4 x 31 1/2 ins / 100 x 80 cm) BEF 45,000. AMSTERDAM, 24 May 2000, *The Green Dress* (oil on panel, 22 x 18 ins / 55 x 46 cm) NLG 4,500. AMSTERDAM, 24 May 2000, *Young Beauty* (1937, oil on canvas, 35 x 31 ins / 90 x 80 cm) NLG 4,800.

BRUSSELS, 18 Dec 2001, *Portraits of African Women* (oil on panel, a pair, 20 x 16 ins / 50 x 40 cm) BEF 70,000. BRUSSELS, 18 Dec 2001, *Portrait of an African Woman at Stanleyville* (1939, oil on canvas, 30 x 26 ins / 75 x 67 cm) BEF 160,000. JOHANNESBURG, 13 May 2002, *Roses in a Glass Vase* (1966, oil on canvas, 31 x 28 ins / 80 x 70 cm) ZAR 19,000. BRUSSELS, 19 Nov 2002, *Two Nudes* (1943, oil on canvas, 43 x 35 ins / 110 x 90 cm) EUR 1,800. JOHANNESBURG, 20 Oct 2003, *Still-life with Roses* (1976, oil on canvas, 20 x 16 ins / 51 x 41 cm) ZAR 19,000. JOHANNESBURG, 3 Dec 2003, *Oriental Girl* (1967, oil on canvas on board, 26 x 19 ins / 67 x 48 cm) ZAR 14,000. ANTWERP, 13 Sept 2004, *Portrait of a Black Woman* (1946, oil on panel, 18 x 15 ins / 45 x 39 cm) EUR 3,600. LYONS, 5 Dec 2004, *African Women at Market* (1967, oil on hardboard, 31 x 28 ins / 80 x 70 cm) EUR 3,000.

SERNER, Heinrich

German, 18th century.

Active in Constance (south-west Germany and Switzerland), in 1754.

Painter (glass).

SERNER, Otto

Swiss, 19th century.

Born 10 April 1854, in Sagan.

Painter. Scenes with figures, landscapes.

Otto Serner studied under Jernberg and Dücker. He travelled to Sicily and brought back many views.

AUCTION RECORDS:

AMSTERDAM, 28 Feb 1989, *Elegant Tourists Admiring the Ruins of Taormino Amphitheatre with Etna in the Background* (1927, oil on canvas, 27 1/2 x 39 1/4 ins / 70 x 100 cm) NLG 1,840. AMSTERDAM, 2 May 1990, *Elegant Tourists Admiring Taormino Amphitheatre in Sicily with Etna in the Background* (1927, oil on canvas, 27 1/2 x 39 1/4 ins / 70 x 100 cm) NLG 2,300.

SERNESI, Raffaelo

Italian, 19th century.

Born 29 December 1838, in Florence, in 1823 according to some sources; died 11 August 1866, in Bolzano (Trentino-Alto-Adige).

Painter, engraver. Portraits, landscapes.

Macchiaioli group.

After the war of 1848-1849, a number of young Florentine painters came together in a group sharing the same political and aesthetic ideals. In parallel with the French Impressionists, they gradually discovered how a patch of pure colour (in Italian *macchia*, giving the group its later name of *Macchiaioli*) could become the object of painting, freeing the artist from servitude to the subject. Giovanni Fattori and Lega were the most important representatives of the group. They used to meet at the Caffè Michelangelo to exchange views about Delacroix and the painters of the Barbizon School. Vincenzo Cabianca's picture of a black pig in front of a white wall, a work that appears to have been a turning point for the group, was painted in about 1855. Revolutionary patriots and often conspirators, these artists were all involved in the War of Italian Independence (1859-1860). Sernesi was wounded in the fighting and died in hospital. It was not until 1862, at an exhibition in Florence, that the group adopted the name of *Macchiaioli*, originally coined by a hostile critic.

Of the *Macchiaioli*, Raffaello Sernesi and Giuseppe Abbatti were to die at a tragically young age, Sernesi from the effects of the war and Abbatti as a result of an accident. Sernesi had been the pupil of Ciseri and produced only a few paintings. He was a restless and idealistic character as passionate about independent Italy as about the new ideas on the liberation of artistic expression through experimentation, with emotion created by colour, where the effect can be experienced instantly by the viewer, before any intellectual explanations. It has been said of him that he was 'the most acute, the most creative colourist of all the *Macchiaioli* '. Like several of his friends in the group, he loved Quattrocento art and often made studies of the works of Filippo Lippi and Botticelli. While his own works share the clear, sunny colours of these 15th-century Florentine artists, they have a very individual poetry in the handling of light and shade, of warm and cold tones, the lightness of touch that make these all-too-rare paintings very attractive.

BIBLIOGRAPHY:

Wittgens, Fernanda, *Dodici opere di Raffaello Sernesi nella raccolta Stramezzi*, Ed. del Milione, Milan, 1951. Intersimone, Giuseppe, *Poetica di Raffaello Sernesi*, Alfieri & Lacroix, Milan, 1968.

MUSEUMS AND GALLERIES:

FLORENCE (Gal. d'Arte Moderna) - ROME (Gal. Nazionale d'Arte Moderna): *Roofs in the Sunlight* (1862-1866).

AUCTION RECORDS:

MILAN, 4 June 1968, *Mountainous Landscape*, ITL 2,000,000. MILAN, 21 Oct 1969, *Landscape*, ITL 1,700,000. ROME, 11 June 1973, *View of a Village*, ITL 2,000,000. MILAN, 5 Nov 1981, *Duel* (pencil, study, 9 3/4 x 7 3/4 ins / 25 x 20 cm) ITL 2,600,000. MILAN, 12 Dec 1985, *Monte alle Croci, Florence* (oil on board, 7 3/4 x 9 3/4 ins / 20 x 25 cm) ITL 11,000,000. NEW YORK, 27 Feb 1986, *The Arno at Roverramo* (oil on board, 6 x 11 1/4 ins / 15.2 x 28.5 cm) USD 18,000. MILAN, 25 Oct 1995, *Green Meadow before a House* (oil on board, 4 3/4 x 7 3/4 ins / 12 x 19.5 cm) ITL 86,250,000. FLORENCE, 4 Oct 1999, *Officer Seen from Behind* (pencil, 9 x 12 ins / 24 x 31 cm) ITL 3,200,000. FLORENCE, 4 Oct 1999, *Study of Seated Female Figure* (pencil on card, 12 x 9 ins / 31 x 24 cm) ITL 3,600,000. MILAN, 28 Oct 2002, *Bridge on the Arno* (oil on canvas, 15 x 28 ins / 37 x 70 cm) EUR 15,000.

SERNUNZAN (Baroness). See **ORTES Elmine d'**

SEROBANCH, Hanns or Hans

German, 15th century.

Active in the Lorraine in 1497.

Painter.

Serobanch was painter to Duke René II.

SERODINE, Bernardino

Swiss, 17th century.

Active in the middle of the 17th century.

Painter.

Serodine painted a fresco in the church of S Maria della Fontana near Ascona, Switzerland.

SERODINE, Giovanni

Italian, 17th century.

Born 1594, in Ascona; died 1631, in Rome.

Painter. Religious subjects, portraits.

Serodine's father and brother Giovanni Battista were sculptors who had joined the circle of Lombard artists working in Rome. Giovanni Serodine followed in their footsteps and became established in Rome in 1615. The climate in which he served his apprenticeship was unquestionably Caravaggesque, judging by two early works attributed to him, *Jesus Calling the Sons of Zebedee* and the *Last Supper at Emmaus*. Although little is known either of his life or the stages of his artistic development, the two pictures he was commissioned to paint for the Roman basilica of S Lorenzo, the *Beheading of St John the Baptist* and the *Charity of St Laurence*, place him at the forefront of the ranks of Lombard painters of the Caravaggesque School. These paintings are sublime, with powerful chiaroscuro reinforcing the sharp outlines of the drawing, and express a profound religious feeling far removed from the pomp of the scenes staged by Counter-Reformation masters. At the same time they are less naturalistic and display a greater awareness of the sacred nature of the subject matter than works by contemporary artists such as

Baburen, Honthorst and Vouet. In terms of religious fervour, Serodine is sometimes reminiscent of Borgianni.

In the few later works extant, such as the *Portrait of the Artist's Father*, Serodine's technique has evolved in a very humanist manner which could be described as pre-Romantic, painted with a light and febrile touch and boldly staged in such a way as to evoke Rembrandt and Impressionism. In 1622, the Pope bestowed on Serodine the title of *cavaliere*. There can be little doubt that the brevity of his career prevented him from achieving his full potential.

Bibliography:

Longhi, R., *Giovanni Serodine*, Florence, 1954. Schoenenberger, W., *Giovanni Serodine pittore di Ascona*, Birkhäuser, Basel, 1957. *Le Caravage et la Peinture italienne du XVIIe siècle*, exhibition catalogue, Musée du Louvre, Paris, 1965. Chiappini, Rudy, *Serodine: la pittura oltre Caravaggio. Catologo delle opere*, catalogue raisonné, exhibition catalogue, Pinacoteca Casa Rusca, Locarno, Electa, Milan, 1987.

Museums and Galleries:

Ascona (Church of SS. Pietro e Paolo): *Jesus Calling the Sons of Zebedee; Last Supper at Emmaus* - Lugano (Mus. civico di belle arti): *Portrait of the Artist's Father* - Veroli (Mus. dell'Abbazia di Casamari): *Charity of St Laurence*.

SERODINE, Giovanni Battista

Italian, 17th century.
Born c. 1587; died c. 1626.
Sculptor.

Giovanni Battista Serodine, the brother of Giovanni Serodine, painted the façade of his family home in Ascona.

SEROFF. See **SEROV**

SERON, Anton von. See **ZERROEN**

SÉRON, Frédéric

French, 20th century.
Sculptor. Figures, animals.

Frédéric Séron was a baker at Pressoir-Prompt (Essonne). He decorated his garden with dozens of cement statues, each one containing a 'soul' - a little coffer filled with objects into which he attempted to impart a powerful magic. Most notable are *Angel of Peace* and *The Skater*, as well as numerous animals. These sculptures are roughly coloured, like much naive art.

SEROUSSI, Doucet

20th century.
Draughtsman. Portraits.

Museums and Galleries:

Mulhouse (MBA): *Portrait of Charles Oulmont*.

SEROUX D'AGINCOURT, Georges

French, 19th century.
Born 1783; died 1843.
Active in Compiègne.
Landscape painter.

Museums and Galleries:

Compiègne (Mus. Antoine Vivenel): *View taken in Sicily*.

SEROV, Iaroslav

Russian, 20th century.
Born 1932, in Leningrad (now St Petersburg).
Painter. Figures, nudes, portraits, scenes with figures.
Socialist Realism.

Serov was a student at the fine arts academy (Repin Institute) in Leningrad. His technique was traditional, oftem making use of the effects of light.

Auction records:

Paris, 18 Feb 1991, *By the Water* (oil on canvas, 30 3/4 x 18 1/2 ins / 78 x 47 cm) FRF 4,500.

SEROV, Valentin Alexandrovitch

Russian, 19th - 20th century.
Born 7 January 1865, in St Petersburg; died 22 November 1911, in Moscow.
Painter, illustrator, engraver. Mythological subjects, genre scenes, portraits, landscapes. Stage sets.
Art Nouveau, Symbolism.
Group: Peredvizhniki (Wanderers). Abramtsevo Artists' Colony.

Valentin Alexandrovitch Serov was related to the composer A. Serov of St Petersburg. He was a student of Carl Koepping in Munich, then of Ilya Repin from 1894 to 1987 (according to some French sources), then of Pavel Tchischakov from 1880 to 1994 at the fine arts academy in St Petersburg. He travelled a great deal, throughout Russia, Germany, France, Italy, the Netherlands, Spain, England and Greece. He ran the portrait and genre painting studio at the fine arts school in Moscow from 1897 to 1909, and was an active member of the St Petersburg fine arts academy from 1903. He was a member of the administrative council of the Tretjakov Gallery in Moscow from 1898 until his death, and greatly helped enrich the collection there.

Serov worked in several categories - illustration, engraving, etching, stage sets - but specialised mainly in historical painting, and owed his reputation to his career as a portrait painter: from 1897, he was overwhelmed with commissions, having been made official portraitist to the court and the aristocracy. He also had a reputation abroad, resulting from his many trips, and notably in Paris, where he may have come under the influence of Bastien-Lepage. In 1887, he painted with a sure hand and a bright and sunny palette of colours the charming *Portrait of Miss Mamontov*, daughter of a wealthy Muscovite, also known as the *The Peach Girl*. This portrait is a good illustration of Serov's role in the evolution of Russian art at a turning point in the country's history. Although he had been a member of the Peredvizhniki (Wanderers) group, which in the 19th century brought together painters who were trying to react against official academicism and other French artists working in the open air, he was also one of the first members of the Mir Izkousstva (World of Art) group, of which Leon and Alexander Benois, who would design sets for Diaghilev ballets, were also members. The group heralded the flowering of the Russian avant garde in the second decade of the 20th century, parallel to that of the Munich secession.

Work by him was shown at the exhibition *L'Art russe au temps de Diaghilev* (*Russian Art at the Time of Diaghilev*) at the Musée des Beaux-Arts in Montreal (2000), and at the group exhibition *Un été russe à Montmartre. Artistes de Saint-Pétersbourg à Paris au début du XXe siècle* (*A Russian Summer in Montmartre. St Petersburg Artists in Paris at the Beginning of the 20th Century*) at the Musée de Montmartre in Paris (2003).

Сѣровъ

Bibliography:

L'Art russe des Scythes à nos jours, exhibition catalogue, Gal. nationales du Grand Palais, Paris, 1967. Halturin, Aleksandr/Hulten, Pontus/Gunar, Karl (ed.), *Paris-Moscou*, group exhibition catalogue, Éd. du Centre Georges-Pompidou, Paris, 1979. Gérard, Raphaël/Essaïan, Sergeï, et al., *Un été russe à Montmartre. Artistes de Saint-Pétersbourg à Paris au début du XXe siècle*, exhibition catalogue, Musée de Montmartre, Éditions Fragments, Paris, 2003.

Museums and Galleries:

Moscow (Rumiantsev Mus.): *Count K. Th. Tolle* - Moscow (State Tretyakov Gal.): *A Grey Day; The Crow; Young Girl with Peaches; The Italian Singer Mazzini; The Painter Levitan; Tatar Village in the Crimea; The Author N. S. Leskoff; Sum-*

mer; Study; Rimsky-Korsakoff; Peter I; Autumn; In the Country - PARIS (Mus. d'Orsay): *Mrs Lvoff* - ST PETERSBURG (Gosudarstvennyj Russkij Muz.): *The Children; The Rape of Europa; Nicholas II; Ida Rubinstein; Princess Orlov; Mrs Mamontova.*

AUCTION RECORDS:

LONDON, 17 July 1968, *Stage Curtain for Sheherezade,* GBP 1,200. NEW YORK, 6 May 1970, *Chaliapin in Judith and Holophernes,* USD 850. LONDON, 14 May 1980, *The Rape of Europa* (1910, watercolour and pencil, 11 1/2 x 18 ins / 29 x 46 cm) GBP 3,500. LONDON, 4 June 1981, *Anna Pavlovna in 'Les Sylphides'* (1909, lithograph, 11 3/4 x 9 1/2 ins / 29.7 x 24.2 cm) GBP 800. LONDON, 27 Nov 1981, *Horsemen in a Landscape* (gouache and watercolour, 11 x 15 1/4 ins / 27 x 39 cm) GBP 1,700. LONDON, 3 Feb 1984, *Portrait of an Elegant Woman with her Dog* (oil on canvas, 31 x 23 ins / 78.6 x 58.5 cm) GBP 1,600. LONDON, 14 Nov 1988, *Portrait of the Industrialist and Philanthropist E. L. Nobel* (1909, oil on canvas, 48 x 35 1/2 ins / 122 x 90 cm) GBP 59,400. LONDON, 10 Oct 1990, *Portrait of Prince Felix Felixovitch Yusupov, Count Suarokov-Elston* (1909, oil on canvas, 35 1/2 x 32 3/4 ins / 90 x 83 cm) GBP 60,500. LONDON, 14 Dec 1995, *Europa and the Bull* (1910, gouache and pencil, 12 x 14 3/4 ins / 30.5 x 37.5 cm) GBP 46,600. LONDON, 19 Dec 1996, *Snowy Landscape* (oil on panel, 6 3/4 x 9 3/4 ins / 17.1 x 25 cm) GBP 3,450. LONDON, 11-12 June 1997, *Horses at the Drinking Trough* (1901, oil on canvas, 13 1/2 x 20 1/4 ins / 34.5 x 51.5 cm) GBP 9,200.

SEROV, Vladimir Aleksandrovich

Russian, 20th century.
Born 1910, in Emmaus, Tver region; died 1968, in Moscow.
Painter. Historical subjects, portraits.
Socialist Realism.

Vladimir Aleksandrovich Serov studied at the academy of arts with Vasili Savinsky and Isaac Brodsky. He taught at the academy of arts (1933 to 1942). He painted scenes and personalities from the October revolution in a style directly derived from 19th century academism. He was People's Artist of the USSR, member of the USSR Academy of Arts, first secretary of the Committee of the R.S.F.S.R. Artists Union (1960 to 1968) and president of the USSR Academy of Arts (1962-1968).

BIBLIOGRAPHY:

L'Art russe des Scythes à nos jours, exhibition catalogue, Gal. nationales du Grand Palais, Paris, 1967.

MUSEUMS AND GALLERIES:

ST PETERSBURG (Gosudarstvennyj Russkij Muz.): *With Lenin.*

SERPA, Fernando Claudio

Italian, 19th century.
Painter. Still-lifes (fruit).

Fernando Claudio Serpa was working c. 1880.

AUCTION RECORDS:

NEW YORK, 18 May 1994, *Still-life with Fruit* (1881, oil on canvas, 18 1/2 x 25 1/4 ins / 46.7 x 64.1 cm) USD 5,750.

SERPA, Yvan

Brazilian, 20th century.
Born 1923, in Rio de Janeiro; died 1973.
Painter.
Neo-Plasticism.

Yvan Serpa studied with Axel Leskochek. In 1957 he was awarded a grant enabling him to spend several years in Europe. He was the leader of the Frente (Front) group, which included both abstract and representational artists and put on exhibitions. Like many other young Latin American artists, he was strongly influenced by Neo-Plasticism, which he followed strictly.

His work was shown in collective exhibitions, including the São Paulo Biennale, where he won the Young Painters' prize. His first solo exhibition was in 1951 at Rio de Janeiro.

MUSEUMS AND GALLERIES:

SÃO PAULO (MAC, Universidade): *Forms* (1951).

SERPAN, Jaroslav, or Iaroslav, Yaroslav

Czech, 20th century.
Born 1922, in Karlstein near Prague, to Russian parents; died 12 May 1976, in the Pyrenées.
Active and naturalised in France.
Painter (including gouache), collage artist, sculptor, engraver.
Nouvelle Figuration.
Paris Surrealist group, Phases. Paris School.

Serpan graduated in biology and mathematics at the Sorbonne in Paris. He started to paint in 1940 and attended his first classes at the Académie de la Grande Chaumière in 1945. He co-founded a number of groups, including La Révolution la nuit (1945 to 1947, with Yves Bonnefoy and Claude Tarnaud) and Rixes (1949 to 1951, with Max Clarac-Sérou and Edouard Jaguer) and was part of the Surrealist group from 1946 to 1948.

In 1947-1948, he was, in his own words, 'committed to freeing the gesture while still placing it at the service of a conscious effort to organise painted structures' and 'achieving a dynamic pictorial space'. With these goals in mind, he created his own personal writing, which comprised small, worm-like strokes that he either grouped in compact masses or distributed across the canvas, in a clear reference to the actual appearance of microbes under the microscope, which he would have known from his training as a biologist. He developed his working procedures around mark making and black lettering, ordering quasi-natural formations into more coherent sets that obeyed clear, simple patterns in which his microscopic worlds were enclosed within well-defined surfaces. In 1964 he stopped painting. When he resumed in 1966, he started to paint his black lettering in white. The following year he switched to red, in an explosion of forms recalling human blood. In 1971, after another hiatus, which lasted five years, he began a new period in which coldly and methodically he deconstructed everyday objects (such as bathrooms) into arrows, circles and triangles and called these pictures *Narrations sans histoire,* and *Natures presque mortes.* With his collages from 1975 his work became more emotionally charged, evoking through its haunting shredded female figures and its scraps of reality taken from the newspapers, a tragic view of existence. He also made a number of wooden and plastic sculptures which he painted in acrylics.

Serpan featured in numerous collective exhibitions in Paris including: *Grande Exposition Internationale du Surréalisme* (1947); Salon des Surindépendants (1946 to 1949); Salon de Mai (1954, 1966, 1969, 1971, 1972 and 1977); Salon Comparaisons (1966, 1967 and 1969). Other collective exhibitions include: Museo Español de Arte Contemporaneo, Madrid (1957); National Museum of Modern Art, Tokyo (1957); Carnegie Institute, Pittsburgh (1958); Tate Gallery, London (1962); Musée d'Art Moderne, Brussels (1962); first Salon des Galerie Pilotes, Musée Cantonal, Lausanne (1963); *Le Mouvement Phases de 1952 à l'horizon 2001* (*The Phases Movement from 1952 to the New Millennium*), Kiosque Centre Culturel, Mayenne and the Centre Noroit, Arras (2000).

Solo exhibitions include: Galerie Breteau, Paris (1951); Galleria del Cavallino, Venice (1953); Galerie Stadler, Paris (1956); Galleria del Naviglio, Milan (1954, 1956); Galleria Spazio, Rome (1955); Palais des Beaux-Arts, Brussels (1957). Posthumous retrospectives include: Abbaye de Beaulieu-en-Rouergue (1977); Fondation nationale des arts graphiques, Paris (1983); and Musée des Beaux-Arts, Lyons (1984). Serpan was also a published poet, (*D'un Regard oubliable pour qu'il soit*), novelist (*Les Roses d'Esfahan*) and author of scientific, critical and theoretical articles, which appeared mainly in Italian magazines.

BIBLIOGRAPHY:

Ier Salon international des Galeries Pilotes, exhibition catalogue, Musée cantonal, Lausanne, 1963. *Serpan, 1922-1976*, exhibition catalogue, Musée des Beaux-Arts, Lyons, 1984. Harambourg, Lydia, *L'École de Paris 1945-1965. Dictionnaire des peintres*, Ides et Calendes, Neuchâtel, 1993.

MUSEUMS AND GALLERIES:

BEAULIEU-EN-ROUERGUE (Abbaye, Centre d'Art Contemporain) - NEW YORK (Solomon R. Guggenheim Mus.): *Saadestakso* (1956).

AUCTION RECORDS:

BRUSSELS, 27 Oct 1976, *Seensha* (1952, oil on canvas, 75 1/2 x 59 ins / 192 x 150 cm) BEF 30,000. PARIS, 21 April 1985, *Keelchun* (1955, oil on canvas, 38 1/4 x 51 1/4 ins / 97 x 130 cm) FRF 22,000. PARIS, 15 June 1988, *Ulesantaas* (1956, oil on canvas, 35 x 46 ins / 89 x 116 cm) FRF 12,000. PARIS, 16 Feb 1989, *Poermaes* (1958, oil on canvas, 51 1/4 x 38 1/4 ins / 130 x 97 cm) FRF 21,000. PARIS, 12 June 1989, *SL STN* (ink and charcoal on paper mounted on canvas, 28 1/4 x 47 1/4 ins / 72 x 120 cm) FRF 24,000. BRUSSELS, 13 Dec 1990, *Mitmesugdet* (1956, oil on canvas, 23 1/2 x 31 1/2 ins / 60 x 80 cm) BEF 91,200. PARIS, 19 April 1991, *Jbarha* (1953, oil on canvas, 43 3/4 x 37 ins / 111 x 94 cm) FRF 36,000. PARIS, 10 July 1991, *ONHMICR* (1967, oil on canvas, 76 3/4 x 51 1/4 ins / 195 x 130 cm) FRF 28,000. NEW YORK, 13 Nov 1991, *Dgrugi* (1958, oil, string and paper collage on canvas, 53 1/4 x 50 3/4 ins / 135.2 x 129 cm) USD 3,850. PARIS, 16 April 1992, *Feuns* (1954, oil on canvas, 36 1/4 x 23 1/2 ins / 92 x 60 cm) FRF 15,000. HEIDELBERG, 15 Oct 1994, *Composition CLK55* (1966, gouache, 19 3/4 x 25 1/2 ins / 50 x 65 cm) DEM 1,700. PARIS, 27 March 1995, *Untitled* (oil on paper, 43 1/4 x 204 3/4 ins / 110 x 520 cm) FRF 16,000. MUNICH, 30 Nov 1999, *Imthsvuun* (oil on canvas, 31 x 25 ins / 79 x 63 cm) DEM 4,200. PARIS, 28 Feb 2003, *Mufftafogee* (1957, oil on canvas, 45 x 57 ins / 114 x 146 cm) EUR 2,900. PARIS, 28 Feb 2003, *Ihun* (1952, oil on canvas, 38 x 51 ins / 97 x 130 cm) EUR 3,000. COLOGNE, 4 June 2004, *Composition* (1963, oil on canvas, 32 x 39 ins / 81 x 100 cm) EUR 1,700. COLOGNE, 4 June 2004, *Imthsvuun* (1957, oil on canvas, 31 x 25 ins / 79 x 63 cm) EUR 1,850.

SERPANTIE
French, 20th century.
Painter. Landscapes.

SERPELL, Susan Watkins. See **WATKINS Susan**

SERPIN, Jean
French, 16th century.
Active at the beginning of the 16th century.
Miniaturist.
Gaillon School.

Serpin painted several miniatures of the famous Breviary of Cardinal Georges d'Amboise for the library of the Château de Gaillon and illuminated the following works: *Valerius the Great, Seneca's Epistles, Three volumes of the Bible written by Soubz, Prior of the Augustinians of Rouen*, two further copies of *The Works of Seneca*, *Proverbs* and *The City of God*. He sometimes worked in collaboration with Robert Baiyon, Nicolas Hiesse and Étienne du Moustier.

SERPLET, Didier
French, 20th - 21st century.
Born 1956, in Barbézieux (Charente).
Painter, sculptor, designer.

Didier Serplet lives and works in Paris. Examples of his work featured in *De Bonnard à Baselitz - Dix Ans d'enrichissements du cabinet des estampes 1978-1988* (*From Bonnard to Baselitz: A Decade of Acquisitions by the Prints Collection 1978-1988*), an exhibition held in 1993 at the Bibliothèque Nationale in Paris.

MUSEUMS AND GALLERIES:

PARIS (BNF, Prints Collection): *Serplet Face Down* (1980).

SERPOTTA, Gaspare
Italian, 17th century.
Died 1669.
Active in Palermo.
Sculptor, stucco artist.

Gaspare Serpotta, the father of Giacomo and Giuseppe Serpotta, executed sculptures and ornaments for the cathedral in Parma.

SERPOTTA, Giacomo
Italian, 17th - 18th century.
Born 1656, in Palermo; died 26 February 1732, in Palermo.
Sculptor, decorative artist.
Sicilian School.

The son of Gaspare and father of Procopio Serpotta, Giacomo Serpotta mainly produced stucco works in marble to decorate numerous churches in Palermo and Sicily, in particular in S Domenico (1710-1717) and at S Zita in Palermo. His Rococo style, light and graceful, was well suited to the churches he decorated.

MUSEUMS AND GALLERIES:

PALERMO (Gal. Regionale della Sicilia): several works.

SERPOTTA, Giuseppe
Italian, 17th - 18th century.
Born 1653; died 1719.
Active in Palermo.
Stucco artist.

Giuseppe Serpotta was the brother of Giacomo Serpotta. He executed works for churches in Palermo.

SERPOTTA, Pietro
Italian, 16th - 17th century.
Sculptor.

Pietro Serpotta worked in Palermo between 1596 and 1623 for churches and the Palazzo Reale in that town.

SERPOTTA, Pietro
Italian, 17th century.
Active in Palermo in the middle of the 17th century.
Sculptor.

Pietro Serpotta executed a balustrade in the church of S Orsola.

SERPOTTA, Procopio
Italian, 18th century.
Born 1679, in Palermo; died 1755, in Caccamo.
Stucco artist.

The son of Giacomo Serpotta, Procopio Serpotta executed decorative works in stucco in several churches in Palermo.

SERR, Jakob or Johann Jakob
German, 19th century.
Born 21 November 1807, in Rodt, near Edenkoben; died 1 May 1880, in Heidelberg.
Painter. Portraits, genre scenes.

Serr attended the academy in Munich. He stayed in Paris and finally settled in Heidelberg.

SERRA, Angela, married name Durazzo
Italian, 19th century.
Died 26 November 1814.
Painter.

Angela Serra worked in Genoa.

SERRA, Antoine
Italian, 20th century.
Born 1908, on Maddalena, Sardinia; died 6 May 1995, in Mouriès, France.

Active in France from 1914.
Painter. Scenes with figures, landscapes.
In 1914, after the death of his father, the young Antoine Serra went with his family to Marseilles. Between 1920 and 1925, he was a student at the École des Beaux-Arts in Marseilles. In the 1930s, he was actively involved in the artistic and cultural life of the town. Called up in 1940, he later joined the Resistance and spent the rest of the period of German occupation in hiding. From 1946, he divided his time between Marseilles and Les Baux de Provence. He was a friend of Ambrogiani, Pignon and Kisling. He painted mainly local subjects and landscapes.

Serra began showing work in 1928 and participated in the Salon d'Automne in Paris (1951). He held solo exhibitions in Marseilles, Paris and Cagliari in Sardinia. A number of retrospective exhibitions have been dedicated to him including: Musée de la Vieille Charité, Marseilles (1984); Musée Paul Valéry, Sète (1985); Abbaye de l'Épau, Le Mans (1987). A posthumous exhibition *A. Serra, peintre des Baux* (*A. Serra, Painter of Les Baux*) was held at the Musée des Baux in 1996.

MUSEUMS AND GALLERIES:
NARBONNE (MAH): *Composition* - PARIS (MAM).

SERRA, Antonio da
Portuguese, 17th - 18th century.
Born 1670, in Lisbon; died November 1728, in Lisbon.
Painter, decorative designer. Ornaments.
Antonio da Serra was the father of Victorino Manoel da Serra.

SERRA, Bartolomeo
Italian, 15th century.
Born in Pinerolo (Piedmont).
Active in 1482.
Painter.

SERRA, Bernardo
Italian, 15th century.
Born in Pinerolo (Piedmont).
Active from 1465 to 1491.
Painter.
Bernard Serra worked for in Turin.

SERRA, Bernardo or Bernat
Spanish, 15th century.
Active in Tortosa and in Morella c. 1423.
Painter.
Bernardo Serra painted altarpieces for the church of S Miguel de la Pobla de Ballestar.

SERRA, Cristoforo
Italian, 17th century.
Died before 1678.
Active in Cesena.
Painter.
Cristoforo Serra was the pupil and imitator of Guercino.

SERRA, Dario
Italian, 20th century.
Painter, watercolourist, mixed media, engraver.
Dario Serra was inspired by the Italian tradition and produced illustrated books, compositions on music manuscript paper and drawings in graphite powder to create a theatrical world evoking the Commedia dell'Arte.

AUCTION RECORDS:
PARIS, 16 Jan 1989, *Ascension of Count Zambeccari's Hot-Air Balloon* (watercolour, pen, ink, sepia and gold powder, 13 1/2 x 11 ins / 34 x 28 cm) FRF 3,000.

SERRA, Enrique. See **SERRA Y AUQUE**

SERRA, Ernesto
Italian, 19th - 20th century.
Born 24 March 1860, in Varallo Sesia (Piedmont); died 1915.
Painter. Genre scenes, landscapes.
Ernesto Serra exhibited in Turin, Florence and Venice.

AUCTION RECORDS:
LONDON, 9 June 1967, *Venetian Wedding*, Gns 550. LONDON, 8 Oct 1986, *Gypsy Woman with a Tambourine* (1883, oil on canvas, 49 x 31 ins / 124.5 x 79 cm) GBP 4,000. LONDON, 11 Oct 1988, *First Communion, Venice*, Gns 650. NEW YORK, 22 May 1991, *Haymaking in the Forest* (oil on canvas, 47 x 66 ins / 119.4 x 167.6 cm) USD 22,000. NEW YORK, 20 Jan 1993, *Spanish Beauty* (oil on canvas, 26 1/4 x 18 ins / 66.7 x 45.7 cm) USD 1,150. LONDON, 18 March 2003, *Young Beauty* (oil on canvas, 28 x 17 ins / 72 x 44 cm) GBP 3,000. FLORENCE, 10 June 2003, *Gentleman Riding Horse* (1899, oil on canvas, 118 x 56 ins / 300 x 143 cm) EUR 6,400.

SERRA, Eudald
Spanish, 20th century.
Born 1911, in Barcelona; died 7 October 2002, in Barcelona.
Sculptor.
Eudald Serra studied under Angel Ferrant at the college of arts and crafts in Barcelona; he lived in Italy, in Paris and, from 1932, in Berlin, Warsaw, Moscow and St Petersburg. In 1935 he set up a studio in Japan, and from 1948 onwards he pursued a career both in Barcelona and in various Eastern countries. His body of work comprises compositions in a Surrealist/Dadaist vein, produced using a variety of modern materials. A typical example of his work is *Caparison*.

Serra exhibited solo in Barcelona in 1934. In 1986 he was one of the few Spanish sculptors selected for an exhibition entitled *Qu'est-ce que la Sculpture Moderne?* (*What is Modern Sculpture?*) at the Centre Georges Pompidou in Paris. A retrospective of his work was held at the Palau de la Virreina in Barcelona in 1998.

BIBLIOGRAPHY:
Catálogo nacional de arte contemporáneo 1990-1991, Ibérico 2Mil, Barcelona, 1990-1991. *Eudald Serra: Rastros de Vida*, exhibition catalogue, Institut de Cultura, Barcelona, 1998 (text in Spanish and English).

SERRA, Francisco
Spanish, 14th century.
Active in Valencia from 1383 to 1396.
Painter.
Francisco Serra painted an altarpiece of the Franciscan monastery at Játiva.

SERRA, Guglielmo
Italian, 15th century.
Born in Pinerolo (Piedmont).
Active in Turin in 1489.
Painter.
Guglielmo Serra was the brother of Bernardo Serra.

SERRA, Jaime, Jaume or Jacobo
Spanish, 14th century.
Died between 1395 and 1396.
Active from 1360 to 1375.
Painter.
Catalan School.
The brother of Pedro Serra, Jaime Serra painted many altarpieces for the churches of Catalonia. A seven-panel altarpiece executed by him in 1361 for the tomb of Fray Martin de Alpartil, canon and treasurer of the Archbishopric of Saragossa, formerly in the monastery of the Holy Sepulchre, is now in the museum in Saragossa. Jaime Serra was the head of a studio in which his two brothers, Pedro and Juan, also worked. A successor to the studio of Rámon Destorrent, Serra's studio was to lead to that of Luis Borrassa, one of Serra's best pupils. The Serra brothers can thus be seen as an important link in the development of Catalan painting. Although it is difficult to be sure of the individual roles

played by the brothers, it seems that it was Jaime who decided on the basic composition of their works. While the technique of the Saragossa altarpiece is still strongly influenced by the Sienese School and the iconography by French art, he and his brothers were able to create a type of Gothic Virgin that is entirely Catalan and exquisitely feminine, as in the *Virgin and Child* in the Palau de Cerdagne attributed to him. His painting is detailed and anecdotal and characterised by light brushstrokes and limpid colours.

BIBLIOGRAPHY:

Les Primitifs méditerranéens, exhibition catalogue, Gal. des Beaux-Arts, Bordeaux, 1952.

MUSEUMS AND GALLERIES:

PALAU DE CERDAGNE: *Virgin and Child* (attributed) - SARAGOSSA (Mus. de Zaragoza): altarpiece of seven panels from the monastery of the Holy Sepulchre (1361).

SERRA, Juan or Joan
Spanish, 14th century.
Active in Catalonia in 1376.
Painter.

Juan Serra was the brother of Jaime Serra.

SERRA, Leonardo de
Italian, 16th century.
Active in Sassari (Sardinia) in 1548.
Painter.

SERRA, Luigi
Italian, 19th century.
Born 18 June 1846, in Bologna; died 11 August 1888, in Bologna.
Painter, watercolourist, draughtsman. Religious subjects, portraits, genre scenes.

Luigi Serra exhibited in Parma, Rome, Turin and Bologna. In 2003, the Galleria d'Arte Moderna in Bologna mounted an exhibition devoted to this artist, *Il segno e il colore: nell'atelier di Luigi Serra* (*Sign and Colour: in Luigi Serra 's Studio*).

MUSEUMS AND GALLERIES:

FLORENCE (Gal. d'Arte Moderna): *San Carlo ai Catinari* - FLORENCE (Palazzo Pitti): *Self-portrait* - ROME (Gal. Nazionale d'Arte Moderna): *Madonna with St Francis and St Bonaventure*; *Al Monte di Pietá*; numerous drawings.

AUCTION RECORDS:

ROME, 30 March 1982, *Portrait of a Woman* (1886, pen and tempera, 19 3/4 x 13 1/2 ins / 50 x 34 cm) ITL 2,800,000.

SERRA, Margherita
Italian, 20th century.
Born 1943, in Brescia.
Sculptor.

Work by Margherita Serra has been shown in collective exhibitions, including the 1995 *Attraverso l'Immagine* (*Through the Image*) at the Centro Culturale in Cremona. She works with marble, alternating smooth and rough surfaces to produce forms derived from living objects and endowed with a degree of sensuality.

BIBLIOGRAPHY:

Attraverso l'immagine, exhibition catalogue, Centro culturale Santa Maria della Pietà, Cremona, 1995.

SERRA, Mario
Italian, 16th century.
Born in Pinerolo (Piedmont).
Active in 1505.
Painter.

SERRA, Matteo
Italian, 15th century.
Active in Pinerolo (Piedmont) in 1443.
Painter.

SERRA, Michel or Miguel. See **SERRE**

SERRA, Pablo
Spanish, 18th century.
Born October 1749, in Barcelona; died 30 May 1796, in Barcelona.
Sculptor.

Pablo Serra was a pupil of S. Gurri, I. Vergara and F. Gutierrez. He executed paintings for churches in Barcelona and for the monastery of Montserrat.

SERRA, Pedro
Spanish, 16th century.
Active in 1513.
Painter.
Catalan School.

Pedro Serra painted the organ case in Valencia Cathedral.

SERRA, Pedro or Pere
Spanish, 14th century.
Born possibly in 1343.
Active in Catalonia from 1363 to 1399.
Painter.
Catalan School.

The brother of Jaime Serra, Pedor Serra worked for the Cathedral and other churches in Manresa (Catalonia). His masterpiece is the altarpiece of the Holy Spirit in the church of Our Lady in Manresa dated 1394 or 1395. It was at about this date that he took over the Serra studio. Of the three brothers, Pedro seems to have been the best draftsman and the one most interested in portraiture. Some of the figures of saints in the predellas produced by the Serra workshop have a true grandeur. Sometimes attributed to Pedro, but also to Jaime, is the altarpiece of the *Mother of God* at the monastery at Sigena.

SERRA, Pietro Antonio
Italian, 18th century.
Painter.

Pietro Antonio Serra worked for the court in Mantua from 1705 to 1717 and also executed altarpieces.

SERRA, Pietro del
Italian, 16th century.
Active from 1583 to 1588.
Sculptor (wood).

Pietro del Serra assisted Lodovico Cardellini in the carving of the ceiling of Volterra Cathedral.

SERRA, Richard
American, 20th century.
Born 2 November 1939, in San Francisco.
Painter, sculptor, draughtsman, engraver, installation artist, performance artist, video artist.
Process Art, Minimal Art.

Richard Serra first studied literature at the University of California in Berkeley and Santa Barbara, working at a steel mill to support himself. He then gained a degree in fine arts and painting at Yale University, where he collaborated on Joseph Albers' work *The Interaction of Color*. Having been awarded a Yale Travelling Fellowship he went to Paris in 1965, where he met Philip Glass, and then to Greece and Turkey. He also spent a year in Florence funded by a Fullbright grant. He settled in New York in 1966, where his circle of friends included contemporary artists who were soon to become noticed, such as Carl Andre, Eva Hesse, Joan Jonas, Bruce Naumann and Robert Smithson, among others. He continued to travel, mainly to supervise the installation of his sculptures, for example to Bilbao and the Basque Country in Spain in 1982, Israel and Japan in 1983, and Greece in 1986.

At the beginning of Serra's career he used a mechanical technique to produce carefully staged acts of painting, filling grids with colours within a specific time period defined by a stopwatch. He discovered the work of Brancusi in Paris in 1965, which greatly interested him. The following year, influenced by Arte Povera, which he discovered in Florence, he began to experiment with volume, abandoning all the traditional rules of sculpture and creating heterogeneous assemblages that combined live animals with stuffed ones in crates and wire cages surrounded by organic material, such as *Live Animal Habitat* of 1963-1964.

The following year he began to exploit the elastic properties of rubber, which he often links with neon lighting, imprinting the shapes of familiar objects into the material but making them difficult to identify, suspending tangled straps of cut-out leather (*Belts*), holding up a plate by its centre (*To Lift*), defining the inherent form of each piece according to its weight. These works, which established new relationships based on the notions of stretching and bending, highlighting both the temporary and uncertain nature of the pieces, were the forerunners of the works he created in 1968 by throwing lead to the ground (*Splash Pieces*) and the huge sculptures that he was to create in the future, conceived for display inside at first and then increasingly for the open air.

When he threw molten lead into the angle between floor and wall in 1967 his main aim was to give expression to the transitional state of solidification that embodies traces of action, tension and an ephemeral gesture. The starting point appears to be the physical action of the artist and the inherent possibilities for movement and balance in the material, essential for a work that is defined as much by its conception and fabrication as its process of evolution; it has been written that 'Serra transforms action, process and language into form'.

Serra made a list of infinitives to describe his work and his activity, including: 'to throw, to mix, to cut, to open, to roll, to turn'. Each work makes a point, sets a scene charged with revealing tensions, imbalance or some potential energy. This use of the weight of the material and the forces of gravity is a constant feature, particularly in his 'prop' work *One Ton Prop (House of Cards)*, four lead plates balanced vertically and held together by their own weight as they lean against one another, not fixed to the floor or to any wall. In these precariously balanced works, built either with the help of friends or using industrial machinery, the latent possibility of collapse and the ensuing danger have been very deliberately exploited. The content of the work appears to be not so much an achievement of equilibrium as a probable imbalance. He replaced the lead, which had a tendency to collapse, with untreated Cor-Ten steel.

Since 1972 Serra has also created huge 'installation drawings', as he calls them, in charcoal or tar on canvas paper (and sometimes on steel), whose format is dictated by the exhibition site. These works give a less aggressive impression than his sculptures, being abstract in style with bold jagged shapes and heavy use of material, but like the latter they intervene physically in their environment, their blackness standing out against the white wall.

His work was at the heart of most of the new developments in American art in the 1970s. Undeniably minimal in his aesthetic choices (factory-produced materials, elementary geometric structures, seriality) he has nevertheless, Rosalind Krauss states, shattered the impenetrable cube of Judd and Tony Smith and placed himself on the fringe of other contemporary trends. Otto Hahn wrote, when attempting to define the multiple aspects of his work, that 'Richard Serra belongs both with the Abstract Expressionists and Minimal Art. But he stands at the crossroads where several current concerns come together. Body Art poses him problems, Land Art interests him.'

Indeed, after 1970, working on an environmental scale, Serra sunk some large steel plates into the ground, the first of which had only a corner remaining visible, while the others emerged progressively, invading the space, inviting the spectator to walk alongside and around them and penetrate the work, compelling him to look, changing his path and his perception of his surroundings. These sculptures owe nothing to chance. The minimal forms (plates and cylinders) in steel, occasionally stone (basalt or granite) or concrete, which are smooth, flat or curved, and neutral in appearance, and are an intrusion, an obstacle in everyday space, are the fruit of long reflection on the part of the artist, of technical, topographical and aesthetic considerations. They reject any sense of the ornamental, creating their impression in the way in which their weight - as much as several hundred tonnes in some cases - and their primitive monolithic architecture intervenes in the environment.

According to Serra his works are site specific and often restructure the organisation of the site both conceptually and perceptually. He is interested in a behavioural space in which the spectator is able to develop a relationship with the sculpture in its context. He is a man with many different preoccupations with a penchant for excess. His works are often so large that galleries do not have the space to accommodate them. They have a very strong physical presence and are truly on an industrial scale, requiring technicians and engineers to install them.

Serra has taken part in many collective exhibitions, including all the major shows dedicated to American sculpture, for example at Yale University Art Gallery in New Haven in 1966, 1973 and 1981; the Noah Goldwosky Gallery, New York, from 1966 until 1968; the Kunsthalle in Cologne in 1968; regularly at the Whitney Museum of Modern Art and the Solomon R. Guggenheim Museum of Modern Art in New York since 1968; *When Attitudes Become Form* at the Kunstalle in Bern in 1969; the Metropolitan Art Gallery in Tokyo in 1970; the Paris Biennale, and *Art & Technology* at the County Museum of Art in Los Angeles in 1971; Documenta in Kassel in 1972, 1977, 1982 and 1987; Centre National d'Art Contemporain, Paris, in 1973 and 1974; National Gallery of Victoria in Melbourne, Walker Art Center in Minneapolis, and *Interventions in Landscapes* at the Massachusetts Institute of Technology in Cambridge in 1974; a travelling exhibition in South America organised by the museum of modern art in Bogotá, and the Smithsonian Institution in Washington in 1975; *Paris-New York* at the Musée National d'Art Moderne in Paris in 1977; *Between Sculpture and Painting* at the Worcester Art Museum in 1978; *The Broadening of the Concept of Reality in the Art of the 80s and 70s* at the Museum Haus Lange in Krefeld in 1979; the Venice Biennale in 1980; *Arte Povera, Antiform, Sculptures 1966-1969* at the Centre d'Arts Plastiques Contemporains in Bordeaux, and *'60'80 Attitudes/Concepts/Images* at the Stedelijk Museum in Amsterdam in 1982; *Sculpture: the Tradition in Steel* at the County Museum of Fine Art in Nassau in 1984; Museum of Fine Arts in Montreal, also in 1984; Palacio Velázquez and Centro de Arte Reina Sofia in Madrid, and *Qu'est-ce-que la sculpture moderne* (*What is Modern Sculpture?*) at the Musée National d'Art Moderne in Paris in 1986; *Philip Glass/Richard Serra: a Collaborative Acoustic Installation* at Ohio State University, 1987; Nationalgalerie in Berlin in 1988; *Skulptur. Projekte in Münster 1997* (*Sculpture. Projects in Münster 1997*), Münster, 1997; *Les Années 70: l'art en cause* (*The 1970s: Art in Question*), Capc-Musée d'Art Contemporain, Bordeaux, in 2002.

Serra has regularly shown his works in solo exhibitions since 1966 in Rome, and has also appeared at the Art Museum, Pasadena, in 1970; regularly at the Leo Castelli Gallery in New York since 1973; the Center for the Visual Arts in Portland in 1975; Galerie M, Bochum, in 1977, 1983 and 1988; the Stedelijk Museum, Amsterdam, in 1977; the Kunsthalle, Tübingen, in 1978; the Kunsthalle, Baden-Baden, in 1978 and 1979; Museum Boymans-Van-Beuningen, Rotterdam, in 1980; the Art Museum, St Louis, in 1982; the Musée National d'Art Moderne, Paris, in 1983; Museum Haus Lange,

Krefeld, in 1985; Museum of Modern Art in New York, and the Louisiana Museum in Hummlebaek in 1986 and 1991; the Westfälisches Landesmuseum für Kunst und Kulturgeschichte in Münster and the Städtische Galerie im Lenbachhaus in Munich in 1987; the Kunsthalle in Basel, the Neuer Kunstverein in Berlin and the Stedelijk Van Abbe Museum in Eindhoven in 1988; the Kunsthaus in Munich and the Musée d'Art Contemporain in Bordeaux in 1990; the Konsthall, Malmö, in 1991; the Museo Nacional Reina Sofia in Madrid, the Kunstsammlung Nordrhein-Westfalen in Düsseldorf and the Tate Gallery and Serpentine Gallery in London in 1992; the Guggenheim Museum SoHo, New York, in 1993; and *Richard Serra Prints* at the Phoenix Art Museum, Phoenix (Arizona) in 2002.

Serra has been awarded many prizes and distinctions, including: the prize from the Skowhegan School of Painting and Sculpture in 1975; the Kaiserring prize for sculpture from the town of Goslar in 1981; the Carnegie Prize in 1985; the Wilhelm-Lehmbruck sculpture prize in Duisburg and Officier de l'Ordre des Arts et des Lettres de l'État Français in 1991; the Sculpture Center Award for distinction in sculpture and member of the Universal Academy of Cultures in 1992. He has also received many public commissions, such as *Sight Point* at the Stedelijk Museum in Amsterdam 1971-1975; *Tilted Arc* on the Federal Plaza in New York in 1981 (a work dismantled in 1989 by the government, who also commissioned it); *Clara-Clara* in the Choisy public gardens in Paris in 1983; *Philibert and Marguerite* in the Cloître de Brou in Bourg-en-Bresse in 1985; *Berlin Junction* in front of the Philharmonic Theatre in Berlin in 1987; *Maillart Extended* on the Grandfey viaduct in Switzerland in 1989; *Afangar* on the island of Videy opposite the port of Reykjavik in 1990; *Octagon for St-Éloi* facing the church in Chagny (Burgundy); *Intersection* on the Theaterplatz in Basel in 1992; and a piece for the Guggenheim Museum in Bilbao in 1999.

BIBLIOGRAPHY:

Richard Serra, exhibition catalogue, Art Museum, Pasadena (CA), 1970. *Richard Serra*, exhibition catalogue, Kunsthalle, Tübingen, Baden Baden, 1978. *Richard Serra*, exhibition catalogue, Musée national d'Art moderne, Éd. du Centre Georges-Pompidou, Paris, 1983. *Richard Serra*, exhibition catalogue, Museum of Modern Art, New York, 1986. Krauss, Rosalind, '*Richard Serra, sculpture*' in *Artstudio* n° 3, periodical, Gal. Templon, Paris, winter 1986-1987. Amman, Jean Christophe/Bois, Yve-Alain/Crimp, Douglas, *Richard Serra*, exhibition catalogue, Westfälisches Landesmuseum für Kunst und Kulturgeschichte, Münster, 1987. Güse, Ernst-Gerhard/Bois, Yve-Alain, *Richard Serra*, exhibition catalogue, Rizzoli International, New York, 1988. Hoppe-Sailer, Richard, *Das druckgraphische Werk, Prints - Catalogue raisonné 1972-1988*, Gal. M, Bochum (DEU), 1988 (text in English and German). *Richard Serra: 10 Sculptures for the van Abbe*, exhibition catalogue, Stedelijk Van Abbemuseum, Eindhoven, 1988. Serra, Richard, *Écrits et entretiens 1970-1989*, Gal. Lelong, Paris, 1990 (English edition, University of Chicago Press, Chicago, 1994). Janssen, Hans, *Richard Serra: Zeichnungen: 1969-1990: Werkverzeichnis*, catalogue raisonné, Benteli, Bern, 1990. Buci Glucksmann, Christine, *Richard Serra: gravures*, exhibition catalogue, Musée d'Art moderne, Céret, 1992. Serra, Richard/Bois, Yve Alain/Germer, Stefan, *Richard Serra*, exhibition catalogue, Museo Nacional Centro de Arte Reina Sofía, Madrid, 1992. Ferguson, R./McCall, A./Weyergraf-Serra, C./Foster, H./Reinartz, D./Sylvester, D./Serra, R., *Richard Serra Sculpture 1985-1998*, exhibition catalogue, The Museum of Contemporary Art, Los Angeles, 1998. '*Richard Serra*' in *3 vol.*, exhibition catalogue, Mercati di Traiano, American Academy in Rome, Rome, 1999 (text in Italian and English). *Richard Serra: Druckgrafik. Werkverzeichnis 1972-1999*, catalogue raisonné, Richter, Düsseldorf, 1999 (text in German, English and French). Foster, Hal (ed.), *Richard Serra*, MIT Press, Cambridge (MA), 2000. *Line Drawings/Richard Serra*, exhibition catalogue, Gagosian Gallery, New York, 2002.

MUSEUMS AND GALLERIES:

BORDEAUX (CAPC-MAC): *Forged Drawings Rectangles* (1992); *Untitled* (1992) - CHICAGO (MCA): *Prop* (1968, lead) - LA JOLLA (MCA of San Diego): from the 'The New York Collection for Stockholm' portfolio (30 artists)*Untitled* (1973, lithograph); *Drawing for Documenta VI* (1976, oil pastel on paper) - MUNICH (Städtische Gal. im Lenbachhaus): *Seven Spaces; Seven Sculptures* - NEW YORK (MoMA): *Circuit; Intersection II* (1992) - NEW YORK (Solomon R. Guggenheim Mus.): *Shafrazi* (1974); *Zadikians* (1974) - NEW YORK (Whitney Mus. of American Art): *Prop* (1968) - PARIS (BNF, Prints Collection): *To Bobby Sands* (1981) - PARIS (MNAM-CCI): *Plinths* (1967); *Hands Scraping* (1968); *Boomerang* (1974); *Corner Prop No7 (For Nathalie)* (1983); *Rue Ligner* (1989); *Comic Opera* (1990); *Decision on the Stone* (1990).

AUCTION RECORDS:

NEW YORK, 21 Oct 1976, *Parallelogram* (1974, painting/paper, 98 x 59 3/4 ins / 249 x 152 cm) USD 8,000. NEW YORK, 23 May 1978, *Untitled* (1968-1972, lead, diam. 20 1/2 ins / 52 cm, h. 2 ins/5 cm) USD 6,500. NEW YORK, 13 Nov 1980, *Untitled* (1974, oil on paper, 113 x 36 ins / 287 x 91.4 cm) USD 15,000. NEW YORK, 5 May 1982, *Untitled* (ink/paper, 60 x 66 ins / 152.4 x 167.6 cm) USD 1,900. NEW YORK, 2 Nov 1984, *T.W.U. No4* (1980, pencil, oil, 49 3/4 x 38 ins / 126.5 x 96.5 cm) USD 7,500. NEW YORK, 7 Nov 1984, *The Moral Majority Sucks* (1981, lithograph, 52 1/4 x 60 3/4 ins / 132.7 x 154.5 cm) USD 1,000. NEW YORK, 6 May 1986, *T.W.U. No49* (1980, pencil, wax, 52 1/2 x 40 1/2 ins / 133.4 x 103 cm) USD 7,500. NEW YORK, 5 May 1987, *Corner Prop* (1976, steel, h. 97 ins / 246.4 cm) USD 110,000. NEW YORK, 6 May 1987, *Untitled* (1972, charcoal/paper, 38 3/4 x 37 1/2 ins / 98.5 x 95 cm) USD 14,000. NEW YORK, 3 May 1989, *T.W.U. 11* (1980, spray paint/paper, 52 1/2 x 40 1/2 ins / 133.5 x 103 cm) USD 30,250. NEW YORK, 23 Feb 1990, *Federal Plaza II* (soft black chalk, fibres and collage of paper/card, 38 x 72 3/4 ins / 96.5 x 185 cm) USD 66,000. NEW YORK, 9 May 1990, *Elevator* (1980, wax crayon/paper, 37 x 59 1/2 ins / 94 x 151 cm) USD 44,000. NEW YORK, 14 Feb 1991, *Untitled* (three sheets of steel, each 24 x 24 x 6 ins / 61 x 61 x 15.2 cm) USD 71,500. NEW YORK, 30 April 1991, *Close Pin Prop* (1969, lead, h. of prop: 98 3/4 ins / 250.7 cm, diam. of prop: 3 3/4 ins/9.5 cm, diam. of tube: 9 3/4 ins/24.7 cm, l. of tube: 40 ins/101.6 cm) USD 231,000. NEW YORK, 13 Nov 1991, *Kitty Hawk* (two plates of steel, height: 48 x 168 x 2 1/2 ins / 121.8 x 426.5 x 6.3 cm, bellow: 48 x 72 x 4 ins/121.8 x 182.8 x 10.2 cm) USD 220,000. NEW YORK, 6 Oct 1992, *Untitled* (1973, ink roll on Arches paper, drawing in 14 parts, each sheet 33 x 49 ins / 83.8 x 124.5 cm) USD 37,400. NEW YORK, 17 Nov 1992, *Square Forged Lever* (forged steel in two parts, 69 x 7 1/2 x 7 1/2 ins / 175.3 x 19.1 x 19.1 cm) USD 170,500. NEW YORK, 19 Nov 1992, *Defence* (1979, laminated steel, 44 1/2 x 24 x 24 ins / 113 x 61 x 61 cm) USD 71,500. NEW YORK, 10 Nov 1993, *Plan of Work* (two steel plates, vertical: 70 x 63 x 3 ins / 177.5 x 160 x 7.6 cm, horizontal 152 3/4 x 64 1/2 x 3 ins/388 x 163.8 x 7.6 cm) USD 112,500. COPENHAGEN, 1 Dec 1993, *Pasolini* (1987, silk screen print, 52 1/4 x 71 ins / 132.5 x 179.5 cm) DKK 11,000. LONDON, 2 Dec 1993, *Model for Three Flat Pieces* (1980, iron and cement, 30 x 22 3/4 x 22 3/4 ins / 76.5 x 57.8 x 57.8 cm) GBP 29,900. PARIS, 17 Oct 1994, *Madness of the Day* (1982, wax crayon/paper, 38 x 50 ins / 96.5 x 127 cm) FRF 80,000. LUCERNE, 20 May 1995, *Philip Glass Porter or Untitled* (silk screen print, 29 1/2 x 41 1/4 ins / 75 x 105 cm) CHF 1,900. NEW YORK, 16 Nov 1995, *Model for Madrid* (beaten steel, 47 x 40 x 30 ins / 119.4 x 101.6 x 76.2 cm) USD 63,000. LONDON, 23 May 1996, *Model for Point of View* (steel, total height 49 1/4 ins / 125 cm) GBP 43,300. NEW YORK, 21 Nov 1996, *Untitled* (1975, black pastel/paper, 50 x 38 ins / 127 x 96.5 cm) USD 17,250. NEW YORK, 7-8 May 1997, *Madrid* (1981, steel, 47 x

34 1/2 x 20 1/2 ins / 119.4 x 87.4 x 52.1 cm) USD 51,750. NEW YORK, 8 May 1997, *Support Indecent and Uncivil Art* (1989, black pastel/paper, two sheets, 76 3/4 x 64 1/4 ins / 195 x 163.5 cm) USD 74,000. NEW YORK, 6 and 7 March 1998, *St Louis* (1982, monotype, 42 1/4 x 31 ins / 107 x 79 cm) USD 1,840. NEW YORK, 20 May 1999, *Model for T.W.U.* (steel, 37 x 17x12 ins / 93 x 43x30 cm) USD 110,000. LOS ANGELES, 14 Dec 1999, *Untitled, Isosceles Triangle* (corten steel, 96 x 96x0 ins / 244 x 244x1 cm) USD 250,000. NEW YORK, 16 May 2000, *Forged Corner, Maastricht* (oil, paintstick and forged steel, two parts, 39 x 24x4 ins / 100 x 60x10 cm) USD 140,000. NEW YORK, 17 May 2000, *Three Lead Coils* (1968, lead, 87 x 87x55 ins / 220 x 220x140 cm) USD 220,000. NEW YORK, 14 Nov 2001, *Untitled* (1984, corten steel, 119 x 144x2 ins / 303 x 366x6 cm) USD 1,100,000. NEW YORK, 15 Nov 2001, *Zappa* (1995, forged steel, two angle bars, 58 x 61x14 ins / 147 x 155x35 cm) USD 400,000. NEW YORK, 14 May 2002, *Plate, Pole, Prop* (1969-1983, steel, 94 x 94x1 ins / 240 x 240x2 cm) USD 300,000. NEW YORK, 15 May 2002, *One Cut Triangle* (1973, oilstick on paper, 50 x 79 ins / 128 x 200 cm) USD 45,000. NEW YORK, 12 Nov 2003, *Corner Block* (1983, hot rolled steel, 11 x 11x36 ins / 28 x 28x91 cm) USD 360,000. NEW YORK, 13 Nov 2003, *Vertical parallelogram* (steel, 49 x 24x24 ins / 124 x 61x61 cm) USD 80,000. NEW YORK, 13 May 2004, *Barge* (1983, oilstick on canvas, 35 x 31 ins / 89 x 79 cm) USD 40,000. NEW YORK, 13 May 2004, *The American Flag is Not an Object of Worship* (1989, paintstick on paper, 113 x 148 ins / 287 x 376 cm) USD 200,000.

SERRA, Rosa
Spanish, 20th century.
Born 1944, in Vic.
Sculptor, draughtswoman. Figures, nudes. Groups, statuettes.

Rosa Serra specialises in monuments, most notably with solid figures, moving women, often involved in sport. She favours curved forms, smooth, shiny surfaces that invite the touch.

She participates in group exhibitions: since 1975 in Gerona, notably at the exhibition of contemporary Catalan art in 1980; 1976 at the Miró foundation in Barcelona; since 1982 at the Arco Arte Contemporáneo in Madrid. She has shown her work in solo exhibitions in Barcelona since 1972, regularly in Olot.

BIBLIOGRAPHY:
Racionero, Lluis, *Rosa Serra*, Àmbit, Barcelona, 1987.

MUSEUMS AND GALLERIES:
BANYOLES - BARCELONA (Mus. of Sport) - CADAQUÉS (Perrot-Moore Art Center) - ELCHE (MAC) - LAUSANNE (Mus. Olympique) - PORRERES (MAC).

AUCTION RECORDS:
AMSTERDAM, 6 Dec 1995, *Torso* (bronze, h. 22 ins / 56 cm) NLG 9,200. AMSTERDAM, 5 June 1996, *Mother and Daughter* (bronze, h. 25 3/4 ins / 65.5 cm) NLG 16,100. AMSTERDAM, 10 Dec 1996, *Volume in Circle* (1991, bronze, h. 9 1/2 ins / 24 cm) NLG 5,535; *Mirada* (bronze, h. 13 3/4 ins / 35 cm) NLG 14,991. AMSTERDAM, 2 Dec 1997, *Nude Seated* (bronze, h. 11 1/2 ins / 29 cm) NLG 10,955.

SERRA, Sebastiano
Italian, 15th century.
Active in Pinerolo (Piedmont) in 1497.
Painter.

SERRA, Vicente
Spanish, 14th - 15th century.
Active from 1399 to 1400.
Sculptor.

Vincente Serra carved the altar in the chapel of St James in Valenica Cathedral.

SERRA, Victorino Manoel da
Portuguese, 18th century.
Born 1692, in Lisbon; died 9 April 1747, in Lisbon.
Painter, decorative designer. Church decoration, ornaments.

Victorino Manoel da Serra was an imitator of V. Baccherelli and the son of Antonio da Serra. He worked for churches in Lisbon.

SERRA DE RIVERA, Xavier
Spanish, 20th - 21st century.
Born 1946, in Sant Joan Despi, Barcelona.
Painter, pastellist. Figures, nudes, scenes with figures, landscapes, still-lifes.

Xavier Serra de Rivera studied at the Sant Jordi school of fine arts and at the book conservatory in Barcelona.

Close to Surrealism, he seems to cultivate the extraordinary, suggesting image games in the tradition of Magritte. He exploits the effect of unusual geometric volumes in a given place and also plays on the exterior/interior ambiguity, opting for hazy lights, using ochres and greens. He frequently uses as the point of departure for his musings all or part of famous paintings.

He has participated in group exhibitions: 1975, São Paulo Biennale and Ljubljana Biennale of design; 1975, Cracow Biennale of design; 1979-80, Salon de Montrouge; 1981, Madrid municipal museum; 1982, Caixa de Pensions de Barcelona foundation; 1986, cultural centre of the city of Madrid; 1987 and 1988, ARCO in Madrid. He has also shown his work in solo exhibitions: 1969, 1971, 1973, 1976, 1980, 1986 and 1988 in Barcelona; 1974 in Valencia; 1978 at the Étienne de Causans gallery in Paris; 1980 and 1984 at the FIAC (Foire Internationale d'Art Contemporain) in Paris.

BIBLIOGRAPHY:
Catálogo nacionál de arte contemporaneo 1990-1991, Ibérico 2Mil, Barcelona, 1990-1991.

MUSEUMS AND GALLERIES:
MADRID (Prado, Prints Collection) - PARIS (MNAM-CCI) - SEVILLE (Centro Andaluz de Arte Contemporáneo).

SERRA DI CALLIANO
Italian, 18th century.
Active during the first half of the 18th century.
Painter.

Serra di Calliano executed works for the abbey in Monferrato. He may have been the same person as the artist known as Pietro Antonio Serra.

SERRA FARNÉS, Pedro
Spanish, 20th century.
Born 31 January 1890, in Barcelona; died 4 October 1974.
Painter. Mountainscapes, landscapes.

Pedro Serra Farnés was a pupil at the Escuela de Bellas Artes in Madrid and featured regularly at the Salón de Otoño in Madrid, where he was a member. He also showed at the Exposición Nacional in Madrid, obtaining a medal in 1922 and in 1926. He only painted landscapes and had a preference for the mountains of Guadarrama, Gredos and Gata.

BIBLIOGRAPHY:
Arnáiz, José Manuel/López Jiménez, Javier/Merchán Díaz, Manuel (ed.), '*Cien años de pintura en Espana y Portugal (1830-1930)*' in vol. X, Antiqvaria, Madrid, 1993.

SERRA MELGOSA, Juan
Spanish, 20th century.
Born 1899, in Lérida (Lleida); died 1970, in Barcelona.
Painter. Figures, landscapes, landscapes with figures, urban landscapes, waterscapes, seascapes, still-lifes.

Juan Serra Melgosa studied at the Escuela de Bellas Artes in Barcelona. Here he was part of the group of 'evolutionists', funded by the businessman José Dalmau. In 1924, he travelled to Paris. He is known for *Avenue of Flowers, Running Aground* and *Part of a Village,* works which enabled him to exploit the potential of colour. He employed broad brushstrokes with a sure touch.

Serra Melgosa featured in various collective exhibitions including: Exposición Nacional, Barcelona (1942 and 1944); Madrid (1944); Sala Parés, Barcelona (1954). He also exhibited in Bilbao, San Sebastián, Paris, London, Pittsburgh, Buenos Aires, Montevideo and Caracas. He was awarded a gold medal in 1950.

BIBLIOGRAPHY:

Arnáiz, José Manuel/López Jiménez, Javier/Merchán Díaz, Manuel (ed.), *'Cien años de pintura en Espana y Portugal (1830-1930)'* in vol. X, Antiqvaria, Madrid, 1993.

MUSEUMS AND GALLERIES:

BARCELONA (MAM del Mus. Nacional d'Art de Catalunya) - MADRID (Mus. de Arte Moderno).

AUCTION RECORDS:

BARCELONA, 11 Dec 1979, *Landscape* (oil on canvas, 14½ x 21¼ ins / 37 x 54 cm) ESP 125,000. BARCELONA, 20 Oct 1981, *Landscape* (oil on canvas, 25¼ x 35¾ ins / 64 x 91 cm) ESP 210,000. BARCELONA, 19 Dec 1984, *Calella de Palafrugell, Patio* (1963, oil on canvas, 32 x 39¼ ins / 81 x 100 cm) ESP 370,000. MADRID, 26 Oct 1999, *Still-life* (oil on canvas, 29 x 39 ins / 73 x 100 cm) ESP 375,000. MADRID, 2 Oct 2001, *Circus Figures* (1959, oil on canvas, 28 x 20 ins / 71 x 51 cm) ESP 1,000,000. MADRID, 2 March 2004, *Still-life with Melon* (oil on canvas, 28 x 39 ins / 72 x 100 cm) EUR 3,500.

SERRA Y AUQUE, Enrique

Spanish, 19th - 20th century.

Born 7 January 1859, in Barcelona; died 16 February 1918, in Rome.

Also active in Italy from 1876.

Painter, illustrator. Religious subjects, figures, portraits, genre scenes, interiors with figures, waterscapes, landscapes, ruins.

Enrique Serra y Auque studied under Ramón Marti y Alsina and Domingo Talarn at the college of fine arts in Barcelona; he was awarded a scholarship in 1876 to continue his studies in Rome, where he spent a large part of his life. He returned to Barcelona in 1879 to recover from a bout of malaria, but by 1895 he had rented a studio in Paris and from then on he divided his time between the French capital and Rome.

Serra was an accomplished and widely respected illustrator who worked on major periodicals such as *La Ilustración Española y Americana* (*Spain and America Illustrated*). His artistic development can be divided in two distinct phases. Up to 1890, he painted mainly Orientalist compositions (*Arab Guarding the Harem, Moor Firing a Gun, Eastern Dance*) directly inspired by the work of Mariano Fortuny and José Villegas. From the 1890s, however, he was influenced by the Naples School and started painting views of lagoons and, above all, interiors and genre compositions which featured in the background his own private collection of carpets, ceramics, Renaissance furniture and antique objets d'art. In that context, mention should be made of *Italian Customs; Sacristan, Reading the News, Welcome Guest, Gypsy Camp, Idyll, Solemn Occasion* and *Wedding Feast*. Pope Leo XIV commissioned him several works for the Vatican. Enrique Serra's work featured at various collective exhibitions including: Sala Parès(on a regular basis from 1879), 1888 Universal Exhibition in Barcelona (gold medal), 1895 National Fine Arts Exhibition in Madrid (bronze medal) and at a retrospective held in Barcelona in 1917.

ENRIQVE SERRA

BIBLIOGRAPHY:

Arnáiz, José Manuel/López Jiménez, Javier/Merchán Díaz, Manuel (ed.), *'Cien años de pintura en Espana y Portugal (1830-1930)'* in vol. X, Antiqvaria, Madrid, 1993.

MUSEUMS AND GALLERIES:

GLASGOW: *Two Clerics.*

AUCTION RECORDS:

PARIS, 4 July 1899, *His Eminence,* FRF 1,800. PARIS, 1 June 1908, *Schoolmaster,* FRF 560. LONDON, 15 May 1911, *Virgin of the Shipwrecked* (1885) GBP 54; *Sacred Tree* (1884) GBP 23; *Artist* (1884) GBP 31. LONDON, 11 Feb 1976, *Divo Imperator* (1896, oil on canvas, 18 x 43½ ins / 46 x 110.5 cm) GBP 450. LONDON, 22 July 1977, *Venetian Wedding* (1885, oil on canvas, 22 x 55 ins / 56 x 139.5 cm) GBP 2,500. LONDON, 15 June 1979, *Pensive Beauty* (oil on canvas, 25¾ x 15½ ins / 65.4 x 39.3 cm) GBP 480. ROME, 19 May 1981, *Marshland Landscape with Young Girl* (1889, oil on canvas, 35¾ x 78¾ ins / 91 x 200 cm) ITL 7,200,000. LONDON, 27 March 1984, *In the Library* (1884, oil on canvas, 22¾ x 32 ins / 58 x 81 cm) GBP 12,000. MONTEVIDEO, 14 Aug 1986, *In the Sacristy* (oil on panel, 9¾ x 8¼ ins / 25 x 21 cm) UYU 710,000. LONDON, 26 Feb 1988, *Young Girl in the Woods* (oil on panel, 5½ x 3½ ins / 14 x 9 cm) GBP 880. ROME, 25 May 1988, *Lake Landscape* (oil on canvas, 30¾ x 23½ ins / 78 x 60 cm) ITL 4,000,000. LONDON, 24 June 1988, *Inundated Ruins* (oil on canvas, 19¾ x 33½ ins / 50 x 85 cm) GBP 3,300. LONDON, 23 Nov 1988, *Wooded Landscape with Ruins and a Pond* (1900, oil on canvas, 27¼ x 41¼ ins / 69 x 105 cm) GBP 2,420. LONDON, 17 Feb 1989, *Ruins at Twilight* (oil on canvas, 37¾ x 30 ins / 96 x 76 cm) GBP 4,620. PARIS, 12 May 1989, *Leo XIII Conducting His First Vatican Mass* (1888, oil on canvas, 16¼ x 26¼ ins / 41.5 x 66.5 cm) FRF 62,000. ROME, 14 Dec 1989, *Small Altar in the Marshes* (oil on canvas, 23¼ x 37½ ins / 59 x 95 cm) ITL 6,900,000. LONDON, 15 Feb 1990, *Admirers* (1885, oil on canvas, 29¼ x 47 ins / 74 x 119.5 cm) GBP 9,900. BERN, 12 May 1990, *Courtesan* (oil on canvas, 28 x 20½ ins / 71 x 52 cm) CHF 5,000. ROME, 31 May 1990, *Lake Landscape* (oil on canvas, 9¾ x 6¼ ins / 24.8 x 15.8 cm) ITL 1,300,000. PARIS, 13 June 1990, *On the Edge of the Pond* (1887, oil on canvas, 10¼ x 16½ ins / 26 x 42 cm) FRF 21,000. ROME, 16 April 1991, *Lakeside Terrace* (oil on canvas, 19¾ x 38¼ ins / 50 x 97 cm) ITL 14,950,000. PARIS, 28 June 1991, *Leo XIII Conducting His First Vatican Mass* (oil on canvas/panel, 26 x 16¼ ins / 66 x 41 cm) FRF 15,000. PARIS, 20 Nov 1991, *Woman at Prayer* (1894, oil on canvas, 32 x 22½ ins / 81 x 57 cm) FRF 11,000. MADRID, 16 June 1992, *Landscape* (oil on panel, 15¼ x 10¼ ins / 39 x 26 cm) ESP 250,000. ROME, 19 Nov 1992, *Fisherman's Hut on Stilts on the Banks of a River* (1890, oil on canvas, 59 x 35½ ins / 150 x 90 cm) ITL 5,520,000. NEW YORK, 15 Oct 1993, *Marsh Landscape at Twilight* (1888, oil on canvas, 44 x 117¾ ins / 111.8 x 299.1 cm) USD 8,050. ROME, 5 Dec 1995, *Reflections in the Water* (oil on canvas, 20½ x 39¼ ins / 52 x 100 cm) ITL 4,125,000. NEW YORK, 2 April 1996, *Evening Reverie* (oil on canvas, 24 x 47¼ ins / 61 x 120 cm) USD 5,750. ROME, 23 May 1996, *Sunset over the Marshes* (oil on canvas, 23½ x 39¼ ins / 60 x 100 cm) ITL 5,750,000. LONDON, 31 Oct 1996, *Fishermen's Boats in a Stormy Sea* (1893, oil on canvas, 33¾ x 30 ins / 86 x 76 cm) GBP 2,415. LONDON, 20 Oct 1998, *The Cardinal's Visit* (1892, oil on panel, 13 x 10 ins / 33 x 25 cm) GBP 7,500. LONDON, 26 March 1999, *Gondola* (1885, oil on canvas, 22 x 55 ins / 56 x 140 cm) GBP 23,000. LONDON, 12 Oct 2000, *Discussions in Library* (1886, oil on panel, 6 x 8 ins / 15 x 20 cm) GBP 5,000. MADRID, 20 March 2001, *Meeting in the Library* (1886, oil on panel, 6 x 8 ins / 15 x 20 cm) ESP 1,600,000. MADRID, 19 June 2001, *Italian Lagoons* (oil on canvas, 24 x 52 ins / 61 x 131 cm) ESP 1,300,000. MADRID, 18 Dec 2002, *Lagoons in Italy* (oil on canvas, 24 x 52 ins / 60 x 131 cm) EUR 7,500. MADRID, 21 Jan 2003, *Travelling Musicians* (oil on canvas, 35 x 50 ins / 89 x 127 cm) EUR 16,000. MADRID, 16 Dec 2003, *St Mary of Ripoll* (oil on canvas,

44 x 24 ins / 113 x 61 cm) EUR 11,000. MUNICH, 17 March 2004, *Ruins by Marsh* (oil on canvas, 22 x 41 ins / 56 x 105 cm) EUR 4,000.

SERRA Y GISBERT, Jaime
Spanish, 19th century.
Born 5 January 1854, in San Ginés de Vilasar; died 28 September 1877, in Barcelona.
Draughtsman, art writer. Architectural views.
Decorative models.

Jaime Serra y Gisbert published models for decorative design.

SERRA Y MIS, Pascual
Spanish, 19th century.
Born in Mataró.
Active during the second half of the 19th century.
Engraver (burin).

Pascual Serra y Mis was a pupil of J. Coromina and J. Adam. He exhibited in Madrid from 1871.

SERRA Y PORSÓN, José
Spanish, 19th century.
Born 1824 or 1828, in Rome, of Spanish parents; died 1910, in Barcelona.
Painter (gouache), watercolourist, draughtsman.
Portraits, genre scenes, interiors with figures, still-lifes (flowers/fruit).

José Serra y Porsón began to study as an artist in Rome before joining the school of fine arts in Madrid. In 1855 he moved to Paris and trained at the studio of William Adolphe Bouguereau. However, his real master was Meissonier, which explains José Serra's introduction of the 'tableautin' or small picture to Spain. He exhibited regularly at the exhibition of the national fine arts society of Madrid and was awarded a bronze medal in 1864. He also exhibited at the Barcelona fine arts exhibitions.

Serra y Porsón painted mainly small genre pieces in the Romantic style characteristic of the 19th-century Catalan School. His works include: *The Artist at Work*; *In Watteau's Studio*; *Studying the Picture*; *The Mysterious Marquis de St Germain*; *Fruit*; *Wildflowers*; and *Duck and Partridge*.

BIBLIOGRAPHY:
Arnáiz, José Manuel/López Jiménez, Javier/Merchán Díaz, Manuel (ed.), *'Cien años de pintura en Espana y Portugal (1830-1930)'* in vol. X, Antiqvaria, Madrid, 1993.

MUSEUMS AND GALLERIES:
BARCELONA (Mus. Nacional d'Art de Catalunya): *A Man from Naples*.

AUCTION RECORDS:
LONDON, 22 June 1988, *The Artist at Work* (1896, oil on panel, 12 1/2 x 9 ins / 31.5 x 23 cm) GBP 3,850. LONDON, 17 Feb 1989, *The Artist's Studio* (1882, oil on panel, 13 1/2 x 10 1/4 ins / 34.3 x 26 cm) GBP 4,950. MADRID, 21 Dec 1999, *Artist's Studio* (1882, oil on panel, 13 x 10 ins / 34 x 26 cm) ESP 550,000. MADRID, 25 Sept 2001, *Painter's Studio* (1882, oil on board, 13 x 10 ins / 34 x 26 cm) ESP 800,000. GRAVENHAGE, 24 April 2002, *Interior with Mother and Child* (1883, oil on canvas, 10 x 8 ins / 26 x 20 cm) EUR 3,000. MADRID, 23 Sept 2002, *Sweet Motherhood* (1883, oil on board, 11 x 9 ins / 29 x 22 cm) EUR 4,750. CALAIS, 16 March 2003, *Suitor Dreaming* (oil on panel, 5 x 4 ins / 13 x 9 cm) EUR 2,400. MADRID, 23 Sept 2003, *Book Lover* (indian ink and gouache, 4 x 3 ins / 11 x 8 cm) EUR 2,750.

SERRA-ZANETTI, Gaetano
Italian, 19th century.
Born 1 May 1807, in Sant'Agata; died 6 March 1862, in Anzola d'Emilia.
Painter.

A pupil of Filippo Pedrini and C. Albesi, Gaetano Serra-Zanetti executed works for churches in Bologna.

MUSEUMS AND GALLERIES:
BOLOGNA (Pinacoteca Nazionale): *Ezzelino da Romano*.

SERRA-ZANETTI, Paola
Italian, 20th century.
Born 5 February 1886, in Budrio (Emilia Romagna).
Painter. Portraits.

Paola Serra-Zanetti studied with Domenico Ferri in Bologna and with Feldbauer in Munich.

SERRACHIONE, Antonio, or Serrachioli
Italian, 17th century.
Born 1611, in Massa Carrara.
Sculptor.

Serrachione worked in Naples from 1636 onwards.

SERRAF, Luc Élysée
French, 20th century.
Born 2 September 1936, in Algiers; died 25 September 1998.
Active in France.
Painter (gouache), draughtsman, sculptor. Landscapes, seascapes.

Luc Élysée Serraf was a student at the school of fine arts in Algiers. He lived and worked in Aubagne. After a Pointillist period that verged on Abstraction, his work developed a representational style that extolled the colours of Provence and, from 1977, of Brittany. From 1969 he showed his works in solo exhibitions in Marseilles and the surrounding area, and in 1988 at the Fondation Vasarely in Aix-en-Provence.

Luc. Élysée SERRAF

MUSEUMS AND GALLERIES:
BOULOGNE-BILLANCOURT (Mus. des Années 1930) - CHÂTEAU-CHINON - LAVAL - MARSEILLES (FRAC Provence-Alpes-Côte d'Azur) - NICE (Mus. d'Art Moderne et d'Art Contemporain).

SERRAILLE, Pierrette
French, 20th - 21st century.
Born 1952, in Lyons.
Engraver, draughtsman.

Pierrette Serraille lives and works in Oullins in the Nord region of France. Examples of her work featured in *De Bonnard à Baselitz - Dix Ans d'enrichissements du cabinet des estampes 1978-1988* (*From Bonnard to Baselitz: A Decade of Acquisitions by the Prints Collection 1978-1988*), an exhibition held in 1993 at the Bibliothèque Nationale in Paris.

MUSEUMS AND GALLERIES:
PARIS (BNF, Prints Collection): *Cyprus* (1986, etching, soft varnish and roller).

SERRALUNGA, Luigi
Italian, 20th century.
Born October 1880, in Turin; died 1940.
Painter. Portraits, still-lifes.

Luigi Serralunga was a pupil of Giacomo Grosso.

AUCTION RECORDS:
MILAN, 6 Nov 1980, *Flowers* (oil on board, 21 3/4 x 30 ins / 55.5 x 76 cm) ITL 1,000,000. NEW YORK, 23 May 1985, *Recumbent Nude* (1917, oil on canvas, 27 1/2 x 66 1/2 ins / 70 x 169 cm) USD 11,000. MILAN, 14 March 1989, *Still-life with Fruit and Flowers* (oil on canvas, 12 1/4 x 15 1/4 ins / 31 x 39 cm) ITL 3,400,000. ROME, 12 Dec 1989, *Portrait of a Woman* (oil on canvas, 28 3/4 x 23 1/2 ins / 73 x 60 cm) ITL 3,400,000. TURIN, 21 March 2000, *Vase of Roses* (oil on board, 19 x 28 ins / 49 x 70 cm) ITL 6,400,000. TURIN, 10 Dec 2002, *Vase with Mimosas* (oil on canvas, 31 x 36 ins / 80 x 91 cm) EUR 2,150. TURIN, 1 Oct 2003, *Vase of Tulips* (oil on board, 30 x 22 ins / 75 x 57 cm)

EUR 1,800. MILAN, 9 Dec 2003, *Vase of Flowers* (oil on canvas, 32 x 21 ins / 81 x 54 cm) EUR 1,800. MILAN, 24 March 2004, *Flowers* (1916, oil on board, 39 x 31 ins / 100 x 80 cm) EUR 3,300.

SERRANIA, Cristóbal
Spanish, 18th century.
Active in Alcora in 1750.
Painter (porcelain).

SERRANIA, Vicente
Spanish, 18th century.
Active from 1728 to 1743.
Painter (porcelain).
Vicente Serrania worked at the Alcora porcelain works.

SERRANO, Diego
Spanish, 15th century.
Painter.
Diego Serrano worked in Naples in 1457.

SERRANO, Emanuele
Italian, 19th century.
Born in Chieti (Abruzzi).
Sculptor.
Emanuele Serrano exhibited in Turin, Milan, Florence and Paris.

SERRANO, Guillermo
Puerto Rican, 20th century.
Painter, engraver, lithographer.
Work by Guillermo Serrana was included in the 1992 exhibition *De Bonnard à Baselitz - Dix ans d'enrichissements du cabinet des estampes 1978-1988* (*From Bonnard to Baselitz: A Decade of Acquisitions by the Prints Collection 1978-1988*) at the Bibilothèque Nationale in Paris. He had a solo exhibition in 1975 at the Galleria de las Americas de San Juan in Puerto Rico.
MUSEUMS AND GALLERIES:
PARIS (BNF, Prints Collection): *Composition in Shades of Blue* (1975, lithograph).

SERRANO, Juan
Spanish, 16th century.
Active in Seville from 1502 to 1506.
Painter.
Juan Serrano worked for various churches in Seville.

SERRANO, Juan
Spanish, 20th century.
Also active in France.
Sculptor.
Equipo 57 group.
Whilst he was living in Paris between 1954 and 1961, Juan Serrano founded Equipo 57 with Agustín Ibarrola, Juan Cuenca and Àngel and José Duarte. This group was very active until its dissolution in 1965. Serrano participated in all the Equipo 57 exhibitions. In 1993, the Museo Centro de Arte Reina Sofía in Madrid organized a retrospective of the group. This was followed in 1996 by another retrospective organized by the two Denise René galleries in Paris.
BIBLIOGRAPHY:
Equipo 57, exhibition catalogue, Museo Nacional Centro de Arte Reina Sofía, Madrid, 1993 (text in Spanish and English). Mérite, Pierre, '*Equipo 57*' in *Art Press* n° 217, periodical, Paris, October 1996.

SERRANO, Lucas
Spanish, 17th century.
Active from 1661 to 1671.
Sculptor.
Lucas Serrano executed the carvings that decorate the high altar of the cathedral of Santiago de Compostela.

SERRANO, Manuel
Mexican, 19th century.
Born 1814; died 1883.
Painter. Local scenes.
Manuel Serrano specialised in the depiction of Mexican country life.
AUCTION RECORDS:
NEW YORK, 27 Nov 1985, *Horse and Rider* (oil on canvas, 25 3/4 x 20 1/4 ins / 65.5 x 51.5 cm) USD 2,500. NEW YORK, 17 May 1994, *Gauchos Lassoing Horses* (oil on canvas, 16 1/2 x 20 ins / 41.9 x 51.1 cm) USD 79,500. NEW YORK, 24-25 Nov 1997, *Pulques Finos* (oil on canvas, 18 x 23 3/4 ins / 45.7 x 60.4 cm) USD 57,500. PARIS, 5 March 1998, *The Inn Kitchen* (oil on canvas, 18 x 23 1/2 ins / 46 x 60 cm) FRF 165,000.

SERRANO, Manuel Gonzalez.
See **GONZÁLEZ-SERRANO Manuel**

SERRANO, Pablo
Spanish, 20th century.
Born 1908, in Crivillen (Aragon); died 1989, in Madrid.
Sculptor. Figures, portraits, animals.
Pablo Serrano studied at the Academia de Bellas Artes in Barcelona, then spent several years in Argentina and Uruguay, where he was a junior lecturer at the University of Montevideo. Up until 1950, his art derived from a Figurative-Expressionist vision which he was able to sustain through various commissions for monuments and portraits of well-known figures such as the *Monument to Miguel de Unamuno* for Salamanca of around 1967 and the *Mask of Antonio Machado* of 1966. He then produced abstract constructions from oxidized iron. Around 1955-1960, he worked the metal into elaborate forms in the tradition of the Russian Constructivists, making careful use of the natural suppleness of specific materials. He progressed to experiment with iron and wood combinations, opposing informality and geometry.

Serrano participated in various collective exhibitions including: Stedelijk Museum, Amsterdam (1968); Museum of Modern Art, New York (1960 and 1967); Venice Biennale (1962); Bochum, Nuremberg and Kunstverein in Berlin (1968); Boymans van Beuningen Museum, Rotterdam and Antwerp (1969); Second Salon of the Galeries Pilotes, Cantonal Museum, Lausanne (1970); Guggenheim Foundation, New York (1985). He gained various awards including: Grand Prix, the Second Hispano-American Biennale, Barcelona (1954); gold medals in Lisbon and Saragossa (1980).
BIBLIOGRAPHY:
IIIe Salon international des Galeries Pilotes, exhibition catalogue, Musée cantonal, Lausanne, 1970. *Catálogo nacional de arte contemporáneo 1990-1991*, Ibérico 2Mil, Barcelona, 1990-1991.
AUCTION RECORDS:
NEW YORK, 14 Dec 1976, *Figure* (patinated bronze, h. 11 1/2 ins / 29.3 cm) USD 450. LONDON, 23 Feb 1989, *Untitled* (bronze, h. 20 ins / 51 cm) GBP 1,210. ROME, 17 April 1989, *Bovids* (1910, bronze, 19 3/4 x 18 x 9 ins / 50 x 46 x 22 cm) ITL 14,000,000. MADRID, 23 March 1999, *Hierros Encontrados y Soldatos* (1957, sculpture, 20 x 10x9 ins / 50 x 25x23 cm) ESP 800,000. MADRID, 19 Feb 2001, *Goya* (1959, bronze, h. 17 ins / 42 cm) ESP 1,800,000. MADRID, 9 April 2002, *Untitled* (bronze, 22 x 19x17 ins / 56 x 47x42 cm) EUR 5,500. MADRID, 25 March 2003, *Bull Scene* (bronze, 7 x 9x12 ins / 19 x 22x31 cm) EUR 2,000. MADRID, 25 March 2003, *Homage to Picasso* (brown-patinated bronze, h. 12 ins / 30 cm) EUR 4,000. MADRID, 26 Jan 2004, *Untitled* (stone and iron, h. 24 ins / 61 cm) EUR 19,000. MADRID, 14 Sept 2004, *Guitar 13* (bronze with iron base, 10 x 10x8 ins / 25 x 25x21 cm) EUR 6,000.

SERRANO, Pedro
Spanish, 17th century.
Active in the middle of the 17th century.
Sculptor (wood).
Working in collaboration with A. de Ortega, Pedro Serrano carved the archbishop's throne at Toledo Cathedral.

SERRÃO, Domingos Vieira
Portuguese, 17th century.
Born in Tomar; died 1645, in Tomar.
Painter, draughtsman.
Domingos Vieira Serrão worked for the church of the Holy Cross in Coimbra and for the Retiro Palace in Madrid. He also made drawings for line engravings.

SERRAO, Luella Varney
American, 19th - 20th century.
Born 11 August 1865, in Angola (New York); died after 1935.
Sculptor. Statues, busts.
Luella Serrao lived and worked in Cleveland.

SERRARIUS, Anton
German, 16th - 17th century.
Died 1632.
Active in Frankfurt am Main in 1598.
Painter. Portraits, interiors.

SERRAT, Jaime
Spanish, 15th - 16th century.
Active in Saragossa from 1492 to 1514.
Painter.
Jaime Serrat painted altarpieces for a number of churches in Catalonia.

SERRATE, José Antonio
Spanish, 20th century.
Of Portuguese origin; died 1911, in Murcia.
Painter.
José Antonio Serrate worked in Murcia. The museum there holds some of his paintings.

SERRATI, Mattia (Fra)
Italian, 16th century.
Active in Consandolo (Emilia Romagna) c. 1505.
Miniaturist.
Fra Mattia Serrati worked at the monastery of S Bartolo near Ferrara. Libanori speaks warmly of his talent.

SERRAZ, Michel
French, 20th century.
Born 1925, in Paris.
Sculptor. Figures, religious subjects. Busts.
Michel Serraz was a pupil at the École des Beaux-Arts in Paris. His teacher from 1947 to 1948 was Marcel Gimond. He worked in wood and stone, creating architectural decorations for the church at Deuil, low relief sculpture, reliefs in copper, sculptures and busts. He was always careful to integrate his work into the everyday architecture at the heart of the city.

He exhibited at the Salon d'Automne, of which he was a member, and at the Société Nationale des Beaux-Arts in Paris, where he won the sculpture prize in 1965. He also took part in the Biennale Formes Humaines at the Musée Rodin, in the Salon Comparaisons, Salon de la Jeune Sculpture, Salon de Dessin and, in public exhibitions: 1964, Galerie Vendôme in Paris; 1966, Musée de St Denis; 1970, *René Iché and Great Sculptors of His Time* at the Musée de Narbonne.
BIBLIOGRAPHY:
René Iché et grands sculpteurs contemporains, exhibition catalogue, Musée de Narbonne, Narbonne, 1970.
MUSEUMS AND GALLERIES:
MAUBEUGE: *Bust of Monsignor Fontenelle*.

SERRE, Alexandre, or Serres
French, 19th century.
Born c. 1850, in Toulouse.
Painter. History painting, mythological subjects, genre scenes, portraits.
A pupil of Jules Garipuy at the École des Beaux-Arts in Toulouse, Alexandre Serre exhibited at the Paris Salon then at the Salon des Artistes Français from 1878.
MUSEUMS AND GALLERIES:
TOULOUSE: *Orpheus and Eurydice*.

SERRE, Charles de
French, 19th century.
Active in Paris during the second half of the 19th century.
Sculptor.
Charles de Serre was a pupil of Girardon.

SERRE, Claude
French, 20th century.
Born 1938, in Sucy-en-Brie; died 13 November 1998.
Draughtsman, engraver.
Claude Serre lived and worked in Lesigny. Mainly an engraver, he also did humorous drawings. In 1992 his work was included in the exhibition *De Bonnard à Baselitz - Dix Ans d'enrichissements du cabinet des estampes 1978-1988* (*From Bonnard to Baselitz: A Decade of Acquisitions by the Prints Collection 1978-1988*) at the Bibliothèque Nationale in Paris.
MUSEUMS AND GALLERIES:
PARIS (BNF, Prints Collection): *Spring* (1978).

SERRE, Denis
French, 20th - 21st century.
Born 1953, in Rabat, Morocco.
Painter, engraver.
Denis Serre spent 1991 at the Künstlerhaus (Artists' House) in Edenkoben. He now lives and works in Lyons. His work ranges across various painting movements, from the figurative (nudes and religious subjects) to the abstract (Minimalism, Expressionism).

He has shown examples of his work at group exhibitions: in 1980 and 1983, at ELAC (Espace Lyonnais d'Art Contemporain) in Lyons and at the FIAC (Foire Internationale d'Art Contemporain) in Paris; in 1986 and 1988, at the Galerie Regards in Paris; in 1988, at the Centre d'Art in St-Priest; in 1990, at the Centre d'Art in Villefranche-sur-Saône; in 1991, at the Centre d'Art International in Mulhouse, the Künstlerhaus in Edenkoben, and at Crédac (Ivry-sur-Seine); in 1994, at the Espace Cordeliers in Lyons; and, in 2004, at the École d'art Gérard Jacot in Belfort.
BIBLIOGRAPHY:
Denis Serre, exhibition catalogue, Crédac centre d'Art contemporain, Ivry-sur-Seine, 1991. Ainardi, Dolène, "*Promenades*' in *Art Press* n° 163, periodical, Paris, November 1991.
MUSEUMS AND GALLERIES:
BOURG-EN-BRESSE (Mus. de Brou) - PARIS (BNF, Prints Collection): *Untitled I* (1987, lithograph) - PARIS (FNAC).

SERRÉ, Gérard
Flemish School, 18th century.
Active in Tournai in 1720.
Painter.
Gérard Serré painted a portrait of *Charles VI* for the city of Tournai.

SERRE, Jean Adam
Swiss, 18th century.
Born 10 November 1704, in Geneva; died 22 March 1788, in Geneva.
Painter, miniaturist.

SERRE, Léopold
French, 19th century.
Died 1890.
Painter. Scenes with figures, genre scenes, landscapes.
Serre worked in Villay. He exhibited at the Salon des Artistes Français in Paris.
MUSEUMS AND GALLERIES:
BOURGES: *Château de Cutan*.

Auction records:
Paris, 23 June 1943, *Countrygirl from the Bourbonnais on her way to the Well,* FRF 1,000.

SERRE, Michel or Miguel, or Serra
French, 17th - 18th century.
Born 10 January 1658, in Tarragona; died 10 October 1733, in Marseilles.
Painter. History painting.

Michel Serre started to study painting at an early age in Marseilles and then moved to Rome. At the age of 17 he was back in Marseilles painting a *Martyrdom of St Peter* in the church of the Dominican friars. Given the age of Serre, this work was a clear measure of his talent and earned him a great number of commissions. On 20 August 1693 he was appointed painter to the king's galley ships, replacing Lecomte who had recommended him. On 6 December 1704 he became a member of the Académie Royale de Peinture in Paris. In order to secure his election, Serre had gone to the capital. He opened a studio there and taught Oudry, whom he sought to entice back to Marseilles. During the 1721 plague epidemic, Serre showed great compassion to the poor and sick and gave away part of his wealth. After the epidemic and though he was nearing 70, he resumed work and painted several scenes of the dark times he had just lived through. He fell foul of the Académie for charging people to view one of these paintings. He was struck off on 21 August 1723, being in breach of the illustrious company's rules, but was reinstated after making amends on 30 October of that year. Serre painted chiefly for the convent of Ste Claire, for the basilica of Ste Marie-Madeleine in St-Maximin-la-Ste-Baume, and for the Carmelites in Aix. His easel paintings are numerous.

Museums and Galleries:
Caen: *Bacchus and Ariadne* - Marseilles: *The Plague in Marseilles; Portrait of the Artist's Wife and Children*; nearly 30 other paintings.

SERRE, Paul Louis Alfred
French, 19th century.
Born in Paris.
Painter, enameller.

A pupil of Pierre Piot and of E. Levasseur, Paul Serre made his debut at the 1869 Salon.

SERRÉ, Yvonne . See **SERMAYER**

SERREAU, Fernand Abel
French, 20th century.
Born 4 September 1885, in Châtellerault (Vienne).
Miniaturist.

Fernand Serreau was a pupil of Bonnet and Luc-Olivier Merson. He was director of the École des Beaux-Arts in Poitiers, and exhibited in Paris at the Salon des Artistes Français from 1907.

SERRERO, Raoul
French, 20th century.
Born in Tiaret, Algeria.
Painter. Flowers.

Raoul Serrero, originally a doctor, taught himself art during his travels in Macedonia, in the East, Germany, Austria, Italy, Switzerland and Spain. He has exhibited in Paris at the Salon d'Automne, the Salon des Indépendants, the Salonde l'Afrique Française, and at Oran, Milan, Paris, and Luxembourg. He has also exhibited privately.

Museums and Galleries:
Mulhouse (MBA): *Flowers* - Oran.

SERRES, Alexandre. See **SERRE**

SERRES, Antony
French, 19th century.
Born 13 February 1828, in Bordeaux; died 1898.
Painter. History painting, genre scenes.

Antony Serres made his debut at the 1859 Salon and became a Member of the Société des Artistes Français.

Museums and Galleries:
Bordeaux: *Tympanistria; Judgement of Joan of Arc.*

Auction records:
Paris, 1882, *Unexpected Return,* FRF 520. Paris, 25 Feb 1901, *Wedding Feast of Pierrot and Columbine,* FRF 105. Paris, 21 Feb 1919, *Lady Bathers Surprised,* FRF 380. Paris, 12 March 1941, *Bathers in the Glade,* FRF 350. Paris, 10 Nov 1944, *Bringing In the Harvest,* FRF 850. Paris, 23 March 1945, *Meeting in the Forest,* FRF 6,100. Paris, 9 July 1945, *Washerwomen,* FRF 1,750. Paris, July 1946, *Farmgirl,* FRF 3,100; *Washerwoman,* FRF 2,600. Paris, 2 Dec 1946, *Washerwomen,* FRF 6,500. Paris, 30 April 1947, *Woman in an Interior,* FRF 2,000. Paris, 25 April 1949, *Shepherdess; Beggar* (two pendants) FRF 5,000. Paris, 10 May 1950, *Woman on a Sofa,* FRF 3,000. Paris, 9 April 1951, *Parish Priest Out for a Walk,* FRF 4,900. London, 11 Feb 1976, *The School Road* (oil on panel, 13 3/4 x 11 ins / 35 x 27 cm) GBP 600. Versailles, 10 June 1979, *Young Girl Dressing* (oil on canvas, 55 x 43 1/4 ins / 140 x 110 cm) FRF 7,800. Copenhagen, 12 Nov 1986, *Venus and Cupid* (oil on canvas, 55 x 41 1/4 ins / 140 x 105 cm) DKK 48,000. Calais, 24 March 1996, *Les Incroyables* (oil on panel, 13 3/4 x 21 ins / 35 x 53.4 cm) GBP 2,200. Paris, 17 Dec 2001, *Arab and his Horse* (oil on panel, 30 x 14 ins / 75 x 36 cm) FRF 88,000. Lund, 16 Nov 2002, *Children with Bird's Nest and Dog* (oil on canvas, 45 x 42 ins / 114 x 106 cm) SEK 45,000. Helsinki, 29 Nov 2003, *The Audience* (oil on canvas, 13 x 16 ins / 32 x 40 cm) EUR 3,600. Neuilly, 6 Oct 2004, *Gallant Scene* (1859, oil on canvas, 16 x 13 ins / 41 x 33 cm) EUR 3,800.

SERRES, Dominique or Dominic, the Elder
French, 18th century.
Born 1722, in Auch; died 6 November 1793, in London.
Painter, watercolourist, draughtsman. Military subjects, seascapes.

Dominique Serres was earmarked by his parents for the priesthood, but this did not appeal to the young man and so he ran off to sea. He was in command of a merchantman captured by the English in 1752 and was brought to London, where he quickly made a name for himself as a painter of seascapes and naval engagements. When the Royal Academy was founded in 1768 Serres was immediately admitted to membership. A few years later King George II retained him as an official naval artist to the Crown. In 1792 Serres was appointed to the post of librarian at the Royal Academy. He exhibited at the Academy on a regular basis.

Museums and Galleries:
Bristol: *First Engagement off the Coast of Sadras; Second Engagement: Off the Ceylon Coast; Fourth Naval Engagement: Off Trincomalee; Fifth Engagement: Off the Portonovo Coast* - Dublin: *View near Torquay* (watercolour) - London (Victoria and Albert Mus.): *Mountain Regions; Village by the Sea; Near Totnes, Devon* (watercolour) - Manchester: *In the Deep* (watercolour).

Auction records:
London, 5 Feb 1910, *Warship Entering Plymouth Harbour,* GBP 7. London, 17 Dec 1926, *View of Quebec and the Attack by General Wolfe; Against the French* (collection) GBP 504. London, 24 Jan 1928, *English Fleet at Anchor,* GBP 399. London, 13 July 1928, *Capture of 'Télémaque' by 'Experiment',* GBP 220. London, 22 Nov 1928, *Vessels off the Dover Coast,* GBP 451. London, 1 Feb 1929, *Maid of Calais,* GBP 294. London, 15 March 1929, *Vessels Discharging a Salvo,* GBP 152. London, 3 May 1929, *Vessels in sight of Plymouth,* GBP 325. London, 13 May 1931, *Sir G. Collier Destroying the American Fleet,* GBP 680. London, 5 April 1935, *Bombardment of Martinique,* GBP 147. London, 25 Feb 1938, *Quebec; General Wolfe to the Attack* (collection) GBP 273. London, 26 July

1940, *The Taking of St Lucia,* GBP 178; *Gorée Island taken from the French,* GBP 178. London, 14 Dec 1945, *Vessels off Belle-Isle,* GBP 131. London, 14 Feb 1951, *Expedition to Havana* (1763) GBP 76. Paris, 2 Dec 1954, *Estuary,* FRF 230,000. London, 31 July 1963, *Commodore James of the 'Protector' with 'Guardian' and 'Bombay Grab',* GBP 400. London, 7 July 1965, *Attack on Moro Castle,* GBP 550. London, 23 Nov 1966, *Seascape,* GBP 1,000. London, 17 Nov 1967, *Frigate Leaving Shore,* Gns 800. London, 3 April 1968, *Warship; 'Victory' at Gibraltar,* GBP 3,500. London, 20 Nov 1970, *View of Plymouth Harbour,* Gns 9,500. London, 10 Dec 1971, *Fort Mahon, Minorca,* Gns 6,000. London, 22 June 1973, *Nelson Reviewing the Fleet,* Gns 7,000. London, 20 March 1974, *Sailing Vessels at Sea* (1780) GBP 4,500. London, 14 July 1976, *Warships at Plymouth* (oil on canvas, 18 1/4 x 33 1/4 ins / 46.5 x 84.5 cm) GBP 1,400. London, 24 June 1977, *Vessels off Gibraltar* (1791, oil on panel, 8 1/2 x 57 ins / 21.6 x 144.8 cm) GBP 5,200. London, 23 March 1979, *Sailing Ships in Rough Seas* (oil on canvas, 29 1/2 x 39 ins / 75 x 99 cm) GBP 2,200. London, 18 March 1980, *Yachts and Fishing Boats drawn up on a Beach* (watercolour and pen, 6 1/2 x 9 ins / 16.5 x 22.8 cm) GBP 1,400. London, 26 June 1981, *Capture of Belle-Isle, 1761* (oil on canvas, series of six, each 14 1/4 x 20 1/4 ins / 36.2 x 51.5 cm) GBP 35,000. New York, 20 April 1983, *English Squadron off Gibraltar* (1770, oil on canvas, 41 x 51 1/2 ins / 104 x 131 cm) USD 7,000. Rome, 20 Nov 1984, *Vessels off the Lisbon Coast* (1779, watercolour and pen, 12 1/2 x 22 1/4 ins / 31.6 x 56.3 cm) GBP 2,200. London, 19 March 1985, *Vessels off the Kent Coast* (1777, watercolour and pen, 12 1/4 x 19 1/2 ins / 31.2 x 49.7 cm) GBP 2,200. London, 18 April 1986, *Siege of Havana on August 14, Two Days prior to the Surrender* (1767, oil on canvas, 32 1/4 x 44 ins / 82.2 x 111.7 cm) GBP 48,000. London, 14 April 1988, *Drover on a Path near a Thatched Cottage in the Woods* (1762, oil on canvas, 12 1/4 x 14 ins / 30.8 x 35.6 cm) GBP 3,300. New York, 10 Jan 1990, *Vice-Admiral Samuel Hood on the Flagship 'Victory' and the English Fleet off Gibraltar in Summer 1790* (oil on canvas, 34 x 17 1/4 ins / 86.5 x 43.5 cm) USD 38,500. London, 14 March 1990, *'Eole', 'Pallas' and 'Brilliant' off the Isle of Man* (1765, oil on canvas, 9 3/4 x 14 3/4 ins / 25 x 37.5 cm) GBP 11,550. London, 20 July 1990, *Drover and Herd near a Thatched Cottage in a Wooded Landscape* (1762, oil on canvas, 12 x 14 ins / 30.5 x 35.5 cm) GBP 3,300. London, 8 April 1992, *Governor's Palace, Quebec; St Lawrence River and the Ruins of the Episcopal City of Quebec* (1760, oil on canvas, pair, each 13 ins / 33 cm 2 1/4 x 20 1/2 ins/6 x 52 cm) GBP 41,800. London, 14 July 1993, *Battle of the Saintes, April 12, 1782* (oil on canvas, 32 1/2 x 49 1/2 ins / 82.5 x 126 cm) GBP 17,250. London, 13 April 1994, *Lord Albemarle's Army Disembarking near Havana, 1762* (1763, oil on canvas, 15 1/4 x 24 1/2 ins / 39 x 62 cm) GBP 8,625. London, 12 April 1995, *Warships of the Royal Fleet: 'Phoenis', 'Roebuck' and 'Tartar' off Fort Washington and Fort Lee and under Fire from the Shore Batteries on the North River, October 9, 1776* (oil on canvas, 24 1/2 x 45 1/2 ins / 62.5 x 115.5 cm) GBP 67,500. London, 14 July 1999, *First Rate off Coast. First Rate Anchor in Bay* (1777, oil on copper, a pair, 6 x 7 ins / 15 x 19 cm) GBP 4,200. Leicester, 18 May 2000, *Captain Montagu of the Pearl Engaging the Spanish Frigate Sancta Monica off the Azores* (1781, oil on canvas, 23 x 35 ins / 58 x 89 cm) GBP 40,000. London, 15 June 2000, *Destruction of the Spanish Floating Batteries at Gibraltar at Night, 13 September 1782* (oil on canvas, 27 x 48 ins / 68 x 121 cm) GBP 15,000. New York, 24 Jan 2001, *Shipping at Portsmouth* (1768, pen and grey wash on paper laid on board, 9 x 19 ins / 22 x 48 cm) USD 2,000. London, 4 July 2001, *View from the Gun Wharf at Portsmouth* (1769, pen, grey ink and grey wash over pencil, 9 x 19 ins / 22 x 48 cm) GBP 4,400. London, 31 Oct 2002, *Squadron of the Red Arriving at their Anchorage* (1774, oil on panel, 11 x 17 ins / 29 x 42 cm) GBP 2,800. London, 22 Jan 2003, *Taking of Belle Isle, 1761, by Commodore Keppel and General Hodgson* (1762, oil on canvas, set of six, 15 x 20 ins / 37 x 52 cm) GBP 120,000. London, 10 Dec 2003, *Panoramic View of Lewes from the South East with Hunting Party* (oil on canvas, 35 x 72 ins / 90 x 182 cm) GBP 72,000. London, 11 June 2004, *View of Portsmouth Harbour with Man o'War and Other Vessels* (1777, oil on panel, 13 x 18 ins / 32 x 46 cm) GBP 23,000. London, 14 Sept 2004, *First Rate Flagship Preparing to Get Underway. Frigate Heaving-to* (1785, pen, ink and watercolour, a pair, 6 x 8 ins / 15 x 20 cm) GBP 5,000.

SERRES, Dominique or Dominic, the Younger

British, 18th century.
Born in England.
Painter, watercolourist, draughtsman. Portraits, landscapes.

Younger brother of Dominique Serres the Elder, Dominique Serres the Younger was known principally as a teacher of drawing and composition. Exhibited at the Royal Academy from 1783 to 1804. Towards the end of his career, Serres suffered a stroke and lodged near his brother John Thomas.

Auction records:

London, 7 Dec 1933, *River Mouth,* GBP 168; *Bay View,* GBP 199. London, 10 May 1939, *Cape of Good Hope* (drawing) GBP 30.

SERRES, Henri Charles de

French, 19th century.
Born 29 October 1823, in Paris; died 1883, in Paris.
Painter, draughtsman. Portraits, genre scenes, mythological subjects, landscapes, still-lifes (flowers).

Henri Charles Serres was a pupil of M. de Rudder; he made his debut at the 1846 Salon.

Museums and Galleries:

Coutances: *Basket of Autumn Flowers* - Rennes: *Basket of Pansies.*

Auction records:

Paris, 23 May 1941, *Fauns and Nymphs in the Forest* (1852) FRF 1,450.

SERRES, John Thomas, called Giovanni

British, 18th - 19th century.
Born December 1759, in London; died 28 December 1825, in London, in prison.
Painter, watercolourist, draughtsman. Seascapes, fishing scenes, harbour views, boats, naval battles.

John Thomas Serres studied under his father Dominique Serres the Elder. He taught drawing and composition at Chelsea Naval College. Serres visited France and Italy in 1790 before following in his father's footsteps in 1793 as naval artist to the Crown (and, concurrently, official Admiralty artist). He exhibited in London between 1780 and 1825, principally at the Royal Academy and the British Institution. He incurred serious debts and was sent to prison, where he died in 1825.

Museums and Galleries:

Bristol: *Fleet off the Coast of Malta* - London (Victoria and Albert Mus.): *Dublin Bay Light and the Yacht 'Dorset'*; six watercolours - Manchester: watercolour.

Auction records:

London, 28 Jan 1911, *Fulham* (1790) GBP 7. London, 26 May 1922, *Warship,* GBP 42. London, 27 June 1924, *Naval Battles* (two canvases) GBP 273. London, 11 June 1926, *Taking of Belle-Isle* (six paintings) GBP 199. London, 15 March 1929, *'Clyde' sinking 'Jason',* GBP 94. New York, 2 April 1943, *'Wasp' and 'Reindeer'* (four watercolours) USD 8,000. London, 31 March 1944, *River Thames and the Port of London,* GBP 357. London, 13 July 1945, *The Royal Yacht,* GBP 210. London, 3 June 1959, *English Fleet Hoisting Sail and Putting out to Sea,* GBP 200. London, 29 March 1963, *View of Naples and Mt Vesuvius,* Gns 280. London, 16 July 1965, *Seascape,*

Gns 350. LONDON, 15 March 1967, *Vessels off Gibraltar; Cape of Good Hope* (two pendants) GBP 1,550. LONDON, 15 Nov 1968, *Seascape*, Gns 1,900. LONDON, 20 Nov 1970, *Warships in Plymouth Harbour*, Gns 900. LONDON, 14 Dec 1971, *Vessels off the Coast* (watercolour on pen outlines) Gns 600. LONDON, 23 June 1972, *Fishermen's Return*, Gns 1,800. LONDON, 22 Nov 1974, *Bay of Naples*, Gns 400. LONDON, 31 March 1976, *Vessels in Genoa Harbour* (oil on canvas, 19 x 34 ins / 48.5 x 86.5 cm) GBP 2,300. LONDON, 25 Nov 1977, *River Thames at Westminster* (1811, oil on canvas, 23 x 33 1/2 ins / 58.3 x 85.1 cm) GBP 5,500. LONDON, 21 March 1979, *Boats on the River Dee* (1798, oil on canvas, 17 1/2 x 23 1/4 ins / 44.5 x 59 cm) GBP 3,800. LONDON, 10 July 1980, *Harbour Entrance, Plymouth* (1794, pen and watercolour, 8 1/4 x 13 3/4 ins / 21 x 35 cm) GBP 2,800. NEW YORK, 18 June 1982, *Battle of Trafalgar* (1824, oil on canvas, 30 x 41 3/4 ins / 76 x 106 cm) USD 12,000. LONDON, 6 July 1983, *English Warship in the Bay of Naples* (1823, oil on canvas, 23 1/4 x 35 1/4 ins / 59 x 89.5 cm) GBP 14,000. LONDON, 21 Nov 1985, *Boating on Virginia Water* (1825, watercolour/pencil outlines, 15 x 30 ins / 38 x 76 cm) GBP 1,600. LONDON, 9 July 1986, *Plymouth Sound* (1786, oil on panel, 14 1/4 x 20 1/2 ins / 36 x 52 cm) GBP 11,800. LONDON, 5 Oct 1989, *Vessels in a Rough Sea off Portland Bill with the Ruins of Weymouth Castle in the Background* (oil on canvas, 19 1/2 x 24 1/2 ins / 49.5 x 62 cm) GBP 3,850. LONDON, 30 May 1990, *Warship in Port* (1825, oil on canvas, 21 1/4 x 30 ins / 54 x 76 cm) GBP 15,400. LONDON, 10 April 1991, *Royal Yacht with George III and Queen Charlotte on Board, leaving Portsmouth to Inspect the Spils of the Glorious First of June* (oil on canvas, 14 1/4 x 22 ins / 36 x 56 cm) GBP 8,140. NEW YORK, 5 June 1992, *Port of Leith* (1825, oil on canvas, 20 x 38 ins / 50.8 x 96.5 cm) USD 11,550. LONDON, 3 Feb 1993, *Estuary Scene with Fishermen Landing their Catch* (oil on canvas, 22 1/2 x 26 3/4 ins / 57 x 68 cm) GBP 1,150. PERTH, 31 Aug 1993, *Port of Leigh* (1825, oil on canvas, 20 x 37 3/4 ins / 51 x 96 cm) GBP 8,050. LONDON, 9 Nov 1994, *Sailing off the Ferrol Coast, Spain* (1815, oil on canvas, 23 1/4 x 35 1/2 ins / 59 x 90 cm) GBP 3,680. NEW YORK, 12 Jan 1996, *View of Florence from the Arno River* (1799, oil on canvas, 19 3/4 x 25 1/2 ins / 50 x 65 cm) USD 23,000. NEW YORK, 17 Feb 1999, *Sir John Borlase Warren's Action with Bompart* (1799, oil on canvas, a pair, 24 x 36 ins / 60 x 91 cm) USD 65,000. LONDON, 13 May 1999, *English Frigate Amidst activity in Bay of Naples* (1823, oil on canvas, 32 x 48 ins / 81 x 122 cm) GBP 56,000. PARIS, 23 March 2000, *View of Livorno Harbour with Many Figures* (oil on canvas, 45 x 59 ins / 115 x 150 cm) FRF 130,000. PARIS, 30 June 2000, *View of the Harbour and Bay of Mahon, Menorca* (c. 1780, oil on canvas, 29 x 38 ins / 74 x 96 cm) FRF 300,000. LONDON, 11 Jan 2001, *River Mersey at Liverpool from the Wallasey Shoreline* (oil on canvas, 24 x 34 ins / 61 x 86 cm) GBP 7,000. LONDON, 24 May 2001, *British and Dutch Frigates Passing in a Heavy Swell* (1787, oil on panel, 15 x 21 ins / 38 x 54 cm) GBP 9,500. LONDON, 16 Jan 2002, *Genoese Frigate Leaving her Home Port* (1797, oil on canvas, 18 x 24 ins / 46 x 61 cm) GBP 16,000. NEW YORK, 29 July 2003, *Shipping off Plymouth from the Coast at Cawsand* (1800, watercolour and ink on board, 7 x 31 ins / 19 x 80 cm) USD 4,800. LONDON, 20 Nov 2003, *Port of Genoa* (pencil and watercolour, 13 x 17 ins / 32 x 44 cm) GBP 1,200. EXETER, 2 Nov 2004, *The Royal Admiral of London at Limehouse* (oil on canvas, 20 x 28 ins / 51 x 71 cm) GBP 7,000. LONDON, 11 Nov 2004, *Barges on a Canal, traditionally identified as the Grand Junction Canal* (1797, oil on canvas, 18 x 24 ins / 45 x 61 cm) GBP 3,000.

SERRES, Olivia, self-styled as Princess of Cumberland
British, 18th - 19th century.
Born 1772; died 21 November 1834.
Painter. Landscapes.

Olivia Serres was the wife of John Thomas Serres. She exhibited in London at the Royal Academy and the British Institution from 1793 to 1811. She claimed to be the illegitimate daughter of Henry Frederick, Duke of Cumberland and arrogated the title 'Princess of Cumberland' (her own father was a house painter named Wilton). Olivia's claim was heard (and rejected) by the House of Commons. Her eccentric ways and extravagance ultimately bankrupted her husband, who died in a debtor's prison.

SERRES, Provin
French, 19th century.
Born in Gaillac (Tarn).
Sculptor.

Provin Serres was a pupil of Moreau and was then entered the École des Beaux-Arts. He made his debut at the 1879 Salon and became a member of the Société de Artistes Français in 1893 and received an honourable mention in 1886.

SERRES, Raoul
20th century.
Painter. Landscapes.

MUSEUMS AND GALLERIES:
LIVERPOOL: *River Mersey*.

AUCTION RECORDS:
PARIS, 7 April 1995, *Mediterranean Landscape* (oil on panel, 22 x 32 1/4 ins / 55 x 82 cm) FRF 5,300.

SERRES, Raoul Jean
French, 19th century.
Born in Cazères-on-Garonne (Haute-Garonne).
Engraver, illustrator.

Raoul Serres was a pupil of J. Jacquet, Debouchet and Bonnat. A member of the Société des Artistes Français from 1906, his work was featured in this Group at the Salon; he received an honourable mention in 1898, a third class medal in 1906 and the Prix de Rome in 1906. He illustrated *La Pécheresse* by Henri de Régnier.

BIBLIOGRAPHY:
Cent-vingt ans de gravure toulousaine, exhibition catalogue, École des beaux-arts de Toulouse, Toulouse, 1982.

SERRET, Charles Emmanuel
French, 19th century.
Born 1824, in Aubenas (Ardèche); died 1900, in Paris.
Painter, watercolourist, pastellist, draughtsman, lithographer. Portraits, genre scenes.

Charles Serret was a pupil of Hippolyte Flandrin, Louis Lamothe, and Charles Comte. He exhibited at the Paris Salon from 1861.

MUSEUMS AND GALLERIES:
PARIS (Mus. des Arts décoratifs): *Children at Play*.

AUCTION RECORDS:
PARIS, 23 June 1900, *Cart* (pastel) FRF 190; *Balloons* (drawing and pastel) FRF 100. PARIS, 7 Dec 1912, *Twin Girls*, FRF 1,300. PARIS, 15-16 Nov 1918, *Front View of a Young Girl; Young Girl Kneeling on a Chair; Young Girl Seated* (three drawings in black pencil) FRF 36. PARIS, 14 March 1945, *Group of Women* (drawing in coloured pencils) FRF 100.

SERRET, Marie Ernestine (Mme).
See **CABART**

SERRET Y COMIN, Nicasio
Spanish, 19th century.
Born 14 December 1849, in Valencia; died 7 July 1880, in Valencia.
Active in Rome from 1876 to 1878.
Painter.

Nicasio Serret y Comin was a pupil of Fr. Domingo.

SERRIER, Georges Pierre Louis
French, 19th - 20th century.
Born in Thionville.
Painter, engraver. Landscapes.

Georges Serrier was a pupil of Oudry and began to exhibit in the Salon of 1876, becoming a member of the Salon des Artistes Français from 1888. He obtained an honourable mention in 1893 and 1894, a third-class medal in 1899 and a bronze medal in 1900 during the Exposition Universelle in Paris.

Museums and Galleries:

Gray: *Landscape.*

Auction records:

Paris, 3 Feb 1919, *Pink Houses by the Water,* FRF 620. Paris, 29 June 1988, *Edge of the Beach* (oil on canvas, 13 x 16 1/4 ins / 33 x 41 cm) FRF 5,000. Paris, 12 June 1992, *Roadmender's Hut* (oil on canvas, 23 1/2 x 31 1/2 ins / 60 x 80 cm) FRF 12,500.

SERRIÈRE, Jean

French, 20th century.
Born in Nancy.
Painter. Religious subjects, figures, portraits, still-lifes, flowers.

Jean Serrière received some teaching from Jacques-Émile Blanche, Desvallières and Laprade, and was known for his delicate interpretations of flowers, the female body, portraits, still lifes, and also for a *Descent from the Cross.* In addition he was a goldsmith and did enamel work. He exhibited in Paris at the Salon d'Automne, of which he was a member. A retrospective exhibition was shown in 1969 in Paris.

Auction records:

Paris, 10 Feb 1932, *Fishing Boats in the Port of Venice,* FRF 65. Paris, 23 Oct 1950, *Parrots* (fan) FRF 400. Paris, 20 May 1955, *Greed* (enamel) FRF 7,000.

SERRITELLI, Giovanni, or Seritelli

Italian, 19th century.
Born 1810, in Naples; died 1860.
Painter. Landscapes, seascapes.

Auction records:

Rome, 4 Dec 1990, *Courtyard of a Neapolitan Farm; Gulf of Naples* (oil on canvas, a pair, each 10 1/4 x 15 3/4 ins / 26 x 40 cm) ITL 17,000,000. Rome, 23 May 1996, *Gulf of Naples* (1856, oil on canvas, 14 1/2 x 25 1/4 ins / 37 x 64 cm) ITL 3,680,000. London, 21 Nov 1996, *Sorrento* (oil on canvas, 30 1/4 x 40 1/4 ins / 77 x 102.2 cm) GBP 10,350. San Francisco, 26 May 1999, *Nocturnal View of the Bay of Naples* (1878, oil on canvas laid on board, 22 x 33 ins / 56 x 85 cm) USD 8,000. Milan, 21 Dec 1999, *View of the Bay of Naples from Posillipo* (oil on canvas, 22 x 35 ins / 57 x 89 cm) ITL 50,000,000. Turin, 21 March 2000, *Taking of Gaeta* (1861, oil on canvas, 27 x 38 ins / 69 x 97 cm) ITL 32,500,000. Berlin, 1 July 2000, *Market Square in Naples* (oil on canvas, 66 x 46 ins / 168 x 117 cm) DEM 74,000. New York, 28 June 2001, *Day at the Market* (oil on canvas, 65 x 46 ins / 166 x 117 cm) USD 36,000. Munich, 17 May 2003, *Northern Italian Mountain Coast. Italian Market Scene* (oil on canvas, 15 x 22 ins / 37 x 55 cm) EUR 12,000. London, 18 June 2003, *Italian Brig and Greek Barque Anchored off the Neapolitan Coast* (oil on canvas, 30 x 40 ins / 75 x 101 cm) GBP 10,000.

SERRO, Jehan

French, 17th century.
Active in Le Mans in 1602.
Sculptor.

Jehan Serro sculpted a font for the church of Crosmières in 1602.

SERRO, Tommaso

Italian, 16th century.
Active in Cagliari (Sardinia) during the first half of the 16th century.
Painter.

Tommaso Serro painted a *Madonna with St John the Baptist and St George* for the church of Nostra Signora delle Grazie in Alcamo in Sicily.

SERROT, Rafael Perez

Painter. Genre scenes.

Serrot is mentioned by Miss Florence Levy.

Auction records:

New York, 14-17 March 1911, *Young Italian Fisherman,* USD 100.

SERRUR, Henry Auguste Calixte César

French, 19th century.
Born 9 or 11 February 1794, in Lambersart; died 2 September 1865, in Paris.
Painter. Historical, religious and mythological subjects, battles, genre scenes, portraits.

Henry Serrur first studied in Lille, then, in 1815, he was awarded an allowance that enabled him to complete his studies in Paris. There he was a pupil of Regnault and studied at the École des Beaux-Arts to which he was admitted on 20 February 1837. He exhibited at the Salon between 1819 and 1850 and was awarded a third class medal in 1836 and a second class medal in 1837.

Museums and Galleries:

Amiens: *Final Farewells of Mary Stuart* - Bordeaux: *Charles X* - Bourges: *Charles X* - Cambrai: *Death of Marat* - Douai: *The French Army leaving Mascara; The Greeks taking Tripolis; Hippolyte Bis; Figure in the Academic Style* - Lille: *Death of Agamemnon; Castor and Pollux Leading their Sister Helen to Menelaes; Ajax; Aug. Dubrunfaut, the Scientist* - Rennes: *Tobias Burying the Dead during the Captivity in Babylon* - Versailles: *Battle Outside the Walls of Nicea; Entry of Louis XV into Strasbourg; Battle for Jaffa; Battle of Coni; Mary Stuart* (two works); *J. de Nettancourt, Count of Vaubecourt; Henry of Lorraine, Marquis of Mony; A. M. de la Trémoille, Pricesse des Ursins; Count J.F.A. Déjean; Count P.F.M.A. Déjean; Le Grand Condé.*

Auction records:

London, 5 Feb 1925, *Game of Billiards,* GBP 49. Paris, 11 March 1974, *Bust of a Young Woman,* FRF 4,400. London, 16 March 1994, *Portrait of a Man in a Park* (1835, oil on canvas, 18 1/2 x 15 ins / 47 x 38 cm) GBP 3,162. Paris, 24 March 1997, *Virgin at Prayer* (oil on canvas, 22 x 18 1/4 ins / 56 x 46.5 cm) FRF 16,000.

SERRURE, Albert

19th - 20th century.
Painter. Still-lifes.

Auction records:

Douai, 26 March 1988, *Still-life* (oil on canvas, 25 1/2 x 32 ins / 65 x 81 cm) FRF 2,800.

SERRURE, Auguste

Belgian, 19th century.
Born 1825, in Antwerp; died 1903, in Schaerbeek (Brussels).
Painter. Genre scenes.

Auguste Serrure was a pupil of Ferdinand Braekelaer.

Museums and Galleries:

Brussels (MBA): *The Agreement.*

Auction records:
New York, 18 Oct 1944, *Empty Gaming Bag*, USD 375. Paris, 22 Sept 1950, *Geographer* (1949) FRF 15,500. London, 22 July 1959, *In the Country*, GBP 420. London, 19 Jan 1968, *Chess Players*, Gns 680. London, 10 Nov 1971, *Departure*, GBP 1,100. Brussels, 10 Dec 1976, *Elegant Woman Fishing* (oil on wood, 11 x 7 ins / 27 x 18 cm) BEF 22,000. London, 16 June 1978, *Backgammon Players* (1847, oil on panel, 21 1/2 x 27 1/2 ins / 54.5 x 70 cm) GBP 1,200. London, 28 Nov 1979, *Woman Selling Flowers* (1873, oil on panel, 35 1/2 x 25 1/2 ins / 90 x 65 cm) GBP 7,500. London, 14 Jan 1981, *Young Woman in a Red Sitting Room; The Magic Box* (1897, oil on panel, a pair, each 15 1/2 x 11 1/2 ins / 39.5 x 29 cm) GBP 1,050. New York, 24 Feb 1983, *Lawyer* (1864, oil on panel, 19 1/4 x 27 1/4 ins / 49 x 69 cm) USD 8,000. Amsterdam, 3 Sept 1988, *Flirting* (1863, oil on panel, 24 3/4 x 15 3/4 ins / 63 x 40 cm) NLG 6,900. New York, 24 May 1989, *Toast on the Arrival of the Victor* (1870, oil on panel, 23 1/4 x 34 ins / 59 x 86.4 cm) USD 16,500. New York, 25 Oct 1989, *Village Gathering round the Church* (1878, oil on panel, 23 1/4 x 34 1/4 ins / 59 x 87 cm) USD 13,200. Paris, 19 Dec 1989, *Victory of the Crossbowman* (1870, oil on panel, 23 1/2 x 33 3/4 ins / 59.5 x 86 cm) FRF 120,000. London, 30 Nov 1990, *Flower Market* (1870, oil on panel, 24 1/2 x 35 1/4 ins / 62 x 89.5 cm) GBP 13,200. London, 18 Nov 1994, *Entertainments* (1882, oil on panel, 20 x 25 1/2 ins / 51.1 x 64.5 cm) GBP 4,600. Lokeren, 11 March 1995, *Lady on the Sofa* (oil on panel, 7 x 9 ins / 17.5 x 22 cm) BEF 28,000. New York, 20 July 1995, *Family Relaxation* (1855, oil on panel, 13 x 16 1/4 ins / 33 x 41.3 cm) USD 3,450. London, 17 Feb 1999, *Portrait of Artist at Work* (1852, oil on panel, 10 x 8 ins / 25 x 21 cm) GBP 2,200. Milan, 9 June 1999, *Skaters* (1863, oil on canvas, 19 x 26 ins / 47 x 66 cm) ITL 13,500,000. London, 4 April 2000, *Winter Outing* (1865, oil on panel, 20 x 28 ins / 50 x 70 cm) GBP 14,000. Antwerp, 11 Dec 2000, *Elegant Figure with Greyhound* (oil on canvas, 26 x 21 ins / 65 x 53 cm) BEF 140,000. Amsterdam, 24 April 2001, *After the Honeymoon* (1862, oil on panel, 15 x 19 ins / 37 x 48 cm) NLG 32,000. London, 23 May 2001, *Garden Party* (1853, oil on panel, 24 x 31 ins / 60 x 78 cm) GBP 6,000. Lille, 20 Oct 2002, *Woman Standing in front of a Piano* (oil on canvas, 28 x 22 ins / 71 x 56 cm) EUR 4,200. Antwerp, 21 Oct 2002, *Chess Game* (1864, oil on panel, 19 x 28 ins / 49 x 70 cm) EUR 135,000. Lyons, 30 March 2003, *Young Romantic Woman in a Gothic Window* (1848, oil on canvas, 40 x 28 ins / 102 x 72 cm) EUR 4,100. Antwerp, 26 May 2003, *Butterfly Hunt* (oil on panel, 6 x 3 ins / 14 x 7 cm) EUR 1,600. St-Germain-en-Laye, 4 April 2004, *Auction* (oil on panel, 5 x 8 ins / 12 x 21 cm) EUR 2,000.

SERRURIER, Louis
German, 18th - 19th century.
Active in Berlin 1790-1800.
Draughtsman, engraver (burin).

Serrurier produced portrait engravings, views of Berlin and illustrations from his own drawings.

SERRUYS, Louis
Dutch, 19th century.
Active in Ostend, c. 1840.
Painter. Landscapes, architectural views.

Louis Serruys was a pupil of P. J. Clays.

Auction records:
Paris, 18 Jan 1950, *Ship at Sea in Heavy Weather* (1859) FRF 1,000. Paris, 27 June 1951, *Frigate and Steamer Sailing in a Rough Sea* (1859) FRF 3,500.

SERRUYS, Yvonne, Mme Mille
Belgian, 20th century.
Born 26 March 1874, in Menin; died 1953, in Paris.
Painter, sculptor.

Yvonne Serruys was a pupil of Egide Rombaux and Emile Claus. She exhibited at the 1887 Salon de la Société Nationale des Beaux-Arts in Paris and at a number of other venues, including the Salon d'Automne, the Salon des Tuileries, the Salon des Artistes Décorateurs, the Exposition des Arts Décoratifs (1925) and the Exposition de la Coloniale (1931). She was a Chevalier of the Légion d'Honneur and of the Order of Leopold.

Museums and Galleries:
Ghent: *Torso of Young Woman* - Nantes: *Bust of a Young Woman* - Paris (former Mus. du Luxembourg): *Youth*.

Auction records:
Enghien-les-Bains, 9 Dec 1979, *Pair of Dancers: Position 1* (black-patinated bronze with green tones, h. 13 1/4 ins / 33.7 cm) FRF 8,000. Lokeren, 25 Feb 1984, *Two Peasant Women Conversing* (oil on canvas, 25 1/2 x 32 1/4 ins / 65 x 82 cm) BEF 140,000. Paris, 27 May 1997, *Woman with Bowl* (c. 1911, light-brown patinated bronze, h. 22 1/2 ins / 57 cm) FRF 29,000. Lokeren, 9 Oct 1999, *Sunlit Garden* (oil on canvas, 19 x 24 ins / 47 x 61 cm) BEF 320,000. Antwerp, 19 Oct 1999, *Woman by a Small Farm in a Landscape* (oil on canvas, 12 x 20 ins / 30 x 50 cm) BEF 140,000. Paris, 16 Nov 2003, *Woman with Cup* (brown patinated bronze, h. 22 ins / 56 cm) EUR 3,000. Paris, 7 July 2004, *Young Female Nude* (patinated bronze, h. 22 ins / 57 cm) EUR 2,000.

SERS, Bernadette
French, 20th century.
Painter, watercolourist, pastellist. Landscapes, seascapes, still-lifes.
Poetic Reality.

Bernadette Sers creates landscapes of Morocco, Spain and Brittany and street and carnival scenes from Venice in lively colour. She takes part in Paris in the Salon Comparaisons, Salon du Dessin et de la Painture à l'Eau, Salon de la Société Nationale des Beaux-Arts, of which she was a member, Salon d'Automne, Salon des Artistes Français, and Salon de la Marine, and also in exhibitions in New York (1960-1989), Brussels (1971). She holds solo exhibitions regularly in Paris, and in Tehran in 1968, Rabat in 1971 and Fez in 1970.

SERSANDERS, Andries
Dutch, 17th century.
Active in 1611.
Engraver (burin).

Andries Sersanders engraved battle scenes.

SERSENDA, Michelangelo
Italian, 18th century.
Active in 1741.
Fresco artist.

Sersenda painted frescoes depicting the *Assumption* in the church in Felonica.

SERT Y BADIA, José María
Spanish, 20th century.
Born 21 December 1874 or 24 December 1876, in Barcelona; died November or December 1945, in Barcelona.
Also active in France from 1900.
Painter, engraver, draughtsman, decorative artist.
Religious subjects, allegorical subjects, nudes, genre scenes. Murals.

José María Sert y Badia started his career in the studio of his father, who was a designer of cartoons for tapestries and fabrics. After a stay in Italy, where he studied the art of fresco painting, he settled and worked for a long period of time in Paris. Here he lived the life of the society painter, frequently mixing in literary circles as well as his own. José María Sert y Badia received several commissions for murals which enabled him to explore colour and eventually evolved towards a more subdued palette. He stopped painting with an easel and executed large murals rather devoid of style in churches, private houses and palaces in Europe and in the USA. Works include: the Waldorf Astoria (1930-1931), the Rockfeller Center (1933) both in New York, and the Council

Chamber at the United Nations in Geneva. He also decorated Vic Cathedral in Catalonia (1904 to 1926) in a style that won him praise. The building was destroyed in 1936 in the Spanish civil war. Sert painted the decoration of the rebuilt cathedral with trompe l'oeil sculptures and low reliefs in 1941. In 1937 he executed *St Theresa, ambassador of divine love in Spain, offers the Spanish Martyrs of 1936 to the Lord* which featured, with works by other artists favourable to the Franco regime, in the Vatican pavilion at the Paris Exposition Universelle. In the same exhibition, artists of a different persuasion featured in the Spanish Republic pavilion including Miró, Julio Gonzáles and Picasso with *Guernica*. Sert also decorated the chapel at the Alcazar in Toledo with panels to the glory of the Franco army. He wrote the preface a special edition of André Gide's *Bethsabée*, executed 12 lithographs for *St Francis of Assisi* the poem by Paul Claudel. José María Sert y Badia is also known as an architect.

He participated in various collective exhibitions in Paris: Exposition Universelle (1900); Salon d'Automne (1907); Musée du Jeu de Paume (1926); Exposition Universelle (1937). He also exhibited in London and New York. In 1929 he was awarded the Great Cross of Alfonso XII and nominated a member of the Escuela de Bellas Artes in Madrid.

BIBLIOGRAPHY:
Castillo Yurrita, Alberto del/Cirici Pellicer, Alejandro, *José Maria Sert, su vida y su obra*, Libreria Ed. Argos, Barcelona, 1947. Monreal y Tejada, Luis, *La Catedral de Vich*, Ed. Aedos, Barcelona, 1948. Claudel, Paul, *L'Œil écoute*, Gallimard, Paris, 1949. *Catálogo nacional de arte contemporáneo 1990-1991*, Ibérico 2Mil, Barcelona, 1990-1991. Arnáiz, José Manuel/López Jiménez, Javier/Merchán Díaz, Manuel (ed.), '*Cien años de pintura en Espana y Portugal (1830-1930)*' in vol. X, Antiqvaria, Madrid, 1993.

AUCTION RECORDS:
PARIS, 18 May 1942, *Two Nudes* (charcoal heightened with chalk) FRF 1,500. PARIS, 18 March 1981, *Departure of the Queen of Sheba* (oil on panel, decor for a ballroom, sixteen panels of 700x455, five panels, 455x137, 455x139, 455x111, two panels 455x239, three panels 455x136, two panels 455x104) USD 4,500. NEW YORK, 22 June 1983, *Minstrels of the Queen of Sheba* (oil and silver leaf/card, 98 x 52 3/4 ins / 249 x 134 cm) USD 4,500. MADRID, 20 June 1985, *The Heroic Defence of the Alcazar of Toledo* (gouache/paper silver, 41 x 46 1/2 ins / 104 x 118 cm) ESP 1,322,500. PARIS, 5 June 1992, ; *Towards the Sky; The Farewells and the Camel* (oil on canvas, two preparatory studies, 48 3/4 x 24 3/4 ins / 124 x 63 cm) FRF 4,500. LONDON, 25 Oct 1995, *Plan for a Decorative Panel* (oil on paper/canvas, 15 3/4 x 7 ins / 40 x 18 cm) GBP 3,680. LONDON, 15 Nov 1995, *Victory Parade* (oil on silver paper and oil on card, design for the Alcazar chapel in Toledo, 41 x 46 1/2 ins / 104 x 118 cm) GBP 6,325. PARIS, 28 June 1999, *Seated Faun* (monochrome oil on canvas, 76 x 40 ins / 192 x 101 cm) FRF 18,000. PARIS, 26 Nov 1999, *Mythological Scene* (mixed media on panel, arched top, 118 x 31 ins / 300 x 79 cm) FRF 20,000. MADRID, 4 April 2000, *Study for Allegory of Labour* (oil and gold leaf on canvas, 24 x 28 ins / 60 x 70 cm) ESP 425,000. MADRID, 22 May 2000, *Figures on Carousel* (oil on panel, 16 x 28 ins / 41 x 72 cm) ESP 4,750,000. MADRID, 3 April 2001, *The Abolition of Slavery* (oil and gold leaf on paper, 20 x 56 ins / 52 x 143 cm) ESP 3,600,000. PARIS, 22 May 2001, *Renowed Trumpter* (oil on canvas, 47 x 26 ins / 120 x 65 cm) FRF 13,000. PARIS, 17 April 2002, *St Peter's Crucifixion* (oil on canvas, 177 x 217 ins / 450 x 550 cm) EUR 16,500. PARIS, 18 Nov 2002, *Project for Decoration* (oil on panel, seven works, 9 x 5 ins / 22 x 12 cm) EUR 8,000. MADRID, 25 March 2003, *Good News for the Shepherds* (oil on canvas, 25 x 31 ins / 63 x 80 cm) EUR 5,500. LONDON, 12 June 2003, *Offering* (oil on plaster/board, 96 x 59 ins / 244 x 149 cm) GBP 75,000.

SERTART
French, 18th century.
Active in Paris in 1760.
Painter, miniaturist. Portraits.

SERTIER
French, 18th century.
Active in Paris.
Sculptor.

Sertier was a member of the Académie de St-Luc and participated in that organisation's exhibitions in 1751 and 1752.

SERTINI DELLA CASA, Michele (Fra)
Italian, 15th century.
Died 1416.
Active in Florence.
Miniaturist.

Fra Michele Sertini was a Dominican monk.

SERTL, Johann
German, 20th century.
Born 21 January 1878, in Schönlind (Bavaria).
Active in Munich.
Sculptor. Religious subjects.

Johann Sertl produced sculptures in wood.

MUSEUMS AND GALLERIES:
LEIPZIG: *Statue of the Virgin*.

SERTL, Johann Peter
Austrian, 18th century.
Active in Vienna, Austria, in 1742.
Sculptor (wood).

Sertl carved the stalls for the church of Hafnererg, Austria.

SERTON VAN ROSWEYDE, Piet A.
Dutch, 20th century.
Born 28 October 1888, in Utrecht; died 30 June 1914, in Utrecht.
Painter.

SERTORIO, Giambattista
Swiss, 19th century.
Died 9 April 1867, in Lugano (Ticino).
Painter. Religious subjects, portraits.

Sertorio attended the art academy of Brera in Milan, Italy.

SERTORIO, Pietro
Swiss, 17th century.
Born in Cimo.
Active during the second half of the 17th century.
Sculptor.

Sertorio produced work for the castle and palaces in Piacenza, Italy.

SERULLAZ, Maurice
French, 20th century.
Born 19 January 1914, in Paris.
Painter. Urban landscapes, landscapes, still-lifes, flowers.

Maurice Serullaz was a nephew of the poet Rollinat and began to paint at the age of 14. He undertook several works for the decorative artist Dumas and was an art historian and chief curator of the Musée du Louvre in Paris.

His original influences are from Laprade, whose painting was inspired by the poetry of Verlaine and Mallarmé. His originality lies in his skill as a colourist - set off by composition in his best works - mostly in harmonies that are difficult to achieve: reds in *Pot of Geraniums* (1935), then whites in *White Lilac* and several Parisian landscapes. In the 1970s, blue monochromes clash with stocks of white used in still-lifes, as in the landscapes of Cannes, while other canvases vigorously detach objects from the discreet and skilful resonance of the backgrounds - a major scale within the minor.

He exhibited for the first time in 1929 and took part in public exhibitions in Paris: 1936 and 1937, Galerie Druet with Marquet, Segonzac, Camoin and Puy; 1937, Exposition de la Vie Parisienne at the Musée d'Art Moderne; 1938, Salon des

Indépendants. In 1951, in London, an exhibition was dedicated to his work.

MUSEUMS AND GALLERIES:

PARIS (MNAM-CCI): *Landscape of the Creuse.*

AUCTION RECORDS:

PARIS, 23 April 1937, *Bouquets of a Variety of Flowers in an Oriental Vase,* FRF 210. PARIS, 23 Feb 1945, *Vase of Flowers* (1937) FRF 500.

SÉRUSIER, Louis Paul Henri, called Paul

French, 19th - 20th century.

Born 1863 or 1864, in Paris; died 6 October 1927, in Morlaix.

Painter. Religious subjects, allegorical subjects, landscapes. Stage sets.

Symbolism.

Nabis group. School of Pont-Aven.

After a good secondary education, Louis Sérusier entered the Académie Julian and attended the Doucet studio. He was enthusiastic, enterprising and a fine speaker, and very active in the academy, which also trained Maurice Denis, Bonnard, Vuillard, K.X Roussel, Ranson, René Piot and Ibels. They used to gather in a restaurant in Brady Passage, where they discussed the aesthetics of Plato and the School of Alexandria, whose esotericism interested Sérusier. In 1895 and 1904 he travelled with Maurice Denis and discovered the Italian and German primitives, absorbing lessons in decoration from some and expressive violence from others. After another journey to Munich in 1907, he became a teacher at the Académie Ranson in Paris from 1908, as a result of which he wrote his *ABC of Painting.* In 1912 he married one of his pupils and withdrew almost totally to Châteauneuf-du-Faou. His wife fell seriously ill in 1921, which overshadowed the last years of Sérusier's life; it was while visiting her at Morlaix, where she was being cared for, that he himself died of a stroke.

With his companions at the Académie Ranson, Sérusier met Gauguin and Émile Bernard painting at Pont-Aven, while travelling to Brittany in 1888. The synthetic art of Gauguin, an admirer of Japanese prints and already searching for that meaningful arabesque, came just in time to provide Sérusier and his friends with a means of expression. Contrary to Bouguereau's example which appeared to them empty, Sérusier returned to the Académie Ranson from Pont-Aven and painted *Landscape of the Wood of Love,* after advice from Gauguin. 'How do you see these trees?' Gauguin had asked. 'They are yellow.' 'All right, so use the yellow, the most beautiful in your palette. This rather blue shadow, paint it with pure ultramarine. These red leaves, do in vermilion...' Sérusier painted, as he was told, on a panel of wood. Not following Gauguin's advice to finish this sketch at the studio, Sérusier kept it as it was and took it to his friends at the Académie Julian.

This little landscape, christened *The Talisman,* became the reference point for the new painting style to be developed by Bonnard, Maurice Denis, Vallotton and Vuillard, later to be joined by Maillol and Émile Bernard - those who would soon be called the Nabis (from the Hebrew Nabim: prophets), a name suggested by one of their Jewish friends, Auguste F. Cazalis. Maurice Denis described how 'they were continually in a state of prophetic enthusiasm.' They also admired the work of Redon and Puvis de Chavannes, and Japanese prints. Sérusier was commissioned to paint the decorations for the Theatre de l'Oeuvre de Lugné-Poe, stronghold of the Symbolist movement. After his journey to Italy in 1905 with Maurice Denis, he painted wall decorations for the church of Châteauneuf-du-Faou, where he spent his summers and, in 1905, translated the *Esthétique de beuron* of father Didier. After the *Talisman* he applied Gauguin's principles on the use of colours to their maximum of symbolic expressivity.

He took part in several public exhibitions, including in 1891, the first Nabi show at the Galerie Barc de Boutteville. After his death his works were in shows dedicated to the Nabis, notably at the Galeries Nationales du Grand Palais in Paris in 1993. He also showed his works in solo exhibitions: 1872, the Town Hall at Pont-Aven; 1909, Galerie Druet in Paris. Then after his death in Paris: 1939, Galerie Zak; 1947, retrospective at the Musée Galliéra; 1984, for the sale of the Boutaric estate; 1985, for the sale of Lebasque-Sérusier; 1988, at the departmental museum of the Prieuré de St-Germain-en-Laye.

BIBLIOGRAPHY:

Sérusier, *ABC de la peinture*, La Douce France, Paris, 1921. Denis, Maurice, *Sérusier, sa vie, son œuvre*, Floury, Paris, 1942 or 1943. Guicheteau, Marcel, *Paul Sérusier*, Éd. SIDE, Paris, 1976. Guicheteau, Marcel/Boutaric, Paule Henriette, '*Paul Sérusier*' in *2 vol.*, Graphedis, Pontoise, 1976-1989. Mauner, G. L., *The Nabis, their History and their Art, 1888-1896*, Garland, New York, 1978. Maurice, Tuchman, *The Spiritual in Art: Abstract painting 1890-1985*, Abbeville Press, New York, 1986. Masson, Henry, *Paul Sérusier: de Pont-Aven à Châteauneuf-du-Faou*, Presses bretonnes, St-Brieuc, 1991. Puget, Catherine/Boyle-Turner, Caroline, *Paul Sérusier et la Bretagne*, exhibition catalogue, Musée de Pont-Aven, Pont-Aven, 1991. *Les Nabis*, exhibition catalogue, Gal. nationales du Grand Palais, Réunion des musées nationaux, Paris, 1993. Boyle-Turner, Caroline, *Sérusier et la Bretagne*, Le Chasse-Marée/ArMen, Douarnenez, 1995. *Gaugain's Nirvana: Painters at Le Pouldu 1889-90*, Wadsworth Atheneum Museum of Art, Hertford, in association with Yale University Press, New Haven, c. 2001.

MUSEUMS AND GALLERIES:

GENEVA (Petit Palais): *Three Bretons* (1893) - LONDON (Tate Collection): *Roof Tops in Paris* (oil on canvas) - MUNICH (Neue Pinakothek): *Breton Women Going Down to the Washing Place* (1890) - OTTAWA (NG. of Canada) - PARIS (BNF, Prints Collection): *Old Woman with a Basket* (1893, lithograph) - PARIS (Mus. d'Orsay): *Talisman; Breton Eve or Melancholy* - PONT-AVEN: *Landscape, End of the Day* (1893, lithograph); *The Sweet Seller with an Umbrella* (1895, lithograph) - QUIMPER (MBA): *Incantation or Sacred Wood* - SENLIS (Mus. d'Art et d'Archéologie): *Workshop of a Breton Weaver* (1888, oil on canvas) - STUTTGART (Staatsgal.): *Rocks at Huelgoat* (1891).

AUCTION RECORDS:

PARIS, 28 March 1918, *Women and Children,* FRF 315. PARIS, 7 April 1924, *Still-life,* FRF 400. PARIS, 3 March 1927, *Pitcher,* FRF 600. PARIS, 8 May 1936, *Still-life,* FRF 300. PARIS, 13 Dec 1940, *Portrait of Naip Chaipp* (1889) FRF 1,050. PARIS, 3 Feb 1943, *Breton Women at the River* (1892) FRF 32,000. PARIS, 24 Feb 1947, *Forest Escapade,* FRF 24,500. PARIS, 22 June 1949, *Chateauneuf du Faou, Finistere* (1924) FRF 90,500. PARIS, 23 Feb 1954, *Breton Woman and Child on the Road,* FRF 500,000. PARIS, 10 June 1958, *Breton Women by the Sea* (oil on card) FRF 820,000. PARIS, 21 June 1961, *Still-life,* FRF 7,000. LONDON, 30 Nov 1962, *Mountain Road,* Gns 4,000. GENEVA, 27 Nov 1965, *Landscape,* CHF 38,000. TOKYO, 3 Oct 1969, *Orchard* (tempera) JPY 400,000. BREST, 17 Dec 1972, *Monts d'Arree in Finistere* (gouache) FRF 7,500. PARIS, 5 Nov 1974, *Christ in Majesty Surrounded by Women in Profile*, FRF 73,000. LONDON, 8 April 1976, *Synchromy in Yellow* (c. 1892, oil on canvas, 31 1/4 x 20 3/4 ins / 79.5 x 53 cm) GBP 7,200. BREST, 18 Dec 1977, *Forest of Love at Pont-Aven* (oil on canvas, 35 1/2 x 22 ins / 90 x 55 cm) FRF 55,000. BREST, 17 Dec 1978, *Stream in the Landscape at Chateauneuf-du-Faou* (pastel, 19 x 23 1/4 ins / 48 x 59 cm) FRF 23,800. NEW YORK, 9 June 1979, *Young Breton Woman Standing* (pen and pencil, 8 x 4 1/4 ins / 20.3 x 11.1 cm) USD 1,500. ENGHIEN-LES-BAINS, 18 Nov 1979, *Breton Women at the Fountain* (1895, oil on canvas, 36 1/4 x 23 1/2 ins / 92 x 60 cm) FRF 165,000. PARIS, 17 Nov 1980, *Old Road from Carhaix to Chateauneuf-du-Faou* (pastel, 22 x 15 ins / 55 x 38 cm) FRF 8,500. BREST, 13 Dec 1981, *Profile of Breton Woman* (drawing with watercolour, 11 x 6 ins / 28 x 15 cm) FRF 8,000. NEW YORK, 21 May 1982, *Woman Telling a Story* (oil on canvas, 34 1/4 x 40 1/4 ins / 87 x 102 cm) USD 37,500. PARIS, 19 June 1984, *Nude Girls Bathing in the Stream* (1890, oil on canvas, 36 1/4 x 28 1/4 ins / 92 x 72 cm) FRF 3,700,000. PARIS, 20 June 1984, *Woman Gleaning* (zincography/yellow paper) FRF 15,000. PARIS, 20 June 1984, *Breton Landscape with Rocks* (watercolour with gouache, 12 1/2 x 19 3/4 ins / 32 x 50 cm) FRF 215,000. PARIS, 20 June 1984, *Marguerite Serusier Reading by the River* (charcoal drawing with pastel, 7 1/4 x 9 ins / 18.5 x 22 cm) FRF 100,000. BREST, 19 May 1985, *Woman in the Forest* (charcoal and pastel, 16 1/4 x 11 ins / 41 x 28 cm) FRF 27,500. PARIS, 8 Dec 1986, *Woman of Kerbrau* (1918, oil on canvas, 51 1/4 x 31 1/2 ins / 130 x 80 cm) FRF 610,000. VERSAILLES, 13 Dec 1987, *Eve Gathering the Apple* (1906, egg and oil on canvas, 32 1/4 x 13 1/2 ins / 82 x 34.5 cm) FRF 120,000. PARIS, 15 April 1988, *Still-life with Green Almonds* (1912, oil on canvas, 5 x 19 3/4 ins / 12.61 x 50 cm) FRF 88,000. CALAIS, 3 July 1988, *Still-life with Pumpkin* (1908, oil on canvas, 23 1/2 x 35 1/2 ins / 60 x 90 cm) FRF 165,000. PARIS, 24 Nov 1988, *Undergrowth in Brittany* (1894, oil on canvas, 17 x 22 ins / 43 x 56 cm) FRF 420,000. LONDON, 29 Nov 1988, *Two Breton Women under an Apple Tree in Blossom* (1890, oil on canvas, 28 x 22 3/4 ins / 71 x 58 cm) GBP 253,000. NEW YORK, 16 Feb 1989, *Autumn Landscape* (oil on card/panel, 10 1/4 x 13 ins / 26.3 x 33 cm) USD 9,350. CALAIS, 26 Feb 1989, *Old Man and Child* (oil on canvas, 35 3/4 x 25 1/2 ins / 91 x 65 cm) FRF 125,000. LONDON, 5 April 1989, *Still-life with Apples* (1915, oil on canvas, 23 1/2 x 28 3/4 ins / 60 x 73 cm) GBP 24,200. PARIS, 27 April 1989, *Chamber Orchestra* (oil on canvas, 13 3/4 x 11 ins / 35 x 27 cm) FRF 55,000. LONDON, 27 June 1989, *Nude with Loincloth* (oil on canvas, 23 1/4 x 35 3/4 ins / 59 x 91 cm) GBP 33,000. LONDON, 25 Oct 1989, *Tetrahedrons* (oil on canvas, 36 x 22 1/2 ins / 91.5 x 57 cm) GBP 27,500. LE TOUQUET, 12 Nov 1989, *Undulating Landscape* (gouache, 13 3/4 x 20 3/4 ins / 35 x 53 cm) FRF 50,000. PARIS, 23 Nov 1989, *Salome Contemplating the Head of St John the Baptist* (oil on canvas, 39 1/4 x 23 1/2 ins / 100 x 60 cm) FRF 200,000. LONDON, 1 Dec 1989, *Woman Spinning with Oak Leaves* (1918, oil on canvas, 36 x 21 1/2 ins / 91.4 x 54.7 cm) GBP 33,000. PARIS, 26 March 1990, *Valkyrie Resting* (1906, oil on canvas, 23 1/4 x 36 ins / 59 x 91.5 cm) FRF 490,000. LONDON, 4 April 1990, *Games of Queen Anne* (oil on canvas, 44 x 73 1/4 ins / 112 x 186 cm) GBP 93,500. NEW YORK, 16 May 1990, *Two Laundry Women* (oil on canvas, 29 x 36 1/2 ins / 73.7 x 92.7 cm) USD 440,000. PARIS, 30 May 1990, *Isolde's Little Dog* (oil on card, 19 x 23 1/4 ins / 48 x 59 cm) FRF 275,000. PARIS, 13 June 1990, *Open Book* (1914, oil on canvas, 23 1/2 x 36 1/4 ins / 60 x 92 cm) FRF 125,000. PARIS, 17 March 1991, *Prayer to the Virgin, Homage to Jean Verkade* (1893, oil on paper, 12 3/4 x 16 ins / 32.5 x 40.5 cm) FRF 175,000. PARIS, 17 Nov 1991, *Still-life with Green Plant and Three Apples* (1903, oil on canvas, 23 3/4 x 28 3/4 ins / 60.5 x 73 cm) FRF 160,000. PARIS, 14 Dec 1992, *Isolde's Little Dog* (mixed media/card/canvas, 19 x 23 1/4 ins / 48 x 59 cm) FRF 105,000. PARIS, 2 June 1993, *Women Carrying Wine* (oil on card, 41 1/4 x 29 1/4 ins / 105 x 74 cm) FRF 155,000. PARIS, 26 Nov 1993, *Vision near the Waterfall or the Fairies' Meeting Place* (1897, oil on canvas, 43 3/4 x 72 ins / 111 x 182 cm) FRF 950,000. BREST, 19 Dec 1993, *Yellow Farm at Pouldu* (oil on canvas, 17 1/4 x 22 ins / 44 x 55 cm) FRF 1,110,000. LONDON, 23-24 March 1994, *Blue Bird* (1908, oil on canvas, 28 3/4 x 19 ins / 73 x 48.5 cm) GBP 17,825. DEAUVILLE, 19 Aug 1994, *Young Woman with Poppy* (1920, gouache and oil on card/canvas, 7 x 5 1/2 ins / 18 x 14 cm) FRF 35,000. NEW YORK, 8 Nov 1994, *Breton Sunday* (oil on canvas, 36 1/4 x 28 3/4 ins / 91.8 x 73.3 cm) USD 233,500. PARIS, 28 Nov 1994, *Rocks in the Forest* (oil on canvas, 37 x 38 1/2 ins / 94 x 97.5 cm) FRF 170,000. AMSTERDAM, 8 Dec 1994, *Country Dance* (gouache/paper/canvas, 23 1/2 x 32 1/4 ins / 60 x 82 cm) NLG 16,100. BREST, 14 May 1995, *Young Breton Women Seated in the Wood* (oil on canvas, 21 1/4 x 25 1/2 ins / 54 x 65 cm) FRF 520,000. PARIS, 2 June 1995, *Silver River in the Wood at Huelgoat (Finistere)* (Indian ink heightened with pastels, 12 1/4 x 9 1/2 ins / 31 x 24 cm) FRF 31,000. PARIS, 23 June 1995, *Village Street, Goose Girl* (1890, oil on canvas, 25 1/2 x 23 1/2 ins / 65 x 60 cm) FRF 850,000. NANCY, 2 July 1995, *Still-life with Mimosa and Apples* (oil on canvas, 19 3/4 x 24 ins / 50 x 61 cm) FRF 95,000. PARIS, 18 March 1996, *Le Pouldu, Cattle Grazing* (oil on canvas, 23 1/2 x 28 3/4 ins / 60 x 73 cm) FRF 1,810,000. PARIS, 28 March 1996, *Young Girl with Flowers* (gouache, 33 x 24 3/4 ins / 84 x 63 cm) FRF 50,000. PARIS, 13 June 1996, *Landscape* (1893, lithograph, 9 1/4 x 12 ins / 23.3 x 30.2 cm) FRF 13,000. LONDON, 25 June 1996, *Haymaker, Homage to Van Gogh* (1892, oil on canvas, 28 1/4 x 35 3/4 ins / 72 x 91 cm) GBP 177,500. LONDON, 2 Dec 1996, *Mother and Child in a Breton Landscape* (1890, oil on canvas, 28 3/4 x 23 1/2 ins / 73.2 x 60 cm) GBP 194,000. PARIS, 16 June 1997, *Portrait of Mai Chaipp* (1889, oil on canvas, 22 x 18 ins / 55 x 46 cm) FRF 185,000. PARIS, 20 Nov 1997, *Two Peasant Women Among the Rocks* (gouache, 6 1/4 x 3 1/2 ins / 16 x 9 cm) FRF 40,000. PARIS, 12 Dec 1997, *Hill with Large Trees* (oil/c, 47 1/4 x 23 1/2 ins / 120 x 60 cm) FRF 83,000. LONDON, 29 June 1999, *Yellow Farm at Pouldu* (1890, oil on canvas, 17 x 22 ins / 44 x 55 cm) GBP 200,000. LONDON, 7 Dec 1999, *Portrait of Mai Chaipp* (1889, oil on canvas, 22 x 18 ins / 55 x 46 cm) GBP 130,000. PARIS, 29 March 2000, *Ile de la Douane, Entree du Trieux* (watercolour heightened with gouache, 13 x 20 ins / 33 x 50 cm) FRF 260,000. NEW YORK, 11 May 2000, *Still-life with Fruit and Vase of Flowers* (oil on canvas, 22 x 15 ins / 56 x 39 cm) USD 30,000. PARIS, 14 Dec 2001, *Breton Women, Meeting in the Sacred Wood* (oil on canvas, 28 x 36 ins / 72 x 92 cm) FRF 2,500,000. BREST, 16 Dec 2001, *Field of Golden Wheat and Buckwheat* (oil on canvas, 41 x 19 ins / 103 x 47 cm) FRF 1,240,000. NEW YORK, 8 May 2002, *Yellow Farm at Pouldu* (1890, oil on canvas, 17 x 22 ins / 44 x 55 cm) USD 380,000. BREST, 12 May 2002, *Harvest of Black Wheat* (1899, oil on canvas) EUR 540,000. NEW YORK, 6 May 2003, *Two Washerwomen by a Waterfall* (c. 1890, oil on canvas, 29 x 37 ins / 74 x 93 cm) USD 550,000. NEW YORK, 11 Dec 2003, *Waiting at the Fountain* (oil on canvas, 43 x 27 ins / 110 x 69 cm) USD 90,000. NEW YORK, 6 May 2004, *Fisherman at the Laita* (1890, tempera on board on panel, 26 x 20 ins / 65 x 50 cm) USD 340,000. LONDON, 22 June 2004, *Woman and Child in a Breton Landscape* (1890, oil on canvas, 29 x 24 ins / 73 x 60 cm) GBP 190,000.

SERUZIER, Jean Gabriel

French, 20th century.

Born 14 December 1905, in Landrecies.

Painter, watercolourist, draughtsman, illustrator.

Portraits, scenes with figures, landscapes, seascapes, still-lifes.

Jean Gabriel Seruzier was a pupil of the École des Arts Décoratifs in Paris. He was a press photographer, reporter and war correspondent who covered many countries before dedicating himself to painting from 1965. He took part in many regional salons as well as the annual Salon des Indépendants in Paris.

He depicted landscapes of Bourbon, Provence and Brittany with characters such as peasants and seed-sowers. He had a lyrical, spontaneous and sometimes naive style, emphasising the effect of colour. He was also a cartoonist, contributing to various journals.

SERVAËS, Albert

Belgian, 20th century.
Born 4 April 1883, in Ghent; died 19 April 1966, in Lucerne.
Active in Switzerland from 1944 (naturalised in 1961).
Painter, draughtsman, illustrator. Religious subjects, portraits, genre scenes, landscapes. Designs for stained glass, designs for tapestries.
Symbolism.
Laethem-St-Martin Group (Second School).

Albert Servaës was a member of the Laethem-St-Martin School along with other first-generation Laethem artists such as Saedeleer and Georges Minne. He took evening courses under Jean Delvin at the fine arts academy in Ghent in 1903. While in Laethem, Servaës - by all accounts a solitary figure - 'found God', declaring that, henceforth, he would 'follow only two masters - the Apostles and Nature'. Servaës became a member of the Royal Flemish Academy of Sciences, Letters and the Arts.

Albert Servaës started by painting sober rustic or religious themes with an overlay of symbolism but subsequently emerged alongside second-generation Laethem artists Gustav de Smet and Constant Permeke as a leading figure in Belgian Expressionism. His subject matter was resolutely religious although he continued to paint landscapes. He was particularly drawn to the depiction of everyday life in Flanders and of its peasants who, to him, embodied naturalness and all that was good. His landscapes and peasant studies formed a platform for his predominantly religious compositions painted in a highly personal and almost sensuous style as he applied colours thickly to bring out the *chiaroscuro* of the Flemish countryside.

Servaës' work proved at times highly controversial, never more so than with respect to his paintings of the Crucifixion, one of which was removed from a church because he had rendered the flesh tones of Christ's face other than in the conventional 'baby' pink. This points to a fundamental problem of contemporary religious art, inasmuch as clerical dogma often precludes artistic innovation. Servaës, a deeply religious man, was pilloried by a scandalised clerical establishment for having dared break with tradition. Yet his profound sense of religious conviction was undoubtedly a major factor in his ability to impart vigour and meaning to his best work.

Servaës first came to the attention of a broader public when he exhibited *Ferryman* - featuring the figure of St Christopher - at the 1908 Salon. A posthumous exhibition devoted to his work was mounted in 1970-1971 at the royal museum in Antwerp.

a. servaes

BIBLIOGRAPHY:

Nisot, Marie Thérèse, *Un peintre flamand, Albert Servaes*, Imprimerie Chantenay, Paris, 1927. Haesaerts, Paul, *Laethem Saint Martin, le village élu de l'Art flamand*, Arcade, Brussels, 1965. *Albert Servaes*, exhibition catalogue, Koninklijk Museum, Antwerp, 1970-1971.

MUSEUMS AND GALLERIES:

ANTWERP: *Peasant Life* (cycle of twelve canvases) - BRUSSELS (Mus. royaux des Beaux-Arts de Belgique): *Pietà* (1920) - GHENT: *Banks of the Lys* (1933) - GRENOBLE (Mus. de Grenoble): *Harvest* (1927).

AUCTION RECORDS:

BRUSSELS, 13-14-15 Oct 1965, *Pietà*, BEF 175,000. ANTWERP, 26 April 1966, *Haystacks*, BEF 120,000. ANTWERP, 23-24 April 1968, *Golden Landscape*, BEF 135,000. ANTWERP, 21 April 1970, *Landscape in the Snow*, BEF 250,000. ANTWERP, 10 Oct 1972, *Gleaners*, BEF 140,000. ANTWERP, 2 April 1974, *Winter Landscape*, BEF 300,000. ANTWERP, 19 Oct 1976, *Harvesting* (1907, oil on canvas, 18½ x 20¾ ins / 47 x 53 cm) BEF 340,000. ANTWERP, 25 Oct 1977, *Harvesters* (1915, oil on canvas, 15¾ x 20¾ ins / 40 x 53 cm) BEF 525,000. ANTWERP, 23 Oct 1979, *Views of Orval* (1929, oil on canvas, 19¾ x 27½ ins / 50 x 70 cm) BEF 100,000. ANTWERP, 22 April 1980, *Monk* (1932, drawing, 35½ x 30 ins / 90 x 76 cm) BEF 240,000; *Portrait of a Man* (1950, pastel, 9 x 6¾ ins / 23 x 17 cm) BEF 40,000. ANTWERP, 29 April 1981, *Peasant* (1935, drawing, 72¾ x 42¼ ins / 185 x 107 cm) BEF 140,000. ANTWERP, 27 April 1982, *Winter Landscape* (1918, oil on canvas, 22 x 25½ ins / 56 x 65 cm) BEF 280,000. LOKEREN, 15 Oct 1983, *Cherry Blossom* (1925, oil on canvas, 26¾ x 33¾ ins / 68 x 86 cm) BEF 360,000. ANTWERP, 25 Oct 1983, *Peasant* (1917, drawing, 30¼ x 28 ins / 77 x 71 cm) BEF 240,000. ANTWERP, 23 April 1985, *Winter Landscape* (1944, oil on canvas, 15¾ x 21¼ ins / 40 x 54 cm) BEF 14,000. LONDON, 23 Oct 1985, *Annunciation* (1931, charcoal, 17¾ x 22½ ins / 45 x 57 cm) GBP 1,400. ANTWERP, 22 April 1986, *St John the Baptist in the River Lys* (1924, oil on canvas, 28¼ x 35½ ins / 72 x 90 cm) BEF 200,000. LOKEREN, 16 May 1987, *Portrait of a Flemish Peasant* (1921, charcoal, 34¼ x 30¾ ins / 87 x 78 cm) BEF 260,000. LOKEREN, 28 May 1988, *Landscape with Poplars* (oil on canvas, 16¼ x 11¼ ins / 41.5 x 28.5 cm) BEF 160,000. AMSTERDAM, 23 May 1991, *Four Seasons* (1938, charcoal/paper, four drawings, each 28¼ x 17 ins / 72 x 43.2 cm) NLG 12,650. BRUSSELS, 7 Oct 1991, *Haystacks* (oil on canvas, 19¾ x 25½ ins / 50 x 65 cm) BEF 170,000. LOKEREN, 21 March 1992, *Landscape in the Snow* (1920, oil on canvas, 32½ x 32½ ins / 82.5 x 82.5 cm) BEF 360,000. LOKEREN, 10 Oct 1992, *Christ on The Cross* (1964, pastel, 20½ x 17½ ins / 52 x 44.5 cm) BEF 90,000; *Harvesters* (1918, oil on canvas, 18 x 24 ins / 46 x 61 cm) BEF 670,000. LOKEREN, 20 March 1993, *Church Interior (St Nicholas, Ghent)* (1915, oil on panel, 26½ x 22¼ ins / 67.5 x 56.5 cm) BEF 90,000. LOKEREN, 20 March 1993, *Snow-Covered Landscape, Laethem* (1920, oil on canvas, 20 x 28 ins / 51 x 71 cm) BEF 330,000. AMSTERDAM, 27-28 May 1993, *House in the Snow* (oil on canvas, 19¾ x 22 ins / 50 x 56 cm) NLG 36,800. LOKEREN, 9 Oct 1993, *Adam and Eve* (1946, pastel, 15¾ x 19¾ ins / 40 x 50 cm) BEF 48,000; *Harvesters* (1920, oil on canvas, 18¼ x 21¼ ins / 46.5 x 54 cm) BEF 750,000. AMSTERDAM, 7 Dec 1994, *Gathering Potatoes* (1928, oil on canvas, 46½ x 68 ins / 118 x 173 cm) NLG 55,200. LOKEREN, 11 March 1995, *Christ on The Cross* (1922, oil on canvas, 36½ x 35½ ins / 93 x 90 cm) BEF 850,000. AMSTERDAM, 5 June 1996, *Landscape with a Farm in the Distance* (oil on card, 15¼ x 20¾ ins / 39 x 53 cm) NLG 4,600. LOKEREN, 5 Oct 1996, *Landscape with Farm* (1919, oil on canvas/panel, 15¼ x 21 ins / 39 x 53.5 cm) BEF 180,000. LOKEREN, 11 Oct 1997, *Landscape at Dusk* (1928, oil on canvas, 21 x 22¼ ins / 52.5 x 56.5 cm) BEF 230,000. LOKEREN, 6 Dec 1997, *Winter* (1923, oil on canvas, 23½ x 23½ ins / 60 x 60 cm) BEF 300,000. ANTWERP, 19 Oct 1999, *The Road to Emmaus* (oil on canvas) BEF 115,000. AMSTERDAM, 4 July 2000, *Christ on the Cross with the Three Marys* (1930, charcoal, 59 x 59 ins / 149 x 149 cm) NLG 34,000. ZURICH, 28 Nov 2000, *Winter in Flanders* (1931, oil on canvas, 44 x 37 ins / 113 x 94 cm) CHF 30,000. LOKEREN, 6 Oct 2001, *Mourners* (1935, charcoal, 39 x 61 ins / 98 x 156 cm) BEF 330,000. LOKEREN, 6 Oct 2001, *Christmas Eve* (1917, oil on canvas, 31 x 39 ins / 80 x 100 cm) BEF 600,000. LOKEREN, 9 March 2002, *Snowy Landscape* (1917, oil on canvas, 22 x 26 ins / 57 x 66 cm) EUR 9,000. ANTWERP, 23 April 2002, *Christ on the Cross* (1921, charcoal, 59 x 59 ins / 150 x 150 cm) EUR 13,000. BRUSSELS, 14 April 2003, *Crucifixion* (1930, mixed media, 59 x 59 ins / 150 x 150 cm) EUR 12,000. ANTWERP, 20 Oct 2003, *Har-*

vest (oil on canvas on panel, 18 x 20 ins / 45 x 52 cm) EUR 8,500. BRUSSELS, 11 Oct 2004, *Countryside in the Snow* (1925, oil on canvas, 20 x 28 ins / 50 x 70 cm) EUR 8,200. BRUSSELS, 6 Dec 2004, *Snowy Landscape with House* (1916, oil on canvas, 17 x 27 ins / 42 x 69 cm) EUR 6,000.

SERVAES, Herman
Flemish School, 17th century.
Born c. 1601, in Antwerp; died 1674 or 1675, in Antwerp.
Painter.

Herman Servaes was a pupil of Van Dyck around 1616. He was in Mechelen in 1630, and in the guild of Antwerp in 1650.

AUCTION RECORDS:
PARIS, 5 March 1945, *Landscape by Night*, FRF 1,700.

SERVAIS, André
Belgian, 20th century.
Born 1937, in Ixelles (Brussels).
Painter, draughtsman, engraver.

André Servais was a lithographer; he worked in the poetic realist vein.

SERVAIS, Franz
Belgian, 20th century.
Born 1904, in Wanfercée.
Painter. Landscapes, still-lifes.

AUCTION RECORDS:
BRUSSELS, 27 March 1990, *Still-life with Accessories* (oil on canvas, 24 x 27 1/2 ins / 61 x 70 cm) BEF 60,000. BRUSSELS, 9 Oct 1990, *Landscape* (oil on panel, 15 1/4 x 23 1/4 ins / 39 x 59 cm) BEF 34,000.

SERVAIS, Joseph
French, 19th century.
Painter. Flowers.

Servais exhibited at the Salon between 1831 and 1839.

SERVALLI, Pietro
Italian, 20th century.
Born 7 October 1883, in Sandino; died 1973.
Painter. Murals.

A fresco painter, Pietro Servalli was a pupil of Ponziano Loverini from Bergamo and Ludwig Herterich from Munich.

MUSEUMS AND GALLERIES:
BERGAMO (Accademia Carrara): *Head of an Old Man.*

SERVAN, Florentin
French, 19th century.
Born 1810, in Lyons; died 1879, in Lyons.
Painter. History painting, portraits, landscapes.

Florentin Servan was a pupil of Augustin Thierriat at the École des Beaux-Arts in Lyons. A nephew of Victor Orsel, he might also have been advised by him in Paris. His work was featured at the Lyons Salon between 1838 and 1867 and at the Paris Salon from 1839.

Most of his paintings are of landscapes in Provence, Italy and the Bugey region of France.

MUSEUMS AND GALLERIES:
LYONS (MBA): *Landscape.*

SERVANDONI, Jean Adrien Claude, or Servandony
French, 18th century.
Born 26 April 1736, in Paris.
Painter. Decorative schemes.

Jean Adrien Claude Servandoni was the son of Jean Nicolas Servandoni.

SERVANDONI, Jean Nicolas or Jean Jérôme or Giovanni Niccolo, or Servandony, Servandon, Servando
French, 18th century.
Born 2 May 1695, in Florence; died 19 January 1766, in Paris.
Painter. Allegorical subjects, landscapes with figures, architectural views.

Jean Nicolas Servandoni studied painting in Piacenza under Giovan Paolo Panini and architecture in Rome under Rossi. He lived in Portugal before going to Paris where he was exceedingly well received. However, his masterpiece, the façade of the church of St Sulpice, has been mercilessly criticized over the years. Less virulent these days, these attacks still have some currency. Yet St Sulpice does not deserve the catalogue of mistakes and bad taste for which it was derided only 50 years ago. People have come to the realisation that it is not without commendable assets besides the Delacroix frescoes (*Jacob Fighting the Angel* and *Heliodorus Driven from the Temple*), the quality of which was never in question. Servandoni was unable to complete the work and it should be remembered that he undertook a difficult project which had defeated architects and sculptors reputedly as talented - or at least as well qualified - as him. Ambition drove him.

For some 20 years there has been an air of mystery around Servandoni, who is now credited with some French extraction and a name Italianised only later in Rome into Servandoni when artists from that nation were the craze in Paris, where he sought to establish himself. There is no solid evidence to back this hypothesis but it might be worthy of a footnote in history books. He became a member of the Académie Royale on 26 May 1731 as an architectural painter. He was also ennobled. In 1749 he went to London where he married. He went on to visit Dresden, Vienna and Württemberg. He exhibited at the Salon from 1737 to 1765.

MUSEUMS AND GALLERIES:
PARIS (Louvre): *Self-portrait* - ROCHEFORT: *Architectural Interior* - VERSAILLES: *Self-portrait.*

AUCTION RECORDS:
PARIS, 1874, *Ruins in a Landscape*, FRF 275. PARIS, 1879, *View of a Temple*, FRF 720. PARIS, 7 Feb 1898, *Plan and Section of a Drawing Room*, FRF 125. PARIS, 17 March 1910, *Pro Pelte di Tre Parti dell' Cortile delle Em. Cardinale di Polignac* (drawing heightened with watercolour) FRF 500. PARIS, 25 Jan 1929, *Italian Landscapes with Ruins* (three canvases) FRF 600. PARIS, 18 June 1943, *The Sabines Interrupting the Fight* (sepia wash) FRF 480; *Allegorical Scenes* (two sepia washes heightened with blue) FRF 1,010. PARIS, 22 March 1950, *Figures among Ruins* (pen and wash, two pendants) FRF 4,000. PARIS, 12 June 1973, *Ruins with Figures*, FRF 26,000. PARIS, 27 March 1992, *Storm near a Coast with Monuments* (oils on canvas, a pair, 18 1/2 x 52 ins / 47 x 132 cm) FRF 82,000. LONDON, 2 July 1996, *Roman Triumph with Prisoners Following a General* (black chalk and ink heightened with white and red gouache/paper with brown finish, 14 1/4 x 25 ins / 36 x 63.6 cm) GBP 862. LONDON, 13 Dec 1996, *Caprice with an Ionic Temple in Ruins and an Obelisk with Peasants* (1724, oil on canvas, 52 x 38 1/2 ins / 132.2 x 98 cm) GBP 51,000. PARIS, 24 March 1999, *Two Views of Imaginary Prisons* (black chalk, colour ink and colour wash heightened with white, a pair, 18 x 24 ins / 46 x 60 cm) FRF 30,000. PARIS, 1 Dec 1999, *River Landscapes* (gouache, three, 15 x 22 ins / 37 x 55 cm) FRF 21,000. PARIS, 16 June 2000, *Three Figures among Roman Ruins* (oil on panel, 8 x 6 ins / 20 x 15 cm) FRF 20,000. VIENNA, 12 June 2001, *Architectural Capriccio* (oil on canvas, 28 x 22 ins / 72 x 56 cm) ATS 120,000. NEW YORK, 24 Jan 2002, *Capriccio of a Ruined Ionic Temple and an Obelisk with Figures* (1724, oil on canvas, 52 x 39 ins / 132 x 98 cm) USD 140,000. PARIS, 27 June 2002, *Architectural Capriccios with Ruins. Women Bathing in a Rocky Landscape. Crossing the Ford* (gouache, set of four, 21 x 30 ins / 53 x 77 cm) EUR 22,000. NEW YORK, 24 Jan 2003, *Capriccio of a Ruined Ionic Temple and an Obelisk with Figures* (1724, oil on canvas, 52 x 39 ins / 132 x 98 cm) USD 120,000.

SERVANES, real name Simone Servanes
French, 20th century.
Born 1918, in Toulon; died September 2000, in Paris.
Painter, sculptor. Architectural integration.
Groups: Espace, GRAV (Groupe de Recherche d'Art Visuel).

Simone Servanes was a pupil at the École des Beaux-Arts in Toulon. She was a painter. She apparently never exhibited before the war, but between 1950 and 1959 she appeared in the Salon des Réalités Nouvelles in Paris. She briefly joined the Espace group, which she left in 1957. In 1960 she appeared in the exhibition *Motus* in Milan. In 1960 she was a founder member of GRAV (Research Centre for Visual Art), where she refused to exhibit and which she left four months later. Up to World War II, Servanes probably painted in a figurative style, fired by Cézanne's example. After the war, often together with Del Marle or other plastic artists and architects (Zehrfuss for the Renault factory at Flins), she devoted the main part of her activity to the building arts, considering the role of multicoloured architecture.

Her ethical view was similar to that of the Russian Productivism of the 1920s, subordinating art to social needs. As for the spatial and constructive - even therapeutic and synaesthetic - potential of colour, in the 1950s Servanes gave up using primary colours of in favour of non-colours: grey, white and black. Between 1949 and 1951 she created all six of her spatial constructions. Mounted on black pedestals and emerging from a cube, they consist of stems of curved metal, glued together and painted, and flat sheets in triangles, circles and rectangular parallelogram blocks, cut in wood, iron or Plexiglas. Individually, these constructions define the potential of the curve, the oblique and the orthogonal. It cannot definitely be said that they materialise geometric figures in space, the curved stems in particular creating less austere volumes. In 1984 she was able to create in true monumental grandeur, within the law of minimum returns, the *Composition* in tubes of curved, multicoloured steel erected at Dijon university, where it rubbed shoulders with other contemporary works such as reliefs by Agam, Jean Gorin and Gottfried Honneger.

BIBLIOGRAPHY:
Orgeval, Domitille d', '*A propos d'acquisitions du musée de Grenoble, les constructions spatiales de Servannes: des éléments pour la synthèse des arts*' in *Revue du Louvre* n° 3 p. 72, periodical, Paris, June 2001.

MUSEUMS AND GALLERIES:
DIJON (FRAC Bourgogne): *Untitled* (1959) - GRENOBLE (Mus. de Grenoble): *Construction n°1* (1949); *Construction n°2* (1949); *Composition* (1950) - VALENCIENNES (MBA): *Polychromies architecturales* (two models).

SERVANG
British, 18th century.
Born in England; died c. 1800, in Cádiz.
Painter. Portraits, landscapes.

Painted stage sets in Lisbon from 1780 to 1790.

SERVANT, André
French, 19th century.
Born in Lyons.
Painter. Portraits, genre scenes, still-lifes.

A. Servant was a pupil of N. S. Cornu. He made his debut at the Salon in 1867.

AUCTION RECORDS:
PARIS, 1891, *Victims of the Young Hunter,* FRF 32.

SERVANT, Jacques
French, 20th century.
Born 29 August 1937, in Bordeaux.
Painter, watercolourist.

Jacques Servant was a pupil at the Académie des Beaux-Arts in Paris. He studied the techniques of the Dutch Masters in the studio of Conrad Kieckert, and then took up watercolour painting from 1974. He spent some time in Mexico. Influenced by Mexican art he worked on geometric, Pantheist motifs, playing with the effects of transparency that allowed him to use Indian ink and watercolour.

He took part in public exhibitions in Paris, notably at the Salon des Indépendants, and showed his works in solo exhibitions from 1989 in Paris, and in 1990 in Mexico and Port-au-Prince.

SERVANT, Josée
French, 20th century.
Born 8 March 1933, in St-Girons.
Painter, potter.

Josée Servant was a pupil at the École des Beaux-Arts in Toulouse up to 1952, and from 1952 to 1955 at the École des Beaux-Arts in Paris. She later worked on ceramics at Vallauris, before returning to Paris in 1957 to take up painting again in 1960. She showed her works in solo exhibitions in Paris in 1970. She later exhibited in Venice, Antwerp, St-Tropez and again in Paris in 1972. Her paintings often have a motorcycle as a subject.

SERVE, Andrée
Belgian, 20th century.
Born 1929, in Ixelles (Brussels).
Painter.

Andrée Serve studied at the fine arts academy in Watermael-Boitsfort near Brussels.

SERVE, Benoît
French, 16th - 17th century.
Active in Lyons.
Sculptor (wood), cabinet maker.

Serve worked for the church of the Collège de la Trinité, Lyons.

SERVE, Joëlle
French, 20th century.
Born 1937, in Paris.
Painter, engraver.

Joëlle Serve lives and works in Paris. She took part in 1992 in the exhibition *De Bonnard à Baselitz - Dix Ans d'enrichissements du cabinet des estampes 1978-1988* (*From Bonnard to Baselitz: A Decade of Acquisitions by the Prints Collection 1978-1988*) at the Bibliothèque Nationale in Paris.

BIBLIOGRAPHY:
'*Joëlle Serve: la fusée à trois étages*' in *Art et Métiers du Livre* n° 198 p. 29-31, periodical, Paris, 1996.

MUSEUMS AND GALLERIES:
PARIS (BNF, Prints Collection): *The Strike* (1983, etching).

SERVEAU, Clément. See **CLÉMENT-SERVEAU**

SERVI, Antonio
Italian, 17th century.
Born in Trevieri, near Ancona; died 1706, in Lucerne.
Painter.

Antonio Servi worked as an artist in almost every country in Europe. He painted two altarpieces for the church of the Madonna del Soccorso in Rovigo.

SERVI, Costantino de'
Italian, 16th - 17th century.
Born 1554, in Florence; died 1622, in Lusignano.
Architect, sculptor, painter.

After working for a time with Santi di Tito, Costantino de' Servi went to Germany where he began to work in the style of Porbus. He owed his reputation mainly to his architectural work although he also made some beautiful mosaics in Florence. He worked as an architect and engineer for the Shah of Persia, the Prince of Wales and Emperor Rudolph II. He had an important influence on a considerable number of young painters whom he encouraged to paint in the style of

Michelangelo but with the latter's severity softened by more graceful contours.

SERVI, Giovanni

Italian, 19th century.
Born 1795 or 1800 (?), in Venice; died 1885, in Milan.
Painter. Genre scenes.

SERVIERES, Eugénie Marguerite Honorée Léthière

Maiden name: Charen
French, 19th century.
Born 1786, in Paris.
Painter. History painting, portraits, genre scenes, landscapes.

Eugénie Servieres was a pupil of Léthière. She exhibited at the Salon between 1808 and 1824 and was awarded medals in 1808 and 1817.

Museums and Galleries:
Versailles (Trianon): *Inès de Castro and her Children at the Feet of the King of Portugal.*

SERVIN

French, 20th century.
Born 1939, in St-Félix-de-Lodez.
Painter, sculptor, engraver.

Servin was a pupil of Raoul Lambert, and lives and works in Brassac. Exhibitions he has taken part in include: 1971, 1975, Museum at Béziers; 1976, Salon de Puteaux; 1978, Bibliothèque Nationale de Paris; 1983, École Nationale des Beaux-Arts in Paris; 1992, *De Bonnard à Baselitz - Dix Ans d'enrichissements du cabinet des estampes 1978-1988* (*From Bonnard to Baselitz: A Decade of Acquisitions by the Prints Collection 1978-1988*), Bibliothèque Nationale, Paris. He has shown in solo exhibitions since 1966: 1966, 1972, Montpellier; 1967, Béziers; 1974, 1975, Nancy; 1986, Paris; 1994, studio Cadres and Lavis, Béziers; and, since 1998, a presentation of sculptures in his garden at Lamontelarie (Tarn). In 1977 and 1980 he received an award from the city of Paris.

Museums and Galleries:
Béziers (MBA) - Paris (BNF, Prints Collection): *Jigsaw of a Nude* (1972, wood) - Paris (Mus. de la Publicité).

SERVIN, Amédée Élie

French, 19th century.
Born 5 September 1829, in Paris; died 1885 or 1886, in Villiers-sur-Morin (Seine-et-Marne).
Painter, engraver. Genre scenes, landscapes, animals.

A. Servin was a pupil of Drolling. Was admitted to the École des Beaux-Arts on 7 April 1848 and made his debut at the Salon in 1850 where he was awarded a second class medal in 1872.

Servin was an artist of great sincerity. He painted scenes from nature with no thought of whether or not they would sell and his work deserves investigation by art lovers.

A.SERVIN.

Museums and Galleries:
Le Mans (Le Mans) - Marseilles: *Balé Windmill* - Melun (Melun) - Paris (Louvre): *My Pork Butcher's Well.*

Auction records:
Paris, 1872, *Balé Windmill,* FRF 5,000. Paris, 13 May 1873, *Sour Wine,* FRF 1,150. Paris, 1875, *My Pork Butcher's Well,* FRF 2,250. Paris, 24 May 1888, *Woodcutters,* FRF 1,050. Paris, 26-27 May 1902, *Archery,* FRF 1,800. Paris, 27 May 1905, *Arrival of the Fishermen,* FRF 1,250. Paris, 10 Nov 1910, *Setting Off for the Park,* FRF 2,000. Paris, 11 June 1926, *Cows Around the Pool,* FRF 420; *Windmill by the Sea,* FRF 200. Paris, 16-17 May 1927, *Drinking Trough,* FRF 1,600; *Entrance to the Village,* FRF 1,650. Paris, 27 May 1943, *Sunken Lane near the Farm,* FRF 2,100. London, 16 Dec 1949, *Housewife Shelling Peas,* GBP 69. Paris, 23 June 1954, *Fish Market,* FRF 15,000. Enghien-les-Bains, 25 Nov 1984, *Joiner's Workshop* (oil on canvas, 23 1/2 x 28 3/4 ins / 60 x 73 cm) FRF 24,500. Amsterdam, 19 Oct 1993, *Windmill at Villiers-sur-Morin* (oil on panel, 17 1/2 x 29 3/4 ins / 44.5 x 75.5 cm) NLG 8,625. London, 17 June 1994, *Windmill at Villiers-sur-Morin* (oil on panel, 17 1/4 x 29 1/4 ins / 43.7 x 74.3 cm) GBP 3,450. Paris, 26 March 2000, *Young Woman by a Fruit Tree* (oil on canvas, 30 x 25 ins / 76 x 64 cm) FRF 39,000. Paris, 26 March 2003, *Evening in a Breton Cottage* (oil on panel, 16 x 22 ins / 40 x 55 cm) EUR 1,800.

SERVITORI, Domingo Maria

Spanish, 18th century.
Active from 1757 to 1773.
Painter, draughtsman. Portraits, religious subjects.

Domigo Maria Servitori was a member of the order of the Knights Hospitaller. He was appointed painter to the king of Spain.

Museums and Galleries:
London (British Mus.): *Portrait of the Artist* (pen drawing); *St Rosalia* (pen drawing).

SERVOISIER, Zénobie Honorine

French, 19th century.
Born 6 April 1821, in Paris.
Painter. Portraits, landscapes.

Zénobie Servoisier was a pupil of L. Cogniet. She exhibited at the Salon in 1857 and 1861.

Museums and Galleries:
Versailles (Mus.): *Portrait of Lt. General Binet, Baron of Marcognet.*

SERVOLINI, Benedetto

Italian, 19th century.
Born 25 February 1805, in Florence; died 7 June 1879, in Florence.
Painter.

A student at the academy in Rome, Servolini worked in Rome and Venice.

Museums and Galleries:
Florence (Gal. dell'Accademia): *Orlando Stealing a Shepherd's Horse when Mad.*

SERVOLINI, Carlo

Italian, 20th century.
Born 5 April 1876, in Livorno; died 12 September 1948, in Collesalvetti (Tuscany).
Painter, watercolourist, draughtsman, engraver.
Religious subjects, scenes with figures, sporting subjects, landscapes.

Carlo Servolini was a self-taught artist with a deep sense of lyricism and exceptional gift for the graphic arts. Guglielmo Micheli, Fattori's favourite pupil, helped him, giving him much good advice. Servolini rejected the imitation of traditional *macchiaiolismo,* becoming one of the few artists working in Livorno to remain truly independent.

A gifted draughtsman, he excelled in the use of colour in his celebrations of wild and primitive nature. In 1935, he became interested in print making, experimenting with engraving and etching. He produced many remarkable plates in which he composed complex and emotionally-charged scenes often dominated by figures in motion. They include his beautiful *Stations of the Cross,* the allegorical series of *Vices* and hunting and sporting scenes. He produced in all some 80 prints, all highly original and often inspired by popular prints of earlier centuries. These do not represent a mere sideline to his main work as a painter; they are rather an indication of the vigorous and strong personality of an artist able to express his tormented imagination equally well in different media. One of the major Italian landscape artists of the first half of the 20th century, he also produced excellent watercolours and lithographs. He participated in the Venice Biennales, the Rome Quadriennales and other the major international exhibitions.

BIBLIOGRAPHY:

Orsini, Giovanni/Servolini, Luigi, *Carlo Servolini*, monograph. Andreucci, Domenico, *'Pittori del primo Novecento: Carla Servolini'* in *Rivista di Livorno*, periodical, Livorno, 1952.

SERVOLINI, Giuseppe

Italian, 18th - 19th century.
Born c. 1770, in Florence; died 1830?.
Painter.

Servolini painted frescoes in churches in Florence.

MUSEUMS AND GALLERIES:

FLORENCE (Uffizi): *Portrait of the Artist.*

SERVOLINI, Luigi

Italian, 20th century.
Born 1 March 1906, in Livorno; died 1981.
Painter, engraver. Religious subjects, landscapes, still-lifes.

The son of Carlo Servolini, like his father Luigi Servolini was self-taught. He taught at the Istituto Reale del Libro in Urbino between 1930 and 1939 when he was appointed director of the Istituto di Belle Arti in Forlì. He also wrote on art.

Luigi Servolini was one of the most important Italian wood-engravers. His works consist in sharply contrasting blacks and whites with no intermediate shades, creating strongly drawn images that seem primitive and often arid and expressionistic. Colour is used in some of the woodcuts (chromoxylographs), each element of the composition outlined in black.

He took part in the Brera Biennale, the Venice Biennale and the Rome Quadriennale.

BIBLIOGRAPHY:

Scrivo, Luigi, *Servolini - Maestro dell'incisione contemporanea*, Incisori Associati, Milan, 1976.

MUSEUMS AND GALLERIES:

AMSTERDAM (Rijksmus.) - ASTI (Pinacoteca e Mus. Civico) - BERLIN (Kupferstichkabinet) - BOSTON (Public Library, Fine Arts Department) - BREMEN (Kunsthalle) - BRUSSELS (Bibliothèque royale Albert Ier, Prints Collection) - BUCHAREST (Bibliothèque de l'Académie, Prints Collection) - BUDAPEST (Magyar Nemzeti Múz.) - BUFFALO (Albright-Knox AG) - CLEVELAND (MA) - COPENHAGEN (Thorvaldsens Mus.) - DARMSTADT (Hessisches Landesmus.) - KHARKOV (MFA) - LISBON (Biblioteca Nacional) - LONDON (British Mus.) - LONDON (Victoria and Albert Mus.) - LOS ANGELES (MMA) - MONTREAL (MAM) - MOSCOW (Pushkin MFA) - MÜNSTER (Westfälischer Kunstverein) - NEW YORK (Metropolitan Mus. of Art) - PALERMO (Gal. d'Arte Moderna) - PARIS (BNF, Prints Collection) - ROME (Prints Collection) - ST PETERSBURG (Hermitage) - TOKYO (National MMA) - TURIN (Gal. Civica d'Arte Moderna e Contemporanea) - VIENNA (Albertina Mus.) - ZURICH (Prints Collection).

SERVONI, Calimero

Italian, 18th century.
Born in Piacenza; died 1733, in Civitavecchia.
Painter. History painting, portraits.

Servoni was active in Rome and Civitavecchia.

SERVRANCKX, Victor

Belgian, 20th century.
Born 26 June 1897, in Dieghem; died 12 December 1965, in Vilvoorde.
Painter, sculptor. Designs for wallpapers and fabrics.
L'Effort Moderne group.

Victor Servranckx, destined to become one of Belgian's leading Abstract painters, claimed to have painted his first 'real' painting at the age of five. He studied between 1913 and 1917 at the Académie Royale des Beaux-Arts in Brussels, working under Crespin and Montald. By 1932, he was teaching at the Ixelles college of decorative and industrial arts. He made frequent trips abroad, notably to the USA and South America. Marcel Duchamp welcomed him to the USA and Laszlo Moholy-Nagy urged him to accept a chair at the Chicago Bauhaus; Servranckx declined.

Like many others, Servranckx started out as a figurative painter influenced by Symbolism. His work became progressively Abstract and Surrealist as he gradually developed a highly personal style which he himself described as 'plastique pure' ('unadulterated plasticity') alternating vertical and horizontal rhythms, blocks of colour and geometrical forms. His compositions were based on the classic 'Golden Mean' principle, overlaid with Futurist components. Around 1920, Servranckx aligned himself with the Paris-based Effort Moderne group around Léonce Rosenberg; the titles he gave to his work from this period attest to his Italian Futurist leanings - *Machine Love, Extended in Space, Stretched to Breaking Point*, etc. His work became increasingly synesthetic, becoming progressively violent and turbulent as his style evolved towards Abstract Expressionism. He was arguably the first Belgian painter to work in this style, although Joseph Lacasse was evolving in that direction about the same time.

Servranckx then turned his attention to the relationship between art, decoration and architecture. He began by designing wallpapers and fabrics and, in 1925, worked alongside architect Huib Oste on the decoration of an exhibition pavilion. He produced a 5,920 square feet (550 square metre) fresco for the Salon de la Radio in Brussels in 1936, a date Fernand Léger would later describe as a 'benchmark year in the history of modern mural art'. He continued to paint the occasional figurative composition, in all probability because his Abstract work enjoyed only modest success. After World War II, however, the situation changed rapidly as the world started to accept and embrace Abstract art.

Servranckx' third and final period was resolutely Abstract and, above all, static and 'pure', recalling the abstractions favoured by Auguste Herbin and Amédée Ozenfant in the 1920s rather than, as some commentators insist, the work of Piet Mondrian.

Servranckx took part in a number of group exhibitions, including that of the Société Anonyme in New York in 1920. He also exhibited from 1947 at the Salon des Réalités Nouvelles in Paris, and examples of his work featured in 1977 at *Aspects Historiques du Constructivisme et de l'Art Concret* (*Historical Aspects of Constructivism and Concrete Art*) at the Musée d'Art Moderne de la Ville de Paris. His first one-man show dates back to 1917 and is widely agreed to have been the first exhibition of Abstract art in Belgium. Major retrospectives were held at the Palais des Beaux-Arts in Brussels in 1947 and at the Musée d'Ixelles in 1965. Servranckx also showed in Paris, Rome, Berlin, Warsaw and New York. He was awarded the Jury Grand Prize and a gold medal at the 1917 *Exposition des Arts Décoratifs* (*Decorative Arts Exhibition*) in Paris.

BIBLIOGRAPHY:

'Servranckx' in *Het Overzicht* n° 21, periodical, Antwerp, 1924. *Servranckx*, exhibition catalogue, Palais des Beaux-Arts, Brussels, 1947. Seuphor, Michel, *L'Art abstrait ses origines, ses premiers maîtres*, Maeght, Paris, 1949. *Collection de la Société Anonyme*, catalogue, Yale University Art Gall., New Haven, 1950.

MUSEUMS AND GALLERIES:

BRUSSELS (Mus. royaux des Beaux-Arts de Belgique): *Opus 47* (1923) - GRENOBLE (Mus. de Grenoble): *Opus 55* (1923); *Velvet Steel* - MONS (MBA).

AUCTION RECORDS:
LONDON, 12 Nov 1970, *Opus 1* (gouache) GBP 2,300. LONDON, 4 July 1973, *Composition* (gouache) GBP 380. ANTWERP, 22 Oct 1974, *Houses at Dusk*, BEF 300,000. ANTWERP, 7 April 1976, *Opus 4* (1955, oil on canvas, 57 1/2 x 32 1/4 ins / 146 x 82 cm) BEF 220,000. LONDON, 8 April 1976, *Composition* (7 1/4 x 14 ins / 18.5 x 35.5 cm) GBP 380. ANTWERP, 17 Oct 1978, *Opus 29* (1923, oil on canvas, 15 x 18 1/2 ins / 38 x 47 cm) BEF 200,000. VERSAILLES, 25 Nov 1979, *Composition* (1922, watercolour, 24 1/2 x 18 1/2 ins / 62 x 47 cm) FRF 12,500. ANTWERP, 22 April 1980, *Sunset* (1923, oil on canvas, 15 1/4 x 27 1/2 ins / 39 x 70 cm) BEF 290,000. ANTWERP, 27 Oct 1981, *Composition* (1922, gouache, 24 3/4 x 19 1/4 ins / 63 x 49 cm) BEF 200,000. BRUSSELS, 30 Nov 1983, *Cubist Composition* (1922, oil on card, 13 x 17 ins / 33 x 43 cm) BEF 90,000. LOKEREN, 5 March 1988, *Wheat* (9 x 11 ins / 22 x 28 cm) BEF 36,000. LONDON, 19 Oct 1989, *Opus 40a* (1922, oil on canvas, 15 1/2 x 27 1/2 ins / 39.4 x 69.7 cm) GBP 41,800. LOKEREN, 9 Oct 1993, *Composition* (1948, dry-point, 12 x 9 ins / 30.5 x 23 cm) BEF 36,000. LOKEREN, 7 Oct 1995, *I Stroke the Women's Horses, I Stroke the Women's Horses* (1941, oil on canvas, 31 1/4 x 27 1/2 ins / 79.5 x 70 cm) BEF 360,000. AMSTERDAM, 25 Oct 1999, *Painting 23-3* (1923, oil on canvas, 15 x 28 ins / 39 x 70 cm) NLG 110,000. AMSTERDAM, 25 Nov 2003, *Opus V* (1963, oil on canvas, 80 x 24 ins / 204 x 60 cm) EUR 14,000. AMSTERDAM, 1 Dec 2004, *Spring in the Orchard* (1931, oil on canvas, 24 x 28 ins / 60 x 72 cm) EUR 5,000.

SERWAZI, Albert B.
American, 20th century.
Painter.

Albert Serwazi took part in exhibitions at the Carnegie Foundation in Pittsburgh.

SERWOUTERS, Philips
Dutch, 17th century.
Born 19 August 1591, in Middelburg; died 7 August 1650, in Amsterdam.
Engraver (wood), draughtsman. Portraits, hunting scenes. Vignettes.

Philips Serwouters was the brother of Pieter van Serwouters. He engraved the portraits of 13 princes on horseback, hunting scenes and vignettes, and was a draughtsman for engravings.

SERWOUTERS, Pieter van, or Perjecouter
Flemish School, 17th century.
Born 28 October 1586, in Antwerp; died 1657; buried 26 September in Amsterdam.
Engraver (burin).

Pieter van Serwouters married Sibella Vooget in 1622 and converted to Catholicism in 1628. He took his inspiration from the style of J. van Londerseel, and engraved in particular several works after Vinckebooms.

PS PS PS

AUCTION RECORDS:
LONDON, 27-28 June 1922, *Portrait of a Gentleman* (pen) GBP 10.

SERY, Olivier
French, 20th century.
Born 18 September 1906, in Le Havre; died 2000.
Painter. Landscapes, seascapes.

Olivier Sery was a pupil at the École de Beaux-Arts in Le Havre, then of the painter Jacques Simon. He practised a traditional style, leaning towards Impressionism. He showed his works in solo exhibitions regularly in Le Havre. He exhibited at the Salon des Artistes Français in Paris, of which he was a member, for several years, and at the Salon d'Automne and Salon d'Hiver. In 1985 he exhibited at the Musée de la Duchesse Anne at Dinan.

BIBLIOGRAPHY:
Boudant, Joël, *Olivier Sery, le peintre du vent*, Éd. Yellow Concept, St-Suliac, 2002.

SERY, Robert de. See **ROBERT Paul Ponce Antoine**

SERZ, J.
American, 19th century.
Born in Saxony; died c. 1878, in Philadelphia.
Engraver (burin).

J. Serz settled in Philadelphia around 1850. He engraved historical and genre scenes.

SERZ, Johann Georg
German, 19th century.
Born 1808, in Nuremberg.
Engraver (burin).

Serz studied under A. Reindel. He settled in America in about 1840.

SESAR, Alois
German, 19th century.
Born 20 December 1825, in Pfaffenhausen; died 27 April 1900, in Augsburg (Bavaria).
Painter.

Sesar studied under Andreas Eigner.

SESBOUE, Suzanne Marie
French, 20th century.
Born 1894, in Mortain (Manche); died 21 May 1927, in Paris.
Painter.

Suzanne Sesboue exhibited in Paris at the Salon des Indépendants.

SESE, Miguel
Spanish, 17th century.
Born 29 March 1662, in Monforte.
Stucco artist, gilder.

Miguel Sese was a member of the Jesuit order. He executed interior decorations for a number of Jesuit churches in Spain.

SESINO
Italian, 18th century.
Active in Casale Monferrato in the first half of the 18th century.
Painter.

Sesino worked for the cathedral in Casale Monferrato.

SESMA, Matias
Spanish, 19th century.
Active in Mélida during the first half of the 19th century.
Sculptor.

Matias Sesma carved the reliquary altar for the abbey church of La Oliva.

SESMA, Raymundo
Mexican, 20th - 21st century.
Born 1954, in San Cristóbal (Chiapas).
Active in Italy from 1980.
Painter, engraver, sculptor, draughtsman, installation artist.

Raymundo Sesma studied painting and silkscreen printing at the Casa de la Cultura in Aguascalientes and xylography in Guadalupe. He also studied painting and design at the university of the Americas in Puebla and in 1977 silk-screen printing and lithography at the Atelier Libre in Toronto. From 1974 to 1975 he taught at the American College in Puebla and from 1974 to 1980 at the Casa de la Cultura in Puebla. Sesma has produced numerous 'artist's books', notably with Jorge Luis Borges and Octavio Paz and has also created installations that incorporate drawings and objects, such as

Muro de los Lamentos (*Wailing Wall*). Sesma has lived and worked in Milan since 1980.

Sesma has taken part in collective exhibitions, including: Casa de la Cultura, Puebla (1976); national fine arts institute, Yucatan (1977); Museo Universitario del Chopo, Mexico City (1981); Palacio de Bellas Artes, Mexico City (1982 and 1983); Italian cultural institute, Prague (1983); Cuba Biennale and the Norway Biennale (1984); Ljubljana Biennale and the international art fair in Stockholm (1985); Centre Georges-Pompidou, Paris (1986); Basel art fair (1987); Bologna art fair (1991); Bibliothèque Nationale de France, Paris (1992). He has also shown his work in solo exhibitions including: Casa de la Cultura, Mexico City (1976); Mexico City arts institute (1977); Museo Universitario del Chopo Mexico City (1980 and 1984); Casa de la Cultura, Aguascalientes (1982); Centro Cultural, Mexico City (1983); Fukuoka museum (1984); Kerr Gallery, New York (1985); Venice Biennale (1986); Calouste Gulbenkian foundation, Lisbon (1990); Monterrey museum, Mexico (1990 and 1991); Museum of Art of the Americas, Washington, Palazzo Reale, Milan and centre for art and culture, Mexico City (1991); Latin-American institute, Rome; and Charlottenburg museum, Berlin (1992).

BIBLIOGRAPHY:

Sesmo: Paintings of silence. Acrylic on canvas, 30 Oct. - 30 Nov., exhibition catalogue, Kerr Gallery, New York, 1985 (Introduction by Gillo Dorfies). Sacca, Lucilla, *Sesma*, exhibition catalogue, Schloss Charlottenburg, Berlin, 1992.

MUSEUMS AND GALLERIES:

BOGOTÁ (MAM) - CALI (MAM La Tertulia) - CARACAS (MAC Sofía Imber) - LISBON (Biblioteca Nacional) - LISBON (Centro de Arte Moderna José de Azeredo Perdigão, Fundação Calouste Gulbenkian) - LONDON (Victoria and Albert Mus.) - MADRID (Biblioteca Nacional) - MEDELLIN (Mus. de Antioquia) - NEW YORK (Metropolitan Mus. of Art) - NEW YORK (Public Library) - PARIS (BNF, Prints Collection): *Manifiesto* (*Manifesto*) (1982, collography) - PARIS (MAMVP) - PUEBLA (RM) - PUERTO RICO (Latin American Mus. of Graphic Arts) - ROME (Biblioteca Nazionale Centrale) - TOKYO (National Library) - TOKYO (National MMA).

SESONI, Francesco, or Sessone
Italian, 18th century.
Born 1705, in Rome.
Engraver.

Francesco Sesoni, the pupil of G.G. Frezza, worked in Naples in 1733.

SESOSTRIS, Vitullo. See **VITULLO Sesostris**

SESSA, Gaetano
Italian, 18th century.
Sculptor, modeller.

Sessa worked in Naples, making figurines for nativity scenes.

SESSA, Nicola
Italian, 19th century.
Active in Naples during the first half of the 19th century.
Painter.

Nicola Sessa painted altarpieces for the church at Monte Cassino and that of S Maria delle Grazie a Toledo in Naples.

SESSAI, real name: Masuyama Masakata, alternate name: Kunsen, artist names: Sessai, Gyokuen, Kan-en, Setsuryo, Choshu, Sekiken Dojin
Japanese, 18th - 19th century.
Born 1755, in Ise Province; died 1820.
Painter.

Sessai, the daimyo of Nagashima in Ise Province, retired from his duties there in 1801 and moved to Edo (now Tokyo) to pursue the artistic life. He made a name for himself as a writer, poet and painter. He worked in the Nagasaki style, specialising in realistic depictions of birds and flowers in the Chinese manner, after Nanbin.

MUSEUMS AND GALLERIES:

TOKYO (National Mus.): *Insects* (four albums).

SESSAI, real name: Tsukioka Shuei, given name: Taikei, artist names: Sessai, Kaikosai
Japanese, 19th century.
Died 1839.
Active in Osaka.
Painter.

A disciple of his father, Settei (1710-1790), Sessai is known as a genre painter of the *ukiyo-e* school. He depicted, with some skill, elegant ladies in kimonos accompanied by their suitors, and created a type of ideal young woman sufficiently linked to the traditional vision to please the Kyoto and Osaka middle classes. In later life, the titles *hokkyo* (bridge of the law) and *hogen* (eye of the law), ecclesiastical titles granted to lay artists, were conferred upon him.

SESSELI, Urs Joseph
Swiss, 19th century.
Born 18 February 1797, in Oensingen; died in Oensingen.
Sculptor.

Sesseli attended the academy in Vienna.

SESSELSCHREIBER, Gilg
German, 15th - 16th century.
Born between 1460 and 1465; died after 1520.
Painter, founder.
Munich School.

Gilg Sesselschreiber lived in Munich, where he worked for the court. He cast several statues after his own sketches for the tomb of Maximilian I in the church of the Innsbruck court.

SESSELSCHREIBER, Stefan
German, 15th century.
Painter.

Stefan Sesselschreiber was a painter of initials. The Österreichische Nationalbibliothek in Vienna has a History of the World in which he collaborated.

SESSHU, real name: Oda, nickname: Sesshu, artist names: Toyo, Beigenzam Shujin, Unkokuken, Yochikaku, posthumous name: Toyo. Commonly known as Sesshu Toyo
Japanese, 15th century.
Born 1420, in Bichu Province (Okayama Prefecture); died 1506.
Painter. Screens.

In the 15th century, the newly imported Chinese technique of ink wash painting (*suiboku*) took root and spread across Japan, thanks in large part to the Kyoto monk painters Josetsu, Shubun and Sotan, who were in the service of the Ashikaga shoguns. Yet the artist who would make this art form into a vehicle for the most profound personal expression, and thus endow it with a national character, would be far removed from the court. He was Sesshu Toyo.

Born into a poor family in the Bichu area (tradition has it that he was born in the village of Akahama, by the shores of the inland sea), Sesshu was probably placed at a very early age in the Hofuku-ji temple at Iyama (now Soja), not far from the family home, and while still very young he entered the Shokoku-ji temple in Kyoto as a novice. There he came under the influence of the monk Shunrin Shuto, who was famous for his piety. At the same time, the presence of the painter Shubun (active in about 1425-1450) at the same monastery would be decisive for his career as an artist. In 1495, Sesshu expressed his debt to both Shubun and Josetsu in an inscription on one of his landscapes, where he described Shubun as ' my painting master '.

Little is known of Sesshu's life or work before he travelled to China in 1467-1469, and in fact none of his work from that time apparently survives. But what is known is that shortly after the death of Shunrin Shuto, Sesshu left the capital to settle near Yamaguchi, in the province of Suo in southwestern Honshu. Under the patronage of the Ouchi family, who had grown rich on trade with mainland Asia, Yamaguchi had become an important cultural centre, and it is not impossible that Sesshu thought that by moving there it would be easier for him to travel to China. There he set up a studio, which he called *Unkoku* (the valley of the clouds), where in 1464-1465 Koshi Eho, a friend of his, visited him, and wrote him a poem praising the maturity of his talent.

Sesshu finally managed to make the crossing to China in 1467, aboard the third ship in the commercial fleet sent by the shogunate to the Ming Emperor. Disembarking in Ningbo, in Zhejiang Province, he stayed for a while in the Ch'an (Zen) monastery of Tianlongsi, where an ecclesiastical title was conferred upon him. Then he accompanied the Japanese embassy up the Grand Canal to Beijing, on the way discovering and becoming familiar with the Chinese countryside, which was very different from what he knew in Japan. His growing understanding of the Chinese landscape then led him to another, deeper understanding: that of the source of Chinese pictorial composition, a discovery that would be of immense importance to his artistic career and that inspired him, at the time, to draw countless sketches of landscapes and scenes from popular life. At the same time, however, as an inscription tells us, if he was also searching for a great master to teach him painting, he found only mediocrities. This did not prevent him from being greatly appreciated in Beijing, for while there he was asked to paint murals for a recently rebuilt official building.

Sesshu's first authentic works to come down to us are a series of four hanging scrolls entitled the *Four Seasons,* signed *Sesshu Toyo, Zen monk from Japan,* now in the National Museum, Tokyo. Sesshu probably painted them while he was in China. In the monumental quality of their composition, they show the influence of the Zhe (Zhejiang) school, which in the Ming dynasty perpetuated the academic style of the Southern Song, and especially that of the painter Li Zai, whom Sesshu met at the court in Beijing. Yet, at the same time they already show the solidity of construction and concision of brushstroke that would be the hallmarks of Sesshu's own style.

Returning to Japan in 1469, he moved to the north of Kyushu to avoid the unrest convulsing the country because of Oei's civil war, finally settling under the patronage of the Otomo family at Oita, where he built a studio, the Tenkaitoga-ro. There, in 1476, he was visited by a friend, the monk Bofu Ryoshin, who has left us a precious account of Sesshu's life as an artist. 'Everybody in the town, from the nobility to the humblest of the humble, admires Sesshu's art and asks him for a work. In his studio, which is set in the midst of the loveliest countryside, he tirelessly depicts his personal universe, while communing now and then with the natural splendour that overlooks the balcony of his studio.' Sesshu seems to have been freeing himself from the clutches of Ming painting by returning to the sources, copying the Song masters Li Tang, Ma Yuan, Xia Gui and Yu Qian, consolidating his own style, and constantly expanding his expressive demesne. This growth can be seen in such works as *Autumn Landscape* and *Winter Landscape* (National Museum, Tokyo). Now his composition is clearer and more solid than before, and married to a sharper sense of the vertical and a highly personal drawing style. Using vigorous, precise brushwork he draws in the rocks, trees and mountains in deep black, highlighting them with a few rougher strokes.

In about 1478-1479, Sesshu set off on a wanderer's life that took him from one Zen monastery to another, providing him with an opportunity to study the Japanese landscape and, by comparing it with his memories of China, to help him absorb its essence. In 1487, he was back in Yamaguchi, where Ouchi Masahiro helped him to rebuild his retreat, the Unkoku-an. To express his gratitude, Sensshu painted for him the famous *Sansui-chokan,* now in the Mori collection, a long landscape scroll depicting the passage of the seasons from spring to winter, a living frieze of astonishing realism through which Sesshu's masterful balancing of empty space and heavily inked areas actually seems to make the air breathe.

Sesshu continued to work, surrounded by his disciples. For one of them, Josui Soen, who in 1495 returned to the Enkaku-ji temple in Kamakura, he painted the *Haboku sansui zu,* in the *pomo* (broken ink) technique. Here the forms, brushed in with rapid washes heightened with dark black strokes, represent a small corner of nature in all its grandeur and stability. In the long inscription above this work, Sesshu pays his respects to his two precursors, Josetsu and Shubun, and states that the painters whom he knew in China taught him little, with the exception of Li Zai and Chang Yousheng (otherwise unknown), who showed him how to apply colour and introduced him to the broken ink technique. At the age of 80, still faithful to his monastic robes, Sesshu painted the *Eka Dampi* (*Huike Cutting off His Arm to Gain the Attention of Bodhiharma*), a well-known episode from the history of Zen Buddhism (now in the National Museum, Kyoto). This rather dry work bears little comparison with the towering masterpiece from his old age, the landscape *Ama-no-Hashidate zu,* in which a life of genius reaches its final, glorious pinnacle.

Bibliography:

Akiyama, Terukazu, *La Peinture japonaise,* Skira, Geneva, 1961. Tanaka, Ichimatsu, *Japanese Ink Painting: Shubun to Sesshu,* Weatherhill, New York, 1972. Paul-David, Madeleine, *'Sesshu Tokyo'* in *Encyclopædia Universalis* vol. XIV, Paris, 1972.

Museums and Galleries:

Bofu (Mori Institute): *Sansui chokan* (dated 1486, ink and colour on paper, handscroll) - Boston (MFA): *Monkeys and Birds in the Trees* (ink on paper, two six-panelled screens, dated 1491) - Kyoto (National Mus.): *Eka Dampi (Huike Cutting off his Arm to Gain the Attention of Bodhidharma)* (dated 1495, ink and light colour on paper, hanging scroll) - Tokyo (Commission For the Protection of Culture): *Ama-no-Hashidate zu* (dated 1502-1506, ink and light colour on paper, hanging scroll) - Tokyo (National Mus.): *Four Seasons* (dated 1467-1469, ink and light colour on silk, four hanging scrolls, signed); *Autumn and Winter Landscapes* (ink on paper, two hanging scrolls); *Haboku sansui (Landscape in Running Style)* (dated 1495, ink on paper, hanging scroll, inscription by the artist) - Washington DC (Freer Gal. of Art): *Landscapes* (ink and light colour on paper, two six-panelled screens); *Birds and Flowers* (colour on paper, six-panelled screen); *Landscape* (handscroll, ink on paper, attributed) -

SESSON. See **SHUKEI Sesson**

SESSON, Shukei, family name: Satake, artist names: Sesson, Shukosai, Shukei, Kakusen-rojin
Japanese, 16th century.
Born c. 1504; died after 1589.
Painter.

During the Muromachi period, monochrome ink *(suiboku)* painting spread to outlying regions east and west of the capital, where the local daimyos, growing in political and economic independence, took artists under their patronage, when they were not artists themselves. Thus we find a very original artist emerge in Tohoku, in northern Japan. He was Sesson Shukei.

Although born at almost exactly the same time that Sesshu was dying at the other end of the country, Sesson claimed to be his spiritual heir, going so far as to write the same character (*setsu* = snow) at the head of his artist name. Sesson spent his entire life in the rustic areas of Aizu (now Fukushima Prefecture) and Hitachi (now Ibaragi Prefecture). He first comes to note during the years when Ashina Moriuji, daimyo of Aizu, was his patron. Later he would build his own studio at Miharu; it stands to this day. He developed as an artist alone, studying the works of the great Chinese and Japanese masters such as Yu Jian and Mu Qi, Shubun and Sesshu. His paintings, however roughly they may seem in execution, are filled with sparkling verve, a sort of reflection of the agitation of his character, itself a reflection of his country, then torn by civil war. In Sesson we find Chinese technique and Japanese sensibility melded together in a uniquely moving match.

MUSEUMS AND GALLERIES:

Tanaka, Ichimatsu, *Japanese Ink Painting: Shûbun to Sesshû*, Weatherhill, New York, 1972.

MUSEUMS AND GALLERIES:

NARA (Mus. Yamato Bunkakan): *Ryodohin (The Taoist Immortal Lu Dongbin)* (ink on paper, hanging scroll); *Self-portrait* (ink and light colour on paper, hanging scroll, poem and four seals of the artist) - TOKYO (National Mus.): *Hawks and Pines* (ink on paper, two signed hanging scrolls, two seals of the artist); *Hama and Tieguai (two Chinese immortals)* (ink on paper, two hanging scrolls, signed, seals of the artist) - WASHINGTON DC (Freer Gal. of Art): *Autumn and Winter Landscapes* (ink and light colour on paper, two six-panel screens).

SESSONE, Francesco. See **SESONI**

SEST, Baptista de

Austrian, 16th century.

Active in Bohemia, in the middle of the 16th century.

Painter.

De Sest was Court Painter to Maximilian II.

SESTER, Marie

French, 20th century.

Painter, sculptor, mixed media.

Marie Sester studied architecture. Her works in paper, enriched and enlarged with varied matter, are built around rectangular figures put together in a geometric structure. These evoke an architectural plan that includes figures. She also creates on wood panels works that resemble reliefs. She shows her works in solo exhibitions: 1991, Galerie Merle-Portalèx at St-Germain-en-Laye; 1996, Centre d'Art Contemporain de Vassivière-en-Limousin.

BIBLIOGRAPHY:

Jover, Manuel, '*Marie Sester*' in *Art Press*, periodical, Paris, September 1991.

SESTI, Giovanni Stefano, or Sesto, or de Sesti, or da Sesto

Italian, 15th - 16th century.

Sculptor.

This artist is probably the same person as, or someone close to, Battista or Giovanni Battista da Sesto. Active between 1491 and 1513, he worked at the Certosa in Pavia, carving statues for the façade of *St Hugh, St Ambrose, St Peter* and *St Paul*.

SESTI, Girolamo

Italian, 16th - 17th century.

Active in Milan and in Recanati (Marche) from 1560 to 1603.

Painter.

Girolamo Sesti painted the altarpiece for a side altar in the church of S Lorenzo in Ancona.

SESTO, Alessandro

Italian, 14th century.

Medallist.

Alessandro Sesto was active in Venice in 1390.

SESTO, Bernardo

Italian, 14th - 15th century.

Medallist, goldsmith.

Bernardo Sesto was active in Venice in 1411 (or perhaps 1311). He was the father of Lorenzo and Marco Sesto.

SESTO, Cesare da, called Il Milanese

Italian, 16th century.

Born 1477, in Sesto Calende (Lombardy); died 27 July 1523, in Milan.

Painter. History painting.

Cesare da Sesto is generally thought to have been the pupil of Leonardo da Vinci. He came under the influence of Raphael after a visit to Rome. He is known also to have been in Naples and Messina but otherwise we have little information about him. The themes of his works show the influence of Leonardo while the figures are more reminiscent of Raphael. His fine landscapes reflect the influence of Dosso Dossi and, probably, Flemish art. An altarpiece formerly attributed to Salvatini in the church of S Trinità della Cova near Salerno is now thought by scholars to be the work of Sesto.

BIBLIOGRAPHY:

Frizzoni, G., '*Certain Studies by Caesare da Sesto in Relation to his Pictures*' in *Burlington Magazine*, vol 26, 1915.

MUSEUMS AND GALLERIES:

BERGAMO (Accademia Carrara): *Virgin and Holy Women* - DIJON: *Virgin and Child* - MADRID (Prado): *Virgin and Child with St Anne* - MILAN (Ambrosiana): *Virgin and Child* - MILAN (Pinacoteca di Brera): *St Jerome; Holy Family with St John; Virgin and Child* - MUNICH: *Virgin* - NAPLES: *The Magi* - ST PETERSBURG (Hermitage): *Holy Family* - STOCKHOLM: *St Jerome* - TURIN: *Madonna* - VATICAN (Mus. Vaticani): *Madonna of the Girdle* - VIENNA: *Portrait of a Young Man* (uncertain); *The Daughter of Herodias*.

AUCTION RECORDS:

PARIS, 1868, *Castor and Pollux*, FRF 5,200. PARIS, 1881, *Circumcision*, FRF 420. LONDON, 1888, *Virgin of the Low Relief*, FRF 63,000. GENOA, 1899, *Virgin and Child with Flower*, FRF 6,500. LONDON, 11 June 1926, *Virgin and Child*, GBP 110. LONDON, 27 Jan 1928, *Virgin and Child*, GBP 99. PARIS, 22 Feb 1937, *Leonardo da Vinci's Servant* (black chalk) FRF 4,000. PARIS, 23 April 1937, *Design for a Fresco* (pen and pencil) FRF 220. PARIS, 26 June 1950, *Head of a Man* (black chalk heightened with white) FRF 45,000. LONDON, 18 Nov 1959, *Madonna and Child*, GBP 700. MILAN, 12-13 March 1963, *Christ and St John as Infants in a Landscape with a Castle in the Background*, ITL 112,500,000. MILAN, 21 May 1970, *Virgin and Child with St John*, ITL 6,000,000. MUNICH, 28 March 2001, *Holy Family* (oil on canvas, 35 x 28 ins / 90 x 70 cm) DEM 5,500.

SESTO, Giovanni Stefano. See **SESTI**

SESTO, Lorenzo

Italian, 14th century.

Medallist.

The son of Bernardo and brother of Marco Sesto, Lorenzo Sesto was active in Venice in 1393. He was one of the first medallists.

SESTO, Marco

Italian, 14th century.

Medallist.

The son of Bernardo and brother of Lorenzo Sesto, Marco Sesto was active in Venice towards the end of the 14th century. He and his brother were early medallists.

SETCH, Terry
British, 20th century.
Born 1936, in Lewisham (London).
Painter, pastellist. Figures.
54 Group.

Terry Setch studied at the Sutton and Cheam School of Art from 1950 to 1954, did National Service in Germany (1954-1956) and returned to study at the Slade School of Fine Art under William Coldstream and Andrew Forge from 1956 to 1960. He has taught at the Leicester College of Art (1960-1964) and was senior lecturer at Cardiff College of Art (South Glamorgan Institute of Higher Education) from 1964. From 1963 to 1969 Setch was organising tutor at the Barry Summer Schools. In 1981 he was visiting lecturer at the Emily Carr College of Art in Vancouver, Canada, and in 1983 he was artist in residence at Victoria College of Art in Melbourne. Setch was elected to the Faculty of Painting of the British School at Rome in 1984 and to the Faculty of Fine Arts in 1987. He has done considerable work as external assessor and examiner for degree courses and is a member of the Association of Artists and Designers in Wales. He acknowledges the influence of Abstract Expressionism on his work, particularly of Jackson Pollock.

Setch lives in Penarth, South Wales, on the Severn Estuary, where he explores the beaches to gather found objects as subjects of his painting. His approach, in which he takes the random detritus of society and assembles it into arrangements to be painted on canvas, deals with humanity's relationship with nature and issues concerning pollution and ecological disaster. His early works, such as *Touch the Earth* (1971), were painted on unstretched canvas which might be dipped into seawater. From the late 1970s, Setch began to use synthetic micro-crystalline wax, which he heated and mixed with turpentine, pigments and dyes to create a paste mimicking mud and sand. In 1978 he started to use the wax in an encaustic heat process, whereby the hot wax was applied directly to the canvas and built up in layers by means of a hot-air gun. Some of his works incorporate found objects into the paintings, as in the 1979 work *Penarth Beach Car Wreck*, in which bits of a wrecked car were wired to the canvas. His important *Once Upon a Time There Was OIL* series from 1981 also involved objects attached to the surface of the works and addressed the issues of pollution and nuclear war on a political level. From 1989, Setch has produced lighter textured paintings on sheets of polypropylene by the use of metallic pigment and white kaolin as a paint filler, as in his 1990/1991 *Above and Below the Tide*, or the 1992 *Rejyarat*. He often seals these paintings on polypropylene between polythene sheets.

Setch's exhibitions include a solo show sponsored by the ORIEL Welsh Arts Council (1992-1993) which toured the National Museum of Wales in Cardiff, the Camden Arts Centre in London and the Talbot Rice Gallery at University of Edinburgh; and solo shows at the Serpentine Gallery, London (1980); Frans Wyman Gallery, Vancouver (1981); Nigel Greenwood Gallery, London (1982); St Paul's Contemporary Art Gallery, Leeds (1987); and the Andrew Knight Gallery, Cardiff (1989). He has also exhibited with the Leicester Group (1964), and at *Which Side of the Fence? Contemporary Art at the Imperial War Museum*, Imperial War Museum, London (1987); *Artists in National Parks*, V & A Museum, London (1988); *Twentieth-Century Welsh Art*, National Museum of Wales (1989, tour to Japan); *Tree of Life*, Royal Festival Hall, London (1989); and the Royal Academy Summer Exhibition (1991). He has received prizes at John Moores Exhibition in Liverpool (1972, 1985) and a Welsh Arts Council Major Artists' Award (1978).

BIBLIOGRAPHY:

Terry Setch, exhibition catalogue, ORIEL, National Museum of Wales, Cardiff, 1992.

MUSEUMS AND GALLERIES:

LONDON (British Council): *Car Wreck Penarth Beach I* (encaustic wax on carpet) - LONDON (Tate Collection): *Wall Split* (1967-1968, screenprint); *Once Upon There Was OIL (Raft)* (1981, pastel and drawing); *Once Upon a Time There Was OIL (Car on Beach)* (1981, pastel); *Once Upon a Time There Was OIL (Car on Beach II)* (1981, pastel and drawing); *Once Upon a Time There Was OIL I-III* (1982, series of three pastels) - LONDON (Victoria and Albert Mus.).

SETCHELL, Sarah
British, 19th century.
Born 1803, in London; died 8 January 1894, in Sudbury (Harrow).
Painter, watercolourist. Portraits, genre scenes, landscapes.

Sarah Setchell made her exhibition debut at the Royal Academy in 1831 and also exhibited at the Suffolk Street Gallery and the New Water-Colour Society (of which she eventually became a member in 1884). She was also a member of the Royal Institute. She continued to show her work until 1887. Some of her compositions were subsequently engraved and proved very popular.

MUSEUMS AND GALLERIES:

LONDON (Victoria and Albert Mus.): *Innocent or Guilty?* (watercolour); *Old Woman and her Daughter* (watercolour).

SETH, Bogarth
Norwegian, 17th century.
Died 1682, in Trondheim.
Painter.

Seth painted for the churches around Trondheim.

SETHER, Gulbrand
Norwegian, 19th - 20th century.
Born 1869; died 1910.
Active in the USA.
Painter. Landscapes, seascapes.

AUCTION RECORDS:

NEW YORK, 16 July 1992, *Norwegian Fishing Port* (oil on canvas, 27 x 39 1/4 ins / 68.6 x 99.7 cm) USD 1,320.

SETLEZKY, Balthazar Sigismond, or Sedletzky
German, 18th century.
Born 1695, in Augsburg, of Polish origin; died 1774, in Augsburg.
Engraver.

Setlezky studied under Johann Andreas Pfeffel the Elder. He engraved in the style of artists such as Jean-Antoine Watteau (1684 - 1721) and the Roos painters.

SETON, Ernest Thompson
British, 19th - 20th century.
Born 14 August 1860, in South Shields; died 23 October 1946, in Seton Village (New Mexico), USA.
Active in the USA.
Draughtsman, illustrator.

Ernest Seton trained under Jean-Léon Gérôme, Bougeureau, Ferrier and Mosler in Paris. He lived and worked in Santa Fe, and was also active as an author, illustrating his own editions of animal stories.

BIBLIOGRAPHY:

SETON, John Thomas
British, 18th - 19th century.
Active in Edinburgh from 1758 to 1806.
Painter. Portraits.

John Thomas Seton was a pupil of Hayman. He exhibited three portraits at the Royal Academy in 1774 (erroneously listed in the exhibition catalogue as 'Seaton').

MUSEUMS AND GALLERIES:

EDINBURGH (Scottish National Portrait Gallery): *Sir Hugh Paterson* (1776, oil on canvas).

AUCTION RECORDS:
LONDON, 1 Dec 1922, *John Hunter*, GBP 37. LONDON, 13 June 1930, *Duana Rochefort and her Children*, GBP 210. LONDON, 2 April 1965, *Sir Robert Chambers surrounded by his Brothers and Sisters*, Gns 1,700. LONDON, 18 Oct 1972, *Portrait of a British Officer*, GBP 320. LONDON, 21 June 1974, *Portrait of Warren Hastings*, Gns 320. LONDON, 19 Nov 1976, *Colonel Ralph Bates and his Wife Anne* (oil on canvas, 38½ x 39½ ins / 97.8 x 100.3 cm) GBP 1,500. LONDON, 16 July 1982, *Group Portrait of Sir James Murray and General Sir John Murray* (oil on canvas, 29¼ x 35¼ ins / 74.2 x 89.5 cm) GBP 7,500. LONDON, 9 July 1986, *Portrait of an Officer* (oil on canvas, 26 x 19¼ ins / 66 x 49 cm) GBP 8,800. LONDON, 15 Nov 1989, *The Wallace Family* (oil on canvas, 52 x 61 ins / 132 x 155 cm) GBP 33,000. NEW YORK, 8 Oct 1993, *Full-length Portrait of a Uniformed Officer and a Civil Servant* (oil on canvas, 36 x 32¼ ins / 91.4 x 81.9 cm) USD 4,140. LONDON, 13 April 1994, *Portrait of a Gentleman and his Secretary (Giles Stibbert and William Hickey?)* (oil on canvas, 35¾ x 32¼ ins / 91 x 82 cm) GBP 4,830. LONDON, 10 July 1996, *Portrait of Christopher Fawcett with his wife Winifred and his son John* (oil on canvas, 37½ x 45¾ ins / 95.5 x 116.5 cm) GBP 8,050. LONDON, 9 Oct 1996, *Portrait of James Johnstone* (oil on canvas, 29¼ x 24¼ ins / 74 x 61.5 cm) GBP 1,955. LONDON, 14 July 1999, *Portrait of Thomas Davis with Wife Elizabeth and Son William* (oil on canvas, 29 x 24 ins / 73 x 62 cm) GBP 2,400. LONDON, 6 Sept 2001, *Portrait of James Johnston* (oil on canvas, 30 x 25 ins / 76 x 63 cm) GBP 1,600. LONDON, 21 March 2002, *Portrait of the Dibdin Family* (oil on canvas, 27 x 35 ins / 69 x 89 cm) GBP 28,000. BAYSWATER, 23 Sept 2002, *Portrait of a Gentleman, Seated in a Landscape* (oil on canvas, 30 x 25 ins / 75 x 63 cm) GBP 3,000.

SETROTTE, Jehan
Flemish School, 15th century.
Active in Tournai during the second half of the 15th century.
Sculptor.
In 1451 Setrotte carved a tabernacle for the church of St Brice.

SETSUZAN, or Setsusan, Sessan, real name: Hirowatari Setsuzan
Japanese, 16th century.
Probably from Hizen, now Nagasaki Prefecture.
Painter.
Setsuzan is supposed to have been a disciple of Shukei Sesson (from c. 1504 until after 1589).

SETTA, Bartolomeo
Italian, 17th century.
Active in Castelli.
Potter.

SETTA, Simone
Italian, 17th century.
Born in Castelli.
Active during the first half of the 17th century.
Painter (glazed earthenware). Murals.
Simone Setta worked on the ceiling in the church of S Donato in Castelli in 1616.

SETTALA, Giorgio
Italian, 20th century.
Born 5 May 1895, in Trieste; died 1960.
Painter. Landscapes, still-lifes.
Giorgio Settala studied at the Accademia di Belle Arti in Vienna.

SETTAN, real name: Hasegawa Munehide or Hasegawa Soshu, original name: Goto, childhood name: Moemon, artist names: Settan, Gangakusai, Ichiyoan, Ichiyosai, Gakutei
Japanese, 19th century.
Born 1778; died 1843.
Active in Edo (now Tokyo).
Print artist.
Settan was a pupil of Hokusai (1760-1849). Examples of his work can be seen in the two illustrated books, the *Edo Meisho-zu-e* (Famous Spots in Edo) and *Toto saijiki* (Annual Festivals of Edo).

SETTE, Francesco Antonio
Italian, 17th century.
Died 1648, in Aquila.
Active in Aquila.
Painter.
Francesco Sette, the pupil of Giuseppe Cesari, painted frescoes in the church of the Madonna in Cascina.

SETTE, Jules
French, 19th century.
Painter, lithographer. Portraits, still-lifes, fruit.
Jules Sette exhibited at the Salon between 1836 and 1846.

SETTEGAST, Joseph Anton
German, 19th century.
Born 8 February 1813, in Koblenz; died 19 March 1890, in Mainz.
Painter. Religious subjects.
Settegast attended the academy in Düsseldorf and studied under Dorothea Veit. He visited Mainz and Rome.
MUSEUMS AND GALLERIES:
FRANKFURT AM MAIN: *Watercolour* - KARLSRUHE (Staatliche Kunsthalle): *Two Children*; *Portrait of the Artist's Father*; *Madonna* - KOBLENZ: *Self-portrait* - MAINZ (Municipal Mus.): *Virgin and Child* - MANNHEIM (Städtische Kunsthalle): *Portrait of Dorothea Veit*.

SETTEI TSUKIOKA. See **TSUKIOKA Settei**

SETTELLA, Manfred
Italian, 17th century.
Born 1600, in Milan; died 1680.
Painter.
Manfred Settella was an engineer who was also well known as a painter. He was director of the academy in Milan.

SETTERINGTON, J.
British, 18th century.
Portrait artist.

SETTEVECCHIE, Geminiano
Italian, 16th century.
Died probably 8 December 1567, in Ferrara.
Painter.
Geminiano was the father of Lodovico Settevecchie.

SETTEVECCHIE, Lodovico di Geminiano da Modena, or Settevecchi
Italian, 16th century.
Born c. 1520, in Modena; died after 3 April 1590.
Painter.
Lodovico Settevecchie executed some paintings in the abbey of S Benedetto in Ferrara.

SETTI, Adamo
Italian, 16th century.
Painter.
Adamo Setti worked at Modena Cathedral between 1518 and 1522.

SETTI, Camillo
Italian, 17th century.
Active in the middle of the 17th century.
Painter.
Camillo Setti painted the picture on the high altar in the church of S Michele in Ferrara.

SETTI, Ercole
Italian, 16th century.
Active in Modena at the end of the 16th century.
Painter.
Ercole Setti painted altarpieces for the church of S Pietro in Modena.
MUSEUMS AND GALLERIES:
MODENA (Gal. Estense): *Coronation of the Virgin*.
AUCTION RECORDS:
LONDON, 22 Oct 1984, *Hunting Scene* (pen and brown ink/outline in black chalk, 9 1/4 x 12 3/4 ins / 23.4 x 32.6 cm) GBP 2,600. PARIS, 3 April 1998, *Martrydom of a Saint* (pen and brown ink, 7 1/4 x 10 ins / 18.5 x 25.7 cm) FRF 7,000.

SETTI, Francesco
Italian, 17th century.
Active in Aquila and in Rome in 1619.
Painter.

SETTI, Francesco or Cecchino
Italian, 15th - 16th century.
Active in Modena from 1495 to 1511.
Painter.
Francesco Setti worked at Modena Cathedral.

SETTI, Simone
Italian, 17th century.
Active in Modena.
Painter.
Simone Setti is said to have been the pupil of G. Gavignani in Carpi.

SETTLE, John
British, 17th century.
Active during the second half of the 17th century.
Sculptor.
John Settle sculpted the tomb of Sir Lumley Robinson in Westminster Abbey.

SETTLE, William Edward Frederick
British, 19th century.
Born 1821, in Hull; died 1897.
Painter, watercolourist. Seascapes.
William Edward Frederick Settle exhibited at the British Institution in 1867.
MUSEUMS AND GALLERIES:
LONDON (Victoria and Albert Mus.): a watercolour.
AUCTION RECORDS:
LONDON, 9 May 1969, *Seascape*, Gns 400. TORQUAY, 13 June 1978, *Ships at Sea* (oil on panel, 6 1/2 x 9 1/4 ins / 16.5 x 23.5 cm) GBP 850. LONDON, 22 Nov 1982, *Ships in the Wind; Ships on a Calm Sea* (1864, oil on panel, a pair) GBP 6,800. LONDON, 5 June 1985, *Men-of-War Getting Under Way* (oil on panel, 6 x 9 ins / 15 x 22 cm) GBP 2,700. LONDON, 22 Nov 1991, *English Frigate and a Coastal Vessel* (1880, oil on panel, 7 1/4 x 10 1/4 ins / 18.3 x 26 cm) GBP 3,850. NEW YORK, 17 Feb 1999, *Naval Scenes* (1851, oil on panel, 6 x 9 ins / 15 x 23 cm) USD 18,000. LONDON, 3 May 2000, *Calm Waters. Rough Seas. Busy Shipping* (watercolour, three, 9 x 13 ins / 22 x 33 cm) GBP 1,700. LEWES, 17 Oct 2000, *Men of War and Other Shipping, Moored in Calm Seas* (1862, oil on canvas, 6 x 9 ins / 15 x 23 cm) GBP 8,000. LONDON, 17 Jan 2001, *Naval Squadron at Sunset* (1879, oil on panel, 12 x 18 ins / 30 x 46 cm) GBP 10,800. LEEDS, 18 June 2002, *Royal Navy Frigate and Other Shipping in a Calm at Sunset* (oil on panel, 4 x 6 ins / 10 x 14 cm) GBP 2,000. DRIFFIELD, 29 Nov 2002, *Warship at Anchor with Fishing Vessels* (watercolour, 8 x 13 ins / 20 x 33 cm) GBP 2,000.

SETTMANN, Karl
German, 19th century.
Active in Cologne during the first half of the 19th century.
Painter.
Settmann studied under P. Cornelius in Düsseldorf, Germany.

SETUBAL, Francisco José de. See **ROCHA Francisco José da**

SEUBERT, Johann Friedrich
German, 19th century.
Born 28 March 1780, in Stuttgart; died 12 July 1859, in Stuttgart.
Painter, watercolourist. Portraits, flowers.
Seubert studied under Heideloff and taught at the Katharinenstift in Stuttgart.

SEUBT, Franz Dominicus
German, 17th century.
Active in Schweidnitz during the second half of the 17th century.
Painter.
Seubt painted portraits of Protestant ministers.

SEUCIAT, Jean, or Senclat
French, 16th century.
Active in 1507.
Painter.

SEUDEINKIN, Sergei. See **SUDEIKIN**

SEUFFERHELD, Heinrich
German, 19th - 20th century.
Born 27 January 1866, in Weinsberg; died 1940.
Painter, engraver.
Heinrich Seufferheld studied at the fine arts academies in Munich, Berlin and Stuttgart. He was primarily a painter, but was also an etcher.

SEUFFERT, Hans Georg
German, 17th century.
Died 17 December 1691, in Bamberg.
Engraver (burin). Portraits, coats of arms.

SEUFFERT, Robert
German, 19th - 20th century.
Born 28 March 1874, in Cologne.
Painter. Religious subjects. Theatre decoration, church decoration.
Robert Seuffert was a pupil of Karl F. Gebhardt and Peter J.T. Janssen; he painted altarpieces and theatre sets.

SEULIN, Philippe, called La Fontaine
French, 17th century.
Died before 1665.
Active in Avon.
Potter.

SEUMEN, Johann Conrad, or Seimen or Zeume
German, 17th - 18th century.
Active in Hildesheim (Lower Saxony) Germany, 1699-1707.
Sculptor.
Seumen produced work for the churches of Hildesheim.

SEUND JA RHEE. See **RHEE Seund Ja**

SEUNTJES, Dirk
Dutch, 18th century.
Active in The Hague during the first half of the 18th century.
Painter, sculptor.
Dirk Seuntjes was a painter in the guild in 1719. He sculpted epitaphs in the churches of Monster and Dreischor.

SEUPEL, Friedrich Daniel
French, 18th century.
Active in Strasbourg in 1788.
Lithographer.
Friedrich Daniel Seupel engraved architectural views and views of cities.

SEUPEL, Jean Adam
French, 17th - 18th century.
Born 1662, in Strasbourg; died 4 February 1714, in Strasbourg.
Painter, engraver (burin). Portraits, landscapes, architectural views.

Jean Adam Seupel engraved portraits, architectural views and landscapes, creating the effects of aquatint with his burin.

MUSEUMS AND GALLERIES:

STRASBOURG (Prints Collection): almost all of Seupel's work.

SEUPEL, Johann Friedrich
German, 18th century.
Active during the second half of the 18th century.
Painter. Animals.

Seupel attended the academy in St Petersburg.

AUCTION RECORDS:

LONDON, 10 July 1992, *Ocelot Keeping a Watchful Eye on a Dead Parrot* (1791, oil on canvas, 40½ x 49½ ins / 102.9 x 125.6 cm) GBP 23,100.

SEUPHOR, Michel, pseudonym of Berckelaers, Ferdinand Louis
Belgian, 20th century.
Born 10 March 1901, in Antwerp; died 12 February 1999, in Paris.
From 1925 active and from 1954 naturalised in France.
Painter, draughtsman, collage artist. Designs for tapestries.
Groupe Cercle et Carré.

In 1921, Michel Seuphor collaborated with Josef Peeters and Geert Pijnenburg to launch in Antwerp a review entitled *Het Overzicht* ('Overview' or 'Panorama') that would run to 25 issues. The periodical was initially devoted to literature but gradually extended to embrace the arts in general, including music. This led to acquaintances with major artists including Robert and Sonia Delaunay, Piet Mondrian, Fernand Léger, Hans and Sophie Taeuber-Arp, Filippo Marinetti and many others.

Seuphor worked in Paris from 1925 and, in 1927, collaborated with Paul Dermée and Enrico Prampolini to publish the *International Documents* of *L'Esprit Nouveau*. 1929 saw Seuphor and Joaquin Torres-Garcia launch the group known as Cercle et Carré ('Circle and Square'), which brought together artists who, while not necessarily Neo-Plasticists like Mondrian, were exponents of 'geometrically abstract' art, be it painting, sculpture, poetry or music. Three issues of the periodical *Cercle et Carré* appeared in 1930 and Seuphor was instrumental in organising group exhibitions, the first of which - in 1930 - featured work by Mondrian, Arp, Sophie Taeuber, Kurt Schwitters, Wassily Kandinski, Antoine Pevsner, Le Corbusier, Sartoris and Fernand Léger.

When Seuphor fell ill and was forced to leave Paris, the Abstraction-Création group, launched in 1932 and spearheaded by Georges Vantongerloo, took up where Cercle et Carré had left off. Abstraction-Création was subsumed in 1939 into Réalités Nouvelles, a grouping which continued to function after World War II and inaugurated the Salon des Réalités Nouvelles in Paris in 1946.

Michel Seuphor was instrumental in organising a large number of exhibitions, including *First Masters of Abstract Art* in 1949; *Fifty Years of Abstract Art* (1958); *Construction and Geometry Painting* (USA, 1959) and the major Mondrian retrospective held at the Musée de l'Orangerie des Tuileries in 1959.

As an artist, Michel Seuphor also took part in numerous group exhibitions both in France and abroad. From 1933, he exhibited solo, notably at the Galerie Berggruen in Paris in 1953; the Denise René Gallery in Paris (1959); the Martano Gallery in Turin (1967); La Chaux de Fonds (municipal museum, 1968); the municipal museum of The Hague (retrospective 1977); the Beaubourg Centre in Paris (also 1977); the Musée de la Bouverie in Liège (1981); the *Treffpunkt Kunst* Gallery in Saarlautern (1986); the Museum of Saarbrücken (retrospective, 1989); *La Galerie* in Paris (1994); and a Michel Seuphor retrospective organised at the Hessenhuis and municipal library in Antwerp in 2001 to celebrate the centenary of his birth.

Seuphor's extensive writings include novels, poems, plays and essays. Specific mention should be made of his Mondrian monograph published in 1956; his *Dictionnaire de la peinture abstraite* (*Dictionary of Abstract Painting*) of 1957; *L'art abstrait, ses origines, ses premiers maîtres* (*Abstract Art: Origins and Leading Exponents*) (1948); *La sculpture de ce siècle* (*Twentieth-Century Sculpture*) (1948); *La peinture abstraite, sa genèse, son expansion* (*Genesis and Evolution of Abstract Painting*) (1962); *Le style et le cri* (*Style and Exclamation*) (1963) and the five benchmark volumes written by him in conjunction with Michel Ragon to chart the history of abstract art (from 1973).

In addition to his drawings and paintings, Seuphor's 'poetry graphics' served as the basis for tapestries. His skills extended to ceramics (he cooperated with the Sèvres Manufacture in 1964) and he also produced illustrations of his own poem *L'autre côté des choses* (*The Other Side of Things*). His Neo-Plastic output dates from 1926, although much of it was never shown. His collages and Indian ink drawings heightened with crisp colours are reminiscent of drawings from the Bauhaus, where Seuphor appeared to 'withhold' specific signs and symbols while in reality including them as 'white silhouettes' or 'negatives' to produce a *chiaroscuro* taken to extremes. His parallel lines are modulated by their respective thickness and different intervals.

Michel Seuphor was a close friend of both Mondrian and Arp and was held in great esteem by them and by others in his circle. His contribution to the history of 20th-century abstract art cannot be overstated.

BIBLIOGRAPHY:

Arp, Jean, *Michel Seuphor, dessins à lacunes*, exhibition catalogue, Gal. Berggruen, Paris, 1953. Hammacher, Abraham Marie, *'Le Dessin de Michel Seuphor'* in *Quadrum* n° 6, periodical, Brussels, 1959. Sartoris, Alberto, *Les Dessins à lacunes de Michel Seuphor*, exhibition catalogue, Gal. Denise René, Paris, 1959. *Michel Seuphor*, exhibition catalogue, Gall. d'Arte Martano, Turin, 1967. *Michel Seuphor*, exhibition catalogue, Musée des Beaux-Arts, La Chaux-de-Fonds, 1968. *Michel Seuphor*, monograph, Mercatorfonds, Antwerp, 1972 (multilingual edition, with previously unpublished material by Michel Seuphor). *Michel Seuphor*, exhibition catalogue, Musée de Besançon, Besançon, 1976 (with previously unpublished notes by Michel Seuphor). Martinez, Carmen/Seuphor, Michel, *Écrits, œuvres, documents et témoignages*, C. Martinez, Paris, 1976. Henkels, H., *Seuphor*, Éd. du Centre Georges-Pompidou, Paris, Fonds Mercator, Antwerp, 1977. Prat, Marie-Aline, *Cercle et carré, peinture et avant-garde au seuil des années 30*, L'Âge d'Homme, Lausanne, 1984. Germoz, Alain, *'L'Irrésistible Jeunesse de Michel Seuphor'* in *Archipel* n° 1, periodical, Antwerp, 1992. Coppel, Georges, *'Michel Seuphor, la jouissance du cercle'* in *Hommage à Michel Seuphor*, exhibition catalogue, La Galerie, Paris, 1994.

MUSEUMS AND GALLERIES:

ANTWERP (Koninklijk Mus. voor Schone Kunsten) - ARNHEM (Provinciehuis Wandtapijt) - BASEL (Kunstmus.) - BESANÇON (MBA et d'Archéologie) - BUFFALO (Albright-Knox AG) - CASTELLANZA (Mus. Pagani): mosaic - CHICAGO (AI) - DEURLE (Mus. Dhondt Dhaenens) - GHENT (Mus. voor Schone Kunsten) - LIÈGE (Mus. of Modern and Contemporary Art) - LÓDZ (Muz. Sztuki) - LOS ANGELES: drawing in 16 parts - LY-

ONS (MBA) - NEWARK (Mus.) - OSTEND (Mus. voor Schone Kunsten): drawing in 16 parts - OTTERLO (Kröller-Müller Mus.): drawing in 16 sections - PARIS (BNF, Prints Collection): *Constellation* - PARIS (MAMVP) - PARIS (MNAM-CCI): *Death of Orpheus* (collage in eight sections) - PARIS (Mus. National de Céramique Sèvres): ceramic - RHEIMS (MBA) - ROTTERDAM (Mus. Boijmans Van Beuningen) - SAARBRÜCKEN (Saarlandmus.): drawing in 16 parts - ST-ÉTIENNE (MAM) - STRASBOURG (MBA) - THE HAGUE (Gemeentemus.) - TURIN (Gal. Civica d'Arte Moderna e Contemporanea).

AUCTION RECORDS:

PARIS, 2 Dec 1979, *Infinite Dialogue* (paint and collage, 29 1/4 x 41 ins / 74 x 104 cm) FRF 3,800. PARIS, 24 March 1986, *Circle and Squares on a Black Ground* (ink and collage, 25 1/4 x 19 1/4 ins / 64 x 49 cm) FRF 5,500. PARIS, 20 March 1988, *Dream of the Grey Square* (ink and collage, 25 1/2 x 19 3/4 ins / 65 x 50 cm) FRF 13,000. PARIS, 18 May 1988, *Game, Rules* (1973, pencil drawing, 12 1/4 x 8 3/4 ins / 31 x 22.5 cm) FRF 25,000. PARIS, 1 June 1988, *Untitled* (ink/paper, 26 x 19 3/4 ins / 66 x 50 cm) FRF 4,700. PARIS, 20-21 June 1988, *Dans chaque instant d'éternité capte la mer à boire* (gouache and collage, 24 x 36 1/4 ins / 61 x 92 cm) FRF 7,600. AMSTERDAM, 9 Dec 1988, *Red Symmetry IV* (1970, ink/paper, 25 1/2 x 19 3/4 ins / 65 x 50 cm) NLG 2,070. PARIS, 12 Feb 1989, *Untitled* (Indian ink drawing, 26 1/2 x 20 ins / 67 x 51 cm) FRF 6,000. PARIS, 3 March 1989, *Lace, Summer Rain, Trill* (1963, ink drawing, 26 3/4 x 19 3/4 ins / 68 x 50 cm) FRF 7,500. PARIS, 29 Sept 1989, *Siren Queen* (1954, Indian ink drawing, 21 1/4 x 14 3/4 ins / 54 x 37.5 cm) FRF 16,000. DOUAI, 11 Nov 1990, *Composition* (1985, ink and collage, 25 3/4 x 19 1/4 ins / 65.5 x 49 cm) FRF 5,600. PARIS, 15 April 1991, *Sacred Wood* (1968, ink/paper, 19 3/4 x 26 ins / 50 x 66 cm) FRF 8,000. LOKEREN, 21 March 1992, *Composition* (1972, ink, 13 1/4 x 9 1/4 ins / 33.5 x 23.5 cm) BEF 36,000. PARIS, 10 April 1992, *Straight and Curved* (Indian ink, 26 1/2 x 20 ins / 67 x 51 cm) FRF 5,200. PARIS, 18 June 1993, *Composition* (mixed media, 26 x 19 3/4 ins / 66 x 50 cm) FRF 6,200. NEW YORK, 29 Sept 1993, *Untitled* (ink/yellow paper, 25 3/4 x 19 1/2 ins / 65.4 x 49.5 cm) USD 978. PARIS, 24 Oct 1993, *My Name is Trapma-Lafla* (Indian ink/paper, 25 1/2 x 19 3/4 ins / 65 x 50 cm) FRF 4,500. LOKEREN, 4 Dec 1993, *Statue of the Voiced Spirit between Heaven and Earth* (1984, ink and collage, 26 x 19 3/4 ins / 66 x 50 cm) BEF 90,000. PARIS, 26 Nov 1994, *Lightness Personnified (sic)* (1949, black ink/vellum, 11 x 15 ins / 28.1 x 38.1 cm) FRF 4,600. LOKEREN, 20 May 1995, *Ironclad Spectacle* (1956, tapestry, 88 1/4 x 66 1/2 ins / 224 x 169 cm) BEF 30,000. PARIS, 3 April 1998, *Frontispiece for Mozart* (1965, Indian ink and collage/paper, 26 x 19 3/4 ins / 66 x 50 cm) FRF 7,500. BRUSSELS, 2 Oct 2001, *Game for Small Tables* (1972, Indian ink, 26 x 20 ins / 66 x 50 cm) BEF 70,000. PARIS, 5 Oct 2001, *Dans chaque instant d'éternité capte la mer à boire* (mixed media collage, 24 x 36 ins / 62 x 91 cm) FRF 13,200. MILAN, 5 June 2002, *Variations in Blue and Red* (1958, mixed media and collage on card, 29 x 20 ins / 73 x 50 cm) EUR 2,200. ANTWERP, 29 April 2003, *Circle and Square* (1967, ink, 26 x 59 ins / 65 x 151 cm) EUR 2,800. LUCERNE, 24 May 2003, *Geometric Fantasy on Blue King with Yellow and Green* (1981, Indian ink, tempera and collage on board, 30 x 20 ins / 75 x 52 cm) CHF 3,600. PARIS, 26 May 2004, *Mondrian's Studio* (1929, gelatin silver photo, 8 x 10 ins / 20 x 25 cm) EUR 3,200. AMSTERDAM, 30 Nov 2004, *Composition no. 8* (1929, gouache, collage, ink and pencil, 30 x 20 ins / 75 x 50 cm) EUR 24,000.

SEURAT, Georges Pierre

French, 19th century.

Born 2 December 1859, in Paris; died 29 March 1891, in Paris.

Painter (including gouache), draughtsman. Genre scenes, figures, portraits, landscapes, landscapes with figures.

Seurat enrolled at the École des Beaux-Arts in the winter of 1877-1878 with his friend, Aman-Jean, and entered the studio of Henri Lehmann. He made many studies of the old masters and antique sculptures in the Louvre. After completing his military service in 1879-1880 he did not return to the École des Beaux-Arts, preferring instead to study the work of Puvis de Chavannes and to start work on a series of sketches executed in conté crayon which Ambroise Vollard reproduced in two exceedingly rare volumes. His early conté drawings display a beauty and resonance achieved by his graduation of tones ranging from dense, velvety matt black to pure white. These studies of Parisian and rural subjects are important because they are forerunners of the principle characteristics of paintings that followed. They display stillness and a sense of atmosphere that had already been seen in the drawings of J.-F. Millet and which would also be found in works by Pissarro.

Seurat's first major paintings date from 1881 with *The Hague, The Invalid* and *The Tramp*. Even though he was painting in the open air in Barbizon and on the banks of the Seine, he was drawn towards conveying the experiences of people who sang in cafés or worked in fairs for a living, and transforming what he saw into studies of light and dark.

The period until 1884 was characterised by the so-called 'balayée' or 'criss-cross' stroke, which was less systematic than the 'divided' stroke later called 'pointillisme'. With his technical and theoretical experiments, Seurat, together with Van Gogh, Gauguin, Cézanne and Toulouse-Lautrec, would provide the impulse from which 20th-century art movements would ensue. Delacroix had already had a presentiment that artistic emotion might, in formal terms, move away from the imitation of nature and explore abstract harmonies generated by lines and colours. He noted: 'You walk into a cathedral, you find yourself standing too far away from the picture to know what it represents, and you are often seized by the magical harmony before you'. This anticipates Maurice Denis' famous 1895 definition of painting as 'a flat surface covered with colours assembled in a certain order'.

In 1882 he painted *Countrygirl Sitting on the Grass, House in a Landscape, Ruins of the Tuileries* and in 1883 he executed several sketches for *Bathers, The Seine at Asnières*, and produced his *Portrait of Aman-Jean*, his childhood friend who was also a painter, and who would make his own contribution to academic Neo-Impressionism.

In 1884, having had works rejected by the Salon, hundreds of artists (including Seurat, Signac, Henri-Edmond Cross and Maximilien Luce) united to found the Salon des Indépendants. On the first exhibition, the objectives of a new movement were apparent although the term Neo-Impressionism was only coined in 1886 by Arsène Alexandre at the time of the Eighth Impressionist Exhibition at 1 Rue Laffite. In 1883-1884 Seurat had painted his large and important work, *Bathers at Asnières*, (re-touched on the right in about 1887), *Canoe, Seamstress* and several sketches for *A Sunday in Summer on the Island of La Grande Jatte*. In 1885 he produced more sketches for *La Grande Jatte*, (*The Seine at Courbevoie, Nurse, Young Girl with a Parasol*). Seurat regarded his numerous, preliminary tonal drawings and oil sketches as fundamentally important for his large works and, finally, in 1886, *La Grande Jatte* was completed. That year the last Impressionist exhibition was mounted.

The schism that would make it impossible for the artists to organise further group exhibitions became permanent. Some newcomers had already demonstrated their independence by establishing the Salon des Indépendants. Signac, having studied Delacroix at the Church of Saint Suplice, and then the Impressionists when they had held their group exhibition on the Boulevard de la Madeleine, was already codifying the new precepts of what would be Neo-Impressionism and Seurat was conducting similar practical experiments. He complemented them with a theoretical study of Chevreul's *Law of Simultaneous Contrast*, published in 1827, which had not escaped Delacroix's attention, and Sutter's *Phenomena of Vision*. Seurat could not have read the works by Père Desiderius (Peter Lenz), the founder of the École d'art religieux in Beuron, because they did not appear until 1895, but he had a thorough knowledge of the golden section, and he had been fired with enthusiasm for Charles Blanc's statement that 'colour, when subjected to firm rules, can be taught in the same way as music'. A subsequent study of established physicists such as Sutter and Rood only encouraged him in the pursuit of his first intuition regarding the definition of strict rules concerning both the harmony of colours and linear composition. After a close reading of Chevreul, he reflected on the various aspects of the law on the 'simultaneous contrast' of colours which 'embraced all the phenomena of modification that objects with different colours appear to convey in the physical composition and the intensity of the tone of their respective colours when viewed simultaneously'.

Having completed the final version of *La Grande Jatte*, in 1886-1887 Seurat was in Honfleur where he painted *La Maria* and several views of Honfleur, including *Honfleur* and *Lighthouse at Honfleur*. Then in 1888, after painting *Les Poseuses (Models)*, he turned his attention to scenes from the circus and the cabaret: *Parade de Cirque, At the Gaîté-Rochechouart, Divan Japonais, Diner*. In spite of its severity of execution, *La Grande Jatte* feels spontaneous when compared with these new works. From now on the new aesthetic would be elaborated in all its detail and its different precepts implemented simultaneously. As Signac pointed out in 1899, this was, broadly speaking, a conscious and logical systematisation of Impressionist concerns. The law of the simultaneous contrast of tones and of optical mixes must no longer be left to the free whim of painters producing scenes from nature, but instead be strictly controlled within the setting of the studio with composition governed by the rationale of the golden section. The analysis that Signac provides of a painting such as *La Parade de Cirque* shows particularly clearly that the entire work, whether in the form of each individual element or when each element is related to the others, is constructed on the precepts of the Golden Section. Seurat's research into the symbolic meaning of the direction of lines within the conventional space of the drawing or of the canvas, can be seen in *La Parade* (1887-1888), with its static assembly of cut-out figures, in which the horizontals and verticals of the drawing convey feelings of sadness, or in *Le Chahut* (1889-1890), or in *Le Cirque* (1890-1891), in which the verticals and diagonals express joyful high spirits.

In the summer of 1890, Seurat summarized his principles in a letter he sent to Maurice Beaubourg. So important is his statement that it is quoted in full:

AESTHETIC

Art is harmony.

Harmony is the analogy between opposites and the analogy between elements similar in *tonal value, colour* and *line* considered in terms of the dominant and under the influence of light, in joyful, calm or sad combinations.

The opposites are:

For *tonal value* a more luminous (lighter) tone against a darker one.

For *colour*, the complementaries, i.e. a certain red contrasted with its complementary, etc. (red-green, blue- orange, yellow violet).

For *line*, those forming a right angle.

Gaiety in terms of tonal value is a luminous, dominant tonality; in terms of colour, a warm dominant colour; in terms of line, lines above the horizontal. Calmness in terms of tonal value is an equal amount of dark and light; in terms of colour, an equal amount of warm and cool; and in terms of line, the horizontal. Sadness in terms of tonal value is a dominant dark tonality; in terms of colour, a cold dominant colour; and in terms of line, downward directions.

TECHNIQUE

Given the phenomena of the duration of a light impression on the retina, synthesis is the unavoidable result. The means of expression is the optical mixture of tonal values and colours (both local colour and the colour of the light source, be it sun, oil lamp, gas etc.) that is to say, the optical mixture of lights and of their reactions (shadows) in accordance with the laws of contrast, gradation, and irradiation.

The harmony of the frame contrasts with that of the tonal values, colours, and lines of the picture.

These ideas found their form in Neo-Impressionism by building on Impressionist immateriality, and brought Seurat the posthumous admiration of the Cubists and Constructivists such as Mondrian.

In 1888 Seurat produced his conté drawing of Paul Alexis; in 1889 he painted views of Le Crotoy, in 1890 *Le Chahut, Young Woman Powdering Herself, Eiffel Tower* and *Portrait of Signac*. In 1891 he painted *Le Cirque, Channel at Gravelines* before he was suddenly struck down by an infectious angina. On his death, an inventory of the works in his studio was compiled by Maximilien Luce and Félix Fénéon, the works numbered in either black or coloured crayon and distributed amongst his family and friends. On that occasion, writing in an impersonal style (a mirror image of the secrecy that surrounded Seurat himself), his friend Félix Fénéon drew up an inventory of the life and works of Seurat: 'On 29 March, at the age of thirty one, Seurat died. Seurat exhibited: at the Salon in 1883; at the Groupe des Artistes Indépendants in 1884; at the Société des Artistes Indépendants in 1884-1885, 1886, 1887, 1888, 1889, 1890 and 1891; at *Les Impressionnistes* in rue Laffitte in 1886; in New York in 1885-1886; in Nantes in 1886; at *Vingt* in Brussels in 1887, 1889 and 1891; at *Blanc et Noir*, Amsterdam in 1886. His catalogue comprised around 6 sketch books, 420 drawings, 170 'boîte à pouce' watercolours and 60 or so canvases (figures, seascapes, landscapes) amongst which: five measuring several metres square and, conceivably, masterpieces (*Bathers, A Sunday at La Grande Jatte, Les Poseuses (Models), Le Chahut, Le Cirque*).

It is therefore difficult to understand Signac's statement: 'At the time of Seurat's death, the critics were acknowledging his talent but found that he had left no paintings'. For some twenty years or so, only a few painters and members of his family kept his memory alive with any fervour; the critics did not even need to forget him, having virtually never noticed him while he was alive. The painter's father and brother dispersed his works, showing nothing but contempt for them. His mother had offered his complete works to the Louvre, which had declined to accept them. The world waited until 1905 before a retrospective exhibition of forty-four of his works was organised at the same time as the Van Gogh retrospective, in the greenhouses at Cours-la-Reine, and Seurat was awarded his true place in modern art. Subsequently, with the works by his childhood friends Ernest Laurent and Aman-Jean, with Le Sidaner and Duhem, and in particular with Albert Besnard and Henri Martin, the Neo-Impressionism of Seurat, Pissarro, Signac, and Cross lost the impulse that had brought the theory to life and became an academic style.

Dead before the age of thirty-two, Seurat nonetheless had had the time to create one of the 19th century's most important art achievements. He was acknowledged as the uncontested leader of the Neo-Impressionists, even though the rules of that School were not formulated into a doctrine until after his death when Signac published *De Delacroix au néo-impressionnisme (From Delacroix to Neo-Impressionism)* (1899). This work discusses Seurat's art as understood at that time while a first-hand account of his life was published by Lucie Cousturier in 1926.

Rigorously planned, Seurat's images can at all times be seen to apply the norms governing both the physical nature of colours and the geometric harmony of shapes.

BIBLIOGRAPHY:

Cousturier, Lucie, *Georges Seurat,* G. Crès, Paris, 1926. Hauke, César M. de, *'Seurat et son œuvre'* in *2 vol.,* Gründ, Paris, 1961. Homer, William Innes, *Seurat and the Science of Painting,* MI.T Press, Cambridge (MA), 1964. Russell, John, *Seurat,* Somogy, Paris, 1966. Chastel, André/Minervino, Fiorella, *L'Œuvre complet de Seurat,* catalogue raisonné, Rizzoli, Milano, Ex Libris, Zurich, 1972 (Flammarion, Paris, 1973). Broude, Norma, *Seurat in Perspective,* Prentice-Hall, Englewood Cliffs (NJ), 1978. Couthion, Pierre, *Seurat,* Thames and Hudson, London, 1989. Rewald, John, *Seurat: a Biography,* Thames and Hudson, London, 1989. Thompson, Richard, *Seurat,* Phaidon, Oxford, 1990. Grenier, Catherine, *'Seurat. Catalogue complet des peintures'* in *coll. Les Fleurons de l'Art,* catalogue raisonné, Bordas, Paris, 1991. Broude, Norma, *Georges Seurat,* Rizzoli International Publications, 1992. Thompson, David, *Life and Work of Georges Seurat: Point Counterpoint,* Phaidon, Oxford, 1995. Smith, Paul, *Seurat and the Avant-garde,* Yale University Press, New Haven, 1997. Thompson, Richard/Leighton, John, et al., *Seurat and the Bathers,* National Gallery, London, 1997. Herbert, Robert L., *Seurat. Drawings and Paintings,* Yale University Press, London, 2001. Flux, Paul, *The Life and Work of Georges Seurat,* Heineman, London, 2002.

MUSEUMS AND GALLERIES:

BRUSSELS (MBA): *Seine at La Grande Jatte* (c. 1885) - BUFFALO (Albright-Knox AG): *Study for Le Chahut* (1889) - CAMBRIDGE, MA (Harvard University): *Head of a Young Girl* - CHICAGO (AI): *Dimanche d' été à La Grande Jatte* (*A Sunday in Summer on the Island of La Grande Jatte*) (1886, oil on canvas) - EDINBURGH (Nat. Gal. of Scotland): *A Study for 'Une Baignade'* (1883, oil/panel) - GLASGOW (AG and Mus.): *Young Peasant Boy Sitting in a Meadow* (c. 1882) - INDIANAPOLIS (MA): *The Channel at Gravelines, Petit Fort-Philippe* (1890) - KANSAS CITY (AM): *Preliminary Sketch for Bathers at Asnières; Seine and Nude Bather Sitting on the Riverbank* (c. 1883) - LONDON (Courtauld Institute of Art): *Man Painting a Boat* (c. 1883, oil/panel); *Horses in the water* (19th century, oil/panel, on long term loan from a private collection); *Bridge at Courbevoie* (1886-1887, oil on canvas); *Young Woman Powdering Herself* (1888-1890, oil on canvas); *Study for 'Le Chahut'* (c. 1889, oil/panel); *Beach at Gravelines* (1890, oil/panel) - LONDON (NG): *Bathers at Asnières* (1884, oil on canvas); *Le Bec du Hoc, Grandcamp* (1885, oil on canvas, on loan from the Tate Collection since 1997); *The Channel of Gravelines, Grand Fort-Philippe* (1890, oil on canvas); several studies - MERION (Barnes Foundation): *Les Poseuses* (*Models*) (1886-1888) - MINNEAPOLIS (IA): *Bridge and Quays at Port-en-Bessin* (1888, oil on canvas) - NEW YORK (Metropolitan Mus. of Art): *A Sunday in Summer on La Grande Jatte, final study* (1884-1885); *La Parade* (1888) - NEW YORK (MoMA): *Port-en-Bessin: Entrance to the Outer Harbour* (1888) - NEW YORK (Solomon R. Guggenheim Mus.): *Peasant Girls at Work* (c. 1882); *Peasant Girl Sitting on the Grass* (1883); *Horse in Harness* (c. 1883); *Farmboy with a Hoe* (c. 1884, several drawings) - NORTHAMPTON, MA (MA, Smith College): *Lady Taking a Dog for a Walk; Preliminary Sketch for La Grande Jatte* (1885) - OTTERLO (Kröller-Müller Mus.): *Corner of the Harbour, Honfleur* (1886); *End of the Jetty, Honfleur* (1886); *Sunday at Port-en-Bessin* (1888); *Le Chahut* (1889-1890); *The Channel at Gravelines towards the Sea* (1890) - PARIS (Louvre): *Women Seated, preliminary sketch for La Grande Jatte* (1884-1885); *Seated model, in profile* (1887); *Model, viewed from the front* (1887); *Model, viewed from the back* (1887); *Port-en-Bessin: The Outer Harbour at High Tide* (1888); *Le*

Cirque (1890-1891) - PRAGUE (Národní Gal. V Praze): *La Maria, Honfleur* (1886) - TOURNAI (MBA): *The Shore at Bas-Butin, Honfleur.*

AUCTION RECORDS:

PARIS, 18-19 May 1903, *Seine at Courbevoie*, FRF 630. PARIS, 24 Feb 1919, *Three Children on the Grass*, FRF 700; *In the Street*, FRF 250; *Wet Nurse* (drawing) FRF 900. PARIS, 8 March 1919, *Fisherman on La Grande Jatte* (drawing) FRF 240. PARIS, 21 March 1919, *On the Stage* (drawing) FRF 310; *Woman Passing By* (pen) FRF 330; *Woman with a Parasol* (drawing) FRF 270. PARIS, 24-25 Nov 1924, *Woman in Black and White* (charcoal) FRF 5,800. PARIS, 12 Dec 1925, *Woman* (charcoal) FRF 1,600. PARIS, 3 March 1927, *Dancer with the Cane* (charcoal) FRF 7,600. PARIS, 29 April 1927, *Young Beggar Sitting on the Floor* (charcoal) FRF 7,500. PARIS, 30-31 May 1927, *Couple out for a Stroll* (lead pencil) FRF 28,000. PARIS, 27 June 1927, *In the Street* (drawing) FRF 7,500. PARIS, 29 Oct 1927, *Woman in a Fur Hat* (drawing) FRF 1,550. PARIS, 15 Dec 1927, *Portrait of the Artist's Mother* (drawing) FRF 11,100. PARIS, 9 May 1928, *The Handcart*, FRF 41,000. PARIS, 3 Dec 1928, *Study of a Woman* (drawing) FRF 35,000; *Man in a Boat*, FRF 58,100. PARIS, 16 May 1929, *Bridge at Courbevoie* (drawing) FRF 68,000; *Landscape*, FRF 20,000; *Landscape*, FRF 40,000. NEW YORK, 25-26 Nov 1929, *Woman Leaning* (drawing) USD 1,300. PARIS, 27 June 1931, *Woman Seated* (drawing) FRF 2,250; *Head* (charcoal drawing) FRF 705. LONDON, 17 Feb 1932, *Landscape*, GBP 160. PARIS, 27 Feb 1932, *Dancer with the Cane* (drawing in black pencil) FRF 5,800. PARIS, 6 May 1932, *The pose* (drawing) FRF 1,000. PARIS, 9 June 1932, *House at Honfleur* (drawing) FRF 15,500; *Artist in his Studio* (drawing) FRF 17,000. PARIS, 17 Nov 1932, *Landscape*, FRF 3,700; *The House at Le Bras Rouge*, FRF 9,900; *Landscape at La Tourelle*, FRF 8,000. PARIS, 16 June 1933, *A Summer Sunday at La Grande Jatte*, FRF 31,000. PARIS, 26-27 Feb 1934, *Hitching Up* (drawing in conté crayon) FRF 2,100. PARIS, 19 June 1934, *Study of a Woman* (charcoal) FRF 800; *Grandmother Reading* (charcoal) FRF 2,700. NEW YORK, 14 Nov 1934, *Fort at La Halle* (drawing) USD 400. NEW YORK, 29 April 1937, *Two Women*, USD 425; *Young Woman seated by an Easel*, USD 5,700; *A Raised Arm* (pencil) USD 2,000. PARIS, 13 March 1939, *The Spring* (drawing, after Ingres) FRF 700. PARIS, 20 June 1941, *Family Gathering* (charcoal) FRF 15,000. PARIS, 4 Dec 1941, *Five Monkeys* (1884, drawing conté crayon, study) FRF 52,000; *Haystacks* (drawing in conté crayon) FRF 50,000; *White Horse* (drawing in conté crayon) FRF 71,000; *Woman with a Basket* (drawing in conté crayon) FRF 100,000; *Tree* (drawing in conté crayon) FRF 70,000; *Foal* (drawing in conté crayon) FRF 45,000; *Man with a Pickaxe* (drawing in conté crayon) FRF 50,000; *Stripes* (drawing in conté crayon) FRF 41,000; *The Swordsman* (drawing in conté crayon) FRF 52,000; *Skirt* (1884-1885; *Study for the Woman with the Monkey on La Jatte* (drawing conté crayon) FRF 10,000; *The Coach Driver* (drawing in conté crayon) FRF 20,000; *Mother and Child* (drawing in conté crayon) FRF 23,500; *Drummer and Other Soldiers* (coloured crayon) FRF 9,500; *Soldier Seated, Another Standing, a Boat* (1879-1880, coloured crayon) FRF 10,000; *Study of drapery* (1877, pencil and chalk, drawing for the Ecole) FRF 10,000; *Study of drapery* (1877, pencil and chalk, drawing for the Ecole) FRF 10,000; *Little Blue Peasant Boy*, FRF 385,000; *Jupiter and Thetis* (c. 1881) FRF 72,000; *Bather with Curtain* (c. 1879) FRF 150,000; *A Sunday in Summer on La Grande Jatte* (study) FRF 200,000; *Seine in Spring* (1885; *Fields, Summer*, FRF 170,000; *Barbizon Forest, Autumn*, FRF 190,000; *Trees, Winter*, FRF 150,000; *Ruins at Grand-Camp* (1885) FRF 140,000; *Afternoon Tea, Three Children on the Grass* (1885) FRF 260,000. PARIS, 30 Nov 1942, *Negress* (pencil) FRF 25,500; *Seamstress* (pencil) FRF 21,000; *Coachman and His Horse* (pencil) FRF 6,100; *Woman Seated with her Back to the Artist* (pencil) FRF 25,000; *Woman Standing* (charcoal) FRF 28,000; *Woman on a Bench* (charcoal) FRF 39,000; *Couple* (charcoal) FRF 42,000; *Groom* (charcoal) FRF 22,400; *Richard Southwell* (pencil, after his portrait by Holbein) FRF 4,000. PARIS, 12 March 1943, *Monsieur Loyal* (conté crayon) FRF 15,500. NEW YORK, 20 April 1944, *The Island of La Grande Jatte*, USD 6,400. NEW YORK, 11 May 1944, *Rehersal* (pencil) USD 1,900; *Ballet Dancers* (pencil) USD 1,900. PARIS, 5 June 1944, *Woman Seated, profile to right* (black lead pencil) FRF 13,000. PARIS, 5 March 1945, *Seamstress* (drawing in black lead pencil) FRF 18,100. PARIS, July 1946, *Portrait of a Man in the Style of Holbein* (black lead pencil, drawing) FRF 1,000. PARIS, 30 April 1947, *Ulysses and the Pretenders to his Title* (black lead pencil) FRF 12,000; *Iphigenia's Cause* (1877, black lead pencil) FRF 9,100; *Clown* (drawing in coloured crayon) FRF 17,500; *Two Draperies* (1877, black lead pencil) FRF 7,000; *Infantryman surrounded by Figures* (charcoal, black lead pencil and coloured crayon) FRF 12,100; *Two Infantrymen and Sketches of Figures* (charcoal, black lead pencil and coloured crayon) FRF 14,000; *Seated Infantryman, together with studies of People and Hands* (charcoal, black lead pencil and coloured crayon) FRF 26,000; *Group of Infantrymen, to left, sketch of a door* (coloured crayon and black lead pencil) FRF 17,200; *Infantryman, head in his Hands, and various sketches of Washerwomen, Soldiers, etc.* (c. 1879, charcoal, black lead pencil and coloured crayon) FRF 8,000; *Breakwater at Port-en-Bessin* (charcoal) FRF 40,000; *Horses, Carriole, Peasant and a Donkey* (drawing) FRF 11,500; *Child with the Scarf* (conté crayon) FRF 53,000; *Woman Standing Wearing a Shawl* (charcoal) FRF 34,500; *Woman Seated on a Bench* (charcoal) FRF 27,000; *Seated Woman with her Hands Crossed* (charcoal) FRF 30,000. PARIS, 30 May 1947, *Study of Snow* (1882-1884) FRF 201,000; *Winter on the Outskirts of Town* (1882-1884) FRF 206,000; *Edge of the Wood in Spring*, FRF 505,000; *Landscape with Pile of Wood (recto); Study in the Style of Puvis de Chavannes' 'The Poor Fisherman' (verso)*, FRF 191,000; *Lying Down* (1882) FRF 400,000; *Outskirts of Town* (1882) FRF 1,300,000; *Pink Wall in the Greenery*, FRF 170,000; *Model (in profile); Model (from the back); Model (seen from the front)* (three studies sold with a painting by Bonnard and three drawings by Seurat) FRF 5,000,000; *Lighthouse at Honfleur* (1886, study) FRF 470,000; *Pinnacle Turrets (recto); Woman Binding Sheaves of Corn (verso)* (charcoal) FRF 75,500; *Two Carriages* (charcoal) FRF 70,000; *Axe* (charcoal) FRF 68,000; *Street Sweeper* (charcoal) FRF 83,000; *Study for Le Cirque* (1890; *The Zone* (charcoal) FRF 140,000; *Factories by Moonlight* (charcoal) FRF 103,000; *At Twilight* (pencil and charcoal) FRF 310,000; *White Cat* (charcoal) FRF 150,000; *Black Horse* (charcoal) FRF 215,500; *Sleeping Man* (c. 1883; *Furnace* (c. 1887, charcoal) FRF 120,000. PARIS, 25 June 1947, *Woman in the Chair* (drawing in black lead pencil) FRF 4,000; *Architectural Motifs* (three drawings) FRF 4,500; *Woman Lying on a Cushion* (drawing) FRF 13,500. PARIS, 19 Nov 1948, *Seamstress* (drawing) FRF 20,000. PARIS, 17 June 1949, *Clown* (1878-1881, coloured crayon) FRF 20,000; *Infantryman Surrounded by Figures* (lead and coloured pencils) FRF 8,300. PARIS, 20 April 1950, *Portrait of a Man in the style of Holbein* (lead pencil) FRF 1,600. PARIS, 21 April 1950, *Seated Woman with her Hands Crossed* (charcoal) FRF 39,000. PARIS, 10 May 1950, *Landscape with Pile of Wood (recto); Study in the style of Puvis de Chavannes' 'The Poor Fisherman' (verso)*, FRF 450,000. PARIS, 5 July 1950, *Woman Leaning* (conté crayon) FRF 41,900. PARIS, 25 Oct 1950, *Group of Infantrymen* (coloured crayon) FRF 20,000. PARIS, 27 Nov 1950, *Circus Scene* (black pencil) FRF 22,000. BRUSSELS, 2 Dec 1950, *Woman Standing* (drawing) BEF 3,000. PARIS, 20 Dec 1950, *Woman Seated* (lead pencil) FRF 12,100; *Small boy, naked* (lead pencil) FRF 10,000; *Virgil* (lead pencil) FRF 10,000. PARIS, 19 March 1951, *Woman Seated on a Prayer Stool* (lead pencil) FRF 16,000. PARIS, 30 April 1951, *Portrait in the Style of Holbein* (lead pencil)

FRF 1,200. PARIS, 27 June 1951, *White Cat* (charcoal) FRF 390,500. PARIS, 23 Feb 1954, *Parasol* (drawing) FRF 1,180,000. LONDON, 10 July 1957, *Reaper*, GBP 22,000; *Stripes* (pencil) GBP 1,300. NEW YORK, 15 Jan 1958, *Haunted House* (pencil) USD 5,000. LONDON, 26 March 1958, *Asnières, Study for a Bather*, GBP 12,000. NEW YORK, 9 Dec 1959, *Ribbon Bonnet* (conté crayon) USD 7,000. LONDON, 7 July 1960, *The Lighthouse at Honfleur* (conté crayon with gouache) GBP 5,000. LONDON, 22 March 1961, *Back View of Nude, feet apart* (pencil) GBP 220. PARIS, 21 June 1961, *Two Sailboats* (drawing) FRF 75,000. NEW YORK, 31 Oct 1962, *On the Banks of a River*, USD 24,000. LONDON, 11 June 1963, *People in a Field*, GBP 34,000. LONDON, 3 Dec 1965, *Fields in Summer*, Gns 36,000. LONDON, 22 June 1966, *Farmworkers at Montfermeil*, GBP 36,000. LONDON, 22 Oct 1970, *Les Poseuses (Models)* (small version) Gns 410,000. LONDON, 21 April 1971, *Stonebreaker*, GBP 42,000. LONDON, 28 Nov 1972, *Summer*, Gns 65,000. LONDON, 2 July 1974, *White Dog, study for La Grande Jatte*, Gns 68,000. LONDON, 6 April 1976, *Study for A Sunday on La Grande Jatte* (c. 1884-1885, oil on panel, 6 1/4 x 9 3/4 ins / 16 x 25 cm) GBP 70,000. PARIS, 9 Dec 1977, *Hayrick* (oil on canvas, 15 x 18 ins / 38 x 45.5 cm) FRF 400,000. NEW YORK, 9 June 1979, *Out for a Stroll* (c. 1881-1882, conté crayon, 12 1/4 x 9 1/4 ins / 31.1 x 23.5 cm) USD 82,000. NEW YORK, 21 Oct 1980, *Workmen Driving in Piles* (1882, oil on panel, 6 x 9 3/4 ins / 15.2 x 24.8 cm) USD 100,000. NEW YORK, 22 May 1981, *Female Torso* (c. 1884, conté crayon, 12 1/4 x 9 1/4 ins / 31 x 23.8 cm) USD 65,000. BERN, 22 June 1984, *Following the Path* (1882-1883, conté crayon, 12 3/4 x 10 ins / 32.5 x 24.5 cm) CHF 275,000. NEW YORK, 24 April 1985, *Study for La Grande Jatte (middle distance, left)* (c. 1884-1885, oil on panel, 6 1/4 x 10 1/4 ins / 15.7 x 26 cm) USD 250,000. NEW YORK, 14 Nov 1985, *Man with the Pick* (c. 1883, conté crayon, 9 3/4 x 12 1/2 ins / 24.7 x 31.7 cm) USD 180,000. NEW YORK, 19 Nov 1986, *Corner of a House (Pink Wall in the Greenery)* (c. 1884, oil on panel, 9 3/4 x 6 ins / 24.7 x 15.5 cm) USD 120,000. PARIS, 20 Nov 1987, *Canoe* (c. 1884/ 1887, oil on panel, study for 'Banks of the Seine at the Island of La Grande Jatte', 7 x 10 1/2 ins / 17.5 x 26.5 cm) FRF 4,300,000. PARIS, 27 Nov 1987, *Woman with Umbrella* (c. 1883, conté crayon, 12 x 8 1/2 ins / 30.5 x 21.5 cm) FRF 1,950,000. LONDON, 2 Dec 1987, *Seated Man Reading on a Terrace* (c. 1884, conté crayon, 12 x 9 1/4 ins / 30.7 x 23.3 cm) GBP 340,000. PARIS, 22 June 1988, *Evening at Port-en-Bessin* (1890, conté crayon, 9 x 11 3/4 ins / 23 x 30 cm) FRF 1,900,000; *Top Hat* (conté crayon, 12 x 9 1/2 ins / 30.5 x 24 cm) FRF 2,000,000; *Tedder or Stonebreaker* (conté crayon, 12 x 9 1/4 ins / 30.5 x 23.5 cm) FRF 2,500,000. PARIS, 24 Nov 1988, *Forest Drive, Barbizon* (c. 1882-1883, oil on panel, 6 1/4 x 9 3/4 ins / 16 x 25 cm) FRF 3,200,000. NEW YORK, 14 Nov 1989, *Peasant Girl Bending Over, her Hands on the Ground* (conté crayon/paper, 9 1/4 x 6 1/2 ins / 23.5 x 16.5 cm) USD 407,000. PARIS, 20 Nov 1989, *Boats Beached at Grandcamp* (1885, oil on panel, 6 1/2 x 10 1/4 ins / 16.5 x 26 cm) FRF 5,200,000. PARIS, 20 March 1990, *Stonebreaker* (c. 1882, oil on canvas, 13 x 16 1/4 ins / 33 x 41 cm) FRF 10,000,000. NEW YORK, 7 May 1991, *General View with the Companion of Woman with Monkey, study for La Grande Jatte* (oil on panel, 6 x 9 3/4 ins / 15.2 x 24.8 cm) USD 1,375,000. PARIS, 17 Nov 1991, *The Reaper* (1881, contécrayon, 11 1/2 x 9 ins / 29 x 23 cm) FRF 4,450,000. LONDON, 4 Dec 1991, *Young Warrior in Helmet* (pencil, 5 3/4 x 7 3/4 ins / 14.7 x 20 cm) GBP 7,700. NEW YORK, 8 Oct 1992, *Ulysses and the Pretenders to his Title* (1876, pencil/paper, 9 1/4 x 12 1/2 ins / 23.2 x 31.7 cm) USD 14,300. NEW YORK, 13 May 1993, *Charlatans* (1880, coloured crayon/paper/card, 5 3/4 x 9 ins / 14.6 x 22.9 cm) USD 14,950. PARIS, 26 Nov 1993, *Hindu Beggar* (lead pencil, 16 1/2 x 10 1/2 ins / 42 x 26.5 cm) FRF 310,000. NEW YORK, 10 May 1995, *Academy* (pencil/paper, 24 1/4 x 18 ins / 61.3 x 45.7 cm) USD 24,150. NEW YORK, 1 May 1996, *Channel at Gravelines: Petit Fort-Philippe* (oil on panel, 6 1/4 x 10 ins / 15.9 x 25.1 cm) USD 2,752,500. NEW YORK, 13 Nov 1996, *Pile of Stones (Stonebreakers)* (c. 1884, oil on canvas, 13 x 16 1/4 ins / 33.2 x 41.3 cm) USD 1,036,500. NEW YORK, 14 Nov 1996, *Helmeted Woman* (1874-1876, black chalk/paper, 18 1/2 x 12 1/4 ins / 47.3 x 31 cm) USD 11,500. LONDON, 2 Dec 1996, *Massive Figure in a Barbizon Landscape* (c. 1882, oil on panel, 6 x 9 3/4 ins / 15.5 x 24.8 cm) GBP 111,500. NEW YORK, 12 May 1997, *Woman at the Water's Edge* (1884-1885, oil on panel, 6 x 9 3/4 ins / 15.5 x 25 cm) USD 1,542,000. NEW YORK, 13-14 May 1997, *Two Handcarts* (c. 1883, chalk/paper, 9 1/2 x 12 1/4 ins / 24 x 31 cm) USD 310,500. PARIS, 18 June 1997, *Shepherd Carrying an Animal* (c. 1877, lead pencil, 24 1/2 x 18 1/2 ins / 62 x 47 cm) FRF 76,000. NEW YORK, 10 May 1999, *Landscape, Ile de la Grande Jatte* (1884, oil on canvas, 26 x 31 ins / 65 x 79 cm) USD 32,000,000. NEW YORK, 11 May 1999, *Pont de Courbevoie* (1886, black crayon, 9 x 12 ins / 24 x 31 cm) USD 700,000. NEW YORK, 23 Feb 2000, *Woman Feeling the Cold, Seen in Profile* (charcoal, 19 x 12 ins / 47 x 30 cm) USD 26,000. NEW YORK, 10 May 2000, *The Hedge - The Clearing* (oil on canvas, 15 x 18 ins / 38 x 46 cm) USD 1,000,000. LONDON, 5 Feb 2001, *Seated Women - Study for Sunday Afternoon on La Grande Jatte* (panel painted c.1881, Oil Painting, 6 x 10 ins / 16 x 25 cm) GBP 980,000. NEW YORK, 7 Nov 2001, *Study on the Island* (1883, oil on panel, 6 x 10 ins / 16 x 25 cm) USD 350,000. LONDON, 9 April 2002, *Pile of Stones* (1884, oil on canvas, 13 x 16 ins / 33 x 41 cm) GBP 780,000. NEW YORK, 5 Nov 2002, *The Two Carts* (c. 1883, conté crayon, 11 x 13 ins / 27 x 33 cm) USD 350,000. LONDON, 6 Feb 2003, *Untitled* (1881, pencil crayon drawing, album, 6 x 4 ins / 14 x 9 cm) GBP 100,000. NEW YORK, 4 Nov 2003, *Seated Women - Study for Sunday Afternoon on the Grande Jatte* (c. 1884-1885, oil on panel, 6 x 10 ins / 16 x 25 cm) USD 1,400,000. LONDON, 2 Feb 2004, *With Trembling Steps* (c. 1884, crayon, 13 x 9 ins / 32 x 24 cm) GBP 250,000.

SEURAT, Jean-Pierre

20th century.

Glassmaker.

AUCTION RECORDS:

PARIS, 6 July 1992, *Imp* (sculpture in polychrome blown glass, h. 12 1/2 ins / 32 cm) FRF 4,600.

SEURRE, Charles Émile Marie

French, 19th century.

Born 22 February 1798, in Paris; died 11 January 1858, in Paris.

Sculptor. Historical figures.

Charles Seurre was brother of Gabriel Bernard and a pupil of Cartellier. He enrolled at the École des Beaux-Arts on 3 March 1814, was awarded second place in the 1822 Prix de Rome and first place in 1824. Seurre exhibited at the Salon in 1831.

MUSEUMS AND GALLERIES:

CHARTRES: *Napoleon I* - PARIS (Louvre): *Boileau* - VERSAILLES: *Admiral Quiéret; Gaston de Foix, Duke of Nemours; Charles VII; Napoleon I.*

SEURRE, Gabriel Bernard

French, 19th century.

Born 11 July 1795, in Paris; died 3 October 1867, in Paris.

Sculptor.

Gabriel Seurre was a pupil of Cartellier. Awarded first prize in 1818 and created Chevalier of the Légion d'Honneur in 1837 Gabriel Seurre was made a Member of the Institute in 1852.

MUSEUMS AND GALLERIES:

VERSAILLES (Mus.): *Portrait of Admiral Behuchet; Portrait of La Fontaine.*

SEUTER. See also **SEUTTER**

SEUTER, Abraham. See **SEUTTER**

SEUTER, Daniel or Joseph Daniel. See **SEITER**

SEUTER, Geoffroy, or Saiter
German, 18th century.
Born 1717, in Augsburg; died 1800.
Painter, engraver.
Seuter studied under Riedinger. He produced engravings of religious, mythological and allegorical subjects, as well as portraits and other subjects.

SEUTER, Johann Gottfried. See **SEUTTER**

SEUTTER, Abraham, or Saiter or Seiter or Seuter or Seyder
German, 18th century.
Born c. 1690, in Augsburg; died 1747.
Painter.

SEUTTER, Albrecht Karl
German, 18th century.
Born 1722, in Augsburg; died 1762.
Draughtsman, engraver (burin). Maps.
Albrecht Seutter was the son of Matthäus. He published topographical maps.

SEUTTER, Bartholomäus
German, 18th century.
Born 1678, in Augsburg; died 1754.
Enameller, painter (porcelain/glazed earthenware), engraver (burin), print publisher.
Seutter produced engravings of portraits.

SEUTTER, Johann
German, 18th century.
Born 1686; died 1719.
Painter, engraver (burin). Portraits, historical subjects.
Johann Seutter was the father of Johann Gottfried.

SEUTTER, Johann Gottfried, or Saiter, Seiter, Seuter or Syder
German, 18th century.
Born 8 August 1717, in Augsburg; died 1800.
Engraver (burin), draughtsman.
Johann Gottfried was the son of Johann Seutter and studied under Johann Elias Ridinger and Georg Martin Preissler in Nuremberg, Germany. He made trips to Italy where he produced engravings of landscapes, and others in the style of the Italian Renaissance masters.

SEUTTER, Martin
German, 18th century.
Born c. 1683, in Augsburg; died 1766.
Engraver (burin and silverpoint).

SEUTTER, Matthäus
German, 18th century.
Born 20 September 1678, in Augsburg; died 1757.
Draughtsman, engraver (burin), geographer. Maps.
Seutter studied under J. B. Homann in Nuremberg, Germany. A geographer and art publisher, he engraved geographical maps, coats of arms and portraits.

SEVAISTRE, Pierre
French, 20th century.
Born 22 March 1879, in Paris.
Painter.
Pierre Sevaistre exhibited at the Salon des Artistes Français from 1907. He won a silver medal in 1924 and a gold medal in 1930 and became a Chevalier of the Légion d'hHonneur Honneur. He also exhibited at the Salon des Indépendants.

SEVAUX, Charles
French, 18th century.
Born 5 May 1751.
Painter. Genre scenes.
Charles Sevaux was a member of the Académie de St-Luc.

SÈVE, Gilbert de, called Sève le Vieux
French, 17th century.
Born 1615, in Moulins; died 9 April 1698, in Paris.
Painter. History painting.
Gilbert de Sève was admitted into the Académie on 1 February 1648 and featured in the exhibition of the Académie Royale in 1673. Many of his portraits of distinguished figures were engraved by Edlinck, Van Schuppen and Masson. He also provided many drawings for the publication of a *History of France* and painted the allegorical paintings adorning Queen Marie-Thérèse's bedroom in Versailles.
AUCTION RECORDS:
PARIS, 1894, *The Last Supper; Jesus among the Doctors* (two pendants) FRF 31.

SÈVE, Jacques de
French, 18th century.
Died after 1790.
Active 1742-1788.
Painter, illustrator.
Jacques de Sève engraved vignettes for the decoration of Classical works.

SÈVE, Jacques Eustache de
French, 19th century.
Born 1790; died 1830.
Active until c. 1815.
Draughtsman, engraver.
Jacques Eustache de Sève was the son of Jacques de Sève. He did burin engravings.
AUCTION RECORDS:
LONDON, 5 July 1993, *Studies of Five Starved Animals* (ink and wash, 9 x 6 1/4 ins / 23 x 16.1 cm) GBP 6,900.

SÈVE, Nicolas
French, 17th century.
Active in Troyes in 1677.
Painter.

SÈVE, Pierre de, the Younger
French, 17th century.
Born 1623, in Moulins; died 9 November 1695, in Paris.
Painter. History painting, genre scenes.
Pierre de Sève the Younger was the brother of Gilbert de Sève. He was admitted into the Académie on 14 April 1663 and exhibited at the Salon of the Académie Royale in 1693.
MUSEUMS AND GALLERIES:
VERSAILLES (Mus.): *Renewal of the Alliance between Switzerland and France in 1663*.
AUCTION RECORDS:
PARIS, 22 Jan 1919, *Cupid Bound by the Graces* (pencil) FRF 67. PARIS, 27 Feb 1919, *Horseman* (study in pencil) FRF 22.

SEVEAU, Georges
French, 20th century.
Born in Poitiers.
Painter. Urban landscapes.
Georges Seveau exhibited in Paris from 1910 at the Salon des Indépendants.
AUCTION RECORDS:
PARIS, 4 Oct 1948, *The Seine at Pont Henri IV*, FRF 1,100.

SEVEHON, Franky Boy. See **FRANCKY BOY Sevehon**

SEVEN SORROWS OF THE VIRGIN ADORED BY THE VAN DE VELDE FAMILY, Master of the. See **ISENBRANT Adriaen**

SEVEN..., Master of. See **MASTERS**

SEVENBOM, Johan, or Saevenbom or Saefvenbom or Säfvenbom or Säfvenboom
Swedish, 18th century.

Born c. 1721, in Närke; died 27 December 1784, in Stockholm.
Painter. Landscapes, architectural views.

Sevenbom was a pupil of Guillaume Thomas Taraval at the Kungliga Akademi för de Fria Konsterna in Stockholm. He painted Swedish castles. Two of his *Views of Paris* are in the museum in Norrköping, and his *Maritime Landscape with Fortress* is in the Nationalmuseum in Stockholm.

SEVER, Anton
Slovene, 20th century.
Born 14 June 1886, in Šencur.
Medallist.

Anton Sever studied with Heinrich Strehblow and Rudolph Marschall. He lived and worked in Ljubljana.

SÉVERAC, Gilbert Alexandre de
French, 19th century.
Born 1834, in St-Sulpice-sur-Leyre; died 1897.
Painter. History painting, portraits, genre scenes, still-lifes, flowers.

Gilbert Séverac was a pupil of Jules Garipuy at the École des Beaux-Arts in Toulouse, then of Léon Cogniet at the École des Beaux-Arts in Paris. Exhibited at the Salon de Paris from 1859 onwards.

MUSEUMS AND GALLERIES:
BÉZIERS: *Bouquet of Roses* - TOULOUSE: *Jules Garipuy; Old Beggars.*

AUCTION RECORDS:
PARIS, 7 Feb 1898, *The Sultana,* FRF 105. PARIS, 25 March 1993, *Young Boy* (1885, charcoal and stump, 7 3/4 x 7 ins / 20 x 18 cm) FRF 3,500.

SÉVERAC, Léon
French, 20th century.
Born in Lodève.
Sculptor.

Léon Séverac exhibited in Paris at the Salon des Artistes Français from 1927 and at the Salon des Indépendants. He won a bronze medal in 1931 and a silver medal in 1944.

SEVERDONCK, Franz van
Belgian, 19th century.
Born 1809, in Brussels; died 1889, in Brussels.
Painter. Genre scenes, landscapes with figures, animals, farmyard scenes, harbour scenes, architectural views.

Franz van Severdonck essentially painted rural landscapes or farmyards with farm animals.

MUSEUMS AND GALLERIES:
BUCHAREST: *Landscape with Animals; Flock of Sheep* - ROUEN: *Sheep* - SÈTE: *Gleaner.*

AUCTION RECORDS:
LONDON, 16 Oct 1968, *Birds in a Landscape,* GBP 600. DORDRECHT, 10 June 1969, *Summer's Day,* NLG 6,500. DORDRECHT, 12 Dec 1972, *Landscape with Figures,* NLG 7,400. NEW YORK, 10 Oct 1973, *Flock of Sheep in a Landscape,* USD 1,500. NEW YORK, 15 Oct 1976, *Sheep and Chickens in a Landscape* (1863, oil on panel, 20 x 28 ins / 51 x 71 cm) USD 3,000. ZURICH, 20 May 1977, *Livestock in Pasture* (1862, oil on panel, 7 x 9 1/2 ins / 17.5 x 24 cm) CHF 3,800. COLOGNE, 20 March 1981, *Sheep Grazing* (1871, oil on wood, 7 x 9 1/2 ins / 18 x 24 cm) DEM 10,000. LONDON, 28 Nov 1984, *Birds in a Landscape* (1869, oil on panel, 17 1/2 x 28 1/2 ins / 44.5 x 72.5 cm) GBP 3,000. LONDON, 29 May 1985, *Sheep in a Stormy Landscape* (1869, oil on canvas, 20 x 27 3/4 ins / 50.5 x 70.5 cm) GBP 2,500. NORFOLK, ENGLAND, 22 Oct 1986, *Sheep, Chickens and Ducks in a Landscape* (1894, oil on panel, 20 1/2 x 27 1/2 ins / 52 x 70 cm) GBP 4,500. NEW YORK, 17 Jan 1990, *Some Sheep on a Hill* (1883, oil on panel, 10 x 15 ins / 25.4 x 38.2 cm) USD 2,750. LONDON, 6 June 1990, *Sheep in a Vast Landscape* (1873, oil on panel, 19 x 25 1/2 ins / 48 x 65 cm) GBP 2,860. NEW YORK, 19 July 1990, *Sheep in a Landscape* (1860, oil on panel, 22 1/4 x 32 1/4 ins / 56.5 x 82 cm) USD 4,675. AMSTERDAM, 6 Nov 1990, *Summer Landscape with Sheep and a Goat near a Pond* (oil on canvas, 14 3/4 x 22 3/4 ins / 37.5 x 58 cm) NLG 7,475. STOCKHOLM, 14 Nov 1990, *Landscape with Sheep Grazing* (oil on panel, 7 1/2 x 9 1/2 ins / 19 x 24 cm) SEK 11,000. AMSTERDAM, 23 April 1991, *Sheep in a Barn* (1853, oil on canvas, 19 1/4 x 26 3/4 ins / 49 x 68 cm) NLG 8,625. NEW YORK, 21 May 1991, *Farm Animals near a Pond* (1865, oil on panel, 21 x 29 1/2 ins / 53.3 x 74.9 cm) USD 6,600. AMSTERDAM, 5-6 Nov 1991, *Livestock in a Meadow* (1864, oil on panel, 8 x 10 1/2 ins / 20.5 x 26.5 cm) NLG 4,600; *Fowls in a Meadow* (1864, oil on panel, 7 x 9 1/2 ins / 17.5 x 24 cm) NLG 3,680. NEW YORK, 16 July 1992, *Sheep and Ducks in a Landscape* (1889, oil on panel, 7 x 10 1/4 ins / 17.8 x 26 cm) USD 3,850. AMSTERDAM, 20 April 1993, *Port of Rotterdam.* EDINBURGH, 13 May 1993, *Feeding Fowls in a Dutch Landscape* (1870, oil on panel, 7 1/4 x 9 1/4 ins / 18.4 x 23.5 cm) GBP 935. NEW YORK, 17 Feb 1994, *Sheep and Fowls beside a Pond* (1874, oil on panel, 18 1/4 x 26 3/4 ins / 46.5 x 68 cm) USD 4,830. PARIS, 15 Dec 1994, *Sheep* (oil on panel, 7 3/4 x 11 3/4 ins / 20 x 30 cm) FRF 7,200. LONDON, 22 Feb 1995, *Sheep and Fowls in a Landscape* (oil on panel, 7 x 9 1/2 ins / 18 x 24 cm) GBP 1,322. LOKEREN, 7 Oct 1995, *Rustic Landscape with Sheep and Ducks* (1883, oil on canvas, 19 3/4 x 27 1/4 ins / 50 x 69 cm) BEF 240,000. AMSTERDAM, 7 Nov 1995, *Sheep in a Sheep Pen* (1886, oil on panel, 10 3/4 x 15 3/4 ins / 27.5 x 40 cm) NLG 1,534. LONDON, 13 March 1996, *Sheep and Ducks in a Landscape* (1880, oil on canvas, 18 1/2 x 26 1/2 ins / 47 x 67 cm) USD 4,600. AMSTERDAM, 16 April 1996, *Sheep and Chickens in a Landscape* (1868, oil on panel, 7 x 9 1/2 ins / 18 x 24 cm) NLG 6,490. LONDON, 31 Oct 1996, *Family of Sheep* (1869, oil on panel, 7 x 9 1/2 ins / 18 x 24 cm) GBP 1,840. LONDON, 22 Nov 1996, *Landscape with a Sheepdog Watching a Flock of Sheep* (oil on panel, 7 x 10 1/2 ins / 17.8 x 26.6 cm) GBP 1,955. NEW YORK, 10 Feb 1998, *Chickens and Ducks beside a Pond* (1883, oil on panel, 7 x 10 1/4 ins / 17.9 x 26 cm) USD 1,840. LOKEREN, 15 May 1999, *In the Warm* (1882, oil on canvas, 20 x 27 ins / 50 x 69 cm) BEF 290,000. LONDON, 28 June 1999, *Chickens and Pigeons in an Open Landscape* (1861, oil on panel, a pair, 7 x 9 ins / 18 x 24 cm) GBP 6,200. WORCESTER, 6 April 2000, *Chickens in Rural Setting* (oil on canvas, a pair, 7 x 10 ins / 18 x 25 cm) GBP 5,000. LOKEREN, 9 Dec 2000, *Flock and Sheepdog* (1886, oil on panel, 7 x 10 ins / 18 x 26 cm) BEF 250,000. BRUSSELS, 23 April 2001, *Rustic Interior with Sheep and Rabbits* (oil on panel, 20 x 24 ins / 50 x 60 cm) BEF 360,000. BRUSSELS, 21 May 2001, *Sheep, Fowl and Ducks in a Landscape* (1873, oil on panel, 19 x 26 ins / 49 x 67 cm) BEF 310,000. ORANGE, 12 Feb 2002, *Sheep and Ducks by a Pond* (oil on board, 10 x 7 ins / 25 x 18 cm) USD 1,650. VLAAMSE KAAI, 26 March 2002, *Cock and Hen* (oil on canvas/panel, 7 x 8 ins / 19 x 20 cm) EUR 11,000. VLAAMSE KAAI, 26 March 2002, *Animals in a Landscape* (oil on panel, 20 x 28 ins / 51 x 71 cm) EUR 12,000. LOKEREN, 15 March 2003, *Landscape with Cock, Chickens, Ducks and Pigeon* (1871, oil on panel, 7 x 9 ins / 17 x 24 cm) EUR 3,600. NEW YORK, 21 May 2003, *Sheep in Stable* (1879, oil on canvas, 20 x 27 ins / 51 x 69 cm) USD 6,000. VIENNA, 27 May 2004, *Sheep and Ducks in Summer Landscape* (oil on canvas, 20 x 28 ins / 51 x 70 cm) EUR 6,500. ANTWERP, 18 Oct 2004, *Hens in a Landscape* (oil on panel, 9 x 12 ins / 23 x 30 cm) EUR 2,200.

SEVERDONCK, Joseph van
Belgian, 19th century.
Born 27 March 1819, in Brussels; died 11 December 1905, in Brussels.
Painter. Military subjects, animals.

Joseph van Severdonck was a pupil of Wappers. He painted military scenes featuring animals, which sometimes causes him to be classified as an animal painter.

MUSEUMS AND GALLERIES:

BRUSSELS: *Lancers on Reconnaissance* - MONTREAL: *Dovecote; Sheep* - TOURNAI: *Princess of Épinoy at the Siege of Tournai* - YPRES: *Episode during the Siege of Ypres.*

AUCTION RECORDS:

NEW YORK, 28 April 1977, *Draught Horses* (1880, oil on canvas, 22½ x 33¾ ins / 57 x 86 cm) USD 2,300. PARIS, 16 April 1986, *Retreat from Russia* (oil on canvas, 57½ x 95 ins / 146 x 241 cm) FRF 52,000. MILFORD, 22 April 1999, *Sheep and Ducks in a Landscape* (oil on panel, 7 x 10 ins / 18 x 25 cm) USD 1,800. LONDON, 29 Nov 2000, *Belgian Hussars* (oil on canvas, 16 x 13 ins / 40 x 32 cm) GBP 1,800. LONDON, 27 March 2001, *Napoleon* (oil on canvas, 29 x 37 ins / 74 x 94 cm) GBP 4,400. BRUSSELS, 5 Nov 2001, *Russia's Retreat* (oil on canvas, 57 x 95 ins / 146 x 241 cm) BEF 1,600,000. LILLE, 10 March 2002, *Hussars' Halt* (oil on panel, 10 x 17 ins / 26 x 42 cm) EUR 4,500. BRUSSELS, 10 June 2002, *Young Italian Woman with Medallion* (1850, oil on canvas, 31 x 26 ins / 80 x 66 cm) EUR 2,200. MUNICH, 5 Nov 2003, *Cavalry Battle* (1871, oil on panel, 11 x 18 ins / 29 x 46 cm) EUR 1,500. BRUSSELS, 23 March 2004, *Busy Street in the Rain* (oil on panel, 15 x 21 ins / 38 x 54 cm) EUR 2,000.

SEVEREN, Dan van

Belgian, 20th century.
Born 8 February 1927, in Lokeren.
Painter, draughtsman.

Dan van Severen studied under Gerard Hermans at the academy of St Luke in Ghent and under Anton Marstboom at the academy in Antwerp. His work has featured at group exhibitions in Belgium, France and Italy and he has exhibited solo in Belgium.

Van Severen is an Abstract painter whose work exhibits an almost Franciscan simplicity and a high degree of spiritual content. He employs crosses, lozenges and squares in neutral colours which are deceptively subtle and sophisticated. He describes his own work as 'a tranquil geometry, an immobile mathematic with icons of silence'. His work represents a non-ecclesiastical approach to modern religious art. His nuanced approach exudes sanctity, particularly in his skilful deployment of delicate shades of browns, greys, blacks, whites and blues.

AUCTION RECORDS:

ANTWERP, 23 April 1985, *Composition* (oil on canvas, 47¼ x 39¼ ins / 120 x 100 cm) BEF 180,000. LOKEREN, 10 Dec 1994, *Cruciform* (1988, pencil, 22 x 16½ ins / 56 x 42 cm) BEF 44,000. LOKEREN, 18 May 1996, *Composition* (1971, oil on canvas, 51¼ x 35½ ins / 130 x 90 cm) BEF 220,000. LOKEREN, 7 Oct 2000, *Cross, Vertical and Horizontal* (1972, three, 30 x 22 ins / 76 x 55 cm) BEF 170,000. ANTWERP, 24 Oct 2000, *Composition* (c. 1972, oil on canvas on panel, 7 x 5 ins / 17 x 13 cm) BEF 75,000. ANTWERP, 24 April 2001, *Composition* (1961, watercolour, 20 x 14 ins / 50 x 35 cm) BEF 75,000. ANTWERP, 24 April 2001, *Composition* (oil on canvas, 47 x 39 ins / 120 x 100 cm) BEF 450,000. ANTWERP, 23 April 2002, *Composition* (1989, drawing, 35 x 26 ins / 88 x 66 cm) EUR 3,000. ANTWERP, 23 April 2002, *Composition* (1989, drawing, 35 x 26 ins / 88 x 66 cm) EUR 3,000. LOKEREN, 11 Oct 2003, *Composition with Diamond* (1977, gouache and Indian ink, 30 x 22 ins / 77 x 55 cm) EUR 3,600.

SEVERI

Italian, 17th century.
Active in Rome in 1667.
Stucco artist.

Severi was commissioned to execute the decorative stucco work in the church of S Agnese in Rome.

SEVERI, Carlo

Italian, 20th century.
Mixed media. Artists' books.

Carlo Severi's work featured in an exhibition of new acquisitions at the Bibliothèque Nationale de France in Paris in 1992, *De Bonnard à Baselitz - Dix Ans d'enrichissements du cabinet des estampes 1978-1988* (*From Bonnard to Baselitz: A Decade of Acquisitions by the Prints Collection 1978-1988*). He produced a number of artists' books.

MUSEUMS AND GALLERIES:

PARIS (BNF, Prints Collection).

SEVERIN, Alexandre

Romanian, 20th century.
Active in France.
Sculptor. Busts.

Alexandre Severin exhibited busts at the Société Nationale des Beaux-Arts, Paris.

SEVERIN, Antoine

Belgian, 19th century.
Active in the middle of the 19th century.
Painter, engraver (etching). Genre scenes, landscapes.

SEVERIN, Juliaan

Belgian, 20th century.
Born 1888, in Bogerhout; died 1975, in Kruibeke.
Painter, pastellist, engraver. Landscapes.

Juliaan Severin studied at the fine arts academy in Brussels and completed his formal studies in Paris.

AUCTION RECORDS:

BRUSSELS, 27 March 1990, *Pointilliste Landscape* (oil on canvas, 25½ x 31½ ins / 65 x 80 cm) BEF 100,000.

SEVERIN, Julius

Italian, 19th century.
Born 29 April 1840, in Rome; died 19 May 1883, in Munich, Germany.
Painter. Genre scenes, landscapes.

Severin was self-taught.

SEVERIN, Mark F.

Belgian, 20th century.
Born 1906, in Brussels; died 1987.
Painter, watercolourist, draughtsman, engraver, medallist, illustrator, designer. Designs for stained glass.

Mark Severin studied in Great Britain before going to teach in Antwerp, notably at the Hoger Instituut voor Schone Kunsten. He was a member of Belgium's royal academy. He worked principally as a woodcut and soft-point engraver and etcher, but also produced paintings and watercolours and a number of stained glass compositions.

BIBLIOGRAPHY:

Mark Severin (1906-1987), Bibliothèque royale de Belgique, Brussels, 1996.

MUSEUMS AND GALLERIES:

ANTWERP (Prentenkabinet).

SEVERIN, Michel-Ange

French, 20th century.
Born 1900, in Marseilles; died 1971, in Marseilles.
Painter (gouache), watercolourist. Portraits, landscapes.

Although Michel-Ange Severin was a pupil at the École des Beaux-Arts in Marseilles, the circumstances of his life did not allow him to follow a career as an artist. He painted all his life but never showed his landscapes - mainly of the old port but also some countryside landscapes. He made rapid and discreet sketches of his subject in watercolour or coloured pencil, then finished the work in oil or gouache at home. His works are very diverse, sometimes in high colour like many Marseillaise painters, sometimes more restrained, evolving into a style between Post-Impressionism and Post-

Cubism. He very often painted self-questioning self-portraits.

SEVERINI, Federico

Italian, 20th century.

Born 31 March 1888, in Pisa; died 13 October 1962, in Pisa.

Painter. Portraits, interiors, architectural views, landscapes, urban landscapes, still-lifes.

Federico Severini also worked as a civil engineer. His canvases, painted with a free touch and often a thick impasto, show glowing landscapes.

His work appeared in many collective exhibitions from 1930 onwards. He held a number of solo exhibitions, particularly in Pisa where a retrospective of his work was mounted in 1972 at the Museo Nazionale San Matteo.

Bibliography:

Federico Severini, Ghelfi, Verona, 1974.

SEVERINI, Gino

Italian, 20th century.

Born 7 April 1883, in Cortona; died 27 February 1966, in Meudon (Hauts-de-Seine), France.

Active in France.

Painter, pastellist, collage artist. Religious subjects, military subjects, figures, still-lifes. Murals, designs for mosaics, stage sets, glass casing.

Futurism.

Les Artistes Italiens de Paris group.

Gino Severini went to Rome, where he held various jobs in the food business while attending evening classes at the Villa Medici art school. In 1901, he met Boccioni, who introduced him to Balla, in whose studio he first encountered Seurat's Divisionism. While there is a tendency to overestimate the influence of Cézanne, since he was so important for the Parisian Cubists, Seurat's major role in the development of European at this period is often overlooked today.

Severini went to Paris for the first time in 1906, perhaps because of his admiration for Seurat and his desire to see more of his work. He lived in a studio in the Impasse Guelma, where Utrillo, Braque and Dufy also had studios. He soon met Modigliani, Max Jacob, Pierre Reverdy, Apollinaire and Picasso. In 1913, he married the daughter of the poet Paul Fort, with Apollinaire acting as witness at the ceremony. In 1923, he converted to Catholicism. He returned to Italy in 1933 and was the only Italian Futurist to be unambiguously condemned by Mussolini's Fascist regime. He stayed in Italy during the war before returning to live in Meudon, near Paris. In 1946, he published the first volume of his memoirs, *Tutta la vita di un pittore* (*A Painter's Life*). In Paris he set up a mosaic school that followed the ancient techniques used in Ravenna in the 6th century.

In the early years of the 20th century, Severini practised a strict Divisionism, a technique that he continued to use during his Cubist and Futurist periods. In 1908-1909, for example, in his *Spring in Montmartre*, the style is pure divisionism with as yet no hint of Fauvism and even less of Cubism. In 1910 - although, as Michel Seuphor relates in his *Le Style et le Cri*, Severini later disputed this fact - he was one of the signatories of the first Futurist manifesto. His works at that time were, however, much closer to Cubism despite their bright colours and use of Divisionism. This can be seen in his painting of *The Boulevard* (1910) where the artist's free interpretation of Cubism anticipated the advent of Synthetic Cubism. It has been suggested by some scholars that it was, in fact, Severini's example that prompted Braque and Picasso to reintroduce colour gradually into their works and that brought about the development towards the greater freedom of the Synthetic period.

Between 1910 and 1914 Severini devoted himself entirely to the Futurist cause, even if he did not attempt to conceal his Cubist leanings. *Pan-Pan Dancing at the Monico* (1910-1911) is rightly considered among the masterpieces of early Futurism. Unable to share the anti-Parisian attitudes stirred up among the Futurists by Marinetti (to whom Severini seems never to have been close) or their declared, but unconvincing, assertion that Cubism had had no influence on Futurism, Severini persuaded them to come to Paris. Here, in 1911, he arranged for Carlo Carrá, Boccioni and Russolo to meet Picasso, Braque, Juan Gris and Robert Delaunay so that the latter artists could explain the current state of painting in Paris. It seems clear that, hitherto, Futurism had done little but express itself in words and intentions and now, coming into contact with Cubist works, was able to find a basis for its formulation. Severini played a decisive role, not so much in the definition of the objectives as of the style of Futurism, at least in its early period. This role was not challenged until 1914. On the occasion of the first Futurist exhibition in 1912, the *Pan-Pan Dancing at the Monico* was held to be the most successful work while the other Futurist painters were still paying homage to neo-Impressionism, now out-moded, and while painters were still studying the rules of construction based on the proportion of the golden number used by Seurat.

Severini now applied his new ease with Futurism to a number of daring portraits, *Self-portrait, Portrait of Mme S.* and, after his painting of Pan-Pan, further dynamic representations of dancers, *Blue Dancer, White Dancer.* As a Futurist, he was interested in ways of recreating the experience of dynamic movement itself. He produced a considerable number of works where he experimented with multiplying a form on the surface of the canvas in order to prolong its existence in time by the time taken by the viewer to read it. He chose scenes of wild rhythmic activity as subjects, doubling the graphic rhythm of the lines and alternating surfaces, and placing contrasting colours in succession. One particularly successful work from this period is his *Dancer at Bal Tabarin* (*Dynamic Hieroglyph of the Bal Tabarin*) (1912). Living in Paris and not sharing the Futurists' hostility towards the Cubists, it was natural that Severini's work should develop along similar lines to those of his Parisian friends into whose society he was completely integrated. He had no hesitation in adopting, for example, the use of collage, first employed by Braque and immediately after that by Picasso, in the three works *Portrait of Arthur Cravan, Homage to My Father* and *Homage to My Mother*. After a last burst of pure Futurism in 1913 with the 'plastic analogies' of the dazzling series known in its entirety as *Spherical Expansion of Centrifugal Light* and the few last works inspired by Futurist dynamism and the World War I (*War, Red Cross Train* of 1914 and *Armoured Train* of 1915), his development culminated in a synthesis of Futurism and Cubism that closely resembled Synthetic Cubism.

Isolated in Paris during the war, Gino Severini was painting in 1917 in a rather unconvinced Synthetic Cubist style, producing mainly still-lifes with musical instruments, moving towards the somewhat lifeless classical perfection of Juan Gris' restrained compositions. He joined, through Gris, Léone Rosenberg's Effort Moderne group which aimed at reconciling the achievements of Cubism with the rigour of classical art. Faithful to the lesson of Seurat and sympathetic to the ideals of classicism, between 1918 and 1920, Severini immersed himself in the study of mathematics and calculations of proportion, publishing, in 1921, his book *From Cubism to Classicism.* While in 1913-1914 Severini had been among the precursors of abstraction with his experiments into the synaesthetic possibilities of painting, in works such as *Dancers* or *Spherical Expansion of Centrifugal Light,* he now produced work that smacked somewhat of academicism with his series of *Harlequins*. He was not alone in this, for it was a tendency appearing in the inter-war period in many parts of Europe.

At the same time, he was working on a series of large frescoes for Castello Montefugoni, outside Florence, using as his motif the traditional masks of the Italian *Commedia dell'Arte*. This commission marked the beginning of a period in which he devoted himself to murals. Up to 1935, he carried out a number of commissions for public and religious bodies, particularly in Switzerland, in Semsales, La Roche, Fribourg and Lausanne. In Italy, he made a mosaic (a technique he knew well) for the reception hall of the palazzo hosting the 1933 Milan Triennale. In 1929, he made some decorative panels for Léonce Rosenberg's house in France. He also worked for the theatre, designing costumes and scenery.

The painter of some of the most important masterpieces of Futurism, Gino Severini was able to avoid the moral compromises made by those Futurists who had remained in Italy during the Fascist period. However, like many other artists in the France of the inter-war period, he turned his back on the adventurous experimentation of the École de Paris in favour of a comfortable bourgeois art. The works produced by Severini at this period do nothing to further his fame. Similarly, the Cubist-Pointilliste and Abstract paintings of his last period appear forced and lifeless. Despite the inglorious conclusion to his career, Severini must be remembered, through his example and his works and through the influence he exercised over those around him, as the instigator of one of the major tendencies in painting at the beginning of the 20th century and, as such, he is one of the creators of modern art.

Gino Severini took part in several collective exhibitions in Paris including: Salon des Indépendants, Salon of the Société Nationale des Beaux-Arts and Salon d'Automne (1908); first Futurist exhibition, Galerie Bernheim Jeune (1912); *Peintre futuristes italiens* (*Italian Futurist Painters*), Rue de la Boétie (1921). Posthumous exhibitions include: *Aspects historiques du constructivisme et de l'art concret* (*Historical Aspects of Constructivism and Concrete Art*), Musée d'Art Moderne de la Ville de Paris (1977); *De Chirico et la peinture italienne de l'entre-deux guerres* (*De Chirico and Italian Painting of the Interwar Period*) Lodève museum and *Aux origines de l'abstraction (1800-1914)* (*The Origins of Abstraction, 1800-1914*), Musée d'Orsay, Paris (2003). He held a number of solo exhibitions including: Galerie Boutet-de-Morvet, Paris (1916); Steiglitz's 291 Gallery, New York (1917); Galerie de l'Effort Moderne, Paris (1919); exhibition of mosaics, Paris (1952); travelling exhibition in Detroit, Los Angeles and Palazzo Venezia in Rome (1961-1962); Musée National d'Art Moderne, Paris (1967); Museum am Ostwall, Dortmund (1971); Galleria Vittorio Emmanuele, Milan (1973); Palazzo Pitti, Florence and Palazzo Casali, Cortona (1983). Gino Severini was awarded the painting prize at the 2nd Rome Quadriennale (1935) and, the Grand Prix at Venice Biennale (1950).

Severini

Gino Severini

Severini

Bibliography:

Severini, Gino, *Les Arts plastiques d'avant-garde et la Science moderne*, Mercure de France, Paris, 1915. Courthion, Pierre, *Gino Severini*, Hoepli, Paris, 1930. Fierens, Paul, *Gino Severini*, Chroniques du jour, Paris, 1936. Bardi, P.M., *Gino Severini*, Stile, Milan, 1942. Wall, Bernard, *Gino Severini*, Harvill Press, London, 1946. Venturi, Lionello, *Gino Severini*, De Luca Editore, Rome, 1961. Lukach, J.M., *'Severini's 1917 Exhibition at Stieglitz's 291'* in *Burlington Magazine, cxiii/817*, 1970. Lukach, J.M., *'A study of Gino Severini's Writings and Paintings of 1916-1917'* in *Critical Art, xx/138*, 1974. Meloni, Francesco, *Gino Severini: tutta l'opera grafica*, catalogue raisonné, Libreria Prandi, Reggio Emilia, 1982. Fagiolo Dell'Arco, Maurizio, *Gino Severini prima e dopo l'opera: documenti, opere ed immagini*, exhibition catalogue, Electa, Florence, 1983. Vescovo, Marisa, *Gino Severini dal 1916 al 1936*, exhibition catalogue, Palazzo Cuttica, Alessandria, Il quadrante, Turin, 1987. Fauchereau, Serge, *'Écrits sur l'art de Severini'* in *coll. Diagonales*, Éd. Cercle d'Art, Paris, 1988. Fonti, Daniela/Fagiolo dell'Arco, Maurizio/Goggioli, Paola/Dorazio, Piero, *Gino Severini: catalogo ragionato*, catalogue raisonné, Arnoldo Mondadori, P. Daverio, Milan, 1988. Amelotti, Enrica/Caffarelli, Maria Luisa/Mantelli, Mario/Serra, Silvana, *Quel mosaico in piazza: Gino Severini al palazzo delle poste di Alessandria*, exhibition catalogue, Palazzo delle Poste, Amnesia, Alessandria, 1990. Fonti, Daniela, *Gino Severini: opere inedite e capolavori ritrovati*, Skira, Milan, 1999. Fonti, Daniela, *Gino Severini: La Danza 1909-1916*, exhibition catalogue, Skira, Milan, 2001. Bonito Oliva, Achille/Iovane, Giovanni/Lista, Giovanni, et al., *De Chirico et la peinture italienne de l'entre-deux guerres*, exhibition catalogue, Musée de Lodève, 2003. Lemoine, Serge/Rousseau, Pascal, et al., *Aux origines de l'abstraction (1800-1914)*, exhibition catalogue, Musée d'Orsay, Paris, 2003.

Museums and Galleries:

Amsterdam (Stedelijk Mus.): *Train for the Wounded* (1914) - Basel (Kunstmus.): *Geometric Study* (1913) - Bergamo (Accademia Carrara): *Landscape in Civray* (1909, oil on canvas) - Florence (Gal. d'Arte Moderna) - Ljubljana (Narodna Gal.) - London (Tate Collection): *Suburban Train Arriving in Paris* (1915, oil on canvas) - Los Angeles (County MA): *Still-life with Playing Cards; Still-life with Ace of Spades* - Madrid (Mus. Thyssen-Bornemisza): *Expansion of Light (Centrifugal and Centripetal)* (1913-1914, oil/corrugated paper) - Milan (Pinacoteca di Brera): *Dynamism of a Dancer* (1912); *Still-life with Fruit Dish; Large Still-life with Marrow; The North-South* - New Brunswick (Beaverbrook AG): *View from a Balcony* (c. 1930, gouache) - New York (MoMA): *Dynamic Hieroglyph of the Bal Tabarin* (1912, oil on canvas); *Armored Train in Action* (1915, oil on canvas) - New York (Solomon R. Guggenheim Mus.): *Red Cross Train Passing a Village* (1915, oil on canvas); *Sea=Dancer* (1914, oil on canvas) - Paris (BNF, Prints Collection) - Paris (MNAM-CCI): *The Bear's Dance at the Moulin Rouge* (1913); *Portraits: Mother and Daughter* (1935); *Green Table* (1947); *Violin* (1959); *Pan-Pan Dancing at the Monico* (replica of the destoyed painting from 1910-1912, made in 1959-1960) - Rome (Gal. Nazionale d'Arte Moderna): *Dynamism of Light-Forms in Space* (1913-1914, oil on canvas) - Rotterdam (Mus. Boijmans Van Beuningen): *Pierrot as Musician* (1924) - San Francisco (FAM): *Still-life with Fish* (1958) - St-Étienne (Mus. d'Art et d'Industrie): *Still-life with the Lacerba Newspaper* (1913) - The Hague (Gemeentemus.): *Two Pierrots* (1922) - Trento (Mus. di Arte Moderna e Contemporanea): *Cannon in Action (Words in Freedom and Forms)* (1914-1915, oil on canvas) - Turin (Galleria Civica d'Arte Moderna e Contemporanea): *Portrait of Miss Signorina Severini (Portrait of Gina Severini, My Daughter)* (1934, oil on canvas) - Venice (Collezione Peggy Guggenheim): *Dancer-Sea* (1913) - Washington DC (Hirshhorn Mus. and Sculpture Garden): *Dynamic Rhythm of a Head in a Bus* (1912, drawing) - West Palm Beach (Norton MA): *Playing Cards and Flask* (c. 1912, collage).

Auction records:

Paris, 11 April 1927, *Still-life* (gouache) FRF 120. Paris, 27-28 Nov 1935, *Guitar Player* (watercolour) FRF 350. Paris, 18 March 1938, *Dance* (lead pencil) FRF 55. Paris, 21 April 1943, *Still-life,* FRF 23,100. Paris, 22 June 1945, *Self-portrait* (1910, pastel) FRF 2,500. Paris, 30 March 1949, *Still-life,* FRF 6,000. New York, 19 March 1958, *Still-life with Doves* (gouache) USD 1,300. London, 13 July 1960, *Mother and Child* (gouache) GBP 250. Milan, 21-23 Nov 1962, *Dancer among Tables* (tempera, pastel, charcoal) ITL 3,600,000. London, 27 Nov 1964, *Dancers* (pastel and Indian ink) Gns 1,300. New York, 13 Dec 1967, *Dancers* (pastel) USD 4,750. London, 7-9 July 1971, *Dancer No. 5,* GBP 12,500. Milan, 29 May 1973, *Dancer* (pastel and Indian ink) ITL 13,500,000. New York, 1 May 1974, *Self-portrait* (mixed media) USD 40,000. Milan, 6 April 1976, *Pienza* (1913, tempera and pastel on board, 29 1/2 x 19 3/4 ins / 75 x 50 cm) ITL 24,000,000. London, 30 June 1976, *Young Woman and Dog on the Beach* (1948, oil on canvas, 25 x 36 ins / 63.5 x 90.5 cm) GBP 12,500. Paris, 23 Feb 1977, *Stele* (enamelled polychrome ceramic, h. 14 ins / 35.5 cm) FRF 3,500. Milan, 5 April 1977, *Still-life: Raw Lobster* (1964, pastel on artboard remounted on panel, 19 3/4 x 25 1/2 ins / 50 x 65 cm) ITL 9,500,000. Milan, 25 Oct 1977, *Readers* (1916-1917, oil on canvas, 51 1/2 x 51 1/4 ins / 131 x 130 cm) ITL 35,500,000. New York, 7 Nov 1979, *North-South Exit* (c. 1912, gouache, pastel and black chalk/brown paper remounted on board, 17 3/4 x 13 3/4 ins / 45 x 34.8 cm) USD 38,000. Rome, 13 Nov 1979, *Still-life* (c. 1946, charcoal drawing with watercolour, 9 x 11 1/2 ins / 23 x 29 cm) ITL 2,100,000. London, 26 Nov 1979, *Cubist Composition* (1916, woodcut, 7 1/2 x 5 ins / 18.9 x 12.9 cm) GBP 1,000. London, 3 Dec 1980, *Still-life with Mandolin* (1918, oil on canvas, 28 x 23 ins / 71 x 58.5 cm) GBP 40,000. New York, 20 May 1982, *Homage to Flaubert* (1915, oil on canvas, 26 3/4 x 28 3/4 ins / 68 x 73 cm) USD 65,000. New York, 5 Nov 1982, *Harlequin* (c. 1950, ceramic, h. 14 ins / 35.5 cm) USD 7,000. Rio de Janeiro, 14 June 1983, *Musicians* (lithograph, 22 x 15 1/4 ins / 56 x 39 cm) BRL 950,000. London, 29 June 1983, *Still-life* (c. 1928, gouache, 21 3/4 x 49 1/2 ins / 55.3 x 125.7 cm) GBP 21,000. Milan, 24 Oct 1983, *Still-life* (1919, oil on canvas, 45 1/4 x 32 ins / 115 x 81 cm) ITL 192,000,000. Milan, 15 Nov 1983, *Study for Plastic Analogy* (1914, Indian ink, 12 1/2 x 9 1/2 ins / 32 x 24 cm) ITL 25,500,000. St-Vincent (Italy), 6 May 1984, *Prismi-Figure* (1952, moulded glass, 15 3/4 x 7 3/4 x 5 ins / 40 x 20 x 13 cm) ITL 5,000,000. San Francisco, 28 Feb 1985, *Still-life with Doves* (gouache, 12 x 9 ins / 30.5 x 23 cm) USD 17,000. London, 26 June 1985, *Seated Woman* (1916, pen and Indian ink, 11 x 8 3/4 ins / 28 x 22.5 cm) GBP 6,200. Paris, 26 June 1986, *Memories of Travel* (oil on canvas, 31 1/2 x 39 1/4 ins / 80 x 99.5 cm) FRF 1,325,000. Paris, 4 Dec 1987, *Futurist Sculpture* (multicoloured ceramic, 14 1/2 x 5 ins / 37 x 13 cm) FRF 27,000. New York, 18 Feb 1988, *Still-life with Nude and Guitar* (gouache/paper, 25 1/2 x 19 1/2 ins / 64.8 x 49.5 cm) USD 37,400. London, 24 Feb 1988, *Still-life* (1943, Indian ink, 10 x 8 1/2 ins / 25.5 x 21.5 cm) GBP 3,300. Paris, 4 May 1988, *Adoration of the Magi* (1927, brown pencil, 14 1/4 x 18 ins / 36 x 46 cm) FRF 18,000. Rome, 15 Nov 1988, *Still-life with Flowers, Onions and an Antique Vase* (oil on canvas, 19 3/4 x 27 1/2 ins / 50 x 70 cm) ITL 55,000,000. New York, 16 Feb 1989, *Still-life* (oil on panel, 18 1/2 x 14 1/4 ins / 47.3 x 36.5 cm) USD 42,900. Milan, 20 March 1989, *Still-life with Pigeon* (stencil, 13 1/4 x 8 1/2 ins / 33.5 x 21.5 cm) ITL 2,400,000; *Villa Passerini near Florence* (1903, oil on panel, 10 1/4 x 15 ins / 26 x 38 cm) ITL 32,000,000. Rome, 21 March 1989, *Still-life with Compass* (1926, gouache on board, 13 3/4 x 9 ins / 35 x 23 cm) ITL 45,000,000. Paris, 17 June 1989, *Still-life with Harmonica* (1948, oil on panel, 13 x 16 1/4 ins / 33 x 41 cm) FRF 400, 000. Paris, 21 June 1989, *Portrait of Madame Declide* (1908, oil on canvas, 28 3/4 x 23 1/2 ins / 73 x 60 cm) FRF 850,000. London, 27 June 1989, *Portrait of Mademoiselle Yvonne Géraud* (1908, pastel/canvas, 36 1/4 x 28 3/4 ins / 92 x 73 cm) GBP 275,000; *Still-life* (oil on canvas, 22 x 18 ins / 55 x 46 cm) GBP 418,000. London, 25 Oct 1989, *Woman Spinning* (1908, oil on canvas, 28 3/4 x 22 1/2 ins / 73.2 x 57 cm) GBP 33,000. Paris, 19 Nov 1989, *Still-life with Fish and Mountains* (1954, tempera on board, 21 1/4 x 38 1/2 ins / 54 x 98 cm) FRF 670,000. New York, 26 Feb 1990, *Still-life* (oil on board, 13 x 18 ins / 33 x 45.6 cm) USD 82,500. Paris, 25 March 1990, *Racing at Merano* (1956, oil on canvas, 19 3/4 x 24 ins / 50 x 61 cm) FRF 2,000,000. New York, 16 May 1990, *Study for Portrait of Madame M. S.* (1912, pastel and charcoal/tinted paper, 19 x 13 3/4 ins / 48.5 x 35 cm) USD 550,000; *Dancer by the Sea* (1951, oil on canvas with metalic disks, 36 1/2 x 29 ins / 92.7 x 73.6 cm) USD 3,630,000. Amsterdam, 22 May 1990, *Harlequin Holding a Horse by the Bridle* (gouache/paper, 5 x 7 ins / 12.8 x 18 cm) NLG 92,000. Milan, 12 June 1990, *Concert* (1930, colour stencil/paper/canvas, 13 x 8 ins / 33 x 20.5 cm) ITL 3,800,000. New York, 14 Nov 1990, *Still-life* (1942, oil on board, 12 1/4 x 16 ins / 30.9 x 40.6 cm) USD 77,000. Paris, 25 Nov 1990, *Dancers* (1962, oil on canvas, 36 1/4 x 25 1/2 ins / 92 x 65 cm) FRF 700,000. Rome, 3 Dec 1990, *Young Woman at her Toilette* (1965, pencil/paper, 12 1/4 x 8 1/4 ins / 31 x 21 cm) ITL 5,750,000. London, 4 Dec 1990, *Seated Christ* (1948, oil on panel, 47 1/4 x 31 1/2 ins / 120 x 80 cm) USD 60,500. London, 20 March 1991, *Mandolin and Fruit Bowl* (1929, tempera/glass, 11 x 13 ins / 27 x 33 cm) GBP 27,500. Rome, 9 April 1991, *Serenade to Pulcinella* (ink/paper, 11 x 8 1/4 ins / 28 x 21.2 cm) ITL 7,000,000. Rome, 13 May 1991, *Still-life with Cakes* (oil/plywood, 14 1/2 x 18 1/2 ins / 37 x 47 cm) ITL 120,750,000. Lugano, 12 Oct 1991, *Still-life with A Jar of Fruit and Cakes* (1942, oil on canvas, 21 x 28 3/4 ins / 53.5 x 73 cm) CHF 165,000. New York, 6 Nov 1991, *Things Become Painting...* (1964, oil on canvas, 25 1/2 x 18 ins / 65 x 46 cm) USD 77,000. Rome, 3 Dec 1991, *Still-life with Bottles and Fruit Bowl* (oil on panel, 9 1/2 x 11 1/4 ins / 24 x 28.5 cm) ITL 73,000,000. Rome, 9 Dec 1991, *Still-life with Musical Instruments, Fruit and a Vase* (1947, tempera/mounted paper, 20 x 14 1/4 ins / 51 x 36 cm) ITL 55,200,000. Milan, 19 Dec 1991, *Still-life* (1940, oil on panel, 17 3/4 x 13 1/2 ins / 45 x 34 cm) ITL 76,000,000; *Light and movement - Ballet at the Opéra* (1953, oil on canvas, 46 x 31 1/2 ins / 116 x 80 cm) ITL 165,000,000. New York, 25 Feb 1992, *Pulcinella and Harlequin* (ink/paper, 11 1/2 x 9 ins / 29.5 x 22.9 cm) USD 8,800. Rome, 12 May 1992, *Rhythm of Objects* (mixed media/paper, 10 x 13 1/4 ins / 25.5 x 33.5 cm) ITL 13,500,000. Milan, 21 May 1992, *Algebraic Poetry* (tempera, 25 1/4 x 19 3/4 ins / 64 x 50 cm) ITL 12,000,000. Paris, 23 Nov 1992, *Still-life with Pigeons* (11 x 13 3/4 ins / 27 x 35 cm) FRF 115,000. New York, 13 May 1993, *Horse Rider Jumping an Obstacle* (watercolour, ink and pencil/paper, 18 3/4 x 26 ins / 47.6 x 66 cm) USD 20,700. Rome, 27 May 1993, *Villa Passerini near Florence* (1903, oil on panel, 9 3/4 x 14 1/2 ins / 25 x 37 cm) ITL 60,000,000. Paris, 11 June 1993, *Composition with Crayfish* (pastel on board, 17 1/4 x 12 ins / 43.5 x 30.5 cm) FRF 66,000. Milan, 22 Nov 1993, *Figure* (pastel/paper/canvas, 24 3/4 x 19 ins / 63 x 48 cm) ITL 176,775,000. London, 1 Dec 1993, *Still-life* (pencil, 19 x 12 1/4 ins / 48.2 x 31.1 cm) GBP 16,675. Rome, 19 April 1994, *Maternity* (1927, oil on panel, 16 1/4 x 12 3/4 ins / 41 x 32.5 cm) ITL 52,900,000. New York, 12 May 1994, *Dancer* (gouache/paper, 25 3/4 x 20 ins / 65.7 x 50.8 cm) USD 29,900. Amsterdam, 31 May 1994, *Still-life in a Landscape* (1922, oil on canvas, 14 1/4 x 32 1/2 ins / 36.5 x 82.5 cm) NLG 241,500. Deauville, 19 Aug 1994, *Dancer* (watercolour, 19 x 11 3/4 ins / 48 x 30 cm) FRF 60,000. Milan, 27 April 1995, *Dancers with a Tambourine* (1913, charcoal and red chalk/paper, 21 1/4 x 18 ins / 54 x 46 cm) ITL 299,000,000. Paris, 4 Dec 1995, *Dancer* (tempera on board, 34 1/4 x 20 3/4 ins / 87 x 53 cm) FRF 212,000. New York, 1 May 1996, *Dancer* (gouache/paper, 25¼ x 19 ins / 64.3 x 48.2 cm) USD 25,300. PARIS, 3 May 1996, *Homage to Sweet Slava* (1958, ball-point pen and pastel, 9 x 11 ins / 23 x 28 cm) FRF 18,000. MILAN, 25 Nov 1996, *Work* (tempera on board, 12¼ x 9¼ ins / 30.8 x 23.5 cm) ITL 28,750,000. LONDON, 2-3 Dec 1996, *Simultaneity of Centrifugal and Centripetal Groups* (1914, oil on canvas, 41¾ x 34¾ ins / 106 x 88.2 cm) GBP 1,871,500; *Cubist Nude with Cat and Guitar* (oil on canvas, 23½ x 18 ins / 60 x 46 cm) GBP 33,350. ROME, 8 April 1997, *Mandolin and Blue Fruit Bowl* (1949, tempera and pastel/paper/canvas, 20½ x 24½ ins / 52 x 62 cm) ITL 25,630,000. MILAN, 19 May 1997, *Dancer* (c. 1960, ink and pastel/paper, 18 x 13 ins / 45.5 x 33 cm) ITL 10,350,000. LONDON, 29 May 1997, *Pulcinella and Harlequin* (c. 1943, pen and ink/paper, 11½ x 9 ins / 29.5 x 23 cm) GBP 4,600. PARIS, 19 Oct 1997, *Boy from Rocca di Papa or Roman Peasant Boy* (1928, graphite/pasted paper, 9 x 7 ins / 23 x 18 cm) FRF 9,000. MILAN, 24 Nov 1997, *Still-life with Fruit Bowl* (1938, oil on board, 28¼ x 36¼ ins / 72 x 92 cm) ITL 144,810,000. PARIS, 8 April 1998, *Portrait of a Girl* (1909, etching and caster) FRF 16,000. LONDON, 28 June 1999, *Woman Dancing* (1913, oil on canvas, 24 x 20 ins / 61 x 50 cm) GBP 1,050,000. LONDON, 21 Oct 1999, *Tulips* (1916, oil and sand on canvas, 24 x 20 ins / 61 x 50 cm) GBP 350,000. PRATO, 25 Nov 2000, *Still-life* (oil on canvas, 20 x 24 ins / 50 x 61 cm) ITL 790,000,000. LONDON, 6 Dec 2000, *Still-life* (1916, oil on canvas, 24 x 20 ins / 61 x 50 cm) GBP 250,000. PARIS, 2 Aug 2001, *Paris-Rome by Plane* (1955, oil on canvas, 26 x 21 ins / 65 x 54 cm) FRF 600,000. LONDON, 22 Oct 2001, *Study for a Painting: Woman Dancing* (1913, oil on canvas, 16 x 12 ins / 41 x 30 cm) GBP 230,000. PRATO, 25 May 2002, *Landscape* (1917, oil on canvas, 32 x 26 ins / 82 x 65 cm) EUR 400,000. LONDON, 21 Oct 2002, *Still-life* (1918, oil on board, 16 x 11 ins / 40 x 28 cm) GBP 95,000. PRATO, 31 May 2003, *Still-life* (1919, oil on canvas, 20 x 24 ins / 50 x 61 cm) EUR 440,000. NEW YORK, 5 Nov 2003, *Woman with Green Plant* (1917, oil and sand on canvas, 39 x 32 ins / 100 x 81 cm) USD 480,000. NEW YORK, 5 May 2004, *Chatelard, Landscape* (1918, oil on canvas, 39 x 29 ins / 100 x 74 cm) USD 340,000. MILAN, 24 May 2004, *Raised on Spikes 1* (1957, oil on canvas, 26 x 18 ins / 65 x 46 cm) EUR 140,000.

SEVERINI, José

Spanish, 19th century.
Active in Madrid from 1852 to 1882.
Engraver (wood).

José Severini was a pupil of F. Batanero.

SEVERINI, Odoardo

Italian, 18th century.
Active in Verona.
Painter.

Severini, the pupil of A. Marchesini, worked in Bologna and Verona. He painted *St Francis Healing a Woman Possessed by the Devil* in the church of St Francis of Paola in Verona.

SEVERINO, Francesco

Italian, 17th century.
Active during the second half of the 17th century.
Painter.

Severino painted *St Anne, St Joachim, St Joseph and St Benedict* for the abbey in Montecassino in 1677.

SEVERINO, Vincenzo

Italian, 19th - 20th century.
Born 10 March 1859; died 22 May 1926, in Afragola near Naples.
Painter. History painting, architectural views.

Vincenzo Severino exhibited in Rome and Naples.

SEVERN, Arthur

British, 19th - 20th century.
Born 14 August 1842; died 23 January 1931, in London.
Painter. Landscapes, seascapes.

Arthur Severn was the son of Joseph Severn. He was a friend of John Ruskin, whose cousin, Joan Agnew, he married. His work featured in the Paris Salons, where he won a jury commendation at the Paris World's Fair of 1889. In 2003 paintings by Severn featured in the exhibition *Ruskin - Turner. Dessins et voyages en Picardie romantique* (*Ruskin - Turner: Drawings and travels in Romantic Picardy*) at the Musée de Picardie in Amiens.

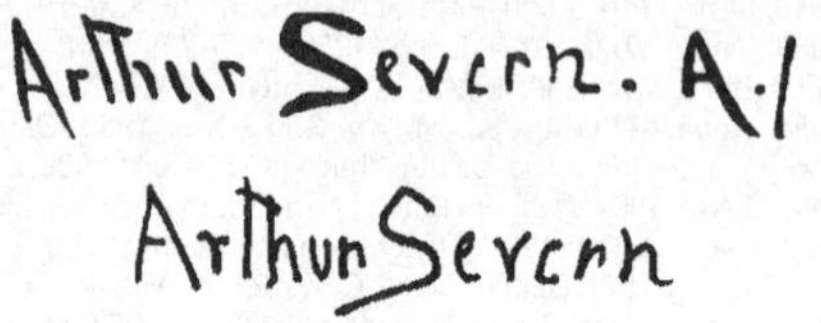

BIBLIOGRAPHY:
Gamble, Cynthia/Wildman, Stephen/Pinete, Matthieu, *Ruskin - Turner. Dessins et voyages en Picardie romantique*, group exhibition catalogue, Musée de Picardie, Amiens, 2003.

MUSEUMS AND GALLERIES:
CARDIFF: *High Tide in Brighton.*

AUCTION RECORDS:
LONDON, 31 Oct 1985, *The Limitation of Nature* (1889, oil on canvas, 26½ x 36¼ ins / 67 x 91.8 cm) GBP 1,800. LONDON, 27 Oct 1987, *The Head of Coniston; In the Lake District* (watercolour, gouache and pencil, 9¾ x 14 ins / 25 x 34.7 cm) GBP 900. GÖTEBORG, 18 May 1989, *Perspective from Ruskin's House Towards the Lake* (1899, oil on canvas, 23½ x 32¼ ins / 60 x 82 cm) SEK 6,000.

SEVERN, Benjamin

British, 18th century.
Active in London during the second half of the 18th century.
Portrait artist.

Benjamin Severn exhibited from 1766 to 1772, principally at the Royal Academy.

SEVERN, Joseph

British, 19th century.
Born 7 December 1793, in Hoxton; died 1879, in Rome.
Painter. History painting, portraits.

Joseph Severn worked in London as an engraver from 1808 to 1815, then attended courses at the Royal Academy, where he was awarded a gold medal in 1818. He settled in Rome in 1820 in the company of the poet John Keats. From 1827 Severn sent paintings from Rome for exhibition at the Royal Academy. He returned to England in 1841 and was awarded a cash prize in 1843 at the competition held to provide decorations for the Houses of Parliament. The years that followed were less rewarding. He exhibited a final time at the Royal Academy in 1868. Severn had returned to Rome in 1861 to serve as English Consul, a post he occupied until 1879, the year of his death. He painted historical, religious and literary themes and also produced miniatures.

BIBLIOGRAPHY:
Pointon, M., '*W.E. Gladstone as an Art Patron and Collector*' in *Victorian Studies*, vol. 19, 1, 1975-1976. Wilson, Michael Claude, *The Enchanted Castle, Acquisition in Focus Series, 1*, exhibition catalogue, National Gallery, London, 1982.

MUSEUMS AND GALLERIES:
LONDON (National Portrait Gal.): *John Hamilton Reynolds* (1818, watercolour/ivory, miniature); *John Keats* (1819, oil/ivory, miniature); *John Keats* (1821-1823, oil on canvas, dated 1821, posthumous portrait) - LONDON (Victoria and Albert Mus.): *Episode from Alexander Pope's 'Eloisa and Abelard'*; *Mary Stuart at Loch Leven Castle*; *Walter Scott*; *Ariel (from Shakespeare's 'The Tempest')*; *Nymph Gathering Honeysuckle*; a watercolour.

AUCTION RECORDS:
LONDON, 6 March 1970, *Portrait of Anne Matthew,* Gns 750. LONDON, 14 Oct 1977, *Anne Matthew* (1846, oil on canvas, 33 3/4 x 44 ins / 86 x 112 cm) GBP 700. NEW YORK, 12 June 1980, *Ariel* (1859, oil on panel, 15 x 20 3/4 ins / 38 x 53 cm) USD 1,700. LONDON, 17 March 1982, *Infant of the Apocalypse saved from the Dragon* (oil on canvas, rounded at the top, 90 x 54 ins / 228.5 x 137 cm) GBP 2,100. LONDON, 26 Nov 1985, *Hermia and Helena* (1834, oil on canvas, 20 x 25 ins / 50.5 x 63.5 cm) GBP 6,000. LONDON, 4 Nov 1994, *Portia and Casket* (oil on canvas, 24 3/4 x 19 1/2 ins / 62.8 x 49.5 cm) GBP 4,600.

SEVERN, Mary or Ann Mary. See **NEWTON**

SEVERN, Walter
British, 19th century.
Born 1830, in Rome; died 22 September 1904, in London.
Painter. Landscapes, seascapes.
Walter Severn was a member of the Royal Cambrian Academy. He exhibited in London from 1853 to 1889.
MUSEUMS AND GALLERIES:
MELBOURNE: *Borrastle Harbour* - SYDNEY: *Cowden Knowes.*
AUCTION RECORDS:
LONDON, 17 Oct 1984, *River Thames at Westminster* (1876, heightened watercolour, 13 1/2 x 19 1/2 ins / 34.3 x 49.5 cm) GBP 750. PARIS, 28 Feb 1997, *Herd Drinking at a Mountain Lake* (1889, watercolour/card, 24 1/2 x 38 3/4 ins / 62.5 x 98.5 cm) FRF 6,000. LONDON, 28 Sept 1998, *Coruisk, Skye* (1894, watercolour, 25 x 39 ins / 63 x 98 cm) GBP 1,800.

SEVERO DA BOLOGNA
Italian, 15th century.
Active in Bologna c. 1460.
Painter.
Severo da Bologna was a pupil of D. Scannabecchi.

SEVERO DA RAVENNA
Italian, 15th century.
Active in Padua during the last quarter of the 15th century.
Sculptor, founder. Religious subjects, mythological figures.
Severo da Ravenna made a statue of *St John* for the church of S Antonio in Padua.
AUCTION RECORDS:
LONDON, 3 May 1977, *Standing Figure of a Satyr* (patinated bronze, h. 8 1/2 ins / 21.7 cm) GBP 5,000. LONDON, 25 June 1980, *Rearing Horse* (bronze, h. 8 ins / 20.5 cm) GBP 14,500. LONDON, 11 Dec 1984, *Kneeling Satyr* (gilded bronze, h. 7 3/4 ins / 19.5 cm) GBP 8,000. LONDON, 24 April 1986, *Boy Taking a Thorn from His Foot* (bronze, h. 7 1/2 ins / 19 cm) GBP 30,000.

SEVERONI, Giuseppe
Italian, 17th century.
Active in Bologna in 1609.
Painter.
Severoni executed the paintings in a chapel in the church of S Prassede in Rome.

SEVESI, Fabrizio
Italian, 19th century.
Died 1837.
Active in Turin.
Painter, decorative designer.
Fabrizio Sevesi was the nephew and pupil of B. Gallari.

SEVESO, Carlos
Uruguayan, 20th - 21st century.
Born 1954.
Painter. Animals.
Carlos Seveso uses an aggressive palette to produce violent depictions of childhood fears such as fear of wolves.

SEVESTE, Charles Émile
French, 19th century.
Born in Lille.
Sculptor.
Charles Seveste was a pupil of Chéret. He made his debut at the Salon in 1878.

SEVESTRE, Jean I
French, 17th century.
Died 18 October 1650.
Active in Paris.
Painter.
Jean Sevestre I was the father of Jean Sevestre II.

SEVESTRE, Jean II
French, 17th century.
Born c. 1623; died 8 August 1694.
Active in Paris.
Painter.
Jean Sevestre II was the son of Jean Sevestre I.

SEVESTRE, Jean III
French, 17th - 18th century.
Born 1676.
Active in Paris.
Painter.
Jean Sevestre III was the son of Jean Sevestre II.

SEVESTRE, Jean IV
French, 18th century.
Died 26 March 1737.
Active in Paris.
Painter.

SEVESTRE, Jules Marie
French, 19th century.
Born 2 February 1834, in Breteuil (Seine-et-Oise); died 9 October 1901, in Paris.
Painter, watercolourist. Portraits, genre scenes.
Jules Sevestre was a pupil of both Corot and Cogniet. He made his debut at the Salon in 1864 and was awarded an honourable mention in 1883.
MUSEUMS AND GALLERIES:
ROUEN: *La Folie du Biblise.*

SEVILL, Luis
Spanish, 19th century.
Active in Jerez de la Frontera in the middle of the 19th century.
Portrait painter.
Luis Sevill was a pupil of J. G. Brücke in Berlin. He worked in Cádiz and Jerez de la Frontera.

SEVILLA, Soledad
Spanish, 20th century.
Born 1944, in Valencia.
Painter, installation artist.
Soledad Sevilla studied at the San Jorge school of fine arts in Barcelona. She lives and works in Granada. She began painting at the end of the 1960s with an approach that was abstract and geometric, but widely poeticised, developing dual themes of materiality/immateriality, day/night, reason/experience, shallow/deep. In the early 1980s she developed her work by incorporating installations. The Instituto Valenciano de Arte Moderno in Valencia held a solo exhibition of her work in 2001.

SEVILLA ROMERO Y ESCALANTE, Juan de. See **JUAN DE SEVILLA Romero y Escalante**

SEVILLA SAEZ, Juan
Spanish, 20th century.
Born 1922, in La Roda (Castile).

Active in France from 1956.
Painter, watercolourist, engraver. Landscapes.
Juan Sevilla Saez was largely self-taught and had been drawn to art from his early childhood. He devoted himself to painting and never swerved from his vocation despite material hardship. He spent only two or three years at the Escuela de Bellas Artes de in San Carlos, Valencia.

He decided to leave Spain for France, where he spent a year taking classes in fine art and perfecting his engraving techniques. He returned to Valencia temporarily in 1954 and settled in France in 1956 for good.

He showed his work for the first time in private exhibitions in Palma, Majorca, and then in Valencia. He participated in many collective exhibitions as well as various Paris Salons. He is a landscape painter whose works are full of poetry, a colourist born with a passion for art and one of the best watercolour artists in Valencia.

SEVILLA Y SÁNCHEZ, Nicasio
Spanish, 19th century.
Born in San Martín de la Vega; died January 1872, in Madrid.
Sculptor.
Nicasio Sevilla y Sánchez was a pupil of J. Piquer. His piece *The Handing over of the Keys of Coimbra* is kept in the Seville museum.

SEVILLE, W.
British, 19th century.
Silhouettist.
Worked in Lancashire around 1821.

SEVIN, Claude
French, 18th century.
Born c. 1750, in Tournon.
Painter.
Claude Sevin was apprenticed to G. F. Doyen in Paris and painted portraits.
MUSEUMS AND GALLERIES:
TOULOUSE: *Alexander and Diogenes*.

SEVIN, Claudius Albert, called Echo
Flemish School, 18th century.
Born in Tournai; died 1776.
Painter. History painting, portraits.
Claudius Albert Sevin worked in Brussels and Liège, as well as in England and Sweden, and in 1755 went to Rome, where he acquired the nickname Echo. The Uffizi in Florence has his *Self-portrait*.

SEVIN, Constant
French, 19th century.
Born 1821; died 1888, in Paris.
Modeller.

SEVIN, Fernand de
French, 20th century.
Painter.
Fernand de Sevin exhibited in Paris at the Salon des Artistes Français, where he won a bronze medal in 1900 and a silver medal in 1937.

SEVIN, François
French, 17th century.
Active in Tournon.
Painter.
François Sevin studied under Horace Le Blanc. He worked for the king and the city of Lyons.

SEVIN, Jean
French, 17th century.
Died 21 March 1702, in Tournon.
Painter.
Jean Sevin was the son of François Sevin.

SEVIN, Jean Baptiste
Flemish School, 18th century.
Active 1739-1758.
Painter.
Jean Baptiste Sevin painted the ceiling of the Notre-Dame de la Chapelle in Brussels in 1752.

SEVIN, Jean Pierre
French, 18th century.
Born c. 1744, in Tournon.
Painter.
Jean Pierre Sevin was the son of François Sevin.

SEVIN, Lucie
French, 20th century.
Sculptor.
Lucie Sevin exhibited in Paris at the Salon des Artistes Français. She won a bronze medal in 1932, a silver medal in 1937 and a gold medal at the Exposition Universelle in Paris the same year.

SEVIN, Nicolas
French, 17th century.
Active in Tournon.
Painter.
Nicolas Sevin may have been the brother of François Sevin.

SEVIN, Pierre Paul
French, 17th - 18th century.
Born 1650, in Tournon; died 2 February 1710, in Tournon, in 1676 according to Bellier.
Painter (gouache), draughtsman. History painting, portraits.
Pierre Paul Sevin worked as a portrait painter in Lyons where he was well regarded. He is reported to have supplied the drawings for several engravings representing the important episodes of Louis XIV's reign. Several of his portraits were engraved, notably that of *Mademoiselle de la Vallière*.
MUSEUMS AND GALLERIES:
CRACOW (Muz. Czartoryskich): *Reception of the Polish Embassador by the Sultan in 1678* - LONDON (Victoria and Albert Mus.): *Turenne on Horseback*.
AUCTION RECORDS:
PARIS, 1756, *Four Cenacles* (miniature after Veronese) FRF 600. PARIS, 1777, *Meal in the House of the Pharisee* (gouache, miniature after Paolo Veronese) FRF 135. PARIS, 1883, *Four Cenacles* (miniature after Veronese) FRF 6,000. PARIS, 10-12 May 1900, *Funerary Monument of Gaston de Foix*, FRF 295. PARIS, 6 Feb 1920, *Carmelite Nun at the Feet of Christ*, FRF 260. PARIS, 26 March 1927, *View of the Town of Arnhem* (gouache, attributed) FRF 25,000. PARIS, 13-15 May 1929, *Grand Opening of the Pont-Royal in Paris* (gouache) FRF 9,500; *To the Glory of Louis XIV, Protector of the Arts* (gouache) FRF 9,000; *Tomb of Marshal Turenne* (gouache) FRF 3,200. PARIS, 24 Nov 1977, *Funerary Decoration: Ceremonial Service in Memory of His Highness the Late Lord Henri de Bourbon*; *Drawing of the Ceremony for the Funeral of his Serene Highness Lord Louis de Bourbon* (two gouaches, 17 x 11 1/2 ins / 43 x 29 cm each) FRF 90,000. VERSAILLES, 25 Feb 1979, *Vanitas* (1681, gouache/vellum, 7 3/4 x 13 ins / 20 x 33 cm) FRF 4,800. PARIS, 18 March 1987, *Grand Opening of the Pont Royal in Paris in 1685* (brown ink and grey wash, 9 1/2 x 6 1/2 ins / 24 x 16.5 cm) FRF 20,000. PARIS, 20 Dec 1988, *Coronation of the Virgin* (1670, oil on canvas, 34 1/4 x 44 1/2 ins / 87 x 113 cm) FRF 142,000. NEW YORK, 11 Jan 1994, *Prince of Turenne Dedicating his Thesis to King Louis XIV at the Collège de Clermont*; *French Army attacking Valence* (1679, black chalk, ink and wash, two projects for the thesis of the Prince of Turenne, 9 1/4 x 6 ins / 23.6 x 15 cm and 9 3/4 x 6 ins/24.7 x 15.4 cm) USD 1,150. PARIS, 26 June 2002, *Padua. St Susanna in Padua* (1672, pen and ink wash, a pair, 6 x 8 ins / 14 x 20 cm) EUR 2,200. PARIS, 26 June 2002, *Modena. Pesaro. Castel Gandolfo* (1661, pen and ink wash,

three, 6 x 7 ins / 14 x 19 cm) EUR 2,400. PARIS, 19 June 2003, *Tomb of Gaston de Foix* (1670, gouache heightened with gold on vellum, 17 x 11 ins / 43 x 29 cm) EUR 3,200.

SEVIN DE LA PENAYE, Charles
French, 18th century.
Born c. 1686, in Fontainebleau; died 9 May 1733, in Paris.
Painter. History painting, portraits.
Charles Sevin de la Penaye was Hyacinthe Rigaud's assistant and they painted a *Portrait of J. B. Bossuet, Bishop of Meaux*, which can be seen at the Louvre in Paris.

SEVKET, Bey
Turkish, 20th century.
Painter. Architectural interiors.
This artist exhibited in Munich in 1909, and at the Salon des Artistes Français in 1933. He specialised in church and mosque interiors.

SEVO, Ferdinando
Italian, 18th century.
Born to a family originally from Piedmont.
Active in Rome c. 1705.
Medallist.

SEVOSTIANOV, Fedor
Russian, 20th century.
Born 1924, in Bryansk.
Painter. Landscapes with figures.
Fedor Sevostianov studied with Boris Ioganson at the Ilya Repin Institute in Leningrad (now St Petersburg) where he later taught. He was a member of the Union of Soviet Artists and Painter Emeritus of the U.S.S.R.
MUSEUMS AND GALLERIES:
MOSCOW (Ministry of Culture) - ST PETERSBURG (Academy) - ST PETERSBURG (Gosudarstvennyj Muz. Istorii).
AUCTION RECORDS:
PARIS, 24 Sept 1991, *Rivalry* (oil on canvas, 43 x 39¾ ins / 109 x 101 cm) FRF 20,500.

SEVRETTE, Jules Adrien
French, 19th century.
Born in Clermont.
Painter, watercolourist, engraver (etching).
Landscapes.
Jules Sevrette was a pupil of A. Cassagne. He exhibited at the Salon from 1868 to 1882 and was a member of the Société des Artistes Français from 1901; he was awarded an honourable mention in 1888.

SEVRIN, Jan Baptista or Joannes Baptist
Belgian, 19th century.
Born 23 October 1817, in Antwerp.
Painter. Genre scenes.
Jan Baptista Sevrin was a pupil of N. de Keyser.
AUCTION RECORDS:
BERN, 26 Oct 1988, *Success* (oil on canvas, 29¼ x 24¾ ins / 74 x 63 cm) CHF 6,000.

SEVRIN, Jeanne. See **DIRMER-SEVRIN**

SEVRYUGIN, Ivan Iliaronovich
Russian, 19th century.
Active during the second half of the 19th century.
Sculptor.
Ivan Iliaronovich Sevryugin studied at the school of art in Moscow.

SEWABENTHALER, Hans.
See **SCHWANTHALER Hans**

SEWAGEN, Heini or Heinrich.
See **SEEWAGEN**

SEWARD, Edwin
British, 19th - 20th century.
Painter. Landscapes, architectural views.
Edwin Seward lived and worked in Cardiff, where he was also active as an architect. He was a member of the Royal Cambrian Academy and the Society of British Architects. He exhibited in London, notably at the Royal Academy, from 1890.
MUSEUMS AND GALLERIES:
CARDIFF: *The Bell-towers of Bruges*.

SEWARD JOHNSON, J.
American, 20th century.
Sculptor.
J. Seward Johnson showed his works in private exhibitions in Europe in 1995, including at the Hotel Le Mirador in Mont-Pèlerin, Switzerland. His life-size sculptures represent figures such as housewives or tourists looking at the countryside.

SEWELL, Amanda, or Lydia Amanda, or Brewster-Sewell
American, 19th century.
Born 24 February 1839, in North Elba; died 1926.
Active in New York.
Painter. Portraits, genre scenes.
Amanda Sewell was the wife of Robert Sewell and studied at the academies in New York and Paris.
AUCTION RECORDS:
NEW YORK, 25 March 1997, *Bacchanalia* (oil on canvas, 60 x 128 ins / 151.5 x 325.1 cm) USD 31,050.

SEWELL, Robert van Vorst
American, 19th - 20th century.
Born 1860, in New York; died 18 November 1924, in Florence.
Painter, decorative designer. Genre scenes.
Robert Sewell studied under Jules Lefèvre and Gustave Boulanger in Paris. He was an associate member of the National Academy in New York and was awarded silver medals in Boston in 1891, Buffalo in 1901 and St Louis in 1904. His works include: *Canterbury Pilgrims* (Georgian Court, Lakenwood, New Jersey) and *Psyche* (Regis Hotel, New York).
AUCTION RECORDS:
NEW YORK, 11 and 12 April 1907, *Bacchante*, USD 525. LOS ANGELES, 28 Nov 1973, *Swimming* (1889) USD 1,800. LOS ANGELES, 15 Oct 1979, *Bacchic Procession* (1896, oil on canvas, 30 x 40 ins / 76.2 x 101.6 cm) USD 3,750. LONDON, 28 May 1981, *Nymph* (oil on canvas, 23¼ x 9 ins / 59 x 23 cm) GBP 1,200. NEW YORK, 22 May 2001, *Nymph* (oil on canvas) USD 3,000. PASADENA, 17 Feb 2004, *Figure in Vegetable Garden* (oil on canvas, 12 x 20 ins / 30 x 51 cm) USD 4,000. PORTSMOUTH, 21 May 2004, *Pre-Raphaelite Painting of a Mounted Knight Flanked by Two Angels* (oil on canvas, 34 x 44 ins / 86 x 112 cm) USD 5,750.

SEWERT, Hans Matthes. See **SEBERT**

SEWOHL, Waldemar
German, 20th century.
Born 28 June 1887, in Wismaz.
Painter. Landscapes.
Waldemar Sewohl was a pupil of W. Blancke.

SEWRENTZ
German, 18th century.
Active in Elbing (now Elblag, Poland).
Sculptor.
Sewrentz painted the altar for the church of Altfelde, Germany in 1711.

SEWRIN-BASSOMPIERRE, Aimé Henry Edmond
French, 19th century.
Born 1 November 1809, in Paris; died October 1896, in Paris.
Painter, pastellist. Portraits, genre scenes.

This artist was a pupil of Hersent and Detouche. He enrolled at the École des Beaux-Arts on 3 April 1830 and exhibited at the Salon from 1832 to 1875. He was awarded a third class medal in 1846.

SEXER, Ginette
French, 20th century.
Born 1913, in Strasbourg.
Painter, engraver.

Ginette Sexer lives and works in Paris. In 1992 she took part in the exhibition *De Bonnard à Baselitz - Dix Ans d'enrichissements du cabinet des estampes 1978-1988* (*From Bonnard to Baselitz: A Decade of Acquisitions by the Prints Collection 1978-1988*) at the Bibliothèque Nationale in Paris.

MUSEUMS AND GALLERIES:
PARIS (BNF, Prints Collection): *Blue Dream* (1986, etching and aquatint).

SEXMINI, Bartolomé
Spanish, 18th century.
Active in the middle of the 18th century.
Sculptor.

Bartolomé Sexmini executed decorative sculptures at Riofrio Palace near Seville.

SEXTO, Francesco
Italian, 15th century.
Active during the second half of the 15th century.
Sculptor.

Francesco Sexto worked in Rome and Toledo.

SEXTON, Fredrick Lester
American, 20th century.
Born 13 September 1887, in Cheshire (Connecticut); died 1975, in New Haven (Connecticut).
Painter. Landscapes, portraits, still-lifes.

Fredrick Sexton studied Fine Art at Yale University, under Sergeant Kendall and John T. Weir. He was a member of the Salamgundi Club.

AUCTION RECORDS:
NEW YORK, 31 March 1994, *Winter in New England* (oil on canvas, 24 x 36 ins / 61 x 91.4 cm) USD 1,380.

SEXTON, Joan
British, 20th century.
Sculptor.

Joan Sexton's work featured in the exhibition of sacred English art held in Paris in 1946.

SEXTRA, Heinrich I
German, 17th century.
Died 1625.
Active in Lübeck.
Sculptor (wood).

Heinrich Sextra I produced carvings for the church of St James in Lübeck.

SEXTRA, Heinrich II
German, 17th century.
Died 1647.
Active in Lübeck.
Sculptor (wood).

Heinrich Sextra II was the son of Heinrich I. He produced staircases and railings for the church of St James in Lübeck.

SEYBOLD, Christian, or Seibold
German, 18th century.
Born 1697, in Mainz; died 19 May or 29 September 1768, in Vienna, Austria.
Painter.

In 1749, Seybold was appointed painter to Maria Theresa, Empress of Germany (succeeded 1740), who was born in 1717 and died in 1780. He painted in the style of Denver.

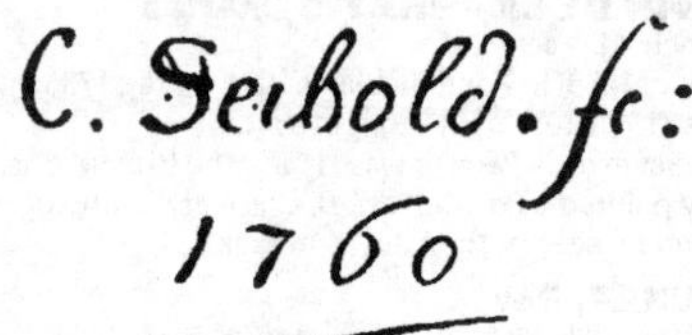

MUSEUMS AND GALLERIES:
BUDAPEST: *The Artist's Daughter*; *Self-portrait*; *Belly of Pork* - DRESDEN: five portraits, including self-portrait - FLORENCE (Uffizi): *Self-portrait* - HANOVER: *Old Woman Laughing* - MAINZ: *Self-portrait* - OSLO: *Portrait of a Man* - PARIS (Louvre): *Self-portrait* - STUTTGART: *Beardless Young Man*; two portraits of men; *Portrait of a Woman*; *Young Man Drawing* - VIENNA (Liechtenstein Mus.): *Self-portrait*; *The Artist's Daughter* - VIENNA (Österreichische Gal. Belvedere, Barockmuseum): *Portrait of a Young Girl* (a pair); *Portrait of a Young Man* - WROCLAW: *Head of an Old Woman*; *Head of an Old Man*.

AUCTION RECORDS:
PARIS, 3-4 May 1923, *A Veteran*, FRF 320. LONDON, 21 Oct 1994, *Woman Teaching a Young Boy to Sing* (oil on canvas, 35 3/4 x 31 1/4 ins / 91.1 x 79.3 cm) GBP 12,075. PARIS, 24 June 1996, *Portrait of the Artist's Wife* (oil/metal, 17 1/4 x 13 1/4 ins / 43.5 x 33.5 cm) FRF 100,000.

SEYBOLD, Egid
German, 19th century.
Born 16 July 1794, in Schwäbisch-Gmünd (Baden-Württemberg); died 13 August 1866, in Schwäbisch-Gmünd.
Painter.

Seybold attended the academies of Munich and Vienna and worked as an interior decorator in Vienna. From 1818, he travelled in southern Germany, and in 1830, was appointed art teacher in Schwäbisch-Gmünd.

SEYBOLD, Georg von
German, 19th century.
Born 20 March 1832, in Schrobenhausen; died 17 October 1900, in Munich.
Painter.

Von Seybold studied in Munich with W. von Kaulbach and in Paris with Couture. He produced a fresco for the former national museum of Bavaria: *Capture of Braunau in 1705 by Plinganser*.

AUCTION RECORDS:
COLOGNE, 12 June 1980, *Mousetrap Seller* (1873, oil on canvas, 33 1/2 x 38 1/2 ins / 85 x 98 cm) DEM 10,000.

SEYBOLD, Karl Jacob
Austrian, 19th century.
Born 1786; died 1844.
Active in Vienna, Austria, 1805-1821.
Painter.

SEYBOLD, Matthias
German, 18th century.
Born 23 February 1696, in Wernfels; died 29 October 1765.
Sculptor. Religious subjects.

A court sculptor and architect, Matthias Seybold is the most important representative of the Rococo style in Eichstätt, Germany. His work was inspired by religion and was produced mainly for the cathedral of Eichstätt.

SEYBOTH, Adolphe
French, 19th - 20th century.
Born 1848, in Strasbourg; died 1907, in Strasbourg.
Draughtsman.

Adolphe Seyboth is the author of plates included in the *Costumes of Women in Strasbourg* (Strasbourg, 1880) and *Costumes of Men in Strasbourg* (Strasbourg, 1881). He was also a historiographer.

MUSEUMS AND GALLERIES:
STRASBOURG: watercolours and drawings.

SEYDEL. See also **SEIDEL** and **SEIDL**

SEYDEL, Christoph Matthäus
German, 17th - 18th century.
Born 1668, in Weissenfels; died 1723, in Berlin.
Draughtsman.

SEYDEL, Eduard Gustav
Luxembourg, 19th century.
Born 18 March 1822, in Luxembourg; died 30 September 1881, in Dresden, Germany.
Active in Dresden.
Painter, watercolourist. Portraits, genre scenes, interiors with figures, landscapes with figures, landscapes.

Eduard Seydel attended the academy in Düsseldorf from 1844 to 1845, and the academy in Antwerp.

MUSEUMS AND GALLERIES:
CHEMNITZ (Municipal Gallery) - DRESDEN (Gemäldegal. Neue Meister): *Self-portrait.*

AUCTION RECORDS:
LONDON, 14 June 1972, *Tavern Scene,* GBP 500. COLOGNE, 15 June 1973, *Broken Wheel,* DEM 4,400. CREWKERNE (ENGLAND), 21 July 1977, *Interior Scene* (1859, oil on canvas, 14 1/4 x 16 3/4 ins / 36 x 42.5 cm) GBP 6,200. COPENHAGEN, 24 April 1979, *Numerous Figures in a Wooded Landscape* (oil on canvas, 20 1/2 x 17 ins / 52 x 43 cm) DKK 30,000. NEW YORK, 29 June 1983, *Hot Drink* (1860, oil on canvas, 13 x 16 3/4 ins / 33 x 42.5 cm) USD 1,600. LONDON, 24 June 1988, *Peddler's Visit* (watercolour, 6 1/2 x 8 1/2 ins / 16.3 x 21.9 cm) GBP 440. NEW YORK, 28 May 1992, *Coffee Time* (1859, oil on canvas, 14 x 16 3/4 ins / 35.6 x 42.5 cm) USD 5,225. HEIDELBERG, 5-13 April 1994, *Village Celebration* (oil on panel, 4 1/2 x 7 1/4 ins / 11.7 x 18.3 cm) DEM 3,800.

SEYDEL, Franz. See **SEITL Franz**

SEYDEL, Hans
German, 19th - 20th century.
Born 18 September 1866, in Karschau (Silesia); died 13 July 1916, in Ober-Arnsdorf.
Painter, engraver. Architectural views, landscapes.

Hans Seydel was a pupil of Otto Brausewetter in Berlin and of William Unger in Vienna; he also worked as a lithographer.

MUSEUMS AND GALLERIES:
WROCLAW: *Cloister.*

SEYDEL, Wilhelm or Christoph Wilhelm. See **SEIDEL**

SEYDELMANN, Appolonie
Italian, 18th - 19th century.
Born 17 June 1767, in Venice, in 1768 in Trieste according to some sources; died 27 June 1840, in Dresden.
Painter, miniaturist.

Appolonie Seydelmann, the wife of Crescentius Josephus Jacob Seydelmann, was a highly talented miniature painter. She produced small sepia copies of the great Italian masters which were much sought after. She was a member of the Dresden academy and in 1789 followed her husband to Rome, where she worked as his assistant.

SEYDELMANN, Crescentius Josephus Jacob
German, 18th - 19th century.
Born July 1750, in Dresden; died 27 March 1829, in Dresden.
Painter, draughtsman, engraver. Historical subjects, allegorical subjects, portraits.

Seydelmann began his studies with Bernardo Bellotti and Casanova. Given a pension by the Elector, he went to Rome to improve his skills, where he formed a friendship with Raffael Mengs who became his mentor. Seydelmann produced a large number of sepia drawings in the style of the great Italian masters, which he sold to foreigners visiting Rome, particularly the English. On his return to Dresden, he was appointed art teacher at the academy, and in 1788, began making copies of works in the gallery for engravers. The following year he went to Rome with his wife, and afterwards to St Petersburg. Several of his painted portraits were engraved.

SEYDER, Abraham. See **SEUTTER**

SEYDEWITZ, Carl Christian
Danish, 19th century.
Born 3 November 1777, in Nortorf (Holstein, Germany); died 10 October 1857, in Copenhagen.
Painter.

Seydewitz was the son of the architect Johan Christoff Heinrich Seydewitz, and the brother of Hans Joachim Seydewitz. He was an officer up until 1815.

AUCTION RECORDS:
MUNICH, 29 Nov 1989, *The Artist's Family* (oil on canvas, 58 1/2 x 46 3/4 ins / 148.5 x 119 cm) DEM 27,500.

SEYDEWITZ, Hans Joachim
Danish, 19th century.
Died 20 May 1842.
Painter.

Hans Seydewitz was an officer.

SEYDEWITZ, Max von
German, 19th - 20th century.
Born 4 April 1862, in Ribnitz.
Painter. Portraits.

Max von Seydewitz studied in Weimar and worked in Malchin, Munich, Dachau and, ultimately, in Riedenburg.

SEYDL, Franz. See **SEITL**

SEYDL, Zdenek
Czech, 20th century.
Born 29 April 1916, in Trebon; died 17 June 1978.
Painter, pastellist, engraver (dry-point), illustrator, ceramicist. Animals, insects. Stage sets, cartoon strips, animated films.

Zdenek Seydl worked in a variety of media, including cartoon strips and puppet films. As painter and dry-point engraver he adapted Jugendstil scrolls and arabesques to the representation of animals and sometimes even the microscopic world of insects, while as an illustrator he often depicted the horrors of fascism and nazism. He was deeply influenced by Chinese art, travelling to that country in 1955 and returning with a deeper understanding of the sources of his own vision. He exhibited with the October 7th Group and took part in the 1962 Venice Biennale.

SEYDLER, J. Joseph
German, 18th century.
Active c. 1715.
Painter.

Museums and Galleries:
Hainfeld (Church): *St Barbara Ascending to Heaven.*

SEYDLITZ, Friedrich Wilhelm von
German, 18th century.
Born 3 February 1721, in Calcar; died 8 November 1773, in Ohlau (now Olawa, Poland).
Active in Prussia.
Painter.
Von Seydlitz was a cavalry general.
Museums and Galleries:
Berlin (Kupferstichkabinet): *Camp and Pillage Scenes* (several watercolours).

SEYDLITZ, Jozef Narcyz Kajetan, or Sejdlitz, Zaidlitz
Polish, 19th century.
Born 23 October 1789, in Warsaw; died June 1845, in Warsaw.
Painter.
Jozef Seydlitz studied with Vogl. In 1803, he continued his studies at the academy of fine arts in Dresden. In 1809, he returned to Warsaw, but soon after went to work for the Karviczi family in Volhynia, where he painted several portraits. He then moved to Krzemieniec (now Kremenets, Ukraine), where he stayed until 1837, working as a teacher of painting. He spent the last ten years of his life in Warsaw. The National Museum in Warsaw and the museum in Poznan own versions of his *View of Krzemieniec.*

SEYDLITZ, Reinhart von
German, 19th century.
Born 20 October 1850, in Berlin.
Painter, writer. Portraits, landscapes.
Von Seydlitz studied under Alex Wagner.

SEYFER, Conrad, or Sifer, Syfer
German, 15th century.
Active near Heidelberg.
Sculptor, architect.
Conrad Seyfer was a brother of Hans. He went to Strasbourg in 1470, where he worked in the cathedral. Three stone busts of prophets from the cathedral and now in the German Museum, Berlin, are attributed to him.
Museums and Galleries:
Berlin (Deutsches Historisches Mus.): *Prophets* (two busts in stone).

SEYFER, Hans, or Seyffer or Syfer, also known as Hans von Heilbronn
German, 15th - 16th century.
Died between 13 and 21 March 1509, in Heilbronn.
Sculptor.
Hans Seyfer was the brother of Conrad and Lienhart. His masterpiece is the *Mount of Olives* in Spire Cathedral. He was influenced by Schongauer.

SEYFER, Lienhart, or Sefer, Seifer, Seiffer
German, 16th century.
Sculptor, founder.
Lienhart Seyfer was the brother of Conrad and Hans and directed a bell foundry in Heidelberg.

SEYFERT
French, 19th century.
Active in Paris.
Painter. Genre scenes.
Seyfert exhibited at the Salon between 1817 and 1822 with landscapes and genre subjects.

SEYFERT, Eloy von (Baron)
or Elegius Baron von Seyfert
German, 18th - 19th century.
Born in Germany.
Active in Metz.
Painter. History painting.
Von Seyfert settled in Metz before the revolution where he was extremely successful, but his connections with the country's nobility, and possibly his personal feelings, made him leave France. In 1802, he returned to Metz and resumed his position as theatre musician, painter and teacher of painting to his many pupils. In 1808, he painted *Francis of Lorraine, Duke of Guise* for one of the rooms in the town hall, later housed in the town's museum. He also produced a number of landscapes, which were in great demand during his lifetime.
Museums and Galleries:
Metz (La Cour D'or): *Francis of Lorraine, Duke of Guise.*

SEYFERT, Johann Gottlieb or Gotthelf, or Seyffert, Seiffert
German, 18th - 19th century.
Born 9 July 1761, in Dresden; died 30 March 1824, in Dresden.
Active in Dresden.
Engraver (burin), draughtsman, pastellist.
Johann Gottlieb Seyfert studied under C. F. Boëtius, J. Casanova and C. F. Stölzel. His collection of graphic work is held in the print room in Dresden.

SEYFERT, Otto
Hungarian, 20th century.
Born 8 December 1884, in Losonc.
Painter, illustrator.
Otto Seyfert lived and worked in Budapest.

SEYFERTH, Jeremias. See **SEIFFERT**

SEYFERTH, Johann Gottfried. See **SEIFFERT**

SEYFFART, Christian Michael
German, 18th - 19th century.
Born 1757, in Dresden; died after 1811.
Active in Dresden.
Painter, draughtsman.

SEYFFART, Conrad Gottfried
German, 18th century.
Died 17 October 1795.
Active in Dorotheenthal.
Potter.

SEYFFARTH, Hans
German, 16th century.
Active in Dresden.
Sculptor (stone).
Seyffarth worked on the construction of the church of Hartenfels Castle, near Torgau.

SEYFFARTH, Louisa (Mrs). See **SHARPE Louisa**

SEYFFER, August
German, 18th - 19th century.
Born 9 August 1774, in Lauffen; died 15 August 1845, in Stuttgart.
Painter, engraver. Landscapes.
Seyffer studied in Stuttgart and Vienna and was curator of engravings in Stuttgart. He produced engravings of landscapes that often depicted views of the areas surrounding Stuttgart and Tübingen in Germany.

SEYFFER, Hans. See **SEYFER**

SEYFFERT, Heinrich Abel
German, 18th - 19th century.
Born 24 April 1768, in Magdeburg (Saxony-Anhalt); died 18 October 1834, in Berlin.
Painter, pastellist, miniaturist. Portraits.
Heinrich Seyffert produced work for the court in Berlin, and from 1793 sent work to exhibitions at the academy there.

Museums and Galleries:
Berlin (Mus. Hohenzollern): *Portrait of Queen Louisa* (miniature); *Portrait of Queen Louisa's Sister* (miniature).

SEYFFERT, Johann Gottlieb or Gotthelf. See **SEYFERT**

SEYFFERT, Leopold Gould
American, 20th century.
Born 6 January 1887, in California (Missouri); died 1956, in Bound Brook (New Jersey).
Painter. Portraits, nudes.
Leopold Gould Seyffert was a member of the American Federation of Arts and the Salmagundi Club. He was a pupil of William M. Chase. He lived in New York and won many gold medals.
Bibliography:
Chambers, Bruce W., *Leopold Seyffert (1887-1956): Retrospective Exhibition*, exhibition catalogue, Berry-Hill Galleries, New York, 1985 (catalogue and essay).
Museums and Galleries:
Chicago (AI) - Detroit - Washington DC (Corcoran Gal. of Art) - Washington DC (Georgetown University): *George Mcneir, ESQ.* (1924, oil on canvas).
Auction records:
San Francisco, 6 Nov 1985, *Fur Stole* (1912, oil on canvas, 60 x 36 ins / 152.5 x 91.5 cm) USD 4,000. New York, 31 March 1993, *Mrs Henry Clews* (oil on canvas, 82 x 40 ins / 208.3 x 101.6 cm) USD 4,600. New York, 3 Dec 1996, *Dutch Girl Sewing* (1912, oil on canvas, 38¼ x 36 ins / 97.2 x 91.5 cm) USD 16,100.

SEYFFERTH, Gustav
German, 19th century.
Born in Schleiz.
Active in Rome, 1875-1876.
Painter. Genre scenes.
Seyfferth attended the academy in Weimar, Germany, from 1868.
Museums and Galleries:
Graz: *Bohemians in the Snow*; *Autumn Celebration in Rome*; *Siesta by the Sea*.

SEYFRIDT, Christoph Wilhelm
Swiss, 17th century.
Active c. 1634.
Miniaturist.

SEYFRIED. See also **SEEFRIED**

SEYFRIED, Ferdinand
German, 18th - 19th century.
Born c. 1750; died 2 January 1828.
Active in Cologne.
Painter, decorative designer.
Ferdinand Seyfried was the son of Norbert. He was a member of the painters' guild from 1787.

SEYFRIED, Johann Felix, or Zeyfried, Siegfried
Polish, 18th century.
Painter.
Johann Seyfried was a painter at the court of Prince A. Sulkowski in Poland from 1768 to 1770.

SEYFRIED, Johann Georg
German, 18th century.
Active in Würzburg (Bavaria).
Sculptor.

SEYFRIED, Johann Heinrich
German, 18th century.
Painter.
Johann Heinrich Seyfried decorated a church in the Gotha (Erfurt) area of Germany in 1701.

SEYFRIED, Johann Heinrich
German, 18th century.
Died 15 May 1771.
Active in Bayreuth-St-George.
Painter (porcelain/glazed earthenware).
Johann Heinrich Seyfried married in Bayreuth-St-George in 1745.

SEYFRIED, Karl
German, 18th century.
Active in Cologne, c. 1797.
Draughtsman.

SEYFRIED, Norbert
Czech, 18th century.
Born to a family originally from Prague, Czechoslovakia.
Painter. Historical scenes.
Norbert Seyfried was the father of Ferdinand, and was active in Bonn, Germany, as court painter to Princes Clement August and Max Friedrich from 1756 to 1782.
Museums and Galleries:
Cologne (Wallraf-Richartz Mus.): several drawings.

SEYFRIED, Wilhelmine
German, 19th century.
Born 1785, in Dresden; died 7 November 1847, in Dresden.
Engraver (burin). Landscapes.
Wilhelmine Seyfried studied under J. A. Darnstedt from 1801. She produced engravings in the style of J. C. Klengel and J. G. Wagner.

SEYKORA, Wenzel or Vaclav, or Sykora
Czech, 19th century.
Born 26 November 1793, in Deutsch-Brod; died 6 April 1856, in Radonitz.
Painter. Architectural views, landscapes.
Wenzel Seykora was a monk at the cloister of Strahow in Prague in 1814. The cloister owns a small number of his paintings and sketches.

SEYL. See **ZYL**

SEYLBERGH, Jaak van den
Belgian, 20th century.
Born 1884, in Antwerp; died 1960.
Painter, pastellist, miniaturist. Landscapes.
Jaak van den Seylbergh studied at the Academie voor Schone Kunsten in Antwerp and painted typical landscapes of the Campine region of Belgium.
Auction records:
Brussels, 27 March 1990, *Orchard in Bloom* (oil on canvas, 25½ x 39¼ ins / 65 x 100 cm) BEF 45,000. Lokeren, 8 March 1997, *Port of Bruges* (pastel/panel, 23½ x 22 ins / 60 x 55 cm) BEF 10,000. Doncaster, 10 Sept 2000, *Still-life with Blue Vase of Japanese Anemones* (pastel, 31 x 28 ins / 80 x 70 cm) GBP 1,100. Doncaster, 17 Dec 2000, *Still-life with Glass Bowl of Dahlias* (pastel, 31 x 39 ins / 79 x 98 cm) GBP 1,100.

SEYLER. See also **SEILER** and **SEILLER**

SEYLER, Johann Christian
German, 17th - 18th century.
Born 1651; died 19 February 1711, in Leipzig.
Engraver (burin).
Seyler produced an engraving of a view of the church of St Matthew in Leipzig.

SEYLER, Johann Georg. See **SEILLER**

SEYLER, Julius
German, 19th - 20th century.
Born 1873, in Munich; died 1958, in Munich.
Painter. Landscapes, animals.
Julius Seyler studied under Ludwig Schmid-Reutte, Wilhelm von Diez and Heinrich Zügel at the fine arts academy in Mu-

nich. From 1913 to 1921 he was in the USA, where he made his living farming.

Museums and Galleries:

Augsburg - Bytom - Munich - Oberschleissheim (Neues Schloss Schleissheim, Staatsgal.) - Pforzheim - Stuttgart - Zurich.

Auction records:

Cologne, 27 June 1974, *Shrimping*, DEM 2,400. Munich, 30 Nov 1978, *Labourer* (oil on paper, 23½ x 31½ ins / 60 x 80 cm) DEM 2,800. Munich, 30 Nov 1979, *Shrimp Fishermen* (oil on canvas, 27½ x 39¼ ins / 70 x 100 cm) DEM 3,300. Bern, 1 May 1980, *Fisherman and Horse* (tempera/panel, 14¼ x 20 ins / 36 x 51 cm) CHF 1,600. Munich, 26 Nov 1981, *Country Road* (oil on paper remounted/panel, 23½ x 31½ ins / 60 x 80 cm) DEM 10,500. Cologne, 22 Oct 1982, *Fishing for Crabs* (tempera, 12¾ x 19¾ ins / 32.5 x 50 cm) DEM 3,000. Cologne, 28 Oct 1983, *Harvesting Potatoes* (oil and tempera, 27½ x 39¼ ins / 70 x 100 cm) DEM 12,000. Vienna, 10 Sept 1985, *Bird and Bouquet of Flowers* (oil on canvas, 23½ x 19¾ ins / 60 x 50 cm) ATS 100,000. Cologne, 20 Oct 1989, *Shrimping* (tempera, 12½ x 17 ins / 32 x 43 cm) DEM 2,400. Cologne, 29 June 1990, *Shrimping on the Dutch Coast* (oil on paper, 19¾ x 27½ ins / 50 x 70 cm) DEM 2,200. Amsterdam, 24 April 1991, *Shrimp Fishermen on the Shore* (oil on card, 27½ x 39¼ ins / 70 x 100 cm) NLG 6,670. Copenhagen, 29 Aug 1991, *Landscape with Tree-Lined Avenue* (1908, oil on canvas, 18½ x 27¼ ins / 47 x 69 cm) DKK 4,000. Munich, 21 June 1994, *Buffalo Hunt* (oil on card, 28¼ x 39¼ ins / 72 x 99.5 cm) DEM 25,300. Munich, 6 Dec 1994, *Road to Diessener* (oil on card, 27½ x 39¼ ins / 70 x 100 cm) DEM 27,600. Munich, 27 June 1995, *Tree-Lined Road; Shrimp Fishermen and Horses on the Shore* (oil on paper and oil on card, pair, 8 x 11¼ ins / 20.5 x 28.5 cm and 9 x 11½ ins/22 x 29.5 cm) DEM 14,950. Munich, 1 Dec 1999, *City View with Harbour* (oil on board, 20 x 28 ins / 50 x 70 cm) DEM 9,500. Munich, 1 Dec 1999, *Fishing Harbour in Brittany* (oil on board, 17 x 28 ins / 44 x 70 cm) DEM 15,000. Stuttgart, 17 March 2000, *Fish Market in Breton Town* (oil on canvas, 25 x 39 ins / 64 x 100 cm) DEM 9,000. Munich, 8 Nov 2000, *Still-life with Flowers* (oil on board, 20 x 26 ins / 50 x 65 cm) DEM 8,500. Munich, 4 July 2001, *Wooded Landscape with Peasants* (oil on board, 20 x 28 ins / 51 x 70 cm) DEM 11,000. Munich, 15 Nov 2001, *Indian* (gouache, double-sided, 25 x 20 ins / 64 x 50 cm) DEM 11,000. Lucerne, 25 May 2002, *Quimper Harbour* (oil on panel, 30 x 41 ins / 77 x 103 cm) CHF 10,000. Munich, 14 Nov 2002, *Red Indians* (dark brown patinated bronze, 13 x 17 ins / 34 x 43 cm) EUR 5,800. Munich, 13 Nov 2003, *Leda and the Swan* (oil on paper on canvas, 12 x 9 ins / 31 x 24 cm) EUR 2,500. Stuttgart, 26 April 2004, *Two Indians on Horseback on a Hill* (oil on board, 14 x 20 ins / 35 x 50 cm) EUR 3,800. Munich, 25 May 2004, *Buffalo Hunt* (oil on board, 27 x 39 ins / 69 x 98 cm) EUR 4,500.

SEYLEVELDT, Antonius van
Dutch, 17th century.
Born 1640, in Amsterdam.
Active in Leiden.
Engraver (burin).

SEYLMAKER, Jacob, or Seilmaker, Seylmaecker
Dutch, 17th century.
Active in Rotterdam.
Painter. Seascapes.

SEYMIRI, Hélène
Turkish, 20th century.
Born in Istanbul.
Painter. Figures, landscapes, flowers.

Hélène Seymiri has exhibited figures, landscapes, flowers and compositions of literary inspiration in Paris. She has a propensity for a fantastical element within a realist structure.

SEYMOUR, Edward
British, 18th century.
Died 1757.
Painter. Portraits.

Painted in the style of Godfrey Kneller.

SEYMOUR, George L.
British, 19th century.
Painter. Local scenes, animals.

George L. Seymour exhibited in London from 1876, principally at the Suffolk Street Gallery.

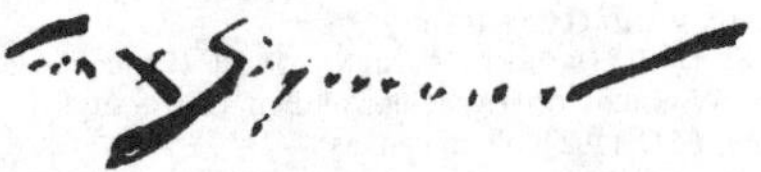

Auction records:

New York, 2 April 1909, *Louisa*, USD 350. London, 28 May 1923, *Female Head*, GBP 36. London, 28 July 1924, *Arab Sentinel*, GBP 48. London, 16 July 1976, *Harem Garden* (oil on panel, 16½ x 10¾ ins / 42 x 27.5 cm) GBP 550. London, 3 Nov 1977, *Snake-Charmer* (oil on canvas, 23½ x 17½ ins / 59.7 x 44.4 cm) GBP 6,500. London, 20 March 1981, *Consecration of Arms* (oil on panel, 14 x 9 ins / 35.6 x 22.9 cm) GBP 7,000. London, 17 June 1999, *Arab Hunter* (oil on panel, 18 x 12 ins / 45 x 30 cm) GBP 32,000.

SEYMOUR, Hariette Anne
British, 19th century.
Born 1830, in the rectory at Marksbury, (Somerset).
Active on Dartmoor.
Painter, watercolourist. Landscapes, seascapes.

SEYMOUR, James
British, 18th century.
Born 1702, in London; died 1752, in London.
Painter, draughtsman. Hunting scenes, sporting subjects, horse racing scenes, animals.

As the son of a banker, James Seymour was sufficiently well-situated financially to try his hand at painting. He emerged as an accomplished draughtsman, with a particular aptitude for drawing horses. Several of his drawings were subsequently engraved. He was a close friend of Peter Lely.

Museums and Galleries:

Cambridge (Fitzwilliam Mus.): *Horse and Groom* (1740s, oil on canvas) - London (British Mus.).

Auction records:

London, 27 Nov 1909, *Flying Childers*, GBP 18. London, 12 March 1910, *Hunting Dogs* (two) GBP 75; *Stag Hunt*, GBP 46. London, 22 Feb 1924, *Chaise Match against Time*, GBP 54. London, 6 May 1927, *Groom Leading a Horse*, GBP 63. London, 9 Dec 1927, *Hunter, Hound and Groom*, GBP 63. London, 14 May 1930, *Hunting Scene*, GBP 360. London, 25 June 1930, *Hunting Scene*, GBP 165. London, 21 Nov 1934, *White Hunter*, GBP 98. London, 21 May 1935, *Hunting Themes*, GBP 135. London, 15 May 1946, *Fox Hunt*, GBP 260. London, 20 July 1951, *Hunt*, GBP 315. London, 15 June 1960, *Horse Race*, GBP 550. London, 16 June 1961, *Ladies and Gentlemen*, GBP 4,200. London, 7 July 1965, *Going to Cover*, GBP 900. London, 23 Nov 1966, *Mr Russell on Horseback*, GBP 3,600. London, 27 Nov 1968, *Hunt Scene, Ashdown Park*, GBP 58,000. London, 20 June 1969, *Portrait of a Horseman*, Gns 13,000. London, 10 Dec 1971, *'Crab' and Jockey*, Gns 14,000. London, 17 March 1972, *Equestrian Portrait of*

Sir Roger Burgoyne, Gns 26,000. LONDON, 31 Oct 1973, *Racehorses Exercising*, GBP 38,000. LONDON, 26 June 1974, *Lord Craven on Horseback*, GBP 9,500. LONDON, 19 Nov 1976, *Exercising Racehorses at Newmarket* (oil on canvas, 34 1/2 x 44 ins / 87.6 x 112 cm) GBP 15,000. LONDON, 24 June 1977, *Hunt Scene* (oil on canvas, 38 1/2 x 49 ins / 97.7 x 124.5 cm) GBP 38,000. LONDON, 18 July 1979, *Racehorse and Jockey* (oil on canvas, 12 x 14 1/4 ins / 30.5 x 36 cm) GBP 7,400. LONDON, 26 June 1981, *Grey with Groom* (1746, oil on canvas, 19 1/2 x 24 1/2 ins / 49.5 x 62.2 cm) GBP 18,000. LONDON, 6 July 1983, *John Warington, Esq of Morden, Surrey on his Dark Bay Hunter* (1746, oil on canvas, 28 1/4 x 27 1/2 ins / 72 x 70 cm) GBP 35,000. LONDON, 20 Nov 1985, *Bay Racehorse and Groom in a Landscape* (1750, oil on canvas, 24 1/2 x 29 1/4 ins / 62 x 74.5 cm) GBP 55,000. ALNWICK, 23 Sept 1986, *Two Racehorses at Exercise on Newmarket Heath* (oil on canvas, 24 1/2 x 35 ins / 62.5 x 89 cm) GBP 20,000. LONDON, 19 Feb 1987, *Horses and Riders* (pencil and red chalk, six studies) GBP 2,300. NEW YORK, 4 June 1987, *Bay Horse and Groom in a Landscape* (1746, oil on canvas, 25 x 30 ins / 63.5 x 76.2 cm) USD 65,000. LONDON, 15 July 1988, *Two Racehorses Stabled and Blanketed, with a Groom and a Dog* (1747, oil on canvas, 23 x 29 ins / 58.4 x 73.6 cm) GBP 154,000. LONDON, 18 Nov 1988, *Landscape with Bay Trotter and Stable Lad* (1742, oil on canvas, 25 1/4 x 29 3/4 ins / 64.1 x 75.8 cm) GBP 13,200. LONDON, 17 Nov 1989, *Thoroughbred and Groom in a Vast Landscape* (1745, oil on canvas, 20 x 24 ins / 50.8 x 61 cm) GBP 17,600. LONDON, 30 Jan 1991, *Dressage Studies* (ink, pair, each 5 3/4 x 6 3/4 ins / 14.5 x 17 cm) GBP 1,265. NEW YORK, 7 June 1991, *'Flying Childers' led by his Stable Lad, Newmarket* (oil on canvas, 40 x 50 ins / 101.6 x 127 cm) USD 50,600. LONDON, 8 April 1992, *Thoroughbred and Jockey, Newmarket* (1741, oil on canvas, 9 1/4 x 11 1/2 ins / 23.5 x 29 cm) GBP 11,000. NEW YORK, 5 June 1992, *Thoroughbred Grey and Jockey Exercising at Newmarket* (oil on canvas, 25 1/4 x 30 1/4 ins / 64.1 x 76.8 cm) USD 36,300. LONDON, 18 Nov 1992, *The Duke of Devonshire's 'Plaistow' beating the Duke of Bolton's 'Doctor', Newmarket, 1735* (oil on canvas, 34 1/2 x 49 ins / 87.5 x 124.5 cm) GBP 7,150. NEW YORK, 4 June 1993, *Thoroughbred and Jockey, Newmarket* (1752, oil on canvas, 28 3/4 x 35 3/4 ins / 73 x 90.8 cm) USD 68,500. LONDON, 14 July 1993, *'Sedbury' led by a Stable Lad followed by another Stable Hand carrying Fodder* (1740, oil on canvas, 28 x 35 ins / 71 x 89 cm) GBP 53,200. LONDON, 9 Nov 1994, *Stable Lad on 'Flying Childers' with other Riders in the Background* (oil on canvas, 38 1/2 x 48 1/2 ins / 98 x 123 cm) GBP 287,500. LONDON, 3 April 1996, *Stable Lad holding 'Sterlin', a Thoroughbred Grey* (1738, oil on canvas, 38 1/2 x 48 1/2 ins / 98 x 123 cm) GBP 419,500. NEW YORK, 12 April 1996, *The Race* (oil on canvas, 25 x 30 1/2 ins / 63.5 x 77.5 cm) USD 68,500. LONDON, 13 Nov 1996, *Stable Lad with the Bay 'Turpin' on the Track* (1744, oil on canvas, 24 x 29 1/2 ins / 61 x 75 cm) GBP 177,500. NEW YORK, 11 April 1997, *Stable Lad with Lord Strange's Bay 'Sportsman'* (1752, oil on canvas, 25 x 29 1/2 ins / 63.5 x 74.9 cm) USD 107,000. LONDON, 9 July 1997, *Thoroughbred and Jockey* (oil on canvas, 27 1/4 x 31 3/4 ins / 69 x 80.5 cm) GBP 67,500; *Mounted Hunter and Hounds in a Landscape* (1745, oil on canvas, 24 1/2 x 29 1/2 ins / 62 x 75 cm) GBP 122,500. LONDON, 12 Nov 1997, *Stable Lad holding a Thoroughbred Grey* (oil on canvas, 24 x 29 1/4 ins / 61 x 74 cm) GBP 43,300. PARIS, 30 March 1998, *Equestrian Portrait of a Young Rider in a Landscape Background* (oil on canvas, 20 3/4 x 25 ins / 53 x 63.5 cm) FRF 500,000. LONDON, 31 March 1999, *Study of Horse and Groom* (1743, watercolour and pencil, 7 x 10 ins / 19 x 26 cm) GBP 3,800. LONDON, 28 May 1999, *Coursing Scene* (1738, oil on canvas, 39 x 49 ins / 98 x 124 cm) GBP 160,000. LONDON, 15 June 2000, *Mr Jolliffe on a Chestnut Hunter with the Hunt Beyond* (oil on canvas, 39 x 48 ins / 98 x 123 cm) GBP 90,000. LONDON, 15 June 2000, *Race over the Beacon Course at Newmarket* (oil on canvas, 35 x 50 ins / 90 x 128 cm) GBP 360,000. LONDON, 4 July 2001, *Regulus, a Bay Racehorse Held by a Groom* (oil on canvas, 25 x 30 ins / 63 x 76 cm) GBP 30,000. LONDON, 29 Nov 2001, *Two Racehorses and their Jockeys Exercising on Newmarket Heath* (oil on canvas, 24 x 35 ins / 62 x 89 cm) GBP 40,000. LONDON, 21 March 2002, *Mr Cotton's Crab* (gouache, 5 x 7 ins / 13 x 17 cm) GBP 10,000. LEEDS, 23 July 2002, *Diana, Got by Lt Portmores Drummer, Nine Years Old* (1744, oil on canvas, 25 x 30 ins / 63 x 76 cm) GBP 78,000. NEW YORK, 18 May 2004, *Racing on Newmarket Heath* (oil on canvas, 39 x 49 ins / 99 x 124 cm) USD 25,000. GODALMING, 20 Oct 2004, *French Captain Riding Post for the Expedition at Dunkirk* (1744, pen and ink) GBP 1,800.

SEYMOUR, Joseph H.

American, 18th - 19th century.

Active in Worcester (Massachusetts) during the 18th and 19th centuries.

Engraver (burin).

Joseph H. Seymour also worked in Boston and Philadelphia between 1791 and 1822.

SEYMOUR, Ralph Fletcher

American, 19th - 20th century.

Born 18 March 1876, in Milan (Illinois); died 1966, in Batavia (Illinois).

Engraver, illustrator.

Ralph Fletcher Seymour studied with Vincent Nowattny and Lewis Meakin in Cincinnati, and also in Paris. He taught decorative illustration at the Chicago Art Institute. He is known mainly for his etchings, a group of which brought him the Cunningham Prize. He visited the American Southwest many times, studying the life of Native Americans, which inspired his woodcut *Snake Dancers*.

Seymour was a member of the Chicago Society of Illustrators and National Arts Club.

MUSEUMS AND GALLERIES:

PARIS (BNF).

SEYMOUR, Robert

British, 19th century.

Born 1798, in Somerset; died 20 April 1836, in London.

Painter, caricaturist, lithographer, engraver. History painting, portraits.

Robert Seymour was an industrial draughtsman by profession. He took up painting and exhibited historical compositions and portraits at the Royal Academy in 1822. He subsequently worked as an illustrator and caricaturist (possibly because his 'serious' work had been less successful than he had anticipated and hoped). He began contributing to a large number of periodicals and other publications, but his principal claim to fame must be his illustrations for Charles Dickens' *Pickwick Papers* and his typology of Dickensian characters Pickwick, Winkle and Tupman. Sadly, Seymour committed suicide before the work was published.

SEYMOUR, Robert George

Irish, 19th century.

Born 20 August 1836, in Dublin; died 31 October 1885, in Clifton.

Painter. Landscapes.

MUSEUMS AND GALLERIES:

DUBLIN (NG of Ireland).

SEYMOUR, Samuel

British, 18th - 19th century.

Born in England.

Painter, watercolourist, engraver, draughtsman. Portraits, local scenes, landscapes.

Samuel Seymour lived from 1797 to 1822 in Philadelphia. He disappeared during an expedition mounted by Major Stephen H. Long.

AUCTION RECORDS:
NEW YORK, 14 Nov 1991, *Two Indian Braves and a Squaw* (1806, watercolour, pencil and sepia ink/paper, 5 x 6 1/4 ins / 12.8 x 16 cm) USD 13,200.

SEYMOUR DAMER, Anna. See **DAMER Anna Seymour**

SEYMOUR HADEN, Francis
British, 19th - 20th century.
Born 16 September 1818, in London; died 1 June 1910, in Alresford.
Painter, engraver. Landscapes.

The son of a celebrated doctor, Francis Seymour Haden studied medicine in London, Paris and Grenoble, and eventually took over his father's London practice. He was appointed consultant surgeon to the Queen's Chapel. He made a number of interesting sketches on a journey to Italy in 1843-1844, and began producing etchings in 1858, thanks to his friendship with Whistler, who was to become his brother-in-law. He established a reputation in France, where an edition of his works contained an admiring foreword by Philippe Burty. English art-lovers soon added their acclaim. Haden took part in the Paris World's Fair of 1889 and the 1900 Exposition Universelle, winning a top prize at each. He founded the Royal Society of Painter-Etchers and Engravers in 1880; he was also a member of the Society of Miniature Painters, and a corresponding member of the Académie des Beaux-Arts in France. Seymour Haden ranked among the leading artists of his day. His bold, powerful handling was inspired by Rembrandt, of whose etchings he was a noted collector, although his compositions and style are highly individual. Haden was the author of a small number of works on the art of etching, and produced a scholarly catalogue for an exhibition of Rembrandt's etchings at the Burlington Fine Arts Club in 1877.

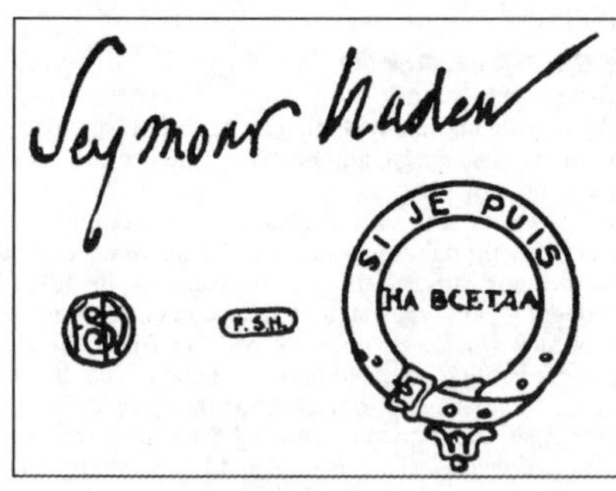

Stamps of sale

Seymour Haden

BIBLIOGRAPHY:
Burty, Philippe, *Études à l'eau-forte par Francis Seymour Haden*, Paris, 1866. Drake, William Richard, *A Descriptive Catalogue of the Etched Works of Francis Seymour Haden*, Macmillan, London, 1880. Schneiderman, Richard S., *Catalogue raisonné of the prints of Sir Francis Seymour Haden*, Garton, London, 1983.

MUSEUMS AND GALLERIES:
LONDON (Victoria and Albert Mus.): selection of 41 proofs - VEVEY (Mus. Jenisch).

AUCTION RECORDS:
NEW YORK, 25 June 1980, *A Sunset in Ireland* (1863, dry-point, 5 1/2 x 8 1/2 ins / 13.8 x 21.5 cm) USD 1,300. NEW YORK, 7 Nov 1984, *A Sunset in Ireland* (1863, dry-point, proof, 5 1/2 x 8 1/2 ins / 14 x 21.6 cm) USD 750.

SEYNES, Alphonse de
French, 19th century.
Born 1786, in Nîmes; died 7 October 1844, in Nîmes.
Painter. Genre scenes.

MUSEUMS AND GALLERIES:
NÎMES: watercolours and drawings.

SEYPPEL, Carl Maria
German, 19th - 20th century.
Born 28 July 1847, in Düsseldorf; died 20 October 1913, in Düsseldorf.
Painter. Portraits, genre scenes.

Carl Maria Seyppel was the father of Hans Seyppel and a pupil of Karl Sohn and Ludwig Knaus; he was noted for his numerous caricatures. He was also an author.

MUSEUMS AND GALLERIES:
BONN: *Flower-Seller* - PHILADELPHIA: *Social Democrat.*

AUCTION RECORDS:
PARIS, 15 June 1934, *Art Lover,* FRF 600. NEW YORK, 18 Oct 1944, *Socialist,* USD 250. ANTWERP, 9-10 May 1967, *Village Mothers,* BEF 46,000. COLOGNE, 21 May 1981, *Moonlit Landscape* (1895, oil on canvas, 8 x 16 ins / 20.5 x 40.5 cm) DEM 4,000. NEW YORK, 31 Oct 1985, *Peasant and Farmhouse* (oil on canvas, 45 1/4 x 34 ins / 115 x 86.5 cm) USD 10,500.

SEYPPEL, Hans
German, 20th century.
Born 10 October 1886, in Düsseldorf.
Active in the Rhineland.
Painter, engraver. Landscapes.

Hans Seyppel was the son of Carl Maria Seyppel; he studied at the fine arts academy in Düsseldorf.

SEYRO, Ramón, or Sieyro
Spanish, 18th century.
Painter.

Ramón Seyro was born without hands. In 1778 he studied at the Real Academia de San Fernando in Madrid with M.S. de Maella and in 1784 became a teacher of the school of drawing in Santiago de Compostela. The bishop's palace and cathedral in Toledo have two paintings by him.

SEYSENEGGER, Jakob. See **SEISENEGGER**

SEYSS, A.
German, 19th century.
Active in Munich, c. 1840.
Lithographer.

SEYSSAUD, René
French, 19th - 20th century.
Born 16 June 1867, in Marseilles; died 26 September 1952, in St-Chamas.
Painter. Landscapes, seascapes, still-lifes, flowers.
Provencal School.

René Seyssaud was born to Vauclusian parents and spent his childhood near Ventoux at Villes-sur-Auzon in an ancestral farm, Pézet house. From a very early age he showed an aptitude for drawing and painting. He entered the École des Beaux-Arts in Marseilles, and from 1885 he went to the studio of Pierre Grivolas at the École des Beaux-Arts in Avignon. He was soon noticed by his teachers for the boldness of his technique and his colouring. He brought back paintings from periods in the Var and the Bouches-du-Rhône. In 1892 he painted a canvas in the Vaucluse, *Chestnut Trees,* using colours in their pure state with broad strokes and a surprising harmony, thus taking his place, along with Valtat, among the precursors of Fauvism. On the 27 April 1901

Thiebault Sisson wrote in *Le Temps*: 'We should give first place here to someone who is like no one else, who is a part of no group and who owes nothing to anyone except himself. Seyssaud, this solitary, unsociable man from Provence, has made himself, a long way from Paris, into a master.'

His work is considerable, having an extraordinary unity of style, almost wild and brutish. It is admired for its richness of colour and for its violence. He also did many large decorative compositions. He settled at Villes-sur-Auzon where for 20 years he painted, while suffering from tuberculosis. In 1904, completely cured, he lived at St-Chamas near Lake Berry and led a hermit's existence dedicated to his art, to simple poetry and to his family. He refused all contracts offered and proposals made, among these an offer from Vollard. Late in life he won the Grand Prix d'Honneur des Provinces Françaises at the Menton Biennale in 1951. He was an Officer of the Légion d'Honneur.

He took part in public exhibitions mainly in Paris: 1892, Salon du Champ de Mars, then at the Salon d'Automne, Salon des Tuileries and the Salon des Indépendants; 1937, *Masters of Independent Art*; 1951, Biennale de Menton. He has been represented posthumously in public exhibitions such as: 2001, *La Femme en Provence et en Méditerranée* (*Women in Provence and the Mediterranean*), Fondation Regards de Provence, Chateau de Borély, Marseilles. He showed his works in solo exhibitions in Paris in 1897 at the Le Barc de Boutteville, from 1899 at the Galerie Vollard and also at the Galerie Bernheim. In 2003 the Musée Zierne at Martigues devoted a show to him under the title *Rene Seyssaud (1867-1952): Another Nature.*

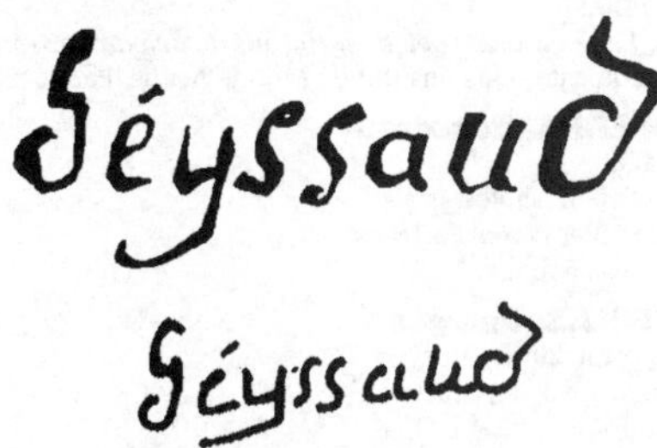

BIBLIOGRAPHY:

Silvestre-Seyssaud, Yvonne/Tourette, Jean (preface), *Seyssaud, documents et souvenirs*, St-Chamas, 1959. Bonicci, Claude, *René Seyssaud: écumes et rivages*, Images en manœuvres, Paris, 2003.

MUSEUMS AND GALLERIES:

MARSEILLES (Mus. Cantini): *St-Chamas, the Old Roofs* - PARIS (MAM) - PARIS (Mus. du Petit Palais).

AUCTION RECORDS:

PARIS, 23 Nov 1910, *Berre Pond,* FRF 60. PARIS, 27 Nov 1919, *Gulf (Gironde),* FRF 220. PARIS, 5 June 1923, *Seascape: Rocks on the Coast at Cassis,* FRF 520. PARIS, 1 March 1926, *Oaks at Sabateri,* FRF 1,000. PARIS, 6 Feb 1929, *Endurance in the Alps,* FRF 140. PARIS, 26-27 Feb 1934, *Provencal Landscape: Banks of the Pond at Berre, Sunset,* FRF 440. PARIS, 4 Feb 1943, *Still-life with Sardines,* FRF 3,000. PARIS, July 1946, *Landscape,* FRF 6,000. MARSEILLES, 18 Dec 1948, *Reapers at St-Chamas* (distemper) FRF 32,000. PARIS, 4 April 1950, *Harvest at Villes-sur-Auzon,* FRF 37,000. PARIS, 21 Feb 1955, *Hillsides of Beaumont,* FRF 245,000. PARIS, 31 March 1960, *Landscape,* FRF 14,000. AIX-EN-PROVENCE, 25 Oct 1965, *Still-life with Bottles,* FRF 14,000. PARIS, 8 June 1970, *Harvest,* FRF 20,000. MARSEILLES, 26 Feb 1972, *Mount Ventoux,* FRF 20,000. ROUEN, 2 May 1974, *Vase of Flowers* (watercolour and gouache) FRF 6,500. TOULOUSE, 15 March 1976, *Red Hillsides* (c. 1920, oil on canvas, 18 x 25 1/2 ins / 46 x 65 cm) FRF 10,500. MARSEILLES, 25 Nov 1977, *Landscape of Vaucluse* (oil on canvas, 35 x 39 1/4 ins / 89 x 100 cm) FRF 29,000. PARIS, 19 June 1978, *Poplars in Summer* (oil on canvas, 23 1/2 x 36 1/4 ins / 60 x 92 cm) FRF 11,000. PARIS, 16 Dec 1979, *Vase of Flowers* (oil on canvas, 23 1/2 x 28 3/4 ins / 60 x 73 cm) FRF 14,500. AVIGNON, 3 May 1981, *Landscape of Vaucluse* (oil on canvas, 11 1/2 x 18 1/2 ins / 29 x 47 cm) FRF 16,000. AVIGNON, 27 March 1983, *Still-life with Fruits and Bunch of Flowers* (oil on card, 40 1/4 x 28 1/4 ins / 102 x 71.5 cm) FRF 21,000. PARIS, 10 Dec 1985, *Still-life with Flowers and Fruits* (1948, oil on canvas, 39 3/4 x 28 3/4 ins / 101 x 73 cm) FRF 25,000. VERSAILLES, 11 June 1986, *Young Women and Children on the Terrace* (oil on canvas, 38 1/4 x 51 1/4 ins / 97 x 130 cm) FRF 83,000. PARIS, 10 Dec 1987, *Country Road* (oil on card). PARIS, 21 April 1988, *Still-life with Fruits* (oil on canvas, 21 1/4 x 25 1/2 ins / 54 x 65 cm) FRF 31,000. PARIS, 23 June 1988, *Oranges* (oil on canvas, 21 1/4 x 25 1/2 ins / 54 x 65 cm) FRF 40,000. PARIS, 22 Nov 1988, *Workers* (oil on canvas, 15 x 18 ins / 38 x 46 cm) FRF 60,000. PARIS, 12 Dec 1988, *Day in the Country* (1900, oil on canvas) FRF 64,000. NEUILLY-SUR-SEINE, 16 March 1989, *Provencal Landscape* (oil on canvas, 21 1/4 x 25 1/2 ins / 54 x 65 cm) FRF 45,000. PARIS, 22 Oct 1989, *Hamlet* (oil on canvas, 12 1/4 x 21 1/4 ins / 31 x 54 cm) FRF 22,000. PARIS, 21 Nov 1989, *Harvesters* (oil on card, 17 1/4 x 23 1/4 ins / 44 x 59 cm) FRF 85,000. PARIS, 19 Jan 1990, *Village on the Midi* (oil on card, 15 1/4 x 21 3/4 ins / 39 x 55.5 cm) FRF 45,000. PARIS, 19 March 1990, *Still-life with Watermelon* (oil on canvas, 19 3/4 x 25 1/2 ins / 50 x 65 cm) FRF 50,000. PARIS, 26 April 1990, *Landscape of the Midi* (oil on canvas, 15 x 24 ins / 38 x 61 cm) FRF 85,000. PARIS, 5 July 1990, *Landscape* (wash and watercolour, 11 1/2 x 14 1/2 ins / 29 x 37 cm) FRF 3,500. PARIS, 17 Oct 1990, *Ladies Walking at Villes-sur-Auzon* (c. 1900, oil on canvas, 18 1/2 x 25 1/2 ins / 47 x 65 cm) FRF 150,000. NEW YORK, 5 Nov 1991, *Harvest at Aurel* (oil on canvas, 23 1/2 x 28 3/4 ins / 60 x 73 cm) USD 14,300. PARIS, 13 Nov 1991, *Landscape with a Tree* (oil on canvas, 22 x 18 ins / 55 x 46 cm) FRF 55,000. AMSTERDAM, 11 Dec 1991, *Landscape with Cherry Trees* (oil on canvas, 18 x 22 ins / 46 x 55 cm) NLG 11,500. LE TOUQUET, 8 June 1992, *Small River Bordered by Trees* (oil on canvas, 22 x 18 ins / 55 x 46 cm) FRF 37,000. NEW YORK, 10 Nov 1992, *Landscape* (oil on card, 12 1/4 x 19 1/2 ins / 30.8 x 49.8 cm) USD 4,180. PARIS, 11 June 1993, *Edge of the Sea* (oil on canvas, 13 x 22 ins / 33 x 55 cm) FRF 29,500. NEW YORK, 29 Sept 1993, *Workers in a Field* (oil on canvas, 22 x 18 ins / 55.9 x 45.7 cm) USD 8,625. PARIS, 18 Nov 1993, *Fishing Fleet Returning* (oil on panel, 64 1/4 x 55 ins / 163 x 139.5 cm) FRF 35,000. NEUILLY, 12 Dec 1993, *Berre Pond at St-Chamas* (1910, oil on canvas, 19 x 20 1/2 ins / 48 x 52 cm) FRF 76,500. PARIS, 22 March 1994, *Plain in Autumn* (watercolour, gouache and oil on card, 15 x 23 3/4 ins / 38 x 60.5 cm) FRF 21,500. PARIS, 22 Nov 1994, *Silhouettes on a Road at La Redonne Near Cassis* (oil on canvas, 23 3/4 x 29 1/4 ins / 60.5 x 74 cm) FRF 110,000. PARIS, 19 April 1996, *Gleaners* (oil on canvas, 13 1/2 x 18 ins / 34 x 46 cm) FRF 22,000. PARIS, 22 Nov 1996, *Chestnut Trees at Villes-sur-Auzon* (oil on canvas, 35 x 51 1/4 ins / 89 x 130 cm) FRF 165,000. PARIS, 12 March 1997, *Reapers with Poppies* (1930, oil on canvas, 22 x 18 ins / 55 x 46 cm) FRF 85,000. CALAIS, 23 March 1997, *Lavender Meadow in Provence* (oil on canvas, 19 3/4 x 24 ins / 50 x 61 cm) FRF 40,000. PARIS, 6 June 1997, *Harvesters at Villes-sur-Auzon* (oil on canvas, 17 3/4 x 23 1/2 ins / 45 x 60 cm) FRF 67,000. PARIS, 11 June 1997, *Still-life with Watermelon* (oil on canvas, 18 1/2 x 22 ins / 47 x 55 cm) FRF 33,000. PARIS, 23 June 1997, *Rocky Inlet* (tempera/paper, 20 x 14 1/4 ins / 51 x 36 cm) FRF 17,000. CANNES, 8 Aug 1997, *Still-life with Flowers and Fruit* (1948, oil on canvas, 39 3/4 x 28 3/4 ins / 101 x 73 cm) FRF 73,000. PARIS, 5 Dec 1997, *Valley of the Touloubre* (1925, oil on canvas, 32 x 39 1/4 ins / 81 x 100 cm) FRF 30,000. PARIS, 22 March 1998, *Sea side in the Midi* (oil on canvas, 4 1/2 x 6 3/4 ins / 11.5 x 17 cm) FRF 7,800. PARIS, 24 March 1999, *Landscape* (oil on canvas, 15 x 21 ins / 37 x 54 cm) FRF 38,000. CALAIS, 23 May 1999, *Ru-*

ral Afternoon Snack in Provence (oil on panel, 18 x 15 ins / 46 x 38 cm) FRF 44,000. PARIS, 19 April 2000, *Still-life with Fruit and Jug* (oil on canvas, 29 x 36 ins / 73 x 92 cm) FRF 49,000. PARIS, 15 Dec 2000, *Toulourbe Valley* (oil on canvas, 25 x 32 ins / 63 x 81 cm) FRF 58,000. CALAIS, 11 Nov 2001, *Still-life with Faience Soup Bowl and Lemons* (oil on canvas, 23 x 31 ins / 58 x 80 cm) FRF 58,000. PARIS, 6 Feb 2002, *Goatherds in Provence* (mixed media, 11 x 12 ins / 27 x 30 cm) EUR 4,400. VERSAILLES, 7 July 2002, *Family Picnic* (1900, oil on canvas, 18 x 23 ins / 46 x 59 cm) EUR 16,000. PARIS, 12 March 2003, *Vaucluse, Peasants in the Fields* (oil on canvas, 20 x 26 ins / 50 x 65 cm) EUR 15,000. CALAIS, 16 March 2003, *Olive Trees in Provence* (oil on canvas, 24 x 32 ins / 61 x 81 cm) EUR 10,200. PARIS, 29 March 2004, *Mediterranean Port* (oil on canvas, 22 x 18 ins / 55 x 46 cm) EUR 6,100. PARIS, 5 May 2004, *Reclining Nude* (oil on canvas, 29 x 46 ins / 73 x 116 cm) EUR 2,600.

SEYSSES, Auguste
French, 20th century.
Born 22 August 1862, in Toulouse.
Sculptor, engraver, medallist.

Auguste Seysses was a pupil of Falguière and took part in Paris from 1884 in the Salon des Artistes Français, becoming a society member and hors concours. He received silver medals at the Exposition Universelle in Paris, first in 1900 asnd then in 1937. He was made a Chevalier of the Légion d'Honneur in 1900 and Officer in 1932. Among his works are: *Theatre Arts* and *The Arts of Drawing* at the Grand Palais in Paris, *Return* at the Jardin des Plantes at Toulouse, *The Marshall Marquis de Villeroy* at the Prefecture in Lyons, the bust of *Augustin de St-Hilaire* in the botanic garden of Rio de Janeiro and the *Monument of Doctor Cabanes* at Gourdon.

MUSEUMS AND GALLERIES:
LONS-LE-SAUNIER: *Pro libertate* (*For Liberty*) - TOULOUSE: *Little Girl with a Tortoise*.

SEYST, Hendrick van
Flemish School, 15th - 16th century.
Died after 1512.
Active in Antwerp.
Painter.
Antwerp School.

Seyst was a pupil of Gillis van Everen in 1481, was a master in Antwerp in 1496 and doyen of the Guild of Painters in 1511 and 1512.

SEYTER, Daniel or Joseph Daniel. See **SEITER**

SEYTON, Filippo. See **SEITON**

SEZAKI
Japanese, 20th century.
Painter.

Sezaki came to Paris before 1939 and exhibited there with his compatriot Suzuki Ryuichi(?). Taking his example from modern French masters, he painted delicate, luminous landscapes in pale colours. His drawing style sometimes recalls Japanese art. He also travelled to Sweden to study the light in the north.

SEZANNE, Augusto
Italian, 19th - 20th century.
Born 1856, in Florence; died 1935, in Venice.
Painter, engraver.

Augusto Sezanne studied at the Accademia di Belle Arti in Bologna and was also an architect. He became a professor at the Accademia di Belle Arti in Venice in 1920. He executed the painted decorations of the meeting hall of Rovereto town council and the Canton dei Fiori House in Bologna.

MUSEUMS AND GALLERIES:
MILAN - ROME.

AUCTION RECORDS:
MILAN, 22 March 1994, *Chioggia* (oil on canvas, 26 1/2 x 37 1/2 ins / 67 x 95 cm) ITL 10,925,000.

SEZENIUS, Valentin
German, 17th century.
Engraver (burin).

Sezenius was an imitator or pupil of Matthias Beutler.

SÉZILLE DES ESSARTS, Auguste Fred Pierre
French, 19th - 20th century.
Born 12 March 1867, in Noyon (Oise).
Painter. Genre scenes, figures.

Auguste Sézille des Essarts was a pupil of Henri Gervex. He painted mainly intimate scenes.

SEZZANO, Giovanni
Italian, 18th century.
Sculptor (wood).

SFEIR, Amine
Lebanese, 20th century.
Born 1931, in Reyfoun (Kesrouan).
Painter. Figures.

Amine Sfeir studied at the Lebanese academy of fine art in Beirut, and then at the Académie des Beaux-Arts and the Académie Grande Chaumière in Paris. He settled in Beirut in 1966, and since then has paid visits to the USA and Europe. He specialises in impressionistic studies of the world of children.

He has exhibited in various public exhibitions in the Lebanon, as well as in the 1964 Biennials in Paris and Alexandria, and in an exhibition organised in New York by the United Nations. He has also held solo exhibitions in the Lebanon.

BIBLIOGRAPHY:
Liban. Le Regard des peintres. 200 ans de peinture libanaise, exhibition catalogue, Institut du Monde Arabe, Paris, 1989.

SFERRA, Benedetto
Italian.
Active in Naples.
Modeller (wax). Portraits.

Sferra was a monk.

SFIKAS, Georges
Cypriot, 20th century.
Born 1943, in Nicosia.
Sculptor.

Sfikas is not linked to any particular school or movement, though it can be said that he flirted with Conceptual Art. His *Curtains* (Blue) reveal his American experiments and his *Corner* follows the line of primary structures, in which austerity is enlivened by the presence of aestheticism. This aesthetic formulation is again emphasised in *Mirror*, where the illusionism of the reflected surface clearly shows his interest in the decorative.

SFONDRATI, or Sfondati
Italian, 16th century.
Active c. 1530.
Painter.

MUSEUMS AND GALLERIES:
VIENNA (Akademie der Bildenden Künste, reserve collection): *Resurrection of Christ with Angels and Saints*.

SFONDRATI, Antonio and Gabriele, or Sfondati
Italian, 16th century.
Born to a family originally from Cremona.
Sculptors.

SFORZA, Alberto
Italian, 18th century.
Born to a family originally from Benevento.
Painter.

Sforza decorated the chapel of Pope Benedict XIII in the Vatican about 1725.

SFORZA, Cesar
Argentinian, 20th century.
Born 1893.
Sculptor.
Cesar Sforza was a pupil at the National Escuela de Bellas Artes in Buenos Aires and exhibited at the Salon from 1914. After winning some lesser prizes, he took a first prize in 1920 with his *Caryatid*. He produced monumental low reliefs.

SFORZA, Francesco
Italian, 15th century.
Born to a family originally from Vicenza.
Painter.
This painter lived in Bassano (Veneto) between 1470 and 1479.

SFORZI, Giuseppe
Italian, 19th century.
Born 1792, in Livorno.
Painter.
Giuseppe Sforzi executed the painted decorations of the municipal theatre in Perugia in 1813.

SFORZOLINI, Domenico
Italian, 19th century.
Born 1810; died 1860.
Active in Gubbio (Umbria).
Painter.
Domenico Sforzolini was a pupil of T. Minardi.

SFRAJO, Vespasiano, or Sfrago
Italian, 15th century.
Active in Paganica (Abruzzi).
Painter.

SGARBI, H.
French, 20th century.
Painter.
H. Sgarbi exhibited in Paris, at the Salon d'Automne.

SGARD, Jean
French, 20th century.
Born 21 March 1891, in Abbeville.
Painter, designer.
Jean Sgard exhibited in Paris at the Salon d'Automne, and received a silver medal at the Salon des Arts Décoratifs in 1925.

SGARGI, Leonardo
Italian, 17th century.
Active in Bologna c. 1684.
Fresco artist.
Sgargi subsequently worked in Vienna.

SGRILLI, Bernardo Sansone, or Desgrilli, Scrilli
Italian, 18th century.
Active in Florence between 1733 and 1755.
Engraver (burin), architect.
Bernardo Sansone Sgrilli was the cousin of Vincenzo Sgrilli.

SGRILLI, Roberto
Italian, 20th century.
Born 23 October 1897, in Florence; died 1985.
Painter, illustrator. Landscapes.
Roberto Sgrilli studied at the Accademia di Belle Arti in Florence with G. Ghini and Augusto Bastianini.
AUCTION RECORDS:
MILAN, 6 June 1991, *Canal in Pisa* (oil on panel, 15 1/4 x 19 1/4 ins / 38.5 x 49 cm) ITL 1,000,000.

SGRILLI, Vincenzo
Italian, 18th century.
Died c. 1720, in Florence, at an early age.
Painter.
Vincenzo Sgrilli was the cousin of Bernardo Sgrilli. The pupil of G. dal Sole and D.F. Gabbiani, he was subsequently attached to the court of Princess Violanta of Tuscany.

SGROOTEN, Christian, or Schrot, Scrot, Scroot
Flemish School, 16th - 17th century.
Born in Sonsbeck; died before 2 April 1609.
Draughtsman, geographer.
From 1557 Sgrooten was official geographer to Philip II of Spain. The National Library of Madrid has an atlas by him that consists of 38 manuscript maps.
MUSEUMS AND GALLERIES:
MADRID (Biblioteca Nacional): *Atlas*.

SGUANCI, Aldo
Italian, 20th century.
Born 1885; died 1933, in Florence.
Sculptor, painter. Portraits.

SGUARI, Giovanni Antonio
Italian, 18th century.
Of Paduan origin.
Painter.
Sguari painted the stations of the cross in the college of St Isidore in Rome between 1701 and 1706.

SGUAZZELLA, Andrea, or Chiazzella
Italian, 16th century.
Born in Florence.
Active in France.
Painter. History painting.
A pupil of Andrea del Sarto, Andrea Sguazzella accompanied his master to France in 1518. When del Sarto returned to Italy the following year, Sguazzella remained in Paris. He painted a number of works for Jacques de Beaune at the chateau of Semblancay but, with the exception of an altarpiece in the chapel, they were all destroyed in 1794. In 1557, he inherited the fortune of his relative Jacopo da Pontorno.
MUSEUMS AND GALLERIES:
FLORENCE (Uffizi): *Holy Family*.

SGUAZZINO. See **PACETTI Giovanni Battista**

SHAAR, Pinchas, or Schaar, pseudonym of Shwarts Pinchas
Polish, 20th century.
Born 15 March 1923, in Lódz; died 1998.
Active in New York from 1975.
Painter, sculptor. Figures, nudes, landscapes. Murals, designs for mosaics.
A painter, mosaicist and fresco artist, Pinchas Shaar received his first lessons at the age of 15 from Wladyslaw Strzeminski, a disciple of Malevich. In 1945, having survived the ghetto and the Holocaust, he found himself in Munich, where he started work once more. In 1948 he moved to Paris, visiting Israel later that year. On returning to Paris, he attended the Académie de la Grande Chaumière. In 1956 he emigrated to Israel and in 1975 finally settled in New York. Of his first, tormented period nothing survives. After 1951 his work becomes more optimistic, with figures and landscapes that seem to have been engraved and then superimposed upon a coloured background. There is a visible affinity between his work and ancient Levantine art, the frescoes of Dura Europos and mosaics from Israel.

Shaar had his first exhibition in Munich in 1947. Thereafter he took part in numerous collective exhibitions including: the Salon des Indépendants and the Salon des Surindépendants (from 1952); the Salon de la Jeune Peinture (from 1954); the Salon d'Automne (from 1955); New York (1954, 1955, 1962, 1963, 1964); annual exhibition of Israeli painters, Tel Aviv (1957 to 1961); Venice Biennale (1960); Salon Art sans frontières, Brussels (1966); *Les Peintres juifs de l'école de Paris*, Paris (1968). Solo exhibition include: Tel Aviv (1951, 1958, 1961, 1968); Paris (1953, 1956, 1965); Brussels (1959, 1965, 1967); Antwerp (1959, 1965); New York and Buffalo (1962); Jewish Museum, New York (1975).

MUSEUMS AND GALLERIES:

CHICAGO (Synagogue): a mosaic.

AUCTION RECORDS:

ANTWERP, 2 April 1974, *Nude on Horseback* (1965) BEF 26,000. LOKEREN, 31 March 1979, *Chariot* (oil on canvas, 18 x 13 ins / 46 x 33 cm) BEF 30,000. ANTWERP, 28 April 1981, *Family* (oil on canvas, 36 1/4 x 25 1/2 ins / 92 x 65 cm) BEF 80,000. PARIS, 27 March 1994, *Bird Trainer* (oil on canvas, 24 x 15 ins / 61 x 38 cm) FRF 6,500. PARIS, 24 March 1996, *Children Riding Donkeys* (1956, oil on canvas, 25 1/2 x 21 1/4 ins / 65 x 54 cm) FRF 8,000.

SHABAKU, artist name: Gessen
Japanese, 16th century.
Active during the second half of the 16th century.
Painter.

Shabaku was a *suiboku* (ink) painter of the Muromachi era. He is supposed to have been a disciple of Shubun (active in the mid-15th century).

SHACKELFORD, Shelby
American, 20th century.
Born 27 September 1899, in Halifax (Virginia); died 1987.
Painter.

Shelby Shackelford was taught by Ross Moffett and Othon Friesz, and married the physicist Richard Threlkeld Fox. She was a member of the Société des Indépendants.

SHACKLETON, Charles
American, 19th - 20th century.
Born 1856, in Mineral Point (Wisconsin); died 2 July 1920, in New Canaan (Connecticut).
Painter.

Charles Shackleton was a pupil of Frederic Clark Gottwald.

SHACKLETON, John
British, 18th century.
Died 16 March 1767.
Painter. History painting, portraits.

John Shackleton succeeded Kent as the official portrait painter at the court of George II, whose portrait he painted on several occasions. In 1755 Shackleton served on a committee set up with the aim of creating an academy of painting. The project was never realised.

MUSEUMS AND GALLERIES:

EDINBURGH (Scottish National Portrait Gallery): *George II* (oil on canvas) - LONDON (National Portrait Gal.): *Henry Pelham* (c. 1752, oil on canvas) - PARIS (Gal. Nationale): *H. Pelham.*

AUCTION RECORDS:

LONDON, 8 April 1911, *Male Portrait; Female Portrait* (1737, two pendants) GBP 13; *Portrait of a Gentleman*, GBP 5. LONDON, 31 May 1935, *Sir Oswald Mosley* (drawing) GBP 31. LONDON, 14 March 1984, *Portrait of George II* (oil on canvas, 86 1/2 x 57 ins / 219.5 x 145 cm) GBP 3,000. LONDON, 18 April 1986, *Portrait of King George II* (oil on canvas, 93 3/4 x 57 3/4 ins / 238.2 x 146.7 cm) GBP 4,800. LONDON, 18 Nov 1988, *Full-length Portrait of Gerard Anne Edward dressed in brown and an embroidered red waistcoat, holding a pamphlet* (1743, oil on canvas, 70 1/4 x 47 ins / 178.5 x 119.3 cm) GBP 60,500. LONDON, 8 April 1992, *Portrait of Jane Pescod, Mrs Carew Mildmay, wearing a White Satin Gown* (oil on canvas, 94 x 57 3/4 ins / 239 x 147 cm) GBP 990. LONDON, 14 June 2000, *Portrait of Gerard Anne Edwards in Brown Coat and Gold Waistcoat, Holding a Pamphlet* (1743, oil on canvas, 70 x 47 ins / 178 x 119 cm) GBP 90,000.

SHACKLETON, Keith Hope
British, 20th century.
Born 16 January 1923, in Weybridge.
Painter, draughtsman, illustrator, writer. Wildlife, seascapes.

Keith Shackleton spent his early years in Australia, then came to Britain and was educated at Oundle School in Northamptonshire. He worked initially in the aviation business, painting in his spare time. He was greatly interested in nature and wildlife and eventually gave up his aviation commitments and became a full-time artist, working at the same time as a broadcaster for the BBC (*Animal Magic* and *Animals in Action*). His occupation as an artist and boatman took him all over the world. His painting was influenced by a wide variety of subjects and places, but he remained principally a marine painter who was perhaps best known for his exciting interpretations of Antarctic wildlife and sea birds.

His work as an illustrator includes contributions to *Birds of the Atlantic Ocean*. He also wrote and illustrated numerous articles for wildlife and yachting magazines as well as a number of books (*Wildlife and Wilderness, An Artist's World, Wild Animals of Britain* and *Ship in the Wilderness*). He lives in London and in south Devon.

A founder member of the Royal Society of Marine Artists and the Society of Wildlife Artists, Keith Shackleton became president of both. His correspondence (c. 1937-1987) with Sir Peter Markham Scott, the wildlife painter, is at Cambridge University in the University Library manuscript and archive department. A retrospective of over 50 years' work was held at the Mall Galleries in London in 1998.

BIBLIOGRAPHY:

Shackleton, Keith, *An Autobiography in Paintings*, Swann Hill Press, 1998.

MUSEUMS AND GALLERIES:

LONDON (National Maritime Mus.) - LONDON (UK Government Art Collection): *Trawlers Fitting Out: Jacobshavn, Greenland; View from the Summit: Paulet Island, Antarctica* - WALLSWORTH HALL, GLOS. (Nature in Art Mus.).

AUCTION RECORDS:

LONDON, 11 May 1973, *Polar Bears* (1965) GNS 120. PERTH, 29 Aug 1989, *Goosanders in Flight* (1947, oil on card, 14 1/2 x 23 1/2 ins / 37 x 60 cm) GBP 770. LONDON, 22 Nov 1995, *Barnacle Goose on a Beach* (1964, oil on card, 17 3/4 x 36 1/4 ins / 45 x 92 cm) GBP 1,725. LONDON, 14 May 1996, *The Marauders: Small Terns above the Waves* (oil on card, 23 1/2 x 5 ins / 59.7 x 12.7 cm) GBP 1,955.

SHACKLETON, William
British, 19th - 20th century.
Born 14 January 1872, in Bradford; died 9 January 1933, in London.
Painter. Genre scenes.

William Shackleton trained in London at the Royal College of Art. A scholarship allowed him to study at the Académie Julian in Paris and to travel to Italy. He exhibited at the New English Art Club, in Liverpool, at the Royal Institute of Fine Art in Glasgow, and at the Royall Academy from 1895 to 1919..

MUSEUMS AND GALLERIES:

LONDON (Tate Collection): *Mackerel Nets* (1913); *The Line of Life* (1915).

AUCTION RECORDS:

LONDON, 19 May 1911, *Genre Scene*, GBP 16. LONDON, 9 April 1980, *A Balcony in Siena* (1899, oil on canvas, 32 1/2 x 44 ins / 82.5 x 112 cm) GBP 2,500. LONDON, 6 Nov 1996, *Lanterns* (1910, gouache and coloured chalks, 17 1/4 x 13 1/2 ins / 44 x 34 cm) GBP 4,025. NEWBURY, 16 May 2001, *Reliquary* (1898, oil on canvas, 21 x 10 ins / 54 x 25 cm) GBP 3,000. LONDON, 19 June 2001, *Lovers* (1899, oil on canvas, 28 x 21 ins / 70 x 54 cm) GBP 8,000.

SHADBOLT, Jack Leonard
Canadian, 20th century.
Born 1909, in England; died 22 November,1998, in British Columbia.
Painter.

Jack Shadbolt moved to Canada as a young child with his parents, who gave him a respect for things well crafted - his mother was a dressmaker, his father a signpainter. Shadbolt's early interest was in technical drawing. After studies at Victoria College and the provincial Normal School, he began to teach art, from 1931 at the Kitsilano High School in Vancouver, and from 1938 at the Vancouver School of Art, a post he held until his retirement in 1966. During World War II he served overseas as a war artist. In 1988, together with his wife Dorris, Shadbolt founded the Vancouver Institute for the Visual Arts, which brings together painters, curators and architects to express the beauty of their region.

Shadbolt's poetic paintings explore a same half-real, half-imagined world. A prolific artist, his work has featured regularly in exhibitions across Canada, the US, Venezuela, Brazil, Great Britain, France, Italy, Spain, Poland, Australia and Japan. Shadbolt was awarded the Order of Canada in 1972 and has received many other awards, including the Gershon Iskowitcz Prize for his contribution to Canadian art.

BIBLIOGRAPHY:
Jack Shadbolt, exhibition catalogue, Vancouver Art Gall., Musée des Beaux-Arts du Canada, Ottawa, 1969. Halpin, Marjorie M., *Jack Shadbolt and the Coastal Indian Image*, University of British Columbia Press, Vancouver, 1986. Wilson, Scott, *Jack Shadbolt*, Douglas & McIntyre, 1990. Ainslie, Patricia, *Jack Shadbolt*, Glenbow, Calgary, 1991.

AUCTION RECORDS:
TORONTO, 17 May 1976, *Red Abstraction* (1960, watercolour/ink, 22 x 30 1/4 ins / 56 x 77 cm) CAD 750. TORONTO, 19 Oct 1976, *Red and White Still-life* (1960, acrylic and ink, 29 1/2 x 22 ins / 75 x 55 cm) CAD 800. TORONTO, 26 May 1981, *Harbour* (1958, watercolour, 9 3/4 x 17 1/2 ins / 25 x 44.4 cm) CAD 2,000. MONTREAL, 17 Oct 1988, *Winter Presences* (1951, mixed media, 26 3/4x20 ins / 68x51 cm) CAD 1,400. TORONTO, 12 June 1989, *The Muskeg Region* (1963, oil on card, sketch, 14 1/2 x 19 3/4 ins / 36.8 x 50.2 cm) CAD 1,750.

SHADE, William Auguste
American, 19th century.
Born 19 November 1848, in New York; died 26 September 1890, in Switzerland, or in 1940 according to some sources.
Painter.

William Auguste Shade studied in Düsseldorf with W. Sohn, and in London and Rome between 1883 and 1888.

AUCTION RECORDS:
LONDON, 20 March 1981, *Fruit of Love* (1881, oil on panel, 13 x 17 1/4 ins / 33 x 44 cm) GBP 1,000. WASHINGTON DC, 12 June 1983, *Mother and Child in an Interior* (oil on canvas, 32 1/4 x 24 1/4 ins / 82 x 61.6 cm) USD 2,500.

SHADILOV, Mikhail, Nicolaievich or Nikitich
Russian, 19th century.
Born 12 September 1815, in St Petersburg; died 1842, in St Petersburg.
Sculptor.

Shadilov was a pupil of Boris Orlovski.

SHAFER, Leon Alaric
American, 19th - 20th century.
Born 17 November 1866, in Genesco (Illinois); died 1940.
Painter, engraver, illustrator.

Leon Alaric Shafer studied at the Art Institute of Chicago and was a member of the American Federation of Arts. He illustrated many war books.

SHAGEN, Simon Adrien
Swiss, 20th century.
Born 26 April 1923, in Geneva.
Active from 1946 in Australia.
Sculptor. Animals.

Simon Shagen studied at the fine arts in Geneva and at the college of arts and crafts in Lucerne. He was noted for his gold, silver and precious metal pieces depicting animals and vegetables.

SHAHABUDDIN
Indian, 20th century.
Painter.

Shahabuddin is an artist of the contemporary Bengal school. He paints bodies in movement with echos of the graphic and pictorial scripts of Vladimir Velickovic.

AUCTION RECORDS:
PARIS, 20 Nov 1988, *Movement* (oil on canvas, 63 1/2 x 51 1/2 ins / 161 x 131 cm) FRF 16,000. PARIS, 9 Feb 1989, *The Leap* (64 1/4 x 63 1/2 ins / 163 x 161 cm) FRF 15,000. PARIS, 18 June 1989, *Start of a Race* (oil on canvas, 34 1/4 x 26 ins / 87 x 66 cm) FRF 8,100. LES ANDELYS, 19 Nov 1989, *The Leap* (oil on canvas, 35 x 46 ins / 89 x 116 cm) FRF 9,800. PARIS, 26 April 1990, *The Leap* (oil on canvas, 51 1/4 x 38 1/4 ins / 130 x 97 cm) FRF 20,000. PARIS, 28 Oct 1990, *Warrior* (oil on canvas, 39 1/4 x 32 ins / 100 x 81 cm) FRF 18,000. PARIS, 4 Oct 1994, *Momentum* (oil on canvas, 25 1/2 x 21 1/4 ins / 65 x 54 cm) FRF 5,500. PARIS, 26 March 1995, *The Samurai* (oil on canvas, 45 x 57 1/2 ins / 114 x 146 cm) FRF 6,800.

SHAHN, Ben
Lithuanian, 20th century.
Born 12 September 1898, in Kovno (now Kaunas); died 14 March 1969, in New York.
Active in the USA.
Painter (including gouache), watercolourist, engraver, photographer. Figures, portraits, scenes with figures, genre scenes, landscapes. Murals.

Ben Shahn was one of the most important painters of his generation. Born in Kaunas, Lithuania, he emigrated with his family to the USA in 1904, when he was eight. Educated as an American and seeing the world through American eyes, he retained little, if anything, of his Lithuanian origins. But his Jewish heritage and his family's social revolutionary beliefs were certainly the main force that drove him to denounce vehemently all forms of injustice whether against individuals or entire communities.

Ben Shahn's family was of very modest means (his father was a carpenter). They settled in Brooklyn. After completing school Ben worked as a lithographer's apprentice until 1930, attending night school at the National Academy of Design (1917 to 1921), the Art Students League and eventually New York University.

He travelled to Europe in 1925 and 1927. During his second visit he attended classes at the Académie de la Grande Chaumière, Paris, and travelled widely in Italy, Spain and North Africa. While in Paris, he must have seen the watered-down post-Cubism then all the rage, but was not tempted: 'Here I am... the son of a carpenter. I like stories and people. The French School is not for me'. Shahn was largely unconcerned by questions of aesthetic theory. What convinced him to become an artist was the deep indignation he felt at injustice. During his travels he painted gouaches.

After returning to the USA, he created in 1930 a series of portraits of the men involved in the 1894 Dreyfus affair in France. In 1931 and 1932 he turned his attention to the Sacco and Vanzetti trial, in which two impoverished Italian anarchists had been executed on very flimsy evidence. Once more, he took up the defence of the victims in his own way, painting 23 gouaches. In 1932-1933, it was the turn of Thomas J. Mooney, a California labour leader who had been wrongfully convicted of bombing in 1916 and who was still in jail, even though the state's case had been shown to have been fabricated. Shahn's paintings were noticed by Diego Rivera, the painter of the Mexican revolution and the Mexican people, then at the height of his fame. At that time Rivera was working on the murals for the Rockefeller Center, New York; he invited the young painter to be his assistant. This is how Ben Shahn learned mural techniques.

Between 1934 and 1942 he received a number of commissions that enabled him to place his art at the service of his socialist convictions: the projected paintings for Rilker's Island Penitentiary, New York, which were never executed; Roosevelt Community Center, N.J (1937 to 1938); the murals for the Bronx Post Office (1938 to 1939), and the murals for the Social Security Building, Washington, DC (1940 to 1942).

Ben Shahn was also known as a photographer. From 1935 to 1938 he travelled through the southern USA for the Farm Security Administration, photographing the lives of the rural poor, notably black cotton pickers and tenant farmers, with uncompromising realism.

During World War II, while continuing to paint, he received commissions from the American Office of War Information to design posters; this enabled him to create works of high graphic quality while continuing to get his convictions across to the public at large. In his words: 'Art is polemic. Its oldest and most honourable privilege is to throw down a challenge at everything that public opinion accepts with the greatest complacency'. Like Georg Grosz and Diego Rivera, Ben Shahn was one of the very few artists who placed his art at the service of his convictions; yet at the same time, his work has unquestionable artistic value.

His career can be divided into two periods, before and after 1945. Before 1945, he painted life on the streets, New York streets with ordinary New Yorkers. He watched them and showed them in their everyday lives, in their distractions and suffering. He made, use of photography in his steadfast refusal to fake reality. His works of this period with their minute details can be quoted as one of the sources of Hyper-Realism in the 1970s. After 1945, Shahn left all this behind, turning toward a richer, more poetical freedom coupled with a varied, inventive technique that played on the effects of perspective and simplification and included geometric motifs. It sometimes recalls Surrealism, but in fact it is much closer to the pictorial language of Paul Klee, whom Shahn particularly admired. During this period he also abandoned anecdotal work for more general themes, such as death, suffering, childhood, loneliness. The aesthetic concerns of his time played no part in Ben Shahn's works. Rather, he liked to think that he operated in the same way as the Italian Primitives, whose work he had discovered on his trips to Europe and whose main concern was the truth and the quality of work.

Collective exhibitions include: São Paulo Biennale (1954 where he was awarded a prize) and the Venice Biennale (1954). Solo exhibitions include: New York (1930 where he showed gouaches from his travels); New York (1932 where he showed the Sacco and Vanzetti paintings); Museum of Modern Art, New York (1947-1948); Fogg Art Museum, Cambridge, Mass (1956-1957). A major posthumous retrospective *Common Man Mythic Vision: The Paintings of Ben Shahn* was held at the Jewish Museum, New York (1998).

BIBLIOGRAPHY:

Soby, James Thrall, '*Ben Shahn. Catalogue raisonné*' in *2 vol.*, New York, 1963. Soby, James Thrall, *Ben Shahn: Paintings*, New York, 1963. Shahn, B.B., *Ben Shahn*, New York, 1972. Prescott, Kenneth Wade, *The Complete Graphic Works of Ben Shahn*, Quadrangle, New York, 1973. Prescott, Kenneth Wade, *The Complete Graphic Works of Ben Shahn*, New York, 1973. Weiss, M. (ed.), *Ben Shahn, Photographer*, New York, 1973. Pratt, D. (ed.), *The Photographic Eye of Ben Shahn*, Cambridge (MA), 1975. Prescott, Kenneth Wade, *Ben Shahn: a retrospective 1898-1969*, exhibition catalogue, The Jewish Museum, New York, The Museum, New York, 1976. *Prints and Posters of Ben Shahn*, New York, 1982. Westerbeck, C., '*Ben Shahn: Artist as Photographer*' in *Connoisseur, vol.212*, no. 848, 1982. Pohl, Frances K., *Ben Shahn: New Deal artist in a cold war climate 1947-1954*, University of Texas Press, Austin (TX), 1989. Chevlowe, Susan, *Common man, mythic vision: the paintings of Ben Shahn*, travelling exhibition catalogue, Jewish Museum, New York, Princeton University Press, Princeton, 1998. Greenfeld, Howard, *Ben Shahn: an artist's life*, biography, Random House, New York, 1998.

MUSEUMS AND GALLERIES:

MONTGOMERY (MFA): *Italian Landscape II, Europa* (1944) - NEW YORK (Metropolitan Mus. of Art) - NEW YORK (MoMA): *Sacco & Vanzetti* (1931-1932); *Handball Game* (1939); *Willis Avenue Bridge* (1940); *Pacific* (1945); *Liberation* (1945); *We Want Peace* (1946); *Violinist* (1947) - NEW YORK (Whitney Mus. of American Art) - PHILADELPHIA (MA): *Miner's Wife* (1948) - ST LOUIS (AM).

AUCTION RECORDS:

NEW YORK, 11 April 1962, *Cybernetic Studies* (gouache and oil on hardboard) USD 2,100. NEW YORK, 19 Oct 1967, *Chicago* (gouache and watercolour) USD 13,000. NEW YORK, 14 March 1968, *Demonstrators in Favour of Sacco and Vanzetti* (gouache on paper mounted on hardboard) USD 8,250. NEW YORK, 7 April 1971, *Three Men* (tempera) USD 13,000. NEW YORK, 14 March 1973, *World's Greatest Comics* (tempera) USD 90,000. NEW YORK, 12 Dec 1974, *Vanity* (tempera) USD 5,250. NEW YORK, 28 Oct 1976, *Portrait of André Malraux* (1955, tempera, 30 x 21 1/2 ins / 76.2 x 54.6 cm) USD 20,000. NEW YORK, 21 April 1977, *Four-piece Orchestra* (1944, tempera on hardboard, 18 x 24 ins / 45.7 x 61 cm) USD 20,000. NEW YORK, 16 Nov 1978, *Paterson* (1953, hand-coloured silk screen print, 31 x 23 ins / 79 x 58.3 cm) USD 2,000. NEW YORK, 16 Feb 1979, *Supermarket* (1957, hand-coloured silk screen print, 16 1/2 x 37 ins / 42 x 94 cm) GBP 2,200. NEW YORK, 20 April 1979, *Study for The Labyrinth* (1952, pen and watercolour, 13 x 10 ins / 33 x 25.4 cm) USD 5,500. NEW YORK, 20 April 1979, *Carnival* (1946, tempera on hardboard, 22 x 29 3/4 ins / 55.9 x 75.5 cm) USD 36,000. NEW YORK, 29 May 1981, *Head on Tricycle* (ink wash and pencil, poster, 34 3/4 x 23 3/4 ins / 88.3 x 60.4 cm) USD 2,600. NEW YORK, 17 Feb 1982, *Flowering Brushes* (1968, colour lithograph, 38 1/4 x 25 ins / 97.2 x 63.5 cm) USD 4,500. NEW YORK, 5 May 1983, *Menorah* (1965, hand-coloured silk screen print with gold leaf, 26 1/2 x 21 ins / 67.5 x 52.5 cm) USD 1,600. NEW YORK, 31 May 1984, *Musicians* (pen, 25 1/2 x 38 ins / 64.8 x 96.5 cm) USD 3,500. NEW YORK, 26 Oct 1984, *Study for Goyescas* (1956, watercolour and Indian ink, 25 1/4 x 29 3/4 ins / 64.2 x 75.5 cm) USD 9,500. NEW YORK, 6 Dec 1985, *Wheatfield* (pen, 25 1/4 x 37 3/4 ins / 64.2 x 96 cm) USD 3,800. NEW YORK, 30 May 1986, *Triple Cone* (brush and black ink and gouache on paper, 23 x 19 ins / 58.4 x 48.5 cm) USD 7,000. NEW YORK, 4 Dec 1986, *Arc de Triomphe* (tempera on panel, 36 x 48 ins / 91.5 x 121.9 cm) USD 22,000. NEW YORK, 1 Oct 1987, *Unemployment* (tempera on paper mounted on hardboard, 13 1/2 x 17 ins / 34.6 x 42.3 cm) USD 45,000. NEW YORK, 24 June 1988, *Apotheosis* (watercolour, gouache and ink on paper, 7 1/2 x 47 1/2 ins / 18.8 x 120.8 cm) USD 19,800. NEW YORK, 1 Dec 1988, *When the Morning Stars* (1959, distemper on gold leaf on panel, 54 x 48 ins / 137.1 x 121.9 cm) USD 55,000. NEW YORK, 16 March 1990, *Ray Bradbury's Playground* (tempera on canvas on synthetic resin, 15 x 14 ins / 38 x 35.5 cm) USD 66,000. NEW YORK, 30 May 1990, *Figure on Public Bench* (oil on canvas, 30 x 40 ins / 76.3 x 101.6 cm) USD 9,350. NEW YORK, 17 Dec 1990, *Portrait of Adlai Stevenson* (ink and wash on paper, 15 3/4 x 10 1/4 ins / 40.1 x 26 cm) USD 8,250. NEW YORK, 15 May 1991, *Father Coughlin* (watercolour and ink on paper, 15 1/2 x 12 ins / 39.4 x 30.5 cm) USD 6,600. NEW YORK, 15 April 1992, *Eyes and Nose* (ink on paper, 4 x 5 1/2 ins / 10.2 x 14 cm) USD 1,320. NEW YORK, 23 Sept 1992, *Picnic at Prospect Park* (oil on canvas, 24 x 32 ins / 61 x 81 cm) USD 8,800. NEW YORK, 3 Dec 1992, *Brick Factory with Chimneys* (gouache on paper, 29 1/2 x 19 3/4 ins / 74.9 x 50.2 cm) USD 13,200. NEW YORK, 31 March 1994, *Oppenheimer* (1955, ink on paper, 17 1/4 x 11 1/4 ins / 43.8 x 28.6 cm) USD 3,738. NEW YORK, 25 May 1994, *Bowery Clothing Factory* (1936, gouache on paper, 10 x 11 1/2 ins / 25.1 x 28.9 cm) USD 20,700. NEW YORK, 29 Nov 1995, *12th St East* (1947, gouache on card, 22 x 30 ins / 55.9 x 76.2 cm) USD 145,500. NEW YORK, 23 May 1996, *F. Scott Fitzgerald and Others* (gouache on paper, 9 3/4 x 12 1/2 ins / 25 x 32 cm) USD 25,300. NEW YORK, 5 Dec 1996, *Why?* (1961, gouache on paper, 19 1/2 x 25 1/2 ins / 49.5 x 64.8 cm) USD 12,650. NEW YORK, 25 March 1997, *On the First Day of Christmas My True Love Gave to Me* (watercolour, ink and pencil on paper, 14 x 19 1/4 ins / 35.6 x 48.6 cm) USD 5,175. NEW YORK, 5 June 1997, *The Physician from the 'Lucky Dragon' series* (tempera on canvas on panel, 52 x 31 ins / 132.2 x 78.8 cm) USD 112,500. NEW YORK, 7 Oct 1997, *Laissez-Faire, from the 'Strike Breakers' series* (watercolour on paper on panel, 11 3/4 x 17 3/4 ins / 29.8 x 45.1 cm) USD 21,850. NEW YORK, 6 and 7 March 1998, *Byzantine Souvenir* (1966, silk screen print, 24 x 17 3/4 ins / 61 x 45 cm) USD 1,265. NEW YORK, 17 Nov 1999, *Man* (gouache and ink wash, 20 x 26 ins / 51 x 66 cm) USD 17,000. NEW YORK, 23 May 2000, *Man Asleep* (oil and gouache, 6 x 17 ins / 15 x 43 cm) USD 11,000. NEW YORK, 23 May 2001, *Detail no.2 Labyrinth* (tempera/paper/baord, 60 x 23 ins / 153 x 58 cm) USD 48,000. NEW YORK, 2 May 2002, *Seward Park* (colour lithograph, 12 x 18 ins / 30 x 45 cm) USD 26,000. NEW YORK, 23 May 2002, *Harvesting Wheat* (1938, fresco, 33 x 44 ins / 84 x 112 cm) USD 22,000. NEW YORK, 5 March 2003, *Credo* (1954, watercolour and gouache, 30 x 22 ins / 77 x 57 cm) USD 16,000. ROME, 10 April 2003, *Sacco and Vanzetti* (ink/paper, 13 x 17 ins / 33 x 44 cm) EUR 27,000. NEW YORK, 11 March 2004, *Atomic Tables* (gouache and gold leaf/paper/panel, 18 x 84 ins / 46 x 213 cm) USD 20,000. NEW YORK, 27 Sept 2004, *Mine Boy* (gouache on cardboard, 8 x 9 ins / 20 x 22 cm) USD 7,500.

SHAHN, Jonathan
American, 20th century.
Born 1938, in Ohio.
Active in Italy since 1970.
Sculptor. Busts.

Jonathan Shahn studied at the Boston Museum Academy and then spent some time in Europe. He creates statues *in situ*. He participated in collective exhibitions such as the Milan Biennale of Art and the Rome Quadriennale in 1977. Solo exhibitions of his work include: New York, 1963 to 1965; University of Illinois, 1969; University of Maine, 1969; Rome, 1972 and 1977; and Palermo, 1975.

BIBLIOGRAPHY:

Shahn, Jonathan, *Jonathan Shahn: Sculpture and Drawings*, Kennedy Galleries, New York, 1972. *Jonathan Shahn*, exhibition catalogue, Gall. delle Ore, Milan, 1977.

SHAIN. See **BUSON**

SHAKIR, Hassan. See **HASSAN AL-SAID Shakir**

SHAKIROF. See **ZAKIROV**

SHALDERS, George
British, 19th century.
Born 1826, in Portsmouth; died 1873, in London.
Painter, watercolourist, draughtsman. Scenes with figures, genre scenes, animals, landscapes.

George Shalders showed his work at the principal exhibitions in London between 1848 and 1873. He was a member of the New Water-Colour Society. His subject matter comprised in the main views of Surrey, Hampshire and Ireland. Shalders died of a stroke in 1873.

MUSEUMS AND GALLERIES:

LIVERPOOL: *Fields near Canterbury* - LONDON (Victoria and Albert Mus.).

AUCTION RECORDS:

LONDON, 17 March 1922, *Sheep by the Roadside* (drawing) GBP 27. LONDON, 8 Dec 1922, *Flock* (drawing) GBP 22. LONDON, 7 March 1924, *Morning* (drawing) GBP 71. LONDON, 20 June 1972, *Flock Drinking*, GBP 450. LONDON, 18 April 1978, *At the Trough at Sunset* (1855, oil on canvas, 23 x 35 ins / 58.5 x 89 cm) GBP 650. LONDON, 25 May 1979, *Wooded Landscape with Mills* (oil on canvas, 32 1/2 x 53 1/2 ins / 82.5 x 135.9 cm) GBP 1,300. LONDON, 18 Sept 1979, *Shepherd in a Wooded Landscape* (watercolour and gouache, 19 x 32 ins / 48.3 x 81 cm) GBP 1,100. LONDON, 1 March 1983, *Evening Glow, Ranmore Common* (1865, gouache, 18 1/2 x 35 ins / 46.7 x 89 cm) GBP 1,700. LONDON, 19 Oct 1983, *Flock Drinking* (1857, oil on canvas, 25 1/4 x 43 ins / 64 x 109 cm) GBP 3,200. LONDON, 1 March 1984, *Shephered tending his Flock* (1861, watercolour heightened with gouache, 11 x 20 ins / 28 x 51 cm) GBP 900. LONDON, 3 June 1988, *A Breath of Fresh Air on a Summer's Day* (oil on canvas, 24 x 42 1/4 ins / 61 x 107 cm) GBP 2,640. NEUILLY-SUR-SEINE, 16 March 1989, *Landscape with Figures* (oil on canvas, 10 1/4 x 16 1/2 ins / 26 x 42 cm) FRF 12,000. LONDON, 13 Dec 1989, *Animals Slaking their Thirst in a Pond* (1860, oil on canvas, 12 1/4 x 22 ins / 31 x 56 cm) GBP 3,080. LONDON, 25-26 April 1990, *Picking Blackberries; Green Pastures* (1865, watercolour and gouache, each 11 1/2 x 19 ins / 29 x 48.5 cm) GBP 11,000. LONDON, 5 March 1993, *Vast Landscape with Shepherd and Flock, Surrey* (1870, watercolour and gouache, 14 1/2 x 30 1/2 ins / 37 x 77.5 cm) GBP 5,520. LONDON, 5 Nov 1993, *Children Picking Blackberries beisde a Shepherd and his Flock* (gouache, 11 1/2 x 19 1/4 ins / 29.2 x 49.1 cm) GBP 4,370. LONDON, 2 Nov 1994, *A Breath of Fresh Air on a Summer's Day* (oil on canvas, 23 3/4 x 42 ins / 60.5 x 106.5 cm) GBP 4,140. LONDON, 5 June 1996, *Noonday Rest* (1865, watercolour and gouache, 18 1/4 x 31 1/2 ins / 46.5 x 80 cm) GBP 8,050; *A Moment's Rest* (1863, watercolour and gouache, 18 x 31 ins / 45.5 x 79 cm) GBP 8,970. LONDON, 6 Nov 1997, *Herdsman in a Mountain Landscape with a Lake* (oil on canvas, 24 x 42 ins / 60.9 x 106.8 cm) GBP 2,990. BILLINGSHURST, 18 May 1999, *The Watering Place* (1856, oil on canvas, 23 x 41 ins / 59 x 105 cm) GBP 4,000. LONDON, 12 July 1999, *Shepherd and Dog with Flock in Landscape - near Holmbury, Dorking* (1870, watercolour and gouache, 11 x 19 ins / 29 x 49 cm) GBP 4,000. LONDON, 8 Feb 2000, *Herding the Flock at Dusk* (1869, watercolour and gouache, 8 x 20 ins / 21 x 52 cm) GBP 2,900. LIVERPOOL, 21 Nov 2000, *Lane and Mountain Scene in North Wales* (1857, oil on canvas, 23 x 41 ins / 58 x 103 cm) GBP 3,000. LEEDS, 13 March 2001, *Rural Scene with Figures beside Lane* (watercolour and gouache heightened with white, 28 x 19 ins / 72 x 47 cm) GBP 2,600. LONDON, 25 Oct 2001, *Shepherd and Sheep in a Wooded Glade* (1861, pencil, watercolour and gouache, 11 x 20 ins / 28 x 50 cm) GBP 3,500. SAN FRANCISCO, 15 May 2002, *Extensive Welsh Landscape with Cattle in the Foreground* (1859, oil on canvas, 22 x 36 ins / 56 x 92 cm) USD 14,000. LONDON, 21 Nov 2002, *Shepherd and his Flock in a Meadow. Returning Home* (1867, pencil, watercolour, gouache and gum arabic, two, 11 x 20 ins / 29 x 50 cm) GBP 2,500. SAN FRANCISCO, 14 May 2003, *Extensive Landscape at Dusk with Cows, Figures and a Dog* (1855, oil on canvas, 24 x 37 ins / 62 x 93 cm) USD 7,500. LONDON, 27 Nov 2003, *Through Woodland Pastures* (1870, watercolour heightened with gouache, 20 x 28 ins / 50 x 71 cm) GBP 8,000. LONDON, 27 May 2004, *Hesitation before Crossing* (oil on canvas, 24 x 34 ins / 61 x 86 cm) GBP 2,000. THOMASTON, 28 Aug 2004, *View in North Wales* (oil on canvas, 18 x 24 ins / 46 x 61 cm) USD 2,750.

SHALER, Frederick R.
American, 20th century.
Born 15 December 1880, in Findlay; died 27 December 1916, in Taormina (Sicily).
Painter.

Frederick R. Shaler was taught by William Chase and F. Du Mond in New York.

SHALER, Lynn
American, 20th - 21st century.
Born 1955, in Detroit (Michigan).
Active in France from 1984.
Engraver, painter.

Lynn Shaler settled in Paris in 1984. She is a painter and engraver as well as a photographer. She took part in the 1992 exhibition: *De Bonnard à Baselitz: Dix Ans d'enrichissements du cabinet des estampes 1978-1988* (*From Bonnard to Baselitz: A Decade of Acquisitions by the Prints Collection 1978-1988*), at the Bibliothèque Nationale, Paris.

BIBLIOGRAPHY:
'*Lynn Shaler: variations*' in *Art et Métiers du Livre* n° 182 p. 43, periodical, Paris, 1993.

MUSEUMS AND GALLERIES:
PARIS (BNF, Prints Collection): *Exits* (1982, etching and aquatint).

SHALLUS, Francis
American, 18th - 19th century.
Born c. 1774, in Philadelphia; died 12 November 1821, in Philadelphia.
Engraver (burin).

SHALOM-OF-SAFED, called the Seigermacher, called Moskowitz of Safed
Israeli, 20th century.
Born 1895; died 1980, in Safed.
Painter (gouache), watercolourist. Scenes with figures, religious subjects.

Shalom-of-Safed was a watchmaker of Polish-Russian exraction who began painting at the age of 60 in order to illustrate the Bible to his grandchildren. His naive creations included graphic elements inspired by tribal art.

In 2001, his work was shown at an exhibition held at the Vienna Kunsthaus, *Die Naibe, aufbruch ins verlorene paradies* (*The Naïve Painters, Journey to a Lost Paradise*), which featured some 200 of his works from the Charlotte Zander Museum in Bönnigheim.

BIBLIOGRAPHY:
Wiesel, Elie/Doron, Daniel, *Images from the Bible: the Paintings of Shalom of Safed*, Overlook Press, New York, 1980. *Die Naive, aufbruch ins verlorene paradies*, exhibition catalogue, Kunsthaus, Vienna, 2001 (text in German and English).

MUSEUMS AND GALLERIES:
BÖNNIGHEIM (Mus. Charlotte Zander).

AUCTION RECORDS:
NEW YORK, 24 Sept 1981, *Rebecca and Eliezer at the Well* (watercolour and gouache, 13 3/4 x 19 3/4 ins / 35 x 50 cm) USD 3,000. TEL AVIV, 16 May 1983, *Exodus* (gouache, 17 1/2 x 22 1/2 ins / 44.5 x 57 cm) ILS 137,760. JERUSALEM, 18 May 1985, *Illustration for a Haggadah* (1957, gouache, series of 20, 19 3/4 x 13 3/4 ins / 50 x 35 cm) USD 54,000. TEL AVIV, 1 Jan 1991, *Rabbi Moshe Alshich, the Blessed* (tempera/paper, 15 3/4 x 9 3/4 ins / 40 x 25 cm) USD 2,640. TEL AVIV, 30 June 1994, *Descending towards Egypt* (gouache, 19 1/2 x 13 1/4 ins / 49.5 x 33.5 cm) USD 2,875. NEW YORK, 10 Oct 1996, *Garden of Eden* (gouache and Indian ink/paper, 19 1/2 x 13 1/2 ins / 49.5 x 34.3 cm) USD 2,875.

SHAMCHIN, Mikhail Nikititch
Russian, 19th century.
Born 15 May 1777; died 24 March 1846.
Portrait artist.

This artist, the father of Petr Mikhailovich Shamchin, studied at the St Petersburg academy.

SHAMCHIN, Petr Mikhailovich
Russian, 19th century.
Born 10 January 1811; died 6 February 1895.
Painter. Religious subjects, portraits, figures, historical figures, scenes with figures.

A pupil at the St Petersburg academy, Shamchin painted a number of religious subjects for churches in St Petersburg.

MUSEUMS AND GALLERIES:
MOSCOW (Rumiantsev Mus.): *Study*; *St Aleksander Nevsky* - MOSCOW (State Tretyakov Gal.): *Portrait of the Daughter of the Painter F.P. Tolstoy*; *Portrait of Countess J.F. Tolstoia*; *Portrait of an Unknown Woman*; *Thraceteverine Dancing* - ST PETERSBURG (Gosudarstvennyj Russkij Muz.): *Holy Family*; *Portrait of the Artist*.

SHAMIRI, Behi
Italian, 20th - 21st century.
Born 1955.
Painter. Interiors with figures.

Behi Shamiri's paintings are figurative, often showing interiors, and explore the interaction of deep perspective and contrasting tones reminiscent of the chromatic range of Cremonini. A good example is *Interior and Light* (1990). Works by Shamiri were shown by the Forni Gallery, Bologna and the International Contemporary Art Fair, Paris (1990).

SHAMS AL-DIN, Ustadh
Persian School, 14th century.
Painter.

Ustadh Shams al-Din was active in the second half of the 14th century. He was the student of Ahmad Mousa and the master of Abd al-Havy and Junayd. A number of other painters also bear the name Shams al-Din. Although nothing remains of his art, he was undoubtedly one of the most important Persian painters of his era. It is known that he illustrated a famous *Shah-Nama* (*Book of Kings*); some have argued that this was the outstandingly rich and beautiful Demotte *Shah-Nama*, but this hypothesis has not met with general acceptance.

SHAN-MERRY, pseudonym of Manoële Antoine
French, 20th century.
Born 26 March 1935, in Paris.
Painter, draughtswoman, watercolourist.

Shan-Merry was trained at the École des Beaux-Arts in Angers and exhibited her work in other places and in various Salons, notably the Salon de la Société Nationale des Beaux-Arts, Salon des Artistes Français, Salon des Indépendants and Salon d'Automne. She is best known for her designs of Hermès scarves.

SHAND, J.
British, 19th century.
Active in London between 1818 and 1820.
Painter. Portraits.

SHANE, Frederick Emanuel
American, 20th century.
Born 2 February 1906, in Kansas City; died 1992.
Painter.

Frederick Shane was a pupil of Randall Davey and a member of the Société des Artistes Indépendants. He won several awards.

SHANG BIN, or Shang Pin
Chinese, 18th century.
Active c. 1760.
Painter.
One of Shang Bin's works, *Autumn Traveller*, signed and dated 1765, is in Cologne.
Museums and Galleries:
Cologne (Mus. für ostasiatische Kunst): *Autumn Traveller* (1765, ink and light colour on paper, handscroll).

SHANG CH'I. See **SHANG QI**

SHANG CHU. See **SHANG ZHU**

SHANG HSI. See **SHANG XI**

SHANG PIN. See **SHANG BIN**

SHANG QI, or Shang Ch'i
Chinese, 14th century.
Born in Caozhou (Shandong Province).
Active at the beginning of the 14th century.
Painter.
Shang Qi was a teacher at court during the reign of Emperor Yuan Chengzong (1295-1307). He later worked in the imperial library. He is known as a bamboo and landscape painter.
Museums and Galleries:
Beijing (Palace Mus.): *Spring Mountains* (ink and greenish colour on silk, handscroll) - Taipei (National Palace Mus.): *Stream with Summer Lotus at the Foot of a Mountain in the Clouds* (signed and dated 1314, after Zhao Lingrang, poem by Wang Da); *Two Crows, One in a Flowering Apricot Tree, the Other in the Water* (signed and dated 1315); *Walker Approaching a Taoist Retreat at the Foot of Mount Song* (signed and dated 1315); *Deep Gorge in the Mountains with Chess-players in a Pavilion Overlooking a Watercourse* (signed).

SHANGRUI, or Shang-jui, sobriquets: Xunjun, Jingrui, style names: Mucun, Pushizi
Chinese, 18th century.
Born in Suzhou (Jiangsu Province); died 1632.
Active 1700-1720.
Painter. Landscapes.
Shangrui was a priest and pupil of Wang Hui (1632-1717).
Museums and Galleries:
Taipei (National Palace Mus.): *10 Landscapes in the Style of the Ancients* (1686, signed album).
Auction records:
New York, 29 May 1991, *Landscapes* (1672, ink and colour on paper, eight-sheet album, each sheet 11 3/4 x 8 ins / 29.8 x 20.2 cm) USD 15,400. New York, 2 Dec 1992, *Landscape* (ink and colour on paper, hanging scroll, 63 1/4 x 43 1/4 ins / 160.6 x 109.8 cm) USD 6,600.

SHANG TSU. See **SHANG ZUO**

SHANG WENBIN, or Shang Wenpin
Chinese, 20th century.
Born 1932, in Jiangsu Province.
Painter. Animals.
Shang Wenbin graduated from the National Taiwan Normal University in 1955, where he had studied under Pu Ru, Huang Junbi and Liao Jichun. He later studied architecture in Belgium at the École Nationale Supérieure. While still abroad, he exhibited at the fifth International Exhibition at São Paulo in 1959 and in 1960 was invited by the Japanese government to take part in a cultural exchange. In 1990, he won first prize at the Montreal International Painting and Print Salon.
Bibliography:
Auction catalogue, Christie's, Hong Kong, March 22, 1993.
Auction records:
Hong Kong, 22 March 1993, *Racoon in Winter Forest* (1990, oil on canvas, 20 3/4 x 28 1/2 ins / 53 x 72.5 cm) HKD 46,000.

SHANG XI, or Shang Hsi, sobriquet: Weiji
Chinese, 15th century.
Born in Puyang (Henan Province).
Active c. 1430-1440.
Painter.
Shang Xi was an officer in the imperial guard and a court painter. He painted tigers, landscapes, figures, and flowers and birds in the style of the Song masters.
Museums and Galleries:
Hakone: *Lao Zi Crossing the Barrier* (ink and light colour on paper, short handscroll, signed) - Taipei (National Palace Mus.): *Man Sitting by a River* (signed and dated 1427, fan); *Emperor Xuanzong's Hunting Party*; *Flowers* (signed and dated 1441, colophon by Wang Guxiang); *Dog, Cat and Birds on Garden Terrace*.

SHANG ZHU, or Shang Chu, sobriquet: Taiyuan, style name: Sunzhai
Chinese, 13th - 14th century.
Active during the Yuan dynasty (1279-1368).
Painter.
Shang Zhu was a landscape painter in the *pomo* (broken ink) style and a painter of rocks. He is known for a handscroll, *Moon over Mountain Village*, signed and dated 1342.

SHANG ZUO, or Shang Tsu
Chinese, 16th - 17th century.
Active at the end of the Ming dynasty (1368-1644).
Painter.
Shang Zuo was the grandson of the painter Shang Xi (active in about 1430-1440). He is known for his pictures of tigers and flowers.
Museums and Galleries:
Taipei (National Palace Mus.): *Hollyhocks in Autumn* (signed).

SHANG-JUI. See **SHANGRUI**

SHANG-KUAN CHOU. See **ZHOU SHANGGUAN**

SHANKS, William Sommerville
British, 19th - 20th century.
Born 1864, in Gourock (Inverclyde), Scotland; died 1951.
Watercolourist, painter (gouache). Genre scenes, interiors with figures, flowers.
William Shanks was a pupil of Benjamin Constant and Jean-Paul Laurens in Paris. He lived and worked in Glasgow, and won a silver medal at the Paris Salon of 1933.

W. S. Shanks

Auction records:
Auchterarder, 30 Aug 1983, *Still-life* (oil on card, 20 x 24 ins / 51 x 61 cm) GBP 1,300. Perth, 27 Aug 1985, *C.E.G.* (oil on canvas, 20 x 24 1/2 ins / 51 x 62 cm) GBP 1,400. Edinburgh, 30 April 1986, *The Green Bottle* (oil on canvas, 14 x 12 ins / 35.4 x 30.5 cm) GBP 3,500. Edinburgh, 22 Nov 1989, *The Small Salon at Rosyth* (oil on card, 12 x 18 ins / 30.5 x 45.7 cm) GBP 1,650. South Queensferry, 1 May 1990, *Secrets* (oil on panel, 11 3/4 x 12 ins / 30 x 30.5 cm) GBP 2,750. Glasgow, 22 Nov 1990, *The Pink Bouquet* (oil on card, 18 1/2 x 12 1/4 ins / 47 x 30.8 cm) GBP 2,200. Edinburgh, 28 April 1992, *Butter-churning* (oil on canvas, 24 x 36 ins / 61 x 91.5 cm) GBP 1,540. Edinburgh, 13 May 1993, *Rhododendrons* (oil on canvas, 25 x 30 ins / 63.5 x 76.2 cm) GBP 6,050. Glasgow, 14 Feb 1995, *Reverie* (watercolour and gouache, 29 1/2 x 21 1/2 ins / 75 x 54.5 cm) GBP 3,450. Edinburgh, 7 April 2000, *Woodland Scene* (oil on panel, 19 x 19 ins / 47 x 48 cm) GBP 1,000. London, 26 Oct 2000, *Still-life with Pears, Apple and Jug* (oil on canvas, 20 x 24 ins / 51 x 61 cm) GBP 16,000. London, 1 Nov

2001, *Still-life with a Lobster on a Platter* (oil on canvas, 20 x 24 ins / 51 x 61 cm) GBP 8,000. LONDON, 6 Dec 2001, *Still-life with Roses* (oil on board, 10 x 14 ins / 25 x 35 cm) GBP 3,500. LONDON, 7 March 2002, *Portrait of a Lady in a White Dress* (oil on canvas, 30 x 25 ins / 76 x 63 cm) GBP 1,600. LONDON, 31 Oct 2002, *Still-life with Roses. Still-life with Oranges* (oil on canvas, a pair, 10 x 14 ins / 25 x 35 cm) GBP 6,000. CAMBRIDGE, 15 Jan 2003, *Red, White and Blue* (oil on canvas, 21 x 17 ins / 54 x 44 cm) GBP 1,600. EDINBURGH, 8 April 2004, *Still-life of Irises and Japanese Prints* (oil on canvas, 30 x 24 ins / 75 x 62 cm) GBP 1,100. EDINBURGH, 18 Aug 2004, *Larder Still-life* (oil on canvas, 25 x 33 ins / 64 x 84 cm) GBP 1,300.

SHANNAN, A. MacFARLANE
British, 19th - 20th century.
Born in Glasgow; died 29 September 1915, in Glasgow.
Sculptor. Figures. Busts.

MUSEUMS AND GALLERIES:
GLASGOW (AG and Mus.): *Bust of G.R. Mather; Bust of H.A. Long; Rev. D. Macrae.*

SHANNON, Charles Haslewood
British, 19th - 20th century.
Born 26 April 1863, in Sleaford (Lincolnshire); died 18 March 1937, in Kew (Surrey).
Painter, draughtsman. Figures, portraits, genre scenes.

Charles Shannon studied engraving at Lambeth School of Art, where he became associated with Charles Ricketts, with whom he founded the Vale Press, a specialist publisher of bibliophile works. He visited Holland and Italy, and was an associate member of the Royal Academy in London in 1911 and 1921 (according to some sources). He took part in numerous British exhibitions from 1885, and illustrated works by Oscar Wilde and Christopher Marlowe.

BIBLIOGRAPHY:

MUSEUMS AND GALLERIES:
BREMEN: *Head of an Old Man* - PARIS (former Mus. du Luxembourg): *Portrait of Mrs Bruce, Sculptress* - VICTORIA: *Souvenir of Van Dyck, Miss Kate Dressed as a Kitchen Boy.*

AUCTION RECORDS:
LONDON, 9 Feb 1923, *Alphonse Legros* (black chalk and white chalk) GBP 11. LONDON, 28 Nov 1933, *The Toilette,* GBP 62. LONDON, 15 May 1942, *Charles Richette* (drawing) GBP 36. LONDON, 12 Oct 1973, *Sea-shell Gatherers,* Gns 5,200. LONDON, 10 May 1974, *The Childhood of Bacchus,* Gns 2,500. LONDON, 25 Oct 1977, *Wood-nymph* (oil on canvas, 43 x 44 ins / 109 x 112 cm) GBP 1,300. LONDON, 8 March 1978, *The Golden Age* (1921-1922, oil on canvas, 56 x 43 ins / 142 x 109.5 cm) GBP 900. LONDON, 8 June 1979, *Swimmers* (oil on canvas, 16 1/2 x 16 1/2 ins / 42 x 42 cm) GBP 460. LONDON, 12 June 1981, *Romantic Landscape* (1904, oil on canvas, 32 3/4 x 31 ins / 83.2 x 79 cm) GBP 2,800. LONDON, 21 June 1983, *The Childhood of Bacchus* (1919-1920, oil on canvas, 48 x 43 ins / 122 x 109 cm) GBP 4,000. LONDON, 13 Nov 1985, *Brown and Silver* (oil on canvas, 13 x 13 ins / 33 x 33 cm) GBP 2,200. SAN FRANCISCO, 12 June 1986, *Golden Angel* (1921-1922, oil on canvas, 56 x 43 1/2 ins / 142 x 110.5 cm) USD 4,500. LONDON, 9 June 1988, *Portrait of a Young Girl in a Black Hat* (1915, oil on canvas, 29 1/2 x 24 1/2 ins / 75 x 62.5 cm) GBP 3,520. LONDON, 27 June 1988, *The Siren* (oil on canvas, 21 1/4 x 23 1/2 ins / 54 x 60 cm) GBP 17,600. LONDON, 25 Jan 1989, *Portrait of a Woman* (coloured chalk, 11 1/2 x 9 1/2 ins / 29 x 24 cm) GBP 462. LONDON, 25-26 April 1990, *Study for Tibullus in the House of Delia* (pastel, 18 x 24 3/4 ins / 46 x 63 cm) GBP 1,045. LONDON, 26 Sept 1990, *Wounded Amazon* (1899, white chalk heightened with red chalk/tinted paper, 15 3/4 x 9 ins / 40 x 23 cm) GBP 825. LONDON, 12 Nov 1992, *Siren* (oil on canvas, 23 1/4 x 21 ins / 59 x 53.5 cm) GBP 11,000. LONDON, 7 June 1995, *Wounded Amazon* (1922, oil on canvas, 40 x 32 1/4 ins / 101.5 x 82 cm) GBP 3,680. LONDON, 24 Sept 2002, *Visitation* (watercolour and gouache, sold with a lithograph, 4 x 5 ins / 11 x 12 cm) GBP 1,100. LONDON, 20 Feb 2003, *Brown and Silver* (oil on canvas, 13 x 13 ins / 32 x 32 cm) GBP 5,500. LONDON, 20 Feb 2003, *Rose and Blanche* (oil on canvas, 42 x 39 ins / 107 x 98 cm) GBP 45,000. LONDON, 24 Nov 2004, *Study for Autumn. Study of a Reclining Figure* (pencil and brown wash, double-sided, 15 x 8 ins / 39 x 21 cm) GBP 4,800.

SHANNON, Howard Johnson
American, 19th - 20th century.
Born 30 May 1876, in Jamaica (New York).
Painter, illustrator.

Howard Johnson Shannon was a pupil of Herbert Adams.

SHANNON, James Jebusa (Sir)
American, 19th - 20th century.
Born 1862, in Auburn; died 6 March 1923, in London.
Active in England from 1878.
Painter. Portraits, genre scenes.

James Jebusa Shannon was from an Irish-American family. At the age of 16 he went to England, where he studied for three years at the South Kensington School under Sir Edward James Poynter, and while he was in London he won a gold medal. He first became known after his *Portrait of Miss Horatia Slopford,* shown at the Royal Academy in 1881. He had intended to return to America, but as a result of his rapid success he decided to stay in London. He received numerous commissions from a wide variety of sources. In 1886 he became a member of the New English Art Club and a member of the Royal Institute of Painters in Watercolours; he became an associate member of the Royal Academy in 1897 and a full member in 1909. He was knighted in 1922, the year before he died.

Shannon's first exhibition was at the Royal Academy in London in 1880, where he won a gold medal. He was noticed by Whistler, his fellow American, and this enabled him to exhibit at the Royal Society of British Artists and at the Société Internationale. He also participated in collective exhibitions in Paris such as the Exposition Universelle in 1889 and 1900, where he won a gold medal the first year and a silver medal the following year.

MUSEUMS AND GALLERIES:
BIRMINGHAM: *Alderman Edward Lawley Parker* - BRADFORD (Cartwright Hall AG): *The Stairs* - CAPE TOWN: *Forbidden Fruit* - CARDIFF: *Green Vase* - LIVERPOOL: *Mgr Nugent; Daydreaming* - LIVERPOOL (Walker AG): *Princess Mary* (1915) - LONDON (Tate Collection): *Young Girl with Flowers.*

AUCTION RECORDS:
LONDON, 17 May 1923, *White Water-lilies,* GBP 33. LONDON, 9 Nov 1976, *Portrait of a Little Girl* (1892, oil on canvas, 57 1/2 x 29 1/2 ins / 146 x 75 cm) GBP 500. LONDON, 18 June 1985, *Mrs Agnes Williamson* (1887, oil on canvas, 67 3/4 x 40 1/4 ins / 172 x 102 cm) GBP 33,000. LONDON, 12 Nov 1986, *Madonna and Child* (oil on canvas, 33 x 27 1/2 ins / 84 x 70 cm) GBP 15,000. NEW YORK, 24 May 1988, *Portrait of a Gentleman at a Hunt Dinner* (1887, oil on canvas, 30 x 17 1/2 ins / 76.2 x 44.4 cm) USD 79,750. LONDON, 2 March 1989, *Portrait of a Young Girl with a White Lawn Cap* (1897, oil on canvas, 24 x 18 1/4 ins / 61.2 x 46.2 cm) GBP 8,800. NEW YORK, 23 May 1989, *Dirkja, Young Dutch Girl* (oil on canvas, 16 1/4 x 12 ins / 41.3 x 30.5 cm) USD 13,200. NEW YORK, 22 May 1990, *Young Woman in Blue, Miss H. Strom* (oil on canvas, 24 3/4 x 20 1/2 ins / 62.9 x 52.1 cm) USD 28,600. NEW YORK, 23 May 1990, *Portrait of*

Ruby Miller (oil on canvas, 77 x 42 ins / 195.6 x 106.7 cm) USD 33,000. NEW YORK, 17 Oct 1991, *Portrait of Miss Annie Beebe* (1886, oil on canvas, 44 3/4 x 34 1/4 ins / 113.7 x 87 cm) USD 33,000. EDINBURGH, 19 Nov 1992, *Young Master and the Little Misses* (oil on canvas, 76 x 58 ins / 193 x 147.2 cm) GBP 11,000. LONDON, 5 Nov 1993, *Lady Dickson-Poynder and her Daughter Joan* (oil on canvas, 72 1/4 x 44 ins / 183.2 x 111.5 cm) GBP 54,300. NEW YORK, 26 May 1994, *Molly, Tim and Dorothy, the Children of James Younger* (oil on canvas, 76 x 58 ins / 193 x 147.3 cm) USD 118,000. LONDON, 5 June 1996, *Portrait of a Little Girl* (1890, oil on canvas, 17 x 14 ins / 43 x 35.5 cm) GBP 3,220. NEW YORK, 10 Feb 1998, *Portrait of a Woman in a Pink and White Dress* (1894, oil on canvas, 36 x 28 ins / 91.5 x 71.1 cm) USD 5,175.

SHANNON, Thomas or Tom
American, 20th - 21st century.
Born 1947.
Sculptor, installation artist, performance artist, video artist.

Thomas Shannon lives and works in New York. Besides his work as an artist he is known for scientific discoveries, especially in the field of astronomy. He portrays magnetic phenomena in his installations evoking space and the universe. They can be spectacular, like the overhead *Compass Moon atom room*, consisting of 270 spheres ranging over various levels between floor and ceiling. He is also inspired by everyday objects which he transforms: a completely flexible electric car, a four-way reversible jacket, a clock showing the time all over the world simultaneously. He also makes videos. Collective exhibitions include: Château d'Orion, Expo 93, Seoul, 1993. Solo exhibitions include: Ronald Feldman Gallery, New York, 1981; Dart Gallery, Chicago, 1984; ARC, Musée d'Art Moderne de la Ville de Paris, 1987; Cincinnati Contemporary Art Centre and Musée de la Marine, Paris, 1993; and Espace Art 04, St-Rémy-de-Provence, 1994.

BIBLIOGRAPHY:
Sans, Jérôme, '*Interview: Thomas Shannon - Une vision globale*' in *Art Press* n° 181, periodical, Paris, June 1993. J., M., '*Shannon, artiste magnétique*' in *Beaux-Arts Magazine* n° 126, periodical, Paris, September 1994.

SHANON, Anna
Polish, 20th century.
Born 1916 or 1920.
Active in Israel, then in France.
Collage artist.

Anna Shanon studied first in Jerusalem, then in Paris, where she settled. She made fragile-looking, earth-coloured collages of delicate geometrical construction that exploited the texture of the paper and its flaws. She took part in various collective exhibitions including: Musée d'Art et d'Industrie, St-Étienne (1964); *Rencontres - Cinquante ans de collages* (*Encounters - Fifty Years of Collage*), Galerie Claudine Lustman, Paris (1991). After 1957 she held regular solo exhibitions in Paris, notably at the Galerie Jaquester (1984 to 1987).

BIBLIOGRAPHY:
Monnin, Françoise, *Rencontres - Cinquante ans de collages*, exhibition catalogue, Gal. Claudine Lustman, Paris, 1991.

AUCTION RECORDS:
PARIS, 16 June 1991, *Untitled* (1975, collage, 24 1/2 x 17 3/4 ins / 62 x 45 cm) FRF 4,500.

SHAO BAO, or Shao Pao, sobriquet: Guoxian, style names: Quanzhai, Erquan
Chinese, 15th - 16th century.
Born 1460; died 1527.
Painter.

Shao Bao was head of the Bureau of Rites and a flower painter. He is not mentioned in the official artists' biographies, and what is known of him comes from the *Chronicle of Wuxi*.

MUSEUMS AND GALLERIES:
TAIPEI (National Palace Mus.).

SHAO FEI
Chinese, 20th - 21st century.
Born 1954, in Beijing.
Painter. Figure compositions, landscapes, animals.

Shao Fei was introduced to painting by her mother, Shao Jingkun, a trained artist of the Socialist Realism school. In 1970, she enlisted in the army and put her artistic gifts at the service of propaganda, designing posters. In 1976, she was appointed member of the Beijing art academy. Although representational, Shao Fei's work is very free and her compositions of geometricised figures and surroundings are full of content and decorative intention. She was involved in the foundation of the *Stars* group, exhibiting with it in 1979-1980. Since then she has taken part in major shows in China and abroad, having her work shown in 1982 at the Central Art Academy Exhibition in Beijing and then in Canada, in 1984-1985 in the travelling show *Contemporary Chinese Painting* in the USA and in 1989 in *Stars: Ten Years* in Taiwan and Hong Kong.

AUCTION RECORDS:
TAIPEI, 22 March 1992, *Dance* (1991, oil on canvas, 28 1/2 x 35 ins / 72.5 x 89.2 cm) TWD 286,000. HONG KONG, 30 March 1992, *Gilded Autumn* (ink and colour on paper, hanging scroll, 36 x 46 1/4 ins / 91.2 x 117.3 cm) HKD 41,800; *Tiger Training* (1990, oil on canvas, 25 3/4 x 31 1/2 ins / 65.4 x 80 cm) HKD 88,000; *Goldfish* (1990, oil on canvas, 39 x 46 ins / 99.3 x 116 cm) HKD 82,500. HONG KONG, 28 Sept 1992, *Sister Flower* (1992, oil on canvas, 30 x 30 ins / 76 x 76 cm) HKD 104,500. HONG KONG, 22 March 1993, *Blessing* (oil on canvas, 39 3/4 x 39 3/4 ins / 101 x 101 cm) HKD 115,000. HONG KONG, 4 May 1995, *Murmurs from the Lotus Pool* (1993, oil on canvas, 31 3/4 x 39 1/4 ins / 80.6 x 99.4 cm) HKD 69,000. HONG KONG, 30 April 1996, *Joy of the Farm* (oil on canvas, 33 1/4 x 42 1/2 ins / 84.5 x 107.9 cm) HKD 51,750. TAIPEI, 18 April 1999, *Modern People* (oil on canvas, 24 x 30 ins / 60 x 76 cm) TWD 100,000.

SHAO GAO, or Shao Kao, sobriquet: Migao
Chinese, 17th century.
Born in Suzhou (Jiangsu Province).
Active c. 1627.
Painter.

Shao Gao was a landscape painter. He is known for a single work, *Landscape with Man in a Pavilion Overlooking a River*, signed and dated 1627.

SHAO JINGKUN
Chinese, 20th century.
Born 1932, in Harbin (Heilongjiang Province).
Painter. Flowers.

Shao Jingkun studied under Xu Beihong and other teachers at the national art academy in Beijing, graduating in 1953. She taught at the academy from that date. In 1962, she went with Dong Xiwen and Wu Guanzhong on a tour of Tibet, bringing back a number of works that were later shown in a travelling exhibition in China. She is the mother of Shao Fei.

AUCTION RECORDS:
HONG KONG, 4 May 1995, *Lilies* (1995, oil on canvas, 29 1/2 x 31 3/4 ins / 75.2 x 80.6 cm) HKD 69,000. HONG KONG, 30 Oct 1995, *Peonies* (1995, oil on canvas, 31 3/4 x 29 1/2 ins / 80.6 x 75.2 cm) HKD 40,250.

SHAO KAO. See **SHAO GAO**

SHAO MI, sobriquet: Sengmi, style names: Guachou, Guanyuansou, etc
Chinese, 17th century.
Born in Suzhou (Jiangsu Province).
Active 1620-1660.
Painter. Landscapes.

Shao Mi was a great poet and calligrapher and one of the Nine Friends of Painting. He painted landscapes in the style of Ni Zan (1301-1374) and Zhao Mengfu (1254-1322). His work is known for the great freedom of its brushwork: sometimes the only detail is in his faces and hands.

MUSEUMS AND GALLERIES:

BEIJING (Palace Mus.): *Figure in a Pavilion Overlooking a River Shaded by Old Trees at the Foot of a High Mountain* (ink and colour on silk, in the manner of Tang Yin, according to an inscription by the artist); *Landscape Studies* (ink and light colour on paper, twelve album sheets) - LONDON (British Mus.): *Bare Trees and Pointed Hills* (signed and dated 1643, album sheet) - NEW YORK (Metropolitan Mus. of Art): *Weeping Willows on an Island* (signed and dated 1640, fan) - SHANGHAI: *Goose* (boneless (meigu) technique, inscription by the artist dated 1630) - TAIPEI (National Palace Mus.): *Guanyin* (signed and dated 1626, ink on paper, hanging scroll); *Two Men Entering a Lake Pavilion* (signed and dated 1637, fan); *Plum Blossom* (signed and dated 1662, ink); *Small 10-sheet Landscape Album (Some after Tang Yin)* (colour); *Landscapes* (two signed album sheets).

AUCTION RECORDS:

TAIPEI, 10 April 1994, *Plum Tree* (ink and colour on gilded paper, fan, 6 3/4 x 19 ins / 17 x 48 cm) TWD 368,000. NEW YORK, 31 May 1994, *Landscape with Fishing Boats* (ink and colour on gilded paper, fan, 5 3/4 x 23 ins / 14.9 x 58.7 cm) USD 5,175. HONG KONG, 25 April 2004, *Landscape* (1634, ink, hanging scroll, 44 x 11 ins / 111 x 29 cm) HKD 95,000.

SHAO PAO. See **SHAO BAO**

SHAPER, Johann. See **SCHAPER**

SHAPIRO, Joël

American, 20th century.

Born 1941, in New York.

Sculptor, engraver, draughtsman, painter (gouache).

New Image (related to).

Joël Shapiro began his visual arts studies at the University of New York in 1964. Living and working in New York, he began in 1970 with small works consisting of 1.5 centimetre sheets of building materials such as concrete, earth, wood and aluminium placed on shelves. Although on the margin of Minimal Art, then at its apogee, the only thing Shapiro's work has in common with this style is the choice of raw material. *Weight Pieces*, magnesium and lead bars of different sizes but the same weight, was created in this vein. The following year, he concentrated on the hand with *Hand Forming Pieces*, and a work emphasising the 'traditional touch' of the artist modelling logs, rolls or balls of clay with his fingers, sculpting bowls in pine and then assembling them on the ground. From 1973, his highly stylised small-scale buildings were based on the theme of the interior (houses, furniture, bridges, coffins). The geometric modules are abstract in shape yet familiar, since a house with bricked-up doors and windows can be discerned at the end of a road, or on a bridge. 'Is it a pentagon or a house?' he asks. He then progressed to more open spaces, comparing interiors and exteriors, flat surfaces and volume. From then on, there is a strong presence of the real in his engravings, as in the 1975 series of etchings of household scenes and in his charcoal drawings and gouaches, which are reminiscent of architectural plans. After this, his work referred to the physical world, and the only remaining reference to Abstraction is the minimalist form of his Constructivist-style hand-made bronze, plaster and wood works. In the 1980s, he returned to large works and introduced long anthropomorphic forms, similar to the figures of Giacometti, whom he admires. There is one recognisable figure in his works, usually assemblages of wooden beams in square section (deal, poplar, pine) or cast in bronze or steel, and also in a rough plaster cast and two hollowed-out parallelipipeds. This figure dances, runs or falls with a body fully engaged in the action. Precariously balanced, seemingly impossible, 'trees' came next. The tree motif was already present in the 1976-1978 reliefs. Set on plinths, branches consisting of layouts of different length painted cylindrical timbers suggest the vital impetus and appear to divide at random in a subtle game of bifurcation and broken angles, which gives the work a unique rhythm.

Shapiro has always occupied an original place in American sculpture, contemporary to but on the margins of Minimal Art, with which it is sometimes compared. While he works from raw materials such as wood, lead and plaster and produces series of geometric forms such as rectangles laid out in paralellipipeds, with variations and permutations on an initial structure, he refuses to present his pieces as they are and reduce them to linear 'primary structures' used for their own qualities. Instead, he chooses to portray them as if at a distance, at eye level on shelves, on the ground, forcing the viewer to approach them and to bend down even further the smaller the pieces are, or on a plinth. He claims their strong power to bring back memories links them with reality, especially with a private world. 'I try to transpose my personal experience so that the work becomes something other than a manufactured object. If it is successful it calls on the memory,' An heir of Rodin, Brancussi and Giacometti, as well as of the Minimalists, Shapiro affirms his desire to express universal, human sentiments, through the abstract signs he uses as metaphors for man.

He has participated in many collective exhibitions, and especially large shows devoted to sculpture, including: *Anti-Illusion: Procedures/Materials*, 1969; *The New Sculpture 1965-1975: Between Geometry and Gesture*, at the Whitney Museum of American Art, New York, 1990. Solo exhibitions include: regular shows at the Paula Cooper Gallery in New York, since 1970; Institute for Art and Urban Resources, New York, 1973; Museum of Contemporary Art, Chicago, 1976; travelling exhibition organised by the Albright Knox Art Gallery, Birmingham, Michigan, 1977; the Whitechapel Art Gallery, London, 1980; Israel Museum, Jerusalem, 1981; a travelling exhibition organised by the Whitney Museum of American Art, New York, 1982; a travelling exhibition organised by the Stedelijk Museum, Amsterdam, 1985; Seattle Art Museum, 1986; Galerie Daniel Templon, Paris, 1986 and 1988; Hirschhorn Museum of Art, Toledo, Ohio, 1989; travelling exhibitions organised by the Des Moines Art Centre and in Europe by the Louisiana Museum of Modern Art, Humlebaek, 1990; Miami Centre for the Fine Arts, 1991; Seoul, 1994; Walker Art Centre and Sculpture Garden, Minneapolis, Galerie Karsten Greve, Paris. He has received many awards and prizes, including: National Endowment for the Arts, 1975; Medal of Merit for Sculpture at the American Academy and the New York Institute of Letters, 1990. In 1994, he became a member of the Swedish Royal Academy of Arts. Public commissions include: the Washington Holocaust Memorial Museum, 1993; Sony Plaza, New York, 1994-1995; Friedrichstadt Passage, Berlin, 1994-1995; Kansas City International Airport, 1996.

BIBLIOGRAPHY:

Joël Shapiro, exhibition catalogue, Museum of Contemporary Art, Chicago, 1976. *Joël Shapiro*, exhibition catalogue, Whitney Museum of American Art, New York, 1982. *Joël Shapiro: Painted Wood*, exhibition catalogue, Hirshhorn Museum and Sculpture Garden, Washington DC, 1987. *Joël Shapiro*, exhibition catalogue, Instituto Valenciano de Arte Moderno (IVAM) Centro Julio González, Valencia, 1990. *Joël Shapiro*, exhibition catalogue, Musée des Beaux-Arts, Calais, 1991. Smulders, Caroline, '*Joël Shapiro - L'Espace métaphorique*' in *Art Press* n° 159, periodical, Paris, June 1991. *Joël Shapiro - Outdoors*, exhibition catalogue, Walker Art Center, Minneapolis, Nelson Atkins Museum of Art, Kansas

City, 1995. Suchère, Éric, *'Joël Shapiro'* in *Art Press* n° 204, periodical, Paris, July-August 1995. Brenson, Michael, *Joël Shapiro*, exhibition catalogue, Pace Wildenstein Gall., Los Angeles, 1996.

MUSEUMS AND GALLERIES:

AMSTERDAM (Stedelijk Mus.) - ATLANTA (High Mus. of Art) - BALTIMORE (MA) - BOSTON (MFA) - BUFFALO (Albright-Knox AG) - CINCINNATI (AM): *Untitled* (bronze); *Untitled No.1* (engraving) - CLEVELAND (MA) - DALLAS (MA): *Untitled* (1975, iron); *Untitled* (1981-1984, bronze) - DENVER (AM) - DES MOINES (Art Center) - DETROIT (IA) - HOUSTON (MFA) - HUMLEBÆK (Louisiana Mus. for Moderne Kunst) - JERUSALEM (Israel Mus.) - LONDON (British Mus.) - LONDON (Tate Collection): *Untitled* (1978 and 1984, bronze, two sculptures) - LOS ANGELES (County MA) - LOS ANGELES (MCA) - MINNEAPOLIS (Walker Art Center) - MUNICH (Städtische Gal. im Lenbachhaus) - NEW YORK (Brooklyn Mus.) - NEW YORK (Metropolitan Mus. of Art) - NEW YORK (MoMA) - NEW YORK (Whitney Mus. of American Art) - PARIS (MNAM-CCI) - PHILADELPHIA (MA) - SAN DIEGO (MA) - ST LOUIS (AM) - STOCKHOLM (Moderna Mus.) - TEL AVIV (MA) - TOLEDO (MA) - TORONTO (AG of Ontario) - VALENCIA (IVAM Centre Julio González) - WASHINGTON DC (Corcoran Gal. of Art) - WASHINGTON DC (Hirshhorn Mus. and Sculpture Garden) - WASHINGTON DC (NGA): *Finger Print Drawing* (1969, finger painting in black ink on paper); *Untitled* (1987, charcoal and black chalk/wove paper) - ZURICH (Kunsthaus).

AUCTION RECORDS:

NEW YORK, 8 Nov 1983, *Untitled* (1979, bronze, 11 1/2 x 11 1/4 x 13 1/2 ins / 29 x 28.5 x 34 cm) USD 22,000. NEW YORK, 6 May 1986, *Untitled JS405* (1980, wood, 8 1/2 x 17 x 4 ins / 21.5 x 43.2 x 10.2 cm) USD 14,000. NEW YORK, 8 Oct 1986, *Untitled* (1975, charcoal, 35 x 46 ins / 88.9 x 116.8 cm) USD 4,000. NEW YORK, 6 May 1987, *Untitled* (1978, charcoal/paper, 22 1/4 x 30 ins / 56.5 x 76.2 cm) USD 6,500. NEW YORK, 9 Nov 1989, *Untitled* (bronze, 9 1/2 x 10 ins / 24 x 25.4 cm) USD 242,000. NEW YORK, 23 Feb 1990, *Untitled* (1972, acrylic/canvas, 8 1/4 x 28 ins / 21 x 71.1 cm) USD 7,700. NEW YORK, 9 May 1990, *Untitled* (1988, pastel/paper, 88 1/2 x 60 ins / 224.8 x 152.3 cm) USD 88,000. NEW YORK, 15 Feb 1991, *Untitled* (gilt-patinated bronze, 9 x 7 x 6 1/2 ins / 23 x 18 x 16.5 cm) USD 27,500. NEW YORK, 1 May 1991, *Untitled* (1974, bronze/wooden base, 12 1/4 x 5 1/4 x 9 1/2 ins / 31.1 x 13.3 x 24.1 cm) USD 49,500. NEW YORK, 13 Nov 1991, *Untitled* (1987, charcoal and coloured chalks/paper, 30 3/4 x 23 ins / 78.1 x 58.4 cm) USD 15,400. LONDON, 26 March 1992, *Untitled* (bronze, 2 1/2 x 2 3/4 x 2 ins / 6.4 x 7.3 x 4.8 cm) GBP 9,900. NEW YORK, 5 May 1992, *Untitled* (bronze, 90 x 6 3/4 x 22 1/4 ins / 228.6 x 17 x 56.5 cm) USD 242,000. NEW YORK, 6 May 1992, *Untitled (JSS 866)* (1989, bronze, 70 x 80 x 30 ins / 177.8 x 203.2 x 76.2 cm) USD 220,000. NEW YORK, 6 Oct 1992, *Untitled* (cast iron on wood, 4 1/2 x 35 x 2 1/4 ins / 11.4 x 88.9 x 5.7 cm) USD 49,500. NEW YORK, 17 Nov 1992, *Untitled* (bronze, 53 x 64 x 45 1/2 ins / 134.6 x 162.6 x 115.5 cm) USD 264,000. NEW YORK, 19 Nov 1992, *Untitled (JS 712)* (oil on wood, 54 1/2 x 12 1/2 x 9 3/4 ins / 138.4 x 31.6 x 24.7 cm) USD 66,000. NEW YORK, 3 May 1993, *Untitled* (bronze, 90 x 67 x 22 1/4 ins / 228.6 x 170.2 x 56.5 cm) USD 233,500. NEW YORK, 5 May 1994, *Untitled (JS 625)* (1985, bronze, 117 x 133 x 72 ins / 297.2 x 337.8 x 182.9 cm) USD 167,500. NEW YORK, 14 Nov 1995, *Untitled* (1989, bronze, 65 x 79 x 50 ins / 165.1 x 200.7 x 127 cm) USD 200,500. NEW YORK, 7 May 1996, *Untitled* (1989, bronze, 90 x 67 x 22 1/4 ins / 228.6 x 170.1 x 56.5 cm) USD 404,000. LONDON, 27 June 1996, *Untitled* (bronze, 60 x 58 x 27 ins / 152.5 x 147.3 x 68.5 cm) GBP 34,500. NEW YORK, 19 Nov 1996, *Untitled* (1981-1984, bronze, 47 x 49 1/4 x 45 3/4 ins / 119.4 x 125.1 x 116.2 cm) USD 118,000. NEW YORK, 20 Nov 1996, *Untitled* (1987, bronze, 15 1/4 x 14 1/4 x 8 ins / 38.7 x 36.2 x 20.3 cm) USD 43,125. NEW YORK, 21 Nov 1996, *Untitled* (1989, charcoal, coloured chalks and graphite on paper, 30 1/2 x 23 ins / 77.5 x 58.4 cm) USD 17,825. NEW YORK, 7 May 1997, *Untitled* (1989, bronze, 39 x 20 1/2 ins / 99.1 x 52.1 cm) USD 21,850. NEW YORK, 7-8 May 1997, *Untitled* (1982-1983, bronze, in three parts, 35 x 19 x 37 ins / 88.8 x 48.2 x 94 cm; 60 1/4 x 31 1/2 x 104 ins/153 x 80 x 264.2 cm and 17 x 43 1/2 x 15 1/2 ins/43.2 x 110.5 x 39.4 cm) USD 607,500. NEW YORK, 8 May 1997, *Untitled* (1986-1987, oil on wood, 64 x 46 x 31 ins / 162.5 x 117 x 79 cm) USD 211,500. NEW YORK, 16 Nov 1999, *Untitled* (1987-1988, bronze, 64 x 38x40 ins / 162 x 96x102 cm) USD 180,000. NEW YORK, 16 Nov 1999, *Untitled* (1995, cast bronze, one of three, 111 x 50x38 ins / 282 x 127x96 cm) USD 190,000. NEW YORK, 18 May 2000, *Untitled* (1986-1987, bronze, one of four, 37 x 20x14 ins / 94 x 51x36 cm) USD 42,000. NEW YORK, 18 May 2000, *Running Man* (1985-1986, bronze, 12 x 9x4 ins / 30 x 24x10 cm) USD 45,000. NEW YORK, 16 May 2001, *Untitled* (1978, bronze and wood, 13 x 25x20 ins / 33 x 63x50 cm) USD 75,000. NEW YORK, 14 Nov 2001, *Untitled - JS 936A-B* (1990-1991, bronze, in two parts, 35 x 50x22 ins / 89 x 128x56 cm) USD 130,000. NEW YORK, 16 May 2002, *Untitled* (1984, bronze, 39 x 28x14 ins / 98 x 72x36 cm) USD 55,000. NEW YORK, 13 Nov 2002, *Untitled* (1980-1981, painted wood, 12 x 13x4 ins / 30 x 32x10 cm) USD 45,000. NEW YORK, 13 Nov 2003, *Untitled* (1985, bronze, 36 x 56x40 ins / 91 x 143x102 cm) USD 150,000. NEW YORK, 13 Nov 2003, *Untitled, JS 354* (1979, cast bronze, one of three, 3 x 24x20 ins / 8 x 62x50 cm) USD 150,000. NEW YORK, 13 May 2004, *Untitled* (1990-1991, dark brown patinated bronze, 2 parts, 9 x 17x11 ins / 24 x 42x29 cm) USD 75,000. LONDON, 25 June 2004, *Untitled* (1975, cast iron, 7 x 7x4 ins / 18 x 19x9 cm) GBP 20,000.

SHAPIRO, Shmuel

American, 20th century.

Born 19 September 1924, in New England; died 1985.

Painter, collage artist.

Shmuel Shapiro studied at the art school in Hartford, Connecticut. In 1948, he joined the Art Students League in New York. He was awarded a scholarship to study in Paris in the mid 1950s.

MUSEUMS AND GALLERIES:

LONDON (Tate Collection): *Gates of Death* (1966-1967, lithograph series).

AUCTION RECORDS:

LUCERNE, 30 Sept 1988, *Untitled* (1970, collage, 11 3/4 x 9 1/2 ins / 30 x 24 cm) CHF 2,800. LUCERNE, 24 Nov 1990, *Winter Morning* (1967, oil on canvas, 19 3/4 x 23 1/2 ins / 50 x 60 cm) CHF 4,500. LUCERNE, 4 June 1994, *Two Compositions* (1967, gouache and pencil/paper, 5 1/2 x 6 ins / 14 x 15 cm) CHF 850. ZURICH, 19 Nov 1997, *Composition* (1967, mixed media, 12 1/2 x 11 1/2 ins / 32 x 29.5 cm) CHF 700. STUTTGART, 2 April 2003, *Composition in Red, Blue and Green* (oil on canvas, 40 x 39 ins / 101 x 100 cm) EUR 2,000.

SHAPIRO, Valentina

Russian, 20th century.

Painter, sculptor, draughtswoman. Figures.

Valentina Shapiro studied in Russia, emigrated to France in 1972, and had solo exhibitions in Paris in 1972 and 1974. She was a figurative painter specialising in figures.

SHAPLEIGH, Frank Henry

American, 19th century.

Born 7 March 1842, in Boston; died 1906.

Painter (gouache). Landscapes.

Frank Henry Shapleigh was taught by Lambinet in Paris.

AUCTION RECORDS:

PORTLAND, 7 April 1979, *New England Inlet* (1878, oil on canvas, 14 x 24 ins / 35.5 x 61 cm) USD 2,000. PORTLAND, 4 April 1981, *Carter Notch from Jackson, New Hampshire* (oil on canvas, 14 x 24 ins / 35.5 x 61 cm) USD 1,900. NEW YORK, 23 June 1983, *Maine Coast* (1872, oil on canvas, 14 x 24 ins / 35.6 x 61 cm) USD 1,500. NEW YORK, 17 March 1988, *Trees in a Forest* (watercolour and charcoal/paper, 24 1/2 x 14 3/4 ins / 62.5 x 37.5 cm) USD 2,310. NEW YORK, 24 Jan 1989, *Crawford*

Valley from Mount Willard (1877, oil on canvas, 21 x 35 1/2 ins / 52.5 x 90 cm) USD 4,675. NEW YORK, 9 Sept 1993, *Wooded Landscape* (1878, gouache/board, 18 1/2 x 33 1/4 ins / 47 x 84.5 cm) USD 1,955. NEW YORK, 12 Sept 1994, *Encampment in the White Mountains* (gouache/paper/board, 12 1/2 x 20 3/4 ins / 31.8 x 53 cm) USD 1,840. CONNECTICUT, 24 May 1999, *View through Barn Door* (oil on canvas, 10 x 16 ins / 25 x 41 cm) USD 3,800. MILFORD, 21 Oct 1999, *Arab Boy with Donkey* (oil on panel, 12 x 9 ins / 30 x 23 cm) USD 4,000. MAINE, 12 Jan 2000, *View of Mt Washington and Carter Notch from Bartlett, NH* (oil on canvas, 14 x 23 ins / 36 x 58 cm) USD 7,250. EAST DENNIS, 4 Aug 2000, *View of the Bay of Naples* (oil on canvas, 34 x 60 ins / 86 x 152 cm) USD 9,000. PITTSFIELD, 8 Sept 2001, *Seine at Sevres* (1874, oil on canvas, 10 x 18 ins / 25 x 46 cm) USD 3,000. NEW ORLEANS, 8 Dec 2001, *Southern Farm Scene with Black Woman* (watercolour, 8 x 5 ins / 20 x 13 cm) USD 1,500. BOSTON, 10 May 2002, *Ellis River, Jackson NH* (oil on canvas, 10 x 19 ins / 25 x 47 cm) USD 5,000. CAMBRIDGE, 17 Nov 2002, *Mt Chacorua from Tamworth* (1886, oil on panel, 7 x 12 ins / 18 x 30 cm) USD 4,700. PHILADELPHIA, 22 June 2003, *Mt Washington from Glenn Road, Jackson NH* (1877, oil on canvas, 20 x 30 ins / 51 x 76 cm) USD 12,000. BOSTON, 21 Nov 2003, *Hospital Street, St Augustine, Florida* (1883, oil on board, 7 x 13 ins / 19 x 32 cm) USD 10,000. TORONTO, 14 June 2004, *In Charlotte Street, St Augustine, Fla* (1891, oil on board, 7 x 12 ins / 18 x 31 cm) CAD 12,500. BOSTON, 10 Sept 2004, *New Hampshire* (1872, oil on canvas, 12 x 7 ins / 30 x 18 cm) USD 6,500.

SHAPOSHNIKOV, Lev or Leon

Russian, 20th century.
Born 5 September 1882, in Rostov.
Painter. Urban landscapes, seascapes.
Symbolism.

Shaposhnikov took part at the Salon des Artistes Indépendants, Salon d'Hiver and the Salon de la Société Nationale des Beaux-Arts in Paris. His landscapes often depict views of Moscow.

SHAQIRI, Ymer

Yugoslav, 20th - 21st century.
Born 1955, in Sveqel (Podujevo).
Engraver, draughtsman.

Shaqiri, who is of Albanian origin, lives and works in Priština, Kosovo.

He took part in 1992 in *De Bonnard à Baselitz - Dix Ans d'enrichissements du cabinet des estampes 1978-1988* (*From Bonnard to Baselitz: A Decade of Acquisitions by the Prints Collection 1978-1988*) at the Bibliothèque Nationale in Paris.

MUSEUMS AND GALLERIES:
PARIS (BNF, Prints Collection): *Door VIII* (1986, etching, aquatint and mezzotint).

SHARADIN, Henry William

American, 19th - 20th century.
Born 22 December 1872, in Kutztown (Pennsylvania); died 1966.
Painter, engraver.

Henry William Sharadin was taught by Carrol Beckwith, Percyval Tudor-Hart in Paris and Nordi in Rome. He was a member of the American Federation of Arts.

SHARAGA MAXY, Mimi. See **KAN Mimi**

SHARAKU, artist names: Sharaku, Toshusai

Japanese, 18th century.
Born c. 1770; died after 1825.
Active in Edo (now Tokyo) 1794-1795.
Print artist, painter.

Next to nothing is known of the life of Sharaku, one of the most striking figures in the story of *ukiyo-e* and a brilliant designer of actor portraits. During the Edo period, portraits of famous actors in their new roles were eagerly sought after by connoisseurs, and it is well known that Shunsho (1726-1792) and his disciples would add a personal note to their prints by making the faces and gestures especially graceful. Standing apart from this tradition, as if deliberately, is a group of some 145 prints, all signed Sharaku and bearing the seal of the publisher Tsutaya Juzaburo. The dates of their appearance have been carefully identified from the names or *mon* (crests) of the actors in question and their roles, and from this chronology it can be shown that, astonishingly, Sharaku started work immediately after the theatre season in the fifth month of 1794 and abandoned all artistic activity early in 1795. His career as an artist thus lasted no more than 10 months, an enigma compounded by the mystery surrounding his existence. To date no one has been able to substantiate the story in the *Shinukiyoe-ruiko* (1869) that Sharaku was a *No* actor named Saito Jurobei in the service of the lord of Awa.

Of Sharaku's works, 141 polychrome prints and some 17 drawings survive, most of them portraits of *kabuki* actors, although there are some sumo wrestlers and a few rare warrior portraits. They fall into four groups, following the development of his art: first, a group of 28 *oban* (15 x 10 in, 38 x 25 cm) *kirara* (mica background) prints, all head-and-shoulders portraits of actors playing in the three *kabuki* theatres (the Miyako-za, Kawarazaki-za and Kiri-za) in Edo during the fifth and sixth months of 1794; second, a group of 38 prints (30 *hosoban* (6.75 x 15 in, 17 x 38 cm) and 8 *oban*), all full-length portraits, sometimes of two figures together, corresponding to the plays during the seventh and eighth months of 1794; third, a series of 61 prints (13 *aiban* (9 x 13 in, 23 x 33 cm), three *oban* and 45 *hosoban*), four of which are portraits of sumo wrestlers, three head-and-shoulders actor portraits and the remainder full-length actor portraits, all from the 11th month of 1794; and finally a group of 14 prints (one *oban*, 10 *hosoban* and three *aiban*), showing full-length actor portraits, warriors and one wrestler, for the new year of 1795.

In the first two, the most remarkable of the four groups, Sharaku appears already at the very height of his powers. Here, especially in his bust portraits, he restricts himself to the barest essentials, to a single, concise, expressive line that evokes the stature, posture and movement of the body with such vigour, such remorseless exaggeration that he seems to be attacking grace and refinement, the very source of the beauty of *ukiyo-e*. His use of colour still further reinforces his unforgettable expressive power and boldness: despite their flatness, his dark tones, cleverly offset with black, succeed in suggesting the volume and mass of the human body, while in his finely outlined faces he needs no more than the eyes, eyebrows and mouth to reveal not just the personality of his actor but also the psychological content of the character he is playing. To heighten the effect, he also places most of these busts against a dark, silvery-grey, mica background that seems to thrust the character forward and whose texture, with its embossing, its relief and its gouged lines, brings out the texture of the actors' robes. The two-figure prints in the second group, too, show great virtuosity in the way the compositions are balanced, with the two contrasting characters complementing or opposing each other. In his later prints, his compositions seem more spread out, and the boldness has gone from his faces. Instead, we find a complexity in the actors' costumes, an abundance of props, and sometimes excessive gesticulation, all of which suggest that Sharaku was looking for decorative qualities. At the same time, his technical subtlety disappears (probably because it was too costly) and his backgrounds are generally in flat yellow. These prints are no longer signed *Toshusai Sharaku ga* but *Sharaku ga*; and with them, he vanishes from the world of art. While he would inspire many imitators, such as Enkyo, Kunimasa and Toyokuni, to carry on the tradition of theatre prints into the 19th century, no one would ever again achieve the dramatic penetration and psychological richness that were part of his sober, virile art.

Bibliography:

Akiyama, Terukazu, *La Peinture japonaise*, Skira, Geneva, 1961. *Six maîtres de l'estampe japonaise au XVIIe siècle*, exhibition catalogue, Musée de l'Orangerie, Paris, 1971. Lion-Goldschmidt, D., '*Sharaku (Toshusai)*' in *Encyclopaedia Universalis* vol. XIV, Paris, 1972. Henderson, Harold G./Ledoux, Louis V., *Saraku's Japanese Theatre Prints: An Illustrated Guide to HIs Complete Work.*, Dover Publications, 1985. Narazaki, Muneshige, *Sharaku: Enigmatic Ukiyo-e Master*, Kodansh Europe, 1995 (tranlated by Bonnie F. Abiko). Guth, Christine, *Japanese Art of the Edo Period*, Calmann & King, London, 1996. Fahr-Becker, Gabriele (ed.), *Japanese Prints*, Taschen, Cologne, 1999.

Auction records:

New York, 21 March 1989, *Portrait of the Actor Arashi Ryuzo II in the Role of the Usurer Ishibe Kinkichi* (Oban Tate-e print, 14 1/2 x 10 ins / 37 x 25.1 cm) USD 286,000; *Portrait of the Actor Sakata Hangoro III in the Role of the Bandit Fujikawa Mizuemon* (Oban Tate-e print, 14 1/2 x 10 ins / 37 x 25.1 cm) USD 462,000. New York, 16 Oct 1989, *Okubi-e Portrait of the Actor Arashi Ryuzo II in the Role of the Usurer Ishibe Kinchiki* (Oban Tate-e print, 15 x 9 3/4 ins / 38 x 25 cm) USD 198,000. New York, 27 March 1991, *Full-length Portrait of the Actor Sakata Hangoro III in the Role of Kosodata no Kanno, Priest of Kannon, in 'The Child Protector'* (Hosoban print, 13 x 5 3/4 ins / 32.1 x 14.9 cm) USD 99,000. Fontainebleau, 4 April 1992, *Portrait of the Actor Arashi Ryuzo* (Hosoban print) FRF 225,000. Paris, 3 June 1992, *Portrait of the Actor Otani Hiroji III* (1794, Hosoban print, 12 1/4 x 5 1/2 ins / 30.8 x 14 cm) FRF 680,000. Paris, 22 March 1995, *Bust of the Actor nakayama Tomasiburo in the Role of Miyagino, Elder Daughter of Matsushita Mikinoshin* (Oban Tate-e print, 15 x 9 3/4 ins / 37.2 x 24.6 cm) FRF 1,300,000. Paris, 25 Nov 2003, *Otani Hiroji III* (1794, colour print, 12 x 6 ins / 31 x 14 cm) EUR 35,560. Paris, 25 Nov 2003, *Nakamura Narazo* (1794, colour print, 13 x 9 ins / 32 x 22 cm) EUR 121,150. New York, 23 March 2004, *Segawa Kikunojo III as Oschizu - Wife of Tanabe Bunzo* (print, 15 x 9 ins / 37 x 24 cm) USD 85,000.

SHARE, Henry Pruett

American, 19th century.
Born 1853, in Los Angeles; died 20 June 1905, in Flatbush.
Painter, journalist.

SHARITS, Paul

American, 20th century.
Born 1943, in Denver (Colorado); died 1999, in Buffalo (New York State).
Video installation artist. Multimedia.

Paul Sharits was a figure in experimental theatre in the USA. He was represented at *Into the Light: The Projected Image in American Art, 1964-1977*, a large exhibition devoted to the moving image (video, installations, cinema), at Cleveland Museum of Art in 2002.

Bibliography:

Iles, Chrissie (ed.), *Into the Light: The Projected Image in American Art 1964-1977*, exhibition catalogue, Cleveland Museum of Art, Cleveland, 2002.

Museums and Galleries:

Paris (BNF, Prints Collection).

SHARKOFF, Pjotr Gherassimovitch.
See **JARKOV Piotr Gerassimovich**

SHARLAMOV, Mikhail Vasilievich

Russian, 19th century.
Sculptor.

Sharlamov was a pupil at the academy of fine arts in St Petersburg.

Museums and Galleries:

St Petersburg (Academy of Fine Art): *Sower*.

SHARLEMAN, Adolf Jossipovich, or Bode-Sharleman

Russian, 19th century.
Born 1826, in St Petersburg; died 1901, in St Petersburg.
Painter, illustrator.

This artist, possibly the son of Iosif Adolovich Sharleman, was the grandson of Jean-Baptiste Baudet-Charlemagne, an artist from Rouen who was summoned to Russia by Catherine the Great and settled there. He was a pupil at the fine arts academy in St Petersburg where he was taught by T. Bruni and Villevalde, and subsequently stayed in Munich and Paris. His notable works include *Suvorov at St Gothard*; *Suvorov Entering Milan*; *Suvorov's Last Night in Switzerland* and *Catherine the Great in Falconnet's Studio*.

Museums and Galleries:

Moscow (State Tretyakov Gal.): *Speech of Tsar Ivan IV at the Place of Execution in 1550*; *Royal Hunt in the 16th Century*.

Auction records:

New York, 24 Feb 1982, *View of St Petersburg* (watercolour and pencil, 14 1/4 x 19 1/4 ins / 36.2 x 48.8 cm) USD 350. London, 6 Oct 1988, *Sleigh Harnessed in Winter in St Petersburg* (gouache/card, oval l. 11 ins / 27 cm) GBP 2,860. London, 14 Nov 1988, *View of the Summer Palace and Gardens from the Neva in St Petersburg* (1855, watercolour, 7 1/2 x 11 1/2 ins / 19 x 29.5 cm) GBP 3,740.

SHARLEMAN, Iosif Adolfovich

Russian, 19th century.
Born 1782; died 1861.
Painter. Landscapes, urban landscapes.

In particular, this artist is noted for a drawing entitled *Distribution of Water in Moscow via Mytichi's System of Canalisation* (1850), in gouache, graphite and Indian ink, depicting fountains against an architectural background.

Auction records:

London, 5 Oct 1989, *View of the Neva* (1804, watercolour and pencil, 6 x 9 1/4 ins / 15 x 23.8 cm) USD 3,520. Stockholm, 23 Nov 1999, *Prussian officer at Cardes de Corps* (1852, watercolour, 13 x 11 ins / 34 x 29 cm) SEK 14,000.

SHARLEMAN, Joseph Adolfovich

Russian, 19th - 20th century.
Born 1880; died 1957.
Painter, draughtsman, illustrator. Urban landscapes, architectural views.

The son of Adolf-Jossifovich Sharleman, Joseph was active in St. Petersburg.

Museums and Galleries:

St Petersburg (Gosudarstvennyj Russkij Muz.): *View of the Mikhailovski Palace*.

Auction records:

Paris, 23 June 1943, *Busy Square* (drawing in lead pencil with highlights) FRF 1,450.

SHARMA, Raja Babu

Indian, 20th - 21st century.
Born 1956, in Jaipur.
Painter.

Raja Babu Sharma is a Tantric painter and works in a studio that has been scrupulously maintained in the traditional manner.

Bibliography:

Martin, Jean-Hubert/Francis, Mark/Magnin, André/Marcadé, Bernard, *Les Magiciens de la terre*, exhibition catalogue, Éd. du Centre Georges-Pompidou, Paris, 1989.

SHAROFF, Shirley

American, 20th century.
Born 1936, in Brooklyn.

Active in France since 1961.
Painter, engraver.

Shirley Sharoff has lived and worked in Paris since 1961. She took part in the 1992 exhibition *De Bonnard à Baselitz: Dix Ans d'Enrichissements du Cabinet des Estampes 1978-1988* (*From Bonnard to Baselitz: A Decade of Acquisitions by the Prints Collection 1978-1988*) at the Bibliothèque Nationale in Paris.

BIBLIOGRAPHY:
'*Grande Muraille*' in *Art et Métiers du Livre* n° 172 p. 48-50, periodical, Paris, 1992.

MUSEUMS AND GALLERIES:
PARIS (BNF, Prints Collection): *Identified Flying Objects Nos. 1 and 8* (1980-1981, two etchings).

SHAROWA, Aleksandra Aleksandrovna. See **JAROVA**

SHARP, Charlotte. See **SHARPE**

SHARP, Christopher
British, 19th century.
Born 1797, in Cambridge.
Engraver (burin).

SHARP, Dorothea
British, 19th - 20th century.
Born 1874, in Dartford (Kent); died 1955.
Active in London and Cornwall.
Painter. Scenes with figures, genre scenes, landscapes, still-lifes.

Dorothea Sharp studied in London, where her teachers included David Murray and George Clausen, and in Paris. She was a member of the Royal Society of British Artists (from 1907), the Royal Institute of Oil Painters (1922) and the Society of Women Artists (1908). She lived in London, working at studios in Maida Vale. In the 1920s and 1930s she travelled in France, Spain, Portugal and Italy, and from 1940 to 1946 she lived in St Ives in Cornwall, where she produced many paintings of beach scenes, notably including children.

DOROTHEA SHARP

BIBLIOGRAPHY:
Wormleighton, Austin, *Morning Tide: John Anthony Park and the Painters of Light, St Ives, 1890-1950*, Stockbridge Books, Stockbridge, 1998.

MUSEUMS AND GALLERIES:
CARDIFF (National Mus. and Gal. of Wales): *At the Seaside* - LEAMINGTON SPA (Mus. and AG): *Where Children Play and Seagulls Fly* (oil on canvas) - TORQUAY (Torre Abbey).

AUCTION RECORDS:
LONDON, 11 Dec 1970, *Children on the Beach*, Gns 180. LONDON, 27 Oct 1972, *Lake Maggiore*, Gns 180. LONDON, 14 Dec 1973, *Promenade*, Gns 400. LONDON, 11 Oct 1974, *Children on the Beach*, Gns 380. GLASGOW, 30 Nov 1976, *Beach Scene* (oil on canvas, 35 1/2 x 41 1/2 ins / 90 x 105.5 cm) GBP 430. LONDON, 31 Jan 1979, *Children on the Beach* (oil on canvas, 17 1/2 x 13 1/2 ins / 44.5 x 34.5 cm) GBP 520. LONDON, 20 June 1983, *The Gooseboy* (oil on canvas, 30 x 35 ins / 76 x 89 cm) GBP 4,600. LONDON, 13 Nov 1985, *Spring* (oil on canvas, 20 x 24 ins / 51 x 61 cm) GBP 9,500. LONDON, 12 Nov 1986, *Children Paddling* (oil on canvas, 38 1/4 x 38 1/2 ins / 97 x 98 cm) GBP 22,000. LONDON, 5 March 1987, *Children Picking Daisies* (oil on canvas, 41 1/4 x 35 1/2 ins / 105 x 90.3 cm) GBP 30,000. LONDON, 9 June 1988, *Still-life with Flowers in a Jug* (oil on card, 17 3/4 x 14 3/4 ins / 45 x 37.5 cm) GBP 9,350; *Baby and Forget-me-nots* (oil on canvas, 24 1/2 x 29 1/2 ins / 62.5 x 75 cm) GBP 20,900. LONDON, 29 July 1988, *Spanish Market* (oil on panel, 10 3/4 x 12 3/4 ins / 27.5 x 32.5 cm) GBP 3,520. BELFAST, 28 Oct 1988, *On the Rocks. Feeding the Ducks* (oil on canvas, double-sided, 25 3/4 x 30 ins / 65.5 x 76.2 cm) GBP 12,100. LONDON, 2 March 1989, *Donkey Ride* (oil on canvas, 29 x 35 ins / 73.5 x 88.7 cm) GBP 37,400. LONDON, 8 March 1990, *The Goose Girl* (oil on panel, 11 1/4 x 15 1/4 ins / 28.6 x 38.8 cm) GBP 11,000. EDINBURGH, 26 April 1990, *Running through Waves* (oil on canvas, 14 x 18 ins / 35.6 x 45.7 cm) GBP 6,600. LONDON, 7 June 1990, *Girl among Blossom* (oil on canvas, 29 1/2 x 24 3/4 ins / 75 x 63 cm) GBP 15,400. LONDON, 7 March 1991, *Summer Flowers* (oil on canvas, 23 1/2 x 19 1/4 ins / 59.5 x 49 cm) GBP 6,820. LONDON, 6 June 1991, *Reading by the Beach* (oil on canvas, 30 x 33 3/4 ins / 76 x 86 cm) GBP 11,000. LONDON, 7 Nov 1991, *Marcella Smith on a Beach in Languedoc* (oil on canvas, 30 1/4 x 38 ins / 77 x 96.5 cm) GBP 9,900. LONDON, 5 June 1992, *Crossing the Étang* (oil on canvas, 36 x 42 1/4 ins / 91.5 x 107 cm) GBP 31,900. LONDON, 6 Nov 1992, *Still-life with Flowers in a Blue Vase* (oil on card, 15 x 12 ins / 38 x 30.5 cm) GBP 2,090. EDINBURGH, 19 Nov 1992, *Summer Flowers* (oil on canvas, 24 x 20 ins / 61 x 50.8 cm) GBP 2,640. ST ASAPH, 2 June 1994, *Mother and Children on a Rocky Shore* (oil on canvas, 24 x 30 ins / 61 x 76 cm) GBP 26,450. NEW YORK, 10 Oct 1996, *Two Girls in a Meadow* (oil on canvas, 24 x 20 1/4 ins / 61 x 51.4 cm) USD 8,625. EDINBURGH, 15 May 1997, *Summer in Italy* (oil on panel, 20 x 24 ins / 50.8 x 61 cm) GBP 4,370. MONTREAL, 17 June 1997, *Young Explorers* (oil on canvas, 24 x 20 ins / 61 x 50.6 cm) CAD 29,000. LONDON, 5 March 1999, *Butterflies* (1916, oil on canvas, 25 x 30 ins / 63 x 76 cm) GBP 32,000. LONDON, 23 June 1999, *Two Girls with Lupins and Poppies* (oil on canvas, 25 x 30 ins / 64 x 76 cm) GBP 42,000. NICE, 28 June 2000, *Two Children by the Sea with Light Effect* (oil on canvas, 35 x 28 ins / 90 x 72 cm) FRF 1,020,000. ST LOUIS, 16 Sept 2000, *Day at the Beach* (oil on canvas, 24 x 20 ins / 61 x 51 cm) USD 60,000. LONDON, 4 July 2001, *Sewing in the Sun* (oil on canvas, 30 x 10 ins / 76 x 25 cm) GBP 48,000. LONDON, 23 Nov 2001, *Gathering Flowers* (oil on canvas, 32 x 33 ins / 81 x 84 cm) GBP 38,000. LEOMINSTER, 28 Aug 2002, *Garden Scene with Three Children Picking Flowers* (1913, oil on canvas, 39 x 32 ins / 99 x 81 cm) GBP 41,000. LONDON, 22 Nov 2002, *Water Babies, Cornish Coast* (oil on canvas, 25 x 30 ins / 63 x 76 cm) GBP 33,000. LONDON, 6 June 2003, *Children Sitting on the Rocks. Trees on a Shoreline* (oil on panel, double-sided, 15 x 18 ins / 38 x 46 cm) GBP 22,000. LONDON, 24 June 2003, *Gathering Daisies* (oil on canvas, 20 x 24 ins / 51 x 61 cm) GBP 18,000. LONDON, 2 June 2004, *Summer Day on the Cliffs* (oil on canvas, double-sided, 35 x 26 ins / 89 x 67 cm) GBP 30,000. LONDON, 19 Nov 2004, *Seaside Joys* (oil on canvas, 32 x 33 ins / 81 x 83 cm) GBP 38,000.

SHARP, Eliza. See **SHARPE**

SHARP, Fraser
British, 20th - 21st century.
Born 1975, in Glasgow.
Painter. Scenes with figures, figures.

Fraser Sharp paints moments from his childhood and family life, simplifying and reducing personal photographs or photographs of unknown people. The Figuration achieved is an almost indiscernible effect in which the viewer is forced to make a kind of reconstruction of fragments of memories of atmosphere, attitude, colour, etcetera.

Sharp has taken part in group exhibitions, including *Picturesque* at the Phillips Contemporary Art Gallery in Manchester in 2002. He has also shown his work in solo exhibitions, including: *It Turns as Milk Does* at Goldsmith's College in London (2000); *Are We Nearly There Yet?* at Inside Space in London (2001); *No Flowers or Grass* at the Galerie Analix Forever in Geneva (2002); and at the Galerie Praz-Delavallade in Paris (2003).

SHARP, George
British, 19th century.
Born 1802, in Dublin; died 5 December 1877, in Dublin.
Painter. Genre scenes.

George Sharp studied under Picot and Couture and went on to teach drawing and composition in Dublin. He was an associate member of the Royal Hibernian Society from 1842 and a full member effective from 1861.

MUSEUMS AND GALLERIES:

DUBLIN (NG of Ireland): *Old Man Sleeping*.

SHARP, John. See **SHARPE**

SHARP, John

British, 18th century.

Died 1768, in Chigwell (Essex).

Engraver (burin).

SHARP, Joseph Henry

American, 19th - 20th century.

Born 27 September 1859, in Bridgeport (Ohio), to Irish parents; died 27 August 1953, in Pasadena (California).

Painter, illustrator. Native Americans, figures, genre scenes, landscapes.

Joseph Henry Sharp moved to Cincinnati at the age of 14 and enrolled in art classes at McMicken School of Drawing and Design. He attended Cincinnati Academy of Art. His studio was in the same building as that of Henry Farny who gave him books on Pueblo Indians. In 1881, he went to Antwerp where he studied history and portrait painting in the realist tradition with Charles Verlat at the Antwerp Academy.

In 1883, after two years in Antwerp, Sharp made his first visit to the American West, going first on a sketching trip that included various pueblos in New Mexico (but not Taos), Santa Fe, Albuquerque, Tucson, and sites in California, and then taking a boat up the West Coast to the Columbia River in the Washington Territory. The sketches he did on that trip were to be the basis for his first Native American portraits.

In 1886, Sharp returned to Europe to study with Karl von Marr at the Munich Art Academy. He also travelled with Frank Duveneck, a Cincinnati artist, through Italy and Spain, spending a great deal of time studying the Spanish masters El Greco, Velázquez, and Goya.

Sharp taught occasional classes at the Cincinnati Art Academy from 1892 to 1902. He visited Taos, New Mexico for the first time in 1893, on a commission from *Harper's Weekly*. The pictures he completed for the commission were well received and led to further illustration work with numerous publications.

From 1895 to 1896 he attended the Académie Julian in Paris where he met Ernest Blumenschein and Bert Phillips, who later joined him in Taos in 1898, and the young painter E.I. Couse. When Sharp returned, President Theodore Roosevelt commissioned him to paint portraits of Native American survivors of Custer's battle site. Sharp travelled throughout the Plains to paint about 200 portraits of living Indians who had been in the battle of Little Big Horn. In 1900, an exhibition of these portraits travelled to Paris and to Washington DC and led to large commissions which made him financially independent. In 1902, he devoted himself to painting full-time and painted in Arizona, California, Wyoming, and Montana. In 1912 Sharp finally moved to Taos permanently, and was a charter member of the Taos Society of Artists formed that same year.

Sharp continued to travel, going frequently to Hawaii and Pasadena, and spending winters in California where he completed numerous floral landscapes. He spent years in Spain, went to Africa twice, to South America, Japan and China. In 1949, the Gilcrease Museum in Tulsa, Oklahoma, mounted a retrospective of Sharp's paintings.

BIBLIOGRAPHY:

Luhan, Mabel Dodge, *Taos and its Artists*, Duell, Sloan and Pearce, New York, 1947. Broder, Patricia Janis, *Taos, A Painter's Dream*, Little Brown, Boston, 1980. Bickerstaff, Laura M., *Pioneer Artists of Taos*, Old West Publishing Co., Denver, 1983. Witt, David L., *The Taos Artists, A Historical Narrative and Biographical Dictionary*, Ewell Fine Art Publications, Denver, 1984. Riebeth, Carolyn Reynolds/Sharp, Joseph Henry, *J.H. Sharp Among the Crow Indians*, Upton, El Segundo, 1985. Eldredge, Charles C., *Art in New Mexico 1900-1945*, National Museum of American Art, Smithsonian Institution, Abbeville Press, New York, 1986.

MUSEUMS AND GALLERIES:

CHICAGO (Terra Foundation for the Arts): *Taos Canyon* (c. 1930) - CINCINNATI (AM) - CORNING (Rockwell Mus. of Western Art): *Prayer to the Spirit of the Buffalo* (1910, oil on canvas) - FORT WORTH (Amon Carter Museum of Western Art) - HOUSTON (MFA) - INDIANAPOLIS (Herron Art Institute) - JERSEY CITY (Jersey City Mus.): *Young America* (1884, chromolithograph) - MADRID (Mus. Thyssen-Bornemisza): *Setting Up Camp, Little Big Horn, Montana* - MISSOULA (Montana Museum of Art & Culture, University of Montana): *Portrait of a Taos Girl* (oil on board); *Taos Garden* (oil on board); *Fall Coloring* (oil on canvas); *Garden of the Copper Bell* (oil on board); *Path to the Mess House* (oil on board); *Winter Landscape* (oil on artist's board); *Winter Landscape #2* (oil on paper); *Taos Landscape* (oil on canvas); *Portrait of a Crow Girl in an Elk Tooth Dress* (oil on board); *Winter Weeds and Seeds* (oil on canvas) - NEW YORK (Metropolitan Mus. of Art): *Wolf Ear, Sioux* (1897) - NORMAN, OK (Fred Jones Jr. Museum of Art, University of Oklahoma): *Fine Bull* (oil on canvas); *Hunting Son* (1926, oil on canvas); *Grand Canyon* (oil on canvas); *Sidi-bou-Said, Tunisia* (oil on masonite) - OKLAHOMA CITY (National Cowboy and Western Heritage Mus.): *Green Maize Ceremony* (1950) - PHILADELPHIA (Academy of Natural Sciences) - SANTA FE (Museum of Santa Fe) - ST LOUIS (Woodcock Museum): *The Bonnet Maker* (1910) - STARK, TX (Stark Museum of Art): *Peonies*; *Coucil of Crows, Montana* - TULSA, OK (Gilcrease Mus.): paintings - WASHINGTON DC (Smithsonian American AM): *Yellow Wings* (1900); *Do-Ree-Tah* (1900); *Wolf Ear* (1900); *Hand* (c. 1900); *Strong Left Hand* (1900); *Running Horse* (1897); *Encampment of Crow Indians* (1908); *Chief American Horse*; *Quinnah* (1902); *The Voice of the Great Spirit* (1906); *White Swan* (1900?); *Little Wolf* (1900); *Chief Flat Iron* (1905); *Spotted Elk, Chief* (c. 1900); *Y-yut-mat* (1900?); *Sunset Dance - Ceremony to the Evening Sun* (1924); *Twilight (Hopi Girl)* (after 1896); *Blackfoot Indian Girl* (1905); *Chief Flat Iron* (1898-1899); *Two Leggins, Crow Chief* (1900); *Two Dogs* (1900?) - YOUNGSTOWN (Butler Institute of American Art): *Ration Day at the Reservation* (1919, oil on canvas).

AUCTION RECORDS:

NEW YORK, 13 May 1966, *River Landscape by Moonlight*, USD 1,400. NEW YORK, 15 April 1970, *Two Indians in an Interior*, USD 2,600. NEW YORK, 13 Sept 1972, *Winter Landscape*, USD 8,000. LOS ANGELES, 4 March 1974, *Indian Camp, Past* (and gouache) USD 8,500. LOS ANGELES, 8 Nov 1977, *Fiesta at Taos* (1931, oil on canvas, 20 x 24 ins / 51 x 61 cm) USD 27,000. LOS ANGELES, 12 March 1979, *Indian Seated* (oil on canvas, 20 x 16 ins / 51 x 40.6 cm) USD 16,000. LOS ANGELES, 24 June 1980, *Indian Camp* (pastel/mounted paper/canvas, 11 x 16 ins / 28 x 40.6 cm) USD 17,500. NEW YORK, 22 Oct 1981, *Elk Foot (Jerry), Taos* (oil on canvas, 25 x 30 ins / 63.5 x 76.2 cm) USD 100,000. NEW YORK, 8 Dec 1983, *Crow Indian Encampment* (oil on canvas, 15 1/2 x 22 1/2 ins / 39.4 x 57.2 cm)

USD 52,500. NEW YORK, 30 May 1985, *Hunting Song - Taos Indians* (oil on canvas, 20 x 24 ins / 50.8 x 61 cm) USD 37,000. NEW YORK, 12 Sept 1985, *Coastal Landscape* (c. 1900-1910, monotype in dark green, 14 x 22 ins / 35.6 x 55.9 cm) USD 1,600. NEW YORK, 22 Jan 1986, *Rhythms of the Waves, Koko Crater Coast, Honolulu* (oil on canvas, 30 x 36 ins / 76.2 x 91.5 cm) USD 6,800. NEW YORK, 4 Dec 1987, *War Bonnet Song* (oil on canvas, 25 x 30 ins / 63.5 x 76.2 cm) USD 70,000. NEW YORK, 1 Dec 1988, *Hunting Son 2* (oil on canvas, 20 x 24 1/4 ins / 50.8 x 61.6 cm) USD 47,300. NEW YORK, 24 May 1989, *Council around the Old Chief* (oil on canvas, 25 1/4 x 30 1/2 ins / 64.1 x 77.5 cm) USD 39,600. NEW YORK, 30 Nov 1989, *Apache Camp in the Aspens* (oil on canvas, 30 1/4 x 25 1/4 ins / 76.8 x 64.1 cm) USD 68,750. NEW YORK, 23 May 1990, *Marigolds and Asters in Chinese Vase* (oil on canvas, 22 x 27 1/4 ins / 56 x 69 cm) USD 16,500. NEW YORK, 29 Nov 1990, *Medicine Man* (oil on card, 18 x 11 ins / 45.7 x 27.9 cm) USD 8,800. NEW YORK, 22 May 1991, *Romero's Gate* (oil on canvas, 20 x 30 ins / 51 x 76 cm) USD 66,000. NEW YORK, 18 Dec 1991, *Western Landscape* (oil on card, 9 3/4 x 13 3/4 ins / 24.8 x 34.9 cm) USD 7,700. NEW YORK, 28 May 1992, *Evening in a Crow Reserve, Montana* (oil on canvas, 12 x 18 ins / 30.5 x 45.7 cm) USD 46,200. NEW YORK, 3 Dec 1992, *Still-life of Flowers* (oil on canvas, 25 x 30 ins / 63.5 x 76.2 cm) USD 13,200. NEW YORK, 4 Dec 1992, *Indians Returning to Winter Camp* (oil on canvas, 20 x 30 ins / 50.7 x 76.4 cm) USD 77,000. NEW YORK, 11 March 1993, *Big Medicine Camp* (oil on canvas, 18 x 26 ins / 45.7 x 66 cm) USD 79,500. NEW YORK, 25 May 1994, *Hunting Son in his Teepee* (oil on canvas, 25 x 30 ins / 63.5 x 76.2 cm) USD 85,000. NEW YORK, 30 Nov 1995, *Indians around the Fire* (oil on canvas, 20 x 30 ins / 50.8 x 76.2 cm) USD 57,500. NEW YORK, 26 Sept 1996, *Indian Encampment in the Woods* (oil on canvas, 12 1/2 x 17 1/4 ins / 31.8 x 43.8 cm) USD 63,000. LONDON, 17 Oct 1996, *Dog in a Kennel in Winter* (1892, oil on canvas, 28 3/4 x 36 ins / 73 x 91.4 cm) GBP 2,070. NEW YORK, 5 June 1997, *Trembles at Hawkeye Creek near Taos* (oil on canvas, 24 x 20 1/4 ins / 61 x 51.4 cm) USD 20,700. NEW YORK, 27 May 1999, *Elk Foot* (oil on canvas, 36 x 24 ins / 91 x 61 cm) USD 220,000. MAINE, 14 Aug 1999, *Hunting Song* (oil on canvas, 30 x 40 ins / 76 x 102 cm) USD 875,000. CINCINNATI, 3 Dec 2000, *Little Big Horn, Indian Encampment* (oil on canvas, 12 x 18 ins / 30 x 46 cm) USD 210,000. LOS ANGELES, 13 Dec 2000, *Grand Bouquet* (oil on canvas, 36 x 40 ins / 91 x 102 cm) USD 90,000. NEW YORK, 24 May 2001, *Crow Reservation in Winter* (oil on canvas, 16 x 24 ins / 41 x 61 cm) USD 120,000. HAYDEN, 28 July 2001, *Careful Shot* (oil on canvas, 25 x 30 ins / 64 x 76 cm) USD 150,000. SANTA FE, 18 May 2002, *The Drummer* (oil on canvas, 20 x 24 ins / 51 x 61 cm) USD 135,000. NEW YORK, 22 May 2002, *Firelight Chant* (oil on canvas, 30 x 36 ins / 76 x 91 cm) USD 230,000. SAN FRANCISCO, 11 June 2003, *Indian Encampment at Sunset* (oil on canvas, 12 x 16 ins / 30 x 41 cm) USD 160,000. PASADENA, 18 Nov 2003, *Taos Indians in the Sunlight* (oil on canvas, 7 x 9 ins / 18 x 24 cm) USD 120,000. HAYDEN, 24 July 2004, *Hunting Son* (oil on canvas, 16 x 12 ins / 41 x 30 cm) USD 140,000. HAYDEN, 24 July 2004, *Squaw Winter* (oil on canvas, 30 x 28 ins / 76 x 71 cm) USD 950,000.

SHARP, Louisa. See **SHARPE**

SHARP, Martin
Australian, 20th century.
Born 1942, in Sydney.
Painter, engraver, draughtsman. Posters.

Martin Sharp is known for his posters for theatres and record sleeves and of rock and roll stars. He was one of the founders of the Australian underground magazine of the 1970s, *OZ*, which came under censorship. Sharp's paintings are often reworkings of the masters which introduce fantastical and often disrespectful elements with a Surrealist touch.

BIBLIOGRAPHY:
Creating Australia: 200 Years of Art 1788-1988, exhibition catalogue, Art Gall. Board of South Australia, Adelaide, 1988.
MUSEUMS AND GALLERIES:
ADELAIDE (AG of South Australia): *Mo* (1978).

SHARP, Mary Anne. See **SHARPE**

SHARP, Michael William
British, 19th century.
Born in London; died 1840, in Boulogne-sur-Mer, France.
Painter. Genre scenes, portraits.

Michael William Sharp studied under Sir W. Beechley and at the Royal Academy Schools. He exhibited portraits at the Academy from 1801 to 1818, when he started submitting genre compositions (until 1836).
MUSEUMS AND GALLERIES:
LONDON (Victoria and Albert Mus.): *Portrait of Miss Duncan*.
AUCTION RECORDS:
LONDON, 4 Feb 1911, *Curiosity*, GBP 13. LONDON, 15 June 1973, *Portrait of an Elegant Young Lady* (1837) Gns 650. ZURICH, 30 Nov 1984, *The New Letter* (oil on canvas, 24 1/4 x 18 ins / 61.5 x 45.5 cm) CHF 13,000. LONDON, 7 Nov 1996, *Chelsea Pensioner; Pensioner General* (oil on canvas and oil on panel, pair, each 15 x 12 ins / 38.2 x 30.4 cm) GBP 2,185.

SHARP, Thomas
British, 19th century.
Active in London.
Sculptor. Religious subjects. Busts.

Thomas Sharp studied in Paris.
MUSEUMS AND GALLERIES:
GLASGOW: *Eve at the Spring* (marble bust).

SHARP, William
British, 18th - 19th century.
Born 29 January 1749, in London; died 25 July 1824, in London.
Draughtsman, engraver.

The celebrated cold-chisel engraver William Sharp was the son of an armourer and was initially apprenticed to a damascene engraver. He also studied heraldic engraving. Sharp spent some time engraving pewter pots for innkeepers, but effectively made his debut as an artist when he engraved an animal portrait of a lion that had been housed for many years in the Tower of London. His reputation spread after he produced prints from Stellard's originals published in the *Novelist's Magazine*, and he was quickly acknowledged as one of the most accomplished engravers of the age. Sharp elected to produce historical and genre portraits, working from originals by the likes of Carracci, Guido Reni and Zampieri. He also engraved portraits of his contemporaries such as Benjamin West, Sir Joshua Reynolds, John Singleton Copley and others. The British Museum houses a comprehensive collection of his work.
MUSEUMS AND GALLERIES:
LONDON (British Mus.) - LONDON (National Portrait Gal.): *Joanna Southcott* (before 1812, pencil); numerous engravings.

SHARP, William
British, 19th century.
Active in London between 1819 and 1831.
Painter, engraver (burin).
AUCTION RECORDS:
NEW YORK, 22 Oct 1982, *Marshall P. Wilder Presiding over the Opening of the United States Agricultural Society in Boston in 1855*, (1855, oil on panel, 40 x 50 1/2 ins / 101.6 x 128.3 cm) USD 7,000.

SHARP, William, pseudonym of Schleifer, Leon
American, 20th century.

Born 1900, in Lemberg, Austria (now Lviv, Ukraine); died 1961, in New York.

Painter, illustrator, lithographer. Urban townscapes.

Leon Schleifer studied art in Austria, Poland and then at the university in Berlin in 1918. He remained in Berlin to work as an illustrator for books, magazines and newspapers. He produced pseudonymous cartoons satirising the Nazis, and the threat of imprisonment led him and his wife to leave Germany for New York in 1934. He changed his name to William Sharp in 1940.

Settling in New York, Sharp resumed his career as a newspaper illustrator, providing sketches for courtroom scenes - including the Lindbergh baby kidnapping trial - and establishing a lasting fame in this genre. He went on to illustrate other famous trials of the 1940s and 1950s. He also produced satirical drawings critical of American society of the time, especially of its treatment of African-Americans. His work appeared in publications such as the New York *Daily Mirror*, *Esquire*, and *Life*.

AUCTION RECORDS:

NEW YORK, 25 Sept 1992, *On the Rooftops of Manhattan* (oil on canvas, 28 x 18 ins / 71.1 x 45.7 cm) USD 715.

SHARPE, Agnes

British, 19th century.

Active between 1850 and 1859.

Draughtswoman.

Sister of Louisa Sharpe.

SHARPE, C. W.

American, 19th century.

Active in Philadelphia c. 1850.

Engraver (burin).

SHARPE, Charles Kirkpatrick

British, 19th century.

Born 15 May 1781, in Hoddam Castle; died 17 March 1851, in Edinburgh.

Painter, watercolourist, engraver.

Charles Kirkpatrick Sharpe initially made his mark painting watercolour portraits of his professors and fellow students at Oxford University. He subsequently settled in Edinburgh, where he worked as an antiquary specialising in Scottish antiques and painting and engraving in his free time. Sharpe produced several vignettes for collections of poetry. Twenty-seven of Sharpe's etchings were published in 1869.

SHARPE, Charles W.

British, 19th century.

Engraver.

Charles W. Sharpe worked in Birmingham, engraving from originals by contemporary artists such as Lepoittevin, Goodall, D. Wilkie, Machise, W. Etty, H.J. Townsend, C.L. Eastlake and T.S. Goode. He exhibited at the Royal Academy from 1858 to 1883.

SHARPE, Charlotte, or Sharp

later Mrs Best Morris

British, 19th century.

Born c. 1799, in London; died 1849.

Painter, draughtsman, watercolourist.

Charlotte Sharpe was the eldest daughter of the engraver William Sharpe. Her remarkable gift for portraiture was evident from a very early age and she started exhibiting her work in 1817. She worked first and foremost in pencil heightened with watercolour. Charlotte Sharpe married the career officer Captain Morris and her subsequent output was constrained by her duties as a wife and mother of two children. She nonetheless exhibited at the Royal Academy from 1822 to 1841 under the name of 'Mrs Best Morris'.

SHARPE, Eliza, or Sharp

British, 19th century.

Born August 1796, in Birmingham; died 11 June 1874, in Burnham Beaches.

Painter. Portraits.

Eliza Sharpe was the daughter of William and sister of Charlotte, Louisa and Mary Anne Sharpe. She was a member of the Society of Painters in Watercolours from 1829 to 1872 and exhibited quite frequently between 1817 and 1869 both at the Society and at the Royal Academy, typically showing portraits. Towards the end of her life she devoted much of her time to copying paintings in the South Kensington (now the Victoria & Albert) Museum.

MUSEUMS AND GALLERIES:

LONDON (British Mus.): *Self-portrait with the Artist's Sisters Louisa and Mary Anne*.

SHARPE, J. F.

British, 19th century.

Active in London and in Southampton.

Painter. Portraits.

J.F. Sharpe exhibited in Southampton between 1826 and 1838.

SHARPE, John, or Sharp

British, 16th century.

Engraver. Seals.

From 1509 to 1547 Sharpe engraved seals at the Tower of London Mint.

SHARPE, Louisa, or Sharp

later Mrs Seyffarth

British, 19th century.

Born 1798, in Birmingham; died 28 January 1843, in Dresden.

Miniaturist, watercolourist. Portraits, genre scenes.

Louisa Sharpe started out painting miniatures but subsequently turned to watercolours. She exhibited in London from 1817 to 1833, showing portraits at the Royal Academy and at the Society of Painters in Watercolours, to membership of which she was admitted in 1829, along with her sister Eliza. She married Dr Seyffarth in 1834 and moved to Dresden. Louisa Sharpe is widely regarded as the most talented of William Sharpe's daughters.

MUSEUMS AND GALLERIES:

NOTTINGHAM (Castle Museum and Art Gallery): *Unexpected Arrival*.

AUCTION RECORDS:

LONDON, 10 Dec 1920, *All Hallow E'en* (drawing) GBP 21.
LONDON, 30 Sept 2004, *Elegant Company. Go-between* (pencil and watercolour heightened with white, a pair, 24 x 30 ins / 60 x 77 cm) GBP 2,200.

SHARPE, Mary Anne, or Sharp

British, 19th century.

Born August 1802, in Birmingham; died 1867.

Painter. Genre scenes, portraits.

Mary Anne Sharp was the youngest daughter of the engraver William Sharpe. First and foremost a portraitist, she exhibited in London from 1819 until her death in 1867, typically at the Royal Academy and the Suffolk Street Gallery. She was admitted to membership of the Society of British Artists in 1830. Mary Anne Sharpe lived with her sister Charlotte and assisted the latter in her work.

SHARPE, Matilda

British, 19th - 20th century.

Born 1830; died 1915.

Painter. Portraits.

MUSEUMS AND GALLERIES:

LONDON (National Portrait Gal.): *Samuel Davidson* (c. 1850-1859, chalk); *Samuel Sharpe* (1868, oil on canvas); *Joseph Bonomi the Younger* (1868, oil on canvas).

SHARPE, William
British, 18th - 19th century.
Engraver.

William Sharpe was active in Birmingham between 1796 and 1802. He worked predominantly as a cold-chisel engraver. His daughters Charlotte, Eliza, Louisa and Mary Anne all went on to become artists in their own right.

SHARPLES, Ellen (Mrs)
Maiden name: Wallace
British, 18th - 19th century.
Born 4 March 1769, in Birmingham; died 14 March 1849, in Bristol.
Painter, pastellist, miniaturist. Portraits.

Ellen Sharples was the wife of James Sharples. While of French origin, she had relatives in America and followed her husband to New York when he moved there in 1796. She worked in pastel and specialised in miniatures and proved as successful as her husband in America. Ellen Sharples exhibited in London between 1783 and 1807, returning to England after the death of her husband and settled in Bristol in 1812, finishing her career there. She made an important contribution to the establishment of the Bristol Fine Arts Academy and subsequently bequeathed to that institution a number of her own paintings together with some of her husband's work.

BIBLIOGRAPHY:

Meschutt, D., *'New Discoveries in American Art'* in *American Art Journal*, vol. 16, 4, New York, 1984. Metz, Kathryn, *'Ellen and Rolinda Sharples: Mother and Daughter Painters'* in *Woman's Art Journal*, vol. 16, 1, 1995.

MUSEUMS AND GALLERIES:

BRISTOL (City Mus. & AG): *North American Indian Chief* (oil on canvas) - LONDON (National Portrait Gal.): *George Washington* (c. 1797, pastel, two versions, by James Sharples, or by Ellen Sharples).

SHARPLES, Félix
British, 19th century.
Born before 1787, in England; died c. 1814, in North Carolina.
Painter. Portraits.

Félix Sharples was the eldest son of James Sharples. He remained behind in America when he mother Ellen returned to England in 1811 following the death of her husband. Sharples enjoyed considerable success in the USA and a large number of his compositions are still owned by some of America's leading families.

SHARPLES, George
British, 19th century.
Born c. 1787, in England; died c. 1849.
Painter. Portraits.

Son of James Sharples Sr.; exhibitor at London's Royal Academy from 1815 to 1823.

SHARPLES, James, the Elder, or Sharpless
British, 18th - 19th century.
Born c. 1751, in England; died 26 February 1811, in New York.
Painter, pastellist, miniaturist. Portraits.

James Sharples Sr. was a Catholic and was originally destined for the priesthood. Instead, he opted to devote his life to painting. Believed to have come from Cambridge, he began exhibiting at the Royal Academy in 1779 and continued to do so until 1785. Sharples married Ellen Wallace, a young painter of French extraction who had relatives in North America. The couple left for the New World, arriving in New York City in 1796. That same year, Sharples came to broad public notice with his life portrait of George Washington (which was subsequently frequently copied by his wife Ellen). His small pastel portraits and miniatures were soon very much in demand and, by all accounts, once he was firmly established, Sharples earned a small fortune. His sons Felix and his daughter Rolinda also became painters in their own right.

BIBLIOGRAPHY:

Meschutt, D., *'Re-identification of a portrait by James Sharples'* in *American Art Journal 16, 4*, 1984. Meschutt, D., *'New Discoveries in American Art'* in *American Art Journal, 16, 4*, New York, 1984.

MUSEUMS AND GALLERIES:

BRISTOL (City Mus. & AG): large collection of portraits - LONDON (National Portrait Gal.): *Joseph Priestley* (c. 1797, pastel, two versions, by or after James Sharples); *George Washington* (c. 1797, pastel, two versions, by James Sharples, or by Ellen Sharples).

AUCTION RECORDS:

NEW YORK, 25-26 March 1931, *Portrait of a Gentleman* (pastel) USD 200. NEW YORK, 26-29 April 1944, *General Elias Dayton* (pastel) USD 250. NEW YORK, 21 May 1970, *Portrait of Alexander Hamilton* (pastel) USD 6,000. NEW YORK, 18 Oct 1972, *Portrait of Dr Elihu Hubbard Smith* (pastel) USD 3,000. NEW YORK, 13 Oct 1983, *Portrait of George Washington* (c. 1800, pastel, 9 x 7 ins / 22.8 x 17.8 cm) USD 6,000. NEW YORK, 4 Dec 1987, *George Washington* (pastel/paper, 9 1/4 x 7 1/2 ins / 23.6 x 19 cm) USD 20,000.

SHARPLES, James, the Younger
British, 19th century.
Born 1789, in Liverpool; died 10 August 1839, in Bristol.
Painter. Portraits.

Son of the portraitist James Sharples, James Sharples the Younger worked in Bristol.

MUSEUMS AND GALLERIES:

BRISTOL: *Portrait of the Artist's Father*; seven still-lifes.

SHARPLES, James
British, 19th century.
Born 1825, in Wakefield (Yorkshire); died 1893.
Painter, engraver.

James Sharples was something of an oddity - a passionate art lover and blacksmith who taught himself to paint and engrave. He was the eldest in a large working-class family. He somehow contrived to attend drawing classes in Bury and, by skimping and saving as best he could, finally managed to acquire some paints and a brush. He painted *Blacksmith's Forge* and proceeded to engrave it by an improvised combination of cold-chisel and mezzotint techniques. Sharples went on to paint a large number of portraits and another notable composition entitled *Blacksmiths*. Despite his love of painting, however, he was never in a position to devote himself completely to his art.

AUCTION RECORDS:

LONDON, 11 June 1923, *Captain Webber* (pastel) GBP 12.

SHARPLES, Rolinda
British, 19th century.
Born 1794, in New York; died 10 February 1838, in Bristol.
Painter. Genre scenes, portraits.

Rolinda Sharples was the daughter of portraitist James Sharples. She was admitted to membership of the Society of British Artists. She exhibited in London from 1820 to 1836, principally at the Royal Academy and the Suffolk Street Gallery. She lived close to her mother, the artist Ellen Sharples.

BIBLIOGRAPHY:

Metz, Kathryn, *'Ellen and Rolinda Sharples: Mother and Daughter Painters'* in *Woman's Art Journal*, vol. 16, 1, 1995.

MUSEUMS AND GALLERIES:

BRISTOL (City Mus. & AG): *Portrait of the Artist's Mother, Mrs Ellen Sharples* (oil on canvas); *Clifton Race Course* (oil on canvas); *Cloakroom in the Clifton Assembly Rooms* (oil on canvas); several other paintings (local scenes, portraits, religious subjects) - BRISTOL (Royal West of England Academy): *Portrait ofthe Artist's Mother, Mrs Ellen Sharples* (oil on canvas).

SHART
20th century.
Born 1927.
Painter. Figures, scenes with figures, landscapes.

Shart is a self-taught artist who produces paintings of landscapes, rural scenes, musicians and carnivals, which reveal naivety and awe of the surrounding world and invite a state of reverie. He has travelled widely and shown in exhibitions in France and abroad, including, since 1954, a number of solo shows.

MUSEUMS AND GALLERIES:
JERUSALEM (Israel Mus.) - L'ISLE-ADAM (MAH Louis-Senlecq) - PONTOISE - VENICE (S Lazzaro Mus.).

SHARVIN, Jakov Vasilievich
Russian, 19th century.
Born 1838; died 1880.
Painter, actor. Genre scenes.

Sharvin was a pupil at the academy in St Petersburg.

MUSEUMS AND GALLERIES:
MOSCOW (State Tretyakov Gal.): *At Mother's Bedside.*

SHATTER, Susan
American, 20th century.
Born 1943.
Painter, draughtswoman, watercolourist.

AUCTION RECORDS:
NEW YORK, 15 Nov 1995, *Canyon Rose* (1986, oil on canvas, 53 x 113 ins / 134.6 x 287 cm) USD 4,600. NEW YORK, 22 Feb 1996, *Untitled, Shadow on the Land* (1976, watercolour and pencil/rice paper, 34 1/2 x 117 ins / 87.6 x 297.2 cm) USD 2,760. BOSTON, 22 March 2002, *Kittery Point, Maine* (1975, watercolour, 21 x 45 ins / 53 x 114 cm) USD 2,000.

SHATTUCK, Aaron Draper
American, 19th - 20th century.
Born 9 April 1832, in Francestown; died 30 July 1928, in Granby (Connecticut).
Painter. Landscapes, animals.

Aaron Draper Shattuck was a pupil of Alexander Ramson, with whom he studied portrait and landscape painting in Boston in 1851. He went on to study at the National Academy of Design in New York, of which he became a member in 1856, and subsequently rented a studio in the famous Tenth Street Studio Building. He was closely associated with the artist John Frederick Kenset. He exhibited regularly in Boston and New York.

MUSEUMS AND GALLERIES:
BUFFALO (Albright-Knox AG).

AUCTION RECORDS:
NEW YORK, 13 Sept 1972, *Landscape*, USD 1,500. NEW YORK, 11 April 1973, *Lake Champlain*, USD 4,000. NEW YORK, 23 March 1974, *The White Hills in October*, USD 4,500. NEW YORK, 20 April 1979, *Lake Champlain* (oil on canvas remounted/panel, 26 1/4 x 2407 1/4 ins / 66.6 x 6114.3 cm) USD 12,000. PORTLAND, 4 April 1981, *Farmongton River, Connecticut* (c. 1865, oil on card, 12 x 16 3/4 ins / 30.5 x 42.5 cm) USD 4,000. NEW YORK, 23 March 1984, *Mount Lafayette* (1857, oil on paper remounted/canvas, 7 1/2 x 15 3/4 ins / 19.3 x 39.9 cm) USD 1,200. NEW YORK, 30 May 1985, *A Memory of the Upper Kanawha* (oil on canvas, 10 x 16 ins / 25.5 x 40.6 cm) USD 4,500. NEW YORK, 24 June 1988, *First Days of Summer* (1860, oil on canvas, 25 1/4 x 42 ins / 64 x 105.8 cm) USD 10,450. NEW YORK, 30 Sept 1988, *Meadow near Granby, Connecticut* (oil on canvas, 12 x 22 1/4 ins / 30.5 x 56.2 cm) USD 3,300. NEW YORK, 24 Jan 1989, *Cattle in a Landscape at Granby in Connecticut* (oil on card, 10 3/4 x 16 ins / 27.5 x 40.7 cm) USD 4,125. NEW YORK, 17 Dec 1990, *Cows on the River Bank* (1880, oil on canvas, 12 x 18 ins / 30.5 x 45.5 cm) USD 2,750. NEW YORK, 24 Sept 1992, *White Mountains in New Hampshire* (1861, oil on card, 10 1/2 x 18 1/2 ins / 26.7 x 47 cm) USD 4,675. NEW YORK, 12 Sept 1994, *Seascape at Nightfall* (oil on canvas, 10 1/4 x 16 ins / 26 x 40.6 cm) USD 3,220.

SHAVER, James Robert
American, 19th - 20th century.
Born 27 March 1867, in Evening Shade (Arkansas); died 1949.
Painter, illustrator.

James Robert Shaver studied at the School of Fine Arts in St Louis and was a member of the Salmagundi Club. He specialised in illustrations for children's books.

SHAVER, Nancy
American, 20th - 21st century.
Born 1946, in Appleton (New York).
Sculptor, assemblage artist, mixed media.

Nancy Shaver was married to Haim Steinbach in the 1980s. She works from junk. From 1987, she participated in collective exhibitions, especially the 1989 *Status of Sculpture*, an exhibition organised by ELAC (Espace Lyonnais d'Art Contemporain), which toured France and Great Britain. She shows her work in solo exhibitions in the USA and in France.

AUCTION RECORDS:
PARIS, 16 Dec 1990, *The American* (1989, mixed media, 17 3/4 x 35 1/2 ins / 45 x 90 cm) FRF 18,000.

SHAW, A.
British, 19th century.
Painter. Architectural views.

A. Shaw lived and worked in London, where he exhibited from 1826 to 1839.

SHAW, Annie Cornelia
American, 19th century.
Born 1852, in Troy (New York); died 1887.
Painter. Landscapes, animals.

Annie Cornelia Shaw studied in Chicago with H.C. Ford. In 1873 she became a member of the academy in Chicago.

MUSEUMS AND GALLERIES:
CHICAGO.

SHAW, Arthur Winter
British, 19th - 20th century.
Born 1869; died 1948.
Painter. Figures, scenes with figures, genre scenes.

AUCTION RECORDS:
LONDON, 8 March 1990, *Mother and Child Beside a Window* (oil on canvas, 21 3/4 x 16 3/4 ins / 55.2 x 42.6 cm) GBP 6,050. NEW YORK, 20 Jan 1993, *The Way Home* (oil on canvas, 11 x 17 1/2 ins / 27.9 x 44.5 cm) USD 2,875. NEW YORK, 16 Feb 1993, *By Candlelight* (oil on canvas, 21 x 17 ins / 53.2 x 43.2 cm) USD 1,100. LONDON, 18 May 2000, *Natures Bath* (1912, watercolour and pencil heightened with white, 20 x 28 ins / 51 x 70 cm) GBP 1,400. GODALMING, 26 July 2000, *Nature's Bath* (1912, watercolour, 20 x 28 ins / 52 x 71 cm) GBP 2,000. LONDON, 4 March 2004, *Domestic Chores* (oil on canvas, 17 x 20 ins / 42 x 52 cm) GBP 1,200.

SHAW, Byam John or John Byam Liston
British, 19th - 20th century.
Born 13 November 1872, in Madras, India, to British parents; died 26 January 1919, in London.
Watercolourist, painter (gouache/mixed media), draughtsman, illustrator. Religious subjects, genre scenes.

John Byam Shaw trained at the St John's Wood School of Art and the Royal Academy, London, where he won the Armitage Prize. A follower of the Pre-Raphaelite movement - as in his acclaimed *Blessed Damosel* (1894-1895) - he was often inspired by the poems of Rossetti. He illustrated several books, including Robert Browning's *Poems* (1897) and Charles Reade's *The Cloister and the Hearth* (1909). His painting *Truth* - showing a woman defiled, bound and blindfolded - served as a cartoon for a tapestry commissioned by Morris & Co. in 1909. He exhibited with the Royal Academy from 1893 to 1917, as well as at the Royal Scottish Academy, the Royal Institute of Oil Painters, the New Gallery in London and the Fine Arts Society in Liverpool.

MUSEUMS AND GALLERIES:

LIVERPOOL (Walker AG): *Love's Baubles* (1897, oil on canvas).

AUCTION RECORDS:

LONDON, 17 Feb 1971, *The Poet and the River*, GBP 500. LONDON, 5 Oct 1973, *The Queen of Hearts*, Gns 1,400. LONDON, 16 Nov 1976, *The Offering* (oil on panel, 17 3/4 x 13 1/2 ins / 45 x 34 cm) GBP 400. LONDON, 14 June 1977, *Truly the Light is Sweet* (1901, oil on panel, 15 3/4 x 11 1/2 ins / 40 x 29 cm) GBP 6,400. LONDON, 14 Feb 1978, *Babes in the Wood* (1896, heightened with gouache, 13 1/4 x 9 1/2 ins / 33.5 x 24 cm) GBP 1,300. LONDON, 1 Oct 1979, *The Start of the Race* (1904, oil on canvas, 29 1/2 x 50 1/2 ins / 75 x 128 cm) GBP 14,000. LONDON, 28 May 1980, *Picnic on a Riverbank* (watercolour and gouache, 9 3/4 x 14 3/4 ins / 25 x 37.5 cm) GBP 650. LONDON, 23 June 1981, *Now is the Pilgrim Year Fair Autumn's Charge* (oil on canvas, 33 1/2 x 47 ins / 85 x 119.5 cm) GBP 22,000. PARIS, 15 Feb 1983, *Despair* (wash gouache, 30 x 17 1/4 ins / 76 x 43.5 cm) FRF 6,000. LONDON, 23 March 1984, *Caged Bird* (1907, oil on canvas, rounded at the top, 37 x 28 ins / 94 x 71 cm) GBP 5,200. MELBOURNE, 26 July 1987, *Diana the Huntress* (1901, watercolour and gouache, 30 x 20 3/4 ins / 76 x 53 cm) AUD 12,000. PARIS, 24 June 1988, *Truth* (1898, canvas remounted/panel, 54 x 61 1/2 ins / 137 x 156 cm) FRF 1,300,000. NEW YORK, 28 Feb 1990, *At the Theatre* (oil on panel, 9 1/4 x 12 ins / 23.8 x 30.5 cm) USD 16,500. LONDON, 11 June 1993, *The Watersprite and the Highlander* (watercolour and gouache, 23 x 18 1/2 ins / 58.4 x 47 cm) GBP 2,070. LONDON, 3 June 1994, *This is a Heart the Queen Leant On* (oil on canvas, 30 x 20 1/4 ins / 76.5 x 51.5 cm) GBP 9,200. LONDON, 10 March 1995, *They Sat Down and Wept* (watercolour and gouache heightened with white, 13 1/2 x 10 ins / 34.3 x 24.5 cm) GBP 4,370. LONDON, 6 Nov 1995, *Who Knoweth the Spirit of Man that Goeth... (Ecclesiastes, III, 21)* (1901, oil on panel, 14 x 9 3/4 ins / 35.6 x 24.8 cm) GBP 4,600. LONDON, 5 Nov 1997, *The New Toy* (1894, oil on canvas, 22 x 29 ins / 56 x 73.5 cm) GBP 5,750. LONDON, 9 June 1999, *Cartoon for Mary's Entry into London as Queen* (charcoal on paper laid on canvas, 76 x 78 ins / 193 x 198 cm) GBP 2,000. GUILDFORD, 14 Dec 1999, *Caged Bird Released* (1907, oil on canvas, arched frame, 37 x 28 ins / 94 x 71 cm) GBP 6,500. LONDON, 30 Nov 2000, *As It Happeneth to the Fool, So It Happeneth Even to Me, and Why Was I More Wise* (1901, oil on canvas, 15 x 11 ins / 39 x 29 cm) GBP 6,000. STOCKHOLM, 5 Dec 2000, *The Regatta* (oil on canvas, 25 x 20 ins / 63 x 50 cm) SEK 125,000. LONDON, 21 March 2001, *While Roses are So Red While Lillies are So White, Shall a Woman Exalt her Face, Brings Delight* (1898, oil on panel, 16 x 11 ins / 40 x 29 cm) GBP 4,600. LONDON, 19 Dec 2001, *Lure* (oil on panel, 24 x 26 ins / 62 x 66 cm) GBP 15,000. LONDON, 13 Feb 2002, *Lovers Seated by Waterfall* (oil on panel, 15 x 10 ins / 37 x 26 cm) GBP 2,800. NEW YORK, 30 Oct 2002, *Cleopatra* (oil on panel, 12 x 10 ins / 30 x 25 cm) USD 12,000. NEW YORK, 24 April 2003, *Angel Before Adam and Eve* (oil on panel, 18 x 13 ins / 46 x 34 cm) USD 9,000. LONDON, 25 Nov 2003, *Time and Chance Happeneth to All I Returned, and Saw Under the Sun* (1901, oil on canvas, 34 x 24 ins / 86 x 61 cm) GBP 24,000.

SHAW, Charles Green

American, 20th century.
Born 1892, in New York; died 1974, in New York.
Painter.
American Abstract Artists (AAA).

Charles Green Shaw studied art in London and Paris as well as at the Art Students League in New York. He was one of the first American painters to tackle Abstraction, creating quite perfunctory works in the 1950s. He was a founder-member of the American Abstract Artists group and also belonged to the Abstract-Creation group in Paris. He is known for works inspired by the linear composition of skyscrapers, the *Plastic Polygon* series based on a montage of structures, and also for reliefs inspired by Jean Arp.

From 1937 onwards, Shaw participated in shows devoted to the American Abstract Artists. Other collective exhibitions in which he participated included the Salon des Réalités Nouvelles in Paris in 1949 and 1950. He also showed his work in solo exhibitions such as in New York in 1934.

BIBLIOGRAPHY:

Charles G. Shaw: Abstractions of the Thirties, Richard York Gallery, New York, 1987. *New York Cubists: Works by A.E. Gallatin, George L.K. Morris and Charles G. Shaw from the Thirties and Forties*, Hirschl and Adler, New York, 1988.

MUSEUMS AND GALLERIES:

SAN FRANCISCO (MoMA): *Space Forms* (1952, oil on canvasboard).

AUCTION RECORDS:

NEW YORK, 25 April 1980, *Blasphemies* (1934, oil on canvas, 28 x 24 ins / 71.1 x 61 cm) USD 5,500. NEW YORK, 29 May 1981, *Abstraction No 4* (1942, oil/hardboard, 10 x 11 1/2 ins / 25.4 x 29.2 cm) USD 4,500. NEW YORK, 21 Oct 1983, *Beach Scene* (oil on mounted card, 9 x 12 ins / 22.8 x 30.5 cm) USD 1,500. NEW YORK, 1 Oct 1986, *Abstraction* (1935, oil on canvas, 39 1/4 x 32 ins / 99.5 x 81.5 cm) USD 8,000. NEW YORK, 17 March 1988, *Harbour* (1954, oil/hardboard, 23 1/2 x 35 1/2 ins / 60 x 90 cm) USD 3,025. NEW YORK, 25 May 1989, *Abstract Seascape* (1941, oil on canvas, 20 x 16 ins / 50.8 x 40.6 cm) USD 16,500. NEW YORK, 28 Sept 1989, *Event 2* (oil on reinforced canvas, 16 x 12 ins / 40.6 x 30.5 cm) USD 1,540. NEW YORK, 16 March 1990, *Draft for a Wall Fountain* (1940, oil on reinforced canvas, 18 x 12 1/4 ins / 45.7 x 31.3 cm) USD 18,700. NEW YORK, 30 May 1990, *Untitled* (1940, oil on card, 16 x 12 ins / 40.7 x 30.5 cm) USD 9,900. NEW YORK, 17 Dec 1990, *Still-life in Plastic* (oil on reinforced canvas, 12 x 15 ins / 30.5 x 38.2 cm) USD 5,500. NEW YORK, 14 March 1991, *Town in Spring* (oil on card, 30 x 22 ins / 76 x 56 cm) USD 8,250. NEW YORK, 26 Sept 1991, *Revolt* (oil on canvas, 50 x 40 1/4 ins / 127 x 102 cm) USD 7,150. NEW YORK, 15 April 1992, *Abstract Composition* (1941, oil on reinforced canvas, 16 x 20 ins / 40.6 x 50.8 cm) USD 8,250. NEW YORK, 25 Sept 1992, *Composition* (1940, oil on card, 20 x 16 ins / 50.8 x 40.6 cm) USD 15,400. NEW YORK, 10 March 1993, *Abstraction* (oil on canvas, 28 x 24 ins / 71.1 x 61 cm) USD 7,475. NEW YORK, 13 Sept 1995, *Abstraction* (oil on card, 12 x 9 ins / 30.5 x 22.8 cm) USD 5,980. NEW YORK, 25 March 1997, *Portrait* (oil on panel, 20 x 15 3/4 ins / 50.8 x 40 cm) USD 3,450. NEW YORK, 4 Oct 2000, *Seated Nude* (oil on canvas, 42 x 30 ins / 107 x 76 cm) USD 6,000. NEW YORK, 4 Oct 2000, *Mannequin* (oil on canvas, 42 x 30 ins / 106 x 76 cm) USD 30,000. NEW YORK, 13 June 2001, *Silhouette Against Yellow* (1968, oil on canvas, 48 x 36 ins / 122 x 91 cm) USD 5,500. NEW YORK, 13 June 2001, *Abstraction* (1940, oil on canvasboard, 14 x 10 ins / 36 x 25 cm) USD 9,500. NEW YORK, 13 Feb 2002, *Abstraction with Red, Blue, Yellow and Green* (oil on canvasboard, 20 x 16 ins / 51 x 41 cm) USD 13,000. NEW YORK, 17 July 2002, *Conflicting Forces* (1966, oil on canvas, 48 x 64 ins / 122 x 163 cm) USD 17,000. NEW YORK, 4 March 2003, *Abstraction with Blue, Brown and Grey Forms* (1941, oil on canvasboard, 16 x 20 ins / 41 x 51 cm) USD 18,000. CHICAGO, 9 Nov 2003, *Still-life with Rye* (oil on board, 11 x 8 ins / 28 x 20 cm) USD 19,000. CHICAGO, 16 May 2004, *Abstract Composition* (painted wood, 11 x 16 ins / 28 x 41 cm) USD 13,000. NEW YORK, 8 Sept 2004, *Façade* (1956, oil on canvas, 24 x 30 ins / 62 x 75 cm) USD 3,200.

SHAW, Evelyn

Maiden name: Pyke-Nott

British, 19th - 20th century.
Painter, miniaturist. Portraits.
Evelyn Shaw was the wife of John Byam Shaw. She studied at the Royal Academy in London from 1899, and lived and worked in London.

SHAW, G. B.
British, 19th century.
Active in London between 1835 and 1850.
Engraver (burin).

SHAW, Harriett, Mrs McCreary
American, 19th - 20th century.
Born 17 March 1865, in Fayettville (Arkansas); died 1934.
Painter, miniaturist.
Harriett Shaw was taught by Magda Heuman, Samuel Richards in Munich and Charles P. Adams in Denver. She was a member of the American Federation of Arts. She won many gold and silver medals for her miniatures on ivory and porcelain and for her portraits.

SHAW, Henry
British, 19th century.
Born 4 July 1800, in London; died 12 June 1873, in Broxbourne (Hertfordshire), England.
Watercolourist, draughtsman, engraver (burin), writer.
Illustrated the Longman edition of the *New Testament.*

SHAW, I.
British, 19th century.
Draughtsman, engraver (burin).

SHAW, James
British, 18th century.
Died c. 1772.
Painter. Animals.
Successful painter of horses; painted from life and exhibited at the Society of Artists in 1761.
AUCTION RECORDS:
LONDON, 19 July 1985, *Preparation for the Gold Cup* (oil on canvas, 37 x 46 ins / 94 x 116.7 cm) GBP 12,000.

SHAW, James
British, 18th century.
Born in Wolverhampton.
Painter. Portraits.
Pupil of Edward Penny; exhibited from 1776 to 1787 and was particularly renowned for his portraiture.

SHAW, James
Australian, 19th century.
Born 1815; died 1881.
Painter. Landscapes.
BIBLIOGRAPHY:
Creating Australia: 200 Years of Art 1788-1988, exhibition catalogue, Art Gall. Board of South Australia, Adelaide, 1988.
MUSEUMS AND GALLERIES:
ADELAIDE (AG of South Australia): *The 'Admella' Wrecked, Cape Banks, August 6, 1859.*

SHAW, Jeffrey
Australian, 20th century.
Born 1944.
Active in the Netherlands.
Performance artist. Multimedia.
Computer Art (Virtual Art).
Jeffrey Shaw's work often has a playful element, for example bringing traffic to a halt using an air cushion. He has taken part in group exhibitions, including at the following; the Festival des Arts Electroniques in Rennes (1986); Berlin (1989); the Frankfurt Art Fair (1991); the 4th Biennale Artifices in St-Denis, where he was guest of honour (1996); and the Cité des Sciences et de l'Industrie in Paris (1996).
BIBLIOGRAPHY:
'Jeffrey Shaw' in *Art Press, special edition: 'Nouvelles Technologies un Art sans Modèle?',* periodical, Paris, 1992.

SHAW, Jim
American, 20th - 21st century.
Born 1952, in Midland (Michigan).
Painter (including gouache), collage artist, draughtsman, mixed media, video artist. Comic strips. Citationism.
Jim Shaw lives and works in Los Angeles. He uses various techniques such as pencil, fluorescent painting, oil and artificial blood on velvet carpet (*Oil on Velvet*), imprints on artificial grass (*Narcissus' Footprints*), and collages in order to give an ironic portrayal of a decadent world. His richly detailed work - comic strips, canvas, objects, collages - borrow from the world of stories, fantasy and religion as well as rock music. He also makes artistic quotations with references to Bosch, Magritte, Dalí and Kollwitz and mixes popular imagery and pictorial culture. He has taken part in collective exhibitions including: *Subréel,* MAC, Galeries Contemporaines des Musées de Marseille, 2002, and *LA Uncool,* Museum of Art, San José, California. Solo exhibitions of his work include: New York, Houston, Milan, 1992; Santa Monica, 1992, 1993; Paris, 1997; *The Rite of the 360 Degree,* Galerie Praz-Delavallade, Paris, 2002; Swiss Institute, New York, 2002; Galerie Massimo de Carlo, Milan, 2002; Magasin, Centre National d'Art Contemporain, Grenoble, 2003.
BIBLIOGRAPHY:
Clearwater, Bonnie, *'Arrêt sur enfance'* in *Art Press* n° 197, periodical, Paris, December 1994. Albertini, Rosanna, *'Jim Shaw, rêveries d'un artiste conceptuel'* in *Art Press* n° 223, periodical, Paris, April 1997.
MUSEUMS AND GALLERIES:
GENEVA (Mamco): *Life and Death: A Non-narrative Narrative* (1981).
AUCTION RECORDS:
NEW YORK, 17 Nov 1992, *Untitled* (graphite, white chalk, charcoal and ink/paper, two drawings, each 14 x 11 ins / 35.6 x 27 cm) USD 2,200. NEW YORK, 8 Nov 1993, *Good Idea (My Mirage Series)* (1987, oil on canvas, 17 x 14 ins / 43.2 x 35.5 cm) USD 3,220. NEW YORK, 19 Nov 1996, *Billy Goes to a Love-in* (1991, gouache and felt/panel) USD 2,875. NEW YORK, 15 Nov 2000, *Seven Dream Drawings* (1993 or 1995, pencil, seven parts, 12 x 9 ins / 30 x 23 cm) USD 3,750. MILAN, 4 June 2002, *Portrait of Man* (1992, pencil on card, 14 x 11 ins / 35 x 27 cm) EUR 7,500. LOS ANGELES, 9 Nov 2003, *Untitled - from the 65 distorted faces* (pencil, 14 x 11 ins / 36 x 28 cm) USD 3,250. NEW YORK, 14 Nov 2003, *Televised Chinese H-Bom. Untitled. Well, it Was Really an Unequal Contest* (graphite, three framed, 17 x 14 ins / 43 x 36 cm) USD 4,200. NEW YORK, 14 May 2004, *Untitled, Bing Crosby. Untitled, Bird Text. Untitled, Dream Drawing* (1995, 2001, 2001, graphite, three, 17 x 14 ins / 43 x 36 cm) USD 4,500. NEW YORK, 10 June 2004, *Dream Drawing. Untitled* (1995. 2001, graphite, pair, 12 x 9 ins / 30 x 23 cm) USD 3,200.

SHAW, Joshua, called Shaw of Bath
British, 19th century.
Born 1776, in Bellingborough; died 1860, in Bordentown (New Jersey), USA.
Painter, draughtsman. Genre scenes, landscapes with figures, waterscapes, mountainscapes, animals, still-lifes.
Joshua Shaw started out as a sign-painter. After serving his apprenticeship he moved to Manchester and married. By this time he had started painting floral compositions, still-lifes and landscapes, on each occasion making a large number of copies. His name features in London exhibition catalogues from 1802 to 1841, notably at the Royal Academy, the British Institution and the Suffolk Street Gallery. On moving to London,

Shaw's work was frequently passed off by art dealers as originals rather than copies of compositions by Berchem or Gainsborough or other leading landscape painters. He then moved to Bath and spent several years there before leaving for the USA in 1817, living for a period in Philadelphia before settling definitively in Bordentown in New Jersey in 1843. The move to the USA effectively represented a new lease of artistic life as Shaw's landscapes and genre compositions - frequently featuring Native American scenes - fired the public imagination. His reputation was further enhanced by a manual on drawing and composition he published in 1819 and by his landscape sketches subsequently engraved by John W. Hill and published in 1820-1821 as the collection *Picturesque Views of the American Landscape*. Shaw fell seriously ill in 1853 and did not paint after that time.

With the notable exception of his masterpiece *The Flood* (often carelessly attributed to Washington Allston), Shaw's canvases are marred by a somewhat uninspired and repetitive compositional approach, leavened however by a delicate touch and his sensitive treatment of light and shade.

Museums and Galleries:

London (Victoria and Albert Mus.): *River Bank with a Young Boy* - New York (Metropolitan Mus. of Art): *The Flood* (1813).

Auction records:

New York, 19 April 1972, *River Landscape at Sunset*, USD 2,500. London, 18 June 1976, *River Landscape* (oil on canvas, 37 1/2 x 50 1/2 ins / 95 x 128 cm) GBP 3,200. New York, 18 Nov 1977, *Sunset on the Mohawk* (oil on canvas, 27 3/4 x 44 1/4 ins / 70.7 x 112.3 cm) USD 3,500. New York, 26 June 1981, *Pennsylvanian Landscape* (1823, oil on canvas, 26 x 36 ins / 65.1 x 91.7 cm) USD 32,000. New York, 2 June 1983, *Peasants on a Country Road* (1851, oil on canvas, 14 x 20 ins / 35.5 x 50.8 cm) USD 8,500. London, 27 Sept 1994, *Mountain Landscape with a Rider walking alongside his Horse and with other Animals* (oil on panel, 15 1/4 x 19 1/2 ins / 38.5 x 49.5 cm) GBP 632.

SHAW, Karen

American, 20th century.
Born 1941.
Mixed media. Artists' books.
Conceptual Art.

Karen Shaw was active in the 1970s. In 1992, she appeared in the exhibition: *De Bonnard à Baselitz: Dix Ans d'enrichissements du cabinet des estampes 1978-1988* (*From Bonnard to Baselitz: A Decade of Acquisitions by the Prints Collection 1978-1988*), at the Bibliothèque National, Paris and in 1998 in *Women of the Book: Jewish Artists, Jewish Themes*, a travelling exhibition in the USA at the La Jolla Athenaeum and the San Diego Centre for Jewish Culture. A solo exhibition of her work was held at the Antwerp International Cultural Centre in 1980.

Bibliography:

Women of the Book: Jewish Artists, Jewish Themes, exhibition catalogue, Florida Atlantic University, Wimberly Library, Boca Raton (FL), 1998.

Museums and Galleries:

Paris (BNF, Prints Collection).

SHAW, Richard Blake

American, 20th - 21st century.
Born 1941, in Hollywood.
Ceramicist.

A pupil of Orange Coast College (1961-1963), Richard Shaw, graduated from San Francisco Art Institute (1965) and the University of California at Davis (1968). He taught at Berkeley in 1987. Since the late 1960s, Shaw has been recreating the world around him in clay, piece by piece. His sculptures mimic everyday objects with an accuracy that belies their medium. Shaw keeps a library of hundreds of moulds in his workshop, a vocabulary of objects that he inverts, varies, and combines in his assemblages and has developed an array of techniques including printmaking, glazing and transfer decals, to increase the realism of his objects.

Shaw is associated with Bay Area Funk, a movement characterised by its irreverent, sometimes surreal assemblage of everyday objects into whimsical and disturbing artworks. However, rather than use readymade found objects, Shaw fashions his pieces. His perfect trompe l'oeil still-lifes include replica books, playing cards, pencil stubs, paint cans, even half-eaten apple cores and a wheel of Brie. An astonishingly skilful evocation of surface and texture, including a seductive patina of age and use, completes the illusion. Ships of all kinds are a recurring theme, a reflection of his childhood fondness for drawing battles at sea. A number of gangly figures, *Mrs Partch* and *Man With Horn* (1985) made of replica junk, suggest portraits made of whatever is handy.

Works include: *Hope* (1991); *Small Card Stack With Book and Bowl* (1996); *Ship Tureen* (1993). His ceramics can be found in major collections in the US, Europe and Japan. Shaw featured in several collective exhibitions throughout the USA, Canada, Mexico, Japan, England, The Netherlands and France. Solo exhibitions include: Braunstein Gallery, San Francisco; Morgan Gallery, Kansas City; Allen Frumkin Gallery, New York; Greenberg Gallery, St Louis, Michael Berger Gallery, Pittsburgh, and Newport Harbor Art Museum.

Bibliography:

Landauer, Susan, *The Lighter Side of Bay Area Figuration*, Kemper Museum of Contemporary Art, Kansas City, 2000.

Museums and Galleries:

Amsterdam (Stedelijk Mus.) - Kansas City (Nelson-Atkins MA) - Lincoln, NE (Sheldon Memorial AG, University of Nebraska): *Mrs Partch* (ceramic with underglaze, glaze and overglaze transfers) - New York (Museum of Contemporary Crafts) - New York (Whitney Mus. of American Art) - Oakland (Mus. of California) - Sacramento, CA (Croker Art Museum) - San Francisco (MA): *Melodious Double Stops* (1980, porcelain with decal overglaze) - Washington DC (Smithsonian American AM): *Secret Hula Book Jar* (porcelain with overglaze).

SHAW, Robert

American, 19th - 20th century.
Born 10 January 1859, in Wilmington; died 18 July 1912, in Wilmington.
Engraver.

Robert Shaw was a self-taught artist. He achieved local fame during his lifetime, also drawing wider national attention for his etchings. He produced detailed depictions of the sights of Delaware.

SHAW, Stephen William

American, 19th century.
Born 15 December 1817, in Windsor (Vermont); died 12 February 1900, in San Francisco.
Painter. Portraits.

SHAW, Sydney Dale

British, 20th century.
Born 16 August 1879, in Walkley.
Painter, engraver. Landscapes.

Sydney Dale Shaw studied at the Art Students League in New York, the Académie Colarossi and the École des Beaux-Arts in Paris. He won numerous prizes in the course of his career.

SHAW, Walter J.

British, 19th century.
Born 1851; died 1933.
Painter. Waterscapes, seascapes.

Walter J. Shaw exhibited in London from 1878, notably at the Royal Academy.

Museums and Galleries:

Bristol: *Salcombe Bar in Bad Weather; Bentham Sands, Devon.*

Auction records:

London, 24 May 1910, *Pentyre Head Padstow,* GBP 9. London, 14 March 1980, *Sailing Boats in Rough Seas* (oil on canvas, 23 1/4 x 35 1/4 ins / 59 x 89.5 cm) GBP 700. Billingshurst, 12 Jan 1999, *A Rough Sea* (1891, oil on canvas, 24 x 36 ins / 61 x 91 cm) GBP 2,300. Clevedon, 23 Nov 2000, *Seascape* (oil on canvas, 36 x 60 ins / 91 x 152 cm) GBP 2,900. Billingshurst, 18 July 2001, *Breaking Waves* (1883, oil on canvas, 36 x 60 ins / 91 x 152 cm) GBP 2,100. Leominster, 25 Sept 2002, *Choppy Sea with Rocky Coastline, possibly Cornwall* (1894, oil on canvas, 40 x 60 ins / 102 x 152 cm) GBP 1,950. Washington, 13 Sept 2003, *Star Point* (oil on canvas, 24 x 42 ins / 61 x 107 cm) USD 2,600.

SHAW, William

British, 18th century.

Born c. 1757; died 1773.

Painter. Animals.

William Shaw exhibited in London between 1760 and 1772.

Auction records:

London, 22 June 1979, *Racehorse and Jockey* (oil on canvas, 14 x 17 ins / 35.4 x 43.1 cm) GBP 700. London, 18 April 1986, *Groom holding a Racehorse* (oil on canvas, 14 1/2 x 17 ins / 36.8 x 43 cm) GBP 3,200. London, 9 Feb 1990, *Stable Lad holding Chestnut Trotter 'Sooty Dun'* (oil on canvas, 25 x 30 ins / 63.5 x 76.2 cm) GBP 5,720. London, 7 April 1993, *Thoroughbred Bay 'Matchem' and Jockey, with its Owner and Trainer at the Finishing Line* (1757, oil on canvas, 40 x 50 ins / 101.6 x 127 cm) GBP 12,650. New York, 1 Dec 1999, *Hunting Conversation, Two Hunters Held by Huntsman with a Couple of Hounds* (oil on canvas, 40 x 51 ins / 102 x 130 cm) USD 19,000. New York, 18 May 2004, *Groom with a Race Horse* (oil on canvas, 28 x 35 ins / 71 x 90 cm) USD 8,500.

SHAW, William. See also **SCHAW**

SHAW, William V.

American, 19th - 20th century.

Born 1842; died 29 December 1909, in Jamaica (New York).

Painter.

SHAW OF BATH. See **SHAW Joshua**

SHAYER, Charles

British, 19th century.

Painter. Genre scenes.

Cited in auction records, Charles Shayer is possibly identical with Charles Waller Shayer.

Auction records:

London, 4 Dec 1909, *Invitation to the Cabaret; Off to Market* (two pendants) GBP 16. London, 24 April 1911, *Gossiping,* GBP 31. London, 9 Dec 1964, *Country Market,* GBP 380. London, 23 April 1974, *Horses and Farm Workers in a Field,* GBP 380. London, 29 Nov 1978, *Well-Earned Rest* (oil on canvas, 11 1/2 x 15 1/4 ins / 29.5 x 38.5 cm) GBP 1,900. London, 12 March 1980, *Well-Earned Rest* (oil on canvas, 14 1/2 x 19 ins / 37 x 48 cm) GBP 850.

SHAYER, Charles Waller

British, 19th - 20th century.

Born 1826; died 1914.

Painter. Landscapes with figures.

The son of William Shayer Senior, Charles Waller Shayer often worked in collaboration with Henry Thring Shayer.

Bibliography:

Stewart, Brian, *The Shayer Family of Painters,* F. Lewis, London, 1981.

Auction records:

London, 10 Nov 1982, *Labourer at Rest* (oil on canvas, 23 1/2 x 35 ins / 59.5 x 89 cm) GBP 3,600. New York, 6 June 1986, *Country Market* (1875, oil on canvas, 23 3/4 x 42 ins / 60.3 x 106.7 cm) USD 13,000. New York, 3 June 1994, *The Melton Mowbray Team* (oil on canvas, 22 x 36 ins / 55.9 x 91.4 cm) USD 13,225. London, 10 March 1995, *In the New Forest* (oil on canvas, in collaboration with Henry Thring Shayer, 19 3/4 x 30 ins / 50.2 x 75.9 cm) GBP 4,370. London, 14 March 1997, *Animals Beside a River* (oil on canvas, in collaboration with Henry Thring Shayer, 30 x 25 1/4 ins / 76.2 x 64.1 cm) GBP 10,120.

SHAYER, Henry Thring

British, 19th century.

Born 1825; died 1894.

Painter. Genre scenes, landscapes with figures.

Son of William Shayer Sr, Henry Thring Shayer frequently worked alongside Charles Waller Shayer and with a William Shayer (possibly his own father).

Bibliography:

Stewart, Brian, *The Shayer Family of Painters,* F. Lewis, London, 1981.

Auction records:

London, 9 July 1980, *At Rest by the Wayside* (1850, oil on card, 12 3/4 x 12 ins / 32.5 x 30.5 cm) GBP 2,300. London, 10 March 1995, *In the New Forest* (oil on canvas, in collaboration with Charles Waller Shayer, 19 3/4 x 30 ins / 50.2 x 75.9 cm) GBP 4,370. London, 14 March 1997, *Cattle Wading in a River* (oil on canvas, in collaboration with Charles Waller Shayer, 30 x 25 1/4 ins / 76.2 x 64.1 cm) GBP 10,120. London, 4 June 1997, *Cattle Watering* (oil on canvas, 18 x 24 ins / 45.5 x 61 cm) GBP 4,830. London, 7 Nov 1997, *Woodcutter Resting* (1865, oil on canvas, in collaboration with William Shayer, 30 x 25 1/4 ins / 76 x 64 cm) GBP 7,475. Nottingham, 10 Dec 1999, *The Sportsman's Return* (oil on canvas, 12 x 16 ins / 30 x 41 cm) GBP 4,800.

SHAYER, William, the Elder

British, 19th century.

Born in Southampton, baptised 14 June 1787 according to some sources, in 1788 according to others; died 21 December 1879, on Shirley, near Southampton.

Painter. Genre scenes, landscapes, landscapes with figures, animals. Escutcheons.

William Shayer married Sarah Lewis Earle in 1810 and fathered William Shayer the Younger, Charles Waller Shayer and Henry Thring Shayer. William Shayer was admitted to membership of the Society of British Artists in 1862 and showed his work at Society exhibitions from 1825 to 1870. He also exhibited at London's Royal Academy and at the British Institution.

William Shayer started out painting furniture in Southampton before leaving for Guildford where he set himself up as a coach-painter. Word soon spread throughout southern England with regard to his skill in painting coats of arms and he was retained to paint the funeral escutcheon of the 4th Earl of Richmond. Shayer continued to paint coats of arms and heraldic devices but started to paint landscapes in his free time. On a visit to Southampton to spend time with his family, Shayer received instruction from the seascape painter Jock Wilson (whom Shayer would soon surpass in terms of their respective ability to paint coastal and sea views). Shayer moved to Bladon Lodge in Shirley, near Southampton, an area renowned for its beautiful skies and rejected all overtures by his peers to return to London.

In essence, William Shayer painted genre compositions featuring fishermen, gamekeepers, gypsies, shepherds, hawkers and the like. He ranks alongside John Frederick

Herring and Thomas Sidney Cooper in the pantheon of 19th-century English landscape art.

W Shayer

BIBLIOGRAPHY:

Stewart, Brian, *The Shayer Family of Painters*, F. Lewis, London, 1981.

MUSEUMS AND GALLERIES:

GLASGOW: two landscapes with cattle; *Gypsy Encampment*; *Young Woman Harvesting Crayfish* - LEICESTER: *Landscape with Figures*; *Hunt* - LONDON (Victoria and Albert Mus.): *Buying Fish*; *Fishermen's Children by the Sea* - MONTREAL (Learmont Collection): *Backyard* - SALFORD (Museum and AG): *Landscape with Gipsy Figures* - SUNDERLAND: *Milking Time*.

AUCTION RECORDS:

NEW YORK, 15-18 April 1909, *Fisherman's Cottage*, USD 175; *New Forest Scene*, USD 600. LONDON, 4 Dec 1909, *Gypsy Family*, GBP 52. LONDON, 18 Dec 1909, *Milking Cows* (1836) GBP 52. LONDON, 29 Jan 1910, *Selling Rabbits*, GBP 71; *Gamekeeper*, GBP 73. LONDON, 5 March 1910, *Farmer with Wife and Daughter*, GBP 73; *Gypsy Woman with Cart* (1846) GBP 50; *Royal Oak Tavern*, GBP 60. LONDON, 12 March 1910, *Back from Market*, GBP 199; *After Work*, GBP 147. LONDON, 23 April 1910, *Village Inn* (1835) GBP 115; *Fisherman's Cottage*, GBP 105. LONDON, 20 Feb 1911, *Gamekeeper*, GBP 19. LONDON, 22 April 1911, *Gypsy with her Child and a White Pony*, GBP 73. LONDON, 17 Feb 1922, *Milking Time*, GBP 52. LONDON, 4-5 May 1922, *Highland Shepherd*, GBP 89. LONDON, 9 June 1922, *Hawkers*, GBP 126. LONDON, 9 June 1922, *Gypsies*, GBP 78. LONDON, 2 Feb 1923, *Village Fair*, GBP 294. LONDON, 23 April 1923, *Harvest Scene*, GBP 73. LONDON, 21 Dec 1923, *Noonday Meal in the Fields*, GBP 262. LONDON, 28 April 1924, *Gypsy Encampment*, GBP 204. LONDON, 13 June 1924, *Selling Rabbits*, GBP 320. LONDON, 21 July 1924, *Peasants and Animals near a Pond*, GBP 241. LONDON, 3 April 1925, *On the South Coast*, GBP 225. LONDON, 3 July 1925, *Fishermen on the Beach*, GBP 102. LONDON, 4 June 1926, *Exterior of the Red Lion Tavern*, GBP 278. LONDON, 2 Dec 1927, *Country Hawkers*, GBP 178. LONDON, 16 Nov 1928, *Working the Land*, GBP 252. LONDON, 16 Nov 1928, *Off to Market*, GBP 231; *Coast Scene*, GBP 162. LONDON, 1 March 1929, *Rustic Scene*, GBP 199. NEW YORK, 10 April 1929, *Fishermen on a Scottish Beach*, USD 575. LONDON, 24 May 1929, *Gypsies' Return*, GBP 304. LONDON, 26 July 1929, *Getting Ready for Market*, GBP 231. NEW YORK, 2 April 1931, *Fishing Port*, GBP 250. LONDON, 26 June 1931, *Wooded Landscape*, GBP 178. NEW YORK, 29 April 1932, *Clearing* (drawing) USD 110. BIRMINGHAM, 15 Nov 1933, *Beach Scene*, GBP 115. NEW YORK, 14 Dec 1933, *Landscape*, USD 410. NEW YORK, 18-19 April 1934, *Landscape*, USD 425. LONDON, 30 Nov 1934, *Gossiping*, GBP 102. LONDON, 2 Dec 1935, *Back from Market*, GBP 325. LONDON, 20 Dec 1935, *Leaving for Market*, GBP 341. LONDON, 23 April 1937, *Figures in front of an Inn*, GBP 257; *Gypsy Encampment*, GBP 210. LONDON, 17 Dec 1937, *Bluebell Inn*, GBP 189. LONDON, 18 Feb 1938, *Itinerant Peasants*, GBP 136. LEEDS, 15-16 April 1942, *Gypsy Encampment*, GBP 173. LONDON, 3 July 1942, *Itinerant Poultry Merchant*, GBP 262. LONDON, 10 Dec 1943, *Quarrel*, GBP 220. NEW YORK, 24 May 1944, *Off to Market*, USD 275. LONDON, 17 Nov 1944, *Resting along the Way*, GBP 120. LONDON, 8 Feb 1945, *Gypsy Repast*, GBP 220. NEW YORK, 28 Feb 1945, *Coast Scene*, USD 350; *Gypsy Encampment*, USD 350. LONDON, 20 April 1945, *Hunters and Peasants* (drawing) GBP 325. LONDON, 15 June 1945, *Boy on a Donkey*, GBP 115. LONDON, 23 Nov 1945, *Fishermen and Horses on a Beach*, GBP 105. LONDON, 12 Dec 1945, *Fieldworkers' Rest*, GBP 115. NEW YORK, 31 Jan 1946, *Fish Market*, USD 500. NEW YORK, 15-16 May 1946, *Back to the Farm*, USD 500. EAXTON, 30-31 May 1946, *Gypsy Encampment*, GBP 235. LONDON, 15 Nov 1950, *Crossroads*, GBP 400. LONDON, 17 Nov 1950, *Peasants and Carts in front of an Inn*, GBP 210. LONDON, 9 Feb 1951, *Landscape with Gypsies, Donkeys and Horses* (1855) GBP 76. MILAN, 28 Feb 1951, *Seaside*, ITL 45,000. LONDON, 20 April 1951, *Flock on a Path*, GBP 121. LONDON, 27 April 1951, *Castle with Peasants in a Forest*, GBP 189. LONDON, 28 March 1958, *Cart with Peasants in front of the Red Lion Inn*, GBP 420. LONDON, 13 March 1959, *Wooded Landscape*, GBP 462. LONDON, 24 Feb 1960, *Fruit-Seller*, GBP 950. LONDON, 29 March 1961, *Tree-Lined Path*, GBP 500. LONDON, 6 March 1963, *Travellers at an Inn*, GBP 880. LONDON, 16 July 1965, *Peasants and Travellers in a Clearing*, Gns 2,000. LONDON, 10 Oct 1969, *Landscape with Figures*, Gns 2,300. LONDON, 19 July 1972, *Breakfast in the Fields*, GBP 6,500. SCOTLAND, 31 Aug 1973, *Gypsy Encampment*, GBP 5,200. LONDON, 26 April 1974, *Halt at the Inn*, Gns 3,200. LONDON, 14 July 1976, *Picnic* (1833, oil on canvas, 27 x 35 1/4 ins / 68.5 x 89.5 cm) GBP 3,100. LONDON, 8 March 1977, *Isle of Wight* (1854, oil on canvas, 21 1/4 x 29 1/4 ins / 54 x 74.5 cm) GBP 2,000. LONDON, 2 Feb 1979, *Halt at the Inn* (1858, oil on canvas, 35 3/4 x 47 3/4 ins / 91 x 121.3 cm) GBP 14,000. LONDON, 7 Oct 1980, *Wayside Inn* (oil on panel, 10 x 12 ins / 25.5 x 30.5 cm) GBP 1,600. LONDON, 5 June 1981, *Fishermen on a Beach* (oil on canvas, 29 1/2 x 39 1/2 ins / 75 x 100.3 cm) GBP 7,500. LONDON, 11 July 1984, *Travellers' Rest* (oil on canvas, 27 x 35 ins / 68.5 x 89 cm) GBP 8,000. NEW YORK, 13 Feb 1985, *Halt at the Inn* (oil on canvas, 30 x 50 ins / 76.2 x 127 cm) USD 31,000. LONDON, 16 May 1986, *Carting Timber in the New Forest* (oil on canvas, 30 1/4 x 41 1/2 ins / 77 x 105.4 cm) GBP 26,000. LONDON, 3 June 1988, *Fishermen in a Coastal Landscape* (oil on canvas, 17 x 23 ins / 43.2 x 58.4 cm) GBP 6,050. LONDON, 15 July 1988, *Fisherfolk Unloading their Catch, with Boats drawn up on the Beach in the Background* (oil on canvas, 39 x 52 ins / 98.8 x 132 cm) GBP 11,000. LONDON, 17 March 1989, *Gypsies Returning Home from Market* (oil on canvas, 20 x 24 ins / 50.8 x 61 cm) GBP 18,700. GÖTEBORG, 18 May 1989, *Seafront House with Figures Gossiping on the Beach* (oil on canvas, 30 1/4 x 40 1/4 ins / 77 x 102 cm) SEK 32,000. LONDON, 2 June 1989, *Gypsy Encampment* (oil on canvas, 18 x 24 ins / 46 x 61 cm) GBP 4,950. LONDON, 27 Sept 1989, *Milking in the Field* (1846, oil on canvas, 14 x 11 1/2 ins / 35.5 x 29 cm) GBP 7,700. LONDON, 17 Nov 1989, *Travellers and Ponies Halting in a Clearing in the New Forest, with the Isle of Wight seen in the Distance* (oil on canvas, 28 x 35 3/4 ins / 71 x 91.1 cm) GBP 15,400. LONDON, 13 Dec 1989, *Village Politicians* (oil on canvas, 40 1/2 x 35 1/2 ins / 103 x 90 cm) GBP 61,600. NEW YORK, 1 March 1990, *Reapers at Shirley, Hampshire* (oil on canvas, 28 1/2 x 36 ins / 72.4 x 91.5 cm) USD 55,000. NEW YORK, 23 May 1990, *Afternoon Break* (oil on canvas, 28 x 36 ins / 71.1 x 91.4 cm) USD 27,500. LONDON, 11 July 1990, *Willagers and their Animals in front of an Inn* (oil on canvas, 19 1/2 x 29 1/2 ins / 49.5 x 75 cm) GBP 18,700. LONDON, 26 Sept 1990, *Village Politicians* (1897, oil on canvas, 40 1/2 x 35 1/2 ins / 103 x 90 cm) GBP 33,000. NEW YORK, 28 Feb 1991, *Gypsies' Return* (oil on canvas, 44 1/4 x 37 1/4 ins / 112.1 x 94.5 cm) USD 14,300. LONDON, 10 July 1991, *Creekl with Fishermen in front of their Homes* (oil on canvas, 32 1/4 x 38 1/4 ins / 82 x 97 cm) GBP 6,600. LONDON, 11 Oct 1991, *Encampment in the New Forest* (oil on canvas, 40 x 33 ins / 101.6 x 83.8 cm) GBP 13,200. NEW YORK, 17 Oct 1991, *Fruit-Seller* (1833, oil on canvas, 28 1/4 x 35 3/4 ins / 71.8 x 90.8 cm) USD 55,000. LONDON, 15 Nov 1991, *Hawking her Wares* (oil on canvas, 30 x 25 ins / 76 x 63.5 cm) GBP 4,950. NEW YORK, 19 Feb 1992, *Unloading the Catch* (1837, oil on canvas, 30 1/4 x 40 1/2 ins / 76.8 x 102.8 cm) USD 17,600. LONDON, 12 June 1992, *Fishermen on the Coast* (oil on canvas, 30 x 40 ins / 76.2 x 101.5 cm) GBP 12,100. LONDON, 13 Nov 1992, *Gypsy Encampment*; *Sluice* (oil on card, pair, each 6 1/4 x 8 1/4 ins / 16 x 21 cm) GBP 7,150.

LONDON, 14 July 1993, *Approaching the Fair* (oil on canvas, 29 1/4 x 39 1/2 ins / 74.5 x 100.5 cm) GBP 28,750. NEW YORK, 12 Oct 1994, *Fisherfolk on the Coast* (1830, oil on canvas, 40 x 50 ins / 101.6 x 127 cm) USD 12,650. LONDON, 12 April 1995, *Coastal Landscape with Figures and Horses on the Foreshore* (oil on panel, 19 1/2 x 23 1/2 ins / 49.5 x 59.5 cm) GBP 6,900. NEW YORK, 1 Nov 1995, *Gypsy Encampment* (oil on canvas, 27 3/4 x 36 ins / 70.5 x 91.4 cm) USD 46,000. LONDON, 6 Nov 1996, *Gathering Bracken* (1839, oil on panel, 13 3/4 x 17 3/4 ins / 35 x 45 cm) GBP 9,200. NEW YORK, 12 Dec 1996, *Gypsy Encampment* (oil on canvas, 28 x 36 ins / 71.1 x 91.4 cm) USD 18,400. LONDON, 13 March 1997, *Valley Landscape with Figures at Rest* (1833, oil on panel, 14 x 11 1/2 ins / 35.6 x 29.2 cm) GBP 6,200. LONDON, 14 March 1997, *Welcome* (oil on canvas, 30 x 25 ins / 76.2 x 63.5 cm) GBP 19,550. LONDON, 4 June 1997, *Harvest* (oil on canvas, 18 x 24 ins / 45.5 x 61 cm) GBP 5,750. LONDON, 7 Nov 1997, *Woodcuitter's Rest* (1865, oil on canvas, in collaboration with Henry Thring Shayer, 30 x 25 1/4 ins / 76 x 64 cm) GBP 7,475. CASTLECOMER, 27 July 1999, *Gypsies Resting by a Woodland Path. Landscape with Figures, Cattle and Sheep* (oil on board, 12 x 12 ins / 30 x 30 cm) IEP 19,000. LEYBURN, 25 Nov 1999, *Gipsy Encampment* (oil on canvas, 23 x 19 ins / 59 x 48 cm) GBP 13,500. DETROIT, 20 Oct 2000, *Figures Along a Coast near Two Masted, Docked Ships, Distant Mountains* (oil on canvas, 30 x 40 ins / 76 x 102 cm) USD 20,000. LONDON, 28 Nov 2000, *Fisherfolk Unloading the Catch on the Isle of Wight* (oil on canvas, 28 x 39 ins / 70 x 100 cm) GBP 13,000. LONDON, 12 June 2001, *Red Lion Inn* (oil on board, 30 x 41 ins / 75 x 103 cm) GBP 27,000. LONDON, 30 Nov 2001, *Itinerant Rabbit Seller* (oil on canvas, 48 x 39 ins / 122 x 100 cm) GBP 31,000. LONDON, 11 June 2002, *Fisherfolk on the Beach* (oil on panel, 24 x 19 ins / 61 x 49 cm) GBP 12,000. LONDON, 19 June 2002, *News from Afar* (oil on canvas, 28 x 36 ins / 71 x 91 cm) GBP 12,000. LONDON, 10 June 2003, *Gypsy Encampment in a Wooded Landscape* (oil on canvas, 28 x 36 ins / 71 x 91 cm) GBP 16,000. LONDON, 10 June 2003, *Summer Landscape with Harvesters* (oil on canvas, 30 x 40 ins / 76 x 102 cm) GBP 24,000. CAMBRIDGE, 21 April 2004, *Itinerant Fishmonger. Interior of a Fisherman's Cottage* (oil on board, a pair, 14 x 17 ins / 35 x 43 cm) GBP 18,000. LONDON, 11 June 2004, *Fisherfolk in a Coastal Landscape* (1838, oil on canvas, 28 x 36 ins / 71 x 92 cm) GBP 15,000.

SHAYER, William or William Joseph, the Younger

British, 19th century.

Born 2 April 1811, in Southampton; died 1892.

Painter. Genre scenes, animals, landscapes.

William Shayer the Younger was the son of William Shayer the Elder. He exhibited in London from 1829 to 1885.

W J Shayer

BIBLIOGRAPHY:

Stewart, Brian, *The Shayer Family of Painters*, F. Lewis, London, 1981.

MUSEUMS AND GALLERIES:

GLASGOW: *Shady Pool*.

AUCTION RECORDS:

LONDON, 4 Dec 1909, *Farmhorse, Donkey and Little Gypsy* (1851) GBP 13. LONDON, 28 May 1923, *Fox Hunt* (pendants) GBP 37. LONDON, 31 March 1926, *Working the Fields; Village Smithy* (two drawings) GBP 42. LONDON, 2 Feb 1927, *Mailcoach*, GBP 155. LONDON, 27 May 1927, *Changing Horses; Mailcoach en Route* (both) GBP 110. LONDON, 15 June 1927, *Two Coaches Meeting; Departure of the Mailcoach* (both) GBP 200. LONDON, 29 June 1927, *Derby Winner* (1836) GBP 100. LONDON, 7 Dec 1928, *London Stage and Brighton Stage Meeting on the Way* (two pendants) GBP 399. NEW YORK, 2 April 1931, *Landscape with Figures*, USD 500. NEW YORK, 20 Nov 1931, *Coast Scene*, USD 200. LONDON, 25 March 1938, *Peasants Drinking*, GBP 173. LONDON, 27 May 1938, *Fieldworkers' Midday Meal*, GBP 136. NEW YORK, 17-21 Nov 1942, *Fox Hunt*, USD 350; *Kenneling*, USD 800. NEW YORK, 24 May 1944, *Fishermen on the Beach*, USD 275. NEW YORK, 28 Feb 1945, *Coach* (two pendants) USD 800. NEW YORK, 20 and 21 Feb 1946, *Gypsy Child*, USD 475. NEW YORK, 23 Feb 1968, *Return from the Hunt*, USD 1,300. LONDON, 11 July 1969, *Small Inn*, Gns 2,600. LONDON, 18 June 1971, *Hunting Scenes* (six canvases) GBP 2,600. LONDON, 9 April 1974, *Resting in the Woods*, GBP 700. LONDON, 14 May 1976, *Gypsies near a Wood* (oil on canvas, 29 1/4 x 39 ins / 74 x 99 cm) GBP 1,200. LONDON, 25 Oct 1977, *Fishermen on the Beach* (oil on canvas, 19 1/2 x 29 1/4 ins / 49.5 x 74 cm) GBP 1,000. LONDON, 21 March 1979, *Woodcutters' Cart* (oil on card, 23 3/4 x 20 ins / 60.5 x 51 cm) GBP 4,200. LONDON, 6 March 1981, *Gypsy Encampment* (oil on canvas, 29 x 38 1/2 ins / 73.6 x 97.8 cm) GBP 2,000. LONDON, 16 Nov 1983, *Shooting Pony* (oil on canvas, 27 1/2 x 35 1/2 ins / 70 x 90 cm) GBP 11,000. LONDON, 19 Nov 1986, *Off to the Races* (1847, oil on canvas, 17 1/2 x 23 1/2 ins / 44.5 x 59.5 cm) GBP 8,500. LONDON, 23 Sept 1988, *Unloading the Catch* (oil on canvas, 28 x 36 ins / 71 x 91.5 cm) GBP 3,960. NEW YORK, 24 Oct 1989, *Red Lion Inn* (1838, oil on canvas, 20 1/4 x 27 1/4 ins / 51.4 x 69.1 cm) USD 4,950. LONDON, 11 July 1990, *The London-Hull Mailcoach; The Lord Nelson London-to-Portsmouth Mailcoach* (1845, oil on canvas, pair, each 15 1/4 x 23 1/2 ins / 39 x 59.5 cm) GBP 8,800. LONDON, 15 Nov 1991, *Landscape with J. Chalmer riding Colonel Pearson's Mount 'Achievement'* (1867, oil on canvas, 14 1/4 x 18 ins / 35.9 x 45.7 cm) GBP 3,300. LONDON, 3 June 1992, *Farmhouse by the Sea* (oil on canvas, 9 x 12 1/2 ins / 23 x 32 cm) GBP 1,980. LONDON, 3 March 1993, *Prizewinning Cow 'Grand Duchess XVII'* (1873, oil on canvas, 24 x 36 ins / 61 x 91.5 cm) GBP 1,955. NEW YORK, 19 Jan 1994, *Travellers' Rest* (oil on canvas, 13 x 12 1/2 ins / 33 x 31.8 cm) USD 3,450. ST ASAPH, 2 June 1994, *Gossiping by the Roadside; Gypsy Encampment* (oil on canvas, pair, each 11 1/4 x 10 ins / 28.5 x 25.5 cm) GBP 6,900. NEW YORK, 9 June 1995, *Travelling by Coach* (1878, oil on canvas, series of four, each 13 x 20 ins / 33 x 50.8 cm) USD 31,050. NEW YORK, 9 April 1999, *Full Cry* (oil on board, a pair, 6 x 9 ins / 16 x 24 cm) USD 30,000. BILLINGSHURST, 18 May 1999, *Hunting Scenes* (oil on board, a pair, diamond shape, 16 x 16 ins / 40 x 40 cm) GBP 8,500. NEW YORK, 6 Dec 2000, *Meet. At the Crossroads* (1884, oil on panel, a pair, 9 x 26 ins / 24 x 67 cm) USD 11,500. NEW YORK, 6 Dec 2000, *Going Out of Kennels. Moving Off. Casting for Scent. Gone Away. Full Cry. Nearing the Kill* (1844, oil on canvas, set of six, 10 x 144 ins / 25 x 365 cm) USD 20,000. LONDON, 14 June 2001, *Two Gentlemen on Hunters with Greyhounds* (oil on canvas, 16 x 16 ins / 40 x 40 cm) GBP 7,500. DORCHESTER, 28 June 2001, *Meet, Gone to Ground. In Full Cry and the Death* (oil on canvas, a pair, 7 x 12 ins / 18 x 30 cm) GBP 8,000. SCARBOROUGH, 10 Sept 2002, *Two Figures with a Grey Pony on a Beach* (oil on canvas, 12 x 9 ins / 30 x 23 cm) GBP 1,250. CRANBROOK, 16 Nov 2003, *Pastoral River Landscape with Milkmaid, Cattle and Distant Tower* (1887, oil on canvas, 14 x 24 ins / 36 x 61 cm) GBP 2,900. DUBLIN, 26 Nov 2003, *On the Beach, Hastings* (oil on canvas, 20 x 26 ins / 51 x 66 cm) EUR 2,800.

SHAYKH MUHAMMAD. See CHEIKH MOHAMMED

SHCHEDRIN, Fedosy Fedorovich

Russian, 18th - 19th century.

Born 1751; died 19 January 1825, in St Petersburg.

Sculptor.

Shchedrin studied at the St Petersburg academy of fine arts, then travelled to Florence, Rome (1773-1774) and Paris, where he worked under Allegrain. He was made academician in 1794 and professor in 1795. From 1818, he was Rector of the academy's sculpture department. His best known works are: *Endymion, Mars* and *Venus* at the Leningrad Academy, *Eve*, a marble statue in the Great Grotto at Peterhof, *Mermaids and Nena* in the waterfall at Peterhof and two caryatids in the entrance to the St Petersburg Admiralty, as well as several other sculptures.

SHCHEDRIN, Semen Fedorovich
Russian, 18th century.
Born 1745, in St Petersburg; died 1 September 1804.
Painter. Landscapes.

The son of a soldier, S.F.Shchedrin studied at the St Petersburg academy of fine arts and in Italy. He became an official painter for Catherine the Great. The Tretyakov Gallery in Moscow and the old Imperial Museums have several works by this artist.

MUSEUMS AND GALLERIES:
MOSCOW (State Tretyakov Gal.): *Landscape with Animals.*

SHCHEDRIN, Silvestr Fedosievich
Russian, 19th century.
Born 2 January 1791, in St Petersburg; died 8 November 1830, in Sorrento.
Also active in Italy.
Painter. Urban landscapes, waterscapes, landscapes.

The son of the sculptor Fedosy Shchedrin, he studied at the St Petersburg academy of fine arts, headed by F.I. Alekseev and M.M. Ivanov, from 1800 to 1811. He then went to perfect his technique in Germany and Italy, where he was resident artist in 1818. He stayed in Rome, Naples, Tivoli and Sorrento enjoying great fame and working for foreign clients. In 2001, his work was shown at the Exhibition *Un Paese incantanto. Italia dipinta da Thomas Jones a Corot* (*An Enchanted Country. Italy Depicted by Artists from Thomas Jones to Corot*) which was held at the Centro internazionale d'Arte e di Cultura di Palazzo Te in Mantua.

He is one of the first Russian landscape painters to paint from life, seascapes and views of Rome, the Gulf of Naples and the Bay of Sorrento. He often paints variations on a theme, thus creating a series, such as that of *Modern Rome* or those of *Terrasses* in which he pays particular attention to the rendering of different effects of light, with a gradation of tones from the silver to the transparent.

BIBLIOGRAPHY:
La Peinture russe à l'époque romantique, exhibition catalogue, Gal. nationales du Grand Palais, Paris, 1976-1977. Ottani Cavina, Anna (ed.), *Un Paese incantato. Italia dipinta da Thomas Jones a Corot*, exhibition catalogue, Electa, Milan, 2001.

MUSEUMS AND GALLERIES:
MINSK: *Modern Rome* (1829) - MOSCOW (Rumiantsev Mus.): *Castel Santangelo, Rome; Moonlight in Naples; Terrasse by the Sea; View of Sorrento; A Terrasse; View of Rome; Near the Gulf of Naples* - MOSCOW (State Tretyakov Gal.): *Modern Rome, Roman Landscape with Castel Santangelo* (1825); *Terrasse by the Sea; View of the Small Harbour at Sorrento, Evening; Ponto del Rosso, in Naples; Self-portrait; Waterfall at Tivoli; Old Rome; Terrasse covered with Vine; Small Port at Sorrento; The Grotto at Sorrento; Large Harbour at Sorrento; Moonlight; The Veranda* (In total a collection of 33 paintings) - ST PETERSBURG (Gosudarstvennyj Russkij Muz.): *The Circus Maximus in Rome; Terrasse; The Temple of Serapis at Pozzuoli* (1828, oil on canvas); *Modern Rome* (1823); *The Outskirts of Naples; Amalfi; Tivoli; Lake Nemi; Sorrento* (In total a collection of 16 paintings) - YEREVAN: *Modern Rome.*

AUCTION RECORDS:
LONDON, 11-12 June 1997, *View of Apuria* (1828, oil on canvas, 9 x 11 3/4 ins / 22 x 30 cm) GBP 11,500.

SHCHERBINOVSKY, Dmitri Anfinovich
Russian, 19th - 20th century.
Born 1867, in Petrovsk; died 1926.
Painter.

Dmitri Anfinovich Shcherbinovsky was a pupil at the academy of fine arts in St Petersburg.

MUSEUMS AND GALLERIES:
HELSINKI (Ateneumin Taidemus.) - MOSCOW (State Tretyakov Gal.) - ST PETERSBURG (Academy).

SHCHESKI, Ivan Vasilevich
Russian, 19th century.
Born 1777, in Mohilev; died 1848, in St Petersburg.
Engraver (burin).

Ivan Shcheski was a member of the Russian imperial academy. He engraved plates for Krussenstern's *Voyage Around the World.*

SHCHESKI, Kosima Vasilevich
Russian, 19th century.
Born 1776; died 1813.
Engraver (burin).

Kosima Shcheski was the brother of Ivan Vasilevich Shcheski and studied at the academy in St Petersburg. He engraved portraits, views and book illustrations.

SHCHIPITSYN, Aleksandr
Russian, 20th century.
Born 1896; died 1944.
Painter.

Aleksandr Shchipitsyn participated in the Russian Art exhibition, Galeries Nationales du Grand Palais, Paris (1967-1968).

SHCHUKIN, Stepan Semionovich.
See **CHUKIN Stepan Semenovich**

SHCHUKIN, Yuri Prokopevich
Russian, 20th century.
Born 1904; died 1935.
Painter.

Yuri Prokopevich Shchukin's painting, *An Airship Above the City*, was included in the exhibition of Russian Art at the Galeries Nationales du Grand Palais, Paris (1967-1968).

SHCHUKSIN, Dimitri Ilich
Russian, 19th century.
Born 12 September 1788.
Miniaturist.

Dimitri Shchuksin studied at the St Petersburg academy.

SHCHUKSIN, Iestafi Ilich
Russian, 19th century.
Born 1780; died 23 July 1817.
Engraver (burin).

Iestafi Shchuksin was the pupil of Klauber. He engraved portraits and book illustrations.

SHDANOFF, Andrej Ossipovitch.
See **JDANOV Andrei Ossipovich**

SHEA, G.
Irish, 18th - 19th century.
Active in Dublin between 1790 and 1814.
Engraver (burin).

SHEA, John
Irish, 18th century.
Active in Dublin c. 1766.
Landscape artist.

SHEA, Judith
American, 20th - 21st century.
Born 1948.
Sculptor.

Judith Shea initially trained as a clothing designer. She works from images of the male and female body, using clothes (coats, dresses) as forms. At first, she worked with fabric alone, but later cast the fabric in metal to produce flowing forms sheathed in bronze or wood, enveloping the absent bodies and set on plinths. In the mid-1980s, she started to experiment with the juxtaposition of figures with forms and with paired figures. Her works include *Post Balzac - Opus Notum Galateae*.

Shea has shown her work in solo exhibitions, including: *Monuments and Statues*, Whitney Museum of American Art at Philip Morris, New York; *Judith Shea: Statues*, John Berggruen Gallery, San Francisco (2004); and *Selected Works: 1979-1994*, Max Protetch Gallery, New York (1994).

Bibliography:

Masséra, Jean Charles, *'Judith Shea'* in *Art Press* n° 169, periodical, Paris, May 1992.

SHEARBOAM ANDREW. See **SHEERBOOM Andries**

SHEARD, Thomas Frederick Mason

British, 19th - 20th century.

Born 16 December 1866, in Oxford; died 4 October 1921, in London.

Painter. Portraits, landscapes.

Orientalism.

Thomas Sheard studied in Paris with Gustave Courtois, Jean André Rixens, Jules Lefebvre and Albert Gabriel Rigolot. He was a professor at Queen's College, London, from 1915. He is noted for his *Portrait of a Man* in Oxford.

Auction records:

London, 15 Oct 1976, *Summer Landscape with Fishermen* (oil on canvas, 35 x 48 ins / 89 x 121 cm) GBP 700. London, 27 Sept 1989, *Riverscape* (oil on canvas, 30 x 22 ins / 76 x 56 cm) GBP 1,045. London, 11 June 1993, *High Summer* (oil on canvas, 19 1/4 x 25 1/2 ins / 49 x 65 cm) GBP 14,375. London, 3 Nov 1993, *Midday Break* (1905, oil on canvas, 15 x 22 ins / 38 x 56 cm) GBP 1,840. London, 14 Dec 1999, *By the River* (oil on canvas, 15 x 18 ins / 38 x 45 cm) GBP 1,200. London, 7 March 2002, *Spirit of Summer* (1887, oil on canvas, 48 x 24 ins / 122 x 61 cm) GBP 1,500.

SHEARER, Christopher H.

American, 19th - 20th century.

Born 1840, in Reading (Pennsylvania); died 1926.

Painter. Landscapes.

Christopher H. Shearer spent time in the studios of F.D. Devlan and J. Heyl as a child, later studying under both artists. He was provided with a studio by his father, who built one on the family farm at Shearertown. He opened a studio in Reading when he was 21 and had considerable success in selling the works he produced.

Auction records:

New York, 8 Feb 1907, *Landscape*, USD 210. New York, 23 March 1984, *Landscape with Wooden Bridge* (1888, oil on canvas, 33 3/4 x 40 3/4 ins / 85.7 x 103.5 cm) USD 3,000. New York, 24 Jan 1989, *Wooded Landscape* (1894, oil on canvas, 22 x 35 1/2 ins / 55 x 90 cm) USD 1,320. New York, 30 May 1990, *Encampment near the River* (1876, oil on canvas, 4 3/4 x 7 3/4 ins / 12 x 20 cm) USD 990. New York, 31 May 1990, *Hillside Village* (1877, oil on canvas, 20 x 36 ins / 50.8 x 91.5 cm) USD 1,650.

SHEBUEV, Vasili Kuz'mich

Russian, 19th century.

Born 2 April 1777, in Kronstadt (now Brasov, Romania); died 28 June 1855, in St Petersburg.

Painter, engraver (burin), lithographer. Religious subjects.

This artist studied at the St Petersburg academy and in Rome. On his return to St Petersburg he was appointed professor at the academy, where he later became director. Notable works include *St Basil the Great, St Gregory* and *St John Chrysostom* in Kazan cathedral, and the *Patriot Igolkin*.

Museums and Galleries:

Moscow (State Tretyakov Gal.): *Angels with Ecclesiastical Objects; Moses with the Ten Commandments; Placing the Deceased in the Coffin; St John the Baptist and the Prophet Ezekiel; Prophet Azor David with Psalteries; Prophets Isaiah and Jonah; Vision of Ezekiel; Transfiguration; Ascension of Christ; St Basil; Portrait of E.M. Shebuyeva, the Artist's Wife; Last Supper; Holy Family*; and numerous drawings - St Petersburg (Gosudarstvennyj Russkij Muz.): *St John the Baptist in the Desert; Last Supper; Brave Deed of the Merchant Igolkin; Assumption of the Virgin; Apostles Peter and John Healing a Lame Man; Grand Duke Aleksander Nevsky, the Orthodox Saint.*

SHEDLIN, Réginald, pseudonym of Schoedelin

French, 20th century.

Born 3 March 1908, in Bayonne; died 22 September 1988, in Lussas.

Painter.

Réginald Shedlin exhibited at the Salon de Mai in Paris. His art tends to the pure abstract.

SHEDROVSKY, Ignatii Stepanovich

Russian, 19th century.

Born 1815; died 25 December 1870, in Moscow.

Painter, lithographer.

It is from drawings by this artist that Bielussov and Umnov printed a series of lithographs portraying the different types of Russian peoples. He also painted portraits of *Nicholas I* and *Alexander II*.

Bibliography:

Suris, B., *I.S. Shchedrovsky*, 1957.

Museums and Galleries:

Moscow (State Tretyakov Gal.).

SHEE, Martin Archer (Sir)

Irish, 18th - 19th century.

Born 20 December 1769, in Dublin; died 19 August 1850, in Brighton.

Painter. Figures, portraits.

Martin Archer Shee took courses in drawing and composition in Dublin before moving to London in 1788 and enrolling at the Royal Academy School in 1790. Times were initially hard and he was obliged to paint portraits to eke out a living. After painting portraits of a number of well-known actors and public figures, however, his reputation quickly grew. He began exhibiting at the Royal Academy and the British Institution in 1789 and continued to submit work until 1845. He was admitted to associate membership of the Royal Academy in 1798 and to full membership in 1800. Following the death of Lawrence, Shee assumed the presidency of the Academy in 1830 and was knighted shortly afterwards.

Shee is remembered for his portraits of the Duke of Clarence, William IV, Queen Adelaide, Queen Victoria and her consort, Prince Albert. He also authored a number of publications, among them *Rhythms or Art* (1805), *Elements or Art* (1809), *Old Court* (a nove, 1829) and *Alasco* (a tragedy, 1809).

Bibliography:

Venning, Barry, *'Turner's Annotated Books: Opie's Lectures on painting and Shee's elements of art (I)'* in *Turner Studies, 2, 1*, 1982. Venning, Barry, *'Turner's Annotated Books: Opie's Lectures on painting and Shee's elements of art (II)'* in *Turner Studies, 2, 2*, 1983. Venning, Barry, *'Turner's Annotated Books: Opie's Lectures on painting and Shee's elements of art (III)'* in *Turner Studies, 3, 1*, 1983.

Museums and Galleries:

Dublin: *Young Peasant Girl; Duke of Leinster* - Glasgow: *Ariane Abandoned* - Liverpool (Walker AG): *Portrait of William Roscoe* (oil on canvas) - London (Corporation of Trinity House): *Captain Sir John Woolmore* (portrait) - London (National Portrait Gal.): *Sir Martin Archer Shee* (1794, oil on canvas); *King William IV* (c. 1800, oil on canvas, portrait in the full-dress uniform); *John Freeman-Mitford, 1st Baron Redesdale* (c. 1802, oil on canvas); *Sir Thomas Picton* (before 1812, oil on canvas); *William Popham* (c. 1814, oil on canvas); *Sharon Turner* (c. 1817, oil on canvas); *Sir Thomas Munro, 1st Bt* (1819, oil on canvas); *Jane, Lady Munro* (1819, oil on canvas); *Sir William Webb Follett* (c. 1820, oil on canvas); *Thomas Denman, 1st Baron Denman* (c. 1832, oil on canvas); *Sir Francis Burdett, 5th Bt* (1843, oil on canvas) - LONDON (NG): *Mr Lewis as the Marquis in 'The Midnight Hour'* (exhibited in 1792, oil on canvas) - LONDON (Tate Collection): *Two Rustic Figures* (c. 1817, watercolour/paper); *A Young Bacchus* (exhibited in 1824, oil on canvas); *Thomas Morton Esq.* (exhibited in 1835, oil on canvas) - NEW YORK (Metropolitan Mus. of Art): *Daniel O'Connell* - SALFORD (Museum and AG): *Madame Malibran.*

AUCTION RECORDS:

LONDON, 1895, *Young Lady,* FRF 4,800. LONDON, 1896, *Portrait of Two Boys,* FRF 12,100. LONDON, 25 Jan 1898, *Portrait of a Lady,* FRF 7,075. LONDON, 1899, *Child Portrait of the Artist's Son,* FRF 4,450. NEW YORK, 12-14 March 1906, *Lady Ashburton,* USD 500; *Portrait of Mrs Hammond,* USD 425. NEW YORK, 22 and 23 Feb 1907, *Portrait of Mrs Douglas,* USD 425. NEW YORK, 1-3 April 1908, *Lady Whitmore,* USD 660. LONDON, 26 Feb 1910, *Child Portrait of Sir Robert Hove Brombey,* GBP 21. LONDON, 20 Dec 1910, *Portrait of Amesley Shee* (sketch) GBP 42. LONDON, 8 April 1911, *Lady in a Smock,* GBP 94. LONDON, 19 June 1911, *Portrait of Charles Keppel, 4th Earl of Albemarke,* GBP 31. LONDON, 14 July 1911, *Portrait of Amesley Shee* (sketch) GBP 25. LONDON, 2 March 1923, *Mrs Mountain as Ophelia,* GBP 168. LONDON, 15 June 1923, *The Ashley Children,* GBP 714. LONDON, 18 July 1924, *Lord Thomas Denman,* GBP 252. LONDON, 8 Oct 1924, *Seated Woman,* GBP 126. LONDON, 12 June 1925, *Lord Spencer,* GBP 115. LONDON, 20 May 1927, *George Romney,* GBP 273. LONDON, 29 June 1928, *Duke of Clarence,* GBP 378; *Duke of Albemarle,* GBP 115. LONDON, 12 July 1929, *Three Young Women of the Worsley Family,* GBP 2,310. LONDON, 19 July 1929, *George O'Shee,* GBP 115. LONDON, 20 Dec 1929, *Young Woman in White,* GBP 315. LONDON, 14 March 1930, *Mrs Reynolds,* GBP 504. LONDON, 9 May 1930, *Andrew Ellis and the Artist,* GBP 115. LONDON, 14 July 1930, *Lady Katherine Frankland,* GBP 236. LONDON, 12 June 1931, *William St-Leger,* GBP 157. NEW YORK, 12 Nov 1931, *Miss Frances Wood,* USD 550. NEW YORK, 14 Dec 1933, *Captain Barnaby,* USD 200. NEW YORK, 18 and 19 April 1934, *Maquis of Thomond,* USD 500. LONDON, 25 May 1934, *Catherine Frankland,* GBP 105. NEW YORK, 26 and 27 March 1943, *Frances Mary Hunter,* USD 400. NEW YORK, 29 April 1943, *Sir Robert Howe Bromley,* USD 975. NEW YORK, 24 May 1944, *Hundu Army Officer,* USD 475. NEW YORK, 28 March 1946, *The Sketcher,* USD 1,200. LONDON, 1 Dec 1961, *The Amesley Children,* Gns 1,000. NEW YORK, 2 April 1976, *Lydia, Countess of Cavan* (oil on canvas, 36 x 28 ins / 91.5 x 71 cm) USD 500. LONDON, 23 Nov 1977, *Rabbi* (oil on canvas, 36 x 27³/₄ ins / 91.5 x 70.5 cm) GBP 1,500. LONDON, 9 July 1980, *Portrait of Lieutenant-General Daniel Burr* (oil on canvas, 55 1/2 x 44 ins / 141 x 112 cm) GBP 1,000. LONDON, 27 March 1981, *Portrait of the Artist's Son* (oil on canvas, 30 1/4 x 25 ins / 77 x 63.5 cm) GBP 4,800. NEW YORK, 19 Jan 1982, *Two Children* (oil on canvas, 56 x 43 ins / 142.5 x 109 cm) USD 4,000. NEW YORK, 20 April 1983, *Portrait of a Lady* (oil on canvas, 93 1/2 x 57 1/2 ins / 237.5 x 146 cm) USD 15,000. LONDON, 19 Nov 1986, *Portrait of James Munro MacNab* (oil on canvas, 92 x 56 ins / 233.5 x 142.5 cm) GBP 30,000. NEW YORK, 1 June 1989, *Portrait of the Artist's Son, Sir John Paul* (oil on canvas, 48 x 38 1/4 ins / 122 x 97 cm) USD 5,500. LONDON, 11 July 1990, *Portrait of a Lady in a Silver Gown and a Yellow Stole, standing next to a Harp and holding an Engraving* (oil on canvas, 93 1/2 x 57 1/2 ins / 237.5 x 146 cm) GBP 23,650. NEW YORK, 26 Oct 1990, *Young Woman holding a Sketchbook* (oil on canvas, 33 3/4 x 26 ins / 85.7 x 66 cm) USD 28,600. DUBLIN, 12 Dec 1990, *Portrait of Lady Hannah Alithea Ellice* (oil on canvas, 30 x 25 ins / 76.2 x 63.5 cm) IEP 500. LONDON, 17 July 1992, *Bust Portrait of a Gentleman dressed in Black and wearing a White Cravat* (oil on canvas, 30 1/4 x 25 ins / 76.8 x 63.5 cm) GBP 1,100. LONDON, 6 Nov 1995, *Rabbi* (oil on canvas, 35 3/4 x 27 1/2 ins / 91 x 70 cm) GBP 7,475. LONDON, 3 April 1996, *Upset Cart* (oil on canvas, 49 1/4 x 39 1/4 ins / 125 x 99.5 cm) GBP 25,300. DETROIT, 10 Dec 1999, *Brother and Sister* (oil on canvas, 34 x 28 ins / 86 x 71 cm) USD 6,000. LONDON, 9 March 2000, *Portrait of Mary Herman, Née Mary Popham, Wearing White Dress and Pearl Necklace, Holding a Crayon* (oil on canvas, 41 x 19 ins / 104 x 48 cm) GBP 13,000. LONDON, 15 June 2000, *Portrait of Two Children* (oil on canvas, 35 x 28 ins / 88 x 72 cm) GBP 5,000. LONDON, 18 May 2001, *Portrait of Frances Sophia Hunter in Landscape* (oil on canvas, 30 x 25 ins / 76 x 63 cm) GBP 25,000. LONDON, 15 June 2001, *Portrait of a Lady in a White Dress, Artist's Palette and Neo-Classical Bust on a Table* (oil on canvas, 94 x 58 ins / 238 x 147 cm) GBP 30,000. CASTLECOMER, 12 Nov 2002, *Portrait of William Fairlie* (oil on canvas, 94 x 57 ins / 238 x 146 cm) EUR 20,000. CASTLECOMER, 12 Nov 2002, *Group Portrait of Margaret Fairlie with Children* (oil on canvas, 94 x 58 ins / 239 x 148 cm) EUR 60,000. LONDON, 12 June 2003, *Portrait of John Russell, 6th Duke of Bedford* (oil on canvas laid on board, 30 x 25 ins / 76 x 63 cm) GBP 11,500. LONDON, 25 Nov 2003, *Portrait of a Lady in a White Dress Holding a Drawstring Purse, by a Tree in a Landscape* (oil on canvas, 50 x 40 ins / 127 x 102 cm) GBP 10,000. NEW YORK, 27 May 2004, *Portrait of Miss Elizabeth Johnson* (oil on canvas, 30 x 25 ins / 76 x 63 cm) USD 8,000. CASTLECOMER, 22 June 2004, *Full Length Portrait of William Senhouse* (oil on canvas, 84 x 59 ins / 213 x 150 cm) EUR 9,000.

SHEE, Michiel Emanuel

Dutch, 18th century.
Died between 18 December 1739 and 30 April 1740.
Active in Amsterdam.
Sculptor.

Michiel Emanuel Shee settled in The Hague in 1721.

AUCTION RECORDS:

LONDON, 15 May 1984, *Cupid and Psyche* (fruit-tree wood, a pair, h. 16 1/2 ins / 42 cm and 18 ins/46 cm) GBP 6,000.

SHEE, Peter

Irish, 18th century.
Died 1767.
Active in Dublin.
Painter.

SHEEHAN, David

Irish, 18th century.
Died 1756.
Active in Dublin.
Sculptor.

David Sheehan worked on the façade of Trinity College, Dublin.

SHEELER, Charles

American, 20th century.
Born 1883, in Philadelphia; died 1965, in New York.
Painter (gouache), watercolourist, draughtsman, photographer. Urban townscapes.
Movement: Precisionism (or Cubist Realism).

Charles Sheeler studied at the Philadelphia Academy of Fine Arts and was then taught by William Merritt Chase in New York. He lived for a time in London, the Netherlands and Spain, and also in Paris, where he came across Cubism and Matisse.

From William Chase, Sheeler learned the technique of quick strokes, inspired by the Munich Expressionists, which was a feature of his early work. As a photographer, he was asked to work on various creations of the industrial age such as factories, buildings, machines and modern ships. His photographic work made him rethink his painting, which from then on concentrated on the mechanical and technological setting of life in developed societies. This required him to change his technique and adopt a style taken from industrial working drawings and adapted to suit his purpose.

In 1946, Sheeler adopted a new technique that gave his work a more pronounced character. His depiction of various building or machinery plans assumed a transparent quality, which enabled him to build up a composition by interlocking and overlapping them with each other. In bringing out the geometric structure of his subjects, he rendered the beauty of their lines and their abstract purity, while avoiding all details. His painting is an extension of Cubism and Purism and is somewhat reminiscent of the painting of another American artist, Lionel Feininger.

Sheeler participated in the major collective exhibitions of Modern American Art, including the Armory Art Show in New York in 1913. Retrospectives of his work were shown at the Museum of Modern Art, New York, 1939; the University of California, 1954; and the University of Iowa, 1963. A posthumous exhibition entitled *The Photography of Charles Sheeler* was held at the Metropolitan Museum of Modern Art, New York.

BIBLIOGRAPHY:

Troyen, Carol/Hirshler, Erica E., *Charles Sheeler, paintings and drawings*, travelling exhibition catalogue, Museum of Fine Arts, Boston, Little Brown, Boston. Rourke, Constance, *Charles Sheeler, artist in the American tradition*, Kennedy Gall., New York, 1969. Friedman, Martin, *Charles Sheeler*, Watson-Guptill, New York, 1975. Lucic, Karen, *Charles Sheeler and the cult of machine*, Harvard University Press, Cambridge (MA), 1991. Mora, Gilles/Stebbins, Theodore E., *Charles Sheeler: une modernité radicale*, Éd. du Seuil, Paris, 2002.

MUSEUMS AND GALLERIES:

CAMBRIDGE, MA (Fogg Art Mus., Harvard University): *Upper Deck* (1929) - NEW YORK (Metropolitan Mus. of Art): *Death of a Miner* (1949) - NEW YORK (MoMA): *Self-portrait* (1923) - NEW YORK (Whitney Mus. of American Art): *Classic Landscape, Factory at Red River* (1932); *Architectural Cadences* (1954) - NORTHAMPTON, MA (MA, Smith College): *Power in Operation* (1939) - PHILADELPHIA (MA): *Cactus* (1931); *Yachts and Yachting* (1922).

AUCTION RECORDS:

NEW YORK, 19 Oct 1967, *Steel-Croton No 2* (tempera) USD 4,500. NEW YORK, 14 Oct 1970, *House and Tree* (gouache) USD 11,000. NEW YORK, 18 Oct 1972, *Industrial Landscape* (watercolour) USD 22,500. NEW YORK, 14 March 1973, *White Sentinels* (tempera) USD 65,000. NEW YORK, 23 May 1974, *Lunenburg* (gouache) USD 13,000. NEW YORK, 6 Feb 1976, *Industrial Series* (1921, lithograph, 8 1/4 x 11 1/4 ins / 21 x 28.3 cm) USD 3,300. NEW YORK, 10 Nov 1977, *Architectural Cadences Number Four* (1954, silk screen print in colour) USD 3,250. NEW YORK, 21 April 1978, *Composition around Red (Pennsylvania)* (1958, tempera/Plexiglas, 6 x 8 ins / 15.2 x 20.3 cm) USD 4,250. NEW YORK, 20 April 1979, *Convolutions* (1952, oil on canvas, 36 x 26 ins / 91.5 x 66 cm) USD 120,000. NEW YORK, 28 Sept 1979, *Yachts* (1924, lithograph, 8 x 10 ins / 20.2 x 25.4 cm) GBP 5,800. NEW YORK, 5 Dec 1980, *Cottage* (1917, charcoal and pencil, 4 1/4 x 6 ins / 11 x 15.3 cm) USD 11,000. NEW YORK, 10 Dec 1981, *Amoskeag Mills No 2* (1948, oil on canvas, 29 x 25 ins / 73.7 x 63.5 cm) USD 170,000. NEW YORK, 13 May 1982, *Yachts* (1924, lithograph, 8 x 9 3/4 ins / 20.1 x 25 cm) USD 6,750. NEW YORK, 2 June 1983, *Tulips* (1931, pencil, 29 1/2 x 29 1/2 ins / 75 x 75.1 cm) USD 190,000. NEW YORK, 2 June 1983, *Classical Landscape* (1931, oil on canvas, 25 x 32 1/4 ins / 63.5 x 81.9 cm) USD 1,700,000. NEW YORK, 8 Dec 1983, *The Spirit of Research* (c. 1955, tempera/Plexiglas, 9 1/2 x 6 ins / 24.1 x 15.2 cm) USD 12,500. NEW YORK, 8 Nov 1984, *Delmonico Building* (1926, lithograph, 9 3/4 x 6 3/4 ins / 24.8 x 17 cm) USD 9,500. NEW YORK, 5 Dec 1985, *Untitled (Yachting)* (c. 1922, pencil, 6 3/4 x 11 ins / 17.1 x 28.1 cm) USD 20,000. NEW YORK, 4 Dec 1986, *Composition around White* (1951, tempera/paper, 6 x 5 1/4 ins / 15.2 x 13.3 cm) USD 45,000. NEW YORK, 3 Dec 1987, *Barn Abstraction* (1946, tempera/paper/card, 21 x 29 1/4 ins / 53.3 x 74.3 cm) USD 220,000. NEW YORK, 26 May 1988, *Grey Barns* (distemper/card, 14 x 20 1/2 ins / 35.6 x 52.1 cm) USD 165,000. NEW YORK, 30 Nov 1989, *Canyons II* (1951, tempera/paper, 5 x 4 1/4 ins / 12.7 x 10.7 cm) USD 44,000. NEW YORK, 1 Dec 1989, *Neighbourhood* (1951, oil on canvas, 18 x 15 ins / 45.7 x 38.1 cm) USD 396,000. NEW YORK, 23 May 1990, *Meta Mold II* (1952, gouache and pencil/paper/card, 8 x 10 ins / 20.4 x 25.3 cm) USD 38,500. NEW YORK, 22 May 1991, *Blue Barn* (1946, tempera and pencil/paper, 9 1/4 x 16 3/4 ins / 23.4 x 42.8 cm) USD 60,500. NEW YORK, 23 Sept 1992, *Untitled (Yachting)* (pencil/paper, 6 3/4 x 11 ins / 17.1 x 28.1 cm) USD 11,000. NEW YORK, 4 Dec 1992, *Industrial Californian Landscape* (1957, oil on canvas, 25 x 33 ins / 63.5 x 83.8 cm) USD 220,000. NEW YORK, 14 Sept 1995, *Dahlias* (1923, pastel and charcoal/paper, 21 x 15 3/4 ins / 53.3 x 40 cm) USD 12,075. NEW YORK, 14 March 1996, *Progress in Transport* (gouache/paper, 8 x 18 ins / 20.3 x 45.7 cm) USD 54,625. NEW YORK, 26 May 1999, *Improvisation on Mill Town* (1949, oil on canvas on board, 29 x 24 ins / 74 x 61 cm) USD 400,000. NEW YORK, 1 Dec 1999, *Ballarvale Revisited* (1949, tempera on board, 15 x 14 ins / 39 x 36 cm) USD 360,000. NEW YORK, 24 May 2000, *San Francisco - Fisherman's Wharf* (1956, oil on canvas, 31 x 22 ins / 80 x 55 cm) USD 340,000. NEW YORK, 31 Oct 2000, *Yachts* (lithograph, 8 x 10 ins / 20 x 26 cm) USD 26,000. NEW YORK, 25 April 2001, *Slag Buggy, Ford Plant, Detroit* (photograph, 9 x 7 ins / 23 x 19 cm) USD 76,000. NEW YORK, 23 May 2001, *Zinnias in a Bowl* (1918, tempera on paper, 13 x 10 ins / 33 x 25 cm) USD 80,000. NEW YORK, 22 Oct 2002, *Pulverzer Buildings, Ford Plant, Detroit* (photograph, 9 x 7 ins / 24 x 19 cm) USD 110,000. NEW YORK, 5 Dec 2002, *Convergence II* (1953, tempera on board, 6 x 4 ins / 15 x 10 cm) USD 240,000. NEW YORK, 21 May 2003, *Plums on a Plate* (c. 1910, oil on panel, 10 x 14 ins / 25 x 35 cm) USD 230,000. NEW YORK, 3 Dec 2003, *Tulip* (pastel and charcoal, 20 x 15 ins / 51 x 38 cm) USD 42,500. NEW YORK, 19 May 2004, *San Francisco - Fisherman's Wharf* (1956, oil on canvas, 31 x 21 ins / 79 x 53 cm) USD 260,000. NEW YORK, 19 May 2004, *Ballarvale Revisited* (1949, tempera on board, 15 x 14 ins / 38 x 36 cm) USD 270,000.

SHEEPSHANKS, John

British, 19th century.

Born 1787, in Leeds; died 5 October 1863, in London.

Draughtsman, watercolourist.

John Sheepshanks was an artist-philanthropist who painted watercolour landscapes and produced some interesting drawings. His principal claim to fame, however, is his magnificent bequest to the nation in the form of 233 oils and 409 drawings and watercolours, presented 'in order to facilitate and advance the study of painting'. The majority of the works concerned are housed in the Victoria and Albert Museum in London.

SHEERBOOM, Andries

Dutch (?), 19th century.

Born 1832; died after 1880.

Painter. Figures, genre scenes, urban landscapes.

AUCTION RECORDS:

LONDON, 5 Dec 1910, (a painting) GBP 2. LONDON, 7 May 1976, *Reapers Resting* (1865, oil on canvas, 24 1/2 x 29 1/2 ins / 62 x 75 cm) GBP 1,200. LONDON, 24 Oct 1978, *A Flower for Daddy* (1869, oil on canvas, 20 x 16 1/4 ins / 51 x 41 cm) GBP 850. LUCERNE, 30 May 1979, *View of a Town beside a Canal* (oil on canvas, 30 x 50 ins / 76.5 x 127 cm) CHF 26,000. LOS ANGELES,

18 June 1979, *Visit to the Future King* (1866, oil on canvas, 32 x 39½ ins / 81.3 x 100.3 cm) USD 1,300. New York, 28 Oct 1982, *Chess Players and Card Players* (oil on canvas, 28 x 36 ins / 71 x 91.5 cm) USD 2,750. New York, 19 Oct 1984, *Visit to the Young Prince* (1870, oil on canvas, 24¼ x 29¼ ins / 61.5 x 74.3 cm) USD 2,800. Montreal, 30 Oct 1989, *The Canterbury Tales* (oil on canvas, 22 x 32 ins / 56 x 81 cm) CAD 2,090. London, 16 Feb 1990, *View of Amsterdam from the Amstel* (1869, oil on canvas, 23½ x 35½ ins / 59.6 x 90.1 cm) GBP 10,120. Amsterdam, 25 April 1990, *Happy Family* (1863, oil on panel, 15¼ x 12 ins / 39 x 30.5 cm) NLG 10,120. Amsterdam, 6 Nov 1990, *Fisherman's Family* (1869, oil on canvas, 13½ x 17¾ ins / 34 x 45 cm) NLG 3,450. Amsterdam, 28 Oct 1992, *Three Generations* (oil on canvas, 22¾ x 19¾ ins / 58 x 50 cm) NLG 5,175. Amsterdam, 9 Nov 1994, *Wine-tasting Cup* (1859, oil on panel, 11½ x 10 ins / 29 x 24.5 cm) NLG 3,910.

SHEERER, Mary Given

American, 19th - 20th century.
Born 1865, in Covington (Kentucky); died 1954.
Painter, engraver.

Mary G. Sheerer studied at the Art Students League in New York and the Pennsylvania Academy of Fine Arts in Philadelphia. She was a member of the American Federation of Arts, New Orleans Art Association, Cincinnati Womens Art Club, Cincinnati Crafters Club, Cincinnati Museum Association and American Ceramic Society. She took part in group exhibitions including those of the New Orleans Art Association, and at the Louisiana Purchase Expo and the 1915 Pan-Pacific Expo, San Francisco.

SHEETS, Millard Owen

American, 20th century.
Born 1907, in Pomona (California); died 1989, in Gualala (California).
Watercolourist, painter (gouache). Landscapes.

Millard Owen Sheets was considered a leading watercolour painter of his time and an exponent of the California School during the Depression era. He painted landscapes, and also depicted scenes of humble people in both rural and urban settings. He took part in exhibitions at the Carnegie Foundation in Pittsburgh.

Museums and Galleries:
Paris (BNF, Prints Collection): *Trees* (c. 1980).

Auction records:
Los Angeles, 6 Nov 1978, *Paradise Cove* (1935, watercolour, 21¾ x 29½ ins / 55.3 x 75 cm) USD 1,500. Los Angeles, 17 March 1980, *Sunlit Landscape* (1929, oil on canvas, 20 x 24 ins / 51 x 61 cm) USD 2,500. Los Angeles, 23 June 1981, *Market at Udaipur, India* (watercolour, 22 x 29½ ins / 56 x 75 cm) USD 2,800. San Francisco, 20 June 1985, *Guadalajara Sunday* (watercolour, 21 x 29 ins / 53.5 x 73.5 cm) USD 3,000. Los Angeles, 9 June 1988, *Plots of Land in Patzcuaro* (watercolour, 25 x 30 ins / 63.5 x 76 cm) USD 8,800. New York, 24 Jan 1990, *Old Circus Ponies* (1936, watercolour/paper, 22¾ x 30½ ins / 57.8 x 77.4 cm) USD 8,800. Los Angeles-San Francisco, 7 Feb 1990, *Foundation of Los Angeles* (oil on canvas, 16¼ x 32½ ins / 41 x 82.5 cm) USD 35,750. Los Angeles-San Francisco, 12 July 1990, *Solitary Tree in a Nocturnal Landscape* (watercolour/paper, 22 x 30 ins / 55 x 76 cm) USD 5,500; *Gaviota Valley* (1932, pencil and watercolour/paper, 15¾ x 18½ ins / 40 x 47 cm) USD 11,000. New York, 27 Sept 1990, *Springtime* (1937, oil on canvas, 30 x 36 ins / 76.5 x 91.5 cm) USD 33,000. Los Angeles-San Francisco, 10 Oct 1990, *Picnic at Asilomar* (1976, watercolour/paper, 22 x 29½ ins / 55 x 75 cm) USD 11,000. New York, 21 May 1991, *Alamos in Mexico* (1940, watercolour and gouache/card, 22 x 30 ins / 55.9 x 76.2 cm) USD 4,400. New York, 14 Sept 1995, *In the Hills of Moorea* (1982, watercolour/paper, 29 x 40 ins / 73.7 x 101.6 cm) USD 13,225. New York, 21 May 1996, *River Canyon* (1937, watercolour and gouache/paper, 22 x 28 ins / 56 x 71 cm) USD 16,100. Los Angeles, 9 Dec 1999, *Harbor of Normandy* (1929, oil on canvas, 18 x 20 ins / 46 x 51 cm) USD 15,000. Los Angeles, 9 Dec 1999, *Hawaiian Fisherman* (oil on canvas, 24 x 32 ins / 61 x 81 cm) USD 26,000. Los Angeles, 3 May 2000, *Protea and Fruit* (1979, acrylic polymer on canvas, 40 x 29 ins / 102 x 73 cm) USD 13,000. New York, 28 June 2000, *Tropical Squall* (oil on canvas, 30 x 44 ins / 76 x 111 cm) USD 8,000. San Francisco, 13 June 2001, *Workers Along the Los Angeles River* (1927, pencil and watercolour, 10 x 13 ins / 25 x 34 cm) USD 5,000. San Francisco, 13 June 2001, *Horses of Chino* (1978, acrylic on canvas, 28 x 36 ins / 71 x 91 cm) USD 22,000. Pasadena, 11 June 2002, *Church Women in Polynesian Scene* (1976, watercolour, 21 x 29 ins / 53 x 74 cm) USD 37,500. Pasadena, 29 Oct 2002, *Ladies of Jaliaza* (1985, watercolour on paper, 22 x 28 ins / 56 x 71 cm) USD 16,000. New York, 19 Dec 2003, *Kahanna Bay* (1935, watercolour, 14 x 23 ins / 35 x 58 cm) USD 18,000. New York, 19 Dec 2003, *Windswept* (1941, watercolour, 22 x 30 ins / 57 x 76 cm) USD 20,000. Pasadena, 15 June 2004, *Connomorra Ponies in Panoramic Landscape* (1969, watercolour, 21 x 29 ins / 53 x 74 cm) USD 14,000. Pasadena, 15 June 2004, *Lava Beach, Hawaii* (1968, watercolour, 22 x 30 ins / 56 x 76 cm) USD 30,000.

SHEETS, Nan, Mrs Fred C. Sheets

American, 20th century.
Born 1885, in Albany (Illinois); died 1976, in Oklahoma City.
Painter, engraver. Landscapes.

Nan Sheets was taught by John Carlson, Robert Reid, Birger Sandzen and Hugh Breckenridge. She was a member of the American Federation of Arts.

Auction records:
Watertown, 5 Nov 2000, *Seaside Garden* (oil on canvas, 20 x 24 ins / 51 x 61 cm) USD 5,200.

SHEFFIELD, George

British, 19th century.
Born 1 January 1839, in Wigton, Cumberland; died 2 October 1892, in Manchester.
Painter, watercolourist, draughtsman. Seascapes, landscapes.

George Sheffield worked initially as an industrial draughtsman in Manchester before devoting himself wholly to painting and settling in Betws-y-Coed in the North Wales. Towards the end of his career he executed oil paintings. Sheffield exhibited in Manchester in 1868 and in London from 1872, particularly at the Royal Academy and the Royal Society of British Artists in Suffolk Street. He became an Associate of the Manchester Academy in 1869 and an Academician in 1871.

G. Sheffield

Museums and Galleries:
Blackburn: drawings - Manchester: *A Hundred Years Ago* (oils) - Montreal: drawings.

Auction records:
London, 27 Feb 1985, *The Canal Lock* (1870, watercolour, 24 x 37 ins / 61 x 94 cm) GBP 5,000. London, 22 Sept 1988, *Storm at Sea* (1879, charcoal, 35½ x 55 ins / 90.2 x 139.7 cm) GBP 440. London, 1 Nov 1990, *Warburton Lock Near Lymm* (watercolour heightened with white, 23¾ x 36¾ ins / 60.3 x 93.5 cm) GBP 1,760. London, 8 Feb 1991, *Boats on a Canal* (1875, watercolour heightened with white/vegetal paper/panel, 32 x 54½ ins / 81.4 x 138.5 cm) GBP 2,640. London, 21 March 2000, *Winter Scene of Horse and Wagons* (1881, pastel, 35 x 55 ins / 90 x 140 cm) GBP 1,500. London, 7 April 2000, *December* (1863, pencil, watercolour and

scratching out, 1 x 13 ins / 2 x 34 cm) GBP 2,200. HASLEMERE, 5 Nov 2003, *Common Scene with Cattle and Sheep. River Landscape with Figures* (1882, on paper, a pair, 24 x 36 ins / 61 x 91 cm) GBP 1,800.

SHEFFIELD, Isaac
American, 19th century.
Born 1798, in Guilford (Connecticut); died 1845.
Painter. Genre scenes, portraits.

Isaac Sheffield was an itinerant portrait painter from Connecticut who went to live in the whale fishing district of New London in 1823. Captains and their families would pose for miniatures and life-size portraits, which were generally three-quarter length. A raised drapery reveals a sailing ship behind each portrait of a man, or a port behind a woman. The captains are usually pictured with their telescopes, while the brooches and earrings of their wives are testament to the glowing health of the Connecticut whale fishing industry. However, most of the sitters wear a pensive or dreamy expression, which is unusual in popular portraiture; the artist captures fleeting expressions that seem to negate the sitters' ornate clothing and surroundings. A good example is his *Lady with Birthmark* with her almost bitter half-smile, which can be seen in the Museum of American Folk Art in New York.

MUSEUMS AND GALLERIES:
NEW YORK (American Folk AM): *Lady with Birthmark*.

AUCTION RECORDS:
NEW YORK, 30 April 1981, *Portrait of Mary Ann Wheeler* (1835, oil on panel, 30 x 24 ins / 76.2 x 61 cm) USD 12,000. NEW YORK, 26 Oct 1985, *Portrait of Captain Skinner* (c. 1835, oil on canvas, 34 1/2 x 27 1/2 ins / 87.5 x 70 cm) USD 37,500. SAN FRANCISCO, 9 June 2002, *Portrait of a Sea Captain* (oil on canvas, 30 x 25 ins / 76 x 63 cm) USD 4,750.

SHEFFIELD, W. E.
British, 18th century.
Active in London.
Painter.

W.E. Sheffield exhibited in London between 1789 and 1792.

SHEGAL, Grigoriy Mikhailovich
Russian, 20th century.
Born 1889, in Kozielsk; died 1956, in Moscow.
Painter. Portraits.
Socialist Realism.

A student at the Moscow Vkhutemas from 1922 to 1925, Grigoriy Mikhailovich Shegal taught at the national academy of fine arts in Moscow from 1937 to 1941. He prodiced paintings in the Academic figurative style and obeyed the principles of Socialist Realism attaching great importance to depicting historical reality, particularly in his scenes of everyday life. One of his works featured in the exhibition *Les Années trente en Europe. Le temps menaçant* (*Europe in the 1930s: The Gathering Storm*), Musée d'Art Moderne de la Ville de Paris (1997).

BIBLIOGRAPHY:
Pagé, Suzanne/Winock, Michel/Michaud, Éric/Vidal, Aline, *Les Années trente en Europe. Le Temps menaçant*, exhibition catalogue, Musée d'Art moderne de la Ville de Paris, Paris musées, Flammarion, Paris, 1997.

MUSEUMS AND GALLERIES:
ST PETERSBURG (Gosudarstvennyj Russkij Muz.): *Leader, Teacher and Friend* (1937).

SHEGOGUE, James Henry
American, 19th century.
Died 1872, in New York.
Painter. Portraits, genre scenes, landscapes.

James Henry Shegogue first exhibited at the National Academy of Design in New York in 1835, and was admitted as a member in 1843.

MUSEUMS AND GALLERIES:
NEW YORK (Metropolitan Mus. of Art): *Portrait of Sequin the Actor*.

SHEIK, Gulam Mohammed
Indian, 20th century.
Born 1937, in Surendranagar (Gujarat).
Painter. Religious subjects, figures, scenes with figures, landscapes, flowers.

Gulam Mohammed Sheik was a student at the fine arts school in Baroda. He subsequently taught art history, and in 1982 was put in charge of the painting department at the fine arts school in Baroda. In 1963, he worked in London on a grant from the Royal College of Art and visited Europe.

Sheik's palette is one of contrasting colours and his style is not naturalistic. His compositions are tinged with naivety and are worked with flat areas of colour and fantastical perspectives. In his street scenes and landscapes, rich compositions full of detail and bringing daily life to life, Sheik manages to establish a dialogue between his native culture and modernity, between the Orient (Indian miniatures) and Western painting (Italian primitivism, Expressionism).

Sheik's work has been shown at collective exhibitions including: exhibition of the 1890 group, of which he was a founder member, Delhi (1963); Paris and Tokyo Biennales (1963); Bombay (now Mumbai) (1979); *Contemporary Indian Art*, London and Hirshhorn Museum in Washington (1982); and *East-West Encounters*, Bombay (1985). Solo exhibitions include: Mumbai (1960, 1969) and Delhi (1963, 1971). In 1962 he was awarded the national prize for painting.

BIBLIOGRAPHY:
Kapur, Geeta, '*Modern Painting since 1935*' in *The Arts of India*, Phaidon, Oxford, 1981. *Gulam Mohammed Sheik - Returning Home*, exhibition catalogue, Éd. du Centre Georges-Pompidou, Paris, 1985.

MUSEUMS AND GALLERIES:
BHOPAL (Roopankar Mus. of Fine Arts): *The Talking Street* (1981); *Winding Roads* (1981) - CHANDIGARTH (Government Mus. and Gal. of Art): *Behind the Wall* (1976) - DELHI (Nat. Gal. of Modern Art): *The Wall* (1976) - LONDON (Victoria and Albert Mus.).

SHEIL, Edward
Irish, 19th century.
Born 1834, in Coleraine; died 11 March 1869, in Cork.
Active in Ireland.
Painter.

SHELDON
British, 18th century.
Active in London.
Painter. Flowers, fruit.

Sheldon may have been related to Alfred Sheldon. He exhibited in London from 1774 to 1775.

SHELDON, Alfred
British, 19th century.
Painter. Hunting scenes, still-lifes.

Alfred Sheldon exhibited in London, particularly at the British Institution and at the Royal Society of British Artists in Suffolk Street from 1844 to 1865.

AUCTION RECORDS:
LONDON, 21 July 1911, *Fox Hunt*, GBP 5. PARIS, 20 March 1944, *Jumping the Bank*, FRF 2,000. PARIS, July 1946, *The Hunt Sets Off*, FRF 3,100. LONDON, 16 Feb 1968, *Fox Hunt* (series of five canvases) Gns 440. VIENNA, 14 Oct 1969, *Fox Hunt* (series of five designs) ATS 35,000.

SHELDRAKE, Timothy
British, 18th century.
Active between 1740 and 1770.
Painter.

Timothy Sheldrake executed a portrait of *David Garrick* in 1749.

SHELFOX, D., or Shilfox
British, 18th century.
Active in London.
Engraver (burin).

D. Shelfox worked in London between 1770 and 1798.

SHELJESNOFF, Michail Ivanovitch.
See **JELIESNOV Michail Ivanovich**

SHELKOVNIKOV, Andrei Mikhailovich
Russian, 19th century.
Born 29 November 1788; died c. 1845.
Engraver (burin), lithographer.

SHELLEY
20th century.
Painter (gouache). Figures.

MUSEUMS AND GALLERIES:
MULHOUSE: *Woman* (1956).

SHELLEY, Samuel
British, 18th century.
Born 1750, in London; died 22 December 1808, in London.
Painter, engraver. Allegorical subjects, portraits.

Samuel Shelley apparently taught himself by copying the works of Sir Joshua Reynolds. His reputation as a miniaturist was considerable and almost equalled those of Cosway and Engleheart. Shelley engraved a number of prints and drew illustrations. He began to exhibit in London in 1773, particularly at the Society of Artists, the Royal Academy, the British Institution and the Society of Painters in Watercolours, of which he was one of the founders. His last submission was in 1808.

MUSEUMS AND GALLERIES:
DUBLIN: *Othello and Desdemona* (watercolour) - LONDON (Victoria and Albert Mus.): *The Huntress; Memory Gathering the Flowers Cut Down by Time* (miniature, allegory).

AUCTION RECORDS:
PARIS, 14 Nov 1946, *Young Woman in a Black Dress with a Wide Lace Collar* (miniature, attributed) FRF 9,500. LONDON, 19 Feb 1987, *Portrait of Lavinia, Countess Spencer* (1788, grey wash, 9 x 7 ins / 22 x 18 cm) GBP 700. LONDON, 21 June 1999, *Young Girl in Loose White Shift, her Dog Beside* (1786, miniature) GBP 3,500. LONDON, 9 Nov 1999, *Portrait of Young Girl in White Dress* (miniature) GBP 3,400. LONDON, 24 May 2000, *Admiral Patrick Drummond in Blue Coat* (1791, miniature) GBP 3,800. LONDON, 24 May 2000, *Peter de Bath in Scarlet Coat* (miniature) GBP 10,000. LONDON, 6 March 2001, *Captain Harvey in Uniform* (miniature) GBP 5,800. LONDON, 30 Oct 2001, *Gentleman in a Brown Coat* (miniature) GBP 5,200. LONDON, 11 April 2002, *Aston Sister* (miniature) GBP 14,000. LONDON, 28 May 2002, *Waldegrave Sisters, Lady Elizabeth Laura, Lady Charlotte Maria and Lady Anna Horatia Seated* (miniature) GBP 11,000. LONDON, 25 June 2003, *Major Perryn in Red Uniform* (c. 1795, miniature) GBP 4,500. LONDON, 18 Dec 2003, *Naval Officer, possibly Archibald, 9th Earl of Dundonald* (miniature) GBP 3,200. DETROIT, 12 March 2004, *Young Girl* (c. 1780, miniature) USD 9,000. LONDON, 17 Nov 2004, *Lady, Seated on a Red Upholstered Chair at a Piano* (miniature) GBP 2,200.

SHELLY, Arthur
British, 19th century.
Born 1841, in Yarmouth; died 1902, in Torquay.
Watercolourist. Landscapes.

MUSEUMS AND GALLERIES:
NORWICH (Castle Mus. and AG): *Chagford, South Devon* (watercolour).

SHELTON, Peter
American, 20th - 21st century.
Born 18 January 1951, in California.
Sculptor, installation artist.

Peter Shelton, who grew up in Tempe, Arizona, studied at Pomona College, Claremont, California, obtaining a bachelor of fine arts in 1973. He proceeded to the Hobart School of Welding Technology, receiving a certificate in 1974; and the University of California in Los Angeles, where he obtained a master's degree in fine arts in 1979. He has lectured in sculpture at Otis/Parsons School of Art and Design (from 1980) and at Claremont Graduate School (from 1981).

Shelton is best known for his large iron, steel and fibreglass sculptures, which often seem to show the figure from both inside and outside at the same time. He says that he wants his work on his sculptures to be physically challenging. He combines his art with his interest in anatomy and biology (he spent a period as a pre-medical student when at Pomona College), seeing his sculptures as an examination of human architecture: bones, intestines, veins, arteries, and internal organs. His *godspipes*, which took five years to complete, is composed of 193 translucent fibreglass and lead pipes which give the impression of limbs, body torsos and joints. His *blackelephanthouse* installation appears to be both a creature and a house-like structure, influenced by his interest in Indian art and Buddhist liturgical buildings such as stupas. The installation *sixtyslippers* comprises 60 cast iron discs suspended from the ceiling in a pattern reminiscent of the form of the human body. Recently Shelton has turned to smaller sculptures, such as the cast bronze works *frenchvent* and *googlelips* (both 2004).

Shelton has received National Endowment for the Arts Fellowships (1980, 1982, 1984); a Young Talent Award, Los Angeles County Museum of Art (1985); a Louis Comfort Tiffany Foundation Grant (1987); a Guggenheim Fellowship (1989); a Flintridge Foundation Visual Artists Award (1999-2000) and a St Gaudens Memorial Fellowship (2000).

His solo exhibitions include *Peter Shelton*, Open Space Gallery, Victoria, BC (1982); *bottlesbonesandthingsgetwet*, Los Angeles County Museum of Art (1994); *oldwetbrickhouse*, Museum of Contemporary Art, San Diego (1997); *sixtyslippers*, University of California, Berkeley (1998-1999); *blackelephanthouse*, Dean Clough, Henry Moore Sculpture Trust, Halifax, UK (1998-1999) and *godspipes*, Irish Museum of Modern Art, Dublin. He has also shown at Artists Space, New York (1982); Musée d'Art Moderne, Paris (1982); the Center for Contemporary Arts, Seattle (1983); Portland Center for Visual Arts (1984); Navy Pier Walk 2003, Chicago International Sculpture Exhibition (2003); *Not-So-Still-life*, San Jose Museum of Art (2003-2004); *Waterworks*, Galleria Cardi and Gian Enzo Sperone Galleries, Milan (2004) and *Monochromos Varaciones sobre el tema*, Museo Nacional Centro de Arte Reina Sofia, Madrid (2004).

BIBLIOGRAPHY:
Peter Shelton, exhibition catalogue, Open Space Gallery, Victoria (CAN), 1982. *Floating Deadman, and Related Work by Peter Shelton*, exhibition catalogue, Wight Art Gallery, University of California, Los Angeles, 1987. Edelamn, Robert G., '*Peter Shelton*' in *Art Press* n° 182, periodical, Paris, July-August 1993. Eliel, Carol S., *Peter Shelton: bottlesbonesandthingsgetwet*, exhibition catalogue, Los Angeles County Museum of Art, Los Angeles, 1994. *Peter Shelton: sixtyslippers*, exhibition catalogue, University of California, Berkeley Art Museum, Berkeley, 1998. Baas, Jacquelynn, *Peter Shelton: Soul Soundings*, exhibition catalogue, Henry Moore Sculpture Trust, Leeds, 1998. Brooks, Rosetta, '*Peter Shelton*' in *Artforum*, journal article, March 1998.

MUSEUMS AND GALLERIES:
ŁÓDZ (MCA) - LOS ANGELES (Broad Art Foundation) - LOS ANGELES (County MA) - LOS ANGELES (Douglas Cramer

Foundation) - LOS ANGELES (Getty Mus.) - LOS ANGELES (Lannan Foundation) - LOS ANGELES (MCA) - LOUISVILLE (J.B. Speed Mus.) - LUGANO (Mus. Cantonale d'Arte) - MINNEAPOLIS (Walker Art Center): *bigflatsack* (1984-1986, iron sculpture) - NEW YORK (MoMA) - NEWPORT BEACH (Orange County MA) - OBERLIN (Allen Memorial Art Museum, Oberlin College): *buglebone* (1990-1993, sculpture) - SAN DIEGO (MCA).

AUCTION RECORDS:

SAN FRANCISCO, 22 April 1999, *shoesandgloves* (1983, brown patinated bronze, h. 9 ins / 22 cm) USD 4,500. LOS ANGELES, 5 Dec 2000, *eightsheader* (1988-1991, green-brown patinated bronze, 19 x 11x4 ins / 49 x 28x11 cm) USD 12,000. NEW YORK, 13 Nov 2002, *whiteshirt* (1984-1986, fibreglass over wire frame, 38 x 57x3 ins / 96 x 146x8 cm) USD 27,500.

SHELTON, William Henry

American, 19th - 20th century.

Born 4 September 1840, in Allen's Hill (New York); died 15 March 1912, in Morristown.

Painter, illustrator.

William Henry Shelton studied at the Art Students League and exhibited at the Brooklyn Art Association, the Boston Art Club, the Pennsylvania Academy, and the Art Institute of Chicago.

SHEMI, Menachem, or Schmidt

Russian, 20th century.

Born 1896 or 1897, in Russia; died 1951, in Safed.

Active in Israel from 1913.

Painter, sculptor. Portraits, landscapes, still-lifes, memorials.

Safed Artists' Colony.

Menachem Shemi was born in Russia. His family emigrated to Palestine in 1913. He studied at the Odessa academy of art and the Bezalel Academy, Jerusalem. In 1920 he co-founded the Association of Painters and Sculptors in Israel and in 1947 was one of the founders of the Safed Artists' Colony. He exhibited in Paris in 1928, 1937 and 1945 and took part in the 1950 Venice Biennale. Retrospectives of his work were held in 1952 in the Tel Aviv Museum and Haifa Museum for Modern Art, and in 1966 in the Israel Museum, Jerusalem.

BIBLIOGRAPHY:

Kolb, E., *Menachem Shemi*, Tel Aviv, 1958. *Menachem Shemi. Permanent display from the collection of the Haifa museum of modern art*, exhibition catalogue, Museum of modern art, Haifa, 1978 (text in English).

AUCTION RECORDS:

TEL AVIV, 16 May 1983, *Street Corner, Acra* (1936, oil on canvas, 23 1/2 x 19 1/4 ins / 60 x 49 cm) ILS 266,900. TEL AVIV, 17 June 1985, *Woman in Courtyard* (1950, oil on canvas, 19 x 15 1/4 ins / 48 x 39 cm) ILS 12,500,000. TEL AVIV, 25 May 1988, *Portrait of the Artist's Wife* (1931, oil on canvas, 12 x 12 ins / 30.5 x 30.5 cm) USD 3,300. TEL AVIV, 3 Jan 1990, *Around Carmel* (oil on canvas, 18 1/2 x 25 3/4 ins / 47 x 65.5 cm) USD 13,750. TEL AVIV, 19 June 1990, *Tiberias* (1942, oil on canvas, 16 1/4 x 22 ins / 41.5 x 55 cm) USD 11,000. TEL AVIV, 12 June 1991, *Carmel Landscape* (oil on canvas, 18 1/2 x 25 3/4 ins / 47 x 65.5 cm) USD 15,400. TEL AVIV, 6 Jan 1992, *Self-portrait* (oil on canvas, 32 x 23 1/2 ins / 81 x 60 cm) USD 18,150. TEL AVIV, 4 Oct 1993, *Still-life with Basket* (1940, oil on canvas, 16 1/4 x 22 ins / 41 x 55 cm) USD 9,200. TEL AVIV, 14 Jan 1996, *An Orthodox Jew and an Arab in a Tarbush Riding Donkeys Meet on the Road* (oil on canvas, 16 x 10 1/4 ins / 40.5 x 26 cm) USD 17,250. TEL AVIV, 7 Oct 1996, *Carob Tree* (1939, oil on canvas, 21 1/4 x 28 3/4 ins / 54 x 73 cm) USD 17,250. TEL AVIV, 12 Jan 1997, *Village in Italy* (1944-1945, oil on canvas, 20 x 15 3/4 ins / 51 x 40 cm) USD 14,950. TEL AVIV, 26 April 1997, *Israeli Landscape* (oil on canvas, 17 1/4 x 20 ins / 44 x 50.7 cm) USD 7,475. TEL AVIV, 25 Oct 1997, *Safed* (1949, oil on canvas, 15 x 21 ins / 38.1 x 53.3 cm) USD 18,400.

SHEMI, Yehiel

Israeli, 20th century.

Born 1922, in Haifa.

Sculptor.

Yehiel Shemi was one of the founders of the Beit Ha-Aravah kibbutz. He travelled to Europe, Egypt and the USA in 1945, and during the late 1950s spent two years in Paris exhibiting with the group Nouveaux Horizons. In the mid-1950s he started making sculptures in welded iron, and in 1958 he produced a monument for Jerusalem.

AUCTION RECORDS:

TEL AVIV, 14 April 1993, *Stretched-out Figure* (welded iron, l. 15 1/4 ins / 39 cm) USD 3,220. TEL AVIV, 4 April 1994, *Tripod* (welded iron, h. 15 1/2 ins / 39.3 cm) USD 2,990. TEL AVIV, 14 Jan 1996, *Composition* (iron, h. 10 1/4 ins / 26 cm) USD 3,450. TEL AVIV, 7 Oct 1996, *Bird* (1954, welded iron, h. 33 1/2 ins / 85 cm) USD 28,750. TEL AVIV, 16 April 2001, *Owl* (1955, welded iron, h. 21 ins / 53 cm) GBP 9, 028. TEL AVIV, 12 June 2001, *Head Armour* (welded iron, h. 26 ins / 65 cm) GBP 18, 571. TEL AVIV, 6 April 2002, *Untitled* (1960, welded iron, h. 7 ins / 19 cm) GBP 2, 817. TEL AVIV, 27 April 2003, *Wounded Bird* (welded metal, h. 20 ins / 52 cm) GBP 8, 824.

SHEMIAKIN, Mikhaïl Fedorovitch.
See **CHEMIAKIN Mihail**

SHEMTSCHUSHNIKOFF, Lew Michailovitch
. See **JEMTCHUNIKOV Lev Mikhailovich**

SHEMYAKIN, Mikhail Fedorovich, or Chemiakin

Russian, 20th century.

Born 1875, in Moscow; died 1944.

Painter. Portraits, genre scenes, still-lifes.

Mikhail Fedorovich Shemyakin studied in Munich for two years, and exhibited in St Petersburg in 1908. He painted mostly portraits of artists, including: *Portrait of the Violinist Liubochitz* and *Portrait of the Poet J. Verkhlitsky*.

MUSEUMS AND GALLERIES:

KLIN (Tchaikovsky Mus.): *Trio; Quartet* - MOSCOW (State Tretyakov Gal.): *Mother and Child*.

AUCTION RECORDS:

LONDON, 18 May 1988, *Head of a Woman* (oil on canvas, 31 3/4 x 27 1/4 ins / 80.5 x 69 cm) GBP 5,060.

SHEMYAKIN, Rebecca Modlen

Russian, 20th century.

Born 1934, in Leningrad (now St Petersburg).

Active in France from 1971, active in Greece from 1979.

Painter (mixed media), sculptor. Figures.

Rebecca Shemyakin studied at the arts school in Leningrad. She married the painter Mikhail Shemyakin, and emigrated with him to Paris in 1971.

She has participated in collective exhibitions, including Art Expo in New York on several occasions. Solo exhibitions include: New York (1982; 1986; Athens (1988); Galerie Altmann and Galerie J.P. Villain, Paris (1989).

SHEN CH'UAN. See **SHEN QUAN**

SHEN CHEN. See **SHEN ZHEN**

SHEN CHIH. See **SHEN ZHI**

SHEN CHO. See **SHEN ZHUO**

SHEN CHOU. See **SHEN ZHOU**

SHEN FENG, sobriquet: Fanmin, style name: Buluo

Chinese, 18th century.

Born in Jiangyin (Jiangsu Province).

Active during the second half of the 18th century.

Painter.

Shen Feng was a seal carver, calligrapher and landscape painter. Several of his works are known, such as *River Panorama, with Pavilion and Trees on an Island*, in the style of Ni

Zan, signed and dated 1751, and *Winter Landscape*, signed and dated 1766.

SHEN GUA, or Shen Kua
Chinese, 11th century.
Born 1031; died 1095.
Art lover, art critic.

After a brilliant career as an official, diplomat and soldier, Shen Gua wrote a monumental work of scholarship, the *Mengqi Bitan* (*Address of the Stream of Dreams*), a veritable Summa of human knowledge encompassing fields as varied as history, politics, music, astrology and astronomy, arts and letters, mathematics, technology and archaeology. This work of genius is not merely a compilation of the works of others but the fruit of original creative thought by an observer, inventor and philosopher. Book 17 is devoted to painting and calligraphy and contains a famous passage in which Sheng Gua comes to the defence of pictorial creation as an autonomous art free from all vulgar concerns of likeness or verisimilitude. 'The wonderful parts (or the mystery) of calligraphy and painting must be realised by the soul; they can hardly be discovered in mere forms,' says Sirén. 'Those who look at paintings are always able to point out faults of form, of likeness, of design and colouring, but I have seldom found people who have penetrated into the mysterious reason and depth of creative activity.... This is because his (the artist Wang Wei's) creative activity and his reason resided in the spiritual part of his nature and because he grasped to the highest degree the idea (inspiration of Heaven). But this is hard to explain to common people.'

BIBLIOGRAPHY:

Sirén, Osvald, *The Chinese on the Art of Painting: Translations and Comments*, H. Vetch, Beijing, 1936. Ryckmans, Pierre, *Les "Propos sur la peinture" de Shitao. Traduction et commentaires pour servir de contribution à l'étude terminologique et esthétique des théories chinoises de la peinture*, Institut belge des hautes études chinoises, Brussels, 1970.

SHEN HAO, sobriquet: Langqian, style name: Shitian
Chinese, 17th century.
Born in Suzhou (Jiangsu Province).
Active c. 1630-1650.
Painter.

Shen Hao was a poet, calligrapher and landscape painter who worked in a style close to that of Shen Zhou (1427-1509). He is mainly known as a critic and theoretician of painting and the author of the *Hua Zhu*, a treatise comprising 13 brief chapters on aesthetics, criticism and technique. Among the usual banalities, such as the inevitable division between the Northern and Southern Schools, the *Hua Zhu* contains some really interesting material and original comments on copying, which Shen Hao regards 'not as simply reproductions of pictures in front of the painter but renderings of their ideas, they must be accomplished in the soul... [The old masters] studied from nature in order to grasp the most intimate aspects of certain landscapes.'

BIBLIOGRAPHY:

Sirén, Osvald, *The Chinese on the Art of Painting: Translations and Comments*, H. Vetch, Beijing, 1936.

MUSEUMS AND GALLERIES:

BEIJING (Palace Mus.): *Scholar in His Study under Old Trees* (inscription of the artist dated 1633) - STOCKHOLM (Nationalmus.): *Philosopher on Rocky Hillside* (signed) - TIANJIN: *Landscape* (colour on paper, album sheet).

SHEN HENG, or Shen Henji, sobriquet: Hengji, style name: Tongzhai
Chinese, 15th century.
Born 1409, in Suzhou; died 1477.
Painter. Landscapes.

Shen Heng was the brother of Shen Zhen and the father of Shen Zhou. He is known as a landscape painter in the style of Du Qiong.

AUCTION RECORDS:

NEW YORK, 2 June 1988, *Cabin in Winter Mountains* (ink on paper, hanging scroll, 41 3/4 x 24 3/4 ins / 106 x 62.8 cm) USD 22,000.

SHEN HSIANG. See **SHEN XIANG**

SHEN HSÜAN. See **SHEN XUAN**

SHEN HUAN
Chinese, 18th century.
Painter. Figures.

Shen Huan was a court painter during the reign of the Qing emperor Qianlong (1736-1796).

SHEN I-CH'IEN. See **SHEN YIQIAN**

SHEN JOU-CHIEN. See **SHEN ROUJIAN**

SHEN JUNG. See **SHEN RONG**

SHEN KUA. See **SHEN GUA**

SHEN NANPIN. See **SHEN QUAN**

SHEN QUAN, or Shen Ch'uan, sobriquet: Hengzhai, style name: Nanpin
Chinese, 18th century.
Born in Wuking (Zhejiang Province).
Painter. Animals, flowers.

Shen Quan is one of the rare Chinese artists who are known beyond doubt to have stayed in Japan, visiting Nagasaki in 1731-1733. During his time there, Shen helped to introduce *wenren hua* (literati painting) techniques, which in Japanese became *bunjinga* or *nanga*. He also left behind him the so-called Nagasaki School, which in reality amounted to little more than a group of minor artists - Chinese who were little known at home, or Japanese. And Shen was in fact only one of the many conduits through which literati painting entered Japan. He is less highly regarded in China than he is in Japan. Most of his works are in Japanese collections.

BIBLIOGRAPHY:

Cahill, James, *Scholar Painters of Japan: the Nanga School*, Asia Society, New York, 1972.

MUSEUMS AND GALLERIES:

LONDON (British Mus.): *Dogs and Peonies* (signed and dated 1750); *Flowers and Birds* (small signed handscroll) - NEW YORK (Metropolitan Mus. of Art): *Two Pheasants on the Branches of a Peach Tree* (signed and dated 1744) - STOCKHOLM (Nationalmus.): *Pair of Mottled Deer beneath a Pine* (dated 1753) - TAIPEI (National Palace Mus.): *Four Wild Geese* (signed); *Two Feng Birds* (signed); *Peacocks* (signed).

AUCTION RECORDS:

NEW YORK, 6 Dec 1989, *Birds and Flowers* (ink and colour on silk, handscroll, 17 1/4 x 384 ins / 43.5 x 975.4 cm) USD 38,500. NEW YORK, 31 May 1990, *Wild Geese* (ink and colour on silk, hanging scroll, 49 x 25 1/4 ins / 124.5 x 64.2 cm) USD 3,575. NEW YORK, 25 Nov 1991, *Deer* (ink and colour on silk, hanging scroll, 90 1/4 x 43 ins / 229.2 x 109.2 cm) USD 29,700. NEW YORK, 31 May 1994, *Two Storks* (ink and colour on silk, 61 1/2 x 18 ins / 156.2 x 44.8 cm) USD 10,350. NEW YORK, 27 March 1996, *Bird and Flower* (ink and colour on paper, hanging scroll, 63 x 37 ins / 160 x 94 cm) USD 34,500. NORTH BETHESDA, 2 April 2001, *Flying Bird among Flowering Branches* (ink and colour on silk) USD 8,500. HONG KONG, 26 Oct 2003, *Cranes of Long Life* (ink and colour on screen, six, 61 x 22 ins / 155 x 56 cm) HKD 1,100,000. LONDON, 13 Nov 2003, *Peonies, Birds and Magnolia* (c. 1750, ink and colour on silk, 75 x 38 ins / 191 x 96 cm) GBP 19,000.

SHEN RONG, or Shen Jung, sobriquet: Shixiang, style name: Oushi
Chinese, 19th century.

Born 1794, in Suzhou (Jiangsu Province); died 1856.
Active c. 1830.
Painter. Landscapes, flowers.
Shen Rong was one of the less important artists o of the Loudong School.
AUCTION RECORDS:
NEW YORK, 31 May 1990, *Flowers* (ink and colour on silk, handscroll, after Yun Shouping, 12 3/4 x 259 1/2 ins / 32.4 x 659.3 cm) USD 6,050.

SHEN ROUJIAN, or Shen Jou-Chien
Chinese, 20th century.
Born 1919, in Fujian.
Painter, wood engraver. Landscapes, seascapes.
Shen Roujian lives and works in Shanghai. His work is typical of post-1949 Chinese wood engraving in its realism, clarity of design and simple colouring, as well as in its subject-matter, boats, bridges, railways and factories under construction, driven by yet another great leap forward.
BIBLIOGRAPHY:
Yonezawa, Yoshiho/Kawakita, Michiaki, *Arts of China: Paintings in Chinese Collections-New Collections*, Kodansha, Tokyo, 1970.
MUSEUMS AND GALLERIES:
PARIS (BNF, Prints Collection): *Snowy Night at Shanghai* (1957, wood).

SHEN SHI, or Shen Shih, sobriquets: Maoxue, Mouxue, Zideng, style name: Qingmen shenren
Chinese, 16th - 17th century.
Born in Hangzhou (Zhejiang Province).
Painter.
Shen Shi was a collector of calligraphy and paintings and is known as a bird-and-flower and landscape painter. The Beijing Palace Museum has a signed, dated handscroll by him entitled *View of Nine Dragon Mountain* (1571 or 1621).
MUSEUMS AND GALLERIES:
BEIJING (Palace Mus.): *View of Nine Dragon Mountain* - TAIPEI (National Palace Mus.): *Flowers* (two fans).

SHEN SHIGENG, or Shen Shih-keng
Chinese, 17th century.
Active c. 1620-1640.
Painter.
Shen Shigeng painted landscapes and figures in the style of Tang Yin (1470-1523).

SHEN SHIH-CH'UNG. See **SHENG SHICHONG**

SHEN SHIH-KENG. See **SHEN SHIGENG**

SHEN T'IEN-HSIANG. See **SHEN TIANXIANG**

SHEN TIANXIANG, or Shen T'ien-hsiang
Chinese, 18th century.
Painter.
Shen Tianxiang was the nephew of the painter Shen Quan (active c. 1725-1780).

SHÊN TSU-YUNG. See **SHEN ZUYONG**

SHEN TSUNG-CH'IEN. See **SHEN ZONGQIAN**

SHEN TSUNG-CHING. See **SHEN ZONGJING**

SHEN XIANG, or Shen Hsiang, sobriquet: Shucheng, style name: Xiaoxia
Chinese.
Born in Shanxi (Zhejiang Province).
Active during the Ming dynasty (1368-1644).
Painter. Plum blossom.

SHEN XINGGONG
Chinese, 20th century.
Born 1943, in Ningbo (Zhejiang Province).
Painter.
Shen Xinggong graduated from the Nanjing art academy in 1981, and went on to become its head (1984-1990) with a permanent teaching position. He visited Japan in 1986 and the USA in 1987. He also taught at Nanyang University, Singapore, as visiting professor.
AUCTION RECORDS:
HONG KONG, 30 Oct 1995, *Season of the Perfume of Flowers* (oil on canvas, 39 1/4 x 32 ins / 100 x 81 cm) HKD 46,000.

SHEN XINHAI
Chinese, 20th century.
Active in the early 20th century.
Painter. Religious subjects.
AUCTION RECORDS:
NEW YORK, 11 April 1990, *The God of Longevity in the Style of Hua Yan* (ink and colour, hanging scroll, 31 3/4 x 15 1/2 ins / 80.7 x 39.4 cm) USD 550.

SHEN XUAN, or Shen Hsüan
Chinese, 14th century.
Active mid-14th century.
Painter.
Shen Xuan painted landscapes in the style of Huang Gongwang (1269-1364).
MUSEUMS AND GALLERIES:
BEIJING (Palace Mus.): *Landscape Study*.

SHEN YAOCHU
Chinese, 20th century.
Born 1908; died 1990.
Active in Taiwan.
Painter. Animals.
Shen Yaochu specialised in painting animals, especially poultry.
AUCTION RECORDS:
HONG KONG, 15 Nov 1989, *Geese* (1988, ink and colour on paper, hanging scroll, 54 x 27 ins / 137 x 68.6 cm) HKD 71,500.
HONG KONG, 31 Oct 1991, *Cock and Hen* (ink and colour on paper, hanging scroll, 34 x 16 1/2 ins / 86.5 x 42 cm) HKD 19,800.

SHEN YINGHUI, or Shen Ying-hui, sobriquet: Langqian, style names: Gengzhai, Yatang
Chinese, 18th century.
Born in Songjiang (Jiangsu Province).
Active c. 1700.
Painter.
Shen Yinghui was a landscape painter and the nephew of Shen Zongjing (1669-1735).

SHEN YINMO
Chinese, 20th century.
Born 1883, in Wuxing (Zhejiang Province); died 1971.
Painter, draughtsman.
Shen Yinmo was also a calligrapher and writer and taught in many universities. He took part in various nationalist movements after World War I and was tortured by Red Guards and forced to burn his work during the Cultural Revolution. In 1946, he showed a calligraphy at the Exposition Internationale d'Art Moderne Ouvert organised by the United Nations at the Musée d'Art Moderne in Paris. In 2002, his work was included in *Brushes with Surprise. The Art of Calligraphy in Modern China* at the British Museum in London.
AUCTION RECORDS:
HONG KONG, 29 Oct 1992, *Bamboo and Rock* (1949, ink on paper) HKD 40,000.

SHEN YIQIAN, or Shen I-ch'ien
Chinese, 20th century.
Born 1908, in Shanghai; reported missing in October 1945.
Painter.

Shen Yiqian studied art at the Shanghai academy. He was one of the group of artists, including Guan Shanyeu, who rediscovered western China during World War II and were captivated by the wild beauty of the Tibetan and Mongolian plateaux and by the local cultures. All Shen did was to record what he saw, and his work is without any great aesthetic interest. He was arrested and disappeared in October 1945.

Bibliography:

Sullivan, Michael, *Chinese Art in the Twentieth Century*, University of California Press, Berkeley, Los Angeles, London, 1959.

SHEN YU

Chinese, 17th century.
Born 1649.
Painter. Landscapes.

Shen Yu was treasurer of the imperial house during the reign of the Qing emperor Kangxi (1662-1722). In 1711, he was commissioned to paint a picture of the summer palace at Jehol. He painted landscapes in the style of Dong Yuan (died 962) and Juran (active c. 960-980).

SHEN YUAN, or Shen Yüan

Chinese, 18th century.
Active c. 1745.
Painter. Figures, scenes with figures, genre scenes.

Shen Yuan was a court painter. Two of his scrolls are in the National Palace Museum, Taipei: *Skating Party on Lake Beihai, Beijing*, with a poem by the Qing emperor Qianlong dated 1746, and *Emperor Qianlong's Music Pavilion on Lake Beihai*, with a colophon by Qianlong.

Museums and Galleries:

Taipei (National Palace Mus.): *Skating Party on Lake Beihai, Beijing*; *Emperor Qianlong's Music Pavilion on Lake Beihai*.

SHEN YUAN

Chinese, 20th - 21st century.
Born 1959, in Xianjou.
Active in Paris since 1990.
Sculptor, installation artist.

Shen Yuan settled in Paris in 1990. She explores the limitations of being a woman, in both Chinese and Western society, and the potential power of the female body. In 2000, she took part in the exhibition *Paris pour escale (Stopover Paris)* at the Musée d'Art Moderne, Paris, and in the São Paulo Biennale. She had solo exhibitions at the Kunsthalle in Bern (*Under the Earth is the Sky*) in 2000 and in England in 2001 at the Arnolfini Gallery, Bristol and the Chisenhale Gallery, London.

Bibliography:

Gao Minglu (ed.), *Inside Out: New Chinese Art*, University of California Press, Berkeley, 1998 (mentioned briefly). Hanru, Hou/Jouanno, Evelyne, et al., *Shen Yuan*, Cornerhouse Publications, London, 2001.

SHEN ZENGZHI

Chinese, 19th - 20th century.
Born 1850; died 1922.
Painter.

Shen Zengzhi was a calligrapher.

Auction records:

Hong Kong, 22 March 1993, *Two Verses* (calligraphy in running script, two hanging scrolls, each 81 x 16 1/2 ins / 205.6 x 42 cm) HKD 36,800. Hong Kong, 3 Nov 1994, *Calligraphy in Cao Shu* (ink on paper, hanging scroll, 51 x 26 1/4 ins / 129.6 x 66.6 cm) HKD 16,100.

SHEN ZHEN, or Shen Chen, sobriquet: Zhenji, style names: Nanzhai, Taoran Daoren

Chinese, 15th century.
Born 1400, in Suzhou (Jiangsu Province); died after 1480.
Painter.

Shen Zhen was the uncle of Shen Zhou (1427-1509). He painted landscapes in the style of Dong Yuan (d. 962). Various signed works of his survive, some of them dated.

SHEN ZHERAI

Chinese, 20th century.
Born 1924, in Tainan.
Painter. Portraits.

Shen Zherai started his training at the Tainan first secondary school before studying under Guo Bochuan and Liao Jichun. He ran the Chinese oil painters' association and was a jury member for provincial exhibitions. He also won several prizes himself.

Auction records:

Taipei, 18 Oct 1992, *Portrait of Lady in Blue* (oil on canvas, 28 3/4 x 20 3/4 ins / 73 x 53 cm) TWD 572,000.

SHEN ZHI, or Shen Chih, sobriquet: Yuean

Chinese, 17th century.
Born 1618, probably in Xiushui (Zhejiang Province).
Painter.

Shen Zhi was a landscape painter. The national museum in Tokyo has a scroll which he painted at the age of 25, *Dwellings of the Immortals at Penglai*, signed and dated 1703 (?).

Museums and Galleries:

Tokyo (National Mus.): *Dwellings of the Immortals at Penglai*.

SHEN ZHOU, or Shen Chou, sobriquet: Qinan, style names: Shitian, Baishiweng, Yutianweng

Chinese, 15th century.
Born 1427, in Suzhou (Jiangsu Province); died 1509.
Painter. Landscapes, flowers, animals.

At the end of the 15th and beginning of the 16th century, a group of painters emerged around the city of Suzhou in the area of Wumen becoming known as the Wu School. They brought an infusion of new blood into literati painting. Although not strictly speaking the founder of the school, Shen Zhou was its dominant figure. He exerted a strong influence on the younger generation and acted as the guiding light of the avant-garde for more than a century to come. Both in the way he lived and in his work, Shen was the embodiment of large parts of the Yuan tradition, which was very different from that of the early Ming.

Shen Zhou was born into an illustrious, wealthy Suzhou family. The family's prosperity dated back to Shen Zhou's great-grandfather, an art lover and friend of Wang Meng. His grandfather had painted and written poetry, and his father and uncle, Shen Heng and Shen Zhen, lived the life of scholars, devoting themselves to poetry and painting in their bamboo studies. Shen Zhou inherited a similar scholarly background from his mother's side, so it is not surprising that he had a thorough classical education and was in contact with the literary and artistic elite of Suzhou, at that time regarded as the capital of the arts and letters, from his early youth. With his natural talent for the arts and all things intellectual he could have made a brilliant career as an official, but he declined to enter public life on the pretext that he had to look after his widowed mother. (She would die in 1506, when Shen Zhou was 80.)

Although he shunned all official honours, he did not follow the example of the Four Masters of Yuan and go into fierce isolation, as would the Qing individualists who succeeded him. He sought purity and independence of spirit instead by living the calm, contemplative life of a scholar devoted to attaining his own spiritual realisation through reading, studying, painting and writing poetry. He spent his life cultivating a group of friends from official circles or from the artistic and literary world. His biographers are unanimous in praising his virtues: his filial piety, his sociability, his modesty and amenity to his peers, his generosity to those more humble than himself. Shen Zhou truly was the perfect example of the high-minded, noble-hearted gentleman scholar who lived the simple life. And his painting is of a piece with his life: its firm, frank, serene touch bears the mark of careful contemplation, a mixture of vigour and the rejection of the facile.

He was taught by his father and uncle perhaps a little later than usual, but his training was slow and thorough. It started with the study of the Old Masters of the Tang, Five Dynasties and Song before moving on to copy the Great Yuan Masters, Huang Gongwang (1269-1354), Ni Zan (1301-1374), Wang Meng (1298-1385) and Wu Zhen (1280-1354). These masters would have a decisive influence: their work would always remain a source of inspiration to him. And the breadth and depth of his culture were such that he could reproduce a prodigious range of models and draw on an astonishing variety of styles. His profound knowledge of the Ancients, and the vitality of his temperament, allowed his pictures to become a sort of free transposition of the originals.

Walking with a Staff, a hanging scroll in the style of Ni Zan is a perfect example of the freedom with which Shen Zhou succeeds in expressing a personal vision through borrowed forms and in turning imitation into a springboard for original creation. He takes Ni's generous contours and texture and replaces them with long, sinuous lines that quiver with subtle tension, while the composition slips into something quite new, a tight, monumental subject filled with dynamism from the instability Shen has given it.

His long, prolific career as an artist (over 300 of his putative works survive, though many are forgeries) can be divided into three periods. His early works, those before 1471 (nothing is known by him that predates 1464, when he reached the age of 37), tend to be small and detailed, with a brushstroke still resembling that of the masters of the 14th and early 15th centuries and painters such as Du Qiong (1396-1474). In these, Shen can already be seen using techniques them that he would develop later, such as placing black inking within vegetation as a sort of echo linking the close to the distant over and above the water or mist or the solid footing of the peaks and mountains, using a firm brush, and constantly repeating his horizontal and vertical marks. Already he generally preferred, as he would always prefer, paper to silk.

With *Lofty Mount Lu*, a large hanging scroll of 1467, he changes both format and style. Now he paints like Wang Meng, his former master and old friend, and indeed this work was intended as a birthday greeting, in which he wished his master a longevity as great as that of the mountains. To do so, he borrows Wang's turbulent handling of rock. But, unlike Wang, he sets his mountains on a solid base and, despite its apparent agitation, his composition is absolutely stable, with greater depth and a more genuine appreciation of distance. Furthermore, the tonality of the picture is autumnal and the interpretation of nature more objective than in Wang.

From 1470 to 1490 come the works of his maturity. Even larger in format, their brushwork even freer, more vigorous, even violent, they display an absolute mastery of the placing of the ink and the differentiation of its various tonal qualities. During this time, he paints a series of album sheets, scenes from the Jiangnan countryside, where he lives, in which he captures intimate, evocative moments of everyday life with a startling freshness that is almost Impressionist. The conciseness of his execution, its fluidity, its naivety remind us of Wu Zhen; but his interpretation is more human, more real, and its ink accents more marked. This album, now in the Nelson-Atkins Museum, Kansas City, is one of his most successful works in this genre. The same search for atmosphere can be found in greater works such as *Celebrating the Mid-autumn Feast*, which can be dated to about 1486. Here the diffuse, diaphonous light of the moon's pale disc is rendered by silvery ink, while visible objects such as the cabin and the rocks are brought out by the subtle addition of light colour. Other marks of his mature art are the dark lines that underscore the buildings, the vigorous lines of texture and contour.

The works of his last years, in which he gives free rein to his thoughts and memories with disconcerting ease, are filled with an immense tenderness. The spontaneous harmony he achieves across his entire register, his luminous quality, his wondering yet always restrained emotions are the hallmarks of this last period when Shen Zhou achieves timelessness. In Shen we see not just subtle introspection but rather an openness to the outside world and a spiritual generosity towards nature.

Shen would have considerable influence over later artists but in most of his disciples classical culture would turn easily toward eclecticism. Some artists, such as Wen Zhenming (1470-1559) and Tang Yin (1470-1523), would strike out along new paths, using Shen's lessons as their starting point. With the individualists, however, the serene vision and the cosmic conception of landscape, of which Shen was one of the last representatives, would disappear altogether.

Bibliography:

Cahill, James, *Chinese Painting*, Skira, Geneva, 1960. Ryckmans, P., *'Chen Tcheou'* in *Encyclopaedia Universalis* vol. IV, Paris, 1969. Pirazzoli-T'Serstevens, Michèle, *Cours de l'École du Louvre*, Paris, 1970-1971. Yang Xin, et al., *Three Thousand Years of Chinese Painting*, Yale Univ. Press, 1997.

Museums and Galleries:

BEIJING (Palace Mus.): *Man in Autumn Wood* (poem by the artist); *Mountain Temple* (signed and dated 1500, ink and colour, painted for Yang Yijing) - BERLIN: *Two Men in a Pavilion Contemplating the Rain and the Wind on the River* (signed handscroll (school work)) - BOSTON (MFA): *Celebrating the Mid-autumn Feast* (ink and colour on paper, handscroll, several inscriptions by the artist including two poems); *Eight-sheet Album, with Poems* (ink and colour on gold-flecked paper, eight signed pages); *Mount Tongguan in the Autumn* (dated 1499, ink on paper, handscroll, five inscriptions) - CHICAGO (AI): *Returning from Stone Lake* (dated 1466, handscroll, poem by the artist) - COLOGNE (Mus. für ostasiatische Kunst): *Landscape in the Style of Juran* (ink on gilded paper, signed fan) - DETROIT (IA): *Pomegranate and Sigua* (hanging scroll, ink and light colour on paper, poem by Wang Ao (1450-1514), two seals of the artist) - HONOLULU (Academy of Arts): *Bird, Bamboo and Banana in the Snow* (inscription of the artist) - INDIANAPOLIS (MA): *Catalpa* - KANSAS CITY (Nelson-Atkins MA): *Solitary Fisher on River in Winter* (dated 1484, ink on paper, hanging scroll, signed poem by the artist, seal of the artist); *Landscapes and Poems* (ink and colour on paper, five signed album sheets made into a handscroll, two colophons, including one by Wen Zhengming); *Hollyhocks* (dated 1475); *Farewell to a Friend* (light colour on paper, small handscroll, poem by the artist) - KYOTO (National Mus.): *Gathering Water Chestnuts* (dated 1466, ink and colour on paper) - LONDON (British Mus.): *Tao Yuan's Haven* (inscription by Wen Zhengming) - MICHIGAN CITY (AG, Western Michigan University): *Pines and Hibiscus* (dated 1489) - NANJING: *Three Cypresses of Yushan* (ink on paper, handscroll, attributed) - NEW YORK (Metropolitan Mus. of Art): *Man in a Boat* (signed fan) - PARIS (Mus. National des Arts asiatiques-Guimet): *Man in a Boat between Rocky Banks* (after Wu Zhen, poem by the artist, inscription by Dong Qichang) - SHANGHAI: *Landscape* (dated 1494, ink and light colour on paper, after Huang Gongwang, hanging scroll, colophon by the artist) - STOCKHOLM (Nationalmus.): *Autumn River* (dated 1500, colophon by Chen Shun); *Winter Landscape* (poems by the artist and by the artist's friends to him, attributed); *Two Crows* (poem by the artist); *Waterside Pavilion* (signed, poem, attributed); *Walking with Staff* (ink on paper, hanging scroll, inscription by the artist); *Studies of Landscapes with Figures* (10 album sheets with poems, the last dated 1482); *Scholar's Retreat at the Foot of the High Mountains* (inscription by the artist dated 1492); *Flowers, Vegetables, Birds, Fish, Various Animals* (signed and dated 1494, ink on paper, 16-sheet album); *Orange and Chrysanthemums* (dated 1502); *Crab* (signed poem by the artist); *Landscape for Liu Jue; Bird on Branch* (signed poem by the artist); *Eight Views of Sanwu* (album sheets, seals of the artist); *Old Pines; Low Pavilions Shaded by Leafy Trees* (ink and light colour on paper, signed album sheet); *View of Suzhou* (colour on paper, signed); *Magnolia and Epidendrons Growing Near a Rock* (inscriptions by Zhu Yunming and Wu Kuan); *Tall Changpu Grass Growing near a Rock; Wild Pigeon on Dead Branch* (signed with a poem by the artist); *Cat and Donkey* (two album sheets with inscriptions by the Qing emperor Qianlong) - TOKYO (National Mus.): *Walking with Staff* (ink on paper) - WASHINGTON DC (Freer Gal. of Art): *Fishing Village near the River* (ink and light colour on paper, handscroll, poem by the artist); *Man Sitting in his Study near the River* (ink and light colour on paper, handscroll dedicated to a friend in 1491, three poems by Qianlong, colophon by the artist); *Mountain Landscape with Pavilions and Streams* (signed and dated 1491, in the style of Wang Meng).

AUCTION RECORDS:

NEW YORK, 2 June 1988, *Crossing the Bridge with a Staff* (ink, hanging scroll, 29 1/4 x 13 1/2 ins / 74.3 x 34.3 cm) USD 41,800; *Haven for a Rainy Night* (ink on paper, hanging scroll, 31 1/2 x 13 1/4 ins / 79.7 x 33.5 cm) USD 77,000. NEW YORK, 31 May 1989, *Hollyhocks and Rocks* (ink and colour on paper, handscroll, 9 x 62 ins / 23 x 157.5 cm) USD 242,000. NEW YORK, 6 Dec 1989, *Crows on Dead Trees* (ink on paper, hanging scroll, 33 3/4 x 10 1/4 ins / 85.8 x 26.3 cm) USD 38,500. NEW YORK, 26 Nov 1990, *Fishing on the Snowy River* (ink on paper, handscroll, 11 1/2 x 59 ins / 28.9 x 149.8 cm) USD 88,000. NEW YORK, 25 Nov 1991, *Riverside Farewell* (ink on paper, handscroll, 12 1/2 x 70 3/4 ins / 32 x 179.7 cm) USD 38,500. NEW YORK, 1 June 1993, *Pine and Rocks* (ink and colour on silk, hanging scroll, 59 x 34 1/2 ins / 149.9 x 87.6 cm) USD 51,750. NEW YORK, 21 March 1995, *Landscape* (ink and colour on paper, seven-part handscroll, each 12 x 20 1/2 ins / 30.2 x 51.8 cm) USD 28,750. NEW YORK, 22 March 1999, *Visiting Friends by Boat* (1494, ink and colour, hanging scroll, 80 x 35 ins / 203 x 90 cm) USD 22,000. HONG KONG, 26 April 1999, *Boating in Autumn River* (ink, hanging scroll, 42 x 23 ins / 106 x 58 cm) HKD 440,000. HONG KONG, 30 Oct 2000, *Landscape of Yanhua Stream, with Accompanying Poem in Running Standard Script Calligraph* (1499, ink, handscroll, 12 x 142 ins / 31 x 361 cm) HKD 300,000. HONG KONG, 28 Oct 2001, *Mountain Forest in Spring* (ink and colour, handscroll, 10 x 104 ins / 26 x 263 cm) HKD 1,000,000. HONG KONG, 6 July 2003, *Landscape of Jin Shan* (ink, handscroll, 11 x 79 ins / 28 x 200 cm) HKD 250,000. HONG KONG, 6 July 2003, *Landscape after Li Cheng* (1502, ink, hanging scroll, 20 x 17 ins / 51 x 44 cm) HKD 400,000. HONG KONG, 25 April 2004, *Bamboo and Plum Blossoms in Ink* (1501, ink, handscroll, 12 x 104 ins / 31 x 264 cm) HKD 350,000.

SHEN ZHUO, or Shen Cho, sobriquet: Zhubin, style name: Mohu waishi
Chinese, 19th century.
Born in Wujiang (Jiangsu Province).
Active c. 1850.
Painter.

After painting portraits and flowers, Shen Zhuo turned to landscape and worked in a style similar to that of Xi Gang (1746-1816).

SHEN ZONGJING, or Shen Tsung-ching, sobriquets: Keting, Nanji, style name: Shifeng
Chinese, 17th - 18th century.
Born 1669, in Songjiang (Jiangsu Province); died 1735.
Painter.

Shen Zongjing was a senior official and poet. He painted landscapes in the style of Juran (active c. 960-980), Huang Gongwang (1269-1354) and Ni Zan (1301-1374).

MUSEUMS AND GALLERIES:

TAIPEI (National Palace Mus.): *Pine Stand in the Mountains* (signed); *Pines in the Spring Mountains* (signed).

SHEN ZONGQIAN, or Shen Tsung-ch'ien, sobriquet: Xiyuan
Chinese, 18th - 19th century.
Born in Wucheng (Zhejiang Province).
Active c. 1770-1817.
Painter. Portraits, landscapes.

Next to nothing is known of Shen Zongqian except that he was the author of the highly important *Jiezhou xue hua bian*, and that he was also a calligrapher. Apparently, he taught himself the art of landscape painting and was probably a professional portrait painter. This, and the fact that portrait painters were afforded no recognition at all, might explain the relative obscurity of his treatise. It only survived because it also appeared in a Japanese edition, yet it was one of the most important books of its time and one of the most eminent studies in the whole history of Chinese painting. This position it owes to its remarkably precise and methodical approach to its subject, for it is one of the few examples of works in this usually rather vague area of literature to follow a real methodology. It is the work of a practising painter and intended for other practising painters, yet it does not overlook the critic's theoretical viewpoint. A very long work, it is divided into four books: the first two discuss landscape, the third portraits and the fourth figures and certain special topics. Each books is divided in turn into chapters.

BIBLIOGRAPHY:

Ryckmans, Pierre, *Les "Propos sur la peinture" de Shitao. Traduction et commentaires pour servir de contribution à l'étude terminologique et esthétique des théories chinoises de la peinture*, Institut belge des hautes études chinoises, Brussels, 1970.

MUSEUMS AND GALLERIES:

BOSTON (MFA): *River and High Mountains* (colophon of the artist).

AUCTION RECORDS:

NEW YORK, 25 Nov 1991, *Four Landscapes* (ink on paper, each 18 1/2 x 9 1/4 ins / 47 x 23.5 cm) USD 2,475.

SHEN ZUYONG, or Shen Tsu-yung, style name: Linyan Laoren
Chinese, 18th century.
Probably active during the 18th century.
Painter.

Shen Zuyong was a landscape painter. Although he is not mentioned in the official biographies, according to an inscription on one of his works he was a sixth-generation descendant of Shen Zhou (1427-1509).

SHENG DAN, or Sheng Tan, sobriquet: Bohan
Chinese, 17th century.
Active in Nanjing c. 1640.
Painter.

Sheng Dan was a landscape painter in the style of Huang Gongwang (1269-1354). Some signed works by his hand survive, such as *Cottage in Bamboos and Trees*, after Tang Di, signed and dated 1638.

SHENG DASHI, or Sheng Ta-shih
Chinese, 19th century.
Born 1771.

Active from 1800.
Painter.
Sheng Dashi was an official, poet and painter who wrote a two-volume treatise on aesthetics entitled *Qishan Woyou Lu*, which appeared in 1822. Typically of the writings of literati painters from the period, it was a rather shapeless collection of the most varied pieces lacking in both intellectual rigour and organisation. In it, technical ideas, aesthetic theories and critical opinions rub shoulders with banalities and quotations from every quarter. The book is representative of the school of Wang Yuanqi (1642-1715) in its thinking and for that reason is of interest as a document.

BIBLIOGRAPHY:

Ryckmans, Pierre, *Les "Propos sur la peinture" de Shitao. Traduction et commentaires pour servir de contribution à l'étude terminologique et esthétique des théories chinoises de la peinture*, Institut belge des hautes études chinoises, Brussels, 1970.

AUCTION RECORDS:

NEW YORK, 2 June 1988, *Village Tucked away in the Mountains* (ink on paper, hanging scroll, 25 x 10 1/2 ins / 63.5 x 26.5 cm) USD 1,980.

SHENG HONG, or Sheng Hongfu, Sheng Hung, sobriquet: Wenyu
Chinese, 14th century.
Born in Hangzhou (Zhejiang Province).
Active in the mid-14th century.
Painter. Figures, landscapes, animals.

Sheng Hong was the father of Sheng Mao (active in about 1310-1360). He mainly painted birds.

MUSEUMS AND GALLERIES:

BEIJING (Palace Mus.): *Narcissi* (1354, with inscriptions by Chen Jiru and the Qing emperor Qianlong).

SHENG MAO, sobriquet: Zizhao
Chinese, 14th century.
Born in Jiaxing (Zhejiang Province).
Active c. 1310-1360.
Painter.

The son of the painter Sheng Hong, Sheng Mao is known for his landscapes, birds and flowers and figure paintings. It was said of his work that although very refined in its beauty, it was sometimes too skilfully wrought. Yet he is also said to have been better known during his lifetime than Wu Zhen (1280-1354), one of the Four Great Masters (Yuan), who was also his neighbour.

Sheng Mao studied with Chen Lin, an academic artist who followed Zhao Mengfu (1254-1322). He then turned towards the style of the Song masters Dong Yuan (d. 962) and Juran (active in about 960-980). More a professional painter than an amateur literatus, like Wu Zhen and the Four Yuan Masters, Sheng seems to lie midway between the style of Zhao Mengfu and certain Southern Song landscape techniques, as can be seen in his *Boating on an Autumn River*, a hanging scroll in ink and colour on paper, with an inscription by the painter Wei Jiuting dated 1361, now in the National Palace Museum, Taipei. Here the boats lying side by side and the passengers chattering on board are drawn in delicately, with refined coloured washes, while the river bank is painted more freely, gaily, the same gaiety as we find in Wu Zhen, whose more relaxed, less elaborate style is far more attractive. Chinese critics place Wu Zhen above Sheng Mao, seeing in his capricious attention to detail a lack of balance and calm.

BIBLIOGRAPHY:

Cahill, James, *Chinese Painting*, Skira, Geneva, 1960. Yonezawa, Yoshiho/Kawakita, Michiaki, *Arts of China: Paintings in Chinese Collections-New Collections*, Kodansha, Tokyo, 1970. Yang Xin, et al., *Three Thousand Years of Chinese Painting*, Yale Univ. Press, 1997.

MUSEUMS AND GALLERIES:

BEIJING (Palace Mus.): *Old Pine Growing out of a Rock Cleft* (ink on paper, inscription by the artist dated 1347); *Landscape in Blue and Green* (signed and dated 1312, album sheet); *Looking for Plum Blossom* (album sheet, seal of the artist) - KANSAS CITY (Nelson-Atkins MA): *Taking Advantage of the Mountain Air* - KYOTO (Hompo-Ji): *Two Large Landscapes with Figures Playing Music under the Woods* (signed) - SHANGHAI: *Clear Song on a Boat in Autumn* (colour on silk, hanging scroll, attributed) - TAIPEI (National Palace Mus.): *Boating on the Autumn River* (ink and colour on paper, handscroll, inscription by Wei Jiuting dated 1361); *Noble Scholar in an Autumn Copse* (ink and light colour on silk, hanging scroll, signed); *Village Artisan* (fan, signed); *Mountain Landscape* (signed and dated 1313, after Zhang Sengyu, album sheet); *Farm in the Trees at the Foot of Snow-covered Mountains* (poem by the artist dated 1322, poem by Qian Weishan dated 1364 and by Qing Qianlong); *Fisherman in Boat Moored by Autumn River* (signed and dated 1344); *Travellers in Summer Mountain Clouds* (signed and dated 1362); *Boating by Moonlight under the Pines* (1423-1495, signed, poem by Yao Shou); *Summer's Day in the Mountains; Swallow Gliding above the Bank in Springtime* (signed); *Mountain Stream with Two Men in Small Boat* (signed); *Scholar and His Servant under the Pines, with Two Cranes* (signed); *Fisherman in Boat on Still Water* (fan, seal of the artist) - WASHINGTON DC (Freer Gal. of Art): *Waiting for the Ferry on an Autumn River* (signed and dated 1351, ink on paper).

SHENG MAOHUA. See **SHENG MAOYE**

SHENG MAOJUN
Chinese.
Active during the Ming dynasty (1368-1664).
Painter.

AUCTION RECORDS:

NEW YORK, 31 May 1990, *Travellers* (ink and colour on paper, 7 1/4 x 20 1/2 ins / 18.1 x 52 cm) USD 2,475. TAIPEI, 10 April 1994, *River Landscape with Fishing Boats* (ink and colour on gilded paper, fan, 6 1/4 x 18 1/4 ins / 16 x 46.5 cm) TWD 207,000.

SHENG MAOYE, or Sheng Maohua, Sheng Mao-yeh, style name: Yanan
Chinese, 17th century.
Born in Suzhou (Jiangsu Province).
Active 1625-1640.
Painter.

Sheng Maoye was a landscape and flower painter. A number of his works survive, such as *Three Laughing Men of Tiger Valley*, a fan in ink and colour on gold-flecked paper, signed and dated 1620 (Museum für Ostasiatische Kunst, Cologne) and *Landscape with Waterfall*, after Ma Yuan, a scroll signed and dated 1640 (National Museum, Stockholm).

SHENG MOU. See **SHENG MAO**

SHENG SHAO-HSIEN. See **SHENG SHAOXIAN**

SHENG SHAOXIAN, or Sheng Shao-hsien, sobriquet: Kezhen
Chinese, 17th century.
Born in Yangzhou (Jiangsu Province).
Active c. 1600.
Painter. Landscapes.

Sheng Shaoxian was a landscape painter.

SHENG SHICHONG, or Sheng Shih-ch'ung, sobriquet: Ziju
Chinese, 17th century.
Born in Huating (Jiangsu Province).
Active c. 1611-1640.
Painter.

After studying with Song Maojin (late 16th century) and Zhao Zuo (active c. 1610-1630), Sheng Shichong went on to absorb a number of different styles, not only those of the Wu School, Shen Zhou (1427-1509) and Song Xu (1523-c. 1605) but also that of Dong Qichang (1555-1636). He is often described as an imitator of Dong, and traces of the Yunjian School style (a school that included many professional artists) can be found in his landscapes. His handscrolls, in the slightly formal style of the literati painters from the late Ming, are the best of his work.

BIBLIOGRAPHY:

Yonezawa, Yoshiho/Kawakita, Michiaki, *Arts of China: Paintings in Chinese Collections-New Collections*, Kondansha, Tokyo, 1970.

MUSEUMS AND GALLERIES:

BEIJING (Palace Mus.): six landscape studies, after the ancient masters (on gold-flecked paper) - BOSTON (MFA): *Landscapes of the Four Seasons* (dated 1633, ink and light colour on paper, handscroll) - COLOGNE (Mus. für ostasiatische Kunst): *Autumn Landscape with Large Trees and River* (signed and dated 1611, ink, light colour on gold-flecked paper, fan) - TAIPEI (National Palace Mus.): *Study in Perfumed Nature* (signed and dated 1623); *Cottage by the River* (signed and dated 1625, small handscroll); *Landscape in the style of Wang Meng* (signed fan) - TIANJIN: *Waterside Residence* (colour on paper, hanging scroll).

SHENG TA-SHIH. See **SHENG DASHI**

SHENG TAN. See **SHENG DAN**

SHENTON, Henry Chawnes, the Elder

British, 19th century.

Born 1803, in Winchester; died 15 September 1866, in London.

Engraver (burin).

Henry Chawnes Shenton the Elder, erroneously referred to as Charles in the handbook written by Charles Le Blan, was a pupil of George Warren and married Warren's daughter. He engraved genre scenes after a number of his contemporaries, and was regarded as one of the finest English burin engravers.

SHENTON, Henry Chawnes, the Younger

British, 19th century.

Born 1825; died 7 February 1846, in London.

Sculptor.

Henry Chawnes Shenton the Younger was the son of Henry Chawnes Shenton the Elder and the brother of William Kernot Shenton. He was a pupil of W. Behnes and studied in Rome. He executed a group representing *Christ and Mary* as well as *The Funeral of the Prince* and a statue of *Archbishop Cranmer*.

MUSEUMS AND GALLERIES:

LONDON (National Portrait Gal.).

SHENTON, William Kernot

British, 19th century.

Born June 1836; died 19 April 1878.

Sculptor.

William Kernot Shenton was the brother of Henry Chawnes the Younger. He worked in London and executed portrait medallions.

SHEPARD, Ernest Howard

British, 20th century.

Born 10 December 1879, in London; died 1976.

Draughtsman, watercolourist, painter (gouache).

Scenes with figures.

Ernest H. Shepard was encouraged while still a child by his father, who was an architect, and by his mother, the daughter of the watercolour painter William Lee. He studied in London at Heatherley's Art School and then at the Royal Academy School from 1897 to 1902. He married his fellow student Florence Chaplin in 1904; she died in 1927, and he eventually married again in 1944, his new wife being Norah Carrol. In 1955, they moved to Lodsworth in Sussex.

Shepard worked as an artist and illustrator of magazines, including the humorous magazine *Punch* from 1907. After World War I broke out, he entered the army in 1915 and was subsequently awarded the Military Cross. As well as producing pictures, both humorous and serious, of life during the war, he continued to send illustrations to *Punch*, and was later appointed to its editorial board in 1921. He contributed to Punch until 1949, and it was due to his position on the editorial board that he met E.V. Lucas, who introduced him to the writer Alan A. Milne. His great fame is founded mainly on his illustrations of Milne's *Winnie-the-Pooh* books, on which he started working during the 1920s.

Shepard ultimately provided illustrations for more than 50 books for both children and adults. In addition to Milne's works, such as *Winnie-the-Pooh* and *The House at Pooh Corner*, he illustrated Kenneth Grahame's *The Wind in the Willows* and two children's books he had written himself, *Betsy and Joe* and *Ben and Brock*. He also produced two illustrated autobiographical works, *Drawn from Memory* and *Drawn from Life*. He continued to provide drawings for further editions of Milne's and Grahame's works, and provided full sets of colour illustrations for both in the 1960s and 1970s.

Shepard's work has been shown in many exhibitions, including: Victoria and Albert Museum, London (1969); University of Kent (1974); a major retrospective in Japan (1980s); *In Celebration: Works of Art from the Collections of Princeton Alumni and Friends of the Art Museum*, Princeton University (1997); and *The Art of E.H. Shepard*, Holburne Museum of Art, Bath (2005). He received various awards and prizes, including a Landseer Scholarship (1898); British Institution Prize (1900); Lewis Carroll Shelf Award (1958, 1962, 1963); and the University of Southern Mississippi Silver Medallion (1970). He received the Order of the British Empire (OBE) in 1972.

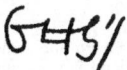

AUCTION RECORDS:

LONDON, 17 June 1977, *Winnie-the-Pooh* (c. 1930, card, oval, 36 x 26½ ins / 91.5 x 67.5 cm) GBP 2,200. LONDON, 20 Sept 1978, *Young Girl Seated in a Flower Bed* (1908, watercolour and pencil heightened with gouache, 13 x 19½ ins / 33 x 49.5 cm) GBP 650. LONDON, 21 July 1982, *Winnie-the-Pooh Standing in front of Owl's Door* (oil on canvas, 35¼ x 41 ins / 89.7 x 104 cm) GBP 1,700. LONDON, 26 July 1984, *Christopher Robin Seated* (pencil, 9 x 7¼ ins / 22.7 x 18.3 cm) USD 2,700. LONDON, 22 July 1986, *Full Moon* (1928, watercolour, gouache, pencil and pen, 13 x 9½ ins / 33 x 24 cm) GBP 2,000. NEW YORK, 24 May 1989, *Christopher Robin up His Tree* (ink heightened with white/card, 10 x 8½ ins / 25.2 x 21.5 cm) USD 14,300. LONDON, 19 April 1999, *All boats have to have a name, so I shall call mine the Floating Bear* (pen and ink, six, 13 x 16 ins / 32 x 40 cm) GBP 21,000. LONDON, 17 Dec 1999, *He nodded and went out, Winnie the Pooh* (pen and ink, 8 x 6 ins / 20 x 15 cm) GBP 70,000. LONDON, 16 June 2000, *Down by the Pond* (pencil, pen and ink heightened with white, six in one frame, 5 x 9 ins / 12 x 22 cm) GBP 15,000. LONDON, 16 June 2000, *But there are twelve pots of honey in my cupboard and they have been calling me for hours* (pencil, pen and ink, 4 x 2 ins / 10 x 5 cm) GBP 42,000. LONDON, 14 June 2001, *Pooh Holding a Sprig of Holly* (1921, pen and ink, sold with original envelope, 8 x 5 ins / 20 x 13 cm) GBP 11,000. LONDON, 6 Dec 2001, *Harold Went Straight in the Right Bush* (pen heightened with white, sold with two others by same hand, 7 x 11 ins / 19 x 27 cm) GBP 1,700. NEW YORK, 11 May 2002, *Menagerie of Fairy Tale Characters lined up to*

Greet Children (pen and ink, 11 x 17 ins / 28 x 43 cm) USD 3,750. LONDON, 4 Dec 2002, *Christopher Robin by the Fireside* (pencil, pen, ink, crayon and watercolour, 6 x 4 ins / 14 x 11 cm) GBP 9,500. LONDON, 12 June 2003, *Look Here I Find I've Left My Purse Behind* (pen and ink, 5 x 4 ins / 13 x 9 cm) GBP 7,500. LONDON, 12 June 2003, *Pooh Singing on a Stepping Stone* (pen, ink and watercolour, 8 x 8 ins / 20 x 20 cm) GBP 18,000. DONCASTER, 29 Feb 2004, *Studies of Pooh, Piglet and Eeyore* (pencil, 9 x 8 ins / 23 x 21 cm) GBP 4,100. LONDON, 1 July 2004, *So Winnie the Pooh Pushed and Pushed. He Started to Shunt Out of the Hole* (pencil and ink, a pair, 6 x 7 ins / 15 x 18 cm) GBP 58,000.

SHEPHARD, F.
British, 19th century.
Active c. 1850.
Painter.

F. Shephard was noted for his *Wellington Reading in his Bedroom at Walmer Castle* and *Wellington at the Window of his Bedroom in Apsley House*.

SHEPHEARD, George, or Shepherd
British, 18th - 19th century.
Born c. 1770, in Guildford; died 1842, in London.
Painter, watercolourist, engraver. Portraits.

George Shepheard worked in London. He engraved numerous portraits and was particularly noted for his *The Attitudes of Lady Hamilton*, 15 plates after Rehberg and *The Fleny Charge* after Morland. There does not seem to be any possible confusion between Shepheard and the similarly named George Shepherd.

AUCTION RECORDS:
LONDON, 13 March 1986, *Selling Fish in the Port of Folkestone* (1837, watercolour heightened with gouache, 17 x 23 1/4 ins / 43 x 59 cm) GBP 1,900.

SHEPHEARD, George Wallwyn
British, 19th century.
Born 1804, in London; died 26 January 1852, in Brighton.
Painter, watercolourist. Landscapes.

George Wallwyn Shepheard was the eldest son of George Shepheard. He visited France, Germany and Italy, and exhibited at the Royal Academy from 1830 to 1852.

SHEPHEARD, Lewis Henry
British, 19th century.
Born 1816, in London; died 1893, in London.
Painter. Landscapes.

Lewis Henry Shepheard was the son of George Shepheard. A number of his sketches were published in 1873, and he exhibited in London - particularly at the Royal Academy and the Royal Society of British Artists in Suffolk Street - from 1844 to 1875.

SHEPHERD, David
British, 20th century.
Born 25 April 1931, in London.
Painter. Animals, aviation subjects, rail subjects, military subjects, landscapes, portraits.

David Shepherd was fascinated by Africa as a child, and set his heart on becoming a game warden. To this end, he travelled to Kenya when he left school to apply for a job in the National Parks; his ambitions were swiftly crushed when he was refused employment. Having attended art classes at school, more as a way of avoiding sports than of expressing any talent, he applied to the Slade School of Fine Arts in London; here, too, he was bluntly rejected. His fortunes took a turn for the better when he met the painter Robert Goodwin, who took him on as a pupil from 1950 to 1953 and gave him an exacting apprenticeship.

Shepherd started out painting aviation pictures in 1953. He received commissions from the Royal Air Force, which flew him to many locations around the world. He went on to depict steam trains, railway settings and military subjects, receiving commissions from the British army and navy. A trip to Kenya in 1960 with the RAF proved to be the turning-point of his career: he received a commission for his first wildlife painting, and this started him off on the path to his greatest fame. Around this time, the sight of 255 zebra poisoned by poachers in Tanzania impelled him to become a conservationist; he felt that the success he was garnering from the depiction of animals in the wild should be repaid by becoming their advocate. At first raising funds from the sale of his paintings, such as *Tiger Fire* in 1973, he went on to set up the David Shepherd Wildlife Foundation in 1984. Reproductions of his paintings - most notably of elephants - have proved extremely popular, beginning with *Wise Old Elephant* (1962).

Although recognised internationally as a leading wildlife artist, Shepherd has also produced landscapes and portraits, his sitters including the former Zambian President, Kenneth Kaunda, and the Queen Mother. He has also written a number of books about his life and art, including *An Artist in Africa* (1967); *The Man who Loves Giants* (1975); *David Shepherd, An Artist in Conservation* (1992); *David Shepherd, My Painting Life* (1995); and *Only One World* (1995). He has been the subject of a number of television programmes about wildlife and steam trains.

Shepherd held his first solo exhibition, which was a great success, in 1962 at the Tryon Gallery in London. His works are frequently exhibited both in Britain and abroad, including in New York in 1967. He has received many awards and honours for his work both as an artist and as a conservationist, including an honorary degree in Fine Arts from the Pratt Institute, New York (1971); the Order of the Golden Ark for his services to conservation (1973); the Order of the British Empire (1979); fellowship of the Royal Society of Arts (1986); the Order of Distinguished Service, from President Kenneth Kaunda of Zambia (1988); fellowship of the Royal Geographical Society (1989); an honorary doctorate in Science from the University of Hertfordshire (1990); and Officer (Brother) of The Order of St John (1996).

David Shepherd

BIBLIOGRAPHY:
Shepherd, David, *David Shepherd, An Artist in Conservation*, Illustrated book, David & Charles, 1992.

AUCTION RECORDS:
LONDON, 16 Nov 1977, *Last Snows* (oil on canvas, 19 1/2 x 29 1/2 ins / 49.5 x 75 cm) GBP 1,000. LONDON, 19 Oct 1979, *Tiger* (1977, oil on canvas, 20 x 34 ins / 51 x 86.5 cm) GBP 7,500. NEW YORK, 1 May 1981, *Leopard and Prey* (1962, oil on canvas, 20 x 28 ins / 51 x 71 cm) USD 18,000. LONDON, 9 Nov 1984, *Elephant* (1974, oil on canvas, 18 x 32 ins / 45.7 x 81.3 cm) GBP 4,200. LONDON, 24 April 1985, *African Elephant* (oil on canvas, 20 x 30 ins / 51 x 76 cm) GBP 3,800. NEW YORK, 6 June 1986, *Zebras in a Landscape* (1964, oil on canvas, 20 x 30 ins / 50.8 x 76.2 cm) USD 8,000. LONDON, 5 Oct 1989, *Comet 4 Over Southampton Docks, R.M.S Queen Elizabeth* (oil on canvas, 28 x 36 ins / 71.2 x 91.4 cm) GBP 4,950. LONDON, 8 March 1990, *Elephant on the Banks of the Luangwa River* (1978, oil on canvas, 8 3/4 x 11 1/2 ins / 22.2 x 29.2 cm) GBP 7,700. LONDON, 8 Nov 1990, *The Heads of the Herd* (1980, oil on canvas, 27 1/2 x 59 1/2 ins / 70 x 151 cm) GBP 36,300. LONDON, 7 March 1991, *In Thick Cover* (oil on canvas, 26 x 52 ins / 66 x 132 cm) GBP 30,800. NEW YORK, 3 June 1994, *Camouflage in a Bush* (1986, oil on canvas, 16 x 28 1/2 ins / 40.6 x 72.4 cm) USD 16,100. NEW YORK, 9 June 1995, *Love under the Baobab* (1962, oil on canvas, 32 x 44 ins / 81.3 x 111.8 cm) USD 51,750. NEW YORK, 12 April 1996, *Bull Elephant* (oil on

canvas, 31 x 29 ins / 78.7 x 73.7 cm) USD 34,500. LONDON, 28 April 1999, *Egrets over Savuti* (oil on canvas, 19 x 39 ins / 48 x 98 cm) GBP 22,000. LONDON, 28 April 1999, *Tiger Haven* (oil on canvas, 23 x 43 ins / 58 x 108 cm) GBP 28,000. HAYDEN, 29 July 2000, *Elephant Ecstasy* (oil on canvas, 30 x 46 ins / 76 x 117 cm) USD 42,500. HAYDEN, 29 July 2000, *Lion Resting* (oil on canvas, 28 x 44 ins / 71 x 112 cm) USD 55,000. BILLINGSHURST, 29 Jan 2001, *Tiger* (1988, oil on canvas, 22 x 37 ins / 55 x 95 cm) GBP 13,000. LONDON, 13 June 2001, *Heavy Freight 67* (1995, oil on canvas, 24 x 42 ins / 61 x 106 cm) GBP 52,000. LONDON, 1 May 2002, *Crested Crane* (oil on canvas, 12 x 20 ins / 30 x 50 cm) GBP 27,000. NEW YORK, 30 May 2002, *Bull Elephant* (1966, oil on canvas, 34 x 62 ins / 86 x 157 cm) USD 55,000. LONDON, 6 June 2003, *Elephants, Amboseli* (1960, oil on canvas, 24 x 36 ins / 61 x 91 cm) GBP 18,000. NEW YORK, 5 Dec 2003, *Bull Elephant* (oil on canvas, 16 x 22 ins / 41 x 56 cm) USD 38,000. LONDON, 19 May 2004, *Elephants* (2002, oil on canvas, 22 x 42 ins / 55 x 106 cm) GBP 18,000. HAYDEN, 24 July 2004, *Resting Tiger* (oil on canvas, 14 x 22 ins / 36 x 56 cm) USD 27,500.

SHEPHERD, Frederick Napoleon

British, 19th century.

Born 1819; died 1878.

Watercolourist.

Frederick Napoleon Shepherd painted several views of London, especially of the city, in wash and watercolour including *Interior of Newly Created Fleet Street Sewer* (1845), *View of a Field Lane Lodging House* (c. 1847), *Holborn* (1840), *Whitecross Street Prison* (c. 1840), *The Old Pied Bull Inn, Essex Road Islington* (c. 1840), *West Smithfield* (c. 1840), *View of Old Merlin's Cave Inn, Skinner Street, Finsbury* (1850), *Fleet Street at the Corner of Clifford's Inn Passage* (1845), *View of the Residence of Titus Oates, Oat Lane* (c. 1845). A number of his works were later engraved. The Guildhall in London houses a large collection of shepherd's watercolours and washes.

MUSEUMS AND GALLERIES:

LONDON (Guildhall Library Print Room): several works.

AUCTION RECORDS:

LONDON, 10 Aug 2000, *Ryde and the Pier from the Parade* (1840, watercolour and scratching out, 7 x 11 ins / 19 x 29 cm) GBP 1,800. EXETER, 15 Oct 2002, *Servant Girl* (oil on canvas, 23 x 19 ins / 59 x 49 cm) GBP 1,550.

SHEPHERD, George. See **SHEPHEARD George**

SHEPHERD, George

British, 19th century.

Painter, watercolourist, draughtsman. Urban landscapes.

George Shepherd painted topographical views of different parts of England, particularly in London, and appears to have enjoyed a certain reputation. His son George Sidney imitated his style. There does not appear to be any possible confusion between Shepherd and the similarly named George Shepheard. He exhibited in London between 1800 and 1830, particularly at the Royal Academy, the British Institution and the Royal Society of British Artists in Suffolk Street.

MUSEUMS AND GALLERIES:

LONDON (British Mus.): drawings - LONDON (Victoria and Albert Mus.): 13 watercolours dated 1809, 1817, 1825, 1827 - MANCHESTER: *London Bridge* - NOTTINGHAM (Castle Mus. & AG): watercolour.

AUCTION RECORDS:

LONDON, 19 Feb 1987, *Buckingham Palace, London* (pencil, 8 x 15¾ ins / 20.5 x 40 cm) GBP 2,400. LONDON, 19 May 1998, *Punters - Eton College* (1827, watercolour heightened with white, 13 x 11 ins / 34 x 28 cm) GBP 1,800. LONDON, 29 Nov 2000, *Star and Garter, Richmond. Cheam Church, Dorking* (1816, watercolour, set of four, 4 x 6 ins / 10 x 16 cm) GBP 2,100.

SHEPHERD, George Sidney or Sydney

British, 19th century.

Born 1784, in London; died c. 1860, in London, in 1858 according to some sources at St Pancras workhouse.

Painter (gouache), watercolourist, draughtsman. Still-lifes, landscapes with figures, urban landscapes.

George Sidney Shepherd was the son of the topographical artist, George Shepherd. He practised watercolour painting in the style of his father, occasionally adding rustic scenes and still-lifes to his portfolio of topographical works. He also painted many views of metropolitan buildings. He exhibited at the Royal Academy between 1830 and 1837, at the Royal Society of British Artists and at the New Water-Colour Society, of which he was a member. Shepherd also provided the illustrations for C. Clarke's *Architectura Ecclesiastica Londini* and W.H. Ireland's *England's Topographer*.

BIBLIOGRAPHY:

Clarke, C., *Architectura Ecclesiastica Londini*, John Booth, London, 1820. Ireland, W.H., *England's Topographer*, G. Virtue, London, 1828-1830 (4 vols).

MUSEUMS AND GALLERIES:

LONDON (Victoria and Albert Mus.): *The Kilns* (1831, watercolour); *Distant View of Greenwich Hospital* (watercolour); *Kings Cross, London: Site of the Great Northern Terminus* (1832, watercolour).

AUCTION RECORDS:

LONDON, 12-16 Nov 1923, *Temple Bar* (watercolour) GBP 102. LONDON, 5 and 6 Nov 1924, *London Bridge* (watercolour) GBP 21. LONDON, 28 May 1926, *Church of St Mary-le-Strand; Somerset House* (two drawings) GBP 44. LONDON, 25 April 1940, *Hampstead Heath* (drawing) GBP 168. LONDON, 12 Feb 1942, *Norfolk Subjects* (six drawings) GBP 52. LONDON, 6 Nov 1973, *View of Lancaster* (watercolour and pencil) Gns 350. LONDON, 13 Dec 1983, *St Mary the Strand, London* (1836, watercolour and pencil heightened with white, 17 x 23 ins / 43 x 57.5 cm) GBP 6,000. LONDON, 21 Nov 1985, *Horseguard's Parade* (1851, watercolour/pencil outlines heightened with gouache, 7¾ x 11 ins / 20 x 27 cm) GBP 2,200. LONDON, 12 March 1987, *Old London Bridge* (1830, watercolour/pencil outlines heightened with white, 11 x 14½ ins / 28 x 37 cm) GBP 9,000. LONDON, 30 Jan 1991, *Exeter High Street* (watercolour and gouache, 6 x 5¾ ins / 15.5 x 14.5 cm) GBP 1,155. LONDON, 13 July 1993, *Beaufoy Vinegar Factory at Cuper's Gardens in Lambeth* (1823, pencil and watercolour, 8½ x 12¼ ins / 21.4 x 31.1 cm) GBP 2,070. HONITON, 9 April 1999, *Celebrations in Honiton High Street with Many Figures* (watercolour, 8 x 11 ins / 20 x 28 cm) GBP 2,050. LONDON, 26 Nov 1999, *Obelisk, St George's Circus, London* (pencil, pen, ink and watercolour with scratching out, 7 x 11 ins / 19 x 27 cm) GBP 2,400. LONDON, 15 June 2000, *Dover Castle from a Market Stall on Castle Street* (watercolour and pencil heightened with gouache and gum arabic, 12 x 15 ins / 31 x 37 cm) GBP 4,600. LONDON, 29 Nov 2000, *The Thames at Greenwich* (watercolour over pencil heightened with gouache and scratching out, 16 x 21 ins / 41 x 53 cm) GBP 5,500. LONDON, 6 Feb 2001, *Figures on a Park Overlooking Greenwich* (1835, watercolour and gouache, 11 x 15 ins / 27 x 37 cm) GBP 1,900. NEWBURY, 28 March 2001, *Numerous Figures with Horsedrawn Carriages in Fleet Street* (oil on canvas, 25 x 35 ins / 63 x 90 cm) GBP 4,400. BLETCHINGLEY, 11 June 2002, *View of Winchester House, Austin Friars* (1811, watercolour, 7 x 8 ins / 18 x 20 cm) GBP 1,500. LONDON, 26 Oct 2004, *Fleet Street towards Temple Bar* (oil on canvas, 24 x 35 ins / 62 x 90 cm) GBP 4,400.

SHEPHERD, James Affleck

British, 19th - 20th century.

Born 29 November 1867, in London; died 1931.

Painter, illustrator. Animals.

James Affleck Shepherd lived and worked at Charlwood (Surrey). He was the brother of Alfred Bryan, and a contributor to *Punch*. Shepherd produced caricatures, illustrations for a number of children's books and was also a writer.

SHEPHERD, Joseph Clinton
American, 20th century.
Born 11 September 1888, in Des Moines (Iowa); died 1975.
Painter, sculptor. Scenes with figures.

Joseph Clinton Shepherd studied at the Art Institute of Chicago and the Institute of Fine Arts in New York. He was a member of the American Artists Professional League.

AUCTION RECORDS:
NEW YORK, 20 April 1979, *The Bulldogger* (1928, greenish-brown-patinated bronze, h. 12 1/2 ins / 31.7 cm) USD 5,000. NEW YORK, 31 March 1994, *Cowboy Fighting a Bull* (bronze, h. 12 ins / 30.5 cm) USD 4,888. SAN FRANCISCO, 9 June 2002, *Native Americans on Horseback in Winter* (oil on canvas, 30 x 20 ins / 76 x 51 cm) USD 2,500. NEW YORK, 9 Nov 2002, *Young Western Woman Making her Way Through Rocky Landscape* (oil on canvas, 38 x 20 ins / 97 x 51 cm) USD 3,250.

SHEPHERD, Juliana or Julia C.
British, 19th century.
Died 1898.
Active in Manchester.
Painter. Genre scenes.

Juliana Shepherd exhibited paintings of flowers in London at the Royal Society of British Artists in Suffolk Street from 1868 to 1870.

MUSEUMS AND GALLERIES:
MANCHESTER: *Young Girl.*

SHEPHERD, Robert. See **SHEPPARD Robert**

SHEPHERD, Robert
British, 17th century.
Born in England.
Active c. 1660.
Engraver.

Robert Shepherd may have been a pupil of David Loggan. He engraved portraits, and was also noted for scaled-down copies of Le Brun's *Alexander's Battles* engraved by Audran.

SHEPHERD, Sarah
British, 19th century.
Died 1814.
Painter.

Sarah Shepherd married the painter Samuel Cotes.

SHEPHERD, Thomas Hosmer
British, 19th century.
Born 1793, in London; died 1864, in London.
Active in London between 1817 and 1840.
Draughtsman, watercolourist.

Little is known about Thomas Hosmer Shepherd, but it appears likely that he was the son of George Shepherd and the brother of George Sydney. He contributed to several topographical works from 1827 to 1831. He exhibited landscapes at the Royal Society of British Artists in Suffolk Street in 1831 and 1832 and executed a considerable number of sketches of old London of which the British Museum has preserved several hundred.

MUSEUMS AND GALLERIES:
LONDON (Victoria and Albert Mus.): six watercolours.

AUCTION RECORDS:
LONDON, 14 June 1968, *The English Coast,* Gns 800. LONDON, 19 July 1973, *Gun Dock* (watercolour) GBP 600. LONDON, 26 Nov 1999, *Fleet Prison. The Poor Debtor's Room, the Chapel. The Room for Refractory Prisoners* (pencil and watercolour, set of three, 6 x 9 ins / 16 x 24 cm) GBP 1,900. LONDON, 29 Nov 2000, *National Gallery, Trafalgar Square, London* (wash over pencil heightened with white, 5 x 9 ins / 12 x 22 cm) GBP 1,200. CLEVEDON, 6 March 2003, *Marquis of Hertford's Villa, Regent's Park* (1826, pencil and sepia wash, 3 x 6 ins / 8 x 15 cm) GBP 1,000. LONDON, 27 Nov 2003, *Views of London* (brown wash over pencil, folio) GBP 12,000. LONDON, 9 March 2004, *Pall Mall* (watercolour, 5 x 7 ins / 12 x 19 cm) GBP 1,500. BURY ST EDMUNDS, 7 April 2004, *Vintner's Hall and St Luke's, Old Street, London* (watercolour, 5 x 8 ins / 12 x 20 cm) GBP 1,000.

SHEPHERD, Valentine Claud
British, 19th century.
Born 1835; died 1888.
Active in London.
Wood engraver.

SHEPHERDS, Master of the. See **MASTERS**

SHEPPARD, Ella, Mrs Gallagher
American, 19th - 20th century.
Born 11 October 1864, in Greenwich (New Jersey).
Painter.

Ella Sheppard was taught by A.W. Drow and was active in South Braintree, Massachusetts. There are similarities between her and Ella Sheppard Bush.

SHEPPARD, G.
British, 18th - 19th century.
Active in London.
Painter, miniaturist. Portraits.

G. Sheppard exhibited in London between 1797 and 1802.

SHEPPARD, Herbert C.
British.
Painter. Seascapes.

MUSEUMS AND GALLERIES:
CARDIFF: *Newton's Banks.*

SHEPPARD, Oliver
Irish, 19th - 20th century.
Born 1865, in Tyrone; died 1941, in London.
Sculptor. Busts, monuments.

Oliver Sheppard was the son of a sculptor noted for his studies of the lost art of polychromy on marble. Sheppard trained initially in Dublin, at the Metropolitan School of Art and the Royal Hibernian Academy's School of Drawing. He became an associate of the Academy in 1898, an academician in 1901 and professor in 1903. Sheppard completed his studies with a bursary enabling him to attend the South Kensington schools in London, and finally a travel scholarship which enabled him to live and work in Paris for a time. He exhibited at the Royal Academy from 1891, and executed several public monuments and a large number of busts.

MUSEUMS AND GALLERIES:
DUBLIN: *Bust of Henry Kirke White* - NOTTINGHAM (Castle Museum and Art Gallery): *Bust of John O'Leary.*

SHEPPARD, Philip
British, 19th century.
Watercolourist, painter. Landscapes.

Philip Sheppard exhibited his work, particularly at the Royal Academy in London in 1861 and 1862 and at the Royal Society of British Artists in Suffolk Street from 1861 to 1866.

MUSEUMS AND GALLERIES:
BLACKBURN: watercolours - LONDON (Victoria and Albert Mus.).

SHEPPARD, Robert, or Shepherd
British, 18th century.
Engraver.

Robert Sheppard engraved most of the portraits of princes and statesmen in Rapin's *History of England* (1732-1737).

SHEPPARD, Warren J. or W.
American, 19th - 20th century.
Born 10 April 1858 or 1859, in Greenwich (New Jersey); died 1937.
Painter. Seascapes.

Warren Sheppard worked with the marine painter Maurice de Haas in New York but mostly taught himself by studying directly from nature. He mainly painted the natural world and paid close attention to the effects of light, such as twilight and moonlight, in a spirit of Post-Romanticism.

MUSEUMS AND GALLERIES:

BUFFALO (Albright-Knox AG): *Seascape* - SPRINGFIELD (Mus. of Art): *The Sea* - TOLEDO (MA): *Seascape.*

AUCTION RECORDS:

NEW YORK, 12 Nov 1909, *Venice,* USD 100. NEW YORK, 30 Nov 1979, *Sailing Ship 'Young America'* (oil on canvas, 25 x 36 1/4 ins / 63.5 x 92.1 cm) USD 3,500. NEW YORK, 22 June 1984, *Sailing Ship at Sunset* (oil on canvas, 19 3/4 x 30 ins / 50.2 x 76.2 cm) USD 3,100. SAN FRANCISCO, 20 June 1985, *View of Venice* (oil on canvas, 16 1/4 x 24 ins / 41 x 61 cm) USD 2,250. NEW YORK, 24 Jan 1989, *Boat Ready to Cast Off* (oil on canvas, 27 1/2 x 22 ins / 70 x 55 cm) USD 1,430. NEW YORK, 16 March 1990, *Sailing Ships at Sea By Moonlight* (1875, oil on canvas, 8 1/2 x 12 ins / 21.6 x 30.5 cm) USD 5,500. NEW YORK, 15 April 1992, *Frigates Off Shore at Twilight* (1894, oil on canvas/card, 24 1/2 x 36 1/4 ins / 62.2 x 92.1 cm) USD 4,400. NEW YORK, 2 Dec 1992, *Sailing Ships in Moonlight* (1884, oil on canvas, 18 x 36 ins / 45.7 x 91.4 cm) USD 1,650. NEW YORK, 31 March 1993, *Venetian Canal* (oil on canvas, 15 3/4 x 26 ins / 40 x 66 cm) USD 3,738. NEW YORK, 9 Sept 1993, *Seascape* (oil on canvas, 20 x 30 ins / 50.8 x 76.2 cm) USD 1,380. NEW YORK, 12 Sept 1994, *Twilight* (oil on canvas, 30 1/2 x 20 1/4 ins / 77.2 x 51.4 cm) USD 8,050. NEW YORK, 9 March 1996, *Sailing Ships at Dawn* (watercolour, gouache and pencil/paper/card, 8 x 11 1/2 ins / 20.2 x 29.3 cm) USD 978. NEW YORK, 23 April 1997, *Venetian Canal* (oil on canvas, 16 1/4 x 24 1/4 ins / 41.3 x 61.5 cm) USD 4,025. WASHINGTON, 22 May 1999, *View of San Giorgio Maggiore, Venice* (oil on canvas, 17 x 14 ins / 43 x 36 cm) USD 3,100. WASHINGTON, 22 May 1999, *View of Houses on Venetian Canal* (oil on board, 16 x 26 ins / 41 x 66 cm) USD 3,900.

SHEPPARD, William

British, 17th century.
Born c. 1602, in England; died c. 1660, in Italy.
Painter. Portraits.

Little is known about William Sheppard, who executed the portrait of the dramatist *Thomas Killigrew* engraved by Faithorne, though he is recorded as having been resident in Venice in 1650.

SHEPPARD, William Ludwell

American, 19th - 20th century.
Born 1833, in Richmond (Virginia); died 27 March 1912, in Richmond.
Sculptor, illustrator.

William Ludwell Sheppard made the *War Memorial* and statue of *General A.P. Hill* in Richmond.

SHEPPERSON, Claude Allin

British, 19th - 20th century.
Born 25 October 1867, in Beckenham (Kent); died 30 December 1921, in London.
Painter, engraver, lithographer, illustrator, draughtsman, stained glass painter. Landscapes.

Claude Shepperson trained in London and Paris, and contributed drawings to numerous publications.

AUCTION RECORDS:

LONDON, 16 Feb 1923, *Grand Piano* (drawing) GBP 18. LONDON, 11 July 1924, *The Carefree Girl* (drawing) GBP 28. LONDON, 11 Oct 1983, *Royal Ascot, June 1914* (black and coloured chalks and watercolour, 13 3/4 x 20 1/2 ins / 35 x 52.3 cm) GBP 700. LONDON, 5 June 1984, *Cupid Pursued* (watercolour and gouache, 8 3/4 x 8 ins / 22.3 x 20.2 cm) GBP 750. LONDON, 7 Oct 2003, *Stage Ball, at the Albert Hall* (mixed media on paper, sold with a letter, 12 x 7 ins / 31 x 19 cm) GBP 1,200.

SHEPPERSON, Matthew

British, 19th century.
Painter, draughtsman. Portraits.

Matthew Shepperson exhibited in London between 1811 and 1821.

SHER-GIL, Amrita, or Sher Gil

Indian, 20th century.
Born 30 January 1913, in Budapest; died 1941, in Lahore.
Active in India since 1921.
Painter. Figures, portraits, scenes with figures. Orientalism.

Amrita Sher-Gil was the daughter of a Sikh nobleman and a Hungarian mother and began studying in Florence. In 1929 she moved to Paris, where she was a pupil of Pierre H. Vaillant at the Académie de la Grande-Chaumière, and of Lucien Simon at the École des Beaux-Arts. In 1934 she returned to India, where she was active in the movement for artistic renewal that was seeking to establish an indigenous but nevertheless totally contemporary Indian art, freed from all British influence.

Until her return to India, Sher-Gil's painting had been bound by the academicism of the École des Beaux-Arts, but as she travelled across India, she discovered her roots. She often painted pictures of young Indian women, in which her sensibilities and personal involvement are apparent, such as *Young Village Girls, The Child Bride* and *The Three Young Girls*. In her own words, she wanted to 'translate into paint the life of the people of India, especially the poor'. Around 1937, during a period spent in a village in the south of the country, Sher-Gil painted traditional scenes from daily life in India: *Farmers Going to Market, The Bride Preparing* and *Group of Priests with their Students*. However, these familiar scenes are not treated as if they were serene images: the bearing of the figures is bowed, they have anxious faces, and the countryside in the background is desolate, a combination of misery and pride. As her art developed, these countryside settings became more and more important for Sher-Gil, the inspiration for them coming from ancient Indian miniatures, and she availed herself of the traditional symbolic values of colours in these settings.

Although Sher-Gil admired the work of Cézanne, Gauguin and Modigliani, as well as the decorative style of the painters Korin and Koetsu, her style was also influenced by Hindu miniatures and sculpture: her drawing was clean and simple, her use of colour expressive and symbolic. Sher-Gil's synthetic style produced hieratic figures reminiscent of Cézanne, Georges de la Tour and Zurbaran, figures whose forms are rigid and reduced to their most basic geometries, like plaques of metal that have been cut out and bent. Sher-Gil was like a bridge between tradition and the contemporary Indian world, and although her work was the subject of controversy among conformists, and despite her sudden and premature death in 1941, many young artists were influenced by the great reputation she had gained. Exhibitions of her work were held in Delhi, Bombay (now Mumbai), Hyderabad, and Allahabad (in 1936). In 1946, her *Elephants Bathing* was shown at the international exhibition organized by UNESCO at the Musée d'Art Moderne in Paris.

BIBLIOGRAPHY:

Khandalavala, K., *Amrita Sher-Gil*, Bombay, 1944. Kaul, Manohar, *Trends in Indian Painting*, Dhoomimal Ramchand, New Delhi, 1961. *Six Indian Painters*, exhibition catalogue, Tate Gallery, London, 1982. *Artistes indiens en France*, exhibition catalogue, Centre national d'Art contemporain, Paris, 1985.

Museums and Galleries:
New Delhi (NGMA): *Portrait of Grandmother (Lady Daljit Singh of Kapurthala)*; numerous works.

SHERAR, Robert
British, 19th - 20th century.
Painter. Interiors with figures.

Robert Sherar exhibited from 1885 to 1903.

Auction records:
London, 17 Nov 1994, *Interior of the Rustic Art Club* (1899, oil on card, 16 3/4 x 31 ins / 42.5 x 77.8 cm) GBP 2,300.

SHERBORN, Charles
British, 18th century.
Born 1716; died 1786.
Engraver. Ex-libris, maps.

Charles Sherborn was active in London. However, there is some confusion with the 18th-century Charles William Sherborn.

SHERBORN, Charles William
British, 19th - 20th century.
Born June 1831, in London; died 10 February 1912, in London.
Painter, engraver, draughtsman.

Charles Sherborn is best known as an engraver of bookplates, but is probably identifiable as the painter of the same name, active in the late 19th and early 20th centuries.

Museums and Galleries:
London (British Mus.): almost complete collection of his bookplates.

SHERBORNE, Robert, or Sherburne
British, 18th century.
Painter, miniaturist. Landscapes.

Robert Sherborne exhibited a miniature at the Society of Artists in London in 1775.

Auction records:
London, 26 Jan 1984, *Indian Camp by Moonlight* (1788, gouache, 18 x 26 3/4 ins / 46 x 68 cm) GBP 900. London, 12 July 1995, *The Ruins of Sherborne Castle; Bridge in Sherborne Park* (1785, oil on canvas, each 18 1/2 x 23 ins / 47 x 58.5 cm) GBP 18,400.

SHEREMETEV, Vasili Vasilievich de
Russian, 19th century.
Born 10 December 1829, in Moscow.
Painter. History painting, genre scenes.

Having been a pupil in St Petersburg of Alekseev, Lomtev, Shil'tsov and Svertchkov, this artist then studied in Paris in 1859 under Couture and Boulanger. He first exhibited at the Paris Salon in 1861, and subsequently exhibited regularly in Paris, in particular with the Cercle de l'Union artistique and at the Salon des Indépendants. His notable works include *Cossack Messenger, Return from the Bear Hunt* and *Cossack Alert*. He decorated a large number of monuments, in particular the Russian church in Paris, which houses his *Flight into Egypt* and *Departure for Emmaus*, the Romanian church in Paris and the Russian embassy in London.

SHERIDAN, Harry
British, 19th century.
Painter. Landscapes.

Harry Sheridan lived in Whitehaven and exhibited at the Royal Academy of Arts in London in 1857.

Museums and Galleries:
London (Victoria and Albert Mus.): *In the Heart of Valais; The Village of Pully.*

SHERIDAN, J.
Irish, 18th century.
Born in County Kilkenny; died 1790, in London.
Painter. Portraits.

J. Sheridan studied in Dublin and went to London where he exhibited at the Royal Academy from 1785 to 1789.

SHERIDAN, James
Irish, 18th - 19th century.
Born 1734; died 1840, in Dublin, at an advanced age.
Miniaturist.

SHERIDAN, Joseph Marsh
American, 20th century.
Born 1897, in Quincy (Illinois); died 1971, in Fresno (California).
Painter.

Joseph Marsh Sheridan was active in San Francisco.

SHERIFF, Charles. See **SHIRREFF**

SHERIFF, John
British, 19th century.
Born 1816; died 1844.
Painter. Animals.

John Sheriff worked in Glasgow. He became a Member of the Royal Scottish Academy in 1839.

Auction records:
London, 18 Nov 1988, *The Chancellor, Black and White Hereford Bull* (oil on canvas, 40 x 50 ins / 101.7 x 127.3 cm) GBP 13,200.

SHERIFF, William Craig
British, 18th century.
Born 26 October 1786, near Haddington; died 17 March 1805, in Edinburgh.
Painter. History painting.

William Craig Sheriff studied at the Trustees' Academy in Edinburgh. He showed great promise, but scarcely had his talent been confirmed by his first painting, *The Escape of Mary Stuart from Loch Leven Castle*, than he died at the age of 19.

SHERINGHAM, George
British, 20th century.
Born 1884, in London; died 11 November 1937, in London.
Painter (gouache), watercolourist, draughtsman, illustrator. Scenes with figures.

George Sheringham was a pupil of Harry Becker. He painted decorative scenes and genre subjects, and illustrated Edmond Rostand's *La Princesse Lointaine* (*The Distant Princess*).

Museums and Galleries:
Paris (Mus. d'Orsay).

Auction records:
Amsterdam, 16 April 1996, *Le lever* (*Upon Rising*) (watercolour and gouache, 6 1/4 x 17 3/4 ins / 16 x 45 cm) NLG 1,888. Philadelphia, 12 Dec 1999, *Emperor and Empress Visit Atelier* (gouache and watercolour on paper laid on canvas, circular) USD 2,100. Lewes, 25 Oct 2002, *Still-life of Chinese Snuff Bottles* (oil on panel, 14 x 8 ins / 36 x 20 cm) GBP 1,600. London, 25 Nov 2004, *The Cauldron of Anwn. Baptism of Dylan. Playing Music. Tale of Kynon. Peredur and the Serpent. Dragon* (watercolour and gouache on silk, set of six, 58 x 23 ins / 148 x 58 cm) GBP 33,000.

SHERINYAN, Elizabeth
Armenian, 20th century.
Born 1877, in Harport; died 1947.
Active in the USA.
Painter, sculptor.

Elizabeth Sherinyan studied under Hermann Dudley Murphy and Philip Leslie Hale at the Boston Museum Art School. She was a member of the American Federation of the Arts.

Museums and Galleries:
Venice (Armenian Monastery): five works.

SHERLOCK, William
British, 18th century.
Born c. 1738, in Dublin.
Painter, miniaturist, engraver. Portraits.

William Sherlock began his studies in London at the St Martin's Lane Academy and went to complete them in Paris under Le Bas. Sherlock executed miniatures and prints of landscapes and portraits. Le Blanc records him as having died in 1795, but this is contradicted by his participation in exhibitions over ten years later. From 1764 to 1797 he exhibited at the Royal Society of Artists, of which he was a Member in the categories for portraits in oils and for portraits in watercolours. He also exhibited at the Royal Academy from 1802 to 1806.

SHERLOCK, William P.
British, 19th century.
Born c. 1780.
Painter, watercolourist, draughtsman, engraver, illustrator. Landscapes.

William P. Sherlock drew inspiration from the style of Richard Wilson and his works were often sold as those of the master. He drew topographical views and also engraved copies of rare engravings and of landscapes after Girtin, Payne and Powell. Sherlock executed some of the illustrations for Dickinson's *Antiquities of Nottinghamshire*. He exhibited at the Royal Academy from 1801 to 1810.

MUSEUMS AND GALLERIES:
LONDON (Victoria and Albert Mus.): two watercolours.

SHERMAN, Albert John
Australian, 20th century.
Born 1882; died 1971.
Painter. Landscapes, still-lifes, flowers.

AUCTION RECORDS:
ROSEBERY, 7 Sept 1976, *Still-life* (oil on canvas, 20 1/2 x 18 ins / 52 x 46 cm) AUD 600. ROSEBERY, 8 March 1977, *Still-life with Flowers* (oil on canvas, 22 x 32 ins / 56 x 81 cm) AUD 2,200. SYDNEY, 21 March 1979, *Basket of Flowers* (oil on canvas remounted, 19 3/4 x 24 3/4 ins / 50 x 63 cm) AUD 1,700. ARMADALE, 11 April 1984, *Bouquet* (oil on card, 21 1/4 x 22 1/2 ins / 54 x 57 cm) AUD 5,500. MELBOURNE, 21 April 1986, *Vase of Flowers and the Book 'The Flower Paintings of Albert Sherman'* (oil on card, 24 x 19 ins / 61 x 48 cm) AUD 7,000. SYDNEY, 3 July 1989, *Still-life with Daisies* (oil on card, 13 x 17 ins / 33 x 43 cm) AUD 5,500. SYDNEY, 16 Oct 1989, *Still-life with Yellow Daisies* (oil on canvas, 17 x 13 ins / 43 x 33 cm) AUD 3,400. LONDON, 30 Nov 1989, *Giant Peonies* (oil on card, 12 x 15 ins / 30.4 x 38.1 cm) GBP 715. SYDNEY, 2 July 1990, *Chinese Lion with Flowers* (oil on card, 16 1/2 x 11 3/4 ins / 42 x 30 cm) AUD 2,800. SYDNEY, 15 Oct 1990, *Flowers* (oil on canvas, 19 3/4 x 15 3/4 ins / 50 x 40 cm) AUD 2,600. SYDNEY, 2 Dec 1991, *A Cottage in the Bush* (oil on canvas, 12 1/4 x 18 ins / 31 x 46 cm) AUD 700. SYDNEY, 29-30 March 1992, *Spring Flowers* (oil on canvas, 22 x 16 1/4 ins / 56 x 41 cm) AUD 2,250. MELBOURNE, 27 April 1999, *White Camellias* (oil on board, 18 x 24 ins / 46 x 61 cm) AUD 4,800. MELBOURNE, 24 Nov 1999, *Still-life with Hydrangeas* (oil on canvas, 30 x 37 ins / 75 x 93 cm) AUD 13,500. SYDNEY, 11 April 2000, *Summer Bouquet in an Oriental Jar* (oil on canvasboard, 29 x 25 ins / 74 x 64 cm) AUD 6,000. MELBOURNE, 3 May 2000, *Daffodils and Clematis in a Derby Vase* (oil on canvas, 20 x 22 ins / 51 x 56 cm) AUD 19,000. SYDNEY, 23 April 2001, *Still-life, Zinnias and Fruit* (oil on canvas, 26 x 31 ins / 67 x 80 cm) AUD 8,000. MELBOURNE, 27 Nov 2001, *Bowl of Flowers* (oil on board, 23 x 26 ins / 58 x 67 cm) AUD 6,000. MELBOURNE, 2 May 2002, *Yellow Vase* (oil on canvas, 20 x 18 ins / 52 x 45 cm) AUD 4,000. VICTORIA, 18 Nov 2002, *Still-life* (oil on board, 21 x 16 ins / 54 x 41 cm) AUD 4,250. SYDNEY, 27 Oct 2003, *Camellias* (oil on canvas, 20 x 26 ins / 51 x 66 cm) AUD 7,500. MELBOURNE, 26 Nov 2003, *Gum Blossom* (1930, oil on canvas laid on board, 20 x 24 ins / 51 x 61 cm) AUD 4,000. MELBOURNE, 10 March 2004, *Zinnias* (oil on canvasboard, 19 x 20 ins / 47 x 52 cm) AUD 3,500. MELBOURNE, 4 May 2004, *White Blossoms in a Chinese Vase* (oil on board, 21 x 17 ins / 53 x 44 cm) AUD 3,800.

SHERMAN, Cindy
American, 20th - 21st century.
Born 19 January 1954, in Glen Ridge (New Jersey).
Photographer. Figures, portraits.
Neo-Conceptual Art, Appropriation Art (Simulationism), Identity Art (Feminist Art).

Cindy Sherman studied painting at State University College, Buffalo, but later gave up painting for photography. She settled in New York. She is best known for her *Untitled Film Stills* series, which she created from 1977 to 1980. In these photographs, she poses as an imaginary blonde actress in stereotypical roles such a sex-kitten, a beautiful librarian, and in 'unguarded' moments at home. Her work addresses the fictional feminity and cultural position of women in post-war America. In other series, with close-ups of her face under stage lighting the aim is visual. A series on fashion for the magazine *Interview*, in 1983, was meant as a parody. A psychological series expressed qualms, anxiety, melancholy and desire. There was a fantastic series with diabolical make-up and monstrous false body parts. An obsessional series in 1987, virtually went outside her own figure in which she substituted a leg, hand, pair of glasses, hat or other accessory personalising some one else, since she always portrays herself as another, with only still-lifes made from junk or repugnant objects, possibly metaphors for the biological fatality of the human body. In the historical series *Historical Portraits*, she dressed and made herself up as figures from history - for example, the self-portrait of Caravaggio's Bacchus in which Caravaggio dresses up - Cindy Sherman appears as Caravaggio and Caravaggio as Bacchus. With this work, photography is only the support and it is not therefore a photographic work. The real subject is the same omnipresent character, Cindy Sherman, and the conclusion appears to be that the artist is questioning herself, in a kind of photo-analysis. As a corollary, the viewer must also ask whether this is a narcissistic contemplation by the artist-creator or, on the other hand, whether dressing up is a form of escape.

Collective exhibitions include: *L'époque, la mode, la morale, la passion* (*Period, Fashion, Morality and Passion*), Georges Pompidou Centre, Paris, 1987; *Présumés innocents: l'art contemporain et l'enfance* (*Presumed Innocent: Contemporary Art and Childhood*), CAPC Musée d'Art Contemporain, Bordeaux, 2000; *Hypermental*, an exhibition on the unreal, the transreal and the reconstruction of reality, at the Kunsthalle, Hamburg, 2001; *Moving Pictures*, an exhibition showing the use of photography, film and video in art since the end of the 1960s, Solomon R. Guggenheim Museum, New York, 2002-2003; *Phantom der Lust: Visionen des Machochismus in der Kunst* (*Phantom of Desire. Visions of Masochism in Art*), an exhibition devoted to Sacher-Masoch, the inventor of masochism, Neue Galerie am Ladesmuseum, Graz, 2003; *Bandes à part: le cinéma dans l'art contemporain* (*On the Fringes: Cinema in Contemporary Art*), an exhibition presented on the occasion of *Trésors publics, 20 ans de création dans les Fonds régionaux d'art contemporain (FRAC)* (*Public Treasury, 20 Years of Creation in the Regional Collection of Contemporary Art*), Musée d'Art Moderne et Contemporain, Strasbourg. She mainly shows her work in solo exhibitions, including: Stedelijk Museum, Amsterdam, 1982; Musée de St-Étienne, 1983; Whitney Museum, New York, 1987; Musée de Périgueux, 1988; Musée de La Roche-sur-Yon and New York, Geneva and Vienna, 1989; Galerie Monika Sprüth, Cologne, 1990; Kunsthalle, Basel, 1991; Turin, 1991; Hamburg, Malmö, Lucerne, 1995; CAPC, Musée d'Art Contemporain, Bordeaux, 1996; Serpentine Gallery, London, 2003.

Bibliography:
Cindy Sherman: An Interview, video, Video Data Bank, Chicago, 1980. Cathcart, L., *Cindy Sherman: Photographs*, exhibition catalogue, Houston, Contemporary Art Museum, Houston, 1980. Caujolle, Christian, *Cindy Sherman*, Musée d'Art moderne, St-Étienne, 1984. *Cindy Sherman*, exhibition catalogue, Schirmer-Mosel, Munich, 1986. *Cindy Sherman*, exhibition catalogue, Whitney Museum of American Art, New York, 1987. Schjeldahl, P./Phillips, L., *Cindy Sherman*, exhibition catalogue, Whitney, New York, 1987. Macdonald, E, *Dis-seminating Cindy Sherman: The Body and the Photograph*, Art Criticism, v/2, New York, 1989. *Cindy Sherman*, exhibition catalogue, Kunsthalle, Basel, Staatsgal., München, Whitechapel, London, 1991. Krauss, Rosalind, *Cindy Sherman 1975-1993*, Rizzoli, New York, 1993. *Cindy Sherman: Photographic Work 1975-1995*, exhibition catalogue, Schirmer Art Books, London, 1995. *Moving Pictures*, exhibition catalogue, Solomon R. Guggenheim Museum, New York, 2002. Steiner, Rochelle/Moore, Lorrie, *Cindy Sherman*, exhibition catalogue, Serpentine Gall., London, 2003. *Cindy Sherman: The Complete Untitled Film Stills*, illustrated book, Museum of Modern Art, New York, 2003. *Cindy Sherman Centerfolds*, exhibition catalogue, Skarstedt Fine Art, New York, 2003.

Museums and Galleries:
AMSTERDAM (Stedelijk Mus.) - BORDEAUX (FRAC Aquitaine): *Untitled No. 67* (1980); *Untitled No. 110* (1982); *Untitled Film Still No. 44* (1979) - LYONS (FRAC Rhône-Alpes): *Untitled* (1982); *Untitled* (1982) - NEW YORK (Solomon R. Guggenheim Mus.): *Untitled, No. 167* (1986, colour photograph) - SYRACUSE (Everson MA): *Untitled* (1986, photograph).

Auction records:
PARIS, 15 Feb 1990, *Untitled No. 95* (1981, colour photograph, 24 x 48 ins / 61 x 121 cm) FRF 105,000. NEW YORK, 23 Feb 1990, *Untitled* (1987, montage of colour photographs/card, 72 x 48 ins / 183 x 122 cm) USD 12,100. NEW YORK, 8 May 1990, *Untitled 10* (1985, photograph and colour, 72 1/2 x 49 1/4 ins / 184.2 x 125.4 cm) USD 19,800. NEW YORK, 5 Oct 1990, *Untitled 132* (1984, montage of colour photos/foam, 70 3/4 x 48 ins / 179.7 x 121.9 cm) USD 9,900. NEW YORK, 2 May 1991, *Untitled* (colour photograph/foam, 71 x 48 ins / 180.6 x 122.2 cm) USD 12,100. NEW YORK, 7 May 1991, *Untitled* (1986, colour photograph, 39 1/2 x 30 ins / 100.3 x 76.2 cm) USD 2,860. PARIS, 4 Dec 1992, *Untitled* (1989, colour photograph on aluminium, 53 1/2 x 46 1/2 ins / 136 x 118 cm) FRF 85,000. NEW YORK, 8 Nov 1993, *Untitled* (colour photographs/foam panel, 46 1/4 x 68 1/4 ins / 117.5 x 173.5 cm) USD 8,050. NEW YORK, 25-26 Feb 1994, *Untitled Film 35* (1979, photograph, 10 x 8 ins / 25.4 x 20.3 cm) USD 26,450. NEW YORK, 2 May 1995, *Untitled, Pose 48* (1979, black and white photograph, 8 x 10 ins / 20.3 x 25.4 cm) USD 40,250. LONDON, 23 May 1996, *Untitled 47* (1985, colour photograph, 47 1/2 x 70 1/2 ins / 120.6 x 179 cm) GBP 12,650. LONDON, 24 Oct 1996, *Untitled No. 160* (1986, colour photograph, series of six, 51 1/2 x 34 ins / 131 x 86.5 cm) GBP 2,875. NEW YORK, 19 Nov 1996, *Untitled 139* (1984, colour photograph/foam, 71 x 48 1/2 ins / 180.4 x 123.2 cm) USD 10,925. NEW YORK, 19 Nov 1996, *Untitled Film Still No. 48* (1979, silver ground, 7 x 9 1/4 ins / 17.6 x 23.8 cm) USD 66,300. NEW YORK, 20 Nov 1996, *Untitled Film Still No. 10* (1978, silver ground, 7 1/4 x 10 ins / 18.4 x 25.4 cm) USD 39,100. NEW YORK, 21 Nov 1996, *Untitled* (1989, colour photograph, 60 3/4 x 46 1/4 ins / 154.3 x 117.7 cm) USD 40,250. LONDON, 6 Dec 1996, *Untitled 154* (1985, colour photograph, 72 1/2 x 49 1/2 ins / 184.3 x 125.5 cm) GBP 9,200. NEW YORK, 6 May 1997, *Untitled (Film Still 57)* (1980, black and white photograph, 8 x 10 ins / 20.3 x 25.4 cm) USD 16,100. NEW YORK, 6-7 May 1997, *Untitled No. 264* (1992, colour photograph, 51 x 76 ins / 129.5 x 193 cm) USD 55,200. NEW YORK, 8 May 1997, *Untitled No. 222* (1990, colour photograph, 60 x 44 ins / 152.3 x 111.7 cm) USD 46,000. NEW YORK, 19 Nov 1997, *Untitled No. 87* (1981, colour photograph, 29 x 52 1/4 ins / 73.6 x 132.7 cm) USD 63,000. NEW YORK, 17 Nov 1999, *Untitled No.87* (1981, colour photo, 5/10, 29 x 52 ins / 74 x 133 cm) USD 110,000. LONDON, 8 Dec 1999, *Untitled Film Still* (1978, gelatin silver print, 1/3, 40 x 30 ins / 102 x 76 cm) GBP 68,000. NEW YORK, 17 May 2000, *Untitled* (1989, colour photo, 57 x 41 ins / 145 x 104 cm) USD 240,000. NEW YORK, 16 Nov 2000, *Untitled No. 92* (1982, colour coupler print, 10/10, 24 x 48 ins / 61 x 122 cm) USD 230,000. NEW YORK, 14 May 2001, *Untitled No. 86* (1981, cibachrome photo, 24 x 48 ins / 61 x 122 cm) USD 150,000. NEW YORK, 17 May 2001, *Untitled Film Still No. 48* (gelatin silver print, 1/10, 8 x 10 ins / 20 x 25 cm) USD 300,000. NEW YORK, 14 May 2002, *Untitled Film Still No. 14* (1978, gelatin silver print, 2/3, 40 x 30 ins / 102 x 76 cm) USD 120,000. NEW YORK, 13 Nov 2002, *Untitled No. 90* (1981, colour coupler print, 5/10, 24 x 48 ins / 61 x 122 cm) USD 110,000. NEW YORK, 11 Nov 2003, *Untitled Film Still No. 54* (1980, gelatin silver print, 8 x 10 ins / 20 x 25 cm) USD 175,000. NEW YORK, 12 Nov 2003, *Untitled Film Still No. 21* (1978, gelatin silver print, 16 x 20 ins / 40 x 51 cm) USD 145,000. NEW YORK, 12 May 2004, *Untitled Film Still No. 48* (1979, black and white photograph, 16 x 20 ins / 41 x 51 cm) USD 280,000. NEW YORK, 13 May 2004, *Untitled No. 211* (1989, c-print, 46 x 40 ins / 117 x 102 cm) USD 85,000.

SHERMAN, Pamela

19th century.

Painter, watercolourist. Botanical subjects, animals.

Pamela Sherman was active around 1860.

Auction records:
NEW YORK, 24 Sept 1992, *Portfolio of 68 botanical and zoological watercolours* (watercolour/paper, from 1 1/2 x 1 1/4 ins / 3.8 x 3.2 cm to 13 x 9 1/2 ins/33 x 24.1 cm) USD 1,980.

SHERMAN, Stuart

American, 20th century.

Born 9 November 1945, in Providence (Rhode Island); died 14 September 2001, in San Francisco.

Sculptor, performance artist, installation artist, video artist, film maker.

Fluxus, Conceptual Art.

Stuart Sherman wrote poems and worked as an actor in the Fluxus group of avant-garde theatre companies in the USA in the 1960s. He was a friend and also later a companion of the writer Carson McCullers. His artistic activity began about 1975 and took him to many cities including Paris, Cairo and St Petersburg. Sherman made objects, sculptures, collages and short films as well as drawing. He also wrote texts and condensed texts, such as the 25-minute *Œdipus Rex*. This idea of brevity runs through his work. He acknowledged Magritte and Buster Keaton as his sources of inspiration. His first performances took place in his exhibition room but later they were in theatres or in the street. In these performances he appeared alone, with no words or hardly any, and used objects he took out of a suitcase as metaphors with which he illustrated the work and invented a crazy world and language. Although always present on the art scene, Sherman was never known to the art buyers. Photographs and films of his performances remain. He was invited to the Salon d'Automne in Paris in 1979, where he performed *The Stations of the Cross or the Passion of Stuart* at the Georges Pompidou Centre.

SHERMAN, Welby

American (?), 19th - 20th century.

Sculptor, engraver.

Welby Sherman sculpted in wood. It is not clear whether he is the same artist as, or is connected to, the Welby Sherman who was a member of the group The Ancients, which included Samuel Palmer and was influenced by William Blake.

SHERRATT, E.
British, 18th century.
Active in London.
Miniaturist, painter. Portraits.
E. Sherratt exhibited miniatures at the Royal Academy in 1787 and 1792.

SHERRATT, Thomas
British, 19th century.
Active in London.
Reproductions engraver.
Thomas Sherratt worked in London between 1860 and 1880.

SHERRIFF-SCOTT, Adam. See **SCOTT Adam Sherriff**

SHERRIN, Daniel
British, 19th - 20th century.
Born 1870; died 1942.
Painter. Landscapes, landscapes with figures, waterscapes, seascapes.
Daniel Sherrin was active from 1895 to 1922. His landscapes, such as *Morning near Reigate Heath; Golden Autumn Days; Summer's Day,* are sensitive depictions of the changing light and atmosphere, according to the time of day or season. Sherrin, also a painter of seascapes, was able to render detailed and informed renditions of ships, as in *Three-master in High Wind; In Full Sail.*

AUCTION RECORDS:
NEW YORK, 8-10 Jan 1908, *Leaving Old Caledonia,* USD 100. LONDON, 15 July 1910, *Coastal Landscape,* GBP 10. LONDON, 18 March 1911, *Golden Autumn Days,* GBP 14. LONDON, 18 May 1976, *Cobham, Surrey* (oil on canvas, 19½ x 29½ ins / 49.5 x 75 cm) GBP 580. LONDON, 12 Dec 1978, *Autumn Evening* (oil on canvas, 19¼ x 29¼ ins / 49 x 74.5 cm) GBP 1,000. LONDON, 20 March 1979, *Dusk* (oil on canvas, 23 x 41 ins / 58.5 x 104 cm) GBP 1,400. LONDON, 3 Oct 1984, *A Hay Barge at Sunset* (oil on canvas, 24 x 42 ins / 61 x 106.7 cm) GBP 2,200. NEW YORK, 24 May 1985, *The Belstone Valley, Dartmoor; Tes Tor, Dartmoor* (gouaches, a pair, 10¼ x 14 ins / 26 x 35.5 cm) USD 1,100. MONTREAL, 25 April 1988, *Landscape with Figures* (oil on canvas, 20 x 30 ins / 51 x 76 cm) CAD 1,800. LONDON, 5 Oct 1989, *Three-master in High Wind* (oil on canvas, 24 x 36 ins / 60.9 x 91.4 cm) GBP 1,760. LONDON, 13 Dec 1989, *Morning near Reigate Heath* (oil on canvas, 20 x 30 ins / 51 x 76.5 cm) GBP 1,430. NEW YORK, 17 Jan 1990, *St Ives* (oil on canvas, 22 x 40 ins / 55.9 x 101.6 cm) USD 2,640. LONDON, 9 Feb 1990, *Wooded Landscape with Figures Gathering Wood* (oil on canvas, 42 x 66½ ins / 106.5 x 169 cm) GBP 3,080. LONDON, 30 May 1990, *In the Southern Seas* (oil on canvas, 24½ x 36¼ ins / 62 x 92 cm) GBP 3,960. LONDON, 13 Feb 1991, *Boat on a Lake* (oil on canvas, 20 x 30 ins / 51 x 76 cm) GBP 902. NEW YORK, 21 May 1991, *Village on the Banks of a River* (oil on canvas, 24¼ x 42¼ ins / 61.6 x 107.3 cm) USD 3,300. PERTH, 26 Aug 1991, *Highland Cattle Beside a Loch* (oil on canvas, 23¾ x 36¼ ins / 60.5 x 92 cm) GBP 3,080. LONDON, 11 Oct 1991, *The Wye Valley* (oil on canvas, 20 x 30 ins / 50.8 x 76.2 cm) GBP 1,540. LONDON, 20 Jan 1993, *In Full Sail* (oil on canvas, 24 x 36 ins / 61 x 91.5 cm) GBP 1,150. LONDON, 3 Feb 1993, *On the Shore of the Silver Sea* (1922, oil on canvas, 21½ x 35½ ins / 54.5 x 90 cm) GBP 920. LONDON, 29 March 1995, *Summer's Day* (oil on canvas, 24 x 42 ins / 61 x 106.5 cm) GBP 2,760. LONDON, 11 March 1999, *Country House at Sunset* (oil on canvas, 42 x 66 ins / 107 x 168 cm) GBP 4,000. LONDON, 10 June 1999, *Evening in the Mole near Dorking* (oil on canvas, 30 x 50 ins / 76 x 127 cm) GBP 3,600. SAN FRANCISCO, 17 May 2000, *Extensive Landscape with Figures Harvesting* (oil on canvas, 24 x 36 ins / 61 x 91 cm) USD 5,000. LONDON, 6 Dec 2000, *Peaceful Waters* (oil on canvas, 24 x 42 ins / 61 x 107 cm) GBP 5,000. SAN FRANCISCO, 16 May 2001, *Extensive River Landscape with Figures by a Cottage* (oil on canvas, 24 x 35 ins / 62 x 89 cm) USD 3,250. SEVENOAKS, 11 July 2001, *Still of Evening* (oil on canvas, 30 x 50 ins / 76 x 127 cm) GBP 1,950. LONDON, 15 April 2002, *Misty Sunshine* (oil on canvas, 40 x 30 ins / 102 x 77 cm) GBP 2,400. LONDON, 28 Aug 2002, *Invernesshire* (oil on canvas, 24 x 42 ins / 61 x 106 cm) GBP 2,800. LONDON, 26 March 2003, *Landscape at Sunset After Rain* (oil on canvas, a pair, 24 x 36 ins / 61 x 91 cm) GBP 1,800. LEYBURN, 10 April 2003, *River Landscape with Figures on the Bank* (oil on canvas, 24 x 42 ins / 61 x 107 cm) GBP 6,000. CHICHESTER, 28 Jan 2004, *Sand Dunes* (oil on canvas, 19 x 30 ins / 49 x 76 cm) GBP 5,000. LEYBURN, 22 July 2004, *Summer's Afternoon, River Landscape with Figures Seated* (oil on canvas, 24 x 42 ins / 61 x 107 cm) GBP 5,000.

SHERRIN, David
British, 19th - 20th century.
Born 1868.
Painter. Landscapes.
David Sherrin may be identifiable as the artist also known as Daniel Sherrin.

BIBLIOGRAPHY:
Johnson, Jane/Greutzner, A., *The Dictionary of British Artists, 1880-1940: an Antique Collectors' Club Research Project Listing 41,000 Artists,* Antique Collectors' Club, Woodbridge, 1976.

AUCTION RECORDS:
MONTREAL, 19 Nov 1991, *Sussex Landscape* (oil on canvas, 20¼ x 30¼ ins / 51.5 x 76.8 cm) CAD 800.

SHERRIN, John
British, 19th century.
Born 1819, in London; died September 1896, in Ramsgate.
Painter (including gouache), watercolourist, draughtsman. Animals, birds, botanical subjects, still-lifes.
John Sherrin took part in the major London exhibitions from 1859. He became a Member of the Royal Institute in 1879, and several of his works were reproduced as colour lithographs. Sherrin specialised in depicting birds.

MUSEUMS AND GALLERIES:
BLACKBURN (Mus. & AG): *Still-life with Bird's Nest* (watercolour) - LONDON (Victoria and Albert Mus.): watercolours.

AUCTION RECORDS:
LONDON, 17 March 1922, *Flowers and Bird's Nest* (drawing) GBP 17. LONDON, 3 April 1922, *Fruit* (drawing) GBP 10. LONDON, 10 July 1922, *Apples; Bird's Nest and Apple Blossom* (two drawings) GBP 31. LONDON, 30 Nov 1923, *Birds' Nests and Roses* (drawing) GBP 15. LONDON, 2 June 1924, *Apple Blossom and Bird's Nest* (drawing) GBP 17. LONDON, 24 May 1984, *Still-life with Fruit* (watercolour and gouache, 8¼ x 11½ ins / 21 x 29 cm) GBP 850. LONDON, 27 Feb 1985, *Two Hares* (watercolour heightened with gouache, 12½ x 18 ins / 32 x 46 cm) GBP 3,800. CHESTER, 9 Oct 1986, *Still-life with Flowers and Bird's Nest* (watercolour heightened with gouache, 12½ x 17½ ins / 32 x 44.5 cm) GBP 2,400. LONDON, 31 Jan 1990, *Still-life with Grapes and Strawberries* (watercolour, 3¼ x 4¼ ins / 8.5 x 11 cm) GBP 660. LONDON, 25-26 April 1990, *Still-life with Apples and Plums* (watercolour and gouache, 12 x 17 ins / 30.5 x 43 cm) GBP 2,090. LONDON, 26 Sept 1990, *Still-life with Apples on a Mossy Bank* (watercolour and gouache, 9 x 11½ ins / 22 x 29 cm) GBP 770. LONDON, 7 Oct 1992, *Still-life with Strawberries and Peas*

(watercolour and gouache, 7 1/4 x 8 3/4 ins / 18.5 x 22.5 cm) GBP 1,100. LONDON, 12 Nov 1992, *Still-life with a Clump of Primroses and a Nest* (watercolour and gouache, 8 x 10 ins / 20.5 x 25.5 cm) GBP 1,540. PERTH, 31 Aug 1993, *Grouse* (1895, watercolour and gouache, 8 3/4 x 12 1/2 ins / 22.5 x 32 cm) GBP 1,495. LONDON, 3 Nov 1993, *Still-life with a Nest and a Clump of Primroses; Still-life with a Nest and a Rosebud* (watercolour and gouache, each 7 x 9 ins / 18 x 22 cm) GBP 5,980. NEW YORK, 20 July 1994, *Still-life with Apples and Grapes* (watercolour and gouache/paper, 7 3/4 x 10 ins / 19.7 x 25.7 cm) USD 2,760. LONDON, 9 Oct 1996, *Festival; No Bread* (watercolour heightened with white, a pair, each 5 3/4 x 8 1/2 ins / 14.5 x 21.5 cm) GBP 1,955. MANCHESTER, 8 Dec 1999, *Still-life with Apples* (watercolour, 6 x 9 ins / 16 x 23 cm) GBP 1,400. LONDON, 8 Dec 1999, *Still-life of Bird's Nest and Shell. Still-life of Bird's Nest, Redcurrants and Rose* (pencil and watercolour heightened with white, a pair, 7 x 10 ins / 19 x 25 cm) GBP 3,000. DUBLIN, 15 Nov 2000, *Bird's Nest with Apple Blossom* (1878, watercolour, 9 x 13 ins / 23 x 32 cm) IEP 3,200. SYDNEY, 27 Nov 2000, *British Plums* (gouache, pencil and watercolour, 13 x 17 ins / 32 x 42 cm) AUD 5,300. LONDON, 25 Oct 2001, *Still-life with Apples and a Plum* (pencil and watercolour heightened with white and gum arabic, 12 x 17 ins / 30 x 43 cm) GBP 1,500. LEWES, 29 Jan 2002, *Still-life of a Pineapple and Three Plums* (watercolour, 11 x 13 ins / 28 x 33 cm) GBP 1,100. LONDON, 25 June 2002, *Still-life of a Bird's Nest and Primroses* (watercolour, 8 x 9 ins / 20 x 23 cm) GBP 1,400. LONDON, 11 March 2003, *Still-life of Plums* (watercolour and gouache, 12 x 17 ins / 30 x 42 cm) GBP 2,000. SALISBURY, 1 Oct 2003, *Still-life of Plums, an Apple and Cobnuts* (watercolour, 10 x 15 ins / 26 x 37 cm) GBP 2,000. CREWKERNE, 14 Jan 2004, *Primroses and a Bird's Nest Against a Mossy Bank* (watercolour heightened with gouache, 12 x 17 ins / 31 x 42 cm) GBP 3,100.

SHERRY, David

British, 20th - 21st century.
Born 1974, in Northern Ireland.
Active in Glasgow.
Performance artist, video artist.

David Sherry has an MA from the Glasgow School of Art. His work criticises 'the systematic processes of everyday life'. For example, his video entitled *Stitching* shows Sherry sewing pieces of wood under the soles of his feet while he talks about what he is doing, like a workman. Other works by Sherry include *Carrying a Bucket of Water about for a Week* and *Avoiding Eye Contact for One Seven Day Period*.

Sherry has taken part in group exhibitions, including *Beck's Futures 2003*, an exhibition presenting the work of the nine artists shortlisted for the Beck's Prize and shown at the ICA in London, the CCA in Glasgow and the Southampton City Art Gallery in 2003.

SHERVUD, Leonid Vladimirovich, or Sherwood

Russian, 19th - 20th century.
Born 28 April 1871, in Moscow; died 23 August 1954, in Leningrad (now St Petersburg).
Sculptor.

The son of the artist and architect Vladimir Osipovich Shervud, Leonid Shervud studied at the St Petersburg academy and completed his training at the Académie Julian (1899 to 1900), where he worked under Auguste Rodin and Emile-Antoine Bourdelle. He had his first national exhibition in 1902 and taught at the painting, drawing and sculpture school in St Petersburg which he and M.D. Bernstein had founded. His work, influenced by Rodin and the Wanderers group, is known through the various monuments he created, notably those to *Pushkin*, the populist writer *G.I. Uspensky* (Volkovo Cemetery, St Petersburg) and *Rosa Luxemburg* (1928). His statue of a border guard *The Sentry* (1933) a plaster, of which there are various versions, is particularly famous.

MUSEUMS AND GALLERIES:

MOSCOW (Central Museum of the Revolution): *Rosa Luxemburg* (1928) - MOSCOW (State Tretyakov Gal.): *The Sentry* - ST PETERSBURG (Gosudarstvennyj Russkij Muz.): *The Sentry; Pushkin*.

SHERWIN, Charles

British, 18th century.
Born 1764; died 1794.
Engraver (burin).

Charles Sherwin was the brother and collaborator of John Keyse Sherwin.

SHERWIN, John Keyse

British, 18th century.
Born 1751, in London; died 20 September 1790.
Painter, engraver, draughtsman.

John Keyse Sherwin was a pupil of Ashley. He engraved portraits, religious subjects, historical subjects and landscapes. He was awarded a Gold Medal by the Royal Academy in 1772 for his oil painting of *Coriolanus Taking Leave of his Family*

MUSEUMS AND GALLERIES:

LONDON (National Portrait Gal.): *David Garrick* (c. 1770?, pencil).

SHERWIN, William

British, 17th - 18th century.
Born 1645, in Wellington; died 1711.
Engraver (mezzotint), draughtsman.

Certain biographers have maintained that William Sherwin was a pupil of Prince Rupert, while others have said that he had no known master. He engraved religious subjects and portraits, and was made Engraver to the King. In 2001 Sherwin's engraved portrait of *Barbara Villiers, Countess of Castlemaine, as a Shepherdess* was included in the exhibition *Painted Ladies. Women at the Court of Charles II* at the National Portrait Gallery in London.

BIBLIOGRAPHY:

MacLeod, Catharine/Marciari Alexander, Julia/Sharpe, Kevin/Dethloff, Diana/Wynne, Sonya, *Painted Ladies. Women at the Court of Charles II*, exhibition catalogue, National Portrait Gall., London, 2001.

SHERWOOD, Mary Clare

American, 19th - 20th century.
Born 18 May 1868, in Lyons (New York); died 1943, in Vicksburg (Mississippi).
Painter.

Mary Clare Sherwood studied at the Art Students League in New York; the circle of women artists in Berlin (where she was taught by Konrad Fehr); and in Paris, where her teacher was F. Edwin Scott. She was a member of the American Federation of Arts.

SHERWOOD, Rosina

Maiden name: Emmett
American, 19th - 20th century.
Born January 1866, in New York; died 1952, in New York.
Painter, watercolourist, draughtswoman. Portraits, genre scenes.

Rosina Sherwood was taught by William Chase in New York and also studied at the Académie Julian in Paris. She exhibited in Paris in 1889 and won a silver medal for drawing at the Exposition Universelle. She won the silver medal in Chicago in 1893 and the bronze medal in 1900, and the silver medal in St Louis in 1904. She became an associate member of the Royal Academy in London in 1906.

Auction records:
Edinburgh, 22 Nov 1989, *Games in the Hay* (1900, watercolour, 26 1/2 x 19 1/4 ins / 67.3 x 48.8 cm) GBP 7,700.

SHERWOOD, Vladimir Ossipovich, or Chervud
Russian, 19th century.
Born 1832, in Isleyevo; died 9 July 1897, in Moscow.
Painter, sculptor, architect. Portraits, genre scenes.
Vladimir Ossipovich Sherwood studied at the school of fine arts in Moscow, and became a member of the academy in 1872. He produced the monument to the Heros of Plevna in Moscow.
Museums and Galleries:
Moscow: *Portrait of the Famous Lover of Painting S.S. Goliachkin; Portrait of Mme K.T. Goliachkina.*

SHERWOOD, William Anderson
American, 19th - 20th century.
Born 13 February 1875, in Middlesex, near Baltimore (Maryland); died 1951.
Also active in Belgium.
Painter, engraver.
William Anderson Sherwood belonged to the American Federation of Arts. His work is displayed in many American museums. He was active in Antwerp and was a member of the Société des Beaux-Arts, the Société Royale des Aquafortistes, and a Chevalier of the Ordre de la Couronne Belge.
Museums and Galleries:
Antwerp - Brussels (Mus. royaux).

SHESTAKOVA, Vera
Russian, 20th century.
Born 1912, in Oriopl.
Painter. Still-lifes, flowers.
Vera Shestakova studied at the academy of fine arts in Leningrad (now St Petersburg). She was a member of the Artists' Union of the USSR.
Museums and Galleries:
Irkutsk (MFA) - Kiev (Mus. of Russian Art) - Moscow (Mus. of the Revolution) - St Petersburg (Gosudarstvennyj Muz. Istorii).
Auction records:
Paris, 26 April 1991, *Lilacs* (oil on canvas, 27 1/2 x 27 1/2 ins / 70 x 70 cm) FRF 5,000. Paris, 15 May 1991, *Roses of the Crimea* (1958, oil on cardboard, 15 x 17 3/4 ins / 38 x 45 cm) FRF 6,300. Paris, 24 Sept 1991, *Blue Vase* (oil on canvas, 39 x 29 1/2 ins / 99 x 75 cm) FRF 4,100.

SHEVCHENKO, Gennadi
Russian, 20th century.
Born 1939, in Orenburg.
Painter. Landscapes.
In Orenburg, Gennadi Shevchenko studied at the agricultural institute until 1962, and then at the polytechnic, graduating in 1966. A member of the Painters' Union of the USSR since 1980, he began exhibiting in 1970. He paints landscapes.
Auction records:
Paris, 11 Dec 1991, *Supporters' Meal* (oil on panel, 39 1/4 x 39 1/4 ins / 100 x 100 cm) FRF 9,000.

SHEVCHENKO, Ivan
Russian, 20th century.
Born 1937.
Painter. Figure compositions.
Ivan Shevchenko studied at the I. Repin Institute and at the academy of fine arts in Leningrad (now St Petersburg). A pupil of Andrei Milnikov, he received the title of Painter Emeritus of the USSR.
Auction records:
Paris, 23 March 1992, *The Milkmaid* (oil on canvas, 34 1/4 x 24 3/4 ins / 87 x 63 cm) FRF 6,300.

SHEVTCHENKO, Jaras Grigorievich
Russian, 19th century.
Born 9 March 1814, in Morintsy, near Kiev; died 10 March 1861, in St Petersburg.
Painter, engraver, poet.
A small museum in this artist's birthplace houses artefacts and paintings by the artist himself in which he recorded the story of his life. Born into serfdom, his freedom was bought by Russian writers who admired his verse; his liberation is the subject of one of his paintings. He was a pupil at the academy in St Petersburg from 1839 to 1849, but returned frequently to the Ukraine. Shevtchenko's opposition to the tsarist regime earned him a prison sentence, followed by exile. On his death, the Ukrainian people erected a monument over his tomb in the form of a heap of large stones, which was subsequently replaced by an official monument of considerably less interest.
Museums and Galleries:
Kiev: several paintings and drawings - Morintsy (Mus. Shevtchenko): *Autobiographical Pictures* - Moscow (Mus. of History): *Self-portrait* (sepia) - Moscow (Mus. of Literature): *several drawings* - Moscow (State Tretyakov Gal.): *Portrait of an Actor and Several Drawings* - St Petersburg (Gosudarstvennyj Russkij Muz.): *Portrait of Lounin and several other drawings* (drawing).

SHGUPAVA, Maria
Russian, 20th century.
Born 1897, in Armavir.
Painter, draughtswoman.
Maria Shgupava studied in Leningrad with Kazimir Severinovich Malevich.

SHI FU
Chinese, 20th - 21st century.
Born 1946.
Painter. Figures, nudes, landscapes with figures.
Shi Fu may be the same artist as Shi Hu.
Auction records:
New York, 2 June 1988, *The Spirits of Hexi (the Western River)* (ink on paper, 26 1/4 x 31 1/4 ins / 66.7 x 79.5 cm) USD 1,320. Hong Kong, 16 Jan 1989, *Girl and Tree* (handscroll, ink and colour on paper, 27 1/4 x 38 1/2 ins / 69 x 98 cm) HKD 16,500. Hong Kong, 30 March 1992, *Nudes and Lotus* (mounted handscroll, ink and diluted colour on paper, 26 1/2 x 52 3/4 ins / 67.3 x 134 cm) HKD 88,000. Hong Kong, 28 Sept 1992, *Prayers for Good Fortune* (1991, three parts, ink and colour on paper, each 56 1/4 x 29 1/2 ins / 143 x 75 cm) HKD 220,000.

SHI FUGUO
Chinese, 20th century.
Born 1935, in Jiangsu Province.
Painter, watercolourist. Urban landscapes.
Shi Fuguo graduated from the Suzhou painting academy in 1954. The winner of many awards, he is an honorary member of the Shanghai watercolour society.
Auction records:
Hong Kong, 30 Oct 1995, *Houses in the City* (1995, watercolour on paper, 40 x 30 ins / 101.6 x 76.2 cm) HKD 17,250.

SHI HU
Chinese, 20th century.
Born 1942, in Xushi (Hebei Province).
Painter. Figures, genre scenes, landscapes with figures.
Auction records:
Hong Kong, 15 Nov 1989, *Album of Figures* (six double sheets, three in ink on paper and three in ink and colour on paper, each 17 3/4 x 27 1/4 ins / 45 x 69 cm) HKD 46,200. Hong Kong, 15 Nov 1990, *Two Figures* (ink and touches of colour on paper, 40 x 39 3/4 ins / 101.5 x 101.2 cm) HKD 55,000. Hong Kong, 2 May 1991, *Spring* (ink on paper, 46 x 56 ins / 117 x 142.5 cm) HKD 59,400. Hong Kong, 30 April 1992, *Abstract*

Figures (ink and diluted colour on paper, 32 x 20 1/2 ins / 81 x 52 cm) HKD 55,000. HONG KONG, 22 March 1993, *Spring Day* (ink and colour on paper, hanging scroll, 54 x 27 1/4 ins / 137 x 69.5 cm) HKD 103,500. HONG KONG, 29 April 1993, *Figures* (ink and colour on paper, 22 1/2 x 23 ins / 57 x 58.5 cm) HKD 29,900. SINGAPORE, 12 Oct 2003, *Three Balinese Girls* (acrylic on paper, 34 x 27 ins / 87 x 69 cm) SGD 18,000. SINGAPORE, 3 April 2004, *Laying a Rainbow* (oil on canvas, 28 x 20 ins / 70 x 51 cm) SGD 15,000.

SHI JIANG, or Shih Chiang, sobriquet: Ruming, style name: Juzhai Daoren
Chinese, 14th century.
Born in Yongqing (Hebei Province).
Active during the first half of the 14th century.
Painter. Figures, birds, landscapes, flowers.

SHI KE, or Shih K'o, sobriquet: Zizhuan
Chinese, 10th century.
Born in Zhendu (Sichuan Province).
Painter. Religious subjects, figures, scenes with figures.

Little is known of the life of this artist, a self-styled *ch'an* Buddhist adept whose extravagant behaviour has passed into legend. According to one document from the first half of the 9th century, Shi Ke was a robust, straightforward fellow who liked to shock people and who preferred to paint rough, jolly rustics. Another text describes him as having absolutely no respect for rules and models. It describes his painting as hideously bizarre - unworthy of attention from civilised people. His work - or at least copies of it - so roundly condemned by the Chinese literati found ready acceptance, even deep appreciation, in Japan. The *Xuanhe huapu* (the Xuanhe or imperial Song painting catalogue) relates that in 965 he was asked to paint murals in the Xiangguo-si temple in the capital, Kaifeng, and to mark the occasion was offered a post in the imperial painting academy, but that he declined the offer and decided instead to return to his home village, dying on the way.

Shi Ke is known as a painter of Buddhist and Taoist figures and one of the most important advocates of monochrome ink painting in the *yipin* (unconstrained) style often associated with *ch'an* painting. Two works are attributed to him (*Two Patriarchs Putting their Spirits in Harmony*), in the National Museum, Tokyo, but they are probably not from the period of the Five Dynasties but rather faithful later copies. Whatever their real age, they are a valuable document of the prickly graphic style of the *yipin* manner as applied to thoroughbred *ch'an* characters. One of the sages, head squat on his shoulders, leans against a tiger that lies sleepily on the ground. The animal's fur and the monk's robes are drawn with a bamboo or frayed straw brush that produces a sort of shredded line, which in turn provokes something like a kinaesthetic sensation as if one can actually feel the painter's hand scratching the paper, halting at an ink mark, pouncing forward, pushing down with his wrist to splay the fibres of the brush out and draw in the stripes on the tiger's skin. These pictures give an unmistakable impression of immediate, spontaneous creation entirely in keeping with the theory of *ch'an* painting.

BIBLIOGRAPHY:

Cahill, James, *Chinese Painting*, Skira, Geneva, 1960.

MUSEUMS AND GALLERIES:

TOKYO (National Mus.): *Two Patriarchs Putting their Spirits in Harmony* (attributed).

SHI LIN, or Shih Lin, sobriquets: Yuxian, Yuruo
Chinese, 16th century.
Born in Nanjing.
Active c. 1520.
Painter. Landscapes.

Shi Lin painted landscapes in the style of the masters of the Yuan dynasty (1276-1368).

SHI LU, formerly known as Feng Yayan
Chinese, 20th century.
Born 1919, in Renshou County (Sichuan Province); died 1982.
Painter. Landscapes, animals, flowers, fruit.

Shi Lu made political woodcuts and *nianhua* (New Years prints) during the Sino-Japanese war. He returned to traditional ink painting in 1960s. He was elected chairman of Shaanxi artists' association after 1957. Persecuted during the Cultural Revolution, he was sentenced to death but escaped from custody and wandered the Qinling Mountains, according to biographers. When the political climate allowed, he returned to Xi'an.

BIBLIOGRAPHY:

Andrews, Julia F., *Painters and Politics in the People's Republic of China: 1949-1979*, University of California Press, Berkeley, 1994. *Collectors' Choice: The Genius of Shi Lu*, Cat Street Galleries, Hong Kong, 1994. Yang Xin, et al., *Three Thousand Years of Chinese Painting*, Yale University Press, 1997.

AUCTION RECORDS:

HONG KONG, 12 Jan 1987, *Hibiscus and Ducks* (ink and colour, hanging scroll, 70 1/2 x 25 1/2 ins / 179 x 64.8 cm) HKD 400,000. NEW YORK, 2 June 1988, *Loquats* (ink on paper, hanging scroll, 58 1/2 x 15 3/4 ins / 148.5 x 40 cm) USD 16,500. HONG KONG, 17 Nov 1988, *Dream Flowers* (ink and colour on paper, 67 x 24 1/2 ins / 170 x 62 cm) HKD 440,000. HONG KONG, 16 Jan 1989, *Peonies* (ink and colour on paper, hanging scroll, 26 1/4 x 13 3/4 ins / 66.6 x 35 cm) HKD 88,000. HONG KONG, 18 May 1989, *Lotus and Memories* (ink and colour, 55 x 27 1/2 ins / 139.7 x 70 cm) HKD 330,000; *Snow on Mount Emei* (ink and colour on paper, hanging scroll, 48 x 19 1/4 ins / 121 x 48.8 cm) HKD 1,650,000. HONG KONG, 15 Nov 1989, *Twilight Mountains* (1959, ink and colour on paper, 52 3/4 x 31 1/4 ins / 134 x 79.3 cm) HKD 506,000. NEW YORK, 4 Dec 1989, *Snow on Mount Hua* (ink and colour on paper, hanging scroll, 71 1/2 x 34 1/2 ins / 181.5 x 87.5 cm) USD 88,000. HONG KONG, 15 Nov 1990, *Pines on Mount Hua* (1972, ink on paper, hanging scroll, 59 1/4 x 26 3/4 ins / 150.5 x 68 cm) HKD 726,000. HONG KONG, 2 May 1991, *Calligraphy* (ink on paper, hanging scroll, 52 x 25 1/2 ins / 132 x 65 cm) HKD 110,000. NEW YORK, 25 Nov 1991, *Peonies* (ink and colour on paper, 35 3/4 x 19 1/2 ins / 90.8 x 49.5 cm) USD 8,800. HONG KONG, 30 March 1992, *Girl Gathering Mulberry Leaves* (ink and colour on paper, handscroll, 26 x 20 1/4 ins / 66 x 51.2 cm) HKD 792,000; *Mount Hua* (ink and colour on paper, hanging scroll, 96 3/4 x 41 3/4 ins / 246 x 106 cm) HKD 1,100,000. HONG KONG, 28 Sept 1992, *Pomegranates* (ink and colour on paper, hanging scroll, 42 3/4 x 39 ins / 108.8 x 98.8 cm) HKD 132,000; *Plum Blossom* (ink and colour on paper, hanging scroll, 38 x 20 1/2 ins / 96.6 x 51.8 cm) HKD 154,000. HONG KONG, 4 Nov 1996, *Red Flowers* (1965, ink and colour on paper, hanging scroll, 26 x 20 1/4 ins / 66 x 51.5 cm) HKD 276,000. HONG KONG, 28 April 2003, *Mother and Daughter* (ink and colour, 11 x 11 ins / 27 x 27 cm) HKD 90,000. HONG KONG, 27 Oct 2003, *Flowers in Bloom* (ink, hanging scroll, 49 x 26 ins / 125 x 67 cm) HKD 260,000. HONG KONG, 26 April 2004, *Lotus* (ink and colour, hanging scroll, 26 x 26 ins / 66 x 65 cm) HKD 120,000. HONG KONG, 26 April 2004, *Plum Blossoms at West Lake* (ink and colour, hanging scroll, 31 x 21 ins / 80 x 54 cm) HKD 200,000.

SHI LU, or Shih Lu
Chinese, 20th century.
Draughtsman (including ink), wood engraver. Scenes with figures.

Shi Lu was a wood engraver with a meticulous, realist yet not unoriginal style who did propaganda work in keeping with the great ideological themes of his time.

BIBLIOGRAPHY:
Yonezawa, Yoshiho/Kawakita, Michiaki, *Arts of China: Paintings in Chinese Collections-New Collections*, Kodansha, Tokyo, 1970.

AUCTION RECORDS:
HONG KONG, 30 Oct 1995, *Three Figures* (1963, ink and colour on paper, 17 1/4 x 12 1/4 ins / 44 x 31 cm) HKD 34,500.

SHI PU, or Shih P'u, sobriquet: Zibo
Chinese, 18th century.
Born in Qiantang (Zhejiang Province).
Active c. 1740.
Painter.

Shi Pu painted landscapes, bamboo and rocks in the style of the great Yuan masters.

SHI QING, or Shih Ch'ing, perhaps known as Rongyang
Chinese, 13th - 14th century.
Active during the Yuan dynasty (1279-1368).
Painter.

Shi Qing is not listed in the official artist biographies. However, he was probably a monk painter whose style was fairly close to that of Tan Zhirui (active early in the 14th century).

SHI QIREN
Chinese, 20th - 21st century.
Born 1946.
Painter. Figures, portraits.

Shi Qiren graduated from the college of art of Shanghai University, where he worked in the oil painting department. He won the bronze medal at the national art exhibition and is associate professor at the Shanghai oil painting and sculpture research centre.

AUCTION RECORDS:
HONG KONG, 30 Oct 1995, *Portrait of Du Fu* (oil on canvas, 69 1/2 x 70 ins / 176.5 x 178 cm) HKD 115,000.

SHI RUI, or Shih Jui, sobriquet: Yiming
Chinese, 15th century.
Born in Qiantang (Zhejiang Province).
Active during the first half of the 15th century.
Painter.

Shi Rui painted landscapes, buildings and figures in the style of Sheng Mao (active from about 1310 to 1360). He was summoned to the imperial palace during the Xuande period (1426-1435). Some of his works are preserved in Japanese museums, such as: *Landscape with Palatial Buildings*, a signed work in the Nezu Museum, Tokyo, and *Ning Qi Mounting an Ox* and *Ni Kuan Working in His Field*, a pair of hanging scrolls in colour on silk, each with the seal of the artist and accompanied by contemporary poems, now in the Tokugawa Museum, Nagoya. These works are listed on the register of important cultural properties.

MUSEUMS AND GALLERIES:
NAGOYA (Tokugawa Art Mus.): *Ning Qi Mounting an Ox*; *Ni Kuan Working in His Field* - TOKYO (Nezu Institute of Fine Arts): *Landscape with Palatial Buildings*.

SHI RUYUAN
Chinese, 20th century.
Born 1944, in Shanxi Province.
Painter. Landscapes with figures, animals, flowers.

Shi Ruyuan works in Chinese colours and with ink on paper. His favourite subjects are birds and flowers.

BIBLIOGRAPHY:
Peintres traditionnels de la République populaire de Chine, exhibition catalogue, Gal. Daniel Malingue, Paris, 1980.

SHI SE, or Shih Se, style name: Nian
Chinese, 17th century.
Active during the second half of the 17th century.
Painter.

Shi Se was Prince Yu, a cousin of the Qing emperor Shunzhi (1644-1661). He painted landscapes in the style of the great masters of Yuan.

MUSEUMS AND GALLERIES:
TAIPEI (National Palace Mus.): *Summer Landscape* (1682, signed and dated).

SHI YANJIE, or Shih Yen-chieh, sobriquet: Ruizi
Chinese, 17th century.
Born in Shaoxing (Zhejiang Province).
Active at the beginning of the Qing dynasty, during the second half of the 17th century.
Painter. Plants.

Shi Yanjie painted bamboo in ink.

MUSEUMS AND GALLERIES:
LONDON (British Mus.): *Bamboo* (ink, after Wu Zhen, signed).

SHI YUAN, or Shih Yüan
Chinese, 18th century.
Born in Yangzhou (Jiangsu Province).
Active c. 1770.
Painter. Animals (donkeys).

Shi Yuan was a famous donkey painter known popularly as Donkey Shi (Shi Luerh).

MUSEUMS AND GALLERIES:
STOCKHOLM (Nationalmus.): *Two Men on Donkeys* (1774, signed and dated).

SHI YUNYU, or Shih Yün-yü, sobriquet: Zhiru, style names: Zhuotang, Zhutang
Chinese, 18th - 19th century.
Born 1756, in Suzhou (Jiangsu Province); died 1837.
Painter.

Shi Yunyu is known as a bamboo painter. He was also a writer and poet.

SHI ZHONG, or Shih Chung, real name: Xu Duanben, sobriquet: Tingzhi, style name: Chiweng
Chinese, 15th - 16th century.
Born 1437, in Nanjing; died c. 1517.
Painter.

Shi Zhong was a friend of Shen Zhou (1427-1509). He painted landscapes in the style of the great masters of the Yuan dynasty.

MUSEUMS AND GALLERIES:
BOSTON (MFA): *Winter Landscape* (dated 1504, ink on paper, handscroll, poem and two seals of the artist) - COLOGNE (Mus. für Ostasiatische Kunst): *Fisherman in Winter Landscape* (signed and dated 1506, ink on silk, handscroll, poem and colophon by the artist, four seals of the artist, two collector's seals) - TAIPEI (National Palace Mus.): *Landscape after Huang Gongwang* (signed and dated 1504, poem and colophon by the artist).

SHI-TSENG. See **CHEN HENGKE**

SHIBA KOKAN. See **KOKAN**

SHIBA SHUN. See **KOKAN**

SHIBAKUNI, artist name: Saikotei
Japanese, 19th century.
Active in the Osaka area c. 1821-1826.
Print artist.

SHIBANOV, Michail or Mihaïl.
See **CHIBANOV Mikhail**

SHIBUTSU, real name: Obuko Gyo, given name: Temmin, childhood name: Ryutaro, artist names: Sobei, Shibutsu, Kozan Sho-oku, Shiseido
Japanese, 18th - 19th century.
Born 1766, in Hitachi (Ibaragi Prefecture); died 1837, in Edo, now Tokyo.
Painter.

Shibutsu was a Nanga School (literati) painter and a friend of Buncho (1763-1840). He is also known as a poet.

SHICHIRO, Enjoji

Japanese, 20th - 21st century.
Born 1950, in Kita Kyushu (Fukuoka Prefecture).
Active in Spain from 1974.
Painter. Still-lifes.

Shichiro Enjoji studied painting in Japan until 1973 and moved to Barcelona the following year. In works such as *Transformer* or *Three Pears on a Plate*, he depicts objects using their distinctive lines of force. Using as his basis a fixed reticule, he develops a more or less elaborate system of small rectangles that he sometimes transforms into lozenges or triangles to the extent that some of his canvases reach a point of total abstraction from the aspects of reality on which they are based. In this respect, Shichiro's approach is reminiscent of Marinetti's dynamism.

He took part in group shows in 1977 at the Basel International Fair; in 1980 at the 3rd biennale of contemporary painting in Barcelona; in 1981 at the Galerie Étienne Causans, Paris; in 1982 at Arco 82, Madrid; in Tarragona; in 1985 at the Sala de la Caixa, Barcelona; in 1985 at the Galería Sébastien Petit, Lérida; in 1988 at Arco 88, Madrid; at the Sala de la Caja, Madrid; and in Barcelona. He has also had a number of one-man shows, including in 1977, 1980, 1982 at the Galería Trece, Barcelona; in 1981 at the Galería Collage, Madrid; at the Fundación Miró, Barcelona; in 1986 at the Galería Maeght, Barcelona. He won the Joan Miró international drawing prize in 1979.

BIBLIOGRAPHY:
Catálogo nacionál de arte contemporaneo 1990-1991, Ibérico 2Mil, Barcelona, 1990-1991.

SHIELDS, Alan

American, 20th century.
Born 1944, in Harrington (Kansas).
Painter (mixed media), engraver.

Alan Shields studied at Kansas State University and the University of Maine Theatre Workshop. He was awarded a Guggenheim study scholarship. His works show great, almost spectacular freedom of craftsmanship. The materials he uses are as varied as they are new, including canvas, wood, paint of all kinds, ribbons, strings of beads and necklaces. While they include grids, pyramids and circular works, the structures are often complex and rarely permit a single head-on view. They are more like woven craftwork than paintings and comprise brightly coloured sections that can only be read in the whole, and therefore the whole work can only be perceived mentally. His creations refer to primitivism and allusions. Borrowings from earlier civilizations, particularly the American Indian civilization, are obvious but intended as out-dated inclusions. Through the natural allure of the simplicity of the craftsmanship, Shields' works can appear to be an ironic parody of American Minimalist austerity or the later stages of Italian arte povera. in France, other artists in the Support-Surface group exploit or exploited the weaving technique, but in the location of his inspiration Shields remains typically American.

The many collective exhibitions in which he has participated include: Paula Cooper Gallery, New York, 1968, where he bacame a frequent exhibitor; *New Acquisitions*, Whitney Museum, New York, 1969, another place where he later exhibited frequently; *Recent Acquisitions*, Guggenheim Museum, New York, 1970, and frequently after that; *Paperworks*, Museum of Modern Art, New York, 1970; Documenta V, Kassel, 1972; 8th Biennale, Paris, 1973; *Soho Scene*, Albright-Knox Gallery, Buffalo, 1975. After his first solo exhibition at the Paula Cooper Gallery, New York, in 1969, followed by others at the same gallery, he has held many others, including: Janie C. Lee Gallery, Dallas, 1970 and 1971; Cleveland, 1971; Galerie Sonnabend, Paris, 1971; Museum of Contemporary Art, Chicago, 1973; Contemporary Arts Museum, Houston, 1973; Musée d'Art et d'Industrie, St-Étienne, 1973; Galerie Daniel Templon, Paris, 1975; as well as Milan, San Francisco, Chicago and Madison.

BIBLIOGRAPHY:
Abadie, Daniel, '*Alan Shields*' in *Art Press* n° 20, periodical, Paris, September-October 1975. Ceysson, Bernard, *Alan Shields*, exhibition catalogue, Musée d'Art et d'Industrie, St-Étienne, 1976 (good documentation).

MUSEUMS AND GALLERIES:
NEW YORK (MoMA) - NEW YORK (Solomon R. Guggenheim Mus.) - NEW YORK (Whitney Mus. of American Art).

AUCTION RECORDS:
NEW YORK, 22 March 1979, *My Ass Hurts* (1973, painting and canvas, 30 x 30 ins / 76.2 x 76.2 cm) USD 1,800. NEW YORK, 21 May 1983, *Untitled* (mixed media and collage/paper, 20 1/2 x 20 1/2 ins / 52 x 52 cm) USD 1,600. NEW YORK, 7 June 1984, *J. & K.* (1972, acrylic and netting/canvas, 108 x 255 ins / 274.3 x 647.8 cm) USD 6,000. NEW YORK, 27 Feb 1990, *Frank P. Biggs (Prison Bars)* (1970, acrylic/canvas and threaded glass beads, 122 x 56 1/2 ins / 310 x 143.8 cm) USD 3,300. NEW YORK, 5 May 1994, *Untitled* (1970, acrylic/canvas and threaded wooden beads, 72 x 108 ins / 182.9 x 274.3 cm) USD 5,463. LOS ANGELES, 14 Dec 1999, *Moon over Miame* (acrylic on canvas with threaded wooden beads, 82 x 82 ins / 208 x 208 cm) USD 5,500. PARIS, 26 March 2003, *Come On Down Billy* (painted fabric, 83 x 126 ins / 211 x 320 cm) EUR 6,000.

SHIELDS, Emma Barbee

American, 19th - 20th century.
Died 16 January 1912, in New York.
Painter.

Emma Barbee Shields was active in Texas and, after 1893, New York.

SHIELDS, Frederic James

British, 19th - 20th century.
Born 14 March 1833, in Hartlepool; died 26 February 1911, in Merton (Surrey).
Painter (including gouache), watercolourist, draughtsman, illustrator, lithographer. Historical subjects, religious subjects, allegorical subjects, figures, genre scenes, interiors with figures. Church decoration.

Frederic Shields was apprenticed to a lithographer, and later became a member of the Royal Society of Painters in Watercolours. He began his career as an illustrator, contributing to the *Sunday Magazine, Once a Week, Punch*. He also illustrated a number of literary works: Daniel Defoe's *A Journal of the Plague Year* in 1862; Bunyan's *Pilgrim's Progress*. He also contributed to the illustration of *The Greyt Eggshibishun; Touches of Nature*. His painting showed the influence of the Pre-Raphaelites, and his last work (1888-1910), an ambitious mural cycle, expresses an overwrought spirituality indicative of his highly-strung and religious temperament. Designed for the chapel of the Ascension in Hyde Park Place in Bayswater, London, the murals were commissioned by Mrs Russell Gurney and designed by Herbert Percy Horne. The complex iconographic programme illustrates major events in the life of Christ and the Apostles, with the overall scheme and style reflecting the art of the High Renaissance. The murals were destroyed in World War II.

BIBLIOGRAPHY:

AUCTION RECORDS:
LONDON, 25 Sept 1979, '*With drooping lids veiling her clean sweet eyes and heavy fall of golden hair unfilleted*' (gouache, 12 x 15 ins / 30.5 x 38 cm) GBP 450. LONDON, 12 July 1984, *William Blake's Workroom at 3 Fountain Court, The Strand* (pencil and grey wash, 9 x 12 3/4 ins / 23 x 32.5 cm) GBP 1,900. LONDON, 29 Oct 1985, *The Peddlar* (1864, watercolour and

pencil, 21 x 17 1/4 ins / 53.5 x 43.5 cm) GBP 3,000. NEW YORK, 31 Oct 1985, *Mary Magdalene* (oil on canvas, 41 1/2 x 19 ins / 105.5 x 48.2 cm) USD 35,000. ENGHIEN-LES-BAINS, 25 Oct 1987, *Mary Magdalene* (1879, watercolour heightened with gouache, 19 1/2 x 11 1/2 ins / 49.5 x 29.5 cm) FRF 54,000. LONDON, 10 March 1995, *Fairy Tale* (1901, oil on canvas, 14 3/4 x 10 ins / 37.5 x 25.5 cm) GBP 2,875.

SHIELDS, Thomas W.
American, 19th - 20th century.
Born 1849 or 1850, in St Johns (New Brunswick), to English parents; died 1920.
Painter. History painting, genre scenes.

Thomas W. Shields was taught by Lemuel Everett Wilmarth in New York and J. Léon Gérome, Carolus Duran and Jules Lefebvre in Paris. He settled in Brooklyn.

MUSEUMS AND GALLERIES:
BROOKLYN, NY: *Mozart Singing his Last Requiem.*

AUCTION RECORDS:
NEW YORK, 17 April 1974, *Mozart Singing his Last Requiem,* USD 3,750. NEW YORK, 22 June 1984, *Mozart Singing his Last Requiem* (1882, oil on canvas, 57 1/4 x 79 1/4 ins / 145.4 x 201.3 cm) USD 8,000. NEW YORK, 24 Jan 1989, *Private Concert* (1887, oil on panel, 8 1/4 x 11 1/2 ins / 21.2 x 29.2 cm) USD 990.

SHIELDS, William
British, 19th century.
Born 1808; died 1852.
Painter. Landscapes with figures, animals.

AUCTION RECORDS:
LONDON, 15 Nov 1991, *Coastal Landscape with a Pony and Two Dogs, a Landseer and a Newfoundland* (oil on canvas, 53 x 75 1/4 ins / 134.6 x 191.1 cm) GBP 7,700.

SHIELLS, Sarah
British, 18th century.
Painter. Portraits.

SHIELS, William
British, 19th century.
Born 1785, in Berwickshire; died 27 August 1857, in Edinburgh.
Painter. Genre scenes, animals.

William Shiels worked in Edinburgh and exhibited at the Royal Academy on a number of occasions between 1813 and 1852.

AUCTION RECORDS:
PERTH, 15 April 1980, *Back from Market* (oil on canvas, 35 1/2 x 47 ins / 90 x 118.5 cm) GBP 3,300. NEW YORK, 11 Feb 1981, *Landscape with Horse and Spaniels* (oil on canvas, 53 1/4 x 75 ins / 135 x 190.5 cm) USD 7,000. LONDON, 26 July 1985, *Ulysses Meeting his Father* (1808, oil on canvas, 50 1/4 x 40 ins / 127.6 x 101.6 cm) GBP 1,900. NEW YORK, 5 June 1986, *Landscape with Pony and Spaniels* (oil on canvas, 53 1/4 x 75 ins / 135 x 190.5 cm) USD 6,000. GLASGOW, 21 Aug 1996, *The Broken Pitcher* (oil on canvas, 12 x 14 ins / 30.5 x 35.5 cm) GBP 1,380. LONDON, 30 Aug 2000, *Fisherman's Cottage, Musselburgh* (1851, oil on canvas, 30 x 36 ins / 76 x 92 cm) GBP 5,000. LONDON, 21 March 2001, *Portrait of Girl in a Landscape, Wearing a White Dress* (oil on canvas, 26 x 21 ins / 65 x 53 cm) GBP 1,800.

SHIERBECK, J. C. See **SCHIERBECK**

SHIERCLIFFE, Edward
British, 18th century.
Active in Bristol between 1765 and 1786.
Miniaturist, enameller.

SHIGANAGA. See **NISHIMURA Shiganaga**

SHIGEFUSA, real name: Terai Shigefusa, artist names: Sesshosai, Shosen, Naofusa
Japanese, 18th century.
Born in Osaka.
Active c. 1740-1760.
Illustrator.

SHIGEFUSA, artist name: Shugansai, personal name: Katsunosuke, given name: Yoshino
Japanese, 19th century.
Print artist.

Shigefusa was active in Osaka between 1829 and 1850.

SHIGEHARU, real name: Yamaguchi Yasuhide or Yamaguchi Kunishige, original name: Takigawa, first artist names: Nagasaki (1821), Kiyosai, Kiyotei, Baigansai, given name: Yamaguchi, artist names: Ryusai (1827-1829 and 1833-1835), Gyokuryutei (1830-1832), Gyokuryusai, childhood names: Yasuhide, Jinjiro
Japanese, 19th century.
Born 1803, in Osaka; died 1853.
Active c. 1821-1841.
Print artist.

SHIGEHIKO, real name: Okamaoto Shigehiko, given names: Gochun, Ichiryusai, childhood name: Sane, artist name: Gokei
Japanese, 19th century.
Born 1808; died 1844.
Active in the Osaka area c. 1850.
Print artist.

SHIGEHIRO, given name: Kikusui, artist names: Shugansai, Shugan, Shuho
Japanese, 19th century.
Active in the Osaka area c. 1865-1878.
Print artist.

SHIGEKATSU, real name: Yamaguchi, artist name: Ukiyo
Japanese, 19th century.
Active in the Osaka area c. 1826.
Print artist.

SHIGEMASA, real name: Kitabatake Shigemasa, given name: Kitao, popular names: Kyugoro, later Sasuke, artist names: Karan, Kosuisai, Tairei, Ichiyosei, Kosuifu, Suiho Itsujin, Hekisui, Kosuiken, Kyukaikyo, Shigureoka Itsumin, Hokusu Dempu, Hokuho
Japanese, 18th - 19th century.
Born 1739; died 1820.
Active in Edo (now Tokyo).
Painter, print artist.

The son of Suharaya Saburobei, an Edo bookseller, Shigemasa studied art from illustrated books. Starting in the 1750s, he designed a number of perspective prints and some *hosoban* (5 x 13 in, 12.5 x 32.5cm) prints of actors and beautiful women, departing from the overwhelming influence that Harunobu had hitherto exercised over this subject-matter and endowing his female figures with realistic, depoeticised expressions. Shigemasa's women stand against plain backgrounds and show off the grace of their bodies and beauty of their clothes quite naturally. He was also a consummate technician. His prints are rare nowadays.

Among illustrated books typical of his work are *Seiro bijin awase sugata kagami* (*A Selection of Beautiful Courtesans before the Mirror*), which he made in 1776 in collaboration with Shunsho. As the founder of the Kitao school, he taught Kitao Masanobu (Sando Kyoden), Masayoshi (Keisai) and Kubo Shunman.

SHIGENAO. See **NOBUKATSU**

SHIGENOBU, real name: Yanagawa Shigenobu, original name: Suzuki, given name: Jubei, artist names: Raito, Kinsai, Reisai, Ushosai
Japanese, 19th century.

Born 1787; died 1832.
Print artist.

SHIGESADA
Japanese, 19th century.
Active in Osaka c. 1830.
Illustrator.
Shigesada illustrated theatre programmes.

SHIGEYOSHI, real name: Hasegawa Shigeyoshi, artist name: Kyosensai
Japanese, 19th century.
Active in Osaka c. 1830.
Print artist.

SHIH CH'ING. See **SHI QING**

SHIH CHIANG. See **SHI JIANG**

SHIH CHUNG. See **SHI ZHONG**

SHIH JUI. See **SHI RUI**

SHIH K'O. See **SHI KE**

SHIH LIN. See **SHI LIN**

SHIH LU. See **SHI LU**

SHIH P'U. See **SHI PU**

SHIH SE. See **SHI SE**

SHIH YEN-CHIEH. See **SHI YANJIE**

SHIH YUAN. See **SHI YUAN**

SHIH YUN-YU. See **SHI YUNYU**

SHIH-T'AO. See **SHITAO**

SHIH-TSU CH'ING. See **QING SHIZU**

SHIHEKI DOJIN. See **KAISEKI**

SHIJAKU, Sali
Albanian, 20th century.
Born 12 March 1933, in Tirana.
Painter, sculptor. Historical subjects, military subjects.
After graduating from the Jordan Misja Arts Lyceum in Tirana in 1954, Sali Shijaku studied from 1957 to 1961 at the academy of arts, Leningrad (now St Petersburg) and the higher institute of art, Tirana (1962). His work, violent, lyrical and passionate, derives its inspiration from revolutionary ideas and depicts action scenes. Among his better known works is *The Hero Vojo Kushi on a Tank*.
MUSEUMS AND GALLERIES:
TIRANA (AG): *Skanderberg's Warrior*; *Vanguard of the 'Vengeance' Partisan Battalion*.

SHIJO. See **IMPO**

SHIKAN, real name: Nakamura Utaemon III
Japanese, 19th century.
Born 1778; died 1838.
Active in Osaka c. 1817.
Actor, print artist.

SHIKANOSUKE, Oka
Japanese, 20th century.
Born 1898, in Tokyo; died 1978.
Also active in France.
Painter. Landscapes.
After graduating from Tokyo fine arts university in 1924, Shikanosuke went to continue his studies in France, remaining there until 1939. He returned to France in 1953 and lived there again from 1959 to 1961. He is the author of two books, *La peinture française* (*French Painting*) and *Les materiaux de la peinture à l'huile* (*The Medium of Oil Painting*).

During his first stay in Paris, he exhibited at the Salon d'Automne, Salon des Indépendants and Salon des Tuileries. While in Japan, he took part in the Japan International Art Exhibition, the 1963 Exhibition of Contemporary Japanese Art in Tokyo and *Masterpieces of Japanese Art*, in conjunction with the Tokyo Olympiad. He has won a number of prizes, including from the ministry of education in 1952; the grand prize for contemporary art in 1956; and the Mainichi Prize in 1957.

SHIKEN, Umekuni, or Bokusen, Ryukosai, Shiosanjin, given name: Taga, artist name: Baikoku
Japanese, 19th century.
Active in Osaka c. 1810-1816.
Print artist.
Shiken was the son of Ryukosai. He is said to have died very young. He is also known as a painter and since one of his artist names, Baikoku, can also be read Umekuni, he may also be the print artist known under this name.

SHIKLER, Aaron
American, 20th - 21st century.
Born 1922, in Brooklyn (New York City).
Painter. Portraits, still-lifes.
Aaron Shikler studied at the Barnes Foundation and the Hans Hofman School. Shikler first obtained a bachelor of Fine Arts and later a Master of Fine Arts from the Tyler School of Art at Temple University. He also studied at the American University in Shrivenham in the United Kingdom. Shikler became an Associate of the National Academy of Design in 1962 and an Academician in 1965.

Shikler is primarily known for his portraits of the Kennedy family and other political figures. His portraits of Jacqueline Kennedy (1970) and Nancy Reagan form part of the White House collection. Jacqueline Kennedy appears in a long white gown against a pale background. As she looks to the side, her dark hair frames her face. Nancy Reagan is shown standing, turned towards the left and looking away from the viewer. She wears a long red dress and is painted against a dark background. In both portraits the emphasis is on the realistic representation of the facial features of the models.
BIBLIOGRAPHY:
Shikler & Levine, Brooklyn Museum, New York, 1971.
MUSEUMS AND GALLERIES:
CHARLOTTE (Mint Museum of Art) - COLUMBUS (The Columbus Museum) - LINCOLN (Shelson Memorial Art Gallery) - MINNEAPOLIS (Frederick R. Weisman AM, University of Minnesota) - NEW BRITAIN (New Britain Museum of American Art) - NEW YORK (Brooklyn Mus.) - NEW YORK (Metropolitan Mus. of Art) - NEW YORK (National Academy of Design Mus.) - SOUTHAMPTON (The Parrish Museum of Art) - WASHINGTON DC (National Portrait Gal.) - WASHINGTON DC (Smithsonian American AM) - WASHINGTON DC (The White House) - WINTERTHUR (Winterthur Museum).
AUCTION RECORDS:
NEW YORK, 24 May 2000, *Study of Jacqueline Kennedy Standing* (1969, pencil, 20 x 15 ins / 51 x 39 cm) USD 5,000. NEW YORK, 13 June 2001, *Sleeping Woman* (1967, pastel on paperboard, 8 x 14 ins / 20 x 36 cm) USD 8,000. NEW YORK, 29 Oct 2002, *Head Study. Seated Female Nude* (1970, one: pencil and red-brown chalk one; the other: oil on paper, 11 x 9 ins / 28 x 23 cm) USD 2,000.

SHIKO, real name: Imamura Jusaburo, artist name: Shiko
Japanese, 20th century.
Born 1880, in Yokohama or Tokyo; died 1916.
Painter. Landscapes.
Shiko studied painting under Matsumoto Fuko, who specialised in historical subjects. In 1914, he crossed China to go to India. He exhibited in shows organised by the imperial art academy and was a member of the Nihon Bijutsu-in (Japan art institute). After completing his studies, he experimented with the use of new techniques to depict traditional subjects in vertical formats with a bold use of space. He would later be influenced by the Impressionists, Van Gogh and Gauguin

before returning towards the end of his life to the more decorative styles of the great Japanese masters Sotatsu (active in about 1630) and Korin (1658-1716).

MUSEUMS AND GALLERIES:

TOKYO (National Mus.): *Eight Views of the Omi River* (1912, colour on paper, hanging scroll); *Sketches from India* (1914).

SHIKO, Watanabe, real name: Watanabe Kyuma, given name: Motome, Sanai, artist names: Shoken, Soshin

Japanese, 18th century.

Born 1683, in Kyoto; died 1755.

Painter.

Watanabe Shiko lived in Kyoto, where he worked in the service of the Konoye family. At first he painted in the Kano School tradition, then in the style of Korin (1658-1716), with whom he studied. Eventually, he would paint in ink and light colour, works much appreciated by Maruyama Okyo (1733-1795).

MUSEUMS AND GALLERIES:

CLEVELAND (MA): *Irises (detail)* (ink and colour on paper).

AUCTION RECORDS:

NEW YORK, 16 Oct 1990, *Chinese Scholars in Landscape* (ink and light colour on gold-leaf on paper, a pair of six-panelled screens, each 59 1/2 x 138 1/4 ins / 151.3 x 351 cm) USD 66,000.

SHIKO MIKUMA. See also **KATEN**

SHILFOX, D.. See **SHELFOX**

SHILLING, Alexander. See **SCHILLING**

SHILLINGOVSKY, Pavel Aleksandrovich, or Chilingovsky

Moldovan, 20th century.

Born 16 February 1887; died 1942.

Painter, engraver.

Pavel Shillinggovsky studied at the academy in St Petersburg where he later taught.

SHIM, Moon-Seup

Korean, 20th century.

Born 1942, in Ch'ong-mo.

Sculptor.

Shim Moon-Seup studied at the Seoul college of fine art and became a teacher at Soodo Women's Teachers College, Seoul. He practised martial arts at a very advanced level. He makes large-scale sculptures using simple forms with great, almost raw simplicity. He worked first in wood for some 10 years, then switched to steel and iron. He also works in terracotta, and juxtaposes these materials. His art may be said to resemble Italian Arte Povera or American Minimalism, but in reality it derives from the Korean tradition of purity of form that in turn comes from Daoism, as witness the title of his exhibition *Opening Up*, which reveals the elemental in all things. He says, 'I try to intervene as little as possible in choosing my subject and even in the act of creating. By limiting the expression of myself to the greatest extent possible I am able to enter into a relationship with the infinite.' The occupation of space to penetrate the universal is not possible without taking the passage of time into account, so Shim works his materials to give them the appearance of ageing, to mark them with the signs of a past that bears within it their future.

He has taken part in numerous group exhibitions, including 1965 to 1972 in Seoul at the national exhibition of Korean art; in 1970 and 1972 in Seoul at the National Museum of Contemporary Art, *Avant garde*; in 1971, 1973 and 1975 at the Paris Biennale; in 1974 at the Seoul Biennale; in 1975 at the São Paulo Biennale and the 9th Paris Biennale; in 1975 and 1995, in Seoul at the National Museum of Contemporary Art, *Seoul School*; in 1976 at the Sydney Biennial; in 1977-1978 in Paris at the 2nd Rencontres Internationales d'Art Contemporain; in 1978, 1980 and 1986 at the National Museum of Modern Art, Seoul; in 1989 and 1992 at the Chicago International Art Exhibition; and in 1994 at the Adelaide Festival.

He has also shown his work in solo exhibitions, including in 1965 in Pusan; in 1972, 1977, 1979, 1982, 1983, 1985, 1989 and 1993 in Tokyo; in 1975, 1980, 1986, 1988, 1990, 1991, 1992, 1993 and 1996 in Seoul; in 1986 in Milan; in 1988 and 1990 in Osaka; in 1989 in Chicago; in 1990 in Hiroshima, Nagoya and Osaka; in 1992 at the Sigma Gallery in New York and at the Galerie Jacqueline Rabouan-Moussion in Paris, which showed him again in 1995, and in 1996, at the Foire Internationale.

BIBLIOGRAPHY:

IXe Biennale de Paris, exhibition catalogue, Idea Books, musée d'Art moderne de la Ville de Paris, Paris, 1975. *Catalogue de la Galerie Hyundai*, Foire internationale d'Art contemporain, Paris, 1995. *Shim Moon-Seup*, exhibition catalogue, Gal. J. Rabouan-Moussion, Paris, Foire internationale d'Art contemporain, Paris, 1996.

MUSEUMS AND GALLERIES:

SEOUL (City Mus. of Art) - SEOUL (NMMA).

SHIMADA, Shizu

Japanese, 20th century.

Born between between 1925 and 1930, in Tokyo.

Painter.

Shizu Shimada studied at Tokyo fine arts university from 1945 to 1949 and lived in Paris in 1958. She paints colourful rhythmic abstracts that during some periods have a lyrical geometric quality.

She has taken part in numerous group exhibitions in Tokyo, including the 1957 Niki Salon, where she won first prize, and the National Exhibition of Young Japanese Artists. Abroad, she took part in the 1965 Salon Comparaisons, in an exhibition at the Dijon Museum and regularly in Paris - in 1959-1960 at the Salon des Indépendants, in 1962-1963 at the Salon des Jeunes Peintres, from 1962 at the Salon d'Automne, in 1962 in *Japanese Painters in Paris* at the Musée Galliéra, and from 1963 at the Salon de Mai. She has also had a number of solo exhibitions - in 1964 in Paris, in 1965 in Luxembourg and twice in Tokyo.

SHIMAMARU

Japanese, 19th century.

Active in Osaka c. 1830.

Print artist.

SHIMAMURA, Homei

Japanese, 19th - 20th century.

Sculptor.

Shimamura Homei was active in Tokyo. As part of the 1900 Exposition Universelle, he exhibited at the Salon des Artistes Français in Paris, where he received an honourable mention.

SHIMAMURA, Kanzan

Japanese, 19th - 20th century.

Painter.

Shimamura Kanzan painted on silk. He was active in Tokyo. As part of the 1900 Exposition Universelle, he exhibited at the Salon des Artistes Français in Paris, where he won a bronze medal.

SHIMIGISHI

Japanese, 20th century.

Painter, lithographer. Flowers.

Shimigishi worked in Paris and took part in various group shows, including *De Bonnard à Baselitz: Dix Ans d'enrichissements du cabinet des estampes 1978-1988* (*From Bonnard to Baselitz: A Decade of Acquisitions by the Prints Collection 1978-1988*) at the Bibliothèque Nationale in Paris in 1992.

Museums and Galleries:
Paris (BNF, Prints Collection): *Flowers I* (c. 1980, lithograph).

SHIMIZU, Momo
Japanese, 20th century.
Born 1944.
Print artist.

Shimizu Momo took part in various group exhibitions from 1969, including in 1969-1970, in Kyoto, *The Independents*; in 1973, in Tokyo, with the Print group; in 1974, in Tokyo, at the Japanese Print Society, and *Art japonais d'aujourd'hui* (*Japanese Art Today*) at the Musée d'Art Contemporain in Montreal.

SHIMIZU, Toshi
Japanese, 20th century.
Born 1896; died 1945.
Painter.

Auction records:
New York, 12 Oct 1989, *Building Site* (oil on canvas, 26½ x 38 ins / 67.5 x 96.5 cm) USD 71,500.

SHIMOMURA, Kanzan, given name: Seizaburo
Japanese, 19th - 20th century.
Born 10 April 1873, in Wakayama; died 10 May 1930, in Tokyo.
Painter. Historical subjects.

Kanzan was the scion of a family of musicians and seal carvers. He moved to Tokyo with his parents in 1881. At the age of nine, he began to learn the techniques of painting with Fujimura Tsuneoki, who quickly arranged for him to go into the studio of Kano Hogai in 1882. Through Hogai, he became a pupil of Hashimoto Gaho in 1886. Three years later, he was admitted to the Tokyo School of Fine Arts, and was appointed as an assistant when he graduated in 1894. By then he had already begun to exhibit. In 1896-1897 he won the first prize at the Japan Painting Society exhibition and one of his works was acquired by the State to be shown at the Exposition Universelle in Paris in 1900. In February 1903, he was sent to Britain with a scholarship to study watercolour techniques. On this occasion, he visited France, Belgium, Holland, Germany and Italy, expressing his interest in the whole of Western painting. From 1917, he was among the number of artists in the circle of the imperial family, and he became a member of the Imperial Academy of Fine Arts. In 1922, he became an associate member of the Salon de la Société Nationale des Beaux-Arts, in Paris, to which he continued to send paintings after the Exposition Universelle, in 1928 receiving an award.

In the final years of the century, he met the American Ernest Fenollosa, who persuaded him to return to the classics. Following his former master Kano Hogai, Kanzan would become one of the important representatives of the classical tradition in the modern era. Abandoning the extremely detailed style of his early works, which depicted historical subjects, he turned to the more impressionistic *morotai* or boneless painting (i.e. wihout outlines), in which the emphasis was on the contrast of light and shade. To him, the problem of colour was fundamental. He founded a study community in Izura, a village north of Tokyo, which he compared to the Barbizon group. The new style, which he dubbed *shikiteki motsu kotsu* (boneless colour), was thus a return to a more traditional genre although overlain with impressionism. He developed steadily as an artist, not permitting himself to be influenced by contemporary movements. In what he called *intai gafu* a relatively academic genre, he used traditional techniques, not being able to reject contours entirely because of his use of colour. Kanzan's restrained and unaudacious style has remained part of the legacy of Japanese classicism.

Bibliography:
Four Artists, Kanzan Shimomura, Aimitsu, Morie Ogiwara, Heihachi Hashimoto, exhibition catalogue, National Museum of Modern Art, Tokyo, 1955. Shin'ichi Nagai, Sentaro Namba, *Kanzan Shimomura, Gyokudo Kawai*, Shueisha, Tokyo, 1976.

Museums and Galleries:
Tokyo (National Mus).

SHIMOMURA, Ryonosuke
Japanese, 20th century.
Born 1923, in Osaka; died 1998.
Painter.

Shimomura Ryonosuke studied at the Kyoto art academy. In 1949 he founded the Real Pan Art Society. In about 1960 he travelled to Europe and India.

SHIMOTANI, Chiharu
Japanese, 20th century.
Born 1934.
Print artist.

Shimotani Chiharu has exhibited at varioius international group shows, including in 1972 and 1973 at the 7th and 8th exhibition of the Japan Art Festival Association; in 1973 at the São Paulo Biennale and in Tokyo and Kyoto at the International Print Biennale; in 1974 in Bradford, England, at the 4th International Print Biennale; and *Art japonais d'aujourd'hui* (*Japanese Art Today*) at the Musée d'Art Contemporain in Montreal.

SHIMOZAWA, Kihachiro
Japanese, 20th century.
Born 1901, in Aomori Prefecture; died 1984.
Print artist.

Shimozawa Kihachiro started exhibiting in 1924 at the imperial painting academy exhibitions in Tokyo, then with the national academy (Kokuga-kai), of which he was a member, winning prizes in 1931, 1933 and 1940, and with the Japan Print Society, of which he was also a member. He won the Van Gogh prize in 1954. He also exhibited at the 1957 International Print Biennale. He is the author of a book entitled *Engraving Techniques*.

SHIN, Moon
Korean, 20th century.
Born 1923, in Masan.
Sculptor.

Shin carves rare and hard wood into hollows and bulges reminiscent of the movement of waterfalls.

Auction records:
Paris, 2 April 1990, *Totem* (rosewood, h. 19½ ins / 49.5 cm) FRF 6,900.

SHIN, Soo Hee
Korean, 20th century.
Born 1944.
Painter.

Shin Soo Hee trained at the fine arts faculty of Seoul National University from 1962 to 1966, and in the monumental art section of the École des Beaux-Arts, Paris, from 1966 to 1968. In 1983 and 1984, she worked in the monotype studio at Stanford University in California. She works in Seoul and Paris.

Her work, almost always gestural rather than geometric, explores a vast range of possibilities within the realm of Abstraction but most often returns to abstract landscape. She has said of her own work that the spontaneity of her gestures, which ultimately derives from calligraphy, seeks to create a spiritual space, and that the colour blue, a constant element in her work, symbolises the vastness of the universal human spirit.

She has taken part in various group exhibitions, including one in 1993 at Levallois (Hauts-de-Seine) and has shown regularly in one-woman shows in Seoul. In 1968 she painted a mural for the Centre de la Jeunesse at Neuilly-sur-Seine.

Bibliography:

Shin Soo-Hee: Blue Paintings, exhibition catalogue, Gall. S. M., Seoul, 1995.

SHIN, Sung Hy

Korean, 20th - 21st century.
Born 1948.
Painter.

Shin Sung Hy studied at the Seoul art school in 1971. He took part in group shows in 1977 at the 4th India Triennale; in 1980 in Paris at the Whanki Foundation; in 1983 in Paris at the Salon de Mai; in Tokyo, Osaka and other cities in Japan; in 1985 at the 13th São Paulo Biennale; in 1987 in Seoul in *Artists of the 1980s* at the Hyundai Gallery; in 1989 and 1991 in Seoul in the Seoul Art Fair at the Hyundai Gallery; in 1995 in Paris at the international contemporary art fair, presented by the Hyundai Gallery, Seoul. He has also had a number of solo exhibitions, including: 1982 Los Angeles; 1988 Seoul, National Museum of Contemporary Art; 1988, 1994 Seoul, Hyundai Gallery; 1992 New York, Sigma Gallery; 1997 Paris, Galerie Baudoin-Lebon.

Bibliography:

Sung Hy Shin, exhibition catalogue, Hyundai Gallery, Seoul, 1995.

SHINAGAWA, Takumi

Japanese, 20th century.
Born 1908, in Niigata Prefecture.
Engraver, draughtsman, photographer.
Sosaku Hanga.
First Thursday Society.

Shinagawa Takumi first studied jewellery at the Tokyo industrial art college before becoming a pupil of Semmin Uno and Koshiro Onchi. His drawings and woodcuts show a constant, original study of his art. He experimented with a variety of media, including photography. Drawing inspiration from the deep colours of traditional *ukiyo-e* woodblock prints, he made his own colours in order to achieve even greater intensity.

He took part in various group shows, including in 1960 in Tokyo, where he was selected for the Tuttle Contemporary Japanese Art Competition, and 1957, 1960 and 1962 in Tokyo at the International Print Biennale. He was a member of the National painting academy and Japan Print Society. He was included in the 2002 exhibition *Japanese Prints under the Allied Occupation, 1945-1952* at the British Museum in London.

Bibliography:

Statler, Oliver, *Modern Japanese Prints: An Art reborn*, Charles E. Tuttle Co., Rutland (USA), Tokyo, 1956. Kawakita, Michiaki, *Contemporary Japanese Prints*, Kodansha International, Tokyo, Palo Alto, (USA), 1967. Smith, Lawrence, *Modern Japanese Prints 1912-1989*, British Museum Press, London, 2002. Smith, Lawrence, *Japanese Prints during the Allied Occupation, 1945-1952: Onchi Koshiro, Ernst Hacker and the First Thursday Society*, exhibition catalogue, British Museum Press, London, 2002.

SHINEN. See HYAKUSEN

SHINGEI. See GEIAMI

SHINKAI

Japanese, 13th century.
Active at the end of the 13th century.
Monk-painter.

Shinkai was a painter of Buddhist subjects, many of which are preserved in the Daigo-ji temple, Kyoto.

SHINKEN

Japanese, 13th century.
Born 1179; died 1261.
Monk-painter.

Shinken was a priest of the Shingon Buddhist sect and a disciple of the monk Seiken. He founded the Jizo-in sanctuary in the Daigo-ji temple, Kyoto, where a number of his Buddhist paintings are preserved.

SHINKO. See ITCHO

SHINN, Everett

American, 19th - 20th century.
Born 6 November 1876, in Woodstown (New Jersey); died 1953, in New York.
Painter, watercolourist, pastellist, draughtsman, illustrator. Figure compositions, figures, nudes, portraits, interiors, urban townscapes, street scenes, landscapes with figures. Murals.
Group: The Eight (Ashcan School).

Everett Shinn studied at the Pennsylvania Academy of Fine Arts in Philadelphia. While still very young, he belonged to a Philadelphia-based group of artists which included William Glackens, John Sloan, George Luks and Robert Henri among its members and acknowledged the authority of Thomas Anshutz, the successor to Thomas Eakins at the Pennsylvania Academy. He moved to New York in 1900.

In 1907, the National Academy of Design rejected all the paintings submitted by Glackens, Sloan and Luks; Robert Henri resigned from the Academy in consequence and the following year brought these painters together in an exhibition which also included Shinn, Prendergast, Ernest Lawson and Arthur B. Davies. Shortly afterwards, the group took the name The Eight. It was led by Robert Henri, who expounded his theories about it in his work *The Art Spirit*. The exhibition, which was unique in so far as the participants never again exhibited together, made a tremendous impact and the group was soon described as the 'Ashcan School'.

From his early days among the Philadelphia artists, the pervasive influence of Thomas Eakins steered Shinn to seek out an art inspired by everyday life, and American life in particular. Until then, American painting had consisted of travelling portrait painters and artists who depicted the folklore of the 'Wild West', often in the Naive style, followed by painting of the *fin de siècle* genre, since the great Impressionists were firmly rooted in Europe. Although they each expressed themselves with their own themes and techniques, in New York the members of The Eight aimed to bring American painting out of the kind of pleasant lethargy originating from the Post-Impressionism portrayed by the National Academy of Design. Referring to the Realist movement that preceded them, as well as to Eakins and Winslow Homer and through them to William Mount and George Bingham, the painters of The Eight claimed to be uniquely American and situated their Realism in 20th-century modernity. Relating their work to industrialisation and its effects on proletarian life in the cities, they aimed to illustrate and at the same time denounce urban life, noise, smells, filth and the dark side of city life. Shinn produced paintings of the industrial life of the great American urban areas, especially in the murals at Trenton Town Hall, New Jersey (1911), as well as depictions of street scenes and brawls.

Shinn was an illustrator for regional newspapers in Pennsylvania, in particular the *Philadelphia Press*. He also worked in New York for the *Herald Tribune*, the *World*, *Harper's*, *Scribner's*, and *McClure's*. He illustrated Hale's *Man Without a Country*, and Oscar Wilde's *The Happy Prince and Other Stories* in 1940, and Moore's *Night before Christmas* in 1942. He also worked as a set designer at the Stuyvesant Theatre in New York. After joining the Theatre, he became very fond of depicting the world of show business, the ballet, music halls, the circus and the actors whose portraits he painted.

Shinn took part in group exhibitions, including the inaugural exhibition of the group that was to become The Eight, at the Macbeth Gallery in New York (1908), and the International Exhibitions at the Carnegie Institute in Pittsburgh.

Bibliography:

DeShazo, Edith, *Everett Shinn 1876-1953: A Figure in His Time*, C.N. Potter, New York, 1974. *City Life Illustrated, 1890-1940: Sloan, Glackens, Luks, Shinn, their Friends and Followers*, exhibition catalogue, DE A. Museum, Wilmington, 1980. Perlman, B.B, *The Immortal Eight and its Influence*, New York, 1983. Forgey, Benjamin, '*The Eight 75 Years Later*' in *The Washington Post*, periodical, Washington DC, January 13, 1983. Yount, S. L., *Consuming Drama: Everett Shinn and the Spectacular City vi/4*, periodical, Amererica Art, Wilmington, Fall 1992.

Museums and Galleries:

Chicago (AI) - Chicago (Terra Foundation for American Art Collection): *Theatre Scene* (1903, oil on canvas) - New York (Metropolitan Mus. of Art) - New York (Whitney Mus. of American Art): *Revue* (1908).

Auction records:

New York, 15-16 Jan 1932, *Ballet* (coloured chalk) USD 255. New York, 9 Oct 1953, *Clown*, USD 3,750. New York, 11 Nov 1959, *Tightrope Walker*, USD 2,750. New York, 21 May 1970, *Music-hall Scene* (pastel) USD 5,500. New York, 16 Oct 1974, *Street Corner, New York* (watercolour and pastel) USD 14,000. New York, 28 Oct 1976, *On the New York Docks* (1895, watercolour and pastel, 22 x 29 1/2 ins / 56 x 75 cm) USD 27,000. New York, 21 April 1977, *Lovers* (1922, pencil and wash, 21 1/2 x 22 ins / 54.6 x 56 cm) USD 3,500. New York, 21 April 1977, *Paris in Winter* (oil on canvas, 20 x 23 3/4 ins / 51 x 60.3 cm) USD 3,300. New York, 27 Oct 1977, *Young Woman Washing Herself* (1900, pastel/brown paper, 5 3/4 x 9 ins / 14.6 x 23 cm) USD 2,750. Portland, 7 April 1979, *Artist and Model* (Conté pencil, 13 x 16 ins / 33 x 40.5 cm) USD 1,800. New York, 20 April 1979, *Is He Home?* (1903, pastel, 10 1/4 x 15 3/4 ins / 26 x 40 cm) USD 5,250. New York, 25 Oct 1979, *Saturday Evening, Ringling Hotel, Sarasota, Florida* (1949, oil on canvas, 24 1/4 x 20 1/4 ins / 61.5 x 51.5 cm) USD 60,000. New York, 2 Dec 1982, *Portrait of Mrs A. Stewart Walker* (1912, red chalk, 17 1/4 x 20 1/2 ins / 43.7 x 52 cm) USD 5,100. New York, 2 Dec 1982, *Polly's Clown* (1946, oil on mounted card, 16 x 12 ins / 40.6 x 30.5 cm) USD 12,500. New York, 18 March 1983, *Nude Getting Dressed* (1907, red chalk, 12 3/4 x 16 1/2 ins / 32.7 x 42 cm) USD 1,400. New York, 8 Dec 1983, *Clown* (1930, oil on canvas, 36 x 42 ins / 91.5 x 106.8 cm) USD 80,000. New York, 23 March 1984, *Vaudeville* (pastel, 12 x 18 ins / 30.3 x 45.8 cm) USD 32,000. New York, 15 March 1985, *Street Scene with Horse and Cart* (1902, Conté pencil, graphite and watercolour, 9 x 6 1/2 ins / 22 x 16.6 cm) USD 1,300. New York, 30 May 1986, *Polly's Clown* (1946, mounted card, 15 3/4 x 12 ins / 40.2 x 30.5 cm) USD 18,000. New York, 28 May 1987, *Docks* (1899, pastel/paper, 22 1/2 x 22 1/2 ins / 57.2 x 57.2 cm) USD 70,000. New York, 26 May 1988, *Parisian Street in Winter* (1910, pastel/canvas, 21 1/4 x 26 ins / 54.2 x 65.2 cm) USD 308,000. New York, 24 June 1988, *The Young King* (watercolour/paper, illustration for Oscar Wilde's 'The Happy Prince', 17 3/4 x 13 1/2 ins / 45 x 34 cm) USD 8,250; *Trapeze Artist* (1949, pastel/paper, 22 x 17 1/4 ins / 55 x 44 cm) USD 8,250. New York, 1 Dec 1988, *Brawl* (1899, watercolour and ink, 8 1/4 x 13 1/4 ins / 21 x 33.6 cm) USD 22,000. New York, 24 Jan 1989, *Prophecy* (1945, watercolour/paper, 15 1/2 x 15 ins / 39.5 x 37.8 cm) USD 990. New York, 1 Dec 1989, *Happy Guy* (1944, oil on canvas, 24 x 20 ins / 61 x 51 cm) USD 52,800. New York, 23 May 1990, *Ballerinas* (oil on canvas/card, 10 x 8 ins / 25.5 x 20.3 cm) USD 24,200. New York, 30 May 1990, *Village Fête* (1906, charcoal/paper, 10 3/4 x 19 1/4 ins / 27.3 x 48.7 cm) USD 2,530. New York, 27 Sept 1990, *Bright Shawl* (1921, oil on card, 32 3/4 x 25 ins / 83 x 63.5 cm) USD 6,600. New York, 29 Nov 1990, *Flower Market in Paris* (pastel and charcoal/canvas, 25 1/2 x 36 1/4 ins / 64.8 x 92 cm) USD 39,600. New York, 30 Nov 1990, *Actress in White on Stage* (oil on canvas, 9 1/4 x 11 ins / 23.2 x 28.2 cm) USD 24,200. New York, 17 Dec 1990, *Nude in a Landscape* (1912, brown pencil/paper, 19 x 16 1/4 ins / 48.1 x 41.3 cm) USD 1,760. New York, 21 May 1991, *Women in a Garden* (oil on canvas, 30 x 35 3/4 ins / 76.2 x 90.8 cm) USD 1,100. New York, 22 May 1991, *Bowling* (1929, watercolour and pencil/paper, 9 1/2 x 14 ins / 24.1 x 35.5 cm) USD 2,420. New York, 6 Dec 1991, *Tightrope Walker* (1904, pastel/card, 12 x 13 ins / 30.5 x 33 cm) USD 88,000. New York, 27 May 1992, *Horse-drawn Omnibus* (1899, pastel/paper, 21 3/4 x 29 1/2 ins / 55.2 x 74.9 cm) USD 20,900. New York, 28 May 1992, *Singer* (1902, oil on canvas, 26 1/2 x 17 1/2 ins / 67 x 44.2 cm) USD 176,000. New York, 23 Sept 1992, *After the Show* (1934, pastel/black paper, 18 x 12 ins / 45.7 x 30.5 cm) USD 24,200. New York, 4 Dec 1992, *Alley Cat* (1933, pastel/card, 19 1/4 x 26 ins / 49.2 x 66 cm) USD 28,600. New York, 26 May 1993, *Rooftop Café* (1925, pastel/blue paper/card, 11 1/4 x 15 1/4 ins / 28.5 x 38.8 cm) USD 66,300. New York, 21 Sept 1994, *Ballerina* (1929, pastel/paper, 15 1/2 x 11 1/4 ins / 39.4 x 28.6 cm) USD 74,000. New York, 22 May 1996, *Young Woman on Stage* (oil on canvas). New York, 27 Sept 1996, *Young French Girl* (oil on canvas/panel, 15 1/4 x 19 ins / 38.5 x 48.3 cm) USD 18,400. New York, 3 Dec 1996, *Nude on a Chair in front of a Bowl* (ink, pencil, gouache and pen/paper, 10 1/2 x 10 1/2 ins / 26.7 x 26.7 cm) USD 1,495. New York, 3 Dec 1996, *Portrait of Paula Shinn* (1935, pastel and charcoal/blue paper, 15 x 18 1/2 ins / 37.8 x 47 cm) USD 2,990. New York, 4-5 Dec 1996, *Recumbent Nude* (oil on panel, 10 x 12 1/4 ins / 25.4 x 31.2 cm) USD 16,100; *Street Scene in Winter* (1936, gouache, watercolour and pencil/paper, 13 1/2 x 10 1/4 ins / 34.3 x 26 cm) USD 23,000. New York, 23 April 1997, *Woman on Stage* (oil on canvas, 12 x 10 ins / 30.4 x 25.4 cm) USD 10,925. New York, 5 June 1997, *Horse-drawn Bus* (1899, pastel/paper, 21 3/4 x 30 ins / 55.3 x 75.3 cm) USD 96,000. New York, 6 June 1997, *Parisian Theatre Scene* (1907, pastel/panel, 15 x 17 1/2 ins / 38.1 x 44.4 cm) USD 96,000. New York, 11 March 1999, *Girl in Bathtub* (1903, pastel, 16 x 14 ins / 41 x 36 cm) USD 50,000. New York, 26 May 1999, *Vaudeville Dancer* (1912, pastel on paperboard, 20 x 17 ins / 51 x 42 cm) USD 290,000. New York, 25 May 2000, *Curtain Call* (1925, oil on canvas, 9 x 11 ins / 23 x 28 cm) USD 110,000. New York, 30 Nov 2000, *Window Shopping* (1903, pastel, 14 x 18 ins / 36 x 46 cm) USD 170,000. New York, 23 May 2001, *Saturday Night* (1905, watercolour and pastel, 18 x 24 ins / 45 x 60 cm) USD 80,000. New York, 23 May 2001, *East River at Night* (1906, pastel, 13 x 21 ins / 33 x 53 cm) USD 130,000. New York, 4 Dec 2002, *Sixth Avenue Elevated After Midnight* (1899, pastel and gouache on board, 8 x 13 ins / 20 x 32 cm) USD 220,000. New York, 4 Dec 2002, *Footlight Flirtation* (1912, oil on canvas, 29 x 36 ins / 74 x 92 cm) USD 3,300,000. New York, 21 May 2003, *Revue* (1929, oil on canvas, 36 x 42 ins / 91 x 107 cm) USD 260,000. San Francisco, 10 Dec 2003, *Backstage at the Start of Act III* (1906, pencil, watercolour and charcoal on paper board, 12 x 20 ins / 30 x 52 cm) USD 105,000. New York, 19 May 2004, *Clown - No Laughs* (1935, oil on canvas, 36 x 42 ins / 91 x 107 cm) USD 55,000. Norwalk, 12 Oct 2004, *Street Scene with Hat Shop* (watercolour on paper on board, 9 x 13 ins / 23 x 33 cm) USD 32,000.

SHINN, Florence Scovel
American, 19th - 20th century.
Born 1869, in Camden (New Jersey); died 17 October 1940, in New York.
Draughtswoman, illustrator.

Florence Scovel Shinn studied at the Pennsylvania Academy of Fine Arts in Philadelphia. She married the artist Everett Shinn in 1898.

Shinn worked on *Century Magazine* and illustrated works including: *Widow O'Callaghan's Boys* (1898); *Four-Masted Catboat* (1899); *Loom of Destiny*; *Autobiography of a Tomboy* (1900); *The Van Dwellers* (1901); Zollinger's *Maggie McLanehan*; *New Boy at Dale* (1903); *Lovey Mary* by Rice; *Mrs Wiggs of the Cabbage Patch*; and Rankin's *Dandelion Cottage* (1904).

BIBLIOGRAPHY:

Osterwalder, Marcus (ed.), *Dictionnaire des illustrateurs 1800-1914*, Ides et Calendes, Neuchâtel, 1989.

SHINNO. See **NOAMI**

SHINODA, Morio
Japanese, 20th century.
Born 1931, in Tokyo.
Sculptor.

Morio Shinoda taught at the Tokyo institute of applied art as an assistant from 1952 and was actively involved with the modern art association from 1955 to 1956. In 1963-1964 he studied at the Art Institute of Chicago. Shinoda's sculpture is reminiscent of the Expressionism of Germaine Richier. From 1963, he exhibited in various group shows, including: 1963 Tokyo, *New Generation of Japanese Sculptors*, in the National Museum of Modern Art, and the Asahi *Exhibition of Masterpieces*; 1964 and 1965 Kyoto, *Trends in Contemporary Japanese Painting and Sculpture*, National Museum of Modern Art; 1965 Tokyo Biennale and the Ube Museum, *Open-air Exhibition of Japanese Sculpture*; 1965-1966 New York, *New Japanese Painting and Sculpture*, Museum of Modern Art; 1966 Venice Biennale and the first exhibition of the Japan Art Festival Association, New York.

MUSEUMS AND GALLERIES:
KAMAKURA (MMA) - MAGAOKA (Mus. of Contemporary Art).

SHINODA, Toko
Japanese, 20th century.
Born 1913, in Manchuria, of Japanese parents.
Painter, draughtsman, calligrapher.

Toko Shinoda started to learn calligraphy from her father at the age of six, continuing at school. She became a member of the Institute for Calligraphy as Art in 1950. She lived in New York from 1956 to 1958 during a visit to the USA. One of the most important representatives of modern Japanese calligraphy, she is the author of *Learn the New Calligraphy in 12 Months*. During her stay in New York, she noted the parallels not only between her own work and that of Franz Kline and Jackson Pollock, but also between her work and contemporary jazz rhythms. Her calligraphic characters resemble sharp-edged, nervous scratches drawn against a background of large signs in white set against dark, warm greys. They are prepared as if for a gestural abstract painting. In her later paintings, such as *Paulownia*, sold at auction in New York in 1994, she juxtaposes strictly defined monochrome flat areas that bring to mind a tendency towards Minimalist Geometric Abstraction.

She exhibited for the first time in Tokyo in 1940. She took part in group shows in 1958 at the Museum of Modern Art, New York and Museum of Modern Art, Tokyo; in 1954 at São Paulo in an exhibition of Japanese calligraphy; in 1955 in Washington, at the Musée Cernuschi in Paris and in Sweden in exhibitions of Japanese calligraphy; in 1959 at the Kröller-Müller Museum in Otterlo, The Netherlands; in 1961 at the Carnegie Institute in Pittsburgh, at the Akademie der Künste in Berlin and at the São Paulo Biennale; in 1962 at the Museum of Modern Art in Tokyo; in 1967 at the Royal Society in Dublin; and in 1979, together with Okada Kenzo and Tsutaka Waichi, in the travelling show *Okada, Shinoda, Tsutaka: Three Pioneers of Abstract Painting in 20th-Century Japan*, which went to the Phillips Collection in Washington, the Columbus Art Gallery, the College of Fine Arts at the University of Texas, Austin, the Indianapolis Art Museum and the Munson-Williams-Proctor Arts Institute in Utica, New York. She has also held numerous one-woman shows, including: Tokyo, Boston (1956), Chicago, Paris (1957), Brussels (1959), Tokyo (1961), and New York (1965, 1968, 1971, 1975, 1977).

MUSEUMS AND GALLERIES:
NEW YORK (Solomon R. Guggenheim Mus.):, 1956) - OTTERLO (Kröller-Müller Mus.) - THE HAGUE (Gemeentemus.) - TOKYO (National MMA).

AUCTION RECORDS:
NEW YORK, 7 May 1991, *Rain* (ink on paper on card, 65 1/2 x 51 ins / 166.3 x 129.8 cm) USD 2,200. NEW YORK, 27 April 1994, *Paulownia* (two panels, ink on paper, each 66 1/2 x 24 1/2 ins / 168.6 x 62.2 cm) USD 24,150. BERN, 1 May 2002, *Phase* (mixed media on silver paper on board, 24 x 17 ins / 60 x 43 cm) CHF 2,400. LONDON, 3 Feb 2003, *Kokord* (ink on platinum ground, 52 x 24 ins / 132 x 62 cm) GBP 1,000. DETROIT, 14 May 2004, *Abstract* (oil on canvas, 51 x 38 ins / 130 x 97 cm) USD 6,000.

SHINPEI
Japanese, 19th century.
Active in Osaka in 1813.
Print artist.

Shinpei may have been born in Kyoto and it is not impossible that he was the same artist as Yukinaga.

SHINSEI. See **KENZAN**

SHINSHO. See **BUSON**

SHINSO. See **SOAMI**

SHINSUI
Japanese, 20th century.
Born 1877; died 1968.
Print artist. Figures, portraits, landscapes.

Shinsui worked in *oban* and *aiban* (large and medium) formats. He may be the same as Ito Shinsui, also known as Ito Hajime.

AUCTION RECORDS:
NEW YORK, 16 April 1988, *Beauty in Snow Storm* (Oban Tate-e print, 17 x 10 3/4 ins / 43.1 x 27.3 cm) USD 7,150. LONDON, 16 June 1988, *Okubi-e Portrait of Young Woman Applying Rouge to Her Lips with Her Finger* (Dai Oban Tate-e print, 17 x 24 ins / 43 x 61.1 cm) GBP 2,420. LONDON, 9 Nov 1988, *Okubi-e Portrait of Young Woman in Profile, Holding her Sleeve to her Cheek* (Oban Tate-e print, 17 x 10 1/2 ins / 43 x 26.5 cm) GBP 1,650. NEW YORK, 20 April 1989, *Young Woman Cutting Her Toenails* (1929, Dai Oban Tate-e print, 17 1/4 x 11 1/4 ins / 43.9 x 28.5 cm) USD 7,700. NEW YORK, 15 June 1990, *Young Woman with Blue Umbrella during a Shower* (Aiban Tate-e print, 14 1/4 x 10 ins / 36 x 25.7 cm) USD 1,540. NEW YORK, 27 March 1991, *Ukimi Temple in Katatade Province* (1918, Aiban Tate-e print, eight views of Omi (Lake Biwa) (a series), 12 3/4 x 8 3/4 ins / 32.3 x 22.2 cm) USD 3,850. NEW YORK, 23 Oct 1991, *Snow Storm* (1932, Dai Oban Tate-e print, 17 1/4 x 11 ins / 43.5 x 27.8 cm) USD 13,200; *Young Woman Squatting and Cutting Her Nails* (1936, Dai Oban Tate-e print, 20 1/4 x 13 ins / 51.2 x 33.3 cm) USD 9,350.

SHINYO, real name: Kitayama, Doryo; given name: Ma; artist name: Shin'yo
Japanese, 18th century.
Died 1801.
Active in Edo (now Tokyo).
Painter.

Shinyo was a Nanga School painter and the father of the painter Kitayama Kangan.

SHINZABURO. See **GIBOKUSAI**

SHINZAI

Japanese, 9th century.
Died 860.
Painter.

Shinzai was a pupil of En-Chin. A painter of religious subjects, he is known for his portrait of Kobo Daishi.

SHIPHAM, Benjamin

British, 19th century.
Born 1806, in Nottingham; died 1872, in Nottingham.
Painter. Landscapes.

Benjamin Shipham was influenced by Henry Dawson. He painted subjects from middle England and Wales, for the most part, and exhibited in London from 1852 to 1872, principally at the Royal Academy, the British Institution and the Royal Society of British Artists in Suffolk Street.

MUSEUMS AND GALLERIES:

GLASGOW: *Landscape with Livestock and Figures* - NOTTINGHAM (Castle Mus. & AG): *Field of Wheat; Near Beddgelert; View of Wilford.*

AUCTION RECORDS:

LONDON, 14 Feb 1978, *Countryfolk Going to Market* (oil on canvas, 17 1/2 x 25 1/2 ins / 44.5 x 65 cm) GBP 1,400. LONDON, 30 March 1982, *The Woodcutters' Cart* (oil on canvas, 22 x 32 ins / 56 x 81 cm) GBP 1,600. LONDON, 29 March 1983, *Bulwell, Nottinghamshire* (oil on canvas, 30 x 39 ins / 76 x 99 cm) GBP 1,500. SHREWSBURY, 10 Nov 1999, *Figures and Animals in Rural Landscape* (oil on canvas, 27 x 39 ins / 69 x 99 cm) GBP 3,800. BILLINGSHURST, 25 May 2000, *Figures in Extensive Landscape, Mountains Beyond* (oil on canvas, 24 x 36 ins / 61 x 92 cm) GBP 1,800.

SHIPLEY, Giorgiana, later Mrs Francis Hare Naylor

British, 18th century.
Died 1806, in Lausanne, Switzerland.
Painter. Portraits.

Giorgiana Shipley exhibited a portrait at the Royal Academy in 1781, at a very early age.

SHIPLEY, William

British, 18th century.
Born 1714; died 28 December 1803, in Manchester.
Painter. Portraits, landscapes.

William Shipley was better known as the founder of a number of art institutions than for his own works. After teaching drawing in Northampton, he moved to London and founded the St Martin's Lane Academy which was initially named Shipley's School. He also founded the Society of Arts.

SHIPSTER, Robert

British, 18th century.
Active in London between 1796 and 1799.
Engraver (burin).

Robert Shipster was a pupil of Francesco Bartolozzi.

SHIQI. See **KUNCAN**

SHIRAGA, Kazuo

Japanese, 20th century.
Born 1924, in Amagasaki, near Osaka (Hyogo Prefecture).
Painter.
Neo-Dadaism, Action Painting.
Groups: Zero, Gutai.

Shiraga Kazuo studied traditional painting at Tokyo fine arts and music university (some sources say the Kyoto art academy). In 1953, together with Kaneyama, Tanaka and Murakami, he founded the Zero group. In 1955, he underwent a conversion to modern western-style painting, and joined the Gutai group, which had been founded in 1954 by Yoshihara Jiro, for the purpose of opening Japanese art to all possible modes of expression, all materials and all attitudes, as well as outdoor events, traditional forums and art galleries. Having won the approval of the critic Michel Tapié in Tokyo, the group went on to make a great impression in Europe and the USA under Tapié's influence, although he did temper some of its showy excesses and directed its members towards abstract art, of which he was then one of the great champions.

Shiraga painted with startling intensity, applying the paint first with his hand, then grinding it in with his foot, pouring, splashing, splattering, trailing it in huge, violent gestures. His work derives as much from oriental calligraphy as it does from Abstract Expressionism.

He started to exhibit with the Zero group at the Shinseisaku Salon. With the Gutai group, he exhibited every year from 1955 to 1970 in Osaka, Kansai and Tokyo. In 1957, he took part in the *World Modern Art Show* in Tokyo and Osaka. In 1959, he exhibited at the Martha Jackson Gallery, New York. In 1962, he had a one-man show and in 1965 took part in a Gutai group show, both at the Galerie Stadler in Paris. In 1988, he took part in the show *Modern Art in Marseilles: The Collection of the Musée Cantini* in Marseilles.

BIBLIOGRAPHY:

Tapié, Michel/Haga, Tôre, *Continuité et avant-garde au Japon*, Ed. d'arte Fratelli Pozzo, Turin, 1961 (text in French). *Ier Salon international des Galeries Pilotes*, exhibition catalogue, Musée cantonal, Lausanne, 1963. *L'Art moderne à Marseille. La Collection du Musée Cantini*, Musée Cantini, Marseilles, 1988. Yamamoto, Atsuo, et al., *Gutai: moments de destruction, moments de beauté*, Blusson, Paris, 2002 (text in French and English).

MUSEUMS AND GALLERIES:

MARSEILLES (Mus. Cantini): *Amagazaki* (1924).

SHIRAI, Akiko

Japanese, 20th century.
Born 1935, in Dairen, Manchuria, of Japanese parents.
Print artist.

Akiko Shirai graduated from the oil painting department of Tokyo fine arts and music university in 1959 and from its print making department in 1964. She then spent a year in the USA on a scholarship. She is a member of the Japan Print Society.

She took part in various group shows from 1962, including the Modern Japanese Art Exhibition in Tokyo in 1962, 1963, 1964 and 1966; the Shell Competition in Tokyo, where she won a prize for excellence, the International Print Biennale and the Asahi *Exhibition of Masterpieces* in 1966; the São Paulo Biennale and the International Colour Print Treinnale in Switzerland in 1967; and the 2nd and 3rd exhibition of the Japan Art Festival Association in 1967 and 1968.

SHIRATAKI, Ikunosuke

Japanese, 19th - 20th century.
Born 1873, in Hyogo Prefecture.; died 1961.
Painter. Landscapes, flowers.

Shirataki Ikunosuke studied under Yamamoto Hosui and Kuroda Seiki, graduating from the Tokyo art school in 1898, whereupon he joined the Hakubakai (White Horse) Circle. From 1904 to 1910, he travelled in Europe and the USA. He was awarded the imperial prize by the Japanese fine art academy in 1921. He is regarded as one of the precursors of the introduction of modern western art into Japan. He took part in various official exhibitions, both Japanese and international, including the Salon des Artistes Français in Paris in 1900 on the occasion of the Exposition Universelle.

AUCTION RECORDS:

NEW YORK, 12 Oct 1989, *Village Street in France* (oil on canvas, 13 1/4 x 18 ins / 33.7 x 45.7 cm) USD 5,500; *Roses in a Vase* (oil on canvas, 16 x 21 ins / 40.8 x 53.2 cm) USD 3,850. NEW YORK, 16 Oct 1990, *Twilight* (oil on panel, 9 1/4 x 13 ins / 23.7 x 33 cm) USD 3,080.

SHIRATO, Francisc
Romanian, 20th century.
Born 1877, in Craiova.
Painter, draughtsman.
Francisc Shirato studied at the Bucharest and Düsseldorf schools of fine art. He later taught at the Bucharest academy. He contributed drawings and critical pieces to many journals and newspapers.

SHIRAYAMA, Masanari
Japanese, 20th century.
Born 22 March 1916, in Tokyo.
Active in France.
Painter (gouache), watercolourist, print artist. Scenes with figures, landscapes, urban landscapes.
Shirayama Masanari painted typical Paris scenes, and scenes with figures from Morocco and the south of France. He exhibited regularly at the Salon de la Société Nationale des Beaux-Arts, Paris.

SHIRIN, Vasili
Russian, 17th century.
Active c. 1610.
Icon painter.
Vasili Shirin was the either the son of Prokopi Shirin or was related to him.
MUSEUMS AND GALLERIES:
MOSCOW (State Tretyakov Gal.): small altarpiece.

SHIRLAW, Walter
British, 19th - 20th century.
Born 6 August 1838, in Paisley, near Glasgow; died 26 December 1909, in Madrid.
Painter, pastellist, engraver, draughtsman, illustrator. Figures, portraits, genre scenes, landscapes. Murals.
Walter Shirlaw was a pupil of Johann Leonhard Raab, Alexander von Wagner, Arthur de Ramberg and Wilhelm von Lindenschmit at the Akademie der Bildenden Künste in Munich. He produced a large number of murals and was active in Chicago in 1861, and in Munich and New York after 1877. He became a member of the National Academy in New York in 1888.

Shirlaw exhibited in the US and Europe, winning medals at the Akademie in Munich, and in Philadelphia in 1876. He won a jury commendation at the Paris World's Fair of 1889, a silver medal in Buffalo in 1901, and a silver medal in St Louis in 1904.

AUCTION RECORDS:
WASHINGTON DC, 30 Sept 1984, *Harvest Scene* (oil on canvas, 28 3/4 x 41 ins / 73 x 103.2 cm) USD 4,500. NEW YORK, 31 March 1994, *The Young Bacchus* (oil on canvas, 19 1/2 x 40 3/4 ins / 49.5 x 103.5 cm) USD 1,840. NEW YORK, 12 Sept 1994, *Good Day!* (oil on canvas, 48 x 29 ins / 121.9 x 73.7 cm) USD 747. NEW YORK, 28 Sept 1995, *Neo-Classical Female Figure* (charcoal and pastel/buff-coloured paper, 54 1/2 x 31 3/4 ins / 138.4 x 80.6 cm) USD 4,887.

SHIRLEY, Henry
British, 19th century.
Died 1870.
Painter. Genre scenes, landscapes with figures, waterscapes, landscapes.
Henry Shirley exhibited at the Royal Academy between 1844 and 1859.
MUSEUMS AND GALLERIES:
GLASGOW: *Scene on a Dutch River.*
AUCTION RECORDS:
LONDON, 22 Nov 1968, *View of a Lake in Wales,* Gns 750. LONDON, 28 Nov 1972, *Figures by the Banks of a River,* GBP 980. LONDON, 27 Jan 1976, *Resting in a Clearing* (oil on canvas, 17 1/4 x 23 ins / 44 x 58.5 cm) GBP 240. LONDON, 14 Feb 1978, *Llanberis Lake, Wales* (1836, oil on canvas, 23 1/2 x 42 1/4 ins / 59.5 x 107 cm) GBP 700. LONDON, 6 June 1980, *The Fishing Party* (oil on canvas, 21 1/2 x 29 1/2 ins / 54.6 x 75 cm) GBP 950. LONDON, 8 Feb 1991, *Young Woman Drawing Under the Trees on Hampstead Heath* (oil on canvas, 24 1/2 x 42 3/4 ins / 62 x 108.5 cm) GBP 5,280. LONDON, 3 Nov 1993, *The Approach of the Storm* (1852, oil on canvas, 18 1/4 x 24 1/4 ins / 46.5 x 61.5 cm) GBP 2,530. LONDON, 10 March 1995, *The Boat-Race* (1864, oil on board, 9 1/4 x 15 1/2 ins / 23.5 x 39.4 cm) GBP 2,070. LONDON, 10 Feb 2000, *Young Sailors* (oil on canvas, 14 x 23 ins / 36 x 58 cm) GBP 2,000.

SHIRLEY-FOX, John. See **FOX John Shirley**

SHIRLOW, Joseph
Australian, 19th - 20th century.
Painter. Landscapes.
AUCTION RECORDS:
NEW YORK, 22 Feb 1911, *After the Storm,* USD 110.

SHIRO-TANAKA, Flavio
Japanese, 20th century.
Born 1928, in Sapporo (Hokkaido).
Active in Brazil from 1931, naturalised in Brazil.
Painter.
Flavio Shiro-Tanaka spent his childhood in the Amazonian jungle before settling in São Paulo. He went to Paris in 1953, where he learned mosaics with Severini, print-making with Friedlander and lithography at the École des Beaux-Arts. His painting falls into the category of Abstract Expressionism or Informal Abstraction, which is less common in Brazil than Geometric Abstraction. Its swirls tend towards a sort of heavy-set calligraphy.

He has taken part in various group shows, mostly in Paris, including the 1961 Biennale and the 1962 Salon des Réalités Nouvelles. He showed work at the 1966 Córdoba Biennale in Argentina. In 1970 he also showed in Rome with *Vision 24,* an exhibition of Latin American painters and sculptors.
BIBLIOGRAPHY:
Vision 24 Pittori et Scultori America Latina, Istituto Italo-Latino Americano, Rome, 1970.

SHIRREFF, Charles, or Sheriff or Sherriff or Shireff
British, 18th century.
Born c. 1750, in Edinburgh.
Painter, miniaturist.
Charles Shirreff studied at the Royal Academy in London from 1768 and was a pupil of Th. Burgess. He worked in London and settled in Bath in 1796. Shirreff travelled to India, where he stayed in Madras and Calcutta, from 1796 to 1809 before returning to end his career in Bath.
MUSEUMS AND GALLERIES:
LONDON (Victoria and Albert Mus.): miniatures.

SHIRREFFS, John
British, 19th - 20th century.
Painter, watercolourist. Genre scenes.
John Shirreffs was active from 1890 to 1937.
AUCTION RECORDS:
EDINBURGH, 2 May 1991, *A Warm Hearth* (1927, watercolour, 14 x 9 3/4 ins / 35.5 x 24.8 cm) GBP 528.

SHIRVING, Archibald. See **SKIRVING**

SHISAN. See **GYOKUSHU**

SHISEI. See **SAN'YO**

SHISHIDO, Tokudo

Japanese, 20th century.
Born 1930, in Tokyo.
Print artist, lithographer.

Shishido Tokudo graduated from the women's college of Tokyo fine arts and music university in 1948 and studied at an arts and crafts school in California in 1952. From 1957 to 1959, she continued her studies at Boston Museum and the art department of Stanford University. On her way home, she stayed in Europe and Southeast Asia. She became a member of the Japan Print Society in 1953 and exhibited with the Graphic Art Club in 1956. She showed etchings, woodcuts and lithographs at the Tokyo International Print Biennale.

SHISHKIN, Ivan Ivanovich

Russian, 19th century.
Born 1831 or 1832; died 1888 or 1898.
Painter, watercolourist. Landscapes with figures, waterscapes.

Ivan Ivanovich Shishkin studied at the college of art in Moscow and later at the art academy in St Petersburg. He was the first Russian landscape painter to appreciate the importance of the open-air study. The central theme of his work is the Russian Landscape.

BIBLIOGRAPHY:

Savinov, A., *Shishkin*, Aurora Art Publisher, Leningrad, 1986.

AUCTION RECORDS:

LONDON, 10 Feb 1978, *Herd in a Landscape with a River* (1869, oil on canvas, 27 x 51 1/2 ins / 68.5 x 130.8 cm) GBP 5,000. LONDON, 14 May 1980, *Clearing* (oil on card, 13 1/2 x 11 3/4 ins / 34 x 30 cm) GBP 1,100. LONDON, 27 Nov 1981, *Trees* (oil on card, 22 1/2 x 16 3/4 ins / 57.1 x 42.5 cm) GBP 1,500. LONDON, 3 March 1982, *In the Forest* (1895, pen, 41 3/4 x 31 3/4 ins / 106 x 80.5 cm) GBP 7,500. NEW YORK, 24 May 1984, *Forest* (1881, oil on canvas remounted on board, 9 1/4 x 13 ins / 23.5 x 33 cm) USD 6,000. LONDON, 13 Feb 1986, *Forest Path at Twilight* (1896, oil on canvas, 62 1/2 x 46 1/2 ins / 159 x 118 cm) GBP 16,000. LONDON, 14 Nov 1988, *Pine Forest* (1880, oil on canvas, 51 1/2 x 31 ins / 130.5 x 79 cm) GBP 8,800; *Figures near a Lake in a Forest* (oil on canvas, 27 1/4 x 20 ins / 69 x 51 cm) GBP 18,700. LONDON, 5 Oct 1989, *Summer Landscape in Valaam* (1858, oil on canvas, 26 x 36 1/2 ins / 65.8 x 93 cm) GBP 38,500. NEW YORK, 16 July 1992, *In the Pine Forest* (oil on canvas, 9 1/4 x 5 3/4 ins / 23.5 x 14.6 cm) USD 1,100. NEW YORK, 26 May 1994, *Gate to the Paddock* (1885, oil on canvas, 77 x 47 1/2 ins / 195.6 x 120.7 cm) USD 68,500. LONDON, 15 June 1995, *Panorama of a Forest Lake* (1886, sepia and watercolour/pencil, 9 1/2 x 13 ins / 24 x 33 cm) GBP 3,680. LONDON, 14 Dec 1995, *Fence* (1885, oil on canvas, 77 x 47 1/2 ins / 195.6 x 120.7 cm) GBP 155,500. LONDON, 17 July 1996, *Study of a Landscape* (1890, oil on canvas, 12 x 19 3/4 ins / 30.5 x 50 cm) GBP 15,525. LONDON, 19 Dec 1996, *Path through a Wood* (oil on canvas, 22 3/4 x 35 ins / 58 x 89 cm) GBP 36,700. LONDON, 11-12 June 1997, *A Hill in Karelia* (oil on canvas, 9 3/4 x 13 ins / 25 x 33 cm) GBP 5,750. LONDON, 29 April 1999, *Fallen Trees* (1889, oil on canvas, 18 x 23 ins / 46 x 58 cm) GBP 11,000. VIENNA, 16 Nov 1999, *Coastal Landscape in Narva* (1887, oil on canvas, 35 x 22 ins / 90 x 57 cm) ATS 220,000. LONDON, 10 May 2000, *Forest Path* (oil on canvas, 23 x 15 ins / 59 x 37 cm) GBP 26,000. LONDON, 10 May 2000, *River Kama, near Yelabuga* (1895, oil on canvas, 77 x 47 ins / 195 x 120 cm) GBP 180,000. LONDON, 23 Nov 2000, *Landscape with Hunter, Valaam Island* (1867, pen and ink, 15 x 21 ins / 37 x 53 cm) GBP 17,000. BERN, 1 May 2002, *Study of a Tree Trunk* (oil on canvas/masonite, oil on canvas, 12 x 9 ins / 31 x 22 cm) CHF 3,900. HELSINKI, 17 May 2003, *Branch. Forest Interior* (1870, oil and pen on paper, 7 x 9 ins / 17 x 24 cm) EUR 3,200. PARIS, 17 Nov 2003, *River Landscape at Twilight* (oil on canvas, 19 x 22 ins / 48 x 55 cm) EUR 12,500.

SHISHKOV, Matvei Andreevich. See **CHICHKOV**

SHISUI. See **KENZAN**

SHITAO, or Shih-t'ao, original name: Zhu Ruoji (Chu Juo-ji); monk's names: Yuan-ji (Yuan-chi), Daoji (Tao-chi)

Chinese, 17th - 18th century.
Born 1641, in Wuzhou (Guangxi); died c. 1719-1720; in 1707 according to some sources.
Painter. Vegetables.

Shitao is the name by which the painter Zhu Ruoji is best known in China, whilst in the west he is more often known by his monk's names Daoji (Tao-chi) or Yuanji (Yuan-chi). He has many sobriquets, of which only the best-known are cited here: Qingxiang laoren (Leftover Man of Qingxiang), Dadizi (Disciple of Great Purity), Kugua Heshang (Monk Bitter Gourd), Xiazunzhe (Venerable Blind Man). He is probably the Chinese painter who is most studied today both in China and overseas.

Shitao was a prolific creator who left an immense body of work of astonishing modernism. In addition, in his inscriptions and theoretical work (the *Hua Yulu (Sayings on Painting,* also known as *Sayings on Painting from Monk Bitter Gourd*), he created a philosophical work, a meditation on aesthetics that goes far beyond the specific domain of Chinese painting.

Born of royal blood, Shitao was descended from the elder brother of Zhu Yuanzhang, the founder of the Ming dynasty who ruled as Emperor Taizu (1368-1399). His father Hengjia, a claimant to the throne, was assassinated in 1645 during the fighting that broke out in southern China among rival factions of Ming loyalists after the Manchu invasion and the establishment of the Qing dynasty. Shitao was saved by a few faithful servants who made him a monk in order to ensure his safety.

His childhood and adolescence were spent in the seclusion of monasteries. The teachings of his Chan Buddhist masters would exert a decisive influence on his philosophical development. But it is difficult to speak in his case of a monastic vocation. When he reached maturity and, thanks to his reputation and social contacts, he was out of danger, he became a layman once more. Indeed, when staying in Beijing (1690-1692), he was not above frequenting Manchu notables and high officials.

Shitao began travelling when he was young and would remain a tireless traveller all his life. He visited the most famous mountains in various provinces, and in particular Mount Huang in Anhui, which he would visit on several occasions; the sketches he made of the mountain would remain a constant source of inspiration for his painting. During these years of wandering, his principal bases were Xuancheng (Anhui), where he stayed from 1666 to 1679, often keeping company with the painter Mei Qing, his elder and his intimate friend; from 1680, Nanjing, where he stayed for nine years; and finally Yangzhou, where he settled permanently in 1693. This city was a thriving artistic centre thanks to the patronage of a rich merchant class, and Shitao enjoyed considerable prestige there, devoting himself to painting. He also laid out gardens (the art of garden creation forms a very important branch of Chinese aesthetics, since it gives birth simultaneously to the creation of a sculptured rhythm and a cosmological vision. This art was developed to a considerable degree in Yangzhou and Suzhou). The date of his death is not known exactly but it may fall somewhere between 1719 and 1720.

Since the information we have at our disposal concerning Shitao's life is fragmentary, it is more difficult to figure out his complex and multi-sided personality. He is particularly Protean in his paintings. In the whole of the history of Chinese painting it would be hard to find an artist with such wide and disconcerting stylistic metamorphoses (transformation is indeed one of the great theoretical themes of his *Sayings on Painting*). Using his technical virtuosity and his classical culture, he imitates the painting of the ancient masters, takes it apart and transforms it, moving deliberately from one extreme to the other in his techniques, from the posed and meticulous to the crude and brutal, from the false naiveties of archaism to the most daring modern innovations. For the teachings of the schools and respect for tradition he substituted the principle of the supreme autonomy of the creative artist: 'The beards and eyebrows of the old masters do grow on my face,' he said, or again, 'the method of not following any method is the best method'.

His radical individualism saw no bounds and the fact that he signed his paintings with more than thirty different names is significant. In his albums he is incomparable, needing only an accidental blot of ink to suggest a microcosm that opens out to inexhaustible riches. Effortlessly he transcends the tradition of ancient values and eccentricities, and yet reconciles the fundamental attributes of ancient cosmology, Confucianism, Daoism and Chan Buddhism to offer a synthetic explanation of the act of painting as a microcosmic pendant to the activity of the creator of the universe.

In the period in which he lived, Shitao's work was not popular, and he was largely appreciated only by the cultural elite of his time, who were mainly concentrated in Yangzhou. In Yangzhou itself, his art would play a direct part in the innovative work in the 18th century of the well-known *Eight Eccentrics of Yangzhou*. In the modern era the fascination that he arouses is more alive than ever. Huang Binhong (1863-1955) and Qi Baishi (1863-1957) have proclaimed their admiration for him, and their works bear witness to his liberating and fertile influence. Zhang Daqian (born 1899) studied his work with ambiguous delight. A large number of Shitao's works in museums and collections are in fact the products of his brush. Fu Baoshi (1904-1965) came under his influence in his painting and studied him as a historian. His monograph remains a basic text. If we add to this the critics, researchers and theoreticians - Chinese as well as Japanese or western - who have leaned towards or are leaning towards this exceptional personality at this very moment, no Chinese artist has ever excited greater interest.

BIBLIOGRAPHY:

Edwards, R. (ed.), *The Painting of Tao-chi*, exhibition catalogue, U.M.I., Anne Arbor, 1967. Chou, Ju-hsi, *In Quest of the Primordial Line: The Genesis and Content of Tao-chi's 'Hua-yu-lu*, dissertation, Princeton University, Princeton (PA), 1969. Ryckmans, Pierre, *Les 'Propos sur la peinture' de Shitao. Traduction et commentaires pour servir de contribution à l'étude terminologique et esthétique des théories chinoises de la peinture*, Institut belge des hautes études chinoises, Brussels, 1970. Yang Xin and others, *Three Thousand Years of Chinese Painting*, Yale University Press, New Haven and London, 1997. Clunas, Craig, *Art in China*, Oxford University Press, Oxford and New York, 1997. Sheng, François, *Shitao. La Saveur du monde*, Phébus, Paris, 2001. Hay, Jonathan, *Shitao: Painting and Modernity in Early Qing China*, Cambridge University Press, Cambridge, 2001. Juliet, Charles, *Shitao et Cézanne*, Échoppe, Paris, 2003.

MUSEUMS AND GALLERIES:

BEIJING (Palace Mus.): *Mountains in Clouds* (dated 1702, signed, long inscription by the artist); *Scholar's Garden on Rocky Riverbank* (inscription by the artist); *Man Seated on Ground Playing a Lute to an Ox* (ink, inscription by the artist); *Man in Boat on River among Large Rocks* (reddish colour on paper, handscroll, signed); *Studies of Landscapes of Mount Huang* (ink and light colour on paper, eight album leaves, inscriptions by the artist); *Mountain Terraces, Bamboo Thicket, Man in Boat* (light colour on paper, four album leaves) - BOSTON (MFA): *Man Going towards Mountain Retreat* (dated 1703, ink on paper, hanging scroll, inscription by the artist); *Bamboo and Rocks* (ink on paper, hanging scroll, inscription by the artist); *Conversion of Hariti to Buddhism* (signed and dated 1683, ink on paper, handscroll); *Rocky River Bank, Pavilions in Trees* (dated 1691, ink on paper, hanging scroll, colophon by Wu Hufan); *Album of Twelve Leaves with Poems and Inscriptions by the Artist* (signed and dated 1703, ink and colour on paper) - CLEVELAND (MA): *Spring on the Min River* (dated 1697, ink and colour on paper, hanging scroll, colophon and seal of the artist); *Orchids, Bamboo and Other Plants* (1662, handscroll, poem by the artist); *Landscapes of Luofushan* (album of 12 leaves, one signed) - HAKONE: *Landscapes of Luofushan* (album of 12 leaves) - PARIS (Mus. national des Arts asiatiques-Guimet): *Landscape: Mountain Retreat and Waterfall* (dated 1671, hanging scroll, signed, colophon of the artist) - SHANGHAI: *Autumn in Welyang* (colour on paper, hanging scroll, long poem by the artist on the history of the city); *Landscape* (dry ink and colour on paper, album leaf); *Large Pavilion in Bamboo Thicket, Scholar Seated on Upper Floor* (dated 1697, inscription by the artist) - STOCKHOLM (Nationalmus.): *Solitary Walker on Mountain Road* (long inscription and seal of the artist); *Bamboo Shoots and Tender Stem* (inscription by the artist); *Two Studies of Rocks and Streams* (two large album leaves, inscriptions and seal of the artist) - WASHINGTON DC (Freer Gal. of Art): *Valley Views with Rocks, Houses and Dead Trees* (dated 1684, handscroll, inscription).

AUCTION RECORDS:

NEW YORK, 31 May 1989, *Hermitage on Mount Tongpo* (ink on paper, hanging scroll, 33 1/2 x 16 1/2 ins / 84.8 x 42 cm) USD 52,250. NEW YORK, 4 Dec 1989, *Vegetables and Praying Mantis* (ink and colour on paper, hanging scroll, 31 1/2 x 24 1/2 ins / 80 x 62 cm) USD 176,000. NEW YORK, 6 Dec 1989, *Roaming in Woods* (ink on paper, hanging scroll, 18 1/2 x 11 3/4 ins / 47 x 30 cm) USD 88,000. NEW YORK, 29 May 1991, *Landscapes* (ink and colour on paper, album of ten leaves, each 9 1/4 x 14 1/2 ins / 23.8 x 36.9 cm) USD 308,000. NEW YORK, 25 Nov 1991, *Flowers, Vegetables and Landscapes* (ink on paper, album of ten leaves, each 13 1/4 x 9 3/4 ins / 33.7 x 24.8 cm) USD 495,000. NEW YORK, 1 June 1992, *Cliff with Waterfall among Pines* (ink and colour on paper, hanging scroll, 88 1/4 x 29 1/2 ins / 224 x 74.9 cm) USD 561,000. NEW YORK, 2 Dec 1992, *Orchid and Rock* (ink on paper, 26 x 14 1/2 ins / 66.3 x 36.7 cm) USD 60,500. NEW YORK, 18 March 1997, *Bamboo, Orchids and Rocks* (1691, ink on paper, handscroll, 10 1/2 x 128 ins / 26.7 x 324.2 cm) USD 211,500. HONG KONG, 26 April 1999, *Vegetables* (ink, hanging scroll, 18 x 15 ins / 46 x 37 cm) HKD 500,000. HONG KONG, 26 April 1999, *Landscapes* (ink and colour, ten in album, 9 x 15 ins / 24 x 37 cm) HKD 5,400,000. HONG KONG, 27 Oct 2003, *Listening to Waterfall* (1684, ink and colour, hanging scroll, 88 x 30 ins / 223 x 76 cm) HKD 5,100,000. HONG KONG, 25 April 2004, *Scenes of Gucheng River* (ink and colour, hanging scroll, 13 x 22 ins / 33 x 55 cm) HKD 280,000. HONG KONG, 25 April 2004, *Landscapes* (1695, ink, ten in album, 9 x 7 ins / 24 x 18 cm) HKD 1,400,000.

SHITNEFF, Jevgenij Ivanovitch. See **JITNEV Evgeni Ivanovich**

SHIUN, real name: Nakasato Michiko
Japanese, 20th century.
Born 23 December 1943, in Nishinomiya (Osaka Prefecture).
Active in France.
Painter. Portraits, landscapes, animals.

Shiun studied literature in her native Japan before moving to Paris, where she studied aesthetics and art. Her style shows the influence of having studied calligraphy as well. She settled in Paris, showing her work at the Grand Palais, at the Georges Pompidou Centre and at UNESCO.

SHIZENG. See **CHEN HENGKE**

SHLAPAK, Anatoly
Ukrainian, 20th century.
Born 1929, in Odessa.
Painter. Landscapes, still-lifes, flowers.

Anatoly Shlapak painted in a style resembling neo-Impressionist pointillism or divisionism.

AUCTION RECORDS:
PARIS, 10 Feb 1991, *Early Spring* (oil on canvas, 24 x 30 ins / 61 x 76 cm) FRF 5,000.

SHLYUSHINSKY, Franz Osipovich
Russian, 20th century.
Died 1 June 1864.
Print artist.

F.O. Shlyushinsky studied at the St Petersburg Academy.

SHMAKOV, Mickail Aleksandrovich
Russian, 19th - 20th century.
Born 1879; died 1906.
Painter.

MUSEUMS AND GALLERIES:
ST PETERSBURG (Gosudarstvennyj Russkij Muz.): two paintings.

SHMAROV, Paul, or Chmaroff Pavel Dimitrevich
Russian, 20th century.
Born 1874, in Voronezh; died 2 July 1950, in Paris.
Active in France.
Painter, draughtsman (red chalk). Figures, animals, landscapes. Decorative panels.

Paul Shmarov studied at the academy in St Petersburg between 1894 and 1899. He was a pupil of the Ilya Repin, and later became his collaborator. A contemporary of the Post-Impressionist movement, he painted the infinite nuances of light. His drawings, particularly those in red chalk, reveal his capacity for observation. A member of the Société Nationale des Beaux-Arts in Paris in 1912, during a stay in Paris, he received advice from Jean Paul Laurens. He won the Grand Prix of the academy of fine arts in St Petersburg, and was named court painter to Nicolas II, the last Tsar. He settled in Paris in 1920, and exhibited at the Salon des Artistes Français until 1939. Several of his works are in the Serge Lifar Collection.

chmaroff

MUSEUMS AND GALLERIES:
TOLEDO.

AUCTION RECORDS:
PARIS, May 1974, *Painting*, FRF 5,200. PARIS, July 1974, *Seated Woman* (pencil) FRF 600; *Reclining Nude* (drawing) FRF 700. HONFLEUR, 18 April 1976, *Swimming* (oil on canvas, 19 1/4 x 28 1/4 ins / 49 x 72 cm) FRF 3,400. HONFLEUR, 16 July 1978, *Young Girl at the River* (oil on canvas, 51 1/4 x 32 ins / 130 x 81 cm) FRF 2,300. VERSAILLES, 25 Feb 1979, *Study of Nude and Face* (drawing, 9 x 11 ins / 22 x 28 cm) FRF 400. PARIS, 22 Oct 1982, *In Front of the Church* (1898, oil on panel, 19 3/4 x 28 3/4 ins / 50 x 73 cm) FRF 6,200. SCEAUX, 18 Nov 1984, *Bathers* (oil on canvas, 23 1/4 x 36 1/4 ins / 59 x 92 cm) FRF 30,000. PARIS, 27 March 1985, *Bathers in Blue* (oil on canvas, 17 3/4 x 24 3/4 ins / 45 x 63 cm) FRF 29,000. LONDON, 6 May 1986, *Bathers* (oil on canvas, 20 x 29 1/4 ins / 50.8 x 74 cm) GBP 1,000. PARIS, 22 March 1989, *Sunbathing* (oil on canvas, 23 1/2 x 36 1/4 ins / 60 x 92 cm) FRF 38,000. PARIS, 27 May 1994, *Bathers* (oil on canvas, 19 3/4 x 28 3/4 ins / 50 x 73 cm) FRF 6,200. PARIS, 3 March 2003, *Woman Bathing in Lake I* (oil on canvas, 24 x 36 ins / 60 x 92 cm) EUR 27,000. LONDON, 19 Nov 2003, *Bathing Beauties* (oil on canvas, 69 x 47 ins / 175 x 120 cm) GBP 21,000. LONDON, 26 May 2004, *Portrait of a Girl with a Cat* (oil on canvas, 46 x 35 ins / 116 x 88 cm) GBP 28,000. PARIS, 16 June 2004, *Still-life with Melon* (oil on canvas, 24 x 36 ins / 60 x 92 cm) EUR 24,000.

SHMELEVSKY, Mikhail Antonovich
Russian, 19th century.
Active during the second half of the 19th century.
Painter, mosaicist.

SHMELKOV, Petr Mikhailovich
Russian, 19th century.
Born 1819; died 1890.
Painter, watercolourist, draughtsman. Genre scenes.

MUSEUMS AND GALLERIES:
MOSCOW (State Tretyakov Gal.): *Nearing Childbirth; Liking Overcomes Restraint; Preparations for a Walk* (watercolour); *In the House of the Departed* (watercolour); *Ivan the Terrible Looking at a Comet* (watercolour); *Nearing Childbirth* (sketch); *The Ivanovskaya Belltower in the Kremlin; Napoleon in Moscow; Before the Execution; An Importunate Guest* (drawing).

AUCTION RECORDS:
NEW YORK, 22 May 1986, *The Letter* (1864, oil on canvas, 45 x 35 1/2 ins / 114.5 x 90 cm) USD 5,250.

SHMIT, Aleksandr
Russian, 20th century.
Born 1911; died 1987.
Painter, watercolourist, pastellist. Figures, nudes, landscapes.

Aleksandr Shmit studied at the Ilya Repin Institute in Leningrad (now St Petersburg) under Kuzma Petrov-Vodkin and Aleksandr Savinov. He exhibited from 1930 and was a member of the Soviet Artists Union.

MUSEUMS AND GALLERIES:
MOSCOW (State Tretyakov Gal.) - OMSK (MFA) - ST PETERSBURG (Academy) - ST PETERSBURG (Gosudarstvennyj Russkij Muz.) - VIBORG (Museum of Contemporary Russian Art).

AUCTION RECORDS:
PARIS, 11 June 1990, *Girl Before Mirror* (1948, gouache and watercolour on card, 17 1/4 x 13 3/4 ins / 44 x 35 cm) FRF 13,000.

SHOAN, artist name: Baian
Japanese, 15th - 16th century.
Painter.

Shoan was a Zen monk and *suiboku* (ink) painter of the Muromachi period. He is reputed to have been a disciple of Shokei (Kei Shoki). He lived in the village of Ota, now in Ibaragi Prefecture.

SHODEJKO, Leonid Florianovich.
See **JODEIKO**

SHOEI, real name: Kano, Tadanobu; popular names: Genshichiro, Oinosuke; artist name and priest name: Shoei
Japanese, 16th century.
Born 1519; died 1592.
Painter.
Kano School.

Shoei was the son of Kano Motonobu (1476-1559), whom he assisted in the family workshops, producing decorative works for temples and palaces. He would later teach his son, Eitoku (1543-1590).

SHOGA, family name: Takuma, priest name: Shoga
Japanese, 12th century.
Active in Kyoto c. 1191.
Painter. Religious subjects.

Shoga painted Buddhist subjects. One of his works survives in the Kyoo Gokoku-ji in Kyoto.

SHOGEN. See **KAIHO Yusho**

SHOGUN, Mampuku
Japanese, 8th century.
Sculptor.

Shogun Mampuku, whose name suggests that he was a naturalised Japanese, was a sculptor of the Nara period. He was involved in producing statues for the western *kondo* (golden hall) of the Kofuku-ji, Nara, which was built on the demand of the empress Komyo in 734. Although the building and its sculptures have disappeared, it may be assumed that Shogun Mampuku's style is recalled in some of the works that do survive in the Kofuku-ji, the *Judai Deshi* (the 10 Great Disciples of the Buddha) and the *Hachibushu* (the Eight Protectors, the eight categories of supernatural being who protect the Buddhist Messengers and the Law).

BIBLIOGRAPHY:
Kuno, Takeshi, *A Guide to Japanese Sculpture*, Mayuyama, Tokyo, 1963.

SHOHAKU, or Kiyu, Shiryu, real name: Soga Kiyu, family name: Miura, given name: Sakonjiro, artist names: Shokaku, Joki, Ranzan, Dasokuken, Kashinsai, Hiran, Kishinshai, Dasokken
Japanese, 18th century.
Born 1730, in Ise; died 1781.
Active in Kyoto.
Painter. Landscapes, scenes with figures.

Soga Shohaku lived and worked in Kyoto. He first learned painting under Takeda Keiho, a Kyoto painter of the Kano School, before studying Sesshu (1420-1506), from whom he would draw much inspiration.

BIBLIOGRAPHY:
Guth, Christine, *Japanese Art of the Edo Period*, Calmann & King, London, 1996.

MUSEUMS AND GALLERIES:
BOSTON (MFA): *Horse* (ink on paper, hanging scroll); *Four Sages of Mount Shang* (ink on paper, two six-panel screens) - KYOTO (Kosho-Ji Temple): *Kanzan and Jittoku* (ink on paper, two hanging scrolls) - WASHINGTON DC (Freer Gal. of Art): *Gama Sennin* (ink on paper, hanging scroll).

AUCTION RECORDS:
NEW YORK, 17 Oct 1989, *Kanzan and Jittoku* (ink on paper, hanging scroll, 49 1/2 x 20 ins / 126 x 50.5 cm) USD 8,800. NEW YORK, 26 March 1991, *Wild Goose* (ink on paper, hanging scroll, 46 1/2 x 22 ins / 118.4 x 55.7 cm) USD 2,200.

SHOHO, nickname: Suga
Japanese, 19th century.
Active in Osaka c. 1810.
Illustrator.

SHOI. See **MATABEI**

SHOKA, real name: Nakae Tocho, nickname: Choko, artist names: Shoka, Kateidojin, Goteki
Japanese, 18th century.
Born in Omi, now Shiga Prefecture.
Active at the beginning of the 18th century.
Painter.

Shoka was a Nanga School (literati) painter who studied landscape under Kyujo and settled in Kyoto after travelling extensively around his native district (including Echigo, Shinano and Edo). He adopted the artist name Goteki, which means 'skilled in the five arts' (seal carving, painting, poetry, calligraphy and music). For this last he played the *koto*.

SHOKA, real name: Watanabe Kai, given name: Shokei, popular name: Shunji, artist name: Shoka
Japanese, 19th century.
Born 1835; died 1887.
Active in Tokyo.
Painter.

Shoka was the son of Kazan (1793-1841) and a painter of the Nanga School (literati). He painted landscapes, birds and flowers.

SHOKADO, real name: Nakanuma, popular name: Shikibu, artist names: Seiseio, Shokado, Shojo
Japanese, 17th century.
Born 1584, in Sakai (Osaka Prefecture); died 1639.
Painter, calligrapher.

Shokado was a calligrapher, and bird and flower painter whose work derives from the Chinese masters of the Song and Yuan dynasties. He became a monk of the Shingon sect and lived at the Hachiman shrine at Otokayama, near Kyoto.

SHOKATSUKAN, real name: Shimizu Kan, given name: Shibun, popular name: Matashiro, artist names: Seisai, Kogado, Shokatsukan
Japanese, 18th century.
Born 1719; died 1790.
Active in Edo (now Tokyo).
Painter.

Shokatsukan was a bird and flower painter. Although he was self-taught, his work contains borrowings from the Chinese masters of the Yuan, Ming and Qing dynasties.

SHOKEI, priest name: Kenko, alternate name: Keishoki: artist name: Hinrakusai
Japanese, 15th - 16th century.
Died probably in 1518.
Painter. Portraits, landscapes, animals.

At the start of the second half of the Muromachi period, a number of *suiboku* (ink) monk-painters emerge who followed the footsteps of Shubun (active in about 1425-1450) and Sesshu (1420-1506) and who were associated with the five great Zen temples of Kamakura, in the Kanto region of eastern Japan. One of these was Shokei, of the Kencho-ji temple, where he would have been a disciple of the monk-painter Chuan Shinko. Shokei is also known as a calligrapher (hence his alternate name, Keishoki, or scribe Kei). In 1478, he went to Kyoto, where he studied painting under Gaiami (1431-1485) and where he would remain for three years before returning to his temple. Shokei's style contains a mixture of elements inherited from the Chinese Ma-Xia School and the Japanese master Shubun. These he would hand on to his own disciples, Keiboku and Keison.

BIBLIOGRAPHY:
Tanaka, Ichimatsu, *Japanese Ink Painting: Shûbun to Sesshû*, Weatherhill, New York, 1972.

MUSEUMS AND GALLERIES:
KYOTO (National Mus.): *Bird on Flowering Branch* (ink and light colour on paper, hanging scroll) - NAGOYA (Tokugawa Art Mus.): *Portraits of Hanshan and Shide* (light colour on paper, two hanging scrolls, attributed); *Landscapes of the Four Seasons* (light colour on paper, six-panel screen, attributed) - TOKYO (Nezu Institute of Fine Arts): *Spring Landscape* (ink and light colour on paper, hanging scroll, two seals of the artist).

AUCTION RECORDS:
NEW YORK, 17 Oct 1989, *Portrait of Su Dongbo* (ink on paper, hanging scroll, 21 3/4 x 10 ins / 55.4 x 25.2 cm) USD 46,200.

SHOKO, or Shokosai, real name: Hanbei
Japanese, 18th - 19th century.
Active in Osaka c. 1795-1809.
Print artist.

Shokosai was a pupil of Ryukosai. He is known for a single print, dated 1798.

SHOMAN, Suha
20th century.
Born February 1944, in Jerusalem.

Active in Jordan.
Painter.

Suha Shoman lived in Paris between 1966 and 1969, where she studied law and took courses in art at the Fahrelnissa Zeid Royal Jordanian Institute of Fine Art. Her painting evokes a universe of galaxies and space in a lyrical blend of natural elements (water, earth and fire), using superimposed and blended colours. They are also characterised by circular or exploding movements, which occasionally reveal figurative subjects such as the silhouettes in the composition *Procession*.

Shoman has taken part in public exhibitions, including: 1981, Cultural Institute, Amman, spring festival of Jordanian painters, Amman and Ankara, Jordanian Culture Week, Moscow; 1981 and 1983, Salon d'Automne, Paris; 1983, *La femme et la créativité* (*Women and Creativity*), Royal Cultural Centre, Amman. She has also held solo exhibitions, including: 1984, *Galaxies d'orient* (*Oriental Galaxies*), Wally Findlay Galleries, Paris.

BIBLIOGRAPHY:

Parinaud, André, *Suha Shoman*, exhibition catalogue, Wally Findlay Gall., Paris, 1984.

SHONBORN, John Lewis

Hungarian, 19th - 20th century.
Born 1852, in Nemora; died 1931, in Gien, France.
Painter, draughtsman. Genre scenes, landscapes, animals.

John Lewis Shonborn emigrated with his parents to Oxford, USA, at a very early age. At the age of 20, he went to France to attend painting courses in various studios, including those of the draughtsman Charles Crauk at Amiens, where he met the painter Francis Tattegrain, and of Léon Bonnat. He fell seriously ill, becoming almost totally deaf and suffering a serious eye condition that obliged him to spend several months each year in the Algerian sun. Several of his works from Algeria were included at the posthumous retrospective held in Senlis in 1965.

Shonborn started by painting scenes of country life, many in the Île-de-France, and especially in the region around Senlis and Montlévêque. He also excelled in painting animals; some of his pictures from Algeria are magnificent studies of Arab thoroughbreds in landscapes bathed in light.

MUSEUMS AND GALLERIES:

AMIENS: *Clearing Heather; Stable Interior.*

AUCTION RECORDS:

LONDON, 21 June 1984, *Arab Encampment* (oil on canvas, 34 x 48 1/2 ins / 85.5 x 123.2 cm) GBP 8,000. PARIS, 18 June 1986, *Two Children Fishing* (oil on canvas, 78 3/4 x 52 3/4 ins / 200 x 134 cm) FRF 50,000. PARIS, 17 June 1988, *Shepherd Watching his Sheep* (oil on canvas, 20 x 15 ins / 51 x 38 cm) FRF 9,000. PARIS, 27 Nov 1989, *Paris Street in the Snow* (oil on canvas, 17 3/4 x 14 3/4 ins / 45 x 37.5 cm) FRF 4,800. PARIS, 22 April 1994, *Kabyle Children Walking* (oil on canvas, 21 1/2 x 17 3/4 ins / 54.5 x 45 cm) FRF 7,800. LONDON, 17 Nov 1994, *Arabs by Shaded Stream* (1909, oil on canvas, 13 x 15 3/4 ins / 32.1 x 40 cm) GBP 2,070. PARIS, 25 June 1996, *Camp* (oil on canvas, 24 x 35 3/4 ins / 61 x 91 cm) FRF 22,000. PARIS, 29 Nov 1999, *South Algeria, Caravan* (oil on canvas, 8 x 13 ins / 21 x 33 cm) FRF 21,500. PARIS, 5 July 2000, *Place a Halfaouine* (oil on canvas, 13 x 16 ins / 32 x 40 cm) FRF 21,000. PARIS, 20 Nov 2000, *Eagle* (oil on canvas on panel, 12 x 10 ins / 30 x 25 cm) FRF 30,000. PARIS, 18 June 2001, *Horsemen by Fortified Town* (oil on canvas, 19 x 30 ins / 49 x 75 cm) FRF 100,000. PARIS, 16 June 2003, *Young Girl at River* (oil on canvas, 15 x 22 ins / 38 x 55 cm) EUR 3,500. PARIS, 15 Dec 2003, *Horses in Camp* (oil on canvas, 29 x 36 ins / 73 x 92 cm) EUR 2,800.

SHONEN, real name: Suzuki Matsutoshi, artist name: Shonen

Japanese, 19th - 20th century.
Born 1849; died 1918.
Active in Kyoto.
Painter. Landscapes.

Shonen was a pupil of Suzuki Hyakunen.

SHONIBARE, Yinka

Nigerian and British, 20th - 21st century.
Born 1962, in London.
Active in London.
Installation artist, painter, photographer.
Young British Artists.

Yinka Shonibare grew up in Lagos but returned to London, his birthplace, at the age of 17. He has received a number of awards, including the Paul Hamlyn Foundation Award for Visual Artists in 1998. He teaches at various art schools, including the School of Oriental and African Art and the Chelsea School of Art.

Although Nigerian, Shonibare was among the artists who took part in the *Sensations* exhibition in 1996-1997, which marked the beginning of media acclaim and commercial success for the 'Young British Artists' and which reflected the vitality and originality of contemporary British art. Shonibare is known for his installations which present 18th-century figures dressed in exotic costumes and colourful native figures. These draw on the European artistic tradition of 'fantasy figures' - men and women dressed in the oriental or Spanish style, for example. One of his best-known installations, *Swing* (2001), actually subverts this art, being an interpretation of Fragonard's *Hasards Heureux de l'Escarpolette* (*The Swing*). Shonibare's approach, which could be seen simply as an attack on Neo-Colonialism, is far more complex. The colourful fabrics symbolise an historically accurate trade, that of cottons manufactured in Europe - in Manchester particularly - and then traded for African slaves. These fabrics, which were in great demand, later paradoxically became a symbol of African identity. By deliberately blurring these clues, Évence Verdier believes that Shonibare 'seeks to create an aesthetic of inter-culturality that is not moralising and manages to produce a fusion between two sides of the same history'. His concept of an aesthetic of hybridization of the cultures is also reflected in the batik motifs he paints and in the thousands of woven and decorated floor plates which he uses in a device which combines minimalism with all-over art, or again in the figure of the rebellious dandy in the photographs in which he himself appears.

Shonibare exhibited at the now historic *Sensations* exhibition at the Royal Academy in London in 1996-1997, organised by Charles Saatchi. He also exhibited at the following: the Johannesburg Biennale in South Africa (1997); *Heaven* at the Kunsthalle in Düsseldorf (1999); *Other Modernities* at the Camberwell College of Art in London (2000); and *Authentic/Ex-centric: Conceptualism in Contemporary African Art* at the 49th Venice Biennale (2001). He has also shown his work in solo exhibitions since 1989, including at the following: the Camden Art Centre in London (2000); the Tate Britain in London (2001); the Israel Museum in Jerusalem (2002); the Kiasma Museum in Helsinki (2003); the Padiglione d'Arte Contemporanea in Milan (2003); and the Boymans van Beuningen Museum in Rotterdam (2004). He was an entrant for the Turner Prize at the Tate Britain, London, in 2004.

BIBLIOGRAPHY:

Enwezor, Okwui, *Yinka Shonibare: dressing down*, exhibition catalogue, Ikon Gallery, Birmingham, 1999. Majo, Elena di/Perrella, Cristina, *Yinka Shonibare: be-muse*, exhibition catalogue, Museo Hendrik Christian Andersen, Rome, 2001. Barber, Anna, *Yinka Shonibare. Double dress*, exhibition catalogue, Israel Museum, Jerusalem, 2002. Verdier, Évence, '*Yinka Shonibare*' in *Art Press*, no. 288, p 29, periodical, Paris, March 2003.

SHONNARD, Eugenie Frederica
American, 20th century.
Born 29 April 1886, in Yonkers (New York); died 1978.
Sculptor.

Eugenie Frederica Shonnard was a student of Antoine Bourdelle and Rodin.

MUSEUMS AND GALLERIES:
NEW YORK (Metropolitan Mus. of Art) - PARIS (Mus. d'Orsay).

AUCTION RECORDS:
NEW YORK, 22 May 1980, *Marabou* (1922, lost-wax bronze with black patina, h. 38 1/2 ins / 97.5 cm) USD 5,500.

SHOO. See **RYUHO I**

SHOOSMITH, Thurston Laidlaw
British, 19th - 20th century.
Watercolourist.

Thurston Shoosmith was active in Northampton. He exhibited in London from 1899.

SHOOTE, John. See **SHUTE**

SHOR, Zvi
Israeli, 20th century.
Born 1898; died 1979.
Painter. Interiors, landscapes, Still-lifes, flowers.

AUCTION RECORDS:
TEL AVIV, 3 May 1980, *Landscape* (oil on canvas, 21 3/4 x 18 1/4 ins / 55.5 x 46.5 cm) ILS 27,000. TEL AVIV, 25 May 1988, *Country Landscape* (oil on canvas, 18 1/4 x 24 1/2 ins / 46.5 x 62.5 cm) USD 1,320. TEL AVIV, 2 Jan 1989, *Landscape* (oil on card, 13 1/4 x 18 3/4 ins / 33.5 x 47.5 cm) USD 1,100. TEL AVIV, 3 Jan 1990, *Neve Zedek* (oil on card, 19 3/4 x 13 1/2 ins / 50 x 34.5 cm) USD 2,970. TEL AVIV, 19 June 1990, *Landscape* (oil on canvas, 21 3/4 x 15 1/4 ins / 55.5 x 38.5 cm) USD 1,540. TEL AVIV, 1 Jan 1991, *Petach Tiqua* (oil on canvas, 15 1/4 x 22 ins / 38.5 x 56 cm) USD 1,540. TEL AVIV, 12 June 1991, *Still-life with Vase of Flowers and Fruit* (oil on canvas, 28 1/2 x 23 1/2 ins / 72.5 x 60 cm) USD 3,300. TEL AVIV, 6 Jan 1992, *Shenkin Gardens in Tel Aviv* (oil on canvas, 13 x 16 1/4 ins / 33 x 41 cm) USD 1,040. TEL AVIV, 12 Jan 1997, *Interior* (1969, oil on canvas, 25 1/2 x 19 3/4 ins / 65 x 50 cm) USD 2,070. TEL AVIV, 4 July 1999, *Road in the Village* (oil on board, 15x22 ins / 38x55 cm) GBP 696. TEL AVIV, 4 July 1999, *Still-life with Vase and Flowers* (oil on canvas, 32x24 ins / 81x61 cm) GBP 1,076. TEL AVIV, 16 Jan 2000, *Hamsin at the Village* (oil on masonite, 18x22 ins / 46x55 cm) GBP 920. TEL AVIV, 16 Jan 2000, *Street in Village* (1976, oil on wood, 14x17 ins / 35x44 cm) GBP 552. TEL AVIV, 15 Jan 2001, *Boulevard with Trees* (oil on canvas, 13x16 ins / 33x41 cm) GBP 685. TORONTO, 16 June 2003, *Laneway with Houses* (oil on canvas, 36x26 ins / 91x65 cm) CAD 3,000. TEL AVIV, 1 Oct 2004, *Landscape* (oil on card, 11 x 14 ins / 27 x 36 cm) GBP 356. TEL AVIV, 1 Dec 2004, *Landscape* (oil on canvas, 13 x 17 ins / 33 x 42 cm) GBP 317.

SHORAKAN. See **KIGYOKU**

SHORAKUSAI, real name: Itoku, artist name: Shoju
Japanese, 19th century.
Active in Osaka c. 1800.
Print artist.

SHORE, Bethea E.
British, 20th century.
Born in Cuttack (India), to British parents.
Painter.

Bethea E. Shore exhibited in Paris from 1906 at the Salon des Indépendants.

SHORE, Henrietta Mary
Canadian, 20th century.
Born 1880, in Toronto; died 1963, in San Jose (California).
Painter.

Henrietta Mary Shore was taught by William Chase and Kenneth Hayes Miller at the Art Students League in New York. She also studied in London and was a member of the Société des Artistes Indépendants. She won many awards.

MUSEUMS AND GALLERIES:
OTTAWA (NG. of Canada).

AUCTION RECORDS:
LOS ANGELES, 18 June 2003, *Fantasy Landscape* (coloured pencil on paper on board, 12 x 17 ins / 31 x 43 cm) USD 9,000.

SHOREY, George H.
American, 19th - 20th century.
Born 9 September 1870, in Hoosick Falls (New York); died 1944.
Painter, illustrator. Religious subjects.

George H. Shorey was a student of Walter Shirlaw, probably in New York, where he too settled. He painted an *Ascension* for the Trinity Church, Grandwood.

SHORT, Frank (Sir), or Schort, Franz
British, 19th - 20th century.
Born 19 June 1857, in London; died 1945.
Watercolourist, draughtsman, engraver.

Frank Short exhibited at the Royal Academy from 1874, and became an associate in 1901 and a full academician in 1911. He taught at the Royal College of Art. He exhibited at the Paris Universal Expositions of 1889 and 1901, winning gold medals on both occasions. He was best known for his work as an engraver, particularly of mezzotints and aquatints, and was President of the Society of Painter-Etchers from 1910 to 1938. He was kinighted in 1911.

MUSEUMS AND GALLERIES:
LONDON (Victoria and Albert Mus.): watercolour.

SHORT, Obediah
British, 19th century.
Born 1803, in Norwich; died 1886, in Norwich.
Painter. Genre scenes.

MUSEUMS AND GALLERIES:
NORWICH (Castle Mus. and AG): *Woman on a Footbridge; Scene on a Highway.*

SHORT, R.
British, 18th century.
Painter, draughtsman. Naval battles, seascapes.

R. Short was noted for 12 scenes depicting naval battles between the French and Spanish forces, engraved by Caroline Watson and published by Boydell.

SHORT, Richard
British, 18th century.
Painter. Landscapes, seascapes.

Richard Short was active in Cardiff. He was a member of the Royal Cumbrian Academy and exhibited in London, particularly at the Royal Academy and the Royal Society of British Artists in Suffolk Street from 1822.

MUSEUMS AND GALLERIES:
CARDIFF: *Stormy Weather; Worm's Head Point, Gower.*

AUCTION RECORDS:
LONDON, 31 May 1989, *The Port of Cardiff* (oil on canvas, 27 x 46 ins / 68.5 x 117 cm) GBP 1,540.

SHORTER
British, 17th century.
Active in Oxford.
Painter.

SHORTER, Edward Swift
American, 20th century.
Born 2 July 1900, in Colombus (Maine).
Painter, engraver.

Edward Swift Shorter studied at the Corcoran Art School and was also taught by Émile Renard in Paris. He was a member of the Société des Artistes Indépendants, the American Artists Professional League and the American Federation of Arts.

SHOSAI. See **ITSUUN**

SHOSEN, real name: Soga Shosen
Japanese, 16th century.
Painter. Figures, landscapes.

The son and disciple of Soga Soyo, Soga Shosen was a *suiboku* (ink) painter of the Muromachi period (early 16th century).

MUSEUMS AND GALLERIES:
TOKYO (Nezu Institute of Fine Arts): *Landscape* (1523, hanging scroll in ink and light colour on paper with an inscription by Gesshû Jukei).

AUCTION RECORDS:
NEW YORK, 23 Oct 1991, *Two Women Crossing a Bridge Lined With Willows under Snow; Two Women Taking Shelter under a Willow during a Summer Shower* (Oban Tate-e print, a pair, each 15 1/4 x 10 1/4 ins / 38.9 x 26 cm) USD 1,430.

SHOSEN'IN, real name: Kano Masanobu, original given name: Eijiro, artist names: Shosen'in, Soshosai, Shoko, Rekido
Japanese, 19th century.
Born 1823; died 1880.
Painter.
Kano School.

Shosen'in was the son and disciple of Yoshin. He ran the Kobikicho Kano studio in Tokyo.

SHOSHO, real name Watanabe Seijiro, original name: Tomika, given name: Genshi, popular name: Kiyojiro, artist names: Seishu, Shusho
Japanese, 19th century.
Born 1821; died 1870.
Active in Osaka c. 1847-1848.
Print artist.

Shosho imitated and deliberately signed in the same style as Sadamasu.

SHOTO, Bokusai, given name: Motsurin (or Botsurin), artist name: Bokusai, alternate name: Judaso
Japanese, 15th century.
Died 1492.
Painter (wash). Portraits, landscapes.

Bokusai belonged to the school of ink painting of the Muromachi period and was probably a pupil of Jasoku, the successor of Hyobu-Bokkei. A Zen priest, he was a disciple of Ikkyu Sojun of the Daitokuji school and became the abbot of the Shuon-an monastery. He lived at Daitoku-ji, Murasakino (Kyoto). An excellent monochrome ink wash (*suiboku-ga*) painter, he painted landscapes as well as the portrait of his master, Ikkyu Sojun.

MUSEUMS AND GALLERIES:
CLEVELAND (MA): *Ants Hauling a Pumpkin* (1400s, ink on paper, hanging scroll, attributed).

SHOU KUN LU. See **LU SHOUKUN**

SHOUBRIDGE, W.
British, 19th century.
Active in London.
Painter. Architectural views.

W. Shoubridge exhibited in London between 1831 and 1853.

SHOUN. See **NANKAI Gion**

SHOUN, real name: Kano Suenobu, original name: Iwamoto, popular name: Ichiemon, artist names: Kano Shoun, Choshinsai
Japanese, 17th century.
Born 1637; died 1702.
Active in Edo (now Tokyo).
Painter.

Shoun was a painter of the Kano School and a disciple of Yasunobu (1613-1685).

SHOUNSAI RISSHI. See **KAZUNOBU**

SHOUT, Robert
British, 18th - 19th century.
Active in Holborn between 1770 and 1830.
Sculptor.

SHOUTE, Hubert Pieter. See **SCHOUTEN**

SHOVER, Edna Mann
American, 20th century.
Born in Indianapolis (Indiana).
Painter, illustrator.

Edna Mann Shover was taught by John or Ludwig Faber, Thomas Scott and Joseph Frank Copeland. She was a member of the American Federation of Arts.

SHOY, Johann Jacob. See **SCHOY**

SHOYOKEN. See **NOBUKADO Takeda**

SHPAGIN, Mikhail
Russian, 20th century.
Born 1940, in Leningrad (now St Petersburg).
Painter. Urban landscapes.

AUCTION RECORDS:
PARIS, 29 Nov 1990, *The Quays of the Fontanka* (oil/synthetic resin, 23 1/4 x 32 1/4 ins / 59 x 82 cm) FRF 3,200.

SHPATARAKU, Constantin
Albanian, 18th century.
Icon painter.

Constantin Shataraku painted the famous *Icon of St Vladimir*. The illustration of the life of this saint contains contemporary scenes (from the 18th century) - the figures are dressed in 18th-century clothes, and it features the Albanian Prince Charles Thopia. The icon dates from 1731, and is now in Lushnjë, in the monastery of Ardenice. The museum of archaeology and ethnography in Tirana also owns works by this artist: *The Last Supper*, and *Crucifixion*, which are both from the church of St Paraskève in Lushnjë.

SHPONKO, Grigori Andreevich
Ukrainian, 20th century.
Born 1926, in Balki, Zaporozhe region.
Painter. Historical subjects, scenes with figures, waterscapes.

Grigori Andreevich Shponko studied in Trohimenko's studio at the Kiev art institute, graduating in 1953. In general, Shponko adhered to the rules of Socialist Realism but, following an accident in which he lost his right arm, he started to work with his left hand and lost some of his precision; he offset this handicap with a keener sense of colour. He lived and worked in Kiev. In 1959 he became a member of the Artists Union. He took part in many exhibitions both in the U.S.S.R. and abroad, including in Poland, Czechoslovakia, Bulgaria and Japan.

MUSEUMS AND GALLERIES:
KIEV (State Historical Museum).

AUCTION RECORDS:
PARIS, 18 March 1991, *Youth* (1973, oil on card, 19 1/4 x 26 3/4 ins / 49 x 68 cm) FRF 6,000; *Bathing the Horses* (1954, oil on canvas, 22 1/2 x 54 ins / 57 x 137 cm) FRF 26,000. PARIS, 19 June 1991, *By the River* (1975, oil on canvas, 25 1/2 x 44 ins / 65 x 112 cm) FRF 4,500.

SHRADER, Edwin Roscoe
American, 19th - 20th century.
Born 14 December 1879, in Quincy (Illinois); died 1960.
Painter, illustrator. Genre scenes, landscapes.

Edwin Roscoe Shrader was a student of Howard Pyle. He was active in Los Angeles.

SHRADY, Henry Merwin
American, 19th - 20th century.
Born 24 October 1871, in New York; died 12 April 1922, in New York.
Sculptor. Animals.

Henry Merwin Shrady was mainly an animal sculptor but he also made equestrian statues, such as that of Washington in Brooklyn and also one of Buffalo Bill.

AUCTION RECORDS:
NEW YORK, 20 April 1972, *Buffalo Bill* (patinated bronze) USD 3,250. NEW YORK, 29 April 1976, *Buffalo* (1900, brown-patinated bronze, h. 22 ins / 56 cm) USD 12,000. NEW YORK, 21 April 1977, *Buffalo* (1900, brown-patinated bronze, h. 21 ins / 53.4 cm) USD 17,000. NEW YORK, 23 May 1979, *Thoroughbred* (1903, patinated bronze, h. 23 ins / 57.5 cm) USD 6,500. NEW YORK, 22 Oct 1982, *Elk Buffalo* (1899, brown-patinated bronze, h. 13 1/2 ins / 34.3 cm) USD 16,000. NEW YORK, 2 June 1983, *Bull Moose* (1900, dark-brown-patinated bronze, h. 19 3/4 ins / 50.2 cm) USD 9,000. NEW YORK, 5 Dec 1985, *The Empty Saddle* (1900, greenish-brown-patinated bronze, h. 11 ins / 27.9 cm) USD 8,750. NEW YORK, 4 Dec 1986, *The Empty Saddle* (dark-brown-patinated bronze, h. 11 ins / 28 cm) USD 10,500. NEW YORK, 26 May 1988, *Monarch of the Plains* (1899, bronze, h. 13 1/4 ins / 33.7 cm) USD 30,800. NEW YORK, 23 May 1990, *Bull Moose* (bronze, h. 20 1/2 ins / 52.1 cm) USD 15,400. NEW YORK, 17 Dec 1990, *Civil War Officer on Horseback* (brown-patinated bronze, h. 19 ins / 48.1 cm) USD 3,575. NEW YORK, 26 May 1993, *Monarch of the Plains* (bronze, h. 14 ins / 35.5 cm) USD 23,000. NEW YORK, 2 Dec 1993, *Hungry Saddle Horse* (bronze, h. 11 ins / 27.9 cm) USD 13,800. NEW YORK, 30 Nov 1995, *Saving the Colours* (1899, bronze, h. 15 3/4 ins / 40 cm) USD 14,950. NEW YORK, 23 May 1996, *Reindeer* (bronze, h. 20 1/2 ins / 52.1 cm) USD 23,000. NEW YORK, 4 Dec 1996, *Monarch of the Plains* (1900, bronze, h. 22 3/4 ins / 58 cm) USD 123,500. NEW YORK, 27 May 1999, *Monarch of the Plains* (1899, dark brown patinated bronze, h. 13 ins / 34 cm) USD 65,000. NEW YORK, 28 June 2000, *Stallion* (1903, green-brown patinated bronze, h. 22 ins / 56 cm) USD 9,750. ST LOUIS, 15 Sept 2001, *Bust of Ulysses S. Grant* (1911, bronze) USD 3,500. NEW YORK, 28 Nov 2001, *Empty Saddle* (greenish patinated bronze, h. 11 ins / 28 cm) USD 27,500. SANTA FE, 9 Nov 2002, *An Empty Saddle* (bronze, h. 11 ins / 28 cm) USD 40,000. NEW YORK, 21 May 2003, *Monarch of the Plains* (reddish-brown patinated bonze, h. 13 ins / 34 cm) USD 80,000.

SHRAMZEV, Vasili
Russian, 19th century.
Active during the first half of the 19th century.
Engraver.

SHRASKY
Russian, 19th century.
Painter. Fruit, still-lifes.

SHRENOV, Aleksandr Sergeevich
Russian, 19th century.
Born in Russia.
Painter, watercolourist.

Member of the Imperial Society of Russian Watercolourists. He exhibited: *We had Searched, Memories of the Past, In the Forest, A Winter's Evening, In Passing.*

SHRIGLEY, David
British, 20th - 21st century.
Born 18 September 1968, in Macclesfield.
Draughtsman, humorist, sculptor, photographer.
Artists' books.

David Shrigley studied at Leicester Polytechnic (1987-1988), and at Glasgow School of Art (1988-1991), where he concentrated on the course in environmental art and obtained a BFA. He lives in Glasgow. He has taught as part-time lecturer at Glasgow School of Art (1997), and as visiting lecturer at the fine art department of Duncan of Jordanstone School of Design, Dundee (1997).

Shrigley's work consists of cartoons and drawings published as books, sculpture and public works. His drawings and texts in books, some published with his own Armpit Press, range in subject matter from a quiz to distinguish television sets from microwaves, to maps and charts. His sculpture is done in a variety of media including steel, polyester and polyurethane foam. His work often contains a strong element of humour and absurdity, focusing on the daily human condition, as in *5 Years of Toenail Clippings* (2002, glass and toenails), or *The Contents of the Gap between the Refrigerator and the Cooker* (1995, plastic). His public artworks include *Millennium Spaces Project*, Possil Park, Glasgow (1999) and *Sous Les Ponts, Le Long de la Rivière*, Casino Luxembourg (2001). In 2002, Shrigley curated the exhibition *Hmmm* for the Scottish National Gallery of Modern Art in Edinburgh.

He has had solo exhibitions at *Map of the Sewer*, Transmission Gallery, Glasgow (1995); Hermetic Gallery, Milwaukee (1997); Stephen Friedman, London (1997); Yvon Lambert, Paris (1998); Camden Arts Centre, London (2002); *Jokes*, Mamco, Geneva (2002); Armand Hammer Museum, University of California, Los Angeles (2002) and Galerie Nicolai Wallner, Copenhagen (2003). Other shows include *Head Shrinker*, Glasgow Green (1990); *Guard Dog*, Willis Tobacco Factory, Glasgow (1991); *In Here*, Transmission Gallery (1992); *Billboard*, Tramway, Glasgow (1993); *Some of My Friends*, Galerie Campbells Occasionally, Copenhagen (1994); *New Art in Scotland*, Centre for Contemporary Arts, Glasgow (1994); *5 Scottish Artists*, Bartok 32 Galéria, Budapest (1995); *The Unbelievable Truth*, Stedelijk Museum, Amsterdam (1996); *Slight*, Norwich Gallery (1997); *New British Photography*, Stadhaus, Ulm (1997); *Surfacing*, Institute of Contemporary Art (1998); *Beck's Futures*, Institute of Contemporary Art, London (2000, tour); *The British Art Show 5*, City Art Centre, Edinburgh (2000, tour); *The Unhomely*, Kettle's Yard, Cambridge (2003); *Splat, Boom, Pow! The Influence of Cartoons in Contemporary Art*, Contemporary Arts Museum, Houston (2003) and *State of Play*, Serpentine Gallery (2004).

BIBLIOGRAPHY:
Shrigley, David, *Slug Trails*, illustrated book, Black Rose, Glasgow, 1991. Shrigley, David, *Merry Eczema*, illustrated book, Black Rose, Glasgow, 1992. Shrigley, David, *Blanket of Filth*, illustrated book, Armpit Press, Glasgow, 1994. Shrigley, David, *Err*, illustrated book, Book Works, London, 1996. Shrigley, David, *Why We Got the Sack from the Museum*, illustrated book, Redstone Press, London, 1998. Bernadac, Marie-Laure/Moisdon-Tremblay, et al., *Présumés innocents: l'art contemporain et l'enfance*, exhibition catalogue, Capc musée d'Art contemporain, Bordeaux, 2000. *Grip/David Shrigley*, Pocketbooks, Morning Star Publications, Edinburgh, 2000. Paul, Frédéric, *David Shrigley*, exhibition catalogue, Centre d'Art contemporain, Domaine de Kerguéhennec, 2002. *David Shrigley*, exhibition catalogue, Center for Curatorial Studies, Bard College, Annandale-on-Hudson, 2002. *David Shrigley*, exhibition catalogue, Kunsthaus, Zurich, 2003.

MUSEUMS AND GALLERIES:
MANCHESTER (Whitworth Art Gallery): *Industrial Estate* (1996, printed wallpaper) - ZURICH (Kunsthaus).

SHRIMP, Master of the. See **CRABBE VAN ESPLEGHEM Frans**

SHRIMPTON, Ada Matilda. See **GILES**

SHRUBSOLE, W. G.
British, 19th century.

Born in Maidstone; died December 1889, in Manchester.
Painter. Landscapes, architectural views.
W.G. Shrubsole exhibited at the Royal Academy of Arts in London from 1881 to 1883 and in 1886.

SHRUCKI, Johann
Lithuanian, 19th century.
Born 1830; died 1870.
Active in Vilna (now Vilnius).
Painter, lithographer.
This artist studied in St Petersburg and soon became a member of its academy. He painted landscapes and portraits.

SHTERENBERG, David Petrovich, or Chternberg
Russian, 20th century.
Born 1881, in Zhitomir; died 1948, in Moscow.
Painter, engraver, illustrator. Landscapes, still-lifes.
From 1906 to 1912, David Petrovich Shterenberg attended the École des Beaux-Arts de Paris and private academies. He returned to Russia in 1917 and from 1918 to 1921 he was director of the IZO Narkompros (the Department of Fine Arts of the People's Commissariat of the Enlightenment). From 1920 to 1930, he was an influential member of Vkhutemas, the Higher Artistic and Technical Studios in Moscow and Leningrad. In 1925, he directed the Russian section of the Exposition Internationale des Arts et Industries Modernes in Paris.

He remained attached to traditional techniques and Academic Realism throughout his career.

He featured in the Art Russe exhibition at the Galeries Nationales du Grand Palais, Paris (1967-1968) and in *Un été russe à Montmartre. Artistes de St-Pétersbourg à Paris au début du XXe siècle* (*A Russian Summer in Montmartre. St Petersburg Artists in Paris at the Beginning of the 20th Century*), Musée de Montmartre, Paris (2003).

BIBLIOGRAPHY:
Gérard, Raphaël/Essaïan, Sergeï, et al., *Un été russe à Montmartre. Artistes de Saint-Pétersbourg à Paris au début du XXe siècle*, exhibition catalogue, Musée de Montmartre, Éditions Fragments, Paris, 2003.

MUSEUMS AND GALLERIES:
MOSCOW (Pushkin MFA): *On the Terrace* (1920); *Port* (1923, etching) - MOSCOW (State Tretyakov Gal.): *Cherries on a Plate* (1918); *Curdled Milk* (1919).

AUCTION RECORDS:
NEW YORK, 3 Nov 1978, *Composition* (c. 1920/21, watercolour and Indian ink, 9 1/2 x 12 3/4 ins / 24 x 32.5 cm) USD 2,000. LONDON, 6 April 1989, *Still-life* (oil on cardboard, 22 x 17 ins / 56 x 43 cm) GBP 20,900. PARIS, 30 April 2002, *Oval Still-life* (watercolour and gouache on paper/panel, 8 x 6 ins / 20 x 16 cm) EUR 4,350. PARIS, 3 July 2002, *Still-life with Oil Lamp* (oil on canvas, 28 x 20 ins / 70 x 50 cm) EUR 6,500. FAIRFIELD, 25 Aug 2004, *Still-life with Green Bottle* (oil on canvas, 27 x 24 ins / 69 x 61 cm) USD 38,000.

SHTILIANOVA, Tzvetana
Bulgarian, 20th century.
Painter.
Tzvetana Shtilianova exhibited a portrait at Salon de la Société Nationale des Beaux-Arts, Paris (1933).

SHU CHIH. See **SHU ZHI**

SHU CHUNGUANG
Chinese, 20th century.
Born 1939.
Painter. Landscapes with figures.
Shu Chunguang became a teacher at the Uighur Autonomous Region art school in Xinjiang. He paints in Chinese ink and colour on paper. His landscapes are often directly inspired by the landscape in north-western China.

BIBLIOGRAPHY:
Peintres traditionnels de la République populaire de Chine, exhibition catalogue, Gal. Daniel Malingue, Paris, 1980.

SHU ZHI, or Shu Chih
Chinese.
Active during the Ming dynasty (1368-1644).
Painter.
Shu Zhi is not mentioned in official artist biographies. He may be the same Ming dynasty artist as Shu Yinzhi.

SHUANG GOULONG, or Shuang Kou-lung
Chinese, 11th century.
Active in Sichuan during the second half of the 11th century.
Painter. Landscapes.
Song dynasty.
Shuang Goulong held the official rank *zhitou* at the Imperial Painting Academy during the reign of Emperor Shanzong (1068-1085).

MUSEUMS AND GALLERIES:
TAIPEI (National Palace Mus.): *River Landscape with Sailing Boats* (inscription by Su Che, younger brother of the poet Su Dongpo).

SHUBIN, Serge, or Choubine
Russian, 20th century.
Born in St Petersburg.
Painter. Portraits, landscapes.
Serge Shubin exhibited in Paris at the Salon d'Automne between 1924 and 1930.

AUCTION RECORDS:
VERSAILLES, 8 July 1990, *Woman on the Path to the House* (oil on canvas, 15 x 18 ins / 38 x 46 cm) FRF 3,500. PARIS, 30 Nov 1994, *Street Scene* (oil on canvas, 25 1/2 x 21 1/4 ins / 65 x 54 cm) FRF 6,200.

SHUBUN, real name: Tokei, alternate name: Tensho, artist names: Ekkei, Shubun
Japanese, 15th century.
Active in Kyoto during the second quarter of the 15th century.
Painter.
The role played by Zen Buddhism in Japan was almost entirely religious until the 14th century. Then, however, its influence started to reach into the arts and culture, and it would go on to inspire not only monk-painters such as Shubun, from whom modern Japanese painting ultimately descends, but also the culture of the five great Zen monasteries in Kyoto, especially the Shokoku-ji, which was founded by Ashikaga Yoshimitsu in 1384. Paintings and other objets d'art start to arrive in these religious centres, as does the academic art of the Southern School with the monochrome landscapes of Li Tang (from around 1050 until after 1130), Ma Yuan and Xia Gui (both active in about 1190-1230). While these monk-painters worked hard to master the ink wash *(suiboku)* technique, they seem to have had trouble in successfully conveying the impression of depth. As a result, they painted somewhat artificial-looking landscapes first on sliding doors and screens, and then, starting in the 15th century, on hanging scrolls above which they would write their own poetry in calligraphic script. The first of these *shigajiku* (poem and picture scrolls) are anonymous, but in time many of them would be attributed to Shubun, for the gradual acceptance of this new kind of landscape was most likely owing to him.

Shubun had a wide range of talents. He not only had control of the financial affairs and administration of the Shokoku-ji but was also highly regarded for his paintings and sculpture. After being sent to Korea in 1423 to acquire Buddhist scriptures, he was asked to sculpt a number of statues for the Shokoku-ji and paint a number of others. In 1438, a prince of the imperial family admired the sliding doors he had decorated, which led to his being appointed master of the Shogun's academy, in which post he would be succeeded in 1465 by his disciple Sotan.

Although not a single authentic work by Shubun survives (the attributions by Tan'yu and Kano Tsunenobu in the 17th century having recently been revised), it may be accepted that he excelled above all in capturing atmospheric quality through delicate black strokes heightened by washes and light colour. In his *Koten en-i* (Distant Views of Heaven and River) in the Nezu Museum, Tokyo, the mode of composition is taken from Ma Yuan (distant mountains bathed in mist balanced in one corner by a more solid foreground) but the picture is imbued with a serenity very distant indeed from the lyricism of the Southern School. Some art historians attach great importance to Shubun's visit to Korea, supposing there to be Korean influence on his painting. It is hard to decide, however, what Shubun may have seen in Korea: would they have been paintings from the early Li, or paintings of the Zhi school, which perpetuated the style of the Southern Song? Yet one cannot deny the way Shubun shines over his time or the fact that he, together with Josetsu, his predecessor at the Shokoku-ji, established ink painting in Japan, which would later be immortalised by Sesshu (1420-1506).

BIBLIOGRAPHY:

Tanaka, Ichimatsu, *Japanese Ink Painting: Shûbun to Sesshû*, Weatherhill, New York, 1972.

SHUBUN, real name: Ri Shubun (or Yi Su Min)
Japanese, 16th century.
Active in Hida (now Gifu Prefecture) in the middle of the 16th century.
Painter.

Shubun was a *suiboku* (ink) painter of the late Muromachi period.

BIBLIOGRAPHY:

Lillehoj, Elizabeth, '*Reconsidering the Identity of Ri Shubun*' in *Artibus Asiae 55*, 1995.

SHUGETSU, real name: Kitagawa Shugetsu
Japanese, 19th century.
Active c. 1820 in Osaka.
Print artist.

SHUGETSU, Tokan, real name: Taki Kanto, childhood name: Gonnokami Takashito, artist names: Shugetsu, Tokan
Japanese, 16th century.
Born 1440; died 1529.
Monk-painter.

Shugetsu was a descendant of the Takaki family of retainers from Satsuma, southern Kyushu. He became a monk and disciple of Sesshu (1420-1506), who presented him with a self-portrait in 1490 as a token of his esteem. Six years later, in 1496, Shugetsu travelled to China and while in Beijing painted a scene of the famous Western Lake. According to a passage in the *Koga-biko* (remarks on ancient paintings) he painted eight landscapes in the style of the Chinese artist Yu Jian, using the *haboku* (broken ink) technique. He lived at Yamaguchi.

SHUGRIN, Anatoly Ivanovich
Russian, 20th century.
Born 1906, in Moscow.
Painter. Figures, genre scenes, landscapes, still-lifes.

Anatoly Shugrin studied under Nikolai Grigorev in 1919 and Mikhail Sokolov in 1920. He was admitted to the Moscow Artists Union in 1930 and although unwilling to toe the Socialist Realist line he became a member of the U.S.S.R. Artists Union in 1945. In the catalogue for *Anatoly Ivanovich Shugrin: Retrospective Exhibition, 1919-1950*, Goldman Fine Arts Gallery, Washington (1982), Norton Dodge has written: 'He was one of the rare Russian artists whose creativity was not maimed, crushed or repressed during the Stalin period. He had found his style in the 1930s and continued to develop it until the 1950s'.

AUCTION RECORDS:

LONDON, 6 April 1989, *Bay* (oil on card, 20 1/2 x 25 3/4 ins / 52 x 65.5 cm) GBP 9,900. LONDON, 24-25 March 1993, *Blue House* (oil on card, 25 1/2 x 16 1/2 ins / 65 x 42 cm) GBP 4,600. TEL AVIV, 14 April 1993, *The Three Graces* (oil on card, 33 3/4 x 26 1/2 ins / 86 x 67 cm) USD 3,220. NEW YORK, 29 Sept 1993, *Artist and his Model* (pencil, ink and wash on paper, 8 1/2 x 9 3/4 ins / 21.6 x 24.8 cm) USD 1,840. NEW YORK, 4 Nov 1993, *Still-life* (oil on canvas on card, 34 3/4 x 26 1/2 ins / 88.3 x 67.3 cm) USD 17,250; *Essence of Grieg* (oil on canvas on card, 35 x 45 ins / 889 x 114.3 cm) USD 31,050. NEW YORK, 24 Feb 1994, *Soldier's Farewell* (oil on panel, 26 1/2 x 34 1/2 ins / 67.3 x 87.6 cm) USD 5,750. NEW YORK, 20 Feb 2002, *Bay* (c. 1945-47, oil on board, 21 x 26 ins / 53 x 66 cm) USD 6,500.

SHUI. See **MUTO Shui**

SHUJU, also known as Joen
Japanese, 14th century.
Born 1318, in Musashi; died 7 July 1373.
Painter.

Shuju was a priest and the disciple of Muso Kokushi.

SHUKALOVICH
Russian, 20th century.
Painter. Landscapes.

AUCTION RECORDS:

PARIS, 10 Feb 1991, *Crimean Landscape* (oil on canvas, 17 3/4 x 26 ins / 45 x 66 cm) FRF 4,000.

SHUKEI, real name: Watanabe Kiyoshi, nickname: Daisuke, artist names: Shukei, Setchosai
Japanese, 19th century.
Born 1778; died 1861.
Active in Nagoya.
Painter.

Shukei was a disciple of Hidenobu, Mitsusada and Tutsugen. He was a member of the Fukko Yamato-e School.

SHUKHAEV, Vasili Ivanovich, or Choukaeff, Shukaev, Choukhaieff, Vassily
Russian, 20th century.
Born 12 January 1887, in Moscow; died 1973.
Also active in France.
Painter (gouache), watercolourist, draughtsman, illustrator. Nudes, portraits, landscapes. Stage costumes and sets.

Vasili Ivanovich Shukhaev was a pupil at the Stroganov College and at the academy of art in St Petersburg between 1906 and 1912. He was a member of the Mir Iskusstva (World of Art) group. Between 1912 and 1914, he travelled in Italy. He emigrated to Paris in 1919, and returned to the USSR in 1945.

In Paris, he exhibited at the Salon des Tuileries and the Salon des Artistes Indépendants (1923 and 1924), and at the Salon d'Automne (1932). He illustrated Alfred de Musset's *Les Deux Maîtresses* (*The Two Mistresses*), Pushkin's *Boris Godunov* and *Queen of Spades*, and Z. Pechkoff's *The Foreign Legion*.

AUCTION RECORDS:

PARIS, 12 March 1985, *Decorative Sketch for the Veliki Gossudar: The Great Sovereign* (gouache and silver, 15 x 21 1/2 ins / 37.8 x 54.7 cm; 14 1/2 x 19 1/4 ins/37 x 49 cm; 13 1/4 x 21 1/4 ins/33.7 x 54.1 cm) FRF 4,800. LONDON, 14 Nov 1988, *Fruit in a Landscape* (1931, gouache, 5 x 15 1/2 ins / 13 x 39.5 cm) GBP 330; *Reclining Nude* (pencil/paper, 24 x 33 3/4 ins / 61 x 86 cm) GBP 572. MILAN, 10 Nov 1992, *Horses and Carriage* (1915, watercolour/paper, 8 1/2 x 13 1/2 ins / 21.5 x 34.5 cm) ITL 1,200,000. NEW YORK, 26 Feb 1993, *Still-life with Teapot*

(1921, oil on canvas, 34 1/2 x 29 ins / 87.6 x 73.7 cm) USD 8,050. LONDON, 29 April 1999, *Drawing Water* (1922, oil on board, 20 x 23 ins / 51 x 59 cm) GBP 3,600. LONDON, 29 April 1999, *Cello* (1921, oil on canvas, 53 x 36 ins / 135 x 91 cm) GBP 15,000. LONDON, 23 Nov 2000, *Reclining Nude* (1964, oil on canvas, 37 x 70 ins / 94 x 177 cm) GBP 10,000. NEW YORK, 21 Oct 2003, *Standing Nude* (1964, red charcoal, 24 x 17 ins / 61 x 44 cm) USD 2,000. LONDON, 26 May 2004, *Picnic in Cassis* (oil on canvas, 24 x 39 ins / 60 x 100 cm) GBP 48,000.

SHUKHVOSTOV, Stepan Mikhailovich
Russian, 19th - 20th century.
Born 1821, in Russia; died 1911.
Painter. Architectural views.

Stepan Mikhailovich Schukhvostov was a pupil at the art school in Moscow, and became a member of the Academy in 1855.

MUSEUMS AND GALLERIES:
MOSCOW (Rumiantsev Mus.): *Cathedral Interior of St Sergius; Monastery Interior in Chudovo; Interior of the Troïtzky Cathedral in the Sergiev Monastery; The Reliquary of St Aleksei, Metropolitan, in the Chudovo Monastery* - MOSCOW (State Tretyakov Gal.): *The Reliquary of St Sergius; The Vestibule of the Cathedral of the Annunciation in Moscow; Interior of the Cathedral of the Annunciation in Moscow.*

SHUKI, real name: Okamoto Hakuki, popular names: Sukenojo, Yunojo, artist names: Shuo, Fujiwara Ryusen
Japanese, 18th - 19th century.
Born 1807, in Edo (now Tokyo); died 1862.
Painter. Flowers, birds.
Nanga School.

Okamoto Shuki was a Nanga School (literati) painter and a disciple of Keisai, on whose death he adopted the style of Kazan (1793-1841). He specialised in painting birds and flowers and was in the service of the Okubo daimyo of Odawara. The Boston Museum has in its possession a two-panel screen of his, *Flowers and Birds*, in ink on paper, signed and dated 1861.

MUSEUMS AND GALLERIES:
BOSTON (MFA): *Flowers and Birds* (1861, two-panel screen).

SHUKIN, Stepan Semenovich. See **CHUKIN**

SHUKLA, Y.K.
Indian, 20th century.
Born 1897, in Calcutta (now Kolkata).
Painter. Religious subjects, figures.

In 1946, Shukla's *Buddha Amleapali* was shown at the international exhibition organized by UNESCO at the Musée d'Art Moderne, Paris.

SHUKO, or Juko, popular name: Murata Mokichi, artist names: Shuko, Dokuryoken, Korakuan, Nansei
Japanese, 15th century.
Born 1422; died 1502.
Active in the second half of the 15th century.
Painter.

Shuko was a *suiboku* (ink) painter of the Muromachi period and disciple of Shubun who lived at Tonomine in Yamato (now Nara Prefecture). A Buddhist priest, he was master of the tea ceremony, for which he established a number of conventions. He received guidance from Ikku Sojun at the Daitoku-ji temple in Kyoto. He specialised in painting *Shoki*, a divinity that defeats demons. The Museum of Fine Art in Boston holds one of his vertical scrolls in ink on paper, representing a monkey.

MUSEUMS AND GALLERIES:
BOSTON (MFA): *Great Bell of Miidera* (ink on paper).

SHUKOFF. See **JUKOV**

SHUKOVSKY, Pavel Vassiliévitch von. See **JOUKOVSKI**

SHUKUYA, real name: Aoki Shummei, alternate names: Daisho, Shitu, popular name: Shoemon, artist names: Shunto, Hachigaku, Yoshukuya, Shukuya
Japanese, 18th century.
Born in Ise; died 1789.
Painter. Genre scenes, landscapes with figures, waterscapes.
Nanga (literati) school.

Shukuya was a disciple of Taiga (1723-1776). On his master's death, he took up residence in his house in Kyoto. Most of his works, landscapes, are in Taiga's style and have little originality.

AUCTION RECORDS:
NEW YORK, 29 March 1990, *Landscape* (ink on paper, hanging scroll, 11 1/2 x 24 1/2 ins / 29.5 x 62 cm) USD 2,200. NEW YORK, 26 March 1991, *Boating on Lake Biwa* (ink and colour on silk, hanging scroll, 36 x 10 3/4 ins / 90.5 x 27.2 cm) USD 12,100.

SHULZ, Ada Walter
American, 19th - 20th century.
Born 21 October 1870, in Terre Haute (Indiana); died 1928, in Nashville (Indiana).
Painter. Genre scenes.

Ada Walter Schulz srudied at the Art Institute of Chicago with John Vanderpoel and Oliver Pennet Grover, and then in Paris at the Académie Vitti. She painted in an Impressionist style, mostly outdoors, producing pictures set in the sunny Indiana landscape and often featuring mothers and children.

MUSEUMS AND GALLERIES:
CHICAGO (AI) - MILWAUKEE (IA).

AUCTION RECORDS:
CINCINNATI, 7 May 2000, *The Yellow Hen* (c. 1926, oil on board) USD 85,000. CINCINNATI, 3 Dec 2000, *Mother and Child* (oil on canvas, 34 x 30 ins / 86 x 76 cm) USD 80,000. OAK PARK, 2 Dec 2001, *Picture Book* (c. 1914, oil on canvas, 24 x 27 ins / 61 x 69 cm) USD 47,500.

SHUMMAN. See **SHUNMAN**

SHUMMEI, real name: Igarashi Shummei or Shunmei, original name: Sano, given name: Hotoku, artist names: Koho, Chikuken, Bokuo, Gempo
Japanese, 18th century.
Born 1700, in Niigata; died 1781, in Niigata.
Painter.
Kano School.

Shummei was a Kano School painter and disciple of Ryoshin. He was also influenced by the styles of Chinese masters such as Liang Kai and Zhang Pingshan. He studied Confucian thought at Kyoto with Yamazaki Anxai. He primarily painted figures.

SHUMPARO. See **KOKAN**

SHUMWAY, Henry Colton. See **SCHUMWAY**

SHUN. See **KOKAN**

SHUN
Japanese, 19th - 20th century.
Born 1868; died 1911.
Painter.

Shun was a painter of the Meiji period.

AUCTION RECORDS:
NEW YORK, 23 Oct 1991, *Edo Flowers Valued at 3,000 Ryo* (ink and colour on silk, hanging scroll, 46 3/4 x 22 ins / 119 x 56 cm) USD 2,420.

SHUN'EI, real name: Katsukawa Shun'ei, original name: Isoda Kyujiro, artist name: Kyutokusai
Japanese, 18th - 19th century.
Born 1762; died 1819.

Active in Edo (now Tokyo).
Print artist. Ukiyo-e prints.
Ukiyo-e (pictures of the floating world).
Katsukawa School.

Shun'ei was one of Shunsho's most important pupils and was Shuntei's master. He may also have influenced Toyokuni I and Sharaku. He designed numerous *hosoban* prints (small format, about 12 x 6 in, 30 x 15 cm) of actors, as single prints, triptychs and pentatychs. His characteristic prints are busts and full-length portraits. He also did some remarkable prints of sumo wrestlers, which have such power than the subjects seem to burst out of the design. He is known in particular for a number of *oshiegata* (fabric motif cut-out) series and a full-length portrait of Arashi Otohachi II in the role of Moronao.

BIBLIOGRAPHY:

Fahr-Becker, Gabriele (ed.), *Japanese Prints*, Taschen, Cologne, 1999.

AUCTION RECORDS:

LONDON, 9 Nov 1988, *Full-length Portrait of the Actor Sawamura Sojuro III* (Oban Tate-e print, 14 3/4 x 9 1/2 ins / 37.3 x 24.3 cm) GBP 4,180. NEW YORK, 21 March 1989, *Large Head Portrait of the Actor Sakata Hangoro III Holding a Fan and Looking at Himself in the Mirror* (Uchiwa-e print, 9 x 9 1/4 ins / 22.9 x 23.8 cm) USD 7,150; *Triple Large Head Portrait of the Actors Sawamura Sojoro, Ichikawa Yaozo and Sagawa Kikunojo in the Play 'Hatsuakebono no kaomise Soga'* (Oban Tate-e print, 14 1/4 x 9 3/4 ins / 36.5 x 25 cm) USD 14,300. NEW YORK, 20 April 1989, *Portrait of the Actor Nakamura Denkuro Holding a Rifle* (Hosoban print, 13 x 5 3/4 ins / 32.9 x 14.5 cm) USD 2,090. NEW YORK, 16 Oct 1989, *Portrait of the Wrestler Kurokomo Otozo Accompanied by a Teahouse Serving Girl* (Oban Tate-e print, 15 1/4 x 10 1/4 ins / 38.8 x 26 cm) USD 3,520. LONDON, 22 March 1990, *The Actor Ichikawa Komazo Standing near a Clump of Reeds with the Bottom of His Robe Tucked into His Sash* (Hosoban print, 12 1/4 x 5 3/4 ins / 31.4 x 14.6 cm) GBP 495. NEW YORK, 15 June 1990, *The Wrestler Nishiki Chogoro Standing* (Oban Tate-e print, 15 1/2 x 10 1/4 ins / 39.1 x 26 cm) USD 1,650. NEW YORK, 27 March 1991, *The Actors Nakayama Raisuke and Ichikawa Yaozo III Flanking Another Actor Playing a Samurai* (Hosoban print triptych, each sheet 12 1/4 x 6 ins / 31.4 x 14.3 cm) USD 4,950. PARIS, 3 June 1992, *Circus Scene* (Hosoban print, 12 3/4 x 6 ins / 32.3 x 14.3 cm) FRF 4,500.

SHUN'YO. See **HOKKEI**

SHUN'YO, real name: Katsukawa Shun'yo
Japanese, 19th century.
Active c. 1822.
Print artist.

SHUN'YOSAI. See **HOKKEI**

SHUN'YU
Japanese, 19th century.
Active in Osaka c. 1817-1822.
Print artist.

SHUN-CHIH CH'ING. See **QING SHIZU**

SHUNBOKU, real name: Ooka Aiyoku, artist names: Shunboku, Jakushitsu
Japanese, 18th century.
Born 1680; died 1763.
Active in Edo (now Tokyo).
Painter.
Kano school.

Shunboku was a Kano School painter and the author of a book on painting entitled *Gashi kaiyo*.

BIBLIOGRAPHY:

Guth, Christine, *Japanese Art of the Edo Period*, Calmann & King, London, 1996 (mentioned in passing).

SHUNCHO, real name: Katsukawa Shuncho, popular name: Kichizaemon, artist names: Yubundo, Toshien, Churinsha, Kichisado
Japanese, 18th century.
Born in Edo, now Tokyo.
Active in Edo c. 1780-1795.
Print artist.
Ukiyo-e (pictures of the floating world).

Shuncho was a disciple of Kiyonaga. Like many ukiyo-e artists he concentrated on two themes: the lives of actors and courtesans. Although lacking Sharaku's depth, he depicted the people of the theatre in greater intimacy behind the screens. He abandoned print making and started a career as a writer of fiction. He was represented in the exhibition *Six Maîtres de l'Estampe Japonaise au XVII siècle* (*Six Masters of the 18th Century Japanese Print*), held in the Musée de l'Orangerie, Paris, in 1971.

BIBLIOGRAPHY:

Succo, Friedrich, *Katsukawa Shunsho*, C.F. Schulz, Plauen, 1922. *Six Maîtres de l'Estampe Japonaise au XVII siècle. Haronubu, Shunshô, Kiyonaga, Shunman, Utamaro, Sharaku*, exhibition catalogue, Réunion des Musées Nationaux, Paris, 1971.

AUCTION RECORDS:

LONDON, 16 May 1988, *Young Boy Dancing before a Lady with His Mother Seated behind Him (Scene from the Play Jaruri)* (print) GBP 418. LONDON, 9 Nov 1988, *Portraits of Okita Naniwaya and Another Actor* (Oban Tate-e print, 15 x 9 3/4 ins / 37.8 x 24.9 cm) GBP 1,540. LONDON, 22 March 1990, *Three Women Carrying a Tsunokakushi on the Balcony of a Teahouse Overlooking the Sumida River* (Oban Tate-e print, 14 1/2 x 10 ins / 37 x 24.5 cm) GBP 1,100. PARIS, 25 Nov 2003, *Shower of Rain* (colour print, triptych, 15 x 10 ins / 38 x 25 cm) EUR 6,500.

SHUNCHO, artist names: Hotta, Harukawa
Japanese, 19th century.
Born in Kyoto.
Active in Osaka c. 1815-1821.
Print artist.

SHUNCHO, artist name: Gajuken
Japanese, 19th century.
Active in Osaka c. 1825.
Print artist.

SHUNCHO. See also **HOKUSHO**

SHUNCHO, Katsukawa. See **SHUNCHO**

SHUNDO, real name: Katsukawa Shundo, artist name: Rantokusai
Japanese, 18th - 19th century.
Painter. Figures, portraits.
Ukiyo-e (pictures of the floating world).

Shundo was one of the many pupils of Shunsho.

SHUNGA
Japanese, 13th century.
Active in Kyoto during the first half of the 18th century.
Monk-painter.

Shunga was a monk-painter who worked in the Jingo-ji and Kozan-ji temples at Takao, near Kyoto. He painted Buddhist subjects.

SHUNGYOSAI I, real name: Hayami Tsuneaki, popular name: Hikosaburo, artist name: Shungyosai
Japanese, 18th - 19th century.
Born c. 1760, in Osaka; died 1823.
Print artist.

Shungyosai I was primarily an illustrator. He also designed a number of prints towards the end of the 1810s, using the Gyokuzan technique.

SHUNGYOSAI II, real name: Gyounsai Shunmin, personal names: Tsuneshige and Taminosuke, given name: Hayami, artist name: Shungyosai
Japanese, 19th century.
Born in Osaka; died 1867.
Active c. 1820-1830.
Print artist.

Shungyosai II was the son of Shungyosai I and may have been a pupil of Hokushu.

SHUNJO, real name: Katsukawa Iwazo, original name: Yasuda, artist name: Shunjo
Japanese, 18th - 19th century.
Print artist. Figures, portraits.
Ukiyo-e (pictures of the floating world).

Shunjo was one of Shunsho's many pupils. He primarily designed prints of scenes from the *kabuki* theatre.

SHUNJO
Japanese, 19th century.
Active in Osaka c. 1832.
Print artist.

From the inscription on a print dated 1832, Shunjo was a pupil of Gatoken Shunshi.

SHUNJU
Japanese, 19th century.
Active in Osaka c. 1828-1829.
Print artist.

From two prints dated 1829, it may be supposed that Shunju was a pupil of Hokuei Shunko. He may also have been the same artist as Hokuju.

SHUNKA
Japanese, 19th century.
Active in Osaka c. 1820-1830.
Print artist.

Shunka worked with Gajuken Shuncho, Shunsei, and Gatoken Shunshi.

SHUNKEI, artist name: Baikosai
Japanese, 19th century.
Active in Osaka c. 1820-1830.
Print artist.

SHUNKI, real name: Shotaro, alternate names: Okamoto, Utagawa, artist names: Nobusada, Harusada II (1849-1867)
Japanese, 19th century.
Born 1830, in Kyoto; died 1887.
Active in Kyoto and Osaka c. 1849-1880.
Print artist.

Under the artist name Nobusada, Shunki designed a number of portraits.

SHUNKIN
Japanese, 19th century.
Active in Osaka c. 1816.
Print artist.

SHUNKIN, real name: Uragami Sen, given name: Hakukyo, popular name: Kiichiro, artist names: Shunkin, Suian, Bunkyotei
Japanese, 19th century.
Born 1779, in Bizen (Okayama Prefecture); died 1846.
Painter.
Nanga School.

Shunkin was a Nanga School (literati) painter and a disciple of his father Gyokudo (1745-1820). He lived in Kyoto. His style differs from that of his father because he also studied the styles of Chinese Yuan and Ming masters.

SHUNKO. See **HOKUEI, HOKUSHU**

SHUNKO, real name: Katsukawa Shunko, original name: Kiyokawa, given name: Denjiro, artist names: Sahitsuan, Sahitsusai
Japanese, 18th - 19th century.
Born 1743; died 1812.
Active in Edo (now Tokyo).
Print artist. Figures, portraits.
Ukiyo-e (pictures of the floating world).

Shunko is regarded the most important pupil of Shunsho. In about 1788 he lost the use of his right hand to paralysis and switched to his left. He designed a large number of *hosoban* prints (small format, about 12 x 6 in, 30 x 15 cm) of actors, most of which are triptychs or pentatychs. His characteristic works are the bust portraits of actors he made during the 1780s, including portraits of Danjuro V, Komazo and Sakata Hangoro.

Bibliography:
Fahr-Becker, Gabriele (ed.), *Japanese Prints*, Taschen, Cologne, 1999.

Auction records:
New York, 20 April 1989, *Portraits of the Actors Ichikawa Danzo and Ichikawa Raizo on Stage* (Hosoban print, 12 3/4 x 6 ins / 32.5 x 15.4 cm) USD 4,400. New York, 15 June 1990, *Okubi-e Portrait of Three Actors* (oban tate-e print, 15 x 10 1/4 ins / 38 x 26.3 cm) USD 770.

SHUNKOSAI. See **HOKUSHU** and **HOKUEI**

SHUNKYO. See **YAMAMOTO Shunkyo**

SHUNMAN, or Shumman, real name: Kubota Yasubei, artist names: Kubo Shunman, Issetsu Senjo, Kozando, Nandakashiran, Shosado, Sashodo
Japanese, 18th - 19th century.
Born 1757, in Edo (now Tokyo); died 1820.
Painter, print artist.

Orphaned at an early age, Shunman was raised by his uncle. He first studied painting under Kantori Nahiko, an artist of the Neo-Confucian school who taught him to paint the *shikunshi* or four plants (orchid, bamboo, plum and chrysanthemum). He then adopted the name Shunman, but since the character *shun* used in the name was the same as that used by Shuncho and the other artists of the Katsukawa School, he changed it to another with the same pronunciation in order to distinguish himself from them. He then studied *ukiyo-e* with Shigemasa and *kyoka* poetry (31 syllable satirical or comic verses) with Ishikawa Gabo, the son of Ishikawa Toyonobu, an early *ukiyo-e* artist. He would later devote himself to poetry and illustration, and was a talented writer of fiction. Sometimes he used the artist name Shosado (*studio that honours the left*), because he painted with his left hand. In addition to his paintings and book illustrations, Shunman designed many *surimono* (limited-edition prints used as announcements and greetings cards) and *ori-hon* (folding books). His most important work is a famous six-sheet polyptych entitled *Mu Tamagawa* (*the six Tamagawa* or crystal rivers).

Shunman's work is that of a refined poet, full of charm yet with an emotional charge unusual in *ukiyo-e*. His painterly qualities can be seen in his prints, where his simplified calligraphy is less prominent than it is with his contemporaries. The celebrated harmony of his silvery grays and deep blacks is his alone, as is his sombre, restrained, delicate palette that sometimes has an almost monochrome effect.

Bibliography:
Six maîtres de l'estampe japonaise au XVIIe siècle, exhibition catalogue, Musée de l'Orangerie, Paris, 1971. Fahr-Becker, Gabriele (ed.), *Japanese Prints*, Taschen, Cologne, 1999.

Auction records:
New York, 16 April 1988, *Beauties near the Kinuta River* (ink and light colour on silk, hanging scroll, 35 x 11 1/2 ins / 88 x 29 cm) USD 14,300. London, 16 June 1988, *Flower Composition with Irises, Roses and Peonies* (Surimono print, 8 x 11 ins / 20.4 x 28.1 cm) GBP 1,320. New York, 21 March 1989, *Songoku, the Magic Monkey* (koban tate-e print, 8 1/4 x 5 1/4 ins / 21 x 13.6 cm) USD 1,650.

SHUNPO, artist name: Gashoken
Japanese, 19th century.
Active in Osaka c. 1825.
Print artist.

SHUNRO. See **HOKUSAI**

SHUNSEI, artist name: Gayuken
Japanese, 19th century.
Active in Osaka c. 1825.
Print artist.

SHUNSEN, real name: Kano Akinobu, artist names: Riunsai, Shunsen
Japanese, 19th century.
Active c. 1804-1817.
Print artist.
Shunsen was a pupil of Katsukawa Shun-ei. He is primarily known for his illustrated books. On the death of Shunko, he is supposed to have adopted the name Shunko II.
Museums and Galleries:
Paris (Mus. National des Arts asiatiques-Guimet).
Auction records:
New York, 27 March 1991, *Full-length Portrait of a Young Woman Holding an Umbrella* (Oban Tate-e print, 14 1/4 x 9 1/2 ins / 36 x 24 cm) USD 1,045.

SHUNSENSAI, or Kiyohide, popular name: Takehara
Japanese, 18th - 19th century.
Born in Osaka.
Active c. 1790-1810.
Print artist.

SHUNSHI, artist names: Shun'yoosai, Seiyosai, Seiyodo, Sunpu
Japanese, 19th century.
Active in Osaka c. 1826-1828.
Print artist.
Shunshi may be an early name of the print artist Hokumyo. His work also shows many similarities to that of Hokkei (active 1818-1820).

SHUNSHI, or Harushiba, artist names: Gatoken, Toryuken, Toryusai
Japanese, 19th century.
Active in Osaka c. 1825.
Print artist.

SHUNSHI, artist name: Gakoken
Japanese, 19th century.
Active in Osaka c. 1825.
Print artist.
Shunshi is said to have been a pupil of Shunshi Gatoken.

SHUNSHI
Japanese, 19th century.
Active in Osaka c. 1830.
Print artist.
Shunshi is said to have been a pupil of Shunshi Gatoken.

SHUNSHIN
Japanese, 19th century.
Active in Osaka c. 1820.
Print artist.
Shunshin is supposed to have been a pupil of Hokushu.

SHUNSHO, real name: Katsukawa Shunsho, original name: Miyagawa, popular name: Yusuke, artist names: Kyokurosei, Yuji, Ririn, Jugasei, Rokurokuan, Shuntei
Japanese, 18th century.
Born 1726; died 1792 or 1793.
Active in Edo (now Tokyo).
Painter, print artist. Figures, portraits, genre scenes.
Ukiyo-e (pictures of the floating world).
Shunsho was a pupil of Miyagawa Shunsui (active in the frist half of the 18th century) who devoted himself to designing *nishiki-e* (brocade pictures) and polychrome woodblock prints. His first works betray the influence of Harunobu (d. 1770). In 1770, he and Buncho (active in the late 18th century) published an illustrated book entitled *Ehon butai no ogi* (*Picture Book of Stage Fans*), which marked a new departure in actor portraits, in which faces were brought to life by means of a few expressive strokes. Thus was born the *nigao-e* (likeness head), which was inspired by the classical *nise-e* (likeness portrait), which in turn goes back to the 13th century. From this point on, Shunsho seems to have been fascinated by the *kabuki* theatre. With both lines and colour showing increasing authority (his blacks and browns stand out in particular), he depicts its actors not only on but also off stage, in harmonious, simple groups. The body of his surviving prints is a priceless document of the organization of the theatre in his day. The same vigorous simplicity returns in his portraits of sumo wrestlers in ceremonial costume or relaxing in their kimonos, in which the ample forms of these popular heroes simply fill the dimensions of the prints.

In his youth, Shunsho used to sign his prints with a *tsubo* (jar-seal) containing the character *hayashi* (forest). For this reason, prints of his with this seal are known as *tsubo Shunsho*. He was also a great *ukiyo-e* painter during the 1770s and 1780s, one of his masterpieces being the *12 Months*, a series depicting women's occupations (now in the Atami Museum). His paintings are broad in conception, with a keen sense of composition and a sureness and subtlety of brushstroke attentive to the slightest detail, a rarity among *ukiyo-e* artists. By about 1780, Shunsho towered over all other painters of his time and trained many artists in his studio, including Katsumata Shunko, Katsumata Shunei, Katsumata Shunjo, Katsumata Shundo, Katsumata Shuncho, Katsumata Shunzan and Katsumata Shunro, later to be famous as Hokusai.
Bibliography:
Smith, Henry, '*Actor Prints: Shunsho, Buncho and the Katsukawa School*' in *Timothy Clark et al, The Actor's Image*, 1995. Guth, Christine, *Japanese Art of the Edo Period*, Calmann & King, London, 1996. Fahr-Becker, Gabriele (ed.), *Japanese Prints*, Taschen, Cologne, 1999.
Museums and Galleries:
Atami: *12 Months* (series).
Auction records:
Paris, 14 Dec 1987, *The Actor Iwai Hanshiro in a Female Role, in a Dark Kimono Holding a Folded Cloth and a Bunch of Flowers* (print) FRF 4,000. London, 16 May 1988, *The Actor Segawa Kikungo in a Female Role* (Hosoban print) GBP 638. London, 9 Nov 1988, *The Actor Ichikawa in the Role of Sanjo Dayu and the Actor Nakamura Tomijuro Wearing a Suit of Armour* (two Hosoban prints, 12 1/4 x 6 ins / 31.1 x 14.3 cm) GBP 825; *Portrait of the Actor Nakamura Riko in a Female Role, from the Series 'Fans of the East' (Bust)* (dai-oban tate-e print, 17 3/4 x 13 ins / 45.2 x 32.9 cm) USD 13,200. New York, 16 Oct 1989, *The Actor Iwai Hanshiro Standing near a Palanquin* (Hosoban print, 12 3/4 x 5 3/4 ins / 32.2 x 14.6 cm) USD 2,420. London, 22 March 1990, *Man Wearing a Hood and Carrying a Sword, Led by a Serving Woman Carrying a Paper Lantern, from the Series 'Eight Views of Fukagawa'* (Chuban Tate-e print, 10 x 7 1/2 ins / 25.3 x 19 cm) GBP 935.

NEW YORK, 15 June 1990, *The Actor Ichikawa Danjuro V with Another Actor Trying to Take a Banner from Him* (Hosoban print (two sheets), each 12 x 5½ ins / 30.4 x 13.7 cm) USD 4,400. NEW YORK, 27 March 1991, *The Actor Nakamura Nakazo I in the Role of Kudo Suketsune in the Spring of the Year Meiwa 8* (1771, Hosoban print, 12½ x 6 ins / 31.8 x 14.3 cm) USD 3,300. PARIS, 3 June 1992, *Samurai on Horseback* (print, 11 x 8 ins / 27.9 x 20.6 cm) FRF 27,000. NEW YORK, 25 March 2003, *Wrestlers Uzgafuchi and Onogawa Kisaburo of the Eastern Group* (colour print, 14 x 10 ins / 36 x 25 cm) USD 3,000. NEW YORK, 25 March 2003, *Portrait of the Actor Nakamura Nazako I as an Itinerant Pilgrim* (colour print, 13 x 6 ins / 32 x 14 cm) USD 4,000.

SHUNSHO. See also **HOKUCHO**

SHUNSHO. See also **SHUNCHO**

SHUNSUI, real name: Katsumiyagawa Shunsui, popular name: Toshiro
Japanese, 18th century.
Print artist.
Ukiyo-e school.

Shunsui was a pupil of his father Miyagawa Choshun. He changed his name to Katsukawa. He was an *ukiyo-e* (pictures of the floating world) artist.

SHUNSUI, real name: Hiranoya Mohei, alternate name: Yoma
Japanese, 19th century.
Born in Kyoto.
Active c. 1880.
Print artist.

SHUNTEI, real name: Katsukawa Shuntei, original name: Yamaguchi Chojoro, artist names: Gibokuan, Shokosai, Shokyuko, Suiho Itsujin, Gachoken
Japanese, 18th - 19th century.
Born 1770.
Active in Osaka c. 1825-1840.
Painter, print artist. Figures, portraits.
Ukiyo-e (pictures of the floating world).

Shuntei was one of the more distinguished pupils of Shun'ei.

SHUNTEI
Japanese, 19th century.
Active in Oasaka c. 1816-1822.
Print artist.

Shuntei may be the same artist as Yasukawa Harusada, the rich Kyoto rice merchant and *ukiyo-e* artist.

SHUNTO. See **SHUKUYA**

SHUNZAN, real name: Katsukawa Shunzan, artist names: Izumi Shoyu, Shoyu
Japanese, 18th - 19th century.
Print artist. Figures, portraits.
Ukiyo-e (pictures of the floating world).

Shunzan was one of Shunsho's many pupils. He was also influenced by Kiyonaga.

AUCTION RECORDS:

NEW YORK, 16 Oct 1989, *Courtesans, Geishas and Other Young Women under Flowering Trees in Ueno Park* (Oban Tate-e print, triptych, each sheet 14½ x 10 ins / 37 x 25.5 cm) USD 5,280.

SHUNZAN, artist name: Hokushinsai
Japanese, 19th century.
Active in Osaka c. 1827-1829.
Print artist.

From a print dated 1829 it would appear that Shunzan was a pupil of Shunkosai Hokushu.

SHUNZHI QING. See **QING SHIZU**

SHUO. See **KAIOKU**

SHURAVLIOFF, Firs Ssegeievitch.
See **JURAVLEV Firs Sergeevich**

SHURIN, family name: Suzuki
Japanese, 18th century.
Active in Osaka c. 1786.
Print artist.

SHURTLEFF, Roswell Morse
American, 19th - 20th century.
Born 14 June 1838, in Rindge; died 6 January 1915, in New York.
Painter, illustrator. Landscapes.

Roswell Morse Shurtleff studied at the Lowell Institute in Boston and the National Academy in New York. He was initially an architect but later became an illustrator. After 1870, he concentrated totally on painting. He took part in collective exhibitions such as those at the National Academy in New York, becoming an associate member of the Academy in 1880 and a member in 1890. In 1901, he won a bronze medal in Buffalo and another in St Louis in 1904.

MUSEUMS AND GALLERIES:

NEW YORK (Metropolitan Mus. of Art): *Mountain Stream* - WASHINGTON DC (Corcoran Gal. of Art): *First Snow* - WASHINGTON DC (Smithsonian American AM): *Photogravure of Painting of a Woodland Scene* (photogravure).

AUCTION RECORDS:

NEW YORK, 15 Feb 1907, *Stream*, USD 135. NEW YORK, 23-24 Feb 1911, *Part of the Review Valley, in the Adirondacks*, USD 125. NEW YORK, 12 Sept 1994, *First Snow* (oil on canvas, 30 x 40 ins / 76.2 x 101.6 cm) USD 2,530.

SHURY, George Salisbury
British, 19th century.
Active in London between 1859 and 1876.
Reproductions engraver.

George Salisbury Shury was the son of the engraver Inigo Shury.

SHURYGIN, Aleksandr Alekseevich
Russian, 19th century.
Painter. Genre scenes.

MUSEUMS AND GALLERIES:

MOSCOW: *Tea*.

SHUSEKI, real name: Watanabe Motoaki, alternate name: Gensho, artist names: Jinjusai, Ran Dojin, Enka, Chikyu, Yuran Dojin
Japanese, 17th century.
Born 1639, in Nagasaki; died 1707.
Painter.
Nanga (literati) school.

Shuseki was a landscape painter and disciple of Itsunen.

SHUSTER, William Howard
American, 20th century.
Born 26 November 1893, in Philadelphia; died 1969, in Albuquerque (New Mexico).
Painter, engraver.

William Howard Shuster was taught by John Sloan, a member of the The Eight, and the Ashcan School. He was a member of the Société des Artistes Indépendants.

AUCTION RECORDS:

NEW YORK, 29 Sept 1999, *Marie of Tesuqe* (1922, oil on canvas, 24 x 20 ins / 61 x 51 cm) USD 7,500. SANTA FE, 1 Nov 2003, *Hyde Park Picnic* (oil on canvas on board, 24 x 18 ins / 61 x 46 cm) USD 8,000.

SHUSTOV, Afinoghen Loghinovich
Russian, 19th century.
Born 20 July 1786; died 26 September 1813.
Painter, draughtsman.

Museums and Galleries:
Moscow (State Tretyakov Gal.): six drawings on a sheet of paper; *Ancient History* (pen and pencil).

SHUSTOV, Nicolai Semenovich, or Shustov
Russian, 19th century.
Born 1835; died 1868.
Painter. Portraits, genre scenes.

Shustov was a member of the Artel which led to the founding of the Wanderers movement; he studied at the St Petersburg academy of fine arts from 1855 to 1863.

Auction records:
Paris, 10-11 March 1941, *Portrait of an Actress*, FRF 240.

SHUTE, John, or Shoote
British, 16th century.
Born in Collumpton; died 25 September 1563.
Painter, architect.

Shute's *The First and Chief Grounds of Architecture* was published in 1563. He was in the service of the Duke of Northumberland, who sent him to Italy in 1550 to complete his studies with the country's masters.

SHUTEI, family name: Tanaka
Japanese, 19th century.
Active c. 1821.
Print artist.

Shutei designed a number of actor prints that were published in Kyoto. He is reputed to have been a pupil of Ueda Kocho.

SHUTER, Thomas
British, 18th century.
Portrait artist.

Thomas Shuter was noted for a portrait which he executed in 1725, in Westwood Park.

SHUTER, William
British, 18th century.
Active in London between 1771 and 1779.
Painter. Flowers.

SHUTOKU, artist name: Ikei
Japanese, 16th century.
Active during the second half of the 15th century.
Painter.

Shutoku was a *suiboku* (ink) painter of the Muromachi period and a monk at the Tofuku-ji temple, Kyoto.

SHUTOV, Sergei
Russian, 20th - 21st century.
Born 1955, in Potsdam (Brandenburg), to Russian parents.
Painter (including mixed media), collage artist.
Sots Art.

Shutov was a member of the graphic arts committee in Moscow, where he settled. He worked from 1978 to 1979 at the Pushkin museum of fine art in Moscow and held the chair of fine arts at the free academy from 1989.

Shutov was one of those Soviet avant-garde artists who could only reveal their artistic bent openly from around 1987 and whose activities were for a long time unknown. His paintings, liberated from the constraints of Socialist Realism, reconciling gestural Abstract elements and figurative, narrative, sometimes Surrealist subjects, are made up of multiple superimposed images, technically treated in different ways. Their mixed subjects are drawn, in the style of American Pop Art (which allies him to the Muscovite 'Sots Art' trend), from snapshots of daily life or from anachronistic, historical and artistic sources, in the spirit of Citationism, for example. He also produced films as a visual artist and protagonist.

Shutov has taken part in collective exhibitions from 1978, notably exhibitions devoted to young Russian visual artists: 1978-1985, Autumn Salon and Spring Salon of the united committee of draughtsmen in Moscow; 1988, central house of visual artists and at the Manege in Moscow; 1989, Kunsthalle in Emden and Modern Art Museum in Fort Worth and San Francisco; and 1990, Albright Knox Art Gallery in New York, Milwaukee Art Museum, Corcoran Galery in Washington and Central House of Visual Artists in Moscow. Solo exhibitions include: 1986, Mayakovsky Museum in Moscow; 1988, Stockholm; and 1989, Galerie Katia Granoff in Paris.

Bibliography:
Serguei Shutov, exhibition catalogue, Gal. Katia Granoff, Paris, 1989.

Auction records:
Moscow, 7 July 1988, *Death to the Assassins* (1987, mixed media/canvas, 51 1/4 x 61 ins / 130 x 155 cm) GBP 4,180. Paris, 17 Dec 1989, *Kasha, Culinary Propaganda* (1988, acrylic and collage/canvas, 39 1/4 x 31 1/2 ins / 100 x 80 cm) FRF 40,000. Paris, 8 April 1990, *Paradise II* (1985, oil, gravel, gilding, glass and collage/canvas, 39 x 51 1/4 ins / 99 x 130 cm) FRF 68,000.

SHÜTTE, Hans. See **SCHUTTE Hans**

SHUTTLEWORTH, Claire
American, 19th - 20th century.
Born 1868 or 1867, in Buffalo (New York State); died 1930, in Buffalo.
Painter. Portraits, landscapes.

Claire Shuttleworth studied at the Académie Vitti in Paris and also with the American painter, Frank Vincent Dumond. While in France, she painted landscapes and genre studies in Brittany and at Pont Aven. When she returned to Buffalo, she continued to paint landscapes, particularly of the Niagara Falls and its surroundings, which brought her international fame.

Auction records:
North Bethesda, 14 Feb 2001, *Confederate Soldier* (oil on canvas, 32 x 21 ins / 81 x 54 cm) USD 4,250.

SHUZAN, real name Kumashiro Akira, alternate name: Hibun, popular name: Zeniya Rizaemon, artist name: Shûzan
Japanese, 18th century.
Engraver.

Shuzan carved wooden *netsuke* (small carved ornaments used to fasten small objects to a sash).

SHVERCHKOV, Nikolai Yegorovich.
See **SVERCHKOV Nikolai Egorovich**

SHWAB, Wladimir, later Walmar
Swiss, 20th century.
Born 1902.
Painter (including gouache).

Wladimir Shwab was born of a Finnish mother and a French father but was adopted at the age of eight by a Swiss family called Shwab. He studied chemistry in Paris between 1920 and 1925 and probably started to paint in his free time. In 1927 he travelled to Germany, where he met Moholy-Nagy and came into contact with the group of artists linked to *Der Sturm* and its gallery. 1930 saw him participating in meetings of the Art Concret Group, although he was not a signatory to the group's manifesto - despite the fact that one of his own compositions featured on the cover. He returned to Switzerland and lived there from 1939 to 1945, working towards his doctorate in chemistry. It was during this period that he formally changed his name from Wladimir to Walmar.

Shwab painted his first Abstract composition in 1926. He made a modest Constructivist film in 1930 and, in 1930-1931, started introducing into his compositions series of curved lines and forms as opposed to the straight lines and rectangles he had favoured. At some point after 1933, Shwab gave up painting and related activities entirely, only to start painting again well after the end of World War II, by which time Abstract art had come into its own.

Shwab's work featured in group exhibitions, including those at the Sacré du Printemps Gallery in Paris (1928) and Der Sturm Gallery in Berlin. He also showed at a Neo-Dadist exhibition at the Studio des Ursulines in Paris; in Amsterdam (1929); and in 1937, after he had stopped painting, at a Guggenheim Foundation exhibition *Art of Tomorrow*. He exhibited solo at the Kunsthaus in Zurich in 1975 and at the Quincampoix Gallery in Paris in 1977.

BIBLIOGRAPHY:

Fabre, Gladys C., *Walmar Shwab*, exhibition catalogue, Kunsthaus, Zurich, 1975. Fabre, Gladys C., *Abstraction-Création 1931-1936*, exhibition catalogue, Westfälisches Landesmuseum für Kunst und Kulturgeschichte, Münster, Musée d'Art moderne de la ville de Paris, Paris, 1978.

AUCTION RECORDS:

PARIS, 20 Nov 1991, *Geometrical Composition* (oil on canvas, 32 3/4 x 24 1/2 ins / 83 x 62 cm) FRF 12,000.

SI MAMMERI

Moroccan, 20th century.

Painter.

Si Mammeri was linked with the group of French painters in Morocco and featured in the Salon de l'Afrique Française in Paris in 1947. He then acquired a central position in Moroccan artistic life.

SI ZIJIE

Chinese, 20th - 21st century.

Born 1956, in Shandong Province.

Painter. Nudes, portraits, genre scenes, landscapes.

Si Zijie graduated from the department of stage design of the central academy of drama in 1982 and has exhibited in numerous oil painting exhibitions in China since 1987. His work, which has been deeply influenced by the Realists and Impressionists, is an attempt to bring the two styles into harmony.

AUCTION RECORDS:

HONG KONG, 22 March 1993, *Beautiful Dream* (1992, oil on canvas, 30 3/4 x 39 1/4 ins / 78 x 100 cm) HKD 57,500.

SI-AI. See **ZHANG XIAI**

SI-KIN KIU-CHE. See **XIJIN JUSHI**

SIALELLI, Catherine

French, 20th century.

Born c. 1940, in Paris.

Painter, pastellist. Murals.

Catherine Sialelli was a pupil at the École des Arts Appliqués, receiving her diploma in 1962. From 1962 to 1965 she trained to be a teacher of drawing. Until 1966 she was a pupil of Maurice Brianchon at the École des Beaux-Arts. She practised as a teacher until 1978. She took part in public exhibitions in a variety of locations. She exhibited privately, chiefly in the exhibitions *Open Doors, Bastille*, and also in 1986 and 1995 in Paris at the Galerie Étienne de Causans. In 1996 she painted three murals for the City of Paris. Her paintings and pastels, with their fluid, gentle harmonies, reconcile an apparently abstract art with suggestions of plant growth.

SIAO HAI-CHAN. See **XIAO HAISHAN**

SIAO K'IEN-TCHONG. See **XIAO QIANZHONG**

SIAO LING-CHO. See **XIAO LINGZHUO**

SIAO TCH'EN. See **XIAO CHEN**

SIAO TCHAO. See **XIAO ZHAO**

SIAO YONG. See **XIAO YONG**

SIAO YU. See **XIAO YU**

SIAO YUN-TS'ONG. See **XIAO YUNCONG**

SIBELIUS, Gerard or J.

Dutch, 18th century.

Born in Amsterdam; died 1785, in England.

Active in England 1775-1785.

Engraver, draughtsman.

Gerard Sibelius engraved several portraits, as well as plates for a work by Sir Joseph Banks on botany and plates for the *Vie de Marianne* (*Life of Marianne*) by Marivaux.

SIBELL, Muriel Vincent

American, 20th century.

Born 3 April 1898, in Brooklyn (New York City); died 1977.

Painter, engraver.

Muriel Vincent Sibell studied at the New York schools of Fine Arts and Applied Arts and the Art Students League. She was a member of the American Federation of Arts and won many awards.

SIBELLATO, Ercole or Eres

Italian, 20th century.

Born 24 December 1881, in Riviera del Brenta (Veneto).

Active in Venice.

Painter, sculptor, illustrator. Figures, portraits, landscapes.

Ercole Sibellato was a pupil of E. Tito.

MUSEUMS AND GALLERIES:

VENICE (Gal. d'Arte Moderna): several paintings.

SIBELLINO, Antonio

Argentinian, 20th century.

Born 1891, in Buenos Aires; died 1962, in Buenos Aires.

Sculptor, painter, draughtsman.

Antonio Sibellino decided on his career at the age of 14 and began his training in a studio in Buenos Aires where the sculptors Tasso (?) and Arturo Dresco were teaching; at the same time he was also studying at the Academia Nacional de Bellas Artes. In 1909 he was awarded a grant to study in Europe. For two years he was a pupil at the Accademia Albertina in Turin. In 1911 he went to Paris, where he remained until the war compelled him to leave in 1915.

Back in Argentina, he exhibited in the national Salons in 1916 and 1918, but in 1923 he displayed a piece which was met with derision (see below) and earned him several years of obscurity and poverty. In 1942 he was at last awarded the first national sculpture prize. In 1945 he was appointed to teach at the Escuela Nacional de Bellas Artes Manuel Belgrano.

When he arrived in Paris in 1911 Sibellino discovered, through Fauvist and Cubist work, the total revolution in the language of fine arts which completely undermined the classical ideals in which he had been trained; he began to work in the Cubist manner. Away from Paris, however, and back in Buenos Aires, he reverted to a classical style and it was not until 1923 that he exhibited a sculpture created under Cubist influence, and it was this caused a furore. When his importance was at last publicly acknowledged in the 1940s, he was already ill and could not take advantage of this new atmosphere to produce the great works he had once planned. In his last 15 years he could do no more than draw and paint. These works show a return to the past. However in 1926 he had created the *Composition of Forms*, a relief informed by the work of Duchamp-Villon and one of the first abstract sculptures conceived in Latin America.

SIBELLINO DA CAPRARA

Italian, 14th century.

Of Bolognese origin.

Active during the second half of the 14th century.

Sculptor.

Sibellino carved the decorations on the tomb of Manfredo Pio in the church of La Sagra in Carpi.

SIBENHARTZ, Hans, or Siebenhartz
Swiss, 16th century.
Active in Zug at the end of the 16th century.
Painter.

Sibenhartz painted altarpieces.

SIBER. See also **SIEBER**

SIBER, Alfons
Austrian, 19th - 20th century.
Born 25 February 1860, in Schwaz; died 8 February 1919, in Hall (Tyrol).
Painter, art restorer. Religious subjects, mythological subjects. Murals.

Alfons Siber studied from 1881 to 1890 at the Akademie der Bildenden Künste in Vienna and moved to Innsbruck, where he painted several murals for churches in the region.

MUSEUMS AND GALLERIES:
INNSBRUCK (Tiroler Landesmus. Ferdinandeum): *Undine in the Inn River.*

SIBER, Gustave
Swiss, 19th - 20th century.
Born 22 November 1864, in Küssnacht, near Zurich.
Sculptor. Figures. Busts.

Gustave Siber spent 18 months working in Richard Kissling's studio in Zurich in 1887-1888 before moving to Paris to complete his studies (1889 to 1891).

MUSEUMS AND GALLERIES:
GENEVA (MAH): *Female Bust.*

SIBER, Hans
German, 15th century.
Born to a family originally from Landshut.
Glass painter.

Siber painted 14 windows for the church of Our Lady, Straubing.

SIBER, Jacob
Swiss, 19th century.
Born 16 July 1807, in Morges; died 7 January 1880, in Lausanne.
Medallist.

SIBER, Johann Baptist
German, 19th century.
Born 1802, near Landsberg.
Active in Wiesbaden, Frankfurt am Main, Ulm; in Vienna, Austria, in 1834; in Munich, Germany, in 1835.
Painter, miniaturist.

Johann Siber attended the academy in Munich from 1823 to 1825 and in 1827.

SIBERDT, Eugène, or Siberth
Belgian, 19th - 20th century.
Born 1851, in Antwerp; died 1931.
Painter. History painting, religious subjects, portraits, genre scenes.

Eugène Siberdt was a pupil of Nicaise de Keyser at the fine arts academy in Antwerp; he taught at the academy in Antwerp from 1883.

MUSEUMS AND GALLERIES:
ANTWERP: *Erasmus and Quentin Metsys.*

AUCTION RECORDS:
AMSTERDAM, 11 Sept 1990, *Portrait of a Little Boy Sitting on a Red Sofa with a Picture Book in his Lap* (1868, oil on canvas, 27 3/4 x 22 ins / 70.5 x 55 cm) NLG 1,840. BRUSSELS, 9 Oct 1990, *Mother Breastfeeding* (1921, oil on canvas, 20 1/2 x 28 ins / 52 x 71 cm) BEF 200,000.

SIBERECHT, Willem van
Flemish School, 17th century.
Painter.

Willem van Siberecht painted an *Italian Landscape* which is in the museum at Liège.

SIBERECHTS, Cornelisz.
Flemish School, 17th century.
Born in Antwerp; died 9 April 1626, in Rome.
Painter.

SIBERECHTS, Jan, or Sibrechts
Flemish School, 17th century.
Born 29 January 1627, in Antwerp; died c. 1703, in London.
Painter. Hunting scenes, landscapes with figures, landscapes.

Jan Siberechts was the son of a sculptor of the same name. He was a pupil of Adriaen de Bye and master of a studio in Antwerp in 1649. In 1652 he married Maria Anna Croes. He went to England in 1672, accompanying the duke of Buckingham who, passing through Flanders, had noted his talent. Siberechts worked for the duke at his residence in Cliveden, painting hunting scenes and panoramic views.

Contrary to most Flemish painters of the 17th century, Siberechts was hardly influenced by the art of Rubens, preferring light to colour. This may be explained by his training, no doubt in Rome, under the influence of the Dutch landscape painters Dujardin and Berchem. However, it was Flemish landscapes that attracted him and led him to paint compositions of which many have as their theme the *Ford*. This subject enabled him to give an anecdotal twist to his work, depicting peasant women driving cows or carts through it, or peasants bathing. It also allowed him to study the various effects of light through trees and reflected on water.

MUSEUMS AND GALLERIES:
ANTWERP: *St Francis of Assisi Preaching to the Animals; Ford* - BERLIN: *Italian Spring* - BORDEAUX: *Landscape with Figures* - BRUSSELS: *Farmyard; Departing for the Hunt* - BUDAPEST: *Ford* - COPENHAGEN (Statens Mus. for Kunst): *Interior* - HANOVER: *Landscape: Canal* - LIÈGE: *Landscape* - LILLE: *Ford; Landscape; Rustic Scene* - MOSCOW (Rumiantsev Mus.): *Landscape with Rainbow* - MUNICH: *Pasture* - PARIS (Louvre): *Rustic Scene* - TOULOUSE: *Pastoral Scene* - VALENCIENNES: *Peasants in front of a Farm.*

AUCTION RECORDS:
PARIS, 1816, *River; Figures Crossing a Ford,* FRF 61. VIENNA, 1827, *Landscape,* FRF 210. PARIS, 1843, *Landscape with Figures,* FRF 620. BRUSSELS, 1850, *Landscape with Figures on Horseback and in a Carriage,* FRF 95. BRUSSELS, 1865, *Views of the Château de Versailles* (two pendants; *View of the Park at Versailles* (collection) FRF 760. PARIS, 1868, *Dutch Landscape with Figures and Animals,* FRF 760; *Landscape with Animals,* FRF 1,420. PARIS, 1877, *Ford,* FRF 850. PARIS, 1881, *Return of the Livestock,* FRF 400. PARIS, 2-3 April 1897, *Crossing a Ford,* FRF 450. PARIS, 30 May 1903, *Ford,* FRF 2,800. PARIS, 1907, *Beside a Ford,* FRF 2,700. PARIS, 12-13

Dec 1923, *Herdswoman*, FRF 12,000. LONDON, 22 July 1925, *Landscape*, GBP 58. LONDON, 12 March 1926, *Figures and Animals in a Fort*, GBP 210. LONDON, 28 March 1927, *Scene near a River*, GBP 577. LONDON, 20 May 1927, *View of Nannan Hall*, GBP 189. LONDON, 22 Dec 1927, *Market Garden Cart*, GBP 525. LONDON, 8 July 1929, *Steep Landscape*, GBP 409. GENEVA, 27 Oct 1934, *Landscape*, CHF 6,600. LONDON, 16 June 1938, *Wooded Landscape*, GBP 115. PARIS, 29 March 1939, *Crossing a Ford*, FRF 5,700. LONDON, 26 June 1946, *Fort*, GBP 420. LONDON, 31 Jan 1951, *Panorama*, GBP 300. PARIS, 5 Dec 1951, *Curious Cow*, FRF 1,100,000. LONDON, 24 June 1959, *Herdswoman and her Daughter*, GBP 5,500. LONDON, 1 April 1960, *Flooded Road*, GBP 6,825. LONDON, 21 June 1961, *Riverscape*, GBP 1,300. LONDON, 11 July 1962, *Landscape with View of Wollaton Park*, GBP 3,200. PARIS, 20 June 1966, *Crossing a Ford*, FRF 25,000. LONDON, 19 April 1967, *Riverscape with Figures*, GBP 8, 000. LONDON, 25 Nov 1970, *Peasants Crossing a Watercourse*, GBP 4,000. LONDON, 11 June 1971, *Livestock Crossing a River*, Gns 3,500. LONDON, 12 Dec 1973, *At the House of an Amateur Art Collector*, GBP 66,000. LONDON, 2 July 1976, *Peasant Woman Going to Market* (1671, oil on canvas, 27 1/2 x 39 ins / 70 x 99 cm) GBP 13,000. LONDON, 2 Dec 1977, *Peasants and Livestock in a Wooded Landscape* (oil on canvas, 39 1/2 x 45 1/2 ins / 100.4 x 115.6 cm) GBP 5,000. LONDON, 21 March 1979, *View of Henley* (oil on canvas, 32 3/4 x 49 3/4 ins / 83 x 126.5 cm) GBP 90,000. NEW YORK, 6 June 1985, *Hunter and Dogs in a Landscape* (1694, oil on panel, 12 x 16 1/4 ins / 30.5 x 41 cm) USD 15,000. LONDON, 19 Nov 1986, *Thames Valley with View of Henley* (1697, oil on canvas, 71 1/4 x 63 1/2 ins / 181 x 161 cm) GBP 50,000. AMSTERDAM, 14 Nov 1988, *Peasant Scene in a Vast Landscape with a Village on Top of a Hill in the Distance* (ink, 5 x 7 ins / 13 x 17.6 cm) NLG 3,680. NEW YORK, 10 Jan 1990, *Peasant Women Crossing a Ford in their Cart with a Windmill in the Background* (oil on canvas, 40 1/4 x 34 ins / 102.5 x 86.5 cm) USD 38,500. LONDON, 11 April 1990, *Haywain Moving down a Canal and a Couple of Peasants Collecting Wood on the Bank* (oil on canvas, 43 x 35 1/2 ins / 109 x 90 cm) GBP 41,800. LONDON, 10 July 1992, *Peasant Woman Crossing a Brook on Horseback with her Livestock at the Edge of a Wood* (oil on canvas, 25 1/2 x 22 1/4 ins / 64.5 x 56.5 cm) GBP 9,350. LONDON, 30 Oct 1997, *Wooded Riverscape with Hunters and their Dogs, and Mountains in the Distance* (1694, oil/copper, 12 1/4 x 15 3/4 ins / 30.8 x 40.3 cm) GBP 20,700. AMSTERDAM, 10 Nov 1997, *Shepherdess on a Donkey Crossing a Torrent with her Flock, with a Village and its Church in the Distance* (1684, oil on canvas, 23 3/4 x 28 3/4 ins / 60.6 x 73.2 cm) NLG 109,554. LONDON, 3-4 Dec 1997, *Coach Drawn by Six Horses Crossing a River* (1671, oil on canvas, 32 1/2 x 38 ins / 82.6 x 96.8 cm) GBP 111,500. NEW YORK, 31 Dec 1997, *Cows Drinking from a Pond near a Mountain on the Edge of a Wood* (1680, oil on canvas, 47 1/4 x 42 1/2 ins / 120 x 108 cm) USD 63,000. LONDON, 31 March 1999, *Landscape with Shooting Party in Foreground* (oil on canvas, 19 x 37 ins / 48 x 94 cm) GBP 20,000. VIENNA, 4 Oct 2000, *Wooded Landscape with Herdsmen, Sheep and Goats* (1679, oil on canvas, 74 x 65 ins / 189 x 165 cm) ATS 450,000. LONDON, 30 Nov 2000, *View of the Thames Valley, with Henley in the Distance* (oil on canvas, 71 x 63 ins / 181 x 161 cm) GBP 420,000. MADRID, 25 April 2001, *Landscape with Farmers and Flock Crossing Stream* (oil on canvas, 74 x 65 ins / 189 x 164 cm) ESP 13,000,000. LONDON, 11 July 2001, *Henley on Thames from Wargrave Road* (1698, oil on canvas, 35 x 47 ins / 90 x 120 cm) GBP 700,000. LONDON, 12 June 2003, *Extensive River Landscape, probably Derbyshire, with Drovers and Cattle* (oil on canvas, 32 x 50 ins / 82 x 128 cm) GBP 100,000. NEW YORK, 22 Jan 2004, *Figures with Cart and Horses Fording Stream* (oil on canvas, 38 x 44 ins / 97 x 112 cm) USD 25,000. BRUSSELS, 16 Feb 2004, *La traie des vaches* (oil on canvas, 23 x 31 ins / 58 x 78 cm) EUR 2,000. LONDON, 21 April 2004, *Departure for Market* (1661, oil on canvas, 63 x 86 ins / 161 x 219 cm) GBP 18,000.

SIBERSMA, G.

Dutch, 18th century.
Engraver (burin).

G. Sibersma is known to have engraved a *Portrait of Baron W. von Imhoff* and *Elevation of William IV to the Throne*.

SIBERT. See also **SIEBERT**

SIBERT, Jean

French, 17th century.
Active in Avignon.
Sculptor. Portraits.

In 1641 Jean Sibert sculpted two statues of saints for the church of Notre-Dame-des-Grâces at Séguret.

SIBERT, Joachim. See **SIWERT**

SIBERT, Johann Martin Jakob. See **SIEBERT**

SIBILE, Joris

Italian, 17th century.
Active in Rome c. 1636.
Painter.

SIBILLA, Gasparo

Italian, 18th century.
Died 1782, in Rome.
Sculptor.

Sibilla became a member of the Accademia di S Luca from 1776 onwards. He sculpted the tomb of Pope Benedict XIV in St Peter's in Rome.

SIBILLA, Gijsbert Jansz., or Sébille

Flemish School, 17th century.
Born c. 1598, in Weesp; died after 1652.
Painter. History painting.

Gijsbert Jansz. Sibilla was the burgomaster of Weesp. For the town hall he painted *The Judgement of Solomon* and *Assembly of the Magistrates in 1652*.

MUSEUMS AND GALLERIES:

DARMSTADT: *Solon before Cresus*.

AUCTION RECORDS:

LONDON, 28 Feb 1990, *Sacrifice of Moses* (oil on canvas, 40 1/4 x 35 ins / 102 x 88 cm) GBP 4,400. LONDON, 20 April 1994, *Visitation* (1645, oil on panel, 19 3/4 x 16 ins / 50.3 x 40.5 cm) GBP 9,200. PARIS, 8 June 1994, *Baptism of the Eunuch of Queen Candice* (oil on oak panel, 21 3/4 x 18 1/4 ins / 55.5 x 46.5 cm) FRF 12,500. LONDON, 7 July 1999, *Sacrifice of Noah* (oil on canvas, 41 x 35 ins / 104 x 90 cm) GBP 6,000.

SIBLEY, Charles

British, 19th century.
Active in London between 1826 and 1847.
Painter.

SIBMACHER, Hans or Johann

German, 17th century.
Died 23 March 1611, in Nuremberg.
Painter, engraver. Portraits, views, hunting subjects, military subjects. Heraldry.

Sibmacher mainly produced heraldic engravings and lace designs. He published several books: the *Book of Heraldry* published in 1605, 1606 and 1612, containing several thousand coats of arms, a book about lace design, *New Book of Patterns*, published in 1604, as well as drawings for book illustration. He possessed a gift for ornamentation and exerted a considerable influence until the 19th century.

SIBOLDT, Samuel. See **SYBOLD**

SIBON

French, 18th century.
Active in Châteaudun.
Sculptor (wood).

Sibon sculpted three great angels and the choir stalls of the church of St-Léger at Sancheville.

SIBON, Joseph
French, 18th century.
Active in Toulon c. 1707.
Painter.

SIBONI, Emma
Danish, 20th century.
Born 29 September 1877, in Denmark.
Active in the USA.
Painter, miniaturist.

Emma Siboni studied at the Kongelige Danske Kunstakademi in Copenhagen and at the Art Institute in Chicago, then under Emile Renard and Madame Lafarge-Charma in Paris, Walter Thor in Munich, and Franz Skarbina in Berlin. she was a member of the American Arts Federation.

SIBONI, Torben
Danish, 20th century.
Born 1928.
Painter.

Torben Siboni studied at colleges and private studios in London, Madrid, Rome and Copenhagen, and travelled extensively throughout Europe, Africa and the Americas. He is related to the opera singer Giuseppe Siboni who established the Danish National Conservatory of Music.

SIBRA, Paul Marie
French, 20th century.
Born 10 September 1889, in Castelnaudary.
Painter.

Paul Marie Sibra exhibited in Paris at the Salon des Artistes Français. In 1924 he became a society member and in 1926 he received a silver medal.

SIBRANDZ, Jelle
Belgian, 17th century.
Painter.

Jelle Sibrandz was a pupil of B. Schendel in Leeuwarden, and went to Italy in 1669. He painted the group of the *Four Daughters of Jac. von dem Waayen* kept in the museum at Verviers.

SIBRAYQUE, Georges, or Siebrecht
French, 17th century.
Sculptor.

Georges Sibrayque worked for Versailles from 1672 to 1682. His statue of *Africa* can be seen in the Parterre du Nord (north flowerbed).

SIBRE, Ernest
French, 19th century.
Born in Paris.
Painter. Genre scenes.

Sibre was pupil of Picot, Giraud and Pils. He exhibited at the Salon in 1867 and 1868.

SIBRECHTS, Jan. See **SIBERECHTS**

SIBRECHTS, Johannes. See **SIEBRECHTS**

SIBRECQ, Bernard and Gérard
French, 17th century.
Active in Lyons 1635-1642.
Sculptors.

SIBSON, Thomas
British, 19th century.
Born March 1817, in Cumberland; died 28 November 1844, in Malta.
Painter, engraver, draughtsman. Genre scenes.

Thomas Sibson went to Edinburgh at a very young age, where he was expected to pursue a career in business, but a marked taste for drawing and painting - in which he was self-taught - took him to London, where he found work as an illustrator; he was among those who executed illustration for the works of Charles Dickens. In 1842 he went to Munich where he worked in Kaulbach's studio, but poor health obliged him to return to England before later leaving for Malta.

SIBUET, Claude
French, 19th century.
Born 1834; died 1879.
Active in Lyons.
Painter. Flowers.

SIBUET, Jocelyne
French, 20th - 21st century.
Born 8 July 1959, in Scionzier (Haute-Savoie).
Painter. Landscapes with figures, mountainscapes.

Jocelyne Sibuet was awarded a painting prize in 1986 to commemorate the bicentenary of the ascent of Mont Blanc. From 1983, her work has consisted primarily of Alpine landscapes inspired by her immediate environment. She has also shown her work in Paris, notably at the Salon International d'Art Naïf.

SIBUSISO, Mbhele
South African, 20th - 21st century.
Born 1964, in Witbank (Transvaal).
Sculptor, assemblage artist.
Art Brut.

Mbhele Sibusiso took part in *Un Art Contemporain d'Afrique du Sud* (*Contemporary Art of South Africa*) at the Galerie de l'Esplanade in La Défense in Paris in 1994.

BIBLIOGRAPHY:

Bolofo, Koto, *Sibusio Mbhele and His Fish Helicopter*, New York, 2002.

SICARD, François Léon
French, 19th - 20th century.
Born 21 April 1862, in Tours; died 1934, in Paris.
Sculptor, draughtsman.

François Sicard was a pupil of Félix Joseph Barrias and Félix Laurent. He won the Prix de Rome in 1891. He appeared at the Salon des Artistes Français in Paris, becoming a member in 1900. He received an honourable mention in 1887, a second-class medal in 1894, a first-class medal in 1897, and a silver medal in 1900 at the Exposition Universelle. He was made a Chevalier of the Légion d'Honneur in 1910 and later an Officer, and named a member of the Institute de France. His notable sculptures in Paris were the *Monument to the Revolution* in the choir of the Pantheon, *The Good Samaritan* in the Jardin des Tuileries, and the statue of *George Sand* in the Jardin du Luxembourg. Other sculptures include the caryatids on the façade of the Hotel de Ville of Tours, and the *Monument to Clemenceau* at Ste-Hermine in the Vendée.

MUSEUMS AND GALLERIES:

PARIS (Mus. d'Orsay): *Oedipus and the Sphinx*; *Apollo and George Sand* - PARIS (Mus. du Petit Palais): *Agar* - TOURS (MBA): studies in red chalk.

AUCTION RECORDS:

PARIS, 23 March 1984, *Oedipus and the Sphinx* (gilded patinated bronze, h. 25 1/2 ins / 65 cm) FRF 46,500. ENGHIEN-LES-BAINS, 28 April 1985, *The Snake Charmer* (bronze, h. 20 3/4 ins / 53 cm) FRF 88,000. LONDON, 10 Dec 2002, *Oedipus and the Sphinx* (gilt bronze, h. 27 ins / 69 cm) GBP 10,000. PARIS, 2 Oct 2003, *St Michel Defeating the Dragon* (brown patinated bronze, h. 45 ins / 115 cm) EUR 12,000. SYDNEY, 15 May 2004, *Oedipus and the Sphinx* (bronze, h. 26 ins / 65 cm) AUD 30,000. LONDON, 9 July 2004, *Winged Victory* (patinated bronze, h. 36 ins / 91 cm) GBP 7,000.

SICARD, Jean Pierre Antoine
French, 18th century.
Active in Toulon.
Painter.

Jean Pierre Antoine Sicard worked for Toulon Cathedral in 1759.

SICARD, Josée
French, 20th - 21st century.
Born c. 1950.
Painter, sculptor, mixed media.

At different stages in her career, Josée Sicard has used various materials ranging from polystyrene to ferro-concrete in a bid to highlight the discrepancy between external bulk and actual weight. In so doing, she has produced work that is geometrically abstract and, at times, akin to Op Art.

She has been involved since 1977 in various group exhibitions in Paris, Marseilles, Toulon, Nice and Quebec. She has also exhibited solo on several occasions: in 1983 in Nuremberg; in 1983 and 1986 in Nice; in 1987 at the Galerie La Tête d'Obsidienne in La Seyne-sur-Mer; in 1987, 1989 and 1990 at the Galerie Macé in Cannes; in 1989 in Marseilles and at the Galerie L'Usine Ephémère in Paris; in 1990 in Nuremberg.

MUSEUMS AND GALLERIES:
TOULON.

SICARD, Louis Apollinaire
French, 19th century.
Born 25 April 1807, in Lyons; died 1881, in Lyons.
Painter, pastellist. Landscapes, flowers.

Sicard was pupil of Berjon, Revoil and Theirat.

MUSEUMS AND GALLERIES:
DIJON (MBA): a canvas; two pastels - LYONS (MBA): four pastels.

AUCTION RECORDS:
NEW YORK, 23 May 1997, *Sunflowers* (1839, oil on canvas, 27½ x 21¼ ins / 70 x 54 cm) USD 68,500.

SICARD, Louis Marie, or Sicardi, Sicardy, Siccardi
French, 18th - 19th century.
Born 1746, in Avignon; died 18 July 1825.
Miniaturist, enameller. Portraits.

Louis Marie Sicard worked in Paris and exhibited at the Salon between 1791 and 1819. The scenes he composed with Pierrot as their chief protagonist reached a large audience through engravings.

MUSEUMS AND GALLERIES:
LONDON (Wallace Collection): *Louis XVI* (1782); *A Young Louis XVI* (miniature); *Young Girl with a Basket of Flowers* (miniature); *Young Woman in a Négligée* (miniature); *Madame Cail as a Bacchante* (miniature); *Lady Dressed in the Style of Late Louis XVI* (miniature); *Young Woman with a Mantilla* (miniature) - PARIS (Louvre): *Louis XVI* (miniature); *Mademoiselle Sicard* (miniature) - PARIS (Mus. Jacquemart-André): *Louis XVI*.

AUCTION RECORDS:
PARIS, 1861, *Miniature* (subject unspecified) FRF 600. PARIS, 1868, *Young Woman Wearing a Turban* (miniature) FRF 405. PARIS, 1872, *Pierrot Holding a Dish with a Sausage Coveted by Columbine* (miniature) FRF 6,020. PARIS, 1874, *Mid-length Portrait of a Young Woman Leaning against a Statue of Cupid* (miniature) FRF 1,300. PARIS, 1 Feb 1877, *Portrait of the Duke of Normandy* (miniature) FRF 520. PARIS, 1886, *Three-quarter Portrait of a Young Woman in a White Bonnet Trimmed with Blue Ribbons* (miniature) FRF 600. PARIS, 1891, *Portrait of the Countess of Jersey* (miniature) FRF 3,300. PARIS, 1897, *Portrait of Madame Lebrun* (miniature) FRF 5,200. PARIS, 1898, *Portrait of a Young Woman* (miniature) FRF 5,100. PARIS, 25-28 March 1898, *Portrait of Madame d'Alembert* (miniature) FRF 4,680; *Portrait of Louis XVI* (miniature) FRF 1,350. PARIS, 12 May 1898, *Portrait of a Woman* (miniature/tortoiseshell box with ring of gold) FRF 2,400. PARIS, 1899, *Portrait of the Artist* (watercolour) FRF 180. LONDON, 5 July 1899, *Portrait of a Lady in White* (miniature) FRF 3,375. PARIS, 8 April 1919, *Portrait of a Young Girl Dressed as a Vestal Virgin* (miniature) FRF 1,950. PARIS, 8 April 1919, *Portrait of a Woman* (miniature) FRF 3,300. PARIS, 8 May 1926, *Portrait of a Man* (miniature) FRF 600. PARIS, 1 June 1928, *O Che Boccone (Tasty Morsel)* (lead pencil) FRF 8,500; *Man in Blue* (miniature) FRF 3,800. LONDON, 29 June 1928, *Group of Five Children Playing in a Garden*, GBP 231. PARIS, 12 June 1929, *Portrait of a Man* (miniature) FRF 4,800; *Portrait of a Woman in a Low-cut Dress* (miniature) FRF 6,900. PARIS, 25 Nov 1936, *Portrait of a Young Woman* (miniature) FRF 5,600. PARIS, 5 March 1937, *Portrait Presumed to be of Mademoiselle Emily Léveillé, from the Comédie-Française, in a White, Very Low-cut Dress* (miniature) FRF 550. PARIS, 18 March 1937, *Portrait of Préville, Actor of the Théâtre-Français, in the Role of Figaro* (pastel) FRF 3,300. PARIS, 18 Dec 1940, *Portrait of a Man* (1772, pastel) FRF 2,400. PARIS, 12 July 1943, *Portrait of Monsieur Warlez, Count of St-Marsault* (1792, miniature) FRF 3,200. PARIS, 28 March 1945, *Woman in a Mauve Dress Wearing a Large Flowery Hat* (1784, miniature) FRF 17,500. PARIS, 1 April 1949, *Portrait of a Man Wearing Purple* (1787, miniature) FRF 16,000. PARIS, 15 Dec 1950, *Young Woman in a Green and Pink Dress* (enamel, attributed) FRF 14,000. PARIS, 11 April 1951, *Woman in a Blue Dress* (miniature) FRF 30,000. PARIS, 21 March 1952, *Portrait of an Actor* (pastel) FRF 140,000. LONDON, 11 Feb 1999, *Lady Leaning Against a Plinth* (miniature) GBP 12,000. FLORENCE, 8 March 1999, *Napoleon and Marie Louise with Emperors of Austria and Russia* (miniature, 17 x 11 ins / 43 x 28 cm) ITL 17,500,000. PARIS, 20 June 2001, *Portrait of a Man in Dark Clothes* (miniature, oval, 2½ x 2 ins / 6 x 5 cm) FRF 16,000. LONDON, 11 April 2002, *Mademoiselle Victorine de Chastenay-Lanty* (miniature, h. 2 ins / 5 cm) GBP 13,000. PARIS, 18 Dec 2002, *Portrait of Antoine Marie* (1811, miniature, oval, 3 x 2 ins / 7 x 5 cm) EUR 2,200. CIRENCESTER, 31 Oct 2003, *Meeting with Tilsitt* (oil on ivory panel, 7 x 6 ins / 19 x 14 cm) GBP 2,000. PARIS, 26 March 2004, *Gentleman Wearing Grey Court Dress* (c. 1770, miniature, oval, 2 x 1½ ins / 5 x 4 cm) EUR 3,100. LONDON, 22 April 2004, *Lady in a White Dress and Corsage* (1790, miniature, h. 2½ ins / 6 cm) GBP 7,000.

SICARD, Nicolas
French, 19th - 20th century.
Born c. 1840, in Lyons; died January 1920.
Painter, watercolourist. Genre scenes, urban landscapes, landscapes with figures, animals.

Nicolas Sicard was a pupil of Victor Vibert and Danguin at the École des Beaux-Arts in Lyons. He began at the Salon de Paris in 1869 and became a member of the Salon des Artistes Français in 1883. He received an honourable mention in 1881 and a bronze medal in 1889 at the Exposition Universelle. He was a Chevalier of the Légion d'Honneur in 1900. He chiefly painted hunting scenes with riders and horses, street scenes and markets, all treated with bright colours.

MUSEUMS AND GALLERIES:
BÉZIERS: *Unhappy Hunter* - LYONS (MBA): *Entry to the Guillotiere Bridge* - NIORT: *Accident* - ST-ÉTIENNE (Mus. d'Art et d'Industrie): *Road on Market Day*.

AUCTION RECORDS:
PARIS, 16-17 May 1897, *Driving off Beggars*, FRF 800. PARIS, 21 June 1919, *Yard of a Country House*, FRF 305. PARIS, 29 June 1927, *Driving off Beggars*, FRF 1,950. PARIS, 18 April 1929, *Arab Riders*, FRF 610. LA VARENNE-ST-HILAIRE, 21 May

1989, *Spanish Marketeer* (oil on canvas, 35 x 46 ins / 89 x 117 cm) FRF 24,000.

SICARD, Pierre
French, 20th century.
Born 30 January 1900, in Paris; died 1980.
Active from 1950 in the USA.
Painter, watercolourist, draughtsman. Figures, portraits, scenes with figures, landscapes, urban landscapes, still-lifes. Designs for tapestries.

Pierre Sicard was the son of the sculptor François Sicard, former Prix de Rome winner and member of the Institute, and a close friend of Georges Clémenceau. He was first a pupil at the École Centrale des Ingénieurs, then left to study architecture and worked on decoration. After working with his father in sculpting, he started to paint in 1924. He travelled in Switzerland and London in 1930, to Spain in 1931, staying two years, to the USA in 1936, and in 1936 and 1937 to the Far East, Hong Kong, Manila, Bali and Angkor. In 1944 he was named Peintre Officiel pour la Guerre, creating projects depicting the glory of the French army. After the war he made frequent journeys to the USA, in 1947 to Los Angeles and New York, and in 1950 he settled in California, where he taught drawing. As an expatriate he tended be forgotten by the French public after 1955.

From 1924 he painted landscapes, soon followed by scenes in bars, dancing and cabaret, and scenes of Parisian life during the 'mad years', all taken from life, which gave him great notoriety during the 1930s. His early admiration for Monet was followed by influences first from Bonnard and Vuillard, and then of the more scripted painting of Matisse and Dufy. Along with the evolution of his technique and his very many travels, he introduced landscapes into his new range of subjects. After settling in the USA, he painted many still-lifes, treated flatly with contrasting colours. He also concentrated on painting views of the wide streets that had fascinated him during the course of his travels and in America. He favoured night views, transposing in a formal but supple geometry and perspective the magical spectacle of the alignment of lit buildings and, crushed in their depths, the uninterrupted flow of the lights of vehicles along the straight streets

While not taking a large part in public exhibitions, he showed collections of his paintings in solo exhibitions: the first in Paris in 1926 at Galerie Durand-Ruel, followed by numerous others, notably at the Galerie Georges Petit. He also exhibited in places during his travels, showing regional scenes.

Pierre Sicard

BIBLIOGRAPHY:
Rémusat, Claude, *Pierre Sicard*, Éd. Pierre Cailler, Geneva, 1955. Rémusat, Claude, *'Pierre Sicard'* in *coll. Documents sur l'Art* n° 66, Éd. Pierre Cailler, Geneva, 1957.

MUSEUMS AND GALLERIES:
LUXEMBOURG (Mus.): *Carmona Seen From the Olive Trees* - PARIS (MNAM-CCI).

AUCTION RECORDS:
NEW YORK, 26 Oct 1960, *Notre-Dame de Paris (Night)*, USD 700. PARIS, 27 Nov 1974, *Versailles, the Chapel*, FRF 7,800. VERSAILLES, 15 May 1977, *Charleston and Trumpet* (oil on canvas, 24 x 18 ins / 61 x 46 cm) FRF 5,000. HONFLEUR, 4 Nov 1979, *Thames in London* (oil on canvas, 24 x 32 ins / 61 x 81 cm) FRF 6,000. PARIS, 29 Jan 1988, *Light in Broadway* (1954, oil on canvas, 32 x 25½ ins / 81 x 65 cm) FRF 3,400; *Notre-Dame, Night* (oil on canvas, 23½ x 32 ins / 60 x 81 cm) FRF 3,000; *Tulips and Fruit* (oil on canvas, 24 x 20 ins / 61 x 51 cm) FRF 2,300. RHEIMS, 13 March 1988, *Pont St-Michel* (oil on canvas, 20 x 25½ ins / 51 x 65 cm) FRF 8,500. VERSAILLES, 24 Sept 1989, *Three Women Bathing* (oil on canvas, 19¾ x 24¼ ins / 50 x 61.5 cm) FRF 4,500. PARIS, 30 May 1990, *View of Manhattan* (oil on canvas, 15 x 18 ins / 38 x 46 cm) FRF 12,000. PARIS, 28 June 2001, *Le Pigall's* (1924, oil on canvas, 24 x 29 ins / 60 x 73 cm) FRF 14,500. PARIS, 28 June 2001, *Dancers at the Cabaret* (oil on canvas, 26 x 36 ins / 65 x 92 cm) FRF 30,000.

SICART, Jean
French, 16th century.
Active in Bourges c. 1523.
Sculptor (wood).

SICCARDI, Giuseppe
Italian, 20th century.
Born 18 July 1883, in Albino (Lombardy).
Painter.

Giuseppe Siccardi was a pupil of Ponziano Loverini.

SICCARDI, Louis Marie. See **SICARD**

SICCIOLANTE, Girolamo da Sermoneta. See **SICIOLANTE Girolamo**

SICCRIST, J. M.. See the entry **SIGRIST Johann**

SICELUS
6th century BC.
Active at the end of the 6th century BC.
Vase painter.
Ancient Greek.

Sicelus is represented by an amphora depicting *Athena and Two Wrestlers* in the museum in Naples.

SICHA, Lukas Georg
Austrian, 17th century.
Active in Prague in 1665.
Engraver (burin). Portraits, book illustrations.

SICHÉ, Paul
French, 20th century.
Born 23 March 1933, in Lyons.
Painter, engraver, lithographer, illustrator, draughtsman. Figures, nudes, village scenes, boats. Murals, stage costumes and sets.

Paul Siché taught himself to paint. He carried out several monumental and theatrical works of decoration. Most notable were: 1973, Lyons, an entrance hall in enamelled concrete; 1975, decoration and costumes for *Through the Looking Glass*, after Lewis Carroll; 1980, 1981, 1982 in the Drôme; 1984, 1987, 1988, painted walls at Lyons (several), Vénissieux, Paris, St-Cyr-au-Mont-d'Or, Belfort. In addition he illustrated several collections of poetry.

After painting carousels in fun fairs, nudes, barges, then paintings of movement including rugby players, he was attracted to non-figurative painting. At the same time, the idea of the crowd becomes a constantly varying theme, to the point of being an army under marching orders.

He took part in public exhibitions including 1960, Menton, selected for the Biennale; 1967, Pontarlier, Salon des Annonciades; from 1975, Salon des Givors (Rhône); 1978-1979 Paris, *L'Estampe Aujourd'hui*, Bibliothèque Nationale. Solo exhibitions include 1966, Pontarlier, guest of honour at the 42nd Salon des Annonciades; 1976, St-Donat-sur-L'Herbasse (Drôme), guest of honour at the 15th J.S. Bach Festival, organised by Marie-Claire Allain; 1977, Metz, guest of honour at the École Nationale d'Ingénieurs; 1980, Limoges, Centre Culturel, and Mézières, Centre Culturel; 1984, New York - East Hampton, Bologna/Landi Gallery; 1985, Belfort, Salle des Fêtes; 1986, Ajaccio; 1988, Rillieux-la-Pape, Espace Baudelaire.

BIBLIOGRAPHY:
'Paul Siché' in *Le Courrier de l'UNESCO*, periodical, Paris, March 1976, October 1978, March 1985, May 1988. *Paul*

Siché, Centre de culture et de communication, Espace Baudelaire, Rillieux-la-Pape, 1988. Boulogne, Daniel, *Actualité du mur peint,* Syros-Alternatives, Paris, 1989.

SICHEL, Ernest Leopold
British, 19th - 20th century.
Born 27 June 1862, in Bradford; died 21 March 1941, in Bradford.
Painter, pastellist, sculptor, worker in precious metals.
Figures, portraits, genre scenes, still-lifes.

Ernest Sichel studied under Alphonse Legros and John Macallan Swan at the Slade School of Fine Art, London. He exhibited with the Royal Academy from 1885, and the New English Art Club from 1891, the year he returned to Bradford, where he worked until his death.

MUSEUMS AND GALLERIES:
BRADFORD (Cartwright Hall AG): *Sir Jacob Behrens; A Child Funeral in the Highlands;* statuette*A Gaul* (bronze); *Portrait of Miss Catherine Howard* (c. 1904, oil on canvas) - LONDON (Tate Collection): *Musical Instruments* (1895-1905).

SICHEL, Nathaniel
German, 19th - 20th century.
Born 8 January 1843, in Mainz; died 4 December 1907, in Berlin.
Painter, engraver. Figures, portraits, local scenes, genre scenes.
Orientalism.

Nathaniel Sichel studied under J. Schrader in Berlin and spent two years in Rome as a Prix de Rome laureate. He visited Paris prior to returning to Berlin, where he was a prolific lithographer.

MUSEUMS AND GALLERIES:
BRUNSWICK: *Yum-Yum* - COLOGNE: *Oriental Woman* - HALLE: *Woman Beggar at the Pont des Arts* - MAINZ: *Sakountala* - ROSTOCK: *Salome.*

AUCTION RECORDS:
LINDAU, 4 May 1983, *Portrait of a Beautiful Nubian Woman* (oil on panel, 21 1/4 x 14 ins / 54 x 35.5 cm) DEM 3,400. LONDON, 22 Nov 1990, *Portrait of a Young Woman with a Veiled Breast* (1895, oil on canvas/panel, 23 x 17 1/4 ins / 58.5 x 44 cm) GBP 1,320. NEW YORK, 16 Feb 1994, *Meditation* (oil on canvas, 28 1/4 x 21 1/2 ins / 71.8 x 54.6 cm) USD 4,313. LONDON, 17 Nov 1994, *Arab Women on a Terrace* (oil on canvas, 38 x 75 1/2 ins / 96.5 x 192 cm) GBP 23,000. LONDON, 10 Feb 1995, *Odalisque* (oil on canvas, 33 x 19 ins / 83.7 x 48.2 cm) GBP 4,600.

SICHEL, Pierre
French, 20th century.
Born 1899; died 21 July 1983, in Paris.
Painter. Figures, nudes, portraits, urban landscapes.

Pierre Sichel showed artistic gifts as a child. He exhibited regularly in Paris at the Salon des Indépendants.

AUCTION RECORDS:
PARIS, 18 May 1947, *Vestal Virgin,* FRF 1,250. PARIS, 24 Dec 1948, *Standing Nude,* FRF 2,500. PARIS, 30 March 1949, *Place de la Concorde,* FRF 1,000; *Pont Alexandre III,* FRF 1,000. PARIS, 15 Feb 1950, *Nude with Raised Arms,* FRF 3,500.

SICHELBART, Ignatius, or Sichelbarth or Sickelpart, also known as Ai Qimeng, Ai Ch'i Meng, Ai K'i-Mong or Ngai K'i-Mong
Bohemian School, 18th century.
Born 26 September 1708, in Neudek, near Karlovy Vary; died 6 October 1780, in Peking (now Beijing), China.
From 1738 active in China.
Painter. Animals.

In 1736 Ignatius Sichelbart entered a religious order, and in 1738 became a missionary in China. He was sent to Peking, where he worked as a painter for the court with the religious father Castiglione.

He specialised in the painting of birds, animals and plants, and was one of Emperor Qianlong's three favourite painters. He helped produced engravings of Qianlong's military conquests; a work carried out in Paris from 1767 to 1774 under Charles-Nicolas Cochin's direction. He may be the same artist as Tadäus Sichbart, who came from Bohemia, and produced four oil paintings for the town hall of Elbogen. In this case, the work would have been carried out before his departure for China.

MUSEUMS AND GALLERIES:
COPPET (Château) - FONTAINEBLEAU (Mus. National du Château) - PARIS (Bibliothèque Mazarine) - PARIS (BNF) - PARIS (Mus. National des Arts asiatiques-Guimet).

SICHELBEIN, Caspar, the Elder
German, 16th - 17th century.
Born in Augsburg; died before 1607, in Memmingen.
Painter.

SICHELBEIN, Caspar, the Younger
German, 17th century.
Died 1621.
Painter.

Caspar Sichelbein the Younger's masterpiece, dating to 1619, is a *Crucifixion.*

SICHELBEIN, Hans Konrad
German, 17th century.
Painter.

Hans Sichelbein was the son of Caspar the Younger. After 1600, he worked for Schloss Zeil (castle) in Germany, and in 1634, in St Gallen, Switzerland. He became a teacher in 1621.

SICHELBEIN, Johann Friedrich
German, 17th - 18th century.
Born 1655; died 1726.
Painter.

Johann Friedrich Sichelbein produced paintings for the church of Memmingen (Bavaria) Germany (*Nativity, Assumption* and *Baptism of Christ*).

MUSEUMS AND GALLERIES:
MEMMINGEN (Antoniter und Strigel Mus.): *The Last Supper; Baptism of Christ; Holy Ghost.*

SICHELBEIN, Johann Friedrich I
German, 17th century.
Born c. 1625; died c. 1690.
Painter.

Johann Friedrich Sichelbein I was the son of Caspar the Younger.

SICHELBEIN, Johann Friedrich II
German, 17th - 18th century.
Born 1648; died 1719.
Painter.

Johann Friedrich Sichelbein II was the son and pupil of Johann Friedrich I. He travelled to Italy.

SICHELBEIN, Joseph Franz
German, 17th century.
Painter.

MUSEUMS AND GALLERIES:
OTTOBEUREN (Klostermus.): several works.

SICHELBEIN, Judas Jacobus
German, 18th century.
Painter.

Judas Jacobus Sichelbein painted casks and the tabernacle in the monastery church of Weingarten, Germany.

SICHELBEIN, Judas Thaddäus
German, 18th century.
Painter.

Judas Thaddäus Sichelbein produced works for the German churches of Säckingen, Ottobeuren and Kissleg.

SICHELBEIN, Tobias
German, 17th century.
Painter.
MUSEUMS AND GALLERIES:
WANGEN (Town Hall): *Last Judgement* (1649).

SICHELL, Ernest Leopold. See **SICHEL**

SICHELSCHMIED, Wolf, or Schmied
German, 16th century.
Born in Heldbourg or Sichelsdorf, near Nuremberg; died 5 February 1597, in Coburg.
Painter.
Sichelschmied painted the *Twelve Apostles* of the choir of the church of Coburg.

SICHEM, Christoffel van, the Elder, or Voschem
Flemish School, 16th - 17th century.
Born c. 1546, probably in Amsterdam; died 20 October 1624, probably in Amsterdam.
Engraver, draughtsman.
Among biographers there is no agreement about the Sichem family. Traditionally there said are to have been four of them: Christoffel the Elder, Christoffel the Younger, Karl and Cornelis. Le Blanc, in his *Manual for the Print Lover*, speaks of the Christoffels as only one artist, and Nagler believes that Christoffel the Younger and Cornelis are identical.

Christoffel the Elder seems to have worked in Basel, Strasbourg and Augsburg. In 1573 *The 13 Locations of the Praiseworthy Confraternity* was published in Basel with woodcuts by him. In 1577, in the same city, Muller von Marpurck's *Portraits of Famous Warriors* was published with 48 of his woodcuts. There are other books published in 1590 and 1600 that contain woodcuts bearing his monogram. Attributed to him are engraved portraits and a series of a dozen historical subjects signed *Ch.-V. Sichem sculp. et exc. Ch.-V. Sichem fecit et Christ. Van Sichem fecit.*

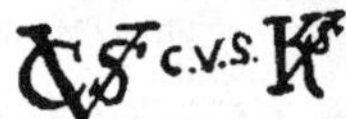

AUCTION RECORDS:
PARIS, 23 May 1928, ; *Faith, Hope and Charity* (drawing) FRF 145.

SICHEM, Christoffel van II, the Younger
Flemish School, 16th - 17th century.
Born c. 1580, in Basel; died 1658, in Amsterdam.
Active in Amsterdam, and in Leiden c. 1603.
Engraver, illustrator.
Christoffel van Sichem the Younger, Carl (or Karl) and Cornelis produced works which are very similar. It seems probable that these three artists were the sons of Christoffel the Elder and worked with him. Christoffel the Younger was a pupil of Goltzius.

His body of work is considerable and includes 797 engravings illustrating the *Biblia Sacra* (*Holy Bible*) (1646).

SICHEM, Cornelis van
Dutch, 16th - 17th century.
Born c. 1580, probably in Delft; died at the beginning of the 17th century, in Amsterdam.
Engraver, print publisher.
Cornelis van Sichem is thought to have been a pupil of H. Goltzius, after whom he engraved on wood several drawings. He also engraved after Bloemart and Mathan.

SICHEM, Karl or Karel
Dutch, 16th century.
Died after 1604.
Engraver (burin).
Perhaps the brother of Christoffel the Younger, Karl or Karel Sichem engraved portraits using his father's technique. Some authors believe he signed with the monogram of three capital letters, K.V.S., and attribute to him 17 plates for the small-folio *Iconica et Historica descriptio Preacipuorum heresiarchum*, which Le Blanc attributes to Christoffel and which contains portraits of the principal reformers.

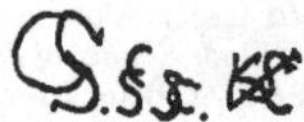

SICHER, Fridolin. See **SIEHER**

SICHLBART, Tadäus. See **SICHELBEIN Judas Thaddäus**

SICHLING, Lazarus Gottlieb
German, 19th century.
Born 1812, in Nuremberg; died 1863, in Leipzig.
Reproductions engraver. Portraits.
Sichling studied under Karl Mayer and Albrecht Reindel. In 1834, he left Nuremberg and lived in Munich and Paris, where he worked for Govard at the Versailles Gallery for nearly two years, and then moved to London. In 1839, he returned to Nuremberg before settling in Leipzig. His numerous portraits include *Beethoven, Gluck* and *Cl. Brentano.*

SICHNIT, Martin
Austrian, 18th century.
Born 3 August 1754, in Vienna; died 13 March 1804, in Vienna.
Painter, engraver.

SICHT, J. J.
German, 17th century.
Active during the first half of the 17th century.
Painter.
MUSEUMS AND GALLERIES:
UTTINGEN (Church): *Christ on the Cross at Magdalene's Feet* (1621).

SICHULSKI, Kazimierz
Polish, 20th century.
Born 17 January 1879, in Lemberg (now Lviv, Ukraine); died 1942, in Lviv.
Painter, caricaturist, engraver. Figures, portraits.
Kazimierz Sichulski first studied philosophy at Cracow University, then painting and decorative art with Leon Wyczolkowski, Jozef Mehoffer and Stanislaw Wyspianski at academy in the same town. Then he went abroad and studied at the academies at Vienna, Paris, Rome and Florence. During World War I he served with the Polish Legion. He taught at Lviv academy from 1920 to 1930 and at Cracow academy from 1930. While in Paris he joined the Salon de la Société Nationale des Beaux-Arts and in 1921 he took part in the exhibition of Polish artists organised by it.

Sichulski was a prolific artist, drawing inspiration from many sources. At the 1921 exhibition he showed *The Three Kings* and *Portrait of Ludwik Solski in the role of Frederick the Great, from the play by Adolf Nowaczynski*. He also executed a series of caricatures of eminent Poles of his time. Many of his works were lost during World War II.

SICILIA, José María
Spanish, 20th - 21st century.
Born 1954, in Madrid.
Active since 1980 in France.
Painter (including mixed media), engraver. Still-lifes, flowers, architectural views, landscapes. Artists' books.
José María Sicilia was a pupil of architecture and then of painting at the Real Academia de Bellas Artes de San

Fernando in Madrid from 1975 until 1979. In 1980 he settled in Paris, where he worked with Miguel Ángel Campano, who had moved there before him. Between 1985 and 1986 he lived in New York.

It was in the climate of calling art into question that prevailed in the Parisian environment that he decided to make a career out of painting. Following the numerous shaky starts that characterised the Parisian artistic context at the end of the war and especially after the social agitation of 1968 and its Neo-Dadaist repercussions, Sicilia joined the movement to return to the materials used in the traditional pictoral style. He immediately concentrated mainly on large formats. His canvases seem to have been painted quickly, spontaneously and quite crudely, a first impression soon contradicted by a closer look. During his early period, each painting is based on a unique subject: a Spanish landscape or a Parisian neighbourhood, then tree trunks, dustbins, sardines, domestic appliances, tools.

During a second period starting in 1985, with a series of square canvases of *Tulips* and *Flowers*, he turns away from the subject, conserving only the colour, the title and above all the dynamic of the lines, three factors still likely to evoke this subject, to develop what is finally an abstract work. He concentrates on the 'inseparable [form] of the background' and uses impasto, white monochromes, colours and stains to create the totality of the square surface as a form.

The artists' books that he has published since 1992 include: *Folded Light* (1984), a book that uses the technique of folding; *You're Alone* (1992), a book that incorporates the style and expression of covering in wax; *The Book of a Thousand and One Nights* (1996) that uses double printing on the front and back of the page; *Impromptu* (1995).

He has participated in group exhibitions: 1982 and 1985, Paris Biennale; 1983, Musée Bonnat, Bayonne; 1984, *Ateliers (Studios)*, ARC of the Musée d'Art Moderne de la Ville de Paris; 1985, Madrid museum of contemporary art, Athens museum of contemporary art; 1986, Venice Biennale; 2001, *Imago Mundi*, an exhibition on the geography of nature, CAPC Musée d'Art Contemporain, Bordeaux.

He has also shown his work in solo exhibitions: 1982 at the Trans Form gallery, Paris; 1984 and 1989 at the Crousel-Hussenot gallery, Paris; 1983 and 1985 at the Christian Laune gallery in Montpellier; 1985, Lisbon; 1985 and 1986, La Máquina Española gallery, Seville; 1985, 1987 and 1990, Blum Helman gallery, New York; 1987, CAPC Musée d'Art Contemporain, Bordeaux; 1987, 1988 and 1997, Velázquez palace, Madrid; 1991, Soledad Lorenzo gallery, Madrid; 2002, *En Flor. Livres, estampes et oeuvres sur papier 1992-2001 (In Flower. Books, Prints and Works on Paper 1992-2001)*, Centre de la Gravure et de l'Image Imprimée, La Louvière.

BIBLIOGRAPHY:

Bonet, Juan Manuel, *Nouvelle Biennale de Paris*, exhibition catalogue, Electa, Le Moniteur, Paris, 1985. *L'Art Moderne à Marseille: La Collection du Musée Cantini*, exhibition catalogue, Musée Cantini, Marseilles, 1988. Peppiatt, Michael, ''*Interview: José María Sicilia - Escaping the Tyranny of Style*' in *Art International* n° 6, periodical, Paris, summer 1989. Tuffeli, Nicole, ''*José María Sicilia: de la tradition en peinture*' in *Artstudio* n° 14, periodical, Gal. Templon, Paris, autumn 1989. *Catálogo nacional de arte contemporáneo 1990-1991*, Ibérico 2Mil, Barcelona, 1990-1991.

MUSEUMS AND GALLERIES:

BORDEAUX (CAPC-MAC) - MARSEILLES (Mus. Cantini): *Sierra Negra* (1984) - PARIS (FNAC): *You're Alone* (1992, artists' book); *Luz Plegada* (1994, artists' book).

AUCTION RECORDS:

NEW YORK, 20 Feb 1988, *Flora* (acrylic/canvas, in four panels 64 1/2 x 64 1/2 ins / 163.6 x 163.6 cm) USD 15,400; *White Frame Flower II* (1986, acrylic/canvas, in two panels 89 x 96 ins / 226 x 244 cm) USD 19,800. NEW YORK, 4 May 1988, *Bastille 2* (1984, oil on canvas, 116 1/4 x 78 ins / 295.1 x 198.3 cm) USD 33,000. NEW YORK, 10 Nov 1988, *Tulip 1* (1985, acrylic/canvas, 102 1/4 x 98 1/2 ins / 260 x 250 cm) USD 41,800. LONDON, 6 April 1989, *Flower 48* (1985, three panel acrylic/canvas, 39 1/4 x 118 ins / 100 x 300 cm) GBP 33,000. PARIS, 16 April 1989, *Scissors* (1984, oil on canvas, 98 1/2 x 94 1/2 ins / 250 x 240 cm) FRF 318,000. NEW YORK, 4 May 1989, *Red Flower* (1986, two acrylic panels/fabric, 95 x 31 1/2 ins / 241.3 x 80 cm) USD 60,500. LONDON, 29 June 1989, *Grey Iron* (1983, acrylic/canvas, 78 3/4 x 74 3/4 ins / 200 x 190 cm) GBP 28,600. NEW YORK, 5 Oct 1989, *Tulip 9* (1985, acrylic/canvas, 98 1/2 x 102 1/4 ins / 250 x 260 cm) USD 55,000. PARIS, 9 Oct 1989, *White Flower XII* (1986, acrylic/canvas, 20 x 20 ins / 51 x 51 cm) FRF 170,000. LONDON, 26 Oct 1989, *Nails* (oil on canvas, 78 3/4 x 63 ins / 200 x 160 cm) GBP 30,800. NEW YORK, 9 Nov 1989, *Tulip 7* (1985, acrylic/canvas, 102 1/2 x 98 1/2 ins / 260.5 x 250 cm) USD 71,500. PARIS, 12 Feb 1990, *Red Flower II* (1988, engraving, 18 x 11 3/4 ins / 45.5 x 30 cm) FRF 4,500. PARIS, 15 Feb 1990, *Black Flower* (1986, mixed media, 19 3/4 x 19 3/4 ins / 50 x 50 cm) FRF 310,000. LONDON, 5 April 1990, *Flower* (1986, acrylic/canvas, four panels 64 1/2 x 64 1/2 ins / 164 x 164 cm) GBP 60,500. NEW YORK, 5 Oct 1990, *Bunch of Yellow Flowers* (oil on canvas, four panels, in all 36 x 36 ins / 91.4 x 91.4 cm) USD 41,800. STOCKHOLM, 5-6 Dec 1990, *Composition* (1985, acrylic/paper, 17 3/4 x 15 ins / 45 x 38 cm) SEK 18,500. NEW YORK, 1 May 1991, *Tulip (flower)* (1985, oil on canvas on four panels, in all 64 x 64 ins / 162.7 x 162.7 cm) USD 44,000. STOCKHOLM, 30 May 1991, *Tulip* (acrylic/paper, 17 3/4 x 15 ins / 45 x 38 cm) SEK 20,000. NEW YORK, 13 Nov 1991, *Flower 13* (acrylic/canvas on four panels, 119 x 80 1/4 ins / 302.2 x 204 cm) USD 33,000. MADRID, 28 April 1992, *Black Flower Line* (1987, acrylic/canvas, 39 1/4 x 39 1/4 ins / 100 x 100 cm) ESP 3,200,000. NEW YORK, 6 May 1992, *Tulip 6* (1985, oil on canvas, 102 1/2 x 98 1/4 ins / 260.3 x 249.5 cm) USD 55,000. NEW YORK, 6 Oct 1992, *Red Flower* (1986, acrylic/canvas, 32 x 96 ins / 81.3 x 243.8 cm) USD 16,500. PARIS, 28 Oct 1992, *Ochre Saw* (1984, oil on canvas, 96 1/2 x 98 1/2 ins / 245 x 250 cm) FRF 120,000. NEW YORK, 19 Nov 1992, *Flower* (1985, oil on canvas in four parts, in all 64 1/4 x 64 3/4 ins / 163 x 164.4 cm) USD 35,200. LONDON, 3 Dec 1993, *Untitled* (1989, acrylic/canvas, 86 1/4 x 87 ins / 219 x 220.8 cm) GBP 6,325. PARIS, 21 March 1994, *Ochre Saw* (1984, oil on canvas, 96 1/2 x 98 1/2 ins / 245 x 250 cm) FRF 93,000. NEW YORK, 3 May 1995, *Red Flower XVI* (1986, acrylic/canvas, in four parts, in all 79 x 79 ins / 200.7 x 200.7 cm) USD 35,650. PARIS, 24 March 1996, *1982* (mixed media/canvas, 76 3/4 x 57 3/4 ins / 195 x 147 cm) FRF 50,000. NEW YORK, 21 Nov 1996, *Place de la Bastille TV 2* (1984, acrylic/canvas, 101 1/2 x 117 1/4 ins / 258 x 298 cm) USD 27,600. LONDON, 5 Dec 1996, *Tulipan 10* (1985, acrylic, wax and plaster/canvas, 26 1/2 x 17 ins / 67 x 43 cm) GBP 23,000. PARIS, 16 March 1997, *Abstract Composition* (1988, mixed media/card, 47 1/4 x 31 1/2 ins / 120 x 80 cm) FRF 14,200. NEW YORK, 6 May 1997, *Black Frame Flower* (1987, acrylic/canvas, 32 x 32 ins / 81 x 80.4 cm) USD 8,625. NEW YORK, 6-7 May 1997, *Black Flower IX* (1986, acrylic/canvas in nine parts, 119 x 119 ins / 302.3 x 302.3 cm) USD 35,650. LONDON, 27 June 1997, *Ochre Flower* (1986, acrylic/canvas in nine parts, 119 x 119 ins / 302.3 x 302.3 cm) GBP 11,500. PARIS, 4 March 1998, *Composition* (1990, wax, 19 1/4 x 13 3/4 ins / 49 x 35 cm) FRF 14,500. NEW YORK, 17 Feb 1999, *Red Flower* (1986, acrylic on canvas, on three panels, 32 x 96 ins / 81 x 244 cm) USD 22,000. MADRID, 22 Nov 1999, *Winter* (1984, oil on canvas, 98 x 102 ins / 250 x 259 cm) ESP 4,250,000. SEVILLE, 7 April 2000, *Untitled IV* (1991, mixed media and chalk on paper, 40 x 40 ins / 101 x 101 cm) ESP 4,000,000. PARIS, 7 June 2000, *Tulip* (1985, mixed media on paper, 87 x 69 ins / 220 x 175 cm) FRF 230,000. NEW YORK, 16 May 2001, *Untitled - The Light that is Extinguished* (1997, oil and beeswax on paper laid on canvas, 40 x 40 ins / 102 x 102 cm) USD 25,000. NEW YORK, 15 Nov

2001, *Flowers* (1997, oil and wax on wood, 79 x 28 ins / 200 x 70 cm) USD 30,000. NEW YORK, 16 May 2002, *Tulip* (1985, oil on canvas, 78 x 61 ins / 197 x 154 cm) USD 32,500. LONDON, 23 Oct 2002, *Tulip 17* (1985, oil on panel, 30 x 36 ins / 75 x 91 cm) GBP 16,000. PARIS, 11 Oct 2003, *Soller* (1989, white titanium and acrylic on canvas laid on panel, 94 x 94 ins / 240 x 240 cm) EUR 25,000. NEW YORK, 12 Nov 2003, *Pivezi Coreen* (1985, oil on canvas, 61 x 78 ins / 155 x 198 cm) USD 36,000. NEW YORK, 13 May 2004, *Flower 16* (1985, acrylic on canvas, in two parts, 131 x 75 ins / 332 x 190 cm) USD 45,000. ZURICH, 23 June 2004, *Blue Sanding Machine* (1983, oil on canvas, 57 x 45 ins / 146 x 114 cm) CHF 26,000.

SICILIANO, Angelo. See **MARINI Angelo**

SICILIANO, Il. See **PLANZONE Filippo**

SICILIANO, Il. See **RODRIGUEZ Luigi**

SICIOLANTE, Girolamo, or Siciolante da Sermoneta
Italian, 16th century.
Born 1521, in Sermoneta (Latium); died 1575.
Painter, fresco artist, draughtsman. Religious subjects, portraits. Murals.

Girolamo Siciolante was first the pupil of Leonardo da Pistoia and then worked with Perino del Vaga both as apprentice and assistant, with the result that his works are often taken for those of Perino. In 1541, he painted a *Virgin and Child with Two Saints* for the church of SS Pietro e Stefano near Sermoneta. He was in Rome in 1543 and, from 1545, worked with Perino del Vaga on the decoration of the Sala Paolina at the Castel Sant'Angelo. Siciolante executed the decoration of the Sala Regia at the Vatican, some frescoes in the church of S Luigi dei Francesi painted in collaboration with Jacopo del Conte depicting the *Baptism of Clovis*, a *Martyrdom of St Catherine* in the church of S Maria Maggiore and a *Nativity* in the church of S Maria della Pace. He worked in Piacenza in 1545 with Pier Luigi Farnese on a *Holy Family with St Michael* now in the gallery in Parma. After the murder of Pier Luigi Farnese, Siciolante went to Bologna where he painted a *Virgin and Child with Saints* for the church of S Martino. On the death of Perino del Vaga, he returned to Rome where he completed a number of his old master's works. In about 1549, he returned to his birthplace where he decorated a chapel in the church of S Giuseppe with a *Virgin and Child* and scenes from the Old and New Testaments. Between 1560 and 1563, he is believed to have returned to Rome to paint a series of frescoes depicting scenes from the life of the Virgin in a chapel of the church of S Maria dell'Anima.

BIBLIOGRAPHY:

Davidson, B., '*Some Early Works by Girolamo Siciolante da Sermoneta*' in *Art Bulletin*, vol 48, 1966. Hunter, J., '*The Drawings and Draughtsmanship in the Middle Years of Girolamo Siciolante da Sermoneta*' in *Master Drawings*, vol 26, 1988.

MUSEUMS AND GALLERIES:

LONDON (British Mus.): study for an apostle - MILAN (Pinacoteca di Brera): *Mary and Jesus* - PARMA (Gal. Nazionale): *Holy Family with St Michael* - POZNAN: *Entombment* - ROME (GA Antica di Palazzo Corsini): *Portrait of a Cardinal; Portrait of Colonna* - ROME (Gal. Colonna): *Virgin, Jesus and St John* - ROME (Mus. e Gal. Borghese): *Virgin, St Elizabeth and St John Offering a Goldfinch to the Infant Jesus; Christ on the Cross; Virgin, Jesus and St John* (two versions) - VIENNA (Albertina Mus.): study for an apostle.

AUCTION RECORDS:

LONDON, 13 July 1923, *Francis II in Armour*, GBP 141. ROME, 15 March 1983, *Portrait of a Cardinal* (oil on panel, 38 1/4 x 30 ins / 97 x 76 cm) ITL 6,000,000. NEW YORK, 16 Jan 1985, *Study for a Prophet (recto)* (pen/red chalk outline/blue paper); *Study of a Girl (verso)* (pen and brown ink, 8 3/4 x 6 ins / 22.3 x 14.4 cm) USD 3,500. LONDON, 9 Dec 1986, *Angel of the Annunciation* (black chalk, pen and wash heightened with white, 13 x 12 ins / 32.8 x 30.3 cm) GBP 16,000. MONTE CARLO, 20 June 1987, *Presentation in the Temple* (pen, brown ink and wash heightened with white/black chalk/faded blue paper, 16 x 10 ins / 40.9 x 25.5 cm) FRF 190,000. ROME, 19 Nov 1990, *Portrait of a Prelate in his Appartments* (oil on panel, 56 3/4 x 42 1/2 ins / 144 x 108 cm) ITL 138,000,000. LONDON, 2 July 1991, *Seated Man with Raised Right Arm* (black chalk, ink and wash heightened with white, 8 1/4 x 5 3/4 ins / 21 x 14.8 cm) GBP 7,700. NEW YORK, 10 Jan 1996, *Study of St Elizabeth for The Visitation* (black chalk heightened with white/blue paper, 9 3/4 x 7 ins / 24.8 x 17.7 cm) USD 23,000. NEW YORK, 28 Jan 1998, *Study for an Apostle* (black chalk, heightened with white/blue paper, 8 1/2 x 8 ins / 21.6 x 20.4 cm) USD 8,050. MUNICH, 29 Sept 1999, *Holy Family with Infant St John the Baptist* (oil on panel, 50 x 38 ins / 128 x 97 cm) DEM 92,000. LONDON, 10 July 2001, *Seated Figure* (black chalk, pen and ink wash heightened with white, 8 x 6 ins / 21 x 15 cm) GBP 9,500.

SICKEL, Alexander and Valentin
German, 16th century.
Active between 1560 and 1590.
Engravers.

SICKELEER, Pieter van. See **SIKKELAER**

SICKELPART. See **SICHELBART**

SICKER, C.
German, 19th century.
Active c. 1856, in Berlin.
Portrait artist.

MUSEUMS AND GALLERIES:

GOTHA (Schloss Friedenstein): *Portrait of Edward VII.*

SICKERT, Bernhard
German, 19th - 20th century.
Born 1862, in Munich; died 2 August 1932, in Jordan.
Painter, engraver. Interiors, landscapes, architectural views.

Bernhard Sickert was the son of Oswald and brother of Walter Sickert.

MUSEUMS AND GALLERIES:

LONDON (Tate Collection): *Old Curiosity Shop, Dieppe* (c. 1895, oil/board).

SICKERT, Johann Jürgen
German, 19th century.
Born 1803, in Flensburg (Schleswig-Holstein); died October 1864, in Altona.
Painter, lithographer.

Johann Jürgen Sickert was the father of Oswald and the grandfather of Walter and Bernhard. He spent part of his career in Copenhagen as decorative painter to King Christian VIII of Denmark, and exhibited in Hamburg from 1837 to 1864.

AUCTION RECORDS:

LONDON, 22 Nov 1978, *Banks of the Elba* (1859, oil on canvas, 24 x 33 ins / 61 x 84 cm) GBP 6,500.

SICKERT, Oswald Adalbert
British, 19th century.
Born 1828, in Altona, Germany; died 1885, in London.
Painter, draughtsman. Genre scenes, urban landscapes, landscapes.

Oswald Adalbert Sickert was British by naturalisation. He was the son of Johann Jurgen Sickert and the father of Walter and Bernhard Sickert. He studied at the Academy of Copenhagen from 1844 to 1846, and at its counterpart in Munich until 1852. He then worked for six months under Couture in Paris.

Museums and Galleries:
Budapest: *Returning from the Harvest.*
Auction records:
London, 22 June 1923, *The Church of Santa Maria della Salute in Venice,* GBP 65.

SICKERT, Walter Richard, sometimes called Sic
German, 19th - 20th century.
Born 31 May 1860, in Munich; died 22 January 1942, in Bathampton (Somerset), England.
From 1866 active and naturalised in England.
Painter, watercolourist, pastellist, draughtsman (including red chalk), engraver (etching/aquatint).
Figures, portraits, nudes, scenes with figures, interiors, landscapes, urban landscapes, street scenes, architectural views, still-lifes.
Camden Town Group.

Walter Richard Sickert was the brother of Bernhard, son of Oswald Adalbert and grandson of Johan Jurgen Sickert. His Danish-German father worked on a satirical journal in Munich (*Fliegende Blätter*). In 1868, following the annexation by Germany of Schleswig-Holstein, the Sickerts moved to England, where the entire family secured British nationality.

Walter Sickert embarked on a career as an actor but in 1881 secured a scholarship which enabled him to study at London's Slade School, thereby following in the family tradition. One of the first to take an interest in Sickert and his work was James Abbott McNeil Whistler, who also encouraged Sickert to take up engraving. In 1883, Whistler entrusted Sickert with the task of conveying his now celebrated *Portrait of the Artist's Mother* to the Paris Salon; he also commended Sickert to his friends Edouard Manet and Edgar Degas. Sickert was unable to meet with the former (who was nearing the end of his life), but he did meet Degas, who befriended him and used him from time to time as a model.

In 1885, despite the opposition of her family, Sickert married Ellen Cobden, daughter of the prominent politician Richard Cobden. The newly-weds set off on their travels, visiting Munich, Vienna, Milan and making a first visit to Dieppe, the French harbour town to which Sickert would return time and again and which was to play such a key role in his career as an artist. Degas, meanwhile, secured Sickert introductions to Elie and Jacques Halévy, Jacques-Emile Blanche, Henri Gervex and others. It would appear that, in 1893, Sickert opened and taught in an *académie libre*; what is certain, however, is that he taught at Westminster Art School until 1918.

In 1895, possibly at Whistler's instigation, Sickert visited Venice. 1899 proved to be a difficult year: Sickert had divorced Ellen and was determined to put England behind him for as long as possible. He joined up with Jacques-Emile Blanche in Dieppe and spent the turn of the century in Paris. He eventually returned to England in 1905 and set himself up in a studio in Bloomsbury, where old friends and new - Lucien Pissarro, George Moore and Augustus John among them - were frequent visitors.

Sickert remarried in 1911 and promptly returned to Dieppe. During the years of World War I, he spent time in Bath (1916 and 1917) but, as soon as the war was over, Sickert hastened back to his beloved Dieppe. In October 1920, tragedy struck when his second wife, Christine, died. Sickert returned to London in 1922. He was elected to membership of the Royal Academy in 1924 and taught there from 1926, devoting himself to the propagation of his approach to painting and contributing significantly to the rejection of sterile academism in English painting. He married for the third time in 1926.

By 1927, Sickert was reputed to have found recognition in some quarters as one of the leading artists in England and was on the point of being elected to the presidency of the Royal Academy; other accounts, arguably more reliable, suggest otherwise, namely that he was elected president of the British Artists Society in 1928 and admitted to Royal Academy membership only in 1934. In any event, he resigned from the Royal Academy the following year and effectively withdrew from London society, exiling himself in Bath, Broadstairs and Brighton.

As early as 1886 or 1888, Sickert had made known his intention to help rid English art of its academic strictures. Accordingly, he had involved himself in the launch of the New England Art Club and exhibited within the framework of that institution. In 1908, he was also involved in the establishment of the Allied Artists Association, a group set up along similar lines to the Salon des Indépendants in Paris. (The first London exhibitions of the work of the French Impressionists were held in 1910.) Then, in 1910-1911, Sickert set up a loose circle of artists known as the Camden Town Group, so called from the district of London Sickert was living in at the time. Little by little, the Camden Town Group revived the ideals postulated by the New England Art Club some twenty-odd years previously, to introduce into English painting some of the notions embraced by late 19th and early 20th-century French artists. Besides Sickert, the principal members of the group were Camille Pissarro's son Lucien, Charles Ginner, Harold Gilman and Spencer Gore; these were the English equivalent of France's Neo-Impressionists. The London Group was set up in 1914 as a successor to the Camden Town Group and most members of the latter gravitated towards the new group.

Sickert's portraiture betrays the influence of Whistler in terms of its sombre colours, whereas his landscapes and seascapes of Dieppe, with their bathers and carefree young women, bear the stamp of Boudin, Manet and the French Impressionists. Sickert's *Loggias* and *Décors* on the other hand, are very much in the mould of Degas, particularly the choice of theme and the off-centre compositional approach. Sickert's range was impressive: Venetian views, Parisian street scenes (*Caf' Conc'*), seascapes, etc.

Up to 1910, Sickert's female figures were, almost without exception, painted indoors as nudes perched on iron bedsteads or as part of a bored couple lounging on a sofa on a Sunday afternoon; in short, his treatment of women verged on misogyny. Around 1910, however, Sickert was commissioned to produce plates for the publication *New Age*, chiefly portraits of men and women; it may be that he was influenced by his remarriage, but his figures suddenly seem less lugubrious. By the time he started painting in Bath around 1916 and 1917, he was at the peak of his powers, painting splendid landscapes and seascapes rendered with an acute perception of changing light effects. Then, after the death of his second wife, he started painting circus and amusement parlour scenes in France, together with scenes of *maisons closes*. He also painted accomplished portraits, including *Victor Lecour* (1922) and *Signor Battistini* (1925). After 1926 and his third marriage, his landscape work became more serene again. Around 1930 and despite his growing infirmity, he set himself to painting stage sets.

Walter Sickert was an excellent painter but, bearing in mind the presence of Turner and Whistler and the overwhelming impact of Ruskin and the Pre-Raphaelites, his salient contribution to the history of English painting may well lie in the fact that he 'brought painting out into the open air'. in any case Sickert dominated the English avant-garde between the years 1907 to 1914 until the advent of the Fauvists and Cubists, when his progressive approach was relegated to the ranks of Post-Impressionism.

Sickert started exhibiting at the Royal Academy in 1915, and his work has featured at a range of group and thematic exhibitions since his death. In 1907 and 1909, Bernheim had organised two solo exhibitions of Sickert's work and a major solo exhibition was mounted at the Stafford Street Gallery in London in 1910, followed in 1913 by a further solo exhibition at the Fairfax Gallery. In 1929 a monumental Sickert retrospective was held at the Leicester Galleries, and in 1941, immediately prior to his death, the National Gallery in London organised a major retrospective. Posthumous retrospectives include *Walter Sickert as Printmaker*, held at the Yale Center for British Art in New Haven in 1979, *James McNeil Whistler and Walter Richard Sickert* at the La Caixa Foundation in Madrid in 1998, and *Richard Sickert: Prints and Drawings*, at the Fitzwilliam Museum in Cambridge, England in 2000.

Sickert

W Sickert

BIBLIOGRAPHY:

Woolf, Virginia, *Walter Sickert: a conversation*, L. and Virginia Woolf at the Hogarth Press, London, 1934. Emmons, Robert, *The Life and Opinions of Walter Richard Sickert*, Faber and Faber, London, 1942. Browse, Lillian/Wilenski, Reginald Howard, *Walter Richard Sickert*, Faber and Faber, London, 1943. Rothenstein, John, *Walter Richard Sickert*, Beaverbrook Newspapers, London, 1961. Sutton, Denys, *Walter Sickert: a biography*, Joseph, London, 1976. Troyen, Aimée, *Walter Sickert as printmaker*, Yale Center for British Art, New Haven, 1979. Jarman, Angela, *Royal Academy Exhibitors, 1905-1970: a Dictionary of Artists and their Work in the Summer Exhibitions*, EP Publishing, Wakefield, 1987. Shone, Richard, *Walter Sickert*, Phaidon, Oxford, 1988. Baron, Wendy/Shone, Richard, *Sickert, paintings*, Royal Academy of Arts, London, 1992. Connett, Maureen, *Walter Sickert and the Camden Town Group*, David & Charles, Newton Abbot, 1992. Greutzner Robins, Anna, *Walter Sickert: Drawings, Theory and Practice*, Scolar Press, Aldershot, 1996. *Walter Sickert: the complete writings on art*, Oxford University Press, Oxford, 2000 (introduction by Anna Gruetzner Robins). Bromberg, Ruth, *Walter Sickert: prints. A catalogue raisonné*, Yale University Press, New Haven and London, 2000. Greutzner Robins, Anna, *Walter Sickert: The Complete Writings on Art*, Oxford University Press, Oxford, 2000. Peters Corbett, David, *Walter Sickert*, Tate Publishing, London, 2001.

MUSEUMS AND GALLERIES:

BRISTOL (City Mus. & AG): *Horses of St Marks, Venice* (oil on canvas); other paintings - DIEPPE: *Royal Hotel, Dieppe*; *St Rémy Church, Dieppe* - GLASGOW (Hunterian AG): *Boutique, Dieppe* (1902) - LEEDS (City AG): *Dieppe Harbour* (oil/panel); *The Laundry Shop* (1885, oil/panel); *Portrait of Ellen Heath* (1896, oil on canvas); *Self Portrait* (c. 1896, oil on canvas); *The Blackbird of Paradise* (c. 1896-1898, oil on canvas, portrait); *Off to the Pub (The Week End)* (1912, oil on canvas); *The Cafe Suisse (Cafe des Arcades, Dieppe)* (1914, oil on canvas); *The New Bedford* (1916-1917, oil on canvas); *Juliet and the Nurse* (c. 1935-1936, oil on canvas); other paintings, two watercolours, drawings - LIVERPOOL (Walker AG): *Bathers, Dieppe* (1902, oil on canvas) - LONDON (National Portrait Gal.): *Charles Bradlaugh* (1890, pencil); *Philip Wilson Steer* (c. 1890, oil on canvas, exhibited at the New English Art Club in 1890); *George Jacob Holyoake* (oil on canvas, exhibition 1892); *Sir Winston Leonard Spencer Churchill* (1927, oil on canvas); *Walter Richard Sickert* (1930, oil on canvas); *William Maxwell Aitken, 1st Baron Beaverbrook* (1935, oil on canvas) - LONDON (Tate Collection): *Café des Tribunaux, Dieppe* (c. 1890, oil on canvas); *George Moore* (1890-1891, oil on canvas); *St Mark's, Venice (Pax Tibi Marce Evangelista Meus)* (1895-1896, oil on canvas); *Interior of St Mark's, Venice* (1896, oil on canvas); *Dieppe, Study No. 2; Facade of St Jacques* (c. 1899, drawing and watercolour/paper); *Les Arcades de la Poissonnerie, Dieppe* (*Fishmarket Arcades, Dieppe*) (c. 1900, oil on canvas); *The Piazzetta and the Old Campanile, Venice* (c. 1901, monotype print with ink wash/paper); *Venice, la Salute* (c. 1901-1903, oil on canvas); *Sketch for 'The Statue of Duquesne, Dieppe'* (c. 1902, carbon paper tracing and watercolour/paper); *Woman Washing her Hair* (1906, oil on canvas); *Ennui* (c. 1914, oil on canvas); *A Marengo* (c. 1903, oil on canvas); *Aubrey Beardsley, 1894, oil on canvas* (1894, oil on canvas); *Miss Gwen Ffrangcon-Davies as Isabella of France* (1932, oil on canvas) - MANCHESTER (City AG): *Beach at Dieppe* (1885) - NEW YORK (MoMA): *Sir Thomas Beecham Conducting* (c. 1935) - OTTAWA (NG. of Canada): *Rue Notre-Dame, Dieppe* (1902) - OXFORD (Ashmolean Mus.): *St Mark's, Venice: the West Front* (oil/paper); *The Lady in the Gondola* (oil on canvas); *The Bridge of Sighs, Venice* (oil on canvas); *Ennui* (c. 1913, oil on canvas); *La Gaieté, Montparnasse* (oil on canvas); *The Bust of Tom Sayers, a self-portrait* (oil on canvas); other paintings; numerous drawings - PARIS (MNAM-CCI): *Boulevard Aguado, Dieppe* - ROUEN (MBA): *Venetian Girl* (c. 1901, major collection of watercolours and drawings).

AUCTION RECORDS:

PARIS, 15 April 1907, *Grand Canal, Venice*, FRF 450. LONDON, 29 April 1911, *Dieppe*, GBP 21. PARIS, 4-5 March 1920, *Santa Maria della Salute, Venice*, FRF 2,020. LONDON, 1 Dec 1925, *Bayadère*, GBP 75; *Little Rachel*, GBP 86; *Daydreaming*, GBP 92. LONDON, 23 March 1928, *Casino, Dieppe*, GBP 420. PARIS, 24 May 1929, *Statue of Tourville, Dieppe*, FRF 15,000. LONDON, 21 June 1929, *Café-Concert*, GBP 420. PARIS, 11 March 1931, *Statue of Duquesne, Place Nationale, Dieppe*, FRF 4,000. PARIS, 26-27 Feb 1934, *Soho Tart* (pastel) FRF 1,500. PARIS, 19 Jan 1945, *Wakening* (pastel) FRF 30,000. LONDON, 29 May 1946, *Cicely Sickert*, GBP 350; *Old Bedford*, GBP 380. PARIS, 7 Feb 1947, *Street Scene with Harnessed Horses*, FRF 29,000. PARIS, 5 June 1950, *Street Scene, Genoa* (1897) FRF 15,000; *Female Study* (heightened red chalk) FRF 4,000. LONDON, 1 Nov 1957, *Statue of Duquesne, Dieppe*, GBP 630. LONDON, 26 April 1961, *Pulteney Bridge, Bath*, GBP 2,200. LONDON, 6 Dec 1963, *St Mark's Basilica and the Campanile*, Gns 2,900. LONDON, 1 May 1968, *L'Eldorado, Paris*, GBP 2,200. LONDON, 14 July 1971, *Nude with Mirror*, GBP 4,000. LONDON, 19 May 1972, *Street Scene (Dieppe)*, Gns 2,400. LONDON, 18 July 1973, *Portrait of a Man with a Moustache*, GBP 16,000. LONDON, 13 March 1974, *New House*, GBP 18,500. LONDON, 17 March 1976, *Place Duquesne, Dieppe* (c. 1900, oil on canvas, 25 1/4 x 20 3/4 ins / 64 x 53 cm) GBP 3,500. LONDON, 11 June 1976, *Santa Maria della Salute, Venice* (c. 1901, watercolour, pencil and chalk, 23 1/4 x 18 ins / 59 x 46 cm) GBP 2,500. LONDON, 16 March 1977, *Giuseppina and Another Little Girl* (c. 1903-1904, black and white chalks/grey paper, 12 1/2 x 15 1/2 ins / 32 x 39.5 cm) GBP 1, 050. LONDON, 17 June 1977, *Horses, St Mark's Square, Venice* (1900, oil on canvas, 20 x 16 ins / 51 x 40.5 cm) GBP 3,200. LONDON, 19 Oct 1979, *Café Suisse, Les Arcades, Dieppe* (watercolour and pen, 10 1/4 x 6 1/4 ins / 26 x 16 cm) GBP 1,800. LONDON, 14 Nov 1979, *Sunday Afternoon* (c. 1912-1913, black chalk, pen and wash, 19 1/2 x 12 1/2 ins / 49.5 x 31.5 cm) GBP 2,500. LONDON, 14 Nov 1979, *The Camden Town Murder* (c. 1908, oil on canvas, 10 x 13 1/2 ins / 24.5 x 34.5 cm) GBP 23,500. LONDON, 14 Oct 1980, *Acting Manager* (1884, etching, 9 1/4 x 9 1/4 ins / 23.8 x 23.6 cm) GBP 650. LONDON, 6 Nov 1981, *Nude with Mirror (Quai Voltaire)* (1906, black chalk and pen heightened with white, 11 x 8 ins / 28 x 20.5 cm) GBP 3,400. LONDON, 12 March 1982, *New Bedford* (c. 1908-1909, oil on canvas, 36 x 14 ins / 91.5 x 35.5 cm) GBP 30,000. LONDON, 10 June 1983, *Music Hall* (black and coloured chalks, 12 x 9 3/4 ins / 30.5 x 24.8 cm) GBP 1,400. LONDON, 2 Nov 1983, *Garden, Neuville* (1911, watercolour/pencil outlines and black chalk, 11 x 15 ins / 28 x 38 cm) GBP 1,000. LONDON, 4 Nov 1983, *Brighton: Clowns* (1915, oil on canvas, 25 x 30 ins / 63.5 x 76.2 cm) GBP 60,000. LONDON, 4 June 1985, *Mogul Tavern, Drury Lane* (1908, etching and aquatint, 9 3/4 x 7 ins / 24.8 x 17.7 cm) GBP 520. LONDON, 8 Oct 1985, *Still-life with Lobster and Bottle* (pen and black and white chalk/grey paper, 9 3/4 x 14 3/4 ins / 25 x 37.5 cm) GBP 2,100. LONDON, 14 Nov 1986, *Comical Lion* (1887, oil on canvas, 20 x 11 3/4 ins / 50.5 x 30 cm) GBP 65,000. LONDON, 3-4 March 1988, *Emily Pavel ('Chicken')* (oil on canvas, 14 3/4 x 12 1/4 ins / 37.5 x 31.2 cm) GBP 27,500; *Camden Town* (1911, pen, brush and brown ink/paper, 12 1/4 x 7 1/2 ins / 31.2 x 19.3 cm) GBP 4,840; *And Now What?* (pencil, 10 3/4 x 10 3/4 ins / 27.5 x 27.5 cm) GBP 1,760. PARIS, 29 April 1988, *St-Jacques Church, Offranville* (oil on panel, 5 1/2 x 4 3/4 ins / 14 x 12 cm) FRF 55,000. LONDON, 9 June 1988, *Vernet's, Dieppe* (pencil, 10 1/4 x 7 1/2 ins / 26.3 x 18.8 cm) GBP 4,180. LOS ANGELES, 9 June 1988, *Declaration* (oil on canvas, 20 x 30 ins / 51 x 76 cm) USD 3,300. LONDON, 9 June 1989, *St-Jacques Church, Dieppe* (oil on canvas, 18 1/2 x 15 1/4 ins / 46.8 x 38.8 cm) GBP 17,600. LONDON, 10 Nov 1989, *Bath Street, London* (oil on canvas, 19 x 31 1/4 ins / 48.1 x 79.5 cm) GBP 26,400. LONDON, 9 March 1990, *Nude and Mirror (Mornington Crescent)* (oil on canvas, 20 x 16 ins / 50.8 x 40.7 cm) GBP 18,150. EDINBURGH, 26 April 1990, *Statue of Duquesne, Dieppe* (oil on canvas, 13 x 9 1/2 ins / 33 x 24.2 cm) GBP 8,800. LONDON, 8 June 1990, *Seated Woman (Granby Street)* (1908, oil on canvas, 20 x 16 ins / 51 x 40.5 cm) GBP 88,000. LONDON, 8 Nov 1990, *Portrait of the Artist's Wife, Thérèse Lessore* (oil on canvas, 29 1/2 x 24 ins / 75 x 61 cm) GBP 23,100. LONDON, 6 June 1991, *La Salute, Venice* (oil on panel, 6 1/4 x 9 1/2 ins / 16 x 24 cm) GBP 7,150. LONDON, 27 Sept 1991, *Maravegie Bridge, San Trovaso, Venice* (pencil/grey paper, 13 x 10 1/2 ins / 33 x 26.5 cm) GBP 770. LONDON, 7 Nov 1991, *Rue Mortier d'Or, Dieppe* (1903, oil on panel, 7 1/2 x 9 1/2 ins / 19 x 24 cm) GBP 18,700. LONDON, 6 March 1992, *Portrait of a Lady* (oil on canvas, 16 x 12 3/4 ins / 40.5 x 32.5 cm) GBP 19,250. LONDON, 12 March 1992, *Old Bedford Grave* (oil on panel, 7 3/4 x 10 ins / 20 x 25.5 cm) GBP 43,300; *Pierrots, Brighton* (1915, oil on canvas, 25 x 30 ins / 63.5 x 76 cm) GBP 221,500. LONDON, 5 June 1992, *Statue of Duquesne, Dieppe* (oil on canvas, 13 x 9 1/2 ins / 33 x 24.2 cm) GBP 8,800. PARIS, 27 April 1994, *Street Scene* (oil on panel, 6 3/4 x 5 ins / 17 x 13 cm) FRF 70,000. ST. ASAPH (ENGLAND), 2 June 1994, *Little Boutique* (oil on card, 9 x 12 ins / 23 x 30.5 cm) GBP 8,050. NEW YORK, 13-14 May 1997, *St-Jacques Church, Dieppe* (c. 1899-1900, oil on canvas, 18 x 15 ins / 45.7 x 38.1 cm) USD 40,250. LONDON, 4 June 1999, *Les Arcades and La Darse, Dieppe* (c. 1898, oil on canvas, 20 x 24 ins / 51 x 61 cm) GBP 27,000. LONDON, 11 Nov 1999, *The Facade of St Mark's, Venice* (1901, oil on canvas, 35 x 28 ins / 90 x 70 cm) GBP 50,000. LONDON, 9 June 2000, *Nude on Couch* (oil on canvas, 16 x 20 ins / 41 x 51 cm) GBP 55,000. LONDON, 24 Nov 2000, *Portrait of a Venetian Woman - la Callera* (c. 1903, oil on canvas, 19 x 15 ins / 49 x 39 cm) GBP 60,000. LONDON, 5 April 2001, *La Maison Blanche, Dieppe* (oil on panel, 7 x 6 ins / 18 x 14 cm) GBP 16,000. LONDON, 8 June 2001, *La Rue Pecquet, Towards St Jacques, Dieppe* (c. 1906-1907, oil on board, 9 x 7 ins / 24 x 19 cm) GBP 26,000. LONDON, 7 June 2002, *Acting Manager of Rehearsal, the End of the Act* (c. 1885-1886, oil on canvas, 24 x 20 ins / 61 x 51 cm) GBP 130,000. LONDON, 4 Dec 2002, *La Grand Duquesne, Dieppe* (oil on canvas, 22 x 18 ins / 55 x 46 cm) GBP 40,000. LONDON, 6 June 2003, *Conversation* (1903=1904, oil on canvas, 18 x 15 ins / 46 x 38 cm) GBP 48,000. LONDON, 21 Nov 2003, *Rio dei Mendicanti, Venice* (c. 1895-1896, oil on canvas, 16 x 11 ins / 41 x 27 cm) GBP 32,000. LONDON, 19 Nov 2004, *The Little Tea-shop, Dieppe* (1885, oil on panel, 9 x 6 ins / 23 x 14 cm) GBP 28,000. LONDON, 19 Nov 2004, *Baccarat* (1920, oil on canvas, 24 x 17 ins / 61 x 44 cm) GBP 120,000.

SICKINGER, Anselm

German, 19th century.
Born 20 April 1807, in Owingen; died 17 October 1873, in Munich.
Sculptor, architect.

Sickinger studied with Konrad Volm in Owingen, and worked for two years in Überlingen before establishing a studio in Munich. He produced work for the church of Our Lady in Munich.

SICKINGER, Franz

German, 15th - 16th century.
Active in Burghausen between 1477 and 1512.
Sculptor. Monuments.

Sickinger carved tombs.

SICKINGER, Grégoire

Swiss, 16th - 17th century.
Born 1558; died 1631.
Active in Solothurn.
Painter, draughtsman, engraver.
Soleure School.

Sickinger married in Solothurn in 1595. It has been established that works signed with the capital letters G and S separated by a cross, a previously unidentified monogram, are in fact by him. Among his works are pen drawings in the Gild of Painters, Solothurn, and some woodcuts in the Albertina, Vienna, that seem to have been intended as models for stained glass windows.

SICKLEER. See **SIKKELAER**

SICKLER, Hans

German, 17th century.
Active c. 1691.
Painter.

SICKLES, Noel

American, 20th century.
Born 24 January 1910, in Chillicothe (Ohio); died 1982.
Painter, illustrator.

Noel Sickles began his art education in 1929 and studied at Ohio State University, the Art Students League in New York and with Julian Clarence Levi at the New School in New York. He exhibited with the New York Society of Illustrators.

SICLERS, Ingelbert Lievin van, or Secliers

Belgian, 18th century.
Born 6 June 1725, in Ghent; died 24 June 1796, in Ghent.
Painter (?).

Ingelbert Lievin van Siclers painted four works which are in the library of the university of Ghent.

SICRE, François

French, 17th century.
Born 1640; died 14 September 1705.
Painter. Portraits.

François Sicre was a member of the Académie de St-Luc in Paris from 1673.

AUCTION RECORDS:

PARIS, 2 Dec 1976, *Portrait of Pierre Corneille* (oil on canvas, round, diam. 30 ins / 76 cm) FRF 35,000.

SICULO, Jacopo

Italian, 16th century.
Active in Spoleto (Umbria).
Painter.

The son-in-law of Lo Spagna, Jacopo Siculo mainly worked in Spoleto, producing work for the cathedral, the Palazzo - where he painted some frescoes in 1538 in the style of Raphael - and the church of S Niccolò. His first authenticated work is a panel in the church of S Mamigliano.

SID ALI HAMS. See **HAMS Sid Ali**

SIDA, Youssef
Egyptian, 20th century.
Born 1922, in Damietta, now Dumyat; died 1994.
Painter. Allegorical subjects.

Youssef Sida was awarded a diploma in applied arts in 1942 and a diploma from the institute of higher education in 1945. In 1950, he won a Fulbright scholarship to pursue his artistic studies at the University of Minnesota. He then followed courses at Columbia University in New York. In 1965, he became a doctor of philosophy at the University of Ohio. He was a professor at the institute of higher art education in Cairo.

Sida's painting associates Arabic calligrapic script with western Gestural Abstraction in a highly energetic manner. The combined or opposing forces of the large and powerful signs give symbolic expression to moral situations and principles: *Friend and Enemy, Right Usurped by Might.* He took part in collective exhibitions, in particular the São Paulo Biennale (1953); the Venice Biennale (1956); *Visages de l'Art Contemporain Égyptien* (*Aspects of Contemporary Egyptian Art*) (1971), Musée Galliera, Paris; as well as in Germany, the USA, and elsewhere. He also had solo exhibitions, including from 1950 to 1952 in the USA and several times in Cairo.

BIBLIOGRAPHY:
Badr El-Din Abou Ghazy, *Visages de l'Art contemporain égyptien*, exhibition catalogue, Musée Galliera, Paris, 1971.

MUSEUMS AND GALLERIES:
ALEXANDRIA (MMA) - CAIRO (Egyptian MMA).

SIDAW, Christian, or Sydau, Sydow
Baltic School, 18th century.
Born 16 August 1682, in Litau (now Jelgava), Latvia.
Painter. Portraits.

Christian Sidaw lived in Litau until 1758.

MUSEUMS AND GALLERIES:
JELGAVA: *Self-portrait.*

SIDAW, Ferdinand Wilhelm
Baltic School, 18th century.
Born 1721; died 19 April 1770.
Active in Mitau (now Jelgava, Latvia).
Painter.

Ferdinand Sidaw was the son of Christian Sidaw.

SIDDAL, Elizabeth or Lizzie Eleanor.
See **ROSSETTI**

SIDEAU, F. G., or Sydow
Swiss, 18th century.
Active in Geneva and St Petersburg, 1782-1784, and in Mitau (now Jelgava, Latvia), in 1786.
Engraver, silhouettist, draughtsman.

Sideau studied under J. D. Huber. He produced silhouettes of members of the tsar's family and the nobility.

MUSEUMS AND GALLERIES:
MOSCOW (Mus. of History): several works - ST PETERSBURG (Hermitage): works.

SIDERIO DA FERMO, Ercole
Italian, 16th century.
Active in Rome.
Painter.

SIDIBÉ, Kalifala
Sudanese, 20th century.
Died 1930.
Painter.

Kalifala Sidibé is said to have been the organiser of a collective exhibition held in Paris in 1929.

SIDLER, Alfred Médard
Swiss, 20th century.
Born 1905, in Lucerne; died 1992.
Painter, draughtsman. Genre scenes, winter landscapes, village views, still-lifes (flowers/fruit).

MUSEUMS AND GALLERIES:
AARAU (Aargauer Kunsthaus): *Flowers in an Earthenware Jug; Fruit outside the Window; Stanstad* (1948); *Resting in the Fields.*

AUCTION RECORDS:
BERN, 26 Oct 1988, *Near St-Rémy* (oil on canvas, 18 x 22 ins / 46 x 56 cm) CHF 1,100. LUCERNE, 24 Nov 1990, *Hasliberg in Winter* (oil on canvas, 19 3/4 x 25 1/2 ins / 50 x 65 cm) CHF 2,800. LUCERNE, 21 Nov 1992, *Still-life with Lemon* (oil on canvas, 13 1/2 x 18 1/2 ins / 34 x 47 cm) CHF 1,500.

SIDLER, J. Ernst
Swiss, 20th century.
Born 13 July 1878, in Zug.
Active in Zug.
Painter.

J. Ernst Sidler was also an author.

SIDLER, Joseph
German, 19th century.
Active in Munich, 1813-1820.
Lithographer.

SIDLER, Zachäus
French, 17th century.
Born to a family originally from Prantut.
Painter. Religious subjects.

Zachäus Sidler painted the Stations of the Cross for the Franciscan monastery in Thann, Alsace.

SIDLEY, Samuel
British, 19th century.
Born 1829, in Manchester; died 9 July 1896, in London.
Painter, illustrator. Genre scenes, portraits, landscapes, flowers.

Samuel Sidley illustrated a number of books. He studied at the Royal Academy schools and began to exhibit from 1855, principally at the Royal Academy and the Royal Society of British Artists in Suffolk Street. He was a Member of the Society of British Artists and a founder member of the Cambrian Academy.

MUSEUMS AND GALLERIES:
LONDON (National Portrait Gal.): *John William Colenso* (1866, oil on canvas).

AUCTION RECORDS:
LONDON, 29 June 1976, *The Allegro* (1866, oil on canvas, 24 1/2 x 19 1/2 ins / 62 x 49.5 cm) GBP 1,800. LONDON, 15 May 1979, *Cheshire Landscape* (1871, oil on canvas, 31 x 48 ins / 79 x 121 cm) GBP 2,500. LONDON, 22 Feb 1985, *Cheshire Landscape* (1871, oil on canvas, 36 1/4 x 48 1/2 ins / 92.3 x 123.2 cm) GBP 3,400. LONDON, 2 June 1989, *Primroses and Bluebells* (oil on canvas, 30 1/4 x 25 1/4 ins / 77 x 64 cm) GBP 17,050. LONDON, 3 Nov 1989, *Please* (1865, oil on canvas, 23 x 19 ins / 58.5 x 48 cm) GBP 3,300. LONDON, 4 Nov 1994, *Bust-length Portrait of a Little Girl* (1862, oil on board, 6 x 6 ins / 15.3 x 15.3 cm) GBP 977. LONDON, 10 March 1995, *Primroses and Bluebells* (oil on canvas, 30 x 25 ins / 76.2 x 63.5 cm) GBP 17,250. LONDON, 26 Nov 2002, *Please* (1865, oil on canvas, oval, 24 x 21 ins / 61 x 53 cm) GBP 4,500. LONDON, 25 Nov 2003, *Challenge* (oil on canvas, 60 x 41 ins / 152 x 103 cm) GBP 20,000.

SIDLÓ, Ferenc
Hungarian, 20th century.
Born 21 January 1882, in Budapest; died 1954, in Budapest.
Sculptor.

Ferenc Sidló trained at Budapest, Munich and Rome. He taught at Budapest art school and was associated with the Gödöllõ artists. Many of his works are in the Magyar Nemzeti Galéria, Budapest. He is particularly known for the bronze statue of St. Stephen at Székesfehérvár.

SIDNELL, Michael
British, 18th century.
Active in Bristol.
Sculptor.
Michael Sidnell executed a number of major works in Bristol such as the tomb of *Edward Colston*, and collaborated with Gibb on his *Architecture* (1728).

SIDNEY, Herbert, called Adams
British, 19th - 20th century.
Born 1858, in London; died 30 March 1923, in London.
Painter. Figures, portraits, animals.
Herbert Sidney (Adams) trained under Nicause de Keyser and Joseph Van Lerius at the Antwerp Academy of fine art. He also studied under Jean-Léon Gérôme in Paris. He should not be confused with the sculptor of portrait busts also known as Herbert Adams.
MUSEUMS AND GALLERIES:
WESTMINSTER (City Hall): *Portrait of R. W. Granville-Smith; Portrait of Booth-Heming.*
AUCTION RECORDS:
LONDON, 12 Oct 1977, *The Sultan's Favourite* (1909, oil on panel, 28 x 14 ins / 71 x 35.5 cm) GBP 750. LONDON, 14 June 1979, *Portrait of Hilda Eckstein* (1897, oil on canvas, 58 x 30 ins / 147.3 x 76.2 cm) GBP 600. LONDON, 21 June 1985, *Fair Rosamond* (1905, oil on canvas, 40 x 24 1/2 ins / 101.5 x 62.2 cm) GBP 8,000. LONDON, 7 Oct 1992, *Rosette Blanche, Japowitz Poodle* (1904, oil on canvas, 30 x 20 ins / 76 x 50.5 cm) GBP 1,320. LUDLOW, 29 Sept 1994, *Ladies of Pompei* (1889, oil on canvas, a pair, each 27 1/4 x 14 ins / 69 x 35.5 cm, ensemble) GBP 6,900. LONDON, 4 June 1997, *Portrait of Mrs Bacher* (1903, oil on canvas, 38 x 20 ins / 96.5 x 50.5 cm) GBP 6,670.

SIDOBRE, Pascal
French, 20th - 21st century.
Born 1964, in Carcassonne.
Painter. Scenes with figures, figures, landscapes.
Pascal Sidobre studied at the École des Beaux-Arts in Toulouse and went on to exhibit primarily in Marseilles and at various venues on the Côte d'Azur. He has been awarded several regional distinctions for his painting which employs Surrealist imagery in its figures and extra-terrestrial landscapes.

SIDOLI, Giuseppe
Italian, 20th century.
Born 4 July 1886, in Piacenza.
Painter, caricaturist. Genre scenes.
The younger brother of Pacifico and Nazzareno Sidoli, Giuseppe Sidoli studied at the Accademia di Belle Arti in Parma and worked in Piacenza.
MUSEUMS AND GALLERIES:
PIACENZA (Gal. d'Arte Moderna Ricci Oddi): *Funeral of a Poet.*

SIDOLI, Nazzareno
Italian, 20th century.
Born 19 July 1879, in Rossoreggio di Piacenza (Emilia Romagna); died 1970.
Painter, fresco artist, pastellist. Religious subjects, figures, nudes, portraits, genre scenes. Murals.
The younger brother of Pacifico and older brother of Giuseppe, Nazzareno Sidoli was a pupil of Bernardino Pollinari and Stefano Bruzzi. As a student, he made a particular study of the artists of the Lombard and Parma Schools. He taught art at the academy in Piacenza.

He specialised in religious compositions in both oils and fresco. He also painted portraits and small easel paintings in the Flemish style, genre subjects and interiors in which he frequently depicted unusual effects of natural or artificial light.
AUCTION RECORDS:
PARIS, 28 March 1949, *Seated Nude* (pastel) FRF 30,000.

SIDOLI, Pacifico
Italian, 19th - 20th century.
Born 17 May 1868, in Rossoreggio di Piacenza (Emilia Romagna); died 1963.
Painter, fresco artist, watercolourist, pastellist.
Religious subjects, portraits. Murals.
The elder brother of Nazzareno and Giuseppe Sidoli, Pacifico Sidoli was first a pupil of Bernardino Pollinari and then completed his studies in Paris. He returned to Piacenza to settle near his brother Nazzareno.

The pastels he produced in Paris were admired for their true feelings and expressions. He painted a *Portrait of Mussolini* for the meeting chamber of the Milan Chamber of Commerce and a powerful composition for the ceiling of the Banca Cattolica in Piacenza.
MUSEUMS AND GALLERIES:
STRASBOURG: two expressive heads.

SIDOROV, Vitali
Russian, 20th century.
Born 1922, in Kursk.
Painter. Flowers, landscapes.
After serving during World War II, Vitali Sidorov studied at Krasnodar art school from 1946 to 1950. A member of the Russian Artists Union, in 1996 was named Honoured Cultural Worker of Kuban. He has exhibited both locally and nationally.
AUCTION RECORDS:
PARIS, 3 June 1992, *Peonies* (oil on canvas, 26 1/4 x 24 1/4 ins / 66.5 x 61.5 cm) FRF 8,000. PARIS, 25 Jan 1993, *Lilac* (oil on canvas, 32 1/2 x 35 1/2 ins / 82.8 x 89.9 cm) FRF 5,000.

SIDOROWICZ, Hanna
Polish, 20th - 21st century.
Born 26 August 1960.
Painter.
Sidorowicz studied at the academy of fine art in Gdansk in 1979. She took part, probably while staying in Paris, in the Salon de Montrouge in 1987 and held a solo exhibition at the Galerie Eolia. She exhibited in 2003 at the Atelier d'Estienne, Espace d'Art Contemporain du Pays de Lorient, Pont Scorff (Morbihan).
AUCTION RECORDS:
PARIS, 14 Oct 1989, *Untitled* (oil and ink/canvas, 55 x 39 1/4 ins / 140 x 100 cm) FRF 17,000.

SIDOROWICZ, Zygmunt
Austrian, 19th century.
Born 1 April 1846, in Lemberg (now Lviv, Ukraine); died 2 May 1881, in Vienna.
Painter. Portraits, landscapes.
Zygmunt Sidorowicz studied at the technical academy in Lemberg, then at the Akademie der Bildenden Künste in Vienna from 1864 to 1868, and later in Munich.
MUSEUMS AND GALLERIES:
CRACOW: *Portrait of a Woman* - LVIV (Municipal Mus.): *Corpus delicti; Road in Autumn* - LVIV (NG): *Self-portrait; The Poet Komorovski* - MUNICH (Schack-Gal.): *Evening Landscape* - WARSAW (Muz. Narodowe): *Gypsy Camp on the Edge of a Forest; Landscape; Head of a Young Woman in 16th-century Costume; Portrait of a Woman.*

SIDOTI, Stanislao
Italian, 19th - 20th century.
Born 5 May 1839, in Lecce (Apulia); died 2 March 1922, in Lecce.
Painter.
Stanislao Sidoti was a pupil of Giuseppe Mancinelli.

SIDOTI, Tindaro
Italian, 18th century.

Active c. 1701.
Painter.

SIDVAL, Amanda Carolina
Swedish, 19th century.
Born 25 July 1844, in Stockholm; died 10 January 1892, in Stockholm.
Painter. Genre scenes, portraits.
Amanda Sidval studied at the Kungliga Akademi för de Fria Konsterna in Stockholm from 1864 to 1871, as well as in Paris. There is a self-portrait by her in the Nationalmuseum in Stockholm. Her *Flower Seller* and *Young Girl From Lapland* are in the Musée du Luxembourg in Paris.

SIÉ, Henri
French, 20th century.
Born 1936, in Toulouse.
Painter. Landscapes.
Henri Sié was a pupil at the École des Beaux-Arts in Toulouse and went to work in Paris as a model maker. When he was 28, he became an opera and concert singer. He settled at St-Tropez and opened his own art gallery. He is a member of the Salon des Peintres de St-Tropez and took part in the Salon des Indépendants in Paris and in various other groups in the area. He uses pencil and brush vigorously in colour with warm tones, and paints landscapes and seascapes of the Midi.

SIE CHE-TCH'EN. See **XIE SHICHEN**

SIE HAI-YEN. See **XIE HAIYAN**

SIE HOUAN. See **XIE HUAN**

SIE KONG-TCHAN. See **XIE GONGZHAN**

SIE LAN-CHANG. See **XIE LANSHENG**

SIE PIN. See **XIE BIN**

SIE PO-CH'ENG. See **XIE BOCHENG**

SIE SOUEI. See **XIE SUI**

SIE SOUEN. See **XIE SUN**

SIE TCH'ENG. See **XIE CHENG**

SIE TCHE-LIEOU. See **XIE ZHILIU**

SIE TS'IU-CHENG. See **XIE QUSHENG**

SIE TSEU-WEN. See **KIE ZIWEN**

SIE TSIN. See **XIE JIN**

SIE YU-K'IEN. See **XIE YUQIAN**

SIE YUAN. See **XIE YUAN**

SIEBE, Christoph
German, 19th - 20th century.
Born 1 May 1849, in Wallenbruck (Westphalia); died 21 April 1912, in Wiedenbrück.
Sculptor, painter, designer.
Christoph Siebe studied at the fine arts in Kassel and decorated the stairwell in the Kassel Art Gallery. He was the father of Wilhelm Siebe.

SIEBE, Wilhelm
German, 20th century.
Born 7 March 1881, in Wiedenbrück.
Sculptor, painter, designer.
Wilhelm Siebe was the son of Christoph Siebe; he was also a poet.

SIEBEL, Franz Anton
German, 19th century.
Born 1777, in Frickenhausen; died 28 January 1842, in Lichtenfels.
Painter (glass and porcelain), silhouettist.
Siebel studied the art of silhouettes in Vienna.

SIEBELIST, Arthur
German, 19th - 20th century.
Born 21 July 1870, in Loschwitz, near Dresden; died 1945.
Active in Hamburg.
Painter, engraver. Portraits, genre scenes.
MUSEUMS AND GALLERIES:
HAMBURG: *Artist and Pupil; Young Girl Doing her Homework; Portrait of Ahlers-Hestermann, Painter; Self-portrait.*

SIEBEN, Gottfried
Austrian, 19th - 20th century.
Born 16 March 1856, in Stockerau; died 1918.
Active in Vienna.
Painter, illustrator, caricaturist.
Gottfried Sieben studied at the Akademie der Bildenden Künste in Vienna; he was renowned for his caricatures.

SIEBENBURGER, Gregor, called Gorgus
French, 16th century.
Active in Schlettstadt (now Sélestat) between 1522 and 1527.
Painter.

SIEBENHAAR, Friedrich Karl Wilhelm
German, 19th century.
Born 12 July 1814, in Warmbrunn; died 22 October 1895, in Warmbrunn.
Engraver (precious stones), modeller.
Friedrich Siebenhaar studied under his uncle O. A. Reichstein, and Benjamin Muller, a precious-stone engraver, in Warmbrunn.
MUSEUMS AND GALLERIES:
WROCLAW (Muz. Narodowe): several works.

SIEBENHAAR, Michael Adolph
German, 18th century.
Active in Wittenberg (Saxony-Anhalt) during the first half of the 18th century.
Painter.
Michael Siebenhaar painted mainly portraits of his contemporaries.

SIEBENHARTZ, Hans. See **SIBENHARTZ**

SIEBENMANN, Minna
Swiss, 19th - 20th century.
Born 1859, in Aarau.
Active in Basel and in Paris.
Painter. Landscapes, flowers.

SIEBENMANN, Selma
Swiss, 20th century.
Born 1884, in Klosters; died 1965.
Active in Basel.
Painter. Landscapes, still-lifes.
Selma Siebenmann was a pupil of Albert Weisgerber, Cuno Amiet and Maurice Denis. She was president of the society of women painters.
MUSEUMS AND GALLERIES:
BASEL: *Ticino Landscape.*

SIEBER
German, 18th century.
Active in Kassel (Hesse).
Draughtsman, engraver (burin).
Sieber provided illustrations for Apell's book *Kassel and its Environs.*

SIEBER, Edward George
American, 19th - 20th century.
Born 1862, in Brooklyn (New York City).
Painter. Landscapes, animals.
Edward G. Sieber was active in New York.

SIEBER, Friedrich
Czech, 20th century.
Born 1925, in Liberec.
Active in Stuttgart.
Painter, graphic artist, engraver.
Group 11.
Friedrich Sieber has exhibited in Belgium, England, Germany and Italy since 1953.

SIEBER, Michael
Bohemian School, 18th century.
Born 24 December 1724; died 27 December 1788, in Lang-Lhota.
Engraver (burin).

SIEBERECHTS, Jan. See **SIBERECHTS**

SIEBERG, Herbert
German, 19th century.
Born 2 May 1798, in Cologne; died 1 March 1829, in Cologne.
Painter, draughtsman.
Herbert Sieberg studied under B. C. Beckenkamp.

SIEBERG, Peter
German, 18th century.
Active in Hamburg, during the second half of the 18th century.
Painter (gouache). Portraits, still-lifes, urban landscapes.
MUSEUMS AND GALLERIES:
HANOVER (Niedersächsisches Landesmus.): four gouaches.

SIEBERT, Adolph
German, 19th century.
Born 1806, in Halberstadt (Saxony-Anhalt); died 1832, in Rome, Italy.
Painter. History painting.
Adolph Siebert, who was a deaf-mute, studied under Wach in Berlin. In 1830, he was awarded the academy prize and won a travel grant for his painting *Jupiter and Mercury Visiting Philemon and Baucis*
AUCTION RECORDS:
LONDON, 20 Feb 1976, *Cynthia* (oil on panel, 9 x 7 ins / 23 x 18 cm) GBP 700.

SIEBERT, C.
German, 19th century.
Active in Darmstadt, c. 1852.
Draughtsman.

SIEBERT, Edward Selmar
American, 19th - 20th century.
Born 1 July 1856, in Washington (District of Columbia); died 1944.
Painter, engraver.
Edward Selmar Siebert was taught by Albert Baur, probably in Weimar; Carl Heinrich Hoff, probably in Karlsruhe; and Wilhelm Diez, probably in Munich. He was active in Rochester, New York.
MUSEUMS AND GALLERIES:
WASHINGTON DC (Corcoran Gal. of Art).

SIEBERT, Franz Julius
German, 19th - 20th century.
Born 18 August 1845, in Rosswein (Saxony); died 10 April 1906, in Eisenach.
Painter. History painting, portraits.
Franz Siebert studied under Schnorr von Karolsfeld and Franz Theodor Grosse at the fine arts in Dresden and under Karl Gussow at the academy in Berlin, before spending five years in Paris and an extended period in England.
MUSEUMS AND GALLERIES:
DRESDEN: *Portrait of Oskar Pletsch, Painter.*

SIEBERT, Georg
German, 20th century.
Born 13 May 1896, in Dresden; died 1984.
Painter, watercolourist. Portraits, landscapes.
Neue Sachlichkeit (New Objectivity).
Georg Siebert studied under Richard Müller at the fine arts academy in Dresden, and was apparently aligned with the *Neue Sachlichkeit* ('New Objectivity') movement.
MUSEUMS AND GALLERIES:
DRESDEN: watercolours - NUREMBERG: watercolours.

SIEBERT, H.
Dutch or German (?), 19th century.
Active 1847-1879.
Pastellist. Portraits.
AUCTION RECORDS:
AMSTERDAM, 24 April 1991, *Three-quarter Portrait of a Young Woman Wearing a White and Blue Dress Standing on a Balcony* (1862, pastel/paper/panel, 170 x 13 1/2 ins / 432 x 34.5 cm) NLG 4,600. AMSTERDAM, 19-20 Feb 1997, *Portrait of a Young Woman in Blue in front of Drapery, with a River in the Background* (1862, pastel/paper, oval, 17 1/2 x 13 3/4 ins / 44.5 x 35 cm) NLG 2,998.

SIEBERT, Johann Christoph
German, 18th century.
Born to a family originally from Ludwigslust, Germany.
Painter (porcelain).
Johann Siebert worked at the porcelain manufactory of Limbach (Saxony) Germany, in 1791.

SIEBERT, Johann Heinrich
German, 18th century.
Born 1760.
Draughtsman, miniaturist, engraver (burin).

SIEBERT, Johann Martin Jakob, or Sibert
German, 19th century.
Born 1804, in Nuremberg.
Active in Nuremberg until 1846.
Engraver (burin).
Johann Martin Siebert attended the academy in Nuremberg from 1822 to 1828.

SIEBERT, Kurt E.G.
German, 20th century.
Born 5 June 1889, in Görlitz.
Active in Berlin.
Engraver.
Kurt Siebert studied architecture under Hans Poelzig in Berlin.

SIEBERT, Selmar
German, 19th century.
Born 4 September 1808, in Lehnin.
Engraver. Maps.
Selmar Siebert studied under C. W. Kolbe the Younger.

SIEBMACHER. See **SIBMACHER**

SIEBMANN, Abraham Gottlieb. See **SIEPMANN**

SIEBRECHT, Georges. See **SIBRAYQUE**

SIEBRECHT, Hans Christian
German, 19th century.
Painter (porcelain).
Hans Christian Siebrecht worked at the porcelain factory in Furstenberg, Germany, at the beginning of the 19th century.

SIEBRECHT, Heinrich
German, 19th century.
Born 1808, in Kassel.
Painter.
Heinrich Siebrecht attended the academy in Kassel, and in Munich from 1832 to 1833.

SIEBRECHT, Philipp
German, 19th century.
Born 1806, in Kassel; died c. 1844, in New Orleans (Louisiana), USA.
Sculptor.
Philipp Siebrecht studied under Johann Christian Ruhl. He travelled to Rome from 1830 to 1831, to Hanau (Hesse), Germany, in 1833, to Frankfurt am Main and later to America. Siebrecht produced the bust of professor *Sylvester Jordan* and the group sculpture of *Paris and Helen*.

SIEBRECHTS, Jan. See **SIBERECHTS**

SIEBRECHTS, Johannes, or Sibrechts
Flemish School, 18th century.
Died probably 1754.
Active in Antwerp.
Painter.

SIEBURG, Friederike
German, 18th century.
Pastellist.
Friederike Sieburg exhibited with her sister Philippine, who produced landscape drawings, in 1788, and in Berlin in 1793 and 1794.

SIEBURG, Georg
German, 20th century.
Painter, sculptor, designer.
Georg Sieburg provided decorative compositions for the Volkstheater in Berlin and the New Theatre in Vienna.

SIEBURGER, Bernhard
Polish, 19th century.
Born 1825, in Danzig (now Gdansk).
Active in Prague.
Painter. History painting, portraits.

SIEBURGER, Frieda, or Sieburgerová
Czech, 19th - 20th century.
Born 1862, in Prague.
Painter. Landscapes.
Frieda Sieburger was one of the founders in November 1906, of the Prague German Women Artists Club.

SIEBURGH
Dutch, 19th century.
Born in Haarlem; died 2 April 1842, in Java.
Painter.

SIECK, Rudolf
German, 20th century.
Born 18 April 1877, in Rosenheim; died 1957.
Painter, engraver, lithographer. Landscapes.
Rudolf Sieck studied at the college of decorative arts in Munich.
MUSEUMS AND GALLERIES:
MUNICH (Neue Pinakothek): *April*.
AUCTION RECORDS:
MUNICH, 28 Nov 1980, *Landscape* (oil on canvas, 23 1/2 x 27 1/2 ins / 60 x 70 cm) DEM 2,300. MUNICH, 23 June 1999, *Autumn Alpine Landscape* (oil on panel, 28 x 31 ins / 71 x 80 cm) DEM 7,000. COLOGNE, 24 Nov 2001, *Early Spring near Rosenheim* (1912, oil on panel, 24 x 28 ins / 60 x 70 cm) DEM 4,600. MUNICH, 11 July 2002, *Figure with Panflute by Water* (1927, watercolour, 11 x 11 ins / 27 x 29 cm) EUR 1,900. KEMPTEN, 11 July 2002, *Spring Meadow with Blossoming Trees* (1906, oil on panel, 23 x 28 ins / 58 x 72 cm) EUR 2,500. NUREMBERG, 20 Nov 2003, *Early Spring* (1944, tempera on canvas, 31 x 28 ins / 80 x 70 cm) EUR 1,800. BREMEN, 26 March 2004, *June Morning B* (oil on panel, 26 x 32 ins / 66 x 81 cm) EUR 5,500. FREIBURG, 1 April 2004, *High Summer Landscape* (oil on canvas, 25 x 28 ins / 63 x 72 cm) EUR 3,200.

SIECKE, Wilhelm
German, 19th - 20th century.
Born 24 September 1844, in Berlin; died January 1917, in Berlin.
Painter. Portraits, genre scenes.
Wilhelm Siecke studied under Jean Lulvès and Max Koner at the fine arts academy in Berlin.

SIEDEN, Andreas
German, 17th century.
Active in Goslar (Lower Saxony).
Sculptor.

SIEDENTOPF, Christian
German, 19th century.
Born 17 May 1818, in Frankfurt am Main; died 28 June 1884, in Frankfurt am Main.
Reproductions engraver.
Siedentopf studied under E. E. Schäffer.

SIEDERSLEBEN, Hermann
German, 20th century.
Born 9 September 1875, in Berlin.
Active in Leipzig.
Painter, engraver. Portraits.

SIEDLECKI, Franciszek Wicenty
Polish, 19th - 20th century.
Born 23 July 1867, in Cracow; died 1 September 1934, in Warsaw.
Painter. Figure compositions, allegorical subjects, portraits.
Symbolism.
Franciszek Siedlecki studied at Cracow University before going on to continue his training in Munich and Paris, where he attended the Académie Colarossi, and travelling to study in Italy and Holland. From 1902 to 1904 he worked in Warsaw. In 1914, he went to Dornach, Switzerland, where he was the director of the glass painting studios. In 1919 he returned to work in Warsaw. He was included in the 1921 Paris exhibition of Polish artists held by the Salon de la Société Nationale des Beaux-Arts, where he exhibited four allegorical works: *Birth* (soft-ground etching), and *Kiss, Procession* and *Portrait of G. Norwid* (etchings).

SIEDOFF, Grigory Semenovich. See **SEDOV**

SIEFERLE, Franz
German, 20th century.
Born 4 October 1875, in Lahr.
Active in Lahr.
Sculptor.
Franz Sieferle studied in Munich, then in Rome (1897-1898) and Karlsruhe (1898-1903).

SIEFERLE, Victor
German, 20th century.
Born 16 July 1881, in Lahr.
Painter.
Victor Sieferle is believed to be Franz Sieferle's brother. He studied in Karlsruhe between 1900 and 1903 and subsequently settled in Lahr.

SIEFERT, Arthur
German, 19th - 20th century.
Born 15 February 1858, in Zörbig.
Painter. Figures.
Arthur Siefert studied at the fine arts academy and lived and worked in Berlin.
AUCTION RECORDS:
LONDON, 19 May 1976, *Young Woman with a Red Shawl* (oil on panel, 7 3/4 x 6 ins / 20 x 15 cm) GBP 1,500.

SIEFFERT, André
French, 20th century.
Painter.

André Sieffert exhibited regularly at the Salon des Artistes Français in Paris and received an honourable mention in 1939, a silver medal in 1943 and a gold medal in 1944. Afterwards he became a member.

SIEFFERT, Eugénie Annette
French, 19th - 20th century.
Born in Paris.
Painter.

Eugénie Sieffert was a pupil of Louis Sieffert, and possibly a relative. She exhibited in Paris, beginning at the Salon des Artistes Français in 1898, and was a member from 1901.

SIEFFERT, Louis Eugène
French, 19th - 20th century.
Born in Paris.
Miniaturist.

Louis Sieffert was a pupil of Justine Marie Lequien. He exhibited in Paris at the Salon des Artistes Français in 1891, received an honourable mention and was a member from 1901.

SIEFFERT, Paul
French, 19th - 20th century.
Born 11 November 1874, in Paris; died 1957, in Paris.
Painter, pastellist, illustrator. Nudes, portraits, genre scenes. Murals, designs for stained glass.

Paul Sieffert was a pupil of Jean Léon Gérôme, Gabriel Guay and Albert Maignan. In 1902 he won the first Grand Prix de Rome. In 1931 he was made a Chevalier of the Légion d'Honneur and in 1937 he received the Diplôme d'honneur for the Exposition Internationale. He exhibited in Paris, mainly at the Salon des Artistes Français, of which he was a member from 1894. He was also a member of the committee and the jury. Although he created some decorative works, cartoons for stained glass, illustrations for books, and even, in his youth, several very Realist subjects (*Dockers, Drunken Slave*) the latter part of his career was devoted to an inexhaustible output of nudes.

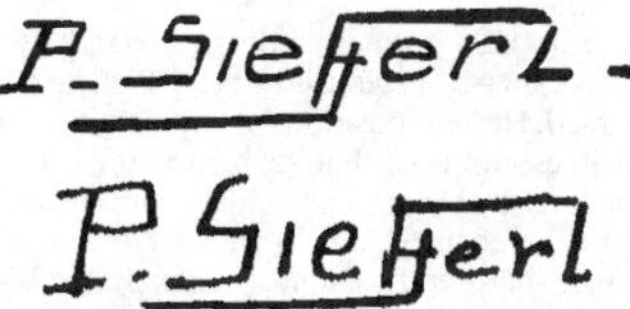

AUCTION RECORDS:
PARIS, 11 Feb 1944, *Young Woman with Low Neckline,* FRF 620. PARIS, 15 May 1944, *Dockers* (1904) FRF 1,100; *Drunken Slave* (1900) FRF 1,500. PARIS, 23 April 1945, *Reclining Nude* (seen from behind) FRF 3,000. PARIS, 12 Nov 1946, *Nude Woman Lying on a Divan, One Leg Bent,* FRF 16,500. NICE, 11-13 Oct 1954, *Nude Woman in Bed,* FRF 11,000. LONDON, 6 May 1977, *Nude in Bed* (oil on canvas, 17 x 34 ins / 43 x 86.4 cm) GBP 600. LONDON, 16 March 1979, *Moroccan Poet* (oil on canvas remounted on board, 21 1/4 x 14 1/2 ins / 54 x 37 cm) GBP 1,900. PARIS, 29 June 1981, *Reclining Nude* (oil on panel, 6 3/4 x 9 ins / 17 x 23 cm) FRF 18,000. PARIS, 27 April 1984, *Nude on a Blue Divan* (oil on canvas, 18 x 25 1/2 ins / 46 x 65 cm) FRF 13,000. LONDON, 21 June 1985, *Axilis at the Stream, Hermione and the Shepherds, Nysa Singing and others* (watercolour, set of 24, 9 x 6 1/2 ins / 23.1 x 16.2 cm) GBP 4,200. LONDON, 26 Nov 1986, *Nude at her Mirror* (oil on canvas, 22 x 18 ins / 55 x 46 cm) GBP 4,200. CALAIS, 3 July 1988, *Seated Nude* (1927, oil on canvas, 9 3/4 x 7 3/4 ins / 25 x 20 cm) FRF 11,000. PARIS, 22 Nov 1988, *Nude with Fur* (oil on canvas, 22 3/4 x 39 1/4 ins / 58 x 100 cm) FRF 40,000. PARIS, 10 April 1989, *Nude* (oil on canvas, 24 x 18 ins / 61 x 46 cm) FRF 9,000. CHARLEVILLE-MÉZIÈRES, 19 Nov 1989, *Potato Peeler* (oil on canvas, 18 x 15 ins / 46 x 38 cm) FRF 13,000. LONDON, 16 Feb 1990, *Reclining Nude* (oil on panel, 6 1/4 x 9 1/4 ins / 15.9 x 23.8 cm) GBP 1,760. PARIS, 20 Feb 1990, *Model on a Blue Sofa* (oil on canvas, 18 x 24 1/2 ins / 46 x 62 cm) FRF 18,000. PARIS, 9 March 1990, *Seated Nude* (pastel, 23 1/2 x 17 3/4 ins / 60 x 45 cm) FRF 6,000. VERSAILLES, 18 March 1990, *Blue Dream* (oil on panel, 6 1/4 x 10 1/4 ins / 16 x 26 cm) FRF 6,500. PARIS, 23 March 1990, *Sensual Delight* (oil on canvas, 38 1/4 x 51 1/4 ins / 97 x 130 cm) FRF 44,000. CALAIS, 8 July 1990, *Reclining Nude* (oil on canvas, 15 x 22 ins / 38 x 56 cm) FRF 12,000. PARIS, 28 June 1991, *Nude with Fur* (oil on canvas, 22 3/4 x 39 1/4 ins / 58 x 100 cm) FRF 30,500. MONTAUBAN, 10 Oct 1993, *Nude on a Sofa* (oil on canvas, 15 x 22 ins / 38 x 55 cm) FRF 7,500. LONDON, 17 June 1994, *Seated Nude* (1926, oil on panel, 11 x 8 1/2 ins / 27 x 21.6 cm) GBP 1,610. CALAIS, 25 June 1995, *Nude Lying on a Bearskin* (oil on canvas, 13 x 22 ins / 33 x 55 cm) FRF 15,500. LONDON, 12 June 1997, *Nude Lying on an Animal Skin* (oil on canvas, 21 3/4 x 31 3/4 ins / 55.2 x 80.7 cm) GBP 5,980. PARIS, 20 Oct 1997, *Nude in Front of Mirror* (oil on canvas, 18 1/4 x 15 ins / 46.5 x 38 cm) FRF 9,500. CHAUMONT, 29 Nov 1997, *Nude Seen from Behind on a Blue Veil* (oil on canvas, 13 x 22 ins / 33 x 55 cm) FRF 23,000. NEW YORK, 3 May 2000, *Reclining Female Nude* (1898, oil on canvas, 35 x 56 ins / 89 x 143 cm) USD 24,000. LONDON, 22 Sept 2000, *Nude with Bearskin* (oil on canvas, 26 x 37 ins / 65 x 95 cm) GBP 10,000. LONDON, 29 March 2001, *Nude from behind with Fur* (oil on canvas, 20 x 26 ins / 51 x 65 cm) GBP 40,000. LONDON, 28 Nov 2001, *Young Girl Doing Her Hair* (oil on canvas, 31 x 23 ins / 79 x 58 cm) GBP 10,500. PARIS, 27 June 2002, *Nude from behind with Fur* (oil on panel, 6 x 9 ins / 15 x 24 cm) EUR 8,000. LONDON, 21 Nov 2002, *Young Tennis Player* (1924, oil on canvas, 36 x 29 ins / 92 x 73 cm) GBP 5,200. STOCKHOLM, 3 Dec 2003, *Reclining Female Nude* (oil on panel, 6 x 10 ins / 16 x 26 cm) SEK 52,000. LONDON, 21 Jan 2004, *Reclining Nude* (oil on canvas, 29 x 39 ins / 74 x 100 cm) GBP 6,000. LONDON, 14 July 2004, *Reclining Nude* (oil on canvas, 21 x 32 ins / 54 x 81 cm) GBP 6,000.

SIEFRIED, Frederic
13th - 14th century.
Active c. 1360.
Painter.

Frederic Siefried is mentioned in Ris-Paquot.

SIEG, Karl
German, 19th century.
Born 4 August 1784, in Magdeburg (Saxony-Anhalt); died 1845, in Magdeburg.
Painter, lithographer.

Sieg attended the academy in Magdeburg; he studied in Paris under J. L. David and in Rome from 1813 to 1815.

MUSEUMS AND GALLERIES:
MAGDEBURG (Kulturhistorisches Mus.): *Portrait of the Preacher Bake; Portrait of the Consistory Adviser Wilhelm Koch.*

SIEGARD, Pär
Swedish, 20th century.
Born 28 December 1887 or 1877, in Hälsingborg; died 1961.
Painter, engraver.

Pär Siegard trained in Stockholm and under Carl Wilhelmson, possibly in Göteborg; he also worked in Paris.

AUCTION RECORDS:
STOCKHOLM, 23 April 1983, *Still-life with Flowers* (1944, oil on panel, 35 x 30 ins / 89 x 76.5 cm) SEK 11,700. LUND, 11 Nov 2000, *Summer Landscape from Hallandsasen* (oil on panel, 15 x 20 ins / 38 x 50 cm) SEK 36,000. MALMÖ, 24 Nov 2001, *Teddy Bears and Ladybird* (oil on canvas, 20 x 24 ins / 52 x 62 cm)

SEK 21,000. STOCKHOLM, 24 April 2002, *St George and the Dragon* (watercolour, 13 x 9 ins / 34 x 24 cm) SEK 19,000. STOCKHOLM, 5 Nov 2002, *Landscape from Halland* (1918, oil on canvas, 22 x 30 ins / 56 x 76 cm) SEK 66,000. STOCKHOLM, 27 April 2004, *Female Circus Rider* (c. 1920, watercolour, 14 x 9 ins / 35 x 24 cm) SEK 16,000.

SIEGEL, Anton. See **SIEGL**

SIEGEL, Christian Heinrich
German, 19th century.
Born 14 May 1808, in Wandsbek; died 1883, in Greece.
Active in Copenhagen and Munich, 1837-1838.
Sculptor.

Siegel studied under Runge in Hamburg. He produced the monument in Nauplia (Greece) that was dedicated to the memory of the Bavarians who fell in Greece.

SIEGEL, Friedrich
German, 20th century.
Born 1931.
Painter (including gouache), draughtsman.

Friedrich Siegel studied under Albert Paris Gütersloh at the Akademie der Bildenden Künste in Vienna, and has exhibited from 1970 at various group and solo exhibitions, notably at the Monika Beck Gallery (1973 onwards). Siegel has created his own universe peopled with organisms that, as the titles he gives his works confirm, address themes of life, death and God.

BIBLIOGRAPHY:
Friedrich Siegel, Éd. Monika Beck, Homburg/Saar, 1983.

SIEGEMUND. See **SIEGMUND** and **SIGISMUND**

SIEGEN, August
German, 19th - 20th century.
Born 1850.
Painter. Urban landscapes, landscapes with figures, waterscapes, architectural views.
Orientalism.

Aug. Siegen

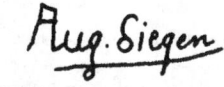

AUCTION RECORDS:
LONDON, 7 May 1976, *Views of Venice* (1880, two oils on canvas, 19½ x 32 ins / 49.5 x 81.5 cm) GBP 1,200. LONDON, 3 Nov 1977, *Street Scene, Cairo* (oil on panel, 20½ x 16 ins / 52 x 40.5 cm) GBP 1,700. NEW YORK, 12 May 1978, *Street Scene, Cairo* (oil on canvas remounted on board, 38½ x 56 ins / 98 x 142 cm) USD 2,000. AMSTERDAM, 19 Sept 1979, *Town by a River* (oil on canvas, 28 x 38¼ ins / 71 x 97 cm) NLG 5,400. VIENNA, 14 March 1984, *View of Stargard* (oil on canvas, 29¼ x 39¼ ins / 74 x 100 cm) ATS 70,000. LONDON, 9 Oct 1985, *Town by a Canal* (oil on canvas, 36¾ x 55 ins / 93.5 x 140 cm) GBP 3,000. COLOGNE, 23 March 1990, *Major German Port with Figures* (oil on canvas, 39½ x 28¾ ins / 100.5 x 73 cm) DEM 5,500. AMSTERDAM, 25 April 1990, *View of Morcote, Lake Lugano* (oil on canvas, 20 x 30¾ ins / 51 x 78 cm) NLG 7,130. PARIS, 23 Oct 1991, *Cairo Street* (oil on canvas, 22¾ x 31½ ins / 58 x 80 cm) FRF 35,000. LONDON, 28 Oct 1992, *Market Scene, Cairo* (oil on panel, 16¼ x 20 ins / 41 x 51 cm) GBP 1,650. MONACO, 2 July 1993, *View of the Piazza dei Signori, Vicenza* (oil on panel, 20¾ x 16¼ ins / 53 x 41.5 cm) FRF 16,650. LONDON, 16 March 1994, *Cairo Street at Sunset* (oil on canvas, 39 x 28¾ ins / 99 x 73 cm) GBP 4,830. PARIS, 22 April 1994, *Oriental Town* (oil on canvas, 37½ x 56¼ ins / 95 x 143 cm) FRF 230,000. NEW YORK, 20 July 1994, *Town Squares* (oil on panel, pair, each 21 x 16¼ ins / 53.3 x 41.3 cm) USD 6,900. LONDON, 10 Feb 1995, *Notre Dame Cathedral, Paris* (1874, oil on canvas, 16½ x 26¼ ins / 42 x 66.5 cm) GBP 2,070. LONDON, 31 Oct 1996, *Arab Market Square* (oil on panel, 15¾ x 20½ ins / 40 x 52 cm) GBP 1,725. NEW YORK, 26 Feb 1997, *Village Harbour* (oil on canvas, 29 x 40 ins / 73.7 x 101.3 cm) USD 3,450.

SIEGEN VON SECHTEN, Ludwig, or Segen
Dutch, 17th century.
Born 1609, in Sechten; died c. 1680, in Wolfenbüttel.
Draughtsman, engraver (mezzotint).

Ludwig Siegen von Sechten deserves recognition as the inventor of engraving in mezzotint, sharing the distinction with the painter Rupert. On his father's side he was of German extraction and was sent to Germany in 1620 to be educated, returning to Holland in 1626. In 1637 he entered the service of the landgrave of Hesse in the rank of lieutenant colonel, but it is not known whether his functions were purely military. In 1641 he travelled back to Holland and spent a year there executing his first plate, the portrait of Landgravine *Amelia Elizabeth of Hesse*. It is certain that he made numerous attempts before trying to apply his process in its entirety. This engraving is not without merit and is very similar to the ones which Prince Rupert executed later, when Siegen had given him his secret. It was dedicated to the princess in 1642. The catalogue of the works of Siegen includes seven pieces, five portraits and two war subjects. He was in the service of the duke of Wolfenbüttel when he died.

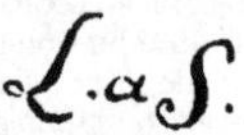

SIEGENTHALER, Albert
Swiss, 20th century.
Born 1938, in Endingen; died 1984.
Installation artist.

Albert Siegenthaler was apprenticed to a stonemason before enrolling at the Kunstgewerbeschule (college of arts and crafts) in Zurich and going on to study at the Beaux-Arts in Paris and London's Royal College of Art. He lived and worked in Stilli.

Beginning in 1964 or thereabouts, Siegenthaler worked primarily with sheets of coloured steel, which he cut, shaped and assembled. His compositions are subject to a number of basic principles, not least that each curvilinear or orthogonal sheet is 'penetrable'. His principal concern was with the juxtaposition of positive and negative elements, interiors and exteriors, solids and vacuums. He exhibited his work in such a way as to bring out the contrast between curved and orthogonal lines and to impart a dynamism as a result of the 'interpenetrability' of the components used. This dynamism is given added value by the use of contrasting interior/exterior/sectional colours. In 1971, Siegenthaler embarked on a series of small sculptures based on these selfsame principles but adapted to a more *intimiste* format, as opposed to the powerful dynamic that characterises the majority of his earlier work.

BIBLIOGRAPHY:
Kneubühler, Theo, *Kunst: 28 Schweizer*, exhibition catalogue, Gal. Raeber, Lucerne, 1972.

MUSEUMS AND GALLERIES:
AARAU (Aargauer Kunsthaus): *Form Entering* (1962); *Form Expelled* (1962, marble).

SIEGER, Fred
Dutch, 20th century.
Born 1902.
Painter. Still-lifes, flowers.

AUCTION RECORDS:
AMSTERDAM, 13 Dec 1989, *Still-life with Onions* (1948, oil on canvas, 15 x 18½ ins / 38 x 47 cm) NLG 1,725. AMSTERDAM, 11 Sept 1990, *Still-life with Summer Flowers in a Vase on a Draped Table* (1945, oil on canvas, 23½ x 18 ins / 59.5 x 45.5

cm) NLG 3,450. AMSTERDAM, 12 Dec 1991, *Composition* (1981, oil on canvas, 19³/4 x 23¹/2 ins / 50 x 60 cm) NLG 3,220. AMSTERDAM, 10 Dec 1992, *Interior with Still-life of a Jug and a Plate of Fruit on a Sideboard* (oil on canvas, 28³/4 x 23¹/2 ins / 73 x 60 cm) NLG 4,025. AMSTERDAM, 1 June 1994, *Improvisation* (1959, oil on canvas, 35¹/2 x 39¹/4 ins / 90 x 100 cm) NLG 7,820.

SIEGER, Marie. See **SCHUSTER-SCHÖRGARN**

SIEGER, Rudolf

German, 19th - 20th century.

Born 23 November 1867, near Magdeburg; died 4 April 1925, in Laage (Mecklenburg).

Painter. Portraits, Still-lifes, flowers.

Rudolf Sieger studied under Vincent Deckers in Düsseldorf and under Lovis Corinth in Munich. He lived and worked successively in Munich (between 1896 and 1902), in Blankenberg (1902-1908), in Doberan (1908-1918) and subsequently in Rostock and Laage. His work has Impressionist undertones, possibly due to the influence of Lovis Corinth.

MUSEUMS AND GALLERIES:

GDANSK: *Portrait of Johann Trojan, Poet* - ROSTOCK: *Self-portrait*; *Still-life*.

AUCTION RECORDS:

NEW YORK, 29 Oct 1992, *Still-life with Peonies in an Oriental Vase* (1916, oil on panel, 28³/4 x 18³/4 ins / 73 x 47.6 cm) USD 8,800.

SIEGER, Viktor

Austrian, 19th century.

Born 17 May 1843, in Vienna, in 1824 according to some sources; died 1905, in Vienna.

Painter, watercolourist, engraver. Genre scenes.

Sieger attended the academies of Vienna and Munich. He produced 101 oil paintings and in excess of 100 watercolours.

Stamp of sale

SIEGERIST. See also **SIGRIST**

SIEGERIST, Johann

Swiss, 19th century.

Born 21 March 1816, in Rafz (Zurich); died 27 August 1885, in Feuerthalen.

Painter (gouache). Landscapes.

SIEGERT, August Friedrich

German, 19th century.

Born 5 March 1820, in Neuwied; died 13 October 1883, in Düsseldorf.

Painter. Genre scenes, harbour scenes, still-lifes.

August Friedrich Siegert attended the academy in Düsseldorf with Th. Hildebrandt and W. von Schadow, and became a teacher there in 1872. He travelled to Antwerp, Paris and Munich.

MUSEUMS AND GALLERIES:

DÜSSELDORF: *Woman Painting Fruits* - HAMBURG: *Devotion* - LIÈGE: *Glass of Wine*.

AUCTION RECORDS:

BREMEN, 20 Oct 1979, *Harbour Scene* (oil on panel, 19 x 15³/4 ins / 48 x 40 cm) DEM 5,000. LONDON, 12 Oct 1984, *The Window Garden* (1878, oil on canvas, 20¹/2 x 15¹/4 ins / 52 x 38.6 cm) GBP 3,400. COLOGNE, 28 June 1985, *Lady Flower Enthusiast* (1878, oil on canvas, 20¹/2 x 15¹/4 ins / 52 x 39 cm) DEM 12,000. COLOGNE, 23 March 1990, *Young Boy Reading in the Library* (1863, oil on canvas, 14³/4 x 11³/4 ins / 37.5 x 30 cm) DEM 8,000. NEW YORK, 19 July 1990, *White Wine and Oysters* (oil on canvas, 11¹/2 x 9¹/2 ins / 29.3 x 24.2 cm) USD 1,650. AMSTERDAM, 5-6 Nov 1991, *Expectation* (1876, oil on canvas, 28¹/4 x 23¹/2 ins / 72 x 60 cm) NLG 13,800. VIENNA, 29-30 Oct 1996, *Soldiers Playing Dice* (1857, oil on canvas, 20 x 25 ins / 51 x 63.5 cm) ATS 322,000. NEW YORK, 2 Nov 1999, *Little Critic* (oil on panel, 7 x 6 ins / 19 x 16 cm) USD 5,750. HATFIELD, 6 March 2002, *Elderly Woman Saying Grace* (oil on canvas, 11 x 9 ins / 28 x 23 cm) USD 1,700. STOCKHOLM, 26 May 2003, *Little Connoisseur of Fine Arts* (oil on canvas, 19 x 17 ins / 49 x 42 cm) SEK 76,000.

SIEGERT, August or Augustin

German, 19th century.

Born 25 December 1786, in Schweidnitz (now Swidnica, Poland); died 12 September 1869, in Jordansmuhl, Poland.

Painter. History painting, portraits, landscapes.

August Siegert studied in Paris under F.A. Vincent and J.L. David. He taught art at the University of Breslau (now Wroclaw, Poland) from 1812, and went to Sicily from 1816 to 1818.

MUSEUMS AND GALLERIES:

WROCLAW: *Landscape*; *Portrait of a Woman*.

AUCTION RECORDS:

ROME, 12 Dec 1989, *The Piazza del Campo in Siena* (oil on panel, 20³/4 x 16³/4 ins / 53 x 42.5 cm) ITL 7,000,000. LONDON, 14 Dec 1999, *Reading the News. Threading a Needle* (oil on canvas, a pair, 12 x 10 ins / 31 x 26 cm) GBP 2,000. ZURICH, 22 March 2002, *Harbour Town* (oil on canvas, 38 x 56 ins / 97 x 143 cm) CHF 8,000.

SIEGERT, Eugen

German, 19th - 20th century.

Born c. 1858; died June 1906.

Painter.

Siegert lived and worked in Berlin.

SIEGERT, Gotthelf

German, 19th century.

Born 1778, in Dresden; died 23 March 1823, in Leipzig.

Painter. Stage sets.

Gotthelf Siegert studied under J. G. Theil.

SIEGFRIED, Arne

Swiss, 20th century.

Born 3 September 1893, in Worb (Bern).

Painter. Figures, portraits.

Arne Siegfried studied fine arts at the Accademia di Belle Arti di Brera in Milan, then in Munich and Paris. He worked initially in Paris before settling in Zurich, where he ran a free academy of painting.

MUSEUMS AND GALLERIES:

BERN: *Self-portrait*.

SIEGFRIED, Heinrich

Swiss, 19th century.

Born 31 December 1814, in Wipkingen, near Zurich; died 22 July 1889, in Wipkingen.

Draughtsman, engraver (aquatint).

Heinrich Siegfried studied under J. R. Dickenmann and engraved views of Zurich and its environs.

SIEGFRIED, Hubert

French, 20th - 21st century.

Born 7 July 1952, in Strasbourg.

Painter, draughtsman, illustrator. Scenes with figures.

Hubert Siegfried studied at the École des Beaux-Arts in Tours. His favourite themes are musicians and dances. He also provides illustrations for the print media.

He has shown his work at group exhibitions, among them: in 1982 at the Salon des Indépendants; from 1985 to 1988 at the Galerie Française; in 1987 at the Salon d'Automne; in 1988 at the Salon Violet; from 1992 to 1996 at the Galerie du Dôme; in 1994 at the Galerie Castiglione; and since 1997 at the Galerie Samagra and the Galerie Artitude in Paris. He exhibited solo in Paris in 1993, 1997, and 1998.

SIEGFRIED, Johann
Swiss, 18th century.
Born in Zofingen.
Active in England.
Painter, decorative designer. Landscapes, flowers, decorative motifs.

As a decorator, Johann Siegfried favoured arabesque work (an interlaced ornamental design that can be floral and/or geometric).

SIEGFRIED, Johann Felix. See **SEYFRIED**

SIEGFRIED, Théodore
French, 19th century.
Born 19 March 1829, in Strasbourg; died after 1884.
Lithographer.

Siegfried engraved portraits and views of Strasbourg; he was a contributor to the humorous magazine *Le Mirliton* from 1882 to 1884.

SIEGFRIED, Wladimir
Romanian, 20th century.
Born 14 October 1909, in Bârlad; died 17 May 1982, in Neuilly, France.
Active in France from 1957.
Painter (including gouache), draughtsman, watercolourist, illustrator, stage-set designer. Figures, nudes, portraits, interiors with figures, landscapes, still-lifes, flowers. Stage costumes, sets.

After training with a Bucharest painter, Siegfried went to Paris, where he studied painting at the Académie d'André Lhote, and theatre décor under Natalya Goncharova and Mikhail Larionov. From 1948 to 1957 he taught stage-set design at the N. Grigorescu Institute of Fine Arts, Bucharest. In 1950 he was appointed artistic director of the Municipal Theatre, Bucharest. In 1953 he organised the Romanian performances at the Warsaw Youth Festival, and in 1954 he went on a tour of China, lecturing on Western theatre.

Siegfried mastered all painting techniques and knew how to convey the psychology of his models, the restrained sensuality of a nude, or the lyricism of the French, Italian or Spanish landscape. He illustrated the works of Voltaire and Mircea Eliade, but he excelled as a stage-set designer. Between 1936 and 1957, he worked on virtually every stage in Bucharest, as well as the Casino de Paris, the Théâtre Mogador, and other theatres in Paris, applying his vast knowledge of the theatre, which ranged from Shakespeare to Giraudoux, to scripts, periods, countries and characters. His set and costume designs, which sometimes he painted in gouache on black paper, and others sketch in pen and ink with watercolour highlights, show remarkable skill. Siegfried mainly held solo exhibitions including: Vienna (1933); Galerie Le Nouvel Essor, Paris (1934); Bucharest (1936, 1944, 1945, 1946); Galerie Marcel Bernheim, Paris (1957); in foyer of the Théâtre Sarah Bernhardt, Paris (1958); Madrid (1971); Marbella, (1972); Hôtel Méridien, Paris (1973, 1974, 1978). Posthumous retrospective include: Neuilly town hall (1984) and Galerie 20, Paris, (1986).

BIBLIOGRAPHY:
Jianou, Ionel, et al., *Siegfried, peintures, dessins, costumes, décors*, Éd. Association des Amis de Siegfried, Neuilly, 1986.
Jianou, Ionel, et al., *Romanian Artists and the West*, American Romanian Academy of Arts and Sciences, Los Angeles, 1986.

SIEGHART, August
Hungarian, 18th century.
Born c. 1677; died 10 May 1734.
Active in Pest.
Painter.

SIEGHART, Johann Simeon Benjamin
German, 18th - 19th century.
Illustrator, calligrapher.

Sieghart studied under A. Fr. Oeser, and taught at the academy in Freiberg (Saxony), Germany, from 1785, where he was still working in 1811.

SIEGL, Anton, or Siegel
Austrian, 18th - 19th century.
Born 1763; died 6 May 1846, in Vienna.
Painter. Portraits, urban landscapes.

MUSEUMS AND GALLERIES:
VIENNA (Historisches Mus.): *View of Vienna* (three watercolours) - VIENNA (University): *Portrait of the Lawyer Franz Anton Edler von Zeiller* (two pictures).

SIEGL, Georg, or Sigl
Austrian, 19th century.
Born 1791; died 1872.
Active in Salzburg, Austria.
Painter.

SIEGL, Karl von
Polish, 19th century.
Born 6 June 1842, in Lancut (Galicia); died 12 April 1900, in Vienna, Austria.
Engraver, draughtsman, engineer.

Von Siegl studied under W. Unger. He illustrated Lutzow's book *Art Sensations of Italy*.

SIEGLÄNDER, Vincenz
Austrian, 19th century.
Born 4 September 1819, in Iglau (now Jihlava, Czech Republic).
Active in Vienna.
Painter, engraver (wood), poet.

SIEGLE, Theo
German, 20th century.
Born 1 July 1902, in Hassloch.
Sculptor. Busts.

Theo Siegle studied at the academy of fine arts, Stuttgart.

SIEGMUND. See also **SIGISMUND**

SIEGMUND, Arnold
Austrian, 20th century.
Born 1883, in Krizba, Transylvania; died 24 June 1914, in Bozen, South Tyrol (now Bolzano, Italy).
Painter. Portraits, landscapes.

SIEGMUND, C. F.
German, 19th century.
Painter. Battles.

C. F. Siegmund exhibited at the academy in Berlin from 1800 to 1810.

SIEGMUND, Christian
German, 19th century.
Born 1788, in Leipzig.
Active in Dresden.
Engraver (including burin), painter (glass).

Christian Siegmund attended the academy in Leipzig.

SIEGMUND, Georg Josef. See **SIGMUND**

SIEGMUND, Johann Jakob
Swiss, 19th century.
Born 1807, in Basel; died 1881, in Basel.
Painter. Landscapes.

Johann Siegmund studied in Karlsruhe (Germany), and travelled in Russia, Germany and the Tyrol (Austria). He produced many paintings of the Bern Oberland in Switzerland.
MUSEUMS AND GALLERIES:
BASEL (Kunstmus.): *The Royal Oak.*

SIEGMUND, Julius Gottfried
Latvian, 19th century.
Born 1 July 1828, in Riga.
Painter. Genre scenes, portraits.
Julius Siegmund studied under O. Berthing, R. Schwede, and at the art academies of Dresden and Leipzig from 1847 to 1850. He worked in Riga from 1850 to 1856, in Antwerp with J. van Lerius and N. de Keyser from 1857 to 1858, and also in Paris, Munich and Rome. From 1859 to 1862, he painted in St Petersburg, and from 1862, in Riga. Many of his portraits are in museums in Riga.
MUSEUMS AND GALLERIES:
RIGA.

SIEGMUND, Rudolph
German, 20th century.
Born 29 March 1881, in Burgel, near Jena.
Painter. Religious subjects, portraits, landscapes.
Rudolph Siegmund studied under Ludwig von Hofmann at the academy of fine arts in Weimar and went on to teach (as of 1914) at the academy in Kassel.

SIEGMUNDT, Ludwig
Austrian, 20th - 21st century.
Born 1960, in Graz.
Painter. Landscapes.
Ludwig Siegmundt trained under Leopold Karl Müller at the Akademie der Bildenden Künste in Vienna. In 1900 he exhibited at the Salon des Artistes Français for the Exposition Universelle in Paris, winning a bronze medal.

SIEGRIST. See **SIGRIST**

SIEGUMFELDT, Hermann Carl
Danish, 19th - 20th century.
Born 18 September 1833, in Esbønderup, near Esrum; died 27 June 1912, in Copenhagen.
Painter. Portraits, genre scenes, interiors with figures, landscapes.
MUSEUMS AND GALLERIES:
COPENHAGEN (Statens Mus. for Kunst): *Portrait of Stephen Emil Dahl, Court Horologist* (1887).
AUCTION RECORDS:
COPENHAGEN, 16 Nov 1994, *Farmhouse Interior with Peasant Woman at her Sewing* (oil on canvas, 15 x 14¼ ins / 38 x 36 cm) DKK 15,000.

SIEGWART, Hugo
Swiss, 19th - 20th century.
Born 25 April 1865; died 1938.
Active in Germany from 1895.
Sculptor, medallist. Allegorical subjects, nudes. Statues.
Hugo Siegwart studied art in Lucerne from 1880 to 1885 before enrolling at the academy of fine arts in Munich (1885-1886), then studying in Paris under Henri Chapu at the Académie Julian and Alexandre Falguière at the École des Beaux-Arts. He lived and worked in Lucerne from 1892 to 1895 before settling definitively in Munich. Siegwart exhibited primarily in his native Switzerland, but also secured a silver medal at the Salon des Artistes Français in Paris, held in 1900 within the framework of that year's Exposition Universelle.
MUSEUMS AND GALLERIES:
BERN: *William Tell and his Son Walter* - LAUSANNE (Cantonal MFA): *Night* (1904, bronze); *Day* (1904, bronze) - LUCERNE (Cantonal College): *Four Seasons.*
AUCTION RECORDS:
LUCERNE, 13 Dec 1986, *Nude Walking* (bronze, h. 24 ins / 61 cm) CHF 3,600.

SIEGWART, M
German, 18th century.
Active in Frankfurt am Main, 1780-1790.
Landscape artist.

SIEGWITZ, Johann Albrecht
German, 18th century.
Born in Bamberg.
Sculptor. Religious subjects.
Siegwitz went to Prague, and Breslau (now Wroclaw, Poland) where he produced work for churches from 1724 to 1756.

SIEHER, Fridolin
Swiss, 16th century.
Died 1546, in St Gall.
Miniaturist, calligrapher, illuminator.
Sieher was a monk in the abbey of St Gall. Attributed to him are a *Missale Diethelmi Blarei* and five other manuscripts mentioned by Haenel, one of which is an *Antiphonary* written in 1544.

SIEKIERZ, Ksawery. See **SZYKIER**

SIEM, Wiebke
German, 20th - 21st century.
Born 1954, in Kiel.
Sculptor (mixed media). Figures.
Wiebke Siem lives and works in Hamburg. She employs specialist sewing and dress design techniques to create mannequins, based on her own measurements, with sometimes just the bust and no head. They wear dresses and come with accessories, hats, shoes and bags. This collection of dressed-up mannequins seems to raise the question of the status of clothing, in this case female clothing, in everyday use.
She has taken part in various group exhibitions including, notably: 1990 Hamburg, Jürgen Becker gallery; 1991 Hamburg, *All around the Dome*, Kampnagelgelände; and Stuttgart, Würtembergischer Kunstverein; 1993 Paris, *Parcours Européen III: Allemagne* (*European Tour III: Germany*), Musée d'Art Moderne de la Ville de Paris. There have also been solo exhibitions: 1990 Hamburg, Westwerk; 1991 Hanover, new art centre; 1993 Paris, Galerie Rüdiger Schöttle; and Cologne, Johnen & Schöttle gallery.
BIBLIOGRAPHY:
Bossé, Laurence/Obrist, Hans-Ulrich, *Parcours européen III Allemagne - Qui, quoi? où? - Un regard sur l'Allemagne en 1992*, exhibition catalogue, Musée d'Art moderne de la ville de Paris, Paris, 1993.
MUSEUMS AND GALLERIES:
DÔLE (FRAC Franche-Comté): *Untitled* (1991).

SIEMENROTH, Konrad
German, 19th - 20th century.
Born 9 December 1854, in Küstrin (now Kostrzyn, Poland).
Painter. History painting, portraits, genre scenes.
Konrad Siemenroth was a pupil of Anton von Werner at the academy of fine arts in Berlin.
AUCTION RECORDS:
LONDON, 8 Nov 1972, *Flautist*, GBP 450.

SIEMERDINK, Johann Bernhard. See **SIMERDING**

SIEMERING, Friedrich Wilhelm
German, 19th century.
Born 1794, in Königsberg (now Kaliningrad, Russia).
Painter, decorative designer.

SIEMERING, Fritz
German, 19th century.

Died 1883, in Munich.
Active in Munich.
Painter. Genre scenes.
Fritz Siemering exhibited from 1872 to 1882.

SIEMERING, Julius
German, 19th century.
Born 1837, in Königsberg (now Kaliningrad, Russia); died 27 April 1908, in Königsberg.
Painter. Landscapes.
Julius Siemering was the brother of Rudolf. He attended the academies of Königsberg and Düsseldorf, and from 1871, settled permanently in Königsberg.

SIEMERING, Rudolf or Leopold Rudolf
German, 19th century.
Born 10 August 1835, in Königsberg (now Kaliningrad, Russia); died 28 January 1905, in Berlin.
Sculptor.
Rudolf Siemering attended the academy in Königsberg and studied under Gustav Bläser in Berlin.
MUSEUMS AND GALLERIES:
BERLIN: *Gotthold Ephraim Lessing* (statuette).

SIEMIANOWSKI, Franciszek Ksawery
Polish, 19th century.
Born 1811, in Sanok; died 1860, in Lemberg (now Lviv, Ukraine).
Painter.
Franciszek Siemianowski was the brother of Maksymilian Siemianowski. He studied at the Akademie der Bildenden Künste in Vienna, and often worked in partnership with his brother.
MUSEUMS AND GALLERIES:
CRACOW (Muz. Narodowe): around 350 drawings and watercolours - LVIV (Lubomirski Mus.): *Vautour Dismembering a Stag.*

SIEMIANOWSKI, Maksymilian
Polish, 19th century.
Born 1810, in Sanol; died 7 April 1878, in Sanok.
Painter.
Maksymilian Siemianowski was the brother and colleague of Franciszek Siemianowski.

SIEMON
German, 18th century.
Painter.
Siemon worked at the porcelain manufactory in Hanau (Hesse), Germany.
MUSEUMS AND GALLERIES:
HAMBURG (Mus. für Kunst und Gewerbe): piggy bank (earthenware).

SIEN-YU-CHOU. See **XIANYU SHU**

SIENA. See **GUIDO DA SIENA**

SIENA, da. See first name

SIEPEN, Adam
German, 19th - 20th century.
Born 1851; died 1904.
Painter.
Adam Siepen lived and worked in Düsseldorf.

SIEPMANN, Abraham Gottlieb, or Siebmann
German, 19th century.
Born 17 January 1780, in Dresden; died 1843?.
Painter, draughtsman. Portraits, genre subjects.
Siepmann attended the academy in Dresden.

SIEPMANN, Heinrich
German, 20th century.
Born 1904.
Painter (including gouache), collage artist.
Marcel Brion refers to Heinrich Siepmann as having been active after World War II, which is to say, between 1945 and 1960 or thereabouts.
BIBLIOGRAPHY:
Brion, Marcel, *La Peinture allemande*, Éd. Pierre Tisné, Paris, 1959.
AUCTION RECORDS:
AMSTERDAM, 9 Dec 1992, *Untitled* (1959, gouache and collage/paper, 19 3/4 x 27 1/4 ins / 50 x 69 cm) NLG 3,450. AMSTERDAM, 8 Dec 1994, *Untitled* (1958, gouache/paper, 29 x 19 3/4 ins / 73.5 x 50 cm) NLG 1,380. AMSTERDAM, 7 Dec 1995, *Untitled* (1958, gouache/paper, 24 x 17 1/2 ins / 61 x 44.5 cm) NLG 1,180. COLOGNE, 28 May 1999, *Composition B 28* (1984, oil on canvas, 39 x 30 ins / 99 x 75 cm) DEM 7,000. COLOGNE, 30 May 2001, *B18/93* (1992, oil on canvas, 20 x 16 ins / 50 x 40 cm) DEM 4,000. COLOGNE, 30 May 2001, *B36/1993* (1993, oil on canvas, 31 x 24 ins / 80 x 60 cm) DEM 6,000. COLOGNE, 28 May 2003, *Untitled - 38* (1983, collage, oil and pencil on board, 19 x 27 ins / 49 x 69 cm) EUR 2,600. COLOGNE, 4 Dec 2003, *Vertically Boxed in* (1960, oil on canvas, 35 x 28 ins / 90 x 70 cm) EUR 1,800. COLOGNE, 2 Dec 2004, *Untitled* (1984, oil on board, 46 x 37 ins / 116 x 94 cm) EUR 4,500. COLOGNE, 2 Dec 2004, *Untitled* (1979, oil on canvas, 59 x 35 ins / 150 x 90 cm) EUR 5,500.

SIER, Wlódzislaw
Polish, 20th century.
Born 1944, in Lódz.
Active in Germany.
Painter, watercolourist, weaver.
Wlódzislaw Sier trained as a painter and weaver under R. Modzelewski and A. Starcewski at Lódz School of Fine Arts from 1965 to 1971. He then went to Belgium before settling in Aachen. His painting is gestural and passionate, making generous use of matter and communicating with colour. As with many eloquent non-figurative works, they hover about the edges of visual memory. He exhibited tapestries and paintings in various countries. In 1991 the Paul Piron Gallery, Spa, Belgium staged a large exhibition of his work, as did the Wegimont Exhibition Pavilion in 1993.

SIERAKOVSKI, Jozef von (Count)
Polish, 18th - 19th century.
Born 1765, in Opole; died 28 May 1831, in Warsaw.
Draughtsman, painter, engraver.
Jozef von Sierakovski began his career in Warsaw in 1789. In 1823, he exhibited a drawing.
MUSEUMS AND GALLERIES:
WARSAW: *Drawings.*

SIERHUIS, Jan
Dutch, 20th century.
Born 1928, in Amsterdam.
Painter (mixed media/gouache). Scenes with figures, figures, portraits, landscapes with figures.
Jan Sierhuis studied at the academy of fine arts in Amsterdam and at the academy of fine arts in Antwerp. He went on to take part in group exhibitions, including the Museo de Bellas Artes in Mexico in 1960, the 1961 São Paulo Biennale and the Municipal Museum in Schiedam in 1962. He exhibited solo for the first time in Amsterdam in 1957.

Like many northern European artists of his generation, Sierhuis was greatly influenced by the aesthetics and principles espoused by the CoBrA Group. Sierhuis was first and foremost an Expressionist, and his Expressionist approach was reinforced following his time spent in Mexico. The influence on his work of Karel Appel and De Kooning is apparent, as is that of the English pop artist Allan Davie, but Sierhuis - particularly after his time in Mexico - imparted a vehemence and violence to his work, notably by his use of vivid colours outlined in heavy black. Like many of his counterparts in the CoBrA era, Sierhuis was oblivious to the figurative/abstract divide and, generally speaking, his work reflects this.

Auction records:
Amsterdam, 9 Dec 1988, *Figures in a Landscape* (1968, black chalk and gouache/paper, 27½ x 35 ins / 70 x 89 cm) NLG 1,265. Amsterdam, 10 April 1989, *Abstract Composition* (1964, gouache, 39 x 27¼ ins / 99 x 69 cm) NLG 3,450; *Mother and Child* (1967, oil on canvas, 39¼ x 51¼ ins / 100 x 130 cm) NLG 5,750. Amsterdam, 22 May 1990, *Personage* (1968, gouache/paper, 28¼ x 38¼ ins / 72 x 97 cm) NLG 2,300. Amsterdam, 12 Dec 1990, *Two Personages* (1971, mixed media/paper, 27½ x 39¼ ins / 70 x 100 cm) NLG 1,725. Amsterdam, 13 Dec 1990, *Untitled* (1963, oil on canvas, 22 x 25½ ins / 55 x 65 cm) NLG 12,650. Amsterdam, 5-6 Feb 1991, *Untitled* (1988, oil on canvas, 27½ x 19¾ ins / 70 x 50 cm) NLG 2,070. Copenhagen, 30 May 1991, *Figure* (1964, oil on canvas, 35½ x 23½ ins / 90 x 60 cm) DKK 10,000. Amsterdam, 12 Dec 1991, *Summer Love* (1960, oil on canvas, 31½ x 33½ ins / 80 x 85 cm) NLG 6,900. Amsterdam, 19 May 1992, *Two Figures* (1964, diptych oil on canvas, each part 23½ x 9¼ ins / 60 x 23.5 cm) NLG 5,175. Amsterdam, 9 Dec 1992, *Portrait* (1964, oil on canvas, 31½ x 27½ ins / 80 x 70 cm) NLG 10,580. Amsterdam, 27-28 May 1993, *Untitled* (1964, oil on paper, 27 x 39 ins / 68.5 x 99 cm) NLG 4,025. Amsterdam, 6 Dec 1995, *Homage to El Greco* (1963, oil and tempera/canvas, 48½ x 39¼ ins / 123 x 100 cm) NLG 4,025. Copenhagen, 12 March 1996, *Composition* (oil on canvas, 41¼ x 45¼ ins / 105 x 115 cm) DKK 14,000. Amsterdam, 1 Dec 1999, *Pandora's Box* (1968, oil and tempera on canvas, 59 x 51 ins / 150 x 130 cm) NLG 7,000. Amsterdam, 4 Dec 2001, *Moonlight* (tempera on canvas, 39 x 28 ins / 100 x 70 cm) EUR 3,000. Amsterdam, 4 Dec 2001, *Composition with Figures* (1967, tempera on canvas, 59 x 51 ins / 150 x 130 cm) EUR 3,000. Amsterdam, 12 March 2002, *Twee Hoofden* (1971, oil and tempera on canvas, 59 x 51 ins / 150 x 130 cm) EUR 2,200. Amsterdam, 26 Nov 2002, *Altarpiece of St Peter the Martyr* (1976, coloured crayon, 29 x 22 ins / 74 x 55 cm) EUR 1,800. Amsterdam, 27 May 2003, *Composition* (1963, oil on canvas, 51 x 59 ins / 130 x 150 cm) EUR 4,200. Amsterdam, 29 Sept 2003, *In the Afternoon* (1963, oil on canvas, 35 x 40 ins / 90 x 102 cm) EUR 3,500.

SIERICH, Ferdinand Karl and Louis. See **SIERIG**

SIERIG, Ferdinand Karl, or Ferdinand Carel Sierich
Dutch, 19th century.
Born 12 March 1839, in The Hague; died 19 October 1905, in The Hague.
Painter. Genre scenes, interiors with figures, landscapes with figures, urban landscapes, winter landscapes.

Ferdinand Karl Sierig was possibly a pupil of Bartholomeus van Hove and without any doubt the pupil of Jacobus E. Josephus van den Berg in The Hague. He took part in the exhibition in The Hague in 1863.

Museums and Galleries:
The Hague (Gemeentemus.): *View of Vlaardingen*.

Auction records:
Lindau, 5 Oct 1983, *Winter Landscape* (oil on panel, 6½ x 10¼ ins / 16.5 x 26 cm) DEM 3,700. Amsterdam, 30 Aug 1988, *Peasants Reading near a Table in a House* (oil on canvas, 7¾ x 11 ins / 20 x 27 cm) NLG 1,035. Amsterdam, 1 Sept 1999, *Children Feeding Goat* (oil on panel, 9 x 11 ins / 22 x 27 cm) NLG 9,000. Amsterdam, 4 Sept 2001, *Bringing Home the Catch* (chalk and watercolour heightened with white, 20 x 15 ins / 50 x 39 cm) EUR 2,200.

SIERIG, Louis, or Sierich
Dutch, 19th - 20th century.
Born 1834; died 1919.
Painter. Genre scenes, landscapes with figures, winter landscapes.

Louis Sierig painted typically Dutch winter scenes, frequently featuring skaters on frozen canals and rivers.

Auction records:
Amsterdam, 8 June 1983, *Figures in a Snow-Covered Landscape* (oil on canvas, 12½ x 17¼ ins / 31.5 x 44 cm) NLG 4,200. Amsterdam, 25 April 1990, *Winter Landscape with Figures on a Frozen River and an Inn* (oil on panel, 12 x 16 ins / 30.5 x 40.5 cm) NLG 5,980. Amsterdam, 22 April 1992, *Landscape with Skaters on a Frozen River near a Château* (oil on panel, 7¾ x 10½ ins / 19.5 x 26.5 cm) NLG 3,680. Amsterdam, 5 Nov 1996, *Winter Landscape with Skaters on a Frozen River* (oil on panel, 7¾ x 10¾ ins / 20 x 27.5 cm) NLG 4,248.

SIERINO, Zuan
Swiss, 16th century.
Active in Malvaglia in 1575.
Sculptor (wood/stone).

Sierino collaborated in carving the ceiling of the church of S Maria di Castello, near Giornico.

SIERPINSKI
Polish, 18th century.
Born in Warsaw; died 1791.
Portrait artist.

Sierpinski studied in Warsaw under I. Grassi. He produced portraits, mostly of women. He committed suicide in 1791.

SIERRA, Felipe de
Spanish, 17th century.
Active in Seville at the beginning of the 17th century.
Painter.

In 1613 Felipe de Sierra worked at the gardens of the Alcázar in Seville.

SIERRA, Francisco Perez. See **PÉREZ SIERRA Francisco**

SIERRA, Tomás de
Spanish, 17th century.
Active at the end of the 17th century.
Sculptor.

In 1693 Tomás de Sierra carved a statue of *St Isidore*.

SIERRA Y PONZANO, Joaquín
Spanish, 19th century.
Born 1821, in Madrid.
Sculptor (wood).

Joaquín Sierra y Ponzano was a pupil of C. de Haes.

SIES, Anton. See **SIESS**

SIES, Hieronymus
Flemish School, 18th century.
Painter, sculptor.

Hieronymus Sies belonged to the Benedictine order in Antwerp. He worked for the monasteries of Corvey and Lamspringe around 1700.

SIES, Philipp
Austrian, 19th century.
Active in Imsterberg, Austria.
Painter.

Sies painted altarpieces and frescoes in the churches of Andria (south Tyrol, Italy), Klagenfurt (Austria), Laas and Untermais (south Tyrol).

SIESBYE, Alev
20th century.
Potter.

AUCTION RECORDS:
COPENHAGEN, 8-9 March 1995, *Earthenware Bowl Painted Blue* (1983, h. 6 ins / 15 cm, diam. 9 3/4 ins/25 cm) DKK 7,000. COPENHAGEN, 7 June 1995, *Stone Bowl Painted Blue* (1987, diam. 9 3/4 ins / 25 cm, h. 6 ins/15 cm) DKK 9,000.

SIESS, Anton, or Sies
Austrian, 18th century.
Active in Sterzing, south Tyrol (now Vitipeno, Italy) in the second half of the 18th century.
Painter.
Siess painted altarpieces for churches in Sterzing and its environs.

SIESS, Johann
Austrian, 19th century.
Painter.
Johann Siess painted altarpieces for the churches of Matsch (Austria) and Sulden (Italy) in 1851.

SIESS, Raimund
Austrian, 18th - 19th century.
Born 3 February 1739, in Lackerhäusern; died 26 February 1811, in Vienna.
Sculptor.

SIESSMAYR, Anton
German, 18th century.
Active in Kissing and in Augsburg in 1754.
Sculptor.
Siessmayr produced sculptures for the church of Fürstenfeldbruck in Germany.

SIESTRZENCEWICZ, Stanislaw Bohusz, or Siestsencevicius, Stanislovas
Lithuanian, 19th - 20th century.
Born 11 November 1869, in Vilnius; died 24 May 1927, in Warsaw.
Painter. Portraits, genre scenes, landscapes.
Stanislaw Siestrzencewicz trained with Gottfried Willewalde at St Petersburg and Josef von Brandt at Munich academy. He was included in the 1921 Paris exhibition of Polish artists held by the Salon de la Société Nationale des Beaux-Arts.

SIETSEMA, Paul
American, 20th - 21st century.
Born 1968, in Los Angeles.
Video installation artist.
Paul Sietsema graduated in 1999 with a Master's degree in Fine Arts from University of California, Los Angeles where he lives and works. He is mainly known as a video installation artist although he has also produced more conventional artwork such as *Taxi*, a mixed media drawing, with graphite, ink, watercolour, gouache, tape and collage on paper (2003).

As a video artist, Sietsema creates by hand all of the scenes and objects he depicts. Emphasising the materiality of film, he makes full use of the of the medium's sensuous qualities and plays with exposures, multiple perspectives and various film processing techniques. *Beautiful Place* (1998) a 19-minute long 16mm movie, uses images of an artificial botany to reflect on vision, time and representation. In it Sietsema shows eight vignettes of artificial flowers and gardens that he meticulously constructed in his studio from paper, foam, wire and paint. *Empire* a 24-minute film that takes its name from Andy Warhol's 1964 film and London's Empire theatre, the first place where in 1896 one could see moving pictures, is concerned with space which it explores through three constructed interiors: a labyrinth, a Rococo room, and Clement Greenberg's New York apartment. The eye of the camera investigates shapes and spatial relationships to study the process of perception from visual information as well as the relationship between the representation of space in painting and sculpture.

Collective exhibitions include: Philomene Magers Projekte, Munich and Sabine Kunst Galerie, Munich (1999); *00*, Barbara Gladstone Gallery, New York (2000); *L.A.* Galerie Monika Spruth & Philomene Magers, Cologne(2000); *The Americans: New Art* Barbican, London (2001); *Sonsbeek 9*, Arnheim, The Netherlands (2001); Aukland Triennale (2001); *Real World. The Dissolving Space of Experience*, Oxford Modern Art Museum, Oxford (2004); *Hyperfocal; 5 From L.A.* Galerie Nelson, Paris. Solo exhibitions include: Regen Projects, Los Angeles (2002, 2004); *Contemporary Series Paul Sietsema: Empire*, 2003 Whitney Museum of American Art, New York.

BIBLIOGRAPHY:
Anton, Saul, *'Paul Sietsema: Whitney Museum of American Art, New York'* in *ArtForum*, journal article, June 2003. Archer, Michael/Cotter, Suzanne, et al., *Real World. Katie Grinnan, Wade Guyton, Christina Mackie, Bojan Sarcevic, Paul Sietsema, Hiroshi Sugito*, illustrated book, Oxford Modern Art Museum, Oxford, 2004 (A companion to the exhibition). Iles, Chrissie, *Empire (2002)*, Book, Whitney Museum of American Art, New York, 2005 (23 illustrations including film and production stills).

MUSEUMS AND GALLERIES:
LOS ANGELES (MCA).

SIETZE, Helene
German, 19th - 20th century.
Born 21 March 1843, in Pomerania; died 3 March 1913, in Berlin.
Painter. Landscapes.
A pupil of Max Schmidt (presumably in Weimar), Helene Sietze exhibited examples of her work in Berlin between 1866 and 1899.

SIEURAC, François Joseph Juste
French, 19th century.
Born 1781, in Cádiz, to French parents; died c. 1832, in Sorèze (Haute-Garonne).
Miniaturist, lithographer.
Sieurac was a student at the Académie in Toulouse and pupil of Augustin. Exhibited at the Salon between 1810 and 1827 and at the Luxembourg Salon in 1830.

AUCTION RECORDS:
PARIS, 22 April 1910, *Portrait of the Duchess of Berry on a chased gold box by Marguerite bearing the inscription given by the Duchess de Berry 'From the Duke de Bordeaux to M. Nicolas Victor Lainé, Grenadier'* (miniature) FRF 3,750. PARIS, 22 March 1945, *Young woman in a Fur Trimmed Red Dress* (1811, miniature) FRF 12,000.

SIEURAC, Henri
French, 19th century.
Born 15 August 1823, in Paris; died 18 December 1863, in Paris.
Painter, draughtsman. History painting, allegorical subjects, mythological subjects, genre scenes.
Henri Sieurac was a pupil of his father, François Joseph Sieurac and of Paul Delaroche. Exhibited at the Salon between 1848 and 1863.

MUSEUMS AND GALLERIES:
AIX: *Triumph of Fabius* - CHALON-SUR-SAÔNE: *Birth of Bacchus* - DIJON: *Faith, Hope and Charity* - TOULOUSE: *The Renaissance of Arts and Letters.*

AUCTION RECORDS:
PARIS, 1880, *Clearing in a Wood; Head of a Young Woman* (silverpoint and lead pencil, a pair) FRF 74. PARIS, 21 March 1898, *The Engagement*, FRF 85; *Feast*, FRF 130. PARIS, 1900, *Love Triumphant*, FRF 50. CHARLEVILLE-MÉZIÈRES, 19 Nov 1989, *Mealtime in the Days of the Renaissance* (oil on canvas, 26 1/2 x 33 3/4 ins / 67 x 86 cm) FRF 23,000. PARIS, 12 June 1990, *Elegant Lady Dressed in Her Jewels* (oil on canvas, 16 1/4 x 13 ins / 41 x 33 cm) FRF 5,500.

SIEVEKING, Elisabeth, or Johanna Elisabeth, or Cramer-Sieveking
Cramer's wife
German, 19th century.
Born 2 June 1825, in Hamburg; died 8 May 1894, in Geneva, Switzerland.
Watercolourist. Architectural views.

SIEVEKING, Louise (Frau). See **MEYER**

SIEVERS. See also **SIVERS**

SIEVERS, August. See **SIVERS**

SIEVERS, Elisabeth Benedicta von
Russian, 18th century.
Born 6 January 1773, in St Petersburg; died 25 July 1799, in Leipzig, Germany.
Active in Dresden, Germany.
Painter.
Von Sievers studied under Casanova. She painted *Portrait of Prince Poutiatine*

SIEVERS, Frederick William
American, 19th - 20th century.
Born 26 October 1872, in Fort Wayne (Indiana); died 1966, in Richmond (Virginia).
Sculptor. Statues, busts.
Frederick William Sievers was taught by Ettore Ferrari at the Accademia di Belle Arti in Rome and also studied at the Académie Julian in Paris. He was active in Richmond. He made statues and busts of many of his contemporaries, and in particular was responsible for many of the statues of American army generals standing in various towns in the USA.
AUCTION RECORDS:
NEW YORK, 18 Dec 1984, *A Pointer* (1905, bronze, l. 28 ins / 71.2 cm) USD 1,800.

SIEVERS, Rudolf
German, 20th century.
Born 19 October 1884, in Brunswick; died 13 October 1918, near Laon.
Painter, draughtsman, engraver, lithographer. Stage sets.
Rudolf Sievers studied at the academy of fine arts in Kassel, and went on to work for the Kassel Theatre. He was also a poet.

SIEVERT, August Wilhelm
German, 18th century.
Died 18 August 1751, in Ludwigsburg (Baden-Württemberg).
Painter, watercolourist, illustrator. Flowers, fruit.
A horticulturist himself, August Sievert painted illustrations for books on horticulture.
MUSEUMS AND GALLERIES:
INNSBRUCK (Tiroler Landesmus. Ferdinandeum): *Flowers* - LUDWIGSBURG (Städtisches Mus.): *Flowers*.
AUCTION RECORDS:
VERSAILLES, 25 Oct 1970, *Floral Composition*, FRF 7,000. NEW YORK, 7 Oct 1993, *Fuchsia, Rose, Tulip, Lily, Honeysuckle, Delphinium and Other Flowers in a Glass Vase on a Pedestal* (oil on canvas, 22 3/4 x 18 1/2 ins / 57.8 x 47.3 cm) USD 34,500. MUNICH, 23 June 1997, *Botanic Studies of Plants, and Cultivated and Wild Fruits* (watercolour/card, four boards, each 8 1/2 x 6 3/4 ins / 21.5 x 17 cm) DEM 26,400.

SIEVERT, Christian Ludwig
German, 18th century.
Died 1795, in Ludwigslust.
Sculptor.
Sievert worked for the manufactory of Ludwigslust from 1758 and produced sculptures for the town's church.

SIEVERT, Katharina
German, 18th century.
Painter.
MUSEUMS AND GALLERIES:
SCHWERIN (Staatliches Mus.): *Landscape with Architectural Views; Still-life* (1754).

SIEVERT, Ludwig
German, 20th century.
Born 17 May 1887, in Hanover.
Painter. Stage sets.
Ludwig Sievert settled in Frankfurt am Main in 1919 and worked in various theatres in Germany.

SIEVIER, Robert William
British, 19th century.
Born 24 July 1794, in London; died 28 April 1865, in London.
Engraver (burin), sculptor.
Robert William Sievier was a pupil of Scriven and Young before attending the Royal Academy schools. He studied modelling, which enabled him to establish himself later as a sculptor with some success; his *Nymph Preparing to Bathe* is an example of his talent in this field. He engraved portraits and genre subjects. Sievier was also a distinguished scholar and was made a Member of the Royal Society in 1840.
MUSEUMS AND GALLERIES:
CAMBRIDGE: *Nymph Preparing to Bathe*.
AUCTION RECORDS:
LONDON, 26 June 1980, *The Earl of Eldon, Lord Chancellor* (1824, white marble, h. 28 1/4 ins / 72 cm) GBP 2,600.

SIEWERT, Clara
German, 19th - 20th century.
Born 9 December 1862, in Buda.
Painter, engraver.
Clara Siewert trained in Berlin and went on to live and work there.
MUSEUMS AND GALLERIES:
ESSEN (Krupp Mus.) - ESSEN (Mus., Prints Collection).

SIEYE, Antoine, or Sieyès
French, 18th century.
Born 16 August 1682, in Fréjus; died 11 June 1757, in La Rochelle.
Portrait artist.

SIEYE, Emmanuel
French, 18th century.
Painter.
Emmanuel Sieye was the son of Vincent Sieye.

SIEYE, Mathieu
French, 18th century.
Active during the second half of the 18th century.
Painter.
Mathieu Sieye was the grandson of Vincent Sieye.

SIEYE, Vincent
French, 18th century.
Active during the first half of the 18th century.
Painter.
Vincent Sieye was the brother of Antoine Sieye.

SIEYÈS. See **SIEYE**

SIEYRO, Ramón. See **SEYRO**

SIFER, Conrad. See **SEYFER**

SIFERWAS, John. See **SIFIRWAS Johannes** or **John**

SIFFAIT DE MONCOURT. See **MONCOURT**

SIFFERT
French, 18th century.
Active in Strasbourg during the first half of the 18th century.
Painter.
Siffert executed paintings in the church of Ebersmunster.

SIFFRE, Achille
French, 19th - 20th century.
Born 16 November 1860, in Paris; died November 1932.
Painter.
Achille Siffre exhibited in Paris at the Salon des Artistes Français, of which he was a member from 1924.

SIFFREDI, Max
French, 20th century.
Born 1941, in Aix-en-Provence.
Sculptor. Nudes.
Max Siffredi is believed to have studied at the École des Beaux-Arts in Aix-en-Provence. He worked as a sculptor in Vauvenargues from 1961 and now lives and works in Vallauris where, until 1976, he was employed as a potter in the Marius Mussarra studio.

He works in baked clay, and also uses a lost-wax technique which enables him to cast in bronze. He has been particularly influenced by primitive art and his sculpture boasts clean lines and sensuous forms. His favourite subject matter is women and motherhood. Some of his sculptures exhibit an abstract approach reminiscent of the work of Henri Laurens.

Siffredi has taken part in group exhibitions since 1987, when he exhibited in Alès before going on to show regularly in Nice, Paris, Passy (1988 Savoy Sculpture Biennale), Bourges, Decize and elsewhere. He also exhibits solo, primarily in Lausanne. He has received several awards and distinctions.

SIFIRWAS, Johannes or John, or Syferwas, Siferwast, Siferwas, Cyfrewas
British, 14th - 15th century.
Miniaturist, illuminator.
Sifirwas was active between 1380 and 1421. He illuminated manuscripts such as the *Sherbourne Abbey Missal*, 1396-1407, a volume that later belonged to the library of the Duke of Northumberland, and the *Lovell Lectionary*, also known as the Lutterell Psalter, commissioned for Salisbury Cathedral. He signed with his name or as a Dominican monk.
MUSEUMS AND GALLERIES:
LONDON (British Mus.): *Lovell Lectionary*; 17 ornate pages.

SIGALON, Antoine
French, 16th century.
Born c. 1524, in Bellegarde, near Nîmes; died 22 April 1590, in Nîmes.
Painter (majolica), potter.
Sigalon invented a new technique for painting majolica on an orange background.
MUSEUMS AND GALLERIES:
LONDON (Victoria and Albert Mus.): a dish.

SIGALON, Xavier or Alexandre François Xavier
French, 19th century.
Born 12 December 1787, in Uzès; died 18 August 1837, in Rome.
Painter, draughtsman. History painting, genre scenes, portraits.
A pupil of Monrose, brother of an actor at the Comédie-Française, Sigalon also trained at the École de Dessin in Nîmes, and worked with Guérin and Souchot in Paris from 1817. His first painting, *Young Courtesan* (the 1822 Salon) was a huge success and was purchased by the State, even though the jury had not thought it worthy of a prize. In 1827 his painting for the Salon entitled *Athalie Ordering the Massacre of her Children* was the subject of violent criticism. Discouraged, he left for Nîmes, where he made his living by giving lessons and painting portraits. The arrival of Thiers at the Ministry of the Interior resulted in a commission for a copy of Michelangelo's *The Last Judgement*. So Sigalon and his pupil, Numa Boucoiran, left for Rome in 1833. Three and a half years later the copy had been completed. Sigalon received 58,000 Francs for his work, a 30,000 Francs allowance and a pension for life of 3,000 francs. Sigalon was preparing to copy the remaining decorations in the Sistine Chapel when he succumbed to a bout of cholera.

X Sigalon.

MUSEUMS AND GALLERIES:
ALÈS: *Courtesan* - AUCH: *Courtesan* - BAGNOLS: *Portrait of Doctor Solimani* - COMPIÈGNE: *Roving Minstrels at Rest* - NANTES: *Athalie ordering the Massacre of the Princes of the Race of David* - NÎMES: *Drawing for Athalie; Portraits of Louis-Philippe and the painter Boucoiran* - PARIS (ENSBA): *The Last Judgement* (in the style of Michelangelo) - PARIS (Louvre): *Young Courtesan; Vision of Saint Jerome* - VERSAILLES: *Portrait of Pellegrino Rossi*.
AUCTION RECORDS:
PARIS, 1897, *Portrait of Schoelcher Senior*, FRF 1,170. PARIS, 9-10 March 1923, *Vagabonds' Debauchery* (pen and wash) FRF 265. PARIS, 22 May 1925, *Portrait of a Woman* (pencil heightened with white) FRF 150. PARIS, 17 March 1947, *Saint Micheal Slaying the Fallen Angels* (attributed) FRF 900. NICE, 24 Feb 1949, *The Holy Family* (attributed) FRF 16,000. NÎMES, 13 April 1991, *The Beauty of Nice* (oil on canvas, $41\frac{3}{4}$ x 33 ins / 106 x 84 cm) FRF 70,000. PARIS, 12 Dec 1994, *Young Courtesan* (1821, oil on canvas, $49\frac{1}{4}$ x $62\frac{1}{4}$ ins / 125 x 158 cm) FRF 75,000. PARIS, 18 Dec 2000, *The Young Courtesan* (oil on canvas, 39 x 51 ins / 98 x 130 cm) FRF 21,000. PARIS, 17 Dec 2003, *Portrait of a Man with a Green Cap* (1817, oil on canvas, 22 x 18 ins / 55 x 46 cm) EUR 2,000.

SIGARD, Louis Appolinaire and Nicolas. See **SICARD**

SIGAUD, Charles
Dutch, 18th century.
Active in Amsterdam.
Sculptor.
Charles Sigaud sculpted the monument to *Jan Nieuwenhuyzen* in the church of Monnikendam.

SIGAUD, Eugenio
Brazilian, 20th century.
Born 1889; died 1979.
Painter. Figures.
Eugenio Sigaud was one of the 'Bernardelli nucleus' which sprang from the changes in teaching at the Escola Nacional de Belas Artes in São Paulo. Members of this group did much to move Brazilian art into modern times.
AUCTION RECORDS:
RIO DE JANEIRO, 8 June 1982, *Construction Workers* (1976, casein, $31\frac{1}{2}$ x $39\frac{1}{4}$ ins / 80 x 100 cm) BRL 1,200,000.

SIGAULT, Jean François
Dutch, 19th century.
Born 1787 (or 1797?); died 20 January 1883, in Amsterdam.

Active in Amsterdam and Haarlem.
Sculptor.

SIGFRIED. See **SIEGFRIED**

SIGG, Emil Karl
Swiss, 20th century.
Born 6 September 1880, in Winterthur.
Painter, lithographer. Landscapes.
Emil Karl Sigg was almost certainly related to Martha Sigg.

SIGG, Irmgard
German, 20th century.
Born 1934, in Bielfeld.
Active in France from 1855.
Sculptor.
Irmgard Sigg lives and works in Paris and has exhibited examples of her work at various group exhibitions, including in Rijeka in 1986, at the FIAC (Foire Internationale d'Art Contemporain) in Paris in 1990 and at the Galerie Darthea Speyer in Paris in 1995. Solo exhibitions have included: those in 1973 at the Galerie Charley Chevalier in Paris; at the Galerie Darthea Speyer in 1984, 1988, 1990, 1994, 1999 and 2002; at the Fernand Léger Gallery in Ivry-on-Seine in 1995; *Irmgard Sigg: Sculpture 1996-1999* at the Château des Ducs de Wurtemberg in Montbéliard in 2001; *Bronzes 1993-1998*, at the Beurnier-Rossel Museum, Montbéliard in 2001; and at the 'Le 19' Regional Centre for Contemporary Art in Montbéliard in 2001.

Irmgard Sigg produces anthropomorphic and zoomorphic symbolist-cum-abstract sculptures in bronze and iron, anonymous mannequin-like figures to which critic Philippe Cyroulnik attributes basic aspects of the human condition such as solidarity, confrontation, loneliness, melancholy and *angst*.

BIBLIOGRAPHY:
Dagbert, Anne, *Irmgard Sigg. Œuvres 1986-1987*, exhibition catalogue, Gal. Darthea Speyer, Paris, 1988. Bataillon, Françoise, *Irmgard Sigg. Les Doubles*, exhibition catalogue, Gal. Darthea Speyer, Paris, 1990. Taillandier, Yvon/Michaud, Yves, *Irmgard Sigg. 'Le Partage des épreuves'*, exhibition catalogue, Crédac-Gal. Fernand Léger centre d'Art contemporain, Ivry-sur-Seine, 1995. Avila, Alin, *Irmgard Sigg. Œuvres 1996-1999*, exhibition catalogue, Gal. Darthea Speyer, Paris, 1999. Cyroulnik, Philippe, *Irmgard Sigg*, exhibition catalogue, Musée du château des Ducs de Wurtemberg, musée Beurnier-Rossel, Centre régional d'Art contemporain Le 19, Montbéliard, 2001.

MUSEUMS AND GALLERIES:
CHAMPIGNY-SUR-MARNE: *L'Ile aux Roches* (1986, fountain sculpture) - CRÉTEIL (FDAC Val-de-Marne): *Façade* (1981, wood).

SIGG, Martha
Swiss, 19th - 20th century.
Born 3 June 1871, in Winterthur; died 1937.
Painter, engraver. Landscapes.
Martha Sigg studied under Hermann Gattiker and Wilhelm Trübner and went on to work as an etcher.

SIGG, Thierry
French, 20th century.
Born 1940, in Paris.
Sculptor, painter.
Thierry Sigg became the art adviser in 1978 of the town of Ivry-sur-Seine, and from 1983 the director of the Galerie Fernand Léger. He has exhibited in *Beware of Painting* (1985), Centre d'Art Contemporain, Cergy-Pontoise (1990), *Design/Drawing of Sculpture II*, Centre d'Art Contemporain, Gennevilliers (1991), FIAC (Foire Internationale d'Art Contemporain), Grand Palais, Stand Darthea Speyer, Paris. He shows his works in solo exhibitions: 1973, Collioure; 1979, Galerie Municipale, Vitry-sur-Seine; 1987, 1990, 1994, 1997, 2001, Galerie Darthea Speyer, Paris; 1999, *Chroniques orbitales*, Centre d'Art, Galerie Fernand Léger, Ivry-sur-Seine; 2003, Galerie Darthea Speyer, Paris.

Up to 1990 he collected materials such as lead, wood and plaster, creating light structures chiefly based on gaps and a sort of transparent occupying of space. Then in painting, he distributed little people, sketchily drawn like graffiti, among abstract interlacings, forming traces of a path. Filled with men and women, animals and chimera, as if suspended in a visual universe made of lines, circles and labyrinths, his very colourful paintings explore the world, seeking form and logic. The use of a large format and the repetition of signs and enigmatic constellations take the idea beyond the imaginary.

BIBLIOGRAPHY:
Bouyeure, Claude, *'Thierry Sigg'* in *Opus international* n° 119, periodical, Paris, May-June 1990. *Thierry Sigg. Peintures 1992-1993*, exhibition catalogue, Gal. Darthea Speyer, Paris, 1994 (conversation with Daniel Dobbels).

SIGHARDT. See **SIEGHART**

SIGHINOLFI, Cesare, or Sighinalfi
Italian, 19th century.
Born 1833, in Modena.
Sculptor.
A pupil of Luigi Mainoni, Cesare Sighinolfi was the author of numerous busts and statues in Modena.

SIGHIZZI. See **SEGHIZZI**

SIGHRAF
Swedish, 12th - 13th century.
Active 1170-1215.
Sculptor.
Sighraf sculpted numerous baptism fonts and low reliefs for Swedish churches.

MUSEUMS AND GALLERIES:
VISBY (Gotlands Konstmus.): two tombstones.

SIGIPOLT
German, 11th century.
Active at Tegernsee (Bavaria) in 1031.
Illuminator.

SIGIS
French, 18th century.
Active in Paris.
Sculptor.
In 1754 Sigis sculpted a low relief representing the *Massacre of the Innocents*.

SIGISMOND III. See **SIGISMUND III, KING OF POLAND**

SIGISMONDI, Pietro
Italian, 17th century.
Died before 1624, in Rome.
Active in Lucca.
Painter.
Sigismondi painted altarpieces for the churches of St Nicholas and St Sebastian in Rome.

AUCTION RECORDS:
MONTE CARLO, 23 June 1985, *Judith and Holofernes* (1615, oil on panel remounted/canvas, 49 x 40 1/2 ins / 124.5 x 103 cm) FRF 18,000. ROME, 20 March 1986, *Judith with the Head of Holofernes* (1615, oil on panel transferred/canvas, 48 3/4 x 40 1/2 ins / 124 x 103 cm) ITL 36,000,000.

SIGISMONDO, Niccolò Alemanno
Italian, 15th century.
Illuminator.
Niccolò Sigismondo illuminated a manuscript now in the Vatican in Rome in the style of Giacomo da Fabriano.

SIGISMONDO DA FIESSO, or da Ferrara
Italian, 16th century.

Active from 1534 to 1535.
Illuminator, miniaturist.
Sigismondo da Fiesso worked for many years on the decoration of Ferrara Cathedral's and Ippolito II d'Este's manuscripts.

SIGISMONDO DE STEFANI
Italian, 16th century.
Died after 14 February 1574.
Painter.
Sigismondo de Stefani was a pupil of Veronese.
MUSEUMS AND GALLERIES:
VERONA (Mus. Civico): *St Lawrence with his Executioners.*

SIGISMUND. See also SIEGMUND

SIGISMUND, Benjamin or Christian Benjamin
German, 18th century.
Born 1717, in Dresden; died 1759.
Painter.
Benjamin was the son of Christian Sigismund. He was court painter in Dresden where he produced ornaments for the stables and horses.

SIGISMUND, Christian, or Siegemund or Siegmund
German, 18th century.
Born c. 1688; died 1737, in Dresden.
Painter.
Christian Sigismund was the father of the painter Benjamin and the portrait artist Christian Gottlob.

SIGISMUND, Christian Gottlob, (the Elder)
German, 18th century.
Died 3 September 1737, in Löbau.
Active in Frieberg (Saxony).
Sculptor. Religious subjects.
Christian Sigismund probably produced the altar for the church of Staucha (Germany) around 1718.

SIGISMUND, Christian Gottlob, (the Younger)
German, 18th century.
Born c. 1719; died 1754.
Painter, miniaturist.
Sigismund was the son of Christian Sigismund; as court painter in Dresden (Germany), he produced miniatures.
MUSEUMS AND GALLERIES:
DRESDEN (Stadtmus.): *Portrait of the Historiographer Ad. Fr. Glafey.*

SIGISMUND III, KING OF POLAND
Polish, 16th - 17th century.
Born 20 June 1566, in Gripsholm; died 30 April 1632, in Warsaw.
Active from the beginning of 1587.
Painter.
King Sigismund III was not only a connoisseur of art, but was himself a painter who produced some important compositions. It is not known if he was assisted in his work. His works include *Mater Dolorosa,* now in Augsburg museum, and an *Allegory at the Foundation of a Jesuit Monastery,* now in the Schleissheim gallery, after being moved from the museum in Düsseldorf. It was previously thought to have been the work of Tintoretto.
MUSEUMS AND GALLERIES:
AUGSBURG: *Mater Dolorosa* - CRACOW: *Boy Being Led by an Old Man* - MUNICH (NM): *Ignatius of Loyola* - STOCKHOLM: *The Christian Religion* - WARSAW: *Triumph.*

SIGL. See SIEGL

SIGLER, Hollis
American, 20th century.
Born 1948, in Gary (Indiana); died 29 March 2001; of breast cancer.
Painter, draughtswoman, printmaker.
Hollis Sigler studied in Philadelphia and Florence before graduating with a Master's Degree from the Art Institute, Chicago (1973). She taught at Columbia College, Chicago from 1978 for 20 years. She lived in the Chicago area. Around the late 1970s Sigler started working in a naive style. A lesbian and a feminist, Sigler set out to convey complex personal emotions in interiors devoid of people and fanciful landscapes with a bright palette, skewed perspectives, intensely agitated brushstrokes and a deceiving, childlike style (*She Always Thought She Was Wrong,* 1982; *Let Me Love You in Fleshy Colors,* 1978; *There is a Doubt She Could Be Right,* 1982; *She Has Been There Since the Beginning,* 1989). She also produced lithographs (including *If She Could Free Her Heart to Her Wildest Desires,* pop up book made of a folded lithograph, 1982).

Sigler was diagnosed with breast cancer in 1985; her mother and great-grandmother had died from the disease. When it metastasised around 1992, she began the series, *The Breast Cancer Journal,* composed of oil paintings, oil pastel drawings, cut paper collages, monotypes and lithographs, incorporating handwritten medical research, personal diary entries directly on the frames and borders. She aimed at conveying her own spiritual and emotional journey as a patient and promoting public awareness (*Being on the Edge of Hope, Each Day Brings Us Closer to Victory,* lithograph).

Sigler featured in *A Distinct Grace,* a collective travelling exhibition showing how artists, men and women, responded to the issues and emotions generated by the disease, and how the making and viewing of art could be an integral part of the healing process (1995) and in *Paint Me a Future,* a documentary film about art therapy (1999). Her work has been shown in hundreds of collective exhibitions in the US including: Akron Art Museum, Akron (1986); Chicago Cultural Center (1987); Museum of Contemporary Art, Chicago (1996). Solo exhibitions include: Museum of Contemporary Art, Chicago (1994); Arkansas Art Center, Little Rock (1996); *Breast Cancer Journals: Walking with the Ghosts of My Grandmothers,* National Museum of Women in the Arts, Washington DC (1998).
BIBLIOGRAPHY:
Sigler, Hollis, *The Breast Cancer Journal,* exhibition catalogue, Museum of Contemporary Art,, Chicago, 1994. Porges, Maria, ' *Hollis Sigler*' in *ArtForum,* journal article, September 1994. Love, Susan M./ Yood, James, *Hollis Sigler's Breast Cancer Journal,* exhibition catalogue, illustrated book, Hudson Hills Press, Manchester (VT), 1999. Sterling, Susan Fisher, '*Hollis Sigler's To Kiss the Spirits*' in *Women in the Arts,* exhibition catalogue, journal article, August 2000.
MUSEUMS AND GALLERIES:
CHICAGO (MCA) - DALLAS (MA) - FORT WAYNE, IN (Fort Wayne MA) - WASHINGTON DC (National Mus. of Women in the Arts): several works.
AUCTION RECORDS:
CHICAGO, 19 Sept 2004, *I've Got This Job of Being a Woman* (oil and pastel on canvas, 26 x 32 ins / 66 x 81 cm) USD 3,600.

SIGMARINGEN COLLECTION, Master of the. See MASTERS

SIGMUND. See SIEGMUND

SIGMUND
German, 15th century.
Active in Freising between 1451 and 1495.
Painter, glass painter.

SIGMUND
German, 15th century.

Active in Landshut.
Painter.

SIGMUND, Benjamin D.
British, 19th century.
Painter (gouache), watercolourist, draughtsman. Genre scenes, landscapes, landscapes with figures, waterscapes.

Benjamin D. Sigmund was a prolific painter who specialised in the landscapes of the English countryside. He was active from 1880 to 1904.

AUCTION RECORDS:
LONDON, 13 Dec 1983, *Primrose Time* (watercolour heightened with white, 14 x 9 3/4 ins / 34.7 x 25 cm) GBP 750. LONDON, 26 Feb 1985, *A Sussex Woman* (watercolour and gouache, 12 1/4 x 16 1/4 ins / 31 x 41 cm) GBP 900. LONDON, 22 July 1986, *Two Young Girls in Front of a Cottage* (watercolour heightened with gouache, 11 x 14 1/2 ins / 27 x 37 cm) GBP 1,400. LONDON, 25 Jan 1988, *Bray-on-Thames* (watercolour, 14 x 20 ins / 35.5 x 51 cm) GBP 4,400. LONDON, 25 Jan 1989, *Scattering Grain for the Hens* (gouache, 10 x 14 1/4 ins / 25.5 x 36 cm) GBP 2,420. LONDON, 26 Sept 1990, *Autumn* (watercolour, 10 x 13 3/4 ins / 25.5 x 35 cm) GBP 1,045. LONDON, 30 Jan 1991, *Scattering Grain for the Chicks* (watercolour and gouache, 10 x 14 ins / 25.5 x 35.5 cm) GBP 880. LONDON, 8 Feb 1991, *Cattle Drinking near Fellows Eyot with Eton College Chapel in the Background* (watercolour heightened with white, 10 1/4 x 20 3/4 ins / 26 x 52.7 cm) GBP 1,100. LONDON, 14 June 1991, *A Little Girl with her Sheep in a Fold near a Cottage* (pencil and watercolour, 10 x 14 1/4 ins / 25.4 x 36.3 cm) GBP 2,640. LONDON, 29 Oct 1991, *Birch Wood, Burnham* (watercolour and gouache, 7 x 10 1/2 ins / 17.8 x 26.7 cm) GBP 990. NEW YORK, 16 July 1992, *Summer Landscape with Sheep in a Meadow* (watercolour/board, 14 1/2 x 21 ins / 36.8 x 53.3 cm) USD 1,430. LONDON, 25 March 1994, *Bray-on-Thames* (pencil and watercolour, 13 1/2 x 20 ins / 34.5 x 51 cm) GBP 3,220. NEW YORK, 10 Feb 1998, *Sheep Grazing near a Cottage* (watercolour/paper) USD 1,150. LONDON, 17 March 1999, *Cattle at Ford* (watercolour, a pair, 7 x 14 ins / 18 x 36 cm) GBP 1,200. LONDON, 9 June 1999, *Almshouses, Bray on Thames* (watercolour heightened with gouache, 14 x 20 ins / 35 x 51 cm) GBP 2,200. LONDON, 3 Feb 2000, *Cattle Watering at the Edge of a Lake. Cattle in a Pasture beside Cottage* (watercolour and gouache, a pair, 14 x 20 ins / 35 x 51 cm) GBP 1,900. BILLINGSHURST, 23 Oct 2000, *Cottage Scenes* (watercolour, a pair, 10 x 14 ins / 25 x 35 cm) GBP 2,000. BILLINGSHURST, 29 Jan 2001, *Bembridge, Isle of Wight* (watercolour, 10 x 14 ins / 25 x 35 cm) GBP 1,400. BILLINGSHURST, 29 Jan 2001, *Girl by a Woodland Pool. Children Playing Beneath a Tree* (1882-1883, oil on canvas laid on board, a pair, 8 x 13 ins / 21 x 33 cm) GBP 2,700. LONDON, 1 May 2002, *Shelley Cottage, Lynmouth, Devon. Devonshire Lane, Near Lynmouth* (watercolour, a pair, 11 x 14 ins / 27 x 36 cm) GBP 1,300. NEWBURY, 14 May 2002, *Stoke Poges, Berks* (watercolour heightened with white, 14 x 20 ins / 35 x 52 cm) GBP 3,000. LONDON, 26 March 2003, *Flower Gathering, Worcestershire. Cottage in Worcestershire Lane* (watercolour, a pair, 10 x 14 ins / 25 x 35 cm) GBP 1,600. WORTHING, 5 Feb 2004, *Girls Feeding Chickens and Calves Beside Cottages* (watercolour, sold with watercolour coastal scene by Shapland, 10 x 14 ins / 25 x 36 cm) GBP 1,100. LONDON, 23 March 2004, *Woman Standing by a Cottage with the Sea Beyond* (1895, watercolour, 13 x 9 ins / 34 x 23 cm) GBP 1,100.

SIGMUND, Georg Josef, or Siegmund
Austrian, 17th - 18th century.
Born 1648; died 17 January 1738.
Painter.

Georg Sigmund exhibited in Salzburg, Austria, from 1692.

SIGNAC, Geneviève Laure Anaïs, called Ginette
French, 20th century.
Born 2 October 1913, in Antibes; died 1 May 1980.
Painter, engraver, draughtsman.

Ginette Signac, daughter of Paul Signac and his second wife Jeanne Selmersheim-Desgrange was quickly initiated into drawing and watercolour, and at the age of 15 was often seen at the Académie de la Grande Chaumière. For a quarter of a century she refused to show her work. Her painting, a close and intimate poetic realism long before that was fashionable, was destined to undergo an abrupt transformation after a long period spent working in the studio of her friend, the sculptor Germaine Richier, where she devoted herself to the technique of etching.

She has drawn 'object-poems' with Alain Borne, Hubert Juin, Michel Habart, Pierre Seghers, Eugène Guillevic and Henri Kréa. She is above all one of those rare artists who confronted the problem of unprincipled industrialisation. Her series of *Scaffolding*, then that of *Petrochemical Industry*, evoke the danger faced by natural beauty face to face with the advancing tide of pollution.

MUSEUMS AND GALLERIES:
ALGIERS (Mus. National des Beaux-Arts) - PARIS (MAMVP) - SALISBURY - SCEAUX (Mus. de l'Île-de-France) - ST-TROPEZ (Mus. de l'Annonciade) - TOULON (MA).

SIGNAC, Paul
French, 19th - 20th century.
Born 11 November 1863, in Paris; died 15 August 1935, in Paris.
Painter, watercolourist, lithographer, draughtsman. Figures, landscapes, seascapes.

In 1880, having left school, Paul Signac contemplated becoming a scholar, his financial independence being assured by his prosperous family. In February 1882, he published a pastiche of Zola's work in the Parisian magazine *Le Chat Noir*, entitled *Une trouvaille* (*Serendipity*), but on seeing reproductions of Monet's work in *La Vie Moderne*, he decided to turn his ambitions to painting. He took lessons with painter Émile Bin in Montmartre, and settled in successive studios in the area. He wrote to Monet, asking his advice, in 1883. In 1884 he met Armand Guillaumin and exhibited work at the Salon des Artistes Indépendants where he was introduced to Georges Seurat, whose *Bathing at Asnières* was a revelation to him. The two artists moved in the same avant-garde literary circles and became close friends. Both were part of the founding committee of the Société des Artistes Indépendants (Signac was it's President from 1909 to 1934 and unceasingly encouraged younger avant-garde artists such as the Fauves and the Cubists). In 1885 Signac met Camille Pissarro at Durand-Ruel's. He met Vincent Van Gogh in 1887 at Père Tanguy's paint shop and the pair remained close friends. He spent summers in various parts of France (Les Andelys and Fécamp in 1886, Comblat-le-Château in Auvergne in 1887, Collioure on the Mediterranean coast, Portrieux in North Brittany in 1888, Cassis in 1889, Italy and Brittany in 1990 and Concarneau in 1891). In 1892 he discovered the little port of St-Tropez where he bought a villa - La Hune - in 1897. He returned there each summer, bringing with him several friends, artists and writers, including Matisse, who worked with Signac and Cross for several months. Signac was constantly searching for new subjects to paint, often travelling to ports such as La Rochelle, Marseilles, Genoa, Rotterdam (1896), Switzerland (1903); Venice (1904 and 1908) and Istanbul (1907). He received the Croix de la Légion d'Honneur in 1911. In 1913, after the birth of his daughter, Ginette, with his mistress Jeanne Selmershein-Desgranges, he separated from his wife and settled in Antibes.

In 1884, Signac discovered the writings of the chemist Michel-Eugène Chevreul, whose pioneering study of colour, *The Law of Simultaneous Contrast (1839)* had been developed by Helmholtz (1878). Signac also read the work of David Sutter, whose articles on the *Phenomena of Sight* were published in 1880 in the review *Art*, and that of Edouard Rood (1881). Signac's views on colour were also influenced by Delacroix, whose *Journal* was published between 1893 and 1895. Signac had a taste for mathematics, and in 1889 worked closely with his friend Charles Henry, a mathematician and physician. Henry was researching mathematical and geometric proportion and their potential application to the industrial arts. Signac was associated with the Symbolists of *La Revue Indépendante*. He was also an admirer of Jules Vallès and Huysmans. He collaborated on the anarchist journal *Le Cri du Peuple* and throughout his life unceasingly expressed his social and political opinions. A competent writer, from 1890 he published various articles on art, provided texts for exhibition catalogues and wrote other publications including a volume on Stendhal (Antibes, December 1913-January 1914) and a monograph on Jongkind (Paris, Crès, 1927) which included a *Traité de l'aquarelle* (*Watercolour treatise*). In 1899 he published *From Delacroix to Neo-Impressionism* (Editions de la Revue blanche, Paris, 1899; H. Floury, Paris, 1911; Hermann, Paris, 1964), in which he analysed the principles of Neo-Impressionism which he had developed with Seurat. He methodically studied the composition and decomposition of light in coloured rays, and quickly established his rôle as the theoretician of the group, which included Henri Edmond Cross, Théo Van Rysselberghe, Maximilien Luce, Henry van de Velde, Hippolyte Petitjean, Lucie Cousturier, Charles Angrand and Albert Dubois-Pillet. Signac illustrated the book, *Cercle Chromatique de M. Charles Henry présentant tous les compléments et toutes les harmonies des couleurs avec une introduciton sur la théorie générale de la dynamogénie, autrement dit du contraste, du rythme et de la mesure* (*Chromatic Circle by M. Charles Henry presenting all colours and colour harmonies with an introduction to the general theory of dynamogeny, otherwise known as contrast, rhythm and measure*) (1888).

Signac painted plein-air paintings with a fiery touch before adopting the pointillist style, based on observation and the direct study of nature as exemplified in Seurat's *Un dimanche à la Grande Jatte* (1886). This so-called Divisionist method, inspired by Michel-Eugène Chevreul's book and developed by Charles Henry, was based on division, colour contrasts and mathematical rhythms. Signac reconciled a naturalist concern for the social reality of the time (*Les Modistes*, 1886) with his own ideological convictions and a new aesthetic inspired by Japanese prints (*Felix Fénéon's portrait*, 1890). A confirmed yachtsman, he applied his new technique to landscapes and seascapes from 1887 to 1895, painting series devoted to the quays of Paris, the port of La Rochelle, and views of St-Raphaël and Antibes. His urge to travel explains the abundance of watercolour in his work, particularly after 1910, and his rapid and exact style. He noted his observations, always searching for the best means of capturing the multiple effects of light and the presence of the sun. Associating his work with musical compositions, until 1893 he designated an opus number to each of his works, sometimes adding musical titles as with the series *La Mer* (1891), allowing visual harmony to coincide with musical and social harmony.

From 1895 to 1897 the pointillist stroke seems to disintegrate and change form in his work, the optical mixing of colours resulting in grey tones; Signac's response is to enlarge the dots with the end of his brush, flattening the brush into a square or rectangle, thus placing brighter colour on the white canvas. In both watercolour and oil, which he used in a very diluted, fluid form, he spread lively and translucent tones on the white of the paper or prepared canvas, leaving the white to appear transparently or at intervals between the strokes of colour. The white has the rôle of giving light and air, and serves as a common link between the many-coloured strokes, thus obtaining an effect of freshness and clarity. The critic Félix Fénéon talked of the 'wild chromatic climbing' of his paintings, and wrote of his art as 'a great decorative development, which sacrifices anecdote to arabesque, nomenclature to synthesis, the fleeting to the permanent...'. Research and experimentation into the recomposition of light and the need to create a particular type of architectural drawing justified working in the studio. Signac applied and adapted a strictly pointillist Divisionism to his own ends. Very small touches of colour, pure and sometimes acid, produced a spectacular brightness. In his second period, he enlarged his colour strokes, making rectangular marks with the brush which structured the form more solidly to the detriment of the optical mix. This Neo-Impressionist technique was highly influential within the many strands of Post-Impressionism and beyond. In 1888, he made his first lithographs for the programme of the Théâtre Libre d'Antoine in Paris. He was also a collector, accumulating around 250 works.

He took part in public exhibitions: in 1884-1895, at the Salon des Artistes Indépendants, Paris; the Salon des Artistes Français, where he exhibited the greater part of his work; in 1885, New York; in 1886 at the 8th and last Impressionist exhibition with Degas, Forain, Gauguin, Pissarro and Seurat; from 1888 at the Salon des Vingt de Bruxelles, a group founded by Octave Maus, of which Signac became a member in 1891; in 1894-1896, Salon de la Libre Esthétique, Brussels; 1901, Galerie Keller et Reiner, Berlin; 1907, Galerie Bernheim-Jeune, Paris; in 1908 at the exhibition of the Zolotoe Runo (Golden Fleece) in Moscow; in 1909-1910 at the Salon Izdebsky at Odessa, Kiev, St Petersburg and Riga; in 1912 at St Petersburg at the Institut Français for the Centennial Exhibition 1812-1912; in 1933 in Paris at the exhibition *Seurat and His Friends*, for which he wrote the catalogue preface. Since his death he has been represented in thematic exhibitions relating to the Post-Impressionist period, including: 1953, *Seurat et ses Amis* (*Seurat and his friends*), Wildenstein Gallery, New York; 1962, *Van Gogh's life in his drawings: Van Gogh's relationship with Signac*, Marlborough Fine Art, London; 1968, *Paul Signac et les Maîtres Suisses du XIXe et XXe siècle*, Galerie Paul Vallotton, Lausanne; 1972, *Seurat and the Neo-Impressionist*, Chuokoron-Sha, Tokyo; 1975, *Paul Signac et ses Amis à Saint-Tropez de 1982 à 1914*, Musée de l'Annonciade, Saint-Tropez; 1994, *Monet to Matisse, Landscape Painting in France, 1874-1914*, National Gallery of Scotland, Edinburgh; 1997, *Signac and the Liberation of Colour, from Matisse to Mondrian*, Musée de Grenoble, Westfälisches Landesmuseum für Kunst und Kulturgeschichte in Münster, Kunstsammlungen in Weimar; 2001, *Signac 1863-1935: Master Neo-Impressionnist*, Grand Palais, Paris, Van Gogh Museum, Amsterdam, Metropolitan Museum of Art, New York.

His works were shown in many individual exhibitions including: 1904, *Paul Signac: Venice, Hollande*, Galerie Druet, Paris; 1923, *Paul Signac: Peintures, Cartons de Tableaux, Dessins, Aquarelles*, Galerie Bernheim-Jeune, Paris; 1950, *Paul Signac: Peintures, aquarelles*, Musée des Beaux-Arts, Mulhouse; 1951, *P. Signac, Musée d'Art moderne*, Paris; 1953, *Watercolors by Paul Signac*, Los Angeles County Museum, Los Angeles; 1954, *Paul Signac, Retrospective Exhibition*, Marlborough Fine Art, London; 1958, *La Création de l'Oeuvre chez Paul Signac*, Marlborough Fine Art, London; 1963, Musée du Louvre, Paris; 1977, *Paul Signac, 1863-1935, Paintings, Watercolors, Drawings and Prints*, Metropolitan Museum of Art, New York; 1986, *Paul Signac: 1863-1935, Watercolours and Drawings*, Marlborough Gallery, London; 1989, Paul Signac: Aquarelles, Musée de Melun; 1992, *Signac et Saint-Tropez*, Musée de l'Annonciade, Saint-Tropez, Musée des Beaux-Arts, Rheims; 2000, *Paul Signac, A Collection of Watercolors and Drawings, 1863-1935*, Arkansas Art Center, Little Rock, and Musée Marmottan, Paris; Fondation Pierre Gianadda, Martigny (Switzerland).

P.Signac 90

P.Signac 96

P.Signac
1897

P.Signac 99

P.Signac

P.S.

BIBLIOGRAPHY:

Herbert, R. L., '*Artist and Anarchism: Unpublished Letters of Pissarro, Signac and Others*' in *Burlington Magazine, cii (1960), pp.473-82, 517-22*. Germain, Alphonse/Christophe, Jules/Fénéon, Félix/Antoine,Jules, in *Peintres novateurs: Chromo-luminaristes*, La Plume, Paris, 1891. Cousturier, Lucie, in *P. Signac*, G. Crès, Paris, 1922. Signac, Paul (preface), *Seurat et ses amis*, exhibition catalogue, La Gazette des beaux-arts, Paris, 1933. Besson, George, in *Paul Signac*, Rombaldi, Paris, 1935. Signac, Paul, '*Fragments de son journal*' in *Gazette des Beaux-Arts*, periodical, Paris, 1949-1953. Besson, Georges, *Signac: dessins*, Braun & Cie, Paris, 1950. Cassou, Jean, *P. Signac*, exhibition catalogue, Musée national d'Art moderne, Paris, 1951. Rewald, John, in *Seurat and his friends*, exhibition catalogue, Wildenstein, New York, 1953. Sandoz, Marc, in *L'Oeuvre de Paul Signac à La Rochelle Croix-de-Vie; Les Sables-d'Olonne de 1911 à 1930*, Soc. de l'histoire de l'art français, Paris, 1956. Sandoz, Marc, in *Le Peintre Paul Signac à la Rochelle et sur les cotes Charentaises et Poitevines*, Marc Texier, Poitiers, 1957. Virault, Simone/Hoog, Michel, in *Le Dessin français de Signac aux abstraits*, Ed. des Musées nationaux, Paris, 1959. Herbert, R. L., in *Les Artistes et l'anarchisme d'après les lettres inédites de Pisaro (sic) Signac et autres*, Les Editions ouvrières, Paris, 1961. Hammacher, A. M., in *Van Gogh's life in his drawings: Van Gogh's relationship with Signac*, exhibition catalogue, Marlborough Fine Art, London, 1962. Lemoyne De Forges, Marie-Thérèse/Bascoul-Gauthier, Pierre, *Signac*, exhibition catalogue, Musée du Louvre, Ministère d'état des Affaires Culturelles, Paris, 1963. Bazin, Germain, in *Signac*, exhibition catalogue, Musée National du Louvre, Paris, 1963. Mura, Anna Maria/Martin, Robert/Pogu, Guy, in *P. Signac*, Hachette, Paris, 1967 (First edition in Italian, Fratelli Fabbri editori, Milan, 1966). Chartrain-Hebbelinck, Marie-Jeanne, in *Les Lettres de Paul Signac à Octave Maus*, Musées royaux des Beaux-Arts de Belgique, Brussels, 1969. Cachin, Françoise, *Paul Signac*, Bibliothèque des Arts, Paris, 1971. Inoue, Yasushi/ Takashina, Shuji, ed., in *Seurat et le néo-impressionnisme*, Chuokoron-Sha, Tokyo, 1972. Kornfeld, Eberhard W./Wick, Peter A., *Catalogue raisonné de l'œuvre gravé et lithographié de Paul Signac*, Kornfeld and Klipstein, Bern, 1974. Signac, Paul, *D'Eugène Delacroix au néo-impressionnisme*, Hermann, Paris, 1974 (First edition 1899, Ed. De la Revue Blanche, Paris). Signac, Ginette, in *Paul Signac et ses amis à Saint-Tropez de 1892 à 1914*, exhibition catalogue, Musée de l'Annonciade, St-Tropez, 1975. Szabo, George (ed.), in *Paul Signac, 1869-1935, paintings, watercolors, drawings and prints: Robert Lehman collection, drawings galleries*, exhibition catalogue, Metropolitan Museum of art, New York, 1977. *Post-Impressionism: Cross-currents in European Painting*, exhibition catalogue, Royal Academy, London, 1979-1980. Bosman, Suzanne, in *Paul Signac: 1863-1935: watercolours and drawings*, exhibition catalogue, Malborough Fine Art, London, 1986. Malpel, Jean (introduction)/Lussiez, Claire/Gelinet, Anette, in *Paul Signac: Aquarelles*, exhibition catalogue, Musée de Melun, Melun, 1989. Monery, Jean-Paul/Ferretti-Bocquillon, Marina/Cachin, Françoise, *Signac et Saint-Tropez, 1892-1913*, exhibition catalogue, Musée Annonciade, St-Tropez, 1992. Ratcliff, Floyd, *Paul Signac and Color in Neo-Impressionism*, Rockerfeller University Press, New York, 1992 (including the first English ed. of 'From Eugène Delacroix to Neo-Impressionism' by Paul Signac, translated by Willa Silverman). Erich, Franz, *Signac et la Libération de la couleur, de Matisse à Mondrian*, exhibition catalogue, Musée de Grenoble, Réunion des musées nationaux, Paris, 1997. Clement, Russell T./Houzé, Annick, in *Neo-impressionist painters: a sourcebook*, Greenwood Press, Westport (CT), London, 1999. *Paul Signac: A Collection of Watercolors and Drawings, 1863-1935*, H. N. Abrams in association with th Arkansas Arts Center, New York, 2000. Ferretti Bocquillon, Marina/Cachin, Charles, in *Paul Signac: dessins et aquarelles*, exhibition catalogue, Ed. de La Martinière, Paris, 2000 (exhibition at Arkansas Arts Center, Little Rock, and Musée Marmottan, Paris). Cachin, Françoise/Ferretti-Bocquillon, Marina, in *Signac: catalogue raisonné de l'oeuvre peint*, catalogue raisonné, Gallimard, Paris, 2000. Ferretti-Bocquillon, Marina, *Signac aquarelliste*, Adam Biro, Paris, 2001. *Paul Signac: Travels in France - Drawings and watercolours from the Arkansas Art Center*, Courtauld Institute Gallery, London, 2001. Faure, Mickaël, et al., '*Signac*' in *Beaux Arts, special issue*, periodical, Paris, 2001 (published for the exhibition 'Signac 1863-1935', Galeries nationales du Grand Palais, 2001). Distel, Anne/Leighton, John/ Stein, Susan Alyson, *Signac, 1863-1935*, exhibition catalogue, Réunion des Museés Nationaux, Paris, 2001 (exhibition at Galeries Nationales du Grand Palais, Paris). Ferretti-Bocquillon, Marina/Cachin, Françoise, in *Signac aquarelliste*, Adam Biro, Paris, 2001. Distel, Anne, in *Signac: au temps d'harmonie*, Gallimard, Réunion des musées nationaux, Paris, 2001. Faton-Boyancé, Jeanne/Distel, Anne/Ferretti-Bocquillon, Marina, '*Signac au Grand Palais*' in *L'Estampille/ L'Objet d'art (Les Dossiers de l'art), special issue*, periodical, Editions Faton, Dijon, March 2001 (published for the exhibition 'Signac 1863-1935', Galeries nationales du Grand Palais, Paris, 2001). Cachin, Françoise/Ferretti-Bocquillon, Marina, in *P. Signac*, exhibition catalogue, Fondation Pierre Gianadda, Martigny, 2003.

MUSEUMS AND GALLERIES:

AMSTERDAM (Van Gogh Mus.): *Railwayjunction near Bois-Colombes* (1885, oil on canvas); *Harbour of Saint-Tropez* (1895, lithograph) - BERGAMO (Accademia Carrara): *The sea.*

Saint-Briac. The Guérin Guard. Saint-Lunaire. Opus 211 (1890, oil on canvas) - BERLIN (Nationalgal.) - BESANÇON (MBA et d'Archéologie): *The Chevet of Notre-Dame* (1925, pencil and watercolour) - BOSTON (MFA): *Port of Saint-Cast* (1890, oil on canvas); *Boats* (1897-98, color lithograph on cream wove paper); *In the Nederlands* (etching); *Sails in Saint-Tropez* (etching); *Bell in St. Topez with Figures* (etching); *Clocher de St. Tropez* (etching); *Flood in Paris* (1922, lithograph) - BRUSSELS (Mus. royaux des Beaux-Arts de Belgique): *Saint-Tropez. The Inlet* (1906, oil on canvas) - BUCHAREST (Muz. National de Arta al României): *Saint-Tropez. The Portrait* (1896, oil on canvas) - CLEVELAND (MA): *Harmonious Times* (1895-96); *Saint-Tropez: The Port* (1897-98); *Evening, The Jetty at Vlissingen* (1898); *Paris, the Pont des Arts with tug-boats* (1927); *Ships near the Trieux River* (1925) - DENAIN (Musée municipal): *The Demolishers* (1897-99) - ESSEN (Folkwang Mus.): *Paris, la Cité* (1912); *The Seine et St-Cloud* (oil on canvas); *Pink Tower (Entry to the Port of Marseilles)* (1913) - GRENOBLE (Mus. de Grenoble): *The Customs Path* (1905); *Saint-Tropez. Sunset on the city. Study* (c. 1896, oil on canvas) - HANOVER (Niedersächsisches): *Venice, Mist* (1908, oil on canvas) - HOUSTON (MFA): *The Bonaventure Pine* (1893, oil on canvas) - LONDON (Courtauld Institute of Art): *St Tropez* (c. 1893, oil and graphite/panel); *Still-life with a Watermelon* (1918, Graphite, watercolour on paper) - LOS ANGELES (County MA): *Saint-Tropez: Evening Sun* (1894, watercolor over traces of graphite); *Lézardrieux: the Coast* (1924, watercolor and pencil) - LYONS (MBA) - MADRID (Museo Thyssen Bornemisza): *Paimpol* (watercolour and pencil); *Port-en-Bessin, The Beach* (oil on canvas) - MARSEILLES (Mus. Cantini): *Entry to the Port of Marseilles* (1918) - MELBOURNE (Nat. Gal. of Victoria): *Gasometers at Clichy* (1886) - MINNEAPOLIS (IA): *Blessing of the Tuna Fleet at Groix* (1923, oil on canvas); *Snow, Boulevard de Clichy, Paris* (1886, oil on canvas); *On The Bank of the River* (watercolor and black chalk on white wove paper); *Le Pont Neuf* (charcoal); *Fishing Boats in La Rochelle* (c. 1919-1921, graphite, watercolor, and opaque white); *Port-en-Bessin* (1888, oil on canvas) - MONTREUIL (Town Hall): *Time of Harmony: The Golden Age is not in the Past it is in the Future* (oil on canvas) - MUNICH (Staatsgemäldesammlungen of Bavaria): *The Seine River in Samois. Etude I, II, III, IV* (1899, oil on canvas, four studies); *River Seine Landscape in Samois* (1899, oil on canvas) - NANCY (MBA): *The demolisher* (1897-99, oil on canvas) - NANTES (MBA) - NEW YORK (Metropolitan Mus. of Art): *Concarneau. Evening stillness. Opus 220 (allegro maestoso)* (1891, oil on canvas); *The Jetty at Cassis* (1889, oil on canvas); *View of the Port of Marseilles* (1905, oil on canvas); *Lighthouse at Groix* (oil on canvas) - NEW YORK (MoMA): *Concarneau, Evening Calm, Opus 220* (1891, oil on canvas); *Setting Sun. Sardine Fishing, Adagio, Opus 221* (1891, oil on canvas); *Port of Saint-Tropez* - OTTERLO (Kröller-Müller Mus.): *Mantes* (1900, oil on canvas); *Port of Collioure* (1887); *Rotterdam. Le moulin. Le canal le matin* (*Rotterdam. The mill. The canal in the morning*) (1906, oil on canvas); *Portrieux* (1888); *The two Cypresses. Opus 241 (mistral)* (1893, oil on canvas) - PARIS (Louvre): *Sketch for Au Temps d'Harmonie* (c. 1893, pink and black wash drawing); *Red sail on the sea* (1906, watercolour); *The Storm* (1895); *Sunset on the Maures* (c. 1905, watercolour) - PARIS (Louvre, Drawings Collection): *Bridge at Asnieres* (watercolour); *Biarritz, the Lighthouse* (1906, pencil and watercolour); *Boats on the Corne d'Or* (1907, pencil and watercolour); *La Salute, Venice* (1914, pencil and watercolour) - PARIS (MNAM-CCI): *Entry to the Port of Marseilles* (1911) - PARIS (Mus. d'Orsay): *Les Andelys, the Bank* (1886, oil on canvas); *River Banks, The River Seine at Herblay* (1889, oil on canvas); *Red Lifebelt* (1895); *The Palace of Popes* (1909, oil on canvas); *Bayonne* (drawing); *Landscapes and Studies* (five); *Portrait of Eric Satie*; *Woman near a Lamp* (1890, oil on wood); *Woman with a Sunshade* (1893, oil on canvas); *Young Provençales near a Well* (*Women near a Well*) (1892, oil on wood, decoration for a panel in half-light); *The Yellow Sail, Venice* (1904, oil on canvas) - PARIS (Musée Marmottan Monet): *Venice* (1908, watercolour) - PITTSBURGH (Museum of Fine Arts Carnegie Institute): *Plane Trees. Opus 242 (place des Lices, Saint-Tropez)* (1893, oil on canvas) - ROTTERDAM (Mus. Boijmans Van Beuningen): *The Meuse at Rotterdam* (1907) - SAN FRANCISCO (FAM): seven works - ST PETERSBURG (Hermitage): *The Harbour at Marseilles* (c. 19061907, oil on canvas); *Square of the Hotel de Ville in Aix-en-Provence* (pencil, watercolour, gouache and white); *Sailboat at a Pier* (c. 1920, pencil, watercolour and gouache on laid paper); *Sailing Ships* (1895, colour lithograph); *Banks of the Seine* (c. 1900, lithographic crayon, watercolour and gouache); *The Large Pine, Saint-Tropez* (c. 1892-93, oil on panel) - ST-TROPEZ (Mus. de l'Annonciade): *Port at St-Tropez* (1894); *Le Pouliguen* (1928, watercolour); *Ornemental pond of Cézanne's house in Jas de Bouffan* (1920, pencil and watercolour); *Sisteron* (1930, pencil and aquarelle); *Bourg-Saint-Andéol* (1930, pencil and watercolour); *View of St-Tropez, Sunset over the Pine Wood* (1896); *St-Tropez, Parasol Pines and Carob Trees* (1897); *Saint-Tropez. Sunset with pinewood* (1896, oil on canvas); *St-Tropez, the Quay* (1899); *The Coastal Path* (c. 1901, watercolour); *Saint-Tropez. The Storm* (1895, oil on canvas) - STUTTGART (Staatsgal.): *The Seine River in Samois. Morning* (1900, oil on canvas on card) - THE HAGUE (Gemeentemus.): *Lunch* (1887); *Cassis* (1889); *Cape Lombardy* (1889) - TOLEDO (MA): *Canal Grande (Venice)* (1905, oil on canvas) - WASHINGTON DC (NGA): *La Rochelle* (c. 1930, watercolor over black chalk on laid paper); *Pont Neuf, Paris* (watercolor over black chalk on laid paper); *Sailboats near a Lighthouse* (pen and brown ink with brown wash over graphite on laid paper); twelve prints - WASHINGTON DC (Smithsonian American AM): *Landscape* (1915, watercolour) - WORCESTER (AM): *Golfe Juan* (1896, oil on canvas) - WUPPERTAL (Von der Heydt Mus.): *Port of St-Tropez* (1893); *Tartans with Flags. Opus 240* (1893, oil on canvas).

AUCTION RECORDS:

PARIS, 9 May 1895, *Seascape* (watercolour) FRF 26. PARIS, 18-19 May 1903, *St-Tropez, Festive Port,* FRF 100. PARIS, 24 Feb 1919, *Venice* (watercolour) FRF 550. PARIS, 28 March 1919, *Mont St-Michel,* FRF 1,050. PARIS, 7 April 1924, *Yellow Sail,* FRF 5,500. PARIS, 18 June 1925, *Portrieux* (watercolour) FRF 1,100. PARIS, 2 June 1926, *Rotterdam* (charcoal) FRF 4,000; *Cliff at Fecamp,* FRF 3,200; *Port at Rotterdam,* FRF 10,500. PARIS, 14 Feb 1927, *Near St-Malo,* FRF 25,100; *Notre-Dame-de-la-Garde at Marseilles,* FRF 18,500. PARIS, 3 Dec 1928, *Bains sur la Seine* FRF 54,000. PARIS, 8 Dec 1928, *Towpath,* FRF 53,000. PARIS, 28 May 1930, *Tulips in Yellow Vase,* FRF 7,550; *Les Andelys,* FRF 40,000. NEW YORK, 18 Jan 1935, *Shore,* USD 650. PARIS, 24 June 1938, *Bridge at Donzere* (watercolour) FRF 1,000. PARIS, 5 Dec 1940, *Bathing in the Seine* (1886) FRF 20,000; *La Rochelle, Boat on the Quay* (1926, watercolour) FRF 2,700. PARIS, 24 Nov 1941, *St-Lunaire* (1885) FRF 45,000. PARIS, 4 Dec 1941, *Le Petit Andely,* FRF 55,000; *Bragozzo, Venice* (1905) FRF 40,000; *Coast, Port-en-Bessin,* FRF 50,000. PARIS, 6 May 1943, *Le Pont des Arts* (*Le Pont des Arts,* FRF 100,000. PARIS, 22 Oct 1943, *Les Andelys* (1887) FRF 81,000. PARIS, 15 Dec 1943, *La Rochelle, Green Tower* (1913) FRF 151,000. NEW YORK, 22 Nov 1944, *Sunset,* USD 1,200. PARIS, 19 March 1945, *Banks of the Seine in Autumn,* FRF 90,500. PARIS, 30 April 1947, *Flushing* (1896, watercolour) FRF 11,000; *Crane at Pont Royal* (1925, charcoal, heightened with watercolour) FRF 35,000. PARIS, 30 May 1947, *Place des Lices at St-Tropez,* FRF 15,000; *Seine at Herblay* (1889) FRF 19,000; *Venetian Boats* (1904, watercolour) FRF 40,000; *Quai Voltaire in Spring* (1923, watercolour) FRF 60,000. PARIS, 24 Feb 1949, *Venice* (1904, watercolour) FRF 21,000. PARIS, 22 June 1949, *Samois, Tugboat* (1901) FRF 221,000; *Le Pont des Arts* (watercolour) FRF 36,100. PARIS, 4 July 1949, *Beach,* FRF 114,000.

STUTTGART, 25 Nov 1949, *Venice* (watercolour and pencil) DEM 1,050. PARIS, 24 Feb 1950, *Tugboats at Rotterdam* (1906) FRF 220,000; *Le Pont des Arts* (1910, watercolour) FRF 37,000. GENEVA, 6 May 1950, *Notre-Dame de Paris* (watercolour) CHF 1,100. PARIS, 26 May 1950, *Bridge, Bourg-St-Andeol* (1926) FRF 346,000. PARIS, 25 Oct 1950, *Collioure,* FRF 410,000. BRUSSELS, 24 Feb 1951, *Notre-Dame de Paris from Pont-Neuf* (1913) BEF 60,000. PARIS, 9 May 1952, *La Bonne-Mere, Marseilles,* FRF 1,600,000. PARIS, 16 May 1955, *Garden of Villa,* FRF 250,000. NEW YORK, 7 Nov 1957, *Beach at St-Brieuc,* USD 31,000. PARIS, 21 March 1958, *River Banks,* FRF 4,910,000. LONDON, 3 Dec 1958, *Green Ray,* GBP 6,200. PARIS, 1 Dec 1959, *Marseilles,* FRF 11,500,000. PARIS, 10 Dec 1959, *Bridge at Grenelle* (1903, oil on canvas/card) FRF 6,200,000. NEW YORK, 16 March 1960, *St-Tropez,* USD 6,500. PARIS, 23 June 1960, *Les Andelys,* FRF 102,000. GENEVA, 19 April 1961, *Landscape* (watercolour) CHF 11,400. LONDON, 28 June 1961, *Sailing Boat,* GBP 9,800. NEW YORK, 30 Oct 1963, *Garden at St-Tropez,* USD 43,000. NEW YORK, 20 Nov 1968, *Portrait of Félix Fénéon on Enamel,* USD 110,000. GENEVA, 7 Nov 1969, *Marseilles,* CHF 390,000. GENEVA, 8 Dec 1970, *La Corne d'Or* CHF 515,000. LONDON, 28 June 1972, *Seine at Herblay, the Colour of the Sun,* GBP 50,000. GENEVA, 29 June 1973, *Port,* CHF 260,000. LONDON, 2 Dec 1974, *Cassis, Cape Canaille* (1889) Gns 69,000. NEW YORK, 17 March 1976, *Brig at Marseilles* (1911, oil on canvas, 32 x 25 3/4 ins / 81.5 x 65.4 cm) FRF 160,000. LONDON, 30 June 1976, *Port of Lezardieux* (watercolour and pencil, 10 3/4 x 17 ins / 27.5 x 43 cm) GBP 3,600. PARIS, 6 Oct 1976, *Les Andelys* (1895, lithograph) FRF 21,500. VERSAILLES, 8 June 1977, *Audierne, Sailing Boats in the Port* (1927, watercolour, 12 x 17 1/4 ins / 30.5 x 43.5 cm) FRF 26,500. LONDON, 27 June 1977, *Concarneau, Morning Calm - Larghetto* (1891, oil on canvas, 25 1/2 x 32 ins / 65 x 81 cm) GBP 105,000. LONDON, 5 April 1978, *Bridge at Lezardrieux* (1925, oil on canvas, 28 3/4 x 36 1/4 ins / 73 x 92 cm) GBP 44,000. NEW YORK, 18 May 1978, *Notre-Dame de Paris* (1910, pencil and watercolour, 11 x 16 1/2 ins / 27 x 42 cm) USD 5,750. NEW YORK, 6 Nov 1979, *Bell-Tower at St-Tropez* (1896, oil on canvas, 32 x 25 1/2 ins / 81 x 65 cm) USD 135,000. LONDON, 26 Nov 1979, *St-Tropez, Port* (1897-1898, lithograph, 17 x 13 ins / 43 x 33 cm) GBP 4,000. HANOVER, 7 June 1980, *La Rochelle* (watercolour and charcoal, 11 x 16 1/2 ins / 28 x 42 cm) DEM 30,000. NEW YORK, 22 Oct 1980, *Port of Constantinople* (ink and wash/brown paper, 31 1/4 x 44 3/4 ins / 79.3 x 113.5 cm) USD 13,000. NEW YORK, 14 Nov 1980, *Les Andelys* (1895, coloured lithograph, 12 x 18 ins / 30.2 x 45.7 cm) USD 14,000. PARIS, 10 Dec 1980, *La Fontaine des Lices at St-Tropez* (1896, oil on canvas, 32 x 25 1/2 ins / 81 x 65 cm) FRF 380,000. NEW YORK, 20 Feb 1981, *Les Andelys* (1895, coloured lithograph, 12 x 18 ins / 30.2 x 45.7 cm) USD 14,000. ENGHIEN-LES-BAINS, 14 June 1981, *Sailing Boats and Fishermen at the Entrance to the Port* (charcoal and watercolour, 4 1/4 x 6 1/2 ins / 10.5 x 16.5 cm) FRF 10,000. LONDON, 2 Dec 1981, *Collioure: les balancelles* (1887, oil on canvas, 18 x 23 1/4 ins / 46 x 59 cm) GBP 178,000. BERN, 25 June 1982, *Bridge on the Rhone* (c. 1910, bistre ink on charcoal outline, 11 x 18 1/4 ins / 28 x 46.4 cm) CHF 22,000; *View of Venice* (1904, watercolour on pencil outlines, 6 3/4 x 9 3/4 ins / 17.2 x 24.8 cm) CHF 25,500. PARIS, 6 Dec 1982, *View of Flessingue* (1896, oil on canvas, 16 1/2 x 22 ins / 42 x 55 cm) FRF 480,000. NEW YORK, 19 May 1983, *Bridge at Constantinople* (pen and wash, 31 1/4 x 44 3/4 ins / 79.3 x 113.5 cm) USD 17,000. HAMBURG, 10 June 1983, *St-Tropez, the Port* (1897-1898, coloured lithograph) DEM 18,000. BERN, 23 June 1983, *Le Pont des Arts in Paris* (1910, watercolour/pencil outlines, 8 1/4 x 10 3/4 ins / 21 x 27.5 cm) CHF 11,000. NEW YORK, 15 Nov 1983, *Port of Portrieux* (1888, oil on canvas, 18 x 22 ins / 46 x 55 cm) USD 360,000. NEW YORK, 2 May 1984, *Lifebelt* (1894, colour lithograph, 16 x 12 3/4 ins / 40.4 x 32.7 cm) USD 17,000. HAMBURG, 9 June 1984, *Footbridge of Billy* (1903, canvas remounted on board, 10 1/2 x 14 ins / 26.7 x 35.5 cm) DEM 90,000. PARIS, 29 Nov 1984, *La Rochelle* (watercolour, 11 1/2 x 17 1/4 ins / 29 x 44 cm) FRF 160,000. PARIS, 4 March 1985, *Application of the Chromatic Circle of M. Ch. Henry* (1888, colour lithograph, programme for the 'Le Théâtre Libre') FRF 1,800. LONDON, 25 June 1985, *Square du Vert-Galant and Pont-Neuf* (watercolour on pencil outlines, 10 3/4 x 17 1/4 ins / 27.5 x 44 cm) GBP 28,000. NEW YORK, 14 Nov 1985, *Port Scene, Antibes* (Indian ink and wash, 31 3/4 x 48 ins / 80.6 x 121.8 cm) USD 21,000. LONDON, 3 Dec 1985, *Brise, Concarneau, Presto* (1891, oil on canvas, 25 1/2 x 32 1/4 ins / 65 x 82 cm) GBP 660,000. CALAIS, 8 Nov 1987, *Sailing Boats at Martigues* (1930, watercolour, 4 1/4 x 6 3/4 ins / 10.5 x 17 cm) FRF 47,500. PARIS, 11 Dec 1987, *St-Beat, Haute Garonne* (brown Indian ink wash, 4 x 5 1/4 ins / 10 x 13.5 cm) FRF 8,500. NEW YORK, 18 Feb 1988, *Neuville-sur-Saone* (watercolour and charcoal, 11 x 17 ins / 27 x 43 cm) USD 19,800. FONTAINEBLEAU, 21 Feb 1988, *Study for Au temps d'harmonie* (oil on panel, double-sided, 14 x 10 1/4 ins / 34.7 x 26.3 cm) FRF 150,000. LONDON, 24 Feb 1988, *Boats in Port* (watercolour and charcoal, 7 1/4 x 9 1/2 ins / 18.5 x 24.4 cm) GBP 9,900. CALAIS, 28 Feb 1988, *Seine at Asnieres* (oil on canvas, 9 1/2 x 12 1/2 ins / 24 x 32 cm) FRF 150,000. PARIS, 21 March 1988, *St-Tropez* (1918, watercolour and gouache, 17 x 13 ins / 43 x 33 cm) FRF 220,000. LONDON, 30 March 1988, *Port at La Rochelle* (1927, watercolour/charcoal, 11 x 17 1/4 ins / 28 x 43.5 cm) GBP 20,900. NEW YORK, 12 May 1988, *Port* (1927, watercolour and charcoal/paper mounted/card, 12 x 16 ins / 30.4 x 40.6 cm) USD 33,000. LOS ANGELES, 9 June 1988, *Croix-de-Vie* (watercolour and charcoal, 11 x 16 1/4 ins / 28 x 41 cm) USD 16,500. L'ISLE-ADAM, 11 June 1988, *Barges and Boats on the Seine* (wash, 17 3/4 x 25 1/2 ins / 45 x 65 cm) FRF 100,000. PARIS, 12 June 1988, *Vaison* (1933, watercolour, 11 1/2 x 17 1/4 ins / 29 x 44 cm) FRF 120,000; *Sailing Boats on the Quay* (watercolour, 9 1/4 x 12 1/2 ins / 23.5 x 31.5 cm) FRF 120,000; *Port of La Rochelle* (1920, watercolour and pencil drawing, 10 3/4 x 15 1/2 ins / 27.5 x 39.5 cm) FRF 130,000. PARIS, 22 June 1988, *St Malo* (1927, watercolour, 12 1/2 x 17 3/4 ins / 31.5 x 45.2 cm) FRF 155,000. LONDON, 28 June 1988, *St-Tropez* (oil/panel, 7 1/2 x 10 1/4 ins / 19 x 26.2 cm) GBP 28,600. PARIS, 29 June 1988, *Asnieres* (1900, watercolour, 6 3/4 x 9 1/2 ins / 17 x 24 cm) FRF 220,000. CALAIS, 3 July 1988, *Seine at Asnieres* (oil on canvas, 9 1/2 x 12 1/2 ins / 24 x 32 cm) FRF 160,000. VERSAILLES, 23 Oct 1988, *Sailing Boats at Volendam* (1896, watercolour, 8 x 10 1/2 ins / 20.5 x 26.5 cm) FRF 66,000. VERSAILLES, 6 Nov 1988, *Boats and Sailing Ship at Quilleboeuf* (1930, watercolour, 3 3/4 x 6 3/4 ins / 9.5 x 17 cm) FRF 24,000. CALAIS, 13 Nov 1988, *Juan-les-Pins* (1914, sepia and gouache, 11 3/4 x 17 3/4 ins / 30 x 45 cm) FRF 75,000. PARIS, 20 Nov 1988, *Barfleur* (1930, watercolour, 11 x 17 ins / 28 x 43 cm) FRF 120,000. PARIS, 21 Nov 1988, *Port of Marseilles* (1903, oil/card, 10 1/2 x 14 ins / 26.5 x 35.5 cm) FRF 920,000. LONDON, 29 Nov 1988, *Bridge of Suresnes* (1883, oil on canvas, 18 x 24 ins / 46 x 61 cm) GBP 198,000.. NEW YORK, 16 Feb 1989, *Port-Louis* (watercolour and chalk/paper/card, 17 x 10 1/4 ins / 43.1 x 26 cm) USD 28,600. CALAIS, 26 Feb 1989, *Port of St Tropez* (sepia, 12 1/2 x 17 ins / 32 x 43 cm) FRF 84,000. LONDON, 3 April 1989, *Bragozzo at Venice* (1905, oil on canvas, 18 1/2 x 22 ins / 47 x 55.6 cm) GBP 770,000. MONACO, 3 May 1989, *Squadron at Golfe-Juan* (watercolour and pencil/paper, 3 3/4 x 7 1/2 ins / 9.5 x 19 cm) FRF 46,620. NEW YORK, 9 May 1989, *Antibes* (1902, oil on canvas, 36 1/2 x 29 1/4 ins / 93 x 74 cm) USD 1,100,000. NEW YORK, 10 May 1989, *Fontaine des Lices at St-Tropez* (1895, oil on canvas, 26 x 32 1/4 ins / 65.8 x 82 cm) USD 1,430,000. LONDON, 26 June 1989, *Quays and Lighthouse at St-Tropez* (1898, oil on canvas, 18 1/2 x 22 ins / 46.8 x 55 cm) GBP 990,000. NEW YORK, 14 Nov 1989, *Sardine Fishing Boat and the Old Town, Concarneau* (1891, oil on canvas, 18 1/2 x 22 ins / 47 x 55.6 cm) USD 2,750,000. PARIS, 20 Nov 1989, *Place des Lices St-Tropez* (1885, oil/panel, 11 x 7 1/2 ins / 27 x 19 cm) FRF 300,000. PARIS, 24 Nov 1989, *Boats at Treguier* (watercolour and graphite, 11 x 18 ins / 28 x 46 cm) FRF 160,000. LONDON, 28 Nov 1989, *Pont des Arts* (1925, oil on canvas, 35 x 46 ins / 89 x 116 cm) GBP 1,595,000. NEW YORK, 26 Feb 1990, *Pont des*

Arts (watercolour and charcoal/paper, 11 1/2 x 17 1/4 ins / 29 x 44 cm) USD 26,400. PARIS, 20 March 1990, *Marseilles* (1907, watercolour and gouache, 11 x 15 1/4 ins / 27 x 39 cm) FRF 250,000. PARIS, 1 April 1990, *Schooner in the Port St-Tropez* (1991, watercolour and graphite, 17 x 13 ins / 43 x 33 cm) FRF 260,000. LONDON, 3 April 1990, *Bank of the Seine at Samois, Morning* (1901, oil on canvas, 25 1/2 x 32 ins / 65 x 81 cm) GBP 715,000. NEW YORK, 16 May 1990, *Still-life with Fruits* (1926, watercolour and charcoal/paper, 12 1/2 x 17 1/4 ins / 31.7 x 43.8 cm) USD 52,800; *Viaduct at Auteuil* (1900, oil on canvas, 18 1/4 x 21 ins / 46.3 x 52.4 cm) USD 506,000. LONDON, 25 June 1990, *La Salute, Venice* (1908, oil on canvas, 28 3/4 x 36 ins / 73 x 91.5 cm) GBP 1,540,000; *Antibes, Pink Cloud* (1916, oil on canvas, 28 3/4 x 36 1/4 ins / 73 x 92 cm) GBP 1,155,000. NEW YORK, 15 Feb 1991, *St-Paul* (watercolour and charcoal/paper, 11 3/4 x 17 1/4 ins / 30 x 44 cm) USD 22,000. PARIS, 25 May 1991, *Tuna Boat Entering Port of La Rochelle at Sunset* (1927, oil on canvas, 28 3/4 x 36 1/4 ins / 73 x 92 cm) FRF 3,000,000. LONDON, 16 Oct 1991, *Montelimar, Little Square* (watercolour and pencil, 5 x 7 3/4 ins / 11.8 x 20 cm) GBP 4,950. NEW YORK, 6 Nov 1991, *Channel at La Rochelle* (1927, oil on canvas, 18 x 22 ins / 46 x 55 cm) USD 275,000. LONDON, 2 Dec 1991, *Port at Constantinople* (1907, oil on canvas, 16 1/4 x 13 ins / 41 x 33 cm) GBP 176,000. PARIS, 2 Dec 1991, *La Rochelle, Lighthouse* (watercolour, 11 x 17 1/4 ins / 28 x 44 cm) FRF 100,000. LONDON, 24 March 1992, *Market at Antibes* (1919, watercolour and pencil/card, 11 1/2 x 16 1/2 ins / 29.5 x 41.8 cm) GBP 23,100. NEW YORK, 12 May 1992, *Antibes, Pink Cloud* (1916, oil on canvas, 28 3/4 x 36 1/4 ins / 73 x 92 cm) USD 660,000. PARIS, 3 June 1992, *La Rochelle* (watercolour, 9 1/2 x 15 1/4 ins / 24 x 39 cm) FRF 136,000. NEW YORK, 5 Oct 1992, *Le Puy* (1912, watercolour, gouache and charcoal/paper, 10 x 15 3/4 ins / 25.7 x 40 cm) USD 17,600. LE TOUQUET, 8 Nov 1992, *Sailing Boat in the Bay* (1904, watercolour, 6 x 9 3/4 ins / 15 x 25 cm) FRF 30,000. PARIS, 25 Nov 1992, *Rotterdam, Smoke* (1906, oil on canvas, 28 1/4 x 36 1/2 ins / 72 x 93 cm) FRF 2,000,000. MUNICH, 1-2 Dec 1992, *Port of La Rochelle* (watercolour and black chalk, 8 x 10 3/4 ins / 20.5 x 27.5 cm) DEM 16,330. NEW YORK, 11 May 1993, *St-Tropez, Port at Sunset* (1892, oil on canvas, 25 3/4 x 32 ins / 65.4 x 81 cm) USD 1,817,500. PARIS, 11 June 1993, *At Flessingue* (1895, lithograph, 9 1/4 x 16 ins / 23.7 x 40.5 cm) FRF 60,000. PARIS, 21 June 1993, *Les Andelys, côte d'aval* (1886, oil on canvas, 23 1/2 x 36 1/4 ins / 60 x 92 cm) FRF 11,100,000. LONDON, 13 Oct 1993, *Church at Penmarch* (watercolour and pencil/paper/card, 10 x 15 ins / 25.4 x 37.8 cm) GBP 6,900. LONDON, 30 Nov 1993, *La Passerelle de Billy* (1903, oil on canvas, 10 1/2 x 14 ins / 26.6 x 35.6 cm) GBP 40,000. NEW YORK, 10 May 1994, *La Maison verte à Venise* (*Green House in Venice*) (1905, oil on canvas, 18 x 21 3/4 ins / 46 x 55.2 cm) USD 530,500. PARIS, 13 June 1994, *La Rochelle, Lighthouse* (1927, oil on canvas, 18 x 22 ins / 46 x 55 cm) FRF 1,490,000. PARIS, 22 June 1994, *Notre-Dame and Ile St-Louis in Sunlight Seen from Quay de la Tournelle* (1884, oil on canvas, 19 3/4 x 31 1/4 ins / 50.3 x 79.3 cm) FRF 3,500,000. PARIS, 27 June 1994, *Marseilles, Old Port and St John's Tower* (1898, oil on canvas, 25 1/2 x 32 ins / 65 x 81 cm) FRF 3,600,000. BOULOGNE-SUR-SEINE, 27 Nov 1994, *Port-Louis* (1922, watercolour, 9 1/2 x 13 3/4 ins / 24 x 35 cm) FRF 81,000. PARIS, 19 Dec 1994, *St-Tropez, le cabanon* (1904, oil on canvas, 25 1/2 x 32 ins / 65 x 81 cm) FRF 2,200,000. PARIS, 13 June 1995, *St-Tropez after the Storm* (1895, oil on canvas, 25 1/2 x 32 ins / 65 x 81 cm) FRF 2,500,000. LONDON, 25 Oct 1995, *Yacht on the Quay* (watercolour and pencil, 8 x 10 ins / 20.5 x 25.5 cm) GBP 12,650. NEW YORK, 8 Nov 1995, *Juan-les-Pins* (1914, oil on canvas, 28 3/4 x 36 1/4 ins / 73 x 92.1 cm) USD 442,500. MAISONS-LAFFITTE, 22 Feb 1996, *Pont des Arts* (watercolour, 9 x 13 1/2 ins / 23 x 34 cm) FRF 52,000. AMSTERDAM, 5 June 1996, *Quimper* (1927, pencil and watercolour/paper, 11 x 18 ins / 28 x 45.5 cm) NLG 43,700. PARIS, 19 June 1996, *Barge at Bank of Cana* (watercolour and pencil/paper, 5 1/2 x 4 1/2 ins / 14 x 11.3 cm) FRF 18,000. LONDON, 2 Dec 1996, *Pont-Royal Autumn* (1930, oil on canvas, 28 3/4 x 36 ins / 73 x 91.5 cm) GBP 353,500. LONDON, 3 Dec 1996, *Regatta* (watercolour and black chalk/paper, 10 1/2 x 16 1/2 ins / 26.5 x 41.8 cm) GBP 21,850. LONDON, 4 Dec 1996, *Boats in Port* (1927, pencil and watercolour/paper, 12 1/4 x 17 3/4 ins / 31 x 45 cm) GBP 12,075. PARIS, 8 Dec 1996, *Sailing Boats in Port* (watercolour and pencil/paper/card, 9 x 11 ins / 22 x 28 cm) FRF 60,000. PARIS, 9 Dec 1996, *Les Andelys, Tugboat on the Seine* (c. 1920, watercolour and pencil/paper, 9 3/4 x 15 3/4 ins / 25 x 40 cm) FRF 105,000. AMSTERDAM, 10 Dec 1996, *Antibes* (1919, lead pencil and watercolour/paper, 10 1/4 x 15 3/4 ins / 26 x 40 cm) NLG 28,830. PARIS, 12 Dec 1996, *Market Scene near Church* (bistre ink wash heightened with charcoal, 11 x 14 1/2 ins / 27 x 37 cm) FRF 18,000. PARIS, 24 March 1997, *Landscape in Brittany, Fishing Boat in Deep Estuary* (watercolour and pencil/paper, 9 x 11 ins / 22 x 28 cm) FRF 62,000. LONDON, 22 Oct 1997, *La Turballe* (22 août 1930, watercolour and pencil/paper) GBP 23,000. PARIS, 24 March 1998, *Avignon, Morning* (1909, oil on canvas, 28 3/4 x 36 1/4 ins / 73 x 92 cm) FRF 2,550,000. PARIS, 8 April 1998, *La Chaîne dans le brouillard* (1900, watercolour, 7 1/2 x 6 3/4 ins / 19 x 17 cm) FRF 25,000. NEW YORK, 11 May 1999, *Clipper, Asnieres* (1887, oil on canvas, 21 x 21 ins / 54 x 54 cm) USD 1,800,000. LONDON, 29 June 1999, *Pont Neuf* (1913, oil on canvas, 35 x 46 ins / 89 x 117 cm) GBP 900,000. NEW YORK, 9 May 2000, *St Tropez, Pines and Sails* (gouache and pencil on silk on board, 11 x 24 ins / 27 x 61 cm) USD 115,000. NEW YORK, 10 May 2000, *Field by the Chateau Cantal* (1887, oil on canvas, 18 x 22 ins / 46 x 55 cm) USD 550,000. PARIS, 22 June 2001, *Marseilles Harbour* (oil on canvas, 29 x 36 ins / 73 x 92 cm) FRF 4,350,000. NEW YORK, 6 Nov 2001, *Edam Mill* (1896, oil on canvas, 26 x 32 ins / 65 x 81 cm) USD 570,000. NEW YORK, 7 May 2002, *Portrieux, Masts, opus 182* (1888, oil on canvas, 18 x 22 ins / 46 x 55 cm) USD 2,400,000. NEW YORK, 8 May 2002, *Rainbow, Venice* (1905, oil on canvas, 29 x 36 ins / 74 x 92 cm) USD 2,000,000. LONDON, 4 Feb 2003, *St-Cloud* (1903, oil on canvas, 18 x 22 ins / 46 x 55 cm) GBP 400,000. NEW YORK, 6 May 2003, *Tuna Boat Entering La Rochelle at Sunset* (1927, oil on canvas, 29 x 36 ins / 73 x 92 cm) USD 1,400,000. LONDON, 2 Feb 2004, *St-Tropez before the Storm* (1895, oil on canvas, 26 x 32 ins / 65 x 81 cm) GBP 740,000. LONDON, 22 June 2004, *Beacons, St-Briac* (1890, oil on canvas, 26 x 32 ins / 65 x 82 cm) GBP 1,550,000.

SIGNAC, Pierre

French, 17th century.

Died 1684.

Active in Sweden 1646-1677.

Miniaturist, enameller. Portraits.

MUSEUMS AND GALLERIES:

HELSINKI: 28 portraits of European sovereigns - STOCKHOLM: *Portrait of Queen Christina*; *Portrait of Queen Ulrika Eleonora*.

SIGNERRE, Guillaume de

French, 16th century.

Active in Rouen c. 1500.

Engraver (wood).

Signerre worked in Milan and founded a printing works. He illustrated G.P. Ferraro's *Mirror of the Soul (Specchio di anima)* with woodcuts.

SIGNOL, Émile

French, 19th century.

Born 8 May 1804, in Paris; died 4 October 1892, in Enghien.

Painter. History painting, religious subjects, portraits, genre scenes.

Signol was a pupil of Baron Gros and of Merry Joseph Blondel at the École des Beaux-Arts in Paris. Was awarded second prize in the 1829 Prix de Rome and first prize in 1830. On his return from Rome he rebelled against Romantisism and became the champion of pure-blooded academic art. This was undoubtedly the result of all the eccentric traits he had developed as a student, and because of the extreme cult devoted to classical traditions. In 1860 was admitted to the Institut de France.

He exhibited at the Salon de Paris from 1824 onwards, being awarded a second class medal in 1834 and a first class medal in 1835 and was promoted to Chevalier of the Légion d'Honneur in 1841 and made an Officer in 1865.

Decorative paintings for numerous churches in Paris, most notably La Madeleine, Saint Roch, Saint Sulpice, Saint Eustache, Saint Séverin and several posthumous portraits for the Palace of Versailles are known by this artist. His canvas entitled *Adulteress* now in the Luxembourg Palace was popularised by the engraving and went on to become his masterpiece. The artist, however, became and more fanatical about his art but it was too conventional to kindle a spark in others. Émile Signol was undoubtedly a skilful artist but his skills were never enough to overcome the dryness of his style. There is no life in his later compositions in which his concerns about design were strongly exaggerated and these disappointed even the majority of his former devotees.

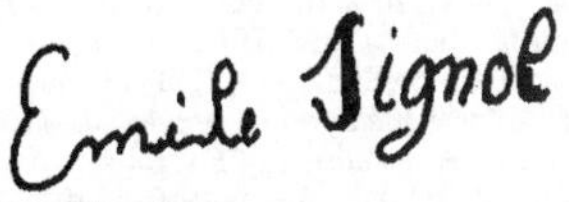

MUSEUMS AND GALLERIES:
AIX-EN-PROVENCE (Mus. Granet): *Noah Cursing his Son* - ANGERS: *Awakening the Just; Awakening the Wicked* - ARRAS: *Scene from the July 1830 Events* - AURILLAC: *The Madonna's Vow* - BAGNOLS-SUR-BIGORRE: *Adulteress* - MARSEILLES: *The Adulteress Before Christ* - MONTARGIS: *Portrait of Dumais* - TOURS: *Portrait of the Artist's Father; Portrait of the Artist; Two Memories of Italy; Two Scenes from Roman History* - VERSAILLES: *Godefroy de Bouillon, King of Jerusalem; Thierry II, also known as Thierry of Chelles; Dagobert I; Louis IX; Tancred on the Mount of Olives; Crossing the Bosphorus in 1097; Scene from the First Crusade; Dagobert II; Clovis II; Childeric II; Thierry I; Preaching the Second Crusade at Vézelay in Burgundy; Philippe-Auguste; Louis VII; Taking Jerusalem; Coronation of Louis XV.*
AUCTION RECORDS:
PARIS, 4 Dec 1922, *Ghosts*, FRF 160.

SIGNOL, Eugène or Louis Eugène
French, 19th century.
Born 17 February 1809, in Lille; died after 1848.
Landscape painter.

Eugène Signol was the brother of Émile. He was a pupil of Picot and exhibited at the Salon between 1837 and 1848.
MUSEUMS AND GALLERIES:
TOURS: *Don Quixote and the Lions.*

SIGNORACCIO, Bernardino del.
See **BERNARDINO D'ANTONIO DEL SIGNORACCIO**

SIGNORACCIO, Paolo del (fra). See **PAOLO DI BERNARDINO DEL SIGNORACCIO**

SIGNORELLI, Francesco
Italian, 16th century.
Died 1559.
Active in Cortona (Tuscany).
Painter. History painting.

Francesco Signorelli was the nephew and pupil of Luca Signorelli and acted as his assistant. He was much influenced by his master's style but was, unfortunately, an inferior artist. One of his works, an *Immaculate Conception*, is in the church of S Francesco in Gubbio. He also painted the *Madonna and Saints* in the Palazzo Pubblico in Cortona and a *Doubting Thomas* and a *Baptism* now in the museum in Città di Castello.

SIGNORELLI, Luca
Italian, 15th - 16th century.
Born 1441 or 1450, in Cortona (Tuscany); died 16 October 1523, in Cortona.
Painter (gouache), fresco artist, engraver, draughtsman. History painting, religious subjects.
Umbrian School.

The son of Egidio di Ventura Signorelli and of a sister of Lazzaro dei Taldi, Luca Signorelli was the grandfather of Vasari. He was a pupil of Piero della Francesca, working with him in Arezzo where he is mentioned in 1472. In 1474 he was in Città di Castello. Between 1476 and 1479 he painted a series of frescoes in the sacristy of the basilica of Loreto, and in 1481 he is recorded as painting two frescoes depicting the *Story of Moses* in the Sistine Chapel. In 1484 he returned to Cortona where, the same year, he painted an altarpiece for the chapel of S Onofrio in Perugia Cathedral. In 1488 Signorelli was granted citizenship of Città di Castello and, the same year, was a member of the governing council of Cortona. Despite a busy career, whenever he was in his home town, Signorelli participated in local affairs throughout his life. From 1482 he received many commissions. For Lorenzo de' Medici he painted a *Madonna* and a *Triumph of Pan* (destroyed in 1944). At the end of the 15th century, Signorelli took on the enormous task of completing the frescoes in the chapel of the Madonna di Brizio in Orvieto Cathedral, left unfinished half a century earlier by Fra Giovanni. A first contract for the work was signed on 5 April 1499 and another on 27 April 1500. Signorelli and his assistant Girolomi Ganga began work. On 15 August 1502 the frescoes were revealed to the admiring gaze of the worshippers. There are four main compositions, *Anti-Christ, Hell, Resurrection* and *Paradise*. In 1508, after visiting Florence as an ambassador, seeking to obtain certain reforms for the commune of Cortona, he went on to Rome to work for Pope Julius II, with Perugino, Pinturicchio and Sodoma, on the decoration of the Vatican. He painted one wall but his work unfortunately disappeared when he and his companions were dismissed and Raphael began painting alone at the Vatican. The last work by Signorelli, the altarpiece in the Collegiata in Foiano, painted when he was over 80, shows a hand as assured as ever.

A few comments will serve to fill in the bare dates outlined above. Signorelli began his studies with Piero della Francesca but, in the view of several scholars, it is likely that he also worked with Antonio Pollaiuolo. His early works certainly show the influence of the latter, as, for example, in the *Flagellation* now at Brera in Milan. It is highly probable that he spent some of his youth in Florence and his work is imbued with the atmosphere and brilliance of that city. First Verrocchio and then Donatello left their mark on the young artist, as can be seen in the emphatic contrasts in the frescoes in the sacristy of the Santa Casa in Loreto. He is skilled in the representation of clothed figures and even more so of nudes. In this respect, one of the strangest paintings of the late 15th century was his *Triumph of Pan* (1490) where the nudes, sharply detached from their background, have a strongly sculptural quality. Signorelli's line looks back to Pollaiuolo and his use of light to Piero della Francesca. He turns away from the light colours of his master, however, in favour of richer, darker hues more like those of the Flemish artists.

It has been suggested that Signorelli's powerful works with their anatomically accurate and daring figures influenced

Michelangelo when he came to design and paint the ceiling of the Sistine Chapel, and he was to Michelangelo what Perugino had been for Raphael. Whether or not this theory is true, it is inconceivable that Michelangelo would have ignored these important works painted ten years before his arrival in the Sistine Chapel. Indubitably, the energy of Signorelli's style and the sculptural forms of his nudes present an awe-inspiring whole that looks forward to the art of Michelangelo.

LVCE·DE CORTONA·P·O

BIBLIOGRAPHY:

Scarpellini, Pietro, *Luca Signorelli*, G. Barbèra, Florence, 1964. Kury, Gloria, *The early work of Luca Signorelli, 1465-1590*, dissertation, Garland, New York, 1978. Kanter, Laurence B., *Orvieto, chapel of San Brizio: Luca Signorelli*, Scala, Florence, 1983. Kanter, Laurence B., *The late works of Luca Signorelli and his followers*, dissertation, New York University, New York, 1989. Bettinzoli, Attilio, *Stanley Meltzoff, Botticelli, Signorelli and Savoranola: theologia poetica and painting from Boccaccio to Poliziano*, Le Lettere, Florence, 1989. Paolucci, Antonio, *Luca Signorelli*, Riverside, New York, 1990. Riess, Jonathan B., *The Renaissance antichrist: Luca Signorelli's Orvieto frescoes*, Princeton university press, Princeton, 1995. Reiss, J., *Luca Signorelli: The San Brizio Chapel, Orvieto*, New York, 1995. Currie, Stuart, *Drawing 1400-1600. Invention and Innovation*, Ashgate, Aldershot, 1998. Henry, T., '*New Documents for Signorelli's Annunciation at Volterra*' in *Burlington Magazine*, vol 140, 1998. Henry, Tom/Kanter, Laurence B./Testa, G., *The Complete Paintings of Luca Signorelli*, monograph, catalogue raisonné, Thames and Hudson, London, 2001.

MUSEUMS AND GALLERIES:

ALTENBURG: nine panels - AREZZO: *Virgin, Female Saint and Prophets* - BERGAMO (Accademia Carrara): *St Roch; Virgin and Child; St Sebastian* - BERLIN: two wings from an altarpiece; *Pan the God of Nature and Lord of Music with his Companions; The Visitation; Portrait of a Man* - BOSTON: *Madonna* - CITTÀ DI CASTELLO: *Martyrdom of St Sebastian* - CITTÀ DI CASTELLO (Church of S Agostino): *Adoration of the Magi* (1482 and 1493, two canvases) - CORTONA (Cathedral): *Dead Christ* (1502) - CORTONA (Diocesan Mus.): *Last Supper* (1512) - DRESDEN: *Archangel Raphael and Tobias, St Jerome and St Bernardino of Siena* (pilaster); *St Bernard, St Onophrius and St Dorothy* (pilaster) - DUBLIN: *Feast at the House of Simon* - FLORENCE (NG): *Virgin and Child* (altar step); *Annunciation; Nativity; Adoration of the Kings; Holy Family* - FLORENCE (Palazzo Pitti): *Holy Family* - FLORENCE (Uffizi): *St Mary Magdalene at the Foot of the Cross* - KASSEL: *Virgin in the Temple* - LONDON (NG): *The Circumcision* (c. 1490-1491, oil on wood transferred to canvas); *The Adoration of the Shepherds* (1496, oil/wood); *The Triumph of Chastity: Love Disarmed and Bound* (c. 1509, fresco/canvas); *The Adoration of the Shepherds* (1510-1515, oil/wood, maybe a fragment of predella); *The Virgin and Child with Saints* (1515, oil/wood) - MILAN (Pinacoteca di Brera): *Flagellation; Virgin and Christ; Virgin, Christ and Saints; Martyrdom of St Catherine* - MONT OLIVETTO DI CHIASURI (Convent): *Life of St Benedict* (large fresco commissioned in 1497) - MUNICH: *Virgin and Child in a Rocky Landscape* - ORLÉANS: *Virgin and Child Seated beneath a Cupola* - OXFORD: *Madonna* - PARIS (Louvre): *Birth of the Virgin; Birth of St John the Baptist; Adoration of the Magi; St Jerome in Ecstasy; Fragment of a Composition* - PARIS (Mus. Jacquemart-André): *Virgin and Child with St John the Baptist and an Aged Saint* (c. 1485-1487) - PÉRIGUEUX: *Annunciation* - PERUGIA: *Madonna* - PERUGIA (Cathedral, Chapel of S Onofrio): altar painting - PRATO: *Crucifixion; Virgin, Christ and Saints* - ROME (Pallavicini-Rospigliosi Gal.): *Virgin and Child with St John the Baptist and St Jerome* (1487-1489) - SAN DIEGO (MA) - VIENNA: a study.

AUCTION RECORDS:

PARIS, 1865, *St George Slaying the Dragon* (red chalk) FRF 140. LONDON, 1874, *Madonna*, FRF 10,765; *Pair of Pilasters*, FRF 6,700; *Story of Coriolanus*, FRF 12,075; *Triumph of Chastity*, FRF 21,000. LONDON, 1882, *Circumcision* (ten life-size figures) FRF 78,700. PARIS, 1889, *Construction of an Italian Villa*, FRF 4,000. LONDON, 1894, *Story of Coriolanus*, FRF 7,870. LONDON, 5 May 1911, *Samson Slaying the Philistines*, GBP 115. PARIS, 21 Feb 1919, *Study for the Figure of the Good Thief* (drawing in black chalk and pierre d'Italie) FRF 1,220. LONDON, 10 July 1925, *Virgin and Child*, GBP 68. LONDON, 22 May 1928, *Young Man* (black chalk) GBP 230. LONDON, 6 Feb 1931, *Virgin and St John the Evangelist*, GBP 120. LONDON, 4 June 1937, *Judith Holding the Head of Holofernes*, GBP 299. NEW YORK, 13 Dec 1949, *The Pilgrims of Emmaus* (two paintings, attributed) USD 5,700. PARIS, 26 June 1950, *Study of a Nude Man from Behind* (red chalk) FRF 6,500. LONDON, 27 March 1963, *St Michael*, GBP 1,000. LONDON, 29 June 1979, *Coronation of the Virgin* (c. 1508, oil on panel, lunette, 50 x 88 1/4 ins / 127 x 223.9 cm) GBP 20,000. LONDON, 11 Dec 1979, *Study of a Man Standing* (black chalk heightened with white gouache, 16 1/4 x 8 1/2 ins / 41 x 21.5 cm) GBP 95,000. MONACO, 21 June 1991, *St Sebastian* (oil on panel, 8 1/2 x 7 3/4 ins / 21.5 x 19.5 cm) FRF 105,450. NEW YORK, 30 Jan 1997, *Prophet Holding a Roll of Parchment* (c. 1490, gold background, tempera/panel, tondo, diam. 7 ins / 17.8 cm) USD 123,500. LONDON, 10 July 2002, *Study for a Seated Prophet* (black chalk partly pricked for transfer, 11 x 8 ins / 29 x 21 cm) GBP 520,000.

SIGNORET, Charles Louis Eugène

French, 19th - 20th century.

Born 19 July 1867, in Marseilles; died 15 September 1932.

Painter. Figures, nudes, landscapes, seascapes.

Charles Signoret was a pupil in Paris of Jules Lefebvre, Benjamin-Constant, Gabriel Ferrier and Jean-Paul Laurens. He exhibited at the Salon des Artistes Français, obtaining an honourable mention in 1898 and becoming a scoiety member in 1900. He won the Prix-Ragnecourt-Guyon in 1910, a silver medal in 1914 and a gold medal in 1920.

AUCTION RECORDS:

PARIS, 28 Dec 1942, *Female Nude Seen from the Back*, FRF 280. PARIS, 27 March 1947, *Boats on the Sea* (1898) FRF 750. LOS ANGELES, 3 May 1982, *Fishermen in a Boat at Dusk* (oil on canvas, 29 x 39 1/2 ins / 73.5 x 100.5 cm) USD 1,700. PARIS, 9 June 2004, *Fishermen at Sunset* (oil on canvas, 29 x 40 ins / 74 x 101 cm) EUR 1,650.

SIGNORET-LEDIEU, Lucie

French, 19th - 20th century.

Born c. 1858, in Nevers; died at the end of 1904.

Sculptor.

Lucie Signoret-Ledieu was a pupil of Jean Gautherin. She exhibited at the Salon de Paris from 1878. In 1883 and 1886 she won honourable mentions at the Salon, by now called the Salon des Artistes Français. Her *Statue of Joan of Arc* stands in St-Pierre-le-Moutier in Nevers.

MUSEUMS AND GALLERIES:
CHAMBÉRY (MBA): *Woman Spinning*.

AUCTION RECORDS:
LONDON, 21 June 1978, *Diana's Nymph* (1891, gilded bronze, h. 26 1/4 ins / 66.5 cm) GBp 900. LONDON, 28 March 1979, *Diana's Nymph* (green-patinated bronze, h. 33 3/4 ins / 86 cm) GBP 1,850. LONDON, 10 Nov 1983, *Diana's Nymph* (c. 1880, patinated bronze, h. 33 3/4 ins / 86 cm) GBP 2,900. LONDON, 20 March 1986, *Spring* (green-brown-patinated bronze, h. 35 ins / 88 cm) GBP 3,200.

SIGNORETTI, Gian Antonio
Italian, 16th century.
Died 1602.
Active in Reggio Emilia.
Medallist.

SIGNORETTI, Paolo
Italian, 17th century.
Active in Rome during the first half of the 17th century.
Painter.
Signoretti was the assistant of H. Regnier in Rome in 1621.

SIGNORI
Italian, 16th century.
Painter.
Signori worked in Casale between 1508 and 1516.

SIGNORI, Alfredo
Italian, 20th century.
Born 1913, in Cremona.
Painter. Figures, interiors, landscapes, urban landscapes, still-lifes.

Whatever the subject of Alfredo Signori's paintings, they are all rendered in restrained, almost colourless greys, sometimes in what seems like a misty atmosphere where planes and forms merge, occasionally brightly lit with strong contrasts between light and shade. His works, reflecting his mood and that of the times, accompany his private diary. Each year, he painted a self-portrait.

He has taken part in a number of collective exhibitions including *Attraverso l'Immagine* (*Through the Image*) held at the Centro Culturale in Cremona in 1995.

BIBLIOGRAPHY:
Attraverso l'immagine, exhibition catalogue, Centro culturale Santa Maria della Pietà, Cremona, 1995.

SIGNORI, Carlo Sergio
Italian, 20th century.
Born 1906, in Milan; died 1988.
Also active in France.
Sculptor.

In 1924, Carlo Signori went to Paris to study art. He studied painting for some years at André Lhote's academy and then, from 1935, sculpture in Malfray's studio at the Académie Ranson. In 1948, he won the competition to choose a sculptor to make the *Monument to the Rosselli Brothers* near Bagnoles-de-l'Orne and lived for a year in Carrara to carry out the commission. He later spent several months of every year there, planning his work according to the marble available.

Until 1945, his works, generally in plaster, were Expressionist in style. He subsequently went through a period of Cubist influence. His first stay in Carrara, which was decisive in his development, coincided with the increasing importance of Brancusi's influence. The marble was treated in a very individual way, reduced to very flat, thin forms that allowed the light to pass through to a greater or lesser degree according to the thickness of the piece. Despite the fact that the sculptures have titles such as *Black Venus* (1950), *Goéland* (1957) and *Venus* (1958), they are in no way figurative. At most, it is possible to see in some of the curving shapes suggestions of anthropomorphic or zoomorphic forms. The surfaces of his works are carefully polished, suggesting perhaps the smoothness of human skin. On the subject of the human forms in Signori's work, Gualtieri di San Lazzaro has written that, whereas Brancusi 'stripped bare the human form, petrifying it in absolute and universal forms, [Signori] seems to have done the opposite, rescuing a few stones to imbue them with humanity'.

Signori's work has often appeared in collective exhibitions in Italy and, in Paris, at the Salon de Mai and the Salon des Réalités Nouvelles. In 1958, a whole room at the Venice Biennale was dedicated to his work. A big retrospective exhibition of all his work was mounted by the Galerie Charpentier in Paris in 1966. He won the Prix de Paris in 1950 for his *Black Venus* and, in 1962, the International Prize awarded by the town of Carrara.

AUCTION RECORDS:
PARIS, 6 June 1974, *Dancer* (marble) FRF 11,000. PARIS, 30 Sept 1996, *Shadows* (black-patinated lost-wax bronze, 21 1/4 x 18 ins / 54 x 46 cm) FRF 23,000. PARIS, 2 Aug 2000, *Study for the Monument to the Brothers Rosselli* (grey marble, 33 x 12x13 ins / 84 x 30x34 cm) FRF 19,000. PARIS, 2 Aug 2000, *Portrait for Raymonde* (green marble, 17 x 14x3 ins / 42 x 36x7 cm) FRF 22,000. PARIS, 31 July 2002, *Leaf* (white marble, h. 15 ins / 37 cm) EUR 3,500. PARIS, 16 June 2003, *Torso of a Woman* (marble, h. 30 ins / 77 cm) EUR 4,000.

SIGNORI, Ilio
Italian, 20th century.
Born 1929, in Aosta.
Sculptor. Figures.

A pupil of Marcel Gimond in Paris, Ilio Signori explored the problems of integrating sculpture with architecture. Having gradually moved away from the influence of his teacher Gimond, Signori produced sculpture that was Expressionist in style and derived from the real world. The sculptor creates violently tortured and contrasting forms, juxtaposing them with smooth and harmonious spaces and areas of light at the heart of solid volumes where harsh shadows accentuate the relief.

AUCTION RECORDS:
NEUILLY, 3 Feb 1991, *Art Lover* (1972, bronze, 22 x 7 3/4 x 7 3/4 ins / 55 x 20 x 20 cm) FRF 32,000. PARIS, 3 June 1991, *Characters* (bronze, 9 3/4 x 10 1/4 ins / 25 x 26 cm) FRF 15,000.

SIGNORINI, Alessandro
Italian, 18th - 19th century.
Born c. 1772; died 13 February 1822.
Active in Cremona.
Painter, designer of ornamental architectural features.

SIGNORINI, Bartolomeo
Italian, 17th - 18th century.
Born 1674, in Verona; died 14 March 1742, in Verona.
Painter.

The pupil of S. Prunati, Bartolomeo Signorini executed numerous paintings for churches in Verona and the surrounding area.

SIGNORINI, Francesco
Italian, 16th century.
Florentine, active in Naples during the second half of the 16th century.
Painter.

Francesco Signorini painted a number of altarpieces for churches in Naples.

SIGNORINI, Fulvio, called il Ninno
Italian, 16th century.
Born 1563.
Sculptor, founder.

Fulvio Signorini executed works for Siena Cathedral and for other churches and palazzi in the same town.

SIGNORINI, Gaetano
Italian, 19th century.
Born 14 September 1806, in Suzzara; died 16 August 1879, in Parma.
Painter.

MUSEUMS AND GALLERIES:
PARMA (Accademia Nazionale di Belle Arti): *Portrait of Count Jacopo Sanvitale.*

SIGNORINI, Giovanni
Italian, 19th century.
Born c. 1808; died after 1858.
Painter. Genre scenes, landscapes.

MUSEUMS AND GALLERIES:
PRATO: *View of the Mercato Nuovo in Florence; Piazza Santa Croce in Florence during the Carnival; Piazza Santa Maria Novella in Florence; Horse Race in Florence; View of a Bridge in Florence.*

AUCTION RECORDS:
PARIS, 21 Oct 1946, *Mule Track,* FRF 4,000. FLORENCE, 13 Oct 1972, *View of Florence,* ITL 2,400,000. LONDON, 19 Jan 1973, *Wine Harvest,* Gns 3,500. LONDON, 19 June 1991, *People Dancing on a Hill Overlooking the Arno in Florence* (1845, oil on canvas, 17 1/2 x 22 ins / 44.5 x 56 cm) GBP 11,550. LONDON, 18 March 1992, *Seascape with Port* (oil on canvas, 32 1/4 x 52 1/4 ins / 82 x 133 cm) GBP 8,250. LONDON, 10 Oct 1996, *Peasant Family Resting by the Roadside with a View of Florence in the Background* (oil on canvas, 13 3/4 x 16 ins / 34.8 x 40.7 cm) GBP 3,500. NEW ORLEANS, 30 Jan 1999, *Travellers on Horseback Crossing a Bridge* (oil on canvas, 26 x 37 ins / 66 x 94 cm) USD 8,500. LONDON, 23 Sept 2004, *Rest on the Journey to Florence* (1832, oil on canvas, 15 x 15 ins / 39 x 39 cm) GBP 6,000.

SIGNORINI, Giovanni Battista
Italian.
Active in Verona.
Painter. Religious subjects.

Giovanni Battista Signorini produced a number of altar paintings.

MUSEUMS AND GALLERIES:
VERONA (Church of S Anastasia): altar paintings - VERONA (Oratory of S Gregorio): altar paintings.

SIGNORINI, Giuseppe or Joseph
Italian, 19th - 20th century.
Born 1847 or 1857, in Rome; died 23 December 1932, in Rome.
Also active in France.
Painter (gouache), watercolourist. Genre scenes, interiors with figures, local scenes.
Orientalism.

Giuseppe Signorini studied at the Accademia di Belle Arti in Rome and with Aurelio Tiratelli. He lived in France for 33 years and a number of his works show that he also spent a long time in North Africa. He exhibited at the Salon des Artistes Français in Paris and was awarded a bronze medal in 1900 at the Exposition Universelle.

AUCTION RECORDS:
NEW YORK, 8-10 April 1908, *The Sultan's Favourite Wife,* USD 200. PARIS, 28 March 1949, *Fruit Sellers* (watercolour) FRF 1,400. LOS ANGELES, 28 Feb 1972, *Departure of the Cardinal* (watercolour) USD 1,100. NEW YORK, 14 Jan 1977, *Last Touch* (1889, watercolour, 16 1/2 x 11 1/2 ins / 42 x 29 cm) USD 1,600. LONDON, 20 Oct 1978, *Gypsy Caravan* (oil on canvas, 39 x 70 ins / 99 x 178 cm) GBP 8,000. NEW YORK, 29 May 1980, *Game of Chess* (oil on panel, 8 1/2 x 6 ins / 21.5 x 15 cm) USD 1,000. NEW YORK, 27 Feb 1982, *Monastery Kitchen* (watercolour and pencil, 23 1/2 x 32 ins / 60 x 81 cm) USD 3,250. NEW YORK, 21 Jan 1983, *Fur Seller* (watercolour, 25 x 17 ins / 63.5 x 43 cm) USD 3,500. ROME, 26 Oct 1983, *View of Florence and the Ponte Vecchio* (oil on canvas, 12 1/2 x 18 1/4 ins / 32 x 46.5 cm) ITL 4,800,000. NEW YORK, 15 Feb 1985, *Old Arab Man Smoking a Pipe* (watercolour/traces of pencil, 28 3/4 x 17 1/4 ins / 73 x 43.5 cm) USD 6,000. MILAN, 11 Dec 1986, *Tournament* (tempera, 36 1/4 x 25 1/2 ins / 92 x 65 cm) ITL 5,400,000. ROME, 31 May 1990, *Antique Dealer* (watercolour/paper, 22 x 17 3/4 ins / 56 x 45 cm) ITL 5,500,000. NEW YORK, 24 Oct 1990, *Fruit Seller in North Africa* (watercolour and gouache/card, 36 1/4 x 28 1/4 ins / 91.8 x 71.5 cm) USD 24,200. ROME, 4 Dec 1990, *Scene in an Interior in Historical Costume* (watercolour/paper, 28 x 17 1/4 ins / 71 x 44 cm) ITL 4,800,000. PARIS, 8 April 1991, *Warrior* (watercolour, 26 3/4 x 16 1/2 ins / 68 x 42 cm) FRF 80,000. LONDON, 4 Oct 1991, *Declaration* (watercolour and gouache/card, 17 3/4 x 23 1/2 ins / 45.1 x 59.7 cm) GBP 4,620. NEW YORK, 17 Oct 1991, *Harem* (watercolour/paper, 34 1/2 x 24 1/2 ins / 87.6 x 62.2 cm) USD 22,000. NEW YORK, 19 Feb 1992, *The Artist's Studio* (watercolour and gouache/card, 17 3/4 x 11 3/4 ins / 45.2 x 30 cm) USD 5,280. PARIS, 13 April 1992, *Prayer* (1879, watercolour, 22 x 15 ins / 55 x 38 cm) FRF 42,000. NEW YORK, 28 May 1992, *Lively Discussion* (watercolour and gouache/card, 27 1/4 x 36 1/2 ins / 69.2 x 92.7 cm) USD 16,500. LONDON, 12 Feb 1993, *Arab Café* (pencil and watercolour/paper/card, 24 1/4 x 34 ins / 61.6 x 86.4 cm) GBP 13,200. NEW YORK, 20 July 1994, *Today's News* (watercolour and pencil/card, 18 x 23 1/2 ins / 45.7 x 59.4 cm) USD 5,750. NEW YORK, 16 Feb 1995, *Frightened Arab* (watercolour/pencil/paper, 38 1/2 x 25 1/2 ins / 97.8 x 64.8 cm) USD 16,100. LONDON, 14 June 1995, *Prayer* (watercolour, 34 1/4 x 23 1/4 ins / 87 x 59 cm) GBP 8,625. PARIS, 18-19 March 1996, *Native Warrior with a Large Straw Hat* (watercolour, 23 1/2 x 15 ins / 60 x 38 cm) FRF 12,000. ROME, 4 June 1996, *On the Water* (pencil/paper, 15 x 20 1/2 ins / 38 x 52 cm) ITL 2,645,000. ROME, 11 Dec 1996, *Arab Warrior* (watercolour/paper, 22 x 15 1/4 ins / 55 x 38.5 cm) ITL 4,660. PARIS, 17 Nov 1997, *Young Oriental Woman with a Striped Scarf* (gouache, 17 1/4 x 13 1/2 ins / 44 x 34 cm) FRF 23,000. NEW YORK, 8 March 2000, *Two Musicians* (watercolour, 30 x 16 ins / 77 x 41 cm) USD 5,000. NEW YORK, 31 Oct 2000, *In the Harem* (watercolour, 23 x 33 ins / 58 x 84 cm) USD 10,000. NEW YORK, 7 Feb 2001, *Cardinal's Audience* (watercolour over pencil heightened with white on paper/board, 19 x 26 ins / 48 x 66 cm) USD 5,250. NEW YORK, 29 Oct 2003, *Serenade* (watercolour and gouache on board, 30 x 21 ins / 77 x 53 cm) USD 10,000.

SIGNORINI, Guido
Italian, 17th century.
Died 1636.
Active in Bologna.
Painter.

Guido Signorini was the pupil of Cignani.

SIGNORINI, Guido
Italian, 17th century.
Died 1644, in Rome.
Active in Bologna.
Painter.

This artist, the nephew and heir of Guido Reni, may have been the Guido Signorini said to have died in 1636.

SIGNORINI, Paolo
Italian, 20th century.
Born 1922, in Chiari.
Painter.

A student at the Accademia Carrara in Bergamo and the Accademia di Brera in Milan, Signorini also obtained a diploma in architecture at the Polytechnicum in Milan. He has taken part in a number of collective exhibitions, including the Menton Biennale of 1972.

SIGNORINI, Telemaco

Italian, 19th century.

Born 18 August 1835, in Florence; died 10 February 1901, in Florence.

Painter, engraver. Figures, portraits, genre scenes, landscapes.

Macchiaioli group.

Although perhaps not the most talented of the group, Signorini was certainly the inspiration and theoretician of the Macchiaioli. This movement has often been associated with Impressionism but was neither as far-reaching nor as technically specific as the French movement. It is connected more closely with the *en plein air* tendency and the painters of the Barbizon School, and with the Realism of Courbet.

Unlike most of the Macchiaioli, who were generally, like Fattori and Lega, of humble origin, Signorini came from a comfortably off, well-educated, liberal family. His father was a painter and in 1852 allowed his son to abandon his academic studies to devote himself to painting. He continued, nevertheless, to take a lively interest in literature. He studied first at the Accademia del Nudo, but before long he was spending most of his time with other Florentine artists at the Caffé Michelangelo discussing revolutionary politics and their equally revolutionary ideas about art. Most of them had taken part in the failed revolution of 1848. They admired the painting of Filippo Lippi, Carpaccio and the Italian Quattrocento, but also the realism and sincerity of Delacroix, Decamps and the Barbizon painters. Rejecting traditional ideas of composition, they sought to celebrate the daily life of the ordinary people, with whom they felt close links, and to observe and record nature and the Italian landscape as faithfully as possible. In their painting they attempted to penetrate the secrets of the changing light of the different seasons and times of day. Fattori, Lega, Sernesi, Abbati and Signorini all took part in the war against Austria in 1859, in which Sernesi lost his life. Signorini wrote of the Macchiaioli: 'After the revolution of 1848... considerable numbers of young people turned away from the constraints of academic teachings. Nature would be their only teacher, nature in all her nakedness, stripped of the scholarly vision.'

For several years, the discussions at the Caffé Michelangelo produced more words than works of art. Finally, in 1855, Vincenzo Cabianca painted a black pig against a white wall, a work that is generally seen as the first statement of the principle of the *macchia* (splash or spot of colour) that was then evolving in the group. It was not until after the war of 1859, however, that the most important works by these artists were painted. It was at the salon in Florence (as important in Italy as the Salon in Paris was for the French) in 1862 that a critic derisively described these artists as *macchiaioli* or 'daubers', thus giving the group its name. Signorini liked the name and was quick to adopt it for himself and his friends. The art critic Vittorio Imbriani has provided a useful definition of the aesthetic ideas behind the *macchia*. 'It is a portrait of the first distant impression of an object or scene; the first impression which impresses itself on the artist's eye, whether he sees the object or scene materially or whether he sees one or the other in a recollection in his imagination... a simple *macchia*, a patch of colour, is capable of provoking a sentiment or feeling in its own right, without determining any kind of object'.

Signorini was invited to teach at the academies of Naples and Florence, and in 1892 he was made an honorary member of the academy of Florence. In 1881, he made the first of several visits to Scotland, where his work was much appreciated.

Of all the Macchiaioli, the educated and well-travelled Severini was the one who best understood the contribution of foreign painters, particularly the French. In 1859, recording the war of that year in which he had fought, he painted one of his most powerful works, *The Cemetery at Solferino*. In it he explores the violent contrasts between dark and indeterminate forms and a stormy and dramatic sky. In 1860, he painted another of his best-known works, *Sunny Day at La Spezia*, sometimes compared to the Intimist works painted by Vuillard in 1900. Like most of the Macchiaioli, he frequently painted the small villages of the Tuscan countryside, usually representing them in the middle of the day when the sun was at its most oppressive. He also painted scenes from the everyday life of ordinary people, often with a social intent. These works are often clearly inspired by literature. He aroused violent controversy with his courageous painting of a scene in a *Hospital for the Female Insane*.

Perhaps as a result of the different influences he experienced during his many journeys abroad, Signorini was the first member of the group to depart from the strict rules of painting in *macchie*. With Lega and Borrani, he formed an autonomous offshoot of the Macchiaioli, the Pergentina School, which followed a more spontaneous and obviously poetic inspiration. In Paris, he had become friends with Manet, Zola and Degas, and the influence of the latter, in particular, is very evident in his varied and marked use of colour and his incisive line. Signorini was the most successful of the Macchiaioli in terms of public and official recognition.

Signorini made his debut in 1860, exhibiting in Turin, Milan, Florence, Venice, Livorno and Bologna as well as abroad, particularly in Paris (where he was awarded a bronze medal at the 1889 Exposition Universelle) and Vienna. In Italy, he was frequently a member of the jury at exhibitions. Since his death, his works have appeared in collective exhibitions including *Dipinti di autori toscani dell'800* (Paintings by 19th-Century Tuscan Artists) held at Farsettiarte, Prato.

TSignorini

TSignorini

TSignorini

BIBLIOGRAPHY:

Sapori, Francesco, *Signorini*, E. Celanza, Turin, 1919. Ojetti, Ugo, *Telemaco Signorini*, Bestetti e Tumminelli, Milan, 1930. Somaré, Enrico, *Signorini*, Istituto nazionale L.U.C.E., Rome, 1931. Troyer, N.G., *The Macchiaioli: Effects of Modern Color Theory, Photography and Japanese Prints on a Group of Italian Painters, 1855-1900*, dissertation, Northwestern University, Evanston (IL), 1978. Masini, Lara-Vinca, *Telemaco Signorini*, Ed. d'Arte il Fiorino, Florence, 1983. Troyer, N.G., *'Telemaco Signorini and Macchiaioli Giapponismo'* in *A. Bull, lxvi, pp. 136-45*, 1984. Broude, Norma, *The Macchiaioli: Italian Painters of the Nineteenth Century*, New Haven and London, 1987. Monti, Raffaele, *Signorini e il naturalismo europeo*, De Luca Editore, Roma, Leonardo, Milan, 1989. Spaletti, Ettore, *Telemaco Signorini*, Ed. dei Soncino, Soncino, 1994. *Telemaco Singorini: una retrospettiva*, exhibition catalogue, Artificio, Florence, 1997. Serafini, P., '*Nuovi contributi su Telemaco Signorini a Piagentina*' in *Ricerche di storia dell'arte* n° 71, periodical, Rome, 2000.

Museums and Galleries:

Florence (Gal. d'Arte Moderna): 17 paintings.

Auction records:

Paris, 18 May 1938, *Banks of a River*, FRF 4,050. Paris, 4 Dec 1941, *Banks of a Canal* (1884) FRF 19,500. Milan, Nov 1949, *Landscape*, ITL 100,000. Milan, May 1950, *Street in Florence*, ITL 170,000. Milan, 3 March 1966, *Island*, ITL 850,000. Milan, 3 Nov 1967, *Flower Garden*, ITL 2,200,000. Florence, 16 Oct 1969, *Villa in Vinci*, GBP 10,000. Milan, 4 June 1970, *Flocks Grazing*, ITL 8,500,000. London, 17 Feb 1971, *Ponte Vecchio, Florence*, GBP 32,000. London, 28 Feb 1973, *Water Carriers*, GBP 11,000. Milan, 28 May 1974, *Village Street*, ITL 15,000,000. Milan, 14 Dec 1976, *Children in the Street in Riomaggiore* (oil on card, 6 3/4 x 11 1/2 ins / 17 x 29 cm) ITL 16,000,000. Milan, 26 May 1977, *Flirtation* (oil on canvas, 18 1/2 x 13 3/4 ins / 47 x 35 cm) ITL 9,500,000. Milan, 12 March 1980, *Country Road* (etching, 11 3/4 x 7 ins / 30 x 18 cm) ITL 800,000. Milan, 16 June 1980, *Seascape near Riomaggiore* (oil on canvas, 9 3/4 x 26 ins / 25 x 66 cm) ITL 28,000,000. Milan, 19 March 1981, *Houses in Riomaggiore* (oil on canvas remounted/card, 6 x 6 3/4 ins / 15 x 17 cm) ITL 21,000,000. Milan, 12 Dec 1983, *Cala dei Fratti* (oil on panel, 9 1/2 x 14 1/4 ins / 24 x 36 cm) ITL 50,000,000. Milan, 27 March 1984, *Head of a Little Girl* (pencil, 7 x 5 1/4 ins / 17.5 x 13.5 cm) ITL 3,000,000. New York, 13 Feb 1985, *Spring* (c. 1870, oil on canvas, 15 x 18 1/2 ins / 38.1 x 47 cm) USD 50,000. Milan, 12 Dec 1985, *Landscape with Tree* (pencil/blue paper, 4 1/4 x 7 1/2 ins / 10.5 x 19 cm) ITL 1,500,000. Milan, 18 March 1986, *Cobbler's Shop in Settignano* (oil on canvas remounted/panel, 5 3/4 x 8 ins / 14.5 x 20.5 cm) ITL 34,000,000. New York, 25 Feb 1987, *Pascoli in Castiglionvello* (oil on canvas, 12 1/2 x 30 1/4 ins / 31.7 x 76.8 cm) USD 55,000. Milan, 31 March 1987, *Portrait of a Little Girl* (pencil, 7 1/4 x 5 1/2 ins / 18.5 x 14 cm) ITL 2,000,000. Milan, 23 March 1988, *Oak Trees in the Cascine, Florence* (oil on card, 14 x 18 ins / 35.5 x 45.5 cm) ITL 60,000,000; *Laughing Man* (oil on canvas, 6 1/2 x 4 1/4 ins / 16.5 x 10.5 cm) ITL 23,000,000. Milan, 14 March 1989, *Portrait of a Peasant Girl* (oil on card, 14 x 10 ins / 35.5 x 24.5 cm) ITL 44,000,000. Milan, 14 June 1989, *Where the Town Meets the Country* (oil on canvas, 5 x 8 1/2 ins / 13 x 21.5 cm) ITL 32,000,000. Milan, 19 Oct 1989, *Square in Settignano with an Old Woman Sitting outside her House* (oil on panel, 5 3/4 x 5 ins / 14.5 x 12.5 cm) ITL 72,000,000. Rome, 14 Dec 1989, *Boy Sitting on a Low Wall* (oil on canvas, 5 x 3 ins / 12.5 x 7.5 cm) ITL 18,400,000. Milan, 8 March 1990, *Street in Edinburgh* (oil on card, 7 x 5 1/4 ins / 18 x 13.5 cm) ITL 58,000,000. Milan, 12 March 1991, *Summer in Settignano* (oil on card, 10 3/4 x 6 1/4 ins / 27.5 x 16 cm) ITL 150,000,000. Milan, 6 June 1991, *Crowd in a Village Square* (oil on card, 3 x 4 3/4 ins / 7.5 x 12 cm) ITL 19,000,000. Rome, 9 June 1992, *Mercato Vecchio, Florence* (etching, 14 1/4 x 6 ins / 36.5 x 15.5 cm) ITL 2,600,000; *Piazza della Fratellanza* (etching, 14 1/4 x 9 1/4 ins / 36.3 x 23.5 cm) ITL 2,600,000. Milan, 16 June 1992, *Crossroads in Settignano* (1884, oil on panel, 11 x 7 3/4 ins / 28 x 19.5 cm) ITL 120,000,000. Milan, 9 Nov 1993, *Sky and Sea* (oil on canvas/card, 4 1/4 x 10 ins / 11 x 24.5 cm) ITL 11,500,000. Milan, 21 Dec 1993, *Lane in Piancastagnaio, Monte Amiata* (oil on panel, 7 1/2 x 11 ins / 19 x 27 cm) ITL 124,200,000. New York, 16 Feb 1995, *Ghetto in Florence* (oil on card, 8 1/2 x 4 1/2 ins / 21.6 x 11.4 cm) USD 23,000. Milan, 14 June 1995, *Farm at Pietramala* (oil on canvas, 13 1/2 x 17 1/4 ins / 34.5 x 44 cm) ITL 184,000,000. Rome, 27 May 1997, *Olive Trees in Settignano* (oil on canvas/panel, 5 x 8 1/4 ins / 13 x 21 cm) ITL 13,800,000. Rome, 2 Dec 1997, *Women in White Darning Clothes* (oil on canvas, 9 x 12 1/4 ins / 23 x 31 cm) ITL 80,400,000. Milan, 29 March 1999, *Two Sisters* (pencil on paper/board, 8 x 11 ins / 20 x 27 cm) ITL 7,000,000. Milan, 16 June 1999, *La cala dei Frati* (1888, oil on canvas, 9 x 14 ins / 23 x 35 cm) ITL 53,000,000. Newbury, 23 Feb 2000, *Italian Street Scene with Market Traders* (oil on canvas, 20 x 14 ins / 51 x 36 cm) GBP 87,000. London, 7 April 2000, *Village* (oil on board, 5 x 7 ins / 12 x 19 cm) GBP 9,600. Milan, 22 May 2001, *Small Place in Riomaggiore* (oil on board, 6 x 11 ins / 15 x 27 cm) ITL 195,000,000. Prato, 16 Nov 2001, *Tuscan Countryside* (oil on canvas, 5 x 8 ins / 13 x 21 cm) ITL 45,000,000. Milan, 22 May 2002, *Broad Street, Bath* (1881, oil on canvas, 14 x 20 ins / 36 x 50 cm) EUR 145,000. Vercelli, 25 May 2002, *At the Park* (oil on cardboard/masonite, 11 x 8 ins / 28 x 20 cm) EUR 40,000. Milan, 14 Oct 2003, *Arcola Street* (pencil and watercolour, 7 x 5 ins / 19 x 12 cm) EUR 3,800. London, 18 Nov 2003, *Towpath* (oil on canvas, 23 x 68 ins / 58 x 173 cm) GBP 2,500,000. Milan, 25 May 2004, *Motherly Love* (oil on canvas/board, 4 x 2 ins / 9 x 6 cm) EUR 7,700. Rome, 10 June 2004, *Settignano* (oil on cardboard, 11 x 7 ins / 27 x 17 cm) EUR 35,000.

SIGNOVERT, Jean

French, 20th century.

Born 24 April 1919, in Paris; died 6 April 1981, in Paris, buried in Ajaccio.

Painter (including gouache), watercolourist, engraver, medallist, lithographer, draughtsman, illustrator.

Jean Signovert had no father and began life with a mechanic's training certificate which he did not even have time to use because he was mobilised into the army in 1939. However, in 1938 he had met Abel Renault who initiated him in engraving. In 1943-1944 he was a pupil at the École des Beaux-Arts in St-Étienne. In 1946 he met the painter Roger Chastel, an important encounter since Chastel introduced him to Aimé Maeght who was opening her gallery in Paris; in 1947 he met Fautrier who sponsored him in 1950 for the Prix Fénéon, and with whom he remained close; he also met Braque in 1949, Jacques Villon in 1951 and Henri-Georges Adam in 1969.

He took part in public exhibitions: in Paris, he began in 1946 and 1947 at the Salon des Moins de Trente Ans and took part in the first two *Les Mains Éblouies* (*Dazzled Hands*), Galerie Maeght; 1946-1947, *Le Noir est une Couleur* (*Black is a Colour*), Galerie Maeght; from 1947 to 1971, Salon de Mai; 1947, *Youth Painting*, Galerie Drouant-David; 1948, third *Les Mains Éblouies*; 1950, Salon des Jeunes Peintres, last *Les Mains Éblouies* and *Sur quatre murs* (*On Four Walls*), also at the Galerie Maeght; 1951, 1952, *Trends*, Galerie Maeght; from 1971 till his death, Salon des Réalités Nouvelles, of which he became a member of the committee in 1973; and others. He also took part in groups in the provinces and abroad: 1950 New York, with *Les Mains Éblouies*, Hugo Gallery; 1952, London, *Paris School*; 1953 São Paulo Biennale.

He also showed in solo exhibitions, including: 1950 Ascona, Galerie La Citadella and Musée de Poitiers, with paintings and engravings; 1953 Paris, Galerie Jeanne Bucher; 1955 Paris, Galerie Diderot; 1958 Brussels, Galerie Ex Libris and Antwerp, Galerie Hans Rodvin; 1963 Paris, Galerie La Hune; 1965 Lausanne, Galerie Melisa; 1970 Paris; Galerie Parnasse; 1972 Paris, Galerie Anne Colin, and Bourges, Maison de la Culture; 1973, Musée de Pontoise; 1974 Paris, Galerie Prouté; 1975 Paris, Galerie Christiane Colin; 1978 Paris, Galerie Arcadia. In 1990, the Galerie Callu Mérite de Paris organised an exhibition *Signovert, Gouaches, Charcoal Drawings, Engravings*.

As an engraver and illustrator he took part in *Masculine Types* in collaboration with Roger Chastel for Paul Éluard's *Bestiary*; in 1950, with Braque for the *Milapera*, Tibetan poet of the eleventh century, and he illustrated *Lizard* by Francis Ponge; in 1951 he illustrated *Five* by Ponge; in 1957 he collaborated with Poliakoff in *Parmenides* by Plato; in 1961, with Esteve in *My Father's Tomb* by André Frénaud. He also collaborated on single engravings, notably for Braque for five years. By his participation in the Galerie Maeght, Jean Signovert identified himself, to the young generation, with a new departure for abstract expression in France. He produced several medals for the Paris mint, notably those of Jean Fautrier, Georges Braque, Alberto Magnelli, Robert Fontené, Roger Chastel. Even though at the beginning of his life it was circumstances that caused him to devote the major part of his activity to engraving, he grew more and more passionate about this technique, willingly showing himself, on occasion, to be an uncompromising censor of any liberties taken with its purity. It is in the hundreds of plates that he engraved that we find the purest of his art. Continuing a rigorous French tradition, he wanted to maintain elements of Cubism and Abstraction.

BIBLIOGRAPHY:

Busse, Jacques, *Discours pour le service funèbre de Jean Signovert,* Paris, 24 April 1981. Yeatman, Evelyne, *Atelier Signovert,* auction catalogue, Nouveau Drouot, Paris, 23 October 1987. *Signovert, gouaches, fusains, gravures,* exhibition catalogue, Gal. Callu Mérite, Paris, 1990. Harambourg, Lydia, *L'École de Paris 1945-1965. Dictionnaire des peintres,* Ides et Calendes, Neuchâtel, 1993.

MUSEUMS AND GALLERIES:

PARIS (BNF, Prints Collection) - PARIS (MNAM-CCI).

AUCTION RECORDS:

PARIS, 1 June 1988, *Composition (Red and Black)* (1958, gouache, 6 1/2 x 4 1/2 ins / 16.5 x 11.5 cm) FRF 1,000. PARIS, 26 Oct 1988, *Composition* (1956, oil on card, 9 x 22 ins / 22 x 55 cm) FRF 6,500. PARIS, 28 Nov 1988, *Trickle* (1955, oil on canvas, 25 1/2 x 32 ins / 65 x 81 cm) FRF 4,200. PARIS, 16 Jan 1989, *Why Not Shed Tears!* (1968, oil on canvas, 27 1/2 x 25 1/2 ins / 70 x 65 cm) FRF 8,100. PARIS, 3 March 1989, *Kyrie* (1957, oil on canvas, 30 x 22 ins / 76 x 55 cm) FRF 8,500; *Composition* (1956, oil on card, 18 1/2 x 23 1/2 ins / 47 x 60 cm) FRF 15,000. PARIS, 26 May 1989, *Composition* (1957, oil on paper, 22 x 14 1/2 ins / 55 x 37 cm) FRF 4,300. PARIS, 11 Oct 1989, *Arabesques* (1967, oil on canvas, 32 x 39 1/4 ins / 81 x 100 cm) FRF 18,000. DOUAI, 3 Dec 1989, *Marriage of the Weightlifter* (1974, oil on canvas, 57 3/4 x 45 1/4 ins / 147 x 115 cm) FRF 30,000. PARIS, 21 June 1990, *Abstract Composition* (oil on canvas, 35 x 28 1/4 ins / 88 x 72 cm) FRF 30,000. PARIS, 1 Oct 1990, *Yellow Composition* (1957, oil on canvas, 34 3/4 x 57 ins / 88.5 x 145 cm) FRF 42,000. DOUAI, 11 Nov 1990, *Composition* (charcoal, 17 3/4 x 22 1/2 ins / 45 x 57 cm) FRF 7,000. LE TOUQUET, 11 Nov 1990, *Composition* (1958, gouache, 12 1/4 x 9 1/2 ins / 31 x 24 cm) FRF 5,000. PARIS, 25 May 1992, *Abstract Composition* (1959, mixed media, 13 x 9 1/4 ins / 33 x 23.5 cm) FRF 6,100. LOKEREN, 10 Oct 1992, *Probable/Possible* (1957, oil on panel, 10 3/4 x 8 1/2 ins / 27.5 x 21.5 cm) BEF 28,000. PARIS, 25 June 1993, *Untitled* (1950, oil on canvas, 31 1/4 x 38 3/4 ins / 79.5 x 98.5 cm) FRF 13,000. PARIS, 12 July 1994, *Arabesque* (1967, oil on canvas, 32 x 39 1/4 ins / 81 x 100 cm) FRF 5,000. PARIS, 4 July 2000, *Cross Tree* (oil on canvas, 51 x 36 ins / 129 x 92 cm) FRF 27,500.

SIGNS OF..., Master of the. See **MASTERS**

SIGNY, Louis

French, 18th century.
Active in Paris 1768-1792.
Painter. Figure compositions.

MUSEUMS AND GALLERIES:

PARIS (Mus. Carnavalet): *Municipal Guards' Parade on the Place de Grève* (two) - PONTOISE: *Panorama of Pontoise* (watercolour).

AUCTION RECORDS:

PARIS, 30 Oct 1928, *Portrait of Buffon* (drawing) FRF 160. PARIS, 10 June 1949, *Landscapes with Figures* (two watercolours) FRF 1,800.

SIGO

French, 11th century.
Active at Fougères in 1055.
Sculptor, illuminator (?).

Sigo was a monk.

SIGOV, Aleksandr or Alexander

Russian, 20th - 21st century.
Born 1955, in Leningrad, now St Petersburg.
Painter. Figures.

Sigov belonged to the 7+1 group. He has exhibited regularly in St Petersburg and Moscow as well as in other major cities of the former USSR.

AUCTION RECORDS:

PARIS, 8 Dec 1990, *Cat Princess* (oil on canvas, 27 1/2 x 23 1/2 ins / 70 x 60 cm) FRF 4,000.

SIGRIST, Anton, or Sigristen

French, 18th century.
Born in Brigue (Alpes-Maritimes), south-east France.
Sculptor. Religious subjects.

In the first half of the 18th century, Sigrist produced many altars for churches in the Swiss cantons of Grisons, Schwyz and Valais.

SIGRIST, Bernhard, or Siegrist

German, 18th - 19th century.
Born 1760, in Mannheim; died 1824, in Mannheim.
Engraver (burin).

Bernhard Sigrist was the father of Wilhelm. He produced stipple engravings (using fine dots as part of an engraving) in the English style.

SIGRIST, Christian, or Siegrist

French, 18th - 19th century.
Born 1746, in Strasbourg; died 7 April 1822, in Strasbourg.
Painter, engraver (etching), draughtsman.

Christian Sigrist studied at the Académie in Paris.

MUSEUMS AND GALLERIES:

STRASBOURG (Prints Collection): *View of Strasbourg*; drawings.

SIGRIST, Edmond

French, 20th century.
Born 1882, in Paris; died February 1947.
Painter, draughtsman. Portraits, landscapes, urban landscapes, waterscapes, flowers.

Edmond Sigrist exhibited at the Salon des Indépendants in Paris from 1910, and later at the Salon d'Automne and the Salon des Tuileries.

He painted landscapes of Provence, the Arles region and the Camargue.

AUCTION RECORDS:

PARIS, 4-5 March 1920, *In Provence,* FRF 145. PARIS, 23 Dec 1927, *St-Cyr-sur-Mer,* FRF 1,280. PARIS, 22 May 1942, *Main Road,* FRF 1,800; *Landscape in the South of France,* FRF 3,000. PARIS, 20 June 1944, *Countryside,* FRF 4,500. PARIS, 18 May 1945, *Bunch of Poppies,* FRF 1,750. PARIS, July 1946, *Landscape in Provence,* FRF 9,000. PARIS, 1 Oct 1946, *Head Portrait of a Child* (pencil drawing) FRF 350. PARIS, 19 Nov 1948, *Road,* FRF 2,500. PARIS, 22 Dec 1989, *The Seine Viewed from Bir-Hakeim Bridge* (oil on canvas, 21 1/4 x 25 1/2 ins / 54 x 65 cm) FRF 7,500.

SIGRIST, Franz, the Younger

Austrian, 18th - 19th century.
Born 1760, in Vienna.
Painter.

Franz Sigrist was the son of Franz the Elder.

SIGRIST, Franz

Austrian, 18th - 19th century.
Born 1773, in Vienna; died 10 February 1836, in Vienna.
Painter.

SIGRIST, Franz or François, the Elder
German, 18th century.
Born 23 May 1727, in Alt-Breisach (Eberfeld); died 21 October 1803, in Vienna, Austria.
Painter, engraver. History painting, religious subjects, mythological subjects. Murals.
Neo-Classical.

Franz Sigrist studied under the Austrian painter Paul Troger (1698 - 1762) at the academy in Vienna and was also influenced by Josef Ignaz Mildorfer (1719 - 1775). From 1754 to 1762, he stayed in Augsburg (Bavaria) Germany. In 1777, by decree, the Prince Elector of Bavaria, Karl Theodor, decided to take control of the arts, calling for more simplicity and putting an end to the magnificent, extravagant displays of the Baroque. Outside Bavaria, however, it continued to be embraced wholeheartedly, particularly by Sigrist. The prince's decree not only triggered the end of the Baroque era; the combined teachings of Johann Joachim Winckelmann (1717 - 1768) and the German painter Anton Raffael Mengs (1728 - 1779) also prompted a return to the canons of antiquity.

Sigrist produced engravings for various projects, including 60 to illustrate a book on the saints, published by J. Giulini in 1753 - 1755, as well as etchings of some of his own religious pictures, such as *Healing of Tobit, Lot and his Daughters*. Other works by him include the choir vault for the church of Seekirchen, Austria, the convent ceiling in Zwiefalten, Germany, and the decoration of the Hall of Ceremonies at Schönbrunn Palace, near Vienna, (illustrating the marriage between Joseph II and Isabella of Parma) to which he contributed. In his ceiling frescoes known as *The Four Faculties*, (representing the four university faculties) painted for the main hall of the Eger Lyceum in Hungary, Sigrist replaced the heavenly profusion of pink, chubby-cheeked angels and holy figures of his predecessors with melancholy scholars and solemn thinkers.

MUSEUMS AND GALLERIES:
BERLIN (National Museum): *Arrival of the Redeemer in Heaven* - NUREMBERG (Germanisches Nationalmus.): *Job Sitting between his Wife and Three Friends* - PRAGUE: *Bacchus and Ariadne*; *Death of Orion* - STUTTGART (Staatsgal.): *St Wilfried Baptising Pagans* - VIENNA (Österreichische Gal. Belvedere): *Death of St Joseph*.

AUCTION RECORDS:
VIENNA, 13 Jan 1976, *Healing the Blind* (oil on canvas, 28 3/4 x 36 ins / 73 x 91.5 cm) ATS 22,000. VIENNA, 13 March 1979, *Zacharias in the Temple* (oil on canvas, fragment, 15 1/4 x 10 1/4 ins / 39 x 26 cm) ATS 110,000. LONDON, 5 July 1984, *Flight into Egypt* (oil/copper, 13 1/2 x 11 ins / 34.5 x 27 cm) GBP 5,000. LONDON, 19 May 1989, *Cupid Playing Soldiers* (oil on panel, 15 x 17 3/4 ins / 37.8 x 45.1 cm) GBP 1,540. NEW YORK, 28 Jan 1998, *Death of Dido* (oil on paper, 6 1/4 x 8 1/4 ins / 15.9 x 21 cm) USD 2,875. VIENNA, 30 March 2000, *Resurrection* (oil on canvas, 9 x 11 ins / 24 x 29 cm) ATS 65,000. VIENNA, 16 June 2004, *Susanna and the Elders* (oil on canvas, 24 x 30 ins / 60 x 77 cm) EUR 6,000.

SIGRIST, Ignaz
Austrian, 18th century.
Active in Vienna, Austria, in the second half of the 18th century.
Painter.

Ignaz Sigrist was probably the son of Franz the Elder.

SIGRIST, Jean Jacques Adolphe
French, 20th century.
Born 22 October 1905, in Münster; died 1 August 1994.
Painter. Figure compositions, figures, nudes, landscapes, seascapes, still-lifes (flowers/fruit).

Jean Jacques Adolphe Sigrist spent his childhood in Chile, returning to France to do his military service. He took evening classes in drawing at the Ville de Paris studios.

He took part in group exhibitions in Paris at the Salon d'Automne from 1942, the Société Nationale des Beaux-Arts from 1943, and the Salon des Surindépendants (of which he became Vice-President) from 1947. He also showed his paintings in solo exhibitions, including in Paris in 1958 at the Galerie Barbizon, in 1975 at the Galerie Cambacérès, and in Colmar in 1971 at the Musée Bartholdi.

He painted a wide range of subjects, and his work has an air of innocence which recalls the celebratory feel in the work of Charles Walch.

BIBLIOGRAPHY:
J. A. Sigrist, auction catalogue, Nouveau Drouot, Paris, 14 October 1985.

AUCTION RECORDS:
BERGERAC, 29 Oct 1988, *The Suresnes Bridge* (oil on canvas) FRF 3,600.

SIGRIST, Johann
Austrian, 18th century.
Born 1756, in Augsburg (Bavaria), Germany; died 14 May 1807, in Vienna.
Painter, engraver.

Probably the son of Franz Sigrist the Elder, Johann Sigrist and J. M. Siccrist (an engraver in Augsburg) may have been one and the same artist.

SIGRIST, Salomon
Swiss, 20th century.
Born 15 October 1880, in Rafz.
Painter, engraver. Portraits, landscapes.

Salomon Sigrist trained in Karlsruhe before going on to live and work in Zurich.

SIGRIST, Wilhelm or Johann Wilhelm, or Siegrist
German, 19th century.
Born 1797, in Mannheim.
Engraver (burin), lithographer. Natural history.

Wilhelm Sigrist was the son of Bernhard Sigrist. He studied under his father and attended the academy in Munich.

SIGRISTE, Guido
Swiss, 19th - 20th century.
Born 10 April 1864, in Aarau; died March 1915, in Pau, France.
Painter. Historical subjects, military subjects.

Guido Sigriste studied in Paris under Gustave Boulanger and Jules Lefebvre and went on to exhibit at the Salon de Artistes Français, where he received an honourable mention in 1905. Sigriste devoted a major portion of his work to the Napoleonic era. His generous style and treatment of light are reminiscent of Edouard Manet.

AUCTION RECORDS:
PARIS, 27 March 1903, *Gendarmes, 1805*, FRF 280. NEW YORK, 25-26 Jan 1911, *Napoleon and his General Staff*, USD 800. PARIS, 8-9 May 1941, *Napoleon at Landgrafenberg in 1805*, FRF 4,000. PARIS, 17 March 1950, *Grenadier*, FRF 33,000. PARIS, 18 March 1955, *Racehorses*, FRF 17,500. LOS ANGELES, 13 Nov 1972, *Napoleon in the Field*, USD 950. LONDON, 2 Nov 1973, *Wellington and Napoleon at Waterloo; French Troops on a Road* (collection) Gns 2,200. PARIS, 16 March 1976, *Scout* (oil on panel, 13 x 9 1/2 ins / 33 x 24 cm) FRF 2,100. ZURICH, 20 May 1977, *Eve of the Battle of Jena* (1806, oil on canvas, 72 x 46 1/2 ins / 182 x 118 cm) CHF 8,000.

Paris, 12 Dec 1979, *Arab Festival* (oil on canvas, 27 x 39 1/4 ins / 68.5 x 100 cm) FRF 8,000. London, 27 Nov 1981, *Napoleon Decorating a Soldier* (1894, oil on panel, 9 1/2 x 12 1/2 ins / 24.2 x 31.7 cm) GBP 3,200. Rouen, 21 March 1982, *Artist's Studio* (1890, watercolour, 14 1/2 x 19 3/4 ins / 37 x 50 cm) FRF 10,500. Lyons, 19 March 1984, *Emperor Napoleon I on Horseback* (oil on canvas remounted on panel, 20 x 28 3/4 ins / 51 x 73 cm) FRF 18,000. Paris, 1 Dec 1989, *Soldiers in a Tavern* (oil on canvas, 17 3/4 x 21 ins / 45 x 53.5 cm) FRF 23,000. Paris, 14 Dec 1990, *Napoleon and his Officers in the Field* (oil on panel, 13 1/2 x 18 ins / 34 x 46 cm) FRF 24,000. New York, 20 Jan 1993, *News from the Front* (oil on panel, 10 1/4 x 6 3/4 ins / 26 x 17.1 cm) USD 1,840. Paris, 27 May 1994, *Napoleon Campaigning* (oil on canvas, 20 x 29 1/4 ins / 51 x 74 cm) FRF 25,000. New York, 16 Feb 1995, *Hussar and Mount* (oil on panel, 10 1/4 x 8 1/4 ins / 26 x 21 cm) USD 5,750. Paris, 19 Oct 1997, *Officers and Mounts* (1891, oil on panel, 9 1/2 x 7 ins / 24 x 18 cm) FRF 12,000.

SIGRISTEN, Anton. See **SIGRIST**

SIGUEIRA, Dom. Ant.. See **SEQUEIRA Domingos Antonio de**

SIGÜENZA Y CHAVARRIETA, Joaquín

Spanish, 19th century.

Born 5 June 1825, in El Peral, near Cuenca (Castile-La Mancha); died 7 July 1902, in Madrid.

Painter. Military subjects, portraits, local scenes, still-lifes.

Joaquín Sigüenza y Chavarrieta studied at the school of fine arts in Madrid and then in Paris at the school of fine arts and in the studios of Léon Cogniet and Horace Vernet. He also travelled to Morocco. He was appointed court painter to Queen Isabella II, curator of the Escorial monastery and drawing teacher at the school of the Escorial. He exhibited at a number of group exhibitions, including the exhibitions of the national fine arts society of Madrid between 1862 and 1897, receiving a commendation in 1864, another in 1867 and a bronze medal in 1892.

He painted mainly historical subjects and is known in particular for *The Glorious Trophies Won in Morocco at the Seizing of Tétouan; The Investiture of Alfonso XII as Grand Master of the Military Orders*; and *The Proclamation of the First Republic at the Puerta del Sol.*

Bibliography:

Arnáiz, José Manuel/López Jiménez, Javier/Merchán Díaz, Manuel (ed.), '*Cien años de pintura en Espana y Portugal (1830-1930)*' in vol. X, Antiqvaria, Madrid, 1993.

SIGÜENZA Y ORTIZ, Mariano

Spanish, 19th century.

Born in Valencia; died 1860, in Valencia.

Painter, copyist, engraver, illustrator. Religious subjects.

Mariano Sigüenza y Ortiz studied at the school of fine arts in Valencia and later taught there. He painted mainly biblical figures including: *Virgin and Child; The Penitent Saints Paul and Anthony*; and *St John the Baptist*, a copy of the painting by Mengs.

As an engraver he made a line engraving of *Infant Jesus* and illustrated the *Biographical Dictionary* by Oliva and the *History of Spain* by Mariana.

Bibliography:

Arnáiz, José Manuel/López Jiménez, Javier/Merchán Díaz, Manuel (ed.), '*Cien años de pintura en Espana y Portugal (1830-1930)*' in vol. X, Antiqvaria, Madrid, 1993.

SIGURDSSON, Sigurdur Arni

Icelandic, 20th century.

Active in France since 1987.

Painter. Landscapes.

Exhibitions of Sigurdsson's landscapes and other works were held in 1995 and 1997 at the Aline Vidal Gallery in Paris. His stylised landscape work permutates naivety, humour and a somewhat unsettling sense of the strange and unreal.

SIGURTA, Antonio

Italian, 18th century.

Active in Milan during the second half of the 18th century.

Painter.

Antonio Sigurta executed works for the cathedrals of Milan and Lodi.

SIGURTA, Luigi

Italian, 18th century.

Active in Venice during the second half of the 18th century.

Painter, engraver (burin).

Luigi Sigurta, who painted altarpieces, exhibited at the Royal Academy in London in 1774.

SIJAKOVIC, Toma

Macedonian, 20th century.

Born 1930, in Kosovo Polje.

Painter.

Toma Sijakovic trained at Ljubljana academy and after graduating travelled in France, Italy, England and Germany. He makes 'cassettes' of distant memories and traditions that recall the *musandra*, the sacred niches in traditional Macedonian houses, but his contain industrially-produced objects. He does not shy away from elegance or decorative effects when using colour or designing geometric ornamentation.

He has taken part in various exhibitions of contemporary Macedonian art, and he had a number of solo exhibitions, in Skopje (1952, 1953, 1962, 1965, 1968), Belgrade (1959) and Kumanovo (1967).

SIJS, Maurice, or Sys

Belgian, 20th century.

Born 27 October 1880, in Ghent; died 1972.

Painter, watercolourist. Portraits, landscapes, urban landscapes, waterscapes, seascapes.

Laethem-St-Martin Group (Second School).

Maurice Sijs studied under Louis Tytgat at the academy of fine arts in Ghent, then under J. de Vriendt at the Fine Arts Institute in Antwerp. Sijs painted views of Flanders and the North Sea coast, together with scenes of the Paris quays and Martigues. The influence of the Impressionists in general and, in particular, of Emile Claus, is most evident in his pure colours and open-air technique.

Museums and Galleries:

Brussels (MBA).

Auction records:

Antwerp, 22 Oct 1974, *Fish, Volendam*, BEF 85,000. Antwerp, 25 Oct 1977, *Artist in his Studio* (1902, oil on canvas, 23 1/2 x 10 1/4 ins / 60 x 26 cm) BEF 38,000. Amsterdam, 28 Nov 1979, *Volendam* (1910, oil on canvas, 13 3/4 x 12 1/4 ins / 35 x 31 cm) NLG 4,000. Amsterdam, 15 Sept 1981, *Fisherman on his Boat* (watercolour, 27 x 28 3/4 ins / 68.5 x 73 cm) NLG 3,800. Antwerp, 27 April 1982, *Fishing Boat* (gouache, 20 1/2 x 33 3/4 ins / 52 x 86 cm) BEF 100,000. Amsterdam, 24 Oct 1983, *Yachts at Anchor* (gouache, 15 1/4 x 26 1/2 ins / 39 x 67 cm) NLG 3,200. Lokeren, 20 Oct 1984, *Fishing Port* (oil on panel, 23 1/2 x 22 ins / 60 x 55 cm) BEF 80,000. Lokeren, 20 April 1985, *Fisherman on his Boat* (1918, gouache, 35 1/2 x 29 1/2 ins / 90 x 75 cm) BEF 170,000. Lokeren, 28 May 1988, *Panoramic View from the Mill at Laethem* (oil on card, 27 1/2 x

23½ ins / 70 x 60 cm) BEF 200,000. LOKEREN, 8 Oct 1988, *Grand'Place, Brussels* (1905, oil on panel, 16¼ x 17¼ ins / 41 x 44 cm) BEF 200,000. AMSTERDAM, 24 May 1989, *River Lys with a Sailing Vessel at Anchor* (1909, oil on canvas, 31¾ x 39¼ ins / 80.5 x 100 cm) NLG 69,000. AMSTERDAM, 6 Nov 1990, *Boats in Port* (oil on canvas/card, 10½ x 15 ins / 26.5 x 38 cm) NLG 4,025. AMSTERDAM, 13 Dec 1990, *Old Corn Market, Ghent* (oil on canvas, 56¾ x 48¼ ins / 144 x 122.5 cm) NLG 115,000. LOKEREN, 21 March 1992, *River Lys and Neighbouring Canal* (1902, watercolour, 8¾ x 14¾ ins / 22.5 x 37.5 cm) BEF 170,000. AMSTERDAM, 21 May 1992, *Boats Aground at Sunset* (1911, oil on canvas, 35½ x 49½ ins / 90 x 126 cm) NLG 36,800. AMSTERDAM, 28 Oct 1992, *Fishing Vessels on the Zuiderzee heading for Volendam* (1919, watercolour and gouache heightened with white/paper, 27¼ x 32¾ ins / 69 x 83 cm) NLG 12,650. LOKEREN, 5 Dec 1992, *Sailing Vessels off Volendam* (gouache, 19¾ x 23½ ins / 50 x 60 cm) BEF 160,000. LOKEREN, 9 Oct 1993, *Sun on the River Lys* (oil on canvas, 23 x 27½ ins / 57.5 x 70 cm) BEF 380,000. LOKEREN, 12 March 1994, *Woman on the Banks of the Lys* (oil on canvas, 32¾ x 42¼ ins / 83 x 107 cm) BEF 440,000. AMSTERDAM, 1 June 1994, *Sunset at Volendam* (1915, oil, gouache and watercolour/card, 24½ x 28 ins / 62 x 71 cm) NLG 28,750. AMSTERDAM, 6 Dec 1995, *Banks of the Lys* (oil on canvas, 22½ x 27½ ins / 57 x 70 cm) NLG 28,750. AMSTERDAM, 4 June 1996, *House near a Watercourse* (oil on canvas, 28¼ x 28¼ ins / 72 x 71.5 cm) NLG 35,400; *Still-life with Flowers and Artist's Tools* (oil on panel, 16½ x 20½ ins / 42 x 52 cm) NLG 16,520. AMSTERDAM, 2-3 June 1997, *Low Tide* (gouache, pastel and oil on paper, 24½ x 28½ ins / 62.5 x 72.5 cm) NLG 35,400. AMSTERDAM, 2 Dec 1997, *Ferryman at Work* (gouache and pastel/panel, 12¼ x 15 ins / 31 x 38 cm) NLG 14,991.

SIJTHOFF, Gijsbertus Jan
Dutch, 19th - 20th century.
Born 1867; died 1949.
Painter. Genre scenes, interiors with figures, urban landscapes.

Gijsbertus Jan Sijthoff painted interiors in the Dutch tradition.

AUCTION RECORDS:

VIENNA, 16 March 1976, *Interior with Woman Knitting* (oil on canvas, 17 x 13 ins / 43 x 33 cm) ATS 22,000. AMSTERDAM, 6 Nov 1990, *Interior with Women Sewing* (oil on canvas, 22 x 26½ ins / 55 x 67 cm) NLG 3,220. AMSTERDAM, 5-6 Nov 1991, *View of Bruges* (oil on canvas, 19 x 23¼ ins / 48 x 59 cm) NLG 2,530. AMSTERDAM, 14 Sept 1993, *Interior with Peasant Woman Feeding a Cat* (oil on canvas, 23¾ x 20 ins / 60.5 x 50.5 cm) NLG 2,185. AMSTERDAM, 9 Nov 1993, *Interior with Mother and Child* (oil on canvas, 37¼ x 29¼ ins / 94.5 x 74 cm) NLG 5,750. AMSTERDAM, 11 April 1995, *Dressmaking Lesson* (oil on canvas, 23¼ x 19¾ ins / 59 x 50 cm) NLG 3,068. AMSTERDAM, 19-20 Feb 1997, *Afternoon Nap* (oil on canvas, 17½ x 19½ ins / 44.5 x 49.5 cm) NLG 4,612. TORONTO, 11 June 1999, *First Lessons* (oil on canvas, 30 x 24 ins / 76 x 62 cm) CAD 3,600. SAN FRANCISCO, 16 May 2001, *Mother and Child in a Cottage Interior* (oil on canvas, 37 x 30 ins / 95 x 76 cm) USD 4,000. AMSTERDAM, 22 Jan 2002, *Teatime* (oil on canvas, 23 x 28 ins / 59 x 70 cm) EUR 2,500. STOCKHOLM, 4 Dec 2002, *Interior Scene with Woman and Child* (oil on canvas, 28 x 24 ins / 70 x 61 cm) SEK 15,000. AMSTERDAM, 1 July 2003, *Tending to the Goat* (oil on canvas, 24 x 18 ins / 60 x 46 cm) EUR 2,500. AMSTERDAM, 19 April 2004, *Larens Interior with a Mother Gazing at a New-born in a Basket* (oil on canvas, 15 x 19 ins / 39 x 49 cm) EUR 2,200.

SIK, József
Hungarian, 20th century.
Born 1922, in Budapest.
Painter.

József Sik exhibited at the Salon de Mai, Paris, in 1953.

SIKA, Jutta
Austrian, 20th century.
Born 17 September 1877, in Linz.
Painter, engraver, designer. Landscapes, flowers.

Sika Jutta trained in Vienna and went on to work in the Austrian capital, exhibiting there and in St-Louis and, in 1925, in Paris.

SIKEMEIER, Johan Hendrik
Dutch, 20th century.
Born 22 April 1877, in Yokohama.
Painter. Portraits.

Johan Hendrik Sikemeier studied at the academy of fine arts in Antwerp and went on to live and work in The Hague.

MUSEUMS AND GALLERIES:

THE HAGUE (Gemeentemus.): *Portrait of Madame Elise von Calcar.*

SIKES. See **SYKES**

SIKIRDJI, Claudie
French, 20th century.
Painter. Landscapes.

Claudie Sikirdji exhibits in France.

She uses a generous amount of paint, in which she cuts deep furrows, and over which she scatters granular trails. Her mysterious landscapes could be described as landscapes of the mind. They feature lines of rubble, expanses of petrified water, and walls covered with indecipherable hieroglyphs.

SIKKELAER, Pieter van, or Sickeleer or Sickeleers, called Saturnus
Flemish School, 17th century.
Engraver (burin).

Pieter van Sikkelaer was the master of a studio in Antwerp in 1674, and engraved allegories.

SIKKER, Anne-Marie
Danish, 20th century.
Born 1941, in Copenhagen.
Active in Belgium.
Painter, collage artist, sculptor, engraver. Wall decorations.

Anne-Marie Sikker trained at the school of industrial art and design and the Kunstakademi in Copenhagen, and at the art academy in Watermael-Boitsfort in Belgium. She spent some time in Latin America.

SIKKINGER. See **SICKINGER**

SIKLÓDY, Lõrinc
Hungarian, 20th century.
Born 1876, in Gyergyo-Borszék.
Sculptor. Figures. Monuments.

Lõrinc Siklódy is known for his war memorials at Gödöllõ and Sopron, as well as genre sculpture.

SIKO, Miklos or Nikolaus
Hungarian, 19th century.
Born 1816, in Sopterpuszta; died 5 May 1900, in Marosvásárhely.
Painter, lithographer. Portraits.

Miklos Siko studied under M. Barabas and also at the art academy in Munich.

SIKORSKI, Jan
Polish, 19th century.
Born 24 December 1804, in Dresden; died 12 February 1887, in Warsaw.
Painter.

Jan Sikorski studied and worked in Warsaw. The Lubomirski museum in Lviv (Ukraine) owns his *Portrait of the Painter A. Lesser.*

SILANION
4th century BC.
Athenian, active 370 to 320 BC.
Sculptor.
Ancient Greek.
Silanion is known chiefly for his portraits of famous people in the world of politics, philosophy and art; he also made statues of athletes and characters from tragedies. His portrait of *Plato* was to become the standard model for portraits of the philosophers. He attempted to reproduce the features of his subjects as expressively and realistically as possible. Most of his works, and particularly the *Satyrus* from Olympia mark a new step towards the art of portraiture in Hellenistic art.

SILAS, Louis
French, 19th century.
Painter. Still-lifes (flowers/fruit).
AUCTION RECORDS:
LONDON, 17 June 1992, *Chrysanthemums, Tulips, Lilies and Delphiniums* (oil on canvas, 41 1/4 x 59 ins / 105 x 150 cm) GBP 3,300. LONDON, 28 Oct 1992, *Still-life with Summer Flowers* (oil on panel, 27 1/2 x 35 ins / 70 x 88 cm) GBP 1,980. LONDON, 27 Oct 1993, *Gentle Reminders of my Lady Friend's Garden* (oil on panel, 23 x 19 ins / 58.5 x 48 cm) GBP 483. AMSTERDAM, 3 Sept 1996, *Still-life with Flowers and Fruit* (oil on panel, 29 1/4 x 46 3/4 ins / 74 x 119 cm) NLG 2,191. STOCKHOLM, 3 Dec 2003, *Scenes with Cupids, Flowers and Parrots* (oil on canvas mounted on screen, in six parts, 81 x 135 ins / 206 x 342 cm) SEK 85,000.

SILBER, Alex, pseudonym of Meyer, Werner Alex
Swiss, 20th - 21st century.
Born 1950, in Basel.
Draughtsman.
Alex Silber plays on the ambiguity between photography and hyperrealist drawing, setting up a narcissistic dialogue between the camera image and mirror image. In 1974 he took part in the exhibition *Transformation, the Look of the Transvestite* at the Kunstmuseum in Lucerne (Switzerland) and Bochum museum (Germany); in 1975 he participated in the 9th Paris Biennale.

SILBERATH
German, 18th century.
Was active in 1769.
Silhouettist.

SILBERBAUER, Fritz
Austrian, 20th century.
Born 4 April 1883, in Leibnitz.
Painter, engraver. Murals.
Fritz Silberbauer studied at the Akademie der Bildenden Künste in Vienna.
MUSEUMS AND GALLERIES:
GRAZ (Landesmus. Joanneum, Neue Gal.).

SILBERBERGER, Stefan
Austrian, 20th century.
Born 16 February 1877, in Reith, near Brixlegg.
Sculptor. Monuments, decorative schemes.
Stefan Silberberger was educated in Dresden and Salzburg; he went on to sculpt war memorials, crucifixes and wall fountains.

SILBEREISEN, Andreas
German, 17th - 18th century.
Born 1673; died 1766, in Augsburg (Bavaria).
Engraver (burin). Maps.

SILBEREISEN, Andreas
German, 18th century.
Born 1713; died 1751, in Augsburg (Bavaria).
Engraver (burin).

SILBERMAN
French.
Glass painter.
The local museum in Épinal has a stained glass window by Silberman from Strasbourg Cathedral.
MUSEUMS AND GALLERIES:
ÉPINAL (Mus. départemental d'Art ancien et contemporain): stained glass window.

SILBERMANN
German, 19th century.
Died 1815.
Active in Dresden.
Painter, miniaturist.
Silbermann studied under G. B. Casanova.

SILBERMANN, Jean Claude
French, 20th century.
Born 31 August 1935, in Boulogne-Billancourt.
Painter, watercolourist, sculptor of assemblages, installation artist. Scenes with figures. Artists' books.
Surrealist group.
Jean Claude Silbermann discovered poetry in 1953 - the year he left school. He was inspired by, in particular, Apollinaire (*Alcools* (*Alcohol*)), Breton, Péret, Char, Rimbaud, Lautréamont and Éluard (*Les Malheurs des Immortels* (*The Misfortunes of the Immortals*)). On returning to Paris after travelling widely, he joined the Surrealist Group in 1955. In 1958, he published a small volume of erotic poems with the Pauvert publishing house, entitled *Au puits de l'Ermite* (*At the Hermit's Well*). He was influenced by Soupault and Charles Trenet, but suffered writer's block. He then experimented, unsuccessfully, with automatic writing.

In 1961 he worked with a Breton painter, Pierre Jaouën, who encouraged him to take up painting and helped improve his technique.

In 1971, the Ministry of Culture commissioned him to develop a teaching programme in line with the unorthodox thinking and artistic practices in the national art schools. He taught at the École National d'Art at Cergy Pontoise from 1981 to 2000.

He authored several artists' books, including: *Testament d'Horus* (*The Testament of Horus*) by José Pierre, *Les Chants de Maldoror* (*Songs of Maldoror*) by Lautréamont, *Poésie* (*Poetry*) by Isidore Ducasse, and *Odor di Femina* by Bernard Marcadé. He also illustrated his own books, including *Chantefables et Chantefleurs* (*Chantefables and Chantefleurs*), the first edition of which contained the entire collection of children's poems by the Surrealist Robert Desnos, and in 2002 *Alice in Wonderland*, both published by Éditions Gründ.

Jean Claude Silbermann's art aims to show how unfamiliar images and objects can interrelate to make a mockery of convention. His imagination is dominated by language and intellectual reflection, which then forms an intimate relationship with painting. Having little interest in 'technique' as such, and feeling constricted within the traditional formats, he began, from 1963, to cut out his painted works, calling them *Artful Signs*. He cited his inspiration as restaurant menu holders. He drew figurative elements on painted plywood panels, then cut them out and overlapped them. This short cut bypassed the problem of integrating the figure with the background. These object paintings, which he first christened *Artful Signs*, are more compact than the simple *Signs* that followed. Silbermann writes of this first series of signs, which are 'all of a piece', that they 'arose from a heraldic type of organisation'. He later added to these paintings (which were increasingly turning into objects), material elements such as abandoned boards or worn-out shoes, as seen in a series of works with the generic title *Run For Your*

Life from 1965, which he defined as a 'commemorative plaque for a looter of shipwrecks'.

Another approach to painting was his experiments with using his left hand in preference to the right hand, which he felt had become desensitised by over-familiarity. This was the theme of a number of exhibitions; *Left Hand, Right Hand* in 1968; *Silbermann, His Life and Work* in 1970. He also singled out certain artefacts in the tradition of Surrealist objects, such as *Inflatable Crutch*, and *Perspective Tamed*, both from 1968. He created installations, in particular *Consumer*, for the exhibition *L'Écart Absolu* (*Stepping Right Out of Line*), the last by the Surrealist group, in 1965.

By fragmentating pictures into several parts, he opened up new spatial approaches, resulting in the environments he created such as *Babble-Babylon*, made up of some forty pieces that he had been working on since the mid 1980s. By blocking out the background of his characters and isolating them, his work concentrates on rendering a vivid image. Silbermann highlights an idea in a subtle play of colours and shapes, unusual for works created in marquetry.

In 1995 his work was presented at the FIAC (Foire Internationale d'Art Contemporain) in Paris by the Galerie Samy. He has shown work in solo exhibitions, including; 1964, *Signs* 1963-1964, Galerie Mona Lisa, the first showing of 'Artful Signs', with foreword by André Breton and José Pierre; 1968, *Right Hand, Left Hand*, Galerie Martin Malburet; 1970, *Silbermann, His Life and Work*, Galerie Lucien Durand, Paris; 1972, Galerie Maya, Brussels, exhibition with foreword by José Pierre; 1973 and 1979, Galerie Mathias Fels, Paris; 1976, *Signs, Poems, Blanks and Anecdotes*, Musée d'Art Moderne de la Ville, Paris; 1980, Galerie Buchholz, Munich; 1984, Galerie Chave, Vence; 1989, Galerie Samy Kinge, Paris; 1994, Palais des Congrès, Paris; 2000, *Babble-Babylon*, Villa Tamaris, La Seyne-sur-Mer; 2002, *Alice at Babble-Babylon*, Maubeuge; 2002, Galerie Les Yeux Fertiles, Paris.

BIBLIOGRAPHY:

Gassiot-Talabot, Gérald, '*J.- Cl. Silbermann*' in *Opus international*, periodical, Paris, June 1969. Pierre, José, '*Enseignes 1971-73*' in *L'Humidité* n° 12, periodical, Paris, 1973. Silbermann, J.-Cl., '*Mais qui a salé la salade de céleri?*' in *Silbermann: enseignes, poèmes, lacunes et anecdotes*, exhibition catalogue, Musée d'Art moderne de la Ville de Paris, Paris, 1976. Silbermann, J.-Cl., *Un bateau autour du cou*, Bordas, Paris, 1985. Silbermann, J.-Cl./Marcadé, Bernard, *Entretien: l'objet du délit*, Éd. Sixtus, Limoges, 1991 (Other texts by Philippe Audoin/André Breton/José Pierre/José Tronche). Strasser, Catherine/Marcadé, Bernard/Semin, Didier/Silbermann, J.- Cl., *Silbermann. Babil-Babylone*, exhibition catalogue, Villa Tamaris, La Seyne-sur-Mer, Éd. Sixtus, Limoges, 2000. Durozoi, Gérard (preface), *Alice à Babil-Babylone*, exhibition catalogue, Idem + Arts, Maubeuge, 2002.

MUSEUMS AND GALLERIES:

PARIS (FNAC): *Les Amants* (*The Lovers*).

AUCTION RECORDS:

PARIS, 6 April 1989, *The Accompanist* (1988, painted wooden sculpture, height 47 1/4 ins / 120 cm) FRF 15,000. PARIS, 8 Nov 1990, *It's Gone* (1985, oil on wood, 40 1/4 x 82 ins / 102 x 208 cm) FRF 22,000. PARIS, 26 Sept 1991, *Unpronounceable* (1968, acrylic/canvas, 35 3/4 x 28 3/4 ins / 91 x 73 cm) FRF 3,800. PARIS, 19 March 1993, *Girl Alone* (1975, painted sign in two parts, 26 3/4 x 42 1/2 ins / 68 x 108 cm and 28 x 21 1/2 ins/71 x 54.5 cm) FRF 7,000. PARIS, 11 June 1993, *Educational Game* (acrylic/canvas, 57 1/2 x 45 ins / 146 x 114 cm) FRF 4,800. PARIS, 12 Oct 1994, *To Be Opened in case of Danger, Objects* (collage and ink/paper in a transparent box, h. 14 1/2 ins / 37 cm, l. 11 ins/27 cm, prof. 3 ins/7.5 cm) FRF 5,000. PARIS, 21 Dec 2001, *Ensign for a Clandestine Passenger* (oil on panel cutout, 51 x 28 ins / 130 x 71 cm) FRF 15,000. PARIS, 15 April 2003, *Voyante* (oil on canvas, 18 x 24 ins / 46 x 61 cm) EUR 4,000. PARIS, 15 April 2003, *Large Tom-cat, Despicable Prince* (oil on wood, 47 x 21 ins / 119 x 54 cm) EUR 7,000.

SILBERMANN, Johann Andreas

French, 18th century.
Born 26 June 1712, in Strasbourg; died 11 February 1783, in Strasbourg.
Painter, draughtsman. Landscapes.

Johann Andreas Silbermann, an organ builder and historian, drew numerous views of Alsace.

SILBERMANN, Malvina

French, 20th - 21st century.
Born 1955, in Paris.
Painter (mixed media).

Malvina Silbermann graduated from the École des Beaux-Arts in Bourges. Her enigmatic pieces, often produced in series, draw inspiration from the animal and vegetable kingdoms.

She has participated in group exhibitions, notably at the Salon des Jeunes Sculpteurs in Paris in 1985 and at the 1989 Salon de Montrouge. She also showed work at an exhibition hosted by Marie-Madeleine Carious in Paris in 1991.

AUCTION RECORDS:

PARIS, 14 Oct 1991, *Lizard* (1991, mixed media/paper, 5 1/2 x 18 1/2 ins / 14 x 47 cm) FRF 3,500.

SILBERMANN, Valentin

German, 16th - 17th century.
Sculptor. Religious subjects. Monuments.
Leipzig School.

Silbermann carved many altars, tombs, pulpits and fountains in Dresden and other towns in Saxony. He also worked in Leipzig from 1584 to 1613.

MUSEUMS AND GALLERIES:

DRESDEN (Stadtmus.): ceremonial buffet.

SILBERNAGEL, Endres

German, 15th century.
Died 2 May 1503, in Fribourg.
Painter.

SILBERNAGEL, Franz

Austrian, 19th century.
Active in Bozen, South Tyrol (now Bolzano, Italy) in the second half of the 19th century.
Painter.

Silbernagel attended the art academy in Munich in 1838.

SILBERNAGEL, Johann Jakob

Austrian, 19th - 20th century.
Born 5 January 1836, in Bozen (now Bolzano, Italy); died 27 March 1915, in Andrian.
Sculptor. Statues, busts.

Silbernagel studied in Vienna under Franz Melnitzky and at the Akademie der Bildenden Künste, and went on to live and work in the Austrian capital.

MUSEUMS AND GALLERIES:

VIENNA (Städtisches Mus.): *Jos. Schreyvogel* (statue).

SILBERNAGEL, Karl

German, 19th century.
Born 1837, in Berlin; died after 1889.
Sculptor.

Silbernagel studied under H. Heidel. He produced two statues for the municipal theatre façade in Halle (Saxony-Anhalt), Germany: *Poetry* and *Truth*.

SILBERSCHLAGK, Hans

German, 16th century.
Active in Erfurt in 1587.
Painter.

SILBERSTEIN, Nathan

Polish, 20th century.

Born 12 May 1884, in Lódz.
Active in Switzerland from 1914.
Painter. Portraits, landscapes.

Nathan Silberstein studied with Angelo Janck at the Munich academy and moved to Zurich in 1914.

SILBERSTEIN, Otto
Austrian, 20th century.
Born 19 September 1876, in Vienna.
Painter, engraver, lithographer. Animals.

Otto Silberstein is noted for paintings and engravings of animals in the Vienna Zoo.

SILBERT, Ben
American, 20th century.
Born 1894, in Gorky; died 1940.
Painter, draughtsman. Landscapes, flowers.

Ben Silbert worked in Europe, especially Spain. He was noticed by Louis Vauxcelles and his work was exhibited by Paul Guillaume, but today he is largely forgotten. In 2003, his work appeared in the collective exhibition *Des Arbres et des Peintres* (*Trees and Painters*) at the Galerie Saphir in Paris.

AUCTION RECORDS:
PARIS, 4 April 1945, *Landscapes* (four drawings, collection) FRF 2,200; *Landscapes, Tree Study* (four drawings, collection) FRF 7,400. PARIS, 22 May 1945, *Segovia* (two oils on canvas, collection) FRF 1,400; *Flowers, Landscape* (two oils on canvas, collection) FRF 1,750.

SILBERT, Marie José Jean Raymond
French, 19th - 20th century.
Born 1862, in Aix-en-Provence; died 1939.
Painter, pastellist. Religious subjects, portraits, genre scenes, local scenes, landscapes, landscapes with figures.

Marie José Jean Raymond Silbert was a student of Jules Lefebvre and Luc Olivier-Merson at the École des Beaux-Arts in Paris. He made several visits to Spain, North Africa and the Far East. His work featured in collective exhibitions in Paris at the Salon des Artistes Français, where he became a member in 1889, and the Salon des Orientalistes Français, between 1908 and 1933. He was made a Chevalier of the Légion d'Honneur in 1908.

Notable works include: *The Legend of St Martin of Dalmatia; The Legend of St Francis of Assisi and the Wolf of Gubbio; Man Displaying Cockatoos; Alima Purveyor of Love.*

MUSEUMS AND GALLERIES:
ALGIERS: *Head of Gypsy* - MARSEILLES (MBA): *Head of Moroccan.*

AUCTION RECORDS:
PARIS, 11 Feb 1919, *Young Peasant Woman Going to Market,* FRF 200; *The Grace, Holland,* FRF 245. MARSEILLES, 18 Dec 1948, *Lydie, Negress of Martinique,* FRF 1,900; *Head of Moroccan* (1917, pastel) FRF 2,100. PARIS, 1 April 1949, *On the Beach,* FRF 4,800. PARIS, 17 June 1988, *Young Berber Woman and her Child* (1914, oil on canvas, 23½ x 19¾ ins / 60 x 50 cm) FRF 20,000. PARIS, 18-19 Nov 1991, *Market at Kairouan* (oil on canvas, 43¼ x 65¾ ins / 110 x 167 cm) FRF 130,000. PARIS, 22 April 1994, *Waterwheel at Kairouan* (1916, oil on canvas, 21¼ x 28½ ins / 54 x 72.5 cm) FRF 13,100. PARIS, 6 Nov 1995, *Morning Prayer in Morocco* (oil on canvas, 36¼ x 28 ins / 92 x 71 cm) FRF 14,500. PARIS, 10-11 June 1997, *Three-Quarter Length Portrait of a Man* (oil on canvas, 12¾ x 10 ins / 32.5 x 25.5 cm) FRF 55,000.

SILBERT, Max
Ukrainian, 19th - 20th century.
Born 29 November 1871, in Odessa.
Active and naturalised in France.
Painter. Genre scenes.

Max Silbert studied in Paris under Jean Léon Gérome and Albert Maignan. In 1907 he joined the Salon des Artistes Français, and exhibited with them thereafter.

AUCTION RECORDS:
PARIS, 28 Feb 1974, *The Tale,* FRF 4,400. NEW YORK, 24 Jan 1980, *Nursery* (oil on canvas, 34½ x 51 ins / 87.6 x 129.4 cm) USD 3,000. LINDAU, 5 Oct 1983, *Night Concert* (oil on canvas, 23½ x 32 ins / 60 x 81 cm) DEM 6,000. NEW YORK, 25 May 1988, *Woman Sewing* (oil on canvas, 32 x 25 ins / 81.3 x 63.5 cm) USD 4,950. LYONS, 13 Nov 1989, *Lace Makers* (oil on canvas, 21½ x 17½ ins / 54.5 x 44.5 cm) FRF 13,000. CHARLEVILLE-MÉZIÈRES, 19 Nov 1989, *Grandmother and Grandchildren* (oil on canvas, 22 x 18 ins / 55 x 46 cm) FRF 15,000. NEW YORK, 1 March 1990, *Shepherdess Watching her Flock by the Sea on a Summer's Day* (oil on canvas, 28 x 38¼ ins / 71.1 x 97.1 cm) USD 12,100. PARIS, 6 April 1993, *Gathering Tulips in Holland* (1912, oil on canvas, 18 x 22 ins / 46 x 55 cm) FRF 11,000.

SILEI, Luisa
Italian, 19th century.
Born 17 February 1825, in Florence; died 6 February 1898, in Rome.
Landscape artist.

Luisa Silei was a pupil of K. Marko.

BIBLIOGRAPHY:
Winspeare, Maddalena Paola, *Donne e colori. Artiste nei Musei Statali Fiorentini,* Firenze Musei, Sillabe, Florence, 2001 (texts in Italian and English).

MUSEUMS AND GALLERIES:
PRATO (Mus. Civico): one work.

SILEIKA, Jonas
Lithuanian, 20th century.
Born 25 June 1883, in Juodagoniai.
Painter. Portraits, landscapes.

Jonas Sileika trained at the Art Institute of Chicago and the academy, in Munich. On his return to Lithuania he settled in Pastas Sakiai.

MUSEUMS AND GALLERIES:
VILNIUS (NG).

SILEM, Ali
Algerian, 20th - 21st century.
Born 1947, in Sfizef.
Painter, engraver, illustrator.

Ali Silem studied at the school of fine arts in Algiers. In 1979, he participated in the execution of a collaborative fresco in Algiers and of sets and costumes for theatrical productions. He has exhibited in Algeria in collective events since 1972 and in solo exhibitions since 1980.

SILER, Matthias or Johann Matthias.
See **SILLER**

SILER, Todd Lael
American, 20th - 21st century.
Born 1953, in Long Island (New York).
Mixed media.

Todd Siler obtained a doctorate from the Massachusetts Institute of Technology, Cambridge, Massachusetts (the first artist to do so) in 1986 with a thesis entitled *Architectonics of Thought: A Symbolic Model of Neuropsychological Processes.* Working at the intersection of science and visual art, and with a wide variety of media and supports, Siler explores creativity and perception and uses abstract art as a tool to study the workings of the human mind. *The Brain Theatre of Mental Imagery* (1989, painting mixed media on synthetic canvas with white light reflection hologram) brings together neurophysiology and nuclear physics to suggest that our thought processes bear a dynamic resemblance to the fusion (merging) and fission (splitting) process that form and shape our universe. *Mind Icon: Connectivity* (1995, mixed media on

Plexiglas) explores the ways in which the human mind naturally connects things to create meaning and to communicate, by depicting various geometries of thought undergoing natural transformations initiated by the process of discovery. *Dream Tree: Metaphorming Life* (2000, mixed media on steel with historic quotations and photographic images installed at the Englewood City Center, Colorado) is a symbolic artwork that pictures the elusive beauty and qualities of 'being human' *Mind Fields* (1999, sculpture, mixed media on steel) remind us that the presence of humankind extends far beyond our mere mortal presence in the environment, and touches everything in nature.

Siler featured in many collective exhibitions since 1972 in the USA, Germany, Canada, Israel, the United Kingdom, The Netherlands, Austria, Brazil and Switzerland. Solo exhibitions from 1978 include: *Changing Minds*, Ronald Feldman Gallery, New York (1997); *Metaphorming Life: adventures in Thinking, Imagination and Innovation*, Museum of Outdoor Arts, Englewood, Colorado (2000); *Metaphormers, Exploration Place*, Whichita, Kansas (2003); *A.R.T. Strings*, Ronald Feldman Gallery, New York (2004).

Siler is also an author, inventor, presenter, educator and consultant. He is the founder and director of *Psi-Phi Communications* and the creator of the *Think Like a Genius* and of *Metaphorming* programmes which aim at helping people think, create and perform at their highest level and realise their full potential.

BIBLIOGRAPHY:

Siler, Todd, *Breaking the Mind Barrier: The Artscience of Neurocosmology*, illustrated book, Simon and Schuster, New York, 1992. Siler, Todd, *Think Like a Genius*, illustrated book, Bantam Books, New York, 1997. Siler, Todd, *A.R.T. Strings: A Guide to the Works of Todd Siler*, illustrated book, Boulder and Englewood, Colorado, 2004.

MUSEUMS AND GALLERIES:

JERUSALEM (Israel Mus.) - MOSCOW (Pushkin MFA) - NEW YORK (Metropolitan Mus. of Art) - NEW YORK (MoMA) - NEW YORK (Solomon R. Guggenheim Mus.) - NEW YORK (Whitney Mus. of American Art) - STUTTGART (Belser Verlag Print Archives).

SILES BADIA, Alfonso

Spanish, 19th - 20th century.

Born 15 March 1872, in Cartagena (Murcia); died 15 April 1956, in Cartagena.

Painter, draughtsman, illustrator, decorative artist. Religious subjects, genre scenes, portraits, urban landscapes, landscapes with figures, seascapes, still-lifes. Murals.

Alfonso Siles Badia was a pupil at the Escuela de Bellas Artes in Madrid and studied with the painter José Lozano. From 1890 he combined his work as a painter with his job as an employee of the Spanish Naval Administration, taking advantage of a voyage to the Philippines to exhibit his work.

In collaboration with Manuel Wessel de Guimbarda he painted the ceiling of the theatre in Cartagena and canvases for the collegiate chapel of St Patrick in Lorca, Murcia. Although he covered a variety subjects in his work, he had a predilection for religious themes and for the streets, squares and everyday life of Cartagena and its surroundings. He is known for: *St Luke, St Matthew, Sailors Receiving the Scapular of their Patron Saint the Virgin of the Carmelites, Ecce Homo, View of the Port of Cartagena, Laundrywoman, All to Port.* Siles Badia took part in various collective exhibitions including: Cartagena (1894); Madrid where he gained an honourable mention (1895) and Manila (1897).

BIBLIOGRAPHY:

Arnáiz, José Manuel/López Jiménez, Javier/Merchán Díaz, Manuel (ed.), *'Cien años de pintura en Espana y Portugal (1830-1930)'* in vol. X, Antiqvaria, Madrid, 1993.

SILFVERBERG, Ida

Finnish, 19th century.

Born 1834; died 1899, in Florence.

Painter, copyist. Portraits, genre scenes.

Ida Silfverberg studied in Helsinki, Dresden and Paris.

MUSEUMS AND GALLERIES:

HELSINKI: *Mother by the Bed of Her Sick Child; Bohemian Violinists; Shepherd Girl; Portrait of the Artist.*

SILFVERSKOG, Joakim, or Silfverskong

Swedish, 18th century.

Active from 1740 to 1753.

Potter.

Silfverskog worked at the porcelain factory in Rörstrand.

SILFVERSTRALE, Gustaf

Swedish, 18th - 19th century.

Born 4 February 1748, in Stockholm; died 11 May 1816, in Lindö.

Draughtsman. Landscapes.

Silfverstrale was a pupil of Jean Eric Rehn. Several of his works are in the Kungliga Akademi för de Fria Konsterna in Stockholm.

SILFWERSPARRE, Sophie

Swedish, 19th century.

Born 1783; died 1815.

Painter, copyist.

SILHOUETTE, Guy

French, 20th century.

Painter. Seascapes.

One of the works of Guy Silhouette is in the Navy Museum in Paris.

AUCTION RECORDS:

PARIS, 6 Dec 1990, *Sailing Boats Racing under Spinnaker, with Le Havre Lightship* (oil on canvas, 21¼ x 32 ins / 54 x 81 cm) FRF 3,800.

SILIGAI, Ferenc

Hungarian, 19th - 20th century.

Born 22 July 1873, in Mocsa; died 4 June 1924, in Budapest.

Painter. Genre scenes, landscapes.

MUSEUMS AND GALLERIES:

BUDAPEST (Fövárosi Képtár).

SILINI, Giuseppe Niccolo di Vincenzo, or Sillini

Italian, 18th - 19th century.

Born 1724, in Siena; died 1814.

Sculptor, stucco artist, architect.

Silini was the pupil of Ercole Lelli. He worked for churches in Siena and Montepulciano.

SILINS, Herberts

Latvian, 20th century.

Born 1926.

Painter. Urban landscapes, landscapes, flowers.

Herberts Silins trained in Belgium and Germany from 1945 to 1948. His work represents views or rather memories of towns and villages, which he paints in highly stylised, elliptical forms tending toward the abstract, in the spirit of the late landscapes of De Staël. After 1948 he took part in numerous exhibitions in Bulgaria, Canada, England, Germany, Greece, Poland, Spain, Sweden and Switzerland. In 1958 he became a member of the Artists Union.

MUSEUMS AND GALLERIES:

COLOGNE (Mus. Ludwig) - MOSCOW (State Tretyakov Gal.) - WARSAW (MCA).

AUCTION RECORDS:

PARIS, 11 July 1990, *Spanish Motif* (1989, oil on canvas, 49¼ x 49¼ ins / 125 x 125 cm) FRF 5,200.

SILINS, Karlis
Latvian, 20th - 21st century.
Born 1959.
Painter. Figure compositions, landscapes, seascapes, still-lifes.

Silins studied at the academy of fine art in Riga until 1984. She was a member of the association of young artists in 1984 and 1989, subsequently becoming a member of the association of Latvian artists. She paints on very varied themes, using a plastic style reminiscent of stylistic formulae that come from Cubism, but which she transposes into a vivid, jovial Expressionism. Her works have appeared in collective exhibitions in Germany, the USA and Turkey.

AUCTION RECORDS:
PARIS, 11 July 1990, *Guitarists Near the Sea* (1990, oil on canvas, 51 1/4 x 51 1/4 ins / 130 x 130 cm) FRF 3,800. PARIS, 14 Jan 1991, *Fishermen* (oil on canvas, 39 1/4 x 39 1/4 ins / 100 x 100 cm) FRF 3,500.

SILIPRANDI, Giuseppe
Italian, 18th century.
Born 28 April 1754; died 1792.
Medallist, engraver (burin).

Siliprandi was a pupil at the academy in Parma, where he studied with Benigno Bossi. He engraved copies of works by Raphael and also produced coats of arms.

SILIUS VON SANTFURT, or Zandvoort
Flemish School, 16th century.
Active in Mechelen in 1563.
Sculptor.

SILIVANOVICH, Nikodim Yureevich
Russian, 19th century.
Born 13 December 1834.
Painter, mosaicist.

Nikodim Yureevich Silivanovich studied at the art academy in St Petersburg. He produced mosaics for the Cathedral of St Isaak in St Petersburg.

SILK
British, 18th century.
Painter.

Silk worked for the Caughley porcelain works and established himself in London as a painter on enamel.

SILK, Thomas
British, 18th century.
Active in London from 1772 to 1780.
Sculptor (wood), designer, draughtsman.

SILL, Émilie
French, 19th - 20th century.
Born in Paris.
Painter. Genre scenes.

Émilie Sill was a student of Henriette de Longchamp and Ernestine de Pelleport. She exhibited in Paris, making her debut in 1882 at the Salon des Artistes Français.

SILLA, Agostino. See **SCILLA**

SILLANI, Sillano
Italian, 17th century.
Active in Rome.
Sculptor.

Sillani executed two statues for the church of S Carlo alle Quattro Fontane in Rome.

SILLANO, Angelo
Italian, 16th century.
Active in 1596.
Painter.

Angelo Sillano is the author of a *Virgin and Child* in the church of S Pietro near Spoleto.

SILLARD VON PREISLINGER, Brigitte
French, 20th century.
Born 1942, in Rennes.
Sculptor, painter, engraver, installation artist.

Brigitte Sillard von Preislinger was awarded the Fondation de France Charles Oulmont Prize in 1995 and the Valloire Ice Sculpture Prize in 1997. She is particularly drawn to signs, symbols and myth. She works in a wide variety of materials, including wood, cement, plaster, stone and especially glass and ice, and also produces pieces with elements in common with Land Art.

She has been involved in various group exhibitions: in 1984 and 1985 at the Salon des Artistes Français in Paris; from 1985 to 1991 at the Salon Figuration Critique in Paris; in 1990 at the Salon d'Automne; in 1992 at the Salon Comparaisons; in 1996 at *Femmes au Pluriel* (*Women in the Plural*) in Roanne; in 1996 at *L'Art du Verre* (*Glass Art*) at the Château Reviers; and in 1997 at MAC, Paris. She has also exhibited solo, notably at the Galerie Ariane in Paris from 1989 to 1992 and at the Centre Cultural in Boulogne in 1994.

SILLAX
5th century BC.
Active in Rhegium c. 468 BC.
Painter.
Ancient Greek.

SILLEMANS, Experiens
Dutch, 17th century.
Born c. 1611, in Amsterdam; died 1653, in Amsterdam.
Painter, draughtsman, engraver. Harbour scenes.

Experiens Sillemans was the son of the Englishman Jeffery Sillemans. He favoured the use of burin, and is remembered for his drawing *View of the Port of Amsterdam*.

AUCTION RECORDS:
LONDON, 30 Oct 1981, *Warships off the Jetty* (1652, oil on panel, grisaille, 6 x 8 1/2 ins / 15 x 21.5 cm) GBP 5,000.

SILLÉN, Herman Gustaf af
Swedish, 19th - 20th century.
Born 20 May 1857, in Stockholm; died 29 December 1908, in Stockholm.
Painter. Seascapes.

Sillén was a naval officer who studied art in Paris and Berlin.

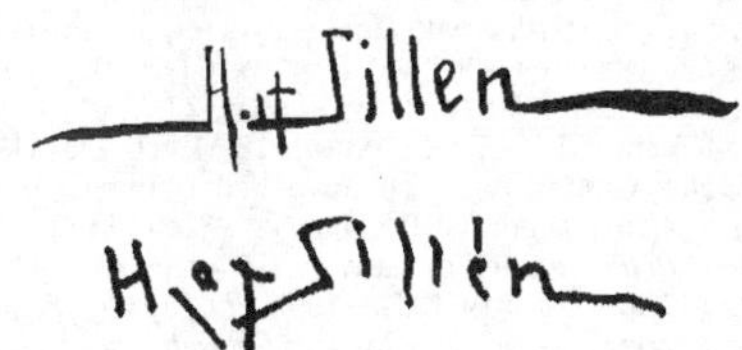

MUSEUMS AND GALLERIES:
STOCKHOLM (Nationalmus.) - WASHINGTON DC (Georgetown University): *Seascape* (oil on canvas).

AUCTION RECORDS:
NEW YORK, 25 Jan 1980, *Fishing Boats at Sea near a Lighthouse* (1897, oil on canvas, 51 1/2 x 41 3/4 ins / 131 x 106 cm) USD 4,250. STOCKHOLM, 26 April 1983, *Seascape* (1892, oil on canvas, 42 1/2 x 74 3/4 ins / 108 x 190 cm) SEK 48,000. STOCKHOLM, 4 Nov 1986, *Fishing Fleet at Sea* (1895, oil on canvas, 35 3/4 x 63 ins / 91 x 160 cm) SEK 105,000. STOCKHOLM, 19 April 1989, *Seascape with Sailing Vessels* (1901, oil on canvas, 40 1/2 x 31 ins / 103 x 79 cm) SEK 115,000. STOCKHOLM, 14 Nov 1990, *Seascape with Sailing Vessels and Fishing Boats in a Storm* (oil on canvas, 11 3/4 x 22 ins / 30 x 55 cm) SEK 14,000. STOCKHOLM, 29 May 1991, *Sailing Vessels and Fishing Boats*

in a Rough Sea (1879, oil on canvas, 11 3/4 x 22 ins / 30 x 55 cm) SEK 15,000.

SILLENBERG. See **SPILLENBERGER**

SILLER, Johann, or Siler
Austrian, 17th (?) century.
Active in Salzburg, Austria.
Painter.

SILLER, Matthias or Johann Matthias, or Siler
Austrian, 18th century.
Born c. 1710, in Salzburg; died in Salzburg.
Painter. Religious subjects.
Matthias Siller produced work for the town hall in Salzburg, and many perspective paintings.

SILLETT, Emma
British, 18th - 19th century.
Died 1880.
Active from the beginning of 1813 in Norwich.
Painter. Flowers, fruit.
Emma Sillett's father was James Sillett.
MUSEUMS AND GALLERIES:
NORWICH (Castle Mus. and AG): *Flowers and Fruit* (1828, watercolour).

SILLETT, James, or Sillet or Selleth
British, 18th - 19th century.
Born 1764, in Norwich; died 6 May 1840, in Norwich.
Painter, miniaturist, illustrator. Still-lifes (flowers/fruit/game). Stage sets.
School of Norwich.
James Sillett was the father of Emma Sillett. He was a pupil at the Royal Academy. Sillett worked in King's Lynn in 1804 before returning to Norwich in 1810, and illustrated Richard's *History of Lynn*. He was one of a group of painters known as the Norwich School who revitalised and transformed the study of nature in a Realist and Romantic vein. Sillett exhibited still-lifes in London from 1797 to 1837, often at the Royal Academy and occasionally at the Royal Society of British Artists in Suffolk Street.
MUSEUMS AND GALLERIES:
NORWICH (Castle Mus. and AG): *Flowers and Fruit* (1827, oil on canvas); *The Winfarthing Oak*; *Double Hawthorn* (watercolour); *Black Grapes* (watercolour); *White Grapes* (watercolour).
AUCTION RECORDS:
LONDON, 19 June 1922, *Flowers and Fruit,* GBP 31. LONDON, 21 March 1979, *Still-life with Game* (1812, oil on panel, 11 3/4 x 18 ins / 30 x 46 cm) GBP 1,000. LONDON, 5 Oct 1984, *Vase of Flowers on a Ledge* (1810, oil on canvas, 23 1/2 x 19 1/2 ins / 59.6 x 49.5 cm) GBP 2,500. LONDON, 12 March 1987, *White Sweetwater Grapes* (watercolour/pencil outlines, 16 3/4 x 12 1/2 ins / 42.5 x 32 cm) GBP 2,200. NEW YORK, 21 Oct 1988, *Still-life with Flowers* (oil on canvas, 17 1/4 x 14 ins / 44 x 35.5 cm) USD 12,100. LONDON, 15 Dec 1993, *Still-life with Peaches, Apples, Grapes, Plums, Cherries and Gooseberries in a Dish with Hazlenuts and a Snail on a Ledge* (1830, oil on panel, 21 1/4 x 26 ins / 54 x 66.3 cm) GBP 8,625. LONDON, 13 Nov 1996, *Auricula Primrose* (oil on panel, study, 13 3/4 x 10 1/4 ins / 35 x 26 cm) GBP 32,200. HASLEMERE, 21 Feb 2001, *Kings Lynn, Norwich and Lynn Stagecoach with Figures and Children* (c. 1810, oil on canvas, 13 x 21 ins / 33 x 53 cm) GBP 5,200. LONDON, 7 March 2002, *Narcissi, Tulips and Other Flowers in a Goblet on a Ledge* (oil on canvas, 14 x 11 ins / 36 x 27 cm) GBP 2,400. LONDON, 28 Nov 2002, *Still-life of Flowers in a Vase* (oil on canvas, 13 x 10 ins / 33 x 26 cm) GBP 3,500. LONDON, 6 March 2003, *Narcissi, Tulips, Carnation and Other Flowers in a Goblet on a Ledge* (oil on canvas, 18 x 15 ins / 46 x 38 cm) GBP 3,000. NEWMARKET, 7 Sept 2004, *Admiral Earl Nelson* (watercolour and gouache on ivory, miniature, after Lemuel Abbott) GBP 9,650. LONDON, 9 Sept 2004, *Figure by a Pond in a Wooded Landscape* (oil on panel, 11 x 16 ins / 29 x 41 cm) GBP 1,000.

SILLEVOORTS, Mathieu
Flemish School, 16th century.
Died 22 September 1603, in Mechelen.
Painter.

SILLEVOORTS, Pierre, or Gillevoorts
Flemish School, 17th century.
Active in Mechelen in 1619.
Painter, sculptor.

SILLIÈRES, Fernand Gérard
French, 19th - 20th century.
Born in Auch (Gers).
Painter.
Fernand Gérard Sillières was a student of Gustave Moreau, Fernand Cormon, Eugène Thirion and François Flameng at the École des Beaux-Arts in Paris. He exhibited regularly at the Salon des Artistes Français in Paris, and won a bronze medal at the Exposition Universelle in 1900.

SILLIG, Viktor von, or Georg Viktor
German, 19th century.
Born 1806, in Dresden.
Painter, engraver (etching). Military subjects, battles, horses.

SILLING, Karl or Christian Karl August
German, 18th century.
Born 11 November 1780, in Dresden; died 4 December 1808, in Dresden.
Draughtsman.

SILLINI, Giuseppe Niccolo di Vincenzo. See **SILINI**

SILLMAN, Sewel
American, 20th century.
Born 24 October 1924, in Savannah (Georgia); died 1992.
Painter, watercolourist, engraver, collage artist.
Sewel Sillman studied at the famous Black Mountain College, North Carolina, with fellow students Robert Rauschenberg and Kenneth Noland. He became Albers' assistant when the latter took over the running of the School of Art and Architecture at Yale University in 1950. He also taught at Rhode Island School of Design in Providence, the University of Michigan at Ann Arbor, New York State University, and the School of Fine Arts at the University of Pennsylvania in Philadelphia. He lived and worked in Connecticut.

In 1955, Sillman went into partnership with the painter Norman Ives to start up *Yves-Sillman*, an art publishing workshop producing prints of Josef Albers, Mondrian, Dubuffet, Willem de Kooning and Richard Lindner, among others. They also published Albers' major theoretical work, *Interaction of Colour*, in 1963.

Sillman's work draws on the strict sources of Constructivism. The colour contrasts work in a similar way to the contrasts of dissonance and consonance in music and, graphically, by using or not using subtle shaded tones. Repetitions and variations, symmetry and asymmetry form complex but planned combinations.

Sillman took part in collective exhibitions at the Sidney Jarvis Gallery in New York. His solo exhibitions include those at the Neuberger Museum, Purchase in New York and the galerie Denise René in Paris in 1987.
MUSEUMS AND GALLERIES:
NEW YORK (MoMA) - NEW YORK (Whitney Mus. of American Art) - PURCHASE (Neuberger Mus. of Art) - WASHINGTON DC (Phillips Collection).

SILLY, Alain
French, 20th century.

Born 4 December 1944, in L'Isle-Adam.

Sculptor of assemblages, mixed media.

Alain Silly collects all manner of objects to produce assemblages. In his sculpture *Sweepings*, for example, he lists the components as including a broom, a brush, a hand brush, a shield, scrawls, hair, a penis, a paintbrush, a palette and daubs.

Silly has been involved in group exhibitions, notably at the second Biennale Européenne de Sculpture de Normandie in 1984. He has exhibited solo, notably at the École Régionale des Beaux-Arts in Rouen in 2001.

Bibliography:

IIe Biennale européenne de sculpture de Normandie, exhibition catalogue, Centre d'Art contemporain, Jouy-sur-Eure, 1984.

SILO, Adam, or Zilo

Dutch, 17th - 18th century.

Born 1674, in Amsterdam; died 1756 or 1760.

Painter, watercolourist, engraver. Portraits, seascapes.

Adam Silo was a sailor and boat builder until 1704. He then worked with Th. van Pee. Peter the Great studied boat building with him and had him paint models of boats and seascapes. His engraved works include: *Calm Sea; Seascape with a Three-master; Storm*; and *Six Seascapes*.

Museums and Galleries:

St Petersburg (Hermitage): *Seascape* - Vienna (Liechtenstein Mus.): *Rough Sea*.

Auction records:

Paris, 24 Jan 1920, *Portrait Presumed to be of Peter the Great*, FRF 200. Paris, 12 Feb 1925, *The Zuyder Zee, Iced over*, FRF 3,020. London, 10 Nov 1967, *Seascape*, Gns 1,000. Amsterdam, 11 May 1971, *Numerous Boats in a Riverscape*, NLG 24,000. Vienna, 18 Sept 1973, *Warships and Boats at Sea*, ATS 220,000. London, 16 April 1980, *Warships Under Way* (oil on canvas, 25 1/4 x 33 ins / 64 x 84 cm) GBP 5,800. Amsterdam, 18 May 1981, *Sailing Ships off the Coast* (oil on canvas, 20 3/4 x 26 3/4 ins / 53 x 68 cm) NLG 14,500. New York, 6 June 1984, *Warship off the Coast* (oil on canvas, 17 1/4 x 24 3/4 ins / 43.8 x 63 cm) USD 3,000. Amsterdam, 26 Nov 1984, *Warships off the Coast* (gouache, 8 1/2 x 12 ins / 21.4 x 30.4 cm) NLG 4,800. Amsterdam, 14 Nov 1988, *The Dutch Frigate Eendracht and Other Vessels Approaching the Coast Under Sail* (watercolour, 7 1/2 x 14 1/4 ins / 19.2 x 36.1 cm) NLG 10,580. London, 15 Dec 1989, *Mouth of a River with a Warship and Other Craft* (oil on canvas, 25 1/2 x 32 1/2 ins / 64.5 x 82.5 cm) GBP 17,600. London, 20 July 1990, *Vessels on the Ij with Amsterdam in the Background; Shipping on the Amstel* (a pair, 22 ins / 55 cm 1 1/4 x 28 3/4 ins/3 x 73 cm) GBP 11,000. St-Brieuc, 26 Nov 1995, *Sailing Ships in a Port; Port Scene; Sailing Ships and Galleons Moving along the Coast; Naval Battle* (four oils on canvas, each 50 x 41 ins / 127 x 104 cm) FRF 460,000. London, 16 April 1999, *Dutch Shipping off Amsterdam* (oil on panel, 7 x 9 ins / 18 x 23 cm) GBP 15,000. Munich, 22 March 2000, *Seascape* (oil on panel, 11 x 14 ins / 29 x 36 cm) DEM 47,500. Munich, 22 March 2000, *Seascape* (oil on panel, 11 x 14 ins / 29 x 35 cm) DEM 47,500. Amsterdam, 5 Nov 2002, *Merchantmen, Kaag and Other Sailing Vessels in a Stiff Breeze* (oil on canvas, 18 x 22 ins / 45 x 55 cm) EUR 11,000. Dorking, 12 July 2003, *Russian Men-o'-war Defeating Enemy in Sea Battle* (9 x 17 ins / 23 x 42 cm) GBP 10,000.

SILOÉ, Diego de, or Siloee or Syloe

Spanish, 16th century.

Born c. 1495, in Burgos (Castilla y León); died 22 October 1563, in Granada.

Sculptor, architect. Religious subjects. Funerary monuments.

The son of Gil de Siloé, Diego worked first in Burgos as his father's pupil. When still very young, he travelled to Italy at a time when Michelangelo was at the peak of his fame and was much influenced by this artist's work. In Naples in 1517, he collaborated with Bartolomé Ordóñez on the altarpiece of the Caracciolo Chapel in the church of S Giovanni in Carbonara. Returning to Spain, he worked mainly in Burgos, between 1519 and 1528 as a sculptor, and Granada as an architect. The tomb of Bishop Don Luis de Acuna in Burgos Cathedral, in a style imitated from Pallaiuolo, is his work. Between 1519 and 1523, he built the gilded staircase at the end of the north transept, a particularly harmonious ensemble, decorated with medallions of children, foliage and fantastic animals. In Burgos, he worked mainly in collaboration with Vigarmy on projects including the St Peter altarpiece and the altarpiece on the principal altar of the chapel of the Constable (1523).

Diego de Siloé's true personality as an architect was not able to flourish until he began to work alone in Granada. Here his first work was to design the cupolas and choir stalls of the church of S Jerónimo. His most important architectural work was to be his participation in the building of Granada Cathedral where he executed for the portals (1531-1534), the rotunda, the ambulatory (1533) and the first level of the tower (1538). Also for Granada Cathedral, he carved several statues of *Virtues, Angels* and *Orantes* and one, in the form of a medallion, representing the *Virgin and Child*. The Renaissance style of Granada cathedral can be found in Málaga and in the east end of the church at Guadix (1541), places where Diego de Siloé must have worked.

Bibliography:

Wethey, Harold Edwin, *Gil de Siloé and his School. A Study of Late Gothic Sculpture in Burgos*, Harvard University Press, Cambridge (MA), 1936. Wethey, *'The Early Works of Bartolomé Ordóñez and Diego de Siloé'* in *Art Bulletin*, vol 22, 1943. Rosenthal, E. E., *The Cathedral of Granada: A Study in the Spanish Renaissance*, Princeton, 1961.

Auction records:

Madrid, 27 Oct 1992, *Pietà* (alabaster, traces of gold and polychrome paint, high-relief, 52 x 39 1/4 ins / 132 x 99.5 cm) ESP 30,000,000.

SILOÉ, Gil de

Spanish, 15th - 16th century.

Died c. 1501.

Sculptor.

Burgos School.

The father of Diego de Siloé, Gil may have come originally from Antwerp although all the examples of his work are concentrated in the Burgos area. For Burgos Cathedral he made the altarpiece in the chapels of St Anne and of the Conception. His most important work can be found at the Carthusian church of Miraflores, Burgos, for which he carved the main altarpiece (1496-1499) with the assistance of his son Diego, the tombs of John of Castile and his wife Isabella of Portugal (1486-1493) and that of their son Don Alfonso. His work is highly decorative and the details of the garments of his figures are rendered with a precision that does not, however, detract from the powerful expressiveness of the whole. He looked forward to the Spanish Renaissance and the direction that was to be pursued and developed by his son.

Bibliography:

Wethey, *'The Early Works of Bartolomé Ordóñez and Diego de Siloé'* in *Art Bulletin*, vol 22, 1943. Rosenthal, E.E., *The Cathedral of Granada: A Study in the Spanish Renaissance*, Princeton, 1961.

Museums and Galleries:
Boston: *St John the Evangelist, St Bartholomew and St Jude Thaddaeus* - Burgos (Mus. de Burgos): *Tomb of Juan de Padilla* - New York (Metropolitan Mus. of Art): *Madonna and Child; St James the Less and Another Saint.*

SILOVSKY, Vladimir

Czech, 20th century.
Born 11 July 1891, in Libán; died 1974, in Prague.
Engraver.

Vladimir Silovsky studied with Max Svabinsky at the Prague academy, where he later taught. He became famous for his etchings and woodcuts of street life. One of his-best known works is *Puppet Theatre* (1925, woodcut).

SILVA, A.

Turkish, 20th century.
Born 3 October 1937, in Istanbul, to Armenian parents.
Active in France.
Painter, sculptor.

A. Silva obtained a diploma at the academy of fine arts in Istanbul and continued her training in Italy. In 1977, she founded the Turkish national committee for fine arts, an organisation connected with UNESCO. In 1980, she settled in France, acquiring French nationality by marriage in 1989. She produces bronzes that combine representation with Abstract elements in a dynamic constructivism that also characterises her paintings.

Silva has taken part in collective exhibitions, particularly in Paris, including the Salon de la Société Nationale des Beaux-Arts (1981); the Salon d'Automne (1981, 1988, 1990-1992); the Salon Comparaisons (1990, 1992); and the Salon Figuration Critique (1990). She has shown her works in solo exhibitions since 1974 in Turkey, Italy and Switzerland, and at the Galerie Ariane in France in 1991.

Museums and Galleries:
Paris (FNAC) - Yerevan (NG).

SILVA, Agostino I

Swiss, 17th century.
Born 1620, in Morbio Inferiore; died 1706.
Sculptor, stucco artist, architect.

Agostino I was the son of Francesco Silva I. He studied in Rome, Urbino, Milan and Turin.

SILVA, Agostino II

Swiss, 18th century.
Born in Morbio Inferiore.
Active in the second half of the 18th century.
Sculptor.

Agostino II was the son of Francesco Silva III. He produced statues for churches in Como, Italy.

SILVA, Alfredo da

Bolivian, 20th century.
Born in Potosí.
Painter.
Kinetic Art.

Work by Alfredo da Silva has been included in numerous exhibitions in North and South America and Europe. In 1959 he won first prize at the Buenos Aires national Salon, and in 1964 third prize at the Biennale in Córdoba in Argentina. He has shown some of his collected productions in solo exhibitions in Bolivia, Chile, Argentina, Uruguay, Peru and the USA.

His paintings of cosmic projections incline to kinetism.

Bibliography:
Lassaigne, Jacques, *Peintres boliviens contemporains*, exhibition catalogue, Musée d'Art moderne de la ville de Paris, Paris, 1973.

Museums and Galleries:
Barranquilla (MAM) - Buenos Aires (MAM) - Caracas (MAM) - La Paz (MMA) - New York (MoMA) - New York (Solomon R. Guggenheim Mus.).

SILVA, Anton

Austrian, 16th century.
Sculptor.

Silva carved the sculptures of the tower of the Brünn Town Hall between 1570 and 1577.

SILVA, Antonio

Italian, 17th century.
Born to a family originally from Vall'Intelvi.
Active at the end of the 17th century.
Sculptor.

Around 1698, this artist sculpted the high altar of the church in Chiavenna.

SILVA, Antonio Caetano da

Portuguese, 18th century.
Died 7 May 1775, in Lisbon.
Active in Lisbon.
Painter.

In collaboration with J. A. Narciso, Antonio Caetano da Silva executed frescoes in the royal foundry in Lisbon.

SILVA, Antonio da

Portuguese, 20th - 21st century.
Born 14 February 1956.
Also active in France.
Painter. Scenes with figures.

Da Silva graduated from the École des Beaux-Arts, in Paris. Elements of the construction of his paintings suggest that he has been influenced by the works of Cremonini, with their precise and yet indeterminate construction, and those of Velickovic, with their effect of the movement of shifting bodies.

He has exhibited at the Salon de Mai and Salon de Montrouge in and around Paris. He exhibited a collection of his work at a solo exhibition at the Maison des Beaux-Arts in Paris in 1985.

SILVA, Benedetto or Carlo Antonio Benedetto

Swiss, 18th century.
Born 1705, in Morbio Inferiore; died 1788.
Sculptor, designer of ornamental architectural features, stucco artist.

Benedetto was the son of Francesco Silva II. He produced work for the Swiss church of Balerna (Ticino) and the Italian churches of Bologna, Città di Castello, Fabriano, Foligno, Orvieto and Perugia.

SILVA, Carlos

Argentinian, 20th century.
Born 1930, in Buenos Aires, in 1910 according to some sources.
Painter.
Op Art.

Carlos Silva had no artistic training other than his work in advertising.

His painting, always abstract, was at first based on strictly circular geometrical forms. Over the years it became more suggestive, making use of the optical illusions of Op Art. Silva in due course created an abstract trompe l'oeil, that is to say a composition of abstract forms involving the now well-recognised effects of volume and depth, of convexity and concavity while retained some touch of fantasy in its creation.

From 1955 onwards Carlos Silva took part in collective exhibitions including the 1960 show at the Museo de Arte Moderno in Buenos Aires and the 1965 exhibition at the Museu de Arte Moderna in Rio de Janeiro.

Bibliography:
Damian Bayon, *Projection et dynamisme, six peintres argentins*, exhibition catalogue, Musée d'Art moderne de la ville de Paris, Paris, 1973.
Museums and Galleries:
Buenos Aires (MAM) - New York (MoMA) - Prague (Národní Muz.).

SILVA, Domingos José da
Portuguese, 20th century.
Born 1783, in Lisbon; died 1863, in Lisbon.
Painter, miniaturist, engraver, medallist.
Domingos José da Silva studied painting and drawing with Eleuterio Manuel de Barros, and engraving with Joaquim Carneiro y Bartolozzi. He was appointed professor at the national academy of fine art in Lisbon in 1836.

SILVA, Francesco I
Swiss, 16th - 17th century.
Born 1560, in Morbio Inferiore; died 1641.
Sculptor, stucco artist.
Francesco Silva I was the father of Agostino Silva I and a pupil of Guglielmo della Porta in Rome. He carved eight statues in the Oratory of Monte Sacro, Varese, and other sculptures for the churches of Locarno and Como.

SILVA, Francesco II or Giovanni Francesco
Swiss, 17th - 18th century.
Born 1668, in Morbio Inferiore; died 1737, in Bonn, Germany.
Sculptor.
Francesco II was the son of Agostino Silva II. He studied in Rome with Ercole Ferrata and produced low reliefs for the church of S Giovanni in Laterano. He also worked in Bologna and Como.

SILVA, Francesco III Antonio
Swiss, 18th century.
Born 1731, in Morbio Inferiore; died after 1784.
Painter.
Francesco III was the son of Benedetto Silva. He studied in Bologna, Italy, and was active in Rome and Como, where he produced frescoes for the church of the Dominicans.

SILVA, Francis Augustus
American, 19th century.
Born 1835, in New York; died 31 March 1886, in New York.
Painter. Landscapes, seascapes.
Hudson River School.
Museums and Galleries:
Brooklyn, NY.
Auction records:
New York, 20 Feb 1969, *Lakeside*, USD 1,600. New York, 10 May 1974, *Riverscape* (1873) USD 4,500. New York, 18 Nov 1976, *Seaside* (1886, oil on canvas, 42¼ x 58 ins / 107 x 147.3 cm) USD 1,500. New York, 27 Oct 1977, *Brace's Rock, Cape Ann, Massachusetts* (1872, oil on canvas, 20 x 36 ins / 51 x 91.5 cm) USD 14,000. New York, 3 Feb 1978, *Seaside* (gouache and watercolour, 11 x 20 ins / 27 x 51 cm) USD 3,600. New York, 23 May 1979, *Seaside, New Jersey* (1883, watercolour, 8 x 14¾ ins / 20.5 x 37.5 cm) USD 4,500. New York, 17 Oct 1980, *Hudson River at Kingston Point* (oil on canvas, 20 x 36 ins / 50.8 x 91.5 cm) USD 77,500. New York, 23 April 1981, *Haverstraw Bay* (oil on canvas, 20 x 36 ins / 50.8 x 91.5 cm) USD 130,000. New York, 6 Dec 1984, *On the Hudson* (1880, oil on canvas, 20 x 36 ins / 50.8 x 91.5 cm) USD 35,000. New York, 31 May 1985, *The Hudson at Dusk* (watercolour, 8 x 12¼ ins / 20.6 x 31.3 cm) USD 13,000. New York, 30 May 1986, *America's Cup Race* (1875-1876, oil on canvas, 31 x 48¼ ins / 78.5 x 122.7 cm) USD 26,000. New York, 4 Dec 1987, *Seabright for Galilee* (1880, oil on canvas, 21 x 42¼ ins / 53.3 x 107 cm) USD 36,000. New York, 30 Sept 1988, *Dunes* (1875, oil on canvas, 10½ x 30 ins / 26.7 x 76.2 cm) USD 9,350. New York, 1 Dec 1988, *Seascape* (oil on canvas, 21 x 28¼ ins / 52.5 x 71.7 cm) USD 27,500. New York, 28 Sept 1989, *Coastal Landscape* (oil on canvas, 14¼ x 24 ins / 36 x 61 cm) USD 8,800. New York, 30 Nov 1989, *Seashore at Dusk* (1874, oil on canvas, 14 x 26 ins / 35.5 x 66 cm) USD 60,500. New York, 29 Nov 1990, *Setting Sun* (oil on canvas, 20 x 36 ins / 50.8 x 91.4 cm) USD 33,000. New York, 17 Dec 1990, *Fishing Boats in the Moonlight* (1880, oil on canvas, 14 x 12 ins / 35.6 x 30.5 cm) USD 6,050. New York, 12 April 1991, *Storm Approaching* (1870, oil on canvas, 14 x 12 ins / 35.6 x 30.5 cm) USD 8,800. New York, 22 May 1991, *Sailing Vessels off Cape Ann* (1872, oil on canvas, 14 x 24 ins / 35.7 x 61.1 cm) USD 15,400. New York, 26 Sept 1991, *Moon Rising over the Sea* (1872, oil on canvas, 14 x 24 ins / 35.5 x 61 cm) USD 35,200. New York, 12 March 1992, *The Hudson at Kingston Point* (oil on canvas, 14 x 24 ins / 35.7 x 61 cm) USD 12,100. New York, 3 Dec 1992, *Summer Dusk* (1881, oil on canvas, 24¼ x 44 ins / 61.6 x 111.8 cm) USD 57,750. New York, 10 March 1993, *On the Hudson near Haverstraw* (1872, oil on canvas, 18 x 30 ins / 45.7 x 76.2 cm) USD 184,000. New York, 23 Sept 1993, *Calm Sea at Dusk* (1873, oil on canvas, 29 x 50 ins / 73.7 x 127 cm) USD 255,500. New York, 14 Sept 1995, *Haverstraw Bay* (oil on canvas, 12 x 24 ins / 30.5 x 61 cm) USD 36,800. New York, 23 April 1997, *Holding her Course* (1883, oil on canvas, 16 x 12 ins / 40.8 x 30.5 cm) USD 8,050. New York, 30 Nov 1999, *Barnegat Bay, New Jersey* (oil on canvas, 12 x 20 ins / 30 x 51 cm) USD 60,000. New York, 30 Nov 1999, *Evening in Gloucester Harbour* (1871, oil on canvas, 20 x 40 ins / 51 x 102 cm) USD 900,000. New York, 24 May 2000, *Cape Ann* (1870, oil on canvas, 20 x 40 ins / 52 x 102 cm) USD 130,000. Milford, 26 Oct 2000, *View on the Hudson River* (1876, oil on canvas, 14 x 12 ins / 36 x 30 cm) USD 160,000. Milford, 26 April 2001, *Sailing at Sunset* (oil on panel, 20 x 16 ins / 51 x 41 cm) USD 65,000. New York, 23 May 2001, *Hudson River looking towards the Catskills* (1871, oil on canvas, 20 x 40 ins / 51 x 102 cm) USD 550,000. Milford, 25 April 2002, *Sunset on the New Jersey Shore* (1883, oil on canvas, 26 x 40 ins / 66 x 102 cm) USD 130,000. New York, 17 July 2002, *Lakeside, Branchport, New York* (1882, gouache, 6 x 13 ins / 16 x 34 cm) USD 11,000. Boston, 16 May 2003, *On the Coast* (1879, oil on canvas, 20 x 40 ins / 51 x 101 cm) USD 250,000. New York, 22 May 2003, *Clearing Off* (oil on canvas, 20 x 38 ins / 51 x 97 cm) USD 100,000. Fairfield, 16 April 2004, *New England Coastline* (watercolour, 12 x 20 ins / 30 x 51 cm) USD 3,500. New York, 18 May 2004, *Hudson River looking toward the Catskills* (1871, oil on canvas, 20 x 40 ins / 51 x 102 cm) USD 480,000.

SILVA, Francisco
Portuguese, 18th century.
Born to a family originally from Portugal.
Active in Seville c. 1775.
Painter. Perspectives.

SILVA, Francisco Domingos da
Brazilian, 20th century.
Painter. Scenes with figures.
The artistic talent of Francisco Domingos da Silva was discovered in 1943 at a time when he was using charcoal and chalk to decorate fishermen's huts in Fortaleza. A basic minimum of material was found for him and he produced several works.

His creations are based on legends of the Amazon and on a fabulous and alarming fauna of giant spiders, dragons and other imaginary monsters.

SILVA, Giovanni
Swiss, 18th century.
Born in Morcote.
Active in the second half of the 18th century.
Painter. History painting. Decorative schemes.
Giovanni Silva studied in Bologna, Italy, from 1758 to 1760.

SILVA, Henrique José da
Portuguese, 18th - 19th century.
Born 1772 or 1773, in Lisbon; died 1834, in Rio de Janeiro.
Painter, engraver, draughtsman, illustrator. Religious subjects, portraits.

Henrique José da Silva studied under P. Alexandrino de Carvalho and was appointed director of the fine arts academy of Rio de Janeiro. He executed religious panels for various churches and painted portraits of distinguished figures of the period, including the king, Don Pedro. He also produced some illustrations (engravings and Indian ink drawings) for literary works.

BIBLIOGRAPHY:

Arnáiz, José Manuel/López Jiménez, Javier/Merchán Díaz, Manuel (ed.), *'Cien años de pintura en Espana y Portugal (1830-1930)'* in vol. X, Antiqvaria, Madrid, 1993.

SILVA, Jeronymo da
Portuguese, 18th century.
Active during the first half of the 18th century.
Painter.

Jeronymo da Silva studied in Rome and painted religious subjects and portraits for churches in Lisbon.

SILVA, João Chrisostome Policarpo da
Portuguese, 18th century.
Born c. 1734, in Merceana; died 20 January 1798, in Lisbon.
Sculptor, painter.

João Chrisostome Policarpo da Silva was a pupil of José de Almeida. He painted religious compositions and made statues for churches in Lisbon. He was a priest.

SILVA, João da
Portuguese, 20th century.
Born 1 December 1880, in Lisbon.
Sculptor, medallist, metal worker.

João da Silva was a pupil of Chaplain and featured in exhibitions in Paris until 1926. He gained an honourable mention in 1900 at the Exposition Universelle.

AUCTION RECORDS:

PARIS, 3 July 1996, *Goat Kid Scratching Itself* (1924, gilt bronze, h. 4 3/4 ins / 12 cm) FRF 3,200.

SILVA, José Antonio da
Brazilian, 20th century.
Born 1909.
Painter. Scenes with figures.

José Antonio da Silva was a farm worker in São José do Rio Preto in São Paulo State and became a painter late in life. He painted the life of peasants in detail and freshness just as he had lived it: harvests, training animals, festivities and invocations to supernatural beings.

AUCTION RECORDS:

SÃO PAULO, 13 Sept 1982, *Devastated Landscape* (1971, oil on canvas, 28 3/4 x 41 1/2 ins / 73 x 105.5 cm) BRL 550,000. SÃO PAULO, 24 Sept 1986, *The Promise* (1955, oil on canvas, 22 x 17 3/4 ins / 55 x 45 cm) BRL 200,000.

SILVA, José Claudio da
Brazilian, 20th century.
Born 1932.
Painter. Figures, landscapes.

José Claudio da Silva came from the north-east region of Brazil where popular tradition flourishes. His tropical landscapes reach out in exuberance, his generously proportioned female forms express sensuality.

SILVA, José Sergio de Carvalho e, or Carvalho e Silva
Portuguese, 19th century.
Born 9 September 1856, in Évora.
Medallist, engraver. Coins.

José Sergio de Carvalho e Silva worked in Lisbon. He signed his work *S. Silva*.

SILVA, Julio Hector
Argentinian, 20th century.
Born 1930, in Entre Rios.
Active in France from 1955.
Sculptor, painter. Figure compositions, figures, landscapes with figures.

Julio Hector Silva arrived in Paris in 1955 and worked as a typist and compositor.

As a painter, his vividly coloured expressionism, graphic and muscular, sometimes tending to the abstract, to which he added his exotic humour, links him to the CoBrA group. Yet he developed a representational world, one with a stylised fauna and flora, mysterious, inspired by the forests of South America, with an atmosphere reminiscent of Wifredo Lam.

As a sculptor, Silva used an abstract style, creating monuments whose baroque manner recalls that of Reinhoud, another artist of the CoBrA group. In Paris he sculpted the group *Pygmalion* in pink Portuguese marble for the Forum at Les Halles, and the *Lady and Moon* in white Carrara marble for the Esplanade de la Défense.

His work featured in very many international collective exhibitions, especially the regular showings in Paris at the Salon de Mai. His solo exhibitions worldwide included a large display of paintings (Paris 1970); sculptures in bronze and brass (Paris 1976); Galerie Héléna Farnatzis (Paris, 1990); *Torano la Notte* at the Galerie Corinne Timsit (Paris, 1995). His exhibitions were described by writers as diverse as Jean-Clarence Lambert, François Mathey, Julio Cortazar, Édouard Jaguer, Hubert Juin and Georges Boudaille, a reflection of the richness of his flourishing work.

BIBLIOGRAPHY:

Saül Yurkievich, *'Julio Silva - Les Engendrements surgissent de la nuit fatale'* in *Artension* n° 18, periodical, Rouen, 1990.

AUCTION RECORDS:

PARIS, Jan 1998, *High Country 2* (1959, oil on canvas, 81 1/2 x 24 ins / 207 x 61 cm) FRF 4,000.

SILVA, Manuel Antonio
Portuguese, 19th century.
Died 1833, in Ajuda near Lisbon.
Painter, draughtsman.

Manuel Antonio Silva worked as a draughtsman at the botanical gardens in Ajuda.

SILVA, Oscar Pereira da
Brazilian, 19th - 20th century.
Born 1867; died 1939.
Painter. Scenes with figures.

Oscar Pereira da Silva paid no attention to Brazilian folk tradition but painted in an antique style.

AUCTION RECORDS:

SÃO PAULO, 3 Dec 1981, *A Brazilian House* (oil on canvas, 15 1/2 x 23 ins / 39.5 x 58.5 cm) BRL 1,750,000. SÃO PAULO, 23 Sept 1986, *Ox-Wagon* (1889, oil on canvas, 12 1/4 x 24 ins / 31 x 61 cm) BRL 90,000. RIO DE JANEIRO, 17 June 2003, *Mangoes* (oil on canvas, 11 x 17 ins / 27 x 44 cm) BRL 9,980. RIO DE JANEIRO, 27 April 2004, *Country Landscape* (oil on canvas, 15 x 36 ins / 37 x 92 cm) BRL 23,000. RIO DE JANEIRO, 27 April 2004, *Portrait of a Slave Girl* (1892, oil on canvas, 17 x 11 ins / 42 x 29 cm) BRL 30,000.

SILVA, Pietro
Italian, 16th century.
Active in Bologna during the second half of the 16th century.
Sculptor (wood).

Pietro Silva carved a confessional for the Jesuit church in Bologna in 1581.

SILVA, Ramon
Argentinian, 20th century.
Born 1890, in Buenos Aires.
Painter. Landscapes.
Ramon Silva was self-taught, and he took no part in the search for a specifically Argentinian art. He travelled in Holland, France, Italy and Spain, and brought back post-Impressionist cosmopolitan landscapes.

SILVA, Vieira da. See **VIEIRA DA SILVA Maria Elena**

SILVA, William Posey
American, 19th - 20th century.
Born 23 October 1859, in Savannah (Maine); died 1948, in Carmel (California).
Painter. Landscapes.
William Posey Silva was taught by Jean-Paul Laurens and Henri Royer at the Académie Julian in Paris. He was active in Carmel, California. He was a member of the American Art Association in Paris and the American Federation of Arts. He won many awards at international collective exhibitions including the Salon des Artistes Français in Paris, where he was awarded an honourable mention in 1922.
AUCTION RECORDS:
LOS ANGELES-SAN FRANCISCO, 10 Oct 1990, *Morning Near Sacramento* (oil on canvas, 16 1/4 x 20 ins / 41 x 51 cm) USD 4,400. NEW YORK, 27 Sept 1996, *Eucalyptus on Carmel Bay* (1924, oil on panel, 16 1/4 x 20 ins / 41.3 x 50.8 cm) USD 5,750. NEW YORK, 25 March 1997, *Sun Rise in Mist, Point Lobos, California* (oil on canvas, 20 x 24 ins / 50.8 x 61 cm) USD 4,887.

SILVA BAZAN Y ARCOS MENESES DE SARMIENTO, Mariana (Doña, Duchess of Huescar y Arcos)
Spanish, 18th century.
Born 14 December 1750, in Madrid; died 17 January 1784, in Madrid.
Painter.
In 1766 Mariana Silva Bazan y Arcos Meneses de Sarmiento was made an honorary member of the Real Academia de San Fernando and later honorary director. She was married three times, on the last occasion to the duke of Arcos. She was also a dramatist and poet.

SILVA GERALDES, Ambrosio José
Portuguese, 18th century.
Active in Lisbon during the second half of the 18th century.
Painter.
Ambrosio José Silva Geraldes was the son and pupil of Antonio da Silva Geraldes.

SILVA GERALDES, Antonio da
Portuguese, 18th century.
Active in Lisbon c. 1750.
Painter.
Antonio da Silva Geraldes painted a religious work for the Resgate hermitage.

SILVA GERALDES, João
Portuguese, 18th century.
Active in Lisbon during the second half of the 18th century.
Painter.
João Silva Geraldes was the son and pupil of Antonio da Silva Geraldes.

SILVA GERALDES, Luis Antonio
Portuguese, 18th century.
Active in Lisbon during the second half of the 18th century.
Painter.
Luis Antonio Silva Geraldes was the nephew of Antonio da Silva Geraldes and a pupil of Nicolas Tolentino Botelho and José Francisco del Cusco.

SILVA GODINHO, Manoel da
Portuguese, 19th century.
Active in Lisbon c. 1800.
Engraver (burin).
Manoel da Silva Godinho was a pupil of J. Carneiro da Silva.

SILVA MOREIRA, Cypriano da
Portuguese, 18th - 19th century.
Born 1754, in Lisbon; died 1826.
Medallist, engraver. Coins.
Cypriano da Silva Moreira was a pupil of João de Figueiredo and worked as a coin engraver to the king.

SILVA OEIRENSE, Francisco Antonio da
Portuguese, 19th century.
Born c. 1797, in Oeiras (Lisbon), Portugal, or in Brazil; died 6 January 1868, in Lisbon.
Painter, engraver (burin).
In 1836 Francisco da Silva Oeirense founded the Lisbon academy. In 1822 he published a collection of 32 portrait engravings.

SILVA PAZ, Lourenço da
Portuguese, 18th century.
Died 10 March 1718.
Active in Lisbon.
Painter.
Lourenço da Silva Paz was painter to the court of Lisbon in 1708.

SILVA PELVIDES, João Paulo da
Portuguese, 18th - 19th century.
Born c. 1751, in Mafra; died 28 December 1821, in Lisbon.
Sculptor.
João Paulo da Silva Pelvides was a pupil of Al. Giusti.

SILVA PORTO, Antonio Carvalho da
Portuguese, 19th century.
Born 1850, in Oporto; died 1893, in Lisbon.
Painter, draughtsman. Portraits, genre scenes, landscapes, waterscapes, animals.
Antonio Carvalho da Silva Porto studied at the school of fine arts in Oporto until 1873, when he was awarded a study bursary for Paris. He joined the Paris school of fine arts and studied there under Alexandre Cabanel and Charles Daubigny. He also spent time in Italy, England, Belgium and Holland. When he returned to Portugal in 1879 he was appointed as a teacher at the school of fine arts in Lisbon.

He exhibited at various group exhibitions, including the Paris Salon (1876 and 1878), the exhibition of the national fine arts society of Lisbon (1880), and the exhibitions of the *Leon Group* (from 1881). He was awarded a medal of honour in 1892.

Silva Porto continued in the tradition of Naturalist painters such as Corot and Millet and of course Daubigny. He painted mainly landscapes, his preferred genre, to which he brought a keen interest in rural folklore.
BIBLIOGRAPHY:
França, José Augusto, *A arte em Portugal no século XIX*, Livraria Bertrand, Lisbon, 1967. Vaz Pacheco, Maria Emília/Canavarro, Pedro, *Silva Porto e o naturalismo em Portugal*, Câmara municipal, Santarém, 1993. Da Silva, Raquel Henriques, *Silva Porto, 1850-1893: exposiçô comemorativa do centenário de sua morte*, exhibition catalogue, Istituto Português de Museus, Lisbon, 1993.
MUSEUMS AND GALLERIES:
LISBON (Mus. do Chiado): *Landscape with View of Sintra*; *Back from the Market*; *Banks of the River Ave* - OPORTO (Mus. Nacional de Soares dos Reis): *The Harvesters*; *Mills of the*

Brotherhood; A Small Misfortune; Child's Head; Entrance to the Village; Banks of the River Oise; Banks of the River Marne; Normandy; Morning in Oise.

SILVA RABELLO, Manuel da
Portuguese, 17th century.
Active in Montemor Velho during the second half of the 17th century.
Painter.
Manuel da Silva Rabello was painter to the court of Lisbon in 1665.

SILVA Y SANTA CRUZ, Mariana de
(Countess). See **WALDSTEIN Maria Anna von**

SILVA Y VELAZQUEZ, Diego Rodriguez de.
See **VELÁZQUEZ Diego Rodríguez da Silva y.**

SILVA-BRUHNS, Ivan da
Brazilian, 20th century.
Born 1880, in Paris, to Brazilian parents; died 17 October 1980, in Cap d'Antibes (Alpes-Maritimes), France.
Painter. Designs for carpets.
Art Deco.
Ivan da Silva-Bruhns settled very young in France. He studied medicine and then became a painter. He knew Maurice Denis, Paul Signac and Jacques Villon. In 1925 he opened a gallery specialising in carpets. He collaborated with great decorative artists, including Ruhlmann. In about 1950 he retired to Cap d'Antibes, where he died just before his hundredth birthday.

He first became known for his expressionist subjects. At the time when he began to make carpets, he was influenced by Cubism, and also by non-European decorative motifs, especially Aztec, Chinese and Persian. His many tapestry cartoons, with their geometric designs in subtle patterns and delicate colours, are clearly abstract.

He exhibited work in Paris from 1907 at the Salons d'Automne and at the Salon des Artistes-Décorateurs. Shortly before 1920 he investigated the technique of tapestry-making, in order to make carpets. He had a retrospective exhibition in 1977 at the Galerie Camard in Paris.

AUCTION RECORDS:
PARIS, 22 Dec 1989, *Abstract Composition* (oil on panel, 20 3/4 x 17 3/4 ins / 53 x 45 cm) FRF 4,200.

SILVAGNI, Giovanni
Italian, 19th century.
Born 1790, in Rome; died 1853.
Painter.
A pupil of G. Landi, Silvagni painted altarpieces for the church of S Sabina in Rome and churches in Ascoli Piceno, Subiaco and Toscanella.

MUSEUMS AND GALLERIES:
PARMA (Gal. Nazionale): *Blind Oedipus* - ROME (Lateran Mus.): *Flagellation of St Anthony.*

AUCTION RECORDS:
PARIS, 5 Nov 1928, *Still-life,* FRF 110. PARIS, 8 March 1929, *St Francis of Assisi,* FRF 250; *Accordion,* FRF 95; *Woman with Parrot,* FRF 500.

SILVAIN, Antoine
French, 17th century.
Died after 1689.
Active in Paris.
Painter.
Antoine Silvain was the son of Edme Silvain and was court painter in 1684.

SILVAIN, Christian, pseudonym of Gohimont
Belgian, 20th - 21st century.
Born 6 March 1950, in Ypres.
Painter (including mixed media/gouache), collage artist, sculptor, engraver, lithographer, screen printer, draughtsman. Scenes with figures, figures, nudes, still-lifes.
Figuration Libre.
Christian Silvain is self-taught, but had contact with Paul Delvaux. His technique has evolved in several phases over the years. He uses a technique that enables him to produce multiples of 50 copies, each of which is different from the others: he starts with a screen-printed drawing, and while the stages of adding colour are the same, different colours are used for each copy.

His early works from the early 1970s were influenced by Surrealism, which was still strong in Belgium. His compositions combine secular, religious and fantasy elements. In 1976 he ventured into sculpture and then music. In 1979, breaking with the Surrealist aesthetic, he went through a Hyperrealist period, producing minutely detailed copies of the façades of dilapidated houses covered in graffiti and ripped posters. Since the late 1980s his work has focused on people with real or imagined mental illnesses, expressing their suffering symbolically. His works, reminiscent of collages, but neatly ordered, present ideograms representing little men (the enemy), different animals, birds (freedom), aircraft (elsewhere), trees (outdoors), cages, bars (inside), pages of children's writing (explaining), red crosses (forbidden), written words (shouting), and a photo of the person who inspired the work of art, as if to authenticate a document. With deliberate clumsiness, he has created a paradoxically very skilled brand of Art Brut.

He has taken part in countless group exhibitions including: 1972, Brussels, Festival d'Art Fantastique; 1982, Basel and Stockholm international art fairs; 1985, London, Art Fair; 1985, 1986 Ghent, Linéart; 1986, Los Angeles and Ghent international art fairs; 1990, Stockholm, Barcelona, New York, Art Fair; 2002, *Mémoires d'autre enfance*, Galerie du Centre, Paris.

There have been many solo exhibitions of his creations, including: 1988 Antwerp and Brussels, Fondation BP; 1990 Aix-en-Provence, Fondation Vasarely; 1990, 1992 Paris, Galerie du Centre; 1992 Aachen, Forum Ludwig; 1993 Knokke-le-Zoute, Guy Pieters gallery.

BIBLIOGRAPHY:
Christian Sylvain, exhibition catalogue, BP Gall., Antwerp, Brussels, 1988. *Christian Sylvain,* exhibition catalogue, Gal. du Centre, Paris, 1990. *Christian Sylvain,* exhibition catalogue, Gal. du Centre, Paris, 1992. *Sylvain 'Paroles d'Autiste',* exhibition catalogue, Knokke-Zoute, 1993 (good documentation). Van Jole, Marcel/Xuriguera, Gérard, *Christian Silvain,* GEV, Eupen, 1997 (text in Dutch, English, French and German).

MUSEUMS AND GALLERIES:
AACHEN (Ludwig Forum für Internationale Kunst) - BARCELONA (MAM del Mus. Nacional d'Art de Catalunya) - BERN (Kunstmus.) - BRUSSELS (Mus. royaux des Beaux-Arts de Belgique) - CHARLEROI (MBA) - COURTRAI (Broelmus.) - HAIFA (MA) - LA LOUVIÈRE (Centre de la Gravure et de L'image Imprimée) - LA LOUVIÈRE (Mus. Ianchelevici) - LAUSANNE (Cantonal MFA) - LIÈGE (Mus. de l'Art wallon) - MONS (MBA) - OSTEND (Mus. voor Moderne Kunst) - PRAGUE (Národní Gal.) - STUTTGART (Neue Stadtgal.) - TOURNAI (MBA) - TROYES (MAM) - VERVIERS (Mus. communal des Beaux-Arts et de la Céramique) - VIENNA (Mus. Moderner Kunst Stiftung Ludwig).

AUCTION RECORDS:
PARIS, 31 Oct 1990, *Matthew and the Black Bird* (1989, mixed media and collage, 39 1/4 x 47 1/4 ins / 100 x 120 cm) FRF 18,000. LOKEREN, 21 March 1992, *Composition with Figures* (1971, mixed media/canvas, 27 1/2 x 31 1/2 ins / 70 x 80 cm)

BEF 38,000. LOKEREN, 23 May 1992, *Large Studio* (1975, oil on panel, 47 1/4 x 31 1/2 ins / 120 x 80 cm) BEF 130,000. LOKEREN, 10 Oct 1992, *Julia-Bird* (1991, mixed media, 41 1/4 x 29 1/2 ins / 105 x 75 cm) BEF 26,000. LOKEREN, 15 May 1993, *Past Time* (1991, mixed media, 18 x 10 1/2 ins / 45.5 x 26.5 cm) BEF 28,000. LOKEREN, 4 Dec 1993, *Blue Star* (1991, mixed media/canvas, 39 1/4 x 27 1/2 ins / 100 x 70 cm) BEF 38,000. LOKEREN, 28 May 1994, *Julia-Bird* (1991, mixed media, 41 1/4 x 29 1/2 ins / 105 x 75 cm) BEF 30,000. LOKEREN, 8 Oct 1994, *Bird-Flower* (1993, various materials, h. 33 3/4 ins / 86 cm) BEF 80,000.

SILVAIN, Edme or Jean Edme, or Silvin or Sylvain
French, 17th century.
Died before 21 September 1683.
Painter.

Edme Silvain was the father of Antoine, Jean and Gabriel Silvain. He worked on the church of the Val-de-Grâce in Paris in 1667 and 1675.

SILVAIN, Gabriel
French, 17th century.
Died 1689; buried 20 July.
Active in Paris.
Painter.

Gabriel Silvain was the son of Edme Silvain. He studied at the Académie Royale in Paris.

SILVAIN, Jean François
French, 17th century.
Baptised 3 November 1664.
Active in Paris.
Painter.

Jean François Silvain was the son of Edme Silvain.

SILVANI, Ferdinando
Italian, 19th century.
Born 16 May 1823, in Parma; died 23 January 1899, in Parma.
Engraver (burin).

Silvani studied at the academy in Parma and with P. Toschi. He made engravings of religious subjects.

SILVANI, Gaetano
Italian, 19th century.
Born 22 September 1798, in Parma; died 6 October 1879, in Parma.
Engraver (burin).

A pupil of A. Isac and P. Toschi, Silvani made engravings of religious subjects, allegories and portraits.

SILVANI, Gherardo
Italian, 17th century.
Born 13 December 1579, in Florence; died 23 November 1675, in Florence.
Sculptor, architect.

The pupil of L. Cigoli and G.B. Caccini, Silvani, who was primarily an architect, pursued his studies in Rome.

SILVANI, Mentore
Italian, 19th century.
Born 1843, in Traversetolo.
Painter, decorative designer. Landscapes, urban landscapes. Stage sets.

Mentore Silvani painted scenery for theatres in Venice.

MUSEUMS AND GALLERIES:
PARMA (GA): *Mill near Ugozzolo; Flood Damage in Parma.*

SILVANUS, C. Silvanus
Active during the Roman age.
Painter.
Ancient Roman.

Silvanus executed the paintings decorating the tomb of Postumius in Carmona (Seville).

SILVEIRA, Belle Silveira. See **GORSKI**

SILVEIRA, Benito
Spanish, 18th century.
Born in San Julián de Cabaleiros; died c. 1790, in Santiago de Compostela.
Sculptor.

Benito Silveira was a pupil of Miguel Romay. He executed sculptures for the gardens of the palace of La Granja and for churches in Mellid, Orense, Pontevedra, Santiago de Compostela and Sobrado.

SILVEIRA, Pedro de
Spanish, 16th century.
Born in La Coruña (Galicia).
Active during the second half of the 16th century.
Sculptor (wood).

In 1566, Pedro de Silveira made several statues for the sculptor Diego Jardin in Santiago de Compostela.

SILVEIRA-SILVA, Claudio
Uruguayan, 20th century.
Born 1935, in Rio Branco.
Painter, engraver, sculptor. Figures, landscapes.

Claudio Silveira-Silva studied at the Montevideo art school. In 1962 he won a grant enabling him to train in the Cami-Bercier studio in the École des Beaux-Arts in Paris and then in the Friedlander studio. In 1974 he was back in Paris.

He was a painter, a wood engraver and a wood carver

His work featured in various collective exhibitions, including the Salón Nacional de Bellas Artes in Montevideo where he won the first prize for engraving (1963); Musée d'Art Moderne in Paris and the *International Engraving Biennale* in Cracow (in the 1970s); *L'Estampe aujourd'hui* (Print-Making Today) at the Bibliothèque Nationale in Paris (1978); Barcelona (1981). He had regular solo exhibitions in Uruguay and in Paris in galleries such as the Paul Prouté, Biren and others.

BIBLIOGRAPHY:
Claudio Silveira Silva, exhibition catalogue, Gal. La Pedrera, Barcelona, 1981.

SILVELA Y CASADO, Mateo
Spanish, 19th - 20th century.
Born 1863, in Madrid.
Painter, watercolourist, draughtsman. Religious subjects, portraits, genre scenes.

Mateo Silvela y Casado was a pupil of Casto Plasencia y Maestro, at the Academia de Bellas Artes in Madrid, then of Léon Gérôme in Paris in 1883. He was awarded a travel scholarship, which he used to further his studies in Rome.

He painted *St Francis of Assisi Feeding the Poor* for the church of S Francisco el Grande in Madrid. He featured in collective exhibitions including; Círculo de Bellas Artes, Madrid (1883); Exposición Nacional de Bellas Artes in Madrid (1887 when he received a second-class medal, 1890, 1892 and 1895).

BIBLIOGRAPHY:
Arnáiz, José Manuel/López Jiménez, Javier/Merchán Díaz, Manuel (ed.), '*Cien años de pintura en Espana y Portugal (1830-1930)*' in vol. X, Antiqvaria, Madrid, 1993.

SILVÉN, Jakob or Jacob or Johan Jacob
Swedish, 19th - 20th century.
Born 31 August 1851, in Sillerud; died 14 March 1924, in Häslö, near Karlskrona.
Painter. Figures, landscapes with figures, landscapes.

Silvén studied at the fine arts academy in Stockholm.

AUCTION RECORDS:
GÖTEBORG, 3 Nov 1982, *Summer Landscape* (1891, oil on canvas, 21 1/4 x 35 1/2 ins / 54 x 90 cm) SEK 13,000. STOCKHOLM, 16 Nov 1983, *Seascape* (oil on canvas, 32 x 48 1/2 ins / 81 x 123 cm) SEK 12,000. STOCKHOLM, 19 April 1989, *Wild Flowers in*

a Meadow with a House in the midst of a Stand of Trees in the Distance (1894, oil on canvas, 20½ x 35 ins / 52 x 88 cm) SEK 34,000. STOCKHOLM, 15 Nov 1989, *Spring Landscape with Red Houses near a Lake* (oil on panel, 6 x 9 ins / 15 x 23 cm) SEK 8,700. STOCKHOLM, 16 May 1990, *Cattle near a Farmhouse on a Swedish Island* (oil on panel, 9½ x 24½ ins / 24 x 62 cm) SEK 16,000.

SILVENA, Bento Coelho da. See **COELHO DA SILVEIRA BENTO**

SILVERA, Eudoro
Panamanian, 20th century.
Born 1917, in Panama.
Painter.
Eudoro Silvera studied painting in Panama and in Munich, and music in New York. In 1953 and 1957 he won the *Ricardo Miró* first prize in Panama.

SILVERIO DE LELLIS. See **LELLIS Silverio de**

SILVERMAN, Burton
20th century.
Born 1928, in Brooklyn (New York City).
Painter (gouache), watercolourist, pastellist, draughtsman, illustrator. Portraits.
Burton Silverman studied at the Pratt Institute and the Art Student's League in New York from 1946 to 1949. He abandoned Modernism and Abstract Expression to concentrate on portrait painting and the classical reproduction of the human figure. His portraits featured in the *New Yorker* magazine have become an institution.

Silverman has shown at numerous exhibitions in the USA and won many awards. He has also written a number of books about his work, including *Breaking the Rules of Watercolor*.

AUCTION RECORDS:
NEW YORK, 15 May 1991, *Fiat 600* (1967, oil on canvas, 37¼ x 37¼ ins / 94.6 x 94.6 cm) USD 3,860. NEW YORK, 3 Dec 1992, *Woman with Beach Hat* (1982, watercolour, gouache and pencil/card, 23½ x 14¼ ins / 59.7 x 36.2 cm) USD 3,850. NEW YORK, 4 Nov 2000, *Two Tailors in Dress-making Shop* (watercolour, 28 x 22 ins / 71 x 56 cm) USD 2, 100. HILTON HEAD ISLAND, 25 Oct 2002, *Silver Medallist* (watercolour, 11 x 10 ins / 28 x 25 cm) USD 800. PHILADELPHIA, 24 Jan 2003, *Black Hat* (oil on panel, 14 x 10 ins / 36 x 25 cm) USD 650. LAMBERTVILLE, 20 Nov 2004, *Woman with Shawl* (watercolour, 13 x 8 ins / 33 x 20 cm) USD 650. BETHESDA, 11 Dec 2004, *Ritual Dance* (pastel, 25 x 17 ins / 64 x 43 cm) GBP 619.

SILVERMAN, Martin
20th - 21st century.
Born 1950.
Sculptor. Local figures.
Martin Silverman's choice of materials and the way he paints his sculptures give them a realistic character, especially those representing normal, everyday people.

AUCTION RECORDS:
NEW YORK, 10 Nov 1988, *Businessman* (1981, bronze, 40 x 18 x 16 ins / 101.6 x 45.7 x 40.7 cm) USD 6,600. NEW YORK, 14 Feb 1989, *Guardian Angel* (bronze, 76¾ x 49 x 32¾ ins / 195 x 124.5 x 83 cm) USD 6,600. NEW YORK, 5 Oct 1989, *Man in a Sleeping Bag* (painted bronze, 10¾ x 15¾ x 5 ins / 27.2 x 40 x 12.7 cm) USD 4,070. NEW YORK, 1 Nov 1994, *Vaudeville Character* (1989, bronze/wood, 71 x 19 x 16 ins / 180.3 x 48.3 x 40.7 cm) USD 1,610.

SILVERTHORNE, Jeanne
French, 20th century.
Sculptor of assemblages, installation artist.
Jeanne Silverthorne's works fall within the Duchamps tradition. They are assemblages of monumental circuits, formed from casts of electrical installations and depicting tentacles invading the space around them in irrational mechanical movements. Works such as *Fear Machine, Tears Machine, Dry Mouth, Irritation,* or *Blink,* create a gripping impression of unease, angst, and invasion of personal space.

In 1994-1995, the Galerie Nathalie Obadia in Paris showed a collection of her assemblages. In 1999 she showed one of her works in the Phillip Morris Annex of the Whitney Museum in New York. In 2002 she showed two large-scale works at the Soshana Wayne Gallery in Santa Monica, Los Angeles.

In 2002 she took part in the exhibition *Chain Reaction: Rube Goldberg and Contemporary Art,* at the Tang Museum in Saratoga Springs, New York State.

MUSEUMS AND GALLERIES:
PARIS (FNAC): *Untitled* (1994, object).

SILVESTER
British, 18th century.
Active in London from 1780 to 1790.
Sculptor (marble), modeller (wax). Busts, statuettes.
Silvester exhibited statuettes in wax in 1782 and 1785, and also executed busts in marble. He and the similarly-named 'sculptor in wax' Sylvester, who died in Dublin, were probably one and the same.

MUSEUMS AND GALLERIES:
LONDON (National Portrait Gal.): *Bust of Wesley.*

SILVESTER. See also **SYLVESTER**

SILVESTER, Lucas, or Silvestre
Flemish School, 16th century.
Sculptor.
Silvester remade the tabernacle that was destroyed in the cathedral of St Bavo, Ghent, in 1566, and worked in Ghent until 1581.

SILVESTRE (Mme)
French, 19th century.
Painter.
A pupil of Regnault, Mme Silvestre made her debut at the Salon de Paris in 1879.

SILVESTRE, Albert
Swiss, 19th - 20th century.
Born 1869, in Geneva.
Painter. Landscapes.
Albert Silvestre exhibited at the Exposition Universelle in Paris in 1900, at the Salon des Artistes Français, where he was awarded a bronze medal.

MUSEUMS AND GALLERIES:
BUCHAREST (Muz. National de Arta al României): *Mondon* - GENEVA (MAH): *Dunes; Ivory.*

AUCTION RECORDS:
NEW YORK, 9 Dec 1982, *On the Beach* (oil on canvas, 18 x 24 ins / 46 x 61 cm) USD 1,600. VEJLE, 16 Jan 2001, *Garden Scene with Flowers* (oil on canvas, 18 x 22 ins / 46 x 55 cm) DKK 16,000. LILLE, 10 March 2002, *Little Pomegranate Seller* (oil on canvas, 60 x 42 ins / 152 x 107 cm) EUR 6,800. SION, 21 June 2003, *Savieze* (oil on canvas, 15 x 18 ins / 37 x 45 cm) CHF 2,200.

SILVESTRE, Alexandre
French, 17th - 18th century.
Born 27 December 1672, in Paris.
Engraver. Religious subjects.
Alexandre Silvestre was one of the sons of Israël Silvestre the Younger. Besides the few engraved works he has left behind, information on Silvestre is scarce. He is known to have taken holy orders and completed a translation of the *Imitation of Christ* into Latin verse, which was published in 1709.

SILVESTRE, Antonin Désiré
French, 19th - 20th century.
Born in Bréhal.
Painter. Genre scenes.

Antonin Désiré Silvestre was a student of Leon Bonnat in Paris. He exhibited at the Salon des Artistes Français, where he won a third-class medal and the Maguebone-Lefebvre-Glaize Prize in 1908. He became a member of the Salon in 1909.

Auction records:

Paris, 3 June 1988, *Musicians* (oil on canvas, 35 1/2 x 47 1/4 ins / 90 x 120 cm) FRF 9,000.

SILVESTRE, Armand

Belgian, 20th century.
Born 1921, in Liège.
Painter.

Armand Silvestre studied at the fine arts academy in Liège. He painted brightly coloured compositions in the lyrical abstract style of the 1950s.

Bibliography:

Conversation avec Léon Wuidar, Tandem, Gerpinnes, 2003.

SILVESTRE, Augustin François de (Baron)

French, 18th - 19th century.
Born 7 December 1762, in Versailles; died 4 August 1851, in Paris.
Painter, draughtsman.

Augustin François de Silvestre studied under his father Jacques Augustin Silvestre. He went to Rome and worked there for four years. The position of drawing master to the king's children, which had been the Silvestres' preserve since Israël Silvestre, had ceased to exist when Augustin returned to France, but he was compensated with the position of deputy librarian and reader to the count of Provence (later to become Louis XVIII). He forsook fine arts for the sciences. During the revolution and the First Empire, he was a high-ranking civil servant. He became a member of the Académie des Sciences in 1809. After the Restoration, he resumed his position as reader to Louis XVIII and then as librarian. He was given the title of Baron. After the 1830 July revolution, the fall of Charles X and the advent of the more populist Louis-Philippe of Orléans, he withdrew from public life and restricted his interests to the sciences.

SILVESTRE, Charles François de

French, 17th - 18th century.
Born 10 April 1667, in Paris; died 8 February 1738 (?), in Versailles.
Painter, draughtsman, engraver (burin).

Charles François de Silvestre was the eldest son of Israël Silvestre the Younger under whom he studied as well as under Charles Le Brun and Joseph Parrocel, completing his studies in Italy. He took over from his father as drawing master to the king's children. He was engraver and painter to the king of Poland and was ennobled by Augustus III. Though 1738 is often given as the year of his death, the fact that he was ennobled along with his brother Louis Silvestre the Younger in 1741 suggests that he died after that date.

He produced landscapes and engravings from his own drawings or from works by his brother Louis. He married Suzanne Thuret, sister of the famous watchmaker Jacques Thuret. Two of his children, Nicolas Charles and Suzanne, were artists.

SILVESTRE, François

French, 17th century.
Born c. 1620, in Nancy.
Draughtsman, engraver.

François Silvestre was the eldest son of Gilles Silvestre. He engraved landscapes. Some biographers believe him to have studied under his father. This seems unlikely as his brother Israël Silvestre the Younger was around the same age as François but, according to a reliable source, was orphaned very young. Gilles Silvestre may, at best, have initiated François' artistic training.

SILVESTRE, François Charles de

French, 18th century.
Born c. 1712, in Paris; died 10 January 1780, in Paris.
Painter.

François Charles de Silvestre was the son of Louis Silvestre the Younger and painter to King Augustus III of Poland, Elector of Saxony. He is mentioned in his father's death certificate on 11 April 1760.

SILVESTRE, Gilles

French, 17th century.
Born c. 1590, in Nancy; died c. 1631, in Nancy.
Stained glass painter.

Gilles Silvestre was a descendant of the Scottish Silvester family who settled in Lorraine in the 16th century. Gilles married Élisabeth Henriet, daughter of Claude Henriet, stained glass painter to the duke of Lorraine. Silvestre was fairly advanced in years when he married, but successfully dedicated himself to painting.

SILVESTRE, Henri

Swiss, 19th century.
Born 4 September 1842, in Geneva; died 20 November 1900, in La Tour-de-Peilz.
Painter, illustrator, director.

Silvestre studied in France and Belgium.

Museums and Galleries:

Geneva (MAH): *A Street in Coppel* (watercolour).

SILVESTRE, Israël, the Elder

Flemish School, 16th century.
Engraver. Portraits.

Silvestre was active in Antwerp about 1542.

SILVESTRE, Israël, the Younger

French, 17th century.
Born 3 August 1621, in Nancy; died 11 October 1691, in Paris.
Engraver, draughtsman.

Israël Silvestre the Younger, orphaned at an early age, went to live in Paris with his uncle and godfather Israël Henriet. Henriet, Jacques Callot's close friend and publisher, had taught Louis XIII drawing. Under his uncle's guidance, Israël Silvestre soon became an outstanding draughtsman and etcher. From 1640 to 1655 he travelled around France and Italy. His exceptional speed of execution enabled him to put together a large number of sketches, many of which he subsequently engraved. In 1661 his uncle died and Silvestre, the sole heir, thereby came into possession of a large part of Callot's work. Silvestre supplemented his collection with the plates still owned by Callot's widow. The plates engraved by Stefano della Bella after his return from Florence as well as those treated by Henriet thus complemented Silvestre's own stock. At about that time he married Henriette Sélincart, whose sister Élizabeth had married the painter Jean Nocret from Nancy. Israël Silvestre had many children, four of whom became artists in their own right: Charles François, Louis the Elder, Alexandre and Louis the Younger. Silvestre was appointed drawing master to the dauphin, heir to the throne of France, who became the godfather of Silvestre's son Louis the Elder on 16 March 1669. Silvestre was also licensed to teach drawing to the pages of both the king's stables.

Having settled in Paris in 1655, he gave up etching for line engraving and a more mannered style. He occupied the middle ground between Callot and Stefano della Bella. At Louis XIV's behest he executed pieces on grand themes: *Courses de Testes et de Bagues* (*Tourney Jousts*) in 1622; *The Delights of the Enchanted Island* in 1664; and, more significantly, engravings of *Royal Estates*, which he elevated from their topographic status, gracing them with the features of landscapes.

BIBLIOGRAPHY:
Faucheux, Louis-Etienne, *Catalogue raisonné de toutes les estampes qui forment l'œuvre d'Israël Silvestre*, F. de Nobele, Paris, 1969.

MUSEUMS AND GALLERIES:
LONDON (British Mus.): drawings - PARIS (Louvre): drawings.

AUCTION RECORDS:
PARIS, 1767, *Becalmed Sea; Storm* (pen) FRF 50. PARIS, 1773, *Arch of Titus; Ruins* (two drawings) FRF 48. PARIS, 1811, *View of the Portal of the Church of St Peter in Rome and Other Monuments* (drawing) FRF 73. PARIS, 1865, *View of the Church of St John in Lyons* (pen drawing) FRF 39. PARIS, 1883, *Perspective View of the Piazza di S Marco in Venice* (pen and Indian ink wash) FRF 105. PARIS, 30 Oct 1928, *Landscapes with Figures* (drawings) FRF 165. BERN, 25 June 1982, *View of Lyons by the Rhône* (c. 1670, pen, 8 1/4 x 10 ins / 21.1 x 25.2 cm) CHF 3,800. BERN, 20 June 1986, *Rome's Stational Churches* (title page and series of 10 etchings) CHF 2,000. LONDON, 2 July 1991, *View of a Fountain in the Park at Fontainebleau* (black chalk, brown ink and grey wash, 4 1/2 x 10 ins / 11.3 x 24.5 cm) GBP 1,430. PARIS, 30 March 1998, *Château de St-Germain-en-Laye* (watercolour, pen, black ink and lead pencil, 4 1/2 x 8 1/2 ins / 11.4 x 21.9 cm) FRF 4,200.

SILVESTRE, Jacques Augustin de
French, 18th century.
Born 1 August 1719, in Paris; died 10 July 1809, in Paris.
Painter, draughtsman.

Jacques Augustin de Silvestre was the son and pupil of Nicolas Charles de Silvestre. He visited Italy and stayed in Rome for three years copying the great masterpieces he found there in abundance. He took over his father's position as drawing master to the king's children. Like his father, he was a dedicated art collector. His splendid collection was sold in 1810.

SILVESTRE, Louis, called Louis the Elder
French, 17th - 18th century.
Born 20 March 1669, in Paris; died 18 April 1740, in Paris.
Painter, draughtsman, engraver (etching). Landscapes.

Louis Silvestre the Elder was the second son of Israël Silvestre the Younger. He is likely to have studied under the same masters as his brother Louis Silvestre the Younger, at least as far as his father and Le Brun are concerned. He was the dauphin's godson. One of his daughters was married to the painter Louis Barerre, member of the Académie de St-Luc and mentioned in Silvestre's death certificate.

SILVESTRE, Louis, the Younger
French, 18th century.
Born 23 June 1675, in Sceaux; died 11 April 1760, in Paris.
Painter. History painting, portraits. Decorative schemes.

Louis Silvestre the Younger was the fourth son of Israël Silvestre the Younger. Having initially studied under his father, he was later taught by Charles Le Brun and Bon Boulogne. In 1701 he went to Italy and worked in Rome with Carlo Muratti. Back in Paris, he was admitted into the Académie Royale on 24 March 1702, where he rose through the hierarchy and finally became its director on 29 July 1752. In 1716 he was called to Dresden by the prince elector of Saxony, son of Augustus II, King of Poland. He became first painter to the king of Poland and in 1727 was appointed head of the academy in Dresden. Two electors of Saxony were elected kings of Poland in succession, and he served them loyally, working both in Dresden and Warsaw, where he decorated the royal palace. He was ennobled by Augustus III of Poland along with his brother Charles François Silvestre in 1741. He exhibited at the Paris Salons in 1704, 1750 and 1757. He also painted the third *Mai* of Notre-Dame in 1703. He decorated several rooms of the Zwinger Palace in Dresden.

Also in Dresden, he decorated the former royal palace with four paintings representing *Perseus and Andromeda, Venus and Vulcan, Bacchus and Ariadne* and *Leto and the Peasants of Lycia*, the latter work being drawn from Jean Jouvenet's painting for the Château de Marly.

BIBLIOGRAPHY:
Weigert, Roger Armand, '*Documents inédits sur Louis de Silvestre, suivis du catalogue de son œuvre*' in *Archives de la Société de l'Art Français*, periodical, Paris, 1932.

MUSEUMS AND GALLERIES:
BRUSSELS: *Legend of St Benedict* (eight paintings) - COMPIÈGNE: *Arion on the Dolphin* - COPENHAGEN (Statens Mus. for Kunst): *Count Jorgen Schell* - CRACOW (Muz. Narodowe): *Countess Branicka; Prince of the Royal House of France* - DESSAU: *Frédéric Henri Eugène, Prince of Anhalt-Dessau* - DRESDEN: *General Jan de Bodt; Nessus and Deïaneira Pursued by Hercules; Meeting of Empress Amelia with her Daughter Maria Josepha and her Husband King Augustus III; Augustus III as a Horseman; Augustus III, Crown Prince; Augustus II the Strong, King of Poland, and Friedrich Wilhelm I of Prussia; Maria Josepha of Austria, Princess of Saxony* - LEIPZIG: *Portrait Presumed to be of the Young Count Heinrich von Brühl* - LEIPZIG (Mus. der Bildenden Künste): *Friedrich Christian, Prince of Saxony* - MADRID (Prado): *Maria Amelia, Princess of Saxony and Queen of Spain* - MONTPELLIER: *Creation of Man by Prometheus* - MUNICH: *Emanuel Franz Joseph of Bavaria; Maria Antonia, Princess of Saxony* - PARIS (Louvre): *Washing of the Feet; Scene from the Life of St Benedict* - ST PETERSBURG (Hermitage): *Marie Louise Élisabeth, Duchess of Berry* - TOURS: *Marie Louise Élisabeth, Duchess of Berry* - VERSAILLES: *Duchess of Berry; Louis XIV Receiving the Elector of Saxony at Fontainebleau (1714); Friedrich Augustus II, King of Saxony (Augustus III, King of Poland); Maria Josepha of Austria, Queen of Poland* - WARSAW (King Stanislas Augustus Gal.): *Portrait of Prince Michel Garlorysk; Portrait of Prince Sulkowski* - WARSAW (Muz. Narodowe): *Negro Tickling a Sleeping Girl; A Pacha and Two Turks; Count Heinrich von Brühl; Portrait of an Unknown Man; Countess Branicka.*

AUCTION RECORDS:
PARIS, 12 Dec 1932, *St Michael Defeating the Dragon* (drawing in red chalk) FRF 550. LONDON, 10-14 July 1936, *The Louvre* (pen and wash) GBP 336. PARIS, 26 June 1981, *Portrait Presumed to be of Count Jacob Heinrich Fleming* (oil on canvas, 98 1/2 x 67 ins / 250 x 170 cm) FRF 72,000. NEW YORK, 12 June 1982, *Scene of Sacrifice* (red chalk, 11 1/4 x 15 ins / 28.7 x 38.2 cm) USD 1,700. MONTE CARLO, 26 June 1983, *Cimon and Ephialtes* (oil on canvas, 25 1/2 x 32 ins / 65 x 81 cm) FRF 28,000. PARIS, 25 Nov 1985, *Rinaldo and Armida* (oil on canvas, 38 1/2 x 51 1/2 ins / 97.5 x 130.5 cm) FRF 57,000. NEW YORK, 17 Jan 1986, *Abduction of Persephone* (oil on canvas, 52 1/2 x 44 1/4 ins / 133.5 x 112.5 cm) USD 25,000. PARIS, 13 Dec 1989, *Rinaldo and Armida* (oil on canvas, 38 1/2 x 50 3/4 ins / 98 x 129 cm) FRF 59,000. PARIS, 9 April 1991, *Latona and the Peasants of Lycia* (oil on canvas, 50 1/2 x 40 ins / 128 x 101.5 cm) FRF 150,000. NEW YORK, 16 Jan 1992, *Portrait of Maria Josepha, Queen of Poland, Electress of Saxony and Archduchess of Austria, in an Embroidered Dress, with the Attributes of Royalty near her and a Parrot Eating Grapes* (oil on canvas, 57 1/2 x 5 ins / 146 x 11.8 cm) USD 46,200. MONACO, 20 June 1992, *St Paul Healing the Paralytic* (black and white chalks/brown paper, 13 3/4 x 11 ins / 35 x 27 cm) FRF 68,820. STUTTGART, 20 June 2002, *Portrait of Christian Graf vom Loss* (oil on canvas, 33 x 26 ins / 84 x 65 cm) EUR 7,500.

SILVESTRE, Lucas. See **SILVESTER**

SILVESTRE, Marie Catherine

French, 18th century.

Born 1680, in Paris; died 15 October 1743, in Dresden.

Painter.

Marie Catherine Silvestre was the wife of Louis Silvestre the Younger. She copied many paintings executed by her husband. The Residenzmuseum in Munich has preserved her portraits of the Princesses Marie Anne, Maria Josepha, and Maria Amalia of Saxony. They could, however, be the work of Marie Maximilienne de Silvestre.

MUSEUMS AND GALLERIES:

MUNICH (Residenzmus.).

SILVESTRE, Marie Maximilienne de

French, 18th century.

Born 1708, in Paris; died 1797, in Paris.

Painter, draughtswoman.

Marie Maximilienne de Silvestre was the daughter of Louis Silvestre the Younger.

MUSEUMS AND GALLERIES:

VERSAILLES (Bibliothèque Municipale): *Portrait of Goldoni* (drawing).

SILVESTRE, Nicolas Charles de

French, 18th century.

Born 7 March 1699, in Versailles; died 30 April 1767, in Valenton.

Painter, engraver, draughtsman. Religious subjects, genre scenes.

Nicolas Charles de Silvestre studied under his father Charles François de Silvestre. He took over his father's position as drawing master to the king's children but had acted for him and enjoyed the title ever since 6 April 1717, the date of his marriage to Marguerite Le Bas, daughter of the famous engraver. He was admitted into the Académie on 30 December 1747 on presentation of a landscape. Mariette apparently deemed him an avid collector of etchings and drawings.

AUCTION RECORDS:

PARIS, 1881, *Subjects and Large Numbers of Views and Landscapes* (oil, sketches and counterproofs in a book) FRF 100. PARIS, 1882, *Landscapes Crossed by Streams with Dwellings and Figures in the Foreground* (four pen drawings) FRF 40. PARIS, 30 April 1924, *Seller of Rat Poison,* FRF 480. PARIS, 20 May 1927, *Reclining Man Leaning his Elbow on a Stone* (heightened red chalk) FRF 17,100. PARIS, 7 Dec 1934, *Portrait Presumed to be of the Artist* (red chalk heightened with white and gouache) FRF 4,800. NEW YORK, 18 Jan 1984, *Landscape with a Palace* (red chalk, 7 3/4 x 12 ins / 19.8 x 30.2 cm) USD 1,400. PARIS, 26 June 1987, *Landscape* (red chalk, 11 1/4 x 15 ins / 28.5 x 38 cm) FRF 12,800. LONDON, 2 July 1991, *Wooded Landscape with Figures in front of a Tavern and the Town in the Background* (drawing within a red chalk circle, 9 1/2 x 9 3/4 ins / 24.4 x 24.6 cm) GBP 7,700. PARIS, 17 June 1994, *Landscape with a Town Entrance* (red chalk, 10 1/4 x 16 1/4 ins / 26.3 x 41.5 cm) FRF 20,000. LONDON, 10 July 2001, *Tower of a Ruined Castle in a Landscape* (red chalk, 8 x 12 ins / 20 x 31 cm) GBP 2,200. LONDON, 10 July 2001, *Wooded Landscape with a Gully. River Landscape with Travellers on a Bridge* (red chalk, two, 9 x 7 ins / 24 x 19 cm) GBP 2,200. LONDON, 8 July 2003, *Extensive Landscape with Fishermen and Travellers on a Bridge, Town in the Background* (red chalk, 10 x 16 ins / 26 x 41 cm) GBP 3,500. NEW YORK, 22 Jan 2004, *Two Shepherds Sitting under a Tree in a Landscape* (red chalk, 14 x 10 ins / 35 x 25 cm) USD 3,200.

SILVESTRE, Paul

French, 20th century.

Born 17 February 1884, in Toulouse.

Sculptor. Genre scenes.

Paul Silvestre studied under Antonin Mercié and Jean Antonin Carlès at the École des Beaux-Arts in Paris. In 1912, he was awarded the Grand Prix de Rome de Sculpture. He exhibited at the Salon des Artistes Français, where he was awarded a commendation in 1910 and a silver medal in 1922. He was made a Chevalier of the Légion d'Honneur in 1926, and received a gold medal in 1930. The Salon awarded him the Hors concours, and he received an honorary diploma at the Exposition Internationale of 1937.

He produced war memorials as well as other sculptures in a lighter vein.

AUCTION RECORDS:

LONDON, 25 Nov 1981, *Fountain Head* (bronze, a pair, each h. 20 ins / 51 cm) GBP 1,100. NEW YORK, 26 March 1983, *Child Bacchus between Two Geese* (black-patinated bronze with tones of grey and green, h. 19 1/2 ins / 49.5 cm and w. 17 3/4 ins/45 cm) USD 1,400. LONDON, 2 May 1985, *Diana the Huntress* (c. 1930, lost-wax bronze, h. 60 ins / 152.4 cm) GBP 6,500. MONTREAL, 23-24 Nov 1993, *Attacked by a Swan* (bronze, h. 7 1/4 ins / 18.3 cm, l. 14 3/4 ins/37.5 cm) CAD 850. PARIS, 14 April 1999, *Rider Controlling Three Horses* (green patinated bronze, 14 x 23 ins / 35 x 58 cm) FRF 29,000. PARIS, 15 Nov 2000, *Rider Driving Three Horses to a Gallop* (aluminium, 14 x 22 ins / 35 x 56 cm) FRF 14,000. NEUILLY, 27 Nov 2001, *Diane* (brown patinated bronze, 30 x 9 ins / 75 x 22 cm) FRF 13,500. PONTOISE, 7 Dec 2002, *Marabout* (brown patinated bronze, 10 x 4x7 ins / 26 x 11x17 cm) EUR 1,600. PARIS, 25 June 2003, *Young Girl with Geese* (green patinated bronze, 19 x 18x9 ins / 48 x 45x24 cm) EUR 2,350. LONDON, 5 Oct 2004, *Satyr and Geese* (bronze, 16 x 33 ins / 40 x 85 cm) GBP 1,800.

SILVESTRE, R. (Mme)

French, 19th century.

Draughtswoman. Landscapes, architectural views.

This artist exhibited at the Salon de Paris between 1837 and 1844.

AUCTION RECORDS:

PARIS, 7 and 8 June 1928, *Landscape with Fountain* (lead pencil) FRF 4,100.

SILVESTRE, Suzanne Élisabeth, later Madame Lemoine

French, 18th century.

Born 14 June 1694, in Paris.

Engraver.

Suzanne Élisabeth Silvestre was the daughter of Charles François de Silvestre and the sister of Nicolas Charles de Silvestre. She studied under her father and married the sculptor Jean Baptiste Lemoine I (not the painter François Lemoine, as asserted in Bellier de la Chavignerie's dictionary). She engraved portraits after Rubens, Van Dyck, Noiret, Largillière, Le Brun and Vivien.

SILVESTRE DU PERRON, Edmond Pierre Henri Adolphe

French, 19th century.

Born 4 January 1823, in Villers-Farlay (Jura); died 14 March 1889, in Salins (Jura).

Painter.

The son or grand-son (?) of Louis François Silvestre du Perron, this artist was a priest.

SILVESTRE DU PERRON, Louis François

French, 18th - 19th century.

Born 1750 (?); died 3 May 1830, in Villers-Farlay (Jura).

Painter. Seascapes.

Louis François Silvestre du Perron was an officer.

MUSEUMS AND GALLERIES:

VILLERS-FARLAY: painting.

SILVESTRI, Carlo
Italian, 19th century.
Born 4 November 1821, in Abbiategrasso (Lombardy); died 29 September 1883, in Milan.
Painter. Genre scenes, portraits.
The father of Oreste Silvestri, Carlo Silvestri studied at the Accademia di Brera in Milan.

SILVESTRI, Ester
Italian, 19th century.
Active during the first half of the 19th century.
Engraver (burin).
A pupil of Anderloni, Ester Silvestri engraved portraits.

SILVESTRI, Gino
Italian, 20th century.
Born 1928, in Belluno near Venice.
Active from 1958 in France.
Painter.
A self-taught artist, Gino Silvestri settled in Paris. His large works, almost always in monochrome, are produced in series in which he explores a single shapeless form that appears sometimes lighter, sometimes darker, than the background. He has shown groups of his works in solo exhibitions in 1991 in Paris at the UNESCO Building and in 1992, also in Paris, at the Foire Internationale d'Art Contemporain under the auspices of the Galerie Weiller.
BIBLIOGRAPHY:
Chalumeau, Jean-Luc, '*Gino Silvestri*' in *Opus international*, no. 129, periodical, Paris, autumn 1992.

SILVESTRI, Guglielmo
Italian, 18th century.
Born 9 July 1763, in Parma.
Engraver (burin).
A pupil at the Accademia di Belle Arti in Parma, Silvestri engraved views of Modena, portraits and religious subjects.

SILVESTRI, Oreste
Italian, 19th - 20th century.
Born 5 September 1858, in Pollone.
Painter, engraver, art restorer. Genre scenes, landscapes.
The son of Carlo Silvestri, Oreste Silvestri was a student at the Accademia di Brera in Milan. He worked in Milan and exhibited in Rome and Turin.

SILVESTRI, Pietro
Italian, 18th century.
Active during the first half of the 18th century.
Medallist.
Pietro Silvestri engraved medals bearing effigies of the cardinals *Pietro Ottoboni* and *Livio Odescalchi.*

SILVESTRI, Tomaso
Italian, 18th century.
Born c. 1748, in Fleims.
Sculptor, engraver (burin).
Tomaso Silvestri worked in Trento and engraved portraits.

SILVESTRI, Tullio
Italian, 20th century.
Born 19 August 1880, in Venice.
Painter. Portraits, genre scenes, landscapes.
A self-taught artist, Tullio Silvestri worked in Zoppola. He also spent some time in Poland and Trieste.

SILVESTRINI, Cosmo or Cosimo. See **SALVESTRINI**

SILVESTRINI, Cristoforo
Italian, 18th - 19th century.
Born 1750, in Rome; died c. 1813.
Engraver (burin).

SILVESTRO, Barbeta di Pietro
Italian, 15th - 16th century.
Active in Venice.
Mosaicist.
Silvestro Barbeta was a follower of Castagno. He made two mosaics for St Mark's Basilica in Venice.

SILVESTRO, Giovanni
Italian, 19th - 20th century.
Born in Montanaro.
Painter, draughtsman. Religious subjects, genre scenes, architectural views. Murals.
The father of Oreste Silvestro, Giovanni Silvestro studied at the Accademia Albertina di Belle Arti in Turin. He executed work in some of the churches in Turin.
AUCTION RECORDS:
PARIS, 1 Feb 1950, *Interior of a Palazzo* (wash and sepia) FRF 1,000. PARIS, 22 Dec 1950, *Val-de-Grâce* (pen and wash) FRF 7,100.

SILVESTRO, Oreste
Italian, 20th century.
Born 27 April 1892, in Montanaro; died 17 November 1917; at the front in World War I.
Painter. Religious subjects. Murals.
The son of Giovanni Silvestro, Oreste Silvestro studied at the Accademia Albertina di Belle Arti in Turin. He painted frescoes for the church of S Grato in Ivrea.

SILVESTRO, Pietro
Italian, 19th - 20th century.
Born 1863, in Montanaro.
Painter, draughtsman. Murals, cartoons (decorative schemes).
The younger brother of Giovanni Silvestro, Pietro Silvestro was the pupil of a Lorenzo Mossello, probably a relation of Placido Mossello of Turin.

SILVESTRO D'OFENA
Italian, 12th century.
Active at the end of the 12th century.
Sculptor.
In 1196 Silvestro d'Ofena sculpted the porch of the church of S Maria a Criptis, near Ofena.

SILVESTRO DA CARATE
Italian, 16th century.
Sculptor, mosaicist.
Silvestro da Carate worked at the Carthusian church (Certosa) in Pavia in 1511.

SILVESTRO DA MELI. See the entry **ROCCO DI SILVESTRO DA MONTEFIASCONE**

SILVESTRO DA SULMONA, or Silvestro di Giacomo di Paolo da Sulmena, called Silvestro dall'Aquila or della Torre or Ariscola
Italian, 15th century.
Born in Sulmona (Abruzzi); died 1504, in L'Aquila (Abruzzi).
Sculptor, painter, architect.
Silvestro da Sulmona in the style of the Florentine School in L'Aquila where, from 1471, he made tombs, statues and low reliefs.

SILVESTRO DALL'AQUILA. See **SILVESTRO DA SULMONA Silvestro di Giacomo di Paolo da Sulmena**

SILVESTRO DEI BUONI
Italian, 15th century.
Born c. 1420, in Naples; died c. 1480.
Painter. History painting.
Silvestro dei Buoni was initially the pupil of his father, Buono dei Buoni, then he transferred to the studio of Zingaro. On the death of Zingaro, he entered the studio of Donzelli. According

to Cavaliere Massimo he made great progress, having a better feel for colour and composition than his master, but it was Antonio Solario who completed Silvestro's education and made him into an artist of great talent. One of his best works is the *St John the Baptist, St John the Evangelist and St John Chrysostomos* in the church at S Giovanni a Mare.

SILVESTRO DEI GHERARDUCCI, or Silvestro Camaldolense
Italian, 14th century.
Died 1399.
Active in Florence.
Miniaturist.

A monk in the monastery of S Maria degl'Angeli in Florence, Silvestro dei Gherarducci was a pupil of Taddeo Gaddi. He worked in collaboration with a fellow monk by the name of Jacopo and together they painted many beautiful illuminated initials for the choir books of their monastery. Their work was greatly admired and particularly by Lorenzo de' Medici. Silvestro is thought to have executed also for the miniatures in a Bible now in the Bibliothèque Nationale in Paris.

AUCTION RECORDS:
LONDON, 5 April 1977, *Prophet: Initial E* (gouache and gold/parchment, 9½ x 7½ ins / 24.2 x 19.2 cm) GBP 1,000.
LONDON, 8 Dec 1981, *St Stephen* (gouache and gold/parchment, initial O, 9 x 9 ins / 23.1 x 22.8 cm) GBP 10,000.

SILVESTRO DELLA SETA
Italian, 15th century.
Active in Verona at the beginning of the 15th century.
Painter.

Silvestro della Seta painted the frescoes in the Palazzo Vecchio and the castle of the Scaligeri family in Verona in 1409.

SILVESTRO DI BERTO
Italian, 15th century.
Active in Carrara (Tuscany) at the end of the 15th century.
Sculptor.

Silvestr di Berto executed a number of decorative sculptures in Pisa Cathedral in 1489.

SILVESTRO DI ORAZIO
Italian, 15th - 16th century.
Glass painter.

Silvestro di Orazio executed the stained glass windows in the church of S Maria Maddelena in Bologna dated 1471 and 1504.

SILVESTRO OF RAVENNA
3rd century.
Painter. Historical subjects, mythological subjects.

Silvestro of Ravenna is mentioned in Ris-Paquot.

MUSEUMS AND GALLERIES:
RHEIMS: *Fall of Phaeton* (drawing).

SILVESTRUCCI, Massimiliano or Massiminiano
Italian, 17th century.
Active at the beginning of the 17th century.
Mosaicist.

Silvestrucci worked on the central portal of Orvieto cathedral in 1612.

SILVIN, pseudonym of Bronckart, Silvin
Belgian, 20th century.
Born 1915, in Liège; died 1970.
Painter, sculptor.
CoBrA group.

Silvin Bronckhardt ('Silvin') studied at St. Luke's in Liège and was attached to the CoBrA Group. He exhibited together with Francine Holley at the 1959 Association des Artistes Wallons in Liège. His work is distinguished by his use of splashes of incandescent colour.

BIBLIOGRAPHY:
Stokvis, Willemijn, *Cobra*, Gallimard, Paris, 2001.

SILVIN, Edme or Jean Edme. See **SILVAIN**

SILVINO
Italian, 18th century.
Died 1724, in Turin, at an early age.
Painter. Architectural views, perspectives.

Silvino studied in Bologna.

SILVIO
Italian, 16th century.
Active in Gubbio during the first half of the 16th century.
Painter.

Silvio and P. Baldinacci painted a banner for the church of S Croce in Gubbio c. 1520.

SILVIO, Giovanni or Giampietro di Marco di Francesco
Italian, 16th century.
Born in Venice.
Active from 1532 to 1549.
Painter.

Giovanni Silvio was perhaps a pupil of Titian. A painting of *St Martin with Sts Peter and Paul and Musicians Angel* by this artist is in the Collegiata di Piove di Sacco near Padua.

SILVIO DA FIESOLE. See **COSINI Silvio**

SILVIUS. See **SYLVIUS**

SILVY
French, 19th century.
Born in Paris.
Miniaturist.

Mme Silvy was a pupil of Augustin and exhibited at the Salon de Paris in 1802.

SILVY-LELIGOIS, Albert
French, 19th - 20th century.
Born 15 April 1873, in Grenoble; died 17 September 1930.
Painter.

Albert Silvy-Leligois studied in Paris under Luc-Olivier Merson and Marcel Baschet.

SILZEMNIEKS, Alberts, or Krumins
Latvian, 20th century.
Born 25 October 1894, in Wolmar.
Painter.

Alberts Silzemnieks was a self-taught painter.

MUSEUMS AND GALLERIES:
RIGA - TUKUMS.

SIMA, Deszö, or Desiderius
Slovak, 20th century.
Born 1880, in Igló (now Spišská Nová Ves); died 1 September 1933, in Spišské Podhradie.
Painter. Landscapes.

Deszö Sima trained in Budapest.

SIMA, Joannes
Dutch, 18th century.
Sculptor.

Joannes Sima worked for the town hall in Amsterdam in 1700.

SIMA, Josef, or Joseph
Czech, 20th century.
Born 19 March 1891, in Jaromer; died 24 July 1971, in Paris.

Active in France from c. 1921; naturalised in 1926.
Painter, engraver, lithographer, draughtsman, illustrator, stained glass artist.
Groups: Devetsil, Grand Jeu.

Josef Sima was born into a family of artists: his grandfather was a sculptor and stonemason, his father a Prague painter and architect who taught at Jaromer School of Arts and Crafts and had Frantisek Kupka among his students. Josef studied at the Prague academy, where he worked in the studio of the Symbolist painter Jan Preisler, who introduced him to the work of Cézanne. In 1911 a Cézanne exhibition had been held in Prague and Cubist exhibitions in 1912 and 1913 had acquainted Sima with Cubism. Later, he studied at the Prague (or Brno) polytechnic, from which he graduated as an engineer. He served during World War I in the Austrian and Czech army. He returned to Brno, where he took up a post as assistant to his former professor at the polytechnic. About 1920 he joined Karel Teige, the leading light in Devetsil, the Czech Surrealist movement, and Roman Jakobsen, the structural linguist. He remained in close contact with Czech avant-garde movements until 1938.

In 1921 he went to work for a stained glass factory in San Sebastian, then settled in France. By 1922 he was in Paris, doing drawings for newspapers and designing fabrics for Dufy and the couturier Paul Poiret. Very soon he met Tristan Tzara and Georges Ribemont-Dessaignes, the Dadaists, and in 1923 married Nadine Germain, a medical student. As correspondent for the Czech magazine *Lidové Novidny* and architectural journal *Stavba*, he was associated with the group Esprit Nouveau, which counted among its members Auguste Perret, Le Corbusier, and the painters Ozenfant, Van Doesburg, and Mondrian. He was also correspondent for Karel Teige's magazine *red chalk*.

Sima mixed with the poets and painters of Montparnasse: Gleizes, Delaunay, and his fellow Czech, Kupka, then with Jean Arp, Miró and Max Ernst, and in 1926 with the Surrealists and Pierre Jean Jouve. He translated the work of Pierre Jean Jouve, Georges Ribemont-Dessaignes and Blaise Cendrars into Czech. In 1926, the Czech poet Richard Weiner introduced him to René Daumal, Roger Vaillant, A. Relland de Renéville, Roger Gilbert-Lecomte and Maurice Henry. Together, these artists and writers formed the group Grand Jeu, which met every Thursday in Sima's studio and in 1928 published a short-lived magazine (it lasted only three issues) for which Sima did the illustrations. In 1929, he broke with the Surrealist movement, even though he had never officially been a member, he and André Breton never got on together, but nonetheless helped to forge close ties between the Surrealists in Paris and in Czechoslovakia. These ties led to the Surrealist exhibitions in Prague, *Poetry 32* in 1932 and *Czech Surrealists* in 1935. In 1931 Grand Jeu ceased activity. During this time Sima was a public figure, recognised by his friends in Grand Jeu and by Paul Éluard, Philippe Soupault, Jacques Prévert, Roger Vitrac and Michel Leiris, and in 1931 *Les Cahiers du Sud* published *Hommage à Sima*. In around 1933, he bought a farm at Yèbles south east of Paris, converting the barn into a studio.

From 1939 to 1950, Sima virtually ceased painting. After the war broke out, he moved to Nice, but also re-established links with Czechoslovakia. In 1945 he returned to Paris, where he lived for the rest of his life, keeping out of the public eye but still continuing to see his literary and artistic friends, whose number was now joined by the philosopher Jean Grenier. During these years he produced the most important part of his work.

Sima was not only a painter but also a stained glass artist and set designer and an illustrator of major significance. As a direct result of his friendship with so many writers, he produced some 600 illustrations for more than 70 books, including *Au temps de Jésus-Christ*, a collection of Czech popular stories translated into French (1922), and *Les amoureux passe-temps*, an anthology of 17th and 18th century love stories selected by Fernand Fleuret (1925). From 1924, Sima was a close friend of the poet Pierre Jean Jouve and the two men worked together on a succession of volumes: *Nouvelles noces* (1926), *Beau Regard* (1927), *La Symphonie à Dieu* (1930), and *Le Paradis Perdu* (not published until 1938, but using drawings by Sima dating from 1924-1925 or 1929). In 1926 he also illustrated Blaise Cendrars' *L'Or*, Apollinaire's *Les Mamelles de Tirésias* and Ribemont-Dessaignes' *Oui et Non*, and designed the décor for Ribemont-Dessaignes' *Le bourreau du Pérou*. In 1952 he illustrated Jouve's *Langue*, in 1960 and 1966 Roger Gilbert-Lecomte's *Sacre et Massacre de l'Amour* and *Monsieur Morphée, empoisonneur public*, and in 1971 René Char's *L'Effroi La Joie*. In 1959, Sima made the acquaintance in Rheims of the stained glass master Charles Marcq, for whom, returning to his original craft, he designed a number of pieces of stained glass and engraved glass. Following this initial contact, the city of Rheims and the Monuments Historiques commissioned a set of stained glass pieces from him and Vieira da Silva for the church of St-Jacques.

Sima once said that all his paintings dated from the time he settled in Paris. As far as his first awareness of painting is concerned, he learned from Cézanne about the material quality itself of the object being painted, just as much as the image being represented; and Roman Jakobsen taught him, that signifier and signified were inseparable. He was also thoroughly impregnated with Czech Baroque sculpture and admired Courbet. In fact, the culture that fed his artistic investigations was so broad that it would be presumptuous to try to identify which influence came to bear at which time.

During his first years in Paris, he painted the banks, bridges and tugs on the Seine in a spontaneous, Expressionist-Fauvist style. It is sometimes claimed that he fell under the influence of Mondrian and Kupka, tending toward a free, coloured geometrical style, a synthesis of purity and dreamlike lyricism (*Blue Landscape* (1921); *Le Havre* (1923)). Yet this claim is belied by the fact that in 1926 he started painting works that go well beyond likeness: *Pink Body, Man of the Earth, Electric tension, Electric Storms*. He very soon came to see that his ideas were very similar to those of his friends in the Grand Jeu: the rejection of all dogmatism, defiance toward the objectivist ambitions inherited from the Cubists, and a preference for the imaginary attainable through a 'philosophy of participation', in which Roger Gilbert-Lecomte saw 'experimental metaphysics... a mystique' that concerned only the viewers. For Sima, this translated into 'vision painting', a sensation, which was related to a spiritualist conception of the universe that he shared with Pierre Jean Jouve, of the 'unity of matter, stones, trees, water, clouds, air and light', a notion not unrelated to alchemy, a subject in which both men were interested. Sima experienced this sensation in the form of sudden, 'inspired' impressions of the profound unity of the great forces of nature, most notably after two huge storms, one in 1922 and the other in 1924-1925, during which it seemed to him that nothing existed except the lightning and the energy of the lightning: 'the world self destructs in the unity of light become matter'. As he explained in an interview with Jean Grenier: 'One stormy night, after the violent light of the lightning, everything, the air, the clouds, the nature of the trees, the earth, the stones, everything seemed to be the sole matter of the world, and Heraclitus' dictum - The thunderbolt directs the course of all things - flashed across my mind'.

At the 1929 Grand Jeu exhibition at the Galerie Bonaparte, Sima showed 10 paintings: in addition to some ghostlike, imaginary portraits of his friends in the group, there were also, and most notably, unreal, universalised landscapes, scenes from which every narrative element had been stripped, a foretaste of his work to come, corresponding to his new perception of the world, which had made him 'dream of matter in order to materialise the imaginary'. Later, symbolic themes appeared, often together.

Sima's paintings from his Grand Jeu period seem to be fluid, abstract landscapes in which the earth, the sky and the sea forever intermingle in vapours and mists to the point that they become confused. Each has universalising, symbolic meaning, while the underlying thought, which is mystical rather than metaphysical, still perhaps implies the existence of beings and the places they inhabit. This is particularly true of the landscapes he painted between 1929 and 1939, when he was working at Yèbles. Here his technique is more intense, his matter sometimes rough, and his themes are the forest, the plain, and fire, and, as war approached, the fall (*Fall of Icarus*). Between 1939 and 1950, he probably only painted two pictures: *Orpheus in Despair* (1943), and *Deucalion's Men* (1944), as a sign of his renunciation.

After the war, Sima resumed activity with a brief period of rather unusual paintings from sketches of the streets of Nice and Paris, landscapes of the Corrèze and the Paris regions, and of his native Czechoslovakia, where he returned in 1947. These were followed by paintings of the labyrinth, once more with his symbolic forest. Shortly after 1950, with *Eurydice* and *Woman and Tree* (1952), he came to the final statement of what had driven him from the very beginning, when he first became aware of the essence of the reality and ambiguity of the human condition, the deep source of his creativity.

His *Orpheus* cycle (from around 1957), named for the poet who dared to descend into the underworld but was not permitted to look back, Sima eliminated every identifiable form, every bodily presence, leaving only light radiating from the hearth at the centre and permeating the entire canvas, creating timeless spaces whose smoky nuances flow into each other.

From 1960, echoing the harmony that rules the universe, Sima pressed these timeless spaces into a geometrical structure, an immaterial web of radiant points tied together by tenuous lines into circles, triangles and polyhedrons, in much the same way that constellations are made up of a number of artificial lines tying together stars far distant from each other. Sima died in 1971 at the age of 80. Until the end he maintained the transcription of his 'light-matter', in which he saw the original energy of the cosmos, the fusion of all things and all life, such as that of his very last work (1971), *Désert de l'amour au regard de cristal* (*Desert of Love with the Crystal Look*).

Collective exhibitions include: Salon des Surindépendants, Paris (1927), at André Breton's invitation; Grand Jeu exhibition, Galerie Bonaparte, Paris (1929); *Hommage à Antonin Artaud*, Galerie Pierre (Loeb) Paris (1947); *Art in France*, San Francisco (1956); *Depuis Bonnard*, Musée National d'Art Moderne, Paris, and the São Paulo Biennale (1957); *Cinquante ans d'art moderne*, Brussels, which coincided with the Exposition Universelle (1958); *French Painting from Gauguin to Our Days*, Warsaw, and Kassel Documenta II (1959); São Paulo Biennale (1961); *Le Surréalisme*, Galerie Charpentier, Paris (1964).

Solo exhibitions (with an hiatus between 1937 and 1952) include: Galerie Joseph Billiet, Paris (1927), where he showed a number of engravings and drawings; Aventinaka Mansarea Gallery, Prague (1928); Galerie Jacques Povolozky, Paris (1929); *Énigme de la face*, Galerie Jacques Povolozky, Paris (1930); Prague (1932-1938); Galerie Jeanne Castel, Paris (1937); retrospective, Prague (1937); Galerie Jeanne Castel, Paris (1952); Galerie Kléber, Paris (1953 showing lithographs); Galerie Kléber, Paris (1954). Studio Facchetti, Paris (1959 and 1960); retrospective of stained glass, engraved glass, and paintings (1927-1930, 1950-1962), Musée de Rheims (1963); retrospectives, Liberec and Hradec-Kralové (1964); Galerie Le Point Cardinal, Paris (1966, the first of a series of exhibitions); retrospective, Musée National d'Art Moderne, Paris and Národní galerie, Prague, which also visited Brno, Bratislava, and Ostrava (1968). Posthumous exhibitions include: Bochum Museum (1974); *Œuvre graphique et amitiés littéraires*, Bibliothèque Nationale, Paris (1979); Grand Jeu exhibition, Musée des Beaux-Arts, Le Havre (1980); complete retrospectives, Musée d'Art Moderne, Paris (1980 and 1992).

Sima

Bibliography:

Gilbert-Lecomte, R., *Sima. Énigme de la face*, exhibition catalogue, Gal. Jacques Povolozky, Paris, 1930. Cassou, Jean/Soupault, Philippe/Jouve, Pierre Jean, *Sima*, exhibition catalogue, Gal. Kléber, Paris, 1954. Wahl, Jean/Ribemont-Dessaignes, *Joseph Sima*, exhibition catalogue, Studio Paul Facchetti, Paris, 1959. Gilbert-Lecomte, R., *Sima*, exhibition catalogue, Musée de Rheims, Rheims, 1963. Grenier, Jean, *Entretiens avec dix-sept peintres non-figuratifs*, Calmann-Lévy, Paris, 1963. Waldberg, P./Faux, Monique, et al., *Sima*, exhibition catalogue, Gal. Le Point Cardinal, Paris, 1966. *Sima. Rétrospective*, exhibition catalogue, Musée national d'Art moderne, Paris, 1968. *Joseph Sima*, exhibition catalogue, Gal. Le Point Cardinal, Paris, 1971. Michel, Jacques, '*La Mort du peintre Joseph Sima*' in *Le Monde*, newspaper, Paris, 29 July 1971. Linhartova, B., *Josef Sima, ses amis, ses contemporains*, Éd. de la Connaissance, Brussels, 1974. *Sima. Œuvre graphique et Amitiés littéraires*, exhibition catalogue, Bibliothèque nationale de France, Paris, 1979. Smejkal, Frantisek, *Joseph Sima*, Prague, 1988 (Éd. Cercle d'Art, Paris, 1991-1992). *L'Art moderne à Marseille. La Collection du Musée Cantini*, exhibition catalogue, Musée Cantini, Marseilles, 1988. *Sima. Rétrospective*, exhibition catalogue, Musée d'Art moderne de la Ville de Paris, Paris, 1992. Lemaire, Gérard-Georges, '*Joseph Sima, l'amant de la littérature*' in *Opus international* n° 128, periodical, Paris, summer 1992. Monod, Luc, *Manuel de l'amateur de livres illustrés modernes 1875-1975*, Ides et Calendes, Neuchâtel, 1992. Henric, Jacques, '*Joseph Sima, impressions d'enfance en Bohême et autres souvenirs*' in *Art Press* n° 168, periodical, Paris, April 1992. Faux, Monique, '*Sima, lumière et matière*' in *Art Press* n° 168, periodical, Paris, April 1992. Harambourg, Lydia, *L'École de Paris 1945-1965. Dictionnaire des peintres*, Ides et Calendes, Neuchâtel, 1993. Snodgrass, Susan, '*Toward a New Bohemia*' in *Art in America*, periodical, April 2000.

Museums and Galleries:

Brno: *Krajina* (1931); *Spanelsko* (1936) - Brussels (Mus. royaux) - Grenoble (Mus. de Grenoble) - Lausanne (Cantonal MFA) - Le Havre (Mus. Malraux) - Litomerice: *Le Havre* (1923) - Lyons (MBA) - Ostrava: *Tun* (1935) - Paris (MAMVP): *On a poem by Pierre Jean Jouve* (1937) - Paris (MNAM-CCI) - Prague (Národní Gal.): *Conflans Ste-Honorine* (1923); *Untitled Picture* (1933); *Return of Theseus* (1933); *Memory of the Iliad* (1934); *Revolution in Spain* (1937, several other works) - Rheims (MBA): *Crystal* (1925); *Portrait of Roger Gilbert-Lecomte* (1929); *Portrait of René Daumal* (1929) - Rouen (MBA) - St-Étienne (Mus. d'Art et d'Industrie) - Valencia: *Grey Shadows* (1960).

Auction records:

Paris, 24 May 1972, *Blue Hurricane*, FRF 18,000. Paris, 27 Nov 1973, *Grey Landscape with Red Mark*, FRF 8,000. Paris, 30 Nov 1974, *Grey Space*, FRF 14,800. Paris, 25 May 1976, *Antaeus* (1958, oil on canvas, 35 3/4 x 28 3/4 ins / 91 x 73 cm) FRF 20,000. Paris, 6 Dec 1979, *Lattice* (1963, oil on paper remounted on canvas, 18 x 21 3/4 ins / 46 x 55.5 cm) FRF 7,000. Paris, 16 April 1982, *Composition* (1955, oil on canvas, 48 x

22¾ ins / 121 x 58 cm) FRF 40,000. PARIS, 21 Nov 1983, *Antaeus* (1958, oil on canvas, 36¼ x 28¾ ins / 92 x 73 cm) FRF 42,500. PARIS, 14 April 1986, *Subterranean Rivers* (1971, oil on canvas, 31½ x 39¼ ins / 80 x 100 cm) FRF 121,000. PARIS, 3 Dec 1987, *Archaeopteryx* (1957, oil on canvas, 9 x 5 ins / 22 x 12.5 cm) FRF 15,000. PARIS, 8 Dec 1987, *Composition* (1957, oil on canvas, 18 x 25½ ins / 46 x 65 cm) FRF 31,500. PARIS, 29 June 1988, *Portrait of a Woman* (oil on canvas, 25¼ x 19 ins / 64 x 48 cm) FRF 22,000. PARIS, 22 Jan 1990, *Composition* (1963, gouache, 15¾ x 19¾ ins / 40 x 50 cm) FRF 41,000. PARIS, 23 April 1990, *Geometric Landscape* (oil on canvas, 19¾ x 25½ ins / 50 x 65 cm) FRF 260,000. BERN, 12 May 1990, *Automobile* (1919, oil on canvas, 15¾ x 19¾ ins / 40 x 50 cm) CHF 8,000. PARIS, 19 June 1990, *Landscape* (1952, oil on canvas, 13½ x 19 ins / 34.5 x 48 cm) FRF 65,000. PARIS, 31 Oct 1990, *Lightscape* (oil on canvas, 22 x 18 ins / 55 x 46 cm) FRF 150,000. PARIS, 10 Feb 1991, *Blue, untitled* (1960, watercolour, 9½ x 7½ ins / 24 x 19 cm) FRF 20,000. ROME, 14 Dec 1992, *Composition* (1960, oil on canvas, 25½ x 35½ ins / 65 x 90 cm) ITL 12,650,000. PARIS, 16 March 1993, *Woman in Fur Coat* (1923, Indian ink, 10½ x 7¾ ins / 26.5 x 19.5 cm) FRF 7,000; *Earth* (1962, oil on canvas, 511¾ x 32 ins / 1300 x 81 cm) FRF 150,000. LONDON, 3 Dec 1993, *Blue Mark Landscape* (1964, oil, pencil and Indian ink on canvas, 46 x 35 ins / 116 x 89 cm) GBP 18,975. PARIS, 24 June 1994, *Moonlit Sky* (1966, oil on canvas, 23½ x 31¾ ins / 59.5 x 80.5 cm) FRF 90,000. PARIS, 26 Nov 1994, *Just Noon* (1958, oil on canvas, 43¼ x 21¼ ins / 110 x 54 cm) FRF 63,000. PARIS, 21 June 1995, *Impasse II* (1968, oil on canvas, 23½ x 32 ins / 60 x 81 cm) FRF 93,000. LONDON, 21 March 1996, *Untitled* (1962, oil on canvas, 36¼ x 28½ ins / 92 x 72.5 cm) GBP 12,650. PARIS, 16 March 1997, *Untitled* (1958, Indian ink and wash, 10½ x 7 ins / 26.5 x 18 cm) FRF 7,500. PARIS, 28 April 1997, *Composition* (1968, watercolour and gouache on paper, 11¼ x 14½ ins / 28.5 x 37 cm) FRF 25,000. PARIS, 23 June 1999, *Green Fabric* (1960, oil on canvas, 35 x 45 ins / 88 x 115 cm) FRF 90,000. PARIS, 23 June 1999, *Bather* (1949, oil on canvas, 31 x 39 ins / 80 x 100 cm) FRF 105,000. PARIS, 29 May 2000, *Composition* (oil on canvas, 24 x 15 ins / 61 x 38 cm) FRF 36,000. PARIS, 21 Dec 2000, *Drops of Lights* (oil on canvas, 32 x 24 ins / 81 x 61 cm) FRF 140,000. PRAGUE, 13 Oct 2001, *Landscape* (1934, oil on canvas, 24 x 32 ins / 60 x 81 cm) CZK 1,100,000. PRAGUE, 13 Oct 2001, *Old Tree in Rocks* (1935, oil on canvas, 32 x 26 ins / 82 x 66 cm) CZK 2,000,000. PARIS, 11 Dec 2002, *Bather* (1949, oil on canvas, 31 x 39 ins / 80 x 100 cm) EUR 32,000. PARIS, 16 Dec 2002, *Cold Sun* (oil on canvas, 24 x 18 ins / 61 x 46 cm) EUR 20,000. PARIS, 24 March 2003, *Blue Landscape, Light I* (1960, oil on canvas, 29 x 36 ins / 73 x 92 cm) EUR 21,500. PARIS, 2 July 2003, *Toile grise-graphique gris* (1960, oil on canvas, 32 x 39 ins / 81 x 100 cm) EUR 18,000. PARIS, 13 Feb 2004, *Earth-Light* (1965, oil on canvas, 39 x 32 ins / 100 x 81 cm) EUR 22,000. PARIS, 21 March 2004, *Untitled* (1957, oil on canvas, 32 x 26 ins / 81 x 65 cm) EUR 22,000.

SIMA, Michel, or real name: Michal Smajewski
Polish, 20th century.
Born 1912, in Slonim (now in Belarus); died 1987.
Active in France.
Sculptor, draughtsman, photographer.

Michal Sima left Poland at the age of 17 and moved to Paris, where he lived in the Grande Chaumière from 1929 to 1932. In 1934-1935 he worked with Zadkine on the Orpheus project, and in 1935-1937, after adopting the name 'Sima', with Brancusi, through whom he met Picasso. In 1942 he was deported to Auschwitz, but survived the camps, and returned to France in 1945, settling in Antibes. From 1959 to his death in 1987, he lived and worked in the Ardèche.

Sima first exhibited his sculpture in 1942, in a joint exhibition with Francis Picabia held in Cannes, but he is primarily known for his photographs, portraits of the great artists of his time, which he took after the war and some of which were published in *21 visages d'artistes* (F. Nathan, 1959). In 2003 an exhibition of his work was held in the Château d'Aubenas.

SIMA, Miron
Israeli, 20th century.
Born 1902, in Israel.
Painter (including gouache). Scenes with figures, local scenes, architectural interiors, landscapes, Still-lifes (flowers/fruit).

Miron Sima worked in Paris and Israel, where he was director of the school of fine art in Jerusalem. His paintings featured scenes from Jewish life, some of which decorated a synagogue in Jerusalem. He was also a driving force behind the new Palestinian School and the Exhibition of Palestinian Artists, which, since 1923, has been held annually in Tel Aviv, Jerusalem and Haifa.

AUCTION RECORDS:

PARIS, 29 Nov 1989, *Young Woman with Doves* (oil on canvas, 76¾ x 48½ ins / 195 x 123 cm) FRF 50,000. TEL AVIV, 6 Jan 1992, *Tower and Trees* (oil on canvas, 19½ x 25½ ins / 49.5 x 65 cm) USD 990; *Still-life with Fruit and Flowers* (gouache, 21 x 14¼ ins / 53.5 x 36.5 cm) USD 880.

SIMA ZHONG, or Ssu-ma Chung, sobriquet: Xiugu
Chinese, 19th century.
Born c. 1800, in Nanjing; died 1860.
Painter. Flowers, birds.

SIMAK, Lev
Czech, 20th century.
Born 3 March 1896, in Kralupy nad Vltavou; died 1989.
Painter, engraver. Landscapes, genre scenes, flowers, interiors with figures.

Lev Simak studied at the Prague academy from 1919 to 1926. He lived and worked in Prague and exhibited widely in his native Czechoslovakia as well as in France, the Soviet Union and Yugoslavia. He painted scenes from country life in a style where the lessons of Cézanne were fully assimilated, sometimes bringing the outside world in through the windows of his interiors.

BIBLIOGRAPHY:

Fifty years of Czechoslovak Painting from the Collections of the Galleries, 1918-1958, exhibition catalogue, Slovenska Narodna Gal., Bratislava, 1968 (in commemoration of the 50th anniversary of the Republic of Czechoslovakia).

SIMAKOV, Ivan Vasilievich
Russian, 20th century.
Born 1877; died 1925.
Painter (gouache), poster designer. Scenes with figures. Socialist Realism.

AUCTION RECORDS:

LONDON, 14 Dec 1995, *The Bolshevik Authorities Compelling the Inhabitants of Burzhui to Perform Community Service* (1920, gouache, 19 x 24½ ins / 48.5 x 62 cm) GBP 1,265.

SIMALUS
3rd century BC.
Active during the first half of the 3rd century BC.
Sculptor.
Ancient Greek.

Simalus is represented by three signatures on pedestals for votive offerings.

SIMANOWITZ, Ludovike von, or Kunigunde Sophie Ludovike
Maiden name: Reichenbach
German, 18th - 19th century.
Born 21 February 1759, in Schorndorf; died 2 September 1827, in Ludwigsburg.
Painter.

Von Simanowitz painted portraits of *Schiller* and the painter *Eberhard Wachter*.
MUSEUMS AND GALLERIES:
STUTTGART: *Portrait of Eberhard Wachter* - VIENNA (Städtisches Mus.): *Portrait of Karl von Reichenbach as a Child with his Mother*.

SIMAO. See also **SECO Simão**

SIMAO PORTUGALOIS. See **PORTUGALOIS Simon**

SIMAR, André
Belgian, 20th century.
Born 1927, in Theux (Liège).
Painter, watercolourist.
Simar studied at the fine arts academy in Liège and at the higher arts institute in Antwerp, and has since gone on to produce spontaneous compositions in various genres.
MUSEUMS AND GALLERIES:
LIÈGE.

SIMAR, Jean Baptiste
German, 18th century.
Sculptor.
Simar produced sculptures for the towns of Aachen (north Rhine, Westphalia, Germany), Metz (north-east France) and Trier (Rhineland-Palatinate, Germany).

SIMARD, Jean
French, 17th century.
Active during the second half of the 17th century.
Sculptor (wood).
Jean Simard was responsible for the execution of a tabernacle in the church of St Maurice in Besançon.

SIMARI, Giacomo
Italian, 15th century.
Active in Naples during the second half of the 15th century.
Painter.
Giacomo Simari decorated the great hall of the Castel Nuovo in Naples in 1472.

SIMARRO OLTRA, Ramón
Spanish, 19th century.
Born in Játiva (Valencia); died 1855, in Játiva.
Painter. Portraits.
Ramón Simarro Oltra studied at the school of fine arts in Madrid, and later in Rome from 1850 to 1855. There was a posthumous retrospective of his work in Valencia in 1855.

SIMART, Pierre Charles or Charles
French, 19th century.
Born 27 June 1806, in Troyes; died 27 May 1857, in Paris.
Sculptor.
Simart was a pupil of Dupaty, Pradier and Ingres. He was admitted to the École des Beaux-Arts in 1824, awarded second prize for sculpture in 1831 and first prize in 1833. Simart exhibited at the Salon de Paris between 1831 and 1855 and won a first class medal in 1840 and again in 1855. Made a Chevalier of the Légion d'Honneur on 5 July 1846, Officer on 14 June 1856, he became a Member of the Institute as a replacement for Pradier in 1852. Simart encountered huge opposition to his artistic leanings from his family. He was left to his own devices and from the age of fifteen he had to fend for himself. This he managed to do by selling drawings of statues on display in Museums. In spite of his scholastic success, he only started to receive serious commissions in around 1840. A statue of *Philosophy* (Salon of 1843), another of *Lyrical Poetry* (Salon of 1845), for the library at the Chambre des Pairs; *The Virgin*, a group executed in marble (Salon of 1845) for Troyes Cathedral, marked the beginning of his prosperity. In addition to these official works there were also four bas-reliefs in bronze (*Faith, Hope, Charity, Bounty*) for the Church of St. Pantaléon in Troyes; two bas-reliefs for the former Hôtel de Ville in Paris, *Architecture and Sculpture, Justice and Industry*, colossal figures, built against the columns of the Place de la Nation, *Art Seeking Its Inspiration from Poetry* (a pediment for the Denon Wing of the Louvre). Simart's crowning work is the decoration of Napoleon's Tomb at Les Invalides which includes ten bas-reliefs: *The Légion d'Honneur, Public Works, Commerce and Industry, The Tax Assizes, The Concordat, The Code, The Council of State, Government*, and *Quelling Unrest*. Simart himself was only able to complete seven and the other three were undertaken by colleagues. He was also commissioned to execute two ceilings for Galleries at the Louvre.
MUSEUMS AND GALLERIES:
PARIS (Louvre): *Venus* - ROUEN: *Oreste* - TROYES: *Faith; Hope; Charity; Charles X; Madame de Chavaudon; City of Troyes; Coronis Dying; Death of Cato of Utica; Bust of Annibal Jourdan; M. Marcotte; Discus Thrower; Architecture; Oreste Taking Refuge at the Altar of Minerva; Harvest; Harvesting the Grapes; Misfortunes of War; City Under Attack; Eglé; The Fates; Venus; Seascape; Vulcan; The Angel consoling Tobias; Orpheus Receiving the Lyre from Apollo, his Father, and Inspiration from his Mother, Calliope; Orpheus Describing the Magnificence of Heaven to Men and Inviting them to Gain Immortality; Mercury placing Eurydice into the Hands of Orpheus; Orpheus in the Underworld melting Pluto's heart so the god will return Eurydice to him; Death of Orpheus; Player of Ruzzica, discus thrower; Tobias and Sarah at Prayer; Napoleon I in Imperial Costume; Head of Napoleon I crowned with a Laurel Wreath; Quelling Civil Unrest; The Concordat; Civil Code; Organisation of Major Public Works; Protection Granted to Commerce and Industry; Creation of the Legion of Honour; Creation of the Council of State; Four Caryatids; Engraving; Painting; Sculpture; Jean Goujon; Pesne; Muse and Spirit of the bas-relief of Pesne; The Awakening of Arts, Industry and Commerce at the Napoleon III Centre; Visconti; M. Félix Dubar; M. Lequeux; Mme Lequeux; M. Lequeux the Younger; Countess of Agout, Daniel Stern; Mme Jay; City of Paris; Minerva; Victory of the Minerva; Shield of the Minerva; Sandals of the Minerva; Creation of Pandora; Mars, Sirius and Bacchus; Apollo, Diana and Vulcan; Tragedy; Elegy; Poetry; Resignation; Mask of Napoleon I; Art Seeking Its Inspiration from Poetry; Coronation of Orpheus; Virgin and the Infant Jesus; A.-F. Arnaud* (sixteen sketches) - VERSAILLES: *Antoine de Bourgogne, Duke of Brabant* - VIRE: *Félix Dubar*.
AUCTION RECORDS:
PARIS, 11 May 1931, *Portrait of Mademoiselle Messager* (drawing heightened with white) FRF 250. PARIS, 9 Oct 1997, *Daniel Stern* (1853, patinated bronze, h. 11 3/4 ins / 30 cm) FRF 8,600.

SIMAY, Imre Karoly, or Emmerich Karl
Hungarian, 19th - 20th century.
Born 16 December 1874, in Budapest; died 1955, in Érd.
Sculptor, painter, engraver. Figures, animals.
Imre Simay studied in Vienna and Munich and taught sculpture and modelling at the school of applied arts in Budapest. He specialised in statues of animals, especially monkeys.
MUSEUMS AND GALLERIES:
BUDAPEST (Magyar Nemzeti Gal.): *Pair of Lions; Horseman*.

SIMBARI, Nicola or Nicolas
Italian, 20th century.
Born 13 July 1927, in San Lucida.
Painter, screen printer. Scenes with figures, figures, genre scenes, landscapes, seascapes, urban landscapes, still-lifes. Murals, stage sets, posters.
Nicola Simbari entered the Accademia di Belle Arti in Rome in 1940 where he first studied architecture before opting for painting. He moved to London in 1958, returning to Grotta-

ferrata near Rome in 1962. In 1953, he designed some stage sets, and in 1958 painted a mural for the Exposition Universelle in Brussels. His work is semi-abstract in style and consists of lively motifs created in fresh, light colours usually applied with a palette knife. He was awarded a gold medal for the best poster in 1954. He began exhibiting regularly in Europe in the 1950s, and in the USA for the first time in 1959.

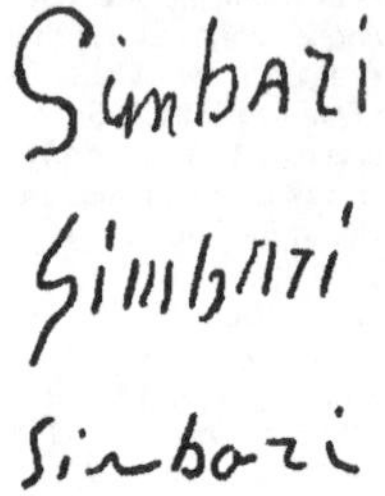

MUSEUMS AND GALLERIES:

PARIS (BNF, Prints Collection): *St-Germain-des-Prés* (1980, lithograph).

AUCTION RECORDS:

NEW YORK, 7 Oct 1972, *Still-life,* USD 850. LOS ANGELES, 6 Nov 1978, *Canal Scene* (1944, oil on canvas, 25 1/2 x 32 ins / 65 x 81 cm) USD 2,700. NEW YORK, 14 Nov 1979, *Boy in Pink* (1965, oil on canvas, 32 3/4 x 40 1/2 ins / 83.2 x 102.8 cm) USD 3,000. NEW YORK, 12 Dec 1981, *Still-life* (1962, oil on canvas, 39 1/4 x 19 3/4 ins / 100 x 50 cm) USD 4,250. ZURICH, 10 Nov 1984, *Rue St-Denis* (oil on canvas, 35 x 39 ins / 89 x 99 cm) CHF 22,000. DETROIT, 31 March 1985, *Girl on a Balcony* (silk screen print, 37 1/2 x 25 1/4 ins / 95 x 64 cm) USD 700. NEW YORK, 18 Dec 1985, *On the Terrace* (1968, oil on canvas, 43 x 47 1/4 ins / 109.5 x 120 cm) USD 5,250. NEW YORK, 7 Oct 1986, *Civita Vecchio* (oil on canvas, 24 x 31 ins / 61 x 79 cm) USD 6,000. NEW YORK, 9 May 1989, *Walk* (oil on canvas, 35 1/2 x 39 1/2 ins / 90 x 100.3 cm) USD 9,350. NEW YORK, 21 Feb 1990, *Young Woman in a Lane* (oil on canvas, 38 1/4 x 51 1/2 ins / 97.2 x 130.8 cm) USD 8,250. NEW YORK, 10 Oct 1990, *Women of Maratea* (1963, oil on canvas, 35 1/2 x 65 1/2 ins / 90.3 x 166.6 cm) USD 11,550. NEW YORK, 13 Feb 1991, *Walking by the Sea* (oil on canvas, 27 1/2 x 39 1/2 ins / 69.8 x 100.4 cm) USD 3,850. NEW YORK, 12 June 1991, *In the Garden* (oil on canvas, 39 1/2 x 47 1/4 ins / 100.3 x 120 cm) USD 9,900. NEW YORK, 5 Nov 1991, *Elfrida at Table* (1967, oil on canvas, 39 3/4 x 43 1/2 ins / 101 x 110.5 cm) USD 6,600. NEW YORK, 9 May 1992, *Memories of the Sea* (1962, oil on canvas, 31 1/2 x 39 1/4 ins / 79.7 x 100 cm) USD 5,500. NEW YORK, 10 Nov 1992, *Flower Arrangement* (1962, oil on canvas, 39 1/4 x 35 1/2 ins / 99.6 x 90 cm) USD 2,420. ROME, 14 Dec 1992, *Untitled* (1956, oil on canvas, 19 3/4 x 15 3/4 ins / 50 x 40 cm) ITL 2,990,000. NEW YORK, 26 Feb 1993, *Yachts on the Riviera* (oil on canvas, 31 1/2 x 39 1/2 ins / 80 x 100.3 cm) USD 12,650. NEW YORK, 24 Feb 1995, *Caterina* (oil on canvas, 35 x 46 ins / 88.9 x 116.8 cm) USD 9,775. NEW YORK, 10 Oct 1996, *Women Bathing* (1983, oil on canvas, 55 x 55 ins / 140 x 139.7 cm) USD 6,325. NEW YORK, 12 Nov 1996, *Sunflowers* (1960, oil on canvas, 39 1/4 x 27 1/2 ins / 99.7 x 69.9 cm) USD 5,175. NEW YORK, 13 May 1997, *Miko Miku* (oil on canvas, 45 x 57 1/2 ins / 114.3 x 146 cm) USD 9,200. NEW YORK, 10 Nov 1999, *White Horse* (oil on canvas, 42 x 62 ins / 106 x 157 cm) USD 9,000. LONDON, 3 Dec 1999, *Romantic Comic Strip* (oil on canvas, 32 x 39 ins / 81 x 100 cm) GBP 4,000. FLORIDA, 18 July 2000, *Sunset on Tirrenian* (1967, oil on canvas, 32 x 39 ins / 81 x 99 cm) USD 6,500. NEW YORK, 20 Feb 2001, *Boulevard de Clichy* (oil on canvas, 31 x 43 ins / 80 x 110 cm) USD 9,000. CHICAGO, 11 June 2001, *Lady by the Ocean* (oil on canvas, 15 x 15 ins / 39 x 39 cm) USD 8,000. FLORIDA, 19 March 2002, *Strange Red Room* (oil on canvas, 38 x 51 ins / 97 x 130 cm) USD 4,750. SAN FRANCISCO, 14 April 2002, *Figures near Rocky Shore* (oil on canvas, 35 x 36 ins / 90 x 91 cm) USD 2,750. FLORIDA, 18 March 2003, *Interior Red and Green* (1964, oil on canvas, 47 x 55 ins / 119 x 140 cm) USD 6,500. NEW YORK, 7 Oct 2003, *Nude in Scarlet* (1983, acrylic on canvas, 51 x 63 ins / 130 x 161 cm) USD 5,500. FLORIDA, 20 Jan 2004, *Port at Ischia* (1966, oil on canvas, 24 x 31 ins / 61 x 79 cm) USD 12,000. NEW YORK, 29 Sept 2004, *Model in the Studio* (acrylic on canvas, 36 x 40 ins / 91 x 101 cm) USD 16,000.

SIMBENATI, Giovanni Antonio
Italian, 17th - 18th century.
Born 1668; died after 1738.
Active in Verona.
Painter.

Simbenati was the pupil of S. Prunati. He was a monk at the monastery of S Zeno in Verona, which he decorated with a large number of paintings.

SIMBERG, Hugo Gerhard
Finnish, 19th - 20th century.
Born 24 June 1873, in Friedrikshamn; died 1917.
Painter (including gouache), watercolourist, engraver.
Genre scenes, portraits.
Symbolism.

Hugo Simberg studied at the fine arts academy in Helsinki and under Akseli Valdemar Gallen-Kellela. He lived for periods in Rome and Paris, exhibiting at the Salon des Artistes Français, where he secured an honourable mention at the Exposition Universelle of 1900. His work was also shown at a number of group and thematic exhibitions, including *Lumières du Nord - La Peinture Scandinave 1885-1905* (*Northern Lights: Scandinavian Painting 1885-1905*) at the Musée du Petit Palais in Paris (1987) and *Les Mondes intérieurs. Le Symbolisme finlandais* (*Inner Worlds: Finnish Symbolism*), held at the Musée d'Ixelles in Brussels in 2002. Simberg drew inspiration from the work of James Ensor and may be credited with having introduced Symbolism to Finnish painting. His work betrays a somewhat macabre sense of humour. As an engraver, he worked predominantly in etching.

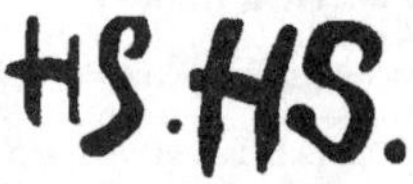

BIBLIOGRAPHY:

Saarikivi, Sakari, *Hugo Simberg*, Porvoo, Helsinki, 1948.

MUSEUMS AND GALLERIES:

HELSINKI: *Portrait of F. Basilier, Painter; Portrait of the Artist* - TURKU: *Young Girl Gathering Potatoes.*

AUCTION RECORDS:

LONDON, 24 March 1988, *Meditation* (1895, watercolour and black pen, 7 1/2 x 6 1/2 ins / 19 x 16.5 cm) GBP 16,500. HELSINKI, 25 April 1999, *The Brothers* (oil on canvas, 44 x 40 ins / 113 x 102 cm) FIM 760,000. HELSINKI, 11 Dec 1999, *Winter Sun* (1900, oil on canvas, 19 x 9 ins / 47 x 23 cm) FIM 340,000. HELSINKI, 13 May 2000, *Boy Playing* (1913, oil on canvas, 17 x 19 ins / 42 x 49 cm) FIM 250,000. LONDON, 27 June 2000, *Winter* (1890, oil on canvas, 10 x 13 ins / 25 x 32 cm) GBP 26,000. HELSINKI, 1 Dec 2001, *Sunday - On the Way to Church* (watercolour and Indian ink, 10 x 9 ins / 26 x 22 cm) EUR 30,275. HELSINKI, 2 Dec 2001, *Carrying Wreaths* (gouache, 9 x 6 ins / 23 x 14 cm) FIM 31,000. LONDON, 13 June 2002, *Seascape in Moonlight* (1900, oil on panel, 13 x 19 ins / 34 x 48 cm) GBP 28,000. HELSINKI, 1 Dec 2002, *Dance on the Jetty* (1904, oil on canvas) EUR 108,000. LONDON, 3 June 2003, *Syksy - Autumn* (1896, pen and black ink, 9 x 6 ins / 23 x 14 cm) GBP 15,000. HELSINKI, 13 Dec 2003, *Beach, Brittany* (1910, oil on canvas, 21 x 27 ins / 54 x 69 cm) EUR 29,000. HELSINKI, 8 May 2004, *Sunny Day in July - Woman Feeding Chicken* (1911, oil on canvas, 88 x 72 ins / 223 x 183 cm) EUR 80,000. HELSINKI, 15 May 2004, *Figure on Skis* (oil on panel, 8 x 6 ins / 20 x 16 cm) EUR 16,000.

SIMBOLI, Igino
Italian, 19th - 20th century.
Born 25 April 1873, in Recanati; died 4 October 1926.
Painter. Religious subjects, portraits, genre scenes. Murals.

A pupil of Luigi Basvecchi and at the Accademia di Belle Arti in Rome, Simboli painted altarpieces and decorative works in churches in Recanati.

SIMBOLI, Raymond
American, 20th century.
Born 1894; died 1964.
Painter. Urban landscapes.

Raymond Simboli emigrated from Italy to Pittsburgh, Pennsylvania, and became a professor of art in the School of Architecture at Carnegie-Mellon University.

AUCTION RECORDS:
NEW YORK, 12 March 1992, *Pittsburgh Factories* (oil on canvas, 30 x 36 ins / 76.2 x 91.4 cm) USD 5,500.

SIMBRECHT, Mathias. See **ZIMPRECHT**

SIMCOCK, T.
British, 18th century.
Active in London from 1779 to 1791.
Enameller.

SIMCOVITS, Giovanni
Hungarian, 19th century.
Active in Budapest.
Sculptor.

The Revoltella museum in Trieste owns a work by Giovanni Simcovits entitled *Loyalty*.

SIMDTHANSEN, Carl Frederik
Norwegian, 19th century.
Born 30 January 1841, in Stavanger.
Painter. Genre scenes.

Simdthansen worked in Düsseldorf, Paris, Christiania (now Oslo), Stockholm and Copenhagen. He settled in Valle, Norway.

MUSEUMS AND GALLERIES:
MUNICH (Pinakothek): *The Village Virtuoso*.

SIME, Sydney Herbert
British, 19th - 20th century.
Born 1867, in Manchester; died 1941, in Worplesdon (Surrey).
Draughtsman, watercolourist, engraver.

Sydney Herbert Sime trained at Liverpool School of Art. He lived and worked in London, where he exhibited at St George's Gallery. He contributed drawings and caricatures to a number of periodicals.

BIBLIOGRAPHY:
AUCTION RECORDS:
LONDON, 23 July 1931, *Forest with Wild Animals,* GBP 52.

SIMECCHI, Gaspero
Italian, 16th century.
Active during the first half of the 16th century.
Sculptor.

Gaspero Simecchi carved an *Assumption* for the choir of Carpi Cathedral some time after 1527.

SIMECEK, François
20th century.
Sculptor. Figures.

MUSEUMS AND GALLERIES:
LAUSANNE (Cantonal MFA): *Adolescent* (1943, Carrara marble).

SIMEK, Ludwig. See **SCHIMECK**

SIMEL, Leonardo
German, 17th century.
Active in Venice, Italy, c.1690.
Painter.

SIMENS, Johann. See **SYMENS**

SIMENSEN, Sigvald
Norwegian, 19th - 20th century.
Died 1920.
Painter. Landscapes.

AUCTION RECORDS:
NEW YORK, 17 Feb 1994, *Village in Winter* (oil on canvas, 31 1/2 x 55 ins / 80 x 139.8 cm) USD 1,495.

SIMEON, Alfred Charles
French, 19th century.
Born in Paris.
Painter. Genre scenes.

Simeon was a pupil of Cogniet and made his debut at the Salon de Paris in 1866.

SIMEON, Fernand
French, 20th century.
Born 1884; died 2 May 1928, in Neuilly-sur-Seine.
Painter, watercolourist, engraver, illustrator. Nudes, scenes with figures, genre scenes, landscapes, seascapes.

Fernand Simeon produced illustrations, paintings and engravings for books by authors from the 17th century to the present, in particular for works by Adalbert de Chamisso, Voltaire and Anatole France.

AUCTION RECORDS:
PARIS, 15 Feb 1930, *Leaving Mass* (watercolour) FRF 200; *Port* (watercolour) FRF 125; *Seated Nude* (watercolour) FRF 210.

SIMÉON, Marie Louise
French, 20th century.
Painter. Landscapes, urban landscapes.

Marie Louise Siméon's work has featured at the Salon des Tuileries in Paris.

MUSEUMS AND GALLERIES:
PARIS (MAM): *Landscape*.

AUCTION RECORDS:
PARIS, 12 Dec 1946, *Landscape,* FRF 2,400. PARIS, 22 March 1998, *View of Paris* (oil on canvas, 18 x 15 ins / 46 x 38 cm) FRF 2,000.

SIMEON, Nikolaus, or Nicholas
American, 19th century.
Died 1876, in Zurich.
Active in New York.
Painter (including porcelain). Landscapes.

Nikolaus Simeon studied porcelain painting in Munich.

SIMEONE, or Simone da Ragusa
Italian, 13th century.
Active in Trani.
Sculptor, architect.

Simeone sculpted the porch of the church of S Andrea, Barletta.

SIMEONE DA CUSIGHE. See **SIMONE da Cusighe**

SIMEONE DI BARTOLOMMEO
Italian, 16th century.
Active in Venice from 1589 to 1590.
Sculptor.

SIMEONOVA, Snejana
Bulgarian, 20th - 21st century.
Born 8 January 1953, in Sofia.
Sculptor.

Simeonova completed her studies in 1976 at the academy of fine art in Sofia, in Professor Ilia Iliev's scupture class. She is a sculptor who has a feeling for the expression of plastic shapes. Her development as an artist has moved from the representation of images inspired by the human body to works in a predominantly Abstract style. She combines different materials, usually stone and bronze, to produce her works.

Simeonova has taken part in collective exhibitions, including: 1988, As Salyam gallery, Cairo; *Interart*, Poznan; Dantesca Biennale, Ravenna; 1989, London Art Fair; 1990, Basel Art Fair; 1993, Paris Biennale, Grand Palais; 1994, *In Pursuit of My Reflected Image*, exhibition rooms of old Plovdiv, Plovdiv, Bulgaria; and 1995, *Bulgarian Art*, Galerie Kornshutte, Lucerne.

Her solo exhibitions include: 1986 and 1993, Balabanovata Kachta gallery, Plovdiv; 1990, Rouski 6 gallery, Sofia; 1991, Linea Galerie, Berlin; 1993 Boyana gallery, Sofia; 1994, *Negative Speeches* (with the collaboration of Adelina Popnedeleva), Studio Spectar Gallery, Sofia; 1995, *Networks*, Studio Spectar gallery, Sofia; and 1996, Haus Heckenried gallery, Meggen. She was awarded the *Art Dialogue* International Association Prize in 1993 in France. She has taken part in Sculpture Symposia in 1990 and 1994, Iserlohn; 1991, Nyíregyháza; Haltern am See; and 1995, Pretoria.

BIBLIOGRAPHY:

Snejana Simeonova, Raumsprache, exhibition catalogue, Gal. HO, Berlin, 1995.

SIMERAY, Alba
French, 20th century.
Born in Damparis.
Painter. Landscapes.

Alba Simeray first exhibited in 1971 in Lons-le-Saunier. In 1973, he showed work at the Salon de Peinture of the Franche Comté in the same town.

He draws his inspiration from nature, painting landscapes of the Jura region of France.

SIMERDING, Arndt
German, 16th century.
Died 1565.
Active in Hanover.
Sculptor.

Simerding carved sculptures in Hanover, including the Old Market Fountain.

SIMERDING, Georg Heinrich
German, 18th century.
Active in Hanover, in 1752.
Sculptor.

SIMERDING, Johann Bernhard, or Siemerdink or Simmerding
German, 18th century.
Died 8 March 1744, in Neunhausen, Luxembourg.
Active in Celle, (Lower Saxony) Germany.
Painter. History painting, portraits.

MUSEUMS AND GALLERIES:

CELLE: *Portrait of Duke Georg Wilhelm of Celle.*

SIMEROVÁ, Ester Martinceková
Maiden name: Fridriková
Slovak, 20th century.
Born 23 January 1909, in Bratislava.
Active in Liptovský Mikuláš from 1954.
Painter, sculptor.

Ester Martinceková-Simerová did her entire artistic training in Paris, where she attended the Académie Julian (1927 to 1929) and the Académie d'Art Moderne de Paris, studying with Fernand Léger, Alexandra Exter, Louis Marcoussis and Amédée Ozenfant (1929 to 1930). On returning to Czechoslovakia she exhibited in major cities, and has since exhibited around the world.

Her work shows a wide variety of influences: in 1930 there are traces of Surrealism; in 1932, Braque's Cubism comes to the fore. In 1935 she started to develop her own, personal style, which although certainly Neo-Cubist and perhaps inspired by the Puteaux group and Jacques Villon concentrated on dreamy, misty colours that are hers and hers alone.

BIBLIOGRAPHY:

Fifty years of Czechoslovak Painting from the Collections of the Galleries, 1918-1958, exhibition catalogue, Slovenska Narodna Gal., Bratislava, 1968 (in commemoration of the 50th anniversary of the Republic of Czechoslovakia).

SIMES, Jorge
Argentinian, 20th century.
Born in Córdoba.
Active in the USA.
Painter, draughtsman, engraver.

Jorge Simes trained in Córdoba before settling in Chicago.

He used an egg tempera medium and placed abstract forms and figures together, painted in intense tones on wooden panels and boxes.

SIMES, Mary Jane
American, 19th century.
Active in Baltimore 1826-1834.
Portrait artist.

SIMESEN, Viggo Rasmus
Danish, 19th - 20th century.
Born 29 July 1864, in Copenhagen.
Painter. Portraits, landscapes.

Viggo Rasmus Simesen studied at the Kongelige Danske Kunstakademi in Copenhagen and under Kroyer; he exhibited as of 1892.

SIMETCHKIN, Pavel Petrovich
Russian, 19th century.
Born 16 January 1815; died 1868.
Watercolourist, lithographer.

Pavel Petrovich Simetchkin studied at the art academy in St Petersburg. He engraved scenes from everyday life.

SIMETI, Turi
Italian, 20th century.
Born 1929, in Alcamo.
Painter.

AUCTION RECORDS:

ZURICH, 26 March 1981, *Ultramarine-Blue* (1970, painting relief, 35 1/2 x 51 1/4 ins / 90 x 130 cm) CHF 4,600. MILAN, 12 June 1990, *Untitled* (1970, blue canvas in relief, diam. 26 3/4 ins / 68 cm) ITL 1,600,000. ZURICH, 18 Oct 1990, *Composition* (1969, acrylic/canvas, 21 1/2 x 17 1/2 ins / 54.5 x 44.5 cm) CHF 950. COPENHAGEN, 20 May 1992, *Composition* (1966, oil on canvas, 31 1/2 x 23 1/2 ins / 80 x 60 cm) DKK 4,000. MILAN, 22 June 1995, *Untitled* (1966, oil on preformed red canvas, 17 x 17 1/4 ins / 43 x 44 cm) ITL 1,380,000. VERCELLI, 23 Nov 2002, *Black* (1988, acrylic on canvas, 35 x 35 ins / 90 x 90 cm) EUR 2,400. AMSTERDAM, 28 May 2003, *Untitled* (1965, oil and wood on canvas, a pair, 16 x 16 ins / 40 x 40 cm) USD 5,000. AMSTERDAM, 28 May 2003, *Oval Forms in Negative* (1966, oil on canvas/panel, 28 x 24 ins / 70 x 60 cm) USD 7,500. MILAN, 20 May 2004, *Untitled* (1966, mixed media on paper/canvas, 29 x 23 ins / 74 x 59 cm) EUR 1,600. MILAN, 20 May 2004, *Untitled* (oil on canvas, 31 x 31 ins / 80 x 80 cm) EUR 3,800.

SIMI, Filadelfo
Italian, 19th - 20th century.
Born 11 February 1849, in Stuzzema; died 5 January 1923, in Florence.
Painter, sculptor, illustrator. Portraits, genre scenes, interiors, landscapes, architectural views.

After studying with Gérôme in Paris, Simi returned to live in Italy. He exhibited in Paris, where he was awarded a bronze medal at the Exposition Universelle of 1889, and in Venice, Florence and Bologna. He contributed illustrations to the Venetian journal *Zig-Zag*. He produced a large number of portraits.

He became very well known in Italy for the liveliness and profundity of his forms and a number of his paintings were critically acclaimed.

MUSEUMS AND GALLERIES:

FLORENCE (Gal. d'Arte Moderna): *Portrait of an Old Woman; Interior in Grenada; Mother-of-Pearl;* six studies of landscapes - ROME (Gal. Nazionale d'Arte Moderna): *Reflection.*

AUCTION RECORDS:

MILAN, 26 Nov 1968, *Portrait of a Little Girl,* ITL 900,000. MILAN, 10 Nov 1982, *Houses in the Country* (oil on panel, 23 1/2 x 14 1/4 ins / 60 x 36 cm) ITL 4,800,000. MILAN, 14 June 1989, *Profile of a Woman* (oil on canvas, 16 1/4 x 11 1/2 ins / 41.5 x 29 cm) ITL 3,600,000. STOCKHOLM, 4 Dec 2001, *Interior Scene with Young Italian Girl* (oil on canvas/panel, 39 x 28 ins / 100 x 70 cm) SEK 36,000. FLORENCE, 4 June 2002, *View of Farms* (oil on canvas, 13 x 9 ins / 32 x 23 cm) EUR 1,700. LONDON, 17 July 2002, *Seamstress* (oil on canvas laid down, 39 x 27 ins / 98 x 69 cm) GBP 3,800.

SIMIAN, Jean

French, 20th century.
Born 2 May 1910, in Algiers; died 1991, in Rueil-Malmaison.
Painter, draughtsman. Military subjects, figures, genre scenes, landscapes, still-lifes.
School of Algiers.

Jean Simian attended the École des Beaux-Arts in Algiers. He also studied in Paris at the Académie Lhote, and later in Ozenfant's studio. In 1954 he was awarded the Casa Velázquez de Madrid Prize, and spent the following year in the Spanish capital.

He first became known as a war artist. He preferred to work on a large scale, drawing his subject matter from reality and interpreting it freely.

He regularly took part in group exhibitions in Paris, including; 1941, Galerie Durand-Ruel; 1946-1947, *Sur 4 murs* (*On Four Walls*) at the Galerie Maeght; from 1958 to 1980 at the Salon d'Automne, where he became a member; from 1946 to 1957 at the Salon de Mai; from 1964 to 1967 at the Salon des Réalités Nouvelles; 1964, Salon des Grands et Jeunes d'Aujourd'hui. He also exhibited in 1955 at the Casa Velázquez de Madrid, and in 1964 at the Musée-Bibliothèque de St-Denis. In 2003 his work featured in the collective exhibition *L'École d'Alger* (*The School of Algiers*) at the Musée des Beaux-Arts in Bordeaux.

He showed work in solo exhibitions, including; 1946, Galerie du Minaret in Algiers; 1951, Galerie Pierre Loeb, Paris; 1956, Galerie Renou et Poyet; 1976, 1978, 1980 and 1982, Galerie Jacques Massol; 1987, Galerie Claude Hemery. He also exhibited in 1953 in Marrakesh, Copenhagen and Brussels, and in 1956 in Bordeaux and Nice.

BIBLIOGRAPHY:

Harambourg, Lydia, *L'École de Paris 1945-1965. Dictionnaire des peintres,* Ides et Calendes, Neuchâtel, 1993. Cazenave, Elisabeth/Dalia, Mahammed-Orfali/Vidal-Bué, Marion, *L'École d'Alger,* exhibition catalogue, Musée des Beaux-Arts, Bordeaux, 2003.

MUSEUMS AND GALLERIES:

ALGIERS (Mus. National des Beaux-Arts) - PARIS (MNAM-CCI).

AUCTION RECORDS:

PARIS, 17 April 1989, *Fun Fair in Spain* (1962, oil on canvas) FRF 18,000. PARIS, 9 June 1989, *Jachia* (1975, oil on canvas, 51 1/4 x 32 ins / 130 x 81 cm) FRF 35,000.

SIMIAND, or Simian

French, 18th century.
Active in Paris 1779-1785.
Sculptor. Portraits.

Simiand exhibited work at the Salon de la Correspondance in Paris in 1781.

AUCTION RECORDS:

PARIS, 23 Oct 1985, *Portrait Presumed to be of Necker* (1784, plaster, h. 29 1/2 ins / 75 cm) FRF 36,000.

SIMIANE, Jeanne Denise, Flora

Maiden name: Bezons
French, 19th century.
Born in Geneva; died 1899.
Painter, pastellist. Genre scenes, portraits, fruit.

A pupil of H. Flandrin, Loyer, Levasseur and E. Martel Jeanne Simiane made her Salon debut in 1864. She was a Member of the Société des Artistes Français.

SIMIC, Pavao or Paul, or Schimitsch

Serb, 19th century.
Born 1818, in Novi Sad; died 18 January 1876, in Novi Sad.
Painter.

Pavao Simic studied under Alois Costani in Novi Sad, and at the art academy in Vienna. He painted icons for churches in Serbia, as well as portraits, and historical and popular scenes.

MUSEUMS AND GALLERIES:

BELGRADE - NEUSATZ.

SIMIER

French, 18th century.
Sculptors, architects.

There were two brothers by the name of Simier but their first names are not known. They produced many sculptures in the churches around Angers between 1770 and 1777, particularly in Montigné, Thouarcé, May, Mazé, Faye, Murs and at the Château de Montgeoffroy.

SIMIL, Alphonse Paul

French, 19th century.
Born 1844.
Painter, watercolourist.

MUSEUMS AND GALLERIES:

PONTOISE: six watercolours.

SIMIL, Emilcar

Haitian, 20th century.
Born 1944.
Painter. Scenes with figures, figures.

AUCTION RECORDS:

NEW YORK, 9 July 1981, *Wealth* (1981, acrylic/hardboard, 24 x 24 ins / 61 x 61 cm) USD 1,800. PARIS, 13 June 1994, *Woman in Blue* (1978, oil on panel, 19 3/4 x 13 3/4 ins / 50 x 35 cm) FRF 7,000. PARIS, 1 April 1996, *The Dream* (oil/hardboard, 75 1/2 x 20 1/2 ins / 192 x 52 cm) FRF 31,000.

SIMIL, Louis Augustin or Auguste

French, 19th century.
Born 5 February 1822, in Nîmes.
Painter. History painting, portraits.

Louis Simil exhibited at the Salon de Paris between 1847 and 1857 and worked in Lunel up until 1857.

SIMIRADZKI, Hendrik or Henryk Ippolitovich, or Semiradsky

Russian, 19th century.
Born 10 October 1843, in Belgorod, near Kharkov; died 23 August 1902, in Strzalkovo.
Painter, watercolourist. History painting, portraits, genre scenes.

Hendrik Ippolitovich Simiradzki studied at the academy of fine arts in St Petersburg. He received a state bursary to con-

tinue his studies at Munich and later in Rome. He was awarded a gold medal at the 1878 Exposition Universelle in Paris, and he was made a chevalier of the Légion d'Honneur in 1898. King Umberto I of Italy awarded him the Commander's Cross of order St Maurice and St Lazarus. He was a member of the academies of St Petersburg, Berlin, Stockholm, and the Accademia de San Luca in Rome. He became a member of the Académie des Beaux-Arts in Paris in 1898.
MUSEUMS AND GALLERIES:
CRACOW (National Museum): *Nero's Torches; Portrait of the Count L. Wodzicki* - HAMBURG (Kunsthalle): *In the Country* - HANOVER: *Vase or Slave?* - LVIV (Municipal Mus.): *Like the Gods; Resting; At the Spring; Greek; Idyll* - MOSCOW (State Tretyakov Gal.): *Sword Dance; Tiberius's Orgy on the Island of Capri* (two other paintings) - POZNAN (Museum of Greater Poland): *Greek* - RIGA (MM): *Portrait of a Young Girl* - ST PETERSBURG (Gosudarstvennyj Russkij Muz.): *Sinner; The Last Judgement* (watercolour); *Massacre of the Innocents* (sepia); *Sodom and Gomorrah; Christ with Martha and Mary; Frina at the Celebration in Eleusis* - WARSAW (Muz. Narodowe): *Two Roman Idylls* (Italian Landscapes); *Last Judgement* - ZAGREB: two Italian landscapes; *Italians*.
AUCTION RECORDS:
NEW YORK, 1-2 April 1902, *The Dance*, FRF 4,375. NEW YORK, 21 Nov 1964, *A New Treasure*, USD 3,200. LONDON, 17 May 1985, *Romans by a Well* (oil on canvas, 20 3/4 x 31 ins / 53 x 79 cm) GBP 8,500. LONDON, 24 Nov 1989, *At the Fountain* (oil on canvas, 21 3/4 x 39 1/2 ins / 55.2 x 100.3 cm) GBP 10,450. NEW YORK, 27 May 1993, *Sunny Afternoon near the Fountain* (oil on canvas, 30 1/2 x 60 1/2 ins / 77.4 x 153.7 cm) USD 29,900. NEW YORK, 13 Oct 1993, *Celebration in Capri* (oil on canvas, 21 x 40 ins / 53.3 x 101.6 cm) USD 19,550. LONDON, 17 March 1995, *Connoisseurs* (oil on canvas, 36 1/2 x 60 3/4 ins / 92.7 x 154.5 cm) GBP 38,900.

SIMKHOVICH, Simka Taibukhovich
Russian, 20th century.
Born 1893; died 1949.
Painter. Scenes with figures, landscapes.

Simka Simkhovich studied at the St Petersburg academy and in 1918 was awarded a prize by the newly-formed Soviet government. Later he emigrated to the USA where he worked under the Fine Arts Program. Among his works are four oil-on-canvas murals in the Post Office in Beaufort, NC.
BIBLIOGRAPHY:
'Simkovitch' in *The New York Times*, periodical, New York, June 21, 1942.
MUSEUMS AND GALLERIES:
ST PETERSBURG (Hermitage).
AUCTION RECORDS:
NEW YORK, 25-26 Nov 1929, *Rainbow*, USD 250; *Family*, USD 300. NEW YORK, 28 Sept 1983, *Island Beach* (1934-1935, oil on canvas, 34 x 56 1/2 ins / 86.4 x 143.5 cm) USD 6,500. NEW YORK, 28 May 1992, *Picnic* (oil on canvas, 44 x 50 ins / 111.8 x 126.8 cm) USD 30,800. NEW YORK, 9 March 1996, *Study for Mr Loyal* (1929, lead pencil and colour on paper, 16 1/2 x 8 1/4 ins / 42 x 21 cm) USD 863. TEL AVIV, 7 Oct 1996, *Russian Dance* (1926, oil on canvas, 37 x 47 ins / 94 x 119.5 cm) USD 14,950.

SIMKIN, Richard
British, 19th - 20th century.
Born 1840; died 1926.
Watercolourist, painter (gouache). Military subjects.

AUCTION RECORDS:
LONDON, 21 Nov 1985, *Second Dragoon Guards: Queen's Bays* (1901-1903, watercolour/pencil outlines heightened with white, 11 1/2 x 20 ins / 29 x 51 cm) GBP 850. LONDON, 30 Jan 1991, *Household Cavalry Regiment* (1878, watercolour heightened with gouache, 13 1/4 x 30 1/4 ins / 33.5 x 77 cm) GBP 990. EDINBURGH, 9 June 1994, *The 8th Royal Irish Hussars on Manoeuvres at Aldershot* (watercolour and gouache, 17 1/4 x 31 ins / 43.8 x 78.8 cm) GBP 2,070.

SIMKINS, Martha
American, 20th century.
Born 1866, in South Carolina; died 1969, in Los Angeles.
Painter.

Martha Simkins studied at the Art Students League in New York and was taught by Chase. She was a member of the Pen and Brush Club. She is best known for her paintings of interiors with figures, still-lifes, and portraits.

SIMKOVICS TARJANI, Jenõ, or Eugen
Hungarian, 20th century.
Born 11 April 1895, in Budapest; died 15 November 1995, in Budapest.
Painter, graphic artist, engraver.

Jenõ Simkovics Tarjani studied in Budapest. He painted and made etchings.

SIMLER, Johann, or Simmler
Swiss, 18th century.
Born 6 January 1693, in Zurich; died 1748, in Stein-am-Rhein.
Painter, engraver (etching). Portraits, flowers.

Simler studied under Pesne in Berlin and Melchior Füssli. He painted portraits of *John Sobieski, King of Poland* and *Prince Eugene*.

SIMLER, Rudolf or Johann Rudolf.
See **SIMMLER**

SIMM, Ananias
Austrian, 19th century.
Born 1799, in Melk.
Painter.

Simm attended the academy in Vienna.
AUCTION RECORDS:
LONDON, 6 Oct 1989, *Young Man Playing the Cello* (1859, oil on panel, 16 1/4 x 12 1/4 ins / 41.5 x 31 cm) GBP 440.

SIMM, Franz Xaver
Austrian, 19th - 20th century.
Born 24 June 1853, in Vienna; died 21 February 1918, in Munich.
Painter, watercolourist, illustrator. Allegorical subjects, figures, portraits, genre scenes, interiors with figures, landscapes with figures. Frescoes.

Franz Simm studied at the Akademie der Bildenden Künste in Vienna. He spent some time in Anselme Feuerbach's studio, and a further two years as a pupil of Eduard von Engerth. Simm lived and worked in Rome between 1881 and 1886, before settling in Munich. Together with his wife, Marie Simm-Mayer, Franz Simm produced a series of frescoes for Tbilisi Museum, Georgia.
MUSEUMS AND GALLERIES:
BERLIN: *Duo* - GRAZ (Landesmus. Joanneum): *Studio Visit* - MUNICH (Neue Pinakothek): *Painting Time* - VIENNA: six watercolour sketches for a ceiling in the Museum of Art and History.
AUCTION RECORDS:
PARIS, 28 March 1949, *Accident*, FRF 70,000. PARIS, 9 May 1949, *Woman Walking in the Park*, FRF 5,000. PARIS, 10 May 1950, *Couple in the Tuileries*, FRF 8,000. COLOGNE, 16 June 1977, *New Frock* (watercolour, 17 x 13 3/4 ins / 43 x 35 cm) DEM 3,000. NEW YORK, 25 Jan 1980, *Baby Portrait* (1889, oil on panel, 13 3/4 x 19 1/4 ins / 35 x 49 cm) USD 35,000. VIENNA, 23 March 1983, *Shepherd and Flock* (1871, oil on canvas, 25 1/4 x 38 1/4 ins / 64 x 97 cm) ATS 40,000. NEW YORK, 13 Dec 1985, *New-Born* (oil on canvas, 16 1/4 x 20 1/4 ins / 41 x 51.5 cm) USD 4,500. VIENNA, 4 Dec 1986, *Woman Fetching Water* (oil on canvas, 15 3/4 x 20 1/2 ins / 40 x 52 cm) ATS 80,000. NEW

YORK, 25 May 1988, *Young Girl in a White Hat* (oil on canvas, 13 x 8 3/4 ins / 33 x 22.2 cm) USD 9,900. PARIS, 10-11 April 1997, *Bachi-Bouzouk and Friends* (oil on canvas, 69 x 52 ins / 175 x 132 cm) FRF 70,000.

SIMM, Joseph
Bohemian, 19th century.
Born 1811, in Reichenberg (now Liberec, Czech Republic); died 1868, in Vienna, Austria.
Painter. Flowers. Church decoration.
Joseph Simm was the father of Franz Xaver.
AUCTION RECORDS:
VIENNA, 16 Nov 1983, *Bouquet of Flowers* (1868, oil on canvas, 27 x 22 ins / 68.5 x 55 cm) ATS 100,000.

SIMM-MAYER, Marie
Maiden name: Mayer
German, 19th - 20th century.
Born 8 June 1851, in Meran (now Merano, Italy); died 25 October 1912, in Munich.
Painter. Portraits, genre scenes. Murals.
Marie Simm-Mayer studied in Munich under Ludwig Löfftz and also in Rome, where she was influenced by Anselme Feuerbach. She assisted her husband Franz Simm on a series of decorative frescoes for the Museum in Tbilisi, Georgia.

SIMMANG, Charles (Junior)
American, 19th - 20th century.
Born 7 February 1874, in Serbin (Texas).
Sculptor, engraver.
Charles Simmang was a pupil of Karl Studenrauch. He was a member of American Federation of Arts.

SIMMEL, Paul
German, 20th century.
Born 1887, in Spandau; died 24 March 1933, in Berlin.
Draughtsman.
Paul Simmel studied at the fine arts academy in Berlin and contributed caricatures to a number of humourous periodicals.

SIMMERDING, Johann Bernhard.
See **SIMERDING**

SIMMERS, Melvin or Robert Melvin
American, 20th century.
Born 28 March 1907, in Hampstead, London; died 1991, in Cape Town, South Africa.
Painter, draughtsman.
Melvin Simmers settled in South Africa, in the Cape, in 1924.
MUSEUMS AND GALLERIES:
CAPE TOWN (South African NG): *Glory of Springtime*; four drawings.

SIMMIAS
6th century BC.
Active in Athens during the Archaic period.
Sculptor.
Ancient Greek.
Simmias made a statue in Athens of *Dionysius*.

SIMMINGER
German, 15th century.
Active at the end of the 15th century.
Sculptor.
Simminger carved a high-relief on the altar of the church of Our Lady, Ingolstadt.

SIMMLER, Franz Joseph
German, 19th - 20th century.
Born 14 December 1846, in Geisenheim; died 2 October 1926, in Offenburg.
Sculptor, illustrator. Religious subjects.
The son of Friedrich K.K. Simmler, Franz Joseph studied at the fine arts academies of Düsseldorf and Munich, and went on to sculpt altars for churches in Baden.

SIMMLER, Friedrich Karl Joseph
German, 19th century.
Born 4 May 1801, in Hanau (Hesse); died 2 November 1872, in Aschaffenburg (Bavaria).
Painter, lithographer, engraver (etching). Animals, genre scenes.
Simmler studied in Munich and Vienna and went on numerous excursions to upper Austria and Syria, studying landscapes and animals from life. He also spent a long period in Italy, notably in Florence, Rome and Venice; in 1829, he returned to Germany, working in Hanover and painting animals in the countryside around Schullen, Bocking and Grieben. The German painters Achenbach and Scheuren sometimes painted the backgrounds of his pictures. He lived in Aschaffenburg from 1862.
MUSEUMS AND GALLERIES:
ASCHAFFENBURG: *Mountain Landscape* - BERLIN (Nationalgal.): *Dangerous Bull* - HANOVER: *Shepherd's Life* - KALININGRAD: *Midday Rest in the Meadow* - POZNAN: *Animals* - WIESBADEN: two paintings of animals.
AUCTION RECORDS:
MUNICH, 21 Sept 1978, *Horse Market* (oil on canvas, 10 x 13 ins / 24.5 x 33 cm) DEM 10,000. PARIS, 26 March 1980, *House in the Trees* (1835, oil on canvas, 13 3/4 x 17 3/4 ins / 35 x 45 cm) FRF 5,100. MUNICH, 25 Sept 2002, *Boy with Cows by Mountain Lake* (oil on panel, 12 x 16 ins / 30 x 40 cm) EUR 2,700. ERLANGEN, 25 Oct 2003, *Romantic Landscape* (oil on canvas, 13 x 15 ins / 32 x 39 cm) EUR 2,600.

SIMMLER, Johann. See **SIMLER**

SIMMLER, Jozef, or Simler
Polish, 19th century.
Born 14 March 1823, in Warsaw; died 1 March 1868, in Warsaw.
Painter, draughtsman. Allegorical subjects, portraits.
Jozef Simmer studied under Pivarski and Dombrovski, and later at the art academies in Dresden and Munich, where he worked with Kaulbach and Schnorr von Carolsfeld. He also worked in Paris with Paul Delaroche. He was one of the founders of the Modern School in Poland. He exhibited a canvas entitled *Woman in a Lilac Dress* at the *Exposition des Artistes Polonais* (*Exhibition of Polish Artists*) held at the Salon de la Société Nationale des Beaux-Arts.

His work is typically Polish, but nonetheless shares certain features with the French School. His palette is warm, rich and lively, with colour combinations that are both sensitive and bold. His composition is simple and skilfull. These qualities are evident in the work *Death of Barbe Radziwill*.
MUSEUMS AND GALLERIES:
CRACOW (Muz. Narodowe): *Cossack with a Parrot* - LVIV (Lubomirski Mus.): *Portrait of K. Podhorski* - LVIV (NG): *The Poetess J. Luszczevska* - WARSAW (Muz. Narodowe): *Portraits of T Tripplin, Two Granddaughters of L. Kronenberg, the Painter J. Kossak, of the Painter E. Petzold, and Mr and Mrs Karski; Allegory of Architecture, Sculpture and Painting.*
AUCTION RECORDS:
MUNICH, 21 June 1994, *A Day of Hunting* (black and brown ink/paper, 23 x 19 ins / 57.5 x 48 cm) DEM 3,450.

SIMMLER, Rudolf or Johann Rudolf, or Simler
Swiss, 17th century.
Born 1633, in Zurich; died 1675.
Painter, engraver (etching).
Rudolf Simmler studied under Konrad Meyer. He produced engravings of animals, ornaments and groups of human heads.

SIMMLER, Wilhelm
German, 19th - 20th century.
Born 6 September 1840, in Geisenheim; died c. 1914.
Painter, illustrator. Mythological subjects, hunting scenes.

The son of Friedrich K.J. Simmler, Wilhelm studied at the fine arts academy in Düsseldorf and went on to paint predominantly hunting scenes.

MUSEUMS AND GALLERIES:
DÜSSELDORF (Kunstmus.): *Faun and Nymph* - WIESBADEN (Wiesbaden Mus.): *Lying in Wait.*

AUCTION RECORDS:
LOS ANGELES, 17 March 1980, *Beggar's Toilette* (1866, oil on canvas, 16 x 13 3/4 ins / 40.7 x 35 cm) USD 2,600. COLOGNE, 20 March 1981, *Hunting Scene* (1867, oil on canvas, 27 1/2 x 37 ins / 70 x 94 cm) DEM 14,000.

SIMMONDS, John. See **SIMMONS**

SIMMONDS, Julius
German, 19th - 20th century.
Born 12 June 1843, in Pyrmont; died 24 April 1924, in Hamburg.
Painter. Portraits, genre scenes, Still-lifes.

MUSEUMS AND GALLERIES:
MÜNSTER (Westfälisches Landesmus.): *Exchanging Secrets; Wedding Day.*

AUCTION RECORDS:
NEW YORK, 26 May 1994, *Hermia and Lysander: A Midsummer Night's Dream* (1870, watercolour and gouache/paper, 36 x 30 1/4 ins / 91.4 x 76.8 cm) USD 43,125.

SIMMONDS, William George
British, 20th century.
Born 3 March 1876, in Constantinople, to English parents; died 23 August 1968.
Sculptor, engraver, illustrator, painter. Genre scenes.

William George Simmonds exhibited genre paintings at the Royal Academy in 1906, and sculptures from 1933 to 1967. He illustrated an edition of Shakespeare's *Hamlet* in 1912.

MUSEUMS AND GALLERIES:
LEICESTER (New Walk Museum and Art Gallery): *Horses at Pasture* - LONDON (Tate Collection): *First Love* (1906); *The Farm Team* (1924-1928); *The Old Horse* (1937?).

SIMMONET, Lucien. See **SIMONNET**

SIMMONS, Edward Emerson
American, 19th - 20th century.
Born 27 October 1852, in Cambridge (Massachusetts); died 17 November 1931, in Baltimore (Maryland).
Painter. Figures, nudes, portraits, genre scenes, landscapes, seascapes. Murals.
Ten American Painters.

Edward Emerson Simmons was a friend of Frank Duveneck. He studied in Boston and was taught by C.R. Boulanger and J.J. Lefebvre at the Académie Julian in Paris from 1879. He specialised in murals and was commissioned to decorate the New York Criminal Court.

Simmons lived in St Ives, Cornwall, from 1887 to 1891 and spent his summers in France at Concarneau, Montreuil and in Fontainebleu forest. In her novel, *Glenn* (1880), Blanche Willis Howard described his life in Concarneau. On his return to the USA, he joined the Ten American Painters, who were named after their first exhibition at Durand-Ruel Galleries in New York in 1898. It was actually a group of 11 painters from New York and Boston who had broken with the Society of American Artists, which they considered too conservative, and who organised annual exhibitions in New York without a jury between 1898 and 1919.

Simmons exhibited in Paris in 1882 (where he was awarded an honourable mention for *Washerwoman*) and in 1889 at the Exposition Universelle (where he was awarded a bronze medal). He won a gold medal in Buffalo in 1901, and exhibited with the Ten in New York from 1898 to 1919. His work has appeared in numerous collective exhibitions such as *Ten American Painters*, Spaniermann Gallery, New York (1990), and *L'Impressionisme Américain 1880-1915* (*American Impressionism 1880-1915*), Fondation de l'Hermitage, Lausanne.

BIBLIOGRAPHY:
Ten American Painters: the first exhibition, exhibition catalogue, Durand-Ruel Galleries, New York, 1898. Gerdts, William H., et al., *Ten American Painters*, exhibition catalogue, Spanierman Gall., New York, 1990. Heisinger, Ulrich, *Impressionism in America: The Ten American Painters*, Prestel, Munich, 1991. Cikovski, Nicolai/Hauptman, William, *L'Impressionnisme américain 1880-1915*, exhibition catalogue, Fondation de l'Hermitage, Lausanne, 2002.

MUSEUMS AND GALLERIES:
CHICAGO (Terra Foundation for American Art Collection) - PHILADELPHIA (Pennsylvania Academy of the Fine Arts Gal.) - ST LOUIS (AM).

AUCTION RECORDS:
NEW YORK, 11-12 April 1907, *Herring Fishermen at St Ives, Cornwall*, USD 215. NEW YORK, 23 May 1979, *Old Woman Peeling an Orange* (oil on canvas, 37 1/2 x 27 1/4 ins / 95 x 69.5 cm) USD 7,000. NEW YORK, 31 May 1984, *Maritime Landscape* (1918, oil on canvas, 28 x 50 ins / 71.1 x 127 cm) USD 10,000. NEW YORK, 25 Oct 1985, *Wash Day* (1883, oil on canvas, 10 3/4 x 16 ins / 27.2 x 40.6 cm) USD 13,500. NEW YORK, 22 Jan 1986, *Night, St Ives Bay* (1889, oil on canvas, 50 1/4 x 65 1/4 ins / 127.5 x 166 cm) USD 50,000. NEW YORK, 29 May 1987, *Awaiting his Return* (1884, oil on canvas, 21 x 15 1/4 ins / 53.4 x 38.7 cm) USD 48,000. NEW YORK, 24 May 1990, *High Sea* (1895, oil on canvas, 39 x 66 1/2 ins / 99 x 168.9 cm) USD 66,000. NEW YORK, 27 Sept 1990, *Nightfall* (oil on canvas, 9 x 18 ins / 23 x 45.7 cm) USD 15,400. NEW YORK, 30 Nov 1990, *Communion Day* (1883, oil on canvas, 16 1/2 x 11 ins / 42 x 28 cm) USD 33,000. PARIS, 19 June 1992, *Rape of Europa* (oil on canvas, 12 3/4 x 16 1/4 ins / 32.5 x 41 cm) FRF 17,500. LONDON, 25 Nov 1992, *Female Nude Playing the Piano* (oil on canvas, 19 3/4 x 23 1/2 ins / 50 x 60 cm) GBP 3,080. NEW YORK, 1 Dec 1994, *Mother and Child* (oil on canvas, 78 x 54 ins / 198.1 x 137.2 cm) USD 34,500. PARIS, 30 May 1997, *Rape of Europa* (oil on canvas, 13 x 16 1/4 ins / 33 x 41 cm) FRF 6,000.

SIMMONS, Franklin
American, 19th - 20th century.
Born 11 January 1839, in Webster; died 8 December 1913, in Rome.
Sculptor. Animals. Monuments, busts.

Franklin Simmons sculpted equestrian monuments and war memorials. He is known for a neo-classical marble *Penelope*. He was decorated by King Umberto of Italy.

MUSEUMS AND GALLERIES:
PORTLAND, ME (MA): *Ulysses S. Grant (1822-1885)* (1894); *Promised Land* (1912); *Penelope.*

AUCTION RECORDS:
NEW YORK, 28 Sept 1989, *Bust of Abraham Lincoln on a Pedestal* (marble, h. 35 ins / 88.9 cm) USD 4,400.

SIMMONS, Gary
American, 20th - 21st century.
Born 1964, in New York.
Draughtsman, sculptor. Scenes with figures.

Gary Simmons obtained a bachelor of fine arts in graphic design and illustration from the School for Visual Arts, New York, in 1988, and a master's degree in fine art from the California Institute of Arts in 1990. He lives and works in New York. He has been influenced by the work of Jackson Pollock. His work particularly addresses issues of race and black identity, using imagery drawn from North American culture, such as cartoons and vernacular architecture. His earliest works showed images of blatant racial stereotypes, such as the crows in the Walt Disney cartoon *Dumbo*.

Simmons is also concerned with the role of pedagogy in culture. He is best known for his *Erasure Drawings*, for which he sketched with chalk on blackboards and walls, then partially erased the work to leave behind ghostly images. He has continued to use blackboards and erasers in his *Chalkboard* series, such as *Black Chalkboards* and *Green Chalkboards* (both 1993), when he used chalk with fixative as a medium; and *Erasure Chair*, a school desk covered with hundreds of chalkboard erasers. The theme of erasure continues in his web-art project *Wake*, in which the movement of the viewer's hand or computer mouse across the screen wipes away the empty whiteness to reveal portions of photographs of empty dance spaces. Simmon's 1997 DVD *Desert Blizzard* documents a skywriting performance as a means of creating temporary imagery.

He has had solo exhibitions at the Whitney Museum of American Art, New York (*The Garden of Hate*, 1992); the Hirshhorn Museum and Sculpture Gardens (*Directions: Gary Simmons*, 1994); the Lannan Foundation (*Gary Simmons: Erasure Drawings*, 1995); the Museum of Contemporary Art, San Diego (*Gary Simmons: Gazebo*, 1997); the St Louis Art Museum (1999) and the Museum of Contemporary Art, Chicago (2002). He has also shown at the 1993 Whitney Biennial, the Fabric Workshop and Museum, Philadelphia (1995); *Wall Drawings*, Kunsthaus, Zurich (1997) and *Flying High: Selections from the Permanent Collection*, Philadelphia Museum of Art (2004).

BIBLIOGRAPHY:

Gary Simmons: The Garden of Hate, exhibition catalogue, Whitney Museum of American Art, New York, 1992. Clearwater, Bonnie, '*Arrêt sur enfance*' in *Art Press* n° 197, periodical, Paris, December 1994. *Gary Simmons: Erasure Drawings*, exhibition catalogue, Lannan Foundation, Los Angeles, 1995. Princenthal, Nancy, '*Gary Simmons: Disappearing Acts*' in *Art & Text*, essay, May-July 1997. Isé, Claudine, '*Gary Simmons*' in *Art Issues*, essay, September/October 1998. *Gary Simmons*, exhibition catalogue, Museum of Contempory Art, Chicago, 2002.

MUSEUMS AND GALLERIES:

MINNEAPOLIS (Walker Art Center): *Everforward...* (1993, mixed media sculpture) - PHILADELPHIA (MA): *Desert Blizzard* (1997, DVD) - SAN DIEGO (MCA): *Gazebo* (1997, paint and chalk on panel).

AUCTION RECORDS:

NEW YORK, 19 May 1999, *Untitled* (1998, chalk on board on masonite, 47 x 60 ins / 119 x 152 cm) USD 4,000. NEW YORK, 15 Nov 2000, *Erasure Series* (1992, charcoal and gouache, 30 x 22 ins / 76 x 56 cm) USD 2,500. NEW YORK, 15 Nov 2000, *Black Chalkboard* (1993, chalk, fixative and slate on painted fibreboard, 48 x 60 ins / 122 x 152 cm) USD 3,750. NEW YORK, 12 Nov 2002, *Erasure Series* (1992, gouache and chalk, two parts, 28 x 20 ins / 70 x 50 cm) USD 2,000. PARIS, 12 May 2004, *Untitled* (mixed media, 48 x 60 ins / 122 x 152 cm) EUR 2,100. PARIS, 12 May 2004, *Composition on a Chalkboard* (1992, oil and charcoal on panel, 45 x 57 ins / 115 x 144 cm) EUR 2,700.

SIMMONS, John, or Simmonds, called Simmons of Bristol

British, 18th century.

Born c. 1715, in Nailsea; died 18 January 1780, in Bristol.

Painter. Religious subjects, portraits.

John Simmons worked as a housepainter and ship's painter in Bristol, but devoted himself with success to painting religious subjects and portraits. He exhibited portraits at the Royal Academy in London from 1772 to 1780. Tradition has it that Hogarth admired his talent.

MUSEUMS AND GALLERIES:

BRISTOL (All Saints Church): altar painting - BRISTOL (City Mus. & AG): *The Annunciation* (oil on canvas) - DEVIZES (St John's): altar painting.

AUCTION RECORDS:

LONDON, 3 April 1996, *Portraits of Mr and Mrs Woodforde* (oil on canvas, a pair, 29 1/4 x 24 1/2 ins / 74 x 62 cm) GBP 4,830.

SIMMONS, John

19th century.

Born 1823; died 1876.

Painter, watercolourist, illustrator. Scenes with figures, landscapes.

John Simmons was a little-known artist who, from 1860 to 1870, painted fantastic subjects - fairies and mythical woodland creatures - which he used to illustrate *A Midsummer Night's Dream*.

AUCTION RECORDS:

LONDON, 23 March 1981, *Summer Stroll through the Fields* (1866, watercolour heightened with white, 20 1/2 x 29 1/4 ins / 52 x 74 cm) GBP 4,200. LONDON, 19 June 1984, *Hermia and Lysander, a Midsummer Night's Dream* (1870, watercolour heightened with gouache, 35 x 29 1/4 ins / 89 x 74 cm) GBP 22,000. LONDON, 21 Jan 1986, *Young Girl Next to a Waterfall* (watercolour heightened with gouache, rounded at the top, 20 x 14 1/4 ins / 51 x 36 cm) GBP 2,000. LONDON, 30 March 1994, *In the Woods* (watercolour heightened with white, 34 1/4 x 26 1/2 ins / 87 x 67 cm) GBP 10,350. KNOWLE, 7 July 1999, *Lady By Sea* (watercolour, 17 x 12 ins / 42 x 31 cm) GBP 340. LONDON, 22 May 2002, *Portrait of a Girl Holding a Lily* (watercolour, 21 x 15 ins / 53 x 39 cm) GBP 3, 000. LONDON, 25 June 2002, *At the Bottom of the Garden* (1871, watercolour heightened with white, arched, 16 x 20 ins / 40 x 51 cm) GBP 5, 800. LONDON, 21 May 2003, *Chance Encounter* (1870, watercolour, 22 x 30 ins / 55 x 77 cm) GBP 1, 500.

SIMMONS, John

British, 20th century.

Died 1943.

Painter. Urban landscapes.

John Simmons exhibited at the Royal Academy in London from 1932 to 1937.

SIMMONS, Laurie

American, 20th - 21st century.

Born 3 October 1949, on Long Island (New York).

Installation artist, photographer. Multimedia.

Neo-Conceptual Art.

Laurie Simmons studied art at the Tyler School of Art in Temple University, Philadelphia, and graduated in 1971. She was awarded a National Endowment for the Arts scholarship in 1984. She lives and works in New York. Although self-taught as a photographer, this is the medium on which her work is based. Her art evokes the psychology of desires and memories. She is often considered a feminist. Collective exhibitions include: Walker Art Centre, Minneapolis, 1987; Octobre des Arts, Lyons, 1987; Cologne, 1989; Galerie Michle Chomette, Paris, 1990; Castello de Rivoli, Centre for Photography, Woodstock, 1991; *L'Esprit de famille* (*Family Spirit*), Villa du Parc, Annemasse, 2001; *Almost Warm and Fuzzy: Childhood and Contemporary Art*, an exhibition recalling childhood in contemporary art, PS.1 Contemporary Art Centre, New York.

BIBLIOGRAPHY:

Schorr, Collier, *Laurie Simmons: photographs 1978-1979*, exhibition catalogue, Skarstedt Fine Art, New York, 2002.

MUSEUMS AND GALLERIES:

GENEVA (Mamco).

AUCTION RECORDS:

NEW YORK, 22 Feb 1996, *Working Hourglass* (1989, black and white photograph framed by the artist, 84 x 48 ins / 213.4 x

121.9 cm) USD 6,900. NEW YORK, 17 Nov 1999, *Talking Ukulele* (cibachrome prints, 1/5, 63 x 46 ins / 161 x 116 cm) USD 10,000. LONDON, 8 Dec 1999, *English Lady* (1987, photographs, 2/5, 36 x 26 ins / 91 x 66 cm) GBP 2,200. NEW YORK, 20 Feb 2002, *Talking Handkerchief* (photographs, 68 x 49 ins / 173 x 125 cm) USD 5,000. NEW YORK, 27 April 2004, *Walking Camera, Jimmy the Camera* (1987, photographs, 2/10, 64 x 48 ins / 163 x 122 cm) USD 16,000.

SIMMONS, W. St Clair
British, 19th century.
Painter. Genre scenes.

W. St Clair Simmons was active from 1878 to 1899.

AUCTION RECORDS:

EDINBURGH, 13 May 1993, *The Ferryman's Call* (1892, oil on canvas, 40 x 28 ins / 101.7 x 71.2 cm) GBP 2,420.

SIMMONS, Will or William Francis Bernard
Spanish, 20th century.
Born 4 June 1884, in Elche de la Sierra (Murcia).
Active in the USA.
Painter, sculptor, engraver. Landscapes, animals.

Will Simmons was a pupil at the Académie Julian in Paris, and was also a writer. He lived and worked in Roxbury and produced engravings, specialising in etchings.

SIMMONS, William Henry
British, 19th century.
Born 11 June 1811, in London; died 6 June 1882, in London.
Engraver (mezzotint).

The celebrated engraver William Henry Simmons studied art at Frelden's Institute. Simmons engraved the works of the most famous modern British painters including Edwin Landseer, Sir John Millais, F. Faed, A. Salomon and Holman Hunt. He also executed some plates dating from 1837. He exhibited at the Royal Academy in London from 1857 to 1880.

SIMMS, Carroll Harris
American, 20th century.
Born 1924, in Bald Knob (Arkansas).
Painter, sculptor (including bronze), ceramicist, jeweller. Religious subjects, figures, animals. Murals, designs for stained glass, mosaics.

Starting in 1944, Carroll Harris Simms studied at Hampton Institute, Hampton, Virginia, the University of Toledo, and the Toledo Museum School of Art. He was the first African-American to graduate from the Cranbrook Academy of Art, Bloomfield Hills, Michigan. He went on to study at the Slade School of Art of the University of London, the Royal College of Art, London, the Swedish Institute, Stockholm, and the Institute of African Studies of the University of Ibadan, Nigeria. From 1949, he taught as part of the faculty of Texas Southern University, Houston (where he joined the artist John Biggers), and he served that institution until he retired in 1987.

Simms took part in various group exhibitions, such as: the *Annual Exhibition of Texas Crafts*, Dallas Museum, Dallas (1952 and 1953); and at the Denver Museum, Colorado (1967). He had a number of solo exhibitions, including one at the Toledo Museum of Fine Arts, Toledo, Ohio (1951). With John Biggers and John Edward Weems, he was the co-author of *Black Art in Houston: The Texas Southern University Experience, Presenting the Art of Biggers, Simms and Their Students* (College Station, London, Texas A&M University Press, 1978).

BIBLIOGRAPHY:

Cederholm, Theresa Dickason, *Afro-American Artists. A Bio-Bibliographical Directory*, Trustees of the Boston Public Library, Boston, 1973. Bearden, Romare/Henderson, Harry, *A History-African-American Artists. From 1792 to the Present*, Pantheon Books, New York, 1993.

MUSEUMS AND GALLERIES:

LOS ANGELES (California African American Mus.).

SIMMS, Charles, or Sims
British, 19th century.
Painter. Seascapes.

Charles Simms exhibited at the Society of British Artists, at the British Institution and at the Royal Academy between 1840 and 1875.

MUSEUMS AND GALLERIES:

LONDON (Victoria and Albert Mus.): *Seashore at Low Tide by Moonlight*.

AUCTION RECORDS:

LONDON, 14 June 1977, *Morning* (oil on panel, 12¼ x 17¼ ins / 31 x 44 cm) GBP 850.

SIMMS, Philip
Irish, 18th century.
Active in Dublin, from 1725 to 1749.
Engraver (burin).

Philip Simms engraved architectural views, portraits, illustrations and ex-libris.

SIMO
Spanish, 15th century.
Active in Valencia at the end of the 15th century.
Painter.

In 1498, Simo painted a curtain for the church of St Martin in Valencia.

SIMO, Ferenc or Franz
Hungarian, 19th century.
Born 11 April 1801, in Odorheiu; died 19 December 1869, in Klausenburg (now Cluj-Napoca, Romania).
Painter, lithographer.

Ferenc Simo studied in Vienna. He produced paintings and miniature portraits. The Magyar Nemzeti Galéria in Budapest owns some portraits by this artist.

SIMO, Juan Baptista, or Simone or Simoni
Spanish, 18th century.
Born in Valencia; died 1717, in Madrid.
Painter, fresco artist. Religious subjects, portraits.

Working in collaboration with Palomino, Juan Baptista Simo painted the frescoes at S Juan del Mercado in 1697. He also worked with Palomino in Madrid at the church of the monastery of S Felipe el Real. The paintings he left unfinished at his death were completed by his son Pedro Simo.

AUCTION RECORDS:

LONDON, 14 Dec 1990, *Portrait of Acisclo Antonio Palomino de Castro y Velasco Painting the Picture Truth and Time with Envy and Discord in a Palace Library* (1726, oil on canvas, 29½ x 25½ ins / 75.2 x 64.8 cm) GBP 30,800.

SIMOËN
French, 20th - 21st century.
Born 1949, in Paris.
Sculptor.

Simoën has shown examples of his work at the Paris Salon de Mai (from 1971) and at the Salon Grands et Jeunes d'Aujourd'hui. He exhibited solo in 1973. He works predominantly in plaster, frequently producing spheres which appear to enclose male figures reduced to the foetal state.

SIMOENS, Hans, or Simons or Symoens
Flemish School, 16th century.
Of German origin.
Sculptor, founder.

Simoens worked in Antwerp and Spain.

SIMOENS, Liévin, or Symoens
Flemish School, 17th century.
Active in Ghent 1651-1669.
Painter.

Liévin Simoens executed two altar paintings for the church of St Saviour in Ghent in 1669.

SIMOENSUERE, Corneille
French, 17th century.
Born in Fontenay-le-Comte.
Active during the first half of the 17th century.
Painter. Religious subjects.
Corneille Simoensuere may have been the artist responsible for 76 painted wood panels depicting biblical scenes.
MUSEUMS AND GALLERIES:
NIORT: *Biblical Scenes* (painted wood panels).

SIMÕES D'ALMEIDA, José, Sobrinho (the nephew)
Portuguese, 20th century.
Born 17 June 1880, in Figueiro dos Vinhos (?), near Thomar.
Sculptor, medallist.
José Simões was the nephew of José Simões d'Almeida and a pupil at the Académie Julian in Paris. He worked for the Mint in Lisbon.

SIMÕES DE ALMEIDA, José
Portuguese, 19th century.
Born 24 April 1844, in Figueiro dos Vinhos; died 13 December 1926.
Sculptor.
José Simões de Almeida studied at the school of sculpture at the naval dockyard in Lisbon where he worked on the decoration of warships. He exhibited in Paris and was awarded a bronze medal in 1878 at the Exposition Universelle and the Grand Prix at the Exposition Universelle of 1889. Among the works he exhibited was one entitled *Young Greek Victorious at the Olympic Games*. He went to Rome where he carved his *Woman Plucking the Petals from a Flower*. He is best known for *Puberty* (marble), *D. Sebastiao* (1875), and *The Duke of Terceira* (1877). He also produced a life-size marble *Statue of Christ* and a *Penitent Magdalene*, also in marble. In 1896 he was appointed as a teacher at the fine arts academy in Lisbon and later became director of the academy. It is possible that he is the same person as the sculptor José de Almeida working at the same period.
BIBLIOGRAPHY:
Exposição José Simões de Almeida e José Veloso Salgado, exhibition catalogue for Academia Nacional de Belas Artes, A Galeria, Lisbon, 1939. França, José-Augusto, *A arte em Portugal no século XIX*, Livranria Bertrand, Lisbon, 1966.
MUSEUMS AND GALLERIES:
LISBON: *Penitent Magdalene* (marble).

SIMOES DE FONSECA, Gaston
Brazilian, 19th - 20th century.
Born 16 October 1874, in Rio de Janeiro; died after 1929.
Active in France.
Painter, illustrator.
Gaston Simoes de Fonseca settled in Paris and was a draughtsman and restorer in the Louvre museum. He exhibited work in Paris at the Salon des Artistes Français, where he won a mention in 1913 and a bronze medal in 1914, and at the Salon des Indépendants from 1937 to 1943. He may have been the artist who showed an abstract composition at the Salon des Réalités Nouvelles in 1954. In 1929 he was made a Chevalier of the Légion d'Honneur.
AUCTION RECORDS:
PARIS, 3 July 1992, *Women Bathing* (oil on canvas, 15 3/4 x 31 1/2 ins / 40 x 80 cm) FRF 3,800. NEW YORK, 25-26 Nov 1996, *Evening* (c. 1910, ink/panel, 23 1/2 x 18 1/2 ins / 59.7 x 47.3 cm) USD 2,645.

SIMON. See **SIMON OF ST ALBANS**

SIMON
French, 14th century.
Active c. 1300.
Painter.
Simon was comissioned to paint two panels for the chapel of the château of Aire, Pas-de-Calais.

SIMON, called Simonet de Lyon
French, 14th century.
Active in the middle of the 14th century.
Painter.
Avignon School.
Simon worked in the Palace of the Popes, Avignon, from 1335 to 1344.

SIMON
French, 15th century.
Active in St-Gobain near Laon during the first half of the 15th century.
Painter.
In 1418 Simon was commissioned to paint seven portraits of saints for the St-Firmin Hospital, Laon.

SIMON
Austrian, 15th century.
Active in Vienna from 1419 to 1458.
Painter.
Simon worked for St Stephen's Cathedral (Stephansdom), Vienna, and the abbey of Klosterneuburg.

SIMON
Hungarian, 15th century.
Sculptor (wood).
Simon sculpted the stalls of the church in Késmark in 1469.

SIMON
Hungarian, 15th - 16th century.
Active from 1499 to 1523.
Painter.
Simon worked in Miskolc and in Kaschau (now Košice, Slovakia).

SIMON, called Simon the Glassmaker or Simon of Lynn or of Lenn
British, 16th century.
Active from 1550 to 1556.
Glass painter.
Simon the Glassmaker painted windows for the chapel of St Stephen, Westminster, and for Ely Cathedral.

SIMON
French, 16th century.
Born in Meaux.
Painter. History painting, portraits.
Simon worked mainly in Lorraine.

SIMON
Dutch, 17th century.
Painter.
Simon painted portraits, possibly in Dordrecht.

SIMON
Dutch, 17th century.
Medallist.
Simon engraved medals bearing the effigies of *Otto Venius* and *Henricus Vroom* in 1635.

SIMON
Swedish, 17th century.
Active in Rättvik, from 1661 to 1671.
Sculptor.
Simon sculpted an altar in the church of Ahl, and a door at the church of Leksand.

SIMON
French, 17th century.
Active 1674-1694.
Painter.
Simon produced paintings for Versailles and Meudon and also worked for the Gobelins manufactory in Paris.

SIMON
Flemish School, 18th century.
Active in Brussels in the middle of the 18th century.
Painter.
Simon worked for the abbey of St Peter in Ghent around 1750.

SIMON
German, 19th century.
Active at the beginning of the 19th century.
Engraver.
Simon engraved a medal bearing the image of *Napoleon in General's Uniform*.

SIMON (père)
French, 19th century.
Sculptor. Religious subjects.
Simon worked for the Church of St. Théodore and the Church of Les Grands Carmes in Marseilles.

SIMON (fils)
French, 19th century.
Sculptor. Busts.
This artist exhibited in Marseilles where he was working on four portraits in 1847.

SIMON, A.
Austrian, 19th century.
Active in Vienna, Austria.
Engraver.
A. Simon produced engravings on steel in the style of Van Dyck and Rembrandt. He published a collection of masterpieces housed in Viennese galleries.

SIMON, Abraham, or Symons or Symonds
British, 17th century.
Born 1617, in London; died 1692, in London.
Modeller (wax), medallist. Portraits.
Abraham Simon's work is often confused with that of his brother Thomas Simon.
MUSEUMS AND GALLERIES:
LONDON (British Mus.): *Portrait of the Artist, by Himself.*

SIMON, Alexander or Karl Wilhelm Alexander, known as Karl Alexander
German, 19th century.
Born 4 November 1805, in Frankfurt an der Oder; died after 1859, in Chile.
Painter, writer, poet.
Alexander Simon attended the academy in Berlin. He was active in Stuttgart and spent time in France.
MUSEUMS AND GALLERIES:
LEIPZIG: *Creation of Man* - WEIMAR: *Self-portrait; Portrait of the Artist's Fiancée; Eight Arabesques for Wieland's 'Oberon'*.

SIMON, André
French, 19th century.
Born in Paris.
Painter.
Pupil of his father and of Millet. Made his debut at the Salon de Paris in 1870.

SIMON, Andrée
French, 20th century.
Painter.
Andrée Simon showed compositions of geometrical abstraction at the Salon des Réalités Nouvelles in 1950, 1952 and 1956. Some of these recalled the synthetic art of Magnelli, while others tended toward greater freedom of expression.

SIMON, Anton
Austrian, 18th century.
Active in the Vorarlberg (Austria) in the middle of the 18th century.
Painter.
Anton Simon painted an altarpiece for the church of Dalaas, Austria, in 1749.

SIMON, Armand
Belgian, 20th century.
Born 3 March 1906, in Pâturages; died 15 June 1981, in Frameries.
Draughtsman, illustrator.
Groups: Rupture, Hainaut Surrealist group.
Armand Simon was a bibliophile and author who took up drawing at a very early age. He aligned himself with the Rupture group in 1936 and with the Hainaut Surrealists group in 1939. He showed his drawings for the first time at the *Surrealism* exhibition held at the Galerie La Boétie in Brussels in 1945. Examples of his work featured at the *Le Surréalisme en Belgique* (*Surrealism in Belgium*) exhibition held at the Isy Brachot Gallery in Paris in 1986. Solo exhibitions were held at the Maison de la Belgique in Cologne in 1973, at the Galerie Véga in Liège in 1974 and at the Galerie La Marée in Brussels in 1975. Armand Simon passed away in June 1981, while a major retrospective of his work was in progress at the Ateliers du Grand Hornu, near Mons. In 2001, the Musée d'Art Ancien in Brussels mounted a tribute exhibition entitled *Armand Simon: prospecteur de l'invisible* (*Armand Simon: Prospecting the Invisible*).

Simon was self-taught and drew his inspiration from his own reading. He illustrated Lautréamont's *Chants de Maldoror*, together with works by Arthur Rimbaud, Gérard de Nerval, Franz Kafka, Lewis Carroll, Herman Melville, Marcel Brion, Irène Hamoir and a host of others. He worked in Indian ink to depict a convoluted and, at times, menacing black-and-white universe.
BIBLIOGRAPHY:
Tendances surréalistes. Delporte, Simon, Graverol, exhibition catalogue, Casino, Knokke, 1978. *Le Surréalisme en Belgique*, exhibition catalogue, Gal. Isy Brachot, Paris, 1986.

SIMON, Arnaud
French, 17th century.
Born in Lyons; died after 1682.
Sculptor.
Arnaud Simon was the son of Mathias Simon. He produced sculptures for the royal chapel of the Brotherhood of White Penitents of Our Lady of Gonfalon in Lyons.

SIMON, Auguste. See **SIMON-AUGUSTE**

SIMON, Brigitte
French, 20th century.
Born 1926, in Rheims.
Painter, stained glass painter, illustrator.
Brigitte Simon's father, Jacques Simon, was a stained glass artist. She began to draw from an early age. From 1945 to 1949 she lived in Paris, where she produced her first stained glass window for Le Corbusier. In 1949 she married the painter Charles Marq, and they took over the stained glass window studio in Rheims, which, from 1956, attracted artists such as Jacques Villon, Roger Bissière, Serge Poliakoff, Vieira da Silva, Raoul Ubac and Marc Chagall.

In 1959 she met Joseph Sima who became a close friend, and in 1963, they created the entire set of windows for the chancel of Rheims Cathedral. She also produced stained glass windows for the cathedrals of Rheims, Nantes and St-Philibert de Tournus, and for many other church buildings. She has illustrated books, including *Lunatics* by René Char and *The End* by Pierre-André Benoit in 1968, and *Spring* by Paul Claudel in 1994. She has held numerous exhibitions in France and abroad, including in 1974 at the Galerie de Seine, Paris, in 1977 and 1982 in London, in 1989 at the Musée des Beaux-Arts in Rheims (a major retrospective exhibition), and in 1995 at the Galerie Herold in Paris (Sima-Simon Exhibition).

The rocky landscapes of the Ardèche exercised a considerable influence on her painting. The mineral world was omnipresent in her imaginary landscapes. Abysses, cliffs, fissures and crystalline structures were prominent features, and her compositions were colourless, as though the absence of colour would ensure pure luminosity. From the 1990s onward, her lines became softer and freer, colour made a tentative appearance (blue or brown washes), and blank areas took on a greater significance. These works aligned the art of Brigitte Simon with the Japanese tradition of landscape painting, as they manifested restraint, a mastery of the use of white space and a poetic and spiritual atmosphere.

Bibliography:

Esteban, Claude, *Brigitte Simon*, exhibition catalogue, Gal. de Seine, Paris, 1974. Chapon, François/Michaux, Henri/Sima, Joseph/Raine, Kathleen, *Joseph Sima, Brigitte Simon: double variation sur champs de rêve*, exhibition catalogue, Gal. Thessa Herold, Paris, 1995.

SIMON, Charles
French, 17th century.
Active in Fontainebleau 1618-1625.
Painter.

Charles Simon copied works by Andrea del Sarto and Titian.

SIMON, Charles
French, 19th century.
Born 6 September 1799, in Paris.
Landscape painter.

Charles Simon was a pupil of Gros. He was admitted to the École des Beaux-Arts on 25 February 1814 and exhibited at the Salon in 1840 and 1841.

SIMON, Christian
German, 17th century.
Active in Leipzig, in 1667.
Painter.

SIMON, Christophe. See **SAINT-SIMON Christophe**

SIMON, Claude
French, 20th century.
Born in Tananarive (Madagascar).
Painter.

Claude Simon exhibited at the Salon d'Automne in Paris, where he was a member.

SIMON, Émile J. J.
French, 20th century.
Born 1890; died 1976.
Painter. Landscapes.

Émile J. J. Simon exhibited regularly at the Salon des Artistes Français in Paris. In 1931 he was awarded a commendation, in 1934 a silver medal and in 1935 a gold medal. He was awarded the Hors concours.

He specialised in painting landscapes of Brittany.

Auction records:

Brest, 14 Dec 1980, *Return of the Fishing Boats* (oil on canvas, 21 1/4 x 25 1/2 ins / 54 x 65 cm) FRF 4,000. Paris, 24 June 1988, *The Little Lighthouse at Kérity* (oil on canvas, 21 1/4 x 28 3/4 ins / 54 x 73 cm) FRF 32,000. Paris, 19 March 1990, *Pardon (Religious Festival) at La Clarté* (oil on panel, 18 x 22 ins / 46 x 55 cm) FRF 30,000. Paris, 25 June 1997, *Breton Market* (oil on canvas, 13 x 16 1/4 ins / 33 x 41 cm) FRF 10,500. Brest, 16 May 1999, *Locronan - Conversation on the Uplands* (oil on canvas) FRF 10,500. Brest, 19 Dec 1999, *Pardon of Penhors in Brittany* (1946, oil on panel, 35 x 21 ins / 90 x 53 cm) FRF 31,500. Brest, 14 May 2000, *Card Party* (oil on canvas, 13 x 16 ins / 33 x 41 cm) FRF 13,000. Brest, 14 May 2000, *La recolte et le brulage du goemon au pays bigouden (The collection and burning of seaweeed in the Bigouden region)* (oil on canvas, 18 x 22 ins / 46 x 55 cm) FRF 28,500. Brest, 20 May 2001, *Chapel and Village of Madeleine near to Penmarch* (oil on panel, 18 x 22 ins / 46 x 55 cm) FRF 16,000. Rennes, 2 Dec 2001, *Wracks of Harvest Yield at St Guenole* (oil on panel, 15 x 18 ins / 38 x 46 cm) FRF 11,200. Brest, 12 May 2002, *Breton in Costume Reading Pardon* (oil on panel, 22 x 18 ins / 55 x 46 cm) EUR 1,800. Brest, 11 May 2003, *Return from Fishing* (oil on canvas, 20 x 25 ins / 52 x 63 cm) EUR 3,600. Brest, 21 Dec 2003, *Pardon of St Anne la Palud* (oil on canvas, 32 x 26 ins / 81 x 65 cm) EUR 5,000. Brest, 16 May 2004, *Market Scene at Douarnenez* (oil on panel, 18 x 21 ins / 45 x 54 cm) EUR 3,200. Brest, 24 July 2004, *Procession in Brittany* (oil on panel, 15 x 18 ins / 38 x 46 cm) EUR 3,000.

SIMON, Erich M.
German, 20th century.
Born 12 April 1892, near Kolberg (now Kolobrzeg, Poland); died April 1978.
Painter, illustrator, engraver, designer. Landscapes.

A pupil of Emil Orlik, Simon painted landscapes and interiors and illustrated books.

SIMON, Ernest Constant
French, 19th century.
Born in Paris; died 1895, in Cairo.
Painter, watercolourist. Genre scenes, local scenes, landscapes.

Father of Jacques Roger Simon, this artist was a pupil of Dardoize and made his debut at the Salon de Paris in 1880.

Auction records:

Paris, 12-15 April 1899, *A Moroccan Cemetery and its Keeper* (watercolour) FRF 550. Paris, 26 Nov 1943, *Egypt: the Water Carrier* (watercolour) FRF 300; *Elephant Island* (watercolour) FRF 550. Paris, 13 Dec 1946, *Mattress Carders in Cairo* (1893) FRF 35050.

SIMON, Francine, known as France Narkis
French, 20th century.
Born 19 March 1930, in Paris.
Painter.

Francine Simon first presented her paintings at the Académie Port-Royal in Paris, then at MacAvoy's studio.

In Paris, she has held regular solo shows from 1982 at the Salon d'Automne and the Salon des Indépendants. She has also held solo shows in New York.

SIMON, François
French, 17th century.
Born 1606, in Tours; died 1671.
Engraver.

François Simon is mentioned by Ris-Paquot.

SIMON, François
French, 19th century.
Born 29 January 1818, in Marseilles; died 14 February 1896, in Marseilles.
Painter. Portraits, genre scenes, animals, landscapes.

François Simon was a pupil of Aubert and Loubon. He made his debut at the Salon de Paris in 1853 and took part in the 1855 Exposition Universelle.

His studies looked in particular to the works of Claude Lorraine and Simon himself painted numerous sunsets.

MUSEUMS AND GALLERIES:
PONTOISE: *Sheep Grazing in the Woods* - ST-ÉTIENNE: *Waiting for Night to Fall on the hill above La Mure, Sheep Grazing; Sheep; Portrait* - STRASBOURG: *Goat and Donkey in the Stable.*
AUCTION RECORDS:
MARSEILLES, 7 Dec 1899, *Horses in the Stable,* FRF 155. PARIS, 12 May 1932, *Calf, Ewe and Lamb in a Landscape,* FRF 85; *Le Cours Mirabeau in Aix-en-Provence,* FRF 500. MARSEILLES, 20 Dec 1946, *Goatherd and his Herd in the Alpilles,* FRF 28,900. MARSEILLES, 18 Dec 1948, *Sheep Grazing, 8 April 1949: Sheep* (two pendants) FRF 1,800. VERSAILLES, 19 Nov 1989, *Shepherd and his Flock Outside the Ramparts* (oil on panel, 17 x 27 1/2 ins / 43 x 70 cm) FRF 11,500. PARIS, 7 April 2000, *Shepherd and his Flock* (oil on panel, 17 x 28 ins / 43 x 71 cm) FRF 13,500. PARIS, 23 Nov 2001, *Shepherd and his Flock* (oil on panel, 13 x 20 ins / 32 x 51 cm) FRF 25,000. NEUILLY, 9 April 2004, *Return of the Flock* (oil on canvas, a pair, 45 x 81 ins / 115 x 207 cm) EUR 7,500.

SIMON, Frank Wotherspoon
British, 19th - 20th century.
Born 1863; died 1933.
Painter. Architectural views, urban landscapes.
Frank Wotherspoon Simon lived and worked in Edinburgh. He exhibited with the Royal Scottish Academy from 1885 to 1892, and was also active as an architect.

SIMON, Franz Anton
Austrian, 18th century.
Active in Feldkirch, Austria, and in Switzerland.
Painter.
Franz Anton Simon painted two altarpieces for the church of Rheinau, Switzerland, in 1744.

SIMON, Frédéric Émile
French, 19th century.
Born 1805, in Strasbourg; died 1886.
Engraver (burin), lithographer.
Frédéric Émile Simon studied as an engraver in Frankfurt am Main and in Munich. He set up a lithography business in Strasbourg with his brother Frédéric Sigismond.

SIMON, Frédéric Sigismond
French, 19th century.
Born 1777; died 1849.
Engraver (burin).
Brother of Frédéric Émile Simon, he worked with him in Strasbourg.

SIMON, Friedrich
German, 19th century.
Born 1809, in Heidelberg; died 1857, in Munich.
Painter. Genre scenes.
Friedrich Simon attended the academy in Munich.
AUCTION RECORDS:
VIENNA, 14 Sept 1976, *The Temptation* (1856, oil on canvas, 20 1/2 x 17 3/4 ins / 52 x 45 cm) ATS 35,000. MUNICH, 26 March 2004, *Peasant Girl Reading the Bible by the Light of an Oil Lamp* (1849, oil on canvas, 9 x 7 ins / 23 x 19 cm) EUR 1,500.

SIMON, Friedrich Rudolf
Swiss, 19th century.
Born 2 February 1828, in Bern; died 16 January 1862, in Hyères (Var), France.
Painter, copyist. Portraits, genre scenes, interiors, landscapes, animals.
Friedrich Rudolf Simon studied initially under Niklauss Senn and Johann Friedrich Dietler. In 1844-1845, his father sent him to Munich to study pharmacy, but Friedrich was enthusiastic about art, and in July 1845, he worked in the studio of the sculptor Max Wedumann. At the end of 1847, Simon left Munich for Geneva, where he studied under Barthélemy Menn (1815 - 1893) and spent time in the studio of the Swiss painter Charles Gleyre (1808 - 1874). Subsequently, he went to Antwerp, then stayed in Paris, Geneva and Hyères. In Antwerp, Simon copied the work of several Flemish masters, including that of the baroque-era painter David Teniers (1610 - 1690), which taught him the intimist style (compositions depicting intimate domestic scenes).
MUSEUMS AND GALLERIES:
BERN: *On the Great Military Road; Towing a Boat on the Thiele, near Lake Biel* - BUCHAREST (Muz. National de Arta al României): *Interior* - GENEVA (MAH): *The Poacher; The Blacksmith; Stagecoach, Night; Italian Shepherds; Landscape near Rome* - NEUCHÂTEL: *Post Horses in Provence.*

SIMON, Gabriel
French, 17th century.
Active in Neufchâteau at the beginning of the 17th century.
Sculptor.
Gabriel Simon worked for Duke Charles III of Lorraine and for the church of the Minims in Épinal.

SIMON, Gabriel Philippe
French, 18th century.
Born 1741, in Paris.
Sculptor.
Gabriel Philippe Simon studied at the Académie Royale. In 1791 he exhibited four plaster busts at the Salon du Louvre.

SIMON, Georges
French, 20th century.
Sculptor.
Georges Simon exhibited at the Salon des Artistes Français in Paris, where he was a member. He was awarded a commendation in 1936, and received a bronze medal in 1939.

SIMON, Georgette
French, 20th century.
Born 11 October 1903, in Besançon.
Painter. Figures, figure compositions, street scenes, animals.
Georgette Simon was a self-taught painter. She began painting in 1949, and exhibited for the first time in 1959 in Paris. She showed her paintings at the Salon d'Automne and the Salon des Artistes Français in Paris, and at the Galerie André Weil and the Galerie Marie de Holmsky.

Her work is figurative, and depicts luminous urban landscapes, plain interiors, and expressive portraits. In general, her style is simple and discreet, and her works have a spiritual atmosphere.
MUSEUMS AND GALLERIES:
BESANÇON (MBA et d'Archéologie): *Portrait of Paul Léautaud* (1961, oil on canvas (46x55)); *Nude* (1951, oil on canvas (31x61)); *Hotel Lutétia* (1952, oil on canvas (55x46)).

SIMON, Gervais
French, 19th century.
Painter. Genre scenes, portraits.
Simon Gervais exhibited at the Salon de Paris in 1812 and again in 1817.

SIMON, Godefroid
Flemish School, 17th - 18th century.
Born c. 1648, in Wavre; died 22 October 1729, in Namur.
Sculptor.
Godefroid Simon sculpted, with Charles Philippe de Rose, the stalls of the church of Our Lady in Namur, and also worked for other churches in that town.

SIMON, Gustav
Austrian, 19th century.
Active in Vienna.
Painter.
Gustav Simon painted a portrait of the Emperor *Ferdinand I* for the town hall in Salzburg, Austria, in 1836.

SIMON, György János, or Jean-Georges, Georg Johann
Hungarian, 20th century.
Born 31 July 1894, in Trieste; died 25 November 1968, in Leeds, and not in Harrogate, where he is buried.
Active from 1930 and naturalised in England.
Painter, watercolourist, draughtsman, engraver, sculptor. Figures, landscapes, still-lifes.
György János Simon studied under István Reti at the Budapest academy from 1913 to 1914, and at various independent academies in Baden Baden and Budapest. About 1920 he lived in Italy and Switzerland. In 1924, he attended the Académie Julian, the École des Beaux-Arts and the Acedémis Colarossi, and worked with Bourdelle. Then he returned to live in Italy and Switzerland, and from 1936 in England. Simon was a Post-Impressionist who was influenced in turn, by Cubism, Expressionism and Futurism. During the 1930s he returned to Realism, and while in England painted a number of Abstracts Collective exhibitions include: *International Modern Art Exhibition*, Geneva (1920-1921); Budapest (regularly from 1923: National Salons,1925 and 1929, and Museum of Fine Arts, 1931, 1940 and 1941); Bern Kunsthalle (1924); Royal Academy, London (1940 and 1951). Solo exhibitions include Budapest (1923, 1927, 1933, 1974); Zurich (1927); Palais des Beaux-Arts, Brussels (1938); City Art Gallery, Wakefield (1973); London (1989); Harrogate (1990). In 1940 the Pál Szinyei Merse Society, Budapest, awarded him its drawing prize.
MUSEUMS AND GALLERIES:
BAJA (Türr István Múzeum) - BUDAPEST (Magyar Nemzeti Gal.) - BUDAPEST (Szépmuvészeti Múz.).

SIMON, H.
German, 18th century.
Active in Göggingen, c. 1750.
Ceramicist.
MUSEUMS AND GALLERIES:
WÜRZBURG (Mainfränkisches Mus.): narrow-necked jug.

SIMON, Henri or Jean Henri
Belgian, 18th - 19th century.
Born 27 July 1752, in Brussels; died 12 March 1834, in Brussels.
Cameo engraver, medallist.
Henri Simon was no doubt the son of Mayer or Jacob Mayer Simon and the father of Jean Marie Amable Henri Simon. He studied in Brussels and was subsequently engraver to Duke Charles of Lorraine and Napoleon.
MUSEUMS AND GALLERIES:
PARIS (Mus. Carnavalet): *Portraits of the Duchess of Orléans and her Children*; *Philippe-Égalité* - THE HAGUE: *Homer* - VIENNA (Kunsthistorisches Mus.): *Joseph II*.

SIMON, Henry
French, 20th century.
Born 28 December 1910, in St-Hilaire-de-Riez (Vendée); died 27 February 1987.
Painter (including gouache), draughtsman, potter, illustrator. Religious subjects, figures, portraits, genre scenes, landscapes, seascapes, still-lifes, flowers.
Henry Simon was a student at the École des Beaux-Arts in Nantes, where he was taught by Émile Simon. He then studied at the École des Beaux-Arts in Paris from 1932, in the studio of Lucien Simon. He was called up to the army in 1939, and taken prisoner the following year. In 1976 he was appointed Chevalier des Arts et des Lettres.
His first exhibits were realist portraits and well-constructed genre scenes. He visited Algeria in 1950, where the quality of the light was a revelation to him. He found a new freedom in the use of colour, and began to favour simpler shapes. From then on he favoured warm, pure, vivid colours, which he applied in flat tints in a manner reminiscent of Matisse and Fauvism. During the 60s he increasingly focused on the effects of movement and light, working with dabs of vivid colour, with less emphasis on the subject. Subsequently he returned to a calmer and more precise style, with scenes of bathing, dancing, concerts, circuses or horse racing, which emanated joie de vivre. From 1937 he received numerous public commissions in the Vendée region, in particular, for frescoes and tableaux for town halls, school and churches.
His work featured in collective exhibitions in Paris, including; 1933, 1936, 1938, 1941, 1942, 1946 and 1961, Salon d'Automne; 1937, Exposition Internationale; 1943, 1946 and 1968, Salon des Peintres Témoins de leur Temps; 1977, Salon Comparaisons; 1949, Salon des Artistes Bretons at the Musée des Beaux-Arts in Nantes; 1982, Musée Municipal de La Roche-sur-Yon.
He regularly showed paintings in solo exhibitions in the Vendée; 1971, Musée Municipal des Sables-d'Olonne; 1978, Palais des Congrès, St-Jean-de-Monts. After his death, an exhibition was held in 1992 entitled *Henry Simon 1910-1987. 60 Years of Painting.*, Conseil Général, Hôtel du Département, La Roche-sur-Yon.
BIBLIOGRAPHY:
Rétrospective Henry Simon, exhibition catalogue, Musée municipal, Les Sables d'Olonne, 1971. *Henry Simon 1910-1987 60 ans de peinture*, exhibition catalogue, Conseil Général de la Vendée-Hôtel du département, La Roche-sur-Yon, 1992. *Henry Simon*, exhibition catalogue, St-Hilaire-de-Riez, 2000.
MUSEUMS AND GALLERIES:
LES SABLES D'OLONNE (Musée de L'Abbaye Ste-Croix): *Woman of the Marais des Monts (Marshes)* (1937); *Young Algerians* (1950).

SIMON, Hervé
Belgian, 20th century.
Born 1888, in Schaerbeek (Brussels).
Painter. Portraits, Still-lifes, flowers.
Hervé Simon studied at the fine arts academy in Brussels.
AUCTION RECORDS:
BRUSSELS, 19 Dec 1989, *Still-life* (oil on canvas, 17 3/4 x 26 3/4 ins / 45 x 68 cm) BEF 30,000. AMSTERDAM, 20 April 1993, *Still-life with Flowers and Fruit* (oil on canvas, 47 1/2 x 36 3/4 ins / 120.5 x 93.5 cm) NLG 11,270. LOKEREN, 12 March 1994, *Still-life with Anemones* (oil on canvas, 19 3/4 x 23 1/2 ins / 50 x 60 cm) BEF 28,000.

SIMON, J. P.
British, 18th century.
Active in London during the second half of the 18th century.
Miniaturist.
J.P. Simon exhibited in London from 1785 to 1786.

SIMON, Jacob Mayer. See **SIMON Mayer** or **Jacob Mayer**

SIMON, Jacques Roger
French, 20th century.
Born 21 November 1875, in Paris; died 1965, in Carolles.
Painter, watercolourist, engraver, illustrator, designer. Genre scenes, landscapes, seascapes, still-lifes.

Jacques Roger Simon worked in the studios of Bouguereau and Ferrier and was taught by Albert Maignan and Charles Cottet. He travelled through Spain, the Maghreb and Egypt before settling in the Villa Abd-el-Tif in Algiers in 1908.

From 1900, he exhibited in Paris at the Salon des Artistes Français, where he became a member, and at the Salon des Indépendants, the Salon des Artistes Décorateurs and the Salon des Orientalistes. He was awarded a third-class medal in 1906, a gold medal in 1928 and a silver medal at the Exposition Internationale of 1937. He was made Chevalier of the Légion d'Honneur in 1928.

He was an engraver and book illustrator, in particular for Raymond Dorgelès, Georges Duhamel (*Fun and Games*), Fromentin and Joseph Kessel. He also produced designs for tapestries and stained glass windows. In addition, he produced designs for the 1931 Colonial Exposition and provided the ceramic décor.

BIBLIOGRAPHY:
Jacques Simon, 1875-1965: peintre graveur, exhibition catalogue, Musée d'Art moderne Richard-Anacréon, Granville, 2001.

MUSEUMS AND GALLERIES:
CHARTRES: *Seascape* - PARIS (former Mus. du Luxembourg): *Port of Algiers; Still-life.*

AUCTION RECORDS:
PARIS, 20 April 1945, *Banks of the Thames: Houses of Parliament* (watercolour) FRF 2,500. PARIS, 11 June 1947, *Still-life with Fish,* FRF 2,200. PARIS, 21 April 1996, *At the Market* (gouache and charcoal/bistre-coloured paper, 7 3/4 x 12 1/2 ins / 20 x 32 cm) FRF 8,000. PARIS, 20 March 1998, *Bridge in Toledo* (oil on canvas, 15 x 22 ins / 38 x 55 cm) FRF 2,400. BAYEUX, 15 Sept 2002, *Landscape with Figures in Carolles* (oil on canvas, 22 x 15 ins / 55 x 38 cm) EUR 1,850. PARIS, 24 March 2003, *Port of Algiers* (oil on canvas, 13 x 16 ins / 33 x 40 cm) EUR 2,800.

SIMON, Jakob
Austrian, 19th century.
Active in 1827.
Miniaturist.

SIMON, Jan
Polish, 19th century.
Born c. 1810; died after 1870.
Portrait artist.
Jan Simon worked in Posen (now Poznan) and in the Ukraine, especially in Odessa.

SIMON, Jan Antoni
Polish, 19th century.
Born 1815; died 1890, in Posen (now Poznan).
Painter.
Jan Antoni Simon painted altarpieces for churches in Posen. He may be the same artist as Jan Simon.

SIMON, Jan de, real name Giovanni Simone
Italian, 17th century.
Died 1627, in Poland.
Sculptor.
Jan de Simon worked in Cracow, and sculpted the portico at the entrance of the convent of the order of St Clare in Stary Sacz in 1603.

SIMON, Janos or Johann
Hungarian, 19th century.
Active in Klausenburg (now Cluj-Napoca, Romania) c. 1800.
Cameo engraver, engraver (burin).

SIMON, Jean
French, 17th century.
Active in Angers 1643-1697.
Sculptor.
Jean Simon was the father of the two sculptors who went under the names Christophe and Jacques St-Simon.

SIMON, Jean
French, 19th century.
Born in Toulon; died 1894.
Painter. Portraits, landscapes.
Jean Simon was a pupil of Morin, Pils and student at the École des Beaux-Arts. He exhibited at the Salon de Paris between 1819 and 1847 and was awarded a third class medal in 1819 and a second class one in 1827.

MUSEUMS AND GALLERIES:
MARSEILLES (MBA): paintings.

AUCTION RECORDS:
PARIS, 16 March 1951, *The Prize Giving,* FRF 7,000.

SIMON, Jean I, called Jean de Bar-sur-Aube
French, 15th century.
Active in Troyes from 1417 to 1440.
Glass painter.
The father of Jean Simon II, Jean Simon I worked for Troyes Cathedral and the city's churches of St-Étienne and Ste-Madeleine.

SIMON, Jean II, called Jean de Bar-sur-Aube
French, 15th century.
Died 1472 or 1473.
Active in Troyes.
Glass painter.
The son of Jean Simon I, Jean Simon II worked for Troyes Cathedral and the city's churches of St Étienne and Ste-Madeleine.

SIMON, Jean Marie Amable Henri
French, 19th century.
Born 28 January 1788, in Paris; died after 1858.
Cameo engraver.
The son of Henri Simon, this artist worked in Brussels and Paris. The Bibliothèque Nationale in Paris has 18 cameos showing kings and princes of his day.

SIMON, Jean or John, or Simons
French, 17th - 18th century.
Born c. 1675, in Normandy; died 22 September 1754, in London.
Engraver (burin/mezzotint).
Jean Simon studied in Normandy and then visited England, where the work of mezzotint engravers persuaded him to adopt this technique. Sir Godfrey Kneller employed him to reproduce several of his portraits. He also engraved religious subjects, genre scenes and portraits after other masters.

SIMON, Jean Pierre
French, 18th century.
Born 1769, in Paris.
Painter, engraver.
Jean Pierre Simon engraved historical subjects, genre scenes, and illustrations for La Fontaine's *Fables.*

AUCTION RECORDS:
PARIS, 21 and 22 Feb 1919, *Self-portrait* (red chalk) FRF 60; *Little Journeyman* (red chalk) FRF 100.

SIMON, Jeanne
Maiden name: Dauchez
French, 20th century.
Born in Paris.
Painter.
Jeanne Simon was the wife of the painter Lucien Simon. She exhibited at the Salon des Artistes Français and Salon des Indépendants in Paris. She was awarded a bronze medal in 1900 at the Exposition Universelle in Paris.

SIMON, Joseph
French, 18th century.
Sculptor.
Joseph Simon worked in Paris and St Petersburg with Nicolas Pineaut.

SIMON, Juan. See **SIMOENS Hans**

SIMON, Julius. See **SIMONY Julius**

SIMON, L.
French, 18th century.
Engraver.
L. Simon engraved after Chardin, favouring the scraper technique.

SIMON, Léon Jean Baptiste or Léon
French, 20th century.
Born 14 June 1836, in Metz; died 23 November 1910, in Vandelainville.
Painter, draughtsman. Landscapes.
Léon Jean Baptiste Simon studied under Jacques M. Hussenot and Auguste K. Migette in Metz. He first became known in Paris, when he exhibited at the 1867 Salon. He showed chiefly drawings, including charcoal drawings.
MUSEUMS AND GALLERIES:
BOURGES: charcoal - PONTOISE: two drawings - STRASBOURG: *Finstingen Marshes*.
AUCTION RECORDS:
NEW YORK, 15-16 Feb 1906, *Landscape*, USD 30.

SIMON, Louis
French, 20th century.
Born in Ernecourt.
Painter.
In Paris, Louis Simon exhibited at the Salon d'Automne, of which he was a member.

SIMON, Louis André
French, 18th - 19th century.
Born 1764, in Paris; died c. 1831.
Painter, decorative designer.
Louis André Simon exhibited a *Portrait of Marie-Antoinette* at the 1817 Salon.

SIMON, Luc
French, 20th century.
Born 16 July 1924, in Rheims.
Painter, watercolourist, lithographer, sculptor, illustrator. Designs for tapestries, designs for stained glass.
Symbolism.
Luc Simon was born into the Simon family, who were masters of stained glass in Rheims for ten generations. He studied at the École des Arts Décoratifs in Paris. He spent some time in Tunisia and travelled across Africa in the steps of Arthur Rimbaud. In 1950, he was awarded the Casa Velázquez Prize and visited Madrid, where he studied the work of Goya. In 1954, he was awarded the Prix Fénéon and in 1963 the Prix de la Critique.

The work of Luc Simon was elusive and indefinable, such was its diverse scope and inspiration, together with the varied techniques and skills he employed. He chose the adaptability of the watercolour medium to cover monumental areas. This was symbolised by his theme of the origin of the world, and to depict it he called on dreams, visions and fantasy. He was a poet, and constantly on the watch. As he put it: 'Something is going to happen. I shall know it when it comes. It will be better than I and I shall be its servant.'

He received numerous commissions from the state and from public and private collections, notably for stained glass windows for the American Church in Paris and for the church at Fère-en-Tardenois

From 1955, he showed his work regularly in collective exhibitions, and exhibited in solo shows in Europe and North America, including in Paris, Brussels, Geneva, Munich, Berlin and New York. Exhibitions included the following; 1962, Galerie Motte, Paris; 1965, H.P.F. Galleries, New York; 1970, Galerie Motte, Geneva; 1973, Galerie Rive Gauche, Paris; 1974, Galerie Contemporaine, Cannes; 1977, Centre Culturel Romain-Rolland, Clamecy; 1978, Galerie Rost, Koblenz; 1979, Maison des Arts et Loisirs, Sochaux; 1982, Galerie Rost, Koblenz. In 1986, he showed a cycle of paintings entitled *Legendary Moralities* at the Musée des Beaux-Arts in Mulhouse, the Städtisches Museum in Gegenbach, the Musée des Beaux-Arts in Rheims, the National Picture Gallery in Athens and the Musée du Château de Belfort. From 1989 to 1991, he showed the watercolour series *L'Allemagne s'échafaude vers des lunes* (*Germany Reaches for the Moon*) and the sculptures of *The Wild Parade* at, among other places, the French Cultural Centre in Berlin, the Musée Arthur Rimbaud in Charleville-Mézières and the Musée du Château de Belfort. In 1994, he exhibited *Thirty Nudes for 'La Dormeuse'*, at the Galerie Natkin-Berta.

BIBLIOGRAPHY:
Chaix, Marie, *Luc Simon: les moralités légendaires 1980-1985*, exhibition catalogue, Musée des Beaux-Arts, Mulhouse, Städtisches Museum, Gegenbach (DEU), Musée des Beaux-Arts, Reims, National Picture Gall., Athinai (Athènes), Musée du Château de Belfort, Belfort, 1986. *L'Allemagne s'échafaude vers des lunes, aquarelles*, exhibition catalogue, Centre culturel français, Berlin, Musée Arthur-Rimbaud, Charleville, Belfort, 1989. *La Parade sauvage, sculptures*, exhibition catalogue, Musée du château de Belfort, 1991. *Luc Simon - Trente nus pour La Dormeuse*, exhibition catalogue, Gal. Natkin-Berta, Paris, 1994.
MUSEUMS AND GALLERIES:
BELFORT (MAH) - CHARLEVILLE-MÉZIÈRES (Mus. Arthur-Rimbaud) - PARIS (MNAM-CCI) - RHEIMS (FRAC Champagne-Ardenne).
AUCTION RECORDS:
PARIS, 18 Nov 1994, *Man is Naked (Hommage to Francis Gruber)* (1957, oil on canvas, 63 x 51 1/4 ins / 160 x 130 cm) FRF 40,000.

SIMON, Lucien J.
French, 19th - 20th century.
Born 18 July 1861, in Paris; died 13 October 1945, in Paris.
Painter (gouache), watercolourist, draughtsman.
Scenes with figures, figures, portraits, genre scenes, waterscapes, seascapes.
Groupe de la Bande Noire.
Lucien J. Simon studied under William Adolphe Bouguereau and Tony Robert-Fleury. He also taught painting, and his students included Bob Humblot, Henri Jannot, Yves Brayer and Georges Rohner.

He specialised in traditional provincial scenes, particularly of Brittany. For the Cercle de la Marine de Toulon, he painted decorative panels inspired by the novels of Pierre Loti. He was also an outstanding portraitist. His drawing was vigorous, his palette warm and colourful, although there was a certain greyness about the light, typical of the region.

From 1931 to 1934 he showed work in exhibitions at the Royal Academy in London, and exhibited regularly at the Salon des Artistes Français in Paris. By the Exposition Universelle of 1900, his reputation was already firmly established, and his contributions were confirmation of this. He was awarded a commendation in 1885, a third-class medal in 1890, a gold medal in 1900, and in 1937 the Grand Prix for the Exposition Internationale. He was made Chevalier of the

Légion d'Honneur in 1900, and an Officer in 1911. He was also appointed a member of the Institut de France in 1927.

Bibliography:
Cariou, André, *Lucien Simon*, Éd. Palantines, Quimper, 2002.

Museums and Galleries:
Boston: *Breton Women* - Bremen: *Portraits of Old Couples* - Brooklyn, NY: *Reconciliation in Brittany* - Budapest: *Lady with her Three Children* - Cairo: *Lady Dressing* - Chicago: *Celebrating Mass in Brittany; Portrait of the Artist* - Colmar: *Quaiside at Audierne* - Detroit: *Breton Inn* - Douai: *The Gayant Family* - Helsinki: *Returning from the Church at Penmarch* - Liège: *Travelling Circus; Skittles Player* - Lyons (MBA): *Portrait of the Artist; Religious Ceremony in Italy* - Mannheim: *Bretons in Church* - Moscow (Mus. of Western Art): *Boatmen; Gust of Wind* - Paris (Mus. Carnavalet): *Welcoming Army Officers at Porte Maillot Station, 14 July 1919* - Paris (Mus. d'Orsay): *Procession; Standing Stone; Summer's Day; Bathing; Thanksgiving* - Paris (Mus. du Petit Palais): *Mendicant Nuns; Visiting* - Rouen (MBA): *Portrait of the Painter J. E. Blanche* - Stockholm: *Evening Chat; Chatting at Twilight* - Venice: *Small Boat; Maundy Thursday Ceremony.*

Auction records:
Paris, 26 April 1899, *Travelling Circus,* FRF 2,150. Paris, 30 May 1910, *Breton Tavern,* FRF 9,200. Paris, 16-17 Dec 1919, *'Pardon' (Religious Procession) in Brittany,* FRF 6,300. Paris, 14 March 1921, *Group of Women from Pont l'Abbé in Traditional Costume* (watercolour) FRF 2,000. London, 22 June 1923, *L'Opéra* GBP 199. Paris, 30 Nov 1925, *Procession,* FRF 9,300. London, 26 March 1929, *Burning Kelp,* GBP 88. Paris, 26-27 Feb 1934, *Church Ceremony in Brittany,* FRF 930. Paris, 8 Dec 1941, *In Church,* FRF 2,200; *Parade in Brittany,* FRF 4,700; *Little Circus,* FRF 3,000. Paris, 11 March 1943, *Brittany: After the 'Pardon',* FRF 14,000; *Family Gathering in Brittany,* FRF 16,800; *Bathers on the Sands* (watercolour) FRF 5,100; *Woman Wearing Headdress of Pont l'Abbé* (watercolour) FRF 5,100; *Women Mending the Nets in Brittany* (watercolour) FRF 10,200. Paris, 25 June 1945, *Chapel at Penhore,* FRF 25,000; *Fancy Dress Festival in Venice,* FRF 22,000. Paris, July 1946, *Tom Pitt Ballet at Le Châtelet* (1905) FRF 13,000; *'Pardon' (Religious Procession) in Brittany* (gouache) FRF 12,200. Paris, 23 May 1951, *Tourists* (watercolour and gouache) FRF 5,800. Paris, 25 Feb 1954, *Circus Horses,* FRF 26,000. Paris, 28 Nov 1973, *Carrioles (Small Open Carriages) in Brittany,* FRF 6,000. London, 11 Feb 1976, *Gondola* (oil on canvas, 52 x 70 3/4 ins / 132 x 180 cm) GBP 700. New York, 11 May 1979, *Reception in a Studio* (1904, oil on canvas, 89 3/4 x 118 ins / 228 x 300 cm) USD 4,500. Paris, 18 Feb 1980, *Moroccan Market* (gouache, 25 1/4 x 39 1/4 ins / 64 x 100 cm) FRF 5,200. New York, 17 July 1981, *Harlequin and Pierrot* (oil on canvas, 93 1/4 x 65 3/4 ins / 237 x 167 cm) USD 2,100. London, 24 June 1983, *Breton Women Gathering Potatoes* (oil on canvas, 40 1/4 x 54 1/4 ins / 102 x 137.5 cm) GBP 2,800. Versailles, 19 Feb 1984, *Threshing the Wheat in Brittany* (gouache and watercolour, 43 1/4 x 57 ins / 110 x 145 cm) FRF 23,000. Brest, 15 Dec 1985, *Regattas in Brittany* (watercolour, 26 x 35 1/2 ins / 66 x 90 cm) FRF 11,000. London, 19 March 1986, *Morning Stroll* (oil on canvas, 33 1/2 x 51 1/4 ins / 85 x 130 cm) GBP 3,000. Paris, 20 June 1988, *Breton Women Bathing* (watercolour, gouache and ink/paper/canvas, 57 3/4 x 41 ins / 147 x 104 cm) FRF 73,000. Versailles, 20 June 1989, *Gathering Wrack* (oil on canvas, 27 1/4 x 39 1/4 ins / 69 x 100 cm) FRF 28,000. New York, 25 Oct 1989, *Street Scene in Paris in Winter* (oil on canvas, 13 x 17 3/4 ins / 33 x 45.1 cm) USD 9,900. Paris, 11 March 1990, *Nude Model* (oil on canvas, 27 1/4 x 21 1/2 ins / 69 x 54.5 cm) FRF 22,000. Paris, 26 April 1990, *Breton Fair* (oil on canvas, 21 1/4 x 28 3/4 ins / 54 x 73 cm) FRF 30,000. Paris, 7 Nov 1990, *Pig Market* (oil on panel, 9 x 7 ins / 23 x 18 cm) FRF 9,000. Paris, 14 June 1991, *Swimming Race* (oil on canvas, 23 1/2 x 33 3/4 ins / 60 x 86 cm) FRF 65,000. New York, 16 July 1992, *In the Studio* (oil on canvas, 21 1/2 x 25 3/4 ins / 54.6 x 65.4 cm) USD 7,700. Paris, 1 Dec 1992, *Fishermen's Wives* (watercolour and gouache, 14 1/2 x 19 3/4 ins / 37 x 50 cm) FRF 4,000. London, 7 April 1993, *Breton Women* (oil on canvas, 37 3/4 x 30 ins / 96 x 76 cm) GBP 5,290. Paris, 18 March 1994, *Carriole (Small Open Carriage) in Brittany* (oil on canvas, 28 3/4 x 23 1/2 ins / 73 x 60 cm) FRF 67,000. Paris, 9 Dec 1994, *Woman Gathering Kelp* (watercolour and gouache, 29 1/2 x 18 ins / 75 x 46 cm) FRF 21,000. Brest, 16 May 1999, *Family Snack* (watercolour and gouache, 43 x 51 ins / 108 x 130 cm) FRF 100,000. Paris, 11 June 1999, *Waiting Room* (oil on canvas, 36 x 41 ins / 91 x 104 cm) FRF 165,000. Paris, 9 June 2000, *Arab Riders under Ramparts* (oil on canvas, 26 x 34 ins / 65 x 87 cm) FRF 53,000. Paris, 7 July 2000, *The Conversation* (oil on canvas, 28 x 30 ins / 70 x 75 cm) FRF 45,000. Paris, 25 March 2001, *Exit from Mass* (1917, oil on canvas, 37 x 51 ins / 93 x 130 cm) FRF 135,000. Brest, 21 July 2001, *Family Scene in Semaphore of Ste-Marine* (watercolour and gouache on paper/canvas, 43 x 52 ins / 110 x 132 cm) FRF 108,000. Brest, 20 July 2002, *Tarare (Winnover)* (oil on canvas, 36 x 47 ins / 92 x 119 cm) EUR 19,000. Brest, 15 Dec 2002, *Brulage de Goemon* (oil on canvas, 58 x 72 ins / 147 x 184 cm) EUR 24,000. Paris, 2 Oct 2003, *Mascarade* (oil on canvas, 52 x 70 ins / 131 x 178 cm) EUR 32,000. Brest, 21 Dec 2003, *Threshing Wheat near Tour Carree at St Guenole, Penmarch* (watercolour and gouache, 43 x 58 ins / 110 x 148 cm) EUR 39,000. Brest, 16 May 2004, *Evening Wedding Party in Brittany* (oil on canvas, 29 x 36 ins / 73 x 92 cm) EUR 27,000. Brest, 16 May 2004, *Procession at Penhors* (oil on canvas, 46 x 77 ins / 116 x 195 cm) EUR 44,000.

SIMON, Lucienne
French, 20th century.
Born 19 October 1905, in Paris.
Painter.

Lucienne Simon studied at a private school of decorative art in Paris. She was given a commission for twelve portraits by French milliners. In Paris she held a solo exhibition of portraits and landscapes. From 1938, she signed herself *Simon-Taugourdeau.*

SIMON, Maria
Argentinian, 20th century.
Born 1922, in Tucuman.
Active in France from 1966.
Sculptor.

Maria Simon was born at the foot of the Andes mountain range, spent her childhood there and learned to deal with solitude. Then in 1963, after ten years' solitary research, she went to London with a grant from the British Council. Later she settled in Paris.

After the bombing of Hiroshima, her horror of which developed into an obsession, she began to model her first boxes, skeletons of dying figures, of horses in agony. The sculptor Libero Badi encouraged her in this work, done in total solitude in Buenos Aires, and set her on the way towards abstraction. In Paris she continued to create boxes in bronze, aluminium, iron, cast aluminium and cardboard. In about 1974 she began to make large pieces, then worked in cast resin, in wood and made bronze casts of everyday items. In collaboration with Michael Horowitz she published the book *Strangers.*

Her work was shown in numerous collective exhibitions: Salon de Mai and the Salon des Réalités Nouvelles (Paris); Buenos Aires Museo de Bellas Artes (Buenos Aires 1966,

1968, 1971); Biennales in Venice and Menton and at the *Engraving Biennale* in Tokyo (1972). Her first solo exhibition was at the Institute of Contemporary Art in London in 1964 and was followed by Galerie Iris Clert (Paris, 1966); Galerie Denise René (Paris, 1973); retrospective at the Galerie Eolia (Paris, 1990). She was awarded the Georges Braque sculpture prize in 1966.

BIBLIOGRAPHY:
Maria Simon. Sculptures, exhibition catalogue, Les Cahiers Eolia, Paris, 1990.

AUCTION RECORDS:
NEW YORK, 30 May 1984, *Celula de Min Mesma* (bronze, h. 10 ins / 25.3 cm) USD 1,800.

SIMON, Mathias
French, 17th century.
Active in Lyons 1639-1662.
Sculptor.

Mathias Simon was the father of Arnaud Simon. He produced the sculptures on the main portal of the town hall in Lyons.

SIMON, Mayer or Jacob Mayer, called Simon de Paris
French, 18th - 19th century.
Born 1746, in Brussels; died 17 March 1821, in Paris.
Engraver.

Mayer Simon carved cameos with effigies of ancient gods and the great figures of his time.

SIMON, Octave
French, 20th century.
Born 10 April 1914, in Lyons; died 1944.
Sculptor, decorative designer. Monuments, low reliefs.

Octave Simon joined the École des Beaux-Arts in Paris at the age of 17, attending classes in the atelier of Jean Boucher. He then studied under Alfred Janniot and later became his assistant. Janniot introduced him to the architect Michel Roux-Spitz who commissioned him to produce low reliefs for a mansion in Brussels and his own villa in Dinard. He exhibited at the Exposition Internationale in 1937, providing the sculpted motifs for the Iraqi pavilion along with two four-metre high decorative figures for the Porte d'Iéna, *L'Art et la Technique* (*Art and Technique*).

A member of the Resistance in 1940, he was arrested and killed in 1944. He was very close to Janniot and greatly admired the sense of monumentality achieved by Bourdelle, something he sought to emulate in his own work.

SIMON, P. Robert
German, 19th century.
Born 1811, in Dresden.
Painter. Portraits, genre scenes, still-lifes.

SIMON, Pedro. See **SIMONS Peeter**

SIMON, Pierre, the Elder
French, 17th - 18th century.
Born c. 1640, in Paris; died after 1710, in Paris.
Painter, engraver, draughtsman. Religious subjects, portraits.
Parisian School.

Pierre Simon the Elder studied under Robert Nanteuil whose manner he emulated. Many of his portraits were executed after his own drawings. He also engraved religious subjects.

BIBLIOGRAPHY:
Meyer, Véronique, '*Pierre Simon (c. 1640-1710)*' in *Nouvelles de l'Estampe*, no. 99, periodical, Paris, July 1988. Meyer, Véronique, '*L'Œuvre de Pierre Simon*' in *Nouvelles de l'Estampe*, no. 103-104, periodical, Paris, 1989.

SIMON, Pierre or Jean Pierre, the Younger
British, 18th - 19th century.
Born before 1750, in London; died c. 1810.
Painter, draughtsman, engraver (burin).

Pierre or Jean Pierre Simon the Younger was one of the collaborators on Boydell's celebrated collection on the works of Shakespeare. He also engraved genre subjects and portraits after the finest painters of his day.

AUCTION RECORDS:
LONDON, 13 Nov 1997, *Tom Jones' Meeting with Sophia After the Reconciliation, and Others* (1789, dry-point engraving, mezzotint and aquatint) GBP 4,140.

SIMON, Pierre Paul
French, 19th century.
Born 1853, in Rheims.
Glass painter. Figures.

A pupil of Luc Olivier Merson, Pierre Simon restored the Great Rose Window in Rheims Cathedral. He was awarded an honourable mention in 1892.

MUSEUMS AND GALLERIES:
RHEIMS: *Old Gardener* (study painted on wood); watercolour.

SIMON, Robert
French, 20th century.
Born 28 June 1889, in Bayeux; died 21 February 1961, in Paris.
Painter, draughtsman, illustrator. Figures, landscapes, seascapes, still-lifes.

Robert Simon studied for entrance to the École des Arts et Métiers in Angers, then became an architect in Caen. In 1911, he settled in Paris, where he embarked on a career in journalism. From 1925, he attended the Académie de la Grande Chaumière, the Académie Julian and the studio of André Lhote. In 1927, he settled in Villiers-sur-Morin (Seine-et-Marne), where he spent time with the painters Kvapil and Jean Pougny and the writer Vercors. He regularly visited the Côte d'Azur and from 1952 to 1958 he travelled in Spain, Italy and Ibiza.

He brought back many canvases from his travels, chiefly in small format. His work evoked the village of Villiers-sur-Morin, his house and the surrounding forest. He applied paint thickly, using dark colours. His habit of returning to his paintings to do further work on them makes dating particularly difficult.

From 1925 to 1961 he exhibited at the Salon d'Automne, where he became a member. From 1932 to 1955 he exhibited at the Salon des Tuileries, and from 1942 to 1945 at the Petit Palais Museum for Prisoners of War and Deportees. A retrospective of his work was presented in 1961 at the museums of Bayeux and Caen, and then the following year at the Galerie Katia Granoff in Paris.

SIMON, Robert
French, 20th century.
Born 1928, in Mulhouse.
Painter, engraver.

Robert Simon was active in Mulhouse. He showed his work in collective exhibitions, including *De Bonnard à Baselitz - Dix Ans d'enrichissements du cabinet des estampes 1978-1988* (*From Bonnard to Baselitz: A Decade of Acquisitions by the Prints Collection 1978-1988*) at the Bibliothèque Nationale in Paris in 1992.

MUSEUMS AND GALLERIES:
PARIS (BNF, Prints Collection): *Winter Sun* (1979, aquatint and dry-point).

SIMON, Romanus
German, 17th century.
Born 1678, in Leipzig; died 10 March 1709, in Leipzig.
Painter.

Simon became a burgher of Leipzig in 1705.

SIMON, Simon
French, 18th century.
Born 1759, in Paris; died 20 November 1807, in Paris.
Engraver (burin).

Simon Simon was a pupil of F. A. David. He engraved illustrations for an edition of La Fontaine's *Fables*.

SIMON, Susana
German, 20th century.
Born 30 September 1913, in Berlin.
Active from 1955 in France.
Painter. Landscapes.

Susana Simon studied painting under Manuel Angeles Ortiz while living in Buenos Aires in 1943. After the war, she moved to Zurich and, subsequently, to Paris. Her work has featured in solo exhibitions in Buenos Aires, Amsterdam, Copenhagen, The Hague, Düsseldorf, Hamburg, London, Paris (notably at the German Cultural Centre in 1977) and Zurich.

Simon's landscapes are painted with rapid and sweeping brushstrokes and exhibit a notational spontaneity that recalls certain forms of Expressionism. As of the 1970s, she was drawn increasingly towards fantasy. She is also noted for her illustrations of the German writer Novalis.

SIMON, Tavik Frantisek
Czech, 20th century.
Born 13 May 1877, in Zeleznice, near Jicin; died 19 December 1942, in Prague.
Painter, watercolourist, engraver. Landscapes, urban landscapes, seascapes.
Mánes Group.

Tavik Frantisek Simon studied at Prague academy and was chairman of the Mánes group. From 1904 to 1912 he lived in Paris, where he rendered familiar scenes with great freshness of vision, such as *Luxemboug Gardens, Boulevard St-Martin in the Snow.* He was also adept at a variety of engraving techniques: aquatint, soft-ground, mezzotint and woodcut. In 1912 he returned to Czechoslovakia. In 1926-1928 he went around the world, and the prints and paintings he produced after returning were shown in an important exhibition in Prague to mark his 50th birthday. In 1928 he was appointed professor of the school of graphic arts at the Prague academy.

Stamp of sale

MUSEUMS AND GALLERIES:
PARIS (MAM) - PRAGUE (Národní Gal.).

AUCTION RECORDS:
LONDON, 25 March 1987, *Beach Scene* (oil on canvas, 29 1/2 x 30 ins / 75 x 76 cm) GBP 27,000. PARIS, 22 Nov 1990, *Beach Scene* (oil on canvas) FRF 39,000. LE TOUQUET, 19 May 1991, *Bathing in the Sea* (oil on canvas, 35 1/2 x 39 1/4 ins / 90 x 100 cm) FRF 20,000. LONDON, 21 June 1991, *Luxembourg Gardens, Paris* (oil on canvas, 26 3/4 x 28 3/4 ins / 68 x 73 cm) GBP 5,280. LONDON, 4 Oct 1991, *Onival beach* (1904, oil on canvas, 18 x 21 1/2 ins / 45.7 x 54.6 cm) GBP 5,500. LONDON, 2 Oct 1992, *View of Dubrovnik* (oil on canvas, 21 1/2 x 29 ins / 54.5 x 73.5 cm) GBP 2,750. NEW YORK, 16 Feb 1993, *Barges in Winter* (oil on canvas, 21 1/4 x 29 1/4 ins / 54.2 x 74.3 cm) USD 2,420. LONDON, 11 Oct 1995, *Greek Ruins on Mediterranean Coast* (1938, oil on canvas, 39 x 31 ins / 99 x 79 cm) GBP 1,955. PRAGUE, 22 May 1999, *Buddhist Temple in Candy, Ceylon* (oil on canvas, 47 x 37 ins / 120 x 95 cm) CZK 380,000. PRAGUE, 20 Nov 1999, *Venetian Shadows* (1903, oil on canvas, 33 x 41 ins / 85 x 105 cm) CZK 250,000. PRAGUE, 18 Nov 2000, *Stairways of Kancy Church, Ceylon* (oil on canvas, 100 x 86 ins / 254 x 218 cm) CZK 380,000. PRAGUE, 18 Nov 2000, *Seashore in France in Summer* (1904, oil on canvas, 158 x 174 ins / 401 x 442 cm) CZK 550,000. PRAGUE, 19 May 2001, *On a Beach* (1916, oil on canvas, 33 x 35 ins / 84 x 90 cm) CZK 120,000. PRAGUE, 17 Nov 2001, *Sleighing on Letna* (oil on canvas, 24 x 29 ins / 60 x 73 cm) CZK 110,000. ZURICH, 26 March 2004, *Sailing Boats - Southern France* (oil on panel, 11 x 16 ins / 28 x 40 cm) CHF 2,800.

SIMON, Thomas, or Symons or Symonds
British, 17th century.
Born 1618, in London; died 1665, in London, of plague.
Draughtsman, engraver, medallist, cameo engraver.
Portraits, animals. Armorials, seals.

Thomas Simon was noted as one of the most skilful engravers of seals and coats of arms in England. He also cut cameos. Simon was a prolific artist under Charles II.

AUCTION RECORDS:
LONDON, 14 July 1987, *Portraits, Figures and Studies of Animals* (pencil or chalk, book of 70 drawings, each 7 3/4 x 5 3/4 ins / 20 x 14.5 cm) GBP 24,000.

SIMON, Wilhelm Te. See **TE SIMON**

SIMON, Wladislaw
Polish, 19th century.
Born 25 January 1816, in Posen (now Poznan); died 30 June 1899, in Posen.
Painter.

Wladislaw Simon studied at the Akademie der Bildenden Künste in Vienna under J. Führich. He painted religious subjects.

SIMON, Yannick
French, 20th century.
Engraver.

In 1992, Yannick Simon's work featured in SAGA (Salon d'Arts Graphiques Actuels) in Paris, presented by the Galerie Metropolis.

SIMON, Yohanan
German, 20th century.
Born 1905, in Berlin; died 1976.
Active in Israel.
Painter. Genre scenes, scenes with figures.

Yohanan Simon studied initially in Berlin and Munich before working with Max Beckmann in Frankfurt and finally moving to Paris, where he lived from 1928 to 1936. In 1934, in the course of a visit to New York, he met and worked alongside Diego Rivera. Simon then emigrated to Israel, where he worked on a kibbutz, painting scenes from everyday life. His work became progressively abstract in his later years.

BIBLIOGRAPHY:
Kampf, Avram, *Chagall to Kitaj: Jewish Experience in 20th Century Art*, Barbican Art Gall., London, 1990.

AUCTION RECORDS:
TEL AVIV, 2 Jan 1989, *Kibbutz* (oil on canvas, 13 1/4 x 10 ins / 33.5 x 24.5 cm) USD 3,960. TEL AVIV, 3 Jan 1990, *Folk Dancing in a Kibbutz* (oil on card, 7 3/4 x 9 3/4 ins / 19.5 x 25 cm) USD 7,920. TEL AVIV, 19 June 1990, *Landscape with Figures at Ma'agan Michael* (1952, oil on canvas, 19 3/4 x 25 1/2 ins / 50 x 64.5 cm) USD 19,250. TEL AVIV, 1 Jan 1991, *Kibbutz with Figures* (1959, oil on canvas, 9 3/4 x 23 3/4 ins / 25 x 60.5 cm) USD 12,100. TEL AVIV, 12 June 1991, *Interior with Woman near a*

Window (1959, oil on canvas, 15 3/4 x 19 3/4 ins / 40 x 50 cm) USD 4,620; *Steelworkers* (1972, oil on canvas, 24 x 28 3/4 ins / 61 x 73 cm) USD 8,250. TEL AVIV, 26 Sept 1991, *Kibbutz Pioneers* (oil on canvas, 21 x 31 1/4 ins / 53.5 x 79.5 cm) USD 8,800. TEL AVIV, 6 Jan 1992, *Landscape with Figures* (1960, oil on canvas, 23 3/4 x 29 ins / 60.5 x 73.5 cm) USD 11,000. TEL AVIV, 14 April 1993, *Composition in Red* (1963, oil on canvas, 28 3/4 x 39 1/4 ins / 73 x 100 cm) USD 13,800. TEL AVIV, 30 June 1994, *Fields at Ma'agan Michael* (1952, oil on canvas, 19 3/4 x 25 1/2 ins / 50 x 64.5 cm) USD 24,150. TEL AVIV, 27 Sept 1994, *Gan Shmuel Kibbutz* (1952, oil on canvas, 25 1/2 x 32 ins / 65 x 81 cm) USD 29,900. TEL AVIV, 12 Oct 1995, *Cliffs in the Negev* (1961, oil on canvas, 28 1/4 x 39 1/2 ins / 72 x 100.5 cm) USD 9,200. TEL AVIV, 14 Jan 1996, *Orchard Workers in a Kibbutz* (1951, oil on canvas, 35 3/4 x 25 1/2 ins / 91 x 65 cm) USD 29,850. TEL AVIV, 30 Sept 1996, *Kibbutz Life* (1943, oil on canvas, 17 x 24 ins / 43.1 x 61 cm) USD 24,150. TEL AVIV, 7 Oct 1996, *Six Days' War* (1967, oil on canvas, 77 1/4 x 46 ins / 196 x 116 cm) USD 18,400. NEW YORK, 10 Oct 1996, *Vegetal Totem* (1972, oil/masonite, 20 x 13 ins / 50.8 x 33 cm) USD 3,162. TEL AVIV, 12 Jan 1997, *Still-life: Interior and Exterior* (1965, oil and mixed media/paper, 14 1/4 x 21 ins / 36.5 x 52.5 cm) USD 8,740; *Figures in a Kibbutz* (1946, gouache, 10 3/4 x 13 1/2 ins / 27.5 x 34 cm) USD 6,900; *Landscape with Red Sun* (1961, mixed media/panel, 15 1/4 x 19 1/4 ins / 38.5 x 49 cm) USD 2,645; *Sea View, Haifa* (1946, gouache and watercolour, 6 x 11 1/2 ins / 15 x 29.5 cm) USD 3,680. TEL AVIV, 26 April 1997, *Gazelle* (1962, oil on canvas, 59 1/4 x 31 3/4 ins / 150.5 x 80.5 cm) USD 7,475. TEL AVIV, 23 Oct 1997, *Landscape* (1962, oil on canvas, 28 x 35 3/4 ins / 71 x 91 cm) USD 17,825.

SIMON DA CORBETTA. See **SIMONE DA CORBETTA**

SIMON DA RAGUSA. See **RAGUSA Simon da**

SIMON DE BAR, or Bari
French, 15th - 16th century.
Born towards the end of the 15th century, in Bar-le-Duc ou Bar-sur-Aube.
Painter, sculptor.

Simon de Bar worked in the Louvre in 1532.

SIMON DE CHÄLONS, or Châlon or Chalon, pseudonym of Simon de Mailly or Malhy
French, 16th century.
Born in Châlons-sur-Marne.
Active in Avignon from 1535 until after 1585.
Painter. Religious subjects.
Avignon School.

Simon de Chälons went to live in Avignon in 1535 and was there a pupil of the Avignon painter Henri Guigo or Guigonis. Simon seems to have produced a considerable number of works during his long life. In 1563 he painted in the church of St Pierre, in addition to several paintings, large grisaille compositions, depicting on one side the 12 Sibyls and on the other the 12 apostles. These paintings were removed in the 18th century to make way for the works of Pierre and Étienne Parrocel. Also among his works are a *Conversion of St Paul* in the Chapelle des Pénitents Gris; two canvases in the sacristy of St-Agricola; a *Nativity* in the church of St Pierre; and *Pentecost* and *The Crowning with Thorns* in St Didier. The refectory of the Great Seminary and the church in Baux, near Le Bedouin, also possess works by him. The Hospice Museum of Villeneuve-lès-Avignon, already the owner of Enguerrand Quarton's *Coronation of the Virgin*, has also an *Entombment* by Simon de Châlon, painted on wood. This picture originally ornamented the funeral chapel of Pierre de Montignac, Cardinal of Pampelune, in the Charterhouse of Villeneuve-lès-Avignon, and is dated 1552. The chapel also houses portraits of Pope Innocent VI and his nephew Pierre de Montignac.

MUSEUMS AND GALLERIES:
AVIGNON: *The Child Jesus Playing with Other Children; Adoration of the Shepherds* (1548); *Descent from the Cross* - PARIS (Louvre): *Doubting Thomas* - ROME (Mus. e Gal. Borghese): *Mourning Madonna; Ecce Homo* - TOULOUSE: *The Evangelists* - VILLENEUVE-LÈS-AVIGNON: *Descent from the Cross; Entombment.*

SIMON DE GURREA. See **GURREA Simon de**

SIMON DE LENN. See **SIMON, called Simon the Glassmaker**

SIMON DE MAILLY. See **SIMON DE CHÄLONS**

SIMON DE NEUFCHASTEL, called Simon l'enlumineur
French, 15th century.
Active in Troyes from 1419 to 1429.
Painter, illuminator.

Simon de Neufchastel painted two cartoons for the tapestries of the church of Ste-Madeleine, Troyes.

SIMON DE PARIS. See **SIMON Mayer** or **Jacob Mayer**

SIMON DE SAN JOSE. See **SAN JOSE Simon de**

SIMON DE SANTIAGO. See **SANTIAGO**

SIMON DE SIENNE. See **MARTINI Simone**

SIMON DE TROYES
French, 15th century.
Born in Troyes; died 1450.
Miniaturist.

From 1422 Simon de Troyes worked for the church of St-Pierre, Troyes.

SIMON OF ST ALBANS
British, 13th century.
Died before 1250.
Painter.

Brother and pupil of Walter of Colchester, he worked in the monastery of St Albans.

SIMON OF WELLS
British, 13th century.
Sculptor (marble).

From 1256 to 1257 Simon sculpted in Westminster Abbey the tomb of Princess Catherine, daughter of Henry VIII.

SIMON PORTUGALOIS. See **PORTUGALOIS Simon**

SIMON VON AMSTERDAM. See **KIES Symon Jansz.**

SIMON VON ASCHAFFENBURG, or Franck, called the Pseudo-Grünewald
German, 16th century.
Painter.

Simon von Aschaffenburg worked in Hall and Aschaffenburg from 1526 to 1549 and was Grünewald's successor at the court of Cardinal Albrecht. A number of paintings of the Cranach School are attributed to him.

SIMON VON GNICHWITZ, or Gnechwicz
German, 14th century.
Active in the second half of the 14th century.
Painter.

Simon von Gnichwitz worked in Breslau (now Wroclaw) for the Diocesan Cathedral.

SIMON VON TAISTEN, or Tästen or Tastenz
Austrian, 15th - 16th century.
Born c. 1460, probably in Taisten (Tyrol); died c. 1530.
Painter.

Simon von Taisten painted frescoes in several churches in the Pustertal Valley (Tyrol). The Ferdinandeum of Innsbruck owns four panels by him from a high altar in Brixen.

Museums and Galleries:
Innsbruck (Tiroler Landesmus. Ferdinandeum): four panels from a high altar in Brixen (Bressanone) - Lienz (Schloss Bruck): altar painting; *Tod Mariens with the Founders Leonhard of Görz and Paola of Gonzaga* (fresco).

SIMON-AUGUSTE, Simon
French, 20th century.
Born 20 April 1909, in Marseilles; died May 1987, in the Roanne region (the Loire Valley).
Painter. Figures, nudes, portraits, scenes with figures, still-lifes.

Simon Simon-Auguste was the son of a cabinetmaker, and began work at the age of twelve in a ceramics factory. In the evenings he studied drawing at the École des Beaux-Arts in Marseilles. He settled in Paris in 1939.

In Paris he showed work at various salons, including the Salon d'Automne and the Salon des Peintres Témoins de leur Temps. He was selected for the exhibition for the first Othon Friesz Prize.

His output was small, as he used a painstaking technique involving the application of successive layers of paint topped with glaze, best suited to human subjects in various poses. His intimate style was particularly appropriate for portraits, the best known of which is *Paul Léautaud*, dated 1956.

Simon-Auguste

Museums and Galleries:
Marseilles (MBA) - Paris (MNAM-CCI) - Paris (Mus. Carnavalet): *Paul Léautaud* (1956) - Sceaux (Mus. de l'Île-de-France).

Auction records:
Versailles, 2 March 1980, *Still-life with Oil Lamp* (oil on panel, 28 3/4 x 45 ins / 73 x 114 cm) FRF 7,000. Zurich, 14 May 1983, *Nude on Blue Divan* (oil on canvas, 9 1/2 x 22 ins / 24 x 55 cm) CHF 3,000. Versailles, 20 March 1988, *Summer in the Garden* (oil on canvas, 22 x 18 ins / 55 x 46 cm) FRF 9,000. Paris, 18 April 1988, *Seated Nude* (oil on canvas, 46 x 35 1/4 ins / 116 x 89.5 cm) FRF 30,000. Paris, 23 June 1988, *The Ball* (oil on canvas, 51 1/4 x 38 1/4 ins / 130 x 97 cm) FRF 40,000. Versailles, 6 Nov 1988, *Child with Cat* (gouache, 12 1/2 x 19 1/4 ins / 32 x 49 cm) FRF 5,500. Paris, 10 April 1989, *Child with Cat* (1909, oil on canvas, 16 1/2 x 25 1/4 ins / 42 x 64 cm) FRF 12,000. Versailles, 22 April 1990, *Nude in Armchair* (graphite and ball-point pen, 19 1/4 x 13 1/2 ins / 49 x 34 cm) FRF 5,800. Versailles, 21 Oct 1990, *At the Beach* (oil on canvas, 11 x 9 ins / 27 x 22 cm) FRF 4,800. Versailles, 9 Dec 1990, *Reading in the Arbour* (oil on canvas, 11 x 9 ins / 27 x 22 cm) FRF 7,300. Calais, 20 Oct 1991, *Still-life with Blue Pitcher* (oil on canvas, 5 1/2 x 16 1/2 ins / 14 x 42 cm) FRF 7,000. Paris, 15 April 1992, *Seated Woman with Blue Headscarf* (oil on canvas, 22 x 13 ins / 55 x 33 cm) FRF 8,000. Paris, 10 June 1992, *Waiting Model* (oil on panel, 12 1/2 x 15 3/4 ins / 32 x 40 cm) FRF 6,000. Calais, 5 July 1992, *Nude in Studio* (oil on canvas, 63 3/4 x 51 1/4 ins / 162 x 130 cm) FRF 22,000. Le Touquet, 14 Nov 1993, *Child* (oil on canvas, 16 1/2 x 5 1/2 ins / 42 x 14 cm) FRF 6,000. Paris, 6 Dec 1993, *Tea Dance* (oil on canvas, 22 x 18 ins / 55 x 46 cm) FRF 8,500. Paris, 20 Nov 1994, *Nude on Divan* (oil on canvas, 51 1/4 x 63 3/4 ins / 130 x 162 cm) FRF 22,000. Paris, 28 March 1996, *Little Girl Drawing* (oil on canvas, 13 x 22 ins / 33 x 55 cm) FRF 7,000.

SIMON-BELLE, Alexis. See **BELLE Alexis Simon**

SIMON-LÉVY
French, 20th century.
Born 29 May 1886, in Strasbourg; died 19 January 1973, in Paris.
Painter, draughtsman. Portraits, landscapes, still-lifes.

Simon-Lévy exhibited in Paris at the Salon des Indépendants, the Salon d'Automne and the Salon des Tuileries.

Museums and Galleries:
Paris (MAM): *Still-life; Roofs* - Strasbourg: *Portrait of the Artist's Father; Beggar.*

Auction records:
Paris, 12 Dec 1946, *Portrait of a Woman,* FRF 6,000. Paris, 24 Nov 1949, *Woman* (pen drawing) FRF 600.

SIMON-REIMS, Jacques Paul
French, 20th century.
Born 10 March 1890, in Rheims.
Painter. Designs for stained glass.

Jacques Paul Simon-Reims was the son of Pierre Paul Simon, who also taught him. In Paris, he exhibited at the Salon des Artistes Français, of which he was a member. In 1920, he was awarded a commendation and made a member of the Légion d'Honneur.

SIMONAU, François, or Simoneau, called the Flemish Murillo
Belgian, 19th century.
Born 1783, in Bornhem; died August 1859, in London. Active in England from 1815.
Painter, lithographer. Figures, portraits, genre scenes.

François Simonau was a pupil of Bernard Friex in Bruges, then of Baron Gros in Paris. In 1815 he set up in London, where he was quickly successful. He exhibited at the Royal Academy in London, and his works were shown at the British Institution from 1818 to 1860.

Simonau painted portraits, but, like all the Belgian artists of the time, he also specialised in lithography, at that time scarcely discovered.

Museums and Galleries:
Brussels (MBA): *Portrait of a Man; Woman Playing the Organ.*

SIMONAU, Gustave Adolphe, or Simoneau
Belgian, 19th century.
Born 10 June 1810, in Bruges; died 10 July 1870, in Brussels.
Painter, watercolourist, lithographer. Landscapes, urban landscapes, architectural views.

Gustave Adolphe Simonau was the nephew of François Simonau. His father was a lithographer in London, but in 1829 Gustave Simonau set up in Brussels. He exhibited in London at the New Water-Colour Society from 1859 to 1870.

Simonau soon abandoned oil painting in favour of watercolour. He painted mainly townscapes and topographical subjects. He lithographed the *Principal Monuments of Europe*, a work which brought him honour.

Museums and Galleries:
Brussels: *View of Brussels; View of Oberstein.*

Auction records:
Paris, 1895, *Banks of the Moselle* (watercolour) FRF 100; *Banks of the Moselle* (watercolour) FRF 220; *Orléans Cathedral* (watercolour) FRF 80. Amsterdam, 2 May 1990, *Village Street with Figures* (1870, watercolour/paper, 28 1/4 x 20 1/2 ins / 72 x 52 cm) NLG 6,900.

SIMONCINI, Francesco. See **SIMONINI**

SIMONCINI, Salvatore
Italian, 19th century.
Born in Palermo.
Painter. Genre scenes, landscapes.

Simoncini took part in all the major Italian salons.

SIMOND, Philippe
French, 18th century.

Active in Paris.
Sculptor.
Philippe Simond exhibited three busts at the 1791 Salon.

SIMONDI, Bernardino
Italian, 15th century.
Born in Venasca (Piedmont); died probably c. 1497 or 1498, in Marseilles.
Painter.
Charles Sterling has shown that Simondi collaborated with Josse Lieferinxe on an altarpiece commissioned by the Priors of the Confraternity of Notre-Dame des Accoules near Marseilles. This piece, made up of seven panels, was for a long time attributed to a certain Master of St Sebastian.

SIMONDS, Charles
American, 20th century.
Born 14 November 1945, in New York.
Sculptor, performance artist. Figures, architectural views.
Charles Simonds studied at the University of California, Berkeley, and then at Rutgers University, New Brunswick, New Jersey. In 1969, he settled in New York and shared a workshop with Gordon Matta Clark. From 1969 to 1971, he taught at Kean College, New Jersey, in Virginia and at Cooper Union, New York. In 1977, he was awarded a DAAD (Deutscher Akadamischen Austauschdienstes) scholarship and spent a year in Berlin. In *Birth*, in 1970, Simonds filmed himself in a quarry, emerging completely, headfirst, followed by the rest of his body, from the clay, the soft, pliable material from which the first man was created. Symbolising man's tie to mother earth, this short film was a forerunner of later work, work that moulds itself and in which humanity and matter are inextricably linked. The following year, he physically revived this act of fusion by building a landscape and a town on his own body, merging himself with the earth. Since then, Simonds has continued building in breaks in walls, abandoned buildings and gutters in deprived areas of cities like New York, Paris and Genoa before a public which had little experience of art, rather than in galleries and museums. He portrayed an imaginary group of nomads in *Little People*, which travelled the world tirelessly creating miniature living areas, *Dwellings*, consisting of dwellings, places for relaxation or worship often arranged over several levels against a cliff. They are made of natural materials, mainly clay, in various colours - red, grey or yellow, for example - together with sand, stones and sometimes seeds that germinate, as in *Growth House*, 1975. Governed by the symbolic forms of the circle, spiral and the labyrinth, these places, created in great detail using miniature bricks assembled with the aid of pliers, were influenced by the Indian buildings of New Mexico and also the ancient world and mythology. Abandoned after construction, they slowly disappear and only the films remain. At the same time, with *Objects*, in 1978, independent sculptures on plinths, Simonds began extracting forms reminiscent of organs of the body, especially sexual organs, from the series *Dwellings*. In the 1980s his towns lost their frozen nature and were animated and tended to be contorted and in a state of collapse. Organic and anthropomorphic forms, especially heads, suddenly appear from the architectural components. A deformed and mistreated face, especially that of his father, becomes the subject of a series called *Smears*, Expressionist works in clay made on a flat surface out of which bulge the distorted lines of a face. Meanwhile, the scale changed in favour of the monumental, as in *Refuge*, in Seoul, which forces the viewer to look twice at disturbing places and figures. Simonds presents an unstable, changing world, which works by analogy from man to nature and from nature to man. Over the years his works have become more complex, metamorphosing places where the components merge with one another but a fantasy or baroque dimension is not ruled out. He also made a sculpture for a Manhattan playground.

He began showing his work in the streets of New York in the early 1970s. His numerous collective exhibitions include: Paris Biennale, 1973 and 1975; Biennale of the Whitney Museum of American Art, New York, 1974 and 1977; Hayden Gallery, MIT, Boston, 1974; Art Institute of Chicago and PS 1 New York, 1975; Venice Biennale, 1976; Museum of Modern Art, New York, 1976; Documenta, Kassel, 1977; Stedelijk Museum, Amsterdam, 1978; *Les Années 70: l'art en cause* (*The 1970s: Art in Question*), CAPC-musée d'Art contemporain, Bordeaux 2002.

Solo exhibitions include: Centre National d'Art Contemporain de Paris, 1975; Albright-Knox Art Gallery, Buffalo, 1977; Westfälischer Kunstverein, Münster, 1978; Ludwig Museum, Cologne and Nationalgalerie, Berlin, Musée de l'Abbaye Ste-Croix des Sables d'Olonne, 1979; first travelling retrospective organised at the Museum of Contemporary Art, Chicago, 1981; Galerie Maeght-Lelong, Paris, 1986; Corcoran Gallery of Art, Washington, 1987; Fondation La Caixa, Barcelona and Galerie Nationale de Jeu de Paume, Paris, 1994; Institut Valencià d'Art Modern, Valencia, 2003; *Charles Simonds, Dwellings*, Musée Les Abattoirs, Toulouse.

BIBLIOGRAPHY:
Charles Simonds, exhibition catalogue, Buffalo Fine Arts Academy, Buffalo (NY), 1977. Lascault, Gilbert, '*Simonds*' in *coll. Repères. Cahiers d'art contemporain* n° 31, Gal. Lelong, Paris, 1986. *Simonds*, exhibition catalogue, Gal. nationale du Jeu de Paume, Paris, 1994-1995. Anfam, David, et al., *Charles Simonds*, exhibition catalogue, Institut Valencià d'Art Modern, Valencia, 2003.

MUSEUMS AND GALLERIES:
BUFFALO (Albright-Knox AG): *Number II (Ritual Furnace)* (1978, clay on a wooden base) - PARIS (MNAM-CCI): *Abandonned Observatory* (1975).

AUCTION RECORDS:
NEW YORK, 5 Oct 1990, *Untitled* (clay, sticks and stones, 12 3/4 x 29 3/4 x 29 3/4 ins / 32.4 x 75.5 x 75.5 cm) USD 10,450.

SIMONDS, George
British, 19th century.
Born 1844 (?), in England.
Sculptor. Mythological subjects, allegorical subjects, figures. Statuettes, busts.
George Simonds exhibited at the Royal Academy from 1866.
MUSEUMS AND GALLERIES:
READING: *Dionysus Riding on a Leopard* (sculpture); *Divine Wisdom* (statuette); *Marble Bust of C.T. Murdoch.*

SIMONE (Fra)
Italian, 14th century.
Painter.
Fra Simone was active in Bologna in the mid-14th century. He restored the altar of St James in the church of S Domenico in c. 1350.

SIMONE
Italian, 16th century.
Born near Lake Como.
Sculptor.
Active between 1519 and 1565, Simone made some pieces for the church at Pellizzano.

SIMONE
Italian, 16th century.
Painter.
Simone executed some altarpieces for the altars in the church of S Leonardo in Baselga di Supramonte.

SIMONE, pseudonym of Toussaint, Simone
Belgian, 20th century.
Born 1940, in Remouchamps.

Painter, draughtsman, engraver. Figures, scenes with figures.

Simone Toussaint studied at the fine arts academy in Namur, and went on to teach. Her own work is vividly coloured and strident, focusing principally on human emotions such as joy or despair.

SIMONE, Antonino or Antonio de

Italian, 17th century.

Sculptor (wood).

Antonino Simone was active in Naples, where he executed sculptures in churches and the cathedral.

SIMONE, Antonio de

Italian, 19th century.

Painter (including gouache). Seascapes, harbour scenes.

Simone was active between 1860 and 1900. He specialised in painting boats and ships, on their own merits rather than for the surrounding sea and Bay of Naples. He can be confused with Tomaso de Simone.

AUCTION RECORDS:

ROME, 25 May 1988, *Steamship in the Port of Naples* (gouache, 16 1/4 x 25 1/4 ins / 41 x 64 cm) ITL 1,800,000. LONDON, 5 Oct 1989, *The Schooner Pilgrim in the Bay of Naples* (1863, oil on canvas, a pair, each 18 x 26 ins / 46 x 66 cm) GBP 4,400. LONDON, 18 Oct 1990, *The Steamer Miranda* (1912, gouache, 18 x 27 ins / 46 x 68.5 cm) GBP 1,980. LONDON, 22 Nov 1991, *The Three-Master Chevy Chase in the Bay of Naples* (gouache, 18 x 24 1/4 ins / 45.7 x 61.5 cm) GBP 1,210. LONDON, 16 July 1993, *The Steamship Jenny Otto in the Bay of Naples* (1879, oil on canvas, 23 x 36 ins / 58.5 x 91.5 cm) GBP 4,025. LONDON, 11 May 1994, *A Steam Yacht in the Bay of Naples* (oil on canvas, 14 x 24 ins / 35.5 x 61 cm) GBP 1,495. LONDON, 3 May 1995, *Warship in the Port of Valetta, Malta* (oil on canvas, 18 x 25 1/2 ins / 45.5 x 65 cm) GBP 3,220.

SIMONE, Antonio di

Italian, 17th - 18th century.

Died 1727.

Painter. Battles, landscapes.

Antonio di Simone was active in Naples about 1656. He is not to be confused with his namesake, the pupil of Luca Giordano.

Apart from his paintings of battles and his landscapes, he occasionally painted figures in some of Niccolo Massaro's pictures.

SIMONE, Battista de

Italian, 17th century.

Sculptor. Religious subjects.

Battista de Simone executed woodcarvings for the churches of S Maria della Sapienza and S Antonio a Posillipo in Naples about 1650.

SIMONE, Battista de. See also **BATTISTA DI SIMONE**

SIMONE, Battista di

Italian, 16th century.

Sculptor. Statues.

Active around 1550, Battista di Simone was commissioned to carve a wooden statue of *St Christopher* for the church dedicated to that saint in Palermo.

SIMONE, Carlo de

Italian, 19th century.

Active in Naples in the middle of the 19th century.

Painter (porcelain/majolica).

The son of Michele de Simone, Carlo de Simone worked at the cathedral of Castelli in 1848.

SIMONE, Francesco de

Italian, 19th century.

Active at the beginning of the 19th century.

Modeller (porcelain).

Francesco de Simone was working at the Capodimonte porcelain factory in Naples in 1803.

SIMONE, Giovanni. See **SIMON Jan de**

SIMONE, Giuseppe de

Italian, 19th century.

Born 1841, in Naples.

Painter. Interiors, architectural views.

MUSEUMS AND GALLERIES:

NAPLES (Gal. dell'Accademia di Belle Arti): *View of the Brancaccio Chapel in the Church of S Angelo a Nilo in Naples.*

SIMONE, Jacovo or Giovanni Jacovo

Italian, 17th century.

Active in Naples during the first half of the 17th century.

Sculptor (wood).

Jacovo or Giovanni Jacovo Simone worked for the church of the Gerolomini family in Naples in 1627.

SIMONE, Juan Baptista. See **SIMO**

SIMONE, Luigi de

Italian, 19th century.

Active at the beginning of the 19th century.

Modeller.

Luigi de Simone worked at the Capodimonte porcelain factory in Naples. He made statuettes of the royal family.

SIMONE, Maria Luisa

Italian, 20th century.

Born 4 July 1938, in Pavia.

Painter. Figures, landscapes, still-lifes.

Maria Luisa Simone studied painting in Venice and obtained a diploma in poster-making at the Scuola Superiore d'Arte Applicata in Milan. She exhibited work in Milan, at the Galleria Cortina in 1968 and the Galleria Diacron in 1971, and held solo exhibitions in Germany and Poland. In 1993, she participated in an exhibition on the themes of still-life painting, *Pittura come Realtà* (*Painting as Reality*), held at the Galleria della Corte in Vignola. Some of her landscapes and paintings of figures show the influence of her travels in Africa.

SIMONE, Michele de

Italian, 19th century.

Miniaturist.

The father of Carlo de Simone, Michele de Simone worked at the Capodimonte porcelain factory in Naples in the first half of the 19th century.

SIMONE, Michele de

Italian, 20th century.

Born 1893, in Barletta; died 1955, in Milan.

Painter. Landscapes, seascapes.

AUCTION RECORDS:

MILAN, 6 Dec 1989, *Walking on the Seafront in Naples* (oil on panel, 5 1/2 x 7 1/4 ins / 14 x 18.5 cm) ITL 1,800,000. ROME, 14 Nov 1991, *Walking on the Seafront* (oil/plywood, 5 1/4 x 7 1/2 ins / 13.5 x 19 cm) ITL 1,840,000. MILAN, 31 May 1999, *Isola Comacina* (oil on panel, 15 x 17 ins / 37 x 42 cm) ITL 6,100,000.

SIMONE, Nicolo da

Italian, 17th century.

Painter. Mythological subjects, religious subjects.

Nicolo da Simone was active in Naples from 1636 to 1677. He belongs to the school of Massimo Stanzioni.

MUSEUMS AND GALLERIES:

NAPLES: *Martyr*; *St Catherine* - ROTTERDAM (Mus. Boijmans Van Beuningen): *St Ursula.*

AUCTION RECORDS:

MILAN, 4 April 1989, *Bacchanale* (oil on canvas, two pendants, each 24 3/4 x 42 1/2 ins / 63 x 108 cm) ITL 55,000,000. ROME, 19 Nov 1990, *Martyrdom of S Gennaro with the Bay of Naples in the Background* (oil on canvas, 45 x 61 ins / 114 x

154 cm) ITL 34,500,000. ROME, 22 Nov 1994, *Half-length Portrait of a Warrior* (oil on canvas, 24 x 19 3/4 ins / 61 x 50 cm) ITL 13,225,000. LONDON, 14 Dec 2001, *Creation of the Golden Calf* (oil on canvas, 68 x 89 ins / 172 x 227 cm) GBP 8,000. ROME, 18 June 2003, *Solomon Adoring the Idols* (oil on canvas, 69 x 93 ins / 174 x 237 cm) EUR 40,000.

SIMONE, Salvatore de
Italian, 19th century.
Born in Naples.
Sculptor. Statues, busts, monuments.

Salvatore de Simone was a pupil of Morelli, Palizzi and Ceparulo.

AUCTION RECORDS:
MONTREAL, 23-24 Nov 1993, *Bust of a Woman* (bronze, h. 18 ins / 45.6 cm) CAD 1,800.

SIMONE, Tomaso de
Italian, 19th - 20th century.
Born 1851; died 1907.
Painter (gouache). Seascapes.

Working between Naples and Malta, Tomaso de Simone specialised in painting ships and boats. He may be the same person as Antonio de Simone.

AUCTION RECORDS:
LONDON, 17 March 1989, *The Steamer Iolaine* (gouache, 16 x 24 1/2 ins / 40.5 x 62 cm) GBP 935. LONDON, 31 May 1989, *The Royal Oak of her Majesty's Fleet off Malta* (1871, oil on canvas, 20 x 30 1/2 ins / 51 x 77.5 cm) GBP 1,650. LONDON, 27 Sept 1989, *Schooner in the Bay of Naples* (1870, oil on canvas, 17 3/4 x 26 3/4 ins / 45 x 68 cm) GBP 1,210. LONDON, 18 Oct 1990, *Ketch in the Bay of Naples; Ketch by Moonlight* (1862, oil on canvas, a pair, each 18 x 26 ins / 46 x 66 cm) GBP 5,500. PARIS, 6 Dec 1990, *The Steam Yacht Namouna in the Bay of Naples* (gouache, 17 x 26 ins / 43 x 66 cm) FRF 26,000. LONDON, 20 Jan 1993, *The Three-Master John Williamson Leaving the Bay of Naples* (1871, oil on canvas, 20 x 30 ins / 51 x 76 cm) GBP 2,760. NEW YORK, 4 June 1993, *The Revenge off Naples* (1862, oil on canvas, 18 x 26 ins / 45.7 x 66 cm) USD 8,050. LONDON, 10 Feb 1995, *The Three-Master Exmouth in the Bay of Naples* (1861, oil on canvas, 10 1/2 x 157 1/4 ins / 26.5 x 399.5 cm) GBP 2,530. LONDON, 17 Aug 1999, *Schooner Lady Cipsey off Naples* (1999, gouache, 15 x 22 ins / 39 x 56 cm) GBP 1,500. LONDON, 11 Nov 1999, *Barque Tarsus approaching Naples* (1868, oil on canvas, 19 x 25 ins / 49 x 63 cm) GBP 3,800. LONDON, 11 May 2000, *Schooner of the Royal Thames Yacht Club at sea. Schooner of the Royal Thames Yacht Club in Heavy Swell* (1850, 1870, oil on canvas, a pair, 18 x 26 ins / 45 x 67 cm) GBP 5,500. LONDON, 11 May 2000, *Schooner Lying at Anchor in the Bay of Naples* (1864, oil on canvas, 18 x 26 ins / 46 x 66 cm) GBP 6,000. LONDON, 5 Sept 2001, *HMS Caesar at Anchor* (1858, oil on canvas, 14 x 20 ins / 35 x 52 cm) GBP 3,800. LONDON, 20 Nov 2001, *Ships from a British Squadron and Other Craft Underway in the Western Reaches of the Bay of Naples* (1862, oil on canvas, 14 x 20 ins / 35 x 52 cm) GBP 2,500. PORTSMOUTH, 17 Aug 2002, *The Susan Hinks, off Naples* (1869, oil on canvas, 22 x 32 ins / 56 x 81 cm) USD 9,500. PENZANCE, 17 Oct 2002, *Steam Assisted Threemaster at Anchor in the Bay of Naples* (1886, gouache, a pair, 12 x 17 ins / 30 x 43 cm) GBP 1,800. DOWNINGTON, 22 Feb 2003, *Portrait of the Steam Yacht Narada* (gouache, 16 x 24 ins / 41 x 61 cm) USD 2,750. LONDON, 12 June 2003, *Squadron of Ships of the Royal Navy's Mediterranean Fleet Lying in Naples Bay* (1886, oil on canvas, a pair, 10 x 26 ins / 26 x 66 cm) GBP 8,000. NEW YORK, 10 Feb 2004, *HMS Exmouth Signalling Her Arrival at Naples* (1862, oil on canvas, 19 x 26 ins / 47 x 66 cm) USD 24,000. LONDON, 17 Feb 2004, *Schooner Rigged Steam Yacht of the Royal Thames Yacht Club, Naples* (gouache, a pair, 15 x 21 ins / 37 x 53 cm) GBP 2,400.

SIMONE, Vincenzo de
Italian, 19th century.
Born 1845, in Naples.
Painter.

Vincenzo de Simone studied under Mancinelli at the Istituto di Belle Arti in Naples. He excelled at painting on pottery and produced some fine work based on imitations of 5th-century art. Unfortunately, his name was not mentioned in the many exhibitions mounted by the factories where he worked and in which his work appeared. He was, however, awarded a silver medal for his amphorae and dishes in the Antique style.

AUCTION RECORDS:
LONDON, 21 March 1980, *English Warship in the Bay of Naples* (1860, oil on canvas, 16 3/4 x 25 1/2 ins / 42.6 x 64.6 cm) GBP 1,700.

SIMONE ANDREA, called Simone Senese
Italian, 14th century.
Sculptor.

Simone Andrea was the son of a master sculptor of Siena, Simone. His work has in the past been confused with that of Andrea Pisano, also known as Andrea da Pontedera.

SIMONE CAMALDOLESE. See **SIMONE DA SIENA**

SIMONE D'ALEMAGNA
Italian, 14th century.
Painter. Religious subjects.

Simone d'Alemagna painted some altarpieces in Milan Cathedral in 1393.

SIMONE D'ANTONIO
Italian, 15th century.
Sculptor (stone/wood).

Simone d'Antonio was active in Siena between 1414 and 1418.

SIMONE D'ARGENTINA
Italian, 15th century.
Painter.

Active in Ferrara, in 1436 Simone d'Argentina painted a *St Jerome* that Antonio da Piacenza presented to Niccolò III d'Este in the same year.

SIMONE D'AVERARA. See **BASCHENIS Simone**

SIMONE DA BOLOGNA. See **SIMONE DEI CROCIFISSI**

SIMONE DA CALDAROLA. See **MAGISTRIS Simone de**

SIMONE DA CAMPIONE
Italian, 16th century.
Active in the middle of the 16th century.
Sculptor.

Simone da Campione carved the throne in the church of S Maria Maggiore in Spello (Umbria) in 1545.

SIMONE DA COLLE. See **COLLE Simone da**

SIMONE DA CORBETTA
Italian, 14th century.
Born in Corbetta (Lombardy).
Active at the end of the 14th century.
Painter.

MUSEUMS AND GALLERIES:
MILAN (Pinacoteca di Brera): *Virgin and Child* (fresco, very damaged).

SIMONE DA CUSIGHE
Italian, 14th - 15th century.
Died before 1416.
Painter. Religious subjects.

This painter was active in Cusighe near Belluno between 1382 and 1409.

MUSEUMS AND GALLERIES:

VENICE (Gal. dell'Accademia): *Virgin* (polyptych); *Eight Scenes from the Life of St Bartholomew* - VENICE (Mus. Civico): *Four Scenes from the Lives of Christ and the Virgin*.

AUCTION RECORDS:

NEW YORK, 22 Oct 1970, *St Anthony with Other Holy Figures*, USD 11,000. LONDON, 10 Dec 1980, *St Anthony with Other Holy Figures* (oil on panel, 27 1/2 x 77 3/4 ins / 69.8 x 197.5 cm) GBP 22,000.

SIMONE DA FIRENZE, called Carigi
Italian, 15th century.
Florentine, active in Pistoia from 1468 to 1470.
Sculptor.

SIMONE DA FIRENZE
Italian, 16th century.
Active in Bologna in 1525.
Sculptor.

SIMONE DA PESARO. See **CANTARINI Simone**

SIMONE DA RAGUSA. See **SIMEONE**

SIMONE DA SIENA, or Camaldolese
Italian, 14th - 15th century.
Illuminator.

Simone da Siena was a monk. He illuminated a missal for the church of S Croce in Florence.

SIMONE DEI CROCIFISSI, also known as Simone di Filippo di Benvenuto, Simone da Bologna, called Il Crocifissajo
Italian, 14th century.
Born c. 1330, in Bologna; died c. 1399, in Bologna.
Painter, fresco artist. Religious subjects.
Bolognese School.

Simone dei Crocifissi is mentioned in Bologna from 1355. He produced many frescoes and religious paintings of which 70 are known today. He was a disciple and imitator of Vitale da Bologna. Despite his nickname *dei Crocifissi* (of the Crucifixes), he specialised in the subject of the Coronation of the Virgin. His style can generally be recognised by the bright colours and the inscrutable expressions of the faces.

BIBLIOGRAPHY:

Van Marle, Raimond, '*The Development of the Italian schools of painting*' in *19 vol*, Martinus Nijhoff, The Hague, 1923-1938 (2nd English edition, Hacker Art Books, New York, 1970). Gibles, Robert, '*Deux familles de peintres à Bologne à la fin du XIVe siècle*' in *Burlington Magazine*, periodical, London, September, 1979.

AUCTION RECORDS:

LONDON, 16 June 1930, *Resurrection*, GBP 15. NEW YORK, 1 June 1989, *Coronation of the Virgin* (tempera/panel with gold background, 43 1/2 x 21 3/4 ins / 110.5 x 55.3 cm) USD 484,000. PARIS, 22 June 1990, *Devotional Tripych* (tempera, gold background/poplar panel, overall size with wings open 24 3/4 x 32 3/4 ins / 63 x 83 cm) FRF 2,550,000. PARIS, 10 Feb 1992, *St Andrew* (tempera/gold background/wood, wing of a polyptych, 20 x 9 1/2 ins / 51 x 24 cm) FRF 150,000. MILAN, 8 June 1995, *Crucifixion* (tempera/panel, 32 1/4 x 21 1/4 ins / 82 x 54 cm) ITL 448,500,000. PARIS, 17 Dec 1997, *Christ and the Instruments of the Passion with a Saint Bishop and a Donor* (tempera/panel, 22 1/2 x 11 3/4 ins / 57 x 30 cm) FRF 160,000. MILAN, 16 May 2001, *Zachariah. Solomon* (tempera on board, a pair, 12 x 9 ins / 30 x 22 cm) ITL 74,000,000. FLORENCE, 11 June 2003, *Crucifixion* (tempera on gold panel, 19 x 11 ins / 48 x 27 cm) EUR 132,000.

SIMONE DEL CAPRINA, or Simone di Gogo del Caprina
Italian, 15th century.
Active in Florence during the second half of the 15th century.
Sculptor.
Florentine School.

Simone del Caprina worked at the church of S Spirito in Florence between 1473 and 1494.

SIMONE DI CINO. See **CINI Simone**

SIMONE DI CORLEONE
Italian, 14th century.
Active in Sicily from 1377 to 1380.
Painter.

SIMONE DI DOMENICO
Italian, 15th century.
Active in Arezzo (Tuscany) from 1413 to 1431.
Painter.

Simone di Domenico worked at Città di Castello in 1431.

SIMONE DI DOMENICO DA FIRENZE
Italian, 15th century.
Florentine, active in Pisa from 1457 to 1462.
Sculptor.

Simone di Domenico made the frames for 24 windows for the Camposanto in Pisa.

SIMONE DI FEDERICO DI VENEZIA
Italian, 15th century.
Active c. 1450.
Sculptor.

SIMONE DI GHERI BULGARINI
Italian, 14th century.
Illuminator.

Active in Siena before 1344, Simone di Gheri Bulgarini was probably related to Bulgarino di Simone who also worked as a miniaturist in Siena in the 14th century.

SIMONE DI GIOVANNI
Italian, 14th century.
Died after 1382.
Active in Siena.
Painter.

Simone di Giovanni painted a fresco in the church at Cerreto Selva near Siena in 1381.

SIMONE DI GOGO DEL CAPRINA. See **SIMONE DEL CAPRINA**

SIMONE DI MARTINO. See **MARTINI Simone**

SIMONE DI MEMMI. See **MARTINI Simone**

SIMONE DI NANNI. See **FERRUCCI Simone di Nanni**

SIMONE DI PAOLO DEL TONDO
Italian.
Active in Perugia (Umbria).
Sculptor (wood).

Simone di Paolo del Tondo sculpted a number of chairs and a banister for Perugia city hall.

SIMONE FIAMMINGO
Italian, 16th century.
Miniaturist.

Simone Fiammingo worked at the court of the duke of Urbino between 1584 and 1589.

SIMONE FIORENTINO. See **FERRUCCI Simone di Nanni**

SIMONE NAPOLITANO. See **PAPA Simone**

SIMONE SENESE. See **SIMONE ANDREA**

SIMONE VENEZIANO. See **PETERZANO Simone**

SIMONE Y LOMBARDO, Enrique
Spanish, 19th - 20th century.
Born 1863 or 1864, in Valencia; died 1927, in Madrid.
Painter, illustrator. Religious subjects, mythological subjects, portraits, genre scenes.

Enrique Simone y Lombardo was a pupil at the Academia de Bellas Artes in Valencia, then a pupil of Bernardo Ferrandiz in Málaga. He went on to study in Madrid. In 1889 he lived for a time in Rome, then travelled to Naples, where he discovered the work of Domenico Morelli. In 1893 he lived in Switzerland and Paris. He taught at the art and business academy in Barcelona between 1904 and 1908, then at the Academia de Bellas Artes in Madrid.

He worked for the publication *La Ilustración Española y Americana* (*Spanish and American Illustration*). He is known for: *The Fortune-Teller, The Decapitation of St Paul, Sappho, The Death of the Centaur Nessus* and *And He Had Her Heart*, a wide range of subjects which gave him the opportunity to exploit the possibilities of light. Enrique Simone participated in many collective exhibitions, gaining various awards including; 1887 third medal at the Exposición Nacional in Madrid; 1896 first medal in Barcelona; 1900 silver medal at the Exposition Universelle in Paris.

BIBLIOGRAPHY:
Arnáiz, José Manuel/López Jiménez, Javier/Merchán Díaz, Manuel (ed.), *'Cien años de pintura en Espana y Portugal (1830-1930)'* in vol. X, Antiqvaria, Madrid, 1993.

MUSEUMS AND GALLERIES:
MADRID (Mus. de Arte Moderno): *Flevit Super Illam*; two portraits.

AUCTION RECORDS:
MADRID, 30 March 1976, *Garden* (oil on canvas, 17 3/4 x 10 1/4 ins / 45 x 26 cm) ESP 30,000. MADRID, 23 Jan 2001, *Oriental Scene* (oil on canvas, 15 x 24 ins / 37 x 62 cm) ESP 2,400,000. MADRID, 17 Dec 2001, *Bedouins in a Lake Landscape* (oil on canvas, 10 x 16 ins / 25 x 40 cm) ESP 740,000. MADRID, 15 Dec 2003, *Procession* (oil on canvas, 19 x 11 ins / 48 x 29 cm) EUR 3,600.

SIMONEAU, Charles
French, 18th century.
Active in Nantes c. 1764.
Sculptor, architect.

SIMONEAU, Charles Louis. See **SIMONNEAU**

SIMONEAU, François. See **SIMONAU**

SIMONEAU, Gustave Adolphe.
See **SIMONAU**

SIMONEAU, Louis, the Younger.
See **SIMONNEAU**

SIMONEAU, Philippe (fils). See **SIMONNEAU**

SIMONELLI, Giuseppe
Italian, 17th - 18th century.
Born c. 1650, in Naples; died c. 1710.
Painter. Mythological subjects, religious subjects.

Initially a domestic servant of Luca Giordano, Simonelli took up painting and produced some remarkable works in the style of his master. He is noted in particular for a *St Nicholas of Tolentino* in the church in Monte Santo.

MUSEUMS AND GALLERIES:
CHAMBÉRY (MBA): *Hercules and Omphale* - NAPLES: *Esther and Ahasuerus*.

AUCTION RECORDS:
LONDON, 31 March 1989, *Tancred and Armida in the Garden of Delights* (oil on canvas, 94 1/2 x 113 1/2 ins / 240 x 288.2 cm) GBP 13,200. NEW YORK, 10 Oct 1990, *King Solomon Sacrificing his Idols* (oil on canvas, 50 x 71 ins / 127 x 180.3 cm) USD 12,100. LONDON, 8 July 1994, *Massacre of the Innocents* (oil on canvas, sketch, 12 3/4 x 21 1/4 ins / 32.2 x 54.2 cm) GBP 2,990. ROME, 28 Nov 1996, *Moses Saved from the Waters of the Nile* (oil on canvas, 48 3/4 x 59 3/4 ins / 124 x 151.6 cm) ITL 28,000,000. MADRID, 20 April 1999, *Madonna Surrounded by Angels* (oil on canvas, 48 x 35 ins / 121 x 90 cm) ESP 950,000. LONDON, 1 Nov 2001, *Massacre of the Innocents* (oil on canvas, 13 x 21 ins / 32 x 54 cm) GBP 5,000. ROME, 12 Dec 2001, *Rinaldo and Armida in the Enchanted Garden* (oil on canvas, 96 x 112 ins / 244 x 285 cm) ITL 125,000,000.

SIMONET. See also **SIMONNET**

SIMONET, Adrien Jacques
French, 19th century.
Born 29 December 1791, in Paris.
Engraver (burin).

Son and pupil of Jean-Baptiste Blaise Simonet, this artist engraved architectural scenes, portraits and vignettes.

SIMONET, Augustine. See **PHILIPPON**

SIMONET, Cécile Charlotte
French, 19th century.
Born in Paris.
Painter. Genre scenes.

Cécile Charlotte Simonet was a pupil of Sarbaud, Donzel and Levasseur. She made her debut at the Salon de Paris in 1876.

AUCTION RECORDS:
VERSAILLES, 18 March 1990, *The Return of the Fishermen* (oil on panel, 10 1/2 x 13 3/4 ins / 26.5 x 35 cm) FRF 8,800.

SIMONET, Claude
French, 15th century.
Born in Bar-le-Duc.
Painter.

Simonet worked for Duke René in 1474.

SIMONET, Jean Baptiste Blaise
French, 18th - 19th century.
Born 1742, in Paris; died after 1813.
Engraver, reproductions engraver. Still-lifes.

Jean Baptiste Blaise Simonet was an engraver of distinction who reproduced in particular many of Greuze's paintings. He also engraved after Moreau the Younger, Baudoin, and Aulery, among others. He collaborated on engraving works from the gallery of the duke of Orléans. He was married to Marie-Françoise Pioleine.

AUCTION RECORDS:
PARIS, 7 Feb 1893, *Still-life: Melon, Basket of Plums, Grapes*, FRF 315.

SIMONET, Jean Jacques François
French, 18th century.
Born in Paris.
Engraver.

Jean Jacques François Simonet exhibited at the 1791 Salon. He practiced line engraving.

SIMONET, John Pierre
Swiss, 19th - 20th century.
Born 1860, in Geneva; died 10 April 1915, in Florence.
Painter, sculptor. Landscapes.

John Pierre Simonet studied painting under Barthélemy Sueur at the fine arts academy in Geneva, and he studied sculpture under Jean Jules Salmson at the College of Applied Arts in Geneva and at the École des Beaux-Arts in Paris. In 1883, he took up painting again, leaving for Algiers, where he lived on and off until 1895, at which juncture he returned to Geneva and settled there. In 1901, together with Hippolyte Coutau and Louis Patru, he founded a private art college that was much frequented. Simonet took part in numerous group exhibitions in Switzerland. In 1896, he was

entrusted with providing decorative compositions for one section of the Swiss National Exhibition in Geneva.
Museums and Galleries:
Geneva (MAH): *Autumn in Sion.*
Auction records:
Bern, 12 May 1990, *Alps* (oil on canvas, 23 1/2 x 28 3/4 ins / 60 x 73 cm) CHF 1,800.

SIMONET, Paul Léon
French, 19th century.
Born in Versailles.
Painter. Fruit.
Paul Simonet was a pupil of Bin and Lavastre. He made his debut at the Salon in 1876.
Auction records:
Paris, 7 Feb 1898, *Fruit,* FRF 315.

SIMONET, Pierre
French, 18th century.
Active in Paris.
Painter.
Pierre Simonet was a member of the Académie de St-Luc. He is mentioned in his children's baptism certificates on 7 June 1769 and 1 January 1772.

SIMONET DE LYON. See **SIMON**

SIMONETTA. See also **SIMONETTI**

SIMONETTA, Carlo, or Simonetti
Italian, 17th century.
Born in Milan; died 3 June 1693, in Milan.
Sculptor. Religious subjects.
From 1660 onwards, Simonetta worked for the cathedral in Milan, where he executed a large number of statues.
Museums and Galleries:
Pavia (Mus. della Certosa): *St Mark* (colossal statue).

SIMONETTA, Silvestro
Italian, 19th century.
Active in Piedmont, during the second half of the 19th century.
Sculptor.
Simonetta worked mainly in Turin, carving portraits and biblical figures.

SIMONETTI
Italian, 19th century.
Active in Australia.
Sculptor. Figures. Statues, busts.
Simonetti lived for many years in Sydney, Australia. His *Statue of Governor Phillip of New South Wales* can be seen in the Sydney Botanical Gardens.
Museums and Galleries:
Sydney: *Bust of Commodore Goodenough.*

SIMONETTI, Alfonso
Italian, 19th century.
Born 29 December 1840, in Naples; died 22 August 1892, in Castrocielo.
Painter, watercolourist. Portraits, genre scenes, landscapes.
Simonetti was a student at the Istituto di Belle Arti in Naples. He exhibited in Turin, Naples, Milan, Venice and abroad, particularly in Paris, London and Melbourne.
Museums and Galleries:
Naples (Mus. di Capodimonte): five paintings.
Auction records:
London, 3 July 1922, *Holidays,* GBP 42. Paris, 25-26 June 1923, *Italian Lighting his Pipe* (watercolour) FRF 100. Amsterdam, 27 April 1976, *Marriage Contract* (1876, oil on panel, 6 1/4 x 10 1/4 ins / 16 x 26 cm) NLG 3,600. Roubaix, 23 Oct 1983, *Fashionable Ladies and a Child Playing in a Park* (1879, oil on canvas, 25 1/4 x 18 ins / 64 x 46 cm) FRF 52,000. Milan, 14 June 1989, *Southern Landscape with Figures* (1876, oil on canvas, 20 x 31 3/4 ins / 50.5 x 80.5 cm) ITL 5,000,000. Rome, 23 May 1996, *Posillipo Seen from Portici; Neapolitan Landscape* (oil on canvas, a pair, each 13 x 19 3/4 ins / 33 x 50 cm) ITL 10,350,000. Billingshurst, 10 Aug 1999, *Musical Duet* (1879, oil on canvas, 21 x 14 ins / 54 x 36 cm) GBP 1,000.

SIMONETTI, Amadeo Momo
Italian, 20th century.
Born 8 April 1874, in Rome; died 22 April 1922, in Rome.
Painter. Landscapes, seascapes.
A student at the Accademia di Belle Arti in Rome, Simonetti was a member of the group I XXV della Campagna Romana (The 25 of the Roman Campagna).
Auction records:
New York, 14 Oct 1978, *The Sultan's Favourite* (watercolour, 20 3/4 x 13 3/4 ins / 53 x 35 cm) USD 1,900. New York, 14 Oct 1993, *The Sultan's Favourite* (1900, watercolour, 20 x 15 ins / 50.8 x 38.1 cm) USD 24,150. New York, 24 May 1995, *Scribe* (watercolour and pencil, 21 1/2 x 15 ins / 54.6 x 38.1 cm) USD 13,800. New York, 18-19 July 1996, *The Sultan's Favourite* (1900, watercolour/paper, 21 1/2 x 14 1/2 ins / 54.6 x 37.1 cm) USD 8,912. New York, 5 May 1999, *Attending the Princess* (1900, watercolour, 21 x 14 ins / 54 x 36 cm) USD 20,000. Delaware, 24 Sept 1999, *Interior with Rug Merchant and Client* (watercolour, 30 x 21 ins / 76 x 53 cm) USD 9,250. Detroit, 14 June 2000, *Four Figures in an Eighteenth Century Viennese Parlour* (oil on canvas, 31 x 24 ins / 79 x 61 cm) USD 2,250. London, 12 Oct 2000, *Rug Merchant* (watercolour and gouache, 29 x 20 ins / 74 x 52 cm) GBP 12,000. Detroit, 12 Jan 2001, *Genre Scene with Cardinal Entertained by the Young Mozart and Pianist* (oil on canvas, 31 x 19 ins / 79 x 48 cm) USD 3,500. Paris, 14 May 2001, *Carpet Sellers* (watercolour, 21 x 14 ins / 53 x 36 cm) FRF 200,000. San Francisco, 15 May 2002, *In the Armory* (pencil and watercolour, 21 x 14 ins / 53 x 36 cm) USD 9,000. Paris, 3 June 2004, *Oriental Woman with Fan* (watercolour, 30 x 21 ins / 76 x 53 cm) EUR 20,000.

SIMONETTI, Attilio
Italian, 19th - 20th century.
Born 13 April 1843, in Rome; died 14 January 1925, in Rome.
Painter (gouache), watercolourist, pastellist, draughtsman. Genre scenes, interiors with figures.
Attilio Simonetti exhibited in Naples and Rome.
Museums and Galleries:
Milan (Gal. d'Arte Moderna) - New York (Metropolitan Mus. of Art).
Auction records:
Paris, 6 March 1893, *Compliment,* FRF 700. New York, 27 April 1906, *War and Peace,* USD 300. Paris, 30-31 March 1910, *Scene in an Interior* (watercolour) FRF 200. Los Angeles, 8 April 1973, *Rendezvous,* USD 2,750. Washington DC, 6 June 1976, *Harem Guard* (1899, watercolour, 26 1/2 x 20 ins / 67.5 x 51 cm) USD 1,300. London, 23 July 1976, *Duo* (1879, oil on canvas, 20 3/4 x 14 ins / 53 x 35.5 cm) GBP 280. New York, 13 Dec 1985, *Checkmate* (watercolour, 21 1/4 x 14 1/2 ins / 53.8 x 37 cm) USD 2,500. London, 19 June 1986, *The Letter* (watercolour, 28 1/4 x 20 1/2 ins / 72 x 52 cm) GBP 2,700. Rome, 14 Dec 1988, *Meditation on Death* (1861, oil on canvas, 19 3/4 x 24 1/4 ins / 50 x 61.5 cm) ITL 2,800,000. Rome, 16 April 1991, *Interior with Lady and Small Dogs* (1882, oil on canvas, 15 3/4 x 19 ins / 40 x 48 cm) ITL 5,750,000. Rome, 10 Dec 1991, *Girl in Regional Costume* (oil on canvas, 21 x 16 1/4 ins / 52.5 x 41 cm) ITL 2,600,000. Milan, 17 Dec 1992, *Last Leaves* (oil on canvas, 18 1/2 x 41 3/4 ins / 47 x 106 cm) ITL 2,000,000. London, 7 April 1993, *Flirtation* (1895, watercolour, 24 x 18 3/4 ins / 61 x 47.5 cm) GBP 1,380. New York, 14 Oct 1993, *Harem Guard* (1899, watercolour/paper, 27 x 20 3/4 ins / 68.5 x 52.7 cm) USD 8,625. London, 13 March 1996, *Washerwomen at San Beneto del Tronto* (oil on panel, 13 1/2 x 8 1/4 ins / 34 x 21

cm) GBP 2,070. London, 21 Nov 1996, *Arabs in an Interior* (1871, pencil, watercolour and gouache/paper/card, 14 x 17 1/4 ins / 35.5 x 43.8 cm) GBP 10,350. San Francisco, 26 May 1999, *Mother's Pride* (1880, watercolour and pencil, 25 x 18 ins / 63 x 46 cm) USD 3,500. Paris, 12 July 1999, *Elegant Lady with Parrot* (oil on canvas, 16 x 13 ins / 41 x 32 cm) FRF 43,000. Rome, 23 May 2000, *Landscape at Sunset* (oil on canvas, 15 x 28 ins / 38 x 70 cm) ITL 4,200,000. New York, 30 Oct 2001, *Musical Interlude* (oil on canvas, 23 x 30 ins / 59 x 77 cm) USD 11,000. Vienna, 29 Nov 2001, *Mother's Pride and Joy* (1877, watercolour, 25 x 18 ins / 64 x 46 cm) ATS 40,000. Florence, 10 June 2003, *View of Temple in Tivoli* (1969, oil on canvas, 24 x 34 ins / 62 x 87 cm) EUR 2,700. Cambridge, 22 Oct 2003, *Duet* (watercolour, 14 x 19 ins / 36 x 48 cm) GBP 1,500. London, 23 Sept 2004, *Playing in the Garden* (1880, watercolour, 24 x 18 ins / 62 x 46 cm) GBP 6,200.

SIMONETTI, Carlo. See **SIMONETTA**

SIMONETTI, Cesare

Italian, 19th - 20th century.
Born in Udine; died 1912, in Florence.
Painter, engraver. Genre scenes.

Cesare Simonetti was a student at the Accademia di Belle Arti in Turin. He exhibited in the city in 1898. As well as painting he made lithographs.

SIMONETTI, Domenico, called Il Magatta

Italian, 18th century.
Born in Ancona.
Painter, watercolourist, draughtsman. Religious subjects, figures, genre scenes.

Simonetti was the pupil of F. Trevisani. He worked for churches, in particular the Suffragio, in Rome. Francesco Appiani was his pupil.

Auction records:

New York, 1876, *Proclamation before the Pantheon,* FRF 13,625. Paris, 1 March 1877, *Italian Peasant Lighting his Pipe* (watercolour) FRF 365; *Italian Peasant Seated Propped against a Wall* (watercolour) FRF 1,050; *Good Bottle of Wine* (watercolour) FRF 345. Paris, 12 Dec 1877, *Turkish Woman,* FRF 1,400. Paris, 1881, *Mandolin Player,* FRF 1,200. Amsterdam, 1884, *In the Garden* (drawing) FRF 1,281. New York, 1888, *Concert* (watercolour) FRF 1,550. Paris, 1893, *Messenger* (drawing) FRF 175.

SIMONETTI, Domenico

Italian, 20th century.
Born 17 January 1893, in Candioa Canavese.
Painter. Portraits, landscapes.

Domenico Simonetti studied at the Accademia di Belle Arti in Turin, and with Giacomo Grosso and Cesare Ferro.

SIMONETTI, Ettore

Italian, 19th century.
Painter (gouache), watercolourist. Genre scenes. Orientalism.

Auction records:

London, 11 Feb 1976, *Musical Soirée* (oil on canvas, 25 3/4 x 35 ins / 65.5 x 89 cm) GBP 3,200. New York, 28 May 1981, *Scene in an Oriental Bazaar* (oil on canvas, 26 1/2 x 35 1/2 ins / 67 x 90 cm) USD 7,500. Los Angeles, 8 Feb 1982, *Oriental Bazaar* (watercolour, 22 x 30 ins / 55 x 76 cm) USD 2,800. New York, 25 Oct 1984, *The Favourite's Lesson* (watercolour/traces of pencil, 19 1/4 x 28 1/2 ins / 49 x 72.5 cm) USD 14,000. New York, 13 Dec 1985, *At the Dressmaker's* (watercolour heightened with white gouache, 29 3/4 x 20 1/2 ins / 75.8 x 51.8 cm) USD 2,600. New York, 25 May 1988, *Baptism* (oil on canvas, 39 3/4 x 29 3/4 ins / 101 x 75.5 cm) USD 33,000. New York, 21 May 1991, *Serenade in a Palace* (watercolour/paper, 22 x 30 ins / 56 x 76.2 cm) USD 4,950. New York, 17 Oct 1991, *Buying Slippers* (watercolour/paper, 30 3/4 x 22 ins / 78.1 x 55.9 cm) USD 22,000. New York, 28 May 1992, *Trying on Slippers* (watercolour/paper, 30 x 21 1/2 ins / 76.2 x 54.6 cm) USD 19,800. New York, 29 Oct 1992, *Carpet Seller* (oil on canvas, 26 1/4 x 35 1/2 ins / 66.7 x 90.2 cm) USD 26,400. London, 16 March 1994, *Making Music* (oil on canvas, 18 x 25 1/4 ins / 46 x 64 cm) GBP 6,900. London, 17 Nov 1994, *Striking a Good Bargain* (pencil and watercolour/paper/card, 30 1/2 x 22 ins / 77.5 x 55.6 cm) GBP 24,150. New York, 24 May 1995, *The New Jewel* (watercolour and gouache/paper/card, 28 x 20 ins / 71.1 x 50.8 cm) USD 20,700. London, 14 June 1996, *Jewellery Box* (pencil and watercolour/paper, 29 3/4 x 21 ins / 75.5 x 53.3 cm) GBP 29,900. Paris, 17 Nov 1997, *Visit to the Secondhand Dealer* (watercolour and gouache, 21 1/4 x 30 ins / 54 x 76 cm) FRF 80,000. London, 17 June 1999, *In St Peter's, Rome* (1877, oil on canvas, 30 x 42 ins / 75 x 107 cm) GBP 6,500. London, 17 June 1999, *In the Dressing Room* (watercolour heightened with white on paper on card, 30 x 21 ins / 76 x 54 cm) GBP 42,000. North Bethesda, 15 April 2000, *Harem Beauty with Attendant* (watercolour on board, 31 x 22 ins / 79 x 56 cm) USD 28,000. London, 21 June 2000, *Music in Harem* (watercolour heightened with white, 21 x 30 ins / 54 x 75 cm) GBP 24,000. Chicago, 11 June 2001, *Graceful Exit* (watercolour, 20 x 28 ins / 51 x 71 cm) USD 4,250. London, 21 June 2001, *In the Dressing Room* (pencil and watercolour heightened with white, 30 x 21 ins / 77 x 54 cm) GBP 50,000. London, 19 Nov 2002, *At the Ball* (oil on canvas, 24 x 38 ins / 60 x 96 cm) GBP 15,000. New York, 29 Oct 2003, *Snake Charmer* (oil on canvas, 22 x 30 ins / 55 x 77 cm) USD 75,000.

SIMONETTI, Francesco. See **SIMONINI**

SIMONETTI, Gianni Emilio

Italian, 20th century.
Born 1940, in Milan or Rome.
Painter.

Gianni Simonetti was a student at Milan University. He is something of a polymath, not only painting but also directing plays, making films and writing scenarios and musical compositions. In touch with all the avant-garde concepts of the day, he is particularly interested in signs and language. Playing on the signifier-signified dualism, he offers a double interpretation, or rather a double decoding, in which images and concepts are superimposed. His work is influenced by the linguistics research of the 1970s.

He has taken part in a number of collective exhibitions, including: 1964 and 1966, in Milan; 1967, at the Carnegie Institute in Pittsburgh and the Museum of Contemporary Art in Chicago; 1968, at the Kunstverein in Frankfurt, in Florence and at the Paris Biennale; 1982, at the Hayward Gallery in London; in Switzerland, England and Holland. He has held regular solo exhibitions in Milan since 1966 as well as, in 1967, in Turin, Geneva, Padua and Brussels and, in 1968, in Trieste.

Auction records:

Milan, 6 April 1976, *Wounded Totem* (1970, mixed media/canvas, 51 1/4 x 35 1/2 ins / 130 x 90 cm) ITL 600,000.

SIMONETTI, Luigi

Italian, 19th century.
Active in Rome in the middle of the 19th century.
Sculptor.

Luigi Simonetti exhibited in Rome in 1844.

Museums and Galleries:

St Petersburg (Academy): *The Sculptor P.A. Stawasser* (bust).

SIMONETTI, Masi

Italian, 20th century.

Died 1971, in Venice.
Active and from 1937 naturalised in France.
Painter. Scenes with figures, landscapes.

Masi Simonetti took part in the Salon des Réalités Nouvelles in Paris in 1946 and 1947. Initially an abstract artist, he worked with Sonia Delaunay, later moving towards figurative art and taking themes from masquerades and the landscape of the Dolomites.

SIMONI, Beniamino

Italian, 19th century.
Born in Saviore (Val Camonica); died at the beginning of the 19th century, in Brescia.
Sculptor (wood), stucco artist.

Simoni executed some 200 statues representing scenes from *The Passion* for the sanctuary of the Via Crucis next to the church of Cerveno in Val Carmonica.

BIBLIOGRAPHY:

Beniamino Simoni, Istituto di Storia dellÁrte, Universita di Parma, Electa, Milan, 2000.

SIMONI, Francesco. See **SIMONINI**

SIMONI, Gustavo

Italian, 19th - 20th century.
Born 5 November 1846, in Rome; died 1926.
Painter, watercolourist. Scenes with figures, local scenes (harems), figures, landscapes.
Orientalism.

A student at the Accademia di San Luca in Rome, Gustavo Simoni also worked in Paris, Spain and Africa. He received an honourable mention at the 1889 Exposition Universelle in Paris.

G Simoni

MUSEUMS AND GALLERIES:

GLASGOW: *Oriental Festival* - LEIPZIG: *Serenade* (watercolour) - MELBOURNE: *Marble Mosque*.

AUCTION RECORDS:

PARIS, 16-17 May 1892, *Watercolour*, FRF 340. FRANKFURT AM MAIN, 1894, *Prayers in the Mosque*, FRF 2,250. PARIS, 1899, *Sleeping Arab* (watercolour) FRF 350. NEW YORK, 8-10 April 1908, *Sorrento* (watercolour) USD 265. PARIS, 23-24 May 1921, *The Young Marquis* (watercolour) FRF 215. LONDON, 20 July 1923, *Chickens Resting* (drawing) GBP 14. NEW YORK, 17-18 May 1934, *Courtyard in a Mosque*, USD 200. NEW YORK, 4 May 1945, *Market Place in Algiers*, GBP 105. PARIS, 12 Dec 1949, *Woman in a Red Dress*, FRF 700. NEW YORK, 9 Oct 1974, *In the Harem*, USD 1,500. WASHINGTON DC, 6 June 1976, *Young Algerian Woman* (1899, watercolour, 25 x 38 1/2 ins / 63.5 x 98 cm) USD 1,000. LOS ANGELES, 17 March 1980, *Interior of the Mosque in Tlemcen* (oil on canvas, 30 x 42 3/4 ins / 76.2 x 108.5 cm) USD 5,500. LONDON, 20 June 1980, *Interior of a Harem* (1881, watercolour, 26 x 17 1/2 ins / 66 x 44.4 cm) GBP 2,500. NEW YORK, 27 Feb 1982, *Horsemen Resting* (1882, watercolour, 14 3/4 x 22 ins / 37.6 x 55.6 cm) USD 2,300. ENGHIEN-LES-BAINS, 26 June 1983, *Musician* (1898, watercolour, 29 1/2 x 22 ins / 75 x 55 cm) FRF 85,000. LONDON, 19 June 1984, *Arabs outside a Palace* (1903, oil on canvas, 46 3/4 x 31 1/2 ins / 119 x 80 cm) GBP 20,000. LONDON, 28 Nov 1985, *Harem Dancer* (1881, watercolour and pencil heightened with white gouache, 13 x 8 1/4 ins / 33 x 21 cm) GBP 5,000. LONDON, 21 March 1986, *Biskra* (oil on canvas, 34 1/2 x 23 1/4 ins / 87.5 x 59 cm) GBP 5,500. LONDON, 24 June 1988, *Street in Biskra* (oil on canvas, 35 x 23 3/4 ins / 88.9 x 60.3 cm) GBP 6,050. NEW YORK, 24 Oct 1989, *Street in Biskra, Algeria* (oil on canvas, 35 x 23 3/4 ins / 88.9 x 60.3 cm) USD 16,500. ROME, 14 Nov 1991, *Odalisque* (1902, watercolour, 20 1/2 x 13 1/2 ins / 52 x 34 cm) ITL 2,300,000. NEW YORK, 20 Jan 1993, *Woman in the Garden of a Villa* (1878, watercolour/paper, 13 3/4 x 10 1/2 ins / 34.9 x 26.7 cm) USD 1,955. NEW YORK, 27 May 1993, *On the Patio* (oil on canvas, 42 1/4 x 28 3/4 ins / 107 x 73 cm) USD 21,850. PARIS, 9 June 1993, *Man Selling Weapons* (1902, watercolour, 20 3/4 x 29 1/2 ins / 53 x 75 cm) FRF 64,000. NEW YORK, 13 Oct 1993, *In the Shop of the Weapons' Seller* (1902, watercolour/paper, 20 3/4 x 29 1/4 ins / 53 x 74 cm) USD 26,450. ROME, 31 May 1994, *Arab in an Interior* (1875, oil on panel, 10 1/2 x 5 3/4 ins / 26.5 x 14.5 cm) ITL 3,064,000. LONDON, 16 Nov 1994, *Carpet Seller* (1896, watercolour, 22 1/2 x 34 1/2 ins / 57 x 87.5 cm) GBP 10,350. LONDON, 15 Nov 1995, *Fêtes Galantes* (1881, oil on canvas, a pair, each 63 x 39 ins / 160 x 99 cm) GBP 17,250. ROME, 5 Dec 1995, *Young Arab and his Donkey* (1905, oil on canvas, 16 1/4 x 13 ins / 41 x 33 cm) ITL 4,714,000. PARIS, 11 Dec 1995, *Palace Guard Inspecting a Sabre* (watercolour, 18 1/4 x 13 1/2 ins / 46.5 x 34.5 cm) FRF 22,000. NEW YORK, 23-24 May 1996, *Waiting for an Audience* (oil on canvas, 23 x 19 3/4 ins / 58.21 x 50.3 cm) USD 21,850. LONDON, 21 March 1997, *Declaration* (1896, pencil, watercolour, gouache and gum arabic/paper, 36 1/4 x 18 ins / 92 x 46 cm) GBP 8,625. NEW YORK, 23 May 1997, *Scene in an Arab Village* (1883, oil on panel, a pair, each 9 x 14 1/4 ins / 22.9 x 36.2 cm) USD 23,000. PARIS, 17 Nov 1997, *Wedding Procession of a Caid* (1898, watercolour, 7 x 11 ins / 18 x 28 cm) FRF 14,500. LONDON, 17 June 1999, *Draughts Players* (1902, watercolour, 13 x 30 ins / 34 x 76 cm) GBP 18,000. NEW YORK, 1 Nov 1999, *Smoking the Hookah* (1880, pencil and watercolour on paper laid on card, 21 x 14 ins / 54 x 36 cm) USD 16,000. PARIS, 12 May 2000, *In the Court* (oil on canvas, 43 x 29 ins / 110 x 74 cm) FRF 180,000. LONDON, 21 June 2000, *Draughts Player* (1893, pencil, watercolour and gum arabic, 27 x 34 ins / 69 x 87 cm) GBP 16,000. NEW YORK, 5 April 2001, *Women in an Orientalist Interior* (1891, watercolour, 40 x 26 ins / 102 x 66 cm) USD 17,000. PARIS, 19 Nov 2001, *Guard with Red Costume* (watercolour, 16 x 10 ins / 40 x 25 cm) FRF 40,000. SHREWSBURY, 24 April 2002, *Interior of a Harem* (1881, watercolour, 14 x 9 ins / 36 x 23 cm) GBP 1,600. ROME, 27 May 2002, *Grottaferrata* (1913, oil on canvas, 20 x 24 ins / 50 x 62 cm) EUR 3,200. DOWNINGTON, 20 Sept 2003, *Busy Market Scene* (1901, watercolour, 21 x 34 ins / 53 x 86 cm) USD 6,000. LONDON, 4 Nov 2003, *Celebrations before an Audience* (1917, watercolour, 17 x 24 ins / 42 x 60 cm) GBP 4,000. NEW YORK, 21 Jan 2004, *Italian Beauty* (watercolour, 17 x 12 ins / 43 x 31 cm) USD 1,800. BERN, 13 May 2004, *Two Women with Clay Jugs* (gouache on board, 7 x 4 ins / 19 x 10 cm) CHF 2,500.

SIMONI, Juan Baptista. See **SIMO**

SIMONI, Luca

Italian, 17th century.
Born in Bologna.
Painter.

Simoni, the pupil of L. Pasinelli, was active about 1680.

SIMONI, M.

French, 20th century.
Painter, watercolourist. Scenes with figures, urban landscapes.

M. Simoni exhibited in Oran. He painted North African subjects.

AUCTION RECORDS:

PARIS, 11 Feb 1919, *Moroccan Concert* (watercolour) FRF 205; *A Street in Biskra* (watercolour) FRF 200.

SIMONI, Paolo A.

Italian, 20th century.
Born 1882; died 1960.
Painter, watercolourist. Scenes with figures.

AUCTION RECORDS:
PARIS, 6 April 1990, *Arab Musicians in a Courtyard* (1912, watercolour/paper, 13 3/4 x 20 1/2 ins / 35 x 52 cm) FRF 18,000. PARIS, 14 May 2001, *Oriental Woman and Her Maid* (watercolour and gouache, 21 x 11 ins / 53 x 27 cm) FRF 28,000.

SIMONIDES
Painter.
Ancient Greek.
Simonides is mentioned as a portrait painter by Pliny.

SIMONIDY, Michel, or Simonidi, Mihail
Romanian, 19th - 20th century.
Born 8 March 1870, in Bucharest; died 1933, in Paris.
Also active in France.
Painter (gouache), watercolourist, pastellist, illustrator.
Historical subjects, figures, nudes, portraits, genre scenes, still-lifes, landscapes with figures, waterscapes, seascapes. Murals.
Michel Simonidy studied with Léon Bonnat, Fernand Humbert and Gabriel Ferrier. He painted murals on a number of ceilings in Bucharest. He exhibited at the Salon des Artistes Français, Paris, obtaining an honourable mention at the 1889 and a silver medal at the 1900 Expositions Universelles. He was made Chevalier de la Légion d'Honneur (1901).

SIMONIDY

MUSEUMS AND GALLERIES:
BUCHAREST (Muz. National de Arta al României): *Death of Mithridates.*
AUCTION RECORDS:
NEW YORK, 1 Feb 1906, *Evening Harmony,* USD 300. PARIS, 4-5 Dec 1918, *On the Cruise,* FRF 580. PARIS, 9 May 1925, *Nude at Seaside,* FRF 2,900; *Nude with Tulips,* FRF 4,000; *Quimperlé, view from viaduct,* FRF 3,800; *Belle-Isle-en-Mer Harbour,* FRF 2,500. PARIS, 15 Dec 1933, *Small Nude against Black Background,* FRF 610; *Standing Nude Holding Grey Housecoat,* FRF 1,050; *Seascape, Alpes-Maritimes,* FRF 610. PARIS, 16-17 May 1939, *Banks of the Danube,* FRF 680. PARIS, 13 March 1942, *Reverie,* FRF 720; *Venetian Woman,* FRF 1,400. PARIS, 5 March 1945, *Woman Gathering Flowers,* FRF 3,000. PARIS, 5 Dec 1946, *Seascape: Hyères Islands* (1927) FRF 14,500. PARIS, 16 Dec 1946, *Bather,* FRF 3,200; *Model on Sofa,* FRF 4,200. PARIS, 8 June 1949, *Still-life with Fruit* (1889) FRF 4,000. PARIS, 15 Nov 1950, *Seaside* (1924) FRF 4,000. PARIS, 25 Feb 1972, *Sleeping Bather* (18 x 22 1/2 ins / 46 x 57 cm) FRF 1,100. VERSAILLES, 11 Feb 1979, *Nude with Drapery* (oil on canvas, 32 x 25 1/2 ins / 81 x 65 cm) FRF 4,200. PARIS, 20 June 1988, *Bathers beneath Peach Tree* (pastel, 22 3/4 x 35 1/2 ins / 58 x 90 cm) FRF 4,000. PARIS, 4 March 1991, *Walk in the Park* (oil on card, 25 1/2 x 19 ins / 65 x 48 cm) FRF 4,200. PARIS, 26 April 1991, *Nude (rear view)* (oil on canvas, 25 1/4 x 20 1/2 ins / 64 x 52 cm) FRF 5,000. NEW YORK, 29 Oct 1992, *Summer* (1901, oil on canvas, 27 x 12 3/4 ins / 68.6 x 32.4 cm) USD 8,800. PARIS, 18 Nov 1993, *Woman with Lilies* (1902, pastel, 31 1/2 x 25 1/4 ins / 80 x 64 cm) FRF 21,500. PARIS, 7 Nov 1994, *Odalisque with Narghile* (gouache and watercolour on card, 12 1/4 x 9 1/4 ins / 31 x 23.5 cm) FRF 6,500. PARIS, 1 April 1996, *The Beautiful Venetian* (oil on canvas, 22 x 18 1/4 ins / 55 x 46.5 cm) FRF 12,000. PARIS, 12 July 2000, *Blue Dress* (oil on canvas, 32 x 26 ins / 82 x 66 cm) FRF 19,000. PARIS, 5 Dec 2003, *Fisherman's Daughter at Quiberon Looking After a Cow* (1916, oil on panel, 18 x 21 ins / 45 x 54 cm) EUR 1,800. PARIS, 26 Jan 2004, *Reading* (1910, oil on canvas, 21 x 26 ins / 54 x 65 cm) EUR 1,800. PARIS, 3 March 2004, *Woman on Sofa* (oil on canvas, 20 x 22 ins / 50 x 55 cm) EUR 2,100.

SIMONIN, called Simonnin de Bar-le-Duc
French, 15th century.
Born in Bar-le-Duc.
Painter.
Simonin worked from 1456 to 1480 in the château of Louppy in the Meuse.

SIMONIN
French, 17th century.
Engraver (burin).
MUSEUMS AND GALLERIES:
PARIS (BNF): *Molière in the Role of Sganarelle.*

SIMONIN, Bonaventure
French, 18th century.
Active in Morteau 1748-1765.
Sculptor.

SIMONIN, Claude
French, 17th century.
Sculptor (wood).
Claude Simonin was working for the duke of Lorraine in Nancy around 1629.

SIMONIN, Claude I
French, 17th - 18th century.
Born c. 1635, in Nantes; died 1721, in Nantes.
Engraver.
Claude Simonin I was the father of Claude Simonin II.

SIMONIN, Claude II
French, 18th century.
Born in Nantes.
Active in the second half of the 18th century.
Engraver.
Claude Simonin II was the son of Claude Simonin I. He was engraver to the king.

SIMONIN, Francine
Swiss, 20th century.
Born 1936, in Lausanne.
Active since c. 1968 in Canada.
Painter, engraver, mixed media.
Francine Simonin's work has featured at group exhibitions, including that at the Michèle Broutta Gallery in Paris within the framework of the *Échange France Québec* (*Franco-Quebec Exchange*). As of 1966, she has been a regular exhibitor in Europe and in Canada. A travelling solo exhibition was held in 1991 in Lausanne, Montreal, Quebec and Essen. Simonin moved to Quebec around 1968 and became preoccupied with various aspects of engraving, starting out with etchings and progressing towards lithography, silk-screen printing and linographics. She uses a spiral technique to offer extremely vivid yet sparse images of the female form.
MUSEUMS AND GALLERIES:
BERN (Schweizerische Landesbibliothek) - GENEVA (MAH, Prints Collection) - MONTREAL (MAC): *Female Zone I and II* (1977) - VEVEY (Mus. Jenisch).
AUCTION RECORDS:
PARIS, 24 May 1992, *Chairs IV* (1986, oil, charcoal and pastel, 22 1/4 x 30 ins / 56.5 x 76.5 cm) FRF 4,600.

SIMONIN, Henri Alexis
French, 19th century.
Born in Paris.
Painter. Portraits, genre scenes, flowers.
Henri Simonin was a pupil of L. Cogniet. He made his Salon debut in 1877.

SIMONIN, Jean Claude
French, 20th century.
Born 1934, in Rheims.
Painter, sculptor, engraver, illustrator.
Jean Claude Simonin was active in Épinal, where he taught at the Collège Jules Ferry. He published several collections of poetry, which he illustrated with wood engravings. He

was one of the illustrators of *Ouverture pour un millénaire*, a book by Jean-Paul Marchal (1983).

He has exhibited regularly in Épinal and the surrounding region. His work has featured in collective exhibitions, including *De Bonnard à Baselitz - Dix Ans d'enrichissements du cabinet des estampes 1978-1988* (*From Bonnard to Baselitz: A Decade of Acquisitions by the Prints Collection 1978-1988*) at the Bibliothèque Nationale in Paris, 1992.

MUSEUMS AND GALLERIES:

PARIS (BNF, Prints Collection): *Le Roi des Aulnes* (1985, wood).

SIMONIN, Raymond

French, 20th century.

Born 1907, in Nancy.

Painter, engraver.

Raymond Simonin lived and worked in Nancy. His work was shown in the collective exhibition *De Bonnard à Baselitz - Dix Ans d'enrichissements du cabinet des estampes 1978-1988* (*From Bonnard to Baselitz: A Decade of Acquisitions by the Prints Collection 1978-1988*) at the Bibliothèque Nationale in Paris in 1992.

MUSEUMS AND GALLERIES:

PARIS (BNF, Prints Collection): *In a Lorraine Village* (wood).

SIMONIN, Solange

French, 20th century.

Draughtswoman, painter (gouache), watercolourist.

Solange Simonin has spent her working life in Chelles (Seine-et-Marne).

In Paris, she has exhibited at the Salon de la Société Nationale des Beaux-Arts, the Salon d'Automne and the Salon de Montrouge.

She creates calligraphic symbols in a style somewhere between abstraction and figuration.

SIMONIN, Victor

Belgian, 20th century.

Born 1877 or 1887, in Brussels; died 1946.

Painter. Landscapes, Still-lifes, flowers.

Victor Simonin studied painting at the fine arts academy in Brussels and music at the Brussels Conservatory. His career as a musician was cut short by an accident to his left hand and he concentrated on painting, taking instruction from the Post-Impressionist Alfred Bastien. Simonin painted landscapes and still-lifes using a sparing technique that elevates his work above the strictly conventional.

V. Simonin

AUCTION RECORDS:

BRUSSELS, 5 Oct 1971, *Studio Corner*, BEF 18,000. BRUSSELS, 15 June 1974, *Still-life*, BEF 14,000. BRUSSELS, 18 June 1980, *Suburb in the Snow* (1931, oil on canvas, 31½ x 39¼ ins / 80 x 100 cm) BEF 28,000. LOKEREN, 28 May 1988, *Still-life with Vase of Flowers* (oil on panel, 18 x 13 ins / 46 x 33 cm) BEF 50,000. BRUSSELS, 19 Dec 1989, *Flowers on a Table* (oil on panel, 29½ x 35½ ins / 75 x 90 cm) BEF 150,000. BRUSSELS, 9 Oct 1990, *Flowers* (oil on canvas, 17¾ x 14½ ins / 45 x 37 cm) BEF 25,000. AMSTERDAM, 13 Dec 1990, *Still-life* (oil on card, 19¼ x 31 ins / 49 x 78.5 cm) NLG 4,370. LOKEREN, 10 Oct 1992, *Still-life* (oil on card/panel, 35¾ x 28 ins / 91 x 71 cm) BEF 44,000. NEW YORK, 22 Feb 1993, *Pitcher of Anemones* (1915, oil on canvas, 32¼ x 23½ ins / 82 x 59.5 cm) USD 1,650. AMSTERDAM, 14 June 1994, *Still-life with a Plate of Apples, Pears and Grapes and a Vase of Flowers on a Draped Table* (oil on card, 23½ x 31½ ins / 60 x 80 cm) NLG 4,830. LOKEREN, 8 Oct 1994, *Still-life with Flowers* (oil on panel, 20½ x 16½ ins / 52 x 42 cm) BEF 48,000. LOKEREN, 9 Dec 1995, *Still-life* (oil on panel, 19¾ x 35 ins / 50 x 88 cm) BEF 28,000. LONDON, 14 Oct 1999, *Summer Flowers with Bowl and a Dish on Table* (oil on panel, 28 x 32 ins / 71 x 81 cm) GBP 2,000. AMSTERDAM, 25 Oct 1999, *Flower Still-life* (oil on canvas, 28 x 24 ins / 70 x 60 cm) NLG 6,500. GRAVENHAGE, 31 Oct 2000, *Table with Bouquets and Tea Pot* (oil on canvas, 28 x 33 ins / 72 x 83 cm) NLG 5,600. BRUSSELS, 20 Feb 2002, *Still-life with Flowers and Fruit* (oil on canvas, 31 x 39 ins / 80 x 100 cm) EUR 1,750. GRAVENHAGE, 6 Nov 2002, *Still-life with Flowers* (oil on panel, 23 x 31 ins / 59 x 78 cm) EUR 3,000.

SIMONINI, Domenico

Italian, 20th - 21st century.

Born 18 October 1952, in Vignola (Modena).

Painter.

Domenico Simonini attended the A. Venturi art college in Modena and the Accademia di Belle Arti in Bologna. He uses traditional subjects and painting methods.

In 1993 his work was shown at the Galleria della Corte in Vignola in the exhibition of still-lifes, *Pittura come realtà* (*Painting as Reality*). He exhibited in the Palazzo Pretorio in Trento, at the Rosmini Serbati centre in Rovereto, at the Vienna cultural institute, in Milan in 1982 at the Galleria Valentini, and in 1983 at the Galleria Carini with the artists who began the 'City and Country' movement. He won several prizes and distinctions, including the first Bice Bugatti painting prize at Nova Milanese in 1984.

SIMONINI, Francesco, or Simoncini or Simonetti or Simoni

Italian, 18th century.

Born 16 June 1686, in Parma; died 1753, in Florence (?).

Painter, engraver. Military subjects, battles.

The pupil of Spolverini, Francesco Simonini worked in Venice at the end of his life.

MUSEUMS AND GALLERIES:

CAEN: *Cavalry Onslaughts* - DARMSTADT: *Cavalry Onslaughts* - NANCY: *Cavalry Onslaughts*.

AUCTION RECORDS:

PARIS, 1776, *Cavalry Detachment Fighting at the Gates of a City* (drawing with brush dipped in bistre) FRF 88. PARIS, 1892, *Horrors of War*, FRF 700. PARIS, 2-3 April 1897, *Horrors of War*, FRF 200. MILAN, 29 Oct 1964, *Battle Scene*, ITL 800,000. PARIS, 24 Nov 1965, *Jesus Healing the Sick; Martyrdom of St Sebastian* (two pendants) ITL 1,400,000. LONDON, 24 Oct 1973, *Coastal Scenes* (two canvases) GBP 8,800. MILAN, 16 May 1974, *Cavalry Engagement*, ITL 3,000,000. NEW YORK, 30 May 1979, *Cavalry Engagement between Turks and Christians* (oil on canvas, 23½ x 38¾ ins / 60 x 98.5 cm) USD 3,500. NEW YORK, 5 June 1979, *Battle Scene* (pen and wash, 15 x 24¾ ins / 38 x 63 cm) USD 2,600. LONDON, 23 June 1982, *Battle Scenes between Christians and Turks* (two oil on canvas, oval, 58¼ x 42½ ins / 148 x 108 cm) GBP 6,200. MILAN, 30 Nov 1982, *Battle Scene* (pen and bistre wash, 10½ x 17 ins / 26.6 x 43 cm) ITL 3,600,000. MILAN, 27 Nov 1984, *Battle Scene* (pen and wash, 16¼ x 24 ins / 41 x 61 cm) ITL 2,800,000. LONDON, 12 Dec 1984, *Battle between Europeans and Turks* (oil on canvas, 37 x 78¾ ins / 94 x 200 cm) GBP 14,000. LONDON, 10 April 1985, *Battle Scene* (pen and wash, 8½ x 13½ ins / 21.6 x 34.2 cm) GBP 700. MILAN, 16 April 1985, *Armistice after the Battle* (oil on canvas, 15 x 19 ins / 38 x 48.5 cm) ITL 3,300,000. MILAN, 4 Dec 1986, *Battle Scene* (pen and colour wash, 19 x 32¾ ins / 48 x 83 cm) ITL 6,000,000. LONDON, 8 Dec 1987, *Cavalry Engagement* (black chalk, pen and wash, 12½ x 19½ ins / 31.6 x 49.5 cm) GBP 2,600. NEW YORK, 14 Jan 1988, *Attack on a Coach in the Mountains* (oil on canvas, 36 x 49¼ ins / 91.5 x 125 cm) USD 49,500. NEW YORK, 21 Oct 1988, *Skirmishes near a Dungeon and Surrounding Walls* (oil on canvas, a pair, each 12¾ x 16¾ ins / 32.5 x 42.5 cm) USD 10,450. NEW YORK, 7 April 1989, *Cavalry Engagement between Occidental and Oriental Sol-*

diers (1665, oil on canvas, 9 x 13 1/4 ins / 23 x 33.5 cm) USD 2, 750. PARIS, 25 April 1989, *Battle Scene* (oil on canvas, 16 1/2 x 13 3/4 ins / 42 x 35 cm) FRF 15,000. ROME, 8 March 1990, *Two Cavalrymen; Two Smugglers Unloading a Barrel from a Boat* (oil on canvas/panel, a pair, diam. each 5 3/4 ins / 14.5 cm) ITL 8,000,000. ROME, 8 May 1990, *Landscape with Attack on a Travellers' Coach* (oil on canvas, 44 x 59 ins / 112 x 149 cm) ITL 78,000,000. NEW YORK, 31 May 1990, *Cavalry Skirmish* (oil on canvas, 6 3/4 x 16 ins / 17 x 40.8 cm) USD 12,100. LONDON, 2 July 1990, *Cavalry Engagement* (ink and wash, 11 1/2 x 17 1/4 ins / 29.3 x 43.7 cm) GBP 2,750. ROME, 19 Nov 1990, *Three Cavalrymen in a Landscape* (oil on canvas, 13 1/2 x 10 ins / 34.5 x 24.5 cm) ITL 16,100,000. LONDON, 14 Dec 1990, *Villa on the Mediterranean Coast with a Galleon Aground and a Horseman and his Dog in the Foreground* (oil on canvas, 24 1/2 x 30 ins / 62.5 x 76 cm) GBP 18,700. PARIS, 24 April 1991, *Cavalrymen Fighting* (pen and wash, 8 1/4 x 13 1/2 ins / 21 x 34.5 cm) FRF 5,000. MILAN, 30 May 1991, *River Landscape with Fishermen and Bathers* (oil on canvas, a pair, 14 1/2 x 22 1/2 ins / 37 x 57 cm) ITL 26,000,000. ROME, 19 Nov 1991, *Cavalry Troop on the March* (oil on canvas, 20 x 28 1/2 ins / 51 x 72.5 cm) ITL 33,000,000. NEW YORK, 16 Jan 1992, *Battle Scene* (oil on canvas, 29 1/4 x 39 ins / 74 x 99.1 cm) USD 18,700. LONDON, 1 April 1992, *Studies of Infantrymen and Cavalrymen* (oil on canvas, a pair, each 22 3/4 x 18 1/2 ins / 58 x 47 cm) GBP 10,450. MONACO, 18-19 June 1992, *Cavalryman Playing the Trumpet* (oil on canvas, 16 1/4 x 12 3/4 ins / 41.5 x 32.5 cm) FRF 33,300. ROME, 24 Nov 1992, *Cavalry Engagement on a Bridge* (oil on canvas, 23 1/2 x 30 1/4 ins / 60 x 77 cm) ITL 29,900,000. MILAN, 3 Dec 1992, *Before the Battle* (oil on canvas, 19 x 28 ins / 48 x 71 cm) ITL 46,000,000. MILAN, 13 May 1993, *Gathering of Soldiers* (oil on canvas, 17 1/4 x 25 1/2 ins / 44 x 65 cm) ITL 34,000,000. PARIS, 29 Nov 1993, *Before the Battle; Battle Scene* (oil on canvas, a pair, each 16 1/2 x 23 1/4 ins / 42 x 59 cm) FRF 110,000. ROME, 10 May 1994, *Military Encampment* (oil on canvas, 28 1/4 x 53 1/4 ins / 72 x 135 cm) ITL 25,300,000. PARIS, 8 June 1994, *After the Battle* (pen, ink and wash, 3 3/4 x 6 ins / 9.8 x 15.1 cm) FRF 5, 000. PARIS, 13 March 1995, *Battle Scene* (brown ink/black chalk, 9 1/4 x 14 1/2 ins / 23.5 x 37 cm) FRF 4,000. PARIS, 7 June 1995, *Battle Scene* (black chalk and wash, 13 3/4 x 23 1/2 ins / 35 x 59.5 cm) FRF 22,000. LONDON, 8 Dec 1995, *Cossacks Crossing the Mouth of a River near a Waterfall* (oil on canvas, 44 x 68 ins / 112 x 172.5 cm) GBP 47,700. NEW YORK, 12 Jan 1996, *Mediterranean Port with Fishermen and Travellers on a Quay* (oil on canvas, 24 x 48 ins / 61 x 121 cm) USD 34,500. MILAN, 21 Nov 1996, *Battle* (watercolour and brown ink, 9 x 15 1/4 ins / 23 x 39 cm) ITL 8,155,000. LONDON, 4 July 1997, *Cavalry Battle* (oil on canvas, 49 1/2 x 25 1/4 ins / 126 x 64.2 cm) GBP 12,075. LONDON, 3-4 Dec 1997, *Cavalry Column Halted on the Approaches to a Town, an Aqueduct and Mountains in the Distance* (oil on canvas, 45 x 63 3/4 ins / 114.5 x 162 cm) GBP 65,300. NEW YORK, 29 Jan 1999, *Mediterranean Port with Levants and Fisherfolk* (oil on canvas, a pair, 23 x 41 ins / 59 x 105 cm) USD 75,000. PARIS, 19 Feb 1999, *River Landscape with Riders and Walkers* (oil on canvas, a pair, 26 x 23 ins / 66 x 58 cm) FRF 310,000. LONDON, 19 April 2000, *Trumpeter on Horseback. Mounted Drummer* (oil on canvas, a pair, 18 x 14 ins / 46 x 36 cm) GBP 12,000. MILAN, 31 May 2000, *Battle Scene* (oil on canvas, a pair, 25 x 34 ins / 63 x 87 cm) ITL 85,000,000. LONDON, 11 July 2001, *Cavalry Battle Outside a Castle, Town Beyond* (oil on canvas, 108 x 92 ins / 275 x 234 cm) GBP 50,000. PARIS, 24 June 2002, *After the Battle* (oil on canvas, 26 x 31 ins / 65 x 80 cm) EUR 27,000. PARIS, 26 June 2002, *Man Riding Horse* (pen and ink wash, 7 x 11 ins / 19 x 27 cm) EUR 4,000. NEW YORK, 23 Jan 2004, *Soldiers in Rocky Landscapes* (oil on canvas, a pair, 19 x 14 ins / 47 x 36 cm) USD 24,000. MILAN, 25 Feb 2004, *Cavalry by Town* (oil on canvas, 46 x 63 ins / 117 x 161 cm) EUR 76,000.

SIMONINI-FULTON, Paola

Italian, 20th century.
Born 14 December 1932, in Brescia, to an American mother and an Italian father.
Active in France.
Painter, engraver.

A student at the Carrara Academy in Bergamo, Paola Simonini Fulton also studied at the school of decorative arts in Geneva. She has taken part in a number of collective exhibitions, particularly in Paris where her works have appeared regularly at the Salon des Indépendants since 1985, at the Salon d'Automne in 1987 and at the Salon des Artistes Français in 1988 and 1989.

SIMONIS, Eugène or Louis Eugène

Belgian, 19th century.
Born 11 July 1810, in Liège; died 11 July 1882, in Kochelberg, near Brussels.
Sculptor.

Eugène Simonis was a pupil of Finallis in Rome and a contemporary of the Geefs brothers and Fraikin, with whom he sometimes collaborated. He sculpted allegories for the fronton of the Théâtre de la Monnaie, and for the Triest Monument in the church of St Gudula. He also executed an equestrian statue of Godefroy de Bouillon erected in the Place Royale in Brussels. These official monuments from a colourless age have scarcely enriched the history of Belgian art. The museum in Brussels has his bust of the sculptor *Mathieu Kessel*, and his *Innocence* and *Unhappy Child*. The museum in Liège has his *Child with a Greyhound* and *Portrait of Mr Frere-Orban*.

SIMONIS, Hélène

Belgian, 20th century.
Born 1898, in Heusy.
Painter. Figures, portraits, interiors, landscapes.

SIMONIS-EMPIS, Catherine Edmée (Mme).
See **EMPIS**

SIMONKA, György, or Georges

Hungarian, 20th century.
Born in Budapest.
Painter. Figures, portraits, genre scenes, landscapes.

György Simonka painted landscapes, especially of Central Europe, portraits and figures, particularly of gypsies, and canvases such as *Return of the Hungarian Prodigal Son*.

MUSEUMS AND GALLERIES:
INNSBRUCK - LINZ - SALZBURG - VIENNA.

SIMONNE, T.

American, 19th century.
Active in New York c. 1815.
Engraver.

SIMONNEAU, Charles Louis, the Elder, or Simoneau

French, 17th - 18th century.
Baptised 3 August 1645 in Orléans; died 22 March 1728, in Paris.
Engraver, draughtsman. Portraits.

Charles Louis Simonneau the Elder was an accomplished engraver who studied under Noël Coypel and Guillaume Chasteau. Originally a burin engraver in the manner of Poilly, he then developed great skill in his use of the needle. He was admitted into the Académie on 28 June 1710.

He engraved many plates, portraits and painting reproductions after contemporary and classical masters.

AUCTION RECORDS:
MONACO, 2 July 1993, *Mountain Landscape and a Wooded Road with Travellers* (black chalk, ink and wash, 6 3/4 x 12 1/2 ins / 17.2 x 31.5 cm) FRF 15,000.

SIMONNEAU, Louis, the Younger, or Simoneau
French, 17th - 18th century.
Baptised 22 May 1654 in Orléans; died 16 January 1727, in Paris.
Draughtsman, engraver.

Louis Simonneau the Younger was the younger brother of Charles Louis Simonneau the Elder. He did burin engravings of portraits and paintings by the French masters. He was admitted into the Académie on 29 May 1706.

A talented draughtsman, he worked in the manner of the Audrans.

SIMONNEAU, Philippe (fils), or Simoneau
French, 18th century.
Born 3 February 1685, in Paris.
Engraver, draughtsman.

Philippe Simonneau was the son and pupil of Charles Louis Simonneau the Elder. He married Anne Langlois. He is mentioned in the death certificates of his uncle (1727) and his father (1728) with the title of draughtsman and engraver to the Académie des Sciences.

He did some engravings after the Italian masters.

SIMONNET. See also **SIMONET**

SIMONNET, Charles
French, 17th century.
Active in Nantes c. 1679.
Sculptor, architect.

SIMONNET, Jeanne
French, 20th century.
Born 10 June 1879, in Paris.
Painter, engraver.

Jeanne Simonnet was taught by her father, Lucien Simonnet, and by Félix Bracquemond. In Paris, she exhibited at the Salon des Artistes Français; she was awarded a commendation in 1908.

AUCTION RECORDS:
VERSAILLES, 21 Jan 1990, *River Banks* (oil on canvas, 22 x 25 1/2 ins / 55 x 65 cm) FRF 4,200.

SIMONNET, Lucien, or Simmonet
French, 19th - 20th century.
Born 22 November 1849, in Paris; died 16 April 1926, in Sèvres.
Painter. Genre scenes, landscapes, mountainscapes, waterscapes.

Lucien Simonnet was the father of Jeanne Simonnet. He was taught by Jules Lefebvre and Gustave Boulanger at the École des Beaux-Arts in Paris. His work featured at the Salon des Artistes Français in Paris from 1887, receiving a third-class medal in 1893, a second-class medal in 1895 and a bronze medal at the Exposition Universelle in 1900. He also received the Rosa Bonheur Prize in 1905.

MUSEUMS AND GALLERIES:
PARIS (Mus. d'Orsay): *Town of Avray, snowscape* - ROCHEFORT: *Sunset at Fouras* - SÈTE: *Picking Blackcurrants in Dijon*.

AUCTION RECORDS:
PARIS, 29 Jan 1945, *Mediterranean Shore; River Bank* (collection) FRF 3,400. PARIS, 21 March 1947, *Snow-Covered Church,* FRF 220. PARIS, 6 July 1951, *Flock of Sheep in Mountainous Landscape,* FRF 2,800. RHEIMS, 23 April 1989, *Small Boat Moored by Shore of Lake* (oil on canvas, 19 3/4 x 25 1/4 ins / 50 x 64 cm) FRF 5,500. PARIS, 1 Feb 1996, *Day in the Country* (1889, oil on canvas, 18 x 24 ins / 46 x 61 cm) FRF 7,500.

SIMONNIN DE BAR-LE-DUC. See **SIMONIN**

SIMONS, Amory Coffin
American, 19th - 20th century.
Born 1869, in Charleston (South Carolina); died 1934, in Santa Barbara.
Active in France.
Sculptor. Animals. Groups, equestrian groups.

Amory Coffin Simons began his artistic education at the Pennsylvania Academy of Fine Arts in Philadelphia. He also studied in Paris with Jean Auguste Dampt and Denis Puech. He was awarded honourable mentions in Paris at the Exposition Universelle (1900), in Buffalo (1901), and at the Salon in Paris (1906), as well as a silver medal in St Louis (1904). He was a member of the American Art Association in Paris.

AUCTION RECORDS:
NEW YORK, 21 May 1996, *Guard at the Villa Borghese (Equestrian Group)* (1913, bronze, h. 15 1/4 ins / 38.5 cm) USD 1,150. NEW YORK, 4 Dec 1996, *Group of Nine Horses* (bronze, h. 14 3/4 ins / 37.5 cm) USD 27,600.

SIMONS, Frans or Jan Frans
Belgian, 19th - 20th century.
Born 4 or 5 September 1855, in Antwerp; died 21 February 1919, in Brussels.
Painter, engraver. Portraits, genre scenes, landscapes, Still-lifes.

Frans Simons studied at the fine arts academy and under Eugeen Joors before settling in Brasschaet and exhibiting in Paris - notably at the Exposition Universelle of 1900, where he was awarded a bronze medal. Frans Simons also produced numerous etchings.

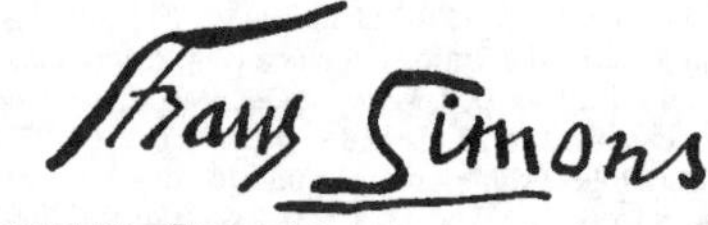

MUSEUMS AND GALLERIES:
ANTWERP: *Sun-Drenched Shore* - TOURNAI.

AUCTION RECORDS:
PARIS, 21 Jan 1924, *Mediterranean Fishing Port,* FRF 135. PARIS, 16 March 1925, *Les Martigues,* FRF 82. LONDON, 20 March 1981, *Wolf and Lamb* (oil on canvas, 32 1/4 x 39 3/4 ins / 82 x 101 cm) GBP 1,500. NEW YORK, 27 Feb 1986, *Wolf and Lamb* (oil on canvas, 32 x 39 3/4 ins / 81.3 x 101 cm) USD 10,500. LOKEREN, 28 May 1988, *Tending the Herd near a Stream* (oil on canvas, 20 x 28 3/4 ins / 51 x 73 cm) BEF 170,000. AMSTERDAM, 5-6 Nov 1991, *Solitude* (oil on canvas, 20 3/4 x 27 1/2 ins / 53 x 70 cm) NLG 1,725. LOKEREN, 20 March 1993, *In the Woods* (oil on canvas, 78 3/4 x 43 1/4 ins / 200 x 110 cm) BEF 190,000. AMSTERDAM, 9 Nov 1993, *Village* (oil on canvas, 27 1/4 x 48 1/2 ins / 69 x 123 cm) NLG 5,750. LOKEREN, 4 Dec 1993, *Returning from the Fields* (1880, oil on canvas, 35 1/2 x 16 1/4 ins / 90 x 41 cm) BEF 55,000. RHEIMS, 18 June 1995, *Deer's Head in the Undergrowth* (oil on canvas, 32 1/2 x 26 1/4 ins / 82.5 x 66.5 cm) FRF 4,000. LOKEREN, 11 Oct 1997, *Respite* (oil on canvas, 16 x 28 1/4 ins / 40.5 x 72 cm) BEF 95,000.

SIMONS, Hans. See **SIMOENS**

SIMONS, J. (Mlle)
French, 18th century.
Active in Paris c. 1786.
Miniaturist.

SIMONS, Jean Baptiste
Flemish School, 18th century.
Active 1743-1777.
Painter.

Jean Baptiste Simons executed two paintings for the church of the Augustinians in Ghent.

SIMONS, Jean or John. See **SIMON**

SIMONS, Leopold
French, 20th century.
Born 22nd February 1901, in Lille; died 17th October 1979, in Lille.

Painter. Scenes with figures.

Simons was proud of his working-class background and loved his native town of Lille, which he portrayed in his work - the everyday life of its cafes and streets - with tenderness and affection. In 1925 he exhibited a *Way of the Cross* at the Salon des Humoristes, in which the figures were all working-class people - factory workers, street urchins, prostitutes - and which was noticed by Forain, who immediately appointed him a member of the Salon. From 1921 to 1923 he worked as a journalist for the paper *L'Echo du Nord*, and from 1930 to 1968 he wrote and acted in his own plays. He also did illustrations for the magazines *Rire* and *Fantasio* and broadcasts for radio and television. He exhibited regularly at the Mischkind Gallery.

Museums and Galleries:

Bailleul - Lille (Hôtel de Ville) - Maubeuge - Wasquehal.

SIMONS, Maria Elisabeth

Dutch, 18th century.

Born c. 1754.

Active in Brussels.

Miniaturist, engraver.

Maria Elisabeth Simons engraved after the Dutch and Flemish masters.

SIMONS, Marie. See **LATOUR Marie de**

SIMONS, Michiel

Dutch, 17th century.

Born c. 1620, in Utrecht (?); died 20 May 1673, in Utrecht.

Painter. Still-lifes.

Michiel Simons may be the same artist as the painter mentioned in several dictionaries of art as M. Simons and about whom it is said that a number of his works are in America.

M. S.

Museums and Galleries:

Aachen - Amsterdam: *Fruit* - Utrecht.

Auction records:

New York, 17-18 March 1909, *Still-life,* USD 250. Paris, 25 Nov 1927, *Dead Game and Accessories,* FRF 700. New York, 26 Nov 1943, *Still-life,* USD 325. Paris, 16 June 1950, *Still-life with Lobster, Dish of Fruit and Game* (1652) FRF 60,000. Paris, 4 June 1958, *Still-life,* FRF 380,000. Paris, 14 June 1961, *Still-life,* FRF 10,000. Cologne, 26 Nov 1970, *Still-life with Fruit,* DEM 16,000. Amsterdam, 22 May 1973, *Still-life,* NLG 36,000. New York, 16 June 1977, *Still-life* (oil on canvas, 37 1/2 x 51 ins / 95 x 129.5 cm) USD 5,500. New York, 10 Jan 1980, *Still-life* (1653, oil on canvas, 36 1/4 x 49 1/2 ins / 92 x 125.5 cm) USD 20,000. New York, 9 June 1983, *Still-life with Fruit and Flowers* (oil on canvas, 24 3/4 x 36 ins / 63 x 91.5 cm) USD 18,000. London, 11 Dec 1985, *Still-life with Fruit and Oysters* (oil on canvas, 38 1/2 x 51 1/4 ins / 97.5 x 130 cm) GBP 18,000. New York, 20 Sept 1986, *Still-life with Flowers and Fruit* (oil on canvas, 20 x 26 ins / 50.8 x 66 cm) USD 30,000. London, 22 April 1988, *Fruit and Roses in a Glazed Earthenware Dish and Wineglass* (1650, 35 3/4 x 46 ins / 91 x 117 cm) GBP 35,200. Milan, 10 June 1988, *Flowers and Fruit* (oil on canvas, 25 1/4 x 30 ins / 64 x 76 cm) ITL 40,000,000. New York, 12 Jan 1989, *Still-life with Basket, Glazed Earthenware Plate and Dish of Fruit, with a Bird Perched on a Plum Branch, on an Entablature Covered with a Cloth* (oil on canvas, 29 1/2 x 39 1/4 ins / 75 x 100 cm) USD 63,250. Amsterdam, 12 June 1990, *Fruit, Game and Dish on a Table Covered with a Cloth* (oil on canvas, 33 x 40 1/2 ins / 83.6 x 102.7 cm) NLG 46,000. New York, 11 April 1991, *Fruit in a Blue and White Dish, a Dish and Different Objects on an Entablature Covered with a Cloth* (oil on canvas, 28 3/4 x 39 ins / 73 x 99 cm) USD 25,300. Amsterdam, 6 May 1993, *Still-life with Fruit, Flowers, Oysters and Game on a Table* (oil on canvas, 27 3/4 x 45 1/2 ins / 70.8 x 115.8 cm) NLG 94,300. New York, 14 Jan 1994, *Still-life with Grapes, Pears and Other Fruit, a Glass of White Wine with a Lemon, and Bread on a Plate on an Entablature in front of a Window* (oil on canvas, 29 x 39 1/4 ins / 73.7 x 99.7 cm) USD 57,500. London, 13 Dec 1996, *Still-life with Grapes, Melon, Peaches, Cherries, Peeled Lemon, Hazelnut, Dish and Pewter Plate on a Table Covered with a Cloth* (oil on canvas, 20 1/4 x 36 1/2 ins / 51.4 x 93 cm) GBP 36,700. Amsterdam, 10 Nov 1997, *Grapes, Peaches, Plums and a Quince on a Wanli Dish with a Melon, Plums, a Peeled Lemon, a Milk Loaf, an Enormous Hock Glass, Cherries and an Apricot on a Pewter Plate, Pears and Mulberries on an Entablature Covered with a Cloth* (oil on canvas, 33 1/4 x 40 3/4 ins / 84.6 x 103.4 cm) NLG 86,490. London, 3 Dec 1997, *Grapes, Peaches, Plums and Apricots in a Wanli Dish, a Peeled Lemon on a Pewter Plate, a Bread Roll, a Hock Glass, Plums, Cherries and Other Fruit on an Entablature Partially Covered with a Cloth* (1667, oil on canvas, 22 1/4 x 28 1/4 ins / 56.5 x 72 cm) GBP 17,250. Paris, 26 May 1999, *Still-life with Birds, Pigeon and Partridge* (oil on canvas, 20 x 26 ins / 52 x 67 cm) FRF 15,000. New York, 25 May 2000, *Fruit in a Porcelain Dish, Flowers in a Vase, Fruit and Wine Glass on a Covered Table* (1653, oil on canvas, 33 x 50 ins / 83 x 126 cm) USD 70,000. New York, 18 Oct 2000, *Still-life with Roemer, Wine Glass, Fruit and Lobster on a Table* (1650, oil on canvas, 33 x 49 ins / 84 x 124 cm) USD 100,000. New York, 26 Jan 2001, *Tulips, Carnations and Other Flowers in a Vase* (oil on canvas, 34 x 45 ins / 87 x 114 cm) USD 100,000. London, 13 Dec 2001, *Still-life with Fruit Tumbling from a Porcelain Bowl on a Wooden Table* (oil on canvas, 32 x 41 ins / 81 x 104 cm) GBP 17,000. Amsterdam, 13 May 2003, *Still-life with Grapes, Apples, Peaches in Bowl, Lobster and Crayfish* (oil on canvas, 29 x 37 ins / 73 x 94 cm) EUR 17,000. Amsterdam, 17 May 2004, *Rose, Various Fruit, Glass Flute, Pheasant and Other Birds on a Table* (oil on canvas, 29 x 41 ins / 73 x 103 cm) EUR 22,000.

SIMONS, P. Marcius. See **MARCIUS-SIMONS Pinckney**

SIMONS, Paul Henri

French, 19th - 20th century.

Born 27 March 1865; died 16 February 1932.

Painter. Landscapes, seascapes.

Paul Henri Simons was a student of Jean Pierre Laurens and Louis Oliver Merson. He specialised in landscapes of Provence.

Auction records:

Paris, 18 Jan 1924, *Canal in Martigues (Provence),* FRF 140. Paris, 20 Feb 1931, *Port of Cassis (Provence),* FRF 120. Paris, 12 April 1943, *Martigues,* FRF 1,600. Paris, 16 March 1944, *Seascape; Landscape* (two canvases) FRF 1,600; *Martigues* (three canvases) FRF 3,200.

SIMONS, Peeter, or Symons

Flemish School, 17th century.

Painter.

Peeter Simons is mentioned as the master of a studio in Antwerp from 1629 to 1637. He painted after sketches by Rubens.

Museums and Galleries:

Madrid (Prado): *Cephalus and Procris.*

SIMONS, Quintijn

Flemish School, 17th century.

Born August 1592, in Brussels.

Painter. History painting.

SIMONS, Tilla

Belgian, 20th century.

Born 1888, in Brasschaat.

Painter. Figures, landscapes, Still-lifes.

Tilla Simons worked alongside her father, Frans Simons.

SIMONSEN, Alfred
Danish, 20th century.
Born 16 December 1906, in Kölstrup, near Kerteminde; died 12 April 1935, in Odense.
Painter, engraver. Landscapes.
Alfred Simonsen studied at the Kongelige Danske Kunstakademi in Copenhagen under Einar Nielsen, Sigurd Wandel and Aksel Jørgensen.

SIMONSEN, Axel Bjerre
Danish, 20th century.
Born 12 October 1884, in Hillerød.
Painter. Landscapes.
Axel Bjerre Simonsen studied at the Kongelige Danske Kunstakademi in Copenhagen.

SIMONSEN, Carl Marius Nikolai
Danish, 19th century.
Born 30 November 1828, in Copenhagen; died 5 December 1902, in Copenhagen.
Lithographer.
Simonsen was a pupil of Lorilleux in Paris.

SIMONSEN, Jess
Danish, 17th century.
Active in 1616.
Sculptor (wood).
Simonsen sculpted the stalls in the church in Sörup.

SIMONSEN, Niels
Danish, 19th century.
Born 10 December 1807, in Copenhagen; died 11 December 1885, in Copenhagen.
Painter, sculptor, engraver. Military subjects, battles, figures, seascapes.
Simonsen was a pupil of Johan Ludwig Lund. He began as a sculptor, before turning to painting. He went to Munich to work as a painter. During his stay in Germany, he travelled to Italy, the Tyrol and Algeria. He returned to Denmark in 1845 and became a member of the Kunstakademi. In 1864, he painted two works on the subject of the War of Slesvig.

N Simonsen
1855

MUSEUMS AND GALLERIES:
COPENHAGEN: *Danish Soldiers Surrounding a Woodshed* - MUNICH: *A Sailor* - OSLO: *A Caravan Overtaken by a Storm in the Desert.*

AUCTION RECORDS:
PARIS, 26 Jan 1944, *Arabian Chief,* FRF 3,100. COPENHAGEN, 30 Aug 1977, *Arabian Horsemen Pursued by the French Cavalry* (1875, oil on canvas, 19 3/4 x 26 1/2 ins / 50 x 67 cm) DKK 10,000. COPENHAGEN, 8 Nov 1979, *Arabian Soldier* (1860, oil on canvas, 22 x 25 1/2 ins / 55 x 65 cm) DKK 17,500. LONDON, 15 March 1983, *Statue of Christ Brought by Thorvaldsen to the Freu Kirke in Copenhagen* (1833-1834, oil on canvas, 16 3/4 x 20 3/4 ins / 42.5 x 53 cm) GBP 25,000. COPENHAGEN, 16 April 1985, *The Pirate Ship* (1868, oil on canvas, 29 1/4 x 37 1/2 ins / 74 x 95 cm) DKK 210,000. COPENHAGEN, 16 April 1986, *The Pirate Ship* (1837, oil on canvas, 32 3/4 x 40 1/2 ins / 83 x 103 cm) DKK 140,000. LONDON, 24 March 1988, *Two Figures Fishing in a Boat* (1869, oil on canvas, 13 x 16 1/4 ins / 33 x 41 cm) GBP 1,100. STOCKHOLM, 19 April 1989, *Old Woman in Regional Costume* (1857, oil on canvas, 20 1/2 x 13 ins / 52 x 33 cm) SEK 5,500. COPENHAGEN, 25 Oct 1989, *Young Moor* (1840, oil on canvas, 11 1/2 x 7 3/4 ins / 29 x 20 cm) DKK 6,000. LONDON, 22 Nov 1989, *Boat, Port-side* (1878, oil on canvas, 13 1/2 x 16 1/2 ins / 34 x 42 cm) GBP 11,000. LONDON, 16 Feb 1990, *Caught!* (1857, oil on canvas, 31 x 41 1/4 ins / 78.8 x 104.8 cm) GBP 4,950. COPENHAGEN, 5 Feb 1992, *View of Lokken From the Coast* (1856, oil on canvas, 13 x 19 3/4 ins / 33 x 50 cm) DKK 11,000. LONDON, 18 March 1992, *The Last Square* (1867, oil on canvas, 30 3/4 x 43 ins / 78 x 109 cm) GBP 17,600. LONDON, 18 June 1993, *Barbaric Boarding of a Boat* (1842, oil on canvas, 27 3/4 x 37 1/4 ins / 70.5 x 94.5 cm) GBP 14,950. NEW YORK, 13 Oct 1993, *The Waiting of the Fishermen* (1869, oil on canvas, 13 1/2 x 16 3/4 ins / 34.3 x 42.5 cm) USD 4,313. PARIS, 22 April 1994, *The Wounded Soldier* (1845, oil on canvas, 36 x 41 3/4 ins / 90.5 x 106 cm) FRF 110,000. COPENHAGEN, 21 May 1997, *Seascape with Yacht and a Boat Off the North African Coast* (1874, 20 3/4 x 33 ins / 53 x 84 cm) DKK 65,000. COPENHAGEN, 1 June 1999, *Landscape with Italian Family Having a Rest* (1871, oil on canvas, 21 x 33 ins / 53 x 83 cm) DKK 50,000. COPENHAGEN, 7 Sept 1999, *Southern Landscape with Soldier Escorting Lady on Horseback* (oil on canvas, 21 x 17 ins / 53 x 43 cm) DKK 50,000. COPENHAGEN, 30 May 2000, *Episode from the Battle at Slesvig 23 April 1848* (1848, oil on canvas, 8 x 13 ins / 20 x 32 cm) DKK 13,000. COPENHAGEN, 27 Nov 2001, *North African Battle Scene* (1861, oil on canvas, 11 x 15 ins / 29 x 37 cm) DKK 55,000. COPENHAGEN, 27 Nov 2001, *North Africans Defending Themselves against the Enemy* (oil on canvas, 35 x 43 ins / 90 x 110 cm) DKK 120,000. COPENHAGEN, 29 May 2002, *A Nomadic Woman Resting under Palm Trees in the Desert* (oil on canvas, 11 x 9 ins / 29 x 24 cm) DKK 28,000. VEJLE, 23 Sept 2002, *Coastal Landscape with Pirates on Way to Sailing Ship* (1847, oil on canvas, 15 x 20 ins / 37 x 51 cm) DKK 33,000. COPENHAGEN, 26 May 2003, *Fisherman's Wife by her Baby's Cradle Waiting for Husband to Return from Sea* (1837, oil on canvas, 18 x 15 ins / 46 x 39 cm) DKK 15,000. LONDON, 12 June 2003, *Faithful Hound* (1856, oil on canvas, 33 x 50 ins / 84 x 127 cm) GBP 1,500. COPENHAGEN, 25 Feb 2004, *Oriental Men Playing Board Game* (1859, oil on canvas, 11 x 14 ins / 27 x 36 cm) DKK 60,000.

SIMONSEN, Peter or Simon Peter
Danish, 20th century.
Born 22 April 1882, in Odense.
Painter. Figures, landscapes.
Peter Simonsen was a pupil of Kristian Zahrtmann and Harald Giersing.

SIMONSEN, Simon Ludvig Ditlev
Danish, 19th - 20th century.
Born 19 January 1841, in Munich; died 27 February 1928, in Copenhagen.
Painter. Figures, animals.
Simon Ludvig Ditlev Simonsen was an animal painter, chiefly of horses and dogs. He studied under his father, Niels Simonsen, then at the Kunstakademi in Copenhagen and under Auguste Bonheur in Chevreuse.

MUSEUMS AND GALLERIES:
HILLERØD (Frederiksborg Slot): *Redoubts at Duppel.*

AUCTION RECORDS:
COPENHAGEN, 7 Dec 1966, *Horse and Basset Hound,* DKK 11,200. COPENHAGEN, 23 Feb 1972, *Prayer,* DKK 8,200. COPENHAGEN, 22 Feb 1973, *Landscape with Hunting Dogs,* DKK 8,900. COPENHAGEN, 21 Nov 1974, *Farmyard,* DKK 7,500. COPENHAGEN, 10 Nov 1976, *Goatherd* (oil on canvas, 26 1/2 x 43 3/4 ins / 67 x 111 cm) DKK 9,000. COPENHAGEN, 30 Aug 1977, *Bitch and Puppies* (1880, oil on canvas, 37 1/2 x 48 1/2 ins / 95 x 123 cm) DKK 16,000. COPENHAGEN, 12 Feb 1980, *Two Young Basset Hounds* (1889, oil on canvas, 11 1/2 x 15 3/4 ins / 29 x 40 cm) DKK 22,000. COPENHAGEN, 22 Sept 1981, *Landscape with Hunter and Dog* (1904, oil on canvas, 28 3/4 x 41 ins / 73 x 104 cm) DKK 14,000. COPENHAGEN, 27 Feb 1985, *Hunting Dog with Prey* (1895, oil on canvas, 33 1/2 x 27 1/4 ins / 85 x 69 cm) DKK 52,000. COPENHAGEN, 20 Aug 1986, *Pointer with Prey* (1895, oil on canvas, 33 1/2 x 27 1/4 ins / 85 x 69 cm) DKK 45,000. COPENHAGEN, 23 March 1988, *Two Horses in a Field* (1864, 12 1/4 x 16 1/4 ins / 31 x 41 cm) DKK

8,000. STOCKHOLM, 19 April 1989, *Dog Guarding Geese* (oil on panel, 13 x 9¾ ins / 33 x 25 cm) SEK 16,000. COPENHAGEN, 25 Oct 1989, *Mule-Drawn Cart* (1868, oil on canvas, 9 x 11 ins / 23 x 28 cm) DKK 4,600. COPENHAGEN, 25-26 April 1990, *Goatherd and Charges on a Rocky Outcrop* (1871, oil on canvas, 7¾ x 11 ins / 20 x 27 cm) DKK 10,000. STOCKHOLM, 14 Nov 1990, *Chickens and Ducks at the Edge of a Wood* (oil on canvas, 15¼ x 10¼ ins / 39 x 26 cm) SEK 4,500. COPENHAGEN, 6 Dec 1990, *Hunting Dog and Young Feeding in a Farmyard* (oil on canvas, 27½ x 33 ins / 70 x 84 cm) DKK 45,000. LONDON, 15 Jan 1991, *Pack of Dogs Chasing a Fox* (1886, oil on canvas/panel, 17¾ x 21¼ ins / 45 x 54 cm) GBP 1,540. COPENHAGEN, 1 May 1991, *Caucasian Rider* (oil on canvas, 11 x 15¼ ins / 28 x 39 cm) DKK 10,500. COPENHAGEN, 29 Aug 1991, *St. Bernard* (1899, oil on canvas, 11½ x 13 ins / 29 x 33 cm) DKK 5,800. LONDON, 7 April 1993, *Dog Portrait (Knar)* (1905, oil on canvas, 20 x 16¼ ins / 51 x 41 cm) GBP 2,185. COPENHAGEN, 5 May 1993, *Horse in a Stableyard* (1895, oil on canvas, 11 x 13¾ ins / 27 x 35 cm) DKK 5,000. COPENHAGEN, 16 Nov 1994, *Three Little Puppies* (1905, oil on canvas/paper, 12½ x 16½ ins / 32 x 42 cm) DKK 16,500. LONDON, 22 Feb 1995, *Dachshunds Resting* (oil on canvas, 15¾ x 22½ ins / 40 x 57 cm) GBP 2,990. LONDON, 17 Nov 1995, *Room in a Country House* (1909, oil on canvas, 13¼ x 10½ ins / 33.4 x 26.4 cm) GBP 3,220. LONDON, 21 March 1997, *A Watchful Eye* (oil on canvas, 9¾ x 14¾ ins / 24.8 x 37.5 cm) GBP 6,670.

SIMONSEN, Søren
Danish, 19th century.
Born 2 May 1843, in Ribe; died 2 May 1900, in Aalborg.
Painter, draughtsman. Religious subjects. Murals.

Simonsen was a pupil at the Kunstakademi in Copenhagen. He taught drawing at the academy in Aarhus. He also worked for the churches there, as well as in Fredericia.

SIMONSON, Anna
British, 20th century.
Died 17 February 1947.
Painter. Interiors, urban landscapes.

Anna Simonson exhibited at the Royal Academy in London.

SIMONSON, David
German, 19th century.
Born 15 March 1831, in Dresden; died 8 February 1896, in Dresden.
Painter.

Simonson attended the academy in Dresden.

MUSEUMS AND GALLERIES:
DRESDEN (Gemäldegal. Neue Meister): *Portrait of his Wife* - DRESDEN (Stadtmus.): *Portrait of the Actor K. Porth the Younger.*

AUCTION RECORDS:
NEW YORK, 24 May 1989, *Portrait of a Man* (1886, oil on canvas, 23¾ x 20½ ins / 60.3 x 52.1 cm) USD 11,000. COLOGNE, 6 April 2000, *Portrait of a Girl with a Red Necklace* (1855, oil on canvas, 19 x 17 ins / 47 x 44 cm) DEM 5,000.

SIMONSON-CASTELLI, Ernst Oskar, or Simonson-Kastelli
German, 19th - 20th century.
Born 20 November 1864, in Dresden; died 29 July 1929, in Dresden.
Painter. Historical subjects, portraits, interiors with figures, landscapes.

Simonson-Castelli studied at the fine arts academy in Munich and under Ferdinand Pauwels.

MUSEUMS AND GALLERIES:
DRESDEN: *Trooping the Colour, Dresden, 23 April 1898; Funeral of Prince Albert of Saxony* - LÜBECK: *Theologian* - MOSCOW (Rumiantsev Mus.): *Hero and Leander* - SCHWERIN: *Gloria Deo; Shaft of Sunlight; Dutch Interior.*

AUCTION RECORDS:
COLOGNE, 19 Oct 1979, *Fishing Boats* (oil on canvas, 27½ x 15¾ ins / 70 x 40 cm) DEM 1,800.

SIMONSSON, Birger Jörgen
Swedish, 20th century.
Born 3 March 1883, in Uddevalla; died 1938.
Painter. Portraits, genre scenes, landscapes, Still-lifes. Unga (Young Ones group).

Birger Simonsson studied under Kristian Zahrtmann in Copenhagen and under Henri Matisse in Paris. His portraiture is conventional, but he deserves his place alongside Isaac Grünewald and Gösta Sandels in the pantheon of the New Swedish School, in view of his unpretentious yet accomplished landscapes, which have a strong emotional content.

AUCTION RECORDS:
GÖTEBORG, 23 March 1976, *Two Young Women on the Beach* (oil on canvas, 47¼ x 39¾ ins / 120 x 101 cm) SEK 7,300. GÖTEBORG, 13 April 1983, *Young Girl with a Cigarette* (1928, oil on canvas, 39¼ x 29½ ins / 100 x 75 cm) SEK 10,500. LONDON, 16 March 1989, *Wooded Landscape near Gothenburg* (oil on panel, 18 x 21¾ ins / 45.5 x 55.5 cm) GBP 2,200. GÖTEBORG, 18 May 1989, *Landscape near Telemark* (oil on canvas, 19¼ x 23¼ ins / 49 x 59 cm) SEK 27,000. STOCKHOLM, 14 June 1990, *Landscape with Reclining Nude Model* (oil on canvas, 24½ x 31 ins / 62 x 79 cm) SEK 24,000. STOCKHOLM, 5-6 Dec 1990, *Landscape near Telemark, Norway* (oil on canvas, 13¾ x 17¾ ins / 35 x 45 cm) SEK 6,700. STOCKHOLM, 27 April 1999, *West Coast Landscape* (oil on canvas, 18 x 21 ins / 46 x 54 cm) SEK 14,000. STOCKHOLM, 27 Nov 2000, *Sunlit Road, View from Cassis* (oil on panel, 18 x 15 ins / 46 x 38 cm) SEK 15,000. STOCKHOLM, 27 Nov 2000, *Towards the Park with Bath-house, Marstrand* (1938, oil on canvas, 32 x 26 ins / 81 x 65 cm) SEK 30,000. STOCKHOLM, 24 April 2002, *By the Wall* (oil on canvas, 26 x 32 ins / 66 x 81 cm) SEK 22,000.

SIMONSZ-HAMERSVELT, Evert.
See **HAMERSVELT Evert Symonsz.**

SIMONSZ., Albert. See the entry **MOSTAERT Jan**

SIMONSZ., Claes Simonsz. and Mouryn Simonsz.. See **WATERLAND**

SIMONT GUILLÉN, José
Spanish, 20th century.
Born 1875, in Barcelona; died 1968, in Caracas (Venezuela).
Also active in France.
Painter, draughtsman, illustrator. Portraits, scenes with figures, genre scenes.

José Simont was a pupil of Nonell and Mir at the Academia de Bellas Artes in Barcelona. He lived in Paris from 1898, then in New York from 1921 to 1932. He returned to France, and later settled for good in his native country of Spain in 1947.

He began his career as an illustrator of short stories and tales for children in the publications *Christmas, The Young Person's News* and *The Illustrated World*. He went on to collaborate on Catholic newspapers and French women's magazines, before moving to work for British and German publications.

BIBLIOGRAPHY:
Arnáiz, José Manuel/López Jiménez, Javier/Merchán Díaz, Manuel (ed.), '*Cien años de pintura en Espana y Portugal (1830-1930)*' in vol. X, Antiqvaria, Madrid, 1993.

AUCTION RECORDS:
VERSAILLES, 4 Oct 1981, *Spanish Couple at a Café in Barcelona* (1898, oil on canvas, 17¼ x 13¾ ins / 43.5 x 35 cm) FRF 15,000.

SIMONY
French, 18th century.
Sculptor. Religious subjects.
Simony produced wood carvings in the palace chapel at Versailles.

SIMONY, Alexandre
French, 18th century.
Born in Coreil.
Active in Nancy in 1748.
Sculptor.

SIMONY, Antal or Anton
Hungarian, 19th century.
Born 1821, in Kecskemét; died 1892, in Budapest.
Painter. Portraits.
Antal Simony studied in Vienna and Paris.

SIMONY, Dominique
French, 18th century.
Active 1704-1724.
Sculptor.
Dominique Simony produced sculptures in Versailles, Paris, and the palaces of St-Germain-en-Laye and Marly.

SIMONY, Julius
German, 19th century.
Born 14 September 1785, in Berlin; died 24 November 1835, in Berlin.
Sculptor.
Simony studied under Gottfried Schadow. He exhibited in Berlin from 1802 and excelled at half-length portraits.

SIMONY, Stefan
Austrian, 19th - 20th century.
Born 26 November 1860, in Vienna; died 1950.
Painter, engraver. Portraits, genre scenes, animals.
Stefan Simony studied at the Akademie der Bildenden Künste in Vienna under Christian Griepenkerl and Josef Huber.
AUCTION RECORDS:
VIENNA, 14 Sept 1976, *Summer's Day at Florisdorf* (1914, oil on canvas, 30 3/4 x 46 3/4 ins / 78 x 119 cm) ATS 90,000. VIENNA, 10 June 1980, *Landscape with Egrets* (oil on panel, 7 3/4 x 10 3/4 ins / 20 x 27.5 cm) ATS 30,000. VIENNA, 15 Sept 1982, *View of Dürnstein* (oil on canvas, 28 x 37 1/2 ins / 71 x 95 cm) ATS 35,000. VIENNA, 5 Dec 1984, *Spitz on the Danube* (1919, oil on canvas, 22 3/4 x 28 3/4 ins / 58 x 73 cm) ATS 90,000. VIENNA, 11 Dec 1985, *Hothouse at Schönbrunn* (1911, oil on canvas, 24 3/4 x 33 3/4 ins / 63 x 86 cm) ATS 80,000. LONDON, 8 Oct 1986, *Figures by a Zoo Lake, Schönbrunn* (1911, oil on canvas, 24 1/2 x 33 ins / 62 x 84 cm) GBP 12,000. LONDON, 11 June 1997, *Figures near a Pond in Schönbrunn Zoo* (1911, oil on canvas, 24 1/2 x 33 ins / 62 x 84 cm) GBP 12,650. VIENNA, 2 Dec 1999, *Summer Residence of Isidore Canevale, Prater* (oil on canvas, 28 x 39 ins / 72 x 100 cm) ATS 200,000. NEW YORK, 2 May 2000, *The Harvesters* (oil on panel, 20 x 30 ins / 51 x 76 cm) USD 7,500. VIENNA, 21 Nov 2001, *Fishing Hut in Durnstein* (oil on board, 19 x 26 ins / 47 x 65 cm) ATS 90,000. VIENNA, 27 May 2003, *Tarrenz in Tyrol* (1923, oil on panel, 21 x 29 ins / 54 x 74 cm) EUR 4,000. VIENNA, 28 Oct 2003, *Schönbrunn* (1912, oil on canvas, 25 x 37 ins / 64 x 94 cm) EUR 9,000. VIENNA, 21 April 2004, *Kaiserpavillion* (1912, oil on board, 8 x 11 ins / 20 x 28 cm) EUR 4,000. VIENNA, 27 May 2004, *Working in the Field with View of the Fortress of Salzburg* (1903, oil on canvas, 29 x 43 ins / 73 x 110 cm) EUR 6,500.

SIMOSSI, Gabriella
French, 20th century.
Sculptor.
Gabriella Simossi created symbolic objects containing elements taken from everyday reality, and disturbing unidentifiable shapes.

SIMOSVIKI, A.
Painter. Genre scenes.
Simosviki is mentioned by Miss Florence Levy.
AUCTION RECORDS:
NEW YORK, 13 Jan 1911, *Good Story*, USD 125.

SIMOTOVÁ, Adriena
Czech, 20th century.
Born 6 July 1926, in Prague.
Engraver, sculptor, collage artist, installation artist.
Figures, scenes with figures.
Adriena Simotová studied in Prague art schools from 1943 to 1950. She lives and works in that city. Her nimble, synthetic lines depict people caught up in unnamed yet urgent occupations. She also makes sculptures out of silk paper and sometimes wrapping paper, creating light, apparently fragile flying objects which she paints in grey tints and then displays alone or in groups on a table top, which serves as a pedestal. Such works include *Small Mirror, Sacred Table, Mask*. Her drawings, in lead or pastel, exploit the qualities of silk paper.

Collective exhibitions include: San Marino Biennale, Monaco Biennale (1965); Konsthallen, Uppsala (1966); Galleria Municipale, Turin and Oslo Museum (1967); Galerie La Hune, Paris (1969); Biennale Internazionale d'Arte Grafica, Florence (1970); Osaka and Kyoto Museums of Modern Art (1981); Centre Georges Pompidou, Paris (1983, 1985); Museum des 20. Jahrhundert, Vienna (1985, 1987); Hirschhorn Museum, Washington, and IVth International Drawing Triennale, Wroclaw (1988); Musée du Luxembourg, Paris (1990). Solo exhibitions include: Prague (1960); and, Chicago (1976); Konsthallen, Uppsala (1978); Ljubljana Print Biennale (1981); Berlin (1982); Galerie de France, Paris (1983 and 1991); Dum umeni mesta (House of Arts), Brno (1986); *L'Œil éphémère. Œuvres sur papier de Jiri Kolar et Adriena Simotova*, as part of the exhibition *Bohemia Magica, a Czech Season In France*, Musée des Beaux-Arts, Dijon (2002).
BIBLIOGRAPHY:
Les Pragois - Les Années de silence, exhibition catalogue, PACA, Présence de l'Art contemporain, Angers, 1990. *Simotova*, exhibition catalogue, Gal. de France, Paris, 1991. *Adriana Simotova, artiste tchèque*, exhibition catalogue, Musée des Beaux-Arts, Dijon, 2002.

SIMOV, Viktor Andreevich
Russian, 19th - 20th century.
Born 14 April 1858, in Moscow; died 21 August 1935, in Moscow.
Painter. Stage sets.
Viktor Simov trained with Vasily Perov, Ilarion Pryanishnikov and Aleksei Savrasov at the academy in St Petersburg, graduating in 1882. He worked in the theatre and designed a number of important productions. He also founded an experimental design studio.
BIBLIOGRAPHY:
Halturin, Aleksandr/Hulten, Pontus/Gunar, Karl (ed.), *Paris-Moscou*, group exhibition catalogue, Éd. du Centre Georges-Pompidou, Paris, 1979.

SIMPKIN, T.
British, 18th century.
Active in London at the end of the 18th century.
Painter. Landscapes, architectural views.
T. Simpkin exhibited *View of the West Front of Peterborough Cathedral* at the Royal Academy of Arts in London in 1786, and *Crowland Abbey* in 1794.

SIMPKINS
British, 18th century.
Active in London in 1780.
Engraver. Ex-libris.

SIMPKINS, Henry John
Canadian, 20th century.
Born 1906; died 1995.
Painter, watercolourist. Landscapes.

Henry John Simpkins was an associate of the Royal Canadian Academy.

AUCTION RECORDS:
MONTREAL, 23-24 Nov 1993, *Montreal from Pine Avenue* (watercolour, 20 x 31¼ ins / 50.6 x 79.6 cm) CAD 800.

SIMPLICE
Italian, 17th century.
Died 1654.
Venetian, active in Rome.
Painter.

Simplice, who was a monk, was the pupil of Brusasorci.

SIMPLICIANO DA PALERMO
Italian, 16th century.
Painter. Religious subjects.

Simplicianoda Palermo was an Augustinian monk.

MUSEUMS AND GALLERIES:
PALERMO (Mus. Nazionale): *Crucifixion* (1514).

SIMPLICIO, Alexandre
Portuguese, 19th century.
Active in Lisbon during the first half of the 19th century.
Painter.

Alexandre Simplicio worked in Lisbon and Rio de Janeiro.

MUSEUMS AND GALLERIES:
VIRE: *Portrait of an Unknown Man* (miniature).

SIMPOL, Claude. See **SAINT-PAUL Claude**

SIMPRONE, Guglielmo
Italian, 17th century.
Active during the first half of the 17th century.
Painter.

Simprone worked in Turin in 1628.

SIMPSON, Agnes
British, 19th century.
Active in London from 1827 to 1848.
Miniaturist. Portraits.

SIMPSON, Charles Walter
British, 20th century.
Born 8 May 1885, in Camberley; died 1971.
Painter (including gouache). Scenes with figures, hunting scenes, landscapes, seascapes, animals.

Charles Simpson originally wished to pursue a military career, but a riding accident forced him to abandon his ambitions and to turn instead to painting. Self-taught to a significant extent, he also studied at the School of Painting in Bushey under Lucy Kemp-Welch, with Alfred Munnings in Norfolk, J. Noble Barlow and Stanhope Forbes in Newlyn (which he first visited in 1903), and finally at the Académie Julian in Paris in 1910. After marrying the portrait-painter Ruth Alison in 1913, he moved first to Newlyn and then in 1921 to St Ives, where the couple ran a painting school. He lived in London from 1924 to 1929, returning in 1930-1931 to Cornwall, where he settled in Penzance and painted local landscapes and seascapes.

Simpson applied a style derived from the French Impressionists to the portrayal of English landscapes and scenes, in works such as the oil painting *Water Meadows at Guildford*. He is best known for his paintings of birds and animals, particularly horses, and of hunting and racing scenes. He also wrote books and articles on hunting and country pursuits as well as on his own art, including *El Rodeo*, based on the sketches he produced at the rodeo held in Wembley in 1924, and *Animals and Bird Painting: The Outlook and Technique of the Artist*. He also provided numerous illustrations for books and magazines, including *Country Life*.

Simpson participated in group exhibitions, including: Royal Academy, London (1907-1953); Laing Gallery, Newcastle upon Tyne (1920); Paris Salon (where he won a silver medal in 1923 and a gold in 1924); Panama Pacific International Exposition, San Francisco (1915, where he won a gold medal); Royal Institute; and Royal Glasgow Institute of Fine Arts. He also held solo exhibitions in London and elsewhere. A retrospective exhibition of his works was held at Penlee House Gallery and Museum, Penzance, in 2005. He became a member of the Royal Institute of Painters in watercolours (1914) and the Royal Institute of Oil Painters (1921).

Charles Simpson

BIBLIOGRAPHY:
Lane, Charles, *Charles Walter Simpson 1885-1971*, British Sporting Art Trust, 1998 ((essay)).

MUSEUMS AND GALLERIES:
LONDON (Victoria and Albert Mus.) - NEWCASTLE UPON TYNE (Laing Art Gallery).

AUCTION RECORDS:
NEW YORK, 7 June 1985, *Before the Derby; After the Derby* (gouache, a pair, 21½ x 30 ins / 54.6 x 76.2 cm) USD 9,000. LONDON, 13 Nov 1986, *Ducks on the Stream at Clapper Mill, Lamorna* (oil on canvas, 21 x 31¼ ins / 53.5 x 79.5 cm) GBP 7,000. LONDON, 13 May 1987, *Ascot* (gouache, 20 x 30 ins / 51 x 76 cm) GBP 22,000. NEW YORK, 9 June 1988, *Hunting* (gouache/paper, 21½ x 28½ ins / 54.6 x 72.4 cm) USD 7,700. LONDON, 9 June 1988, *Wardley Wood* (gouache, 26 x 39 ins / 66.3 x 98.8 cm) GBP 1,980. LONDON, 8 March 1990, *The Farndale on Blakey Ridge, Yorkshire* (gouache, 20½ x 28½ ins / 52.1 x 72.5 cm) GBP 5,500. LONDON, 27 Sept 1991, *Jumping the Fence at the Grand National* (oil on canvas, 28 x 40¼ ins / 71 x 102 cm) GBP 2,200. LONDON, 15 March 1994, *Studies of Ducks* (gold, silver and oil paint on panel, screen in three parts, in all 60 x 83 ins / 152.4 x 210.8 cm) GBP 1,725. LONDON, 13 Nov 1996, *The Coronation Stakes at Ascot* (1928, gouache, 20¾ x 29½ ins / 53 x 75 cm) GBP 4,600. LONDON, 18 Dec 1997, *In Full Cry* (gouache, 15 x 21¾ ins / 38.1 x 55.3 cm) GBP 1,092. LONDON, 28 May 1999, *Pinto* (oil on canvas, 18 x 24 ins / 46 x 61 cm) GBP 2,300. LONDON, 30 Sept 1999, *Portrait of Phyllis Cunningham* (1920, oil on canvas, 24 x 20 ins / 61 x 51 cm) GBP 3,500. LONDON, 5 April 2000, *Phyllis and Vera Cunningham on a Cornish Beach* (1919, oil on canvas, 20 x 24 ins / 51 x 61 cm) GBP 32,000. MARKET HARBOROUGH, 5 Sept 2000, *Sir Julian Cahn, with the Fernie Hounds at Standford Park* (oil on canvas, 45 x 60 ins / 115 x 153 cm) GBP 21,000. NEW YORK, 8 March 2001, *Polo Players* (1920, oil on board, 41 x 50 ins / 104 x 127 cm) USD 8,000. LONDON, 25 Sept 2001, *Herring Season* (gouache, 22 x 31 ins / 55 x 78 cm) GBP 5,200. LONDON, 12 March 2002, *Mallard Drakes and Aylesbury Ducks* (oil on canvas, 24 x 30 ins / 61 x 76 cm) GBP 4,200. LONDON, 7 Aug 2002, *Jockeys Mounting Up* (oil on canvas, 20 x 24 ins / 51 x 61 cm) GBP 3,000. LEYBURN, 10 April 2003, *Grand National, Bechers Brook* (oil on canvas, 28 x 36 ins / 71 x 92 cm) GBP 6,000. CREWKERNE, 15 May 2003, *Loading the Hay Cart* (oil on canvas, 27 x 35 ins / 69 x 90 cm) GBP 4,400. LONDON, 15 June 2004, *The Tent* (oil on canvas, 20 x 24 ins / 51 x 61 cm) GBP 16,000. TORONTO, 22 Nov 2004, *Horse and Cutter* (1941, oil on canvas, 20 x 26 ins / 51 x 66 cm) CAD 5,500.

SIMPSON, Charles Walter
Canadian, 20th century.
Born 1878; died 1942.
Painter. Landscapes.

AUCTION RECORDS:
TORONTO, 17 May 1976, *Wolfe's Cove, Quebec* (oil on panel, 9¾ x 13 ins / 25 x 33 cm) CAD 450. LONDON, 17 Sept 1980, *On*

the Way to the Paddock (gouache, 14 1/4 x 21 ins / 36 x 52.5 cm) GBP 420.

SIMPSON, Clara D. (Mrs). See **DAVIDSON**

SIMPSON, Edna, Mrs Huestis
American, 20th century.
Born 26 November 1882, in Troy (New York); died 1964, in New York.
Miniaturist.

Edna Simpson studied at the Art Students League in New York and was a member of the American Federation of Arts.

SIMPSON, Eugénie
British, 19th century.
Active in Hackney.
Painter.

Eugénie Simpson exhibited in London, particularly at the Royal Academy and the Royal Society of British Artists in Suffolk Street from 1882 to 1887. She exhibited paintings of flowers for the most part.

MUSEUMS AND GALLERIES:
CAPE TOWN: *Lichfield Cathedral* (watercolour).

SIMPSON, Francis
British, 19th century.
Born 1796; died 29 July 1865, in Stamford.
Draughtsman.

The antiquary Francis Simpson published a volume of drawings of baptismal fonts.

SIMPSON, G.
British, 18th century.
Active in London.
Painter, miniaturist. Portraits.

G. Simpson exhibited at the Royal Academy in London from 1799 to 1806.

SIMPSON, Henry
British, 19th - 20th century.
Born 1853, in Nacton (Suffolk); died 31 August 1921, in London.
Painter. Genre scenes.

Henry Simpson exhibited at the Royal Academy in London from 1886 to 1888.

MUSEUMS AND GALLERIES:
THE HAGUE (Mesdag Museum): *Head of a Young Girl.*

AUCTION RECORDS:
LONDON, 6 Nov 1985, *The Doorway to the Mosque* (1898, watercolour, 13 3/4 x 8 1/4 ins / 35 x 21 cm) GBP 750.

SIMPSON, Herbert W.
British, 20th century.
Born 23 February 1875, in Chelsea; died 19 February 1958, in Madrid.
Active in Spain.
Painter. Portraits, landscapes.

Herbert W. Simpson lost his father at the age of nine, and began work aged 14 while studying art at evening classes at Westminster and Lambeth Art Schools, where he was encouraged by William Mouat Loudan. He settled in Cornwall and, from 1936, in Spain. He spent time in Dalmatia in 1941. Simpson exhibited with the Royal Institute of Painters, the Royal Society of British Artists, and the Royal Academy. He received numerous portrait commissions, and painted landscapes (including Spanish views) from 1922.

AUCTION RECORDS:
MADRID, 19 Dec 1974, *Portrait of Pio Baroia,* ESP 95,000.

SIMPSON, John
Irish, 18th century.
Painter. Landscapes.

John Simpson was active in Dublin from 1745 to 1750. He was also an art dealer.

SIMPSON, John
British, 19th century.
Born 1782, in London; died 1847, in London.
Painter. Portraits.

John Simpson was the father of Philip Simpson. He studied at the Royal Academy, and for a considerable period of time he was the assistant of Thomas Lawrence. Simpson was painter to the King of Portugal in 1834, and exhibited in London, particularly at the Royal Academy, the British Institution and the Royal Society of British Artists in Suffolk Street, from 1807 to 1847.

MUSEUMS AND GALLERIES:
DUBLIN: *King William IV* - EDINBURGH (Scottish National Portrait Gallery): *Sir Charles Napier Admiral* (oil on canvas) - LISBON (Mus. Nacional): *Auguste, Duke of Leuchtenberg; Maria II da Glória, Queen of Portugal; Dom Pedro I, Emperor of Brazil* - LONDON (National Portrait Gal.): *Frederick Marryat* (engraved in 1826, oil on canvas); *Sir Herbert Taylor* (exhibited in 1833, oil on canvas) - LONDON (Tate Collection): *Head of a Negro* (c. 1827, oil on canvas, exhibited at the British Institution in 1829).

AUCTION RECORDS:
PARIS, 20 Feb 1931, *Portrait of Maria da Gracia, Queen of Portugal* (attributed) FRF 380. LONDON, 18 Nov 1988, *Portrait of Miss Mary Simpson Wearing a Short Pink Jacket Over a White Dress* (oil on canvas, 30 x 25 ins / 76 x 63.5 cm) GBP 6,600. CANTERBURY, 11 April 2000, *Portrait of Harrriet Leonard Bull Wearing Black Silk Dress* (oil on canvas, 24 x 20 ins / 61 x 51 cm) GBP 2,200. LONDON, 8 June 2000, *Drover Resting with Sheep and Cattle in a Meadow* (1836, oil on canvas, 20 x 26 ins / 51 x 65 cm) GBP 2,200.

SIMPSON, John
British, 19th century.
Active in London.
Painter, miniaturist. Portraits.

John Simpson exhibited in London from 1831 to 1871. He exhibited miniatures on enamel for the most part.

SIMPSON, Joseph, the Elder
British, 17th - 18th century.
Engraver (burin). Portraits, seascapes. Coats of arms.

Joseph Simpson the Elder was active in London towards 1710. He executed burin engravings, mainly of seascapes, after Monamy, Vandevelde, Wootton and Wyke as well as a number of portraits and coats of arms.

SIMPSON, Joseph, the Younger
British, 18th century.
Died 1736.
Engraver.

Joseph Simpson the Younger was the son of Joseph Simpson the Elder.

SIMPSON, Joseph
British, 20th century.
Born 1879, in Carlisle; died 1939.
Painter, draughtsman, illustrator, engraver. Portraits, landscapes.

Joseph Simpson exhibited in London from 1897, and at the Royal Scottish Academy from 1898-1915. He was one of the leading caricaturists of his day.

MUSEUMS AND GALLERIES:
EDINBURGH: a landscape - EDINBURGH (Scottish National Portrait Gallery): *Edward VII* (coloured woodcut).

AUCTION RECORDS:
EDINBURGH, 26 April 1990, *The Green Turban* (oil on canvas, 19 x 16 ins / 48.2 x 40.5 cm) GBP 7,700.

SIMPSON, Lorna
American, 20th - 21st century.
Born 1960, in Brooklyn (New York City).

Engraver, photographer, mixed media, installation artist.

Conceptual Art, Identity Art.

Lorna Simpson studied at the University of San Diego and then at the New York School of Visual Arts. She started out as a photo-journalist and her work has retained a connection between the photograph and text. She is an African American artist who works from texts and photographs and sometimes makes sound installations. She portrays the black female body and questions the usual stereotypes, as in the series *Guarded Conditions*, (1989-1990). This series shows, for example, a photograph of a black woman dressed in large night shirt or cotton dress. The model is shown six times, while a text printed as a caption alternates the words 'sex attack' with the words 'skin attacks', inferring that the woman has been sexually attacked because of the colour of her skin and that the condition of the Black woman predisposes her to becoming a rape victim. In addition to the feminist idea, the photographs are also a metaphor for the condition of Black people in the USA. The economy of means, black and white photography and a simple text typed on a typewriter and stuck on, gives the work an objective coldness accentuated by the fact that the subject's back is turned away from the viewer. Affirmation of the feminine presence together with denunciation of injustices in American society are part of the approach of Afro-American artists between 1980 and 1990, all of whom took the photography in conjunction with text as their main medium. This combination also comes from Afro-American narrative tradition and here develops into a political debate.

Simpson's work appeared in numerous collective exhibitions from 1982, including: Allen Memorial Art Museum, Oberlin, 1984; New Museum of Contemporary Art, New York, regularly from 1987; Institute of Contemporary Art, Boston, 1988; Venice Biennale, 1990; Whitney Museum of American Art, New York, 1991; Institut du Monde Arabe, Paris, 1992; Art Prospekt, Frankfurt, 1993. Solo exhibitions have been held regularly since 1985 and include: San Diego, 1985; Toronto, 1988; Wadsworth Atheneum Museum, Hartford, Connecticut, 1989; New York Museum of Modern Art and Denver and Portland Art Museums, 1990; Centre for Exploratory and Perceptual Art, Buffalo, 1991; Houston Contemporary Arts Museum, 1993; Whitney Museum of American Art, New York, 1994; Albrecht Kemper Museum, St Joseph, 1995; Dade County Art Museum, Miami, 1997.

Bibliography:

Jones, Kellie, *Lorna Simpson*, Phaidon, London, 2002.

Museums and Galleries:

La Jolla (MCA of San Diego): *Guarded Conditions* (1989, mixed media) - New York (Whitney Mus. of American Art).

Auction records:

New York, 11 Nov 1993, *Water Carrier* (photograph and acrylic/Plexiglas, installation, 54 1/2 x 81 ins / 138.4 x 205.7 cm) USD 19,550. New York, 23 Feb 1994, *Untitled* (1989, two black and white engravings on a polyester background framed by the artist with two plastic plaques with printed text, 43 1/2 x 37 1/2 ins / 110.5 x 95.3 cm) USD 6,900. New York, 5 May 1994, *Reading Proofs* (1989, gelatine silver print photograph with plastic in four parts, 42 x 42 ins / 106.7 x 106.7 cm) USD 8,050. New York, 8 May 1996, *Landscape/Parts of the Body II* (1992, montage of two polaroid engravings with engraved Plexiglas in a frame by the artist, 49 1/2 x 20 1/2 ins / 125.7 x 52.1 cm) USD 5,175. New York, 17 Feb 1999, *The Bed* (1995, serigraph on felt, in four parts, 35 x 22 ins / 89 x 56 cm) USD 9,000. New York, 18 Nov 1999, *Haze* (1998, serigraph on felt, in eight parts, 68 x 69 ins / 173 x 175 cm) USD 8,500. New York, 17 Nov 2000, *Car* (serigraph on felt with text panel, 102 x 104 ins / 259 x 264 cm) USD 8,000. New York, 15 May 2001, *Untitled - Tondos and Words* (two photographs and eleven plastic plaques, 38 x 90 ins / 96 x 229 cm) USD 8,000. New York, 18 May 2001, *1978-88* (four photographs and thirteen engraved plastic plaques, 48 x 67 ins / 123 x 170 cm) USD 9,000. New York, 26 Sept 2002, *Haze* (1998, serigraph, six panels, 68 x 69 ins / 173 x 175 cm) USD 5,500. New York, 12 Nov 2003, *Bed* (1995, acrylic on felt, four panels, 35 x 20 ins / 90 x 51 cm) USD 4,800. New York, 13 May 2004, *Myths* (1991, photographs, four parts, 43 x 137 ins / 109 x 347 cm) USD 13,000.

SIMPSON, Matthew

British, 17th century.

Painter, miniaturist.

After teaching drawing to the children of Charles I, Matthew Simpson went to work in Sweden. He signed his work *M.S.*.

SIMPSON, Merton

American, 20th century.

Born 20 September 1928, in Charleston (South Carolina).

Painter (mixed media), art dealer. Portraits, landscapes. Spiral Group.

Merton Simpson studied with William Baziotes at New York University and Robert Gwathney at the Cooper Union. From 1951 to 1954, he served with the US Air Force in Cheyenne, Wyoming, where he painted portraits, including one of General Eisenhower. After being discharged from the Air Force, he returned to New York, where he joined the Spiral. This was a group of African-American artists who met in Romare Bearden's studio to discuss 'their responsibilities as artists at a time when racial violence was reaching a peak'. He opened a gallery on Madison Avenue, the Merton D. Simpson Gallery of Primitive and Modern Art, which specialises in primitive art. He also played the saxophone.

During the 1950s, Simpson made collages with paper on canvas, applying colour in coats of pigment. He painted abstract landscapes in blues, greys and browns. After the Harlem riots and until 1969, he concentrated on political themes, such as in the 22 canvases of his *Confrontation* series (1964), with their mask-like faces that invade the canvas, painted in rough black and white brushstrokes. In the 1970s, he turned to jazz, painting abstracts based on the expression of rhythm. In the 1990s, he drew inspiration from African art, of which he became an important collector. His collages often use a particular fabric that comes from Mali, which he tears up and then sticks on the canvas before applying a number of coats of varnish. He also includes shells, string and other objects.

Simpson has taken part in various group exhibitions, such as: the *Eighth Annual Exhibition of Painting, Sculpture and Prints by Negro Artists*, Atlanta University, Georgia (1949); *Younger American Painters*, Guggenheim Museum, New York (1954); *Black Artists/South*, Huntsville Museum, Huntsville, Alabama (1979); and *Since the Harlem Renaissance. 50 Years of Afro-American Art*, Center Gallery of Bucknell University, Lewisburg, Pennsylvania (1986). He had his first solo exhibition in 1955 at the Bertha Schaeffer Gallery, New York, and, since then, he has had a number of shows, including: at the College of Charleston, South Carolina (1984); and at Twining Gallery in New York (1990).

Bibliography:

Honig Fine, Elsa, *The Afro-American Artist*, Holt, Rinehart and Winston, New York, 1971. Hollingsworth, Alvin, '*Merton Simpson, Artist*' in *Black Art. An International Quarterly* vol. III n° 2, periodical, Los Angeles, 1979. *Since the Harlem Renaissance. 50 Years of Afro-American Art*, group exhibition catalogue, Center Gall. of Bucknell University, Lewisburg (PA), 1986. *Merton D. Simpson: The Journey of An Artist*, Carolina Art Association/Gibbes Museum of Art, Charleston, 1995.

Museums and Galleries:
Charleston (Gibbes Mus. of Art): three paintings - Chicago (Scott Field Mus.) - Columbia (MA) - Columbia (South Carolina Arts Commission): *Confrontation #20* (1968, oil on canvas) - New York (Solomon R. Guggenheim Mus.).

SIMPSON, Mrs (Miss). See **BURT Maria E.**

SIMPSON, Philip
British, 19th century.
Active in London at the beginning of the 19th century.
Painter. Genre scenes, portraits.

Philip Simpson was the son of John Simpson. He exhibited at the Royal Academy, the British Institution and the Society of British Artists from 1824 to 1837.

Museums and Galleries:
London (Victoria and Albert Mus.): *I Want to Fight*.

SIMPSON, Sylvia Salazar
American, 20th century.
Assemblage artist. Artists' books.

Sylvia Salazar Simpson produces artists' books. She has participated in collective exhibitions such as *De Bonnard à Baselitz: Dix Ans d'Enrichissements du Cabinet des Estampes 1978-1988* (*From Bonnard to Baselitz: A Decade of Acquisitions by the Prints Collection 1978-1988*) at the Bibliiothèque Nationale in Paris in 1992.

Museums and Galleries:
Paris (BNF, Prints Collection).

SIMPSON, T.
British, 18th - 19th century.
Active in London from 1790 to 1815.
Engraver (burin).

T. Simpson engraved hunting scenes and portraits.

SIMPSON, T. M.
British, 19th century.
Active in London during the first half of the 19th century.
Painter. Genre scenes, portraits.

T.M. Simpson exhibited in London from 1804 to 1821.

SIMPSON, Thomas
British, 18th century.
Active in London from 1765 to 1778.
Engraver (burin), watercolourist.

SIMPSON, W. Graham
British, 19th century.
Miniaturist.

W. Graham Simpson exhibited in London, particularly at the Royal Academy and the Royal Society of British Artists in Suffolk Street from 1878.

SIMPSON, William
British, 17th century.
Active from 1635 to 1646.
Engraver (burin).

SIMPSON, William
British, 19th century.
Born 28 October 1823, in Glasgow; died 17 August 1899, in Willesden.
Painter, watercolourist, engraver, draughtsman.
Military subjects, battles.
Orientalism.

William Simpson was initially an apprentice lithographic printer and then an apprentice draughtsman. In 1851 he moved to London and was employed to execute views of the Universal Exhibition. In 1854 Simpson went to Crimea where he executed drawings for the Colmagny company, who used them to publish 80 colour lithographs. Queen Victoria commissioned him to execute a painting of the Battle of Balaclava, and subsequently to paint a considerable number of watercolours depicting the important events of her reign. In 1859 he went to India and brought back 250 watercolours on the subject of the great uprising, though only 50 of these were reproduced in the album *India Ancient and Modern* (1867). In 1866 Simpson was employed to execute illustrations for the *Illustrated London News*. Simpson visited Moscow with the Princess and Prince of Wales (the future King Edward VII), and in 1868 he accompanied the expedition to Abyssinia. He followed operations during the war of 1870-1871 and spent the period of the Paris Commune in Paris itself. Simpson also followed the Afghanistan war of 1878. Simpson was elected a Member of the Royal Institute in 1874 and frequently took part in its exhibitions. He left a considerable oeuvre.

Wm. Simpson.

Museums and Galleries:
Cape Town: *Near Grahamstown* - Edinburgh (Nat. Gal. of Scotland, Print Room): *Division Camp, Crimea* (watercolour) - Glasgow: *View of Glasgow* (c. 1840) - London (Victoria and Albert Mus.): 44 watercolours of the Indies - Nice: *Queen Victoria and Prince Albert Visiting the Resolute, Commanded by a Descendant of Franklin*.

Auction records:
London, 9 May 1979, *Indian Landscape* (1884, watercolour and pencil heightened with white, 14 1/2 x 21 1/2 ins / 37 x 54.5 cm) GBP 800. London, 6 May 1981, *The Pyramids at Dusk* (1875, watercolour heightened with white, 18 3/4 x 27 1/4 ins / 47.5 x 69 cm) GBP 1,100. London, 26 Jan 1984, *Parnassus and Helicon from Corinth* (1870, watercolour/pencil outlines, 14 3/4 x 23 1/2 ins / 37.5 x 59.5 cm) GBP 3,200. London, 29 Oct 1985, *Glassalt Shiel, Loch Muick: Queen Victoria Driving in her Carriage* (1882, watercolour heightened with white, 10 x 17 ins / 25.3 x 43 cm) GBP 7,000. London, 13 March 1986, *The Nikolsky Gate, The Kremlin, Moscow* (1883, watercolour/pencil outlines heightened with gouache, 15 x 10 3/4 ins / 38 x 27.5 cm) GBP 2,400. London, 12 March 1987, *Durbar* (1860, watercolour and gouache/pencil outlines, 13 1/2 x 18 ins / 34 x 45.5 cm) GBP 1,500. Tel Aviv, 4 Oct 1993, *Jerusalem* (1880, watercolour heightened with white, 7 3/4 x 11 1/4 ins / 19.5 x 28.3 cm) USD 10,350. Perth, 30 Aug 1994, *Episode of the Crimean War: the Charge of the Light Brigade* (1854, watercolour and pencil, 10 1/2 x 16 1/4 ins / 26.5 x 41.5 cm) GBP 1,495. London, 31 March 1999, *Panoramic View of Inkerman. Panoramic View of Sebastapol* (watercolour over pencil heightened with gouache, two, 7 x 4 ins / 17 x 10 cm) GBP 3,800. London, 29 April 1999, *Seven Abyssinian Studies* (1868, pen, ink and watercolour, 9 x 14 ins / 23 x 35 cm) GBP 3,500. London, 8 June 2000, *View of Udaipur in Rajputana, India* (1862, watercolour and pencil heightened with white, 13 x 19 ins / 34 x 49 cm) GBP 9,000. London, 8 June 2000, *View of Amber, the Ancient Capital of Jaipur, India* (1883, watercolour and pencil heightened with gouache, 13 x 20 ins / 34 x 50 cm) GBP 12,000. London, 28 Sept 2001, *Prinsep's Ghat, Calcutta* (1875, pencil and watercolour heightened with white, 11 x 17 ins / 27 x 42 cm) GBP 4,000. London, 21 Nov 2001, *Great Wall of China* (1891, pencil and watercolour heightened with white, 12 x 18 ins / 31 x 46 cm) GBP 8,000. London, 31 Oct 2002, *Graves on Cathcart's Hill of the Officers of the Fourth Division* (pencil and watercolour, 18 x 28 ins / 45 x 70 cm) GBP 3,400. Malmö, 27 Nov 2002, *Landscape from Cheetore, Town near Udaipur, North India* (1866, watercolour, 10 x 14 ins / 26 x 36 cm) SEK 32,000. London, 29 April 2003, *Great Wall of China* (1874, watercolour over pencil heightened with white, 21 x 30 ins / 53 x 75 cm) GBP 29,000. London, 24 Sept 2003, *Buddhist Rock Cut Temple, Ajanta* (1875, pencil and watercolour heightened with white, 13 x 20 ins / 33 x 51 cm) GBP 13,000. London, 27 April 2004, *Chittor-*

garth, India (1863, watercolour, 14 x 20 ins / 36 x 51 cm) GBP 5,300.

SIMPSON, William H.
American, 19th century.
Born c. 1818, in Buffalo; died 1872, in Boston.
Painter.

William H. Simpson was apprenticed to the painter Matthew Wilson then settled in Boston in 1854 and there acquired a certain renown as a portrait painter. He was publicised by William Wells Brown, author of *The Rising Sun, or the Antecedents and Advancement of the Colored Race*, (1876) who also collected together most of the biographical material on the artist. He is above all known for his portraits of the Loguen (Jermain, a former slave who became bishop of the African Methodist Episcopal Church in New York, and his wife Caroline). In these he showed a sensitive touch, giving his designs a dignified and serene presence. After the fashion of other Afro-American painters of the first half of the 19th century, the black people that he painted seem to be totally integrated into the society of their times, both in their attitude and in their costume. It is possible to see in the portraits the wish of the painter to assert himself according to contemporary aesthetic criteria as well as the wish of the designs to consolidate or to acquire social recognition. William Simpson appeared in thematic group exhibitions on Afro-American artists, such as: 1941, *American Negro Art, 19th and 20th Centuries*, Downtown Gallery, New York, 1945, 1967, Howard University, Washington DC.

BIBLIOGRAPHY:
Greene, Caroll Jr., "*Perspective: The Black Artist in America*' in *Art Gallery Magazine*, periodical, New York, April 1970. Dickason Cederholm, Theresa (ed.), *Afro-American Artists. A Bio-Bibliographical Directory*, Trustees of the Boston Public Library, Boston, 1973. Lewis, Samella, *African American art and artists*, periodical, University of California Press, Berkeley, 1994.

MUSEUMS AND GALLERIES:
WASHINGTON DC (GA, Howard University): *Bishop Jermain Wesley Loguen* (1835, oil on canvas).

SIMROCK-MICHAEL, Margarete
German, 19th - 20th century.
Born 19 May 1870, in Leipzig.
Painter. Portraits.

Simrock-Michael was a pupil of Karl Gussow, Franz Skarbina and Moritz Müller; he lived and worked in Altenburg.

SIMS, Charles
British, 19th - 20th century.
Born 28 January 1873, in Islington (London); died 13 April 1928, in St Boswells (Roxburgh).
Painter, engraver. Portraits, genre scenes, landscapes.

Charles Sims studied under Lefebvre and Constant in Paris. He entered the Royal Academy Schools in 1893, winning a silver medal in 1893, and the Landseer Prize in 1895. He became an associate member in 1909. Sims travelled to the US in 1925 and 1926. He exhibited at the Paris Salon and won a third-class medal in 1900. His earlier works were inspired by fantastical themes and legends. Sims's fine, craftsmanlike style earned him considerable success as a portrait painter, but he subsequently returned to mystical subjects bordering on abstraction, before committing suicide.

SIMS

MUSEUMS AND GALLERIES:
LEEDS (City AG): *'What are these to me and you who deeply drink of wine'* (1895, oil on canvas); *'And the Fairies ran away with their Clothes'* (oil on canvas) - LONDON (Tate Collection): *The Fountain; The Wood beyond the World* - PARIS (former Mus. du Luxembourg): *Childhood.*

AUCTION RECORDS:
LONDON, 27 Jan 1922, *The Henwife*, GBP 46. LONDON, 16 Feb 1923, *The Waders* (drawing) GBP 33. LONDON, 5 March 1926, *Water Babies*, GBP 204. LONDON, 29 April 1927, *Kent Landscape*, GBP 105. LONDON, 20 July 1928, *Some Pass By*, GBP 336. NEW YORK, 5 May 1932, *Fantastical Landscape*, USD 200. PARIS, 6 July 1950, *Nuns Out Walking* (watercolour) FRF 1,500. LONDON, 18 July 1969, *The Beautiful is Fled*, Gns 1,100. LONDON, 9 April 1980, *Chasing Butterflies* (oil on canvas, 48 x 53 1/2 ins / 121 x 136 cm) GBP 15,500. LONDON, 19 May 1982, *Mother and Children Chasing Butterlfies* (c. 1903, oil on canvas, 46 x 51 1/2 ins / 117 x 131 cm) GBP 7,000. LONDON, 27 Nov 1984, *Love and the Student* (1898, oil on canvas, 32 x 46 ins / 81 x 117 cm) GBP 9,500. NEW YORK, 23 May 1985, *Landscape with Children* (oil on canvas remounted on hardboard, 28 x 36 ins / 71.1 x 91.4 cm) USD 4,000. LONDON, 12 Nov 1986, *A Mother and Her Young Boy Catching Butterflies* (oil on canvas, 45 1/4 x 51 1/4 ins / 115 x 130 cm) GBP 13,000. LONDON, 29 July 1988, *I Am the Darkness and the Light* (charcoal and black chalk/wash, study, 28 1/4 x 36 3/4 ins / 72 x 93.5 cm) GBP 792. LONDON, 3 May 1990, *Nymphs in a Pastoral Landscape* (gouache and pencil, 13 1/2 x 17 1/4 ins / 34.5 x 44 cm) GBP 1,815. LONDON, 7 Oct 1992, *Maternal Joys* (mixed media/card, 15 1/2 x 21 ins / 39.5 x 53.5 cm) GBP 1,540. LONDON, 9 Nov 1992, *Kent Landscape* (oil on canvas, 14 x 39 ins / 35.5 x 99 cm) GBP 1,980. LONDON, 13 Nov 1992, *The Awakening of Titanis* (1896, oil on canvas, 27 1/4 x 14 ins / 69.2 x 35.6 cm) GBP 15,950. LONDON, 3 March 1993, *Adoration of the Child* (oil on canvas, 14 x 17 ins / 35.5 x 43 cm) GBP 4,715. NEW YORK, 15 Oct 1993, *Bathers* (oil on canvas, 25 x 30 1/4 ins / 63.5 x 76.8 cm) USD 1,840. LONDON, 10 March 1995, *Romance* (oil on canvas/card, 19 1/2 x 23 ins / 49.6 x 58.4 cm) GBP 3,450. NEWBURY, 17 Feb 1999, *Portrait of Mrs Agnes Helen Sims, née Mac Whirter* (1898, oil on canvas, 54 x 36 ins / 137 x 92 cm) GBP 3,200. LONDON, 11 Nov 1999, *Portrait of Young Woman* (oil on canvas, 25 x 30 ins / 63 x 76 cm) GBP 2,200. STOCKHOLM, 31 Jan 2000, *Seated Woman with Parasol* (oil on canvas, 35 x 28 ins / 90 x 70 cm) SEK 14,000. LONDON, 20 June 2000, *Summer* (tempera on board, 15 x 22 ins / 38 x 55 cm) GBP 2,900. LONDON, 4 July 2001, *Wood Beyond the World* (1913, oil on canvas, 37 x 51 ins / 94 x 129 cm) GBP 1,800. LONDON, 21 Nov 2001, *Spring Song* (oil on canvas, 36 x 28 ins / 91 x 71 cm) GBP 9,200. LOTS ROAD, 28 May 2002, *Fountain* (oil on canvas, 30 x 25 ins / 76 x 63 cm) GBP 1,500. LOTS ROAD, 18 June 2002, *Muses* (watercolour and gouache, 21 x 30 ins / 54 x 75 cm) GBP 1,400. LONDON, 3 July 2003, *Rebel Powers that Three Array* (oil on canvas, 36 x 28 ins / 91 x 71 cm) GBP 4,200. LONDON, 26 Nov 2003, *Sunshine* (oil on panel, 16 x 20 ins / 40 x 51 cm) GBP 6,800.

SIMS, Charles. See also **SIMMS**

SIMS, George
British, 19th century.
Died 1840, in London.
Painter, watercolourist. Landscapes.

G. Sims was a Member of the New Water-Colour Society. He exhibited in London from 1829 to 1840.

MUSEUMS AND GALLERIES:
DUBLIN: *Pasture.*

SIMS, William
British, 19th century.
Active in London.
Painter. Portraits, landscapes.

William Sims exhibited in London from 1821 to 1867.

SIMSON, David
British, 19th century.
Born 1803, in Dundee; died 27 March 1874, in Edinburgh.
Painter, modeller. Landscapes.

David Simson was the brother of George and William Simson.
MUSEUMS AND GALLERIES:
EDINBURGH (Scottish National Portrait Gallery): *William Simson, Artist* (plaster, bust).

SIMSON, George
British, 19th century.
Born 1791, in Dundee; died 1862, in Edinburgh.
Painter, engraver. Portraits, genre scenes.
George Simson was the brother of David and William Simson. He was a member of the Royal Scottish Academy in 1862.
MUSEUMS AND GALLERIES:
EDINBURGH (Royal Scottish Academy): *The Girl at the Well* (c. 1831, oil/panel).
AUCTION RECORDS:
PERTH, 19 April 1977, *Wooded Landscape With River and Fisherman* (oil on canvas, 29 1/2 x 24 1/2 ins / 75 x 62 cm) GBP 700. EDINBURGH, 13 April 2001, *Dundee from the South East* (oil on canvas, 16 x 39 ins / 41 x 100 cm) GBP 3,800.

SIMSON, John
British, 16th century.
Painter. Murals.
Simson worked in the Westminster Hall, London, in 1552.

SIMSON, Margaret and Theodore Spicer.
See **SPICER-SIMSON**

SIMSON, William
British, 19th century.
Born 1800, in Dundee; died 29 August 1847, in London.
Painter, watercolourist. Genre scenes, landscapes, seascapes.
William Simson was the brother of David and George Simson. He was a pupil at the Trustees' Academy in Edinburgh and was elected member of the Royal Scottish Academy in 1829. After spending a period of three years in Italy, he settled in London in 1838.
MUSEUMS AND GALLERIES:
EDINBURGH (Nat. Gal. of Scotland): *A Scene in Holland* (oil on panel); *Solway Moss: Evening* (oil on canvas); *Passage Boats Becalmed on the Maas at Dort* (oil/panel); *A Goatherd's Cottage* (oil/panel) - EDINBURGH (Royal Scottish Academy): *Landscape* (1934, oil on canvas) - LONDON (National Portrait Gal.): *John Burnet* (1841, oil on canvas) - LONDON (Victoria and Albert Mus.): watercolours.
AUCTION RECORDS:
LONDON, 4 Feb 1972, *The Arrest of William Tell,* Gns 380. LONDON, 16 July 1976, *Boats on the River Maas* (oil on canvas, 20 1/2 x 30 1/2 ins / 52 x 77.5 cm) GBP 900. LONDON, 20 July 1979, *Waiting for the Gondola* (1837, oil on panel, 31 x 44 ins / 78.6 x 111.6 cm) GBP 1,500. LONDON, 22 April 1983, *The End of the Day: William Scrope on a White Pony with his Keepers, and the Day's Bag* (oil on canvas, 35 1/4 x 45 1/2 ins / 89.5 x 115.6 cm) GBP 15,000. GLASGOW, 5 Feb 1986, *A Dutch Family* (1838, oil on canvas, 44 x 56 ins / 112 x 142 cm) GBP 3,000. LONDON, 14 March 1990, *Cart Harnessed to a Goat in Kensington Gardens* (1846, oil on board, 14 1/2 x 18 1/4 ins / 37 x 46.5 cm) GBP 8,580. NEUILLY, 15 Dec 1991, *The Grand Canal in Venice* (1837, oil on panel, 33 x 46 1/4 ins / 84 x 117.5 cm) FRF 80,000. AUCHTERARDER, 26 Aug 1997, *The Rubens Château* (1840, oil on panel, 19 3/4 x 24 ins / 50 x 61 cm) GBP 10,350. VIENNA, 14 June 2000, *Colombo Asking for Water for his Son* (1840, oil on panel, 35 x 43 ins / 90 x 109 cm) ATS 40,000. LONDON, 4 March 2004, *Death of Edward V and his Brother Richard, Duke of York, in the Tower, 1483* (oil on panel, 36 x 50 ins / 91 x 127 cm) GBP 5,500.

SIMUNOVIC, Frano
Croat, 20th century.
Born 1908, in Dicmo.
Painter. Landscapes.
Frano Simunovic studied at Zagreb academy, before travelling in France, Spain and Italy. He painted austere landscapes inspired by the bleak hills of the Dalmatian Zagora, landscapes that tend toward Abstraction and that convey both its beauty and geological structure.

SIMUS I
3rd century BC.
Born in Cyprus.
Active in the second half of the 3rd century BC.
Sculptor.
Ancient Greek.
Simus is represented by two marble pedestals, now in the Louvre in Paris, made to support statues of Hippomachus and Dionysus.

SIMUS II
2nd century BC.
Sculptor.
Ancient Greek.
Simus made sculptures of *Callistratus* and *The Aristandrides, Father and Son*.

SIMUS III
Painter.
Ancient Greek.
Pliny mentions three paintings by Simus, who may be the same person as the sculptor of the same name.

SIMYAN, Victor Étienne
French, 19th century.
Born 18 September 1826, in St-Gengoux (Saône-et-Loire); died 1886, in London (?).
Sculptor.
Victor Simyan was a pupil of Jouffroy and Pradier. He exhibited at the Salon between 1855 and 1861 and was awarded a third class medal in 1857. He set up an art pottery factory in London.
MUSEUMS AND GALLERIES:
AVIGNON: *Etruscan Art represented by a Seated Woman* (marble statue) - TOURNUS: *Bust of J. B. Greuze; Souvenir.*

SINAEV-BERNSTEIN, Leopold Semenovich
Russian, 19th century.
Born in Vilnius.
Sculptor.
Leopold Semenovich Sinaev studied under Dalou. His work featured in the Paris Salons, where he was awarded a commendation in 1893. He received a silver medal in 1900 at the Exposition Universelle in Paris. He was made a chevalier of the Légion d'Honneur in 1903, and received a third class medal in the same year.
MUSEUMS AND GALLERIES:
ST PETERSBURG (Gosudarstvennyj Russkij Muz.): *Slumber.*

SINAI, Samuel
Turkish, 20th century.
Born 1 May 1915, in Smyrna, now Izmir.
Active and naturalised in France.
Painter. Urban landscapes, still-lifes.
Samuel Sinai attended the École des Beaux-Arts in Marseilles from 1933 to 1939, when he was mobilised for World War II and subsequently taken prisoner. On his release, he entered the École des Beaux-Arts in Paris, in Souverbie's studio. He specialises in still-lifes and views of Paris. He has exhibited in Paris at the Salon d'Automne, the Salon des Artistes Français and the Salon des Indépendants, of which he has been a member since 1948.
MUSEUMS AND GALLERIES:
BEIT URI.

SINAVE
Flemish School, 18th - 19th century.

Active in Loo.
Sculptor.
Sinave sculpted an *Equestrian Statue of Joseph II* in the town hall of Furnes.

SINAYSKY, Viktor Aleksandrovich
Russian, 20th century.
Born 1893, in Mariupol'; died 1968, in Leningrad (now St Petersburg).
Sculptor. Busts.
Viktor Sinaysky trained at Odessa art school and worked at the Leningrad Vkhutemas, where he later taught. He also taught at the Leningrad academy. Sinaysky executed the *Bust of Lassalle* for the Nevsky Prospekt, St Petersburg.
BIBLIOGRAPHY:
Halturin, Aleksandr/Hulten, Pontus/Gunar, Karl (ed.), *Paris-Moscou*, group exhibition catalogue, Éd. du Centre Georges-Pompidou, Paris, 1979.
MUSEUMS AND GALLERIES:
ST PETERSBURG (Gosudarstvennyj Russkij Muz.): *Bust of Lassalle* (1918, granite, copy).

SINCLAIR, Alexander Gordon
British, 19th - 20th century.
Born 1859; died 1930.
Painter. Portraits, landscapes.
Alexander Sinclair was a member of the Society of Eight in Edinburgh, together with other leading Scottish painters of his day. From 1883 to 1931 he exhibited regularly at the Royal Scottish Academy.
AUCTION RECORDS:
GLASGOW, 11 Dec 1996, *Old Street, Loch Auray; Beside Loch Auray* (oil on panel and oil on canvas, a pair, each 25 x 27 1/4 ins / 63.5 x 69 cm) GBP 920. LONDON, 15 April 1997, *The Road to the Isles* (oil on canvas, 60 1/2 x 84 ins / 153.5 x 213.5 cm) GBP 6,440.

SINCLAIR, Alfredo. See **SINCLAIR BALLESTROS**

SINCLAIR, Archie
British, 20th century.
Born 19 February 1895, in Pitlochry, Scotland; died 17 December 1967, in London.
Painter, engraver. Landscapes.
Archie Sinclair was a pupil of John H. Dixon and Clyde Leon Keller. He was a member of the Society of Independent Artists.

SINCLAIR, Irving
American, 20th century.
Born 1895, in British Columbia, Canada; died 1969, in San Francisco.
Active from 1917 in the USA.
Painter. Portraits, genre scenes.
Irving Sinclair settled in San Francisco in 1917. He worked as art director for Fox during the 1920s He is best known for his portraits of Hollywood stars, and of US presidents F.D. Roosevelt and D.D. Eisenhower.
AUCTION RECORDS:
NEW YORK, 23 Sept 1992, *The Poker Game* (oil on canvas, 54 x 78 1/4 ins / 137 x 198.5 cm) USD 7,700.

SINCLAIR, J. P.
British, 19th century.
Painter.
AUCTION RECORDS:
PARIS, 23 Dec 1949, *Sheepfold*, FRF 2,300.

SINCLAIR, Max
British, 19th - 20th century.
Painter. Landscapes, seascapes.
Max Sinclair was active from 1881-1910.
AUCTION RECORDS:
PERTH, 13 April 1976, *Landscape* (1884, oil on canvas, 17 x 25 ins / 43 x 63.5 cm) GBP 280. LONDON, 12 July 1977, *The Fishermen's Return* (oil on canvas, 20 x 30 ins / 51 x 76 cm) GBP 850. LONDON, 2 Nov 1979, *Boats in Rough Sea* (oil on canvas, 19 1/2 x 29 1/2 ins / 49.6 x 75 cm) GBP 1,500. PERTH, 1 Sept 1992, *Lake Callender* (oil on canvas, 24 x 36 ins / 61 x 91.5 cm) GBP 1,980. LONDON, 27 Sept 1994, *Waiting to Pass the Barrier; Running for Shelter* (oil on canvas, a pair, 12 x 17 3/4 ins / 30.5 x 45 cm) GBP 1,725. KNOWLE, 17 March 1999, *Ships Loading at Dusk. Shipping on Thames by Moonlight* (1889, oil on canvas, a pair, 24 x 20 ins / 60 x 50 cm) GBP 4,200. CHESTER, 10 June 1999, *Tantallon Castle Scotland* (oil on canvas, 16 x 24 ins / 41 x 61 cm) GBP 1,040. LONDON, 9 Nov 2000, *Awaiting the Turn of the Tide* (1887, oil on canvas, 13 x 17 ins / 34 x 44 cm) GBP 1,050. LONDON, 8 Feb 2001, *In the River. Just Home* (oil on canvas, a pair, 12 x 16 ins / 30 x 41 cm) GBP 2,300. CHICAGO, 11 June 2001, *On the Coast of Cornwall* (oil on canvas, 20 x 30 ins / 51 x 76 cm) USD 3,000. NEW YORK, 5 June 2002, *Calm Waters* (1884, oil on canvas, 20 x 30 ins / 51 x 76 cm) USD 1,700. EXETER, 2 July 2002, *In Harbour. Last Cheers* (1881, oil on canvas, a pair, 15 x 23 ins / 38 x 58 cm) GBP 3,500. UPPSALA, 28 May 2004, *Carrick Castle, Loch Goil* (oil on canvas, 17 x 24 ins / 42 x 61 cm) SEK 32,000. BATH, 26 July 2004, *Crossing the Bar, Mantcamen. Home Again, Glaucus* (oil on canvas, a pair, 13 x 20 ins / 34 x 52 cm) GBP 2,300.

SINCLAIR, Muriel
French, 20th century.
Born in Paris.
Painter, engraver.
Muriel Sinclair exhibited her works in Paris in 1962, 1967, 1971 and 1973, and in Vence. From 1958, she concentrated on painting. She was equally at home using oils, wax, pastel, burin or etching needle. With swift brush-strokes, she created a kind of visionary universe.

SINCLAIR, Olga
Panamanian, 20th - 21st century.
Born 1957, in Panama.
Painter. Scenes with figures.
AUCTION RECORDS:
NEW YORK, 21 Nov 1989, *Nostalgia for the Rendez-Vous* (1988, oil on canvas, 48 x 60 ins / 122 x 152.5 cm) USD 6,600. NEW YORK, 20-21 Nov 1990, *Ines's Mantilla* (1986, acrylic/canvas, 60 x 48 ins / 152.5 x 122 cm) USD 4,400.

SINCLAIR, Peter
British, 20th - 21st century.
Born 1962, in Walberswick.
Active in Nîmes.
Installation artist, performance artist.
Peter Sinclair studied at the École des Beaux-Art in Nîmes from 1980 to 1985, and settled there. He is also a musician who plays in rock bands and integrates his love of music into sound installations, usually working with compressed air which, when released, produces sound from wind instruments.

He has taken part in group exhibitions at the following: the Miró Foundation in Barcelona (1983); the charterhouse of Villeneuve-lès-Avignon and the Centre Georges-Pompidou in Paris (1986); the Cité des Sciences et de l'Industrie de la Villette in Paris and the Institute of Contemporary Art in London (1987); the FRAC (Regional Contemporary Art Foundation) PACA in Marseilles and the CNAP (National Fine Arts Centre) in Paris (1988); and the Maison des Expositions in Genas (1989). He has also shown his work in solo exhibitions at the following: Nîmes (1984); Parvis 2 in Tarbes (1987); the Maison du Boulanger in Troyes (1988); and Montpellier and Groningen (1989).
BIBLIOGRAPHY:
Peter Sinclair, exhibition catalogue, Maison des Expositions, Genas, 1989.

MUSEUMS AND GALLERIES:
PARIS (FNAC): *Bellow and Roar Door* (1987).

SINCLAIR BALLESTROS, Alfredo

Panamanian, 20th century.
Born 1915, in Panama.
Painter, engraver.

Alfredo Sinclair Ballestros trained at the Buenos Aires art school. He lived and worked in Panama. His work was featured in collective exhibitions in South America, the USA and elsewhere, also in the exhibition *De Bonnard à Baselitz - Dix Ans d'enrichissements du cabinet des estampes 1978-1988* (*From Bonnard to Baselitz: A Decade of Acquisitions by the Prints Collection 1978-1988*) at the Bibliothèque Nationale in Paris in 1992.

MUSEUMS AND GALLERIES:
PARIS (BNF, Prints Collection): *Reflection* (1978, silk screen print).

SINDGREN, Amélie

Swedish, 19th century.
Born 1814, in Stockholm.
Painter.

Sindgren was the daughter of a well-known Swedish writer. She drew from instinct, without a professor, when Gvarnahon spotted her rare talent and had her attend the Kungliga Akademi för de Fria Konsterna in Stockholm. Having won a travel grant in 1850, she went to Düsseldorf and to Paris, where she worked under the direction of Leon Cogniet and Ange Tissier until 1854. She then visited Munich and Rome, and stayed again in Paris from 1855 to 1856. Her portraits and paintings of popular scenes are distinct in their broad and energetic execution, their fresh palette, and in their exquisite, natural feeling. Sindgren was an honorary member of the Association of Women Artists in London.

MUSEUMS AND GALLERIES:
COPENHAGEN: *Spring Day on the Lofoten Islands* - MUNICH: *Young Bathers* - OSLO: *View of Queen in Lofoten* - STOCKHOLM: *The Outer Reef, Summer Night on the Norwegian Coast.*

SINDING, Elisabeth

Norwegian, 19th - 20th century.
Born 16 March 1846, in Nes, near Romerike; died 24 November 1930, in Oslo.
Painter. Animals.

Elisabeth Sinding was a pupil of Johann F. Eckersberg, Johannes S. Dahl and Gustav A. Friedrich.

MUSEUMS AND GALLERIES:
OSLO (Nasjonalgal.): *Horses.*

AUCTION RECORDS:
LONDON, 12 June 1996, *Three Dogs* (1882, oil on canvas, 36 1/4 x 45 1/4 ins / 92 x 115 cm) GBP 11,500.

SINDING, Johanna

Norwegian, 19th century.
Born 13 June 1854, in Trondheim.
Sculptor.

Sinding was the sister of Otto and the aunt of Sigmund Sinding. She was a pupil of Albert Wolff.

SINDING, Knud

Danish, 20th century.
Born 27 August 1875, in Aarhus; died 1946.
Painter. Scenes with figures, figures, landscapes.

Knud Sinding studied under Kristian Zahrtmann at the Kunstakademi in Copenhagen and went on to live and work in the Danish capital.

MUSEUMS AND GALLERIES:
KOLDING - MARIBO - ODENSE - RANDERS.

AUCTION RECORDS:
COPENHAGEN, 23 March 1988, *Italians near a Village* (27 1/2 x 40 1/4 ins / 70 x 102 cm) DKK 6,500. LONDON, 24 June 1988, *Interior* (oil on canvas, 17 x 22 1/2 ins / 43.1 x 57.2 cm) GBP 6,600. LONDON, 16 March 1989, *Hilltop View* (oil on canvas, 28 x 40 1/4 ins / 71 x 102 cm) GBP 1,650. COPENHAGEN, 25-26 April 1990, *Shepherd, Italy* (oil on canvas, 31 1/2 x 39 1/4 ins / 80 x 100 cm) DKK 4,500. LONDON, 22 Feb 1995, *Farmyard* (1895, oil on canvas, 22 x 27 1/4 ins / 55 x 69 cm) GBP 575. LONDON, 12 May 1999, *Interior with Pieter Brueghel's Parable of Blind* (oil on canvas, 23 x 24 ins / 59 x 60 cm) GBP 1,000. COPENHAGEN, 1 June 1999, *Sunday Morning in a Farmhouse* (1927, oil on canvas, 31 x 47 ins / 80 x 120 cm) DKK 31,000. LONDON, 7 Dec 2000, *Setting the Table* (1912, oil on canvas, 24 x 33 ins / 62 x 84 cm) GBP 1,500. COPENHAGEN, 5 March 2001, *From the Artist's Sitting-room with his Paintings on the Wall* (1944, oil on canvas, 31 x 43 ins / 80 x 110 cm) DKK 13,000. COPENHAGEN, 5 March 2001, *Peasant Pamily from West Jylland Moving* (1926, oil on canvas, 37 x 51 ins / 95 x 130 cm) DKK 14,000. HAMBURG, 8 May 2002, *Woman Knitting in Interior* (oil on canvas, 31 x 34 ins / 79 x 86 cm) EUR 1,800. ULLERSLEV, 22 Sept 2002, *Young Female Students on the Way to the Dunes* (1904, oil on canvas, 47 x 52 ins / 120 x 132 cm) DKK 15,000.

SINDING, Otto Ludvig

Norwegian, 19th century.
Born 20 December 1842, in Königsberg (now Kaliningrad, Russia); died 23 November 1909, in Munich.
Painter, illustrator. History painting, landscapes, seascapes.

Otto Sinding was the father of the painter Sigmund Sinding. After studying law, he turned to painting in 1867. He attended the art school of Johan F. Eckersberg, and then the Kunstakademi in Karlruhe. A friend of Eilif Peterssen, he accompanied him to the Kunstakademi in Munich, where he then settled. He travelled to Italy in 1880, and then worked in Christiania (now Oslo) during the 1890s. He was also a poet and playwright.

He painted dramatic landscapes and illustrated popular Norwegian fables. His style is resolutely realist, but it underwent a transition in the 1890s, demonstrating his taste for grandiose landscapes and elaborate compositions. He was included in the exhibition *Da Dahl a Munch. Romanticismo, realismo e simbolismo nella pittura di paesaggio norvegese* (*From Dahl to Munch: Romanticism, Realism and Symbolism in Norwegian Landscape Painting*) in 2001, at the Palazzo dei Diamanti in Ferrara.

BIBLIOGRAPHY:
Muther, R., *The History of Modern Painting III*, monograph, Henry and Co., London, 1896. *Kunstnerbrodrene: maleren Otto Sinding, billedhuggeren Stephan Sinding, komponisten Christian Sinding*, exhibition catalogue, Stiftelsen Modums, Blaafarveværk, 2000. Lange, Marit (ed.), *Da Dahl a Munch. Romanticismo, realismo e simbolismo nella pittura di paesaggio norvegese*, exhibition catalogue, Palazzo dei Diamanti, Ferrara Arte editore, Ferrara, 2001.

MUSEUMS AND GALLERIES:
BERGEN (Kunstmus.): *Winter Day in the Lofotens; Forest Landscape* - COPENHAGEN (Statens Mus. for Kunst): *Spring Day in the Lofotens* - MUNICH (Neue Pinakothek): *Children in the Bath* - OSLO (Nasjonalgal.): *Queen Mitif in the Lofotens* (1883, oil on canvas, two seascapes); *Landscape Near Mjøsen*

- STOCKHOLM (Nationalmus.): *On the Outer Islands of the Norwegian Coast.*

AUCTION RECORDS:

COLOGNE, 23 March 1973, *Mountain Landscape,* DEM 3,000. LONDON, 11 Feb 1977, *First Rays of Sunlight* (1885, oil on canvas, 90 1/2 x 133 3/4 ins / 230 x 340 cm) GBP 1,000. NEW YORK, 26 Jan 1979, *Bathing in a Fjord* (c. 1889, oil on canvas, 38 x 55 1/2 ins / 96.5 x 141 cm) USD 7,000. VIENNA, 16 May 1984, *Fishing Boats Off Venice* (oil on canvas, 31 1/2 x 50 1/2 ins / 80 x 128 cm) ATS 48,000. VIENNA, 19 March 1985, *Children Bathing* (oil on canvas, 25 1/2 x 21 1/2 ins / 65 x 54.5 cm) ATS 38,000. LONDON, 25 March 1987, *The Young Bathers* (pastel, 17 x 19 ins / 43 x 48.5 cm) GBP 7,000. LONDON, 16 March 1989, *The Stone Bridge at Rapallo* (1904, oil on canvas, 12 x 15 3/4 ins / 30.5 x 40 cm) GBP 3,300. STOCKHOLM, 14 Nov 1990, *A Fjord in Winter* (1906, oil on canvas, 53 1/4 x 82 3/4 ins / 135 x 210 cm) SEK 77,000. LONDON, 19 June 1991, *The Tarantella* (1905, oil on canvas, 41 1/4 x 81 1/4 ins / 105 x 206.5 cm) GBP 8,250. NEW YORK, 27 May 1993, *Half-light After the Storm* (1875, oil on canvas, 29 1/2 x 41 1/2 ins / 75 x 105.4 cm) USD 6,900. LONDON, 18 June 1993, *The Tarantella* (1905, oil on canvas, 41 1/2 x 80 3/4 ins / 105.7 x 205.2 cm) GBP 7,015. COPENHAGEN, 16 Nov 1994, *Little Girl Reading* (1877, oil on canvas, 15 x 11 1/2 ins / 38 x 29 cm) DKK 20,000. COPENHAGEN, 14 Feb 1996, *Northern Mountain Landscape* (oil on canvas, 28 x 43 3/4 ins / 71 x 111 cm) DKK 13,000. VEJLE, 11 Aug 1999, *La Tarentella* (1880, oil on canvas, 39 x 79 ins / 100 x 200 cm) DKK 75,000. OSLO, 22 Nov 1999, *Approaching Storm* (oil on canvas, 38 x 54 ins / 96 x 137 cm) NOK 42,000. OSLO, 25 May 2000, *Ploughing with Horse* (oil on paper/canvas, 15 x 20 ins / 38 x 50 cm) NOK 38,000. OSLO, 18 Dec 2000, *Anna by the Water* (1878, oil on canvas, 26 x 18 ins / 65 x 45 cm) NOK 120,000. BOSTON, 11 May 2001, *Mermaid* (pastel, 44 x 22 ins / 112 x 55 cm) USD 9,000. OSLO, 22 May 2001, *Fishmarket* (oil on canvas, 15 x 20 ins / 38 x 50 cm) NOK 52,000. COPENHAGEN, 27 Aug 2002, *Ullensvang in Hardanger, Mountains and Sheep* (oil on canvas, 15 x 20 ins / 38 x 50 cm) DKK 16,000. OSLO, 17 Dec 2002, *Fishing Village in Lofoten* (oil on canvas, 15 x 20 ins / 38 x 50 cm) NOK 26,000. OSLO, 19 Nov 2003, *Spring Day in Svolvær* (1882, oil on canvas, 25 x 40 ins / 64 x 101 cm) NOK 88,000. OSLO, 19 Nov 2003, *Storm* (1875, oil on canvas, 33 x 56 ins / 83 x 143 cm) NOK 125,000. OSLO, 25 May 2004, *Snow Fall, View from Svolvaer, Lofoten* (oil on canvas, 37 x 50 ins / 95 x 126 cm) NOK 90,000. LONDON, 16 June 2004, *La Tarantella* (1880, oil on canvas, 39 x 74 ins / 100 x 187 cm) GBP 7,000.

SINDING, Paul

Danish, 20th century.

Painter. Military subjects, seascapes.

MUSEUMS AND GALLERIES:

LONDON (Corporation of Trinity House): *Barque off Elsinore* (1943).

AUCTION RECORDS:

COPENHAGEN, 2 Oct 1979, *Frigates at Sea* (1944, oil on canvas, 39 x 45 ins / 99 x 114 cm) DKK 6,500. LONDON, 11 May 1994, *Frigate 'Jutland'* (oil on canvas, 39 3/4 x 51 1/2 ins / 101 x 131 cm) GBP 1,552. NEW YORK, 19 Jan 1995, *Battle of Koge Bay, 1 July 1677* (oil on canvas, 40 x 40 ins / 101.6 x 101.6 cm) USD 4,312. LONDON, 3 May 2000, *Heavy Seas* (1948, oil on canvas, 28 x 31 ins / 70 x 80 cm) GBP 1,500. VEJLE, 7 Aug 2001, *The Swedish Man-o-war Svaerdet in Battle at Oland 1 July 1676* (oil on canvas, 39 x 52 ins / 99 x 131 cm) DKK 12,000. LANDSKRONA, 12 May 2002, *The Battle at Helgoland, 9 May 1864* (1945, oil on canvas, 39 x 43 ins / 98 x 110 cm) SEK 26,000. COPENHAGEN, 27 Aug 2002, *The Battle in Koge Bay* (1944, oil on canvas, 48 x 39 ins / 121 x 98 cm) DKK 13,000.

SINDING, Sigmund

Norwegian, 20th century.

Born 23 May 1875, in Munich, to Norwegian parents; died 3 March 1936, in Oslo.

Painter. Portraits, interiors, landscapes, Still-lifes.

Sigmund Sinding was the son of the painter Otto Ludwig Sinding. He exhibited in Paris on a number of occasions, notably at the Exposition Universelle of 1908, when he received an honourable mention.

MUSEUMS AND GALLERIES:

OSLO (Nasjonalgal.): *Interior.*

SINDING, Stephan Abel or Stephan

Norwegian, 19th - 20th century.

Born 4 August 1846, in Drontheim; died 23 January 1922, in Paris.

Active from 1884; naturalised in Denmark from 1890; and active in France from 1911.

Sculptor. Figures.

Stephan Sinding studied under A. Wolf in Rome and under Paul Dubois, Louis E. Barrias and Marius J.A. Mercié in Paris. He exhibited in the French capital, notably at the 1878 and 1889 Expositions Universelles (he was awarded the Grand Prix at the latter). When in Rome, he made his mark with *Barbarian Mother Removing her Son's Dead Body from the Field of Battle,* undoubtedly his most accomplished painting. His other - equally dramatic - compositions tend to be more wooden. He is also noted for his commemorative monuments to the sailors of the Île d'Yeu and the Danish volunteers at Rueil.

MUSEUMS AND GALLERIES:

COPENHAGEN (Ny Carlsberg Glyptotek): *First-Born; Joie de Vivre; The Nourishing Earth; Slave; Two Men* - COPENHAGEN (Statens Mus. for Kunst): *Widow* (1892) - OSLO (Nasjonalgal.): *Two Humans* (1889); *Imprisoned Mother.*

AUCTION RECORDS:

COLOGNE, 19 Oct 1979, bronze, h. 30 1/4 ins / 77 cm) DEM 3,500. CHESTER, 9 March 1983, *The Embrace* (brown patinated bronze, h. 19 ins / 48 cm) GBP 2,800. LONDON, 21 March 1985, *Young Woman with Arms Raised* (c. 1905, patinated bronze and ivory, h. 28 1/4 ins / 72 cm) GBP 3,500. LONDON, 24 March 1988, *The Valkyrie* (bronze, h. 28 1/4 ins / 71.5 cm) GBP 4,180. LONDON, 16 March 1989, *The Lovers* (wood, h. 11 ins / 28 cm) GBP 2,750. LONDON, 29 March 1990, *The Valkyrie* (bronze, h. 22 ins / 56 cm) GBP 2,860. LONDON, 17 May 1991, *The Valkyrie* (bronze, h. 22 ins / 56 cm) GBP 2,530.

SINDING LARSEN, Kristoffer Andreas Lange

Norwegian, 20th century.

Born 3 April 1873, in Christiania (now Oslo).

Painter, engraver. Portraits, landscapes.

Sinding Larsen studied in Christiania and under Kroyer in Copenhagen. He exhibited variously in Paris, notably at the Exposition Universelle of 1900, where he received a mention.

MUSEUMS AND GALLERIES:

OSLO (Nasjonalgal.): *Portrait of the Artist's Sister.*

SINDLER, Johann Georg

Austrian, 17th - 18th century.

Born c. 1669, in Styria; died 19 October 1732, in Rome, Italy.

Modeller (wax).

Sindler settled in Rome from 1713.

SINDONI, Turillo

Italian, 19th - 20th century.

Born 24 December 1870, in Messina.

Sculptor.

Sindoni worked in South America, New York and the Far East.

SINDRAM. See **SINTRAM**

SINÉ
French, 20th century.
Born 31 December 1928, in Paris.
Cartoonist.

Siné has contributed to many periodicals, especially *L'Express; Arts et Spectacle; Lui; Hara Kiri; L'Événement du Jeudi.* In 1962, he created his own periodical: *Siné-Massacre.* His work earned him frequent court appearances. Despite this, he was awarded the Grand Prix for Black Humour in 1957, and the Daumier Prize in 1984.

AUCTION RECORDS:
PARIS, 27 Nov 1993, *No Caption (Eroticised Album)* (black ink/paper, 6 x 6 3/4 ins / 15.5 x 17 cm) FRF 5,000. PARIS, 25 Sept 1999, *Pharmacist* (watercolour, 47 x 31 ins / 120 x 80 cm) FRF 13,500.

SINELL, Bruno
German, 20th century.
Born 26 September 1879, in Berlin.
Painter, sculptor.

Bruno Sinell studied under Arthur Lewin-Funke and Martin Körte, and at the fine arts academy in Berlin.

SINEMUS, Wilhelmus Friedrich or Wim
Dutch, 19th - 20th century.
Born 1903, in Amsterdam; died 1987.
Painter.

Wilhelmus ('Wim') Sinemus studied at the fine arts academy in The Hague and went on to live and work in the Dutch capital as a member of the Vrij Beelden ('Free Artists') Group. He visited Paris in 1928 and exhibited at the Salon des Réalités Nouvelles in 1950. In 2002, examples of his work featured at *Focus Paris, Bekering tot abstract* (*Focus Paris: The Turn towards Abstraction*), an exhibition held at the CoBrA Museum for Modern Art in Amstelveen to honour the members of the Vrij Beelden and Creatie ('Creation') groups of artists, whose work was influenced by their time spent in Paris and their exposure to the French abstract movement.

Wim Sinemus' first works date from 1937. As a calligrapher and graphic artist, his style is not dissimilar to that of Hans Hartung.

BIBLIOGRAPHY:
Focus Paris, die Hinwendung zum Abstrakte, exhibition catalogue, Cobra Museum voor Moderne Kunst, Amstelveen, 2002.

AUCTION RECORDS:
AMSTERDAM, 10 April 1989, *Bird* (1942, ink and watercolour, 12 1/2 x 9 ins / 31.5 x 22 cm) NLG 1,380. AMSTERDAM, 12 Dec 1991, *Untitled* (1963, gouache and pastel/paper, 25 1/4 x 19 1/2 ins / 64 x 49.5 cm) NLG 3,910. AMSTERDAM, 5 June 1996, *Composition* (1953, mixed media and collage/paper, 22 3/4 x 18 ins / 58 x 46 cm) NLG 4,025. AMSTERDAM, 7 June 2000, *Untitled* (mixed media, 28 x 21 ins / 70 x 53 cm) NLG 7,500. AMSTERDAM, 25 Nov 2003, *Abstract Composition* (1966, pastel, 27 x 20 ins / 68 x 50 cm) EUR 1,500.

SINET, André
French, 19th - 20th century.
Born 19 February 1867, in Villennes-sur-Seine.
Painter, pastellist, draughtsman. Portraits, genre scenes, landscapes with figures, urban landscapes, waterscapes.

André Sinet painted several portraits of famous people of the time, including Anatole France and Yvette Guilbert. He also painted scenes from the life of the society woman, and views of Paris and its surroundings.

MUSEUMS AND GALLERIES:
BORDEAUX (MBA): *Twilight in Paris.*

AUCTION RECORDS:
PARIS, 8 Dec 1894, *Acacia Avenue in April* (pastel) FRF 260. PARIS, 8 Dec 1895, *Sketch for Portrait of Yvette Guilbert,* FRF 240. PARIS, 1 June 1899, *Game,* FRF 1,000; *Woman Getting Up,* FRF 190; *Singing Lesson,* FRF 380; *Nude Woman beside the Water,* FRF 290; *Spring,* FRF 450. PARIS, 14 April 1943, *Seaside Resort,* FRF 750. PARIS, July 1946, *Dancer and Dresser* (pastel) FRF 2,100. PARIS, 15 March 1950, *Champs-Élysées* (pastel) FRF 1,100. PARIS, 24 Nov 1950, *Bougival* (1902, pastel) FRF 1,000. PARIS, 6 July 1951, *Champs-Élysées in the Evening* (1901, pastel) FRF 750. ST-BRIEUC, 7 Nov 1977, *Beach* (1902, pastel, 9 1/2 x 15 3/4 ins / 24 x 40 cm) FRF 750. PARIS, 7 Dec 1987, *Glass of Absinthe* (oil on canvas, 12 1/2 x 8 1/4 ins / 32 x 21 cm) FRF 4,000. NEW YORK, 19 Feb 1992, *At the Opera* (1896, pastel, 15 3/4 x 10 3/4 ins / 40 x 27.3 cm) USD 14,300.

SINET, Louis René Hippolyte
French, 19th century.
Born in Péronne (Somme).
Painter. Portraits, genre scenes.

Sinet was a pupil of Couture and Binnoury and made his Salon debut in 1859.

SINÉVI, Saadi
Turkish, 20th century.
Born 1902; died 1987.
Active in Lebanon.
Painter. Landscapes.

Saadi Sinévi worked for the Lebanese government, organising collective exhibitions at the parliament and then at the UNESCO building. He was president of the association of Lebanese artists, painters and sculptors. He was a landscape painter who privileged sensation over realism.

SING, Johann Kaspar
Austrian, 17th - 18th century.
Born 1651, in Braunau-on-Inn; died 16 February 1729, in Munich, Germany.
Painter. Religious subjects.

Sing was court painter in Munich. He produced altar paintings for many Bavarian churches.

AUCTION RECORDS:
LONDON, 16 May 1984, *David with the Head of Goliath* (1686, oil on canvas, 67 1/2 x 41 1/4 ins / 171.5 x 104.5 cm) GBP 1,300.

SING, Thiemo
Austrian, 17th century.
Born 24 March 1639, in Braunau-on-Inn; died 27 August 1666, in Salzburg.
Active in Salzburg.
Painter.

Sing produced work for the monastery of St Peter in Salzburg, including the altar paintings for its church.

SINGDAHLSEN, Andreas
Norwegian, 19th century.
Born 31 March 1855, in Moss.
Painter. Landscapes.

Singdahlsen was a pupil of Christian Krohg and Fritz Thaulow. One of his paintings is in the Nasjonalgaleriet in Oslo.

MUSEUMS AND GALLERIES:
OSLO (Nasjonalgal.).

SINGELAAR, Cornelis, or Cingelaer
Dutch, 17th - 18th century.
Active in Rotterdam at the end of the 17th century.
Painter. Genre scenes.

Cornelis Singelaar was a pupil of Fr. Verwilt. He may have been the same person as Melchior Cingelaer.

SINGELANDT, Pieter Cornelisz. van.
See **SLINGELAND**

SINGENDONCK, Diederick Jan
Dutch, 19th century.
Born 1784; died 10 December 1833.
Active in Utrecht.
Painter, engraver (etching). Still-lifes.

AUCTION RECORDS:
AMSTERDAM, 26 May 1970, *Still-lifes* (two pendants) NLG 13,000. GRAVENHAGE, 7 Nov 2001, *Still-life with Fruit, Shells and Oyster Shells* (oil on panel, 13 x 18 ins / 34 x 45 cm) NLG 15,000.

SINGER, Albert
German, 19th - 20th century.
Born 23 November 1869, in Munich; died 20 March 1922, in Schlierbach.
Painter. Sporting subjects, landscapes.
Albert Singer was a pupil of Johann C. Herterich and Alexander von Wagner; he favoured hunting scenes.

SINGER, Clyde
American, 20th century.
Born 1908, in Malvern (Ohio); died 1999, in Canfield (Ohio).
Painter.
Clyde Singer studied at the Columbus Art School in Ohio. In 1933, he was awarded a scholarship to the Art Students League in New York, where he studied with Kenneth Hayes Miller, John Stuart Curry, Alexander Brook, Bridgman, Lahey, Ivan Olinsky, DuMond, and Thomas Hart Benton. He subsequently became a teacher and curator at the Butler Institute.

Singer produced Regionalist paintings in a Social Realist style; he portrayed people in various everyday settings - carnivals, standing in bars, on street corners, celebrating holidays, in picture galleries. He participated in group exhibitions from 1935, including: the Whitney Museum annual; the Corcoran Biennial; the National Academy of Design; and the Carnegie Foundation in Pittsburgh.

C. Singer

AUCTION RECORDS:
NEW YORK, 31 Jan 1985, *Old Chicago* (1939, oil on canvas, 21 x 36 ins / 53.3 x 91.5 cm) USD 2,100. NEW YORK, 24 Jan 1989, *Corner of 57th and 7th* (1967, casein/synthetic resin, 35 1/2 x 38 ins / 90 x 96.8 cm) USD 7,700. NEW YORK, 18 Dec 1991, *44th Street at Night* (1963, oil on card, 21 3/4 x 27 3/4 ins / 55.2 x 70.5 cm) USD 1,760. NEW YORK, 17 May 2001, *USA Work Programme, WPA, Florida* (1939, watercolour, 16 x 20 ins / 40 x 51 cm) USD 4,000. FAIRFIELD, 25 Aug 2004, *Flower Vendor* (1947, oil on board, 9 x 20 ins / 23 x 51 cm) USD 3,550.

SINGER, Emil
Austrian, 20th century.
Born 17 August 1881, in Gaya (Moravia).
Painter, engraver.
Emil Singer lived and worked in Vienna.

SINGER, Emmi, Mrs Hiessleitner
Austrian, 20th century.
Born 8 September 1884, in Voitsberg.
Painter, engraver.
Emmi Singer studied art in Graz and under Oskar Graf in Munich. Singer lived and worked in Graz.

SINGER, Franz
Austrian, 20th century.
Born 1886, in Reutte.
Painter. Landscapes.
Franz Singer was responsible for restoring frescoes in churches in Hall, where he lived and worked.

SINGER, Franz. See also **SIGRIST**

SINGER, Gail
American, 20th century.
Born 1924, in Galveston (Texas); died 1983.
Active in France from 1955.
Painter, watercolourist, engraver.
Gail Singer studied in St Louis and then at the School of Fine Arts at the University of Washington, where she won a scholarship to travel in Europe in 1952. She settled in Paris in 1955 and worked in S.W. Hayter's Atelier 17. Her work has been compared to that of Arshile Gorky, in her preference for brightly coloured abstract forms presented in isolation from each other in the space of the canvas.

Singer participated in many collective exhibitions of engravings throughout the world, particularly at the Salon des Réalités Nouvelles in Paris, which paid tribute to her in 1984. Solo exhibitions of her work were held in Paris, such as those at the Galerie Le Soleil dans la Tête in 1961 and the Galerie Rive Gauche in 1975.

BIBLIOGRAPHY:
Pieyre de Mandiargues, André, *Gail Singier - Gravures*, exhibition catalogue, Gal. Le Soleil dans la tête, Paris, 1961. de Mandriargues, A. Pieyre/Hayter, S.W., *Gail Singer*, exhibition catalogue, Gal. Rive Gauche, Paris, 1975.

AUCTION RECORDS:
PARIS, 22 Nov 1995, *Devil* (oil on canvas, 28 3/4 x 36 1/4 ins / 73 x 92 cm) FRF 4,300.

SINGER, Gérard
French, 20th century.
Born 1929, in Paris.
Painter, pastellist, sculptor.
Gérard Singer studied at the École des Beaux-Arts in Paris, where he learnt the different techniques of painting, fresco, and sculpture by direct carving.

He first showed his paintings in Paris at the Salon d'Automne, Salon de Mai and Salon des Peintres Témoins de leur Temps. In 1964 he exhibited at the Exposition des Jeunes Artistes de Tokyo. He was an award winner at the Biennale des Jeunes Artistes in 1961.

After having been taught in the tradition of David, he was prepared, when the moment came, to practice the strict academic precepts laid down by the Social Realism favoured in post-war Communist circles, although he never really felt at home with this technique. He then gave up painting, tried his hand at relief, and finally took up sculpture. Using tinted synthetic resins, and elements that could be assembled, he conceived a system of organised spaces that invited penetration. The topography of the structure appeared completely arbitrary. It was simply open to be entered, seen and touched at whim. In the same spirit, he was given the opportunity by some young architects to design the area between the various buildings of the Lycée de la Source (a girls' school). His solution was a series of graduated elevations, alternating with small amphitheatres in the hollows between them.

BIBLIOGRAPHY:
Bouret, Jean, *VIe Salon des peintres témoins de leur temps 'Le Sport'*, exhibition catalogue, Musée Galliera, Paris, 1957. '*Voyage en Epoxy*' in *Chroniques de l'Art Vivant* n° 1, periodical, Maeght, Paris, November 1968. Abadie, Daniel/Ceysson, Bernard/Daval, Jean Luc, *Gérard Singier*, Skira, Geneva, 1996.

AUCTION RECORDS:
PARIS, 25 Feb 1996, *Composition* (1966, pastel, 29 1/2 x 19 3/4 ins / 75 x 50 cm) FRF 7,200. PARIS, 28 April 1997, *Composition* (1957, watercolour and ink/paper/card, 15 x 11 ins / 38 x 28 cm) FRF 14,000. PARIS, 4 Oct 1997, *Tree in the Morning* (1963, oil on canvas, 36 1/4 x 28 3/4 ins / 92 x 73 cm) FRF 29,000.

SINGER, Halsey William
American, 20th - 21st century.
Born 1957, in Philadelphia.
Active in France from 1970.
Engraver, draughtsman.
Halsey William Singer settled in Vence, on the French Riviera. Collective exhibitions include: *De Bonnard à Baselitz:*

Dix Ans d'enrichissements du cabinet des estampes 1978-1988 (*From Bonnard to Baselitz: A Decade of Acquisitions by the Prints Collection 1978-1988*), at the Bibliothèque National, Paris, 1992.

MUSEUMS AND GALLERIES:

PARIS (BNF, Prints Collection): *From the Same Desert* (1986, burin).

SINGER, Hans, or Singher, Zinger, called Hans de Deuytscher
German, 16th century.
Born 1510, in Marburg; died 1558, in Marburg.
Painter.
Antwerp School.

Hans Singer entered the Antwerp Guild of Painters in 1543 and became a master in 1549. He may have been an ancestor of the Duyts family. He painted landscapes and drew many cartoons for tapestries.

SINGER, Janos Mihaly or Johann Michael
Hungarian, 18th century.
Sculptor.

Janos Mihaly Singer worked for the town hall in Eger in 1738.

SINGER, Johann Ambros
Austrian, 18th century.
Active in Styria, Austria.
Painter.

Johann Singer painted architectural views for Schloss Oberkindberg (castle) in Austria in 1763.

SINGER, Johann Georg
Austrian, 18th century.
Active in the Tyrol, Austria, c. 1738.
Painter. Mountain landscapes.

Johann Georg Singer studied under Johann Georg Grasmair.

AUCTION RECORDS:

NEW YORK, 6 Feb 1997, *Mountain River Landscape with Figures* (1780, oil on canvas, 15 1/4 x 11 ins / 38.7 x 27.9 cm) USD 4,600.

SINGER, Johann Michael
German, 18th century.
Active in Bavaria at the end of the 18th century.
Painter. Religious subjects.

Johann Michael Singer produced some ceiling paintings for the churches of Hofgiebing and Waal in Germany.

SINGER, Johann Paul
German, 19th century.
Born 1823, in Nuremberg.
Engraver (burin/steel). Portraits, illustrations for missals.

Johann Paul Singer studied under Friedrich Wagner.

SINGER, Michal
Czechoslovak, 20th - 21st century.
Born 22 March 1959, in Prague.
Painter (including gouache), watercolourist, draughtsman, illustrator, lithographer, writer.

Michal Singer was awarded a degree in philosophy at the University of Prague in 1984. He was a writer, journalist and illustrator of the weekly *Respekt* from 1989. He taught himself to paint and dedicated himself to it from 1993. He settled in Prague.

He is inspired by ancient Shamanist myths and, in this frame of mind, regularly paints a cat that he uses as a guide for the journey into the hereafter. Through this he seeks the attainment of self-knowledge. He creates works in contrasting colours.

He has taken part in collective exhibitions, including: *The Czech Alternative*, ULUV Gallery, Prague, 1990. He has had solo exhibitions, in particular: *Trip on an Aspirin Tablet*, Navratil Gallery, Prague, 2002; *Temple of the Red Cat*, Centre Culturel Tchèque, Paris, 2003.

SINGER, Sebald
German, 16th century.
Active in Nuremberg during the first half of the 16th century.
Painter.
Cracow School.

Sebald Singer was in the service of the Polish court in Cracow and worked for the city's cathedral.

SINGER, William Earl
American, 20th century.
Born 10 July 1910, in Chicago.
Painter, sculptor. Busts, monuments.

William Earl Singer studied at the Art Institute of Chicago and then went to Europe, where he worked in André Lhote's studio. He made the *Vincent Van Gogh* statue for the town of Arles and painted portraits of political and literary figures of his time, including Winston Churchill, Thomas Mann and Einstein.

Singer exhibited in Australia, Colombia, Israel, America and Europe. He won a gold medal in 1968, was made a chevalier des Arts et des Lettres in France in 1969, and became a member of the Institut des Arts et des Lettres in Geneva. He won many prizes and awards in the USA.

SINGER, William Henry, Jr.
American, 19th - 20th century.
Born 5 July 1868, in Pittsburgh; died 1943, in Norway.
Active in the Netherlands from 1922.
Painter. Landscapes.

William Henry Singer studied at the Académie Julian in Paris and then settled in Laren in the Netherlands. In the summer, he used to stay regularly in Norway, where he eventually died. He painted landscapes of the Netherlands and Norway in the Impressionist style. He was a member of the American Federation of Arts and the Association of American Artists in Paris. As an art collector, he was particularly keen on 19th-century French and Dutch works.

BIBLIOGRAPHY:

Vries, R.W.P. de/Mauclaire, Camille, *William Henry Singer, jr.: de mens en de Kunstenaar [the man and the artist]*, F. G. Kroonder, Bussum, 1950. *William H. Singer*, exhibition catalogue, Washington County Museum of Fine Arts, Hagerstown (MD), 1981.

MUSEUMS AND GALLERIES:

AMSTERDAM - ANTWERP - MEMPHIS - MUNICH (Neue Pinakothek) - NEW YORK (Metropolitan Mus. of Art) - OSLO (Nasjonalgal.) - PARIS (former Mus. du Luxembourg) - PORTLAND, ME (MA): *The Coming of Night* - THE HAGUE.

AUCTION RECORDS:

NEW YORK, 10 July 1980, *First Snow* (1933, oil/hardboard, 24 x 15 3/4 ins / 60.1 x 40 cm) USD 1,700. WASHINGTON DC, 26 Sept 1982, *Summer Landscape* (1926, oil on canvas, 32 x 33 3/4 ins / 81.5 x 86 cm) USD 2,500. SAN FRANCISCO, 20 June 1985, *My Garden* (oil on canvas, 42 1/4 x 40 1/2 ins / 107 x 103 cm) USD 22,500. NEW YORK, 15 March 1986, *Peace Divine* (pastel/card, 17 3/4 x 21 1/2 ins / 45 x 54.5 cm) USD 2,700. PARIS, 6 June 1988, *Pine Tress* (1930, pastel, 21 1/4 x 17 3/4 ins / 54 x 45 cm) FRF 10,500. NEW YORK, 30 May 1990, *Solitude* (1923, oil on canvas, 33 1/2 x 31 1/2 ins / 85.4 x 80.3 cm) USD 3,850. AMSTERDAM, 9 Dec 1992, *Pines* (1936, coloured chalk/card, 22 x 18 ins / 55 x 46 cm) NLG 7,475. NEW YORK, 23 Sept 1993, *Morning Mist* (1926, oil on canvas, 39 1/2 x 41 1/2 ins / 100.3 x 105.4 cm) USD 2,875. AMSTERDAM, 31 May 1994, *September Morning* (1931, oil on canvas, 21 1/4 x 25 1/2 ins / 54 x 65 cm) NLG 3,220. NEW YORK, 20 March 1996, *Oldenmeld in Norway in Winter* (oil on canvas, 39 3/4 x 41 3/4 ins / 101 x 106 cm) USD 1,725. AMSTERDAM, 18 June 1996, *Landscape with a Ditch* (1918, oil on card, 15 3/4 x 18 1/4 ins / 40 x 46.5 cm) NLG

1,840. AMSTERDAM, 19-20 Feb 1997, *View over the Dunes* (oil on card, 13 x 16¼ ins / 33 x 41 cm) NLG 3,690. AMSTERDAM, 5 Sept 2000, *Torrent in Norwegian Landscape* (oil on panel, 18 x 22 ins / 45 x 55 cm) NLG 8,000. OSLO, 18 Dec 2000, *Night in Winter* (oil on canvas, 26 x 22 ins / 65 x 55 cm) NOK 26,000.

SINGER-SCHINNERL, Susi or Selma
Austrian, 20th century.
Born 27 October 1895, in Vienna.
Painter, sculptor, potter.

Susi Singer-Schinnerl studied at the Akademie der Bildenden Künste in Vienna. Her ceramics have as their favourite themes portraits of children or of young girls with flowers and fruit.

MUSEUMS AND GALLERIES:
NEW YORK (Metropolitan Mus. of Art): two statuettes.

SINGH, Arpita
Indian, 20th century.
Born 1937, in Bara Nagar (Bengal).
Painter, watercolourist, draughtswoman. Scenes with figures.

Arpita Singh studied art at the New Delhi Polytechnic, then worked as a stylist in Calcutta and New Delhi before dedicating herself totally to painting. Singh works with juxtaposition, putting together decorative motifs, maily flowers, geometric elements, figures, vegetables, animals, stars, vehicles (aeroplanes) and objects (sofas) on the same plane with generously applied paint. Her vision of life is naive: she brings to the viewer a world liberated from the laws of gravity and perspective, an invitation to daydream.

From 1960 onwards, her work was shown at numerous collective exhibitions: Art Heritage Gallery, New Delhi and at the New Delhi Triennales (1975 and 1982); *Festival of India* at the Royal Academy of Art, London (1982); *Indian Artists* exhibition, Istanbul and Ankara (1985); Centre Georges-Pompidou, Paris (1986); in Bombay (now Mumbai; 1987, 1988, 1990); Sydney (1993); and Monde de l'Art, Paris (1995).

BIBLIOGRAPHY:
Kapur, G., *Pictorial space: A point of view on contemporary Indian Art*, Rabindra Bhavan, New Delhi, 1977. *Arpita Singh*, exhibition catalogue, Éd. du Centre Georges-Pompidou, Paris, 1986.

SINGH, Rao Gobind
Indian, 18th century.
Painter.

SINGHER, Jan. See **SINGER Hans**

SINGIER, Gustave or Georges
Belgian, 20th century.
Born 11 February 1909, in Warneton (Flanders); died 5 May 1984, in Paris.
Active from 1919 and naturalised in France from 1947.
Painter (gouache), watercolourist, engraver, illustrator. Stage costumes and sets, murals, designs for mosaics, tapestries, and stained glass windows.

Gustave Singier's childhood was spent in war-torn Belgium under the German occupation. His father was a cabinetmaker and his mother a weaver. He started to paint in 1923, at the age of 14. He studied for three years at the École Boulle before going on to work (until 1936) as an interior architectural draughtsman and furniture designer, while painting in his free time. He met the painter Charles Walch, who encouraged him in his work and opened his eyes to his own potential as an artist painting from nature. He taught at the Académie Ranson in Paris from 1951 to 1954, then at the École des Beaux-Arts from 1967 to 1978.

Gustave Singier took part in various Salons, notably the Salon des Indépendants (1936 to 1939); the Salon d'Automne (1937 to 1949), of which he became a member in 1942; the Salon des Tuileries (1939 to 1942); the May Salon (as of 1945), of which he was a founder and committee member; and various other group exhibitions in Paris, including *Vingt Peintres de tradition française* (*Twenty French Traditional Painters*), an exhibition held in 1941 at the Galerie Braun that brought together the majority of those young French artists who would go on to make a name for themselves - and was a direct and double challenge, incidentally, to the occupying German forces on the one hand and, on the other, to the National Socialist concept of modern art as 'degenerate'. Singier's work was also shown in 1943 at *Douze Peintres d'aujourd'hui* (*Twelve Painters of Today*), an exhibition that featured works by many of the artists highlighted in the 1941 exhibition. This was followed by *Le Moal, Manessier, Singer* at the Galerie de France (1945) and the Galerie Drouin (1946) and a further exhibition at the Musée de Luxembourg (in 1949). Singier also exhibited abroad, notably at *La Jeune Peinture française* (*Recent French Painting*) at the Palais des Beaux-Arts in Brussels in 1945; at the Kunsthalle in Bern (1951-1952); the Stedelijk Museum in Amsterdam (1953); the 1954 Venice Biennale; the Carnegie Institute in Pittsburgh (1955, 1958); the Brussels Universal Exhibition of 1958; in Grenoble, Ljubljana and Paris in 1959; the Turin and Toyko Biennales in 1961; the Tate Gallery in London in 1962; and the São Paulo Biennale of 1963. Solo exhibitions of Singier's work were held in Paris (Galerie Billiet-Caputo, 1949, 1950; and at the Galerie de France on a regular basis from 1952 to 1972); Stockholm (1950); Brussels (1951); Turin (1953); Hanover (Kestner Gesellschaft), Lübeck, Duisburg, Elberfeld and Hamburg (1957); Brunswick (1958); Copenhagen (1961); New York (1962); Bern (1963); Caen and Rennes (1973); and at the École des Beaux-Arts in Paris in 1982. Numerous posthumous exhibitions of Singier's work were scheduled, including those at the Salon de Vitry in 1984 (*Hommage à Singier* (*Homage to Singier*)), the Arnoux and Couvrat-Desvergnes galleries in Paris in 1988, and a 1942-1984 retrospective organised at the Association Noroit-Arras in 1992.

As a painter, Gustave Singier's range was as wide as his output was prolific. By way of illustration, mention might be made of his *Miracle of the Loaves and Fishes* mural for the refectory of the Dominicains de la Glacière in Paris in 1946; his tapestries, including *Summer* (1946) and a *Departure of the Sailing Ships* of 1950, together with others for the Court of Appeal buildings in Paris (1954), two monumental compositions for the Paris church of St. Marcel (1969) and a further one for the Lycée Pré-Olympique at Font-Romeu; his stained glass for the Dominican Chapel of Monteils (1952); his mosaics for the Lycée in Argelès (1959) and the maison de la Radio in Paris (1964); his costumes for the production of Monteverdi's *Orfeo* at Aix-les-Bains (1955); his costumes and sets for the production of *Pelleas and Mélisande* at the Brussels Opera and his costumes for Monteverdi's *Tancred and Clorinde* at the Provins Festival (both in 1971); his chisel-point engravings for Camille Bourniquel's *Quatrains* (1947) or his colour lithographs for Julien Gracq's *Un Balcon en Forêt* of 1972.

Gustave Singier started out as an Expressionist and soon forged a reputation (as of his beginnings, around 1936). He found kindred spirits in the likes of Manessier and Le Moal, and his own style repeatedly intersected over the years with that of the former. Both artists - Manessier and Singier - were united in their rejection of 'pure abstraction', insisting that a work was ultimately based on or drawn from some aspect of reality. In effect, both drew freely from Impressionist and Cubist models, and it can be argued that both belong to that generation of French artists who were preoccupied with achieving a synthesis rather than being innovative for innovation's sake. This synthesis embraced Seurat and Cézanne on the one hand, as much as it did Matisse and Picasso on the other. Moreover, as of the immediate post-war years, Kandinsky, Klee and Mondrian would prove additional influences. In his later work, however, Singier follows a completely different route from that adopted by Manessier. The carefully constructed mosaics of his earlier years give way to compositions that are free-flowing and almost *tachiste*, reminiscent of the watercolours at which Singier also excelled. Some critics have taken him to task on account of a surfeit of elegance and daintiness, but these qualities are surely no grounds for reproach.

BIBLIOGRAPHY:

Bourniquel, Camille, *Trois peintres: Le Moal, Manessier, Singier*, Éd. du Chêne, Paris, 1946. Marester, Guy, *'Singier et la Sérénité'* in *XXe siècle*, periodical, Paris, 1952. Charbonnier, Georges, *'Singier'* in *coll. Musée de Poche*, Georges Fall, Paris, 1957. Schmücking, Rolf, *Das graphische Werk*, Städtisches Museum, Braunschweig, 1958. Charbonnier, Georges, *Le Monologue du peintre*, Éd. Julliard, Paris, 1959. Bourniquel, Camille, *Hommage à Singier*, Bibliothèque nationale de France, Paris, 1986. Harambourg, Lydia, *L'École de Paris 1945-1965. Dictionnaire des peintres*, Ides et Calendes, Neuchâtel, 1993. Le Burghe, Philippe, *Gustave Singier*, Ides et Calendes, Neuchâtel, 2002.

MUSEUMS AND GALLERIES:

ARLES (Mus. Réattu) - BRUSSELS (Mus. royaux) - ESSEN: *Morning* (1956) - HAMBURG: *Hillsides, Collioure* (1956) - LA CHAUX-DE-FONDS (MBA) - LE HAVRE (Mus. Malraux) - LONDON (Tate Collection): *Provence I* (1957, oil on canvas) - MONTREAL (MAC): *Matinal Nereids* (1968) - NEW YORK (Solomon R. Guggenheim Mus.): *Dutch Town* (1952) - PARIS (BNF, Prints Collection): *Composition on a Blue-Green Ground* (1978, lithograph) - PARIS (MAMVP) - PARIS (MNAM-CCI): *Summer* (1947); *Christmas Eve* (1950) - PITTSBURGH (Carnegie MA): *Open Door on the Garden* (1944, oil on canvas); *Composition* (1953, lithograph in five colours); several other works - SKOPJE (Muzej na Sovremena Umetnost).

AUCTION RECORDS:

PARIS, 8 July 1954, *Red Interior*, FRF 80,000. PARIS, 8 Dec 1959, *Morning at the Window*, FRF 400,000. NEW YORK, 18 May 1960, *Old Town in Provence*, USD 600. STUTTGART, 3-4 May 1962, *Springtime in Paris*, DEM 13,200. GENEVA, 18 June 1966, *Navigable Space*, CHF 12,000. PARIS, 9 March 1972, *By the Lighthouse*, FRF 10,100. VERSAILLES, 2 Dec 1973, *Tub*, FRF 9,100. PARIS, 29 Oct 1974, *Abstract Composition*, FRF 17,000. VERSAILLES, 9 Feb 1976, *Composition* (17 1/4 ins / 44 cm, 2 x 22 1/4 ins/5 x 56.5 cm) FRF 4,000. PARIS, 25 Oct 1976, *Autostrade* (1951, oil on panel, 7 1/2 x 12 3/4 ins / 19 x 32.5 cm) FRF 2,100. PARIS, 22 March 1977, *Near the Lighthouse* (1954, oil on canvas, 32 x 39 1/4 ins / 81 x 100 cm) FRF 11,000. ZURICH, 30 May 1979, *Solar Migration* (1962, mixed media/paper, 17 1/4 x 22 ins / 44 x 55 cm) CHF 3,800. NEW YORK, 18 Jan 1980, *Composition in Red* (1952, oil on canvas, 11 3/4 x 19 ins / 29.9 x 48.2 cm) USD 1,500. PARIS, 25 Oct 1982, *Grid* (1944, oil on canvas, 28 3/4 x 21 1/4 ins / 73 x 54 cm) FRF 10,500. PARIS, 13 Dec 1983, *Tree in the Morning* (1963, oil on canvas, 36 1/4 x 28 3/4 ins / 92 x 73 cm) FRF 11,800. PARIS, 6 Dec 1986, *Couple and the Sea* (1965, oil on canvas, 76 3/4 x 51 1/4 ins / 195 x 130 cm) FRF 96,000. LONDON, 25 Feb 1988, *Departure of the Sailing Vessels* (1950, oil on panel, 30 1/4 x 26 ins / 77 x 66 cm) GBP 12,100. PARIS, 29 April 1988, *Composition* (1973, watercolour, 22 x 17 1/2 ins / 56 x 44.5 cm) FRF 13,200. NEUILLY, 20 June 1988, *Composition* (1968, ink drawing, 17 3/4 x 22 ins / 45 x 56 cm) FRF 10,500; *Untitled* (1973, watercolour, 22 1/4 x 17 1/2 ins / 56.5 x 44.7 cm) FRF 15,000; *Untitled* (1965, pastel, 22 x 17 3/4 ins / 56 x 45 cm) FRF 12,000. PARIS, 20-21 June 1988, *Composition* (1947, oil on panel, 9 1/2 x 14 1/4 ins / 24 x 36 cm) FRF 26,000. PARIS, 24 June 1988, *Awakening* (1949, oil on canvas, 28 3/4 x 23 1/2 ins / 73 x 59.7 cm) FRF 170,000. LONDON, 20 Oct 1988, *Interior behind Closed Shutters* (1949, oil on canvas, 51 1/4 x 38 1/4 ins / 130 x 97 cm) GBP 19,800. PARIS, 28 Oct 1988, *House by the Roadside* (1945, ink/paper, 8 1/2 x 7 1/2 ins / 21.5 x 19 cm) FRF 7,000. NEUILLY, 22 Nov 1988, *Theseus* (1981, watercolour, 17 1/4 x 22 ins / 44 x 56 cm) FRF 22,000. NEUILLY, 16 March 1989, *Dazzled Bather* (1964, oil on canvas, 76 3/4 x 51 1/4 ins / 195 x 130 cm) FRF 290,000. PARIS, 19 March 1989, *Composition* (wax crayon) FRF 18,000. LONDON, 29 June 1989, *Siesta* (1943, oil on canvas, 51 1/4 x 38 1/4 ins / 130 x 97 cm) GBP 59,400. DOUAI, 2 July 1989, *Bather with Flower* (oil on canvas, 18 x 15 ins / 46 x 38 cm) FRF 94,000. PARIS, 8 Oct 1989, *Moors (Night No. 1)* (1961, oil on canvas, 32 x 39 1/4 ins / 81 x 100 cm) FRF 240,000. LE TOUQUET, 12 Nov 1989, *Composition* (1965, pastel and gouache, 22 x 17 3/4 ins / 56 x 45 cm) FRF 28,000. DOUAI, 3 Dec 1989, *Portrait of Edouard Pignon* (1963, ink, 22 1/4 x 18 ins / 56.5 x 45.5 cm) FRF 21,000; *From the Bull's Perspective* (1952, oil on canvas, 11 x 16 1/4 ins / 27 x 41 cm) FRF 240,000. PARIS, 18 Feb 1990, *Traveller* (1954, oil on paper, 13 x 22 ins / 33 x 55 cm) FRF 330,000. LONDON, 22 Feb 1990, *Child with Plant* (1947, oil on canvas, 28 3/4 x 23 1/2 ins / 73 x 60 cm) GBP 49,500. PARIS, 7 March 1990, *Untitled* (watercolour, 12 1/2 x 9 ins / 32 x 22 cm) FRF 23,000. PARIS, 8 April 1990, *Moors; Night II* (1961, oil on canvas, 32 1/4 x 39 1/4 ins / 82 x 100 cm) FRF 270,000. PARIS, 26 April 1990, *Composition* (watercolour/paper, 11 3/4 x 9 ins / 30 x 23 cm) FRF 25,000. NEUILLY, 10 May 1990, *Hydra-Meridian I* (1970, oil on canvas, 36 1/4 x 28 3/4 ins / 92 x 73 cm) FRF 200,000. PARIS, 11 June 1990, *Composition* (gouache/paper, 17 1/4 x 22 ins / 43.5 x 56 cm) FRF 45,000. PARIS, 22 June 1990, *Humid Garden* (1951, oil on canvas, 32 x 23 1/2 ins / 81 x 60 cm) FRF 315,000. ST-GERMAIN-EN-LAYE, 8 Dec 1991, *Footbridge* (1944, oil on canvas, 28 x 20 3/4 ins / 71 x 53 cm) FRF 191,000. LONDON, 26 March 1992, *Houseboats at Clichy* (1950, watercolour/paper/card, 9 1/2 x 12 1/2 ins / 24.3 x 31.5 cm) GBP 1,870. PARIS, 9 July 1992, *Composition* (1965, pastel/paper, 22 x 17 1/4 ins / 55 x 44 cm) FRF 17,500. LONDON, 15 Oct 1992, *Still-life* (1944, oil on canvas, 13 3/4 x 10 1/2 ins / 35 x 26.7 cm) GBP 4,840. PARIS, 9 Dec 1992, *Tub* (oil on canvas, 39 1/4 x 32 ins / 100 x 81 cm) FRF 75,000. PARIS, 24 Oct 1993, *Moors (Night I)* (1961, oil on canvas, 32 x 39 1/4 ins / 81 x 100 cm) FRF 125,000. COPENHAGEN, 3 Nov 1993, *Composition* (1966, watercolour, 22 x 17 3/4 ins / 56 x 45 cm) DKK 13,000. LONDON, 3 Dec 1993, *Interior behind Closed Shutters* (1949, oil on canvas, 51 1/4 x 37 3/4 ins / 130 x 96 cm) GBP 19,550. PARIS, 11 April 1994, *White Collar* (1946, oil on canvas, 36 1/4 x 28 3/4 ins / 92 x 73 cm) FRF 85,000. PARIS, 28 Oct 1995, *Blue Interiors with figures* (1971, oil on canvas, 63 3/4 x 51 1/4 ins / 162 x 130 cm) FRF 95,000. LONDON, 21 March 1996, *Butterflies of the Night* (1949, pastel/paper, 9 1/2 x 12 1/4 ins / 24 x 31.3 cm) GBP 1,150. PARIS, 3 May 1996, *Sands* (1973, watercolour, 17 3/4 x 22 ins / 45 x 56 cm) FRF 5,500. NEW YORK, 10 Oct 1996, *Marine Garden II* (1959, oil on canvas, 35 x 46 ins / 88.9 x 116.8 cm) USD 21,850. PARIS, 29 Nov 1996, *Composition* (1963, engraving, 14 1/2 x 17 3/4 ins / 37 x 45 cm) FRF 32,500. PARIS, 5 Dec 1997, *Abstract Composition* (1966, watercolour) FRF 5,000. PARIS, 23 March 1998, *Bathers-Traces IV* (1968, oil on canvas, 33 x 12 3/4 ins / 84 x 32.5 cm) FRF 31,000.

SINGKNECHT, Christoph Gregor

German, 17th century.

Active in Königsberg (now Kaliningrad, Russia), during the first half of the 17th century.

Painter.

Singknecht produced paintings for the town hall and former stock exchange in Königsberg.

SINGLETON, H. (Mrs)
British, 19th century.
Active in London.
Miniaturist.

Mrs Singleton exhibited in London, particularly at the Royal Academy and the British Institution, from 1807 to 1822. She married the history painter Henry Singleton.

SINGLETON, Henry
British, 18th - 19th century.
Born 19 October 1766, in London; died 15 September 1839, in London.
Painter, engraver, illustrator. History painting, portraits.

Henry Singleton was an orphan, and was taught by his uncle the miniaturist Joseph Singleton. He was subsequently a pupil of the Royal Academy schools, and exhibited at the Royal Academy from 1780 to 1839. Singleton was awarded a Gold Medal in 1788, and his work was highly regarded by Sir Joshua Reynolds. His ready skill and easy fluency enabled him to produce a substantial oeuvre both as an illustrator and as a painter; his work was extremely popular. Singleton's works included a series of small paintings of scenes from Shakespeare, a number of which were reproduced as engravings.

This easy success was short-lived, however, and he was never elected to the Royal Academy. After his death his works fell very much out of favour.

Museums and Galleries:

Coire: *Portrait of General Suvorov* - Edinburgh (Scottish National Portrait Gallery): *James Boswell and his Family* (oil on canvas) - Frankfurt am Main (Städel): *Vicar Receiving the Tithe* - Leicester: *Manto and Tiresias* - London (National Portrait Gal.): *Richard Howe, 1st Earl Howe* (engraved in 1799, oil on canvas) - London (Royal Academy of Arts): *Portrait of Thomas Sandby* (1793, oil on canvas); *The Royal Academicians in General Assembly* (1795, oil on canvas) - London (Tate Collection): *Manto and Tiresias* (exhibited in 1792, oil on canvas); *Palemon and Lavinia* (c. 1792, oil on canvas, inspired by 'Seasons', a poem by James Thomson); *Ariel on a Bat's Back* (exhibited in 1819, oil on canvas, inspired by Shakespeare's 'The Tempest') - London (Victoria and Albert Mus.): *At the Inn Door* - Paris (Louvre): *Rivals*.

Auction records:

Paris, 10 June 1893, *The Two Rivals*, FRF 580. Paris, 18-25 March 1901, *The Two Rivals*, FRF 1,020. London, 19 May 1911, *West Coast; East Side of a Town* (two pendants) GBP 598. London, 6 May 1926, *Interiors with figures* (black chalk) GBP 22. London, 16 Dec 1927, *Col. Bragge Prowse Primm*, GBP 50. London, 21 Feb 1930, *The Husband's Return; The Soldier's Return* (both) GBP 147. London, 19 March 1942, *View of the Indies* (three paintings) GBP 126. New York, 20 and 21 Feb 1946, *Work; Idleness* (two pendants) USD 2,000. London, 23 March 1966, *The Submission of the Two Sons of Tipu Sultan, Seringapatam*, GBP 550. New York, 25 Sept 1968, *War and Peace* (two pendants) USD 2,300. London, 10 Dec 1971, *Portrait of a Woman*, Gns 500. London, 23 June 1972, *Young Woman Offering a Helmet to a Gentleman*, Gns 750. London, 21 June 1974, *Interior With Family Group*, Gns 450. London, 18 June 1976, *The Death of Captain Strangeways, 16th of July 1796* (oil on canvas, 19 1/2 x 25 1/2 ins / 49.5 x 65 cm) GBP 480. London, 23 Nov 1977, *The Hostages* (oil on canvas, 20 x 25 ins / 51 x 63.5 cm) GBP 2,400. London, 11 April 1980, *Returning from Market* (oil on canvas, 13 1/4 x 11 1/4 ins / 33.6 x 28.6 cm) GBP 1,000. London, 26 June 1981, *The Helmet Sent by Isabel to Sir Bertram* (oil on canvas, 49 1/2 x 62 1/4 ins / 125.6 x 158 cm) GBP 1,700. London, 27 April 1983, *The Helmet Sent by Isabel to Sir Bertram* (oil on canvas, 49 1/2 x 62 1/4 ins / 126 x 158 cm) GBP 1,600. London, 26 May 1989, *Interior With Elegant Couple Dancing* (oil on canvas, 14 x 12 ins / 35.6 x 30.4 cm) GBP 1,650. London, 18 Oct 1989, *Angels* (oil on canvas, 49 3/4 x 39 1/2 ins / 126.5 x 100.5 cm) GBP 1,650. London, 31 Oct 1990, *Officer of the East India Company Dictating to a Scribe* (oil on canvas, 15 1/4 x 11 3/4 ins / 39 x 30 cm) GBP 2,640. London, 7 Oct 1992, *Portrait of a Mother Reading to her Child* (oil on canvas, 50 x 40 ins / 127 x 101.5 cm) GBP 1,540. London, 18 Nov 1992, *The Death of Nelson* (oil on canvas, 24 1/2 x 33 1/2 ins / 62 x 85 cm) GBP 6,600. London, 12 April 1995, *Peace and War* (oil on canvas, a pair, and two engravings after the paintings, each 29 1/4 x 24 ins / 74 x 61 cm) GBP 8,625. London, 10 July 1996, *Arviragus, Belarius, Guiderius and Imogen in the Forest* (oil on canvas, 24 1/2 x 29 1/4 ins / 62 x 74 cm) GBP 4,140. London, 11 June 1999, *Returned from Market* (oil on canvas, 14 x 12 ins / 36 x 31 cm) GBP 3,500. London, 11 Nov 1999, *Death of Nelson at the Battle of Trafalgar* (oil on canvas, 25 x 34 ins / 63 x 86 cm) GBP 14,000. London, 8 March 2001, *Cottage Door* (oil on canvas, 30 x 25 ins / 76 x 63 cm) GBP 2,800. London, 21 March 2001, *Volumnia and Virgilla Pleading before Coriolanus* (oil on canvas, 23 x 31 ins / 59 x 79 cm) GBP 2,500. London, 9 July 2003, *Storming of the Bastille* (oil on canvas, 18 x 24 ins / 46 x 61 cm) GBP 6,500. London, 26 March 2004, *Portrait of Benjamin Franklin* (pencil, 9 x 7 ins / 23 x 17 cm) GBP 1,500. London, 11 June 2004, *West End of the Town. East End of the Town* (oil on canvas, a pair, 15 x 17 ins / 38 x 44 cm) GBP 35,000.

SINGLETON, J.
British, 18th century.
Engraver. Portraits.

SINGLETON, Joseph
British, 18th century.
Active in London.
Miniaturist. Portraits.

Joseph Singleton was the brother of William Singleton. He exhibited 30 miniatures at the Royal Academy between 1773 and 1788.

SINGLETON, Maria
British, 19th century.
Active in London.
Painter, miniaturist. Military portraits, portraits.

Maria Singleton was the sister of Henry and Sarah Macklarinan Singleton. She exhibited at the Royal Academy from 1808 to 1820.

SINGLETON, R.
British, 18th century.
Active c. 1760.
Sculptor.

R. Singleton sculpted a tomb in Norwich Cathedral together with G. Bottomley.

SINGLETON, Sarah Macklarinan
British, 18th - 19th century.
Active in London.
Miniaturist, painter. Portraits.

Sarah Macklarinan Singleton was the sister of the history painter Henry Singleton. She exhibited 74 miniatures at the Royal Academy between 1787 and 1813.

SINGLETON, Thomas
British, 18th century.
Active from 1750 to 1780.
Sculptor.

Thomas Singleton was probably the brother of R. Singleton. He executed tombs in Hampstead and in Horringer (also - and formerly - known as Horningsheath, in Suffolk), in Redenhall (Norfolk) and in Norwich.

SINGLETON, William
British, 18th century.
Died 1793.
Active in London.

Miniaturist, enameller. Portraits.
William Singleton exhibited at the Royal Academy between 1770 and 1790.
AUCTION RECORDS:
PARIS, 8 April 1919, *Portrait of Lady Hamilton, Dressed as a Bacchante* (miniature after Sir J. Reynolds) FRF 2,100. LONDON, 10 April 2002, *Child, in a White Dress* (miniature) GBP 1,000.

SINGLETON COPLEY, John. See **COPLEY John Singleton**

SINGRY, Eulalie. See **DORUS**

SINGRY, J.
French, 19th century.
Died 1824.
Miniaturist.
J. Singry was a pupil of Isabey and Vincent. He exhibited at the Salon between 1806 and 1824.
MUSEUMS AND GALLERIES:
LONDON (Wallace Collection): *Portrait of the Marchioness of Conyngham; Lady in Restoration Costume.*
AUCTION RECORDS:
PARIS, 18-22 April 1910, *Portrait of Dupaty* (miniature) FRF 305. PARIS, 18 Dec 1922, *Portrait of a Man; Portrait of a Woman* (two miniatures) FRF 400. PARIS, 19 March 1924, *Portrait of Mademoiselle de St-Aubin, the actress* (miniature) FRF 2,850. PARIS, 10 Dec 1927, *Young woman in a Low-Cut Red Bodice* (miniature) FRF 1,820. PARIS, 31 March 1950, *Mme Adèle shown Rising from her Bed* (miniature) FRF 45,000.

SINGRY, Jean Baptiste
French, 19th century.
Born 1 March 1782, in Nancy; died 7 August 1824, in Paris.
Miniaturist, lithographer. Portraits.
Son of Nicolas Singry and father of Eulalie Dorus, this artist was a pupil of Vincent and Isabey.
MUSEUMS AND GALLERIES:
LONDON (Wallace Collection): two portraits.

SINGRY, Jean Pierre
French, 18th century.
Active in Nancy during the second half of the 18th century.
Sculptor.
Jean Pierre Singry worked at the church of St-Nicolas in Nancy in 1771.

SINGRY, Nicolas
French, 18th century.
Active in Nancy during the second half of the 18th century.
Painter.
Nicolas Singry was the father of Jean Baptiste Singry. He produced a portrait of *General Drouot.*

SINHA, Abani
Indian, 20th century.
Draughtsman.
Sinha produced images inspired by the Indian epic poem, the *Ramayana.*

SINIA, Cornelia Maria
Dutch, 20th century.
Born 14 February 1878, in Hoorn.
Painter, watercolourist. Landscapes.
Cornelia Maria Sinia was self-taught.
MUSEUMS AND GALLERIES:
HAARLEM (Teylers Mus.).

SINIA, Oscar
Belgian, 20th century.
Born 8 May 1877, in Ghent.
Sculptor, medallist. Religious subjects.
Oscar Sinia studied at the academy of St Luke in Ghent and went on to provide sculptures for various towns in Flanders, notably religious statuary and decorative compositions for public buildings.
MUSEUMS AND GALLERIES:
GHENT: *Parting Kiss.*

SINIAVER, Osip
Ukrainian, 20th century.
Born 1899, in Odessa.
Active in Belgium.
Painter, draughtsman, watercolourist, illustrator. Scenes with figures.
Osip Siniaver studied at the Gent academy.

SINIBALDI. See also **MONTELUPO**

SINIBALDI, Jean Paul or Paolo
French, 19th - 20th century.
Born 17 May 1857, in Paris; died January 1909, in Bourg (Ain).
Painter. Genre scenes.
Jean Paul Sinibaldi studied under Cabanel and Alfred Stevens. He exhibited in Paris at the Salon des Artistes Français. He was awarded a commendation in 1886, a travelling scholarship in 1888, a bronze medal at the Exposition Universelle of 1889, a second-class medal in 1898 and a silver medal at the Exposition Universelle of 1900. He was made a Chevalier of the Légion d'Honneur in 1900.

MUSEUMS AND GALLERIES:
AMIENS: *Manon Lescaut; Mist Clearing Away; Stable Interior* - GRAY: *Procession* - MULHOUSE: *Conseil* - SÈTE: *Claudius Proclaimed Emperor.*
AUCTION RECORDS:
PARIS, 8 Nov 1918, *Village in Seine-et-Marne,* FRF 70. PARIS, 17-18 Oct 1919, *On a Bench,* FRF 30. PARIS, July 1946, *Oriental Woman,* FRF 250. PARIS, 20 June 1951, *Landscape,* FRF 3,000. PARIS, 18 March 1977, *Studio* (oil on canvas, 44 x 32 3/4 ins / 112 x 83 cm) FRF 7,600. NEW YORK, 24 Jan 1980, *Louis XIII and Richelieu Receiving an Ambassador* (1899, oil on canvas, 29 x 34 1/2 ins / 73.7 x 87.6 cm) USD 4,000. NEW YORK, 11 Feb 1981, *Cardinal's Blessing* (oil on canvas remounted on board, 18 x 26 1/4 ins / 46 x 66.5 cm) USD 7,000. NEW YORK, 24 May 1984, *Festival of Dancing* (oil on canvas, 19 1/4 x 31 1/4 ins / 49 x 79.5 cm) USD 5,000. LONDON, 21 June 1985, *Art Lover* (oil on panel, 22 x 14 1/2 ins / 56 x 37 cm) GBP 5,500. VERSAILLES, 7 Dec 1986, *Young Woman in a Boat on the River* (oil on panel, 11 x 16 1/4 ins / 27 x 41 cm) FRF 36,000. LONDON, 16 Feb 1990, *Capri* (oil on canvas, 42 3/4 x 51 1/4 ins / 108.9 x 130 cm) GBP 4,620. BERN, 12 May 1990, *Still-life with Basket of Apples, Carafe and Bottle of Champagne* (oil on canvas, 15 x 18 ins / 38 x 46 cm) CHF 2,400. NEW YORK, 22 May 1990, *Elegant Woman in Paris Street* (oil on panel, 12 1/4 x 10 3/4 ins / 31.1 x 27.3 cm) USD 20,900. PARIS, 25 March 1992, *Portrait of Seated Woman in White Dress* (oil on canvas, 32 x 25 1/2 ins / 81 x 65 cm) FRF 25,000. NEW YORK, 12 Oct 1994, *On the Terrace in Capri* (oil on canvas, 19 x 12 3/4 ins / 48.3 x 32.4 cm) USD 5,750. PARIS, 16 March 1998, *Young Woman* (oil on canvas, 16 x 11 ins / 40.5 x 27 cm) FRF 9,200.

SINIBALDI, Lorenzo
Italian, 17th century.

Active in Todi and in Rome in 1611.
Painter.
Sinibaldi worked as the assistant of Agostino Tassi.

SINIBALDI Y MONTELEYRO, Rafael
Spanish, 16th century.
Active in Castile.
Sculptor.
Rafael Sinibaldi y Monteleyro was Italian in origin but brought to Spain by Giovanni da Fiesole to assist him in the construction of the mausoleum raised to the memory of the cardinal of Burgos

SINIBALDO DA PERUGIA. See **IBI Sinibaldo**

SINICKI, René
French, 20th century.
Painter. Still-lifes, flowers.
AUCTION RECORDS:
NEW YORK, 15 Nov 1990, *Flowers* (oil on canvas, 8½ x 4¾ ins / 21.5 x 12 cm) USD 2,090. PARIS, 23 April 1993, *Lobster* (oil on canvas, 7½ x 9½ ins / 19 x 24 cm) FRF 3,000. LUCERNE, 26 Nov 1994, *Still-life with Two Pictures* (oil on card, 7 x 9½ ins / 18 x 24 cm) CHF 1,100. MONTREAL, 15 Dec 2003, *Woman on a Divan* (oil on canvas, 24 x 20 ins / 61 x 50 cm) CAD 3,800.

SININGER, Leonhard. See **SINNIGER**

SINJEUR, Govert
Dutch, 17th century.
Born 1655; died 27 February 1702, in Rotterdam.
Active in Rotterdam.
Painter.
Govert Sinjeur painted in the style of Ph. Wouwermann.

SINKEL, Henricus Johannes or Heinrich Johann
Dutch, 19th century.
Born 6 January 1835, in Almelo; died 15 January 1908, in Düsseldorf.
Painter. History painting, portraits.
Henricus Johannes Sinkel was a student at the academy in Düsseldorf. He executed more than 450 portraits from 1880, of which the museum in Düsseldorf has one: *Portrait of the Painter Ittenbach*

SINKO, Armand
French, 20th century.
Born 3 May 1934, in Grasse.
Painter.
Although his first application to enter the École des Beaux-Arts in Nice in 1948 was unsuccessful, Armand Sinko was accepted two months later, and studied there until 1952. He enrolled at the École des Beaux-Arts in Paris in 1953, where he worked in the Brianchon studio. He obtained a bursary from the school in 1955. In 1956, he visited the Villa Médicis in Rome. He did no painting at all between 1964 and 1967 - when he spent a year as teacher of drawing at the Lycée Français in Rome. He gave up teaching in 1968 to concentrate on painting.

He showed his work in group exhibitions, notably in Vence in 1952. From 1958, he regularly held solo shows in Los Angeles, Paris and Rome. He prefers to paint using an easel.

SINKOVICS, Dezsö, or Sinkovich Desiderius
Hungarian, 20th century.
Born 5 June 1888, in Timisoara; died 1933, in Timisoara.
Painter.

SINKWITZ, Karl
German, 20th century.
Born 9 April 1886, in Dresden; died 1933, in Dresden.
Painter, engraver. Architectural views, landscapes.
MUSEUMS AND GALLERIES:
BAUTZEN - GÖRLITZ - ZITTAU.

SINN
German, 18th century.
Active in Bayreuth (Bavaria) c. 1750.
Painter.

SINNER, Abraham
Swiss, 17th - 18th century.
Born 1670; died 25 January 1737.
Active in Bern.
Painter.

SINNER, Michel
Luxembourg, 19th century.
Born 1826, in Ettelbruck; died 1882, in Ettelbruck.
Painter, pastellist, illustrator. Figure compositions.
Michel Sinner studied under Jean-Baptiste Fresez from 1844 to 1846. He continued his studies at the academy in Antwerp, then studied under the Swiss painter Charles Gleyre (1808 - 1874) in Paris. He also made frequent trips to Germany, Belgium, France and England. Sinner's work drew on the romanticism inherent in the national character of the Grand Duchy, particularly in the painting *Death of John the Blind Man* (c.1845). He also produced illustrations for *Les Misérables* by French poet, dramatist, novelist and leader of the French Romantic movement, Victor Hugo (1802 - 1885).

In 1989, Sinner's works were featured at the exhibition *150 Ans d'Art Luxembourgeois au Musée National d'Histoire et d'Art* (*150 Years of Luxembourg Art at the Musée National d'Histoire et d'Art*).
BIBLIOGRAPHY:
Cent cinquante ans d'Art luxembourgeois, exhibition catalogue, Musée national d'Histoire et d'Art, Luxembourg, 1989.
MUSEUMS AND GALLERIES:
LUXEMBOURG (Mus. national d'histoire et d'art): *Death of John the Blind Man* (c. 1845); *Portrait of Two Young Ladies* (1854); *Portrait of Doctor Moris* (1864).

SINNIGER, Leonhard, or Sininger
German, 16th century.
Sculptor. Monuments.
Active in Ingolstadt from 1528 to 1546, Sinniger carved mainly tombs.

SINNOCK, John Ray
American, 20th century.
Born 8 July 1888, in Raton (New York); died 1947, in Staten Island (New York).
Painter, medallist. Murals.
John Ray Sinnock studied at the Pennsylvania Museum School of Industrial Art. He was appointed chief engraver of the United States Mint in Philadelphia. His portrait medals include those of President Herbert Hoover, Charles Dickens, Henry Morgenthau and Thomas Edison. As a painter, he specialised in murals. He was a member of the American Federation of Arts, the Philadelphia Sketch Club, and the Philadelphia Alliance. He exhibited medals at the Pennsylvania Academy.

SINNOTT, Kevin
British, 20th - 21st century.
Born 1947.
Painter. Sporting subjects.
BIBLIOGRAPHY:
Cohen, Carolyn/Lucie-Smith, Edward/Higgins, Judith, *The New British Painting*, Phaidon, Oxford, 1990. Sinnot, Kevin, *Kevin Sinnott: Bernard Jacobson Gallery*, Bernard Jacobson Gallery, London, 1990.
AUCTION RECORDS:
LONDON, 26 March 1993, *Joker and Ice Skaters* (oil on canvas, 69 x 92¼ ins / 175 x 234 cm) GBP 2,185. LONDON, 25 Nov

1993, *Hectic Days* (1988, oil on canvas, 68 x 17 1/2 ins / 173 x 44.5 cm) GBP 2,530. LONDON, 20 Nov 2002, *Wishing* (oil on canvas, 27 x 51 ins / 69 x 130 cm) GBP 2,800. LONDON, 3 Dec 2002, *Adam and Eve* (oil on canvas, 68 x 57 ins / 173 x 144 cm) GBP 2,000.

SINOPICO, Primo, pseudonym of Chareun Covrias, Raoul de
Italian, 20th century.
Born 16 December 1889, in Cagliari.
Painter, illustrator. Landscapes, still-lifes. Stage sets.

After studying in Milan at the Accademia di Brera, Sinopico continued to live and work there. His name began to be known after his solo exhibition in Milan in 1918. His canvases often feature aspects of contemporary life, as in, for example, *Electricity* and *Radio Station*. He also painted some landscapes.

MUSEUMS AND GALLERIES:
NOVARA (Gal. d'Arte Moderna Giannoni).

SINOQUET, Jean Baptiste
French, 19th century.
Painter, miniaturist.

J.B. Sinoquet exhibited at the Salon de Paris in 1848.

SINOVIEFF, Georgi Terentevich.
See **ZINOVEV**

SINQUIN, René
French, 20th century.
Born 1933.
Painter. Scenes with figures, seascapes, still-lifes.

René Sinquin was trained at the École des Beaux-Arts in Lorient.

SINSSON, Jacques Nicolas, or Sisson
French, 18th - 19th century.
Active 1781-1845.
Painter (porcelain), decorative designer. Flowers. Ornaments.

Jacques Nicolas Sinsson worked for the Sèvres porcelain manufactory.

SINSSON, Louis, or Sisson
French, 19th century.
Born 1815.
Painter (porcelain), decorative designer. Flowers. Ornaments.

Worked at the Sèvres porcelain factory from 1839 until 1885.

SINSSON, Nicolas, or Sisson
French, 18th century.
Painter (porcelain), designer of ornamental architectural features. Flowers.

Nicolas Sinsson worked for the Sèvres porcelain manufactory from 1773 to 1799.

SINSSON, Pierre Antoine, or Sisson
French, 19th century.
Born 1808.
Painter (porcelain), designer of ornamental architectural features. Flowers.

Pierre Antoine Sinsson worked at the Sèvres porcelain factory until 1848.

SINT-JANS. See **GEERTGEN TOT SINT JANS**

SINTENIS, Renée
German, 20th century.
Born 20 March 1888, in Glatz (now Klodzko, Poland); died 1965, in Berlin.
Sculptor, medallist, engraver. Portraits, animals. Busts.

Renée Sintenis studied at the fine arts academy in Stuttgart and, from 1908 to 1911, at the Berlin College of Arts and Crafts. She was married to the sculptor Emil Rudolf Weiss. In 1929, she was elected to membership of the Prussian academy of fine arts, but her membership was discontinued when the National Socialists came to power. A large part of her work was destroyed in 1944, as a result of bombing. In 1947, she was admitted to a teaching post at the Berlin fine arts academy. A retrospective of her work was held in 1958 at the Haus am Waldsee in Berlin, to commemorate her 70th birthday. Sintenis participated in group exhibitions, including *Der Andere Blick: Künstlerinnen des 20. Jahrhunderts* (*A Different Perspective: Women Artists of the 20th Century*), held at the Diocese Museum in Trier.

Sintenis was an animal sculptor who invariably portrayed her subjects in full flow, imparting a sense of movement. She also produced a number of portrait busts and medals, notably several self-portraits, a bust of her husband and a further bust of the author André Gide.

BIBLIOGRAPHY:
Kiel, Hanna, *Renée Sintenis*, Rembrandt, Berlin, 1956. Buhlmann, Britta E., *Renée Sintenis. Werkmonographie der Skulpturen*, Wissenschaftliche Buchgemeinschaft, Darmstadt, 1987. *Der andere Blick: Künstlerinnen des 20. Jahrhunderts*, exhibition catalogue, Diözesanmuseum, Trier, 1998.

AUCTION RECORDS:
STUTTGART, 3-4 May 1962, *Young Donkey* (bronze) DEM 9,000. HAMBURG, 18 Nov 1967, *Donkey* (bronze) DEM 16,000. MUNICH, 11 Dec 1969, *Child on a Pony* (bronze) DEM 10,000. HAMBURG, 5 June 1970, *Little Daphne*, DEM 8,000. COPENHAGEN, 18 May 1971, *Daphne*, DKK 19,000. HAMBURG, 16 June 1973, *Nurmi* (bronze) DEM 6,200. NEW YORK, 6 June 1974, *Foal* (patinated silver) USD 2,000. HAMBURG, 4 June 1976, *Flautist* (1953, bronze, h. 12 ins / 30.4 cm) DEM 8,000. COLOGNE, 3 Dec 1977, *Donkey of Selow* (1927, bronze, h. 30 1/4 ins / 77 cm, w. 27 1/2 ins/70 cm) DEM 15,000. MUNICH, 24 Nov 1978, *Little Donkey* (1925, bronze, h. 5 1/4 ins / 13.5 cm) DEM 5,200. NEW YORK, 16 May 1979, *Polo Player* (1929, reddish-brown patinated bronze, h. 17 ins / 43.2 cm) USD 11,000. COLOGNE, 30 May 1981, *Young Girl Bathing* (etching, 11 x 7 ins / 27 x 18 cm) DEM 2,800. LONDON, 6 Oct 1982, *Runner* (c. 1924, bronze, h. 15 3/4 ins / 40 cm) GBP 2,600. NEW YORK, 16 Nov 1983, *Foals* (1932, grey-patinated bronze, h. 41 1/4 ins / 105 cm) USD 17,000. NEW YORK, 14 Nov 1985, *Crouching Fawn* (c. 1930, brown-patinated bronze, h. 20 ins / 51 cm) USD 6,500. LONDON, 5 Dec 1986, *Crouching Doe* (c. 1930, patinated bronze, h. 20 ins / 51 cm) GBP 8,000. MUNICH, 13 Dec 1989, *Horse Looking Over its Shoulder* (bronze, h. 3 3/4 ins / 9.4 cm) DEM 14,300. MUNICH, 31 May 1990, *Bear Cub* (bronze, h. 5 1/2 ins / 14 cm) DEM 16,500. TEL AVIV, 1 Jan 1991, *Foal at Rest* (bronze, h. 2 ins / 5 cm) USD 1,760. NEW YORK, 5 Nov 1991, *Leaping Foal* (brown-patinated bronze, h. 5 1/2 ins / 13.7 cm) USD 7,700. NEW YORK, 12 June 1992, *Fawn* (bronze, h. 5 ins / 12.7 cm) USD 8,250. NEW YORK, 22 Feb 1993, *Erich Brandl, Boxer* (brown-patinated bronze, h. 16 ins / 40.5 cm) USD 7,700. NEW YORK, 26 Feb 1993, *Foal* (1928, dark-patinated bronze, h. 4 ins / 10.2 cm) USD 8,050. NEW YORK, 4 Nov 1993, *Nurmi* (1924, bronze, h. 16 1/2 ins / 41.9 cm) USD 12,650. NEW YORK, 7 Nov 1995, *Pony at Rest* (bronze, l. 5 ins / 12.7 cm) USD 5,520. BERN, 20-21 June 1996, *Little Boy Carrying a Lamb* (1949, bronze, h. 11 1/2 ins / 29.5 cm) CHF 13,500. NEW YORK, 10 Oct 1996, *Young Dog* (bronze, h. 3 1/2 ins / 8.9 cm) USD 4,887. COLOGNE, 13 Nov 1999, *Flautist* (patinated bronze, 5 x 7x4 ins / 13 x 17x11 cm) DEM 28,500. BERLIN, 27 Nov 1999, *Elephant Running - African Elephant* (1954, brown patinated bronze, 4 x 6x2 ins / 10 x 14x6 cm) DEM 45,000. BERLIN, 27 May 2000, *Running Elephant* (brown patinated bronze, 4 x 6x2 ins / 11 x 15x6 cm) DEM 49,000. COLOGNE, 11 Nov 2000, *African Elephant* (patinated bronze, h. 4

ins / 11 cm) DEM 44,000. NEW YORK, 23 Feb 2001, *Little Daphne* (brown patinated bronze, h. 11 ins / 29 cm) USD 8,000. BERLIN, 30 Nov 2001, *Small Daphne* (brown patinated bronze, 11 x 2x2 ins / 29 x 5x5 cm) DEM 30,000. COLOGNE, 4 Dec 2002, *Elephant Running* (bronze, h. 4 ins / 10 cm) EUR 17,000. HAMBURG, 7 Dec 2002, *Young Elephant* (bronze, 4 x 6x2 ins / 9 x 15x6 cm) EUR 19,000. BERLIN, 30 May 2003, *Donkey of Seelow* (yellow-brown patinated bronze, h. 31 ins / 78 cm) EUR 45,000. BERLIN, 30 May 2003, *Great Daphne* (brown patinated bronze, h. 57 ins / 144 cm) EUR 150,000. BERLIN, 11 June 2004, *Rearing Pony* (greyish green patinated bronze, h. 46 ins / 116 cm) EUR 82,000. MUNICH, 11 Nov 2004, *Ram* (bronze, h. 29 ins / 73 cm) EUR 45,000.

SINTENIS, Walter
German, 19th - 20th century.
Born 20 July 1867, in Zittau; died 15 November 1911, in Dresden.
Sculptor (stone). Nudes. Statuettes, busts.

Walter Sintenis studied under Robert Diez at the fine arts academy in Dresden, then in Brussels under Constantin Meunier and Jules Lagae.

MUSEUMS AND GALLERIES:
BAUTZEN (Stadtmus.): *Crouching Bather* - DRESDEN (Albertinum): *Bust of a Southern French Woman* (1905).

SINTES, Giovanni Battista
Italian, 18th century.
Born c. 1680; died c. 1760.
Active in Rome.
Engraver.

Sintes was the pupil of B. Farjat.

SINTÈS, Joseph
French, 19th - 20th century.
Born 1829, in Aleyor; died 1913, in Algiers.
Painter. Scenes with figures, rustic scenes, landscapes with figures, urban landscapes.
Orientalism.
School of Algiers.

Joseph Sintès was one of the leaders of the Algiers School, with Alfred Chataud and Émile Aubry. His canvases capture the yellows and ochres of the Mediterranean light.

He featured in *Les Peintres de l'autre rive. Alger 1830-1930* (*Painters from the Other Shore. Algiers 1830-1930*) an exhibition organised as part of 'Djazaïr, a Year of Algeria in France' at the Musée de la Castre, Cannes (2003). That same year, he was also included in *L'École d'Alger* (*The School of Algiers*), Musée des Beaux-Arts, Bordeaux.

BIBLIOGRAPHY:
Barrucand, Victor, *L'Algérie et les Peintres orientalistes*, B. Arthaud éditeur, Grenoble, 1930. Vidal-Bué, Marion, *Alger et ses peintres: 1830-1960*, Paris-Méditerranée, 2000. Vidal-Bué, Marion, *Les Peintres de l'autre rive. Alger 1830-1930*, exhibition catalogue, Musée de la Castre, Cannes, 2003. Cazenave, Elisabeth/Dalia, Mahammed-Orfali/Vidal-Bué, Marion, *L'École d'Alger*, exhibition catalogue, Musée des Beaux-Arts, Bordeaux, 2003.

MUSEUMS AND GALLERIES:
ALGIERS (Mus. National des Beaux-Arts): *The Route of the Qaddous*.

AUCTION RECORDS:
PARIS, 22 June 1992, *Narrow Street in the Casbah of Algiers* (oil on canvas, 15 3/4 x 10 1/4 ins / 40 x 26 cm) FRF 10,000. PARIS, 8 Nov 1993, *The Surrounds of the Sidi Abdelrahmane Mosque* (oil on canvas, 9 3/4 x 7 1/2 ins / 25 x 19 cm) FRF 6,500. PARIS, 10-11 June 1997, *At the Fountain* (oil on panel, 19 1/2 x 14 1/4 ins / 49.5 x 36.5 cm) FRF 7,000.

SINTHOS
Swiss, 17th century.
Active in Geneva.
Painter. Religious subjects, figures.

MUSEUMS AND GALLERIES:
AVIGNON: *St Lawrence Distributing Gold Vases to the Poor; Warrior Condemned to be Beheaded*.

SINTRAM
French, 12th century.
Active in Marbach (Alsace).
Illuminator.

The Library of the Great Seminary of Strasbourg possesses a manuscript illuminated by this artist. A canon in the Augustinian monastery of Murbach, he painted his illustrations in 1154, including in them many scenes of daily life.

SINTRAM, or Sindrammus or Sindram
Swiss, 9th - 10th century.
Active in St Gall in the 9th and 10th centuries.
Illuminator.

Sintram was one of the most important illuminators of his time and was active from 885. He illuminated the initials of the *Evangelium Longum*.

SINTZENICH, Elisabeth, or Sinzenich
German, 19th century.
Born c. 1778, in Mannheim.
Draughtswoman, painter.

Elisabeth Sintzenich was the daughter of Heinrich Sintzenich. Her father engraved portraits from her drawings and paintings.

MUSEUMS AND GALLERIES:
ZURICH (Kunsthaus): *Anthony and Cleopatra* (watercolour).

SINTZENICH, Friedrich Heinrich, or Sinzenich
German, 19th century.
Born c. 1780, in Mannheim.
Engraver (burin). Historical scenes, portraits.

Friedrich Sintzenich was the son and pupil of Heinrich Sintzenich.

SINTZENICH, Gustav
British, 19th century.
Active in London during the first half of the 19th century.
Painter. Flowers, fruit.

Gustav Sintzenich exhibited at the Royal Academy from 1809 to 1836.

SINTZENICH, Gustavus Ellinthorpe
British, 19th century.
Active in London in the middle of the 19th century.
Painter. History painting.

Gustavus Ellinthorpe Sintzenich exhibited in London from 1844 to 1856.

SINTZENICH, Heinrich or Henri, or Sinzenich
German, 18th - 19th century.
Born 1 December 1752, in Mannheim; died 1812, in Munich.
Engraver (burin/mezzotint/stippling).

After studying at the art academy in Mannheim, Heinrich Sintzenich went to London to complete his education in the studio of Italian engraver Francesco Bartolozzi (1727 - 1815). On his return to Mannheim, he was appointed court engraver and produced prints based on the English method. He was a member of the academies of Munich and Berlin.

MUSEUMS AND GALLERIES:
BERLIN (Kupferstichkabinet): *Two Caricatures; Landscape with Flocks and Shepherds* - MUNICH: *Portrait of a Child* - RIGA (Municipal Mus.): *Bonaparte, Consul and General, Dedicated to Mars from Birth*.

SINTZENICH, Peter, or Sinzenich
German, 18th century.

Active in Mannheim, in the second half of the 18th century.
Engraver (burin). Landscapes, portraits.
Peter Sintzenich was the brother of Heinrich and attended the academy in Dresden. He settled in London in 1785.

SINYAVSKY, Nikolai Alekseevich or Aleksandrovch
Russian, 18th - 19th century.
Born 1 May 1771.
Painter. Portraits, landscapes.
Nikolai Alekseevich Sinyavsky studied at the art academy in St Petersburg.

SINZ, Karl Rudolf
Swiss, 19th century.
Born 5 May 1818, in St Gall; died 25 April 1896.
Draughtsman, painter.
Sinz settled in Zurich, Switzerland, c. 1860. He was a doctor.
MUSEUMS AND GALLERIES:
ST GALL (Kunstmus.): *Views of Southern Italy and Sicily.*

SINZENICH. See **SINTZENICH**

SIOERTSMA, Anthonie Heeres, or Siourtsma
Dutch, 17th century.
Born c. 1626, in Amsterdam.
Engraver (burin).
Anthonie Heeres Sioertsma was a pupil of Crispin de Passe and engraved architectural views.

SIOFFEL, Joseph
Luxembourg, 20th century.
Born 1911.
Painter (gouache). Nudes.
Sioffel worked predominantly in gouache. He is noted, above all else, for his nudes.

SIOMASH, Iuri
Ukrainian, 20th - 21st century.
Born 20 February 1948, in Belgiansk.
Painter. Scenes with figures.
Siomash graduated from the academy of fine art in Leningrad (now St Petersburg). Initially a Realist in the Russian convention of the Soviet years, he then participated in a 1980s revival of interest in Fantastic art. His work, though imbued with fantasy, is supported by a traditional detailed technique.
MUSEUMS AND GALLERIES:
GRUYÈRES (Château, Salle d'Art Fantastique): *Water Tower.*

SION, Ion Theodoresco
Romanian, 20th century.
Born 1882, in Janca (Braila); died 1939.
Painter, draughtsman. Military subjects.
Ion Theodoresco Sion trained in Bucharest and then at the École des Beaux-Arts, Paris. He was appointed Inspector General of the Arts in 1933. He is probably the same Theo Sion who, together with Demetre de Berea, founded the Ileana Free Academy in Bucharest. During World War I he served at the front, sending back drawings from life. He won the gold medal at the 1910 Bucharest Salon and the national painting prize in 1937.

SION, Peeter
Flemish School, 17th century.
Died 21 August 1695, in Antwerp.
Painter. Still-lifes.
Peeter Sion was a pupil of F. Lanckveelt. He was a master in the guild of St Luke from 1649 to 1650.
AUCTION RECORDS:
MUNICH, 30 Sept-1 Oct 1964, *Still-life*, DEM 6,000. LONDON, 5 July 1985, *Still-life* (oil on canvas, 25 1/4 x 31 1/2 ins / 64.2 x 80 cm) GBP 10,000. LONDON, 27 Oct 1999, *Joseph Lowered into a Well by His Brothers* (oil on copper, 24 x 30 ins / 61 x 77 cm) GBP 4,000.

SION, Zbysek
Czechoslovak, 20th century.
Born 12 April 1938, in Policka.
Painter.
Zbysek Sion studied at technical schools in Brno from 1955 to 1958 and at art schools in Prague from 1958 to 1964. He belongs to the current of Surrealism and fantasy art that is by now traditional in Czech art. Frantisek Smejkal has said of him: 'Out of Zbysek Sion's delirious imagination are born monsters, an expression of human abjection'. He has taken part in various collective exhibitions, especially those of young Czech artists and including in Paris (1969). He has also shown his work in solo exhibitions in his home country.
BIBLIOGRAPHY:
Smejkal, Frantisek, *Sept jeunes peintres tchécoslovaques*, exhibition catalogue, Gal. Lambert, Paris, 1969.

SIONAC, Henri de
French, 19th century.
Born 1832; died 30 August 1904, in St-Sulpice-sur-Lèze (Haute-Garonne).
Landscape painter.

SIOT-DECAUVILLE, E.
French, 19th century.
Died 1909.
Sculptor.
A member of the Société des Artistes Français and Chevalier of the Légion d'Honneur, by the end of his career Siot-Decauville was spending most of his time editing items about sculpture.

SIOTTO, Pio
Italian, 19th century.
Born 3 May 1824, in Rome.
Cameo engraver.
Siotto was a pupil of Tenerani and Bartolomeo Rinaldi.

SIOURTSMA, Anthonie Heeres. See **SIOERTSMA**

SIOUX, the Elder
French, 18th century.
Born 1716.
Painter (porcelain). Flowers, fruit.
Sioux the Elder worked for the Sèvres porcelain manufactory from 1752 to 1792.

SIOUX, the Younger
French, 18th century.
Born 1718.
Painter (porcelain). Flowers, fruit.
Sioux the Younger worked for the Sèvres porcelain manufactory from 1752 to 1759.

SIPEK, Viktor
Slovene, 20th century.
Born 16 February 1896, in Donja Stubica.
Painter, watercolourist. Landscapes.
Viktor Sipek studied in Zagreb and Munich.

SIPKES, Joseph
Dutch, 19th century.
Active in Amsterdam c. 1840.
Painter. Seascapes.
AUCTION RECORDS:
AMSTERDAM, 8 June 1982, *Naval Battle* (1846, oil on canvas, 33 3/4 x 43 1/4 ins / 86 x 110 cm) NLG 8,000.

SIPMANN, Gerhard, or Sippmann
German, 19th century.
Born 1790, in Düsseldorf; died 30 December 1866, in Munich.

Painter. History painting, portraits, landscapes.
Decorative schemes.

Gerhard Sipmann attended the academy in Düsseldorf and studied under J. P. Langer and Cornelius in Munich. He painted the arabesques for the Glyptothek in Munich with Cornelius.

SIPMANN, Karl
German, 19th century.
Born 1802, in Düsseldorf.
Painter.

Carl Sipmann was the brother of Gerhard and studied under Cornelius. He produced decorative paintings and murals; later he painted figures, flowers and fruits.

SIPONTINUS
Italian, 12th century.
Active in Puglia.
Sculptor, illuminator, goldsmith.

SIPORIN, Mitchell
American, 20th century.
Born 1910, in New York; died 1976, in Newton (Massachusetts).
Painter. Scenes with figures, figures.

Mitchell Siporin was stationed in Italy with the Army Art Corps during World War II. After the war, he won a Guggenhein Fellowship and the Prix de Rome. He was very prominent in the USA, and painted complex compositions with numerous figures, often inspired by contemporary events, in a Modernist style. He participated in the exhibitions of the Carnegie Institute in Pittsburgh.

AUCTION RECORDS:
NEW YORK, 19 Oct 1967, *Figures round a Fountain,* USD 1,000. NEW YORK, 16 May 1973, *End of an Era,* USD 2,250.

SIPOS, Bela
Slovak, 20th century.
Born 14 December 1888, in Jernye.
Illustrator.

Bela Sipos, an architect, also produced drawings for the *Leipziger Illustrierte.*

SIPOS, David
Hungarian, 18th century.
Born 1762, in Chidea.
Sculptor, cabinet maker, architect.

He worked mostly in Cluj, where he produced sculptures and low reliefs for churches in and around the town.

SIPPMANN. See **SIPMANN**

SIQUEIROS, David Alfaro
Mexican, 20th century.
Born 29 December 1896, in Chihuahua; died 6 January 1974, in Cuernavaca.
Painter, draughtsman. Figures, scenes with figures. Murals.
Muralism.

David Alfaro Siqueiros grew up in an educated family. He was interested in Mexican archaeology and folk art, believed passionately in the independence of Mexico, and at the age of 15 entered the San Carlo art school in Mexico and also the Santa Anita school of open air painting. The revolution, however, put an end to his studies. In 1913 he joined the party of General Venustiano Carranza. When Carranza became president of Mexico, Siqueiros was sent to Europe on a task involving both art and diplomacy. He met Diego Rivera in Paris; and in Florence he saw Renaissance frescoes, which profoundly affected him. Returning to Mexico, in 1922 he became leader of the Union of Workers, Technicians, Painters and Sculptors, and in 1924 he and Orozco founded the pamphlet-style review *El Machete.* He became more and more active as a Marxist-Stalinist, earning promotion, prison or exile according to the fluctuations in the Mexican government. In 1932-1933 he was in Argentina, then in California at Los Angeles where he worked on new pictorial techniques, mechanised materials and dynamic composition, and taught at the Chouinard School of Art. In 1938 he fought as a republican lieutenant-colonel in the Spanish Civil War. Back in Mexico, there is evidence that he was closely involved in the penultimate attempt in 1939 on the lives of Trotsky and his wife, who were being sheltered by Diego Rivera. Trotsky miraculously escaped this attempt on his life, apparently ordered over the telephone by Stalin, but was killed in 1940. Siqueiros was arrested again but went into exile, returning to Mexico in 1944.

From 1918 onwards Siqueiros developed a new idea of painting in relation to the changes in social structures for which he fought politically. In Madrid he founded a review in which he published a *First Manifesto to the Artists of America.* In this he stated his refusal to bow to the authority of European criteria and advocated the creation of a specific, monumental art accessible to all, not to a few privileged collectors alone; a human art of the people founded on pre-Columbian traditions and on present-day folk art, dealing with social struggles and the lives of ordinary people. In Mexico in 1922 he published a *Second Manifesto, Social, Political and Aesthetic,* which redefined the aims of the mural-painters. In the same year he produced his first mural painting, *The Elements,* close in style to the paintings by Orozco in the National Preparatory School in Mexico. His early murals were a symbolic expression of a social message, marked by religiosity and only partially supporting the muralist programme that demanded a 'monumental and heroic art in the great prehispanic traditions of America'. After 1924 his painting became much more strongly linked to his revolutionary plans, and some of his works were even destroyed in the conservative reaction. In 1933 while in Buenos Aires, he discovered how to use synthetic resins to enhance and add relief to the surfaces of his paintings, producing concave and convex effects. In 1935 in New York he set up an experimental studio, with Pollock as a pupil, for the study of materials for mural work. During his exile in Chile in 1941 he created huge mural compositions, including *Death to the Invader,* in the high school in Chillan, often thought to be his masterpiece. In Cuba in 1943 he painted his *Allegory of Racial Equality.* Back in Mexico once more he continued to paint the small easel pictures he had become accustomed to work with while in prison. In 1941, recognised as the 'national painter', he was given the opportunity to decorate a large number of public buildings. He had gradually worked out his own personal theory of muralism. With the intention of dramatising the events he was recording, he now used exaggerated perspectives, surrealist symbols, assemblages in depth and even optical appliances which led him to the idea of 'sculpto-painting'. During this period he produced among other pieces *The Mexican Revolution,* a fresco in the National Museum of Anthropology and History, and *Scenic Art in Social Life* for the theatre of the National Association of Actors in Mexico. He began these in about 1960 but did not finish them until after 1965, having been once again imprisoned, this time purely because of his communist opinions. After his release he and team worked on the gigantic *March of Humanity* inside and outside the Hotel de Mexico, Mexico City. This work covers 5380 square yards (4,600 square metres) and unites elements of architecture, painting and sculpture. The titles reveal the didactic and moralistic nature of Siqueiros' work. Because of his adherence to Stalinist Communism one would expect a strict observance of the precepts of socialist realism, but through his own extremism, his inner folk memories, his faith in the prehispanic tradition, Siqueiros, like Rivera and Orozco, created his own language. Following Rivera's example, he and Orozco produced a specifically Mexican movement, known as muralism, which was one of the most important movements in modern art of the 1920s in South America.

He showed work in collective exhibitions: Venice Biennale, winning second prize for foreign painters (1950); Galeria del Centenario in Mexico (1962). Solo exhibitions included Museo Universitario do Ciencas y Arte in Mexico (1967); Tokyo Central Museum (1972). Among his posthumous exhibitions are: Palace of Fine Art in Mexico (1975); Palazzo Vecchio in Florence (1977); Hirshhorn Museum and Sculpture Garden in Washington (1978); Arvil Gallery in Mexico, jointly with Pollock (1995); Whitechapel Art Gallery (1997). He received the National Prize for Mexican Art in 1996 and the Lenin Peace Prize in 1967.

SIQUEIROS

BIBLIOGRAPHY:

Rogovin, M., '*The March of Humanity: An Expression in Public Art*' in *Alumni Bulletin, 26*, 1969 (memoir of a team member who worked on the Poliforum Siqueiros). Goldman, S.M., '*Siqueiros and Three Early Murals in Los Angeles*' in *Art Journal xxxiv/33*, periodical, New York, 1974. Hurlburt, L.P., '*The Siqueiros Experimental Workshop: New York, 1936*' in *Art Journal, xxxvi/35*, periodical, New York, 1976. De Micheli, Mario (ed.), *David Alfaro Siqueiros e il muralismo*, exhibition catalogue, Museo d'Arte moderna, Messico, Palazzo Vecchio, Firenze, Conti tipocolor, Calenzano, 1976. Hurlburt, L.P., '*David Alfaro Siqueiros' Portrait of the Bourgeoisie*' in *Artforum, xv/6*, periodical, 1977. Siqueiros, David Alfaro, *Me llamaban el Coronelazo: memorias*, Grijalbo, Mexico, 1977 (2nd edition, 1986). Rochfort, D., *The Development of a Revolutionary Public Mural Art in the Work of David Alfaro Siqueiros, 1896-1975*, dissertation, London Royal College of Art, 1986. Hurlburt, L.P., *The Mexican Muralists in the United States*, Albuquerque, 1989. Desmond, Rochfort, *Mexican muralists: Orozco, Rivera, Siqueiros*, L. King, London, 1993. White, Anthony D., *Siqueiros: a biography*, Floricanto Press, Encino (USA, CA), 1994. Stein, Philip, *Siqueiros: His Life and Works*, International Publishers, New York, 1994. Harten, Jürgen, *Siqueiros/Pollock, Pollock/Siqueiros*, exhibition catalogue, Kunsthalle, Düsseldorf, Dumont, Cologne, 1995. *David Alfaro Siqueiros: Portrait of a Decade, 1930-1940*, exhibition catalogue, Mexico City, Mus. N. A.; London, Whitechapel Art Gallery;, 1996-1997. *Otras rutas hacia Siqueiros: un simposio*, symposium proceedings, Instituto Nacional de Bellas Artes, Mexico, 1996. Rochfort, D., *Mexican Muralists: Orozco, Rivera and Siqueiros*, London, 1997. Tibol, Raquel/Goldman, Shifra M./Arteaga, Agustín, *Los murales de Siqueiros*, Instituto Nacional de Bellas Artes, Mexico, 1998.

MUSEUMS AND GALLERIES:

MEXICO CITY (MMA): *Rotation* (1934); *Figure* (1935); *Our Present Image* (1947); *The Devil in the Church* (1947) - MEXICO CITY (Mus. de Arte Carrillo Gil): *Rocky Landscape with Figure* (1947); *May Day* (1952); *Zapata* (1966) - MEXICO CITY (Mus. del Palacio de Bellas Artes): *New Democracy, War Victim* (1944); *New Democracy, Victim of Fascism* (1944) - NEW YORK (MoMA): *Echo of a Cry* (1937) - NEW YORK (Solomon R. Guggenheim Mus.): *Portrait of Sternberth* (1932) - PHILADELPHIA (MA) - RIO DE JANEIRO (MAM) - SANTA BARBARA (MA): *Two Native American Women* (1930, oil on canvas); *The Hill of the Dead* (1944, duco/board); *Portrait of Present Day Mexico* (1932, fresco).

AUCTION RECORDS:

NEW YORK, 26 April 1961, *El Caromilozo* (work/paper) USD 1,250. NEW YORK, 24 Nov 1962, *Portrait of a Woman*, USD 875. NEW YORK, 20 Oct 1966, *Portrait of the Artist's Wife*, USD 4,250. NEW YORK, 13 Dec 1967, *Nude* (gouache) USD 2,400. NEW YORK, 8 Oct 1969, *Pinto*, USD 5,500. NEW YORK, 4 Feb 1970, *The Lovers*, USD 6,250. LOS ANGELES, 8 May 1972, *Composition*, USD 3,000. NEW YORK, 20 Jan 1973, *Three Men*, USD 8,750. NEW YORK, 3 May 1974, *Dolor*, USD 19,000. NEW YORK, 22 Oct 1976, *Visit to a Peasant* (1930, oil on canvas, 37 x 28 3/4 ins / 94 x 73 cm) USD 25,500. NEW YORK, 26 May 1977, *Portrait of a Woman* (1937, oil on panel, 30 1/2 x 24 ins / 77.5 x 61 cm) USD 15,000. NEW YORK, 5 April 1978, *Portrait of Ione Robinson* (1931, oil on canvas, 34 x 22 3/4 ins / 86.5 x 58 cm) USD 20,000. NEW YORK, 11 May 1979, *Zapata* (1930, lithograph, 21 x 15 3/4 ins / 53.5 x 40 cm) USD 2,600. NEW YORK, 17 Oct 1979, *Head of a Woman* (oil and gouache/card, 14 3/4 x 19 3/4 ins / 37.5 x 50.2 cm) USD 14,000. NEW YORK, 8 May 1981, *Portrait of a Woman* (1956, oil/hardboard, 46 1/2 x 37 1/2 ins / 118 x 95.3 cm) USD 17,000. NEW YORK, 12 May 1983, *Head of a Man* (gouache/paper, 25 1/2 x 19 3/4 ins / 65 x 50 cm) USD 5,500. NEW YORK, 27 Nov 1984, *The Two Americas* (1952, oil/hardboard, 27 3/4 x 49 3/4 ins / 70.5 x 126.5 cm) USD 50,000. NEW YORK, 26 Nov 1985, *Eagle* (1952, gouache/mounted paper/card, 24 1/2 x 19 ins / 62.3 x 48.3 cm) USD 3,800. NEW YORK, 25 Nov 1986, *Huelga* (acrylic/hardboard, 63 x 47 1/4 ins / 160 x 120 cm) USD 75,000. NEW YORK, 21 Nov 1988, *Mexican Peasants* (1959, oil/synthetic resin, 33 1/4 x 27 1/2 ins / 84.7 x 70 cm) USD 71,500; *Lorca's Women* (1938, pyroxyline/panel, 20 x 29 1/4 ins / 51 x 74 cm) USD 66,000. NEW YORK, 17 May 1989, *Exodus* (1963, pyroxyline/panel, 18 x 23 3/4 ins / 45.7 x 60.5 cm) USD 27,500. NEW YORK, 21 Nov 1989, *Child-Mother* (1936, encaustic/panel, 30 x 24 ins / 76.5 x 61 cm) USD 363,000. NEW YORK, 1 May 1990, *Landscape* (acrylic/synthetic resin, 23 1/2 x 33 3/4 ins / 60 x 86 cm) USD 46,200. NEW YORK, 2 May 1990, *Horsemen of the Revolution* (duco/panel, study for a mural decoration, 33 1/2 x 27 1/2 ins / 85 x 70 cm) USD 154,000. NEW YORK, 20-21 Nov 1990, *Portrait of Two Little Girls, One Alive, One Dead* (1931, oil on canvas, 39 1/4 x 29 3/4 ins / 100 x 75.5 cm) USD 66,000. NEW YORK, 8 May 1991, *Peasant* (1929, oil on canvas, 15 3/4 x 11 3/4 ins / 40 x 30 cm) USD 23,100. NEW YORK, 15-16 May 1991, *Rest* (1963, acrylic/panel, 17 x 12 1/2 ins / 43 x 32 cm) USD 33,000. NEW YORK, 19 Nov 1991, *Two Heads* (1957, pyroxyline/synthetic resin, 35 x 23 1/4 ins / 89 x 59 cm) USD 88,000. NEW YORK, 18-19 May 1992, *Portrait of Blanca Luz* (1931, oil on sacking coated in gesso, 36 1/4 x 27 1/4 ins / 92.1 x 69.2 cm) USD 88,000. NEW YORK, 19-20 May 1992, *Slave, Symbol of a Fighter Sacrificed* (1948, acrylic/canvas/synthetic resin, 39 3/4 x 26 ins / 101 x 65.1 cm) USD 104,500. NEW YORK, 24 Nov 1992, *Life* (1965, acrylic/panel, 34 1/2 x 15 3/4 ins / 87.6 x 40 cm) USD 27,500. NEW YORK, 18 May 1993, *Green Landscape* (1965, acrylic/synthetic resin, 25 x 47 ins / 63.5 x 119.5 cm) USD 90,500. NEW YORK, 18-19 May 1993, *Father of the First Victim of the Cananea Strike* (1961, acrylic/paper, 32 x 23 3/4 ins / 81.3 x 60.3 cm) USD 68,500. NEW YORK, 17 May 1994, *The Machete, Self Portrait* (1968, pyroxyline/treated card, 48 x 45 1/4 ins / 121.9 x 114.9 cm) USD 178,500. NEW YORK, 20 Nov 1995, *Study of Detail for Mural Painting at Chapultepec* (1964, pyroxyline/panel, 32 x 24 ins / 81.3 x 61 cm) USD 63,000. NEW YORK, 25-26 Nov 1996, *Woman* (1945, pyroxyline/masonite, 31 x 24 ins / 78.7 x 61 cm) USD 211,500. PARIS, 10 Dec 1996, *Poems from Canto General* (1968, lithograph, book with ten illustrations, 23 1/2 x 21 ins / 60 x 52.5 cm) FRF 4,000. NEW YORK, 28 May 1997, *Portrait of a Woman* (1949, oil on panel, 35 3/4 x 26 1/2 ins / 90.8 x 67 cm) USD 63,000. NEW YORK, 29-30 May 1997, *Peasant Prisoner* (1930, oil on canvas, 18 x 14 ins / 45.7 x 35.6 cm) USD 34,500. NEW YORK, 24-25 Nov 1997, *Rocks* (c. 1960, pyroxyline/panel, 36 x 47 1/2 ins / 90.5 x 120.7 cm) USD 79,500. NEW YORK, 2 June 1999, *Mountain* (pyroxyline on panel, 31 x 35 ins / 80 x 90 cm) USD 65,000. NEW YORK, 22 Nov 1999, *Laconesa* (1958, pyroxyline on masonite, 48 x 67 ins / 122 x 170 cm) USD 140,000. NEW YORK, 1 June 2000, *Revelucionario* (c. 1945, pyroxyline on panel, 31 x 25 ins / 79 x 63 cm) USD 100,000. NEW YORK, 1 June 2000, *Plan for the Mural in Porphyria of the Revolution in Castillo de Chapultepec* (1958, pyroxyline on masonite, 48 x 67 ins / 122 x 169 cm) USD 170,000. NEW YORK, 30 May 2001, *People from the University* (1951, oil on vinyl and masonite, 48 x 143 ins / 122 x 363 cm) USD 240,000. NEW YORK, 19 Nov 2001, *Pumpkin* (1953, pyroxyline on masonite, 23 x 30 ins / 58 x 76 cm) USD 65,000. NEW YORK, 19 Nov 2002, *Head of Man* (1935, pyroxyline on copper, 14 x 12 ins / 36 x 30 cm) USD 80,000. NEW YORK, 20 Nov 2002, *Geographic Architecture* (1959, pyroxyline on board, 48 x 36 ins / 123 x 92 cm) USD 90,000. NEW YORK, 28 May 2003, *Self-portrait* (1934, black crayon and white tempera on zinc plate, 19 x 11 ins / 47 x 29 cm) USD 65,000. NEW YORK, 19 Nov 2003, *Untitled* (1965, pyroxyline on panel, 31 x 24 ins / 80 x 61 cm) USD 150,000. FLORIDA, 20 Jan 2004, *Spirit* (1965, acrylic on board, 39 x 26 ins / 99 x 66 cm) USD 17,000. NEW YORK, 26 May 2004, *Spirit* (1965, acrylic and mixed media on paper and wood, 40 x 26 ins / 102 x 66 cm) USD 25,000.

SIR, Franz
Austrian, 19th century.
Died 1865, in Prague.
Painter, lithographer. Portraits.

SIR L., pseudonym of Aradian, Lévon
Lebanese, 20th century.
Born 1932, in Beirut, to Armenian parents.
Active in France from 1951.
Painter, draughtsman, pastellist, illustrator. Nudes, portraits, landscapes.
Symbolism.
Armenian Fine Artists group.

Sir L. is a self-taught painter from Armenia, who began his artistic career in Paris in 1972. In 1982, he claimed to have created a new classicism based on a modernisation of the Classical style. He has also been involved in founding artists' groups, including the Artistes Plasticiens Arméniens de France (Armenian Plastic Artists of France) in 1986.

He paints fantastic-erotic nudes inspired by both Classicism and Surrealism in a Symbolist style - drawings, pastels, paintings and, occasionally, coloured crayon drawings are all created with concern for line, creating an atmosphere of strangeness, hedonism and pseudo innocence. Since the 1990s he has turned towards the naive representation of landscapes and flowers. He illustrated an encyclopedia of sexuality in 1980-1981 (compiled by Gilbert Akoka).

Since 1975, Sir L. has participated in a number of exhibitions: 1975-1977, Salon de la Jeune Peinture, Paris; 1992, *De Bonnard à Baselitz - Dix Ans d'enrichissements du cabinet des estampes 1978-1988* (*From Bonnard to Baselitz: A Decade of Acquisitions by the Prints Collection 1978-1988*), Bibliothèque Nationale, Paris; 1995, *L'Artiste et la transformation du monde* (*The Artist and the Transformation of the World*), École Nationale des Beaux-Arts, Paris.

Since 1977 he has held a number of solo exhibitions, including: 1989, *Hymn to Aphrodite*, Pléiade Gallery, Athens; 1992, *For Armenia*, Athens Centre of Culture, Greece; 1993, *Nuages et Fleurs* (*Clouds and Flowers*), Galerie Liliane François, Paris; The International Fair of Contemporary Art, Seoul, Korea; 2001, *Ciels et fleurs en Berry* (*Sky and Flowers in Berry*), St-Vic Museum, St-Amand-Montrond.

BIBLIOGRAPHY:
Xuriguera, Gérard, *Regard sur la peinture contemporaine*, reference work, Arted, Paris, 1983. Xuriguera, Gérard, *Les figurations de 1960 à nos jours*, reference work, Mayer, Paris, 1985. Xuriguera, Gérard, *Le Dessin, le pastel, l'aquarelle dans l'art*, reference work, Mayer, Paris, 1987. Katchatrian, Chahen, *Artistes arméniens en France*, Anahid, Erevan (ARM), 1991.

MUSEUMS AND GALLERIES:
PARIS (BNF, Prints Collection): *Female Centaur* (1974, lithograph).

SIRACUSA, Federico
Italian, 18th - 19th century.
Born in Trapani.
Sculptor.

The pupil of I. Marabitti, Federico Siracusa sculpted statues for the churches of Cagliari, Palermo and Trapani.

SIRACUSA, Leopoldo Borbone di (Count)
Italian, 19th century.
Born 22 May 1813, in Naples; died 4 October 1860, in Pisa.
Sculptor.

Leopoldo Borbone di Siracusa was the son of Francis I, King of the Two Sicilies. He carved statues and marble groups for the cemetery in Naples.

SIRACUSA, Santi, or Siragusa
Italian, 18th century.
Active in Messina in 1712.
Sculptor (wood).

SIRACUSANO, Giovanni
Italian, 16th - 17th century.
Active in Messina from 1583 to 1628.
Sculptor (wood).

Giovanni Siracusano carved a *Madonna* for the high altar of the church of the Candelore in Castroreale in Sicily in 1602.

SIRAG, Karel
Dutch, 20th - 21st century.
Born 1948, in Driebergen.
Painter, miniaturist. Urban landscapes, architectural views.

Karel Sirag's works, which are very small in size, show urban scenes in minute, precious detail, both banks of a river, or both sides of a street, often adding a peculiar detail depicted on a different scale: matches, a bowl and a spoon, for example. He has taken part in the following group exhibitions: 1996, *Celestial Acts*, Lieve Hemel gallery in Amsterdam; 2002, Colectie Pan-Amsterdam 2002, Lieve Hemel gallery, Amsterdam; 2003, *The Destiny of Man*, Lieve Hemel gallery, Amsterdam. This gallery also mounted a solo exhibition of his works in 1997.

BIBLIOGRAPHY:
Nieuwendijk, Koen, *Met engelengeduld (The patience of an angel)*, exhibition catalogue, Gal. Lieve Hemel, Amsterdam, 1995.

SIRANI, Anna Maria
Italian, 17th - 18th century.
Born 1645; died 1715.
Active in Bologna.
Painter.

Anna Maria Sirani was the pupil of her father, Giovanni Andrea Sirani, and her sister, Elisabetta. She painted saints, Madonnas and religious subjects and worked mainly in Bologna.

SIRANI, Barbara, or Sirani Borgognoni
Italian, 17th century.
Active in Bologna.
Painter.

Barbara Sirani was the pupil of her father, Giovanni Andrea Sirani, and her sister, Elisabetta. She painted altarpieces for churches in Bologna.

SIRANI, Elisabetta
Italian, 17th century.
Born 8 January 1638, in Bologna, in 1628 according to some sources; died 28 August 1665, in Bologna, murdered.
Painter, engraver, draughtswoman. Religious subjects, allegorical subjects, portraits.

Elisabetta Sirani's father, Giovanni Andrea Sirani, was her first master. She showed remarkable natural aptitude from a very early age and began painting for the public in 1655. She is noted in particular for a *Baptism of Christ* in La Certosa, and for other works in the Zampierri Caprera and Bacari palaces in Bologna and in the Palazzo Corsini and the Palazzo Bolognetta in Rome.

Although she may have been barely 27 years old when she died, poisoned by her servant woman, she left a considerable body of work. Her paintings were in the style of Guido Reni.

MUSEUMS AND GALLERIES:

BESANÇON: *Mary Magdalene in the Wilderness* - BOLOGNA (Pinacoteca Nazionale): *St Anne, the Virgin and the Infant Jesus; Head of Christ; St Elizabeth with the Virgin and the Infant St John; Mary Magdalene Worshipping the Crucifix; Head of Christ Crowned with Thorns; Madonna of the Rose; Heads of St Joseph and St Philip; St Anthony of Padua and the Infant Jesus; Madonna of the Turtle Dove; Infant Jesus and Saints* - CAEN: *Portrait of the Artist* - COMPIÈGNE (Mus. national du Château): *Cupid Sleeping* - DRESDEN: *The Spring; Portrait of Anna Maria Cagnuoli; Allegories* - DUBLIN: *Mary Magdalene* - EDINBURGH (Nat. Gal. of Scotland): *The Infant St John the Baptist in the Wilderness* (oil on canvas) - LEIPZIG: *Cupid Sleeping* - MOSCOW (Rumiantsev Mus.): *Virgin and St Joseph Finding Jesus in the Temple* - PESARO (Mus. Civico): *Release of St Peter* - RENNES: *Death of Abel* - ROHRAU (Schlossmus., Graf Harrach'sche Familiensammlung): *Virgin* - ST PETERSBURG (Hermitage): *Holy Family; Infant Jesus* - TOURS: *Marriage of St Catherine* - VICENZA: *Immaculate Virgin* - VIENNA: *Martha Reprimanding her Sister.*

AUCTION RECORDS:

PARIS, 1756, *Baptism of Our Lord* (three drawings) FRF 52. PARIS, 1891, *Virgin and St Joseph in Adoration* (miniature) FRF 50. VENICE, 1894, *Holy Family, the Infant St John and an Angel,* ITL 2,550. LONDON, 24 March 1922, *Woman as Sainte Agnes* GBP 31. LONDON, 4-7 May 1923, *Mary Magdalene,* GBP 31. LONDON, 30 Nov 1966, *Painting and Music,* GBP 600. MILAN, 18 April 1972, *Virgin and Child,* ITL 5,000,000. MILAN, 6 June 1973, *Mary Magdalene,* ITL 1,900,000. LONDON, 9 July 1976, *Cleopatra* (oil on canvas, 34 x 28 1/2 ins / 86.5 x 72.5 cm) GBP 1,600. MILAN, 5 Dec 1978, *Portrait of Guido Reni* (oil on panel, 9 x 7 ins / 23 x 18 cm) ITL 2,400,000. LONDON, 11 July 1980, *Mystical Marriage of St Catherine* (1664, oil on canvas, 46 1/2 x 61 1/2 ins / 118 x 156.2 cm) GBP 4,500. LONDON, 20 Feb 1981, *Mystical Marriage of St Catherine* (1664, oil on canvas, 46 1/2 x 61 1/2 ins / 118 x 156.2 cm) GBP 5,500. LONDON, 3 April 1984, *Head of a Young Girl* (black, red and white chalk/grey paper, 11 1/4 x 11 ins / 28.7 x 27.9 cm) GBP 4,200. LONDON, 11 Dec 1984, *Portia Piercing her Thigh* (1664, oil on canvas, 39 3/4 x 54 1/4 ins / 101 x 138 cm) GBP 18,000. MONTE CARLO, 23 June 1985, *Charity* (oil on canvas remounted/panel, 50 1/2 x 41 3/4 ins / 128 x 106 cm) FRF 28,000. LONDON, 1 April 1987, *A Bishop and Three Monks Kneeling before a Statue of the Virgin* (red chalk and brown wash, 6 1/2 x 3 3/4 ins / 16.5 x 9.6 cm) GBP 700. LONDON, 10 July 1987, *Holy Family with St Teresa of Avila* (1664, oil on canvas, 48 x 61 1/2 ins / 121 x 156 cm) GBP 17,000. LONDON, 21 July 1989, *Holy Family with Saints Elizabeth and Zacharias* (oil on canvas, 30 1/4 x 40 1/4 ins / 77 x 102.5 cm) GBP 6,050. ROME, 27 Nov 1989, *Infant Bacchus Inventing Wine* (1664, oil on canvas, 23 x 16 1/4 ins / 58.5 x 41.5 cm) ITL 29,900,000. LONDON, 8 Dec 1989, *Young Woman Personifying Music before a Group of Stringed Instruments in a Music Room* (1659, oil on canvas, 37 1/2 x 29 3/4 ins / 95.3 x 75.7 cm) GBP 60,500. ROME, 8 March 1990, *St Jerome Writing.* NEW YORK, 15 Jan 1993, *Infant St John the Baptist* (oil on panel, 27 1/2 x 19 ins / 69.9 x 48.3 cm) USD 43,125. NEW YORK, 19 May 1993, *Cleopatra* (oil on canvas, 34 3/4 x 29 1/4 ins / 88.3 x 74.3 cm) USD 46,000. ROME, 9 May 1995, *Death of Cleopatra* (oil on canvas, 29 1/2 x 39 1/4 ins / 75 x 100 cm) ITL 51,750,000. LONDON, 2 July 1996, *Woman at her Toilette* (black chalk, brown ink and wash, 10 x 7 1/2 ins / 25.5 x 19.3 cm) GBP 5,750. VENICE, 22 June 1997, *S Joseph with the Infant Jesus* (oil on canvas, 39 x 29 1/4 ins / 99 x 74 cm) ITL 7,000,000. ROME, 1 June 1999, *St John the Baptist* (1654, oil on canvas, 41 x 31 ins / 105 x 79 cm) ITL 32,000,000. VIENNA, 6 Oct 1999, *Madonna and Child with the Young St John* (oil on canvas, 40 x 32 ins / 102 x 81 cm) ATS 200,000. NEW YORK, 27 Jan 2000, *Porcia* (oil on canvas, 33 x 27 ins / 83 x 68 cm) USD 28,000. NEW YORK, 25 May 2000, *Venus and Cupid* (oil on canvas, 43 x 36 ins / 110 x 92 cm) USD 30,000. NEW YORK, 25 Jan 2001, *Personification of Music* (1659, oil on canvas, 37 x 29 ins / 95 x 74 cm) USD 50,000. MILAN, 12 June 2001, *Dido Abandoned by Aeneas* (oil on canvas, 25 x 34 ins / 64 x 87 cm) ITL 185,000,000. NEW YORK, 23 Jan 2002, *Head of a Young Woman* (red chalk, double-sided, 11 x 8 ins / 29 x 20 cm) USD 1,800. LONDON, 12 Dec 2002, *Cupid, Holding a Flaming Torch and Bow, Seated on a Shell* (1661, oil on canvas, 36 x 28 ins / 91 x 71 cm) GBP 24,000. LONDON, 10 July 2003, *Pandora* (oil on canvas, 36 x 30 ins / 92 x 76 cm) GBP 25,000. VENICE, 21 Sept 2003, *Cupid* (oil on canvas, 46 x 58 ins / 117 x 147 cm) EUR 27,000. VIENNA, 24 March 2004, *St Jerome* (oil on canvas, 40 x 33 ins / 102 x 84 cm) EUR 7,500. MILAN, 26 May 2004, *Putto in Seascape* (oil on canvas, 35 x 28 ins / 89 x 70 cm) EUR 95,000.

SIRANI, Giovanni Andrea or Jean André

Italian, 17th century.

Born 4 September 1610, in Bologna; died 21 May 1670, in Bologna.

Painter, engraver, draughtsman. Religious subjects.

Giovanni Andrea Sirani was the pupil of Guido Reni, whose style he imitated in the early part of his career. He engraved a number of plates which he signed *G.A.S.* or *I.A.S.* His daughter Elisabetta was a famous painter.

After the death of his master, Sirani was chosen to complete several of his works, in particular the painting of St Bruno in La Certosa. He later adopted a more powerful style, closer to that of Caravaggio.

MUSEUMS AND GALLERIES:

BERGUES: *Portrait of a Man* - BOLOGNA: *Presentation in the Temple* - BOLOGNA (Church of S Giorgio): *Marriage of the Virgin* - BOLOGNA (Church of S Martino): *Crucifixion* - BOLOGNA (Mus. della Certosa): *Meal at the House of Simon the Pharisee* - CHAMBÉRY (MBA): *Head of David* - FLORENCE: *The Artist* - STOCKHOLM: *Head of an Angel; Head of the Virgin* - VENICE: *Madonna.*

AUCTION RECORDS:

PARIS, 1785, *Holy Family* (red chalk) FRF 36. PARIS, 1860, *Virgin and Child,* FRF 630. PARIS, 23 March 1921, *Lot and his Daughters,* FRF 400. VIENNA, 9 June 1970, *Virgin and Child with St Anne,* ATS 60,000. LONDON, 2 July 1984, *Head of a Black Youth* (red chalk and touches of white chalk/pale blue paper, 9 x 6 1/2 ins / 22.8 x 16.2 cm) GBP 3,800. LONDON, 10 April 1985, *Angel and Putto* (red chalk, 6 3/4 x 8 1/4 ins / 17.3 x 20.7 cm) GBP 2,400. LONDON, 2 July 1991, *Apotheosis of St Francis Surmounted by Angels Making Music* (red chalk, ink and wash, design for the dome of an apse, 11 x 16 ins / 27 x 40.5 cm) GBP 8,800. NEW YORK, 27 Jan 1999, *Apotheosis of St Francis, Surrounded by Angels* (pen and brown ink wash over red chalk, 11 x 16 ins / 27 x 41 cm) USD 12,500. VENICE, 14 May 1999, *Mary Magdalene* (oil on canvas, 29 x 24 ins / 73 x 60 cm) ITL 6,800,000. ZURICH, 15 March 2000, *Mary with Child* (oil on canvas, 28 x 22 ins / 70 x 55 cm) CHF 34,000. ROME, 4 Dec 2000, *Diana and Endymion* (oil on canvas, 114 x 83 ins / 290 x 210 cm) ITL 180,000,000. ROME, 22 May 2001, *Lucrecia* (oil on canvas, 35 x 28 ins / 88 x 71 cm) ITL 30,000,000. NEW YORK, 23 May 2001, *Fortune with a Purse* (oil on canvas, 64 x 51 ins / 162 x 130 cm) USD 40,000. LONDON, 12 Dec 2002, *Esther before Ahasuerus* (oil on canvas, 41 x 56 ins / 104 x 142 cm) GBP 16,500. LONDON, 10 April 2003,

Cimon and Pero (oil on canvas, 40 x 33 ins / 102 x 84 cm) GBP 13,000. MADRID, 2 March 2004, *Holy Family* (oil on canvas, 39 x 29 ins / 99 x 73 cm) EUR 12,000. LONDON, 8 July 2004, *Allegory of Astrology* (oil on canvas, 46 x 30 ins / 116 x 75 cm) GBP 15,000.

SIRASCER, Jerónimo (Fray), or Gerónimo Siraster
Spanish, 17th century.
Engraver.
Jerónimo Sirascer was a monk at the Franciscan monastery in Valladolid around 1602 (1613 according to some sources). He engraved plates for *Historia del Monte Celia de Nuestra Señora de la Salieda* (*History of Monte Celia de Nuestra Señora de la Salieda*) by Don Fr. Pedro Gonzálvez de Mendoza, archbishop of Granada.

SIRAT, Joseph
French, 19th - 20th century.
Born 24 December 1869, in Toulouse.
Painter, draughtsman.
Joseph Sirat was well known for his caricatures.

SIRATO, Francisc
Romanian, 20th century.
Born 15 August 1877, in Craiova; died 1953.
Painter, illustrator. Landscapes, genre scenes.
Group of Four.
After a brief period in 1898 in a Düsseldorf lithography workshop, Francisc Sirato studied at Bucharest fine arts school from 1900 to 1905. In 1917 he was appointed curator of the Romanian National Folk Art Museum and from 1933 taught at the academy. He also wrote on art. Sirato exhibited with various Romanian groups and associations, including Artistic Youth, Romanian Art and the Group of Four.
MUSEUMS AND GALLERIES:
BUCHAREST (Muz. National de Arta al României): *Return from Market* - IASI (Muzeul de Arta): *Meeting*.

SIRAUT, Marcel
Belgian, 20th century.
Born 1942, in St-Pieters-Woluwe.
Painter, draughtsman, pastellist, watercolourist.
Marcel Siraut trained at the St-Lucas Academie in Ghent. He also worked as an advertising draughtsman.

SIRBEREGOVIC, Kemal. See **KEMAL**

SIRCANA, Giovanni
Italian, 20th century.
Born in Olbia (Sardinia).
Painter.
Sircana lived and worked in Livorno. He participated in many exhibitions and won several prizes.

SIRCEUS. See **SOYE Philipp de**

SIRCH, Joseph
German, 18th century.
Active in Augsburg (Bavaria).
Miniaturist.
Joseph Sirch was the father of Wolfgang Joseph.

SIRCH, Wolfgang Joseph
German, 18th - 19th century.
Born c. 1745; died c. 1810, in Augsburg (Bavaria).
Painter.
Wolfgang was the son of Joseph Sirch. He painted portraits and watercolours and worked on enamel.

SIRCIO. See **SOYE Philipp de**

SIRE, Balthazar
French, 18th century.
Active at the beginning of the 18th century.
Sculptor.
Balthazar Sire sculpted an altarpiece and some statues of saints for the church of Maîche in 1710.

SIRE, Blaise
French, 17th - 18th century.
Sculptor.
Blaise Sire worked for the church of Ste-Bénigne in Pontarlier and for the churches of Estavayer, Frasne and Orgelet.

SIRE, Hugonin, or Syre
Swiss, 15th century.
Died March 1476, in Fribourg.
Painter, stucco artist. Decorative schemes.
Hugonin Sire worked in Fribourg, Switzerland, from 1453.

SIRE, Le. See **LESIRE**

SIREE, Clementina. See **ROBERTSON**

SIRENA, Giuseppe
Italian, 16th century.
Active in Palermo from 1579 to 1582.
Painter.
Perhaps the pupil of Vincenzo di Pavia, Giuseppe Sirena painted an altarpiece for the church of S Eulalia dei Catalani in Palermo.

SIRET, Nicolas
French, 16th century.
Born in Lons-le-Saulnier.
Glass painter.

SIRGA, Master of. See **MASTERS**

SIRI, Sisto. See **SYRI Sixtus**

SIRIES, Carlo
Italian, 19th century.
Died 29 October 1854.
Active in Florence.
Cameo engraver.
Carlo Siries was the son of Luigi Siries.

SIRIES, Cosimo
Italian, 18th century.
Active in Florence from 1759 to 1789.
Cameo engraver.
Cosimo Siries was the son of Louis Siries, whom he succeeded at the workshops producing 'pietre dure' mosaics in Florence.

SIRIES, Louis
Italian, 18th century.
Died 29 October 1754, in Florence.
Cameo engraver, goldsmith.
The father of Cosimo and Violante Beatrice Siries, Louis Siries was active in Florence from 1722 onwards.
MUSEUMS AND GALLERIES:
VIENNA (Kunsthistorisches Mus.): *Francesco I of Tuscany with his Family* (cameo in onyx).

SIRIES, Luigi
Italian, 18th - 19th century.
Born 28 June 1743, in Florence; died 15 October 1811.
Cameo engraver.
Luigi Siries was the son of Cosimo Siries.

SIRIES, Violante Beatrice, later Signora Cerroti
Italian, 18th century.
Born 26 January 1709, in Florence; died 1783.
Painter, pastellist, watercolourist. Historical subjects, portraits, group portraits, flowers, fruit.
The daughter of Louis Siries, Violante Siries initially studied pastel and watercolour painting with Giovanna Fratellini. She then went to Paris, where she studied with Hyacinthe Rigaud and François Boucher. Although she painted a number of historical subjects, flowers and fruit, her talent was most evident in portraiture. She is noted in particular for a

group portrait of the family of the grand duke, painted on her return to Florence. Her self-portrait is in the collection of the Uffizi in Florence.

AUCTION RECORDS:

LONDON, 11 Dec 1992, *Half-length Portraits of Young Women* (1753, oil on canvas, a pair, both oval 13 1/2 x 10 ins / 34 x 25.4 cm) GBP 2,970.

SIRIEZ DE LONGEVILLE, G.
French, 20th century.
Born in Boulogne-sur-Mer.
Painter, draughtsman.

G. Siriez de Longeville spent his working life in Paris. He was made a Chevalier of the Légion d'Honneur. He specialised in portraits set against a hazy background.

SIRIGATTI, Ridolfo
Italian, 16th - 17th century.
Active in Florence.
Sculptor.

The master of P. Bernini, Ridolfo Sirigatti carved a bust of *Francesco I, Duke of Tuscany* in 1594.

SIRINE-REAL, Ernestine
French, 20th century.
Sculptor.

Ernestine Sirine-Real exhibited at the Salon des Artistes Français in Paris. She was awarded a commendation in 1928, a bronze medal in 1936 and a silver medal in 1941.

SIRK, Albert
Italian, 20th century.
Born 26 May 1887, in Santa Croce, near Trieste.
Painter, illustrator.

Sirk was a pupil of Ettore Tito.

SIRLETTI, Flavio, or Sirleto or Sirletto
Italian, 18th century.
Born in Ferrara; died 15 August 1737, in Rome.
Cameo engraver.

Flavio Sirletti, the father of Francesco and Raimondo Sirletti, copied Roman antiquities. He is noted for a *Laocoön* on amethyst.

SIRLETTO. See also **SIRLETTI**

SIRLETTO, Francesco, or Sirleto or Sirletto
Italian, 18th century.
Born c. 1714; died November 1788.
Cameo engraver.

Francesco Sirletto was the son of Flavio Sirletti.

SIRLETTO, Raimondo, or Sirleto or Sirletto
Italian, 18th century.
Died soon after 1737.
Cameo engraver.

Raimondo Sirletto was the son of Flavio Sirletto.

SIROKY, Jósef
Czech, 18th century.
Active in Krumau.
Sculptor (wood).

Jósef Siroky sculpted the altar of the church in Husinec in 1731.

SIROMBO, Giovanni
Italian, 20th century.
Born 9 August 1885, in Milan.
Painter. Landscapes.

Sirombo was a self-taught painter.

AUCTION RECORDS:

MILAN, 19 Dec 1995, *Island of San Giorgio* (oil on panel, 18 x 23 1/2 ins / 46 x 60 cm) ITL 1,150,000. MILAN, 18 Dec 1996, *Lagoons near Lerici* (oil on card, 27 1/2 x 37 1/2 ins / 70 x 95 cm) ITL 2,330,000.

SIRON, André
20th century.
Born 1926.
Painter.

MUSEUMS AND GALLERIES:

AARAU (Aargauer Kunsthaus): *No title* (1979).

SIRONI, Mario
Italian, 20th century.
Born 12 May 1885, in Tempio Pausania, Sardinia; died 1961, in Milan.
Painter (gouache), illustrator, draughtsman, decorative designer, sculptor. Figures, portraits, urban landscapes. Murals, stage sets.
Futurism, Novecento Italiano.
Milanese School.

Mario Sironi was studying mathematics in Rome with the intention of becoming an engineer when he decided to enrol in the academy of fine art. He met Severini and Boccioni who introduced him to Balla. After 1914, he moved to Milan, his parents' home town. He was not only an artist but also a writer on art and an architect.

Sironi's paintings depict a variety of subjects, often including faces, and seek to portray the wretchedness of the human condition in urban society. He was only briefly associated with Futurism, in 1915. Often using a collage technique applied to coloured paper, he produced works with broad contrasting planes 'on the modern myths of machines and speed' with titles like *Aeroplane; Harlequin; Lorry; Cyclist; Dancer; Helix; Workshop of Wonders*, all dating from 1915-1916. Nevertheless, his predilection for Expressionism was always clear, as can be seen from the covers and illustrations relating to the war that he provided for the journal *Gli Avvenimenti* (*Events*) in 1916. After World War I, he drew illustrations for another journal, *Popolo d'Italia* (*People of Italy*). His brief interest in Futurism soon faded and he returned to working in the Expressionist style, which came more naturally to him. With his series of *Urban Landscapes* he returned to the subject of his earlier works, the fate of individuals trapped in industrial city life, depicting it in muted colours and disturbing spaces revealed by dim gleams of light. In 1922, he was one of the founding members of the semi-official Novecento (20th Century) group. A reflection of the political and historical context - Mussolini's Fascist Italy - in which it was formed, the group declared its opposition to the experimentation of the avant-garde and advocated a return to 'traditional' Roman values.

Sironi himself stood apart from the worst of the prevailing Realist and Academic styles by virtue of the quality of his work, in which the image is reduced to its essence and rendered with a robust, unpolished power. In the 1930s, he concentrated on monumental compositions, which clearly reveal his political sympathies. These works were executed in fresco and mosaic and include *Labour* of 1933, created for the 5th Milan Triennale. He also designed decorative ceramic work, including that for the Pavilion of Fascist Italy at the 1937 Exposition Universelle. After World War II, he concentrated almost exclusively on designing theatre sets.

He took part in a large number of collective exhibitions from 1905 onwards. From 1914, he exhibited regularly in Rome: in 1914, at the *Free Futurist Exhibition*; 1919, at the *Great Futurist Exhibition*; 1925, at the International Exhibition of Fine Art. Outside Rome, he exhibited in Paris in 1921 at the *Exposition des peintres futuristes italiens* (*Exhibition of Italian Futurist Painters*), from 1924, regularly at the Venice Biennale and in Milan at the *First Exhibition of the Italian Novecento Group* held in 1926. Other exhibitions include: at the Rath Museum in Geneva in 1927; at the Stedelijk Musdeum in Amsterdam, also in 1927; at the Kunsthalle in Basel in 1930; at the Carnegie Institute in Pittsburgh in 1931; at the Musée du Jeu de Paume in Paris in 1935; at the Musée des

Beaux-Arts in Lyons in 1938; at the Musée des Beaux-Arts in La Chaux-de-Fonds in 1947; at the Museum of Modern Art in New York and the Musée Nationale d'Art Moderne in Paris in 1949; at the Zurich Kunsthalle in 1950; at Documenta in Kassel in 1955. After his death in 1961, there were other exhibitions which included works by him: at Documenta in Kassel in 1964; at the museum of modern art in Mexico in 1966; at the Galleria Nazionale d'Arte Moderna in Rome in 1968; at the Palazzo Reale in Milan in 1973 and 1992; at the Kunsthalle in Düsseldorf in 1974; at the Galleria d'Arte Moderna in Bologna in 1978 and 1980; at Palazzo Grassi in Venice in 1979, 1986 and 1989; at the Centre Georges Pompidou in Paris in 1980 in an exhibition entitled *Les Réalismes* (*Realisms*); at the Villa Medici in Rome in 1987 and 1989; at the Royal Academy in London in 1989 in the exhibition entitled *Italian Art in the 20th Century*; at the Tate Gallery in London in 1990; at the museum in Lodève in 2003 in the exhibition entitled *De Chirico et la peinture italienne de l'entre-deux guerres* (*De Chirico and Italian Painting of the Interwar Period*).

He held regular solo exhibitions in Milan and Rome from 1919 onwards. Other solo exhibitions include those of 1953 at the Institute of Contemporary Art in Boston and 1954 at the Baltimore Museum of Art. Posthumous retrospectives include: 1969, the Palazzo Corsini in Florence; 1972, the Galleria Civica d'Arte Moderna in Palazzo dei Diamante in Ferrara; 1973 and 1985, the Palazzo Reale in Milan; 1984, Palazzo Grassi in Venice; 1988, the Städtische Kunsthallen in Düsseldorf and Baden Baden; 1989, the Galleria Civica d'Arte Contemporanea in Marsala; 1990, the Montrouge Salon; 1991, the Uffizi Galleries in Florence (in the Prints and Drawings Collection). In 1961, he was awarded the Premio Milano.

Sironi

BIBLIOGRAPHY:

Mario Sironi, exhibition catalogue, Palazzo Reale, Electa, Milan, 1973. Bellonzi, F., *Catalogue raisonné de l'œuvre gravé*, Electa, Milan, 1985. Penelope, Mario, *Sironi*, De Luca Editore, Roma, Mondadori, Milan, 1985. *Mario Sironi*, exhibition catalogue, DuMont, Cologne, 1988. Bonito Oliva, Achille/Iovane, Giovanni/Lista, Giovanni, et al., *De Chirico et la peinture italienne de l'entre-deux guerres*, exhibition catalogue, Musée de Lodève, 2003.

MUSEUMS AND GALLERIES:

BUFFALO (Albright-Knox AG) - CAMBRIDGE (Kettle's Yard, University of Cambridge): about 70 drawings - FLORENCE (Gal. d'Arte Moderna) - LAUSANNE (Cantonal MFA) - LONDON (Tate Collection): *The Syphon* (1916, gouache and mixed media/paper); *Mountains* (c. 1928, oil on canvas) - MADRID (Mus. de Arte Moderno) - MILAN (Gal. d'Arte Moderna): *Self-portrait* (1913) - PARIS (MNAM-CCI): *Mountain Lake* (1928) - ROME (Gal. Nazionale d'Arte Moderna): *Solitude* (1926); *Family* (1930) - TOLEDO (MA) - TRIESTE (Civico Mus. Revoltella) - ZURICH (Kunsthaus).

AUCTION RECORDS:

NEW YORK, 18 May 1960, *Composition*, USD 1,300. MILAN, 22 Nov 1961, *Cyclist*, ITL 8,500,000. MILAN, 1 Dec 1964, *Composition* (tempera) ITL 1,300,000. MILAN, 29 Nov 1966, *Myth*, ITL 9,000,000. MILAN, 4 Dec 1969, *Figure* (tempera) ITL 1,000,000. ROME, 28 Nov 1972, *Composition*, ITL 7,000,000. MILAN, 29 May 1973, *Family*, ITL 32,500,000. MILAN, 4 June 1974, *Symbols* (tempera) ITL 13,000,000. MILAN, 16 March 1976, *Builders* (pastel and tempera, 39 x 19 3/4 ins / 99 x 50 cm) ITL 3,200,000. ROME, 9 Dec 1976, *Workers* (1932, oil on canvas, 47 1/4 x 65 ins / 120 x 165 cm) ITL 16,500,000. ROME, 19 May 1977, *Suburban Tram* (oil on mounted card, 10 1/4 x 16 3/4 ins / 26 x 42.5 cm) ITL 5,500,000. MILAN, 19 Dec 1978, *Composition* (tempera/paper mounted/canvas, 11 1/2 x 13 3/4 ins / 29 x 35 cm) ITL 1,700,000. MILAN, 26 June 1979, *Composition with Figures* (oil on canvas, 43 1/4 x 36 1/4 ins / 110 x 92 cm) ITL 13,500,000. MILAN, 12 March 1980, *Portrait of a Woman* (soft chalk, 9 1/2 x 8 ins / 24 x 20.2 cm) ITL 1,900,000. MILAN, 24 June 1980, *Origins of Tragedy* (1952, mixed media/canvas, 39 x 32 ins / 99 x 81 cm) ITL 22,000,000. MILAN, 26 Feb 1981, *Composition* (1956, oil on canvas, 31 1/2 x 39 1/4 ins / 80 x 100 cm) ITL 38,000,000. MILAN, 21 Dec 1982, *Annunciation* (1935, charcoal, ink and wash/mounted card, three panels, 93 3/4 x 93 ins / 238 x 236 cm) ITL 18,000,000. MILAN, 13 June 1984, *Workers* (1928, charcoal, 18 1/2 x 23 1/4 ins / 47 x 59 cm) ITL 11,000,000. MILAN, 15 Nov 1984, *Townscape* (mixed media, 12 1/4 x 17 3/4 ins / 31 x 45 cm) ITL 18,000,000. ROME, 4 Dec 1984, *Portrait of Matilde the Artist's Wife* (1919, oil on panel, 35 x 29 1/4 ins / 89 x 74 cm) ITL 70,000,000. MILAN, 19 Dec 1985, *Figure* (soft chalk, 10 x 9 1/2 ins / 25.5 x 24 cm) ITL 6,500,000. MILAN, 28 Oct 1986, *The Great Miracle* (1956, oil on canvas, 33 1/2 x 45 1/4 ins / 85 x 115 cm) ITL 130,000,000. MILAN, 8 June 1988, *Mural Composition* (1936, mixed media, 15 1/4 x 20 3/4 ins / 39 x 53 cm) ITL 4,400,000. NEW YORK, 6 Oct 1988, *Composition* (1950, gouache and watercolour, 13 3/4 x 19 3/4 ins / 35 x 50.1 cm) USD 6,820. LONDON, 19 Oct 1988, *Composition* (oil on canvas, 27 3/4 x 23 3/4 ins / 70.4 x 60.5 cm) GBP 18,700. ROME, 15 Nov 1988, *Sunday Football Match* (1921, distemper/paper/canvas, 41 x 30 ins / 104 x 76 cm) ITL 11,000,000. LONDON, 22 Feb 1989, *Composition* (oil on canvas, 23 1/2 x 19 3/4 ins / 60 x 50 cm) GBP 23,100. MILAN, 20 March 1989, *Mountain* (1955, oil on canvas, 19 3/4 x 23 1/2 ins / 50 x 59.5 cm) ITL 40,000,000. MILAN, 7 Nov 1989, *Urban Landscape* (mixed media/paper/canvas, 13 1/2 x 20 ins / 34.5 x 51 cm) ITL 53,000,000. NEW YORK, 26 Feb 1990, *Composition* (1953, Indian ink and gouache/paper/canvas, 25 1/2 x 17 1/2 ins / 64.5 x 44.5 cm) USD 33,000. MILAN, 27 March 1990, *Fishing* (1928, oil on canvas, 59 1/2 x 47 1/4 ins / 151 x 120 cm) ITL 535,000,000. NEW YORK, 16 May 1990, *Composition* (gouache and pencil/tinted paper mounted/material, 19 x 12 1/2 ins / 48.3 x 32 cm) USD 330,000. LONDON, 17 Oct 1990, *Figure on a Daybed* (tempera, gouache and charcoal/paper/card, 17 x 19 ins / 43 x 48 cm) GBP 8,800. MILAN, 24 Oct 1990, *Vertical Composition* (1958, oil on canvas, 43 1/4 x 35 1/2 ins / 110 x 90 cm) ITL 170,000,000. MILAN, 26 March 1991, *Composition* (oil on canvas, 15 3/4 x 19 3/4 ins / 40 x 50 cm) ITL 45,000,000. ROME, 9 April 1991, *Composition with Two Figures* (mixed media/paper/canvas, 19 1/4 x 26 3/4 ins / 49 x 68 cm) ITL 56,000,000. ROME, 13 May 1991, *Nude* (1930, oil on canvas, 39 1/4 x 32 3/4 ins / 100 x 83 cm) ITL 216,200,000. NEW YORK, 12 June 1991, *Composition* (gouache and ink/paper, 11 1/4 x 19 1/4 ins / 28.3 x 48.6 cm) USD 18,700. LUGANO, 12 Oct 1991, *Female Nude* (ink/paper, 4 1/4 x 3 1/4 ins / 11 x 8.4 cm) CHF 3,700. MILAN, 14 Nov 1991, *Composition* (1944, oil on canvas, 20 3/4 x 26 3/4 ins / 53 x 68 cm) ITL 205,000,000. ROME, 9 Dec 1991, *Small Houses High in the Mountains* (oil on canvas, 14 1/2 x 19 3/4 ins / 37 x 50 cm) ITL 63,250,000. MILAN, 19 Dec 1991, *Composition* (1957, oil on canvas, 35 1/2 x 38 1/4 ins / 90 x 97 cm) ITL 160,000,000. NEW YORK, 25 Feb 1992, *Landscape* (1952, oil on card/canvas, 18 x 15 1/4 ins / 45.7 x 38.7 cm) USD 35,200. MILAN, 14 April 1992, *Composition* (mixed media/card, 13 1/2 x 21 ins / 34 x 53.5 cm) ITL 23,000,000. ROME, 25 May 1992, *Untitled* (ink and tempera/paper/canvas, 9 3/4 x 8 3/4 ins / 25 x 22.5 cm) ITL 16,675,000. LUGANO, 10 Oct 1992, *Figures in a Landscape* (mixed media/mounted paper, 29 1/2 x 22 1/2 ins / 75 x 57 cm) CHF 26,000. MILAN, 9 Nov 1992, *Urban Landscape* (1942, tempera/card, 14 1/2 x 12 3/4 ins / 37 x 32.5 cm) ITL 36,000,000. MILAN, 15 Dec 1992, *Composition with Urban Landscape* (mixed media, 30 x 19 3/4 ins / 76 x 50 cm) ITL 56,000,000. NEW YORK, 23-25 Feb 1993, *Man Drinking* (gouache/paper/canvas, 11 x 9 1/4 ins / 27.9 x 23.5 cm) USD 4,140. MILAN, 16 Nov 1993, *Brown Composition* (1958, oil on canvas, 22 3/4 x 31 ins / 58 x 79 cm) ITL 62,100,000. ROME, 19 April 1994, *Venetian Woman* (1926, tempera and white lead/paper, 6 3/4 x 6 ins / 17 x 15.5 cm) ITL 10,925,000. MILAN, 5 May 1994, *Symbol* (1952, mixed media/paper, 52 x 43 1/4 ins / 132 x 110 cm) ITL 92,000,000. PARIS, 8 June 1994, *Composition with Sleeping Figures* (lead pencil and gouache, 6 1/2 x 10 1/4 ins / 16.2 x 26 cm) FRF 28,000. MILAN, 27 April 1995, *Metaphysical Composition* (mixed media/mounted paper, 56 x 48 1/2 ins / 142 x 123 cm) ITL 201,250,000. NEW YORK, 3 May 1995, *Untitled Abstract* (ink and gouache/canvas, 13 1/4 x 19 1/4 ins / 33.7 x 48.9 cm) USD 3,450. LONDON, 28 Nov 1995, *Composition* (oil on panel, 27 1/2 x 22 ins / 70 x 55 cm) GBP 17,250. MILAN, 19 March 1996, *Urban Landscape* (1932, oil on canvas, 27 1/4 x 31 ins / 69 x 79 cm) ITL 195,500,000. MILAN, 20 May 1996, *Wooded Landscape* (c. 1949, oil on canvas, 15 1/2 x 23 1/2 ins / 39.5 x 60 cm) ITL 19,245,000. MILAN, 23 May 1996, *Study for Fiat 500* (1936, ink and soft chalk/paper, 13 x 16 3/4 ins / 33 x 42.5 cm) ITL 12,075,000. NEW YORK, 10 Oct 1996, *Three Men* (charcoal/ripped paper, 7 1/4 x 14 1/2 ins / 18.1 x 36.8 cm) USD 1,035. MILAN, 25 Nov 1996, *Composition in Two Sections* (1954, tempera/paper/canvas, 11 1/2 x 18 ins / 29 x 46 cm) ITL 9,200,000; *Composition with Kneeling Nude Figure* (1972, oil on card, 14 1/4 x 21 1/4 ins / 36 x 54 cm) ITL 39,100,000. MILAN, 10 Dec 1996, *Two Trees* (1930, oil on canvas, 27 1/2 x 31 1/2 ins / 70 x 80 cm) ITL 45,435,000. MILAN, 18 March 1997, *Justice* (c. 1935, oil on panel, 23 1/2 x 19 3/4 ins / 60 x 50 cm) ITL 81,550,000. MILAN, 19 May 1997, *Calling of St Peter* (oil on canvas, 23 1/2 x 27 1/2 ins / 60 x 70 cm) ITL 36,800,000. MILAN, 15 April 1999, *Urban Landscape with Letters and Aeroplanes* (1918, collage and tempera, 12 x 9 ins / 30 x 22 cm) ITL 74,000,000. MILAN, 22 June 1999, *Urban Landscape* (1932, oil on canvas, 27 x 31 ins / 69 x 79 cm) ITL 127,000,000. MILAN, 15 Nov 2000, *Composition* (1949, mixed media on paper/canvas, 20 x 28 ins / 51 x 72 cm) ITL 45,000,000. PRATO, 25 Nov 2000, *Composition with Lorry* (oil and collage on canvas, 21 x 21 ins / 53 x 53 cm) ITL 190,000,000. PRATO, 26 May 2001, *Landscape with Three Trees* (mixed media on paper/canvas, 22 x 35 ins / 57 x 88 cm) ITL 54,000,000. ZURICH, 4 Dec 2001, *Poor Fisherman* (oil on canvas, 40 x 30 ins / 102 x 76 cm) CHF 720,000. VERCELLI, 2 March 2002, *St Joan* (1928, mixed media on paper/canvas, 37 x 25 ins / 95 x 63 cm) EUR 30,000. MILAN, 21 May 2002, *Fisherman and Sailing Boat* (1929, oil on canvas, 35 x 31 ins / 90 x 80 cm) EUR 180,000. PRATO, 31 May 2003, *Saddled Horse* (1917, oil and collage on paper/canvas, 35 x 28 ins / 90 x 72 cm) EUR 560,000. MILAN, 16 Dec 2003, *Little Theatre* (mixed media on paper/canvas, 17 x 19 ins / 43 x 49 cm) EUR 36,000. PRATO, 29 May 2004, *Figure and Wall* (1939-1940, oil on canvas, 33 x 36 ins / 84 x 92 cm) EUR 85,000. LONDON, 19 Oct 2004, *Motorcyclist* (oil on canvas, 26 x 23 ins / 66 x 59 cm) GBP 280,000.

SIROT, Guillaume
French, 18th century.
Active in Nantes 1757-1781.
Painter.

Guillaume Sirot was the son of Pierre Sirot.

SIROT, Jacques
French, 20th century.
Born 1944, in Saintes.
Painter, draughtsman.

Jacques Sirot lives and works in Paris. Examples of his work featured in *De Bonnard à Baselitz - Dix Ans d'enrichissements du cabinet des estampes 1978-1988* (*From Bonnard to Baselitz: A Decade of Acquisitions by the Prints Collection 1978-1988*) in 1993 at the Bibliothèque Nationale in Paris.

MUSEUMS AND GALLERIES:
PARIS (BNF, Prints Collection).

SIROT, Patrick
French, 20th - 21st century.
Born 15 July 1962, in Moulins (Allier).
Painter, draughtsman, assemblage artist, installation artist, video artist.

Patrick Sirot lives and works in Toulon. His assemblages bring together disparate everyday objects and subject them to innovative artificial light effects.

He exhibited solo in 1992 at the Le Creux d'Enfer Art Centre in Thiers and, in 1995, in Toulon.

SIROT, Pierre
French, 18th century.
Born c. 1700, in Nantes; died 6 March 1756, in Nantes.
Painter.

SIROT, Sophie
French, 20th century.
Painter.

AUCTION RECORDS:
PARIS, 25 Nov 1990, *The Kiss* (acrylic/canvas, 13 1/2 x 11 ins / 34 x 27 cm) FRF 7,000.

SIROTKIN, Vladimir
Russian, 20th - 21st century.
Born 1950, in Moscow.
Painter. Genre scenes.

Sirotkin studied at the school of art in Moscow. He is a member of the International Federation of Painters in Moscow, where he regularly takes part in exhibitions.

AUCTION RECORDS:
PARIS, 14 Nov 1992, *Troika Race* (oil on canvas, 18 x 15 ins / 46 x 38 cm) FRF 4,200. PARIS, 19 April 1993, *Small Courtyard in Pskov* (oil on panel, 11 3/4 x 15 3/4 ins / 30 x 40 cm) FRF 4,000.

SIROUY, Achille Louis Joseph
French, 19th century.
Born 29 November 1834, in Beauvais; died January 1904, in Paris.
Painter, lithographer.

A pupil of M. E. Lassalle, Sirouy was admitted to the École des Beaux-Arts on 31 March 1853, and made his Salon debut in 1853. He was awarded third class medals in 1859, 1861 and 1863 and was a member of the Committee of the Société des Artistes Français.

MUSEUMS AND GALLERIES:
AURILLAC: *Prodigal Son*.

SIRRICH, Christian
German, 17th century.
Active in Liegnitz (now Legnica, Poland).
Sculptor.

Sirrich also worked in Leipzig, Germany from 1682 to 1684.

SIRRY, Gazbeya
Egyptian, 20th century.
Born 1925, in Cairo.
Painter. Figures, scenes with figures.

Gazbeya Sirry taught painting at the institute of higher art education in Cairo. She won a scholarship for six years, and in 1952 she made a study trip to Rome. Her painting is representational, with a primitive tendency.

Sirry has taken part in collective exhibitions, including the São Paulo Biennale (1953, 1963); the Venice Biennale (1952, 1956, 1958, receiving the prize of honour in 1956); the Alexandria Biennale (1963, receiving the first prize for oil painting in the Egyptian section); and *Visages de l'Art Contemporain Égyptien* (*Aspects of Contemporary Egyptian Art*) at the Musée Galliera in Paris (1971). She often shows her works in solo exhibitions, such as in 1989 in Cairo.

BIBLIOGRAPHY:
Badr El-Din Abou Ghazy, *Visages de l'Art contemporain égyptien*, exhibition catalogue, Musée Galliera, Paris, 1971.

MUSEUMS AND GALLERIES:
ALEXANDRIA (MMA) - CAIRO (Egyptian MMA).

SIRTAINE, Albert
Belgian, 19th - 20th century.
Born 1868, in Verviers; died 1959.
Painter. Portraits, landscapes.
Sirtaine studied under Carpentier at the royal academy of fine arts in Liège and went on to exhibit his work at the Liège fine arts circle between 1892 and 1932.

Alb Sirtaine

MUSEUMS AND GALLERIES:
LIÈGE (Mus. de l'Art wallon): *Haystacks* - VERVIERS.

SIRUGO, Salvatore
Italian, 20th century.
Born 1920, in Sicily.
Painter.
Salvatore Sirugo served in the American army during the period 1942-1948. He has taken part in a number of group exhibitions, including: 1952, the Whitney Annual organised by the Whitney Museum of American Art in New York; 1953, Pennsylvania Academy Annual; 1958, Art Festival of Provincetown. He has also exhibited at the Museum of Contemporary Art in Houston, at the Howard Wise Gallery in Cleveland and the Art Institute in Kansas City. He was awarded the Emily Lowe Prize in 1951 and the Woodstock Foundation Prize in 1952.

SIRY, Sixtus. See **SYRI Sixtus**

SÍS, Peter
Czech, 20th - 21st century.
Born 1949, in Brno.
Active in the USA from 1982; naturalised US citizen.
Illustrator, film maker.
Peter Sís studied film-making and painting at the Prague academy of applied arts and the Royal College of Art, London. He began his career as a film maker, winning a Golden Bear at the 1980 West Berlin Film Festival. In 1982 he was sent by his government to Los Angeles to make a film for the 1984 Olympics. After the film was cancelled he was ordered to return home but decided to stay in the USA and applied for asylum. Moving to New York, he turned his talents to illustrating children's books and became an internationally honoured figure in that field. He also produced illustrations for magazines in the USA and abroad. In addition to his work as illustrator, Peter Sís designed posters and stage sets, and created murals. His work has been exhibited in Prague, London, Zurich, Hamburg, Los Angeles, and New York.

SISA, Jaime
Italian, 15th century.
Died 19 May 1489, in Messina.
Active in Barcelona.
Sculptor.

SISANTE, Juan
Spanish, 15th century.
Painter.
Active in Oropesa, New Castile, Juan Sisante also worked in Valencia in 1401.

SISCARA, Angela
Italian, 18th century.
Painter.
Angela Siscara was the daughter of Matteo Siscara and worked as Solimena's assistant.

SISCARA, Matteo
Italian, 18th century.
Born 1705, in Naples; died 1765.
Painter.
Matteo Siscara, the father of Angela Siscara and pupil of Andrea Asta, painted historical subjects and portraits.

SISCO, Louis Hercule, or Sixo
French, 19th century.
Born 1778, in Paris; died 24 September 1861, in Paris.
Engraver, illustrator.
Sisco was a pupil of R. F. Ingouf and P. Guérin. Using a burin on steel, he engraved works by Guérin, Gros and Menjaud; he also engraved vignettes and illustrations from the Classics. This artist exhibited at the Salon de Paris between 1824 and 1843.

SISCO VIDAL. See **VIDAL Francisco**

SISEL. See **ZIESEL**

SISLA, Master of La. See **MASTERS**

SISLEY, Alfred
British, 19th century.
Born 30 October 1839, in Paris, to British parents; died 29 January 1899, in Moret-sur-Loing (Seine-et-Marne).
Active in France.
Painter, engraver, lithographer. Landscapes.
Impressionist group.
Alfred Sisley's father, William Sisley, and his mother, Felicia Sell, were both English, and he retained British nationality throughout his life even though he spent little time in his country of origin. His father was a haberdashery import-export agent established in France who enjoyed a comfortable level of affluence and paid for his three children to have an excellent middle-class education. When Sisley was 18, his father directed him initially towards a career in commerce and sent him to London to improve his knowledge of English and begin to learn how to manage business affairs.

On his return to France, his father allowed him to frequent Gleyre's studio, where he met and became friends with Claude Monet, Auguste Renoir and Frédéric Bazille. Their meeting marked the beginning, for Sisley, of an artistic adventure of infinite consequence. Like Monet, Bazille and Renoir, he felt absolutely no affinity with Gleyre and merely passed through the school. Monet's strong personality and independence were the initial motivating force behind the decision of all four to leave Gleyre's studio. After one occasion on which Gleyre had rebuked him in a manner which he considered unjustified, Monet brought his friends together: 'Let us be off, away from here', he told them, 'this place is noxious, people here have no sincerity'. Sisley remained in close contact with his three fellow students. On Easter Day 1863, he went with them to Chailly near Fontainebleau; in 1865 he was to be found, like his three friends and Cézanne, at the Lejoisne Salon. They worked together, and together they admired Corot, Delacroix, Millet and Rousseau. One of Sisley's paintings, entitled *Chestnut Tree Walk at La Celle St-Cloud*, which dates from 1865 and is now preserved in the Petit Palais Museum, shows that in terms of technical skill he was capable of rivalling Corot and Daubigny even at this youthful stage; however, when the painting was exhibited at the 1866 Salon it went unnoticed.

In 1866 Sisley was in Marlotte, where he was joined by Renoir, and in 1867 he was in Honfleur, where Bazille painted his portrait. That same year he entered the Salon as a pupil of Corot. Durand-Ruel exhibited two of Sisley's paintings in London in 1871. At the heart of the new school which was gradually emerging, centred around the close-knit group of friends, Sisley nevertheless stood out for the intimacy of feeling in his paintings and for a palette that subtly recalled his British origins. He had initially practised painting as a pleasure rather than a profession, unconcerned with any idea of selling his work and cutting a privileged figure among his more needy friends because he had other sources of money. But in 1870 his father died suddenly and penniless, leaving Sisley without an allowance and with no resources other than what he could earn from his painting. A time of financial difficulty now began in which Sisley, who was married and had children, sought to provide for his family and himself, living in poverty from this point until his death.

The innovative nature of Sisley's work, like that of his friends, gradually became so apparent and so openly declared that these young artists could no longer think of presenting their works to the Salon, knowing full well in advance that they would never get through the door. Sisley and his friends then founded a society of 30 artists, taking the name Société anonyme des artistes peintres, sculpteurs et graveurs (The Limited Company of Artists: Painters, Sculptors and Engravers) and deciding to hold an independent exhibition at their own expense. The premises they chose comprised a suite of vast rooms occupied by the photographer Nadar at 35, Boulevard des Capucines in Paris. The group exhibition opened there on 15 April 1875 and created a public scandal. It marked a crucial date in the history of modern art, as it was at this point that a hostile columnist - aiming the term at the painters of the new school as an insult - gave them the sobriquet of *Impressionnistes,* a name they themselves then retained and wore as a badge of honour. Prior to this, their movement had only been known in artistic circles as the Batignolles School or the Café Guerbois Group (from the name of a café in Clichy where the painters used to meet before the war of 1870). Having become the Impressionists, and now more unsaleable than ever, the artists organised a public sale of their works in Paris the following year. This sale, held on 24 March 1875, was another event that has remained a red-letter day in the annals of history. The sale included 21 of Sisley's canvases, presented to the public in a catalogue with an introduction by Philippe Burty and expert assessment by Pillet. The event was accompanied by scenes which would be almost unbelievable today; on the day of the exhibition and during the sale Pillet requested police protection, fearing that the public's fury would render the auction impossible, and the proceedings were howled down by a roused and angry mob. Sisley's paintings found buyers only among a small circle of friends and at very low prices; the 21 canvases made 2,455 francs altogether between them, giving an average of little more than 100 francs for each. A second exhibition of these young painters' work, organised in 1876, was given the same disastrous reception as the first: every art critic, every wit and well-known journalist of the day inveighed against the new school as if with a single voice. Albert Wolff, an eminent contributor to a fashionable paper (*Le Figaro* of 3 April 1876) gave an account of the exhibition in these terms: 'The rue Le Peletier is surely a street of misfortune. After the fire at the Opéra, disaster has stuck the neighbourhood once more. An exhibition has just opened at Durand-Ruel's of *something that calls itself painting.* Some five or six madmen - including one madwoman - have come together to exhibit their work here; there are those who cannot contain their laughter at these things, but for my part I can scarcely contain my anguish'. The unhappy Impressionists, still hoping for a reversal of opinion, tried several more group exhibitions: in 1877 'in a large apartment on the first floor at 6, Rue Le Peletier' (*The Memoirs of Durand-Ruel*); in 1879 in the Avenue de l'Opéra; and in 1880 in the Rue des Pyramides. Sisley took part in every exhibition. The most turbulent was the 1877 exhibition, which was the occasion of an extraordinary explosion of hilarity and indignation. In order to understand the public's protracted rejection of this new art-form to which they were so opposed, one has to consider the spirit of the day and see the events through very different eyes. Painting such as this seemed in those days, to bring even politics into question, these innovators appeared to the public to be the disciples of Courbet - even though their style was the antithesis of realism as it was understood at the time - and Courbet's works were at that time (after the Commune of 1871) being violently rejected. Political passions inflamed a desire to discredit any works that even seemed to draw on his example. People felt that this young school, the Impressionists, were imbued with a subversive spirit and constituted a danger to society.

Moreover, this new painting surprised; it terrified the eye with the unaccustomed clarity and brightness of its tones and thus plunged the public into genuine confusion and dismay. Art critics strove for ten years to discover or formulate an acceptable definition and explanation of this new art without ever succeeding in doing so. The essential escaped them - proof of which could be found in the fact that the definitions they proposed differed from one aesthetician to another; each explanation contradicted the next and nothing specific ever emerged with any clarity from the morass of discussion. It was rare for anyone to see Sisley and Monet as they were to be perceived later, or to see them for what they really were - as the precursors of Seurat, of Fauvism and of Informal art, and as the liberators of the interrelations of colours. One art critic and writer, Armand Silvestre, did nevertheless write of the Impressionists as early as 1873 that 'their secret lies wholly in the minute observation of the relations between tones'.

And what of Sisley himself amidst all this tumult? He came close to dying in the most abject poverty, and was so destitute that he was reduced to selling his canvases for 25 or 30 francs. He was fortunate enough to count among his friends a confectioner and restaurateur named Murer who had an establishment on the Boulevard Voltaire and who loved painting, giving painters a warm welcome. Sisley and Renoir found the restaurant's doors were always open to them, and they paid their patron and provider in paintings for the meals he gave them. But for Murer, Sisley would have gone hungry. Fragments of correspondence, in which his misery and despair can be read between the lines of his British discretion and reserve, reveal that in 1878 he sought an art lover or enlightened art dealer 'who would give him 500 francs a month to live on for six months'; he offered 30 canvases in exchange, thus setting the price of each one at 100 francs - but he found no one to accept such a deal. The business world was in economic crisis at the time and Durand-Ruel was in difficulties, forcing him to abandon his artist friends; at the Hoschedé sale held by court order on 5 and 6 June 1878 the 13 Sisleys offered for sale were knocked down at prices ranging from 21 to 251 francs. They included one of the paintings of the *Flood at Port-Marly.* As always with Impressionist painting at this time, the public who attended the sale were loud and unruly, and to cap it all - whether by bad luck or malice, on purpose or by accident - a number of the canvases, which no one had even troubled to frame, were presented to the public back-to-front and upside-down: 'it was fashionable at the time to maintain that they were just as incomprehensible one way up as the other', wrote Durand-Ruel in his *Memoirs.*

During these years, Sisley never went far from Paris; the sites of Île-de-France were certainly his favourite subject matter and, in thrall to their finely shaded skies, he almost always lived either near the capital or in Paris itself. Before the 1870 war he lived at Louveciennes and Bougival, then after the war and until 1877 in Marly. His views of the Seine at Port-Marly date from this period, together with his paintings of the orchards and lanes of Louveciennes - the works in which his talent reached its greatest heights. From 1877 to 1879 Sisley lived in Sèvres, where he painted the Seine by Meudon and by St Cloud, the river banks, water and more water. In 1879 he settled in Moret, where he remained almost all the time thereafter, although he did leave Moret for Les Sablons on 24 August 1883.

Sisley's travels included a trip to England in 1874 in the company of Faure, baritone at the Opéra, from which he returned with views of the Thames at Hampton Court. In 1894 he painted in Normandy, near Rouen, and then in 1897 he went to Britain again from May to October and stayed on the Welsh coast near Swansea and Cardiff, in Longland and in Pennant where he painted the cliffs and the sea. These were tourist trips and brief stays, however - Sisley only felt at home in France and did not much care for crossing the Channel. In 1895 he decided to apply for French nationality by naturalisation and took the first steps towards this, but his file was incomplete and a number of documents concerning his civil status were missing. The application was shelved, and Sisley died before he could become French by law even though in his heart he was French already.

His financial situation improved somewhat during the 1880s and his work began to sell better. After 1883 Durand-Ruel, his fortunes re-floated by his success in New York, took an interest in the Impressionists once more and took their work in hand again, but he now held only successive individual exhibitions of his painters' work - the days of the great group exhibitions were definitely over. Sisley was attached to the Salon exhibition structure, however, and turned towards the new, nonconformist society called the Société Nationale des Beaux-Arts (National Society of Fine Arts) that had just been founded outside the purview of the Société des Artistes Français and which was holding a sort of second Salon for the first time at the Champ de Mars in 1890. He was given a favourable reception, and presented groups of seven or eight paintings at each of the 1894, 1895, 1896 and 1898 exhibitions, becoming significantly better known by taking part in these popular exhibitions.

Sisley left some notes on the art of landscape painting as he saw it which he wrote in 1892 to his friend Tavernier: 'there is always *a best-loved corner* in a canvas', he wrote to Tavernier, and according to Sisley 'this is the where the centre of the theme is, and this is, in a way, the point to which the artist must *lead* the spectator. Life and movement are necessary; they depend on the emotion of the artist who must modify his style in accordance with this emotion and not always use the same style indiscriminately. The sky is made up of planes - foreground, middle distance and background - *just as the ground is*, and contributes to the painting's movement and effect.' The style that Sisley created for himself in the 1870s was eminently well-suited to conveying riverside landscapes, the surface of the water and soft-clouded mother-of-pearl skies. He was the consummate poet of the open air; with his limited means and in his minor order, he achieved an elusive, absolute perfection. Later, after the year 1880, Sisley depicted themes and subject matter with a little more dark around them, less bathed in light. Some of the views of the *Bridge at Moret* or the *Moret Church* of 1894, housed in the Detroit Museum, are excellent examples of this second style. His need for a strong, dynamic element now found favoured subject matter in the form of architectural motifs, approached with an insistence that sometimes bordered on dryness. The contrast between two views of the Loing, dating from 1892 and housed in the Louvre in Paris, shows the uneven success that characterised his last works: one (in the Camondo Collection) is a beautiful painting in which intense colours cleverly balance light and shade, while the other is pretty and precious but stylistically too evasive. The paintings Sisley executed during the last years of his life are generally considered - however favourably inclined the analysis - to be poorer in quality than those he executed between 1870 and 1880. He became more concerned with issues of technique, with abiding by the rules of some unknown pictorial system to which he confined himself. Rather as occurred with the ageing Pissarro, the freshness and vigour of Sisley's earlier works faded, though his eye always remained that of a colourist. In his hermitage at Moret he remained until the end, despite his failing powers, the most exquisite poet of poplar trees, village rooftops and bridges mirrored in running water. He lived a very isolated life.

Relatively little is known about Sisley's character and personal life. It is true that towards the end of his life he broke off all contact with Durand-Ruel, and it is also true that he complained on a number of occasions about a cabal organised against him after 1890 - particularly in a letter addressed to Mirbeau and dated 25 May 1892: 'you have made yourself the champion of a coterie who would be well-pleased to see me utterly cast down. They will not have that pleasure, and you will be well-served for your unjust and deceitful criticism' (Mirbeau had devoted an unpleasant critique to Sisley in *Le Figaro*). Gustave Geoffroy left an account of a visit he made to Sisley in Moret in 1894, where he found him full of a dignified sadness, relinquishing his disappointed hopes. Once more it was Tavernier who proved to be the critic closest to him in his last years, and who most nurtured his memory after Sisley's death: 'I could not desire a better critical appreciation than you have made of me, and I shall never be interpreted with as much talent...', Sisley wrote to him.

A private exhibition of Sisley's work was held in Georges Petit's gallery in 1897 and public favour seemed to smile on him at last. Art lovers and faithful friends such as Charpentier, Decap and Viau loaned paintings that belonged to them in order to complete the ensemble, and the critics in the press were less stinting with their praise than before. But these were the last months of Sisley's life; he was suffering from throat cancer and could no longer move his head due to 'the swelling of his neck, the oesophagus, the gullet and near the ear' (letter to Georges Viau dated 31 December 1898); he felt 'at the end of his strength' and asked for a doctor but was tormented by the worry of the fee 'which must not exceed 100 to 200 francs'. Viau took a doctor Marie to see him and ineffectual treatment was prescribed. On 13 January 1899 Monet answered a call to come and make his farewells as Sisley was dying. He died on 29 January. His death went unnoticed, and his funeral was attended by Monet, Renoir, Cazin and Tavernier.

Sisley's death, however, triggered an abrupt change in the fortune of his works. Three months after his death, 27 canvases were sold on behalf of his heirs at the Salle Petit in rue de Sèze: for the first time, art lovers fought over them and the auction was so lively that the prices of the paintings rose to give a sum total of over 110,000 francs. Immediately, collectors began to display a passion for Sisley's paintings and prices inflated with unheard-of speed. On 6 March 1900 when Tavernier's collection was sold, one of his landscapes, *The Flood*, was sold at 43,000 francs (the Count of Camondo, who bought it, later donated it to the Louvre).

Sisley is frequently represented in group or thematic exhibitions, including: *Impression: Painting Quickly in France, 1860-1890* at the National Gallery in London in 2000. Of the individual exhibitions, the most noteworthy include a major retrospective of his work in 1992 which was organised jointly by the Royal Academy of Arts in London, the Musée d'Orsay in Paris and the Walters Art Gallery in Baltimore, and another Sisley exhibition held at the Museum of Fine Arts in Lyons in 2002.

Sisley. 72.

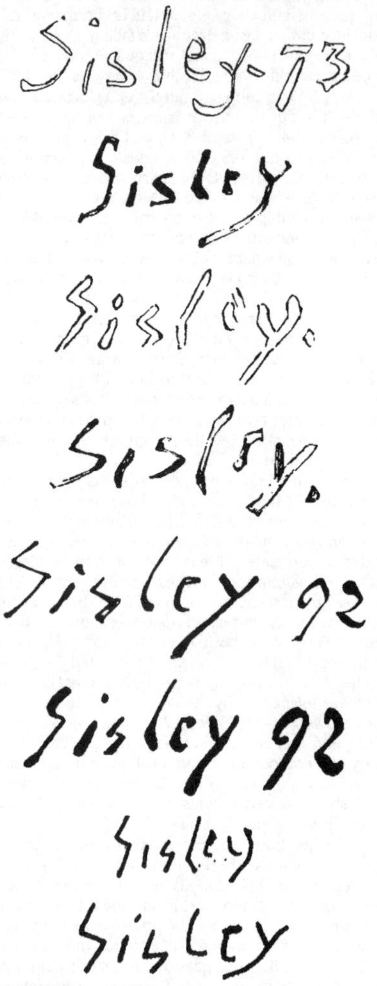

BIBLIOGRAPHY:

Watson, F., *Alfred Sisley*, The Arts, London, 1921. Geffroy, Gustave, *Alfred Sisley*, G. Crès, Paris, 1923. Sisley, C., *'Alfred Sisley'* in *Burlington Magazine*, periodical, London, 1949. Gotthard, Jedlicka, *Alfred Sisley*, periodical, A. Scherz, Bern, 1949. Daulte, F./Durand-Ruel, Ch., *Catalogue raisonné de l'œuvre peint d'Alfred Sisley*, periodical, Gal. Durand-Ruel, Paris, 1959. Daulte, F., *Alfred Sisley. Catalogue raisonné de l'œuvre peint*, Gal. Durand-Ruel, Lausanne, 1959. Daulte, F., *Sisley. Paysages*, La Bibliothèque des Arts, Paris, 1968. Lassaigne, Jacques/Patin, S., *Alfred Sisley*, Nouvelles Éditions Françaises, Paris, 1983. *Alfred Sisley*, exhibition catalogue, Yale University Press, London, Réunion des musées nationaux, Paris, 1992. *Frédéric Bazille et ses amis impressionnistes*, exhibition catalogue, Musée Fabre, Montpellier, Réunion des musées nationaux, Paris, 1992. Dampérat, M.H./Cahn, I./Richet, L., *'Alfred Sisley. L'Exposition du musée d'Orsay'* in *Beaux-Arts Magazine, special issue*, periodical, Paris, 1992. *Alfred Sisley*, exhibition catalogue, Musée d'Orsay, Paris, 1992. Couldrey, Vivienne, *Alfred Sisley: The English Impressionist*, David & Charles, Newton Abbot, 1992. Shone, Richard, *Sisley*, Phaidon, London, 1992. *Alfred Sisley, 1839-1899*, Yale University Press/Royal Academy of Arts, New Haven and London, 1992. Bretell, Richard R., *Impression: Painting Quickly in France, 1860-1890*, exhibition catalogue, Yale University Press, New Haven, 2000. *Alfred Sisley*, exhibition catalogue, Musée des Beaux-Arts, Lyons, 2002. Shone, Richard, *Sisley*, Phaidon, Paris, 2004.

MUSEUMS AND GALLERIES:

AGEN: *September Morning* - ALGIERS: *Moret Bridge in Winter* - BERLIN (Nationalgal.): *Snow in a Village* - BERN (Kunstmus.): *Langland Bay Storrs Rock, Morning* (1897) - BREMEN (Kunsthalle): *A Lane near a Small Town* - BRUSSELS (MAM): *Landscape* (1885) - BUCHAREST (Muz. National de Arta al României): *Moret Church* - CHARLOTTENLUND (Ordrupgaard): *Idle Barges on the Loing Canal at St Mammès* (1874) - COLOGNE (Wallraf-Richartz Mus.): *Hampton Court Bridge* (1874) - COPENHAGEN: *Ferry to the Ile-de-la-Loge - Flood* (1872); *The Machine at Marly* (1873) - DENVER (AM): *The Seine Grenelle* - DETROIT: *Moret Church* - DOUAI: *Banks of the Loing River* - FORT WORTH (Kimbell AM): *Drying Nets* (1872, oil on canvas) - FRANKFURT AM MAIN (Städel): *Banks of the Seine in Autumn* - GENEVA (MAH): *At St Mammès* (1884); *The Loing at St Mammès* (1885) - GRENOBLE (Mus. de Grenoble): *View of Montmartre, from the Cité des Fleurs, Les Batignolles* - HAMBURG (Kunsthalle): *The Wheat-Field* (1873) - HANOVER: *View of the English Coast* - LE HAVRE (Mus. Malraux): *Barges on a Canal* - LILLE (MBA): *The Seine at Suresnes* (1880) - LONDON (Courtauld Institute of Art): *Snow at Louveciennes* (c. 1874, oil on canvas) - LONDON (Tate Collection): *The Bridge at Sèvres* (1877, oil on canvas); *The Path to the Old Ferry at By* (1880, oil on canvas); *The Small Meadows in Spring* (1880, oil on canvas) - LOS ANGELES (Getty Mus.): *The Road from Versailles to St Germain* (1875, oil on canvas) - LYONS: *Landscape* (1870); *The Seine at Marly* (1876) - MANNHEIM (Städtische Kunsthalle): *A Road in Marly* (1871); *Market Place* (1876) - MELBOURNE (Nat. Gal. of Victoria): *Hills Behind St Nicaise; Straw Ricks at Moret* (1891) - NANTES (MBA): *The Banks of the Loing* - NEW YORK (Metropolitan Mus. of Art): *The Bridge at Villeneuve-la-Garenne* (1872); *Sahurs Meadows in the Morning Sun* (1894) - OTTERLO (Kröller-Müller Mus.): *The Brickworks; Landscape Near Paris* (1879) - PARIS (Mus. d'Orsay): *Little Square in Argenteuil; Banks of the Seine; Still-life with Heron* (1867); *View of the Canal St Martin* (1870); *Footbridge in Argenteuil* (1872); *Square in Argenteuil* (1872); *Island of La Grande-Jatte* (1873); *The Sèvres Road* (1873); *Boats at Bougival Lock* (1873); *The Village of Voisins* (1874); *Regatta at Molesey* (1874); *The Forge at Marly-le-Roi* (1875); *Snow at Marly-le-Roi* (1875); *The Flood at Port-Marly* (1876); *The Boat During the Flood* (1876); *The Seine at Suresnes* (1877); *The Snow at Louveciennes* (1878); *Resting on the Banks of the Stream* (1878); *The Banks of the Loing* (c. 1879); *The Seine Seen From the Hillsides of By* (1881); *A Street in Louveciennes* (1883); *St Mammès* (1885); *An Edge of the Forest in Spring* (1885); *Trembles et Acacias* (1889); *The Loing Canal* (1892); *The Bridge at Moret* (1893); *Landscape: Riverbank* (1897, pastel) - PARIS (Mus. de l'Orangerie): *The Maubuisson Road at Louveciennes* (1875) - PARIS (Mus. du Petit Palais): *The Tug; Avenue of Chestnut Trees near La Celle St Cloud* (1865); *The Church at Moret, Evening* (1894) - PORTLAND, ME, USA (MA): *Moret-sur-Loing* (1888) - RENNES (MBA): *The Seine at St Cloud* - RHEIMS (MBA): *La Rade de Cardiff* (1897) - RIEHEN (Fondation Beyeler): *Banks of the Loing* (1890) - ROUEN (MBA): *The Church at Moret, Bright Sunlight* (1893); *The Path by the Edge of the Water in Sahurs, Normandy: Evening* (1894); *The Flood* - ST PETERSBURG (Hermitage): *Village by the Seine* (1872); *The Embankment at St Mammès* (1884) - WASHINGTON DC (NGA): *Flood at Port-Marly* (1872, oil on canvas); *Boulevard Héloïse, Argenteuil* (1872, oil on canvas); *The Banks of the Oise* (1877-1878, oil on canvas) -

WINTERTHUR (Kunstmus.): *Under Hampton Court Bridge* (1874) - WUPPERTAL (Von der Heydt Mus.): *The Canal.*

AUCTION RECORDS:

PARIS, 1874, *Bougival,* FRF 380. PARIS, 13 Jan 1874, *St Germain Road, Near Bougival,* FRF 575; *The Weir at Marly,* FRF 520. PARIS, 1877, *Boat Unloading Cargo of Coal,* FRF 126; *Boat at Bas-Meudon,* FRF 130; *Banks of the Seine,* FRF 120. PARIS, 1888, *Riverbank,* FRF 350; *The Winding Road,* FRF 365. PARIS, 29 April 1889, *The Loing at Moret* (pastel) FRF 2,995; *The Railway Tracks* (pastel) FRF 820. PARIS, 1890, *The Orchard* (1872) FRF 1,150; *The Bridge at Moret,* FRF 300; *Banks of the Loing,* FRF 300. PARIS, 1890, *Île St Denis,* FRF 1,700; *View of the Seine,* FRF 290; *Effet de neige (Snow Effect,* FRF 380; *The Seine at Suresnes,* FRF 400. PARIS, 1892, *The Seine Near Paris,* FRF 1,300. PARIS, 1892, *The Flood,* FRF 1,000. PARIS, 1893, *The Loing at St Mammès,* FRF 3,050; *Line Fisherman,* FRF 2,500; *The Bridge at Sèvres,* FRF 1,420; *At the Entrance to the Woods,* FRF 1,110. PARIS, 1894, *View of the Seine at Marly,* FRF 1,550; *View of the Thames at Hampton Court,* FRF 1,350; *Evening,* FRF 1,100. NEW YORK, 1895, *The Gué de l'Épine,* FRF 1,025; *Ruins of Fortifications at Moret,* FRF 1,025. PARIS, 1895, *The Weir at St Mammès,* FRF 760; *Gardens,* FRF 650; *Morning, Edge of the Woods in June,* FRF 600; *The Weir at Suresnes, in Spate,* FRF 710; *White Frost,* FRF 710; *Autumn Landscape,* FRF 860; *View of Moret,* FRF 610. PARIS, 1897, *The Flood,* FRF 3,100; *The Bridge at Moret,* FRF 1,250; *Louveciennes Road, Snow,* FRF 4,600; *The First Snow,* FRF 1,150; *Between Moret and St Mammès,* FRF 1,650; *Effet de neige (Snow,* FRF 2,200; *Autumn,* FRF 2,500. PARIS, 10 May 1897, *The Seine at Suresnes,* FRF 2,350; *The Machine at Marly,* FRF 980. PARIS, 1899, *The First White Frost,* FRF 9,000; *Effet de neige (Snow,* FRF 6,050; *The Meadow,* FRF 6,000; *The Setting Sun,* FRF 6,550. COLOGNE, 1899, *Banks of the Seine,* FRF 3,937. PARIS, 1899, *The Seine at Billancourt,* FRF 6,000. PARIS, 1899, *Bridge on the Briare Canal: Hoarfrost,* FRF 4,500; *The Bridge at Moret and Mills: Snow,* FRF 5,000; *The Old Gretz Road, Evening,* FRF 4,000; *An Avenue in Moret,* FRF 5,150; *Moret at Sunset,* FRF 5,700; *Huts by the Loing, Evening,* FRF 9,000; *Sunrise in November,* FRF 6,020; *Boats from Berry, on the Loing Canal in Spring,* FRF 4,600; *La Rade de Cardiff* FRF 4,050; *Lady's Cove Before the Storm,* FRF 3,550; *The Goose Pond* (drawing) FRF 650; *The Cowherd* (drawing) FRF 400. PARIS, 1899, *Road Near Marly,* FRF 9,300; *The Bell-Tower in Noisy-le-Roi,* FRF 8,500; *The Bridge at Suresnes,* FRF 5,700; *Near Louveciennes: Snow,* FRF 5,600; *The Wooden Bridge in Marly,* FRF 4,700. PARIS, 25 March 1899, *View of St Cloud, Banks of the Seine,* FRF 4,000. PARIS, 24 April 1899, *Snow,* FRF 3,700. PARIS, 29 April 1899, *The Railway Tracks* (pastel) FRF 820. PARIS, 1900, *Spring Sunshine, a Bend in the Loing,* FRF 11,600; *Rainy Spring,* FRF 3,700; *The Embankment at Moret* (pastel) FRF 660. PARIS, 1900, *A Road in Louveciennes,* FRF 7,000; *A View of Moret in Winter,* FRF 6,900. PARIS, 1900, *The Flood at Port-Marly,* FRF 15,350; *Moret,* FRF 15,000; *The St Germain Road,* FRF 8,000; *The Terrace at St Germain,* FRF 12,000; *The Highroad,* FRF 6,800. PARIS, 6 March 1900, *The Flood,* FRF 43,000; *Street in Ville-d'Avray,* FRF 6,600; *Straw Rick in October,* FRF 7,100; *Sèvres Road,* FRF 7,600; *Versailles Road,* FRF 8,050; *The Banks of the Loing,* FRF 9,050. PARIS, 27 April 1900, *The Loing in Spate at Moret, Snowy Weather,* FRF 6,100; *The Seine at Bougival,* FRF 4,305; *The Banks of the Loing, Near Moret,* FRF 10,100. PARIS, 15 June 1900, *The Bridge at Moret,* FRF 3,905. PARIS, 23 June 1900, *Moret,* FRF 10,000; *The Field,* FRF 7,000. PARIS, 7 Feb 1901, *The Woodcock Reserve,* FRF 4,600. PARIS, 3 May 1901, *St Cloud,* FRF 8,500; *Hampton,* FRF 8,700; *The Bridge at Moret,* FRF 10,100; *White Frost,* FRF 15,100; *Marly Bridge Before the Flood,* FRF 13,000; *The Flood,* FRF 8,900. PARIS, 27-28 May 1902, *The Bridge,* FRF 9,100. PARIS, 8 June 1903, *Winter,* FRF 9,000; *Setting Sun,* FRF 11,000. PARIS, 8-9 May 1904, *The Hillsides of Argenteuil,* FRF 40,100; *Watering Place at Marly,* FRF 12,500. PARIS, 4 May 1906, *The Bridge at Moret,* FRF 10,100. PARIS, 3 May-1 June 1906, *View of Moret, Summer,* FRF 11,000; *The Watering Place at Marly,* FRF 8,000; *Snow in Argenteuil,* FRF 16,000. PARIS, 1-2 March 1920, *Villeneuve-la-Garenne,* FRF 37,200; *St Martin's Summer,* FRF 16,300; *Gennevilliers Road,* FRF 14,100; *The Village at the Edge of the Wood, Autumn,* FRF 17,500; *Street in Louveciennes,* FRF 19,000. PARIS, 4-5 March 1921, *The Bridge at Moret,* FRF 40,100; *On the St-Mammès Road, Morning,* FRF 25,000; *The Apple Tree in Flower,* FRF 19,100; *The Bridge at Moret,* FRF 20,100; *The Bridge at Sèvres,* FRF 24,100; *View of Moret,* FRF 21,000; *The Seine at Billancourt,* FRF 20,600; *The Alley,* FRF 15,000; *Houses Beside the Highroad,* FRF 15,100; *The Rowers,* FRF 30,000. PARIS, 18 April 1921, *Spring Landscape,* FRF 9,600; *The Bridge at Moret,* FRF 11,000; *The Inn,* FRF 16,500; *Village Street in Dull Weather,* FRF 26,900; *The Loing at Moret,* FRF 25,000. PARIS, 30 June 1921, *Moret,* FRF 31,000; *Coastline in Wales,* FRF 10,200; *The Bridge at Moret, Snow,* FRF 21,000; *The Banks of the Loing,* FRF 25,700; *Coasts of England,* FRF 10,500; *The Banks of the Seine,* FRF 24,500; *View of a Village in Winter* (pastel) FRF 3,500; *Cows Grazing by the Seine* (pastel) FRF 1,220. PARIS, 26 Oct 1922, *Countrywoman, Facing Away; A Winding Road; Beating Down the Nuts* (three pastels) FRF 520. PARIS, 20 Nov 1922, *The Hillsides of La Bouille; Sahurs Meadow,* FRF 16,100; *The Banks of the Loing, in Summer,* FRF 14,000; *The Quarry,* FRF 3,350. PARIS, 25 May 1923, *The Lesson,* FRF 5,300; *Summer Afternoon,* FRF 34,000; *Willows and Poplar Trees on the Banks of the Loing, Morning,* FRF 25,500; *Path Beside the Water,* FRF 25,000; *September Morning,* FRF 30,500; *Riverbanks,* FRF 17,500; *The Loing and Moret Church,* FRF 29,000; *The Steamboats,* FRF 55,000; *Summer Day,* FRF 19,100; *Village by the Water,* FRF 10,000; *Moret,* FRF 50,000; *The Footbridge, Morning in Late September,* FRF 30,000; *Lighters on the Loing,* FRF 26,500; *The Banks of the Loing,* FRF 30,000; *The Bridge at Moret,* FRF 37,000; *A Clearing,* FRF 12,500; *The Village Road,* FRF 19,100; *The Bridge at Moret,* FRF 15,100; *The Loing at Moret,* FRF 42,100; *St Cloud,* FRF 43,100; *Between Veneux and By, December Morning* (1882, oil on canvas, 21 1/4 x 28 3/4 ins / 54 x 73 cm) FRF 26,100. PARIS, 11 June 1924, *Barge on the Seine at St Mammès,* FRF 33,700. PARIS, 6 Nov 1924, *Landscape at Louveciennes,* FRF 20,500; *Morning in Moret, in May,* FRF 49,000; *The Orvanne Bridge in Moret,* FRF 78,000. PARIS, 14-15 Dec 1925, *The Orvanne and the Loing Canal in Winter,* FRF 35,500. PARIS, 7 May 1926, *Geese by the River, Summer Landscape* (pastel) FRF 9,200. PARIS, 10 May 1926, *Near Moret, Autumn,* FRF 12,600; *The Highroad in Autumn, Near Moret,* FRF 16,900. PARIS, 2 June 1926, *The House in Moret,* FRF 43,000. PARIS, 25 April 1927, *The Kitchen Garden,* FRF 1,380. LONDON, 29 April 1927, *Riverbanks,* GBP 525; *The Sèvres Bridge,* GBP 840. LONDON, 13 May 1927, *Riverbanks in Moret,* GBP 367. PARIS, 30-31 May 1927, *Sunrise over the Loing in Flood Season,* FRF 50,000. PARIS, 1-3 June 1927, *By the Sea,* FRF 24,000. PARIS, 3 June 1927, *The Village,* FRF 5,800. PARIS, 9 June 1927, *Riverbanks, Snow,* FRF 34,100. PARIS, 29-30 June 1927, *The Seine at St Mammès,* FRF 37,100. LONDON, 28-29 July 1927, *Snowy Weather,* GBP 504. PARIS, 29 Oct 1927, *Landscape,* FRF 2,200. PARIS, 21 Jan 1928, *Landscape, View Taken on the Banks of the Seine Between Moret and St Mammès,* FRF 60,000. PARIS, 23 June 1928, *Moret Church,* FRF 111,000; *Snowy Weather in Veneux,* FRF 115,000; *Landscape with Hillsides, Near Paris,* FRF 54,000. PARIS, 3 Dec 1928, *Interior, Farmhouse,* FRF 10,500. PARIS, 20 April 1929, *Five Drawings,* FRF 7,800. PARIS, 24 May 1929, *The Mill at Moret,* FRF 55,000. PARIS, 6 June 1929, *St Pierre Church,* FRF 4,400. PARIS, 29 Nov 1929, *Moret Landscape,* FRF 47,000. PARIS, 6 Feb 1930, *The Bois des Roches (Rock Wood),* FRF 58,100. PARIS, 11 March 1931, *The Loing at Moret,* FRF 78,000; *The Seine near St Cloud,* FRF 61,000.

NEW YORK, 12 Nov 1931, *View of Moret*, USD 1,300. PARIS, 13 Feb 1932, *The House at Moret*, FRF 24,500. LONDON, 11 May 1932, *Stream Running Down to the Valley*, GBP 110. PARIS, 25 May 1932, *Moret-sur-Loing, Dull Weather*, FRF 36,000. PARIS, 15 Dec 1932, *Village by the Seine*, FRF 41,000; *Frost*, FRF 31,000; *Indian Summer, by the Sea*, FRF 24,000. PARIS, 2 June 1933, *Landscape, View Taken Beside the Seine*, FRF 44,300. PARIS, 18 Nov 1933, *At Pasture* (watercolour) FRF 1,700. PARIS, 15 Dec 1933, *The Mill at Moret, November Morning*, FRF 12,000. PARIS, 18 Jan 1934, *The Road from Moret to St Mammès*, FRF 23,100; *The Canal Banks at St Mammès*, FRF 4,500. PARIS, 16 May 1934, *Watering Place at Marly, in Winter*, FRF 17,600; *Meadow Beside the Loing*, FRF 23,050; *The Veneux-Nadon Road in Spring*, FRF 31,100. PARIS, 9 March 1935, *Houses Beside the Loing, Morning, Overcast Weather*, FRF 21,000. PARIS, 20 March 1935, *The Duck Pond in Louveciennes*, FRF 20,500; *Banks of the Seine at La Roche-Guyon* (pastel) FRF 9,600. PARIS, 28 June 1935, *The Seine at Sahurs, Near Rouen, Summer Morning*, FRF 4,400. PARIS, 10 Feb 1936, *Beside the Loing*, FRF 16,900; *Snow, View Taken from the Station in Moret* (pastel) FRF 9,200; *Garden in Moret in Winter* (pastel) FRF 6,350; *The Loing Canal at St Mammès*, FRF 36,500. PARIS, 17 March 1936, *Summer Afternoon*, FRF 60,000; *September Morning in St Mammès*, FRF 53,100. PARIS, 23 June 1936, *Lady's Cove Before the Storm*, FRF 17,500. LONDON, 9 Dec 1936, *March Snow*, GBP 140. PARIS, 23 April 1937, *The Goose Pond* (pastel) FRF 10,350. LONDON, 23 June 1937, *River Scene*, GBP 210. PARIS, 23 Nov 1937, *Moret*, FRF 45,000. PARIS, 29 Nov 1937, *Moret - Sunrise*, FRF 45,000. PARIS, 1 June 1938, *Les Noyers, Sunset, November*, FRF 58,000. PARIS, 9 June 1938, *The Apple Orchard* (colouring pencil) FRF 2,600. PARIS, 18 Feb 1939, *Bridge at Moret in Autumn*, FRF 150,500. PARIS, 13 March 1939, *Winter Afternoon in Les Sablons*, FRF 45,000. PARIS, 12 May 1939, *Canal-Boat Harbour in St Mammès*, FRF 60,000; *The Bridge at Moret*, FRF 60,000. PARIS, 19 Jan 1940, *View of the Seine*, FRF 136,500. PARIS, 7 Feb 1941, *Lighters at St Mammès* (1885) FRF 108,000. PARIS, 5 March 1941, *In the Fields* (two drawings in colouring pencil) FRF 780; *Strolling* (drawing in colouring pencil) FRF 480. PARIS, 20 June 1941, *Strolling* (pastel) FRF 350. LONDON, 26 June 1941, *St Maurier Boat Yard*, GBP 315. PARIS, 6 March 1942, *Riverbank*, FRF 508,000. LONDON, 27 March 1942, *Riverbank*, GBP 504. NEW YORK, May 1942, *The Loing Canal*, USD 3,500. PARIS, 11 May 1942, *The Garden*, FRF 308,000. PARIS, 24 June 1942, *Washerwoman; Countryman; Countrywoman* (three sketches in colouring pencil) FRF 5,000; *The Seine Valley Seen from the Terraces of St Germain-en-Laye* (1875) FRF 995,000. NEW YORK, 10 Oct 1942, *The Loing and the Hillsides of St Nicaise*, USD 2,800. NEW YORK, 3 Dec 1942, *The Bridge at Moret*, USD 2,700. PARIS, 11 Dec 1942, *The Loing at Moret* (1885) FRF 1,205,000; *St Mammès Road* (1895) FRF 1,200,000; *White Frost, Evening* (1888) FRF 700,000. NEW YORK, 25 Feb 1943, *The Plain*, USD 1,600; *The Bridge at Moret*, USD 2,300. PARIS, 12 March 1943, *The Seine Seen from the Hillsides of By*, FRF 361,000; *Waves* (colouring pencil) FRF 4,100. PARIS, 7 April 1943, *The Artist's House at Moret-sur-Loing* (1892, drawing) FRF 27,600. PARIS, 21 May 1943, *Winter*, FRF 86,100. PARIS, 2 June 1943, *Flood in Moret* (1889, lead pencil) FRF 6,700. PARIS, 23 June 1943, *The Dale*, FRF 460,000. PARIS, 20 March 1944, *The Artist's House in Marly* (pastel, from the Dietsh-Sisley succession) FRF 30,100; *The Little Lodge* (pastel, same provenance) FRF 30,100. NEW YORK, 20 April 1944, *The Loing as it Meets the Seine*, USD 4,100. LONDON, 28 June 1944, *Spring Landscape*, GBP 295. NEW YORK, 22 Nov 1944, *Landscape at Moret*, USD 1,700. PARIS, 8 Feb 1945, *The Garden in Autumn*, FRF 800,000. PARIS, 26 Feb 1945, *Gypsy Hovels Near the Loing* (1896) FRF 500,000. NEW YORK, 12 April 1945, *The Fountain Walk at Veneux-Nadon*, USD 5,000. NEW YORK, 17 May 1945, *The Railway Embankment*, USD 3,000; *At Louveciennes*, USD 2,800; *The St Germain Road*, USD 4,000; *Remains of Old Fortifications at Moret*, USD 1,250. PARIS, 25 May 1945, *The Painters in the Forest* (c. 1870, painting) FRF 90,000. PARIS, 25 June 1945, *The Artist's Garden* (1892, watercolour) FRF 23,100. NEW YORK, 1 May 1946, *St Mammès* (pastel) USD 825; *Bridge on the Orvanne*, USD 900. PARIS, July 1946, *Orchard Near Louveciennes* (1873) FRF 560,000. PARIS, 18 June 1947, *The Exhibition of '89* (pen drawing) FRF 20,000. PARIS, 8 Dec 1948, *Study of Barge and Horse* (colouring pencil) FRF 7,800. PARIS, 22 Dec 1948, *Washerwomen* (drawing heightened with pastel) FRF 8,500. PARIS, 29 April 1949, *Reading by Lamplight* (drawing) FRF 18,000. PARIS, 22 June 1949, *Geese and Countrywomen* (pencil, pages of sketches) FRF 10,000. GENEVA, 5 Nov 1949, *Sisley's Garden* (pastel) CHF 1,600. PARIS, 17 Nov 1949, *Path in the Countryside in Autumn* (1885) FRF 1,005,000. PARIS, 28 Nov 1949, *Riverbank* (pastel) FRF 105,000; *Houses Beside the River* (pastel) FRF 98,000. NEW YORK, 16 Dec 1949, *The Quai Malaquais (Malaquais Quay), Paris* (1873) USD 1,600. PARIS, 20 March 1950, *Foggy Morning, the Welsh Coast* (colouring pencil) FRF 41,000. NEW YORK, 20 April 1950, *Fortifications at Moret* (1888) USD 2,000. PARIS, 21 April 1950, *Riverbank* (colouring pencil) FRF 52,000. PARIS, 5 July 1950, *Barges; Tow-Horse* (lead and coloured pencil, study) FRF 8,000. GENEVA, 17 May 1951, *House Beside the Loing* (1875) CHF 22,000. PARIS, 21 May 1951, *The Pink House*, FRF 1,200,000. NEW YORK, 23 May 1951, *The Rowers* (1877) USD 7,700. PARIS, 14 May 1952, *The Banks of the Loing at Moret, in the Morning*, FRF 4,800,000. PARIS, 4 April 1957, *The Highroad, Morning*, FRF 3,600,000. LONDON, 10 July 1957, *The Seine in Paris, Pont de Grenelle*, GBP 9,000. NEW YORK, 7 Nov 1957, *The Loing at Moret*, USD 37,000. PARIS, 10 June 1958, *Cottage in Les Sablons*, FRF 5,000,000. NEW YORK, 8 Nov 1958, *Canal*, USD 1,800. PARIS, 18 March 1959, *The Path to the Meadows, Morning* (1891) FRF 5,600,000. NEW YORK, 15 April 1959, *The Edge of the Forest of Fontainebleau, Morning*, USD 32,500. LONDON, 6 May 1959, *La Jonction du Loing et de la Seine* GBP 11,500. PARIS, 25 May 1960, *Geese by the Water* (pastel) FRF 4,700. LONDON, 6 July 1960, *The Washerwomen* (1876) GBP 11,000. PARIS, 21 June 1961, *The Flood*, FRF 785,000. LONDON, 28 June 1961, *The Snow in Louveciennes*, GBP 22,000. PARIS, 30 Nov 1961, *The Bridge at Moret, with the River in Spate*, FRF 630,000. PARIS, 29 March 1962, *Gooseherd on the Banks of the Loing; Banks of the Loing* (two pastels) FRF 65,000. LONDON, 1 July 1964, *Banks of the Seine at La Roche-Guyon* (pastel) GBP 5,500. LONDON, 27 Nov 1964, *Bouquet of Flowers*, Gns 34,000. LONDON, 3 Dec 1965, *The Loing at Moret, in Summer*, Gns 32,000. LONDON, 22 June 1966, *The Loing at St Mammès*, GBP 4,000. LONDON, 7 Dec 1966, *Hunters at the Edge of the Forest of Marly in Autumn*, GBP 33,000. LONDON, 28 June 1967, *Winter in Veneux-Nadon* (1881, oil on canvas, 21 x 28 ins / 52.5 x 71 cm) GBP 37,000. GENEVA, 10 Nov 1967, *Geese* (pastel) CHF 86,000. PARIS, 27 June 1968, *Boatyard at St Mammès*, FRF 520,000. LONDON, 3 July 1968, *Snow-covered Landscape in Sunshine* (pastel) GBP 11,200. GENEVA, 7 Nov 1969, *Barges on the Loing*, CHF 58,000. LONDON, 30 June 1970, *A Highroad in Seine-et-Marne*, Gns 50,000. NEW YORK, 21 Oct 1971, *Along the Wood in Autumn, Fontainebleau*, USD 105,000. MARSEILLES, 25 Nov 1972, *The Loing at Moret* (pastel) FRF 115,000. LONDON, 29 Nov 1972, *Moret Bridge in Summer*, GBP 70,000. LONDON, 2 April 1974, *The Flood at Port-Marly*, GBP 111,000. GENEVA, 6 June 1974, *The Station at Moret-sur-Loing* (pastel) GBP 3,000. PARIS, 21 June 1976, *Geese at St Mammès* (pastel). LONDON, 6 Dec 1977, *Hillsides Near Paris* (1879, oil on canvas, 19¾ x 25½ ins / 50 x 65 cm) GBP 28,000. BERN, 22 June 1979, *Riverbanks, or, The Geese* (1897, coloured lithograph/Chine collé) CHF 7,800. VERSAILLES, 21 Oct 1979, *Landscape* (1885, pastel, 11½ x 15¼ ins / 29 x 39 cm) FRF 70,000. NEW YORK, 6 Nov 1979, *The Sèvres Bridge*

(c. 1877, oil on canvas, 15 x 18 ins / 38 x 46 cm) USD 190,000. NEW YORK, 15 May 1980, *An Orchard* (1885, coloured chalks, 6 1/2 x 9 1/2 ins / 16.5 x 24.2 cm) USD 4,750. LONDON, 2 Dec 1981, *Peasant at Work* (c. 1894, pencil and pastel, study, 6 1/2 x 10 ins / 16.5 x 24.5 cm) GBP 3,400. ENGHIEN-LES-BAINS, 13 Dec 1981, *Pasture Beside the Seine* (pastel, 9 3/4 x 14 1/4 ins / 25 x 36 cm) FRF 84,000. LONDON, 29 June 1983, *The Geese* (pastel, 7 1/2 x 10 ins / 19 x 24.5 cm) GBP 17,500. NEW YORK, 16 Nov 1983, *The Seine at Auteuil* (pen and wash, 6 1/2 x 8 ins / 16.5 x 20.2 cm) USD 12,000. NEW YORK, 16 May 1984, *Spring in Veneux* (1880, oil on canvas, 28 3/4 x 35 1/2 ins / 73 x 90 cm) USD 350,000. MONTEVIDEO, 16 May 1984, *Riverbanks, or, The Geese* (1897, coloured lithograph/chine collé, 8 1/2 x 12 1/2 ins / 21.5 x 32 cm) USD 7,500. NEW YORK, 24 April 1985, *The Machine at Marly, and the Weir* (1875, oil on canvas, 15 x 18 ins / 38 x 46 cm) USD 260,000. RAMBOUILLET, 20 Oct 1985, *Village Street* (colouring pencil and wax crayon, 5 1/2 x 9 ins / 14 x 22 cm) FRF 92,000. PARIS, 18 March 1986, *On the Canal Bank in the Spring, Evening* (1897, oil on canvas, 21 1/4 x 25 1/2 ins / 54 x 65 cm) FRF 2,420,000. ZURICH, 21 Nov 1986, *View of St Cloud* (1876, oil on canvas, 21 1/4 x 28 3/4 ins / 54 x 73 cm) CHF 900,000. NEW YORK, 10 Nov 1987, *Sunrise at St Mammès* (1880, oil on canvas, 19 1/2 x 26 ins / 49.5 x 65.1 cm) USD 680,000. PARIS, 9 Dec 1987, *The Seine at St Cloud* (oil on canvas, 15 x 22 ins / 38 x 55 cm) FRF 2,030,000. LONDON, 24 Feb 1988, *Three Little Girls (Palmire, Théodine, Olympe)* (pastel and pencil, 6 1/4 x 10 ins / 16 x 24.5 cm) GBP 5,500. LONDON, 28 June 1988, *The Bridge at Moret at Sunset* (1892, oil on canvas, 23 1/2 x 28 3/4 ins / 60 x 73 cm) GBP 396,000. CALAIS, 3 July 1988, *The Washerwomen*. VERSAILLES, 6 Nov 1988, *Young Girl, Seated* (colouring pencil, 3 3/4 x 2 1/2 ins / 9.5 x 6.5 cm) FRF 17,000. LONDON, 29 Nov 1988, *The Loing at the Bridge at Moret* (1892, oil on canvas, 29 x 36 1/2 ins / 73.6 x 92.7 cm) GBP 1,375,000. PARIS, 16 Dec 1988, *Bend in the Loing* (1897, painting/canvas, 21 1/4 x 25 1/2 ins / 54 x 65 cm) FRF 3,490,000. PARIS, 16 Jan 1989, *A Street (Probably the Rue des Saules in Montmartre)* (oil on panel, 3 1/2 x 2 3/4 ins / 9 x 7 cm) FRF 550,000. LONDON, 3 April 1989, *Banks of the Loing at Sunset* (1891, oil on canvas, 15 x 18 ins / 38 x 46 cm) GBP 352,000. NEW YORK, 9 May 1989, *Banks of the Loing* (1890, oil on canvas, 18 x 22 ins / 46 x 56 cm) USD 715,000. NEW YORK, 10 May 1989, *The Road to Hampton Court* (1874, oil on canvas, 15 1/4 x 21 3/4 ins / 38.5 x 55.5 cm) USD 2,640,000. LONDON, 27 June 1989, *The Plain of Champagne from the Heights of Roches-Courtaut* (1880, oil on canvas, 19 3/4 x 25 1/2 ins / 50 x 65 cm) GBP 858,000. NEW YORK, 18 Oct 1989, *The Poplar Walk in Moret* (1888, oil on canvas, 21 1/4 x 28 3/4 ins / 54 x 73 cm) USD 3,410,000; *Moret-sur-Loing* (1891, oil on canvas, 25 1/2 x 36 1/4 ins / 65 x 92 cm) USD 2,530,000. LONDON, 28 Nov 1989, *August Afternoon in Veneux* (1881, oil on canvas, 21 1/4 x 28 3/4 ins / 54 x 73 cm) GBP 1,320,000. PARIS, 20 March 1990, *The Donkey, or, Master Aliboron* (c. 1890-1892, pastel on paper, 7 1/2 x 10 ins / 19 x 24.5 cm) FRF 220,000. LONDON, 3 April 1990, *The Matrat Boatyard at Moret-sur-Loing* (1888, oil on canvas, 15 1/4 x 18 ins / 39 x 46 cm) GBP 616,000. NEW YORK, 15 May 1990, *Morning Sun in St Mammès* (1884, oil on canvas, 19 1/4 x 25 1/2 ins / 49 x 65 cm) USD 1,650,000. AMSTERDAM, 6 Nov 1990, *A Boat on a Lake* (pastel, 5 1/2 x 9 1/4 ins / 14.2 x 23.7 cm) NLG 10,350. NEW YORK, 13 Nov 1990, *The Rowers* (1877, oil on canvas, 18 1/4 x 22 ins / 46.5 x 56 cm) USD 1,485,000. PARIS, 19 Nov 1990, *Studies of Barges* (colouring pencil/paper, 7 1/2 x 10 1/4 ins / 19 x 26 cm) FRF 100,000. PARIS, 21 Oct 1991, *Cliffs in Wales* (1897, oil on canvas, 23 1/2 x 36 1/4 ins / 60 x 92 cm) FRF 2,900,000. NEW YORK, 5 Nov 1991, *Street in Veneux* (1883, oil on canvas, 21 1/2 x 29 ins / 54.6 x 73.7 cm) USD 550,000. NEW YORK, 6 Nov 1991, *Spring in Veneux* (1880, oil on canvas, 28 3/4 x 36 ins / 73 x 91.5 cm) USD 797,500. NEW YORK, 13 May 1992, *Village Street in Dull Weather* (1874, oil on canvas, 15 x 22 ins / 38.1 x 55.9 cm) USD 660,000. NEW YORK, 11 Nov 1992, *Farm in Les Sablons in Bright Sunshine* (1885, oil on canvas, 21 1/4 x 28 3/4 ins / 53.7 x 73 cm) USD 605,000. PARIS, 24 Nov 1992, *The Road from Veneux to Thomery, Beside the Water, Evening* (1880, oil on canvas, 19 3/4 x 25 1/2 ins / 50 x 65 cm) FRF 3,100,000. LONDON, 30 Nov 1992, *Barges on the Loing* (1896, oil on canvas, 13 x 16 1/4 ins / 33 x 41 cm) GBP 121,000. LONDON, 21 June 1993, *The Family* (pencil on paper, 9 1/4 x 13 ins / 23.3 x 33 cm) GBP 9,200. NEW YORK, 2 Nov 1993, *The Loing Below the Bridge at Moret* (1892, oil on canvas, 29 x 36 1/2 ins / 73.6 x 92.7 cm) USD 1,102,500. LONDON, 29 Nov 1993, *The Factory at Sèvres* (1879, oil on canvas, 23 1/2 x 29 ins / 60 x 73.4 cm) GBP 771,500. NEW YORK, 10 May 1994, *Moret, View of the Loing on a May Afternoon* (1888, oil on canvas, 19 3/4 x 25 1/2 ins / 50 x 65 cm) USD 1,652,500. PARIS, 22 June 1994, *Rocky Coast of Lady's Cove, Langland Bay* (1897, pastel on paper, 10 x 13 1/2 ins / 25.5 x 34 cm) FRF 105,000. PARIS, 12 May 1995, *Riverbanks, or, The Geese* (1897, coloured lithograph, 8 1/2 x 12 1/2 ins / 21.5 x 32 cm) FRF 19,000. LONDON, 27 June 1995, *The Seine Seen from the Quay at Daybreak* (1878, oil on canvas, 21 1/4 x 25 3/4 ins / 54 x 65.5 cm) GBP 386,500. NEW YORK, 7 Nov 1995, *Snow Effect in Argenteuil* (1874, oil on canvas, 21 1/4 x 25 1/2 ins / 54 x 65 cm) USD 1,982,500. PARIS, 21 Nov 1995, *The Embankment at St Mammès* (oil on canvas, 21 1/4 x 28 3/4 ins / 54 x 73 cm) FRF 1,600,000. PARIS, 19 March 1996, *Near Les Sablons, Dull Weather* (1886, oil on canvas, 23 1/2 x 28 3/4 ins / 60 x 73 cm) FRF 4,100,000. NEW YORK, 30 April 1996, *The Bridge at Moret in the Sun* (1892, oil on canvas, 25 1/2 x 32 ins / 65 x 81 cm) USD 1,212,500. NEW YORK, 12 Nov 1996, *Moret-sur-Loing* (1888, oil on canvas, 23 1/2 x 28 3/4 ins / 60 x 73 cm) USD 1,762,000. LONDON, 2 Dec 1996, *The Weir at St Mammès* (1885, oil on canvas, 18 x 33 1/2 ins / 46 x 85 cm) GBP 573,500. LONDON, 3 Dec 1996, *Plum Trees and Walnut Trees in the Spring* (1889, oil on canvas, 23 1/2 x 28 3/4 ins / 60 x 73 cm) GBP 958,500. NEW YORK, 14 May 1997, *The Boats* (1885, oil on canvas, 21 1/2 x 15 1/4 ins / 54.7 x 38.5 cm) USD 772,500. PARIS, 16 June 1997, *Canal Banks* (pastel on paper, 10 3/4 x 15 1/4 ins / 27.5 x 38.5 cm) FRF 425,000. LONDON, 24 June 1997, *Bridge on the Orvanne Near Moret* (1883, oil on canvas, 20 3/4 x 25 1/2 ins / 53 x 65 cm) GBP 408,500. NEW YORK, 13 Nov 1997, *Chevreuil (Roe Deer) Lake* (c. 1888, oil on canvas, 19 1/4 x 25 3/4 ins / 49 x 65.5 cm) USD 662,500. PARIS, 24 March 1998, *Eight Geese on the Bank of the Loing* (oil on canvas, 9 1/2 x 18 ins / 24 x 46 cm) FRF 1,200,000. NEW YORK, 16 Nov 1998, *The Loing at St-Mammes* (1885, oil on canvas, 18 x 22 ins / 46 x 55 cm) USD 820,000. LONDON, 28 June 1999, *The Loing at Moret* (1886, oil on canvas, 21 x 29 ins / 54 x 73 cm) GBP 920,000. LONDON, 8 Dec 1999, *Children Playing in the Prairy* (1873, oil on canvas, 20 x 29 ins / 50 x 73 cm) GBP 560,000. NEW YORK, 8 May 2000, *The Seine at Bougival* (1873, oil on canvas, 21 x 29 ins / 54 x 73 cm) USD 1,800,000. NEW YORK, 11 May 2000, *A Garden in Louveciennes, Étarche Path* (1973, oil on canvas, 25 x 18 ins / 64 x 46 cm) USD 3,200,000. NEW YORK, 7 May 2001, *Watering Place at Marly, Washerwomen* (1875, oil on canvas, double-sided, 15 x 22 ins / 39 x 56 cm) USD 1,200,000. NEW YORK, 7 Nov 2001, *Morning in Moret in May* (1886, oil on canvas, 21 x 28 ins / 54 x 72 cm) USD 780,000. NEW YORK, 5 Nov 2002, *The Loing at Moret* (1886, oil on canvas, 22 x 29 ins / 55 x 74 cm) USD 1,300,000. NEW YORK, 6 Nov 2002, *Banks of the Seine at Bougival* (1876, oil on canvas, 15 x 22 ins / 39 x 57 cm) USD 900,000. LONDON, 23 June 2003, *The Bridge in Moret and Windmills, Winter Effect* (1890, oil on canvas, 21 x 26 ins / 54 x 65 cm) GBP 340,000. LONDON, 21 June 2004, *Road in Louveciennes* (1874, oil on canvas, 26 x 21 ins / 65 x 54 cm) GBP 1,400,000. LONDON, 2 Feb 2004, *Route de Marly-le-Roi* (1875, oil on canvas, 24 x 29 ins / 60 x 73 cm) GBP 1,300,000.

SISMORE, Charles Porter

British, 20th century.

Painter. Seascapes.

AUCTION RECORDS:
LONDON, 22 Sept 1988, *American Ships on the Mersey* (oil on canvas, 21 x 26 ins / 53.5 x 66 cm) GBP 3,520; *Dutch Sailing-ship in an Estuary* (oil on canvas, 12 x 18 ins / 30.5 x 45.7 cm) GBP 770.

SISQUELLA ORIOL, Alfredo
Spanish, 20th century.
Born 1900, in Barcelona; died 1964, in Sitges (Catalonia).
Painter. Figures, portraits, landscapes.
Alfredo Sisquella Oriol was a pupil at the Academia de Bellas Artes in Barcelona. He is known for *Figure at Table* and *Woman Thinking*. He took part in various collective exhibitions in Barcelona including: Academia de Bellas Artes exhibition (1919, 1923); Salón de Otoño (1922); Sala Parès (1940 onwards). A posthumous retrospective of his work was organized in Sitges in 1985.
BIBLIOGRAPHY:
Arnáiz, José Manuel/López Jiménez, Javier/Merchán Díaz, Manuel (ed.), '*Cien años de pintura en Espana y Portugal (1830-1930)*' in vol. X, Antiqvaria, Madrid, 1993.
MUSEUMS AND GALLERIES:
BARCELONA (MAM del Mus. Nacional d'Art de Catalunya).
AUCTION RECORDS:
BARCELONA, 28 Feb 1980, *Reverie* (oil on canvas, 29 1/4 x 24 1/4 ins / 74 x 61.5 cm) ESP 400,000. BARCELONA, 2 June 1982, *Seascape* (oil on canvas, 20 3/4 x 24 3/4 ins / 53 x 63 cm) ESP 325,000. BARCELONA, 19 Dec 1984, *Still-life* (oil on canvas, 23 1/2 x 28 3/4 ins / 60 x 73 cm) ESP 420,000. LONDON, 23 Nov 1988, *Undulating Mediterranean Landscape* (oil on canvas, 32 x 25 1/2 ins / 81 x 65 cm) GBP 3,850. BERN, 5 May 1999, *Harbour Scene under Cloudy Skies* (oil on canvas, 15 x 22 ins / 38 x 55 cm) CHF 6,500. MADRID, 19 Dec 2000, *Still-life with Cards and Mask* (oil on canvas, 24 x 29 ins / 60 x 73 cm) ESP 540,000.

SISSOEV, Nikolai, or Sisoyev, Sissoyev
Russian, 20th century.
Painter.
Nikolai Sissoev is known for the picture *Lenin and Krupskaya at the Village of Gorki*.

SISSOIEV, Vadim
Russian, 20th - 21st century.
Born 1966.
Painter. Still-lifes.
Sissoiev graduated from the Vladimir Serov school of fine art in St Petersburg, where he lives and works. He has participated regularly in exhibitions, including: 1989, *Forty Years of the Avant-Garde in Leningrad*; and 1992, *Contemporary Russian Painting* at the Kunsthaus in Cologne and the Holman gallery in Düsseldorf.

В. Сысоев

AUCTION RECORDS:
PARIS, 1 June 1994, *Still-life with Guitar, Music Series* (oil on canvas, 24 x 19 3/4 ins / 61 x 50 cm) FRF 8,800.

SISSON. See also **SINSSON**

SISSON, Auguste
French, 19th century.
Painter. History painting, portraits.
Auguste Sisson exhibited at the Salon in 1848 and 1849.

SISSON, Richard
Irish, 18th century.
Died April 1767, in Dublin.
Miniaturist, engraver (mezzotint). Portraits.
Richard Sisson was a pupil of Francis Bindon, and worked in Dublin and London. His style was similar to that of Denner.

SISTI, Francesco
Italian, 17th century.
Active in Ferrara in 1631.
Painter.
Francesco Sisti painted the fresco depicting *Jesus Aged Twelve Years in the Temple* above the portal in the church of St Joseph in Ferrara.

SISTIAGA, José Antonio
Spanish, 20th century.
Born 4 May 1932, in San Sebastián.
Painter, film maker.
Gaur Group.
José Antonio Sistiaga was essentially self-taught, having entered the École des Beaux-Arts in Paris in 1955 only to drop out a month and a half later. In 1965, in collaboration with the painter Amable and the sculptor Oteiza, he created the Gaur group (meaning 'today' in Basque) whose aim was to protect the identity of Basque culture.

Since 1974 he has lived and worked in Ciboure in the Basque region. In 1988-1989 he made the film *Impressions of the Upper Atmosphere*, painted on to film using the Imax-Omnimax system, which was shown several times at the Géode in Paris and at the Auditorium of the Louvre to celebrate the centenary of the birth of cinema.

Although Sistiaga was initially a figurative artist, his encounters with the works of Kandinsky, De Stael and Fautrier towards the end of the 1950s caused a major shift in his artistic direction. His painting became informal but remained lyrical and extremely colourful. The use of cinema enabled him to create even deeper resonances with colour. His first film is the only abstract feature film in the history of cinema.

As a film maker he made his name in 1970 with a feature film *Ere erera baleibu izik subua aruaren*, in which he coloured all the images by hand. This won him the prize for experimental cinema at the 10th International Biennale for documentary films held in Bilbao in 1968. The film then went on to be shown at the International Underground Film Festival in London. Sistiaga showed his work in a private exhibition in 1998 at the Galeria Berta Belaza in Bilbao.
BIBLIOGRAPHY:
'*José Antonio Sistiaga*' in *Chroniques de l'Art Vivant*, periodical, Maeght, Paris, December 1970. *Sistiaga, pintura, dibujos eroticos, films, 1958-1996*, exhibition catalogue, Rekalde, Bilbao, 1996.
MUSEUMS AND GALLERIES:
BILBAO (MBA) - MADRID (Mus. Nacional Centro de Arte Reina Sofía): *Wave and Cloud* (1972-1974).

SISTIC, Johann
Slovene, 17th century.
Died 29 August 1666, in Ljubljana.
Painter.

SISTO DA ALATRI
Italian, 14th century.
Active during the second half of the 14th century.
Sculptor (marble).
Sisto da Alatri carved some decorative sculptures in the church and abbey of Montecassino in 1380.

SISTO DI ENRICO. See **SYRI Sixtus**

SISTORI, Pablo
Spanish, 18th century.
Active in Murcia from 1767 to 1792.
Painter.
Pablo Sistori painted altarpieces for churches in Cartagena and Murcia.

SISTRIER, Marie
French, 20th century.
Born 8 May 1908, in Hazebrouck.
Painter. Flowers.

Marie Sistrier exhibited in Paris, Boulogne-sur-Mer, Arras, Lille, St-Quentin, Montpellier, Amiens, Le Touquet and Nice. She was awarded a prize in Vichy in 1965, and another in Le Touquet in 1969. Her paintings have been shown abroad, in the United Kingdom, Germany, Norway and elsewhere.

SITA, Pietro
Italian, 18th century.
Active in Ferrara in 1738.
Painter.
Pietro Sita executed altarpieces for the church of SS Cosimo e S Damiano and Sant'Uffizio in Ferrara.

SITAU, Michael. See **ZITTOZ**

SITCHY, M. A.
Austrian, 19th century.
Born 1829; died 1906.
Painter. Genre scenes.
Sitchy was active in Russia where he was court painter.
MUSEUMS AND GALLERIES:
MOSCOW (Rumiantsev Mus.): *The Devil and Tamar* - MOSCOW (State Tretyakov Gal.): *The Grandmother.*
AUCTION RECORDS:
PARIS, 28 June 1928, *Nude Woman* (red chalk) FRF 580.

SITHIUM, Michael. See **ZITTOZ Miguel**

SITIENS. See **SOYE Philipp de**

SITIUS. See **SOYE Philipp de**

SITJE, Joronn
Maiden name: Mohr
Norwegian, 20th century.
Born 30 April 1897, in Telemark.
Painter. Figures, landscapes.
Joronn Sitje was a pupil of Henrik Sörensen. Sitje moved to Kenya in 1929.
MUSEUMS AND GALLERIES:
GÖTEBORG: *Female Head* - OSLO (Nasjonalgal.): *Negress; Landscape*; two studies.

SITNIKOV, Aleksandr or Alexander
Russian, 20th century.
Born 1945, in Iva-Golitsyno.
Painter (mixed media).
Sitnikov studied at the Surikov Institute in Moscow, where he lives and works. He became a member of the association of Soviet artists. He produces Abstract compositions dominated by colour, which consist of Figurative elements inspired by Russian tradition, notably icons, Cyrillic characters and fantastic bestiaries. He took part in 1987 in the exhibition *Art Soviétique Contemporain* (*Contemporary Soviet Art*) at the Galerie de France in Paris. He has exhibited his works in solo exhibitions from 1975 in the USSR and abroad from 1982.
AUCTION RECORDS:
MOSCOW, 7 July 1988, *Black Bull* (1986, mixed media/canvas, 59 x 55 ins / 150 x 140 cm) GBP 8,250.

SITNIKOV, Vasili
Russian, 20th century.
Born 1915; died 1987.
Painter.
A non-conformist artist, Vasili Sitnikov is known for the private art school and studio he ran in Moscow in the 1960s and for his unorthodox teaching practices.
AUCTION RECORDS:
PARIS, 14 May 1990, *Woman's Freedom* (1970, oil on canvas, 23 1/2 x 41 1/4 ins / 60 x 105 cm) FRF 13,500.

SITOLEUX, Jacques
French, 20th century.
Born 1930, in Paris.
Draughtsman, engraver.
Jacques Sitoleux lives and works in Mareil-Marly. He has exhibited in collective exhibitions, including *De Bonnard à Baselitz - Dix Ans d'enrichissements du cabinet des estampes 1978-1988* (*From Bonnard to Baselitz: A Decade of Acquisitions by the Prints Collection 1978-1988*) at the Bibliothèque Nationale in Paris, 1992.
MUSEUMS AND GALLERIES:
PARIS (BNF, Prints Collection): *Flowering Hedge* (etching and burin).

SITTE, Artus
Dutch, 17th century.
Active in Berlin 1666-1673.
Sculptor.
Artus Sitte worked for the court of Brandenburg.

SITTE, Camillo
Austrian, 19th century.
Born 17 April 1843, in Vienna; died 16 November 1903, in Vienna.
Painter, architect, writer.
Sitte produced decorative paintings.

SITTE, Willi
German, 20th century.
Born 1945; died 1982.
Painter. Scenes with figures.
In 2003 Willi Sitte's work featured in *Berlin-Moscow/Moscow-Berlin 1950-2000* at the Martin-Gropius-Bau in Berlin and the Tretyakow Gallery in Moscow, an exhibition/survey following on from the one covering the period 1900-1950, and examining Germano-Russian artistic and cultural links over a 50-year period marked by political transformation. Solo exhibitions have included 1982 Bremen, and 1986 Altes Museum in Berlin.
BIBLIOGRAPHY:
Hutte, Wolfgang, *Willi Sitte*, Kunsthalle, Rostock, 1971. Kaufman, Frölich, *Willi Sitte*, exhibition catalogue, Staatliche Kunsthalle, Berlin, 1982. *'Berlin-Moskau/Moskau-Berlin 1950-2000'* in *2 vol*, exhibition catalogue, Martin-Gropius-Bau, Berlin, 2003 (text in German).

SITTEL, Constant
French, 19th century.
Active in Paris.
Painter, engraver. Portraits.
Sittel exhibited at the Salon in 1849.

SITTER, Inger
Norwegian, 20th century.
Born 1929, in Trondheim.
Painter, assemblage artist. Murals.
Inger Sitter started painting when she was only a child. She went on to study from 1945 to 1949 at the Fine Arts Academies of Oslo and Antwerp, before completing her studies in Paris under André Lhote and at Hayter's Atelier 17. As of 1950, she visited Paris on a regular basis and also spent time in Spain.

Sitter featured at numerous group exhibitions in Norway and elsewhere. She also exhibited solo, notably in Oslo (as of 1955) and in Stockholm (1959). In 1963, Sitter was awarded the Copenhagen Nordic Biennale Youth Prize. She started out as a realist, but her work became increasingly abstract as of 1954-1955. She also produced a number of plastic and metal 'assemblies'. In 1958, for Government House in Oslo, she completed decorative compositions using a process of engravings etched into concrete.

SITTERICH, Jacobus or Jacob
Dutch, 18th century.
Died 25 August 1757.
Active in Roermond.
Painter.

Jacobus Sitterich was a citizen of Roermond in 1714. He is noted for *Emperor Charles VI as Duke of Guelder* in the town hall at Roermond (1719) and *Assumption of the Virgin* in Roermond Cathedral.

SITTHIKET, Vasan
Thai, 20th - 21st century.
Born 1957, in Nakhorn Swan.
Painter (mixed media). Multimedia.

Vasan Sitthiket studied in Bangkok. His work is rooted in a particular socio-political context. As well as painting, Sitthiket produces video works and installations.

He has had solo exhibitions including: *Hell* (1991); *Buddha Returns to Bangkok '92; I Love Thai Culture* and *No Future* (1995).

SITTICH, Balthasar, or Neitsch
German, 17th century.
Died September 1626, in Dresden.
Painter.

Sittich worked for the court in Saxony, Germany, and painted coats of arms.

SITTIG, Georg Heinrich
German, 19th - 20th century.
Born 23 March 1863, in Sindlingen am Main.
Painter. Portraits, landscapes. Designs for stained glass.

Georg Sittig studied at the Städel Institute in Frankfurt am Main and at the academy of fine arts in Karlsruhe.

MUSEUMS AND GALLERIES:
BERN.

AUCTION RECORDS:
ZURICH, 29 Oct 1983, *Mountain Landscape* (1903, oil on canvas, 36 1/4 x 46 ins / 92 x 116 cm) CHF 2,800.

SITTINGER. See **SUTTINGER**

SITTMANN, Leonhard Hubert
German, 19th century.
Born 1802, in Cologne; died 1 February 1840, in Cologne.
Painter, draughtsman.

Sittmann studied under P. von Langer in Munich.

MUSEUMS AND GALLERIES:
BERLIN (Nationalgal.): *Portrait of Franz Brulliot* (drawing).

SITTMANN, Mathilde
German, 20th century.
Born 7 December 1878, in Darmstadt.
Painter. Portraits, flowers.

Sittmann was the pupil of Wilhelm J. Bader.

SITTOW, Michael. See **ZITTOZ Miguel**

SITZMANN, Johann
German, 19th century.
Born 6 December 1854; died 9 July 1901.
Active in Schlaifhausen, Switzerland.
Sculptor.

Johann Sitzmann was the son of Urban Sitzmann. He produced decorative sculptures, crucifixes and tombstones for several churches in Franconia.

SITZNPERGER, Hieronymus
Austrian, 16th century.
Born in Vienna; died 23 October 1510.
Miniaturist.

Sitznperger was a canon of the abbey of Klosterneuburg and worked there from 1469.

SIU CHE-TCH'ANG. See **XU SHICHANG**

SIU FANG. See **XU FANG**

SIU HI. See **XU XI**

SIU JONG. See **XU RONG**

SIU KIE-MIN. See **XU JIEMIN**

SIU LIN. See **XU LIN**

SIU MEI. See **XU MEI**

SIU MEOU-WEI. See **XU MOUWEI**

SIU PEI-HONG. See **XU BEIHONG**

SIU PEN. See **XU BEN**

SIU T'AI. See **XU TAI**

SIU TAN. See **XU DAN**

SIU TAO-NING. See **XU DAONING**

SIU TCH'ONG-KIU. See **XU CHONGJU**

SIU TCH'ONG-SSEU. See **XU CHONGSI**

SIU WANG-HIONG. See **XU WANGXIONG**

SIU WEI. See **XU WEI**

SIU WEI-JEN. See **XU WEIREN**

SIU YANG. See **XU YANG**

SIU YEN-SOUEN. See **XU YANSUN**

SIU YUAN. See **XU YUAN**

SIU YUAN-WEN. See **XU YUANWEN**

SIU YUANWEN. See **HSU YU-JEN**

SIUAN-TSONG MING. See **XUANZONG MING**

SIUDA, Ferdinand, or Nandor
Hungarian, 20th century.
Born 1893, in Budapest.
Painter. Landscapes.

SIUDMAK, Wojtek
Polish, 20th - 21st century.
Born 10 October 1972.
Painter, collage artist.

Siudmak re-established the imagery of everyday life in the same vein as the Pop artists, taking his documents from the realities of magazines and advertising material. However, he then extricated himself from a language that had become commonplace to express his own view of the world with its own moods and anger. His collage technique, backed up by drawn and painted insertions, is reminiscent of Rauschenberg. He received attention while still young in a Paris exhibition in which he appeared with Kurt Sønderborg, Harold Cousins, and others. In 2003, his work was exhibited at a solo exhibition in the town hall in St Avold, Moselle.

W.SIUDMAK

BIBLIOGRAPHY:
Guimard, Jacques/Béart, Guy, *L'Art hyperréaliste fantastique de Wojtek Siudmak*, Éd. du Cygne, Paris, 1978.

SIUE SIUAN. See **XUE XUAN**

SIUE SOU-SOU. See **XUE SUSU**

SIUE WONG. See **CHEN ZHIFO**

SIUE WOU. See **XUE SUSU**

SIUE-KIEN. See **XUEJIAN**

SIUE-YAI. See **XUEYA**

SIVADE, André, or Sivad Dréo
French, 20th century.
Born 1883, in Nice; died 1950, in Paris.
Painter. Portraits, landscapes.

André Sivade exhibited at the Salon des Indépendants in Paris from 1909 to 1930. He was influenced by Fauvism.

SIVALLI, Luigi
Italian, 19th century.
Born 10 December 1811, in Cremona; died 5 January 1887, in Parma.
Engraver (burin).
A pupil of P. Toschi, Sivalli made engravings after works by Correggio.

SIVARD, Robert
American, 20th century.
Born 1914, in New York; died 1990, in Washington DC.
Painter. Murals.
Robert Sivard studied painting at the Pratt Institute and the National Academy of Design in New York, and then at the Académie Julian in Paris. He was in turn a fresco painter and artistic director of several American publications and international advertising agencies in Geneva, Paris and Washington.

Despite his academic training and varied artistic practice, Sivard can be allied to the Naive painters. He painted many psychologically acute portraits, and produced work that is full of humour and affection for the many surprises offered by the Paris streets or types such as *Madame Celesta, Clairvoyant*, in the door of her caravan; a *Caretaker*, in a vest and old slippers in front of his lodge, topped with a bust of Napoleon; and, in *Tribute to Victor Guimard*, a nun coming out of an Art Nouveau-style Metro station wearing a wimple in the same shape as the glass roof.

Sivard's first solo exhibition was held in France in 1953. Others followed in New York, the Musée d'Art Moderne de la Ville de Paris, and numerous American art galleries, especially the 1967 retrospective at the Philadelphia Art Alliance.

SIVED, G.
British, 18th century.
Active in London in 1780.
Painter.

SIVEL, Joseph
French, 19th century.
Painter.
Sivel exhibited at the Salon in 1848 and 1850.

SIVELL, Robert
British, 20th century.
Born 1888; died 1958.
Painter. Figures, portraits.
Robert Sivell exhibited regularly, notably at the Royal Academy in London, from 1918 to 1959.
AUCTION RECORDS:
GLASGOW, 23 Sept 1997, *A Cloudy Day* (oil on card, 10 1/2 x 14 1/2 ins / 26.7 x 36.8 cm) GBP 276. LONDON, 2 March 1999, *Head of Boy* (oil on panel, 12 x 10 ins / 31 x 26 cm) GBP 1,050. LONDON, 30 Oct 2003, *Portrait of a Young Girl* (oil on canvas, 40 x 30 ins / 101 x 75 cm) GBP 2,000.

SIVERS, August, or Sievers
German, 19th century.
Born 1816, in Hardenberg.
Painter.
August Sivers attended the academy in Munich.

SIVERS, August
German, 19th century.
Active in Munich.
Glass painter.
August Sivers exhibited stained glass windows in Paris in 1855.

SIVERS, Clara von
Maiden name: Krüger
German, 19th century.
Born 29 October 1854, in Pinneberg (Schleswig-Holstein).
Painter. Still-lifes (flowers).
Clara von Sivers studied in Copenhagen, Paris, Lyons, Stuttgart and Dresden. She settled in Kiel (Germany), where she married a naval officer.
MUSEUMS AND GALLERIES:
CHEMNITZ: *Flowers*.
AUCTION RECORDS:
COLOGNE, 18 March 1983, *Spring* (oil on canvas, 29 1/4 x 17 ins / 74.5 x 43 cm) DEM 13,000. AMSTERDAM, 2 May 1990, *Carnations in a Glass with Apples, Pears and Grapes in a Plate on a Table with Drapery* (oil on canvas, 20 3/4 x 15 3/4 ins / 53 x 40 cm) NLG 6,325. NEW YORK, 13 Oct 1993, *Still-life with Delphiniums, Poppies, Phlox and Daisies in a Watering Can* (oil on canvas, 31 x 39 ins / 78.7 x 99.1 cm) USD 14,950. MUNICH, 2 Dec 1997, *Still-life with Wild Flowers in a Chinese Vase* (oil on canvas, 35 x 43 1/2 ins / 89 x 110.5 cm) DEM 21,600. AMSTERDAM, 27 April 1999, *Still-life with Lilacs and Violets on a Draped Guilt Rococo Table* (oil on canvas, 35 x 44 ins / 90 x 113 cm) NLG 14,000. COPENHAGEN, 1 June 1999, *Still-life with Flowers* (oil on canvas, 35 x 44 ins / 88 x 111 cm) DKK 35,000. AMSTERDAM, 4 July 2000, *Forest Landscape with Roses in a Wicker Basket* (oil on canvas, 20 x 32 ins / 51 x 81 cm) NLG 20,000. AHLDEN, 28 Sept 2001, *Still-life* (oil on canvas, 34 x 43 ins / 86 x 110 cm) DEM 9,000. COLOGNE, 24 Nov 2001, *Eaves - Flowers round Water in a Stone Gutter* (oil on canvas, 26 x 16 ins / 65 x 40 cm) DEM 14,000. VIENNA, 16 May 2002, *Autumnal still-life with Cut Melon, Grapes and Twigs in a Copper Jug* (oil on canvas, 35 x 44 ins / 89 x 113 cm) EUR 11,000. VIENNA, 28 Nov 2002, *Flower Arrangement with White Lilac in a Chinese Vase* (oil on canvas, 46 x 35 ins / 118 x 88 cm) EUR 8,000. TOESTORF, 8 Nov 2003, *Still-life with Roses* (1886, oil on canvas/board, 9 x 13 ins / 24 x 34 cm) EUR 5,500. AMSTERDAM, 21 April 2004, *Morning Dew on Pink Roses* (1880, oil on canvas/cardboard, 9 x 13 ins / 24 x 34 cm) EUR 2,800. AMSTERDAM, 21 April 2004, *Colourful Zinnias in a Copper Pot* (oil on canvas, 35 x 43 ins / 88 x 110 cm) EUR 4,500.

SIVERS, Peter Felix von
Estonian, 19th century.
Born 12 March 1807, in Eusekül1; died 10 March 1853, in Wiborg, Germany.
Portrait artist.
Peter von Sivers attended the academies of Düsseldorf and Dresden, Germany. He settled in Dorpat (now Tartu, Estonia).

SIVERT, Joachim. See **SIWERT**

SIVERTSEN, Jan
Danish, 20th century.
Painter.
AUCTION RECORDS:
COPENHAGEN, 30 Nov 1988, *Composition* (1983, acrylic/paper, 29 1/2 x 55 ins / 75 x 140 cm) DKK 4,400. COPENHAGEN, 6 Sept 1993, *U. Title* (1989, oil on canvas, 51 1/4 x 35 ins / 130 x 89 cm) DKK 5,000. COPENHAGEN, 3 Nov 1993, *Musician - B 68* (1991, oil on canvas, 86 1/2 x 57 1/2 ins / 220 x 146 cm) DKK 13,000. COPENHAGEN, 6 Dec 1994, *1001 Lives and Virtues* (1986, oil on canvas, 25 1/2 x 19 3/4 ins / 65 x 50 cm) DKK 4,000. COPENHAGEN, 12 March 1996, *Untitled No. B 28* (1986, acrylic/canvas, 57 x 38 1/4 ins / 145 x 97 cm) DKK 10,000. COPENHAGEN, 22-24 Oct 1997, *Composition* (1984, oil on canvas, 76 3/4 x 51 1/4 ins / 195 x 130 cm) DKK 13,000. COPENHAGEN, 5 Oct 2004, *Figure Coming out of a Column* (1998, oil on canvas, 57 x 44 ins / 145 x 113 cm) DKK 14,000.

SIVERTSEN, Lars
Norwegian, 18th century.
Active during the first half of the 18th century.
Sculptor (wood).

Sivertsen was a pupil of Christopher Ridder. He finished an altarpiece begun by his master in the church of the Saviour in Oslo.

SIVIERO, Carlo
Italian, 20th century.
Born 22 July 1882, in Naples; died 1953, on Capri.
Painter, pastellist, sculptor. Portraits, genre scenes, flowers.
A pupil of Bernardo Celentano, Michele Cammarano and Domenico Morelli, Siviero also wrote about art. He lived and worked in Rome.
MUSEUMS AND GALLERIES:
FLORENCE (Uffizi): *Self-portrait* - ROME (Gal. Nazionale d'Arte Moderna): *Flowers; Astraia and Irene.*
AUCTION RECORDS:
COMO, 1 June 1971, *Abyssinian Warrior,* ITL 3,200,000. ROME, 14 Dec 1988, *Orphan* (1917, pastel/paper, 37 1/2 x 17 1/2 ins / 95 x 44.5 cm) ITL 2,000,000. ROME, 7 June 1995, *Portrait of a Lady* (oil on canvas, 15 x 11 ins / 38 x 28 cm) ITL 1,035,000.

SIVORI, Eduardo
British, 19th century.
Born 13 October 1847.
Painter.
Eduardo Sivori was a pupil of J.P. Laurens in Paris, and studied at the Académie Colarossi. He exhibited at the 1887 Paris Salon.

SIWERT, Joachim, or Sivert or Sibert
German, 17th century.
Painter.
Siwert was court painter in Brandenburg, Germany, c. 1630, where he produced portraits of the reigning family.

SIX, Mathias
German, 17th century.
Sculptor (wood).
Six carved an altar in 1619 and a tabernacle in 1628 for the church of Kelheim, Germany.

SIX, Michaël
Austrian, 20th century.
Born 23 September 1894, in Weng (Braunau-am-Inn).
Sculptor, medallist. Statues.
Six studied in Salzburg and Vienna before settling in the Austrian capital. He is noted for numerous commemorative medals, plaques and statues.

SIX, Nicolaus, or Syx
Dutch, 18th century.
Born 1694 or 1695, in Haarlem; died 10 May 1731, in Haarlem.
Painter, engraver (etching), collector. Religious subjects, figures.
Nicolaus Six was a pupil of Carel de Moor. In 1715 he entered the guild of Haarlem and was deputy mayor of that town. The museum of Bremen has a canvas by him entitled *Little Girl Reading.* He engraved the two plates *Flautist* and *Mary Magdalene.*

SIXDENIERS, Alexandre Vincent
French, 19th century.
Born 23 December 1795, in Paris; died 10 May 1846, in Paris, drowned.
Engraver (burin/mezzotint).
Sixdeniers was a pupil of Villerey; he exhibited at the Salon between 1822 and 1846. He engraved portraits, historical subjects, primarily using a burin, then genre scenes using the mezzotint technique. He gained a considerable reputation, particularly for the works produced using this process.

SIXDENIERS, Christian
Flemish School, 16th century.
Sculptor, glass painter.
Also an architect, between 1529 and 1541 Sixdeniers carved sculptures and painted windows for the chapel of the Holy Blood, Bruges.

SIXE, Antoine
French, 17th century.
Active in St-Martin-de-l'Aigle during the second half of the 17th century.
Painter, gilder.

SIXET, Louis Antoine de (Chevalier), or Sixe or Sixce
French, 18th century.
Born 3 January 1704, in L'Aigle; died 13 April 1780, in Évreux.
Painter. Self-portraits, figures, historical portraits, portraits.
Louis Antoine de Sixet studied under Oudry and worked for Henri Louis de la Tour d'Auvergne, Count of Évreux.
MUSEUMS AND GALLERIES:
ÉVREUX: *Portrait of Charles Godefroy de la Tour d'Auvergne; Portrait of the Duchess of Bouillon; Self-portrait* - LOUVIERS: *Woman Reading.*
AUCTION RECORDS:
PARIS, 4 Dec 1920, *Portrait of a Lady of Quality,* FRF 920. PARIS, 28 Oct 1931, *The Pick of the Game* (1773) FRF 2,800. NEW YORK, 21 Oct 1997, *Chinoiserie with an Elegant Lady in Chinese Dress Holding a Parrot, Two Servants at her Side* (1751, oil on canvas, in grisaille, 22 x 27 1/2 ins / 56 x 70 cm) USD 11,500.

SIXO, Louis Hercule. See **SISCO**

SIXT VON STAUFEN, or Han Sixt von Staufen
Swiss, 16th century.
Active in Fribourg from 1515 to 1537.
Sculptor.
Sixt von Staufen carved the retable of the Virgin in Fribourg Cathedral and statues for a house in the city.

SIXTO Y BACARO, Tomás
Spanish, 19th century.
Born 11 June 1778, in Cádiz; died 17 December 1826, in Medina Sidonia.
Painter.

SIXTUS, Ernst Philipp
Swiss, 19th century.
Active in the first half of the 19th century.
Lithographer.
Sixtus engraved eight *Views of the Carthusian Monastery near Thun* in 1826.

SJAMAAR, Pieter Geerard or Gerardus, or Sjamar
Dutch, 19th century.
Born 22 February 1819, in The Hague; died 19 September 1876, in The Hague.
Painter, architect. Genre scenes, landscapes.
MUSEUMS AND GALLERIES:
PONTOISE: *Mussels Eater* - THE HAGUE (Gemeentemus.): *Evening Market in front of the Town Hall in The Hague.*
AUCTION RECORDS:
PARIS, 18 June 1943, *Game of Cards,* FRF 7,000. PARIS, 13 Oct 1943, *Hermit,* FRF 1,000. PARIS, 17 Nov 1950, *Meal by Candlelight,* FRF 12,000. PARIS, 16 Feb 1951, *Meal of Mussels,* FRF 8,200. NEW YORK, 30 April 1970, *Dinner by Candlelight,* USD 1,000. LONDON, 28 Feb 1973, *Young Servant Girl,* GBP 500. LONDON, 13 June 1974, *Young Girl Serving Oysters,* Gns 600. LONDON, 11 Feb 1976, *Oyster Supper* (oil on panel, 17 1/4 x 23 3/4 ins / 43.5 x 60.5 cm) GBP 1,800. NEW YORK, 24 Jan 1980, *Tavern Scene* (oil on panel, 17 x 22 ins / 43.2 x 56 cm) NLG 1,700. AMSTERDAM, 15 May 1984, *Game of Cards by*

Candlelight (oil on panel, 17 3/4 x 24 1/2 ins / 45 x 62.2 cm) NLG 6,000. AMSTERDAM, 10 Feb 1988, *Merry Company Playing Cards and Drinking by Candlelight* (oil on panel, 17 3/4 x 25 1/4 ins / 45 x 64 cm) NLG 6,325. STOCKHOLM, 15 Nov 1988, *Interior Lit by a Candle with a Woman Preparing a Meal* (oil, 11 3/4 x 9 1/4 ins / 30 x 23.5 cm) SEK 23,000. AMSTERDAM, 11 Sept 1990, *Interior with Grandfather Reading to the Family by the Light of a Candle* (oil on panel, 17 x 19 3/4 ins / 43 x 50 cm) NLG 6,325. LONDON, 5 Oct 1990, *Mussels Festival* (oil on panel, 17 1/4 x 23 3/4 ins / 43.9 x 60.3 cm) GBP 1,980. AMSTERDAM, 24 April 1991, *Peasants Chatting round a Candle in an Interior* (oil on panel, 8 x 10 1/2 ins / 20.5 x 26.5 cm) NLG 2,530. AMSTERDAM, 14-15 April 1992, *Man near a Window Eating Fish* (1860, oil on panel, 13 1/2 x 10 3/4 ins / 34 x 27.5 cm) NLG 6,900. LONDON, 16 March 1994, *Animated Discussion* (oil on panel, 15 3/4 x 19 1/4 ins / 40 x 49 cm) GBP 3,220. AMSTERDAM, 21 April 1994, *Supper by Candlelight in an Interior* (oil on panel, 11 3/4 x 16 1/4 ins / 30 x 41.5 cm) NLG 9,775. AMSTERDAM, 18 June 1996, *Night Market in The Hague* (oil on panel, 11 x 9 ins / 28 x 22 cm) NLG 6,325. AMSTERDAM, 19-20 Feb 1997, *Recital by Candlelight* (oil on panel, 9 1/4 x 12 1/4 ins / 23.5 x 31 cm) NLG 6,919. AMSTERDAM, 2 July 1997, *Merry Company Playing Cards in an Interior Lit by a Candle* (oil on canvas, 16 1/4 x 19 1/2 ins / 41.5 x 49.5 cm) NLG 7,495. NEW YORK, 15 June 1999, *Moonlit Market Scene* (oil on panel, 17 x 22 ins / 43 x 56 cm) USD 2,800. NORTH BETHESDA, 22 Jan 2000, *Merrymaking* (oil on panel, 11 x 15 ins / 28 x 38 cm) USD 2,000. LYONS, 19 Nov 2000, *Women in Candlelit Interior* (oil on panel, 11 x 9 ins / 28 x 23 cm) FRF 15,500. NEW ORLEANS, 8 Dec 2000, *Evening Market* (oil on panel, 12 x 9 ins / 30 x 23 cm) USD 3,000. GRAVENHAGE, 24 April 2002, *Interior with Card Players* (oil on panel, 9 x 11 ins / 22 x 28 cm) EUR 2,400. GRAVENHAGE, 6 Nov 2002, *Musicians and Dance Company by Candlelight* (oil on canvas, 10 x 14 ins / 25 x 35 cm) EUR 2,100. AMSTERDAM, 1 July 2003, *Evening at the Inn* (oil on panel, 12 x 17 ins / 31 x 42 cm) EUR 3,200. KEMPTEN, 10 July 2003, *Men Playing Draughts by Candlelight* (oil on panel, 14 x 17 ins / 35 x 44 cm) EUR 2,000. AMSTERDAM, 27 Sept 2004, *Men Drinking, Smoking and Playing Checkers in a Candlelit Interior* (oil on panel, 13 x 17 ins / 34 x 44 cm) EUR 2,400.

SJÖBERG, J. Axel

Swedish, 19th - 20th century.
Born 1866; died 1950.
Painter, pastellist, watercolourist. Landscapes, animals.

Sjöberg exhibited in Paris, notably at the Exposition Universelle of 1900, where he was awarded a silver medal.

MUSEUMS AND GALLERIES:

COPENHAGEN (Statens Mus. for Kunst): *Onset of Winter* - GÖTEBORG: *Spring at the Coast* - STOCKHOLM: *Frozen Lake.*

AUCTION RECORDS:

STOCKHOLM, 6 April 1951, *Trial* (1892) DKK 1,500. STOCKHOLM, 27 Oct 1981, *Seaside* (oil on canvas, 35 1/2 x 48 3/4 ins / 90 x 124 cm) SEK 30,000. STOCKHOLM, 20 April 1983, *Winter Landscape* (watercolour, 18 x 23 1/2 ins / 46 x 60 cm) SEK 7,700. STOCKHOLM, 24 April 1984, *Seagulls* (oil on canvas, 43 1/4 x 61 ins / 110 x 155 cm) SEK 15,000. LONDON, 24 March 1988, *Summer Day at Sandhamm* (1942, pencil and watercolour, 17 1/4 x 23 3/4 ins / 43.9 x 60.3 cm) GBP 2,420. STOCKHOLM, 14 Nov 1990, *Rocky Inlet* (pastel, 19 1/4 x 25 1/4 ins / 49 x 64 cm) SEK 12,500. STOCKHOLM, 10-12 May 1993, *First Signs of Thaw on a Winter Morning* (watercolour, 20 3/4 x 28 1/4 ins / 53 x 72 cm) SEK 20,000. STOCKHOLM, 30 Nov 1993, *Daybreak in the Fields at the End of Winter* (watercolour, 20 3/4 x 28 1/4 ins / 53 x 72 cm) SEK 18,000. STOCKHOLM, 26 May 1999, *Potato Pickers* (1905, oil on canvas, 36 x 49 ins / 92 x 125 cm) SEK 31,000. MALMÖ, 8 April 2000, *Storm Approaching* (1912, oil on canvas, 45 x 62 ins / 115 x 157 cm) SEK 15,000. STOCKHOLM, 22 May 2000, *Fiske* (oil on canvas, 35 x 48 ins / 90 x 123 cm) SEK 15,000. STOCKHOLM, 28 May 2002, *Small Girl Wearing Large Straw Hat* (c. 1890, oil on canvas, 13 x 11 ins / 34 x 28 cm) SEK 26,000. STOCKHOLM, 4 June 2003, *Seascape with Ducks* (oil on canvas, 28 x 35 ins / 70 x 90 cm) SEK 26,000. STOCKHOLM, 4 June 2003, *Swans, Sandhamn* (1905, oil on canvas, 37 x 50 ins / 95 x 127 cm) SEK 38,000. STOCKHOLM, 25 May 2004, *Archipelago* (1903, oil on canvas, 40 x 57 ins / 101 x 145 cm) SEK 43,000.

SJÖHOLM, Adam

Swedish, 20th century.
Born 1923, in Budapest, to Swedish parents.
Active from 1950 in France.
Sculptor.

Adam Sjöholm studied at the fine arts academy in Budapest. He left Hungary for Sweden in 1948, before finally settling in Paris. His work featured at numerous group exhibitions in Paris, notably at the Salon Comparaisons, the Salon de la Jeune Sculpture and the Salon des Réalités Nouvelles. He also showed at a *L'Hommage à Brancusi* (*Tribute to Brancusi*) and at the first Salon des Galeries Pilotes at the Cantonal Museum of Lausanne in 1963. Solo exhibitions of his work were held variously in London, Munich, Paris and elsewhere.

Adam Sjöholm went through an initial figurative phase, but rapidly developed a technique and approach that served him in good stead over two decades. He stopped working in stone, opting instead to work with metal sheets that he rolled and assembled into a form of leafage.

BIBLIOGRAPHY:

Ier Salon international des Galeries Pilotes, exhibition catalogue, Musée cantonal, Lausanne, 1963.

SJÖHOLM, Charles

Swedish, 20th century.
Born 1933.
Painter (mixed media). Scenes with figures, genre scenes, urban landscapes.

AUCTION RECORDS:

STOCKHOLM, 28 Oct 1991, *Café Victoria; Matsalar, Stockholm* (1970, oil on canvas, 35 3/4 x 25 1/4 ins / 91 x 64 cm) SEK 9,500. STOCKHOLM, 13 April 1992, *Café at Norrmälarstrand, Stockholm* (mixed media, 17 x 23 1/2 ins / 43 x 60 cm) SEK 4,900. STOCKHOLM, 25 April 2000, *Couples Dancing at Mosebacke* (oil on canvas, 39 x 63 ins / 99 x 160 cm) SEK 15,000.

SJÖLANDER, Waldemar

Swedish, 20th century.
Painter. Landscapes with figures, fishing scenes.
Mec Art.

Waldemar Sjölander's work featured at the Biennale des Jeunes in Paris in 1967. He is an exponent of 'Mec Art' (mechanical art), using multiples of photographic clichés that are worked entirely or in part before being positioned on emulsified sheet metal. He also directs short animated films (cartoons).

AUCTION RECORDS:

GÖTEBORG, 18 May 1989, *Tehuana Fishing - Juchitan, Mexico* (1948, oil on canvas, 15 3/4 x 33 ins / 40 x 84 cm) SEK 13,000. STOCKHOLM, 22 May 1989, *Composition* (1967, oil on canvas, 37 1/2 x 37 3/4 ins / 95 x 96 cm) SEK 6,000. STOCKHOLM, 6 Dec 1989, *Sombre Men - Mexico* (1958, oil on canvas, 74 3/4 x 53 1/4 ins / 190 x 135 cm) SEK 11,500. STOCKHOLM, 14 June 1990, *Landscape with Mexican Houses and Figures* (1955, oil on canvas, 19 3/4 x 28 3/4 ins / 50 x 73 cm) SEK 12,500. STOCKHOLM, 13 April 1992, *Women in a Sunny Street* (oil on canvas, 37 1/2 x 37 1/2 ins / 95 x 95 cm) SEK 3,600. STOCKHOLM, 4 Nov 2003, *Summer Flowers in Evening Sunshine* (1941, oil on canvas, 43 x 41 ins / 110 x 105 cm) SEK 42,000.

SJOLLEMA, Dirck Pieter

Dutch, 18th - 19th century.
Born 6 July 1760, in Terbantsterchans; died 23 December 1840, in Heerenaval.
Painter. Landscapes, seascapes.

Dirck Pieter Sjollema specialised in painting Frisian subjects. The museum of Leiden has his *Foundations in Friesland* painted in 1825, and the museum in Louvain has two landscapes by him.

SJOLLEMA, Joop
Dutch, 20th century.
Born 1900; died 1991.
Painter. Portraits.

AUCTION RECORDS:
AMSTERDAM, 10 Dec 1992, *Portrait of Martinus Nijhoff* (oil on canvas, 16 x 11 3/4 ins / 40.5 x 30 cm) NLG 8,625.

SJÖLUND, Stig
Swedish, 20th - 21st century.
Born 1955.
Painter (mixed media).

AUCTION RECORDS:
STOCKHOLM, 30 May 1991, *Composition* (1983, mixed media, 35 x 35 ins / 89 x 89 cm) SEK 5,500.

SJOSTRAND, Carl or Karl Lucas
Finnish, 19th century.
Born 1828; died 1906.
Sculptor.

Sjostrand was one of the precursors of Finnish statuary. In 1864, he executed a monumental statue of the historian Porthan in Åbo (Turku).

MUSEUMS AND GALLERIES:
HELSINKI: *Kullervo as a Child Tearing Out His Tongues; Death of Kullervo* (two); *Sotkottaret; Monument of Porthan* (in miniature); *J.A. Munck; H. Gabr. Porthan; M. Calonius; J.L. Russeberg; T. Lonnroth; E.J. Lofgren; Fr. de Sjastrom; J. Kuntson; O. Kleinch; F. Berndtson; H. Munsterhjelm; F. Cygnaeus; J. Topenis; Th. Höijer; Kyllikli*; study.

SJÖSTRAND, Helmi
Finnish, 19th - 20th century.
Born 1864; died 1957.
Painter. Scenes with figures, urban landscapes.

AUCTION RECORDS:
LONDON, 15 March 1989, *Market Scene, Copenhagen* (1917, oil on canvas, 25 1/2 x 34 1/4 ins / 65 x 87 cm) GBP 45,000. STOCKHOLM, 15 Nov 1989, *Country House near a Lake* (oil, 19 3/4 x 15 3/4 ins / 50 x 40 cm) SEK 6,500. HELSINKI, 25 April 1999, *From Stockholm Harbour* (oil on canvas, 30 x 23 ins / 76 x 58 cm) FIM 25,000. HELSINKI, 2 Dec 2001, *Southern Mountain Landscape* (oil on canvas, 38 x 56 ins / 97 x 141 cm) FIM 11,000.

SJOSTROM, Fr. Anat.
Finnish, 19th century.
Watercolourist. Landscapes.

Sjostrom's watercolour, *View of Djurgården Park*, is in the museum in Helsinki.

SKADE, Fritz
German, 20th century.
Born 17 June 1898, in Freital; died 1971.
Painter. Portraits.

Skade was the pupil of Otto Gussmann.

AUCTION RECORDS:
ROME, 18 May 1983, *Portrait* (1925, pencil, 22 1/2 x 16 1/4 ins / 57 x 41 cm) ITL 1,200,000. LONDON, 18 Oct 2000, *Young Woman* (c. 1925, watercolour and pencil, 19 x 13 ins / 48 x 32 cm) GBP 1,500. BERLIN, 30 June 2001, *Female Nude* (watercolour, 19 x 13 ins / 48 x 32 cm) DEM 5,400.

SKADOVSKY, Nikolai L'vovich
Russian, 19th century.
Born 1846; died 1892.
Painter. Genre scenes.

MUSEUMS AND GALLERIES:
MOSCOW (State Tretyakov Gal.): *Reading the Newspaper* (drawing); *The Orator*; another painting.

SKAER, Lucy
British, 20th - 21st century.
Born 1975, in Cambridge.
Active in Glasgow.
Performance artist, draughtswoman.
Henri VIII's Wives.

Lucy Skaer completed a Master of Arts degree at the Glasgow School of Art. She belongs to the Henry VIII's Wives group of artists. She draws on a number of disciplines and always works in a public space. In *Public Project* (2001) she left a diamond and a scorpion side by side on a pavement in Amsterdam.

Skaer has taken part in group exhibitions, including *Beck's Futures 2003*, an exhibition presenting the work of the nine artists shortlisted for the Beck's Prize and shown at the ICA in London, the CCA in Glasgow and the Southampton City Art Gallery in 2003. She has also shown her work in solo exhibitions, including *Like a Circle in a Spiral* at the Transmission Gallery in Glasgow, and at the Kaganmartos Gallery in New York.

SKAHLE, Johann, or Skale
German, 17th century.
Active in Gottorf, in 1634.
Painter. Horses.

SKAIFE, T.
British, 19th century.
Active in Liverpool.
Miniaturist.

T. Skaife exhibited six miniatures at the Royal Academy in London between 1846 and 1852.

SKALA, Frantisek
Czech, 19th century.
Active in Pisek c. 1850.
Miniaturist.

Frantisek Skala was the father of Jan Skala.

SKALA, Jan
Bohemian School, 19th century.
Active in Prague during the second half of the 19th century.
Painter.

Jan Skala was the son of Frantisek Skala.

SKALA, Jaroslav
Czech, 20th century.
Born 27 December 1881, in Pardubice; died 11 January 1919, in Pardubice.
Sculptor.

Jaroslav Skala trained under Stanislav Sucharda and Josef V. Myslbek.

SKALA, Jósef
Bohemian School, 19th century.
Born 1802, in Breznitz, Bohemia.
Engraver (burin).

Jósef Skala studied at the academy in Prague and worked in Prague until 1838.

SKALIKS, Wilhelm
German, 20th century.
Born 18 December 1886, in Bruissen.
Painter. Portraits, landscapes, animals.

Skaliks studied under Heinrich Wolff and Ludwig Dettman at the fine arts academy in Königsberg (now Kaliningrad,

Russia) and under Willy Jaeckel in Berlin. He went on to live and work in Königsberg.
Museums and Galleries:
Kaliningrad: *Bulldog.*

SKALINGER, Nicola, or Scalinger
Italian, 19th century.
Died 26 November 1889, in Naples.
Painter. Stage sets.
Skalinger designed scenery for the San Carlo theatre in Naples.

SKALKIN, Viktor
Russian, 20th century.
Born 1938, in Moscow.
Painter. Figures.
Viktor Skalkin was a member of the Artists Union. He lives and works in Moscow.
Museums and Galleries:
Moscow (State Tretyakov Gal.).
Auction records:
Paris, 17 Nov 1990, *Woman and Child* (1989, oil on canvas, 47 1/4 x 70 3/4 ins / 120 x 180 cm) FRF 4,800.

SKALL
French, 20th - 21st century.
Born 1960, in Paris.
Sculptor of assemblages.
Skall works with a range of unusual materials, including straw, artificial flowers, rugs and electric sockets.
Examples of Skall's work have featured at various group exhibitions: in 1984 and 1985, at the Salon de Montrouge; in 1985, in New York and at the Musée d'Art Moderne de la Ville de Paris; and, in 1989, at the Musée de la Poste in Paris and the Amsterdam Contemporary Arts Fair. Solo exhibitions by Skall include those in Amsterdam in 1987 and 1988; in 1987, at Groningen Museum; and, in 1989, at the French Institute in London.
Museums and Galleries:
Groningen - Paris (Mus. de la Poste).
Auction records:
Paris, 7 March 1990, *Lewitt Floor Covering* (1990, rubber rug, hinges, electric sockets, silk, recto/verso, 23 1/2 x 45 1/4 x 4 ins / 60 x 115 x 10 cm) FRF 6,000.

SKANBERG, Carl Emmerik
Swedish, 19th century.
Born 12 June 1850, in Norrköping; died 24 January 1883, in Stockholm.
Painter. Landscapes with figures, landscapes, seascapes.
Skanberg was a pupil at the Kungliga Akademi för de Fria Konsterna in Stockholm. He also stayed in Paris. He painted mostly motifs of Stockholm, in addition to Dutch and Venetian landscapes.
Museums and Galleries:
Oslo: *The Rising of the Moon over Venice* - Stockholm: *The Grand Canal in Rainy Weather; Port in Venice.*
Auction records:
Stockholm, 25-27 Sept 1935, *Roses,* DKK 1,360. Stockholm, 22 Nov 1950, *Yachts in Holland,* DKK 2,010. Stockholm, 30 March 1966, *Winter Landscape,* SEK 10,000. Stockholm, 8 Nov 1972, *Snowy Landscape,* SEK 9,000. Malmö, 2 May 1977, *Village Street Under the Snow* (oil on canvas, 31 1/2 x 47 1/4 ins / 80 x 120 cm) SEK 34,500. Stockholm, 28 Oct 1980, *Italian Landscape* (1882, oil on panel, 6 1/2 x 10 3/4 ins / 16.5 x 27.5 cm) SEK 15,100. Stockholm, 27 Oct 1981, *Naval Site in Dordecht* (1880, oil on canvas, 20 3/4 x 35 3/4 ins / 53 x 91 cm) SEK 30,500. Stockholm, 11 April 1984, *Gondolas on the Lagoon, Venice* (1882, oil on canvas, 19 3/4 x 32 ins / 50 x 81 cm) SEK 45,000. Stockholm, 24 April 1984, *View of Venice* (1882, watercolour, 9 3/4 x 13 3/4 ins / 25 x 35 cm) SEK 9,000. Stockholm, 29 Oct 1985, *Winter Landscape* (1876, oil on canvas, 41 x 72 ins / 104 x 182 cm) SEK 65,000. Stockholm, 22 April 1986, *Boats in Port, Venice* (1882, oil on canvas, 12 1/2 x 21 1/4 ins / 32 x 54 cm) SEK 76,000. Stockholm, 15 Nov 1988, *Dawn in Danviken* (oil, 9 x 11 3/4 ins / 23 x 30 cm) SEK 34,000. Göteborg, 18 May 1989, *Landscape with Houses at Dusk* (oil on canvas, 9 1/2 x 12 1/2 ins / 24 x 32 cm) SEK 16,000. Stockholm, 15 Nov 1989, *View From Danviken in the Evening* (oil on canvas, 9 x 11 3/4 ins / 23 x 30 cm) SEK 28,000. Stockholm, 14 Nov 1990, *The Port of Venice* (oil on canvas, 11 1/4 x 19 ins / 28.5 x 48 cm) SEK 55,000. Stockholm, 10-12 May 1993, *Marine with People Beaching a Boat* (oil on panel, 9 x 13 1/2 ins / 22 x 34 cm) SEK 9,000. Stockholm, 30 Nov 1993, *Busy Paris Street* (oil on canvas, 16 1/4 x 11 ins / 41 x 27 cm) SEK 22,000. Malmö, 10 April 1999, *Winter* (oil on canvas, 41 x 72 ins / 103 x 183 cm) SEK 61,000. Stockholm, 24 Nov 1999, *Venetian Scene* (oil on canvas, 22 x 17 ins / 55 x 43 cm) SEK 56,000. Stockholm, 29 May 2000, *Harbour with Sailing Vessel* (oil on canvas, 16 x 23 ins / 40 x 59 cm) SEK 25,000. Stockholm, 28 Nov 2000, *Moonlight over the Sea* (oil on canvas, 13 x 22 ins / 33 x 55 cm) SEK 15,000. Stockholm, 28 Nov 2001, *Town by Water* (oil on canvas, 9 x 13 ins / 22 x 32 cm) SEK 17,500. Stockholm, 28 Nov 2001, *Venetian Harbour Scene* (oil on panel, 7 x 13 ins / 19 x 32 cm) SEK 21,000. Stockholm, 4 Dec 2002, *Venice* (oil on canvas, 13 x 21 ins / 33 x 54 cm) SEK 80,000. Stockholm, 26 May 2003, *Venice* (oil on panel, 16 x 13 ins / 41 x 32 cm) SEK 28,000. Stockholm, 3 Dec 2003, *Canal Scene, Venice* (oil on canvas/board, 18 x 13 ins / 45 x 34 cm) SEK 32,000. Stockholm, 26 May 2004, *Summer Landscape with Lady on Shore* (oil on canvas, 28 x 42 ins / 70 x 107 cm) SEK 16,000. Stockholm, 26 May 2004, *Coastal Landscape with Reeds, Summer* (oil on canvas, 7 x 13 ins / 19 x 34 cm) SEK 21,000.

SKAPINAKIS, Nikias
Portuguese, 20th century.
Born 1931, in Lisbon.
Painter.
Nikias Skapinakis exhibited in Paris and Lisbon. His popular erotic paintings stand on the margins of poetic realism.
Museums and Galleries:
Lisbon (Centro de Arte Moderna José de Azeredo Perdigão, Fundação Calouste Gulbenkian).

SKARBEK, Fryderyk de (Count)
Polish, 19th century.
Born 15 February 1792, in Torun; died 25 November 1866, in Warsaw.
Painter, writer.
The Mielzynski museum in Poznan owns *Stormy Landscape, The Tamka District in Warsaw,* and *Chopin's Birch Tree at Zelazowa Wola* by Fryderyk de Skarbek.

SKARBINA, Franz or Frantz
German, 19th - 20th century.
Born 24 February 1849, in Berlin; died 18 May 1910, in Berlin.
Painter, engraver. Landscapes.
Franz Skarbina was an etcher who studied initially at the fine arts academy in Berlin, before going on to complete his studies in Paris from 1855 to 1856. Skarbina's work featured at major exhibitions in the French capital, including the Exposition Universelle of 1900, where he was awarded a bronze medal (having already received an honourable mention in 1886).

F Skarbina

F. Skarbina

Museums and Galleries:
Aachen: *Cloister Chapel, Aachen* - Berlin: *Lacemaking, Bruges; Evening in the Village; Morning Ablutions* - Dresden: *Interior with Belgian Peasants* - Hamburg (Kunsthalle): *Three Views of Old Hamburg* - Leipzig (Mus. der Bildenden Künste): *Church at Furnes; Mourning* - Munich: *Farmyard in Picardy* - Wuppertal (Von der Heydt Mus.): *Opera Ball.*
Auction records:
Cologne, 24 Nov 1971, *Fishermen's Wives,* DEM 3,000. Cologne, 24 March 1972, *Farmyard,* DEM 3,000. Cologne, 25 June 1976, *Smithy* (1881, oil on canvas remounted on board, 15 3/4 x 21 1/4 ins / 40 x 54 cm) DEM 3,300. Munich, 30 May 1979, *Canal View, Berlin* (1894, pastel, 9 x 12 1/4 ins / 23 x 31 cm) DEM 2,100. Cologne, 21 May 1981, *Two Monks Contemplating a Painting* (oil on canvas, 27 1/2 x 22 ins / 70 x 56 cm) DEM 6,800. London, 19 March 1986, *Evening Stroll* (oil on canvas, 17 3/4 x 11 1/2 ins / 45 x 29.5 cm) GBP 10,500. London, 17 March 1989, *Canal Walk* (oil on canvas, 44 x 23 1/2 ins / 112 x 60 cm) GBP 41,800. Munich, 29 Nov 1989, *Moonlight* (1899, oil on canvas, 62 1/2 x 42 1/4 ins / 159 x 107 cm) DEM 143,000. London, 22 June 1990, *Children Skating in a Berlin Street* (oil on canvas/card, 25 3/4 x 20 1/4 ins / 65.7 x 51.7 cm) GBP 8,360. Amsterdam, 5-6 Nov 1991, *Dunkirk Beach and Figures* (oil on canvas, 13 1/2 x 19 1/4 ins / 34 x 49 cm) NLG 10,350. Amsterdam, 19 Oct 1993, *Afternoon Moment* (oil on canvas/panel, 12 1/2 x 10 ins / 31.5 x 24.5 cm) NLG 11,500.

SKARICZA, Maté or Mathäus
Hungarian, 16th century.
Born 1544, in Ráckeve; died c. 1606.
Draughtsman.
Maté Skaricza was also a theologian.

SKARNOS, Georg
Slovene, 17th century.
Active in Ljubljana during the first half of the 17th century.
Sculptor.
Georg Skarnos was commissioned to produce the altar of St Michael in the church of St Peter in Ljubljana.

SKARPA, George, or Djordje
Croat, 20th century.
Born 29 November 1881, in Starigrad (Hvar Island).
Sculptor. Religious subjects.
George Skarpa studied at Vienna and Zagreb. He lived and worked in Zagreb, where he sculpted tombs and an *Entombment* for the Church of Our Lady.

SKAT, Niels
Danish, 16th century.
Active probably c. 1550.
Painter (?).

SKEAF, D.
British, 19th century.
Active in London from 1807 to 1819.
Painter.

SKEAK, Edmund
British, 18th century.
Active in London c. 1790.
Painter.

SKEAPING, John Rattenbury
British, 20th century.
Born 9 June 1901, in South Woodford (Essex); died 1980.
Painter (including gouache), sculptor, watercolourist, pastellist, draughtsman. Portraits, sporting subjects, equestrian subjects, horse racing scenes, animals, nudes.
John Rattenbury Skeaping was the son of a painter, who was his first teacher, and studied at Goldsmith's College, followed by the Central School of Art and Design in London from 1917 to 1919, and the Royal Academy from 1919 to 1920. He won the Prix de Rome in 1924, and married the sculptress Barbara Hepworth in Florence the same year. He was a member of the 7&5 Society in 1932, and the London Group from 1928 to 1934. Skeaping was an Official War Artist during World War II. He was active in Mexico from 1949 to 1950. He became an associate of the Royal Academy in 1950. He taught at the Royal College of Art from 1948, and was Professor of Sculpture from 1953 to 1959.

He exhibited at the Royal Scottish Academy, and held his first show with Barbara Hepworth in 1928. The couple were divorced in 1932. He was the author of *Animal Drawing* (1936), *How to Draw Horses* (1941) and the *Great Trees of Mexico* (1952). He is best known for his animal sculpture, and was influenced by Cubism.

JOHN SKEAPING

Bibliography:
Skeaping, John Rattenbury, *The Art of Drawing Dainty Decoration... Third Thousand*, London and New York, 1915. Skeaping, John Rattenbury, *An Exhibition of Sculpture by John Skeaping and Barbara Hepworth*, London, 1930. Skeaping, John Rattenbury, *Animal Drawing*, periodical, The Studio, London, 1936.
Museums and Galleries:
London (Tate Collection): *Racehorse* (1929); *Horse* (1934).
Auction records:
London, 26 April 1972, *Deauville,* GBP 500; *Violin* (wood and marquetry) GBP 500. London, 5 March 1976, *The Races at Deauville* (1963, oil on canvas, 29 1/4 x 36 ins / 74 x 91.5 cm) GBP 380. London, 21 May 1980, *Passing the Post* (1964, watercolour heightened with gouache, 21 1/2 x 29 1/2 ins / 54.5 x 75 cm) GBP 750. New York, 4 June 1982, *The Finish at Saratoga* (1969, oil on canvas, 25 x 31 ins / 63.4 x 79 cm) USD 3,400. London, 14 July 1982, *Standing Nude* (1928, stone, h. 24 1/2 ins / 62 cm) GBP 2,300. London, 21 Sept 1983, *Horserace* (1972, coloured chalk, 25 x 29 1/4 ins / 63.5 x 74 cm) GBP 850. New York, 11 April 1984, *The Finish at Saratoga* (1969, oil on canvas, 25 x 31 ins / 63.5 x 79 cm) USD 4,200. London, 23 May 1984, *Portrait of a Dancer* (bronze, h. 27 ins / 68.5 cm) GBP 2,000. London, 18 July 1984, *An Encounter in the Desert* (1965, watercolour and gouache, 22 x 29 1/4 ins / 56 x 74 cm) GBP 2,200. London, 6 Feb 1985, *Horserace* (pastel, 18 x 22 ins / 46 x 56 cm) GBP 2,600. London, 22 July 1986, *Flamencos* (1934, watercolour and pen, 9 1/4 x 9 ins / 23.5 x 22 cm) GBP 1,100. London, 14 Nov 1986, *Serpent Form IV* (1936, stone, l. 7 3/4 ins / 20 cm) GBP 3,500. London, 12 Nov 1987, *Heavy Going, Arlington Park* (1967, watercolour and gouache, 21 x 28 1/2 ins / 53.5 x 72.7 cm) GBP 3,200. New York, 9 June 1988, *Photo Finish* (oil on canvas, 23 x 35 ins / 58.4 x 88.8 cm) USD 1,980. London, 9 June 1988, *The Trial Run* (1964, gouache, 22 x 29 1/2 ins / 55 x 75 cm) GBP 3,520. Nîmes, 25 Feb 1989, *Stable Boy and Horses* (oil on canvas, 32 x 46 ins / 81 x 116 cm) FRF 25,000. London, 21 Sept 1989, *Blue Bird* (sculpture in lapis lazuli, h. 2 1/2 ins / 6.3 cm) GBP 2,420. London, 9 Nov 1990, *The Jump* (1976, brown-patinated bronze, h. 12 1/2 ins / 32 cm) GBP

4,950. LONDON, 25 Jan 1991, *Greyhound Race* (1957, pencil and pastel, 14 1/4 x 22 ins / 36 x 56 cm) GBP 1,210. LONDON, 7 March 1991, *Jockey at the Gallop* (1956, pastel, 14 1/4 x 20 1/4 ins / 36 x 51.5 cm) GBP 1,430. LONDON, 8 March 1991, *Holly, the Artist's Greyhound* (1979, brown-patinated gilded bronze, l. 44 ins / 112 cm) GBP 11,550. LONDON, 2 May 1991, *Crouching Nude* (pencil and ink, 16 x 11 1/4 ins / 40.5 x 28.5 cm) GBP 550. NEW YORK, 7 June 1991, *Returning to the Stable Surrounded by Crowds* (1962, oil on canvas, 43 x 37 1/2 ins / 109.2 x 95.3 cm) USD 6,600. NEW YORK, 26 May 1992, *The Pureblood Bay Kenneth Rowntree During a Race* (oil on panel, 20 x 30 ins / 50.8 x 76.2 cm) USD 1,650. EDINBURGH, 13 May 1993, *Study of a Siamese Cat on the Alert* (1955, pencil and watercolour, 13 x 18 ins / 33 x 46 cm) GBP 2,090. LONDON, 13 Nov 1996, *In the Saddle* (1977, pastel/grey paper, 14 x 22 ins / 35.5 x 56 cm) GBP 1,092; *At the Finish* (1949, watercolour and gouache, 20 1/2 x 28 ins / 52 x 71 cm) GBP 4,140; *At the Finish* (1966, watercolour and gouache, 20 3/4 x 29 1/4 ins / 53 x 74 cm) GBP 6,325; *Over the Hedge* (dark-brown patinated bronze, h. 10 ins / 25.4 cm; l. 14 ins/35.6 cm) GBP 2,875; *Five Racehorses* (1977, bronze, group, h. 11 3/4 ins / 30 cm, l. 35 ins/89 cm) GBP 16,675. LONDON, 12 Nov 1997, *The Pureblood Bay Royal Palace* (1969, brown-patinated bronze, l. 17 1/4 ins / 44 cm) GBP 11,500. LONDON, 4 June 1999, *Galloping Horse* (1977, brown patinated bronze, 10 x 15 ins / 26 x 39 cm) GBP 9,000. LEYBURN, 25 Nov 1999, *Horse, with Head Down and One Foot Raised* (1978, bronze, h. 19 ins / 48 cm) GBP 4,000. LONDON, 22 March 2000, *Easy Win* (colour chalk, 18 x 15 ins / 46 x 39 cm) GBP 1,200. LONDON, 15 June 2000, *The Last Furlong* (1977, pastel on grey paper, 18 x 24 ins / 46 x 62 cm) GBP 1,600. LONDON, 20 March 2001, *Dog* (wood, h. 19 ins / 47 cm) GBP 4,300. LONDON, 28 June 2001, *Mill Reef* (1974, brown patinated bronze, h. 10 ins / 25 cm) GBP 33,000. LONDON, 2 July 2002, *Cat* (wood, 5 x 10 ins / 12 x 26 cm) GBP 5,200. LONDON, 6 Nov 2002, *Over the Hedge* (1970, brown patinated bronze, 15 x 10 ins / 37 x 25 cm) GBP 4,000. LONDON, 22 May 2003, *Group of Five Race Horses* (1977, brown patinated bronze, l. 36 ins / 91 cm) GBP 21,000. LONDON, 19 Nov 2003, *Mill Reef* (brown patinated bronze, 10 x 13 ins / 25 x 32 cm) GBP 25,000. CREWKERNE, 14 Jan 2004, *Horse and Jockey, Arles* (colour chalk, ink and brush, 13 x 19 ins / 33 x 48 cm) GBP 1,400. LONDON, 21 Sept 2004, *The Family* (wood, h. 9 ins / 24 cm) GBP 1,900.

SKEATS, Leonard Frank
British, 19th - 20th century.
Born 9 June 1874, in Southampton; died 13 September 1943.
Painter. Portraits, figures.

Leonard Skeats exhibited with the Royal Academy from 1906 to 1909.

SKEIBROCK, Mathias Severin Berntsen
Norwegian, 19th century.
Born 1 December 1851; died 22 March 1896, in Christiania (now Oslo).
Sculptor.

Skeibrock studied in Copenhagen and then lived in Paris, developing an appreciation for the academic art of Jerichau. His tormented and vigorous *Ragnar Lodbrog in the Snakepit* earned him notice in 1878. His *Fatigue*, currently in the Nasjonalgaleriet in Oslo, received mention at the Salon de Paris during the Exposition Universelle in 1889.

MUSEUMS AND GALLERIES:

BERGEN: *Ragnar Lodbrog in the Snakepit; Statuette of Ludwig Holberg; In Full Torment; Snorri Recounting the Legends of Norwegian Kings* - OSLO (Nasjonalgal.): *Ragnar Lodberg in the Snakepit; The Old Mother* (marble); *Fatigue; Busts of Søren Jaabæk and Bjørnstjerne Bjørnson.*

SKELBYE, Poul
Danish, 20th century.
Born 1919, in Kastrup.
Active from 1952 in Sweden.
Painter, illustrator.

Poul Skelbye studied architecture and civil engineering in Copenhagen before making his debut as a painter in 1943. He went on to work as an illustrator and typesetter and also designed exhibition stands. He took part in group exhibitions in Scandinavia, as well as exhibiting solo - initially in 1944, and subsequently also in Copenhagen, Malmö and Paris (1971).

Skelbye's work became progressively abstract as of 1946. His background as an architect and civil engineer left a taste for 'pure' and precise mechanical forms and his compositions are precisely that - essentially, blueprints painted in extremely smooth and suave colours.

SKELL. See **SCKELL**

SKELLY
British, 18th century.
Active at the end of the 18th century.
Painter.

Skelly painted views, and exhibited at the Royal Academy in London in 1792 and 1794. He was an officer.

SKELTON, James
British, 18th century.
Born 1758, in Rome, of British origin.
Painter.

MUSEUMS AND GALLERIES:

LONDON (Victoria and Albert Mus.): two views.

AUCTION RECORDS:

LONDON, 13 May 1925, *Rome* (drawing); *Tivoli* (drawing, collection) GBP 27; *Castel Gandolfo; Tivoli* (two drawings) GBP 45; *Rochester; Rochester Castle and Bridge; Near Rochester Castle* (three drawings) GBP 45. LONDON, 17 Oct 1968, *View of Tivoli* (watercolour) GBP 520. LONDON, 11 Nov 1969, *The Edge of the Wood* (watercolour) Gns 700.

SKELTON, Joseph
British, 19th century.
Born c. 1785; died after 1850.
Engraver (burin).

Joseph Skelton was the brother of William Skelton. He worked in London and Paris. He executed views, architectural engravings and portraits.

SKELTON, Joseph Ratcliffe
British, 19th century.
Born 1865, in Newcastle upon Tyne; died 1927, in North Kensington (London).
Painter, watercolourist. Figures, illustrations, genre scenes.

Joseph Skelton lived in London. He exhibited at the Royal Academy, at the Royal Institute of Painters in Watercolours, at the Royal Institute of Oil Painters and at the Royal West of England Academy, of which he was a member.

SKELTON, Leslie James
Canadian, 19th - 20th century.
Born 27 April 1848, in Montreal; died 10 January 1929, in Colorado Springs.
Painter. Landscapes.

Leslie James Skelton studied in Montreal and Paris.

MUSEUMS AND GALLERIES:

COLORADO SPRINGS (Fine Arts Center): *Sunrise on the Peak* (oil on canvas) - OTTAWA (NG. of Canada).

AUCTION RECORDS:

NEW YORK, 15 March 1985, *Mountain Lake* (oil on canvas, 16 1/4 x 24 1/4 ins / 41 x 61.5 cm) USD 2,200.

SKELTON, Perceval
British.
Painter.

Joseph Skelton engraved in the style of Perceval Skelton.

SKELTON, William
British, 18th - 19th century.
Born 14 June 1763, in London; died 13 April 1848, in London.
Engraver (burin).
William Skelton was a pupil of James Basire and William Sharp. He worked principally for Boydell and the Society of Dilettanti, for whom he executed his finest engravings. He enjoyed great success with his portraits of the British royal family from George III to Queen Victoria.

SKENE, James, known as Skene of Rubislaw
British, 18th - 19th century.
Born 7 March 1775, in Aberdeen; died 1864, in Oxford.
Active in Europe 1802-1816; in Edinburgh 1816-1837; in Greece 1838 to 1845.
Painter, watercolourist, draughtsman, etcher.
Architectural views, landscapes.
James Skene was the younger son of the laird of Rubislaw. He depicted scenes of Edinburgh and landscapes in Europe in watercolours and drawings. He was a friend of Sir Walter Scott and the two of them planned to portray the changing face of Edinburgh in a publication, but Scott encountered financial difficulties and the project was dropped in 1826. Between 1817 and 1837, Skene produced over two hundred views of Edinburgh, including *Guard-House and Black Turnpike* and *Parliament House*. Examples of these formed part of two exhibitions: *O Caledonia! Sir Walter Scott and the Creation of Scotland* at the Scottish National Portrait Gallery in 1999 and *From Castle to Palace: Artists and the Royal Mile* at the City Art Centre, Edinburgh in 2004.

Skene lived on the continent between 1802 and 1816, returning in 1834 to live in Greece until 1844 where he painted many landscapes and views of classical Greek architecture, for example, *Road to Phyle, Mount Parnos* (1840). He also travelled in Asia Minor painting as he went, for example *Ephesus* (1838) and *Constantinople: the Seraglio Point from the Descent to Galata*. An exhibition of Skene's Greek work - *Views of Greece by James Skene* - was held by the Anglo-Hellenic League in 1963.

BIBLIOGRAPHY:
Skene, James, *A Series of Sketches of the Existing Localities Alluded to in the Waverley Novels*, Edinburgh, 1829 (etched from original drawings). Skene, James, *Italian Journey: Being Excerpts from the Pre-Victorian Diary of James Skene of Rubislaw*, International Publishing Co., London, 1937. *Views of Greece by James Skene*, exhibition catalogue, Anglo-Hellenic League, London, 1963 (to mark the jubilee 1913-1963). Viles, M., *James Skene 1775-1864: Watercolours and Drawings by the Artist, Traveller and Scholar*, Arts Council, 1964. Tsigakou, Fani-Maria, *James Skene: Monuments and Views of Greece 1838-1845*, National Historical Museum, Athens, 1987. Tsigakou, Fani-Maria, *British Images of Greece from the Benaki Museum Collections*, Benaki Museum, Athens, 1995. Cannizzion, Jean, *O Caledonia! Sir Walter Scott and the Creation of Scotland*, exhibition catalogue, CD-ROM, National Galleries of Scotland, Edinburgh, 1999.

MUSEUMS AND GALLERIES:
ATHENS (National Historical Museum): various Greek landscapes - EDINBURGH (City Libraries): over 200 views in and around Edinburgh.

AUCTION RECORDS:
LONDON, 17 Oct 2001, *Road to Phyle, Mount Parnos* (1840, watercolour, 11 x 18 ins / 28 x 46 cm) GBP 2,200. LONDON, 16 Dec 2003, *Interior of the Parthenon* (1841, watercolour, 13 x 23 ins / 33 x 59 cm) GBP 3,000.

SKERL, Friedrich Wilhelm
German, 18th - 19th century.
Born 1752, in Brunswick; died 13 July 1810, in Dresden.
Painter, engraver (etching), lithographer.
Friedrich Skerl was the father of Paul Anton. He engraved portraits, horses and views.

MUSEUMS AND GALLERIES:
DRESDEN (Stadtmus.): *Portrait of the Flautist P.G. Buffardin; Portrait of Martin Luther* (engraving after Lucas Cranach).

SKERL, Paul Anton
German, 19th century.
Born 1787, in Dresden; died 1852, in Dresden.
Engraver (burin), lithographer. Portraits, views, architectural views.
Paul Anton Skerl studied under C. A. Lindner at the academy in Dresden.

MUSEUMS AND GALLERIES:
DRESDEN (Prints Collection): several portraits.

SKETCHLEY
British, 18th century.
Active in London in 1783.
Painter. Flowers.

SKEYSERT, Clara de. See **KEYSERE**

SKIDMORE
British, 19th century.
Sculptor.
Skidmore sculpted the choir screen in Lichfield Cathedral towards 1860.

SKIDMORE, Lewis Palmer
American, 19th - 20th century.
Born 3 September 1877, in Bridgeport; died 1955.
Painter, engraver.
Lewis Palmer Skidmore was taught by John H. Niermeyer, Jean-Paul Laurens and Léon Bonnat in Paris. He lived and worked in Brooklyn. As an engraver, he specialised in etching.

SKIDMORE, Thornton D.
American, 20th century.
Born 2 June 1884, in Brooklyn (New York City); died 1956.
Painter, illustrator.
Thornton D. Skidmore was taught by Howard Pyle and Eric Pape. He is best known for his street and harbour scenes.

SKIKKILD, Chresten
Danish, 20th century.
Born 2 January 1885, in Ringköbing; died 15 November 1927, in Vordingborg.
Sculptor.
Skikkild studied under August Saabye and at the Kongelige Danske Kunstakademi in Copenhagen, and went on to carve altars and provide stained glass compositions for churches in Esbjerg.

SKILL, Edward
Swedish, 19th century.
Born 23 June 1831, near London; died 5 May 1873, in Stockholm.
Sculptor (wood).
Skill engraved mostly portraits.

SKILL, Frederick John
British, 19th century.
Born c. 1824; died 8 March 1881, in London.
Painter. Portraits, landscapes, rustic scenes.
Frederick John Skill was a member of the New Water-Colour Society. He exhibited in London from 1858 to 1881, par-

ticularly at the Royal Academy, the Royal Society of British Artists in Suffolk Street and the New Society. He also exhibited in Paris, where he stayed on numerous occasions.

Museums and Galleries:

London (National Portrait Gal.): *Men of Science Living in 1807-8* (c. 1857-1862, pencil and wash, in collaboration with Sir John Gilbert, Elizabeth and William Walker) - London (Victoria and Albert Mus.): three watercolours - London (Wallace Collection): *Sheep in a Turnip Field; In Winter; Walmer Castle; Breton Byre* (1867).

SKILLIN, Samuel

Irish, 19th century.

Born c. 1819, in Cork; died 27 January 1847, in Cork.

Painter, engraver (etching). Figures, portraits.

Samuel Skillin was a pupil at the Dublin Academy. He exhibited a *Portrait of John Clarke* and *Scenes from the Marriage of Figaro* at the Dublin Academy in 1842.

SKILLMAN, William

British, 17th century.

Active c. 1660.

Engraver.

SKILOYANNIS, Georgios

Greek, 20th - 21st century.

Born 20 June 1950, in Amphissa.

Active in France from 1981.

Assemblage artist, sculptor.

Skiloyannis studied at the school of fine art in Athens, then studied in Paris. He produces assemblages from time-worn wooden planks. He took part in collective exhibitions in 1985 and 1988, Salon de Montrouge; 1985, Pinakotheke in Rodos, Centre Georges Pompidou in Paris; 1986, Musée de Cagnes-sur-Mer; 1987, Pinakotheke in Athens; 1988, Institut du Monde Arabe in Paris; 1989, French Institute in Athens; and 1990, Musée d'Art Moderne in St Étienne. Solo exhibitions include those in 1985 in Athens and in 1989 in the Chapelle de Vallauris.

SKILTERS, Gustavs

Latvian, 19th - 20th century.

Born 3 November 1874, in Rujiena; died 1954.

Painter, sculptor, etcher, book designer.

Rukis (The Gnome).

Gustavs Skilters studied at the Stieglitz Institute in St Petersburg and was at that time he was a member of Rukis, an association of Latvian artists and art students in the capital that promoted realism and national identity through art. He obtained a study grant from the Institute, which enabled him to visit Paris, where he received advice from Rodin. From 1905 to 1908 he taught at the Institute and later at the Latvian academy of art. Skilters carved a number of monuments, mostly in Latvia. He was a renowned Art Nouveau book designer and etcher. His relief sculptures can be seen in Hotel Bergs, Riga.

Museums and Galleries:

Riga (MM) - Riga (Valsts makslas muz.).

SKINNER, Jacob

British, 18th century.

Died 9 November 1754, in Bath.

Engraver.

Jacob Skinner engraved ex-libris.

SKINNER, John

British, 18th century.

Miniaturist.

John Skinner exhibited two miniatures at the Royal Academy between 1776 and 1787.

SKINNER, Martin

Irish, 17th century.

Died before 1702.

Painter. Portraits.

Martin Skinner was a member of the Dublin Guild from 1698.

SKINNER, Matthew

British, 18th century.

Engraver.

Matthew Skinner was active in Exeter from 1750 to 1760. He engraved ex-libris.

SKIPPE, John or J. B. or Jean

British, 18th - 19th century.

Born 1742, in Ledbury; died 8 April 1811, in Overbury.

Painter, watercolourist, engraver. Scenes with figures, genre scenes, landscapes.

John Skippe came from a wealthy family and practised art for his own pleasure. He studied landscape with Joseph Vernet and engraving with John Baptiste Jackson. He practised wood engraving using burin, etching and chiaroscuro. Inspired by the beautiful wood engraving executed by Ugo da Carpi in chiaroscuro after a study drawn by Raphael for his tapestry, *The Miraculous Draught of Fishes*, Skippe engraved in chiaroscuro several drawings by Raphael, Parmigianino and Correggio among others, which he published between 1770 and 1811. He also executed watercolours.

Museums and Galleries:

London (Victoria and Albert Mus.): *Huntresses and Dogs Asleep in a Wood* (watercolour); *Group of Trees on the Flank of a Hill* (watercolour).

SKIPWORTH, Frank Markham or Markbam

British, 19th - 20th century.

Born 1854; died 1929.

Painter. Figures, portraits, genre scenes.

Frank Markham Skipworth lived and worked in London where he exhibited at the Royal Academy and Suffolk Street from 1882 to 1916.

Museums and Galleries:

Liverpool (Walker AG): *Portrait of Marshall Roberts.*

Auction records:

New York, 18-20 April 1906, *Best friend,* USD 126. New York, 17-18 March 1909, *Young girl and her dog,* USD 60. London, 16 Nov 1976, *Roman holiday* (1889, oil on canvas, 50 x 40 1/4 ins / 127 x 102 cm) GBP 1,200. Los Angeles, 18 June 1979, *Young girl playing the tambourine* (1889, oil on canvas, 60 x 44 ins / 152.3 x 112 cm) USD 3,900. New York, 24 Oct 1989, *Indolence* (1884, oil on canvas, 24 1/4 x 35 1/4 ins / 61.5 x 89.5 cm) USD 88,000. London, 13 June 1990, *Head of a Young Woman* (1887, oil on panel, 8 1/4 x 6 1/4 ins / 21 x 16 cm) GBP 1,650. New York, 19 Feb 1992, *The Lesson* (oil on canvas, 25 3/4 x 34 1/4 ins / 65.4 x 87.3 cm) USD 17,600. London, 3 Nov 1993, *The Mirror* (1911, oil on canvas, 21 1/2 x 27 1/2 ins / 54.5 x 70 cm) GBP 6,670. London, 11 Oct 1995, *Ball gown* (1904, oil on card, 12 3/4 x 7 3/4 ins / 32.5 x 19.5 cm) GBP 1,897. London, 6 Nov 1996, *A moment's rest* (1913, oil on canvas, 20 3/4 x 27 1/4 ins / 53 x 69 cm) GBP 2,530.

SKIRA, Pierre

French, 20th century.

Born 1938, in Paris.

Painter, draughtsman.

Nouvelle Figuration.

Pierre Skira showed his work at the Paris Biennale in 1965, 1967 and 1969, and also exhibited in Amsterdam, Paris and Milan. In 1977, during the Festival d'Automne in Paris, his work appeared in *Papier sur nature* (*Paper on Nature*), an exhibition organised by Jean Clair during the controversy about the return to drawing and figuration.

Bibliography:

Mauriès, Patrick, *Traité d'incertitude*, Le Promeneur, Paris, 2002.

SKIRMUNT, Helena
Polish, 19th century.
Born 5 November 1827, in Kolodno; died 13 February 1874, in Amélie-les-Bains, France.
Sculptor, painter.
Helena Skirmunt studied under W. Dmochowski in Vilnius, J. Cesar in Vienna and P. Galli in Rome. The National Museum in Cracow owns a bust that she sculpted of *The Grand Duke Gedymine*, and medallion portraits of *H. Rodziewicz, H. Plawinski* and *Josephine Butrymowicz*.

SKIRMUNT, Szymon
Polish, 19th century.
Born 1835, in Molodow; died 1902, in Paris.
Painter. History painting.
Szymon Skirmunt studied at the art academy in St Petersburg. He travelled in Italy and France.
AUCTION RECORDS:
NEW YORK, 24 May 1984, *The Unexpected Visitor* (oil on canvas, 36 1/4 x 58 ins / 92 x 147.3 cm) USD 2,000.

SKIROTETIS, Aldona
Lithuanian, 20th century.
Born 1932, in Vilnius.
Engraver.
From the work shown in the exhibition *L'Art russe des Scythes à nos jours*, Grand Palais, Paris (1967), it can be concluded that Aldona Skirotetis made allegorical linocuts illustrating the official line.
BIBLIOGRAPHY:
L'Art russe des Scythes à nos jours, exhibition catalogue, Gal. nationales du Grand Palais, Paris, 1967.

SKIRVING, Archibald, or Shirving
British, 18th - 19th century.
Born 1749, in Haddington; died 1819, in Inverness.
Miniaturist.
Archibald Skirving studied in Rome. His miniatures were remarkable for the sharpness and clarity of their drawing, and the beauty of their colouring and expression. He gave up miniatures to devote himself mainly to expressive portraits in pencil.
He exhibited miniatures at the Royal Academy in London from 1778 to 1799.
MUSEUMS AND GALLERIES:
EDINBURGH (Mus. of Scotland): *Portrait of a Man* - EDINBURGH (Nat. Gal. of Scotland, Print Room): *Janet Skirving, Mrs John Carnegie of Edrom Newton* (pastel) - EDINBURGH (Scottish National Portrait Gallery): *Robert Burns* (1796-1798, drawing); *Rev. Alexander Carlyle* (oil on canvas); *Adam Skirving, the Artist's Father* (oil on canvas); other portraits (drawings).

SKJELBORG, Axel
Danish, 20th century.
Born 19 June 1895, in Molgjer.
Painter. Animals.
Skjelborg studied at the Kongelige Danske Kunstakademi in Copenhagen. He was influenced by Théodore Philpsen.
MUSEUMS AND GALLERIES:
ESBJERG - HORSENS - KOLDING.

SKJÖLDEBRAND, Anders Fredrik, or Anders Friedrich
Swedish, 19th century.
Born 1757, in Sweden; died 1835.
Painter, watercolourist, engraver. Landscapes.
In 1799, Skjöldebrand went to Cape North with Acerbin. Upon his return, he published a book about his voyage. In 1804, he published a volume on the waterfalls of Trollättan.
AUCTION RECORDS:
STOCKHOLM, 19 May 1992, *Cascatellerna Near Tivoli* (watercolour/wash, 16 x 11 1/2 ins / 40.5 x 29.5 cm) SEK 3,500.

SKJÖLDEBRAND, E.
Swedish, 19th century.
Painter. Portraits.
Skjöldebrand was active around 1850. He painted the portrait of *Friederika Dorothea Wilhelmina of Baden, Queen of Sweden*.

SKLAVOS, Gerasimos, or Gerassimos, Yerasimos, Yerassimos
Greek, 20th century.
Born 10 September 1927, in Domata, Kefallonia; died 28 January 1967, in Levallois-Perret, France, as the result of an accident.
Active in France.
Sculptor, painter, draughtsman.
Gerasimos Sklavos graduated in sculpture from the Athens school of fine arts in 1956 and was awarded a travel grant by the Greek government, which he used the following year to go to Paris, where he studied in the atelier of Marcel Gimond at the École des Beaux-Arts and with Osip Zadkin at the Académie de la Grande Chaumière.
Sklavos' early work, when still a student in Athens, was traditional, but once he arrived in Paris, he started to experiment with techniques and content, in particular questioning his attachment to figurative art. Soon, little was left of it but the occasional allusion, and very quickly he came into his stride, attaining technical mastery and his own definitive way of expressing himself. At first he worked in wood, iron, and cement, a medium little used in his time but in which he created a considerable number of well-finished works. Finally, he turned to the hardest stones, to attack which he developed a special technique using metal-working tools. He would in fact use an oxy-acetylene torch to cut grooves and hollows in the stone, hacking it back until it reached the essential form and volume he wanted, always bearing in mind the specific qualities of each new stone, and leaving the scars and marks of his creative aggression to enliven its surface.
Sklavos developed smoothly from metaphoric figurative work to pure Abstraction. Although clearly an artist of his time, he was also part of the Greek tradition, and while removing all human likeness from his creations, he endowed them with all the elegance, the vital force, and the draped sensuousness of the Goddesses of the ancient world.
He preferred to work on the monumental scale. Returning one day to his studio to work he tripped on his *Pygmalion* which fell and crushed him to death.
Collective exhibitions include: Panhellenic Exhibition, Athens and Festival of Youth, Moscow (1957); Salon d'Automne, Paris (1958, 1960); Salon de la Jeune Sculpture, Salon des Réalités Nouvelles, Salon de Mai (from 1959); Salon Comparaisons (from 1960); Biennale voor Beeldhouwkunst, Middelheim Park, Antwerp (1961); São Paulo Biennale (1961); Biennale des Jeunes, Paris (1961), winning the jury and exhibiters' prizes; *Artistes grecs vivant à Paris*, Musée d'Art moderne, Paris (1962); *L'Objet - Antagonismes II*, Musée des Arts décoratifs, Paris (1962); *Petits bronzes*, Musée d'Art moderne, Paris (1962); Carnegie International Exhibition, Pittsburgh (1964); Premier Symposium de Sculpture d'Amérique du Nord, Montréal (1964); Salon Grands et Jeunes d'Aujourd'hui, Paris (1964-1966); Sculpture Panatheneum, Athens (1965); IIIe Exposition internationale de la Sculpture contemporaine, Musée Rodin, Paris (1966). Posthumous exhibitions include: Salon de Mai (1967); Paris Biennale, then at the Greek Pavilion of Expo 67, Montréal, and at *L'Art Grec Contemporain*, Musée Rath, Geneva (1967); *Hommage à Christian et Yvonne Zervos*, Grand Palais, Paris (1970); National Art Gallery, Athens (1972, 1992); Musée des Beaux-Arts, Calais (1976); Musée de la Monnaie, Paris (1985, 1988); *Peintres et sculpteurs grecs contemporains en France* (*Greek Sculptors and Painters in France*), Maison de l'Eu-

rope, Paris (1994). Solo exhibitions include: Galerie Cahiers d'art, Paris (1961); Lausanne (1962); major solo show at the Paris Biennale (1963), as winner of the Jury Prize at the previous Biennale; Paris (1965); Athens (1966). Posthumous retrospectives include: Musée Rodin and the Galerie Cahiers d'Art, Paris (1968); City Hall, Ist Arrondissement, Paris (1979); Centre culturel, Toulouse (1980); Institut français, Athens (1980); Cultural Centre, Hasselt, Belgium (1982); European Cultural Centre, Delphi (1984); Cultural Centre, Thessaloniki (1999).

BIBLIOGRAPHY:

Boudaille, Georges, '*Sklavos, sculpteur grec*' in *Studio International*, periodical, London, April, 1965. Lipsi, Jeanine, '*Sklavos*' in *Quadrum* vol. XIII, periodical, Brussels, 1966. Zervos, Christian, '*Peut-on être moderne et classique?*' in *Hommage à Sklavos*, exhibition catalogue, Musée Rodin, Paris, 1968. '*Hommage à Sklavos*' in *Cahiers d'art*, periodical, Paris, 1968. Boudaille, Georges, '*Sensibilité de Sklavos*' in *XXe Siècle* n° 31, periodical, Paris, December 1968. Béatrice, Andia, *Sklavos*, exhibition catalogue, Éd. de la ville de Paris, Paris, 1979. Fioravantes, Spyrovassilis, *L'œuvre du sculpteur Y. Sklavos: analyse esthétique et questions théoriques*, dissertation, Université René-Descartes Paris V, Paris, 1986. Fioravantes, Vassilis, *Sklavos - Monographie*, Parousia, Athens, 1994. Iliopoulou-Rogan, Dora, *Sklavos*, Nation al Bank of Greece, Athens, 1998 (English edition). Sklavos, Nicolas, *Sklavos. Sculpteur, peintre 1927-1967*, 2002 (study by the artist's brother).

MUSEUMS AND GALLERIES:

ATHENS (Ethnikí Pinakothíki): *Icarus* (1956); *Elevation* (1962); *Passer-By* (1965) - CALAIS (MBA et de la Dentelle): *New Creation Toward Space* (1961) - DELPHI (Mun.): *Light of Delphi* (1965) - DIJON (MBA): *Column with Triumphant Breasts* (1961); *Whirlwind* (1965); *Eye* (1965) - MONT-DE-MARSAN (Mus. Despiau-Wlérick): *Three Figures* (1962) - MONTREAL (Centre de Sculpture Mont-Royal): *Cardinal Sisters* (1964) - MONTREAL (MAC): *Télélumière* (1964) - MOUNTAINVILLE (Storm King Art Center): *Eyes of the Sky* (1964) - PARIS (CNAC): *Birth; Three Figures* (engraving) - PARIS (MNAM-CCI): *Soul* (1961, sculpture, in the sculpture garden of the Parc floral, Paris); *Flight in Space* (1962, drawing); *The Friend who Didn't Stay* (1966) - PARIS (Mus. de la Monnaie): medal of the Paris Biennale (1967); *Cyclades* (1963); *Couple de forces lumineuse* (*Luminous Force Couple*) (1962); *Flight in Space* (1965) - SÃO PAULO (MAC): *Fertile Man* (1961) - VÉZELAY (Municipal collection): several works.

AUCTION RECORDS:

PARIS, 12 June 1986, *Cosmic Light* (1964, stone, 11 1/2 x 7 1/2 x 5 1/2 ins / 29 x 19 x 14 cm) FRF 51,000. PARIS, 6 Dec 1986, *Bonds of Tenderness* (1959, wood, h. 62 1/2 ins / 159 cm) FRF 75,000. PARIS, 25 Oct 1987, *Earth Light* (1965, marble, 12 1/2 x 6 x 4 ins / 32 x 15 x 10 cm) FRF 21,000. PARIS, 20 March 1988, *Overture* (1961, quartzite stone, 9 x 7 x 9 ins / 22 x 18 x 22 cm) FRF 22,000. PARIS, 16 Oct 1988, *Composition: everyday objects* (1960, iron, 31 1/2 x 23 1/2 x 14 1/4 ins / 80 x 60 x 36 cm) FRF 15,000. PARIS, 16 April 1989, *Transmutation* (1961, stone, 26 x 12 1/4 x 9 3/4 ins / 66 x 31 x 25 cm) FRF 100,000. PARIS, 5 Feb 1990, *Project: Girl no 2* (1964, 7 x 5 x 1 1/2 ins / 18 x 13 x 4 cm) FRF 17,000. PARIS, 3 Feb 1992, *Swallow* (1965, bronze, 6 1/4 x 6 1/4 x 4 3/4 ins / 16 x 16 x 12 cm) FRF 7,000. PARIS, 20 June 1997, *Poetry* (1966, antique green-patinated bronze, 15 x 10 1/4 ins / 38.3 x 26 cm) FRF 21,000. PARIS, 19 Oct 1997, *Spatial Plant* (1966, antique green-patinated bronze, 17 1/4 x 11 x 9 ins / 43.5 x 27 x 22 cm) FRF 25,000. PARIS, 23 Nov 1997, *Virgin* (1964, brown-patinated bronze with shades of purple, 20 1/2 x 5 x 2 ins / 52 x 13 x 5 cm) FRF 30,000. PARIS, 22 March 1998, *Whirlwind* (1965, antique-green-patinated bronze, 17 3/4 x 6 1/4 x 4 ins / 45 x 16 x 10 cm) FRF 18,000.

SKLENÁR, Zdenek

Czech, 20th century.

Born 5 April 1910, in Leština; died 19 April 1986, in Prague.

Painter, illustrator, graphic artist, engraver. Figures, still-lifes, flowers.

Mánes Group.

Zdenek Sklenár was the son of a schoolmaster. He studied under Arnost Hofbauer and Zdenek Kratochvil at the Prague school of applied arts from 1929 to 1935 and later taught there as assistant professor from 1945 to 1950. He belonged to the Mánes group from 1943. In 1955 he went to China, a visit that had a profound influence on his art.

In 1943, Emanuel Moravec, a Czech pro-Nazi collaborator who was appointed Minister of Education in German-occupied Czechoslovakia from 1942 to 1945, condemned modern Czech art as degenerate (using the same criteria as the Nazis had in 1937), and Sklenár was deported to a labour camp in Germany. After the war he returned to Prague but the new government accorded him no recognition, so he went to work for the art departments of various newspapers, designed posters and illustrated books, and gradually made a name for himself in Czechoslovakia and in exhibitions abroad, winning a number of prizes. At the same time, he continued to paint, though his work was little appreciated. His first, hesitant, paintings, from 1943, show the influence of the School of Paris, in a sort of synthesis, very common in Europe of that time, of Post-Cubism, Matisse style drawing and Picasso style Expressionism. To this Sklenár added a Surrealist dimension of the sort that had earlier been strongly represented in Czechoslovakia by Stryrsky, Toyen and Hudecek, which gave some of his works a charming air of unreality. By 1945, his graphic style had characteristic, endless arabesque curves curling back upon themselves, while his paintings were starting to take on the quality of enamels. From 1948, these characteristics had taken hold and Sklenár was in full flight as an artist of sure originality. After his visit to China, his work attains greatness: in its colour and matter, floating somewhere between the figurative and the abstract, it has the richness of enamels. The bewildering mosaic of disparate figures and objects all heaped together in these works sometimes recall the soldiers in Altdorfer or Brueghel armies, or again the real or imaginary fruit-and-vegetable figures of Arcimboldo, the court painter of Rudolph II, who at one point had lived in Prague. In their dense, elaborate graphic style, their jewel-like material quality of their colours and their explosions of chiaroscuro, Sklenár's works also recall some of the periods in the work of Max Ernst.

After the great generation of Kupka, Filla, Kubista, Sima, and the others, Sklenár is one of the few pioneers in Czech art. Yet his work was also part of a broader, progressive pattern that announced the liberalisation of Socialist Realism, and it was only in 1965, that is, within this broader scheme, that he was finally recognised as one of Czechoslovakia's leading artists. When the end of the Prague Spring came in August 1968 and the Soviets invaded Czechoslovakia to crush Alexander Dubcek's reforms and re-establish orthodox communism, Sklenár was rumoured to have committed suicide. But he continued on through the 1970s, teaching at the academy of applied arts in Prague and designing postage stamps, bookplates, and so on; the calligraphic style he had learned in China never abandoned him.

He took part in the Mánes group's exhibitions and in foreign exhibitions of Czechoslovak art including: Paris, Brussels, Antwerp and Liège (1946); Kunstmuseum Lucerne (1947); Beijing, Nanjing, Shanghai and Canton (1955); Venice Biennale and *Modern Czechoslovak Art*, London (1962); *Czechoslovak Art Today*, Stadtmuseum Bochum, Staatliche Kunsthalle, Baden Baden and Kunsthaus, Hamburg (1965); *International Surrealist Exhibition*, São Paulo and Rio de Janeiro (1965); Folkwang Museum,Essen and Stedelijk Museum Amsterdam (1966). After 1940, he also showed his work regularly at solo exhibitions in Prague. 1965 was a turning point in his career. That year retrospectives of his work, including all his paintings, drawings, illustrations, prints and other works were held in 16 galleries around the country and various other places abroad. The Prague show came as a revelation to the public that a hitherto unknown artist of such stature had been in their midst all along.

BIBLIOGRAPHY:

Fifty years of Czechoslovak Painting from the Collections of the Galleries, 1918-1958, exhibition catalogue, Slovenska Narodna Gal., Bratislava, 1968 (in commemoration of the 50th anniversary of the Republic of Czechoslovakia).

SKLERIUS, Kajetonas, or Sklerys

Lithuanian, 20th century.

Born 1876; died 1932.

Painter, watercolourist.

Lithuanian Watercolour School.

Kajetonas Sklerius studied at St Petersburg and was the director of the Kaunas Art School. He is known as one of the main figures in the Lithuanian watercolour school.

MUSEUMS AND GALLERIES:

VILNIUS (Lithuanian Art Museum).

SKLYAROV, Prokopi Alekseevich

Russian, 19th - 20th century.

Born 1862.

Painter. Landscapes with figures, seascapes.

MUSEUMS AND GALLERIES:

MOSCOW (Mus. of Western Art) - MOSCOW (State Tretyakov Gal.): *Boats on the Dnepr* - PARIS (BNF, Prints Collection): *Return of the bandits* (c. 1920, wood heightened with watercolour).

SKOBL, Mikhail, or Scobl

Slovene, 17th century.

Painter.

Mikhail Skobl painted altarpieces for churches in Slovenigradec from 1638 to 1663.

SKOCZYLAS, Wladyslaw, or Ladislas, Vladislas

Polish, 20th century.

Born 4 April 1883, in Wieliczka; died 8 April 1934, in Warsaw.

Painter, illustrator, print artist (woodcuts). Folklore, historical subjects, figures, scenes with figures, genre scenes, landscapes, urban landscapes.

Rytm (Rhythm) Group.

Wladyslaw Skoczylas studied at the Kunstgewerbeschule, Vienna (1901-1904) before going on to study painting at the academy of fine arts in Cracow (1904-1907) and sculpture with Antoine Bourdelle in Paris (1910-1911). Between 1908 and 1918 he taught drawing and sculpture at the Lumber Industry School, in Zakopane. He was one of the founding members of the Podhale Arts Society (1909) and the Kilim Cooperative in Zakopane. In 1922 he co-founded the Rytm (Rhythm) Group of painters, working with it until its demise in 1932.

Because of a skin condition, Skoczylas was unable work in oils. Consequently, he turned to watercolours and printmaking, starting with drypoint and etching. In 1913 he went to the Graphic Arts Academy in Leipzig to learn woodcut techniques.

Skoczylas is regarded as the father of the modern Polish woodcut. He drew his subject matter from Polish folk woodcuts and glass paintings and from the legends and customs of the mountain folk of southern Poland. While he is known for his cycle *Mountain Bandits*, he also painted pale, romantic landscapes and genre scenes from the southern mountains.

After moving to Warsaw in 1918, Skoczylas had a distinguished career in teaching and public life. He was also a writer, penning reviews and other articles for Polish and foreign journals and newspapers.

Skoczylas first exhibited in 1903 and had his first solo show in 1908 with the Friends of the Fine Arts Society, Cracow. In 1910 and 1914 he took part in the Henryk Grohman Graphic Arts Contest, in Zakopane and Warsaw, winning twice, first prize. Between 1917 and 1922 he exhibited with the Formists, and in 1921 at the *Art Polonais* (*Polish Art*) exhibition held by the Salon de la Société Nationale des Beaux-Arts, Paris. In 1925 he won a gold medal and an honourable mention at the International Decorative Arts Exhibition, Paris, and in 1929 the grand gold medal at the Universal National Exhibition, Poznan. In 1955, five of his watercolours, including *Small Town in Poland, Old Warsaw Street, Village Church* and *Young Peasant Women in Meadow* were shown in the Polish section of the Salon d'Automne, which had been organised by the Franco-Polish Society for Literary and Artistic Exchanges.

MUSEUMS AND GALLERIES:

MOSCOW (Mus. of Western Art) - PARIS (BNF, Prints Collection): *Return of the bandits* (c. 1920, wood heightened with watercolour).

SKODA, Jules de

French, 19th century.

Painter. Genre scenes.

Jules de Skoda exhibited at the Salon in 1842 and 1847.

SKODA, Vladimir or Wladimir

Czechoslovak, 20th century.

Born 22 November 1942, in Prague.

Active in France from 1968 and naturalised in 1975.

Sculptor, engraver, draughtsman.

Skoda, a wood-turner and cutter in Prague, took evening classes in drawing from 1960. He spent some time in France in 1967 and decided to study there. The following year he lived in Grenoble on a grant and took painting classes at the École des Arts Décoratifs. Having decided to settle permanently in France, he studied sculpture at the École des Beaux-Arts in Paris from 1969 to 1973 in the workshops of Georges Jeanclos, Pierre Carron, Pierre Faure, Robert Couturier, and then César. He spent two years in Rome with his wife, Marie Claude Brunet, who shared the Villa Medici Prize with him.

Skoda taught at the École d'Art in Le Havre from 1979 to 1985, the École d'Art de Luminy in Marseilles from 1986 to 1994, and at the École des Arts Décoratifs in Strasbourg from 1994. In 1991, a grant from the ministry of culture enabled him to spend time in the USA. He has completed public commissions in Thiers (1987), Le Havre (1988), and Nantes (1990) and a *Tribute to Jean Moulin* in Chartres. He lives and works in Paris.

A painter in his early years, Skoda took up sculpture from 1972 with figurative shapes in twisted wire, exploring the link between the designer, the tool and the material. He continued this study with *Hand (Transformation in Volume)*, a conceptual work consisting of 13 photographs showing in close-up the various stages in the design of copper balls by a pair of hands: seven balls are lined up on the ground under the plates.

Skoda's now abstract work uses industrial materials and simple geometrical shapes laid on the ground, with no base.

Manually working the steel in a forge to begin with, he produces varied works alternating plates and bars from the same volume of material. He then 'attacks' the material with a hydraulic hammer in an industrial forge. His works embody various geometrical elements associated with drawings, then simple volumes with smooth or hammered surfaces, cubes with blunt edges, spirals, plates, and balls. He concentrates on a self-contained shape (since 1988, the sphere). Each sculpture is; punched, incised, hammered, decorated with lines (copper or brass wire), in steel sometimes combined with silver, the parts placed randomly but according to the place they reflect when polished, are reminiscent of the astronomical chart.

Skoda has taken part in collective exhibitions, including: Salon de la Jeune Sculpture, Paris (1972); Galleria Blun, Milan (1975, 1976); International Contemporary Art Fair, Bari (1975); FIAC (Foire Internationale d'Art Contemporain), Paris (1976); International Contemporary Art Fair, Bologna (1976, 1979); Centre Culturel, Villeparisis (1978, 1982); Musée des Beaux-Arts, Le Havre (1981, 1984); Musée d'Art Moderne de la Ville de Paris (1982); 1st Sculpture Biennale, Belfort (1985); Prospekt 86, Frankfurt (1986); Foire Internationale d'Art Contemporain, Paris (1987); French Institute, Prague (1994); and Galerie Baudoin Lebon, Paris (2003).

Solo exhibitions include: Rome (1975, 1989); Novara (1976); Florence (1977); Regensburg (1980, 1984); Bremen (1982, 1992); Munich (1985, 1988, 1992); Galerie Montenay-Delsol in Paris, Crédac d'Ivry-sur-Seine (1986); ARC Musée d'Art Moderne de la Ville de Paris, Halle d'Art Contemporain La Criée in Rennes, Centre d'Action Culturelle in Montbéliard (1987); Musée des Beaux-Arts in Le Havre, Musée Ziem in Martigues (1988); École des Beaux-Arts, Valence (1989); Berlin (1990); Prague (1991, 1994, 1995); Maison d'Art Contemporain Chaillioux, Fresnes (1993); gallery at the École des Arts Décoratifs, La Chaufferie in Strasbourg (1994); Centre d'Art Contemporain, Vassivière (1995); Poznan, Wilhelm Hack Museum in Ludwigshafen, Musée des Beaux-Arts in Mulhouse (1996); *Les États de la Sculpture* (*Sculpture States*), Centre d'Art Contemporain, Montbéliard (1998); Galerie Baudoin Lebon, Paris (2001); and Le 19 Centre d'Art Contemporain, Montbéliard (2002). He has been awarded many prizes and honours, including: sculpture prize from the Salon de Montrouge (1977); and monumental art grant from Ivry (1985).

Bibliography:

L'Art moderne à Marseille - La Collection du Musée Cantini, Musée Cantini, Centre de la Vieille Charité, Marseilles, 1988. Lemaire, Gérard-Georges, *Skoda Constellations*, exhibition catalogue, Centre d'Art contemporain de Vassivière en Limousin, Beaumont-du-Lac, Gal. Rudolfinum, Praha [Prague], Gal. de l'École des Arts Décoratifs, Strasbourg, 1995. Védrenne-Careri, Élisabeth, *'Dans la sphère de Skoda'* in *Beaux-Arts Magazine*, n° 147, periodical, Paris, July-August 1996. Greff, Jean-Pierre/Mengden, Lida von/Van de Leemput, Henri/Skoda, Vladimir, *Vladimir Skoda, Atelier 340*, travelling exhibition catalogue, Gal. Miejska Arsenal, Poznan, Wilhelm-Hack-Museum, Ludwigshafen, Villa Steinbach, Mulhouse, Atelier 340, Brussels, 1998 (text in French, Dutch, English and German).

Museums and Galleries:

Belfort (MAH) - Dôle (FRAC Franche-Comté) - Limoges (FRAC Limousin) - Marseilles (FRAC Provence-Alpes-Côte d'Azur) - Marseilles (Mus. Cantini) - Montpellier (FRAC Languedoc-Roussillon) - Paris (BNF, Prints Collection): two aquatints - Paris (FNAC): *Untitled* (1982); *Large Black Hole* (1992) - Paris (MAMVP) - Paris (MNAM-CCI) - Sélestat (FRAC Alsace): *Untitled* (1984).

Auction records:

Paris, 30 Jan 1989, *Sculpture* (block in forged steel, H.9 3/4 ins / 25 cm and diam.11 3/4 ins/30 cm) FRF 20,500.

SKOGLUND, Jean

Swedish, 20th century.
Born 1908; died 1948.
Painter. Landscapes.

Auction records:

Stockholm, 15 Nov 1989, *Winter Landscape with Frosted Trees and a Frozen Lake* (1948, oil on canvas, 23 1/4 x 28 1/4 ins / 59 x 72 cm) SEK 25,000.

SKOGLUND, Sandy

American, 20th - 21st century.
Born 1946, in Boston (Massachusetts).
Sculptor, installation artist.

Sandy Skoglund creates room-size installations with a Surrealistic dreamlike quality, created over months and painted in bright colours, such as pink for floors and yellow for walls. They are furnished with familiar and repeating objects modelled from clay and painted, such as coat hangers, spoons, chewing gum, foxes, squirrels or cats. When the installation is finished, Skoglund photographs it with people in it, and the photograph is considered the end result of her work. She describes her work as 'a Frankensteinian model where the human beings have created a world that is out of control and turns on them'. She taught at the University of Hartford Art School in Connecticut (1973-1976) and began teaching photography as well as installation and multi-media art at Rutgers University in 1976. She has participated in collective and themed exhibitions such as *Almost Warm and Fuzzy: Childhood and Contemporary Art*, PS.1 Contemporary Art Centre, New York. Solo exhibitions include: Tokyo, 1984; New York, 1987; Paris, 1989; Denver Art Museum and Eastman House, Rochester, 1990; a retrospective in Erlangen, Frankfurt, Bremen, Zurich and Barcelona (Fondation La Caixa), 1991-1992; Yvonamort Palix Art Area, Paris, 1997.

Bibliography:

Roegiers, Patrick, *'Sandy Skoglund - Du Syndrome de la sucromanie'* in *Art Press* n° 171, periodical, Paris, July-August 1992. *Sandy Skoglund. Reality under siege. A retrospective*, exhibition catalogue, Smith College Museum of Art, Northampton (MA), 1998. Loke, Margaret, *'Sandy Skoglund'* in *ARTNews*, journal article, April 1999.

Auction records:

New York, 25-26 Feb 1994, *Untitled* (1988, painted bronze, 11 1/2 x 20 x 18 ins / 29.2 x 50.8 x 45.7 cm) USD 3,163. Amsterdam, 7 June 2000, *Walking on Eggshells* (1999, photograph, 47 x 60 ins / 120 x 152 cm) NLG 11,000. New York, 12 Oct 2000, *Revenge of the Goldfish* (photograph, 28 x 35 ins / 71 x 90 cm) USD 15,000. London, 28 June 2001, *Walking on Eggshells* (photograph, 18/30, 48 x 60 ins / 121 x 152 cm) GBP 3,400. New York, 17 April 2002, *Fox Games* (1989, photograph, 46 x 63 ins / 117 x 160 cm) USD 12,000. New York, 17 April 2002, *Revenge of the Goldfish* (1981, photograph, 27 x 35 ins / 69 x 89 cm) USD 14,000. New York, 24 April 2003, *Coathangers* (1980, photographs, 26 x 33 ins / 65 x 83 cm) USD 4,000. New York, 20 Oct 2003, *Fox Games* (dye-destruction print, 47 x 63 ins / 119 x 161 cm) USD 14,000. London, 4 Feb 2004, *Walking on Eggshells* (1997, photograph, 48 x 60 ins / 121 x 152 cm) GBP 3,000. New York, 16 Oct 2004, *Revenge of the Goldfish* (1980, oversized photograph, 27 x 35 ins / 69 x 89 cm) USD 14,000.

SKÖLD, Otte

Swedish, 20th century.
Born 14 July 1894, in Wuchang; died 1958.
Painter, engraver. Figures, portraits, landscapes, Still-lifes.

Otte Sköld studied in Paris, Italy and Spain and worked for many years as curator of Stockholm's National Museum. He participated in the *Art in Sweden* exhibition, held in Paris in 1929.

Sköld was profoundly influenced by Cubism, as exemplified by works in the Tetzen-Lund Collection in Copenhagen. His own *Changing of the Guard in Copenhagen* carries strong echoes of Roger de la Fresnaye. Sköld played a pivotal role in the development of Swedish painting between the two world wars.

AUCTION RECORDS:
STOCKHOLM, 11-12 April 1935, *Dance,* SEK 1,600. STOCKHOLM, 22 Nov 1950, *Still-life,* SEK 2,475. STOCKHOLM, 6 April 1951, *Twilight,* SEK 2,850; *Still-life,* SEK 2,150. GÖTEBORG, 8 Nov 1978, *Madame Douareau* (1920, oil on panel, 18 x 14 1/2 ins / 46 x 37 cm) SEK 6,800. STOCKHOLM, 26 April 1983, *Still-life* (oil on panel, 7 3/4 x 9 3/4 ins / 20 x 25 cm) SEK 12,500. STOCKHOLM, 28 Oct 1991, *Still-life with Carnations in a Vase* (oil/glass, 28 1/4 x 15 1/4 ins / 72 x 39 cm) SEK 5,500. STOCKHOLM, 27 April 1999, *Moonlight, Rue Boulard* (1922, oil on copper, 8 x 11 ins / 21 x 29 cm) SEK 75,000. STOCKHOLM, 17 May 1999, *Woman on Couch* (oil on canvas, 35 x 47 ins / 89 x 120 cm) SEK 155,000. STOCKHOLM, 7 Nov 2000, *Rooftops, Paris* (1926, mixed media on paper, 5 x 8 ins / 13 x 21 cm) SEK 49,000. STOCKHOLM, 27 Nov 2000, *Closed Window Shutters* (oil on metal, 15 x 11 ins / 37 x 28 cm) SEK 100,000. STOCKHOLM, 2 May 2001, *Café Oriental* (oil on copper, 8 x 11 ins / 21 x 27 cm) SEK 350,000. STOCKHOLM, 27 Nov 2001, *Street Corner in Tunisia* (oil on panel, 10 x 13 ins / 26 x 32 cm) SEK 47,000. STOCKHOLM, 5 Nov 2002, *Still-life* (oil on canvas, 31 x 34 ins / 79 x 86 cm) SEK 95,000. STOCKHOLM, 5 Nov 2002, *Men on Horseback* (oil on canvas, 35 x 29 ins / 88 x 74 cm) SEK 410,000. STOCKHOLM, 28 April 2003, *Torget, Strömstad - the Market* (1923, oil on panel, 11 x 19 ins / 28 x 49 cm) SEK 140,000. STOCKHOLM, 4 Nov 2003, *Model Wearing Red Dress* (1930, oil on canvas, 18 x 17 ins / 46 x 42 cm) SEK 100,000. STOCKHOLM, 2 Nov 2004, *Horse Transport* (oil on panel, 14 x 26 ins / 36 x 65 cm) SEK 29,000. STOCKHOLM, 2 Nov 2004, *Riders* (c. 1917, oil on canvas, 24 x 18 ins / 62 x 46 cm) SEK 65,000.

SKOLLE, John
American, 20th century.
Born 1903, in Plauen (Saxony).
Painter.
John Skolle participated in exhibitions at the Carnegie Foundation in Pittsburgh.

SKOOG, Karl Frederick
Swedish, 20th century.
Born 3 November 1878.
Active in the USA.
Painter, sculptor. Busts, monuments.
Karl Frederick Skoog was the pupil of Bela L. Prat. He lived and worked in Cambridge, Massachusetts (USA) and sculpted numerous portrait busts and memorials.

SKOOGAARD. See **SKØVGAARD**

SKOPALIK, Franz
Austrian, 19th - 20th century.
Born 1863, in Uhricice (Moravia).
Painter. Architectural views.
Skopalik studied at the fine arts academy in Munich and went on to live and work in Vienna.

SKOPAS. See **SCOPAS**

SKOPTSOV, Semen Sergeevich
Russian, 20th century.
Born 1917, in Rostov-on-Don.
Painter. Landscapes.
Semen S. Skoptsov trained under Sergei V. Gerassimov at the V.I. Surikov Institute, Moscow, graduating in 1948. He was admitted to the Union of Soviet Artists and settled in Rostov.
AUCTION RECORDS:
GLASGOW, 4 Dec 1991, *Lake on a Cloudy Day* (1954, oil on card, 19 3/4 x 28 1/4 ins / 50 x 72 cm) GBP 550.

SKOPTSOVA, Ludmila
Maiden name: Savelievna
Russian, 20th century.
Born 1929, in Rostov-on-Don.
Painter. Interiors, still-lifes, flowers.
Ludmila Skoptsova attended the M. B. Grekov School of Art in Rostov, graduating in 1950, and was admitted to the Union of Soviet Artists in 1958. She lives and works in Rostov.
AUCTION RECORDS:
GLASGOW, 4 Dec 1991, *Autumn Bouquet* (1957, oil on canvas, 31 1/2 x 39 1/4 ins / 80 x 100 cm) GBP 495.

SKORIKOV, Ivan Dmitrievich
Russian, 19th century.
Born 15 May 1812; died 1842.
Painter. Landscapes.
Ivan Dmitrievich Skorikov studied at the art academy in St Petersburg.
MUSEUMS AND GALLERIES:
MOSCOW (State Tretyakov Gal.): *View of Pargolov.*

SKORIKOV, Yuri
Russian, 20th century.
Born 1924, in Nalchik.
Painter. Figures, landscapes.
Yuri Skorikov studied under Mikhail Avilov at the Repin Institute in Leningrad (now St Ptersburg). He later taught there and was a member of the Union of Soviet Artists.
AUCTION RECORDS:
PARIS, 18 Feb 1991, *Horseman* (oil on canvas) FRF 4,200.

SKOROBOGATOV, Igor
Russian, 20th century.
Born 1920.
Painter. Figure compositions, animals.
Igor Skorobogatov studied under Osip Brodsky and Rudolf Frents at the Repin Institute in Leningrad (now St Petersburg). He was a member of the Union of Soviet Artists and was named People's Artist. He often painted dogs and horseracing scenes. During the 1940s he exhibited regularly in the Soviet Union and from 1968 alternately in the USSR and abroad. He was represented in the exhibition *Art of Leningrad,* which was held in Tokyo from 1968 to 1974 and in Osaka in 1978, and other group shows held in Montréal (1980), London (1982) and Madrid (1985).
BIBLIOGRAPHY:
L'École de Léningrad, auction catalogue, Drouot, Paris, 19 November 1990.
MUSEUMS AND GALLERIES:
BRATISLAVA (Slovenská Národná Gal.) - DRESDEN (Gemäldegal.) - MOSCOW (Ministry of Culture) - MOSCOW (State Tretyakov Gal.) - OSAKA (Gallery of Soviet Art) - ST PETERSBURG (Gosudarstvennyj Russkij Muz.) - TOKYO (Gallery of Contemporary Art).
AUCTION RECORDS:
PARIS, 19 Nov 1990, *The Last Straight Line* (1951, oil on canvas, 31 1/2 x 45 ins / 80 x 114 cm) FRF 10,500.

SKORODOMOFF. See **SCORODUMOV**

SKOROJEVIC, Markus
Bosnian, 17th century.
Active in Bosnia.

Miniaturist.
Markus Skorojevic painted coats of arms.

SKOTCHOVSKY, Michael
German, 18th century.
Modeller.
Skotchovsky worked for the earthenware factory at Proskau (now Proszków, Poland), in 1770.

SKOTEINOS, Giorgos, or Skotinos, George, Yorko
Cypriot, 20th century.
Born 1937, in Limassol, (other sources say in Famagusta).
Painter. Allegorical subjects.
Giorgos Skoteinos has painted since he was very young. During the liberation struggle (1955-1959) he was imprisoned in England, where he took his first lessons in painting and ceramics. After being released, he went to Athens, where he studied art and drama at the National School of Drama (1961-1964), and to New York, where he studied film-making (1964-1967). Following the Turkish invasion of 1974, he was compelled to abandon his studio in Famagusta.

He settled in Protaras. His work, which is influenced by a popular expressionist tradition, uses allegory to represent the dislocation of the Cypriot people, often in starkly tragic terms.

Skoteinos has exhibited in New York (1966), Edinburgh (1971), Tel Aviv (1973), Athens (1974), Basel and Vienna (1975), Moscow (1990), Hamburg (1991), and his native Cyprus, as well as at the 1967 Paris, 1968 Alexandria, 1969 Venice and 1970 São Paulo Biennales, winning an honourable mention at the Alexandria Biennale, and the gold medal at the 1982 India Triennale.

SKOTNICKI, Jan
Polish, 20th century.
Born 29 August 1876, in Bobrowniki; died 1968, in Podkowa Lesna.
Painter, print artist.
Jan Skotnicki studied with L. Bakst at the St Petersburg Academy, with J. Malczewski and J. Mehoffer at the Cracow Academy, and in Paris. He painted historical and legendary subjects.
MUSEUMS AND GALLERIES:
LVIV (Picture Gallery) - VIENNA (Österreichische Gal. Belvedere) - WARSAW (Polish Military Mus.): *Druga Brigada* (1915).

SKOTNICKI, Michal von (Count)
Polish, 18th century.
Born c. 1775, in Warsaw; died 25 April 1808, in Florence.
Painter.
In 1800, Michal von Skotnicki studied in Dresden with Grassi.

SKOTNIKOV, Egor Ossipovich, or Skotnikov
Russian, 19th century.
Born c. 1780; died 10 March 1843, in Moscow.
Engraver (burin).
Egor Ossipovich Skotnikov studied under Klauber at the art academy in St Petersburg and later became a member of it. He engraved portraits, illustrations, reproductions of paintings, and vignettes. His works include a *Christ on the Cross* from a work by Le Brun.

SKOTTE, Odis
Norwegian, 16th century.
Active in Bergen.
Sculptor.
In 1548 Skotte carved a statue of *St John* in Bergen Cathedral.

SKOTTE-OLSEN, Wiliam, called WSO
Danish, 20th century.
Painter, engraver. Figures, scenes with figures.
In 1983, the Danish Embassy in Paris organised an exhibition at the Maison du Danemark, entitled *WSO un expressionniste danois - peintures et eaux-fortes 1966-1982* (*WSO: A Danish Expressionist*), featuring examples of Skotte-Olsen's paintings and etchings from the years 1966 through 1982. Skotte-Olsen's 'trademarks' - distorted features, exaggerated use of vivid colours, haggard features and hallucinating eyes - situate his work fairly and squarely in the mainstream of Scandinavian Expressionism.
AUCTION RECORDS:
COPENHAGEN, 7 April 1976, *Composition* (oil on canvas, 74 x 86 1/2 ins / 188 x 220 cm) DKK 5,200. COPENHAGEN, 13-14 Feb 1991, *Composition* (1983, oil on canvas, 59 x 52 ins / 150 x 132 cm) DKK 7,000. COPENHAGEN, 3 June 1993, *Composition with Figures* (1970, oil on canvas, 59 x 70 3/4 ins / 150 x 180 cm) DKK 5,800. COPENHAGEN, 6 Sept 1993, *Figure* (paint/plywood, 70 3/4 x 38 1/2 ins / 180 x 98 cm) DKK 4,000. COPENHAGEN, 15 June 1994, *Portrait* (oil on canvas, 59 x 39 1/4 ins / 150 x 100 cm) DKK 4,800.

SKOTTI. See **SCOTTI**

SKOTTI, Mikhail Ivanovich, or Scotti
Russian, 19th century.
Born 17 October 1814; died 1861.
Painter. History painting, portraits.
MUSEUMS AND GALLERIES:
MOSCOW (State Tretyakov Gal.): *Jesus Before the People*; *Portrait of the Sculptor N.S. Pimenov*; three canvases; a drawing; *Scene near a Fountain in Constantinople* - ST PETERSBURG (Gosudarstvennyj Russkij Muz.): *Three Neapolitans*; Other works.

SKOTTI, Pietro or Piotr Ivanovich, or Scotti
Russian, 18th - 19th century.
Born 21 September 1768; died 13 August 1838.
Painter and decorative artist. Perspectives.
Pietro Skotti was the son of Ivan Skotti.

SKOTTOWE, Charles
Irish, 19th century.
Born 1793, in Cork.
Portrait artist.
Charles Skottowe worked in Cork, and from 1834 to 1842 in London.
MUSEUMS AND GALLERIES:
LONDON (National Maritime Mus.): *Admiral Sir William Parry*.

SKOV, Marius or Anders Marius Hansen
Danish, 20th century.
Born 11 July 1885, in Skodborg.
Painter. Landscapes.
Skov studied at the Kongelige Danske Kunstakademi in Copenhagen.
MUSEUMS AND GALLERIES:
AALBORG - ESBJERG.

SKOVGAARD. See **SKOOGAARD**

SKØVGAARD, Hjalte, or Skoogaard
Danish, 20th century.
Born 25 October 1899, in Copenhagen.
Painter, designer. Landscapes.
Hjalte was the son of Niels Skøvgaard. He studied at the Kongelige Danske Kunstakademi in Copenhagen.
MUSEUMS AND GALLERIES:
KOLDING: *Landscape*.

SKØVGAARD, Joaquim, or Skoogaard, Joakim Frederik
Danish, 19th - 20th century.

Born 18 November 1856, in Copenhagen; died 9 March 1933, in Copenhagen.

Painter, sculptor, potter, engraver, illustrator. Religious subjects, genre scenes. Designs for mosaics, murals.

Joaquim Skøvgaard was the son of Peter Kristian Skøvgaard. He exhibited on various occasions in Paris, most notably at the Expositions Universelles of 1889 and 1900, where he was awarded bronze and silver medals, respectively. He is noted for Byzantine-inspired frescoes and altarpieces in numerous cathedrals and churches in Norway, Denmark and other Scandinavian countries, and, in particular, for his fresco work in Finland's Viborg Cathedral.

Museums and Galleries:

Copenhagen: *Portrait of the Artist's Wife; Feeding Maria; Model Bear Spouting Water; Italian Landscape; Portrait of a Boy; Tisvild Beach on an Overcast Day; Mother Suckling her Infant* - Oslo: *Bethesda Pond.*

Auction records:

Copenhagen, 25 April 1963, *Adam and Eve in the Garden of Eden,* DKK 8,200. Copenhagen, 17 Feb 1970, *Landscape with Young Italian Woman,* DKK 11,000. Copenhagen, 11 April 1972, *Sunday Afternoon at Civita d'Antino,* DKK 9,500. Copenhagen, 5 Sept 1974, *Landscape with Horses,* DKK 6,800. Copenhagen, 4 May 1976, *Wooded Landscape* (1845, gouache, 9 1/2 x 14 1/4 ins / 24 x 36.5 cm) DKK 4,500. Copenhagen, 10 Nov 1976, *Two Young Italian Women with Baskets on their Heads* (1883, oil on canvas, 13 3/4 x 22 1/2 ins / 35 x 57 cm) DKK 24,000. Copenhagen, 24 Nov 1977, *Reaper* (1918, oil on canvas, 31 1/2 x 48 ins / 80 x 122 cm) DKK 10,500. Copenhagen, 30 May 1979, *Washerwomen* (1886, oil on canvas, 15 1/4 x 23 1/2 ins / 39 x 60 cm) DKK 16,000. Copenhagen, 2 Oct 1984, *Summer Day* (1884, oil on canvas, 9 1/4 x 13 1/2 ins / 23.5 x 34 cm) DKK 13,000. London, 16 March 1989, *Woodsmen* (1880, oil on canvas, 14 x 21 ins / 34.7 x 53.4 cm) GBP 2,420. Copenhagen, 5 April 1989, *Garden Walk, Classens Have* (1898, oil on canvas, 15 x 24 3/4 ins / 38 x 63 cm) DKK 15,000. Copenhagen, 21 Feb 1990, *Road to Civita d'Antino* (1883, oil on canvas, 17 x 22 3/4 ins / 43 x 58 cm) DKK 36,000. Copenhagen, 6 March 1991, *Floral Branches* (1898, oil on canvas, 22 x 19 ins / 55 x 48 cm) DKK 5,000. Copenhagen, 18 Nov 1992, *Roman Tavern* (1883, oil on canvas, 20 1/2 x 25 1/2 ins / 52 x 65 cm) DKK 38,000; *Returning Hunters, Civita d'Antino* (oil on canvas, 32 3/4 x 50 ins / 83 x 127 cm) DKK 50,000. London, 18 March 1994, *Returning from the Hunt* (oil on canvas, 33 1/4 x 49 3/4 ins / 84.4 x 126.4 cm) GBP 13,800. Copenhagen, 21 May 1997, *Summer Landscape with Cattle* (1878, 18 x 27 1/2 ins / 46 x 70 cm) DKK 14,000.

SKØVGAARD, Johan Thomas, or Skoogaard

Danish, 20th century.

Born 29 August 1888, in Copenhagen.

Painter, designer. Religious subjects.

Johan Thomas was the son of (and assistant to) Joachim (Joaquim) Skøvgaard. He studied under Holger Grönvold and at the Kongelige Danske Kunstakademi in Copenhagen. Skøvgaard took part in group exhibitions, including the Menton Biennale of 1972. He painted various altarpieces and frescoes for churches throughout Denmark.

SKØVGAARD, Nils or Niels Kristian, or Skoogaard

Danish, 19th century.

Born 2 November 1858, in Copenhagen.

Painter, sculptor, engraver, illustrator. Figures, landscapes.

Skøvgaard was the brother of Joaquim Skøvgaard and the son of Peter Kristian Skøvgaard. He exhibited in Paris at the Exposition Universelle of 1900, receiving a bronze medal. He also worked in ceramics.

Museums and Galleries:

Aalborg - Aarhus - Copenhagen: *Willow Trees in the Prairie at Nyso; Woman's Dance in Megar; Old Constructions Attached to a Manor; Aage and Else* (sculpture) - Helsinki: *Cbaand in Haland* - Kolding - Maribo - Odense - Oslo - Randers - Ribe - Rønne - Stockholm: *Tall Beeches on the Dagsas Church Hill.*

Auction records:

Copenhagen, 11 Feb 1976, *September Morning* (1886, oil on canvas, 31 x 48 3/4 ins / 79 x 124 cm) DKK 7,500. Copenhagen, 18 Nov 1992, *Dune Landscape* (oil on canvas, 23 1/2 x 24 ins / 60 x 61 cm) DKK 7,500. Copenhagen, 6 Sept 1993, *Landscape in Ostroo* (oil on canvas, 11 3/4 x 17 ins / 30 x 43 cm) DKK 7,500. Copenhagen, 6 Sept 2000, *Forester in Ellemose, Halland in November* (1881, oil on canvas, 28 x 25 ins / 72 x 64 cm) DKK 48,000. Copenhagen, 10 April 2002, *Wooded Landscape* (1924, oil on canvas, 28 x 39 ins / 72 x 100 cm) DKK 15,000. Copenhagen, 3 June 2002, *Misty Morning at Megara, Greece* (1889, oil on canvas, 15 x 27 ins / 38 x 69 cm) DKK 17,000. Vejle, 10 March 2003, *Children Playing Outside* (1883/1902, oil on canvas, 24 x 31 ins / 62 x 78 cm) DKK 18,000. Vejle, 10 May 2004, *Swedish Landscape with Elks* (1915, oil on canvas, 25 x 41 ins / 64 x 103 cm) DKK 13,000.

SKØVGAARD, Peter Kristian Thomsen, or Skoogaard

Danish, 19th century.

Born 4 April 1817, in Hammershus, near Ringsted; died 13 April 1875, in Copenhagen.

Painter. Figures, landscapes, landscapes with figures, waterscapes.

Skøvgaard first studied with his mother. At the age of 15, he went to the Kunstakademi in Copenhagen. He received acclaim from 1836 on, and King Christian VIII bought a painting from him. He travelled to Italy, stopping in Rome and Naples to copy Claude Lorraine and Titian. In 1864, he was accepted into the Kunstakademi in Copenhagen. He was included in the exhibition *Twee gouden eeuwen: schilderkunst uit Nederland en Denemarken (Two Golden Ages: Masterpieces of Dutch and Danish Painting)* at the Rijksmuseum in Amsterdam in 2001.

Bibliography:

Sommerrejsen til Vejby 1843: J.Th. Lundbye og P.C. Skovgaard, exhibition catalogue, Statens Museum for Kunst, Copenhagen, 1989. Monrad, K., et al., *Two Golden Ages: Masterpieces of Dutch and Danish Painting,* Waanders, Amsterdam and Copenhagen, 2001.

Museums and Galleries:

Copenhagen (Davids Samling): *View of Nordskoven Near Jægerspris, Zealand* (1843) - Copenhagen (Statens Mus. for Kunst): *Two Landscapes; Young Girl; A Blacksmith and His Wife; Several Landscapes; The Cliff at Moen; In the Forest of Tisvilde; Forest Area of Joegerspris; The Outskirts of a Village; Lake Gurn; The Mill of the Queen (Sjælland); View of a Lake; Delhoved Forest; Summer Day in the Zoological Garden; Path at Vognserup Castle; Portrait of a Lady; Dusk in the Forest; View of the Sjælland Coast; Evening by Lake Bonde; Stormy Summer Day in the Zoological Garden; Stormy Weather; Afternoon in Nyso; Autumn Evening; September Evening; Alevano; Laundress Bleaching in a Clearing;* three studies - Hillerød (Frederiksborg Slot).

Auction records:

Copenhagen, 7 Dec 1950, *Return From the Fields* (1852) DKK 7,350. Copenhagen, 7 Feb 1951, *The Flooded Forest* (1844) DKK 3,800. Copenhagen, 5 April 1951, *Italian Landscape, Olevano* (1870) DKK 7,000. Copenhagen, 25 April 1951, *House in the Trees* (1860) DKK 2,350. Copenhagen, 3 Oct 1956, *Landscape,* DKK 7,000. Copenhagen, 9 Sept 1966, *Stags in an Underbrush,* DKK 7,500. Copenhagen, 19 March 1969, *Young Women in a Garden,* DKK 48,000. Copenhagen, 3

May 1971, *Landscape With Trees*, DKK 34,000. COPENHAGEN, 11 April 1972, *Seashore*, DKK 24,000. COPENHAGEN, 4 Sept 1974, *A Tree-lined Path*, DKK 28,000. COPENHAGEN, 4 May 1976, *Landscape with Pond* (1865, oil on canvas, 13 3/4 x 21 1/4 ins / 35 x 54 cm) DKK 26,000. COPENHAGEN, 3 May 1977, *Landscape with Pond* (1845, gouache and pen, 9 x 12 ins / 22 x 30.5 cm) DKK 6,500. COPENHAGEN, 27 Sept 1977, *Wooded Landscape* (oil on canvas, 16 1/2 x 25 1/2 ins / 42 x 65 cm) DKK 10,000. COPENHAGEN, 12 June 1979, *Wooded Landscape* (oil on canvas, 9 x 16 1/4 ins / 23 x 41 cm) DKK 10,000. COPENHAGEN, 10 June 1981, *Winter Landscape* (oil on canvas, 36 1/4 x 43 ins / 92 x 109 cm) DKK 21,000. COPENHAGEN, 2 May 1984, *View of Frederiksborg Castle* (oil on canvas, 8 3/4 x 11 ins / 22.5 x 27 cm) DKK 75,000. COPENHAGEN, 12 Aug 1985, *View of Frederiksborg Castle* (1842, oil on canvas, 13 1/2 x 23 1/4 ins / 34 x 59 cm) DKK 90,000. STOCKHOLM, 15 Nov 1988, *Lush Landscape with Waterfall* (1859, oil, 15 1/4 x 18 1/2 ins / 39 x 47 cm) SEK 12,000. COPENHAGEN, 5 April 1989, *Summer Day in Dyrehaven* (1841, oil on canvas, 15 1/4 x 22 ins / 39 x 55 cm) DKK 33,000. LONDON, 5 May 1989, *Vast Mountain Landscape* (oil on canvas, 30 x 44 ins / 76 x 112 cm) GBP 3,520. COPENHAGEN, 25 Oct 1989, *Landscape Study* (oil on canvas, 16 1/4 x 17 ins / 41 x 43 cm) DKK 5,600. COPENHAGEN, 21 Feb 1990, *Trees and Bushes By a Lake* (oil on canvas, 14 1/2 x 23 1/2 ins / 37 x 60 cm) DKK 8,000. COPENHAGEN, 25-26 April 1990, *Forest* (oil on canvas, 15 1/4 x 15 3/4 ins / 39 x 40 cm) DKK 4,000. COPENHAGEN, 29 Aug 1990, *The Cliffs of Moens* (1852, oil on canvas, 49 1/2 x 73 1/4 ins / 126 x 186 cm) DKK 67,000. COPENHAGEN, 6 March 1991, *Landscape Study with Lake* (oil on canvas, 9 3/4 x 15 1/4 ins / 25 x 39 cm) DKK 5,500. COPENHAGEN, 29 Aug 1991, *Italian Mountain Landscape* (oil on canvas, 7 1/2 x 10 1/4 ins / 19 x 26 cm) DKK 5,500. COPENHAGEN, 5 Feb 1992, *Dusk in Knabstrup* (1874, oil on canvas, 9 x 15 ins / 23 x 38 cm) DKK 11,000. COPENHAGEN, 6 May 1992, *Peasant Woman in the Hellebæk Region* (1852, oil on canvas, 22 3/4 x 30 3/4 ins / 58 x 78 cm) DKK 30,000. COPENHAGEN, 10 Feb 1993, *View From the Ballustrade of the Dome of the Cathedral in Milan with Snow-covered Mountains in the Background* (1870, oil on canvas, 14 1/2 x 22 3/4 ins / 37 x 58 cm) DKK 26,000. COPENHAGEN, 15 Nov 1993, *Stags in Dyrehaven at Sunset* (1863, oil on canvas, 74 3/4 x 106 1/4 ins / 190 x 270 cm) DKK 72,000. LONDON, 17 Nov 1993, *The Moen Cliff in Denmark* (1852, oil on canvas, 49 1/2 x 73 1/4 ins / 126 x 186 cm) GBP 5,290. COPENHAGEN, 2 Feb 1994, *Farmyard in Winter with Children Playing with a Sleigh in the Foreground* (1849, watercolour, 13 3/4 x 11 ins / 35 x 28 cm) DKK 9,000. COPENHAGEN, 7 Sept 1994, *Landscape with Cows in a Field Near Vejby in Summer* (1843, oil on canvas, 10 1/4 x 13 1/2 ins / 26 x 34 cm) DKK 42,000. COPENHAGEN, 16 Nov 1994, *View of the Fields in Summer from the Underbrush* (1851, oil on canvas, 7 3/4 x 9 3/4 ins / 20 x 25 cm) DKK 46,000. COPENHAGEN, 14 Feb 1996, *View of Dyrehaven From Øresund* (1847, oil on canvas, 14 1/2 x 22 ins / 37 x 55 cm) DKK 18,000. COPENHAGEN, 29 Feb 2000, *Sketch for Decoration of H. C. Aggerborg's Dining Room* (oil on canvas, 13 x 15 ins / 32 x 37 cm) DKK 40,000. COPENHAGEN, 6 Sept 2000, *Landscape near Aabenraa* (oil on canvas, 15 x 23 ins / 39 x 59 cm) DKK 75,000. VEJLE, 7 Aug 2001, *The Coast at Seravezza* (1854, oil on canvas, 13 x 27 ins / 34 x 68 cm) DKK 135,000. COPENHAGEN, 27 Nov 2001, *Beached Boats on the Shores near Serravezza* (1854, oil on canvas, 13 x 27 ins / 34 x 68 cm) DKK 200,000. COPENHAGEN, 6 Feb 2002, *Hay Harvest in Vejleaadalen* (1857, oil on canvas, 13 x 21 ins / 32 x 54 cm) DKK 54,000. COPENHAGEN, 4 March 2002, *Landscape from Iselinge Forest with Mr and Mrs Aagaard and their Daughters and Dog* (1861, oil on canvas, 48 x 39 ins / 122 x 98 cm) DKK 1,000,000. COPENHAGEN, 26 May 2003, *Study of Clouds near the Sea* (c. 1839, oil on canvas, 10 x 15 ins / 25 x 39 cm) DKK 105,000. COPENHAGEN, 9 Dec 2003, *Landscape with Clouds at Jyderup* (oil on canvas, 9 x 13 ins / 22 x 33 cm) DKK 100,000. COPENHAGEN, 2 March 2004, *View of the Sea at Moens Klint* (oil on canvas, 13 x 20 ins / 34 x 50 cm) DKK 18,000. NEW YORK, 23 April 2004, *Village Pond at Hellebæk* (oil on canvas, 31 x 39 ins / 78 x 98 cm) USD 9,000.

SKOVRONSKI, Grzegorz

Polish, 18th century.
Active in Cracow during the first half of the 18th century.
Engraver (wood).

SKOWRON, Roman

Polish, 20th century.
Born 1937, in Sroda.
Painter.

Roman Skowron became a teacher at the Cracow Academy, where he also studied. Among the group exhibitions in which he has taken part was the 1972 Menton Biennale.

SKRAM, Johan Jørgen

Norwegian, 18th century.
Active in Christiania (now Oslo) c. 1700.
Sculptor.

Skram studied in Hamburg.

SKRAMLIK, Jan Rytir

Czech, 19th - 20th century.
Born 1 July 1860, in Prague; died 1936.
Painter. Figures, portraits.

Jan Skramlík studied under Wilhelm Lindenschmit at the Munich Academy, in Paris, and later with Vaclav Brozik in Prague.

MUSEUMS AND GALLERIES:

PRAGUE (Národní Gal.).

AUCTION RECORDS:

LOS ANGELES, 23 June 1980, *Reading the Newspaper* (oil on canvas, 25 x 31 ins / 63.5 x 78.7 cm) USD 2,600. SAN FRANCISCO, 28 Feb 1985, *Reading the News* (oil on canvas, 25 x 31 1/2 ins / 63.5 x 80 cm) USD 2,500. PRAGUE, 8 March 2003, *Knight and Innkeeper* (oil on canvas, 32 x 24 ins / 81 x 60 cm) CZK 60,000.

SKRAMSTAD, Ludvig or Ludwig

Norwegian, 19th - 20th century.
Born 30 December 1855, in Hamar; died 26 December 1912, in Munich.
Active in Munich.
Painter, draughtsman. Waterscapes, landscapes.

Skramstad studied in Oslo, Düsseldorf and Munich. He lived and worked in the Bavarian capital.

MUSEUMS AND GALLERIES:

BERGEN: *Landscape with Lake*; *Landscape* - OSLO (Nasjonalgal.): drawings.

AUCTION RECORDS:

COPENHAGEN, 24 April 1979, *Fjord* (oil on canvas, 45 1/4 x 70 ins / 115 x 178 cm) DKK 8,000. MUNICH, 17 May 1984, *Winter Landscape* (oil on canvas, 28 1/4 x 43 1/4 ins / 72 x 110 cm) DEM 5,500. COPENHAGEN, 12 Nov 1986, *Mountain Landscape with Trees* (oil on canvas, 47 1/4 x 78 3/4 ins / 120 x 200 cm) DKK 40,000. STOCKHOLM, 15 Nov 1989, *Winter Landscape at Dusk, with a Building near a Road* (oil, 15 3/4 x 22 3/4 ins / 40 x 58 cm) SEK 15,000. COPENHAGEN, 6 Sept 1993, *Landscape with Cattle* (oil on canvas, 15 3/4 x 24 3/4 ins / 40 x 63 cm) DKK 12,500. LONDON, 27 Oct 1993, *Pine Trees on the Slopes above a Fjord* (oil on canvas, 25 1/2 x 38 1/4 ins / 65 x 97 cm) GBP 1,725. VIENNA, 29-30 Oct 1996, *Pond in the Forest* (oil on canvas, 32 x 53 1/4 ins / 81.5 x 135 cm) ATS 74,750.

SKREDSVIG, Christian Eriksen

Norwegian, 19th - 20th century.
Born 12 March 1854, in Modum; died 19 January 1924, in Eggedal.
Painter, draughtsman. Scenes with figures, landscapes.

Christian Skredsvig studied under Johan F. Eckersberg in Munich in 1875 and, around this time, met Heinrich Zugel.

He moved to Paris and then to Rome. He exhibited in the French capital and was awarded a bronze medal in 1881. He also exhibited out of competition at the Exposition Universelle of 1889, the same year he was made a Chevalier of the Légion d'Honneur. Skredsvig was also an author.

In 2001, examples of Skredsvig's work featured at *Da Dahl a Munch. Romanticismo, realismo e simbolismo nella pittura di paesaggio norvegese* (*From Dahl to Munch: Romanticism, Realism and Symbolism in Norwegian Landscape Painting*), an exhibition held at the Palazzo dei Diamanti in Ferrara.

Painted while he was living in France, Skredsvig's landscapes of Normandy betray the influence of Jean François Millet. He spent the summers of 1886-1888 at Fleskum on Lake Daehli near Baerum in the company of Kielland, Hans Backer, Erik Werenskiold and Gerard Münthe. He worked, above all, in the Eggedal region of Norway at a time when Norwegian Romanticism was coming into its own and liberating itself from Swedish and Danish influences.

BIBLIOGRAPHY:

Reed Thomsen, Ingrid, '*Christian Skredsvig (1854-1924): lig og verk med hovedvekt pa Menneskens son (1891) og det religiose maleri*' in *3 vol.*, Universitetet i Oslo, Oslo, 1986. Reed Thomsen, Ingrid, *Christian Skredsvig*, Grondahl Dreyer, Oslo, 1995. Hurley, Karen Lynn, '*Christian Skredsvig'paintings, 1879-1885: an evaluation of his artistic development and the signifiance of his experience in France*' in *2 vol*, Universitetet i Oslo, K. L. Hurley, Oslo, 2000. Lange, Marit (ed.), *Da Dahl a Munch. Romanticismo, realismo e simbolismo nella pittura di paesaggio norvegese*, exhibition catalogue, Palazzo dei Diamanti, Ferrara Artę editore, Ferrara, 2001.

MUSEUMS AND GALLERIES:

COPENHAGEN (Statens Mus. for Kunst): *Midsummer's Eve in Norway* (1886) - OSLO (Nasjonalgal.): *Birthplace of the Poet Aasmund Olafsa Vinje, Telemark; Normandy Landscape; Father's Son; Children's Party, Eggedal; Still-life; Animal Study* (11 landscapes) - PARIS (former Mus. du Luxembourg): *Villa Bacciochi, Ajaccio* - RHEIMS: *Farm in Normandy*.

AUCTION RECORDS:

COPENHAGEN, 17 April 1970, *At Pasture*, DKK 5,900. COPENHAGEN, 28 Sept 1976, *River Landscape* (1890, oil on canvas, 31 1/2 x 25 1/4 ins / 80 x 64 cm) DKK 21,000. LONDON, 25 Nov 1983, *River Landscape, Eggedal* (1890, oil on canvas, 25 1/2 x 22 ins / 65 x 55 cm) GBP 6,000. LONDON, 24 June 1987, *Orange Seller* (1883, oil on canvas, 31 x 26 ins / 79 x 66 cm) GBP 34,000. LONDON, 23 March 1988, *Marshland Meadow at Twilight* (oil on canvas, 25 1/2 x 37 1/2 ins / 65 x 95 cm) GBP 9,350. LONDON, 27-28 March 1990, *Midsummer Night* (1888, oil on canvas, 15 x 28 ins / 38 x 71 cm) GBP 68,200. LONDON, 17 June 1992, *Modern Life* (oil on canvas, 7 1/4 x 11 3/4 ins / 18.5 x 30 cm) GBP 7,700. LONDON, 15 March 1996, *Midsummer's Eve, Norway* (1887, oil on canvas in grisaille, 16 x 28 3/4 ins / 40.5 x 73 cm) GBP 8,625. OSLO, 26 Nov 1998, *Woodland Tarn, Summer Evening* (1997, oil on canvas, 37 x 47 ins / 94 x 120 cm) NOK 200,000. OSLO, 22 Nov 1999, *Autumn in my Garden* (oil on canvas, 25 x 39 ins / 63 x 99 cm) NOK 280,000. OSLO, 23 Oct 2000, *Midsummer's Night - Figures in Rowing Boat* (1888, oil on canvas, 15 x 29 ins / 38 x 73 cm) NOK 740,000. OSLO, 22 May 2001, *After Sunset, Eggedal with Woman and Cattle* (1896, oil on canvas, 37 x 47 ins / 94 x 120 cm) NOK 320,000. OSLO, 6 Nov 2001, *From the Blue Sitting Room, Fleskum with Lady at Table* (1890, oil on canvas, 19 x 26 ins / 49 x 65 cm) NOK 1,200,000. OSLO, 30 May 2002, *Morning at Holmvassbu - Landscape with Milkmaid and Cattle* (oil on canvas, 39 x 53 ins / 100 x 135 cm) NOK 155,000. OSLO, 19 Nov 2003, *Beautiful Norefjell, Pastoral Landscape* (1903, oil on canvas, 40 x 50 ins / 101 x 127 cm) NOK 240,000. OSLO, 25 May 2004, *Spring in Eggedal* (oil on canvas, 25 x 19 ins / 63 x 48 cm) NOK 250,000. LONDON, 15 June 2004, *Norwegian Poetry* (1897, oil on canvas, 47 x 37 ins / 120 x 95 cm) GBP 25,000.

SKREIBROK, Mathias. See **SKEIBROCK Mathias Severin Berntsen**

SKRETA, Franz Leopold

Czech, 18th century.
Born 23 November 1685.
Painter.

Franz Leopold was the son of Mathias Skreta. He worked for the Prince Polyxena of Lobkowitz.

SKRETA, Karl or Karel. See **SCRETA**

SKRETA, Mathias

Czech, 17th century.
Active during the second half of the 17th century.
Painter.

Mathias Skreta was the father of Franz Leopold Skreta. He worked for the Prince of Lobkowitz. He painted a *St Rosalia* for the church in Podiebrad.

SKRETA, Michael, or Screto

Czech, 17th century.
Painter.

Michael Skreta painted portraits of princes.

SKRIABIN, Vladimir

Russian, 20th century.
Born 1927; died 1989.
Painter. Nudes, scenes with figures.
Socialist Realism.

Vladimir Skriabin was an academic, post-impressionist painter. He studied under Boris Ioganson at the Repin Institute in Leningrad (now St Petersburg) and was a member of the USSR Artists Union and a People's Artist. He exhibited both at home and abroad after 1950.

BIBLIOGRAPHY:

L'École de Léningrad, auction catalogue, Drouot, Paris, 19 November 1990.

MUSEUMS AND GALLERIES:

ARKHANGELSK (Regional Fine Art Museum) - BRATISLAVA (Slovenská Národná Gal.) - DRESDEN (Gemäldegal.) - MOSCOW (Ministry of Culture) - MOSCOW (State Tretyakov Gal.) - PETROZAVODSK (MFA) - PSKOV (MFA) - ST PETERSBURG (Academy) - ST PETERSBURG (Gosudarstvennyj Russkij Muz.).

AUCTION RECORDS:

PARIS, 11 June 1990, *Little Girl Sitting in the Garden* (oil on canvas, 19 3/4 x 31 1/2 ins / 50 x 80 cm) FRF 13,000. PARIS, 19 Nov 1990, *Girls Reading* (oil on canvas, 26 3/4 x 22 1/2 ins / 68 x 57 cm) FRF 15,500. PARIS, 4 March 1991, *Wheatfield* (1968, oil on card, 19 1/4 x 27 1/2 ins / 49 x 70 cm) FRF 3,500. PARIS, 25 March 1991, *Morning* (1978, oil on canvas, 33 3/4 x 56 1/4 ins / 86 x 143 cm) FRF 5,000.

SKRIBANEK, A.

Austrian, 19th century.

Active in Vienna, Austria, during the second half of the 19th century.
Painter. Seascapes.
Skribanek exhibited in Vienna in 1867.

SKRIDE, Arijs
Latvian, 20th century.
Born 24 September 1906, in Verane (Madona); died 1987.
Painter. Landscapes.
Arijs Skride studied under Vilhelms Purvitis in Riga until 1932. He won the Culture Fund prize in 1933 and 1937.
MUSEUMS AND GALLERIES:
RIGA.

SKRIMSHIRE, Alfred J.
British, 19th century.
Active at the end of the 19th century.
Engraver (burin/mezzotint).
Alfred J. Skrimshire exhibited at the Royal Academy in London from 1899.

SKRYPITZIN, Oleg
French, 20th century.
Born in Marseilles.
Painter. Landscapes.
In 1923, at the Salon des Indépendants in Paris, Oleg Skrypitzin exhibited a landscape of New York's East River, which was praised by Paul Éluard.

SKRZICZIEK
Czech, 15th century.
Active at the beginning of the 15th century.
Illuminator.

SKRZYCKI, Mauryci
Lithuanian, 19th century.
Active in Vilnius at the beginning of the 19th century.
Engraver (burin).
Mauryci Skrzycki was a member of the Carmelite order.

SKUBER, Berty
Italian, 20th century.
Painter.
Berty Skuber lives and works in Bolzano. She has taken part in collective exhibitions including *De Bonnard à Baselitz - Dix Ans d'enrichissements du cabinet des estampes 1978-1988* (*From Bonnard to Baselitz: A Decade of Acquisitions by the Prints Collection 1978-1988*) held at the Bibliothèque Nationale in Paris in 1992. She has produced artists' books.
MUSEUMS AND GALLERIES:
PARIS (BNF, Prints Collection): *Transparent Snakes* (1981, book).

SKUBKO, Sergei Mikhailovich
Russian, 20th century.
Born 1918.
Painter. Landscapes.
S.M. Skubko is known for *Winter at Suzdal*.
AUCTION RECORDS:
PARIS, 25 Jan 1993, *The Spaso-Evfimiev Monastery, Suzdal* (1972, oil on canvas, 31 3/4 x 25 1/2 ins / 80.5 x 65 cm) FRF 5,000.

SKUFAS, Philotheos
Greek, 17th century.
Active during the second half of the 17th century.
Painter.
Philotheos Skufas was a priest at the church of St Giorgio in Venice and later a monk on the Island of Zakynthos.
MUSEUMS AND GALLERIES:
ZÁKINTHOS (Mus.): *The Divine Liturgy; The Battle of Naupaktos.*

SKUIN, Elena Petrovna
Russian, 20th century.
Born 2 April 1908, in Ekaterinodar; died 1986.
Painter. Landscapes, portraits, genre scenes, still-lifes, scenes with figures.
Elena Petrovna Skuin studied under Aleksandr Osmerkin at the Repin Institute in Leningrad (now St Petersburg), graduating in 1939 and exhibiting in major cities in the USSR ever since. She had a solo exhibition in Leningrad in 1978. She is a member of the Soviet Artists Union (now the Russian Artists Union) and was named People's Artist.
MUSEUMS AND GALLERIES:
IRKUTSK (Mus. of Contemporary Russian Art) - MOSCOW (Pushkin MFA) - MOSCOW (State Tretyakov Gal.) - PSKOV (Fine Arts Museum) - ST PETERSBURG (Academy) - ST PETERSBURG (Gosudarstvennyj Russkij Muz.) - VLADIMIR (MFA).
AUCTION RECORDS:
PARIS, 25 March 1991, *Girl Playing* (1962, oil on card, 19 1/4 x 22 ins / 49 x 55 cm) FRF 9,600. PARIS, 15 May 1991, *Still-life* (1960, oil on canvas, 20 1/2 x 17 3/4 ins / 52 x 45 cm) FRF 4,000. PARIS, 20 May 1992, *At the Piano* (1957, oil on canvas, 31 1/2 x 41 3/4 ins / 80 x 106 cm) FRF 9,000.

SKULASON, Thorvaldur
Icelandic, 20th century.
Born 1906, in Bordeyri; died 1984.
Painter.
Thorvaldur Skulason studied at the fine arts academy in Oslo and travelled extensively in Italy, Switzerland, the Low Countries and England. He spent some time in Paris, living there between 1931 and 1933 and, again, between 1938 and 1940.

Skulason took part in numerous group exhibitions in Scandinavia, Brussels, New York, Rome and elsewhere. His first geometrical abstracts date from 1938, and he ranks as the first abstract artist in Iceland.
AUCTION RECORDS:
COPENHAGEN, 2 June 1983, *Composition with Mask* (oil on canvas, 39 1/4 x 26 ins / 100 x 66 cm) DKK 32,000. COPENHAGEN, 15 Oct 1985, *Interior with Still-life* (oil on canvas, 23 1/2 x 19 3/4 ins / 60 x 50 cm) DKK 22,000. COPENHAGEN, 2 March 1988, *Composition* (37 1/2 x 29 1/2 ins / 95 x 75 cm) DKK 100,000. COPENHAGEN, 8 Feb 1989, *Composition* (1960, oil on canvas, 51 1/4 x 38 1/4 ins / 130 x 97 cm) DKK 68,000. COPENHAGEN, 10 May 1989, *Composition* (1947, oil on canvas, 27 1/2 x 31 1/2 ins / 70 x 80 cm) DKK 42,000. COPENHAGEN, 22 Nov 1989, *Composition* (1953, oil on canvas, 39 1/4 x 31 1/2 ins / 100 x 80 cm) DKK 56,000. COPENHAGEN, 21-22 March 1990, *Composition* (1980, oil on canvas, 43 1/4 x 31 1/2 ins / 110 x 80 cm) DKK 15,000. COPENHAGEN, 30 May 1990, *Composition No. 1* (1959, oil on canvas, 51 1/4 x 39 1/4 ins / 130 x 100 cm) DKK 40,000. COPENHAGEN, 30 May 1991, *Composition* (1947, oil on canvas, 30 3/4 x 24 3/4 ins / 78 x 63 cm) DKK 34,000. COPENHAGEN, 22-24 Oct 1997, *Composition* (1945, oil on canvas, 35 1/2 x 29 1/2 ins / 90 x 75 cm) DKK 34,000. COPENHAGEN, 9 Feb 2000, *Composition* (oil on canvas, 39 x 25 ins / 98 x 64 cm) DKK 23,000. COPENHAGEN, 9 Feb 2000, *Composition No. 7* (1958, oil on canvas, 34 x 28 ins / 86 x 72 cm) DKK 43,000. COPENHAGEN, 29 May 2002, *Mountain Landscape, Iceland* (oil on canvas, 24 x 29 ins / 60 x 74 cm) DKK 16,000. COPENHAGEN, 18 Sept 2002, *Composition* (1954, oil on canvas, 39 x 31 ins / 100 x 80 cm) DKK 34,000. COPENHAGEN, 1 April 2003, *Composition in Yellow and Brown* (1958, oil on canvas, 51 x 39 ins / 130 x 100 cm) DKK 50,000. COPENHAGEN, 29 March 2004, *Model* (c. 1935, oil on canvas, 37 x 26 ins / 95 x 65 cm) DKK 35,000. COPENHAGEN, 29 March 2004, *Mountain Landscape, Iceland* (1931, oil on canvas, 25 x 31 ins / 64 x 78 cm) DKK 36,000.

SKULME, Dzemma
Latvian, 20th century.
Born 1925.
Painter. Figure compositions.

Dzemma Skulme graduated from the Riga Academy in 1949 and the Repin Institute in Leningrad (now St Petersburg) in 1955. Starting in 1949, she exhibited in Riga, Moscow, Vilnius and other Soviet capitals, as well as in Canada, Germany, Italy, Sweden, Switzerland and the USA. She was elected member of the USSR Artists Union in 1977 and has been the President of the Latvian Artists Union since 1983. In 1984 she was awarded the USSR Prize and in 1992 she was elected Honorary member of the Latvian Academy of Sciences.

MUSEUMS AND GALLERIES:
COLOGNE (Mus. Ludwig) - MOSCOW (State Tretyakov Gal.) - RIGA (Ministry of Culture) - RIGA (Valsts makslas muzejs/State Art Museum).

AUCTION RECORDS:
PARIS, 11 July 1990, *Heritage* (1989, oil on panel, 59 x 67 ins / 150 x 170 cm) FRF 15,000. PARIS, 14 Jan 1991, *Girl* (oil on canvas, 31½ x 35½ ins / 80 x 90 cm) FRF 4,000.

SKULME, Marta
Maiden name: Liepina
Latvian, 20th century.
Born 13 May 1890, in Malpils; died 1962.
Sculptor.
Rigas Makslinieku Grupa (Riga Artists Group).

Marta Liepina-Skulme was the wife of Oto Skulme. She studied at Kazan Art School and under Leonid Shervud at the St Petersburg Academy. In 1933 she was awarded a Culture Fund prize. Her work was influenced by synthetic cubism.

SKULME, Oto, or Otto
Latvian, 20th century.
Born 8 August 1889, in Jekabpils; died 22 March 1967, in Riga.
Painter, set designer, graphic artist.
Rigas Makslinieku Grupa (Riga Artists Group).

Oto Skulme was the husband of Marta Liepina-Skulme. He studied under Janis Rozentals in Riga (1906-1907) and Stanislav Zhukovsky in Moscow (1907-1908), and graduated from the decorative and stage design class at Stiglitz's Central School for Technical Drawing in St Petersburg in 1914. From 1920 to 1938 he was a member of the Riga Artists Group and was its chairman from 1923 to 1938. From 1919 he worked as a set designer in various theatres in Latvia. At the same time, he painted, exhibiting his works in Latvia, the USSR, and other countries. His work was realist and bears all the marks of the New Objectivity then current in Latvia. Skulme was Rector of the Latvian Academy of Arts (1940-1941) and again from 1944 to 1961, and was Head of the Monumental Painting Workshop from 1944 to 1956. In 1933 he was awarded the Culture Fund prize.

MUSEUMS AND GALLERIES:
KARLSTAD - MOSCOW - RIGA.

SKULME, Uga
Latvian, 20th century.
Born 21 May 1895, in Jekabpils; died 6 November 1963, in Moscow.
Painter, print artist.
New Objectivity.
Rigas Makslinieku Grupa (Riga Artists Group).

Uga Skulme studied architecture at Petrograd Academy from 1914 to 1916 and painting under Kuzma Petrov-Vodkin in 1918. He was a member of the Riga Artists Group from 1921 to 1939. From 1923 to 1927 he ran a private drawing studio and from 1924 to 1927 was head of the drawing studio at Riga People's High School (1924-1927). He was awarded Culture Fund prizes in 1925 and 1927. Skulme was also an art critic who actively promoted the New Objectivity both in his writings and in his work as an artist, and an editorial staff member of the Latvian Encyclopedia (1928-1940) and Professor at the Latvian State Academy of Arts (1941, 1945-1963).

MUSEUMS AND GALLERIES:
RIGA - SERDBOSK - TALLINN.

SKULYARI, Mikhail Nikolaevich
Ukrainian, 20th century.
Born 1905, in Odessa; died 1985.
Painter. Still-lifes.

M.N. Skulyari was educated in Siberia after his family moved there to escape the revolutionary turmoil in Russia. He trained at the Leningrad Academy from 1926, after spending some time in the Cadets. A man of wide general culture, he worked in the studios of Kuzma Petrov-Vodkin, Arkady Rylov and Vladimir Filimonov.

AUCTION RECORDS:
PARIS, 9 Oct 1995, *Still-life with Lemon* (watercolour, 25¼ x 17¼ ins / 64 x 43.5 cm) FRF 4,000.

SKUM, Nils Nilsson
Swedish, 19th - 20th century.
Born 1872; died 1951.
Painter, draughtsman. Scenes with figures, landscapes.

AUCTION RECORDS:
STOCKHOLM, 30 Oct 1979, *Landscape with Reindeer Herd* (1941, coloured chalk, 10½ x 13½ ins / 26.5 x 34 cm) SEK 7,000. STOCKHOLM, 30 Oct 1979, *Reindeer-Drawn Sleigh with Two Figures* (painted wood, h. 15¼ ins / 38.5 cm, l. 12¼ ins/31 cm) SEK 15,100. STOCKHOLM, 26 April 1982, *Landscape* (1944, pencil and coloured chalk, 9¾ x 13½ ins / 25 x 34 cm) SEK 9,100. STOCKHOLM, 1 Nov 1983, *Landscape with Reindeer Herd* (1942, pencil, 11¾ x 16½ ins / 30 x 42 cm) SEK 9,000. STOCKHOLM, 1 Nov 1983, *Reindeer Harnessed to a Sled* (1941, painted wood, h. 12¼ ins / 31 cm and l. total 35½ ins/90 cm) SEK 9,000. STOCKHOLM, 27 May 1986, *Lapp Landscape* (1942, coloured chalks, 11¾ x 15¼ ins / 30 x 39 cm) SEK 10,000. STOCKHOLM, 21 Nov 1988, *Landscape with Young Boys* (pencil and chalks, 9 x 11¾ ins / 22 x 30 cm) SEK 8,500. STOCKHOLM, 22 May 1989, *Trappers and Reindeer beside a Watercourse in a Broad Valley* (1946, oil on panel, 20¾ x 25¼ ins / 53 x 64 cm) SEK 60,000. STOCKHOLM, 16 May 2000, *Laplanders' Camp and Reindeer in the Mountains* (oil on panel, 22 x 28 ins / 56 x 70 cm) SEK 52,000. STOCKHOLM, 5 Dec 2000, *Driving the Reindeer* (1949, pencil and crayon, 10 x 13 ins / 25 x 34 cm) SEK 16,000. STOCKHOLM, 29 May 2001, *Herd of Reindeer* (1944, 18 x 22 ins / 46 x 55 cm) SEK 29,000. STOCKHOLM, 4 Dec 2001, *Herding the Reindeer* (1949, oil on panel, 19 x 30 ins / 49 x 77 cm) SEK 30,000. STOCKHOLM, 3 Dec 2002, *Moving the Reindeer Flock* (1947, chalk and pencil, 10 x 14 ins / 25 x 35 cm) SEK 18,500. STOCKHOLM, 3 Dec 2002, *Outdoor Painting by Kaukirjaure* (1940, oil on panel, 21 x 26 ins / 53 x 65 cm) SEK 42,000. STOCKHOLM, 26 May 2004, *Mountain Landscape with Flock of Reindeer* (1945, pencil and coloured chalk, 10 x 13 ins / 26 x 32 cm) SEK 19,000. STOCKHOLM, 30 Nov 2004, *Laplander in Sleigh Pulled by Reindeer* (1939, chalk and pencil, 9 x 12 ins / 24 x 31 cm) SEK 21,000.

SKUPINSKI, Bogdan Kazimierz
Polish, 20th century.
Born 16 July 1942, in Pabianice (Lódz).
Active in the USA from 1971 and naturalised in 1976.
Engraver, draughtsman.

Skupinski studied at the academy of fine art in Cracow and then in Paris.

He has taken part in collective exhibitions regularly between 1965 and 1969 in Poland and in 1974 at the arts museum in São Paulo. He exhibited his works in solo exhibitions for the first time in 1967 in Cracow then in 1972 at the University of New York, in 1975 at the International Exhibition of Graphic Arts in Ljubljana, in 1977 at the International exhibition of Graphic Arts at the Albertina Museum in Vienna and then in Leipzig. He has been awarded very many prizes and honours.

SKURAWY, Friedrich
Austrian, 20th century.
Born 6 August 1894, in Paris, to Austrian parents.
Engraver.

Skurawy was a woodcut engraver who studied at the academy of fine arts in Paris and went on to live and work in Vienna.

SKURJENI, Matija, Mato
Croat, 20th century.
Born 1898, in Veternica; died 1990, in Zapresic.
Painter. Figures, flowers, architectural views, landscapes.

Matija Skurjeni worked as a railwayman, miner and house painter, which is where he first learned how to paint. He started painting in 1924 and in 1945 took evening courses at the Vinko Jedjut Workers' Cultural Association. Thereafter he painted without seeking further advice, taking his subject matter where he chose: nature, buildings, the ruins of ancient castles. His landscapes are often monotonous or heavy.

Skurjeni first exhibited in 1947, and was a regular exhibitor at shows of Yugoslav primitive art. In 1962 his work, with its mix of dreams and menace, anxiety and demons, attracted the attention of the Paris Surrealists around André Breton, and he is now regarded as the only Surrealist painter among the Naïves. In 2001 his work was included in the show *Die Naïve, Aufbruch ins verlorene Paradies* (Vienna Kunsthaus), which included 200 works from the collection of the Museum Charlotte Zander.

BIBLIOGRAPHY:
Bihalji-Merin, Oto, *Les Peintres naïfs*, Delpire, Paris, 1960. Skurjeni, Matija/Kelemen, Boris, *Matija Skurjeni: retrospektiva 1924-1975*, exhibition catalogue, Galerija primitivne umjetnosti, Zagreb, 1977. Maxim, Julia/Crnkovic, Vladimir, *Matija Skurjeni*, exhibition catalogue, Museum Charlotte Zander, Wachter, Bönnigheim, 1998 (text in German and English).

MUSEUMS AND GALLERIES:
BÖNNIGHEIM (Mus. Charlotte Zander).

SKURLA, Hans Martin
German, 19th - 20th century.
Born 3 November 1872, in Berlin.
Painter. Portraits, landscapes.

Hans Martin Skurla lived and worked in Heide.

SKURRY, E. (Miss)
British, 18th - 19th century.
Active in London.
Miniaturist.

E. Skurry exhibited a miniature at the Royal Academy in 1800.

SKURSZKY, Georg or György
Hungarian, 18th century.
Active during the second half of the 18th century.
Sculptor.

Georg Skurszky was a member of the Franciscan order. He sculpted a *Calvary* for the Franciscan church in Vác.

SKUTECKY, Dominik, or Skuteczki Döme or Dominik
Slovak, 19th - 20th century.
Born 9 February 1850, in Kisgajar; died 14 March 1921, in Banská Bystrica.
Painter. Genre scenes.

Dominik Skutecky studied at Vienna and Venice. In 1885 he settled in Neusohl (now Banská Bystrica). He exhibited on more than one occasion in Paris, receiving an honourable mention at the 1900 Paris Exposition Universelle. There is a permanent exhibition of his work in Banská Bystrica.

MUSEUMS AND GALLERIES:
BUDAPEST (Magyar Nemzeti Gal.).

AUCTION RECORDS:
VIENNA, 15 June 1971, *Young Women Praying in Church*, ATS 22,000. NEW YORK, 26 Jan 1979, *Garland of Flowers* (1879?, oil on canvas remounted on hardboard, 23 1/2 x 16 1/2 ins / 60 x 42 cm) USD 2,400. LONDON, 24 Nov 1982, *Woman and Child Praying in San Marco's, Venice* (1887, oil on canvas, 34 x 25 3/4 ins / 85.5 x 65.5 cm) GBP 3,000. MADRID, 21 May 1985, *Woman and Child Praying in San Marco's, Venice* (1887, oil on canvas, 34 x 25 3/4 ins / 85.5 x 65.5 cm) ESP 1,300,000. NEW YORK, 29 Oct 1986, *Foundry* (1899, oil on canvas, 41 1/4 x 60 1/2 ins / 105 x 153.7 cm) USD 15,000.

SKYLAX. See **SCYLAX**

SKYLLIS. See **SCYLLIS**

SKYMNOS. See **SCYMNUS**

SKYNEAR
American, 20th century.
Painter.

Skynear lived and worked in Prescott, Arizona. He participated in numerous regional collective exhibitions at which he received many prizes and awards. Since 1975, his work has been shown regularly in solo exhibitions in the USA, such as those at the Contemporary Gallery in Dallas (1975-1977) and at the Masur Museum of Art in Monroe, Louisiana (1977).

SKYNKE, James
British, 15th century.
Glass painter.

Skynke worked for St George's Chapel, Windsor, in 1479.

SKYTHES. See **SCYTHES**

SKYTT, Jost. See **SCHUTZE Jost** or **Joost**

SLABBAERT, Karel, or Slabbard
Dutch, 17th century.
Born c. 1619, in Zierikzee; died 1654; buried 6 November in Middelburg.
Painter, engraver (etching).

Karel Slabbaert is said by certain biographers to have been a pupil of Gérard Dou. He was in Amsterdam in 1645 and was a member of the guild in Middelburg the same year, becoming its dean in 1653.

MUSEUMS AND GALLERIES:
AMSTERDAM: *Lunch* - BRUNSWICK: *Boy with a Bird* - CAMBRIDGE (Fitzwilliam Mus.): *Child Drinking* (attributed) - COPENHAGEN: *Botanist at his Desk* - FRANKFURT AM MAIN: *Portrait of a Painter* - THE HAGUE: *Scene in a Camp*.

AUCTION RECORDS:
VIENNA, 9 June 1970, *Portrait Presumed to be of Rembrandt*, ATS 45,000.

SLABBINCK, Franck
Belgian, 20th century.
Painter. Figures, animals.

Slabbinck exhibited in Belgium, predominantly with uncommonly elegant images inspired by carnivals and animals.

AUCTION RECORDS:

LOKEREN, 5 Oct 1996, *Three Birds* (oil on canvas, 35 1/2 x 27 1/2 ins / 90 x 70 cm) BEF 28,000.

SLABBINCK, Rik

Belgian, 20th century.

Born 1914, in Bruges; died 1991.

Painter, draughtsman. Portraits, nudes, landscapes, Still-lifes.

Jeune Peinture Belge.

Rik Slabbinck studied in his native Bruges before enrolling at academy of St Luke in Ghent. He was involved in the establishment of the La Jeune Peinture belge (Young Belgian Painters) movement and was also a member of Belgium's royal academy. Slabbinck taught at the school of architecture in Antwerp. In 1987, he was awarded the national fine arts prize. He exhibited at the Venice Biennale (in 1948 and 1953), the São Paulo Biennale (in 1951) and the Menton Biennale (in 1953). An exhibition of his work was organised in 2002 at the Candelaershuys in the Brussels suburb of Uccle.

Constant Permeke's influence on Slabbinck was decisive, although he did contrive to develop a personal style based essentially on his individual use of pure and violent colours, similar to those employed by the German Expressionists and the Fauves.

BIBLIOGRAPHY:

Gyselen, Gaby, *Rik Slabbinck*, Lannoo, Tielt, 1979. *Rik Slabbinck*, exhibition catalogue, Halle, Gemeentekrediet S. l., Bruges, 1993.

AUCTION RECORDS:

LONDON, 12 Nov 1970, *Sunset*, GBP 350. ANTWERP, 12 Oct 1971, *Still-life*, BEF 50,000. ANTWERP, 18 April 1972, *Landscape with Red Sky*, BEF 65,000. ANTWERP, 3 April 1973, *Landscape at Sissewege*, BEF 120,000. ANTWERP, 22 Oct 1974, *Landscape with Church Tower*, BEF 110,000. LOKEREN, 13 March 1976, *Still-life* (oil on canvas, 51 1/4 x 38 1/4 ins / 130 x 97 cm) BEF 130,000. BRUSSELS, 23 March 1977, *Sun-Drenched Landscape* (oil on canvas, 19 x 28 1/4 ins / 48 x 72 cm) BEF 75,000. BRUSSELS, 24 Oct 1979, *Red Landscape (Summer)* (oil on canvas, 19 3/4 x 29 1/4 ins / 50 x 74 cm) BEF 75,000. ANTWERP, 28 April 1981, *Still-life* (oil on canvas, 23 1/2 x 28 3/4 ins / 60 x 73 cm) BEF 85,000. BRUSSELS, 26 Oct 1983, *Still-life* (oil on canvas, 51 1/4 x 31 1/2 ins / 130 x 80 cm) BEF 85,000. ANTWERP, 23 April 1985, *Synthesis* (1957, oil on canvas, 51 1/4 x 38 1/4 ins / 130 x 97 cm) BEF 200,000. LOKEREN, 28 May 1988, *Beautiful Summer* (oil on canvas, 23 1/4 x 29 1/2 ins / 59 x 75 cm) BEF 130,000. PARIS, 27 Oct 1988, *Landscape* (oil on canvas, 23 3/4 x 32 ins / 60.5 x 81 cm) FRF 10,000. LOKEREN, 21 March 1992, *Evening at Sea* (oil on canvas, 25 1/2 x 39 1/4 ins / 65 x 100 cm) BEF 160,000. LOKEREN, 23 May 1992, *Working the Fields* (1945, oil on canvas, 31 3/4 x 39 1/4 ins / 80.5 x 100 cm) BEF 120,000; *Blue Flasks* (oil on canvas, 23 1/2 x 28 3/4 ins / 60 x 73 cm) BEF 120,000. LOKEREN, 10 Oct 1992, *Evening at Sea* (oil on canvas, 25 1/2 x 39 1/4 ins / 65 x 100 cm) BEF 120,000. LOKEREN, 5 Dec 1992, *Still-life* (oil on canvas, 51 1/4 x 38 1/4 ins / 130 x 97 cm) BEF 200,000. AMSTERDAM, 9 Dec 1992, *Village View* (acrylic/canvas, 28 3/4 x 36 1/2 ins / 73 x 92.5 cm) NLG 12,650. LOKEREN, 20 March 1993, *Working the Fields* (1945, oil on canvas, 31 3/4 x 39 1/4 ins / 80.5 x 100 cm) BEF 140,000. LOKEREN, 9 Oct 1993, *Josef Cantre in his Studio* (oil on canvas, 51 1/4 x 39 1/4 ins / 130 x 100 cm) BEF 110,000. AMSTERDAM, 9 Dec 1993, *Landscape* (oil on canvas, 15 x 22 ins / 38 x 55 cm) NLG 3,450. LOKEREN, 8 Oct 1994, *Blue Flasks* (oil on canvas, 23 1/2 x 28 3/4 ins / 60 x 73 cm) BEF 140,000. LOKEREN, 10 Dec 1994, *Landscape* (oil on canvas, 38 1/4 x 51 1/4 ins / 97 x 130 cm) BEF 300,000. AMSTERDAM, 31 May 1995, *Landscape* (oil on canvas, 23 1/2 x 31 1/2 ins / 60 x 80 cm) NLG 3,540. LOKEREN, 7 Oct 1995, *Still-life* (oil on canvas, 36 1/4 x 28 3/4 ins / 92 x 73 cm) BEF 130,000. LOKEREN, 9 March 1996, *Reclining Nude* (oil on canvas, 31 1/2 x 46 ins / 80 x 116 cm) BEF 200,000. LOKEREN, 18 May 1996, *Champagne Bottle* (1975, oil on canvas, 15 x 22 ins / 38 x 55 cm) BEF 160,000; *Landscape with Orange-Tinted Sky* (oil on canvas, 28 3/4 x 36 1/4 ins / 73 x 92 cm) BEF 270,000. AMSTERDAM, 3 Sept 1996, *Landscape with Red Sky* (oil on canvas, 25 1/2 x 39 1/4 ins / 65 x 100 cm) NLG 10,378. LOKEREN, 8 March 1997, *Seascape* (oil on panel, 5 1/2 x 10 1/4 ins / 14 x 26 cm) BEF 15,000; *Landscape with Yellow Fields* (oil on canvas, 25 1/2 x 39 1/4 ins / 65 x 100 cm) BEF 240,000. LOKEREN, 11 Oct 1997, *Still-life* (dry-point, 19 3/4 x 25 1/2 ins / 50 x 65 cm) BEF 14,000. LOKEREN, 9 Oct 1999, *Landscape* (oil on canvas, 29 x 36 ins / 73 x 92 cm) BEF 260,000. LOKEREN, 11 Dec 1999, *The Blue House* (oil on canvas, 24 x 28 ins / 60 x 70 cm) BEF 260,000. ANTWERP, 4 April 2000, *In the Studio* (1947, oil on canvas, 48 x 36 ins / 123 x 92 cm) BEF 340,000. BRUSSELS, 9 May 2000, *Vase of Flowers* (oil on canvas, 36 x 29 ins / 92 x 73 cm) BEF 220,000. LOKEREN, 6 Oct 2001, *Road Near Coast* (oil on canvas, 29 x 36 ins / 73 x 92 cm) BEF 220,000. ANTWERP, 22 Oct 2001, *Still-life with Bananas* (oil on canvas, 31 x 39 ins / 80 x 100 cm) BEF 280,000. LOKEREN, 9 March 2002, *Road to Blankenberge* (1948, oil on canvas, 31 x 39 ins / 80 x 100 cm) EUR 6,000. ANTWERP, 23 April 2002, *Yellow Tablecloth* (oil on canvas, 51 x 37 ins / 130 x 95 cm) EUR 6,200. LOKEREN, 17 May 2003, *Reclining Nude* (oil on canvas, 24 x 39 ins / 60 x 100 cm) EUR 7,500. LOKEREN, 11 Oct 2003, *Black Clouds* (oil on canvas, 38 x 51 ins / 97 x 130 cm) EUR 8,500. ANTWERP, 25 Oct 2004, *Summer Landscape* (oil on canvas, 20 x 29 ins / 50 x 73 cm) EUR 5,000. ANTWERP, 7 Dec 2004, *Spring* (oil on canvas) EUR 5,000.

SLABY, Frantisek or Franz

Austrian or Hungarian, 19th - 20th century.

Born 1863, in Sazená; died 22 June 1919, in Sazená.

Painter, illustrator. Figures, landscapes.

Slaby studied at the fine arts academy in Prague. His work was featured at various exhibitions in Paris, notably at the Exposition Universelle of 1900, where he received an honourable mention.

AUCTION RECORDS:

LONDON, 31 Oct 1996, *Hunter and Hound* (1892, 16 1/4 x 23 1/2 ins / 41.5 x 60 cm) GBP 2,530.

SLACIK, Anne

French, 20th - 21st century.

Born 1959, in Narbonne.

Painter.

Anne Slacik studied visual arts at the University of Provence and went on to teach between 1982 and 1990 while painting in her free time. She was awarded the Fénéon Prize in 1991.

Her paintings are predominantly juxtapositions of colour but nonetheless exhibit a certain formal structure. She works in acrylics and pigments mixed with soil and very fine sand to produce a thick, rich and naturally coloured surface texture. She shows a preference for natural colours in large paintings such as her *Gardens*, where she opts for a nuanced colour palette comprising blacks, blues, white, greens and ochres. She frequently works as an illustrator in conjunction with various poets, a prime example being her collaboration with Anise Koltz on *Chants de Refus*, published by the Lucien Schweitzer Gallery in Luxembourg.

Slacik's work has featured at various group exhibitions, including in 1986 at Galerie L'Aire du Verseau in Paris; in 1987, 1988, 1990, 1994 and 2000 at MAC, Paris; and at other venues both in France and abroad, including the St'Art Contemporary Arts Fair in Strasbourg. She has also exhibited solo on numerous occasions: in 1990 at the Museum of Modern Art in Vilnius, Lithuania; in 1991 and 1992 at the Galerie Phal in Paris; in 1992 at Galeria El Diente del Tiempo in Valencia; in 1995 at the Schweitzer Gallery in Luxembourg; in 1995 at the Galerie Anne Bourdier in Rouen; in 1995, 1997 and 2003 at the Galerie Hélène Trintignan in Montpellier; in 1996 at the Galerie Jacob in Paris; in 1996 at the Schweitzer Gallery in Luxembourg; in 1998 at *Grandes peintures, livres peints* (*Large Paintings and Illustrated Books*) at the Galerie du Théâtre in St-Quentin d'Yvelines; in 2000 at *Les Écritures croisées d'Anne Slacik* (*Anne Slacik: Calligraphies*) in the library of the Carré d'Art in Nîmes; in 2000 at *Figures de l'air* (*Figures in the Air*) at the Galerie Sabine Puget in Paris; and in 2001 at *Figures in the Water* at the Schweitzer Gallery in Luxembourg.

BIBLIOGRAPHY:

Demarcq, Jacques, *Anne Slacik, peintures récentes*, exhibition catalogue, Gal. Phal, Paris, 1991. Albiach, Anne-Marie, *Anne Slacik. La Noce La Desconocido...*, exhibition catalogue, Gal. El Diente del Tiempo, Valencia, 1992 (text in French, Spanish and English). Minière, Claude/Cosculluela, Jean-Gabriel, *Anne Slacik. Jours, Traversées*, exhibition catalogue, Gal. municipale Édouard-Manet, Gennevilliers, Gal. Jacob, Paris, 1997. Noël, Bernard/Terrail, Jean, *Anne Slacik. Roman de la fluidité, grandes peintures, livres peints*, exhibition catalogue, Gal. du Théâtre de Saint-Quentin-en-Yvelines, St-Quentin-en-Yvelines, 1998. *Les écritures croisées d'Anne Slacik*, exhibition catalogue, Carré d'Art-bibliothèque, Nîmes, 2000.

MUSEUMS AND GALLERIES:

GENNEVILLIERS (Fonds d'Art Contemporain) - PARIS (BNF).

AUCTION RECORDS:

PARIS, 14 April 1991, *Naxos* (1990, oil on canvas, 51 1/4 x 51 1/4 ins / 130 x 130 cm) FRF 12,000.

SLADE, Adam or Frank

British, 19th - 20th century.

Born 20 January 1875, in Croydon.

Painter, illustrator. Landscapes.

Adam Slade was the father of the painter Anthony Slade. He exhibited with the Royal Academy from 1928 to 1935.

SLADE, Anthony

British, 20th century.

Born 1908, in London.

Painter, illustrator. Landscapes.

Anthony Slade is the son of the painter Adam Slade.

SLADE, Caleb Arnold

American, 20th century.

Born 2 August 1882, in Acushnet (Massachusetts); died 1961, in Truro (Massachusetts).

Painter. Religious subjects, portraits, genre scenes, landscapes, seascapes.

Caleb Arnold Slade studied in New York and at the Académie Julian in Paris, where he was advised by Frank V. Dumond, Jean-Paul Laurens, François Schommer and Marcel A. Baschet. He tackled every genre, including seascapes, landscapes, religious compositions and genre paintings.

MUSEUMS AND GALLERIES:

ÅLLTEBORO - BOSTON - BROOKLYN, NY - MILWAUKEE.

AUCTION RECORDS:

BOSTON, 9 March 2001, *Etaples, Autumn Scene* (oil on canvas, 13 x 15 ins / 34 x 37 cm) USD 2,900. BOSTON, 9 March 2001, *Moonlight at Etaples* (oil on canvas, 19 x 24 ins / 49 x 61 cm) USD 4,250. BOLTON, 11 July 2002, *Hagia Sophia* (oil on canvasboard, 3 x 4 ins / 8 x 10 cm) USD 2,200. NEW YORK, 10 Dec 2002, *Notre Dame* (oil on board, 9 x 13 ins / 23 x 33 cm) USD 2,750. EAST DENNIS, 28 March 2003, *Self-portrait of Caleb Arnold Smith with Harbour Scene* (oil on canvas, 16 x 13 ins / 41 x 33 cm) USD 4,600. EAST DENNIS, 31 July 2003, *Couple Harvesting Wheat* (oil on canvas, 17 x 22 ins / 44 x 56 cm) USD 5,000. CAMBRIDGE, 16 May 2004, *Boats on La Conche, France* (1914, oil on board, 13 x 16 ins / 33 x 41 cm) USD 4,250.

SLADEK, Karel

Czechoslovak, 20th - 21st century.

Born 20 October 1952, in Prague.

Painter. Scenes with figures.

Sladek studied in Prague at the secondary art school between 1968 and 1972, then took classes at the academy of fine art from 1973 to 1979, teaching there from 1983. 'The Philosophy of Life's Banal Truths' and 'The Relative Relationships of Morals and Ethics' are the two themes dominating his art. His disjointed figures, half-way between Naive Art and a stylisation reminiscent of film or circus show posters of the 1920s, are sustained by strong, contrasting colours.

Sladek took part in several collective exhibitions regularly between 1977 and 1989 in Prague, in Bulgaria in 1978, Moscow in 1985, and the International Painting Festival in Cagnes-sur-Mer in 1987. He has held solo exhibitions in 1981 in Czechoslovakia and Poland, 1982 in Bucharest, 1984 in Sofia and 1988 in Swedt (Germany).

SLADER, Samuel M.

British, 19th century.

Died after 1861.

Active in London.

Engraver (wood).

SLAGE, Hendrik

Dutch, 17th century.

Active in Rotterdam in 1665.

Painter.

SLAGER, Corry, later Mrs Van Dam

Dutch, 20th century.

Born 6 May 1883, in 's Hertogenbosch.

Painter. Still-lifes, flowers.

Corry Slager studied under her father, Petrus Marinus Slager, and her brother, Piet Slager.

SLAGER, Frans

Dutch, 20th century.

Born 23 April 1876, in 's Hertogenbosch; died 1953, in Meerhout.

Active in Belgium.

Painter, draughtsman, engraver. Landscapes, architectural views.

Frans Slager was the son and pupil of the painter Petrus Marinus Slager. He also studied under Frans van Leemputten.

AUCTION RECORDS:

AMSTERDAM, 24 Sept 1992, *Capture* (1933, oil on canvas, 33 x 41 ins / 84 x 104 cm) NLG 1,207. AMSTERDAM, 21 Jan 1998, *Young Girl with Flowing Tresses* (1939, oil on canvas, 18 1/2 x 14 1/4 ins / 47 x 36 cm) NLG 5,996. AMSTERDAM, 9 March 1999, *View of 's Hertogenbosch in Winter with Horse-drawn Cart* (1922, oil on canvas, 20 x 16 ins / 50 x 40 cm) NLG 7,000. ROTTERDAM, 20 April 1999, *Harbour Workers on Horseback on the Quay, Antwerp* (1906, oil on canvas, 59 x 85 ins / 150 x 215 cm) NLG 11,000. AMSTERDAM, 21 Oct 2003, *The Old Sacristy, 's Hertogenbosch Cathedral* (1911, oil on canvas, 17 x 26 ins / 43 x 67 cm) EUR 2,500. AMSTERDAM, 20 April 2004, *Malle Jan in the Snow* (1946, oil on canvas, 22 x 40 ins / 56 x 101 cm) EUR 3,200. AMSTERDAM, 27 Sept 2004, *View of Den Bosch* (oil on canvas, 19 x 30 ins / 48 x 77 cm) EUR 1,600.

SLAGER, Jeannette

French, 20th century.

Born 14 July 1881, in 's Hertogenbosch, the Netherlands; died 1945.

Painter. Still-lifes, flowers.

Jeannette Slager was the daughter of Petrus Marinus, who also taught her. Another of her teachers was her brother Piet Slager.

AUCTION RECORDS:
AMSTERDAM, 17 Sept 1991, *Poppies in a Copper Pot* (oil on canvas, 28 1/4 x 40 1/4 ins / 71.5 x 102 cm) NLG 2,070.

SLAGER, Petrus Marinus or Piet
Dutch, 19th - 20th century.
Born 4 December 1841, in 's Hertogenbosch; died 10 November 1912, in 's Hertogenbosch.
Painter. Portraits, genre scenes.
Petrus Marinus Slager studied at the fine arts academy in Antwerp.

MUSEUMS AND GALLERIES:
HAARLEM (Frans Halsmus.): *Young Woman from North Brabant.*

AUCTION RECORDS:
AMSTERDAM, 5-6 Feb 1991, *Portrait of an Elegant Lady Dressed in Pink and with a Dog* (oil on canvas, 26 1/2 x 20 ins / 67.5 x 50.5 cm) NLG 1,725. AMSTERDAM, 5-6 Nov 1991, *Two Little Nude Girls by the Fireside* (oil on panel, 9 x 6 3/4 ins / 23 x 17 cm) NLG 3,910.

SLAGER, Piet
Dutch, 19th - 20th century.
Born 12 November 1871, in 's Hertogenbosch.
Painter. Portraits, figures.
Piet Slager was the son and pupil of Petrus Marinus Slager. He also studied at the fine arts academy in Antwerp.

SLAGER VAN GILSE
Dutch, 19th - 20th century.
Painter, engraver.
Slager van Gilse was the wife of Piet Slager.

SLAGER-VELSEN, Suze
Dutch, 20th century.
Born 1883; died 1964.
Painter, engraver. Still-lifes.
Suze Slager-Velsen was the wife of Frans Slager.

AUCTION RECORDS:
AMSTERDAM, 16 April 1996, *Still-life with Roses in a Vase* (oil on canvas, 15 3/4 x 19 3/4 ins / 40 x 50 cm) NLG 1,121.

SLAKTA, Janos, or Johann
Hungarian, 19th - 20th century.
Born 18 July 1873, in Jászárokszállás.
Painter. Landscapes.

SLAMA, André
Belgian, 20th century.
Born 1941, in Liège.
Painter, draughtsman.

MUSEUMS AND GALLERIES:
BRUSSELS (Bibliothèque royale Albert Ier, Prints Collection) - BRUSSELS (Mus. d'Art Wallon).

SLANEY, Margaret Noel
British, 20th century.
Born 1915.
Painter. Portraits, interiors, still-lifes.
Margaret Noel Slaney lived and worked in Glasgow. She exhibited a *Still-life* at the Royal Academy in 1940, and from 1939 to 1968 exhibited at the Royal Academy in London.

AUCTION RECORDS:
PERTH, 29 Aug 1989, *In the Studio* (oil on card, 30 x 40 1/4 ins / 76 x 102 cm) GBP 880. GLASGOW, 14 Feb 1995, *Still-life with Flowers in a Jug* (oil on card, 22 1/4 x 18 ins / 56.5 x 46 cm) GBP 920.

SLANGENBURGH, Karel or Carel Jacob Baar van
Dutch, 19th century.
Born 2 October 1783, in Leeuwarden; died c. 1850.
Painter. Portraits, genre scenes.
Karel Slangenburgh was a pupil of H.W. Beckkerk, J.H. Nicolai and W.B. van der Kool. He lived in Louvain, Haarlem, Utrecht and Delft.

SLANN, Robert
British, 19th century.
Active in London c. 1820.
Engraver.
Robert Slann was an assistant to Holloway.

SLAOUI, Hassan
Moroccan, 20th - 21st century.
Born 1946, in Fez.
Sculptor, potter.
Hassan Slaoui was a ceramicist by training, then abandoned this traditional technique to undertake experimental sculpture. Along with other young Moroccan and North African artists of his generation, he grappled with the problem of creating a post-colonial sociological identity, in the artistic domain as elsewhere, and of liberating themselves from western academic models.

When he turned to sculpture, Slaoui took an innovative approach. Initially, he presented the unique formations of upturned roots, with little modification, as sculptures, a procedure somewhat similar to that of Étienne-Martin. He continued to work with wood, but cut into panels and patinated on which he produced various forms of low relief encrusted with bone and metallic threads (a reference to Arabic decoration of clothing, furniture and jewellery, which uses gold and silver threads). He is also interested in the potential of other materials, such as leather, wool and soil, which allow a form of artistic intervention that enables them to be constituted in a contemporary creation that is nevertheless connected with traditional origins.

BIBLIOGRAPHY:
M' Rabet, Khalil, *Peinture et identité - L'Expérience marocaine*, L'Harmattan, Rabat, apr. 1986.

SLAPNICKA, Jan
Bohemian School, 19th century.
Born 1831; died 17 March 1872, in Prague.
Draughtsman, engraver (wood).

SLARS, Hans
Austrian, 16th century.
Died 29 September 1532, in Vienna.
Sculptor.

SLATER, Edwin Crowther
American, 20th century.
Born 22 December 1884, in New Jersey.
Painter, decorative designer.
Edwin Crowther Slater was taught by William M. Chase, Hugh Breckenridge, Herman D. Murphy and Walter Priggs. He was a member of the Salmagundi Club and lived and worked in New York.

SLATER, George. See **BARKENTIN**

SLATER, John Falconar
British, 19th - 20th century.
Born 1857; died 1937.
Painter. Landscapes, seascapes.
John Falconar Slater exhibited with the Royal Academy from 1905-1936.

JF Slater

AUCTION RECORDS:
LONDON, 3 June 1979, *Farmyard* (oil on canvas, 15 1/2 x 21 1/2 ins / 39.5 x 54.5 cm) GBP 450. LONDON, 6 June 1984, *On the Tyne* (oil on canvas, 24 x 36 ins / 61 x 91.5 cm) GBP 1,300. GÖTEBORG, 1 Oct 1988, *Landscape with a Canal and Windmill*

(oil on canvas, 16 1/4 x 24 ins / 41 x 61 cm) SEK 3,400. CHESTER, 20 July 1989, *Watermill* (oil on card, 35 x 50 ins / 89 x 127 cm) GBP 1,430. LONDON, 3 March 1993, *Fishing-boats at Dusk* (oil on card, 20 3/4 x 30 3/4 ins / 53 x 78 cm) GBP 1,035.

SLATER, Joseph
British, 18th century.
Born c. 1750.
Painter, designer. Portraits, landscapes.

Joseph Slater was most noted as a landscape painter and designer. He worked particularly at Mereworth Castle and in Stowe. He exhibited in London at the Royal Academy and the Free Society from 1772 to 1787.

MUSEUMS AND GALLERIES:
LONDON (National Portrait Gal.): *Edward Irving* (c. 1825, pencil).

SLATER, Joseph W. or Isaac? W.
British, 19th century.
Died 1847.
Active in London.
Miniaturist, painter. Portraits.

Joseph W. Slater exhibited 67 miniatures at the Royal Academy between 1803 and 1836. Brian's Dictionary cites a miniaturist named J.W. Slater who successfully established himself in Dublin before returning to England and exhibiting at the Royal Academy in 1786 and 1787, but Graves Dictionary makes no mention of any miniaturist named Slater exhibiting at these dates. It is possible that these two J.W. Slaters are in fact one and the same artist. The National Portrait Gallery has two drawings by this artist (or possibly by his brother (?) Josuah Slater).

MUSEUMS AND GALLERIES:
LONDON (National Portrait Gal.): two drawings.

AUCTION RECORDS:
LONDON, 10 July 1925, *Landscape with Young Girl* (drawing) GBP 15.

SLATER, Josiah, the Younger
British, 19th century.
Born 178 1/2; died 1847.
Active during the first half of the 19th century.
Painter.

Josiah Slater the Younger exhibited in London from 1808 to 1818.

SLATER, Josuah or Josiah
British, 19th century.
Active in London.
Miniaturist.

Josuah Slater appears to have been very regarded in his day. He exhibited no fewer than 130 miniatures at the Royal Academy between 1806 and 1833.

SLATER, Peter
British, 19th century.
Born 1809.
Active in the middle of the 19th century.
Sculptor. Portraits.

Peter Slater exhibited at the Royal Academy in London from 1846 to 1870.

MUSEUMS AND GALLERIES:
EDINBURGH (Scottish National Portrait Gallery): *Professor Macvey Napier* (ink and wash); *Andrew Duncan* (porcelain, bust, after Benjamin Cheverton).

SLATER, T.
British, 17th century.
Engraver (burin).

SLATER, William James
British, 19th century.
Active in Manchester.
Painter. Landscapes, animals.

William James Slater was a Member of the Royal Cambrian Academy. He exhibited in London, particularly at the Royal Academy from 1877.

MUSEUMS AND GALLERIES:
MONTREAL: *Landscape with Livestock.*

SLATNI, Youcef
Algerian, 20th century.
Sculptor.

Youcef Slatni held a solo exhibition at the Centre Culturel Algérien in Paris in 1991.

SLATTERY, John Joseph
Irish, 19th century.
Active in Dublin between 1846 and 1858.
Painter. Portraits.

MUSEUMS AND GALLERIES:
DUBLIN: *Portrait of W. Carleton.*

AUCTION RECORDS:
LONDON, 27 March 1973, *Mrs Keogh and Her Children,* GBP 1,300. CELBRIDGE, 29 May 1980, *Portrait of Jeremiah Hodges Mulcahy* (oil on canvas, 45 x 31 1/4 ins / 114.3 x 79.4 cm) GBP 400.

SLAUGHTER, Mary
British, 18th century.
Active in London during the second half of the 18th century.
Modeller (wax).

Mary Slaughter was the sister of Stephen Slaughter. She sculpted portrait-medallions.

SLAUGHTER, Stephen
Irish, 18th century.
Born 1697, in Ireland; died 15 May 1765, in Kensington (London).
Painter. Portraits.

Stephen Slaughter worked in Ireland between 1730 and 1750. He was made Keeper of the King's Pictures.

MUSEUMS AND GALLERIES:
DUBLIN: *Portrait of John Hoadly, Archbishop of Armagh; Bishop Michael Cox; Anne O'Brien* - LONDON (National Portrait Gal.): *Sir Hans Sloane, Bt* (1736, oil on canvas) - LONDON (Tate Collection): *The Betts Family* (c. 1746, oil on canvas, attributed to Hogarth for some time); *Sir George Lee* (1753, oil on canvas, portrait).

AUCTION RECORDS:
LONDON, 20 Sept 1909, *Portrait of a Lady in a White Dress* (1745) GBP 22. LONDON, 1 May 1959, *Three Gentlemen Drinking and Conversing in a Library,* GBP 399. LONDON, 17 June 1966, *Portrait of Sir Robert Walpole,* Gns 350. LONDON, 26 March 1976, *Interior With Family Group* (oil on canvas, 39 x 49 ins / 99 x 124.5 cm) GBP 1,300. LONDON, 10 July 1985, *Portrait of the Hon. John Spencer* (1739, oil on canvas, 92 1/4 x 56 ins / 234 x 142 cm) GBP 3,800. LONDON, 19 Nov 1986, *Ladies Gathering Fruit* (oil on canvas, 48 1/2 x 39 1/4 ins / 123 x 99.5 cm) GBP 42,000. LONDON, 29 Jan 1988, *Portrait of a Naval Officer* (oil on canvas, 50 1/4 x 40 ins / 127.7 x 101.6 cm) GBP 1,650. LONDON, 15 Nov 1989, *Portrait of Two Little Girls* (oil on canvas, 24 1/2 x 29 1/2 ins / 62.5 x 75 cm) GBP 5,500. LONDON, 17 July 1992, *Portrait of Lord Bowes of Clonlyon in his Lord Chancellor's Robes* (oil on canvas, 50 x 40 ins / 127 x 101.6 cm) GBP 5,500. LONDON, 9 Nov 1994, *Portrait of a Young Boy; Portrait of a Young Girl* (oil on canvas, a pair, each 35 x 27 1/4 ins / 89 x 69 cm) GBP 17,250. CASTLECOMER, 14 Oct 1999, *Portrait of Gentleman in Brown Coat* (oil on canvas, 30 x 25 ins / 76 x 63 cm) IEP 17,000. LONDON, 17 May 2001, *Portrait of a Gentleman Seated at a Table. Portrait of Two Gentlemen Raising a Toast* (1746, oil on canvas, a pair, 14 x 12 ins / 35 x 30 cm) GBP 35,000. LONDON, 18 May 2001, *Portrait of William Fitzmaurice, 2nd Earl and 21st Baron of*

Kerry (1744, oil on canvas, 50 x 40 ins / 127 x 101 cm) GBP 65,000.

SLAVICEK, Antonín

Czech, 19th - 20th century.

Born 16 May 1870, in Prague; died 1 February 1910, in Prague.

Painter, pastellist. Landscapes, landscapes with figures, urban landscapes, architectural views, still-lifes.

Antonín Slavícek studied under Julius Marák at the Prague Academy from 1887 to 1891 and again from 1894 to 1897, but later followed Antonín Chittussi. In 1900 he won a bronze medal at the Salon des Artistes Français in connection with the Exposition Universelle, and visited Paris in 1907 and Dalmatia in 1909, the latter for health reasons.

During the 1890s, Slavícek painted pictures of fields and meadows, seeking to render the effects of light in an impressionist fashion, before turning to a more symbolist approach, capturing the strength and harshness of the countryside of southern Bohemia and later Moravia in sombre, sober colours. He also succeeded in capturing the drama of the life of the city, its lively bustle, in nervous, luminous brushstrokes. At this point in his career he was working with such intensity that he had a stroke and the misery that ensued caused him to take his own life.

Antonín Slavícek is regarded as one of the greatest of all Czech landscape painters. He had a decisive influence on Czech landscape painting at the turn of the 20th century. He marks the end of the dominance of the Mánes group and points the way to a new perception of nature. He was the father of Jan Slavícek.

BIBLIOGRAPHY:

Hovorkova, Marie, *Antonín Slavícek, 1870-1910. Soupis díla*, Státní Nakladatelství Krásné Literatury a Umení, Prague, 1965. Tomes, Jan, *Antonín Slavícek*, Odeon, Prague, 1966.

MUSEUMS AND GALLERIES:

MORAVSKÁ OSTRAVA - PLZEN - PRAGUE (Národní Gal.): *Irises* (1893); *In Bechyne Game Park* (1895); *Autumn at Veltrusy* (1896); *Impression with Birches* (1897); *Walking in Hvezda Park* (1897); *Hostisov* (1902); *Our Kamenicky* (1904); *Elisabeth Bridge* (1906); *Garden Bower* (1907); *Sketch of Prague from Ladvi* (1908); *St Vitus Cathedral* (1908); *Sea at Dubrovnik* (1909); *Road at Zamberk* (1909); *Still-life with Fruit* (1910) - ROUDNICE.

SLAVICEK, Antonín Vaclav

Czech, 20th century.

Born 2 January 1895, in Rozsec; died 1938, in Zlin.

Print artist, illustrator. Urban landscapes.

Antonín Vaclav Slavicek studied in Prague. He lived and worked in Telc.

AUCTION RECORDS:

BERN, 26 Oct 1988, *Prague Old City* (oil on canvas, 28 x 39 1/4 ins / 71 x 100 cm) CHF 2,600.

SLAVICEK, Jan

Czech, 20th century.

Born 22 January 1900, in Prague.

Painter. Landscapes.

Mánes Group.

Jan Slavicek was the son of the painter Antonín Slavícek. He studied under Vratislav Nechleba at the Prague Academy from 1916 to 1925. After 1922 he was part of the Mánes group. He travelled widely in Europe.

Jan Slavícek's work shows clear evidence of the influence of the School of Paris, with its mix of coloured arabesques in the manner of Matisse, and Post-Cubism stemming from Cézanne. The work of André Derain also comes to mind. Later in his career he painted landscapes in the Post-Impressionist style of his father.

Slavícek took part in many group exhibitions in both Czechoslovakia and abroad, including 1936, Pittsburgh and Brussels; 1937, Exposition Universelle, Paris; 1954, Moscow; 1955, Warsaw, Budapest; and 1958, Moscow and New York, where he was awarded a Guggenheim prize. From 1933, he also held solo exhibitions in various towns in Czechoslovakia.

BIBLIOGRAPHY:

Fifty years of Czechoslovak Painting from the Collections of the Galleries, 1918-1958, exhibition catalogue, Slovenska Narodna Gal., Bratislava, 1968 (in commemoration of the 50th anniversary of the Republic of Czechoslovakia).

MUSEUMS AND GALLERIES:

PRAGUE (Národní Gal.).

SLAVIK, Otakar

Czechoslovak, 20th century.

Born 18 December 1931, in Pardubice.

Painter. Portraits.

In 1948, Otakar Slavik went to technical school and from 1952 to 1955 he attended teacher training courses in Prague.

Slavík is representative of young Czech painters during the 1960s. He has an unusual style in which the brushstrokes resemble mosaic tesserae or patches of colour that have passed through a vast printer's screen. During the Prague Spring, he painted Alexander Dubcek's portrait many times in this fashion.

He has taken part in numerous group exhibitions, including the 1968 International Symposium, Vela Luka; 1969 Salon de Mai, Paris; and 1970 International Symposium, Roudnice-nad-Labem (north of Prague). He has also shown his work in solo exhibitions, mainly in Prague.

SLAVIK, Vassiliew or Wassilieff

Estonian, 20th century.

Born 6 January 1920, in Tallinn.

Active and naturalised in France since 1930.

Painter, designer. Tapestry designs.

Slavik arrived in France at the age of ten and studied decorative arts in Paris. He soon developed a taste for the Italian baroque and has used it as a foil for his French culture and a source of ideas for his work. Apart from his work as a painter and designer, he sought to bring artists back to designing *objets de luxe*. In addition to the baroque, Slavik incorporated elements of dream Surrealism in his quest for the unusual. During the 1960s he was much in demand as a decorator and was especially distinguished for his tapestries *Paris ma fête* and *Noble Pantomime*.

SLAVINSKY, Ivan

Russian, 20th - 21st century.

Born 1968.

Painter. Still-lifes.

AUCTION RECORDS:

PARIS, 28 Nov 1993, *Pendulum and Hooks* (oil on canvas, 13 x 9 1/2 ins / 33 x 24 cm) FRF 5,800. PARIS, 19 June 1994, *Still-life: Five-to-Two* (oil on canvas, 13 x 9 1/2 ins / 33 x 24 cm) FRF 7,200.

SLAVON, Guillaume

Flemish School, 18th century.

Sculptor.

Guillaume Slavon sculpted a communion table for Antwerp Cathedral in the middle of the 18th century, and an altar for the church of St Andrew in the same city.

SLAVONA, Maria, pseudonym of Schorer, Maria

German, 19th - 20th century.

Born 14 March 1865, in Lübeck; died 10 May 1931, in Berlin.

Painter. Portraits, landscapes, flowers.

Maria Slavona studied in Berlin and Munich and spent much of her life in Paris.

Museums and Galleries:
Düsseldorf: *Bouquet of Flowers* - Kiel: *Old Corridor, Lübeck* - Leipzig: *Study for a Portrait* - Lübeck: *Study for a Portrait; Storm Landscape; Flowers.*

SLAVYANSKY, Th. or Fedor Mikhailovich
Russian, 19th century.
Born c. 1818 or 1819; died 18 February 1876.
Painter. Portraits, genre scenes.
Slavyansky studied under Venezianov whose portrait he painted.
Museums and Galleries:
Moscow (State Tretyakov Gal.): *The Room of the Painter A.G. Venezianov*; two other paintings - St Petersburg (Gosudarstvennyj Russkij Muz.): *Portrait of K.M. Beliayev.*

SLEAP, Joseph Axe
British, 19th century.
Born 30 May 1808, in London; died 16 October 1859, in London.
Painter. Urban landscapes, landscapes.
Joseph Axe Sleap lived in poverty, dying just as he was about to become well known.
Museums and Galleries:
London (Victoria and Albert Mus.): *Lake Maggiore* - Sheffield: *View of St Paul's Yard on the Thames.*
Auction records:
London, 19 Dec 1924, *The Doges' Palace, Venice; The Dogana, Venice* (two drawings) GBP 28.

SLEATOR, James Sinton
Irish, 20th century.
Born 1889; died 1950.
Painter. Interiors with figures, still-lifes.
Auction records:
London, 2 March 1979, *Still-life* (oil on canvas, 30 x 25 ins / 76.3 x 63.5 cm) GBP 550. Dublin, 12 Dec 1990, *A Dublin Interior* (oil on canvas, 23 1/4 x 12 1/2 ins / 59.2 x 31.7 cm) IEP 18,000. London, 28 April 1999, *Self-portrait with Hat* (oil on board on panel, double-sided, 21 x 17 ins / 53 x 42 cm) GBP 2,600. Belfast, 4 Oct 2000, *Still-life of Flowers* (oil on board, 16 x 12 ins / 41 x 30 cm) GBP 1,000. London, 17 May 2001, *Still-life with Apples and Pears* (1936, oil on canvas, 20 x 24 ins / 51 x 61 cm) GBP 7,000. Belfast, 4 June 2003, *Still-life* (oil on canvas, 20 x 16 ins / 50 x 40 cm) GBP 1,800. London, 14 May 2004, *Young Girl in Blue* (oil on board, 17 x 12 ins / 42 x 30 cm) GBP 1,500. London, 14 May 2004, *Still-life with Flowers in a Vase* (oil on board, 28 x 21 ins / 70 x 54 cm) GBP 7,000.

SLEETH, L. Macdonald
American, 20th century.
Born 24 October 1864 or 1860, in Croton, or in Edina (Missouri); died 1951, in Laguna Beach (California).
Painter, sculptor. Busts.
L. Macdonald Sleeth was taught by James A. Whistler, Frederick W. Macmonnies and Sören E. Carlsen.
Museums and Galleries:
Washington DC (Corcoran Gal. of Art): *Bust of General John M. Wilson.*

SLEIGH, Bernard
British, 19th - 20th century.
Born 1872, in Birmingham; died 1954.
Painter, engraver. Religious subjects, genre scenes.
Bernard Sleigh trained at Birmingham College of Art in 1885, and became a member of the Birmingham Group. His paintings were influenced by Burne-Jones, from whom he borrowed certain motifs, especially those used in his tapestry cartoons. Sleigh was principally active as a painter, but also produced wood-cuts.
Auction records:
London, 27 April 1982, *Beatrice* (1899, watercolour heightened with gouache, 10 x 6 1/2 ins / 25.5 x 16.5 cm) GBP 850. London, 29 March 1984, *Allegory of Love* (oil on panel, 14 1/2 x 30 1/4 ins / 37 x 77 cm) GBP 1,200. London, 29 March 1996, *The Annunciation* (tempera/panel, 9 x 9 ins / 22.8 x 22.8 cm) GBP 4,140. London, 10 Nov 1999, *Elaine* (1902, oil on canvas, semi-circle, 30 x 51 ins / 75 x 129 cm) GBP 4,800. London, 28 Nov 2000, *Annunciation* (oil on canvas, 9 x 9 ins / 23 x 23 cm) GBP 4,200. London, 21 March 2001, *Wood of the Dryads* (1927, oil on canvas, 15 x 27 ins / 38 x 68 cm) GBP 4,600. London, 21 March 2001, *Legend of Saint George and the Dragon* (some watercolour heightened with gouache, 26 plates framed, 28 x 32 ins / 71 x 82 cm) GBP 10,000. London, 25 Nov 2003, *Garden of Enna* (tempera on board, 12 x 15 ins / 30 x 39 cm) GBP 2,000.

SLEIGH, William
Irish, 18th century.
Active in Cork in 1776.
Painter.

SLEIJSER, Harry
Belgian, 20th century.
Born 1926, in Brussels; died 1992.
Painter, watercolourist, draughtsman, engraver.

SLEIN, Johan
Swedish, 17th century.
Active in Sweden in the middle of the 17th century.
Painter.

SLENDRINSKI, Ludomir. See **SLENDZINSKI**

SLENDZINSKI, Aleksander
Polish, 19th century.
Painter. Genre scenes.
Aleksander Slendzinski was the father of Vincent Slendzinski. He studied in Vilnius under Rustem.

SLENDZINSKI, Ludomir
Polish, 20th century.
Born 16 December 1889, in Wilno (now Vilnius, Lithuania); died 1980.
Painter, sculptor. Portraits.
Ludomir Slendzinski was the son of the painter Wincenty Slendzinski. He studied at the St Petersburg Academy. He exhibited two portraits of men in the Polish section of the 1928 Salon d'Automne, Paris, which had been organised by the Franco-Polish Society for Literary and Artistic Exchanges and the Circle of Polish Artists in Paris. Slendzinski was the head of the Vilnius school. His work is representative of Polish neo-classicism.

SLENDZINSKI, Wincenty, or Slendrinski
Lithuanian, 19th century.
Born 1 January 1837, in Screbihy; died July 1909, in Vilnius.
Painter. Figures, portraits.
Wincenty Slendzinski was the father of Lubomir Slendzinski. He studied at the school of fine arts in Moscow. He then worked in Nizni-Novgorod and Kharkhov. From 1872, he worked in Dresden for several years, before settling in Vilnius.
Museums and Galleries:
Cracow: *An Orphan Girl; Portrait of A. Mickiewicz; Portrait of A. Kirkor* - Poznan (Mielzynski Mus.): *An Orphan Girl.*

SLEPYSHEV, Anatoli
Russian, 20th century.
Born 1932, in Moscow.
Painter. Figures.
Anatoli Slepyshev studied at the Surikov Institute in Moscow and was a member of the Union of Soviet Artists. He has exhibited in Russia and abroad. His work is non-realist figurative, barely suggesting forms. His palette is sober and his technique very bold. He shows a preference for group

scenes, crowds in the subway in the countryside or on the street.

AUCTION RECORDS:

PARIS, 29 Nov 1990, *Peasant* (oil on canvas, 5 1/2 x 9 ins / 14 x 22 cm) FRF 3,200.

SLESENZOV, Fedor Gravilovich

Russian, 18th century.

Active at the end of the 18th century.

Painter, miniaturist. History painting, portraits.

Fedor Gravilovich Slesenzov studied at the art academy of St Petersburg.

SLESINSKA, Alina

Polish, 20th century.

Sculptor.

Alina Slesinska is noted for her habitable sculptures. She exhibited in London in 1959 and at the Biennale Internazionale Dantesca in 1977 and 1979.

SLEVOGT, Max

German, 19th - 20th century.

Born 8 October 1868, in Landshut; died 20 September 1932, in Neukastel (Rhineland Palatinate).

Painter, engraver, draughtsman, illustrator. History painting, scenes with figures, religious subjects, mythological subjects, genre scenes, local scenes, portraits, landscapes, Still-lifes, animals. Murals.

Berliner Secession group. Dachau Artists' Colony##.

Max Slevogt studied under Wilhelm Diez at the fine arts academy in Munich, before spending 1889 to 1890 in Paris, where he was enrolled at the Académie Julian. He moved to Berlin in 1891 and taught there at the fine arts academy. As of 1896, he was a contributor to the periodicals *Jugend* ('Youth') and *Simplicissimus.*

Slevogt made his exhibition debut alongside fellow artist Corinth at the 1899 Secession in Berlin, then presided over by Max Liebermann. In 2003, the Municipal Gallery im Lenbachhaus in Munich devoted an exhibition to the work of Corinth and Slevogt.

Max Slevogt started out as a Realist who owed a debt of gratitude to the elegance and refinement of Manet and those around him, assimilating their exuberant colours; for all that, he stopped short of breaking down their colour tones, and he remained very close to the real without undertaking transposition, as is so evident in the work of Renoir. Like the Impressionists as a whole, however, he thought that painting should draw on everyday life and, unlike Odilon Redon for example, Slevogt never painted solely from his imagination. In effect, his style was much closer to that of artists such as Raffaelli. At the same time, he appears to have been largely uninfluenced by Cézanne.

Max Slevogt was, to all intents and purposes, a devotee of Manet, and it was the Manet of the *Olympia* that influenced his work, as well as other turn-of-the-century German painters such as Max Liebermann. The freer painting style of Manet and others of the French School was frowned upon, to some extent, in Germany, despite the fact that many painters had enthusiastically espoused the Manet model. (Adolf von Menzel was still a beacon at this juncture, although it should be pointed out that, in addition to his historical subject matter, Menzel also painted the occasional 'everyday' subject - theatre scenes and views of public parks and the like.)

Max Slevogt was a prolific painter of figures, views, animals in Frankfurt Zoo and landscapes. In short, he was open to every aspect of modern life, be it horse racing, landscapes or scenes from the Nile Delta, where he spent some time in 1913. And, in everything he did, he showed an originality and a vigorous sense of his own personality - including in his lithographs. He belonged to a generation of German painters who have come to be regarded as leading exponents of their art. Unlike the French Impressionists, they were, perhaps, not great innovators, but the sheer quality of their work justifies their place of honour in the pantheon of painters of the latter half of the 19th century.

BIBLIOGRAPHY:

Waldmann, Emil Albert, *Max Slevogts graphische Kunst,* Ernst Arnold, Dresden, 1921. Sievers, Johannes/Waldmann, Emil/Imiela, Hans Jürgen, *'Max Slevogt: das druckgraphische Werk, Radierungen, Lithographien, Holzschnitte 1890-1914'* in vol. I, Heinz Moos, Heidelberg, Berlin, 1962 (text in English, Alan Wofsy Fine Arts, San Francisco, 1990). Imiela, Hans-Jürgen, *Max Slevogt. Eine Monographie,* G. Braun, Karlsruhe, 1968. With, C., *'The Emperor, the National Gallery and Max Slevogt'* in *Zeitschrift des deutschen Vereins für Kunstwissenschaft,* vol. 30, no. 1-4, pp. 86-94, 1976. *Printed graphics. Max Liebermann 1847-1935, Max Slevogt 1868-1932, Lovis Corinth 1858-1925,* Institut für Auslandbeziehungen, Stuttgart, 1979. Imiela, Hans-Jürgen/Harthausen, Hartmut, *Max Slevogt als Illustrator,* exhibition catalogue, Kunstverein, Speyer, 1982. *German impressionism and expressionism: paintings by Slevogt, Purrman and Weisgerber from the Moderne Galerie des Saarland-Museums, Saarbrücken, Germany, 19 June - 21 August 1983,* Leicestershire Museums, Art Galleries and Records Service, Leicester, 1983. *Slevogt und Mozart,* exhibition catalogue, Landesmuseum, Mainz, 1991. Berthold, Roland/Alten, Wilken von/Imiela, Hans-Jürgen, *Max Slevogt: Pfälzische Landschaften,* Hirmer, Munich, 1991. Sievers, Joannes, *Max Slevogt: the graphic work, 1890-1914: etchings, lithographs, woodcuts,* Alan Wofsy Fine Arts, San Francisco, 1991 (text in English). Güse, Ernst-Gerhard/Dittmann, Lorenz, *Max Slevogt: Gemälde, Aquarelle, Zeichnungen,* exhibition catalogue, Saarland-Museum, Saarbrücken, 1992. *Max Slevogt. Bilder aus Ägypten,* exhibition catalogue, Niedersächsisches Landesmuseum, Hanover, 1997.

MUSEUMS AND GALLERIES:

BERLIN (Nationalgal.): *Self-portrait; Portrait of Madame Volle and Daughter; Horse Racing; Funeral Mass for the Knights of St. George; View of Neu-Cladox; Don Juan in the Cemetery; Scene from Mozart's 'Magic Flute'; Palatinate Landscape; Still-life with Lemons; Vines in Flower; Sardanapale; Portrait of Stumpf; Portrait of Sudermann; Portrait of Schmitt-Ott* - BERLIN (Staatliche Mus.): *Homo Sapiens* - BREMEN (Kunsthalle): *Black Panthers* (1901); *Portrait of a Lady; Country House; Portrait of the Musician Ansorge; Fernando Cortez before Montezuma in Mexico; Hunters on the Hillside; Black Panthers; Strawberries* - CHEMNITZ: *Lady in Brown* - COLOGNE (Wallraf-Richartz Mus.): *French Dragoon on Horseback* - DRESDEN: *Knight and Ladies of the Harem; Marietta Dancer; Portrait of Fuchs; Pavlova Danser* (17 views of Egypt) - DÜSSELDORF: *Nude Study seen from above* - ERFURT: *Godramstein* - ESSEN: *Palatinate Landscape* - FRANKFURT AM MAIN (Städel): *Madame Aventiure; Lilacs in Flower; Midsummer Night's Dream* - HALLE (MM): *Portrait of Ph. von Fischer* - HAMBURG: *Senator Oswald; Silvan Landscape; River Flet, Hamburg; Professor Karl Voll in his Sunday Best* - HANOVER: *View of Frankfurt am Main* - KAISERSLAUTERN: *Palatinate Landscape* - KARLSRUHE (Staatliche Kunsthalle): *Stuffed Pig* - KREFELD: *Portrait of Baron Schirnding* - LEIPZIG: *Portrait of the Artist; Godramstein* - LINZ (Neue Gal. der Stadt) - MANNHEIM (Städtische Kunsthalle): *Tiger at Rest; Palatinate Landscape; Portrait of Kohl with the Artist; Gardener and his Mallows; Landscape in Early Spring; Widow; Country View; Forest Clearing with Stocks* - MUNICH: *Siesta; Scheherazade; Portrait of Karl Voll; Portrait of Madame von Tschudi; Portrait of Prince Regent Luitpold of Bavaria* (four); *Portrait of G.*

Conrad with the Artist; Church Scene; Uniforms; Horsel Hill; Entrance to the Port of Syracuse; Fruit; Terrace at Neukastel - MUNICH (Neue Pinakothek): *Sunny Corner of the Garden* - MUNICH (Städtische Gal. im Lenbachhaus): *Danae; Madame Papenhagen* - NUREMBERG (Municipal Gal.): *Portrait of the Artist; Still-life with Salmon; Huldschinsky Auction* - POZNAN: *Equestrian Portrait* - STUTTGART (Staatsgal.): *Prodigal Son* (1868); *Andrade Performing 'Don Juan'* (1902); *Champagne Song; Chair (study); Bather* - SZCZECIN: *Portrait of the Artist; Portrait of Conrad Ansorge* - VIENNA (Österreichische Gal. Belvedere): *Child in the Bath* - WIESBADEN (Wiesbaden Mus.): *Portrait of Max Liebermann* - WROCLAW (Muz. Narodowe): *Rider; Palatinate Landscape; Lady in Blue* - WUPPERTAL: *Portrait of Madame Erler.*

AUCTION RECORDS:

LONDON, 23 March 1962, *Masked Ball,* Gns 850. VIENNA, 22 Sept 1964, *Sketchbook* (set of 15 watercolours and drawings) DEM 17,000. COLOGNE, 8-9 Dec 1966, *Vase of White Lilacs,* DEM 40,000. MUNICH, 1 Dec 1972, *Portrait of General von Sichart,* DEM 46,000. DÜSSELDORF, 20 June 1973, *Summer Landscape,* DEM 98,000. MUNICH, 29 Nov 1974, *Still-life with Oranges,* DEM 60,000. MUNICH, 28 May 1976, *Autumn Storm* (c. 1927, oil on canvas, 35 3/4 x 43 1/4 ins / 91 x 110 cm) DEM 83,000. MUNICH, 26 Nov 1977, *Siesta* (c. 1910, oil on canvas, 24 1/2 x 29 1/2 ins / 62 x 75 cm) DEM 63,000. COLOGNE, 5 Dec 1979, *Red Carnations* (1904, oil on canvas, 30 1/2 x 24 1/2 ins / 77.5 x 62 cm) DEM 36,000. HEIDELBERG, 18 Oct 1980, *Amazon* (c. 1908, Indian ink and watercolour, 12 3/4 x 16 1/2 ins / 32.5 x 42 cm) DEM 4,200. COLOGNE, 5 Dec 1981, *Wine Festival* (1902, oil on card, 11 1/4 x 19 ins / 28.5 x 48.5 cm) DEM 12,000. ZURICH, 13 May 1982, *Landscape* (watercolour and pencil, 8 1/4 x 11 1/4 ins / 21.1 x 28.4 cm) CHF 4,300. MUNICH, 26 Nov 1982, *Trotting Race* (c. 1911-1912, chalk heightened with white, 6 x 9 1/2 ins / 15.5 x 24 cm) DEM 3,200. COLOGNE, 2 June 1984, *Man with Parrot* (1901, oil on canvas, 39 1/4 x 32 ins / 100 x 81 cm) DEM 800,000. HAMBURG, 5 June 1985, *Trotting Race* (1923, lithograph/porcelain, set of 13, 14 x 17 1/4 ins / 35.6 x 43.5 cm) DEM 8,000. LONDON, 3 Dec 1985, *Sada Yakko and the Japanese Child* (1906, oil on canvas, 52 x 43 1/2 ins / 131.2 x 110.2 cm) GBP 21,000. COLOGNE, 31 May 1986, *Self-portrait at Work* (c. 1895, oil on canvas, 19 3/4 x 25 1/2 ins / 50 x 65 cm) DEM 96,000. LONDON, 29 June 1987, *Garden, Godramstein* (1910, oil on canvas, 39 1/4 x 32 ins / 100 x 81 cm) GBP 180,000. LONDON, 21 Oct 1988, *Cavalry Charge* (1899, ink/paper, 8 x 7 1/4 ins / 20.3 x 18.5 cm) GBP 1,045; *Landscape* (oil on canvas/card, 17 1/4 x 19 1/4 ins / 43.8 x 49 cm) GBP 7,150. MUNICH, 26 Oct 1988, *Cat Sleeping beside its Young* (oil on canvas, 18 x 21 1/4 ins / 46 x 54 cm) DEM 55,000. LONDON, 27 Nov 1989, *Road to Godramstein* (1909, oil on canvas, 25 x 31 ins / 63.5 x 78.8 cm) GBP 198,000. MUNICH, 31 May 1990, *Stone Quarry with Cart* (1910, oil on canvas, 24 1/2 x 30 1/2 ins / 62.5 x 77.5 cm) DEM 156,200. BERLIN, 30 May 1991, *Portrait of Helen Lewin* (1917, oil on canvas, 14 1/4 x 9 3/4 ins / 36 x 25 cm) DEM 22,200. BERLIN, 29 May 1992, *Hunter amid the Conifers* (oil on canvas, 19 3/4 x 23 1/2 ins / 50 x 60 cm) DEM 49,720. BERLIN, 27 Nov 1992, *Self-portrait* (1906, oil on card, 8 1/2 x 6 3/4 ins / 21.5 x 17.3 cm) DEM 39,550. LONDON, 20 May 1993, *Bosquet, Neuchâtel* (1921, oil on canvas, 29 1/2 x 37 1/4 ins / 75 x 94.5 cm) GBP 89,500. PARIS, 20 Dec 1993, *Woman Seated in a Wicker Chair* (1921, oil on canvas/panel, 35 1/2 x 43 1/4 ins / 90 x 110 cm) FRF 270,000. MUNICH, 27 June 1995, *White Horse* (1903, oil on wood, 25 3/4 x 25 1/2 ins / 65.5 x 65 cm) DEM 23,000. LONDON, 11 Oct 1995, *Butterflies and Grasses* (1917, oil on canvas, 29 1/4 x 30 3/4 ins / 74.3 x 78.2 cm) GBP 56,500. LONDON, 9 Oct 1996, *Entrance to the Frankfurt Zoo* (1901, oil on canvas, 25 1/2 x 30 3/4 ins / 65 x 78 cm) GBP 188,500. COPENHAGEN, 21 May 1997, *Euriolus, 31 March 1914* (watercolour, 5 1/2 x 8 1/4 ins / 14 x 21 cm) DKK 17,000. MUNICH, 27 Feb 1999, *Miss Meissner as Pierrette* (oil on canvas, 41 x 33 ins / 105 x 85 cm) DEM 80,000. NEW YORK, 5 May 1999, *Artist in Landscape* (oil on canvas, 30 x 37 ins / 75 x 95 cm) USD 170,000. LONDON, 17 Oct 2000, *Neukastel* (1930, oil on canvas, 26 x 22 ins / 65 x 57 cm) GBP 65,000. LONDON, 17 Oct 2000, *Finding of Moses - Antonie by the Pond* (1913, oil on canvas, 29 x 24 ins / 74 x 62 cm) GBP 120,000. BERLIN, 29 June 2001, *Still-life with Aspargus and Radishes* (oil on card, 15 x 19 ins / 37 x 49 cm) DEM 70,000. HAMBURG, 8 Dec 2001, *Portrait of Young Woman with Violin* (oil on canvas, 63 x 43 ins / 160 x 110 cm) DEM 54,000. COLOGNE, 4 June 2002, *Still-life* (1903, oil on canvas, 19 x 28 ins / 49 x 72 cm) EUR 85,000. HAMBURG, 28 Sept 2002, *Woman in Punt* (oil on canvas, 13 x 17 ins / 32 x 42 cm) EUR 12,000. BERLIN, 31 May 2003, *Black D'Andrade - Study* (oil on board, 21 x 15 ins / 54 x 39 cm) EUR 9,000. COLOGNE, 13 Dec 2003, *Summer Landscape in the Pfalz* (1930, oil on canvas, 27 x 35 ins / 69 x 88 cm) EUR 90,000. LONDON, 3 Feb 2004, *Path to the Summerhouse* (1912, oil on canvas, 24 x 30 ins / 62 x 77 cm) GBP 75,000. HAMBURG, 10 June 2004, *Dance of Morgiane with Dolche* (watercolour, Indian ink and gouache heightened with gold, 7 x 12 ins / 17 x 31 cm) EUR 6,200.

SLEWINSKI, Wladyslaw, or Ladislas, Vladyslav
Polish, 19th - 20th century.
Born 1854, in Bialynin; died 24 March 1918, near Paris.
Painter. Figures, portraits, genre scenes, landscapes, urban landscapes, waterscapes, seascapes, still-lifes.
School of Pont-Aven.

Wladyslaw Slewinski studied at Wojciech Gerson's drawing school in Warsaw and from 1883 to 1885 at the Cracow academy. In 1896 he would return there to work as an instructor. He then continued his studies in Paris, where he attended the Académie Julian (1888) and the Grande-Chaumière. He worked with Carolus-Duran from 1885. In 1888, he met Paul Gauguin, and accompanied him to Pont-Aven in 1890. He spent his summers in Brittany until 1896, when he settled in nearby Pouldu. From 1895 he frequented the Russian artists who formed the 'L'Atelier' club. In 1905 he returned to Poland, where he taught at the Warsaw school of fine arts and founded an artistic group. In 1907 he went to Munich. He returned to France in 1910, settling in Brittany once more, this time for good, at Douëlan. He was a member of the Munich Kunstverein and the Sztuka artists' association.

Slewinski painted over 300 works, including many views of Paris, in particular the banks of the Seine, and ordinary people from Brittany or the Tatra. At first he drew inspiration from the new laws of painting (synthetisme and cloisonnisme) being formulated at Pont-Aven, simplifying his motifs and using flat areas of strong, expressive colour outlined in black. Then his palette lightened and his touch became firmer, with a hesitant period during his return to Poland, when he adopted temporarily what Gérald Schürr described as 'the foggy grisaille typical of Slav colourists'.

Several of his works were included in group shows such as the Champ de Mars, Paris (from 1890), the 1921 exhibition of Polish art organised by the Salon de la Société Nationale des Beaux-Arts, Paris, and the 2001 exhibition *L'Avant-printemps. Pologne 1880-1920* held in the Palais des Beaux-Arts, Brussels. A posthumous retrospective of his work was held in Pont-Aven in 1961 and another in the Vannes Museum in 1966.

BIBLIOGRAPHY:

Jaworska, Wladyslawa, *Wladyslaw Slewinski, 1854-1918: wystawa monograficzna,* Muzeum narodowe, Warsaw, 1983. Jaworska, Wladyslawa, *Wladyslaw Slewinski,* Krajowa Agencja Wydawnicza, Warsaw, 1991. Morawinska, Agnieszka/Clegg, Elisabeth/Poprzecka, Maria/Crugten, Alain van, *L'Avant-printemps. Pologne 1880-1920,* exhibition catalogue, Palais des Beaux-Arts, Tempera, Brussels, 2001.

MUSEUMS AND GALLERIES:
BYDGOSZCZ - CRACOW (Muz. Narodowe): *Portrait of Stanislaw Ignacy Witkiewicz* (c. 1911, oil on canvas) - KATOWICE - WARSAW (Muz. Narodowe): *Self-portrait with Straw Hat* (1894, oil on canvas); *Woman with Cat* (c. 1896, oil on canvas); *Masks and Books* (c. 1897, oil on canvas); *Two Breton Women with Basket of Apples* (c. 1897, oil on canvas); *Woman Dressing her Hair* (1897, oil on canvas); *Anemonies* (c. 1905, oil on canvas); *The Orphan of Poronin (The Little Orphan)* (c. 1906, oil on canvas); *Isolated Rock in the Sea* (1907, oil on canvas).
AUCTION RECORDS:
VERSAILLES, 18 June 1972, *Still-life with Apples and Glass* (oil on canvas, 11 x 17 1/4 ins / 28 x 44 cm) FRF 4,000. LONDON, 29 June 1972, *Autumn Landscape,* GBP 500. LONDON, 4 July 1974, *Still-life,* GBP 800. PARIS, 20 Oct 1982, *Tugs and Stevedores on the Banks by the Pont des Arts, Paris* (oil on canvas, 10 1/4 x 13 1/2 ins / 26 x 34 cm) FRF 20,000. LONDON, 20 May 1987, *Head of Breton Woman* (crayon with black pencil outlines, 13 3/4 x 17 ins / 35 x 43 cm) GBP 4,800. PARIS, 16 Oct 1988, *Quays of the Seine* (oil on canvas, 9 3/4 x 13 ins / 25 x 33 cm) FRF 13,500. WARSAW, 5 Oct 2000, *Vase of Roses* (oil on canvas, 18 x 13 ins / 45 x 33 cm) PLN 125,000. NEW YORK, 8 Nov 2000, *Ile de Croix* (oil on canvas, 17 x 25 ins / 43 x 63 cm) USD 38,000. BREST, 12 May 2002, *Composition with Fruit* (oil on canvas, 17 x 26 ins / 44 x 65 cm) EUR 36,000. LONDON, 18 Nov 2003, *Still-life of Fruit* (oil on canvas, 19 x 24 ins / 49 x 60 cm) GBP 30,000. WARSAW, 14 Dec 2003, *Jug with Flowers* (c. 1909, oil on canvas, 24 x 20 ins / 61 x 50 cm) PLN 250,000.

SLEZER, John
British, 18th century.
Of Dutch origin; died 24 June 1714, in Scotland.
Engraver (burin), draughtsman.

John Slezer settled in Scotland in 1669. He was an officer.

SLIMANI, Kheira
Algerian, 20th - 21st century.
Born 1964, in Algiers.
Painter.

Kheira Slimani uses ink, acrylic paint and oil paint in equal measure to produce large-scale Abstract works that privilege gesture and colour. She has taken part in several cultural events in Algeria. Her first solo exhibition was held in Algiers in 1989.

SLINGELAND, Cornelis van, or Slingelant or Slingerlant, Zeehaan
Dutch, 17th century.
Born c. 1635; died 1686; buried 16 April in Dordrecht.
Active in Dordrecht.
Painter.

Cornelis van Slingeland was a cook, he went to Rome by sea twice, and was a member of the guild of St Pietersheeren in 1669.

SLINGELAND, Lambert van, or Slingelandt
Dutch, 17th century.
Died before 1662.
Active in The Hague and Dordrecht.
Landscape painter.

SLINGELAND, Pieter Cornelisz. van, or Singelandt, Slinglandt, Slingerland, Slingelandt or Slingelant
Flemish School, 17th century.
Born 20 October 1640, in Leiden; died 7 November 1691, in Leiden.
Painter, draughtsman. Figures, portraits, genre scenes, interiors with figures. Miniatures.

Pieter Cornelisz. van Slingeland was a pupil of Gérard Dou, whose style he imitated. He entered the guild in Leiden in 1661 and became its dean in 1691. He had as his pupils Jacob van der Huys and Jan Frelius. Slingeland was his master's equal when it came to the 'finish' of the execution of his paintings.

He was represented at the exhibition *Twee gouden eeuwen: schilderkunst uit Nederland en Denemarken* (*Two Golden Ages: Masterpieces of Dutch and Danish Painting*) at the Rijksmuseum in Amsterdam in 2001.
MUSEUMS AND GALLERIES:
AIX: *Seamstress* - AMSTERDAM: *Singing Rehearsal; Portrait of a Man; Portrait of a Young Man and a Woman* (with miniatures by W. van Mieris) - BERLIN: *Portrait of a Young Man; Child Angling* - CAEN: *Dutch Woman* - COPENHAGEN (Statens Mus. for Kunst): *Wealthy Dutch Interior* (1663); *Young Girl with Parrot* (1663) - DRESDEN: *Music Lesson; Old Man Offering a Cockerel to a Young Woman; Woman at a Harpsichord Singing* - DUBLIN: *Portrait of a Woman; Portrait of a Man* - FLORENCE: *Soap Bubbles* - GLASGOW: *Doctor's Visit; Musical Gathering* - HELSINKI: *Man with a Glass of Wine* - LEIPZIG: *Drinker* - LIÈGE: *Dinner* - MUNICH: *Woman Sewing* - PARIS (Louvre): *Dutch Family; Portrait of a Man; Kitchen Utensils; Mary Magdalene; St Jerome* - RENNES: *Cat Watching a Bird* - ROTTERDAM: *Johannes van Crombrugge* - SCHWERIN: *Shoemaker's Workshop; Violinist; Old Beggar* - ST PETERSBURG (Hermitage): *Lunch* - STOCKHOLM: *Young Woman with a Pumpkin* - VALENCIENNES: *Kitchen Interior* - VIENNA (Czernin'sche Gemäldegal.): *Richly Dressed Lady, Child and Female Servant.*
AUCTION RECORDS:
AMSTERDAM, 1706, *Woman Preparing Pancakes,* FRF 240; *Woman Sorting Beetroot,* FRF 410. PARIS, 1771, *Kitchen Interior,* FRF 4,220. PARIS, 1817, *Interior of a Dutch Bedroom,* FRF 6,300. PARIS, 1837, *Dutch Interior,* FRF 5,250. PARIS, 1843, *Dutch Interior,* FRF 2,630. PARIS, 1858, *Dutch Interior,* FRF 4,000. PARIS, 1861, *Music Lesson,* FRF 5,000. PARIS, 1862, *School,* FRF 1,625. PARIS, 6-9 March 1872, *Music Lesson,* FRF 5,200. PARIS, 1873, *Portrait of a Lady and her Little Daughter,* FRF 3,550. AMSTERDAM, 1881, *Lace Maker,* FRF 16,800; *Woman Making Cakes; Little Messenger* (collection) FRF 7,875. PARIS, 1889, *Lace Maker,* FRF 26,500. LONDON, 1896, *Two Boys, a Cat and a Bird in a Cage,* FRF 8,920. PARIS, 25 May 1905, *Kitchen Interior,* FRF 4,200. NEW YORK, 21 March 1906, *Music Lesson,* USD 225. PARIS, 11 and 12 March 1908, *Woman and Child,* FRF 3,100. LONDON, 8 June 1910, *Interior: Gentleman near a Table,* GBP 29. PARIS, 12 June 1919, *Portrait of a Woman,* FRF 10,600. LONDON, 31 May 1922, *Interior of an Office,* GBP 42. LONDON, 27 and 28 June 1922, *Cornelius van Dalen* (black chalk) GBP 20. LONDON, 2 March 1923, *Hermit Reading,* GBP 62. LONDON, 20 April 1923, *Interior with Peasants Drinking,* GBP 57. LONDON, 4-7 May 1923, *Woman with Mandolin,* GBP 367. LONDON, 30 May 1930, *Interior with Woman Sewing,* GBP 210. PARIS, 15 May 1931, *Message,* FRF 27,100. PARIS, 16 June 1932, *Music Lesson,* FRF 1,600. PARIS, 4 June 1937, *Lace Maker,* FRF 35,100. PARIS, 4 June 1941, *Woman Selling Poultry* (attributed) FRF 6,800. PARIS, 5 Nov 1941, *Three Figures in a Barn Playing with an Owl* (attributed) FRF 3,600. LONDON, 13 Feb 1946, *Jan Musschenbrock and his Wife,* GBP 1,800. PARIS, 8 Dec 1948, *Portrait of a Young Woman* (attributed) FRF 52,000. PARIS, 4 April 1949, *Young Girl with Parrot* (attributed) FRF 10,100. PARIS, 11 April 1951, *Hurdy-gurdy Player* (attributed) FRF 60,000. AMSTERDAM, 1 May 1951, *Kitchen Interior,* NLG 2,000. PARIS, 1 June 1951, *Young Woman in her Kitchen* (attributed) FRF 60,000. PARIS, 24 March 1955, *Lace Maker,* FRF 275,000. LONDON, 25 Nov 1970, *Instrument Maker Jan van Musschenbroek with his Wife in an Interior,* GBP 3,000. PARIS, 20 Dec 1973, *Young Woman and Young Boy in a Kitchen,* FRF 24,000. LONDON, 29 Nov 1974, *Young Boy Seated in a Niche,* Gns 7,500. AMSTERDAM, 31 Oct 1977, *Return from Church* (oil on panel, 16 1/4 x 13 3/4 ins / 41.3 x 35 cm) NLG 100,000. LONDON, 28 March 1979, *Two Young Boys at a Win-*

dow (oil on panel, 10½ x 7¾ ins / 26.5 x 20 cm) GBP 15,000. AMSTERDAM, 18 Nov 1980, *Young Boy Filling a Jug* (black chalk and traces of red chalk heightened with white/blue paper, 11¾ x 7½ ins / 30 x 19 cm) NLG 4,200. BRUSSELS, 17 June 1982, *Departing for the Hunt* (oil on canvas, 38¼ x 37 ins / 97 x 94 cm) BEF 100,000. COPENHAGEN, 7 Nov 1984, *Young Woman with a Parrot at a Window* (oil on panel, 9½ x 7 ins / 24 x 18 cm) DKK 80,000. PARIS, 13 May 1985, *Half-length Portrait of a Child* (1671, lead pencil/parchment, 7 x 5½ ins / 17.5 x 14 cm) FRF 28,000. LONDON, 11 Dec 1985, *Lace Maker* (oil/copper, 11 x 8½ ins / 28 x 21.5 cm) GBP 8,000. LONDON, 8 July 1987, *Hermit Seated at the Foot of a Tree, Reading* (oil on panel, 16¾ x 14¼ ins / 42.5 x 36 cm) GBP 20,000. STOCKHOLM, 15 Nov 1989, *Couple Seated near a Table* (oil, 6¾ x 5 ins / 17 x 13 cm) SEK 190,000. PARIS, 22 May 1992, *Bust Portrait of a Woman* (wash of black and grey ink /vellum, 6½ x 5¼ ins / 16.5 x 13.2 cm) FRF 7,500. LONDON, 8 July 1992, *Lady and her Child in the Courtyard of a Country Residence* (1681, oil on panel, 12¼ x 9½ ins / 31.4 x 24.1 cm) GBP 30,800. NEW YORK, 14 Oct 1992, *Portrait of a Lady in a Satin Skirt Holding a Book in her Lap* (1683, oil on panel, rounded at the top, 9 x 6½ ins / 22.9 x 16.5 cm) USD 8,800. LONDON, 11 Dec 1992, *Young Woman Peeling Turnips in a Kitchen* (oil on panel, 9½ x 8½ ins / 24.2 x 21.7 cm) GBP 11,000. LONDON, 3-4 Dec 1997, *Interior with a Woman, her Child and her Servant* (oil on panel, 15¼ x 13¼ ins / 38.9 x 33.6 cm) GBP 17,250. LONDON, 14 Dec 2000, *Portrait of a Lady in Pink Holding a Rose* (oil on panel, 7 x 7 ins / 19 x 17 cm) GBP 24,000. COLOGNE, 28 June 2001, *Young Woman Cleaning Carrots* (oil on canvas, 16 x 13 ins / 41 x 34 cm) DEM 6,000. LONDON, 8 July 2004, *Portrait of a Man* (1668, oil on copper, 6 x 5 ins / 16 x 12 cm) GBP 23,000.

SLINGELANDT, Pieter Jansz.

Dutch, 17th century.
Active in Amsterdam in 1678.
Sculptor.

SLINGELANDT, Quirin Ponsz. van

Dutch, 17th century.
Landscape painter.

Quirin Ponsz. van Slingelandt was a member of the guild in The Hague in the middle of the 17th century.

SLINGELANT, Pieter Cornelisz. van. See **SLINGELAND**

SLINGENEYER, Ernest or Ernst

Belgian, 19th century.
Born 29 May 1820, in Lochristi (East Flanders); died 27 April 1894, in Brussels.
Painter. Religious subjects, figures, portraits.

Ernest Slingeneyer was a pupil of Gustave Wappers in Antwerp, and subsequently visited North Africa. He took advantage of being elected to the Chamber of Representatives in 1884 to lead a campaign against the group called the Société Libre des Beaux-Arts, which he considered to be revolutionary. He advocated history painting. He was a member of the Académie de Bruxelles, and was decorated with the Order of Leopold.

Slingeneyer is particularly remembered for 12 important compositions, kept at the Académie des Beaux-Arts in Brussels, recounting the principal events in the history of Belgium.

MUSEUMS AND GALLERIES:

ANTWERP: *Christian Martyr; Woman Bathing* - BRUSSELS (MBA): *Battle of Lepanto; The Painter F.A. Bossuet; The Composer F.J. Fétis* - COLOGNE: *Wreck of Le Vengeur* - TOURNAI: *General Renard; Laure and Adolphe van Cutsen; Baroness van der Linden d'Hoogoorst.*

AUCTION RECORDS:

BRUSSELS, 1886, *Memories of the Desert*, FRF 410. PARIS, 24 June 1926, *Revolt of Gaul; Battle of Tolbiac* (two studies) FRF 1,000. PARIS, 8 Oct 1980, *Moroccan Woman at the Well* (oil on panel, 36¼ x 23¼ ins / 92 x 59 cm) FRF 11,500. LONDON, 17 Nov 1994, *Two Arabs in Ambush* (1852, oil on canvas, 36¼ x 29 ins / 92.1 x 73.4 cm) GBP 8,050. PARIS, 12 June 1995, *Bedouin Woman* (oil on canvas, 43¼ x 31¾ ins / 110 x 80.5 cm) FRF 125,000. LOKEREN, 9 Oct 1999, *Kaptein Jacobsen brengt zyn bedreigde schip voor Oostende* (1844, oil on canvas, 49 x 61 ins / 125 x 154 cm) BEF 310,000. BRUSSELS, 10 June 2002, *Stolen Kiss* (oil on panel, 26 x 21 ins / 66 x 53 cm) EUR 2,100. NEW YORK, 24 April 2003, *Proud Fisherman* (1854, oil on canvas, 83 x 49 ins / 212 x 125 cm) USD 30,000. ANTWERP, 8 March 2004, *At the Forge* (oil on panel, 28 x 20 ins / 70 x 52 cm) EUR 2,000.

SLINGERLAND. See also **SLINGELAND**

SLINGERLAND, Adrianus

Dutch, 20th century.
Born 1893, in Zoeterwoude.
Painter. Landscapes with figures, urban landscapes.

Adrianus Slingerland was a naive painter whose subject matter was drawn from his native village and the surrounding countryside. He also tried his hand at decorative compositions, producing highly-detailed and almost lace-like images of birds and trees (much in the same vein as the naive Nantes painter Loirand.

BIBLIOGRAPHY:

Gans, Louis, *Meesters der Europese naïven*, exhibition catalogue, Centraal Museum, Utrecht, 1970.

SLIWICKI, Walenty

Polish, 18th - 19th century.
Born c. 1765; died 20 September 1857, in Warsaw.
Painter, lithographer.

Walenty Sliwicki studied under M. Bacciarelli. He engraved portraits of famous Poles and local people, and produced illustrations for books.

SLIWINSKI, Robert

Polish, 19th century.
Born November 1840, in Lissa (now Leszno); died 5 September 1902, in Breslau (now Wroclaw).
Lithographer. Landscapes, mountain landscapes, architectural views.

Sliwinski studied under Brauner in Breslau and attended the Städel Institute in Frankfurt am Main, Germany. He settled in Breslau.

MUSEUMS AND GALLERIES:

WROCLAW (Muz. Narodowe): *Mountain Landscape; Schweinhaus Castle.*

SLIWINSKI, Stanislaw

Polish, 20th century.
Born 21 April 1893, in Warsaw; died 1940.
Painter. Landscapes, architectural views. Stage sets.

Stanislaw Sliwinski studied at Warsaw and Cracow Academy and worked with the Polish Theatre in Warsaw.

MUSEUMS AND GALLERIES:

CRACOW - POZNAN - PRAGUE.

SLIZIEN, Rafal

Polish, 19th century.
Born 27 June 1804, in Bartniki Poloneczka; died 20 May 1881, in Wolna or Lubow.
Painter, medallist, architect.

Rafal Slizien studied under Rustem. He painted portraits.

SLOAN, John

American, 19th - 20th century.

Born 2 August 1871, in Lock Haven (Pennsylvania); died 7 September 1951, in Hanover (New Hampshire).

Painter, engraver, illustrator. Figures, nudes, landscapes, landscapes with figures.

Group: The Eight (Ashcan School).

John Sloan studied at the Pennsylvania Academy of Fine Arts, Philadelphia, from 1892 to 1894. He sold his first canvas at the age of 14. He regularly worked as an illustrator for newspapers such as the *Philadelphia Inquirer* and the *Philadelphia Press,* but he also designed advertising and taught himself the technique of engraving. On the advice of Robert Henri, he moved to New York in 1904 and subsequently became a member of The Eight. Sloan was politically active and joined the Socialist Party in 1910; he stood for election to the New York State Assembly the same year but was defeated and stood again in 1915. He trained at the Art Students League in New York in 1916 and was elected president in 1931 but resigned the following year in order to join the Archipenko School of Art. He joined the League again in 1935. In 1929, he was elected to the National Institute of Arts and Letters. His teaching has influenced a whole generation of artists.

John Sloan's first paintings were portraits, dating from 1896-1897. Robert Henri, considered to be the leader of a new generation of painters, had a great influence on him. Sloan intended to take up Eakins' Realist tradition and relate art to contemporary life; his paintings - like his engravings, of which he was one of the main exponents of his time - portray realistically the sometimes wretched aspects of daily life. When in 1907 the National Academy of Design refused to show his works, or those of other painters such as Luks and Glackens, Robert Henri, who was a member of the Academy at the time, withdrew his own works in protest. The following year, these same artists together with a few others exhibited together in the only exhibition held by this group, which became known as The Eight, and which was derisively nicknamed the Ashcan School by New York art critics. Besides Robert Henri, William J. Glackens, George Luks and John Sloan, the members were Everett Shinn, Arthur B. Davies, Ernest Lawson and Maurice Prendergast. The Eight was a very diverse group, but Sloan specialised in pictures of street life. In *Election Night in the Herald Square* (1907), the muted shades and visible strokes depict the crowd and its movement. The same is true of *Fifth Avenue* (1909). *Woman's Work* (1911) is typical of the subjects taken from everyday life: a woman laying out washing on a windy day. *Sunday, Girls Drying their Hair* (1912) is in the same vein, young girls drying their long hair in the open air on the roof of a building. This picture was shown at the Armory Show in 1913. In 1914, Sloan settled in a popular district of Manhattan where he observed and sketched his neighbours.

John Sloan's paintings and engravings rejected conventional subjects and the conformism prevailing at the turn of the 20th century, and instead 'democratised' painting by giving expression to the vitality of real-life everyday occupations. His Realism is nevertheless a reflection on painting itself, as suggested by the modern advances, that he was aware of and participated in, at the 1913 Armory Show in New York.

Sloan participated in collective exhibitions such as: Pennsylvania Academy Annual, 1901; Allan Gallery, New York (with Robert Henri, among others), 1901; Society of American Artists, 1903; Carnegie Foundation, Pittsburgh, 1905 and regularly after that; *The Eight,* New York Gallery, 1908; and the Armory Show, New York, 1913. In 2001 he was represented at the exhibition *L'Héroïque et le Quotidien: Les Artistes Américains, 1820-1920* (*The Heroic and the Everyday: American Artists, 1820-1920*) at Musée d'Art Américain in Giverny.

Solo exhibitions include: H.P. Whitney's studio in New York, 1916; Hudson Guild Social Center, New York, 1916; Kraushaar Gallery, New York, where he exhibited regularly after 1917; an exhibition of engravings at the Whitney Museum, New York, 1936; a retrospective of engravings at the Kraushaar Gallery, New York, 1937; a retrospective at the Addison Gallery of American Art, New York, 1938; Wanamaker Galleries, New York, 1939; New Mexico Museum, 1941 and a retrospective at the Whitney Museum of American Art, New York.

From 1905 onwards Sloan received many awards including a bronze medal for engraving at the San Francisco Pan-Pacific Exposition in 1915; a gold medal for engraving in 1926; a gold medal for painting awarded by the Pennsylvania Academy of Fine Arts in Philadelphia in 1931 and another in 1950 from the Academy of Arts and Letters.

John Sloan

BIBLIOGRAPHY:

Gallatin, Albert, *Joan Sloan,* E. P. Dutton, New York, 1925. Goodrich, Lloyd, *John Sloan,* Macmillan Co., New York, 1952. Scott, David, *John Sloan. Paintings, Prints, Drawings,* Watson-Guptill, New York, 1953. Morse, Peter, *John Sloan's Prints. A Catalogue Raisonné of the Etchings, Lithographs and Posters,* Yale University Press, New Haven and London, 1969. McGarth, R. (ed.), *John Sloan. Paintings, Prints, Drawings,* exhibition catalogue, Hood Museum of Art, Dartmouth College, Hanover (NH), 1981. Elzea Rowland, *John Sloan's Oil Paintings: a Catalogue Raisonné,* Associated University Presses, London, University of Delaware Press, Newark (DE), 1991. Loughery, John, *John Sloan: painter and rebel,* Holt, New York, 1995.

MUSEUMS AND GALLERIES:

ANDOVER, MA (Addison Gal. of American Art): *Sunday: Women Drying their Hair* (1912) - ANN ARBOR (University of Michigan Mus. of Art): several drawings - BOSTON (MFA): *Pigeons* - CHICAGO (Terra Foundation for American Art Collection): *A Brass Band in the Garden* (1907, monotype); *Under the Lamp* (c. 1907, monotype) - HARTFORD (Wadsworth Atheneum): *Hairdresser's Window* (1907, oil on canvas) - NEW YORK (Metropolitan Mus. of Art): *Dust Storm, Fifth Avenue* - NEW YORK (Whitney Mus. of American Art): *Nude with Nine Apples* (1937) - ROCHESTER (Memorial AG, Rochester University): *Election Night in Herald Square* (1907) - SAN DIEGO (MA): *Italian Procession, New York* (1913-1925, oil on canvas) - SYRACUSE (Everson MA): *Helen Taylor Sketching* (1916, oil on canvas) - WASHINGTON DC (National Portrait Gal.): *Portraits* - WASHINGTON DC (NGA): , 1922, oil on canvas) - WASHINGTON DC (Smithsonian American AM): *Gwendolyn* (c. 1918, oil on canvas); *Travelling Carnival, Santa Fe* (1924, oil on canvas) - WILMINGTON, DE (Delaware AM): *Self-portrait* (oil on canvas); *Wet Night, Washington Square* (oil on canvas); *Spring Rain* (oil on canvas); *Walnut Street Theater, Philadelphia* (oil on canvas); around 300 paintings, 2500 works/paper.

AUCTION RECORDS:

NEW YORK, 20 April 1944, *Gossips,* USD 925. NEW YORK, 11 Oct 1961, *Play on Rocks,* USD 3,000. NEW YORK, 27 Jan 1965, *Carol with Blue Ribbons,* USD 4,100. NEW YORK, 16 March 1967, *Seaside,* USD 5,500. NEW YORK, 10 Dec 1970, *Family Going to Church in a Cart,* USD 9,000. NEW YORK, 8 Dec 1971, *Seafood Dinner,* USD 7,500. NEW YORK, 24 May 1972, *Drive in the Car,* USD 52,500. NEW YORK, 12 Dec 1974, *Portrait of Aline Rhone,* USD 1,200. NEW YORK, 21 April 1977, *Painter at his Easel in a Landscape* (1907, oil on card, 8 3/4 x 10 3/4 ins / 22.3 x 27.3 cm) USD 4,750. NEW YORK, 2 May 1979, *Seated Nude* (colouring pencil and graphite, 12 x 9 ins / 30.5 x 22.8 cm) USD 1,300. NEW YORK, 28 Sept 1979, *Bath* (c. 1915, monotype, 8 3/4 x 6 3/4 ins / 22.2 x 17.2 cm) USD 5,000. NEW YORK, 25 April 1980, *Spring Flowers: Greenwich Village* (1913, oil on canvas, 26 x 32 ins / 66 x 81.3 cm) USD 130,000. NEW YORK, 8 Aug 1980, *Mrs Wellington Shrieked and Stood Transfixed...* (1906, graphite and Conté pencil, 14 1/2 x 20 ins / 37 x 51 cm) USD 3,300. NEW YORK, 24 Sept 1981, *The Making of an Actress* (1908, charcoal heightened with white, 15 3/4 x 12 1/2 ins / 40 x 31.8 cm) USD 1,800. NEW YORK, 4 June 1982, *Tree by Yellow Chama* (oil on canvas, 38 1/4 x 37 ins / 97 x 94 cm) USD 14,000. NEW YORK, 27 Jan 1984, *The Inspiration of Perot* (1906, pen and wash, 17 x 21 3/4 ins / 43.1 x 55.2 cm) USD 5,000. NEW YORK, 15 March 1984, *Night Windows* (1910, etching, 5 1/4 x 7 1/4 ins / 13.6 x 18.1 cm) USD 3,000. NEW YORK, 30 May 1985, *Guadelupe Church and Moonlight* (1920, oil on canvas, 20 x 16 ins / 50.8 x 40.6 cm) USD 27,000. NEW YORK, 30 Sept 1985, *Roof Carpenter* (pencil and graphite, 14 1/2 x 20 1/4 ins / 36.6 x 51.6 cm) USD 1,600. NEW YORK, 4 Dec 1986, *Play on the Rocks* (1916, oil on canvas, 20 x 24 ins / 50.8 x 61 cm) USD 48,000. NEW YORK, 28 May 1987, *At a Window Overlooking Greenwich Village* (1913, oil on canvas, 23 3/4 x 20 ins / 60.6 x 50.8 cm) USD 60,000. NEW YORK, 1 Oct 1987, *Young Girl Dressing Herself* (1914, Conté pencil, 7 3/4 x 9 1/2 ins / 20 x 24 cm) USD 1,700. NEW YORK, 26 May 1988, *Young Girl Daydreaming* (oil on canvas, 16 x 21 3/4 ins / 40.7 x 55.5 cm) USD 12,100. NEW YORK, 24 June 1988, *Two Figures in a Landscape* (oil on canvas, 9 1/4 x 11 1/4 ins / 23.5 x 28.8 cm) USD 7,975. NEW YORK, 30 Sept 1988, *Milliner's Hat* (1935, oil on card, 26 x 18 ins / 66.2 x 45.6 cm) USD 19,800. NEW YORK, 1 Dec 1988, *Rocks, Reefs and Sea* (1917, oil on canvas, 26 x 32 ins / 66 x 81.3 cm) USD 33,000. NEW YORK, 24 May 1989, *Rocky Islets near Gloucester* (oil on canvas, 20 x 24 ins / 50.8 x 61 cm) USD 16,500. NEW YORK, 28 Sept 1989, *Reddy in a Deep Rocky Inlet* (oil on canvas, 20 x 24 ins / 51 x 61 cm) USD 26,400. NEW YORK, 30 Nov 1989, *Crossing Gloucester* (1917, oil on canvas, 24 1/4 x 20 1/4 ins / 61.6 x 51.4 cm) USD 209,000. NEW YORK, 23 May 1990, *Woman with a Brass Bowl* (oil/synthetic resin, 17 1/4 x 27 3/4 ins / 43.8 x 70.3 cm) USD 14,300. NEW YORK, 30 May 1990, *Rosina* (oil/synthetic resin, 24 x 20 ins / 61 x 50.8 cm) USD 13,200. NEW YORK, 26 Sept 1990, *Summery Landscape* (1908, oil on canvas, 9 x 11 ins / 22.8 x 27.9 cm) USD 11,000. NEW YORK, 15 May 1991, *Therese Fell on Rossignol* (ink/card, 10 1/4 x 7 1/2 ins / 26 x 19.1 cm) USD 1,540. NEW YORK, 23 May 1991, *Play on the Rocks* (1916, oil on canvas, 20 x 24 ins / 50.8 x 61 cm) USD 50,600. NEW YORK, 6 Dec 1991, *Seated Nude Glancing Back* (oil on canvas, 32 x 26 ins / 81.3 x 66 cm) USD 60,500. NEW YORK, 23 Sept 1992, *Santa Fé Landscape* (oil on panel, 15 3/4 x 20 1/4 ins / 40.3 x 51.5 cm) USD 24,200. NEW YORK, 27 May 1993, *Pink and Blue* (oil on canvas, 24 x 20 ins / 61 x 50.8 cm) USD 19,550. NEW YORK, 12 Sept 1994, *Angry Man* (lead pencil/paper, 12 1/2 x 10 ins / 31.8 x 25.4 cm) USD 2,645. NEW YORK, 25 May 1995, *Bleecker Street on Saturday Evening* (oil on canvas, 26 1/4 x 32 ins / 66.7 x 81.3 cm) USD 855,000. NEW YORK, 22 May 1996, *Nude Sleeping on a Lavender Blanket* (1936, 22 x 24 ins / 55.9 x 61 cm) USD 12,650. NEW YORK, 5 Dec 1996, *Wonson Rocks and Ten Pound Island* (oil on canvas, 20 x 24 ins / 50.8 x 61 cm) USD 87,750. NEW YORK, 3 Dec 1997, *Fishing Port, Gloucester* (oil on canvas, 20 x 24 ins / 50.8 x 61 cm) USD 90,500. NEW YORK, 11 Nov 1999, *The Barber Shop* (sepia etching, 10 x 12 ins / 25 x 30 cm) USD 12,000. NEW YORK, 30 Nov 1999, *Mountains, September* (oil on canvas, 20 x 24 ins / 51 x 61 cm) USD 60,000. NEW YORK, 24 May 2000, *Bleeker Street, Saturday Night* (oil on canvas, 26 x 32 ins / 67 x 81 cm) USD 2,000,000. NEW YORK, 30 Nov 2000, *Our Red Cottage, Gloucester* (1916, oil on canvas, 16 x 20 ins / 41 x 51 cm) USD 80,000. NEW YORK, 28 Nov 2001, *Neighbour's Garden* (1916, oil on canvas, 20 x 24 ins / 51 x 61 cm) USD 40,000. NEW YORK, 5 Dec 2001, *Dolly in White, Rocks and Sea* (oil on canvas, 20 x 24 ins / 51 x 61 cm) USD 160,000. NEW YORK, 4 Dec 2002, *Gray and Brass* (1907, oil on canvas, 22 x 26 ins / 55 x 67 cm) USD 2,100,000. NEW YORK, 5 Dec 2002, *Bench on the Palisades* (1906, oil on canvas, 9 x 11 ins / 23 x 28 cm) USD 70,000. NEW YORK, 21 May 2003, *Easter Eve* (1907, oil on canvas, 32 x 26 ins / 81 x 66 cm) USD 2,700,000. NEW YORK, 3 Dec 2003, *High Tide, Gloucester* (1914, oil on canvas, 20 x 24 ins / 51 x 61 cm) USD 110,000. MILFORD, 6 May 2004, *Willows and Rocks* (oil on canvas, 16 x 20 ins / 41 x 51 cm) USD 16,000. NEW YORK, 19 May 2004, *Blonde Rock and Blue Sea* (1914, oil on canvas, 20 x 24 ins / 51 x 61 cm) USD 60,000.

SLOANE, Eric

American, 20th century.

Born 1910 or 27 February 1905, in New York; died 1985, in New York.

Painter. Figures, genre scenes, landscapes with figures, waterscapes, mountainscapes.

Eric Sloane painted landscapes in which he paid close attention to light at different times of the day and in the different seasons.

MUSEUMS AND GALLERIES:

OKLAHOMA CITY (National Cowboy and Western Heritage Mus.): *Taos Morada*.

AUCTION RECORDS:

NEW YORK, 23 May 1979, *Autumn Landscape* (oil on card, 15 3/4 x 23 3/4 ins / 40 x 60.5 cm) USD 3,200. NEW YORK, 29 Jan 1981, *Sailing Ships and Clouds* (oil/hardboard, 20 1/2 x 22 3/4 ins / 52 x 57.9 cm) USD 2,800. NEW YORK, 26 Oct 1984, *Fall Foliage* (oil/hardboard, 24 x 30 ins / 61 x 76.2 cm) USD 6,250. NEW YORK, 24 April 1985, *Pompanoosue Bridge, Vermont* (oil/hardboard, 23 x 26 3/4 ins / 58.5 x 68 cm) USD 4,400. NEW YORK, 17 March 1988, *Flight of Geese over a Lake* (oil on canvas, 15 3/4 x 19 3/4 ins / 40 x 50 cm) USD 2,970. NEW YORK, 24 June 1988, *Above the Clouds* (1939, oil/synthetic resin, 18 3/4 x 27 1/2 ins / 47.5 x 70 cm) USD 1,870; *Jungfrau* (oil on canvas, 35 1/2 x 47 1/4 ins / 90 x 120 cm) USD 4,675. NEW YORK, 24 Jan 1989, *Autumn Gold* (oil/synthetic resin, 16 1/4 x 44 1/4 ins / 41.2 x 112.5 cm) USD 7,150. NEW YORK, 28 Sept 1989, *Skiing Downhill* (oil on panel, 36 x 47 3/4 ins / 91.5 x 121.3 cm) USD 9,350. NEW YORK, 27 Sept 1990, *Covered Bridge* (oil/synthetic resin, 20 x 24 1/4 ins / 51 x 61.5 cm) USD 8,800. NEW YORK, 17 Dec 1990, *Four Skiers* (oil on reinforced canvas, 20 x 23 3/4 ins / 50.8 x 60.3 cm) USD 4,675. NEW YORK, 14 March 1991, *Barn at Sunset* (oil/synthetic resin, 23 x 34 1/4 ins / 58.5 x 87 cm) USD 9,350. NEW YORK, 26 Sept 1991, *Slope* (oil on reinforced canvas, 20 x 24 ins / 51 x 61 cm) USD 3,850. NEW YORK, 6 Dec 1991, *Barn in Berkshire* (oil/synthetic resin, 24 x 40 ins / 61 x 101.5 cm) USD 19,800. NEW YORK, 2 Dec 1992, *Late Fall* (oil on card, 23 1/2 x 25 ins / 59.7 x 63.5 cm) USD 4,620. NEW YORK, 31 March 1993, *Pennsylvania Barn* (oil/synthetic resin, 22 x 28 ins / 55.9 x 71.1 cm) USD 10,350. NEW YORK, 27 May 1993, *Fishing Season* (oil/synthetic resin, 35 1/2 x 45 3/4 ins / 90.2 x 116.2 cm) USD 19,550. NEW YORK, 22 Sept 1993, *Bringing Home the Christmas Tree* (oil/synthetic resin, 23 1/2 x 32 3/4 ins / 59.6 x 83.4 cm) USD 36,800. NEW YORK, 13 Sept 1995, *Nostalgic Summer* (oil/synthetic resin, 24 x 42 ins / 61 x 106.7 cm) USD 24,150. NEW YORK, 22-23 May 1996, *End of Summer* (oil/Masonite, 24 x 47 ins / 61 x 119.4 cm) USD 20,700; *Barn in Autumn* (oil on card, 21 3/4 x 35 ins / 55.2 x 88.8 cm) USD 19,550. NEW YORK, 26 Sept 1996, *Late Afternoon in Autumn* (oil/Masonite, 24 x 45 ins / 61 x 114.3 cm) USD 19,550. NEW YORK, 3 Dec 1996, *Mad River* (oil/Masonite, 17 3/4 x 24 ins / 45 x 61 cm) USD 5,520; *Davos Slopes* (oil/Masonite, 47 1/2 x 35 3/4 ins / 120.5 x 91 cm) USD 9,200. NEW YORK, 25 March 1997, *Swiss Slope* (oil/Masonite, 28 x 37 1/4 ins / 71.1 x 94.9 cm) USD 3,737. NEW YORK, 23 April 1997, *Red Barn in Autumn* (oil/Masonite, 17 1/4 x 23 ins / 43.8 x 58.5 cm) USD 6,900. NEW YORK, 7 Oct 1997, *Red Barn* (oil/Masonite, 24 x 33 ins / 61 x 83.7 cm) USD 17,250. NEW YORK, 1 Dec 1999, *Barn and Sky* (oil on masonite, 32 x 40 ins / 81 x 102 cm) USD 42,500. NEW YORK, 1 Dec 1999, *Hilltop Farm* (oil on masonite, 24 x 40 ins / 61 x 102 cm) USD 42,500.

New York, 15 March 2000, *Barn in Landscape* (oil on masonite, 24 x 36 ins / 61 x 91 cm) USD 22,000. New York, 30 Nov 2000, *Harvest Eve* (oil on masonite, 20 x 46 ins / 51 x 117 cm) USD 25,000. New York, 14 March 2001, *Great Point Beach, Nantucket* (oil on masonite, 17 x 36 ins / 43 x 91 cm) USD 25,000. Portland, 8 Aug 2001, *Morning on the Farm* (oil on masonite, 23 x 34 ins / 58 x 86 cm) USD 28,000. Santa Fe, 18 May 2002, *Old Still River Bridge 1838* (oil on canvas, 24 x 36 ins / 61 x 91 cm) USD 19,000. Los Angeles, 19 June 2002, *Pennsylvania Barn* (oil on masonite, 18 x 45 ins / 46 x 114 cm) USD 22,000. Santa Fe, 23 May 2003, *Cornwall Bridge, Conn* (oil on board, 24 x 42 ins / 61 x 107 cm) USD 35,000. Portland, 8 Aug 2003, *Autumn Shadows* (oil on masonite, 24 x 36 ins / 61 x 91 cm) USD 25,000. Santa Fe, 15 May 2004, *Taow Recollection* (oil on board, 13 x 43 ins / 33 x 109 cm) USD 23,000. Hayden, 24 July 2004, *Kansas Sky* (oil on board, 24 x 36 ins / 61 x 91 cm) USD 37,500.

SLOANE, Mary Annie
British, 19th century.
Born in Leicester.
Painter, engraver, illustrator. Landscapes.

Mary Annie Sloane studied under Frank Short. She took part in exhibitions in Paris, receiving an honourable mention in 1902. She exhibited landscapes in London from 1889.

Museums and Galleries:
London (Victoria and Albert Mus.) - Ottawa (NG. of Canada).

SLOANE, Michael or Michel
British, 19th century.
Active at the beginning of the 19th century.
Engraver.

Michael Sloane studied under Bartolozzi. He engraved genre scenes and historical subjects.

SLOB, Jan Jansz.
Dutch, 17th century.
Born c. 1643 (?), in Edam.
Active in Hoorn.
Glass painter.

Jan Jansz. Slob was a pupil of Jos. Oostfries.

SLOBO, pseudonym of Slobodan Jevtic
Yugoslav, 20th century.
Born 1934, in Valjevo (now in Serbia).
Active in France since 1965.
Painter.

Slobo (Slobodan Jevtic) studied scenography with M. Serban at the academy of applied arts and architecture at the University of Belgrade. He moved to France in 1965 and settled in the Auvergne. Since 1984 he has been director of the Association pour le Musée d'Art Contemporain, Chamalières. Slobo paints the infinite world of the stars and the iridescent Milky Way in white, yellow, blue and ochre, or fantastic landscapes structured around pyramids, circles or trompe-l'œil buildings, evoking the coalescence of time. The catalogue for his Issoire exhibition contains illustrations of all his trompe-l'oeil walls.

Slobo has exhibited since 1957. Among his solo exhibitions are: 1971, National Museum, Valjevo; 1977, Museum of Modern Art, Dubrovnik; 1980, Maison des Congrès et de la Culture, Clermont-Ferrand; 1984, Galerie du Musée d'Art Contemporain, Chamalières; 1986, Galerie Utopia, Saint-Étienne; 1988, a retrospective (1958-1988) at the European Parliament, Strasbourg; and 1999, Centre Pomel, Issoire. He has also taken part in various group shows, including the Salon Comparaisons in Paris and the Salon d'Auvergne in Clermont-Ferrand.

Bibliography:
Liris, Robert, *Slobo 1958-1988*, exhibition catalogue, Association Musée d'Art contemporain, Chamalières, 1988. *Slobo*, exhibition catalogue, Ville d'Issoire, 1999.

SLOCOMBE, Alfred
British, 19th century.
Active in London from 1865 to 1886.
Painter, engraver (etching), watercolourist. Flowers.

Alfred Slocombe was a member of the Royal Cambrian Academy. He exhibited his work in London, including at the Royal Academy, the British Institution, Suffolk Street and at the Society of Painters in Watercolours, from 1862 until 1887.

SLOCOMBE, Charles Philip
British, 19th century.
Born 1832; died 24 September 1895.
Painter, watercolourist, engraver. Scenes with figures, landscapes.

Charles Philip Slocombe devoted a large part of his life to teaching in Somerset House and South Kensington. He mainly produced original engravings, particularly of landscapes, and reproductions after Rembrandt, J. Pettie, Frank Holl and other artists. He took part in the main London exhibitions from 1850 until 1882.

Museums and Galleries:
London (Victoria and Albert Mus.): two watercolours.

Auction records:
Paris, 8 Dec 1987, *Medieval Scene* (1872, watercolour, 20 x 28 1/4 ins / 51 x 72 cm) FRF 14,500. Paris, 11 June 1993, *Medieval Scene* (1872, watercolour/paper, 21 1/4 x 29 3/4 ins / 54 x 75.5 cm) FRF 12,000.

SLOCOMBE, Edward
British, 19th - 20th century.
Born 1850, in London.
Painter, engraver (etching), watercolourist.

Edward Slocombe was a member of the Royal Society of Painter-Etchers. He exhibited his work in London from 1868 until 1904.

Auction records:
London, 22 Oct 1986, *Harem Dancer* (1897, watercolour heightened with gouache, 19 x 28 ins / 48 x 71 cm) GBP 1,800. Billingshurst, 24 July 2000, *Nymphs in a Bluebell Wood* (1899, watercolour, 15 x 28 ins / 39 x 72 cm) GBP 1,300.

SLOCOMBE, Frederick Albert
British, 19th - 20th century.
Born 1847, in London; died c. 1920.
Painter (gouache), watercolourist, engraver.
Mythological subjects, genre scenes, landscapes.

Frederick Albert Slocombe was the brother of Charles Philip Slocombe. He was a member of the New Water-Colour Society and the Royal Society of Painter-Etchers, and was a member of the Committee in 1909. He exhibited his work, particularly his etchings, in London from 1866 until 1916.

Auction records:
New York, 24 May 1985, *Perseus and Andromeda* (watercolour and gouache, 23 1/2 x 17 1/2 ins / 59.8 x 44.5 cm) USD 4,500. New York, 24 May 1989, *Blackberry Picking* (1879, oil on canvas, 30 x 56 ins / 76.4 x 142.5 cm) USD 12,100. New York, 18-19 July 1996, *Perseus and Andromeda* (watercolour and gouache/paper, 23 3/4 x 17 1/2 ins / 60.3 x 44.5 cm) USD 4,600.

SLODKI, Marcel, or Slodky
Polish, 20th century.

Born 11 November 1892, in Lódz, possibly of Ukrainian origin; died 1943, in Auschwitz.

Painter, print artist. Landscapes, portraits.

Dadaism.

Marcel Slodki was born into a well-to-do family and studied painting in Munich. In 1913, after working in a Berlin theatre, he went to Paris. In 1914, when war broke out, he went to Switzerland, where he took part in the *Dada* exhibition held in 1916 in the Cabaret Voltaire, Zurich, for which he designed the exhibition poster and contributed to the magazine. In 1917 he exhibited at the Dada Gallery. This marked the end of his involvement in the movement. Following that, his work was mainly influenced by German Expressionism and to a lesser extent by Post-Impressionism. In 1923 he returned to Paris and in the following years had a number of exhibitions, mostly in Switzerland but also in Paris, London and Warsaw. During World War II he took refuge first in central France, then near Chambéry, and after Italy capitulated in 1943 he went into hiding in the mountains but was betrayed to the Gestapo and then sent to Auschwitz.

Bibliography:

Dorival, Bernard/Hoog, Michel, *Dada*, exhibition catalogue, National Art Museum moderne, Paris, 1966. Nieszawer, Nadine/Boyé, Marie/Lanzmann, Claude (preface), *Peintres juifs de l'école de Paris 1905-1939*, Denoël, Paris, 2001.

Museums and Galleries:

Warsaw (Muz. Narodowe).

SLODTZ, Dominique François

French, 18th century.

Born 20 May 1711, in Paris; died 11 December 1764, in Paris.

Painter. Landscapes.

Dominique François Slodtz was the eighth son of Sébastien Slodtz and his twelfth child. No work by him is recorded. He was painter to the king's *Menus Plaisirs* and a councillor of the Académie de St-Luc. He showed in the Académie's 1761 exhibition. He is reported to have lived on Rue St-Lazare and was the last artist in the Slodtz family.

SLODTZ, Jean Baptiste

French, 18th century.

Born 11 August 1699, in Paris; died 9 September 1759, in Paris.

Painter. Landscapes.

Jean Baptiste Slodtz was the fourth son of Sébastien Slodtz and his seventh child. Nothing is known of his works. On 21 November 1752 he was certified as keeper of the paintings of the duke of Orléans with the title of supernumerary painter. He married Marie Barbe Carlier with whom he had three daughters. He lived on the Quai de la Mégisserie. In 1771 his widow married Pierre Schoevaerts, Chevalier de Valcour, painter and gentleman-in-waiting to Archduchess Maria Elisabeth, Governess of The Netherlands.

SLODTZ, Paul Ambroise

French, 18th century.

Born 2 July 1702, in Paris; died 16 December 1758, in Paris.

Sculptor, draughtsman.

Paul Ambroise Slodtz was the sixth son of Sébastien Slodtz and his ninth child. He studied under his father and was approved by the Académie on 27 May 1741 and admitted as an Académicien on 29 November 1743. Initially an assistant professor, he obtained a chair on 6 July 1745. At the Salon in 1741 and 1742 he exhibited a bronze *Angel* destined for the high altar of a church in Sens, and from 1745 to 1750 showed the *Assumption of the Virgin*, a silver statue for a convent in La Flèche. He produced some works in the churches of St-Barthélemy, St-Sulpice, Notre-Dame and St-Merri. Upon the death of his brother Sébastien Antoine Slodtz, he was certified to continue the office of 'dessinateur de la chambre et du cabinet du roi'. He lived on the Rue de Grenelle-St-Honoré.

Museums and Galleries:

Versailles: *Versailles Opera Hall: Section and Decoration Plan* (drawing).

SLODTZ, René Michel, called Michel-Ange

French, 18th century.

Born 27 September 1705, in Paris; died 26 October 1764, in Paris.

Sculptor.

René Michel Slodtz was the seventh son of Sébastien Slodtz and his tenth child. He shone at the Académie Royale where his fellow students had already nicknamed him Michel-Ange (Michelangelo), a moniker he was to keep all his life. In January 1722 he won a third prize, in January 1723 a second prize, and in 1724 he received the second-place Prix de Rome. (Bellier de la Chavignerie is mistaken when he asserts that the first-place Prix de Rome went to him in 1726 for there were no awards that year or in 1729.) In 1725 Jean Baptiste Lemoyne had been awarded the first prize for sculpture. When students were selected for the Académie de Rome, Lemoyne's father Jean Louis Lemoyne, by then aged and frail, appealed to Duke d'Antin to keep Jean Baptiste at his side in France. The duke decided on Slodtz as a replacement (see *Correspondence of the Directors of the Académie de Rome*, vol. VII, p 398).

The document making Slodtz a *pensionnaire* is dated 12 March 1728, the year in which Slodtz arrived in Rome. Wenghels repeatedly praises him in his letters to D'Antin and his reputation grew enough to earn him some commissions. Two busts by him were particularly admired: *Head of Calchas* and *Head of Iphigenia*. For the church of St Peter in Rome Slodtz sculpted a *Statue of St Bruno Refusing the Rank of Bishop*. In the church of S Giovanni dei Fiorentini he executed the *Tomb of Marquis Capponi*. His reputation reached Paris, where students back from Rome praised his skills, adding that Bouchardon would have to watch out for the competition.

Slodtz was in Paris in 1743, according to Cochin, living with his brothers who were much more comfortably off than himself. In 1747 (the date supplied by Diderot and subsequently adopted by biographers) he returned from the Dauphiné. Before his return, he had been to Carrara to select marble blocks for the king of France. Around that time he received a commission from Cardinal d'Auvergne for a monument in Vienne Cathedral intended for the remains of the cardinal and his predecessors. Slodtz designed the model for it in Rome in 1742 and, on the way home, stayed in the Dauphiné to complete this important piece. Nicolas Cochin blames Count Caylus for stalling the sculptor's progress which, given the engraver's natural benevolence, should be noted. It is clear that Slodtz did not live up to expectations. He was approved by the Académie on 31 December 1749 but never became a fully-fledged Académicien.

In 1750 he won the important commission for *The Tomb of the Parish Priest Jean Baptiste Longuet de Gergy* for the church of St-Sulpice, for which he also sculpted the great figures in the porch, some of his most significant works. Diderot praised it effusively. In 1755 Slodtz received a pension of 600 francs from the king. This was raised to 800 francs on 25 August 1762. He took over the position of 'dessinateur de la chambre et du cabinet du roi' after the death of his brother Paul Ambroise Slodtz. Slodtz also had the honour of training Houdon and left his pupil 300 francs in his will with the observation that for eight years he had worked under Houdon's direction.

Bibliography:

Souchal, François, *Les Slodtz. Sculpteurs et décorateurs du roi (1685-1764)*, De Boccard, Paris, 1968. Scherf, Guilhelm,

'*Un sculpteur qui dessine: Michel-Ange Slodtz*' in *Dessins Français au XVIIe et XVIIIe Siècles*, symposium proceedings, École du Louvre, Paris, 2003 (symposium 15 and 24 June 1999).

MUSEUMS AND GALLERIES:

PARIS (Mus. Jacquemart-André): *Bust of Nicolas Wleughem* - ROME (Church of S Luigi dei Francesi): low relief - VERSAILLES: *St Louis Attending to the Poor* (low relief).

AUCTION RECORDS:

PARIS, 1765, *Tombs; St Bruno* (four drawings) FRF 247. PARIS, 1884, *Supper* (drawing in Indian ink wash) FRF 2,300; *Ball* (drawing in Indian ink wash) FRF 2,260. PARIS, 1894, *May Ball* (watercolour, attributed) FRF 3,800. PARIS, 25 June 1931, *Dancers in their Ballet Costumes* (pen and wash) FRF 950. PARIS, 7 Nov 1997, *Plan for a Funeral Urn with Two Chained Lions* (pen and brown ink, 8 1/2 x 5 1/2 ins / 21.5 x 14.2 cm) FRF 5,500.

SLODTZ, Sébastien

French, 17th - 18th century.

Born 1655, in Antwerp; died 8 May 1726, in Paris.

Sculptor.

Sébastien Slodtz arrived in Paris very young, apparently having travelled through Rome where he is reported to have worked. He was apprenticed to Girardon and worked for Versailles and Trianon in 1688. He was a member of the Académie de St-Luc of which he became director. He is noted particularly for the following works: *Statue of Faith* and the low relief *Clemency and Misericord* for the palace chapel at Versailles; a marble vase decorated with flowers; *Aristeus and Proteus*, a marble group after Girardon; the statue of *Hannibal* for the Tuileries Garden, finished in 1720 and now at the Louvre; a statue of *Vertumnus* for Marly; and a statue of *St Ambrose* and a low relief of *St Louis Sending Missionaries into the East* for the church of the Invalides.

According to Jal, Sébastien Slodtz married Madeleine Cucci around 1689. She was the daughter of Domenico Cucci, a leading cabinet-maker who worked for the Gobelins manufactory. They had 13 children: Madeleine (died aged 5); Sébastien René (sculptor who died before 1726 - he does not figure among the brothers on his father's death certificate); a second Madeleine (died in 1705); Antoine Sébastien (sculptor); Marie Françoise (goddaughter of Girardon); Jean; Jean Baptiste (painter); Guillaume (died aged 2); Paul Ambroise (sculptor and draughtsman); René Michel (godson of his brother Antoine Sébastien and of Catherine, the daughter of the sculptor René Chauveau); Madeleine Denise (died in her first year, goddaughter of the wife of the painter Louis Michel Dumesnil); Dominique François (painter); and Jules Charles.

Sébastien Slodtz had lodgings at the Louvre around 1699. Before that he lived on Rue Froid-Manteau then on Rue du Coq (later Marengo). On 16 July 1715 he married his daughter Marie Françoise to the Flemish landscapist Carel van Valeus.

MUSEUMS AND GALLERIES:

PARIS (Louvre): *Hannibal*.

SLODTZ, Sébastien Antoine

French, 18th century.

Born c. November 1695, in Paris; died 25 September 1754, in Paris.

Sculptor.

Sébastien Antoine Slodtz was the second son of Sébastien Slodtz and his fourth child. He was apprenticed to his father. In 1726 he figures in his father's death certificate as a sculptor. There is no record of works by him. Bellier de la Chavignerie, who wrongly credits him with the *Statue of Hannibal* that was sculpted by his father, says he worked on the decorations for state celebrations. Slodtz occupied the position of 'dessinateur de la chambre et du cabinet du roi', which was passed on to his brother Paul Ambroise Slodtz at his death.

SLODTZ, Sébastien René

French, 18th century.

Born c. 1693, in Paris; died before 1726.

Sculptor.

Sébastien René Slodtz was the first son of Sébastien Slodtz and his second child. He was apprenticed to his father and worked as a sculptor. There is no record of his work and it is generally thought that he died very young.

SLOM, André, or Slomszynski

French, 19th century.

Of Polish origin; died 27 December 1909, in Paris.

Painter, draughtsman.

André Slom worked for various Parisian periodicals.

AUCTION RECORDS:

PARIS, 1895, *Eiffel Tower* (drawing) FRF 27.

SLOM, Olga, or Slomszynska

Swiss, 20th century.

Born 29 March 1881, in Vevey; died 29 July 1941, in Paris.

Painter. Genre scenes, landscapes with figures, landscapes, waterscapes.

Olga Slom studied under her father André Slom and under E. Grasset and J.B. Duffaud. She was a member of the Société des Artistes Français and an exhibitor at Society salons. Slom was the recipient of numerous awards and distinctions, including an honourable mention in 1912, a silver medal and the Maria Bashkirtseff Prize in 1912, and the Hyde Prize awarded by the Société des Peintres Orientalistes Français. Works by Slom were acquired by the French State in 1910, 1912, 1914, etc.

Olga Slom travelled extensively in search of her favourite themes: sea views, lakeside views and seaside resorts. She painted the banks of the Lavaux (Switzerland) on many occasions. Her style is distinctive and highly personal, with a lightness of touch that is fully commensurate with her pleasing subject matter.

SLOMAN, Joseph

American, 20th century.

Born 30 December 1883, in Philadelphia.

Painter (gouache), sculptor, draughtsman, illustrator. Portraits, genre scenes.

Joseph Sloman was taught by Howard Pyle, B.W. Clinedinst and Clifford Grayson.

AUCTION RECORDS:

NEW YORK, 24 June 1988, *Adele* (1968, oil on card, 23 1/2 x 15 3/4 ins / 60 x 40 cm) USD 1,100. NEW YORK, 18 Dec 1991, *Passenger on the Metro* (gouache and pencil/newsprint); *Portrait of Ruth* (oil/synthetic resin, 24 x 18 ins / 61 x 45.8 cm) USD 1,320.

SLOMINSKI, Andreas

German, 20th - 21st century.

Born 1959, in Meppen.

Installation artist.

Conceptual Art.

Andreas Slominski lives and works in Hamburg. One of his series of works is on the theme of the trap. Visual, mental and physical traps are represented by real traps (*Trap* in German). In doing so, he highlights the relationship between the artist and the public, a relationship based around the meaning of an object which seems out of place as an exhibit in an art gallery. German critics often call him a *Fallensteller*, or setter of traps. He also uses objects like bicycles and everyday objects in installations aimed at destabilising cultural conventions.

Group exhibitions in which he has taken part include: 1988, Aperto 88, Venice Biennale; 1989, Berlin March; 1990,

Berlin; 1991, Centre d'Art Contemporain, Le Magasin, Grenoble; 1993, *Parcours Européen III: Allemagne* (*European Tour III: Germany*), Musée d'Art Moderne de la Ville de Paris; 1997, Musée d'Art Moderne de la Ville de Paris; 1997, Venice Biennale; 2003, *L'État des Choses* (*The State of Things*), an examination of the status of the everyday object in contemporary art, an exhibition forming part of *Trésors publics, 20 ans de création dans les Fonds régionaux d'art contemporain (FRAC)* (*Public Treasury, 20 Years of Creation in the Regional Collection of Contemporary Art*) at the Musée des Beaux-Arts, Nantes.

Solo exhibitions of his works have included: 1987, 1989, Produzentengalerie, Hamburg; 1988, 1991, Kabinett für aktuelle Kunst, Bremerhaven; 1998, Kunsthalle, Zurich; 1999, Deutsche Guggenheim, Berlin; 2003, Fondazione Prada, Milan.

Bibliography:

BiNationale, exhibition catalogue, Kunsthalle, Düsseldorf, 1988 (conversation with the artist). Bossé, Laurence/Obrist, Hans-Ulrich, *Parcours européen III Allemagne - Qui, quoi? où? - Un regard sur l'Allemagne en 1992*, group exhibition catalogue, Musée d'Art moderne de la Ville de Paris, Paris, 1993. Schorr, Collier/Spector, Nancy, *Andreas Slominski*, exhibition catalogue, Deutsche Guggenheim, Berlin, 1999 (text in German and English). Zahm, Olivier (preface), et al., *Trésors publics, 20 ans de création dans les Fonds régionaux d'art contemporain*, Flammarion, Paris, 2003 (text in French and English).

Museums and Galleries:

Dunkirk (FRAC Nord-Pas de Calais): *Falle* (*Trap*) (1992, sculpture).

SLOOT, Jentje Van der

Dutch, 20th century.
Born 1881; died 1963.
Painter.

Jentje van der Sloot came of humble stock and worked variously as a shopkeeper, café owner and peasant farmer. His paintings feature the Dutch countryside with its watercourses and coastal views. Remarkably - for a naive painter - he exhibited a strong compositional sense and a fondness for chiaroscuro light effects.

Bibliography:

Gans, Louis, *Meesters der Europese naïven*, exhibition catalogue, Centraal Museum, Utrecht, 1970.

SLOOTH, Jan

Dutch, 17th century.
Painter.

Jan Slooth was an apprentice of Paulus Moreelse in 1619.

SLOOTS, Jan

Flemish School, 17th century.
Born 1636, in Mechelen; died 23 January 1690, in Mechelen.
Painter. Animals.

Jan Sloots was a pupil of F. van Orsagghem. He specialised in painting birds and other small animals.

Auction records:

London, 16 May 1984, *Kitchen Interior* (oil on canvas, a pair, 10 1/4 x 15 1/4 ins / 26 x 39 cm) GBP 2,500.

SLOOVERE, Georges de

Belgian, 20th century.
Born 4 August 1873, in Bruges; died June 1970, in Bruges.
Painter. Portraits, genre scenes, landscapes.

Georges de Sloovere studied at the Fine Arts Academies of Bruges and Brussels. He lived and worked in the Belgian capital but remained a leading figure in his native Bruges in the years between the First and Second World Wars. He taught in the academy in Bruges and painted landscapes in which trees and undergrowth feature strongly.

Museums and Galleries:

Bruges.

Auction records:

Lokeren, 10 Oct 1992, *Flowers* (oil on canvas, 23 1/2 x 19 3/4 ins / 60 x 50 cm) BEF 65,000. Lokeren, 20 March 1993, *Peasant Farmer on his Land* (oil on canvas, 39 1/4 x 25 1/4 ins / 100 x 64 cm) BEF 60,000. Lokeren, 15 May 1993, *Azaleas* (oil on canvas, 39 1/4 x 31 1/2 ins / 100 x 80 cm) BEF 480,000. Brussels, 19 April 1999, *Dreve in Sunshine* (oil on canvas, 29 x 21 ins / 73 x 54 cm) BEF 70,000. Lokeren, 7 Dec 2002, *Still-life of Flowers* (oil on canvas, 24 x 20 ins / 60 x 50 cm) EUR 1,900. Brussels, 1 Dec 2003, *Little Girl Leaning on a Rail by a Canal in Bruges* (oil on canvas, 24 x 28 ins / 60 x 70 cm) EUR 1,500.

SLOTHAUSEN, Ferdinand

German, 17th century.
Active in Marsberg and Fritzlar in 1682.
Painter.

SLOTHOUWER, H. J.

Dutch, 19th century.
Born 1809, in Thiel.
Portrait artist.

H. J. Slothouwer was a pupil of Oosterhoudt. He worked in Amersfoort, Nijmegen, Rotterdam and Utrecht, and, from 1841, in Germany.

SLOTT-MÖLLER, Agnes

Maiden name: Rambusch
Danish, 20th century.
Born 10 June 1862, in Copenhagen; died 11 June 1937, in Løgismose.
Painter, sculptor, designer, writer. History painting, mythological subjects.

Agnes was the wife of Harald Slott-Möller and the pupil of P.S. Kroyer in Copenhagen. She was influenced by the work of the Pre-Raphaelites; she is noted for a drawing of Georg Brandes.

Museums and Galleries:

Aalborg - Maribo - Odense - Randers - Ribe - Tondern.

Auction records:

Copenhagen, 20 Feb 1979, *Festival Time* (1904, oil on canvas, 33 x 53 1/4 ins / 84 x 135 cm) DKK 13,000. Copenhagen, 27 Jan 1981, *Henrik Harpestreng Picking Flowers* (oil on canvas, 55 x 39 1/4 ins / 140 x 100 cm) DKK 6,500. Copenhagen, 16 April 1985, *Rider in an Enchanted Forest* (oil on canvas, 41 3/4 x 60 1/4 ins / 106 x 153 cm) DKK 32,000. Stockholm, 15 Nov 1988, *Danish Landscape near a Lake in Summer* (oil, 20 1/2 x 40 1/4 ins / 52 x 102 cm) SEK 14,000. Copenhagen, 25 Oct 1989, *Meadow in Summer* (1916, oil on canvas, 18 x 23 1/2 ins / 46 x 60 cm) DKK 7,000. Stockholm, 19 May 1992, *Danish Archipelago in Summer* (oil on canvas, 20 1/2 x 40 1/4 ins / 52 x 102 cm) SEK 10,000. Copenhagen, 7 Sept 1994, *Popular Festival with Young Couple* (1922, oil on canvas, 24 x 16 1/4 ins / 61 x 41 cm) DKK 4,000. London, 17 Nov 1995, *Drawing Room Portrait of the Artist's Family on an Evening* (1885, oil on canvas, 30 1/2 x 36 1/2 ins / 77.5 x 92.5 cm) GBP 4,600. Copenhagen, 14 Feb 1996, *Embarking for Flensborg Fjord* (1925, oil on canvas, 27 1/2 x 48 ins / 70 x 122 cm) DKK 9,000. Copenhagen, 1 June 1999, *Flowering Roses in the Park at Lovenholm* (1922, oil on canvas, 31 x 20 ins / 80 x 50 cm) DKK 15,000. Copenhagen, 29 Feb 2000, *Niels Ebbesen on Horseback* (oil on canvas, 31 x 38 ins / 78 x 97 cm) DKK 40,000. Havnen, 25 Nov 2000, *Christening Surrounded by Tree of Life* (oil on canvas, 27 x 27 ins / 69 x 69 cm) DKK 13,000. Copenhagen, 5 March 2001, *Oluf on Horseback in Elverhoj* (oil on canvas, 21 x 33 ins / 53 x 85 cm) DKK 22,000. Vejle, 25 Sept 2001, *Tristan. Isolde* (1907, oil on canvas, a pair, 17 x 11 ins / 43 x 27 cm) DKK 14,500. Copenhagen, 3 June 2002, *Queen Margrete I and Erik of Pomerania* (oil on canvas, 55 x

35 ins / 140 x 90 cm) DKK 130,000. LONDON, 17 June 2004, *Dying Betrothed* (1906, oil on canvas, 32 x 53 ins / 82 x 135 cm) GBP 48,000.

SLOTT-MÖLLER, Harald or Georg Harald
Danish, 19th - 20th century.
Born 1864; died 1937.
Painter, designer, art writer. Portraits, genre scenes. Symbolism.

Harald was the husband of Agnes Slott-Möller. An idealist and neo-Romantic who was strongly influenced by the English Pre-Raphaelites, Harald Slott-Mötter is noted for several portraits of the Danish writer and literary critic Georg Brandes.

BIBLIOGRAPHY:
Agnes og Harald Slott-Møller: mellem kunst og idealer, exhibition catalogue, Kunstforeningen, 1988.

MUSEUMS AND GALLERIES:
AALBORG: two portraits - COPENHAGEN: *Destitute* - COPENHAGEN (Den Hirschsprungske Samling): *Spring* (1896) - FLORENCE (Uffizi): *Portrait of the Artist* - HILLERØD (Frederiksbörg Slot): *Portrait of the Writer Helge Rode* - MARIBO: *Portrait of the Artist's Fiancée.*

AUCTION RECORDS:
COPENHAGEN, 21 Nov 1974, *Landscape with Young Woman*, DKK 6,200. COPENHAGEN, 3 June 1980, *St. Hans Nat* (oil on canvas, 26 x 33 ins / 66 x 84 cm) DKK 11,000. COPENHAGEN, 25 Jan 1984, *Young Woman Picking Flowers* (1924, oil on canvas, 18 x 32¼ ins / 46 x 82 cm) DKK 12,000. LONDON, 28 Nov 1986, *Young Woman at a Window* (oil on canvas, 33½ x 27¼ ins / 85 x 69 cm) GBP 13,500. LONDON, 24 March 1988, *Fallow Deer at Nightfall* (1901, oil on canvas, 17½ x 27¾ ins / 44.5 x 70.5 cm) GBP 6,600. COPENHAGEN, 5 April 1989, *Fjord in Summer (Landscape Study)* (oil on wood, 16¼ x 27½ ins / 41 x 70 cm) DKK 4,000. LONDON, 29 March 1990, *Billiard Room* (1908, oil on canvas, 16¼ x 24 ins / 41 x 61 cm) GBP 14,850. LONDON, 29 Nov 1990, *Georg Bandes at Copenhagen University* (1889, oil on canvas, 36¼ x 32 ins / 92 x 81 cm) GBP 36,300. COPENHAGEN, 6 March 1991, *Landscape with Three Children* (oil on canvas, 28 x 35½ ins / 71 x 90 cm) DKK 10,000. LONDON, 17 May 1991, *On the Beach* (1907, oil on canvas, 18¾ x 33¼ ins / 47.8 x 84.5 cm) GBP 8,800. NEW YORK, 20 Feb 1992, *Poet Holger Drachman surrounded by his Muses* (oil on canvas, 47 x 79 ins / 119.4 x 200.7 cm) USD 11,000. COPENHAGEN, 6 Sept 1993, *Interior with View of Lake Garda* (1910, oil on canvas, 19¼ x 24¾ ins / 49 x 63 cm) DKK 32,000. LONDON, 19 Nov 1993, *Desenzano* (1910, oil on canvas, 18¾ x 25 ins / 47.9 x 62.6 cm) GBP 5,750. NEW YORK, 20 July 1994, *Noli Me Tangere* (oil on canvas, 68¾ x 59½ ins / 174.6 x 151.1 cm) USD 3,450. COPENHAGEN, 1 June 1999, *Midsummer Night* (oil on canvas, 26 x 33 ins / 66 x 84 cm) DKK 100,000. VEJLE, 11 Aug 1999, *Beach Scene with Girls Bathing* (oil on canvas, 26 x 32 ins / 66 x 81 cm) DKK 40,000. COPENHAGEN, 6 Sept 2000, *Summer Morning - Young Girl Opening Window to Garden* (1918, oil on canvas, 22 x 22 ins / 57 x 57 cm) DKK 110,000. COPENHAGEN, 4 Dec 2000, *Two Young Girls Paddling* (1888, oil on canvas, 48 x 70 ins / 123 x 178 cm) DKK 300,000. COPENHAGEN, 5 March 2001, *Two Birds on the Terrace of Hotel Munkebjerg in Vejle* (1914, oil on canvas, 17 x 29 ins / 43 x 73 cm) DKK 32,000. VEJLE, 13 Nov 2001, *Belgian Mares - Two Horses at Logismose* (1931, oil on canvas, 39 x 56 ins / 100 x 142 cm) DKK 36,000. COPENHAGEN, 25 Feb 2002, *Midsummer Night - Three Girls by Sea* (oil on canvas, 29 x 35 ins / 73 x 90 cm) DKK 145,000. COPENHAGEN, 3 June 2002, *Morning Sun in Garden Room at Engelsholm with Daughter of the House by Door* (oil on canvas, 28 x 40 ins / 72 x 101 cm) DKK 52,000. COPENHAGEN, 26 May 2003, *Italian Terrace by the Sea* (1928, oil on canvas, 28 x 37 ins / 72 x 95 cm) DKK 80,000. HAVNEN, 30 Aug 2003, *Summer's Day in the Wood with Mrs Myllius and Mrs Scholl* (1917, oil on canvas, 25 x 30 ins / 64 x 75 cm) DKK 22,000. COPENHAGEN, 8 Sept 2004, *Young Woman, Possibly the Artist's Wife, Looking at the Sunset* (oil on canvas, 24 x 20 ins / 62 x 50 cm) DKK 42,000.

SLOTZ. See **SLODTZ**

SLOUKA
Czech, 19th century.
Born in Moravia; died 11 March 1868, in Prossnitz.
Painter. Religious subjects.

Slouka painted several altarpieces for churches in Prossnitz, Moravia.

SLOUS, George
British, 18th - 19th century.
Active in London from 1791 to 1839.
Painter, miniaturist.

George Slous was the father of Henry Courtney Slous. He painted portraits, genre pictures and landscapes.

SLOUS, Henry Courtney, or Selous
British, 19th century.
Born 1811, in Deptford; died 24 September 1890, in Beaworthy.
Painter, engraver. Allegorical subjects, portraits, genre scenes, landscapes.

Henry Courtney Slous was the son of George Slous and studied under J. Martin. He painted views of Switzerland, England and the Rhine, historical scenes and illustrations for Shakespearean tragedies. He exhibited at the Royal Academy under the name Slous from 1818 until 1831, and under the name of Selous from 1838 until 1885. He produced many line engravings.

MUSEUMS AND GALLERIES:
LIVERPOOL: *Swiss Valley* - LONDON (Victoria and Albert Mus.): *Opening of the Universal Exhibition in Hyde Park, London, in 1851* - SHEFFIELD: *Two Lovers.*

AUCTION RECORDS:
NEW YORK, 23 May 1990, *Allegories of Purity and Vanity* (oil on canvas, a pair, each 36 x 15¾ ins / 91.5 x 40.3 cm) USD 23,100. LONDON, 15 June 1990, *Flower Market near the Columns of St Theodore in St Mark's Square, Venice* (oil on canvas, 25½ x 22 ins / 65 x 55 cm) GBP 5,500.

SLOVNIK, Josef
Slovene, 20th century.
Born 9 February 1881, in Sentvid, near Ljubljana.
Active in Germany.
Painter, designer, art writer.

Josef Slovnik studied in Düsseldorf and Karlsruhe. He created altarpieces for the churches in Dübislar, Elberfeld and Erkrath.

SLUCE, J.A.
British, 19th century.
Active in London.
Painter.

J.A. Sluce exhibited his work at the Royal Academy from 1833-1835 and also in 1837.

SLUIJTER. See **SLUYTER**

SLUIJTERS, Georges Joseph van.
See **FEURE Georges de**

SLUIJTERS, Johannes Bernardus Carolus, called Jan, or Sluyters
Dutch, 20th century.
Born 17 December 1881, in 's Hertogenbosch; died 1957, in Amsterdam.
Painter (gouache), watercolourist, draughtsman. Figure compositions, figures, nudes, portraits, interiors with figures, Still-lifes, flowers, landscapes.

Johannes ('Jan') Sluijters studied at the fine arts academy in Amsterdam, where he was a Rome Prize laureate in 1904. He duly travelled to Italy in 1906 to 1907, also visiting Spain and

France. His friendship with Piet Mondrian dated from 1906, and the two artists often painted side by side out of doors. Sluijters settled in Amsterdam in 1911, although he spent 1915 to 1916 in Staphorst, where he met Le Fauconnier. He exhibited alongside Mondrian at the Stedelijk Museum in Amsterdam in 1909 (at a juncture when Mondrian was still some way from his subsequent Neo-Plasticism). Then, in 1910, Sluijters joined with Cornelis Spoor, Jan Toorop and Mondrian to establish the Moderne Kunstring art circle. His work has featured at recent group exhibitions, including *Art, Pays-Bas, XXe siècle - La Beauté exacte, de Van Gogh à Mondrian* (*Dutch 20th Century Art: Beauty in Precision, from Van Gogh to Mondrian*) held at the Musée d'Art Moderne de la Ville de Paris in 1994, and, in 2003, at *De blijvende verlokking: Nederlandse kunstenaars in Italië, 1806-1940* (*Lasting Attraction: Dutch Artists in Italy, 1806-1940*), an exhibition held in Rotterdam to illustrate the impact of Italy on Dutch artists. Sluijters' first major solo exhibition was held at the Stedelijk Museum in Amsterdam in 1927. In 2003, the Kunsthal Museum in Rotterdam mounted a comprehensive retrospective of his work.

Typically for his day, Jan Sluijters started out as a Post-Impressionist, but he was quickly drawn to Van Gogh and the Expressionist currents that were then sweeping northeast Europe, and to Fauvism. From that point onwards, his colours became and remained clear and vivid. Sluijters was also aware of Gauguin and current developments in Cubism and Futurism and, in effect, did not shy away from incorporating certain elements into his own body of work. His preferred subject matter included nudes, portraits, interiors and landscapes - particularly by moonlight. During his sojourn in Staphorst in 1915 to 1916, he produced what many consider to be his best (or, at all events, his most sensitive) work; this took the form of compositions depicting the everyday life of the Dutch countryside, capturing the visual expressions of its inhabitants in dark brown tones punctuated by patches of chiaroscuro not dissimilar to Van Gogh's series of Nuenen paintings. From that point onwards and until his death, Sluijters' work became softer and more serene, although he continued to exploit the Fauvist/Expressionist colour palette. Overall, he remains a major figure from the beginning of Dutch Expressionism.

Bibliography:

Art, Pays-Bas, XXe Siècle - La Beauté exacte, de Van Gogh à Mondrian, exhibition catalogue, Musée d'Art moderne de la ville de Paris, Paris, 1994. *De blijvende verlokking: Nederlandse kunstenaars in Italië, 1806-1940*, exhibition catalogue, Kunsthal, Rotterdam, 2003.

Museums and Galleries:

Amsterdam (Stedelijk Mus.): *Portrait of Madame J. van der Vurst de Vries-Godin* (1914); *Self-portrait* (1924); *Joy of Painting* (1946) - Antwerp (Koninklijk Mus. voor Schone Kunsten) - Eindhoven (Van Abbe Mus.): *Landscape* (1910); *Reading* (1911); *Portrait of Germ de Jong* (1933) - Haarlem (Frans Halsmus.): *Peasants at Staphorst* (1917) - Otterlo (Kröller-Müller Mus.): *Factory Land at Twilight* (1908); *Flower in a Vase* (1912); *Female Nude (back view)* (1919); *Lamentation of Christ* (1925); *Don Quixote* (1939) - The Hague (Gemeentemus.): *Child's Bedroom* (1910); *Sunset at Laren II* (1911); *Portrait of the Artist's Family* (1922); *Chrysanthemums* (1925); *Nude* (1933); *Still-life with Full-length Nude* (1933).

Auction records:

London, 23 April 1971, *Village in the Snow*, Gns 380. Amsterdam, 27 April 1976, *Reclining Nude* (watercolour, 10¼ x 18¼ ins / 26 x 46.5 cm) NLG 6,200. Amsterdam, 7 Sept 1976, *Leda and the Swan* (1903, oil on canvas, 20¾ x 37 ins / 53 x 94 cm) NLG 4,200. Amsterdam, 26 April 1977, *Still-life with Flowers* (oil on canvas, 19½ x 15½ ins / 49.5 x 39.5 cm) NLG 16,000. Amsterdam, 28 June 1977, *Seated Nude* (watercolour, 14¼ x 13½ ins / 36 x 34 cm) NLG 4,000. Amsterdam, 24 April 1979, *Summer Landscape with Cyclists* (c. 1910, oil on canvas, 19¾ x 27½ ins / 50.3 x 70 cm) NLG 50,000. Amsterdam, 2 Oct 1981, *Reclining Nude* (oil on canvas, 41 x 31½ ins / 104 x 80 cm) NLG 50,000. Amsterdam, 6 June 1983, *Seated Nude* (oil on canvas, 30½ x 22 ins / 77.2 x 56 cm) NLG 26,000. Amsterdam, 24 Oct 1983, *Motherhood* (watercolour, 17 x 13 ins / 43 x 33 cm) NLG 4,800. Amsterdam, 5 June 1984, *Seated Nude* (1916, black chalk and wash, 17 x 12¾ ins / 43 x 32.5 cm) NLG 3,000. Amsterdam, 18 March 1985, *Still-life with Flowers* (oil on canvas, 29½ x 26½ ins / 75 x 67.5 cm) NLG 10,500. Amsterdam, 8 Dec 1988, *Portrait of a Girl on a Balcony* (oil on canvas, 18¾ x 13 ins / 47.5 x 33 cm) NLG 3,220; *Bouquet of Summer Flowers in a Vase* (oil on canvas, 28¼ x 22¾ ins / 71.5 x 58 cm) NLG 16,100; *Gladioli and Summer Flowers in a Vase* (oil on canvas, 36 x 31½ ins / 90.5 x 80 cm) NLG 55,200. Amsterdam, 10 April 1989, *Flowers in a Vase* (oil on canvas, 41¼ x 36½ ins / 105 x 93 cm) NLG 34,500. Amsterdam, 24 May 1989, *Moonlight* (1912, oil on canvas, 31½ x 49½ ins / 80 x 126 cm) NLG 1,092,500. Amsterdam, 13 Dec 1989, *Sculptor's Atelier* (1909, oil on canvas, 41¼ x 36½ ins / 105 x 92.5 cm) NLG 276,000. Amsterdam, 10 April 1990, *Dune Landscape* (1909, oil on canvas, 16 x 19¾ ins / 40.4 x 50.2 cm) NLG 178,250. Amsterdam, 22 May 1990, *Seated Nude (three-quarter view)* (1912, oil on canvas, 30 x 27½ ins / 76.5 x 70 cm) NLG 322,000. Amsterdam, 12 Dec 1990, *Portrait of Dora Schrama, Seated (three quarters)* (1952, oil on canvas, 32¼ x 24½ ins / 82 x 62.5 cm) NLG 13,800; *Still-life with Flowers* (1912, oil on canvas, 50½ x 37 ins / 128 x 94 cm) NLG 322,000. Amsterdam, 5-6 Feb 1991, *Women Dancing* (oil/treated canvas, 78¾ x 212¼ ins / 200 x 539 cm) NLG 3,450. Amsterdam, 22 May 1991, *Interior with Two Female Nudes* (oil on canvas, 19 x 20¾ ins / 48 x 53 cm) NLG 71,300. Amsterdam, 17 Sept 1991, *Portrait of Ysbrand Hiddes Galema* (1946, oil on canvas, 39¼ x 33½ ins / 100 x 85 cm) NLG 8,050. Amsterdam, 11 Dec 1991, *Moonlight* (1910, oil on canvas, 16¼ x 13¼ ins / 41 x 33.5 cm) NLG 69,000. Amsterdam, 12 Dec 1991, *Reclining Nude* (ink and gouache/paper, 8 x 10¾ ins / 20.5 x 27.5 cm) NLG 1,725. Amsterdam, 19 May 1992, *Cubist Female Portrait* (oil on canvas, 42¼ x 37½ ins / 107 x 95 cm) NLG 172,500. Amsterdam, 10 Dec 1992, *Largo II* (oil on canvas, 25¾ x 20¼ ins / 65.5 x 51.5 cm) NLG 115,000. Amsterdam, 26 May 1993, *Half-Nude Seated Female* (oil on canvas, 48½ x 37 ins / 123 x 94 cm) NLG 69,000. Amsterdam, 14 Sept 1993, *Portrait of a Young Child* (charcoal and watercolour/paper, 17 x 13½ ins / 43 x 34 cm) NLG 1,725. Amsterdam, 8 Dec 1993, *Carriage in the Evening* (1911, oil on canvas, 13¼ x 16¼ ins / 33.5 x 41 cm) NLG 132,250. Amsterdam, 1 June 1994, *Portrait of a Black* (oil on canvas, 57½ x 42 ins / 146 x 106.5 cm) NLG 23,000. Amsterdam, 31 May 1995, *Portrait of Greet van Cooten* (1910, oil on canvas, 16½ x 13¼ ins / 42 x 33.5 cm) NLG 115,319. Amsterdam, 4-5 June 1996, *Landscape with Trees* (c. 1908, oil on canvas, 16 x 12¾ ins / 40.5 x 32.2 cm) NLG 37,760; *Interior* (lead pencil and colour/paper, 10¼ x 7¾ ins / 26 x 20 cm) NLG 2,530; *Regatta* (oil on card, 10 x 28¼ ins / 25.5 x 72 cm) NLG 63,250. Amsterdam, 10 Dec 1996, *Nude* (pencil and watercolour/paper, 10¼ x 7¾ ins / 26 x 19.5 cm) NLG 4,612; *Greet van Cooten wearing a Hat* (c. 1910, oil on canvas, 20¾ x 16½ ins / 53 x 42 cm) NLG 69,192. Amsterdam, 17-18 Dec 1996, *Sloterdijk Station* (1909, oil on canvas, 16¾ x 20½ ins / 42.5 x 52 cm) NLG 35,400. Amsterdam, 2-3 June 1997, *Nude* (1911, oil on canvas, 35¾ x 24½ ins / 91 x 62 cm) NLG 584,100. Amsterdam, 2-3 June 1997, *Female Portrait* (oil on canvas, 23½ x 19¾ ins / 60 x 50 cm) NLG 70,800. Amsterdam, 4 June 1997, *Floral Still-life* (c. 1936, oil on canvas, 43¼ x 37½ ins / 110 x 95 cm) NLG 138,384. Am-

STERDAM, 1 Dec 1997, *Montreux on Lake Geneva, by Night* (1954, oil on canvas, 25 1/2 x 31 ins / 64.5 x 78.5 cm) NLG 330,400. AMSTERDAM, 2 Dec 1997, *Nude Reading* (c. 1908-1910, pencil and pastel/paper, 5 x 9 3/4 ins / 12.5 x 25 cm) NLG 11,532; *Elegant Lady with a Black Chain* (1915, oil on canvas, 35 3/4 x 26 ins / 91 x 66 cm) NLG 172,980. AMSTERDAM, 10 June 1999, *Mills in Dazzling Sunlight, Zaagmolens in Amsterdam* (1907, oil on card, 10 x 8 ins / 26 x 20 cm) NLG 170,000. AMSTERDAM, 1 Dec 1999, *Standing Nude with White Drapery* (oil on canvas, 46 x 32 ins / 116 x 82 cm) NLG 260,000. STOCKHOLM, 15 May 2000, *Still-life of Flowers* (oil on canvas, 24 x 29 ins / 60 x 73 cm) SEK 245,000. AMSTERDAM, 8 June 2000, *Black Man in Armour* (oil on canvas, 43 x 37 ins / 108 x 95 cm) NLG 110,000. AMSTERDAM, 13 June 2001, *Seated Nude* (oil on canvas, 35 x 27 ins / 89 x 68 cm) NLG 370,000. AMSTERDAM, 3 Dec 2001, *Three Women Bathing* (c. 1926, oil on canvas, 57 x 65 ins / 145 x 166 cm) NLG 320,000. AMSTERDAM, 28 May 2002, *Farmhouse in Brabant* (1907, oil on canvas, 16 x 24 ins / 40 x 60 cm) EUR 78,000. AMSTERDAM, 3 Dec 2002, *View on the Pont Neuf, Paris* (1906, oil on canvas, 11 x 14 ins / 27 x 35 cm) EUR 55,000. AMSTERDAM, 27 May 2003, *Corner of Studio with Model* (c. 1912, oil on canvas, 34 x 26 ins / 86 x 66 cm) EUR 130,000. AMSTERDAM, 27 May 2003, *Nude with Pearls* (c. 1925, oil on canvas, 38 x 26 ins / 96 x 66 cm) EUR 130,000. AMSTERDAM, 30 Nov 2004, *Nude with Flowers* (oil on canvas, 20 x 16 ins / 50 x 40 cm) EUR 50,000. AMSTERDAM, 1 Dec 2004, *Hemelse en aardse lifede* (1912, oil on canvas, 20 x 25 ins / 50 x 63 cm) EUR 220,000.

SLUIS, Jacobus or Jacob van der, or Sluys
Flemish School, 17th - 18th century.
Born c. 1660, in Leiden; died 1732; buried 15 September in Leiden.
Painter. Allegorical subjects, portraits, genre scenes, interiors with figures.

Jacobus van der Sluis was a pupil of A. de Voys and P. van Huixeland, entering the guild in Leiden in 1685. He is noted for two *Allegories* and a portrait.

MUSEUMS AND GALLERIES:
LEIDEN: *Nymphs Bathing.*

AUCTION RECORDS:
AMSTERDAM, 18 May 1707, *A Lord and a Young Lady,* FRF 38. PARIS, 1888, *Inn Interior,* FRF 3,050. STOCKHOLM, 29 May 1991, *Salesman Flaunting Coins* (oil on panel, 7 1/2 x 7 1/2 ins / 19 x 19 cm) SEK 15,000. BRUSSELS, 13 Sept 1999, *At the Tobacconist's* (oil on canvas, 13 x 11 ins / 33 x 27 cm) BEF 800,000. UPPSALA, 7 Dec 2003, *At the Fishmarket* (oil on panel, 11 x 9 ins / 28 x 24 cm) SEK 28,000.

SLUITER, Pieter, or Sluyter
Dutch, 17th - 18th century.
Born possibly in 1675, in Amsterdam; died probably after 1713, in Amsterdam.
Engraver (burin).

Pieter Sluiter was probably a pupil of Petrus Schenk. He engraved portraits and book illustrations.

SLUITER, Willy
Dutch, 20th century.
Born 24 May 1873, in Amersfoort; died 1949.
Painter, engraver. Genre scenes, horse racing scenes.

Willy Sluiter studied at the academy in Rotterdam and went on to exhibit in Paris, earning a bronze medal at the Exposition Universelle of 1900.

Willy Sluiter

MUSEUMS AND GALLERIES:
DORDRECHT: *Wise Men of Dordrecht* - ROTTERDAM (Mus. Boijmans Van Beuningen): *At the Beach* - THE HAGUE: *Portrait of the Sculptor Ch. van Wijk.*

AUCTION RECORDS:
LONDON, 13 March 1980, *Cart in the Dunes* (watercolour and gouache, 10 1/2 x 13 1/2 ins / 26.7 x 34.3 cm) GBP 420. NEW YORK, 11 Feb 1981, *Fishermen Setting Forth* (gouache, 16 1/2 x 20 3/4 ins / 42 x 53 cm) USD 2,100. AMSTERDAM, 4 April 1988, *Fisherman's Wife Sewing by the Window, Volendam* (18 1/4 x 18 3/4 ins / 46.5 x 47.5 cm) NLG 3,220. AMSTERDAM, 3 Sept 1988, *Interior with Still-life of Tulips in a Black Vase* (oil on canvas, 26 x 20 ins / 66 x 51 cm) NLG 1,150. PARIS, 21 Nov 1988, *Scheveningen Beach* (oil on canvas, 15 x 17 3/4 ins / 38 x 45 cm) FRF 27,000. AMSTERDAM, 19 Sept 1989, *Showjumping* (charcoal and coloured chalk/paper, 14 3/4 x 12 ins / 37.5 x 30.5 cm) NLG 1,495. AMSTERDAM, 13 Dec 1989, *Bridge at Dordrecht* (1912, oil on canvas, 21 3/4 x 25 3/4 ins / 55.5 x 65.5 cm) NLG 8,050. AMSTERDAM, 10 April 1990, *Gathering Shellfish on the Beach* (watercolour/paper, 19 1/4 x 25 1/4 ins / 49 x 64 cm) NLG 2,990. AMSTERDAM, 6 Nov 1990, *Harbour, Volendam* (oil on canvas, 78 3/4 x 59 ins / 200 x 150 cm) NLG 19,550. AMSTERDAM, 24 April 1991, *Fisherman's Wife and Child Waiting in the Dunes* (ink and watercolour, 4 1/4 x 5 1/4 ins / 11 x 13.5 cm) NLG 1,955. AMSTERDAM, 5-6 Nov 1991, *Little Girl in Regional Dress, Volendam* (1911, oil on panel, 17 x 13 ins / 43 x 33 cm) NLG 3,680. AMSTERDAM, 14-15 April 1992, *Figures on a Terrace, Scheveningen* (1939, watercolour, 18 1/2 x 25 1/4 ins / 47 x 64 cm) NLG 10,350. AMSTERDAM, 2-3 Nov 1992, *Riding* (pastel, 11 3/4 x 15 1/4 ins / 30 x 39 cm) NLG 1,150. AMSTERDAM, 9 Dec 1992, *Boxing Match* (gouache and pencil/paper/card, 24 1/2 x 30 ins / 62 x 76 cm) NLG 2,300. AMSTERDAM, 21 April 1993, *Wind* (oil on canvas, 31 1/2 x 39 1/4 ins / 80 x 100 cm) NLG 7,475. AMSTERDAM, 19 April 1994, *Young Girl in Traditional Dress, Volendam* (1905, pastel, 17 1/4 x 15 ins / 43.5 x 38 cm) NLG 3,680. AMSTERDAM, 7 Nov 1995, *Young Rascals* (1914, oil on panel, 15 1/2 x 18 1/2 ins / 39.5 x 47 cm) NLG 3,540. AMSTERDAM, 16 April 1996, *Mother and Child Walking in the Buitenhof in The Hague* (oil on canvas, 15 x 18 ins / 38 x 46 cm) NLG 17,700. AMSTERDAM, 3 Sept 1996, *Volendam* (oil on canvas, 25 x 25 ins / 63.5 x 63.5 cm) NLG 2,883. AMSTERDAM, 19-20 Feb 1997, *Buziau the Clown* (1935, oil on canvas/panel, 23 1/2 x 19 3/4 ins / 60 x 50 cm) NLG 4,382; *Elegant Figures on Monte Pincio, Rome* (1900, lead pencil and colour/paper, 14 1/4 x 20 1/2 ins / 36 x 52 cm) NLG 5,189. AMSTERDAM, 21 Jan 1998, *Swell* (black chalk and pastel/paper, together with two other pastels by the same artist, 10 x 6 1/2 ins / 24.5 x 16.5 cm) NLG 4,036. AMSTERDAM, 27 April 1999, *Portrait of Volendam Knitter* (watercolour and gouache, 19 x 15 ins / 47 x 38 cm) NLG 7,500. AMSTERDAM, 18 April 2000, *Awaiting the Fleet, Katwijk aan Zee* (1907, oil on canvas, 31 x 39 ins / 80 x 100 cm) NLG 60,000. JOHANNESBURG, 8 May 2000, *Pulling in the Boats* (1898, watercolour, 14 x 27 ins / 36 x 69 cm) ZAR 46,000. AMSTERDAM, 30 Jan 2001, *Town Views and Figure Studies* (pencil drawings, seven sketchbooks) NLG 14,000. AMSTERDAM, 4 Sept 2001, *Volendam Harbour in Autumn* (oil on canvas, 48 x 40 ins / 121 x 101 cm) EUR 6,500. GRAVENHAGE, 24 April 2002, *Hyde Park* (oil on canvas, 19 x 26 ins / 49 x 65 cm) EUR 17,000. AMSTERDAM, 25 Nov 2002, *Children Playing on the Beach* (1898, oil on canvas, 9 x 11 ins / 22 x 28 cm) EUR 8,000. AMSTERDAM, 29 April 2003, *Modern Times - Promenading on Scheveningen Boulevard* (1932, oil on canvas, 59 x 39 ins / 151 x 100 cm) EUR 75,000. GRAVENHAGE, 7 May 2003, *Three Fisherboys from Volendam* (oil on canvas, 25 x 31 ins / 64 x 78 cm) EUR 10,000. AMSTERDAM, 20 April 2004, *Coachdriver Waiting for Passengers* (1904, pastel and black chalk, 9 x 11 ins / 23 x 29 cm) EUR 4,500. GRAVENHAGE, 3 Nov 2004, *Elegant Pair Dining in a Train* (1910, pastel, 12 x 15 ins / 31 x 39 cm) EUR 12,000.

SLUKA, Robert
Austrian, 20th century.
Born 28 April 1893, in Oderberg.
Painter. Figures, portraits, landscapes.
Robert Sluka studied at the Akademie der Bildenden Künste in Vienna and under Josef Jungwirth.

SLUPSKI, Felix
Polish, 20th century.
Born 1 May 1870, in Skolimow.
Painter. Portraits, genre scenes, landscapes.
Felix Slupski studied at the Académie Julian, Paris. He exhibited in Warsaw in 1923 and Poznan in 1937.

SLUPSKI, Jelita Cyprian
Polish, 20th century.
Born 16 September 1864, in Warsaw; died 1918, in Warsaw.
Painter. Portraits, landscapes, architectural views.
Cyprian Slupski studied in Warsaw, Prague and Dresden.

SLUTER, Claes or Claus. See **SLUYTER**

SLUTSKAIA, Liya
Russian, 20th century.
Born 16 May 1899, in Usun-Ada.
Active in Switzerland.
Painter, graphic artist, print artist.
Liya Slutskaia studied at the Munich academy and went to live in Switzerland in 1914.

SLUTZ, Helen Beatrice
American, 20th century.
Born in Cleveland (Ohio).
Painter.
Helen Beatrice Slutz studied at the Cleveland School of Art and was a member of the American Federation of Arts.

SLUYS, Gilles or Gillis or Gilleken van der, or Versluys
Flemish School, 15th - 16th century.
Sculptor.
Sluys carved a statue of *St Matthew* for the church of Our Lady, Antwerp, in 1484.

SLUYS, Jacobus or Jacob van der. See **SLUIS**

SLUYS, Théo van. See **MAES Eugène Remy**

SLUYSE, Carolus Jos Joan or Charles Joseph Jean van der
Flemish School, 18th century.
Active in Heusden.
Painter.
Carolus Jos Joan van der Sluyse was director of the academy in Antwerp in 1784, having been a student there in 1773.

SLUYSWACHTER
Dutch, 17th century.
Active in Utrecht in 1621.
Cameo engraver.

SLUYTER, Claes or Claus, or Sluter or de Slutere or Seluster or Sluter or Celoistre or Celustre or Celuister
Flemish School, 14th century.
Born probably, in Haarlem; died between 24 September 1405 and 30 January 1406, in Dijon.
Sculptor.
Claes Sluyter was the major figure in the Burgundian School of sculpture which resulted from the coming together of artists from Flanders, France and Italy in the late 14th century. It was centred on the Valois, and especially the court of Philip the Bold. A native of Holland, Sluyter had been a member of the Brussels Guild of Sculptors before setting off to seek his fortune at the Dijon court. From the moment of his arrival there, his attention was engaged completely by the Charterhouse of Champnol being constructed for the Duke of Burgundy, Philip the Bold. It was for this building that he carried out his most important works: the porch of the chapel, the tomb of Philip the Bold and the Well of Moses. The porch of the Charterhouse that was to be the site of Philip the Bold's tomb had been begun by Jean de Marville (a former collaborator with Hennequin of Liège), to whom is attributed the Virgin above the pier; the four other statues, *Duke Philip the Bold*, *St John the Baptist* who presents him, and the *Duchess* and *St Catherine*, are certainly by Sluyter. They have the relief and power that are the marks of his work. The kneeling Duke is especially remarkable, his face ecstatic, but treated nevertheless with unflinching realism, the folds of his robe full and noble in proportion. The Duke's tomb remained in the chapel of the Charterhouse of Champnol until the French Revolution and is now in the Guard Room of the Ducal Palace of the Musée des Beaux-Arts in Dijon. Jean de Marville began the tomb in 1385 and worked on it until his death in 1398, Sluyter worked on it from 1404, and it was finished by his nephew, Claus de Werve. Although not every detail of it is by Sluyter, it was he who was responsible for the overall design and who imagined, for example, the procession of 41 figures that runs around the base. There are choristers, cantors, monks, and officers and servants of the Duke in a wide variety of attitudes that show clearly through the folds of their garments, despite the fact that the figures are mainly hooded. These *Weepers* from the tomb of Philip the Bold can be found again around the tomb of his son, John the Fearless, which was carved by Jean de la Huerta and which has been placed next to that of his father in the Guard Room of the Ducal Palace in Dijon. This procession of *Weepers* was to become a mark of French funerary sculpture until the 16th century and reached its fullest expression in the tomb of Philippe Pot, formerly in Dijon but now in the Louvre. However, Sluyter's masterpiece is without doubt the *Well of Moses* from the Charterhouse. This monument consists of a hexagonal base forming a pedestal on the surface of which stand statues of the six Prophets who announced the Passion of Christ. Above them are six weeping angels, their outstretched wings meeting to support a platform on which there once rose a Calvary that is today missing. 'The most surprising of these statues,' wrote J.K. Huysmans in *The Oblate*, 'the one that immediately overcomes us with the unexpected vehemence of its glance, is that of Moses. Wrapped in a gown that appears as flexible as real material, supple folds flowing in wave movement from the waist to the feet... The head is large and has long hair, the forehead swells with two bumps that are almost horns and is wrinkled with circumflex accents above eyes that are screwed up in an almost insolent look; the double-forked beard falls from the cheeks to breast, but leaves visible an eagle-beaked nose and an imperious and pitiless mouth. An implacable, uplifted face pushes through the wild mane. It is the face of a judge and a despot, of a bird of prey... The stormy figure that one feels is almost on the point of exploding is almost superhuman.'
MUSEUMS AND GALLERIES:
DIJON: *The Tomb of Philip the Bold*.

SLUYTER, Dirk, or Sluijter
Dutch, 19th century.
Born 19 January 1790, in Amsterdam; died 17 June 1852, in Amsterdam.
Engraver (burin).
Dirk Sluyter engraved views and book illustrations.

SLUYTER, Dirk Juriaen or Jurriaan
Dutch, 19th century.
Born 14 February 1811, in Amsterdam; died 29 May 1886, in Amsterdam.
Painter, engraver (burin/wood).

Dirk Juriaen Sluyter was the son of Dirk Sluyter and a pupil of André Benoît Barreau Taurel. He specialised in engraving subjects from everyday life after the Dutch masters of the 17th century.

SLUYTER, Hendrik D. Jzoon
Dutch, 19th - 20th century.
Born 16 June 1839, in Amsterdam; died 26 February 1931, in Abkoude.
Engraver (burin).
Hendrik D. Jzoon Sluyter was the son and pupil of Dirk Juriaen Sluyter. He studied at the academy in Amsterdam and went on to engrave portraits and reproductions of paintings.

SLUYTER, Pieter. See **SLUITER**

SLUYTERMAN VON LANGEWEYDE, Georg
German, 20th century.
Born 13 April 1903, in Essen; died 5 January 1978.
Painter, draughtsman, engraver.
Georg Sluyterman von Langeweyde entered the Essen arts and crafts school in 1920, studying graphic art and decorative painting under Wilhelm Poetter and wood-engraving under Hermann Kätelhön. He went on to study at the Düsseldorf academy with Fritz Mackensen before setting up as a graphic artist in Düsseldorf. He joined the Nazi party on 1 May 1928 and began to produce pro-Nazi illustrations. He executed engravings of rural life in Lower Saxony, portraits (including one of Adolf Hitler) and murals. Following World War II, in which he fought and was captured, he continued in the field of commercial illustration and also began painting in the 1950s. In 1970, he received a gold award from the far-right Deutsches Kulturwerk Europäischen Geistes organisation.
BIBLIOGRAPHY:
Monzat, René, '*La Culture graphique de la nouvelle droite*' in *Art Press* n° 223, periodical, Paris, April 1997.

SLUYTERS. See also **FEURE Georges de**

SLUYTERS, Georges Joseph van. See also **FEURE Georges de**

SLUYTERS, Jan. See **SLUIJTERS Johannes Bernardus Carolus**

SLY, F.
Dutch, 17th century.
Active in 1642.
Painter.
F. Sly painted in the style of Jan Martszen the Younger or Palamedes. He may have been the same artist as Thomas Sly.

SLY, Thomas
Dutch, 17th century.
Active in Haarlem in 1643.
Painter.
Thomas Sly may have been the same artist as F. Sly.

SLYTER, Hendrik. See **SLUYTER Hendrik D. Jzoon**

SMACHTENS, Charles
French, 19th century.
Born in Paris.
Engraver.
Works by this artist featured at the Salon des Artistes Français where he received an honourable mention in 1899.

SMACK, Gerrit van der
Dutch, 17th - 18th century.
Born 1671 (?); died 1727, in Rotterdam.
Painter, draughtsman.
Gerrit van der Smack sketched subjects from Rotterdam.

SMADJA, Alex
French, 20th century.
Born 1897, in Mestghanem, Algeria; died 8 November 1977, in St-Léger-en-Bray (Oise).
Painter, poet, writer.
After World War I, Alex Smadja moved to Paris, where he earned his living as a cartoonist.

A self-taught artist, he worked alone. During World War II he was stationed in Toulouse.

In 1945, he began to practise Abstraction, taking an active part in the movement for 'Non-Figurative Expressionism' or 'Lyrical Abstraction' (alongside Atlan, Hartung, Soulages, Schofer and others). He gave many lectures in defence of this movement, both in Paris, especially in the studio of the musician and painter Valensi, and also in Rouen and Beauvais. His painting was characterised by strong blacks and subtle greys set against luminous whites and punctuated by vivid colours.

He first exhibited in 1920 at the Paris Salons. Later exhibitions included; 1929, Salon d'Automne; 1930-1939, Salon des Indépendants, Salon des Tuileries and Salon des Surindépendants; 1947, Salon des Réalités Nouvelles; 1948, Salon de Mai; 1958, Salon Comparaisons and Salon de la Jeune Peinture. In 1957 his works were shown at the exhibition *L'École de Paris* (*The Paris School*) at the Galerie Charpentier in Paris, and on a number of occasions at the Maison de la Pensée Française. He exhibited in 1940 at the Musée des Augustins in Toulouse with other World War II painters from Paris and also; 1949, Salon Corner in Copenhagen; Salon Comparaisons in Cannes, and in Tokyo, Mexico, Rio de Janeiro, Algiers, Bonn and Israel.

His solo exhibitions included; 1941, Galerie Chappe-Lautier, Toulouse; 1948, Galerie Breteau, Paris; 1957, Galerie Ex-Libris, Brussels; 1957, 1959 and 1965, Brussels; 1958, Galerie Birch, Copenhagen. After his death, an exhibition was held in 1985 at the Galerie Jacques Barbier in Paris; and in 1989 a retrospective of his work dating from the 1950s was held at the Galerie La Pochade in Paris.
BIBLIOGRAPHY:
Alex Smadja, exhibition leaflet, Gal. Jacques Barbier, Paris, 1985. Zeitoun, Jacques, *Smadja 1897-1977*, Gal. La Pochade, Paris, 1989. Harambourg, Lydia, *L'École de Paris 1945-1965. Dictionnaire des peintres*, Ides et Calendes, Neuchâtel, 1993.
AUCTION RECORDS:
PARIS, 23 Oct 1985, *Composition* (oil on canvas, 51 1/4 x 35 ins / 130 x 89 cm) FRF 17,000. PARIS, 3 March 1988, *Composition* (oil on canvas, 51 1/4 x 35 ins / 130 x 89 cm) FRF 26,000. PARIS, 11 Oct 1988, *Composition* (oil on panel, 18 1/2 x 15 ins / 47 x 38 cm) FRF 17,300. PARIS, 26 Oct 1988, *Sicyoni* (1970, oil on canvas, 36 1/4 x 25 1/2 ins / 92 x 65 cm) FRF 13,500. PARIS, 3 March 1989, *Composition* (1951, oil on canvas, 36 1/4 x 24 3/4 ins / 92 x 63 cm) FRF 12,500. DOUAI, 2 July 1989, *Composition* (oil on canvas, 17 3/4 x 12 1/4 ins / 45 x 31 cm) FRF 49,000. PARIS, 29 Nov 1989, *Composition* (1961, oil on hardboard, 12 3/4 x 9 3/4 ins / 32.5 x 25 cm) FRF 6,200. PARIS, 11 March 1990, *Magnetisation* (1955, oil on canvas, 51 1/4 x 35 ins / 130 x 89 cm) FRF 52,000. PARIS, 27 March 1990, *Mauve Bath; The Circumcision on 1 January* (two canvases, each 45 x 56 ins / 114 x 142 cm) FRF 45,000. COPENHAGEN, 30 May 1990, *Composition* (oil on canvas, 22 x 18 ins / 55 x 46 cm) DKK 5,000. PARIS, 6 Nov 1990, *Composition* (1955, oil on canvas, 36 1/4 x 25 1/2 ins / 92 x 65 cm) FRF 25,000. PARIS, 11 Dec 1991, *Composition* (charcoal and oil on paper/card, 16 1/4 x 12 1/4 ins / 41 x 31 cm) FRF 15,000. PARIS, 16 April 1992, *Composition* (oil on canvas, 46 x 32 ins / 116 x 81 cm) FRF 12,000. PARIS, 23 April 1993, *Composition* (1960, oil on canvas, 25 1/2 x 19 3/4 ins / 65 x 50 cm) FRF 6,000. PARIS, 30 Jan 1995, *Untitled* (oil on canvas, 51 1/4 x 38 1/4 ins / 130 x 97 cm) FRF 16,000. PARIS, 4 Oct 1997, *Composition* (c. 1950, oil on canvas, 46 x 32 ins / 116 x 81.5 cm) FRF 7,500.

SMAELEN, L.
19th century.
Active at the end of the 19th century.
Painter. Animals.
Smaelen is mentioned in F. Spar's public auctions yearbook.
AUCTION RECORDS:
PARIS, 5 Feb 1951, *Farmyard* (two pendants) FRF 5,000; *Sheep* (two pendants) FRF 3,700.

SMAJIC, Petar
Croat, 20th century.
Born 1910, in Donji-Dolac, near Split; died 1985, in Ernestinovo.
Active near Osijek.
Sculptor.
Petar Smajic lived the life of a peasant with his family. As a carter, he learned woodworking; during his free moments he would carve Gula, ornamental heads for a one-string musical instrument. In 1935, once art lovers started to take an interest in his work, he gave up this sort of woodcarving and took up carving heads and figures in wood. He took part in exhibitions of primitive art in Yugoslavia and in 1958 was one of the artists exhibited in the Yugoslav pavilion at the Brussels Universal Exhibition. In 2001 some of his works were included in *Die Naïve, Aufbruch ins verlorene Paradies* (Vienna, Kunsthaus).
BIBLIOGRAPHY:
Bihalji-Merin, Oto, *Les Peintres naïfs*, Delpire, Paris, 1960. Kelemen, Boris, *Petar Smajic*, exhibition catalogue, Galerija Primitivne Umjetnosti, Zagreb, 1980 (text in Serbo-Croat and English). *Die Naïve, Aufbruch ins verlorene Paradies*, exhibition catalogue, Kunsthaus, Vienna, 2001 (text in German and English).
MUSEUMS AND GALLERIES:
BÖNNIGHEIM (Mus. Charlotte Zander).

SMAK GREGOOR, Gilles
Dutch, 18th - 19th century.
Born 10 January 1770, in Dordrecht; died 4 December 1843, in Dordrecht.
Painter. Landscapes.
Gilles Smak Gregoor was a pupil of his uncle Van Stry and of Versteeg and Van Leen. He was no doubt related to the Dordrecht painter Pieter Martinus Gregoor.
MUSEUMS AND GALLERIES:
BRUSSELS - DORDRECHT - LA FÈRE: *Landscape with Animals*.
AUCTION RECORDS:
AMSTERDAM, 30 Oct 1996, *Milkmaid and her Livestock near a Farm on a Sunny Afternoon* (oil on panel, 25½ x 32¼ ins / 64.5 x 81.7 cm) NLG 10,378.

SMALE, H.. See **SCHMALE**

SMALL, David
British, 19th - 20th century.
Born 1846; died 1927.
Watercolourist. Landscapes.
MUSEUMS AND GALLERIES:
GLASGOW: a watercolour.

SMALL, Florence Véric Hardy
British, 19th - 20th century.
Born c.1860, in Nottingham; died 1933, in London.
Painter. Genre scenes, flowers, fruit.
Florence Small trained in Paris under Bouguereau, Deschamps and Robert Henry. She exhibited at the Salon des Artistes Français, winning a jury commendation in 1909, and at the Royal Academy in London from 1881.

SMALL, May. See **MOTT-SMITH May**

SMALL, William
British, 19th - 20th century.
Born 27 May 1843, in Edinburgh; died 23 December 1929, in Worcester.
Painter (gouache), watercolourist, illustrator. Genre scenes, landscapes.
William Small studied at the Royal Scottish Academy in Edinburgh before settling in London where he became a member of the Royal Society of Painters in Watercolours and the New Water-Colour Society. From 1869 he exhibited in London, notably at the Royal Academy. Small enjoyed a solid reputation, and illustrated a number of literary works: Arthur's *Words for the Wise* in 1864, Blackmore's *Lorna Doone* in 1883, and *Picture Book* of 1879. He also contributed illustrations to a number of other works, including: *Poems* by Ingelow, and *Spirit of Praise*. His drawings were also published in periodicals, including *The Quiver*, *Good Words* and *Sunday Magazine*.

BIBLIOGRAPHY:
MUSEUMS AND GALLERIES:
LEICESTER: *The Good Samaritan* - LIVERPOOL: *Summer in the Highlands* - LONDON (Tate Collection): *The Last Match* - MANCHESTER: *A Wreck*.
AUCTION RECORDS:
NEW YORK, 3-4 Aug 1898, *Chariot Race*, FRF 625. SLANE CASTLE, 13 May 1980, *Striking a Bargain, Connemara* (1877, watercolour heightened with gouache, 20 x 27 ins / 51 x 68.5 cm) GBP 420. LONDON, 6 Nov 1995, *After the Storm* (1877, oil on canvas, 38 x 6¼ ins / 96.5 x 15.8 cm) GBP 14,950.

SMALLFIELD, Frederick
British, 19th - 20th century.
Born 1829, in Homerton; died 1915, in Finchley (London).
Painter, watercolourist, draughtsman. Portraits, genre scenes.
Frederick Smallfield studied at the Royal Academy in London, where he exhibited from 1849 until 1886. Very little biographical information is available on him. He studied at the Royal Academy School in the 1840s. In the 1850s he was greatly influenced by the Pre-Raphaelite artists. John Ruskin drew attention to his work, when he gave an enthusiastic review of his exhibits on display at the Society of British Artists in 1857. He was also a member of the Young Engravers Club and in 1858 he was one of the artists commissioned to illustrate the poems of Thomas Hood. His work includes several watercolours and engravings inspired by these poems.
MUSEUMS AND GALLERIES:
MANCHESTER (City AG): *First Love*.
AUCTION RECORDS:
LONDON, 31 May 1927, *Angel Comforting a Blind Man* (drawing) GBP 22. LONDON, 19 May 1978, *Inventor of Sails* (1877, oil on canvas, 32 x 41 ins / 81.2 x 104 cm) GBP 600. LONDON, 1 June 1983, *Arab Smoking Hookah* (1859, watercolour on pencil outlines, round, diam. 9 ins / 23 cm) GBP 1,550. LONDON, 25 March 1994, *Little Girl Picking Raspberries* (1868, pencil and watercolour heightened with gouache, 25 x 17 ins / 63.7 x 43 cm) GBP 5,750. NEW YORK, 20 July 1994, *Tartini* (1863, watercolour and gouache/paper/card, 16 x 26½ ins / 40.6 x 67.3 cm) USD 6,612. LONDON, 3 June 1999, *Lunchtime* (1860, oil on board, 8 x 6 ins / 21 x 15 cm) GBP 5,000. LONDON, 7 June 2001, *Still-life with a Pear, Quinces and Beechnuts* (pencil, watercolour and gum arabic heightened with gouache, 9 x 11 ins / 24 x 29 cm) GBP 1,200. ZURICH, 5 Sept 2001, *Still-life with Flowers and Glass* (1848, oil on board, 18 x 14 ins / 45 x 36 cm) CHF 2,800. LONDON, 13 Feb 2002, *Vase of Flowers with Self-portrait* (1848, oil on board, 18 x 14 ins /

45 x 35 cm) GBP 2,400. LONDON, 1 May 2002, *Preparing for a Nightmare* (1859, watercolour, 10 x 13 ins / 25 x 34 cm) GBP 2,600. SYDNEY, 15 May 2004, *Tartini* (1863, watercolour, 16 x 27 ins / 40 x 68 cm) AUD 17,000.

SMALLWOOD, William Frome

British, 19th century.

Born 24 June 1806, in London; died 22 April 1834, in London.

Draughtsman, watercolourist, architect. Architectural views.

William Frome Smallwood studied under Cottingham. He exhibited sketches at the Royal Academy and Suffolk Street from 1826 until his death.

MUSEUMS AND GALLERIES:

LONDON (Victoria and Albert Mus.): a watercolour.

SMARGIASSI. See also **CIAFFERI**

SMARGIASSI, Agostino. See **CIAFFERI Agostino**

SMARGIASSI, Gabriele

Italian, 19th century.

Born 22 July 1798, in Vasto; died 12 May 1882, in Naples.

Painter. Genre scenes, landscapes with figures, landscapes, seascapes.

Smargiassi exhibited at the Paris Salon between 1827 and 1837.

MUSEUMS AND GALLERIES:

CHANTILLY: *Landscape; Palace of Caserta* - NAPLES (Pinacoteca): *The Conscript's Farewell* - VERSAILLES (Trianon): *View of Palermo.*

AUCTION RECORDS:

PARIS, 11-12 Feb 1924, *Bay of Naples at Sunset,* FRF 600. LONDON, 14 Nov 1973, *Italian Coast,* GBP 1,650. MILAN, 15 March 1977, *Seascape* (oil on canvas, 11 x 15 1/2 ins / 27 x 39.5 cm) ITL 1,200,000. LONDON, 19 June 1981, *Ruins of a Temple of Venus on the Edge of a Bay* (1832, paper/remounted/canvas, 19 x 25 1/2 ins / 48.3 x 64.8 cm) GBP 1,200. ROME, 19 May 1987, *View of Casamicciola* (pencil, 8 1/4 x 10 3/4 ins / 21 x 27.5 cm) ITL 1,500,000. MILAN, 19 Oct 1989, *Fortified Farm with Peasants and Animals* (oil on panel, 9 x 15 ins / 23 x 38 cm) ITL 5,000,000. ROME, 28 May 1991, *Cabin by the Sea* (oil on canvas, oval, 12 3/4 x 15 1/4 ins / 32.5 x 39 cm) ITL 7,500,000. ROME, 19 Nov 1992, *Landscape with Shepherds and Flocks* (oil on card, 13 x 24 1/2 ins / 33 x 62.5 cm) ITL 5,520,000. ROME, 6 Dec 1994, *Rocky Landscape with Figures* (1850, oil on canvas, 25 1/2 x 20 1/2 ins / 65 x 52 cm) ITL 5,893,000. ROME, 5 Dec 1995, *Gulf of Naples Seen from the Hills* (1850, oil on canvas, 15 3/4 x 20 3/4 ins / 40 x 53 cm) ITL 5,893,000. ROME, 23 May 2000, *Woman with Tambourine* (oil on canvas, 19 x 14 ins / 47 x 35 cm) ITL 4,000,000. COPENHAGEN, 3 Sept 2001, *View of the Bay of Naples with the Pagoda near Posillipo* (oil on canvas, 13 x 17 ins / 32 x 44 cm) DKK 22,000. LONDON, 5 June 2003, *Villagers at a Monument Overlooking the Neapolitan Coast* (1833, oil on canvas, 15 x 26 ins / 39 x 67 cm) GBP 5,000. ROME, 11 June 2003, *Landscape with Trees* (watercolour on cardboard, 12 x 17 ins / 30 x 42 cm) EUR 3,000. MILAN, 25 May 2004, *Landscape* (1839, oil on canvas, 9 x 7 ins / 24 x 19 cm) EUR 2,400.

SMARGIASSO, Pietro. See **CIAFFERI**

SMART, Borlase

British, 20th century.

Born 11 February 1881, in Kingsbridge; died 1947.

Painter, engraver, draughtsman. Seascapes.

Borlase Smart studied under Julius Olsson.

MUSEUMS AND GALLERIES:

LONDON: drawings - PLYMOUTH: drawings.

SMART, Claus

British, 18th century.

Died 1739.

Cameo engraver.

Claus Smart studied under Karl Reisen, possibly in London. He was in Paris around 1722.

SMART, Dorothy

British, 20th century.

Born 19 August 1879, in Tresco; died November 1970, in the Channel Islands.

Painter, miniaturist. Portraits, landscapes.

Dorothy Smart was a member of the Royal Society of Miniaturists.

SMART, Douglas Ion

British, 20th century.

Born 1879; died 1970.

Engraver, watercolourist.

Douglas Ion Smart lived and worked in London.

SMART, Frank Jeffrey Edson

Australian, 20th century.

Born 1921, in Adelaide.

Painter. Scenes with figures, landscapes.

Frank Smart is noted for his painting *Holiday resort* of 1946, evoking a sense of vacuity and desolation with great economy of motifs and means, and a faded colour palette.

BIBLIOGRAPHY:

Creating Australia: 200 Years of Art 1788-1988, exhibition catalogue, Art Gall. Board of South Australia, Adelaide, 1988.

AUCTION RECORDS:

SYDNEY, 6 Oct 1976, *The Inspector* (oil on canvas, 23 1/2 x 32 ins / 59.5 x 81 cm) AUD 1,600. SYDNEY, 10 March 1980, *Man on a Balcony* (oil on card, 15 3/4 x 12 1/2 ins / 40 x 32 cm) AUD 2,800. MELBOURNE, 7 Nov 1984, *Lungamere* (1966, oil on canvas remounted on board, 24 3/4 x 31 1/4 ins / 63 x 79.5 cm) AUD 9,000. MELBOURNE, 20-21 Aug 1996, *The Sculptor and his Work in Situ* (1984-1985, acrylic and oil on canvas, 39 x 47 ins / 99 x 119.5 cm) AUD 112,500. MELBOURNE, 27 April 1999, *Sculptor with Work in Situ* (1984-1985, acrylic and oil on canvas, 39 x 47 ins / 99 x 119 cm) AUD 208,000. MELBOURNE, 22 Nov 1999, *Man with Bouquet* (synthetic polymer and oil on canvas, 35 x 30 ins / 90 x 75 cm) AUD 165,000. MELBOURNE, 3 May 2000, *Over the Flaminia* (oil on canvas, 33 x 43 ins / 85 x 109 cm) AUD 150,000. MELBOURNE, 28 June 2000, *Steps, Parma* (1965, oil on canvas, 24 x 30 ins / 62 x 77 cm) AUD 170,000. MELBOURNE, 9 May 2001, *End of the Autostrada 1968* (oil on canvas, 31 x 39 ins / 80 x 100 cm) AUD 230,000. MELBOURNE, 27 Nov 2001, *Arezzo Turn Off II* (1973, oil and acrylic on canvas, 47 x 32 ins / 120 x 81 cm) AUD 320,000. MELBOURNE, 5 March 2002, *Over the Flaminia* (oil on canvas, 33 x 43 ins / 85 x 109 cm) AUD 220,000. MELBOURNE, 27 Aug 2002, *Stadium I* (1967-1968, oil on canvas, 25 x 31 ins / 64 x 80 cm) AUD 200,000. MELBOURNE, 4 March 2003, *Holiday Resort* (1946, oil on canvas, 20 x 24 ins / 51 x 61 cm) AUD 205,000. SYDNEY, 27 Aug 2003, *Near Pisa Airport* (oil on canvas, 39 x 30 ins / 98 x 75 cm) AUD 340,000. MELBOURNE, 10 March 2004, *Skaters 1999* (oil on canvas, 26 x 33 ins / 65 x 85 cm) AUD 170,000. PADDINGTON, 24 Aug 2004, *Plastic Garden, Filling Station* (1970, oil on canvas, 31 x 35 ins / 79 x 89 cm) AUD 200,000.

SMART, Henry

British, 15th century.

Active in Winchester during the second half of the 15th century.

Glass painter.

SMART, John
British, 19th century.
Painter. History painting, portraits.

John Smart exhibited his work in London from 1822 until 1850.

SMART, John
British, 19th century.
Born 16 October 1838, in Leith (Edinburgh); died 1 June 1899, in Edinburgh.
Painter. Figures, landscapes with figures, architectural views.

John Smart was the son of a lithographer and engraver. He studied at the Schools of the Board of Manufactures, then with MacCulloch. He made his debut in 1860 at exhibitions held by the Royal Scottish Academy in Edinburgh and then exhibited in London in 1870. In 1871 he was made an associate of the Royal Scottish Academy and became an academician in 1877. He also exhibited at the Glasgow Institute and was a member of the Society of British Artists.

He particularly liked to paint the Scottish lochs and the most picturesque areas of Wales.

Museums and Galleries:

Edinburgh (Royal Scottish Academy): *'Far from the Busy World'* (1879, oil on canvas) - Glasgow: *Gloom of Glen Ogle* - Liverpool: *Cateran Pass* - Melbourne (Nat. Gal. of Victoria): *Seny Crossing.*

Auction records:

London, 4 Sept 1909, *Sheep* (1873) GBP 54. London, 3 June 1910, *Landscape* (1872) GBP 5. London, 17 June 1910, *Halfway Home* (1882) GBP 115. London, 22 April 1911, *View of a Fort* (1868) GBP 9. London, 26 Nov 1937, *Artist in a Green Coat* (drawing) GBP 270. London, 24 July 1973, *Gypsies in a Wooded Landscape,* GBP 540. Perth, 19 April 1977, *Salmon Fisherman* (1865, oil on canvas, 21 1/2 x 35 1/2 ins / 54.5 x 90 cm) GBP 750. Edinburgh, 2 July 1981, *Glencoe* (1874, oil on canvas, 27 1/2 x 53 1/2 ins / 70 x 136 cm) GBP 900. Auchterarder, 30 Aug 1983, *Drawing the Salmon Nets on the Teith* (1865, oil on canvas, 22 x 36 ins / 56 x 91.5 cm) GBP 1,600. Auchterarder, 28 Aug 1984, *Kilchurn Castle, Loch Awe* (1888, watercolour, 24 1/4 x 38 1/4 ins / 61.5 x 97.1 cm) GBP 850. Orchardleigh Park (Somerset), 21 Sept 1987, *Miss Goulburn* (watercolour, h. 2 1/4 ins / 5.7 cm) GBP 2,200. London, 23 Sept 1988, *On the Road between Ballingluig and Pitlochrie* (1879, oil on canvas, 22 x 27 1/2 ins / 56 x 70 cm) GBP 1,320. Stockholm, 15 Nov 1988, *On the Banks of the Stream in Strathyre* (oil on canvas, 22 1/2 x 13 3/4 ins / 57 x 35 cm) SEK 5,500. Toronto, 30 Nov 1988, *Children in a Wood in Perthshire* (1872, oil on canvas, 19 1/2 x 25 1/2 ins / 49.5 x 64.5 cm) CAD 1,000. Glasgow, 7 Feb 1989, *Flock on a Steep-sided Path near Callander* (1886, oil on canvas, 26 x 45 ins / 66 x 114 cm) GBP 1,045. South Queensferry, 1 May 1990, *Light and Shadow at Strathyre in Perthshire* (1883, oil on canvas, 30 x 50 ins / 76 x 127 cm) GBP 1,980. New York, 29 Oct 1992, *Pool Island on the Orchy* (1889, oil on canvas, 21 3/4 x 36 1/4 ins / 55.3 x 92.1 cm) USD 1,650. Edinburgh, 23 March 1993, *Herding the Sheep* (1872, oil on canvas, 32 3/4 x 60 3/4 ins / 83 x 154.5 cm) GBP 2,645. Edinburgh, 2 Sept 1999, *Children on Woodland Path* (1874, oil on board, 6 x 5 ins / 15 x 12 cm) GBP 1,550. London, 28 Oct 1999, *Extensive Landscape with Figures in the Foreground* (1894, pencil and watercolour heightened with white, 15 x 25 ins / 38 x 63 cm) GBP 1,000. London, 5 Sept 2001, *In Pandy Plaw Two More, Musselburgh* (1889, watercolour heightened with gouache, 18 x 29 ins / 45 x 73 cm) GBP 44,000. Ottawa, 22 Nov 2001, *Troon Links* (1889, watercolour and gouache, 19 x 30 ins / 47 x 75 cm) CAD 72,500. London, 1 Sept 2004, *On the Grouse Moor* (1873, oil on canvas, 27 x 48 ins / 68 x 122 cm) GBP 7,000.

SMART, John I
British, 18th - 19th century.
Born 1 May 1741, in Norfolk, near Norwich; died 1 May 1811, in London.
Painter, miniaturist, draughtsman.

John Smart, who is considered to be one of the master miniaturists of the 18th century in England, studied first at St Martin's Lane Academy and then under Soniel Door. He may also have been taught by Richard Cosway. He made his debut at the Society of Artists at an early age, appearing in its London exhibitions from 1762. He subsequently became its director and vice-president, and sent 107 works to be exhibited there. He then appeared at the Royal Academy, where he took part in exhibitions until 1813, the year in which 41 of his works were exhibited posthumously. He married Edith Vere when he was very young and settled in Russell Place, Fitzroy Square. He left for the West Indies in 1788 and stayed there for five years. On his return to London he took up work again, enjoying as much success as he had previously.

Smart differed from most of his contemporaries in that he had an expert knowledge of the human face. He drew his portraits and studied his figures. He researched his pencil portraits in as much detail as the ones he painted.

Two different styles can be distinguished in his work. The miniatures he produced before 1770, which were generally on a small scale, are painted with extreme care and are quite similar to enamels. Those painted at the end of his career are larger.

Museums and Galleries:

London (British Mus.): *Portraits of Hindu Princes* (two drawings) - London (National Portrait Gal.): *James Bruce* (1776, watercolour and bodycolour/ivory) - London (Victoria and Albert Mus.) - New York (Metropolitan Mus. of Art) - Nottingham (Castle Mus. & AG): *Portrait of a Lady in a Blue Dress.*

Auction records:

Paris, 1895, *Portrait of a Lady in an Orange Dress* (miniature) FRF 2,925; *Portrait of a Lady in a White Dress* (miniature) FRF 4,050. Paris, 1898, *Portrait of the Countess of Jersey* (miniature) FRF 6,750; *Portrait of a Lady* (miniature) FRF 6,625. London, 29 Feb 1928, *Mr Shakespeare in Green* (drawing) GBP 57; *Mrs Shakespeare* (drawing) GBP 78; *Mr Fitz Herbert* (drawing) GBP 52; *Mrs Bailey* (drawing) GBP 42; *Mrs Lloyd* (drawing) GBP 58; *Portrait of a Gentleman* (drawing) GBP 48. London, 17 Dec 1936, *Artist Drawing,* GBP 152. Paris, 29 May 1937, *Portrait thought to be of Emily, Countess of Bellamont* (miniature) FRF 3,900; *Portrait thought to be of H.R.H. Princess Amelia* (miniature) FRF 330. Paris, 12 May 1939, *Bust of Girl Dressed in White* (miniature) FRF 4,200. Paris, 22 March 1945, *Lady Wearing a Low-cut Blue Dress* (1760, miniature) FRF 9,000. London, 15 March 1967, *Harriet, Eleanor and Anne Wigram,* GBP 500. London, 14 June 1983, *Portrait of Colonel Kidd* (1790, pencil, oval, 5 1/2 x 5 ins / 14 x 12.7 cm) GBP 2,000. London, 24 May 2000, *Gilbert Ford in Blue Velvet Coat* (1765, miniature, oval) GBP 18,000. London, 21 Nov 2000, *Young Gentleman in Brown Coat* (1804, miniatures, oval) GBP 22,000. London, 2 July 2001, *Joseph Francois Louis, Comte de Lautour* (1793, miniature, oval) GBP 15,000. London, 6 Nov 2001, *Dr James Anderson in a Dark Coat with Gold Buttons* (1800, miniature, oval) GBP 22,000. London, 28 May 2002, *Elizabeth Anne Oakes* (1786, miniature) GBP 32,000. London, 28 May 2002, *Young Gentleman in a Blue Coat* (1793, miniature) GBP 36,000. London, 9 Dec 2003, *Miss Twining* (1801, miniature, oval) GBP 22,000. London, 9 Dec 2003, *Young Lady* (1776, miniature) GBP 22,000. London, 22 April 2004, *Peeress, in Ermine-trimmed Mauve Satin Robe* (1775, miniature, oval) GBP 35,000. London, 25 May 2004, *Mrs John Richardson, in White Dress and Green Sash* (miniature) GBP 32,000.

SMART, John II, the Younger
British, 18th - 19th century.

Died June 1809, in Madras.
Miniaturist.

John Smart II was the son and student of John Smart I. He exhibited his work in London at the Society of Artists, the Free Society of Artists, the Free Society and the Royal Academy from 1775 until 1811.

AUCTION RECORDS:
LONDON, 31 Oct 2000, *Young Lady in Brown Dress* (miniature, oval) GBP 1,400. LONDON, 21 Nov 2000, *Horatio Townshend of Bridgemount, Co. Cork, in Blue* (1801, miniature, oval) GBP 15,000. LONDON, 5 Nov 2002, *Sir John Doyle Wearing Scarlet Coat with Gold Aiguilette Black Facings* (miniature, after James Ramsey, oval) GBP 5,000.

SMART, Rowley

British, 20th century.
Born 26 January 1887, in Manchester; died 9 August 1934, in Longnor.
Painter, watercolourist, lithographer. Landscapes, architectural views.

Rowley Smart trained at Manchester School of Art from 1901-1903, and in Liverpool from 1903 to 1906 under John Burridge; in Liverpool he was influenced by Augustus John. He then continued his studies at Manchester Academy of Fine Art from 1906-1907, and the École des Beaux-Arts in Paris. He was a member of the Sandon Society in Liverpool in 1907, and a founder of the Society of Modern Painters in Manchester in 1912. He served in France during World War I, after which he suffered ill-health for the rest of his life. He settled with Augustus John in Dorset, and later lived mainly in France while continuing to travel to Cornwall and Sweden for his health. He exhibited his first painting in 1908.

MUSEUMS AND GALLERIES:
BIRKENHEAD - LONDON (Tate Collection): *Pines in the Snow* (1934) - MANCHESTER (Whitworth Art Gallery) - SOUTHPORT.

SMART, Samuel Paul

British, 18th century.
Active in London during the second half of the 18th century.
Miniaturist, painter.

Samuel Smart exhibited his work in London between 1769 and 1787.

SMART, T.

British, 19th century.
Active in London in the middle of the 19th century.
Painter. History painting, portraits, genre scenes.

T. Smart exhibited his work in London from 1835 until 1855.

SMED, Nikolaus. See SCHMID

SMEDLEY, William Thomas

American, 19th - 20th century.
Born 26 March 1858, in Chester County (Pennsylvania); died 26 March 1920, in Bronxville (New York).
Painter, decorative designer, illustrator. Portraits, genre scenes, landscapes.

William Thomas Smedley studied at the Pennsylvania Academy of Fine Arts and was a student of Jean-Paul Laurens in Paris. At the turn of the 20th century, the village of Bronxville, north of Manhattan, became the centre of a small community of artists. Otto Bacher was the first to settle there in 1896, followed by Will Hicock Law. Smedley settled there in 1898 along with Milne Ramsey. He was a member of the American New Water Color Society, the National Association of Portrait Painters, the National Institute of Arts and Letters and the National Academy of New York in 1905.

Smedley began his career in 1880 as an illustrator for Harper. He illustrated a number of works including: Bangs' *A Rebellious Heroine*, and Page's *In Ole Virginia*, with other illustrators (1896); Twain's *A Dog's Tale* (1904); and H. James' *Julia Bride* (1909). He also worked for *Scribner's*. He won a bronze medal in Paris in 1900 at the Exposition Universelle, a bronze and a silver medal at Buffalo in 1901, and the Carnegie Prize in 1907.

BIBLIOGRAPHY:
Osterwalder, Marcus (ed.), *Dictionnaire des illustrateurs 1800-1914*, Ides et Calendes, Neuchâtel, 1989.

MUSEUMS AND GALLERIES:
NEW YORK (Metropolitan Mus. of Art): *Portrait of the Artist's Mother* - SYDNEY: several drawings - WASHINGTON DC (Smithsonian American AM): *One Day in June* (c. 1880-1885, oil on canvas).

AUCTION RECORDS:
SYDNEY, 10 Sept 1979, *Melbourne Cup from Members' Stand* (1887, gouache, 14 1/4 x 22 ins / 36 x 56 cm) AUD 1,800. NEW YORK, 28 Sept 1995, *Public Sale* (1893, watercolour/paper, 15 1/2 x 13 1/2 ins / 39.4 x 34.3 cm) USD 1,265. NEW YORK, 30 Nov 1995, *White Dress: Portrait of a Young Woman in a Park* (1903, oil on canvas, 50 x 26 ins / 127 x 66 cm) USD 16,100.

SMEDT, Antoni de. See SMETS

SMEDT, Jan de

Belgian, 20th century.
Born 7 February 1905, in Mechelen; died 17 September 1954, in Mechelen.
Painter, watercolourist, sculptor (clay), draughtsman. Portraits, self-portraits, genre scenes, interiors with figures, landscapes, seascapes, flowers.

Jan de Smedt was a pupil of Henri van Perck and Theo Blickx at the Academie voor Beeldende Kunsten in Mechelen from 1928 to 1930, and of Egide Rombaux and Victor Rousseau at the Académie des Beaux Arts in Brussels from 1930 to 1934. He made numerous study trips to Amsterdam, Paris and London, during which he was particularly influenced by Rembrandt, Rodin and Turner. He lived for a time in Zeeland, then on the Belgian coast and in Switzerland, bringing back canvases, sketches and watercolours. His signature is occasionally followed by *v(an) M(echelen)* (*f(rom) M(echelen)*).

De Smedt had a remarkable gift for rendering light effects and capturing atmosphere, and his colour palette was rich and nuanced. His approach leaned towards the Classical, although some of his seascapes verge on Expressionism and Abstraction. He was a talented portrait artist with an *intimiste* technique and a distinct ability to render facial tonalities. In addition to 11 extant self-portraits, he repeatedly painted portraits of his wife Camille and their son Raphaël. As a sculptor, he produced nudes, portraits and children's heads in terracotta, his favourite medium.

De Smedt took part in group exhibitions from 1929, notably in Brussels, Ghent, Mechelen and Namur. He exhibited solo on three occasions - in Antwerp and Mechelen in 1946 and Dendermonde in 1948.

BIBLIOGRAPHY:
Huldetentoonstelling Jan de Smedt (1905-1954), exhibition catalogue, Mechelen, 1973. *Retrospectieve tentoonstelling Jan de Smedt, 1905-1954*, exhibition catalogue, Cultureel Centrum, Mechelen, 1979. Contryn, J., *Jan de Smedt of de bezielde eenvoud*, Cimelia Jan de Smedt Van Mechelen, Mechelen, 1985. Turkry, René, *De sculptuur Van Jan de Smedt*, Cimelia Jan de Smedt Van Mechelen, Mechelen, 1990. *De sfeer Van intimiteit. Schilderijen en beelden Van de Belg Jan de Smedt (1905-1954)*, exhibition catalogue, Museum Kempenland, Eindhoven, 1990. Smets, F., *Jan de Smedt als marineschilder*, Cimelia Jan de Smedt Van Mechelen, Mechelen, 1991. Hellens, F., *Jan de Smedt, artiste malinois*, Cimelia Jan de Smedt Van Mechelen, Mechelen, 1992. Buckinx, P.G., *De serene tragiek Van Jan de Smedt*, Cimelia Jan de Smedt Van Mechelen, Mechelen, 1993. De Smedt, R., *Jan de Smedt en Nijvel*, Cimelia Jan de Smedt Van Mechelen,

Mechelen, 1994. Blickx, A., *Herinneringen aan mijn oom Jan de Smedt,* Cimelia Jan de Smedt Van Mechelen, Mechelen, 1995. Puydt, R.M. de/Danneels, Godfried, *Het religieuze motief bij Jan de Smedt,* Cimelia Jan de Smedt Van Mechelen, Mechelen, 1996. Verhesen, Fernand/Hennart, Marcel, *L'Univers intime de Jan de Smedt,* exhibition catalogue, Musées des Beaux-Arts, Verviers et Tournai, 1996-1997. De Smedt, R., *Jan de Smedt of het getemperde zomerlicht,* exhibition catalogue, Cultureel Centrum, Mechelen, 1997. Smets, F., *Het doodsmotief bij Jan de Smedt,* Cimelia Jan de Smedt Van Mechelen, Mechelen, 1997. Vaeck, A./Paulus, Camille, *Jan de Smedt en het Vrijbroekpark,* Cimelia Jan de Smedt Van Mechelen, Mechelen, 1998.

MUSEUMS AND GALLERIES:

ANTWERP (Prentenkabinet): *View over Antwerp* - BRUSSELS (Bibliothèque royale Albert Ier, Prints Collection): *Self-portrait with Raphaël Playing with Blocks* - BRUSSELS (Ministère de la Culture): *Young Girl in Blue* - LOUVAIN (Stedelijk Mus. Vander Kelen-Mertens): *After the Storm* - MECHELEN (Stedelijk Mus. Hof van Busleyden): *Botanical Gardens; Mother and Child; Savoy Cabbage* - MECHELEN (Town Hall): *King Albert I* - TOURNAI (MBA): *Still-life with Apples* - VERVIERS (Mus. communal des Beaux-Arts et de la Céramique): *Sunflowers.*

SMEDT, Jos de

Belgian, 20th century.

Born 1894, in Antwerp.

Painter, sculptor. Religious subjects, historical subjects, figures, nudes. Church decoration.

Jos de Smedt studied at the fine arts academies of Antwerp, Mechelen and Brussels, and went on to contribute to the decoration of the Armenian church of the Prado in Marseilles.

AUCTION RECORDS:

LOKEREN, 19 Oct 1985, *Reclining Nude* (1915, oil on canvas, 39 3/4 x 47 1/4 ins / 101 x 120 cm) BEF 180,000. LOKEREN, 7 Oct 1995, *Costumed Dancers* (oil on panel, 23 1/2 x 15 3/4 ins / 60 x 40 cm) BEF 26,000.

SMEDT, Liévin de

Flemish School, 16th century.

Sculptor.

De Smedt was commissioned to carve a crucifix for the Town Hall of Grammont in 1558.

SMEDT, Th. de. See **DESMEDT**

SMEERS, Frans

Belgian, 20th century.

Born 1873, in Brussels; died 1960.

Painter. Portraits, landscapes, seascapes.

Frans Smeers studied under J. Portaels and Stallaert at the Académie Royale des Beaux Arts in Brussels.

Fr. Smeers

MUSEUMS AND GALLERIES:

THE HAGUE (Gemeentemus.): *Landing Stage in Scheveningen; Boulevard, Scheveningen.*

AUCTION RECORDS:

ANTWERP, 15 Oct 1969, *Ostend Harbour,* BEF 100,000. BRUSSELS, 16 Nov 1971, *Little Girl and Young Woman on the Landing Stage,* BEF 170,000. ANTWERP, 23 Nov 1973, *Young Woman on the Beach,* BEF 180,000. ANTWERP, 22 Oct 1974, *On the Beach,* BEF 110,000. ANTWERP, 7 April 1976, *On the Beach* (oil on canvas, 31 1/2 x 39 1/4 ins / 80 x 100 cm) BEF 300,000. BREDA, 26 April 1977, *Beach at Cannes* (1921, oil on canvas, 22 x 27 1/2 ins / 55 x 70 cm) NLG 15,000. LOKEREN, 15 Oct 1983, *Children on the Beach* (oil on canvas, 28 x 32 ins / 71 x 81 cm) BEF 280,000. LOKEREN, 14 April 1984, *On the Beach* (oil on canvas, 33 1/2 x 50 1/2 ins / 85 x 128 cm) BEF 400,000. LOKEREN, 20 April 1985, *Young Girl on the Beach* (oil on panel, 11 1/2 x 16 1/2 ins / 29 x 42 cm) BEF 110,000. LONDON, 8 Oct 1986, *Jardin des Tuileries* (1906, oil on canvas, 19 1/4 x 29 1/4 ins / 49 x 74 cm) GBP 7,000. LONDON, 27 June 1989, *Little Girl with a Pail* (1906, oil on canvas, 28 1/4 x 23 ins / 72 x 57.5 cm) GBP 13,200. BRUSSELS, 19 Dec 1989, *Portrait* (drawing, 13 x 14 1/4 ins / 33 x 36 cm) BEF 36,000. BRUSSELS, 27 March 1990, *Women and a Child on the Beach* (oil on panel, 11 3/4 x 17 3/4 ins / 30 x 45 cm) BEF 400,000. AMSTERDAM, 30 Oct 1990, *Reflective Moment* (1918, oil on canvas, 23 1/2 x 14 1/2 ins / 60 x 37 cm) NLG 8,625. NEW YORK, 23 May 1991, *Day at the Beach* (oil on panel, 13 1/2 x 17 3/4 ins / 34.3 x 45 cm) USD 13,200. LOKEREN, 10 Oct 1992, *Vindictivekaai, Ostend* (1926, oil on canvas, 19 1/2 x 24 ins / 49.5 x 61 cm) BEF 180,000. LOKEREN, 18 May 1996, *Beached Boats* (oil on canvas, 19 3/4 x 24 ins / 50 x 61 cm) BEF 33,000. AMSTERDAM, 5 June 1996, *Little Girl with a Pail* (1906, oil on canvas, 28 1/4 x 23 ins / 72 x 57.5 cm) NLG 7,475. AMSTERDAM, 2-3 June 1997, *Mending Nets on the Quayside* (1921, oil on canvas, 22 x 25 1/2 ins / 55 x 65 cm) NLG 20,060. LOKEREN, 11 Dec 1999, *The Beach at Scheveningen* (1915, pastel, 17 x 24 ins / 42 x 60 cm) BEF 320,000. LOKEREN, 11 Dec 1999, *Woman on the Dike* (1922, oil on canvas, 21 x 26 ins / 54 x 65 cm) BEF 520,000. BRUSSELS, 9 May 2000, *Beach Scene* (oil on canvas, 16 x 24 ins / 40 x 60 cm) BEF 420,000. BRUSSELS, 19 Dec 2000, *Evening in the Dunes, or Margot and Francine on the Beach* (oil on canvas, 20 x 24 ins / 51 x 60 cm) BEF 300,000. LOKEREN, 10 March 2001, *The Red Jacket* (1925, oil on canvas, 20 x 23 ins / 50 x 59 cm) BEF 750,000. BRUSSELS, 17 Sept 2001, *Portrait of Mariette Smeers in a Red Dress in the Dunes* (1907, panel, 18 x 11 ins / 45 x 27 cm) BEF 190,000. BRUSSELS, 15 April 2002, *Choosing the Jewels* (oil on canvas, 24 x 18 ins / 60 x 45 cm) EUR 4,200. LOKEREN, 11 May 2002, *Fishing Port in Nieuport* (1931, oil on canvas, 19 x 24 ins / 49 x 60 cm) EUR 4,400. NEW YORK, 24 April 2003, *Flower Gatherers* (oil on canvas, 24 x 20 ins / 61 x 50 cm) USD 15,000. AMSTERDAM, 21 Oct 2003, *Girl Leaning Out of the Window* (oil on panel, 18 x 15 ins / 46 x 38 cm) EUR 8,000. BRUSSELS, 11 Oct 2004, *Children on the Beach by the Bathing Huts* (1920, oil on canvas laid on panel, 19 x 35 ins / 49 x 88 cm) EUR 9,000. ANTWERP, 7 Dec 2004, *Woman Seated* (1916, oil on canvas, 24 x 20 ins / 60 x 50 cm) EUR 5,500.

SMEES, Jan

Dutch, 18th century.

Died at the beginning of 1729.

Active in Amsterdam.

Painter, engraver (etching). Landscapes.

Jan Smees engraved plates in the style of Jan Both.

MUSEUMS AND GALLERIES:

LONDON (British Mus.): five etchings depicting Italian landscapes with ruins - POMMERSFELDEN: *View of a Castle* - VIENNA (Schönborn-Buckheim): *Landscape with Ruins.*

SMEESTERS

Flemish School, 18th century.

Active in Brussels during the second half of the 18th century.

Painter. Landscapes.

AUCTION RECORDS:

BRUSSELS, 1847, *Landscape on the Banks of the Meuse,* FRF 26; *Landscape: View near Huy,* FRF 30.

SMEETON, Burn

British, 19th century.

Active in Paris from 1840 to 1860.

Engraver (wood).

SMEJKAL, Jan

Czech, 20th - 21st century.

Born 1948, in Beroun.

Painter, watercolourist, installation artist.
Jan Smejkal studied in Prague in 1967-1968 and then in the Städelschule in Frankfurt am Main from 1968 to 1973. He works from handwritten notes, processing the ambient information of his daily life, and transposes them into a sort of 'painted writing'. He exhibited at Art Affairs in Amsterdam in 1993.

SMEKENS, Gérard Joseph Charles
Belgian, 19th century.
Born 30 March 1812, in Antwerp.
Painter. Landscapes.

SMELKOFF, Petr Mikhailovich.
See **SHMELKOV**

SMELLICH, Johann
Hungarian, 17th century.
Active during the first half of the 17th century.
Painter.
Johann Smellich painted an *Adoration of the Kings* in the church in Aranyosmarot in 1618.

SMELTZING, Arent, or Schmeltzing
Dutch, 18th century.
Died 4 October 1710, in Leiden.
Active in Leiden.
Medallist, engraver. Seals.

A Smet AS
A.S. 1667

SMELTZING, Jan, or Schmeltzing
Dutch, 17th century.
Born in Nijmegen; died 1703, in Leiden.
Medallist, sculptor. Figures. Statuettes.
MUSEUMS AND GALLERIES:
AMSTERDAM (Rijksmus.): *Boy* (clay, statuette); *Little Girl* (clay, statuette).

SMELTZING, Jan I, or Schmeltzing
Dutch, 17th century.
Born 3 August 1656, in Leiden; died 18 October 1693, in Leiden.
Medallist.
Jan Smeltzing I executed medals with the effigies of numerous political personalities of his time.

SMELTZING, Jan II, or Schmeltzing
Dutch, 17th - 18th century.
Born 5 July 1668, in Leiden.
Medallist.
Jan Smeltzing II was the son of Arent Smeltzing. He was engraver to the town of Leiden from 1695 to 1709.

SMELTZING, Martin, or Schmeltzing
Dutch, 18th century.
Died 1714, in Leiden.
Medallist.
Martin Smeltzing was the brother of Jan Smeltzing II. He worked in Leiden and Amsterdam for several princes in Europe.

SMELZ, Guillaume
Flemish School, 16th century.
Active in Liège in 1591.
Glass painter.

SMERALDI, Antonio
Italian, 18th century.
Active in the middle of the 18th century.
Painter (porcelain).
Antonio Smeraldi was employed at the porcelain works in Doccia, near Florence, about 1750.

SMERALDI, Ettore
Italian, 17th century.
Born 11 October 1577; died before 1 February 1636.
Painter, engraver (burin).
Most of Ettore Smeraldi's engravings are of allegories, architectural views and religious subjects.

SMERALDO DI GIOVANNI
Italian, 14th - 15th century.
Born 1366; died 26 August 1444.
Active in Florence.
Painter and decorative artist. Frescoes.
Assistant to Giovanni del Ponte, Smeraldo di Giovanni painted frescoes and decorated chests.

SMEREKAR, Hinko, or Heinrich
Slovene, 20th century.
Born 1883, in Ljubljana.
Painter, print artist, graphic artist, illustrator, art writer. Religious subjects, portraits, landscapes.
Hinko Smerekar studied in Vienna and Munich. He illustrated popular fiction and designed cartoons.

SMERIGLIO, Mariano. See **SMIRIGLIO**

SMET, Adriaen de
Flemish School, 16th century.
Active in Oudenaarde at the end of the 16th century.
Sculptor.
In 1593 Adriaen de Smet carved a tabernacle and statues of *St Anne* and *St Agnes* for the Hospital of Our Lady, Oudenaarde.

SMET, Cornelio, or Smit
Flemish School, 16th century.
Died c. 1592, in Naples.
Painter. Religious subjects.
Cornelio Smet settled in Naples before 1574 and painted many altarpieces for the churches of the city and the surrounding area.

SMET, Cornelis or Corneille de
Belgian, 18th - 19th century.
Born 1742, in Termonde; died 5 April 1815, in Antwerp.
Sculptor (terracotta/wood).
Cornelis Smet served his apprenticeship with Jacob Hozef van der Neer in Antwerp, and attended courses at the academy in Antwerp. He was admitted as a freeman of the guild of St Luke in Antwerp on 11 May 1770, was appointed assistant director of the academy in 1780 and professor of sculpture in 1796.

Smet received numerous commissions from the bourgeoisie. He also sculpted the Evangelists in the choir of Brussels Cathedral, and other statues in Antwerp Cathedral. His body of work shows the influence of both Classicism and the Flemish Baroque of the 17th century.
MUSEUMS AND GALLERIES:
BRUSSELS (Mus. royaux des Beaux-Arts de Belgique): wooden sculpture; *St Elizabeth* (terracotta); *Allegory of the City of Antwerp* (terracotta).

SMET, Cornelis van der, or Smit
Flemish School, 16th century.
Sculptor.
Cornelis van der Smet worked for the Town Hall and Market of Bruges.

SMET, Frédéric de
Belgian, 20th century.
Born 13 March 1876, in Ghent; died 1948.
Painter, sculptor, art critic. Seascapes.

Frédéric de Smet studied at the Academie voor Schone Kunsten in Ghent and under Albrecht de Vriendt at the Academie voor Schone Kunsten in Antwerp; he also worked as an art critic. He exhibited statues and seascapes in Brussels in 1903 and in Ghent in 1909.

Museums and Galleries:
Ghent.

SMET, Fredy de. See **DESMET**

SMET, Gust

Belgian, 20th century.
Born 1911, in Sint-Niklaas.
Painter.

Gust Smet studied under Alfons Proost at the academy in Sint-Niklaas.

SMET, Gustaaf de

Belgian, 20th century.
Born 21 January 1877, in Ghent; died 8 October 1943, in Deurle-sur-Lys.
Painter (including gouache), pastellist, draughtsman (including charcoal), engraver. Figures, nudes, portraits, fishing scenes, interiors with figures, landscapes, landscapes with figures, urban landscapes, still-lifes.
Laethem-St-Martin Group (Second School).

Gustaaf de Smet initially worked alongside his younger brother Léon, also a painter, with his father, the photographer and decorative artist Jules de Smet. He then studied under Jules van Biesbroek and Jean Delvin at the Koninklijke Academie voor Schone Kunsten in Ghent from 1889 to 1895. He settled in Laethem-St-Martin in 1901, but he also spent time in Deurle and was back again in Ghent in 1911. At the outbreak of World War I, he sought refuge in the Netherlands.

De Smet's brother Léon was with him in Laethem, and the two met Permeke, van den Berghe and Servaes, with whom they would subsequently form the nucleus of the second-generation Laethem School, which was significantly more aligned with the Flemish Expressionist tradition that preceded it and closer to the Social Realism (Vérisme Social) of the Barbizon School. While in the Netherlands, he also met the Dutch painter Sluyters, who was strongly influenced by Fauvism and Expressionism, and the French artist Le Fauconnier, whose style has been described as 'post-Cubist rustic'. From 1918, he and the art critics P. van Hecke and André de Ridder set up the Galerie Sélection, which would prove to have a substantive influence on contemporary Belgian painting. He returned to Belgium in 1920 and settled in Afsnée the following year, although he spent short periods in Deurle (1935) and in France (1940).

De Smet's early work was tentatively Impressionist but, following his return to Belgium in 1920 and his exposure in Laethem to the work of Permeke and van den Berghe, he proclaimed himself a member of the Belgian Expressionists. His work shared with Expressionism a heavy colour palette and a taste for popular subject-matter. His browns, brick reds and pinks exude warmth, but his figures are puppet-like, his animals and farm buildings of the 'doll's house' variety. These features distance him considerably from the general run of the Expressionists. He appears to have learned from Le Fauconnier how to treat spatial volumes and this may justify his inclusion among the ranks of latter-day Cubists. The Flemish tradition of 'village fair' painting found expression in De Smet as a mildly poetic verisimilitude, with traces of caricature such as one finds in the work of Marc Chagall.

De Smet's work featured at solo exhibitions, including those held in 1914 at the Regnard & Co gallery in Amsterdam; in 1916, at the Heysteet-Smith gallery, also in Amsterdam; in 1919, at the Galerie Giroux in Brussels; and in 1921, at the Galerie Sélection in Brussels. A De Smet retrospective was mounted at the Palais des Beaux-Arts in Brussels in 1936. Following his death, his work was exhibited at the De Vuyst gallery in Lokeren, notably in 2003.

Gust De Smet

GDS

Bibliography:
Van Puyvelde, Leo, *Een expressionistisch schilder: Gustaaf de Smet*, Onze Kunst, Antwerp, Amsterdam, 1918. Huebner, Friedrich Markus, '*Gustaaf de Smet*' in *Nieuwe Kunst* vol. XI, Van Munster, Amsterdam, 1921. Van Hecke, Paul-Gustave, '*Gustave de Smet*' in *Sélection*, March 1924. Haesaerts, Luc/Haesaerts, Paul, '*Dans l'univers de Gustave de Smet*' in *Gustave de Smet*, retrospective exhibition catalogue, Palais des Beaux-Arts, Brussels, 1936. Van Hecke, Paul-Gustave/Langui, Émile, *Gustave de Smet. Sa vie et son œuvre*, Éd. Lumière, Brussels, 1945. Van Puyvelde, Leo, *Gustave de Smet*, De Sikkel, Antwerp, 1949. Haesaerts, Paul, *Laethem-Saint-Martin, le village élu de l'Art flamand*, Brussels, 1965. Boyens, Piet, *Gustave de Smet*, Antwerp, 1989. Boyens, Piet, *Flemish Art: Symbolism to Expressionism at Sint-Martens-Latem*, Lannoo/Art Book Co, Tielt/St-Martens-Latem, 1992.

Museums and Galleries:
Amsterdam (Stedelijk Mus.): *Blue Table* (1915) - Antwerp (Koninklijk Mus. voor Schone Kunsten): *Pally* (1922); *Eating Mussels* (1923); *Little Girl in Pink* (1937); *Still-life with Herrings* (1938) - Basel (Kunstmus.): *Sleeping Woman* (1919); *Bouquet of Dark Flowers* (1919); *Poacher* (1925) - Brussels (Mus. royaux des Beaux-Arts de Belgique): *Women at Katwijk* (1918); *Béatrice I* (1923); *Young Woman in Blue* (1935); *Self-portrait* (1937); *Nocturnal Landscape* (1941) - Deinze (Mus. van Deinze): *Woman* (1928); *Straw Hat* (1938) - Eindhoven (Van Abbe Mus.): *Dance-Hall* (1922); *Woman and Child* (1922); *Landscape* (1937); *Barebreasted Young Woman* (1937-1938) - Ghent (Mus. voor Schone Kunsten): *Church at Afsnée* (1906); *Interior with Porcelain Figures* (before 1914) - Grenoble: *Circus II* (1926) - Ixelles: *Dovecot* (1920); *Parade* (1922) - Liège (Mus. of Modern and Contemporary Art): *Still-life* (1940) - The Hague (Gemeentemus.): *White Chrysanthemums* (1914); *Farmhouse* (1914); *Moonlit Landscape in the Snow* (1918); *Female Figure* (1919); *Loggia II* (1928).

Auction records:
Amsterdam, 23 Oct 1958, *Winter Landscape*, NLG 5,500. Brussels, 25 April 1959, *Still-life*, BEF 50,000. Brussels, 12 March 1960, *Seated Nude*, BEF 40,000. Milan, 21 Nov 1961, *Farm at Sunset*, ITL 1,900,000. Antwerp, 13 and 15 Oct 1964, *Fisherman's Wife*, BEF 160,000. Antwerp, 30 and 31 March 1965, *Young Woman in Pink*, BEF 210,000. Antwerp, 26 April 1966, *Nude with Goldfish*, BEF 420,000. Antwerp, 11-13 April 1967, *Dance-Hall* (gouache) BEF 350,000. London, 12 Nov 1970, *Chestnut Trees*, GBP 4,500. Antwerp, 27 April 1971, *Portrait of a Young Woman*, BEF 340,000. Antwerp, 23 Oct 1973, *View of Amsterdam* (pastel) BEF 85,000. Antwerp, 22 Oct 1974, *Interior with Portrait of the Artist's Wife*, BEF 400,000. Antwerp, 6 April 1976, *Gardener* (1929, oil on canvas, 36 1/4 x 28 ins / 92 x 71 cm) BEF 900,000. Amsterdam, 26 April 1977, *Three Figures at Table* (1921, oil on canvas, 33 1/2 x 39 ins / 85 x 99 cm) NLG 66,000. Antwerp, 17 Oct 1978, *Bedroom* (gouache, 14 1/2 x 18 1/2 ins / 37 x 47 cm) BEF 80,000. London, 4 April 1979, *Quayside* (oil on card, 12 1/2 x 15 3/4 ins / 32 x 40 cm) GBP 3,000. Antwerp, 23 Oct 1979, *Hunter* (pastel, 11 x 9 ins / 28 x 23 cm) BEF 180,000. Lokeren, 25 April

1981, *Green Cupola, Amsterdam* (1920, oil on canvas, 41 3/4 x 51 1/2 ins / 106 x 131 cm) BEF 1,400,000. BRUSSELS, 30 Nov 1983, *Seated Woman* (drawing, 20 1/2 x 16 1/4 ins / 52 x 41 cm) BEF 120,000. LOKEREN, 25 Feb 1984, *Angler* (c. 1925, oil on panel, 18 1/2 x 20 1/2 ins / 47 x 52 cm) BEF 600,000. LONDON, 26 June 1985, *Circus* (gouache, 28 1/4 x 20 1/2 ins / 72 x 51.8 cm) GBP 3,800. BRUSSELS, 29 Oct 1986, *Woman with Blue Corsage* (oil on canvas, 26 x 21 ins / 66 x 52.5 cm) BEF 2,600,000. LOKEREN, 16 May 1987, *Béatrice* (1923, charcoal, 9 3/4 x 7 3/4 ins / 25 x 20 cm) BEF 95,000. LOKEREN, 28 May 1988, *View of Amsterdam* (pastel, 24 3/4 x 20 1/2 ins / 63 x 52 cm) BEF 380,000. LOKEREN, 8 Oct 1988, *In the Garden* (1912, oil on canvas, 42 x 51 1/4 ins / 106.5 x 130 cm) BEF 3,800,000. AMSTERDAM, 8 Dec 1988, *Winter Landscape* (1915, oil on canvas, 11 x 10 ins / 28 x 24.5 cm) NLG 29,900. AMSTERDAM, 10 April 1989, *Fishing Boats in Harbour* (oil on card, 10 1/2 x 12 3/4 ins / 26.5 x 32.5 cm) NLG 13,800. AMSTERDAM, 24 May 1989, *Field of Flax in Bloom* (1912, oil on canvas, 17 x 42 1/2 ins / 43 x 108 cm) NLG 94,300. LONDON, 24 May 1989, *Village* (oil on canvas, 10 3/4 x 13 1/4 ins / 27.4 x 33.6 cm) GBP 13,200. LONDON, 28 June 1989, *Blue Sofa* (1928, oil on canvas, 57 x 45 1/4 ins / 145 x 115 cm) GBP 550,000. LONDON, 19 Oct 1989, *Beach at Ooidonck* (oil on canvas, 55 1/2 x 47 1/4 ins / 141 x 120 cm) GBP 49,500; *Young Peasant Woman* (oil on panel, 26 1/4 x 19 ins / 66.7 x 48.2 cm) GBP 60,500. AMSTERDAM, 13 Dec 1989, *Evening View of Laren* (1916, oil on canvas, 40 1/2 x 52 ins / 103 x 132 cm) NLG 230,000. PARIS, 3 April 1990, *Landscape* (oil on card, 17 1/4 x 23 1/4 ins / 44 x 59 cm) FRF 140,000. AMSTERDAM, 22 May 1990, *Two Boats Heading Out to Sea* (oil on card, 14 3/4 x 20 ins / 37.5 x 50.8 cm) NLG 25,300. LONDON, 23 May 1990, *Beguine Convent, Bruges* (1906, oil on canvas, 24 x 41 1/4 ins / 61 x 105 cm) GBP 16,500. BRUSSELS, 12 June 1990, *Landscape with Church and Goats* (oil on panel, 15 3/4 x 13 ins / 40 x 33 cm) BEF 6,500,000. PARIS, 15 June 1990, *Part of Castle Borlut at St-Denijs-Westrem, Ghent* (c. 1911-1912, oil on canvas, 55 x 46 ins / 140 x 117 cm) FRF 730,000. AMSTERDAM, 12 Dec 1990, *Houses at Zaandam* (oil on canvas, 16 1/4 x 14 1/2 ins / 41 x 37 cm) NLG 40,250. LONDON, 20 March 1991, *Japanese Still-life* (1914, oil on canvas, 24 3/4 x 20 1/2 ins / 63 x 52 cm) GBP 16,500. AMSTERDAM, 11 Dec 1991, *Landscape with a Goat on a Riverbank* (oil on canvas, 19 1/2 x 27 ins / 49.5 x 68.5 cm) NLG 43,700. LONDON, 24 March 1992, *Orchard at Sunset* (oil on panel, 15 3/4 x 20 1/2 ins / 40 x 52 cm) GBP 9,020. AMSTERDAM, 19 May 1992, *Fishermen's Return* (oil on canvas, 27 1/2 x 31 ins / 70 x 79 cm) NLG 55,200. LONDON, 1 Dec 1992, *Banks of the Lys* (oil on canvas, 35 x 41 1/4 ins / 89 x 105 cm) GBP 44,000. AMSTERDAM, 9 Dec 1992, *Farmyard with Mare and Foal* (oil on card, 23 x 24 1/2 ins / 57.5 x 62.2 cm) NLG 57,500. LOKEREN, 15 May 1993, *Still-life with Cactus* (1935, oil on canvas, 20 x 16 ins / 51 x 40.5 cm) BEF 380,000. LOKEREN, 9 Oct 1993, *Sailboats* (1908, oil on canvas, 23 1/2 x 33 1/2 ins / 59.5 x 85 cm, 2 ins/5 cm) BEF 1,100,000. AMSTERDAM, 9 Dec 1993, *Village Beauty* (1929, oil on card, 35 x 24 3/4 ins / 88 x 62.7 cm) NLG 281,750. LOKEREN, 10 Dec 1994, *Winter at Deurle* (oil on canvas, 39 1/4 x 47 1/4 ins / 100 x 120 cm) BEF 3,300,000. AMSTERDAM, 31 May 1995, *Summer on the River Lys* (1911, oil on canvas, 19 1/2 x 27 ins / 49.5 x 68.5 cm) NLG 47,200. LOKEREN, 7 Oct 1995, *Farmhouse with Peasant* (charcoal and watercolour, 20 3/4 x 19 1/4 ins / 53 x 49 cm) BEF 180,000. LOKEREN, 18 May 1996, *Village* (1916, charcoal, 19 x 25 1/2 ins / 48 x 65 cm) BEF 180,000. AMSTERDAM, 4 June 1996, *Female Portrait* (oil on card, 18 3/4 x 16 3/4 ins / 47.5 x 42.5 cm) NLG 14,160. LOKEREN, 5 Oct 1996, *Country Road near a Mill* (1891, oil on canvas, 24 x 20 ins / 61 x 51 cm) BEF 130,000. LONDON, 4 Dec 1996, *Castle Borlut Gardens* (c. 1911-1912, oil on canvas, 55 x 46 ins / 140 x 117 cm) GBP 56,500. LOKEREN, 7 Dec 1996, *Cattle near a Village* (1934, oil on canvas, 25 1/2 x 39 1/4 ins / 65 x 100 cm) BEF 1,500,000. AMSTERDAM, 4 June 1997, *Still-life with Flowers* (c. 1917, oil on panel, 15 x 19 ins / 38 x 48 cm) NLG 50,740. LONDON, 25 June 1997, *Landscape* (oil on canvas, 21 1/4 x 19 3/4 ins / 54 x 50 cm) GBP 25,300. AMSTERDAM, 1 Dec 1997, *Boat on a Canal, Amsterdam* (oil on canvas, 19 3/4 x 23 ins / 50 x 58.5 cm) NLG 40,120. AMSTERDAM, 25 Oct 1999, *Daydreams* (oil on canvas, 36 x 29 ins / 92 x 74 cm) NLG 860,000. PARIS, 22 Nov 1999, *Fairground People* (oil on canvas, 32 x 26 ins / 82 x 65 cm) FRF 1,750,000. LONDON, 22 Nov 2000, *Seascape* (c. 1930, oil on canvas, 19 x 25 ins / 49 x 63 cm) GBP 16,000. AMSTERDAM, 30 Nov 2000, *Chapel* (1904, oil on canvas, 24 x 40 ins / 60 x 101 cm) NLG 80,000. BRUSSELS, 5 Nov 2001, *The Lys at Deurle* (oil on canvas, 18 x 22 ins / 45 x 56 cm) BEF 1,200,000. AMSTERDAM, 4 Dec 2001, *Potato Harvest* (c. 1930, oil on paper laid on board, 18 x 25 ins / 45 x 63 cm) EUR 70,000. LONDON, 22 Oct 2002, *Garden at Saint Martens Latem* (c. 1910, oil on canvas, 13 x 17 ins / 32 x 44 cm) GBP 7,000. LONDON, 5 Feb 2003, *Woman by a Rosebush* (1912, oil on canvas, 42 x 52 ins / 107 x 131 cm) GBP 220,000. AMSTERDAM, 25 Nov 2003, *At the Window* (c. 1931, gouache and charcoal on card, 25 x 19 ins / 64 x 49 cm) EUR 100,000. ANTWERP, 26 Oct 2004, *Chestnut Tree in Blossom* (oil on panel, 29 x 24 ins / 74 x 60 cm) EUR 36,000. AMSTERDAM, 1 Dec 2004, *Flowers* (oil on card/panel, 18 x 14 ins / 45 x 36 cm) EUR 40,000.

SMET, Hans. See the entry **MARBOCH Henni**

SMET, Henri de
Flemish School, 16th century.
Active in Louvain in the first half of the 16th century.
Painter. Designs for tapestries.

SMET, Jan de
Flemish School, 15th century.
Active in Brussels.
Glass painter.

Jan de Smet painted a window for the church of Notre-Dame du Sablon, Brussels, and for the church of Hal.

SMET, Jean de
Flemish School, 16th century.
Active in Bruges in 1562.
Sculptor.

SMET, Joos de. See **SMIT Joos Woutersz.**

SMET, Léon de
Belgian, 20th century.
Born 20 July 1881, in Ghent; died 9 September 1966, in Deurle.
Painter. Nudes, portraits, landscapes, still-lifes.
Laethem-St-Martin Group (Second School), Vie et Lumière Group.

Léon de Smet studied, as did his brother Gustaaf, at the Academie voor Schone Kunsten in Ghent, where his mentor was Jean Joseph Delvin. Although he lived in Laethem-St-Martin between 1906 and 1913, he was not a member of the Laethem Expressionist group, being primarily influenced by Impressionism. He became a member of the Luminist Vie et Lumière (Life and Light) Group alongside Theo van Rysselberghe. In 1914, while his brother Gustaaf was in self-imposed exile in the Netherlands after the outbreak of World War I, Léon de Smet moved to Germany. He returned to Brussels after the war and finally settled in Deurle in 1926.

Spending some time in England, de Smet painted chiefly portraits of authors, including those of *John Galsworthy, George Bernard Shaw* and *Joseph Conrad*, as well as portraits of London society figures. Immediately after the war, he flirted briefly with Expressionism but soon reverted to his Impressionist style with which, unlike his Expressionist counterparts, he celebrated predominantly 'happy moments', as exemplified by his *Bath-time* and *Harmony in White* (1909), *Interior* (1912), *Deurle in the Snow* (1938) and *Intimacy* (1941).

De Smet's work featured at the 1909 Venice Biennale, and he also exhibited at the Leicester Galleries in London. Following his death, his work was shown at the De Vuyst gallery in Lokeren, most notably in 2003.

MUSEUMS AND GALLERIES:
ANTWERP (Mus. Flamand): *Portrait of Herman Teirlinck; Portrait of Auguste Vermeylen; Portrait of Styn Streuvels* - BRUSSELS (Mus. royaux) - DEURLE (Mus. Leon De Smet) - IXELLES (MBA).

AUCTION RECORDS:
LONDON, 25 Feb 1929, *Flowers and Still-life,* GBP 50. PARIS, 4 Dec 1950, *Vase of Flowers* (1917) FRF 1,900. ANTWERP, 13 and 15 Oct 1964, *Interior,* BEF 68,000. LONDON, 24 June 1966, *River Thames at Runnymede,* Gns 700. ANTWERP, 13 and 14 April 1967, *Woman at the Window,* BEF 85,000. ANTWERP, 22 April 1969, *Interior,* BEF 150,000. LONDON, 12 Nov 1970, *Carnival,* GBP 4,000. ANTWERP, 18 April 1972, *Flowers,* BEF 110,000. LOKEREN, 23 March 1974, *Landscape with Bridge* (pastel) BEF 65,000. ANTWERP, 2 April 1974, *Interior,* BEF 700,000. LONDON, 1 Dec 1976, *Vase of Zinnias* (1927, oil on canvas, 27¼ x 31¼ ins / 69.5 x 79.5 cm) GBP 3,400. BREDA, 26 April 1977, *Garden* (oil on canvas, 23½ x 22½ ins / 60 x 57 cm) NLG 16,000. ANTWERP, 8 May 1979, *Still-life with Vegetables* (oil on canvas, 27½ x 35½ ins / 70 x 90 cm) BEF 260,000. LOKEREN, 16 Feb 1980, *Self-portrait* (1946, red chalk, 19¾ x 15¾ ins / 50 x 40 cm) BEF 60,000. ANTWERP, 27 Oct 1981, *Undergrowth* (oil on canvas, 19¾ x 22¾ ins / 50 x 58 cm) BEF 200,000. LONDON, 28 March 1984, *Self-portrait* (1914-1918, pastel, 18¾ x 24 ins / 47.6 x 61 cm) GBP 3,200. LONDON, 24 Oct 1984, *Still-life with Flowers* (1931, oil on canvas, 35¾ x 27¾ ins / 90.7 x 70.5 cm) GBP 5,500. LOKEREN, 16 Feb 1985, *Young Woman, Seated* (1917, charcoal, 28¼ x 22 ins / 72 x 56 cm) BEF 65,000. LONDON, 26 March 1985, *Harbour* (1924, oil on canvas, 32 x 39 ins / 81.2 x 99 cm) GBP 20,000. LONDON, 2 Dec 1986, *Bouquet of Flowers* (1925, oil on canvas, 28½ x 32¼ ins / 72.5 x 82 cm) GBP 30,000. LOKEREN, 21 Feb 1987, *Seated Nude* (1922, black chalk, 32¼ x 47¼ ins / 82 x 120 cm) BEF 200,000. LONDON, 1 July 1987, *Bouquet of Flowers and Japanese Screen* (1924, oil on canvas, 20¾ x 23½ ins / 53 x 60 cm) GBP 39,000. LONDON, 24 Feb 1988, *Vase of Flowers* (1915, oil on canvas, 18 x 14¼ ins / 46 x 36 cm) GBP 13,200. PARIS, 3 March 1988, *Woman on a Balcony* (oil on canvas, 16¼ x 13 ins / 41 x 33 cm) FRF 9,800. LOKEREN, 28 May 1988, *Interior with the Figure of the Artist's Wife Reading 'Sélection'* (1927, oil on canvas, 44¼ x 56¾ ins / 112.5 x 144 cm) BEF 1,300,000. LOKEREN, 8 Oct 1988, *Red Beech* (oil on canvas, 30¼ x 38¼ ins / 77 x 97 cm) BEF 600,000. LONDON, 19 Oct 1988, *Riverbank* (1908, oil on canvas, 28 x 24 ins / 71.1 x 60.8 cm) GBP 18,700. LONDON, 22 Feb 1989, *Interior* (oil on canvas, 28 x 32 ins / 71 x 81 cm) GBP 16,500. DOUAI, 23 April 1989, *Seated Woman* (1920, oil on canvas, 2898 ins / 7360 cm) FRF 42,000. AMSTERDAM, 24 May 1989, *Trees in a Garden near a House* (1910, oil on canvas, 23½ x 32 ins / 60 x 81 cm) NLG 149,500; *Still-life with a Vase of Dahlias and a Chinese Porcelain Sugar Bowl on a Table* (1926, oil on canvas, 28 x 31½ ins / 71 x 80 cm) NLG 126,500. LONDON, 28 June 1989, *Woman at the Window* (1909, oil on canvas, 37¾ x 40¼ ins / 96 x 102 cm) GBP 170,500. LONDON, 19 Oct 1989, *Little Grey Dress* (1917, oil on canvas, 28 x 22 ins / 71.2 x 55.8 cm) GBP 41,800. NEW YORK, 26 Feb 1990, *Rocky Coast* (oil on card, 16½ x 21 ins / 41.6 x 52.4 cm) USD 8,800. LONDON, 3 April 1990, *Ostend Harbour* (1924, oil on canvas, 32¼ x 39½ ins / 81.9 x 100.4 cm) GBP 44,000. AMSTERDAM, 10 April 1990, *Landscape* (charcoal/paper, 13 x 17¼ ins / 33 x 44 cm) NLG 4,600. LONDON, 23 May 1990, *Still-life* (1929, oil on canvas, 26½ x 31¼ ins / 67 x 79.5 cm) GBP 39,600. LONDON, 16 Oct 1990, *Garden View, Wingstone* (1914, oil on canvas, 30¼ x 25 ins / 76.8 x 63.5 cm) GBP 16,500. LONDON, 17 Oct 1990, *Flowers and Shellfish on a Table* (1924, oil on canvas, 24½ x 29½ ins / 62 x 75 cm) GBP 28,600. AMSTERDAM, 13 Dec 1990, *Vase of Flowers* (oil on canvas, 36 x 31¼ ins / 90.5 x 79.5 cm) NLG 103,500. LONDON, 19 March 1991, *Still-life with Tulips and Daffodils* (1936, oil on canvas, 24 x 20 ins / 61 x 50.8 cm) GBP 8,250. LONDON, 24 March 1992, *Bust of Woman Holding a Rose* (1925, oil on canvas, 27¼ x 22 ins / 69.5 x 56 cm) GBP 9,350. LOKEREN, 23 May 1992, *Winter Landscape* (oil on canvas, 19¼ x 22¾ ins / 49 x 58 cm) BEF 380,000. AMSTERDAM, 27-28 May 1993, *Still-life* (oil on canvas, 43¼ x 47¼ ins / 110 x 120 cm) NLG 97,750. LOKEREN, 9 Oct 1993, *Interior with Still-life* (1932, oil on canvas, 37½ x 48 ins / 95.5 x 121 cm) BEF 900,000. LONDON, 30 Nov 1993, *Full-length Nude* (oil on canvas, 52¼ x 26 ins / 133 x 66 cm) GBP 13,800. LONDON, 29 Nov 1994, *Still-life with Azaleas* (oil on canvas, 34 x 47¼ ins / 86.3 x 119.7 cm) GBP 29,900. AMSTERDAM, 8 Dec 1994, *Thameside Wharfs* (1915, oil on canvas, 21¾ x 27 ins / 55.3 x 68.5 cm) NLG 48,300. LOKEREN, 10 Dec 1994, *Woman with a Blue Shawl* (1925, oil on canvas, 28¾ x 23½ ins / 73 x 60 cm) BEF 900,000. LOKEREN, 20 May 1995, *Still-life* (1929, oil on canvas, 26½ x 31½ ins / 67 x 80 cm) BEF 900,000. LONDON, 25 Oct 1995, *Garden Terrace* (oil on canvas, 25½ x 31½ ins / 65 x 80 cm) GBP 20,700. LOKEREN, 9 March 1996, *Woman Seated at a Mirror* (oil on canvas, 23½ x 27½ ins / 60 x 70 cm) BEF 380,000. NEW YORK, 2 May 1996, *Vase of Flowers and Japanese Print* (1917, oil on canvas, 30¼ x 25 ins / 76.8 x 63.5 cm) USD 79,500. LOKEREN, 18 May 1996, *River Landscape* (c. 1895, oil on canvas, 19¾ x 29½ ins / 50 x 75 cm) BEF 85,000; *Large White Lilies* (1925, oil on canvas, 24 x 27 ins / 61 x 68.8 cm) BEF 1,700,000. LONDON, 25 June 1996, *Woman Brushing her Hair at a Window* (1919, oil on canvas, 29½ x 25 ins / 75 x 63.5 cm) GBP 34,500. PARIS, 16 Oct 1996, *Landscape with Farmhouses* (1907, oil on canvas, 21 x 19¾ ins / 53.5 x 50 cm) FRF 96,000. LOKEREN, 7 Dec 1996, *Interior* (1944, oil on canvas, 39¼ x 47¼ ins / 100 x 120 cm) BEF 1,100,000. AMSTERDAM, 10 Dec 1996, *Flowers* (oil on canvas, 40½ x 26¼ ins / 103 x 66.5 cm) NLG 27,676. LOKEREN, 8 March 1997, *Woman Reading at Sunset* (1910, oil on canvas, 41¾ x 53¼ ins / 106 x 135 cm) BEF 2,200,000. LONDON, 9 Dec 1997, *Bathers* (1910, oil on canvas, 63 x 55 ins / 160 x 140 cm) GBP 95,000. LONDON, 26 March 1999, *Vase of Flowers in an Interior on a Yellow Chest of Drawers* (1922, oil on canvas, 27 x 24 ins / 68 x 61 cm) GBP 21,000. LOKEREN, 13 May 2000, *The Letter* (oil on canvas, 30 x 33 ins / 75 x 85 cm) BEF 900,000. LONDON, 28 June 2000, *Vase of Flowers* (1916, oil on canvas, 24 x 20 ins / 60 x 50 cm) GBP 20,000. LONDON, 27 June 2001, *Young Woman in an Interior* (1919, oil on canvas, 57 x 72 ins / 144 x 182 cm) GBP 20,000. LOKEREN, 6 Oct 2001, *Nude and Vase of Flowers* (1922, oil on canvas, 50 x 60 ins / 127 x 153 cm) BEF 1,700,000. LOKEREN, 11 May 2002, *Still-life with Flowers* (1910, oil on canvas, 26 x 22 ins / 67 x 55 cm) EUR 36,000. LOKEREN, 5 Oct 2002, *View of the Middelland Sea* (oil on canvas, 26 x 31 ins / 65 x 80 cm) EUR 41,000. AMSTERDAM, 3 June 2003, *Odalisque with Bunch of Roses and Fruit Dish* (c. 1924, oil on canvas, 36 x 79 ins / 92 x 200 cm) EUR 70,000. LONDON, 24 June 2003, *Vase of Flowers* (1916, oil on canvas, 20 x 32 ins / 51 x 81 cm) GBP 50,000. BRUSSELS, 10 May 2004, *Composition with Vase of Flowers and Precious Objects on an Engraved Background* (oil on canvas, 26 x 30 ins / 65 x 75 cm) EUR 27,000. NEW YORK, 5

Nov 2004, *Table with Flowers* (oil on canvas, 26 x 30 ins / 66 x 75 cm) USD 40,000.

SMET, Mathieu de
Flemish School, 16th century.
Active in the first half of the 16th century.
Sculptor.
Mathieu de Smet worked with Jean de Smytere on the tomb of Isabella of Austria in the church of St Peter, Ghent.

SMET, Pierre de
Flemish School, 16th century.
Glass painter.
In 1593 Pierre de Smet painted windows depicting *The Virgin* and *St Peter* for the church of Meirelbeke, near Ghent.

SMET, René Louis
Belgian, 20th century.
Born 1929, in Brussels.
Painter, engraver, lithographer.
René Louis Smet studied at the Académie Royale des Beaux Arts in Brussels. His painting conjures up a silent and pallid personal universe. He travelled extensively, notably to Brazil, where he first exhibited in São Paulo in 1956 and 1957. He went on to exhibit in Rome, Paris, Brussels and Washington DC.

SMET, Roger de, called Le Fèvre
Flemish School, 15th century.
Born probably in Tournai; died 1502 or 1503, in Courtrai.
Sculptor.
Roger de Smet worked on the baptismal chapel of the church of St Martin, Courtrai.

SMET, Roger de
Flemish School, 16th century.
Died February 1510, in Courtrai.
Sculptor.
Roger de Smet carved several statues for the churches of Courtrai.

SMET, Roger de
Flemish School, 16th century.
Died c. 1545, in Courtrai probably.
Sculptor (stone/wood).
Roger de Smet worked in Bruges and Courtrai and carved ceilings, retables and statues.

SMET, Roger de, or Roeger
Flemish School, 16th century.
Died c. 1520, probably in Courtrai.
Painter, sculptor.
Roger de Smet carved a coat-of-arms for the ramparts of Courtrai.

SMET, Wolfgang de
Flemish School, 17th century.
Active in Louvain during the second half of the 17th century.
Painter.
Wolfgang de Smet painted an *Interior of the Church of St Peter in Louvain*, dated 1667, which is in the museum of Louvain Museum

SMET, Yves de
Belgian, 20th - 21st century.
Born 1946, in Ghent.
Painter.
Yves de Smet won the grand prize of the Association Belge des Critiques d'Art in 1977. He teaches at the Académie St-Lucas in Ghent. He moved from Constructivism to Conceptual Art.

MUSEUMS AND GALLERIES:
BRUSSELS (MAM) - GHENT (Stedelijk Mus. voor Actuele Kunst).

SMETANA, Jan
Czechoslovak, 20th century.
Born 3 October 1918.
Painter.
Jan Smetana studied architecture in Prague from 1936 to 1939. From 1941 to 1943 he studied at the school of applied arts. He painted industrial landscapes, not from the point of view of the modern world but rather as picturesque subjects. He exhibited in Paris and Belgium in 1946, and in many other exhibitions of modern Czech art.
BIBLIOGRAPHY:
Fifty years of Czechoslovak Painting from the Collections of the Galleries, 1918-1958, exhibition catalogue, Slovenska Narodna Gal., Bratislava, 1968 (in commemoration of the 50th anniversary of the Republic of Czechoslovakia).

SMETANA, Léopold
French, 20th century.
Born in Tonnerre.
Painter. Genre scenes.
Léopold Smetana exhibited at the Salon des Indépendants in Paris from 1912.

SMETANIN, Vladimir Dimitrievich
Russian, 20th century.
Born near Moscow.
Painter. Urban landscapes, landscapes with figures, village views.
Vladimir Dimitrievich Smetanin studied at Moscow school of fine arts from 1969 to 1973. Smetanin works in tempera, painting scenes of Russian towns and villages; but he only paints those parts that have remained traditional, utterly refusing to paint modern buildings. Moreover, despite his academic training, he prefers to paint in a naive style, which he sees as consistent with his rejection of modernity.

His work was included in the travelling exhibition *Contemporary Works*, which was organised by the Soviet Ministry of Culture and which travelled around the USA in 1991-92. In 1992, he had a solo exhibition in a Paris gallery.

SMETH, Henri de, or Hendrick, or Rik
Belgian, 19th - 20th century.
Born 31 October 1865, in Antwerp; died 1940, in Brasschaat.
Painter, illustrator. Genre scenes, interiors with figures, landscapes.
Henri de Smeth was a pupil of August de Lathouwer and H. F. Joseph Hendrickx, and a friend of Romain Looymans. He was a co-founder of the Group of XIII. He was preoccupied with the effects of light, and is noted for his illustrations for works by Henri Conscience. He died blind. He exhibited in Paris, where he was awarded a bronze medal at the 1889 Exposition Universelle.

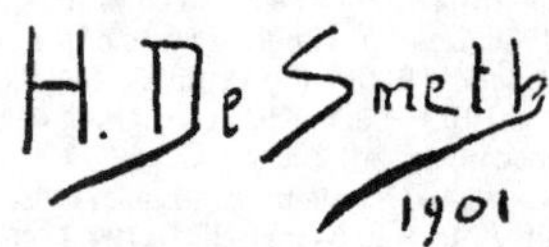

MUSEUMS AND GALLERIES:
ANTWERP: *Dressmaker's Account*; *Sacristy* - BRUSSELS - TOURNAI.
AUCTION RECORDS:
LONDON, 14 Feb 1990, *Cowgirl* (1896, oil on canvas, 18 x 22 ins / 45.5 x 56 cm) GBP 3,520. AMSTERDAM, 14-15 April 1992, *Visit* (1901, oil on canvas, 19 x 14 3/4 ins / 48 x 37.5 cm) NLG 3,450. LOKEREN, 6 March 1999, *Young Girl in Landscape* (1899, oil on canvas, 21 x 14 ins / 54 x 36 cm) BEF 110,000.

ANTWERP, 27 March 2001, *Mother by a Cradle* (1967, oil on canvas, 28 x 31 ins / 70 x 80 cm) BEF 260,000. JOHANNESBURG, 16 Oct 2001, *Painter's Workshop* (oil on panel, 18 x 15 ins / 45 x 37 cm) ZAR 24,000. LOKEREN, 11 May 2002, *Young Knitter in Zeeland* (1905, oil on canvas, 18 x 26 ins / 45 x 65 cm) EUR 4,000. AMSTERDAM, 19 April 2004, *Gentleman Sitting in a Neo-Renaissance Interior* (1901, oil on canvas, 19 x 15 ins / 48 x 37 cm) EUR 2,600. ANTWERP, 8 June 2004, *At the Inn* (oil on canvas, 36 x 28 ins / 91 x 70 cm) EUR 5,500.

SMETH, Louis Antoine de
Belgian, 20th century.
Born 5 October 1883, in Brussels.
Sculptor, medallist.

Louis Antoine de Smeth had some of his works featured at the Exposition Universelle in Brussels in 1910.

SMETHAM, James
British, 19th century.
Born 9 September 1821, in Yorkshire; died 6 February 1889, in Stoke Newington.
Painter (gouache), watercolourist, pastellist, engraver (etching). Mythological subjects.

James Smetham started out as an art teacher at the Normal College. He wrote various works, including essays on Reynolds and Blake. He exhibited at the Royal Academy and Suffolk Street from 1851 until 1876, but his works were not popular with the public. However, he was held in great esteem and warmly supported by men such as Ruskin, Madox-Brown and Rossetti. His works were more popular after he died.

J-SMETHAM

MUSEUMS AND GALLERIES:
LONDON (Tate Collection): *Naboth in his Vineyard* (1856, oil on wood); *Saul Hiding* (oil/wood) - LONDON (Victoria and Albert Mus.): *Landscape* - NOTTINGHAM (Castle Mus. & AG): *Scene by Milton*.

AUCTION RECORDS:
LONDON, 30 Oct 1964, *Knight's Bride*, Gns 360. LONDON, 2 July 1971, *Shepherd and Shepherdess in a Landscape*, Gns 1,800. LONDON, 14 July 1972, *Shepherds Guiderius and Arviragus Mourning Imogen*, Gns 2,000. LONDON, 13 March 1973, *Eventide* (watercolour) Gns 2,200. LONDON, 25 Jan 1974, *Lycidas*, Gns 1,300. LONDON, 14 May 1976, *Sir Belvedere Fighting Excalibur* (oil on card, 4 1/4 x 12 ins / 10.5 x 30.5 cm) GBP 2,600. LONDON, 19 March 1979, *Knight's Bride* (1864, oil on panel, 9 x 6 1/4 ins / 23 x 16 cm) GBP 2,000. NEW YORK, 3 June 1981, *In the Garden of Gethsemane* (coloured chalks/two sheets remounted/canvas, 36 x 27 3/4 ins / 90.6 x 70.5 cm) USD 2,700. LONDON, 15 June 1982, *Death of Earl Siward* (1861, oil on canvas, 27 1/4 x 17 ins / 69 x 43 cm) GBP 2,200. LONDON, 26 July 1985, *And their Ears are Dull of Hearing* (oil on canvas, 18 x 25 1/2 ins / 45.8 x 64.8 cm) GBP 2,400. LONDON, 16 Oct 1986, *Woman Playing a Mandolin* (watercolour heightened with gouache, 18 x 14 ins / 46 x 35.5 cm) GBP 3,000. LONDON, 3 June 1988, *Bureau de Change* (1864, oil on panel, 4 1/2 x 7 1/2 ins / 11.5 x 18.8 cm) GBP 715. LONDON, 23 Sept 1988, *Pandora* (oil on canvas, 30 x 24 1/2 ins / 76.5 x 62 cm) GBP 8,580. LONDON, 26 Sept 1990, *Miranda* (1856, oil on canvas, 24 x 20 ins / 61 x 51 cm) GBP 770. LONDON, 12 Nov 1992, *Traveller* (pastel, 4 3/4 x 13 1/2 ins / 12 x 34.5 cm) GBP 1,870. LONDON, 6 Nov 1996, *Procession in Summer* (1869, oil on panel, 11 3/4 x 16 ins / 30 x 40.5 cm) GBP 2,415. LONDON, 6 June 1997, *Playing the Bagpipes down in the Valley* (oil on panel, 4 1/2 x 12 ins / 11.5 x 30.6 cm) GBP 2,530; *Hard at Work* (1864, oil on panel, 7 1/4 x 5 ins / 18.5 x 12.4 cm) GBP 1,725. LONDON, 6 Sept 2001, *Call of the Prophet Amos* (1875, oil on canvas, 10 x 24 ins / 25 x 62 cm) GBP 3,500. LONDON, 8 Oct 2002, *Christ Preaching to the Fishermen* (oil on panel, 9 x 16 ins / 24 x 41 cm) GBP 1,800.

SMETS, Antoni, or de Smedt
Dutch, 17th century.
Active in The Hague in 1665.
Painter.

SMETS, Christian or Chrétien
Flemish School, 16th century.
Born in Mechelen.
Painter.

Christian Smets worked in France for Henri d'Albret, King of Navarre, in 1550 and returned to the Netherlands in 1557.

SMETS, Jacob
Dutch, 17th century.
Born c. 1630.
Active until 1666.
Painter.

SMETS, Jacques
Flemish School, 16th century.
Active in Tournai from 1561 to 1575.
Painter. Coats of arms, figurines.

SMETS, Jacques
Flemish School, 17th - 18th century.
Born 1680, in Mechelen; died 1764, in Auch.
Painter.

Jacques Smets was a pupil of J. Smeyers in Mechelen. He executed paintings for the churches and town of Auch.

MUSEUMS AND GALLERIES:
AUCH: *St Jerome in the Vestments of a Cardinal, with his Lion.*

AUCTION RECORDS:
PARIS, 9 Dec 1979, *Still-life* (1720, oil on canvas, 39 x 51 1/2 ins / 99 x 131 cm) FRF 58,000.

SMETS, Jean Baptiste or Jean Bernard
French, 18th century.
Active in Auch 1746-1781.
Painter. Portraits.

Jean Baptiste Smets was the son of Jacques Smets.

MUSEUMS AND GALLERIES:
AUCH: *Portrait of Father Ambroise de Lombez.*

SMETS, John Charles
Belgian, 20th - 21st century.
Born 21 December 1958, in Vilvoorde.
Painter, engraver. Figures, landscapes.

John Smets trained at the Institut St-Luc in Brussels between 1981 and 1985. His paintings, figurative in style, use intense, contrasting colours.

SMETS, Léon
Belgian, 20th century.
Born 1895, in Mechelen.
Painter, engraver.

Léon Smets studied at the academies of Antwerp and Berchem and subsequently worked in a variety of styles, including Impressionism, Abstraction and Constructivism.

MUSEUMS AND GALLERIES:
ANTWERP (Prentenkabinet) - BRUSSELS (Bibliothèque royale Albert Ier, Prints Collection).

SMETS, Louis
Dutch, 19th century.
Painter. Local scenes, scenes with figures, landscapes, winter landscapes.

Louis Smets painted Dutch folk in winter scenes. He was the same artist as Louis Smits.

AUCTION RECORDS:
LONDON, 29 Oct 1976, *Winter Landscape* (oil on canvas, 23 x 30 1/2 ins / 58.5 x 77.5 cm) GBP 3,000. LONDON, 23 Feb 1977, *Winter Landscape with Figures* (oil on panel, 19 x 26 1/4 ins /

48 x 66.5 cm) GBP 2,300. CHESTER, 22 July 1983, *Winter Landscape with Skaters* (oil on canvas, 17 x 23 ins / 43 x 58.5 cm) GBP 2,000. NEW YORK, 30 Oct 1985, *Figures in a Winter Landscape* (oil on canvas, 24 1/4 x 33 1/4 ins / 61.5 x 84.3 cm) USD 6,000. AMSTERDAM, 16 Nov 1988, *Sleigh, Skaters and Villagers Gathering Wood on a Frozen Canal* (1861, oil on canvas, 28 x 45 1/4 ins / 71 x 115 cm) NLG 21,850. BRUSSELS, 12 June 1990, *Skaters* (1859, oil on panel, 13 x 17 ins / 33 x 43 cm) BEF 120,000. NEW YORK, 29 Oct 1992, *Skaters on a Frozen River* (1865, oil on canvas, 22 1/2 x 31 1/4 ins / 57.2 x 79.4 cm) USD 4,950. LONDON, 15 Nov 1995, *Skating Scene in Holland* (1862, oil on canvas, 15 1/4 x 19 ins / 39 x 48 cm) GBP 3,220. AMSTERDAM, 16 April 1996, *Winter Landscape with Skaters on a Frozen River* (1864, oil on canvas, 13 1/2 x 22 ins / 34 x 55 cm) NLG 5,900. AMSTERDAM, 30 Oct 1996, *Landscape of a Frozen River with Skaters Refreshing themselves near an Iced-up Boat* (oil on canvas/panel, 18 3/4 x 25 ins / 47.8 x 63.5 cm) NLG 11,532. COLOGNE, 25 March 1999, *Numerous Figures with Sledges on a Frozen River near a Town* (oil on canvas, 32 x 46 ins / 81 x 118 cm) DEM 26,000. LEAMINGTON SPA, 12 Oct 2000, *Winter Landscape with Skaters on a Frozen River* (1860, oil on canvas, 23 x 33 ins / 59 x 83 cm) GBP 17,000. LONDON, 27 Oct 2000, *Skaters on a Frozen River* (oil on canvas, 24 x 34 ins / 62 x 86 cm) GBP 11,000. CALAIS, 10 Dec 2000, *Skaters on a Canal* (oil on canvas, 13 x 16 ins / 34 x 41 cm) FRF 25,000. BRUSSELS, 23 April 2001, *Winter Landscape with Skaters* (1847, oil on canvas, 19 x 24 ins / 47 x 60 cm) BEF 360,000. NEW YORK, 30 Oct 2001, *Figures and Skaters on a Frozen Lake* (oil on canvas, 28 x 41 ins / 72 x 104 cm) USD 10,000. AMSTERDAM, 3 Sept 2002, *Horse-drawn Sledge on a Frozen Waterway* (oil on panel, 12 x 15 ins / 30 x 38 cm) EUR 3,000. LEYBURN, 22 July 2004, *Frozen Winter Landscape with Figures Skating on the Ice* (1857, oil on canvas, 18 x 25 ins / 46 x 63 cm) GBP 6,000. LONDON, 23 Sept 2004, *Figures by a Bridge, Dutch Hamlet* (oil on canvas, 18 x 24 ins / 46 x 61 cm) GBP 2,000.

SMETS, Mattheus. See **HEYNS Mattheus**

SMETSENS, Arnold. See **SMITSEN**

SMEYERS, Abraham

Flemish School, 17th century.

Active in Antwerp in the first half of the 17th century.

Sculptor.

Abraham Smeyers was a pupil of Peeter Seuns.

SMEYERS, Egide or Gilles, the Elder

Flemish School, 17th - 18th century.

Born 1637, in Mechelen; died 1710; buried 30 August in Mechelen.

Painter. Religious subjects, group portraits.

Egide Smeyers the Elder was the son of Nicolas Smeyers and a pupil of Jean Verhoeren. In 1657 he married Elisabeth Herregouts, by whom he had three sons who were painters: Jean-Louis, Justin, and perhaps a Nicolas. In 1657 he was exempt from payments to the guild and in 1682 he was its treasurer. After the death of Franchoys II, he completed an *Assumption* by that artist.

He is particularly noted for his *The Holy Trinity* in the church of St John in Mechelen, and his *Raising of Lazarus* at the seminary.

MUSEUMS AND GALLERIES:

MECHELEN: *The Members of the Guild of Tailors in 1695.*

SMEYERS, Egide or Gilles Joseph, the Younger

Flemish School, 18th century.

Baptised 6 August 1694 in Mechelen; died 11 April 1771, in Mechelen.

Painter. History painting, portraits, landscapes.

Egide Smeyers the Younger is said to have been the son of a Nicolas Smeyers, who may have been one of the three sons of Egide Smeyers the Elder. At first he showed a taste for the study of history, and did not devote himself to painting until the age of 21. He went to Düsseldorf in 1715 and worked for three years in the studio of J.F. Douven. He was obliged to return to Mechelen as his parents had become blind. He focused on decoration and became a writer, notably by providing Descamps with contributions for his history of Flemish painters. He also published a supplement to the work by Van Mander, with contributions on the Mechelen painters. In spite of considerable effort, he lived in poverty and had to sell his library to pay for a hospital bed in Mechelen. He produced the following works in Mechelen: *Portrait of Canon de Laet* (in the large seminary); *Story of St Dominic* (church of St Rombaut); *Pentecost* (convent of the Black Sisters); *Allegorical Groups* (convent of the Maricole sisters); and various other works in the museum. Also mentioned are several paintings in the church of Osselie and portraits of children in the church of Our Lady of Hanswyck.

MUSEUMS AND GALLERIES:

BRUSSELS: *St Norbert Ordaining; Death of St Norbert* - MECHELEN: *The Masters of the Guild of Tailors in 1735* - SIBIU: *Jacob Receiving Joseph's Clothes.*

SMEYERS, Jacques

Flemish School, 17th - 18th century.

Baptised 8 October 1657 in Mechelen; died 6 December 1732, in Mechelen.

Painter. History painting, portraits, genre scenes.

Jacques Smeyers was a pupil of his brother Egide Smeyers the Elder. He was master of a studio in 1688, the same year that he married Catherine Capellamans. Some time after 1715 he went blind. He produced the following works in Mechelen: *Temptation of St Anthony* and *A Holy Family* in the church of St Catherine; and *Nuns Adoring the Trinity* at the convent of the Black Sisters.

MUSEUMS AND GALLERIES:

LIÈGE: *Old Man Counting his Money and an Old Woman* (1710).

SMEYERS, Jean Louis

Flemish School, 17th century.

Born 1663, in Mechelen.

Painter.

Jean Louis Smeyers was the son and pupil of Egide Smeyers the Elder. He was a member of the guild in Mechelen, but no works by him are known to have survived.

SMEYERS, Justin or Guillaume Juste

Flemish School, 17th century.

Born 1669, in Mechelen.

Painter.

Justin Smeyers was the son and pupil of Egide Smeyers the Elder. He was a member of the guild in Mechelen.

SMEYERS, Nicolas

Flemish School, 17th century.

Died 27 November 1645.

Painter.

Nicolas Smeyers was the pupil of Lucas Franchoys the Elder in 1630, and the master of a studio in Mechelen in 1632. He was the father of Egide Smeyers the Elder and Jacques Smeyers.

SMIADECKI

Russian, 17th century.

Painter, miniaturist. Portraits.

An artist of this name studied under either Samuel or Alexander Cooper in Sweden, and was active in around 1650. He may be the same as Franciszek Smiadecki.

MUSEUMS AND GALLERIES:

STOCKHOLM: *Portrait (Identity Unknown).*

SMIADECKI, Franciszek, or Sniadecki, Szniadecki
Polish, 16th - 17th century.
Painter, miniaturist, engraver. Portraits.

Franciszek Smiadecki was active from 1596 to 1616. He produced mostly wood engravings.

MUSEUMS AND GALLERIES:
STOCKHOLM: *Portrait of a Man* (painted on a silver medal).

SMIBERT, John, or Smybert
American, 18th century.
Born 2 April 1688, in Edinburgh; died 2 March 1751, in Boston.
Painter. Portraits.

John Smibert holds an important place in the history of American painting, not for his exceptional talent, but because he was the first painter with a formal European training to emigrate to the USA. The nature of the art and techniques he took with him were based on a long pictorial tradition that was quite different from the American Naive painting of the time.

In 1709 Smibert was working as an apprentice to a decorative painter in London, and while he was earning money decorating coaches and copying old masters, he also studied art. He continued his artistic education in Italy from 1717 to 1720, then again from 1720 to 1728. In 1728 he was working as a painter and, despite having a provincial clientele, was well known in London as a portraitist and received an invitation from Bishop George Berkeley to accompany him to Bermuda. Berkeley was planning to set up a higher education college there and invited Smibert along with him to take up the post of art teacher. Smibert accepted immediately and headed for America with the rest of the group. On the way they were forced to stop at Newport while they waited for additional funds to arrive. It turned out to be a long wait, which gave Smibert time to paint the members of the expedition, whom he depicted grouped around a table. In this painting, entitled *Bermuda Group*, Smibert marries the techniques of portraiture with a quest for composition, and renders the silks and velvets with confident skill. Although it is a work of quality and not of genius, it was significant in being the first painting by an artist with a formal European training to arrive in America. The most demonstrable proof of its importance can be seen in the group portrait of Isaac Royall and his family, painted by the American artist Robert Feke, which follows the exact same compositional format as the *Bermuda Group*.

The expedition to Bermuda eventually fell through, and in 1730 Smibert married a rich woman named Mary Williams who was 20 years younger than he. The couple moved to Boston, where he earned a reputation as a great portrait artist. His studio became the first museum of American painting. Smibert had a working relationship with Pelham, who made engravings of his portraits before they were sold. Towards the end of his life, Smibert's sight failed considerably, so he gave up portraiture and took up landscape painting instead.

BIBLIOGRAPHY:
Wilder Foote, Henry, *John Smibert, Painter*, Harvard University Press, Cambridge (MA), 1950.

MUSEUMS AND GALLERIES:
BOSTON: *Aunt Blaney; Edmund Quincy; Mrs Hannah Gardiner McSparren; John Turner* - BROOKLYN, NY: *Martha Dandridge* - BUFFALO: *James Crawford* - DUBLIN: *Bishop Berkeley, his Wife and his Friends* - LONDON (National Portrait Gal.): *George Berkeley* (1730, oil on canvas) - NEW HAVEN: *Bishop Berkeley, his Wife and his Friends* - NEW YORK (Metropolitan Mus. of Art): *Nathaniel Byfield; Lieutenant Governor W. Taylor* - WORCESTER, MA (AM): *Portrait of Elizabeth Ferne* (1724); *Portrait of Henry Ferne* (1727).

AUCTION RECORDS:
LONDON, 8 July 1910, *Portrait of Robert Gay Esquire*, GBP 189. LONDON, 24 June 1965, *Portrait of a Gentleman*, Gns 450. LONDON, 10 Dec 1971, *Portrait of Lady Anne Jacqueline*, Gns 5,500. NEW YORK, 27 Jan 1983, *Mr and Mrs David Miln* (c. 1722-1725, oils on canvas, a pair, 49 3/4 x 39 3/4 ins / 126.4 x 101 cm) USD 4,750. NEW YORK, 29 May 1986, *Portrait of a Gentleman* (1723, oil on canvas, 21 1/4 x 16 ins / 54 x 40.6 cm) USD 26,000. NEW YORK, 16 June 1999, *Portrait of a Lady in a Red Dress* (oil on canvas, 30 x 21 ins / 76 x 53 cm) USD 1,800. PORTSMOUTH, 6 Aug 2004, *Portrait of Captain John Gerrish* (oil on canvas, 30 x 25 ins / 76 x 64 cm) USD 20,000.

SMIBERT, Nathaniel
American, 18th century.
Born 20 January 1734, in Boston; died 3 November 1756, in Boston.
Portrait artist.

Nathaniel Smibert was the son and pupil of John Smibert. He died before he could fully develop his artistic talents.

SMICCA. See **MANNI Giannicola di Paolo**

SMICHÄUS, Anton, or Schmigäus or Smicheus or Smigäus
Czech, 18th century.
Born 1704, in Prague; died 1770, in Laun, Austria.
Painter.

Anton Smichäus studied in Prague. He produced paintings and frescoes for the church of Unter-Rotschow, Czechoslovakia.

SMICHÄUS, Franz, or Schmigäus
Austrian, 18th century.
Active in Laun, Austria, from 1746 to 1761.
Painter.

Franz Smichäus painted altarpieces for the churches of Liblin (west Bohemia, Czechoslovakia) and a *Calvary* for the church of Peruc (Czechoslovakia).

SMICHÄUS, Johann Jakob
Austrian, 17th - 18th century.
Active in Laun, Austria, 1694-1734.
Painter. Religious subjects.

Johann Smichäus was the father of Franz Smichäus.

SMICRUS
6th century BC.
Athenian, active c. 500 BC.
Vase painter.
Ancient Greek.

MUSEUMS AND GALLERIES:
LONDON (British Mus.): *Heroes Wrestling* (vase painting).

SMIDS, Ludolf
Flemish School, 18th century.
Active in 1715.
Draughtsman.

Ludolf Smids sketched a *Pilgrimage to Laaren* which is kept in the museum of Brussels.

SMIDT. See also **SCHMIDT** or **SMIT**

SMIDT, A. de
19th century.
Painter.

MUSEUMS AND GALLERIES:
CAPE TOWN: *Knysna Heads*.

SMIDT, Abraham. See **SMIT**

SMIDT, Aernout or Johann Arnold. See **SMIT**

SMIDT, Agnes
Danish, 20th century.
Born 4 October 1874, in Lundsmark; died 18 April 1952, in Erritsø.

Painter. Portraits, landscapes.
Agnes Smidt studied in Copenhagen under Vilhelm Klein and Niels Vinding Dorph and went on to paint altarpieces.
MUSEUMS AND GALLERIES:
HADERSLEBEN - TONDERN.

SMIDT, Andres
Flemish School, 17th century.
Active in Antwerp in 1687.
Painter.
Andres Smidt may have been the same person as Andres Smit.

SMIDT, Carl Martin
Danish, 20th century.
Born 15 October 1872, in Thyregod, near Vejle; died 21 November 1947, in Kongens Lyngby.
Painter.
Carl Martin Smidt studied at the Kunstakademi in Copenhagen and under Kristian Zahrtmann. He also worked as an architect and archaeologist.

SMIDT, Eduardo
German, 19th century.
Active in Berlin.
Painter. Seascapes.
MUSEUMS AND GALLERIES:
TRIESTE (Civico Mus. Revoltella): one piece of work.

SMIDT, Emil
German, 20th century.
Born 7 March 1878, in Hamburg; died 1945.
Painter, engraver.
Emil Smidt studied at the fine arts academies in Stuttgart and Munich and at the Académie Julian in Paris.
MUSEUMS AND GALLERIES:
HAMBURG (Kunsthalle): *Geese Market; Rue Royale, Paris; Portrait of the Artist.*

SMIDT, Georges
Belgian, 20th century.
Born 1917; died 15 February 1964, in Schaerbeek.
Painter.
Georges Smidt was a professor at the Académie Royale des Beaux Arts in Brussels.

SMIDT, Hans Jacob, or Smith
Danish, 18th century.
Active in Copenhagen from 1706 to 1728.
Painter. Landscapes. Decorative schemes.

SMIDT, Hanson. See **SCHMIDT**

SMIDT, Jacob or Johann Jacob, or Schmidt
Danish, 18th century.
Born c. 1764, probably in Copenhagen; died 15 June 1804, probably in Copenhagen.
Modeller.
Smidt studied at the Kunstakademi in Copenhagen, and went on to work at the royal porcelain factory in Copenhagen. Several of his figurines are in the Kunstindustrimuseet in Copenhagen.

SMIDT, Jacques or Jacobus de, or Smit
Flemish School, 18th century.
Died 10 July 1787.
Active in Bruges.
Painter.
Jacques Smidt executed the altar painting for the church of St Saviour in Bruges (in the chapel of Our Lady of the Seven Sorrows) from 1756 to 1759.

SMIDT, Jakob or Peder J. Nielsen.
See **SMITH**

SMIDTH, Anna
Danish, 19th - 20th century.
Born 5 April 1861, in Rønnede; died after 1915.
Painter. Landscapes, flowers, fruit.
Anna Smidth was a pupil of Luplau and E. Mundt. She worked at the royal Copenhagen porcelain factory from 1885 to 1915.

SMIDTH, Hans Ludvig
Danish, 19th - 20th century.
Born 2 October 1839, in Nakskov; died 5 May 1917, in Frederiksberg.
Painter, illustrator. Figures, genre scenes, interiors with figures, landscapes with figures, landscapes.
Hans Ludvig Smidth studied under N. Simonsen and V. Kyhn at the Kunstakademi in Copenhagen. He painted landscapes of Jutland and was one of the first artists, together with Frederik Vermehren, Julius Exner and Christen Dalsgaard, to produce scenes of rural life in Denmark. In that vein, he also illustrated several works by the author Steen Steensen Blicher. Smidth was less attentive to detail than his aforementioned fellow artists, and his vision of rural life tended to be somewhat coarse and at times rather bleak.
BIBLIOGRAPHY:
Sthyr, Jörgen, *Malerier af Hans Smidth*, Copenhagen, 1933.
Nørregård-Nielsen, Hans Edvard, *Hans Smidth*, Skive Museum, Skive Folkeblad, 1989.
MUSEUMS AND GALLERIES:
AALBORG - AARHUS - COPENHAGEN - COPENHAGEN (Den Hirschsprungske Samling): *Scene from Steen Steensen Blicher's 'The Knitting Room'* (1898) - MARIBO - ODENSE - RANDERS - RIBE - RØNNE - STOCKHOLM.
AUCTION RECORDS:
COPENHAGEN, 16 May 1950, *Broom*, DKK 8,500. COPENHAGEN, 6 Oct 1950, *Riding in the Landes*, DKK 5,000. COPENHAGEN, 7 Dec 1950, *Cart*, DKK 1,640. COPENHAGEN, 23 Jan 1951, *Peasant and Daughter Going to Church*, DKK 3,000. COPENHAGEN, 5 April 1951, *Peasants in the Polders*, DKK 5,800. COPENHAGEN, 19 March 1969, *Village Street*, DKK 9,000. COPENHAGEN, 9 Feb 1972, *Landscape with Winged Creatures*, DKK 10,000. COPENHAGEN, 21 Nov 1974, *Warriors*, DKK 16,000. COPENHAGEN, 4 May 1976, *Ferry* (1914, oil on canvas, 32 x 49 1/4 ins / 81 x 125 cm) DKK 38,000. COPENHAGEN, 27 Sept 1977, *School Road* (1882, oil on canvas, 15 3/4 x 13 1/2 ins / 40 x 34 cm) DKK 19,000. COPENHAGEN, 2 Oct 1979, *Burning Thatch* (1916, oil on canvas, 24 1/2 x 37 1/2 ins / 62 x 95 cm) DKK 25,000. COPENHAGEN, 22 Sept 1981, *Interior with Peasants* (oil on canvas, 20 3/4 x 30 ins / 53 x 76 cm) DKK 24,000. COPENHAGEN, 8 May 1984, *Village Street* (1903, oil on canvas, 17 1/4 x 28 ins / 44 x 71 cm) DKK 43,000. COPENHAGEN, 27 Feb 1985, *Market Scene* (1894, oil on canvas, 33 x 50 1/2 ins / 84 x 128 cm) DKK 150,000. COPENHAGEN, 20 Aug 1986, *Hunter* (1913, oil on canvas, 16 1/4 x 23 1/4 ins / 41 x 59 cm) DKK 40,000. COPENHAGEN, 5 April 1989, *Figure in a Garden* (oil on canvas, 15 1/4 x 10 1/4 ins / 39 x 26 cm) DKK 6,000. COPENHAGEN, 25 Oct 1989, *Barn Interior* (1916, oil on canvas, 15 x 19 1/4 ins / 38 x 49 cm) DKK 22,000. COPENHAGEN, 29 Aug 1990, *Woman and Three Small Girls in the Courtyard of an Old Farmhouse* (oil on canvas, 21 1/4 x 17 3/4 ins / 54 x 45 cm) DKK 16,000. COPENHAGEN, 6 Dec 1990, *Woman and Three Small Girls in the Courtyard of an Old Farmhouse* (oil on canvas, 21 1/4 x 17 3/4 ins / 54 x 45 cm) DKK 15,000. COPENHAGEN, 6 March 1991, *Gaggle of Geese* (oil on canvas, 14 1/4 x 17 3/4 ins / 36 x 45 cm) DKK 7,000. COPENHAGEN, 1 May 1991, *Young Farmer's Wife Walking on the Foreshore* (oil on canvas, 12 1/2 x 16 1/4 ins / 32 x 41 cm) DKK 12,500. COPENHAGEN, 29 Aug 1991, *Road along the Foreshore* (oil on canvas, 11 3/4 x 22 ins / 30 x 55 cm) DKK 4,500. COPENHAGEN, 18 Nov 1992, *Interior with Flowers on a Window Sill*. COPENHAGEN, 6 Sept 1993, *Young Fishermen, Limfjorden* (oil on canvas, 22 3/4 x 33 ins / 58 x 84 cm) DKK 23,000. COPENHAGEN, 8 Feb 1995, *Inte-*

rior with Peasant Reading (oil on canvas, 235 3/4 x 20 ins / 599 x 51 cm) DKK 6,000.

SMIDTS, Heinrich or Hendrick
Flemish School, 17th century.
Active in 1676.
Painter, engraver (burin).
Heinrich Smidts executed a *View of St Mark's Square in Venice* and a *Panorama of the Siege of Vienna by the Turks in 1683*.

SMIDTS, Johannes. See **SMITS**

SMIED, Anton
German, 17th century.
Active in Wismar (Mecklenburg, west Pomerania).
Painter.
Smied painted *Beheading of St John the Baptist* and *Jesus with St Peter on the Sea* for the church of St Nicholas of Greifswald, Germany, from 1640 to 1655.

SMIES, Jacob
Dutch, 18th - 19th century.
Born 11 June 1764, in Amsterdam; died 11 August 1833, in Amsterdam.
Painter, draughtsman, caricaturist.
Jacob Smies was a pupil of J.G. Walforp and J. Ekel the Younger. He specialised in caricatures and was influenced by Rowlandson.
AUCTION RECORDS:
PARIS, 22 Nov 1991, *Villagers' Entertainment* (Indian ink and watercolour, 3 x 5 3/4 ins / 7.8 x 14.9 cm) FRF 3,800.

SMIGÄUS, Anton. See **SMICHÄUS**

SMIGELSCHI, Octavian, or Oktáv
Romanian, 19th - 20th century.
Born 21 March 1866, in Ludos; died 10 November 1912, in Budapest.
Painter.
Octavian Smigelschi studied at Budapest Academy. He painted popular characters from Transylvania, portraits and landscapes, and together with Arthur Coulin painted the frescoes in Sibiu Cathedral.
MUSEUMS AND GALLERIES:
BUDAPEST (Magyar Nemzeti Gal.) - SIBIU (Muz. National Brukenthal).

SMIJTERS, Anna de. See **SMYTERS**

SMILIS
6th century BC.
Active in Aegina in the Archaic period.
Sculptor.
Ancient Greek.
Smilis worked on the temple of Samos, specialising in statues of Hera. He is said by Pausanias to have been a contemporary of the legendary Daedalus.

SMILLIE, George Frederick Cumming
American, 19th - 20th century.
Born 22 November 1854, in New York; died 1924.
Engraver.
George Frederick Cumming Smillie was James Smillie's nephew. He was a burin engraver who mainly worked on bank notes.

SMILLIE, George Henry
American, 19th - 20th century.
Born 29 October 1840, in New York; died 10 November 1921, in New York.
Painter (including gouache), watercolourist, draughtsman. Landscapes, landscapes with figures, waterscapes, harbour scenes.
George Henry Smillie was the son of the engraver James Smillie and younger brother of the landscape painter James D. Smillie. He travelled to the Rocky Mountains and Yosemite Valley in 1871 and then visited Florida. In 1864, he was an associate member of the National Academy and became a full member in 1882. He was also a member of the American Watercolors Society.
MUSEUMS AND GALLERIES:
NEW YORK (Metropolitan Mus. of Art) - WASHINGTON DC (Corcoran Gal. of Art).
AUCTION RECORDS:
NEW YORK, 25-26 March 1909, *Autumn in Upper Delaware*, USD 100. NEW YORK, 21 May 1909, *Landscape*, USD 100. NEW YORK, 14-17 March 1911, *Harvest in Normandy*, USD 100. NEW YORK, 4 March 1937, *In the Berkshires*, USD 300. NEW YORK, 13 Sept 1972, *Landscape*, USD 1,400. LOS ANGELES, 5 March 1974, *Fluvial Landscape*, USD 2,000. NEW YORK, 28 Oct 1976, *Catskill Mountains* (1865, oil on canvas, 11 x 18 ins / 27 x 45.7 cm) USD 1,200. NEW YORK, 27 Oct 1977, *Summer Landscape* (1904-1910, oil on canvas, 20 x 30 ins / 51 x 76.2 cm) USD 4,500. NEW YORK, 23 May 1979, *Wooded Landscape* (1890, oil on canvas, 26 x 36 ins / 66 x 91.5 cm) USD 1,800. NEW YORK, 24 Oct 1979, *East Gloucester, Mass.* (1889, watercolour, 9 1/2 x 13 1/2 ins / 24 x 34 cm) USD 1,800. NEW YORK, 19 June 1981, *Massachusetts Landscape* (1884, oil on canvas remounted on board, 7 1/4 x 15 ins / 18.3 x 38.1 cm) USD 4,750. NEW YORK, 3 Dec 1982, *Landscape Around Elizabethtown* (1868, oil on canvas, 28 x 52 1/4 ins / 71.2 x 132.9 cm) USD 11,000. NEW YORK, 2 June 1983, *Massachusetts Coast in Autumn* (1884, oil on canvas, 16 x 24 ins / 40.6 x 61 cm) USD 7,500. NEW YORK, 23 March 1984, *Lake George* (watercolour/mounted paper/card, 13 3/4 x 20 3/4 ins / 35 x 52.8 cm) USD 1,100. NEW YORK, 24 Jan 1989, *View from his Favourite Tree* (oil on canvas, 9 1/4 x 6 1/2 ins / 23.5 x 16.5 cm) USD 3,850. NEW YORK, 30 Nov 1990, *Water's Edge* (1868, oil on canvas, 12 x 20 ins / 30.6 x 51 cm) USD 14,300. NEW YORK, 17 Dec 1990, *Repose by the River's Edge* (oil on canvas, 16 x 24 ins / 40.7 x 61 cm) USD 3,575. NEW YORK, 22 May 1991, *Blocked Harbour* (1893, gouache and pencil/paper/card, 10 x 14 ins / 25.3 x 35.5 cm) USD 4,400. NEW YORK, 18 Dec 1991, *Spring* (oil on canvas, 20 x 30 ins / 50.8 x 76.2 cm) USD 6,050. NEW YORK, 9 Sept 1993, *Unionville Connecticut* (1892, pencil and watercolour, 10 1/2 x 15 ins / 26.7 x 38.1 cm) USD 1,495. NEW YORK, 13 Sept 1995, *Meadows in Vermont* (1885, oil on canvas, 15 1/4 x 24 ins / 38.7 x 61 cm) USD 10,350. NEW YORK, 30 Oct 1996, *Pastoral Landscape* (oil on canvas, 20 x 30 ins / 50.8 x 76.2 cm) USD 5,750.

SMILLIE, Helen Sheldon Jacobs
American, 19th century.
Born 14 September 1854, in New York; died 1926.
Painter.
Helen Sheldon Jacobs Smillie was a pupil of James David Smillie and the wife of George Henry Smillie.

SMILLIE, James
British, 19th century.
Born 23 November 1807, in Edinburgh; died 4 December 1885, in Poughkeepsie (New York), USA.
Active in the USA.
Engraver (steel/burin). Banknotes.
James Smillie was apprenticed to a metal engraver when he was 12 years old, worked with Edward Mitchell for a time and went to America when he was 14. At first he worked as a jeweller in Quebec in the company founded by his father and brothers. However, thanks to the sponsorship of Lord Dalhousie, he was able to return to Europe and worked with Andrew Wilson for five months. When he returned to America he settled in New York and worked on the production of banknotes. He subsequently developed a reputation as one of the best metal engravers in America. He became an Associate of the National Academy of New York in 1832 and an academician in 1851.

SMILLIE, James David
American, 19th - 20th century.
Born 16 January 1833, in New York; died 14 September 1909, in New York.
Painter, watercolourist, engraver, draughtsman.
Landscapes, landscapes with figures, mountainscapes.
James David Smillie was the son of the engraver James Smillie. He initially intended to follow his father's profession, but gave up engraving in burin and etching in 1864 and took up landscape painting, especially mountain views. He visited Europe in 1876. He was a founder-member of the American Society of Painting in Watercolours, its secretary, treasurer and from 1873 to 1878, its president. He produced an important body of work.
AUCTION RECORDS:
NEW YORK, 22 Jan 1908, *In the High Sierra,* USD 60. PORTLAND, 10 Nov 1979, *Yosemite Valley, No 2* (oil on canvas, 20 x 14 ins / 51 x 35.5 cm) USD 2,000. NEW YORK, 1 June 1984, *Mountainous Landscape* (1868, oil on canvas, 9 x 14 1/2 ins / 23 x 37 cm) USD 3,200. NEW YORK, 22 June 1984, *The Home of George G. van Walkenburgh* (1872, watercolour/mounted paper/card, 15 1/2 x 22 1/2 ins / 39.4 x 57.1 cm) USD 7,500. NEW YORK, 30 Sept 1985, *Breton Village* (1885, charcoal, 12 x 18 3/4 ins / 30.7 x 47.7 cm) USD 900. NEW YORK, 28 Sept 1989, *Madison Square Garden* (oil on canvas, 40 x 24 ins / 101.7 x 61.1 cm) USD 20,900. NEW YORK, 9 March 1996, *William Smillie's House on the Hudson River* (1876, watercolour and pencil/paper, 15 x 21 3/4 ins / 38.1 x 55.2 cm) USD 5,175. NEW YORK, 23 April 1997, *October in the Hills* (1871, oil on paper/panel, 7 x 7 1/4 ins / 17.8 x 18.4 cm) USD 3,220.

SMILLIE, William Cumming
British, 19th century.
Born 1813, in Edinburgh.
Engraver (burin).
William Cumming Smillie was the brother of James Smillie. He engraved designs for banknotes and worked for the Canadian government.

SMILLIE, William Maine
American, 19th century.
Born 1835, in New York; died 1888, in New York.
Engraver (burin).
William Maine Smillie was the brother of James David Smillie. He mostly engraved banknotes.

SMILOWSKI, Jean
French, 20th century.
Born 1927, of Polish origin; died 1989.
Painter, assemblage artist, draughtsman. Figures. Furniture.
Art Brut.
Jean Smilowski lived and worked in Lille at his cabin 'le Ranch', located on the Vaubon fortifications. He filled it with his creations. In 2001 he was represented in the group exhibition *La Planète exilée* (*The Exiled Planet*) held at the Musée d'Art Moderne of the municipality of Lille, Villeneuve d'Ascq, and in 2002 this museum organised a solo exhibition of his works.

SMILTNIEKS, Zanis
Latvian, 20th century.
Born 27 April 1893, near Mitau (now Jelgava, Latvia); died 28 April 1931, in Riga.
Sculptor, painter.
Zanis Smiltnieks studied at the Petrograd and Riga Academies.
MUSEUMS AND GALLERIES:
RIGA (Valsts makslas muzejs/National Art Museum).

SMIRIGLIO, Mariano, or Smeriglio
17th century.
Died 19 September 1636, in Palermo.
Painter, architect.
Mariano Smiriglio executed works for churches in Palermo and Salemi.

SMIRKE, Mary
British, 19th century.
Active in London during the first half of the 19th century.
Painter. Landscapes, waterscapes, architectural views.
Mary Smirke was the daughter of Robert Smirke. She exhibited at the Royal Academy of Arts in London in 1809 and from 1812 until 1814. Her works include *View of Arundel Castle* and *Cottage near Blackheath*.

SMIRKE, Richard
British, 18th - 19th century.
Born 1778, in London; died 5 May 1815, in London.
Painter, draughtsman.
Richard Smirke was the father of the famous architect Sir Robert Smirke. He studied at the schools of the Royal Academy. He concentrated mostly on producing pictures of antiquities and was frequently employed by the Society of Antique Dealers in London to carry out this type of work for them.

SMIRKE, Robert
British, 18th - 19th century.
Born 1752, in Wighton, near Carlisle; died 5 January 1845, in London.
Painter, illustrator. History painting, genre scenes, portraits.
Robert Smirke studied at the schools of the Royal Academy. He seems to have had a difficult start to his career and is said to have painted coats of arms on coaches. He exhibited his work in London from 1775 until 1834 at the Society of Artists, of which he was a member, the Royal Academy and occasionally on Suffolk Street. He became an associate of the Royal Academy in 1791 and an academician in 1793.

He took his subjects from the Bible, English history, Shakespeare, *Don Quixote*, the *Thousand and One Nights* and was particularly successful with humorous compositions.
MUSEUMS AND GALLERIES:
LONDON (Victoria and Albert Mus.): *Scene from the Capricious Officer (Duel); Illustration of Beaumont and Fletcher; Sidrophel and the Widow (Hudibras)* - NOTTINGHAM (Castle Mus. & AG): *Scandal; Scipio and the Hermit; Gil Blas; Launa and Grizelda Playing Cards; Grenadier Sergeant and Officer.*
AUCTION RECORDS:
LONDON, 1805, *Shakespeare's Seven Ages of Man,* FRF 6,300. PARIS, 1886, *Scene from The Heiress by Burgogne,* FRF 210. NEW YORK, 14-15 Jan 1909, *Juliet and her Nurse,* USD 200. LONDON, 26 Feb 1910, *Midday,* GBP 4. PARIS, 10 June 1925, *Meeting in a Garden* (pen and wash) FRF 360. LONDON, 1 June 1928, *Scene from Busybody,* GBP 105. LONDON, 18 June 1976, *Hunch-Back and the Tailor; Christian Merchant* (oil on canvas, pendants, 21 3/4 x 18 ins / 55.5 x 46 cm) GBP 550. NEW YORK, 3 Nov 1983, *Fortune Teller* (oil on canvas, 48 1/4 x 38 ins / 122.5 x 96.5 cm) USD 6,500. LONDON, 10 July 1984, *Design for the New Hall, Windsor Castle* (1824, watercolour and pen heightened with white, 12 1/2 x 11 ins / 32 x 27 cm) GBP 700. MONACO, 17 June 1989, *Queen Labe's Incantation* (oil on canvas, 16 1/2 x 12 1/2 ins / 42 x 31.5 cm) FRF 24,420. LONDON, 12 July 1989, *Fortune Teller* (oil on canvas, 47 x 37 1/4 ins / 118.5 x 94.5 cm) GBP 7,150. LONDON, 15 Nov 1991, *Portrait of Sir Thomas Horsley Curties in Uniform* (1833, oil on canvas, 44 x 34 ins / 112 x 86.5 cm) GBP 2,200. LONDON, 6 April 1993, *Visit to a Lawyer* (oil on canvas, 17 3/4 x 22 ins / 45 x 56 cm) GBP 2,185. LONDON, 4 July 2001, *Scene from Shakespeare* (oil on canvas, six on one canvas, 11 x 9 ins / 29 x 22 cm) GBP 1,800.

SMIRKE, Sydney
British, 19th century.
Born 1798 or 1799, in London; died 8 December 1877, in Tunbridge.
Draughtsman, architect. Architectural views.
Sydney Smirke studied at the Royal Academy in London.

SMIRNOFF, Boris
French, 19th - 20th century.
Born at the end of the 19th century.
Painter, watercolourist. Figures, portraits, scenes with figures.
Boris Smirnoff trained at the studio of Lucien Simon at the École des Beaux-Arts in Paris, and also studied portraiture with Fujita. He exhibited in Paris, London, Lisbon, New York, Stockholm, Bern, Geneva, Cairo, Palermo, Rome, Nice and Cannes. His principal residence was at Cagnes-sur-Mer in the Alpes-Maritimes. He designed some features of the Italian Embassy in Tokyo.
AUCTION RECORDS:
PARIS, 24 Nov 1932, *Composition* (watercolour) FRF 50; *Bathing,* FRF 70; *Bathers,* FRF 100; *Dancers,* FRF 100. PARIS, 20 June 1947, *Compositions* (watercolour, a pair) FRF 300. NEW YORK, 29 May 1980, *Salome* (1886, oil on canvas, 55 1/2 x 38 1/2 ins / 141 x 98 cm) USD 2,250. LONDON, 2 April 1987, *Russian Fair* (watercolour and pencil, 18 3/4 x 21 1/2 ins / 47.5 x 54.5 cm) GBP 1,100.

SMIRNOV, Boris, or Smirnoff
Russian, 20th century.
Born 1926; died 1982.
Painter, graphic artist. Portraits, nudes, interiors, genre scenes, urban landscapes, urban views.
Boris Smirnov was a member of the Union of Soviet Artists. He liked to paint in sombre, cold colours with a delicate touch.
AUCTION RECORDS:
PARIS, 24 Nov 1987, *Portrait of a Man* (crayon on paper, 19 x 22 1/2 ins / 48 x 57 cm) FRF 2,500. DOUAI, 3 Dec 1989, *Town Views* (two oils on canvas, 7 x 9 ins / 18 x 23 cm) FRF 3,500. PARIS, 26 March 1990, *Reclining Nude* (oil on panel, 8 3/4 x 13 ins / 22.5 x 33 cm) FRF 8,000. PARIS, 18 May 1990, *Young Engineers* (oil on canvas, 31 1/2 x 28 ins / 80 x 71 cm) FRF 5,200. PARIS, 29 Nov 1990, *Old Man* (oil on canvas, 43 1/4 x 32 ins / 110 x 81 cm) FRF 3,000.

SMIRNOV, Nikolai
Russian, 20th century.
Born 20 October 1939, in Aleshkovo (Kostroma).
Painter. Genre scenes, landscapes with figures, landscapes.
Nikolai Smirnov attended the Kostroma school of fine arts from 1956 to 1961 before going on to the Surikov Institute, Moscow. He is a member of the Union of Russian Painters. He lives and works in Kostroma, and exhibits both in Russia and abroad.
AUCTION RECORDS:
PARIS, 14 Dec 1993, *Winter Festival* (1986, oil on canvas, 37 1/2 x 51 1/4 ins / 95 x 130 cm) FRF 7,200.

SMIRNOV, Nikolai Nikolaevich
Russian, 20th century.
Born 1938, in Moscow.
Painter.
N.N. Smirnov works from photographs. He became known in France in 1987.

SMIRNOV, Samson Ivanovich
Russian, 18th century.
Born 28 May 1781; died 10 November 1803.
Medallist.

SMIRNOV, Sergei
Russian, 20th - 21st century.
Born 1954.
Painter. Local scenes, urban landscapes, landscapes with figures.
Smirnov studied at the V. Surikov School of Fine Art in Moscow under Dmitri Mochalsky. His main source of inspiration is the Russia of the end of the 19th century. He has exhibited from 1977 in Russia and abroad.
MUSEUMS AND GALLERIES:
GENEVA (Petit Palais): *Apple Market.*
AUCTION RECORDS:
PARIS, 23 March 1992, *First Snow in Moscow* (oil on canvas, 43 1/4 x 55 ins / 110 x 140 cm) FRF 13,000. PARIS, 5 Nov 1992, *Fair Day* (oil on canvas, 19 3/4 x 27 1/2 ins / 50 x 70 cm) FRF 8,000. PARIS, 18 Oct 1993, *Apple Market in Moscow* (oil on canvas, 33 3/4 x 25 1/2 ins / 86 x 65 cm) FRF 17,000. PARIS, 1 June 1994, *Toy Seller* (oil on canvas, 19 3/4 x 15 3/4 ins / 50 x 40 cm) FRF 8,000. PARIS, 20 Nov 1994, *Apple Market in Moscow* (oil on canvas, 33 3/4 x 25 1/2 ins / 86 x 65 cm) FRF 50,000. MADRID, 21 Feb 2000, *Fruit Market* (oil on canvas, 26 x 20 ins / 65 x 50 cm) ESP 350,000.

SMIRNOV, Vasili Sergeevitch
Russian, 19th century.
Born 1858; died 1890.
Painter. History painting.
Vasili Sergeevitch Smirnov studied at the art academies in Moscow and St Petersburg.
MUSEUMS AND GALLERIES:
MOSCOW (State Tretyakov Gal.): *Byzantine Empress at the Tomb of her Ancestors* - ST PETERSBURG (Gosudarstvennyj Russkij Muz.): *The Death of Nero.*

SMIRNOV, Yuri
Ukrainian, 20th century.
Born 1925, in Kharkov; died 1998.
Painter. Figures, still-lifes.
Yuri Smirnov attended Kharkov art school and Kharkov art academy, graduating in 1951, and joined the Ukraine Artists Union in 1961. He exhibited his work in Zaporozhe in 1958 and 1979. Smirnov's work was traditional, part of the school of Socialist Realism.
AUCTION RECORDS:
PARIS, 13 March 1992, *Bouquet of Phlox* (oil on canvas, 46 1/2 x 26 ins / 118 x 66 cm) FRF 5,000. PARIS, 25 Jan 1993, *Lenin and his Supporters* (oil on canvas, 65 x 55 ins / 165 x 140 cm) FRF 4,000.

SMIRNOVA, Galina
Russian, 20th century.
Born 1929, in Soligalich (Kostroma).
Painter. Portraits, still-lifes.
Galina Smirnova studied at Kostroma School of Fine Arts before going on to the Repin Institute in Leningrad (now St Petersburg), where she studied under Y. Neprintsev. She paints traditional subjects but with visible brushwork.
MUSEUMS AND GALLERIES:
KIEV (Museum of Russian Art) - MOSCOW (Pushkin MFA) - ST PETERSBURG (Academy) - ST PETERSBURG (Gosudarstvennyj Muz. Istorii).
AUCTION RECORDS:
PARIS, 18 Feb 1991, *Market Scene* (oil on canvas, 31 1/2 x 41 1/4 ins / 80 x 105 cm) FRF 7,600. PARIS, 26 April 1991, *Study for 'October Eve'* (1955, oil on canvas, 39 x 23 1/4 ins / 99 x 59.3 cm) FRF 6,500. PARIS, 29 May 1991, *Mandolin Player* (1953, oil on canvas, 42 1/4 x 32 1/2 ins / 107 x 82.5 cm) FRF 7,000.

SMIRNOVA, Olga
Russian, 20th - 21st century.
Born 1954, in Leningrad, now St Petersburg.
Painter. Landscapes, flowers, fruit.
Smirnova studied at the Repin Institute.

Museums and Galleries:
St Petersburg (Gosudarstvennyj Muz. Istorii).
Auction records:
Paris, 13 Dec 1993, *In the Garden* (oil on canvas, 31 1/2 x 33 1/4 ins / 80 x 84.6 cm) FRF 9,200. Paris, 27 March 1994, *Flowers and Fruit* (oil on canvas, 31 1/2 x 33 1/2 ins / 80 x 85 cm) FRF 9,000. Paris, 30 Jan 1995, *Poppies* (oil on canvas, 27 1/2 x 29 1/2 ins / 70 x 75 cm) FRF 12,000.

SMIRNOVSKI, Ivan
Russian, 19th century.
Born before 1783; died after 1822.
Portrait artist.

SMIRSCH, Johann Karl
Austrian, 19th century.
Born 1801, in Vienna; died 18 September 1869, in Vienna (?).
Painter. Still-lifes, flowers.

Smirsch attended the academy in Vienna and exhibited from 1820 to 1844.
Auction records:
London, 15 Feb 1978, *Still-life with Flowers* (oil on canvas, 15 1/4 x 12 1/4 ins / 39 x 31 cm) GBP 1,850. Bath, 12 April 1999, *Still-life with Flowers and Pomegranate on a Stone Ledge* (1856, oil on panel, 13 x 10 ins / 32 x 25 cm) GBP 4,200.

SMISEK, Johann Christoph
Austrian, 17th century.
Active in Prague from 1654 to 1695.
Engraver (burin). Portraits, book illustrations, frontispieces.

Johann Christoph Smisek was the son of Johann Smisek.

SMISEK, Johann or Hans, or Schmischeck or Schmisek or Zwischegg
Czech, 17th century.
Born before 1585, in Prague.
Active in Innsbruck, Munich and Prague.
Engraver (burin). Landscapes, religious subjects, hunting scenes.

SMISSAERT, Frans
Dutch, 19th - 20th century.
Born 1862, in The Hague; died 1944.
Painter. Fishing scenes.

Frans Smissaert studied at the Academie van Beeldende Kunsten in The Hague and under W. Roelof.
Auction records:
Amsterdam, 24 Sept 1992, *Mending Fishing Nets in the Dunes* (1900, oil on canvas, 19 x 25 1/4 ins / 48.5 x 64 cm) NLG 1,380.

SMISSEN, Cornelis van der
Dutch, 17th century.
Active in Amsterdam 1632-1635.
Painter.

SMISSEN, Dominicus van der
German, 18th century.
Born 28 April 1704, in Altona; died 6 January 1760, in Altona.
Active in Altona, Hamburg, London, Brunswick and Dresden.
Painter. Portraits, landscapes, still-lifes.

Van der Smissen studied under Balthasar Denner.
Museums and Galleries:
Berlin (Bodemus.): *Portrait of a Man* - Brunswick: *Self-portrait; Bust of a Woman* - Hamburg (Kunsthalle): *Brockes, Senator and Poet; Still-life; Friedrich Hagedorn; Self-portrait; Mayor M. Widow; Mrs Widow; Portrait of a Captain* - Hamburg (Mus. für Hamburgische Geschichte): *Portrait of Friedrich Hagedorn* - Kiel: *Senator Brockes.*
Auction records:
London, 9 Dec 1992, *Self-portrait* (1750, oil on canvas, 16 1/2 x 14 3/4 ins / 42.2 x 37.7 cm) GBP 10,780. Cologne, 19 May 2001, *Portrait of Man* (oil on canvas, 33 x 28 ins / 85 x 72 cm) DEM 4,800. London, 29 Oct 2001, *Portrait of a Lady in a Green Dress Holding a Book* (1759, oil on canvas, 50 x 40 ins / 127 x 102 cm) GBP 1,200.

SMISSEN, Frans van der
Belgian, 20th century.
Born 1894, in Dendermonde.
Sculptor.

Frans van der Smissen was the brother of Léo van der Smissen and a pupil of Fonteyne, Pickery and Rotsaert.

SMISSEN, Jacob
German, 18th - 19th century.
Born 23 December 1735, in Altona; died 19 May 1813, in Altona.
Painter. Portraits, landscapes.

Jacob Smissen was the son and pupil of Dominicus.

SMISSEN, Léo van der
Belgian, 20th century.
Born 1900, in Dendermonde.
Painter. Urban landscapes, landscapes, still-lifes.

Bibliography:
Bruyn, J.P. de, *L'École de Dendermonde*, Dendermonde, 1994.
Auction records:
Brussels, 19 Dec 1989, *Village in the Sun* (oil on canvas, 25 1/2 x 29 1/2 ins / 65 x 75 cm) BEF 28,000. Lokeren, 20 May 1995, *Autumn on a Canal Bank in Bruges* (oil on canvas, 78 3/4 x 94 1/2 ins / 200 x 240 cm) BEF 180,000. Lokeren, 13 March 2004, *Returning Farmer with Cows* (oil on canvas, 67 x 79 ins / 170 x 200 cm) EUR 2,000.

SMIT. See also **SMET** and **SMITS**

SMIT, A.
Dutch, 18th century.
Active in Amsterdam 1767-1792.
Engraver (burin), portrait artist.

SMIT, Abraham, or Smidt or Smith
Dutch, 17th century.
Died 1672; buried 30 April in Amsterdam.
Active in Lokeren.
Painter.

SMIT, Aernout or Johann Arnold, or Smidt
Flemish School, 17th - 18th century.
Born c. 1641, in Amsterdam; died 1710, in Amsterdam.
Painter. Seascapes.

Aernout Smit was a pupil of Jan Teunisz. Blankhof. He painted in the style of L. Backhuysen, but in darker tones. He is thought to be identical to the painter Andreas mentioned as painting seascapes at about the same period and having one work in the Berlin Gallery.

A Smit

Museums and Galleries:
Bonn (Rheinisches Landesmus.): *Seascape* - Compiègne (Mus. national du Château): *Storm* - Darmstadt: *Rough Sea* - Hamburg: *Storm at Sea* - Mannheim: *Seascape* - Oslo: *Seascapes* - Schwerin: *Seascape* - Utrecht: *Italian Port.*
Auction records:
New York, 20 Jan 1911, *Seascape*, USD 225. Paris, 28 Feb 1919, *Return from Fishing*, FRF 430. Paris, 20 March 1940,

Seascape, FRF 720. LONDON, 9 July 1976, *Boats in a Heavy Sea* (oil on canvas, 46½ x 58½ ins / 118 x 148.5 cm) GBP 2,000. LONDON, 22 April 1977, *Sailing Boats at Anchor* (oil on canvas, 20½ x 24 ins / 52 x 61 cm) GBP 4,000. AMSTERDAM, 18 May 1981, *Boats and Sailing Ships on the Zuider Zee* (oil on canvas, 20 x 27¾ ins / 51 x 70.5 cm) NLG 17,000. ST-DIÉ, 20 March 1988, *Seascape with a Rough Sea* (13 x 18½ ins / 33 x 47 cm) FRF 16,000. LONDON, 17 June 1988, *Vessels in a Storm* (oil on canvas, a pair, each 16 x 21¼ ins / 40.6 x 54 cm) GBP 13,200. AMSTERDAM, 12 June 1990, *Fishing Boats Sheltering near a Jetty at the Approach of a Storm, with a Three-master at Anchor* (oil on canvas, 43¼ x 62 ins / 110 x 157.5 cm) NLG 63,250. PARIS, 31 Jan 1991, *Dutch Boats in a Storm* (oil on canvas, 18½ x 24¼ ins / 47 x 61.5 cm) FRF 85,000. AMSTERDAM, 2 May 1991, *Small Tug Approaching a Three-master Sailing in a Storm* (oil on canvas, 26¼ x 35 ins / 66.7 x 89 cm) NLG 17,250. LONDON, 6 Dec 1995, *Dutch Warships Including the Flagship Firing a Salvo, with a Merchant Ship and an English Boat in a Rough Sea* (oil on canvas, 39¼ x 57 ins / 99.8 x 144.5 cm) GBP 21,850. LONDON, 13 Dec 1996, *Boats under Way* (oil on canvas, 18 x 27 ins / 46 x 68.3 cm) GBP 13,225. PARIS, 5 Dec 2001, *Seascape with Dutch Ships* (oil on canvas, 30 x 41 ins / 76 x 103 cm) FRF 125,000. LONDON, 10 July 2002, *Coastal Nocturne with Ship Ablaze on the Shore, Other in a Calm beyond* (oil on canvas, 41 x 61 ins / 105 x 154 cm) GBP 20,000. AMSTERDAM, 5 Nov 2003, *Man-o'-war, possibly Het Wapen van Utrech, and a Wijdschip in a Stiff Breeze* (1671, oil on canvas, 34 x 44 ins / 86 x 112 cm) EUR 35,000. LONDON, 19 Nov 2003, *Dutch Admiralty* (oil on canvas, 15 x 18 ins / 37 x 45 cm) GBP 1,500. AMSTERDAM, 3 Feb 2004, *Threemaster in a Gale off a Rocky Coast* (oil on canvas, 24 x 36 ins / 62 x 91 cm) EUR 4,200. SAN FRANCISCO, 18 May 2004, *Shipping Offshore in Rough Seas* (oil on panel, 9 x 12 ins / 23 x 30 cm) USD 4,000.

SMIT, Andres
Flemish School, 17th century.
Active in Spain from the end of the 17th century.
Painter.
Andres Smit was also active in Rome in the middle of the 17th century. He accompanied Velázquez to Madrid and remained in Spain.

SMIT, Andries
Flemish School, 17th - 18th century.
Born c. 1674.
Active in Amsterdam.
Painter.

SMIT, Arie
20th century.
Born 1916, in Zaandam, the Netherlands.
Painter, engraver. Figures, scenes with figures.
Arie Smit studied at the Rotterdam academy of art. Influenced by Impressionism, he depicted graceful figures in a setting of luxurious, colourful vegetation. In 1938 he travelled to Indonesia to work for Batavia's topographic service and as a lithographer. He was appointed Professor of Art in Bandung and settled on the island of Bali in 1956, setting up a School for Young Artists and encouraging his pupils to adopt a modern approach to art.
AUCTION RECORDS:
AMSTERDAM, 7 Nov 1995, *Balinese Dancers* (oil on card, 20½ x 10 ins / 52 x 24.5 cm) NLG 7,670. SINGAPORE, 5 Oct 1996, *Rest* (1986, oil on canvas, 19¾ x 15 ins / 50 x 38 cm) SGD 10,350. SINGAPORE, 3 Oct 1999, *In a Balinese Temple* (1991, acrylic, 28x38 ins / 71x97 cm) SGD 20,000. SINGAPORE, 3 Oct 1999, *Entrance to the Village* (oil on canvas, 24x24 ins / 60x60 cm) SGD 12,000. SINGAPORE, 1 Oct 2000, *Lagoon, North Bali* (1986, oil on board, 11x15 ins / 29x39 cm) SGD 4,500. SINGAPORE, 1 Oct 2000, *Red Pura, Red Temple* (1989, oil on board, 8x11 ins / 20x29 cm) SGD 6,500. SINGAPORE, 30 Sept 2001, *Flowers in the Garden* (1991, acrylic, 28x30 ins / 71x75 cm) SGD 30,000. SINGAPORE, 30 Sept 2001, *Woman on the Way to the Market* (1984, acrylic, 14x17 ins / 35x42 cm) SGD 8,500. HONG KONG, 27 Oct 2002, *Pura-temple* (1997, acrylic, 16x20 ins / 40x51 cm) HKD 90,000. HONG KONG, 27 Oct 2002, *Joyful Life of Flowers* (1989, acrylic, 46x33 ins / 116x83 cm) HKD 200,000. HONG KONG, 26 Oct 2003, *Temple* (1972, oil on canvas, 22x22 ins / 56x56 cm) HKD 75,000. HONG KONG, 26 Oct 2003, *Coastal Landscape* (1972, oil on canvas, 24x19 ins / 60x48 cm) HKD 60,000. HONG KONG, 31 Oct 2004, *Tropical Landscape* (1990, oil on canvas, 28 x 33 ins / 72 x 84 cm) HKD 220,000. HONG KONG, 31 Oct 2004, *Green Landscape* (1961, acrylic, 25 x 36 ins / 63 x 91 cm) HKD 220,000.

SMIT, Cornelio. See **SMET**

SMIT, Cornelis van der. See **SMET**

SMIT, D.
Flemish School, 17th century.
Painter. Figures, portraits.
D. Smit painted a portrait of a sailor, dated 1681.

SMIT, Dirk
Dutch, 17th (?) century.
Painter. Landscapes, seascapes.
Dirk Smit is noted for his landscapes in the style of Ruysdael.

SMIT, Gerrit
Dutch, 18th century.
Active in Rotterdam.
Painter.
Gerrit Smit also worked in Amsterdam at the beginning of 1702.

SMIT, Jacobus
Dutch, 17th century.
Born c. 1659, in Amsterdam; died 1694, in Amsterdam.
Painter.
Jacobus Smit was the brother of Pieter Smit.

SMIT, Jacques or Jacobus de. See **SMIDT**

SMIT, Jan
Dutch, 17th century.
Born 1662 or 1663, in Amsterdam.
Engraver. Religious subjects, landscapes.

SMIT, Jan Borritsz., or Smith
Dutch, 17th century.
Born 1598, in Amsterdam; died before 1644.
Painter. Seascapes.
Jan Borritsz. Smit painted a *Calm Sea* which is in the Nostitz Museum in Prague.
AUCTION RECORDS:
PARIS, 17 June 1924, *Rough Sea*, FRF 1,400.

SMIT, Jan Borritsz.
Dutch, 18th century.
Born 1721; died 1768.
Painter, engraver, draughtsman. Landscapes with figures, seascapes.
Jan Borritsz. Smit executed views of Amsterdam, Zaandam and Rosendal.
AUCTION RECORDS:
NEW YORK, 3 June 1988, *Estuary with Dutch Vessels and Figures on the Jetty* (oil on panel, 15½ x 27 ins / 39.5 x 68.5 cm) USD 49,500.

SMIT, Jan or Johannes
Dutch, 18th century.
Died 9 February 1720, in Amsterdam.
Painter. Designs (wallpapers).
Jan Smit set himself up in Amsterdam and specialised in producing wallpapers.

SMIT, Johann Arnold. See **SMIT Aernout** or **Johann Arnold**

SMIT, Joos Woutersz., or Smet
Flemish School, 14th - 15th century.
Born in Antwerp; died c. 1515.
Painter.

Joos Woutersz. Smit worked in Antwerp and Bruges.

SMIT, Pieter
Dutch, 17th century.
Born c. 1663, in Amsterdam.
Active in Amsterdam.
Painter.

Pieter Smit was the brother of Jacobus Smit.

SMIT, Rombout
Flemish School, 16th century.
Active in Antwerp.
Glass painter.

Rombout Smit was a pupil of Dingemans in Antwerp in 1543 and was burned at the stake as an Anabaptist in 1555.

SMIT, Samuel Pietersz.. See **SMITS**

SMIT LE BENEDICTE, Jean Claude
Belgian, 20th - 21st century.
Born 1947, in Ukkel.
Draughtsman, illustrator.

Jean Claude Smit Le Benedicte specialises in drawing urban landscapes.

SMITH
British, 18th - 19th century.
Active in London.
Painter. Landscapes, architectural views.

Smith was the sister of Emma Smith. She exhibited her work at the Royal Academy from 1799 until 1804.

SMITH. See also **SMYTH**

SMITH, A. or Abraham
British, 18th century.
Engraver, illustrator.

Abraham Smith was active in the second half of the 18th century. He produced burin engravings of views and book illustrations.

SMITH, A. R.. See **SMITH Reginald** or **A. R.**

SMITH, Abraham. See **SMIT**

SMITH, Adam
British, 18th century.
Active in London during the second half of the 18th century.
Draughtsman, engraver (burin).

Adam Smith exhibited his work in London from 1768 until 1770.

SMITH, Albert
Austrian, 19th century.
Painter. Seascapes.

Smith exhibited in Vienna from 1844 to 1852.

SMITH, Albert Talbot
British, 19th - 20th century.
Born 20 July 1877, in Canton.
Illustrator, caricaturist.

SMITH, Albert, or Albert Delmont
American, 20th century.
Born 1896, in New York, 14 February 1886 according to some sources; died 1940, in Sallanches (Haute-Savoie), France.
Painter, draughtsman, engraver, watercolourist.
Portraits, scenes with figures, landscapes.

Albert Smith studied at the Art Students League and was taught by Du Mond and Chase. He was a member of the Salmagundi Club. He dealt with a number of themes in a wide variety of techniques and styles. His subjects included scenes of grape harvests, dancing, boxing, the circus, bullfighting as well as many portraits, town views and some rural landscapes.

BIBLIOGRAPHY:
Atelier Albert Smith, Auction catalogue, Paris, 27 November 1991.

MUSEUMS AND GALLERIES:
DETROIT: *Portrait of the Artist*.

AUCTION RECORDS:
PARIS, 27 Nov 1991, *Cabaret* (1932, oil on canvas, 25 1/2 x 20 ins / 65 x 51 cm) FRF 6,500.

SMITH, Alexis Patricia Anne
American, 20th - 21st century.
Born 1949, in Los Angeles.
Mixed media collage artist. Murals.

Alexis Smith originally trained to be a French teacher until she began taking art classes and realised what she could do with art. She lives and works in Los Angeles and has taught at the University of Hawaii, the J. Paul Getty Center, the University of California, Los Angeles, and the Carnegie Mellon University. Alexis Smith uses magazine covers, newspapers, billboards, book jackets and a range of kitsch and found objects to create collages using 'easy' images with which people are familiar, to make the viewer think about society's ills, like consumerism and the objectification of women, with irony and wit. Quotations from a range of authors (including Walt Whitman, Jack Kerouac, Raymond, Chandler, Francis Scott Fitzgerald, Gertrude Stein, John Dos Passos) and scientists ('imagination is more important than knowledge', Einstein) are often incorporated in her work. Images of women appear frequently as in *Men Seldom Make Passes at Girls Who Wear Glasses*, a vast collage in which Marilyn Monroe wears glasses that are uniquely shaped picture frames inside which are football players making passes. She also incorporates maps to explore the 'romance of travel'.

Smith has executed murals like the 560 feet (170 m) long *Snake Path* (1992), University of California, La Jolla and *Same Old Paradise*, now in the lobby of Brooklyn Museum, New York showing fields, orange trees, mountains and a road that ends as a curled-up snake.

Solo exhibitions include: *Alexis Smith: Public Works*, University of California, La Jolla (1991); *Alexis Smith*, Whitney Museum of American Art (1991); *Words to Live By* Margo Leavin Gallery, Los Angeles (1999); *An Embarrassment of Riches*, Lawrence Rubin Greenberg Van Doren Fine Art, New York (2000); *Fools Rush In*, Ameringer Howard, Boca Raton (2000); *The Sorcerer's Apprentice*, with Amy Gerstler, Museum of Contemporary Art, San Diego and Miami Art Museum, Miami (2001); *Alexis Smith-Real World; Collage Works 1981-2002*, Modernism, San Francisco (2002);

Collective exhibitions include: *Beau Monde: Toward a Redeemed Cosmopolitanism*, Santa Fe (2001) and *100 Artists See God*, Institute of Contemporary Art, London (2004).

BIBLIOGRAPHY:
Armstrong, Richard, *Alexis Smith*, exhibition catalogue, Whitney Museum of American Art, New York, 1991. Drohojowska, Hunter, *Alexis Smith, Public Works*, exhibition catalogue, University of California, La Jolla (CA), 1991. Smith, Alexis, *Snake Path*, University of California, La Jolla (CA), 1997 (videorecording).

MUSEUMS AND GALLERIES:
DENVER (AM) - LA JOLLA (Start Collection) - ŁÓDZ (Muz. Sztuki) - LOS ANGELES (Getty Center): *Taste* (1997, permanent wall installation) - NEW YORK (Whitney Mus. of American Art) - SAN DIEGO (MCA): *Men Do Not Make Passes at Girls Who Wear Glasses* (1985).

AUCTION RECORDS:
SAN FRANCISCO, 26 Oct 1999, *Christmas Eve, 1943 No 12 Desperado* (mixed media and ready made objects on paper, 22 x 17 ins / 55 x 44 cm) USD 2,250. LOS ANGELES, 14 Dec 1999, *Shell Shock* (mixed media on paper, 24 x 20 ins / 61 x 51 cm) USD 9,000. LOS ANGELES, 7 June 2000, *Alone* (mixed media and printed paper collage, sixteen pieces, two panels, 13 x 71 ins / 32 x 181 cm) USD 4,500. NEW YORK, 14 May 2003, *Cinephilia* (printed paper, candy box, feather, ribbon and bob pins collage, 44 x 34x4 ins / 111 x 87x9 cm) USD 9,000.

SMITH, Alfred
French, 19th century.
Born July 1853, in Bordeaux.
Painter. Portraits, landscapes, landscapes with figures, architectural views, still-lifes.

Alfred Smith was a pupil of H. Pradelles and L. Chalery. He made his Salon debut in 1880 and was given an honourable mention in 1886, a third class medal in 1888, a bronze medal at the Exposition Universelle held in 1889 and again in 1900. He was appointed a Chevalier of the Légion d'Honneur in 1894 and his work was also shown at the Salon des Tuileries.

MUSEUMS AND GALLERIES:
BORDEAUX: *Gondola; Undergrowth; Evening scene of the Quayside in Bordeaux* - PARIS (former Mus. du Luxembourg): *Summer Harmony; Seamstress.*

AUCTION RECORDS:
PARIS, 1890, *In the Spring,* FRF 50. PARIS, 12 May 1923, *A Snowy Morning,* FRF 80. PARIS, 8 Jan 1943, *Landscape,* FRF 1,200. PARIS, 24 May 1943, *Undergrowth,* FRF 180. PARIS, 2 Dec 1946, *Sheep Grazing in the Woods,* FRF 1,000. LONDON, 18 July 1973, *Still-life with Apples and Pears,* GBP 800. FONTAINEBLEAU, 16 May 2004, *Barat Mill at Crozant* (oil on canvas, 19 x 22 ins / 47 x 56 cm) EUR 2,200. LONDON, 26 May 2004, *Arc de Triomphe* (1894, oil on canvas, 30 x 20 ins / 75 x 52 cm) GBP 4,000.

SMITH, Alfred E.
American, 19th - 20th century.
Born 27 May 1863, in Lynn; died 1955.
Painter.

Alfred E. Smith studied at the Académie Julian in Paris and in the studios of Boulanger, Lefebvre, E. Constant and Doucet.

AUCTION RECORDS:
NEW YORK, 4 Dec 1986, *Farmhouse, Sunny Morning* (1888, oil/hardboard, 29 1/2 x 44 1/2 ins / 75 x 113.1 cm) USD 14,500. PARIS, 25 March 1990, *Evening in the Creuse* (oil on canvas, 18 x 22 ins / 46 x 55 cm) FRF 50,000. PARIS, 27 April 1990, *In the Creuse, in Autumn* (oil on canvas, 18 x 22 ins / 46 x 55 cm) FRF 5,800. PARIS, 13 June 1990, *Creuse at Crozant in Winter* (oil on canvas, 23 1/2 x 32 ins / 60 x 81 cm) FRF 7,500. PARIS, 4 Dec 1995, *Chevet of Notre-Dame and the Rive Banks* (1886, oil on canvas, 28 1/4 x 35 3/4 ins / 72 x 91 cm) FRF 60,000.

SMITH, Alice Ravenel Huger
American, 19th - 20th century.
Born 14 July 1876, in Charleston (South Carolina); died 1958, in Charleston.
Painter.

Alice Ravenel Huger Smith was mainly self-taught as an artist, studying Japanese ukiyo-e prints and producing woodblock prints in accordance with the same principles. She was a leading figure in the renaissance of art taking place in Charleston between 1915 and 1940, and became a member of the American Federation of Arts.

AUCTION RECORDS:
BOSTON, 14 May 1999, *Flying Egrets* (watercolour, 20 x 16 ins / 52 x 40 cm) USD 22,000. NEW YORK, 7 Dec 1999, *Two Grey Trees* (watercolour, 20 x 13 ins / 51 x 33 cm) USD 15,000. BOSTON, 10 Nov 2000, *Egrets Perched in a Tree* (watercolour, gouache and graphite, 22 x 17 ins / 55 x 43 cm) USD 56,000. BOSTON, 11 May 2001, *Poetry* (watercolour, 29 x 22 ins / 74 x 55 cm) USD 51,000. BOSTON, 11 May 2001, *Misty Moon* (watercolour, 15 x 21 ins / 39 x 53 cm) USD 55,000. NEW ORLEANS, 22 Feb 2002, *Launching of the Ship* (watercolour, 3 x 4 ins / 7 x 9 cm) USD 2,000. HATFIELD, 10 Sept 2003, *Dusk Landscape of Cypress Swamp, Buildings with Lighted Windows in Distance* (watercolour, 21 x 12 ins / 53 x 30 cm) USD 27,500. BOSTON, 12 Sept 2003, *Southern Pines* (watercolour and gouache, 21 x 14 ins / 54 x 35 cm) USD 30,000. NEW YORK, 29 Sept 2004, *Herons in the Bayou* (watercolour on board, 22 x 11 ins / 55 x 29 cm) USD 37,500.

SMITH, Allan
American, 19th century.
Born 1810; died 1890.
Active in Cleveland.
Painter. Portraits, landscapes.

MUSEUMS AND GALLERIES:
CLEVELAND: *Portrait of the Artist's Mother.*

SMITH, Amanda Banks
American, 19th - 20th century.
Born 1846; died April 1924, in Greenwich (Connecticut).
Painter.

SMITH, Anders or Andrew Lauritzen
Norwegian, 17th century.
Born in Scotland; died c. 1694, in Sola (near Stavanger).
Sculptor, painter.

Anders Smith was the father of Knud Smith and a pupil of Peter Negelsen in Bergen. He worked for churches in Bergen and Stavanger.

SMITH, Anker
British, 18th - 19th century.
Born 1759, in London; died 23 June 1819, in London.
Engraver, miniaturist.

Anker Smith studied under Taylor and Bartolozzi. He collaborated with James Heath. He engraved many pretty vignettes, including those for Bell's edition of English poets. He also produced work with Boydell for the Shakespeare Gallery. He became an Associate of the Royal Academy in 1797.

SMITH, Anne
Maiden name: Wyke
Irish, 19th century.
Miniaturist.

Anne Smith was the wife of Stephen Catterson Smith the Elder.

SMITH, Archibald Cary
American, 19th - 20th century.
Born 4 September 1837, in New York; died December 1911, in Bayonne (New Jersey).
Painter. Seascapes.

Archibald Cary Smith was a naval yacht designer and marine artist. Among the yachts he designed were the *Mischief,* which defended the Americas Cup in 1881, the *Meteor,* the *Iroquois,* the *Resolute,* and the *Fortuna.* His seascapes often presented the dangerous, immense and uncontrollable aspects of the ocean, in the spirit of 19th century Romanticism.

AUCTION RECORDS:
NEW YORK, 24 March 1844, *Yachting Scenes* (matching pair) USD 310. NEW YORK, 1 Feb 1986, *The Yacht 'Dauntless'* (1880, oil on canvas, 24 x 36 ins / 60.9 x 91.4 cm) USD 14,000. NEW YORK, 30 Sept 1997, *Ships off the Coast at Sunrise* (1874, oil on canvas, 12 x 23 ins / 30.5 x 58.4 cm) USD 2,587.

SMITH, Benjamin
British, 19th century.
Died 1833, in London.
Engraver.

Benjamin Smith studied under Bartolozzi. He produced work for Boydell's Shakespeare Gallery. He also produced many engravings after English painters of his time using stippling and the crayon manner.

SMITH, Bentley
British.
Landscape artist.

MUSEUMS AND GALLERIES:
CARDIFF: *Meadows.*

SMITH, Bernhard
British, 19th century.
Born 1820; died 1885.
Active in London from 1842 to 1848.
Sculptor. Medallions.

MUSEUMS AND GALLERIES:
LONDON (National Portrait Gal.): *Sir John Richardson* (1842, plaster, casting of a medallion); *Sir James Clark Ross* (1843, plaster, casting of a medallion).

SMITH, Brian Reffin
British, 20th - 21st century.
Born 1946, in Sudbury (Suffolk).
Active in France and in Germany.
Installation artist. Multimedia.

Brian Smith studied at Brunel University and the Royal College of Art in London. He has taught in France at the École Nationale des Beaux-Arts in Bourges since 1986. His first French exhibition at the Galeries des Beaux-Arts in Nantes in 1992 was entitled *Vers une politique de l'art/ordinateur* (*Towards a politics of art/computer*). The show highlighted the aesthetic ambiguities of the treatment and manipulation of images through computer technology, using portraits taken from a book published by the Nazis.

SMITH, Bryce
British, 19th century.
Active in London.
Miniaturist.

Bryce Smith exhibited 13 miniatures at the Royal Academy in London between 1843 and 1861.

SMITH, C. H.
American, 19th century.
Active in Philadelphia and New York 1855-1860.
Engraver (burin).

SMITH, C.H.
British, 19th century.
Active in London.
Miniaturist.

C.H. Smith exhibited 13 miniatures and landscapes at the Royal Academy in London between 1836 and 1875.

SMITH, Carl or Carlo Frithjof
Norwegian, 19th - 20th century.
Born 5 April 1859, in Christiania (now Oslo); died 11 October 1917, in Weimar.
Painter. Portraits, genre scenes, landscapes, landscapes with figures.

Carl Smith studied from 1880 to 1884 under Löfftz at the academy in Munich, then worked in Paris under Gude. He was in Weimar in 1890. He exhibited at the Paris Salon, where he received an honourable mention in 1887.

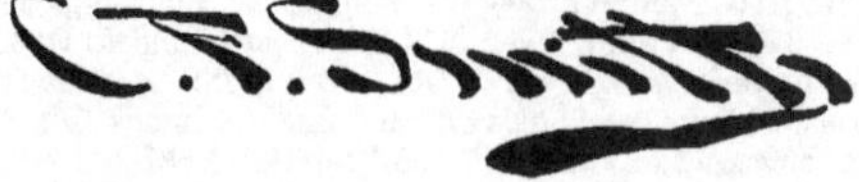

MUSEUMS AND GALLERIES:
BORDEAUX: *October Evening, Norway* - COLOGNE: *Fishermen's Return* - LA ROCHELLE: *Net* - LILLE: *Steamboat Dock, Norway* - MONTPELLIER: *Home from Work* - RHEIMS: *Summer Night, Norway* - ROUEN: *Fishermen* - THE HAGUE (Gemeentemus.): *Evening; Village Church* (1885) - TRIESTE: *After Communion* - WEIMAR: *Portrait of Henrik Johan Ibsen.*

AUCTION RECORDS:
PARIS, 7 Feb 1891, *Seascape,* FRF 150. NEW YORK, 11 Feb 1981, *Hospital Garden* (oil on canvas, 70 3/4 x 116 1/2 ins / 180 x 296 cm) USD 15,000. LONDON, 25 March 1987, *Portrait of a Little Girl* (pastel, 20 x 15 1/4 ins / 51 x 39 cm) GBP 4,000. STOCKHOLM, 15 Nov 1989, *Lake Landscape with Figures, Yachts and Mountains in the Distance* (1884, oil, 26 1/2 x 38 1/2 ins / 67 x 98 cm) SEK 35,000.

SMITH, Carl Wilhelm Daniel Rohl. See **ROHL-SMITH Carl Wilelm Daniel**

SMITH, Carlton Alfred
British, 19th - 20th century.
Born 1853, in London; died 1946.
Painter, watercolourist, draughtsman. Genre scenes.

Carlton Alfred Smith studied in France and at the Slade School in London. He married the painter Martha Sarah King and lived in London and Surrey, visiting India from 1916. He exhibited at the Royal Academy, the Royal Institute of Painters in Watercolours, the Royal Society of British Artists and the Royal Institute of Painters in Oil Colours. He painted cottage interiors and scenes of rural life.

MUSEUMS AND GALLERIES:
LONDON (Victoria and Albert Mus.): *Young Girl Destroying Old Letters* (watercolour) - MELBOURNE: *Christmas Eve* - SUNDERLAND: *News at Christmas.*

AUCTION RECORDS:
LONDON, 18 Nov 1921, *Cullaby* (drawing) GBP 15. LONDON, 3 July 1922, *Little Favourite* (drawing) GBP 42. LONDON, 29 Feb 1924, *Playtime* (drawing) GBP 56. LONDON, 6 July 1928, *When the Work is Done* (drawing) GBP 39. LONDON, 19 May 1971, *Young Woman under an Apple Tree in Blossom,* GBP 480. LONDON, 20 March 1979, *The Love Letter* (1887, oil on panel, 12 1/4 x 9 ins / 31 x 23 cm) GBP 750. LONDON, 24 June 1980, *Looking after the Baby* (1885, watercolour, 17 1/4 x 23 1/2 ins / 44 x 59.5 cm) GBP 750. LONDON, 5 June 1981, *Private View* (1879, oil on canvas, 16 1/4 x 24 1/4 ins / 41.2 x 61.6 cm) GBP 1,200. CHESTER, 13 Jan 1984, *Home* (1904, oil on canvas, 29 1/2 x 49 3/4 ins / 75 x 126.5 cm) GBP 6,000. CHESTER, 12 July 1985, *Christmas Preparations* (1903, watercolour, 17 x 25 1/4 ins / 43 x 64 cm) GBP 4,500. LONDON, 16 Dec 1986, *First Lesson* (1897, watercolour heightened with white, 21 1/2 x 14 3/4 ins / 54.6 x 37.7 cm) GBP 7,000. LONDON, 29 April 1987, *Little Girls Picking Flowers in a Field* (1892, watercolour/pencil outlines, 14 1/2 x 12 3/4 ins / 37 x 32.5 cm) GBP 4,200. LONDON, 25 Jan 1988, *Summertime* (1909, watercolour, 21 x 14 1/4 ins / 53.5 x 36 cm) GBP 6,050; *Morning Nap: Young Woman and Child Asleep* (1908, watercolour, 12 3/4 x 9 ins / 32.5 x 23 cm) GBP 7,700. NEW YORK, 25 May 1988, *The Artist's Daughter* (1909, watercolour and gouache, 14 1/2 x 10 1/2 ins / 36.7 x 26.4 cm) USD 9,350. PARIS, 22 Nov 1988, *Forest Interior in Beaulieu* (oil on canvas, 30 x 21 3/4 ins / 76 x 55.5 cm) FRF 28,000. PARIS, 16 Dec 1988, *At Monceau Park* (1891, oil on paper remounted/canvas, 22 x 15 ins / 55 x 38 cm) FRF 17,000. LONDON, 31 Jan 1990, *The New Favourite* (1895, watercolour, 21 x 14 1/4 ins / 53.5 x 36 cm) GBP 14,850. LONDON, 25-26 April 1990, *Fairytale* (1896, watercolour, 15 1/2 x 22 1/2 ins / 39.5 x 57 cm) GBP 5,500. LONDON, 15 June 1990, *Bedtime* (1896, oil on

panel, 12 x 9 1/4 ins / 30.5 x 23.5 cm) GBP 4,180. LONDON, 30 Jan 1991, *Little Girl Cradling her Puppy* (1903, watercolour, 14 1/2 x 9 1/2 ins / 37 x 24 cm) GBP 6,050. LONDON, 5 June 1991, *Moment's Wait* (1901, watercolour, 29 1/4 x 46 1/2 ins / 74 x 118 cm) GBP 13,200. LONDON, 29 Oct 1991, *Jewel Box* (1897, pencil and watercolour, 19 1/4 x 14 ins / 48.9 x 34.7 cm) GBP 5,500. LONDON, 3 June 1992, *Christmas Holly* (1901, watercolour, 29 1/2 x 48 1/2 ins / 75 x 123 cm) GBP 9,900. NEW YORK, 30 Oct 1992, *The Three Sisters* (1902, watercolour, 30 1/2 x 10 1/4 ins / 77.5 x 25.8 cm) USD 12,100. LONDON, 11 June 1993, *Will you Have a Taste?* (pencil and watercolour, 18 3/4 x 26 1/2 ins / 47.6 x 67.3 cm) GBP 9,200. EDINBURGH, 9 June 1994, *Sweets* (1906, watercolour, 18 x 27 ins / 45.7 x 68.6 cm) GBP 8,625. LONDON, 6 Nov 1995, *When the Work Is Done* (1895, watercolour, 31 x 48 ins / 78.8 x 121.9 cm) GBP 16,100. LONDON, 6 Nov 1996, *News from Home* (oil on panel, 13 1/2 x 8 1/4 ins / 34 x 21 cm) GBP 2,070. LONDON, 3 June 1999, *Two Girls in an Interior Winding a Skein of Wool* (1899, pencil and watercolour heightened with gouache, 13 x 21 ins / 33 x 53 cm) GBP 12,500. LONDON, 9 June 1999, *Pot Luck* (1898, oil on canvas, 18 x 26 ins / 46 x 66 cm) GBP 17,000. NEWBURY, 6 Sept 2000, *Two Figures in an Interior Winding Wool* (watercolour, 12 x 18 ins / 30 x 46 cm) GBP 13,000. LONDON, 30 Nov 2000, *Best Friends* (oil on canvas, 24 x 17 ins / 61 x 42 cm) GBP 21,000. LONDON, 26 Sept 2001, *Young Girls* (1886, oil on panel, a pair, 13 x 8 ins / 34 x 21 cm) GBP 13,000. LONDON, 5 Nov 2001, *The Knitting Lesson* (1893, watercolour, 29 x 49 ins / 74 x 124 cm) GBP 19,000. LEYBURN, 21 Nov 2002, *Young Girl Holding a Doll and an Orange* (1892, oil on panel, 13 x 8 ins / 34 x 20 cm) GBP 3,800. VICTORIA, 13 Oct 2003, *Broken Hoop* (watercolour, 18 x 26 ins / 46 x 66 cm) AUD 25,000. LONDON, 19 Nov 2003, *Blackberry Picking* (1904, oil on canvas, 30 x 20 ins / 77 x 51 cm) GBP 11,000. LONDON, 8 June 2004, *Shelling Peas* (1892, watercolour, 15 x 11 ins / 39 x 28 cm) GBP 8,500. LONDON, 16 June 2004, *Shelling Peas* (1892, oil on canvas, 30 x 20 ins / 77 x 51 cm) GBP 13,000.

SMITH, Catterson. See **SMITH Stephen Catterson, the Elder** and **the Younger**

SMITH, Charles
British, 18th - 19th century.
Born c. 1749, in the Orkney Islands; died 19 December 1824, in Leith (Edinburgh), Scotland.
Painter, engraver. Mythological subjects, portraits.

Charles Smith studied art in London. He is known to have been living in Edinburgh in 1793. He then went to the East Indies, where he became painter to the great Mongol. He returned to London in 1796, where he exhibited paintings entitled *Andromeda, Cyneus* and *Iphigenia*. He took part in London exhibitions at the Society of Artists and particularly at the Royal Academy from 1776. He etched a self-portrait.

AUCTION RECORDS:
LONDON, 4 March 1911, *Lacemaker* (1803) GBP 11; *Basket Maker* (1804) GBP 9.

SMITH, Charles
British, 19th century.
Active in London.
Sculptor.

Charles Smith was the son of James Smith. He exhibited his work in London from 1820 until 1833. He produced scenes for Durham Cathedral.

SMITH, Charles
British, 19th century.
Active in London during the first half of the 19th century.
Painter.

Charles Smith exhibited his work in London from 1815 until 1829.

SMITH, Charles
British, 19th - 20th century.
Painter. Landscapes with figures, landscapes.

Charles Smith was active in Greenwich. He exhibited his work in London from 1857 until 1908.

AUCTION RECORDS:
LONDON, 3 June 1988, *Fisherman on the Banks of a Welsh River* (oil on canvas, 19 x 24 ins / 48 x 61 cm) GBP 550. NEW YORK, 26 May 1992, *Peasant Woman near a Stream* (1881, oil on canvas/card, 19 1/4 x 24 1/4 ins / 48.8 x 61.4 cm) USD 1,320. LONDON, 9 June 1994, *Salisbury Bridge* (oil on card, 12 x 18 ins / 30.5 x 45.5 cm) GBP 1,150. CHESTER, 6 Nov 2002, *Valley in North Wales* (1867, oil on canvas, 24 x 33 ins / 61 x 85 cm) GBP 1,700. LONDON, 29 May 2003, *Devon Coast* (oil on canvas, 16 x 40 ins / 41 x 102 cm) GBP 1,900.

SMITH, Charles Hamilton (Lt. Col.)
British, 19th century.
Born 1776, in Vrommenhofen (East Flanders); died 1859, in Plymouth.
Draughtsman, watercolourist. Military subjects, costume studies.

Charles Hamilton Smith was an officer. He drew uniforms, costumes, arms and antiquities.

MUSEUMS AND GALLERIES:
LONDON (Victoria and Albert Mus.): several drawings.

SMITH, Charles Harriot
British, 19th century.
Born 1792; died 27 October 1864.
Active in London.
Sculptor, architect.

Charles Harriot Smith studied at the Royal Academy in London. He exhibited busts in London from 1809 until 1824.

SMITH, Charles John
British, 19th century.
Born 1803, in Chelsea; died 23 November 1838, in Chelsea.
Engraver (burin).

Charles John Smith studied under Charles Pye. He built up a solid reputation for himself and found plenty of work, notably with contemporary topographical publications. In 1828 he produced a number of autographs of famous people from the reign of Richard II to that of Charles II. He was a member of the London Antique Dealers Association.

SMITH, Charles Loraine
British, 18th - 19th century.
Born 1751; died 1835.
Active in Enderby.
Painter. Hunting scenes, horses.

AUCTION RECORDS:
LONDON, 22 Feb 1935, *Dick Knight of the Pytchley*, GBP 57.

SMITH, Charles Raymond
British, 19th century.
Active from 1842 to 1876.
Sculptor.

Charles Raymond Smith carved monuments and commemorative plaques.

SMITH, Charles William
American, 20th century.
Born 22 June 1893, in Lofton (Virginia); died 1987.
Painter, illustrator.

Charles William Smith was taught by Richard N. Brook, Sergeant Kendall and M. Ligeron in Paris. He was a member of the American Artists Professional League.

SMITH, Clifford
British, 19th century.
Active in London.
Miniaturist.

Clifford Smith exhibited five miniatures at the Royal Academy from 1823 until 1855.

SMITH, Colvin
British, 19th century.
Born 1795, in Brechin; died 21 July 1875, in Edinburgh.
Painter.

Colvin Smith studied at the schools of the Royal Academy in London, then went to perfect his skills in Belgium and Italy. On his return he settled in Edinburgh as a portrait painter, where he was very successful. He was a member of the Royal Scottish Academy. He exhibited his work in London from 1830 until 1871.

One of his best-known works is a portrait of *Walter Scott*, which he had to reproduce more than 20 times.

MUSEUMS AND GALLERIES:
EDINBURGH (Scottish National Portrait Gallery): *Sir Ralph Abercromby* (oil on canvas); *Sir James Mackintosh* (oil on canvas); *Robert Saunders Dundas, 2nd Viscount Melville* (oil on canvas); *Sir Walter Scott* (oil on canvas) - GLASGOW: *Elisabeth Steven, Dolmadie and Bellahouston; Lord Jeffrey; Moses Steven, Dolmadie and Bellahouston* - MONTREAL (Learmont): *Sir Walter Scott* - OXFORD (Ashmolean Mus.): *Walter Scott* (painting).

AUCTION RECORDS:
LONDON, 14 June 1911, *Portrait of the Duke of Gordon,* GBP 25. LONDON, 9 May 1996, *Head and Shoulder Portrait of Francis, Lord Jeffery, in a Black Suit* (oil on canvas, 36 x 28 ins / 91.5 x 71 cm) GBP 2,185. LONDON, 21 March 2001, *Portrait of Francis Lord Jeffrey Wearing a Black Coat and White Stock* (oil on canvas, 35 x 28 ins / 90 x 70 cm) GBP 3,000. EDINBURGH, 28 May 2004, *Full Length Portrait of George Patrick Skene and his Son with Guns and Dog* (oil on canvas, 94 x 60 ins / 240 x 152 cm) GBP 6,500.

SMITH, Constance J.
British, 19th century.
Active in Bath.
Miniaturist.

Constance J. Smith exhibited her work in London, particularly at the Royal Academy from 1890.

SMITH, Constant or Constantin Louis Félix
French, 19th century.
Born 18 November 1788, in Paris; died 10 September 1873, in Paris.
Painter. History painting, portraits, genre scenes.

C. Smith was admitted to the École des Beaux-Arts on 16 November 1813 and was a pupil of David and Girodet. He exhibited at the Salon from 1817 to 1827 and was awarded a medal in 1817.

MUSEUMS AND GALLERIES:
AMIENS: *Andromach at the Tomb of Hector* - ORLÉANS: *Italian Landscape* - VERSAILLES: *Amerigo Vespucci; Amerigo Vespucci; Marie Adélaïde of Savoy, Duchess of Bourgogne.*

SMITH, Dana
American, 19th century.
Born in New Hampshire; died 1901.
Painter.

Dana Smith lived in Franklin and painted scenes of local life, often with panoramic views, in a style dubbed 'Naive'.

SMITH, David
British, 18th century.
Active in Edinburgh in 1769.
Engraver.

SMITH, David Roland
American, 20th century.
Born 9 March 1906, in Decatur (Indiana); died 23 May 1965, in Bolton Landing (New York State), in a car accident.
Sculptor, painter, draughtsman.
Group: American Abstract Artists (AAA). School of New York.

David Roland Smith took evening classes at the Art Students League in New York in 1926. He studied painting and engraving there full-time from 1927 to 1932 and was taught by Jan Mayulka (until 1931), Allan Lewis, John Sloan and Kimon Nicolaides. He married the painter Dorothy Dehner in 1927. Although he worked as an illustrator on several magazines, he was forced by circumstances to have various jobs unrelated to art until 1945, including working on oil tankers in the navy and assembling parts for tanks and locomotives during World War II.

In 1930, Smith met the Russian-born American artist John Graham, who introduced him to European avant-garde art. In 1935-1936 he visited Europe, working for a time in Stanley Hayter's studio in Paris, and also visiting Greece, Crete, London and Russia. In 1937, he became a member of the American Abstract Artists (AAA) and worked for the Works Project Administration Federal Arts Project from 1937 to 1939. He met Robert Motherwell in 1947, and Helen Frankenthaler and Kenneth Noland in 1950. In 1961, he refused the third prize at the Carnegie Institute Pittsburgh international exhibition. During his life he gave numerous lectures in various art schools and institutions. He won the Creative Arts Award from Brandeis University in 1964.

Around 1930, Smith was still painting in an Abstract Surrealist style. After making collages that were halfway between painting and sculpture, he began in 1932 to sculpt in polychrome wood, using coral and metal wire; in 1933 he used soldering in his metal sculptures for the first time. He was the first sculptor to work in this way in the USA. From that time on, his work had its roots both in the Expressionist Cubism of Picasso and the metallic sculptures of Gonzalez, whom he met in 1930 on the magazine *Cahiers d'Art*, and also a little in Surrealism.

Smith produced a number of works in a more traditional style, protesting against institutional violence, as in the series of *Medals of Dishonor* (1937-1940), and a few small bronzes such as *The Rape* (1945). However, he continued until about 1960 to be linked to the use of a minimal figuration borrowed from Picasso and the Surrealists. From the point of view of form, his sculptures of the 1930s and 1940s were still created from assemblages of metal *objets trouvés* (wheels, various instruments) - particularly in the series *Agricola* (1950) - the principle of collage or addition remaiing a constant, reworked in different materials. Pieces like *Song of an Irish Blacksmith* (1949-1950) or *Hudson River Landscape* (1951, interpreted as a synthesis of his travels between the towns of Albany and Poughkeepsie) emphasise the flexibility of the metal line. Later *Tanks-Totems*, about 1955, would develop garlands of small symbols in space giving the impression of man in a dialectic relationship with heavy masses.

Smith's work became more monumental after 1960. The first of his work in this new style, *Zigs*, created in 1961 from assemblages of steel sheets, returned to the problem of integrating colour and form. It was followed by the 27 pieces in the *Voltri* series, created in 30 days in Italy in 1962; and finally the famous *Cubis* series (28 pieces produced between 1961 and 1965), in which the Constructivist heritage can be seen. Always of the opinion that metal was the material of the 20th century and global industrialisation, in *Cubis*, Smith piles up parallelepipeds in unstable equilibrium, cubes or rectangles enclosed in polished stainless steel, whose extremely reduced weight is in contradiction with the sensations of heavy mass that they communicate. He was a very prolific artist, producing an estimated 600 sculptures between 1931 and 1965 (some in soldered metal, others carved in marble, bronze, and slate), as well as thousands of drawings and paintings.

Smith participated in collective exhibitions, including: the Print Club, Philadelphia (1930); American Abstract Artists, Fine Arts Galleries, New York, (1938); New York World's Fair (1939); Annual Exhibition, Whitney Museum of American Art (1941); São Paulo Biennale (1951); *Douze Peintres et Sculpteurs Américains Contemporains* (*Twelve Contemporary American Painters and Sculptors*), Musée National d'Art Moderne, Paris (1953); Venice Biennale (1954, 1958); Exposition Internationale de Sculpture Contemporaine, Musée Rodin, Paris (1956); Documenta II, Kassel (1959); and *The Art of Assemblage*, MoMA, New York. Posthumous exhibitions include: *L'Art du Réel aux USA 1948-1968* (*The Art of the Real, USA, 1948-1968*), at the Centre National d'Art Contemporain, Paris, in 1968.

The first solo exhibition of Smith's work was held at the East River Gallery, New York in 1938. This was followed by shows at: the St Paul Gallery and School of Art, New York (1940); Willard Gallery, New York (1940-1943, 1950-1954, 1956); Skidmore College, Saratoga Springs, New York (1942, 1947); travelling exhibition (1947); MoMA, New York (1957); Carnegie Institute, Pittsburgh (1961); and the Institute of Contemporary Art, University of Pennsylvania, Philadelphia (1964).

Posthumous solo exhibitions include: County Museum, Los Angeles (1965); Rijksmuseum Kröller-Müller in Otterlo, Tate Gallery in London, Kunsthalle in Basel, Kunsthalle in Nuremberg and Wilhelm-Lehmbruck Museum in Duisburg (1966); Solomon R. Guggenheim Museum, New York, and Museum of Art, Dallas (1969); Corcoran Gallery of Art, Washington (1970); Staatsgalerie, Stuttgart (1976); Hirshhorn Museum and Sculpture Garden, and National Gallery of Art, Washington (1982); Whitechapel Art Gallery, London (1986); Institut d'Art Moderne, Valence (1996); and *Dessins de David Smith. Un Choix d'Alain Kirili* (*Drawings by David Smith. Chosen by Alain Kirili*), at the Chapelle des Petits-Augustins, Paris (2003).

Bibliography:

Goossen, E.C., *'David Smith'* in *Arts Magazine*, periodical, New York, March, 1956. *David Smith*, exhibition catalogue, Marlborough-Gerson Gall., New York, 1964. *David Smith 1906-1965*, exhibition catalogue, The Harvard University Art Museums-Fogg Art Museum, Cambridge (MA), 1966. Goossen, E.C., *L'Art du réel, U.S.A., 1948-1968*, exhibition catalogue, Gal. nationales du Grand Palais, Paris, 1968. *'David Smith'* in *L'Art Vivant*, periodical, Maeght, Paris, June 1969. Krauss, Rosalind E., *The Sculpture of David Smith. A catalogue Raisonné*, Garland, New York, London, 1977. Wilkin, Karen, *David Smith*, Abbeville Press, New York, 1984. Freas, J., *David Smith: Drawings of the Fifties*, Anthony d'Offay Gall., London, 1988. *David Smith in Italy*, Prada Milano Arte, Milan, 1995. *Dessins de David Smith. Un chois d'Alain Kirili*, exhibition catalogue, École des Beaux-Arts, Paris, 2003. Smith, David, *David Smith. Related Clues: Drawings, Paintings and Sculptures 1931-1964*, Gagosian Gallery, New York, 2004.

Museums and Galleries:

Boston (MFA): *Cubi XVIII* (1964, polished stainless steel) - Buffalo (Albright-Knox AG): *Cubi XVI* - Cambridge, MA (Fogg AM, Harvard University) - Canberra (Nat. Gal. of Australia): *25 Planes* (1958) - Chicago (AI): *Cubi VII* - Cleveland (MA) - Cologne (Mus. Ludwig) - Dallas (MA): *Untitled* (1962, spray paint on paper); *Cubi XVII* (1963, polished steel) - Detroit (IA): *Cubi I* - Houston (MFA): *Two Circles Sentinel* (1961) - Indianapolis (MA): *Egyptian Barnyard* (sculpture) - Jerusalem (Israel Mus.): *Cubi VI* - London (Tate Collection): *Cubi XIX* (1964, stainless steel, sculpture) - Los Angeles (County MA): *Cubi XXIII* - Minneapolis (Walker Art Center): *Cubi IX* (1961, stainless steel) - New York (Metropolitan Mus. of Art): *Becca* (1965) - New York (MoMA): *Cubi X*; *Sentinelle* (1961) - New York (Solomon R. Guggenheim Mus.): *Cubi XXVII* - New York (Whitney Mus. of American Art): *Lectern Sentinel* (1961) - Otterlo (Kröller-Müller Mus.) - Philadelphia (MA): *Two Box Structures* (1961) - Pittsburgh (Carnegie MA): *Cubi XXIV* (1964, sculpture) - San Francisco (California Palace of the Legion of Honor): *Untitled* (1962, spray enamel/paper) - San Francisco (De Young Mus.): *Zig V* (1961, painted steel) - San Francisco (MoMA): *Noon Sun* (1959, steel); *Untitled (Brooklyn)* (c. 1935, gelatin silver print) - Seattle (AM): *Fifteen Planes* (1958) - St Louis (AM): *Cubi XIV* - Toronto (AG of Ontario): *Untitled* (1964) - Washington DC (Hirshhorn Mus. and Sculpture Garden): *Sentinel II* (1956-1957, stainless steel); *Cubi XII* (1963, stainless steel) - Washington DC (NGA): *Sentinel I* (1956, steel); *Circle I* (1962, painted steel); *Cubi XXVI* (1965, steel) - Washington DC (Smithsonian American AM): *Europa and Calf* (1956-1957, bronze/poured and hammered/stone base); *Untitled* (c. 1951, ink and tempera/paper).

Auction records:

New York, 11 Dec 1963, *Agricola* (steel) USD 8,750. New York, 27 Jan 1966, *Low Landscape* (bronze) USD 3,500. New York, 18 Nov 1970, *Amusement Park* (iron) USD 25,000. New York, 17 Nov 1971, *Composition* (iron) USD 20,000. New York, 26 Oct 1972, *Zig II* (steel) USD 80,000. New York, 4 May 1973, *Interior* (painted iron and bronze) USD 33,000. New York, 3 May 1974, *Structure of Arches* (steel and copper) USD 52,500. New York, 20 Oct 1977, *Composition* (1953, wrought iron, h. 21 1/2 ins / 54.5 cm, w. 40 1/2 ins/103 cm) USD 35,000. New York, 3 Nov 1978, *Jurassic Bird* (1945, steel, 25 1/2 x 35 1/4 x 7 1/2 ins / 65 x 89.5 x 19 cm) USD 75,000. New York, 8 Nov 1979, *Voltri II* (1962, steel, 77 3/4 x 27 1/4 x 9 1/4 ins / 197.4 x 69.2 x 23.7 cm) USD 135,000. New York, 10 Nov 1982, *2 Doors* (1964, polished steel, 111 x 93 1/2 x 17 1/2 ins / 281 x 237.5 x 44.5 cm) USD 520,000. New York, 11 May 1983, *Untitled* (1952, brush, black ink and tempera/paper, 15 3/4 x 20 1/4 ins / 40 x 51.5 cm) USD 9,500. New York, 1 Nov 1984, *Circles and Angles* (1959, polished and wrought steel, 25 3/4 x 41 1/2 x 8 1/2 ins / 65.5 x 105.5 x 21.5 cm) USD 155,000. New York, 1 May 1985, *The Forest* (1950, forged and painted steel, 40 x 38 x 4 3/4 ins / 101.5 x 96.5 x 12 cm) USD 240,000. New York, 6 Nov 1985, *Untitled* (1963, ink/paper, 16 x 20 1/2 ins / 39.8 x 52 cm) USD 3,500. New York, 6 May 1986, *VB XXIII* (1963, forged steel, 69 1/2 x 29 x 24 ins / 176.5 x 72.8 x 61 cm) USD 1,200,000. New York, 11 Nov 1986, *Two Circles on Yellow and Green* (1959, oil on canvas, 106 x 49 ins / 269.2 x 124.5 cm) USD 28,000. New York, 4 May 1987, *8 Planes 7 Bars* (1957-1958, stainless steel, 124 3/4 x 77 x 22 3/4 ins / 316.9 x 195.6 x 57.8 cm) USD 900,000. New York, 20 Feb 1988, *Untitled* (1953, ink/paper, 16 x 20 1/2 ins / 39.8 x 52.1 cm) USD 7,150. New York, 4 May 1988, *Untitled* (1959, 17 1/2 x 11 1/2 ins / 44.6 x 29.1 cm) USD 6,050. New York, 8 Oct 1988, *Untitled* (1959, ink and egg tempera/paper, 26 x 39 1/2 ins / 66.1 x 100.3 cm) USD 13,200. New York, 14 Feb 1989, *Medal of Dishonor: Bombed Hospital and Ships full of Refugees* (1939, bronze plaque fixed on a wooden panel, 13 3/4 x 15 1/4 x 1 ins / 35 x 39 x 2.7 cm) USD 31,900. New York, 3 May 1989, *Woman on Horseback* (1940, bronze, h. 8 ins / 20.2 cm) USD 49,500. New York, 23 Feb 1990, *Torso* (1937, iron on a wooden plinth, 15 3/4 x 4 1/4 x 8 ins / 40.3 x 10.8 x 20.3 cm) USD 93,500. New York, 4 Oct 1990, *Musician* (1944, painted welded steel, 179 x 9 x 6 ins / 454.7 x 22.8 x 15.2 cm) USD 148,500. New York, 12 Nov 1991, *Albany IX* (1960, oil/welded steel, 17 3/4 x 20 1/4 x 4 3/4 ins / 45 x 51.5 x 12 cm) USD 88,000. New York, 6 May 1992, *Ritual* (forged steel, 9 3/4 x 10 1/2 x 4 ins / 24.7 x 26.6 x 10.2 cm) USD 28,600. New York, 17 Nov 1992, *Untitled* (1937, welded iron, 16 1/2 x 7 3/4 x 5 ins / 42.2 x 19.7 x 12.7 cm) USD 93,500. New York, 3 May 1993, *Construction No 35* (steel, 6 1/2 x 11 1/4 x 3 1/4 ins / 16.5 x 28.6 x 8.5 cm) USD 60,250; *Voltrix IX* (steel, 78 1/2 x 32 x 11 3/4 ins / 199.4 x 81.3 x 29.8 cm) USD 233,500. New York, 9 Nov 1993, *Coastguard Ship* (1960, painted steel, 93 3/4 x 33 1/2 x 26 ins / 238 x 85.4 x 66.3 cm) USD

816,500. NEW YORK, 4 May 1994, *Cubi V* (1963, polished stainless steel, 96 x 73 x 22 ins / 243.8 x 185.4 x 55.9 cm) USD 4,072,500. NEW YORK, 2 May 1995, *Three Circles and Planes* (1959, stainless steel, 112 1/2 x 41 1/2 x 17 1/4 ins / 285.8 x 105.4 x 44.1 cm) USD 1,982,500. NEW YORK, 3 May 1995, *Chinese Restaurant* (1959, spray paint/canvas, 101 1/4 x 50 ins / 257.2 x 127 cm) USD 145,500. NEW YORK, 15 Nov 1995, *Compass Circle* (1962, steel, 31 1/4 x 18 x 6 ins / 79.4 x 45.7 x 15.2 cm) USD 233,500. NEW YORK, 8 May 1996, *Construction of a Still-life* (1938, iron, 14 x 15 1/4 x 8 ins / 35.6 x 38.7 x 20.3 cm) USD 222,500. NEW YORK, 19 Nov 1996, *Untitled* (1938, pen, black ink, watercolour/paper/Masonite, 5 x 3 3/4 ins / 12.7 x 9.5 cm) USD 4,600. NEW YORK, 19 Nov 1996, *Agricola X* (1952, red painted steel, 35 x 13 x 27 ins / 88 x 32.1 x 68.3 cm) USD 310,500. NEW YORK, 20 Nov 1996, *Forging VI* (1955, stainless steel, 79 x 9 x 9 ins / 200.7 x 22.8 x 22.8 cm) USD 272,000. NEW YORK, 7 May 1997, *Family Totem* (1951, painted steel, 32 x 22 x 6 ins / 81.3 x 55.9 x 15.2 cm) USD 409,500. NEW YORK, 8 May 1997, *To be a Golden Harbour* (1959, spray/canvas, 91 ins / 231 cm, 3 1/4 x 51 3/4 ins/8 x 131.4 cm) USD 57,500. NEW YORK, 18 Nov 1997, *Puritan Landscape* (1946, welded steel, bronze, iron and nickel, 28 1/2 x 15 x 10 ins / 72.4 x 38.1 x 25.4 cm) USD 123,500. NEW YORK, 18-19 Nov 1997, *Puritan Landscape* (1946, steel, bronze, iron and nickel, 28 1/2 x 15 x 10 ins / 72.4 x 38.1 x 25.4 cm) USD 123,500. NEW YORK, 18 May 1999, *Untitled* (1933, oil on canvas, 26 x 35 ins / 65 x 90 cm) USD 14,000. NEW YORK, 18 May 1999, *Perfidious Albion* (1945-1946, green patinated bronze, 14 x 7x4 ins / 36 x 17x11 cm) USD 220,000. NEW YORK, 9 May 2000, *Tempus Fugit* (1951, welded iron, 29 x 11x10 ins / 74 x 29x25 cm) USD 180,000. NEW YORK, 18 May 2000, *Untitled* (spray paint on paper, 13 x 19 ins / 33 x 48 cm) USD 8,000. NEW YORK, 16 May 2001, *Untitled* (1956, ink, 11 x 8 ins / 27 x 21 cm) USD 6,000. NEW YORK, 16 May 2001, *Untitled - Circle Studies* (1962, ink and pencil, 11 x 8 ins / 27 x 21 cm) USD 17,000. NEW YORK, 15 May 2002, *Untitled* (1959, ink, 27 x 40 ins / 69 x 101 cm) USD 26,000. NEW YORK, 26 Sept 2002, *Untitled* (1959, spray enamel on paper, 17 x 11 ins / 44 x 29 cm) USD 17,000. NEW YORK, 11 Nov 2003, *Family Totem* (1951, painted steel, 32 x 22x6 ins / 81 x 56x15 cm) USD 1,100,000. NEW YORK, 12 Nov 2003, *Walking Dida* (1959, green patinated bronze, 28 x 21x5 ins / 72 x 53x13 cm) USD 1,300,000. NEW YORK, 11 May 2004, *Little Albany IX* (1960, painted steel, 18 x 20x4 ins / 46 x 52x11 cm) USD 800,000. NEW YORK, 12 May 2004, *Untitled* (1960, welded steel, 99 x 35x9 ins / 251 x 88x22 cm) USD 2,700,000.

SMITH, Duncan
American, 20th century.
Born 21 October 1877, in Charlottesville (Virginia); died 1934, in Charlottesville.
Painter, decorative designer, illustrator.

Duncan Smith was a student of Cox, Twatchtmann and De Camp.

SMITH, E. Boyd
American, 19th - 20th century.
Born 1860, in St John (New Brunswick); died 1943.
Draughtsman, writer.

E. Boyd Smith studied in France. He wrote and illustrated several works including: the *Story of Pocahontas and Captain John Smith*, 1906; *Story of Noah's Ark*, 1909; *Railroad Book*, 1913; *In the Land of Make Believe*, 1916; *After They Came Out of the Ark*, 1918; and *Country Book*, 1924. He also illustrated other works such as: Harris' *Plantation Pageants*, 1899; Defoe's *Robinson Crusoe*, 1909; Brown's *John of the Woods*, 1909; and Scott's *Ivanhoe*, 1913.

BIBLIOGRAPHY:

Osterwalder, Marcus (ed.), *Dictionnaire des illustrateurs 1800-1914*, Ides et Calendes, Neuchâtel, 1989.

AUCTION RECORDS:

NEW YORK, 24 June 1988, *Late Afternoon in Summer* (oil on canvas, 14 3/4 x 21 1/2 ins / 37.5 x 54.6 cm) USD 16,500. NEW YORK, 14 Feb 1990, *Young Girl Reading under a Tree* (oil on canvas/synthetic resin, 16 3/4 x 9 3/4 ins / 42.5 x 24.7 cm) USD 2,860. NEW YORK, 3 Dec 1996, *Commerce* (oil on canvas, 52 x 39 ins / 132 x 99 cm) USD 3,680. MAINE, 11 Sept 1999, *Haying, Brittany* (c. 1890, oil on canvas, 10 x 12 ins / 25 x 30 cm) USD 2,900. MILFORD, 11 May 2000, *Resting by River, France* (oil on canvas on board, 18 x 14 ins / 46 x 36 cm) USD 16,000. NEW YORK, 28 Nov 2000, *Haystacks in a Green Field* (oil on canvas, 13 x 22 ins / 33 x 56 cm) USD 4,500. CINCINNATI, 7 Sept 2003, *Haystacks near Auvers* (oil on canvas on board, 12 x 14 ins / 30 x 36 cm) USD 1,700.

SMITH, Edith Heckstall
British, 19th century.
Painter, watercolourist. Landscapes with figures.

Edith Heckstall Smith exhibited her work from 1827.

MUSEUMS AND GALLERIES:

LONDON (Victoria and Albert Mus.): *Stormy Landscape with Ruins and Rider*.

AUCTION RECORDS:

LONDON, 25 Jan 1989, *Young Shepherd and his Flock* (watercolour, 29 1/4 x 19 1/2 ins / 74 x 49.5 cm) GBP 990.

SMITH, Edward, or Smyth
Irish, 18th - 19th century.
Born 1746, in County Meath; died 2 August 1812, in Dublin.
Sculptor.

Edward Smith was the father of the sculptor John Smith. He studied under Verpyle in Dublin. His first important work was a statue of Dr Lucas at the Dublin Stock Exchange in 1772. This piece established his reputation, but until 1802 he had very little opportunity to produce anything other than decorative ornaments for the homes of the Irish upper classes. This situation changed as a result of the influence of the architect Gordon. Among other projects he produced 12 figures representing the rivers of Ireland to decorate the Dublin Customs Office. He also carved *Clemency, Justice, Moses, Pardon* and *Minerva* for the law courts, works which are very highly regarded pieces in the collection of Irish art. He also created a very remarkable collection of cherubs' heads to decorate the ceiling of the chapel in Dublin castle. He earned a great deal of money, but did not save any of it, which forced him to accept the post of sculpture teacher at the Dublin school in 1806.

MUSEUMS AND GALLERIES:

DUBLIN: *George II* (bust).

SMITH, Edward
British, 19th century.
Active in Liverpool.
Painter.

MUSEUMS AND GALLERIES:

LIVERPOOL: *Edward Rushton*.

AUCTION RECORDS:

LONDON, 21 March 1979, *Portrait of Katherine Stackhouse, later Mrs Jonathan Rashleigh* (oil on canvas, 29 1/2 x 24 1/2 ins / 75 x 62 cm) GBP 1,100.

SMITH, Edward
British, 19th century.
Active in London from 1823 to 1851.
Engraver (burin).

Edward Smith engraved portraits and reproductions of paintings.

SMITH, Edward Blount
British, 19th century.
Died 19 June 1899, in London.
Painter. Landscapes.

Edward Blount Smith exhibited his work in London from 1877.

SMITH, Edwin Dalton
British, 19th century.
Born 23 October 1800, in London; died c. 1847.
Miniaturist. Flowers.

Edwin Dalton Smith was the son and student of Anker Smith. He exhibited 66 miniatures at the Royal Academy, 13 on Suffolk Street and 3 at the New Water-Colour Society. He is possibly the same person as Edwin Dalton.

SMITH, Elliza D. (Mrs). See **ADERS Eliza**

SMITH, Émile Joseph
French, 19th century.
Born in Paris.
Painter. Genre scenes.
Orientalism.

A pupil of Cornuet and Lobbedez, Émile Smith made his Salon debut in 1876.

SMITH, Emma
British, 18th - 19th century.
Born 1783, in London.
Painter, watercolourist, miniaturist. Historical subjects.

Emma Smith was the daughter of John Raphael Smith. She was member of the Society of Artists in Watercolours. She exhibited 33 miniatures at the Royal Academy from 1799 until 1808.

SMITH, F.
British, 19th century.
Painter. Landscapes.

SMITH, Ferdinand David
Irish, 19th century.
Born 1830; died 18 October 1855, in Dublin.
Painter. Genre scenes.

SMITH, Francis
Portuguese, 20th century.
Born 1881, in Lisbon; died 1961, in Paris.
Also active in France.
Painter (gouache), draughtsman, watercolourist. Genre scenes, still-lifes, landscapes, waterscapes, urban landscapes.

Francis Smith was a pupil of J. Ribeiro the Younger, Luciano Freire and Constantino Fernandes in Lisbon, then of Jean-Paul Laurens at the Académie Julian in Paris. Although he lived in Paris, he retained his Portuguese nationality and made many visits to his native country.

He featured in many collective exhibitions including: *Free Art*, Lisbon (1911, 1934); Exposition Universelle, Paris (1937); *Portugal in the work of Francis Smith*, Portuguese Cultural Centre, Gulbenkian Foundation, Paris (1969); drawings, Casa de Portugal, Paris (1972). He also participated in the Salon d'Automne, Salon des Tuileries and Salon des Peintres Témoins de leur Temps (Salon for Contemporary Painters), in Paris. A Francis Smith Prize has been created in his memory.

He painted the shores of the Mediterranean where he spent so much time, and scenes portraying the joy of life itself in is own naive style. His native Portugal played an important role in his work.

Bibliography:

Les Cahiers de la peinture, Presses artistiques, Paris, 1963. *Le Portugal dans l'œuvre de Francis Smith*, Presses des procédés d'art graphique, Paris, 1969. Warnod, Jeanine, *Dessins de Francis Smith*, Casa de Portugal, Paris, 1972. Arnáiz, José Manuel/López Jiménez, Javier/Merchán Díaz, Manuel (ed.), '*Cien años de pintura en Espana y Portugal (1830-1930)*' in vol. X, Antiqvaria, Madrid, 1993.

Museums and Galleries:

Lisbon (MM) - Lisbon (Mus. do Chiado) - Paris (Mus. des Arts d'Afrique et d'Océanie) - Paris (Mus. du Petit Palais).

Auction records:

Paris, 29 Oct 1925, *Street in Lisbon*, FRF 1,650. Paris, 2 Dec 1938, *Landscape in Portugal*, FRF 420; *Vase of Flowers*, FRF 110. Paris, 30 Nov- 1 Dec 1942, *Landscape in Portugal* (gouache) FRF 6,000. Paris, July 1946, *Steep Street and Village Church, Portugal* (watercolour and gouache) FRF 4,200. Paris, 6 April 1951, *Figure Before the Entrance to a Park* (1930, gouache) FRF 4,300. Paris, 28 May 1954, *View of Portugal*, FRF 25,100. Paris, 15 June 1970, *Lane in Portugal* (gouache) FRF 5,100. Paris, 3 Dec 1972, *Street in Portugal* (watercolour) FRF 6,000. Paris, 16 May 1973, *Village Scene in Portugal*, FRF 17,000. Versailles, 29 Feb 1976, *Meadow in Flower* (oil on panel, 12 1/2 x 16 1/2 ins / 32 x 42 cm) FRF 6,000. Versailles, 7 Nov 1976, *Portuguese Motherhood* (gouache, 19 x 24 3/4 ins / 48 x 63 cm) FRF 5,000. Paris, 6 April 1979, *Village in Portugal* (gouache, 18 x 15 ins / 46 x 38 cm) FRF 4,200. Versailles, 7 May 1980, *White Houses in Portugal* (1932, oil on canvas, 21 1/2 x 18 ins / 54.5 x 46 cm) FRF 8,000. Versailles, 29 Nov 1981, *Young Women on the Terrace Before the Village in Portugal* (oil on paper remounted/canvas, 59 x 39 3/4 ins / 150 x 101 cm) FRF 24,000. Paris, 15 June 1983, *Courtyard in Portugal* (1927, oil on canvas, 25 1/2 x 19 3/4 ins / 65 x 50 cm) FRF 21,100. Paris, 12 June 1985, *Village in Portugal* (gouache, 19 x 15 3/4 ins / 48 x 40 cm) FRF 13,000. La Varenne-St-Hilaire, 23 Oct 1988, *Young Women and Children in the Courtyard of the Hacienda* (oil on canvas, 24 x 19 3/4 ins / 61 x 50 cm) FRF 66,000. Paris, 22 Nov 1988, *Seashore* (1927, oil on canvas, 28 3/4 x 23 1/2 ins / 73 x 60 cm) FRF 140,000. Paris, 18 May 1989, *Courtyard of a Hacienda* (oil on panel, 18 x 15 ins / 46 x 38 cm) FRF 6,800. Strasbourg, 29 Nov 1989, *In the Garden* (Indian ink, 10 1/4 x 7 ins / 26 x 18 cm) FRF 6,500. Paris, 20 Feb 1990, *Library* (oil on panel, 19 1/4 x 13 3/4 ins / 49 x 35 cm) FRF 53,000. Paris, 13 June 1990, *Country Festival* (oil on canvas, 18 x 22 ins / 46 x 55 cm) FRF 100,000. Calais, 9 Dec 1990, *Grey Weather by the Coast* (1927, oil on panel, 13 x 16 1/2 ins / 33 x 42 cm) FRF 41,000. Nancy, 24 Nov 1991, *Village in Portugal* (oil on canvas, 24 3/4 x 20 1/2 ins / 63 x 52 cm) FRF 82,500. Paris, 18 May 1992, *Garden in Portugal* (gouache, 9 x 12 1/4 ins / 23 x 31 cm) FRF 13,000. Calais, 5 July 1992, *Lively Lane in Portugal* (oil on canvas, 16 1/4 x 13 ins / 41 x 33 cm) FRF 51,000. L'Isle-Adam, 20 Dec 1992, *Paris, Street Scene* (oil on canvas, 28 3/4 x 23 1/2 ins / 73 x 60 cm) FRF 130,000. Calais, 14 March 1993, *Clown* (watercolour and gouache, 9 1/2 x 7 1/2 ins / 24 x 19 cm) FRF 22,200. Paris, 2 June 1993, *Nanny, Garden in Portugal* (oil on canvas, 24 x 19 3/4 ins / 61 x 50 cm) FRF 62,000. Paris, 16 Dec 1993, *Mocking Harlequin* (1934, gouache, diam. 19 ins / 48 cm) FRF 20,000. Calais, 13 March 1994, *Picnic in Portugal* (oil on canvas, 25 1/2 x 21 1/4 ins / 65 x 54 cm) FRF 108,000. Lucerne, 26 Nov 1994, *Guitarist by the Canal* (oil on canvas, 14 1/2 x 17 3/4 ins / 37 x 45 cm) CHF 11,500. Le Touquet, 21 May 1995, *Sunday Afternoon* (oil on panel, 11 x 9 ins / 28 x 23 cm) FRF 24,000. Calais, 7 July 1996, *Small Path Overlooking the Bay* (oil on canvas, 18 1/2 x 22 ins / 47 x 55 cm) FRF 66,500. New York, 10 Oct 1996, *The Nativity* (oil on canvas, 24 x 20 ins / 61 x 50.5 cm) USD 12,650. Paris, 24 March 1997, *Farmyard* (oil on panel, 7 1/2 x 9 1/2 ins / 19 x 24 cm) FRF 21,000. New York, 13 May 1997, *Village* (oil on canvas, 28 3/4 x 21 1/4 ins / 73 x 54 cm) USD 17,250. New York, 9 Oct 1997, *Village* (oil on canvas, 28 3/4 x 23 1/2 ins / 73 x 60 cm) USD 21,850. Paris, 6 April 1998, *The Flight into Egypt* (watercolour, 9 3/4 x 7 3/4 ins / 25 x 20 cm) FRF 23,000. New York, 28 May 1999, *View of Mount Vesuvius* (oil on canvas, 26 x 54 ins / 67 x 136 cm) USD 95,000. Paris, 15 Oct 1999, *Leaving Church* (gouache, 12 x 9 ins / 31 x 23 cm) FRF 28,000. Calais, 12 March 2000, *Streets with Figures in Portugal* (oil on panel, 18 x 15 ins / 46 x 38 cm) FRF 226,000. Paris, 15 Dec 2000, *Land-*

scape with Church (oil on card, 16 x 13 ins / 41 x 33 cm) FRF 95,000. PARIS, 31 May 2001, *Portuguese Village* (1928, oil on canvas, 26 x 21 ins / 66 x 54 cm) FRF 300,000. PARIS, 31 May 2001, *Le Petit Cognet* (1955, oil on canvas, 32 x 39 ins / 81 x 100 cm) FRF 500,000. PARIS, 19 March 2002, *Stroll Out of Town* (oil on canvas, 24 x 20 ins / 61 x 50 cm) EUR 34,000. PARIS, 10 April 2002, *Petit Coignet par Brignol, Var* (oil on canvas, 20 x 24 ins / 50 x 61 cm) EUR 35,000. CALAIS, 9 Nov 2003, *Street with Figures, Montmartre, Paris* (oil on canvas, 15 x 22 ins / 38 x 55 cm) EUR 19,000. PARIS, 2 Dec 2003, *Seaside* (1930, gouache and oil on board, 24 x 18 ins / 62 x 46 cm) EUR 22,000. CALAIS, 14 March 2004, *Pink House at Montmartre* (stump, 15 x 22 ins / 38 x 55 cm) EUR 14,000. PARIS, 15 March 2004, *Street with Figures, Lisbon* (1924, gouache on card, 18 x 15 ins / 46 x 38 cm) EUR 18,000.

SMITH, Francis Drexel

American, 20th century.

Born 11 June 1874, in Chicago; died 1956.

Painter.

Francis Drexel Smith studied at the Art Institute of Chicago and was taught by John Vanderpoel, John F. Carlson and Everett L. Warner. He was a member of the American Federation of Arts.

SMITH, Francis Hopkinson or Francis Hopkins

American, 19th - 20th century.

Born 23 October 1838, in Baltimore; died 7 April 1915, in New York.

Painter, illustrator. Landscapes.

Francis Hopkinson Smith worked without a teacher. He was also a writer and an engineer.

MUSEUMS AND GALLERIES:

BUFFALO - ST LOUIS - WASHINGTON DC (National Portrait Gal.): *Elihu Vedder* (c. 1882).

AUCTION RECORDS:

WASHINGTON DC, 7 Dec 1980, *Canal Scene, Venice* (watercolour heightened with white, 18 x 25 1/2 ins / 46 x 65 cm) USD 2,500. NEW YORK, 28 Sept 1983, *Street Scene in Seville* (1882, watercolour, gouache and pencil, 14 1/4 x 24 3/4 ins / 36.5 x 63 cm) USD 4,200. NEW YORK, 30 Sept 1985, *Canal Scene in Summer* (watercolour and pencil, 14 3/4 x 23 3/4 ins / 37.5 x 60.5 cm) USD 6,000. NEW YORK, 28 May 1987, *Inn of William the Conqueror* (gouache, watercolour and charcoal, 23 1/4 x 35 1/2 ins / 59.1 x 90.2 cm) USD 31,000. NEW YORK, 26 May 1988, *Canal Scene* (watercolour, gouache and pencil/paper, 24 1/2 x 14 1/2 ins / 62.5 x 36.8 cm) USD 8,800. NEW YORK, 30 Sept 1988, *Market Day* (watercolour and gouache/paper, 14 1/4 x 25 1/4 ins / 36.2 x 64.2 cm) USD 3,300; *Venice: Fishing Port* (watercolour/paper, 14 1/2 x 24 1/2 ins / 37 x 62.2 cm) USD 8,250. NEW YORK, 1 Dec 1988, *Afternoon at the Inn of William the Conqueror in Dives in Normandy* (1905, gouache/paper, 23 1/4 x 35 1/2 ins / 59 x 90.2 cm) USD 34,100. NEW YORK, 24 May 1989, *Sunny Day in Italy* (gouache and charcoal/paper, 21 1/2 x 14 1/4 ins / 54.6 x 36.2 cm) USD 14,300. NEW YORK, 30 Nov 1989, *Courtyard of the Inn of William the Conqueror* (gouache, watercolour and charcoal/paper, 27 x 19 ins / 68.5 x 48.2 cm) USD 11,000. NEW YORK, 14 March 1991, *Venetian Staircase* (gouache and charcoal/blue paper/card, 19 1/2 x 29 1/4 ins / 49.5 x 74 cm) USD 8,800. NEW YORK, 26 Sept 1991, *Interior Courtyard of an Italian House* (1911, watercolour and gouache/tinted paper/card, 14 1/2 x 25 ins / 37 x 63.5 cm) USD 6,600. NEW YORK, 14 Nov 1991, *Battery Park in New York City* (watercolour, charcoal and gouache/brown paper, 13 1/2 x 24 1/2 ins / 34.2 x 62.2 cm) USD 3,300. NEW YORK, 18 Dec 1991, *Picnic on the Bank of a Stream* (1875, watercolour and gouache/paper, 25 1/2 x 18 1/4 ins / 64.8 x 46.4 cm) USD 2,200. NEW YORK, 12 March 1992, *Summer Morning at the Inn of William the Conqueror* (gouache and charcoal/paper, 23 1/2 x 35 3/4 ins / 59.4 x 91 cm) USD 16,500. NEW YORK, 3 Dec 1992, *Fluvial Landscape* (watercolour, charcoal and gouache/paper/card, 18 1/4 x 26 3/4 ins / 46.4 x 67.9 cm) USD 7,700. NEW YORK, 10 March 1993, *Fashionable Young Women* (1906, gouache/paper, 17 x 23 ins / 43.2 x 58.4 cm) USD 9,200. NEW YORK, 17 March 1994, *Porta della Carta* (watercolour and gouache/paper, 26 1/4 x 18 ins / 66.7 x 45.7 cm) USD 14,950. NEW YORK, 30 Oct 1996, *Bridge of Sighs, Venice* (watercolour and gouache/paper/card, 15 x 26 ins / 37.2 x 65.1 cm) USD 3,450. LONDON, 31 Oct 1996, *View of the Salute* (gouache, 13 1/2 x 22 3/4 ins / 34 x 58 cm) GBP 3,680. NEW YORK, 25 March 1997, *Canal View* (gouache/paper, 14 1/2 x 24 1/4 ins / 36.8 x 61.6 cm) USD 4,600.

SMITH, Francis or Francesco

British, 18th century.

Born possibly in Naples; died before 1780, in London.

Painter. Urban landscapes, local scenes, landscapes. Orientalism.

Francis Smith exhibited views of Vesuvius, Naples and Constantinople in London from 1768 until 1780. He travelled a lot, visiting Italy and the Orient with Lord Baltimore. At the end of his career he produced views of London.

AUCTION RECORDS:

BURNHAM, 18 March 1969, *View of London*, GBP 5,500.

SMITH, Frank E.

American, 20th century.

Born 1939, in Chicago.

Painter, engraver (including linocuts), ceramicist. AfriCobra Group.

Frank E. Smith studied at the University of Illinois, Chicago, and at Howard University, Washington DC (where he also taught from 1970 to 2002). In 1970, he joined AfriCobra (the African Commune of Bad Relevant Artists). Smith's work, consistent with the AfriCobra tradition, draws its inspiration from African iconography. He uses bright colours and sometimes includes objects, paper and pieces of cloth in his work.

Smith has taken part in various group exhibitions, such as: *Since the Harlem Renaissance: 50 Years of Afro-American Art*, Bucknell Center Gallery, Bucknell University, Lewisburg, Pennsylvania (1985); 1988, National Museum of Fine Arts, Kinshasa (The Democratic Republic of Congo); *AfriCobra: The First Twenty Years*, Nexus Contemporary Art Center, Atlanta, Georgia (1990); and *Narratives of African Art and Identity, The David C. Driskell Collection*, High Museum of Art, Atlanta (1998).

BIBLIOGRAPHY:

Narratives of African Art and Identity. The David C. Driskell Collection, group exhibition catalogue, High Museum of Art, Atlanta, 1998. Harris, Michael D., *Colored Pictures: Race and Visual Representation*, University of North Carolina Press, Chapel Hill, 2003.

SMITH, Frank Hill

American, 19th century.

Born 1841, in Boston; died 1904, in Boston.

Painter, draughtsman. Figures, portraits, genre scenes, landscapes.

Frank Hill Smith joined together his middle name and surname, thereby changing his name to Frank Hillsmith. His granddaughter was Fannie Hillsmith, and the two artists are sometimes confused because of their initials. Smith was a pupil of Léon Bonnat in Paris. He co-founded the Boston Museum School in 1877, and later became an interior designer. One of his paintings is a portrait of his wife, whose maiden name was Fay, entitled *Woman with a Parasol* (1877). The work is reminiscent of the solitary figures on seashores painted by Winslow Homer.

His work was featured in the 1977 exhibition *Art in Transition: A Century of the Museum School* at the Boston Museum of Fine Arts, which celebrated the centenary of the Boston Museum School.

BIBLIOGRAPHY:

Art in Transition: A Century of the Museum School, group exhibition catalogue, Museum of Fine Arts, Boston, 1977. *'Fannie Hillsmith'* in *Black Mountain College Dossiers*, no. 2, periodical, Black Mountain College Museum and Arts Center, Black Mountain (NC), 1996.

AUCTION RECORDS:

NEW YORK, 20 March 1996, *View of Venice* (1886, oil on canvas, 23¾ x 39½ ins / 60.3 x 100.3 cm) USD 1,725. MILFORD, 11 May 2000, *Sewing on the Veranda* (1875, oil on canvas, 17 x 25 ins / 43 x 64 cm) USD 4,600.

SMITH, Frank Vining

American, 19th - 20th century.

Born 25 August 1879, in Whitman (Massachusetts); died 30 July 1967, in Hingham (Massachusetts).

Painter. Seascapes.

Frank Vining Smith studied with Frank W. Benson and Edmund C. Tarbell at the Boston Museum of Fine Arts. He also studied at the Central Ontario School of Design in Toronto and the Art Students League of New York. He worked as an illustrator for various papers and periodicals, including the Boston *Globe*, *Field and Stream*, and *Outing*. He was mainly a painter of the sea, coast and ships - whaling ships, schooners, yachts, and clippers. He was a keen angler and fowler, and painted sporting subjects, such as waterfowl in flight.

Smith exhibited maritime subjects at the Pennsylvania Academy of the Fine Arts in 1918 and may also have exhibited at the National Academy of Design in 1917.

AUCTION RECORDS:

NEW YORK, 18 Nov 1977, *Sailing Ship in a Breeze* (oil on canvas, 34 x 40 ins / 86.3 x 101.5 cm) USD 3,500. NEW YORK, 29 Jan 1981, *Three Master at Sea* (oil on canvas, 30 x 40 ins / 76.2 x 101.6 cm) USD 3,750. BOLTON, 17 Nov 1983, *Wild Ducks in Full Flight* (oil on canvas, 28 x 31½ ins / 71.2 x 80 cm) USD 2,400. NEW YORK, 20 June 1985, *Two Sailing Ships at Sea* (oil on canvas, 25 x 34 ins / 63.5 x 86.4 cm) USD 3,200. NEW YORK, 31 March 1993, *Shipping in High Seas* (oil on canvas, 28 x 36 ins / 71.1 x 91.4 cm) USD 3,335. NEW YORK, 9 Sept 1993, *Shipping in Tropical Seas* (oil on canvas, 30 x 40 ins / 76.2 x 101.6 cm) USD 4,313. NEW YORK, 28 Sept 1995, *Seascape* (oil on canvas, 40¼ x 34 ins / 102.2 x 86.4 cm) USD 3,680. NEW YORK, 21 May 1996, *Coastal Land* (1924, oil on canvas, 22 x 26 ins / 56 x 66 cm) USD 1,150. CONNECTICUT, 22 Feb 1999, *Ship at Sea* (oil on board, 22 x 28 ins / 56 x 71 cm) USD 4,500. DETROIT, 11 June 1999, *Two American Three Masted Sailing Ships Passing at Sea* (oil on board, 24 x 50 ins / 61 x 127 cm) USD 8,500. BOSTON, 10 March 2000, *The Seventh Wave* (oil on canvas, 40 x 60 ins / 101 x 152 cm) USD 15,000. BOSTON, 23 May 2000, *Ducks Landing in a Marsh* (oil on board, 22 x 16 ins / 56 x 41 cm) USD 3,000. PORTSMOUTH, 3 Nov 2001, *Square Rigger* (oil on canvas, 28 x 35 ins / 71 x 89 cm) USD 15,000. PORTSMOUTH, 3 Nov 2001, *Passing Clippers* (oil on canvas, 30 x 40 ins / 76 x 102 cm) USD 15,000. PORTSMOUTH, 17 Aug 2002, *Sunlit Seas* (oil on board, 34 x 41 ins / 86 x 104 cm) USD 13,500. PORTSMOUTH, 17 Aug 2002, *Full Sail Under a Cloud of Canvas* (oil on canvas, 34 x 40 ins / 86 x 102 cm) USD 15,000. LONDON, 21 May 2003, *Knight of Malta and P&O Passenger Liners in Grand Harbour, Valetta* (pencil and watercolour, a pair, 19 x 30 ins / 48 x 76 cm) GBP 6,000. EAST DENNIS, 21 Nov 2003, *American Clipper Ship Under Sail* (oil on board, 24 x 30 ins / 61 x 76 cm) USD 8,200. BOSTON, 14 May 2004, *Clipper Ship* (oil on canvas, 26 x 42 ins / 67 x 107 cm) USD 13,000. FLORIDA, 18 Sept 2004, *Pintails in Flight* (oil on masonite, 18 x 26 ins / 46 x 66 cm) USD 2,000.

SMITH, Frederick Carl

American, 20th century.

Born 7 September 1868, in Cincinnati (Ohio); died 1955.

Painter.

Frederick Carl Smith studied at the Cincinnati Art School, the Ohio Mechanics' Institute, and at the Académie Julian in Paris with Bouguereau, Ferrier and Constant. He was a member of the American Art Association in Paris. He worked in Washington DC as a portrait painter for 17 years before moving to Pasadena in California in 1917; he became active in the Laguna Beach art community and a founder-member of its Art Association. He painted seascapes as well as portraits.

AUCTION RECORDS:

OAK PARK, 22 Oct 2000, *Californian Landscape* (c. 1930, oil on canvas, 20 x 24 ins / 51 x 61 cm) USD 1,800. MAINE, 4 Aug 2002, *Snow Capped Sierras* (oil on canvas, 24 x 42 ins / 61 x 107 cm) USD 3,000. PASADENA, 17 June 2003, *Landscape, Along the Carmen Coast* (oil on board, 12 x 16 ins / 30 x 41 cm) USD 3,250. PASADENA, 18 Nov 2003, *Flowers of the Desert Antelope Valley, Mojave, Calif* (oil on board, 16 x 22 ins / 41 x 56 cm) USD 3,000. PASADENA, 17 Feb 2004, *Lingering Snow - High Sierras* (oil on canvas, 25 x 30 ins / 64 x 76 cm) USD 2,250. PASADENA, 15 June 2004, *Coastal Landscape* (oil on masonite, 18 x 24 ins / 46 x 61 cm) USD 2,750.

SMITH, Frederick Richard

British, 19th - 20th century.

Born 30 December 1876, in Harescombe.

Painter, designer. Genre scenes, landscapes, seascapes.

Frederick Richard Smith studied in London and Rome.

SMITH, Frederick William

British, 19th century.

Born 25 August 1797, in London; died 18 January 1835, in Shrewsbury.

Sculptor.

Frederick William Smith was the son of Anker Smith and brother of Herbert Luther Smith. He exhibited 40 works at the Royal Academy from 1818 until 1828.

SMITH, Frederik Coke

British, 19th century.

Born c. 1820; died 13 May 1839.

Watercolourist. Architectural views.

Frederik Coke Smith spent a long time in Turkey, then went to Canada. J.F. Louis engraved views of Constantinople in his style.

MUSEUMS AND GALLERIES:

EDINBURGH: *Doges' Palace in Venice; Catholic Church in Dresden.*

SMITH, G.

British, 18th - 19th century.

Active in London.

Miniaturist.

G. Smith exhibited a miniature at the Society of Artists and 37 at the Royal Academy in London from 1789 until 1805.

SMITH, G. Ormerod

British, 19th century.

Painter.

G. Ormerod Smith was in Rome in 1857.

MUSEUMS AND GALLERIES:

LIVERPOOL: *Seraphine* (1857).

SMITH, Gabriel

British, 18th century.

Born 1724, in London; died 1783, in London.

Engraver.

Gabriel Smith began his studies in London and went to Paris to refine his skills. He studied pencil style engraving there among other things. He worked in collaboration with Ryland. He engraved religious subjects and genre scenes.

SMITH, Gar
Canadian, 20th - 21st century.
Born 1946.
Sculptor.

Gar Smith studied at the University of Toronto School of Architecture from 1965 to 1968. He gave up his architectural studies to take up light sculpture. Then, discovering 'that sunlight outdid all artificial light', he started to draw up a system of notes on natural light.

SMITH, Garden Grant
British, 19th - 20th century.
Born 1860, in Aberdeen; died 24 August 1913, in Hammersmith (London).
Painter.

Garden Grant Smith trained at Edinburgh School of Art and under Carolus Duran, in Paris.

AUCTION RECORDS:
GLASGOW, 25 Aug 1997, *Hay-making* (1882, oil on canvas, 24 x 15 ins / 61 x 38.2 cm) GBP 1,150.

SMITH, Gaspar. See **SMITZ**

SMITH, George, or Smithe, called Smith of Chichester
British, 18th century.
Born 1714, in Chichester; died 17 September 1776, in Chichester.
Painter, engraver. Genre scenes, landscapes, landscapes with figures, still-lifes.

George Smith soon became popular after Woollett had produced engravings of his works. His likeable nature and his skills as a poet and musician also contributed to his success. He exhibited in London from 1760 until 1774 and sent no less than 103 works to the exhibitions of the Free Society. His works include about 50 plates that he engraved with his brother John, taken from their landscapes.

He studied nature when painting the area around his home town and was inspired by the classical conception of Claude Lorraine and Poussin.

MUSEUMS AND GALLERIES:
DUBLIN: *Landscape* - LONDON (Tate Collection): *Classical Landscape* (1760-1770, oil on canvas); *Landscape* (oil on canvas) - LONDON (Victoria and Albert Mus.): *Waterfall and Fishermen; Shores of a Lake, Boat and Fishermen.*

AUCTION RECORDS:
NEW YORK, 22-24 March 1911, *Landscape*, USD 52. PARIS, 7 March 1951, *Cowshed in the Snow* (1774) FRF 7,500. LONDON, 20 Nov 1963, *Picking Hops*, GBP 680. LONDON, 18 March 1970, *River Landscape*, GBP 700. LONDON, 10 Dec 1971, *Wooded Landscape*, Gns 650. LONDON, 28 Nov 1973, *Winter Landscape*, GBP 4,000. LONDON, 22 Nov 1974, *Wooded River Landscape* (1769) Gns 2,800. LONDON, 18 June 1976, *Winter Landscape* (oil on canvas, 16 1/2 x 24 ins / 42 x 61 cm) GBP 1,600. LONDON, 18 March 1977, *Cottage in a Landscape* (1754, oil on canvas, 16 x 24 1/2 ins / 40.6 x 62.2 cm) GBP 1,800. LONDON, 18 July 1979, *Still-life of Bread and Wine* (1754, oil on canvas, 24 3/4 x 30 ins / 63 x 76 cm) GBP 3,600. LONDON, 26 June 1981, *Shepherd and Flock in Wooded River Landscape* (1770, oil on canvas, 42 x 66 3/4 ins / 106.7 x 169.5 cm) GBP 6,000. LONDON, 16 April 1982, *Italian Landscape* (1755, oil on canvas, 42 1/2 x 43 1/2 ins / 108 x 110.5 cm) GBP 5,000. LONDON, 16 March 1984, *Angler in a Wooded River Landscape* (oil on canvas, 19 1/4 x 23 ins / 49 x 58.5 cm) GBP 2,600. LONDON, 20 Nov 1985, *Travellers Resting; Landscape with Ruined Castle* (1769, oil on canvas, 32 x 43 1/2 ins / 81.5 x 110.5 cm) GBP 17,500. LONDON, 18 April 1986, *Wooded River Landscape with Angler and Flock* (oil on canvas, 15 1/2 x 48 ins / 39.4 x 121.9 cm) GBP 9,500. LONDON, 18 Nov 1988, *Wooded Landscape with River and Folly on a Promontory* (oil on canvas, 16 3/4 x 25 ins / 42.6 x 63.5 cm) GBP 6,600. LONDON, 15 Nov 1989, *Winter Landscape with Cattle near a Frozen Stream* (oil on canvas, 17 x 24 1/2 ins / 43 x 62 cm) GBP 8,580. LONDON, 20 April 1990, *Vast Landscape with the Ruins of a Castle and the Village of Chichester in the Distance* (1765, oil on canvas, 45 3/4 x 72 1/2 ins / 116.2 x 184.3 cm) GBP 28,600. LONDON, 8 April 1992, *Still-life with Bread and Cheese near a Carafe on a Table Covered with a White Cloth* (oil on canvas, 24 1/2 x 29 1/4 ins / 62 x 74.5 cm) GBP 4,400. NEW YORK, 22 May 1992, *Vast Landscape with the Isle of Wight in the Distance* (1750, oil on canvas, 25 1/4 ins / 64 cm, 3 1/4 x 42 ins/8 x 106.7 cm) USD 11,000. LONDON, 7 April 1993, *Vast Landscape with Anglers near a Bridge and Cottages in the Background* (oil on canvas, 31 1/2 x 39 1/2 ins / 80 x 100.4 cm) GBP 10,350. NEW YORK, 6 Oct 1995, *Vast Landscape with Fishermen and Shepherds near a Pond and a Castle in the Background* (oil on canvas, 45 1/4 x 57 1/2 ins / 114.9 x 146.1 cm) USD 90,500. NEW YORK, 12 April 1996, *Classical River Landscape with Fishermen in the Foreground and a Castle in the Background* (oil on canvas, 25 1/4 x 41 3/4 ins / 64.1 x 106 cm) USD 17,250. LONDON, 5 Sept 1996, *Still-life of Cheese, Beer and Bread* (oil on canvas, 25 x 30 1/4 ins / 63.5 x 76.8 cm) GBP 6,900. LONDON, 12 Nov 1997, *Farm; Landscape with Figures Resting near a Lake* (1775, oil on canvas, a pair, each 16 1/2 x 24 3/4 ins / 42 x 63 cm) GBP 6,325.

SMITH, George
British, 19th century.
Born 1802, in London; died 15 October 1838, in London.
Painter. History painting, genre scenes, figures.

George Smith originally went into commerce, but gave it up to study at the schools of the Royal Academy. His success earned him a travel scholarship to Rome. When he returned to England his works were not very popular and after struggling for several years he became discouraged and gave up. He exhibited in London from 1828 until 1836.

MUSEUMS AND GALLERIES:
LONDON (Birmingham): *Village School Teacher* - LONDON (Victoria and Albert Mus.): *Scipio the African Receiving his Son.*

AUCTION RECORDS:
MONTREAL, 30 Oct 1989, *Rival* (oil on panel, 11 3/4 x 15 3/4 ins / 30 x 40 cm) CAD 3,190.

SMITH, George
British, 19th century.
Born 18 April 1829, in London; died 2 January 1901, in London.
Painter. Genre scenes, landscapes with figures, landscapes.

George Smith studied under Cary and at the schools of the Royal Academy in 1854. He worked as an assistant to C.W. Cope on the frescoes for Parliament. He was a protégé of Prince Albert, Queen Victoria's husband. He exhibited his work in London from 1847 until 1887.

He mainly painted genre scenes in a similar style to that of Webster.

MUSEUMS AND GALLERIES:
LONDON (Victoria and Albert Mus.): *Young Boy Fishing and Little Girl; Temptation, a Display of Fruit; Children Picking Wild Flowers* - NOTTINGHAM (Castle Mus. & AG): *Country Road and Cottage.*

AUCTION RECORDS:
LONDON, 4 Sept 1909, *First Grapes of the Season,* GBP 21. LONDON, 4 March 1911, *My Dolly* (1856) GBP 21. LONDON, 9 June 1911, *Rustic Lovers* (1877) GBP 22. LONDON, 19 May 1971, *Art Lovers,* GBP 450. LONDON, 20 June 1972, *Morning Post,* GBP 1,200. LONDON, 9 April 1974, *Figures in an Interior; True Heir,* GBP 900. LONDON, 14 May 1976, *Child Playing the Flute* (1857, oil on card, 13 1/2 x 9 1/2 ins / 34.2 x 24 cm) GBP 1,200. LONDON, 14 June 1977, *Love Letter* (1862, oil on panel, 9 1/2 x 7 1/2 ins / 24 x 19 cm) GBP 2,400. LONDON, 20 March 1979, *Lesson* (1866, oil on panel, 15 x 11 1/2 ins / 38 x 29 cm) GBP 5,200. LONDON, 24 March 1981, *Child's Rattle* (1878, oil on canvas, 23 1/2 x 19 1/2 ins / 60 x 49.5 cm) GBP 2,800. LONDON, 13 June 1984, *Grandfather's Visit* (1876, oil on panel, 17 x 20 3/4 ins / 43 x 53 cm) GBP 7,500. LONDON, 12 April 1985, *Gallant Country Policeman* (oil on canvas, 19 1/4 x 29 1/4 ins / 49 x 74 cm) GBP 7,500. LONDON, 16 April 1986, *Reading the Letter* (oil on panel, 24 x 36 ins / 61 x 91.5 cm) GBP 12,500. LONDON, 15 June 1988, *Reading with Grandmother* (1854, oil on panel, 14 x 11 1/2 ins / 35.5 x 29 cm) GBP 2,750. GLASGOW, 7 Feb 1989, *Cattle Drinking from the River* (oil on canvas, 16 1/4 x 20 ins / 41 x 51 cm) GBP 2,090. GÖTEBORG, 18 May 1989, *Peasant with Cows* (oil on panel, 12 1/4 x 16 1/4 ins / 31 x 41 cm) SEK 3,000. LONDON, 2 June 1989, *Waiting* (1861, oil on panel, 16 x 14 ins / 40.5 x 35.5 cm) GBP 7,920. LONDON, 13 Dec 1989, *Lesson* (1866, oil on panel, 15 1/4 x 12 ins / 39 x 30.5 cm) GBP 12,650. GLASGOW, 6 Feb 1990, *Woodcutters* (oil on card, 12 x 16 1/4 ins / 30.5 x 41.5 cm) GBP 1,760. LONDON, 15 June 1990, *Potential Rival* (oil on panel, 12 x 16 ins / 30.6 x 40.6 cm) GBP 1,980. GLASGOW, 5 Feb 1991, *Harvest* (oil on card, 12 x 15 3/4 ins / 30.5 x 40 cm) GBP 990. STOCKHOLM, 29 May 1991, *Little Girl and her Doll on the Doorstep* (oil on panel, 9 3/4 x 8 1/4 ins / 25 x 21 cm) SEK 11,500. PERTH, 26 Aug 1991, *Rounding up Calves in a Meadow* (oil on card, 25 x 30 ins / 63.5 x 76 cm) GBP 4,400. LONDON, 12 June 1992, *Sketch for 'The Lottery'* (1868, oil on panel, 8 3/4 x 14 ins / 22.2 x 35.5 cm) GBP 3,850. LONDON, 3 June 1994, *Picking Grapes* (1875, oil on panel, 20 x 15 1/2 ins / 50.8 x 39.4 cm) GBP 8,050. LONDON, 10 March 1995, *Sewing Lesson by the Fire* (1867, oil on panel, 13 3/4 x 18 ins / 35 x 45.7 cm) GBP 6,670. LONDON, 29 March 1996, *Picking Grapes* (1875, oil on panel, 20 x 15 1/2 ins / 50.8 x 39.4 cm) GBP 9,200. LONDON, 11 March 1999, *Straw Plaiting* (1854, oil on panel, 12 x 14 ins / 30 x 36 cm) GBP 1,800. LONDON, 30 Nov 1999, *Country Courtship* (oil on panel, 15 x 13 ins / 39 x 34 cm) GBP 9,000. LONDON, 22 March 2000, *Lace Making* (1866, oil on panel, 16 x 14 ins / 40 x 35 cm) GBP 18,000. VICTORIA, 16 Oct 2000, *Mother Watching Child* (1877, oil on canvas, 23 x 19 ins / 58 x 48 cm) CAD 21,000. LONDON, 7 June 2001, *Dinner Time* (oil on panel, 8 x 7 ins / 21 x 17 cm) GBP 3,000. LONDON, 14 June 2001, *Home, 'Be It Ever So Humble'* (1867, oil on canvas, 28 x 36 ins / 71 x 91 cm) GBP 65,000. GODALMING, 29 May 2002, *Mother and Child in a Farmhouse* (oil on panel, 6 x 8 ins / 15 x 20 cm) GBP 3,400. LONDON, 11 June 2002, *Visitor* (1896, oil on canvas, 25 x 20 ins / 64 x 51 cm) GBP 10,500. LONDON, 20 Feb 2003, *Rightful Heir. Coming of Age* (oil on panel, a pair, 10 x 16 ins / 26 x 41 cm) GBP 14,000. LONDON, 12 June 2003, *Nibble* (oil on canvas, 25 x 32 ins / 63 x 81 cm) GBP 5,000. LONDON, 4 March 2004, *Straw Plaiting* (1854, oil on panel, 12 x 14 ins / 31 x 36 cm) GBP 1,800. LONDON, 16 June 2004, *Lacemaker* (1865, oil on panel, 24 x 20 ins / 61 x 50 cm) GBP 12,500.

SMITH, George
British, 19th - 20th century.
Born 2 February 1870; died 1934.
Painter. Landscapes, animals.

MUSEUMS AND GALLERIES:
VENICE (Gal. d'Arte Moderna).

AUCTION RECORDS:
GLASGOW, 19 April 1984, *Flower Market* (oil on canvas, 22 1/2 x 15 1/2 ins / 57.1 x 39.3 cm) GBP 2,600. PERTH, 27 Aug 1985, *Shrimp Fishers, Brittany* (oil on canvas, 27 1/2 x 35 1/2 ins / 70 x 90 cm) GBP 4,000. LONDON, 21 Sept 1989, *Feeding the Cattle* (oil on canvas, 28 x 35 1/2 ins / 71.2 x 90.3 cm) GBP 3,080. EDINBURGH, 9 June 1994, *Driving the Herd* (oil on canvas, 28 x 36 ins / 71.2 x 91.4 cm) GBP 2,760. GLASGOW, 16 April 1996, *Throughbred Horses* (oil on reinforced canvas, 11 3/4 x 16 ins / 30 x 40.5 cm) GBP 1,265. GLASGOW, 11 Dec 1996, *Loading the Waggon* (oil on canvas, 14 1/4 x 18 1/4 ins / 36 x 46.5 cm) GBP 1,840. LONDON, 28 Oct 1999, *Collecting Seaweed* (oil on canvas, 28 x 36 ins / 72 x 91 cm) GBP 3,000. LONDON, 28 Oct 1999, *Farmer with his Herd, East Lothian* (oil on board, 16 x 20 ins / 41 x 51 cm) GBP 3,500. LONDON, 30 Aug 2000, *Hay Wagon* (oil on canvas laid on board, 11 x 15 ins / 29 x 39 cm) GBP 2,800. LONDON, 26 Oct 2000, *Killin Flower Market* (oil on canvas, 12 x 16 ins / 30 x 40 cm) GBP 4,000. EDINBURGH, 24 Aug 2001, *Cattle Watering in a Continental Farmyard* (oil on canvas, 28 x 35 ins / 70 x 90 cm) GBP 4,000. AUCKLAND, 11 Dec 2001, *Return from Pasture* (oil on canvas, 28 x 36 ins / 72 x 92 cm) NZD 13,000. EDINBURGH, 22 Aug 2002, *Little Cowherd* (oil on canvas laid on board, 12 x 16 ins / 30 x 40 cm) GBP 1,900. EDINBURGH, 13 Sept 2002, *Heavy Horses Ploughing* (oil on canvas, 16 x 20 ins / 41 x 51 cm) GBP 2,800. LONDON, 30 Oct 2003, *Arrival at the Fair* (oil on board, 27 x 35 ins / 68 x 88 cm) GBP 2,600. CHICAGO, 7 Dec 2003, *Arrival at Blenheim Palace* (oil on canvas, 26 x 20 ins / 66 x 51 cm) USD 3,600. EDINBURGH, 18 Aug 2004, *Bringing Home the Herd* (oil on canvas, sold with a companion, 11 x 15 ins / 29 x 39 cm) GBP 3,200. LONDON, 1 Sept 2004, *Hay Loft* (oil on canvas, 28 x 36 ins / 71 x 92 cm) GBP 3,000.

SMITH, George Armfield. See **ARMFIELD**

SMITH, George Girdler
American, 19th century.
Born 1795, in Danvers (Massachusetts); died 1859, in Boston.
Engraver (burin). Portraits. Banknotes.

SMITH, George Melville
American, 19th - 20th century.
Born 1879, in Chicago.
Painter. Interiors with figures. Murals.

George Melville Smith created murals in various public buildings during the 1930s under the auspices of the Work Project Administration. He often exhibited at the Art Institute of Chicago and the New York Society of Independent Artists.

AUCTION RECORDS:
NEW YORK, 15 May 1991, *Studio Interior* (oil on canvas, 29 1/2 x 22 1/2 ins / 74.9 x 57.2 cm) USD 2,750. NEW YORK, 24 Sept 1992, *The Land Yields Her Increase* (tempera/panel, 24 x 43 ins / 61 x 109.2 cm) USD 3,300.

SMITH, George V.
British, 19th century.
Active in 1863.
Painter. Landscapes.

MUSEUMS AND GALLERIES:
LONDON (Victoria and Albert Mus.): *Penmoyle on the Severn.*

SMITH, Georges
French, 19th century.
Born in Le Havre.
Painter. Landscapes.

Georges Smith was a pupil of Achard and made his Salon debut in 1876.

SMITH, Grace Cossington
Australian, 20th century.
Born 1892; died 1984.
Painter. Interiors, urban landscapes, still-lifes.

Grace Cossington Smith exhibited with the Contemporary Group. Her work is characterised by quick sketches of everyday subjects, and by vividly coloured paintings which seek, like those of Van Gogh, to both absorb and radiate colour and light.

BIBLIOGRAPHY:

Thomas, Daniel, *'Colour-Worship'* in *Creating Australia: 200 Years of Art 1788-1988*, exhibition catalogue, Art Gall. Board of South Australia, Adelaide, 1988.

MUSEUMS AND GALLERIES:

SYDNEY (AG of New South Wales): *Troops Marching* (1917); *The Lacquer Room* (1936).

AUCTION RECORDS:

ROSEBERY, 29 June 1976, *Still-life* (1971, oil on card, 25¼ x 17 ins / 64 x 43 cm) AUD 1,100. SYDNEY, 4 Oct 1977, *The Salon* (1940, card, 19¾ x 16½ ins / 50 x 42 cm) AUD 3,400. SYDNEY, 20 Oct 1980, *Boatshel* (oil on card, 18 x 11¾ ins / 45.5 x 30 cm) AUD 2,800. MELBOURNE, 7 Nov 1984, *The Garden* (1938, oil on card, 15¼ x 13½ ins / 39 x 34 cm) AUD 3,000. LONDON, 20 Nov 1986, *Still-life with Bottles of Wine, Oranges and a Candlestick* (1947, oil on card, 13½ x 9 ins / 34.3 x 22.8 cm) GBP 6,500. LONDON, 28 Nov 1991, *Still-life with Leaves* (1953, oil on canvas/card, 20¾ x 17 ins / 52.7 x 43.2 cm) GBP 9,900. MELBOURNE, 20-21 Aug 1996, *Still-life with Teapot* (oil on panel, 15¼ x 13¾ ins / 39 x 35 cm) AUD 34,500. MELBOURNE, 29 April 1997, *Interior with Flag* (1941, oil on panel, 13 x 11½ ins / 33.1 x 29 cm) AUD 23,000. MELBOURNE, 23 Aug 1999, *Interior with Windows* (1940, oil on board, 19 x 17 ins / 49 x 42 cm) AUD 50,000. MELBOURNE, 23 Nov 1999, *Still-life with Jugs* (1963, oil on board, 31 x 21 ins / 79 x 54 cm) AUD 150,000. MELBOURNE, 15 Aug 2000, *Blossom in Earthenware Jug* (1939, oil on board, 19 x 15 ins / 48 x 37 cm) AUD 32,000. MELBOURNE, 28 Nov 2000, *Sofa in the Corner* (1963, oil on board, 13 x 10 ins / 33 x 26 cm) AUD 49,000. PADDINGTON, 3 June 2001, *Still-life with Red Vase* (1962, oil on board, 24 x 35 ins / 62 x 90 cm) AUD 145,000. PADDINGTON, 27 Aug 2001, *Sofa in the Room* (1960, oil on composition board, 36 x 24 ins / 91 x 60 cm) AUD 155,000. MELBOURNE, 28 Aug 2002, *Wildflowers in a Glass* (c. 1943, oil on board, 24 x 20 ins / 62 x 51 cm) AUD 80,000. PADDINGTON, 17 Nov 2002, *Centre of a City* (1935, oil on canvas, 33 x 28 ins / 83 x 71 cm) AUD 300,000. MELBOURNE, 6 May 2003, *Blue Glass* (1937, oil on board, 18 x 14 ins / 46 x 36 cm) AUD 85,000. MELBOURNE, 26 Nov 2003, *Winter Tree, Turramurra* (1935, oil on board, 24 x 20 ins / 61 x 51 cm) AUD 110,000. MELBOURNE, 3 May 2004, *Still-life with Jugs* (1963, oil on board, 31 x 21 ins / 79 x 54 cm) AUD 170,000. MELBOURNE, 8 Sept 2004, *Bush and River* (1954, oil on canvas laid on board, 21 x 15 ins / 53 x 39 cm) AUD 34,000.

SMITH, H. R.

British, 19th century.
Portrait artist.

H.R. Smith exhibited in London from 1839 until 1856. It appears that this is probably the same person as Harriet C. Smith, whose works, are mentioned in the annual auction records.

MUSEUMS AND GALLERIES:

SYDNEY: *Portrait of Lieutenant-Colonel George Johnston.*

AUCTION RECORDS:

PARIS, 20 Oct 1950, *Wargrave Ferre; Near Wargrave* (1861, two pendants) FRF 4,100.

SMITH, Hans

Danish.
Painter. Genre scenes.

MUSEUMS AND GALLERIES:

COPENHAGEN: *A Stranger Asks the Way; At the Door of the Foodseller.*

SMITH, Hans Jacob. See SMIDT

SMITH, Harriet Frances

American, 19th - 20th century.
Born 28 July 1873, in Worcester; died 1935.
Painter.

Harriet Frances Smith was taught by Denmann W. Ross, E.W.D. Hamilton, Henry B. Snelle and C.H. Woodbury. She was a member of the American Federation of Arts.

SMITH, Hélène

Swiss, 20th century.
Born c. 1867.
Draughtswoman, watercolourist.

Hélène Smith's work is known exclusively from reproductions published in 1900 by Professor Flournoy of Geneva in his collection entitled *Des Indes à la Planète Mars* (*From the Indies to the Planet Mars*). Smith was a shop assistant with no artistic training who painted and drew visions of Mars while under hypnosis. She also produced 'visions' of plants and architectural motifs, purported to have been first experienced by Chinese or Japanese artists of the early dynastic period.

SMITH, Henry. See SCHMIDT

SMITH, Henry Pember

American, 19th century.
Born 20 February 1854, in Waterford, USA; died 16 October 1907, in Ashbury Park (New Jersey).
Painter. Landscapes, seascapes.

Henry Pember Smith learned to paint without a teacher and acquired a reputation as an accomplished landscape painter fairly early in his career. He took an extended trip to Venice, and subsequently produced many interesting works on subjects he had encountered there. Smith also painted numerous views of New Jersey. He was a member of the American Watercolor Society.

MUSEUMS AND GALLERIES:

BROOKLYN, NY - CINCINNATI.

AUCTION RECORDS:

PARIS, 23 April 1897, *Sunny Path*, FRF 300. NEW YORK, 2 and 3 Feb 1906, *Late Afternoon*, USD 400. NEW YORK, Jan 1907, *Along the Grand Canal*, USD 175. NEW YORK, 13 and 14 Feb 1908, *Old Oak*, USD 310; *Summer's Day in New Jersey*, USD 310. NEW YORK, 7 March 1911, *Oak in Autumn*, USD 330. NEW YORK, 6 Nov 1968, *Oaks*, USD 950. NEW YORK, 1 Oct 1969, *Connecticut Landscape*, USD 2,000. LOS ANGELES, 22 May 1973, *View of Venice*, USD 1,800. NEW YORK, 29 April 1976, *Landscape with Fishermen* (1881, oil on panel, 9½ x 13¾ ins / 24.2 x 35 cm) USD 2,500. NEW YORK, 18 Nov 1977, *October Landscape* (oil on canvas, 20¼ x 28¼ ins / 51.5 x 71.7 cm) USD 3,750. NEW YORK, 2 Feb 1979, *Deal Lake, New Jersey* (oil on canvas, 20 x 28 ins / 51 x 71.2 cm) USD 3,800. NEW YORK, 23 May 1979, *Venice* (1884, watercolour, 10 x 14 ins / 25.5 x 35.5 cm) USD 2,500. NEW YORK, 18 April 1984, *Fishing Boats on a Beach* (watercolour, 13 x 19¼ ins / 33 x 48.8 cm) USD 850. NEW YORK, 7 Dec 1984, *Path to the River* (oil on canvas, 14¼ x 20 ins / 36 x 50.9 cm) USD 3,500. NEW YORK, 20 June 1985, *Landscape with Pond and a Boat* (oil on canvas, 20½ x 28½ ins / 52.1 x 72.4 cm) USD 5,250. NEW YORK, 14 March 1986, *Summer Afternoon* (oil on canvas, 20¼ x 28¼ ins / 51.5 x 71.5 cm) USD 7,500. NEW YORK, 17 March 1988, *Cottage by the Water's Edge* (oil on canvas, 14 x 20½ ins / 35.6 x 51.8 cm) USD 6,050. NEW YORK, 30 Sept 1988, *Hacienda* (oil on canvas, 20¼ x 29 ins / 51.4 x 73.7 cm) USD 2,200. NEW YORK, 24 Jan 1989, *Morning over Lake Como* (oil on canvas, 19¾ x 27½ ins / 50 x 70 cm) USD 4,400. NEW YORK, 28 Sept 1989, *Gray Morning* (1883, oil on canvas, 18¼ x 28 ins / 46.2 x 71.1 cm) USD 8,250. NEW YORK, 14 Feb 1990, *Old Orchard near a Forest* (oil on canvas, 20 x 28 ins / 51 x 71 cm) USD 4,400. NEW YORK, 17 Dec 1990, *Venice* (oil on canvas, 16 x 12 ins / 40.7 x 30.5 cm) USD 4,400. NEW YORK, 14 March 1991, *House by a River* (oil on canvas, 12¼ x 16¼ ins / 31 x 41 cm) USD 5,500. NEW YORK, 22 May 1991, *Lighthouse off Sandy Hook in New Jersey* (1879, oil on canvas, 12 x 16 ins / 30.5 x 40.6 cm) USD 6,050. NEW YORK, 14 Nov 1991, *Cottage near a Clearing* (oil on canvas, 19 x 29¼ ins / 48.5 x 74.3 cm) USD 4,950. New York, 25 Sept 1992, *Day in September* (oil on canvas, 14 x 20 ins / 35.6 x 50.8 cm) USD 3,575. New York, 15 Nov 1993, *Spanish Village by the Edge of a River* (oil on canvas, 20 x 28 ins / 50.9 x 71.1 cm) USD 2,990. New York, 31 March 1994, *In a Boat on a Pond* (oil on canvas, 20 x 28¼ ins / 50.8 x 71.8 cm) USD 4,945. New York, 14 March 1996, *Old Turnpike Road in New England* (oil on canvas, 20 x 28 ins / 50.8 x 71.1 cm) USD 12,650. New York, 30 Sept 1997, *Fishing in a River* (1881, oil on canvas, 15¼ x 12 ins / 38.7 x 30.5 cm) USD 10,350. Boston, 12 March 1999, *Country Lane* (1880, oil on canvas, 12 x 20 ins / 31 x 51 cm) USD 6,000. Los Angeles, 9 Dec 1999, *River Landscape in Summer, 1880* (oil on canvas, 17 x 28 ins / 43 x 71 cm) USD 17,000. Smithville, 23 March 2000, *View of Venice* (oil on canvas) USD 13,500. New York, 4 Oct 2000, *Morning at Hamilton, Bermuda* (watercolour over pencil on board, 11 x 7 ins / 28 x 19 cm) USD 9,000. San Francisco, 13 June 2001, *Spring in New Jersey* (oil on canvas, 20 x 28 ins / 51 x 72 cm) USD 9,000. Pittsfield, 8 Sept 2001, *Boaters and Ducks near a Marshland Cottage in Summer* (oil on canvas, 12 x 16 ins / 30 x 41 cm) USD 5,500. Milford, 25 April 2002, *Old Homestead* (watercolour and gouache, 17 x 28 ins / 43 x 71 cm) USD 5,000. New York, 17 July 2002, *Early Summer at East Lyme, Connecticut* (oil on canvas, 20 x 28 ins / 51 x 71 cm) USD 8,000. Milford, 23 Oct 2003, *Last Gleam, East Lyme, Connecticut* (oil on canvas, 20 x 28 ins / 51 x 71 cm) USD 5,500. New York, 19 Dec 2003, *Spring Morning* (oil on canvas, 20 x 28 ins / 51 x 71 cm) USD 7,000. New York, 26 May 2004, *Venetian Canal* (oil on canvas, 35 x 25 ins / 89 x 64 cm) USD 12,000. Portland, 6 Aug 2004, *Farm by the River* (watercolour, 10 x 14 ins / 25 x 36 cm) USD 3,000.

SMITH, Henry T.

American, 19th century.

Painter. Portraits, genre scenes.

Henry T. Smith exhibited in Philadelphia from 1861 to 1867.

SMITH, Herbert Luther

British, 19th century.

Born 1811, in London; died 13 March 1870, in London.

Painter. History painting, portraits.

Herbert Luther Smith was the son of Anker Smith and studied at the Royal Academy. He exhibited his work in London from 1830 until 1854. He produced copies for Queen Victoria.

SMITH, Hezekiah Wright

American, 19th century.

Born 1828, in Edinburgh.

Active in Boston and Philadelphia.

Engraver (burin). Portraits.

SMITH, Hobbe

Dutch, 19th - 20th century.

Born 7 December 1862, in Witmarsum; died 1942.

Painter. Genre scenes, landscapes, waterscapes, seascapes, still-lifes (including flowers).

Hobbe Smith studied at the academy in Amsterdam and under C. Verlat. He exhibited in Rome in 1911.

Auction records:

New York, 10-11 Jan 1907, *Trouble,* USD 100. Amsterdam, 24 April 1968, *River Amstel, Amsterdam,* NLG 3,600. Amsterdam, 27 April 1976, *Sailing Vessel on the Zuiderzee* (oil on canvas, 16¼ x 21¼ ins / 41.5 x 54 cm) NLG 8,000. Amsterdam, 9 March 1978, *Sailing Vessels off the Coast* (oil on canvas, 29¼ x 38¾ ins / 74 x 98.5 cm) NLG 4,000. London, 20 April 1979, *Banks of the River Meuse* (oil on canvas, 14½ x 10 ins / 36.8 x 25.4 cm) GBP 800. Amsterdam, 19 May 1981, *View of Amsterdam* (oil on canvas, 37 x 29¼ ins / 94 x 74 cm) NLG 10,500. Amsterdam, 14 March 1983, *Vessels off the Coast, Amsterdam* (oil on canvas, 27 x 44¼ ins / 68.5 x 112.5 cm) NLG 5,000. Amsterdam, 10 Feb 1988, *Embarking in the Breeze* (oil on canvas, 8½ x 12 ins / 21.5 x 30.5 cm) NLG 1,725. London, 26 Feb 1988, *Dutch Town with Moored Houseboats* (oil on canvas, 14½ x 10½ ins / 37 x 26.5 cm) GBP 1,320. Amsterdam, 11 Sept 1990, *Pacific Ocean* (oil on canvas, 30 x 37¾ ins / 76 x 96 cm) NLG 8,625. Amsterdam, 6 Nov 1990, *Still-life with Violets in a Jar* (oil on panel, 11¾ x 7¾ ins / 30 x 20 cm) NLG 4,370. Amsterdam, 24 April 1991, *Wooded River Landscape at Twilight with Moored Vessels* (oil on canvas, 25¼ x 35½ ins / 64 x 90 cm) NLG 4,370. Amsterdam, 24 Sept 1992, *Sailing Vessels on the?, Amsterdam* (oil on canvas, 18¾ x 14¼ ins / 47.5 x 36 cm) NLG 3,450. Amsterdam, 20 April 1993, *View of the?, Amsterdam* (oil on canvas, 23½ x 31¾ ins / 60 x 80.5 cm) NLG 10,120. Amsterdam, 11 April 1995, *View of St Nikolaaskerk, Amsterdam* (oil on canvas, 16½ x 21¼ ins / 42 x 54 cm) NLG 7,788. Amsterdam, 18 June 1996, *River Landscape with Boats Moored near a Windmill* (oil on canvas, 16¼ x 22¼ ins / 41.5 x 56.5 cm) NLG 4,370. Amsterdam, 30 Oct 1996, *Vessels Moored near a Swingbridge on the Amstel River* (oil on canvas, 31½ x 45¼ ins / 80 x 115 cm) NLG 18,451. Amsterdam, 5 Nov 1996, *View of Montelbaanstoren* (oil on canvas, 29¾ x 37¾ ins / 75.5 x 96 cm) NLG 5,192. Gravenhage, 28 April 1999, *Man of Volendam Smoking Pipe on Top of a Dune* (watercolour, 15 x 9 ins / 37 x 23 cm) NLG 6,500. Amsterdam, 7 July 1999, *Shipping on Ij, Amsterdam with Koepelkerk and Westerkerk Beyond* (oil on canvas, 30 x 37 ins / 75 x 95 cm) NLG 32,000. Amsterdam, 19 April 2000, *Moored Sailing Boats in Dordrecht Harbour* (oil on canvas, 16 x 22 ins / 40 x 55 cm) NLG 16,000. Staufen, 22 Sept 2000, *Dutch Town with Fishing Boats* (oil on canvas, 50 x 78 ins / 126 x 198 cm) DEM 14,000. North Bethesda, 14 Feb 2001, *Village with Windmill* (oil on canvas, 16 x 24 ins / 41 x 60 cm) USD 1,600. Gravenhage, 25 April 2001, *Nettenboeter* (oil on canvas, 49 x 39 ins / 124 x 100 cm) NLG 16,000. Amsterdam, 23 April 2002, *View of the Montelbaanstoren, Amsterdam* (oil on canvas, 19 x 13 ins / 49 x 32 cm) EUR 5,500. Amsterdam, 21 Oct 2002, *Floralia* (1898, triptych, h. 83 ins / 212 cm) EUR 44,000. Gravenhage, 7 May 2003, *Sailing Ship* (oil on panel, 12 x 19 ins / 31 x 48 cm) EUR 4,600. Amsterdam, 2 Sept 2003, *Koepelkerk on the Singel, Amsterdam* (oil on canvas, 17 x 14 ins / 43 x 35 cm) EUR 3,200. Amsterdam, 3 Feb 2004, *Portrait of a Girl, Said to be the Artist's Daughter* (1886, oil on canvas, 16 x 12 ins / 40 x 30 cm) EUR 1,700. Amsterdam, 21 April 2004, *Festive Fleet on the Zuiderzee* (oil on canvas, 90 x 72 ins / 228 x 184 cm) EUR 12,000.

SMITH, Holmes

British, 19th - 20th century.

Born 9 May 1863, in Keighley.

Painter, watercolourist.

Holmes Smith was a watercolour specialist, and a member of the American Arts Federation.

SMITH, Houghton Cranford

American, 20th century.

Born 1887, in Arlington (New Jersey); died 1983, in New York.

Painter.

Houghton Cranford Smith studied at the Art Students League in New York, the Cape Cod School of Art in Provincetown, Massachusetts, and in France, where his teachers included André Lhote. He travelled extensively: both abroad, visiting France, Spain, Chile, and Bermuda, and across the USA. His work appeared in exhibitions at the Carnegie Foundation in Pittsburgh.

Bibliography:
Houghton Cranford Smith 1887-1983, Grace Borgenicht Gallery, New York, 1990. *Houghton Cranford Smith: The Purist Landscapes*, Richard Cork Gallery, New York, 1996. *Houghton Cranford Smith: Explorations in Colour*, Richard Cork Gallery, New York, 1998.

SMITH, Howard Everett
American, 20th century.
Born 27 April 1885, in West Windham; died 1970, in Carmel (California).
Painter, illustrator.

Howard Everett Smith was a student of Howard Pyle and was active in Boston. He exhibited widely and won prizes in Boston, Philadelphia, and San Francisco.

Auction records:
New York, 11 March 1981, *Young Girl Reading* (oil on canvas, 29 1/2 x 24 3/4 ins / 75 x 63 cm) USD 2,500. Boston, 27 Oct 2002, *Two Bailey's Ice Cream Paintings* (oil on canvas on aluminium, two, 56 x 28 ins / 142 x 71 cm) USD 7,500.

SMITH, Hugh Bellingham.
See **BELLINGHAM-SMITH Hugh**

SMITH, Isabel E.
American, 20th century.
Born in Smith's Landing (Oklahoma).
Painter.

Isabel E. Smith was taught in Paris by Lhermitte, Delance and Callot. She was a member of the Club d'Art Feminine in Paris.

SMITH, Ismael. See **SMITH Y MARI**

SMITH, J. (Miss)
British, 18th - 19th century.
Miniaturist.

J. Smith exhibited 13 miniatures at the Royal Academy in London from 1802 until 1809.

SMITH, J. F.
British.
Painter. Genre scenes.

Museums and Galleries:
Nottingham: *Fishmonger* (drawing).

SMITH, J. John
British, 18th - 19th century.
Born c. 1775, in London.
Engraver (etching). Village scenes, landscapes.

J. John Smith exhibited occasionally at the Royal Academy between 1813 and 1833. He engraved village scenes.

SMITH, Jack Martin
British, 20th century.
Born 18 June 1928, in Sheffield.
Painter.
Symbolism.
Kitchen Sink School.

Jack Martin Smith spent his childhood in Sheffield and subsequently trained at the Sheffield College of Art (1994-1946), St Martin's School of Art (1948-1950) and the Royal College of Art in London (1950-1953). He made study trips to Spain and Italy in 1954 and 1955. His early works inspired the sobriquet 'Kitchen Sink School', coined by the critic David Sylvester to characterise the realist trend in 1950s painting in Britain. Smith's subsequent works remained figurative, but were more Symbolist in inspiration. His later work explored the concept of synaesthesia: canvases were covered with coloured hieroglyphics or invented calligraphic signs, seeking to find synaesthetic equivalents for a range of sensations, including the experience of illumination and displacement.

His work has been the subject of a number of solo exhibitions since 1953: annually (with a few exceptions) in London; 1958, 1962, New York; 1959, retrospective, London; 1977 retrospective, Sunderland Arts Centre. Smith won first prize at the John Moores Exhibition in Liverpool in 1956.

Museums and Galleries:
Leeds (City AG): *Still-life with Bowl of Cherries* (1954-1955, oil/panel) - London (Tate Collection).

Auction records:
London, 26 Sept 1984, *Child Writing* (1954, oil on canvas, 59 3/4 x 48 ins / 152 x 122 cm) GBP 2,200. London, 7 June 1985, *Painted Relief* (1962, oil on panel relief, 24 x 26 1/2 ins / 61 x 67.5 cm) GBP 1,700. London, 29 July 1988, *Objects on a Table* (1959, oil on canvas, 35 1/2 x 35 1/2 ins / 90 x 90 cm) GBP 1,375. New York, 15 Nov 1990, *Model of a House with a Swimming-pool* (gouache/card, 15 1/2 x 22 3/4 ins / 39.4 x 57.9 cm) USD 4,400. London, 26 March 1993, *Sensation of Noise 1977* (1977, oil, drawing pins, wood and graph paper, 15 1/2 x 15 1/2 x 4 ins / 39.4 x 39.4 x 10 cm) GBP 1,552. London, 25 Nov 1993, *Snowy Landscape from a Train* (1956, oil on card, 29 1/2 x 23 1/2 ins / 75 x 59.7 cm) GBP 2,530. London, 6 Dec 2000, *Still-life* (1958, oil on canvas, 48 x 48 ins / 122 x 122 cm) GBP 1,000. London, 6 Dec 2000, *21 Elements on a Grid* (1968, oil on canvas, 41 x 42 ins / 105 x 107 cm) GBP 1,900. London, 2 June 2004, *Baby in Sink* (oil on board, 43 x 50 ins / 109 x 126 cm) GBP 43,000. London, 24 Nov 2004, *Side to Side No. 2* (1963, oil on canvas, 60 x 60 ins / 152 x 152 cm) GBP 1,900.

SMITH, Jack Wilkinson
American, 20th century.
Born 1873, in Paterson (New Jersey); died 1965, in Monterey Park (California).
Painter. Landscapes.

Jack Wilkinson Smith studied at the Cincinnati Academy of Art and the Art Institute of Chicago. He was a member of the Salmagundi Club and received numerous awards.

Auction records:
New York, 15 March 1985, *Mountainous Landscape* (oil on canvas, 28 x 34 1/4 ins / 71 x 86.7 cm) USD 7,000. London, 14 July 1987, *The Wye below the New Weir* (1788, watercolour and pencil, 5 x 8 1/2 ins / 13 x 21.3 cm) GBP 1,800. Los Angeles, 9 June 1988, *Mountain Lake* (oil on canvas, 30 x 40 1/4 ins / 76 x 102 cm) USD 17,600. Los Angeles-San Francisco, 7 Feb 1990, *High Sierras* (oil on canvas, 20 x 24 ins / 51 x 61 cm) USD 24,750. Los Angeles-San Francisco, 12 July 1990, *Rocky Shore* (oil on card, 18 x 24 ins / 46 x 61 cm) USD 8,250. New York, 25 March 1997, *Crashing Waves on the Rocks* (oil on canvas, 20 x 24 ins / 50.8 x 61 cm) USD 5,750. New York, 23 April 1997, *Malibu Canyon* (oil on panel, 12 x 16 ins / 30.5 x 40.5 cm) USD 3,680. Maine, 14 Aug 1999, *High Sierra Trail* (oil on canvas, 26 x 34 ins / 66 x 86 cm) USD 85,000. Los Angeles, 28 Oct 1999, *Crashing Surf* (oil on board, 18 x 24 ins / 46 x 61 cm) USD 10,000. San Francisco, 14 June 2000, *Mountain Pool, High Sierra* (oil on canvas, 20 x 24 ins / 51 x 61 cm) USD 16,000. San Francisco, 14 June 2000, *Pacific Coast* (oil on canvas, 40 x 50 ins / 102 x 127 cm) USD 100,000. Pasadena, 13 Feb 2001, *Snow Blocked Trail* (oil on board, 25 x 30 ins / 64 x 76 cm) USD 22,500. Los Angeles, 2 May 2001, *Rocky Shore* (oil on canvas, 30 x 40 ins / 76 x 102 cm) USD 30,000. Los Angeles, 19 June 2002, *High Sierra Pack Trip* (oil on canvas, 26 x 34 ins / 67 x 86 cm) USD 80,000. New York, 4 Dec 2002, *Riders in the High Sierras* (1945, oil on canvas, 28 x 34 ins / 71 x 86 cm) USD 25,000. Los Angeles, 29 Oct 2003, *Silver Surf* (oil on canvas, 28 x 34 ins / 71 x 86 cm) USD 15,000. San Francisco, 10 Dec 2003, *Winter Solitude, High Sierras* (oil on canvas, 24 x 30 ins / 61 x 76 cm) USD 18,000. Pasadena, 17 Feb 2004, *The Sentinel of the Coast* (oil on canvas, 24 x 30 ins / 61 x 76 cm) USD 27,500. Los Angeles, 28 April 2004, *Along the Pacific Coast* (1922, oil on canvas, 33 x 42 ins / 83 x 106 cm) USD 160,000.

SMITH, Jacob
British, 18th century.

Active in London c. 1730.
Engraver.

Jacob Smith engraved portraits. His works include a print engraved with a single line, in the genre of those of Mellou.

SMITH, Jakob or Peder J. Nielsen, or Smidt
Danish, 19th century.
Born 16 October 1792, in Hals; died 28 June 1825, in Copenhagen.
Portrait artist.

Smith was a pupil at the Kunstakademi and of Christopher Wilhelm Eckersberg.

SMITH, James
British, 18th century.
Active in 1733.
Engraver (burin).

James Smith engraved portraits of the kings of England.

SMITH, James
British, 18th century.
Active in London.
Miniaturist.

James Smith is known to have exhibited a miniature at the Society of Artists, a miniature at the Free Society and 24 miniatures at the Royal Academy in London from 1773 until 1789.

SMITH, James
British, 18th - 19th century.
Born 1772; died 25 April 1815, in London.
Sculptor.

James Smith was the father of the sculptor Charles Smith and student of G.B. Locatelli. He created monuments for Westminster Abbey.

SMITH, James Bennet H.
British, 19th century.
Active in London during the first half of the 19th century.
Painter.

James Bennet H. Smith exhibited his work in London at the Royal Academy from 1830 until 1847.

SMITH, James Bonaventure
British, 19th century.
Born 1816; died December 1846.
Portrait artist.

James Bonaventure Smith studied under David d'Angers in Paris.

SMITH, James Burrell
British, 19th century.
Born 1822; died 1897, in London.
Painter, watercolourist. Landscapes.

James Burrell Smith painted landscapes in many parts of England, for example *Rydal Mount, Westmorland* (1869) and *View of Launceston, Cornwall* (1851). He also travelled on the Continent, producing river views such as *Cologne of the Rhine* (1865).

Museums and Galleries:
Newcastle upon Tyne (Laing Art Gallery): *Mountainous Landscape* (1850, watercolour on paper); *Harrier Hill* (watercolour on paper).

Auction records:
Tokyo, 27 May 1969, *Landscape with Waterfall*, GBP 502. London, 2 July 1971, *River Landscape with Waterfall*, Gns 320. New York, 12 Jan 1974, *Waterfall*, USD 1,000. London, 3 Feb 1978, *Landscape with Waterfall* (1894, oil on canvas, 35 1/4 x 25 1/4 ins / 89.5 x 64 cm) GBP 750. London, 20 March 1979, *Alpine Landscape* (watercolour and gouache, 21 x 35 1/4 ins / 53.5 x 89.5 cm) GBP 850. London, 29 Feb 1980, *Wooded River Landscape* (1882, oil on canvas, 19 3/4 x 14 3/4 ins / 50.2 x 37.5 cm) GBP 1,700. London, 19 Feb 1981, *Brinkburn Priory on the Coquet, Northumberland* (1862, watercolour heightened with gouache, 16 x 27 1/4 ins / 40.5 x 69 cm) GBP 600. London, 27 Feb 1985, *Cumberland Landscape* (watercolour heightened with gouache, 16 1/2 x 27 1/4 ins / 42 x 69 cm) GBP 900. London, 25 Jan 1988, *Twisel Castle and the Bridge over the Till between Berwick and Coldstream* (1887, watercolour, 5 x 7 ins / 13 x 17.5 cm) GBP 638. New York, 25 Feb 1988, *Figures near a River in Northumberland* (1859, watercolour, 16 1/4 x 28 ins / 41.3 x 71.2 cm) USD 1,540. Edinburgh, 22 Nov 1989, *View of Princes Street Gardens and the National Gallery in Edinburgh* (1885, watercolour and gouache, 19 1/4 x 12 3/4 ins / 48.8 x 32.3 cm) GBP 3,520. London, 30 Jan 1991, *House on the Bank of a Stream on the Isle of Wight* (1891, watercolour heightened with white, 11 x 15 3/4 ins / 28 x 40 cm) GBP 605. London, 14 June 1991, *Figures on the Banks of the Rhine, with Marksburg Castle in the Background* (1863, pencil and watercolour, 8 1/2 x 20 3/4 ins / 21.3 x 52.7 cm) GBP 1,595. Perth, 20 Aug 1996, *Loch in the Highlands* (1852, watercolour, 7 3/4 x 13 1/2 ins / 20 x 34 cm) GBP 517. London, 28 Oct 1999, *Loch Katrine, Perthshire* (1853, pencil and watercolour heightened with gouache and scratching out, 24 x 37 ins / 60 x 94 cm) GBP 2,800. Dublin, 8 Dec 1999, *Killarney* (1890, watercolour, 13 x 20 ins / 33 x 51 cm) IEP 2,400. Newbury, 23 Feb 2000, *Betws y Coed, Waterfalls* (1875, oil on canvas, a pair, 14 x 18 ins / 35 x 46 cm) GBP 2,700. London, 29 Nov 2000, *Balmoral Castle from across the River Dee* (watercolour over pencil heightened with gouache and stopping out, 13 x 17 ins / 33 x 44 cm) GBP 3,000. London, 5 Nov 2001, *Deer by a Sunlit Lake* (watercolour heightened with scratching out, stopping out and white, 22 x 35 ins / 56 x 89 cm) GBP 1,500. London, 1 May 2002, *On the Rhine* (1866, watercolour heightened with gouache, 9 x 21 ins / 24 x 53 cm) GBP 2,100. London, 21 Nov 2002, *View of Windsor Castle from across the Thames* (1884, pencil, watercolour, gum arabic and gouache with scratching out, 13 x 20 ins / 34 x 50 cm) GBP 2,000. Leeds, 4 Feb 2003, *Cattle on a Bridge above Loch Fyne* (1879, watercolour heightened with white, 17 x 27 ins / 42 x 68 cm) GBP 2,100. London, 12 June 2003, *Derwentwater with Bassenthwaite Beyond, Cumbria* (1868, watercolour and gouache, 21 x 41 ins / 54 x 105 cm) GBP 2,200. Bletchingley, 8 June 2004, *Extensive Rural Landscape with Figure Crossing a Stone Bridge* (oil on canvas, 11 x 24 ins / 28 x 61 cm) GBP 1,900.

SMITH, James Calvert
American, 20th century.
Born 1878; died 1962.
Illustrator.

James Calvert Smith was a member of the Salmagundi Club.

SMITH, James P.
American, 19th century.
Born 1803; died 1888, in Philadelphia.
Active in Philadelphia.
Miniaturist, painter. Portraits.

SMITH, Jan
Dutch, 17th century.
Painter.

Jan Smith painted the portrait of *Adam van Vianen*, which was engraved by Th. van Kessel.

SMITH, Jan Borritsz.. See **SMIT**

SMITH, Jessie Wilcox
American, 19th - 20th century.
Born 1863, in Philadelphia; died 1935, in Philadelphia.
Painter, illustrator.

Jessie Wilcox Smith studied at the Pennsylvania Academy of Fine Arts in Philadelphia, where she was taught by Thomas Eakins, and at the Drexel Institute, where she was taught by Howard Pyle. She was a member of the American Federation of Arts.

Smith specialised in painting and illustrating for children and also produced a number of covers for *Good Housekeeping* magazine. The works she illustrated include: Scribner's *A Child's Garden of Verses*, 1905; Coussens' *The Everyday Fairy Book*, 1911; Brown's *Little Women*, 1915; and Scribner's *The Children of Dickens*, 1925. She also produced illustrated books such as *A Child's Book of Old Verses*, 1910, and *The Little Mother Goose*, 1918. She won many prizes including a silver medal at the 1904 exhibition in St Louis and another one at the 1915 Panama-Pacific Exposition in San Francisco.

BIBLIOGRAPHY:

Schnessel, S. Michael, *Jessie Willcox Smith*, Crowell, New York, 1977. Mitchell, Gene, *The Subject Was Children: The Art of Jessie Willcox Smith*, Dutton, New York, 1979. Nudelman, Edward D., *Jessie Willcox Smith: A Bibliography*, Pelican Pub. Co, Gretna, 1989. Nudelman, Edward D., *Jessie Willcox Smith: American Illustrator*, Pelican Pub. Co, Gretna, 1990.

AUCTION RECORDS:

BOLTON, 20 Nov 1980, *Mowgli* (oil and charcoal/mounted paper/card, 21 x 18 ins / 52.5 x 46 cm) USD 2,300. NEW YORK, 20 April 1982, *Night of the Fourth* (1896, oil on canvas, 22 x 16 ins / 56 x 40.8 cm) USD 2,000. NEW YORK, 28 Sept 1989, *Rebecca from Sunny Brook Farm* (oil and charcoal/card, 18 1/2 x 16 1/2 ins / 46.7 x 41.6 cm) USD 16,500. NEW YORK, 26 May 1993, *Jack and Jill* (gouache and charcoal/card, 19 x 26 1/4 ins / 48 x 66.7 cm) USD 18,400. NEW YORK, 22 Sept 1993, *It was the Night Before Christmas* (ink and watercolour/card, 9 1/2 x 14 1/4 ins / 24.2 x 36.3 cm) USD 5,980. THOMASTON, 30 Oct 1999, *Little Red Riding Hood* (mixed media on paper, illustration for calendar) USD 60,000. LOS ANGELES, 9 Dec 1999, *Woman Surrounded by Children* (watercolour, gouache and pencil on paperboard, 34 x 23 ins / 86 x 58 cm) USD 135,000. NEW YORK, 14 March 2001, *Young Girl with Doll* (charcoal, pencil and gouache, 9 x 23 ins / 22 x 58 cm) USD 16,000. NEW YORK, 10 Nov 2001, *Boy Seated under an Apple Tree* (oil, charcoal and watercolour on board, 7 x 10 ins / 18 x 25 cm) USD 70,000. NEW YORK, 11 May 2002, *Young Girl Standing in the Corner, a Doll on the Floor* (charcoal and watercolour, 14 x 9 ins / 36 x 23 cm) USD 34,000. NEW YORK, 9 Nov 2002, *Little Red Riding Hood Approaching Grandmother* (charcoal, oil and watercolour, 25 x 16 ins / 64 x 41 cm) USD 65,000. NEW YORK, 15 Nov 2003, *The Goose Girl* (oil and charcoal on board, 22 x 14 ins / 56 x 36 cm) USD 110,000. PHILADELPHIA, 7 Dec 2003, *Young Tennis Player* (oil, mixed media and charcoal on board, 21 x 15 ins / 53 x 38 cm) USD 60,000. BOSTON, 5 March 2004, *In the Garden* (oil, gouache and charcoal on board, 23 x 15 ins / 59 x 39 cm) USD 110,000. NEW YORK, 15 May 2004, *Little Bo Peep Has Lost Her Sheep* (oil and charcoal on board, 18 x 25 ins / 46 x 64 cm) USD 80,000.

SMITH, Joachim

British, 18th - 19th century.
Active in London.
Sculptor, modeller, cameo engraver. Medallions.

Joachim Smith exhibited his work in London from 1760 until 1814.

MUSEUMS AND GALLERIES:

LONDON (National Portrait Gal.): *Thomas Bentley* (c. 1773 (1922), Wedgwood ceramic, medallion).

SMITH, Joachim Becher

Danish, 20th century.
Born 15 March 1851, in Copenhagen; died 31 December 1926, in Copenhagen.
Sculptor.

Joachim Becher Smith studied at the Kunstakademi in Copenhagen and under J. A. Jerichau.

MUSEUMS AND GALLERIES:

AALBORG.

SMITH, Johan

Dutch, 17th century.
Portrait artist.

SMITH, John

British, 17th - 18th century.
Born c. 1652, in Daventry; died 17 January 1742, in Northampton.
Painter, draughtsman, engraver (mezzotint).

John Smith was the son of an engraver, but was apprenticed to a painter at first. He was then employed by Isaac Becket to prepare his plates. He was also advised by J. Van der Vaart. Sir Joseph Kneller supported him and got him to reproduce many of his works. He painted and drew a number of portraits.

SMITH, John, the Younger

British, 18th century.
Born 1717, in Chichester; died 29 July 1764, in Chichester.
Engraver (etching/burin). Landscapes, seascapes.

John Smith was the brother of George Smith of Chichester. He depicted landscapes and seascapes.

SMITH, John, called Warwick Smith and Smith the Italian

British, 18th - 19th century.
Born 26 July 1749, in Irthington; died 22 March 1831, in London.
Painter, watercolourist, draughtsman. Landscapes.

John Warwick Smith was educated at St Beels. He was a topographical painter and draughtsman and one of the first watercolourists to follow Paul Sandly. He accompanied Lord Warwick to Italy, which earned him his nicknames. He exhibited his work in London from 1807 until 1823, joined the Society of Painters in Watercolours as an associate in 1805, becoming a member in 1807 and its president in 1814, 1817 and 1818.

In 2001 he was represented in the exhibition *Un Paese incantato. Italia dipinta da Thomas Jones a Corot* (*An Enchanted Country. Italy Depicted by Artists from Thomas Jones to Corot*) at the Centro Internazionale d'Arte e di Cultura de Palazzo Te in Mantua, Italy.

BIBLIOGRAPHY:

Ottani Cavina, Anna (ed.), *Un Paese incantato. Italia dipinta da Thomas Jones a Corot*, exhibition catalogue, Electa, Milan, 2001.

MUSEUMS AND GALLERIES:

LONDON (British Mus.): *View of Naples from Capodimonte* (watercolour/paper); *Villa Medici* (watercolour/paper) - LONDON (Victoria and Albert Mus.): eight watercolours - MANCHESTER: *Lake Lugano* (watercolour).

AUCTION RECORDS:

LONDON, 22 Oct 1970, *View of Ostia* (watercolour) GBP 340. LONDON, 2 March 1971, *View of Tivoli* (watercolour) Gns 580. LONDON, 14 Dec 1972, *View of Ludlow* (watercolour) GBP 600. LONDON, 4 June 1974, *Landscape with St Peter's in Rome in the Background* (watercolour) Gns 1,000. VERSAILLES, 7 Nov 1976, *Portuguese Motherhood* (gouache, 19 x 24 3/4 ins / 48 x 63 cm) FRF 5,000. LONDON, 22 Nov 1977, *Auckland Castle* (watercolour and pencil, 13 3/4 x 20 1/2 ins / 35 x 52 cm) GBP 600. LONDON, 13 Dec 1979, *View of Naples* (1781, watercolour and pencil, 13 3/4 x 20 1/4 ins / 35 x 51.5 cm) GBP 2,800. LONDON, 30 March 1983, *View of Naples* (1800, watercolour on pencil outlines, 21 x 32 3/4 ins / 52.5 x 83 cm) GBP 3,200. LONDON, 20 Nov 1986, *Cascatelli in Tivoli at Dusk* (watercolour/pencil outlines heightened with white, 19 1/2 x 28 3/4 ins / 49.5 x 73 cm) GBP 3,200. LONDON, 14 July 1987, *Lake Nemi* (watercolour and pencil, 12 1/4 x 17 1/2 ins / 31 x 44.7 cm) GBP 2,800. LONDON, 31 Jan 1990, *Mount Snowdon in Caernarvonshire* (1797, watercolour, 5 x 9 ins / 12.5 x 22 cm) GBP 1,870. YORK, 12 Nov 1991, *Italian Landscape with a Building at the Roadside* (watercolour, 12 1/2 x 17 3/4 ins / 32 x 45 cm) GBP 1,100. LONDON, 8 June 1999, *View of Fonthill Abbey, Wiltshire* (pencil and watercolour, 9 x 12 ins / 22 x 30 cm) GBP 2,900. BILLINGSHURST, 19 Oct 1999, *Clynnog Fawr on the Bay of Caernarfon* (watercolour over pencil, 5 x 9 ins / 12 x 22 cm) GBP 3,000. SEVENOAKS, 18 July 2000, *Church and Mountain Hamlet of Festiniog, Merionethshire* (1786, watercolour over pencil, 5 x 9 ins / 13 x 22 cm) GBP 1,000. SEVENOAKS, 18 July 2000, *View to Llangollen and Castle Dinas Bran* (watercolour over pencil, 5 x 9 ins / 13 x 22 cm) GBP 1,200. LONDON, 10 April 2001, *Lake of Nemi, Italy* (watercolour over pencil, 12 x 18 ins / 31 x 45 cm) GBP 3,000. LONDON, 7 Nov 2001, *Mansel Lacy House, Foxley. Foxley Woods, Herefordshire* (watercolour over pencil, a pair, 5 x 9 ins / 13 x 22 cm) GBP 2,400. LONDON, 17 Oct 2002, *Coast of Sorrento* (pencil and watercolour, 10 x 15 ins / 26 x 37 cm) GBP 2,600. LONDON, 28 Nov 2002, *Sailing Vessels off the Island of Elba* (watercolour over pencil and scratching out, 6 x 9 ins / 15 x 22 cm) GBP 2,600. LONDON, 22 Jan 2003, *Tintern Abbey by Moonlight* (pencil, watercolour and scratching out, 5 x 8 ins / 13 x 21 cm) GBP 10,000. LONDON, 20 Nov 2003, *View Near the Head of Lake Thun, Switzerland* (1788, pencil and watercolour heightened with gouache, 14 x 20 ins / 35 x 52 cm) GBP 3,800. LEWES, 9 March 2004, *Pass from Tyrol into Italy, near Verona. Cortona* (watercolour, a pair, 7 x 12 ins / 18 x 30 cm) GBP 2,000. LONDON, 9 Nov 2004, *Cortona, Tuscany, Pass from the Tyrol into Italy, near Verona* (watercolour, two, 7 x 13 ins / 18 x 33 cm) GBP 3,600.

SMITH, John, or Smyth
Irish, 18th - 19th century.
Born c. 1773, in Dublin; died March 1840, in Dublin.
Sculptor.

John Smith studied under his father, the sculptor Edward Smith, whom he succeeded as teacher at the school of sculpture in Dublin.

He was an interesting artist, whose works are a good indication of the Irish conception of art.

SMITH, John
British, 19th century.
Engraver.

John Smith was active in Edinburgh from 1800 until 1830. He produced a burin engraving of *William Hunter* after Joshua Reynolds.

SMITH, John
British, 19th century.
Born c. 1798.
Engraver.

Smith studied at the Royal Academy in London. He created burin engravings and engravings on steel of landscapes and views of towns.

SMITH, John Brandon
British, 19th century.
Died 1884.
Painter. Landscapes with figures, landscapes, waterscapes.

John Brandon Smith exhibited his work regularly at the Royal Academy in London from 1860 until 1874.

His favourite subjects were waterscapes, landscapes of Scottish and Welsh rivers and especially waterfalls and mountain lakes, sometimes including the figure of a local inhabitant on a bridge, or a fisherman beside a stream. He also painted views of various English counties. His themes are characteristic of the great Romantic trend in Europe.

AUCTION RECORDS:

LONDON, 15 Oct 1976, *Waterfall* (oil on canvas, 17 1/2 x 13 1/2 ins / 44.5 x 34.3 cm) GBP 750. LONDON, 14 June 1977, *Riverside Road* (1870, oil on canvas, 19 1/2 x 29 1/2 ins / 49.5 x 75 cm) GBP 750. LONDON, 9 Oct 1979, *Fishermen beside a Waterfall* (1881, oil on canvas, 39 x 49 1/2 ins / 99 x 126 cm) GBP 2,600. LONDON, 8 May 1981, *Waterfalls* (1881, painting/card, a pair, each 14 x 12 1/4 ins / 35.6 x 31 cm) GBP 1,700. AUCHTERARDER, 28 Aug 1984, *Falls at Hespe, North Wales* (1895, oil on canvas, 20 x 16 ins / 50.8 x 40.6 cm) GBP 1,900. LONDON, 2 Oct 1985, *Landscape with Waterfall* (1883, oil on canvas, a pair, 17 3/4 x 13 1/2 ins / 45 x 34 cm) GBP 4,500. LONDON, 17 Dec 1986, *Waterfalls* (1867, oil on canvas, a pair, 18 x 14 ins / 46 x 35.5 cm) GBP 3,200. LONDON, 15 June 1988, *Waterfall* (1874, oil on canvas, 12 x 10 ins / 30.5 x 25.5 cm) GBP 2,090. TORONTO, 30 Nov 1988, *Welsh Peasant on a Bridge at Nightfall* (1876, oil on canvas, 13 1/4 x 17 1/2 ins / 33.5 x 44.5 cm) CAD 2,400. LONDON, 27 Sept 1989, *Waterfall; Footbridge over a Rocky River* (1879-1880, oil on canvas/card, a pair, each 13 x 17 ins / 33 x 43 cm) GBP 6,380. LONDON, 9 Feb 1990, *Mountain Lake* (1873, oil on canvas, 37 x 27 1/2 ins / 94 x 70 cm) GBP 1,980. LONDON, 15 June 1990, *Waterfall* (1888, oil on card, 8 x 10 ins / 20.3 x 25.4 cm) GBP 2,860. LONDON, 8 Feb 1991, *Highland Waterfall* (1883, oil on canvas, 18 1/4 x 14 ins / 46.4 x 35.6 cm) GBP 2,200. LONDON, 14 June 1991, *Fishermen near a Waterfall on the River Conway in North Wales* (1881, oil on canvas, 34 3/4 x 10 1/2 ins / 88.3 x 26.4 cm) GBP 9,900. LONDON, 12 Nov 1992, *Waterfall* (1881, oil on canvas, 14 x 12 ins / 35.5 x 30.5 cm) GBP 1,980. MONTREAL, 23-24 Nov 1993, *View of Waterfalls* (oil on canvas, 18 x 14 ins / 45.6 x 35.5 cm) CAD 2,400. LONDON, 9 June 1994, *Waterfall* (1877, oil on canvas, 20 1/4 x 26 1/2 ins / 51.5 x 67 cm) GBP 6,670. LONDON, 10 March 1995, *The Lynn in Devon* (1878, oil on canvas, 14 x 18 ins / 35.6 x 45.8 cm) GBP 2,875. LONDON, 6 Nov 1995, *Waterfall; Fishing in a Stream* (oil on card, a pair, each 13 1/2 x 17 1/4 ins / 34 x 44 cm) GBP 6,440. LONDON, 7 June 1996, *Fishing in the Stream* (1878, oil on canvas, 20 x 27 ins / 50.8 x 68.6 cm) GBP 3,450. NEW YORK, 18-19 July 1996, *Waterfall in a Landscape* (1874, oil on canvas, a pair, each 18 x 14 ins / 45.7 x 35.6 cm) USD 9,775. LONDON, 12 March 1997, *On the Llugwy, North Wales* (1879, oil on canvas, 20 x 27 1/4 ins / 51 x 69 cm) GBP 5,750. EDINBURGH, 15 May 1997, *Tummel Falls, Perthshire* (1871, oil on canvas, 18 x 14 ins / 45.8 x 35.5 cm) GBP 3,450. LONDON, 4 June 1997, *On the Lledr, North Wales* (oil on canvas, 14 x 18 ins / 35.5 x 46 cm) GBP 3,220. LONDON, 28 June 1999, *Waterfall* (oil on canvas, 24 x 20 ins / 61 x 51 cm) GBP 2,800. LEYLAND, 3 Nov 1999, *Angler by Scottish River with Bridge and Mountains Beyond* (oil on canvas, 18 x 32 ins / 46 x 81 cm) GBP 2,800. LONDON, 22 March 2000, *Waterfall* (1881, oil on canvas, 18 x 14 ins / 46 x 35 cm) GBP 7,000. LEEDS, 14 Nov 2000, *Waterfall Scene with Trees, Possibly High Force, Upper Teesdale* (oil on canvas, 13 x 17 ins / 33 x 44 cm) GBP 6,500. LONDON, 23 May 2001, *On the Lledr, North Wales. Waterall, Valley of Neath South Wales* (1871, oil on canvas, a pair, 18 x 14 ins / 46 x 35 cm) GBP 6,200. MALMÖ, 24 Nov 2001, *Stone Path of the Clyde - Waterfall in Green Landscape* (1887, oil on canvas, 20 x 27 ins / 51 x 69 cm) SEK 70,000. LONDON, 26 March 2002, *Skelwith Force, Langdale. Colwith Force, Langdale* (1872, oil on canvas, a pair, 18 x 14 ins / 46 x 36 cm) GBP 8,200. LONDON, 11 June 2002, *Mountain Landscape with Waterfall. Fisherman Beside a Waterfall* (1892, oil on canvas, a pair, 24 x 36 ins / 61 x 92 cm) GBP 7,000. OXFORD, 2 Sept 2003, *Falls of the Parthen, South Wales, Waterfall with a Plunge Pool in a Landscape* (1880, oil on canvas, 18 x 13 ins / 45 x 34 cm) GBP 5,800. LONDON, 1 Oct 2003, *Waterfall near Onllwyn, South Wales* (1879, oil on canvas, 17 x 13 ins / 44 x 34 cm) GBP 3,800. LONDON, 4 March 2004, *Figures by a Waterfall* (1874, oil on canvas, 26 x 20 ins / 66 x 51 cm) GBP

3,600. EDINBURGH, 28 May 2004, *Near Capel Curig, North Wales* (1872, oil on canvas, a pair, 18 x 14 ins / 46 x 36 cm) GBP 4,800.

SMITH, John Francis
American, 19th - 20th century.
Born 23 June 1868, in Chicago; died 27 December 1941, in San Diego.
Painter.

John Francis Smith was taught by Gregori, Boulanger, Lefebvre and Constant in Paris. He was a member of the American Art Association in Paris.

SMITH, John Guthrie Spence
British, 20th century.
Born 1880; died 1951.
Painter. Landscapes, landscapes with figures, seascapes, harbour views.

AUCTION RECORDS:
EDINBURGH, 26 April 1990, *Springtime in Angus* (oil on panel, 25 x 30 ins / 63.5 x 76.2 cm) GBP 1,870. GLASGOW, 5 Feb 1991, *Windmill and Hayricks* (1910, oil on panel, 14 3/4 x 17 3/4 ins / 37.5 x 45 cm) GBP 770. PERTH, 26 Aug 1991, *The Quaysides at Etaples* (oil on card, 20 x 23 1/2 ins / 51 x 60 cm) GBP 1,100. EDINBURGH, 23 March 1993, *Chickens in an Orchard* (oil on card, 20 x 24 ins / 50.5 x 61 cm) GBP 1,840. GLASGOW, 11 Dec 1996, *On a Country Road* (oil on canvas, 30 x 25 ins / 76 x 63.5 cm) GBP 713. TORONTO, 17 May 1999, *Young Girl and Ducks on Sun Dappled Road* (oil on canvas, 25 x 30 ins / 63 x 76 cm) CAD 4,200. TORONTO, 17 May 1999, *Mother and Child on a Rural Path* (oil on canvas, 33 x 28 ins / 84 x 71 cm) CAD 4,800. LONDON, 10 April 2000, *The Old Stone Bridge* (oil on canvas, 26 x 32 ins / 66 x 82 cm) GBP 1,200. LONDON, 30 Aug 2000, *Corner at Ceres, Fife* (oil on board, 20 x 24 ins / 51 x 61 cm) GBP 2,000. EDINBURGH, 11 April 2002, *Valley of the Tay* (oil on canvasboard, sold with a companion, 11 x 15 ins / 29 x 39 cm) GBP 2,000. LONDON, 15 April 2002, *Playing in the Woods* (oil on canvas, 40 x 30 ins / 102 x 76 cm) GBP 1,700.

SMITH, John Henry
British, 19th century.
Active in London during the second half of the 19th century.
Painter. Genre scenes, animals.

John Henry Smith exhibited his work in London from 1852 until 1893.

SMITH, John Henry
American, 19th - 20th century.
Born 1879.
Sculptor (including wood/stone), ceramicist.

John Henry Smith was self-taught. His work seems to have been in circulation during the first exhibitions of African-American artists in the USA, which were held in the 1940s. Like other black artists of the time, such as Beauford Delaney and Palmer Hayden, he worked as a janitor. Little else is known of his life, and even the date of his death is unknown.

Works by John Henry Smith have been included in group exhibitions, including: at the Society of Independent Artists, New York (1938); and *American Negro Art: 19th and 20th Centuries*, Downtown Gallery, New York (1941). He made realistic portraits in wood, granite and ceramics, such as *Tough Boy* (1938), the face of a black man, lined deep with fatigue and life's trials.

BIBLIOGRAPHY:
'*John Smith: Janitor and Sculptor*' in *Ebony*, periodical, New York, February 1950. Dickason Cederholm, Theresa, *Afro-American Artists. A Bio-bibliographical Directory*, Trustees of the Boston Public Library, Boston, 1973. Fine, Elsa Honig, *The Afro-American Artist*, Holt, Rinehart and Winston, New York, 1973.

SMITH, John Orrin
British, 19th century.
Born 1799, in Colchester; died 15 October 1843, in London.
Engraver (wood).

John Orrin Smith studied under S. Williams and W. Harvey. He engraved illustrations of classical authors.

SMITH, John Raphael
British, 18th - 19th century.
Born 1752, in Derby; died 2 March 1812, in Doncaster.
Painter, pastellist, engraver, draughtsman. Portraits, genre scenes.

John Raphael Smith was the son of Thomas Smith of Derby. He began his working life as an apprentice to a cloth manufacturer, but it is more than likely that he also learned to draw and paint from his father. He went to London when he was very young and became a shop assistant. He painted miniatures to supplement his income. It is not known who taught him to engrave, but he published a print entitled *The Public Ledger Open to All Parties*, which was so successful that it determined his future career. He was considered to be one of the most skilful English engravers after 1778. His success earned him the royal warrant of the Prince of Wales. At the height of his success as an engraver he began to try out his skills at painting and portraiture. He had exhibited at the Society of Artists and the Free Society since 1773, but from 1779 until 1805 he frequently sent works to the Royal Academy, particularly pencil portraits. His paintings were of genre subjects. He left London and settled in turn in York, Sheffield, Doncaster and other cities.

He was very skilful, but the extreme ease with which he carried out his work, and perhaps also the need for money, led him to complete his pieces very quickly, which compromised their quality. He could paint or draw a portrait from start to finish in an hour. His collection of this type of work is considerable; however, he produced about 150 prints and it is these that show his true artistic worth.

MUSEUMS AND GALLERIES:
LONDON (National Portrait Gal.): *George Morland* (c. 1792, two versions, an oil on canvas and a pastel); *Thomas Morton* (c. 1803, pastel); *John Raphael Smith* (c. 1807, pastel); *Sir Francis Leggatt Chantrey* (1818?, pastel).

AUCTION RECORDS:
LONDON, 4 and 5 May 1922, *Sir Francis Burdett* (pastel) GBP 10. LONDON, 22 June 1922, *Mary and Charlotte Hart* (drawing) GBP 64; *Julius Cesar Ibbetson* (drawing) GBP 20; *Chalybeate Well* (drawing) GBP 46. LONDON, 8 April 1925, *Proverbs* (two coloured chalks) GBP 110. LONDON, 7 May 1926, *The Byng Family*, GBP 346. LONDON, 18 Nov 1927, *Wedding Plans*, GBP 199. LONDON, 8 June 1928, *Portrait of Woman* (pastel) GBP 131. LONDON, 11 June 1928, *Fortune Teller* (drawing) GBP 54. LONDON, 29 June 1928, *Master Rowsby* (pastel) GBP 131. LONDON, 14 July 1939, *Woman in Blue Dress*, GBP 136. LONDON, 3 April 1968, '*What you will*', GBP 900. LONDON, 11 Nov 1969, *Portrait of Emma Smith* (pastel) Gns 350. LONDON, 9 Nov 1971, *Major John Tempest* (pastel) Gns 500. LONDON, 27 July 1979, *George Prince of Wales* (coloured mezzotint, 26 x 18 ins / 65.9 x 45.8 cm) GBP 520. LONDON, 27 June 1980, *Portrait of Charles James Fox* (1808, oil on canvas, 55 1/4 x 46 ins / 140.2 x 117 cm) GBP 500. LONDON, 20 March 1984, *Portrait of Elegant Woman in a Hat with a Feather* (pencil, red chalk and wash, oval, 7 1/2 x 6 1/2 ins / 19.2 x 16.5 cm) GBP 580. LONDON, 10 July 1984, *Portrait of Charles James Fox* (pastel, 24 1/2 x 17 ins / 62.5 x 43.4 cm) GBP 1,800. LONDON, 19 Nov 1986, *A Visit to Grandfather* (oil on canvas, 30 x 24 1/2 ins / 76.5 x 62.5 cm) GBP 18,000. EDINBURGH, 23 May 1996, *Moralist* (oil on canvas, 24 x 19 3/4 ins / 61 x 50.2 cm) GBP 7,475. LONDON, 13 Nov 1997, *Lady in Milton's 'Comus'*; *Indian Chief's Widow Looking at her Dead Husband's Weapons* (1789, mezzotint, a pair, each 1 3/4 x 2 1/4

ins / 4.55 x 5.6 cm) GBP 6,440. SAUGERTIES, 10 Jan 1999, *Portrait of Gentleman* (c. 1800, pastel, 9 x 8 ins / 23 x 20 cm) USD 1,700. LONDON, 31 March 1999, *Portrait of Samuel Athawes* (pastel, 24 x 17 ins / 62 x 42 cm) GBP 5,200. LONDON, 8 March 2001, *Winter, Portrait of a Lady in a Blue Dress with Pink Wrap and Black Hat, in a Landscape* (oil on canvas, 30 x 25 ins / 76 x 63 cm) GBP 10,000. SALISBURY, 30 Oct 2001, *Soldier's Farewell* (oil on canvas, 15 x 11 ins / 37 x 29 cm) GBP 3,000. LONDON, 9 July 2002, *Soldier's Farewell on the Eve of a Battle* (oil on canvas, 15 x 13 ins / 38 x 32 cm) GBP 2,800. MELBOURNE, 26 Nov 2002, *Portrait of John Glover* (coloured crayon, 5 x 5 ins / 13 x 12 cm) AUD 12,000. TIMONIUM, 18 March 2004, *Soldier's Farewell on the Eve of a Battle* (oil on wood panel, sold with a framed print, 15 x 12 ins / 38 x 30 cm) USD 8,200. LONDON, 3 June 2004, *Portrait of the Right Honourable Charles James Fox MP Seated in his Study* (pastel, 24 x 17 ins / 61 x 44 cm) GBP 7,000.

SMITH, John Rowson
American, 19th century.
Active in New York in 1844.
Painter. Panoramas.

John Rowson Smith was the son of John Rubens Smith.

SMITH, John Rubens
British, 18th - 19th century.
Born 23 January 1775; died 21 August 1849, in New York.
Painter, engraver (burin), art writer. Portraits, genre scenes, landscapes.

John Rubens Smith was the son of John Raphael Smith. He exhibited 48 works, mainly portraits, at the Royal Academy from 1796 until 1811.

BIBLIOGRAPHY:
Smith John, '*Catalogue raisonné of the Works of the Most Eminent Dutch, Flemish and French Painters*' in *9 vol.*, S.n., London, 1829-1936.

AUCTION RECORDS:
NEW YORK, 15 Nov 1967, *Strade's Mill, Pennsylvania* (watercolour) USD 1,300.

SMITH, John Thomas
British, 18th - 19th century.
Born 23 June 1766, in London; died 8 March 1833, in London.
Engraver (etching), draughtsman, painter, art writer. Landscapes, topographical views.

John Thomas Smith was the son of the sculptor Nathaniel Smith. He first studied under the sculptor Nollekens, then became a student at the schools of the Royal Academy, before studying under the engraver Sherwin. He exhibited landscapes at the Royal Academy in 1787 and in 1788 he became an art teacher. Between 1791 and 1800 he also prepared and published an important work on the antiquities of London and the surrounding area. *Antiquities of Westminster*, a large work comprising 246 engravings, appeared next, followed by a supplement. He then published *Ancient Topography of London*, 32 prints reminiscent of Piranesi because of their breadth of technique, which he completed in 1815. He was appointed Curator of Prints at the British Museum. He also produced a book on the beggars of London, illustrated with etchings, and a critical work entitled *Nollekens and his Time*.

SMITH, Jori
Canadian, 20th century.
Born 1907, in Montreal.
Painter, watercolourist. Figures, portraits, interiors with figures, still-lifes.

Jori Smith studied at the School of Fine Arts in Montreal from 1923 to 1928 and then worked for Edwin Holgate. She was an active member of the Eastern Group and of the Contemporary Art Society at the end of the 1930s. She also worked in the studio of the Bouchard sisters. She stayed in the South of France and Sardinia in 1980.

While Smith's painting aimed to reflect the difficult social conditions of her time, it also evoked tenderness and nostalgia, which is particularly evident in the heads of women or children, still-lifes and interior scenes. She used harmonious materials and colours, which often blurred the form. Although she took part in the revival of French-Canadian painting in the 1930s, her work was not recognised until the beginning of the 1980s. Since then, her painting has undergone changes marked by preoccupations with light both in the use of colours and in the symbolic expression.

Smith participated in the Exposition des Indépendants in Montreal in 1941. Solo exhibitions of her work were held in the Dominion and Kastel Galleries in Montreal.

MUSEUMS AND GALLERIES:
MONTREAL (MAC): *Sister of Vitaline* (1952).

AUCTION RECORDS:
MONTREAL, 17 Oct 1988, *Portrait* (1945, oil on canvas, 20 x 16 1/4 ins / 51 x 41 cm) CAD 1,100. TORONTO, 15 Nov 2000, *Still-life with Pineapple* (1954, oil on board, 20 x 30 ins / 51 x 76 cm) CAD 4,500. TORONTO, 16 May 2001, *Portrait of Vitaline Simard* (oil on masonite, 24 x 20 ins / 61 x 50 cm) CAD 3,750. MONTREAL, 26 June 2001, *Untitled* (1946, oil on canvas, 24 x 30 ins / 61 x 76 cm) CAD 2,600. TORONTO, 14 May 2002, *Seated Young Girl* (oil on board, 22 x 19 ins / 57 x 49 cm) CAD 4,200. OTTAWA, 21 Nov 2003, *Village Scene, St Urbain* (1936, oil on board, 7 x 9 ins / 19 x 24 cm) CAD 3,500.

SMITH, Joseph
British, 19th century.
Active from 1820 to 1837.
Portrait artist.

SMITH, Joseph Clarendon
British, 18th - 19th century.
Born 1778, in London; died August 1810, in England.
Painter, watercolourist, engraver (burin).
Topographical views.

Joseph Clarendon Smith started out as a ship's boy, and was then placed as an apprentice to an engraver. He went on to produce topographical watercolours. One of his best engraved works is *Topography* by Killarney.

MUSEUMS AND GALLERIES:
LEICESTER: *Waltham Cross* - LONDON (Victoria and Albert Mus.): six watercolours - MANCHESTER: a watercolour.

SMITH, Joseph Lindon
American, 19th - 20th century.
Born 11 October 1863, in Pawtucket (Rhode Island); died 1950.
Painter, lithographer. Wall decorations.

Joseph Lindon Smith studied at the Boston School of Art and the Académie Julian in Paris, where he was taught by Boulanger and Lefebvre. He was a member of the American Federation of Arts. He painted murals at Boston library, and one of his works is in the École du Louvre.

MUSEUMS AND GALLERIES:
BOSTON - CHICAGO - PARIS (Mus. National des Arts asiatiques-Guimet) - WASHINGTON DC.

AUCTION RECORDS:
NEW YORK, 31 May 1990, *Egyptian Figure - Wall Relief* (oil on canvas, 36 x 27 ins / 91.5 x 68.6 cm) USD 1,430. CAMBRIDGE, 11 Nov 2000, *Profile Portrait of Exotic Woman* (oil on board, 16 x 12 ins / 41 x 30 cm) USD 1,600. BOSTON, 2 Dec 2001, *Egyptian Sculpture Site* (watercolour and pencil, 21 x 14 ins / 53 x 36 cm) USD 7,000. NEW YORK, 13 June 2002, *God Amun Enthroned* (oil on canvas, 36 x 24 ins / 91 x 60 cm) USD 3,500. BOSTON, 5 March 2004, *Egyptian Figure, Tomb of Siptah, Valley of the Kings* (oil on canvasboard, 27 x 23 ins / 69 x 59 cm)

USD 4,000. BOSTON, 10 Sept 2004, *Amalfi Coast* (1889, oil on canvas, 35 x 23 ins / 89 x 58 cm) USD 4,000.

SMITH, Judson

American, 20th century.

Born 4 July 1880, in Grand Haven; died 1962.

Painter.

Judson Smith was taught by John La Farge, Twachtman and Kenyon Cox. He worked at Woodstock. He executed monumental decoration according to Cubist principles. He won first prize at the Detroit Institute of Art in 1926 and a first award at the Carnegie Foundation International Exhibition in 1931.

MUSEUMS AND GALLERIES:

NEW YORK (Whitney Mus. of American Art): *Along the Hudson.*

AUCTION RECORDS:

NEW YORK, 3 Dec 1996, *Along Old Saginaw Turnpike* (tempera/paper/card, 18 3/4 x 44 1/4 ins / 47.6 x 112.3 cm) USD 4,025.

SMITH, Jules Andre

American, 20th century.

Born 1880, in Hong Kong; died 1959.

Engraver, painter, architect, writer.

Jules Andre Smith studied architecture at Cornell University. However, he soon turned to etching as a means of artistic expression. He served in the Army camouflage section in World War I and became one of the eight artists commissioned to record the activities of American Expeditionary Forces. He took an innovative approach to art, exploring new areas in a number of media - painting, sculpture, and print-making. He lived and worked in Pine Orchard, and served as director of the Research Studio in Maitland, Florida, which sought to encourage artistic experimentation. He exhibited his work, winning a gold medal in San Francisco for his etching.

AUCTION RECORDS:

NEW ORLEANS, 8 June 2002, *Palm Shade, Eatonville, Florida* (watercolour, 13 x 19 ins / 33 x 48 cm) USD 1,550.

SMITH, Kiki

American, 20th - 21st century.

Born 18 January 1954, in Nuremberg, Germany.

Sculptor (mixed media), graphic artist.

Kiki Smith was born in Germany, but grew up in New Jersey. Her father was the sculptor Tony Smith, and as a child she helped him make cardboard models for his geometric models, thereby learning about Formalism and Minimalism. She studied at Hartford Art School (1974-1976), and has also trained in industrial baking and as an Emergency Medical Technician. She has lived in New York since 1976 and was associated with Collaborative Projects Inc. there through the early 1980s. Influences on her work include Eva Hesse, Louise Bourgeois and Lee Bontecou.

Since the late 1970s, her work has focused on the human body, ranging from fragments of the body to whole figures. Some of her works are cast from live models. Her sculptures challenge public stereotypes of the (particularly female) body in relation to our private perceptions of our bodies and sexuality, and seek to express the interface between body and soul.

In the late 1970s, Smith's work had a particular focus on the skin, while by the 1980s she began to make sculptures and drawings based on the human nervous system, internal organs and cellular forms. She has since broadened her subject matter to include animals, domestic objects, classical and biblical mythology, and Egyptian figures. She has created sculptures in bronze, plaster, paper, wood and wax, as well as printing by photolithography, photogravure and silkscreen. In 1985, she first began to work with glass at the New York Experimental Glass Workshop.

She has a particular interest in the vulnerability of the body, as in how the skin is simultaneously protective and fragile. In *Blood Pool* (1992), broken bones protrude from the figure. Bodily fluids (sweat, blood, tears, saliva) are a particular subject, as in her beeswax sculpture *Untitled* (1992), where milk and semen leak from a naked couple, and in other works such as *Sperm* (1988-1990) and *Digestive System.*

Smith received the Skowhegan Medal for Sculpture (2000). Her work is held in the collections of the Art Institute of Chicago; the Brooklyn Museum; the Fogg Art Museum, Harvard University; the Los Angeles County Museum of Art; the Moderna Museet, Stockholm; the Museum of Modern Art, New York; the Tate Gallery, London; the Toledo Museum of Art, Ohio; the V & A Museum, London; Yale University Art Gallery; the Whitney Museum of American Art, New York; the Cleveland Museum of Art; and the Corcoran Gallery of Art, Washington DC.

Smith has exhibited at *Désordres,* Galerie Nationale du Jeu de Paume, Paris (1992); a solo exhibition at the Irish Museum of Modern Art, Dublin (1997); *Directions - Kiki Smith: Night,* Hirshhorn Museum and Sculpture Garden (1998); *Botanica: Contemporary Art and the World of Plants,* Tuxedo Museum of Art, Duluth (1999); *My Nature: Works with Paper by Kiki Smith,* St Louis Art Museum, Missouri (1999); *Kiki Smith: Small Sculptures and Large Drawings,* Ulmer Museum, Ulm, Germany (2001); the 2002 Whitney Biennial; *Retrospective of Prints and Multiples,* Museum of Modern Art, New York (2003-2004); *Mostly Photography and Signs and Signals: Art Since 1980 from the Collection,* Williams College Museum of Art, Williamstown, MA (2004).

BIBLIOGRAPHY:

Kiki Smith: Unfolding the Body, exhibition catalogue, Brandeis University, Rose Art Museum, Waltham, 1992. Shearer, Linda, *Kiki Smith,* exhibition catalogue, Williams College of Art, Williamstown, 1992. *Kiki Smith: Prints and Multiples,* exhibition catalogue, Barbara Kradow Gallery, Boston, 1994. Bradley, Jessica, *Kiki Smith,* exhibition catalogue, Power Plant, Toronto, 1994. Haenlein, Carl (ed.), *Kiki Smith: All Creatures Great and Small,* exhibition catalogue, Scalo, New York, 1999. *Kiki Smith: Telling Tales,* exhibition catalogue, International Center of Photography, New York, 2001. Reinhardt, Brigitte (edition), *Kiki Smith: small sculptures and large drawings,* exhibition catalogue, Hatje Cantz, Ostfildern-Ruit, 2001 (catalogue of the exhibition at the Ulmer Museum, text in English and German).

MUSEUMS AND GALLERIES:

BOSTON (MFA): *Lilith* (1994, bronze sculpture); *Untitled* (1990, paper and wood sculpture) - BRUNSWICK, ME (MA, Bowdoin College): *Immortal (Monkey)* (1999, print) - BUFFALO (Albright-Knox AG): *Born* (2002, bronze sculpture) - LONDON (Tate Collection): *Untitled* (1990, lithograph/paper); *Worm* (1992, etching and collage/paper) - LONDON (Victoria and Albert Mus.) - NEW YORK (Guggenheim Mus.): *Ribs* (1987, terracotta sculpture) - NEW YORK (Metropolitan Mus. of Art): *Lilith* (1994); *Nest and Trees* (1997, Iris print) - NEW YORK (MoMA) - OBERLIN (Allen Memorial Art Museum, Oberlin College): *Untitled IV (Shield)* (1990, plaster sculpture) - ST LOUIS (Mildred Lane Kemper AM, Washington University): *Tidal* (1998, photogravure, photolithography, silk screen) - STOCKHOLM (Moderna Mus.): *Sperm* (1988-1990) - TOLEDO (MAC) - TULSA, OK (Fred Jones Jr. MA, University of Oklahoma): *Las Animas* (1997, photogravure) - VIENNA (Österreichisches Mus. für Angewandte Kunst).

AUCTION RECORDS:

NEW YORK, 9 May 1992, *For Mr G* (1984, black ink and silver paint on tinted sacking, 31 1/2 x 66 ins / 80 x 167.6 cm) USD 2,860. NEW YORK, 16 Nov 1995, *Untitled* (1993, mixed media/paper, 30 x 19 3/4 ins / 76.2 x 50.2 cm) USD 8,050. NEW YORK, 8 May 1996, *Untitled* (1981, oil on panel, 13 x 20 ins / 33 x 50.8 cm) USD 6,325. NEW YORK, 21 Nov 1996, *Untitled* (1986, 12 glass bottles, each 19 1/4 x 10 1/2 x 10 1/2 ins / 48.9 x 26.7 x 26.7 cm) USD 57,500. NEW YORK, 6-7 May 1997, *Urinating Body* (1992, wax and glass beads, 27 x 28 x 28 ins / 68.6 x 71.1 x 71.1 cm) USD 233,500. NEW YORK, 16 Nov 1999, *Mary Magdalene* (1994, silicone, bronze and forged steel, 60 x 20x22 ins / 152 x 52x55 cm) USD 160,000. NEW YORK, 17 Nov 1999, *Worm* (1992, etching, aquatint and collage, 42 x 62 ins / 106 x 157 cm) USD 3,200. NEW YORK, 17 May 2000, *Untitled* (1993, graphite on metho-cellulose, 63 x 19x54 ins / 160 x 47x137 cm) USD 160,000. NEW YORK, 17 Nov 2000, *Mother* (rice paper and papier mâché, 104 x 16x20 ins / 264 x 41x51 cm) USD 65,000. NEW YORK, 15 May 2001, *Rib Drawing* (1955, watercolour, 26 x 21 ins / 65 x 53 cm) USD 2,400. NEW YORK, 16 May 2001, *Trough* (1990, plaster and steel, 14 x 63x19 ins / 36 x 159x48 cm) USD 15,000. LONDON, 27 June 2002, *Untitled: Standing Female Nude with Bird* (1999, ink, pencil and collage, 78 x 30 ins / 198 x 77 cm) GBP 8,000. NEW YORK, 12 Nov 2002, *Untitled: Head with Tongue* (1999, phosphorous and bronze, two parts, 8 x 9x6 ins / 21 x 23x16 cm) USD 30,000. NEW YORK, 14 May 2003, *Untitled: Hands* (1994, paint on silver leafed vintage Japanese paper, 23 x 76 ins / 59 x 193 cm) USD 18,000. NEW YORK, 14 May 2003, *Flock* (1998, white tombasil bronze, 71 parts) USD 70,000. STOCKHOLM, 17 Feb 2004, *Scapula* (1987, mixed media, 10 x 7 ins / 25 x 18 cm) SEK 23,000. STOCKHOLM, 17 Feb 2004, *Head* (1988, watercolour, 21 x 17 ins / 54 x 43 cm) SEK 54,000.

SMITH, Knud

Norwegian, 17th century.

Born c. 1670, in Stavanger; died in Scotland.

Sculptor, painter.

Smith's *Portrait of Lauritz Smith, Brother of the Artist* is in the Kunstindustrimuseet in Oslo.

SMITH, Lawrence Beall

American, 20th century.

Born 1902 or 1909, in Washington DC; died 1989, in Cross River (New York).

Painter, lithographer, illustrator, sculptor (stone).

Urban landscapes.

Lawrence Beall Smith studied at the Art Institute of Chicago and at the University of Chicago, gaining a PhD degree in 1931. He also studied in Boston and Gloucester, Massachusetts, with Ernest Thurn, Charles Hopkinson and Harold Zimmerman. He established his reputation with a solo exhibition at the Whitney Museum of American Art, New York, in 1941.

AUCTION RECORDS:

NEW YORK, 31 May 1990, *Looking Towards His Future* (1942, oil on card, 40 x 28 3/4 ins / 101.6 x 73 cm) USD 3,850. NEW YORK, 26 Sept 1990, *Corner in Carolina* (1942, oil/synthetic resin, 20 x 29 ins / 50.8 x 73.6 cm) USD 35,200. NEW YORK, 14 March 1996, *Back Back Bay Stairway* (1937, oil on canvas, 28 x 22 ins / 71.1 x 55.9 cm) USD 13,800. NEW YORK, 21 May 1996, *Spring 1941* (1941, oil/synthetic resin, 8 1/4 x 13 3/4 ins / 20.9 x 35.2 cm) USD 4,370.

SMITH, Leon Polk

American, 20th century.

Born 1906, in Ada or Chikasha (Oklahoma); died 1996.

Painter, sculptor.

Leon Polk Smith lived on a ranch before going to Oklahoma State College, from which he graduated in 1934. He went on to study at the Teachers College of the University of Columbia, New York, graduating from there in 1938. He travelled to Europe in 1939, and on his return to the USA taught in various colleges, including Mills College, New York. He lived in New York from 1939 to 1945.

Smith was always a strictly geometric Abstract painter, and his work was often similar to the Neo-Plasticism of Mondrian. He also incorporated some of the latter's principles into his sculpture. He soon found that the curved line enabled him to 'liberate Mondrian's idea of space', defining new form/colour fields with the help of 'shaped canvas'. These canvases took various forms: two surfaces juxtaposed and cut into rounds and ovals, covered by the same curved line; or the side of a pictures extending beyond the space by means of a black stick.

Smith used basic geometric forms - rectangles, triangles, squares, lozenges - in different colours and on various materials. The extreme asceticism of the forms and colours in his paintings and their obvious rejection of any possible association with reality makes him one of the originators of *Hard Edge* and, with Yougermann and Kelly, one of the precursors of the ascetic approach of Minimal Art in the 1960s.

Smith's work appeared in collective exhibitions, including: *Post Mondrian Painters*, New York, 1949; *Construction and Geometry in Painting*, New York, 1960; *Geometric Abstraction in America*, Whitney Museum of American Art, New York, 1962; *Post Mondrian Abstraction in America*, Museum of Contemporary Art, Chicago, 1979; and *Paris-New York*, George Pompidou Centre, Paris. From 1940 onwards, solo exhibitions were held in many towns across the USA, and a handfull in France: two exhibitions at the Musée de Peinture et de la Sculpture, Grenoble, 1989; and *Leon Polk Smith Collages 1954-1986*, 1998.

BIBLIOGRAPHY:

Ratcliff, Carter, *Leon Polk Smith: 5 Decades of Geometric Inventions*, Di Laurenti Gallery, New York, 1987. Ratcliff, Carter, *Leon Polk Smith: American Painter*, Brooklyn Museum, Brooklyn, 1996. *Leon Polk Smith: Paintings of the Nineties*, Jason McCoy Inc, New York, 1996.

MUSEUMS AND GALLERIES:

NEW YORK (MoMA) - NEW YORK (Whitney Mus. of American Art).

AUCTION RECORDS:

NEW YORK, 12 Nov 1982, *Collage: Red-Black* (1962, collage/coloured paper, 32 x 21 ins / 81.5 x 52.5 cm) USD 4,000. NEW YORK, 7 June 1984, *Tondo* (painted wood, diam. 10 3/4 ins / 27.6 cm) USD 900. NEW YORK, 2 Nov 1984, *Correspondence Violet-Yellow Deep* (1964, oil on canvas, 50 1/4 x 40 1/4 ins / 127.5 x 102.3 cm) USD 4,800. NEW YORK, 2 May 1989, *Correspondence Blue and Yellow* (1963, oil on canvas, 36 x 30 ins / 91.5 x 76.2 cm) USD 13,200. NEW YORK, 23 Feb 1990, *Beyond Blue* (1981, two panels of oil on canvas, 97 x 183 3/4 ins / 246.5 x 467 cm) USD 44,000. NEW YORK, 3 Oct 1991, *Correspondence* (1962, oil on canvas, 68 x 43 ins / 172.7 x 109.3 cm) USD 17,600. NEW YORK, 27 Feb 1992, *'Caddo'* (1958, oil and metallic paint/canvas, 25 x 20 ins / 63.8 x 51.1 cm) USD 4,950. NEW YORK, 5 May 1994, *Untitled* (1965, collage/paper, 32 x 46 1/2 ins / 81.3 x 118.1 cm) USD 5,750. NEW YORK, 3 Nov 1994, *Constellation - Yellow Arch* (1971, acrylic/cut canvas, 82 x 90 ins / 208.2 x 228.6 cm) USD 20,700. NEW YORK, 15 Nov 1995, *Correspondence Orange-Red* (1968, acrylic/canvas, 85 x 65 3/4 ins / 216 x 167 cm) USD 11,500. NEW YORK, 22 Feb 1996, *No 7809* (acrylic/cut canvas, diam. 80 ins / 203.2 cm) USD 9,200. LONDON, 23 Oct 1997, *Full Black-Red* (1961, oil/Masonite/painted wood, 14 x 10 ins / 35.5 x 25.2 cm) GBP 4,025. NEW YORK, 17 Feb 1999, *Untitled* (1976, collage, 40 x 26 ins / 102 x 66 cm) USD 5,000. NEW YORK, 23 Feb 1999, *Constellation Curved* (1973, acrylic on panel, on two panels, oval, 95 x 48 ins / 241 x 122 cm) USD 4,500. NEW YORK, 1 May 2000, *Untitled* (paper collage) USD 4,500. NEW YORK, 13 Nov 2002, *Constellation Levelling, Blue, Green* (1967, oil on shaped canvas, 42 x 24 ins / 107 x 62 cm) USD 8,000. CHICAGO, 14 Sept 2003, *Untitled* (oil on canvas, 42 x 20 ins / 107 x 51 cm) USD 12,000. NEW YORK, 13 Nov 2003, *Constellation No. 12, purple, orange streak* (1973, acrylic on canvas, two parts, 116 x 60 ins / 295 x 152 cm) USD 42,500. NEW YORK, 12 Feb 2004, *Untitled* (1960, cut paper collage, 40 x 26 ins / 101 x 66 cm) USD 2,500.

SMITH, Letta Crapo
American, 19th - 20th century.
Born 1862, in Flint (Michigan); died 17 March 1921, in Boston.
Painter.
Letto Crapo Smith was taught by Chase, Rolshoven, and Hitchcock, and also studied at the Académie Julian in Paris.

SMITH, Lucien Louis Jean Baptiste.
See **SCHMIDT**

SMITH, Lucy, later Mrs Bentley
British, 19th - 20th century.
Active in London.
Miniaturist.
Lucy Smith exhibited in London from 1879 to 1904.

SMITH, Ludvig August
Danish, 19th century.
Born 22 November 1820, in Copenhagen; died 12 November 1906, in Copenhagen.
Painter, engraver, illustrator. Portraits, genre scenes.
Ludwig Smith studied at the Kunstakademi in Copenhagen and with Christopher Wilhelm Eckersberg.
MUSEUMS AND GALLERIES:
COPENHAGEN - HILLERØD (Frederiksborg Slot).
AUCTION RECORDS:
LONDON, 22 June 1983, *The Grandmother's Favourite* (oil on canvas, 18 1/4 x 20 1/2 ins / 46.5 x 52 cm) GBP 1,300. LONDON, 6 June 1990, *Childhood* (1845, oil on canvas, 13 1/2 x 12 1/4 ins / 34 x 31 cm) GBP 3,080.

SMITH, M. Hannah E.
British, 19th century.
Active in London.
Miniaturist.
Hannah Smith exhibited her work in London from 1888.

SMITH, M.A.
British, 18th - 19th century.
Active in London.
Miniaturist.
M.A. Smith exhibited six miniatures at the Royal Academy from 1804 until 1816. She is possibly the same person as Margaret Smith.

SMITH, Madeleine
French, 19th century.
Born in Paris.
Painter. Portraits, genre scenes.
Madeleine Smith was a pupil of Roederstein. She joined the Société des Artistes Français from 1890 and her work featured in that group at the Salon; she was awarded a third class medal in 1895 and a bronze medal at the Exposition Universelle in 1900.

SMITH, Margaret, also known as Lucan, later Mrs Bingham
British, 18th - 19th century.
Born 1740; died c. 1815.
Miniaturist.
Margaret Smith was an amateur artist who managed to acquire the same talent as the most skilled professionals. Her best known work is the five-volume illustrated collection of the complete works of Shakespeare, completed in 1806.

SMITH, Maria. See **ROSS Maria**

SMITH, Matilda (Miss)
British, 19th century.
Active in London.
Miniaturist.
Matilda Smith exhibited miniatures at the Royal Academy in 1823 and 1824.

SMITH, Matthew (Sir)
British, 20th century.
Born 22 October 1879, in Halifax (Yorkshire); died 29 September 1959, in London.
Painter. Figures, nudes, landscapes, still-lifes.
Matthew Smith studied technical drawing at Manchester School of Art from 1900 to 1904, and continued his training at the Slade School of Fine Art, London, from 1905 to 1907. He attended Henri Matisse's Paris studio for a brief period in 1910. Smith lived and worked in London, but frequently returned to France in the inter-war years, especially to Provence. Smith's ethereal drawing and rich colours were inspired by Fauvism, and particularly by Matisse, from as early as 1914 - for instance in *Fitzroy Street Nude No. 1* (1916) and *Cornish Landscapes.* Broad swathes of rich, unctuous colour, voluptuous arabesques and the painted landscapes of Cornwall, around 1920, are characteristic of his talented output, which proved highly influential for English painting in the post-war years. Smith also painted a number of scenes depicting World War II.

He exhibited for the first time with the London Group in 1915. In 1938 an exhibition of his work featured at the Venice International Exposition. In 1946 works by Smith featured in the exhibition of modern British paintings from the Tate Gallery, London, organised by the Musée du Jeu de Paume in Paris: *Cyclamens, Peonies, Peaches,* and a still-life. Retrospectives of his work have been held in 1953, Tate Gallery, London; 1960, Royal Academy, London; 1972, Arts Council of Great Britain; 1983, Barbican Art Gallery. Smith was knighted in 1954.

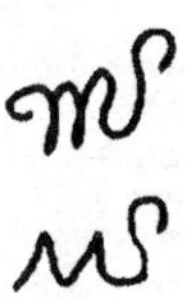

BIBLIOGRAPHY:
A Memorial Exhibition of Works by Sir Matthew Smith CBE, 1897-1959, exhibition catalogue, Royal Academy of Arts, London, 1960. Keene, Alice, *The Two Mr Smiths: the Life and Work of Sir Matthew Smith, 1879-1959,* Lund Humphries, London, 1995. Yorke, Malcolm, *Matthew Smith: His Life and Reputation,* Faber and Faber, London, 1997.
MUSEUMS AND GALLERIES:
BRISTOL (City Museum and Art Gallery): *Three Pears* (oil on canvas) - LEEDS (City AG): *Lilies* (1913-1914, oil on canvas) - LONDON (Courtauld Institute of Art): *Still-life* - LONDON (Tate Collection): *Nude; Apples on a Dish* (1919) - OTTAWA (Nat. Gal. of Canada) - OXFORD (Ashmolean Mus.): *Flowers* (painting).
AUCTION RECORDS:
LONDON, 25 Nov 1931, *Iris,* GBP 68; *Cyclamen,* GBP 105; *Seated Woman,* GBP 75. LONDON, 12 June 1940, *Seated Young Girl,* GBP 160. LONDON, 12 June 1940, *Mont Ste-Victoire,* GBP 200; *Colour of a Rose,* GBP 200. LONDON, 23 April 1941, *Pottery,* GBP 120. LONDON, 19 March 1943, *Red Road,* GBP 120. LONDON, 16 April 1943, *Young Woman,* GBP 115. LONDON, 18 April 1951, *Portrait of Augustus John, of the Royal Academy,* GBP 600; *Reclining Model,* GBP 500; *Peaches,* GBP 420; *House Covered with Roses* (1925) GBP 400. LONDON, 28 March 1958, *Still-life with a White Bowl,* GBP 420. LONDON, 4 Nov 1959, *The Mougins Road,* GBP 1,550. LONDON, 14 Dec 1960, *Landscape near Antibes,* GBP 1,100. LONDON, 26 April 1961, *Reclining Nude No. 1,* GBP 800. LONDON, 13 Dec 1961, *Red Roses in a Green Vase with Two Apples on a Table,* GBP 1,100. LONDON, 13 Nov 1964, *Landscape near Aix-en-Provence,* Gns 800. LONDON, 14 Dec 1966, *Vase of Red Roses,* GBP 1,100. LONDON, 3 Nov 1967, *Still-life with*

Pears, Gns 1,400. LONDON, 15 Dec 1971, *Stil-life*, GBP 1,600. LONDON, 19 Dec 1972, *Still-life with Flowers and Fruit*, Gns 3,200. LONDON, 18 July 1973, *Flowers and Fruit*, GBP 5,800. LONDON, 10 May 1974, *Reclining Nude (Sunita)* (1931) Gns 6,000. LONDON, 17 March 1976, *Vase of Flowers* (oil on canvas, 29½ x 15½ ins / 75 x 39.5 cm) GBP 900. LONDON, 16 March 1977, *St-Paul-du-Var* (c. 1935, oil on canvas, 15 x 22 ins / 38 x 55 cm) GBP 1,450. LONDON, 18 Nov 1977, *Still-life with Flowers and Fruit* (watercolour, 17½ x 14 ins / 44.5 x 35.5 cm) GBP 620. LONDON, 14 March 1979, *Reclining Nude* (1926, oil on canvas, 28¼ x 45 ins / 72 x 114 cm) GBP 3,700. LONDON, 12 March 1982, *Tulips and Daffodils* (oil on canvas, 30 x 25 ins / 76.2 x 63.5 cm) GBP 8,500. LONDON, 9 Nov 1984, *Still-life with Fruit* (oil on canvas, 36 x 28 ins / 91.5 x 71.2 cm) GBP 8,000. LONDON, 21 May 1986, *Reclining Nude* (oil on canvas, 26 x 33 ins / 66 x 84 cm) GBP 17,000. LONDON, 9 June 1988, *Reclining Nude* (oil on canvas, 21¼ x 25¼ ins / 53.8 x 63.9 cm) GBP 24,200. LONDON, 9 June 1989, *Red still-life with a Delphinium in a Vase* (oil on canvas, 23¼ x 19 ins / 59 x 48.1 cm) GBP 17,600. LONDON, 10 Nov 1989, *Lyons* (1922, oil on canvas, 14½ x 18 ins / 37 x 45.5 cm) GBP 16,500. LONDON, 9 March 1990, *Still-life with a Clay Figurine* (oil on canvas, 28 x 45 ins / 71.2 x 114.3 cm) GBP 24,200. LONDON, 8 June 1990, *Apples and Pears* (oil on canvas, 14½ x 17¾ ins / 37 x 45 cm) GBP 17,600. LONDON, 20 Sept 1990, *Sunflowers in a Blue Vase* (watercolour, 14½ x 10 ins / 37 x 25.5 cm) GBP 1,760. LONDON, 7 March 1991, *Vase of Roses* (oil on canvas, 18 x 21½ ins / 46 x 54.5 cm) GBP 11,000. LONDON, 5 June 1992, *Coastal Landscape* (1911, oil on panel, 8½ x 10½ ins / 21.5 x 26.5 cm) GBP 3,850. LONDON, 12 March 1993, *Reclining Nude* (1952, oil on canvas, 25 x 30 ins / 63.5 x 76 cm) GBP 15,525. ST ASAPH, 2 June 1994, *Still-life with Flowers* (oil on canvas, 23 x 19 ins / 58.5 x 48 cm) GBP 18,400. LONDON, 29 May 1997, *Tulips and Daffodils* (c. 1940, oil on canvas, 30 x 25 ins / 76 x 63.5 cm) GBP 17,250. LONDON, 5 March 1999, *Flowers in Blue Jug* (1925, oil on canvas, 22 x 18 ins / 55 x 46 cm) GBP 15,000. LONDON, 23 June 1999, *Landscape near Cagnes* (oil on canvas, 15 x 18 ins / 38 x 46 cm) GBP 28,000. LONDON, 9 June 2000, *Landscape, South of France* (oil on canvas, 15 x 22 ins / 39 x 55 cm) GBP 26,000. LONDON, 21 June 2000, *Pink Roses in Blue Jug* (oil on canvas, 24 x 20 ins / 61 x 51 cm) GBP 29,000. LONDON, 5 April 2001, *Still-life with Flowers and Fruit on a Table* (oil on canvas, 36 x 24 ins / 92 x 61 cm) GBP 28,000. LONDON, 8 June 2001, *Still-life with Fruit and Pitcher* (1955, oil on canvas, 28 x 36 ins / 71 x 91 cm) GBP 26,000. LONDON, 7 June 2002, *Nude with Mauve Drapery* (c. 1931, oil on canvas, 24 x 32 ins / 61 x 81 cm) GBP 19,000. LONDON, 22 Nov 2002, *Tulips and Mimosa in a Brown Jug* (1933, oil on canvas, 26 x 26 ins / 65 x 65 cm) GBP 24,000. LONDON, 25 March 2003, *Flowers in a Jug, Red Background* (oil on canvas, 31 x 24 ins / 80 x 60 cm) GBP 22,000. LONDON, 3 Dec 2003, *Barn with Trees, Varengeville* (oil on canvas, 22 x 18 ins / 55 x 46 cm) GBP 35,000. LONDON, 17 Nov 2004, *The Plaster Cast* (1913, oil on canvas, 29 x 38 ins / 74 x 96 cm) GBP 28,000. LONDON, 17 Nov 2004, *Quinces and Pomegranates* (oil on canvas, 25 x 30 ins / 63 x 76 cm) GBP 55,000.

SMITH, Minna, Mrs Walker
American, 20th century.
Born 29 March 1883, in New Haven.
Painter.

Minna Smith studied at Yale School of Fine Arts and was a member of the American Federation of Arts.

SMITH, Nathaniel
British, 18th century.
Born 1740 or 1741.
Active in London.
Sculptor, miniaturist.

Nathaniel Smith was the father of John Thomas Smith. He exhibited his work at the Royal Academy from 1772 until 1773.

MUSEUMS AND GALLERIES:
LONDON (Victoria and Albert Mus.): two models.

SMITH, Ole Jørgen. See **SCHMIDT**

SMITH, Olga Marie
Danish, 19th - 20th century.
Born 24 July 1866, in Frederiksberg; died 7 March 1930, in Hørsholm.
Painter. Portraits, interiors, landscapes.

Olga Marie Smith painted compositions for the convent at Gisselfeld and the church in Hovborg.

SMITH, Patti
American, 20th - 21st century.
Born 1946, in Chicago.
Draughtswoman.

Patti Smith is known as a rock singer (album *Horses*, 1975) but she also draws and writes poetry. Photographer Robert Mapplethorpe was a major influence. She creates hybrid figures, reminiscent of Cocteau's for *La Belle et la Bête* (*Beauty and the Beast*). The fine lines and delicate colour of her drawings can be submerged by text from her own poems or by other authors. Her 2003 show boasted about 100 drawings, including those inspired by the destruction of the Twin Towers in the September 11th terrorist attack on New York interwoven with a reworking of the *Tower of Babel* (*Tour de Babel*) by Pieter Brueghel. Her drawings have been shown in Paris and in 2003, in the exhibition *Strange Messenger: The Work of Patti Smith*, mounted in co-operation with the Andy Warhol Museum in Pittsburgh, which went on show at the Haus der Kunst in Munich.

MUSEUMS AND GALLERIES:
NEW YORK (MoMA).

AUCTION RECORDS:
NEW YORK, 31 Oct 1989, *Death of a Spanish Animal* (graphite and colouring pencil/paper, 11 x 8½ ins / 28 x 21.5 cm) USD 770.

SMITH, Percy John
British, 20th century.
Born 11 March 1882, in London; died 1948.
Engraver, illustrator.

Percy John Smith was active as a book illustrator.

SMITH, Ray
South American, 20th - 21st century.
Born 1949 or 1959.
Painter. Figure compositions, figures.

Ray Smith's approach can be figurative and painstaking, naive, but also meticulously realistic. His work is complex, a little extravagant and populated by unusual figures and minor characters, while full of an acid humour that can be difficult to grasp. His world is that of the great but torrid South American novelists of the late 20th century. Ray Smith took part in a collective exhibition in Paris in 1955 at the Vidal-Saint Phalle gallery. In Paris in 1977 he took part in the *Artistes Latino-Américains* (*Latin American Artists*) exhibition at the Daniel Templon gallery; this gallery also held a solo exhibition of Smith's work in 1998.

RAY SMITH

AUCTION RECORDS:
NEW YORK, 19 Nov 1992, *Untitled* (1989, oil on panel, 35¾ x 47¾ ins / 91.1 x 121.3 cm) USD 11,000. NEW YORK, 23-25 Feb 1993, *Pancho* (1986, acrylic/canvas, 50½ x 50 ins / 128.3 x 127 cm) USD 5,750. NEW YORK, 23 Feb 1994, *Maria de la Cruz according to Chocmol* (1988, oil on panel, in four panels 96 x 192 ins / 243.9 x 487.7 cm) USD 11,500. NEW YORK, 3 May

1994, *Diplomacy* (1990, oil and encaustic on six wooden panels, 73 1/4 x 168 ins / 186 x 426.7 cm) USD 32,200. NEW YORK, 21 Nov 1995, *Joie de Vivre* (oil/four panels, altogether 96 x 196 ins / 243.8 x 497.6 cm) USD 13,800. NEW YORK, 8 May 1996, *Peras y Perones* (1987, oil on canvas, 54 1/4 x 35 ins / 137.7 x 88 cm) USD 10,350. NEW YORK, 19 Nov 1996, *Diego* (1987, oil on canvas, 60 x 40 1/2 ins / 152.4 x 102.9 cm) USD 5,750. NEW YORK, 29-30 May 1997, *The Monkey Man* (1989, oil and charcoal/panel, collection of four panels, total 83 3/4 x 142 ins / 212.7 x 360.7 cm) USD 20,700. NEW YORK, 24-25 Nov 1997, *T.S. Eliot* (1993, oil on panel, triptych, total 90 x 80 ins / 228.6 x 203.2 cm) USD 21,850.

SMITH, Reginald or A. R.

British, 19th - 20th century.

Born 1870; died c. 1925.

Painter. Landscapes, seascapes.

Reginald Smith lived and worked in Bristol. He exhibited in London, notably at the Royal Academy from 1872.

MUSEUMS AND GALLERIES:

BRISTOL: *The Sea*; two marines, watercolour - LONDON (Victoria and Albert Mus.): a watercolour - SYDNEY: *Seascape* (watercolour).

AUCTION RECORDS:

LONDON, 1 March 1984, *Animals on the Beach* (watercolour heightened with white, 30 x 48 ins / 76 x 122 cm) GBP 650. LONDON, 22 Sept 1988, *Coastal Landscape and Cornwall* (oil on canvas, each, a pair, 12 x 20 ins / 30.5 x 51 cm) GBP 385. LONDON, 12 May 1993, *View from a Hill* (watercolour, 8 x 15 ins / 20.5 x 38 cm) GBP 690.

SMITH, Richard

British, 19th century.

Active in London in the middle of the 19th century.

Miniaturist, painter.

Richard Smith exhibited his work from 1837 until 1855.

AUCTION RECORDS:

LONDON, 30 June 1977, *Fool's Blue* (1970, acrylic and graphite/canvas, 131 x 200 x 20 3/4 ins / 333 x 508 x 53 cm) GBP 1,800.

SMITH, Richard

British, 20th century.

Born 27 October 1931, in Letchworth (Hertfordshire).

Painter, sculptor.

Situation Group.

Richard Smith trained at Luton and St Albans Schools of Art, and at the Royal College of Art in London from 1954 to 1957. He won a Harkness scholarship in 1959, and studied in New York from 1959 to 1961. Smith was a member of the Situation group. He has taught in numerous schools, including St Martin's School of Art in London from 1961 to 1963 and UCLA in 1968.

Richard Smith's work is closely similar in appearance to that of American Minimalism and the broader category of post-Mondrian abstract painting in general - compositional structures based on primary forms incorporating colours deployed in a neutral context, devoid of any psychological associations. However, Smith's personal aesthetic is essentially derived from the Pop Art influences of his early artistic career, which he subsequently developed to the brink of abstraction. His exploration of elementary visual phenomena (the concept of the square, the sensation of blue or red, etc.) focuses primarily on the role of these elementary forms in the context of communication. Later works, influenced by Stephen Buckley - with whom he worked in close collaboration, and whose work he influenced in turn - are comparable to paintings by the artists of the French group Support-Surface. Smith's analysis of painterly materials and the act of painting itself has led to the creation of successive series of works, beginning with canvases on stretchers of different shapes, highlighting the arbitrary nature of traditional formats. A subsequent series is based on canvases fixed to their stretchers by a variety of different means; a third features canvases devoid of any support, and free to be hung or fixed in space in different ways. The surfaces of each series feature separate styles: striped, multicoloured brushstrokes or simple areas of flat colour. Smith's compositions are all subdivided on a straightforward grid pattern, quite unlike Mondrian's proportional grilles. The elements fixing the canvas to the support are often visible on the recto of the painting, forming an integral part of the composition.

His work has featured in a number of major international exhibitions, including: 1961, 2nd Biennale des Jeunes, Paris; 1966, Whitechapel Art Gallery, London; 1967, University of Virginia, Charlottesville; 1970, 35th Venice Biennale (British pavilion); 1973, *Peinture anglaise aujourd'hui* (*English Painting Today*), Musée d'Art Moderne de la Ville de Paris. Smith's work has also been the subject of a number of solo exhibitions, including: 1968, retrospective, Jewish Museum, New York. He won the 1966 Robert C. Skull Prize at the 33rd Venice Biennale. In 1967 he won the Grand Prix at the 9th São Paulo Biennale.

BIBLIOGRAPHY:

Lynton, Norbert, '*American Pop'Art and Richard Smith*' in *Art International*, periodical, Zurich, February, 1964. *Richard Smith: British Pavilion*, XXXV Venice Biennale, 1970. Lassaigne, Jacques, *Peinture anglaise aujourd'hui*, exhibition catalogue, Musée d'Art moderne de la ville de Paris, Paris, 1973. Smith, Richard, *Drawings and Prints by Richard Smith, 1966-1975*, Arts Council of Great Britain, London, 1975. *Smith, Richard: Paintings 1960-1963*, exhibition catalogue, Knoedler Gallery, London, 1990.

MUSEUMS AND GALLERIES:

LONDON (Tate Collection): *Tailspan*.

AUCTION RECORDS:

LONDON, 5 July 1973, *Map*, GBP 5,000. LONDON, 3 April 1974, *Mandarin* (1970) GBP 2,000. LONDON, 1 July 1976, *Untitled* (c. 1968, polyurethane on canvas, 15 3/4 x 15 3/4 ins / 40 x 40 cm) GBP 280. LONDON, 6 April 1989, *Untitled* (1982, colouring pencil, acrylic and watercolour/paper, 30 1/4 x 44 ins / 77 x 111.5 cm) GBP 1,045. MILAN, 19 Dec 1989, *'Pitman'* (1969, blue and mauve shaped canvas, 15 3/4 x 15 3/4 ins / 40 x 40 cm) ITL 4,500,000. LONDON, 8 June 1990, *Valentine 1959* (1959, oil on canvas, 30 x 30 ins / 76 x 76 cm) GBP 6,600. NEW YORK, 6 Nov 1990, *MM* (1959, oil on canvas, 36 x 36 ins / 91.4 x 91.4 cm) USD 8,800. LONDON, 9 Nov 1990, *A Whole Year and Half a Day No. 6* (1966, acrylic/canvas, 60 x 60 ins / 152.5 x 152.5 cm) GBP 2,420. NEW YORK, 12 June 1991, *Untitled (blue square on blue ground)* (1975, pastel and string/paper, 25 x 24 3/4 ins / 63.5 x 62.9 cm) USD 2,200. LONDON, 17 Oct 1991, *Album* (1962, oil on canvas, 72 x 48 ins / 183 x 122 cm) GBP 7,700. LONDON, 11 June 1992, *Malaya* (1969, oil on canvas, 96 x 78 x 14 1/4 ins / 244 x 198 x 36 cm) GBP 4,400. LONDON, 3 June 1999, *A Whole Year and Half a Day No. 8* (1966, acrylic on canvas and aluminium sheets, 60 x 60 ins / 152 x 152 cm) GBP 1,700. LONDON, 26 Nov 1999, *Quiet Waters, Resting Salmon* (1989, oil on board, 31 x 44 ins / 79 x 112 cm) GBP 1,000. LONDON, 28 April 2000, *First Birthday* (1972, acrylic and twine on canvas, 54 x 118 ins / 136 x 300 cm) GBP 1,200. MIAMI, 16 Jan 2001, *Triptych* (acrylic on shaped canvas, 70 x 55 ins / 178 x 140 cm) USD 1,600. LONDON, 6 Sept 2001, *A Whole Year and Half a Day No. 6* (acrylic on canvas, 60 x 60 ins / 152 x 152 cm) GBP 1,100. CHICAGO, 15 Dec 2003, *You Was Never Lovlier* (oil on canvas, 35 x 35 ins / 89 x 89 cm) USD 2,400. LONDON, 24 Nov 2004, *For the Birds 2* (1957, oil on canvas, 48 x 48 ins / 122 x 122 cm) GBP 1,900.

SMITH, Robert

British, 16th century.

Died 1555.

Active in Windsor.

Painter.

SMITH, Robert (Captain)
Irish, 19th century.
Born 14 September 1792, in Dublin; died 26 November 1882, in Dublin.
Painter. Portraits, landscapes.
Robert Smith mainly painted Italian and Indian landscapes.
AUCTION RECORDS:
LONDON, 28 Nov 1973, *View of the North Beach, Prince of Wales Island,* GBP 3,000. LONDON, 31 March 1978, *View of Prince of Wales Island* (1826, oil on canvas, 21 x 36 ins / 53.5 x 91.5 cm) USD 950. LONDON, 18 Nov 1988, *Purana Kila near Delhi* (1830, oil on canvas, 25 1/4 x 40 ins / 64 x 101.6 cm) GBP 57,200; *Explosion at the Ammunition Factory in Baratpur* (1845, oil on canvas, 25 1/2 x 42 ins / 64.8 x 106.4 cm) GBP 13,200.

SMITH, Robert Catterson
Irish, 19th century.
Born 24 February 1853, in Dublin.
Painter.
AUCTION RECORDS:
BELFAST, 24 April 2002, *Thoughts too Deep for Words* (watercolour, 21 x 15 ins / 53 x 38 cm) GBP 3,200. BELFAST, 24 April 2002, *In the Bosom of a Leafy Wood* (tempera on paper, 28 x 20 ins / 71 x 51 cm) GBP 4,000.

SMITH, Russell William Thompson
American, 19th century.
Born 1812, in Glasgow; died 1896 or 1898, in Edge Hill.
Painter. Figures, landscapes, mountainscapes. Stage sets.
Russell William Thompson Smith studied with J.P. Lambdin in Philadelphia, and then worked for the city's theatres.
AUCTION RECORDS:
LOS ANGELES, 27 May 1974, *Old Man of the Mountain,* USD 2,250. NEW YORK, 30 Jan 1980, *Norristown* (1863, oil on board, 9 x 13 ins / 22.9 x 33 cm) USD 2,000. NEW YORK, 29 Jan 1982, *Mouth of the Wissahickon* (1836, oil on canvas, 20 1/4 x 30 ins / 51.4 x 76.2 cm) USD 3,200. NEW YORK, 21 Oct 1983, *At Edge Hill; Moel Hebog* (oils on canvas, a pair, 12 x 18 ins / 30.5 x 45.7 cm) USD 3,100. NEW YORK, 14 June 1985, *Old Bridge on the Juniatta* (oil on mounted paper/canvas, 12 x 18 ins / 30.5 x 45.8 cm) USD 2,000. NEW YORK, 29 May 1986, *Valley Landscape* (oil on canvas, 24 x 36 ins / 61 x 91.5 cm) USD 6,000. NEW YORK, 30 May 1990, *Rockhill Park in Branchtown* (1844, oil on panel, 16 1/2 x 23 3/4 ins / 42 x 60.3 cm) USD 3,300. NEW YORK, 27 Sept 1990, *King of the Grove* (1863, oil on canvas, 21 x 31 3/4 ins / 53.6 x 80.8 cm) USD 6,600. NEW YORK, 21 May 1991, *Jocoy Creek near Chelten Hills* (oil on canvas, 20 1/4 x 16 1/4 ins / 51.4 x 41.3 cm) USD 2,200. NEW YORK, 22 May 1991, *Lafayette College in Easton, Pennsylvania* (oil on canvas, 18 x 27 1/4 ins / 45.9 x 68.9 cm) USD 5,500. NEW YORK, 14 Nov 1991, *Lafayette College in Easton, Pennsylvania* (oil on canvas, 18 x 27 1/4 ins / 45.9 x 68.9 cm) USD 7,700. NEW YORK, 12 Sept 1994, *Mountains in Tunnkahannock* (1839, oil on paper, 8 x 12 ins / 20.3 x 30.2 cm) USD 1,725. NEW YORK, 29 Nov 1995, *Chocorua Peak, New Hampshire* (oil on canvas, 30 x 50 1/4 ins / 76.2 x 127.6 cm) USD 17,250. NEW YORK, 23 May 1996, *Riverscape* (1867, oil on canvas, 34 x 12 3/4 ins / 86.4 x 32.6 cm) USD 16,100. DOWNINGTON, 23 April 1999, *Time's Triumph, Allegorical Scene with Old Man in a Temple Ruin* (oil on canvas, 48 x 34 ins / 122 x 86 cm) USD 6,000. DOWNINGTON, 23 April 1999, *Basilica of Constantine, Rome, Victorian Figures in Ruins* (oil on canvas, 28 x 38 ins / 71 x 97 cm) USD 6,500. NEW YORK, 4 Oct 2000, *Llyn Dinas near Beddgelert, North Wales* (1852, oil on canvas, 26 x 39 ins / 66 x 99 cm) USD 4,200. WASHINGTON, 9 Dec 2000, *Old Holliday Street Theater, Baltimore* (1839, oil on canvas, 16 x 9 ins / 41 x 23 cm) USD 17,000. MILFORD, 26 April 2001, *Day on a Farm* (1868, oil on canvas, 24 x 36 ins / 61 x 91 cm) USD 16,000. NORTH BETHESDA, 6 Oct 2001, *Mount Vernon* (oil on canvas, 29 x 19 ins / 74 x 48 cm) USD 17,000. NEW ORLEANS, 7 Dec 2002, *Half a Mile from Sestri, Genoese Coast* (oil on canvas, 20 x 30 ins / 51 x 76 cm) USD 4,600. PHILADELPHIA, 8 Dec 2002, *Pennypack Park* (oil on canvas, 12 x 18 ins / 30 x 46 cm) USD 6,000. NEW YORK, 9 Oct 2003, *Corn Sheaves and Buggy* (1868, oil on paper, 8 x 12 ins / 20 x 30 cm) USD 4,000. EAST DENNIS, 21 Nov 2003, *Near Mt Loudon* (oil on canvas, 12 x 18 ins / 30 x 46 cm) USD 4,000. NEW YORK, 3 March 2004, *View of a Valley, Springtime* (oil on canvas, 12 x 18 ins / 30 x 46 cm) USD 14,000. PORTLAND, 6 Aug 2004, *Down by the River* (oil on canvas, 18 x 27 ins / 46 x 69 cm) USD 5,000.

SMITH, Samuel
British, 18th century.
Active in London during the second half of the 18th century.
Painter. Landscapes, architectural views.
Samuel Smith exhibited his work in London from 1768 until 1776.

SMITH, Samuel
British, 18th century.
Born c. 1745, in London; died c. 1808, in London.
Engraver.

SMITH, Samuel Mountjoy
British, 19th century.
Active in London from 1830 to 1857.
Painter. Portraits, genre scenes, landscapes.

SMITH, Samuel S.
British, 19th century.
Born c. 1809; died 1879, in London.
Engraver.

SMITH, Seton
American, 20th century.
Active in France from c. 1985.
Sculptor, photographer. Multimedia.
Seton Smith uses large but unframed and even blurred photographs shown in groups of two or as a triptych, or accompanied by sculptural or architectural samples, to show the symbolic relationships between nature and humankind. She lives in Paris.

Smith has participated in collective exhibitions, including *Ateliers 88* at l'ARC (Art Recherche Confrontation) at the Musée d'Art Moderne de la Ville de Paris, in 1988. Solo exhibitions include: Tom Cugliani Gallery, New York; Galerie Jule Kewenig, Cologne, 1991; Galerie Urbi et Orbi, Paris, 1991; Musée des Beaux-Arts, Nantes, 1994; and Galerie Cent8, Paris, 1994.
BIBLIOGRAPHY:
Jonas Storsve, '*Seton Smith*' in *Art Press* n° 165, periodical, Paris, January 1992.

SMITH, Sidney Lawton
American, 19th century.
Born 15 June 1845, in Foxboro (Massachusetts); died after 1906.
Active in Boston.
Engraver (burin/etching), painter.
Sidney Lawton Smith mostly made ex-libris. He also painted decorations for Trinity Church in Boston.

SMITH, Sophia
British, 18th - 19th century.
Active in Bath.
Miniaturist, painter.
Sophia Smith was the sister of Emma Smith. She is known to have exhibited four miniatures at the Society of Artists and eight at the Royal Academy between 1800 and 1804.
MUSEUMS AND GALLERIES:
LONDON (Victoria and Albert Mus.): *Portrait of Man* (1765).

SMITH, Stephen Catterson, the Elder
Irish, 19th century.
Born 12 March 1806, in Shipton-in-Craven; died 30 May 1872, in Dublin.
Painter.

Stephen Catterson Smith studied at the schools of the Royal Academy in London. In 1840 he went to Ireland to paint the portrait of the *Lord Lieutenant*, and he was offered so many commissions there that he decided to settle in Dublin. He was elected as a member and then president of the Hibernian Academy. He exhibited in London from 1828 until 1858.

MUSEUMS AND GALLERIES:
DUBLIN: *Self-portrait*; *Will. Gargan*; *Peter Pureell*; *Sir Philip Crampton Bart*; *Count of Bessborough*; *James Henthorn Todd* - LONDON (Victoria and Albert Mus.): *Viscount Dungannon.*

AUCTION RECORDS:
LONDON, 11 July 1984, *Bathers* (oil on canvas, 44 1/2 x 58 1/4 ins / 113 x 148 cm) GBP 4,500. LONDON, 15 April 1988, *Portrait of a Young Socialite, Seated* (1864, oil on canvas, 22 1/4 x 18 1/2 ins / 56.2 x 47 cm) GBP 2,860. NEW YORK, 28 Feb 1990, *Princess Victoria, Aged 9, in a Landscape* (1828, oil on panel, 15 1/2 x 12 ins / 39.4 x 30.5 cm) USD 27,500. LONDON, 2 June 1995, *Portrait of the Hon. Richard Ponsonby, Archbishop of Derry and Raphoe, Sitting in a Red Armchair Holding his Glasses and a Letter* (oil on canvas, 22 1/2 x 17 3/4 ins / 57 x 45 cm) GBP 1,495. LONDON, 14 May 2004, *Portrait of Marianne Gage, Full-length, Seated on a Red Cloak, Feeding a Dog* (oil on canvas, 61 x 48 ins / 154 x 122 cm) GBP 16,500.

SMITH, Stephen Catterson, the Younger
Irish, 19th - 20th century.
Born 19 June 1849, in Dublin; died 24 November 1912, in Dublin.
Painter. Portraits, landscapes with figures.

Stephen Smith was the son of Stephen Catterson Smith the Elder. He was a member of the Royal Hibernian Academy.

MUSEUMS AND GALLERIES:
DUBLIN: *Portrait of William J. Fitzpatrick.*

AUCTION RECORDS:
LONDON, 5 March 1976, *Landscape with a hunter and his dog* (oil on canvas, 12 x 17 3/4 ins / 30.5 x 45 cm) GBP 90. LONDON, 15 June 1988, *Elegant ladies out for a stroll* (1869, oil on panel, 16 1/2 x 11 ins / 42 x 27 cm) GBP 2,640.

SMITH, Sydney Ure, or Sydney George
Australian, 20th century.
Born 1887, in London.
Painter, watercolourist. Landscapes.

Sydney Ure Smith was vice president of the Australian Academy of Art and president of the Society of Australian Artists. He often took his inspiration from Rushcutter's Bay, Sydney.

SMITH, T.
British, 18th century.
Cameo engraver.

SMITH, Theophilus or Thomas
British, 19th century.
Born in Sheffield.
Sculptor. Busts.

Theophilus Smith exhibited his work in London from 1827 until 1877. He worked using wax models.

MUSEUMS AND GALLERIES:
SHEFFIELD: *Marble Bust of Samuel Roberts.*

SMITH, Thomas
American, 17th century.
Active during the second half of the 17th century.
Painter. Portraits.

Thomas Smith was a poet and military captain as well as a portrait painter. He may have been the same person as the artist Thomas Smith who was active between 1650 and 1690.

SMITH, Thomas
American, 17th century.
Active 1650-1690.
Painter. Portraits.

Thomas Smith was a former sailor - a fact that is mentioned in his will (dated 1688). There is also an entry in an accounting records book, which states that Major Thomas Smith received payment for a portrait he painted for Harvard College in New England on 2 June 1680. This evidence, along with the remarkable *Self-portrait* in the Worcester Art Museum, are among the earliest records of American art. Painted around 1690, the *Self-portrait* seems to sum up the artist's life against the background of a naval battle.

MUSEUMS AND GALLERIES:
WORCESTER, MA (AM): *Self-portrait* (c. 1680, oil on canvas).

SMITH, Thomas, called Smith of Derby
British, 18th century.
Died 12 September 1767, in Bristol.
Painter, engraver. Sporting subjects, landscapes, landscapes with figures.

Thomas Smith taught himself by observing nature. Many of his works have been engraved by Vivares, Mason and Elias. He is an important English landscape artist.

MUSEUMS AND GALLERIES:
BRISTOL (City Mus. & AG): *View of St Vincent's Rocks* (oil on canvas) - MANCHESTER: *The Avon at Clifton.*

AUCTION RECORDS:
LONDON, 15 July 1983, *View of Chatsworth, Derbyshire* (oil on canvas, 32 1/2 x 42 1/2 ins / 82.5 x 108 cm) GBP 12,000. LONDON, 10 April 1992, *Vast Landscape of an Estuary and Peasants*; *Vast River Landscape with Figures and a Bridge in the Background* (oil on canvas, a pair, each 18 1/4 x 40 1/4 ins / 46.5 x 102.5 cm) GBP 9,900.

SMITH, Thomas
British, 18th century.
Active in London.
Miniaturist.

Thomas Smith exhibited four miniatures at the Society of Artists and six at the Royal Academy from 1773 until 1788.

SMITH, Thomas
French, 18th - 19th century.
Born 1779, in Rome.
Active mostly in Paris.
Engraver (burin). Natural history.

Thomas Smith engraved illustrations for travel accounts and natural history works.

SMITH, Thomas (Revd.)
British, 19th century.
Died 1831.
Active from 1823 to 1836.
Landscape artist, topographer.

SMITH, Thomas Correggio
British, 18th century.
Died at the beginning of the 19th century, in Uttoxeter.
Miniaturist.

Thomas Correggio Smith was the elder son of Smith of Derby. He exhibited miniatures and small pencil portraits at the Royal Academy from 1767 until 1788.

SMITH, Thomas Herbert
American, 20th century.
Born 31 October 1877, in New York.
Painter.

Thomas Herbert Smith was a pupil of George Bellows. He was a member of the Society of Independent Artists and the

American Arts Federation. He lived and worked in New York.

AUCTION RECORDS:

NEW YORK, 25 Sept 1992, *Landscape with a Fisherman on a Lake* (oil on canvas, 24 x 20 ins / 61 x 50.8 cm) USD 2,860.

SMITH, Thomas Lochlan

British, 19th century.

Born 1835, in Glasgow; died 1884, in the USA.

Active in the USA.

Painter. Winter landscapes.

Thomas Lochlan Smith studied under G.H. Boughton in Albany. His favourite subjects were winter landscapes.

AUCTION RECORDS:

NEW YORK, 20 March 1969, *Winter Landscape*, USD 900.

SMITH, Thomas Reynolds

British, 19th - 20th century.

Born 1839, in Newcastle upon Tyne; died 1910, in London (?).

Sculptor (ivory), miniaturist.

SMITH, Thomas Stuart

British, 19th century.

Born 1813, in London; died 1869, in Avignon, France.

Painter. Genre scenes, portraits.

Thomas Stuart Smith was self-taught and learned his skills in Italy. He was active in London, Nottingham and Glassingall.

AUCTION RECORDS:

PARIS, 2 April 1997, *View of Naples* (oil on panel, 15 x 21 1/4 ins / 38 x 54 cm) FRF 24,000.

SMITH, Tom, called Squire Smith

British, 18th century.

Died 1785; young.

Engraver (burin).

Tom Smith studied under Charles Crignion and was Charles White's assistant.

SMITH, Tony

American, 20th century.

Born 1912, in South Orange (New Jersey); died 26 December 1980, in New York.

Sculptor, painter, architect.

Tony Smith took evening classes at the Art Students League in New York from 1933 to 1936, then during 1937-1938 he studied at the New Bauhaus in Chicago. In 1938 he worked as assistant to the architect Frank Lloyd Wright on projects such as *Taliesin East* and the *Ardmore Experiment*. It was while working for Wright that he became aware of the modular, on which he bases his sculpture, enabling him to use more complex relationships than the straightforward 90° angle. In the 1940s and 1950s he worked as an architect and designer. The influence of Le Corbusier and Rietveld is evident in is creations, especially the building of a house based on hexagonal modules, and projects - the most famous being a church for which Pollock was to paint pictures. A close friend of Pollock, Newman and Rothko, Smith taught in art schools at various times: 1946-1950, New York University; 1950-1953, Cooper Union and Pratt Institute, New York; 1957-1958, Pratt Institute, New York; 1958-1961, Bennington College, Bennington, Vermont; 1962-1974 and 1979-1980, Hunter College, New York and 1975-1978, Princeton University, New Jersey. He has received a number of public commissions, including: *Gracehoper*, Institute of Fine Art, Michigan; *The Snake is Out*, Albany, New York; *Moses*, Princeton University, New Jersey and *Source*, Banque Lambert, Brussels.

From the end of the 1930s until his death, Tony Smith returned periodically to painting. He went through an Abstract Expressionist period in the 1940s, followed by a geometric period during which he gradually reduced his formats so that he could more or less use them as modules. In fact, he had confronted geometrical questions of form and structure very early on. As a child convalescing from tuberculosis, he made a model of a Pueblo village out of cardboard boxes. When he was 12, he was already reading Jay Hambidge's *Elements of Dynamic Symmetry*. He did not immediately go on to create sculptures. His first attempts remained experimental or were carried out with students in the course of his teaching. They were based on the classical proportions and architectural values of geometric shapes, particularly the cube, but also the hexagon, the tetrahedron and the octahedron, which gradually led him to think in terms of pure form. *The Black Box*, 1962, is a seminal piece for the works that were to come, a black metal parallelepiped, not made up of modular elements. *Free Ride*, dating from the same year, is formed from three edges of a cube, this time open in an arrangement that multiplies the possible openings and directions. Other sculptures were completed from models dating back to well before *The Black Box* because, on his own admission, it was impossible to imagine them in his mind. Better known than the first two sculptures is the piece *Die*, 1962, a cube of 6 feet (1,8m). It was exhibited in the Grand Palais in 1968 at the exhibition *L'Art du Réel* (*The Art of the Real*). Its human size, determined by the Leonardo da Vinci drawing *the Vitruvian Man*, is neither a monument that escapes the spectator's view nor an object that this same spectator could see over the top of. After that, constructions based on irregular polygons, tetrahedra or octahedra, in bronze that is either painted matt black or left in a natural rust colour, allowed him to diversify the lines subtending the volume contained by the planes, creating a more complex rhythm, a more marked virtual exchange in the extrinsic space of the sculpture. Smith also created groups of works such as *Ten*, which correspond to one another, and several land art projects such as cutting a triangle shape into the side of a mountain.

Tony Smith's sculptures have an organic, even anthropomorphic, element running counter to a unique formalist interpretation. According to its creator, *Die* evoked 'six feet underground'. Elsewhere, when commenting on the piece entitled *Willy*, Smith said of it: 'It looks like some crawling thing that was not designed to crawl.' Among the ambivalent features of his work, that of the rationality of geometry in the face of the abundance of possible meanings is absolutely central. So his work should not be included under the heading of Minimalist Art, even though he has often been described as foreshadowing this trend. His work pre-dates that of the Minimalists.

He took part in group exhibitions including: 1958, Documenta IV, Kassel and Venice Biennale; 1968, *L'Art du Réel aux USA 1948-1968* (*The Art of the Real, USA, 1948-1968*), Centre d'Art Contemporain, Paris; 1976, *Two Hundred Years of American Sculpture*, Whitney Museum of American Art, New York; 2001, *Abstracción: El Paradigma Amerindio* (*Abstraction: The American-Indian Paradigm*), IVAM Centro Julio González, Valencia.

He had solo shows of his work, including 1966, Wadsworth Atheneum, Hartford, Connecticut; 1967, *Tony Smith and Minimalist Sculpture*, Walker Art Center, Minneapolis, Minnesota; 1968, Galerie Renée Ziegler, Zurich and Galerie Yvon Lambert, Paris; 1970, travelling exhibition in the USA; 1971, Museum of Modern Art, New York City; 1979, Pace Gallery, New York. Posthumous exhibitions: 1983, Pace Gallery, New York; 1986, Galerie Templon, Paris; 1985, 1989 and 1991, Paula Cooper Gallery, New York; 1993, Musée d'Art Contemporain, Geneva; 1995, Musée d'Art Moderne, St-Étienne; 1993, Louisiana Museum, Denmark and 2002, IVAM Institute of Modern Art in Valencia.

BIBLIOGRAPHY:
Wagstaff, Samuel Jr., *'Talking with Tony Smith'* in *Artforum*, periodical, New York, December, 1966. Libbard, Lucy R., *'Tony Smith: the Ineluctable Modality of the Visible'* in *Art International*, periodical, Zurich, Summer 1967. Smith, Tony, *'Homage to the Square'* in *Art in America*, periodical, New York, July-August, 1967. Green, Eleanor, *Tony Smith, painting and sculpture*, exhibition catalogue, College Park, University of Maryland Art Gall., Maryland, 1974. Hunter, Sam, *Tony Smith. Ten elements and throwback*, exhibition catalogue, Pace Wildenstein Gall., New York, 1979. Hobbs, Robert, *Tony Smith, Paintings and Sculpture*, exhibition catalogue, Pace Wildenstein Gall., New York, 1983. Criqui, Jean-Pierre, *'Trictrac pour Tony Smith'* in *Artstudio* n° 6, periodical, Gal. Templon, Paris, 1987. Meschede, Friedrich/Pachner, Joan, *Tony Smith, Skulpturen und Zeichnungen 1961-1969*, exhibition catalogue, Westfälische Landesmuseum, Münster, 1988 (text in German and English). *Tony Smith*, exhibition catalogue, Louisiana Museum, Louisiana, 1995-1996. Drathen, Doris von, *'À l'écart des catégories. Un autre regard sur Tony Smith et Carl André'* in *Art Press* n° 224, periodical, Paris, May 1997. Storr, Robert/Keenen, John/Pachner, Joan, *Tony Smith, architect, painter, sculptor*, exhibition catalogue, Museum of Modern Art, New York, 1998. Paternosto, César/Frame, Mary/Lippard, Lucy R., et al., *Abstracción: El paradigma amerindio*, exhibition catalogue, Instituto Valenciano de Arte Moderno (IVAM), Valencia, 2001. *Tony Smith: Paintings and Sculpture, 1960-65*, exhibition catalogue, Mitchell-Innes and Nash/Matthew Marks Gallery, New York, 2001. *Louisenberg: Tony Smith*, exhibition catalogue, Mitchell-Innes and Nash/Matthew Marks Gallery, New York, 2003.

MUSEUMS AND GALLERIES:
BUFFALO (Albright-Knox AG) - DALLAS (MA): *Willy* (1962, produced later, steel) - DETROIT (IA) - HARTFORD (Wadsworth Atheneum): *Amaryllis* (steel, sculpture); *Spit Ball* (marble) - HOUSTON (The Menil Collection): *The Snake is out* (1962); *Spitball* (1962) - MINNEAPOLIS (Walker Art Center) - NEW YORK (Metropolitan Mus. of Art) - NEW YORK (MoMA): *Gracehoper* (1961); *Black Box* (1962); *Snake is Out* (1962); *Cigarette* (1961) - NEW YORK (Solomon R. Guggenheim Mus.) - NEW YORK (Whitney Mus. of American Art) - OTTAWA (Nat. Gal. of Canada) - OTTERLO (Kröller-Müller Mus.) - PHILADELPHIA (ICA, University of Pennsylvania) - SAN FRANCISCO (MoMA): *Throwback* (1976, painted aluminium); *Spitball* (1961, marble) - ST LOUIS (AM) - WASHINGTON DC: *The Black Box* (1962) - WASHINGTON DC (Corcoran Gal. of Art) - WASHINGTON DC (Hirshhorn Mus. and Sculpture Garden) - WASHINGTON DC (NGA): *Untitled* (1962, acrylic/canvas); *Moondog* (1964 (model) 1998/1999 (final version), painted aluminium); *Wandering Rocks* (1967, painted steel, five elements) - WASHINGTON DC (Smithsonian American AM): *She Who Must Be Obeyed* (1975, assembled and painted fiberboard).

AUCTION RECORDS:
NEW YORK, 11 Nov 1982, *The Yellow Bird* (c. 1965, painted steel, 30 x 45 x 20 ins / 76 x 114.5 x 51 cm) USD 18,000. NEW YORK, 8 May 1984, *Black Box* (1962, steel painted black, 22½ x 33 x 25 ins / 57 x 84 x 63.5 cm) USD 16,000. NEW YORK, 3 May 1988, *Black Box* (steel, 22½ x 33 x 25¼ ins / 57 x 84 x 64 cm) USD 40,700. NEW YORK, 10 Nov 1988, *Model of Cigarette* (sanded steel, 13 x 22 x 17 ins / 33.3 x 55.9 x 43.2 cm) USD 27,500. NEW YORK, 3 May 1989, *Throwback* (steel painted black, 13½ x 32 x 16¼ ins / 34.6 x 81.2 x 41 cm) USD 44,000. NEW YORK, 31 Oct 1989, *The Louisenberg no. 5* (oil on canvas, 19½ x 39½ ins / 49.8 x 100.4 cm) USD 16,500. NEW YORK, 7 Nov 1989, *Throne* (welded steel, 31 x 40½ x 32½ ins / 78.8 x 103 x 82.5 cm) USD 165,000. NEW YORK, 14 Feb 1991, *One Two Three* (bronze, three objects, 5 x 14 x 7½ ins / 13 x 35.6 x 19 cm; 10 x 13½ x 13½ ins/25.4 x 34.3 x 34.3 cm; 10 x 21 x 13½ ins/25.4 x 53.3 x 34.3 cm) USD 38,500. NEW YORK, 1 May 1991, *We Lost* (bronze, 18 x 17¾ ins / 45.7 x 45 cm; 2¾ x 18 ins/7 x 45.7 cm) USD 33,000. NEW YORK, 13 Nov 1991, *Marriage* (1961, bronze, 20 x 20 x 24 ins / 50.8 x 50.8 x 61 cm) USD 35,200. PARIS, 26 June 1992, *Tau* (1965, bronze, 23½ x 15¼ x 12¼ ins / 60 x 39 x 31 cm) FRF 110,000. NEW YORK, 24 Feb 1993, *We Lost* (1962, bronze, 18 x 18 x 18 ins / 45.7 x 46 x 45.7 cm) USD 16,500. NEW YORK, 4 May 1993, *For V.T.* (bronze, 29 x 40 x 40 ins / 73.7 x 101.6 x 101.6 cm) USD 32,200. NEW YORK, 9 Nov 1993, *Throne* (1956, welded steel, 28 x 44 x 32 ins / 71.1 x 111.8 x 81.3 cm) USD 85,500. NEW YORK, 5 May 1994, *Tau* (1965, painted aluminium, 45 x 70 x 42¾ ins / 114.3 x 177.8 x 108.6 cm) USD 85,000. NEW YORK, 22 Feb 1996, *Yellow Bird* (varnish/steel, 30¼ x 44 x 30 ins / 76.8 x 111.8 x 76.2 cm) USD 18,975. NEW YORK, 8 May 1996, *Trap* (1968, black-patinated bronze, 10 x 55 x 55 ins / 25.3 x 139.7 x 139.7 cm) USD 34,500. LUCERNE, 8 June 1996, *New Piece* (black lacquered wood, 18½ x 19 ins / 47 x 48 cm) CHF 1,300. NEW YORK, 21 Nov 1996, *Moondog* (1967, black-patinated bronze, 33 x 32 x 27 ins / 83.7 x 81.3 x 68.6 cm) USD 27,600. NEW YORK, 7 May 1997, *Marriage* (1961, black-patinated bronze, 20 x 24 x 20 ins / 50.8 x 61 x 50.8 cm) USD 29,900. NEW YORK, 8 May 1997, *Gracehoper* (1967, bronze, 33½ x 64 x 43 ins / 85.1 x 162.6 x 109.3 cm) USD 85,000. NEW YORK, 18-19 Nov 1997, *Spitball* (1947-1950, black granite, 12¼ x 14½ x 15 ins / 30.8 x 36.8 x 38.1 cm) USD 22,425. NEW YORK, 13 May 1999, *The Snake is Out* (1962, sculpture, 15 x 24x14 ins / 37 x 60x35 cm) USD 40,000. NEW YORK, 15 Feb 2000, *Spitball* (1961, black marble, 12 x 14x14 ins / 30 x 35x35 cm) USD 4,800. NEW YORK, 17 May 2001, *Tau* (1965, black patinated bronze, 14 x 23x19 ins / 36 x 58x47 cm) USD 28,000. NEW YORK, 17 May 2001, *Playground* (1962, black patinated bronze, 16 x 32x16 ins / 41 x 82x41 cm) USD 38,000. NEW YORK, 5 Nov 2002, *Untitled* (c. 1957, oil on canvas, 48 x 60 ins / 122 x 152 cm) USD 22,000. NEW YORK, 12 Nov 2002, *Mistake* (black patinated bronze, 12 x 12x8 ins / 30 x 30x20 cm) USD 15,000. NEW YORK, 23 Sept 2003, *Duck* (black patinated bronze, 11 x 13x9 ins / 27 x 32x22 cm) USD 38,000. NEW YORK, 12 Nov 2003, *Tau* (1965, painted aluminium, 45 x 70x43 ins / 114 x 178x109 cm) USD 120,000. LONDON, 6 Feb 2004, *Marriage* (1961, black patinated bronze, 20 x 20x24 ins / 51 x 51x61 cm) GBP 26,000. NEW YORK, 15 Sept 2004, *Untitled* (1970, ink, 14 x 22 ins / 35 x 56 cm) USD 32,000.

SMITH, Vincent DaCosta

American, 20th century.
Born 1929, in Brooklyn (New York City); died December 2003.
Painter, draughtsman, engraver, illustrator. Portraits, genre scenes, street scenes. Murals.

Vincent D. Smith was born into a family of Barbadian origin. He studied at the Skowhegan School of Painting and Sculpture in Maine and at the Brooklyn Museum Art School, New York, and took his degree at the age of 50 from Empire State College, State University of New York, Saratoga, New York. He taught at the Whitney Museum Art Resources Center, New York, and was one of the artists who worked in Robert Blackburn's Printmaking Workshop. He lived and worked in New York.

Smith divided his own work into two periods: his urban period (1953-1973), during which he kept a chronicle of daily life among African-Americans in New York, and his second period (1974-1994), during which he used African motifs in works such as *Fry Bones (Fire from the Diaspora)*. In paintings constructed around stylised perspective, whose figures are distorted in expressionist manner, and whose colours remain warm, juxtaposed in contrasts, and applied in thick strokes, he unceasingly condemned racism and violence in American society. He also painted murals, such as the West Indian carnival scene *Jonkonnu Festival Wid the Frizzly Rooster Band* (1991), which was created for the Oberia D.

Dempsey Multi-Service Center of Central Harlem, New York, and for the 116th Street Subway station in Harlem.

Vincent Smith took part in various group exhibitions, including: *Tradition and Conflict: Images of a Turbulent Decade, 1963-1973*, Studio Museum in Harlem, New York (1985); *Narratives of African Art and Identity: The David C. Driskell Collection*, High Museum of Art, Atlanta (1998); and *Slave Routes, The Long Memory*, Kenkeleba Gallery, New York (1999). He had a number of solo exhibitions: at the Brooklyn Museum Art School Gallery, Brooklyn, New York (1955); at the Studio Museum in Harlem, New York (1969 and 1974); at the Whitney Museum Art Resources Center, New York (1972 and 1976); at the Brooklyn Museum of Art, Brooklyn, New York (1977); in a travelling exhibition, Henry Street Settlement, Abrons Arts Center, New York (1990); at N'Namdi Gallery, Birmingham, Michigan (1991 and 1998); and at Alexandre Gallery, New York (2000).

BIBLIOGRAPHY:

Patton, Sharon F., *Vincent D. Smith: riding on a blue note: monoprints and works on paper on jazz themes*, Henry Street Settlement, New York, 1990. Patton, Sharon F., *African-American Art*, Oxford University Press, New York, 1998.

MUSEUMS AND GALLERIES:

BALTIMORE (MA) - BOSTON (MFA) - CHAPEL HILL (Ackland Art Mus.) - CHICAGO (AI) - COLUMBUS, OH (MA) - DETROIT (MA) - NEW HAVEN (AG, Yale University) - NEW YORK (Brooklyn Mus.) - NEW YORK (MoMA) - NEWARK (Mus.).

SMITH, W.
American, 18th century.
Active in 1760.
Engraver. Ex-libris plates.

SMITH, W. Armfield
British, 19th century.
Active in London from 1832 to 1849.
Painter.

W. Armfield Smith exhibited at the Royal Academy several times between 1832 and 1849. He may have been the brother of George Armfield.

SMITH, W. Boase
British, 19th century.
Born 1842; died 24 January 1896, in Falmouth.
Painter. Landscapes, seascapes.

W. Boase Smith settled in Falmouth and became a member of the Society of Western England. He took an active part in exhibitions throughout the country, including in Birmingham, Manchester and Liverpool.

SMITH, W.A.
British, 18th century.
Active from 1787 to 1793.
Miniaturist.

MUSEUMS AND GALLERIES:

LONDON (British Mus.): *Portrait of a Lady*.

SMITH, W.R.
British, 19th century.
Active in London during the first half of the 19th century.
Engraver (burin).

W.R. Smith engraved views and landscapes.

SMITH, Walter Granville, called Granville-Smith
American, 19th - 20th century.
Born 26 January 1870, in South Granville (New York); died 1938.
Painter, watercolourist, draughtsman, illustrator. Landscapes.

Walter Granville Smith studied with Walter Satterlee, Carrol Beckwith and Willard Metcalf and at the Art Students League in New York. He also studied in Europe. He was a member of the Salmagundi Club and the American Federation of the Arts. He received many awards, including a bronze medal in Charleston, several from the Salmagundi Club and a Carnegie prize of 500 dollars in 1927. He specialised in landscapes.

AUCTION RECORDS:

NEW YORK, 13-15 Feb 1907, *Drawing Day*, USD 140. NEW YORK, 21 Nov 1945, *On the River*, USD 525. NEW YORK, 10 May 1974, *Family Scene*, USD 1,400. NEW YORK, 30 April 1980, *Montauk Point* (oil on canvas, 45 x 60 ins / 114.3 x 152.4 cm) USD 2,500. SAN FRANCISCO, 8 Oct 1980, *The Inside Passage to Alaska* (oil on card, 12 x 18 ins / 30.5 x 45.5 cm) USD 500. NEW YORK, 23 Sept 1981, *The Promenade* (1897, watercolour/mounted paper/card, 17 3/4 x 28 1/2 ins / 45.1 x 72.4 cm) USD 2,400. NEW YORK, 7 Dec 1984, *Regatta Day* (1915, oil on canvas, 36 x 43 3/4 ins / 91.2 x 111.4 cm) USD 30,000. NEW YORK, 6 Dec 1985, *Lady Boarding a Yacht* (1895, watercolour/mounted paper/card, 19 1/4 x 30 ins / 49 x 76.2 cm) USD 5,500. NEW YORK, 15 March 1986, *Priming the Hull* (oil on canvas, 12 1/4 x 16 1/4 ins / 31 x 41 cm) USD 6,250. NEW YORK, 24 Jan 1990, *Woman in a Hat* (watercolour and gouache/green paper, 11 3/4 x 8 1/2 ins / 29.8 x 21.5 cm) USD 3,190. NEW YORK, 30 May 1990, *On Board* (1893, watercolour and gouache/paper, 20 x 16 ins / 50.8 x 40.7 cm) USD 5,225. NEW YORK, 12 March 1992, *Skating near a Mill* (1938, oil on canvas, 30 x 40 ins / 76.2 x 101.6 cm) USD 5,500. NEW YORK, 10 June 1992, *Fishing off Coast* (oil on canvas, 5 x 12 ins / 12.8 x 30.5 cm) USD 2,200. NEW YORK, 31 March 1993, *Fly Fisherman* (1930, watercolour and pencil/card, 10 x 13 ins / 25.4 x 33 cm) USD 633. NEW YORK, 9 Sept 1993, *The Water's Edge* (pencil and watercolour heightened with white/card, 19 1/2 x 13 ins / 49.8 x 33 cm) USD 1,150. NEW YORK, 28 Sept 1995, *Landscape with a Pond* (1919, oil on canvas, 18 x 24 1/4 ins / 45.7 x 61.3 cm) USD 3,680. NEW YORK, 27 Sept 1996, *Willows, Bellport, New York State* (1920, oil on canvas, 16 x 22 ins / 40.6 x 55.8 cm) USD 3,450. DOWNINGTON, 14 Sept 2001, *Interior Scene of a Doctor Attending to a Black Family* (watercolour, pen and ink, 9 x 13 ins / 23 x 33 cm) USD 3,500.

SMITH, Warwick. See **SMITH John, called Warwick Smith**

SMITH, Wells
British, 19th century.
Active in London.
Painter. Genre scenes.

Wells Smith exhibited his work at the Suffolk Street Gallery in the Exhibition of the Society of British Artists from 1870 until 1875.

AUCTION RECORDS:

LONDON, 5 March 1910, *Young Tradeswoman*, GBP 5. LONDON, 11 March 1999, *Fisherman's Tale* (1882, oil on canvas, 28 x 36 ins / 71 x 91 cm) GBP 3,000.

SMITH, Wilhelm
Swedish, 19th - 20th century.
Born 25 April 1867, in Karlshamn.
Painter. Portraits, genre scenes, landscapes.

Wilhelm Smith studied under Bonnat in Paris. He is best known for his winter landscapes. He exhibited at the Paris Salon, where he was awarded an honourable mention in 1891 for his painting *Three Against One*.

MUSEUMS AND GALLERIES:

BUDAPEST - GÖTEBORG - STOCKHOLM: *Italian Blacksmiths; Winter Day at Dalarna; Italian Tavern*.

SMITH, William, called Smith of Chichester
British, 18th century.
Born 1707, in Guildford; died 4 October 1764, in Shopwyke, near Chichester.
Painter, engraver. Portraits, landscapes, still-lifes (fruit).

William Smith was the elder brother of George Smith, and was known as Smith of Chichester. He exhibited in London from 1761.

Auction records:

London, 26 March 1976, *Italian Landscape* (1753, oil on canvas, 27¼ x 35 ins / 69 x 89 cm) GBP 350. London, 17 Feb 1984, *Still-life of Fruit* (oil on canvas, a pair, 12 x 14 ins / 30.5 x 35.5 cm) GBP 1,300. New York, 17 Jan 1990, *Vast Landscape with Shepherds near Thatched-Roofed Houses* (1757, oil on canvas, a pair, 13 x 19 ins / 33.1 x 48.1 cm) USD 5,500. London, 27 Sept 1994, *Classical Landscape with Shepherds* (oil on panel, 7¾ x 11¾ ins / 19.5 x 30 cm) GBP 552.

SMITH, William
British, 18th - 19th century.
Active in London.
Miniaturist, engraver (burin/mezzotint).

William Smith studied under W. Pether. He exhibited his work in London in 1774 and 1802.

SMITH, William
British, 19th century.
Painter. Portraits, landscapes with figures, animals.

William Smith exhibited his work in London from 1813 until 1859.

Auction records:

London, 20 Nov 1985, *Sir Rowland Hill of Hawkstone in Shropshire with Otter Hounds* (1837, oil on canvas, 19¼ x 23½ ins / 49 x 59.5 cm) GBP 18,000. London, 18 Oct 1989, *Landowners with a Prize Bull in a Landscape* (oil on canvas, 29½ x 36 ins / 75 x 91.5 cm) GBP 7,040. Amsterdam, 3 Nov 1992, *Shepherd in a Meadow with his Flock* (1844, oil on panel, 13¾ x 17 ins / 35 x 43 cm) NLG 4,140.

SMITH, William Collingwood
British, 19th century.
Born 1815, in Greenwich, London; died 15 March 1887, in London.
Painter, watercolourist, draughtsman. Seascapes, landscapes.

William Collingwood Smith was self-taught except for taking some advice from J.D. Harding. He made his debut at the Royal Academy in 1836 with a view of Westminster Abbey and continued to take part in exhibitions there, as well as in those held at the British Institution and on Suffolk Street. In 1843 he became an associate of the Society of Painters in Watercolours, becoming a member in 1849 and treasurer from 1854 until 1879. He made frequent visits to France, Switzerland and Italy and brought back numerous paintings.

He produced a considerable collection of works, especially watercolours. He is often confused with William Collingwood; however, he is not thought to be the same artist.

Museums and Galleries:

London (Victoria and Albert Mus.): three watercolours.

Auction records:

London, 28 Jan 1924, *Lake Geneva* (drawing) GBP 24. London, 6 Feb 1973, *Entrance to the Grand Canal, Venice* (watercolour) GBP 520. London, 21 Dec 1982, *The Dreadnought, Seamen's Hospital Ship off Greenwich* (watercolour heightened with white, 10¾ x 14¼ ins / 27.5 x 36 cm) GBP 950. New York, 29 Feb 1984, *La Piazzetta, Venice* (watercolour, 31½ x 53¼ ins / 80 x 135 cm) USD 3,250. London, 22 Oct 1986, *View of Constantinople from the Bosphorus* (watercolour/pencil outlines heightened with white, 11¾ x 16¼ ins / 30 x 41.5 cm) GBP 1,100. London, 25 Jan 1989, *Small Waterfall* (watercolour and gouache, 13¼ x 19¾ ins / 33.5 x 50 cm) GBP 440. London, 12 June 1992, *View of Haddon Hall from the River* (pencil and watercolour, 9¼ x 21¾ ins / 23.2 x 55.3 cm) GBP 1,210. New York, 29 Oct 1992, *Italian Village beside a River* (watercolour/paper/card, 8¼ x 11¼ ins / 21 x 28.6 cm) USD 660. London, 12 May 1999, *Swiss Peasants by Lake with Mountains Beyond* (watercolour over pencil heightened with gouache and gum arabic, 13 x 29 ins / 33 x 74 cm) GBP 2,200. London, 11 Nov 1999, *Opening Encounter at Trafalgar, HMS Royal Sovereign Engaging the Spanish Flagship Santa Ana* (pencil and watercolour heightened with white and scratching out, 28 x 40 ins / 71 x 102 cm) GBP 39,000. London, 29 Nov 2001, *Woman and Child Walking by a River* (watercolour over pencil heightened with gouache, 13 x 19 ins / 34 x 48 cm) GBP 1,200. London, 19 March 2002, *Bay of Uri, Lake Lucerne, Switzerland, near William Tell's Chapel* (watercolour heightened with white, 30 x 51 ins / 76 x 129 cm) GBP 4,200. London, 27 Nov 2003, *Bay of Uri, Lake Lucerne from the Left Bank* (watercolour heightened with gouache and scratching out, 30 x 51 ins / 76 x 129 cm) GBP 8,500. London, 26 March 2004, *Dogana and the Church of Santa Maria Della Salute, Venice* (watercolour over pencil heightened with gouache, 6 x 17 ins / 14 x 42 cm) GBP 3,600.

SMITH, William D.
American, 19th century.
Active in Newark and New York 1829-1850.
Engraver (burin).

SMITH, William Good
American, 19th century.
Active in New York 1844-1856.
Miniaturist. Portraits.

SMITH, William Harding Collingwood
British, 19th - 20th century.
Born 1848; died 9 January 1922.
Active in London.
Painter. Genre scenes.

Harding Smith was the son and pupil of William Collingwood.

SMITH, William James
British, 19th century.
Active in London c. 1825.
Engraver (etching).

William James Smith produced engravings after Rembrandt.

SMITH, William Russel. See **SMITH Russel William Thompson**

SMITH, Wuanita
American, 19th - 20th century.
Born 1 January 1866, in Philadelphia; died 1959.
Painter, illustrator.

Wuanita Smith studied at the Academy of the Fine Arts in Philadelphia and the Art Students League in New York. She also studied in Paris. She was a member of the American Federation of the Arts, and won a number of prizes. She illustrated many books, including Grimms' *Fairy Tales* and Swift's *Gulliver's Travels*.

SMITH, Xanthus Russell
American, 19th - 20th century.
Born 1838, in Philadelphia; died 2 December 1929, in Weldon.
Painter. Landscapes, landscapes with figures, naval battles, boats.

Xanthus Russell Smith is known for his scenes of naval battles.

Museums and Galleries:

Columbia, SC (MA): *Coast of South Carolina* - Philadelphia (Union League): *The Monitor and the Merrimac* (1875, oil on canvas).

Auction records:

New York, 21 April 1977, *Opening of the Battle of Gettysberg and the Death of General Reynolds, July 1st* (1863, oil on canvas, 15 x 25 ins / 38 x 63.5 cm) USD 4,250. New York, 30 April 1980, *Admiral du Pont's Naval Machine Shop* (1865, oil on canvas, 12¼ x 18 ins / 31.1 x 45.7 cm) USD 15,000. NEW YORK, 6 Dec 1984, *A Blockade Runner Beached* (1867, oil on canvas, 12¼ x 18¼ ins / 31.1 x 46.3 cm) USD 26,000. NEW YORK, 31 May 1985, *U.S.S. Kearsarge Sinking the Alabama* (oil on canvas, 35¾ x 21 ins / 91 x 53.3 cm) USD 32,000. NEW YORK, 6 Dec 1991, *Abandoned* (1880, oil on canvas, 20¼ x 30½ ins / 51.2 x 77.4 cm) USD 12,100. NEW YORK, 18 Dec 1991, *The American Falls* (1879, oil on canvas/synthetic resin, 8 x 12 ins / 20.3 x 30.5 cm) USD 2,475. NEW YORK, 12 March 1992, *The Lizzie Driscoll at Dock* (1878, oil on canvas, 15¼ x 23½ ins / 38.7 x 59.4 cm) USD 6,600. NEW YORK, 31 March 1993, *Mountainous Landscape with Cottage and Figures Herding Livestock* (1898, oil on canvas, 14½ x 21 ins / 36.8 x 53.3 cm) USD 1,725. LONDON, 12 May 1993, *Chalets at Zwing Uri in the Reuss Valley in Switzerland* (1882, oil on canvas, 14 x 22½ ins / 35.5 x 57 cm) GBP 920. NEW YORK, 22 Sept 1993, *The Old Man's Basin at Franconia Notch* (1876, oil on canvas, 12 x 18 ins / 30.5 x 46 cm) USD 5,520. NEW YORK, 12 Sept 1994, *Shipwrecked Sailors being Rescued at Cape May* (1875, oil on paper/card/panel, 5¾ x 12¾ ins / 14.6 x 32.4 cm) USD 3,105. NEW YORK, 30 Oct 1996, *Salvaging a Wreck, Cape May, New Jersey* (oil on canvas, 16 x 27 ins / 40.6 x 68.6 cm) USD 3,450.

SMITH DE COST

American, 19th - 20th century.

Born 1864, in Skaneateles; died 1911, in Amenia (New York).

Painter.

De Cost Smith was a student of Boulanger and Lefebvre. He became a member of the Salmagundi Club in 1901. He painted scenes of Native American life.

AUCTION RECORDS:

LOS ANGELES, 24 June 1980, *Moving Camp* (pen and wash, in grisaille, 14½ x 20¾ ins / 37 x 53 cm) USD 1,500. NEW YORK, 4 Dec 1986, *The Last Stand* (1892, oil on canvas, 26 x 46 ins / 66 x 116.8 cm) USD 13,000. NEW YORK, 2 Dec 1992, *War Cry* (1909, oil on canvas, 45 x 34 ins / 114.3 x 86.4 cm) USD 3,520. NEW YORK, 4 March 2003, *Indian Warrior* (1903, oil on canvas, 24 x 18 ins / 62 x 46 cm) USD 11,000.

SMITH OF CHICHESTER, George. See **SMITH George, called Smith of Chichester**

SMITH OF DERBY. See **SMITH Thomas, called Smith of Derby**

SMITH STONE (Mrs)

British, 18th century.

Painter. Animals.

Mrs Smith Stone exhibited in London between 1780 and 1791.

SMITH Y MARI, Ismael

Spanish, 20th century.

Born 16 or 17 July 1886, in Barcelona; died 1972, in White Plains (New York).

Active in the USA from 1919.

Painter, sculptor, engraver, draughtsman, illustrator.

Religious subjects, portraits, genre scenes, landscapes.

Ismael Smith y Mari was a pupil of R. Casella in Barcelona; he then continued his studies in Paris at the École des Arts Décoratifs from 1910 to 1914. During World War I, he returned to his hometown of Barcelona, before settling permanently in the USA in 1919. He began his career illustrating Spanish magazines. He also worked in Paris as a fashion designer and made a number of bust portraits in Barcelona, but it was as an engraver that he was most productive. Among his many etchings, most notable are: *Woman of Fashion, Man Out Walking, Waves, Adam and Eve* and *Bull Race*. Ismael Smith y Mari took part in various collective exhibitions including: Salon d'Automne and Georges Petit Gallery, Paris (1913); Salon de la Société Nationale des Beaux-Arts de Paris, London (1914); New York (1919). He was a member of the Salmagundi Club.

BIBLIOGRAPHY:

Arnáiz, José Manuel/López Jiménez, Javier/Merchán Díaz, Manuel (ed.), '*Cien años de pintura en Espana y Portugal (1830-1930)*' in vol. X, Antiqvaria, Madrid, 1993.

MUSEUMS AND GALLERIES:

BARCELONA (MAM del Mus. Nacional d'Art de Catalunya): several engravings - LONDON (British Mus., Department of Prints and Drawings): several engravings.

SMITH-HALD, Bjørn

Norwegian, 20th century.

Born 1883, in Paris; died 1964.

Painter. Genre scenes.

Bjørn Smith-Hald studied under his father, Frithjof Smith-Hald, and in Paris. He went on to paint in a conventional style before adopting a more personal expressive style.

AUCTION RECORDS:

LONDON, 29 March 1990, *Promenading in Paris* (coloured crayons and watercolour/brown paper, 40½ x 29¼ ins / 103 x 74.3 cm) GBP 4,180. LONDON, 19 June 1991, *Modern Life* (ink and watercolour, 29¼ x 39¼ ins / 74 x 100 cm) GBP 5,500. LONDON, 16 Nov 1994, *Fishermen* (1887, oil on canvas, 38¾ x 59 ins / 98.5 x 149 cm) GBP 10,350.

SMITH-HALD, Frithjof

Norwegian, 19th century.

Born 13 September 1846, in Kristiansand; died 9 March 1903, in Chicago (Illinois).

From 1879 also active in France.

Painter. Genre scenes, landscapes with figures, landscapes, waterscapes.

Smith-Hald was the father of Bjørn Smith. He was a pupil of J.F. Eckersberg in Christiania (now Oslo). He received a bursary, and continued his studies in Karlsruhe and at the Kunstakademi in Düsseldorf. He later travelled to Berlin and London. In 1879, he settled in Paris. He participated in several collective exhibits, including Lyons, 1881, where he received a second place medal; Versailles, 1882, where he received a first place medal; and the national art exhibitions in Madrid of 1884, 1887 and 1890. He painted numerous scenes of Norwegian peasants and fishermen.

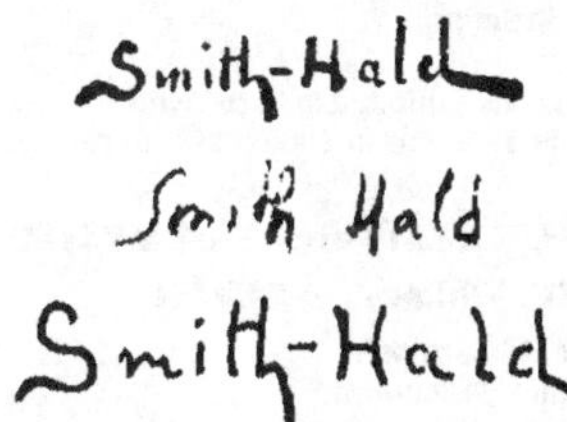

BIBLIOGRAPHY:

Arnáiz, José Manuel/López Jiménez, Javier/Merchán Díaz, Manuel (ed.), '*Cien años de pintura en Espana y Portugal (1830-1930)*' in vol. X, Antiqvaria, Madrid, 1993.

MUSEUMS AND GALLERIES:

BERGEN: *Two Landscapes* - BORDEAUX (MBA): *October Evening in Norway* - COLOGNE: *Return of the Fisherman* - GÖTEBORG: *Two Landscapes in Winter* - LA ROCHELLE: *The Net* - LILLE: *Landing* - MONTPELLIER (Mus. Fabre): *Return From Work* - RHEIMS (MBA): *Summer Night in Norway* - ROUEN (MBA): *Moon Rising Over the Sea* - THE HAGUE: *Winter Evening by the Shore* - TRONDHEIM: *Winter Afternoon Near Ulrikken.*

AUCTION RECORDS:

PARIS, 24 Nov 1922, *View From Holland,* FRF 310. PARIS, 16-17 May 1927, *A Boat Arriving at Port,* FRF 2,000. PARIS, 10

Feb 1950, *Fishing Women* (1888) FRF 10,000. PARIS, 15 May 1950, *Landscape in the Moonlight*, FRF 53,100. PARIS, 22 Nov 1950, *Village By the Sea in the Moonlight*, FRF 46,000. NEW YORK, 2 May 1979, *Awaiting the Ferryboat* (oil on canvas, 35 x 56 1/2 ins / 89 x 143.5 cm) USD 4,250. STOCKHOLM, 24 April 1984, *Scene by the Sea* (1891, oil on canvas, 48 3/4 x 78 3/4 ins / 124 x 200 cm) SEK 61,000. LONDON, 20 March 1985, *The Bank of a Fjord with Figures on a Summer Evening* (1874, oil on canvas, 41 x 66 1/4 ins / 104 x 168 cm) GBP 7,000. LONDON, 23 March 1988, *Family of Fishermen Watching the Boats* (oil on canvas, 49 1/4 x 82 ins / 125 x 208 cm) GBP 24,200. COLOGNE, 23 March 1990, *Summer Evening on the Coast of Cornouailles* (oil on canvas, 18 1/2 x 29 1/2 ins / 47 x 75 cm) DEM 17,000. LONDON, 27-28 March 1990, *Children in the Snow* (1880, oil on canvas, 30 1/4 x 46 3/4 ins / 77 x 119 cm) GBP 12,100. LONDON, 22 May 1992, *Hamlet in a Snowy Landscape* (oil on canvas, 16 1/2 x 20 1/2 ins / 42 x 52 cm) GBP 2,200. PARIS, 21 June 1995, *Women Walking on the Road of a Seaside Village* (oil on canvas, 39 x 61 3/4 ins / 99 x 157 cm) FRF 23,500. LONDON, 25 March 1999, *Waiting for the Ferry* (oil on canvas, 35 x 57 ins / 88 x 144 cm) GBP 11,000. OSLO, 16 Dec 1999, *Winter Landscape with Woman and Children Fishing* (1902, oil on canvas, 32 x 51 ins / 81 x 129 cm) NOK 45,000. OSLO, 10 April 2000, *Artists Painting Outdoors, Possibly Sinding and Grimelund* (oil on canvas/board, 22 x 17 ins / 56 x 42 cm) NOK 380,000. OSLO, 4 Dec 2000, *Mending Fishing Nets* (oil on canvas, 46 x 70 ins / 118 x 179 cm) NOK 105,000. LONDON, 29 March 2001, *Waiting for the Ferry* (oil on canvas, 35 x 58 ins / 90 x 147 cm) GBP 3,500. OSLO, 29 Oct 2001, *Mother and Child Looking Out to Sea* (oil on canvas, 35 x 59 ins / 90 x 150 cm) NOK 85,000. OSLO, 2 Dec 2002, *Woman and Children Watching Fishing Boats Leaving* (oil on canvas, 19 x 30 ins / 47 x 75 cm) NOK 40,000. OSLO, 26 May 2003, *Northern Landscape with Seabirds, Norway* (oil on canvas, 23 x 31 ins / 58 x 79 cm) NOK 29,000. OSLO, 19 Nov 2003, *Young Boys Fishing* (oil on canvas, 24 x 39 ins / 60 x 100 cm) NOK 190,000.

SMITH-HARDER, Hans Georg. See **HARDER Hans Georg**

SMITH-KIELLAND, Per Axel. See **KIELLAND Per Axel Smith**

SMITH-LEWIS, John

American, 19th century.

Born in Burlington.

Painter.

John Smith-Lewis exhibited in Paris, where he was awarded an honourable mention in 1886 and a third-class medal in 1897.

SMITHE, Lionel Percy. See **SMYTHE**

SMITHE, William. See **SMITH**

SMITHER, James

American, 18th century.

Active 1768-1797.

Engraver.

James Smither's engravings of small portraits, cards and industrial plates were used to illustrate numerous books and magazines. He also engraved ex-libris, certificates and a large map of Philadelphia decorated with views of several buildings, which was published in 1786.

SMITHS, Heinrich. See **SCHMITZ**

SMITHSON

British, 19th century.

Active in England.

Miniaturist.

Smithson exhibited a miniature on Suffolk Street in 1830.

SMITHSON, Robert

American, 20th century.

Born 1938, in Passaic (New Jersey); died 20 July 1973, in Amarillo (Texas), as the result of an accident.

Painter, draughtsman, collage artist, assemblage artist, installation artist.

Land Art, Process Art, Conceptual Art.

Robert Smithson was a leading exponent of the Land Art movement. His drawings from the early 1960s and his collages, combining mythology and religion with dinosaurs, astronauts and King Kong, were influenced by a number of movements, but especially Expressionism and Pop Art. His oils and small assemblages - already making use of glass, mirrors and slate - were more like a kind of Optical Art. He also directed films with his friends Bob Fiore, Barbara Jarvis and his wife Nancy Holt. When articles appeared in art journals, Smithson wrote formal theoretical reflections, which are considered an essential companion to help understand his work. A collection of these writings was published in 1979 at the instigation of Nancy Holt.

Smithson started producing three-dimensional work in 1966. He displayed *Nonsites*, samples of mineral or vegetable material taken outside their natural situation, and *Sites* or *Earthworks*, works created outside the context of the gallery or museum, on the site of the geographical or geological environment chosen by the artist. These were later than the *Nonsites*, which were generally shown with an arrangement aligned to the ground with the aid of metallic structures or mirrors in a style similar to that of Minimal Art.

Smithson used mirrors in an effort to enlarge the traditional perspective and to play with perception, altering the relation of the 'seen' and the 'unseen'. The outside series of *Mirror Displacements*, followed by *Paths of Mirrors*, were ephemeral works because the mirrors were re-used: all that remains are photographs. *Adventures of Travels with Mirrors in the Yucatan*, on which *Artform* published an article and photo-reportage in 1969, relate nine stages, nine installations of mirrors in sand, earth, seaweed and other bases. These 'displacements' disrupt the natural site with the help of mirrors.

The *Sites* are generally places scarred by the oblivion of post-industrial neglect. In his writings, Smithson is very insistent on the idea of 'entropic landscape', consisting of the sense of a process of fossilised disintegration. He discovered this entropy in the natural landscapes themselves, and also in the relationship between humanity and nature. These on-site operations are accessible either through visual images in the form of films or because they have been preserved at the request of the local people (*Broken Circle*, 1971; *Spiral Hill*, 1971). One of the best known, *Asphalt Rundown*, (1969), consists of a huge flow of asphalt tipped from the back of a truck on the slope of an abandoned Roman quarry. *Spiral Jetty* (1970) is a spiral winding towards the left, built on the great red salt lake in Utah from local materials such as silt, rocks and salt crystals. Two years later the work was engulfed when the lake water rose.

Robert Smithson's radical protest against the art market and art institutions, as well as the 'ecological' interpretation of his work since his death, have made a legend of this artist who died prematurely at the age of 35 in an aeroplane accident.

Smithson participated in many collective exhibitions, such as: Jewish Museum, New York, 1966; *Earth Art*, New York, Stedelijk Museum, Amsterdam, Junsthalle, Bern, *Prospect*, Düsseldorf, and Museum of Contemporary Art, Chicago, 1969; 3rd Salon International des Galeries Pilotes, Musée Cantonal, Lausanne, 1970; Documenta V, Kassel, 1972; *L'Art Conceptuel, une Perspective* (*Conceptual Art: A Perspective*), Musée d'Art Moderne de la Ville de Paris, 1989; *Moving Pictures*, Solomon R. Guggenheim Museum, New York, 2002-2003; *Les Années 70: L'Art en Cause* (*The 1970s: Art in Question*), at Capc-Musée d'Art Contemporain, Bordeaux, 2002;

and *Paysages* (*Landscapes*), part of *Trésors Publics, 20 Ans de Création dans les Fonds Régionaux d'Art Contemporain (FRAC)* (*Public Treasury, 20 Years of Creation in the Regional Collection of Contemporary Art*), Centre Européen d'Actions Artistique Contemporaines, Strasbourg, 2003. Solo exhibitions include: New York, 1966, 1968, 1969 and Düsseldorf, 1968. Posthumous retrospectives were held at the Musée Contemporain de Marseille and the palais des Beaux-Arts, Brussels in 1994.

BIBLIOGRAPHY:

Smithson, Robert, '*Entropy and the New Monuments*' in *Artforum*, periodical, New York, June, 1966. Smithson, Robert, '*Quasi-infinities and the Wanting of Space*' in *Arts Magazine*, periodical, New York, November, 1966. Smithson, Robert, '*Towards the Development of an Air Terminal Site*' in *Artforum*, periodical, New York, June, 1967. Smithson, Robert, '*The Monument of Passaic*' in *Artforum*, periodical, New York, December, 1967. Parent, Béatrice, '*Land Art*' in *Opus international*, periodical, Paris, March 1971. Hobbs, Robert, *Robert Smithson: Sculpture*, Cornell University Press, Ithaca (NY), 1981. Ligwood, James/Gilchrist, Maggie/Larson, Kay/Brouwer, Marianne/Criqui, Jean-Pierre/Gintz, Claude, *Robert Smithson. Le Paysage entropique, 1960-1973*, exhibition catalogue, Musée d'Art contemporain, Marseilles, 1994 (with essays by Robert Smithson). *Earthwards: Robert Smithson and Art after Babel*, University of California Press, 1995. Conley, Brian (ed.), *Robert Smithson: a collection of writings*, exhibition catalogue, Pierogi 2000, New York, 1997. *Robert Smithson retrospective: works 1955-1973*, National Museum of Contemporary Art, Oslo, 1999. *Moving Pictures*, exhibition catalogue, Solomon R. Guggenheim Museum, New York, 2002. Roberts, Jennifer, L., *Mirror-Travels: Robert Smithson and History*, Yale University Press, New Haven, 2004.

MUSEUMS AND GALLERIES:

CHÂTEAUGIRON (FRAC Bretagne): *Movie Treatment, Sulfur Island, Texas* (1970); *Mounds* (1973) - NEW YORK (Solomon R. Guggenheim Mus.): *Hotel Palenque* (1969, photos and audio CD); *Yucatan Mirror Displacements (1-9)* (1969, photos).

AUCTION RECORDS:

NEW YORK, 23 July 1976, *Site Uncertain, Non Site* (1968, seven steel compartments containing coal, 15 x 90 x 90 ins / 38 x 228.5 x 228.5 cm) USD 13,500. NEW YORK, 13 Nov 1980, *The City of Glue* (1969, pen, 10 x 7 3/4 ins / 25.5 x 20 cm) USD 1,000. NEW YORK, 16 Feb 1984, *Vortex* (1966, colouring pencil, 16 3/4 x 14 ins / 42.5 x 35.5 cm) USD 900. NEW YORK, 1 Nov 1984, *Vortex* (1965, stainless steel and mirror, 16 3/4 x 9 x 8 ins / 42.5 x 22.7 x 20.3 cm) USD 7,250. NEW YORK, 1 Oct 1985, *Vortex* (1966, red pencil/paper, 16 3/4 x 13 3/4 ins / 42.5 x 35 cm) USD 1,000. NEW YORK, 5 May 1987, *Leaning Mirror* (1968; *Earth Mirror* (1969, pencil, two drawings, 22 x 18 ins / 56 x 45.8 cm and 21 1/2 x 17 1/2 ins/54.7 x 44.5 cm) USD 3,500. NEW YORK, 20 Feb 1988, *Untitled* (mirror, 7 x 12 1/4 x 12 1/4 ins / 17.8 x 30.8 x 30.8 cm) USD 5,280. NEW YORK, 8 Oct 1988, *Museum of Space* (pencil/paper, 18 x 24 1/4 ins / 45.5 x 61.3 cm) USD 4,400. NEW YORK, 7 May 1990, *Untitled* (1966, painted aluminium, 15 x 19 x 19 ins / 38 x 48.3 x 48.3 cm) USD 28,600. NEW YORK, 8 May 1990, *Corner Mirror with Coral* (1969, three mirrors and coral, 36 x 36 x 36 ins / 91.5 x 91.5 x 91.5 cm) USD 165,000. NEW YORK, 6 Nov 1990, *Demons and Angels* (1962, ink/paper/card, 24 x 18 ins / 61 x 45.8 cm) USD 1,650. NEW YORK, 2 May 1991, *Mirror/Chasm* (1965, stainless steel and mirror, 16 3/4 x 9 1/4 x 7 1/2 ins / 42.5 x 23.5 x 19 cm) USD 13,200. NEW YORK, 2 May 1991, *Spiral Hill, White Sand and Blocks of Peat, Emmen Holland* (graphite and ink/paper, 15 1/2 x 12 1/2 ins / 39.3 x 32 cm) USD 15,400. LONDON, 26 March 1992, *Madrone Spiral* (1972, pencil/paper, 23 3/4 x 19 ins / 60.5 x 48 cm) GBP 6,050. NEW YORK, 6 Oct 1992, *Mirror Thicket (Inside-Outside)* (1969, pencil/paper, 14 x 17 ins / 35.6 x 43.2 cm) USD 7,150. NEW YORK, 4 May 1993, *Earth Mirror* (1968, pencil/paper, 24 x 19 ins / 61 x 48.3 cm) USD 7,475. NEW YORK, 3 May 1994, *Four-sided Vortex* (1967, stainless steel and mirror, 35 1/2 x 28 x 28 ins / 90.2 x 71.1 x 71.1 cm) USD 36,800. NEW YORK, 9 May 1996, *Island of Coal* (1969, pencil and marker pen/paper, 17 3/4 x 23 3/4 ins / 45.4 x 60.6 cm) USD 10,350. NEW YORK, 10 Nov 1997, *Spiral Film Plan for Island of Broken Glass* (1969, graphite/card, 17 3/4 x 24 ins / 45 x 60.8 cm) USD 27,600. NEW YORK, 19 Nov 1997, *Museum at the World Fair (Japan)* (1969, graphite/panel, 16 3/4 x 13 3/4 ins / 42.5 x 35 cm) USD 14,950. NEW YORK, 18 May 1999, *Petrified Coral with Mirrors* (1971, limestone and three mirrors, 31 x 31x31 ins / 79 x 79x79 cm) USD 130,000. LONDON, 27 June 2000, *Untitled* (painted steel Plexiglas mirrors, 15 x 100x6 ins / 38 x 254x16 cm) GBP 50,000. LONDON, 28 June 2000, *Spiral Mangrove* (1971, pencil and crayon, 19 x 24 ins / 48 x 61 cm) GBP 14,000. NEW YORK, 13 May 2004, *Island of Coal* (1969, colour marker, colour crayons and pencil, 18 x 24 ins / 45 x 61 cm) USD 30,000. NEW YORK, 13 May 2004, *Spiral Jetty, Great Salt Lake - Movie Treatment* (1970, pencil on paperboard, two parts, 28 x 24 ins / 72 x 60 cm) USD 70,000.

SMITHWICK, J. G.

American, 19th century.

Active during the second half of the 19th century.

Engraver (wood).

J. G. Smithwick worked with Frank French and provided engravings for magazines.

SMITS, Alexander

Dutch, 17th century.

Active in the middle of the 17th century.

Painter.

Alexander Smits was the son of Samuel Smits.

SMITS, Eugène or Eugeen Joseph Henri

Belgian, 19th - 20th century.

Born 22 May 1826, in Antwerp; died 4 December 1912, in Brussels.

Painter, watercolourist, engraver, draughtsman.

Religious subjects, mythological subjects, portraits, genre scenes, landscapes, still-lifes, flowers.

Société Libre des Beaux-Arts.

Eugène Smits was the son of a senior civil servant. An art-lover and an admirer of the work of Rubens in particular, Smits - together with Willem Herreyns - was charged with the recovery of works of art 'liberated' by Napoleon. As an artist, he took instruction from François Navez and was involved in the launch of the Société Libre des Beaux-Arts in 1868. His finest work was *Changing Seasons*. Examples of his work featured at the Salon des Artistes Français in Paris, where he was awarded a bronze medal at the Exposition Universelle of 1889. *Changing Seasons* was exhibited at the retrospective *L'Art Belge Ancien et Moderne* (*Belgian Art, Past and Present*) held at the Musée du Jeu de Paume in Paris in 1923.

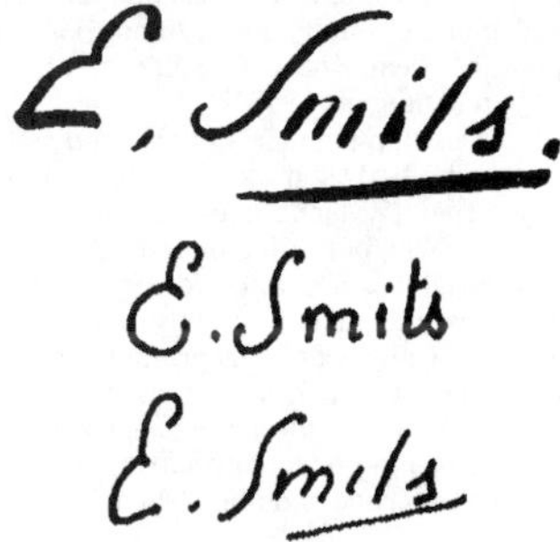

Museums and Galleries:
Antwerp: *Happiness and Sadness* - Brussels (MBA): *Changing Seasons; Roma; Diana; Wounded Lansquenet; Venice; Judgment of Paris; Letter to Metella; Flowers* - Ghent: *Pietà* - Ixelles - Louvain.
Auction records:
Paris, 1881, *Young Woman* (watercolour) FRF 600. Paris, 6 April 1891, *Siesta*, FRF 1,100. Paris, 26 March 1904, *Reading*, FRF 340; *Letter to Metella*, FRF 760. Paris, 1 May 1940, *Young Italian Woman with an Orange*, FRF 200. Paris, 4 May 1942, *Italia* (pen drawing) FRF 200. Brussels, 2 Dec 1950, *Flora*, BEF 5,000. Amsterdam, 23 April 1980, *Portrait of a Young Woman* (oil on canvas, 17¾ x 13½ ins / 45 x 34 cm) NLG 3,600. Brussels, 17 June 1982, *Chaste Susanna* (1857) BEF 75,000. London, 25 March 1988, *Changing Seasons* (watercolour, 20¾ x 24 ins / 53 x 61 cm) GBP 2,750. Amsterdam, 2 May 1990, *Cherries on a Plate on a Wooden Table* (oil on panel, 9½ x 12½ ins / 24 x 32 cm) NLG 4,025. Lokeren, 28 May 1994, *Young Woman* (oil on panel, 18 x 14¼ ins / 46 x 36.5 cm) BEF 33,000. New York, 9 Jan 1997, *Washing Day* (oil on canvas, 23 x 18 ins / 58.4 x 45.7 cm) USD 8,625. Lokeren, 6 Dec 1997, *On the Beach* (oil on canvas, 9¾ x 18¼ ins / 24.8 x 46.5 cm) BEF 90,000.

SMITS, François or Frans Marcus
Dutch, 18th - 19th century.
Born 1760, in Antwerp; died 15 March 1833, in Antwerp.
Painter. Portraits.

François Smits was a student at the academy in Antwerp in 1779, and a pupil of A.B. de Quertenmont. He lived and died in penury. He is noted for his portrait of the painter *William J. Herreyns*, kept in Antwerp.

SMITS, Gaspar or Casparus. See **SMITZ Gaspar**

SMITS, Hyacinthe
Belgian, 20th century.
Born 1866, in Brussels.
Painter. Landscapes.

SMITS, Jakob or Jacobs
Dutch, 19th - 20th century.
Born 9 July 1855, in Rotterdam; died 15 February 1928, in Moll (Kempen).
Active then naturalised in Belgium.
Painter, watercolourist, pastellist, draughtsman (charcoal/red chalk), engraver (etching). Religious subjects, figures, portraits, genre scenes, interiors with figures, architectural views, landscapes.

Jakob Smits studied at the fine arts academies of Rotterdam, Brussels (under Portaels), Munich, Vienna and Rome, and went on to serve as principal of the college of decorative arts in Haarlem. In 1885, he left his wife and family to move to Drente, where he met the Naturalist painter Neuhuys. In 1889, he settled in the countryside at Achterbos near Antwerp and spent the greater part of his life there as a recluse. He took Belgian nationality in 1902.

Smits did not take up painting until around 1900, having previously worked chiefly in pastels and in charcoal. He also worked as an etcher. His landscapes, portraits and interiors have a rustic simplicity bordering on the naive. Throughout his career, he exhibited a predilection for Biblical themes (where his figures are almost invariably depicted in peasant garb and wearing clogs). His art is primitive to the point of Expressionism, but it also has an aura of simplicity and something approaching mysticism. He applied his colours in layers to achieve a coarse texture akin to that of a rough-cast wall. His figures are crude and unpolished, his treatment of light theatrical.

A commemorative exhibition of Smits' work was organised at the Koninklijk Museum voor Schone Kunsten in Antwerp in 1955.

Bibliography:
Haesaerts, Paul, *Jacob Smits*, De Sikkel, Antwerp, 1948. Lebeer, Louis/Nave, Francine de, *Jakob Smits. Etser en lithograaf*, De Gulden Roos Pandora, Antwerp, 1997.

Museums and Galleries:
Brussels: *End of the Day; Condemned Man's Father; Emblem of the Kempen Rehion; Mater Dolorosa* - Courtrai: *Woman Knitting* - Ghent: *Pietà* - Rotterdam: *Rotterdam, Cradle of the Fine Arts*.
Auction records:
Brussels, 12 May 1934, *Woman with Dog* (watercolour) BEF 8,000; *Motherhood*, BEF 6,000. Brussels, 11 Dec 1937, *Blindness*, BEF 8,000. Brussels, 25 March 1938, *Abandoned Mill*, BEF 4,200. Brussels, 17 and 18 March 1939, *Interior in Kempen*, BEF 3,200; *Woman with Dog*, BEF 6,500. Brussels, 15 April 1939, *Old Mill*, BEF 10,000; *Motherhood* (drawing) BEF 2,100. Brussels, 8 Feb 1950, *No Man's Land* (1918) BEF 40,000. Brussels, 21 Oct 1950, *Near the Frontier*, BEF 36,000. Brussels, 1951, *Peeling Potatoes* (gouache) BEF 17,000; *Weavers* (watercolour) BEF 12,000. Brussels, 24 Feb 1951, *Harvesting the Crop/Cloud* (1901) BEF 55,000; *Dressmaking* (watercolour) BEF 8,500. Brussels, 21 May 1951, *Seated Woman* (drawing) BEF 2,000. Brussels, 8 and 9 Dec 1965, *Interior in the Campine*, BEF 650,000. Antwerp, 26 April 1966, *Brightly-lit Interior*, BEF 640,000; *Interior in Kempen* (watercolour) BEF 220,000. Brussels, 23 and 24 April 1968, *Interior in Kempen*, BEF 850,000. Brussels, 12 Oct 1971, *Large Landscape*, BEF 340,000. Brussels, 24 Oct 1972, *Landscape in Kempen*, BEF 240,000. Antwerp, 23 Oct 1973, *Cloud*, BEF 460,000. Brussels, 2 April 1974, *Female Portrait* (pastel) BEF 220,000. Antwerp, 19 Oct 1976, *Little Church* (oil on panel, 5 x 6¼ ins / 13 x 16 cm) BEF 55,000. Breda, 26 April 1977, *Condemned Man's Father* (watercolour, 15¾ x 11½ ins / 40 x 29 cm) NLG 20,000. Brussels, 26 Oct 1977, *Mill at Achterbos* (1918, oil on canvas, 35½ x 39¼ ins / 90 x 100 cm) BEF 425,000. Antwerp, 17 Oct 1978, *Mater Amabilis* (watercolour, 25½ x 22 ins / 65 x 55 cm) BEF 600,000. Antwerp, 8 May 1979, *Interior in Kempen* (oil on canvas, 31½ x 39¼ ins / 80 x 100 cm) BEF 1,200,000. Lokeren, 13 Oct 1979, *Interior with Woman Sewing near a Cradle* (charcoal, study, 7½ x 9½ ins / 19 x 24 cm) BEF 110,000. Brussels, 24 Oct 1979, *Young Peasant Woman Daydreaming* (watercolour, 26¾ x 19¾ ins / 68 x 50 cm) BEF 380,000. Lokeren, 25 April 1981, *Thatched Cottages* (charcoal, 9 x 11 ins / 22 x 28 cm) BEF 45,000. Lokeren, 16 Oct 1982, *Marguerite* (oil on canvas, 28¾ x 23½ ins / 73 x 60 cm) BEF 850,000. Lokeren, 23 April 1983, *Portrait* (red chalk, 8¼ x 7½ ins / 21 x 19 cm) BEF 65,000. Brussels, 28 March 1984, *Women Peeling Potatoes* (watercolour, 19 x 24¾ ins / 48 x 63 cm) BEF 440,000. Antwerp, 3 April 1984, *Child with Doll* (oil on canvas remounted/panel, 52¼ x 42½ ins / 133 x 108 cm) BEF 1,900,000. Brussels, 27 March 1985, *Bust of a Young Girl* (red chalk, 5 x 4¼ ins / 12.5 x 11 cm) BEF 160,000. Antwerp, 21 Oct 1986, *Hamlet* (c. 1903, oil on canvas, 48 x 56 ins / 121 x 142 cm) BEF 2,000,000. Lokeren, 5 March 1988, *Landscape* (oil on canvas, 11 x 11 ins / 27 x 28 cm) BEF 440,000. Lokeren, 28 May 1988, *Malvina* (oil on canvas, 17¾ x 15¼ ins / 45 x 39 cm) BEF 480,000. Lokeren, 8 Oct 1988, *Young Peasant* (oil on panel, 9¼ x 7¾ ins / 23.3 x 19.5 cm) BEF 330,000. London, 28 Nov 1989, *Mill at Haechterbroek* (oil on canvas, 23½ x 23½ ins / 59.5 x 59.5 cm) GBP 30,800. London, 16 Oct 1990, *Interior in Kempen* (oil on canvas, 27½ x 29¾ ins / 69.8 x 75.5 cm) GBP 44,000. Amsterdam, 6 Nov 1990, *Cradle* (oil on canvas, 15¾ x 19¾ ins / 40 x 50 cm) NLG 40,250. Paris, 20 Nov 1991, *Child Wearing a Beret* (oil on canvas, 14¼ x 11 ins / 36 x 28 cm) FRF 27,000. Lokeren, 21 March 1992, *Interior with Peasant and Young Woman Reading* (black chalk,

24 1/2 x 18 1/2 ins / 62 x 47 cm) BEF 500,000; *Dressmaker* (oil on canvas, 27 1/4 x 33 ins / 69 x 84 cm) BEF 1,250,000. AMSTERDAM, 9 Dec 1992, *Summer Sunset in the Country* (oil on canvas, 27 1/4 x 36 1/2 ins / 69 x 93 cm) NLG 34,500. LOKEREN, 15 May 1993, *Portrait of a Young Boy (Boby)* (oil on canvas, 14 1/4 x 10 3/4 ins / 36 x 27.5 cm) BEF 380,000. AMSTERDAM, 8 Dec 1993, *Clear Night* (oil on panel, 10 1/4 x 11 ins / 26 x 28 cm) NLG 16,100. LOKEREN, 8 Oct 1994, *Peasant Woman Sitting and Stroking her Dog* (lead pencil and pastel, 15 x 13 1/2 ins / 38 x 34 cm) BEF 260,000. LOKEREN, 7 Oct 1995, *Malvina* (oil on canvas/panel, 14 x 10 3/4 ins / 35.5 x 27.5 cm) BEF 440,000. LOKEREN, 9 March 1996, *Gust Loos, Gardener* (oil on canvas, 19 x 12 1/2 ins / 48 x 32 cm) BEF 480,000. LOKEREN, 18 May 1996, *Interior in Kempen* (black chalk, 8 x 9 3/4 ins / 20.5 x 25 cm) BEF 50,000; *Summer Landscape with a Hay Wain* (oil on panel, 8 x 11 ins / 20.4 x 28 cm) BEF 160,000. LOKEREN, 5 Oct 1996, *Stable Interior* (watercolour, 8 1/2 x 12 1/4 ins / 21.5 x 31 cm) BEF 170,000. LOKEREN, 7 Dec 1996, *War-Blinded* (1918, oil on canvas, 39 3/4 x 42 ins / 101 x 106.5 cm) BEF 1,700,000. LOKEREN, 8 March 1997, *Sewing by the Window (recto)/Peeling Potatoes (verso)* (chalk, 9 x 11 1/2 ins / 23 x 29 cm) BEF 33,000; *Mills* (oil on canvas, 15 3/4 x 17 3/4 ins / 40 x 45 cm) BEF 460,000. AMSTERDAM, 4 June 1997, *Two Trees* (oil on panel, 20 3/4 x 22 3/4 ins / 53 x 58 cm) NLG 69,192. AMSTERDAM, 1 Dec 1997, *Adoration of the Magi* (1905, oil on canvas, 51 1/4 x 57 ins / 130 x 145 cm) NLG 141,600. LOKEREN, 6 Dec 1997, *Two Children* (1935, pencil, 8 3/4 x 7 ins / 22.5 x 18 cm) BEF 180,000. LOKEREN, 10 Oct 1998, *Interior with Mother and Child in Campine* (oil on canvas, 39 x 43 ins / 100 x 110 cm) BEF 2,400,000. LOKEREN, 9 Oct 1999, *Campine Landscape with Farm* (1927, oil on panel, 20 x 20 ins / 50 x 50 cm) BEF 1,000,000. LOKEREN, 7 Oct 2000, *Annunciation in Campine* (oil on canvas, 37 x 40 ins / 95 x 101 cm) BEF 2,850,000. NEUILLY, 5 April 2001, *Woman Praying* (oil on panel, 10 x 9 ins / 25 x 22 cm) FRF 67,000. LOKEREN, 9 March 2002, *Mother with Child in Crib in Interior* (oil on canvas, 22 x 24 ins / 55 x 60 cm) EUR 48,000. ANTWERP, 29 April 2003, *Family in Interior* (oil on canvas, 39 x 41 ins / 100 x 105 cm) EUR 55,000. BRUSSELS, 7 June 2004, *Rue in a Hamlet* (oil on canvas, 47 x 55 ins / 120 x 140 cm) EUR 64,000.

SMITS, Johan Gerard or Jan Geerard
Dutch, 19th - 20th century.
Born 14 February 1823, in The Hague; died 8 September 1910, in The Hague.
Painter, watercolourist. Figures, genre scenes, landscapes.

Johan Gerard Smits was a pupil of Salomon Leonardus Verveer.

MUSEUMS AND GALLERIES:
THE HAGUE (Gemeentemus.): *Magistrates' Bench in the Town Hall in The Hague; View of Bergen, near Alkmaar; Fun on the Beach*; watercolour.

AUCTION RECORDS:
NEW YORK, 19 April 1977, *Skating* (hardboard, 13 1/4 x 19 ins / 33.5 x 48.2 cm) USD 2,000. AMSTERDAM, 28 Feb 1989, *Village in an Undulating Landscape* (1886, oil on panel, 7 3/4 x 11 3/4 ins / 19.5 x 30 cm) NLG 1,150; *Elegant Couple Speaking to a Coachman near a Town Postern* (1841, oil on canvas, 17 3/4 x 19 ins / 45 x 48.5 cm) NLG 5,750. NEW YORK, 9 Jan 1991, *Children near a House by a Canal in Winter* (1853, watercolour/paper, 6 x 7 3/4 ins / 14.3 x 19.7 cm) USD 880. AMSTERDAM, 24 April 1991, *View of Bergen near Alkmaar* (1893, oil on canvas, 31 1/2 x 49 1/4 ins / 80 x 125 cm) NLG 4,370. AMSTERDAM, 18 Feb 1992, *View of the Groenburgwal, Amsterdam* (oil on canvas, 22 x 33 1/2 ins / 55 x 85 cm) NLG 2,875. AMSTERDAM, 14-15 April 1992, *Dunes at Scheveningen* (1908, watercolour, 10 1/4 x 17 1/4 ins / 26 x 44 cm) NLG 3,795. AMSTERDAM, 28 Oct 1992, *Little Milkmaid* (oil on panel, 12 1/4 x 10 ins / 31 x 24.5 cm) NLG 4,600. AMSTERDAM, 2-3 Nov 1992, *Town Scene* (watercolour, 11 1/2 x 8 3/4 ins / 29.5 x 22.5 cm) NLG 3,450. NEW YORK, 26 May 1993, *Market Day* (oil on canvas, 32 1/4 x 23 1/4 ins / 81.9 x 59.1 cm) USD 5,750. AMSTERDAM, 8 Feb 1994, *Figures on a Path through the Dunes at Sunset, with Boats Anchored off the Coast* (1856, oil on canvas, 17 1/2 x 19 ins / 44.5 x 48.5 cm) NLG 5,750. AMSTERDAM, 21 Jan 1998, *Fisherman's Family* (pencil, pen, brown ink and watercolour/paper, 7 3/4 x 6 1/4 ins / 20 x 16 cm) NLG 1,153.

SMITS, Johannes, or Smidts
Dutch, 17th century.
Active in 1660.
Painter.

Johannes Smits is noted for a still-life and *Diogenes with the Lantern*.

SMITS, Johannes
Dutch, 20th century.
Born 1916, in Amsterdam.
Painter. Figures, interiors with figures, still-lifes.

Johannes Smits was a coffee-house owner and part-time painter. His interiors with figures are highly detailed, virtually ethnological compositions.

BIBLIOGRAPHY:
Gans, Louis, *Meesters der Europese naïven*, exhibition catalogue, Centraal Museum, Utrecht, 1970.

AUCTION RECORDS:
VERSAILLES, 28 Nov 1982, *Creel of Herrings* (oil on canvas, 19 x 23 ins / 48 x 57.5 cm) FRF 10,500.

SMITS, Louis
Belgian, 19th century.
Born in Antwerp.
Painter, engraver. Genre scenes.

Louis Smits was a pupil of J. Ruyten. He executed etchings. He was the same artist as Louis Smets.

AUCTION RECORDS:
LONDON, 6 Oct 1989, *Dutch Landscape with Skaters on a Frozen River* (1860, oil on canvas, 24 1/4 x 35 ins / 61.5 x 88 cm) GBP 30,800. COLOGNE, 28 Oct 1999, *Dutch River Landscape in Winter with Figures Skating* (oil on canvas, 16 x 24 ins / 40 x 61 cm) DEM 9,500.

SMITS, Marcel
Belgian, 20th century.
Born 1888, in Brussels.
Painter. Figures, portraits, landscapes, still-lifes.

Marcel Smits studied at the Académie Royale des Beaux Arts in Brussels.

SMITS, Nicolas or Johannes
Dutch, 17th - 18th century.
Born 1672, in Breda; died 1731.
Painter. History painting, portraits.

Nicolas Smits worked at the castle of Houselardyk and in The Hague. His works are rare.

SMITS, Rémi
Belgian, 20th century.
Born 1921, in Ixelles (Brussels).
Painter, draughtsman. Murals, designs for tapestries, designs for mosaics, and stained glass windows.

Rémi Smits studied at the academy in Brussels.

SMITS, René
Dutch, 20th century.
Born 1925, in Antwerp.
Sculptor, draughtsman.

René Smits studied at the Academie voor Schone Kunsten in Antwerp and went on to teach drawing and composition at the Academie voor Beeldende Kunsten in Mechelen and sculpture at the Academie in Sint-Niklaas. His sculptures, although essentially abstract, are clearly anthropomorphic. His style aspires to a simplicity and purity of line and curve, reminiscent of Hans (Jean) Arp. He also produces stand-alone drawings which are not merely roughs for his sculpture.

SMITS, Samuel Pietersz., or Smit
Dutch, 17th century.
Died 1652.
Active in The Hague.
Painter. History painting, portraits.

Samuel Pietersz. Smits was the father of Alexander Smits, and was a member of the guild in The Hague in 1650. The Hermitage Museum in Leningrad has his *Allegory of Fortune*.

SMITS, Theodor. See **SMITZ Gaspar**

SMITSEN, Arnold, or Smitsens or Smytsens or Smetsens
Flemish School, 18th century.
Born c. 1687, in Liège; died 27 April 1744, in Liège.
Painter. Still-lifes.

Arnold Smitsen painted hunting trophies.

AUCTION RECORDS:
PARIS, 4 May 1945, *Still-life with Game in a Landscape*, FRF 5,300.

SMITTERS, Anna de. See **SMYTERS**

SMITZ, Gaspar, or Smith or Smits Theodor, also known as Theodorus Hartcamp
Flemish School, 17th century.
Born c. 1635; died c. 1707 or 1689, in Dublin.
Painter, engraver. Religious subjects, portraits, still-lifes.

Gaspar Smitz moved from The Hague to England shortly after the restoration of Charles II, where he was nicknamed 'Magdalene Smith' because of the large number of paintings of Mary Magdalene he executed. He went to Ireland and made his name. He had as his pupils Maubert and Gawdy of Exeter. He engraved some original prints.

MUSEUMS AND GALLERIES:
BERLIN: *Still-life with Crayfish, Oysters, etcetera* - COLOGNE (Peltzer Collection): *Still-life*.

AUCTION RECORDS:
LONDON, 18 May 1990, *Still-life with a Peeled Lemon, Shellfish, Grapes and Peaches round a Glass* (oil on panel, 13 1/2 x 18 1/4 ins / 34.2 x 46.4 cm) GBP 13,750. STOCKHOLM, 5 Dec 2000, *Vanitas Still-life* (oil on canvas, 19 x 15 ins / 47 x 38 cm) SEK 120,000. LONDON, 14 Dec 2001, *Vanitas Still-life with Candle, Vase of Flowers and Skull on Partially Draped Table* (oil on canvas, 19 x 16 ins / 49 x 40 cm) GBP 5,500. LONDON, 13 Dec 2002, *Roemer with Peaches, Crabs, Oysters, Pipe and a Knife on a Stone Shelf* (oil on canvas, 9 x 13 ins / 24 x 32 cm) GBP 13,000. COLOGNE, 1 July 2004, *Still-life* (oil on canvas, 19 x 16 ins / 49 x 40 cm) EUR 4,500.

SMMER, Christoph
German, 16th century.
Active c. 1536 or 1540.
Engraver.

Smmer is referred to by Ris-Paquot.

SMOCZYNSKI, Mikolaj
Polish, 20th - 21st century.
Born 1955, in Lublin.
Installation artist.

Smoczynski studied at the school of fine arts in Lódz, at the University of Lublin and at the academy of fine art in Warsaw. His work consists of revealing the memory of walls, highlighting the layers of old paint and the technique of this 'skin' in large rectangular-shaped pictures. He has shown his works in solo exhibitions in Warsaw, Lódz and Lyons (Galerie Ollave) and also in 1991 at the San Diego State University Art Gallery and the Wschodnia Gallery in Lódz.

SMOGERER, Wendel
German, 15th century.
Active in Görlitz, from 1488 to 1494.
Painter.

SMOKOWSKI, Franciszek
Lithuanian, 19th century.
Died c. 1840, in Dubosnia.
Sculptor, painter.

Franciszek Smokowski studied at the school of art in Vilnius. He produced decorative paintings and sculptures in the castle at Vilnius and the Dubosnia palace in Vilnius.

SMOKOWSKI, Wincenty
Polish, 19th century.
Born c. 1797, in Vilna (now Vilnius, Lithuania); died 19 February 1876, in Krykiany.
Painter, engraver (wood), lithographer, art writer.

Wincenty Smokowski studied in Vilna and St Petersburg. He revived the art of wood engraving in Poland.

MUSEUMS AND GALLERIES:
CRACOW (Muz. Narodowe): *Several Drawings* - LVIV (NG): *Portrait of a Man in Polish Costume* - POZNAN (Mielzynski Mus.): *Portrait of J. I.Kraszewski and K. W. Wojcicki* - WARSAW (Muz. Narodowe): *The Lake at Troki with Ruins*.

SMOL, Bernard
French, 20th century.
Born 1897; died 1969.
Painter.

Bernard Smol was an artist of the Neo-Impressionist School. Using shimmering colours, he produced paintings with the brilliance of enamel. His subjects were chiefly dream-like characters; harlequins, dancers, clowns, poets, Bohemians and mystical figures, drifting through parkland and cloaked in deep shadow. His work has been compared to that of Monticelli. The powerful effect of his works stems from the range of tones employed, from sparkling to dull, and the opulence and fantasy of the subject matter.

AUCTION RECORDS:
PARIS, 28 Dec 1949, *At the Races*, FRF 4,300. VERSAILLES, 10 Dec 1989, *Landscape with Large Trees* (oil on canvas, 39 1/4 x 28 3/4 ins / 100 x 73 cm) FRF 3,800.

SMOLDERS, Michel
Belgian, 20th century.
Born 1929, in Ixelles (Brussels).
Sculptor.

Michel Smolders produced organically Abstract sculptures in wood, granite and bronze.

SMOLDERS, Paul
Belgian, 20th century.
Born 1921.
Painter, watercolourist, draughtsman.

Paul Smolders is principally known for portraits of children, usually girls.

AUCTION RECORDS:
LOKEREN, 13 March 1976, *Child Playing* (oil on canvas, 22 x 17 3/4 ins / 55 x 45 cm) BEF 80,000. LOKEREN, 5 Nov 1977, *Child Portrait* (oil on canvas, 22 x 17 3/4 ins / 55 x 45 cm) BEF 65,000. LOKEREN, 17 Feb 1979, *Child with Flowers* (oil on canvas, 23 1/2 x 19 3/4 ins / 60 x 50 cm) BEF 70,000. LOKEREN, 25

April 1981, *Little Girl Seated* (charcoal, 16 1/4 x 12 1/4 ins / 41 x 31 cm) BEF 33,000. LOKEREN, 15 Oct 1983, *Little Girl Seated* (coloured chalk and watercolour, 33 1/2 x 25 1/2 ins / 85 x 65 cm) BEF 45,000. LOKEREN, 20 Oct 1984, *Young Woman* (pastel, 30 x 21 1/4 ins / 76 x 54 cm) BEF 50,000. LOKEREN, 5 March 1988, *Terrace* (oil on canvas, 19 3/4 x 23 1/2 ins / 50 x 60 cm) BEF 95,000. LOKEREN, 23 May 1992, *Little Girl Wearing a Coat* (watercolour, 20 3/4 x 11 3/4 ins / 53 x 30 cm) BEF 26,000. LOKEREN, 5 Dec 1992, *Little Girl with Flowers* (oil on canvas, 19 3/4 x 15 3/4 ins / 50 x 40 cm) BEF 85,000. LOKEREN, 4 Dec 1993, *Terrace* (oil on canvas, 17 3/4 x 19 3/4 ins / 45 x 50 cm) BEF 80,000. LOKEREN, 11 March 1995, *Child Wearing a Hat* (oil on canvas, 15 3/4 x 13 3/4 ins / 40 x 35 cm) BEF 85,000. ANTWERP, 19 Oct 1999, *Terrace on the Groenplaats* (oil on canvas, 20 x 24 ins / 50 x 60 cm) BEF 120,000. ANTWERP, 12 Dec 2000, *Small Children Playing* (oil on canvas, 18 x 20 ins / 45 x 50 cm) BEF 90,000. ANTWERP, 24 April 2001, *Ballerina Resting* (oil on canvas, 28 x 20 ins / 72 x 50 cm) BEF 100,000. ANTWERP, 24 April 2001, *Harlequin* (oil on canvas, 22 x 13 ins / 55 x 32 cm) BEF 130,000. ANTWERP, 22 April 2002, *Portrait of a Girl* (oil on canvas, 27 x 21 ins / 69 x 53 cm) EUR 2,000. LOKEREN, 11 May 2002, *Child Playing* (oil on canvas, 20 x 22 ins / 50 x 55 cm) EUR 2,600. ANTWERP, 17 March 2003, *Terrace on the Dike* (oil on canvas, 23 x 27 ins / 58 x 68 cm) EUR 3,400. ANTWERP, 21 Oct 2003, *Harlequin* (oil on canvas, 27 x 19 ins / 68 x 48 cm) EUR 3,400. LOKEREN, 11 Dec 2004, *Ballerina* (watercolour and gouache, 38 x 27 ins / 96 x 68 cm) EUR 1,700.

SMOLIK, Vincenc Rupert
Bohemian School, 19th century.
Born 18 October 1857, in Sychrov; died 30 June 1902, in Prague.
Sculptor.

Vincenc Smolik studied at the art academy in Munich. He worked in Prague from 1887.

SMOLKO, Janek
Polish, 15th century.
Active in Cracow c. 1466.
Painter.

SMOLKY, Athanasius
Hungarian, 19th century.
Born 1775, in Komárom.
Miniaturist.

A portrait artist, Athanasius Smolky was apparently in Paris in 1811.

SMONT. See also **SMOUT**

SMONT, Lucas I, or Smout
Flemish School, 17th century.
Born 3 February 1620, in Antwerp; died at the beginning of 1674, in Antwerp.
Painter. History painting, portraits.

Lucas Smont I was the father of Lucas Smont II and a pupil of Lucas Wolfaert in 1631. He became master of a studio in 1653, and in 1654 married Anna Maria Tyssens.

L. Smout.

SMONT, Lucas II, or Smout
Flemish School, 17th - 18th century.
Born 27 February 1671, in Antwerp; died 8 April 1713, in Antwerp.
Painter, draughtsman. Genre scenes, landscapes, landscapes with figures, seascapes, architectural views.

Lucas Smont II was the son of Lucas Smont I and a pupil of Hendrick van Minderhout in 1685.

MUSEUMS AND GALLERIES:
ANTWERP: *Beach at Scheveningen* - DIJON: *Fish Market* - DRESDEN: *Seaport near a Gulf*; *Beggar at the Door of a Church* - SCHWERIN: *Seascape* (two).

AUCTION RECORDS:
PARIS, 17 and 18 March 1927, *Road with Figures and Animals near a Village* (pen) FRF 280. HAMBURG, 7 June 1979, *Seaside Scene* (oil on panel, 8 x 8 1/2 ins / 20.2 x 21.6 cm) DEM 3,200. COPENHAGEN, 28 April 1981, *Village Celebrations* (oil on panel, 8 1/4 x 11 1/4 ins / 21 x 28.5 cm) DKK 27,000. LONDON, 9 April 1986, *Imaginary View of Paris with Figures on the Banks of the Seine* (oil on canvas, 7 3/4 x 11 ins / 20 x 28 cm) GBP 4,000. PARIS, 13 April 1992, *Fish Market* (oil on canvas, 15 1/4 x 20 1/4 ins / 39 x 51.5 cm) FRF 7,500. NEW YORK, 6 Oct 1994, *Coastal Landscape with Fishermen Selling their Catch on the Shore and Boats in Fine Weather in the Background* (oil on canvas, 16 1/4 x 21 1/4 ins / 41 x 54 cm) USD 3,450. PARIS, 16 June 1995, *Resting near a Waterfall* (oil on oak panel, 13 x 11 ins / 33 x 27 cm) FRF 5,000. NEW YORK, 23 May 2000, *Cavalry Skirmish in Village* (oil on canvas, 16 x 22 ins / 40 x 56 cm) USD 2,400. LONDON, 10 Dec 2003, *Elegant Figures Inspecting the Catch on a Beach with Sailing Barges and Shipping beyond* (oil on canvas, 16 x 21 ins / 40 x 54 cm) GBP 2,600.

SMORENBERG, Dirk
Dutch, 20th century.
Born 4 September 1883, in Alkmaar; died 1960.
Painter. Landscapes.

AUCTION RECORDS:
AMSTERDAM, 12 Dec 1990, *Boat in the Water* (oil on canvas, 35 1/2 x 23 1/2 ins / 90 x 60 cm) NLG 2,760. AMSTERDAM, 17 Sept 1991, *Water-lilies* (oil on canvas, 20 x 15 3/4 ins / 50.5 x 40 cm) NLG 1,150. AMSTERDAM, 12 Dec 1991, *View of Lake Geneva* (1912, oil on canvas, 25 1/2 x 35 1/2 ins / 65 x 90 cm) NLG 17,250. AMSTERDAM, 18 Feb 1992, *Water-lilies* (oil on canvas, 16 1/2 x 25 1/2 ins / 42 x 65 cm) NLG 6,900. AMSTERDAM, 21 May 1992, *Water-lilies* (oil on canvas, 21 1/4 x 28 3/4 ins / 54 x 73 cm) NLG 8,625. AMSTERDAM, 9 Dec 1992, *Winter Landscape* (oil on canvas, 18 x 28 1/2 ins / 45.5 x 72.5 cm) NLG 7,475. AMSTERDAM, 10 Dec 1992, *Landscape with Water-lilies, with the Town of Hilversum in the Distance* (oil on canvas, 19 3/4 x 23 1/2 ins / 50 x 60 cm) NLG 3,450. AMSTERDAM, 11 Feb 1993, *Mountain Chalet in Winter* (1929, oil on canvas, 16 1/4 x 23 1/2 ins / 41 x 60 cm) NLG 4,830. AMSTERDAM, 27-28 May 1993, *Winter Landscape* (oil on canvas, 16 x 20 ins / 40.5 x 50.5 cm) NLG 3,910; *Still-life with Anemones* (oil on canvas, 21 3/4 x 26 ins / 55.5 x 66 cm) NLG 4,600. AMSTERDAM, 14 June 1994, *Water-lilies* (oil on canvas, 23 1/4 x 23 1/2 ins / 59 x 60 cm) NLG 8,050. AMSTERDAM, 31 May 1995, *Water-lilies* (1958, oil on canvas, 28 1/2 x 36 1/4 ins / 72.5 x 92 cm) NLG 5,192. AMSTERDAM, 19-20 Feb 1997, *Water-lilies* (oil on canvas, 19 3/4 x 17 3/4 ins / 50 x 45 cm) NLG 4,843. AMSTERDAM, 2-3 June 1997, *Forest* (oil on canvas, 18 x 28 3/4 ins / 46 x 73 cm) NLG 5,310. AMSTERDAM, 2 July 1997, *Stand of Trees in a Polder Landscape* (oil on canvas, 14 3/4 x 18 1/2 ins / 37.5 x 47 cm) NLG 10,955. AMSTERDAM, 10 June 1999, *Flowering Amaryllis* (oil on canvas, 31 x 21 ins / 79 x 54 cm) NLG 14,000. AMSTERDAM, 1 Sept 1999, *Waterlilies in Loosdrechse Plassen* (oil on canvas, 17 x 26 ins / 44 x 65 cm) NLG 12,000. AMSTERDAM, 4 July 2000, *White Water Lilies in the Loosdrechtse Plassen* (oil on canvas, 20 x 28 ins / 50 x 70 cm) NLG 25,000. AMSTERDAM, 4 July 2000, *Water Lilies in the Loosdrechtse Plassen* (1923, oil on canvas, 22 x 31 ins / 55 x 80 cm) NLG 28,000. AMSTERDAM, 30 Jan 2001, *Waterlillies in the Loosdrechtse Plassen, Kortenhoef in the Distance* (oil on canvas, 20 x 16 ins / 50 x 40 cm) NLG 20,000. AMSTERDAM, 12 June 2001, *Farm in a Snow-covered Winter Landscape* (1912, oil on canvas, 24 x 46 ins / 62 x 116 cm) NLG 20,000. AMSTERDAM, 3 Dec 2002, *Waterlilies* (oil on canvas, 16 x 20 ins / 40 x 50 cm) EUR 5,500. AMSTERDAM, 3 Dec 2002, *Willows Along a Canal* (1914, oil on canvas, 16 x

20 ins / 40 x 50 cm) EUR 10,000. AMSTERDAM, 27 May 2003, *Still-life with Flowers* (1925, oil on canvas, 22 x 28 ins / 55 x 70 cm) EUR 8,500. AMSTERDAM, 2 Dec 2003, *Water Landscape* (oil on canvas, 17 x 26 ins / 42 x 65 cm) EUR 10,000. AMSTERDAM, 3 Feb 2004, *Waterlilies* (oil on canvas, 18 x 20 ins / 45 x 50 cm) EUR 10,000. AMSTERDAM, 30 Nov 2004, *Loosdrechtse Plassen* (oil on canvas, 28 x 46 ins / 70 x 117 cm) EUR 26,000.

SMORROV, Konstantin Vladimirovich.
See **SUVAROV**

SMOUT, Dominikus
Flemish School, 17th - 18th century.
Active in Antwerp.
Painter. History painting.

Dominikus Smout was the son of Lucas Smont I and a pupil of Godefried Maes.

AUCTION RECORDS:
PARIS, 13 Dec 1982, *Goldsmith*; *Miser and his Treasures* (oil on canvas, a pair, 25 1/2 x 32 ins / 65 x 81 cm) FRF 28,600. PARIS, 7 Nov 1984, *Goldsmith*; *Miser and his Treasures* (oil on canvas, two pendants, 25 1/2 x 31 1/2 ins / 64.5 x 80 cm) FRF 65,000. LONDON, 24 May 1985, *Artist's Studio* (oil on canvas, 26 3/4 x 33 ins / 68 x 83.8 cm) GBP 3,500. NEW YORK, 3 Oct 1996, *Figures Surrounded by Precious Objects in an Elegant Interior* (oil on canvas, 26 3/4 x 33 3/4 ins / 68 x 85.7 cm) USD 6,900.

SMOUT, Lucas I and Lucas II. See **SMONT**

SMOUT, Vuillequin, Willequin, Willem or Gauthier, or Semonst or Smont
Flemish School, 14th century.
Sculptor. Religious subjects.

An assistant of Claus Sluter in the Charterhouse of Champmol, Smout worked in Brussels in the second half of the 14th century. He was in Mechelen in 1385.

SMUDJA, Gradimir
Yugoslav, 20th - 21st century.
Born 1956, in Novi Sad (now in Serbia).
Active since 1995 in Italy.
Painter, draughtsman. Comic strips.

Gradimir Smudja studied at the academy of fine art in Belgrade. He left Yugoslavia for Italy, where he lives and teaches drawing in Lucca. His drawings were displayed in 1999 at the Karikatur & Cartoon Museum in Basel.

He portrays his favourite artists Van Gogh, Toulouse-Lautrec and Velázquez, telling semi-parodic, semi-historical stories imbued with tenderness. He attracted attention in France with the publication in 2002 of *Vincent and Van Gogh* (Paris, Delcourt).

MUSEUMS AND GALLERIES:
BASEL (Karikatur & Cartoon Mus.): *Brothel of the Muses* (drawing).

SMUGGLER PARKER. See **PARKER Henry Perle** or **Perlee**

SMUGLEVICH, Feliks Fedorovich, or Smuglevitch
Russian, 19th century.
Active in the middle of the 19th century.
Painter. History painting.

Feliks Fedorovich Smuglevich studied at the art academy of St Petersburg from 1847 to 1852.

SMUGLEVITCH, Antoni
Polish, 18th - 19th century.
Born c. 1740; died c. 1810, in Vilna (now Vilnius, Lithuania).
Painter.

Antoni Smuglevitch was the son and the student of Lucasz Smuglevitch. He painted mostly mural decorations for King Stanislas August. The Mielzynski museum in Poznan owns some landscapes by this artist, featuring ruins, and the National Museum in Warsaw owns some of his drawings.

SMUGLEVITCH, Filip
Polish, 18th century.
Born c. 1752 (?).
Painter.

Filip Smuglevitch was the son of Lucasz Smuglevitch. He painted frescoes.

SMUGLEVITCH, Franciscus or Franciszek or Francissek, or Smuglewicz
Polish, 18th century.
Born 6 October 1745, in Warsaw; died 18 September 1807, in Vilna (now Vilnius, Lithuania).
Painter.

Franciscus Smuglevitch was the son of Lucasz Smuglevitch. He studied with Czechovitch. In 1763 he went to Rome, where he worked with Mengs. He was awarded the first prize at the Accademia di S Luca. In 1785, he returned to Poland on the request of King Stanislas August. The King commissioned him to produce paintings for several churches. He later went to Vilna (now Vilnius, Lithuania) where he produced several historical and religious paintings. On returning to Warsaw, he founded a school of painting. In 1797, he was appointed a teacher at the art academy in Vilna, and in 1800 he was invited to St Petersburg by the Emperor Paul to decorate the St Michael palace. A *Portrait* by this painter featured in the *Exposition d'Art Polonais* in 1921 at the Salon de la Société Nationale des Beaux-Arts in Paris.

MUSEUMS AND GALLERIES:
CRACOW (Muz. Narodowe): *The Battle of Chocim in 1673*; *King Stanislas August at the Court of Lublin*; *Polish Peasants at the Dinner Table* - LVIV (Lubomirski Mus.): *Persian Ambassadors before the Sultan of Morocco*; *Scythian Ambassadors Visiting Darius* - POZNAN (Mielzynski Mus.): *Polish Peasants at the Dinner Table*; *Kosciuszko's Oath in Cracow*; *Two Italian Genre Scenes* - WARSAW (Muz. Narodowe): *Alexander's Victory over Darius*; *Two Scenes from the Legend of St Basil*; *The Bishop J.S. Gedroyé*; *The Family of K. Prozor*.

AUCTION RECORDS:
LONDON, 16 April 1982, *Portrait of Philip Yorke, 3rd Earl of Hardwicke with Colonel Wettenstein* (oil on canvas, 22 x 18 ins / 56 x 45.6 cm) GBP 8,500. PARIS, 22 Nov 2000, *Submission of the Defeated before a Sovereign* (pen, grey wash and ink, 12x15 ins / 30x37 cm) FRF 4,800.

SMUGLEVITCH, Jósef
Polish, 19th century.
Born 1784.
Draughtsman.

Jósef Smuglevitch was the son of Philip Smuglevitch, and studied under Franciscus Smuglevitch in Vilna (now Vilnius, Lithuania).

SMUGLEVITCH, Konstanty
Polish, 18th century.
Born c. 1755 (?).
Painter.

Konstanty Smuglevitch was the son of Lucasz Smuglevitch. He worked in Torun and painted mostly views. The National Museum in Warsaw owns his *Dominican Monks Arriving in Torun in the 17th Century*.

SMUGLEVITCH, Lucasz or Lukasz
Polish, 18th century.
Born 1709, in Poland; died 26 October 1780, in Warsaw.
Painter, fresco artist. Portraits.

Lucasz Smuglevitch was appointed as a painter at the court of King August III. He painted portraits and decorative panels. He was the father of Antoni, Franciscus, Lucjan, Philip and Konstanty Smuglevitch.

SMUGLEVITCH, Lucjan, or Smugleviez
Polish, 18th century.
Born c. 1750 (?).
Active in Warsaw.
Painter.
Lucjan Smuglevitch was the son and the student of Lucasz Smuglevitch. In about 1794, he was invited to work at the palace of Princess Isabelle Lubomirski in Lancut, and produced several works there. He decorated several ceilings in the palace with frescoes. He also produced paintings for the church in Lancut, and for other churches in Poland.

SMUKROVICH, Petr
Russian, 20th century.
Born 1928, in Leningrad (now St Petersburg); died 1998.
Painter. Figure compositions.
Petr Smukrovich studied under Boris Ioganson at the Repin Institute in Leningrad (now St Petersburg). He was a member of the Leningrad Artists Union and was named People's Painter of the USSR. He was a regular exhibitor in Moscow and Leningrad, afterwards St Petersburg.
MUSEUMS AND GALLERIES:
KHARKOV (State Museum of Fine Arts) - KIEV (National Art Museum) - YAROSLAVL (Mus. of Russian Art).
AUCTION RECORDS:
PARIS, 25 Nov 1991, *Revisions* (1953, oil on canvas, 24 3/4 x 31 1/2 ins / 63 x 80 cm) FRF 11,000. PARIS, 27 Jan 1992, *Lenin's Funeral* (oil on canvas, 23 1/4 x 43 3/4 ins / 58.8 x 111.2 cm) FRF 5,000. PARIS, 25 Jan 1993, *On the Dnepr* (oil on canvas, 33 x 43 ins / 84 x 109.5 cm) FRF 4,800.

SMUKROVICH, Vitold
Russian, 20th - 21st century.
Born 1967, in Leningrad, now St Petersburg.
Painter.
Smukrovich was admitted to the Repin Institute in 1987 and worked in B. Ugarov's workshop.
AUCTION RECORDS:
PARIS, 27 Jan 1992, *On the Balcony* (oil on canvas, 23 3/4 x 27 1/2 ins / 60.2 x 70.1 cm) FRF 5,600.

SMULLYAN SLOAN, Robert
American, 20th century.
Born 1915, in New York.
Painter, draughtsman. Genre scenes.
Robert Smullyan Sloan was a student at the City College of Art in New York, graduating in 1936. He continued to study art and art history at the New York Institute of Fine Art. He started to earn his living as an artist in 1940. He produced illustrations for Time, Coronet and Colliers. During the war he made his artistic talents available to the army. He uses a technique deliberately inspired by the Dutch 'bambochades' of the 17th century. He has taken part in group exhibitions including the Corcoran Biennale and the Carnegie International. He has had solo exhibitions in New York and, in 1999, at the Instituto de Bellas Artes de San Miguel de Allende in Mexico. Since 1946, he has had a career as a painter of portraits and genre scenes.

SMUTH, Tomas Valentin. See **SCHMUTH**

SMUTNY, Joseph S.
American, 19th century.
Born 1835, in Bohemia; died 15 January 1903, in New York.
Portrait artist.
Joseph S. Smutny studied in Vienna and settled in New York around 1888.

SMUTNY, Oldrich
Czech, 20th century.
Born 17 June 1925, in Debr, near Mlada Boleslav.
Painter.
Oldrich Smutny studied music and at various art schools in Prague until 1954. He settled in Prague. He had his first exhibition in 1957 in Prague and since then has exhibited widely in the Czech Republic and around the world. He also took part in group exhibitions of young Czechoslovak artists. His work, playful in its graphic forms, shows the influence of Far Eastern calligraphy.

SMUTZ, J. R.
Painter. Portraits.
Smutz is mentioned in *Art Prices Current*.
AUCTION RECORDS:
LONDON, 5 Dec 1910, *Portrait of the Actor William Penkethman*, GBP 6.

SMYBERT, John. See **SMIBERT**

SMYTERE, Jan de
Flemish School, 16th century.
Born in Ghent (?); died before 6 August 1528, in Ghent (?).
Sculptor. Statues, monuments.
Ghent School.
Smytere worked for the churches of Ghent and is probably identical with Jehan Semettre, a sculptor in Lille. He carved tombs, low reliefs and statues, but none of his work has survived.

SMYTERS, Anna de, or Smytere or Smijters
Dutch, 16th century.
Active in Ghent.
Miniaturist.
De Smyters was a pupil and the wife of Jan de Heere, and had a son, Lucas de Heere.

SMYTH. See also **SMITH**

SMYTH, Coke
British, 19th century.
Active in London.
Painter.
Coke Smyth exhibited his work at the Royal Academy in London from 1842 until 1867.

SMYTH, Daniel Kinahan
Irish, 19th century.
Born 1811; died 2 September 1871, in Dublin.
Landscape artist.

SMYTH, Emily R.
British, 19th century.
Painter. Genre scenes, landscapes, animals.
Emily R. Smyth was active in Ipswich and exhibited her work in London from 1850 until 1874.
AUCTION RECORDS:
LONDON, 12 March 1969, *Landscape*, GBP 500.

SMYTH, Hervey
British, 18th - 19th century.
Born 1734; died 1811.
Watercolourist. Seascapes.
Hervey Smyth was an officer who was a committed amateur painter. He was the aide-de-camp to General Wolfe and took part in the British conquest of Quebec. His watercolours, which he painted from life, were published in 1760 by Thomas Jefferys in London under the title *Six Elegant Views of the Most Remarkable Places in the River and Gulf of St Laurence*.
MUSEUMS AND GALLERIES:
LONDON (National Portrait Gal.): *James Wolfe* (pencil, by Harold Lee-Dillon after a drawing by Sir Harvey Smith).
AUCTION RECORDS:
COPENHAGEN, 25-26 April 1990, *Seascape with a Sailing Ship near the Coast* (oil on canvas, 26 1/2 x 36 1/4 ins / 67 x 92 cm) DKK 8,200.

SMYTH, John. See also **SMITH**

SMYTH, John Talfourd
British, 19th century.
Born 1819, in Edinburgh; died 18 May 1851, in Edinburgh.
Engraver.
John Talfourd Smyth studied under William Allan.

SMYTH, Olive Carleton
British, 20th century.
Born 11 December 1882, in Glasgow; died 1949.
Painter, designer, engraver.
Olive Smyth lived and worked in Cambuslang, near Glasgow.
Museums and Galleries:
Tokyo - Toronto.
Auction records:
London, 9 Dec 1980, *Guardians* (gouache/parchment remounted on board, 12 1/2 x 9 1/2 ins / 32 x 24 cm) GBP 720. Glasgow, 19 April 1984, *'The Seventh Day'* (watercolour, gouache and silver, 17 x 28 ins / 43.1 x 71.1 cm) GBP 1,300. London, 5 Sept 2001, *Scheherazade* (gouache and gold paint over pen and ink on vellum, 10 x 9 ins / 25 x 23 cm) GBP 3,000. London, 5 Sept 2001, *Eastern Goddess* (1916, pen, ink, watercolour and wash on vellum heightened with gold, 12 x 7 ins / 30 x 18 cm) GBP 3,000.

SMYTH, William or William Henry (Captain)
Irish, 19th century.
Born 12 November 1813, in Dublin; died 5 March 1878, in London.
Watercolourist, writer. Landscapes.
Auction records:
London, 18 March 1982, *On the Point of Portsmouth* (1857, watercolour and pencil, 12 x 18 ins / 30.5 x 45.5 cm) GBP 750. London, 24 April 1986, *Landscapes of Switzerland and Italy* (1860-1861, watercolour/pencil outlines, 29-page album, 11 x 15 ins / 27 x 38 cm) GBP 1,450.

SMYTHE, Francisco
Chilean, 20th century.
Born 17 April 1952, in Puerto Montt; died 22 November 1998, in Santiago.
Painter (mixed media).
Conceptual Art.
Francisco Smythe used photographic documents and written texts in his art seeking to form a synthesis between traditional art and the new technologies.

SMYTHE, H.
British, 19th century.
Painter. Landscapes, waterscapes.
H. Smythe was active at the beginning of the 19th century. His works include *View of the River Usk in Brecon, South Wales*, which he exhibited at the Royal Academy in 1845.
Auction records:
London, 8 April 1992, *Landscape of the Towy Valley* (oil on canvas, 27 1/2 x 35 1/2 ins / 70 x 90 cm) GBP 5,280.

SMYTHE, Lionel Percy, or Smithe
British, 19th - 20th century.
Born 4 September 1839, in London; died 10 July 1918, in Wimereux, France.
Painter, watercolourist, draughtsman. Figures, genre scenes, landscapes.
Lionel Smythe was an associate of the Royal Scottish Academy and a member of the Royal Society of Painters in Watercolours. He exhibited in London, notably at the Royal Academy and at Suffolk Street, from 1860. Smythe also exhibited in Paris, winning a bronze medal at the Paris Exposition of 1889 and a silver medal in 1900.
Museums and Galleries:
Glasgow: *Children Returning Home from School* - Liverpool: *In a Wheatfield* - London (Tate Collection): *Germinal* - Melbourne: *Bread-winners.*
Auction records:
London, 30 April 1910, *The Field in its Golden Robe* (1884) GBP 120. London, 11-14 Nov 1922, *The Shepherdess,* GBP 38. London, 22 June 1923, *In the Wheatfields,* GBP 31. London, 16 May 1924, *Young Fisherwoman* (drawing) GBP 35. London, 8 Oct 1924, *Wimereux* (drawing) GBP 26. London, 28 Nov 1924, *Gleaners Returning from the Fields* (drawing) GBP 29; *Playmates* (drawing) GBP 16. London, 17 June 1927, *In the Woods* (drawing) GBP 29. London, 12 March 1974, *Young Woman on a Barge* (1872) GBP 320. New York, 2 May 1979, *Winter Landscape; Summer Landscape* (oil on canvas, a pair, 12 x 18 ins / 30.6 x 45.8 cm) USD 5,750. London, 21 July 1981, *Fishermen at Boulogne* (1893, print, watercolour and pencil heightened with white, 16 3/4 x 31 1/2 ins / 42.5 x 80 cm) GBP 4,200. London, 25 Jan 1988, *The Fruits of Love* (1910, watercolour, 31 x 22 ins / 79 x 56 cm) GBP 8,800. Amsterdam, 24 April 1991, *Children Feeding Pigeons in a Farmyard* (watercolour/paper/card, 7 x 7 1/2 ins / 18 x 19 cm) NLG 1,840. New York, 21 May 1991, *Gloucestershire Landscape* (oil on panel, 21 1/2 x 35 1/2 ins / 54.8 x 90.1 cm) USD 3,740. New York, 16 July 1992, *Buttercups and Daisies* (1883, watercolour and gouache/paper/card, 8 1/2 x 12 1/4 ins / 21.3 x 31.1 cm) USD 1,100. London, 27 March 1996, *Gathering Flowers in the Fields* (oil on canvas, 13 3/4 x 9 3/4 ins / 35 x 25 cm) GBP 5,750. London, 6 Nov 1996, *Laura* (1907, watercolour heightened with gouache, 9 1/2 x 6 ins / 24 x 15 cm) GBP 1,725.

SMYTHE, Richard
British, 19th century.
Born 13 February 1863, in Cromford.
Painter, engraver (burin/mezzotint).
Richard Smythe was active in London.

SMYTHE, Thomas, called Smythe of Ipswich
British, 19th - 20th century.
Born 1825; died 1907.
Painter. Genre scenes, landscapes with figures.
Thomas Smythe was brought up in Ipswich with his elder brother, Edward Robert Smythe, also an artist. In the 1840s he set up as a landscape and animal painter in Brook Street, Ipswich, where he painted some of his finest pictures. In addition to working on canvas, he also worked with wood panels, some of which have an enamel-like quality. In 1868 the Ipswich Art Society awarded him a silver medal. Smythe visited Cumberland in 1876 and London in 1898, which occasioned many paintings of these locations. In his final years he moved to London to be with his family. Smythe's best-known paintings depict everyday scenes and subjects, which he rendered with great feeling and simplicity.

T Smythe

Auction records:
London, 29 June 1976, *Horse Market* (oil on canvas, 26 1/2 x 41 ins / 67 x 104 cm) GBP 2,000. London, 2 Oct 1979, *Sparrow-trap* (oil on canvas, 11 1/2 x 17 1/4 ins / 29 x 44 cm) GBP 2,800. London, 29 Oct 1981, *Snowball Fight* (oil on panel, 11 1/2 x 21 1/4 ins / 29.5 x 54 cm) GBP 5,800. London, 6 May 1983, *Countrymen, Donkeys and a Horse in Front of a Farm* (oil on canvas, 20 x 30 1/4 ins / 50.8 x 76.8 cm) GBP 4,000. London, 10 July 1985, *A Village at the Ferry Crossing* (oil on canvas, 19 1/4 x 29 1/4 ins / 49 x 74 cm) GBP 10,000. London, 1 Oct 1986, *Carriage Halted Outside an Inn, in Winter* (oil on panel, 13 x 24 ins / 33 x 61 cm) GBP 13,000. London, 15 June 1988, *Labourer's Rest* (oil on canvas, 12 x 16 ins / 30.5 x 40.5 cm)

GBP 1,760. LONDON, 23 Sept 1988, *A Gusty Day* (oil on panel, 10 3/4 x 14 1/2 ins / 27.5 x 37 cm) GBP 3,740. LONDON, 27 Sept 1989, *The White Swan Inn; The Butcher's Cabin* (oil on canvas, a pair, each 12 x 18 ins / 30.5 x 46 cm) GBP 7,920. LONDON, 31 Oct 1990, *Traveller in Front of the Black Swan Inn* (oil on panel, 11 3/4 x 15 1/4 ins / 30 x 39 cm) GBP 1,100. LONDON, 13 Feb 1991, *Resting Beside a Road* (oil on panel, 6 3/4 x 8 ins / 17 x 20.5 cm) GBP 825. LONDON, 3 June 1992, *At the Cottage Door* (oil on canvas, 9 x 13 ins / 23 x 33 cm) GBP 7,700. NEW YORK, 5 June 1992, *Midday Rest* (oil on canvas, 18 x 24 ins / 45.7 x 61 cm) USD 8,250. LONDON, 25 March 1994, *East Anglian Village Scene* (oil on canvas, 15 1/4 x 21 1/4 ins / 38.7 x 54 cm) GBP 2,530. LONDON, 7 June 1996, *On the Road to Market* (oil on panel, 11 3/4 x 17 1/2 ins / 29.8 x 44.5 cm) GBP 6,900. LONDON, 10 July 1996, *Gypsy Encampment with Donkeys and Horses* (oil on card, 10 x 15 1/4 ins / 25.5 x 38.5 cm) GBP 1,725. LONDON, 14 March 1997, *Farmer at Rest; Home from the Market* (oil on canvas, a pair, each 18 1/4 x 24 1/4 ins / 46.1 x 61.3 cm) GBP 8,970. LONDON, 5 Nov 1997, *On the Road to Market* (oil on canvas, 12 x 18 ins / 30.5 x 46 cm) GBP 3,450.

SMYTSENS, Arnold. See **SMITSEN**

SNABILLE, Maria Geertruida or Geertruida, or Snabilie

Dutch, 18th - 19th century.

Born 1776; died 7 February 1838, in Haarlem.

Painter. Flowers.

Maria Geertruida Snabille was the wife of Pieter Bartholomeusz. Barbiers.

AUCTION RECORDS:

VIENNA, 14 Sept 1976, *Bouquet of Flowers* (1838, oil on canvas, 25 x 20 ins / 63.5 x 51 cm) ATS 250,000.

SNACK, Johan

Swedish, 18th century.

Active in Stockholm from 1782 to 1783.

Draughtsman, engraver (burin).

Snack engraved portraits.

SNAFFLES, pseudonym of Payne, Charles Johnstone

20th century.

Born 1884; died 1964.

Painter (including gouache), watercolourist. Military subjects.

AUCTION RECORDS:

LONDON, 1 March 1983, *Soldiers* (watercolour and pencil heightened with white/grey paper, 20 1/2 x 26 ins / 52 x 66 cm) GBP 1,200. LONDON, 9 June 1994, *Prettiest Sight in Europe* (watercolour and gouache, a pair, 8 3/4 x 17 ins / 22.5 x 43 cm) GBP 14,375. NEW YORK, 11 April 1997, *Great Military Gold Cup of 1911* (watercolour, gouache and black chalk on traces of pencil/panel, 17 3/4 x 25 ins / 45.1 x 63.5 cm) USD 9,200.

SNAGG, Thomas

Irish, 18th - 19th century.

Born 28 February 1746, in London; died 1 February 1812, in Dublin.

Painter, miniaturist, actor. Portraits, landscapes.

Thomas Snagg painted a *Miniature Portrait of Catherine II* in St Petersburg.

SNAPE, Martin

British, 19th - 20th century.

Born 31 December 1852, in Gosport (Hampshire); died 24 November 1930.

Painter, watercolourist. Landscapes, animals.

Martin Snape was the son of the artist Alfred C. Snape. His sister and four brothers were also painters, the most notable, besides Martin, being William. Snape frequently painted scenes in and around his home town of Gosport, Portsmouth Harbour and south Hampshire and made regular trips to paint in the Meon valley. His landscapes are varied, for example *Early Morning Calm on the Solent Looking Towards the Isle of Wight; English River Landscape with Swans* (1910) and *Estuary Scene with a Mother and Child and Other Figures by a Lock*. In 1922, he was commissioned to design a seal for the newly created borough of Gosport.

Snape exhibited at the Royal Academy between 1874 and 1901, including *The Gamekeeper's Museum*, (1883) and *Forton Creek*, (1890). He also exhibited at the Royal Society of British Artists and the Grosvenor Gallery.

The Gosport Gallery held an exhibition, *Martin Snape*, in 1999 and the Richard Martin Gallery included some of his works in their annual exhibition in 2004.

BIBLIOGRAPHY:

Pavière, Sydney Herbert, *A Dictionary of British Sporting Painters*, F. Lewis, Leigh on Sea, 1965.

MUSEUMS AND GALLERIES:

GOSPORT (Gosport Discovery Centre): several works - GOSPORT (Town Hall): *Forton Creek* (1890, oils).

AUCTION RECORDS:

SAN FRANCISCO, 26 May 1999, *Estuary Scene with Mother and Child* (oil on canvas, 24 x 36 ins / 60 x 91 cm) USD 14,000. BILLINGSHURST, 2 July 2001, *Nelson's Victory* (1920, oil on canvas, 10 x 15 ins / 26 x 39 cm) GBP 1,700.

SNAPHAEN, Abraham de, or Schnaphan, Snaphaan, Snaphan

Dutch, 17th century.

Born 2 November 1651, in Leiden; died 1 September 1691, in Dessau.

Painter. History painting, portraits, genre scenes.

Abraham de Snaphaen was painter to the court of Dessau.

MUSEUMS AND GALLERIES:

BERLIN (Bodemus.): *Toilette* - DESSAU: *Prince Johann Georg I of Anhalt and his Wife* - HELSINKI: *Portrait of a Man in a Dressing Gown*.

AUCTION RECORDS:

VIENNA, 15 June 1971, *Young Woman with a Parrot*, ATS 45,000.

SNAYERS. See also **SNYDERS** and **SNYERS**

SNAYERS, Eduaert

Flemish School, 17th century.

Active in Antwerp 1616-1659.

Painter. Battles.

Eduaert Snayers was probably the brother of Pieter Snayers.

SNAYERS, Hendrik. See **SNYERS**

SNAYERS, Pieter or Peeter

Flemish School, 17th century.

Baptised 24 November 1592 in Antwerp; died 1667, in Brussels.

Painter. Battles, portraits, genre scenes, hunting scenes, landscapes, winter landscapes.

Pieter Snayers was a pupil of Sebastian Vranx. He was master of a studio in Antwerp in 1613, becoming a member of the guild in Brussels in 1628. In 1618 he married Anna Schut. He was painter to the courts of Isabella, Cardinal Infante Ferdinand, Leopold William and Don Juan of Austria, and worked for Prince Piccolomini. He also painted portraits to order, and picaresque subjects depicting the episodic adventures of rogues. His pupil A.F. van der Meulen, who continued so brilliantly the great tradition of painting battles.

If Snayers had to capture on canvas the disposition of the battles won by his powerful protectors, he also liked painting hunting scenes and even landscapes, forests or snow effects, showing in his works that, in other circumstances, he could have aspired to an art form wider and more universal than the single speciality of battles. However, in his chosen speciality he amply proved his gifts as a painter by the clarity of his exposition, the ease of his movements and a certain sense of the poetic grandeur of the panorama. Perhaps through historical necessity, detail is adhered to, down to the buttons on the uniforms, without in any way harming the work as a whole.

1667

-Pieter· snayers ·c· i· pictor

PETRVS SNAYERS. PICTOR
DEL S" C.I S ANNO 1650

MUSEUMS AND GALLERIES:

AIX: *Brigandage Scene; Return from Hunting* - AMSTERDAM: *View of a Battle; Siege of Gulik (?)* - ANTWERP: *Battle of Calloo; Ceremonial Entry of Prince Cardinal Ferdinand of Austria into Antwerp on 17 April 1635* - BERLIN: *Hunting in a Forest, and Traveller* - BRUSSELS: *Battles of White Mountain, Wimpfen, Hoechst and Calloo; Siege of Courtrai; Hôtel de Branonville and Panorama of Brussels; Archduke Leopold William, Governor of The Netherlands; St Anne's Fountain and Panorama of Brussels* - BUDAPEST: *Soldiers in Camp* - DOUAI: *Entrance to a Forest; Northern Landscape* - DRESDEN: *Cavalry Skirmish near a Windmill; Cavalry Skirmish near a Gibbet; Pillage of a Village; Brigands in a Forest; Brigands in front of a Village; Landscape with Horsemen* (two) - DUNKIRK: *Large Landscape with Horsemen* - KASSEL: *Winter Scene* - LILLE: *Camp* - MADRID (Prado): *The Cardinal Infante Returning from Hunting; Hunting Bears and Wild Boar; Fight between Spanish and Dutch Cavalrymen; Philip IV's Hunt* (two); *Siege of Gravelines; Night Attack during the Siege of Lille; Capture of Ypres; Capture of s'-Hertogenbosch; Capture of St-Venau; Capture of Breda Square; Capture of a Fort; Siege of St-Omer; Attack on Aire by the Cardinal Infante; Surrender of Ostende; View of Breda* - OBERSCHLEISSHEIM (Neues Schloss Schleissheim, Staatsgal.): *Battle of White Mountain; Skirmish between Spaniards and Dutchmen* - ORLÉANS: *Attack on a Town by the Imperial Troops* - ROHRAU (Schlossmus., Graf Harrach'sche Familiensammlung): *Siege of Presburg* - STOCKHOLM: *Episode in the Battle of Nordlingen (Possibly of Molenaer)* - TOULOUSE: *Portrait of a Bishop* - VALENCIENNES: *Wooded Landscape; Landscape with Attack by Robbers* (two) - VIENNA: *Troop of Cavalrymen; Battlefield; Large Battlefield; Cavalry Skirmish; Landscape with Castle* - VIENNA (Czernin'sche Gemäldegal.): *Cavalry Skirmish* - VIENNA (Liechtenstein Mus.): *Skirmish near a Wood.*

AUCTION RECORDS:

BRUSSELS, 1833, *Battle in front of Antwerp,* FRF 80. PARIS, 1840, *Meeting of Enemies,* FRF 1,500. PARIS, 1867, *Battle,* FRF 4,500; *Siege of the Town of Courtrai in Flanders,* FRF 3,700; *Routing of Halberstadt,* FRF 4,500; *Defeat of the Palatine Troops in Bavaria,* FRF 4,550. PARIS, 1881, *Sack of a Town in Holland,* FRF 920. PARIS, 8 June 1896, *Sack of a Village; Sack of a Village* (two paintings) FRF 2,700. PARIS, 9-11 April 1902, *Cavalry Skirmish,* FRF 250. PARIS, 29 June 1905, *Cavalry Skirmish,* FRF 820. BRUSSELS, 12 and 13 July 1905, *Cavalry Clash,* FRF 110. LONDON, 11 and 12 May 1911, *Bandits in a Landscape,* GBP 132. LONDON, 1 June 1911, *Siege of a Town by Land and Sea,* GBP 18. PARIS, 8-11 Dec 1920, *Skirmish of Cavalry against a Troop of Infantry,* FRF 500. PARIS, 10 June 1925, *Hermit in the Mountains,* FRF 2,500. PARIS, 19 June 1925, *Skirmish,* FRF 850. PARIS, 26 May 1933, *Attack on a Military Convoy,* FRF 780. PARIS, 30 June and 1 July 1941, *Cavalry Clash,* FRF 420. PARIS, 29 April 1942, *Brigands Attacking a Convoy,* FRF 29,100. PARIS, 16 Nov 1942, *Presumed Entry of Alexander Farnèse into the City of Antwerp, 27 August 1585,* FRF 70,000. PARIS, 20 Dec 1943, *Attack on a Waggon,* FRF 8,000. PARIS, 12 Jan 1944, *Brigandage Scene,* FRF 5,100. PARIS, 16 Feb 1944, *Cavalry Clash* (attributed) FRF 3,100. PARIS, 24 Dec 1948, *Troops Occupying a Village* (attributed) FRF 40,000. PARIS, 1 June 1949, *Cavalry Clash* (attributed) FRF 5,000. PARIS, 15 June 1949, *Military Procession in a Public Square* (attributed) FRF 65,000. PARIS, 24 Nov 1949, *Cavalry Battle* (attributed) FRF 5,200. PARIS, 25 April 1951, *A Fight,* FRF 215,000. LONDON, 15 Oct 1965, *Street Scene in a Small Dutch Town,* Gns 700. BRUSSELS, 18-20 April 1967, *Siege of Tehran,* BEF 240,000. LONDON, 10 July 1968, *Horseman in a Landscape* (in collaboration with Jan Wildens) GBP 2,900. PARIS, 11 Dec 1969, *Battle Scene,* FRF 30,000. LONDON, 8 Dec 1971, *Winter,* GBP 9,000. BRUSSELS, 27 Oct 1976, *Undulating Landscape with Figures* (oil on canvas, 45 1/4 x 76 3/4 ins / 115 x 195 cm) BEF 950,000. LONDON, 30 March 1979, *Ambush* (oil on canvas, 40 1/2 x 72 1/4 ins / 102.8 x 183.6 cm) GBP 14,000. LONDON, 10 April 1981, *Ambush in a Wooded Landscape* (oil on canvas, 40 1/2 x 72 1/4 ins / 102.8 x 183.6 cm) GBP 12,000. LONDON, 12 Dec 1984, *Siege of Dixmude; Siege of Armentières* (oil on canvas, a pair, 40 1/4 x 52 3/4 ins / 102 x 134 cm) GBP 55,000. LONDON, 14 May 1986, *Horsemen in a Village Street* (oil on canvas, 46 x 60 1/4 ins / 116 x 153 cm) GBP 13,500. NEW YORK, 15 Oct 1987, *Scene beside a River* (oil on canvas, 27 x 43 1/4 ins / 68.5 x 110 cm) USD 50,000. PARIS, 7 July 1988, *Landscape with Skirmish* (oil on canvas, 33 3/4 x 57 1/2 ins / 86 x 146 cm) FRF 75,000. PARIS, 3 April 1990, *Brigandage Scene* (oil on panel, 19 x 25 3/4 ins / 48.5 x 65.3 cm) FRF 82,000. LONDON, 17 April 1991, *Cavalry Engagement* (oil on canvas, 27 1/4 x 40 1/2 ins / 69.5 x 103 cm) GBP 9,350. LONDON, 3 July 1991, *Landscape with Soldiers Pillaging a Village* (oil on panel, 29 x 41 1/4 ins / 73.5 x 104.5 cm) GBP 20,900. LONDON, 5 July 1991, *Transport of Merchandise in a Waggon Covered with a Tarpaulin Escorted by Soldiers on the Edge of a Wood* (oil on canvas, 44 1/4 x 63 1/4 ins / 112.7 x 160.7 cm) GBP 13,200. NEW YORK, 15 Jan 1993, *Military Engagement in a Wooded Landscape* (oil on panel, 19 1/4 x 25 ins / 48.9 x 63.5 cm) USD 23,000. AMSTERDAM, 7 May 1993, *Cavalry Skirmish* (oil on panel, 19 x 29 ins / 48.5 x 73.5 cm) NLG 15,525. NEW YORK, 12 Jan 1994, *Defeat of the Spanish and the Imperial Troops by France and Savoy in October 1635 at Valenza del Po* (oil on canvas, 65 x 75 1/2 ins / 165 x 192 cm) USD 184,000. PARIS, 16 Dec 1994, *Capture of a Town in the North by the Spanish* (oil on canvas, 23 x 33 1/4 ins / 58.5 x 84.5 cm) FRF 57,000. PARIS, 3 April 1995, *La Bataille de Cobdé sur Escaut* (oil on canvas, 49 1/2 x 51 1/4 ins / 125.5 x 130 cm) FRF 200,000. NEW YORK, 16 May 1996, *Bandits Attacking a Caravan in a Vast Landscape* (oil on panel, 21 1/2 x 30 ins / 54.6 x 76.2 cm) USD 19,550. LONDON, 14 Dec 1999, *Cavalry Skirmish in front of a Windmill* (oil on panel, 12 x 19 ins / 30 x 49 cm) GBP 5,800. MADRID, 18 Feb 2000, *Battle* (oil on copper, 24 x 31 ins / 60 x 80 cm) ESP 3,900,000. LONDON, 17 April 2002, *Landscape with Cavalry Battle* (oil on panel, 29 x 41 ins / 73 x 104 cm) GBP 25,000. MADRID, 21 Jan 2003, *Battle Scene* (oil on board, 29 x 41 ins / 74 x 104 cm) EUR 45,000. NEW YORK, 23 Jan 2004, *Conversion of St Paul* (oil on copper, 28 x 35 ins / 71 x 89 cm) USD 11,000. LONDON, 8 July 2004, *Landscape with Cavalry Engagement* (oil on canvas, 31 x 42 ins / 80 x 107 cm) GBP 19,000.

SNEDEN, Eleanor Antoinette
American, 20th century.
Born 1876, in New York.
Sculptor.

Eleanor Sneden was a pupil of Geneviève Granger in Paris. She sculpted portraits and medallions. She lived and worked in Avon by the Sea.

SNEIS, Frans. See **SNYDERS**

SNEL, Jan, or Snell
Flemish School, 15th century.
Died 1504.
Active in Antwerp.
Painter.

Snel was admitted to the Antwerp Guild of Painters in 1483.

SNELL, Éric
British, 20th - 21st century.
Born 1953, in Guernsey.
Active in Guernsey.
Sculptor, draughtsman.

Éric Snell studied at the Birmingham Polytechnic and Hornsey College of Art in London. During the 1980s, he fashioned instruments by using magnetic forces, magnets and compasses. During the 1990s he returned to prehistory and drew in wood charcoal the shadows of objects (such as a chair, table or ladder) which he had previously burnt. These installations, based around the notion of the appearance and disappearance of objects, comprise the series known as *Burnt Wood Wall Drawings*. The notion of energy, both natural and artificial (magnetic fields, electricity, fire, light) is at the heart of Snell's work because it has the capacity to transform objects and forms and serves as a place or tool for the transition from light to shade and from the invisible to the visible.

Snell has taken part in group exhibitions, including: *Numbering* at the Hamilton Art Gallery in Ontario (1990); at the Kunsthalle in Liestal in Switzerland, the Folkwang Museum in Essen and the San Diego Museum of Contemporary Art (1991); *Open Door* at the fine art academy in Budapest (1996); *L'Abstraction et ses Territoires* (*Abstraction and its Territories*) at Le 19 at the Centre Régional d'Art Contemporain in Montbéliard (1998); and at the Bauhaus in Dessau (1999). His solo exhibitions include those at the following: the Jordan Gallery in London (1978); the Crédac in Ivry-sur-Seine (1989); the Galerie Bernard Jordan in Paris (1988, 1990, 1992); the Neuer Berliner Kunstverein in Berlin (1990); the 360o Gallery in Tokyo (1992, 1993, 1994, 1996); the Roswell Museum and Art Center in New Mexico (2000); and *De la Réalité à l'Abstraction* (*From Reality to Abstraction*) at Le 19 at the Centre Régional d'Art Contemporain in Montbéliard (2001).

Bibliography:
Buhlmann, Britta E./Gooding, Mel, *Blick über den Ärmelkanal... via Guernsey. John Carter, Norman Dilworth, Michael Kidner, Éric Snell, Gary Woodley*, exhibition catalogue, Pfalzgalerie, Kaiserslautern, 1994 (text in German and English).

Museums and Galleries:
Paris (FNAC): *Magnetic Drawing Number 38* (1985).

SNELL, Florence Francis
American, 19th century.
Painter.

Florence Francis Snell was married to Henry Bayley Snell.

SNELL, Henry Bayley
American, 19th - 20th century.
Born 29 September 1858, in Richmond (England); died 1943.
Painter, watercolourist. Seascapes, landscapes, architectural views.

Henry Bayley Snell studied in New York and won a number of prizes in competitions in America. He received an honourable mention in Paris at the 1900 Exposition Universelle, silver medals in Buffalo in 1901 and Saint Louis in 1904, and a prize from the Salmagundi Club in 1918. He was a member of the New York Watercolor Club.

Auction records:
New York, 21 Nov 1945, *Gloucester Harbour*, USD 650. Los Angeles, 8 Nov 1977, *Old Windjammer* (oil on canvas, 34 x 44 1/4 ins / 86.4 x 112.4 cm) USD 2,750. New York, 14 Feb 1990, *Moored at Moonlight* (oil on canvas/card, 11 1/2 x 13 1/2 ins / 29.1 x 34 cm) USD 2,200. New York, 14 March 1991, *Along Shore* (oil on canvas, 18 1/4 x 24 1/4 ins / 46.3 x 61.5 cm) USD 6,050. New York, 12 March 1992, *Low Tide* (oil on canvas, 34 x 44 ins / 86.2 x 111.8 cm) USD 38,500. New York, 15 Nov 1993, *Gloucester* (oil on canvas, 25 x 30 ins / 63.5 x 76.2 cm) USD 8,050. New York, 14 Sept 1995, *Beached Boats* (oil on canvas, 25 x 30 ins / 63.5 x 76.2 cm) USD 12,650.

SNELL, James Herbert
British, 19th - 20th century.
Born 1861; died 1935.
Painter. Landscapes, waterscapes.

James Snell was a member of the Royal Society of British Artists. He exhibited in London from 1879.

Museums and Galleries:
Melbourne (Nat. Gal. of Victoria): *Lock on the River Coln in Hertfordshire*.

Auction records:
London, 25 March 1911, *Apples Trees and a Marsh* (two pendants) GBP 1. Stockholm, 15 Nov 1988, *Landscape Showing a Plain Beneath Cloudy Skies* (oil, 7 x 10 ins / 18 x 25.5 cm) SEK 8,000. London, 25 March 1994, *Harvest Time* (oil on canvas, 22 x 30 ins / 55.9 x 76.2 cm) GBP 4,370. London, 16 Sept 1999, *Mediterranean Harbours* (oil on canvas, two, 14 x 20 ins / 35 x 51 cm) GBP 1,000. Aarhus, 6 March 2001, *Sunset, Late Summer Evening near Burnham, Forest is Beautiful, Dark and Deep* (oil on canvas, 13 x 9 ins / 33 x 24 cm) DKK 13,000. Washington, 8 Dec 2001, *River Landscape with Cows and Sheep in a Pasture* (1895, oil on canvas, 24 x 36 ins / 61 x 91 cm) USD 3,000. London, 5 Sept 2002, *Morning in the Meadows* (oil on canvas, 36 x 48 ins / 91 x 122 cm) GBP 3,200. London, 6 March 2003, *Mirror of the Woods* (oil on canvas, 36 x 48 ins / 91 x 122 cm) GBP 1,900.

SNELL, Rudolf
Swiss, 19th century.
Born 1823, in Basel; died 8 March 1898, in Bern.
Painter. Landscapes, mountain landscapes.

Museums and Galleries:
Bern (Kunstmus.): *Schmadribach Waterfall, Lauterbrunnen Valley*.

Auction records:
Zurich, 20 May 1977, *Landscape* (1890, oil on canvas, 30 x 41 3/4 ins / 76 x 106 cm) CHF 2,000.

SNELLAERT, Abraham
Dutch, 17th century.
Born 1646, in Haarlem; died 1693; buried 5 December in Haarlem.
Sculptor (stone/wood).

Abraham Snellaert was a pupil of Jacob de Weth in 1661, and was in the guild of Haarlem from 1668 to 1692. He worked for the churches in Haarlem.

SNELLAERT, Claes or Nicholas
Flemish School, 16th century.
Born c. 1540, in Courtrai; died before 15 January 1602, in Dordrecht.
Painter. Mythological subjects, portraits, architectural views.
Dordrecht School.

Son of Willem Snellaert, Claes or Nicholas Snellaert was a pupil of his father and Carel van Yperen. He settled in Dordrecht and became a member of the Guild in 1586. He married his second wife, Emerenta van Spertsenberg, in 1588.

SNELLAERT, Hans
Dutch, 16th century.
Died 1603.
Active at the beginning of the 16th century.
Painter.
Hans Snellaert was the son of Claes Snellaert and a pupil of Giles van Bree in Haarlem.

SNELLAERT, Jan
Flemish School, 15th century.
Died before 1480.
Active in Antwerp.
Painter.
Antwerp School.
Jan Snellaert was Regent of the Antwerp Guild in 1454, probably Court Painter to Maria of Burgundy, and may be the Jan Snellaert who was painting in Tournai in 1453. However, it is possible there were two painters of this name. There was a Jan Snellaert who was a pupil in Tournai in 1462, 1466, 1474 and 1476, and a Jan Snellaert who was doyen of the Antwerp Guild in 1458, 1465 and 1477. He is considered to be the founder of the Antwerp School.

SNELLAERT, Jan
Flemish School, 15th century.
Painter.
Jan Snellaert was a master in Antwerp in 1483.

SNELLAERT, Willem
Flemish School, 16th century.
Active in Courtrai.
Painter, watercolourist.
Willem Snellaert was the father of Claes Snellaert and is thought to have been Pieter Vierick's first master.

SNELLE
French, 17th century.
Died 1643, in Nice.
Painter. History painting.
Snelle was a friend of Poussin.
MUSEUMS AND GALLERIES:
ORLÉANS: *Pope Nicholas V Having the Vault Opened which Contains the Remains of Francis of Assisi.*

SNELLEBRAND, Cornelis Rog'aar.
See **ROG'AAR SNELLEBRAND Cornelis**

SNELLEN, T.
Dutch, 17th century.
Draughtsman.
T. Snellen is noted for a drawing depicting *The Visitation*.

SNELLGRAVE, T., or Snellgrove
British, 18th - 19th century.
Active in London.
Miniaturist.
T. Snellgrave exhibited 14 miniatures at the Royal Academy from 1800 until 1827.

SNELLINCK, Abraham, or Snellincx
Flemish School, 17th century.
Baptised 13 August 1597 in Antwerp; died 1661.
Painter. Landscapes.
Abraham Snellinck was the son and pupil of Jan Snellinck I, or possibly of Jan Snellinck II. He was master of a studio in 1638 and married Anna Maria Richardi the same year. They had a son, Frans, who was a painter and became a monk in 1669.

SNELLINCK, Andrea or Andries, or Snellincx
Flemish School, 17th century.
Baptised 28 January 1587 in Antwerp; died 12 September 1653, in Antwerp.
Painter. Still-lifes.
Andrea Snellinck was a pupil of his father Jan Snellinck II. He married Maria Claessens in 1609 and became an art dealer in 1620.

SNELLINCK, Cornelis
Dutch, 17th century.
Died 1669.
Active in Rotterdam.
Painter. Landscapes with figures, landscapes.
Cornelis Snellinck was probably the son of Jan Snellinck II and was certainly the father of Jan Snellinck III. He is credited with the landscapes signed: *S. Snellik*. These are in the museum of Prague and the Liechtenstein Gallery in Vienna.
AUCTION RECORDS:
LONDON, 22 April 1977, *Wooded Landscape with Village* (oil on panel, 23 x 35 1/4 ins / 58.5 x 89.5 cm) GBP 4,000. LONDON, 8 Dec 1995, *Wooded Landscape with a Couple of Shepherds on a Track with their Flock near a Village* (oil on panel, 52 1/2 x 39 1/2 ins / 133.3 x 100.3 cm) GBP 16,100. LONDON, 19 April 2000, *River Landscape with Figures before a Cottage and a Man Buying Fish* (1643, oil on panel, 15 x 19 ins / 37 x 49 cm) GBP 6,500. AMSTERDAM, 9 May 2001, *Fruit Market in Rotterdam at Night* (oil on panel, 15 x 19 ins / 37 x 49 cm) NLG 24,000. VIENNA, 23 Sept 2002, *Landscape with Figures and Windmill* (oil on panel, 22 x 36 ins / 57 x 91 cm) EUR 9,000.

SNELLINCK, Daniel I
Flemish School, 16th century.
Painter.
Mechelen School.
Daniel Snellinck I was master in Mechelen in 1531 or 1544.

SNELLINCK, Daniel II
Flemish School, 16th century.
Painter.
Mechelen School.
Daniel Snellinck II was doyen of the Mechelen Guild in 1581.

SNELLINCK, Daniel III
Flemish School, 16th - 17th century.
Born 1576; died 20 July 1627.
Painter.
Daniel Snellinck III was the son of Jan Snellinck I. He entered the guild of Antwerp in 1606 and married Angela del Gondi the same year. One of their sons, Steven Snellinck, was a painter.

SNELLINCK, David
Flemish School, 17th century.
Born 13 June 1591, in Antwerp.
Painter.
David Snellinck was the son of Jan Snellinck I.

SNELLINCK, Geeraert
Flemish School, 16th century.
Baptised 3 July 1577 in Antwerp.
Painter. Battles.
Antwerp School, Brussels School.
Son of Jan Snellinck I, Geeraert Snellinck was a master in Brussels in 1603 and in Antwerp in 1608. He married Maria de Lares.

MUSEUMS AND GALLERIES:
PRAGUE: *Children in front of a Fruit Stall* - VIENNA (Liechtenstein Mus.): *Landscape*.

SNELLINCK, Jan I, Hans or Joan, or Snellincx or Snellinx
Flemish School, 16th - 17th century.
Born c. 1549, in Mechelen; died 1 October 1638, in Antwerp.
Painter, fresco artist. Religious subjects, genre scenes, battles.
Antwerp School.

Jan Snellinck I became a burgher of Antwerp about 1597 and entered the city's Guild in 1617. In 1574 he married Helena de Jode, and in 1587 Paulina Cuypers. He was the father of Jan II, Daniel III, Geeraert, Andrea, and perhaps Abraham. He was Court Painter to Albert and Isabella, who appreciated his deep Catholic piety and his Mannerist style, and to the Count Mansfield. Among his pupils, in addition to his children, were A. Mor in 1577, Ad. Vranx in 1582, Abraham Janssens in 1585, Cornelis van den Sande in 1586, Antoine van den Steen in 1596, Jan de Crustere in 1599, Gauth. Vervoot in 1600, Machabee Bommaert in 1601, and Jan Wiets, François Symons, Jan de Kiermaker and Ed. Caymocx in 1602.

He drew cartoons for tapestries and in 1610 painted frescoes for the Confraternity of Nobles in Antwerp. He also painted retables for the churches of Mechelen, Oudenaarde and Antwerp.

JVAN SNELLINCK
1.5.9.7.

MUSEUMS AND GALLERIES:
ANTWERP: *Christ between the Two Thieves* - ANTWERP (Church of St James): *Mary and St Cecilia* - MECHELEN (Church of St Catherine): *Pentecost* - MECHELEN (Sint-Rombouts Kathedraal): *Resurrection of Christ* (triptych) - OUDENAARDE (Church of Notre-Dame): *Creation of Man* (triptych) - OUDENAARDE (Church of St Walburge): *Transfiguration of the Virgin*.

AUCTION RECORDS:
PARIS, 1881, *Return to the Castle*, FRF 800. PARIS, 15 Dec 1922, *Entry of the Maskers*, FRF 1,000. LONDON, 20 April 1988, *Crucifixion* (oil on panel, 29 1/4 x 19 3/4 ins / 74.5 x 50 cm) GBP 2,200. AMSTERDAM, 17 Nov 1993, *Christ on the Cross, with Mary Magdalene* (oil on panel, 14 3/4 x 11 ins / 37.5 x 27 cm) NLG 5,980.

SNELLINCK, Jan II, or Hans, or Snellincx or Snellinx
Flemish School, 17th century.
Born 1575 or 1580, in Antwerp; died after 1627.
Painter. Landscapes.

Jan Snellinck II was the elder son of Jan Snellinck I. In 1606 he was in the guild of Antwerp, and in 1614 he is mentioned as being in Rotterdam, whilst in 1627 he was in Amsterdam. He married Adriana Caymocx. He was possibly the father of Abraham and probably the father of Cornelis Snellinck.

SNELLINCK, Jan III, or Snellincx
Dutch, 17th century.
Baptised 9 April 1640 in Rotterdam; died before 1691, in Rotterdam.
Painter. Genre scenes, landscapes with figures.

Jan Snellinck III was a pupil of his father Cornelis Snellinck.

J snellinck

MUSEUMS AND GALLERIES:
ROTTERDAM: *Landscape*.

AUCTION RECORDS:
PARIS, 2 Dec 1927, *Fishermen Bringing in their Hoop Nets*, FRF 2,500. AMSTERDAM, 10 Nov 1997, *Peasants Returning from Market in a Wooded Italian Landscape* (oil on panel, 14 x 19 1/4 ins / 35.5 x 49 cm) NLG 10,378. AMSTERDAM, 5 Nov 2002, *Wooded Landscape with Travellers Resting* (oil on panel, 14 x 19 ins / 36 x 49 cm) EUR 4,500.

SNELLINCK, Joh., or Snellinks
Dutch, 17th century.
Born 9 April 1642, in Rotterdam.
Painter. Landscapes.

Joh. Snellinck was a pupil of his father Cornelis Snellinck, and may have been the same artist as Jan Snellinck III.

SNELLINCK, Paul
Flemish School, 17th century.
Born 23 October 1615; died 1669.
Active in Antwerp.
Painter.

Paul Snellinck was the son of Geeraert Snellinck.

SNELLINCK, Steven
Flemish School, 17th century.
Active in Mechelen in the first half of the 17th century.
Painter.

Steven Snellinck was the son of Daniel Snellinck III.

SNELLING, Mathew
British, 17th century.
Active in London c. 1650.
Miniaturist. Historical figures.

Mathew Snelling is known to have painted portraits of women in the reign of Charles II, and also a portrait of *Charles I*, dated 1647.

MUSEUMS AND GALLERIES:
LIVERPOOL: *Portrait of Charles I; Portrait of Queen Henrietta Maria; Portrait of Catherine Sedley, Countess of Dorchester*.

SNELLINGH. See **SNELLINCK**

SNELLINGH, Pieter
Dutch, 17th century.
Active in Amsterdam in 1634.
Painter.

SNELLMANN, Eero Juhani
Finnish, 20th century.
Born 1890, in Helsinki.
Painter.

Eero Juhani Snellmann studied in Helsinki and Prague and went on to co-ordinate the Finnish pavilion at the Exposition Internationale in Paris in 1937. Two of his paintings hang in the Athenaeum museum in Helsinki.

MUSEUMS AND GALLERIES:
HELSINKI (Ateneumin Taidemus.).

SNELS, Abraham
Dutch, 18th century.
Active in 1770.
Engraver. Architectural views.

SNELSON, Kenneth
American, 20th - 21st century.
Born 29 June 1927, in Pendleton (Oregon).
Sculptor, photographer.

Kenneth Snelson studied drawing and painting at the Corcoran School of Art in Washington DC from 1945 to 1946 and at the University of Oregon in Eugene, Oregon from 1946 to 1948. In 1948 he enrolled at Black Mountain College, North Carolina, to study art theory with Josef Albers. There he met Buckminster Fuller whose theories of structural design helped him turn from painting to sculpture. Snelson's earliest sculptures were carefully balanced Calderesque stabile-like structures. Ultimately, Snelson was drawn to Fuller's pioneering concepts of structural engineering. To understand the physics of Fuller's complex structures better, Snelson took engineering courses at Oregon State College in 1949. He left his studies with a fresh sculptural aesthetic based on the fundamental forces of tension and compression, or tensegrity. While he was experimenting and developing his structural concepts and ideas from 1952 to 1968, he supported himself as a cinematographer. His sculptural experiments consisted of rigid metal elements being held in suspension by wires instead of being connected by bolts or welding. After 1960 he produced his characteristic gravity-defying sculptures which were self-supporting and formed from highly polished aluminium tubing, suspended and connected in space by stainless steel cables.

His first solo exhibition was in 1966 at the Dwan Gallery in New York, and he appeared in group exhibitions at the Whitney Museum of American Art and in Los Angeles County Museum of Art's *Sculpture of the Sixties* exhibition in 1967. By the late 1960s, he had gained considerable recognition, with additional solo exhibitions in New York, Holland and Germany. He also earned a number of prominent commissions including the 18-meter high outdoor installation, *Needle Tower* (1968) at the Hirshhorn Sculpture Garden in Washington DC.

Snelson's many honours and awards include a National Endowment for the Arts Award in 1974, the American Institute of Architects Medal in 1981, membership of the American Academy of Arts and Letters in 1994, a Lifetime Achievement Award from the International Sculpture Center in 1999 and the Elizabeth Watrous Prize from the National Academy of Design in 2002. Snelson is also known for his panoramic photographs where he explores concepts of competing and complementary forces within the urban townscape.

BIBLIOGRAPHY:

Coplans, John, *'An Interview with Kenneth Snelson'* in *Artforum,* 1967. Kurtz, Stephan, *'Kenneth Snelson: The Elegant Solution'* in *Art News,* October 1968. *IIIe Salon international des Galeries Pilotes,* exhibition catalogue, Musée cantonal, Lausanne, 1970. Donadio, Emmie, *'Kenneth Snelson'* in *Arts Magazine,* February 1975. Perlberg, Deborah, *'Snelson and Structure'* in *Artforum,* May 1977. Fox, Howard, *Kenneth Snelson: Portrait of an Atomist,* exhibition catalogue, Hirshhorn Museum, 1981. Fox, H.N., *Kenneth Snelson,* exhibition catalogue, Albright-Knox Art Gallery, Buffalo (NY), 1981. Whelan, Richard, *'Kenneth Snelson: Straddling the abyss between art and science'* in *Art News,* February 1981. Hagen, Charles, *'Full Circle'* in *Camera Arts Magazine,* January-February 1982. *Kenneth Snelson Exhibition: The Nature of Structure,* exhibition catalogue, The New York Academy of Sciences, New York, 1989.

MUSEUMS AND GALLERIES:

AMSTERDAM (Rijksmus.) - AMSTERDAM (Stedelijk Mus.) - BUFFALO (Albright-Knox AG) - CANBERRA (Australian National Gallery) - CHICAGO (AI) - CLEVELAND (MA) - DALLAS (MA) - DUISBURG (Wilhelm Lehmbruck Museum) - GRENOBLE (Mus. de Grenoble) - MINNEAPOLIS (Walker Art Center) - NEW YORK (Metropolitan Mus. of Art) - NEW YORK (MoMA) - NEW YORK (Whitney Mus. of American Art) - OTTERLO (Rijksmuseum Kroller-Muller) - PALO ALTO, CA (Stanford University) - PITTSBURGH (Museum of Art, Carnegie Institute) - SEATTLE (AM): *Centreville, Westside Highway, New York* (1979, gelatin silver print) - SHIGA, JAPAN (Museum of Modern Art) - WASHINGTON DC (Hirshhorn Mus. and Sculpture Garden): *Needle Tower* (1968, aluminium and stainless steel).

AUCTION RECORDS:

NEW YORK, 12 May 1977, *Untitled* (1967, stainless steel, 46 x 96 ins / 117 x 244 cm) USD 8,000. NEW YORK, 19 Oct 1979, *Some Date* (1975, aluminium, 27 x 33 ins / 68.6 x 83.8 cm) USD 8,250. NEW YORK, 21 May 1983, *Untitled* (c. 1967-1969, aluminium, 14 1/2 x 14 1/2 x 14 1/2 ins / 36.9 x 36.9 x 36.9 cm) USD 2,600. NEW YORK, 27 Feb 1985, *Untitled* (1970, aluminium, 22 1/4 x 13 ins / 56.5 x 33 cm) USD 4,250. NEW YORK, 4 May 1989, *Maquette for Osaka Piece* (1969, steel tube and cable, 77 x 46 3/4 x 47 1/4 ins / 195.6 x 118.7 x 119.8 cm) USD 46,200. NEW YORK, 8 May 1990, *Untitled* (sculpture in aluminium and copper wire, 15 x 22 x 22 ins / 38.1 x 55.9 x 55.9 cm) USD 8,250. NEW YORK, 6 Nov 1990, *King's Axe* (1972, sculpture in aluminium and wire, 6 x 38 1/2 x 24 ins / 15.2 x 97.8 x 61 cm) USD 8,250. NEW YORK, 1 May 1991, *Untitled* (1968, stainless steel and wire, 134 x 134 x 134 ins / 340.5 x 340.5 x 340.5 cm) USD 66,000. NEW YORK, 7 May 1993, *Untitled* (1967, aluminium tubes and wire, 14 1/2 x 14 1/2 x 14 1/2 ins / 37 x 37 x 37 cm) USD 3,450. NEW YORK, 11 Nov 1993, *Bee Tree II* (1980, aluminium and stainless steel, 32 x 38 x 38 ins / 81.3 x 96.5 x 96.5 cm) USD 16,100. NEW YORK, 14 June 1995, *Green Guide* (chrome, steel and wire, h. 17 1/4 ins / 43.8 cm) USD 5,750. HOUSTON, 25 June 1999, *Double Shell Form* (1979, aluminium and stainless steel, 35 x 35 ins / 89 x 89 cm) USD 2,250. NEW YORK, 5 Nov 2002, *Leda No. 7634* (1969, aluminium and wire, 20 x 28 ins / 51 x 72 cm) USD 3,750. NEW YORK, 5 Nov 2002, *Easy K* (1971, aluminium and wire, 9 x 61 ins / 24 x 156 cm) USD 4,500. CHICAGO, 15 Dec 2003, *Untitled* (porcelainized aluminium and stainless steel, four models, 14 x 14x14 ins / 36 x 36x36 cm) USD 7,500. NEW YORK, 12 Feb 2004, *East River Drive* (1980, gelatin, silver print and felt tip pen, 20 x 117 ins / 50 x 297 cm) USD 4,250. NEW YORK, 29 June 2004, *Stage Five* (1966, aluminium coated wire, 36 x 12 ins / 92 x 30 cm) USD 8,000.

SNEYD, Eleonor F.
British, 19th century.
Active in London.
Miniaturist.

Eleonor F. Sneyd exhibited her work in London, particularly at the Royal Academy, from 1892.

SNEYDERS, Frans. See **SNYDERS**

SNEYDERS, Levinus. See **SNYDERS**

SNEYERS. See **SNAYERS, SNYDERS** and **SNYERS**

SNIADECKI, Franciszek. See **SMIADECKI**

SNICKARE, Jon. See **STRÖM Johan**

SNIER, Giovanni. See **SNYERS Johannes** or **Giovanni**

SNIGIREVSKI, Aleksandr Vasilievich
Russian, 19th century.
Born 1840.
Sculptor.

Aleksandr Vasilievich Snigirevski studied at the art academy in St Petersburg from 1858 to 1870.

SNIJDERS. See also **SNYDERS**

SNIJDERS, Ben
Dutch, 20th century.
Born 1943, in Almelo.
Painter. Figures, nudes, portraits, still-lifes (flowers/fruit).

Ben Snijders' paintings, in which he employs the techniques of the Dutch masters, depict various subjects, including decorative still-lifes. His work has featured in group exhibitions including those held in 2002 and 2003, Lieve Hemel gallery, Amsterdam. There have also been solo exhibitions including one in 1996 at the Lieve Hemel gallery in Amsterdam.

BIBLIOGRAPHY:

Nieuwendijk, Koen, *Met engelengeduld (The patience of an angel),* exhibition catalogue, Gal. Lieve Hemel, Amsterdam, 1995.

AUCTION RECORDS:

AMSTERDAM, 31 May 1994, *Reclining Nude* (1992, oil on paper, 11 x 17 3/4 ins / 28 x 45 cm) NLG 9,200. AMSTERDAM, 6

Dec 1995, *Still-life* (1975, oil on card, 7 1/2 x 9 1/2 ins / 19 x 24 cm) NLG 8,625.

SNIKARE, Urban. See **SCHULTZ Urban**

SNIKER, Peter. See **SCHNITKER**

SNISCHEK, Max
Austrian, 20th century.
Born 24 August 1891, in Dürnkrut.
Designer, draughtsman.
Max Snischek studied at the college of applied arts in Vienna and went on to work as a fashion designer.

SNITKER, Johann. See **GRONINGEN Johann von**

SNOCK, Jeremias, or Snoek
Dutch, 18th century.
Active in Rotterdam 1792-1795.
Painter, engraver, draughtsman. Allegorical subjects.
Jeremias Snock is noted for *Allegories on Liberty, Equality and Fraternity*, and *J.M. Boon* after G. v. d. Berg. He did burin engravings.

SNOECK, Alphonse
Belgian, 20th century.
Born 1942, in Aubel.
Sculptor.
Alphonse Snoeck trained at the Instistut St-Luc in Liège. He created several works for architectural structures in Brussels, Liège and Verviers.

SNOECK, C. A.
Belgian, 19th century.
Active in Brussels during the first half of the 19th century.
Lithographer.
C.A. Snoeck engraved travel journals, monuments and castles.

SNOECK, H. E.
Dutch, 17th century.
Active in 1674.
Painter.
H.E. Snoeck painted a portrait of a lady, dated 1674.

SNOECK, J.
20th century.
Painter. Genre scenes.
Snoeck showed at the Royal Glasgow Institute of Fine Art in 1909. He was probably the same artist as Jacob Cornelis Snoeck.
AUCTION RECORDS:
NEW YORK, 18 Sept 1980, *Mother and Child in a Rural Interior* (oil on canvas, 25 3/4 x 16 1/4 ins / 65.5 x 41 cm) USD 1,200. ANTWERP, 19 Nov 2001, *Church Interior* (oil on canvas, 29 x 23 ins / 74 x 59 cm) BEF 18,000.

SNOECK, Jacob Cornelis, called Jac
Dutch, 20th century.
Born 2 January 1881, in The Hague; died 8 December 1921, in Laren.
Painter. Church interiors, genre scenes, interiors with figures, architectural views, still-lifes.
Snoeck was a pupil of F. C. Sierig.
MUSEUMS AND GALLERIES:
THE HAGUE (Gemeentemus.): *Interior*.
AUCTION RECORDS:
LONDON, 30 June 1911, *Mother and Child*, GBP 18; *Church Interior*, GBP 31; *Interior of Thatched Cottage*, GBP 21. LONDON, 9 May 1924, *Industry*, GBP 37. NEW YORK, 15 Oct 1976, *Young Woman Sewing on the Doorstep* (oil on canvas, 15 x 18 1/2 ins / 38 x 47 cm) USD 1,000. AMSTERDAM, 28 Feb 1989, *Still-life with Apples and other Fruit on a Pewter Plate and a Copper Pan on a Table* (oil on canvas, 20 1/4 x 24 1/2 ins / 51.5 x 62 cm) NLG 1,380. LONDON, 28 Oct 1992, *Preparing the Meal* (oil on panel, 12 1/4 x 9 ins / 31 x 22 cm) GBP 770. AMSTERDAM, 14 Sept 1993, *Interior with Peasant Woman Cooking* (oil on canvas, 11 1/2 x 14 1/4 ins / 29.5 x 36.5 cm) NLG 1,840. LONDON, 7 Oct 1999, *The Nursery* (oil on canvas, 24 x 20 ins / 61 x 51 cm) GBP 4,000. EDINBURGH, 13 Oct 2000, *Dutch Girl Sewing by Window* (oil on canvas, 11 x 16 ins / 29 x 40 cm) GBP 1,450.

SNOECK, Pieter Jansz.. See the entry **BONTEPAERT Dirk Pietersz**

SNOEK, Jan
Dutch, 18th century.
Active in The Hague.
Painter. Genre scenes.
Jan Snoek was a pupil of A. Schouman and may be identical to J.W. Snoek, who worked at the academy in The Hague.

SNOEK, Jeremias. See **SNOCK Jeremias**

SNOEK, Paul, pseudonym of Schietekat, Edmond
Belgian, 20th century.
Born 1934, in St Niklaas (Waes); died 1981, in Egem (Tielt).
Painter.
Snoek was a self-taught painter, better known for his poetry.

SNOUCKPOL DE. See **DESNOUCKPOL**

SNOW, Edward Taylor
American, 19th - 20th century.
Born 13 March 1844, in Philadelphia; died 26 September 1913, in Philadelphia.
Painter, illustrator. Landscapes.
Edward Taylor Snow was a pupil of Christian Schussele and also studied at the Pennsylvania Academy of the Fine Arts in Philadelphia and in France. He exhibited at the Pennsylvania Academy of the Fine Arts in 1883, 1884 and from 1899 to 1904, at the Boston Art Club in 1901 and 1906, and at the American Art Society in Philadelphia in 1902.

SNOW, John Wray
British, 19th century.
Born 1801; died 1854.
Painter. Sporting subjects, animals.
John Wray Snow was active from 1832 until 1840.
AUCTION RECORDS:
LONDON, 22 June 1979, *Racehorse Harkaway with his Owner in a Landscape* (1830, oil on canvas remounted on board, 27 1/2 x 35 ins / 70 x 89 cm) GBP 650. LONDON, 11 July 1990, *Pedigree Bay Retriever with its Trainer* (1839, oil on canvas, 32 3/4 x 44 ins / 83 x 112 cm) GBP 3,960.

SNOW, Michael James A.
Canadian, 20th - 21st century.
Born 1929, in Toronto.
Active in Toronto, but active in USA 1964-1972.
Painter, sculptor, collage artist, lithographer, video installation artist.
Conceptual Art.
Michael James Snow was a student at the Ontario College of Art in Toronto from 1948 and graduated in 1953. He spent time in Europe in 1954-1955. He also made a name for himself as a jazz musician. He mainly chooses the most ordinary subjects and objects from everyday life, which he empties of their usual significance in order to transmute them by making their place in space and time perceptible. His early works were figurative, interiors and figures. However, from 1961, he particularly exploited the theme of the woman walking in the series *Walking Woman*, portraying her in many different ways and using many different materials. Most notable is the group of eleven sculptures on this theme, exhibited in the Ontario Pavilion at the Montreal Expo in 1967, a work he produced in various versions, one of which was for the ex-

hibition *Canada, Art d'Aujourd'hui* (*Art Today in Canada*) at the Musée d'Art Moderne in Paris in 1968. Snow used this walking woman, who is both the form and content of the work and was his sole subject from 1961 to 1967, to analyse the mechanisms of painting, especially the relationships between the outline and the background. In 1967, with *Snow Storm, 8 February 1976,* he adopted a position closer to conceptual art by presenting photographs of snowfalls on enamelled panels pierced with rectangles. It is this conceptual approach to landscape that he revealed in his films, especially in *The Central Region,* in which he systematically filmed the same landscape from all angles. Film and photography appear to Snow to provide an objective means of systematically analysing pictorial representation. As a musician, Snow is one of the few painters to turn to the cinema who also produces the sound accompanying his films.

One of Snow's most widely known works is Flight Stop, a sculptural installation of Canada Geese suspended from the ceiling in the Eaton Centre in Toronto. Snow is a Member of the Order of Canada and a Chevalier of the Order of Arts and Letters in France He has taken part in many group exhibitions, including 1956, *Four Young Canadians* with William Ronald, Gerald Scott and Robert Varvarande in Toronto; 1970 Venice Biennale; 2002, *Les Années 70: l'Art en Cause* (*The 1970s: Art in Question*), CAPC Musée d'Art Contemporain, Bordeaux and *Sans Commune Mesure. Image et texte dans l'Art Actuel* (*Without Common Measure: Image and Text in Contemporary Art*), Le Fresnoy Studio International des Arts Contemporains, Tourcoing. His solo and retrospective exhibitions include 1970, Art Gallery of Ontario, Toronto, and 2002, Musée National d'Art Moderne, Paris.

BIBLIOGRAPHY:

Michael Snow: A Survey, exhibition catalogue, Art Gallery of Toronto, Toronto, 1970. *About 30 works by Michael Snow,* exhibition catalogue, The Gallery, Ottawa, 1972. *Michael Snow,* Éd. du Centre Georges-Pompidou, Paris, 1978. Cornwell, Regina, *Snow seen: the films and photographs of Michael Snow,* New York Zoetrope, New York, 1980. *Walking Woman Works: Michael Snow 1961-1967, New Representational Art and its Uses,* exhibition catalogue, Herbert F. Johnson Museum of Art, Cornell University, Ithaca (NY), 1983. Reid, Dennis, *A Concise History of Canadian Painting,* Oxford University Press, Toronto, 1988. *The collected writings of Michael Snow,* Wilfrid Laurier University Press, Waterloo (CAN), 1994. Sheddon, Jim (ed.), *Presence and Absence: the Films of Michael Snow, 1956-1991,* Art Gallery of Ontario, Toronto, 1995 (illustrated book). Roberts, Catsou/Steeds, Lucy (ed.), *Michael Snow: Almost Cover to Cover,* exhibition catalogue, Arnolfini, Bristol, 2001. Fréruchet, Maurice, et al., *Les Années soixante-dix: l'art en cause,* exhibition catalogue, Cap musée d'Art contemporain, Bordeaux, 2002. Durand, Régis, et al., *Sans commune mesure. Image et texte dans l'art actuel,* exhibition catalogue, Éd. Léo Scheer, Paris, 2002. Bouhours, Jean-Michel (ed.), *Michael Snow. Des Écrits 1958-2001,* École nationale supérieure des beaux-arts, Paris, 2002. Kellman, Kila Landon, *Figuring Redemption: Resighting My Self in the Art of Michael Snow,* Wilfrid Laurier University Press, Waterloo, 2002 (illustrated book).

MUSEUMS AND GALLERIES:

KITCHENER (Kitchener-Waterloo AG): *Crossing* (1961, oil on cardboard) - LONDON, CANADA: *Beach-hcaeb* (1963) - MONTREAL (MAC): *Headline (Sketch for News)* (1959); *1956, a Videoprint* (1974) - MONTREAL (MBA): *Door* (1979) - OTTAWA (Nat. Gal. of Canada): *Clear Lake* - PARIS (FNAC): *Egg* (object) - TORONTO (AG of Ontario): *Venus Simultaneous* (1962, oil); *Duol* (oil) - WASHINGTON DC (Hirshhorn Mus. and Sculpture Garden): *27 Ladies (Women)* (1962, oil and collage); *Noctambulation (Death Walk)* (1961, oil); *A Falling, Walking Woman* (1961, oil and pencil).

SNOW, Peter

British, 20th century.

Painter.

Peter Snow's exploration of synthetic abstraction is reminiscent of the Impressionists. His work is also influenced by Mexican art.

SNOWDEN, George Holburn

American, 20th century.

Born 17 December 1902, in Yonkers (New York); died 1990.

Sculptor.

George Holburn Snowden was a pupil of Male and Adolphe Alexander Weinman at the Beaux-Arts Institute, New York. He won the American Prix de Rome in 1927.

SNOWMAN, Isaac

British, 19th - 20th century.

Born 1874, in London.

Active in Israel.

Painter. Figures, portraits, genre scenes.

Isaac Snowman trained at the Royal Academy Schools in London and under Bouguereau and Benjamin Constant in Paris. He painted portraits of the English kings *George V* and *Edward VII,* and exhibited at the Royal Academy from 1898 to 1919. He settled in Palestine in the 1920s, and was among the first artists to render the atmosphere of the Holy Land while at the same time depicting its ordinary people.

AUCTION RECORDS:

PARIS, 8 Feb 1950, *Young Woman Opening her Shutters* (1917; *Love's Trust* (two pendants) FRF 10,500. LONDON, 18 Sept 1973, *The Love Letter,* GBP 420. LONDON, 31 May 1977, *Vesta* (1895, oil on canvas, 31 x 24 1/2 ins / 79 x 62 cm) GBP 900. LONDON, 18 June 1985, *Slumber* (oil on canvas, 27 1/2 x 35 1/2 ins / 70 x 90 cm) GBP 30,000. LONDON, 13 Feb 1986, *The Wailing Wall, Jerusalem* (1922, oil on canvas, 28 x 36 ins / 71 x 91.5 cm) GBP 12,000. TEL AVIV, 26 May 1988, *The Wailing Wall* (1927, oil on panel, 15 3/4 x 12 1/4 ins / 40.3 x 30.8 cm) USD 8,800. LONDON, 15 June 1988, *Margot* (1919, oil on canvas, 36 x 28 ins / 91.5 x 71 cm) GBP 2,200. LONDON, 27 Sept 1989, *Portrait of a Young Woman of the World, very probably Madeleine Lemaire* (1918, oil on canvas, 36 x 28 1/2 ins / 91.5 x 72.5 cm) GBP 2,420. LONDON, 30 March 1994, *The Bracelet* (oil on canvas, 50 x 40 ins / 127 x 101.5 cm) GBP 20,700. TEL AVIV, 26 April 1997, *The Shores of Lake Galilee* (1909, oil on canvas, 26 3/4 x 42 1/2 ins / 68 x 108 cm) USD 31,050.

SNUFFELAER. See **LAAR Pieter Jacobsz. van,** and **MARSEUS VAN SCHRIECK Otto**

SNYDER, H. W.

American, 18th - 19th century.

Active in New York and Boston 1797-1816.

Engraver (stippling).

SNYDER, Joan

American, 20th - 21st century.

Born 16 April 1940, in Highland Park (New Jersey).

Active in Brooklyn (New York).

Painter (mixed media), printmaker.

Joan Snyder began painting in her final year at Douglas College in New Brunswick, New Jersey, and received a Master of Fine Arts degree in 1966 from Rutgers University. In the late 1960s, she painted landscapes and portraits, but in the 1970s, fuelled by feminist politics, Snyder and other artists, including Jennifer Bartlett, Susan Rothenberg and Elizabeth Murray, responded to the reductive aesthetic and modernist abstraction of the 1960s by reintroducing content in an expressionist and highly personal vein. In the early 1970s, her paintings were loosely brushed, gestural and were still concerned with formalist issues such as the integrity of the picture plane, the grid, and the edge of the canvas. These so-called 'stroke' paintings were well-received, but Snyder soon rejected her analytic and formulaic approach and sought more expressive and personal forms. By 1974, her work included scrawled notes and childlike drawings of landscapes and stick figures which eventually evolved to include feminist subject matter. In 1974, she was awarded a National Endowment for the Arts Fellowship, and in 1983 was awarded a John Simon Guggenheim Memorial Fellowship. In the mid-1980s, landscape resurfaced as a theme in her so-called 'field paintings'. Throughout the 1980s, her work included more autobiographical subject matter and expressed a strong identification of the female body with the earth and fertility.

Snyder has taught or been an artist-in-residence extensively at numerous schools throughout the USA, including: Rutgers University; State University of New York, Stony Brook; University of Colorado, Boulder; Princeton University; Atlanta College of Art; San Francisco Art Institute; and Parsons School of Design.

Snyder has exhibited extensively throughout the USA and in Hamburg, Germany. In 1994, the *Joan Snyder* exhibition held at Brandeis University's Rose Art Museum, Waltham, Massachusetts was awarded First Prize for the Best Regional Exhibition by the International Association of Art Critics.

BIBLIOGRAPHY:

Tucker, Marcia, '*The Anatomy of a Stroke: Recent Paintings by Joan Snyder*' in *Artforum*, 19 May 1971. Baker, Kenneth, *Joan Snyder and Pat Steir*, Institute of Contemporary Art, Boston, 1974. Herrera, Hayden, *Joan Snyder: Seven Years of Work*, Neuberger Museum, State University of New York, Purchase (NY), 1978. Rubinstein, Charlotte Streifer, *American Women Artists from Early Indian Times to the Present*, 1982. Baker, John, *Joan Snyder*, Hirschl & Adler Modern, New York, 1985 (introduction). Herrera, Hayden, *Joan Snyder Collects Joan Snyder*, Santa Barbara Contemporary Arts Forum, Santa Barbara (CA), 1988. Ashton, Dore, *Joan Snyder*, Nielsen Gallery, Boston, 1991. Belz, Carl, *Joan Snyder Painter 1969 to Now*, exhibition catalogue, Rose Art Museum, Brandeis University, Waltham (MA), 1994. Diehl, Carol, *Joan Snyder New Paintings*, Locks Gallery, Philadelphia, 1995.

MUSEUMS AND GALLERIES:

ATLANTA (High Mus. of Art) - BOSTON (MFA): *Resurrection* (1977, oil and collage on canvas) - CAMBRIDGE, MA (Fogg AM, Harvard University) - DALLAS (MA) - NEW YORK (Brooklyn Mus.): paintings - NEW YORK (Metropolitan Mus. of Art) - NEW YORK (MoMA) - NEW YORK (Whitney Mus. of American Art) - NORTHAMPTON, MA (MA, Smith College): *My Temple My Totems* (1983-1984, mixed media) - OBERLIN, OH (Allen Art Museum, Oberlin College) - WASHINGTON DC (Corcoran Gal. of Art) - WASHINGTON DC (National Mus. of Women in the Arts): *Can We Turn Our Rage to Poetry?* (1985, mixed media on canvas) - WASHINGTON DC (The Phillips Collection) - WORCESTER, MA (Art Museum).

AUCTION RECORDS:

NEW YORK, 13 May 1981, *Country Landscape* (1977, mixed media and oil on canvas, 32 1/2 x 65 1/2 ins / 82.5 x 166.4 cm) USD 6,250. NEW YORK, 2 Nov 1984, *Paint the House* (1970, coloured chalk, ink and gouache, 30 x 22 ins / 76.5 x 55.9 cm) USD 750. NEW YORK, 8 Oct 1986, *Moonshine Ford D.L. and M.* (1973, mixed media/canvas, 60 x 164 ins / 152.4 x 416.6 cm) USD 12,000. NEW YORK, 10 Nov 1988, *Victory* (mixed media, 48 x 96 ins / 122.1 x 244 cm) USD 20,900. NEW YORK, 4 May 1989, *Little Symphony for Women II* (1976, three acrylic panels, coloured chalks, graphite and collage of painting/canvas, one 23 3/4 x 23 3/4 ins / 60.2 x 60.2 cm and the others 24 x 24 ins/61.2 x 61.2 cm) USD 24,200. NEW YORK, 17 Nov 1992, *Cantata No. 2* (1988, acrylic, nails, wire, fabric and oil on paper, 36 x 19 3/4 ins / 91.4 x 50.2 cm) USD 5,280. NEW YORK, 28 June 2000, *Untitled* (oil and acrylic on canvas, 60 x 120 ins / 152 x 305 cm) USD 22,000.

SNYDER, William Henry

American, 19th - 20th century.

Born 1829, in Brooklyn; died 4 October 1910, in Brooklyn.

Painter. Figures, genre scenes, landscapes.

AUCTION RECORDS:

NEW YORK, 16 Oct 1974, *Old Black Woman Darning Socks* (1885) USD 1,300. NEW YORK, 24 Oct 1979, *The Black Cook* (1887, oil on canvas, 14 1/4 x 18 ins / 36 x 46 cm) USD 3,500.

SNYDERS. See also **SNAYERS** and **SNYERS**

SNYDERS, Frans, or Sneyders, Snyers, Sneis, or Snijders

Flemish School, 16th - 17th century.

Baptised 11 November 1579 in Antwerp; died 19 August 1657, in Antwerp.

Painter, draughtsman. Religious subjects, mythological subjects, genre scenes, hunting scenes, animals, dogs, interiors, flowers, fruit, still-lifes (including game). Antwerp School.

Franz Snyders studied with Pieter Breughel the Younger in 1593 and perhaps with Hinrock van Balen. He was made a master of the Antwerp guild in 1602, and went to Italy in 1608, returning to Antwerp from Milan the following year. He married Margaretha de Vos, the sister of Cornelis and Pieter de Vos, and soon acquired a reputation. Van Dyck considered him the best of the collaborators of Rubens. Among his pupils were Paul de Vos, Jan Fyt, Nicasius Bernaert, Pieter Bols and Jurian Jacobsz. He painted mainly still-lifes at first and then devoted himself to hunting scenes. He collaborated with Rubens and Jordaens and was associated with 'Velvet' Brueghel.

Initially he painted flowers, fruit, and genre or open-air scenes, and the idyllic character of these paintings is quite different from that of his hunting scenes. They were peaceful subjects such as *The Animals Entering the Ark, Creation of the Animals: Quadrupeds and Birds, The Earthly Paradise*; subjects that 'Velvet' Brueghel painted, but treated very differently from Snyders. He also painted interiors such as kitchens and market stalls. His easel paintings are few and highly prized. In addition to these paintings Snyders is usually attributed with 16 aquatints, depicting animals. However, some critics believe that these aquatints are not by Snyders but Jan Fyt, and that the name was only added after the first printing to help them sell. Brussels has one of the best paintings of this peaceful genre, overflowing with animals, fruit, vegetables, game and fish, and thus very much in the Flemish style. A large number of his works are to be found in Spain.

Snyders applied to all his works the criteria of history painting, both in terms of size and treatment: he painted fights between animals with all the effect of a human battle. Rubens and Snyders often painted figures in each other's pictures. Nevertheless, Snyder's own paintings are of the highest order. He belongs unquestionably to the School of Rubens and adopts Rubens' procedures, but his own personality shines through and it would be unjust to categorise him merely as an assistant of Rubens. His still-lifes, hunting scenes and other luxuriant compositions are powerful and skilful.

Fr. Snyders. pinx. 1646.

F. Snijders. fecit.

F Sneyders 1632

F·Snyders fecit
F·Snÿders. fecit. 16..

Bibliography:

Buschmann, P., *F. Snyders*, Bibliographie Nationale XXIII, Brussels, 1921-1924. Hairs, Marie-Louise, *Les Peintres de fleurs flamands au XVIIe siècle*, Lefebvre et Gillet, Brussels, 1985. Robels, Hella, *frans Snyders. Stilleben und Tiermaler 1579-1657*, Deutscher Kunstverlag, Munich, 1989. Koslow, Susan, *Frans Snyders: Stilleven, en dierenschilder*, Fonds Mercator Paribas, Antwerp, 1995.

Museums and Galleries:

Aix: sketch; *Bear Attacked by a Pack of Hounds* - Ajaccio: *Boar Hunt* - Amiens: *Game, Vegetables and Fruit; Dog; Large Still-life* - Amsterdam: *Still-life; Game* - Angers: *Skaters; Crushed Dog* - Antwerp (Koninklijk Mus. voor Schone Kunsten): *Swans and Dogs; Still-life; Still-life with Fish* (disputed) - Arras: *Wolf Hunt; Boar Hunt* - Berlin: study; *Still-life with Fruit; Still-life with Chicken; Cock Fight* - Besançon: *Wounded Dog; Fruit; Fruit and Flowers* - Bonn (Rheinisches Landesmus.): *Still-life* - Bordeaux: *An Old Lion; Fox Hunt* - Bremen: *Still-life* - Brunswick: *Boar Hunt; Three Hares* - Brussels: *Two Larders* (figures by Backhort); *Kitchen Interior; Crown of Fruit and Vegetables; Stag Hunt* (landscape by Wildens); study; *Animals and Fruit* - Budapest: *Vulture and Chicken* - Caen: *Interior of a Pantry* - Cambrai: *Still-life and Figures* - Chaumont: *Hunting Picture* (six) - Cherbourg: *Neptune, Thetis and Two Sailors* - Cologne: *Still-life* - Copenhagen (Statens Mus. for Kunst): *Game and Fruit; Fruit on a Table* - Dresden: *Lady Holding a Parrot; Still-life with Bitch and her Puppies; Still-life with Monkey and Parrot; Large Still-life with Two Peasants; Still-life with Bitch and her Puppies, Cook and Kitchenmaid; Boar Hunt* - Dunkirk: *Fruit, Flowers and Two Figures* - Edinburgh: *Portrait of a Gentleman; Boar Hunt; Wolf Hunt* - Edinburgh (Nat. Gal. of Scotland): *Mischievous Monkeys* (oil on canvas) - Florence: *Boar Hunt* - Frankfurt am Main: *Stag Hunt; Still-life and Kitchen* - Geneva (MAH): *Dog Seizing a Heron* - Grenoble: *Parrots; Dog and Cat* - Hamburg: *Game and Fruit* - Hanover: *Still-life* - Kassel: *Food; Group of Birds; Still-life* - La Fère: *Two Still-lifes* - Leipzig: *Game Seller* - Lille: *Boar Hunt; Great Dane*; a sketch - London (Wallace Collection): *Pantry Scene with a Page* (1615-1620, oil on canvas) - Lyons: *Kitchen Table Covered with Game* - Madrid: *Boar Hunt; Dogs Stealing Food; Dog with its Prey; Fox Hunt; Fable of the Hare and the Tortoise; Stork and Other Animals; The Fox and the Cat; Fable of the Lion and the Rat; Fruit; Birds Singing in a Tree; Boar Attacked by Dogs at the Edge of a Wood* (two); *Game Fighting over Their Prey; Bird Chorus; Bull Overcome by Dogs; Cock Fight; Kitchenmaid Holding a Chicken; Goat Suckling; Inn, with Table and Fruit*; same subject; *Stag Hunt; Poultry Seller* - Milan (Pinacoteca di Brera): *Stag Hunt* - Moscow (Rumiantsev Mus.): *Butcher's Shop; Fruit; Monkeys, Cup and Fruit; Parrot and Flowers* - Munich: *Fruit and Vegetable Shop; Kitchen; Lioness Killing a Boar; Two Young Lions Pursuing a Deer; Boar Hunt; Still-life, Fruit and Flowers; Still-life* - Nancy: *Fox Eating a Chicken* - Oldenburg: *Large Still-life; Bird Chorus* - Orléans: *Horse Being Eaten by Wolves* - Paris (Louvre): *The Earthly Paradise; Entry of the Animals into Noah's Ark; Stag Pursued by a Pack of Hounds; Boar Hunt; Fish Sellers; Dogs in a Pantry; Fruit and Animals; Fish Shop; Game Seller; Stag Drinking; Birds; Fruit; Basket of Fruit* - Rennes: *Wounded Mastiff* - Rohrau (Schlossmus., Graf Harrach'sche Familiensammlung): *Stag Hunt* - Rouen: *Boar Hunt* - St Petersburg (Hermitage): *Fruit Seller's Shop; Woman Selling Vegetables; Fish Seller; Game Seller; Pantry* (two); *Still-life; Fish Stall; Dog Fight; Battle between a Domestic Cock and a Turkey-Cock; Study of a Cat; Bird Chorus* - Stockholm: *Two Dogs Fighting Over the Flayed Head of a Bullock; Dead Game; Bowl of Fruit in a Niche; Reynard at the Meal with the Heron* - Tarbes: *Boar Hunt* - The Hague: *Game* - Valenciennes: *Store-Cupboard* - Vienna: *Boar Fighting Dogs; Paradise; Fish Market* (two); *Fox Hunt; Hunt; Head of Medusa* (with Rubens) - Vienna (Czernin'sche Gemäldegal.): *Vultures and Snake Fighting Over a Dead Wolf; Fox and Dogs* - Vienna (Liechtenstein Mus.): *Squirrel with a Grape; Stag Hunt* (two); *Dead Deer* - Wroclaw: *Battle for the Prey* - Ypres: *Game Seller* (with Rubens).

Auction records:

Amsterdam, 1703, *Birds*, FRF 150. Amsterdam, 18 May 1706, *An Eagle and Several Other Birds*, FRF 800. Haarlem, 1711, *Bear Hunt*, FRF 1,100. London, 30 Jan 1768, *Boar Hunt*, FRF 2,365. Ghent, 1837, *Fight between Dogs and Wolves*, FRF 875; *Fight between Bears and Dogs*, FRF 1,200; *Stag Hunt*, FRF 950. London, 1844, *Fruit and Game*, FRF 1,265. Paris, 1846, *Dispute over a Chicken; Boar Hunt* (collection) FRF 7,620; *Lion Pursuing a Deer*, FRF 1,686. Paris, 1853, *Groups of Birds* (four paintings, collection) FRF 8,575. Paris, 1859, *Bears and Dogs*, FRF 2,943; *Man Disembowelling a Deer*, FRF 2,800. Paris, 1867, *Game Seller*, FRF 6,000; *Fruit with Still-life*, FRF 10,200; *Cats and Dogs*, FRF 4,600. Paris, 1875, *Kites and Cockerels*, FRF 5,800; *Fight between a Cockerel and a Turkey*, FRF 6,200; *Game Seller*, FRF 6,300. Brussels, 1882, *Pantry*, FRF 8,700; *Owl Hunt*, FRF 1,700. Paris, 1884, *Pantry*, FRF 16,700. London, March 1892, *Interior of an Oven*, FRF 13,120. Le Havre, 1898, *Pantry*, FRF 15,000. Brussels, 1899, *Still-life*, FRF 6,700. Paris, 16 June 1899, *Fish Stall*, FRF 4,000. Vienna, 1900, *Woman Selling Fruit*, FRF 5,150. London, 18 Dec 1909, *Wolf Hunt*, GBP 21. London, 19 Feb 1910, *Boar Hunt*, GBP 89; *Stag Hunt*, GBP 65. London, 19 Nov 1910, *Dog and Dead Game*, GBP 63. London, 14 July 1911, *Dead Game, Lobster, Fruit and a Boar's Head*, GBP 546. Paris, 25-28 March 1912, *At the Market*, FRF 43,000. Paris, 18 Dec 1919, *Still-life*, FRF 1,150. Paris, 15 Dec 1920, *Fishmonger's Stall*, FRF 4,100. London, 28 April 1922, *Wolf Hunt*, GBP 42. London, 26 May 1922, *Fruit and Dead Birds*, GBP 126. Paris, 4 Dec 1922, *Still-life*, FRF 6,900. London, 4-7 May 1923, *The Stork and the Fox*, GBP 157. London, 13 July 1923, *Still-life*, GBP 131. Paris, 22 and 23 May 1924, *Monkey, Birds and a Basket of Fruit*, FRF 8,500. Paris, 12 Feb 1925, *Birds, Fruit and Game*, FRF 9,900. London, 27 March 1925, *Stag Hunt*, GBP 136. London, 26 June 1925, *Still-life with Fruit*, GBP 231. London, 10 July 1925, *Dead Game and Fruit*, GBP 168; *Still-life in a Kitchen*, GBP 199. London, 17 July 1925, *Basket of Fruit*, GBP 141. Paris, 9 May 1927, *Study of Dogs*, FRF 17,900. London, 8 July 1927, *Back-Kitchen Scene*, GBP 131. Paris, 8 Nov 1928, *Dogs Eating Provisions*, FRF 2,600. Paris, 1 Dec 1930, *Pantry*, FRF 23,000. New York, 22 Jan 1931, *Still-life*, USD 900. Paris, 26 Feb 1931, *Dog and Game*, FRF 1,850. London, 11 March 1931, *Still-life*, GBP 220. London, 10 July 1931, *Fruit, Monkey and Parrot*, GBP 120. Geneva, 27 Oct 1934, *Still-life*, CHF 3,350. Paris, 28 Nov 1934, *Monkey and Gander*, FRF 18,200. Brussels, 17-18 Dec 1934, *Still-life*, BEF 12,000. Geneva, 7 Dec 1935, *Still-life with Fruit*, CHF 15,750. Paris, 17 Dec 1935, *Fruit-Loving Monkey* (pen and wash) FRF 950. London, 4 June 1937, *Fruit and Vegetables*, GBP 588; *Game Stall*, GBP 189. Brussels, 21-22 Feb 1938, *Fish Stall*, BEF 11,000; *Still-life*, BEF 11,000. London, 23 Feb 1938, *Fox with Dead Chicken*. London, 1 July 1938, *Stag Hunt*, GBP 110. Paris, 30 June-1 July 1941, *Dog and Cats Fighting over a Leg of Mutton* (school of Frans Snyders) FRF 560. Paris, 29 April 1942, *Still-life* (attributed) FRF 10,500. London, 10 June 1942, *Flock of Macaws on a Tree*, GBP 180. Paris, 29 Oct 1942, *Game and Dead Birds* (school of Frans Snyders) FRF 11,000. Paris, 16 Dec 1942, *Fishwife* (attributed) FRF 58,000. Paris, 18 Jan 1943, *Cat and Game* (school of Frans Snyders) FRF 9,000. Par-

IS, 24 Feb 1943, *Kill of the Boar* (attributed) FRF 16,000. PARIS, 12 March 1943, *Bowl of Grapes and Fruit* (school of Frans Snyders) FRF 4,300. PARIS, 12 April 1943, *Game and Animals* (school of Frans Snyders) FRF 15,000. NICE, 15 Nov 1943, *Interior Scene* (school of Frans Snyders) FRF 30,700. PARIS, 19 Nov 1943, *Dog Nosing Out a Heron, with Small Dead Birds* (attributed) FRF 1,600. PARIS, 14 Feb 1944, *Boar Attacked by Dogs; Bear Attacked by Dogs* (two pendants) FRF 26,000. PARIS, 31 March 1944, *The Earthly Paradise*, FRF 300,000. PARIS, 24 April 1944, *Hares* (two pencil drawings) FRF 380. PARIS, 5 May 1944, *Fishwife* (attributed) FRF 16,000. PARIS, 22 March 1945, *Basket of Fruit* (workshop of Frans Snyders) FRF 240,000. NEW YORK, 18-19 May 1945, *Still-life*, USD 750. NEW YORK, 15-16 May 1946, *Stag Hunt*, USD 460. PARIS, July 1946, *Game Seller* (1641) FRF 280,000. PARIS, 20 Dec 1946, *Fishwife* (school of Frans Snyders) FRF 69,000. PARIS, 13 March 1947, *Paying Court to the Housewife* (school of Frans Snyders) FRF 12,500. PARIS, 21 May 1947, *Boar Attacked by Dogs; Wolf Taking Ducks by Surprise* (two pendants, attributed) FRF 51,000. PARIS, 18 Oct 1948, *Fruit and Game* (attributed) FRF 51,000. PARIS, 25 May 1949, *Table Laid with Food*, FRF 780,000; *Three Parrots*, FRF 560,000. PARIS, 10 June 1949, *Two Women in front of a Game Stall (recto); Stag Attacked by a Dog (verso)* (pen and wash) FRF 2,800. PARIS, 19 Dec 1949, *Basket of Fruit* (attributed) FRF 240,000. BRUSSELS, 4 Dec 1950, *Still-life with Game and Poultry*, BEF 55,000. PARIS, 25 April 1951, *Still-life with Books* (attributed) FRF 260,000. LONDON, 4 May 1951, *Interior of a Kitchen*, GBP 420. LONDON, 23 May 1951, *Still-life with Dead Game* (1652) GBP 140. LONDON, 13 July 1951, *Fruit and Dead Game* (in collaboration with Jacob Jordaens) GBP 336. LONDON, 24 June 1959, *Landscape with the Fable of the Fox and the Heron*, GBP 1,600. PARIS, 3 Dec 1959, *Still-life with a Basket of Fruit and a Vase of Flowers*, FRF 1,900,000. LONDON, 23 March 1960, *Interior of a Food Storage Cupboard*, GBP 7,600. LONDON, 30 June 1961, *Red and Green Macaws*, GBP 2,730. LONDON, 28 Nov 1962, *Still-life*, GBP 4,800. LONDON, 23 June 1967, *Bird Chorus*, Gns 2,200. PARIS, 7 Dec 1970, *Pantry*, FRF 35,000. LONDON, 14 May 1971, *Still-life with Fruit and Flowers*, Gns 3,800. LONDON, 6 Dec 1972, *Still-life*, GBP 14,000. LONDON, 19 June 1973, *Large Still-life with Seated Young Woman and Young Man* (in collaboration with Cornelis de Vos) Gns 36,000. LONDON, 9 July 1976, *Still-life with Intertwined Bowl* (oil on canvas, 59 x 82 ins / 149.8 x 208.2 cm) GBP 7,200. AMSTERDAM, 9 June 1977, *Still-life* (oil/panel, 26¼ x 36¼ ins / 66.5 x 92 cm) NLG 90,000. LONDON, 14 April 1978, *Still-life* (oil on canvas, 47½ x 81 ins / 120.6 x 205.7 cm) GBP 11,000. LONDON, 12 Dec 1979, *Still-life with Fruit and Monkeys* (26¼ x 37 ins / 66.5 x 94 cm) GBP 16,000. LONDON, 10 Dec 1980, *Still-life with Fruit and Birds* (1616, oil/panel, 28 x 20¼ ins / 71 x 51.5 cm) GBP 45,000. LONDON, 2 Dec 1983, *Still-life with Fruit* (oil on canvas, 43¼ x 68 ins / 110 x 173 cm) GBP 35,000. ROUEN, 16 Dec 1984, *Still-life with Porcelain Bowl* (oil on wood, 18 x 25¼ ins / 46 x 64 cm) FRF 400,000. LONDON, 29 Oct 1986, *Still-life with Flowers and Fruit* (oil/panel, 20 x 26¼ ins / 50.5 x 66.5 cm) GBP 32,000. MONTE CARLO, 20 June 1987, *Fishmonger and his Stall* (oil on canvas, 80¼ x 132¾ ins / 204 x 337 cm) FRF 1,000,000. NEW YORK, 14 Jan 1988, *Still-life with Game, Flowers and Fruit* (oil on canvas, 20 x 26¼ ins / 51 x 66.5 cm) USD 77,000. NEW YORK, 15 Jan 1988, *Wolf Hunt* (oil on canvas, 63 x 118½ ins / 160 x 301 cm) USD 33,000. PARIS, 26 June 1989, *Study of Heads of Lion Cubs* (oil on canvas, 24¼ x 29¼ ins / 61.5 x 74.5 cm) FRF 910,000. LONDON, 27 Oct 1989, *A Poodle Playing with a Ratter next to a Spit of Dead Birds* (oil on canvas, 33¾ x 48 ins / 85.6 x 121 cm) GBP 6,820. MONACO, 2 Dec 1989, *Dogs Feeding* (oil on canvas, 41¾ x 65¼ ins / 106 x 166 cm) FRF 72,150. LONDON, 9 April 1990, *Peasants Going to Market* (oil on canvas, 89 x 110 ins / 226 x 279.5 cm) GBP 330,000. LONDON, 7 Feb 1991, *Two Mastiffs Fighting Over an Upturned Bucket and some Food Scraps* (oil on canvas, 41 x 55¼ ins / 104.2 x 140.3 cm) GBP 2,640. STOCKHOLM, 29 May 1991, *An Elegant Couple and their Servants at the Fish Market* (oil on canvas, 6¼ x 87½ ins / 16 x 222 cm) SEK 200,000. LONDON, 2 July 1991, *Boar Surrounded by Dogs in a Clearing* (black chalk, brown ink and wash, 11½ x 17¾ ins / 29 x 45 cm) GBP 44,000. MONACO, 5-6 Dec 1991, *Still-life* (ink and wash, 10½ x 14 ins / 26.9 x 35.4 cm) FRF 56,610. NEW YORK, 16 Jan 1992, *Still-life of Dead Game on a Table, with a basket of fruit and two dogs attached to the table* (oil on canvas, 90¼ x 66¼ ins / 229.2 x 168.3 cm) USD 110,000. LONDON, 9 Dec 1992, *Still-life of fruit and almonds in baskets and bowls, with a monkey and a squirrel on the table* (oil on canvas, 61 x 76¼ ins / 155 x 193.5 cm) GBP 88,000. PARIS, 16 June 1993, *Still-life with basket of fruit, game and shrimps*. ORLÉANS, 23 Oct 1993, *Still-life with Lobster* (oil on panel, 28¾ x 48 ins / 73 x 121 cm) FRF 205,000. AMSTERDAM, 17 Nov 1993, *Still-life with a basket of fruit, game, vegetables and a dead squirrel* (oil on canvas, 30 x 48 ins / 76.5 x 121 cm) NLG 109,250. LONDON, 8 July 1994, *Dogs Attacking a Boar* (oil on canvas, 82 x 135½ ins / 208 x 344 cm) GBP 73,000. NEW YORK, 11 Jan 1995, *Hunting Picture with a rabbit, a pheasant, a woodcock and other perching birds, Wanli porcelain bowls, grapes in a basket and copper cooking pots with a chicken, a cockerel and pigeons* (oil on panel, 37½ x 49½ ins / 95.5 x 125.6 cm) USD 222,500. LONDON, 5 July 1995, *Still-life with grapes, pears, apricots, gooseberries and cherries on a stand, wild strawberries on a blue and white plate decorated with a pink and an opened nut on the table* (oil/copper, 13½ x 19¾ ins / 34 x 50 cm) GBP 188,500. PARIS, 27 Nov 1995, *Cook in the Pantry* (oil on canvas, 56 x 82¾ ins / 142 x 210 cm) FRF 420,000. NEW YORK, 11 Jan 1996, *Fruit and Vegetable Seller* (1627, oil on canvas, 65¼ x 95¼ ins / 165.7 x 241.9 cm) USD 1,542,500. VIENNA, 29-30 Oct 1996, *Prunes in a bowl, nuts on a plate, strawberries in a basket and a squirrel on the table* (oil on panel, 33 x 19¾ ins / 84 x 50 cm) ATS 1,070,000. PARIS, 31 March 1998, *Still-life with a bowl of grapes, shrimps and hunting trophies* (1613, oil on oak panel) FRF 720,000. LONDON, 16 Dec 1999, *Swags of Fruit with Infants Christ and St John the Baptist Playing* (oil on canvas, 67 x 96 ins / 170 x 243 cm) GBP 75,000. MADRID, 24 Jan 2000, *Monkey and Cat* (oil on canvas, 45 x 33 ins / 115 x 85 cm) ESP 2,250,000. MADRID, 4 July 2000, *Still-life with Pheasant and Rabbit* (oil on canvas, 25 x 33 ins / 63 x 85 cm) ESP 1,900,000. MADRID, 25 April 2001, *Vase with Flowers* (oil on canvas, 23 x 20 ins / 59 x 51 cm) ESP 11,000,000. LONDON, 12 July 2001, *River Landscape with Hounds Attacking Wolves, Huntsmen Emerging from a Wood Beyond* (oil on canvas, 84 x 136 ins / 213 x 346 cm) GBP 60,000. LONDON, 9 Dec 2002, *Still-life with Game, Fruit, an Artichoke and Lobster* (pen/ink wash, 8 x 11 ins / 20 x 29 cm) GBP 9,000. MUNICH, 24 Sept 2003, *Heron in Reeds* (oil on canvas, 52 x 46 ins / 132 x 116 cm) EUR 14,000. LONDON, 10 Dec 2003, *Melon, Grapes, Apples and Pears with Other Fruit in a Basket, Wine Glass and a Diana Monkey on Table* (oil on canvas, 38 x 58 ins / 96 x 147 cm) GBP 160,000. LONDON, 7 July 2004, *Deer, Fawn and Other Dead Game Suspended on Hooks* (oil on canvas, 70 x 54 ins / 178 x 137 cm) GBP 170,000. LONDON, 7 July 2004, *Still-life of Fruit with Bowls and Sparrow* (oil on panel, 21 x 33 ins / 54 x 85 cm) GBP 200,000.

SNYDERS, Levinus, or Sneyders
Flemish School, 18th century.
Active in Middelburg 1725-1761.
Painter, sculptor.

SNYDERS, Michael
Flemish School, 17th century.
Born c. 1588; died c. 1630.
Active in Antwerp.
Engraver, print publisher. Allegorical subjects, insects, flowers.
Antwerp School.

Michael Snyders was in the guild of Antwerp in 1611 and was still a member in 1630.

SNYERS. See also **SNAYERS** and **SNYDERS**

SNYERS, Frans. See **SNYDERS**

SNYERS, Hendrik, or Snayers

Flemish School, 17th century.

Born c. 1612, in Antwerp.

Engraver (burin).

Hendrik Snyers was a pupil of M. Lauwers in 1636. He imitated the style of Bolswert and had a considerable reputation. He engraved after Rubens, Van Dyck and Jordaens, as well as after the great Italian masters. He signed his plates: *Henrick Snyers* and *H. Snyers*.

SNYERS, Isabelle

Belgian, 19th century.

Born c. 1802, in Antwerp; died after 1841.

Active in Brussels.

Painter. Portraits, genre scenes.

Isabelle Snyers was a pupil of F.G. Kinssen in Paris in 1826. She visited London.

SNYERS, Jacques Joseph

Flemish School, 18th - 19th century.

Born 13 April 1754, in Mechelen; died 28 February 1832, in Antwerp.

Engraver (burin).

Jacques Joseph Snyers was a pupil of P.F. Martenasie.

SNYERS, Johannes or Giovanni, or Snier

Flemish School, 16th century.

Of Flemish origin.

Active at the end of the 16th century.

Painter.

Snyers was in Naples in 1597.

SNYERS, Petrus Johannes

Flemish School, 18th century.

Born 1696, in Antwerp; died 21 September 1757, in Antwerp.

Painter. Still-lifes.

Petrus Johannes Snyers was a pupil of his uncle Peter Snyers and was dean of the guild in Antwerp in 1734. Certain biographers state that he abandoned painting at about the age of 20, in 1715, which does not seem compatible with the function he fulfilled 19 years later.

SNYERS, Pieter or Peter or Petrus, called The Saint

Flemish School, 17th - 18th century.

Born 30 March 1681, in Antwerp; died 4 May 1752, in Antwerp.

Painter, engraver. Portraits, genre scenes, landscapes, still-lifes, flowers.

Pieter Snyers was a pupil of Alexander van Bredael in 1694. He was master of a studio in Brussels in 1705 and in Antwerp in 1707. There is reason to believe that he was in England between 1720 and 1726, where he painted numerous portraits of gentlemen. He returned to Antwerp, married Maria Catharina van der Boven the same year, and bought a house in 1739. He was a great collector of Flemish and Dutch paintings. His nickname 'The Saint' came from his great piety.

His very varied subjects are treated in an archaistic style. He produced some original prints, as well as prints after the masters.

P·Snyers

MUSEUMS AND GALLERIES:

ABBEVILLE: *Pilgrim* - AMSTERDAM: *Tradeswoman* - ANTWERP: *Nest*; two still-lifes - BRUSSELS: *Two Plants and Fruit* - LIÈGE: *Stag Devouring the Head of an Ox* - LONDON (NG): *A Still-life with Fruit, Vegetables, Dead Chickens and a Lobster* (oil on canvas) - NUREMBERG: *Birds*.

AUCTION RECORDS:

PARIS, 30 May 1903, *Still-life*, FRF 190; *Family Celebrating*, FRF 25,050. LONDON, 18 Dec 1909, *Peacock and Flowers in a Garden*, GBP 33. LONDON, 27 Jan 1928, *The Months of the Year* (five oils on canvas) GBP 231. PARIS, 1 April 1963, *Two Hunting Trophies* (painting/metal, forming a pair) FRF 13,000. PARIS, 7 June 1974, *Dream Landscape*, FRF 31,000. LONDON, 10 Dec 1980, *Still-life with Game* (oil/metal, 14¼ x 11 ins / 36.5 x 27 cm) GBP 4,600. LONDON, 17 Nov 1982, *Four Months of the Year: January, March, July and December* (1727, four oils on canvas, 33 x 27 ins / 84 x 68.5 cm) GBP 20,000. LONDON, 1 May 1984, *Still-life with Flowers and Shellfish with a Woman Standing Holding a Broom* (oil/copper, 12½ x 15½ ins / 32 x 39.3 cm) GBP 30,000. LONDON, 10 Dec 1986, *Still-life with Flowers, a Bundle of Asparagus, Radishes and Gherkins* (oil on canvas, oval, 27½ x 23 ins / 70 x 58.5 cm) GBP 22,000. NEW YORK, 12 Jan 1989, *Marsh Mallow and Poppies with a Mink on a Horse's Skull; Wild Flowers: Mallow, Thistles and Common Mullein* (two oils on canvas, pair of studies of plants, each 52¼ x 38 ins / 133 x 96.5 cm) USD 132,000. NEW YORK, 12 Oct 1989, *Young Savoyard Playing with a Marmot* (oil on canvas, 17¼ x 13¼ ins / 44 x 33.5 cm) USD 4,950. LONDON, 15 Dec 1989, *Vegetables and Fruit Laid out at the Foot of a Tree with a Man Pressing Grapes in the Background* (oil/copper/wood, 7¼ x 11½ ins / 18.5 x 29.5 cm) GBP 8,800. LONDON, 11 Dec 1991, *Woman near a Still-life of Flowers in a Vase, Shellfish, a Bird of Paradise and a Jar with a Snake on a Desk* (oil/copper, 13 x 16 ins / 33 x 40.5 cm) GBP 38,500. ROME, 28 April 1992, *Pheasant in a Still-life of Flowers and Fruit in a Wood* (oil on canvas, 44 x 33¼ ins / 112 x 84.5 cm) ITL 30,000,000. LONDON, 8 July 1992, *Still-life of Fruit and Vegetables with a Rabbit in a Landscape* (oil/copper, 7½ x 11¾ ins / 19 x 30 cm) GBP 9,680. NEW YORK, 19 May 1993, *Vase of Flowers, Jars with a Snake, a Reptile and Shellfish on a Table, a Basket of Fruit on a Casket and Shellfish, a Chestnut and a Snake in a Jar* (oil/copper, a pair, each 8½ x 6½ ins / 21.3 x 16.5 cm) USD 57,500. LONDON, 5 July 1993, *Portrait of a Collector (Self-portrait)* (1747, oil on panel, 12 x 10¾ ins / 30.2 x 27.2 cm) GBP 11,500. NEW YORK, 11 Jan 1995, *Two Months of the Year: June and November* (oils on canvas, a pair, each 33½ x 26½ ins / 85.4 x 67.6 cm) USD 63,000. NEW YORK, 22 May 1997, *Young Artist Drawing a Still-life of Fruit and Vegetables in a Garden with a Sculpture of a Monumental Fountain Decorated with Reliefs* (oil on canvas, 31½ x 25½ ins / 80 x 64.8 cm) USD 20,700. NEW YORK, 29 Jan 1998, *Two Months of the Year: December with a Peasant Woman and a Chestnut Seller; March with Women and Children at a Market, and a Village Behind* (two oils on canvas, 33¼ x 26¾ ins / 84.5 x 68 cm) USD 48,300. AMSTERDAM, 9 May 2000, *Peaches, Plums, Medlar, Figs on a Vine and Apple on a Forest Floor* (oil on canvas, 17 x 14 ins / 43 x 35 cm) NLG 28,000. ZURICH, 22 Sept 2000, *Market Scene* (oil on canvas, 39 x 32 ins / 98 x 82 cm) CHF 15,000. LONDON, 25 April 2001, *Plums on the Branch, Peaches, Apricots, Fruit, a Nest with Eggs and a Goldfinch* (oil on canvas, 28 x 31 ins / 70 x 80 cm) GBP 14,000. LONDON, 14 Dec 2001, *Wooded Landscape with Ladies and Gentleman Resting after the Chase* (oil on canvas, 26 x 33 ins / 67 x 85 cm) GBP 5,000. LONDON, 18 April 2002, *Still-life with Fruit and Ivory Tankard* (oil on canvas, 28 x 31 ins / 72 x 78 cm) GBP 6,000. PARIS, 6 June 2002, *Still-life with Artichokes and Other Vegetables* (oil on copper, 8 x 10 ins / 20 x 26 cm) EUR 15,000. AMSTERDAM, 4 Nov 2003, *Flower Garland surrounding a German Silver-gilt and Ivory Tankard* (oil on canvas, 37 x 30 ins / 93 x 77 cm) EUR 10,000. COPENHAGEN, 9 Dec 2003, *Still-life with Dead Game and Guns in a Landscape* (oil on canvas, 43 x 68 ins / 110 x 173 cm) DKK 160,000. LONDON, 22 April 2004, *Courtship Scene with Young Lady being Presented with Flowers by Young Men* (oil on canvas, 33 x 27 ins / 85 x 68 cm) GBP 15,000. COPENHAGEN, 9 June 2004, *Battle Scene from the Thirty Years War* (oil on canvas, 29 x 24 ins / 74 x 62 cm) DKK 35,000. BETHESDA, 18 Sept 2004, *Dance of the Seven Veils* (oil on canvas, 79 x 47 ins / 201 x 119 cm) USD 7,000.

SNYKENS, Henri
Belgian, 19th century.
Born 3 September 1854, in Brussels.
Painter.

Henri Snykens studied in Düsseldorf.

SO, Shiseki, real name: Kusumoto Kohachi, alternate name: Kunkaku, artist names: Sekkei, Katei, Sogaku, Sekko, So Shiseki
Japanese, 18th century.
Born 1712; died 1786.
Painter.

So Shiseki painted bamboo, birds and flowers in the style of the Nagasaki School. He is said to have been a disciple of the Chinese painter Song Ziyan, who was there at the time.

BIBLIOGRAPHY:
Guth, Christine, *Japanese Art of the Edo Period*, Calmann & King, London, 1996.

AUCTION RECORDS:
NEW YORK, 17 Oct 1989, *Birds on a Snow-covered Flowering Branch* (ink and colour on silk, hanging scroll, 48 1/2 x 17 ins / 123 x 42.3 cm) USD 9,900.

SO, Shizan, real name: Kusmoto Hakkei, popular names: Kunshaku, Manju, artist names: Taikei, Sekko
Japanese, 18th century.
Born 1733; died 1805.
Painter.

The son and disciple of So Shiseki (1712-1786), So Shizan belonged to the Nagasaki School and worked in Edo (now Tokyo).

AUCTION RECORDS:
NEW YORK, 26 March 1991, *Cock during a Shower* (ink and colour on silk, hanging scroll, 38 3/4 x 17 1/4 ins / 98.4 x 44 cm) USD 13,200.

SOAMI, real name: Nakao Shinso, artist names: Soami, Kangaku, Shosetsusai
Japanese, 16th century.
Born possibly in 1485; died 1525.
Active in Kyoto.
Painter.

During the Muromachi period, the Ami family, which was in the service of the Ashikaga shogunate, distinguished itself in *suiboku* (ink) and wash painting. Soami was one of the major figures in the family. The son of Geiami (1431-1485) and grandson of Noami (1397-1471), he was celebrated as a landscape painter. Following in the footsteps of his ancestors, he contributed to the *Kundaikan so choki*, the famous notebook of the Shogun's art secretary, which listed the names of the principal Chinese painters and classified them in accordance with the taste of the time. Like that of his family, Soami's work gradually freed itself from the Chinese stamp while still remaining faithful to the ink wash tradition. His are the magnificent landscapes on the sliding doors of the Daisen-in sub-temple of the Daitoku-ji temple in Kyoto, where nature, in all its grandeur, its misty effects delicately conveyed by subtle washes, evokes an authentically Japanese serenity of spirit. These ink-on-paper landscapes are now mounted as scrolls. They are kept in the National Museum in Kyoto and are listed on the register of important cultural properties.

MUSEUMS AND GALLERIES:
TOKYO (National Mus.).

SOAR, Thomas
British, 18th century.
Active in Derby c. 1790.
Painter (porcelain).

Thomas Soar was also a gilder.

SOARDI, Giovanni Battista
Italian, 18th century.
Active during the second half of the 18th century.
Sculptor (wood).

Soardi worked for churches in Celentino and Vermiglio.

SOARES, Agostin Floriano, or Suárez
Portuguese, 17th century.
Active c. 1640.
Engraver (burin).

SOARES, Antonio
Portuguese, 20th century.
Born 1894; died 1978.
Painter, draughtsman.

Antonio Soares worked in a range of muted tones, rich in subtle gradations. He is known for *Natacha, Portrait of the Artist's Sister* and *Lisbon*. He took part in group exhibitions including: Sociedade Nacional das Belas Artes, Lisbon (where he won a medal) and the 1937 Exposition Universelle, Paris.

BIBLIOGRAPHY:
Arnáiz, José Manuel/López Jiménez, Javier/Merchán Díaz, Manuel (ed.), '*Cien años de pintura en Espana y Portugal (1830-1930)*' in vol. X, Antiqvaria, Madrid, 1993.

MUSEUMS AND GALLERIES:
LISBON (Mus. do Chiado).

SOARES, Francisco
Portuguese, 16th century.
Born in Braga.
Active in Galicia, Spain during the second half of the 16th century.
Painter.

Francisco Soares worked for the church of the Trinity in Orense and the cathedral of Santiago de Compostela.

SOARES, Luis
Portuguese, 20th century.
Born in Mozambique.
Painter.

In his painting, Luis Soares blends African icononography and stylistic devices with Western forms of expression. He mounted an exhibition of his work in Belgium in 1991.

SOARES, Luiz
Brazilian, 20th century.
Born 1876, in Pernambuco.
Painter, watercolourist. Genre scenes.

Luiz Soares, a representative of the modern Brazilian school, exhibited in London and Paris. At the 1946 exhibition put on in the Musée d'Art Moderne in Paris by the United Nations Organisation, he showed his *Pastoral, Brazilian Dance* and *The Circus*.

SOARES, Ruy
Portuguese, 16th century.
Active in the middle of the 16th century.
Painter.

Ruy Soares decorated the queen of Portugal's litter with paintings in 1551.

SOAVE, Carlo
Italian, 19th century.
Born 2 January 1844, in Alessandria (Piedmont); died 11 June 1881, in Turin.
Painter, illustrator, lithographer.

A pupil of A. Gastaldi, Soave painted an altarpiece for the church of SS Pietro e Paolo in Turin.

SOAVE, Raffaele. See **SUA**

SOAVI, Giuseppe
Italian, 17th century.
Active in Montecassino towards the end of the 17th century.
Miniaturist.

MUSEUMS AND GALLERIES:
MONTECASSINO (Biblioteca): miniature (1686).

SOBA, Bernardo
Italian, 16th century.
Active in 1574.
Engraver (wood).

Bernardo Soba specialised in portraits.

SOBAJIC, Ilija
Montenegrin, 20th century.
Born 15 August 1876, in Danilovgrad.
Painter. Figures, portraits, landscapes.

Ilija Sobajic studied in Vienna and Paris. He worked at the court of Montenegro. In 1946 he took part in the inaugural exhibition of the Artists' Association of Montenegro.

SOBAJIC, Milos
Yugoslav, 20th century.
Born 1945, in Belgrade (now in Serbia).
Active in France.
Painter.

Sobajic, the son of an ambassador, travelled beyond the borders of his own country from an early age. He lived for some years in Istanbul and for a year in Israel, but still managed to study at the school of fine art in Belgrade, from which he graduated in 1970. He settled in Paris in 1972.

Sobajic is of the generation of Dado, Ljuba and Velickovic, and they have the same rapid style of drawing in common. Like them, he expresses the absurdity and horror of the world. Men clustered together, organised and oppressed, seem to keel over in a world of waste. An atmosphere of permanent upheaval, of exile and a state of perpetual anxiety prevail in his painting. In an extensive register of colours, he suggests shapes with a few nimble strokes. Only a few details are more heavily laboured.

Sobajic has participated in group exhibitions including in 1955 at the Venice Biennale. Solo exhibitions include: 1972, Galerie Lambert, Paris; from 1973, F.V. Gallery, New York; 1983, Arts Centre, Belgrade; 1985, Galerie Alain Blondel, Paris; 1988, Galerie du Dragon, Paris; 1994, Narodni Muzej and Muzej Savremene Umetnosti, Belgrade; 1999, 2000, *Art Paris*, Frank Pages Art Galerie, Carousel du Louvre, Paris.

BIBLIOGRAPHY:
Handke, Peter, *Milos Sobaïc*, La Différence, Paris, 2002.

MUSEUMS AND GALLERIES:
AMSTERDAM (Miniatuur Mus.) - ATHENS (Gal.) - BELGRADE (Muz. savremene umetnotsi) - BELGRADE (Narodni Muz.) - NOVI SAD (Muzej Vojvodine) - THESSALONICA (Makedoniko Mouseío Synchronis Technis/Macedonian Museum of Contemporary Art).

SOBEJANO Y LOPEZ, José María
Spanish, 19th - 20th century.
Born 1852, in Murcia; died 1918, in Murcia.
Painter. Genre scenes.

José María Sobejano was a pupil of F. Bushell, then of Dubois and Rosales. He completed his training as an artist by copying the Old Masters in the Prado Museum in Madrid. He specialised in genre painting, favouring the depiction of scenes of everyday life in the Murcia region, with great attention to detail and the use of an intense light. He is notable for *Quiet Conversation* and *Water Carrier*. He exhibited in Murcia from 1873 to 1883. A retrospective of his work was held at the Círculo de Bellas Artes in Murcia in 1926.

BIBLIOGRAPHY:
Arnáiz, José Manuel/López Jiménez, Javier/Merchán Díaz, Manuel (ed.), *'Cien años de pintura en Espana y Portugal (1830-1930)'* in vol. X, Antiqvaria, Madrid, 1993.

SOBEL, Janet
Maiden name: Lechovsky
American, 20th century.
Born 1894, near Kiev; died 1968, in New York.
Painter.

Little known outside the USA, Janet Sobel may have been the first artist ever to paint all-over drip paintings. Born in the Ukraine, she emigrated with her mother and two brothers to New York in 1908, after her father died in a pogrom. Entirely self-taught, she started to paint in 1937, naive gouaches of still-life reminiscent of Chagall. By 1943, however, her work had moved to a spontaneous form of Abstract Expressionism that attracted much admiration from major figures in the art world.

Her first solo exhibition was at the Puma Gallery, New York, in 1944. In 1945 she was included in the *Women Show* at Peggy Guggenheim's Art of this Century, where her work caught the attention of Clement Greenberg and Jackson Pollock, and in 1946 she was given a solo exhibition at *Art of this Century*, at which she showed her drip paintings.

MUSEUMS AND GALLERIES:
NEW YORK (MoMA).

SOBIAC, Milos. See **SOBAJIC**

SOBICO, Johann
Austrian, 15th century.
Active in Prague in 1410.
Miniaturist.

SOBIESKI, Jean
French, 20th century.
Born 1937, in Cannes.
Painter.

Jean Sobieski studied architecture at the École des Beaux-Arts in Paris. He was based in the Beaudoin Studio. However, he only stayed for two years, leaving to concentrate on painting. From 1967 to 1970, he divided his time between Paris and Rome, taking acting jobs to make ends meet and to enable him to continue to paint.

The first individual exhibition of his works was in 1969.

In Paris, he founded the Réalisme Mutant group. The aim of the group was to demonstrate visually that to grasp the reality of our time means grasping a vanishing reality. His paintings, which appear cold, convey a vision of the world and of human life that haunts our generation. Taking his cue from the laboratory experiments of Fraenkel Conrad and Robley Williams at Berkeley, this artist depicts life recreated in the laboratory as a chemical complex. His work shows us a mineral world with geometric lines and smooth surfaces. The technical drawing skills he learned when studying architecture are in evidence here.

SOBIESKI, Jeanne. See **GILLET Jeanne**

SOBINSKI, Kasimierz
Polish, 18th century.
Active at the end of the 18th century.
Miniaturist, painter (porcelain).

Kasimierz Sobinski studied under J. Peszka. He was the director of the porcelain factory in Korzec.

SOBISSO. See **PIETRO DI BERNARDINO**

SOBKOWIAK, Tadeusz
Polish, 20th - 21st century.
Born 1955.
Painter.

Sobkowiak is a graduate of the university of fine art in Poznan. His works appear in museums in the USA, Sweden and Denmark. He has taken part in many exhibitions featuring Polish painters.

SOBLEAU, Michele de. See **DESUBLEO Michele**

SOBOLEV, Andrei
Russian, 18th century.
Born 1745.
Painter (porcelain), mosaicist.

Andrei Sobolev studied at the art academy of St Petersburg.

SOBOLEV, Dmitri Mikhailovich
Russian, 19th century.
Born c. 1784, in Moscow.
Portrait artist.

Dmitri Mikhailovich Sobolev studied under Anton Gradd in Dresden.

SOBOLEV, Ivan
Russian, 17th century.
Active at the beginning of the 17th century.
Icon painter.

Ivan Sobolev was a member of the Stroganov school.

SOBOLEV, Yuri
Russian, 20th century.
Born 1928, in Moscow; died 14 December 2002.
Painter, graphic artist, animations director, theatre director.

Yuri Sobolev studied at the Moscow polygraphic institute (1947 - 1953). He then worked in a variety of fields - graphic art, painting, cartoons, film, and theatre - and was responsible for the foundation of various artistic groups, including Hermitage in Moscow and Interstudio (International Studio of Theatre of Synthesis and Animation) in St Petersburg. Sobolev was one of the non-official Soviet artists who, despite a lack of recognition by the authorities and the incomprehension of the general public, continued to explore the limits of artistic expression.

He took part in a large number of group exhibitions in Russia and elsewhere from 1962, including: 1962, *Studio Artists Exhibition* under El Belyutin, Taganka, Moscow; Yunost Hotel, Moscow; Central Exhibition Hall (Manège) Moscow; 1965, *Actual Alternative - 2*, Castello Spaniolo, L'Aquila, Italy; *Nine Russian Artists*, Gdansk; 1979, 20th Anniversary of Unofficial Soviet Art, Bochum; and an exhibition of Vladimir Tarasov's private collection, State Art Museum, Vilnius, Lithuania; 1990, *Art Mass*, Basel; Domberger Gallery, Stuttgart; Seltz Gallery, Düsseldorf; 1991, *Another Art*, State Tretyakov Gallery, Moscow. He also had solo exhibitions in Moscow and Zurich in 1985, 1988 and 1993.

SOBOLEVSKI, Andrei Petrovich
Russian, 19th century.
Born 1789; died 1867.
Portrait artist.

SÖBORG, Paul
German, 19th century.
Born 22 October 1852, in Berlin.
Painter. Landscapes, architectural views.

Söberg studied under Chr. Wilberg and E. Bracht. He was married to Josephine Söborg-Merz.

SÖBORG-MERZ, Josephine
German, 19th - 20th century.
Born 29 June 1861, in Halberstadt.
Painter. Portraits, genre scenes, landscapes.

Josephine Söborg-Merz was married to Paul Söborg. She was a pupil of Gussow, Skarbina and L. Deschamps.

SOBOROVA, Alexandra
Russian, 20th century.
Poster artist.

Works by Alexandra Soborova were included in the exhibition *Paris-Moscou* held in the Centre Georges Pompidou, Paris, in 1979. She produced posters and decors for propaganda trains.

SOBRE, François Hyacinthe
French, 19th century.
Born 7 March 1793, in Paris.
Sculptor.

The father of Hyacinthe Phileas Sobre, this artist was admitted to the École des Beaux-Arts on 4 October 1821. He was a pupil of Cartellier and exhibited at the Salon between 1827 and 1859.

SOBRE, Hyacinthe Phileas
French, 19th century.
Born 3 February 1826, in Paris; died 9 February 1902, in Paris.
Sculptor.

Son of François Hyacinthe Sobre. Hyacinthe Phileas Sobre was a pupil of Ramey the Younger and Dumont. Was admitted to the École des Beaux-Arts on 2 October 1844 and made his Salon debut in 1850. He won the Prix de Rome in 1851 and an honourable mention in 1858.

SOBREIRA, Gregorio de
Spanish, 17th century.
Active in Orense during the first half of the 17th century.
Painter.

Gregorio de Sobreira worked for churches in Nogueira and Beira.

SOBREMAZAS, Pedro de
Spanish, 16th century.
Active in Valladolid at the end of the 16th century.
Painter.

Around 1590, Pedro de Sobremazas completed an altarpiece in Burgos Cathedral left unfinished by Gregorio Martínez. He also collaborated on the high altar.

SOBRERO, Emilio
Italian, 20th century.
Born 10 December 1890, in Turin; died 1964, in Rome.
Painter, draughtsman, writer. Figures, portraits, landscapes, still-lifes.

A student at the Accademia di Belle Arti in Turin, Emilio Sobrero exhibited in Venice in 1928 and in Turin in 1930. His work, which is variable in quality, includes landscapes, for example *Roman Countryside*, still-lifes in natural light, such as *Objects in a Window*, studies of women including *Toilette*, *Female Nude* and *Woman on a Terrace*, portraits and self-portraits.

AUCTION RECORDS:

ROME, 15 Nov 1988, *Landscape near the Village of Pazzi* (1950, oil on panel, 11 1/2 x 15 3/4 ins / 29 x 40 cm) ITL 1,700,000. ROME, 17 April 1989, *Valtournanche Woods* (1929, oil on panel, 15 3/4 x 12 1/4 ins / 40 x 31 cm) ITL 2,000,000. ROME, 28 Nov 1989, *Lovers* (oil on canvas, 39 1/4 x 55 ins / 100 x 140 cm) ITL 12,500,000. ROME, 25 March 1993, *Nude Figure of a Child* (1940, oil on canvas, 19 3/4 x 25 1/2 ins / 50 x 65 cm) ITL 4,400,000. ROME, 30 Nov 1993, *Sleeping Girl* (1938, oil on canvas, 22 x 29 1/2 ins / 55 x 75 cm) ITL 3,910,000. ROME, 19 April 1994, *Grape Harvest* (1919, oil on canvas, 28 3/4 x 27 1/2 ins / 73 x 70 cm) ITL 5,750,000. ROME, 28 March 1995, *Journey by Night* (1936, oil on canvas, 43 1/4 x 61 ins / 110 x 155 cm) ITL 11,500,000. MILAN, 2 April 1996, *Grape Harvest* (1919, oil on canvas, 80 x 77 1/2 ins / 203 x 197 cm) ITL 8,050,000. ROME, 18 April 2002, *Still-life with Jug* (1923, oil on canvas, 24 x 20 ins / 60 x 50 cm) EUR 2,300.

SOBRERO, Ettore
Italian, 20th century.
Born 7 August 1924, in Turin.
Painter.

The subject of Ettore Sobrero's work is space travel. Painted in acrylic on wood, his compositions use thick materials and an agitated graphism, the rhythm of which evokes the sky and stars. The glowing colours are highlighted with red and blue. He has taken part in many group exhibitions and has held a number of solo exhibitions, including: 1963, Pistoia; 1963, Prato; 1964 and 1971, Turin; 1965, Biella; 1968, Bari; 1969, Venice; 1971, Paris; 1973, Bologna.

BIBLIOGRAPHY:

Gli alti cieli di sobrero, exhibition catalogue, Gal. Sanvitale, Bologna, 1973.

SOBRINO, Cecilia

Maiden name: Morillas or Sicilia y Enriquez de Morillas
Spanish, 16th century.
Born 1538; died 21 October 1581, in Madrid.
Sculptor (wood), painter.

It was said of Cecilia Sobrino that she had a vast knowledge of the different branches of science. She is supposed to have made a number of remarkable terrestrial globes and some geographical maps. Her son José and her daughters Cecilia and Maria were painters.

SOBRINO, Cecilia

Spanish, 17th century.
Died 7 April 1646, in Valladolid.
Painter.

Cecilia Sobrino was the daughter of Cecilia Sobrino née Morillas. She was a member of the Carmelite order where she was known as Cecilia del Nacimiento. She lived at the Carmelite convent in Valladolid and was responsible for some of the convent's decorations.

SOBRINO, Francisco

Spanish, 20th century.
Born 1923 or 1932, in Guadalajara (Castille-La Mancha).
Active in France from 1959.
Painter, sculptor.
Kinetic Art.
GRAV (Groupe de Recherche d'Art Visuel).

Francisco Sobrino lived in Argentina from 1949 to 1958, where he studied at the school of fine art in Buenos Aires. He qualified as a teacher of art and engraving. After exhibiting in Argentina, he was involved in the foundation of the GRAV, where he remained active until its dissolution in 1968.

As a Kinetic artist, Sobrino was the first to use interfering elements in his work: transparent, tinted or opaque materials, Perspex, aluminium or steel, juxtaposed or superimposed so as to enable the viewer to see one element through another, while the movements of the spectator created the apparent displacement of one element from another and modified its relative appearance. In order to emphasise the viewer's participation, Sobrino also created works that could be dismantled and reassembled. Among his best-known works are: *Opposing Rotations* of 1966 to 1967 in Perspex and wood, and *In the Wind*, exhibited at the Paris Biennale in 1967, which required the involvement of the viewing public. Sobrino participated in numerous shows put on by the GRAV group, notably in Spain, Germany, France, Italy, Belgium, Holland and New York.

BIBLIOGRAPHY:

Popper, Frank, *L'Art cinétique*, Gauthier-Villars, Paris, 1970.
Aupetitallot, Yves/Popper, Frank/Hohfeldt, Marion, *GRAV. Groupe de recherche d'art visuel*, Centre d'Art contemporain, Grenoble, 1998.

SOBRINO, José

Spanish, 17th century.
Painter.

José Sobrino was the son of Cecilia Sobrino née Morillas. He was a priest.

SOBRINO, María, or Sobrino y Morillas, religious name: María de San Alberto
Maiden name: Morillas
Spanish, 17th century.
Died 1640, in Valladolid.
Painter (?).

María Sobrino was the daughter of Cecilia Sobrino and was a member of the Carmelite order.

SOBRINO BUHIGAS, Carlos

Spanish, 20th century.
Born 18 March 1885, in Pontevedra (Galicia); died 4 December 1978.
Painter. Religious subjects, genre scenes, landscapes with figures, waterscapes.

Carlos Sobrino Buhigas was a pupil of Alejandro Ferrant and Eliseo Meifren, then continued his studies in London and Paris. He taught at the school of art and crafts in Vigo. He mainly painted genre paintings, women working and scenes from the life of fishermen. He is known, among others, for *Seaside Festival, Muros Fishermen,* and *Village Woman with Cows*. He took part in various collective exhibitions, including: Salon de la Société Nationale des Beaux-Arts de Paris (1908, 1910 and 1915 when he received a third-class medal); Salon Iturriz, Madrid (1913) and Universal Exhibition, Panama (1926).

BIBLIOGRAPHY:

Arnáiz, José Manuel/López Jiménez, Javier/Merchán Díaz, Manuel (ed.), '*Cien años de pintura en Espana y Portugal (1830-1930)*' in vol. X, Antiqvaria, Madrid, 1993.

SOC, John

British, 13th century.
Painter.

A pupil of Master William, he worked in the chapel of Windsor Castle from 1252 to 1253.

SOCARD, Edmond

French, 19th - 20th century.
Born 1 July 1869, in Troyes.
Stained glass painter.

Edmond Socard was the father of Jacques and Tony Socard. He painted stained glass windows for the churches of St-Charles de Paris, Ste-Madeleine de Troyes and Notre-Dame d'Épernay.

SOCARD, Jacques

French, 20th century.
Born 14 December 1903, in Paris.
Stained glass painter.

Jacques Socard was the son of Edmond Socard. He exhibited at the Salon des Artistes Décorateurs in Paris, and received a gold medal in 1925. He produced stained glass windows for the Église Notre-Dame in Épernay.

SOCARD, Tony

French, 20th century.
Born 26 September 1901, in Paris.
Stained glass painter.

Tony Socard was the son of Edmond Socard. He exhibited at the Salon des Artistes Décorateurs in Paris. He was awarded a gold medal in 1925.

SOCCI, Antonio

Italian, 17th century.
Born in Modena; died in Modena, at an early age.
Painter.

Antonio Socci executed works for churches in Modena.

SOCCI, Jacopo

Italian, 17th century.
Active at the beginning of the 17th century.
Sculptor.

The statue of *St John the Baptist* in the baptistery in Settignano is the work of Jacopo Socci.

SOCCORSI, Angelo or Gianangelo, or Soccorso
Italian, 18th century.
Active in Rome c. 1716.
Painter.
Soccorsi painted a picture for the chapel of the Madonna of the Rosary in the church of S Prassede in Rome.

SOCCORSI, Camille
French, 20th century.
Born 21 October 1919, in Bourg-St-Andéol.
Sculptor, painter. Figures, animals.
Camille Soccorsi has spent his working life in Tarascon. He has taken part in many public events, winning awards and regional prizes.

He is best known as a sculptor and a creator of traditional figures designed to be put on show in shops and fairgrounds. He has also produced sculptures of horses and bulls for public spaces in Beaucaire and Mollégès.

SOCHACZEWSKI, Alexander, also known as Sander Leib
Polish, 19th - 20th century.
Born May 1843, in Ilow, near Lowicz; died June 1923, in Vienna.
Painter.
Alexander Sochaczewski studied in Warsaw. He is known for his paintings of political exiles in Siberia, where he spent two years of his life. He was also imprisoned in the Warsaw Citadel.
MUSEUMS AND GALLERIES:
LVIV (Municipal Mus.): *Farewell; Europe!; Self Portrait* (two); 125 other works.

SOCHER, Johann
German, 18th century.
Active in Sonthofen, during the second half of the 18th century.
Sculptor (wood).
Socher carved an altar for the church of Bernbach (Germany) and a tabernacle for the church of Sonthofen in 1794.

SOCHER, Johann. See also **SCHOR Hans**

SOCHET, Auguste
French, 19th century.
Born in Vendeuvre-sur-Barse.
Sculptor.
Sochet was a pupil of Cavalier and made his Salon debut in 1878

SOCHOR, Eduard
Czech, 19th century.
Born 23 September 1802, in Vlcí u Loun.
Architect, painter. Topographical views.
Eduard Sochor studied at the Akademie der Bildenden Künste in Vienna.

SOCHOR, Vaclav
Czech, 19th - 20th century.
Born 7 October 1855, in Obora u Loun; died 23 February 1935, in Prague.
Painter, sculptor.
Vaclav Sochor studied in Prague before going to the Munich School. He exhibited at the Paris Expositions Universelles, winning an honourable mention in 1886 and a silver medal in 1889.

SOCHOS, Antonios
Greek, 20th century.
Born 1880, on Tinos.
Sculptor. Monuments.
Antonios Sochos studied in Athens and Paris. He sculpted monuments. Some of his wood carvings and plaster casts are in the Antonios Sochos Museum on Tinos.

SOCHOS, Lazaros, or Lazare
Greek, 19th - 20th century.
Born 6 January 1862, on Tinos; died 1911, in Athens.
Sculptor. Statues, monuments.
Lazaros Sochos first took drawing lessons from the French master Guillemet in Constantinople (now Istanbul). He then went to Paris, where he worked under Cavelier and Antonin Mercié at the École des Beaux-Arts, and stayed in the city from 1881 to 1901, exhibiting at the Paris Expositions Universelles and winning an honourable mention in 1889 and a gold medal in 1900.

Sochos is known for his monumental statues. He created mausoleums and monuments to the dead in Athens, Constantinople and Paris. His most important work is *Greece Protecting the Antiquities*, which was exhibited in Paris in 1900.

SOCKH, Michael, or Sock or Sockher
Austrian, 17th century.
Died 1615, in Kremnitz (now Kremnica, Slovakia).
Active in Kremnitz.
Medallist.

SOCKL, Sophie
Austrian, 19th century.
Active during the first half of the 19th century.
Painter. Portraits, birds.
Sophie Sockl exhibited in Vienna in 1837.

SOCKL, Theodor Benedikt
Austrian, 19th century.
Born 16 April 1815, in Vienna; died 24 December 1861, in Vienna.
Active in Hermannstadt (Sibiu, Romania) and Vienna.
Painter, art restorer.
Theodor Sockl attended the academy in Vienna.
MUSEUMS AND GALLERIES:
SIBIU (Muz. National Brukenthal): *Portrait of an Unknown Person; Portrait of a Lady; Councillor Friedrich Soterius von Sachsenheim; Mrs Justine Soterius von Sachsenheim; Mrs Klara Soterius von Sachsenheim, née Miller von Milborn.*

SÖCKLER
German, 17th century.
Active in Cologne.
Engraver (burin).
Söckler produced an engraving entitled *The Virgin of Kevelaer* in 1640.

SÖCKLER, Bernhard
German, 18th century.
Born c. 1700; died before 1 April 1767, in Augsburg (Bavaria).
Engraver (burin). Religious subjects, views.
Bernhard Söckler was the father of Johann Michael.

SÖCKLER, Johann Michael
German, 18th century.
Born 9 November 1744, in Augsburg; died 7 April 1781, in Munich.
Engraver (burin). Portraits, religious subjects, views, book illustrations.
Johann Michael was the son of Bernhard Söckler and studied under Franz Xaver Jungwierth.

SOCLET, Arthur Louis
French, 19th century.
Born in Paris.
Painter, watercolourist. Genre scenes, landscapes.
Soclet was a pupil of Ch. Lhullier. Made his Salon debut in 1879.

MUSEUMS AND GALLERIES:
LE HAVRE: *Vauban Quay at le Havre* (watercolour); *Old Fishmarket, le Havre* (gouache).
AUCTION RECORDS:
PARIS, 30 April 1919, *Harlequin's Lunch,* FRF 36.

SOCLUS
5th century BC.
Active in Alopece in Attica.
Sculptor.
Ancient Greek.
Soclus was one of the sculptors working on the pediment of the Erechtheum on the Acropolis in Athens in 408-407 BC.

SOCQUET, or Soqui
French, 18th century.
Painter.
Socquet worked during the second half of the 18th century for the porcelain works of Sèvres, Plymouth, Worcester and Bristol.

SOCQUET, Jeanne
French, 20th century.
Born 24 November 1928, in Paris.
Painter, draughtswoman, watercolourist. Designs for mosaics.
Jeanne Socquet studied drawing, painting and sculpture at classes held by the Ville de Paris. She continued her studies at the Académie de la Grande Chaumière, the free studios at the École des Beaux-Arts in Paris and Souverbie's Académie de la Section d'Or. She visited Spain in 1951. She was active in Paris.

In the early 1960s, Jeanne Socquet began to depict older women; lonely figures on the margins of society who failed to conform to the norms of youth, beauty or wealth. Later, her main interest was the artistic representation of such people in series. Examples of this are; Arms and Vamps (1970), Drag Artists of the Alcazar (1971), Women in Red (1973), Heads and Contorted Faces (1974), Women Bound (1977). A human concern is always strongly present in her work, regardless of its subject. Coloration was an important feature of her work, ranging from monochrome to a process of superimposition and veiling, the end result being a series of delineated shapes. She also produced two series of drawings and paintings produced in psychiatric hospitals depicting madness and incarceration.

She has taken part in collective exhibitions, including; 1959, *Confrontation de la Peinture Italienne et de la Peinture Française* (*Confrontation between Italian and French Painting*), Château de Blois; 1961, *Peintres Français à Teheran* (*French Painters in Tehran*); 1966-1967, Sélection du Salon Comparaisons, Paris. She also showed work at the following Paris salons; Salon de la Jeune Peinture, Salon d'Automne, Salon des Peintres Témoins de leur Temps, Salon Comparaisons, Salon des Réalités Nouvelles. She also showed work at an exhibition entitled, *Painters on the Telephone* in 1985 at the Galerie Pierre Lescot in Paris; and during the 1990s, Groupe 109 in Paris.

She has shown her works in solo exhibitions, including; 1958, 1959, 1962 and 1965, Galerie Dauphine, Paris; 1968, Galerie J.-C. Bellier, Paris; 1969, Galerie St-Placide Jean Rumeau, Paris; 1970, 1971, 1973, 1974 and 1975, Galerie Valérie Schmidt, Paris; 1981 and 1984, Galerie Jacques Massol, Paris; 1981, Galerie Arcadia, Paris. In 1982, Jeanne Socquet's work was shown at the International Contemporary Art Fair in Paris by the Jacques Massol Gallery. Further exhibitions included; 1989, Galerie Pierette Morda, Paris; 1992, Librairie des Océanes, Pornichet; 1993, Galerie Philippe Gand, Paris; 1996, Galerie Béatrice Soulié, Paris. She was awarded the Prix Barbizon in 1963 and the Prix Drouant in 1981.

BIBLIOGRAPHY:
Leenhardt, Jacques, *Connaître la peinture de Jeanne Socquet,* 1986. Cheval, Jean-Claude/Bilot, Alain, '*Entretien avec Jeanne Socquet*' in *Jeanne Socquet,* exhibition catalogue, Librairie des Océanes, Pornichet, 1992.

SOCRATE, Carlo
Italian, 20th century.
Born 12 March 1889, in Mezzana Bigli (Pavia); died 1967, in Rome.
Painter, decorative designer. Figures, landscapes, animals, still-lifes.
A pupil of Giovanni Costetti at the Scuola Libera del Nudo, Carlo Socrate began exhibiting in 1911. In 1914, he settled in Rome. He was involved with a tour of Diaghilev's Ballets Russes as scenery designer.

Stylistically, Socrate moved gradually from a moderate Cubism towards the aesthetic espoused by the journal *Valori Plastici,* which involved a re-evaluation of the painters of the Italian Renaissance; an art that was more Classical than that of the avant-garde. Socrate's work, mainly paintings of figures, also has elements of the mystical realist, particularly in a work like *Ecstasy of St Francis,* in which the figure of the saint is set against a natural background painted with the skill of a landscape artist.

His work was represented in the collective exhibition *De Chirico et la peinture italienne de l'entre-deux guerres* (*De Chirico and Italian Painting of the Interwar Period*) held in Lodève in 2003.

BIBLIOGRAPHY:
Longhi, Roberto, *Storia di Socrate,* Vita artistica, Rome, 1926. Quesada, Mario/Briganti, Giuliano, *Carlo Socrate: opere dal 1910 al 1946,* exhibition catalogue, Nuova Editrice Romana, Rome, 1988. Bonito Oliva, Achille/Iovane, Giovanni/Lista, Giovanni, et al., *De Chirico et la peinture italienne de l'entre-deux guerres,* exhibition catalogue, Musée de Lodève, 2003.

MUSEUMS AND GALLERIES:
ROME (Gal. Nazionale d'Arte Moderna) - ROME (Municipal Mus.).
AUCTION RECORDS:
MILAN, 29 Nov 1966, *Maternity,* ITL 2,800,000. ROME, 23 Nov 1981, *Still-life* (1933, oil on canvas, 18 x 23 1/2 ins / 45.5 x 60 cm) ITL 3,200,000. ROME, 18 May 1983, *Vase of Wild Flowers* (1932, oil on canvas, 23 1/2 x 18 ins / 60 x 45.5 cm) ITL 3,200,000. ROME, 7 April 1988, *Anchovies* (1930, oil on canvas, 9 3/4 x 15 ins / 25 x 38 cm) ITL 7,500,000. ROME, 15 Nov 1988, *Villa Strohl Fern* (oil on canvas, 11 3/4 x 9 3/4 ins / 30 x 25 cm) ITL 5,800,000. ROME, 17 April 1989, *Flora* (1942, oil on canvas, 39 1/4 x 30 1/2 ins / 100 x 77.5 cm) ITL 15,500,000. ROME, 28 Nov 1989, *Piazza del Popolo* (oil on canvas, 11 3/4 x 15 3/4 ins / 30 x 40 cm) ITL 12,000,000. ROME, 10 April 1990, *Still-life with Fish and Artichokes* (1927, oil on panel, 18 3/4 x 23 1/2 ins / 47.5 x 60 cm) ITL 16,500,000. ROME, 12 May 1992, *Female Figure Asleep* (oil on canvas, 11 3/4 x 15 1/2 ins / 30 x 39.5 cm) ITL 11,000,000. ROME, 19 Nov 1992, *Still-life with Green Pears* (oil on card, 11 3/4 x 15 3/4 ins / 30 x 40 cm) ITL 8,500,000. ROME, 8 Nov 1994, *Piazza del Popolo* (oil on canvas, 15 3/4 x 19 3/4 ins / 40 x 50 cm) ITL 7,475,000. ROME, 14 Nov 1995, *Still-life with Musical Instruments* (1965, oil on canvas, 19 3/4 x 27 1/2 ins / 50 x 70 cm) ITL 6,900,000. VENICE, 7-8 Oct 1996, *Female Figure* (oil on canvas, 16 x 11 3/4 ins / 40.5 x 30 cm) ITL 3,455,000. MILAN, 25 March 1997, *View of the Tiber with Castel Sant'Angelo and St Peter's* (oil on canvas, 22 1/4 x 32 ins / 56.5 x 81 cm) ITL 27,960,000. MILAN, 24 Nov 2003, *Double Portrait* (1949, oil on canvas, 31 x 28 ins / 80 x 70 cm) EUR 4,000.

SOCRATES I
5th century BC.
Active during the first half of the 5th century BC.

Sculptor.
Ancient Greek.
Socrates made a statue of the *Mother of the Gods* for a sanctuary at Thebes.

SOCRATES II
5th century BC.
Active in Athens from 470 to 460 BC.
Sculptor.
Ancient Greek.
Socrates worked on the Acropolis. Traditionally, this sculptor was identified with the famous philosopher of the same name.

SOCRATES III
4th century BC.
Painter.
Ancient Greek.
Socrates was a pupil of Pausias.

SOCTANER, Jaime
Spanish, 16th century.
Active at the beginning of the 16th century.
Glass painter.
Jaime Soctaner worked on the stained glass windows of Valencia Cathedral in 1501.

SODAR, André
Belgian, 19th century.
Born 1829; died 1903, in Dinant.
Painter. Landscapes.

SODAR, Franz
Belgian, 19th century.
Born 1827, in Dinant-sur-Meuse; died January 1900, in Assisi, Italy.
Painter. Historical subjects, religious subjects, portraits, genre scenes, landscapes, architectural views.
Franz Sodar was a painter of historical subjects and portraits at the start of his career, but he then devoted himself to sacred art. He travelled to Palestine, from where he brought back studies of the holy places for canvases which he painted at Assisi. He received the gold medal of Christian artists from Pope Leo XIII.

SODE, Charlotte or Caroline Charlotte
Danish, 19th - 20th century.
Born 16 April 1859, in Vævergård (Bornholm); died 5 December 1931, in Copenhagen.
Painter. Portraits, genre scenes, flowers.
Charlotte Sode lived and worked in Copenhagen, where she taught drawing and painting.

SODEMANN, Karl
German, 20th century.
Born 10 February 1888, in Berlin.
Painter, engraver. Landscapes.
Karl Sodemann lived and worked in Kieselbach.

SODEN, John Edward
British, 19th century.
Painter. Genre scenes.
John Edward Soden exhibited his work in London from 1861 until 1887.
AUCTION RECORDS:
LONDON, 7 June 1995, *Wrong Note* (oil on panel, 15 3/4 x 20 ins / 40 x 51 cm) GBP 2,990. LONDON, 3 Dec 2002, *Smoking by the Fireside* (1862, oil on paper on canvas, 12 x 14 ins / 30 x 35 cm) GBP 1,200.

SODEN, Susannah
British, 19th century.
Born in Broerston.
Active during the second half of the 19th century.
Painter. Flowers, fruit.
Susannah Soden exhibited her work in London from 1866 until 1890.

SODER, Alfred
Swiss, 20th century.
Born 18 July 1880, in Basel.
Engraver, lithographer.
Alfred Soder studied at the fine arts academy in Munich and under J. Herterich and P. Halm. He was an etcher known principally for his *ex libris* designs.

SÖDERBERG, Gustaf or Gösta
Swedish, 19th century.
Born 8 April 1799, in Norrköping; died 3 November 1875, in Stockholm.
Painter, lithographer. Landscapes, figures.
Söderberg studied in France and Italy, and was an officer. He painted views of Stockholm and of the castles of the King of Sweden. In 2001, several of his landscapes were included in the exhibition *Un Paese incantato. Italia dipinta da Thomas Jones a Corot* (*An Enchanted Country. Italy Depicted by Artists from Thomas Jones to Corot*), at the Centro Internazionale d'Arte e di Cultura di Palazzo Te, in Mantua.
BIBLIOGRAPHY:
Ottani Cavina, Anna (ed.), *Un Paese incantato. Italia dipinta da Thomas Jones a Corot*, exhibition catalogue, Electa, Milan, 2001.
MUSEUMS AND GALLERIES:
STOCKHOLM (Nationalmus.): *View of Vesuvius From the Bridge of San Gennaro in Naples* (oil on paper); *Rome, From the Campidoglio*.

SÖDERBERG, P.
Swedish, 18th century.
Active in Stockholm during the second half of the 18th century.
Sculptor (wood).
Söderberg sculpted for the Adolf Frederik church in Stockholm, from 1773 until 1774.

SÖDERDAHL, Olof
Swedish, 18th century.
Sculptor (wood).
Söderdahl sculpted a chair for the Ekeby church in 1741.

SODERINI, Antonio
Italian, 17th century.
Painter.
Soderini painted the altarpiece depicting the *Death of St Joseph* in the church of S Piero in Gattolino.

SODERINI, Francesco
Italian, 17th - 18th century.
Born 1673; died 1735.
Active in Florence.
Painter.
Francesco Soderini, the father of Mauro Soderini and pupil of A. Gherardini, painted altarpieces for churches in Florence.

SODERINI, Mauro
Italian, 18th century.
Born 15 January 1704, in Florence; died after 1739.
Painter. History painting.
Mauro Soderini was the pupil of G.G. del Sole. His painting of the *Miracle of St Zenobius* can be seen in the church of S Stefano in Florence.

SÖDERLUND, Charles or Carl Gustaf
Swedish, 19th - 20th century.
Born 8 January 1860, in Stockholm.
Engraver.
Charles Söderlund studied under Courtry and Cormon. He engraved works by Rembrandt and Vermeer. He exhibited

in Paris, where he secured an honourable mention in 1894 and a silver medal at the Exposition Universelle of 1900.

SÖDERMAN, Anders
Swedish, 18th century.
Active in Stockholm at the beginning of the 18th century.
Painter.

Söderman executed paintings on wood for the Häverö church.

SÖDERMAN, Carl August
Swedish, 19th century.
Born 26 August 1835, in Örebro; died 22 April 1907, in Stockholm.
Sculptor.

Carl Söderman was a pupil at the Kungliga Akademi för de Fria Konsterna in Stockholm. He sculpted busts and medallions.

SÖDERMARK, Johan Olaf or Olaf Johan
Swedish, 19th century.
Born 11 May 1790, in Landskrona; died 15 October 1848, in Stockholm.
Painter. Portraits, genre scenes.

An officer in the Swedish army until 1819, Södermark fought in several military campaigns. He left the army in 1819 and went to study in Munich and Rome. He met with great success. His last work was a portrait of the celebrated singer, *Jenny Lind*.

BIBLIOGRAPHY:

Loostrom, L., *Olaf Johan Sodermark*, monograph, Loostroom and Komp, Stockholm, 1879. C. Laurin, et al., *Scandinavian Art*, American-Scandinavian Foundation, New York, 1922. Kent, N., *The Triumph of Light and Nature: Nordic Art 1740-1940*, monograph, Thames and Hudson, London, 1987.

MUSEUMS AND GALLERIES:

GÖTEBORG: *Greek; The Painter Hj. Mörner* - NORRKÖPING: *Roman Woman* - ÖREBRO: *Counsellor C. J. af Nordin* - STOCKHOLM: *The Artist's Father* (medallion); *Grazia; The Painter Franz Riepenhausen; A. van Hartmanskork; Caroline Bygler, Model of the Sculptor Bystrom* - VERSAILLES: *The Writer Henri Beyle, Known as Stendhal.*

AUCTION RECORDS:

LONDON, 19 Nov 1969, *Portrait of Jenny Lind*, GBP 2,000. AMSTERDAM, 19 Sept 1989, *Two Young Italian Women Talking on a Terrace* (1839, oil on canvas, 30¼ x 37½ ins / 77 x 95 cm) NLG 8,625.

SÖDERMARK, Per or Johan Per
Swedish, 19th century.
Born 3 June 1822, in Mossebo, near Karlsberg; died 26 November 1889, in Stockholm.
Painter. Military subjects, portraits.

Södermark was the son of Johan Olaf Södermark. He became a soldier but abandoned a career in the army to accompany his father to Italy in 1845. He then became a pupil at the Kungliga Akademi för de Fria Konsterna in Stockholm and in Düsseldorf, as well as of Couture in Paris. He was elected into the Kungliga Akademi för de Fria Konsterna in Stockholm in 1874. His *Portrait of the Painter W. Hohnberg* is in the Ateneumin Taidemuseo in Helsinki.

SODINI, Dante
Italian, 19th - 20th century.
Born 29 August 1858, in Florence; died 31 December 1934, in Florence.
Sculptor, decorative designer. Religious subjects. Busts.

Dante Sodini was involved in the decoration of the cathedral in Florence and sculpted a large number of busts. His work was exhibited at the Expositions in Paris and he was awarded a gold medal at the Exposition Universelle of 1889.

MUSEUMS AND GALLERIES:

ROME (Gal. Nazionale d'Arte Moderna): *Faith.*

SODOMA, IL, real name: Bazzi Giovanni Antonio
Italian, 16th century.
Born 1477, in Vercelli (Piedmont); died 15 February 1549, in Siena.
Painter, fresco artist. Religious subjects, mythological subjects, portraits.
Lombard School, School of Rome.

Although later he claimed to belong to the noble Tizzoni family of Piedmont, Bazzi, known as Il Sodoma, was in reality the eldest son of a shoemaker. He was apprenticed for a term of seven years in 28 November 1490 to a stained glass maker of Casale, Martino Spanzotti. At the end of this period, he went to Milan. Although there is no evidence to prove that he was the pupil of Leonardo da Vinci, he was certainly influenced by Leonardo's work. He was summoned to Siena in about 1500 by the Spannocchi family of rich Sienese merchants. Siena was to become the main centre of Bazzi's career. Attributed to this period is *The Deposition*, now in the Accademia in Siena but painted for the church of S Francesco. He also decorated the convent of S Anna in Creta near Pienza with frescoes representing the miracle of the loaves and fishes. In 1505, he was asked to complete the frescoes in the convent of Monte Oliveto begun by Luca Signorelli and showing scenes from the *Life of St Benedict*. The highly imaginative elements that he introduced into some of his compositions earned him the nickname of *Il Maltaccio* (The Eccentric). In 1507, Julius II summoned him to Rome to assist in the decoration of the Vatican. He painted, in particular, the ceiling of the Camera della Signatura, later partly repainted by Raphael. In 1515, after a period in Siena, Bazzi returned to Rome and, for the rich banker Agostino Chigi, painted frescoes portraying the *Life of Alexander* in the Villa Farnesina, the most famous of which is that of the *Wedding of Roxana and Alexander* painted in a Renaissance style emphasised by the presence of nudes and cupids. Back in Siena once more, in 1517 he painted a *Flagellation* for the convent of S Francesco, a fragment of which is preserved in the gallery in Siena. In 1518, together with Girolamo del Pacchia and Domenico Beccafumi, he worked on the decoration of the Oratorio di San Bernardino. His contribution was three scenes from the life of the Virgin: *The Presentation in the Temple, The Visitation* and *The Assumption*. Other works worth mentioning include an *Adoration of the Magi* and *The Death of Lucretia*, a painting presented to Leo X and for which Bazzi was ennobled. He is thought to have returned to work in Lombardy between 1518 and 1525. Later we find in Siena again, now painting the famous fresco of the *Life of St Catherine*. In the following years he was to enjoy great renown. Unfortunately, despite all his labours and perhaps because of his character, his career ended less gloriously and he died very poor. It is generally thought that Vasari's description of Bazzi's vices is exaggerated. He was, rather, an eccentric. Vasari's views that he was an artist without talent are contradicted by the evidence of his surviving works.

BIBLIOGRAPHY:

Hauvette, H., *Le Sodoma*, H. Laurens, Paris, 1911. Hayum, W., *Giovanni Antonio Bazzi, 'il Sodoma*, New York, 1976. Loseries, W., *'Sodoma's Holy Family in Baltamore: The 'Lost' Arduini Tondo'* in *Burlington Magazine*, vol 136, 1994. Zambrano, P., *'A New Scene by Sodoma from the Ceiling of Palazzo Chigi at Casato di Sotto, Siena'* in *Burlington Magazine*, vol 136, 1994.

MUSEUMS AND GALLERIES:

BERGAMO: *Madonna* - BERLIN: *Charity; St Catherine* - BONN: *Christ Crowned with Thorns* - BUDAPEST: *Flagellation* - CHIUSURE (Abbazia di Monte Oliveto Maggiore): *Scenes of St Benoit's Life* (1505-1508, frescoes) - FLORENCE: *Portrait of a*

Man; Arrest of Christ - FLORENCE (Palazzo Pitti): *Banner with the Virgin and St Sebastian; Self-portrait; Ecce Homo* - HANOVER: *Virgin and Child* - LILLE: *Eternal Father* - LONDON (NG): *The Madonna and Child with Sts Peter and Catherine of Siena and a Carthusian Donor* (1540-1549, oil/wood); *Head of Christ* (c. 1525-1550, oil/wood, attributed) - MILAN (Municipal Mus.): *St Michael* - MILAN (Mus. Poldi Pezzoli): *Madonna and Child with the Lamb* - MILAN (Pinacoteca di Brera): *Madonna and Child* - MONTEPULCIANO (Pinacoteca P.F. Crociani): *Holy Family* - MONTPELLIER (Mus. Fabre): *Virgin and Child with St John* - MUNICH: *Head of the Archangel Michael; Virgin and Child Seated beneath a Red Canopy* - NANCY: *Deposition* - NAPLES (Mus. di Capodimonte): *Resurrection* - NEW YORK (Metropolitan Mus. of Art): *Mars and Venus in Vulcan's Net* - PARIS (Louvre): *Love and Chastity* - PISA (Mus. Civico): *Madonna and Saints* - ROME (Mus. e Gal. Borghese): *Holy Family; Virgin with the Dead Christ in her Lap* - SIENA: *Christ on the Mount of Olives; Christ's Descent into Limbo; St Bernard Tolomei; Resurrection; Deposition; Adoration of the Christ Child; Holy Family; Judith* - STOCKHOLM: *Pietà* - STRASBOURG: *Holy Family* - TURIN: *Holy Family; Madonna and Saints; Death of Lucretia* - VERCELLI: *Adoration of the Christ Child* - VIENNA: *Holy Family; Apollo and Daphne; Group of Three figures*.

AUCTION RECORDS:

PARIS, 1876, *Deposition*, FRF 5,200. NEW YORK, 1909, *Judgement of Paris*, USD 180. LONDON, 11 April 1924, *Holy Family*, GBP 73. LONDON, 15 July 1927, *Holy Family*, GBP 819. PARIS, 21 and 22 May 1928, *Virgin and Child with St Joseph and St John*, FRF 28,000. NEW YORK, 27 and 28 March 1930, *Christ at the Column*, USD 500. LONDON, 26 Nov 1958, *Holy Family with St Clare*, GBP 700. LONDON, 8 July 1959, *Holy Family with St Clare*, GBP 400. LONDON, 8 Dec 1972, *Virgin and Child*, Gns 17,000. NEW YORK, 4 April 1973, *Crucifixion*, USD 4,000. NEW YORK, 10 Jan 1980, *Holy Family with St John the Baptist in a Landscape* (oil on panel, diam. 30 ins / 76.2 cm) USD 36,000. NEW YORK, 16 Jan 1985, *Christ Carrying the Cross (recto)* (pen and wash heightened with white/outline in black chalk); *Resurrection (verso)* (pen and brown ink heightened with white/outline in black chalk, ochre paper, 7 1/2 x 8 1/2 ins / 18.8 x 21.5 cm) USD 20,000. LONDON, 11 Dec 1985, *Holy Family with the Infant St John the Baptist in a Landscape* (oil on panel, round, diam 30 ins / 76.2 cm) GBP 20,000. MONTE CARLO, 20 June 1987, *Head of a Man Looking to the Left* (black chalk and red chalk, 12 1/4 x 8 ins / 31.1 x 20.1 cm) FRF 800,000. LONDON, 6 July 1994, *Mars and Venus Ensnared by Vulcan* (oil on canvas, 12 x 27 ins / 30.5 x 68.7 cm) GBP 23,000. COLOGNE, 29 June 2000, *Apostles' Farewell* (oil on canvas, 48 x 32 ins / 122 x 81 cm) DEM 70,000. VENICE, 9 Feb 2002, *Holy Family* (oil on board, oval, 26 x 25 ins / 66 x 64 cm) EUR 17,000.

SODRE, Adir

Brazilian, 20th century.
Painter.

Adir Sodre lived and worked in the Mato Grosso. He painted vigorous Still-lifes.

SØDRING, Frederik Hansen

Danish, 19th century.
Born 31 May 1809, in Aalborg; died 18 April 1862, in Lille Mariendal, near Hellerup.
Painter, watercolourist. Landscapes, waterscapes.

Sødring studied at the Kunstakademi in Copenhagen and with J. P. Møller.

MUSEUMS AND GALLERIES:

AARHUS - COPENHAGEN.

AUCTION RECORDS:

COPENHAGEN, 24 Nov 1979, *A Street in Copenhagen* (1839, oil on canvas, 9 1/2 x 12 1/2 ins / 24 x 32 cm) DKK 9,500. COPENHAGEN, 9 Nov 1983, *Damhusseon* (1828, oil on canvas, 20 x 24 3/4 ins / 51 x 63 cm) DKK 29,000. COPENHAGEN, 12 Nov 1986, *Landscape* (1829, oil on canvas, 26 3/4 x 41 3/4 ins / 68 x 106 cm) DKK 105,000. COPENHAGEN, 25 Oct 1989, *Boat on a Pond* (1843, oil on canvas, 12 1/4 x 17 1/4 ins / 31 x 44 cm) DKK 34,000. COPENHAGEN, 6 Dec 1990, *Nordic Landscape with Chalets by a Fjord* (1857, oil on canvas, 37 1/2 x 61 1/2 ins / 95 x 156 cm) DKK 40,000. COPENHAGEN, 6 March 1991, *Panorama of the Environs of Christiania (Oslo) in Norway* (1833, oil on canvas, 22 3/4 x 37 1/2 ins / 58 x 95 cm) DKK 28,000. COPENHAGEN, 10 Feb 1993, *Norwegian Landscape with Trees and Rocks* (1841, oil on canvas, 12 1/4 x 22 ins / 31 x 56 cm) DKK 5,000. COPENHAGEN, 16 Nov 1994, *Boat on a Pond in the Forest in Summer* (1847, oil on canvas, 11 3/4 x 17 1/4 ins / 30 x 44 cm) DKK 18,000. COPENHAGEN, 23 May 1996, *Castle in Ruins* (1833, oil on canvas, 15 x 23 1/2 ins / 38 x 60 cm) DKK 23,000. COPENHAGEN, 10-12 Sept 1997, *Chapel* (1837, watercolour, 12 3/4 x 19 ins / 32.5 x 48 cm) DKK 17,000. COPENHAGEN, 2 March 1999, *Landscape with Horse and Cart Crossing Bridge, Dramatic Sky* (1833, oil on canvas, 8 x 12 ins / 20 x 31 cm) DKK 11,500. COPENHAGEN, 31 Aug 1999, *Sunshine Breaking Through Clouds* (1833, oil on canvas, 8 x 12 ins / 20 x 30 cm) DKK 16,000. COPENHAGEN, 31 Aug 1999, *Landscape from Lilleland in Telemark, Norway* (1834, oil on canvas, 24 x 37 ins / 60 x 93 cm) DKK 34,000. HAMBURG, 7 June 2000, *Siebengebirge am Rhein* (1840, oil on canvas, 14 x 24 ins / 35 x 62 cm) DEM 17,000. COPENHAGEN, 6 Sept 2000, *Shepherdess with Sheep in Rocky Landscape with River* (1831, oil on canvas, 20 x 31 ins / 50 x 80 cm) DKK 70,000. COPENHAGEN, 3 Sept 2001, *Norwegian Landscape with Sawmill by Waterfall* (oil on canvas, 10 x 10 ins / 26 x 25 cm) DKK 30,000. COPENHAGEN, 27 Nov 2001, *From Marmorpladsen - Mattresses being Aired in the Sunshine* (oil on canvas, 19 x 19 ins / 49 x 48 cm) DKK 45,000. COPENHAGEN, 27 Aug 2002, *Romantic Landscape with Young Traveller Resting* (oil on canvas, 16 x 24 ins / 41 x 61 cm) DKK 40,000.

SØDRING, Henriette Marie

Maiden name: de Bang
Danish, 19th century.
Born 17 October 1809, in Sparresholm; died 6 November 1855, in Lille Mariendal, near Hellerup.
Landscape artist.

Henriette Marie Sødring was the wife of Frederik Hansen Sødring. Her romantic landscapes are currently in Sparresholm castle.

SOE, Engelbert op der

German, 16th century.
Active during the first half of the 16th century.
Sculptor (wood).

In 1521 Soe carved the stalls in the former Dominican church of Dortmund.

SØEBORG, Axel

Danish, 20th century.
Born 22 November 1872, in Viborg; died 20 June 1939, in Silkeborg.
Painter. Portraits, landscapes, still-lifes.

Axel Søeborg studied under L. Tuxen and P.A. Schou at the Kongelige Danske Kunstakademi in Copenhagen.

MUSEUMS AND GALLERIES:

AABENRAA - AALBORG.

AUCTION RECORDS:

COPENHAGEN, 26 Feb 1976, *Interior with Woman Knitting* (1916, oil on canvas, 19 1/4 x 20 1/2 ins / 49 x 52 cm) DKK 3,000.

SØEBORG, Knud Christian

Danish, 19th - 20th century.
Born 31 May 1861, in Viborg; died 4 September 1906, in Frederiksberg.
Painter, illustrator. Portraits, interiors with figures.

Knud Christian Søeborg was the brother of Axel Søeborg. He studied at the Kongelige Akademiet for de Skønne Kunster in Copenhagen and went on to work as an illustrator on art periodicals.

Auction records:

London, 24 March 1988, *Reading next to the Table* (1891, oil on canvas, 16 x 13 ins / 40.8 x 33 cm) GBP 2,200.

SOEDA, Toshiko
Japanese, 20th century.
Born in Hamacho (Nihonbashi).
Painter.

Toshiko Soeda studied print making under Yoshitoshi Mori. She works in a traditional spirit, yet with her own personal style, introducing spontaneous, coloured abstract figures. Now working in textiles, she has pioneered the combination of traditional and modern techniques. During the 1970s she took part in the Japan-France exhibitions held in the Grand Palais, Paris. She has also shown her work in solo exhibitions, such as at the galerie Marcel Bernheim, Paris, in 1981.

SOEDER, August
German, 20th century.
Born 21 November 1892, in Darmstadt.
Painter. Portraits, landscapes, industrial landscapes.

August Soeder studied in Darmstadt and Munich and also worked as an architect.

SOEFFRENS, Nicolas
Latvian, 17th - 18th century.
Born 4 June 1662, in Windau; died 5 August 1710, in Windau.
Sculptor (wood).

Soeffrens carved a lavishly decorated altar for the church of St Anne of Libau (Latvia), as well as altars and pulpits for churches in Courlande (Kurzeme), Latvia.

SOEHLKE
German, 18th century.
Active in Hamburg, c. 1725.
Painter.

Soehlke mainly painted theatre sets.

SOEHNITZ, M.
German, 19th century.
Born 1811, in Dresden; died 1870, in Dresden.
Medallist, cameo engraver.

Soehnitz engraved medals bearing the image of King *Frederick August II of Saxony* and the poet *Ch. A. Tiedge*.

SOELDTNER, Erasmus
German, 18th century.
Born c. 1715; died after 1785.
Active in Munich.
Miniaturist.

Soeldtner also painted coats of arms and certificates.

SOELLNER, Oscar Daniel
American, 20th century.
Born 8 April 1890, in Chicago; died 1952.
Painter, engraver.

Oscar Daniel Soellner was a member of the American Federation of the Arts and the American Artists Professional League.

SOEMEREN, Barent van. See **SOMER Bernard** or **Barent van**

SOEMMERING, Margaretha. See **GRUNELIUS Margaretha**

SOEN, nickname: Josui (or Nyosui)
Japanese, 15th century.
Active in Kamakura at the end of the 15th century.
Monk-painter.

A monk-painter at the Enkaku-ji temple, Kamakura, Soen was a disciple of Sesshu (1420-1506) and worked for many years in his studio, only returning to his own temple in 1495. He is one of the *suiboku* (ink) painters of the Muromachi period.

SOENS, Eric van
Belgian, 20th century.
Born 1939, in Ixelles (Brussels).
Painter, draughtsman. Figures, landscapes, architectural views. Murals.

Eric van Soens started painting in 1960 after attending the Ixelles and Molenbeek academies. He paints in a typically Flemish mode, notably architectural interiors and imaginary cathedrals, almost invariably from an unusual perspective and with lightly outlined figures. He has exhibited solo on several occasions, most notably at the Centre Artistique in Tournai in 1967; the Westrand cultural centre in Dilbeek in 1978; the Hutse gallery in Brussels in 1979, 1982, 1984, 1986, 1990 and 1994; the Oasis cultural centre in Brussels-Evere in 2001; and the Abbaye de Forest in Brussels in 2004.

Bibliography:

Coune, Dominique, *'Rêve, délire et fantaisie avec le Bruxellois Éric Van Soens'* in *La Meuse*, 15 October 2002.

SOENS, Jan or Hans, or Saens or Sonsis, called il Flammingo
Flemish School, 16th - 17th century.
Born 1547 or 1548, in s' Hertogenbosch; died 1611 or 1614, in Parma or in Cremona.
Active in Italy.
Painter, fresco artist. Religious subjects, mythological subjects, landscapes.

Soens was first a pupil of Jakob Bron, then of Gillis Mostaert in Antwerp. He worked in Rome for Pope Gregory XIII about 1575 and went to Parma in 1580 with Alessandro Farnese, whose successor, Rannuccio I, appointed him Court Painter. He was in Parma in 1581, when he decorated the organs of the Steccato and the Palazzo del Giardino. He settled in Cremona in about 1600. His landscapes show the influence of the Bril brothers and also of Correggio. Towards the end of his life he seems to have responded to Emilian Mannerism.

Museums and Galleries:

Naples: *Christ on the Mount of Olives; Ascension; Poseidon and Amphitrite; Pan and Silenus; Jupiter and Antiope; Cybele, Cronus and Phylira* - Parma (Gal. Nazionale): *Resurrection; Story of the Creation* (six paintings) - Valenciennes: *Ceres and the Nymph Cyane; The Rape of Proserpina.*

Auction records:

Brussels, 8 Dec 1966, *Orpheus Enchanting the Animals,* BEF 55,000. Vienna, 18 June 1968, *Noah's Ark,* ATS 55,000. Brussels, 28 Oct 1969, *The Earthly Paradise,* BEF 180,000. London, 10 Dec 1982, *Behold the Lamb of God* (oil on canvas, 36 1/2 x 35 1/2 ins / 92.8 x 90.1 cm) GBP 3,200. London, 24 April 1988, *Meeting of Christ and St John the Baptist* (oil on canvas, 35 x 35 ins / 88 x 88 cm) GBP 9,900. Milan, 13 Dec 1989, *Virgin and Child* (oil on panel, 15 x 10 3/4 ins / 38 x 27.5 cm) ITL 24,000,000. London, 8 Dec 1993, *St Jerome in a Wooded River Landscape* (oil on canvas, 28 1/2 x 36 1/2 ins / 72.2 x 92.7 cm) GBP 11,500.

SOER, Christiaan, called Chris
Dutch, 20th century.
Born 1882; died 1961.
Painter. Landscapes with figures, waterscapes, urban landscapes.

Auction records:

Amsterdam, 5-6 Feb 1991, *Peasant Woman in a Garden in Summer* (oil on card, 7 3/4 x 10 ins / 19.5 x 24.5 cm) NLG 1,610. Amsterdam, 18 Feb 1992, *River Landscape with a Peasant in a Boat Moored near a Field* (oil on canvas, 16 1/4 x 23 1/2 ins /

41 x 60 cm) USD 2,185. AMSTERDAM, 11 Feb 1993, *Canal View, Bruges (?)* (oil on canvas, 15 3/4 x 11 3/4 ins / 40 x 30 cm) NLG 1,380. AMSTERDAM, 14 June 1994, *Farm* (oil on canvas, 23 1/2 x 31 1/2 ins / 60 x 80 cm) NLG 1,150. AMSTERDAM, 18 June 1996, *Flower Market* (oil on canvas, 15 3/4 x 19 3/4 ins / 40 x 50 cm) NLG 1,495. AMSTERDAM, 2 Sept 1997, *Moonlit Landscape with Poplars and Shrubs* (oil on canvas, 10 x 17 3/4 ins / 25.5 x 45 cm) NLG 1,729. AMSTERDAM, 21 Jan 1998, *View of Scheveningen* (oil on canvas, 9 3/4 x 7 1/4 ins / 25 x 18.5 cm) NLG 2,537. AMSTERDAM, 19 Jan 1999, *The Wynhaven, Dordrecht* (oil on canvas, 24 x 39 ins / 62 x 100 cm) NLG 7,000. AMSTERDAM, 19 April 2000, *The Weststraat in Winter, Brussels* (oil on canvas, 24 x 20 ins / 60 x 50 cm) NLG 7,700. GRAVENHAGE, 24 April 2002, *Farmer's Wife in Farmyard with Geraniums* (oil on canvas, 15 x 19 ins / 39 x 49 cm) EUR 2,000. GRAVENHAGE, 7 May 2003, *View of Bruges in the Winter* (oil on canvas, 23 x 34 ins / 59 x 87 cm) EUR 3,200. GRAVENHAGE, 12 May 2004, *View of the Town of The Hague* (oil on canvas, 15 x 11 ins / 39 x 29 cm) EUR 4,800. GRAVENHAGE, 12 May 2004, *View of the Town of The Hague with The Hague Post Office* (oil on canvas, 15 x 11 ins / 39 x 29 cm) EUR 5,000.

SOEREN, Gerrit Jacobus van

Dutch, 19th century.

Born 20 June 1859, in Amsterdam; died 9 March 1888, in Amsterdam.

Painter. Genre scenes, animals.

MUSEUMS AND GALLERIES:

AMSTERDAM: *Scourge of the Land (Monkeys in a Cage).*

SOERENSEN. See **SORENSEN**

SOEST, Aert Willemsz. van

Dutch, 17th century.

Active in Soest 1611-1627.

Painter.

Aert Willemsz. van Soest was a member of the guild of St Luke in Utrecht in 1611.

SOEST, Conrad von. See **CONRAD VON SOEST**

SOEST, Franciscus van

Flemish School, 17th - 18th century.

Active in Antwerp 1689-1722.

Illuminator.

SOEST, Gerard van, or Soeste or Zoest or Zoust

British, 17th century.

Born 1637, in Westphalia, c. 1600 in Soest, near Utrecht, according to some sources; died 11 February 1681, in London.

Painter. Portraits.

Gerard van Soest is traditionally said to have come from Soest in Westphalia, though some sources state he was almost certainly Dutch by birth and training. He probably came to London in the late 1640s and his earliest works show the influence of William Dobson. Unlike Lely, Soest painted his sitters in contemporary dress and also paid great attention to their hands. John Riley was a pupil of Soest's.

BIBLIOGRAPHY:

Talley, M.K., *Portrait Painting in England: Studies in the Technical Literature before 1700,* Paul Mellon Center for Studies in British Art, New Haven, 1981. MacLeod, Catharine/Marciari Alexander, Julia/Sharpe, Kevin/Dethloff, Diana/Wynne, Sonya, *Painted Ladies. Women at the Court of Charles II,* exhibition catalogue, National Portrait Gall., London, 2001.

MUSEUMS AND GALLERIES:

EDINBURGH (National Portrait Gallery): *Marquess of Tweeddale* - LONDON (Dulwich Picture Gal.): *Aubre de Vere, 20th Earl of Oxford* - LONDON (National Portrait Gal.): attributed*Unknown Man, Formerly Thought to be Sir Henry Vane the Younger* (c. 1650, oil on canvas); *Thomas Stanley* (1660, oil on canvas); *Samuel Butler* (1670s, oil on canvas); *Unknown Man, Formerly Thought to be Thomas Blood* (1670s, oil on canvas) - LONDON (Tate Collection): on loan from the National Portrait Gallery since 1958*Portrait of a Lady as a Shepherdess* (c. 1670, oil on canvas); *Portrait of a Gentleman with a Dog, Probably Sir Thomas Tipping* (c. 1660, oil on canvas); *Double Portrait of Viscount Fairfax and his Wife* (1645-1648, oil on canvas, on loan from the National Portrait Gallery since 1976).

AUCTION RECORDS:

LONDON, 26 Feb 1910, *Portrait of a Girl,* GBP 54. LONDON, 19 Nov 1910, *William Chiffuch, Page to Charles II,* GBP 31. LONDON, 16 May 1924, *The Earl of Pembroke,* GBP 294. LONDON, 15 June 1928, *Portrait of a Gentleman,* GBP 94. LONDON, 13 July 1945, *Portrait of a Child,* GBP 126. LONDON, 17 Nov 1967, *Lord John Hay and the Marquess of Tweedale as Boys,* Gns 3,800. LONDON, 24 Nov 1972, *Monsieur de Grand Pré at 27,* Gns 1,000. LONDON, 27 June 1980, *Portrait of a Young Gentleman* (oil on canvas, 32 1/2 x 24 1/4 ins / 82.5 x 61.5 cm) GBP 800. LONDON, 14 March 1984, *Portrait of an Officer, Possibly Sir Ralph Hare, 1st Bt of Stow Bardolf, Norfolk* (1637, oil on canvas, 56 x 44 ins / 142 x 112 cm) GBP 5,000. LONDON, 20 Nov 1985, *Portrait of Mr Tipping* (c. 1655, oil on canvas, 37 x 45 1/4 ins / 94 x 115 cm) GBP 16,000. LONDON, 29 Jan 1988, *Portrait of a Lady in a Grey Dress* (oil on canvas, 29 1/2 x 24 1/2 ins / 75 x 62.5 cm) GBP 770. LONDON, 20 April 1990, *Portrait of a Gentleman, Thought to be Constantin Lyttleton, in Armour, with his Wife in a Blue Dress and Orange Stole* (oil on canvas, a pair oval, 30 x 26 ins / 76.5 x 66.2 cm and 30 x 25 ins/76.5 x 63.5 cm) GBP 11,000. LONDON, 24 Nov 1999, *Portrait of Admiral Sir John Pennington, Wearing a Breastplate* (oil on canvas, 29 x 24 ins / 73 x 61 cm) GBP 9,000. LONDON, 22 March 2000, *Portrait of Captain Robert Hartland* (oil on canvas, painted cartouche, 30 x 25 ins / 76 x 64 cm) GBP 5,800. NEW YORK, 19 Oct 2000, *Portrait of Dame Ann Robinson* (oil on canvas, 29 x 24 ins / 73 x 62 cm) USD 4,500. PORTSMOUTH, 3 Nov 2001, *Portrait of a Girl* (c. 1670, oil on canvas, 30 x 25 ins / 76 x 64 cm) USD 3,800. LONDON, 25 Nov 2003, *Double Portrait of a Lady and her Son with his Arm Resting on a Hound, in a Landscape* (oil on canvas, 57 x 48 ins / 146 x 121 cm) GBP 10,000. LONDON, 13 Oct 2004, *Portrait of a Gentleman, said to be James Usher* (oil on canvas, 15 x 12 ins / 39 x 30 cm) GBP 1,500.

SOEST, Johann Wilhelm

German, 17th century.

Active in Cologne, 1628-1647.

Painter.

SOEST, Louis Willem van

Dutch, 19th - 20th century.

Born 5 April 1867, in Purworejo (Java); died 1948.

Painter. Landscapes with figures, landscapes.

Louis Willem van Soest was a self-taught artist who quickly emerged as one of the best Dutch modernists. He lived and worked in The Hague. He should probably be attributed with a painting in Munich museum of *Winter* by a Willem van Soest. He secured a medal in Brussels and a silver medal in Paris at the Exposition Universelle of 1900.

MUSEUMS AND GALLERIES:

MONTREAL: *Winter in Holland* - PARIS (Louvre): *Winter Morning.*

AUCTION RECORDS:

PARIS, 16 Dec 1927, *Fisherman Tying Up his Boat* (watercolour) FRF 170. LONDON, 5 Oct 1979, *Town View in Winter* (oil on canvas, 23 1/4 x 27 1/4 ins / 59 x 69 cm) GBP 600. AMSTERDAM, 5 June 1990, *Autumn* (oil on canvas, 31 1/2 x 43 1/4 ins / 80 x 110 cm) NLG 3,220. AMSTERDAM, 17 Sept 1991, *Stream in a Forest in Winter* (1910, oil on canvas, 25 3/4 x 23 3/4 ins / 65.5 x 60.5 cm) NLG 2,760. AMSTERDAM, 21 April 1993, *Village by a River in Winter* (oil on canvas, 26 x 30 1/2 ins / 66 x 77.5 cm) NLG 6,900. MONTREAL, 23-24 Nov 1993, *Winter in Holland* (oil on canvas, 24 x 31 3/4 ins / 61 x 80.6 cm) CAD 1,800. AMSTERDAM, 19-20 Feb 1997, *Horses Standing in a Snow-Covered Street* (oil on canvas, 29 1/2 x 47 1/2 ins / 75 x 120.5 cm) NLG 2,306. AMSTERDAM, 5 Sept 2000, *Moonlit Forest Track* (1944, oil on canvas, 31 x 35 ins / 78 x 88 cm) NLG 7,000. AMSTERDAM, 5 Sept 2000, *Birches in Extensive Snowy Landscape* (oil on canvas, 31 x 35 ins / 78 x 88 cm) NLG 8,000. AMSTERDAM, 11 Feb 2001, *Stream in a Snowy Forest* (oil on canvas, 24 x 31 ins / 60 x 80 cm) NLG 6,500. AMSTERDAM, 3 Sept 2002, *Sunny Day in Winter* (oil on canvas, 20 x 28 ins / 51 x 71 cm) EUR 2,500. ROTTERDAM, 5 Nov 2002, *Winter Landscape* (oil on canvas, 30 x 59 ins / 75 x 150 cm) EUR 5,000. AMSTERDAM, 30 June 2003, *In the Snow of Amsterdam* (oil on canvas, 26 x 30 ins / 66 x 77 cm) EUR 3,000. AMSTERDAM, 21 April 2004, *Atmospheric Winter's Day* (oil on canvas, 39 x 48 ins / 99 x 121 cm) EUR 6,500.

SOEST, Pierre van

Dutch, 20th century.
Born 1930, in Venlo.
Painter.

AUCTION RECORDS:
AMSTERDAM, 13 Dec 1990, *Untitled* (1963, oil on canvas, 20 x 23 3/4 ins / 50.5 x 60.5 cm) NLG 3,680. AMSTERDAM, 21 May 1992, *Untitled* (1964, acrylic/canvas, 46 x 38 1/4 ins / 116 x 97 cm) NLG 5,290. AMSTERDAM, 9 Dec 1992, *Untitled* (1962, oil on canvas, 39 1/4 x 51 ins / 99.5 x 129.5 cm) NLG 4,945. AMSTERDAM, 17-18 Dec 1996, *Untitled* (1962, oil on canvas, 35 1/4 x 39 1/4 ins / 89.5 x 100 cm) NLG 7,080.

SOEST, Pieter Cornelisz. van

Dutch, 17th century.
Died c. 1667; probably in Amsterdam.
Painter. Battles, seascapes.

Pieter Cornelisz. van Soest was a citizen of Amsterdam in 1642.

MUSEUMS AND GALLERIES:
ABBEVILLE: *Great Naval Battle.*

AUCTION RECORDS:
LONDON, 1 March 1991, *Dutch Attack on the English Fleet in the Medway* (oil on panel, 22 1/2 x 40 1/4 ins / 57.2 x 102.2 cm) GBP 4,950. LONDON, 30 Oct 1996, *The Four Days' Battle* (1666, oil on panel, 19 x 25 1/2 ins / 48.2 x 64.5 cm) GBP 17,250. LONDON, 31 Oct 2002, *Dutch Fleet Entering the Sound and Passing Kronberg Castle, 29 October 1858* (oil on canvas, 22 x 27 ins / 57 x 68 cm) GBP 8,000. STOCKHOLM, 26 May 2003, *Naval Battle by Oland's Northern Foreland 1566* (oil on panel, 20 x 37 ins / 51 x 94 cm) SEK 92,000. LONDON, 19 Nov 2003, *Dutch Attack on English Fleet in the Medway* (oil on canvas, 27 x 43 ins / 69 x 110 cm) GBP 95,000.

SOETE. See also **ZUTMAN**

SOETE, Adolphe

Belgian, 19th century.
Born 27 August 1819, in Courtrai; died 18 July 1862, in Montevideo.
Painter. Landscapes, architectural views.

Adolphe Soete was a pupil of J.-B. Daveloose. The museum at Courtrai has his *View of the Area around Tournai.*

SOETE, Arnestus de

Flemish School, 17th century.
Active in Ghent in 1662.
Landscape painter.

SOETEBOOM, Hendrik Jacobsz.

Dutch, 17th century.
Engraver (etching).

Hendrik Jacobsz. Soeteboom engraved frontispieces and illustrations for books.

SOETENS, Michael

Dutch, 17th century.
Born in The Hague.
Painter. Genre scenes, landscapes.

Michael Soetens travelled in the Tyrol and Italy with Six van Chandelier, and also spent time in Rome. He is noted for a portrait dated 1631.

SOETERIK, Theodor

Dutch, 19th century.
Born 12 January 1810, in Utrecht; died 20 August 1883, in Utrecht.
Painter, watercolourist. Landscapes with figures.

Theodor Soeterik was a pupil of C. van Gelen and B. van Straaten. He was also an art dealer.

MUSEUMS AND GALLERIES:
BRUSSELS: a watercolour - UTRECHT: *Landscape by Moonlight.*

AUCTION RECORDS:
PARIS, 6 Feb 1929, *Winter Landscape in Holland,* FRF 880. COLOGNE, 12 June 1980, *Outskirts of a Town in Winter* (oil on panel, 18 3/4 x 21 ins / 47.5 x 53.5 cm) DEM 18,000. AMSTERDAM, 6 Nov 1990, *Summer Landscape with Figures on a Track* (oil on panel, 14 1/4 x 19 1/4 ins / 36 x 49 cm) NLG 4,830. AMSTERDAM, 14 Sept 1993, *Winter: Figures Walking on a Snow-covered Path near Ruins* (oil on canvas, 33 x 26 1/2 ins / 84 x 67.5 cm) NLG 3,680. AMSTERDAM, 14 June 1994, *Traveller Talking to a Small Boy near a House in a Wooded Landscape* (1837, oil on panel, 9 1/4 x 12 1/2 ins / 23.5 x 31.5 cm) NLG 2,185. AMSTERDAM, 19-20 Feb 1997, *Wooded Landscape with Figures on a Path, and a Village in the Distance* (oil on panel, 10 x 13 ins / 24.5 x 33 cm) NLG 2,306. AMSTERDAM, 21 Jan 1998, *Wooded Landscape with a Young Boy and his Dog on a Raft* (oil on canvas, 31 1/2 x 23 ins / 80 x 57.5 cm) NLG 5,189.

SOETERMANS, Justus. See **SUSTERMAN Justus, Joest, Josse, Jodocus, Giusto**

SOFALVI, Antal or Anton

Hungarian, 19th century.
Painter. Portraits.

In 1846, Antal Sofalvi painted the portrait of the writer *G. Döbrentei,* now in the academy of sciences in Budapest.

SOFFICI, Ardengo

Italian, 20th century.
Born 7 April 1879, in Rignano sull'Arno (Florence); died 1964, in Forte dei Marmi (Lucca).
Painter, collage artist, monotype artist, watercolourist, engraver, writer, art critic. Figures, portraits, landscapes, still-lifes.
Futurism, Novecento Italiano.

Ardengo Soffici was a pupil of the Academy of Fine Arts in Florence. From 1900 to 1907 he was in Paris during which time he lived at la Ruche and joined with Apollinaire, Max Jacob, le Dounaier Rousseau and others. During this period he made drawings for *Assiette au beurre* (*Plate of Butter*), in *Rire* (*Laughter*) and for Apollinaire's review *Plume* (*Pen*). He returned to Italy and settled in Florence. He enlisted in the army in 1915 to take part in World War I. In 1939 he entered the Academy of Italy. In 1944 he was arrested for collaboration and interned in a concentration camp.

With Giovanni Papini and Prezzolini he became one of the animators of the avant-garde review *La Voce* (*The Voice*). After two exhibitions of the Futurists in Milan at the beginning of 1911, Soffici violently criticised in his review the attitude of those Futurists who despite appearances, stated their complete independence from the Cubists, and he accused them of boasting and Italian provincialism. Blows were exchanged. However, Soffici remained with Futurism in 1912 and joined the group until 1915 when, still more so than Severini he showed the contribution of French Cubism. He organised an exhibition on Futurism in the premises of the review *La Voce* (*The Voice*) in Florence. His paintings from that time (many still-lifes and 'syntheses' of landscapes) responded to the aesthetic demands of the movement while including the rigorous construction of Cubism and the technique of collage. Soffici founded with Papini the bimonthly review *Lacerba* in which he defended the Futurist argument. Careful to situate it in the European cultural scene, he even wrote two theoretical works *Cubismo e Futurismo*, 1913; *Primi Principi di una estetica futurista* (*First Principles of a Futurist Aesthetic*), 1920. He exhibited regularly with the Futurists from 1913, then after his break with the group he returned to classical representation, rejoining the reactionary academicism of the group Novocento (New Century), and painting mainly landscapes and portraits, consulting the Macchiaioli and in particular Fattori, that is to say those who took the place of the Impressionists in the Italy of the second half of the 19th century, adopting in his turn a position of Italian provincialism, similar to that which he had reproached the Futurists for earlier. Beyond his writings on Futurism, he compiled biographies on *Carlo Carrà* (1928) and *Menardo Rosso* (1929), the literary works *Ignoto Toscano* (*Unknown Tuscany*) (1909), *Arlechino* (*Harlequin*) (1914), and a autobiographical novel, *Lemmorio Boreo* (1911). He also did etchings.

Soffici's work was included in the following group exhibitions: 1926, 1929 exhibition of the *Novecento Italiano* (*Italian New Century*); 1928, 1934, 1936, Biennale; 1931, Quadrenniale de Rome (Prize); 2003, *De Chirico et la peinture italienne de l'entre-deux guerres* (*De Chirico and Italian Painting of the Interwar Period*), Musée de Lodève; 2003, *Futurismo 1909-1926. La bellezza della velocità* (*Futurism 1909-1926: The Beauty of Speed*) Musée d'Ixelles, Brussels; 2003, *Aria di Parigi: tre toscani a La Ruche; Soffici, Modigliani, Viani* (*Air of Paris: Three Tuscans at La Ruche; Soffici, Modigliani, Viani*), Galleria d'Arte Frediano Farsetti, Cortina D'Ampezzo; and 2004, *L'estate incantata: la Versilia nelle opere di Dazzi, Carrà, Soffici* (*The Enchanted Summer: La Versilia in the works of Dazzi, Carrà, Soffici*), Il Fortino, Forte dei Marmi. Posthumous solo exhibitions included in 1975, *Ardengo Soffici: l'artista e lo scrittore nella cultura del '900* (*Ardengo Soffici: The Artist and the Writer in the Culture of 1900*), Villa Medicea, Poggio a Caiano; 1976, *The Artist and the Writer in the Culture of 1900*, Villa Medicea, Poggio a Caiano; 1980, *Soffici: immagini e documenti* (*Soffici: Images and documents*), Galleria Il Castello, Milan; 1982, *Ardengo Soffici: lavori per affresco* (*Ardengo Soffici: works for fresco*), Castello di Volpaia, Radda in Chianti; 1994, *Ardengo Soffici - Arte e storia* (*Ardengo Soffici - art and history*), Villa di Petriolo, Rignano sull'Arno; 1994, *Ardengo Soffici. Un percorso d'arte* (*Ardengo Soffici. A Journey in Art*), Villa Medicea, Poggio a Caiano; 2000, *Ardengo Soffici - un itinerario plastico* (*Ardengo Soffici - a plastic itinerary*), Galleria Arte Sansrasmo, Milan; 2000, *Ardengo Soffici, ambienti e figure fra luce e tenebre* (*Ardengo Soffici, Ambience and Figures through Light and Darkness*), Galleria Patrizia Poggi, Ravenna; 2001, *Ardengo Soffici. Un'arte toscana per l'Europa* (*Ardengo Soffici. A Tuscan Art for Europe*), Galleria Pananti, Florence; and 2003, *Ardengo Soffici: poesia nel paesaggio* (*Ardengo Soffici: Poetry in Landscape*), Villa la Delfiniana at Montepiano, Palazzo Communale at Vernio.

Bibliography:

Raimondi, G./Cavallo, L., *Ardengo Soffici*, Vallecchi, Florence, 1967. Bartolini, Sigfrido, *Ardengo Soffici: l'opera incisa con appendice e iconografia*, catalogue raisonné, Emilia Prandi, Reggio, 1972. Parronchi, Alessandro, *Ardengo Soffici*, Editalia, Rome, 1976. Soffici, Ardengo, *L'Artista e lo scrittore nella cultura del 1900*, Villa Medicea, Poggio a Caiano, 1976. Cavallo, Luigi/Moretti, Marco/Nuti, Nicola, *Ardengo Soffici. Un percorso d'arte*, exhibition catalogue, Villa Medicea, Poggio a Caiano, Mazzotta, Milan, 1994. Bonito Oliva, Achille/Iovane, Giovanni/Lista, Giovanni, et al., *De Chirico et la peinture italienne de l'entre-deux guerres*, exhibition catalogue, Musée de Lodève, Lodève, 2003. Masoero, Ada/Miracco, Renato (ed.), *Futurismo 1909-1926. La bellezza della velocità*, group exhibition catalogue, Musée d'Ixelles, Bruxelles, Mazzotta, Milan, 2003. Fergonzi, Flavio, *La Collezione Mattioli: capolavori dell'avanguardia italiana*, catalogue, Peggy Guggenheim Collection, Venezia, Skira, Ginevra, 2003.

Museums and Galleries:

Florence (Gal. d'Arte Moderna) - London (Estorick Collection): *Scomposizione dei piani di un lume* (*Decomposition of Planes of Light*) (1912-1913, oil on canvas) - Milan (Gal. d'Arte Moderna) - Rome (Gal. Nazionale d'Arte Moderna): *Autumn Landscape* (1913) - Turin (Gal. Civica d'Arte Moderna e Contemporanea) - Venice (Collezione Peggy Guggenheim): *Frutta e liquori* (*Fruit and Liqueurs*) (1915); *Trofeino* (*Small Trophy*) (1915) - Winterthur (Kunstmus.): *Natura morta* (*Still-life*) (1914-1915, oil on canvas).

Auction records:

Milan, 21 and 23 Nov 1962, *Melon and Divine Physician*, ITL 6,000,000. Milan, 4 and 5 Dec 1969, *Compositions*, ITL 13,500,000; *Still-life with Bottle* (watercolour) ITL 14,000,000. Milan, 2 Dec 1971, *Undergrowth*, ITL 4,200,000. London, 28 Nov 1972, *Synthesis of an Autumnal Landscape*, Gns 16,000. Milan, 16 Oct 1973, *Caffè Apollo* (tempera and collage) ITL 12,000,000. Rome, 27 Nov 1973, *April*, ITL 8,000,000. Rome, 20 May 1974, *Houses*, ITL 6,500,000. Rome, 26 Nov 1974, *Dusk* (pastel) ITL 5,300,000. Rome, 9 Dec 1976, *Still-life with Bottles* (1914, oil on canvas, 26 x 21½ ins / 66 x 54.5 cm) ITL 17,000,000. Rome, 24 May 1977, *Landscape* (oil on canvas, 19¾ x 23½ ins / 50 x 60 cm) ITL 4,800,000. London, 4 juil 1979, *Synthesis of an Autumnal Landscape* (1912, oil on canvas, 18 x 17 ins / 45.5 x 43 cm) GBP 17,000. Rome, 2 Dec 1980, *Study of a Nude* (1909-1910, pencil and charcoal, 15¼ x 12½ ins / 39 x 32 cm) ITL 1,800,000. Rome, 11 June 1981, *Tuscan Landscapes (recto)* (1907; *Dancers (verso)* (1911, oil on card, 36¼ x 28¾ ins / 92 x 73 cm) ITL 43,500,000. Rome, 18 May 1983, *Forte dei Marmi* (1963, watercolour/mounted paper/card, 12¾ x 9½ ins / 32.5 x 24 cm) ITL 8,500,000. Rome, 5 May 1983, *Landscape* (1906, oil on card re-mounted/canvas, 25½ x 19¾ ins / 65 x 50 cm) ITL 35,000,000. Milan, 13 May 1985, *Modern Frenchman; Wait for the Reader to...* (two drawings, ink, the first one with blue pastel, 12¾ x 9¾ ins / 32.5 x 25 cm) ITL 3,400,000. Milan, 19 June 1986, *Spring Rain* (1938, oil on canvas, 22 x 27¾ ins / 55 x 70.5 cm) ITL 36,000,000. Rome, 28 April 1987, *Portrait of Carlo Carra* (1927, pen and sepia ink, 10 x 7 ins / 25.5 x 17.5 cm) ITL 1,900,000. Versailles, 21 Feb 1988, *Conversation* (pencil and Indian ink, 11½ x 9¼ ins / 29 x 23.5 cm) FRF 9,000. Rome, 7 April 1988, *Cheese and Pears* (distemper/card, 27½ x 17¾ ins / 70 x 45 cm) ITL 33,000,000. London, 19 Oct 1988, *Still-life* (1911, oil on canvas, 10 x 14 ins / 25.5 x 35.5 cm) GBP 46,200. Rome, 15 Nov 1988, *Mistress and Maidservant Asleep* (1927, oil on canvas, 55 x 46 ins / 140 x 116 cm) ITL 128,000,000. Milan, 6 June 1989, *Still-life* (1916, oil on canvas, 24¼ x 20 ins / 61.5 x 50.5 cm) ITL 450,000,000. Milan, 27 March 1990, *Composition of Plastic Planes* (1913, oil on card, 13¼ x 9¼ ins / 33.5 x 23.5 cm) ITL 410,000,000. Milan, 20 June 1991, *Haystacks* (1943, oil on panel, 13¾ x 15½ ins / 35 x 39.5 cm) ITL 35,000,000. MILAN, 23 June 1992, *Landscape near Poggio di Caiano* (1947, oil on paper/canvas, 19³/₄ x 13³/₄ ins / 50 x 35 cm) ITL 30,000,000. MILAN, 15 Dec 1992, *Landscape* (1945, oil on strong paper/card, 15¹/₄ x 12¹/₂ ins / 39 x 31.5 cm) ITL 20,000,000. MILAN, 6 April 1993, *Green Bottle and Fruit* (1949, oil on card, 20¹/₂ x 14¹/₂ ins / 52 x 37 cm) ITL 41,000,000. MILAN, 5 May 1994, *Landscape* (pencil, ink and watercolour/paper, 10 x 8¹/₄ ins / 24.5 x 21 cm) ITL 5,750,000. MILAN, 26 Oct 1995, *Houses at Poggio a Caiano* (1947, oil on mounted card, 27 x 19³/₄ ins / 68.5 x 50 cm) ITL 40,250,000. MILAN, 28 May 1996, *Beach* (1927, oil on canvas/card, 17³/₄ x 25¹/₂ ins / 45.2 x 65 cm) ITL 75,880,000. MILAN, 26 Nov 1996, *Farmhouse* (1923, oil on paper, 25 x 19 ins / 63.5 x 48 cm) ITL 74,750,000. ROME, 27 April 1999, *Discomposition of the Planes of a Bottle* (1913, oil on board laid on panel, 15 x 13 ins / 39 x 34 cm) ITL 300,000,000. PRATO, 25 Nov 2000, *Still-life* (oil on cardboard, 14 x 20 ins / 35 x 50 cm) ITL 56,000,000. PRATO, 25 Nov 2000, *Landscape* (oil on canvas/cardboard, 24 x 31 ins / 60 x 78 cm) ITL 185,000,000. PRATO, 16 Nov 2001, *Love Letter* (1931, bronze, h. 15 ins / 39 cm) ITL 5,000,000. MILAN, 20 Nov 2001, *Still-life with Red Egg* (1914, oil, tempera and collage on canvas, 18 x 15 ins / 46 x 38 cm) ITL 320,000,000. FLORENCE, 16 May 2002, *Study for Woman Holding Plate* (1932, ink on paper/board, 63 x 35 ins / 160 x 90 cm) EUR 11,500. MILAN, 19 Nov 2002, *Berna's House* (1950, oil on cardboard, 20 x 29 ins / 51 x 74 cm) EUR 56,000. PRATO, 31 May 2003, *Landscape* (watercolour, 9 x 12 ins / 23 x 31 cm) EUR 10,500. PRATO, 31 May 2003, *Trofeino* (tempera on board, 26 x 20 ins / 65 x 50 cm) EUR 80,000. PRATO, 29 May 2004, *Sunset in Tuscan Countryside* (1923, oil on cardboard, 25 x 19 ins / 64 x 48 cm) EUR 95,000. PRATO, 11 June 2004, *If You Want Them, What Will You Give Me First?* (1904, pencil, pastel and watercolour, 11 x 9 ins / 29 x 22 cm) EUR 9,000.

SOFIANOPULOS, Caesar
Italian, 20th century.
Born 28 May 1889, in Trieste.
Painter. Portraits, figures.

Sofianopulos was a pupil of A. Jank and F. von Stuck in Munich and J. P. Laurens in Paris.

MUSEUMS AND GALLERIES:
TRIESTE (Civico Mus. Revoltella): *Masks.*

SOFRONOVA, Antonina Fedorovna
Russian, 20th century.
Born 1892, in Droskovo, Orlov; died 1966.
Painter (including gouache), graphic artist, illustrator.
Constructivism.

Antonina Fiodorovna Sofronova studied at F.I. Rerberg's art school and I.I. Mashkov's studio in Moscow from 1910 to 1917. In 1914 she joined the Bubnovy Valet (Jack of Diamonds) group. In 1917 she took part in the Mir Iskusstva (World of Art) exhibition in Moscow. In 1920-21 she taught at the Tver State studios and became interested in Constructivism. On returning to Moscow in 1922 she embarked on a major series of Constructivist drawings in pencil, charcoal and coloured ink. She was also active as a graphic artist, illustrating books such as Nikolai Tarabukin's *From the Easel to the Machine*. Later, in the 1930s, like many other artists, she turned to landscape and was closely associated with Aleksandr Drevin and Lev Zhegin. Her work did not become widely known until after her death.

AUCTION RECORDS:
LONDON, 23 May 1990, *Compositions* (blue ink pen, a pair, each 7 x 4¹/₄ ins / 17.7 x 10.6 cm) GBP 3,300. MILAN, 10 Nov 1992, *Composition* (1927, tempera/paper, 11¹/₂ x 8 ins / 29 x 20.5 cm) ITL 4,500,000. NEW YORK, 17 Feb 1999, *Two Compositions* (coloured ink, two, 7 x 4 ins / 18 x 10 cm) USD 2,200.

SOGA, Soyo. See **JASOKU**

SOGA CHOKUAN. See **CHOKUAN**

SOGA KIYU. See **SHOHAKU**

SOGARI, Prospero. See **SPANI**

SOGARO, Oscar
Italian, 20th century.
Born 1888, in Dolo, near Venice; died 1967, in Venice.
Painter. Portraits, landscapes.

Sogaro was a pupil of Domenico Ferri.

MUSEUMS AND GALLERIES:
VENICE (Mus. Civico): *St Francis in the Desert.*

AUCTION RECORDS:
MILAN, 20 Dec 1994, *One End of Piazza San Marco in Venice* (1935, oil on card, 9 x 10³/₄ ins / 22 x 27.5 cm) ITL 1,380,000.

SOGENE OU. See **WU ZUOREN**

SOGENES
Active in Paros.
Sculptor.
Ancient Greek.

Sogenes was the son of Socrates of Paros; he made statues.

SOGGETTI, Gino Giuseppe
Italian, 20th century.
Painter, watercolourist, illustrator.
Futurism.

BIBLIOGRAPHY:
Lista, Giovanni, *Le Livre futuriste: de la libération du mot au poème tactile*, Panini, Modena, 1984 (text in French).

AUCTION RECORDS:
MONACO, 17 June 1990, *Aurora* (1920, watercolour/paper, 11 x 13¹/₂ ins / 28 x 34 cm) FRF 42,180. ROME, 25 Nov 1999, *Mechanical Dynamism* (1920, tempera on board, 14 x 12 ins / 35 x 30 cm) ITL 7,000,000.

SOGGI, Niccolò
Italian, 15th - 16th century.
Born c. 1474 or 1480, in Arezzo; died 12 July 1552, in Arezzo.
Painter. Religious subjects.
Florentine School.

A pupil of Pietro Perugino, Niccolò Soggi imitated his master's style. Most of his career was spent in Florence although in 1550 he worked for the Pope in Rome.

MUSEUMS AND GALLERIES:
FLORENCE (Church of the Madonna delle Lagrime): *Nativity* - FLORENCE (Palazzo Pitti): *Virgin and Child and Four saints; Annunciation.*

AUCTION RECORDS:
NEW YORK, 30 May 1991, *Virgin and Child with a Female Saint Offering Fruit* (oil on panel, tondo, diam. 33¹/₂ ins / 85 cm) USD 159,500.

SOGLIANI, Bartolommeo
Italian, 16th century.
Born c. 1559, in Florence; died 7 September 1589, in Rome.
Painter.

SOGLIARI, Giovanni Antonio, or Giovannantonio di Francesco, or Sogliani
Italian, 16th century.
Born 1492, in Florence; died 1544, in Florence.
Painter. Religious subjects.
Florentine School.

Giovanni Antonio Sogliari was a pupil of Lorenzo di Credi with whom he worked until around 1515 when he set up his own studio. One of his earliest works is a *St Martin* in the church of S Michele in Florence. In 1521, he painted a *Martyrdom of St Arcadius* in the church of S Lorenzo. He collaborated with Andrea del Sarto and Sodoma on the decoration of the high altar of Pisa Cathedral. In general he imitated the style of his master Lorenzo di Credi although, in some of his works, the influence of Fra Bartolommeo and Andrea del Sarto (for whom he 'finished' an incomplete work) can be seen. He should not, however, be written off as a mere imitator. Vasari tells how one of his designs for an altarpiece was rejected on the grounds that it was too modern.

MUSEUMS AND GALLERIES:

FLORENCE: *Virgin, Christ and St John; St Bridget with Nuns and Monks* - KASSEL: *Adoration of the Shepherds* - PISA: *Nude of a Child or a Genius; Virgin and Child in Glory; Sts Andrew, Nicholas of Bari and Anthony Abbot* - PRATO: *Virgin and St Thomas; Virgin, Christ and Two Saints* - TOULON: *Virgin and Child with the Infant St John.*

AUCTION RECORDS:

LUCERNE, 21-27 Nov 1961, *Virgin and Child,* CHF 19,000. LONDON, 11 Dec 1979, *Woman's head in profile* (black chalk/paper, 8 x 6 1/2 ins / 20.5 x 16.4 cm) GBP 1,300. LONDON, 25 March 1982, *Virgin and Child with Tobias and the Angel* (pen and wash, 9 x 8 1/2 ins / 22.7 x 21.4 cm) GBP 3,000. LONDON, 1 July 1986, *Standing Saint* (black and white chalk/watermarked paper, 16 x 11 ins / 40.9 x 27 cm) GBP 38,000. MONTE CARLO, 20 June 1987, *Standing Saint holding a Cross* (black chalk heightened with white/grey paper, 11 3/4 x 5 3/4 ins / 30 x 14.5 cm) FRF 300,000. PARIS, 25 June 1991, *The Holy Family* (oil on panel, 52 x 40 1/2 ins / 132 x 103 cm) FRF 780,000. NEW YORK, 11 Jan 1995, *Madonna and Child with Landscape* (oil on panel, 31 1/2 x 22 ins / 80 x 55 cm) USD 107,000. NEW YORK, Jan 1998, *The Holy Family and St Françis* (oil on panel, 30 x 22 3/4 ins / 76.2 x 57.8 cm) USD 46,000. LONDON, 6 July 1999, *St Lucy Holding a Dish and Palm in Profile. Studies of the Christ-child* (chalk, double-sided, 9 x 6 ins / 23 x 14 cm) GBP 3,600. LONDON, 11 July 2001, *Head of a Bearded Man. Study for Madonna and Child with Saints* (black chalk heightened with white chalk, double-sided, 13 x 9 ins / 32 x 22 cm) GBP 32,000. PARIS, 21 March 2002, *Young Woman Looking Left* (chalk, 13 x 8 ins / 33 x 21 cm) EUR 60,000. LONDON, 10 July 2002, *Study of a Male Saint Holding a Cross* (black chalk heightened with white chalk, 12 x 6 ins / 30 x 14 cm) GBP 25,000. VIENNA, 27 March 2003, *Madonna and Child with St John the Baptist* (oil on panel, 24 x 18 ins / 60 x 46 cm) EUR 28,000.

SÖGMÜLLER, Andreas

German, 18th century.
Active in Rosenheim.
Painter, sculptor.

Sögmüller produced a sculpture of *St John the Baptist* for the font in the church of Prien on Lake Chiemsee (Bavaria), Germany.

SOGNI, Giuseppe

Italian, 19th century.
Born 18 May 1795, in Robbiano Giussano; died 11 August 1874.
Painter. History painting, portraits.

Sogni studied at the academy in Milan.

MUSEUMS AND GALLERIES:

FLORENCE (Uffizi): *Self-portrait, Portraits of Emperor Franz Joseph I and Empress Elizabeth of Austria* - MILAN (Gal. d'Arte Moderna): *Susanna Bathing; Abduction of Giselde.*

AUCTION RECORDS:

LONDON, 19 Nov 1997, *Adam and Eve Expelled from the Garden of Eden* (oil on canvas, 82 x 62 1/4 ins / 208 x 158 cm) GBP 80,700.

SOGNO, Anna

Italian, 20th century.
Born in the second half of the 20th century.
Painter.

Anna Sogno studied at the Accademia di Brera in Milan. She exhibited in Milan in 1957, 1958 and 1968, in Paris in 1959 and 1970, in Philadelphia in 1961, in New York in 1961 and 1963, and in Washington in 1965.

SOGNO, Bruno

French, 20th century.
Painter.

Bruno Sogno sees himself as belonging to the tradition of French Abstract painting, which, according to Jean Bazaine, takes its starting point from the perceptible and visible: 'The world, if it is not represented, must be present'. In Bruno Sogno's paintings, it is light, in its infinite variations, that represents the world.

In 1996, the Centre Van Gogh in St-Rémy-de-Provence presented an exhibition of his paintings.

SOGOYAN, Vera Semenova

Armenian, 20th century.
Born 1925, in Armenia; died 1988, in Kiev.
Painter. Figures, portraits, still-lifes.

Vera Sogoyan studied with N. Sharikov at Krasnadar and with Grigorev at the Kiev fine arts institute. She was a member of the Artists Union. Sogoyan painted men and women in scenes of everyday life in a bright, traditional style but exhibited little.

AUCTION RECORDS:

PARIS, 18 March 1991, *Near the Gate* (1956, oil on canvas, 31 1/2 x 24 1/2 ins / 80 x 62 cm) FRF 7,500; *Still-life with Plaster Bust* (1959, oil on canvas, 25 1/2 x 39 1/4 ins / 65 x 100 cm) FRF 6,800.

SOGUES, Martin

French, 16th century.
Active in Tours in 1585.
Sculptor.

SOHAJ, Slavko

Croat, 20th century.
Born 1908, in Zagreb.
Painter, stained glass artist. Still-lifes, religious subjects.

Slavko Sohaj is known for his religious paintings as well as his still-lifes. He is a participating artist at the Stanisic Stained Glass Studio, Sombor.

MUSEUMS AND GALLERIES:

ZAGREB (Museum of Contemporary Art).

SOHE, Albert

Belgian, 20th century.
Born 1873, in Hoeilaert; died 1927, in Turnhout.
Painter. Landscapes, still-lifes.

MUSEUMS AND GALLERIES:

TURNHOUT.

SOHEI, real name: Takahashi, U; popular name: Genkichi; artist names: Takumin, Sohei

Japanese, 19th century.
Born 1802, in Kitsuki, Bungo Province (now Oita Prefecture); died 1833.
Painter.
Nanga (literati) school.

Sohei was a Nanga School (literati) painter of birds and flowers and landscapes. He joined Tanomura Chikuden (1777-1835) at the age of 19, becoming his principal disciple. Indeed, Chikuden regarded him as his future heir, but unfortunately Sohei died before his master, who mourned this talent lost before it could mature. Sohei's style resembles that of Chikuden. It has little obvious originality, and his paintings, once popular among the merchant classes, add little of any significance to the glory of the Nanga School.

BIBLIOGRAPHY:

Cahill, James, *Scholar Painters of Japan: the Nanga School,* Asia Society, New York, 1972.

SOHIER (the Elder)

French, 19th century.
Painter. Genre scenes.

Sohier exhibited at the Paris Salon in 1812 and 1819.

SOHIER, Charlotte Joséphine. See **RICHARD**

SOHIER, Jean, or Soier, Soyer or Soyere
Flemish School, 14th century.
Died probably soon after 1325.
Painter. Portraits.

Sohier painted portraits of the counts of Flanders for the Town Hall of Ypres.

SOHIER, Ulrich Louis
French, 19th century.
Born in Versailles.
Painter. Genre scenes.
Orientalism.

Ulrich Sohier was a pupil of Marquerie. Made his debut at the 1881 Salon.

SOHL, Joseph. See **SOLL Joseph** or **Franz Joseph**

SOHLBERG, Harald Oscar
Norwegian, 19th - 20th century.
Born 29 November 1869, in Christiania (now Oslo); died 19 June 1935, in Oslo.
Painter. Architectural views, landscapes.
Symbolism.

Harald Oscar Sohlberg studied under Sven Jørgensen in Christiania and at the Kongelige Akademiet for de Skønne Kunster in Copenhagen under P.H. Kristian Zahrtmann, before completing his studies in Paris and Weimar. Among his better-known works are *Night Visions, Winter Night* and *Afternoon Sun*. His work was included in the group exhibitions *Lumières du Nord: La Peinture Scandinave 1885-1905* (*Northern Lights: Scandinavian Painting 1885-1905*) at the Petit Palais in Paris (1987); and *Da Dahl a Munch. Romanticismo, Realismo e Simbolismo nella Pittura di Paesaggio Norvegese* (*From Dahl to Munch: Romanticism, Realism and Symbolism in Norwegian Landscape Painting*) at the Palazzo dei Diamanti in Ferrara (2001).

Sohlberg

BIBLIOGRAPHY:
Stenseng, Arne, *Harald Sohlberg: en kunstner utenfor allfarvei*, Oslo, 1963. Bjerke, Oivind Storm, *Harald Sohlberg: ensomhetens maler*, Glydendal, Oslo, 1991. Bjerke, Oivind Storm, *Edvard Munch and Harald Sohlberg: landscapes of the mind*, National academy of Design, New York, 1995. Lange, Marit (ed.), *Da Dahl a Munch. Romanticismo, realismo e simbolismo nella pittura di paesaggio norvegese*, exhibition catalogue, Palazzo dei Diamanti, Ferrara Arte editore, Ferrara, 2001.

MUSEUMS AND GALLERIES:
OSLO (Nasjonalgal.): *Afternoon Sun* (1895, oil on canvas).

AUCTION RECORDS:
LONDON, 25 March 1987, *Winter Night in the Mountains* (oil on canvas, 30 1/2 x 33 1/2 ins / 77.5 x 85 cm) GBP 210,000. LONDON, 24 March 1988, *Summer Night on Oslo Fjord* (1926, oil on canvas, 35 x 44 1/2 ins / 88 x 113 cm) GBP 132,000. LONDON, 16 March 1989, *Winter at Hvalsbakken* (1926, oil on canvas, 16 x 23 ins / 40.7 x 58.5 cm) GBP 66,000. LONDON, 27-28 March 1990, *Bay of Nærsnes* (1930, oil on canvas, 15 1/4 x 23 1/4 ins / 39 x 59 cm) GBP 20,900. LONDON, 15 June 1994, *'Graaveir'* (oil on canvas, 25 1/2 x 20 3/4 ins / 65 x 53 cm) GBP 17,250. LONDON, 28 June 1999, *Oslo, Fra Akershus* (1933, oil on canvas, 37 x 49 ins / 94 x 125 cm) GBP 485,000. OSLO, 6 Dec 1999, *From Nærsnes Bay* (1930, oil on canvas, 20 x 26 ins / 51 x 66 cm) NOK 900,000. LONDON, 7 April 2000, *The House at Maridalen* (1930, oil on canvas, 17 x 24 ins / 43 x 60 cm) GBP 40,750. OSLO, 23 Oct 2000, *Midsummer Night from Kjerringvik* (oil on canvas, 22 x 28 ins / 55 x 70 cm) NOK 910,000. OSLO, 3 April 2001, *Winter Night in Rondane* (1917, colour lithograph, 20 x 23 ins / 51 x 59 cm) NOK 65,000. OSLO, 11 June 2001, *Vestre Slidre in Valdres* (1894, gouache and Indian ink, 8 x 11 ins / 20 x 28 cm) NOK 20,000. OSLO, 2 Dec 2002, *Winter Night in Rondane* (colour lithograph, 20 x 24 ins / 52 x 60 cm) NOK 100,000. OSLO, 17 Dec 2002, *Winter's Night at Rondane* (1917, colour lithograph, 23 x 24 ins / 58 x 62 cm) NOK 96,000. OSLO, 17 March 2003, *Winter Night in Rondane* (1917, colour lithograph, 20 x 24 ins / 52 x 60 cm) NOK 110,000. OSLO, 17 March 2003, *From Ranviken - Midsummer Night* (1910, oil on canvas, 14 x 21 ins / 36 x 54 cm) NOK 580,000. OSLO, 7 June 2004, *Winter Night in Rondane* (1917, colour lithograph, 20 x 24 ins / 52 x 60 cm) NOK 54,000. OSLO, 6 Dec 2004, *View Across Oslo Fjord* (1926, oil on canvas, 20 x 26 ins / 50 x 66 cm) NOK 432,000.

SÖHLE, Meno Heinrich
German, 19th century.
Born 1807; died 1899, in Lockstedt.
Painter.

SOHLEMANN, Hans
German, 20th century.
Born 26 February 1874, in Hildesheim.
Watercolourist, designer.

Hans Sohlemann was a pupil of Anton Burger. He also worked as an architect.

SOHLERN, Karl Ernst von (Freiherr)
German, 19th - 20th century.
Born 25 October 1866, in Johannishof, near Königshofen; died 26 October 1950, in Gössweinstein.
Painter. Landscapes.

Karl Ernst von Sohlern studied under Anton Burger and went on to work in Munich and in Gossweinstein castle, Switzerland.

SÖHLKE, Gerhard
German, 19th century.
Active in Berlin.
Painter. Portraits, genre scenes, landscapes, architectural views.

Söhlke exhibited in Berlin from 1848 to 1877.

SOHMANN, Alexander Hieronymus
German, 18th century.
Active in Hamburg.
Sculptor.

Sohmann worked on the portals of the church of St Michael of Hamburg from 1742 to 1744.

SOHN, André Erasmus. See **ANDRESOHN Erasmus**

SOHN, Andreas
German, 19th - 20th century.
Born 1847; died 1920.
Active in Zizenhausen (near Stockach).
Sculptor.

Andreas Sohn was the son of Theodor Sohn.

SOHN, Anton
German, 18th - 19th century.
Born 28 August 1769, in Kimratshofen; died 1841, in Zizenhausen, near Stockach.
Active in Basel.
Painter. Religious subjects.

Anton was the son of Joseph Sohn. He produced groups, popular figures and costumes modelled in terracotta.

SOHN, August Wilhelm or Johann August Wilhelm or Wilhelm
German, 19th century.

Born 29 August 1830, in Berlin; died 16 March 1899, in Pützchen, near Bonn.

Painter. History painting, religious subjects, portraits, genre scenes.

August Wilhelm Sohn went to Düsseldorf, where he studied under his uncle Karl Sohn in 1847 and settled there, becoming a teacher at the art academy in 1874. He exhibited in Paris where he won a medal in 1867.

MUSEUMS AND GALLERIES:

BERLIN (Nationalgal.): *The Last Supper* - DRESDEN: *Bust of an 18th-Century Warrior* - DÜSSELDORF: *Jesus and his Disciples on a Rough Sea; Flemish Woman; Head of a Man*; a sketch - KALININGRAD: *Hungarian Gypsy* - LEIPZIG: *The Consultation; Romany Woman with her Dog* - TOUL: *Table Covered with Fruit* - WIESBADEN: *Various Paths of Life.*

AUCTION RECORDS:

COLOGNE, 24 June 1983, *St Boniface Preaching* (oil on canvas, 20 1/4 x 30 ins / 51.5 x 76 cm) DEM 8,500. BRUSSELS, 19 Dec 1989, *Back Street with Figures in North Africa* (oil on canvas, 24 x 16 ins / 61 x 40.5 cm) BEF 22,000. AMSTERDAM, 23 April 1991, *Portrait of a Lady* (oil on canvas, 18 1/2 x 14 1/2 ins / 47 x 37 cm) NLG 6,670. NEW YORK, 29 Oct 1992, *Lady in Black* (oil on canvas, 16 1/2 x 12 1/2 ins / 41.9 x 31.8 cm) USD 2,640. HEIDELBERG, 15 Oct 1994, *Silent Companion* (oil on canvas, 13 1/2 x 10 1/2 ins / 34.5 x 26.5 cm) DEM 1,200. AUCKLAND, 3 April 2001, *Portrait of a Seated Woman* (1876, oil on canvas, 23 x 18 ins / 59 x 45 cm) NZD 5,000. PENZANCE, 25 Oct 2001, *Glamorous Lady Seated in an Interior* (1876, oil on canvas, 24 x 17 ins / 60 x 44 cm) GBP 2,500. NEW YORK, 29 Oct 2003, *Elegant Lady with Fan in a Black Shawl* (oil on canvas, oval, 53 x 40 ins / 135 x 101 cm) USD 14,000.

SOHN, Dong-Chin

Korean, 20th century.

Born 1921, in Kyungjou.

Active in France.

Painter. Murals.

Sohn Dong-Chin trained in the Yasui studio in Tokyo and from 1955 to 1959 at the École des Beaux-Arts, Paris, where he worked in the Souverbie studio, which specialised in fresco painting. He began teaching in the faculty of art of Se Jong University in 1964. Sohn's work is symbolic in style. It draws from European medieval frescoes and traditional Korean popular decorative arts, evoking an unreal world peopled with masked figures and fabulous animals and fish.

He took part in the contemporary art exhibition at the Musée d'Art Moderne, Paris in 1956; the international fine art exhibition, Deauville in 1957; an international exhibition in Montreal in 1967; the São Paulo Biennale in 1968; the contemporary art exhibition in Seoul in 1976; and an exhibition at the Museum of Modern Art, Seoul in 1979. He had a number of solo exhibitions, most often in Seoul, and one in 1980 at the Galerie Katia Granoff, Paris. He won the grand prize at the Korea Salon in 1943.

MUSEUMS AND GALLERIES:

SEOUL (Nat. Mus. of the Republic of Korea) - SEOUL (NMCA) - TOKYO (Holi Mus.).

SOHN, Else, or Sohn-Rethel

German, 19th century.

Active during the second half of the 19th century.

Painter.

Else Sohn was the daughter of Alfred Rethel and the wife of Karl Rudolph Sohn.

MUSEUMS AND GALLERIES:

AACHEN: drawings - DÜSSELDORF: drawings.

SOHN, Hermann

German, 20th century.

Born 5 April 1895, in Mettingen, near Esslingen.

Painter.

Hermann Sohn studied at the Akademie der Bildenden Künste in Stuttgart and went on to produce decorative compositions.

MUSEUMS AND GALLERIES:

STUTTGART (Staatsgal.): *Painter and Model; Still-life with Tomato.*

SOHN, Joseph or Franz Joseph

German, 18th century.

Born c. 1739; died 1802, in Kimratshofen, near Kempten (Bavaria).

Sculptor. Low reliefs.

Joseph Sohn produced terracotta low reliefs and statuettes for cribs.

SÖHN, Karl

German, 19th - 20th century.

Born 14 May 1853, in Barmen; died 27 November 1925, in Munich.

Painter, designer. Portraits, genre scenes, landscapes. School of Düsseldorf.

Karl Söhn was the father of Richard Söhn-Skuwa. He studied at the Akademie der Bildenden Künste in Düsseldorf and worked in Munich as a set designer.

SOHN, Karl or Karl Ferdinand

German, 19th century.

Born 10 December 1805, in Berlin; died 25 November 1867, in Cologne.

Painter, engraver (etching). History painting.

School of Düsseldorf.

Karl Ferdinand Sohn was the father of Karl Rudolph. He attended the academy in Berlin studying under W. Schadow, and in 1826, followed his master to Düsseldorf where he settled. After a trip to Holland, he went to Italy in 1830. In 1832, he was appointed a teacher at the academy in Düsseldorf, and in 1838, a professor. He mainly produced historical pictures, but was also a highly esteemed portrait painter.

C Sohn 1849

MUSEUMS AND GALLERIES:

AACHEN: *Amalie Else Suermondt, née Cockerill* - BERLIN: *Woman Playing the Lute* - BONN (Stadtmus.): *Mathilde Wesendonck and Johanna Muckemeyer* - BREMEN: *Study of a Head* - COLOGNE: *Countess Monts; Karl Windscheidt; M. Kühlwetter* - DÜSSELDORF: *Torquato Tasse and Leonora d'Este; The Painter Christian Köhler; Mrs Wiegmann; Mrs Adele Preyer; Countess Bocholt; Renaud and Armide; The Painter Henry Ritter* - FRANKFURT AM MAIN (Städel): *Johann Karl Klotz and Mrs Anna Christine Dorothea Klotz* - KALININGRAD: *Lady with Mirror* - KARLSRUHE (Staatliche Kunsthalle): *Portrait of a Young Girl* - LEIPZIG: *Donna Diana* - MANNHEIM: *Spring* - OSLO: *Torquato Tasse and Leonora d'Este* - POZNAN: *The Two Leonoras.*

AUCTION RECORDS:

NEW YORK, 1899, *Diana and her Nymphs*, FRF 1,500. LONDON, 3 June 1983, *A Long Wait* (oil on panel, 7 1/2 x 4 3/4 ins / 19 x 12 cm) GBP 850. MILFORD, 22 April 1999, *Beautiful Young Woman* (1836, oil on canvas, 16 x 13 ins / 41 x 33 cm) USD 7,000. HEIDELBERG, 9 Dec 2000, *Young Woman with Mirror* (1843, oil on canvas, 44 x 36 ins / 111 x 91 cm) DEM 9,000.

SOHN, Karl Rudolph

German, 19th century.

Born 21 July 1845, in Düsseldorf; died 29 August 1908, in Düsseldorf.

Painter. Figures, portraits, still-lifes.

Karl Rudolf Sohn was the son of Karl Ferdinand; his sons Alfred, Karl Ernst and Otto Sohn-Rethel were also painters. He studied under his nephew August Wilhelm and painted portraits of European princes.

C Sohn

Museums and Galleries:
Toul: *Still-life.*
Auction records:
New York, 25 Oct 1984, *Dessert* (1881, oil on canvas, 25¾ x 32¾ ins / 65.4 x 83.2 cm) USD 8,500. Cologne, 23 March 1990, *Young Girl Wearing a Red Hat and Shawl* (1880, oil on panel, 11 x 8¾ ins / 28 x 22.5 cm) DEM 3,000. London, 17 Nov 1995, *The Two Leonoras* (1834, oil on canvas, 68½ x 52¼ ins / 174 x 132.7 cm) GBP 58,700. New York, 18 Oct 2000, *Welcome Interruption* (1881, oil on canvas, 22 x 30 ins / 57 x 77 cm) USD 25,000. New York, 28 June 2001, *Little Green Friend* (1895, oil on canvas, 30 x 22 ins / 77 x 57 cm) USD 11,000.

SOHN, Karli. See **SOHN-RETHEL Carl Ernst**

SOHN, Richard or Paul Eduard Richard
German, 19th - 20th century.
Born 11 November 1834, in Düsseldorf; died 8 March 1912, in Düsseldorf.
Painter. Genre scenes, portraits.
Richard Sohn was the son and pupil of Carl Ferdinand Sohn. He also studied under Rudolf Jordan at the Akademie der Bildenden Künste in Düsseldorf.
Auction records:
New York, 15 Jan 1937, *Amusement of the Baby,* USD 450.

SOHN, Theodor
German, 19th century.
Died 1876.
Active in Zizenhausen (near Stockach).
Sculptor.
Theodor Sohn was the son of Anton and worked in terracotta. He exhibited in Karlsruhe, Germany, in 1846.

SOHN-RETHEL, Alfred
German, 20th century.
Born 8 February 1875, in Düsseldorf; died 1955.
Painter.
Alfred Sohn-Rethel was the son of Carl Rudolph Sohn. He studied in Düsseldorf and Paris.
Museums and Galleries:
Düsseldorf (Kunstmus.): *Market in Nowogrodek.*

SOHN-RETHEL, Carl Ernst, called Sohn Karli
German, 20th century.
Born 8 May 1882, in Düsseldorf; died 1966.
Painter.
Carl Ernst Sohn-Rethel was the son of Carl Rudolph Sohn. He studied at the Akademie der Bildenden Künste in Düsseldorf and Dresden and spent an extended period in Indonesia.
Museums and Galleries:
Aachen: *Watching a Nocturnal Feast in Bali* - Cologne (Wallraf-Richartz Mus.): *Roman Landscape.*
Auction records:
Cologne, 21 May 1976, *Landscape with Mule* (oil on card, 13¾ x 17¾ ins / 35 x 45 cm) DEM 1,800.

SOHN-RETHEL, Else. See **SOHN Else**

SOHN-RETHEL, Otto
German, 20th century.
Born 18 January 1877, in Düsseldorf.
Painter.
Worpswede Artists' Colony.
Otto Sohn-Rethel was the son of Carl Rudolph Sohn. He studied in Düsseldorf, Worpswede, Paris and Rome.

Museums and Galleries:
Wuppertal: *Dutch Peasants.*

SÖHN-SKUWA, Richard
German, 20th century.
Born 2 March 1887, in Munich.
Painter. Figures, portraits, landscapes.
Richard Söhn-Skuwa was the son of Karl Söhn and the pupil of A. Jank.

SÖHNGEN, Andreas Bernhard
German, 19th - 20th century.
Born 14 February 1864, in Oberlahnstein; died 1920, in Frankfurt am Main.
Painter, engraver, lithographer. Landscapes, still-lifes.
Andreas Bernhard Söhngen studied under E. von Steinle and at the Städelsche Kunstinstitut in Frankfurt am Main. He engraved scenes of Frankfurt old town.

SÖHNHOLD, Wilhelm or Karl Wilhelm
German, 19th century.
Born 1789, in Leipzig; died 26 July 1818, in Rome, Italy.
Painter.
Söhnhold attended the academy in Leipzig and settled in Rome in December 1817.

SÖHNLE, Gottlieb Jakob
German, 18th century.
Active in Heilbronn (Baden-Württemberg), in 1788.
Sculptor.
Museums and Galleries:
Heilbronn (Städtische Mus.): *Most Holy Mary of Pity.*

SOHOS, Lazare. See **SOCHOS Lazaros**

SOIA, Bartolomeo
Italian, 17th century.
Born in Cadore.
Active during the first half of the 17th century.
Painter.
Soia produced altarpieces for the churches in the Fassa valley.

SOIDAS
5th century BC.
Active in Naupactus.
Sculptor.
Ancient Greek.
Soidas collaborated with Menaechmus I on the statue of *Artemis the Huntress* at Calydon.

SOIER, Jean. See **SOHIER**

SOIGNIE, Jacques Joachim
Flemish School, 18th century.
Born 28 March 1720, in Mons; died 20 May 1783, in Mons.
Painter. Religious subjects, genre scenes.
Jacques Joachim Soignie studied in Paris, worked in Lyons, and then returned to Mons.
Museums and Galleries:
Mons: *Annunciation; Adoration of the Shepherds; Episodes in the Life of Mme de Chantal.*

SOINARD, François Louis
French, 19th century.
Painter, engraver (stippling). History painting, landscapes, architectural views.
Soinard exhibited at the Paris Salon in 1824 then again between 1834 and 1839.

SOIRON, François David
British, 18th century.
Born 12 October 1764, in Geneva.
Engraver (stippling).
Little is known about François Soiron, who is not mentioned in any of the principal English directories of artists. Howev-

er, his work appears to have been in demand, as he produced engravings of popular paintings, and his prints, particularly those in colour, are still very sought after. His works include *Military Subjects in Uniform*, a series of seven pieces, *Edwin and Ethelinde, A. Pioneer* and *Patience in a Punt*, after Bunbury; *Promenade in St James's Park*, after E. Dayes; *St James's Park* and *Tea Garden*, two pendants after G. Morland; *Flora* after Singleton; and *Weary Sportsman* after Wheatley.

AUCTION RECORDS:

LONDON, 24 June 1938, *Interesting Reading* (drawing) GBP 39. LONDON, 13 Nov 1997, *St James's Park; Open-Air Tea Room* (1790, dry-point engraving, a pair, each 1³/4 x 2¹/4 ins / 4.7 x 5.4 cm) GBP 6,210.

SOIRON, François or Jean François, called Soiron père
French, 18th - 19th century.
Born 18 August 1756, in Geneva; died 1813, in Paris.
Enameller.

François Soiron exhibited at the Salon between 1800 and 1810, mostly portraits of Napoléon and Joséphine, winning a first class medal in 1808. He worked in particular for the duchess of Berry. His son Philippe David Soiron painted on porcelain.

MUSEUMS AND GALLERIES:

GENEVA (MAH): *Portrait of a Young Man* - LONDON (Wallace Collection): *Madame Récamier* (after Gérard) - PARIS (Louvre): *Napoléon and Joséphine*.

AUCTION RECORDS:

PARIS, 1872, *Portrait of Peter the Great* (enamel, miniature) FRF 3,000. PARIS, 16 May 1950, *Portrait of a Man in Blue* (1799, enamel, miniature) FRF 155,000. LONDON, 24 May 2000, *Madame Popp in Low-cut Black Dress* (1802, enamel on copper, miniature) GBP 2,500.

SOIRON, Isaac Daniel
French, 19th century.
Born 11 November 1778, in Geneva.
Enameller.

This artist was the son of François Soiron.

SOIRON, Jacques
French, 18th century.
Born in Mens (Dauphiné, now Rhône-Alpes).
Active in Geneva, Switzerland, 1747-1791.
Engraver.

Jacques Soiron was the father of François David.

SOIRON, Philippe David, or Soiron fils
French, 19th century.
Born 10 February 1783, in Geneva; died after 1857, in Paris (?).
Painter (porcelain/enamel).

Philippe David Soiron was the son and pupil of François Soiron. He worked for the Court of Napoleon 1st and for King Jerome in Kassel.

SOISSON, Jacques
French, 20th century.
Born 1928, in Paris.
Also active in the USA.
Painter, sculptor, engraver.

Jacques Soisson studied at the École des Beaux-Arts in Montpellier in the painting and sculpture studios between 1948 and 1951. From 1952 to 1962, he taught drawing in Sétif and Oran in Algeria. He joined the Compagnie de l'Art Brut in 1969 and was a member of the Société de Psychopathologie de l'Expression. He created a number of monumental works for educational institutions or residences. He also wrote a number of articles on art brut.

His works have featured in group exhibitions, notably at the Menton Biennale and, in 1977, at the *Furniture-Paintings* exhibition at the Centre Georges Pompidou in Paris.

He has held solo exhibitions of his works, including; 1954, Galerie Art Décoration, Montpellier; 1955, Cercle Lelian, Algiers; 1959, Hôtel de Ville, Sétif; 1965, Galerie Denise Mansion, Le Havre; 1973, Galerie Regards, Paris; 1975, Galerie Lahumière, Paris; 1978, Galerie Bonafous Murat, Paris; 1978, Kunstmuseum in Denmark; 1980, Galerie Art et Décoration, Montpellier; 1986, Key West, USA.

His canvases are inspired by fantasy and are totemic in form. This artist is just as much at home bringing life to monumental sculpture as he is when working with canvas and easel.

BIBLIOGRAPHY:

Cazaubiel, Michel, *An Outsider Soisson*, video film, Cinémage. *Cahier de l'Herne*, Éd. de l'Herne, Paris, 1976. Delteil, Joseph, *Le Sacré Corps*, Grasset, Paris, 1976.

AUCTION RECORDS:

LA VARENNE-ST-HILAIRE, 16 June 1990, *Head* (1979, multiple in laminated wood, 20³/4 x 18¹/2 ins / 53 x 47 cm) FRF 5,000. PARIS, 25 Jan 1998, *Double Split* (1973, oil on canvas, 28³/4 x 39¹/4 ins / 73 x 100 cm) FRF 2,200.

SOITER, Daniel. See **SEITER Daniel** or **Joseph Daniel**

SOITOUT, Jean François or Jean Baptiste, or Soitoux
French, 19th century.
Born 5 September 1816, in Besançon; died 21 May 1891, in Paris.
Sculptor.

Soitout was a pupil of David d'Angers and of J. J. Feuchère. He completed several statues for public places in Paris (one, *République*, erected in 1880 in front of the Palais de l'Industrie in Paris has now disappeared), as well as for the Louvre and for various cemeteries. He was a member of the Société des Artistes Français and was made Chevalier of the Légion d'Honneur.

MUSEUMS AND GALLERIES:

BLOIS: *Silène; Gambetta; Robert Houdin; Denis Papin; Affert* (medallion).

SOJA, Anton
Swiss, 19th - 20th century.
Born 13 December 1860, in Bologna.
Draughtsman, engraver. Portraits, landscapes.

Anton Soja lived and worked in Zurich and Küssnacht.

SOJARO, Il. See **GATTI Bernardino, GATTI Gervasio** and **GATTI Uriele**

SOJC, Ivan
Slovene, 20th century.
Born 10 May 1879, in Ljubnica, near Vitanje.
Sculptor.

Ivan Sojc lived at Maribor. He sculpted altars, busts, low reliefs and tombs in wood and stone.

SOJO. See **SOYE Philipp de**

SOJO, Eduardo
Spanish, 19th century.
Born 1849, in Madrid.
Painter, illustrator.

Eduardo Sojo was a pupil of E. Alvarez Durmont. Under the pen-name Democrito he drew caricatures for humorous magazines.

SOJUN. See **IKKYU**

SOK, Ap
Dutch, 20th century.
Born in Rotterdam.

Engraver.
Ap Sok was an etcher whose output, like that of many Dutch engravers, is said to have been influenced by the work of Hercule Seghers.

SOKEI, Oguri. See **SORITSU**

SOKEMAWOU
Guinean, 20th - 21st century.
Born 1960.
Sculptor.
Sokemawou exhibits examples of his work at the 1990 Salon de la Jeune Peinture in Paris and has also exhibited solo in Lomé. His sculptures are fetish-like pieces representing human figures, such as a mother and child.

SOKEN, or Sojun, real name: Yamaguchi Soken (or Sojun), alternate names: Hakugo, Hakuryo, popular name: Takejiro, artist name: Sansai
Japanese, 18th - 19th century.
Born 1759; died 1818.
Active in Kyoto.
Painter.
Soken was a disciple of Maruyama Okyo (1733-1795). He specialised in paintings of beautiful women.
AUCTION RECORDS:
NEW YORK, 17 Oct 1989, *Beauty* (ink and colour on silk, hanging scroll, 36 3/4 x 12 1/2 ins / 93.5 x 31.7 cm) USD 3,300.

SOKHÄTNUKH, Marx or Marcus.
See **SCHOKOTNIGG**

SOKOL, Jano
Yugoslav, 20th century.
Born 1909, in Kovacica, near Pancevo (now in Serbia and Montenegro).
Painter.
In 1938, Jano Sokol met the peasant painter Martin Paluska, who taught him the rudiments of painting. In 1952, he founded the Kovacica peasant painters group, following the example of many other villages in Yugoslavia, where painting by ordinary people was enjoying a singular success. In 1953, a professional painter by the name of Trumic came to Kovacica from Pancevo and encouraged the peasant painters not simply to copy what they saw other people doing but to paint everyday life in their own village. Sokol followed this advice to the letter. He liked painting wedding preparations. In his work he seeks to capture the moment and imbue it with the atmosphere of bygone years.
BIBLIOGRAPHY:
Bihalji-Merin, Oto, *Les Peintres naïfs*, Delpire, Paris, 1960.

SOKOL, Koloman
Slovak, 20th century.
Born 12 December 1902, in Liptovský Mikuláš; died 12 January 2003, in Tucson (Arizona).
Active in the USA.
Painter, print artist, graphic artist.
Koloman Sokol studied in Eugen Kron's graphic school in Košice in 1921, Gustav Mally's painting school in Bratislava and the Prague Academy, where he studied under Max Svabinsky and T.F. Simon from 1924 to 1932. He went to France on a study trip in 1932. In 1937 he went to Mexico and was one of the co-founders of the Escuela de Las Artes Del Libro in Mexico City. He was appointed professor of graphic art at the Escuela Nacional de Artes Plásticas of the University of Mexico. From 1942 to 1946, Sokol lived in New York, taking part in cultural events in support of the Czechoslovakian resistance. In 1946 he returned to Czechoslovakia on the invitation of the Foreign Ministry to take up a position as professor of graphics at the Prague Academy, which he held until he went to teach in the department of drawing and painting at the Slovak Technical College in Bratislava. In 1947 he was awarded the Slovak National Art Prize. In 1948 he emigrated to the USA, settling in Arizona. In 1962 the Slovak National Gallery held a retrospective of his work, and in 1960 another major solo exhibition.
BIBLIOGRAPHY:
Fifty years of Czechoslovak Painting from the Collections of the Galleries, 1918-1958, exhibition catalogue, Slovenska Narodna Gal., Bratislava, 1968 (in commemoration of the 50th anniversary of the Republic of Czechoslovakia).

SOKOL, Rudolf
Austrian, 20th century.
Born 1887, in Altstadt (now Stará Ves, Slovakia).
Landscape artist.
Rudolf Sokol exhibited in Brünn (now Brno, Czech Republic) in 1928.

R Sokol

SOKOLNICKI, Michal
Polish, 18th - 19th century.
Born 1760; died 1816, in Warsaw.
Painter, engraver.
Michal Skolnicki was a general and painted a *Portrait of President Thomas Jefferson*.

SOKOLOFF, Pierre Théodore. See **SOKOLOV Petr Fedorovitch**

SOKOLOV, Aleksandr Petrovich
Russian, 19th - 20th century.
Born 29 October 1829; died 19 November 1913, in St Petersburg.
Painter. Portraits, genre scenes.
A.P. Sokolov was the son of P.F. Sokolov. He studied at the St Petersburg Academy.
MUSEUMS AND GALLERIES:
MOSCOW (State Tretyakov Gal.): *Portrait of the Artist's Wife*; *Portrait of a Lady* - ST PETERSBURG (Gosudarstvennyj Russkij Muz.): *Portraits of ladies* (four); *A Moment's Hesitation*.

SOKOLOV, Aleksei, or Alyosha (?)
Russian, 20th century.
Born 1922.
Painter. Genre scenes, landscapes.
Aleksei Sokolov attended the Repin Institute, where he studied under Grabar, Oreshnikov and A. Milnikov. He later taught at the Institute, was a member of the Union of Soviet Artists, and was named People's Artist.
AUCTION RECORDS:
PARIS, 5 Oct 1992, *Fishing Village* (1965, oil on canvas, 43 1/4 x 68 1/2 ins / 110 x 174 cm) FRF 19,000.

SOKOLOV, Ivan
Russian, 20th century.
Born 1914.
Painter. Still-lifes.
Ivan Sokolov studied at the Leningrad Academy. He painted in traditional style, and is particularly known for his bouquets of flowers.
AUCTION RECORDS:
PARIS, 23 March 1992, *Bouquet against Drapery* (oil on canvas, 23 1/2 x 30 3/4 ins / 60 x 78 cm) FRF 3,800.

SOKOLOV, Ivan Alekseevich
Russian, 18th century.
Born 1717; died 1757, in St Petersburg.
Engraver.
Ivan Alekseevich Sokolov studied under O. Elliger the Younger and Wortmann. He worked for the Russian court

and executed burin engravings of portraits and contemporary scenes, as well as views of St Petersburg and Moscow.

SOKOLOV, Ivan Ivanovich
Russian, 19th century.
Born 1823, in Astrakhan; died 1910 or 1918.
Painter. Genre scenes, landscapes.
Ivan Ivanovich Sokolov studied at the art academy in St Petersburg.
MUSEUMS AND GALLERIES:
MOSCOW (State Tretyakov Gal.): *The Morning after the Wedding; Picking Cherries in the Garden of a Landlord; Near Constantinople; Inhabitants of Little Russia.*

SOKOLOV, Lev
Russian, 20th - 21st century.
Born 1949.
Painter. Urban landscapes, still-lifes.
Sokolov's cityscapes distort traditional perspective and are steeped in a strange atmosphere. He is a member of the association of artists of the former USSR.

SOKOLOV, Mikhail
Russian, 20th century.
Born 1931, in Moscow.
Painter. Urban landscapes, landscapes.
Mikhail Sokolov began his training in 1951 at the Repin Institute, going on to the Surikov Institute, Moscow, where he studied from 1952 to 1957. He was a member of the USSR Artists Union. He first exhibited in 1954 and has since had solo exhibitions at Moscow, Uglich and Pushkinskie Gory. Sokolov travelled widely throughout the Soviet Union, visiting the north, Siberia and the Caucasus, and bringing back a large number of landscape sketches. In 1974 and 1978 he visited France, where he also made a number of landscapes.
BIBLIOGRAPHY:
Tableaux soviétiques, auction catalogue, Salle Drouot, Paris, 3 October 1990.
AUCTION RECORDS:
PARIS, 3 Oct 1990, *Sverdlov Square, Moscow* (oil on reinforced canvas, 9 1/2 x 13 3/4 ins / 24 x 35 cm) FRF 6,000.

SOKOLOV, Nikolai Aleksandrovich
Russian, 20th century.
Born 1903, in Moscow; died 2000.
Painter, graphic artist, caricaturist, illustrator. History painting, landscapes. Posters, stage sets.
Kukryniksy Group.
Nikolai Aleksandrovich Sokolov studied at PROLETKULT art studio, Rybinsk, from 1920 to 1923 and under Vladimir Favorski at the Moscow Vkhutemas/Vkhutein from 1923 to 1929. He was a member of the Kukryniksy Group and was active in Moscow. Sokolov painted landscapes, scenes from history and the revolution, and designed political posters and cartoons. He exhibited widely in Russia and abroad, including 1960 in Berlin and Budapest He was made a Soviet academician in 1947, was awarded Stalin prizes in 1942, 1947, 1949, 1950 and 1951 (all as a member of the Kukryniksy), and two Orders of Lenin.
MUSEUMS AND GALLERIES:
MOSCOW (Russian Mus.) - MOSCOW (State Tretyakov Gal.).
AUCTION RECORDS:
PARIS, 9 Dec 1991, *Night on the Grand Canal* (1963, oil on card, 9 3/4 x 13 3/4 ins / 25 x 35 cm) FRF 25,000. PARIS, 12 Oct 1992, *In Venice* (1958, oil on canvas/card, 6 x 8 1/2 ins / 15 x 21.5 cm) FRF 8,200. PARIS, 5 Nov 1992, *Apple Trees in Blossom* (oil on card, 5 x 6 3/4 ins / 13 x 17 cm) FRF 10,500. PARIS, 16 Nov 1992, *Goat* (1937, oil on panel, 7 x 10 3/4 ins / 18 x 27.5 cm) FRF 7,200. PARIS, 12 Dec 1992, *Dacha at Polenovo* (1948, oil on canvas, 11 1/2 x 19 1/4 ins / 29 x 49 cm) FRF 11,500; *The Appian Way near Rome* (1956, oil on canvas, 9 1/2 x 13 3/4 ins / 24 x 35 cm) FRF 12,500. PARIS, 20 March 1993, *Roman Carriages* (oil on canvas/card, 6 x 8 1/2 ins / 15 x 21.5 cm) FRF 5,800.

SOKOLOV, Nikolai Fedorovich (?)
Russian, 20th century.
Born 1921, in Verkhoki (Ulyanovsk).
Painter. Figure compositions, landscapes with figures.
Not to be confused with Nikolai Aleksandrovich Sokolov, Nikolai (Fedorovich) Sokolov settled in Orenburg, had his first exhibition in 1943 in Vladivostok, and has been a member of the Artists Union since 1969. Among his works are pictures of forest interiors in light colours and with visible brushwork, with figures in them posing, sitting on benches.
AUCTION RECORDS:
PARIS, 15 May 1991, *Pine Parasol* (1956, oil on canvas, 19 1/4 x 27 1/4 ins / 49 x 69 cm) FRF 12,900. PARIS, 11 Dec 1991, *Blast Furnaces* (1968, oil on canvas, 39 1/4 x 35 1/2 ins / 100 x 90 cm) FRF 4,000. PARIS, 13 April 1992, *In Prague* (1954, oil on canvas, 13 3/4 x 19 1/4 ins / 35 x 49 cm) FRF 11,500. PARIS, 20 May 1992, *Small Street in Italy* (1963, oil on card, 13 3/4 x 9 3/4 ins / 35 x 25 cm) FRF 18,500.

SOKOLOV, Nikolai Ivanovich
Russian, 18th century.
Born 6 December 1767, in St Petersburg.
Engraver (burin).
Nikolai Ivanovich Sokolov studied at the art academy in St Petersburg, under Skorodumov. He engraved mainly portraits.

SOKOLOV, Pavel Petrovich
Russian, 18th - 19th century.
Born 1765; died 1831, in St Petersburg.
Sculptor.
Pavel Petrovich Sokolov studied at the art academy in St Petersburg. He sculpted busts, as well as statues for churches and bridges.

SOKOLOV, Pavel Petrovich
Russian, 19th century.
Born 1826; died 2 October 1905, in St Petersburg.
Painter (gouache), watercolourist, illustrator. Genre scenes, figures.
Pavel Petrovich Sokolov was the son of Piotr Fedorovich Sokolov: he studied at the art academy in St Petersburg.
MUSEUMS AND GALLERIES:
ST PETERSBURG (Gosudarstvennyj Russkij Muz.): several watercolours.
AUCTION RECORDS:
LONDON, 15 June 1995, *Board Game* (1881, gouache, 11 1/2 x 14 3/4 ins / 29 x 37.5 cm) GBP 1,150. LONDON, 14 Dec 1995, *Artist and Model* (1870, gouache, 8 3/4 x 13 ins / 22.5 x 33 cm) GBP 1,207.

SOKOLOV, Petr Fedorovitch
Russian, 19th century.
Born 1791; died 1847 or 1848, in St Petersburg.
Painter (gouache), watercolourist, draughtsman. Portraits.
MUSEUMS AND GALLERIES:
MOSCOW (State Tretyakov Gal.): *Mme Lisogonle; The Poet K.N. Bationchkov; N. Pally; The Count P. Tiesenhausen; The Countess Tiesenhausen; Portrait of a Woman* (two versions); *Count Benkendorf, Police Chief; Portrait of Prince Trubetsky; Portrait of Aleksandra Osipovno Smirnova* - ST PETERSBURG: *Portrait of Princess Cherkasskaya; Portrait of the Singer Pauline Viardot.*

AUCTION RECORDS:
LONDON, 5 Oct 1989, *Portrait of the Poet Pushkin* (pencil and watercolour heightened with white/paper, 8 1/2 x 6 3/4 ins / 21.8 x 17.1 cm) GBP 44,000. MUNICH, 8 Nov 2000, *Man with Blue Coat* (gouache, miniature, 2 x 2 ins / 6 x 5 cm) DEM 5,500. MUNICH, 8 Nov 2000, *Portrait of an Officer* (1821, watercolour, miniature, oval, 6 x 4 ins / 14 x 10 cm) DEM 13,000. HELSINKI, 1 Dec 2002, *Young Man* (1818, watercolour, 10 x 8 ins / 26 x 20 cm) EUR 3,000.

SOKOLOV, Petr Ivanovich

Russian, 18th century.
Born 1752, in St Petersburg; died 20 April 1791, in St Petersburg.
Painter. Mythological subjects.

Petr Ivanovich Sokolov studied under Batoni in Rome. He became a non-certified teacher at the art academy in St Petersburg.

MUSEUMS AND GALLERIES:
ST PETERSBURG (Gosudarstvennyj Russkij Muz.): *Mercury and Argus*.

SOKOLOV, Petr Petrovich

Russian, 19th century.
Born 1821, in Tsarskoye-Selo; died October 1899, in Tsarskoye-Selo.
Painter, watercolourist, decorative artist. Portraits, genre scenes, hunting scenes.

Petr Petrovich Sokolov was a talented artist who enjoyed success within his lifetime. He was a member of the art academy of St Petersburg and was awarded a gold medal in Paris in 1889 at the Exposition Universelle.

MUSEUMS AND GALLERIES:
MOSCOW (State Tretyakov Gal.): *In the Office of the Director of the Saburov Theatre; Peasant Funerals; Giving Birth in the Field; Horse Fair; Wolf Hunting*.

AUCTION RECORDS:
Troika (watercolour, no forename given) FRF 165. PARIS, 1895, *Wolf Hunting* (watercolour) FRF 141. PARIS, 29 June 1895, *Sledging through the Snow* (watercolour) FRF 130. PARIS, 14 June 1923, *Fisherwomen* (watercolour) FRF 600. WASHINGTON DC, 4 March 1984, *Couple in a Troika* (1898, oil on canvas, 26 x 33 1/4 ins / 66 x 84.5 cm) USD 1,900. PARIS, 5 April 1990, *Horse Fair* (1869, watercolour, 20 3/4 x 27 1/4 ins / 53 x 69 cm) FRF 50,000. COLOGNE, 24 Nov 2001, *Caucasian Procession* (1895, oil on canvas, 49 x 31 ins / 125 x 80 cm) DEM 5,500. LONDON, 21 May 2003, *Tales of the War* (1859, watercolour, 6 x 8 ins / 16 x 21 cm) GBP 1,200. NEW YORK, 4 June 2003, *Wolf Attack* (oil on canvas, 20 x 32 ins / 51 x 81 cm) USD 19,000.

SOKOLOV, Vasili

Russian, 18th century.
Engraver.

Vasili Sokolov was active in the second half of the 18th century and studied under Johan Stenglin. He engraved portraits.

SOKOLOV, Vasili

Russian, 20th century.
Born 1915, in Petrograd (now St Petersburg).
Painter. Figure compositions, interiors, landscapes, seascapes.

Vasili Sokolov studied under Boris Ioganson at the Repin Institute in Leningrad (now St Petersburg) and went on to make a career as a professor there. He was a member of the USSR Artists Union. His diploma piece, The Breakthrough of the Red Army into Novgorod (1946), was highly praised.

MUSEUMS AND GALLERIES:
MOSCOW (Ministry of Culture) - MOSCOW (State Tretyakov Gal.) - ST PETERSBURG (Academy) - ST PETERSBURG (Gosudarstvennyj Russkij Muz.).

AUCTION RECORDS:
PARIS, 24 Sept 1991, *Beach in Crimea* (1949, oil on canvas, 38 1/2 x 30 3/4 ins / 98 x 78 cm) FRF 5,000. PARIS, 25 Nov 1991, *Reading* (1965, oil on card, 19 x 13 ins / 48 x 33 cm) FRF 9,500. PARIS, 6 Dec 1991, *Young Dreamer* (1960, oil on canvas, 19 x 13 ins / 48 x 33 cm) FRF 7,500. PARIS, 5 April 1992, *Pushkin Park* (1956, oil on canvas, 53 1/2 x 35 1/2 ins / 136 x 90 cm) FRF 18,000.

SOKOLOV, Viktor

Russian, 20th century.
Born 1923; died 1985.
Painter. Figure compositions, landscapes.

Viktor Sokolov studied at the Surikov Institute, Moscow. He was a member of the Union of Soviet Artists and exhibited widely in the USSR and abroad from 1946.

MUSEUMS AND GALLERIES:
MOSCOW (State Tretyakov Gal.) - ODESSA (Museum of Western and Eastern Art) - ST PETERSBURG (Gosudarstvennyj Russkij Muz.).

AUCTION RECORDS:
PARIS, 16 June 1991, *Harvest* (1957, oil on canvas, 23 1/2 x 31 1/2 ins / 60 x 80 cm) FRF 5,200.

SOKOLOV, Vladimir

Russian, 20th century.
Born 1923, in Theodossia.
Painter. Genre scenes, landscapes.

Vladimir Sokolov studied with Bogazhevski in 1940-41 and at the Simferopol school of fine arts in 1949-52.

MUSEUMS AND GALLERIES:
KIEV (Ministry of Culture) - SIMFEROPOL (Art Museum).

AUCTION RECORDS:
PARIS, 3 June 1992, *Gathering Roses* (oil on card, 13 3/4 x 19 3/4 ins / 35 x 50 cm) FRF 4,000. PARIS, 16 Nov 1992, *Steps in Venice* (1960, oil on canvas, 30 x 22 1/2 ins / 76 x 57 cm) FRF 4,000. PARIS, 12 Dec 1992, *Fishing Village* (1964, oil on card, 9 3/4 x 19 ins / 25 x 48 cm) FRF 4,200. PARIS, 23 April 1993, *Park at Tsarskoe Selo* (oil on canvas, 29 1/4 x 47 1/4 ins / 74.6 x 119.8 cm) FRF 7,000. PARIS, 13 Dec 1993, *Before Sailing* (oil on canvas, 30 1/4 x 39 3/4 ins / 77 x 101 cm) FRF 5,500.

SOKOLOV, Vladimir Ivanovich

Russian, 20th century.
Born 1872.
Painter, print artist. Genre scenes, landscapes.

MUSEUMS AND GALLERIES:
MOSCOW (State Tretyakov Gal.): *In the Park at Dusk; Old Metairie*.

SOKOLOVA, Anastassia

Russian, 20th - 21st century.
Born 1967.
Painter. Nudes, interiors with figures, landscapes, architectural views.

Sokolova studied at the V. Surikov School of Fine Art in Moscow. She worked under Salakhov and Nikolai Sokolov, a member of the 'Kukryniksy' artists' collective. She is a member of the association of painters in Moscow and has taken part in many exhibitions in the former USSR and abroad from 1990.

MUSEUMS AND GALLERIES:
MOSCOW (Ministry of Culture).

AUCTION RECORDS:
PARIS, 15 May 1991, *Pont d'Arcole* (oil on canvas, 11 1/2 x 19 1/4 ins / 29 x 49 cm) FRF 4,800. PARIS, 25 Nov 1991, *Summer's Afternoon* (oil on canvas, 25 1/2 x 32 ins / 65 x 81 cm) FRF 18,000. PARIS, 9 Dec 1991, *Dacha at the Edge of the Lake*

(oil on canvas, 28¾ x 23½ ins / 73 x 60 cm) FRF 22,000. PARIS, 23 March 1992, *Lunch* (oil on canvas, 24 x 19¾ ins / 61 x 50 cm) FRF 8,800; *Grandmother's Chest of Drawers* (oil on canvas, 32 x 23½ ins / 81 x 60 cm) FRF 26,500. PARIS, 13 April 1992, *Still-life with China Vase* (oil on canvas, 36¼ x 25½ ins / 92 x 65 cm) FRF 28,000. PARIS, 20 May 1992, *Flowers in the Garden* (oil on canvas, 35¾ x 22 ins / 91 x 56 cm) FRF 30,000. PARIS, 5 Nov 1992, *Orange Tablecloth* (oil on canvas/card, 25½ x 19¾ ins / 65 x 50 cm) FRF 15,000. PARIS, 20 March 1993, *Lovers* (oil on canvas/card, 17¼ x 14¼ ins / 44 x 36 cm) FRF 6,500.

SOKOLOVA, Elena Ilinichna

Russian, 20th century.
Born 1919, in Petrograd (now St Petersburg).
Painter. Genre scenes.

Elena Sokolova studied under Boris Ioganson at the Repin Institute in Leningrad (now St Petersburg), in about 1947.

AUCTION RECORDS:
PARIS, 27 May 1992, *A Cup of Tea* (1990, oil on canvas, 27¼ x 27½ ins / 69 x 70 cm) FRF 6,500.

SOKOLOVA, Tatyana

Russian, 20th - 21st century.
Born 1958, in Leningrad, now St Petersburg.
Painter. Scenes with figures, still-lifes, flowers, fruit.

Sokolova studied at the school of fine art in Leningrad (now St Petersburg) and at the Repin Institute. She is a member of the association of painters of the former USSR.

AUCTION RECORDS:
PARIS, 18 Feb 1991, *Dish of Bilberries* (oil on canvas, 25½ x 35½ ins / 65 x 90 cm) FRF 6,500; *Bluebells* (oil on canvas, 31½ x 33 ins / 80 x 84 cm) FRF 7,000. PARIS, 23 March 1992, *Bathers* (oil on canvas, 39¼ x 51¼ ins / 100 x 130 cm) FRF 7,200.

SOKOLOVSKI, Beleslas

French, 19th century.
Born in Paris.
Painter. Genre scenes, portraits.

Sokolovski made his debut at the 1876 Salon. His watercolours are particularly outstanding.

SOKOLOVSKI, Jakob

Polish, 19th century.
Born 1784, in Wyczolki; died 1837, in Bukova.
Draughtsman, engraver (etching), lithographer, watercolourist. Historical figures.

Jakob Sokolovski studied under E. Pinck.

MUSEUMS AND GALLERIES:
CRACOW (Muz. Narodowe) - WARSAW (Muz. Narodowe): *Prince Constantin on Horseback*; 17 watercolours of servicemen.

SOKOLOVSKI, Zygmunt or Sigmond

Polish, 19th century.
Born 1859, near Posen (now Poznan); died 1888, in Paris.
Painter.

The museum in Cracow owns Zygmunt Sokolovski's *David Playing the Harp*.

SOKOR

Bohemian School, 19th century.
Born in Bohemia.
Painter.

Sokor is considered one of the pioneers of modern concepts in art which originated in France.

SOKOTNIK, Marx or Marcus.
See **SCHOKOTNIGG**

SOKOV, Leonid Petrovich

Russian, 20th century.
Born 11 October 1941, in Mikhailevo (Kalinin).
Active in the USA from 1979.
Sculptor.
Sots Art.

Sokov was one of the artists who, with Komar, Melamid and Kosolapov, used the heroic imagery of the USSR Socialist State by twisting it, and whose works were described by the art critics as 'Sots Art' or 'Soc Art'.

Sokov is the sculptor of Sots Art; he matched the artistic forms of Russian folklore with those of Socialist Realism. His *History of the USSR: Leaders* (1983) forms a series each work consisting of small wooden figurines installed one on top of the other in the shape of a pyramid. Interchangeable, they represent Soviet and international leaders on which the protective figure of Stalin holds court. He lives and works in New York.

Sokov appeared in 2003 at *Berlin-Moscow/Moscow-Berlin 1950-2000*, a panoramic exhibition which, following on from a previous exhibition on the period from 1900-1950, provided material for discussion on 50 years of Germano-Russian artistic and cultural relations influenced by the political changes at the Martin-Gropius-Bau in Berlin and at the Tretyakov Gallery in Moscow.

BIBLIOGRAPHY:
'Berlin-Moskau/Moskau-Berlin 1950-2000' in *2 vols.*, exhibition catalogue, Martin-Gropius-Bau, Berlin, 2003 (text in German).

SOL, Agricole

French, 19th century.
Born in Paris.
Painter. Genre scenes.

Sol was a pupil of Pils and Corot and made his Salon debut in 1877.

SOLA, Antonio

Spanish, 19th century.
Born 1787, in Barcelona; died 7 June 1861, in Barcelona.
Sculptor.

Antonio Sola studied in Barcelona and Rome. There are examples of his work in Barcelona, Havana and Rome.

BIBLIOGRAPHY:
Marin Medina, J., *La escultura española contemporánea 1800-1978: Historia y evolución crítica*, Edarcón, Madrid, 1978.

MUSEUMS AND GALLERIES:
MADRID: *Charity*; *Blaseo de Garay*; *Pius VII*.

SOLA, Léon

French, 20th century.
Painter. Figures, landscapes, still-lifes.

AUCTION RECORDS:
PARIS, 22 Jan 1921, *Figure*, FRF 95; *Children at the Port*, FRF 100. PARIS, 22 Nov 1922, *Seated Young Woman: Nude Study*, FRF 100. PARIS, 29 Dec 1927, *Village beside the River*, FRF 280. PARIS, 16 March 1929, *Young Girl with Jug*, FRF 130. PARIS, 15 Feb 1930, *Still-life with Fish*, FRF 30. PARIS, 30 May 1945, *Still-life with Apples*, FRF 120.

SOLAKOV, Nedko

Bulgarian, 20th - 21st century.
Born 28 December 1957, in Cherven Bryag.
Installation artist.
Conceptual Art.

Solakov completed his studies at the academy of fine art in Sofia in 1982 in Mito Ganovski's monumental painting class. He went on to study in Belgium in 1985-1986 at the Nationaal Hoger Instituut voor Schone Kunsten in Antwerp. He was one of the founders in 1986-1987 of the art group City, which played a vital part until 1992 in the development of informal aesthetic movements in the context of Bulgarian plastic art. He worked as a scholar in Zurich in 1992 at the Artest Foundation and then in Austria in 1993 at the Kultur Kontakt in Vienna. He went to the Künstlerhaus Bethanien in Berlin in 1994-1995, having received a grant from the Philip Morris Foundation.

Solakov works exclusively in the field of installation. His works are monumental narrative productions that develop on several levels: narrative line combining several themes, disturbing plastic forms, vivid details suggesting a plausible effect of the whole, and playful elements catching the spectator's attention. His installations invade the spectator's senses.

He has taken part in collective exhibitions, including: 1993, *Aperto 93* at the Venice Biennale; *Exchange II*, Schedhalle, Zurich; 1994, *Europa 94*, Munich; 22nd São Paulo Biennale; 1995, *Club Berlin-Kunstwerke* (*Berlin Works of Art Club*) at the Venice Biennale; *Orient-ation* at the 4th Biennale in Istanbul; 1996, *Beyond Belief*, Museum of Contemporary Art, Chicago; at the Institute of Contemporary Art in Philadelphia; *The Sense of Order*, Moderna Galeria, Ljubljana; *Manifesto I*, Rotterdam; *Inclusion: Exclusion*, Steirischer Herbst '96, Graz; and *Scream/Borealis'8*, Arken Museum for Moderne Kunst, Copenhagen.

Solo exhibitions include: 1993, *Good Luck*, Medizinhistorisches Museum, Zurich; *Adventures of François de Bergeron*, French Institute, Sofia; 1994, *The Superstitious Man*, Museum of Contemporary Art, Skopje; Center for Curatorial Studies, Bard College, New York; 1995, *Mr Curator, Please...*, Künstlerhaus Bethanien, Berlin; 1995, *Touching Antiquity*, Galerie Ata-Ray, Sofia; 1996, *Graffitis*, National Gallery of Fine Art, Sofia; *Desires*, Galerie Arndt & Partner, Berlin; and 2004, Casino Luxembourg - Contemporary Art Forum.

BIBLIOGRAPHY:

Barsch, Barbara, *Nedko Solakov*, exhibition catalogue, Ifa-Galerie Friedrichstrasse, Stuttgart, 1992. *Eran Schaerf, Peter Wüthrich, Nedko Solakov, Anders Widoff, Nathalie Tison*, exhibition catalogue, Shedhalle, Zurich, 1993 (text in German and English). *Nedko Solakov: the collector of art*, exhibition catalogue, Ludwig Múzeum, Budapest, 1994. Fricke, Harald, '*Nedko Solakov*' in *Flash Art*, periodical, Milan, December, 1995.

SOLANA, José Gutiérrez

Spanish, 20th century.

Born 1886, in Madrid; died 24 June 1945, in Madrid.

Painter, engraver, draughtsman. Religious subjects, portraits, scenes with figures, genre scenes, still-lifes, animals.

Symbolism, Magical Realism.

A descendant of an ancient but penniless family from which he inherited no more than certain bizarre character traits, Solana was almost entirely self-educated, teaching himself to paint and write in order to express the strangeness of the passions which enveloped him. His teachers were García del Valla and Diez Palma and he studied at the Escuela de Bellas Artes in Madrid from 1900 to 1904. He lived in Paris from 1937 to 1939. On his return to Madrid, like Toulouse-Lautrec in Paris, he spent nearly all his time in the most obscure quarters of the city or visited the villages of Castille and the ports of the Bay of Biscay, mingling with the local people and taking part in their festivals in search of the lost traces of a former proud tradition.

Solana was an outsider who cannot be easily categorized; he embraced his Hispanic soul almost to the point of caricature. He continued the denunciation of the flaws in Spanish society begun by Isidro Nonell in the Goya tradition, but, though in the same generation as Picasso, he never positioned himself in the international evolution of pictorial expression. Ever the provincialist, he deliberately dedicated his art to all things Spanish. Jacques Lassaigne, an astute commentator on Spain, has written: 'Writers of the *Generation of 98* (a literary group]) like Unamuno and Ganivet Ortega analysed the causes of the decadence in Spain in order to seek the remedies. Solana, on the other hand, feels no need to denounce a heritage whose misery he regards with fondness and which holds, according to him, hidden and vital significance'.

By 1898, with the decay of the Spanish Empire setting in for good, the first social uprisings started to clash with the forces of repression. The noble aims of the Anarchists were gaining the attention of young intellectuals. In his paintings and in the two volumes of *Scenes and Customs of Madrid*, which he published in 1912 and 1918, as well as in *Black Spain* of 1920, Solana effectively drew up a list of the country's failings with *The Choir, The Return of the Indian, The Bishop's Visit* and *The Destitute*. Technically, the only thing that concerned him was using the most direct and violent forms of expression using a robust realism derived from combining powerful volumetric drawing with accentuated contrasts of light and shade. This method links him closely to Spanish artistic tradition as seen in the works of El Greco, Velázquez, Ribera and Goya, but also invites comparison with the principles of the German Neue Sachlichkeit Group, in particular those of Otto Dix. When not attending the low-life festivals of rundown areas, Solana would escape to scour the stalls of the Rastro, Madrid's main flea market, bringing back the pathetic vestiges of a once exotic but now outmoded past, including wax dolls in old-fashioned costumes, silent witnesses of bygone days. On a trip to Paris, he was not fired by the revolutionary new aspects of painting which were influencing artists across the world, but was inspired by the display cases at the Musée Grevin, the waxworks museum, which prompted him to execute several compositions including *Charlotte Corday* and *Madame Roland*. Jacques Lassaigne has noted that Solana imbued his groups of painted figures with a rigidity normally only used for objects and arranged them by affinity or profession as if to classify them. In contrast, however, he breathed new life into the remnants of the past. All his life, Solana behaved like an anarchic outsider, less glamorous but no less appealing than Gauguin or Van Gogh.

Solana was first spotted at an exhibition of the Círculo de Bellas Artes, Madrid (1907). Major exhibitions soon spread awareness of his unique talent across the world. He participated in several collective exhibitions including: National Society for the Fine Arts, Madrid (1917 where he was awarded a third class medal); Royal Academy, London (1920); Salón de Otoño, Madrid (from 1920); Venice Biennale (1922 to 1942); Humorists Salon, Madrid (1923 and 1924); Brooklyn Museum, New York and Carnegie Institute, Pittsburgh (1925, 1926); Círculo de Bellas Artes, Madrid (1928 to 1945 with a gold medal in 1943); Exposición Internacional, Barcelona (1929 with a first class medal); Musée du Jeu de Paume, Paris (1936); Exposition Universelle, Paris (1937).

He also showed his work in solo exhibitions including: Santander High School (1921, 1928 and 1934); Museo d'Arte Moderno, Madrid (1927 and 1929); Bernheim-Jeanne Gallery, Paris (1928); Estilo Gallery, Madrid (1943). Solana won most of the principal official distinctions of his country, despite the arrogant impropriety of his chosen themes.

J. Solana

BIBLIOGRAPHY:

Arnáiz, José Manuel/López Jiménez, Javier/Merchán Díaz, Manuel (ed.), '*Cien años de pintura en Espana y Portugal (1830-1930)*' in vol. X, Antiqvaria, Madrid, 1993.

Museums and Galleries:
Barcelona (MAM del Mus. Nacional d'Art de Catalunya): *The Choir* (c. 1922) - Bilbao (MBA): *Women of the World* - Madrid (Mus. de Arte Moderno): *The Pombo Group* (1920) - Paris (MNAM-CCI): *Young Female Bullfighters.*
Auction records:
London, 24-27 June 1925, *Village Carnival,* GBP 63. London, 7 July 1971, *Village Carnival,* GBP 15,000. Madrid, 4 June 1978, *Poor People* (etching, 11 x 83/4 ins / 27 x 22.5 cm) ESP 32,000. London, 1 Dec 1980, *Picador and Bull* (oil on canvas, 241/2 x 281/2 ins / 62.2 x 72.5 cm) GBP 18,000. London, 30 Oct 1981, *Portrait of a Venetian Woman in a Black Dress* (oil on panel, 93/4 x 71/2 ins / 24.6 x 19 cm) GBP 1,500. Madrid, 22 Feb 1983, *Portrait of an Old Peasant Woman* (chalk/paper, 26 x 18 ins / 66 x 46 cm) ESP 800,000. Paris, 21 Nov 1983, *Plants* (oil on canvas, 39 x 483/4 ins / 99 x 124 cm) FRF 222,000. Madrid, 24 Oct 1984, *Maniqui* (oil on canvas, 381/4 x 251/2 ins / 97 x 65 cm) ESP 2,250,000. Madrid, 20 May 1985, *Three Women* (oil on canvas, 321/4 x 261/4 ins / 82 x 66.5 cm) ESP 8,900,000. London, 24 June 1986, *Hairdressers* (c. 1937, oil on canvas, 641/4 x 431/4 ins / 163 x 110 cm) GBP 82,000. Madrid, 17 March 1987, *The Revolutionary Tribunal at the Musée Grevin: Madame Roland before the Judges* (1928-1929, oil on canvas, 44 x 56 ins / 112 x 142 cm) ESP 12,000,000. Madrid, 5 Nov 1987, *Masks in the Meadows* (1930-1933, pen, wash and pencil, 9 x 61/2 ins / 23 x 16.5 cm) ESP 1,520,000. New York, 23 May 1990, *Blind Street Singer* (oil on card, 213/4 x 18 ins / 55.2 x 45.7 cm) USD 101,750. Romans-sur-Isère, 8 July 1990, *Procession - the Judas Kiss* (1932, oil on canvas, 893/4 x 82 ins / 228 x 208 cm) FRF 2,600,000. Madrid, 22 Nov 1990, *Old Woman from the Mountains* (charcoal, 26 x 18 ins / 66 x 46 cm) ESP 3,360,000. Madrid, 28 Jan 1992, *Masquerade (The Cook)* (pencil/paper, 173/4 x 111/4 ins / 45 x 28.5 cm) ESP 1,176,000. Madrid, 24 March 1992, *Still-life with Cauliflower* (oil on canvas, 243/4 x 283/4 ins / 63 x 73 cm) ESP 14,000,000. Madrid, 16 June 1992, *Mask* (oil on canvas, 27 x 21 ins / 68.5 x 53.5 cm) ESP 12,500,000.

SOLANAS
Spanish, 15th century.
Active in Saragossa at the beginning of the 15th century.
Sculptor (wood).
Solanas was commissioned in 1413 to carve the two lions at the base of the lectern in Saragossa Cathedral.

SOLANES, Andrés de
Spanish, 17th century.
Active in Valladolid.
Sculptor.
Andrés de Solanes was a pupil of Gregorio Fernandez. He carved a very fine retable, the painted elements of which were executed by the French painter Reynaldo de Valdelante, justifiably renowned for his perspective work.

SOLANGE, Marthe
French, 20th century.
Painter, pastellist, watercolourist. Still-lifes (flowers/fruit).
Auction records:
Paris, 22 Dec 1941, *Mandarin Oranges* (1923, pastel) FRF 300; *Garden* (1925, gouache) FRF 405. Paris, 14 May 1943, *Basket of Fruit* (pastel) FRF 130. Paris, 19 Jan 1949, *Fruit* (1923, pastel) FRF 280.

SOLANO, Juan
Spanish, 15th century.
Active in Saragossa at the beginning of the 15th century.
Painter.
Juan Solano painted a number of altarpieces for churches in Aragon between 1401 and 1407.

SOLANO, Juan
Spanish, 16th century.
Active in Toledo.
Sculptor.
Juan Solano was the son of Pedro. The two men made a marble base for the choir grille in Toledo Cathedral.

SOLANO, Nicolás
Spanish, 15th century.
Active in Saragossa at the beginning of the 15th century.
Painter.
Nicolás Solano collaborated with his brother Juan in the execution of altarpieces.

SOLANO, Pedro
Spanish, 16th century.
Active from 1539 to 1548.
Sculptor.
Pedro Solano carried out work in the choir of Toledo Cathedral.

SOLANO, Susana
Spanish, 20th - 21st century.
Born 25 July 1946, in Barcelona.
Sculptor.
Solano studied at the Escuela de Bellas Artes in Barcelona, where she teaches sculpture. She lives and works in Sant Just Desvern near Barcelona. Solano initially carved in wood, before subsequently using materials such as sheet metal. Working in metal, she has produced cage-like objects, particularly with wire mesh, which confines and visualises the external and internal volume and space of the object. While there is an element of minimalism in her work, her sculptures should not be 'read' in a strictly formal manner. She incorporates a timeless existential and metaphysical dimension into her work, by way of traditional and modern shapes. She has exhibited at group exhibitions including *Preliminar,* a travelling exhibition in Spain in 1983, *En Tres Dimensiones* (*In Three Dimensions*) at Fundación Caixa de Pensions in Madrid in 1984, *Peintres et Sculpteurs Espagnols* at Fondation Cartier in Jouy-en-Josas in 1986, *Documenta 8* in Kassel in 1987, the XIX São Paulo Biennale in 1987, *Espagne 87. Dynamiques et Interrogations* at ARC, Musée d'Art Moderne in Paris in 1987, and in the Spanish pavillion at the Venice Biennale in 1988. She has also given solo exhibitions including at Fundació Joan Miró in Barcelona in 1980, at Galeria Ciento in Barcelona in 1983, at Galeria Fernando Vijande in Madrid in 1986, at Capc Musée d'Art Contemporain in Bordeaux in 1987, in Maastricht in 1988, at Städtisches Museum Abteiberg in 1989 and at Galerie Lelong in Paris in 1991.
Bibliography:
Poinsot, J.- M., *La Sculpture de Susana Solano,* Capc musée d'Art contemporain, Bordeaux, 1987. Francblin, Catherine, '*Les Sculptures pièges de Susana Solano*' in *Artstudio* no. 14, periodical, Gal. Templon, Paris, autumn 1989. *Catálogo nacional de arte contemporáneo 1990-1991,* Ibérico 2Mil, Barcelona, 1990-1991. Garcia, Aurora, '*Susana Solano. Portrait*' in *Beaux-Arts Magazine,* periodical, Paris, October 1991.
Museums and Galleries:
Paris (FNAC): *No te pases no 2* (*Steady on No 2*) (1988).
Auction records:
Paris, 8 Oct 1989, *Studies* (1986, Indian ink/paper, 251/2 x 193/4 ins / 65 x 50 cm) FRF 3,800. Paris, 18 Feb 1990, *Landscape for Richard Serra* (welded iron, 331/2 x 223/4 ins / 85 x 58 cm) FRF 130,000. Madrid, 26 Nov 1992, *Patena de Transit No 2* (iron, 2 x 19 x 131/2 ins / 5 x 48 x 34 cm) ESP 1,288,000. Paris, 19 March 1993, *Untitled* (1987, charcoal, wash and gouache/paper, 271/4 x 19 ins / 69.5 x 48.5 cm) FRF 3,500. Madrid, 10 June 1993, *Patena de Transit No 6* (iron, 11/4 x 17 x 15 ins / 3 x 43 x 38 cm) ESP 1,150,000. London, 27 Oct 1994, *Recession 3* (1983, bronze, 11/2 x 193/4 x 81/4 ins / 4 x 50 x 21

cm) GBP 2,530. NEW YORK, 7-8 May 1997, *Shadow Deposit 12* (1984, steel, 20 x 59 x 40 ins / 50.8 x 150.1 x 101.6 cm) USD 9,775. NEW YORK, 17 Nov 1999, *Object and Cause* (1988, galvanized steel, 59 x 127 ins / 150 x 322 cm) USD 22,000. MADRID, 8 May 2000, *Untitled* (metal and aluminium sheet, 15 x 11x6 ins / 39 x 29x15 cm) ESP 1,000,000. NEW YORK, 13 Nov 2002, *Charity, no. 5* (1988, iron and wood, 72 x 70x18 ins / 183 x 179x45 cm) USD 17,000. NEW YORK, 14 May 2003, *Stanca no. 2* (1986, steel construction, 30 x 54x54 ins / 76 x 138x138 cm) USD 15,000. NEW YORK, 12 Nov 2003, *Que Duda Cabe no. 3* (1987, steel and lead, 30 x 30x31 ins / 77 x 75x79 cm) USD 12,000. MADRID, 6 Oct 2004, *Maze IV* (1986, iron, 11 x 28x29 ins / 28 x 70x74 cm) EUR 20,000.

SOLAR, Xul, or Xul Solar Alejandro, pseudonym of Solari Oscar Schulz
Argentinian, 20th century.
Born 1887; died 1963, in Buenos Aires.
Painter, draughtsman, watercolourist. Figure compositions, figures, landscapes, landscapes with figures, urban landscapes.

Xul Solar was keenly interested in the occult, in philology and astrology. He lived in the Far East, and in various countries in Europe, where he had exhibitions, notably in Milan in 1920.

Until 1930 his paintings displayed a fresh humorous quality like that of a child's drawing; after that date they are burdened with heavy symbolism. His style, reminiscent of that of Paul Klee, includes stylised figures, a quantity of symbolic items, especially ladders, and draws on the universe of signs. It was not at first recognised in Europe. Solar painted an important series of imaginary landscapes and buildings. His friend and admirer Jorge Luis Borges said that, 'He told me he was a realist painter in the sense that his painting was not an arbitrary combination of forms and figures but showed what he had seen in his visions'.

His work was shown in collective exhibitions, including in 2000 the *Machine Vision*, which featured the 'seeing machines' used by artists and architects, at the Musée des Beaux-Arts in Nantes. Among retrospectives were the Museo de Bellas Artes in Buenos Aires (1968); Musée d'Art Moderne de la Ville de Paris (1977); *The Architectures* at the Courtauld Institute in London (1994); Palacio Episcopal, Malaga (1998).

BIBLIOGRAPHY:

Gradowczyk, Mario H., *Alejandro Xul Solar*, Ediciones Alba, Buenos Aires, 1994 (English edition, Abrams, New York, 1994). *Vision machine*, exhibition catalogue, Musée des Beaux-Arts, Nantes, Somogy, Paris, 2000.

AUCTION RECORDS:

NEW YORK, 7 May 1981, *Casi Plantas* (1946, watercolour and gouache, 13 3/4 x 19 1/4 ins / 35 x 49.2 cm) USD 2,300. NEW YORK, 18 Nov 1987, *Composition* (1930, tempera/mounted paper/card, 12 1/2 x 18 1/4 ins / 32 x 46.5 cm) USD 8,500. NEW YORK, 17 May 1988, *Masks* (1924, watercolour/card, 6 x 7 3/4 ins / 15 x 19.5 cm) USD 20,900. NEW YORK, 17 May 1989, *Mansilla 2936* (1920, watercolour/paper, 5 1/2 x 7 1/4 ins / 13.7 x 18.6 cm) USD 24,200. NEW YORK, 21 Nov 1989, *Axende Encurvas Miflama Hasta el Sol* (1922, pencil, gouache and ink/paper, 8 1/4 x 5 ins / 21 x 12.6 cm) USD 22,000. NEW YORK, 1 May 1990, *International* (1923, watercolour and collage/paper, 8 1/4 x 10 ins / 21 x 25.5 cm) USD 28,600. NEW YORK, 20-21 Nov 1990, *Egyptian Souls* (1923, gouache/paper/card, 6 x 8 1/4 ins / 15 x 21.2 cm) USD 25,300. NEW YORK, 20 Nov 1991, *Shadow of a Railwayman* (oil on panel, 8 1/4 x 8 1/4 ins / 21 x 21 cm) USD 35,200. NEW YORK, 18-19 May 1992, *National Festivity* (1925, watercolour and ink/paper, 11 x 15 ins / 28 x 38 cm) USD 55,000. NEW YORK, 24 Nov 1992, *Motherland B* (1925, watercolour, colouring pencil and graphite, 13 1/2 x 11 ins / 34 x 28 cm) USD 38,500. NEW YORK, 18 May 1993, *Landscape with Five Pagodas* (1949, watercolour/paper/card, 15 1/4 x 12 1/2 ins / 38.5 x 32 cm) USD 51,750. NEW YORK, 16 Nov 1994, *Six Faces* (1922, watercolour, tempera and graphite/paper/paper construction, 4 x 9 1/4 ins / 10.2 x 23.5 cm) USD 17,250. NEW YORK, 15 May 1996, *Saints Dancing* (1925, watercolour and graphite/paper/card, 9 1/4 x 12 ins / 23.5 x 30.5 cm) USD 43,700. NEW YORK, 29-30 May 1997, *Criol Pajaros* (1927, watercolour, gouache and graphite/paper, 13 x 10 ins / 32.1 x 25.1 cm) USD 36,800.

SOLARI. See **LOMBARDO Aurelio, Girolamo** and **Lodovico**

SOLARI. See also **SOLARIO, SOLARO**

SOLARI, Achille
Italian, 19th century.
Born 9 October 1835, in Naples.
Painter. Landscapes.

A student at the Instituto di Belle Arti in Naples, Solari exhibited in Turin, Naples and London.

AUCTION RECORDS:

LONDON, 7 May 1980, *View of Sorrento* (oil on panel, 7 1/2 x 12 3/4 ins / 19 x 32.5 cm) GBP 450. LONDON, 11 July 1983, *Views of the Bay of Naples* (oil on panel, series of four, 4 1/4 x 9 ins / 11 x 22 cm) GBP 950. ROME, 13 Dec 1994, *Gulf of Pozzuoli; Cabins on a Beach* (oil on canvas, a pair, each 10 1/2 x 16 ins / 26.5 x 40.5 cm) ITL 14,950,000. LONDON, 15 March 1996, *Panorama of Sorrento* (oil on panel, 7 x 12 1/2 ins / 18 x 32 cm) GBP 4,600. LONDON, 13 March 1997, *Capri Seen from Massa Lubrente; Coast of Sorrento; Bay of Naples; Sorrento* (oil on panel, series of four, 12 x 5 ins / 30.5 x 12.5 cm) GBP 3,450. NEW YORK, 28 March 2000, *Neapolitan Views* (oil on panel, a pair, 13 x 7 ins / 33 x 18 cm) USD 2,200. BILLINGSHURST, 6 June 2000, *Napoli da Posilipo. Napoli di Posilipo Eppetto di Sera* (oil on panel, a pair, 13 x 7 ins / 33 x 18 cm) GBP 2,100. VIENNA, 20 Nov 2001, *Gulf of Sorrento from Capodimonte* (oil on canvas, 11 x 16 ins / 28 x 40 cm) ATS 50,000. VIENNA, 29 Nov 2001, *Naples with Vesuvius* (oil on board, 9 x 10 ins / 22 x 25 cm) ATS 40,000. LONDON, 21 March 2002, *Two Views of Naples* (oil on panel, a pair, 13 x 7 ins / 32 x 18 cm) GBP 1,300. STUTTGART, 18 Sept 2003, *Landscape near Naples* (oil on canvas, 11 x 19 ins / 28 x 48 cm) EUR 1,500. ROME, 10 Dec 2003, *Naples from Sorrento. Capri from Sorrento* (oil on canvas, a pair, 11 x 16 ins / 27 x 40 cm) EUR 8,200.

SOLARI, Andrea. See **SOLARIO**

SOLARI, Andrea, or Andrea da Carona
Italian, 15th century.
Active in Carona (Lombardy) from 1444 to 1445.
Sculptor.

Andrea Solari was the brother of Filippo.

SOLARI, Andrea
Austrian, 18th century.
Active in Luditz, Bohemia, 1700-1704.
Sculptor.

SOLARI, Angelo
Italian, 19th century.
Born 12 December 1775, in Caserte; died 6 April 1846, in Naples.
Sculptor.

Angelo Solari produced work for several churches, first in Caserte and then in Naples.

SOLARI, Antonio
Italian, 17th century.
Active in Genoa in 1628.
Sculptor.

Antonio Solari executed part of the fountain in front of the ducal palace in Genoa.

SOLARI, Antonio
Italian, 18th century.
Active in the Netherlands.
Sculptor.
A pharmacist in Leeuwarden commissioned a statue of Aesculpius by Antonio Solari.

SOLARI, Antonio. See also **SOLARI Ignazio** and **LOMBARDO Antonio I** and **Aurelio**

SOLARI, Bartolomeo. See **SOLARO**

SOLARI, Bartolomeo Antonio
Italian, 19th century.
Born 1807, in Figgino di Barbengo; died 1868.
Painter.
A student of the academy in Milan, Bartolomeo Solari executed a number paintings for palazzi, town halls and churches in northern Italy.

SOLARI, Bernardino
Italian, 16th century.
Active in Carona (Lombardy).
Sculptor.
Bernardino Solari worked in Genoa in 1548.

SOLARI, Bernardo
Italian, 17th century.
Active during the first half of the 17th century.
Sculptor (wood).
Bernardo Solari carved eagles and garlands on the façade of St Peter's in Rome in 1611.

SOLARI, Cristoforo, or Solario
Italian, 16th century.
Born in Carona (Lombardy).
Sculptor.
Cristoforo Solari worked in Genoa between 1579 and 1583, particularly for Andrea Doria.

SOLARI, Cristoforo da, called il Gobbo (the Hunchback)
Italian, 15th - 16th century.
Born c. 1460, probably in Angera, on Lake Maggiore; died 1527, in Milan.
Sculptor. Religious subjects.
The father of Paolo Emilio and brother of Andrea Solari, Cristoforo Solari was both a sculptor and an architect. In 1490 he made figures of *Eve* and *St George* for the Carità in Venice. Between 1497 and 1499, he carved the effigies for the tombs of *Ludovico il Moro* and *Beatrice d'Este*. Appointed sculptor for Milan Cathedral, he made statues of *Adam* and *Eve* for the exterior in 1502.

As an architect he worked mainly in Milan where he built the cupola of S Maria della Passione and the church of S Maria della Fontana. He also completed the church of S Ambrogio begun by Bramante.
MUSEUMS AND GALLERIES:
PAVIA (Mus. della Certosa): *Ludovico il Moro*; *Beatrice d'Este* (funerary effigies).

SOLARI, Domenico
Italian, 15th century.
Sculptor.
Active in Sonvico, Domenico Solari worked in Siena in 1476-1477.

SOLARI, Domenico di, or Solario
Italian, 15th century.
Sculptor.
Active in Pavia, Domenico di Solari worked in marble.

SOLARI, Filippo
Italian, 15th century.
Died before 1477.
Active in Carona (Lombardy).
Sculptor.
The brother of Andrea Solari, Filippo Solari worked in Lombardy in Melido and Milan, and in Venice.
BIBLIOGRAPHY:
Schulza, Anne M., *'A Venetian sculpture by Lombard sculptors: Filippo Solari, Andrea da Carona, and the Franco altarpiece for S Pietro di Castello, Venice'* in *Burlington Magazine*, vol 139, 1997.

SOLARI, Francesco, or Solaro or Solario
Italian, 16th - 17th century.
Born in Claino (Lombardy).
Active in Rome from 1580 to 1619.
Sculptor (stone/wood).
Francesco Solari worked at St Peter's Basilica in Rome.

SOLARI, Francesco, or Solario
Italian, 17th century.
Born 21 May 1618, in Rome; died 29 August 1664, in Rome.
Painter.
The son of Giovanni Antonio Solari, Francesco Solari was a member of the Accademia di S Luca about 1636.

SOLARI, Francesco di, or Solario
Italian, 15th century.
Born in Carona (Lombardy); died 2 January 1470, in Milan.
Sculptor, architect.
Francesco di Solari executed work in the small cloister of the Carthusian convent in Pavia and at the Cathedral and the Ospedale Maggiore both in Milan.

SOLARI, Francesco or Franzio. See **SOLARO**

SOLARI, Giambattista
Italian, 19th century.
Active in Genoa.
Medallist.
Solari engraved a medal with a portrait of *Columbus* dated 1837.

SOLARI, Giorgio
Italian, 17th century.
Active in Carona (?) during the first half of the 17th century.
Sculptor.
Giorgio Solari worked on the portal of the church in Grosotto in 1639.

SOLARI, Giorgio de', or Solario
Swiss, 15th century.
Active in Solario (Tessin).
Sculptor.
From 1403 to 1404 Giorgio de'Solari worked for Milan Cathedral, where he carved a *St George* and two statues of prophets.

SOLARI, Giovanni Antonio
Italian, 17th century.
Born c. 1581, in Milan; died 8 March 1666, in Rome.
Painter.
Giovanni Antonio Solari was the father of Francesco Solari.

SOLARI, Giovanni Domenico
Italian, 16th century.
Born in Piumazzo (Emilia Romagna).
Sculptor.
Giovanni Solari worked in Genoa between 1538 and 1550.

SOLARI, Guiniforte or Boniforte
Italian, 15th century.
Born 1429; died early January 1481, in Milan.
Sculptor, architect.
The father of Pietro Antonio Solari,Guiniforte Solari worked at Milan Cathedral and the Carthusian convent in Pavia.

SOLARI, Ignazio
Austrian, 17th century.
Died after 1646, probably en 1650.
Active in Salzburg, Austria.
Painter.
Ignazio Solari painted a *Crucifixion* for the church of St Peter in Salzburg and several frescoes for the cathedral of Salzburg.

SOLARI, Michele
Italian, 16th century.
Born in Carona (Lombardy).
Sculptor.
Michele Solari worked in Genoa occasionally with Giacomo della Porta.

SOLARI, Oscar Schulz. See **SOLAR Xul**

SOLARI, Paolo Emilio
Italian, 16th century.
Sculptor.
The son of Cristoforo Solari, Paolo Emilio worked at Milan Cathedral between 1515 and 1521.

SOLARI, Philippe
French, 19th - 20th century.
Born 1840, in Aix-en-Provence; died 1906, in Aix-en-Provence.
Sculptor.
Philippe Solari was a student of Jouffroy. He made his first appearance at the Salon in 1867. He created a bust of *Émile Zola*, which was unveiled at the Montmartre Cemetery on 21 May 1904.

SOLARI, Pietro, or Solario
Italian, 18th century.
Died 1790, in Caserta.
Sculptor.
Pietro Solari, the son and pupil of Tommaso Solari I, sculpted statues in the park of the palace at Caserta.

SOLARI, Pietro. See also **LOMBARDO Pietro and Tullio**

SOLARI, Pietro Antonio, or Solario
Italian, 15th century.
Born after 1450, possibly in Milan; died 1493, in Moscow.
Sculptor, architect.
The son and pupil of Guiniforte Solari, Pietro Antonio worked at the Cathedral and the Ospedale Maggiore in Milan. He settled in Moscow in 1490 where he carried out work at the Kremlin.

SOLARI, Pompeo. See **SOLARO**

SOLARI, Raymond
French, 20th - 21st century.
Born 22 September 1947, in Marseilles.
Painter. Figures, landscapes.
Raymond Solari studied at the École des Beaux-Arts in Marseilles before enrolling at the École des Beaux-Arts in Paris. He has worked as a set designer for television productions. His style derives from Fauvism and features bold and generously applied contrasting colours which yield contorted landscapes and figures.

Solari's work has featured at various group exhibitions, notably from 1970 at the Salon des Artistes Français in Paris (he became a member of the Society in 1987) and from 1970 regularly at the Salon d'Automne. He has exhibited solo in Paris and Lyons and in the USA.

SOLARI, Santino or Santini, known as Santin, or Solario
Swiss, 17th century.
Born 1576, in Verna, near Lugano; died 10 April 1646, in Salzburg, Austria.
Sculptor, architect.
Santino Solari worked for the archbishops of Salzburg, producing buildings and architectural sculptures from 1612.

SOLARI, Tommaso I
Italian, 18th century.
Died 1779, in Caserta.
Active in Genoa.
Sculptor.
Most of the works of Tommaso Solari I, the father of Pietro and Angelo Solari, were carried out for the royal palace and park at Caserta.

SOLARI, Tommaso II
Italian, 19th century.
Born 4 September 1820, in Naples; died 2 December 1897, in Naples.
Sculptor.
The son of Angelo Solari, Tommaso Solari II studied in Naples and Rome. He carved many statues for churches and public buildings in Naples.
MUSEUMS AND GALLERIES:
NAPLES (Mus. di Capodimonte): *Bacchante*.

SOLARI, Tullio
Italian, 17th century.
Born c. 1577; died 1626, in Rome.
Sculptor.
Tullio Solari executed sculptures in the Sistine Chapel and the churches of S Maria Maggiore, S Maria della Scala and S Maria della Pace in Rome.

SOLARI, Tullio. See also **LOMBARDO Pietro and Tullio**

SOLARIO. See also **SOLARI** and **SOLARO**

SOLARIO, Andrea, or Solari
Italian, 15th - 16th century.
Born c. 1470, in Solario or in Milan; died 1524, in Milan or Pavia.
Painter. Religious subjects, portraits, landscapes.
Because some of the works by Andrea Solario are signed *Andreas Mediolanensis*, they have sometimes been confused with those of another Andrea from Milan, Solaino or Salai, a pupil of Leonardo da Vinci. Andrea Solario has sometimes been given the nickname *il Gobbo* (the Hunchback) but in reality this name was used to refer to his brother the sculptor Cristoforo. According to the most recent research, Andrea Solario came from a family of artists who had moved from Solario to Milan in the first half of the 15th century. Andrea apparently was born in Milan in about 1460 but remained there for only three years. It is not known if he studied with any master. He went to Venice in 1490 with his elder brother Cristoforo, a sculptor, remaining there for three years. He probably received at this time a commission for his *The Holy Family with St Jerome*, also known as *Virgin and Child with Two Saints*, for the church of S Pietro in the island of Murano (now in the Brera in Milan). Two works, a *Crucifixion* of 1503 (Louvre) and an *Annunciation* of 1506, both show the fusing of the influences of Leonardo and Dürer, particularly in the case of the latter work where Leonardo's sfumato is particularly apparent. At this same period he also produced a number of portraits including: *Gentleman* (Boston), *Gentleman with a Pink* (London), *Portrait of a Man by a Balustrade* (1500, Brera) and *Cristoforo Longoni* (1505, Brera).

Not long after, Andrea Solario was summoned to France by Cardinal Charles d'Amboise to work on the decoration of the cardinal's chateau at Gaillon. The accounts recording the work provide specific details. Solario left Milan on 6 August 1507; he travelled on horseback, accompanied by a valet or assistant referred to as 'his man', and received 70 gold pieces. He worked at the chateau until the end of 1509, during which time he painted the chapel, destroyed unfortunately in 1793. As well as this work, he also painted a number of pictures. An inventory of the chateau drawn up in 1550 mentions 'a beautiful painting of the Nativity of Our Lord', a painting that subsequently disappeared. The count of Pourtalés had in his collection a *Madonna and Child,* signed and dated 1507, similar in every detail to the painting in the Louvre known as the *Virgin with the Green Cushion*. According to Félibien, this was acquired by Marie de' Medici in 1619 from the convent of the Cordeliers in Blois who had been given it by Cardinal d'Amboise. Dating from the same period is a *Pietà*, a *Head of St John the Baptist* (1507), an *Ecce Homo, Christ Carrying the Cross* and a *Salome Presenting the Head of St John the Baptist* which gave rise to numerous copies. It has been suggested that Jean Clouet's early portraits were influenced by the works produced by Solario at this time.

In 1514, Solario was in Rome and then, in 1515, in Milan where he painted *Rest on the Flight into Egypt*, a *Pietà* (Washington) and some portraits including *Lady with a Lute* (Rome). The last known work by this artist is an *Assumption of the Virgin,* commissioned in 1515 for the sacristy of the Carthusian church in Pavia. He died before he could finish it and it may have been completed in 1576 by Bernardino Compi.

It is possible to detect in Solario's work a variety of influences: Leonardo, the Venetians around Giovanni Bellini, other artists such as Antonello da Messina, Verrocchio, Boltrafio, Alvise Vivarini, Dürer and the Flemish School, since it is possible that Solario visited Antwerp during the time he was in France. But as an artist Solario had his own personality, particularly in his portraits among which can be included his extraordinary *Heads of St John the Baptist.* Solario painted these as still-lifes, on a fruit dish on a pedestal, replacing all the horror of the event with an unexpected resignation and gentleness; the severed head is reduced to a decorative painting conveying a message of serenity.

·ANDREAS·D·
·SOLARIO·
F
·1505

A: SOLARIO.
·F·

BIBLIOGRAPHY:

Davis, M., *National Gallery Catalogues: The Earlier Italian Schools,* London, 1961. Brown, D.A., *Andrea Solario*, Milan, 1987.

MUSEUMS AND GALLERIES:

BERGAMO (Accademia Carrara): *Virgin and Child; Ecce Homo; Redemption* - BERLIN: *Portrait of a Man* - BOSTON: *Portrait of a Gentleman* - BRESCIA: *Christ Carrying the Cross; Moses Adoring the Cross* - DIJON: *Holy Family* - DUBLIN: *Portrait of an Italian Gentleman* - GRENOBLE: *Christ Carrying the Cross* - LONDON (NG): *A Man with a Pink* (c. 1495, tempera/wood, formerly known as 'Venetian Senator'); *Giovanni Cristoforo Longoni* (1505, oil/wood, portrait) - MILAN (Ambrosiana): *Penitent St Jerome* - MILAN (Pinacoteca di Brera): *Virgin and Christ; The Redeemer; Holy Family and St Jerome* (1495); *Portrait of a Man by a Balustrade* (1500); *Portrait of Cristoforo Longoni* (1505) - NANTES: *Christ Carrying the Cross* - PARIS (Louvre): *Crucifixion* (1503); *Annunciation* (1506); *Virgin with the Green Cushion* (1507); *Charles d'Amboise* (c. 1507); *Head of St John the Baptist* (1507) - ROME (Gal. Nazionale d'Arte Antica di Palazzo Barberini): *Lady with a Lute* - ROME (Mus. e Gal. Borghese): *Jesus with the Pharisees* - ROME (Palazzo Doria Pamphili): *Christ Carrying the Cross* - VIENNA: *Christ Carrying the Cross* - WASHINGTON DC (NGA): *Lamentation* (c. 1505-1507, oil/panel).

AUCTION RECORDS:

PARIS, 1767, *Virgin Suckling the Infant Jesus,* FRF 403. PARIS, 1800, *Salome holding the Head of St John the Baptist,* FRF 1,105. PARIS, 1855, *Virgin and Child,* FRF 600. PARIS, 1861, *Virgin and Child in a Landscape,* FRF 1,105. PARIS, 1865, *Head of St John the Baptist on a Raised Silver Dish,* FRF 2,700. PARIS, 1870, *Virgin and Christ,* FRF 4,520. PARIS, 1881, *Diana,* FRF 4,108. PARIS, 3-5 June 1907, *Virgin and Child,* FRF 4,200. NEW YORK, April 1910, *Annunciation,* FRF 56,500. LONDON, 18 Dec 1925, *Man of Sorrows,* GBP 96. LONDON, 3 May 1929, *Portrait of a Poet,* GBP 325. NEW YORK, 24 April 1930, *Mater Dolorosa,* USD 200. NEW YORK, 4 and 5 Feb 1931, *Mater Dolorosa,* USD 1,150. PARIS, 21 May 1941, *Annunciation* (1506) FRF 650,000. LONDON, 22 June 1960, *Salome,* GBP 1,700. LONDON, 2 July 1965, *Virgin Suckling the Infant Jesus,* Gns 1,000. LONDON, 21 April 1982, *Salome Receiving the Head of St John the Baptist* (oil on canvas, 22 x 18 1/4 ins / 56 x 46.5 cm) GBP 4,000. MILAN, 13 Dec 1989, *Ecce Homo* (oil on panel, 12 x 8 1/2 ins / 30.5 x 21.5 cm) ITL 14,500,000. ROME, 26 May 1993, *The Sea at Palermo* (oil on card, a pair, 11 1/4 x 23 1/4 ins / 28.5 x 59 cm) ITL 1,600,000. NEW YORK, 19 May 1994, *Virgin and Child with St Roch* (tempera and oil on panel, 14 3/4 x 12 3/4 ins / 37.5 x 32.4 cm) USD 222,500. PARIS, 27 June 1994, *Christ of the Reed* (oil on panel, 20 3/4 x 16 1/4 ins / 53 x 41.5 cm) FRF 4,500,000. NEW YORK, 27 Jan 2000, *Madonna and Child* (tempera on panel, 17 x 13 ins / 44 x 33 cm) USD 260,000.

SOLARIO, Antonio di Giovanni di Pietro,
called Lo Zingaro (the Gypsy)
Italian, 16th century.
Painter. Religious subjects.
Neapolitan School.

According to one story, possibly borrowed from the life of Quentin Metsys, Antonio Solario was a blacksmith who fell in love with the daughter of Colantonio del Fiore at the age of 17 and became a painter to impress her. Active between 1502 and 1514, he was a pupil of Dalmasii in Bologna, subsequently studying with Vivarini in Venice, Bieci in Florence and Galassi in Ferrara. Returning to Naples, he married his beloved and became a famous painter. Among his works in Naples are 20 frescoes in a courtyard at the convent of S Severino depicting scenes from the *Life of St Benedict* and an *Ascension* in the church of Monte Oliveto. Solario appears also to have worked in Venice.

BIBLIOGRAPHY:

Falcke, S., '*A Triptych by Antonio da Solario*' in *Burlington Magazine,* vol 69, 1936. Schulza, Anne M., '*A Venetian sculpture by Lombard sculptors: Filippo Solari, Andrea da Carona, and the Franco altarpiece for S Pietro di Castello, Venice*' in *Burlington Magazine,* vol 139, 1997.

MUSEUMS AND GALLERIES:

BRISTOL (City Museum & AG): *St Catherine of Alexandria* (panel, on loan from the National Gallery in London); *St Ursula* (1514, panel, on loan from the National Gallery in London); altarpiece - GENEVA (Mus. Ariana): *Annunciation* - LONDON (NG): *The Virgin and Child with Saint John* (1500-1510, oil on wood transferred to canvas) - MILAN (Ambrosiana): *Head of St John the Baptist* - NAPLES: *Madonna and Child* - ROME (Gal. Doria Pamphili): *Salome with the Head of St John the Baptist; Woman Playing a Violin.*

AUCTION RECORDS:

COLOGNE, 1862, *St Anne Seated on a Throne with the Virgin and Child in her Lap,* FRF 265. MONACO, 16 June 1989, *Virgin and Child* (oil on panel, 49 1/2 x 27 1/2 ins / 126 x 70 cm) FRF 888,000.

SOLARIO, Balzarino
Italian, 15th century.
Active during the second half of the 15th century.
Sculptor.
Balzarino Solario worked at Milan Cathedral from 1460 to 1488 and at the church of S Zaccaria in Venice in 1463.

SOLARIO, Cristoforo da. See **SOLARI Cristoforo**

SOLARIO, Domenico de or di. See **SOLARI Domenico di**

SOLARIO, Francesco. See **SOLARI**

SOLARIO, Francesco di. See **SOLARI**

SOLARIO, Giorgio de'. See **SOLARI**

SOLARIO, Pietro Antonio. See **SOLARI**

SOLARIO, Santino or Santini. See **SOLARI Santino** or **Santini, known as Santin**

SOLARIO, Simone
Italian, 17th century.
Painter and sculptor.
Simone Solario sculpted an *Adoration of the Kings* for the town hall in Atri in 1665.

SOLARO. See also **SOLARI** and **SOLARIO**

SOLARO, Antonio, or Solari
Italian, 17th century.
Active in Naples from 1618 to 1644.
Sculptor.
Antonio Solaro produced capitals, low reliefs and tombs for churches in Naples.

SOLARO, Bartolomeo, or Solari
Italian, 18th century.
Born in Carrara.
Sculptor.
Having studied in Turin with Simone Martinez as well as in Rome, Bartolomeo Solaro executed statues for the sanctuary at Visa, near Mondovi.

SOLARO, Carlo
Italian, 17th century.
Born 1615, in Genoa (?); died 4 December 1680, in Genoa (?).
Sculptor.
The father of Daniello Solaro, Carlo Solaro worked in the Carignano basilica in Genoa.

SOLARO, Daniello
Italian, 17th century.
Born 1634, in Genoa; died 1698; after 1702 according to some sources.
Sculptor.
The son of Carlo Solaro, Daniello was the pupil and assistant of Puget and worked mostly in Genoa.

SOLARO, Francesco. See also **SOLARI**

SOLARO, Francesco or Franzio, or Solari
Italian, 15th century.
Active in Campione (Lombardy) during the first half of the 15th century.
Sculptor, painter. Figures.
Lombard School.
Francesco Solaro worked at Milan Cathedral between 1427 and 1451.

SOLARO, Giovanni
Italian, 17th century.
Died 1657 or 1658, in Genoa.
Painter.
Giovanni Solaro was the pupil and imitator of Giovacchino Assereto.

SOLARO, Martino
Italian, 17th century.
Sculptor.
Active in Lugano, Martino Solaro was active in Turin in the second half of the 17th century. He executed numerous sculptures on the façade of the church of St Francis of Paola in Turin.

SOLARO, Mattia
Italian, 17th century.
Active in Lugano (Ticino), Switzerland.
Sculptor.
Mattia Solara worked on the Palazzo Reale in Turin from 1659 to 1665.

SOLARO, Pompeo
Italian, 17th century.
Born to a family originally from Carona.
Sculptor.
Pompeo Solaro collaborated with Antonio Solaro on the cloisters of the church of the Madonna del Carmine, and also decorated an altar in Cremona cathedral.

SOLAROLA, Jacopo, or Solarolo, called Rosso
Italian, 15th century.
Active during the second half of the 15th century.
Miniaturist.
In 1459, Jacopo Solarola illuminated a *Breviary* and a *Missal* for Duke Borso d'Este. He also produced a treatise on birds and a number of other books including two volumes of *Legends of the Holy Fathers* in 1462 and 1469, and *Cento Morelli* in 1467.

SOLATI, Bartolomeo
Italian, 17th century.
Painter.
Bartolomeo Solati, the pupil of Guercino, painted altarpieces for the churches of Ferrara about 1630.

SOLAVAGIONE, Piero
Italian, 20th century.
Born 18 June 1899, in Carmagnola, near Turin.
Painter. Landscapes.
Solavagione was a pupil of Giacomo and Cesare Ferro.

SOLAZZINO, Giuliano. See **GIULIANO DI GIOVANNI DE' CASTELLANI DA MONTELUPO**

SOLBACH, Andreas, or Solpach
Austrian, 17th century.
Active in Bozen, South Tyrol (now Bolzano, Italy), during the first half of the 17th century.
Painter.

SOLBACH, David
Austrian, 16th century.
Died 24 May 1591, in Brixen, South Tyrol (now Bressanone, Italy).
Painter.
Solbach worked for the Bishop of Brixen, mainly in his castle at Velturns.

SOLBACH, Wilhelm
German, 19th century.
Born 3 July 1812, at Brenzingen Castle; died 19 April 1891, in Cologne.
Painter, art dealer. Landscapes, religious subjects.

SOLBES, Rafael. See **EQUIPO CRONICA**

SOLBRIG, Johann, or Solbrich
Austrian, 19th century.
Born 1780; died 12 August 1828, in Vienna.
Engraver (burin).

SOLBRIG, Johann Gottlieb or Gottlob, or Sollbrig
German, 18th - 19th century.
Born 1765, in Marienthal, Zwickau, (Saxony) Germany; died 1842 (?).
Miniaturist.

Johann Gottlieb Solbrig was a portrait and silhouette artist.

SOLBRIG, Konrad Hieronymus, or Solbrich
Austrian, 19th century.
Born 1792; died 29 April 1822, in Vienna.
Engraver (burin).

SOLDAINI, Raffaello
Italian, 19th century.
Painter.

A pupil of Pietro Benvenuti, Soldaini worked at the Certosa (Carthusian church) outside Parma in 1844. He was a monk.

SOLDAINI, Santi
Italian, 19th century.
Born in the first half of the 19th century, in Pisa.
Painter, draughtsman. Historical subjects. Wall decorations.

Santi Soldaini drew scenes of contemporary history and decorated the ceilings of Palais Eynard in Geneva.

SOLDAN, Melle
Finnish, 19th century.
Born in Finland.
Painter.

Soldan exhibited at the Expositions Universelles in Paris, receiving an honourable mention in 1889 and a bronze medal in 1900.

SOLDAN, Philipp
German, 16th century.
Born c. 1500; died after 1569.
Active in Frankenberg (Hesse).
Sculptor (stone/wood), painter, architect.

Soldan carved many works for the churches and houses of Hesse.

MUSEUMS AND GALLERIES:
KASSEL (Hessisches Landesmus.): *Town Councillor's Chair* - MARBURG: *Plaster ornament.*

SOLDAN-BROFELT, Venny or Vendla Irene
Finnish, 20th century.
Born 2 November 1863, in Helsinki; died 10 October 1945.
Painter. Portraits, genre scenes.

Venny Soldan-Brofelt's work includes a *Portrait of the Painter Juhani Aho, Husband of the Artist.* She exhibited in Paris and was awarded the Grand Prix at the Exposition Universelle of 1900.

MUSEUMS AND GALLERIES:
HELSINKI: *Old Woman.*

SOLDANI, Massimiliano or Benzi
Italian, 17th - 18th century.
Born 1658, in Florence; died 23 February 1740, in Montevarchi.
Sculptor, medallist.

The pupil of Ciro Ferri and Ercole Ferrata, Massimiliano Soldani worked for Cosimo III, Christina of Sweden and Louis XIV.

MUSEUMS AND GALLERIES:
FLORENCE (Gal. Corsini): *Saint before the Crucifix* - FLORENCE (NG): *Mercury Slaying Argos; Faun with a Small Goat; Ecstasy of St Teresa; Death of St Joseph; Death of St Francis Xavier* - SEATTLE (AM): *Lamentation over the Dead Christ* (c. 1730-1740, bronze/marble base).

AUCTION RECORDS:
LONDON, 21 April 1982, *Florence Triumphing over Pisa* (bronze, after Giambologna, h. 11 1/2 ins / 29 cm) GBP 9,500. LONDON, 8 June 1999, *Apotheosis of Manoel de Vilhena. Manoel de Vilhena* (1725, one wax low relief, one bronze tondo, 34 x 24 ins / 86 x 62 cm) GBP 36,000. LONDON, 14 Dec 2001, *Figure of the Dancing Faun* (bronze, h. 13 ins / 32 cm) GBP 14,000. LONDON, 14 Dec 2001, *Figure of a Nude Athlete* (brown patinated bronze, h. 12 ins / 31 cm) GBP 15,000.

SOLDATENKO, Igor
Russian, 20th century.
Born 1934.
Painter. Landscapes.

Igor Soldatenko studied at the Surikov Institute, Moscow, where he later taught. He was a member of the Union of Soviet (later Russian) Artists.

AUCTION RECORDS:
PARIS, 6 Feb 1993, *Borovsk Monastery* (oil on canvas, 35 1/2 x 39 1/4 ins / 90 x 100 cm) FRF 4,600.

SOLDATI, Agostino
Swiss, 19th century.
Born 1 December 1792, in Neggio; died 7 June 1831, in the same area.
Active in Bergamo and Borgomanero, Italy, and in Neggio.
Painter.

Agostino Soldati attended the art academy in Cararra at Bergamo.

SOLDATI, Atanasio
Italian, 20th century.
Born 25 August 1896, in Parma; died 27 August 1953, in Parma.
Painter, pastellist.
Groups: Abstraction-Création, MAC (Movimento Arte Concreta).

After qualifying as an architect from the school of fine art in Parma in 1920, Atanasio Soldati settled in Milan in 1925. In 1935, he was a member of the Abstraction-Création in Paris. With Dorflès, Monnet and Munari he founded the Movimento Arte Concreta (Concrete Art Movement) in Milan immediately after the war to defend abstract art in Italy.

When he began painting in 1928 his main influence was Cézanne, and he was later inspired too by Klee and Kandinsky. He did not start painting entirely abstract works until 1949. As his career developed, he met with much opposition from the official painters of the Fascist regime. While he pursued his artistic journey from Cézanne to abstraction with courage and determination, the final result was attractive work with little originality. His sharply defined and elegantly articulated forms, somewhat reminiscent of Magnelli, are painted in vivacious colours outlined in black.

He took part in several collective exhibitions, including: 1932 in Forlì; 1933 at the Mostra Internazionale in Florence; 1934, an exhibition of contemporary art in Lausanne; 1936, an exhibition of modern Italian art entitled *Bianco e Nero* (*Black and White*) at Villa Olmo in Como; 1939, the 3rd Rome Quadriennale; 1948 and 1952, the Venice Biennale; 1971, the exhibition *Arte Concreta* at the Westfälischer Kunstverein in Münster; 2003, the exhibition *De Chirico et la peinture italienne de l'entre-deux guerres* (*De Chirico and Italian Painting of the Interwar Period*) at the museum in Lodève.

He held a number of solo exhibitions, including: 1931 at the Galleria del Milione in Milan (his debut) and again in 1933 and 1935; at the Galleria Bompiani in Milan in 1951; at the Galleria Civica d'Arte Moderna in Rome in 1970.

SOLDATI

BIBLIOGRAPHY:
Dorfles, *soldati*, Arti Visive, Rome, 1952. Venturi, Lionello, *Soldati*, Gall. Bergamini, Milan, 1954. Bonito Oliva, Achille/Iovane, Giovanni/Lista, Giovanni, et al., *De Chirico et la peinture italienne de l'entre-deux guerres*, exhibition catalogue, Musée de Lodève, 2003.
MUSEUMS AND GALLERIES:
MILAN (Gal. d'Arte Moderna) - ROME (Gal. Nazionale d'Arte Moderna): *At the Sign of the Goldfish*.
AUCTION RECORDS:
MILAN, 13 and 15 Nov 1962, *Metaphysical Still-life*, ITL 1,300,000. MILAN, 1 Dec 1964, *Up to the Right*, ITL 1,300,000. MILAN, 29 Nov 1966, *Captive Dove* (tempera) ITL 1,000,000. MILAN, 22 June 1970, *Composition*, ITL 5,800,000. MILAN, 25 May 1971, *31 July 1951*, ITL 4,700,000. ROME, 28 Nov 1972, *Composition (Locomotive)*, ITL 10,000,000. MILAN, 29 May 1973, *Composition*, ITL 6,500,000. MILAN, 11 June 1973, *Composition* (tempera) ITL 750,000. ROME, 26 Nov 1974, *Composition with Locomotive* (1939) ITL 15,000,000. MILAN, 21 Dec 1976, *Big Field* (1951, oil on canvas, 32 x 39¼ ins / 81 x 100 cm) ITL 11,000,000. MILAN, 7 June 1977, *Pastoral* (1950, oil on canvas, 21½ x 28¾ ins / 54.5 x 73 cm) ITL 10,000,000. MILAN, 24 June 1980, *Still-life* (tempera/mounted paper/canvas, 12¼ x 9 ins / 31 x 22 cm) ITL 2,500,000. MILAN, 24 June 1980, *Analogy* (1949-1950, oil on canvas, 32 x 39¼ ins / 81 x 100 cm) ITL 22,000,000. MILAN, 16 June 1981, *Composition* (oil on panel, 11¾ x 13¾ ins / 30 x 35 cm) ITL 8,500,000. MILAN, 9 Nov 1982, *Composition* (gouache, 13 x 9¾ ins / 33 x 24.7 cm) ITL 3,600,000. LONDON, 7 Dec 1983, *Composition* (gouache, 9¼ x 9¼ ins / 23.5 x 23.5 cm) GBP 1,000. ROME, 22 May 1984, *Still-life (Trumpet)* (1943, oil on canvas, 19¾ x 23½ ins / 50 x 60 cm) ITL 17,000,000. ROME, 4 Dec 1984, *Composition* (1951, tempera, 7 x 8¼ ins / 17.5 x 21 cm) ITL 3,000,000. MILAN, 24 March 1988, *Still-life* (1934, oil on panel, 23½ x 19¾ ins / 60 x 50 cm) ITL 44,000,000. MILAN, 8 June 1988, *Composition* (1950, oil on canvas, 6¾ x 9 ins / 17 x 22 cm) ITL 11,500,000. MILAN, 20 March 1989, *Seascape* (oil on canvas, 19¾ x 23½ ins / 50 x 60 cm) ITL 32,000,000. MILAN, 6 June 1989, *Composition* (1934, oil on panel, 72 x 46 ins / 183 x 116 cm) ITL 160,000,000. ROME, 28 Nov 1989, *Geometry* (1943, oil on canvas, 23½ x 20 ins / 60 x 50.5 cm) ITL 70,000,000. MILAN, 20 June 1991, *Composition* (1944, oil/chipboard, 4 x 5 ins / 10 x 13 cm) ITL 9,000,000. MILAN, 14 Nov 1991, *Composition with Fish* (1947, oil on canvas, 21¼ x 28¾ ins / 54 x 73 cm) ITL 78,000,000. MILAN, 23 June 1992, *Composition* (1934, tempera/card, 12¾ x 9 ins / 32.5 x 23 cm) ITL 19,000,000. MILAN, 20 May 1993, *Figure* (1957, tempera/card, 3½ x 5½ ins / 9 x 14 cm) ITL 5,000,000. MILAN, 22 Nov 1993, *Small Composition* (1950, oil on canvas, 16¼ x 11 ins / 41 x 27 cm) ITL 29,462,000. MILAN, 9 March 1995, *Composition* (oil on canvas, 18 x 13 ins / 46 x 33 cm) ITL 46,000,000. MILAN, 26 Oct 1995, *Composition* (oil on canvas, 21¼ x 32 ins / 54 x 81 cm) ITL 69,000,000. MILAN, 23 May 1996, *Untitled* (1949, pastel/paper, 3½ x 7 ins / 9 x 17.5 cm) ITL 4,255,000. MILAN, 25 Nov 1996, *Pessimism* (oil on panel, 11¾ x 13¾ ins / 30 x 35 cm) ITL 26,450,000. MILAN, 18 March 1997, *Landscape with Hills* (c. 1941, oil on canvas, 21¼ x 28¾ ins / 54 x 73 cm) ITL 51,260,000. MILAN, 15 April 1999, *Untitled* (1953, tempera on paper, 4 x 3 ins / 11 x 8 cm) ITL 4,200,000. MILAN, 9 Nov 1999, *Composition* (oil on panel, 12 x 14 ins / 30 x 35 cm) ITL 30,000,000. PRATO, 25 Nov 2000, *On Brown Background* (oil on board, 15 x 22 ins / 38 x 55 cm) ITL 56,000,000. MILAN, 28 Nov 2000, *Composition* (1934, tempera on cardboard, 13 x 9 ins / 32 x 23 cm) ITL 7,000,000. MILAN, 29 May 2001, *Composition* (1933, oil on canvas, 18 x 22 ins / 46 x 55 cm) ITL 66,000,000. MILAN, 5 Dec 2001, *Composition* (watercolour, 7 x 6 ins / 17 x 15 cm) ITL 6,500,000. FLORENCE, 16 May 2002, *Abstract Composition* (1952, oil on canvas, 21 x 29 ins / 54 x 73 cm) EUR 30,000. VERCELLI, 22 June 2002, *Untitled* (1946-1947, oil on canvas, 15 x 18 ins / 38 x 46 cm) EUR 25,000. TURIN, 26 June 2003, *Composition* (mixed media, 3 x 3 ins / 7 x 7 cm) EUR 1,600. TURIN, 17 Nov 2003, *Composition* (1940-1943, oil on canvas, 20 x 20 ins / 50 x 50 cm) EUR 34,000. MILAN, 11 March 2004, *Landscape* (colour pencil, 6 x 8 ins / 16 x 20 cm) EUR 5,000. PRATO, 29 May 2004, *Composition* (1950, oil on board, 21 x 12 ins / 54 x 31 cm) EUR 22,000.

SOLDATI, Sebastiano
Swiss, 18th century.
Born 1682; died 1748.
Active in Neggio.
Painter.

Sebastiano Soldati produced paintings for the church of Our Lady of Magliasina, Switzerland, in 1740.

SOLDÉ, Alexandre
French, 19th century.
Born 1822, in Angers; died 2 June 1893, in Paris.
Painter, watercolourist, draughtsman, copyist.
Historical subjects, allegorical subjects, figures, portraits, genre scenes, hunting scenes (hunting with hounds), interiors, landscapes, urban landscapes, urban views, animals. Fans.

This artist was a pupil of Léon Cogniet at the École des Beaux-Arts in Paris. Exhibited at the Paris Salon between 1844 and 1868; several of his drawings were included in the Exhibition *Pilgrimage to Watteau* held in 1977 at the Hôtel de la Monnaie in Paris. He painted fans and sketched numerous copies of Watteau's *L'Indifférent* (*The Casual Lover*).
AUCTION RECORDS:
PARIS, 1875, *People who Love Fans* (fan) FRF 275. PARIS, 1888, *Line Fishing*, FRF 155. PARIS, 1889, *Riding to Hounds in the Middle Ages (recto); Cupid Firing a Dart at a Young Girl (verso)* (fan) FRF 800. PARIS, 2 June 1924, *View of an Italian Town with a River Flowing under a Bridge* (watercolour and gouache) FRF 190. PARIS, 2-3 June 1926, *Dead Game at the Foot of a Tree* (two oil on canvas) FRF 6,500. PARIS, 21 March 1949, *View of Brittany* (1880, watercolour) FRF 400. PARIS, 22 Sept 1992, *The Painter and his Admirers* (1864, watercolour and gouache, fan shaped, 6¾ x 22¼ ins / 17 x 56.5 cm) FRF 6,800. PARIS, 12 April 1996, *Series of Drawings showing Studies of Animals* (pencil, pen and watercolour, 42 plates) FRF 14,000. PARIS, 24 June 2004, *Hunting Trophies* (1877, oil on canvas, 75 x 86 ins / 191 x 218 cm) EUR 32,000.

SOLDENHOFF, Alexander Jules Jakob Joseph von
Swiss, 19th century.
Born 8 July 1849, in Widma; died 1 August 1902, in Zurich.
Painter, decorative designer. Genre scenes, landscapes.

Von Soldenhoff studied in Cracow and Munich and was influenced by Böcklin. He produced decorative paintings for the Château Rouge in Zurich, as well as theatre decorations.
AUCTION RECORDS:
BERN, 22 Oct 1976, *Valais Landscape* (1880, oil on canvas, 18 x 29½ ins / 45.5 x 75 cm) CHF 1,000. LONDON, 30 Nov 1977, *Conversation in the Drawing Room* (1873, oil on canvas, 26¾ x 35 ins / 68 x 88 cm) GBP 800. LONDON, 5 Oct 1979, *Young Lover* (1873, oil on canvas, 26½ x 33¾ ins / 67.2 x 85.7 cm) GBP 700.

SOLDENHOFF, Alexander Leo von
Swiss, 20th century.
Born 13 September 1882, in Geneva; died 1951.
Painter, engraver. Portraits, landscapes, still-lifes.

Alexander Leo von Soldenhoff was the son of Alexander von Soldenhoff. He studied in Zurich.
MUSEUMS AND GALLERIES:
AARAU (Aargauer Kunsthaus): *Dreamer*; *Head of a Bearded Man* (1940) - FRANKFURT AM MAIN (Städel): *Flowers*; *Portrait*

of the Artist in Soldier's Uniform - GLARIS: *Evening Walk; Dahlias; Melancholia; Portrait of the Artist and his Wife* - MANNHEIM (Städtische Kunsthalle) - WINTERTHUR - ZURICH.

AUCTION RECORDS:

ZURICH, 18 Nov 1976, *Springtime in the Mountains* (1932, oil on canvas, 29 3/4 x 37 1/2 ins / 75.5 x 95.5 cm) CHF 2,000. ZURICH, 30 Oct 1980, *Still-life with Flowers* (1942, oil on canvas, 32 1/4 x 24 1/2 ins / 82 x 62 cm) CHF 1,800. ZURICH, 15 May 1981, *Three Women* (1943, oil on canvas, 61 1/2 x 48 3/4 ins / 156 x 124 cm) CHF 4,300. ZURICH, 8 June 1983, *Hans Vaterlaus, Singer* (1920, oil on canvas, 37 3/4 x 25 1/2 ins / 96 x 65 cm) CHF 4,000. LONDON, 23 May 1985, *Sunny Landscape with Reclining Nude* (oil on canvas, 27 1/2 x 47 1/4 ins / 70 x 120 cm) CHF 11,000. ZURICH, 26 Nov 1986, *Vase of Flowers* (oil on canvas, 23 1/2 x 21 1/4 ins / 60 x 54 cm) CHF 8,500. LUCERNE, 30 Sept 1988, *Full Field* (oil on panel, 14 1/4 x 17 3/4 ins / 36 x 45 cm) CHF 1,000. LUCERNE, 21 Nov 1992, *Three Women* (1943, oil on canvas, 31 3/4 x 23 3/4 ins / 80.5 x 60.5 cm) CHF 4,400. ZURICH, 3 April 1996, *Female Nude with Cat* (oil on canvas, 55 x 41 1/4 ins / 140 x 105 cm) CHF 2,800. ZURICH, 12 Nov 1996, *Young Woman with Flowers* (oil on canvas, 53 1/4 x 41 1/4 ins / 135 x 105 cm) CHF 5,000. ZURICH, 8 April 1997, *La Petite Cocotte* (oil on canvas, 55 x 39 1/4 ins / 140 x 100 cm) CHF 6,500. ZURICH, 8 Dec 1999, *Asters - Book, Apple, Sunflowers* (1936, oil on canvas, 24 x 20 ins / 60 x 50 cm) CHF 3,800. ZURICH, 7 June 2000, *Sunflowers in Vase* (1939, oil on canvas, 35 x 24 ins / 90 x 60 cm) CHF 4,000. ZURICH, 7 June 2000, *Boat with Bathers* (oil on canvas, 45 x 59 ins / 115 x 150 cm) CHF 7,000. ZURICH, 11 Dec 2001, *Still-life of Flowers in Jug* (oil on canvas, 24 x 20 ins / 60 x 50 cm) CHF 2,500. ZURICH, 11 Dec 2001, *Still-life of Flowers* (oil on canvas, 25 x 19 ins / 63 x 48 cm) CHF 4,000. ZURICH, 3 June 2002, *Rape of the Sabine Women* (oil on canvas, 24 x 19 ins / 60 x 48 cm) CHF 4,800.

SOLDERA, Erminion

Italian, 20th century.

Born 14 December 1874, in Capella Maggiore.

Painter. Figures, portraits, landscapes.

Soldera was a pupil of Cesare Tollone and Pietro Pajetta.

SOLDEVILA Y TREPAT, Ramón

Spanish, 19th century.

Born 31 December 1828, in Barcelona; died 1873.

Painter, draughtsman. Historical subjects, figures, portraits, scenes with figures. Wall decorations, church decoration.

Ramón Soldevila y Trepat studied at the school of fine arts in Barcelona and was appointed as a teacher at the school of fine arts in Valencia in 1858 and in Madrid in 1861. He exhibited in Valencia in 1860. He painted many portraits, including *The Duke of Tétouan, Don Francisco de Paula Vasallo, The Duke of San Ricardo,* and *Queen Isabella II and her Husband Visiting the Maundy Thursday Monument in the Church of Sta Maria.* He also made a drawing of *The Courtyard of S Gregorio in Valladolid* and two pictures illustrating the African war: *The Capture of a Black Corporal* and the *Battle of Tétouan.* He produced various paintings for Valencia town hall and for the chapel of the Loreto college.

BIBLIOGRAPHY:

Arnáiz, José Manuel/López Jiménez, Javier/Merchán Díaz, Manuel (ed.), *'Cien años de pintura en Espana y Portugal (1830-1930)'* in vol. X, Antiqvaria, Madrid, 1993.

SOLDEVILLA, Dolorès. See **LOLO**

SOLDEVILLA VALLS, Miguel

Spanish, 20th century.

Born 1885, in San Andreu de Palomar, near Barcelona; died 1956, in Barcelona.

Painter, enameller. Religious subjects, portraits, landscapes.

Miguel Soldevilla Valls studied at the Escuela de Bellas Artes in Barcelona. He worked in Rome from 1936 for several years, producing commissions for the Vatican. Among his most notable works are: *Countess of Godo, Francisco Cambo, Immaculate Virgin,* and *The Virgin Mary and the Sleeping Child.* He dedicated himself to enamelling in 1925. Miguel Soldevilla participated in various collective exhibitions including: Exposición Internacional, Barcelona (1907); Sala Parès, Barcelona (1913 and 1946 obtaining a gold medal).

BIBLIOGRAPHY:

Arnáiz, José Manuel/López Jiménez, Javier/Merchán Díaz, Manuel (ed.), *'Cien años de pintura en Espana y Portugal (1830-1930)'* in vol. X, Antiqvaria, Madrid, 1993.

MUSEUMS AND GALLERIES:

BARCELONA (MAM del Mus. Nacional d'Art de Catalunya).

SOLDI, Andrea or Andrew

Italian, 18th century.

Born c. 1703, in Florence; died after 1771, in London.

Painter. History painting, figures, portraits.

Andrea Soldi visited the Holy Land and then in 1735 went to England, where he settled. Elected a member of the Incorporated Society of Artists in 1766, he took part in its exhibitions until 1769.

MUSEUMS AND GALLERIES:

EDINBURGH (Nat. Gal. of Scotland): *Portrait of a Gentleman* (oil on canvas) - LONDON (Dulwich Picture Gal.): portrait*Louis François Roubiliac* (1751, oil on canvas).

AUCTION RECORDS:

LONDON, 10 April 1970, *Michael Rysbrack in his Studio,* Gns 8,000. LONDON, 18 March 1977, *Portrait of an Architect* (1758, oil on canvas, 38 x 32 ins / 96.5 x 81.3 cm) GBP 6,000. LONDON, 27 March 1981, *Portrait of Philip, Count of Harborough* (oil on canvas, 50 x 40 ins / 126.9 x 101.6 cm) GBP 3,800. LONDON, 13 July 1984, *Portrait of a Musician* (oil on canvas, 35 1/4 x 28 ins / 89.6 x 71.1 cm) GBP 13,000. LONDON, 26 April 1985, *Portrait of a Gentleman* (oil on canvas, 65 1/2 x 54 ins / 166.3 x 137.1 cm) GBP 6,000. LONDON, 8 July 1988, *Portrait of a Man in Oriental Dress, Propping his Elbows on a Piece of Furniture* (oil on canvas, 36 1/2 x 29 1/4 ins / 93 x 74.5 cm) GBP 49,500. NEW YORK, 28 Oct 1988, *Portrait of a Man in Oriental Dress* (oil on canvas, 49 x 38 1/2 ins / 124.5 x 98 cm) USD 49,500. LONDON, 12 July 1989, *Portrait of a Gentleman Seated in an Armchair, Wearing a Blue Suit and Red Waistcoat* (oil on canvas, 64 1/2 x 52 3/4 ins / 164 x 134 cm) GBP 6,600. LONDON, 24 May 1991, *Three-quarter-length Portrait of John Michael Rysback, Dressed in a Plum Suit over a Red Waistcoat and Wearing a Purple Hat, Pointing to a Terracotta Statuette Representing Hercules* (oil on canvas, 44 x 35 3/4 ins / 112 x 91 cm) GBP 143,000. LONDON, 13 April 1994, *Three-quarter-length Portrait of Richard Bendyshe, Dressed in a Brown Suit and Red Waistcoat, with his Dog* (1751, oil on canvas, 49 1/4 x 39 ins / 125 x 99 cm) GBP 11,500. LONDON, 28 May 1999, *Portrait of Richard Bendyshe of Barrington Hall, Cambridgeshire* (1751, oil on canvas, 51 x 41 ins / 130 x 104 cm) GBP 14,000. LONDON, 22 Sept 1999, *Group Portrait of Arthur Jones Nevill, Eleanor Parker and Mrs Hogshawe* (oil on canvas, 59 x 72 ins / 151 x 182 cm) GBP 16,000. PARIS, 5 Dec 2001, *Portrait of Gentleman with Fur Collar* (oil on canvas, 24 x 19 ins / 60 x 48 cm) FRF 135,000. DUBLIN, 25 Nov 2003, *Portrait of Lady, Seated* (oil on canvas, 68 x 40 ins / 172 x 101 cm) EUR 14,000. COPENHAGEN, 25 Feb 2004, *Portrait of Gentleman* (1755, oil on canvas, 24 x 20 ins / 61 x 50 cm) DKK 16,500.

SOLDI, Antenore

Italian, 19th century.

Born 14 June 1844, in Florence; died 30 December 1877, in Turin.

Painter, engraver (etching). Portraits, genre scenes, landscapes.

School of Rivara.
A pupil of Andrea Gastaldi, Soldi was a member of the Scuola di Rivara (Rivara School).

SOLDI, Baldassare
Italian, 17th century.
Active in 1626.
Painter.
Baldassare Soldi painted the portrait of the notary Giacomo Bosisio in the Ospedale Maggiore in Milan.

SOLDI, Émile Arthur, or Soldi-Colbert
French, 19th century.
Born 27 May 1846, in Paris; died 14 March 1906, in Rome.
Sculptor, engraver. Statues, busts.
Soldi was a pupil of Farochon, Lequesne and Dumont and was awarded first place at the Prix de Rome in 1869 (engravings on medals). He made his debut at the 1872 Salon and won a third class medal in 1873. He was made a Chevalier of the Légion d'Honneur in 1878.

He also carved cameos, engraved medals and wrote about art.

BIBLIOGRAPHY:
Catalogue sommaire illustré des sculptures, Musée d'Orsay, Paris, 1986.

MUSEUMS AND GALLERIES:
ALGIERS: *Guillaumet* - BESANÇON: *Actéon* - LE MANS: *Bust of Louis David, the painter* - PARIS (Louvre): *Flora* - RHEIMS: *The Weapons of Perseus and Bellerophon.*

AUCTION RECORDS:
PARIS, 8-13 May 1892, *Portrait of the sculptor Richbrach,* FRF 220. PARIS, 15-17 Feb 1897, *Negligence Perceived,* FRF 150. ENGHIEN-LES-BAINS, 2 Dec 1984, *Dance Steps* (bronze, lustrous bronze patina, h. 32 3/4 ins / 83 cm) FRF 39,000. LONDON, 6 Nov 1986, *Ballerina* (c. 1870, patinated bronze, h. 32 ins / 81 cm) GBP 2,500. NEW YORK, 16 Feb 1994, *Gallia* (bronze, h. 29 1/2 ins / 74.9 cm) USD 1,150.

SOLDI, Giacomo
Italian, 19th century.
Born 18 September 1806, in Botticino; died 1836, in Brescia.
Painter, lithographer.
A pupil of Teosa and Vantini, Giacomo Soldi executed the painted decoration in the choir of the church at Iseo.

SOLDI, Raul
Argentinian, 20th century.
Born 1905, in Buenos Aires.
Painter, pastellist, scenographer. Figures, landscapes. Stage sets, frescoes.
Raul Soldi lived and worked in Buenos Aires. He studied at the Accademia di Belle Arti di Brera in Milan; in Italy he joined the group Il Milione and exhibited at the Rome Quadriennale. He returned to Buenos Aires, and then had a grant to go to the USA, where he studied scenography. In 1958 he won the São Paulo Biennale prize. He painted scenery for the Teatro Colón in Buenos Aires, and frescoes for the chapel in Glew in Buenos Aires province.

His work featured in collective exhibitions, including: 1960, when he was guest of honour at the *Interamerican Biennale* in Mexico; and in 1960, *150 Years of Argentinian Art.* After returning to Buenos Aires from Italy he had several exhibitions there, and one in 1958 in Paris.

AUCTION RECORDS:
NEW YORK, 11 June 1982, *Landscapes* (1941, oil on panel, double-sided, 11 3/4 x 16 1/2 ins / 29.9 x 42.2 cm) USD 1,500. NEW YORK, 25 Nov 1992, *Harlequins* (1952, pastel/paper, 40 1/4 x 27 1/4 ins / 102 x 69.5 cm) USD 12,100. NEW YORK, 17 Nov 1994, *Harlequins* (1952, pastel/paper, 40 1/4 x 27 1/4 ins / 102 x 69.5 cm) USD 17,250. MONTEVIDEO, 5 Jan 1999, *Bahia Street Scene* (c. 1971, oil on board, 11 x 8 ins / 29 x 21 cm) USD 5,000. BUENOS AIRES, 25 June 1999, *Musician* (oil on canvas, 48 x 46 ins / 122 x 117 cm) USD 80,000. BUENOS AIRES, 1 June 2004, *Girl with Scarf* (oil on canvas, 22 x 18 ins / 55 x 45 cm) USD 80,000. BUENOS AIRES, 2 Nov 2004, *Theatre Figures* (mixed media on card, 19 x 27 ins / 48 x 68 cm) USD 31,500.

SOLDIERI, Lorenzo
Italian, 17th century.
Active in Naples at the beginning of the 17th century.
Painter.
Lorenzo Soldieri painted altarpieces in the churches of St John and the Holy Annunciation in Pescopagnano.

SOLDINI, Antonio
Italian, 19th century.
Born 23 September 1839, in Ligornetto (Ticino); died 26 July 1879, in the same area.
Sculptor. Monuments.
A pupil of V. Vela, Soldini carved funerary monuments.

SOLDINI, Antonio
Swiss, 19th century.
Born 1854, in Chiasso.
Sculptor.
Soldini studied under Lorenzo Vela. He produced monuments in Bern and Locarno, Switzerland, as well as tombs at the Monumental Cemetery in Milan (Cimitero Monumentale) and the Père-Lachaise Cemetery in Paris.

SOLDINI, Arnoldo or Arnaldo
Italian, 19th - 20th century.
Born 18 November 1862, in Brescia; died 1936.
Painter. Landscapes with figures, urban landscapes, landscapes.
Arnoldo Soldini was a pupil of Luigi Campini.

MUSEUMS AND GALLERIES:
TRIESTE (Civico Mus. Revoltella): *Alpine Landscape.*

AUCTION RECORDS:
MONACO, 21 April 1990, *Sitting in the Sun outside the House in Brescia* (oil on canvas, 28 1/4 x 18 ins / 72 x 46 cm) FRF 33,300. ROME, 16 April 1991, *Old Quarter of Brescia* (oil on canvas, 38 1/2 x 25 1/2 ins / 98 x 65 cm) ITL 40,250,000. MILAN, 8 June 1994, *Mountain Stream* (oil on canvas, 44 1/2 x 31 ins / 113 x 79 cm) ITL 16,100,000. MILAN, 22 March 2000, *Landscape* (1898, oil on panel, 25 x 18 ins / 63 x 46 cm) ITL 7,000,000. ROME, 27 May 2002, *Mountainous Landscape* (1901, oil on canvas, 39 x 61 ins / 100 x 155 cm) EUR 25,000.

SOLDINI, Luigi Domenico
French, 18th century.
Born 1715, in Florence (?); died after 1772.
Painter. Genre scenes.
Luigi Domenico Soldini was a member of the Académie de St-Luc in Paris. He exhibited at the 1756 Salon.

MUSEUMS AND GALLERIES:
DIJON: *Country Scene; Children Playing; Joys of Fishing; La Balançoire.*

AUCTION RECORDS:
PARIS, 30 March 1942, *Park with Figures* (1764, pen and watercolour wash) FRF 410. VERSAILLES, 20 July 1976, *Shepherd* (1772, oil on canvas, 21 x 25 1/2 ins / 53.5 x 64.5 cm) FRF 17,000. ROME, 20 March 1986, *Allegories* (oils on canvas, a pair, 34 1/4 x 49 1/4 ins / 87 x 125 cm) ITL 40,000,000. PARIS, 18 Dec 1996, *Portrait of Monsieur de Gennes de Lambert* (1752, oil on canvas, 39 1/2 x 31 3/4 ins / 100.5 x 80.5 cm) FRF 45,000.

SOLDINI, Paolo
Italian, 14th century.
Active in Florence during the second half of the 14th century.
Illuminator.

Paola Soldini and Simone da Siena illuminated a manuscript, now in the Biblioteca Laurenziana in Florence, for the church of S Pancrazio.

SÖLDNER, Karl
German, 20th century.
Born 14 June 1871, in Nördlingen.
Draughtsman. Landscapes.
Karl Söldner lived and worked in Munich, where he practised as an architect.

SOLDO, Gaudenzio
Italian, 17th century.
Active in the Como region.
Sculptor.
Gaudenzio Soldo was the pupil of D. Bussola.

SOLDO, Rina
Italian, 20th century.
Born 1899, in Chiari; died 1982, in Salò.
Painter. Landscapes with figures, urban landscapes.
Rina Soldo painted the landscape around Rome, Venice, Milan and Turin. Her work featured in a number of collective exhibitions, including *Attraverso l'Immagine (Through the Image)* held at the Centro Culturale in Cremona in 1995.

BIBLIOGRAPHY:

Attraverso l'immagine, exhibition catalogue, Centro culturale Santa Maria della Pietà, Cremona, 1995.

SOLDT, Jacobus van, or Solt
Dutch, 17th century.
Born 8 June 1628, in Amsterdam; died 2 April 1649, in The Hague.
Engraver (etching). Landscapes.
MUSEUMS AND GALLERIES:
AMSTERDAM (Rijksprentenkabinet): a landscape.

SOLE, Achille. See **SOLI**

SOLE, Angelo
Italian, 15th century.
Active in Naples.
Sculptor.
Angelo Sole was a pupil of Andrea del Verrocchio.

SOLE, Giovanni Antonio del
Italian, 18th century.
Painter.
Active in Milan, Giovanni Antonio del Sole painted religious subjects.

SOLE, Giovanni Antonio Maria dal
Italian, 17th century.
Born 1606, in Bologna; died 1684.
Painter, engraver. Landscapes.
Giovanni Antonio Maria dal Sole was a pupil in the school of Francesco Albani, and an excellent landscapist. He always worked left-handed, which earned him the nickname 'Il mancino dei Paesi'. His legacy includes prints, religious subjects, battle scenes and portraits. He was the father of Giovanni Giuseppe dal Sole.

SOLE, Giovanni Battista del
Italian, 17th - 18th century.
Died 1719.
Painter, engraver (burin).
The son of Pietro del Sole, Giovanni Battista del Sole executed numerous paintings in churches in Milan and Varese.

SOLE, Giovanni Giuseppe dal, or Giovan Gioseffo
Italian, 17th - 18th century.
Born 10 October 1654, in Bologna; died 22 July 1719, in Bologna.
Painter, engraver, draughtsman. Religious subjects, landscapes, landscapes with figures.
The son of Giovanni Antonio Maria dal Sole, Giovanni Giuseppe dal Sole was first taught drawing by his father; he then became the disciple of Domenico-Maria Ganuti and finally the pupil of Lorenzo Pasinelli. For some time he adopted a style inspired by Pasinelli and drew attention to himself by the immense elegance with which he rendered certain details such as hair and angels' wings, accessories, veils and armour. He embellished his compositions with landscapes and architectural motifs, and in this respect appears to have surpassed his master. His finest landscapes are to be found in the Jappi palace in Imola.

Held in high esteem by his contemporaries, he was employed by Italian or foreign noblemen and was also summoned to the courts of Poland and England. The most highly regarded works by dal Sole include his *Incredulity of St Thomas* (in the church of the Madonna di Galieri) and the *Annunciation* (in the church of St Gabriel). Having been accused of being incapable of working at a quicker pace, dal Sole painted a *Bacchus* and an *Ariadne* in a single week for the illustrious Giusti family in Verona, which were recognised as having great merit. Once completed, he obliterated the works, repainting them to his own taste. Having proved he was capable of satisfying others in terms of speed, he said he now wished to please himself by means of the care he lavished on his work.

Two styles are apparent in the work of this artist. The first, which receives most attention, resembles that of Pasinelli, while the second is reminiscent of Guido Reni. Dal Sole came close to being the equal of this master, which is why he is often called the 'modern Guido'.

MUSEUMS AND GALLERIES:
BOLOGNA (Pinacoteca Nazionale): *Virgin Reading a Missal; St Mary Magdalene Repentant; St Francis of Assisi in Ecstasy; Adoration of the Shepherds; Birth of Christ; Mary Magdalene* (drawing) - BORDEAUX: *Landscape with Three Allegorical Figures* - BURGHAUSEN: *Stigmatisation of St Mary Magdalene* - CHAMBÉRY (MBA): *St Mary Magdalene* - DRESDEN: *Hercules and Omphale* - FLORENCE (Uffizi): *Self-portrait* - IMOLA (Jappi Palace): *Evening; Night; Aurora* - MODENA (Gal. Estense): *St Mary Magdalene* - ROME (Gal. Nazionale): *Death of St Mary Magdalene.*

AUCTION RECORDS:
VIENNA, 28 Nov 1967, *Mary Magdalene*, ATS 32,000. MILAN, 28 Nov 1974, *Tarquin and Lucretia* (tempera) ITL 900,000. MILAN, 27 Nov 1984, *Communion of a Saint* (oil on paper remounted/canvas, 16 1/4 x 10 3/4 ins / 41.5 x 27.5 cm) ITL 2,600,000. LONDON, 2 July 1990, *Study of a Seated Bishop* (black chalk heightened with white, 12 x 10 1/2 ins / 29.6 x 26.5 cm) GBP 1,705. NEW YORK, 30 May 1991, *Allegory with a Woman Seated in a Landscape Welcoming Putti Bearing a Garland of Fruit (Pomona in Autumn?)* (oil on canvas, 22 3/4 x 18 1/2 ins / 58 x 47 cm) USD 220,000. LONDON, 1 Nov 1991, *Personification of the Visual Arts Appearing to the Pope* (oil on paper/canvas, 10 x 14 ins / 25.5 x 35.5 cm) GBP 9,900. LONDON, 8 July 1992, *Diana and Endymion* (oil on canvas, 26 1/2 x 38 3/4 ins / 67 x 98.5 cm) GBP 41,800. LONDON, 5 July 1995, *Mary Magdalene Repentant* (oil on canvas, 48 x 38 1/2 ins / 121 x 98 cm) GBP 17,250. VENICE, 25 May 1997, *Mary Magdalene Meditating* (oil on canvas, 31 1/2 x 23 1/2 ins / 80 x 60 cm) ITL 9,500,000. VENICE, 25 May 1997, *Mary Magdalene at Prayer* (oil on canvas) ITL 4,500,000. NEW YORK, 28 Jan 2000, *Penitent Magdalene* (oil on canvas, 35 x 33 ins / 90 x 83 cm) USD 55,000. PARIS, 18 Dec 2000, *Lucrecia* (oil on canvas, 40 x 30 ins / 102 x 76 cm) FRF 30,000. NEW YORK, 24 Jan 2002, *Diana and Endymion* (oil on canvas, 26 x 39 ins / 67 x 98 cm) USD 60,000. ROME, 16 June 2004, *Ariadne Abandoned* (oil on canvas, 20 x 20 ins / 50 x 51 cm) EUR 20,000.

SOLE, Lombardo dal
Italian, 17th century.
Sculptor.
Lombardo dal Sole, a Venetian, worked in Udine about 1670.

SOLE, Pietro del
Italian, 17th century.
Died after 1700.
Painter.
The father of Giovanni Battista del Sole, Pietro del Sole painted frescoes in Milan.

SOLE, Stelio
Venezuelan, 20th century.
Born 1932, in Caracas.
Active from 1955 in Canada.
Painter, sculptor.
Stelio Sole trained in the Brera art school in Milan, then in Venice, then studied archaeology in Florence and carried out research in Mexico. Finally he studied sculpture with Giacomo Manzú and Arturo Martini.

What he was trying to do in his paintings, sculptures and plexiglass murals was to set matter, space and light in relation to each other by means of geometrical forms.

From 1959 onwards he regularly showed work in collective exhibitions, including 1975, 1981, 1984, at the Salon de Montrouge in Paris; 1981,1987, 1988, at the Salon Grands et Jeunes d'Aujourd'hui in Paris. Among his solo shows were Milan (1959); Rome (1960); New York (1961); Quebec (1964 to 1970); Barcelona (1968); General Delegation of Quebec in Paris (1982).

MUSEUMS AND GALLERIES:
MILAN (Gal. d'Arte Moderna) - PARIS (MAM).

AUCTION RECORDS:
PARIS, 24 May 1992, *Porta dorata con finestra 2* (1991, oil pigments and gold/canvas, 55 x 30¾ ins / 140 x 78 cm) FRF 25,000.

SOLEIL, Alexandre François
French, 19th century.
Painter (including gouache). Genre scenes, flowers, fruit.
Laexandre Soleil made his debut at the 1877 Salon. He worked mainly with gouache.

SOLEMACKER. See **SOOLMAKER**

SOLENGHI, Giuseppe
Italian, 20th century.
Born 3 May 1879, in Milan; died 1944, in Cernobbio.
Painter. Portraits, landscapes.
Solenghi was a pupil of C. Tallone, E. Bazzaro and Giuseppe Mentessi.

He specialised in landscapes painted in the Italian Alps and the Lombard countryside.

AUCTION RECORDS:
MILAN, 28 March 1974, *Sad Return*, ITL 1,000,000. MILAN, 28 Oct 1976, *Corso Vittorio Emanuele in the Snow; Ship in a Snowstorm* (two works, oil on panel, 7 x 5½ ins / 18 x 14 cm) ITL 950,000. MILAN, 21 April 1983, *My Girls* (oil on canvas, oval, 24½ x 18 ins / 62.5 x 46 cm) ITL 2,200,000. MILAN, 4 June 1985, *Fishermen in a River Landscape* (oil on canvas, 26¾ x 19¾ ins / 68 x 50 cm) ITL 3,300,000. ROME, 14 Dec 1988, *Snowfall* (oil on canvas, 19 x 26¾ ins / 48.5 x 68 cm) ITL 2,200,000. MILAN, 14 June 1989, *The Park in Monza under Snow* (1934, oil on panel, 21¼ x 15¾ ins / 54 x 40 cm) ITL 2,200,000. ROME, 31 May 1990, *Winter on the Canal* (oil on canvas, 27¼ x 39 ins / 69.5 x 99 cm) ITL 8,000,000. MILAN, 21 Nov 1990, *The Alps* (oil on canvas, 8½ x 17 ins / 21.5 x 43 cm) ITL 800,000. MILAN, 7 Nov 1991, *Midnight Mass* (oil on panel, 11¾ x 19¾ ins / 30 x 50 cm) ITL 3,300,000. MILAN, 21 Dec 1993, *Lombard Landscape* (oil on card, 11 x 8 ins / 28 x 20.5 cm) ITL 1,092,000. ROME, 31 May 1994, *Canal in Chioggia* (oil on canvas/card, 15¾ x 19¾ ins / 40 x 50 cm) ITL 4,714,000. MILAN, 8 June 1994, *Vegetable Market in Chioggia* (oil/plywood, 38¼ x 47½ ins / 97 x 120.5 cm) ITL 6,900,000. MILAN, 19 Dec 1995, *Car in the Snow in Milan; Snow in Milan* (oil on panel, a pair, each 6½ x 4½ ins / 16.5 x 11.5 cm) ITL 2,875,000. ROME, 23 May 1996, *Mending the Nets* (oil on canvas, 19 x 27½ ins / 48 x 70 cm) ITL 3,800,000. ROME, 2 Dec 1997, *Via Vallone in Milan* (1929, oil on canvas, 39¼ x 27½ ins / 100 x 70 cm) ITL 18,400,000. MILAN, 20 Oct 1999, *Figures in a Landscape* (oil on canvas, 28 x 39 ins / 70 x 100 cm) ITL 5,951,000. MILAN, 15 June 2000, *Chioggia* (oil on panel, 19 x 23 ins / 48 x 58 cm) ITL 5,000,000. MILAN, 4 Dec 2000, *View of Milan* (oil on board, 16 x 12 ins / 40 x 30 cm) ITL 4,000,000. MILAN, 23 Oct 2002, *Getting Down in a Rush* (1931, oil on board, 26 x 20 ins / 66 x 50 cm) EUR 2,600. MILAN, 27 May 2003, *Market in Chioggia* (oil on canvas, 24 x 31 ins / 60 x 80 cm) EUR 1,500. TURIN, 22 March 2004, *Chioggia* (1920, oil on canvas, 31 x 43 ins / 80 x 110 cm) EUR 6,500. MILAN, 25 May 2004, *Old Milan with Carriages* (oil on board, 7 x 5 ins / 17 x 12 cm) EUR 1,500.

SOLER, Jean
Dutch (?), 20th century.
Painter. Figures, genre scenes, landscapes with figures.

AUCTION RECORDS:
AMSTERDAM, 11 Sept 1990, *Lady Crossing a Busy Street in Paris* (oil on canvas/panel, 13¼ x 16¼ ins / 33.5 x 41.2 cm) NLG 5,520. AMSTERDAM, 30 Oct 1990, *Lady and Fishmonger on the Beach* (oil on card, 12¾ x 16 ins / 32.5 x 40.5 cm) NLG 2,300. AMSTERDAM, 24 Sept 1992, *Young Lady Carrying a Hat-Box in a Paris Street* (oil on panel, 11 x 8¾ ins / 27 x 22.5 cm) NLG 1,150. AMSTERDAM, 14 June 1994, *Beach Crocquet* (oil on canvas/card, 13¾ x 17¾ ins / 35 x 45 cm) NLG 1,725.

SOLER, Jean-Paul
French, 20th century.
Born in Algeria.
Painter.
The paintings of Jean-Paul Soler are surrealist and mystical, and are intended as a reflection of the human soul.

SOLER, Jorge
20th - 21st century.
Born 1946.
Active in France.
Painter.
Jorge Soler has lived in Paris since 1946. His works feature figures or simple outlines of figures in the background. He has shown at the Salon Comparaisons, the Salon de la Jeune Peinture and Mac 2000.

BIBLIOGRAPHY:
Jorge Soler: à propos de musique, exhibition catalogue, Festival de musique de Besançon Franche-Comté, Besançon, 1999.

SOLER, José
Spanish, 19th century.
Active in Alicante from 1860 to 1870.
Painter.

SOLER, Juan
Spanish, 15th century.
Active in Valencia during the first half of the 15th century.
Painter.
Juan Soler was commissioned to paint a curtain decorated with coats of arms in 1418.

SOLER, Juan
Spanish, 19th century.
Active in Catalonia.
Sculptor.
Juan Soler executed paintings for the church of St Augustine in Barcelona and for churches in Pallea and Villafranca

del Penedés. He has sometimes been confused with Juan Roig y Soler.

SOLER, Pedro
Spanish, 15th century.
Active in Valencia from 1404 to 1429.
Miniaturist.

SOLER, Peter Lorenz
Swiss, 18th century.
Died 28 October 1718, in Truns.
Active in Igels (?).
Sculptor (wood).
Soler produced sculptures for the monastery church of Dissentis, Switzerland.

SOLER, Roberto
French, 20th century.
Born 8 December 1928, in Paris, of Spanish parentage.
Painter.
Alicante Group.
Roberto Soler was taught by Federico Bertran Masse at the Académie Espagnole in Paris in 1943. He attended the Académie de Valence in 1945, before entering the École des Beaux-Arts in 1947. He visited Spain in 1952 and exhibited with the Alicante Group. He then worked on stage sets. He was a member of the jury that assessed final qualifications and diplomas at the École des Arts Appliqués in Paris.

Until about 1959, he painted a variety of subjects, often clowns, in an anecdotal manner. From 1959 to 1964, he followed the movement of the Paris School in the direction of abstract landscape. From 1965, he introduced a swirling rhythmic structure evocative of solar ejecta, which sometimes recalled the gestural lyricism of an artist like Mathieu.

His work has been shown at collective exhibitions, including at the Salon de Mai in Paris in 1961 and 1962. His first solo exhibition was held in 1955 in the Foyer des Artistes in Montparnasse. Other solo exhibitions included; 1955, Foyer des Artistes, Paris; 1963, Vence; 1971, Méribel-les-Allues; 1972, Galerie Tourtour, Paris; 1984, Palais de Justice, Paris; 1985, Galerie de Nesle, Paris.

BIBLIOGRAPHY:
Vorms, Anne, *Roberto Soler: itinéraire d'un peintre de 1950 à 2002*, L'Œil du Myp, Paris, 2002.

SOLER, Tomás
Spanish, 18th century.
Active during the second half of the 18th century.
Sculptor.
Tomás Soler worked at Valencia Cathedral from 1777 to 1779.

SOLER, Urbici
Spanish, 20th century.
Born 1890, in Farrán (Catalonia).
Active in Barcelona.
Sculptor.
Urbici Soler was a pupil of P. Carbonnell and Ad. Von Hildebrand. He worked in Barcelona and in South America.

SOLER GILL, Domingo
Spanish, 19th - 20th century.
Born 24 October 1871, in Sabadell (Catalonia); died 26 November 1951, in Barcelona.
Painter. Landscapes with figures, waterscapes, seascapes, landscapes.
Domingo Soler Gill was a pupil at the Escuelas de Bellas Artes in Sabadell and Barcelona. He continued his studies in Rome and Paris.

He took part in various collective exhibitions in Barcelona including: Salón Nacional de la Sociedad Nacional de Bellas Artes (1891); Salon for industrial arts (1892); Sala Parès (1911); Exposición Internacional de Bellas Artes (1911 and 1918). A retrospective of his work was held in Sabadell in 1947. Soler Gill won a number of awards.

BIBLIOGRAPHY:
Arnáiz, José Manuel/López Jiménez, Javier/Merchán Díaz, Manuel (ed.), *'Cien años de pintura en Espana y Portugal (1830-1930)'* in vol. X, Antiqvaria, Madrid, 1993.

AUCTION RECORDS:
BARCELONA, 28 Feb 1980, *Landscape* (oil on canvas, 31 1/2 x 39 ins / 80 x 99 cm) ESP 92,000. MADRID, 25 May 1993, *View of the Paseo de Gracia in Barcelona* (oil on canvas, 25 1/2 x 19 1/2 ins / 65 x 49.5 cm) ESP 345,000. MADRID, 3 April 2000, *Castilian Landscape with the Monserrat Mountain* (oil on canvas, 28 x 39 ins / 70 x 98 cm) ESP 550,000. MADRID, 10 Dec 2003, *Lady and Girl* (1918, oil on canvas, 28 x 20 ins / 70 x 50 cm) EUR 1,500.

SOLER JORBA, Vicente, or Solé Jorba
Spanish, 20th century.
Born 1904, in Olot, near Gerona; died 1949, in El Brull (Catalonia).
Painter. Figures, portraits, landscapes, landscapes with figures, still-lifes.
Vincente Soler Jorba studied at the Escuela de Bellas Artes in Olot. He is known for: *Rainy Day, Pilgrimage* and *Afternoon Clouds*. He participated in collective exhibitions including: Salón de la Primavera, Olot (1936); Exposicións Nacionals de Bellas Artes, Sala Parès and Pinacoteca, Barcelona (1942 and 1944); Bilbao Salon.

BIBLIOGRAPHY:
Arnáiz, José Manuel/López Jiménez, Javier/Merchán Díaz, Manuel (ed.), *'Cien años de pintura en Espana y Portugal (1830-1930)'* in vol. X, Antiqvaria, Madrid, 1993.

AUCTION RECORDS:
BARCELONA, 23 May 1984, *At the Feria, Olot* (1940, oil on canvas, 17 3/4 x 23 1/2 ins / 45 x 60 cm) ESP 280,000. BARCELONA, 28 Nov 1985, *Landscape* (1944, oil on canvas, 32 x 46 ins / 81 x 116 cm) ESP 600,000. MADRID, 10 July 2000, *Olot Landscape* (1939, oil on canvas, 20 x 26 ins / 50 x 65 cm) ESP 320,000.

SOLER PÉREZ, Rigoberto
Spanish, 20th century.
Born 1 February 1896, in Alcoy (Valencia); died 1968, in Barcelona.
Painter, engraver. Portraits, genre scenes, landscapes with figures, waterscapes.
Rigoberto Pérez was a pupil at the Escuela de Bellas Artes in Valencia and also of José Mongrell. He taught at the Escuela de Bellas Artes in Barcelona, then settled in Ibiza in 1925. He mainly focused on genre paintings and seashore landscapes, inspired by the Balearic Islands, where he exploited the changing effects of the natural light.

Rigoberto Pérez participated in various collective exhibitions: Valencia (1916); Exposición Nacional, Barcelona (1917 onwards receiving medals in 1917 and 1926); Escuela de Bellas Artes in Barcelona (1918); Pinacoteca, Barcelona (1947 and 1951). He also showed his work in private exhibitions: Valencia (1926); Barcelona (1927) and Madrid (1930).

BIBLIOGRAPHY:
Arnáiz, José Manuel/López Jiménez, Javier/Merchán Díaz, Manuel (ed.), *'Cien años de pintura en Espana y Portugal (1830-1930)'* in vol. X, Antiqvaria, Madrid, 1993.

AUCTION RECORDS:
LONDON, 22 June 1988, *Two Children in an Interior with a Basket of Grapes* (1922, oil on canvas, 23 1/2 x 19 3/4 ins / 60 x 50 cm) GBP 15,400; *On the Terrace* (1928, oil on canvas, 15 1/2 x 19 3/4 ins / 39.5 x 50 cm) GBP 4,400. LONDON, 23 Nov 1988, *Couple on a Terrace* (1934, oil on canvas, 47 1/4 x 35 3/4 ins / 120 x 91 cm) GBP 8,800. LONDON, 22 Nov 1989, *Among the Flowers* (1952, oil on canvas, 35 x 28 3/4 ins / 89 x 73 cm) GBP 18,700. LONDON, 22 June 1990, *Water Carriers* (1935, oil on canvas, 23 1/2 x 27 1/2 ins / 60 x 70 cm) GBP 9,680. MADRID, 16

April 2002, *Young Woman in Landscape* (1942, oil on canvas, 46 x 35 ins / 116 x 88 cm) EUR 5,500. MADRID, 22 Oct 2002, *Morning Light* (1931, oil on canvas, 24 x 28 ins / 60 x 70 cm) EUR 20,000.

SOLER PUIG, Juan
Spanish, 20th century.
Born 1906, in Barcelona; died 1984.
Painter, draughtsman. Portraits, landscapes, urban landscapes, waterscapes.

Juan Soler Puig was a pupil at the Escuela de Bellas Artes in Barcelona, then continued his studies in Madrid and Paris, where he lived for 20 years. He was appointed professor at the Escuela de Bellas Artes in Barcelona.

He mainly painted landscapes in which he exploited the possibilities of colour. He is known, among other works, for: *Montmartre, St Vincent's Creek* and *House in the Country*. He featured in both collective and private exhibitions including: Busquets Gallery, Barcelona (from 1929); Salón de la Primavera, Barcelona (1935); Vic (1945); Madrid (1948); Pinacoteca, Barcelona (1951). He also showed his work at the Charpentier Gallery, Paris; in Munich and in Palma de Majorca.

BIBLIOGRAPHY:
Arnáiz, José Manuel/López Jiménez, Javier/Merchán Díaz, Manuel (ed.), *'Cien años de pintura en Espana y Portugal (1830-1930)'* in vol. X, Antiqvaria, Madrid, 1993.

SOLER ROVIROSA, Francisco
Spanish, 19th century.
Born 24 June 1836, in Barcelona; died November 1900, in Barcelona.
Painter, decorative designer. Landscapes, architectural views.

Francisco Soler Rovirosa was a pupil of Lorenzo Ferrer. He travelled in England, Belgium and France. In Paris he studied perspective under Louis Ricquier and worked in the studios of René Philastre and Félix Cagé. He returned to his native city in 1865.

Ferrer painted for Barcelona's theatres, providing the sets for plays, operas and ballets including *Romeo and Juliet, Macbeth, La Traviata, Don Juan, Samson and Delilah, Tristan and Isolde*, and *Jesus of Nazareth*. He also wrote a treatise entitled *The Art of Theatrical Production*.

BIBLIOGRAPHY:
Arnáiz, José Manuel/López Jiménez, Javier/Merchán Díaz, Manuel (ed.), *'Cien años de pintura en Espana y Portugal (1830-1930)'* in vol. X, Antiqvaria, Madrid, 1993.

SOLER Y LLOPIS, L. Eduardo
Spanish, 19th - 20th century.
Born 1 April 1840, in Alcoy (Valencia); died 26 February 1928, in Valencia.
Painter. Religious subjects, portraits.

Eduardo Soler y Llopis studied at the Escuela de Bellas Artes in Valencia. He was appointed professor at the Escuela de Bellas Artes in Cádiz in 1867, then at the school in Valencia.

He painted various religious works including: *First Mass of St John of the Cross*, for the Carmelite convent in Valencia; *Burial of St Vincent the Martyr* and *Burial of the Franciscan Martyrs* in the church of St Bartolomé in Valencia. He is also known for: *Presentation of the Virgin, Pope Pius IX* and *Burial of the Pope St Stephen in the Catacombs*. Eduardo Soler featured in the Exposición Nacional in 1864, obtaining a third class medal.

BIBLIOGRAPHY:
Arnáiz, José Manuel/López Jiménez, Javier/Merchán Díaz, Manuel (ed.), *'Cien años de pintura en Espana y Portugal (1830-1930)'* in vol. X, Antiqvaria, Madrid, 1993.

MUSEUMS AND GALLERIES:
MADRID: *St Stephen after his Martyrdom* - VALENCIA (SFA): various portraits.

AUCTION RECORDS:
NEW YORK, 17 Jan 1990, *Studies after Several Old Masters* (oil on canvas/card, 32 3/4 x 25 ins / 83.3 x 63.5 cm) USD 3,300.

SOLER Y OLIVERAS, José or Josep
Spanish, 19th century.
Born 1808, in Manresa; died 1840.
Painter.

José Soler y Oliveras painted religious subjects and portraits.

SOLERI, Giorgio, or Solero
Italian, 16th century.
Born in Alessandria (Piedmont); died 1587, in Turin.
Active in Spain.
Painter, sculptor.

Giorgio Soleri is thought to have been a pupil of Bernardino Lassini whose daughter he married. Called to Spain, he worked for Philip II at the Escorial Palace. His pictures include an altarpiece in the church of the convent at Alessandria and a painting in the Dominican church in Casale, signed and dated 1573. Soleri was also a talented portrait painter.

SOLERI, Raffaello Angelo
Italian, 16th century.
Active in Turin.
Painter.

The son of Giorgio Soleri, Raffaello Soleri painted an *Adoration of the Magi* in the church of S Francesco in Acqui (Piedmont).

SOLERI-BRANCALEONI, Giuseppe
Italian, 18th century.
Died 22 December 1806, in Rimini.
Active in Rimini.
Painter.

Giuseppe Soleri-Brancaleoni executed altarpieces for several churches in Rimini.

SOLERO, Pio
Italian, 20th century.
Born 3 March 1881, in Sappada Cadore.
Painter. Landscapes.

MUSEUMS AND GALLERIES:
PADUA: *Alpine Landscape*.

SOLESMES, Jehan de. See **GOURBEILLON Eugène**

SOLFAROLO. See **GRUEMBROECH Johann**

SOLFERINI, E.
Italian (?), 19th century.
Miniaturist.

E. Solferini may be the same person as Giuseppe Solferini.

AUCTION RECORDS:
PARIS, 18 Dec 1946, *Three Cherubs with a Young Woman Breaking One of their Bows*.

SOLFERINI, Giuseppe
Italian, 19th century.
Active in Trieste during the first half of the 19th century.
Painter.

Giuseppe Solferini studied at the Accademia di Belle Arti in Venice.

MUSEUMS AND GALLERIES:
TRIESTE (Civico Mus. Revoltella): *Cain*.

SOLI, Achille, or Sole
Italian, 16th century.
Born in Siena.
Painter, engraver (etching), draughtsman. Architectural views.

Achille Soli produced views of Pisa, Siena, Jerusalem and the island of Malta.

SOLI, Cesare
Italian, 20th century.
Born 1926, in Vignola.
Painter.
The uncle of the sculptor Ivo Soli, Cesare Soli studied at the Venturi school of fine art in Modena. In 1993, he participated in the exhibition on still-life painting held at the Galleria della Corte in Vignola, *Pittura come Realtà* (*Painting as Reality*). He had a solo exhibition in 1981 at the castle in Vignola. He was awarded the Anno Santo (Holy Year) Prize in 1950.

SOLI, Giuseppe Maria
Italian, 18th - 19th century.
Born 23 June 1747, in Vignola; died 20 December 1823, in Modena.
Painter.
Giuseppe Maria Soli studied at the Accademia di Belle Arti in Bologna. As well as being a painter and architect, he was also a historian and architectural critic.

SOLIBES, Francisco, or Solives
Spanish, 15th - 16th century.
Active in Banyoles (Gerona).
Painter.
Francisco Solibes painted the altarpiece in the church of San Llorens dels Morunys in 1480.

SOLIERE, Jean. See **SOHIER**

SOLIGNAC, Alexandre
French.
Born in St-Germain-du-Teil (Aveyron).
Sculptor. Figure compositions.
Solignac won the Crozatier Prize in 1867.
MUSEUMS AND GALLERIES:
LE PUY-EN-VELAY: *Nude Men Sitting.*

SOLIGNAC, Jean
French, 17th century.
Sculptor (wood).
Jean Solignac sculpted the altarpiece for the church at Ouveillan near Béziers in 1619 and 1620.

SOLIGNON, Armand Louis, called Armand
French, 18th century.
Sculptor (wood).
Armand Solignon produced part of the door of the church of St-Louis des Invalides in Paris in 1709.

SOLIMA, Pietro. See **SOLLIMA**

SOLIMAN, Guillermo Martinez
Argentinian, 20th century.
Born 1900, in La Plata.
Active in Belgium.
Painter. Landscapes.
Guillermo Martinez Soliman travelled to Europe to study in 1925. He showed work in Belgium where he principally worked.

SOLIMAN, Hassan
Egyptian, 20th century.
Born 1928.
Painter. Landscapes with figures, still-lifes.
Hassan Soliman studied at the faculty of fine arts in Cairo. He won a study scholarship to train at the studio in Luxor. He evokes scenes from Egyptian rural life in his painting, using simplified forms in a multiple perspective. He has taken part in collective exhibitions, in particular the Venice Biennale (1966), and *Visages de l'Art Contemporain Égyptien* (*Aspects of Contemporary Egyptian Art*) at the Musée Galliera in Paris (1971). He has also shown his works in solo exhibitions.
BIBLIOGRAPHY:
Badr El-Din Abou Ghazy, *Visages de l'Art contemporain égyptien*, exhibition catalogue, Musée Galliera, Paris, 1971.
MUSEUMS AND GALLERIES:
CAIRO (Egyptian MMA).

SOLIMAN, Johann Franz de (Count)
Italian, 18th century.
Born c. 1716; died 1784, in Venice.
Painter. History painting, religious subjects.
Soliman, who was influenced by Tiepolo, painted altarpieces.
MUSEUMS AND GALLERIES:
VENICE (Mus. Civico): *Madonna with Guardian Angel and St Francis.*

SOLIMANI, Niccolò
Italian, 15th century.
Active in Verona.
Painter.
Niccolò Solimani painted a *Madonna* in the Ognissanti church in Mantua in 1465.

SOLIMENA, Angelo
Italian, 17th - 18th century.
Born c. 1630, in Canale di Serino; died c. 1716, in Nocera.
Painter. Religious subjects.
Angelo Solimena, the father of Francesco, was the pupil of Fr Guarini. Works by both father and son were shown in the exhibition *Angelo e Francesco Solimena: due culture a confronto* (*Angelo and Francesco Solimena: Two Cultures Compared*) at the Convento di Sant'Anna in Nocera Inferiore.
BIBLIOGRAPHY:
Vega De Martini, Antonio Braca, *Angelo e Francesco Solimena: due culture a confronto,* Fiorentino, Naples, 1994 (1990 exhibition catalogue).
MUSEUMS AND GALLERIES:
NAPLES (Churches): several altarpieces - NOCERA (Churches).
AUCTION RECORDS:
ROME, 21 Nov 1995, *Mary Magdalene Repenting* (oil on canvas, 49 1/4 x 39 3/4 ins / 125 x 101 cm) ITL 17,678,000.

SOLIMENA, Francesco, called l'abbate Ciccio
Italian, 17th - 18th century.
Born 4 October 1657, in Canale di Serino; died 5 April 1747, in Barra.
Painter. Religious subjects, allegorical subjects, portraits.
Francesco was the son and pupil of Angelo Solimena. Initially, his father wanted to steer him towards the study of literature, but thanks to the intervention of Cardinal Orsini, later Pope Benedict XIII, Francesco was allowed to give his enthusiasm for painting free rein. After two years' study with his father, he went in 1674 to Naples to work with Francesco di Maria, then with Giacomo del Po. He continued his studies in Rome, copying the works of Pietro da Cortona, Guido Reni and Carlo Maratti.

He worked at the churches of S Maria Donna Regina in 1684 and S Paolo Maggiore in 1689. Between 1697 and 1708 he took part in the monumental decorative works at the abbey at Montecassino, where he executed frescoes for two chapels and four major canvases for the chancel. In 1708, he received a commission for three paintings for the Senate chamber in Genoa, executed between 1715 and 1717; these paintings were destroyed in 1777, but a number of preparatory sketches survive. Although most of his working life was spent in Naples, he also visited Spain, where Philip V asked him to execute several paintings for the royal chapel in Madrid, and made two trips to Rome, where he painted his celebrated *Heliodorus Driven from the Temple* (1725) at the church of Gesù Nuovo. An outstanding Baroque artist, Solimena was first inspired by the style of Luca Giordano, to which he brought a solidity and more dramatic contrastive effects. While Luca Giordano's *Madonna del Baldacchino* is an insubstantial work, Solimena's *Virgin and Child with SS Peter and Paul,* constructed on the same principles of composition, is a more dramatic work in which contrast is used to accentuate form clearly. These dramatic luminous effects are undoubtedly borrowed from Preti, while Solimena's perspectival effects derive from the style of Lanfranc. Solimena's work might therefore be said to be a true synthesis of all the elements in the Neapolitan Baroque, merged in luminous scenography. In his mature work, he continued in the measured rhythm of the Baroque, fiercely resisting the Rococo and leaning towards more academic painting. He exerted considerable influence on painters in subsequent generations, both in Naples and in Europe as a whole, and he and Luca Giordano ushered in the era of 18th-century Neapolitan art with their respective decorative works in the Cappella del Tesoro in S Martino. He was also a poet, architect and musician.

Collective thematic exhibitions in which his work has featured include *Cieux en gloire* (*Celestial Glories*) at the Fesch museum in Ajaccio in 2002, an evocation of the great Roman decorative commissions during the Baroque period using sketches ('bozzetti' and 'modelli'), and *The Mysteries of Naples. The Sublime and the Trivial: Neapolitan Painting* at the Fesch museum in 2003; *Angelo e Francesco Solimena: due culture a confronto* (*Angelo and Francesco Solimena: Two Cultures Compared*), featuring works by both father and son, was mounted in 1990 at the Convento di Sant'Anna at Nocera Inferiore.

Solimena
Francesco

BIBLIOGRAPHY:

Ruiz, Vergnet, ''*Sur quelques peintures de Solimena*' in *Revue des Arts* vol. VIII, periodical, Paris, 1958. Bologna, Ferdinando, *Francesco Solimena*, periodical, L'Arte tipografica, Naples, 1958. Bologna, F., '*Solimena's 'Solomon worshipping Pagan Gods'* in *A. Q. xxxi*, periodical, 1968 (35-62). Sica, Manfredi, *Inediti di Francesco Solimena e d'altri pittori meridionali*, periodical, Dehoniane, Naples, 1974. Spinosa, Francesco, ''*More unpublished works by Francesco Solimena'* in *Burlington Magazine* n° 912, p. 211-220, periodical, London, 1979. Bologna, F., ed. C. Whitfield/Martineau, J., *Painting in Naples, 1606-1705: From Caravaggio to Giordano*, exhibition catalogue, Royal Academy, London; NGA, Washington; Grand Palais, Paris; Fond. Agnelli, Turin, 1982-1983 (245-248). Spinosa, N., *A Taste for Angels: Neapolitan Painting in North American Collections (1650-1750)*, exhibition catalogue, l, Yale University Press, New Haven, 1987. De Martini, Vega/Braca, Antonio, *Angelo e Francesco Solimena: due culture a confronto*, exhibition catalogue, Fiorentino, Naples, 1994 (1990 exhibition catalogue, Convento di Sant'Anna, Nocera Inferiore). Olivesi, Jean-Marc (ed.), *Cieux en gloire*, exhibition catalogue, periodical, Musée Fesch, Ajaccio, 2002. Spinosa, Nicolà, et al., *Les Mystères de Naples. Sublime et triviale: la peinture napolitaine*, group exhibition catalogue, Musée Fesch, Ajaccio, 2003.

MUSEUMS AND GALLERIES:

AJACCIO (Mus. Fesch): *Departure of Rebecca* (oil on canvas) - AMIENS: *St John the Baptist Preaching in the Desert* - ANGERS: *Annunciation* - AVIGNON: *Bronze Serpent* - BESANÇON: *Godefroy de Bouillon Wounded* - BÉZIERS: *Coronation of the Virgin* - BONN: *Paradise* - BORDEAUX: *Joseph Interpreting Dreams in Prison* - CAEN: *Death of Archimedes* - CHAMBÉRY (MBA): *Descent from the Cross* - CHERBOURG: *Jacob's Ladder* - COMPIÈGNE: *Portrait of a Man; Rough Sketch* - DIJON: *Death of St Joseph; Assumption* - DRESDEN: *Centaurs and Lapiths in Combat; Virgin and Infant Jesus in the Clouds; Angel with Violin Appearing to St Francis; Mater Dolorosa; Sophonisba Receiving Poison from her Husband's Messengers; Juno and Io Turned into a Cow; Abduction of Women* - FLORENCE: *The Artist; Diana Bathing with her Nymphs* - GLASGOW: *Justice and Peace* - HANOVER: *St Thomas Aquinas; Know Thyself* (allegory) - LA FÈRE: *Death of the Virgin* - LE HAVRE: *Simon the Magician* - LE PUY-EN-VELAY: *Baptism of Jesus* - LILLE: *Legend of St Thomas Aquinas* - LONDON (NG): *An Allegory of Louis XIV* (c. 1700, oil on canvas, sketch); *Dido receiving Aeneas and Cupid disguised as Ascanius* (1720s, oil on canvas) - MADRID (Prado): *Prometheus in Chains in the Caucasus; St John the Baptist; Portrait of a Man; Portrait of the Artist; St Joachim and St Anne* - MARSEILLES: *Christ on the Cross* - MILAN (Pinacoteca di Brera): *St Leo on his Way to Meet Attila; Conference of the Order of St Benedict* - MONTAUBAN: *Allegory of Life* - MOSCOW (Rumiantsev Mus.): *St Martin Giving his Garments to Beggars; Philogeniture* - MULHOUSE: *Assumption* - NAPLES: *Portia and Brutus; Death of Virginia; Venus Surrounded by the Divinities of Love; Allegories* (two); *St Roch; Massacre of the Giustiniani Family; Transfiguration of the Madonna* (two); *Madonna and Child; Death of Filippo Neri; Vision of Pius V; Expulsion of Heliodorus from the Temple* - NEW HAVEN (Knights of Columbus Mus.): *The Virgin Immaculata or Allegory of Purity* - PARIS (Louvre): *Heliodorus Driven from the Temple* - ROHRAU (Schlossmus., Graf Harrach'sche Familiensammlung): *Virgin, Infant Jesus and St John* (two); *Virgin and Infant Jesus; Deborah; Christ on a Rock; Veneration of St Januarius; Allegory of Sovereignty* - ROME (Gal. Nazionale): *Liberation of St Peter; Madonna and Child; Portrait of a Young Man* - ROME (Palazzo Doria Pamphili): *Personification of Europe, America, Asia and Africa* - ROUEN: *Christopher Columbus Receiving Papal Bulls; St Remigius, Archbishop of Rheims* - SALFORD (Museum and AG): *Christ Appearing to Mary Magdalen* - SORRENTO: *Portrait of a Woman* - SPEYER: *Madonna with Child and St John* - ST PETERSBURG (Hermitage): *Allegory of Religion* - STUTTGART (Staatsgal.): *Rebecca at the Well* - TARBES: *Wise and Foolish Virgins* - THE HAGUE: *Annunciation* - TOULON: *Abdication of Charles V; St Benedict Healing the Sick* (a sketch) - TOULOUSE: *Portrait of a Woman* - TRAPANI: *Assumption* - VATICAN (Mus. Vaticani): *St Michael Vanquishing the Devil* - VENICE (Gal. dell'Accademia): *Rebecca and Eliezer; Jacob and Rebecca* - VIENNA (Kunsthistorisches Mus.): *Emperor Charles VI and Count Gundaker Althann* - VIENNA (Österreichische Gal. Belvedere): *Abduction of Oreithyia; Descent from the Cross* - WASHINGTON DC (Georgetown University): *The Departure of Rebecca* (c. 1710, oil on canvas).

AUCTION RECORDS:

LONDON, 23 April 1910, *Bacchante* (1885) GBP 24. LONDON, 30 April 1910, *Butterfly*, GBP 54. LONDON, 13 May 1911, *St Peter Denying Christ* (1883) GBP 48; *Delilah* (1887) GBP 25. LONDON, 5 June 1924, *Convalescence*, GBP 63. LONDON, 24 Nov 1926, *Hermann A de Stern as a Child*, GBP 231. LONDON, 27 Jan 1976, *Woman of the Harem* (1887, oil on canvas, 66 1/4 x 48 ins / 168 x 122 cm) GBP 420. LONDON, 15 May 1979, *Delilah* (1887, oil on canvas) GBP 700. LONDON, 6 March 1981, *Portrait of a Young Girl* (oil on card, 20 x 14 ins / 50.8 x 35.5 cm) GBP 1,500. LONDON, 25 Nov 1983, *Portrait of Violet, Lady Metchett, with her Two Daughters* (oil on canvas, 81 x 42 ins / 205.7 x 106.7 cm) GBP 7,000. LONDON, 29 Nov 1985, *Laus Deo* (oil on canvas, rounded at the top, 93 x 68 ins / 236.5 x 173 cm) GBP 11,000. LONDON, 8 July 1987, *Holy Family* (1731, oil on canvas, 22 x 15 ins / 55 x 38 cm) GBP 22,000. NEW YORK, 23 May 1989, *Lucille* (1890, oil on canvas, 24 x 20 ins / 61 x 51 cm) USD 9,900. NEW YORK, 28 Feb 1990, *In the Kitch-*

en Garden (oil on canvas, 24 x 20 ins / 61 x 50.8 cm) USD 35,200. LONDON, 8 Feb 1991, *Study for Eve* (oil on canvas, 27½ x 22¼ ins / 69.8 x 56.4 cm) GBP 4,180. NEW YORK, 13 Oct 1993, *God be Praised!* (oil on canvas, 96¼ x 69½ ins / 244.2 x 176.5 cm) USD 57,500. LONDON, 5 Nov 1993, *Study for the Birth of Love* (red chalk, 18 x 10¼ ins / 45.5 x 26.3 cm) GBP 2,760. LONDON, 7 June 1995, *Portrait of a Small Child with a Birdcage* (1902, oil on canvas, 25 x 20 ins / 63.5 x 51 cm) GBP 3,910. NEW YORK, 30 Jan 1998, *Noli me tangere* (between 1710 and 1720, oil on canvas, 26 x 19½ ins / 66 x 49.5 cm) USD 79,500. NEW YORK, 28 May 1999, *Education of the Virgin* (oil on canvas, oval, 30 x 23 ins / 76 x 58 cm) USD 45,000. LONDON, 17 Dec 1999, *Study for Personification of Charity* (oil on canvas, 19 x 30 ins / 49 x 77 cm) GBP 30,000. MILAN, 31 May 2000, *Sacrifice of Ephigenia* (oil on canvas, 40 x 50 ins / 102 x 128 cm) ITL 160,000,000. LONDON, 2 Nov 2000, *Madonna and Child Enthroned, with Sts Augustine, Monica and Attendant Angels* (oil on canvas, arched top, 25 x 16 ins / 64 x 41 cm) GBP 7,500. NEW YORK, 25 Jan 2001, *Priam in the Tent of Achilles and Venus with Iapis Curing Aeneas of Wounds Suffered During the War* (oil on canvas, a pair, 19 x 39 ins / 49 x 100 cm) USD 150,000. NEW YORK, 25 Jan 2001, *Zeuxis and the Maidens of Croton* (oil on canvas, 46 x 66 ins / 116 x 168 cm) USD 200,000. LONDON, 9 July 2002, *St Felix of Cantalice* (oil on canvas, 20 x 24 ins / 50 x 60 cm) GBP 13,000. LONDON, 11 Dec 2002, *Triumph of King Charles of Naples* (oil on canvas, 57 x 47 ins / 144 x 120 cm) GBP 180,000. NEW YORK, 30 May 2003, *Royal Hunt of Dido and Aeneas* (oil on canvas, 29 x 30 ins / 74 x 77 cm) USD 95,000. ROME, 17 Dec 2003, *Elijah* (oil on canvas, 40 x 30 ins / 102 x 77 cm) EUR 46,000. LONDON, 21 April 2004, *Noli me Tangere* (oil on canvas, 27 x 20 ins / 68 x 50 cm) GBP 43,000. NAPLES, 19 May 2004, *Education of the Virgin* (oil on copper, 22 x 20 ins / 56 x 50 cm) EUR 68,000.

SOLIMENA, Giulio
Italian, 17th - 18th century.
Born c. 1667, in Naples; died 25 December 1722, in Rome.
Painter.

MUSEUMS AND GALLERIES:
ROME (Gal. dell'Accademia Nazionale di S Luca): *Massacre of the Innocents* (1702).

SOLIMENA, Orazio
Italian, 18th century.
Active in Naples during the first half of the 18th century.
Painter, engraver (burin).

The nephew and pupil of Francesco Solimena, Orazio painted religious subjects in St Dominic's church in Barra; he was also an architect.

SOLINGEN, Gottschalk von.
See **SOLLINGEN**

SOLINGEN, Johannes van
Dutch, 18th century.
Born 1712 or 1713, in Leiden.
Engraver (burin).

Johannes van Solingen studied in Leiden. He engraved views.

SOLINI, Tommaso. See **SALINI Tommaso, called Mao**

SOLIS
Spanish, 17th century.
Sculptor (wood).

Solis was a pupil of Montanés and assisted him in 1617 and 1618 with the sculptural work he executed for Sta Maria de las Cuevas in Seville.

MUSEUMS AND GALLERIES:
SEVILLE (Mus.): *Justice; Strength; Old Age; Youth* (wood).

SOLIS, Alonso de
Spanish, 16th century.
Painter.

Alonso de Solis worked in Seville and emigrated to America in 1556.

SOLIS, Andreas or Endres
German, 16th century.
Born 20 September 1550; died 23 June 1592.
Painter.

Andreas Solis was a son of Virgil Solis the Elder and brother of Hans. He worked in Nuremberg.

SOLIS, Diego de
Spanish, 16th century.
Active during the second half of the 16th century.
Sculptor.

Diego de Solis carved the choir stalls in Orense Cathedral in 1580.

SOLIS, Fernando or Hernardo
Spanish, 16th century.
Active in Valladolid c. 1598.
Engraver (burin).

SOLIS, Francisco de
Spanish, 17th century.
Born 1629, in Madrid; died 25 September 1684, in Madrid.
Painter, engraver (burin). History painting.

Francisco de Solis was the son of the painter Juan de Solis. He was originally destined to join the church but after demonstrating his talent as an artist at an early age he was allowed to become a painter. Philip IX was so impressed by the young artist's work that he had Francisco write his age (he was 18) on one of his paintings. He collaborated on the decorations for the ceremonial entry of Queen Louise of Orléans, executing 12 paintings of Hercules. Francisco de Solis was also a great friend of the arts. He opened an academy where young people could learn to draw free of charge. He wrote a *Life of Spanish Painters, Sculptors and Architects*, the manuscript of which has unfortunately been lost. He also gathered together a remarkable collection of books, engravings and drawings which he intended to bequeath to the Spanish nation, although his early death prevented this.

BIBLIOGRAPHY:
Bermudez, C., *Diccionario histórico de los más ilustres profesores de las bellas artes en España*, Madrid, 1800. Brown, J., *Painting in Spain 1500-1700*, Yale University Press, New Haven and London, 1998.

SOLIS, Georg
German, 16th century.
Born 23 November 1573; died before 9 June 1608.
Active in Nuremberg.
Painter.

Georg Solis was the son of Andreas Solis.

SOLIS, Hanns, or Sallis
German, 17th century.
Active in Nuremberg in 1525.
Painter.

Hanns Solis was probably the father of Virgil Solis, known as the Elder.

SOLIS, Hans
German, 16th - 17th century.
Died before 26 December 1616.
Painter, illustrator.
Nuremberg School.

Hans Solis was a son of Andreas Solis the Elder and brother of Andreas. He worked in Nuremberg and Frankfurt am Main. He painted illustrated messages.

SOLIS, Juan
Spanish, 17th century.
Born 1595; died 1654.
Active in Segovia.
Painter.
Juan Solis was the father of Francisco de Solis.

SOLIS, Nicolas, Nikolaus or Niclas
German, 16th century.
Born c. 1542, in Nuremberg; died 1584, in Augsburg.
Painter, engraver.
Nicolas Solis was a son of Virgil Solis the Elder. He did burin and aquatint engravings and made drawings for woodcuts. He engraved 15 sheets depicting the marriage of Duke Wilhelm V to Renée of Lorraine in 1568.

SOLIS, Virgil or Virgilius, the Elder
German, 16th century.
Born 1514, in Nuremberg; died 1 August 1562, in Nuremberg.
Illuminator, painter, draughtsman, engraver (burin/etching/wood/copper). Religious subjects, mythological subjects, portraits, hunting scenes, animals. Ornaments.
Nuremberg School.
Virgil Solis, the father of Andreas and Hans, left a large number of engravings. It is known that he was also a remarkable illuminator, but little of his work in this genre has survived. Nagler mentions a Frankfurt Bible of 1561 that contains a portrait.

He engraved religious and mythological subjects, portraits, animals, hunting scenes and decorations on wood or copper, usually after his own well-executed drawings, and he produced more than 2,000 plates.

In 2003 he was represented in the exhibition *Les Dieux comme les Hommes. Gravures rhénanes du XVIè siècle. (Gods as Men. Rhineland Engravings of the 16th Century)*, which showed the collections of the Prints and Drawings Department of the Musée des Beaux-Arts, Strasbourg.

BIBLIOGRAPHY:
La Gravure allemande à la Renaissance, group exhibition catalogue, Musée des Beaux-Arts, Caen, 1999. Schefer, Jean Louis/Haus, Anny-Claire/Hergott, Fabrice (preface), et al., *Les Dieux comme les Hommes. Gravures rhénanes du XVIe siècle*, group exhibition catalogue, Musée des Beaux-Arts, Strasbourg, 2003. Jover, Manuel, '*Les Petits Maîtres de Nuremberg*' in *L'Œil* n° 544, periodical, Paris, February 2003.
MUSEUMS AND GALLERIES:
STRASBOURG (MBA, Prints Collection): *Bear Hunt*.
AUCTION RECORDS:
PARIS, 1864, *Two Pen Drawings with Watercolour Wash*, FRF 50. PARIS, 1896, *Mythological Scene. Battle in the Clouds*. (pen drawing) FRF 55. PARIS, 21 May 1928, *Lansquenet* (pen) FRF 780. PARIS, 28 Nov 1934, *King David Watching from his Palace Bathsheeba Bathing* (pen) FRF 380. LONDON, 13 Dec 1984, *Design for a Frieze* (1537, pen and black ink, 4 1/2 x 12 3/4 ins / 11.3 x 32.4 cm) GBP 2,400. LONDON, 10 July 2001, *Dog in Profile to the Left in a Landscape* (1549, pen/ink, 4 x 6 ins / 9 x 15 cm) GBP 4,000.

SOLIS, Virgil or Virgilius II, called the Younger
German, 16th century.
Born 14 November 1551, in Nuremberg.
Painter, watercolourist, draughtsman. Mythological subjects.
Prague School.
A son of Virgil the Elder, Virgil Solis the Younger worked in Prague for the Emperor Rudolph II and made plans of the areas of the city.
AUCTION RECORDS:
HEIDELBERG, 11 April 1992, *Diana and her Followers Setting Out for the Hunt* (watercolour and ink, 7 3/4 x 8 1/4 ins / 19.9 x 20.8 cm) DEM 2,600.

SOLIS ÁVILA, Antonio
Spanish, 20th century.
Born 27 September 1898, in Madroñera (Extremadura); died 21 December 1967, in Madrid.
Painter, draughtsman, illustrator. Figures, portraits, landscapes with figures.
Antonio Solis Ávila took part in various collective exhibitions including: Exposición Internacional, Barcelona (1930); Sociedad Nacional de Bellas Artes, Madrid (1930 and 1948 when he was awarded a third class medal); he also exhibited in New York. He collaborated on several Spanish magazines.
BIBLIOGRAPHY:
Arnáiz, José Manuel/López Jiménez, Javier/Merchán Díaz, Manuel (ed.), '*Cien años de pintura en Espana y Portugal (1830-1930)*' in vol. X, Antiqvaria, Madrid, 1993.

SOLISMEO. See **SOLOSMEO**

SOLITARIO, Ernesto
Italian, 19th century.
Born July 1838, in San Giorgio Lamulara.
Sculptor.
A student at the Accademia di Belle Arti in Naples, Solitario produced works for the churches at Baia and Saviano.
MUSEUMS AND GALLERIES:
NAPLES (Mus. di Capodimonte): *Charles III* (colossal bust).

SOLIVA, Jacobus
Swiss, 18th century.
Active during the first half of the 18th century.
Painter.
Jacobus Soliva painted altarpieces for the chapel of St Anne in Truns in 1717.

SOLIVA, Joaquín
Spanish, 18th century.
Painter.
Joaquín Soliva worked as a painter at the Alcora porcelain works from 1783 to 1789.

SOLIVA, Louis
French, 19th century.
Born in Paris.
Sculptor.
Soliva's work featured at the Salon des Artistes Français. He won an honourable mention in 1893.

SOLIVA, Miguel
Spanish, 18th century.
Died 1755, in Alcora.
Active in Conca.
Painter (porcelain), earthenware maker.
Miguel Soliva worked for the Alcora porcelain works from 1727 to 1750.

SOLIVES, Francisco. See **SOLIBES**

SÖLKNER, Franz
Austrian, 18th century.
Sculptor.
Franz Sölkner produced sculptures for the high altar of Hallein church in 1799.

SOLL, Gottfried
German, 19th century.
Active in Trostberg.
Painter.
Son of Ignaz Soll II.

SOLL, Ignaz I
German, 19th century.
Born 1780, in Trostberg; died 1841, in Trostberg.
Painter.
Son of Joseph Soll. He painted religious pictures.

SOLL, Ignaz II, real name Kirchbichler
German, 19th century.
Born 23 December 1805, in Seeon; died 1866, in Trostberg.
Painter.
Father of Gottfried, Ignaz Soll III, Josef and Xaver Soll. Adoptive son of Ignaz Soll I. He worked in Munich and was a friend of Ludwig Schanthaler.

SOLL, Ignaz III
German, 19th century.
Died 1903, in Trostberg.
Painter.
Son of Ignaz Soll II.

SOLL, Josef
German, 19th - 20th century.
Died 1921, in Trostberg.
Painter.
Josef Soll was the son of Ignaz Soll II.

SOLL, Joseph or Franz Joseph, or Söll
German, 18th century.
Born in Fridingen an der Donau; died 9 February 1798, in Trostberg.
Painter. Religious subjects.
Father of Ignaz Soll I. He painted altarpieces for churches at Alzgern, Feichten, Ostaig, Kirchweidach, Lauterbach, Obereschelbach, Siegsdorf, Tacherting and Trostberg.

SOLL, Xaver
German, 19th century.
Active in Trostberg.
Painter.
Son of Ignaz Soll II.

SOLLAZZINO, Giuliano. See **GIULIANO DI GIOVANNI DE' CASTELLANI DA MONTELUPO**

SOLLBRIG, Johann Gottlieb or Gottlob. See **SOLBRIG**

SOLLENER, Johann. See **SOLLERER**

SÖLLER, Anton
German, 19th century.
Born 6 January 1807, in Cologne; died 9 December 1875, in Mülheim.
Painter, art restorer. Portraits, landscapes.
Anton Söller trained at art academies in Düsseldorf and Munich. He worked in Mülheim am Rhein.

SOLLERER, Johann, or Sollener
Austrian, 18th century.
Born 30 April 1747; died 28 June 1809, in Vienna.
Miniaturist.
Johann Sollerer trained at the art academy in Vienna.

SOLLERIO. See **SOLARI**

SOLLET, François
French, 16th century.
Active in Paris in 1566.
Sculptor.

SOLLEWYN, Hendrina A.
Dutch, 19th century.
Born 1784, in Haarlem.
Painter. Flowers, fruit.
Hendrina A. Sollewyn was a pupil of W. Hendriks.

SOLLFLEISCH, Johann Anton
German, 18th century.
Active in Cham.
Painter.
Johann Anton Sollfleisch produced works for churches in Miltach and Weissenregen.

SOLLI, Giuseppe
Italian, 18th century.
Born c. 1753, in Florence.
Engraver, designer of ornamental architectural features.
Giuseppe Solli was the pupil of Vincenzo Meucci.

SOLLIER
French, 18th century.
Painter.
Sollier studied at the Académie Royale and was awarded medals in 1751 and 1752.

SOLLIER, Claude Florentin
French, 18th century.
Died 23 January 1784.
Active in Paris.
Painter, art dealer.
Claude Florentin Sollier was a member of the Académie de St-Luc in 1774, where he exhibited a still-life.

SOLLIER, Clémence Marie Louise
French, 19th century.
Died 1849.
Painter, pastellist. Portraits, figures, genre scenes.
Clémence Sollier exhibited at the Salon between 1842 and 1849.

SOLLIER, Eugène or Paul Louis Eugène
French, 20th century.
Born in Paris; died April 1915.
Sculptor, medallist.
Eugène Sollier, or Paul Louis Eugène, was a student of Cordier. He exhibited at the Salon from 1869 to 1909. He was a member of the Société des Artistes Français from 1883, receiving commendations in 1881 and 1883.

SOLLIER, Henri Alexandre
French, 20th century.
Born 7 December 1886, in Bagnolet; died 1966, in Paris.
Painter, watercolourist, draughtsman. Landscapes, architectural views.
Henri Alexandre Sollier was a student of François Flameng, François Schommer and J. Adler. He worked in Dakar for three years. Some of his works reveal the influence of this period.

Before 1914, he began exhibiting regularly at the Salon des Artistes Français in Paris, where in 1920 he was awarded a commendation. In 1922, he received the Prix de l'Afrique Occidentale Française. He won a silver medal in 1930 and golds in 1934 and 1937 at the Exposition Internationale.

After 1957, he worked in Auvergne, Haute-Savoie, Provence and then Italy. He was a member of the committee and the jury of the Artistes Français in 1937. He was principally a landscape artist, but also painted architectural subjects. The former Musée des Colonies in Paris owns some of his work.

H. Sollier

BIBLIOGRAPHY:
Vente Henri Sollier, auction catalogue, Maître Pierre-Marie Rogeon, Paris, 1972.

MUSEUMS AND GALLERIES:
CASABLANCA.
AUCTION RECORDS:
PARIS, 18 Feb 1980, *Market in Senegal* (1923, oil on canvas, 51 1/4 x 63 3/4 ins / 130 x 162 cm) FRF 31,000. PARIS, 7 June 1988, *Bambara Woman* (1922, oil on panel, 13 3/4 x 11 ins / 35 x 27 cm) FRF 3,500. LONDON, 21 Oct 1988, *Breton Women after Mass* (oil on canvas, 25 1/2 x 32 ins / 65 x 81 cm) GBP 1,980. BREST, 14 May 2000, *Day of Pardon and Showman Fete near the Chapel in Brittany* (oil on canvas, 24 x 19 ins / 61 x 47 cm) FRF 17,500. BREST, 14 May 2000, *Vegetable Market at Pont l'Abbe* (oil on canvas, 21 x 26 ins / 54 x 65 cm) FRF 19,000. BREST, 20 May 2001, *Livestock Market at Pont-l'Abbe* (oil on canvas, 20 x 29 ins / 50 x 73 cm) FRF 37,000. MUNICH, 4 July 2001, *Bath-time* (oil on canvas, 38 x 51 ins / 97 x 130 cm) DEM 7,500. LONDON, 18 July 2002, *Plastic Greek. High-relief* (oil on canvas, a pair, 36 x 27 ins / 91 x 68 cm) GBP 1,900. BREST, 20 July 2002, *Showman Fete* (oil on canvas, 18 x 24 ins / 46 x 61 cm) EUR 3,300. BREST, 11 May 2003, *Young Girl from Plougastel at Church* (oil on canvas, 30 x 20 ins / 75 x 50 cm) EUR 1,550.

SOLLIER D'APT, Joseph Noël Eleazar
French, 19th century.
Born 25 December 1810, in Apt (Vaucluse).
Sculptor.

Sollier was a pupil of David d'Angers. He exhibited at the Salon between 1841 and 1843 with busts, bronze statuettes and allegorical figures and created a fountain in Saignon (Vaucluse).

SOLLIGER, Andres. See **SALGEN**

SOLLIMA, Pietro, or Solima
Italian, 17th century.
Active in Messina c. 1650.
Painter.

The pupil of Quagliata, Sollima was later influenced by Dürer.

SOLLINGEN, Gottschalk von, or Solingen
German, 16th - 17th century.
Active in Cologne from 1572 to 1605.
Painter.

SOLLITTO, Carlo. See **SELLITTO**

SOLLMANN, Paul
German, 20th century.
Born 15 September 1886, in Coburg (Bavaria).
Painter, watercolourist, engraver. Landscapes, architectural views.

Paul Sollmann studied in Munich, Rome and Paris. He subsequently lived and worked in Rothenburg ober der Tauber.
MUSEUMS AND GALLERIES:
COBURG: several watercolours.

SOLLY, Arthur. See **SOLY**

SOLMANS, Alden
American, 19th - 20th century.
Born 1835; died 29 April 1930, in South Norwalk.
Painter.

SOLMAR, Jacob
German, 19th century.
Born c. 1799, in Ludwigslust; died May 1832.
Portrait artist.

Pupil of Fr Lenthe and of the art academies in Berlin and Dresden.

SOLMI, Valentino
Italian, 19th century.
Born 1810; died 1866.
Active in Bologna.
Painter. Architectural views.

MUSEUMS AND GALLERIES:
BOLOGNA (Pinacoteca Nazionale): *Byzantine Church; Portal of the Aracoeli Church in Rome*.

SOLMS, F.C. von (Count)
German, 18th century.
Active at the beginning of the 18th century.
Engraver (etching).

F.C. de Solms produced an engraved landscape in 1705.

SOLMS, Friedrich Wilhelm Maximilian von (Count)
German, 18th century.
Active c. 1770.
Engraver (etching).

MUSEUMS AND GALLERIES:
DRESDEN (Prints Collection): two vignettes.

SOLMS, Jacobus von
German, 17th century.
Died after 1623.
Active in Cologne.
Painter.

MUSEUMS AND GALLERIES:
DORTMUND (Mus. für Kunst und Kulturgeschichte): *Crucifixion*.

SOLMS, Marie Studolmine de
Maiden name: Wyse
French, 19th century.
Born 21 (?) July 1833, in Waterford; died 6 February 1902, in Paris.
Caricaturist, writer.

She was a great niece of Napoleon Bonaparte

SOLMS-LAUBACH, Christiane Louise von (Countess)
German, 18th - 19th century.
Born 1754, in Laubach; died 1815.
Painter.

She exhibited in Kassel in 1781 and in Berlin in 1786.

SOLNON, Daniel
French, 20th century.
Painter.

Daniel Solnon began painting in the Abstract style, but later became well known as one of France's specialists in trompe l'oeil painting.

His solo shows included the 1995 exhibition entitled *Dijon as seen by Daniel Solnon*, at the Palais des Ducs de Bourgogne, Dijon.

SOLNZEV, Egor Grigorievich, or Solnzeff
Russian, 19th century.
Born 12 April 1812; died 31 December 1864, in St Petersburg.
Painter, mosaicist. Landscapes.

MUSEUMS AND GALLERIES:
MOSCOW: *View of Italy*.

SOLNZEV, Fedor Grigorievich
Russian, 19th century.
Born 14 April 1801, near Yaroslavl; died 3 March 1892, in St Petersburg.
Painter.

Fedor Grigorievich Solnzev studied at the art academy in St Petersburg. He made educational visits to the main artistic centres in Europe. He painted several historical canvases in Moscow for Tsar Nicholas. In 1876, he was appointed to a teaching post at the art academy in St Petersburg.
MUSEUMS AND GALLERIES:
MOSCOW (State Tretyakov Gal.): *An Angel Appearing to Pontiff Zacharias* - ST PETERSBURG (Gosudarstvennyj Russkij Muz.): *Meeting of Sviataslav and Zimisus*.

SOLOBRIN, Jérôme
Italian, 15th - 16th century.
Of Italian origin.
Active in Amboise from 1494 to 1502.
Ceramicist.

SOLODOVNIKOV, Aleksei Pavlovich
Ukrainian, 20th century.
Born 1928, in Tokarevo (Yaroslavl).
Painter. Figure compositions.

A.P. Solodovnikov studied at Yaroslavl art college from 1943 to 1948 and Kiev Art Institute (1948-1956), where he worked under Grigorev. He settled in Kiev and his work is often reproduced in books on Ukrainian art.

MUSEUMS AND GALLERIES:
KIEV (National Art Museum) - MOSCOW (Pushkin MFA).

AUCTION RECORDS:
PARIS, 19 June 1991, *Poster* (1965, oil on canvas, 45 1/4 x 60 1/4 ins / 115 x 153 cm) FRF 7,000. PARIS, 16 Nov 1992, *Snowbound Road* (oil on canvas, 19 1/2 x 31 ins / 49.5 x 78.5 cm) FRF 3,200.

SOLOGUB, Leonid Romanovich, or Sologoub
Russian, 20th century.
Born 1884, in Erik.
Painter, architect.

L.R. Sologub studied at the Academy in Petrograd (now St Petersburg). He exhibited in The Hague and Rotterdam, at the Salon des Indépendants and the Salon d'Automne in Paris, and in Russia.

SOLOMATKIN, Leonid Ivanovich
Russian, 19th century.
Born 1837; died 1883.
Painter. Genre scenes.

MUSEUMS AND GALLERIES:
MOSCOW (State Tretyakov Gal.): *In the Cellar.*

AUCTION RECORDS:
LUCERNE, 20 May 1980, *Russian Peasants in an Interior* (1860, oil on canvas, 8 1/4 x 11 1/2 ins / 21 x 29 cm) CHF 2,600. LONDON, 19 Dec 1996, *Greeting the Civil Servant* (1867, oil on canvas, 7 3/4 x 11 1/4 ins / 20 x 28.5 cm) GBP 9,200. LONDON, 23 Nov 2000, *Welcoming the Official* (oil on canvas, 8 x 11 ins / 21 x 29 cm) GBP 17,500.

SOLOMBRE, Jean
French, 20th - 21st century.
Born 1948, in Paris.
Painter, engraver, illustrator.

Jean Solombre lives and works in Boulogne-Billancourt. The essential feature of his technique is the formal reduction of figures, objects and landscapes to silhouettes scattered about the surface of his canvases.

His engravings have been used to illustrate several publications, among them *Le Coeur Mémorable* (*Memorable Heart*), (text by Jean Solombre, 1978); *Carnival* (text by Michel Haas, 1979); *Straits* (text by Julien Gracq, 1980); *Exile* (text by Jean Solombre, 1981); *Road* (text by Julien Gracq, 1981); and *Mornings on the Earth* (text by Kenneth White, 1981).

Solombre has shown examples of his work at various group exhibitions in France, notably at the Salon Grands et Jeunes d'Aujourd'hui, and abroad, including international art fairs in Chicago, Basel, Washington, New York, London and Frankfurt. His solo exhibitions have included those in 1979 at the Galerie Jean-Marie Cupillard in Grenoble; in 1980 at the Galerie Lahumière in Paris; in 1981, at Montbrison Museum; in 1982 at the Galerie Michel Broutta in Paris; and a retrospective at the Artothèque in Mulhouse in 1989.

BIBLIOGRAPHY:
White, Kenneth (preface), *Jean Solombre*, Éd. Art Extension, Éd. Natiris, Cébazat, 1988.

MUSEUMS AND GALLERIES:
ATLANTA (MMA) - CHICAGO (AI) - PARIS (BNF) - PARIS (FNAC) - PARIS (MAMVP).

AUCTION RECORDS:
PARIS, 7 March 1990, *Movable Earth* (acrylic/canvas, 39 1/4 x 32 ins / 100 x 81 cm) FRF 12,000. PARIS, 23 Nov 1992, *Generations* (1990, acrylic/canvas, 57 1/2 x 45 ins / 146 x 114 cm) FRF 8,000. LONDON, 23 Oct 1996, *Music Room* (tapestry, 72 3/4 x 89 ins / 185 x 226 cm) GBP 805.

SOLOMBRINO, Eleucadio
Italian, 16th century.
Active in Forlì during the second half of the 16th century.
Painter.

Eleucadio Solombrino specialised in painting on ceramics.

MUSEUMS AND GALLERIES:
BERLIN (Palace Mus.): *Marriage of Hercules and Dejanira* - BOLOGNA (Mus. Civico): *St Mary Magdalene Washing Christ's Feet* - RAVENNA (Mus. Nazionale): *Ecce Homo.*

SOLOME, Anton
German, 19th century.
Active in Riedenburg in the middle of the 19th century.
Painter. Portraits, figures.

Trained at the art academy in Munich.

SOLOMIN, Nikolai
Russian, 20th century.
Born 1907.
Painter. Figures.

Nikolai Solomin was a member of the USSR Artists Union.

AUCTION RECORDS:
PARIS, 14 May 1990, *Portrait of a Gypsy* (oil on canvas, 29 1/4 x 23 1/4 ins / 74 x 59 cm) FRF 8,000.

SOLOMIN, Nikolai
Russian, 20th century.
Born 1940.
Painter. Figure compositions, portraits, landscapes with figures.

Nikolai Solomin graduated from the Surikov Institute Moscow in 1965, where he had studied with V.G. Tsyplakov. He was a member of the Artists Union, a People's Artist, and Secretary of the Russian Union of Artists.

AUCTION RECORDS:
PARIS, 15 May 1991, *Winter in Moscow* (1975, oil on canvas, 22 x 25 1/2 ins / 55 x 65 cm) FRF 4,500.

SOLOMKO, Serge de
French, 20th century.
Illustrator.

Serge de Solomko has illustrated: *Nymphs Dancing with Satyrs*, by René Boylesve; *Adophe*, by Benjamin Constant; *Balthazar, Speech at the Unveiling of the Statue of Renan at Tréguier, The Corinthian Weddings, The Procurator of Judaea*, by Anatole France; *Mlle de Maupin*, by Théophile Gautier; *The Three Kings*, by Émile Gebhart; *The Trophies*, by José Maria de Hérédia; *La Princesse de Clèves* (*The Princess of Cleves*), by Mme de La Fayette; *Les Nuits* (*Nights*), by Alfred de Musset; *The Prayer on the Acropolis*, by Ernest Renan; *On the Sides of the Vase*, by Albert Samain; *Anna Pavlova*, by V. Snétlow; *Les Fêtes Galantes*, by Paul Verlaine.

SOLOMON, Abraham
British, 19th century.
Born May 1824, in London; died 19 December 1862, in Biarritz, France.
Painter. Portraits, genre scenes, animals.

Abraham Solomon was the brother of Simeon Solomon. He studied at the Bloomsbury Art School in 1838, then at the Royal Academy in 1839. He took part in exhibitions held by the British Institute and the Royal Academy. His works include *Awaiting the Verdict*. Engraving increased the popularity of his works.

His early works were inspired by his Jewish background, but later, when working with his brother, he became interested in the rites of orthodox Christian and Catholic religions.

MUSEUMS AND GALLERIES:

LEICESTER: *Escape from Lucknow* - MONTREAL: *Acquittal* - SHEFFIELD: *Timid Suitor*.

AUCTION RECORDS:

LONDON, 20 Dec 1909, *Departure of the Stagecoach; Biarritz*, GBP 6. LONDON, 16 Dec 1924, *Rival Beauties*, Gns 70. LONDON, 20 May 1925, *Rival Beauties*, GBP 136. LONDON, 20 March 1963, *First Class Coach Travel*, GBP 2,500. LONDON, 15 Dec 1972, *Awaiting the Verdict*, Gns 2,800. LONDON, 16 March 1973, *Amorous Lion*, Gns 3,000. LONDON, 9 April 1974, *Awaiting the Verdict* (1857) GBP 2,700. LONDON, 25 Oct 1977, *Portrait from Memory* (1851, oil on canvas, rounded at the top, 11 1/2 x 13 1/2 ins / 29 x 34 cm) GBP 3,000. LONDON, 25 May 1979, *Amorous Lion* (oil on canvas, rounded at the top, 28 x 35 1/2 ins / 71.1 x 90.1 cm) GBP 7,500. NEW YORK, 29 Oct 1981, *First Class* (1854, oil on canvas, rounded at the top, 27 x 38 ins / 68.5 x 96.5 cm) USD 120,000. LONDON, 30 Nov 1984, *Awaiting the Verdict; Acquittal* (1859, oil on canvas, a pair, 24 x 29 1/2 ins / 61 x 75 cm) GBP 30,000. LONDON, 18 June 1985, *Contrast* (1855, oil on canvas, 41 1/4 x 59 1/2 ins / 105 x 151 cm) GBP 60,000. LONDON, 31 Oct 1986, *Mad Blaiz* (1857, oil on canvas, 20 x 24 ins / 51 x 61 cm) GBP 3,000. LONDON, 19 Dec 1991, *Drunken Evening* (oil on card, 8 x 6 ins / 20.3 x 15.2 cm) GBP 2,640. LONDON, 12 Nov 1992, *Amorous Lion* (oil on canvas, rounded at the top, 28 x 36 1/4 ins / 71 x 92 cm) GBP 27,500. LONDON, 11 June 1993, *Female Visiter* (1853, oil on panel, 9 x 7 ins / 22.9 x 17.5 cm) GBP 6,325. LONDON, 30 March 1994, *Young Acolyte* (1842, oil on canvas, 26 x 14 1/4 ins / 66 x 36 cm) GBP 8,625. LONDON, 10 March 1995, *Portrait of Miss Rowley* (oil on canvas, 24 1/4 x 20 ins / 61.3 x 51.1 cm) GBP 3,680. LONDON, 12 May 1999, *New Hat* (1850, oil on board, 11 x 9 ins / 28 x 23 cm) GBP 2,200. LONDON, 17 Sept 2002, *William Shakespeare, As You Like It, Act III, Scene VII* (oil on canvas, 30 x 25 ins / 76 x 64 cm) GBP 4,000. LONDON, 20 Feb 2003, *Sketch from Memory* (1851, oil on canvas, 12 x 14 ins / 30 x 36 cm) GBP 15,000.

SOLOMON, Harry

American, 20th century.
Born 1873, in New York.
Painter. Portraits.

Harry Solomon studied in Paris. He lived and worked in New York.

SOLOMON, Hyde

American, 20th century.
Born 1911, in New York; died 1982.
Painter, sculptor.

Hyde Solomon was a student at the Pratt Institute from 1923 to 1933. He spent eight years studying sculpture before turning to painting. He benefited from a MacDowell Scholarship in 1951, and Yaldo Scholarships in 1956-1959. He was first influenced by French Impressionism and German Expressionism. Then after helping to organise a private gallery in 1944, the pupils of Hans Hofmann, with whom he came into contact, led him towards Abstraction. In 1950, he showed an abstract composition with geometric tendencies, precise, airy and classically balanced, at the Salon des Réalités Nouvelles in Paris. He has taken part in many group exhibitions, notably at the Whitney Museum in New York and the Salon des Réalités Nouvelles in Paris.

SOLOMON, J. Solomon or Joseph Solomon

British, 19th - 20th century.
Born 16 September 1860, in London; died 27 July 1927, in Birchington.
Painter. History painting.

Joseph Solomon trained at the Royal Academy School in 1877, and under Cabanel in Paris in 1879. After an extended study tour of Italy, Germany, Holland, Spain and Morocco, he returned to Cabanel's studio for another nine months before settling in London. He was a member of the Royal Institute, became an associate of the Royal Academy in 1894, and an academician in 1906. He exhibited in London from 1881, and won a third class medal at the Paris Exposition of 1889.

MUSEUMS AND GALLERIES:

LEEDS (City AG): *The Awakening* (1891, oil on canvas) - LIVERPOOL (Walker AG): *Samson* (oil on canvas) - LONDON (Royal Academy of Arts): *St George* (c. 1906, oil on canvas) - VICTORIA: *Lord Provost Longair*.

AUCTION RECORDS:

LONDON, 23 April 1910, *Bacchante* (1885) GBP 24. LONDON, 30 April 1910, *Butterfly*, GBP 54. LONDON, 13 May 1911, *St Peter Denying Christ* (1883) GBP 48; *Delilah* (1887) GBP 25. LONDON, 5 June 1924, *Convalescence*, GBP 63. LONDON, 24 Nov 1926, *Hermann A. de Stern as a Child*, GBP 231. LONDON, 27 Jan 1976, *Woman of the Harem* (1887, oil on canvas, 66 1/4 x 48 ins / 168 x 122 cm) GBP 420. LONDON, 15 May 1979, *Delilah* (1887, oil on canvas) GBP 700. LONDON, 6 March 1981, *Portrait of a Young Girl* (oil on card, 20 x 14 ins / 50.8 x 35.5 cm) GBP 1,500. LONDON, 25 Nov 1983, *Portrait of Violet, Lady Metchett, with her Two Daughters* (oil on canvas, 81 x 42 ins / 205.7 x 106.7 cm) GBP 7,000. LONDON, 29 Nov 1985, *Laus Deo* (oil on canvas, rounded at the top, 93 x 68 ins / 236.5 x 173 cm) GBP 11,000. NEW YORK, 24 Feb 1987, *Portrait of Mrs Alfred Mond and her Two Daughters* (oil on canvas, 81 x 42 ins / 205.7 x 106.7 cm) USD 47,500. NEW YORK, 23 May 1989, *Lucille* (1890, oil on canvas, 24 x 20 ins / 61 x 51 cm) USD 9,900. NEW YORK, 28 Feb 1990, *In the Kitchen Garden* (oil on canvas, 24 x 20 ins / 61 x 50.8 cm) USD 35,200. LONDON, 8 Feb 1991, *Study for Eve* (oil on canvas, 27 1/2 x 22 1/4 ins / 69.8 x 56.4 cm) GBP 4,180. NEW YORK, 13 Oct 1993, *God be Praised!* (oil on canvas, 96 1/4 x 69 1/2 ins / 244.2 x 176.5 cm) USD 57,500. LONDON, 5 Nov 1993, *Study for the Birth of Love* (red chalk, 18 x 10 1/4 ins / 45.5 x 26.3 cm) GBP 2,760. LONDON, 7 June 1995, *Portrait of Young Child with a Birdcage* (1902, oil on canvas, 25 x 20 ins / 63.5 x 51 cm) GBP 3,910. LONDON, 18 March 1999, *The Young Artist* (oil on panel, 18 x 10 ins / 45 x 26 cm) GBP 1,700. NEWBURY, 18 Sept 2002, *Portrait of Kate Leon Seated on a Branch Reading a Book* (oil on canvas, 22 x 18 ins / 56 x 45 cm) GBP 3,600. LONDON, 20 Feb 2003, *Study for 'Equipped'* (oil on canvas, 36 x 24 ins / 91 x 62 cm) GBP 8,000.

SOLOMON, J.J.

British, 19th century.
Active in London from 1854 to 1856.
Painter. Architectural views.

J.J. Solomon painted motifs of Bruges and Antwerp.

SOLOMON, J.W.

British, 19th century.
Active in London from 1827 to 1849.
Painter. History painting, portraits, genre scenes.

SOLOMON, Lance Valben

Australian, 20th century.
Born 1913, in Liverpool, Australia; died 1989.
Painter. Landscapes, landscapes with figures.

Lance Solomon trained at the Royal Academy in London, where he won the landscape prize in 1939.

AUCTION RECORDS:

LONDON, 11 May 1976, *Landscape and Pond* (oil on card, 12 x 10 ins / 30.5 x 25.5 cm) GBP 250. SYDNEY, 29 June 1981, *On the Farm* (oil on card, 15 3/4 x 23 1/2 ins / 40 x 60 cm) AUD 1,700. SYDNEY, 4 July 1988, *Kangaroo Valley* (1938, oil on canvas, 11 1/2 x 14 1/4 ins / 29 x 36 cm) AUD 700. SYDNEY, 16 Oct 1989, *A Road in Summer* (oil on canvas, 11 3/4 x 14 1/4 ins / 30 x 36 cm) AUD 2,700. SYDNEY, 26 March 1990, *Cattle in a*

Landscape (watercolour, 7¾ x 9¾ ins / 20 x 25 cm) AUD 1,000. SYDNEY, 2 July 1990, *Spring Morning* (oil on card, 11¾ x 9¾ ins / 30 x 25 cm) AUD 3,000. SYDNEY, 29-30 March 1992, *Cattle at Pasture Beside a Creek* (oil on card, 18 x 15¾ ins / 46 x 40 cm) AUD 2,600. PADDINGTON, 26 Aug 2002, *Morning on the Farm* (c. 1966, oil on board, 30 x 35 ins / 75 x 90 cm) AUD 4,200. MELBOURNE, 2 April 2003, *Little Farm House near Coffs Harbour* (oil on canvas laid on board, 23 x 19 ins / 58 x 49 cm) AUD 3,000. MELBOURNE, 16 June 2004, *Along the Creek* (oil on canvas laid on board, 24 x 30 ins / 61 x 76 cm) AUD 3,000.

SOLOMON, Rebecca (Miss)
British, 19th century.
Born 1832; died 1886.
Painter. History painting, portraits.

Rebecca Solomon was the sister of Abraham Solomon. She exhibited her work at the Royal Academy from 1852 until 1869.

AUCTION RECORDS:

LONDON, 11 July 1969, *Jesus in the House of his Parents* (in collaboration with John Everett Millais) Gns 1,200. LONDON, 3 Feb 1978, *A Fashionable Couple* (oil on canvas, 19 x 21 ins / 48.2 x 53.3 cm) GBP 900. LONDON, 3 July 1979, *Reprimand* (1865, oil on canvas, 26¼ x 31¼ ins / 66.5 x 79.5 cm) GBP 900. LONDON, 18 March 1983, *Elegant Couple* (oil on canvas, 19 x 21 ins / 48.2 x 53.3 cm) GBP 1,800. NEW YORK, 24 May 1985, *Secret; Lesson in Using a Fan* (oil on card, an oval-shaped pair, 8¼ x 6¼ ins / 20.9 x 15.9 cm) USD 2,000. LONDON, 14 March 1997, *Friend in Need* (1850, oil on canvas, curved at the top, 38¼ x 31¼ ins / 97 x 79.5 cm) GBP 7,820. LONDON, 13 June 2000, *Peg Woffington's Visit to Triplet* (1860, oil on canvas, 34 x 44 ins / 86 x 112 cm) GBP 15,000. LONDON, 20 Feb 2003, *Fashionable Couple* (oil on canvas, 19 x 21 ins / 48 x 53 cm) GBP 7,500. LONDON, 20 Feb 2003, *Love Letter* (1861, oil on canvas, 21 x 17 ins / 53 x 42 cm) GBP 17,000.

SOLOMON, Simeon
British, 19th century.
Born 9 October 1840, in London; died 14 August 1905, in London.
Painter (gouache), watercolourist, draughtsman. Symbolism.
Pre-Raphaelite (related to).

Simeon Solomon studied at Cary's Academy in Bloomsbury then at the schools of the Royal Academy. He also took advice from his elder brother Abraham Solomon. When he was very young he was a friend of the Pre-Raphaelites Dante Gabriel Rossetti and Burne-Jones. He exhibited a drawing at the Royal Academy in 1858 and a painting entitled *Moses* in 1860. He also exhibited frequently at the Dudley Gallery. In 1866 he made his first visit to Italy and studied Luini and Sodoma in particular while he was there. He exhibited at the Royal Academy for the last time in 1871. He was awarded a bronze medal at the Exposition Universelle in Paris in 1889 and as well as a silver medal in 1900. He published a work entitled *A Vision of Love Revealed in Sleep* in 1871. He died in a rest home.

He belonged to Gabriel Rossetti's circle of artist friends in the 1860s, and his works are characterised by the refinement of their lines and colour. Gerald Schurr, who contributed to his revival from general obscurity, described his pictures as precious, with decorative harmonies, whose melancholy tone, troubled atmosphere and spiritualism were greatly appreciated by Oscar Wilde.

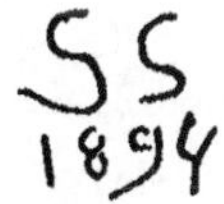

MUSEUMS AND GALLERIES:

BIRMINGHAM (Mus. and AG): *Bacchus* (1867, oil/paper/canvas); *Greek Acolyte* (1867-1868, watercolour); *Dawn* (1871, oil on canvas); allegory*Night and Sleep* (1888, pastel) - BOSTON: *Night* - DUBLIN (Civic Mus.): *Moses Saved from the Waters* - LONDON (Victoria and Albert Mus.): *In the Temple of Venus* (watercolour); *Portrait of Tennyson*.

AUCTION RECORDS:

LONDON, 17 Feb 1922, *Love between Jew and Christian* (coloured chalk) GBP 10. LONDON, 10 July 1970, *Ruth; Naomi and Child*, Gns 500. LONDON, 1 Oct 1973, *Priestess of the Sun* (watercolour and gouache) Gns 1,100. LONDON, 16 July 1976, *Woman's Head in Profile* (1892, oil on panel, 17¼ x 15 ins / 43.5 x 38 cm) GBP 250. MUNICH, 27 May 1977, *Rosa Mystica* (1867, oil on canvas, 19¾ x 14¾ ins / 50 x 37.5 cm) DEM 3,000. LONDON, 14 June 1977, *Shadrach, Meshach and Abednego* (1863, gouache, 12¾ x 9 ins / 32.5 x 23 cm) GBP 4,200. LONDON, 1 Oct 1979, *Air* (1894, blue chalk, 19¾ x 9½ ins / 50 x 24 cm) GBP 4,500. LONDON, 9 April 1980, *Sapho and Erinna in the Garden of Mytelene* (1864, oil on canvas, 13 x 14½ ins / 33 x 37 cm) GBP 4,200. LONDON, 6 Oct 1980, *In the Summer Twilight* (1869, watercolour heightened with white, 20 x 28¾ ins / 51 x 73 cm) GBP 9,500. LONDON, 23 June 1981, *Ruth and Boaz* (1862, watercolour heightened with gouache/paper, 9½ x 7 ins / 24 x 18 cm) GBP 2,800. NEW YORK, 28 Oct 1982, *Love in Autumn* (1866, oil on canvas, 33 x 26 ins / 84 x 66 cm) USD 45,000. LONDON, 1 March 1983, *Shadrach, Meshach and Abednego in the Burning Fiery Furnace* (1873, watercolour heightened with white, 13 x 9 ins / 33 x 22.8 cm) GBP 9,000. LONDON, 16 Feb 1984, *Sleep* (1886, black and blue pencil, 10 x 9 ins / 25.3 x 22 cm) GBP 4,500. LONDON, 27 Nov 1984, *Marguerite* (1866, oil on canvas, 16 x 14 ins / 40.5 x 35.5 cm) GBP 4,000. LONDON, 30 May 1985, *Meditation* (1873, graphite and red pencil, 9¾ x 11 ins / 25 x 28 cm) GBP 1,400. NEW YORK, 30 Oct 1985, *Mercury* (oil on card, 24 x 19¾ ins / 61 x 50.2 cm) USD 14,000. LONDON, 22 May 1986, *Pope from the Orthodox Church* (1874, gouache, 12 x 8½ ins / 30.5 x 21.5 cm) GBP 4,000. ENGHIEN-LES-BAINS, 25 Oct 1987, *Ave Maria* (pastel, 19 x 12½ ins / 48 x 32 cm) FRF 25,000. PARIS, 20 March 1989, *Archangel Gabriel* (1896, watercolour heightened with gouache/paper, 13¾ x 9½ ins / 35 x 24 cm) FRF 11,000. NEW YORK, 23 May 1990, *Good News* (1884, pencil/paper, 11 x 18 ins / 28 x 45.5 cm) USD 16,500. LONDON, 26 Sept 1990, *Woman's Head* (1890, red chalk/tinted paper, 16 x 11½ ins / 40.5 x 29 cm) GBP 1,045. LONDON, 12 June 1992, *Quia Multum Amavit (Gospel According to St Luke)* (1892, red chalk, 14 x 16 ins / 35.8 x 40.7 cm) GBP 3,080. NEW YORK, 29 Oct 1992, *Beauty of Death* (1884, blue and red chalks and pencil/paper, 17¼ x 12½ ins / 43.7 x 31.7 cm) USD 3,080. LONDON, 13 Nov 1992, *Woman's Head* (1892, oil on card, 17¾ x 15 ins / 45 x 38.2 cm) GBP 3,300. LONDON, 11 June 1993, *Bacchus* (1867, watercolour and gouache, 19¾ x 14¾ ins / 50.2 x 37.5 cm) GBP 32,200. NEW YORK, 20 July 1994, *Head of Young Girl* (watercolour and ink/paper, 11 x 8½ ins / 27.9 x 21.6 cm) USD 2,415. LONDON, 4 Nov 1994, *Symbolist Face* (1894, red chalk, 11½ x 9¼ ins / 28.9 x 23.5 cm) GBP 4,140. LONDON, 9 May 1996, *Youth at Dawn* (1884, oil on card, 19 x 13½ ins / 48 x 34.5 cm) GBP 1,725. LONDON, 5 June 1996, *Ophelia* (1890, red chalk, 14 x 11¼ ins / 35.5 x 28.5 cm) GBP 3,450. LONDON, 6 Nov 1996, *Marguerite* (1866, oil on canvas, 16 x 14 ins / 40.5 x 35.5 cm) GBP 12,075; *Amor* (1877, black chalk, 9 x 6¾ ins / 22 x 17 cm) GBP 1,840. LONDON, 8 Nov 1996, *St John the Baptist* (1898, watercolour, 9½ x 13¼ ins / 24.2 x 33.4 cm) GBP 3,500. LONDON, 12 March 1997, *Twilight in Summer* (1866, coloured chalks and pencil heightened with white, study, 16½ x 24¼ ins / 42 x 61.5 cm) GBP 4,025. LONDON, 4 June 1997, *Twilight in Summer* (1869, watercolour heightened with white and gum arabic, 20½ x 29 ins / 52 x 73.5 cm) GBP 34,500; *Portrait of Woman* (watercolour and gouache, oval, 10½ x 9 ins / 26.5 x 22 cm) GBP 2,990. LONDON, 6 June 1997, *She Who Loved so Much* (1892, red chalk, 14 x 16 ins / 35.8 x 40.7 cm) GBP 4,370. LONDON, 5 Nov 1997, *Drought* (1866-1872, watercolour heightened with gouache, 15 1/4 x 7 3/4 ins / 39 x 20 cm) GBP 2,990; *Young Girl* (1863, oil on panel, round, diam. 7 3/4 ins / 20 cm) GBP 14,950. LONDON, 30 Nov 2001, *Young Musician Employed in the Temple Service* (1861, oil on canvas, 24 x 18 ins / 61 x 46 cm) GBP 50,000. LONDON, 19 Dec 2001, *Angel of Light* (1885, coloured chalk, 17 x 13 ins / 42 x 32 cm) GBP 5,800. LONDON, 6 June 2002, *Portrait of a Woman* (pencil and red chalk, 14 x 10 ins / 36 x 25 cm) GBP 6,500. LONDON, 25 June 2002, *Portrait of a Youth* (1889, red chalk, sold with five others by the same hand, 17 x 13 ins / 44 x 32 cm) GBP 9,500. LONDON, 20 Feb 2003, *Heliogabalus, High Priest of the Sun* (1866, pencil and watercolour heightened with gouache, gum and scratching out, 19 x 11 ins / 48 x 29 cm) GBP 22,000. LONDON, 20 Feb 2003, *Deacon* (1863, oil on canvas, 14 x 10 ins / 35 x 25 cm) GBP 34,000. LONDON, 26 March 2004, *Ophelia* (ink and wash, 16 x 18 ins / 41 x 46 cm) GBP 9,800. LONDON, 25 Nov 2004, *Night* (1890, oil on board, 20 x 17 ins / 52 x 42 cm) GBP 13,000.

SOLOMON, William Ewart Gladstone
British, 20th century.
Born 1880, in Sea Point, near Capetown.
Painter, illustrator. Figures, portraits.

William Solomon trained in London. He produced illustrations for books about India, and was also a writer on art.

SOLOMONS
British, 18th century.
Active in London in 1782.
Portrait artist.

SOLOMONS, Richard
British, 19th century.
Active in Liverpool during the first half of the 19th century.
Painter. Seascapes.

Richard Solomons exhibited his work in London in 1823.

SOLOMOUKHA, Anton
Ukrainian, 20th century.
Born 1945, in Kiev.
Active in France.
Painter. Figures.

Solomoukha is a graduate of the academy of fine art in Kiev. He left the former USSR in 1979 and settled in Paris. He generally practises quotation art or interprets ancient myths (*Susannah and the Elder*, 1989), blending different representational styles in the same painting.

Solomoukha has taken part in collective exhibitions, including: 1982, Salon de la Jeune Peinture, Paris; 1985, *Travaux sur Papier* (*Works on Paper*), Salon de Villeparisis, and Octobre des Arts, Lyons; 1986, Génie de la Bastille, Paris; 1989, Salon de Montrouge; and 1990, Foire Internationale d'Art Contemporain, Galerie du Génie, Paris. He has shown his works in solo exhibitions, notably at the Galerie Philippe Gravier in Paris.

AUCTION RECORDS:
PARIS, 31 Oct 1990, *RARANOM* (1989, mixed media/canvas and collage, 59 3/4 x 49 1/4 ins / 152 x 125 cm) FRF 40,000. PARIS, 25 June 1993, *Untitled* (1989, mixed media/canvas, 58 1/4 x 54 ins / 148 x 137 cm) FRF 3,200. PARIS, 28 Jan 1994, *Wrestler* (oil on canvas, 59 1/2 x 49 1/4 ins / 151 x 125 cm) FRF 4,800.

SOLON, Harry
American, 20th century.
Born 5 June 1873, in San Francisco; died 1958, in New York.
Painter. Portraits.

Harry Solon studied at the Art Institute of Chicago, the Académie Julian, and with Henri Royer and Richard Muller in Paris. He was a member of the American Federation of the Arts. He painted many portraits of his compatriots.

SOLON, Léon Victor
British, 20th century.
Born 1872, in Stoke-on-Trent; died 1957, in New York.
Active then naturalised in the USA.
Painter, illustrator, potter, poster artist.

Léon Victor Solon was the son of the sculptor Marc Louis Emmanuel Solon (1835-1913). He was also a writer. He lived in England for a number of years, and was artistic director of the Minton porcelain factory from 1897 to 1909. He subsequently settled in Florida and finally New York. Solon executed the decorative wall-paintings for the Philadelphia Museum of Fine Art. His fine, highly original illustrations are similar in style to the work of Alphonse Mucha. He was the author and illustrator of a number of works, including *The Ancient Art of Stoneware* (1892), *Old French Faïence* (1903) and *Ceramic Literature* (1910). Solon was also a contributor to the periodicals *The Parade* and *The Studio*.

BIBLIOGRAPHY:

SOLON, Marc Louis Emmanuel
French, 19th - 20th century.
Born 1835, in Montauban; died 23 June 1913, in Stoke-on-Trent.
Active in the UK and in France.
Potter, painter (porcelain), draughtsman, engraver (etching), collector, writer.

Marc Louis Emmanuel Solon was the father of Leon Victor Solon. He used the pseudonym of Milès. He worked in porcelain factories in Sèvres and Stoke-on-Trent.

MUSEUMS AND GALLERIES:
HAMBURG (Mus. für Kunst und Gewerbe) - LIMOGES (Mus. national Adrien-Dubouché) - LONDON (Victoria and Albert Mus.).

SOLON, Marie Jeanne
French, 19th century.
Born 1836, in Montauban.
Painter, miniaturist. Portraits.

Marie Solon was a pupil of Belloc; she made her Salon debut in 1857.

MUSEUMS AND GALLERIES:
MONTAUBAN: *Portrait of a Woman* (miniature/ivory).

SOLON I
2nd century BC.
Active in Myrina.
Sculptor.
Ancient Greek.

Solon made a statue of *Aristomenes* at Telos.

SOLON II
Cameo engraver. Mythological subjects.
Ancient Greek.

MUSEUMS AND GALLERIES:
LONDON (British Mus.): *Medusa (Strozzi Medusa)* - NAPLES (Mus. Nazionale): *Heracles*.

SOLONYER, Franz. See **SALONIER Franz**

SOLORZANO, Andrés
Spanish, 16th century.
Active during the first half of the 16th century.
Sculptor.

Andrés Solorzano worked on the high altar of Toledo Cathedral in 1503-1504.

SOLORZANO, Esteban
Spanish, 16th century.
Active in Huesca.
Painter.

Probably the pupil of Pedro de Aponte, Esteban Solorzano executed works for the cathedral and the church del Carmen in Huesca between 1520 and 1557.

SOLOSMEO, Antonio di Giovanni da Settignano, or Solismeo
Italian, 16th century.
Active in Florence from 1525 to 1536.
Painter, sculptor.

Antonio Solosmeo studied sculpture under Andrea Sansovino and painting with Andrea del Sarto. One of his works, a *Virgin and Child with Saints* signed *Antonius Solusmeus Scultor, M. D. XXVII*, can be seen at the Badia di S Fedele in Poppi (Tuscany).

SOLOTAREFF, Boris
Russian, 20th century.
Born 23 October 1889, in Bendare, Romania; died 1966, in New York.
Active in Lausanne, Paris and New York.
Painter. Portraits, landscapes, still-lifes, horses, urban landscapes.

Boris Solotareff studied at the Russian art school, Odessa, before going to the academy in Munich, which he attended from 1907 to 1914. From 1914 to 1920 he lived and worked in Lausanne. He then moved to Paris, where he was a member of the Salon des Indépendants until 1937, when he moved to New York. In 1949 he became a naturalised American citizen. Solotareff's work was in the mainstream of Eastern European Expressionism, with influences of Art Deco from the time when he lived in Paris.

SOLOTAROV, Dorotei Ermolaevich
Russian, 17th century.
Active during the second half of the 17th century.
Painter.

Dorotei Ermolaevich Solotarov studied under S. Lopuzki and Daniel Wuchter. He produced decorative paintings for the court in Moscow.

SOLOTAROV, Karp Ivanovich
Russian, 17th century.
Active during the second half of the 17th century.
Icon painter.

Karp Ivanovich Solotarov studied under Bogdan Saltanov. He worked for the court in Moscow.

SOLOVEV, Sergei
Russian, 20th century.
Born 1915, in Noginsk.
Painter. Portraits, genre scenes.
Socialist Realism.

Sergei Solovev studied under Sergei Gerassimov at the Surikov Institute, Moscow, graduating in 1941. During World War II he painted military subjects. He was admitted to the Union of Soviet Artists in 1943, and taught art at the secondary fine arts school, Moscow. Solovev adhered strictly to the tenets of Socialist Realism. He painted many canvases of the war and war heroes, as well as pictures of workers. He later turned to more intimate portraits.

BIBLIOGRAPHY:
Tableaux soviétiques, auction catalogue, Salle Drouot, Paris, 3 October 1990.

MUSEUMS AND GALLERIES:
ALMA-ATA - KURGAN - MOSCOW (State Tretyakov Gal.).

AUCTION RECORDS:
PARIS, 12 Dec 1992, *Navvies* (1960, oil on card, 8 1/4 x 9 1/2 ins / 21 x 24 cm) FRF 4,500.

SOLOVIEV, Dmitri
Russian, 18th century.
Painter. Religious subjects, figures. Designs for tapestries.

Dmitri Soloviev was active in the first half of the 18th century. He worked at the carpet factory in St Petersburg as a carpet designer, and produced paintings at the palaces of Peterhof and Monplaisir, as well as in the St Paul Cathedral in St Petersburg.

MUSEUMS AND GALLERIES:
MOSCOW (State Tretyakov Gal.): *Cobblers*.

SOLOVYOVA, Irina
Russian, 20th - 21st century.
Born 1966.
Painter. Flowers.

Solovyova studied at the school of fine art in Moscow. She worked under Olga Pasternak.

AUCTION RECORDS:
PARIS, 12 Dec 1992, *Chrysanthemums* (oil on canvas, 25 1/2 x 21 1/4 ins / 65 x 54 cm) FRF 4,000; *Buttercups* (oil on canvas, 19 3/4 x 24 ins / 50 x 61 cm) FRF 4,800. PARIS, 20 March 1993, *First Tulips* (oil on canvas, 19 3/4 x 19 3/4 ins / 50 x 50 cm) FRF 4,500. PARIS, 18 Oct 1993, *Yellow Bouquet* (oil on canvas, 25 1/2 x 21 1/4 ins / 65 x 54 cm) FRF 4,500.

SOLPACH, Andreas. See **SOLBACH**

SOLSERNUS, or Solsternus
Italian, 13th century.
Active in Spoleto (Umbria) in 1267.
Mosaicist.

There is a large mosaic in the Byzantine style by this artist on the façade of Spoleto Cathedral. It depicts *Christ Enthroned, the Virgin and St John*.

SOLT, Jacobus van. See **SOLDT**

SOLTAN, Anna de (Countess). See **RÖMER Anna von**

SOLTAU, Hermann Wilhelm
German, 19th century.
Born 9 July 1812, in Hamburg; died 14 May 1861, in Hamburg.
Painter, engraver, draughtsman. Portraits, genre scenes, architectural views.

Soltau studied in Hamburg under Gerdt Hardorff the Younger, then in Munich and Paris. He produced etchings and lithographs.

MUSEUMS AND GALLERIES:
HAMBURG (Altonaer Mus.): *Ipkenwarft on the Isle of Hooge; The Kremper Polder; Shallows near Büsum* - HAMBURG (Kunsthalle): *Portrait of Carsten Wilhelm Soltau* - KIEL (Prints Collection): *Painter Asleep in front of his Easel; The Hoptrup Meeting; Cobblers in their Workshop; Pastor in his Study* - MUNICH (Bayerisches Nationalmus.): *Portraits of Bavarian Princes of the 13th to 15th centuries* (gouache, 26 works) - MUNICH (Municipal Mus.): *Artists' Carnival* (five lithographs).

AUCTION RECORDS:
VIENNA, 29-30 Oct 1996, *Happy Family in the Countryside* (oil on canvas, oval, 53 1/2 x 71 1/4in/136 x 181cm) ATS 172,000.

SOLTAU, Otto
German, 20th century.
Born 27 March 1885, in Arnis an der Schlei.
Painter. Figures, portraits, horses.

Otto Soltau studied in Hanover and Munich and under Georg Greve-Waldhausen. He exhibited in Berlin in 1911.

AUCTION RECORDS:
LONDON, 24 March 1988, *Two Botanical Studies* (pencil and watercolour, 10 1/4 x 7 ins / 26 x 18 cm) GBP 880.

SOLTAU, Pauline
Maiden name: Suhrlandt
German, 19th century.
Born 30 June 1833, in Ludwigslust; died 13 April 1902, in Schwerin.
Painter. Portraits, genre scenes.

Pauline Soltau was taught by her father Rudolf Suhrlandt and by E. Dubufe in Paris.

Museums and Galleries:
Rudolstadt: *The Grand-Duchess Marie von Mecklenburg-Schwerin* - Schwerin: *Portrait of the Intendant of Wolzogen.*
Auction records:
New York, 28 May 1992, *Mother's Favourite* (oil on canvas, 45 3/4 x 35in/116.2 x 88.9cm) USD 8,800.

SOLTMANN, Hans
German, 20th century.
Born 4 December 1876, in Breslau (now Wroclaw, Poland).
Painter, engraver, lithographer, illustrator.
Hans Soltmann studied at the Akademie der Bildenden Künste in Berlin and Karlsruhe before settling in Berlin, where he worked as a woodcut engraver and produced numerous illustrations for children's books.

SOLUTUS, or Soluti
Italian, 16th century.
Active in 1555.
Painter.
Work by Solutus shows the influence of D. Capriolo.
Museums and Galleries:
Treviso (Mus. Civico L. Bailo): *Adoration of the Shepherds.*

SOLVAIN, Jean
French, 17th century.
Born 1600, in Le Puy; died 1664.
Painter.
Museums and Galleries:
Le Puy-en-Velay: *Portrait of Gaspard de Chabron, Doctor and Barrister at the Riom Courts.*

SOLVEEN, Henri
German, 20th century.
Born 3 January 1891, in Strasbourg; died 9 May 1956, in Strasbourg.
Painter, engraver. Landscapes.
Henri Solveen studied in Strasbourg and Leipzig and founded the Arc Group. He was also a writer.
Museums and Galleries:
Strasbourg: *Portrait of Lothar von Seebach.*

SOLVES, Jean-Michel
French, 20th - 21st century.
Born 1955, in Paris.
Painter (mixed media).
Jean-Michel Solves studied at the École des Beaux-Arts in Paris. His work, typically incorporating metal elements set in relief, exhibits a distinct compositional rigour without being uncompromisingly geometric.

He has shown his work at various group exhibitions, including in 1987 and 1988 at the Salon de Montrouge in Paris and in 1989 at the Biennale de la Jeune Peinture in Cannes. His solo exhibitions include those at the Galerie Loft in 1988 and the Galerie Pierre Lescot in 1989.

SOLVYNS, Balthazar or Frans Balthazar
Belgian, 18th - 19th century.
Born 6 July 1760, in Antwerp; died 10 October 1824, in Antwerp.
Painter, engraver (etching). Seascapes.
Balthazar Solvyns was a pupil of Quartenmont in Antwerp, then of Vincent in Paris. An ethnographer, he departed for the Indies in 1789 for several years, and there collected the elements of an important work on the customs, festivals and costumes of the Hindus, covering 300 plates. He was the harbourmaster of the port of Antwerp. His paintings are rare.

Auction records:
Paris, 4 April 1997, *Two Natives Named Oorni and Kurtaul* (heightened engraving, a pair, 14 1/2 x 9 3/4 ins / 37 x 25 cm) FRF 6,700.

SOLY, Arthur, or Solly
British, 17th century.
Died c. 1695.
Active c. 1683.
Engraver, draughtsman.
Arthur Soly engraved portraits and worked for Robert White.

SOLYMOS, Beatrix, Bea
Hungarian, 20th century.
Born 4 March 1889, in Mitrovica; died 1974, in Budapest.
Painter. Portraits, still-lifes.

SOLZIUS, H.
Sculptor. Mythological subjects. Low reliefs.
Museums and Galleries:
Sydney: *Banquet of the Gods* (low relief).

SOM, Carl de, or Desom Carl
German, 17th century.
Painter.
He worked at Weingarten monastery.

SOM, Laurens, or Soon
Dutch, 18th century.
Sculptor (ivory).
Museums and Galleries:
Amsterdam (Stedelijk Mus.): miniature dolls' house utensils (ivory sculpture).

SOM, Ludwig
German, 18th century.
Active in Lindau from 1705 to 1720.
Engraver (burin).
Museums and Galleries:
Lindau (Town Hall Mus.): several works.

SOMACCHINI. See **SAMACHINI**

SOMAGLIA, Rossane (Contessa)
Italian, 18th - 19th century.
Born 3 February 1751, in Piacenza; died 16 April 1827.
Draughtswoman.
Most of Somaglia's work comprises architectural views. She was also a translator.

SOMAINI, Francesco
Italian, 19th century.
Born 14 May 1795, in Maroggia; died 13 August 1855, in Milan.
Sculptor. Religious subjects. Statues, busts, low reliefs.
Francesco Somaini worked with Camillo Paccetti and was a student at the Accademia di Brera in Milan. He worked in many parts of northern Italy.

SOMAINI, Francesco
Italian, 20th century.
Born 1926, in Lomazzo, near Como.
Sculptor (bronze/steel). Monuments.
While studying for a degree in law, Francesco Somaini also attended classes at the Accademia di Brera in Milan. His early work was generally figurative in style, but after periods travelling in Europe between 1944 and 1948, when he saw new developments in international modern art, his work changed. With a series of sculptures inspired by horses' skulls he began to free himself from the restrictions of realism, and from 1950 his work became entirely abstract. From 1954, a desire to produce something on a monumental scale led him to experiment with steel, which he used (in 1966-1967) for the *Monument to Italian Sailors* for Corso Ventidue

di Marzo in Milan. His sculptures seem to leap up into space in a series of Baroque plant-like forms, their elegantly jagged edges enclosing areas of space.

He has taken part in many group exhibitions, including: the São Paulo Biennale of 1959, at which he received the prize for the best foreign sculptor; the 1960 Venice Biennale, when a whole room was given over to his works; the Biennale of Sacred Art in Rome in 1968, at which he won first prize for sculpture; the 2nd European Sculpture Biennale held in the Centre d'Art Contemporain in Jouy-sur-Eure, Normandy in 1984. He held solo exhibitions in Florence (1956) and Milan (1959, 1962 and 1968).

BIBLIOGRAPHY:

Apollonio, U./Tapié, Michel, *Francesco Somaini*, Éd. du Griffon, Neuchâtel, 1960. *IIe Biennale européenne de sculpture de Normandie*, exhibition catalogue, Centre d'Art contemporain, Jouy-sur-Eure, 1984.

AUCTION RECORDS:

NEW YORK, 19 May 1966, *Horizontal* (bronze) USD 2,500. NEW YORK, 4 April 1968, *Horizontal* (patinated bronze) USD 3,500. LONDON, 25 Oct 1974, *Design for a Monument* (bronze) USD 1,200. NEW YORK, 22 Oct 1976, *Sea Story* (1961-1962, grey-patinated bronze, Long. 19 ins / 48.2 cm) USD 750. NEW YORK, 8 Oct 1988, *Wave* (bronze, 26 x 51 x 20 ins / 66 x 129.5 x 50.7 cm) USD 2,475. NEW YORK, 10 Oct 1990, *Sculpture* (silver-patinated bronze, h. 10 ins / 25.4 cm) USD 1,760. MILAN, 16 Nov 1993, *Untitled* (steel, 7 3/4 x 17 x 6 1/4 ins / 20 x 43 x 16 cm) ITL 3,450,000. ROME, 18 Dec 2002, *Untitled* (bronze, 15 x 10x14 ins / 39 x 25x35 cm) EUR 3,000. MILAN, 24 Nov 2003, *Untitled* (1977, bronze and concrete, 11 x 19x15 ins / 29 x 48x39 cm) EUR 12,000.

SOMAINI, Giuseppe

Italian, 19th century.
Sculptor.

Giuseppe Somaini was pupil of Francesco Somaini.

SOMAIO, Giovanni Francesco de

Italian, 15th century.
Died between 1477 and 1481.
Active in Vicenza.
Painter.

Giovanni Francesco de Somaio worked in Vicenza from 1453.

SOMARE, Sandro

Italian, 20th century.
Born after 1925.
Painter.

Somare's work was shown in Brussels in 1969 at an exhibition organised by Patrick Waldberg entitled *Signes d'un renouveau surréaliste* (*Signs of a Surrealist Revival*), which featured little-known new young artists.

SOMAZZI, Arlette

Maiden name: Van den Bilcke
French, 20th century.
Born 27 October 1921, in Villié-Morgon.
Painter, sculptor, medallist. Figure compositions, figures, portraits.

After studying briefly at the École des Beaux-Arts in Lyons, Arlette Somazzi enrolled at the Académie de la Grande-Chaumière in Paris, where she studied painting under Yves Brayer and sculpture under Charles Despiau. She then moved to the former (1910-1958) French territories in west-central Africa called French Equatorial Africa. She lived there from 1945 to 1947, exhibiting in Leopoldville (now Kinshasa), and Brazzaville. From 1949 to 1954 in lived in Polynesia, Tahiti and the Leeward Islands, where she made a film entitled *Té Poé Moana* (*The Pearl of the Great Ocean*).

She subsequently settled in Menton, where she exhibited in 1964. In mainland France, she produced several medals for the Paris Mint, depicting Fernand Gregh, Josephine Baker and Henri Guillemin. She produced many other medals, including commissions from the Principality of Monaco and the town of Menton. She produced medals depicting Marcel Pagnol, Jean Cocteau and Nietzsche, among others. She has sculpted a great many busts and masks of writers, including Arthur Miller, René Huyghe, of musicians such as Karl Münchinger, Samson François and Henri Dutilleux, dancers such as Serge Lifar and Rudolf Nureyev, actors such as André Luguet, and other celebrities, including Prince Rainier III and Alexander Onassis, and Prince Albert of Monaco. As Arlette Somazzi light-heartedly commented: 'I've done all comers, provided they were strong characters. I have a need for intense dialogue with them.'

Exhibitions of her work included; 1966 and 1968, Monte Carlo; 1972, sculpture collection in the atrium of the Monte Carlo Opera, with an introduction by Armand Lanoux; 1982, Menton Palais de l'Europe; 1987, Galerie F. Muller, Paris, with an introduction by Alain Decaux; 1994, ten busts in the Jardin de Sculpture of the Musée des Beaux-Arts, Menton; 1997, *Sculptures and Drawings*, Musée des Beaux-Arts, Menton.

BIBLIOGRAPHY:

Lanoux, Armand (preface), *Bustes et masques d'Arlette Somazzi*, exhibition catalogue, Opéra de Monte-Carlo, Monte Carlo, 1972. Decaux, Alain, *Arlette Somazzi, ses personnages*, Gal. F. Muller, Paris, 1987.

MUSEUMS AND GALLERIES:

MENTON (MBA): *Prince Rainier III; Prince Louis of Polignac; Samson François; Arthur Miller; Serge Lifar; Rudolf Nureyev;* other busts and masks - MONACO: *Prince Louis of Polignac* - NICE (MBA Jules-Chéret): *François Didier Gregh* - PARIS (MAMVP).

SOMAZZO, Bernardo

Italian, 15th century.
Painter.

Bernardo Somazzo painted some frescoes in the church of S Giacomo in Livo, near Gravedona, in 1412.

SOMEBODY, P.

British, 18th century.
Active in England c. 1780.
Engraver.

P. Somebody was the pseudonym of a burin engraver, whose works include a *Portrait of General Wolfe* after Benjamin West.

SOMEDA, Domenico

Italian, 19th - 20th century.
Born in Udine.
Painter. History painting, genre scenes, landscapes.

Someda made his debut in Venice in about 1885 with his painting *Invasion of the Magyars*.

SOMELLI, Guido

Italian, 20th century.
Born 1881, in Florence.
Painter. Figures, landscapes.

SOMENZIO, Francesco

Italian, 16th century.
Died soon after 1580.
Active in Cremona.
Painter.

A pupil of Bernardo Campi, Francesco Somenzio worked at Cremona Cathedral.

SOMENZIO, Pietro Martire

Italian, 16th century.
Active in Cremona.
Miniaturist, calligrapher.

SOMER, Bernard or Barent van, or Someren or Soemeren
Dutch, 16th - 17th century.
Born c. 1572, in Antwerp; died 1632, in Amsterdam.
Painter, engraver (burin), picture dealer.

Bernard or Barent van Somer was the brother of Paul van Somer and a pupil of P. Lisart in 1588. He married Leonora, the daughter of Arnold Mystens, and in 1626 A. Brauwer was living with him.

AUCTION RECORDS:
PARIS, 1 March 1920, *Portrait of a Gentleman of Quality* (Indian ink) FRF 195.

SOMER, Hendrick van, or Someren or Zomeren
Flemish School, 17th century.
Born 1615, in Amsterdam; died at the end of 1684, in Amsterdam, at the beginning of 1685 according to some sources.
Painter, draughtsman. Religious subjects, figures, landscapes, flowers.

Hendrick van Somer was the son of Bernard van Somer.

MUSEUMS AND GALLERIES:
LONDON (British Mus.): *Family* (drawing).

AUCTION RECORDS:
NEW YORK, 7 June 1978, *St Jerome Translating the Bible* (1651, oil on canvas, 38 1/2 x 48 1/2 ins / 98 x 123 cm) USD 13,000. NEW YORK, 17 Jan 1985, *St Jerome Translating the Bible* (1651, oil on canvas, 38 1/2 x 48 1/2 ins / 98 x 123 cm) USD 21,000. NEW YORK, 31 May 1989, *St Jerome* (1654, oil on canvas, 51 x 41 1/4 ins / 129.3 x 105 cm) USD 71,500. NEW YORK, 18 May 1994, *St Jerome* (oil on canvas, 51 1/4 x 41 1/4 ins / 130.2 x 104.8 cm) USD 19,550. VIENNA, 3 Oct 2001, *St Paul the Hermit* (oil on canvas, 47 x 38 ins / 119 x 96 cm) ATS 160,000. VIENNA, 3 Oct 2001, *St Jerome* (oil on canvas, 40 x 29 ins / 101 x 73 cm) ATS 160,000. LONDON, 11 July 2002, *St Jerome* (oil on canvas, 45 x 66 ins / 115 x 168 cm) GBP 38,000. NEW YORK, 22 Jan 2004, *John the Baptist* (oil on canvas, 73 x 59 ins / 185 x 151 cm) USD 70,000.

SOMER, Jan van, or Someren
Dutch, 17th century.
Born 1645, in Amsterdam (?); died after 1699, in Amsterdam (?).
Engraver (mezzotint), painter.

Jan van Somer was the brother of Paul van Somer. He engraved a large number of portraits and subjects from everyday life, after the masters of his time.

AUCTION RECORDS:
LONDON, 27 June 1984, *Bringer of Letters* (mezzotint/watermarked paper, 14 1/2 x 11 1/4 ins / 36.6 x 28.6 cm) USD 1,250.

SOMER, Mathias van, or Someren or Sommern
Dutch, 17th century.
Draughtsman, engraver. Portraits.

Mathias van Somer was working in 1650 in Amsterdam, then up to 1670 in Cologne, Regensburg and Nuremberg. He engraved portraits.

M.V.S. VS fecit
VS f MSimus F

SOMER, Melchior
German, 17th century.
Active during the first half of the 17th century.
Sculptor (wood).

Somer worked in Ghent. Thieme and Becker list him as German.

SOMER, Paul van, or Someren
Flemish School, 16th - 17th century.
Born c. 1576, in Antwerp; died between 27 June and 10 October 1621, in London.
Painter. History painting, portraits.

Paul van Somer worked in 1604 in Antwerp and followed Van Mander to Amsterdam, where he painted numerous portraits with his brother Bernard. In 1600 he was in London and in 1617 in Brussels, where he painted the portraits of *Albert and Isabella*. He returned to London and completed his career there, and many of his works are to be found in England.

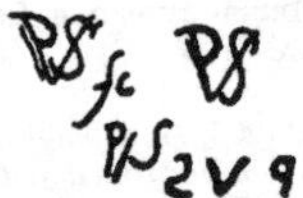

MUSEUMS AND GALLERIES:
COPENHAGEN (Statens Mus. for Kunst): *Charles I of England* - HOUSTON (MFA): *Elizabeth, Viscountess Falkland* (c. 1620, oil on canvas) - LONDON: *Francis Bacon; Elizabeth Vernon, Countess of Southampton; Henry, Prince of Wales; James I* - LONDON (National Portrait Gal.): *Lodovick Stuart, 1st Duke of Richmond, and 2nd Duke of Lennox* (c. 1620, oil on canvas); *The 1st Earl of Monmouth and his family* (c. 1617, oil on canvas, attributed); several engravings - LONDON (Tate Collection): *Lady Elizabeth Grey, Countess of Kent* (c. 1619, oil/wood) - MADRID (Prado): *King James I of England* (oil on canvas).

AUCTION RECORDS:
NEW YORK, 22-23 Feb 1906, *Portrait of Sir Francis Leigh*, USD 250. LONDON, 11 Dec 1909, *Portrait of Henry Frederick; Prince of Wales; Son of James I*, GBP 220. LONDON, 26 Feb 1910, *Portrait of Sir Edward Hales as a Child*, GBP 25. LONDON, 25-26 May 1911, *Portrait of a Gentleman and a Lady* (two pendants) GBP 441. LONDON, 10-11 Nov 1911, *Young Boy*, GBP 68. LONDON, 3 Feb 1922, *Head of a Woman*, GBP 31. LONDON, 18 June 1924, *Earl of Pembroke and Earl of Montgomery*, GBP 99. LONDON, 27 June 1924, *Prince of Wales*, GBP 231. LONDON, 4 Dec 1925, *Lady Musgrave*, GBP 220. LONDON, 27 Nov 1968, *Portrait of James I of England*, GBP 1,800. LONDON, 17 March 1972, *Portrait of a Woman*, Gns 1,400. LONDON, 21 March 1979, *Portrait of Robert Carey, First Earl of Monmouth, with his Wife* (oil on canvas, 89 1/2 x 85 ins / 227.5 x 216 cm) GBP 7,500. NEW YORK, 4 Nov 1986, *Portrait of Henry, 18th Earl of Oxford, High Chamberlain of England* (oil on canvas, 85 1/2 x 47 1/2 ins / 217 x 120.8 cm) USD 21,000. CALAIS, 3 July 1994, *Pastoral Scenes in Classical Ruins* (pen and wash, a pair, each 7 1/2 x 11 ins / 19 x 28 cm) FRF 14,000.

SOMER, Paul van, or Someren
Dutch, 17th century.
Born c. 1649, in Amsterdam; died c. 1694 (?), in London.
Painter, engraver (burin/mezzotint).

Paul van Somer was the brother of Jan van Somer. He was in Paris from 1671 to 1675, then in London. He engraved religious and mythological subjects, scenes from everyday life and portraits.

MUSEUMS AND GALLERIES:
AMSTERDAM (Rijksprentenkabinet): *Moses Saved from the Waters* - VIENNA (Albertina Mus.): *The Last Supper*.

AUCTION RECORDS:
PARIS, 1844, *Dog Bringing back a Duck to its Master*, FRF 55; *Empty-handed Hunter*, FRF 85. GHENT, 1856, *Singing Lesson*, FRF 200. PARIS, 1886, *Portrait of Henry, Prince of Wales, Son of James I*, FRF 4,350. LONDON, 9 Oct 1928, *Richard De-*

ring, GBP 210. LONDON, 2 May 1929, *King James I,* GBP 157. NEW YORK, 18 Dec 1929, *Portrait of a Woman,* USD 430. LONDON, 29 May 1931, *James I of England,* GBP 189. KINGSTON-ON-THAMES, 25 July 1934, *Earl of Essex,* GBP 600. LONDON, 28 July 1939, *Lady Arabella Stuart,* GBP 131.

SOMEREN. See **SOMER**

SOMERS, Francine
Belgian, 20th century.
Born 1923, in Ghent.
Painter, engraver, medallist, draughtswoman. Scenes with figures.

Francine Somers produced highly stylised medals using the lost-wax casting technique.

SOMERS, Frans
Flemish School, 17th - 18th century.
Active in Antwerp.
Sculptor.

Frans Somers was a pupil of Cornelis Maes.

SOMERS, Frans
Flemish School, 18th century.
Active in Antwerp.
Sculptor.

Frans Somers was probably the son of Frans Somers I. The museum of Brussels has his *Jesus and the Samaritan Woman.*

SOMERS, Guillaume
Belgian, 19th century.
Born 12 December 1819, in Antwerp.
Painter. Historical subjects, genre scenes, interiors.

Guillaume Somers was a pupil of Gustave Wappers at the Koninklijke Academie voor Schone Kunsten in Antwerp.

SOMERS, Louis Jean
Belgian, 19th century.
Born 25 November 1813, in Antwerp; died 3 June 1880, in Antwerp.
Painter. History painting, genre scenes.

Louis Jean Somers was a pupil of Ferdinand de Braeckeleer and was also influenced by Félix de Vigne.

Louis Somers ft Antwerpen

MUSEUMS AND GALLERIES:
ANTWERP: *Librarian; Correcting the Proof* - BREMEN: *Brotherhood (Scene in a Monastery)* - LEIPZIG: *Cromwell Discovering a Conspiracy against his Life* - LIÈGE: *Monks' Plainsong* - MECHELEN: *Waiting* - STRASBOURG: *Three Drinkers.*

AUCTION RECORDS:
PARIS, 13-14 March 1929, *The Collector,* FRF 1,400. BRUSSELS, 26 April 1971, *The Music Lesson,* BEF 40,000. LONDON, 23 March 2000, *Awaiting a Ride* (oil on canvas, 17 x 24 ins / 44 x 60 cm) GBP 4,500. ANTWERP, 15 Oct 2001, *Courting Couple with Farm beyond* (oil on panel, 24 x 18 ins / 61 x 46 cm) BEF 100,000. BRUSSELS, 18 Feb 2002, *The Artist's Workshop* (oil on panel, 18 x 15 ins / 46 x 38 cm) EUR 2,300. AMSTERDAM, 29 April 2003, *Entertaining Conversation* (oil on panel, 20 x 17 ins / 52 x 43 cm) EUR 5,000. LOKEREN, 13 March 2004, *Chat* (oil on panel, 25 x 19 ins / 63 x 47 cm) EUR 3,000. BRUSSELS, 7 June 2004, *Musical Party in an Inn* (oil on panel, 15 x 18 ins / 38 x 46 cm) EUR 3,000.

SOMERSALO, Jaakko
Finnish, 20th century.
Born 3 September 1916, in Kuhmoinen; died 9 September 1966.
Painter, engraver.

Jaakko Somersalo started out as a figurative woodcut engraver who coloured his compositions by adding layers of coloured film. Over time, his stylised approach to engraving evolved in the direction of Abstraction as he developed a concise style that exhibited a distinct oriental touch. His paintings are also characterised by a special colouring technique which features superimposed glazes, frequently using red lacquers.

SOMERSCALES, Thomas Jacques
British, 19th - 20th century.
Born 30 October 1842, in Hull; died 27 June 1927, in Hull.
Painter, watercolourist. Historical subjects, genre scenes, harbour views, landscapes, seascapes, boats.

Thomas Somerscales exhibited at the Royal Academy in London in 1901. He seems to have travelled extensively and for long periods of time in South America, certainly in 1895, 1907, 1909, 1910, 1912, 1913 and 1918, and the coasts and bays of America are depicted in many of his works. Somerscales also painted reconstructions of events in maritime history.

MUSEUMS AND GALLERIES:
BRISTOL: *The Caravels of Christopher Columbus; Waiting for the Pilot* - LIVERPOOL: *A Man Overboard* - LONDON (Tate Collection): *Leaving Valparaiso.*

AUCTION RECORDS:
LONDON, 21 March 1910, *Leaving Valparaiso* (1895) GBP 15. LONDON, 28 April 1924, *In Full Sail,* GBP 32. LONDON, 10 July 1939, *Homeward Bound,* GBP 80. PARIS, 17 Jan 1951, *Landscape of South America* (1912 and 1913, two watercolours, collection) FRF 280. LONDON, 6 Feb 1973, *Sailing-ships at Sea,* GBP 1,250. LONDON, 15 Oct 1976, *The Bay of Valparaiso* (1909, oil on canvas, 42 1/4 x 72 ins / 107 x 183 cm) GBP 3,200. LONDON, 6 Feb 1980, *Boat Offshore at Valparaiso* (oil on panel, 11 1/2 x 15 3/4 ins / 29 x 40 cm) GBP 3,200. NEW YORK, 8 May 1981, *View of the Andes, Chile* (1906, oil on canvas, 24 x 36 ins / 61 x 91.5 cm) USD 22,000. NEW YORK, 29 May 1984, *In the Doldrums* (1910, oil on canvas, 23 3/4 x 41 ins / 60.3 x 104 cm) USD 14,000. LONDON, 2 Oct 1985, *A Three-master* (oil on canvas, 22 3/4 x 32 1/4 ins / 58 x 82 cm) GBP 5,800. LONDON, 20 Nov 1986, *The Harbour at Valparaiso* (1882, oil on card, 14 x 20 ins / 35.6 x 50.8 cm) GBP 8,000. LONDON, 31 May 1989, *Journey's End - The Bay at Valparaiso* (1907, oil on canvas, 18 x 14 ins / 46 x 35.5 cm) GBP 11,550. LONDON, 2 June 1989, *Panoramic View of Robin Hood's Bay* (1918, oil on canvas, 15 1/4 x 19 ins / 39 x 48 cm) GBP 1,650. LONDON, 30 May 1990, *Change of Course* (oil on canvas, 18 x 12 ins / 46 x 30.5 cm) GBP 4,950. LONDON, 20 Jan 1993, *Off the Coast of Rio* (1910, oil on canvas, 14 x 20 3/4 ins / 35.5 x 53 cm) GBP 15,870. LONDON, 29 May 1997, *White-topped Waves off Tenerife* (1905, oil on canvas, 32 x 48 ins / 81.5 x 122 cm) GBP 49,900.

SOMERSET, Isabel, Lady Henry
British, 19th - 20th century.
Died 12 March 1921.
Sculptor, painter. Figures.

Isabel Somerset was also active as a writer.

MUSEUMS AND GALLERIES:
MELBOURNE: *Mother and Child* (plaster, statuette).

SOMERSET, Richard Gay
British, 19th - 20th century.
Born 1848, in Manchester; died 1928.
Painter. Landscapes with figures, landscapes, seascapes, architectural views.

Richard Gay Somerset exhibited at the Royal Academy of Arts in London in 1876-1877, 1879-1884, 1886-1889, 1896 and 1902. He painted English landscapes and also views of Capri and the Bay of Naples and views of Venice.

MUSEUMS AND GALLERIES:
ROCHDALE (Art Gallery): *Mountain Pasture, Snowdonia.*

SOMERVILLE, or Sommervaille
British, 18th - 19th century.

Active c. 1800.
Cameo engraver.

SOMERVILLE, Andrew
British, 19th century.
Born 1808, in Edinburgh; died January 1834, in Edinburgh.
Painter. Genre scenes.

Andrew Somerville studied at the Trustees' Academy in Edinburgh and settled in the city. He achieved rapid success, was made an associate of the Royal Scottish Academy in 1831 and became an academician in 1832.

MUSEUMS AND GALLERIES:
EDINBURGH (Nat. Gal. of Scotland): *Cottage Children* (oil on canvas).

SOMERVILLE, Charles
British, 19th - 20th century.
Born 29 July 1870, in Falkirk.
Painter. Figures, portraits, landscapes.

SOMERVILLE, Daniel
British, 18th - 19th century.
Born c.1780, in Dalkeith; died 1834.
Active in Edinburgh from 1798 to 1825.
Engraver (burin), lithographer.

SOMERVILLE, Howard
British, 19th - 20th century.
Born 1873, in Dundee.
Painter, illustrator. Portraits, interiors, still-lifes.

Howard Somerville settled in London, where he worked for *Punch*.

MUSEUMS AND GALLERIES:
LIVERPOOL (Walker AG): *Joyce*; *A Manila Scarf*.

AUCTION RECORDS:
BOLTON, 15 May 1985, *Portrait of J. Page Laughlin* (oil on canvas, 30 1/2 x 25 ins / 77.5 x 63.5 cm) USD 2,300.

SOMERVILLE, Peggy Scott, or Margaret
British, 20th century.
Born 2 June 1918, in Ashford (Middlesex); died 29 June 1975.
Painter, graphic artist. Landscapes, flowers, figures.

Peggy Somerville was a remarkable child prodigy, exhibiting her watercolours at the age of three at the thirty-third annual exhibition of the Royal Drawing Society at the Guildhall in London. She progressed to oil painting by age five. In 1926, her *Happy Days by the Sea* was selected for the New Irish Salon exhibition in Dublin by judges unaware of her age. By the age of fourteen she had had three solo shows in London, attracting the attention of established artists such as Walter Sickert and John Lavery. She initially learned to paint from her father Charles Somerville, an artist and collector, and was encouraged by her mother, the writer Rose Anne Chantrey. Her brother Stuart was also an artist. The Somerville family lived at Ashford until 1931, when they moved to Suffolk. They visited The Netherlands for six months in 1936, during which time Somerville painted Dutch subjects. Her only formal art training was at the Royal Academy Schools for a six-week period in 1939. She served in the Women's Land Army in World War II. After the war, she made visits to France, the Pembroke Coast in Wales and Cornwall, and moved house with her mother a number of times, finally settling at Middleton in 1964.

Somerville's earliest paintings as a child were highly imaginative, as in her 1921 watercolour *Figures in a Pink Landscape*. By about 1925 she began to try a more realistic style, painting from direct visual experience, such as the watercolour *Cows in a Meadow* (1926), or the oil *The Lane in Spring* (1927). From 1955 to 1970, pastel was her favoured medium, although she also returned to oils and watercolour in her final years. Somerville was noted for her sense of composition, for her use of tonal values, and as a fine colourist, as in her pastel *Orange, Chair, Fruit and Flowers*, or the pastel *Conversation* (c. 1960). She seldom dated her paintings and did not always sign them; her signature was variously *Margaret Scott Somerville, Margaret S. Somerville, MSS, Peggy, Peggy Somerville*, and *PS*.

Somerville's first solo exhibition took place at the Claridge Gallery in 1929, followed by another in 1932 at Beaux Arts Gallery, London. She exhibited with the Royal Society of British Artists, the Royal Institute of Oil Painters and the Royal Hibernian Academy. In the 1960s she sold most of her work locally in Suffolk and severed her ties with London galleries. Since her death, retrospective shows have included the Aldeburgh Festival (1977, 1994); Norwich Castle Museum (1985); Gainsborough's House, Sudbury (1986); Stephen Reiss Fine Art, Norwich (1987); International Monetary Fund, Washington DC (1990); David Messum Gallery (1991); and Christchurch Mansion, Ipswich (1997). Fifty-six of her works were bequeathed to the Norwich Castle Museum in 1977 and 1985.

BIBLIOGRAPHY:
Reiss, Stephen, *The Child Art of Peggy Somerville*, illustrated book, Herbert Press, London, 1990. Reiss, Stephen, *Peggy Somerville: An English Impressionist*, illustrated book, Antique Collectors' Club, Woodbridge, 1996.

MUSEUMS AND GALLERIES:
NORWICH (Castle Museum): *Happy Days by the Sea* (1926, oil); *The Fair at Aldeburgh* (1957, pastel); *Peggy* (c. 1960, pastel); *Summer, Aldeburgh* (c. 1960, oil); *Green Parasol* (c. 1960, pastel); *Head of a Girl* (c. 1973, biro and pastel).

AUCTION RECORDS:
BURY ST EDMUNDS, 28 Sept 2000, *Figures on a Beach* (pastel, 10 x 14 ins / 26 x 35 cm) GBP 2,600. BURY ST EDMUNDS, 28 Sept 2000, *Walberswick* (oil on canvas, 25 x 30 ins / 63 x 76 cm) GBP 6,200. NORFOLK, 14 June 2001, *Flowers in a Glass Vase* (pastel, 15 x 10 ins / 37 x 26 cm) GBP 1,000. NORFOLK, 14 June 2001, *Cockerel* (1959, pastel, 12 x 9 ins / 31 x 23 cm) GBP 1,200. IPSWICH, 30 Sept 2002, *Harvest Landscape, Suffolk* (oil on canvas, 22 x 33 ins / 57 x 84 cm) GBP 6,500. BURY ST EDMUNDS, 16 Dec 2002, *Still-life with Flowers in a Blue Vase* (oil on board, 20 x 16 ins / 50 x 40 cm) GBP 1,000. BURY ST EDMUNDS, 6 Oct 2004, *Dutch Landscape with Windmill* (1939, oil on panel, 14 x 18 ins / 35 x 46 cm) GBP 1,250.

SOMERVILLE, Stuart Scott
British, 20th century.
Born 1908; died 1983.
Painter, pastellist. Figures, nudes, landscapes with figures, still-lifes (flowers).

AUCTION RECORDS:
LONDON, 29 July 1988, *Bouquet of Flowers in a Vase* (pastel, 19 3/4 x 14 1/4 ins / 50 x 36.2 cm) GBP 968. LONDON, 2 March 1989, *Apple Blossom* (1931, oil on canvas, 23 1/2 x 19 3/4 ins / 60 x 50 cm) GBP 5,280. LONDON, 12 May 1989, *Standing Nude in a Garden* (pastel, 22 1/4 x 15 1/4 ins / 56.2 x 38.7 cm) GBP 1,650. LONDON, 12 May 1993, *Summer Flowers in a Vase* (oil on card, 14 x 10 ins / 35.5 x 25.5 cm) GBP 1,035. AYLSHAM, 19 Feb 1999, *Still-life of Mixed Summer Flowers in Glass Vase* (oil on canvas, 13 x 15 ins / 33 x 38 cm) GBP 1,600. LEEDS, 30 June 1999, *Still-life of Flowers in Glass Vase* (oil on canvas, 24 x 20 ins / 60 x 50 cm) GBP 1,350. BURY ST EDMUNDS, 9 May 2001, *Boats in an Estuary* (oil on canvas, 11 x 16 ins / 28 x 41 cm) GBP 1,050. BURY ST EDMUNDS, 9 May 2001, *April Day, Suffolk* (oil on board, 11 x 17 ins / 28 x 44 cm) GBP 1,050. LONDON, 23 May 2002, *Scottish Panelled Hall* (1929, oil on canvas, 30 x 25 ins / 76 x 63 cm) GBP 2,500. IPSWICH, 30 Sept 2002, *Ornamental Birds Amidst Flowering Vases with Decorative Border* (1928, oil on canvas, four-fold screen, 72 x 137 ins / 183 x 348 cm) GBP 3,100. GODALMING, 30 July 2003, *Mixed Flowers in a Vase on a Marble Ledge* (1949, oil on canvas, two, 24 x 20 ins / 61 x 51 cm) GBP 1,000.

SOMIS
Sculptor.
Ancient Greek.
Somis made a sculpture of a victor at Olympia.

SOMIS, Lorenzo, called l'Ardi or l'Ardito
Italian, 18th century.
Born 1702, in Turin; died 29 November 1775, in Turin.
Painter.
Lorenzo was the brother of Prospero Somis. He was both a painter and a violinist.

SOMIS, Prospero
Italian, 18th century.
Born c. 1693.
Painter.
Prospero Somis was the brother of Lorenzo Somis.

SOMLO, Jenö, or Eugen
Hungarian, 20th century.
Born 1894, in Budapest.
Painter. Figures.

SOMLO, Lili
Hungarian, 20th century.
Born 1887, in Budapest.
Painter. Figures, landscapes.

SOMLO-HLAVATHY, Sari, or Charlotte
Hungarian, 20th century.
Born 7 March 1886, in Arad.
Sculptor, poet. Monuments.
Charlotte Somlo-Hlavathy studied in Budapest and sculpted tombs in that city. She was also a poet.
MUSEUMS AND GALLERIES:
BUDAPEST (Fövárosi Képtár).

SOMM, Henry or Henri, pseudonym of François Clément Sommier
French, 19th century.
Born 1844, in Rouen; died 15 March 1907, in Paris.
Painter, watercolourist, engraver, illustrator, silhouettist. Figures, genre scenes.
Impressionist group.
After studies in Rouen, Henri Somm arrived in Paris in 1870, where he perfected his drawing technique. In 1879 and 1889 took part in the Impressionists Exhibitions held at Durand-Ruel in Paris. An illustrator, he contributed to the following presses: *Le Chat noir, La Charge, La Cravache, Chronique Parisienne, High-Life, Frou-Frou, Le Rire,* where he had a humorous sketch column. He published several albums: 1870 *La Rapinéïde ou L'Atelier (Den of Thieves or The Studio)*; 1885 *La Berline de l'émigré (The Emigré's Berline)*; 1886 *L'Escalier (The Staircase)*; 1908 in the collection *Les maîtres humorists (Masters of Humour)*: *Henry Somm*. Contributed to the illustration of *Sérénités* by A. Tinchant. Illustrated numerous literary works including: *Journal d'un nègre à l'Exposition de 1900 (Journal of a Negro at the 1900 Exhibition)* by G. Bergeret; *Tanzaï et Néadarné* by Crébillon the Younger; *La Maison de fous (The Mad House)* by R. Lesclide; Montassier's *Rose tendre et vert foncé (Soft Pink and Dark Green)*; *Solutions conjugales, Histoires conjugales, Ce qu'on n'ose pas dire (Conjugal Solutions, Conjugal Stories, Words you Never Dared Utter)* by A. Saulière. In 1911 the Berthe Weill Gallery in Paris devoted a special exhibition to his works. In 1933 his work was featured in the exhibition *The Décor under the Third Republic* held at the Louvre Museum. Since that time his works have been shown in many galleries in London, Düsseldorf, Paris (Prouté Gallery, 1983 and 1986).

Initially deeply influenced by the Japanese School, he wanted the Government to send him on a mission to Japan. But the war of 1870 prevented it and he then resolved to devote himself to what would bring him his greatest success: scenes showing the people of Paris of that time. This became his speciality and he exercised it with talent as shown in several watercolours which Arsène Alexandre described in 1897 as 'alluring by their very subject' and elegant, inspired, lively, spiritual drawings that sometimes verged on satire. These works were often much more than mere fashion illustrations, and they have echoes of the art of Constantin Guys or Toulouse-Lautrec, or even, in some ways, of Monet or Renoir. Henry Somm has left a large number of sketch books filled with sketches of doubtless merit. He jotted down the briefest of notes which show great artistic quality. These drawings, which lay undiscovered for a long time, make it all the more regrettable that he should have been forced to spend time working on humorous journals in order to be make ends meet. His possibilities as a painter of talent were never explored to the full. In 1897, in the preface to a sales catalogue, Roger-Milès wrote: 'Henry Somm is one of those people for whom art, which appears so transient, has such solid qualities; he had an inner vitality which refuses to fade away'.

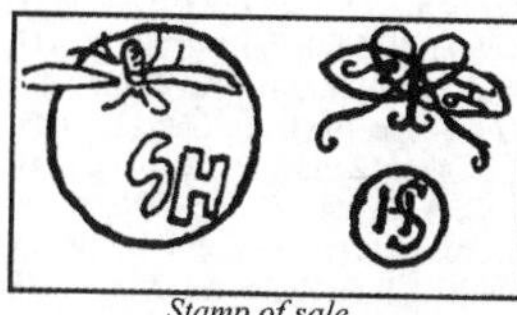

Stamp of sale

H Somm

BIBLIOGRAPHY:
Osterwalder, Marcus (ed.), *Dictionnaire des illustrateurs 1800-1914*, Ides et Calendes, Neuchâtel, 1989.
MUSEUMS AND GALLERIES:
AUVERS-SUR-OISE (Mus. Daubigny) - KANSAS CITY (Nelson-Atkins MA) - PARIS (Louvre) - PARIS (Mus. d'Orsay): *Illustrated Japanese Grammar* (drawing) - ROUEN (MBA): *Red Overcoat* (watercolour) - WASHINGTON DC (NGA): *Program for Theatres l'Athénée* (1881, dry-point/paper).
AUCTION RECORDS:
PARIS, 1898, *Trio*, FRF 85. PARIS, 3 March 1898, *To Your Very Good Health* (watercolour) FRF 70. PARIS, 26 Feb 1900, *Head and Torso of Young Woman in Elegant Attire* (drawing) FRF 163. PARIS, 8 Feb 1919, *Parisienne* (watercolour) FRF 26. PARIS, 27 March 1919, *Woman with a Toy Dog* (watercolour) FRF 34. PARIS, 13 Feb 1924, *Young Woman with a Fan* (watercolour) FRF 160. PARIS, 14 Nov 1927, *Ladies out for a Stroll* (watercolour) FRF 270. PARIS, 12-13 Nov 1928, *At the Circus* (watercolour) FRF 105. PARIS, 17 Feb 1937, *Strolling along the Boulevards* (watercolour) FRF 75. PARIS, 1 April 1942, *Parisienne in the Wood* (watercolour) FRF 600. PARIS, 17 June 1942, *Ladies out for an Evening Walk* (watercolour) FRF 210. PARIS, 30 Oct 1942, *Woman Seated in front of a Japanese Decoration* (fan-shaped gouache) FRF 1,000. PARIS, 2 June 1943, *Woman in the Wood* (watercolour) FRF 1,300. PARIS, 17 Dec 1943, *Parisienne in the Countryside* (Indian ink and watercolour) FRF 700. PARIS, 18 July 1944, *Parisienne* (watercolour) FRF 3,100. PARIS, 23 March 1945, *Woman with a Bouquet* (watercolour) FRF 2,400; *A Heart Torn Between Them* (watercolour) FRF 2,350; *The Follower* (watercolour) FRF 2,300. PARIS, July 1946, *At the Moulin Rouge, a gentleman alone, Valentin le Désossé and L'Asperge* (watercolour) FRF 3,000; *A Loose Woman in Conversation with a Man Strolling around the Jardin de Paris* (watercolour) FRF 5,550. PARIS, 11 June 1947, *Young Parisienne in her Apartment*; *Young Parisienne in a Winter Garden* (two watercolours) FRF 3,000. NICE, 24 Feb 1949, *Scenes of Parisian Life* (four pen and ink draw-

ings heightened with watercolour) FRF 6,100. PARIS, 5 May 1949, *Woman and Two Puppets* (watercolour) FRF 2,300. PARIS, 9 June 1949, *Parisienne Sitting in the Bullier Gardens* (India ink wash heightened with gouache) FRF 6,500. PARIS, 28 June 1950, *An Elegant Woman* (watercolour) FRF 2,100. PARIS, 5 March 1951, *Woman in a Blue Dress* (watercolour) FRF 3,200; *Woman in a Yellow Dress* (watercolour) FRF 3,100. PARIS, 30 April 1951, *Elegant Woman Walking in the Woods* (watercolour) FRF 3,000. PARIS, 28 May 1951, *Young Girl with a Fan* (watercolour) FRF 3,200. PARIS, 23 Nov 1953, *Elegant Women in Conversation and Gentlemen* (watercolour and gouache) FRF 21,000. PARIS, 20 Nov 1972, *The Cup of Coffee,* FRF 4,500. LONDON, 6 Dec 1973, *At the bar* (gouache) GBP 1,000. LONDON, 8 Dec 1977, *In the Wings* (c. 1878-1880, watercolour and pencil, 17 1/2 x 11 1/2 ins / 44.5 x 29.2 cm) GBP 1,000. LONDON, 4 April 1979, *Young Woman in front of a Bookshop* (watercolour, gouache and pencil, 9 x 5 3/4 ins / 23 x 14.5 cm) GBP 900. LONDON, 26 March 1980, *Young Woman Seated* (charcoal and coloured crayon, 18 3/4 x 12 ins / 47.5 x 30.5 cm) GBP 1,100. VERSAILLES, 21 Feb 1982, *Elegant Ladies out for a Stroll* (1899, wash and sepia, 11 3/4 x 9 ins / 30 x 23 cm) FRF 14,000. PARIS, 22 March 1982, *An Elegant Woman* (watercolour, 19 x 13 1/2 ins / 48 x 34 cm) FRF 14,000. LONDON, 7 Dec 1983, *An Elegant Woman* (watercolour/pen strokes, 17 x 12 ins / 43.2 x 30.5 cm) GBP 1,150. ENGHIEN-LES-BAINS, 1 Dec 1985, *An Elegant Woman on Les Grands Boulevards* (watercolour and Indian ink, 8 x 5 1/2 ins / 20.5 x 14 cm) FRF 8,000. PARIS, 12 Oct 1986, *Portrait of Leo Tolstoy* (pen, 11 3/4 x 7 1/2 ins / 30 x 19 cm) FRF 5,500. PARIS, 3 June 1987, *An Elegant Woman with a Bouquet* (watercolour, 8 1/4 x 6 ins / 21 x 15 cm) FRF 10,100. TROYES, 24 Nov 1987, *The Dance Card* (watercolour and wash, 12 x 9 1/4 ins / 30.5 x 23.5 cm) FRF 21,500. PARIS, 22 March 1988, *An Elegant Woman in the Garden* (watercolour, 11 1/2 x 8 1/2 ins / 29.5 x 21.5 cm) FRF 10,500; *An Elegant Woman* (watercolour, 8 3/4 x 6 ins / 22.5 x 15.5 cm) FRF 5,500. PARIS, 9 Dec 1988, *An Elegant Woman* (watercolour, 11 3/4 x 7 ins / 30 x 18 cm) FRF 14,000. PARIS, 22 Dec 1989, *Elegant Women 1900* (ink and watercolour, 7 3/4 x 10 ins / 20 x 25.5 cm) FRF 4,000. CALAIS, 4 March 1990, *Elegant Woman on the Banks of the River* (watercolour, 9 x 6 1/4 ins / 23 x 16 cm) FRF 10,500. LA VARENNE-ST-HILAIRE, 20 May 1990, *Elegant Woman with a Fan* (watercolour, 8 x 6 1/4 ins / 20.5 x 16 cm) FRF 9,000. PARIS, 6 Oct 1990, *Elegant Woman in a Japanese-style Interior* (watercolour, 7 3/4 x 5 1/2 ins / 19.5 x 14 cm) FRF 5,300. PARIS, 26 June 1991, *Elegant Woman at the Museum* (watercolour, 19 1/4 x 12 1/2 ins / 49 x 32 cm) FRF 21,500. PARIS, 28 Oct 1991, *Elegant Woman on the Banks of the River* (pen and watercolour, 9 x 6 ins / 23 x 15.5 cm) FRF 5,500. PARIS, 24 April 1992, *In the Studio* (watercolour, 7 3/4 x 10 3/4 ins / 20 x 27.5 cm) FRF 8,200. CALAIS, 4 July 1993, *Foyer of the Montmartre Theatre* (watercolour, 7 3/4 x 6 ins / 20 x 15 cm) FRF 6,500. PARIS, 15 Dec 1994, *Woman in a Windblown Landscape* (watercolour, 7 3/4 x 5 3/4 ins / 19.5 x 14.5 cm) FRF 7,600. PARIS, 27 Jan 1995, *Japonaise* (watercolour and gouache, 19 x 12 1/4 ins / 48 x 31 cm) FRF 5,500. PARIS, 4 Feb 1998, *La Japonaise* (pen and watercolour, 10 1/2 x 7 1/2 ins / 26.5 x 19 cm) FRF 7,500. PARIS, 27 Oct 1999, *Elegant Lady* (watercolour, 9 x 6 ins / 23 x 15 cm) FRF 11,000. PARIS, 1 Dec 2000, *Japanese Woman with Fan* (watercolour, 8 x 6 ins / 20 x 15 cm) FRF 18,500. PARIS, 3 June 2002, *Elegant Lady* (1895, watercolour, 19 x 12 ins / 49 x 31 cm) EUR 1,600. PARIS, 2 July 2002, *Woman with a Letter* (pastel and wax crayon, 21 x 17 ins / 53 x 44 cm) EUR 3,800. NEUILLY, 19 Dec 2002, *Party in the Country* (watercolour and ink, 12 x 24 ins / 30 x 60 cm) EUR 4,500. LONDON, 22 Oct 2003, *Elegant Lady on the Beach in the Wind* (1883, watercolour, 12 x 7 ins / 30 x 17 cm) GBP 2,100. NEW YORK, 29 Jan 2004, *Elegantly Dressed Woman at a Door* (watercolour, 10 x 8 ins / 25 x 20 cm) USD 2,800. FONTAINEBLEAU, 6 June 2004, *Elegant Ladies at the Hatter's* (oil on canvas, 22 x 15 ins / 55 x 38 cm) EUR 5,400.

SOMMA, G.
Italian, 18th century.
Active in Naples during the second half of the 18th century.
Sculptor.

G. Somma modelled figurines for nativity scenes.

SOMMA, Nicola
Italian, 18th century.
Active in Naples during the second half of the 18th century.
Sculptor.

Nicola Somma sculpted nativity figurines.

SOMMARIVA, Emilio
Italian, 20th century.
Born 8 December 1883, in Lodi.
Painter. Landscapes.

Sommariva was pupil of Giuseppe Mentessi.

SOMMARUGA, Napoleone
Italian, 19th century.
Born 1848, in Milan; died 4 June 1906, in Milan.
Painter. Architectural views, church interiors.

SOMMARUGA, Renzo
Italian, 20th century.
Born 1917, in Milan.
Draughtsman, engraver (wood/etching/lino). Figures, nudes, landscapes, urban landscapes.

Until the end of the 1930s, Sommaruga was a violinist and composer. He put aside these activities to devote himself to painting and, particularly, engraving and drawing. His works include linocuts, woodcuts and etchings. The style varies according to the technique, but the lines are usually cursive and sharply defined.

He took part in collective exhibitions, including *Attraverso l'Immagine* (*Through the Image*) held in 1995 at the Centro Culturale in Cremona.

BIBLIOGRAPHY:

Attraverso l'immagine, exhibition catalogue, Centro culturale Santa Maria della Pietà, Cremona, 1995.

SOMMATI DI MOMBELLO, Giulio
Italian, 19th - 20th century.
Born 1858, in Chieri.
Painter. Landscapes, architectural views.

Sommati di Mombello was a pupil of Andrea Gastaldi and Pier Celestino Gilardi. He worked in Turin.

SOMMAVILLA, Goffredo
Italian, 19th - 20th century.
Born 23 June 1850, in Belluno.
Active in Uruguay.
Painter. Figures, portraits, genre scenes.

Goffredo Sommavilla exhibited in Milan and Turin before going to live in Uruguay.

SOMME, Charles de
French, 17th century.
Born January 1637, in Brussels; died 11 July 1673, in Paris.
Painter. Flowers, fruit.

Charles de Somme was painter to the queen.

SOMME, Félicité
Belgian, 19th century.
Born in Antwerp.
Painter. History painting, portraits, genre scenes.

Félicité Somme exhibited in Ghent, Brussels and Paris from 1826 to 1849.

SØMME, Jacob Kielland
Norwegian, 19th - 20th century.
Born 2 May 1862, in Stavanger.
Painter (including porcelain), illustrator, designer.
Portraits, genre scenes, interiors with figures.

Jacob Kielland Sømme studied under Wilhelm von Lindenschmidt the Younger, at the Akademie der Bildenden Künste in Munich, then under Pascal Dagnan-Bouveret at the Académie Colarossi in Paris.

MUSEUMS AND GALLERIES:
BERGEN (Kunstmus., Billedgal.): *Little Girl Picking Flowers* - OSLO (Nasjonalgal.): *Portrait of the Artist's Mother; Lamp-lit Interior.*

SOMME, Pierre Nicolas
French, 18th century.
Goldsmith.

Somme became a master goldsmith in 1760.

MUSEUMS AND GALLERIES:
PARIS (Mus. des Arts décoratifs).

SOMME, Théophile François
French, 19th - 20th century.
Born 7 September 1871, in Nancy.
Sculptor.

Théophile François Somme exhibited in Paris, at the Salon des Artistes Français, where he was a member from 1899. In 1902 he was awarded a commendation and in 1924 he won a silver medal. In 1925 he won a gold medal followed by another gold at the Exposition Internationale of 1937, where he was awarded the hors concours.

AUCTION RECORDS:
FRANKFURT AM MAIN, 24 June 1978, *Inspiration* (c. 1900, bronze and ivory, h. 18 3/4 ins / 47.5 cm) DEM 4,200. BREST, 14 Dec 1980, *Young Breton Woman at Prayer* (bronze and ivory, h. 11 ins / 28 cm) FRF 6,800. PARIS, 10 April 1981, *Woman with Muff* (patinated bronze and ivory, h. 9 3/4 ins / 25 cm) FRF 10,000. PARIS, 7 Dec 1983, *Inspiration* (bronze and ivory, h. 16 1/2 ins / 42 cm) FRF 27,500. LOKEREN, 20 April 1985, *Birds-Nesting for Eagles' Eggs* (dark-brown patinated bronze, h. 37 1/2 ins / 95 cm) BEF 260,000. PARIS, 17 April 1991, *Seated Oriental Woman* (chryselephantine sculpture, h. 7 3/4 ins / 20 cm) FRF 20,000. PARIS, 17 Nov 2000, *Young Breton at Prayer* (gilt bronze and ivory, h. 11 ins / 29 cm) FRF 15,000. PARIS, 10 Dec 2001, *Woman with Harp* (patinated bronze and ivory, 18 x 9x2 ins / 45 x 22x5 cm) FRF 16,000. CRANBROOK, 15 Dec 2002, *Semi-draped Young Beauty* (bronze) GBP 1,000. STUTTGART, 27 March 2003, *Inspiration* (bronze and ivory, h. 18 ins / 46 cm) EUR 4,500. LONDON, 25 Nov 2003, *Figure of a Maiden* (gilt bronze, h. 13 ins / 34 cm) GBP 2,400. TOKYO, 20 March 2004, *Woman* (marble) JPY 240,000.

SOMMEDEVILLE, Melchior
Flemish School, 16th century.
Active in Bruges in 1563.
Painter.

Sommedeville was a pupil of Marc Gérards.

SOMMER. See also **SOMER**

SOMMER, A.
Austrian, 19th century.
Of Bohemian origin.
Active at the beginning of the 19th century.
Draughtsman.

Sommer trained at the art academy in Leipzig. He exhibited two landscapes in Dresden in 1802 and 1805.

SOMMER, Alois. See **SONNE VON SONNEFELD**

SOMMER, August or Carl Wilhelm August
German, 19th - 20th century.
Born 5 March 1839, in Coburg; died 15 September 1921, in Coburg.
Sculptor. Mythological subjects.

August Sommer studied in Stuttgart, Munich, Vienna and Budapest. He travelled to Rome in 1875 before returning to settle in Coburg.

MUSEUMS AND GALLERIES:
BERLIN (Nationalgal.): *Sleeping Siren; Faun with Otter* - BUCHAREST (Muz. National de Arta al României): *Bacchante.*

AUCTION RECORDS:
NEW YORK, 24 May 1979, *Landscape with Traveller and his Dog* (oil on canvas, 28 x 42 1/4 ins / 71.2 x 107 cm) USD 1,000.

SOMMER, Carl August
German, 19th century.
Born 1829, in Veitlahm.
Painter, lithographer. Landscapes, mountainscapes.

Carl August Sommer worked in Altona and exhibited landscapes from 1872 to 1894.

AUCTION RECORDS:
NEW YORK, 30 April 1980, *Mountain Landscape at Dusk* (oil on canvas, 20 x 36in/50.8 x 91.4cm) USD 1,300. HAMBURG, 24 Oct 2003, *Holstein* (oil on canvas, 26 x 40 ins / 66 x 102 cm) EUR 4,500. BERLIN, 12 Dec 2003, *Hudson High Mountains. Sunset in New York* (oil on canvas, a pair, 9 x 12 ins / 22 x 31 cm) EUR 1,500.

SOMMER, Eberhard
German, 17th century.
Active in the middle of the 17th century.
Sculptor (wood), architect.

Eberhard Sommer produced altar sculptures for the monastery at Schöntal an der Jagst.

SOMMER, Ed
Swiss, 20th century.
Born 1932.
Sculptor.
Kinetic Art.

Ed Sommer studied commerce and worked in industry between 1952 and 1965. He started studying art in 1959 and attended courses under Max Bense. In 1964, he started producing pieces fashioned by heat-forming his favourite medium, Plexiglas. Between 1965 and 1969 he was an art critic for the periodical *Art International*. Some of his transparent Plexiglas compositions feature mobile elements which can be interpreted in a number of different ways. These helped inspire him to work in cinema and produce animated features for television. He demonstrates both elegance and ingenuity in working his chosen material.

Sommer participated in numerous group exhibitions of Kinetic Art when it was at the height of its popularity. He also exhibited solo, including in 1966 in Esslingen, Cologne and Kassel; in 1967 in Milan, Rome, Bern and Frankfurt am Main; in 1968 in Bologna, Esslingen, Düsseldorf and Cologne; in 1969 in Cologne, Amsterdam, Nuremberg and Hamburg; and in 1970 in Krefeld and Frankfurt am Main.

BIBLIOGRAPHY:
Popper, Frank, *L'Art cinétique*, Gauthier-Villars, Paris, 1970. *Ed Sommer*, exhibition catalogue, Gal. Appel und Fertsch, Frankfurt am Main, 1970.

SOMMER, Elias
German, 18th century.
Died 23 March 1717, in Leipzig.
Active in Zeitz.
Painter.

Elias Sommer produced paintings for churches and the town hall in Zeitz.

SOMMER, Eugénie. See **HAUPTMANN Eugénie**

Printed and bound in Italy
by G. Canale & C. S.p.A. - Borgaro T. se (Torino)
February 2006